2012 STANDARD POSTAGE STAMP CATALOGUE

ONE HUNDRED AND SIXTY-EIGHTH EDITION IN SIX VOLUMES

VOLUME 4
COUNTRIES OF THE WORLD
J-M

EDITOR	James E. Kloetzel
ASSISTANT EDITOR	Charles Snee
ASSISTANT EDITOR /NEW ISSUES & VALUING	Martin J. Frankevicz
ASSOCIATE EDITORS	David Akin, Donna Houseman
VALUING ANALYST	Steven R. Myers
ADMINISTRATIVE ASSISTANT/CATALOGUE LAYOUT	Eric Wiessinger
PRINTING AND IMAGE COORDINATOR	Stacey Mahan
CREATIVE DIRECTOR	Mark Potter
ADVERTISING	Angela Nolte
CIRCULATION/PRODUCT PROMOTION MANAGER	Tim Wagner
VICE PRESIDENT/EDITORIAL AND PRODUCTION	Steve Collins
PRESIDENT	William Fay

Released July 2011
Includes New Stamp Listings through the May 2011 *Linn's Stamp News Special Edition* Catalogue Update

Scott Publishing Co.

911 Vandemark Road, Sidney, OH 45365-0828
A division of AMOS PRESS, INC., publishers of *Linn's Stamp News, Linn's Stamp News Special Edition, Coin World* and *Coin World Special Edition.*

Table of Contents

See Volume 1 for United States, United Nations and Countries of the World A-B
See Volume 2, 3, 5, 6 for Countries of the World, C-I, N-Z.

Volume 2: C-F
Volume 3: G-I
Volume 5: N-Sam
Volume 6: San-Z

Scott Publishing Mission Statement

The Scott Publishing Team exists to serve the recreational, educational and commercial hobby needs of stamp collectors and dealers.

We strive to set the industry standard for philatelic information and products by developing and providing goods that help collectors identify, value, organize and present their collections.

Quality customer service is, and will continue to be, our highest priority. We aspire toward achieving total customer satisfaction.

Copyright Notice

Trademark Notice

ISBN 0-89487-463-2

Library of Congress Card No. 2-3301

Scott Publishing Co.

SCOTT 911 VANDEMARK ROAD, SIDNEY, OHIO 45365 937-498-0802

Dear Scott Catalogue User:

Where are the value changes in the 2012 Volume 4?

Many thousands of value changes appear in the 2012 edition of Volume 4 of the *Scott Standard Postage Stamp Catalogue*. This volume covers countries of the world alphabetically J through M. The number of changes is in line with the numbers seen each year for about the past decade. There are value changes in almost every country in the volume.

The countries with the most value changes in the Volume 4 Standard catalogue are Malaya and Malaysia. More than 3,200 changes appear, almost equally split between the two entities. Other countries with a large number of changes are Libya, with 1,227 value changes, followed by Morocco (813), Martinique (699), Montenegro (548), and Macedonia (540).

The Scott editors do not count in their total value changes the new values that are added to stamps that previously were not valued. Along these lines, it should be mentioned that values have been added in 2012 for the used stamps of Laos between Scott 317 and 1381. Appropriate notes have been added to indicate which issues are valued postally used as opposed to canceled to order. The total number of additional values entered for Laos is 1,075.

Value changes in the Federated Malay States are numerous and are a mixture of increases and decreases. In the Federation of Malaya period, a similar mixture is seen, with some noticeable drops in value but also some significant increases. This is seen most clearly in the postage due listings, and also in the occupation issues. A notable increase in value is seen in the 1942 set of 1c-12c occupation postage dues, Scott NJ8-NJ13, which jumps to $75.50 mint, never hinged and $128.50 used, from $51.50 mint, never hinged and $106.50 used in the 2011 Volume 4. On the other hand, the 1943 1c-15c Thai occupation issue, Scott 2N1-2N6, drops in value a bit more than 10 percent, both mint, never hinged and used.

In Malaysia, the general trend is to slightly lower values. There are occasional increases. This trend is seen through the late 1990s, at which time values stabilize or often rise somewhat. This is consistent with trends the editors have seen for a great many countries, where the scarcity of stocks of quite modern material has resulted in rising prices.

The general weakness in worldwide economies has continued throughout the past year, and that certainly has dampened most upward pressure on values. The results of a weak United States economy, from the perspective of U.S. catalogue editors, are threefold. First, economic weakness harms hobby-related fields generally because it is relatively easy to put hobby expenses on hold for a period of time, whereas it is not possible to put necessities such as food and housing on hold. It follows that the more common philatelic material in the marketplace would be expected to show a pretty lethargic sales pattern, and that is what we have been seeing. Nothing terribly upsetting, but also very little showing strength in the market.

Second, as usual during such uncertain periods, true rarities and condition rarities show strength.

The third pattern we see often during difficult economic times is a swing in the relative value for different currencies. If all countries experienced the same weakness, currencies could be expected to remain relatively stable in relation to each other. That pattern, however, is seldom the case. There are strong currencies and there are weak currencies, and with Scott being a retail-value catalogue, these relative shifts have an impact on values. If an important country experiences a stronger currency in relation to the United States dollar's value, it will tend to cause prices to rise in the United States, because more dollars are needed to compete with the stronger home-country currency.

What's happening on the editorial side?

Many of the listing changes made to this Volume 4 relate to issues of North Korea. While no stamps have been added or deleted, the listings have been brought into closer adherence to normal Scott listing style. Collectors and dealers who have labeled their collections or their stocks will want to check the Number Additions, Deletions & Changes list carefully this year. These are one-time changes, and further changes of this nature are not expected for this country.

Many lettered minor listings have been added in several countries in Volume 4. In Jordan, numerous overprint errors have been added in the Scott 113 to 129 and J2-J5 issues. Similar additions have been made in early Lebanon airmails.

A great number of interesting varieties receive lettered minor listings in the Malaya area. There is a differentiation between ordinary and chalky papers for Scott J21, J23 and J27. The first occupation stamps of Malaya, Scott NJ1-NJ7, have been broken down by overprint color, because there are substantial value differences between the scarce red and brown overprints, versus the more common black overprints.

In Martinique, Scott 177a has been added for the 5fr ultramarine Tercentenary of French Possessions in the West Indies issue. The normal stamp was printed in brown, Scott 177.

New major numbers appear for the first time in Libya, Macao and Mexico. In Libya, the 1986 50d-2500d issue for Khadafy has been listed as Scott 1286-1297. This set apparently was on sale for only two hours on January 1, 1986. The stamps are valued at $20 each, mint, never hinged or used. Macao sees the addition of a 1981 postal tax stamp, Scott RA20A. In Mexico, it was found that the catalogue inadvertently failed to list a 25c blue revenue stamp used for postage, and that has been added to the 1c to 10c revenues used for postage starting in July 1914, Scott 393A-393E. The new 25c stamp is Scott 393F.

To see these and all other listing changes that have been made this year, consult the 2012 Volume 4 Number Additions, Deletions & Changes list. In this volume, it is on page 1308.

Final thoughts.

Dr. Hsien-Ming Meng, a great Scott friend and benefactor, passed away Feb. 8, 2011, at age 84. Longtime catalogue users might recognize his name. When Scott began digitally scanning stamps for our catalogue images in 2001, we began by scanning all of the stamps in our own reference collection. But this left a huge number of earlier stamps in the old black and white velox format, often fuzzy in appearance. Recognizing the benefit of Scott's scanning project, Dr. Meng stepped forward with an offer to loan us his massive collection of unused stamps for scanning purposes. The time and effort saved by having this immense resource made available proved invaluable, and the Scott catalogues began appearing in full color much sooner than they otherwise would have. We will forever remember the kindness and generosity shown by this wonderful Ohio collector.

And speaking of our color project, there are only 52 images in this Volume 4 remaining to be converted to color. Most of these are stamps with overprints of one kind or another. Other volumes have more or fewer images remaining to be found. We still have staff and outside contributors on the lookout for the stamps not currently shown in color.

A hobby is a great gift. Happy collecting.

James E. Kloetzel

James E. Kloetzel/Catalogue Editor

Acknowledgments

Our appreciation and gratitude go to the following individuals who have assisted us in preparing information included in this year's Scott Catalogues. Some helpers prefer anonymity. These individuals have generously shared their stamp knowledge with others through the medium of the Scott Catalogue.

Those who follow provided information that is in addition to the hundreds of dealer price lists and advertisements and scores of auction catalogues and realizations that were used in producing the catalogue values. It is from those noted here that we have been able to obtain information on items not normally seen in published lists and advertisements. Support from these people goes beyond data leading to catalogue values, for they also are key to editorial changes.

A special acknowledgment to Liane and Sergio Sismondo of The Classic Collector for their extraordinary assistance and knowledge sharing that has aided in the preparation of this year's Standard and Classic Specialized Catalogues.

A. R. Allison (Orange Free State Study Circle)
Roland Austin
Robert Ausubel (Great Britain Collectors Club)
Jack Hagop Barsoumian (International Stamp Co.)
George G. Birdsall
John Birkinbine II
Roger S. Brody
Keith & Margie Brown
Mahdi Bseiso
Paul Buchsbayew
Bernard Bujnak
Timothy Bryan Burgess
Mike Bush (Joseph V. Bush, Inc.)
Tina & John Carlson (JET Stamps)
Richard A. Champagne (Richard A. Champagne, Inc.)
Henry Chlanda
Bob Coale
Leroy P. Collins III (United Postal Stationery Society)
Frank D. Correl
Tom Cossaboom
Francis J. Crown, Jr.
Tony L. Crumbley (Carolina Coin & Stamp, Inc.)
Stephen R. Datz
Tony Davis
Kenneth E. Diehl
Bob Dumaine
Sister Theresa Durand
Mark Eastzer (Markest Stamp Co.)
Esi Ebrani (Iran Philatelic Study Circle)
Paul G. Eckman
George Epstein
Mehdi Esmaili
Leon Finik
Robert A. Fisher
Geoffrey Flack
Jeffrey M. Forster
Ken Fowler
Ernest E. Fricks (France & Colonies Philatelic Society)
Phillip F. Gallagher
Bob Genisol (Sultan Stamp Center)
Stan Goldfarb
Daniel E. Grau
Jan E. Gronwall
Bruce Hecht (Bruce L. Hecht Co.)
Robert R. Hegland
Clifford O. Herrick (Fidelity Trading Co.)
Peter Hoffman
Armen Hovsepian
Philip J. Hughes
Doug Iams
Thomas Jackson (Stamp Parlor)
N. M. Janoowalla
Peter Jeannopoulos
Stephen Joe (International Stamp Service)
Richard A. Johnson
Allan Katz (Ventura Stamp Co.)
Stanford M. Katz
Lewis Kaufman
Patricia A. Kaufmann
William V. Kriebel
Dr. Ingert (Ihor) Kuzych-Berlzovsky
Frederick P. Lawrence
John R. Lewis (The William Henry Stamp Co.)
Ulf Lindahl
Pedro Llach (Filatelia Llach S.L.)
George Luzitano
Dennis Lynch
Robert L. Markovits (Quality Investors, Ltd.)
Marilyn R. Mattke
Robert Maushammer
William K. McDaniel
Gary McLean
Mark S. Miller (India Study Circle)
Allen Mintz (United Postal Stationery Society)
Gary Morris (Pacific Midwest Co.)
Peter Mosiondz, Jr.
Bruce M. Moyer (Moyer Stamps & Collectibles)
Richard H. Muller
Gregg Nelson
Robert Odenweller
Marc Parren
John E. Pearson (Pittwater Philatelic Service)
Donald J. Peterson (International Philippine Philatelic Society)
Stanley M. Piller (Stanley M. Piller & Associates)
Todor Drumev Popov
Peter W. W. Powell
Stephen Radin (Albany Stamp Co.)
Siddique Mahmudur Rahman
Dr. Reuben A. Ramkissoon
Ghassan D. Riachi
Eric Roberts
Omar Rodriguez
Michael Rogers (Michael Rogers, Inc.)
Robert G. Rufe
Michael Ruggiero
Andrew Sader
Mehrdad Sadri (Persiphila)
Alex Schauss (Schauss Philatelics)
Jacques C. Schiff, Jr. (Jacques C. Schiff, Jr., Inc.)
Bernard Seckler (Fine Arts Philatelists)
Guy Shaw
Jeff Siddiqui
Sergio & Liane Sismondo (The Classic Collector)
Jay Smith
Frank J. Stanley, III
Alfred E. Staubus
Peter Thy
Scott R. Trepel (Siegel Auction Galleries)
Philip T. Wall
Giana Wayman
William R. Weiss, Jr. (Weiss Expertizing)
Ed Wener (Indigo)
Don White (Dunedin Stamp Centre)
Kirk Wolford (Kirk's Stamp Company)
Robert F. Yacano (K-Line Philippines)
Ralph Yorio
Val Zabijaka
Michal Zika
Alfonso G. Zulueta, Jr.

Grand Imperial
Jacoona Amrita
SIX PENCE
U.S. POSTAGE

Addresses, Telephone Numbers, Web Sites, E-Mail Addresses of General & Specialized Philatelic Societies

Collectors can contact the following groups for information about the philately of the areas within the scope of these societies, or inquire about membership in these groups. Aside from the general societies, we limit this list to groups that specialize in particular fields of philately, particular areas covered by the Scott Standard Postage Stamp Catalogue, and topical groups. Many more specialized philatelic society exist than those listed below. These addresses are updated yearly, and they are, to the best of our knowledge, correct and current. Groups should inform the editors of address changes whenever they occur. The editors also want to hear from other such specialized groups not listed.

Unless otherwise noted all website addresses begin with http://

American Philatelic Society
100 Match Factory Place
Bellefonte PA 16823-1367
Ph: (814) 933-3803
www.stamps.org
E-mail: apsinfo@stamps.org

American Stamp Dealers Association, Inc.
Joe Savarese
217-14 Northern Blvd.
Bayside NY 11361
Ph: (718) 224-2500
www.asdaonline.com
E-mail: asda@erols.com

National Stamp Dealers Association
Dick Keiser, president
2916 NW Bucklin Hill Rd #136
Silverdale WA 98383-8514
Ph: (800) 875-6633
www.nsdainc.org
E-mail: gail@nsdainc.org

International Society of Worldwide Stamp Collectors
Joanne Berkowitz, MD
P.O. Box 19006
Sacramento CA 95819
www.iswsc.org
E-mail: executivedirector@iswsc.org

Royal Philatelic Society
41 Devonshire Place
London, W1G 6JY
UNITED KINGDOM
www.rpsl.org.uk
E-mail: secretary@rpsl.org.uk

Royal Philatelic Society of Canada
P.O. Box 929, Station Q
Toronto, ON, M4T 2P1
CANADA
Ph: (888) 285-4143
www.rpsc.org
E-mail: info@rpsc.org

Young Stamp Collectors of America
Janet Houser
100 Match Factory Place
Bellefonte PA 16823-1367
Ph: (814) 933-3820
www.stamps.org/ysca/intro.htm
E-mail: ysca@stamps.org

Philatelic Research Resources

(Scott editors are encouraging any additional research organizations to submit data for inclusion in this new listing category)

The Western Philatelic Library
P.O. Box 2219
1500 Partridge Avenue
Sunnyvale CA 94087
Ph: (408) 733-0336
www.fwpf.org

Groups focusing on fields or aspects found in worldwide philately (some may cover U.S. area only)

American Air Mail Society
Stephen Reinhard
P.O. Box 110
Mineola NY 11501
www.americanairmailsociety.org
E-mail: sreinhard1@optonline.net

American First Day Cover Society
Douglas Kelsey
P.O. Box 16277
Tucson AZ 85732-6277
Ph: (520) 321-0880
www.afdcs.org
E-mail: afdcs@aol.com

American Revenue Association
Eric Jackson
P.O. Box 728
Leesport PA 19533-0728
Ph: (610) 926-6200
www.revenuer.org
E-mail: eric@revenuer.com

American Topical Association
Vera Felts
P.O. Box 8
Carterville IL 62918-0008
Ph: (618) 985-5100
www.americantopicalassn.org
E-mail: americantopical@msn.com

Christmas Seal & Charity Stamp Society
John Denune
234 East Broadway
Granville OH 43023
Ph: (740) 587-0276
http://www.charityseals.org
E-mail: jdenune@roadrunner.com

Errors, Freaks and Oddities Collectors Club
Don David Price
5320 Eastchester Drive
Sarasota FL 34134-2711
Ph: (717) 445-9420 Nor. Am. Phone No.
www.efocc.org
E-mail: ddprice98@hotmail.com

First Issues Collectors Club
Kurt Streepy, Secretary
3128 E. Mattatha Drive
Bloomington IN 47401
www.firstissues.org
E-mail: secretary@firstissues.org

International Society of Reply Coupon Collectors
Peter Robin
P.O. Box 353
Bala Cynwyd PA 19004
E-mail: peterrobin@verizon.net

The Joint Stamp Issues Society
Richard Zimmermann
124, Avenue Guy de Coubertin
Saint Remy Les Chevreuse, F-78470
FRANCE
www.jointstampissues.net
E-mail: contact@jointstampissues.net

National Duck Stamp Collectors Society
Anthony J. Monico
P.O. Box 43
Harleysville PA 19438-0043
www.ndscs.org
E-mail: ndscs@ndscs.org

No Value Identified Club
Albert Sauvanet
Le Clos Royal B, Boulevard des Pas Enchantes
St. Sebastien-sur Loire, 44230
FRANCE
E-mail: alain.vailly@irin.univ nantes.fr

The Perfins Club
Jerry Hejduk
P.O. Box 490450.
Leesburg FL 34749-0450
Ph: (352) 326-2117
E-mail: flprepers@comcast.net

Postage Due Mail Study Group
John Rawlins
13, Longacre
Chelmsford, CM1 3BJ
UNITED KINGDOM
E-mail: john.rawlins2@ukonline.co.uk.

Post Mark Collectors Club
Beverly Proulx
7629 Homestead Drive
Baldwinsville NY 13027
Ph: (315) 638-0532
www.postmarks.org
E-mail: stampdance@yahoo.com

Postal History Society
Kalman V. Illyefalvi
869 Bridgewater Drive
New Oxford PA 17350-8206
Ph: (717) 624-5941
www.stampclubs.com
E-mail: kalphyl@juno.com

Precancel Stamp Society
Jerry Hejduk
P.O. Box 490450.
Leesburg FL 34749-0450
Ph: (352) 326-2117
www.precancels.com
E-mail: psspromosec@comcast.net

United Postal Stationery Society
Stuart Leven
P.O. Box 24764
San Jose CA 95154-4764
www.upss.org
E-mail: poststat@gmail.com

United States Possessions Philatelic Society
Geoffrey Brewster
6453 E. Stallion Rd.
Paradise Valley AZ 85253
Ph: (480) 607-7184
www.uspps.com
E-mail: patlabb@aol.com

Groups focusing on U.S. area philately as covered in the Standard Catalogue

Canal Zone Study Group
Richard H. Salz
60 27th Ave.
San Francisco CA 94121-1026

Carriers and Locals Society
Martin Richardson
P.O. Box 74
Grosse Ile MI 48138
www.pennypost.org
E-mail: martinr362@aol.com

Confederate Stamp Alliance
Patricia A. Kaufmann
10194 N. Old State Road
Lincoln DE 19960
Ph. (302) 422-2656
www.csalliance.org
E-mail: csaas@comcast.net

Hawaiian Philatelic Society
Kay H. Hoke
P.O. Box 10115
Honolulu HI 96816-0115
Ph: (808) 521-5721

Plate Number Coil Collectors Club
Gene Trinks
16415 W. Desert Wren Ct.
Surprise AZ 85374
Ph: (623) 322-4619
www.pnc3.org
E-mail: gctrinks@cox.net

Ryukyu Philatelic Specialist Society
Laura Edmonds, Secy.
P.O. Box 240177
Charlotte NC 28224-0177
Ph: (704) 519-5157
www.ryukyustamps.org
E-mail: secretary@ryukyustamps.org

United Nations Philatelists
Blanton Clement, Jr.
P.O. Box 146
Morrisville PA 19067-0146
www.unpi.com
E-mail: bclemjr@yahoo.com

United States Stamp Society
Executive Secretary
P.O. Box 6634
Katy TX 77491-6631
www.usstamps.org
E-mail: webmaster@usstamps.org

U.S. Cancellation Club
Roger Rhoads
6160 Brownstone Ct.
Mentor OH 44060
http://bob.trachimowicz.org/indfk.html
E-mail: rrrhoads@aol.com

U.S. Philatelic Classics Society
Rob Lund
2913 Fulton
Everett WA 98201-3733
www.uspcs.org
E-mail: membershipchairman@uspcs.org

Groups focusing on philately of foreign countries or regions

Aden & Somaliland Study Group
Gary Brown
P.O. Box 106
Briar Hill, Victoria, 3088
AUSTRALIA
E-mail: garyjohn951@optushome.com.au

American Society of Polar Philatelists (Antarctic areas)
Alan Warren
P.O. Box 39
Exton PA 19341-0039
www.polarphilatelists.org
E-mail: alanwar@att.net

Andorran Philatelic Study Circle
D. Hope
17 Hawthorn Dr.
Stalybridge, Cheshire, SK15 1UE
UNITED KINGDOM
apsc.free.fr
E-mail: apsc@free.fr

Australian States Study Circle of The Royal Sydney Philatelic Club
Ben Palmer
GPO 1751
Sydney, N.S.W., 2001
AUSTRALIA

Austria Philatelic Society
Ralph Schneider
P.O. Box 23049
Belleville IL 62223
Ph: (618) 277-6152
www.austriaphilatelicsociety.com
E-mail: rschneider39@charter.net

American Belgian Philatelic Society
Edward de Bary
11 Wakefield Dr. Apt. 2105
Asheville NC 28803
E-mail: belgam@charter.net

Bechuanalands and Botswana Society
Neville Midwood
69 Porlock Lane
Furzton, Milton Keynes, MK4 1JY
UNITED KINGDOM
www.nevsoft.com
E-mail: bbsoc@nevsoft.com

Bermuda Collectors Society
Thomas J. McMahon
P.O. Box 1949
Stuart FL 34995
www.bermudacollectorssociety.org
E-mail: science29@comcast.net

Brazil Philatelic Association
William V. Kriebel
1923 Manning St.
Philadelphia PA 19103-5728
Ph: (215) 735-3697
E-mail: kriebewv@drexel.edu

British Caribbean Philatelic Study Group
Dr. Reuben A. Ramkissoon
11075 Benton Street #236
Loma Linda CA 92354-3182
www.bcpsg.com
E-mail: rramkissoon@juno.com

The King George VI Collectors Society (British Commonwealth)
Brian Livingstone
21 York Mansions, Prince of Wales Drive
London, SW11 4DL
UNITED KINGDOM
www.kg6.info
E-mail: livingstone484@btinternet.com

British North America Philatelic Society (Canada & Provinces)
David G. Jones
184 Larkin Dr.
Nepean, ON, K2J 1H9
CANADA
www.bnaps.org
E-mail: shibumi.management@gmail.com

British West Indies Study Circle
John Seidl
4324 Granby Way
Marietta GA 30062
Ph: (770) 642-6424
www.bwisc.org
jseidl@mindspring.com

Burma Philatelic Study Circle
Michael Whittaker
1, Ecton Leys, Hillside
Rugby, Warwickshire, CV22 5SL
UNITED KINGDOM
www.burmastamps.homecall.co.uk
E-mail: whittaker2004@btinternet.com

Cape and Natal Study Circle
Dr. Guy Dillaway
P.O. Box 181
Weston MA 02493
www.nzsc.demon.co.uk

Ceylon Study Group
R. W. P. Frost
42 Lonsdale Road, Cannington
Bridgewater, Somerset, TA5 2JS
UNITED KINGDOM
E-mail: rodney.frost@tiscali.co.uk

Channel Islands Specialists Society
Moira Edwards
86, Hall Lane, Sandon,
Chelmsford, Essex, CM2 7RQ
UNITED KINGDOM
www.ciss1950.org.uk
E-mail: membership@ciss1950.org.uk

China Stamp Society
Paul H. Gault
P.O. Box 20711
Columbus OH 43220
www.chinastampsociety.org
E-mail: secretary@chinastampsociety.org

Colombia/Panama Philatelic Study Group (COPAPHIL)
Thomas P. Myers
P.O. Box 522
Gordonsville VA 22942
www.copaphil.org
E-mail: tpmphil@hotmail.com

Association Filatelic de Costa Rica
Giana Wayman
c/o Interlink 102, P.O. Box 52-6770
Miami, FL 33152
E-mail: scotland@racsa.co.cr

Society for Costa Rica Collectors
Dr. Hector R. Mena
P.O. Box 14831
Baton Rouge LA 70808
www.socorico.org
E-mail: hrmena@aol.com

International Cuban Philatelic Society
Ernesto Cuesta
P.O. Box 34434
Bethesda MD 20827
www.cubafil.org
E-mail: ecuesta@philat.com

Cuban Philatelic Society of America
P.O. Box 141656
Coral Gables FL 33114-1656
www.cubapsa.com
E-mail: cpsa.usa@gmail.com

Cyprus Study Circle
Colin Dear
10 Marne Close, Wem
Shropshire, SY4 5YE
UNITED KINGDOM
www.cyprusstudycircle.org/index.htm
E-mail: colindear@talktalk.net.

Society for Czechoslovak Philately
Phil Rhoade
905 E. Oakside St.
South Bend IN 46614
www.csphilately.org
E-mail: philip.rhoade@mnsu.edu

Danish West Indies Study Unit of the Scandinavian Collectors Club
Arnold Sorensen
7666 Edgedale Drive
Newburgh IN 47630
Ph: (812) 480-6532
www.scc-online.org
E-mail: valbydwi@hotmail.com

East Africa Study Circle
Jonathan Smalley
1 Lincoln Close
Tweeksbury, B91 1AE
UNITED KINGDOM
easc.org.uk
E-mail: jpasmalley@tiscali.co.uk

Egypt Study Circle
Mike Murphy
109 Chadwick Road
London, SE15 4PY
UNITED KINGDOM
Dick Wilson: North American Agent
egyptstudycircle.org.uk
E-mail: egyptstudycircle@hotmail.com

Estonian Philatelic Society
Juri Kirsimagi
29 Clifford Ave.
Pelham NY 10803
Ph: (914) 738-3713

Ethiopian Philatelic Society
Ulf Lindahl
21 Westview Place
Riverside CT 06878
Ph: (203) 866-3540
home.comcast.net/~fbheiser/ethiopia5.htm
E-mail: ulindahl@optonline.net

Falkland Islands Philatelic Study Group
Carl J. Faulkner
Williams Inn, On-the-Green
Williamstown MA 01267-2620
www.fipsg.org.uk
Ph: (413) 458-9371

Faroe Islands Study Circle
Norman Hudson
40 Queenís Road, Vicarís Cross
Chester, CH3 5HB
UNITED KINGDOM
www.faroeislandssc.org.
E-mail: jntropics@hotmail.com

Former French Colonies Specialist Society
BP 628
75367 Paris, Cedex 08
FRANCE
www.colfra.com
E-mail: clubcolfra@aol.com

France & Colonies Philatelic Society
Edward Grabowski
111 Prospect St., 4C
Westfield NJ 07090
www.franceandcolonies.org
E-mail: edjjg@alum.mit.edu

Germany Philatelic Society
P.O. Box 6547
Chesterfield MO 63006
www.gps.nu

Gibraltar Study Circle
David R. Stirrups
34 Glamis Drive
Dundee, DD2 1QP
UNITED KINGDOM
E-mail: drstirrups@dundee.ac.uk

Great Britain Collectors Club
Steve McGill
10309 Brookhollow Circle
Highlands Ranch CO 80129
www.gbstamps.com/gbcc
E-mail: steve.mcgill@comcast.net

International Society of Guatemala Collectors
Jaime Marckwordt
449 St. Francis Blvd.
Daly City CA 94015-2136
www.guatemalastamps.com

Haiti Philatelic Society
Ubaldo Del Toro
5709 Marble Archway
Alexandria VA 22315
www.haitiphilately.org
E-mail: u007ubi@aol.com

Hong Kong Stamp Society
Ming W. Tsang
P.O. Box 206
Glenside PA 19038

Society for Hungarian Philately
Robert Morgan
2201 Roscomare Rd.
Los Angeles CA 90077-2222
www.hungarianphilately.org
E-mail: bwilson1951@aol.com

India Study Circle
John Warren
P.O. Box 7326
Washington DC 20044
Ph: (202) 564-6876
www.indiastudycircle.org
E-mail: warren.john@epa.gov

Indian Ocean Study Circle
Mrs. S. Hopson
Field Acre, Hoe Benham
Newbury, Berkshire, RG20 8PD
UNITED KINGDOM

Society of Indo-China Philatelists
Ron Bentley
2600 North 24th Street
Arlington VA 22207
www.sicp-online.org
E-mail: ron.bentley@verizon.net

Iran Philatelic Study Circle
Mehdi Esmaili
P.O. Box 750096
Forest Hills NY 11375
www.iranphilatelic.org
E-mail: m.esmaili@earthlink.net

Eire Philatelic Association (Ireland)
David J. Brennan
P.O. Box 704
Bernardsville NJ 07924
eirephilatelicassoc.org
E-mail: brennan704@aol.com

Society of Israel Philatelists
Michael Bass
P.O. Box 507
Northfield OH 44067
www.israelstamps.com
israelstamps@gmail.com

Italy and Colonies Study Circle
Andrew DíAnneo
1085 Dunweal Lane
Calistoga CA 94515
www.icsc.pwp.blueyonder.co.uk
E-mail: audanneo@napanet.net

International Society for Japanese Philately
William Eisenhauer
P.O. Box 230462
Tigard OR 97281
www.isjp.org
E-mail: secretary@isjp.org

Korea Stamp Society
John E. Talmage
P.O. Box 6889
Oak Ridge TN 37831
www.pennfamily.org/KSS-USA
E-mail: jtalmage@usit.net

Latin American Philatelic Society
Jules K. Beck
30 1/2 Street #209
St. Louis Park MN 55426-3551

Liberian Philatelic Society
William Thomas Lockard
P.O. Box 106
Wellston OH 45692
Ph: (740) 384-2020
E-mail: tlockard@zoomnet.net

Liechtenstudy USA (Liechtenstein)
Paul Tremaine
410 S. W. Ninth St.
Dundee OR 97115
Ph: (503) 538-4500
www.liechtenstudy.org
E-mail: editor@liechtenstudy.org

Lithuania Philatelic Society
John Variakojis
3715 W. 68th St.
Chicago IL 60629
Ph: (773) 585-8649
http://lithuanianphilately.com/lps
E-mail: variakojis@sbcglobal.net

Luxembourg Collectors Club
Gary B. Little
7319 Beau Road
Sechelt, BC, VON 3A8
CANADA
lcc.luxcentral.com
E-mail: gary@luxcentral.com

Malaya Study Group
David Tett
P.O. Box 34
Wheathampstead, Herts, AL4 8JY
UNITED KINGDOM
www.m-s-g/org/uk
E-mail: davidtett@aol.com

Malta Study Circle
Alec Webster
50 Worcester Road
Sutton, Surrey, SM2 6QB
UNITED KINGDOM
E-mail: alecwebster50@hotmail.com

Mexico-Elmhurst Philatelic Society International
David Pietsch
P.O. Box 50997
Irvine CA 92619-0997
E-mail: mepsi@msn.com

Asociacion Mexicana de Filatelia AMEXFIL
Ave. 16 de Septiembre #6-401, Col. Centro
Mexico City DF, 06000
MEXICO
www.amexfil.org.mx
E-mail: carlosfet@prodigy.net.mx

Society for Moroccan and Tunisian Philately
206, bld. Pereire
75017 Paris
FRANCE
members.aol.com/Jhaik5814
E-mail: splm206@aol.com

Nepal & Tibet Philatelic Study Group
Roger D. Skinner
1020 Covington Road
Los Altos CA 94024-5003
Ph: (650) 968-4163
fuchs-online.com/ntpsc/
E-mail: colinhepper@hotmail.co.uk

American Society for Netherlands Philately
Hans Kremer
50 Rockport Ct.
Danville CA 94526
Ph: (925) 820-5841
www.angelfire.com/ca2/asnp
E-mail: hkremer@usa.net

New Zealand Society of Great Britain
Keith C. Collins
13 Briton Crescent
Sanderstead, Surrey, CR2 0JN
UNITED KINGDOM
www.cs.stir.ac.uk/~rgc/nzsgb
E-mail: rgc@cs.stir.ac.uk

Nicaragua Study Group
Erick Rodriguez
11817 S.W. 11th St.
Miami FL 33184-2501
clubs.yahoo.com/clubs/nicaraguastudygroup
E-mail: nsgsec@yahoo.com

Society of Australasian Specialists/Oceania
Stuart Leven
P.O. Box 24764
San Jose CA 95154-4764
Ph: (408) 978-0193
www.sasoceania.org
E-mail: sas_oceania@yahoo.com

Orange Free State Study Circle
J. R. Stroud
28 Oxford St.
Burnham-on-sea, Somerset, TA8 1LQ
UNITED KINGDOM
orangefreestatephilately.org.uk
E-mail: richardstroudph@gofast.co.uk

Pacific Islands Study Circle
John Ray
24 Woodvale Avenue
London, SE25 4AE
UNITED KINGDOM
www.pisc.org.uk
E-mail: info@pisc.org.uk

Pakistan Philatelic Study Circle
Jeff Siddiqui
P.O. Box 7002
Lynnwood WA 98046
E-mail: jeffsiddiqui@msn.com

Centro de Filatelistas Independientes de Panama
Vladimir Berrio-Lemm
Apartado 0823-02748
Plaza Concordia Panama,
PANAMA
E-mail: panahistoria@gmail.com

Papuan Philatelic Society
Steven Zirinsky
P.O. Box 49, Ansonia Station
New York NY 10023
Ph: (718) 706-0616
www.communigate.co.uk/york/pps
E-mail: szirinsky@cs.com

International Philippine Philatelic Society
Donald J. Peterson
7408 Alaska Ave., NW
Washington DC 20012
Ph: (202) 291-6229
www.theipps.info
E-mail: dpeterson@comcast.net

Pitcairn Islands Study Group
Dr. Everett L. Parker
249 NW Live Oak Place
Lake City FL 32055-8906
Ph: (386) 754-8524
www.pisg.net
E-mail: eparker@hughes.net

Polonus Philatelic Society (Poland)
Chris Kulpinski
9350 E. Palm Tree Dr.
Scottsdale AZ 85255
Ph: (480) 585-7114
www.polonus.org
E-mail: ctk@kulpinski.net

International Society for Portuguese Philately
Clyde Homen
1491 Bonnie View Rd.
Hollister CA 95023-5117
www.portugalstamps.com
E-mail: cjh1491@sbcglobal.net

Rhodesian Study Circle
William R. Wallace
P.O. Box 16381
San Francisco CA 94116
www.rhodesianstudycircle.org.uk
E-mail: bwall8rscr@earthlink.net

Rossica Society of Russian Philately
Edward J. Laveroni
P.O. Box 320997
Los Gatos CA 95032-0116
www.rossica.org
E-mail: ed.laveroni@rossica.org

St. Helena, Ascension & Tristan Da Cunha Philatelic Society
Dr. Everett L. Parker
249 NW Live Oak Place
Lake City FL 32055-8906
Ph: (386) 754-8524
www.atlanticislands.org
E-mail: eparker@hughes.net

St. Pierre & Miquelon Philatelic Society
James R. (Jim) Taylor
2335 Paliswood Rd. SW
Calgary, AB, T2V 3P6
CANADA

Associated Collectors of El Salvador
Joseph D. Hahn
1015 Old Boalsburg Rd. Apt G-5
State College PA 16801-6149
www.elsalvadorphilately.org
E-mail: joehahn2@yahoo.com

Fellowship of Samoa Specialists
Donald Mee
23 Leo Street
Christchurch, 8051
NEW ZEALAND
www.samoaexpress.org
E-mail: donanm@xtra.co.nz

Sarawak Specialists' Society
Stu Leven
P.O. Box 24764
San Jose CA 95154-4764
Ph: (408) 978-0193
www.britborneostamps.org.uk
www.s-s-s.org.uk
E-mail: stulev@ix.netcom.com

Scandinavian Collectors Club
Donald B. Brent
P.O. Box 13196
El Cajon CA 92020
www.scc-online.org
E-mail: dbrent47@sprynet.com

Slovakia Stamp Society
Jack Benchik
P.O. Box 555
Notre Dame IN 46556

Philatelic Society for Greater Southern Africa
Alan Hanks
34 Seaton Drive
Aurora, ON, L4G 2KI
CANADA
Ph: (905) 727-6993
www.psgsa.thestampweb.com
Email: alan.hanks@sympatico.ca

Spanish Philatelic Society
Robert H. Penn
1108 Walnut Drive
Danielsville PA 18038
Ph: (610) 767-6793
E-mail: roberthpenn@aol.com

Sudan Study Group
c/o North American Agent
Richard S. Wilson
53 Middle Patent Road
Bedford NY 10506
www.sudanstamps.org
E-mail: dadu1@verizon.net

American Helvetia Philatelic Society (Switzerland, Liechtenstein)
Richard T. Hall
P.O. Box 15053
Asheville NC 28813-0053
www.swiss-stamps.org
E-mail: secretary2@swiss-stamps.org

Tannu Tuva Collectors Society
Ken Simon
513 Sixth Ave. So.
Lake Worth FL 33460-4507
Ph: (561) 588-5954
www.tuva.tk
E-mail: yurttuva@yahoo.com

Society for Thai Philately
H. R. Blakeney
P.O. Box 25644
Oklahoma City OK 73125
E-mail: HRBlakeney@aol.com

Transvaal Study Circle
J. Woolgar
P.O. Box 379
Gravesend, DA11 9EW
UNITED KINGDOM
www.transvaal.org.uk

Ottoman and Near East Philatelic Society (Turkey and related areas)
Bob Stuchell
193 Valley Stream Lane
Wayne PA 19087
www.oneps.org
E-mail: rstuchell@msn.com

Ukrainian Philatelic & Numismatic Society
George Slusarczuk
P.O. Box 303
Southfields NY 10975-0303
www.upns.org
E-mail: Yurko@frontiernet.net

Vatican Philatelic Society
Sal Quinonez
1 Aldersgate, Apt. 1002
Riverhead NY 11901-1830
Ph: (516) 727-6426
www.vaticanphilately.org

British Virgin Islands Philatelic Society
Giorgio Migliavacca
P.O. Box 7007
St. Thomas VI 00801-0007
www.islandsun.com/FEATURES/bviphil9198.html
E-mail: issun@candwbvi.net

West Africa Study Circle
Dr. Peter Newroth
Suite 603
5332 Sayward Hill Crescent
Victoria, BC, V8Y 3H8
CANADA
www.wasc.org.uk/

Western Australia Study Group
Brian Pope
P.O. Box 423
Claremont, Western Australia, 6910
AUSTRALIA
www.wastudygroup.com
E-mail: black5swan@yahoo.com.au

Yugoslavia Study Group of the Croatian Philatelic Society
Michael Lenard
1514 North 3rd Ave.
Wausau WI 54401
Ph: (715) 675-2833
E-mail: mjlenard@aol.com

Topical Groups

Americana Unit
Dennis Dengel
17 Peckham Rd.
Poughkeepsie NY 12603-2018
www.americanaunit.org
E-mail: info@americanaunit.org

Astronomy Study Unit
John W. G. Budd
29203 Coharie Loop
San Antonio FL 33576-4643
Ph: (352) 588-4706
www.astronomystudyunit.com
E-mail: jwgbudd@earthlink.net

Bicycle Stamp Club
Tony Teideman
P.O. Box 90
Baulkham Hills, NSW, 1755
AUSTRALIA
members.tripod.com/~bicyclestamps
E-mail: tonimaur@bigpond.com

Biology Unit
Alan Hanks
34 Seaton Dr.
Aurora, ON, L4G 2K1
CANADA
Ph: (905) 727-6993

Bird Stamp Society
Graham Horsman
23 A East Main Street
Blackburn West Lothian
Scotland, EH47 7QR
UNITED KINGDOM
www.bird-stamps.org/bss
E-mail: graham_horsman7@msn.com

Canadiana Study Unit
John Peebles
P.O. Box 3262, Station ìBî
London, ON, N6A 4K3
CANADA
E-mail: c.s.u@sympatico.ca

Captain Cook Study Unit
Brian P. Sandford
173 Minuteman Dr.
Concord MA 01742-1923
www.captaincooksociety.com
E-mail: US@captaincooksociety.com

Casey Jones Railroad Unit
Dr. Roy Menninger
85 SW Pepper Tree Lane
Topeka KS 66611-2072
www.uqp.de/cjr/index.htm
E-mail: roymenn@sbcglobal.net

Cats on Stamps Study Unit
Mary Ann Brown
3006 Wade Rd.
Durham NC 27705
www.catsonstamps.org
E-mail: mabrown@nc.rr.com

Chemistry & Physics on Stamps Study Unit
Dr. Roland Hirsch
20458 Water Point Lane
Germantown MD 20874
www.cpossu.org
E-mail: rfhirsch@cpossu.org

Chess on Stamps Study Unit
Ray C. Alexis
608 Emery St.
Longmont CO 80501
E-mail: chessstuff911459@aol.

Christmas Philatelic Club
Linda Lawrence
312 Northwood Drive
Lexington KY 40505
www.web.295.ca/cpc/
E-mail: stamplinda@aol.com

Christopher Columbus Philatelic Society
Donald R. Ager
P.O. Box 71
Hillsboro NH 03244-0071
ccps.maphist.nl/
Ph: (603) 464-5379
E-mail: meganddon@tds.net

Collectors of Religion on Stamps
Verna Shackleton
425 North Linwood Avenue #110
Appleton WI 54914
www://my.vbe.com/~cmfourl/coros1.htm
E-mail: corosec@sbcglobal.net

Dogs on Stamps Study Unit
Morris Raskin
202A Newport Rd.
Monroe Township NJ 08831
Ph: (609) 655-7411
www.dossu.org
E-mail: mraskin@cellurian.com

Earth's Physical Features Study Group
Fred Klein
515 Magdalena Ave.
Los Altos CA 94024
epfsu.jeffhayward.com

Ebony Society of Philatelic Events and Reflections, Inc (African-American topicals)
Manuel Gilyard
800 Riverside Drive, Ste 4H
New York NY 10032-7412
www.esperstamps.org
E-mail: gilyardmani@aol.com

Europa Study Unit
Donald W. Smith
P.O. Box 576
Johnstown PA 15907-0576
www.europastudyunit.org/
E-mail: eunity@aol.com or donsmith65@msn.com

Fine & Performing Arts
Deborah L. Washington
6922 So. Jeffery Boulevard
#7 - North
Chicago IL 60649
E-mail: brasslady@comcast.net

Fire Service in Philately
Brian R. Engler, Sr.
726 1/2 W. Tilghman St.
Allentown PA 18102-2324
Ph: (610) 433-2782
www.firestamps.com

Gay & Lesbian History on Stamps Club
Joe Petronie
P.O. Box 190842
Dallas TX 75219-0842
www.glhsc.org
E-mail: glhsc@aol.com

Gems, Minerals & Jewelry Study Unit
George Young
P.O. Box 632
Tewksbury MA 01876-0632
Ph: (978) 851-8283
www.rockhounds.com/rockshop/gmjsuapp.txt
E-mail: george-young@msn.com

Graphics Philately Association
Mark H Winnegrad
P.O. Box 380
Bronx NY 10462-0380
www.graphics-stamps.org
E-mail: indybruce1@yahoo.com

Journalists, Authors & Poets on Stamps
Ms. Lee Straayer
P.O. Box 6808
Champaign IL 61826
E-mail: lstraayer@dcbnet.com

Lighthouse Stamp Society
Dalene Thomas
8612 West Warren Lane
Lakewood CO 80227-2352
Ph: (303) 986-6620
www.lighthousestampsociety.org
E-mail: dalene@lighthousestampsociety.org

Lions International Stamp Club
John Bargus
108-2777 Barry Rd. RR 2
Mill Bay, BC, V0R 2P2
CANADA
Ph: (250) 743-5782

Mahatma Gandhi On Stamps Study Circle
Pramod Shivagunde
Pratik Clinic, Akluj
Solapur, Maharashtra, 413101
INDIA
E-mail: drnanda@bom6.vsnl.net.in

Mask Study Unit
Carolyn Weber
1220 Johnson Drive, Villa 104
Ventura CA 93003-0540
E-mail: cweber@venturalink.net

Masonic Study Unit
Stanley R. Longenecker
930 Wood St.
Mount Joy PA 17552-1926
Ph: (717) 669-9094
E-mail: natsco@usa.net

Mathematical Study Unit
Estelle Buccino
5615 Glenwood Rd.
Bethesda MD 20817-6727
Ph: (301) 718-8898
www.math.ttu.edu/msu/
E-mail: montystrauss@gmail.com

Medical Subjects Unit
Dr. Frederick C. Skvara
P.O. Box 6228
Bridgewater NJ 08807
E-mail: fcskvara@optonline.net

Military Postal History Society
Ed Dubin
One South Wacker Drive, Suite 3500
Chicago IL 60606
www.militaryPHS.org
E-mail: dubine@comcast.net

Mourning Stamps and Covers Club
James Bailey, Jr.
P.O. Box 937
Brownwood TX 76804
E-mail: jfbailey238@earthlink.net

Napoleonic Age Philatelists
Ken Berry
7513 Clayton Dr.
Oklahoma City OK 73132-5636
Ph: (405) 721-0044
www.nap-stamps.org
E-mail: krb2@earthlink.net

Old World Archeological Study Unit
Caroline Scannel
11 Dawn Drive
Smithtown NY 11787-1761
www.owasu.org
E-mail: editor@owasu.org

Petroleum Philatelic Society International
Dr. Chris Coggins
174 Old Bedford Road
Luton, England, LU2 7HW
UNITED KINGDOM
E-mail: WAMTECH@Luton174.fsnet.co.uk

Philatelic Computing Study Group
Robert de Violini
P.O. Box 5025
Oxnard CA 93031-5025
www.pcsg.org
E-mail: dviolini@adelphia.net

Philatelic Lepidopterists' Association
Alan Hanks
34 Seaton Dr.
Aurora, ON, L4G 2K1
CANADA
Ph: (905) 727-6933
E-mail: alan.hanks@sympatico.ca

Rotary on Stamps Unit
Gerald L. Fitzsimmons
105 Calla Ricardo
Victoria TX 77904
rotaryonstamps.org
E-mail: glfitz@suddenlink.net

Scouts on Stamps Society International
Lawrence Clay
P.O. Box 6228
Kennewick WA 99336
Ph: (509) 735-3731
www.sossi.org
E-mail: lclay3731@charter.net

Ships on Stamps Unit
Les Smith
302 Conklin Avenue
Penticton, BC, V2A 2T4
CANADA
Ph: (250) 493-7486
www.shipsonstamps.org
E-mail: lessmith440@shaw.ca

Space Unit
Carmine Torrisi
P.O. Box 780241
Maspeth NY 11378
Ph: (917) 620-5687
stargate.1usa.com/stamps/
E-mail: ctorrisi1@nyc.rr.com

Sports Philatelists International
Margaret Jones
705 S Laclede Station Rd S, Apt 163.
St. Louis MO 63119-4969
www.sportstamps.org

Stamps on Stamps Collectors Club
Alf Jordan
156 West Elm Street
Yarmouth ME 04096
www.stampsonstamps.org
E-mail: ajordan1@maine.rr.com

Windmill Study Unit
Walter J. Hollien
P.O. Box 346
Long Valley NJ 07853-0346
Ph: (862) 812-0030
E-mail: whollien@earthlink.net

Wine On Stamps Study Unit
Bruce L. Johnson
115 Raintree Drive
Zionsville IN 46077
www.wine-on-stamps.org
E-mail: indybruce@yahoo.com

Women on Stamps Study Unit
Hugh Gottfried
2232 26th St.
Santa Monica CA 90405-1902
E-mail: hgottfried@adelphia.net

Zeppelin Collectors Club
Cheryl Ganz
P.O. Box 77196
Washington DC 20013
www.americanairmailsociety.org

Expertizing Services

The following organizations will, for a fee, provide expert opinions about stamps submitted to them. Collectors should contact these organizations to find out about their fees and requirements before submiting philatelic material to them. The listing of these groups here is not intended as an endorsement by Scott Publishing Co.

General Expertizing Services

American Philatelic Expertizing Service (a service of the American Philatelic Society)
100 Match Factory Place
Bellefonte PA 16823-1367
Ph: (814) 237-3803
Fax: (814) 237-6128
www.stamps.org
E-mail: ambristo@stamps.org
Areas of Expertise: Worldwide

B. P. A. Expertising, Ltd.
P.O. Box 137
Leatherhead, Surrey, KT22 0RG
UNITED KINGDOM
E-mail: sec.bpa@tcom.co.uk
Areas of Expertise: British Commonwealth, Great Britain, Classics of Europe, South America and the Far East

Philatelic Foundation
70 West 40th St., 15th Floor
New York NY 10018
Ph: (212) 221-6555
Fax: (212) 221-6208
www.philatelicfoundation.org
E-mail:philatelicfoundation@verizon.net
Areas of Expertise: U.S. & Worldwide

Philatelic Stamp Authentication and Grading, Inc.
P.O. Box 56-2111
Miami FL 33256-2111
Customer Service: (305) 345-9864
www.stampauthentication.com
E-mail: info@stampauthentication.com

Professional Stamp Experts
P.O. Box 6170
Newport Beach CA 92658
Ph: (877) STAMP-88
Fax: (949) 833-7955
www.collectors.com/pse
E-mail: pseinfo@collectors.com
Areas of Expertise: Stamps and covers of U.S., U.S. Possessions, British Commonwealth

Royal Philatelic Society Expert Committee
41 Devonshire Place
London, W1N 1PE
UNITED KINGDOM
www.rpsl.org.uk/experts.html
E-mail: experts@rpsl.org.uk
Areas of Expertise: All

Expertizing Services Covering Specific Fields Or Countries

China Stamp Society Expertizing Service
1050 West Blue Ridge Blvd
Kansas City MO 64145
Ph: (816) 942-6300
E-mail: hjmesq@aol.com
Areas of Expertise: China

Confederate Stamp Alliance Authentication Service
Gen. Frank Crown, Jr.
P.O. Box 278
Capshaw AL 35742-0396
Ph: (302) 422-2656
Fax: (302) 424-1990
www.csalliance.org
E-mail: csaas@knology.net
Areas of Expertise: Confederate stamps and postal history

Errors, Freaks and Oddities Collectors Club Expertizing Service
138 East Lakemont Dr.
Kingsland GA 31548
Ph: (912) 729-1573
Areas of Expertise: U.S. errors, freaks and oddities

Estonian Philatelic Society Expertizing Service
39 Clafford Lane
Melville NY 11747
Ph: (516) 421-2078
E-mail: esto4@aol.com
Areas of Expertise: Estonia

Hawaiian Philatelic Society Expertizing Service
P.O. Box 10115
Honolulu HI 96816-0115
Areas of Expertise: Hawaii

Hong Kong Stamp Society Expertizing Service
P.O. Box 206
Glenside PA 19038
Fax: (215) 576-6850
Areas of Expertise: Hong Kong

International Association of Philatelic Experts
United States Associate members:

Paul Buchsbayew
119 W. 57th St.
New York NY 10019
Ph: (212) 977-7734
Fax: (212) 977-8653
Areas of Expertise: Russia, Soviet Union

William T. Crowe
P.O. Box 2090
Danbury CT 06813-2090
E-mail: wtcrowe@aol.com
Areas of Expertise: United States

John Lievsay
(see American Philatelic Expertizing Service and Philatelic Foundation)
Areas of Expertise: France

Robert W. Lyman
P.O. Box 348
Irvington on Hudson NY 10533
Ph and Fax: (914) 591-6937
Areas of Expertise: British North America, New Zealand

Robert Odenweller
P.O. Box 401
Bernardsville NJ 07924-0401
Ph and Fax: (908) 766-5460
Areas of Expertise: New Zealand, Samoa to 1900

Sergio Sismondo
10035 Carousel Center Dr.
Syracuse NY 13290-0001
Ph: (315) 422-2331
Fax: (315) 422-2956
Areas of Expertise: British East Africa, Camerouns, Cape of Good Hope, Canada, British North America

International Society for Japanese Philately Expertizing Committee
132 North Pine Terrace
Staten Island NY 10312-4052
Ph: (718) 227-5229
Areas of Expertise: Japan and related areas, except WWII Japanese Occupation issues

International Society for Portuguese Philately Expertizing Service
P.O. Box 43146
Philadelphia PA 19129-3146
Ph: (215) 843-2106
Fax: (215) 843-2106
E-mail: s.s.washburne@worldnet.att.net
Areas of Expertise: Portugal and Colonies

Mexico-Elmhurst Philatelic Society International Expert Committee
P.O. Box 1133
West Covina CA 91793
Areas of Expertise: Mexico

Ukrainian Philatelic & Numismatic Society Expertizing Service
30552 Dell Lane
Warren MI 48092-1862
Areas of Expertise: Ukraine, Western Ukraine

V. G. Greene Philatelic Research Foundation
P.O. Box 204, Station Q
Toronto, ON, M4T 2M1
CANADA
Ph: (416) 921-2073
Fax: (416) 921-1282
E-mail: vggfoundation@on.aibn.com
www.greenefoundation.ca
Areas of Expertise: British North America

Information on Catalogue Values, Grade and Condition

Catalogue Value

The Scott Catalogue value is a retail value; that is, an amount you could expect to pay for a stamp in the grade of Very Fine with no faults. Any exceptions to the grade valued will be noted in the text. The general introduction on the following pages and the individual section introductions further explain the type of material that is valued. The value listed for any given stamp is a reference that reflects recent actual dealer selling prices for that item.

Dealer retail price lists, public auction results, published prices in advertising and individual solicitation of retail prices from dealers, collectors and specialty organizations have been used in establishing the values found in this catalogue. Scott Publishing Co. values stamps, but Scott is not a company engaged in the business of buying and selling stamps as a dealer.

Use this catalogue as a guide for buying and selling. The actual price you pay for a stamp may be higher or lower than the catalogue value because of many different factors, including the amount of personal service a dealer offers, or increased or decreased interest in the country or topic represented by a stamp or set. An item may occasionally be offered at a lower price as a "loss leader," or as part of a special sale. You also may obtain an item inexpensively at public auction because of little interest at that time or as part of a large lot.

Stamps that are of a lesser grade than Very Fine, or those with condition problems, generally trade at lower prices than those given in this catalogue. Stamps of exceptional quality in both grade and condition often command higher prices than those listed.

Values for pre-1900 unused issues are for stamps with approximately half or more of their original gum. Stamps with most or all of their original gum may be expected to sell for more, and stamps with less than half of their original gum may be expected to sell for somewhat less than the values listed. On rarer stamps, it may be expected that the original gum will be somewhat more disturbed than it will be on more common issues. Post-1900 unused issues are assumed to have full original gum. From breakpoints in most countries' listings, stamps are valued as never hinged, due to the wide availability of stamps in that condition. These notations are prominently placed in the listings and in the country information preceding the listings. Some countries also feature listings with dual values for hinged and never-hinged stamps.

Grade

A stamp's grade and condition are crucial to its value. The accompanying illustrations show examples of Very Fine stamps from different time periods, along with examples of stamps in Fine to Very Fine and Extremely Fine grades as points of reference. When a stamp seller offers a stamp in any grade from fine to superb without further qualifying statements, that stamp should not only have the centering grade as defined, but it also should be free of faults or other condition problems.

FINE stamps (illustrations not shown) have designs that are quite off center, with the perforations on one or two sides very close to the design but not quite touching it. There is white space between the perforations and the design that is minimal but evident to the unaided eye. Imperforate stamps may have small margins, and earlier issues may show the design just touching one edge of the stamp design. Very early perforated issues normally will have the perforations slightly cutting into the design. Used stamps may have heavier than usual cancellations.

FINE-VERY FINE stamps will be somewhat off center on one side, or slightly off center on two sides. Imperforate stamps will have two margins of at least normal size, and the design will not touch any edge. For perforated stamps, the perfs are well clear of the design, but are still noticeably off center. *However, early issues of a country may be printed in such a way that the design naturally is very close to the edges. In these cases, the perforations may cut into the design very slightly.* Used stamps will not have a cancellation that detracts from the design.

VERY FINE stamps will be just slightly off center on one or two sides, but the design will be well clear of the edge. The stamp will present a nice, balanced appearance. Imperforate stamps will be well centered within normal-sized margins. *However, early issues of many countries may be printed in such a way that the perforations may touch the design on one or more sides. Where this is the case, a boxed note will be found defining the centering and margins of the stamps being valued.* Used stamps will have light or otherwise neat cancellations. This is the grade used to establish Scott Catalogue values.

EXTREMELY FINE stamps are close to being perfectly centered. Imperforate stamps will have even margins that are slightly larger than normal. Even the earliest perforated issues will have perforations clear of the design on all sides.

Scott Publishing Co. recognizes that there is no formally enforced grading scheme for postage stamps, and that the final price you pay or obtain for a stamp will be determined by individual agreement at the time of transaction.

Condition

Grade addresses only centering and (for used stamps) cancellation. *Condition* refers to factors other than grade that affect a stamp's desirability.

Factors that can increase the value of a stamp include exceptionally wide margins, particularly fresh color, the presence of selvage, and plate or die varieties. Unusual cancels on used stamps (particularly those of the 19th century) can greatly enhance their value as well.

Factors other than faults that decrease the value of a stamp include loss of original gum, regumming, a hinge remnant or foreign object adhering to the gum, natural inclusions, straight edges, and markings or notations applied by collectors or dealers.

Faults include missing pieces, tears, pin or other holes, surface scuffs, thin spots, creases, toning, short or pulled perforations, clipped perforations, oxidation or other forms of color changelings, soiling, stains, and such man-made changes as reperforations or the chemical removal or lightening of a cancellation.

Grading Illustrations

On the following two pages are illustrations of various stamps from countries appearing in this volume. These stamps are arranged by country, and they represent early or important issues that are often found in widely different grades in the marketplace. The editors believe the illustrations will prove useful in showing the margin size and centering that will be seen on the various issues.

In addition to the matters of margin size and centering, collectors are reminded that the very fine stamps valued in the Scott catalogues also will possess fresh color and intact perforations, and they will be free from defects.

Examples shown are computer-manipulated images made from single digitized master illustrations.

Stamp Illustrations Used in the Catalogue

It is important to note that the stamp images used for identification purposes in this catlaogue may not be indicative of the grade of stamp being valued. Refer to the written discussion of grades on this page and to the grading illustrations on the following two pages for grading information.

Fine-Very Fine

SCOTT CATALOGUES VALUE STAMPS IN THIS GRADE

Very Fine

Extremely Fine

Fine-Very Fine

SCOTT CATALOGUES VALUE STAMPS IN THIS GRADE

Very Fine

Extremely Fine

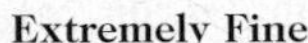

Fine-Very Fine

SCOTT CATALOGUES VALUE STAMPS IN THIS GRADE

Extremely Fine

Fine-Very Fine

SCOTT CATALOGUES VALUE STAMPS IN THIS GRADE

Very Fine

Extremely Fine

For purposes of helping to determine the gum condition and value of an unused stamp, Scott Publishing Co. presents the following chart which details different gum conditions and indicates how the conditions correlate with the Scott values for unused stamps. Used together, the Illustrated Grading Chart on the previous pages and this Illustrated Gum Chart should allow catalogue users to better understand the grade and gum condition of stamps valued in the Scott catalogues.

Gum Categories:	**MINT N.H.**	**ORIGINAL GUM (O.G.)**				**NO GUM**
	 **Mint Never Hinged** *Free from any disturbance*	 **Lightly Hinged** *Faint impression of a removed hinge over a small area*	 **Hinge Mark or Remnant** *Prominent hinged spot with part or all of the hinge remaining*	**Large part o.g.** *Approximately half or more of the gum intact*	**Small part o.g.** *Approximately less than half of the gum intact*	 **No gum** *Only if issued with gum*
Commonly Used Symbol:	★★	★	★	★	★	(★)
Pre-1900 Issues (Pre-1881 for U.S.)	*Very fine pre-1900 stamps in these categories trade at a premium over Scott value*			Scott Value for "Unused"		Scott "No Gum" listings for selected unused classic stamps
From 1900 to break-points for listings of never-hinged stamps	Scott "Never Hinged" listings for selected unused stamps	Scott Value for "Unused" (Actual value will be affected by the degree of hinging of the full o.g.)				
From breakpoints noted for many countries	Scott Value for "Unused"					

Never Hinged (NH; ★★): A never-hinged stamp will have full original gum that will have no hinge mark or disturbance. The presence of an expertizer's mark does not disqualify a stamp from this designation.

Original Gum (OG; ★): Pre-1900 stamps should have approximately half or more of their original gum. On rarer stamps, it may be expected that the original gum will be somewhat more disturbed than it will be on more common issues. Post-1900 stamps should have full original gum. Original gum will show some disturbance caused by a previous hinge(s) which may be present or entirely removed. The actual value of a post-1900 stamp will be affected by the degree of hinging of the full original gum.

Disturbed Original Gum: Gum showing noticeable effects of humidity, climate or hinging over more than half of the gum. The significance of gum disturbance in valuing a stamp in any of the Original Gum categories depends on the degree of disturbance, the rarity and normal gum condition of the issue and other variables affecting quality.

Regummed (RG; (★)): A regummed stamp is a stamp without gum that has had some type of gum privately applied at a time after it was issued. This normally is done to deceive collectors and/or dealers into thinking that the stamp has original gum and therefore has a higher value. A regummed stamp is considered the same as a stamp with none of its original gum for purposes of grading.

Understanding the Listings

On the opposite page is an enlarged "typical" listing from this catalogue. Below are detailed explanations of each of the highlighted parts of the listing.

1 Scott number — Scott catalogue numbers are used to identify specific items when buying, selling or trading stamps. Each listed postage stamp from every country has a unique Scott catalogue number. Therefore, Germany Scott 99, for example, can only refer to a single stamp. Although the Scott catalogue usually lists stamps in chronological order by date of issue, there are exceptions. When a country has issued a set of stamps over a period of time, those stamps within the set are kept together without regard to date of issue. This follows the normal collecting approach of keeping stamps in their natural sets.

When a country issues a set of stamps over a period of time, a group of consecutive catalogue numbers is reserved for the stamps in that set, as issued. If that group of numbers proves to be too few, capital-letter suffixes, such as "A" or "B," may be added to existing numbers to create enough catalogue numbers to cover all items in the set. A capital-letter suffix indicates a major Scott catalogue number listing. Scott generally uses a suffix letter only once. Therefore, a catalogue number listing with a capital-letter suffix will seldom be found with the same letter (lower case) used as a minor-letter listing. If there is a Scott 16A in a set, for example, there will seldom be a Scott 16a. However, a minor-letter "a" listing may be added to a major number containing an "A" suffix (Scott 16Aa, for example).

Suffix letters are cumulative. A minor "b" variety of Scott 16A would be Scott 16Ab, not Scott 16b.

There are times when a reserved block of Scott catalogue numbers is too large for a set, leaving some numbers unused. Such gaps in the numbering sequence also occur when the catalogue editors move an item's listing elsewhere or have removed it entirely from the catalogue. Scott does not attempt to account for every possible number, but rather attempts to assure that each stamp is assigned its own number.

Scott numbers designating regular postage normally are only numerals. Scott numbers for other types of stamps, such as air post, semi-postal, postal tax, postage due, occupation and others have a prefix consisting of one or more capital letters or a combination of numerals and capital letters.

2 Illustration number — Illustration or design-type numbers are used to identify each catalogue illustration. For most sets, the lowest face-value stamp is shown. It then serves as an example of the basic design approach for other stamps not illustrated. Where more than one stamp use the same illustration number, but have differences in design, the design paragraph or the description line clearly indicates the design on each stamp not illustrated. Where there are both vertical and horizontal designs in a set, a single illustration may be used, with the exceptions noted in the design paragraph or description line.

When an illustration is followed by a lower-case letter in parentheses, such as "A2(b)," the trailing letter indicates which overprint or surcharge illustration applies.

Illustrations normally are 70 percent of the original size of the stamp. Oversized stamps, blocks and souvenir sheets are reduced even more. Overprints and surcharges are shown at 100 percent of their original size if shown alone, but are 70 percent of original size if shown on stamps. In some cases, the illustration will be placed above the set, between listings or omitted completely. Overprint and surcharge illustrations are not placed in this catalogue for purposes of expertizing stamps.

3 Paper color — The color of a stamp's paper is noted in italic type when the paper used is not white.

4 Listing styles — There are two principal types of catalogue listings: major and minor.

Major listings are in a larger type style than minor listings. The catalogue number is a numeral that can be found with or without a capital-letter suffix, and with or without a prefix.

Minor listings are in a smaller type style and have a small-letter suffix or (if the listing immediately follows that of the major number) may show only the letter. These listings identify a variety of the major item. Examples include perforation and shade differences, multiples (some souvenir sheets, booklet panes and se-tenant combinations), and singles of multiples.

Examples of major number listings include 16, 28A, B97, C13A, 10N5, and 10N6A. Examples of minor numbers are 16a and C13Ab.

5 Basic information about a stamp or set — Introducing each stamp issue is a small section (usually a line listing) of basic information about a stamp or set. This section normally includes the date of issue, method of printing, perforation, watermark and, sometimes, some additional information of note. *Printing method, perforation and watermark apply to the following sets until a change is noted.* Stamps created by overprinting or surcharging previous issues are assumed to have the same perforation, watermark, printing method and other production characteristics as the original. Dates of issue are as precise as Scott is able to confirm and often reflect the dates on first-day covers, rather than the actual date of release.

6 Denomination — This normally refers to the face value of the stamp; that is, the cost of the unused stamp at the post office at the time of issue. When a denomination is shown in parentheses, it does not appear on the stamp. This includes the non-denominated stamps of the United States, Brazil and Great Britain, for example.

7 Color or other description — This area provides information to solidify identification of a stamp. In many recent cases, a description of the stamp design appears in this space, rather than a listing of colors.

8 Year of issue — In stamp sets that have been released in a period that spans more than a year, the number shown in parentheses is the year that stamp first appeared. Stamps without a date appeared during the first year of the issue. Dates are not always given for minor varieties.

9 Value unused and Value used — The Scott catalogue values are based on stamps that are in a grade of Very Fine unless stated otherwise. Unused values refer to items that have not seen postal, revenue or any other duty for which they were intended. Pre-1900 unused stamps that were issued with gum must have at least most of their original gum. Later issues are assumed to have full original gum. From breakpoints specified in most countries' listings, stamps are valued as never hinged. Stamps issued without gum are noted. Modern issues with PVA or other synthetic adhesives may appear ungummed. Unused self-adhesive stamps are valued as appearing undisturbed on their original backing paper. Values for used self-adhesive stamps are for examples either on piece or off piece. For a more detailed explanation of these values, please see the "Catalogue Value," "Condition" and "Understanding Valuing Notations" sections elsewhere in this introduction.

In some cases, where used stamps are more valuable than unused stamps, the value is for an example with a contemporaneous cancel, rather than a modern cancel or a smudge or other unclear marking. For those stamps that were released for postal and fiscal purposes, the used value represents a postally used stamp. Stamps with revenue cancels generally sell for less.

Stamps separated from a complete se-tenant multiple usually will be worth less than a pro-rated portion of the se-tenant multiple, and stamps lacking the attached labels that are noted in the listings will be worth less than the values shown.

10 Changes in basic set information — Bold type is used to show any changes in the basic data given for a set of stamps. These basic data categories include perforation gauge measurement, paper type, printing method and watermark.

11 Total value of a set — The total value of sets of three or more stamps issued after 1900 are shown. The set line also notes the range of Scott numbers and total number of stamps included in the grouping. The actual value of a set consisting predominantly of stamps having the minimum value of twenty cents may be less than the total value shown. Similary, the actual value or catalogue value of se-tenant pairs or of blocks consisting of stamps having the minimum value of twenty cents may be less than the catalogue values of the component parts.

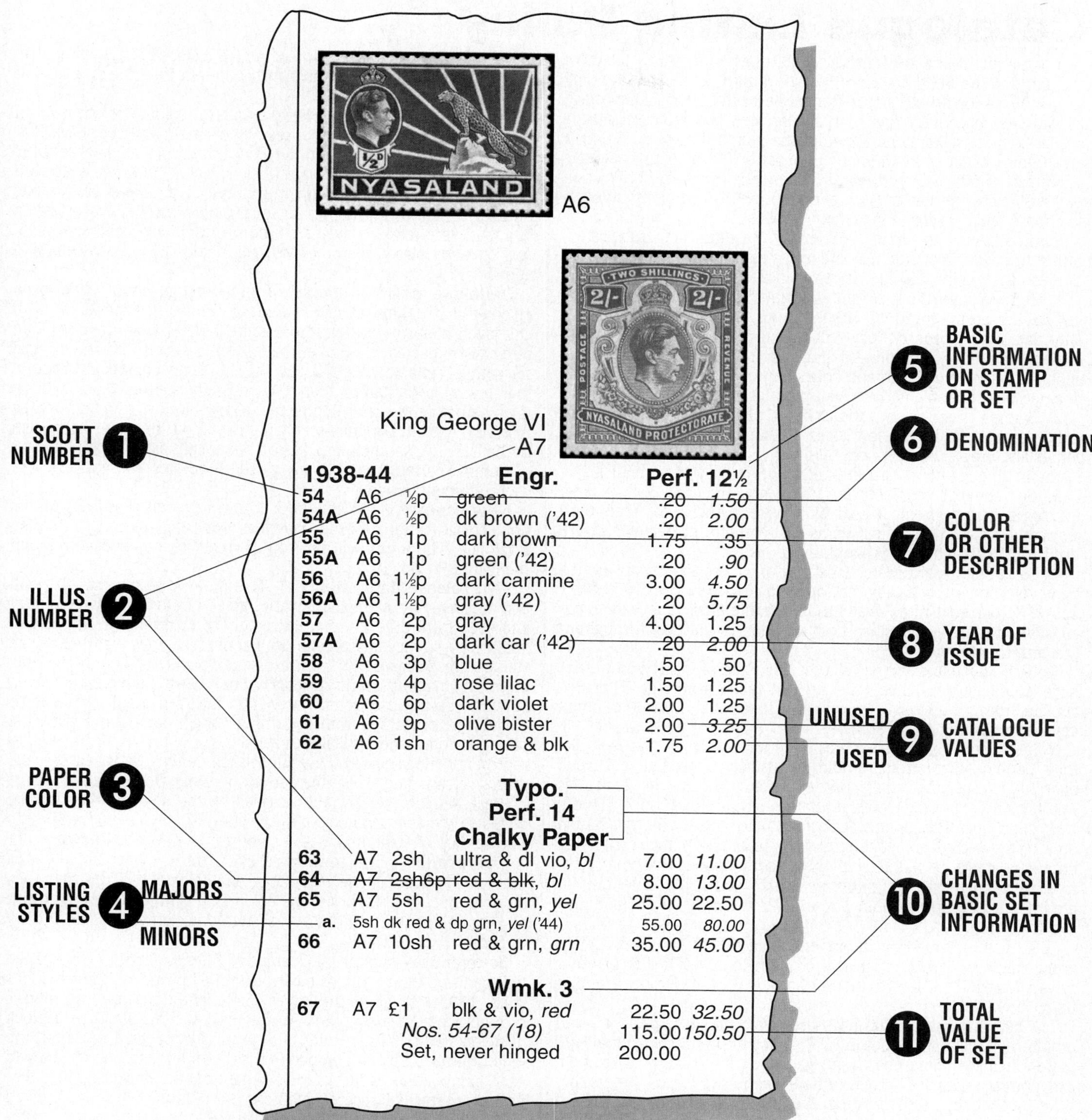
NYASALAND
A6
TWO SHILLINGS
2/- 2/-
POSTAGE REVENUE
NYASALAND PROTECTORATE
King George VI
A7
1938-44 Engr. Perf. 12½
54 A6 ½p green .20 1.50
54A A6 ½p dk brown ('42) .20 2.00
55 A6 1p dark brown 1.75 .35
55A A6 1p green ('42) .20 .90
56 A6 1½p dark carmine 3.00 4.50
56A A6 1½p gray ('42) .20 5.75
57 A6 2p gray 4.00 1.25
57A A6 2p dark car ('42) .20 2.00
58 A6 3p blue .50 .50
59 A6 4p rose lilac 1.50 1.25
60 A6 6p dark violet 2.00 1.25
61 A6 9p olive bister 2.00 3.25
62 A6 1sh orange & blk 1.75 2.00
Typo.
Perf. 14
Chalky Paper
63 A7 2sh ultra & dl vio, bl 7.00 11.00
64 A7 2sh6p red & blk, bl 8.00 13.00
65 A7 5sh red & grn, yel 25.00 22.50
a. 5sh dk red & dp grn, yel ('44) 55.00 80.00
66 A7 10sh red & grn, grn 35.00 45.00
Wmk. 3
67 A7 £1 blk & vio, red 22.50 32.50
Nos. 54-67 (18) 115.00 150.50
Set, never hinged 200.00
SCOTT NUMBER 1
ILLUS. NUMBER 2
PAPER COLOR 3
LISTING STYLES 4
MAJORS
MINORS
5 BASIC INFORMATION ON STAMP OR SET
6 DENOMINATION
7 COLOR OR OTHER DESCRIPTION
8 YEAR OF ISSUE
UNUSED
USED
9 CATALOGUE VALUES
10 CHANGES IN BASIC SET INFORMATION
11 TOTAL VALUE OF SET

Catalogue Listing Policy

It is the intent of Scott Publishing Co. to list all postage stamps of the world in the *Scott Standard Postage Stamp Catalogue*. The only strict criteria for listing is that stamps be decreed legal for postage by the issuing country and that the issuing country actually have an operating postal system. Whether the primary intent of issuing a given stamp or set was for sale to postal patrons or to stamp collectors is not part of our listing criteria. Scott's role is to provide basic comprehensive postage stamp information. It is up to each stamp collector to choose which items to include in a collection.

It is Scott's objective to seek reasons why a stamp should be listed, rather than why it should not. Nevertheless, there are certain types of items that will not be listed. These include the following:

1. Unissued items that are not officially distributed or released by the issuing postal authority. If such items are officially issued at a later date by the country, they will be listed. Unissued items consist of those that have been printed and then held from sale for reasons such as change in government, errors found on stamps or something deemed objectionable about a stamp subject or design.

2. Stamps "issued" by non-existent postal entities or fantasy countries, such as Nagaland, Occusi-Ambeno, Staffa, Sedang, Torres Straits and others. Also, stamps "issued" in the names of legitimate, stamp-issuing countries that are not authorized by those countries.

3. Semi-official or unofficial items not required for postage. Examples include items issued by private agencies for their own express services. When such items are required for delivery, or are valid as prepayment of postage, they are listed.

4. Local stamps issued for local use only. Postage stamps issued by governments specifically for "domestic" use, such as Haiti Scott 219-228, or the United States non-denominated stamps, are not considered to be locals, since they are valid for postage throughout the country of origin.

5. Items not valid for postal use. For example, a few countries have issued souvenir sheets that are not valid for postage. This area also includes a number of worldwide charity labels (some denominated) that do not pay postage.

6. Intentional varieties, such as imperforate stamps that look like their perforated counterparts and are usually issued in very small quantities. Also, other egregiously exploitative issues such as stamps sold for far more than face value, stamps purposefully issued in artificially small quantities or only against advance orders, stamps awarded only to a selected audience such as a philatelic bureau's standing order customers, or stamps sold only in conjunction with other products. All of these kinds of items are usually controlled issues and/or are intended for speculation. These items normally will be included in a footnote.

7. Items distributed by the issuing government only to a limited group, club, philatelic exhibition or a single stamp dealer or other private company. These items normally will be included in a footnote.

The fact that a stamp has been used successfully as postage, even on international mail, is not in itself sufficient proof that it was legitimately issued. Numerous examples of so-called stamps from non-existent countries are known to have been used to post letters that have successfully passed through the international mail system.

There are certain items that are subject to interpretation. When a stamp falls outside our specifications, it may be listed along with a cautionary footnote.

A number of factors are considered in our approach to analyzing how a stamp is listed. The following list of factors is presented to share with you, the catalogue user, the complexity of the listing process.

Additional printings — "Additional printings" of a previously issued stamp may range from an item that is totally different to cases where it is impossible to differentiate from the original. At least a minor number (a small-letter suffix) is assigned if there is a distinct change in stamp shade, noticeably redrawn design, or a significantly different perforation measurement. A major number (numeral or numeral and capital-letter combination) is assigned if the editors feel the "additional printing" is sufficiently different from the original that it constitutes a different issue.

Commemoratives — Where practical, commemoratives with the same theme are placed in a set. For example, the U.S. Civil War Centennial set of 1961-65 and the Constitution Bicentennial series of 1989-90 appear as sets. Countries such as Japan and Korea issue such material on a regular basis, with an announced, or at least predictable, number of stamps known in advance. Occasionally, however, stamp sets that were released over a period of years have been separated. Appropriately placed footnotes will guide you to each set's continuation.

Definitive sets — Blocks of numbers generally have been reserved for definitive sets, based on previous experience with any given country. If a few more stamps were issued in a set than originally expected, they often have been inserted into the original set with a capital-letter suffix, such as U.S. Scott 1059A. If it appears that many more stamps than the originally allotted block will be released before the set is completed, a new block of numbers will be reserved, with the original one being closed off. In some cases, such as the U.S. Transportation and Great Americans series, several blocks of numbers exist. Appropriately placed footnotes will guide you to each set's continuation.

New country — Membership in the Universal Postal Union is not a consideration for listing status or order of placement within the catalogue. The index will tell you in what volume or page number the listings begin.

"No release date" items — The amount of information available for any given stamp issue varies greatly from country to country and even from time to time. Extremely comprehensive information about new stamps is available from some countries well before the stamps are released. By contrast some countries do not provide information about stamps or release dates. Most countries, however, fall between these extremes. A country may provide denominations or subjects of stamps from upcoming issues that are not issued as planned. Sometimes, philatelic agencies, those private firms hired to represent countries, add these later-issued items to sets well after the formal release date. This time period can range from weeks to years. If these items were officially released by the country, they will be added to the appropriate spot in the set. In many cases, the specific release date of a stamp or set of stamps may never be known.

Overprints — The color of an overprint is always noted if it is other than black. Where more than one color of ink has been used on overprints of a single set, the color used is noted. Early overprint and surcharge illustrations were altered to prevent their use by forgers.

Se-tenants — Connected stamps of differing features (se-tenants) will be listed in the format most commonly collected. This includes pairs, blocks or larger multiples. Se-tenant units are not always symmetrical. An example is Australia Scott 508, which is a block of seven stamps. If the stamps are primarily collected as a unit, the major number may be assigned to the multiple, with minors going to each component stamp. In cases where continuous-design or other unit se-tenants will receive significant postal use, each stamp is given a major Scott number listing. This includes issues from the United States, Canada, Germany and Great Britain, for example.

Special Notices

Classification of stamps

The *Scott Standard Postage Stamp Catalogue* lists stamps by country of issue. The next level of organization is a listing by section on the basis of the function of the stamps. The principal sections cover regular postage, semi-postal, air post, special delivery, registration, postage due and other categories. Except for regular postage, catalogue numbers for all sections include a prefix letter (or number-letter combination) denoting the class to which a given stamp belongs. When some countries issue sets containing stamps from more than one category, the catalogue will at times list all of the stamps in one category (such as air post stamps listed as part of a postage set).

The following is a listing of the most commonly used catalogue prefixes.

Prefix... Category
C .... Air Post
M....... Military
P........ Newspaper
N .... Occupation - Regular Issues
O .... Official
Q....... Parcel Post
J......... Postage Due
RA ..... Postal Tax
B........ Semi-Postal
E........ Special Delivery
MR .... War Tax

Other prefixes used by more than one country include the following:
H .... Acknowledgment of Receipt
I......... Late Fee
CO..... Air Post Official
CQ..... Air Post Parcel Post
RAC ... Air Post Postal Tax
CF...... Air Post Registration
CB ..... Air Post Semi-Postal
CBO... Air Post Semi-Postal Official
CE ..... Air Post Special Delivery
EY...... Authorized Delivery
S........ Franchise
G .... Insured Letter
GY ..... Marine Insurance
MC .... Military Air Post
MQ.... Military Parcel Post
NC..... Occupation - Air Post
NO..... Occupation - Official
NJ ...... Occupation - Postage Due
NRA... Occupation - Postal Tax
NB ..... Occupation - Semi-Postal
NE ..... Occupation - Special Delivery
QY ..... Parcel Post Authorized Delivery
AR ..... Postal-fiscal
RAJ .... Postal Tax Due
RAB ... Postal Tax Semi-Postal
F........ Registration
EB...... Semi-Postal Special Delivery
EO ..... Special Delivery Official
QE ..... Special Handling

New issue listings

Updates to this catalogue appear each month in the *Linn's Stamp News Special Edition* magazine. Included in this update are additions to the listings of countries found in the *Scott Standard Postage Stamp Catalogue* and the *Specialized Catalogue of United States Stamps*, as well as corrections and updates to current editions of this catalogue.

From time to time there will be changes in the final listings of stamps from the *Linn's Stamp News Special Edition* to the next edition of the catalogue. This occurs as more information about certain stamps or sets becomes available.

The catalogue update section of the *Linn's Stamp News Special Edition* is the most timely presentation of this material available. Annual subscriptions to *Linn's Stamp News* are available from Linn's Stamp News, Box 926, Sidney, OH 45365-0926.

Number additions, deletions & changes

A listing of catalogue number additions, deletions and changes from the previous edition of the catalogue appears in each volume. See Catalogue Number Additions, Deletions & Changes in the table of contents for the location of this list.

Understanding valuing notations

The *minimum catalogue value* of an individual stamp or set is 20 cents. This represents a portion of the cost incurred by a dealer when he prepares an individual stamp for resale. As a point of philatelic-economic fact, the lower the value shown for an item in this catalogue, the greater the percentage of that value is attributed to dealer mark up and profit margin. In many cases, such as the 20-cent minimum value, that price does not cover the labor or other costs involved with stocking it as an individual stamp. The sum of minimum values in a set does not properly represent the value of a complete set primarily composed of a number of minimum-value stamps, nor does the sum represent the actual value of a packet made up of minimum-value stamps. Thus a packet of 1,000 different common stamps — each of which has a catalogue value of 20-cents — normally sells for considerably less than 200 dollars!

The *absence of a retail value* for a stamp does not necessarily suggest that a stamp is scarce or rare. A dash in the value column means that the stamp is known in a stated form or variety, but information is either lacking or insufficient for purposes of establishing a usable catalogue value.

Stamp values in *italics* generally refer to items that are difficult to value accurately. For expensive items, such as those priced at $1,000 or higher, a value in italics indicates that the affected item trades very seldom. For inexpensive items, a value in italics represents a warning. One example is a "blocked" issue where the issuing postal administration may have controlled one stamp in a set in an attempt to make the whole set more valuable. Another example is an item that sold at an extreme multiple of face value in the marketplace at the time of its issue.

One type of warning to collectors that appears in the catalogue is illustrated by a stamp that is valued considerably higher in used condition than it is as unused. In this case, collectors are cautioned to be certain the used version has a genuine and contemporaneous cancellation. The type of cancellation on a stamp can be an important factor in determining its sale price. Catalogue values do not apply to fiscal, telegraph or non-contemporaneous postal cancels, unless otherwise noted.

Some countries have released back issues of stamps in canceled-to-order form, sometimes covering as much as a 10-year period. The Scott Catalogue values for used stamps reflect canceled-to-order material when such stamps are found to predominate in the marketplace for the issue involved. Notes frequently appear in the stamp listings to specify which items are valued as canceled-to-order, or if there is a premium for postally used examples.

Many countries sell canceled-to-order stamps at a marked reduction of face value. Countries that sell or have sold canceled-to-order stamps at *full* face value include United Nations, Australia, Netherlands, France and Switzerland. It may be almost impossible to identify such stamps if the gum has been removed, because official government canceling devices are used. Postally used copies of these items on cover, however, are usually worth more than the canceled-to-order stamps with original gum.

Abbreviations

Scott Publishing Co. uses a consistent set of abbreviations throughout this catalogue to conserve space, while still providing necessary information.

COLOR ABBREVIATIONS

amb .amber
anil ..aniline
ap ....apple
aqua.aquamarine
az.....azure
bis....bister
bl .....blue
bld ...blood
blk ...black
bril...brilliant
brn...brown
brnshbrownish
brnz .bronze
brt....bright
brnt..burnt
car ...carmine
cer ...cerise
chlky chalky
cham chamois
chnt .chestnut
choc.chocolate
chr ...chrome
cit ....citron
cl .....claret
cob...cobalt
cop...copper
crim .crimson
cr .....cream
dk ....dark
dl .....dull
dp ....deep
db ....drab
emer emerald
gldn .golden
grysh grayish
grn ...green
grnsh greenish
hel ...heliotrope
hn ....henna
ind ...indigo
int....intense
lav....lavender
lem ..lemon
lil .....lilac
lt......light
mag..magenta
man .manila
mar ..maroon
mv ...mauve
multi multicolored
mlky milky
myr ..myrtle
ol .....olive
olvn .olivine
org ...orange
pck...peacock
pnksh pinkish
Prus .Prussian
pur...purple
redsh reddish
res....reseda
ros ...rosine
ryl ....royal
sal ....salmon
saph .sapphire
scar ..scarlet
sep ...sepia
sien ..sienna
sil.....silver
sl......slate
stl.....steel
turq..turquoise
ultra .ultramarine
Ven ..Venetian
ver ...vermilion
vio ...violet
yel....yellow
yelsh yellowish

When no color is given for an overprint or surcharge, black is the color used. Abbreviations for colors used for overprints and surcharges include: "(B)" or "(Blk)," black; "(Bl)," blue; "(R)," red; and "(G)," green.

Additional abbreviations in this catalogue are shown below:

Adm............Administration
AFL.............American Federation of Labor
Anniv. ....Anniversary
APS.............American Philatelic Society
Assoc. ....Association
ASSR............Autonomous Soviet Socialist Republic
b..................Born
BEP.............Bureau of Engraving and Printing
Bicent. ....Bicentennial
Bklt.............Booklet
Brit. ....British
btwn. ....Between
Bur. ....Bureau
c. or ca.........Circa
Cat...............Catalogue
Cent.............Centennial, century, centenary
CIO..............Congress of Industrial Organizations
Conf.............Conference
Cong............Congress
Cpl...............Corporal
CTO.............Canceled to order
d..................Died
Dbl...............Double
EDU.............Earliest documented use
Engr. ....Engraved
Exhib. ....Exhibition
Expo. ....Exposition
Fed. ....Federation
GB ....Great Britain
Gen..............General
GPO.............General post office
Horiz............Horizontal
Imperf..........Imperforate
Impt.............Imprint
Intl..............International
Invtd............Inverted
L..................Left
Lieut., lt. ......Lieutenant
Litho. ....Lithographed
LL ....Lower left
LR................Lower right
mm ....Millimeter
Ms. ....Manuscript
Natl..............National
No. ....Number
NY ....New York
NYC.............New York City
Ovpt. ....Overprint
Ovptd...........Overprinted
P..................Plate number
Perf. ....Perforated, perforation
Phil. ....Philatelic
Photo. ....Photogravure
PO ....Post office
Pr. ....Pair
P.R. ....Puerto Rico
Prec. ....Precancel, precanceled
Pres..............President
PTT..............Post, Telephone and Telegraph
Rio ....Rio de Janeiro
Sgt. ....Sergeant
Soc...............Society
Souv. ....Souvenir
SSR ....Soviet Socialist Republic, see ASSR
St. ....Saint, street
Surch. ....Surcharge
Typo.............Typographed
UL ....Upper left
Unwmkd......Unwatermarked
UPU.............Universal Postal Union
UR ....Upper Right
US................United States
USPOD ....United States Post Office Department
USSR............Union of Soviet Socialist Republics
Vert. ....Vertical
VP................Vice president
Wmk............Watermark
Wmkd..........Watermarked
WWI............World War I
WWII...........World War II

Examination

Scott Publishing Co. will not comment upon the genuineness, grade or condition of stamps, because of the time and responsibility involved. Rather, there are several expertizing groups that undertake this work for both collectors and dealers. Neither will Scott Publishing Co. appraise or identify philatelic material. The company cannot take responsibility for unsolicited stamps or covers sent by individuals.

All letters, E-mails, etc. are read attentively, but they are not always answered due to time considerations.

How to order from your dealer

When ordering stamps from a dealer, it is not necessary to write the full description of a stamp as listed in this catalogue. All you need is the name of the country, the Scott catalogue number and whether the desired item is unused or used. For example, "Japan Scott 422 unused" is sufficient to identify the unused stamp of Japan listed as "422 A206 5y brown."

Basic Stamp Information

A stamp collector's knowledge of the combined elements that make a given stamp issue unique determines his or her ability to identify stamps. These elements include paper, watermark, method of separation, printing, design and gum. On the following pages each of these important areas is briefly described.

Paper

Paper is an organic material composed of a compacted weave of cellulose fibers and generally formed into sheets. Paper used to print stamps may be manufactured in sheets, or it may have been part of a large roll (called a web) before being cut to size. The fibers most often used to create paper on which stamps are printed include bark, wood, straw and certain grasses. In many cases, linen or cotton rags have been added for greater strength and durability. Grinding, bleaching, cooking and rinsing these raw fibers reduces them to a slushy pulp, referred to by paper makers as "stuff." Sizing and, sometimes, coloring matter is added to the pulp to make different types of finished paper.

After the stuff is prepared, it is poured onto sieve-like frames that allow the water to run off, while retaining the matted pulp. As fibers fall onto the screen and are held by gravity, they form a natural weave that will later hold the paper together. If the screen has metal bits that are formed into letters or images attached, it leaves slightly thinned areas on the paper. These are called watermarks.

When the stuff is almost dry, it is passed under pressure through smooth or engraved rollers - dandy rolls - or placed between cloth in a press to be flattened and dried.

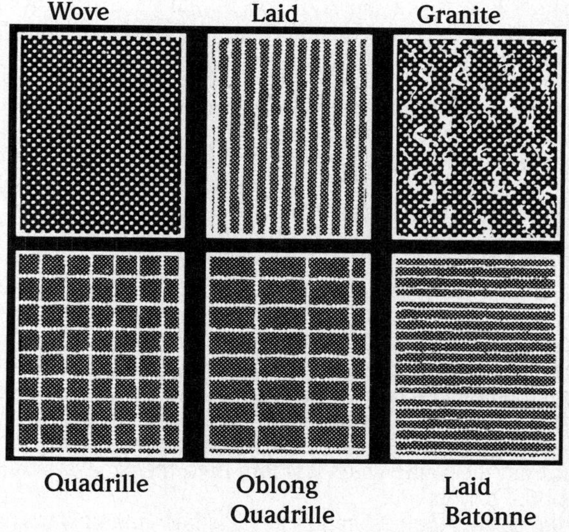

Stamp paper falls broadly into two types: wove and laid. The nature of the surface of the frame onto which the pulp is first deposited causes the differences in appearance between the two. If the surface is smooth and even, the paper will be of fairly uniform texture throughout. This is known as *wove paper*. Early papermaking machines poured the pulp onto a continuously circulating web of felt, but modern machines feed the pulp onto a cloth-like screen made of closely interwoven fine wires. This paper, when held to a light, will show little dots or points very close together. The proper name for this is "wire wove," but the type is still considered wove. Any U.S. or British stamp printed after 1880 will serve as an example of wire wove paper.

Closely spaced parallel wires, with cross wires at wider intervals, make up the frames used for what is known as *laid paper*. A greater thickness of the pulp will settle between the wires. The paper, when held to a light, will show alternate light and dark lines. The spacing and the thickness of the lines may vary, but on any one sheet of paper they are all alike. See Russia Scott 31-38 for examples of laid paper.

Batonne, from the French word meaning "a staff," is a term used if the lines in the paper are spaced quite far apart, like the printed ruling on a writing tablet. Batonne paper may be either wove or laid. If laid, fine laid lines can be seen between the batons.

Quadrille is the term used when the lines in the paper form little squares. *Oblong quadrille* is the term used when rectangles, rather than squares, are formed. Grid patterns vary from distinct to extremely faint. See Mexico-Guadalajara Scott 35-37 for examples of oblong quadrille paper.

Paper also is classified as thick or thin, hard or soft, and by color if dye is added during manufacture. Such colors may include yellowish, greenish, bluish and reddish.

Brief explanations of other types of paper used for printing stamps, as well as examples, follow.

Pelure — Pelure paper is a very thin, hard and often brittle paper that is sometimes bluish or grayish in appearance. See Serbia Scott 169-170.

Native — This is a term applied to handmade papers used to produce some of the early stamps of the Indian states. Stamps printed on native paper may be expected to display various natural inclusions that are normal and do not negatively affect value. Japanese paper, originally made of mulberry fibers and rice flour, is part of this group. See Japan Scott 1-18.

Manila — This type of paper is often used to make stamped envelopes and wrappers. It is a coarse-textured stock, usually smooth on one side and rough on the other. A variety of colors of manila paper exist, but the most common range is yellowish-brown.

Silk — Introduced by the British in 1847 as a safeguard against counterfeiting, silk paper contains bits of colored silk thread scattered throughout. The density of these fibers varies greatly and can include as few as one fiber per stamp or hundreds. U.S. revenue Scott R152 is a good example of an easy-to-identify silk paper stamp.

Silk-thread paper has uninterrupted threads of colored silk arranged so that one or more threads run through the stamp or postal stationery. See Great Britain Scott 5-6 and Switzerland Scott 14-19.

Granite — Filled with minute cloth or colored paper fibers of various colors and lengths, granite paper should not be confused with either type of silk paper. Austria Scott 172-175 and a number of Swiss stamps are examples of granite paper.

Chalky — A chalk-like substance coats the surface of chalky paper to discourage the cleaning and reuse of canceled stamps, as well as to provide a smoother, more acceptable printing surface. Because the designs of stamps printed on chalky paper are imprinted on what is often a water-soluble coating, any attempt to remove a cancellation will destroy the stamp. *Do not soak these stamps in any fluid.* To remove a stamp printed on chalky paper from an envelope, wet the paper from underneath the stamp until the gum dissolves enough to release the stamp from the paper. See St. Kitts-Nevis Scott 89-90 for examples of stamps printed on this type of chalky paper.

India — Another name for this paper, originally introduced from China about 1750, is "China Paper." It is a thin, opaque paper often used for plate and die proofs by many countries.

Double — In philately, the term double paper has two distinct meanings. The first is a two-ply paper, usually a combination of a thick and a thin sheet, joined during manufacture. This type was used experimentally as a means to discourage the reuse of stamps.

The design is printed on the thin paper. Any attempt to remove a cancellation would destroy the design. U.S. Scott 158 and other Banknote-era stamps exist on this form of double paper.

The second type of double paper occurs on a rotary press, when the end of one paper roll, or web, is affixed to the next roll to save time feeding the paper through the press. Stamp designs are printed over the joined paper and, if overlooked by inspectors, may get into post office stocks.

Goldbeater's Skin — This type of paper was used for the 1866 issue of Prussia, and was a tough, translucent paper. The design was printed in reverse on the back of the stamp, and the gum applied over the printing. It is impossible to remove stamps printed on this type of paper from the paper to which they are affixed without destroying the design.

Ribbed — Ribbed paper has an uneven, corrugated surface made by passing the paper through ridged rollers. This type exists on some copies of U.S. Scott 156-165.

Various other substances, or substrates, have been used for stamp manufacture, including wood, aluminum, copper, silver and gold foil, plastic, and silk and cotton fabrics.

Watermarks

Watermarks are an integral part of some papers. They are formed in the process of paper manufacture. Watermarks consist of small designs, formed of wire or cut from metal and soldered to the surface of the mold or, sometimes, on the dandy roll. The designs may be in the form of crowns, stars, anchors, letters or other characters or symbols. These pieces of metal - known in the paper-making industry as "bits" - impress a design into the paper. The design sometimes may be seen by holding the stamp to the light. Some are more easily seen with a watermark detector. This important tool is a small black tray into which a stamp is placed face down and dampened with a fast-evaporating watermark detection fluid that brings up the watermark image in the form of dark lines against a lighter background. These dark lines are the thinner areas of the paper known as the watermark. Some watermarks are extremely difficult to locate, due to either a faint impression, watermark location or the color of the stamp. There also are electric watermark detectors that come with plastic filter disks of various colors. The disks neutralize the color of the stamp, permitting the watermark to be seen more easily.

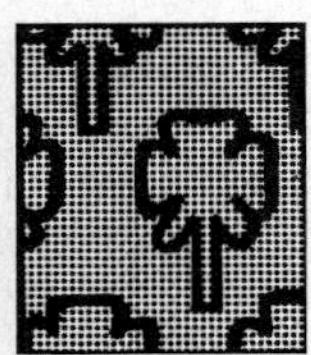

Multiple watermarks of Crown Agents and Burma

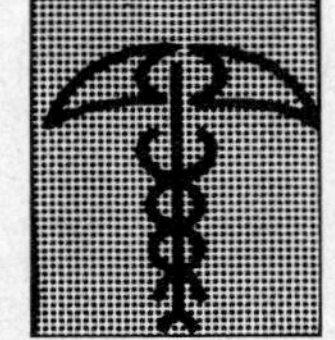

Watermarks of Uruguay, Vatican City and Jamaica

WARNING: Some inks used in the photogravure process dissolve in watermark fluids (Please see the section on Soluble Printing Inks). Also, see "chalky paper."

Watermarks may be found normal, reversed, inverted, reversed and inverted, sideways or diagonal, as seen from the back of the stamp. The relationship of watermark to stamp design depends on the position of the printing plates or how paper is fed through the press. On machine-made paper, watermarks normally are read from right to left. The design is repeated closely throughout the sheet in a "multiple-watermark design." In a "sheet watermark," the design appears only once on the sheet, but extends over many stamps. Individual stamps may carry only a small fraction or none of the watermark.

"Marginal watermarks" occur in the margins of sheets or panes of stamps. They occur on the outside border of paper (ostensibly outside the area where stamps are to be printed). A large row of letters may spell the name of the country or the manufacturer of the paper, or a border of lines may appear. Careless press feeding may cause parts of these letters and/or lines to show on stamps of the outer row of a pane.

Soluble Printing Inks

WARNING: Most stamp colors are permanent; that is, they are not seriously affected by short-term exposure to light or water. Many colors, especially of modern inks, fade from excessive exposure to light. There are stamps printed with inks that dissolve easily in water or in fluids used to detect watermarks. Use of these inks was intentional to prevent the removal of cancellations. Water affects all aniline inks, those on so-called safety paper and some photogravure printings - all such inks are known as *fugitive colors. Removal from paper of such stamps requires care and alternatives to traditional soaking.*

Separation

"Separation" is the general term used to describe methods used to separate stamps. The three standard forms currently in use are perforating, rouletting and die-cutting. These methods are done during the stamp production process, after printing. Sometimes these methods are done on-press or sometimes as a separate step. The earliest issues, such as the 1840 Penny Black of Great Britain (Scott 1), did not have any means provided for separation. It was expected the stamps would be cut apart with scissors or folded and torn. These are examples of imperforate stamps. Many stamps were first issued in imperforate formats and were later issued with perforations. Therefore, care must be observed in buying single imperforate stamps to be certain they were issued imperforate and are not perforated copies that have been altered by having the perforations trimmed away. Stamps issued imperforate usually are valued as singles. However, imperforate varieties of normally perforated stamps should be collected in pairs or larger pieces as indisputable evidence of their imperforate character.

PERFORATION

The chief style of separation of stamps, and the one that is in almost universal use today, is perforating. By this process, paper between the stamps is cut away in a line of holes, usually round, leaving little bridges of paper between the stamps to hold them together. Some types of perforation, such as hyphen-hole perfs, can be confused with roulettes, but a close visual inspection reveals that paper has been removed. The little perforation bridges, which project from the stamp when it is torn from the pane, are called the teeth of the perforation.

As the size of the perforation is sometimes the only way to differentiate between two otherwise identical stamps, it is necessary to be able to accurately measure and describe them. This is done with a perforation gauge, usually a ruler-like device that has dots or graduated lines to show how many perforations may be counted in the space of two centimeters. Two centimeters is the space universally adopted in which to measure perforations.

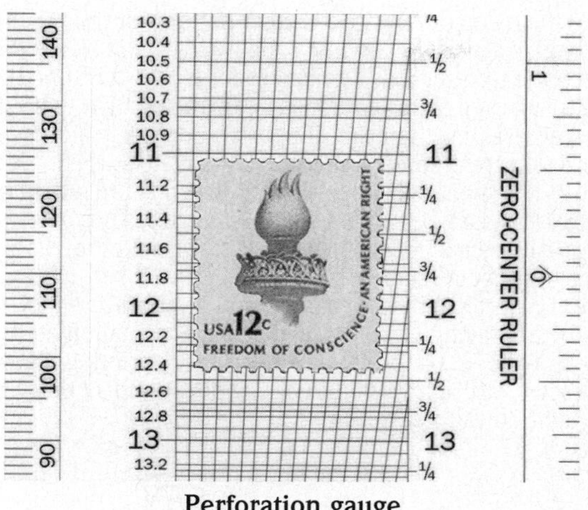

Perforation gauge

To measure a stamp, run it along the gauge until the dots on it fit exactly into the perforations of the stamp. If you are using a graduated-line perforation gauge, simply slide the stamp along the surface until the lines on the gauge perfectly project from the center of the bridges or holes. The number to the side of the line of dots or lines that fit the stamp's perforation is the measurement. For example, an "11" means that 11 perforations fit between two centimeters. The description of the stamp therefore is "perf. 11." If the gauge of the perforations on the top and bottom of a stamp differs from that on the sides, the result is what is known as *compound perforations.* In measuring compound perforations, the gauge at top and bottom is always given first, then the sides. Thus, a stamp that measures 11 at top and bottom and 10 1/2 at the sides is "perf. 11 x 10 1/2." See U.S. Scott 632-642 for examples of compound perforations.

Stamps also are known with perforations different on three or all four sides. Descriptions of such items are clockwise, beginning with the top of the stamp.

A perforation with small holes and teeth close together is a "fine perforation." One with large holes and teeth far apart is a "coarse perforation." Holes that are jagged, rather than clean-cut, are "rough perforations." *Blind perforations* are the slight impressions left by the perforating pins if they fail to puncture the paper. Multiples of stamps showing blind perforations may command a slight premium over normally perforated stamps.

The term *syncopated perfs* describes intentional irregularities in the perforations. The earliest form was used by the Netherlands from 1925-33, where holes were omitted to create distinctive patterns. Beginning in 1992, Great Britain has used an oval perforation to help prevent counterfeiting. Several other countries have started using the oval perfs or other syncopated perf patterns.

A new type of perforation, still primarily used for postal stationery, is known as microperfs. Microperfs are tiny perforations (in some cases hundreds of holes per two centimeters) that allows items to be intentionally separated very easily, while not accidentally breaking apart as easily as standard perforations. These are not currently measured or differentiated by size, as are standard perforations.

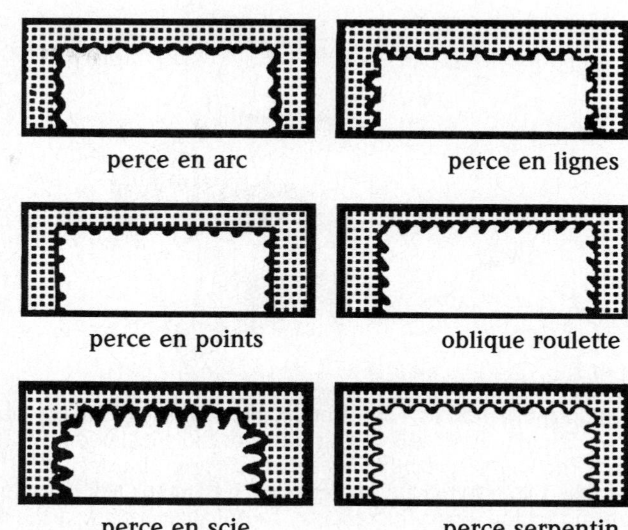

perce en arc | perce en lignes

perce en points | oblique roulette

perce en scie | perce serpentin

ROULETTING

In rouletting, the stamp paper is cut partly or wholly through, with no paper removed. In perforating, some paper is removed. Rouletting derives its name from the French roulette, a spur-like wheel. As the wheel is rolled over the paper, each point makes a small cut. The number of cuts made in a two-centimeter space determines the gauge of the roulette, just as the number of perforations in two centimeters determines the gauge of the perforation.

The shape and arrangement of the teeth on the wheels varies. Various roulette types generally carry French names:

Perce en lignes - rouletted in lines. The paper receives short, straight cuts in lines. This is the most common type of rouletting. See Mexico Scott 500.

Perce en points - pin-rouletted or pin-perfed. This differs from a small perforation because no paper is removed, although round, equidistant holes are pricked through the paper. See Mexico Scott 242-256.

Perce en arc and *perce en scie* - pierced in an arc or saw-toothed designs, forming half circles or small triangles. See Hanover (German States) Scott 25-29.

Perce en serpentin - serpentine roulettes. The cuts form a serpentine or wavy line. See Brunswick (German States) Scott 13-18.

Once again, no paper is removed by these processes, leaving the stamps easily separated, but closely attached.

DIE-CUTTING

The third major form of stamp separation is die-cutting. This is a method where a die in the pattern of separation is created that later cuts the stamp paper in a stroke motion. Although some standard stamps bear die-cut perforations, this process is primarily used for self-adhesive postage stamps. Die-cutting can appear in straight lines, such as U.S. Scott 2522, shapes, such as U.S. Scott 1551, or imitating the appearance of perforations, such as New Zealand Scott 935A and 935B.

Printing Processes

ENGRAVING (Intaglio, Line-engraving, Etching)

Master die — The initial operation in the process of line engraving is making the master die. The die is a small, flat block of softened steel upon which the stamp design is recess engraved in reverse.

Master die

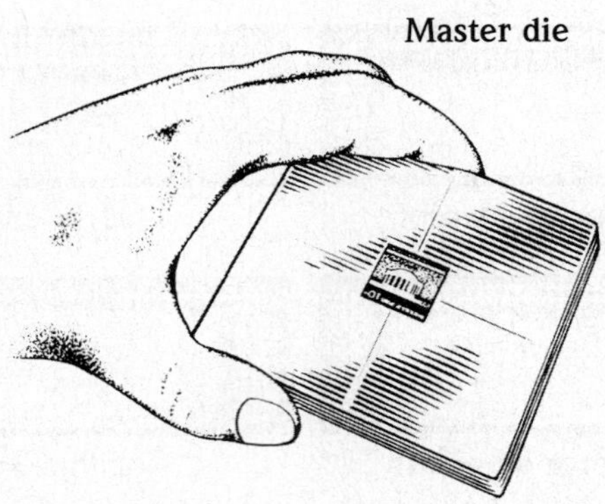

Photographic reduction of the original art is made to the appropriate size. It then serves as a tracing guide for the initial outline of the design. The engraver lightly traces the design on the steel with his graver, then slowly works the design until it is completed. At various points during the engraving process, the engraver hand-inks the die and makes an impression to check his progress. These are known as progressive die proofs. After completion of the engraving, the die is hardened to withstand the stress and pressures of later transfer operations.

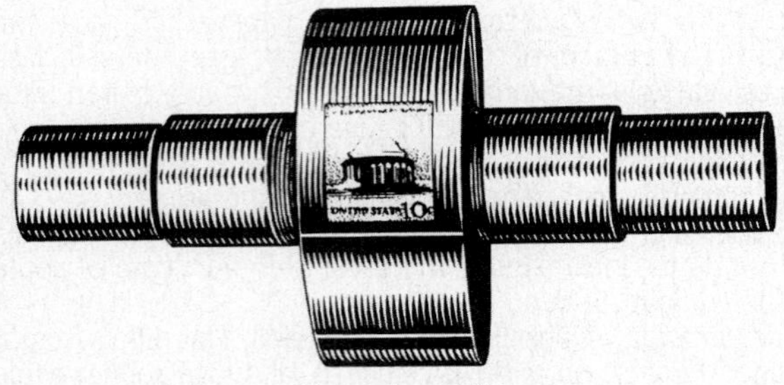

Transfer roll

Transfer roll — Next is production of the transfer roll that, as the name implies, is the medium used to transfer the subject from the master die to the printing plate. A blank roll of soft steel, mounted on a mandrel, is placed under the bearers of the transfer press to allow it to roll freely on its axis. The hardened die is placed on the bed of the press and the face of the transfer roll is applied to the die, under pressure. The bed or the roll is then rocked back and forth under increasing pressure, until the soft steel of the roll is forced into every engraved line of the die. The resulting impression on the roll is known as a "relief" or a "relief transfer." The engraved image is now positive in appearance and stands out from the steel. After the required number of reliefs are "rocked in," the soft steel transfer roll is hardened.

Different flaws may occur during the relief process. A defective relief may occur during the rocking in process because of a minute piece of foreign material lodging on the die, or some other cause. Imperfections in the steel of the transfer roll may result in a breaking away of parts of the design. This is known as a relief break, which will show up on finished stamps as small, unprinted areas. If a damaged relief remains in use, it will transfer a repeating defect to the plate. Deliberate alterations of reliefs sometimes occur. "Altered reliefs" designate these changed conditions.

Plate — The final step in pre-printing production is the making of the printing plate. A flat piece of soft steel replaces the die on the bed of the transfer press. One of the reliefs on the transfer roll is positioned over this soft steel. Position, or layout, dots determine the correct position on the plate. The dots have been lightly marked on the plate in advance. After the correct position of the relief is determined, the design is rocked in by following the same method used in making the transfer roll. The difference is that this time the image is being transferred from the transfer roll, rather than to it. Once the design is entered on the plate, it appears in reverse and is recessed. There are as many transfers entered on the plate as there are subjects printed on the sheet of stamps. It is during this process that double and shifted transfers occur, as well as re-entries. These are the result of improperly entered images that have not been properly burnished out prior to rocking in a new image.

Modern siderography processes, such as those used by the U.S. Bureau of Engraving and Printing, involve an automated form of rocking designs in on preformed cylindrical printing sleeves. The same process also allows for easier removal and re-entry of worn images right on the sleeve.

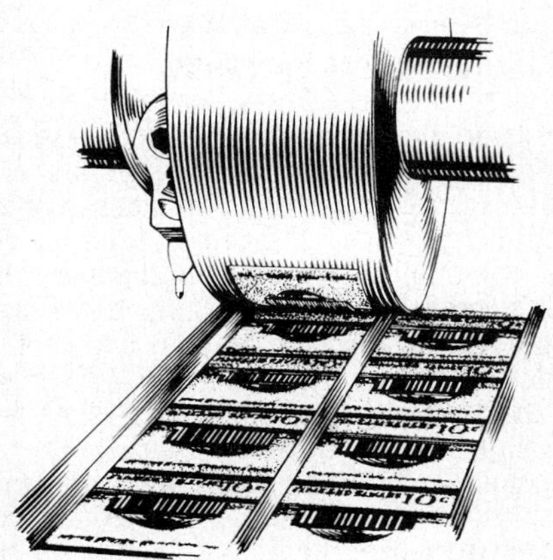

Transferring the design to the plate

Following the entering of the required transfers on the plate, the position dots, layout dots and lines, scratches and other markings generally are burnished out. Added at this time by the siderographer are any required *guide lines, plate numbers* or other *marginal markings.* The plate is then hand-inked and a proof impression is taken. This is known as a plate proof. If the impression is approved, the plate is machined for fitting onto the press, is hardened and sent to the plate vault ready for use.

On press, the plate is inked and the surface is automatically wiped clean, leaving ink only in the recessed lines. Paper is then forced under pressure into the engraved recessed lines, thereby receiving the ink. Thus, the ink lines on engraved stamps are slightly raised, and slight depressions (debossing) occur on the back of the stamp. Prior to the advent of modern high-speed presses and more advanced ink formulations, paper had to be dampened before receiving the ink. This sometimes led to uneven shrinkage by the time the stamps were perforated, resulting in improperly perforated stamps, or misperfs. Newer presses use drier paper, thus both *wet* and *dry printings* exist on some stamps.

Rotary Press — Until 1914, only flat plates were used to print engraved stamps. Rotary press printing was introduced in 1914, and slowly spread. Some countries still use flat-plate printing.

After approval of the plate proof, older *rotary press plates* require additional machining. They are curved to fit the press cylinder. "Gripper slots" are cut into the back of each plate to receive the "grippers," which hold the plate securely on the press. The plate is then hardened. Stamps printed from these bent rotary press plates are longer or wider than the same stamps printed from flat-plate presses. The stretching of the plate during the curving process is what causes this distortion.

Re-entry — To execute a re-entry on a flat plate, the transfer roll is re-applied to the plate, often at some time after its first use on the press. Worn-out designs can be resharpened by carefully burnishing out the original image and re-entering it from the transfer roll. If the original impression has not been sufficiently removed and the transfer roll is not precisely in line with the remaining impression, the resulting double transfer will make the re-entry obvious. If the registration is true, a re-entry may be difficult or impossible to distinguish. Sometimes a stamp printed from a successful re-entry is identified by having a much sharper and clearer impression than its neighbors. With the advent of rotary presses, post-press re-entries were not possible. After a plate was curved for the rotary press, it was impossible to make a re-entry. This is because the plate had already been bent once (with the design distorted).

However, with the introduction of the previously mentioned modern-style siderography machines, entries are made to the preformed cylindrical printing sleeve. Such sleeves are dechromed and softened. This allows individual images to be burnished out and re-entered on the curved sleeve. The sleeve is then rechromed, resulting in longer press life.

Double Transfer — This is a description of the condition of a transfer on a plate that shows evidence of a duplication of all, or a portion of the design. It usually is the result of the changing of the registration between the transfer roll and the plate during the rocking in of the original entry. Double transfers also occur when only a portion of the design has been rocked in and improper positioning is noted. If the worker elected not to burnish out the partial or completed design, a strong double transfer will occur for part or all of the design.

It sometimes is necessary to remove the original transfer from a plate and repeat the process a second time. If the finished re-worked image shows traces of the original impression, attributable to incomplete burnishing, the result is a partial double transfer.

With the modern automatic machines mentioned previously, double transfers are all but impossible to create. Those partially doubled images on stamps printed from such sleeves are more than likely re-entries, rather than true double transfers.

Re-engraved — Alterations to a stamp design are sometimes necessary after some stamps have been printed. In some cases, either the original die or the actual printing plate may have its "temper" drawn (softened), and the design will be re-cut. The resulting impressions from such a re-engraved die or plate may differ slightly from the original issue, and are known as "re-engraved." If the alteration was made to the master die, all future printings will be consistently different from the original. If alterations were made to the printing plate, each altered stamp on the plate will be slightly different from each other, allowing specialists to reconstruct a complete printing plate.

Dropped Transfers — If an impression from the transfer roll has not been properly placed, a dropped transfer may occur. The final stamp image will appear obviously out of line with its neighbors.

Short Transfer — Sometimes a transfer roll is not rocked its entire length when entering a transfer onto a plate. As a result, the finished transfer on the plate fails to show the complete design, and the finished stamp will have an incomplete design printed. This is known as a "short transfer." U.S. Scott No. 8 is a good example of a short transfer.

TYPOGRAPHY (Letterpress, Surface Printing, Flexography, Dry Offset, High Etch)

Although the word "Typography" is obsolete as a term describing a printing method, it was the accepted term throughout the first century of postage stamps. Therefore, appropriate Scott listings in this catalogue refer to typographed stamps. The current term for this form of printing, however, is "letterpress."

As it relates to the production of postage stamps, letterpress printing is the reverse of engraving. Rather than having recessed areas trap the ink and deposit it on paper, only the raised areas of the design are inked. This is comparable to the type of printing seen by inking and using an ordinary rubber stamp. Letterpress includes all printing where the design is above the surface area, whether it is wood, metal or, in some instances, hardened rubber or polymer plastic.

For most letterpress-printed stamps, the engraved master is made in much the same manner as for engraved stamps. In this instance, however, an additional step is needed. The design is transferred to another surface before being transferred to the transfer roll. In this way, the transfer roll has a recessed stamp design, rather than one done in relief. This makes the printing areas on the final plate raised, or relief areas.

For less-detailed stamps of the 19th century, the area on the die not used as a printing surface was cut away, leaving the surface area raised. The original die was then reproduced by stereotyping or electrotyping. The resulting electrotypes were assembled in the required number and format of the desired sheet of stamps. The plate used in printing the stamps was an electroplate of these assembled electrotypes.

Once the final letterpress plates are created, ink is applied to the raised surface and the pressure of the press transfers the ink impression to the paper. In contrast to engraving, the fine lines of letterpress are impressed on the surface of the stamp, leaving a debossed surface. When viewed from the back (as on a typewritten page), the corresponding line work on the stamp will be raised slightly (embossed) above the surface.

PHOTOGRAVURE (Gravure, Rotogravure, Heliogravure)

In this process, the basic principles of photography are applied to a chemically sensitized metal plate, rather than photographic paper. The design is transferred photographically to the plate through a halftone, or dot-matrix screen, breaking the reproduction into tiny dots. The plate is treated chemically and the dots form depressions, called cells, of varying depths and diameters, depending on the degrees of shade in the design. Then, like engraving, ink is applied to the plate and the surface is wiped clean. This leaves ink in the tiny cells that is lifted out and deposited on the paper when it is pressed against the plate.

Gravure is most often used for multicolored stamps, generally using the three primary colors (red, yellow and blue) and black. By varying the dot matrix pattern and density of these colors, virtually any color can be reproduced. A typical full-color gravure stamp will be created from four printing cylinders (one for each color). The original multicolored image will have been photographically separated into its component colors.

Modern gravure printing may use computer-generated dot-matrix screens, and modern plates may be of various types including metal-coated plastic. The catalogue designation of Photogravure (or "Photo") covers any of these older and more modern gravure methods of printing.

For examples of the first photogravure stamps printed (1914), see Bavaria Scott 94-114.

LITHOGRAPHY (Offset Lithography, Stone Lithography, Dilitho, Planography, Collotype)

The principle that oil and water do not mix is the basis for lithography. The stamp design is drawn by hand or transferred from engraving to the surface of a lithographic stone or metal plate in a greasy (oily) substance. This oily substance holds the ink, which will later be transferred to the paper. The stone (or plate) is wet with an acid fluid, causing it to repel the printing ink in all areas not covered by the greasy substance.

Transfer paper is used to transfer the design from the original stone or plate. A series of duplicate transfers are grouped and, in turn, transferred to the final printing plate.

Photolithography — The application of photographic processes to lithography. This process allows greater flexibility of design, related to use of halftone screens combined with line work. Unlike photogravure or engraving, this process can allow large, solid areas to be printed.

Offset — A refinement of the lithographic process. A rubber-covered blanket cylinder takes the impression from the inked lithographic plate. From the "blanket" the impression is *offset* or transferred to the paper. Greater flexibility and speed are the principal reasons offset printing has largely displaced lithography. The term "lithography" covers both processes, and results are almost identical.

EMBOSSED (Relief) Printing

Embossing, not considered one of the four main printing types, is a method in which the design first is sunk into the metal of the die. Printing is done against a yielding platen, such as leather or linoleum. The platen is forced into the depression of the die, thus forming the design on the paper in relief. This process is often used for metallic inks.

Embossing may be done without color (see Sardinia Scott 4-6); with color printed around the embossed area (see Great Britain Scott 5 and most U.S. envelopes); and with color in exact registration with the embossed subject (see Canada Scott 656-657).

HOLOGRAMS

For objects to appear as holograms on stamps, a model exactly the same size as it is to appear on the hologram must be created. Rather than using photographic film to capture the image, holography records an image on a photoresist material. In processing, chemicals eat away at certain exposed areas, leaving a pattern of constructive and destructive interference. When the phororesist is developed, the result is a pattern of uneven ridges that acts as a mold. This mold is then coated with metal, and the resulting form is used to press copies in much the same way phonograph records are produced.

A typical reflective hologram used for stamps consists of a reproduction of the uneven patterns on a plastic film that is applied to a reflective background, usually a silver or gold foil. Light is reflected off the background through the film, making the pattern present on the film visible. Because of the uneven pattern of the film, the viewer will perceive the objects in their proper three-dimensional relationships with appropriate brightness.

The first hologram on a stamp was produced by Austria in 1988 (Scott 1441).

FOIL APPLICATION

A modern tecnique of applying color to stamps involves the application of metallic foil to the stamp paper. A pattern of foil is applied to the stamp paper by use of a stamping die. The foil usually is flat, but it may be textured. Canada Scott 1735 has three different foil applications in pearl, bronze and gold. The gold foil was textured using a chemical-etch copper embossing die. The printing of this stamp also involved two-color offset lithography plus embossing.

COMBINATION PRINTINGS

Sometimes two or even three printing methods are combined in producing stamps. In these cases, such as Austria Scott 933 or Canada 1735 (described in the preceding paragraph), the multiple-printing technique can be determined by studying the individual characteristics of each printing type. A few stamps, such as Singapore Scott 684-684A, combine as many as three of the four major printing types (lithography, engraving and typography). When this is done it often indicates the incorporation of security devices against counterfeiting.

INK COLORS

Inks or colored papers used in stamp printing often are of mineral origin, although there are numerous examples of organic-based pigments. As a general rule, organic-based pigments are far more subject to varieties and change than those of mineral-based origin.

The appearance of any given color on a stamp may be affected by many aspects, including printing variations, light, color of paper, aging and chemical alterations.

Numerous printing variations may be observed. Heavier pressure or inking will cause a more intense color, while slight interruptions in the ink feed or lighter impressions will cause a lighter appearance. Stamps printed in the same color by water-based and solvent-based inks can differ significantly in appearance. This affects several stamps in the U.S. Prominent Americans series. Hand-mixed ink formulas (primarily from the 19th century) produced under different conditions (humidity and temperature) account for notable color variations in early printings of the same stamp (see U.S. Scott 248-250, 279B, for example). Different sources of pigment can also result in significant differences in color.

Light exposure and aging are closely related in the way they affect stamp color. Both eventually break down the ink and fade colors, so that a carefully kept stamp may differ significantly in color from an identical copy that has been exposed to light. If stamps are exposed to light either intentionally or accidentally, their colors can be faded or completely changed in some cases.

Papers of different quality and consistency used for the same stamp printing may affect color appearance. Most pelure papers, for example, show a richer color when compared with wove or laid papers. See Russia Scott 181a, for an example of this effect.

The very nature of the printing processes can cause a variety of differences in shades or hues of the same stamp. Some of these shades are scarcer than others, and are of particular interest to the advanced collector.

Luminescence

All forms of tagged stamps fall under the general category of luminescence. Within this broad category is fluorescence, dealing with forms of tagging visible under longwave ultraviolet light, and phosphorescence, which deals with tagging visible only under shortwave light. Phosphorescence leaves an afterglow and fluorescence does not. These treated stamps show up in a range of different colors when exposed to UV light. The differing wavelengths of the light activates the tagging material, making it glow in various colors that usually serve different mail processing purposes.

Intentional tagging is a post-World War II phenomenon, brought about by the increased literacy rate and rapidly growing mail volume. It was one of several answers to the problem of the need for more automated mail processes. Early tagged stamps served the purpose of triggering machines to separate different types of mail. A natural outgrowth was to also use the signal to trigger machines that faced all envelopes the same way and canceled them.

Tagged stamps come in many different forms. Some tagged stamps have luminescent shapes or images imprinted on them as a form of security device. Others have blocks (United States), stripes, frames (South Africa and Canada), overall coatings (United States), bars (Great Britain and Canada) and many other types. Some types of tagging are even mixed in with the pigmented printing ink (Australia Scott 366, Netherlands Scott 478 and U.S. Scott 1359 and 2443).

The means of applying taggant to stamps differs as much as the intended purposes for the stamps. The most common form of tagging is a coating applied to the surface of the printed stamp. Since the taggant ink is frequently invisible except under UV light, it does not interfere with the appearance of the stamp. Another common application is the use of phosphored papers. In this case the paper itself either has a coating of taggant applied before the stamp is printed, has taggant applied during the papermaking process (incorporating it into the fibers), or has the taggant mixed into the coating of the paper. The latter method, among others, is currently in use in the United States.

Many countries now use tagging in various forms to either expedite mail handling or to serve as a printing security device against counterfeiting. Following the introduction of tagged stamps for public use in 1959 by Great Britain, other countries have steadily joined the parade. Among those are Germany (1961); Canada and Denmark (1962); United States, Australia, France and Switzerland (1963); Belgium and Japan (1966); Sweden and Norway (1967); Italy (1968); and Russia (1969). Since then, many other countries have begun using forms of tagging, including Brazil, China, Czechoslovakia, Hong Kong, Guatemala, Indonesia, Israel, Lithuania, Luxembourg, Netherlands, Penrhyn Islands, Portugal, St. Vincent, Singapore, South Africa, Spain and Sweden to name a few.

In some cases, including United States, Canada, Great Britain and Switzerland, stamps were released both with and without tagging. Many of these were released during each country's experimental period. Tagged and untagged versions are listed for the aforementioned countries and are noted in some other countries' listings. For at least a few stamps, the experimentally tagged version is worth far more than its untagged counterpart, such as the 1963 experimental tagged version of France Scott 1024.

In some cases, luminescent varieties of stamps were inadvertently created. Several Russian stamps, for example, sport highly fluorescent ink that was not intended as a form of tagging. Older stamps, such as early U.S. postage dues, can be positively identified by the use of UV light, since the organic ink used has become slightly fluorescent over time. Other stamps, such as Austria Scott 70a-82a (varnish bars) and Obock Scott 46-64 (printed quadrille lines), have become fluorescent over time.

Various fluorescent substances have been added to paper to make it appear brighter. These optical brighteners, as they are known, greatly affect the appearance of the stamp under UV light. The brightest of these is known as Hi-Brite paper. These paper varieties are beyond the scope of the Scott Catalogue.

Shortwave UV light also is used extensively in expertizing, since each form of paper has its own fluorescent characteristics that are impossible to perfectly match. It is therefore a simple matter to detect filled thins, added perforation teeth and other alterations that involve the addition of paper. UV light also is used to examine stamps that have had cancels chemically removed and for other purposes as well.

Gum

The Illustrated Gum Chart in the first part of this introduction shows and defines various types of gum condition. Because gum condition has an important impact on the value of unused stamps, we recommend studying this chart and the accompanying text carefully.

The gum on the back of a stamp may be shiny, dull, smooth, rough, dark, white, colored or tinted. Most stamp gumming adhesives use gum arabic or dextrine as a base. Certain polymers such as polyvinyl alcohol (PVA) have been used extensively since World War II.

The *Scott Standard Postage Stamp Catalogue* does not list items by types of gum. The *Scott Specialized Catalogue of United States Stamps* does differentiate among some types of gum for certain issues.

Reprints of stamps may have gum differing from the original issues. In addition, some countries have used different gum formulas for different seasons. These adhesives have different properties that may become more apparent over time.

Many stamps have been issued without gum, and the catalogue will note this fact. See, for example, United States Scott 40-47. Sometimes, gum may have been removed to preserve the stamp. Germany Scott B68, for example, has a highly acidic gum that eventually destroys the stamps. This item is valued in the catalogue with gum removed.

Reprints and Reissues

These are impressions of stamps (usually obsolete) made from the original plates or stones. If they are valid for postage and reproduce obsolete issues (such as U.S. Scott 102-111), the stamps are *reissues.* If they are from current issues, they are designated as *second, third,* etc., *printing.* If designated for a particular purpose, they are called *special printings.*

When special printings are not valid for postage, but are made from original dies and plates by authorized persons, they are *official reprints. Private reprints* are made from the original plates and dies by private hands. An example of a private reprint is that of the 1871-1932 reprints made from the original die of the 1845 New Haven, Conn., postmaster's provisional. *Official reproductions* or imitations are made from new dies and plates by government authorization. Scott will list those reissues that are valid for postage if they differ significantly from the original printing.

The U.S. government made special printings of its first postage stamps in 1875. Produced were official imitations of the first two stamps (listed as Scott 3-4), reprints of the demonetized pre-1861 issues (Scott 40-47) and reissues of the 1861 stamps, the 1869 stamps and the then-current 1875 denominations. Even though the official imitations and the reprints were not valid for postage, Scott lists all of these U.S. special printings.

Most reprints or reissues differ slightly from the original stamp in some characteristic, such as gum, paper, perforation, color or watermark. Sometimes the details are followed so meticulously that only a student of that specific stamp is able to distinguish the reprint or reissue from the original.

Remainders and Canceled to Order

Some countries sell their stock of old stamps when a new issue replaces them. To avoid postal use, the *remainders* usually are canceled with a punch hole, a heavy line or bar, or a more-or-less regular-looking cancellation. The most famous merchant of remainders was Nicholas F. Seebeck. In the 1880s and 1890s, he arranged printing contracts between the Hamilton Bank Note Co., of which he was a director, and several Central and South American countries. The contracts provided that the plates and all remainders of the yearly issues became the property of Hamilton. Seebeck saw to it that ample stock remained. The "Seebecks," both remainders and reprints, were standard packet fillers for decades.

Some countries also issue stamps *canceled-to-order (CTO),* either in sheets with original gum or stuck onto pieces of paper or envelopes and canceled. Such CTO items generally are worth less than postally used stamps. In cases where the CTO material is far more prevalent in the marketplace than postally used examples, the catalogue value relates to the CTO examples, with postally used examples noted as premium items. Most CTOs can be detected by the presence of gum. However, as the CTO practice goes back at least to 1885, the gum inevitably has been soaked off some stamps so they could pass as postally used. The normally applied postmarks usually differ slightly from standard postmarks, and specialists are able to tell the difference. When applied individually to envelopes by philatelically minded persons, CTO material is known as *favor canceled* and generally sells at large discounts.

Cinderellas and Facsimiles

Cinderella is a catch-all term used by stamp collectors to describe phantoms, fantasies, bogus items, municipal issues, exhibition seals, local revenues, transportation stamps, labels, poster stamps and many other types of items. Some cinderella collectors include in their collections local postage issues, telegraph stamps, essays and proofs, forgeries and counterfeits.

A *fantasy* is an adhesive created for a nonexistent stamp-issuing authority. Fantasy items range from imaginary countries (Occusi-Ambeno, Kingdom of Sedang, Principality of Trinidad or Torres

Straits), to non-existent locals (Winans City Post), or nonexistent transportation lines (McRobish & Co.'s Acapulco-San Francisco Line).

On the other hand, if the entity exists and could have issued stamps (but did not) or was known to have issued other stamps, the items are considered *bogus* stamps. These would include the Mormon postage stamps of Utah, S. Allan Taylor's Guatemala and Paraguay inventions, the propaganda issues for the South Moluccas and the adhesives of the Page & Keyes local post of Boston.

Phantoms is another term for both fantasy and bogus issues.

Facsimiles are copies or imitations made to represent original stamps, but which do not pretend to be originals. A catalogue illustration is such a facsimile. Illustrations from the Moens catalogue of the last century were occasionally colored and passed off as stamps. Since the beginning of stamp collecting, facsimiles have been made for collectors as space fillers or for reference. They often carry the word "facsimile," "falsch" (German), "sanko" or "mozo" (Japanese), or "faux" (French) overprinted on the face or stamped on the back. Unfortunately, over the years a number of these items have had fake cancels applied over the facsimile notation and have been passed off as genuine.

Forgeries and Counterfeits

Forgeries and counterfeits have been with philately virtually from the beginning of stamp production. Over time, the terminology for the two has been used interchangeably. Although both forgeries and counterfeits are reproductions of stamps, the purposes behind their creation differ considerably.

Among specialists there is an increasing movement to more specifically define such items. Although there is no universally accepted terminology, we feel the following definitions most closely mirror the items and their purposes as they are currently defined.

Forgeries (also often referred to as *Counterfeits*) are reproductions of genuine stamps that have been created to defraud collectors. Such spurious items first appeared on the market around 1860, and most old-time collections contain one or more. Many are crude and easily spotted, but some can deceive experts.

An important supplier of these early philatelic forgeries was the Hamburg printer Gebruder Spiro. Many others with reputations in this craft included S. Allan Taylor, George Hussey, James Chute, George Forune, Benjamin & Sarpy, Julius Goldner, E. Oneglia and L.H. Mercier. Among the noted 20th-century forgers were Francois Fournier, Jean Sperati and the prolific Raoul DeThuin.

Forgeries may be complete replications, or they may be genuine stamps altered to resemble a scarcer (and more valuable) type. Most forgeries, particularly those of rare stamps, are worth only a small fraction of the value of a genuine example, but a few types, created by some of the most notable forgers, such as Sperati, can be worth as much or more than the genuine. Fraudulently produced copies are known of most classic rarities and many medium-priced stamps.

In addition to rare stamps, large numbers of common 19th- and early 20th-century stamps were forged to supply stamps to the early packet trade. Many can still be easily found. Few new philatelic forgeries have appeared in recent decades. Successful imitation of well-engraved work is virtually impossible. It has proven far easier to produce a fake by altering a genuine stamp than to duplicate a stamp completely.

Counterfeit (also often referred to as *Postal Counterfeit* or *Postal Forgery*) is the term generally applied to reproductions of stamps that have been created to defraud the government of revenue. Such items usually are created at the time a stamp is current and, in some cases, are hard to detect. Because most counterfeits are seized when the perpetrator is captured, postal counterfeits, particularly used on cover, are usually worth much more than a genuine example to specialists. The first postal counterfeit was of Spain's 4-cuarto carmine of 1854 (the real one is Scott 25). Apparently, the counterfeiters were not satisfied with their first version, which is now very scarce, and they soon created an engraved counterfeit, which is common. Postal counterfeits quickly followed in Austria, Naples, Sardinia and the Roman States. They have since been created in many other countries as well, including the United States.

An infamous counterfeit to defraud the government is the 1-shilling Great Britain "Stock Exchange" forgery of 1872, used on telegraph forms at the exchange that year. The stamp escaped detection until a stamp dealer noticed it in 1898.

Fakes

Fakes are genuine stamps altered in some way to make them more desirable. One student of this part of stamp collecting has estimated that by the 1950s more than 30,000 varieties of fakes were known. That number has grown greatly since then. The widespread existence of fakes makes it important for stamp collectors to study their philatelic holdings and use relevant literature. Likewise, collectors should buy from reputable dealers who guarantee their stamps and make full and prompt refunds should a purchased item be declared faked or altered by some mutually agreed-upon authority. Because fakes always have some genuine characteristics, it is not always possible to obtain unanimous agreement among experts regarding specific items. These students may change their opinions as philatelic knowledge increases. More than 80 percent of all fakes on the philatelic market today are regummed, reperforated (or perforated for the first time), or bear forged overprints, surcharges or cancellations.

Stamps can be chemically treated to alter or eliminate colors. For example, a pale rose stamp can be re-colored to resemble a blue shade of high market value. In other cases, treated stamps can be made to resemble missing color varieties. Designs may be changed by painting, or a stroke or a dot added or bleached out to turn an ordinary variety into a seemingly scarcer stamp. Part of a stamp can be bleached and reprinted in a different version, achieving an inverted center or frame. Margins can be added or repairs done so deceptively that the stamps move from the "repaired" into the "fake" category.

Fakers have not left the backs of the stamps untouched either. They may create false watermarks, add fake grills or press out genuine grills. A thin India paper proof may be glued onto a thicker backing to create the appearance an issued stamp, or a proof printed on cardboard may be shaved down and perforated to resemble a stamp. Silk threads are impressed into paper and stamps have been split so that a rare paper variety is added to an otherwise inexpensive stamp. The most common treatment to the back of a stamp, however, is regumming.

Some in the business of faking stamps have openly advertised foolproof application of "original gum" to stamps that lack it, although most publications now ban such ads from their pages. It is believed that very few early stamps have survived without being hinged. The large number of never-hinged examples of such earlier material offered for sale thus suggests the widespread extent of regumming activity. Regumming also may be used to hide repairs or thin spots. Dipping the stamp into watermark fluid, or examining it under longwave ultraviolet light often will reveal these flaws.

Fakers also tamper with separations. Ingenious ways to add margins are known. Perforated wide-margin stamps may be falsely represented as imperforate when trimmed. Reperforating is commonly done to create scarce coil or perforation varieties, and to eliminate the naturally occurring straight-edge stamps found in sheet margin positions of many earlier issues. Custom has made straight-edged stamps less desirable. Fakers have obliged by perforating straight-edged stamps so that many are now uncommon, if not rare.

Another fertile field for the faker is that of overprints, surcharges and cancellations. The forging of rare surcharges or overprints began in the 1880s or 1890s. These forgeries are sometimes difficult to detect, but experts have identified almost all. Occasionally, overprints or cancellations are removed to create non-overprinted stamps or seemingly unused items. This is most commonly done by removing a manuscript cancel to make a stamp resemble an unused example. "SPECIMEN" overprints may be removed by scraping and repainting to create non-overprinted varieties. Fakers use inexpensive revenues or pen-canceled stamps to generate unused stamps for further faking by adding other markings. The quartz lamp or UV lamp and a high-powered magnifying glass help to easily detect removed cancellations.

The bigger problem, however, is the addition of overprints, surcharges or cancellations - many with such precision that they are very difficult to ascertain. Plating of the stamps or the overprint can be an important method of detection.

Fake postmarks may range from many spurious fancy cancellations to a host of markings applied to transatlantic covers, to adding normally appearing postmarks to definitives of some countries with stamps that are valued far higher used than unused. With the increased popularity of cover collecting, and the widespread interest in postal history, a fertile new field for fakers has come about. Some have tried to create entire covers. Others specialize in adding stamps, tied by fake cancellations, to genuine stampless covers, or replacing less expensive or damaged stamps with more valuable ones. Detailed study of postal rates in effect at the time a cover in question was mailed, including the analysis of each handstamp used during the period, ink analysis and similar techniques, usually will unmask the fraud.

Restoration and Repairs

Scott Publishing Co. bases its catalogue values on stamps that are free of defects and otherwise meet the standards set forth earlier in this introduction. Most stamp collectors desire to have the finest copy of an item possible. Even within given grading categories there are variances. This leads to a controversial practice that is not defined in any universal manner: stamp *restoration.*

There are broad differences of opinion about what is permissible when it comes to restoration. Carefully applying a soft eraser to a stamp or cover to remove light soiling is one form of restoration, as is washing a stamp in mild soap and water to clean it. These are fairly accepted forms of restoration. More severe forms of restoration include pressing out creases or removing stains caused by tape. To what degree each of these is acceptable is dependent upon the individual situation. Further along the spectrum is the freshening of a stamp's color by removing oxide build-up or the effects of wax paper left next to stamps shipped to the tropics.

At some point in this spectrum the concept of *repair* replaces that of restoration. Repairs include filling thin spots, mending tears by reweaving or adding a missing perforation tooth. Regumming stamps may have been acceptable as a restoration or repair technique many decades ago, but today it is considered a form of fakery.

Restored stamps may or may not sell at a discount, and it is possible that the value of individual restored items may be enhanced over that of their pre-restoration state. Specific situations dictate the resultant value of such an item. Repaired stamps sell at substantial discounts from the value of sound stamps.

Terminology

Booklets — Many countries have issued stamps in small booklets for the convenience of users. This idea continues to become increasingly popular in many countries. Booklets have been issued in many sizes and forms, often with advertising on the covers, the panes of stamps or on the interleaving.

The panes used in booklets may be printed from special plates or made from regular sheets. All panes from booklets issued by the United States and many from those of other countries contain stamps that are straight edged on the sides, but perforated between. Others are distinguished by orientation of watermark or other identifying features. Any stamp-like unit in the pane, either printed or blank, that is not a postage stamp, is considered to be a *label* in the catalogue listings.

Scott lists and values booklet panes. Modern complete booklets also are listed and valued. Individual booklet panes are listed only when they are not fashioned from existing sheet stamps and, therefore, are identifiable from their sheet stamp counterparts.

Panes usually do not have a used value assigned to them because there is little market activity for used booklet panes, even though many exist used and there is some demand for them.

Cancellations — The marks or obliterations put on stamps by postal authorities to show that they have performed service and to prevent their reuse are known as cancellations. If the marking is made with a pen, it is considered a "pen cancel." When the location of the post office appears in the marking, it is a "town cancellation." A "postmark" is technically any postal marking, but in practice the term generally is applied to a town cancellation with a date. When calling attention to a cause or celebration, the marking is known as a "slogan cancellation." Many other types and styles of cancellations exist, such as duplex, numerals, targets, fancy and others. See also "precancels," below.

Coil Stamps — These are stamps that are issued in rolls for use in dispensers, affixing and vending machines. Those coils of the United States, Canada, Sweden and some other countries are perforated horizontally or vertically only, with the outer edges imperforate. Coil stamps of some countries, such as Great Britain and Germany, are perforated on all four sides and may in some cases be distinguished from their sheet stamp counterparts by watermarks, counting numbers on the reverse or other means.

Covers — Entire envelopes, with or without adhesive postage stamps, that have passed through the mail and bear postal or other markings of philatelic interest are known as covers. Before the introduction of envelopes in about 1840, people folded letters and wrote the address on the outside. Some people covered their letters with an extra sheet of paper on the outside for the address, producing the term "cover." Used airletter sheets, stamped envelopes and other items of postal stationery also are considered covers.

Errors — Stamps that have some major, consistent, unintentional deviation from the normal are considered errors. Errors include, but are not limited to, missing or wrong colors, wrong paper, wrong watermarks, inverted centers or frames on multicolor printing, inverted or missing surcharges or overprints, double impressions, missing perforations, unintentionally omitted tagging and others. Factually wrong or misspelled information, if it appears on all examples of a stamp, are not considered errors in the true sense of the word. They are errors of design. Inconsistent or randomly appearing items, such as misperfs or color shifts, are classified as freaks.

Color-Omitted Errors — This term refers to stamps where a missing color is caused by the complete failure of the printing plate to deliver ink to the stamp paper or any other paper. Generally, this is caused by the printing plate not being engaged on the press or the ink station running dry of ink during printing.

Color-Missing Errors — This term refers to stamps where a color or colors were printed somewhere but do not appear on the finished stamp. There are four different classes of color-missing errors, and the catalog indicates with a two-letter code appended to each such listing what caused the color to be missing. These codes are used only for the United States' color-missing error listings.

FO = A *foldover* of the stamp sheet during printing may block ink from appearing on a stamp. Instead, the color will appear on the back of the foldover (where it might fall on the back of the selvage or perhaps on the back of the stamp or another stamp). FO also will be used in the case of foldunders, where the paper may fold underneath the other stamp paper and the color will print on the platen.

EP = A piece of *extraneous paper* falling across the plate or stamp paper will receive the printed ink. When the extraneous paper is removed, an unprinted portion of stamp paper remains and shows partially or totally missing colors.

CM = A misregistration of the printing plates during printing will result in a *color misregistration*, and such a misregistraion may result in a color not appearing on the finished stamp.

PS = A *perforation shift* after printing may remove a color from the finished stamp. Normally, this will occur on a row of stamps at the edge of the stamp pane.

Measurements – When measurements are given in the Scott catalogues for stamp size, grill size or any other reason, the first measurement given is always for the top and bottom dimension, while the second measurement will be for the sides (just as perforation gauges are measured). Thus, a stamp size of 15mm x 21mm will indicate a vertically oriented stamp 15mm wide at top and bottom, and 21mm tall at the sides. The same principle holds for measuring or counting items such as U.S. grills. A grill count of 22x18 points (B grill) indicates that there are 22 grill points across by 18 grill points down.

Overprints and Surcharges — Overprinting involves applying wording or design elements over an already existing stamp. Overprints can be used to alter the place of use (such as "Canal Zone" on U.S. stamps), to adapt them for a special purpose ("Porto" on Denmark's 1913-20 regular issues for use as postage due stamps, Scott J1-J7) or to commemorate a special occasion (United States Scott 647-648).

A *surcharge* is a form of overprint that changes or restates the face value of a stamp or piece of postal stationery.

Surcharges and overprints may be handstamped, typeset or, occasionally, lithographed or engraved. A few hand-written overprints and surcharges are known.

Personalized Stamps — In 1999, Australia issued stamps with se-tenant labels that could be personalized with pictures of the customer's choice. Other countries quickly followed suit, with some offering to print the selected picture on the stamp itself within a frame that was used exclusively for personalized issues. As the picture used on these stamps or labels vary, listings for such stamps are for *any* picture within the common frame (or any picture on a se-tenant label), be it a "generic" image or one produced especially for a customer, almost invariably at a premium price.

Precancels — Stamps that are canceled before they are placed in the mail are known as precancels. Precanceling usually is done to expedite the handling of large mailings and generally allow the affected mail pieces to skip certain phases of mail handling.

In the United States, precancellations generally identified the point of origin; that is, the city and state. This information appeared across the face of the stamp, usually centered between parallel lines. More recently, bureau precancels retained the parallel lines, but the city and state designations were dropped. Recent coils have a service inscription that is present on the original printing plate. These show the mail service paid for by the stamp. Since these stamps are not intended to receive further cancellations when used as intended, they are considered precancels. Such items often do not have parallel lines as part of the precancellation.

In France, the abbreviation *Affranchts* in a semicircle together with the word *Postes* is the general form of precancel in use. Belgian precancellations usually appear in a box in which the name of the city appears. Netherlands precancels have the name of the city enclosed between concentric circles, sometimes called a "lifesaver." Precancellations of other countries usually follow these patterns, but may be any arrangement of bars, boxes and city names.

Precancels are listed in the Scott catalogues only if the precancel changes the denomination (Belgium Scott 477-478); if the precanceled stamp is different from the non-precanceled version (such as untagged U.S. precancels); or if the stamp exists only precanceled (France Scott 1096-1099, U.S. Scott 2265).

Proofs and Essays — Proofs are impressions taken from an approved die, plate or stone in which the design and color are the same as the stamp issued to the public. Trial color proofs are impressions taken from approved dies, plates or stones in colors that vary from the final version. An essay is the impression of a design that differs in some way from the issued stamp. "Progressive die proofs" generally are considered to be essays.

Provisionals — These are stamps that are issued on short notice and intended for temporary use pending the arrival of regular issues. They usually are issued to meet such contingencies as changes in government or currency, shortage of necessary postage values or military occupation.

During the 1840s, postmasters in certain American cities issued stamps that were valid only at specific post offices. In 1861, postmasters of the Confederate States also issued stamps with limited validity. Both of these examples are known as "postmaster's provisionals."

Se-tenant — This term refers to an unsevered pair, strip or block of stamps that differ in design, denomination or overprint.

Unless the se-tenant item has a continuous design (see U.S. Scott 1451a, 1694a) the stamps do not have to be in the same order as shown in the catalogue (see U.S. Scott 2158a).

Specimens — The Universal Postal Union required member nations to send samples of all stamps they released into service to the International Bureau in Switzerland. Member nations of the UPU received these specimens as samples of what stamps were valid for postage. Many are overprinted, handstamped or initial-perforated "Specimen," "Canceled" or "Muestra." Some are marked with bars across the denominations (China-Taiwan), punched holes (Czechoslovakia) or back inscriptions (Mongolia).

Stamps distributed to government officials or for publicity purposes, and stamps submitted by private security printers for official approval, also may receive such defacements.

The previously described defacement markings prevent postal use, and all such items generally are known as "specimens."

Tete Beche — This term describes a pair of stamps in which one is upside down in relation to the other. Some of these are the result of intentional sheet arrangements, such as Morocco Scott B10-B11. Others occurred when one or more electrotypes accidentally were placed upside down on the plate, such as Colombia Scott 57a. Separation of the tete-beche stamps, of course, destroys the tete beche variety.

Currency Conversion

Country	Dollar	Pound	S Franc	Yen	HK $	Euro	Cdn $	Aus $
Australia	0.9979	1.5971	1.0253	0.0120	0.1280	1.3518	1.0111	—
Canada	0.9869	1.5795	1.0140	0.0118	0.1266	1.3369	—	0.9890
European Union	0.7382	1.1815	0.7585	0.0088	0.0947	—	0.7480	0.7398
Hong Kong	7.7955	12.477	8.0093	0.0934	—	10.560	7.8990	7.8119
Japan	83.473	133.60	85.763	—	10.708	113.08	84.581	83.649
Switzerland	0.9733	1.5578	—	0.0117	0.1249	1.3185	0.9862	0.9753
United Kingdom	0.6248	—	0.6419	0.0075	0.0801	0.8464	0.6331	0.6261
United States	—	1.6005	1.0274	0.0120	0.1283	1.3546	1.0133	1.0021

Country	Currency	U.S. $ Equiv.
Jamaica	dollar	.0117
Japan	yen	.0120
Jordan	dinar	1.413
Kazakhstan	tenge	.0068
Kenya	shilling	.0123
Kiribati	Australian dollar	1.0021
Korea (South)	won	.0009
Korea (North)	won	.0077
Kosovo	euro	1.3546
Kuwait	dinar	3.569
Kyrgyzstan	som	.0211
Laos	kip	.0001
Latvia	lat	1.923
Lebanon	pound	.0007
Lesotho	maloti	.1374
Liberia	dollar	.0140
Liechtenstein	Swiss franc	1.0274
Lithuania	litas	.3904
Luxembourg	euro	1.3546
Macao	pataca	.1245
Macedonia	denar	.0221
Malagasy Republic	ariary	.0005
Malawi	kwacha	.0066
Malaysia	ringgit (dollar)	.3275
Maldive Islands	rafiyaa	.0781
Mali	Community of French Africa (CFA) franc	.0021
Malta	euro	1.3546
Marshall Islands	U.S. dollar	1.00
Mauritania	ouguiya	.0035
Mauritius	rupee	.0341
Mayotte	euro	1.3546
Mexico	peso	.0831
Micronesia	U.S. dollar	1.00
Moldova	leu	.0838
Monaco	euro	1.3546
Mongolia	tugrik	.0008
Montenegro	euro	1.3546
Montserrat	East Caribbean dollar	.3724
Morocco	dirham	.1209
Mozambique	metical	.0386

Source: ***Wall Street Journal*** *Feb. 12, 2011. Figures reflect values as of Feb. 11, 2011.*

COMMON DESIGN TYPES

Pictured in this section are issues where one illustration has been used for a number of countries in the Catalogue. Not included in this section are overprinted stamps or those issues which are illustrated in each country.

EUROPA
Europa, 1956

The design symbolizing the cooperation among the six countries comprising the Coal and Steel Community is illustrated in each country.

Belgium	496-497
France	805-806
Germany	748-749
Italy	715-716
Luxembourg	318-320
Netherlands	368-369

Europa, 1958

"E" and Dove — CD1

European Postal Union at the service of European integration.

1958, Sept. 13

Belgium	527-528
France	889-890
Germany	790-791
Italy	750-751
Luxembourg	341-343
Netherlands	375-376
Saar	317-318

Europa, 1959

6-Link Enless Chain — CD2

1959, Sept. 19

Belgium	536-537
France	929-930
Germany	805-806
Italy	791-792
Luxembourg	354-355
Netherlands	379-380

Europa, 1960

19-Spoke Wheel CD3

First anniversary of the establishment of C.E.P.T. (Conference Europeenne des Administrations des Postes et des Telecommunications.) The spokes symbolize the 19 founding members of the Conference.

1960, Sept.

Belgium	553-554
Denmark	379
Finland	376-377
France	970-971
Germany	818-820
Great Britain	377-378
Greece	688
Iceland	327-328
Ireland	175-176
Italy	809-810
Luxembourg	374-375
Netherlands	385-386
Norway	387
Portugal	866-867
Spain	941-942
Sweden	562-563
Switzerland	400-401
Turkey	1493-1494

Europa, 1961

19 Doves Flying as One — CD4

The 19 doves represent the 19 members of the Conference of European Postal and Telecommunications Administrations C.E.P.T.

1961-62

Belgium	572-573
Cyprus	201-203
France	1005-1006
Germany	844-845
Great Britain	383-384
Greece	718-719
Iceland	340-341
Italy	845-846
Luxembourg	382-383
Netherlands	387-388
Spain	1010-1011
Switzerland	410-411
Turkey	1518-1520

Europa, 1962

Young Tree with 19 Leaves CD5

The 19 leaves represent the 19 original members of C.E.P.T.

1962-63

Belgium	582-583
Cyprus	219-221
France	1045-1046
Germany	852-853
Greece	739-740
Iceland	348-349
Ireland	184-185
Italy	860-861
Luxembourg	386-387
Netherlands	394-395
Norway	414-415
Switzerland	416-417
Turkey	1553-1555

Europa, 1963

Stylized Links, Symbolizing Unity — CD6

1963, Sept.

Belgium	598-599
Cyprus	229-231
Finland	419
France	1074-1075
Germany	867-868
Greece	768-769
Iceland	357-358
Ireland	188-189
Italy	880-881
Luxembourg	403-404
Netherlands	416-417
Norway	441-442
Switzerland	429
Turkey	1602-1603

Europa, 1964

Symbolic Daisy — CD7

5th anniversary of the establishment of C.E.P.T. The 22 petals of the flower symbolize the 22 members of the Conference.

1964, Sept.

Austria	738
Belgium	614-615
Cyprus	244-246
France	1109-1110
Germany	897-898
Greece	801-802
Iceland	367-368
Ireland	196-197
Italy	894-895
Luxembourg	411-412
Monaco	590-591
Netherlands	428-429
Norway	458
Portugal	931-933
Spain	1262-1263
Switzerland	438-439
Turkey	1628-1629

Europa, 1965

Leaves and "Fruit" CD8

1965

Belgium	636-637
Cyprus	262-264
Finland	437
France	1131-1132
Germany	934-935
Greece	833-834
Iceland	375-376
Ireland	204-205
Italy	915-916
Luxembourg	432-433
Monaco	616-617
Netherlands	438-439
Norway	475-476
Portugal	958-960
Switzerland	469
Turkey	1665-1666

Europa, 1966

Symbolic Sailboat — CD9

1966, Sept.

Andorra, French	172
Belgium	675-676
Cyprus	275-277
France	1163-1164
Germany	963-964
Greece	862-863
Iceland	384-385
Ireland	216-217
Italy	942-943
Liechtenstein	415
Luxembourg	440-441
Monaco	639-640
Netherlands	441-442
Norway	496-497
Portugal	980-982
Switzerland	477-478
Turkey	1718-1719

Europa, 1967

Cogwheels CD10

1967

Andorra, French	174-175
Belgium	688-689
Cyprus	297-299
France	1178-1179
Germany	969-970
Greece	891-892
Iceland	389-390
Ireland	232-233
Italy	951-952
Liechtenstein	420
Luxembourg	449-450
Monaco	669-670
Netherlands	444-447
Norway	504-505
Portugal	994-996
Spain	1465-1466
Switzerland	482
Turkey	B120-B121

Europa, 1968

Golden Key with C.E.P.T. Emblem CD11

1968

Andorra, French	182-183
Belgium	705-706
Cyprus	314-316
France	1209-1210
Germany	983-984
Greece	916-917
Iceland	395-396
Ireland	242-243
Italy	979-980
Liechtenstein	442
Luxembourg	466-467
Monaco	689-691
Netherlands	452-453
Portugal	1019-1021
San Marino	687
Spain	1526
Turkey	1775-1776

Europa, 1969

"EUROPA" and "CEPT" CD12

Tenth anniversary of C.E.P.T.

1969

Andorra, French	188-189
Austria	837
Belgium	718-719
Cyprus	326-328
Denmark	458
Finland	483
France	1245-1246
Germany	996-997
Great Britain	585
Greece	947-948
Iceland	406-407
Ireland	270-271
Italy	1000-1001
Liechtenstein	453
Luxembourg	475-476
Monaco	722-724
Netherlands	475-476
Norway	533-534
Portugal	1038-1040
San Marino	701-702
Spain	1567
Sweden	814-816

Switzerland 500-501
Turkey 1799-1800
Vatican 470-472
Yugoslavia 1003-1004

Europa, 1970

Interwoven Threads CD13

1970

Andorra, French 196-197
Belgium 741-742
Cyprus 340-342
France 1271-1272
Germany 1018-1019
Greece 985, 987
Iceland 420-421
Ireland 279-281
Italy 1013-1014
Liechtenstein 470
Luxembourg 489-490
Monaco 768-770
Netherlands 483-484
Portugal 1060-1062
San Marino 729-730
Spain 1607
Switzerland 515-516
Turkey 1848-1849
Yugoslavia 1024-1025

Europa, 1971

"Fraternity, Cooperation, Common Effort" CD14

1971

Andorra, French 205-206
Belgium 803-804
Cyprus 365-367
Finland 504
France 1304
Germany 1064-1065
Greece 1029-1030
Iceland 429-430
Ireland 305-306
Italy 1038-1039
Liechtenstein 485
Luxembourg 500-501
Malta 425-427
Monaco 797-799
Netherlands 488-489
Portugal 1094-1096
San Marino 749-750
Spain 1675-1676
Switzerland 531-532
Turkey 1876-1877
Yugoslavia 1052-1053

Europa, 1972

Sparkles, Symbolic of Communications CD15

1972

Andorra, French 210-211
Andorra, Spanish 62
Belgium 825-826
Cyprus 380-382
Finland 512-513
France 1341
Germany 1089-1090
Greece 1049-1050
Iceland 439-440
Ireland 316-317
Italy 1065-1066
Liechtenstein 504
Luxembourg 512-513
Malta 450-453
Monaco 831-832

Netherlands 494-495
Portugal 1141-1143
San Marino 771-772
Spain 1718
Switzerland 544-545
Turkey 1907-1908
Yugoslavia 1100-1101

Europa, 1973

Post Horn and Arrows CD16

1973

Andorra, French 219-220
Andorra, Spanish 76
Belgium 839-840
Cyprus 396-398
Finland 526
France 1367
Germany 1114-1115
Greece 1090-1092
Iceland 447-448
Ireland 329-330
Italy 1108-1109
Liechtenstein 528-529
Luxembourg 523-524
Malta 469-471
Monaco 866-867
Netherlands 504-505
Norway 604-605
Portugal 1170-1172
San Marino 802-803
Spain 1753
Switzerland 580-581
Turkey 1935-1936
Yugoslavia 1138-1139

Europa, 2000

CD17

2000

Albania 2621-2622
Andorra, French 522
Andorra, Spanish 262
Armenia 610-611
Austria 1814
Azerbaijan 698-699
Belarus 350
Belgium 1818
Bosnia & Herzegovina (Moslem) 358
Bosnia & Herzegovina (Serb) 111-112
Croatia 428-429
Cyprus 959
Czech Republic 3120
Denmark 1189
Estonia 394
Faroe Islands 376
Finland 1129
Aland Islands 166
France 2771
Georgia 228-229
Germany 2086-2087
Gibraltar 837-840
Great Britain (Guernsey) 805-809
Great Britain (Jersey) 935-936
Great Britain (Isle of Man) 883
Greece 1959
Greenland 363
Hungary 3699-3700
Iceland 910
Ireland 1230-1231
Italy 2349
Latvia 504
Liechtenstein 1178
Lithuania 668
Luxembourg 1035
Macedonia 187
Malta 1011-1012
Moldova 355
Monaco 2161-2162
Poland 3519
Portugal 2358
Portugal (Azores) 455
Portugal (Madeira) 208

Romania 4370
Russia 6589
San Marino 1480
Slovakia 355
Slovenia 424
Spain 3036
Sweden 2394
Switzerland 1074
Turkey 2762
Turkish Rep. of Northern Cyprus 500
Ukraine 379
Vatican City 1152

The Gibraltar stamps are similar to the stamp illustrated, but none have the design shown above. All other sets listed above include at least one stamp with the design shown, but some include stamps with entirely different designs. Bulgaria Nos. 4131-4132 and Yugoslavia Nos. 2485-2486 are Europa stamps with completely different designs.

PORTUGAL & COLONIES

Vasco da Gama

Fleet Departing CD20

Fleet Arriving at Calicut — CD21

Embarking at Rastello CD22

Muse of History CD23

San Gabriel, da Gama and Camoens CD24

Archangel Gabriel, the Patron Saint CD25

Flagship San Gabriel — CD26

Vasco da Gama — CD27

Fourth centenary of Vasco da Gama's discovery of the route to India.

1898

Azores 93-100
Macao 67-74
Madeira 37-44
Portugal 147-154
Port. Africa 1-8
Port. Congo 75-98
Port. India 189-196
St. Thomas & Prince Islands 170-193
Timor 45-52

Pombal
POSTAL TAX
POSTAL TAX DUES

Marquis de Pombal — CD28

Planning Reconstruction of Lisbon, 1755 — CD29

Pombal Monument, Lisbon — CD30

Sebastiao Jose de Carvalho e Mello, Marquis de Pombal (1699-1782), statesman, rebuilt Lisbon after earthquake of 1755. Tax was for the erection of Pombal monument. Obligatory on all mail on certain days throughout the year. Postal Tax Dues are inscribed "Multa."

1925

Angola RA1-RA3, RAJ1-RAJ3
Azores RA9-RA11, RAJ2-RAJ4
Cape Verde RA1-RA3, RAJ1-RAJ3
Macao RA1-RA3, RAJ1-RAJ3
Madeira RA1-RA3, RAJ1-RAJ3
Mozambique RA1-RA3, RAJ1-RAJ3
Nyassa RA1-RA3, RAJ1-RAJ3
Portugal RA11-RA13, RAJ2-RAJ4
Port. Guinea RA1-RA3, RAJ1-RAJ3
Port. India RA1-RA3, RAJ1-RAJ3
St. Thomas & Prince Islands RA1-RA3, RAJ1-RAJ3
Timor RA1-RA3, RAJ1-RAJ3

Vasco da Gama CD34

Mousinho de Albuquerque CD35

Dam CD36

Prince Henry the Navigator CD37

Affonso de Albuquerque CD38

Plane over Globe CD39

1938-39

Angola 274-291, C1-C9
Cape Verde 234-251, C1-C9
Macao 289-305, C7-C15
Mozambique 270-287, C1-C9
Port. Guinea 233-250, C1-C9
Port. India 439-453, C1-C8
St. Thomas & Prince Islands ... 302-319, 323-340, C1-C18
Timor 223-239, C1-C9

Lady of Fatima

Our Lady of the Rosary, Fatima, Portugal — CD40

1948-49

Angola	315-318
Cape Verde	266
Macao	336
Mozambique	325-328
Port. Guinea	271
Port. India	480
St. Thomas & Prince Islands	351
Timor	254

A souvenir sheet of 9 stamps was issued in 1951 to mark the extension of the 1950 Holy Year. The sheet contains: Angola No. 316, Cape Verde No. 266, Macao No. 336, Mozambique No. 325, Portuguese Guinea No. 271, Portuguese India Nos. 480, 485, St. Thomas & Prince Islands No. 351, Timor No. 254. The sheet also contains a portrait of Pope Pius XII and is inscribed "Encerramento do Ano Santo, Fatima 1951." It was sold for 11 escudos.

Holy Year

Church Bells and Dove CD41

Angel Holding Candelabra CD42

Holy Year, 1950.

1950-51

Angola	331-332
Cape Verde	268-269
Macao	339-340
Mozambique	330-331
Port. Guinea	273-274
Port. India	490-491, 496-503
St. Thomas & Prince Islands	353-354
Timor	258-259

A souvenir sheet of 8 stamps was issued in 1951 to mark the extension of the Holy Year. The sheet contains: Angola No. 331, Cape Verde No. 269, Macao No. 340, Mozambique No. 331, Portuguese Guinea No. 275, Portuguese India No. 490, St. Thomas & Prince Islands No. 354, Timor No. 258, some with colors changed. The sheet contains doves and is inscribed 'Encerramento do Ano Santo, Fatima 1951.' It was sold for 17 escudos.

Holy Year Conclusion

Our Lady of Fatima — CD43

Conclusion of Holy Year. Sheets contain alternate vertical rows of stamps and labels bearing quotation from Pope Pius XII, different for each colony.

1951

Angola	357
Cape Verde	270
Macao	352
Mozambique	356
Port. Guinea	275
Port. India	506
St. Thomas & Prince Islands	355
Timor	270

Medical Congress

CD44

First National Congress of Tropical Medicine, Lisbon, 1952. Each stamp has a different design.

1952

Angola	358
Cape Verde	287
Macao	364
Mozambique	359
Port. Guinea	276
Port. India	516
St. Thomas & Prince Islands	356
Timor	271

Postage Due Stamps

CD45

1952

Angola	J37-J42
Cape Verde	J31-J36
Macao	J53-J58
Mozambique	J51-J56
Port. Guinea	J40-J45
Port. India	J47-J52
St. Thomas & Prince Islands	J52-J57
Timor	J31-J36

Sao Paulo

Father Manuel da Nobrega and View of Sao Paulo — CD46

Founding of Sao Paulo, Brazil, 400th anniv.

1954

Angola	385
Cape Verde	297
Macao	382
Mozambique	395
Port. Guinea	291
Port. India	530
St. Thomas & Prince Islands	369
Timor	279

Tropical Medicine Congress

CD47

Sixth International Congress for Tropical Medicine and Malaria, Lisbon, Sept. 1958. Each stamp shows a different plant.

1958

Angola	409
Cape Verde	303
Macao	392
Mozambique	404
Port. Guinea	295
Port. India	569
St. Thomas & Prince Islands	371
Timor	289

Sports

CD48

Each stamp shows a different sport.

1962

Angola	433-438
Cape Verde	320-325
Macao	394-399
Mozambique	424-429
Port. Guinea	299-304
St. Thomas & Prince Islands	374-379
Timor	313-318

Anti-Malaria

Anopheles Funestus and Malaria Eradication Symbol — CD49

World Health Organization drive to eradicate malaria.

1962

Angola	439
Cape Verde	326
Macao	400
Mozambique	430
Port. Guinea	305
St. Thomas & Prince Islands	380
Timor	319

Airline Anniversary

Map of Africa, Super Constellation and Jet Liner — CD50

Tenth anniversary of Transportes Aereos Portugueses (TAP).

1963

Angola	490
Cape Verde	327
Mozambique	434
Port. Guinea	318
St. Thomas & Prince Islands	381

National Overseas Bank

Antonio Teixeira de Sousa — CD51

Centenary of the National Overseas Bank of Portugal.

1964, May 16

Angola	509
Cape Verde	328
Port. Guinea	319
St. Thomas & Prince Islands	382
Timor	320

ITU

ITU Emblem and the Archangel Gabriel — CD52

International Communications Union, Cent.

1965, May 17

Angola	511
Cape Verde	329
Macao	402
Mozambique	464
Port. Guinea	320
St. Thomas & Prince Islands	383
Timor	321

National Revolution

CD53

40th anniv. of the National Revolution. Different buildings on each stamp.

1966, May 28

Angola	525
Cape Verde	338
Macao	403
Mozambique	465
Port. Guinea	329
St. Thomas & Prince Islands	392
Timor	322

Navy Club

CD54

Centenary of Portugal's Navy Club. Each stamp has a different design.

1967, Jan. 31

Angola	527-528
Cape Verde	339-340
Macao	412-413
Mozambique	478-479
Port. Guinea	330-331
St. Thomas & Prince Islands	393-394
Timor	323-324

Admiral Coutinho

CD55

Centenary of the birth of Admiral Carlos Viegas Gago Coutinho (1869-1959), explorer and aviation pioneer. Each stamp has a different design.

1969, Feb. 17

Angola	547
Cape Verde	355
Macao	417
Mozambique	484
Port. Guinea	335
St. Thomas & Prince Islands	397
Timor	335

Administration Reform

Luiz Augusto Rebello da Silva — CD56

Centenary of the administration reforms of the overseas territories.

1969, Sept. 25

Angola 549
Cape Verde 357
Macao 419
Mozambique 491
Port. Guinea 337
St. Thomas & Prince Islands 399
Timor 338

Marshal Carmona

CD57

Birth centenary of Marshal Antonio Oscar Carmona de Fragoso (1869-1951), President of Portugal. Each stamp has a different design.

1970, Nov. 15

Angola 563
Cape Verde 359
Macao 422
Mozambique 493
Port. Guinea 340
St. Thomas & Prince Islands 403
Timor 341

Olympic Games

CD59

20th Olympic Games, Munich, Aug. 26-Sept. 11. Each stamp shows a different sport.

1972, June 20

Angola 569
Cape Verde 361
Macao 426
Mozambique 504
Port. Guinea 342
St. Thomas & Prince Islands 408
Timor 343

Lisbon-Rio de Janeiro Flight

CD60

50th anniversary of the Lisbon to Rio de Janeiro flight by Arturo de Sacadura and Coutinho, March 30-June 5, 1922. Each stamp shows a different stage of the flight.

1972, Sept. 20

Angola 570
Cape Verde 362
Macao 427
Mozambique 505
Port. Guinea 343
St. Thomas & Prince Islands 409
Timor 344

WMO Centenary

WMO Emblem — CD61

Centenary of international meterological cooperation.

1973, Dec. 15

Angola 571
Cape Verde 363
Macao 429
Mozambique 509
Port. Guinea 344
St. Thomas & Prince Islands 410
Timor 345

FRENCH COMMUNITY

Upper Volta can be found under Burkina Faso in Vol. 1

Madagascar can be found under Malagasy in Vol. 3

Colonial Exposition

People of French Empire CD70

Women's Heads CD71

France Showing Way to Civilization CD72

"Colonial Commerce" CD73

International Colonial Exposition, Paris.

1931

Cameroun 213-216
Chad 60-63
Dahomey 97-100
Fr. Guiana 152-155
Fr. Guinea 116-119
Fr. India 100-103
Fr. Polynesia 76-79
Fr. Sudan 102-105
Gabon 120-123
Guadeloupe 138-141
Indo-China 140-142
Ivory Coast 92-95
Madagascar 169-172
Martinique 129-132
Mauritania 65-68
Middle Congo 61-64
New Caledonia 176-179
Niger 73-76
Reunion 122-125
St. Pierre & Miquelon 132-135
Senegal 138-141
Somali Coast 135-138
Togo 254-257
Ubangi-Shari 82-85
Upper Volta 66-69
Wallis & Futuna Isls. 85-88

Paris International Exposition Colonial Arts Exposition

"Colonial Resources" CD74 CD77

Overseas Commerce CD75

Exposition Building and Women CD76

"France and the Empire" CD78

Cultural Treasures of the Colonies CD79

Souvenir sheets contain one imperf. stamp.

1937

Cameroun 217-222A
Dahomey 101-107
Fr. Equatorial Africa 27-32, 73
Fr. Guiana 162-168
Fr. Guinea 120-126
Fr. India 104-110
Fr. Polynesia 117-123
Fr. Sudan 106-112
Guadeloupe 148-154
Indo-China 193-199
Inini 41
Ivory Coast 152-158
Kwangchowan 132
Madagascar 191-197
Martinique 179-185
Mauritania 69-75
New Caledonia 208-214
Niger 72-83
Reunion 167-173
St. Pierre & Miquelon 165-171
Senegal 172-178
Somali Coast 139-145
Togo 258-264
Wallis & Futuna Isls. 89

Curie

Pierre and Marie Curie CD80

40th anniversary of the discovery of radium. The surtax was for the benefit of the Intl. Union for the Control of Cancer.

1938

Cameroun B1
Cuba B1-B2
Dahomey B2
France B76
Fr. Equatorial Africa B1
Fr. Guiana B3
Fr. Guinea B2
Fr. India B6
Fr. Polynesia B5
Fr. Sudan B1
Guadeloupe B3
Indo-China B14
Ivory Coast B2
Madagascar B2
Martinique B2
Mauritania B3
New Caledonia B4
Niger B1
Reunion B4
St. Pierre & Miquelon B3
Senegal B3
Somali Coast B2
Togo B1

Caillie

Rene Caillie and Map of Northwestern Africa — CD81

Death centenary of Rene Caillie (1799-1838), French explorer. All three denominations exist with colony name omitted.

1939

Dahomey 108-110
Fr. Guinea 161-163
Fr. Sudan 113-115
Ivory Coast 160-162
Mauritania 109-111
Niger 84-86
Senegal 188-190
Togo 265-267

New York World's Fair

Natives and New York Skyline CD82

1939

Cameroun 223-224
Dahomey 111-112
Fr. Equatorial Africa 78-79
Fr. Guiana 169-170
Fr. Guinea 164-165
Fr. India 111-112
Fr. Polynesia 124-125
Fr. Sudan 116-117
Guadeloupe 155-156
Indo-China 203-204
Inini 42-43
Ivory Coast 163-164
Kwangchowan 121-122
Madagascar 209-210
Martinique 186-187
Mauritania 112-113
New Caledonia 215-216
Niger 87-88
Reunion 174-175
St. Pierre & Miquelon 205-206
Senegal 191-192
Somali Coast 179-180
Togo 268-269
Wallis & Futuna Isls. 90-91

French Revolution

Storming of the Bastille CD83

French Revolution, 150th anniv. The surtax was for the defense of the colonies.

1939

Cameroun B2-B6
Dahomey B3-B7
Fr. Equatorial Africa B4-B8, CB1
Fr. Guiana B4-B8, CB1
Fr. Guinea B3-B7
Fr. India B7-B11
Fr. Polynesia B6-B10, CB1
Fr. Sudan B2-B6
Guadeloupe B4-B8
Indo-China B15-B19, CB1
Inini B1-B5
Ivory Coast B3-B7

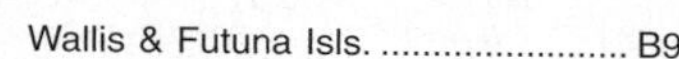

Kwangchowan B1-B5
Madagascar B3-B7, CB1
Martinique B3-B7
Mauritania B4-B8
New Caledonia B5-B9, CB1
Niger B2-B6
Reunion B5-B9, CB1
St. Pierre & Miquelon B4-B8
Senegal B4-B8, CB1
Somali Coast B3-B7
Togo B2-B6
Wallis & Futuna Isls. B1-B5

Plane over Coastal Area CD85

All five denominations exist with colony name omitted.

1940

Dahomey C1-C5
Fr. Guinea C1-C5
Fr. Sudan C1-C5
Ivory Coast C1-C5
Mauritania C1-C5
Niger C1-C5
Senegal C12-C16
Togo C1-C5

Defense of the Empire

Colonial Infantryman — CD86

1941

Cameroun B13B
Dahomey B13
Fr. Equatorial Africa B8B
Fr. Guiana B10
Fr. Guinea B13
Fr. India B13
Fr. Polynesia B12
Fr. Sudan B12
Guadeloupe B10
Indo-China B19B
Inini B7
Ivory Coast B13
Kwangchowan B7
Madagascar B9
Martinique B9
Mauritania B14
New Caledonia B11
Niger B12
Reunion B11
St. Pierre & Miquelon B8B
Senegal B14
Somali Coast B9
Togo B10B
Wallis & Futuna Isls. B7

Colonial Education Fund

CD86a

1942

Cameroun CB3
Dahomey CB4
Fr. Equatorial Africa CB5
Fr. Guiana CB4
Fr. Guinea CB4
Fr. India CB3
Fr. Polynesia CB4
Fr. Sudan CB4
Guadeloupe CB3
Indo-China CB5
Inini CB3
Ivory Coast CB4
Kwangchowan CB4
Malagasy CB5
Martinique CB3
Mauritania CB4
New Caledonia CB4
Niger CB4
Reunion CB4
St. Pierre & Miquelon CB3
Senegal CB5
Somali Coast CB3
Togo CB3
Wallis & Futuna CB3

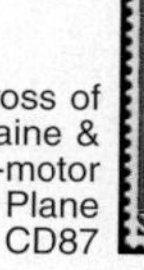

Cross of Lorraine & Four-motor Plane CD87

1941-5

Cameroun C1-C7
Fr. Equatorial Africa C17-C23
Fr. Guiana C9-C10
Fr. India C1-C6
Fr. Polynesia C3-C9
Fr. West Africa C1-C3
Guadeloupe C1-C2
Madagascar C37-C43
Martinique C1-C2
New Caledonia C7-C13
Reunion C18-C24
St. Pierre & Miquelon C1-C7
Somali Coast C1-C7

Transport Plane CD88

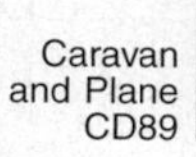

Caravan and Plane CD89

1942

Dahomey C6-C13
Fr. Guinea C6-C13
Fr. Sudan C6-C13
Ivory Coast C6-C13
Mauritania C6-C13
Niger C6-C13
Senegal C17-C25
Togo C6-C13

Red Cross

Marianne CD90

The surtax was for the French Red Cross and national relief.

1944

Cameroun B28
Fr. Equatorial Africa B38
Fr. Guiana B12
Fr. India B14
Fr. Polynesia B13
Fr. West Africa B1
Guadeloupe B12
Madagascar B15
Martinique B11
New Caledonia B13
Reunion B15
St. Pierre & Miquelon B13
Somali Coast B13
Wallis & Futuna Isls. B9

Eboue

CD91

Felix Eboue, first French colonial administrator to proclaim resistance to Germany after French surrender in World War II.

1945

Cameroun 296-297
Fr. Equatorial Africa 156-157
Fr. Guiana 171-172
Fr. India 210-211
Fr. Polynesia 150-151
Fr. West Africa 15-16
Guadeloupe 187-188
Madagascar 259-260
Martinique 196-197
New Caledonia 274-275
Reunion 238-239
St. Pierre & Miquelon 322-323
Somali Coast 238-239

Victory

Victory — CD92

European victory of the Allied Nations in World War II.

1946, May 8

Cameroun C8
Fr. Equatorial Africa C24
Fr. Guiana C11
Fr. India C7
Fr. Polynesia C10
Fr. West Africa C4
Guadeloupe C3
Indo-China C19
Madagascar C44
Martinique C3
New Caledonia C14
Reunion C25
St. Pierre & Miquelon C8
Somali Coast C8
Wallis & Futuna Isls. C1

Chad to Rhine

Leclerc's Departure from Chad — CD93

Battle at Cufra Oasis — CD94

Tanks in Action, Mareth — CD95

Normandy Invasion — CD96

Entering Paris — CD97

Liberation of Strasbourg — CD98

"Chad to the Rhine" march, 1942-44, by Gen. Jacques Leclerc's column, later French 2nd Armored Division.

1946, June 6

Cameroun C9-C14
Fr. Equatorial Africa C25-C30
Fr. Guiana C12-C17
Fr. India C8-C13
Fr. Polynesia C11-C16
Fr. West Africa C5-C10
Guadeloupe C4-C9
Indo-China C20-C25
Madagascar C45-C50
Martinique C4-C9
New Caledonia C15-C20
Reunion C26-C31
St. Pierre & Miquelon C9-C14
Somali Coast C9-C14
Wallis & Futuna Isls. C2-C7

UPU

French Colonials, Globe and Plane — CD99

Universal Postal Union, 75th anniv.

1949, July 4

Cameroun C29
Fr. Equatorial Africa C34
Fr. India C17
Fr. Polynesia C20
Fr. West Africa C15
Indo-China C26
Madagascar C55
New Caledonia C24
St. Pierre & Miquelon C18
Somali Coast C18
Togo C18
Wallis & Futuna Isls. C10

Tropical Medicine

Doctor Treating Infant CD100

The surtax was for charitable work.

1950

Cameroun B29
Fr. Equatorial Africa B39
Fr. India B15
Fr. Polynesia B14
Fr. West Africa B3
Madagascar B17
New Caledonia B14
St. Pierre & Miquelon B14
Somali Coast B14
Togo B11

Military Medal

Medal, Early Marine and Colonial Soldier — CD101

Centenary of the creation of the French Military Medal.

1952

Cameroun 322
Comoro Isls. 39
Fr. Equatorial Africa 186
Fr. India 233
Fr. Polynesia 179
Fr. West Africa 57
Madagascar 286
New Caledonia 295
St. Pierre & Miquelon 345
Somali Coast 267
Togo 327
Wallis & Futuna Isls. 149

Liberation

Allied Landing, Victory Sign and Cross of Lorraine — CD102

Liberation of France, 10th anniv.

1954, June 6

Cameroun C32
Comoro Isls. C4
Fr. Equatorial Africa C38
Fr. India C18
Fr. Polynesia C22
Fr. West Africa C17
Madagascar C57
New Caledonia C25
St. Pierre & Miquelon C19
Somali Coast C19
Togo C19
Wallis & Futuna Isls. C11

FIDES

Plowmen CD103

Efforts of FIDES, the Economic and Social Development Fund for Overseas Possessions (Fonds d' Investissement pour le Developpement Economique et Social). Each stamp has a different design.

1956

Cameroun 326-329
Comoro Isls. 43
Fr. Equatorial Africa 189-192
Fr. Polynesia 181
Fr. West Africa 65-72
Madagascar 292-295
New Caledonia 303
St. Pierre & Miquelon 350
Somali Coast 268
Togo 331

Flower

CD104

Each stamp shows a different flower.

1958-9

Cameroun 333
Comoro Isls. 45
Fr. Equatorial Africa 200-201
Fr. Polynesia 192
Fr. So. & Antarctic Terr. 11
Fr. West Africa 79-83
Madagascar 301-302
New Caledonia 304-305
St. Pierre & Miquelon 357
Somali Coast 270
Togo 348-349
Wallis & Futuna Isls. 152

Human Rights

Sun, Dove and U.N. Emblem CD105

10th anniversary of the signing of the Universal Declaration of Human Rights.

1958

Comoro Isls. 44
Fr. Equatorial Africa 202
Fr. Polynesia 191
Fr. West Africa 85
Madagascar 300
New Caledonia 306
St. Pierre & Miquelon 356
Somali Coast 274
Wallis & Futuna Isls. 153

C.C.T.A.

CD106

Commission for Technical Cooperation in Africa south of the Sahara, 10th anniv.

1960

Cameroun 339
Cent. Africa 3
Chad 66
Congo, P.R. 90
Dahomey 138
Gabon 150
Ivory Coast 180
Madagascar 317
Mali 9
Mauritania 117
Niger 104
Upper Volta 89

Air Afrique, 1961

Modern and Ancient Africa, Map and Planes — CD107

Founding of Air Afrique (African Airlines).

1961-62

Cameroun C37
Cent. Africa C5
Chad C7
Congo, P.R. C5
Dahomey C17
Gabon C5
Ivory Coast C18
Mauritania C17
Niger C22
Senegal C31
Upper Volta C4

Anti-Malaria

CD108

World Health Organization drive to eradicate malaria.

1962, Apr. 7

Cameroun B36
Cent. Africa B1
Chad B1
Comoro Isls. B1
Congo, P.R. B3
Dahomey B15
Gabon B4
Ivory Coast B15
Madagascar B19
Mali B1
Mauritania B16
Niger B14
Senegal B16
Somali Coast B15
Upper Volta B1

Abidjan Games

CD109

Abidjan Games, Ivory Coast, Dec. 24-31, 1961. Each stamp shows a different sport.

1962

Chad 83-84
Cent. Africa 19-20
Congo, P.R. 103-104
Gabon 163-164, C6
Niger 109-111
Upper Volta 103-105

African and Malagasy Union

Flag of Union CD110

First anniversary of the Union.

1962, Sept. 8

Cameroun 373
Cent. Africa 21
Chad 85
Congo, P.R. 105
Dahomey 155
Gabon 165
Ivory Coast 198
Madagascar 332
Mauritania 170
Niger 112
Senegal 211
Upper Volta 106

Telstar

Telstar and Globe Showing Andover and Pleumeur-Bodou — CD111

First television connection of the United States and Europe through the Telstar satellite, July 11-12, 1962.

1962-63

Andorra, French 154
Comoro Isls. C7
Fr. Polynesia C29
Fr. So. & Antarctic Terr. C5
New Caledonia C33
Somali Coast C31
St. Pierre & Miquelon C26
Wallis & Futuna Isls. C17

Freedom From Hunger

World Map and Wheat Emblem CD112

U.N. Food and Agriculture Organization's "Freedom from Hunger" campaign.

1963, Mar. 21

Cameroun B37-B38
Cent. Africa B2
Chad B2
Congo, P.R. B4
Dahomey B16
Gabon B5
Ivory Coast B16
Madagascar B21
Mauritania B17
Niger B15
Senegal B17
Upper Volta B2

Red Cross Centenary

CD113

Centenary of the International Red Cross.

1963, Sept. 2

Comoro Isls. 55
Fr. Polynesia 205
New Caledonia 328
St. Pierre & Miquelon 367
Somali Coast 297
Wallis & Futuna Isls. 165

African Postal Union, 1963

UAMPT Emblem, Radio Masts, Plane and Mail
CD114

Establishment of the African and Malagasy Posts and Telecommunications Union.

1963, Sept. 8

Cameroun C47
Cent. Africa C10
Chad C9
Congo, P.R. C13
Dahomey C19
Gabon C13
Ivory Coast C25
Madagascar C75
Mauritania C22
Niger C27
Rwanda 36
Senegal C32
Upper Volta C9

Air Afrique, 1963

Symbols of Flight — CD115

First anniversary of Air Afrique and inauguration of DC-8 service.

1963, Nov. 19

Cameroun C48
Chad C10
Congo, P.R. C14
Gabon C18
Ivory Coast C26
Mauritania C26
Niger C35
Senegal C33

Europafrica

Europe and Africa Linked — CD116

Signing of an economic agreement between the European Economic Community and the African and Malagasy Union, Yaounde, Cameroun, July 20, 1963.

1963-64

Cameroun 402
Chad C11
Cent. Africa C12
Congo, P.R. C16
Gabon C19
Ivory Coast 217
Niger C43
Upper Volta C11

Human Rights

Scales of Justice and Globe
CD117

15th anniversary of the Universal Declaration of Human Rights.

1963, Dec. 10

Comoro Isls. 58
Fr. Polynesia 206
New Caledonia 329
St. Pierre & Miquelon 368
Somali Coast 300
Wallis & Futuna Isls. 166

PHILATEC

Stamp Album, Champs Elysees Palace and Horses of Marly
CD118

Intl. Philatelic and Postal Techniques Exhibition, Paris, June 5-21, 1964.

1963-64

Comoro Isls. 60
France 1078
Fr. Polynesia 207
New Caledonia 341
St. Pierre & Miquelon 369
Somali Coast 301
Wallis & Futuna Isls. 167

Cooperation

CD119

Cooperation between France and the French-speaking countries of Africa and Madagascar.

1964

Cameroun 409-410
Cent. Africa 39
Chad 103
Congo, P.R. 121
Dahomey 193
France 1111
Gabon 175
Ivory Coast 221
Madagascar 360
Mauritania 181
Niger 143
Senegal 236
Togo 495

ITU

Telegraph, Syncom Satellite and ITU Emblem
CD120

Intl. Telecommunication Union, Cent.

1965, May 17

Comoro Isls. C14
Fr. Polynesia C33
Fr. So. & Antarctic Terr. C8
New Caledonia C40
New Hebrides 124-125
St. Pierre & Miquelon C29
Somali Coast C36
Wallis & Futuna Isls. C20

French Satellite A-1

Diamant Rocket and Launching Installation — CD121

Launching of France's first satellite, Nov. 26, 1965.

1965-66

Comoro Isls. C15-C16
France 1137-1138
Fr. Polynesia C40-C41
Fr. So. & Antarctic Terr. C9-C10
New Caledonia C44-C45
St. Pierre & Miquelon C30-C31
Somali Coast C39-C40
Wallis & Futuna Isls. C22-C23

French Satellite D-1

D-1 Satellite in Orbit — CD122

Launching of the D-1 satellite at Hammaguir, Algeria, Feb. 17, 1966.

1966

Comoro Isls. C17
France 1148
Fr. Polynesia C42
Fr. So. & Antarctic Terr. C11
New Caledonia C46
St. Pierre & Miquelon C32
Somali Coast C49
Wallis & Futuna Isls. C24

Air Afrique, 1966

Planes and Air Afrique Emblem — CD123

Introduction of DC-8F planes by Air Afrique.

1966

Cameroun C79
Cent. Africa C35
Chad C26
Congo, P.R. C42
Dahomey C42
Gabon C47
Ivory Coast C32
Mauritania C57
Niger C63
Senegal C47
Togo C54
Upper Volta C31

African Postal Union, 1967

Telecommunications Symbols and Map of Africa — CD124

Fifth anniversary of the establishment of the African and Malagasy Union of Posts and Telecommunications, UAMPT.

1967

Cameroun C90
Cent. Africa C46
Chad C37
Congo, P.R. C57
Dahomey C61
Gabon C58
Ivory Coast C34
Madagascar C85
Mauritania C65
Niger C75
Rwanda C1-C3
Senegal C60
Togo C81
Upper Volta C50

Monetary Union

Gold Token of the Ashantis, 17-18th Centuries — CD125

West African Monetary Union, 5th anniv.

1967, Nov. 4

Dahomey 244
Ivory Coast 259
Mauritania 238
Niger 204
Senegal 294
Togo 623
Upper Volta 181

WHO Anniversary

Sun, Flowers and WHO Emblem
CD126

World Health Organization, 20th anniv.

1968, May 4

Afars & Issas 317
Comoro Isls. 73
Fr. Polynesia 241-242
Fr. So. & Antarctic Terr. 31
New Caledonia 367
St. Pierre & Miquelon 377
Wallis & Futuna Isls. 169

Human Rights Year

Human Rights Flame — CD127

1968, Aug. 10

Afars & Issas 322-323

Comoro Isls. 76
Fr. Polynesia............................243-244
Fr. So. & Antarctic Terr. 32
New Caledonia 369
St. Pierre & Miquelon......................382
Wallis & Futuna Isls. 170

2nd PHILEXAFRIQUE

CD128

Opening of PHILEXAFRIQUE, Abidjan, Feb. 14. Each stamp shows a local scene and stamp.

1969, Feb. 14

Cameroun C118
Cent. Africa C65
Chad C48
Congo, P.R. C77
Dahomey C94
Gabon C82
Ivory Coast C38-C40
Madagascar C92
Mali C65
Mauritania C80
Niger C104
Senegal C68
Togo C104
Upper Volta C62

Concorde

Concorde in Flight CD129

First flight of the prototype Concorde supersonic plane at Toulouse, Mar. 1, 1969.

1969

Afars & Issas C56
Comoro Isls. C29
France C42
Fr. Polynesia C50
Fr. So. & Antarctic Terr. C18
New Caledonia C63
St. Pierre & Miquelon C40
Wallis & Futuna Isls. C30

Development Bank

Bank Emblem — CD130

African Development Bank, fifth anniv.

1969

Cameroun 499
Chad 217
Congo, P.R. 181-182
Ivory Coast 281
Mali 127-128
Mauritania 267
Niger 220
Senegal 317-318
Upper Volta 201

ILO

ILO Headquarters, Geneva, and Emblem — CD131

Intl. Labor Organization, 50th anniv.

1969-70

Afars & Issas 337
Comoro Isls. 83
Fr. Polynesia 251-252
Fr. So. & Antarctic Terr. 35
New Caledonia 379
St. Pierre & Miquelon......................396
Wallis & Futuna Isls. 172

ASECNA

Map of Africa, Plane and Airport CD132

10th anniversary of the Agency for the Security of Aerial Navigation in Africa and Madagascar (ASECNA, Agence pour la Securite de la Navigation Aerienne en Afrique et a Madagascar).

1969-70

Cameroun 500
Cent. Africa 119
Chad 222
Congo, P.R. 197
Dahomey 269
Gabon 260
Ivory Coast 287
Mali 130
Niger 221
Senegal 321
Upper Volta 204

U.P.U. Headquarters

CD133

New Universal Postal Union headquarters, Bern, Switzerland.

1970

Afars & Issas 342
Algeria 443
Cameroun 503-504
Cent. Africa 125
Chad 225
Comoro Isls. 84
Congo, P.R. 216
Fr. Polynesia 261-262
Fr. So. & Antarctic Terr. 36
Gabon 258
Ivory Coast 295
Madagascar 444
Mali 134-135
Mauritania 283
New Caledonia 382
Niger 231-232
St. Pierre & Miquelon 397-398
Senegal 328-329
Tunisia 535
Wallis & Futuna Isls. 173

De Gaulle

CD134

First anniversary of the death of Charles de Gaulle, (1890-1970), President of France.

1971-72

Afars & Issas 356-357
Comoro Isls. 104-105
France 1322-1325
Fr. Polynesia 270-271
Fr. So. & Antarctic Terr. 52-53
New Caledonia 393-394
Reunion 377, 380
St. Pierre & Miquelon 417-418
Wallis & Futuna Isls. 177-178

African Postal Union, 1971

UAMPT Building, Brazzaville, Congo — CD135

10th anniversary of the establishment of the African and Malagasy Posts and Telecommunications Union, UAMPT. Each stamp has a different native design.

1971, Nov. 13

Cameroun C177
Cent. Africa C89
Chad C94
Congo, P.R. C136
Dahomey C146
Gabon C120
Ivory Coast C47
Mauritania C113
Niger C164
Rwanda C8
Senegal C105
Togo C166
Upper Volta C97

West African Monetary Union

African Couple, City, Village and Commemorative Coin — CD136

West African Monetary Union, 10th anniv.

1972, Nov. 2

Dahomey 300
Ivory Coast 331
Mauritania 299
Niger 258
Senegal 374
Togo 825
Upper Volta 280

African Postal Union, 1973

Telecommunications Symbols and Map of Africa — CD137

11th anniversary of the African and Malagasy Posts and Telecommunications Union (UAMPT).

1973, Sept. 12

Cameroun 574
Cent. Africa 194
Chad 294
Congo, P.R. 289
Dahomey 311
Gabon 320
Ivory Coast 361
Madagascar 500
Mauritania 304
Niger 287
Rwanda 540
Senegal 393
Togo 849
Upper Volta 297

Philexafrique II — Essen

CD138

CD139

Designs: Indigenous fauna, local and German stamps. Types CD138-CD139 printed horizontally and vertically se-tenant in sheets of 10 (2x5). Label between horizontal pairs alternately commemoratives Philexafrique II, Libreville, Gabon, June 1978, and 2nd International Stamp Fair, Essen, Germany, Nov. 1-5.

1978-1979

Benin C285-C286
Central Africa C200-C201
Chad C238-C239
Congo Republic C245-C246
Djibouti C121-C122
Gabon C215-C216
Ivory Coast C64-C65
Mali C356-C357
Mauritania C185-C186
Niger C291-C292
Rwanda C12-C13
Senegal C146-C147
Togo C363-C364

BRITISH COMMONWEALTH OF NATIONS

The listings follow established trade practices when these issues are offered as units by dealers. The Peace issue, for example, includes only one stamp from the Indian state of Hyderabad. The U.P.U. issue includes the Egypt set. Pairs are included for those varieties issued with bilingual designs se-tenant.

Silver Jubilee

Windsor Castle and King George V CD301

Reign of King George V, 25th anniv.

1935

Antigua 77-80
Ascension 33-36
Bahamas 92-95
Barbados 186-189
Basutoland 11-14
Bechuanaland Protectorate 117-120
Bermuda 100-103
British Guiana 223-226
British Honduras 108-111
Cayman Islands 81-84
Ceylon 260-263
Cyprus 136-139
Dominica 90-93
Falkland Islands 77-80
Fiji 110-113
Gambia 125-128

Gibraltar...100-103
Gilbert & Ellice Islands...33-36
Gold Coast...108-111
Grenada...124-127
Hong Kong...147-150
Jamaica...109-112
Kenya, Uganda, Tanganyika...42-45
Leeward Islands...96-99
Malta...184-187
Mauritius...204-207
Montserrat...85-88
Newfoundland...226-229
Nigeria...34-37
Northern Rhodesia...18-21
Nyasaland Protectorate...47-50
St. Helena...111-114
St. Kitts-Nevis...72-75
St. Lucia...91-94
St. Vincent...134-137
Seychelles...118-121
Sierra Leone...166-169
Solomon Islands...60-63
Somaliland Protectorate...77-80
Straits Settlements...213-216
Swaziland...20-23
Trinidad & Tobago...43-46
Turks & Caicos Islands...71-74
Virgin Islands...69-72

The following have different designs but are included in the omnibus set:

Great Britain...226-229
Offices in Morocco...67-70, 226-229, 422-425, 508-510
Australia...152-154
Canada...211-216
Cook Islands...98-100
India...142-148
Nauru...31-34
New Guinea...46-47
New Zealand...199-201
Niue...67-69
Papua...114-117
Samoa...163-165
South Africa...68-71
Southern Rhodesia...33-36
South-West Africa...121-124

249 stamps

Coronation

Queen Elizabeth and King George VI CD302

1937

Aden...13-15
Antigua...81-83
Ascension...37-39
Bahamas...97-99
Barbados...190-192
Basutoland...15-17
Bechuanaland Protectorate...121-123
Bermuda...115-117
British Guiana...227-229
British Honduras...112-114
Cayman Islands...97-99
Ceylon...275-277
Cyprus...140-142
Dominica...94-96
Falkland Islands...81-83
Fiji...114-116
Gambia...129-131
Gibraltar...104-106
Gilbert & Ellice Islands...37-39
Gold Coast...112-114
Grenada...128-130
Hong Kong...151-153
Jamaica...113-115
Kenya, Uganda, Tanganyika...60-62
Leeward Islands...100-102
Malta...188-190
Mauritius...208-210
Montserrat...89-91
Newfoundland...230-232
Nigeria...50-52
Northern Rhodesia...22-24
Nyasaland Protectorate...51-53
St. Helena...115-117
St. Kitts-Nevis...76-78
St. Lucia...107-109
St. Vincent...138-140
Seychelles...122-124
Sierra Leone...170-172
Solomon Islands...64-66
Somaliland Protectorate...81-83
Straits Settlements...235-237
Swaziland...24-26
Trinidad & Tobago...47-49
Turks & Caicos Islands...75-77
Virgin Islands...73-75

The following have different designs but are included in the omnibus set:

Great Britain...234
Offices in Morocco...82, 439, 514
Canada...237
Cook Islands...109-111
Nauru...35-38
Newfoundland...233-243
New Guinea...48-51
New Zealand...223-225
Niue...70-72
Papua...118-121
South Africa...74-78
Southern Rhodesia...38-41
South-West Africa...125-132

202 stamps

Peace

King George VI and Parliament Buildings, London CD303

Return to peace at the close of World War II.

1945-46

Aden...28-29
Antigua...96-97
Ascension...50-51
Bahamas...130-131
Barbados...207-208
Bermuda...131-132
British Guiana...242-243
British Honduras...127-128
Cayman Islands...112-113
Ceylon...293-294
Cyprus...156-157
Dominica...112-113
Falkland Islands...97-98
Falkland Islands Dep...1L9-1L10
Fiji...137-138
Gambia...144-145
Gibraltar...119-120
Gilbert & Ellice Islands...52-53
Gold Coast...128-129
Grenada...143-144
Jamaica...136-137
Kenya, Uganda, Tanganyika...90-91
Leeward Islands...116-117
Malta...206-207
Mauritius...223-224
Montserrat...104-105
Nigeria...71-72
Northern Rhodesia...46-47
Nyasaland Protectorate...82-83
Pitcairn Island...9-10
St. Helena...128-129
St. Kitts-Nevis...91-92
St. Lucia...127-128
St. Vincent...152-153
Seychelles...149-150
Sierra Leone...186-187
Solomon Islands...80-81
Somaliland Protectorate...108-109
Trinidad & Tobago...62-63
Turks & Caicos Islands...90-91
Virgin Islands...88-89

The following have different designs but are included in the omnibus set:

Great Britain...264-265
  Offices in Morocco...523-524
Aden
  Kathiri State of Seiyun...12-13
  Qu'aiti State of Shihr and Mukalla...12-13
Australia...200-202
Basutoland...29-31
Bechuanaland Protectorate...137-139
Burma...66-69
Cook Islands...127-130
Hong Kong...174-175
India...195-198
  Hyderabad...51
New Zealand...247-257
Niue...90-93
Pakistan-Bahawalpur...O16
Samoa...191-194
South Africa...100-102
Southern Rhodesia...67-70
South-West Africa...153-155
Swaziland...38-40
Zanzibar...222-223

164 stamps

Silver Wedding

King George VI and Queen Elizabeth
CD304 CD305

1948-49

Aden...30-31
  Kathiri State of Seiyun...14-15
  Qu'aiti State of Shihr and Mukalla...14-15
Antigua...98-99
Ascension...52-53
Bahamas...148-149
Barbados...210-211
Basutoland...39-40
Bechuanaland Protectorate...147-148
Bermuda...133-134
British Guiana...244-245
British Honduras...129-130
Cayman Islands...116-117
Cyprus...158-159
Dominica...114-115
Falkland Islands...99-100
Falkland Islands Dep...1L11-1L12
Fiji...139-140
Gambia...146-147
Gibraltar...121-122
Gilbert & Ellice Islands...54-55
Gold Coast...142-143
Grenada...145-146
Hong Kong...178-179
Jamaica...138-139
Kenya, Uganda, Tanganyika...92-93
Leeward Islands...118-119
Malaya
  Johore...128-129
  Kedah...55-56
  Kelantan...44-45
  Malacca...1-2
  Negri Sembilan...36-37
  Pahang...44-45
  Penang...1-2
  Perak...99-100
  Perlis...1-2
  Selangor...74-75
  Trengganu...47-48
Malta...223-224
Mauritius...229-230
Montserrat...106-107
Nigeria...73-74
North Borneo...238-239
Northern Rhodesia...48-49
Nyasaland Protectorate...85-86
Pitcairn Island...11-12
St. Helena...130-131
St. Kitts-Nevis...93-94
St. Lucia...129-130
St. Vincent...154-155
Sarawak...174-175
Seychelles...151-152
Sierra Leone...188-189
Singapore...21-22
Solomon Islands...82-83
Somaliland Protectorate...110-111
Swaziland...48-49
Trinidad & Tobago...64-65
Turks & Caicos Islands...92-93
Virgin Islands...90-91
Zanzibar...224-225

The following have different designs but are included in the omnibus set:

Great Britain...267-268
  Offices in Morocco...93-94, 525-526
Bahrain...62-63
Kuwait...82-83
Oman...25-26
South Africa...106
South-West Africa...159

138 stamps

U.P.U.

Mercury and Symbols of Communications — CD306

Plane, Ship and Hemispheres — CD307

Mercury Scattering Letters over Globe CD308

U.P.U. Monument, Bern CD309

Universal Postal Union, 75th anniversary.

1949

Aden...32-35
  Kathiri State of Seiyun...16-19
  Qu'aiti State of Shihr and Mukalla...16-19
Antigua...100-103
Ascension...57-60
Bahamas...150-153
Barbados...212-215
Basutoland...41-44
Bechuanaland Protectorate...149-152
Bermuda...138-141
British Guiana...246-249
British Honduras...137-140
Brunei...79-82
Cayman Islands...118-121
Cyprus...160-163
Dominica...116-119
Falkland Islands...103-106
Falkland Islands Dep...1L14-1L17
Fiji...141-144
Gambia...148-151
Gibraltar...123-126
Gilbert & Ellice Islands...56-59
Gold Coast...144-147
Grenada...147-150
Hong Kong...180-183
Jamaica...142-145
Kenya, Uganda, Tanganyika...94-97
Leeward Islands...126-129
Malaya
  Johore...151-154
  Kedah...57-60
  Kelantan...46-49
  Malacca...18-21
  Negri Sembilan...59-62
  Pahang...46-49
  Penang...23-26
  Perak...101-104
  Perlis...3-6
  Selangor...76-79
  Trengganu...49-52
Malta...225-228
Mauritius...231-234
Montserrat...108-111
New Hebrides, British...62-65
New Hebrides, French...79-82
Nigeria...75-78
North Borneo...240-243
Northern Rhodesia...50-53
Nyasaland Protectorate...87-90
Pitcairn Islands...13-16
St. Helena...132-135
St. Kitts-Nevis...95-98
St. Lucia...131-134
St. Vincent...170-173

Sarawak....176-179
Seychelles....153-156
Sierra Leone....190-193
Singapore....23-26
Solomon Islands....84-87
Somaliland Protectorate....112-115
Southern Rhodesia....71-72
Swaziland....50-53
Tonga....87-90
Trinidad & Tobago....66-69
Turks & Caicos Islands....101-104
Virgin Islands....92-95
Zanzibar....226-229

The following have different designs but are included in the omnibus set:

Great Britain....276-279
Offices in Morocco....546-549
Australia....223
Bahrain....68-71
Burma....116-121
Ceylon....304-306
Egypt....281-283
India....223-226
Kuwait....89-92
Oman....31-34
Pakistan-Bahawalpur 26-29, O25-O28
South Africa....109-111
South-West Africa....160-162

319 stamps

University

Arms of University College CD310

Alice, Princess of Athlone CD311

1948 opening of University College of the West Indies at Jamaica.

1951

Antigua....104-105
Barbados....228-229
British Guiana....250-251
British Honduras....141-142
Dominica....120-121
Grenada....164-165
Jamaica....146-147
Leeward Islands....130-131
Montserrat....112-113
St. Kitts-Nevis....105-106
St. Lucia....149-150
St. Vincent....174-175
Trinidad & Tobago....70-71
Virgin Islands....96-97

28 stamps

Coronation

Queen Elizabeth II — CD312

1953

Aden....47
Kathiri State of Seiyun....28
Qu'aiti State of Shihr and Mukalla....28
Antigua....106
Ascension....61
Bahamas....157
Barbados....234
Basutoland....45
Bechuanaland Protectorate....153
Bermuda....142
British Guiana....252
British Honduras....143
Cayman Islands....150
Cyprus....167
Dominica....141
Falkland Islands....121
Falkland Islands Dependencies....1L18
Fiji....145
Gambia....152
Gibraltar....131
Gilbert & Ellice Islands....60
Gold Coast....160
Grenada....170
Hong Kong....184
Jamaica....153
Kenya, Uganda, Tanganyika....101
Leeward Islands....132
Malaya
Johore....155
Kedah....82
Kelantan....71
Malacca....27
Negri Sembilan....63
Pahang....71
Penang....27
Perak....126
Perlis....28
Selangor....101
Trengganu....74
Malta....241
Mauritius....250
Montserrat....127
New Hebrides, British....77
Nigeria....79
North Borneo....260
Northern Rhodesia....60
Nyasaland Protectorate....96
Pitcairn....19
St. Helena....139
St. Kitts-Nevis....119
St. Lucia....156
St. Vincent....185
Sarawak....196
Seychelles....172
Sierra Leone....194
Singapore....27
Solomon Islands....88
Somaliland Protectorate....127
Swaziland....54
Trinidad & Tobago....84
Tristan da Cunha....13
Turks & Caicos Islands....118
Virgin Islands....114

The following have different designs but are included in the omnibus set:

Great Britain....313-316
Offices in Morocco....579-582
Australia....259-261
Bahrain....92-95
Canada....330
Ceylon....317
Cook Islands....145-146
Kuwait....113-116
New Zealand....280-284
Niue....104-105
Oman....52-55
Samoa....214-215
South Africa....192
Southern Rhodesia....80
South-West Africa....244-248
Tokelau Islands....4

106 stamps

Royal Visit 1953

Separate designs for each country for the visit of Queen Elizabeth II and the Duke of Edinburgh.

1953

Aden....62
Australia....267-269
Bermuda....163
Ceylon....318
Fiji....146
Gibraltar....146
Jamaica....154
Kenya, Uganda, Tanganyika....102
Malta....242
New Zealand....286-287

13 stamps

West Indies Federation

Map of the Caribbean CD313

Federation of the West Indies, April 22, 1958.

1958

Antigua....122-124
Barbados....248-250
Dominica....161-163
Grenada....184-186
Jamaica....175-177
Montserrat....143-145
St. Kitts-Nevis....136-138
St. Lucia....170-172
St. Vincent....198-200
Trinidad & Tobago....86-88

30 stamps

Freedom from Hunger

Protein Food CD314

U.N. Food and Agricultural Organization's "Freedom from Hunger" campaign.

1963

Aden....65
Antigua....133
Ascension....89
Bahamas....180
Basutoland....83
Bechuanaland Protectorate....194
Bermuda....192
British Guiana....271
British Honduras....179
Brunei....100
Cayman Islands....168
Dominica....181
Falkland Islands....146
Fiji....198
Gambia....172
Gibraltar....161
Gilbert & Ellice Islands....76
Grenada....190
Hong Kong....218
Malta....291
Mauritius....270
Montserrat....150
New Hebrides, British....93
North Borneo....296
Pitcairn....35
St. Helena....173
St. Lucia....179
St. Vincent....201
Sarawak....212
Seychelles....213
Solomon Islands....109
Swaziland....108
Tonga....127
Tristan da Cunha....68
Turks & Caicos Islands....138
Virgin Islands....140
Zanzibar....280

37 stamps

Red Cross Centenary

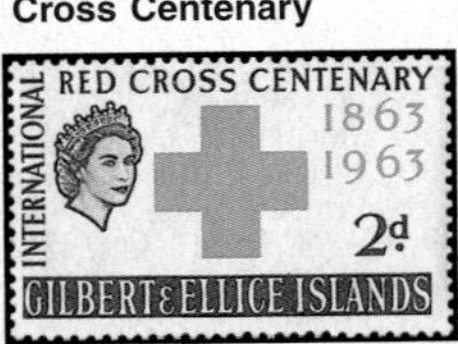

Red Cross and Elizabeth II CD315

1963

Antigua....134-135
Ascension....90-91
Bahamas....183-184
Basutoland....84-85
Bechuanaland Protectorate....195-196
Bermuda....193-194
British Guiana....272-273
British Honduras....180-181
Cayman Islands....169-170
Dominica....182-183
Falkland Islands....147-148
Fiji....203-204
Gambia....173-174
Gibraltar....162-163
Gilbert & Ellice Islands....77-78
Grenada....191-192
Hong Kong....219-220
Jamaica....203-204
Malta....292-293
Mauritius....271-272
Montserrat....151-152
New Hebrides, British....94-95
Pitcairn Islands....36-37
St. Helena....174-175
St. Kitts-Nevis....143-144
St. Lucia....180-181
St. Vincent....202-203
Seychelles....214-215
Solomon Islands....110-111
South Arabia....1-2
Swaziland....109-110
Tonga....134-135
Tristan da Cunha....69-70
Turks & Caicos Islands....139-140
Virgin Islands....141-142

70 stamps

Shakespeare

Shakespeare Memorial Theatre, Stratford-on-Avon — CD316

400th anniversary of the birth of William Shakespeare.

1964

Antigua....151
Bahamas....201
Bechuanaland Protectorate....197
Cayman Islands....171
Dominica....184
Falkland Islands....149
Gambia....192
Gibraltar....164
Montserrat....153
St. Lucia....196
Turks & Caicos Islands....141
Virgin Islands....143

12 stamps

ITU

ITU Emblem CD317

Intl. Telecommunication Union, cent.

1965

Antigua....153-154
Ascension....92-93
Bahamas....219-220
Barbados....265-266
Basutoland....101-102
Bechuanaland Protectorate....202-203
Bermuda....196-197
British Guiana....293-294
British Honduras....187-188
Brunei....116-117
Cayman Islands....172-173
Dominica....185-186
Falkland Islands....154-155
Fiji....211-212
Gibraltar....167-168
Gilbert & Ellice Islands....87-88
Grenada....205-206
Hong Kong....221-222
Mauritius....291-292
Montserrat....157-158
New Hebrides, British....108-109
Pitcairn Islands....52-53
St. Helena....180-181
St. Kitts-Nevis....163-164
St. Lucia....197-198
St. Vincent....224-225
Seychelles....218-219
Solomon Islands....126-127
Swaziland....115-116
Tristan da Cunha....85-86
Turks & Caicos Islands....142-143
Virgin Islands....159-160

64 stamps

Intl. Cooperation Year

ICY Emblem CD318

1965

Antigua 155-156
Ascension 94-95
Bahamas 222-223
Basutoland.................................103-104
Bechuanaland Protectorate......204-205
Bermuda....................................199-200
British Guiana............................295-296
British Honduras.........................189-190
Brunei 118-119
Cayman Islands..........................174-175
Dominica....................................187-188
Falkland Islands 156-157
Fiji 213-214
Gibraltar.....................................169-170
Gilbert & Ellice Islands............104-105
Grenada.....................................207-208
Hong Kong 223-224
Mauritius....................................293-294
Montserrat 176-177
New Hebrides, British 110-111
New Hebrides, French 126-127
Pitcairn Islands 54-55
St. Helena 182-183
St. Kitts-Nevis............................165-166
St. Lucia 199-200
Seychelles 220-221
Solomon Islands.........................143-144
South Arabia 17-18
Swaziland 117-118
Tristan da Cunha............................87-88
Turks & Caicos Islands 144-145
Virgin Islands.............................161-162

64 stamps

Churchill Memorial

Winston Churchill and St. Paul's, London, During Air Attack CD319

1966

Antigua 157-160
Ascension 96-99
Bahamas 224-227
Barbados 281-284
Basutoland.................................105-108
Bechuanaland Protectorate......206-209
Bermuda....................................201-204
British Antarctic Territory.............16-19
British Honduras........................191-194
Brunei 120-123
Cayman Islands.........................176-179
Dominica...................................189-192
Falkland Islands 158-161
Fiji 215-218
Gibraltar....................................171-174
Gilbert & Ellice Islands............106-109
Grenada....................................209-212
Hong Kong 225-228
Mauritius...................................295-298
Montserrat 178-181
New Hebrides, British 112-115
New Hebrides, French 128-131
Pitcairn Islands 56-59
St. Helena 184-187
St. Kitts-Nevis..........................167-170
St. Lucia 201-204
St. Vincent................................241-244
Seychelles 222-225
Solomon Islands.......................145-148
South Arabia 19-22
Swaziland 119-122
Tristan da Cunha..........................89-92
Turks & Caicos Islands 146-149
Virgin Islands............................163-166

136 stamps

Royal Visit, 1966

Queen Elizabeth II and Prince Philip CD320

Caribbean visit, Feb. 4 - Mar. 6, 1966.

1966

Antigua 161-162
Bahamas 228-229
Barbados 285-286
British Guiana............................299-300
Cayman Islands.........................180-181
Dominica...................................193-194
Grenada....................................213-214
Montserrat 182-183
St. Kitts-Nevis...........................171-172
St. Lucia 205-206
St. Vincent................................245-246
Turks & Caicos Islands 150-151
Virgin Islands............................167-168

26 stamps

World Cup Soccer

Soccer Player and Jules Rimet Cup CD321

World Cup Soccer Championship, Wembley, England, July 11-30.

1966

Antigua 163-164
Ascension 100-101
Bahamas 245-246
Bermuda....................................205-206
Brunei 124-125
Cayman Islands.........................182-183
Dominica...................................195-196
Fiji 219-220
Gibraltar....................................175-176
Gilbert & Ellice Islands............125-126
Grenada....................................230-231
New Hebrides, British 116-117
New Hebrides, French 132-133
Pitcairn Islands 60-61
St. Helena 188-189
St. Kitts-Nevis..........................173-174
St. Lucia 207-208
Seychelles 226-227
Solomon Islands.......................167-168
South Arabia 23-24
Tristan da Cunha..........................93-94

42 stamps

WHO Headquarters

World Health Organization Headquarters, Geneva — CD322

1966

Antigua 165-166
Ascension 102-103
Bahamas 247-248
Brunei 126-127
Cayman Islands.........................184-185
Dominica...................................197-198
Fiji 224-225
Gibraltar....................................180-181
Gilbert & Ellice Islands............127-128
Grenada....................................232-233
Hong Kong 229-230
Montserrat 184-185
New Hebrides, British 118-119
New Hebrides, French 134-135
Pitcairn Islands 62-63
St. Helena 190-191
St. Kitts-Nevis..........................177-178
St. Lucia 209-210
St. Vincent................................247-248
Seychelles 228-229
Solomon Islands.......................169-170
South Arabia 25-26
Tristan da Cunha........................99-100

46 stamps

UNESCO Anniversary

"Education" — CD323

"Science" (Wheat ears & flask enclosing globe). "Culture" (lyre & columns). 20th anniversary of the UNESCO.

1966-67

Antigua 183-185
Ascension 108-110
Bahamas 249-251
Barbados 287-289
Bermuda....................................207-209
Brunei 128-130
Cayman Islands.........................186-188
Dominica...................................199-201
Gibraltar....................................183-185
Gilbert & Ellice Islands............129-131
Grenada....................................234-236
Hong Kong 231-233
Mauritius...................................299-301
Montserrat 186-188
New Hebrides, British 120-122
New Hebrides, French 136-138
Pitcairn Islands 64-66
St. Helena 192-194
St. Kitts-Nevis..........................179-181
St. Lucia 211-213
St. Vincent................................249-251
Seychelles 230-232
Solomon Islands.......................171-173
South Arabia 27-29
Swaziland 123-125
Tristan da Cunha.......................101-103
Turks & Caicos Islands 155-157
Virgin Islands............................176-178

84 stamps

Silver Wedding, 1972

Queen Elizabeth II and Prince Philip — CD324

Designs: borders differ for each country.

1972

Anguilla.....................................161-162
Antigua 295-296
Ascension 164-165
Bahamas 344-345
Bermuda....................................296-297
British Antarctic Territory.............43-44
British Honduras........................306-307
British Indian Ocean Territory......48-49
Brunei 186-187
Cayman Islands.........................304-305
Dominica...................................352-353
Falkland Islands 223-224
Fiji 328-329
Gibraltar....................................292-293
Gilbert & Ellice Islands............206-207
Grenada....................................466-467
Hong Kong 271-272
Montserrat 286-287
New Hebrides, British 169-170
Pitcairn Islands 127-128
St. Helena 271-272
St. Kitts-Nevis..........................257-258
St. Lucia 328-329
St.Vincent.................................344-345
Seychelles 309-310
Solomon Islands.......................248-249
South Georgia 35-36
Tristan da Cunha.......................178-179
Turks & Caicos Islands 257-258
Virgin Islands............................241-242

60 stamps

Princess Anne's Wedding

Princess Anne and Mark Phillips — CD325

Wedding of Princess Anne and Mark Phillips, Nov. 14, 1973.

1973

Anguilla.....................................179-180
Ascension 177-178
Belize 325-326
Bermuda....................................302-303
British Antarctic Territory.............60-61
Cayman Islands.........................320-321
Falkland Islands 225-226
Gibraltar....................................305-306
Gilbert & Ellice Islands............216-217
Hong Kong 289-290
Montserrat 300-301
Pitcairn Island 135-136
St. Helena 277-278
St. Kitts-Nevis..........................274-275
St. Lucia 349-350
St. Vincent................................358-359
St. Vincent Grenadines....................1-2
Seychelles 311-312
Solomon Islands.......................259-260
South Georgia 37-38
Tristan da Cunha.......................189-190
Turks & Caicos Islands 286-287
Virgin Islands............................260-261

44 stamps

Elizabeth II Coronation Anniv.

CD326

CD327

CD328

Designs: Royal and local beasts in heraldic form and simulated stonework. Portrait of Elizabeth II by Peter Grugeon. 25th anniversary of coronation of Queen Elizabeth II.

1978

Ascension 229
Barbados 474
Belize 397
British Antarctic Territory....................71
Cayman Islands.................................404
Christmas Island 87
Falkland Islands 275
Fiji 384
Gambia 380
Gilbert Islands 312
Mauritius...464
New Hebrides, British 258
St. Helena 317
St. Kitts-Nevis...................................354
Samoa 472

Solomon Islands.................368
South Georgia.....................51
Swaziland.........................302
Tristan da Cunha...............238
Virgin Islands....................337

20 sheets

Queen Mother Elizabeth's 80th Birthday

CD330

Designs: Photographs of Queen Mother Elizabeth. Falkland Islands issued in sheets of 50; others in sheets of 9.

1980

Ascension.........................261
Bermuda...........................401
Cayman Islands..................443
Falkland Islands.................305
Gambia.............................412
Gibraltar...........................393
Hong Kong........................364
Pitcairn Islands..................193
St. Helena........................341
Samoa.............................532
Solomon Islands.................426
Tristan da Cunha...............277

12 stamps

Royal Wedding, 1981

Prince Charles and Lady Diana — CD331

CD331a

Wedding of Charles, Prince of Wales, and Lady Diana Spencer, St. Paul's Cathedral, London, July 29, 1981.

1981

Antigua...........................623-625
Ascension.........................294-296
Barbados..........................547-549
Barbuda...........................497-499
Bermuda...........................412-414
Brunei.............................268-270
Cayman Islands..................471-473
Dominica..........................701-703
Falkland Islands.................324-326
Falkland Islands Dep...........1L59-1L61
Fiji..................................442-444
Gambia.............................426-428
Ghana..............................759-761
Grenada...........................1051-1053
Grenada Grenadines............440-443
Hong Kong........................373-375
Jamaica............................500-503
Lesotho............................335-337
Maldive Islands..................906-908
Mauritius..........................520-522
Norfolk Island....................280-282
Pitcairn Islands..................206-208
St. Helena........................353-355
St. Lucia..........................543-545
Samoa.............................558-560
Sierra Leone......................509-517
Solomon Islands.................450-452
Swaziland.........................382-384
Tristan da Cunha...............294-296
Turks & Caicos Islands........486-488
Caicos Island.....................8-10
Uganda............................314-316
Vanuatu...........................308-310
Virgin Islands....................406-408

Princess Diana

CD332

CD333

Designs: Photographs and portrait of Princess Diana, wedding or honeymoon photographs, royal residences, arms of issuing country. Portrait photograph by Clive Friend. Souvenir sheet margins show family tree, various people related to the princess. 21st birthday of Princess Diana of Wales, July 1.

1982

Antigua...........................663-666
Ascension.........................313-316
Bahamas...........................510-513
Barbados..........................585-588
Barbuda...........................544-546
British Antarctic Territory.......92-95
Cayman Islands..................486-489
Dominica..........................773-776
Falkland Islands.................348-351
Falkland Islands Dep...........1L72-1L75
Fiji..................................470-473
Gambia.............................447-450
Grenada...........................1101A-1105
Grenada Grenadines............485-491
Lesotho............................372-375
Maldive Islands..................952-955
Mauritius..........................548-551
Pitcairn Islands..................213-216
St. Helena........................372-375
St. Lucia..........................591-594
Sierra Leone......................531-534
Solomon Islands.................471-474
Swaziland.........................406-409
Tristan da Cunha...............310-313
Turks and Caicos Islands......530A-534
Virgin Islands....................430-433

250th anniv. of first edition of Lloyd's List (shipping news publication) & of Lloyd's marine insurance.

CD335

Designs: First page of early edition of the list; historical ships, modern transportation or harbor scenes.

1984

Ascension.........................351-354
Bahamas...........................555-558
Barbados..........................627-630
Cayes of Belize...................10-13
Cayman Islands..................522-525
Falkland Islands.................404-407
Fiji..................................509-512
Gambia.............................519-522
Mauritius..........................587-590
Nauru..............................280-283
St. Helena........................412-415
Samoa.............................624-627
Seychelles........................538-541
Solomon Islands.................521-524
Vanuatu...........................368-371
Virgin Islands....................466-469

Queen Mother 85th Birthday

CD336

Designs: Photographs tracing the life of the Queen Mother, Elizabeth. The high value in each set pictures the same photograph taken of the Queen Mother holding the infant Prince Henry.

1985

Ascension.........................372-376
Bahamas...........................580-584
Barbados..........................660-664
Bermuda...........................469-473
Falkland Islands.................420-424
Falkland Islands Dep...........1L92-1L96
Fiji..................................531-535
Hong Kong........................447-450
Jamaica............................599-603
Mauritius..........................604-608
Norfolk Island....................364-368
Pitcairn Islands..................253-257
St. Helena........................428-432
Samoa.............................649-653
Seychelles........................567-571
Solomon Islands.................543-547
Swaziland.........................476-480
Tristan da Cunha...............372-376
Vanuatu...........................392-396
Zil Elwannyen Sesel............101-105

Queen Elizabeth II, 60th Birthday

CD337

1986, April 21

Ascension.........................389-393
Bahamas...........................592-596
Barbados..........................675-679
Bermuda...........................499-503
Cayman Islands..................555-559
Falkland Islands.................441-445
Fiji..................................544-548
Hong Kong........................465-469
Jamaica............................620-624
Kiribati.............................470-474
Mauritius..........................629-633
Papua New Guinea..............640-644
Pitcairn Islands..................270-274
St. Helena........................451-455
Samoa.............................670-674
Seychelles........................592-596
Solomon Islands.................562-566
South Georgia....................101-105
Swaziland.........................490-494
Tristan da Cunha...............388-392
Vanuatu...........................414-418
Zambia.............................343-347
Zil Elwannyen Sesel............114-118

Royal Wedding

Marriage of Prince Andrew and Sarah Ferguson CD338

1986, July 23

Ascension.........................399-400
Bahamas...........................602-603
Barbados..........................687-688
Cayman Islands..................560-561
Jamaica............................629-630
Pitcairn Islands..................275-276
St. Helena........................460-461
St. Kitts............................181-182
Seychelles........................602-603
Solomon Islands.................567-568
Tristan da Cunha...............397-398
Zambia.............................348-349
Zil Elwannyen Sesel............119-120

Queen Elizabeth II, 60th Birthday

Queen Elizabeth II & Prince Philip, 1947 Wedding Portrait — CD339

Designs: Photographs tracing the life of Queen Elizabeth II.

1986

Anguilla...........................674-677
Antigua...........................925-928
Barbuda...........................783-786
Dominica..........................950-953
Gambia.............................611-614
Grenada...........................1371-1374
Grenada Grenadines............749-752
Lesotho............................531-534
Maldive Islands..................1172-1175
Sierra Leone......................760-763
Uganda............................495-498

Royal Wedding, 1986

CD340

Designs: Photographs of Prince Andrew and Sarah Ferguson during courtship, engagement and marriage.

1986

Antigua...........................939-942
Barbuda...........................809-812
Dominica..........................970-973
Gambia.............................635-638
Grenada...........................1385-1388
Grenada Grenadines............758-761
Lesotho............................545-548
Maldive Islands..................1181-1184
Sierra Leone......................769-772
Uganda............................510-513

Lloyds of London, 300th Anniv.

CD341

Designs: 17th century aspects of Lloyds, representations of each country's individual connections with Lloyds and publicized disasters insured by the organization.

1986

Ascension.........................454-457
Bahamas...........................655-658
Barbados..........................731-734
Bermuda...........................541-544
Falkland Islands.................481-484
Liberia.............................1101-1104
Malawi.............................534-537
Nevis...............................571-574
St. Helena........................501-504
St. Lucia..........................923-926
Seychelles........................649-652
Solomon Islands.................627-630

South Georgia 131-134
Trinidad & Tobago 484-487
Tristan da Cunha.....................439-442
Vanuatu 485-488
Zil Elwannyen Sesel 146-149

Moon Landing, 20th Anniv.

CD342

Designs: Equipment, crew photographs, spacecraft, official emblems and report profiles created for the Apollo Missions. Two stamps in each set are square in format rather than like the stamp shown; see individual country listings for more information.

1989

Ascension Is. 468-472
Bahamas 674-678
Belize.......................................916-920
Kiribati 517-521
Liberia 1125-1129
Nevis.......................................586-590
St. Kitts 248-252
Samoa 760-764
Seychelles 676-680
Solomon Islands.......................643-647
Vanuatu 507-511
Zil Elwannyen Sesel 154-158

Queen Mother, 90th Birthday

CD343

CD344

Designs: Portraits of Queen Elizabeth, the Queen Mother. See individual country listings for more information.

1990

Ascension Is. 491-492
Bahamas 698-699
Barbados 782-783
British Antarctic Territory..........170-171
British Indian Ocean Territory 106-107
Cayman Islands.......................622-623
Falkland Islands 524-525
Kenya.......................................527-528
Kiribati 555-556
Liberia 1145-1146
Pitcairn Islands........................336-337
St. Helena 532-533
St. Lucia 969-970
Seychelles 710-711
Solomon Islands.......................671-672
South Georgia 143-144
Swaziland 565-566
Tristan da Cunha......................480-481
Zil Elwannyen Sesel 171-172

Queen Elizabeth II, 65th Birthday, and Prince Philip, 70th Birthday

CD345

CD346

Designs: Portraits of Queen Elizabeth II and Prince Philip differ for each country. Printed in sheets of 10 + 5 labels (3 different) between. Stamps alternate, producing 5 different triptychs.

1991

Ascension Is. 505-506
Bahamas 730-731
Belize.......................................969-970
Bermuda...................................617-618
Kiribati 571-572
Mauritius..................................733-734
Pitcairn Islands........................348-349
St. Helena 554-555
St. Kitts 318-319
Samoa 790-791
Seychelles 723-724
Solomon Islands.......................688-689
South Georgia 149-150
Swaziland 586-587
Vanuatu 540-541
Zil Elwannyen Sesel 177-178

Royal Family Birthday, Anniversary

CD347

Queen Elizabeth II, 65th birthday, Charles and Diana, 10th wedding anniversary: Various photographs of Queen Elizabeth II, Prince Philip, Prince Charles, Princess Diana and their sons William and Henry.

1991

Antigua 1446-1455
Barbuda 1229-1238
Dominica..............................1328-1337
Gambia 1080-1089
Grenada...............................2006-2015
Grenada Grenadines............1331-1340
Guyana 2440-2451
Lesotho...................................871-875
Maldive Islands....................1533-1542
Nevis.......................................666-675
St. Vincent...........................1485-1494
St. Vincent Grenadines 769-778
Sierra Leone........................1387-1396
Turks & Caicos Islands 913-922
Uganda 918-927

Queen Elizabeth II's Accession to the Throne, 40th Anniv.

CD348

CD349

Various photographs of Queen Elizabeth II with local Scenes.

1992 - CD348

Antigua 1513-1518
Barbuda 1306-1309
Dominica..............................1414-1419
Gambia 1172-1177
Grenada...............................2047-2052
Grenada Grenadines............1368-1373
Lesotho...................................881-885
Maldive Islands....................1637-1642
Nevis.......................................702-707
St. Vincent...........................1582-1587
St. Vincent Grenadines 829-834
Sierra Leone........................1482-1487
Turks and Caicos Islands.........978-987
Uganda 990-995
Virgin Islands..........................742-746

1992 - CD349

Ascension Islands 531-535
Bahamas 744-748
Bermuda..................................623-627
British Indian Ocean Territory 119-123
Cayman Islands.......................648-652
Falkland Islands 549-553
Gibraltar..................................605-609
Hong Kong 619-623
Kenya.......................................563-567
Kiribati 582-586
Pitcairn Islands........................362-366
St. Helena 570-574
St. Kitts 332-336
Samoa 805-809
Seychelles 734-738
Solomon Islands.......................708-712
South Georgia 157-161
Tristan da Cunha.....................508-512
Vanuatu 555-559
Zambia.....................................561-565
Zil Elwannyen Sesel 183-187

Royal Air Force, 75th Anniversary

CD350

1993

Ascension 557-561
Bahamas 771-775
Barbados 842-846
Belize 1003-1008
Bermuda..................................648-651
British Indian Ocean Territory 136-140
Falkland Is. 573-577
Fiji 687-691
Montserrat 830-834
St. Kitts 351-355

Royal Air Force, 80th Anniv.

Design CD350 Re-inscribed

1998

Ascension 697-701
Bahamas 907-911
British Indian Ocean Terr 198-202
Cayman Islands.......................754-758
Fiji 814-818
Gibraltar..................................755-759
Samoa 957-961
Turks & Caicos Islands 1258-1265
Tuvalu 763-767
Virgin Islands......................... 879-883

End of World War II, 50th Anniv.

CD351

CD352

1995

Ascension 613-617
Bahamas 824-828
Barbados 891-895
Belize 1047-1050
British Indian Ocean Territory 163-167
Cayman Islands.......................704-708
Falkland Islands 634-638
Fiji 720-724
Kiribati 662-668
Liberia 1175-1179
Mauritius.................................803-805
St. Helena 646-654
St. Kitts 389-393
St. Lucia 1018-1022
Samoa 890-894
Solomon Islands.......................799-803
South Georgia & S. Sandwich Is. 198-200
Tristan da Cunha.....................562-566

UN, 50th Anniv.

CD353

1995

Bahamas 839-842
Barbados 901-904
Belize 1055-1058
Jamaica 847-851
Liberia 1187-1190
Mauritius.................................813-816
Pitcairn Islands........................436-439
St. Kitts 398-401
St. Lucia 1023-1026
Samoa 900-903
Tristan da Cunha.....................568-571
Virgin Islands..........................807-810

Queen Elizabeth, 70th Birthday

CD354

1996

Ascension 632-635
British Antarctic Territory..........240-243
British Indian Ocean Territory 176-180
Falkland Islands 653-657
Pitcairn Islands........................446-449
St. Helena 672-676
Samoa 912-916
Tokelau 223-227
Tristan da Cunha.....................576-579
Virgin Islands..........................824-828

Diana, Princess of Wales (1961-97)

CD355

1998

Ascension.......696
Bahamas.......901A-902
Barbados.......950
Belize.......1091
Bermuda.......753
Botswana.......659-663
British Antarctic Territory.......258
British Indian Ocean Terr.......197
Cayman Islands.......752A-753
Falkland Islands.......694
Fiji.......819-820
Gibraltar.......754
Kiribati.......719A-720
Namibia.......909
Niue.......706
Norfolk Island.......644-645
Papua New Guinea.......937
Pitcairn Islands.......487
St. Helena.......711
St. Kitts.......437A-438
Samoa.......955A-956
Seycelles.......802
Solomon Islands.......866-867
South Georgia & S. Sandwich Islands
.......220
Tokelau.......252B-253
Tonga.......980
Niuafo'ou.......201
Tristan da Cunha.......618
Tuvalu.......762
Vanuatu.......719
Virgin Islands.......878

Wedding of Prince Edward and Sophie Rhys-Jones

CD356

1999

Ascension.......729-730
Cayman Islands.......775-776
Falkland Islands.......729-730
Pitcairn Islands.......505-506
St. Helena.......733-734
Samoa.......971-972
Tristan da Cunha.......636-637
Virgin Islands.......908-909

1st Manned Moon Landing, 30th Anniv.

CD357

1999

Ascension.......731-735
Bahamas.......942-946
Barbados.......967-971
Bermuda.......778
Cayman Islands.......777-781
Fiji.......853-857
Jamaica.......889-893
Kirbati.......746-750
Nauru.......465-469
St. Kitts.......460-464
Samoa.......973-977
Solomon Islands.......875-879
Tuvalu.......800-804
Virgin Islands.......910-914

Queen Mother's Century

CD358

1999

Ascension.......736-740
Bahamas.......951-955
Cayman Islands.......782-786
Falkland Islands.......734-738
Fiji.......858-862
Norfolk Island.......688-692
St. Helena.......740-744
Samoa.......978-982
Solomon Islands.......880-884
South Georgia & South Sandwich Islands.......231-235
Tristan da Cunha.......638-642
Tuvalu.......805-809

Prince William, 18th Birthday

CD359

2000

Ascension.......755-759
Cayman Islands.......797-801
Falkland Islands.......762-766
Fiji.......889-893
South Georgia.......257-261
and South Sandwich Islands
Tristan da Cunha.......664-668
Virgin Islands.......925-929

Reign of Queen Elizabeth II, 50th Anniv.

CD360

2002

Ascension.......790-794
Bahamas.......1033-1037
Barbados.......1019-1023
Belize.......1152-1156
Bermuda.......822-826
British Antarctic Territory.......307-311
British Indian Ocean Territory.......239-243
Cayman Islands.......844-848
Falkland Islands.......804-808
Gibraltar.......896-900
Jamaica.......952-956
Nauru.......491-495
Norfolk Island.......758-762
Papua New Guinea.......1019-1023
Pitcairn Islands.......552
St. Helena.......788-792
St. Lucia.......1146-1150
Solomon Islands.......931-935
South Georgia & So. Sandwich Is.......
.......274-278
Swaziland.......706-710
Tokelau.......302-306
Tonga.......1059
Niuafo'ou.......239
Tristan da Cunha.......706-710
Virgin Islands.......967-971

Queen Mother Elizabeth (1900-2002)

CD361

2002

Ascension.......799-801
Bahamas.......1044-1046
Bermuda.......834-836
British Antarctic Territory.......312-314
British Indian Ocean Territory.......245-247
Cayman Islands.......857-861
Falkland Islands.......812-816
Nauru.......499-501
Pitcairn Islands.......561-565
St. Helena.......808-812
St. Lucia.......1155-1159
Seychelles.......830
Solomon Islands.......945-947
South Georgia & So. Sandwich Isls.....
.......281-285
Tokelau.......312-314
Tristan da Cunha.......715-717
Virgin Islands.......979-983

Head of Queen Elizabeth II

CD362

2003

Ascension.......822
Bermuda.......865
British Antarctic Territory.......322
British Indian Ocean Territory.......261
Cayman Islands.......878
Falkland Islands.......828
St. Helena.......820
South Georgia & South Sandwich Islands.......294
Tristan da Cunha.......731
Virgin Islands.......1003

Coronation of Queen Elizabeth II, 50th Anniv.

CD363

2003

Ascension.......823-825
Bahamas.......1073-1075
Bermuda.......866-868
British Antarctic Territory.......323-325
British Indian Ocean Territory.......262-264
Cayman Islands.......879-881
Jamaica.......970-972
Kiribati.......825-827
Pitcairn Islands.......577-581
St. Helena.......821-823
St. Lucia.......1171-1173
Tokelau.......320-322
Tristan da Cunha.......732-734
Virgin Islands.......1004-1006

Prince William, 21st Birthday

CD364

2003

Ascension.......826
British Indian Ocean Territory.......265
Cayman Islands.......882-884
Falkland Islands.......829
South Georgia & South Sandwich Islands.......295
Tokelau.......323
Tristan da Cunha.......735
Virgin Islands.......1007-1009

Cover Supplies

COVER SLEEVES

Protect your covers with clear polyethylene sleeves.
Sold in packages of 100.

U.S. POSTAL CARD

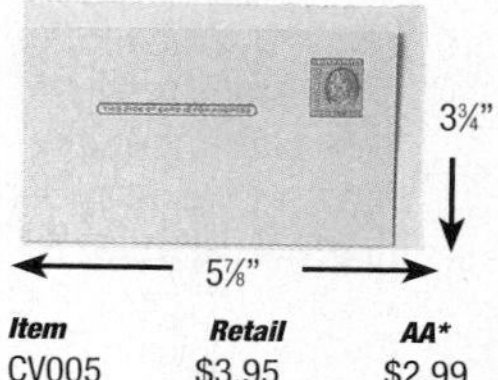

3¾" × 5⅞"

Item	Retail	AA*
CV005	$3.95	$2.99

U.S. FIRST DAY COVER #6

4" × 6¾"

Item	Retail	AA*
CV006	$3.95	$3.10

CONTINENTAL POSTCARD

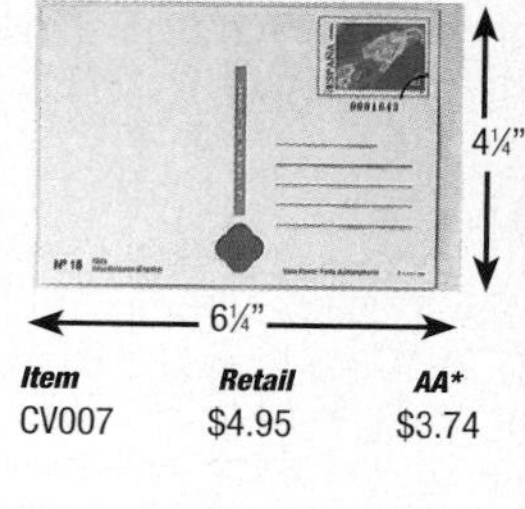

4¼" × 6¼"

Item	Retail	AA*
CV007	$4.95	$3.74

EUROPEAN FIRST DAY COVER

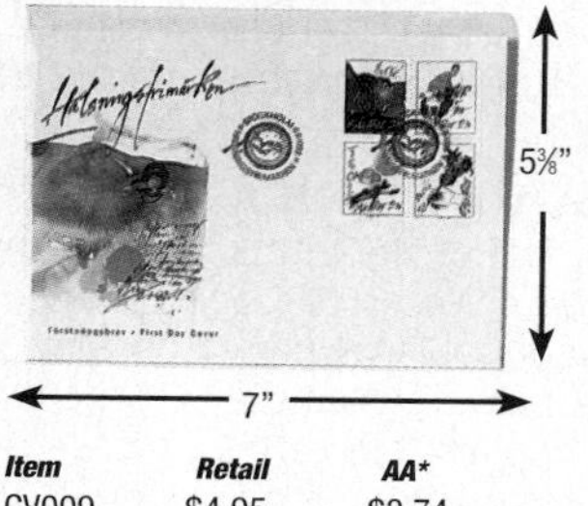

5⅜" × 7"

Item	Retail	AA*
CV009	$4.95	$3.74

#10 BUSINESS ENVELOPE

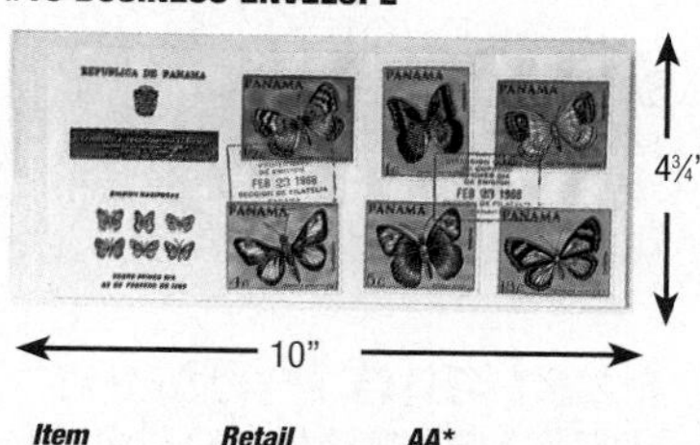

4¼" × 10"

Item	Retail	AA*
CV010	$5.95	$4.49

COVER BINDERS AND PAGES

Padded, durable, 3-ring binders will hold up to 100 covers. Features the "D" ring mechanism on the right hand side of album so you don't have to worry about creasing or wrinkling covers when opening or closing binder. Cover pages sold separately. Available in black with 1 or 2 pockets. Sold in packages of 10.

Item		Retail	AA*
CBRD	Burgundy	$11.99	$9.59
CBBL	Blue	$11.99	$9.59
CBCA	Candy Apple	$11.99	$9.59
CBGY	Gray	$11.99	$9.59
CBBK	Black	$11.99	$9.59
SS2PGB	Pgs. 2-Pock.	$4.95	$4.50
SS2PG1B	Pgs. 1-Pock.	$4.95	$4.50

MINT SHEET BINDERS & PAGES

Keep those mint sheets intact in a handsome, 3-ring binder. Just like the cover album, the Mint Sheet album features the "D" ring mechanism on the right hand side of binder so you don't have to worry about damagaing your stamps when turning the pages.

Item			Retail	AA*
MBRD	Red (Burgundy)		$18.99	$15.25
MBBL	Blue		$18.99	$15.25
MBGY	Gray		$18.99	$15.25
MBBK	Black		$18.99	$15.25
SSMP3B	Mint Sheet Pages	(Black 12 per pack)	$8.75	$7.95
SSMP3C	Mint Sheet Pages	(Clear 12 per pack)	$8.75	$7.95

PRINZ CORNER MOUNTS

Clear, self-adhesive corner mounts are ideal for postal cards and covers. Mounts measure ⅞" each side and are made from transparent glass foil. There are 250 mounts in each pack.

Item	Retail	AA*
ACC176	$9.95	**$7.96**

1. AA* prices apply to paid subscribers of *Linn's and orders placed online.*
2. Prices, terms and product availability subject to change.
3. **Shipping & Handling:**
   United States: 10% of order total. Minimum charge $6.99 Maximum charge $45.00.
   Canada: 15% of order total. Minimum charge $19.99 Maximum charge $50.00.
   Foreign orders are shipped via FedEx Intl and billed actual freight. Credit cards only.

Call 1-800-572-6885

www.amosadvantage.com

British Commonwealth of Nations

Dominions, Colonies, Territories, Offices and Independent Members

Comprising stamps of the British Commonwealth and associated nations.

A strict observance of technicalities would bar some or all of the stamps listed under Burma, Ireland, Kuwait, Nepal, New Republic, Orange Free State, Samoa, South Africa, South-West Africa, Stellaland, Sudan, Swaziland, the two Transvaal Republics and others but these are included for the convenience of collectors.

1. Great Britain

Great Britain: Including England, Scotland, Wales and Northern Ireland.

2. The Dominions, Present and Past

AUSTRALIA

The Commonwealth of Australia was proclaimed on January 1, 1901. It consists of six former colonies as follows:

New South Wales
Queensland
South Australia
Victoria
Tasmania
Western Australia

The following islands and territories are, or have been, administered by Australia: Australian Antarctic Territory, Christmas Island, Cocos (Keeling) Islands, Nauru, New Guinea, Norfolk Island, Papua.

CANADA

The Dominion of Canada was created by the British North America Act in 1867. The following provinces were former separate colonies and issued postage stamps:

British Columbia and Vancouver Island
New Brunswick
Newfoundland
Nova Scotia
Prince Edward Island

FIJI

The colony of Fiji became an independent nation with dominion status on Oct. 10, 1970.

GHANA

This state came into existence Mar. 6, 1957, with dominion status. It consists of the former colony of the Gold Coast and the Trusteeship Territory of Togoland. Ghana became a republic July 1, 1960.

INDIA

The Republic of India was inaugurated on January 26, 1950. It succeeded the Dominion of India which was proclaimed August 15, 1947, when the former Empire of India was divided into Pakistan and the Union of India. The Republic is composed of about 40 predominantly Hindu states of three classes: governor's provinces, chief commissioner's provinces and princely states. India also has various territories, such as the Andaman and Nicobar Islands.

The old Empire of India was a federation of British India and the native states. The more important princely states were autonomous. Of the more than 700 Indian states, these 43 are familiar names to philatelists because of their postage stamps.

CONVENTION STATES

Chamba
Faridkot
Gwalior
Jhind
Nabha
Patiala

FEUDATORY STATES

Alwar
Bahawalpur
Bamra
Barwani
Bhopal
Bhor
Bijawar
Bundi
Bussahir
Charkhari
Cochin
Dhar
Dungarpur
Duttia
Faridkot (1879-85)
Hyderabad
Idar
Indore
Jaipur
Jammu
Jammu and Kashmir
Jasdan
Jhalawar
Jhind (1875-76)
Kashmir
Kishangarh
Kotah
Las Bela
Morvi
Nandgaon
Nowanuggur
Orchha
Poonch
Rajasthan
Rajpeepla
Sirmur
Soruth
Tonk
Travancore
Wadhwan

NEW ZEALAND

Became a dominion on September 26, 1907. The following islands and territories are, or have been, administered by New Zealand:

Aitutaki
Cook Islands (Rarotonga)
Niue
Penrhyn
Ross Dependency
Samoa (Western Samoa)
Tokelau Islands

PAKISTAN

The Republic of Pakistan was proclaimed March 23, 1956. It succeeded the Dominion which was proclaimed August 15, 1947. It is made up of all or part of several Moslem provinces and various districts of the former Empire of India, including Bahawalpur and Las Bela. Pakistan withdrew from the Commonwealth in 1972.

SOUTH AFRICA

Under the terms of the South African Act (1909) the self-governing colonies of Cape of Good Hope, Natal, Orange River Colony and Transvaal united on May 31, 1910, to form the Union of South Africa. It became an independent republic May 3, 1961.

Under the terms of the Treaty of Versailles, South-West Africa, formerly German South-West Africa, was mandated to the Union of South Africa.

SRI LANKA (CEYLON)

The Dominion of Ceylon was proclaimed February 4, 1948. The island had been a Crown Colony from 1802 until then. On May 22, 1972, Ceylon became the Republic of Sri Lanka.

3. Colonies, Past and Present; ControlledTerritory and Independent Members of the Commonwealth

Aden
Aitutaki
Antigua
Ascension
Bahamas
Bahrain
Bangladesh
Barbados
Barbuda
Basutoland
Batum
Bechuanaland
Bechuanaland Prot.
Belize
Bermuda
Botswana
British Antarctic Territory
British Central Africa
British Columbia and Vancouver Island
British East Africa
British Guiana

British Honduras
British Indian Ocean Territory
British New Guinea
British Solomon Islands
British Somaliland
Brunei
Burma
Bushire
Cameroons
Cape of Good Hope
Cayman Islands
Christmas Island
Cocos (Keeling) Islands
Cook Islands
Crete,
British Administration
Cyprus
Dominica
East Africa & Uganda
Protectorates
Egypt
Falkland Islands
Fiji
Gambia
German East Africa
Gibraltar
Gilbert Islands
Gilbert & Ellice Islands
Gold Coast
Grenada
Griqualand West
Guernsey
Guyana
Heligoland
Hong Kong
Indian Native States
(see India)
Ionian Islands
Jamaica
Jersey
Kenya
Kenya, Uganda & Tanzania
Kuwait
Labuan
Lagos
Leeward Islands
Lesotho
Madagascar
Malawi
Malaya
Federated Malay States
Johore
Kedah
Kelantan
Malacca
Negri Sembilan
Pahang
Penang
Perak
Perlis
Selangor
Singapore
Sungei Ujong
Trengganu
Malaysia
Maldive Islands
Malta
Man, Isle of
Mauritius
Mesopotamia
Montserrat
Muscat
Namibia
Natal
Nauru
Nevis
New Britain
New Brunswick
Newfoundland
New Guinea
New Hebrides
New Republic
New South Wales
Niger Coast Protectorate
Nigeria
Niue
Norfolk Island
North Borneo
Northern Nigeria
Northern Rhodesia
North West Pacific Islands
Nova Scotia
Nyasaland Protectorate
Oman
Orange River Colony
Palestine
Papua New Guinea
Penrhyn Island
Pitcairn Islands
Prince Edward Island
Queensland
Rhodesia
Rhodesia & Nyasaland
Ross Dependency
Sabah
St. Christopher
St. Helena
St. Kitts
St. Kitts-Nevis-Anguilla
St. Lucia
St. Vincent
Samoa
Sarawak
Seychelles
Sierra Leone
Solomon Islands
Somaliland Protectorate
South Arabia
South Australia
South Georgia
Southern Nigeria
Southern Rhodesia
South-West Africa
Stellaland
Straits Settlements
Sudan
Swaziland
Tanganyika
Tanzania
Tasmania
Tobago
Togo
Tokelau Islands
Tonga
Transvaal
Trinidad
Trinidad and Tobago
Tristan da Cunha
Trucial States
Turks and Caicos
Turks Islands
Tuvalu
Uganda
United Arab Emirates
Victoria
Virgin Islands
Western Australia
Zambia
Zanzibar
Zululand

POST OFFICES IN FOREIGN COUNTRIES

Africa
East Africa Forces
Middle East Forces
Bangkok
China
Morocco
Turkish Empire

Colonies, Former Colonies, Offices, Territories Controlled by Parent States

Belgium

Belgian Congo
Ruanda-Urundi

Denmark

Danish West Indies
Faroe Islands
Greenland
Iceland

Finland

Aland Islands

France

COLONIES PAST AND PRESENT, CONTROLLED TERRITORIES

Afars & Issas, Territory of
Alaouites
Alexandretta
Algeria
Alsace & Lorraine
Anjouan
Annam & Tonkin
Benin
Cambodia (Khmer)
Cameroun
Castellorizo
Chad
Cilicia
Cochin China
Comoro Islands
Dahomey
Diego Suarez
Djibouti (Somali Coast)
Fezzan
French Congo
French Equatorial Africa
French Guiana
French Guinea
French India
French Morocco
French Polynesia (Oceania)
French Southern & Antarctic Territories
French Sudan
French West Africa
Gabon
Germany
Ghadames
Grand Comoro
Guadeloupe
Indo-China
Inini
Ivory Coast
Laos
Latakia
Lebanon
Madagascar
Martinique
Mauritania
Mayotte
Memel
Middle Congo
Moheli
New Caledonia
New Hebrides
Niger Territory
Nossi-Be
Obock
Reunion
Rouad, Ile
Ste.-Marie de Madagascar
St. Pierre & Miquelon
Senegal
Senegambia & Niger
Somali Coast
Syria
Tahiti
Togo
Tunisia
Ubangi-Shari
Upper Senegal & Niger
Upper Volta
Viet Nam
Wallis & Futuna Islands

POST OFFICES IN FOREIGN COUNTRIES

China
Crete
Egypt
Turkish Empire
Zanzibar

Germany

EARLY STATES

Baden
Bavaria
Bergedorf
Bremen
Brunswick
Hamburg
Hanover
Lubeck
Mecklenburg-Schwerin
Mecklenburg-Strelitz
Oldenburg
Prussia
Saxony
Schleswig-Holstein
Wurttemberg

FORMER COLONIES

Cameroun (Kamerun)
Caroline Islands
German East Africa
German New Guinea
German South-West Africa
Kiauchau
Mariana Islands
Marshall Islands
Samoa
Togo

Italy

EARLY STATES

Modena
Parma
Romagna
Roman States
Sardinia
Tuscany
Two Sicilies
  Naples
  Neapolitan Provinces
  Sicily

FORMER COLONIES, CONTROLLED TERRITORIES, OCCUPATION AREAS

Aegean Islands
  Calimno (Calino)
  Caso
  Cos (Coo)
  Karki (Carchi)
  Leros (Lero)
  Lipso
  Nisiros (Nisiro)
  Patmos (Patmo)
  Piscopi
  Rodi (Rhodes)
  Scarpanto
  Simi
  Stampalia
Castellorizo
Corfu
Cyrenaica
Eritrea
Ethiopia (Abyssinia)
Fiume
Ionian Islands
  Cephalonia
  Ithaca
  Paxos
Italian East Africa
Libya
Oltre Giuba
Saseno
Somalia (Italian Somaliland)
Tripolitania

POST OFFICES IN FOREIGN COUNTRIES

"ESTERO"*
Austria
China
  Peking
  Tientsin
Crete
Tripoli
Turkish Empire
  Constantinople
  Durazzo
  Janina
Jerusalem
Salonika
Scutari
Smyrna
Valona

*Stamps overprinted "ESTERO" were used in various parts of the world.

Netherlands

Aruba
Netherlands Antilles (Curacao)
Netherlands Indies
Netherlands New Guinea
Surinam (Dutch Guiana)

Portugal

COLONIES PAST AND PRESENT, CONTROLLED TERRITORIES

Angola
Angra
Azores
Cape Verde
Funchal
Horta
Inhambane
Kionga
Lourenco Marques
Macao
Madeira
Mozambique
Mozambique Co.
Nyassa
Ponta Delgada
Portuguese Africa
Portuguese Congo
Portuguese Guinea
Portuguese India
Quelimane
St. Thomas & Prince Islands
Tete
Timor
Zambezia

Russia

ALLIED TERRITORIES AND REPUBLICS, OCCUPATION AREAS

Armenia
Aunus (Olonets)
Azerbaijan
Batum
Estonia
Far Eastern Republic
Georgia
Karelia
Latvia
Lithuania
North Ingermanland
Ostland
Russian Turkestan
Siberia
South Russia
Tannu Tuva
Transcaucasian Fed. Republics
Ukraine
Wenden (Livonia)
Western Ukraine

Spain

COLONIES PAST AND PRESENT, CONTROLLED TERRITORIES

Aguera, La
Cape Juby
Cuba
Elobey, Annobon & Corisco
Fernando Po
Ifni
Mariana Islands
Philippines
Puerto Rico
Rio de Oro
Rio Muni
Spanish Guinea
Spanish Morocco
Spanish Sahara
Spanish West Africa

POST OFFICES IN FOREIGN COUNTRIES

Morocco
Tangier
Tetuan

Dies of British Colonial Stamps

DIE A

DIE B

DIE A:
1. The lines in the groundwork vary in thickness and are not uniformly straight.
2. The seventh and eighth lines from the top, in the groundwork, converge where they meet the head.
3. There is a small dash in the upper part of the second jewel in the band of the crown.
4. The vertical color line in front of the throat stops at the sixth line of shading on the neck.

DIE B:
1. The lines in the groundwork are all thin and straight.
2. All the lines of the background are parallel.
3. There is no dash in the upper part of the second jewel in the band of the crown.
4. The vertical color line in front of the throat stops at the eighth line of shading on the neck.

DIE I

DIE II

DIE I:
1. The base of the crown is well below the level of the inner white line around the vignette.
2. The labels inscribed "POSTAGE" and "REVENUE" are cut square at the top.
3. There is a white "bud" on the outer side of the main stem of the curved ornaments in each lower corner.
4. The second (thick) line below the country name has the ends next to the crown cut diagonally.

DIE Ia.	DIE Ib.
1 as die II.	1 and 3 as die II.
2 and 3 as die I.	2 as die I.

DIE II:
1. The base of the crown is aligned with the underside of the white line around the vignette.
2. The labels curve inward at the top inner corners.
3. The "bud" has been removed from the outer curve of the ornaments in each corner.
4. The second line below the country name has the ends next to the crown cut vertically.

British Colonial and Crown Agents Watermarks

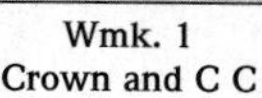
Wmk. 1
Crown and C C

Wmk. 2
Crown and C A

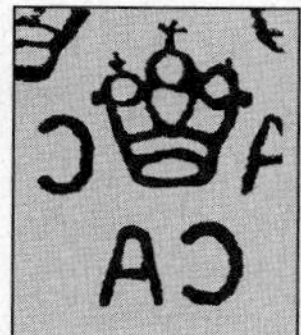
Wmk. 3
Multiple Crown and C A

Wmk. 4
Multiple Crown and Script C A

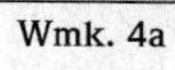
Wmk. 4a

Wmk. 314
St. Edward's Crown and C A Multiple

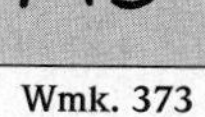
Wmk. 373

Wmk. 384

Wmk. 406

Watermarks 1 to 4, 314, 373, 384 and 406, common to many British territories, are illustrated here to avoid duplication.

The letters "CC" of Wmk. 1 identify the paper as having been made for the use of the Crown Colonies, while the letters "CA" of the others stand for "Crown Agents." Both Wmks. 1 and 2 were used on stamps printed by De La Rue & Co.

Wmk. 3 was adopted in 1904; Wmk. 4 in 1921; Wmk. 314 in 1957; Wmk. 373 in 1974; Wmk. 384 in 1985; Wmk 406 in 2008.

In Wmk. 4a, a non-matching crown of the general St. Edwards type (bulging on both sides at top) was substituted for one of the Wmk. 4 crowns which fell off the dandy roll. The non-matching crown occurs in 1950-52 printings in a horizontal row of crowns on certain regular stamps of Johore and Seychelles, and on various postage due stamps of Barbados, Basutoland, British Guiana, Gold Coast, Grenada, Northern Rhodesia, St. Lucia, Swaziland and Trinidad and Tobago. A variation of Wmk. 4a, with the non-matching crown in a horizontal row of crown-CA-crown, occurs on regular stamps of Bahamas, St. Kitts-Nevis and Singapore.

Wmk. 314 was intentionally used sideways, starting in 1966. When a stamp was issued with Wmk. 314 both upright and sideways, the sideways varieties usually are listed also – with minor numbers. In many of the later issues, Wmk. 314 is slightly visible.

Wmk. 373 is usually only faintly visible.

album accessories

ADVANTAGE STOCK SHEETS

Advantage stock sheets fit directly in your 2-post or 3-ring National or Specialty album. Available with 1 to 8 pockets.

Sheets are sold in packages of 10.

- Stock sheets match album pages in every respect, including size, border, and color.
- Punched to fit perfectly in binder.
- Ideal for storing minor varieties and collateral material. A great place to keep new issues until the next supplement is available.
- Provides the protection of clear acetate pockets on heavyweight pages.

NATIONAL BORDER

Item			Retail	AA*
AD11	1 Pocket	242mm	$19.99	$17.99
AD12	2 Pockets	119mm	$19.99	$17.99
AD13	3 Pockets	79mm	$19.99	$17.99
AD14	4 Pockets	58mm	$19.99	$17.99
AD15	5 Pockets	45mm	$19.99	$17.99
AD16	6 Pockets	37mm	$19.99	$17.99
AD17	7 Pockets	34mm	$19.99	$17.99
AD18	8 Pockets	31mm	$19.99	$17.99

SPECIALTY BORDER

Item			Retail	AA*
AD21	1 Pocket	242mm	$19.99	$17.99
AD22	2 Pockets	119mm	$19.99	$17.99
AD23	3 Pockets	79mm	$19.99	$17.99
AD24	4 Pockets	58mm	$19.99	$17.99
AD25	5 Pockets	45mm	$19.99	$17.99
AD26	6 Pockets	37mm	$19.99	$17.99
AD27	7 Pockets	34mm	$19.99	$17.99
AD28	8 Pockets	31mm	$19.99	$17.99

BLANK PAGES

Ideal for developing your own album pages to be integrated with your album.

SPECIALTY SERIES PAGES (BORDER A)

(20 per pack)

Item		Retail	AA*
ACC110		$8.99	$6.99
ACC111	Quadrille*	$13.99	$11.99

* Graph pattern printed on page.

SPECIALTY/NATIONAL SERIES BINDERS

National series pages are punched for 3-ring and 2-post binders. The 3-ring binder is available in two sizes. The 2-post binder comes in one size. All Scott binders are covered with a tough green leatherette material that is washable and reinforced at stress points for long wear.

3-RING BINDERS & SLIPCASES

With the three ring binder, pages lay flat and the rings make turning the pages easy. The locking mechanism insure that the rings won't pop open even when the binder is full.

Item			Retail	AA*
ACBR01	Small 3-Ring Binder	Holds up to 100 pages	$39.99	$32.99
ACBR03	Large 3-Ring Binder	Holds up to 250 pages	$39.99	$32.99
ACSR01	Small 3-Ring Slipcase.		$32.50	$26.99
ACSR03	Large 3-Ring Slipcase.		$37.50	$26.99

LARGE 2-POST BINDER & SLIPCASE

For the traditional Scott collector, we offer the standard hinge post binder. Scott album pages are punched with rectangular holes that fit on rectangular posts. The posts and pages are held by a rod that slides down from the top. With the post binder pages do not lie flat. However, filler strips are available for a minimal cost.

Item			Retail	AA*
ACBS03	Large 2-Post Binder	Holds up to 250 pages	$54.99	$46.99
ACSS03	Large 2-Post Slipcase		$37.50	$26.99

ALBUM PAGE DIVIDERS

Postage, air post, semi-postals; they're all right at your fingertips with Specialty Album Page Dividers. The dividers are a great way to keep your albums organized and save wear and tear on your pages.

Item		Retail	AA*
ACC145	Package of 10	$4.49	$3.49

NATIONAL SERIES PAGES (BORDER B)

(20 per pack)

Item		Retail	AA*
ACC120		$8.99	$6.99
ACC121	Quadrille*	$13.99	$11.99

PAGE PROTECTORS

Protect your stamps and album pages with a clear archival quality plastic sleeve. Sleeves fits over the entire page and protects pages from creases, fingerprints and tears. Scott Page protectors are pvc free and thin enough that they won't make your binder bulge. Page Protectors are available in two sizes. Sold in packages of 25.

2-Post Minuteman/International Pg Protectors

Item	Retail	AA*
ACC165	$13.99	$11.75

National/Specialty Series Pg Protectors*

Item	Retail	AA*
ACC166	$13.99	$11.75

*Punched to fit 2-post and 3-ring binder.

To Order Call 1-800-572-6885

www.amosadvantage.com

1. AA* prices apply to paid subscribers of *Linn's* and orders placed online.
2. Prices, terms and product availability subject to change.
3. **Shipping & Handling:**
   United States: 10% of order total. Minimum charge $6.99 Maximum charge $45.00.
   Canada: 15% of order total. Minimum charge $19.99 Maximum charge $50.00.
   Foreign orders are shipped via FedEx Intl. and billed actual freight. Credit cards only.

JAMAICA

jə-'mā-kə

LOCATION — Caribbean Sea, about 90 miles south of Cuba
GOVT. — Independent state in the British Commonwealth
AREA — 4,411 sq. mi.
POP. — 2,652,443 (1999 est.)
CAPITAL — Kingston

Jamaica became an independent state in the British Commonwealth in August 1962. As a colony, it administered two dependencies: Cayman Islands and Turks and Caicos Islands.

12 Pence = 1 Shilling
20 Shillings = 1 Pound
100 Cents = 1 Dollar (1969)

Catalogue values for unused stamps in this country are for Never Hinged items, beginning with Scott 129 in the regular postage section and Scott B4 in the semi-postal section.

Watermarks

Wmk. 45 — Pineapple

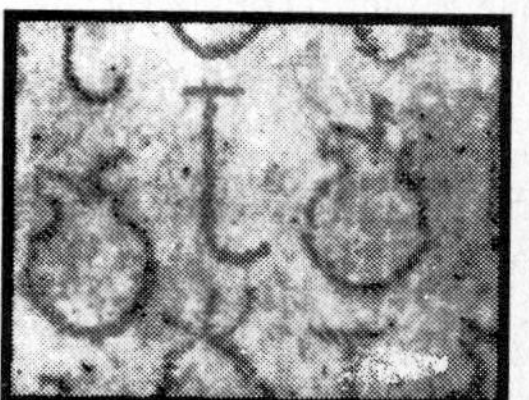

Wmk. 352 — J and Pineapple, Multiple

Values for unused stamps are for examples with original gum as defined in the catalogue introduction. Very fine examples of Nos. 1-12 will have perforations touching the design on at least one side due to the narrow spacing of the stamps on the plates. Stamps with perfs clear on all four sides are scarce and will command higher prices.

Queen Victoria
A1 A2

A3

A4

A5 A6

1860-63 Typo. Wmk. 45 ***Perf. 14***

1 A1 1p blue 65.00 15.00
 a. Diagonal half used as ½p on cover 825.00
 b. 1p deep blue 140.00 35.00
 c. 1p pale blue 77.50 19.00
 d. 1p pale greenish blue 100.00 24.00
2 A2 2p rose 160.00 65.00
 a. 2p deep rose 240.00 65.00
3 A3 3p green ('63) 160.00 32.50
4 A4 4p brown org 250.00 62.50
 a. 4p orange 250.00 27.50
5 A5 6p lilac 225.00 27.50
 a. 6p deep lilac 1,050. 65.00
 b. 6p gray lilac 350.00 40.00
6 A6 1sh brown 225.00 35.00
 a. 1sh lilac brown 700.00 30.00
 b. 1sh yellow brown 575.00 32.50

All except No. 3 exist imperforate.

1870-71 **Wmk. 1**

7 A1 1p blue 75.00 .90
8 A2 2p rose 80.00 .85
 a. 2p brownish rose 100.00 1.10
9 A3 3p green 110.00 9.25
10 A4 4p brown org ('72) 210.00 12.00
 a. 4p red orange 450.00 6.50
11 A5 6p lilac ('71) 80.00 6.00
12 A6 1sh brown ('73) 27.50 9.50
 Nos. 7-12 (6) 582.50 38.50

The 1p and 4p exist imperf.
See Nos. 17-23, 40, 43, 47-53.

A7

A8

A9

A10

1872, Oct. 29

13 A7 ½p claret 16.00 3.75
 a. ½p deep claret 21.00 6.00

Exists imperf. See No. 16.

1875, Aug. 27 ***Perf. 12½***

14 A8 2sh red brown 45.00 22.50
15 A9 5sh violet 100.00 *160.00*

Exist imperf.
See Nos. 29-30, 44, 54.

1883-90 Wmk. 2 ***Perf. 14***

16 A7 ½p blue green ('85) 5.75 1.25
 a. ½p gray green 1.10 .20
17 A1 1p blue ('84) 350.00 6.00
18 A1 1p carmine ('85) 55.00 .65
 a. 1p rose 70.00 1.75
19 A2 2p rose ('84) 215.00 4.50
20 A2 2p slate ('85) 95.00 .65
 a. 2p gray 140.00 6.00
21 A3 3p ol green ('86) 2.75 1.40
22 A4 4p red brown 2.25 .40
 a. 4p orange brown 440.00 24.00
23 A5 6p orange yel ('90) 6.00 5.00
 a. 6p yellow 30.00 8.00
 Nos. 16-23 (8) 731.75 19.85

Nos. 18 and 20 exist imperf. Perf. 12 stamps are considered to be proofs.
For surcharge, see No. 27.

1889-91

24 A10 1p lilac & red vio 6.00 .20
25 A10 2p deep green 14.00 6.50
 a. 2p green 25.00 3.75
26 A10 2½p lilac & ultra ('91) 6.25 .75
 Nos. 24-26 (3) 26.25 *7.45*

No. 22 Surcharged in Black

1890, June

27 A4 2½p on 4p red brn 37.50 13.50
 b. Double surcharge 350.00 250.00
 d. "PFNNY" 100.00 70.00
 f. As "d," double surcharge

Three settings of surcharge.

1897

28 A6 1sh brown 7.00 *7.00*
29 A8 2sh red brown 32.50 24.00
30 A9 5sh violet 65.00 *92.50*
 Nos. 28-30 (3) 104.50 *123.50*

The 2sh exists imperf.

Llandovery Falls
A12

Arms of Jamaica
A13

1900, May 1 Engr. Wmk. 1

31 A12 1p red 5.75 .30

1901, Sept. 25

32 A12 1p red & black 6.00 .25
 a. Pair, imperf. horiz. 12,000.
 b. Bluish paper 120.00 110.00

1903-04 Typo. Wmk. 2

33 A13 ½p green & black 1.75 .40
 b. "SERv ET" for "SERVIET" 45.00 *50.00*
34 A13 1p car & black ('04) 2.25 .20
 b. "SERv ET" for "SERVIET" 35.00 40.00
35 A13 2½p ultra & black 4.25 .45
 a. "SERv ET" for "SERVIET" 70.00 *85.00*
36 A13 5p yel & black ('04) 17.50 *26.00*
 a. "SERv ET" for "SERVIET" 850.00 *1,050.*
 Nos. 33-36 (4) 25.75 *27.05*

1905-11 Chalky Paper Wmk. 3

37 A13 ½p green & black 5.00 .20
 b. "SERv ET" for "SERVIET" 32.50 *45.00*
38 A13 1p car & black 20.00 1.00
39 A13 2½p ultra & blk ('07) 3.25 *5.50*
40 A4 4p black, *yel* ('10) 8.50 *55.00*
41 A13 5p yel & black ('07) 65.00 *75.00*
 a. "SERv ET" for "SERVIET" 1,300. *1,500.*
42 A13 6p red vio & vio ('11) 14.00 15.00
43 A6 1sh black, *green* ('10) 7.00 *9.25*
44 A8 2sh vio, *blue* ('10) 8.50 3.75
45 A13 5sh vio & black 50.00 50.00
 Nos. 37-45 (9) 181.25 214.70

1905-11 Ordinary Paper

46 A13 2½p ultra ('10) 3.75 1.40
47 A3 3p sage green ('07) 6.50 4.00
 a. 3p olive green ('07) 7.00 4.25
48 A3 3p pale purple, *yel* ('10) 5.50 3.75
 a. 3p vio, *yel*, chalky paper ('10) 2.10 1.60
49 A4 4p red brn ('08) 75.00 80.00
50 A4 4p red, *yel* ('11) 1.60 *8.50*
51 A5 6p dull vio ('09) 30.00 *50.00*
52 A5 6p org yel ('09) 29.00 *65.00*
 a. 6p orange ('06) 17.00 27.50
53 A6 1sh brown ('06) 20.00 *40.00*
54 A8 2sh red brn ('08) 110.00 *160.00*
 Nos. 46-54 (9) 281.35 *412.65*

Nos. 48 and 51 also come on chalky paper.

A14

A15

1906

58 A14 ½p green 4.00 .25
 a. Booklet pane of 6
59 A15 1p carmine 1.60 .20

For overprints see Nos. MR1, MR4, MR7, MR10.

Edward VII
A16

George V
A17

1911, Feb. 3

60 A16 2p gray 4.75 *15.00*

1912-20

61 A17 1p scarlet ('16) 3.50 .80
 a. 1p carmine ('12) 1.75 .20
 b. Booklet pane of 6
62 A17 1½p brown org ('16) 1.10 .70
 a. 1½p yellow orange 15.00 1.25
63 A17 2p gray 2.25 *2.00*
64 A17 2½p dp br blue .75 *1.25*
 a. 2½p ultra ('13) 1.75 .20

Chalky Paper

65 A17 3p violet, *yel* .60 .50
66 A17 4p scar & blk, *yel* ('13) .60 *4.00*
67 A17 6p red vio & dl vio 4.00 2.50
68 A17 1sh black, *green* 2.60 2.25
 a. 1sh blk, *bl grn*, olive back ('20) 2.60 *6.25*
69 A17 2sh ultra & vio, *blue* ('19) 18.00 *29.00*
70 A17 5sh scarlet & green, *yel* ('19) 80.00 *100.00*

Surface-colored Paper

71 A17 3p violet, *yel* ('13) .65 .45
72 A17 4p scar & black, *yel* ('14) 1.00 *4.50*
73 A17 1sh black, *green* ('15) 2.50 *5.50*
 Nos. 61-73 (13) 117.55 *153.45*

See Nos. 101-102. For overprints see Nos. MR2-MR3, MR5-MR6, MR8-MR9, MR11.

Exhibition Buildings of 1891 — A18

Arawak Woman Preparing Cassava — A19

World War I Contingent Embarking for Overseas Duty — A20

King's House, Spanish Town — A21

Return of Overseas Contingent, 1919 — A22

Columbus Landing in Jamaica — A23

Cathedral in Spanish Town — A24

Statue of Queen Victoria — A26

Memorial to Admiral Rodney — A27

Monument to Sir Charles Metcalfe — A28

Woodland Scene — A29

King George V — A30

1919-21 Typo. Wmk. 3 *Perf. 14*
Chalky Paper

75 A18 ½p ol grn & dk grn ('20) 1.10 1.10
76 A19 1p org & car ('21) 2.40 2.00

Engr.
Ordinary Paper

77 A20 1½p green .45 1.10
78 A21 2p grn & bl ('21) 1.25 *4.50*
79 A22 2½p blue & dk blue ('21) 15.00 3.50
80 A23 3p blue & grn ('21) 1.75 *2.75*
81 A24 4p green & dk brown ('21) 2.75 *10.00*
83 A26 1sh brt org & org ('20) 4.25 *9.00*
a. Frame inverted 30,000. 22,500.
As "a," revenue cancel 3,000.
84 A27 2sh brn & bl ('20) 15.00 *30.00*
85 A28 3sh org & violet ('20) 22.50 *110.00*
86 A29 5sh ocher & blue ('21) 62.50 *92.50*
87 A30 10sh dk myrtle grn ('20) 85.00 *175.00*
Nos. 75-87 (12) 213.95 *441.45*

See note after No. 100.

A 6p stamp depicting the abolition of slavery was sent to the Colony but was not issued. "Specimen" examples exist with wmk. 3 or 4. Value $750 each.

Without "Specimen," values: wmk. 3, $30,000; wmk. 4, $50,000.

Port Royal in 1853 A31

1921-23 Typo. Wmk. 4 *Perf. 14*
Chalky Paper

88 A18 ½p ol grn & dk grn ('22) .60 .60
a. Booklet pane of 4
89 A19 1p orange & car ('22) 1.75 .20
a. Booklet pane of 6

Engr.
Ordinary Paper

90 A20 1½p green 1.50 .55
91 A21 2p grn & blue 7.50 .90
92 A22 2½p bl & dk bl 6.50 2.00
93 A23 3p bl & grn ('22) 2.75 .80
94 A24 4p grn & dk brn 1.10 .35
95 A31 6p bl & blk ('22) 15.00 2.25
96 A26 1sh brn org & dl org 2.00 .90
97 A27 2sh brn & bl ('22) 3.75 .75
98 A28 3sh org & violet 13.50 11.00
99 A29 5sh ocher & bl ('23) 35.00 29.00
a. 5sh orange & blue 70.00 *80.00*
100 A30 10sh dk myrtle green ('22) 60.00 80.00
Nos. 88-100 (13) 150.95 129.30
Set, never hinged 350.00

No. 89 differs from No. 76 in having the words "Postage and Revenue" at the bottom.

On No. 79 the horizontal bar of the flag at the left has a broad white line below the colored line. On No. 92 this has been corrected and the broad white line placed above the colored line.

Watermark is sideways on #76-77, 87, 89-90.

Type of 1912-19 Issue

1921-27 Typo. Wmk. 4

101 A17 ½p green ('27) 2.75 .20
a. Booklet pane of 6
102 A17 6p red vio & dl vio 11.50 4.50

No. 102 is on chalky paper.

A32

Type I

Type II

Type II — Cross shading beneath "Jamaica."

1929-32 Engr. *Perf. 13½x14, 14*

103 A32 1p red, type I 7.50 .20
a. 1p red, type II ('32) 9.00 .20
b. Booklet pane of 6, type II
104 A32 1½p brown 4.50 .20
105 A32 9p violet brown 5.50 1.25
Nos. 103-105 (3) 17.50 1.65
Set, never hinged 22.00

The frames on Nos. 103 to 105 differ.

Coco Palms at Columbus Cove — A33

Scene near Castleton, St. Andrew — A34

Priestman's River, Portland Parish — A35

1932 *Perf. 12½*

106 A33 2p grn & gray blk 29.00 3.25
a. Vertical pair, imperf. between *6,500.*
107 A34 2½p ultra & sl blue 6.00 1.75
a. Vertical pair, imperf. between *17,500. 17,500.*
108 A35 6p red vio & gray black 29.00 3.00
Nos. 106-108 (3) 64.00 8.00
Set, never hinged 70.00

Common Design Types pictured following the introduction.

Silver Jubilee Issue
Common Design Type

1935, May 6 *Perf. 11x12*

109 CD301 1p car & blue .55 .25
a. Booklet pane of 6 *175.00*
110 CD301 1½p black & ultra .75 *1.75*
111 CD301 6p indigo & grn 10.00 *19.50*
112 CD301 1sh brn vio & ind 6.50 *12.00*
Nos. 109-112 (4) 17.80 33.50
Set, never hinged 27.50

Coronation Issue
Common Design Type

1937, May 12 *Perf. 13½x14*

113 CD302 1p carmine .20 .20
114 CD302 1½p gray black .40 .30
115 CD302 2½p bright ultra .60 *.70*
Nos. 113-115 (3) 1.20 1.20
Set, never hinged 2.25

King George VI — A36

Coco Palms at Columbus Cove — A37

Scene near Castleton, St. Andrew — A38

Bananas A39

Citrus Grove A40

Priestman's River, Portland Parish — A41

Kingston Harbor A42

Sugar Industry A43

Bamboo Walk — A44

Woodland Scene — A45

King George VI — A46

1938-51 *Perf. 13½x14*

116 A36 ½p dk blue grn 1.40 .20
a. Booklet pane of 6 9.00
b. Wmkd. sideways
117 A36 1p carmine 1.00 .20
a. Booklet pane of 6 13.00
118 A36 1½p brown 1.00 .20

Perf. 12½, 13x13½, 13½x13, 12½x13

119 A37 2p grn & gray blk, perf. 12½ 1.00 1.00
a. Perf. 13x13½ ('39) 2.25 .60
b. Perf. 12½x13 ('51) 1.00 .20
120 A38 2½p ultra & sl bl 2.25 *2.25*
121 A39 3p grn & lt ultra .90 *1.75*
122 A40 4p grn & yel brn .45 .20
123 A41 6p red vio & gray blk, perf. 13½x13 ('50) 2.00 .20
a. Perf. 12½ 5.50 .35
124 A42 9p rose lake .55 .55
125 A43 1sh dk brn & brt grn 5.75 .25
126 A44 2sh brn & brt bl 20.00 1.25

Perf. 13, 14

127 A45 5sh ocher & bl, perf. 13 ('50) 5.50 4.25
a. Bluish paper, perf. 13 ('49) 5.00 3.50
b. Perf. 14 11.50 4.00
128 A46 10sh dk myrtle grn, perf. 14 9.00 *10.50*
a. Perf. 13 ('50) 10.00 *8.00*
Nos. 116-128 (13) 50.80 22.80
Set, never hinged 100.00

See Nos. 140, 148, 149, 152.

Catalogue values for unused stamps in this section, from this point to the end of the section, are for Never Hinged items.

Courthouse, Falmouth A47

Kings Charles II and George VI A48

House of Assembly, 1762-1869 A50

Institute of Jamaica — A49

Allegory of Labor and Learning — A51

Constitution and Flag of Jamaica A52

Perf. 12½

1945, Aug. 20 Engr. Wmk. 4

129 A47 1½p brown .20 .35
a. Booklet pane of 4 37.50
b. Perf. 12½x13½ ('46) 6.00 .60
130 A48 2p dp grn, perf. 12½x13½ .35 *.55*
a. Perf. 12½ 11.00 1.10
131 A49 3p bright ultra .20 *.55*
a. Perf. 13 ('46) 3.00 *3.25*
132 A50 4½p slate black .35 .35
a. Perf. 13 ('46) 4.00 *4.00*
133 A51 2sh chocolate .50 .50
134 A52 5sh deep blue 2.25 1.10
135 A49 10sh green 2.25 *2.60*
Nos. 129-135 (7) 6.10 *6.00*

Granting of a new Constitution in 1944.

Peace Issue

Common Design Type

1946, Oct. 14 Wmk. 4 *Perf. 13½*

136 CD303 1½p black brown .30 *2.50*
a. Perf. 13½x14 2.75 .20

Perf. 13½x14

137 CD303 3p deep blue 4.50 1.50
a. Perf. 13½ .60 *5.00*

Silver Wedding Issue

Common Design Types

1948, Dec. 1 Photo. *Perf. 14x14½*

138 CD304 1½p red brown .35 .25

Engr.; Name Typo.

Perf. 11½x11

139 CD305 £1 red 30.00 *70.00*

Type of 1938 and

Tobacco Industry A53

1949, Aug. 15 Engr. *Perf. 12½*

140 A39 3p ultra & slate blue 3.50 1.25
141 A53 £1 purple & brown 50.00 35.00

UPU Issue

Common Design Types

Perf. 13½, 11x11½

1949, Oct. 10 Wmk. 4

142 CD306 1½p red brown .20 .20
143 CD307 2p dark green 1.40 2.75
144 CD308 3p indigo .45 *1.25*
145 CD309 6p rose violet .55 *1.75*
Nos. 142-145 (4) 2.60 5.95

University Issue

Common Design Types

1951, Feb. 16 *Perf. 14x14½*

146 CD310 2p brown & gray blk .35 .35
147 CD311 6p rose lilac & gray blk .60 .50

George VI Type of 1938

1951, Oct. 25 *Perf. 13½x14*

148 A36 ½p orange 1.75 .35
a. Booklet pane of 6 12.00
149 A36 1p blue green 2.25 .20
a. Booklet pane of 6 20.00

Boy Scout Emblem with Map — A54

Map and Emblem A55

Perf. 13½x13, 13x13½

1952, Mar. 5 Typo. Wmk. 4

150 A54 2p blk, yel grn & blue .30 .20
151 A55 6p blk, yel grn & dk red .70 .60

1st Caribbean Boy Scout Jamboree, 1952.

Banana Type of 1938

1952, July 1 Engr. *Perf. 12½*

152 A39 3p rose red & green 4.25 .40

Coronation Issue

Common Design Type

1953, June 2 *Perf. 13½x13*

153 CD312 2p dk green & black 1.50 .20

Type of 1938 with Portrait of Queen Elizabeth II and Inscription: "ROYAL VISIT 1953"

1953, Nov. 25 *Perf. 13*

154 A37 2p green & gray black .55 .20

Visit of Queen Elizabeth II and the Duke of Edinburgh, 1953.

Warship off Port Royal A56

Designs: 2½p, Old Montego Bay. 3p, Old Kingston. 6p, Proclaiming abolition of slavery.

1955, May 10 Engr. *Perf. 12x12½*

Center in Black

155 A56 2p olive green .75 .20
156 A56 2½p light ultra .25 .35
157 A56 3p deep plum .25 .30
158 A56 6p rose red .30 .20
Nos. 155-158 (4) 1.55 1.05

300th anniv. of Jamaica's establishment as a British territory.

Palm Trees — A57

Blue Mountain Peak — A58

Arms of Jamaica — A59

Arms of Jamaica — A60

1p, Sugar cane. 2p, Pineapple. 2½p, Bananas. 3p, Mahoe flower. 4p, Breadfruit. 5p, Ackee fruit. 6p, Streamer (hummingbird). 1sh, Royal Botanic Gardens, Hope. 1sh6p, Rafting on the Rio Grande. 2sh, Fort Charles.

1956 Wmk. 4 *Perf. 12½*

159 A57 ½p org ver & black .20 .20
a. Booklet pane of 6 .30
160 A57 1p emer & blk .20 .20
a. Booklet pane of 6 .50
161 A57 2p rose red & blk .20 .20
a. Booklet pane of 6 .85
162 A57 2½p lt ultra & black .75 .55
a. Booklet pane of 6 4.50
163 A57 3p brown & green .25 .20
164 A57 4p dk blue & ol grn .25 .20
165 A57 5p ol green & car .25 2.75
166 A57 6p car & blk 2.50 .20

Perf. 13½

167 A58 8p red org & brt ultra .40 .20
168 A58 1sh blue & yel grn 1.25 .20
169 A58 1sh6p dp cl & ultra 1.00 .20
170 A58 2sh ol grn & ultra 9.00 2.50

Perf. 11½

171 A59 3sh blue & black 1.75 *2.50*
172 A59 5sh carmine & blk 4.25 *5.50*
173 A60 10sh blue grn & blk 32.50 *20.00*
174 A60 £1 purple & blk 32.50 *20.00*
Nos. 159-174 (16) 87.25 55.60

For overprints see Nos. 185-196. For types overprinted see Nos. 208-216.

West Indies Federation

Common Design Type

Perf. 11½x11

1958, Apr. 22 Engr. Wmk. 314

175 CD313 2p green .65 .20
176 CD313 5p blue 1.25 *3.00*
177 CD313 6p carmine rose 1.25 .45
Nos. 175-177 (3) 3.15 3.65

Britannia Plane over 1860 Packet Boat A61

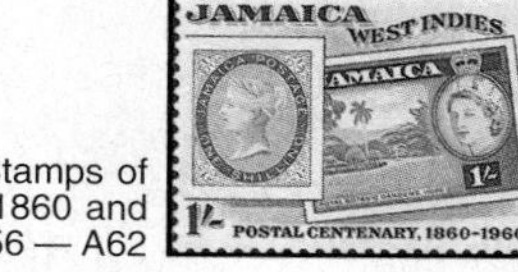

1sh Stamps of 1860 and 1956 — A62

6p, Victorian post cart and mail truck.

1960, Jan. 4 *Perf. 13x13½*

178 A61 2p lilac & blue .55 .20
179 A61 6p ol grn & car rose .55 .50

Perf. 13

180 A62 1sh blue, yel grn & brn .55 .55
Nos. 178-180 (3) 1.65 1.25

Centenary of Jamaican postal service.

Independent State

Zouave Bugler and Map of Jamaica A63

1sh6p, Gordon House (Legislature) & hands of three races holding banner. 5sh, Map & symbols of agriculture & industry.

1962, Aug. 8 Photo. *Perf. 13*

181 A63 2p multicolored 1.75 .20
182 A63 4p multicolored 1.00 .20
a. Yellow omitted
183 A63 1sh6p red, black & brn 5.00 1.00
184 A63 5sh multicolored 7.00 *4.00*
Nos. 181-184 (4) 14.75 5.40

Issue of 1956 Overprinted:

a

b

Perf. 12½

1962, Aug. 8 Wmk. 4 Engr.

185 A57(a) ½p org ver & blk .20 *1.00*
186 A57(a) 1p emer & blk .20 .20
187 A57(a) 2½p lt ultra & blk .20 *1.50*
188 A57(b) 3p brn & grn .20 .20
189 A57(b) 5p ol grn & car .25 *.80*
190 A57(b) 6p car & black 3.00 .20

Perf. 13½

191 A58(b) 8p red org & brt ultra .30 .20
192 A58(b) 1sh bl & yel grn .30 .20
193 A58(b) 2sh ol green & ultra 1.25 *1.75*

Perf. 11½

194 A59(a) 3sh blue & blk 1.40 *1.75*
195 A60(a) 10sh bl grn & blk 4.00 *5.00*
196 A60(a) £1 pur & black 4.00 *6.00*
Nos. 185-196 (12) 15.30 *18.80*

Nos. 181-196 issued to commemorate Jamaica's independence.

"Independence" measures 17½x1½mm on #185-187; 18x1mm on #194-196.

See Nos. 208-216.

Weight Lifting, Soccer, Boxing and Cycling A64

Designs: 6p, Various water sports. 8p, Running and jumping. 2sh, Arms and runner.

Perf. 14½x14

1962, Aug. 11 Photo. Wmk. 314

197 A64 1p car & dk brown .20 .20
198 A64 6p blue & brown .20 .20
199 A64 8p olive & dk brown .25 .20
200 A64 2sh multicolored .45 *.75*
Nos. 197-200 (4) 1.10 1.35

IX Central American and Caribbean Games, Kingston, Aug. 11-25.

A souvenir sheet containing one each of Nos. 197-200, imperf., was sold exclusively by National Sports, Ltd., at 5sh (face 3sh3p). The Jamaican Post Office sold the entire issue of this sheet to National Sports at face value, plus the printing cost. The stamps are postally valid. The sheet has marginal inscriptions and simulated perforations in ultramarine. Value $14.

Freedom from Hunger Issue

Man Planting Mango Tree and Produce A65

Perf. 12½

1963, June 4 Unwmk. Litho.

201 A65 1p blue & multi .30 .20
202 A65 8p rose & multi .95 .60

See note after CD314, Common Design section.

Red Cross Centenary Issue

Common Design Type

1963, Sept. 2 Wmk. 314 *Perf. 13*

203 CD315 2p black & red .25 .20
204 CD315 1sh6p ultra & red .75 1.40

Carole Joan Crawford — A66

Unwmk.

1964, Feb. 14 Photo. *Perf. 13*

205 A66 3p multicolored .30 .20
206 A66 1sh olive & multi .50 .20
207 A66 1sh6p multicolored .80 .80
a. Souvenir sheet of 3 2.75 2.75
Nos. 205-207 (3) 1.60 1.20

Carole Joan Crawford, Miss World, 1963.

No. 207a contains one each of Nos. 205-207 with simulated perforations. Issued May 25. Sold for 4sh.

Types of 1956 Overprinted like 1962 Independence Issue

Wmk. 314

1963-64 Engr. *Perf. 12½*

208 A57(a) ½p org ver & blk .20 .20
209 A57(a) 1p emer & blk ('64) .20 *1.75*
210 A57(a) 2½p lt ultra & blk ('64) .55 *3.00*
211 A57(b) 3p brn & grn .30 .20
212 A57(b) 5p ol grn & car ('64) .85 *3.00*

Perf. 13½

213 A58(b) 8p red org & brt ultra ('64) .50 *.90*
214 A58(b) 1sh bl & yel grn .75 .75
215 A58(b) 2sh ol grn & ultra ('64) 1.25 *7.50*

Perf. 11½

216 A59(a) 3sh bl & blk ('64) 4.00 *5.25*
Nos. 208-216 (9) 8.60 22.55

Overprint is at bottom on Nos. 214-215, at top on Nos. 192-193.

Lignum Vitae, National Flower, and Map — A67

1½p, Ackee, national fruit, and map. 2p, Blue Mahoe, national tree, and map, vert. 2½p, Land shells (snails). 3p, Flag over map. 4p, Murex antillarum, sea shell. 6p, Papilio homerus. 8p, Streamer (hummingbird). 9p, Gypsum industry. 1sh, Stadium and statue of runner. 1sh6p, Palisadoes International Airport. 2sh, Bauxite mining. 3sh, Blue marlin and boat. 5sh, Port Royal exploration of sunken city, map, ship and artifacts. 10sh, Coat of arms, vert. £1, Flag and Queen Elizabeth II.

Perf. 14½, 14x14½

1964, May 4 Photo. Wmk. 352

Size: 26x22mm, 22x26mm

217 A67 1p bis, vio bl & green .20 .20
a. Booklet pane of 6 .35
218 A67 1½p multicolored .20 .20
219 A67 2p multicolored .20 .20
a. Booklet pane of 6 .85
220 A67 2½p multicolored 1.10 .65
221 A67 3p emer, yel & black .20 .20
a. Booklet pane of 6 3.00
222 A67 4p violet & buff .55 .20
223 A67 6p multicolored 2.50 .20
a. Ultramarine omitted 70.00
224 A67 8p multicolored 2.75 1.75
a. Red omitted 140.00

Perf. 14½x14, 13½x14½, 14x14½

Size: 32x26mm, 26x32mm

225 A67 9p blue & yel 1.75 .35
226 A67 1sh yel brn & blk .25 .20
a. Yellow brown omitted 2,250.
b. Black omitted 1,800.
227 A67 1sh6p sl, buff & bl 4.50 .20
228 A67 2sh bl, brn red & black 3.00 .35
229 A67 3sh grn, saph & dk bl, perf. 14½x14 .50 *.70*
a. Perf. 14x14½ 1.75 1.25
230 A67 5sh bl, blk & bis 1.40 1.25
231 A67 10sh multicolored 1.40 1.50
a. Blue ("Jamaica" etc.) omitted 375.00
232 A67 £1 multicolored 2.00 1.25
Nos. 217-232 (16) 22.50 9.40

See Nos. 306-318. For overprints & surcharges see Nos. 248-251, 279-291, 305.

Scout Hat, Globe, Neckerchief — A68

Scout Emblem, American Crocodile — A69

Design: 3p, Scout belt buckle.

Perf. 14½x14, 14

1964, Aug. 27 Wmk. 352

233 A68 3p pink, black & red .20 .20
234 A68 8p ultra, black & olive .20 *.25*
235 A69 1sh ultra & gold .25 *.45*
Nos. 233-235 (3) .65 *.90*

6th Inter-American Scout Conference, Kingston, Aug. 25-29.

Gordon House, Kingston, and Commonwealth Parliamentary Association Emblem — A70

6p, Headquarters House, Kingston. 1sh6p, House of Assembly, Spanish Town.

1964, Nov. 16 Photo. *Perf. 14½x14*

236 A70 3p yel green & blk .20 .20
237 A70 6p red & black .30 .20
238 A70 1sh6p ultra & black .50 .25
Nos. 236-238 (3) 1.00 .65

10th Commonwealth Parliamentary Conf.

Eleanor Roosevelt — A71

1964, Dec. 10 Wmk. 352

239 A71 1sh lt green, blk & red .25 .20

Eleanor Roosevelt (1884-1962) on the 16th anniv. of the Universal Declaration of Human Rights.

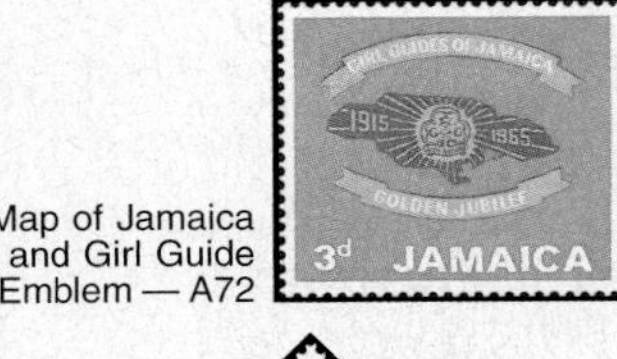

Map of Jamaica and Girl Guide Emblem — A72

Girl Guide Emblems — A73

Perf. 14x14½, 14

1965, May 17 Photo. Wmk. 352

240 A72 3p lt blue, yel & yel grn .20 .20
241 A73 1sh lt yel grn, blk & bis .25 .30

50th anniv. of the Girl Guides of Jamaica.

Salvation Army Cap — A74

1sh6p, Flag bearer, drummer, globe, vert.

Perf. 14x14½, 14½x14

1965, Aug. 23 Photo. Wmk. 352

242 A74 3p dp blue, yel, mar & blk .25 .20
243 A74 1sh6p emerald & multi .55 .40

Centenary of the Salvation Army.

Paul Bogle, William Gordon and Morant Bay Court House A75

1965, Dec. 29 Unwmk. *Perf. 14x13*

244 A75 3p vio blue, blk & brn .20 .20
245 A75 1sh6p yel green, blk & brn .25 .20
246 A75 3sh pink & brown .40 *.75*
Nos. 244-246 (3) .85 1.15

Cent. of the Morant Bay rebellion against governor John Eyre.

ITU Emblem, Telstar, Telegraph Key and Man Blowing Horn — A76

Perf. 14x14½

1965, Dec. 29 Photo. Wmk. 352

247 A76 1sh gray, black & red .45 .25

Cent. of the ITU.

Nos. 221, 223, 226-227 Overprinted: "ROYAL VISIT / MARCH 1966"

Perf. 14½, 14½x14

1966, Mar. 3 Photo. Wmk. 352

Size: 26x22mm

248 A67 3p emer, yel & black .30 .20
249 A67 6p multicolored 2.75 .35

Size: 32x26mm

250 A67 1sh yel brown & blk .90 .20
251 A67 1sh6p slate, buff & blue 4.00 2.25
Nos. 248-251 (4) 7.95 3.00

See note after Antigua No. 162.

Winston Churchill A77

1966, Apr. 18 *Perf. 14, 14x14½*

252 A77 6p olive green & gray .60 .35
253 A77 1sh violet & sepia .95 .95

Sir Winston Leonard Spencer Churchill (1874-1965), statesman and WWII leader.

Runner, Flags of Jamaica, Great Britain and Games' Emblem A78

Designs: 6p, Bicyclists and waterfall. 1sh, Stadium. 3sh, Games' Emblem.

Perf. 14½x14

1966, Aug. 4 Photo. Wmk. 352

254 A78 3p multicolored .25 .20
255 A78 6p multicolored .40 .20
256 A78 1sh multicolored .25 .20
257 A78 3sh gold & dk vio blue .40 .45
a. Souvenir sheet of 4 6.50 6.50
Nos. 254-257 (4) 1.30 1.05

8th British Empire and Commonwealth Games, Aug. 4-13, 1966.

No. 257a contains 4 imperf. stamps with simulated perforations similar to Nos. 254-257. Issued Aug. 25, 1966.

Bolivar Statue, Kingston, Flags of Jamaica and Venezuela — A79

1966, Dec. 5 *Perf. 14x14½*

258 A79 8p multicolored .40 .20

150th anniv. of the "Bolivar Letter," written by Simon Bolivar, while in exile in Jamaica.

Jamaican Pavilion — A80

1967, Apr. 28 *Perf. 14½x14*

259 A80 6p multicolored .20 .20
260 A80 1sh multicolored .20 .20

EXPO '67 Intl. Exhibition, Montreal, Apr. 28-Oct. 27.

Donald Burns Sangster — A81

Perf. 13x13½

1967, Aug. 28 Unwmk.

261 A81 3p multicolored .20 .20
262 A81 1sh6p multicolored .25 .25

Sir Donald Burns Sangster (1911-1967), Prime Minister.

Traffic Police and Post Office A82

Designs: 1sh, Officers representing various branches of police force in front of Police Headquarters. 1sh6p, Constable, 1867, Old House of Assembly, and 1967 constable with New House of Assembly.

Perf. 13½x14

1967, Nov. 28 Photo. Wmk. 352

Size: 42x25mm

263 A82 3p red brown & multi .50 .20

Size: 56½x20½mm

Perf. 13½x14½

264 A82 1sh yellow & multi .50 .20

Size: 42x25mm

Perf. 13½x14

265 A82 1sh6p gray & multi .80 *.90*
Nos. 263-265 (3) 1.80 1.30

Centenary of the Constabulary Force.

A Human Rights set of three (3p, 1sh, 3sh) was prepared and announced for release on Jan. 2, 1968. The Crown Agents distributed sample sets, but the stamps were not issued. On Dec. 3, Nos. 271-273 were issued instead. Designs of the unissued set show bowls of food, an abacus and praying hands. Value, $160.

Wicketkeeper, Emblem of West Indies Cricket Team — A82a

Designs: No. 266, Wicketkeeper and emblem of West Indies Cricket Team. No. 267, Batsman and emblem of Marylebone Cricket Club. No. 268, Bowler and emblem of West Indies Cricket Team.

1968, Feb. 8 Photo. *Perf. 14*

266 A82a 6p multicolored .50 *.65*
267 A82a 6p multicolored .50 *.65*
268 A82a 6p multicolored .50 *.65*
a. Horiz. strip of 3, #266-268 2.00 2.25
Nos. 266-268 (3) 1.50 1.95

Visit of the Marylebone Cricket Club to the West Indies, Jan.-Feb. 1968.

Sir Alexander and Lady Bustamante — A83

1968, May 23 *Perf. 14½*

269 A83 3p brt rose & black .25 .20
270 A83 1sh olive green & black .25 .20

Labor Day, May 23, 1968.

Human Rights Flame and Map of Jamaica A84

Designs: 1sh, Hands shielding Human Rights flame, vert. 3sh, Man kneeling on Map of Jamaica, and Human Rights flame.

1968, Dec. 3 Wmk. 352 *Perf. 14½*

271 A84 3p multicolored .30 .20
a. Gold (flame) omitted 130.00
272 A84 1sh multicolored .30 .20
273 A84 3sh multicolored .50 *.90*
a. Gold (flame) omitted 160.00
Nos. 271-273 (3) 1.10 1.30

International Human Rights Year.

ILO Emblem A85

Unwmk.

1969, May 23 Litho. *Perf. 14*

274 A85 6p black & orange yel .20 .20
275 A85 3sh black & brt green .30 .30

50th anniv. of the ILO.

WHO Emblem, Children and Nurse — A86

Designs: 1sh, Malaria eradication, horiz. 3sh, Student nurses.

1969, May 30 Photo. *Perf. 14*

276 A86 6p org, black & brown .20 .20
277 A86 1sh blue grn, blk & brn .20 .20
278 A86 3sh ultra, black & brn .25 *.90*
Nos. 276-278 (3) .65 1.30

WHO, 20th anniv.

Nos. 217-219, 221-223, 225-232 Surcharged with New Value and: "C-DAY 8th SEPTEMBER 1969"

1969, Sept. 8 Wmk. 352 *Perf. 14½*

Size: 26x22mm, 22x26mm

279 A67 1c on 1p multi .20 .20
280 A67 2c on 2p multi .20 .20
281 A67 3c on 3p multi .20 .20
282 A67 4c on 4p multi 1.40 .20
283 A67 5c on 6p multi 1.40 .20
a. Blue (wing dots) omitted *70.00*

Perf. 14½x14, 13½x14½, 14x14½

Size: 32x26mm, 26x32mm

284 A67 8c on 9p multi .20 .20
285 A67 10c on 1sh multi .20 .20
286 A67 15c on 1sh6p multi .55 *1.00*
287 A67 20c on 2sh multi 1.75 *2.00*
288 A67 30c on 3sh multi 2.25 *3.00*
289 A67 50c on 5sh multi 1.40 *3.25*
290 A67 $1 on 10sh multi 1.40 *7.00*
291 A67 $2 on £1 multi 1.50 *7.00*
Nos. 279-291 (13) 12.65 24.65

Introduction of decimal currency.

The old denomination is obliterated by groups of small rectangles on the 1c and 3c, and with a square on the 2c, 4c and 8c; old denominations not obliterated on others.

Madonna and Child with St. John, by Raphael — A87

Christmas (Paintings): 2c, The Adoration of the Kings, by Vincenzo Foppa. 8c, The Adoration of the Kings, by Dosso Dossi.

1969, Oct. 25 Litho. *Perf. 13*

292 A87 2c vermilion & multi .20 .40
293 A87 5c multicolored .25 .40
294 A87 8c orange & multi .25 .40
Nos. 292-294 (3) .70 1.20

First Jamaica Penny — A88

Design: 3c, First Jamaica halfpenny.

1969, Oct. 27 *Perf. 12x12½*

295 A88 3c brt pink, blk & silver .20 .20
296 A88 15c emerald, blk & silver .20 .20

Centenary of the first Jamaican coinage.

George William Gordon — A89

Crucifixion, by Antonello da Messina — A90

Portraits: 3c, Sir Alexander Bustamante (1884-1977). 5c, Norman W. Manley (1893-1969). 10c, Marcus M. Garvey (1887-1940). 15c, Paul Bogle (1820-1865).

Perf. 12x12½

1970, Mar. 11 Photo. Unwmk.

297 A89 1c lt violet & multi .20 .20
298 A89 3c lt blue & multi .20 .20
299 A89 5c lt gray & multi .20 .20
300 A89 10c pale rose & multi .20 .20
301 A89 15c pale green & multi .30 .25
Nos. 297-301 (5) 1.10 1.05

National heroes connected with Jamaica's independence.

1970, Mar. 23

Easter: 3c, Christ Appearing to St. Peter, by Annibale Carracci. 20c, Easter lily.

302 A90 3c pink & multi .20 .20
303 A90 10c gray green & multi .20 .20
304 A90 20c gray & multi .30 *.60*
Nos. 302-304 (3) .70 1.00

No. 219 Surcharged

1970, July 16 Wmk. 352 *Perf. 14½*

305 A67 2c on 2p multicolored .40 .30

Type of Regular Issue, 1964
Values in Cents and Dollars

Designs: 1c, Lignum vitae and map. 2c, Blue mahoe and map, vert. 3c, Flag over map. 4c, Murex antillarum, sea shell. 5c, Papilio homerus. 8c, Gypsum industry. 10c, Stadium and statue of runner. 15c, Palisadoes International Airport. 20c, Bauxite mining. 30c, Blue marlin and boat. 50c, Port Royal exploration of sunken city, map, ship and artifacts. $1, Coat of arms, vert. $2, Flag and Queen Elizabeth II.

1970 Wmk. 352 Photo. *Perf. 14½*

Size: 26x22mm, 22x26mm

306 A67 1c bister & multi .85 *1.00*
307 A67 2c gray grn & multi .35 .20
308 A67 3c emer, yel & black .55 *.80*
309 A67 4c violet & buff 3.00 .35
310 A67 5c green & multi 3.50 .70

Perf. 14½x14, 13½x14½, 14x14½

Size: 32x26mm, 26x32mm

311 A67 8c blue & yellow 2.50 .20
312 A67 10c yel brn & black .70 .25
313 A67 15c multicolored 3.00 3.00
314 A67 20c multicolored 1.40 *3.00*
315 A67 30c multicolored 4.50 *6.75*
316 A67 50c multicolored 1.40 *4.00*
317 A67 $1 multicolored 1.25 *5.75*
318 A67 $2 multicolored 1.50 *4.25*
Nos. 306-318 (13) 24.50 30.25

Issued: #306-312, 9/7; #313-318, 11/2.

Bright's Cable Gear on "Dacia" A91

Designs: 3c, Telegraph cable ship "Dacia." 50c, Double current Morse key, 1870, and map of Jamaica.

1970, Oct. 12 Litho. *Perf. 14½*

319 A91 3c red orange & multi .20 .20
320 A91 10c blue green & multi .25 .20
321 A91 50c emerald & multi 1.25 1.25
Nos. 319-321 (3) 1.70 1.65

Centenary of telegraph service.

Bananas, Citrus Fruit, Sugar Cane and Tobacco — A92

1970, Nov. 2 Wmk. 352 *Perf. 14*

322 A92 2c brown & multi .20 .20
323 A92 10c black & multi .45 .35

Jamaica Agricultural Society, 75th anniv.

"The Projector," 1845 — A93

Locomotives: 15c, Engine 54, 1944. 50c, Engine 102, 1967.

1970, Nov. 21 Litho. *Perf. 13½*

324 A93 3c green & multi .20 .20
325 A93 15c org brown & multi 1.00 1.00
326 A93 50c multicolored 3.50 3.50
Nos. 324-326 (3) 4.70 4.70

125th anniv. of the Jamaican railroad.

Kingston Cathedral — A94

30c, Arms of Jamaica Bishopric. 10c, 20c, like 3c.

1971, Feb. 22 *Perf. 14½*

327 A94 3c lt green & multi .20 .20
328 A94 10c dull orange & multi .20 .20
329 A94 20c ultra & multi .40 .40
330 A94 30c gray & multi .60 .60
Nos. 327-330 (4) 1.40 1.40

Centenary of the disestablishment of the Church of England.

Henry Morgan, Ships in Port Royal Harbor A95

Designs: 15c, Mary Read, Anne Bonny and pamphlet on their trial. 30c, 18th century merchantman surrendering to pirate schooner.

1971, May 10 Litho. Wmk. 352

331 A95 3c red brown & multi 1.25 .20
332 A95 15c gray & multi 1.75 .50
333 A95 30c lilac & multi 2.75 1.75
Nos. 331-333 (3) 5.75 2.45

Pirates and buccaneers.

Dummer Packet Letter, 1705 — A96

Designs: 5c, Stampless cover, 1793. 8c, Post office, Kingston, 1820. 10c, Modern date cancellation on No. 312. 20c, Cover with stamps of Great Britain and Jamaica cancellations, 1859. 50c, Jamaica No. 83a, vert.

1971, Oct. 30 *Perf. 13½*

334 A96 3c dk carmine & black .20 .20
335 A96 5c lt ol grn & black .20 .20
336 A96 8c purple & black .20 .20
337 A96 10c slate, black & brn .25 .25
338 A96 20c multicolored .50 .50
339 A96 50c dk gray, blk & org 1.25 1.25
Nos. 334-339 (6) 2.60 2.60

Tercentenary of Jamaica Post Office.

Earth Station and Satellite — A97

1972, Feb. 17 *Perf. 14x13½*

No.	Type	Denom.	Description	Unused	Used
340	A97	3c	red & multi	.20	.20
341	A97	15c	gray & multi	.40	.40
342	A97	50c	multicolored	1.10	1.10
			Nos. 340-342 (3)	1.70	1.70

Jamaica's earth satellite station.

Bauxite Industry — A98

National Stadium A99

Perf. 14½x14, 14x14½

1972-79 **Litho.** **Wmk. 352**

No.	Type	Denom.	Description	Unused	Used
343	A98	1c	Pimento, vert.	.20	.20
344	A98	2c	Red ginger, vert.	.20	.20
345	A98	3c	shown	.20	.20
346	A98	4c	Kingston harbor	.20	.20
347	A98	5c	Oil refinery	.20	.20
348	A98	6c	Senate Building, Univ. of the West Indies	.20	.20
			Perf. 13½		
349	A99	8c	shown	.40	.20
350	A99	9c	Devon House, Hope Road	.20	.20
351	A99	10c	Stewardess and Air Jamaica plane	.25	.20
352	A99	15c	Old Iron Bridge, vert.	2.50	.20
353	A99	20c	College of Arts, Science & Technology	.35	.20
354	A99	30c	Dunn's River Falls, vert.	.70	.20
355	A99	50c	River raft	2.00	.50
356	A99	$1	Jamaica House	1.00	*1.50*
357	A99	$2	Kings House	1.10	*1.50*

Perf. 14½x14

Size: 37x26½mm

No.	Type	Denom.	Description	Unused	Used
358	A99	$5	Map and arms of Jamaica ('79)	1.75	1.75
			Nos. 343-358 (16)	11.45	7.65

For overprints see Nos. 360-362, 451.

Nos. 345, 351, 355 Overprinted: "TENTH ANNIVERSARY INDEPENDENCE 1962-1972"

1972, Aug. 8 *Perf. 14½x14, 13½*

No.	Type	Denom.	Description	Unused	Used
360	A98	3c	multicolored	.30	.30
361	A99	10c	multicolored	.30	.20
362	A99	50c	multicolored	.95	*1.50*
			Nos. 360-362 (3)	1.55	2.00

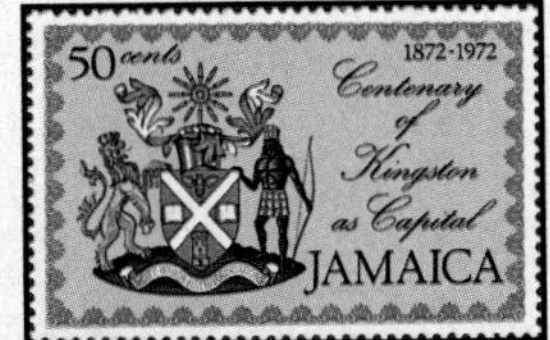

Arms of Kingston — A100

Design: 5c, 30c, Arms of Kingston, vert.

1972, Dec. 4 *Perf. 13½x14, 14x13½*

No.	Type	Denom.	Description	Unused	Used
363	A100	5c	pink & multi	.25	.20
364	A100	30c	lemon & multi	.40	.35
365	A100	50c	lt blue & multi	.60	*1.75*
			Nos. 363-365 (3)	1.25	2.30

Centenary of Kingston as capital.

Mongoose and Map of Jamaica A101

40c, Mongoose & rat. 60c, Mongoose & chicken.

Perf. 14x14½

1973, Apr. 9 **Litho.** **Wmk. 352**

No.	Type	Denom.	Description	Unused	Used
366	A101	8c	yel green & blk	.20	.20
367	A101	40c	blue & black	.85	.85
368	A101	60c	salmon & black	1.60	1.60
a.			Souvenir sheet of 3, #366-368	3.75	3.75
			Nos. 366-368 (3)	2.65	2.65

Centenary of the introduction of the mongoose to Jamaica.

Euphorbia Punicea — A102

Flowers: 6c, Hylocereus triangularis. 9c, Columnea argentea. 15c, Portlandia grandiflora. 30c, Samyda pubescens. 50c, Cordia sebestena.

1973, July 9 *Perf. 14*

No.	Type	Denom.	Description	Unused	Used
369	A102	1c	dp green & multi	.25	.20
370	A102	6c	vio blue & multi	.35	.20
371	A102	9c	orange & multi	.45	.30
372	A102	15c	brown & multi	.65	.45
373	A102	30c	olive & multi	1.25	1.25
374	A102	50c	multicolored	1.90	*2.25*
			Nos. 369-374 (6)	4.85	4.65

Broughtonia Sanguinea — A103

Orchids: 10c, Arpophyllum jamaicense, vert. 20c, Oncidium pulchellum, vert. $1, Brassia maculata.

1973, Oct. 8 *Perf. 14x13½, 13½x14*

No.	Type	Denom.	Description	Unused	Used
375	A103	5c	multicolored	.60	.25
376	A103	10c	multicolored	.80	.25
377	A103	20c	slate & multi	2.00	.50
378	A103	$1	ultra & multi	4.00	*4.50*
a.			Souv. sheet of 4, #375-378, perf 12	8.00	8.00
			Nos. 375-378 (4)	7.40	5.50

Mailboat "Mary" (1808-1815) — A104

Designs: Mailboats.

Perf. 13½ (5c, 50c), 14½ (10c, 15c)

1974, Apr. 8 **Wmk. 352**

No.	Type	Denom.	Description	Unused	Used
379	A104	5c	shown	.95	.20
a.			Perf. 14½	2.50	1.25
380	A104	10c	"Queensbury" (1814-27)	.95	.35
381	A104	15c	"Sheldrake" (1829-34)	1.25	.55
382	A104	50c	"Thames" (1842)	2.75	2.75
a.			Souv. sheet of 4, #379-382, perf 13½	6.50	6.50
			Nos. 379-382 (4)	5.90	3.85

Jamaican Dancers — A105

Designs: Dancers.

1974, Aug. 1 **Litho.** *Perf. 13½*

No.	Type	Denom.	Description	Unused	Used
383	A105	5c	green & multi	.20	.20
384	A105	10c	black & multi	.20	.20
385	A105	30c	brown & multi	.50	.40
386	A105	50c	lilac & multi	.75	.65
a.			Souvenir sheet of 4, #383-386	3.00	3.00
			Nos. 383-386 (4)	1.65	1.45

National Dance Theatre.

Globe, Letter, UPU Emblem A106

1974, Oct. 9 *Perf. 14*

No.	Type	Denom.	Description	Unused	Used
387	A106	5c	plum & multi	.20	.20
388	A106	9c	olive & multi	.20	.20
389	A106	50c	multicolored	.85	.85
			Nos. 387-389 (3)	1.25	1.25

Centenary of Universal Postal Union.

Senate Building and Sir Hugh Wooding A107

10c, 50c, Chapel & Princess Alice. 30c, like 5c.

1975, Jan. 13 **Wmk. 352**

No.	Type	Denom.	Description	Unused	Used
390	A107	5c	yellow & multi	.20	.20
391	A107	10c	salmon & multi	.20	.20
392	A107	30c	dull orange & multi	.35	.35
393	A107	50c	multicolored	.60	.60
			Nos. 390-393 (4)	1.35	1.35

University College of the West Indies, 25th anniversary.

Commonwealth Symbol — A108

Commonwealth Symbol and: 10c, Arms of Jamaica. 30c, Dove of peace. 50c, Jamaican flag.

1975, Apr. 29 **Litho.** *Perf. 13½*

No.	Type	Denom.	Description	Unused	Used
394	A108	5c	buff & multi	.20	.20
395	A108	10c	rose & multi	.20	.20
396	A108	30c	violet blue & multi	.40	.40
397	A108	50c	multicolored	.60	.60
			Nos. 394-397 (4)	1.40	1.40

Commonwealth Heads of Government Conference, Jamaica, Apr.-May.

Graphium Marcellinus A109

Koo Koo, "Actor-boy" A110

Butterflies: 20c, Papilio thoas melonius. 25c, Papilio thersites. 30c, Papilio homerus.

1975, Aug. 25 **Litho.** *Perf. 14*

No.	Type	Denom.	Description	Unused	Used
398	A109	10c	lt green & multi	1.90	.40
399	A109	20c	lt green & multi	1.90	1.40
400	A109	25c	lt green & multi	2.60	*2.75*
401	A109	30c	lt green & multi	3.00	*3.75*
a.			Souvenir sheet of 4, #398-401	10.00	10.00
			Nos. 398-401 (4)	9.40	*8.30*

See Nos. 423-426, 435-438.

1975, Nov. 3 **Litho.** **Wmk. 352**

Christmas: 10c, Red "set-girls." 20c, French "set-girls." 50c, Jawbone or "House John Canoe." Festival dancers drawn by I. M. Belisario in Kingston, 1837.

No.	Type	Denom.	Description	Unused	Used
402	A110	8c	multicolored	.20	.20
403	A110	10c	olive & multi	.20	.20
404	A110	20c	ultra & multi	.40	.40
405	A110	50c	multicolored	1.10	1.40
a.			Souv. sheet of 4, #402-405, perf. 13½	2.75	2.75
			Nos. 402-405 (4)	1.90	2.20

See Nos. 416-418.

Map of Jamaica, by Benedetto Bordone, 1528 — A111

Maps of Jamaica by: 20c, Tommaso Porcacchi, 1576. 30c, Theodor DeBry, 1594. 50c, Barent Langenes, 1598.

1976, Mar. 12 *Perf. 13½x14*

No.	Type	Denom.	Description	Unused	Used
406	A111	10c	brown, buff & red	.35	.20
407	A111	20c	bister & multi	.65	.40
408	A111	30c	lt blue & multi	.90	.90
409	A111	50c	multicolored	1.40	*1.75*
			Nos. 406-409 (4)	3.30	3.25

See Nos. 419-422.

Olympic Rings — A112

1976, June 14 **Litho.** *Perf. 13½x14*

No.	Type	Denom.	Description	Unused	Used
410	A112	10c	black & multi	.20	.20
411	A112	20c	blue & multi	.30	.30
412	A112	25c	red & multi	.40	.40
413	A112	50c	green & multi	.70	.70
			Nos. 410-413 (4)	1.60	1.60

21st Olympic Games, Montreal, Canada, July 17-Aug. 1.

Map of West Indies, Bats, Wicket and Ball A112a

Prudential Cup — A112b

1976, Aug. 9 Unwmk. *Perf. 14*

414	A112a	10c lt blue & multi	.35	.30
415	A112b	25c lilac rose & blk	.75	.70

World Cricket Cup, won by West Indies Team, 1975.

Christmas Type of 1975

Belisario Prints, 1837: 10c, Queen of the "set-girls." 20c, Band of Jawbone John Canoe. 50c, Koo Koo, "actor-boy."

1976, Nov. 8 Wmk. 352 *Perf. 13½*

416	A110	10c brick red & multi	.20	.20
417	A110	20c bister & multi	.35	.30
418	A110	50c tan & multi	.90	1.10
a.		Souv. sheet of 3, #416-418, perf. 14	1.50	1.75
		Nos. 416-418 (3)	1.45	1.60

Christmas.

Map Type of 1976

Maps of Jamaica by: 9c, Edmund Hickeringill, 1661. 10c, John Ogilby, 1671. 25c, House of Visscher, 1680. 40c, John Thornton, 1689.

1977, Feb. 28 Litho. *Perf. 13*

419	A111	9c lt blue & multi	.35	.30
420	A111	10c buff & multi	.55	.55
421	A111	25c multicolored	1.00	1.00
422	A111	40c multicolored	1.25	*2.50*
		Nos. 419-422 (4)	3.15	4.35

Butterfly Type of 1975

10c, Eurema elathea. 20c, Dynamine egaea. 25c, Atlantea pantoni. 40c, Hypolimnas misippus.

1977, May 9 Wmk. 352 *Perf. 13½*

423	A109	10c black & multi	.75	.30
424	A109	20c black & multi	1.40	1.00
425	A109	25c black & multi	2.10	2.10
426	A109	40c black & multi	3.25	*4.75*
a.		Souv. sheet of 4, #423-426, perf. 14½	8.00	8.00
		Nos. 423-426 (4)	7.50	8.15

Scout Emblem, Doctor Bird, Outline of Jamaica — A113

1977, Aug. 5 Litho. *Perf. 14*

427	A113	10c multicolored	.60	.20
428	A113	20c multicolored	.90	.35
429	A113	25c multicolored	1.25	.50
430	A113	50c multicolored	1.50	*1.75*
		Nos. 427-430 (4)	4.25	2.80

6th Caribbean Jamboree, Hope Gardens, Kingston, Aug. 3-17.

Trumpeter A114

10c, 2 clarinetists and oboist. 20c, kettle drummer and oboist, vert. 25c, Cellist and trumpeter, vert.

1977, Dec. 19 Litho. *Perf. 14*

431	A114	9c multicolored	.25	.20
432	A114	10c multicolored	.30	.20
433	A114	20c multicolored	.70	.50
434	A114	25c multicolored	.85	.85
a.		Souvenir sheet of 4, #431-434	3.50	3.50
		Nos. 431-434 (4)	2.10	1.75

Jamaica Military Band, 50th anniversary.

Butterfly Type of 1975

Butterflies: 10c, Callophrys crethona. 20c, Siproeta stelenes. 25c, Urbanus proteus. 50c, Anaea troglodyta.

1978, Apr. 17 Litho. *Perf. 14½*

435	A109	10c black & multi	.70	.25
436	A109	20c black & multi	1.25	.40
437	A109	25c black & multi	1.50	1.00
438	A109	50c black & multi	2.75	*3.25*
a.		Souvenir sheet of 4, #435-438	7.00	7.00
		Nos. 435-438 (4)	6.20	4.90

Half Figure with Canopy — A115

Norman Manley Statue — A116

Arawak Artifacts, found 1792: 20c, Standing figure. 50c, Birdman.

1978, July 10 Litho. *Perf. 13½x13*

439	A115	10c multicolored	.20	.20
440	A115	20c multicolored	.30	.25
441	A115	50c multicolored	.80	.80
a.		Souv. sheet of 3, #439-441, perf. 14	1.25	1.50
		Nos. 439-441 (3)	1.30	1.25

1978, Sept. 25 Litho. Wmk. 352

Designs: 20c, Alexander Bustamante statue. 25c, Kingston coat of arms. 40c, Gordon House Chamber, House of Representatives.

442	A116	10c multicolored	.20	.20
443	A116	20c multicolored	.25	.20
444	A116	25c multicolored	.35	.25
445	A116	40c multicolored	.40	*.50*
		Nos. 442-445 (4)	1.20	1.15

24th Commonwealth Parliamentary Conf.

Salvation Army Band A117

Designs: 20c, Trumpeter. 25c, "S" and Cross entwined on pole of Army flag. 50c, William Booth and Salvation Army shield.

1978, Dec. 4 *Perf. 14*

446	A117	10c multicolored	.20	.20
447	A117	20c multicolored	.40	.25
448	A117	25c multicolored	.40	.30
449	A117	50c multicolored	.80	*.90*
		Nos. 446-449 (4)	1.80	1.65

Christmas; Salvation Army centenary.

"Negro Aroused," by Edna Manley — A118

Arawak Grinding Stone, c. 400 B.C. — A119

1978, Dec. 11 *Perf. 13*

450	A118	10c multicolored	.40	.20

International Anti-Apartheid Year.

No. 351 Overprinted: "TENTH / ANNIVERSARY / AIR JAMAICA / 1st APRIL 1979"

1979, Apr. 2 Litho. *Perf. 13½*

451	A99	10c multicolored	.50	.50

1979, Apr. 23 *Perf. 14*

Arawak Artifacts (all A.D.): 10c, Stone implements, c. 500, horiz. 20c, Cooking pot, c. 300, horiz. 25c, Serving boat, c. 300, horiz. 50c, Storage jar fragment, c. 300.

452	A119	5c multicolored	.20	.20
453	A119	10c multicolored	.20	.20
454	A119	20c multicolored	.20	.20
455	A119	25c multicolored	.20	.25
456	A119	50c multicolored	.40	.50
		Nos. 452-456 (5)	1.20	1.35

Jamaica No. 183, Hill Statue A120

Hill Statue and Stamps of Jamaica: 20c, No. 83a. 25c, No. 5. 50c, No. 271.

1979, Aug. 13 Litho. *Perf. 14*

457	A120	10c multicolored	.25	.20
458	A120	20c multicolored	.25	.20
a.		Souvenir sheet of 1	.75	.75
459	A120	25c multicolored	.25	.20
460	A120	50c multicolored	.45	*.75*
		Nos. 457-460 (4)	1.20	1.35

Sir Rowland Hill (1795-1879), originator of penny postage.

Children, IYC Emblem A121

International Year of the Child: 20c, Doll, vert. 25c, "The Family." 25c, "House on the Hill." 25c, 50c are children's drawings.

1979, Oct. 1

461	A121	10c multicolored	.20	.20
462	A121	20c multicolored	.20	.20
463	A121	25c multicolored	.20	.20
464	A121	50c multicolored	.30	.35
		Nos. 461-464 (4)	.90	.95

Tennis, Montego Bay — A122

Jamaican Tody — A123

Designs: 2c, Golfing, Tryall Hanover. 4c, Horseback riding, Negril Beach. 5c, Old Waterwheel, Tryall Hanover. 6c, Fern Gully, Ocho Rios. 7c, Dunn's River Falls, Ocho Rios. 10c, Doctorbird. 12c, Yellow-billed parrot. 15c, Hummingbird. 35c, White-chinned thrush. 50c, Jamaican woodpecker. 65c, Rafting Martha Brae Trelawny. 75c, Blue marlin fishing, Port Antonio. $1, Scuba diving. Ocho Rios. $2, Sail boats, Montego Bay.

Wmk. 352

1979-80 Litho. *Perf. 13½*

465	A122	1c multicolored	.80	.80
466	A122	2c multicolored	2.50	2.50
467	A122	4c multicolored	.60	*2.50*
468	A122	5c multicolored	1.40	.35
469	A122	6c multicolored	1.75	*2.50*
470	A122	7c multicolored	.60	.35
472	A123	8c multicolored	1.25	1.25
473	A123	10c multicolored	1.25	.25
474	A123	12c multicolored	1.25	*2.25*
475	A123	15c multicolored	1.25	.35
476	A123	35c multicolored	1.75	.35
477	A123	50c multicolored	2.00	.35
478	A122	65c multicolored	2.00	*3.25*
479	A122	75c multicolored	2.25	2.25
480	A122	$1 multicolored	2.25	2.25
481	A122	$2 multicolored	2.50	.75
		Nos. 465-481 (16)	25.40	22.30

Issued: #465-470, 11/26/79; #472-481, 5/80.

For surcharges see Nos. 581-582, 665-666.

Institute of Jamaica Centenary — A124

1980, Feb. 25 Litho. *Perf. 13½*

484	A124	5c shown	.20	.20
485	A124	15c Institute building, 1980	.20	.20
486	A124	35c "The Ascension" on microfilm reader, vert.	.35	.30
487	A124	50c Hawksbill and green turtles	.60	.60
488	A124	75c Jamaican owl, vert.	2.25	2.25
		Nos. 484-488 (5)	3.60	3.55

Don Quarrie, 1976 Gold Medalist, 200-Meter Race, Moscow '80 Emblem A125

1952 4x400-meter Relay Team: a, Arthur Wint. b, Leslie Laing. c, Herbert McKenley. d, George Rhoden.

1980, July 21 Litho. *Perf. 13*

489	A125	15c shown	.50	.25
490		Strip of 4	3.25	3.25
a.-d.	A125	35c any single	.75	.75

22nd Summer Olympic Games, Moscow, July 19-Aug. 3.

Parish Church, Kingston A126

1980, Nov. 24 Litho. *Perf. 14*

491	A126	15c shown	.20	.20
492	A126	20c Coke Memorial	.20	.20
493	A126	25c Church of the Redeemer	.20	.20
494	A126	$5 Holy Trinity Cathedral	2.00	2.00
a.		Souvenir sheet of 4, #491-494	3.00	3.00
		Nos. 491-494 (4)	2.60	2.60

Christmas.

Tube Sponge A127

1981, Feb. 27 Wmk. 352 *Perf. 14*

495	A127	20c Blood cup sponge, vert.	.20	.20
496	A127	45c shown	.45	.40
497	A127	60c Black coral, vert.	.60	.60
498	A127	75c Tire reef	.75	.75
		Nos. 495-498 (4)	2.00	1.95

See Nos. 523-527.

Indian Coney A128

Designs: b, Facing left. c, Eating. d, Family.

1981, May 25 Wmk. 352 ***Perf. 14***

499 Strip of 4 1.10 1.10
a.-d. A128 20c any single .25 .25

Royal Wedding Issue
Common Design Type

1981, July 29 Litho. ***Perf. 15***

500 CD331 20c White orchid .20 .20
501 CD331 45c Royal coach .20 .20
502 CD331 60c Couple .30 .25

Perf. 13½

503 CD331 $5 St. James' Palace .75 .50
a. Souvenir sheet of 1 1.75 1.75
b. Bklt. pane of 4, perf 14x14½ 2.00
Nos. 500-503 (4) 1.45 1.15

Also issued in sheets of 5 + label, perf. 13½.

Intl. Year of the Disabled A129

1981, Sept. 14 Wmk. 352 ***Perf. 13½***

504 A129 20c Blind weaver .25 .20
505 A129 45c Artist .45 .45
506 A129 60c Learning sign language .60 .60
507 A129 1.50 Basketball players 2.75 2.75
Nos. 504-507 (4) 4.05 4.00

World Food Day — A130

Perf. 13x13½, 13½x13

1981, Oct. 16 Litho. Wmk. 352

508 A130 20c No. 218 .50 .20
509 A130 45c No. 76, vert. .90 .45
510 A130 $2 No. 121 2.50 1.50
511 A130 $4 No. 125 3.75 2.50
Nos. 508-511 (4) 7.65 4.65

Bob Marley (1945-1981), Reggae Musician — A131

Portraits of Bob Marley and song titles.

1981, Oct. 20 Wmk. 373 ***Perf. 14½***

512 A131 1c multicolored 1.00 *1.25*
513 A131 2c multicolored 1.00 *1.25*
514 A131 3c multicolored 1.00 *1.25*
515 A131 15c multicolored 3.75 .40
516 A131 20c multicolored 4.00 .40
517 A131 60c multicolored 5.25 4.00
518 A131 $3 multicolored 9.00 *13.00*
Nos. 512-518 (7) 25.00 21.55

Souvenir Sheet

519 A131 $5.25 multicolored 10.00 10.00

Christmas A132

1981, Dec. 11 Wmk. 352 ***Perf. 14***

520 A132 10c Webb Memorial Baptist Church .20 .20
521 A132 45c Church of God .40 .20
522 A132 $5 Bryce United Church 2.75 2.75
a. Souvenir sheet of 3, #520-522, perf. 12½x12 4.50 4.50
Nos. 520-522 (3) 3.35 3.15

See Nos. 547-549.

Marine Life Type of 1981

1982, Feb. 22 Litho. ***Perf. 14***

523 A127 20c Gorgonian coral, vert. .60 .20
524 A127 45c Hard sponge .95 .30
525 A127 60c Sea cow 1.25 .55
526 A127 75c Plume worm 1.40 .65
527 A127 $3 Coral-banded shrimp 3.75 2.00
Nos. 523-527 (5) 7.95 3.70

Scouting Year — A133

Princess Diana, 21st Birthday — A134

20c, 45c, 60c, Various scouts. $2, Baden-Powell.

1982, July 12 Litho. ***Perf. 13½***

528 A133 20c multicolored .75 .20
529 A133 45c multicolored 1.25 .45
530 A133 60c multicolored 1.60 1.00
531 A133 $2 multicolored 2.50 2.50
a. Souvenir sheet of 4, #528-531 8.50 8.50
Nos. 528-531 (4) 6.10 4.15

1982, Sept. 1 ***Perf. 14½***

532 A134 20c Lignum vitae .40 .20
533 A134 45c Couple in coach .60 .45
534 A134 60c Wedding portrait .85 .70
a. Booklet pane of 3, #532-534 2.00
535 A134 75c Saxifraga longifolia 1.50 *3.00*
536 A134 $2 Diana 2.40 3.25
537 A134 $3 Viola gracilis major 2.40 *3.50*
a. Booklet pane of 3, #535-537 7.50
Nos. 532-537 (6) 8.15 11.10

Souvenir Sheet

538 A134 $5 Honeymoon 4.50 4.50

Nos. 535, 537 in sheets of 5.

Nos. 532-538 Overprinted: "ROYAL BABY / 21.6.82"

1982, Sept. 13

539 A134 20c multicolored .35 .20
540 A134 45c multicolored .50 .45
541 A134 60c multicolored .75 .60
a. Booklet pane of 3, #539-541 2.00
542 A134 75c multicolored 1.25 *2.00*
543 A134 $2 multicolored 2.10 2.10
544 A134 $3 multicolored 2.40 *2.50*
a. Booklet pane of 3, #542-544 7.00
Nos. 539-544 (6) 7.35 7.85

Souvenir Sheet

545 A134 $5 multicolored 4.50 4.50

Birth of Prince William of Wales, June 21.

Lizard Cuckoo Capturing Prey — A135

Designs: b, Searching for prey. c, Calling. d, Landing. e, Flying.

1982, Oct. 25

546 Strip of 5 11.00 11.00
a.-e. A135 $1 any single 1.75 1.75

Christmas Type of 1981

Perf. 13x13½

1982, Dec. 8 Wmk. 352

547 A132 20c United Pentecostal Church .80 .25
548 A132 45c Disciples of Christ Church 1.50 .35
549 A132 75c Open Bible Church 2.25 *2.75*
Nos. 547-549 (3) 4.55 3.35

Visit of Queen Elizabeth II — A136

1983, Feb. 14 Litho. ***Perf. 14***

550 A136 $2 Queen Elizabeth II 5.00 4.00
551 A136 $3 Arms 6.00 *7.00*

A136a

1983, Mar. 14 Litho. Wmk. 352

552 A136a 20c Dancers .20 .20
553 A136a 45c Bauxite mining .50 .50
554 A136a 75c Map .70 .70
555 A136a $2 Arms, citizens 1.60 *1.75*
Nos. 552-555 (4) 3.00 3.15

Commonwealth Day.

25th Anniv. of Intl. Maritime Org. A137

1983, Mar. 17 Litho. ***Perf. 14***

556 A137 15c Cargo ship 1.25 .35
557 A137 20c Cruise liner 1.90 .50
558 A137 45c Container vessel 2.75 .95
559 A137 $1 Intl. Seabed Headquarters 4.25 *5.75*
Nos. 556-559 (4) 10.15 7.55

21st Anniv. of Independence A138

Prime Ministers Alexander Bustamante and Norman Washington Manley.

1983, July 25 Litho. ***Perf. 14***

560 A138 15c blue & multi .20 .20
561 A138 20c lt green & multi .20 .20
562 A138 45c yellow & multi .40 .40
Nos. 560-562 (3) .80 .80

World Communications Year — A139

1983, Oct. 18 Wmk. 352 ***Perf. 14***

563 A139 20c Ship-to-shore radio 1.00 .20
564 A139 45c Postal services 1.60 .50
565 A139 75c Telephone communication 2.00 *3.50*
566 A139 $1 TV satellite 2.50 *4.00*
Nos. 563-566 (4) 7.10 8.20

Christmas 1983 A140

Paintings: 15c, Racing at Caymanas, by Sidney McLaren. 20c, Seated Figures, by Karl Parboosingh. 75c, The Petitioner, by Henry Daley, vert. $2, Banana Plantation, by John Dunkley, vert.

1983, Dec. 12 Litho. ***Perf. 13½***

567 A140 15c multicolored .20 .20
568 A140 20c multicolored .20 .20
569 A140 75c multicolored .75 .50
570 A140 $2 multicolored 1.75 *4.00*
Nos. 567-570 (4) 2.90 4.90

Alexander Bustamante (1884-1977), First Prime Minister — A141

1984, Feb. 24 Litho. ***Perf. 14***

571 20c Portrait 1.10 1.10
572 20c Blenheim (birthplace) 1.10 1.10
a. A141 Pair, #571-572 2.50 *3.50*

Sea Planes A142

1984, June 11 Litho. ***Perf. 14***

573 A142 25c Gypsy Moth 2.25 .35
574 A142 55c Consolidated Commodore 2.75 1.00
575 A142 $1.50 Sikorsky S-38 5.00 5.00
576 A142 $3 Sikorsky S-40 5.75 5.75
Nos. 573-576 (4) 15.75 12.10

1984 Summer Olympics A143

1984, July 11

577 A143 25c Bicycling 2.50 .60
578 A143 55c Relay race .85 .35
579 A143 $1.50 Running 2.50 *5.50*
580 A143 $3 Women's running 2.25 *4.50*
a. Souvenir sheet of 4, #577-580 8.00 8.00
Nos. 577-580 (4) 8.10 10.95

Nos. 469, 474 Surcharged

1984, Aug. 7 Litho. ***Perf. 13½***

581 A122 5c on 6c #469 .55 .45
582 A123 10c on 12c #474 1.60 .60

Early Steam Engines — A144

1984, Nov. 16 Litho. ***Perf. 13½***

583 A144 25c Enterprise, 1845 2.10 .35
584 A144 55c Tank Locomotive, 1880 2.75 .85
585 A144 $1.50 Kitson-Meyer Tank, 1904 4.50 4.25

586 A144 $3 Superheater, 1916 5.50 *5.75*
Nos. 583-586 (4) 14.85 11.20

See Nos. 608-611.

Christmas — A145

Local sculptures: 20c, Accompong Madonna, by Namba Roy. 25c, Head, by Alvin Marriott. 55c, Moon, by Edna Manley. $1.50, All Women are Five Women, by Mallica Reynolds.

1984, Dec. 6 Wmk. 352 *Perf. 14*
587 A145 20c multicolored .35 .20
588 A145 25c multicolored .40 .20
589 A145 55c multicolored 1.40 .50
590 A145 $1.50 multicolored 2.50 2.50
Nos. 587-590 (4) 4.65 3.40

Jamaican Boas — A146

1984, Oct. 22 Litho. *Perf. 14½*
591 A146 25c Head of boa *13.00* .80
592 A146 55c Boa over water *16.00* *1.75*
593 A146 70c Boa with young *18.50* *6.75*
594 A146 $1 Boa on branch *27.50* *7.25*
a. Souv. sheet of 4, #591-594 *15.00* *15.00*
Nos. 591-594 (4) 75.00 16.55

Stamps in #594a do not have WWF emblem.

Brown Pelicans — A147

1985, Apr. 15 Wmk. 352 *Perf. 13*
595 A147 20c multicolored 1.25 .20
596 A147 55c multicolored 2.25 .45
597 A147 $2 multicolored 3.50 3.50
598 A147 $5 multicolored 5.00 5.00
a. Souvenir sheet of 4, #595-598 12.00 12.00
Nos. 595-598 (4) 12.00 9.15

Birth bicentenary of artist and naturalist John J. Audubon (1785-1851).

Queen Mother 85th Birthday
Common Design Type

1985, June 7 Litho. *Perf. 14½x14*
599 CD336 25c Holding photograph album, 1963 .60 .20
600 CD336 55c With Prince Charles, Windsor Castle, 1983 .80 .25
601 CD336 $1.50 At Belfast University 1.25 1.25
602 CD336 $3 Holding Prince Henry 2.25 *3.25*
Nos. 599-602 (4) 4.90 4.95

Souvenir Sheet
603 CD336 $5 With limousine 4.25 4.25

Maps of Americas and Jamaica, IYY and Jamboree Emblems A148

1985, July 30 Litho. *Perf. 14*
604 A148 25c multicolored 1.50 .20
605 A148 55c multicolored 1.75 .35
606 A148 70c multicolored 2.00 1.60
607 A148 $4 multicolored 4.00 *7.00*
Nos. 604-607 (4) 9.25 9.15

Intl. Youth Year and 5th Pan-American Scouting Jamboree.

Locomotives Type of 1984

1985, Sept. 30 Size: 39x25mm
608 A144 25c Baldwin 1.90 .35
609 A144 55c Rogers 2.60 .40
610 A144 $1.50 Projector 3.75 3.50
611 A144 $4 Diesel 5.00 *6.50*
Nos. 608-611 (4) 13.25 10.75

The Old Settlement, by Ralph Campbell — A149

Christmas (Paintings by local artists): 55c, The Vendor, by Albert Hiue, vert. 75c, Road Menders, by Gaston Tabois. $4, Woman, Must I Not Be About My Father's Business? by Carl Abrahams, vert.

1985, Dec. 9
612 A149 20c multicolored .20 .20
613 A149 55c multicolored .20 .20
614 A149 75c multicolored .25 .25
615 A149 $4 multicolored 1.50 1.50
Nos. 612-615 (4) 2.15 2.15

Birds — A150

A151

1986, Feb. 10 Litho. *Perf. 14*
616 A150 25c Chestnut-bellied cuckoo 1.25 .20
617 A150 55c Jamaican becard 1.50 .30
618 A150 $1.50 White-eyed thrush 2.00 2.00
619 A150 $5 Rufous-tailed flycatcher 4.00 4.00
Nos. 616-619 (4) 8.75 6.50

Queen Elizabeth II 60th Birthday
Common Design Type

Designs: 20c, With Princess Margaret, 1939. 25c, Leaving Liverpool Street Station for Sandringham with Princes Charles and Andrew, 1962. 70c, Visiting the Montego Bay war memorial, Jamaica, 1983. $3, State visit to Luxembourg, 1976. $5, Visiting Crown Agents' offices, 1983.

1986, Apr. 21 *Perf. 14½*
620 CD337 20c scar, blk & sil .20 .20
621 CD337 25c ultra & multi .20 .20
622 CD337 70c green & multi .20 .20
623 CD337 $3 violet & multi 1.00 1.00
624 CD337 $5 rose vio & multi 1.60 1.60
Nos. 620-624 (5) 3.20 3.20

1986, May 19

AMERIPEX '86: 25c, Bustamante Childrens Hospital. 55c, Vacation cities. $3, Norman Manley Law School. $5, Exports.

625 A151 25c multicolored .80 .20
626 A151 55c multicolored 3.00 .45
627 A151 $3 multicolored 1.50 1.50
628 A151 $5 multicolored 8.75 8.75
a. Souvenir sheet of 4, #625-628 13.50 13.50
Nos. 625-628 (4) 14.05 10.90

Royal Wedding Issue, 1986
Common Design Type

Designs: 30c, At the races. $4, Andrew addressing the press.

Perf. 14½x14
1986, July 23 Wmk. 352
629 CD338 20c multicolored .25 .20
630 CD338 $5 multicolored 2.00 2.00

Boxing Champions A152

Champions: 45c, Richard "Shrimpy" Clarke, 1986 Commonwealth flyweight. 70c, Michael McCallum, 1984 WBA junior middleweight. $2, Trevor Berbick, 1986 WBC heavyweight. $4, Clarke, McCallum and Berbick.

1986, Oct. 27 Litho. *Perf. 14*
631 A152 45c multicolored .30 .20
632 A152 70c multicolored .45 .30
633 A152 $2 multicolored 1.00 *1.25*
634 A152 $4 multicolored 2.25 *3.00*
Nos. 631-634 (4) 4.00 4.75

Flowers A153

1986, Dec. 1 *Perf. 14*
635 A153 20c Heliconia wagneriana, vert. .20 .20
636 A153 25c Heliconia psittacorum .20 .20
637 A153 55c Heliconia rostrata, vert. .30 .30
638 A153 $5 Strelitzia reginae 3.00 *3.75*
Nos. 635-638 (4) 3.70 4.45

Christmas. See Nos. 675-678, 706-709.

Shells — A154

1987, Feb. 23 Litho. *Perf. 15*
639 A154 35c Crown cone .70 .20
640 A154 75c Measled cowrie .85 .65
641 A154 $1 Trumpet triton 1.00 *1.10*
642 A154 $5 Rooster-tail conch 2.00 *4.00*
Nos. 639-642 (4) 4.55 5.95

Prime Ministers A155

Natl. Coat of Arms A156

Designs: 1c-9c, 55c, Norman Washington Manley. 10c-50c, 60c-90c, Sir Alexander Bustamante.

1987-94 *Perf. 12½x13*

No inscription below design unless noted
643 A155 1c dull red .20 *.55*
644 A155 2c rose pink .20 *.55*
645 A155 3c light olive .20 *.55*
646 A155 4c dull green .20 *.55*
647 A155 5c slate blue .40 *.50*
a. Inscribed "1988" .40 *.50*
648 A155 6c ultramarine .25 *.55*
649 A155 7c dull magenta .80 *.55*
650 A155 8c red lilac .30 .20
651 A155 9c brown olive .80 .20
652 A155 10c deep rose .35 *.45*
a. Inscribed "1993" .35 *.45*
b. Inscribed "1994" .35 *.45*
653 A155 20c bright org .65 .20
a. Inscribed "1988" .65 .20
b. Inscribed "1989" .65 .20
c. Inscribed "1992" .65 .20
d. Inscribed "1993" .65 .20
e. Inscribed "1994" .65 .20
654 A155 30c emerald .65 .20
a. Inscribed "1994" .65 .20
655 A155 40c lt blue green .40 .25
a. Inscribed "1991" .40 .25
b. Inscribed "1992" .40 .25
c. Inscribed "1994" .40 .25
656 A155 50c gray olive .80 .25
a. Inscribed "1991" .80 .25
b. Inscribed "1992" .80 .25
c. Inscribed "1993" .80 .25
d. Inscribed "1994" .80 .25
656A A155 55c olive brown inscr. "1994" 1.50 .20
657 A155 60c light ultra .40 .25
658 A155 70c pale violet .40 .30
659 A155 80c violet .80 .40
660 A155 90c light brown 1.25 .70
a. Inscribed "1992" 1.25 .70
b. Inscribed "1993" 1.25 .70
661 A156 $1 dull brn & buff .80 .45
a. Inscribed "1991" .80 .45
b. Inscribed "1992" .80 .45
c. Inscribed "1993" .80 .45
d. Inscribed "1997" .80 .45
661A A156 $1.10 dull brn & buff, inscr. "1994" 2.50 .65
662 A156 $2 orange .90 .90
a. Inscribed "1997" .90 .90
663 A156 $5 gray olive & greenish buff 1.25 1.25
a. Inscribed "1997" 1.25 1.25
664 A156 $10 royal blue & pale blue 2.25 1.75

Perf. 13x13½
664A A156 $25 vio & pale vio, inscr. "1991" 3.75 1.75
664B A156 $50 lilac & pale lilac, inscr. "1991" 6.25 3.00
Nos. 643-664B (26) 28.25 17.15

Issued: $25, $50 (dated "1991"), 10/9/91; 55c, $1.10 (dated "1994"), 10/10/94; others (undated), 5/18/87.

Reprints issued: No. 647a, 653a, 6/6/88; 653b, 1989; 645a, 656a, 2/12/91; 661a, 6/6/91; 661b, 1992; 653c, 655b, 656b, 660a, 5/92; 653d, 656c, 660b, 661c, 1993; 652a, 11/93; 654d, 655c, 656c, 1994; 652b, 654a, 10/10/94; 661d, 662a, 663a, 4/30/97.

Nos. 477-478 Surcharged

1986, Nov. 3 *Perf. 13½*
665 A123 5c on 50c multi 3.00 3.00
666 A122 10c on 65c multi 2.00 2.00

A157

Wmk. 352
1987, July 27 Litho. *Perf. 14*
667 A157 55c Flag, sunset 2.00 .75
668 A157 70c Flag, horiz. 2.00 2.00

Natl. Independence, 25th anniv.

A158

1987, Aug. 17

669 25c Portrait 1.90 *2.00*
670 25c Statue 1.90 *2.00*
a. A158 Pair, #669-670 4.25 *4.50*

Marcus Mosiah Garvey (1887-1940), natl. hero. No. 670a has a continuous design.

Salvation Army in Jamaica, Cent. A159

Designs: 25c, School for the Blind. 55c, Col. Mary Booth, Bramwell-Booth Memorial Hall. $3, "War Chariot," 1929. $5, Arrival of col. Abram Davey on the S.S. Alene, 1887.

1987, Oct. 8 *Perf. 13*

671 A159 25c multicolored 2.25 .40
672 A159 55c multicolored 2.25 .40
673 A159 $3 multicolored 6.00 6.00
674 A159 $5 multicolored 7.25 *8.50*
a. Souvenir sheet of 4, #671-674 19.00 19.00
Nos. 671-674 (4) 17.75 15.30

Flower Type of 1986

1987, Nov. 30 Litho. *Perf. 14½*

675 A153 20c Hibiscus hybrid .25 .20
676 A153 25c Hibiscus elatus .25 .20
677 A153 $4 Hibiscus cannabinus 3.50 3.50
678 A153 $5 Hibiscus rosa sinensis 4.00 4.00
Nos. 675-678 (4) 8.00 7.90

Christmas. Nos. 675-678 vert.

Birds — A160

Designs: No. 679, Chestnut-bellied cuckoo, black-billed parrot, Jamaican euphonia. No. 680, Jamaican white-eyed vireo, rufous-throated solitaire, yellow-crowned elaenia. No. 681, Snowy plover, little blue heron, great white heron. No. 682, Common stilt, snowy egret, black-crowned night heron.

1988, Jan. 22 Litho. *Perf. 14*

679 45c multicolored 2.60 2.60
680 45c multicolored 2.60 2.60
a. A160 Pair, #679-680 6.00 *7.00*
681 $5 multicolored 6.50 *7.00*
682 $5 multicolored 6.50 *7.00*
a. A160 Pair, #681-682 14.00 *15.00*
Nos. 679-682 (4) 18.20 19.20

Nos. 680a, 682a have continuous designs.

Marine Mammals A161

1988, Apr. 14 Litho. *Perf. 14*

683 A161 20c Blue whales 3.50 .85
684 A161 25c Gervais's whales 3.50 .85
685 A161 55c Killer whales 5.25 1.00
686 A161 $5 Common dolphins 8.00 *9.50*
Nos. 683-686 (4) 20.25 12.20

Cricket A162

Bat, wicket posts, ball, 18th cent. belt buckle and batsmen: 25c, Jackie Hendriks. 55c, George Headley. $2, Michael Holding. $3, R.K. Nunes. $4, Allan Rae.

1988, June 6 Litho. *Perf. 14*

687 A162 25c multicolored 2.50 .60
688 A162 55c multicolored 2.50 .60
689 A162 $2 multicolored 4.50 4.00
690 A162 $3 multicolored 5.00 5.00
691 A162 $4 multicolored 5.75 5.75
Nos. 687-691 (5) 20.25 15.95

Intl. Red Cross and Red Crescent Organizations, 125th Annivs. — A163

Anniversary emblem, Jamaica Red Cross emblem and: 55c, Ambulances. $5, Jean-Henri Dunant, 1828-1910, treating the wounded after the Battle of Solferino, 1859.

1988, Aug. 8 Litho. *Perf. 14½*

692 A163 55c multicolored .75 .40
693 A163 $5 multicolored 3.75 3.75

1988 Summer Olympics, Seoul A164

1988, Aug. 24 Wmk. 352 *Perf. 14*

694 A164 25c Boxing .50 .20
695 A164 45c Cycling 2.00 .75
696 A164 $4 Women's running 2.50 2.50
697 A164 $5 Hurdling 2.50 2.50
a. Souvenir sheet of 4, #694-697 8.00 8.00
Nos. 694-697 (4) 7.50 5.95

No. 697a sold for $9.90. For surcharges see Nos. B4-B7.

Natl. Olympic Bobsled Team A165

1988, Nov. 4 Litho. *Perf. 14*

698 A165 25c Team members 1.00 1.00
699 A165 25c Two-man bobsled 1.00 1.00
a. Pair, #698-699 2.75 *3.00*
700 A165 $5 Team members, diff. 3.00 3.00
701 A165 $5 Four-man bobsled 3.00 3.00
a. Pair, #700-701 7.00 *8.00*
Nos. 698-701 (4) 8.00 8.00

Nos. 699a, 701a have continuous designs.

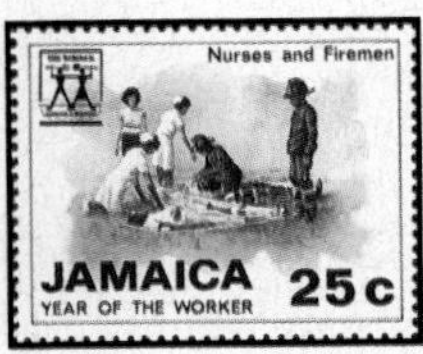

Labor Year — A166

Perf. 14½x14

1988, Nov. 24 Wmk. 352

702 A166 25c Medicine, fire fighting 1.00 .50
703 A166 55c Handicrafts 1.00 .50
704 A166 $3 Garment industry 2.00 2.00
705 A166 $5 Fishing 2.50 2.50
Nos. 702-705 (4) 6.50 5.50

Flower Type of 1986

1988, Dec. 15

706 A153 25c Euphorbia pulcherrima, vert. .90 .20
707 A153 55c Spathodea campanulata 1.00 .25
708 A153 $3 Hylocereus triangularis, vert. 2.25 1.75
709 A153 $4 Broughtonia sanguinea 2.75 2.00
Nos. 706-709 (4) 6.90 4.20

Christmas.

Methodist Church in Jamaica, Bicent. — A167

25c, Old York Castle School. 45c, Parade Chapel, Kingston, Rev. Thomas Coke. $5, Fr. Hugh Sherlock, St. John's Church.

1989, Jan. 19 *Perf. 13½*

710 A167 25c multicolored .40 .20
711 A167 45c multicolored .50 .20
712 A167 $5 multicolored 4.00 4.00
Nos. 710-712 (3) 4.90 4.40

Indigenous Moths — A168

Wmk. 352

1989, Aug. 30 Litho. *Perf. 14*

713 A168 25c *Syntomidopsis variegata* 1.00 .20
714 A168 55c *Himantoides undata-perkinsi* 1.75 .30
715 A168 $3 *Hypercompe nigriplaga* 3.00 3.00
716 A168 $5 *Sthenognatha toddi* 4.75 4.75
Nos. 713-716 (4) 10.50 8.25

See #725-728, 752-755. For surcharges & overprints see #729-732, 756-759.

A169

A171

Discovery of America, 500th Anniv. (in 1992): 25c, Arawak spear fisherman. 70c, Smoking tobacco. $5, Ferdinand and Isabella inspecting caravels. $10, Columbus studying chart.

1989, Dec. 22 *Perf. 13½*

717 A169 25c multicolored .30 .20
718 A169 70c multicolored .60 .40
719 A169 $5 multicolored 4.00 4.00
720 A169 $10 multicolored 7.00 *8.50*
a. Souvenir sheet of 4, #717-720, perf. 12½ 25.00 25.00
Nos. 717-720 (4) 11.90 13.10

No. 720a exists imperf.

Wmk. 352

1990, June 28 Litho. *Perf. 14*

721 A171 45c multicolored 2.00 .40
722 A171 55c multi, diff. 2.00 .40
723 A171 $5 multi, diff. 7.25 *9.00*
Nos. 721-723 (3) 11.25 9.80

Girl Guides of Jamaica, 75th anniv.

Indigenous Moths type of 1989

Wmk. 352

1990, Sept. 12 Litho. *Perf. 14*

725 A168 25c Eunomia rubripunctata 1.50 .50
726 A168 55c Perigonia jamaicensis 2.00 .50
727 A168 $4 Uraga haemorrhoa 4.25 4.25
728 A168 $5 Empyreuma pugione 4.25 4.25
Nos. 725-728 (4) 12.00 9.50

Nos. 725-728 Ovptd. in Black

1990, Sept. 12

729 A168 25c No. 725 1.50 .45
730 A168 55c No. 726 2.25 .45
731 A168 $4 No. 727 4.25 4.25
732 A168 $5 No. 728 4.25 4.25
Nos. 729-732 (4) 12.25 9.40

Expo '90, International Garden and Greenery Exposition, Osaka, Japan.

Intl. Literacy Year A172

Wmk. 352

1990, Oct. 10 Litho. *Perf. 14*

733 A172 55c shown 1.10 .35
734 A172 $5 Mathematics class 6.25 6.25

Christmas — A173

Children's art.

Perf. 13½x14

1990, Dec. 7 Litho. Wmk. 352

735 A173 20c To the market .70 .20
736 A173 25c Untitled (houses) .70 .20
737 A173 55c Jack and Jill .85 .25
738 A173 70c Untitled (market) 1.10 .50
739 A173 $1.50 Lonely (beach) 2.75 2.75
740 A173 $5 Market woman, vert. 4.75 4.75
Nos. 735-740 (6) 10.85 8.65

See Nos. 760-763.

Discovery of America, 500th Anniv. (in 1992) A174

Maps of Columbus' voyages.

1990, Dec. 19 *Perf. 14*

741 A174 25c First, 1492 2.00 .70
742 A174 45c Second, 1493 2.50 .70
743 A174 $5 Third, 1498 7.00 7.00
744 A174 $10 Fourth, 1502 10.00 *11.00*
Nos. 741-744 (4) 21.50 19.40

Souvenir Sheet

745 Sheet of 4 18.00 18.00
a. A174 25c Cuba, Jamaica 1.25 1.25
b. A174 45c Hispaniola, Puerto Rico 1.50 1.50
c. A174 $5 Central America 5.00 5.00
d. A174 $10 Venezuela 9.00 9.00

Souvenir sheet also exists imperf. Value, $25.

See Nos. 764-767.

Natl. Meteorological Service — A175

1991, May 20 Litho. Wmk. 352

746 A175 50c multicolored 1.00 .25
747 A175 $10 multicolored 9.00 9.00

11th World Meteorological Congress.

Intl. Council of Nurses Council of Natl. Representatives, Jamaica — A176

Wmk. 352

1991, June 24 Litho. *Perf. 13½*

748 A176 50c Mary Seacole 1.50 .35
749 A176 $1.10 Mary Seacole House 3.00 3.00

Souvenir Sheet

750 A176 $8 Hospital at Scutari 5.50 5.50

Cyclura Collei (Jamaican Iguana) — A177

Designs: a, Head pointed to UR. b, Facing right. c, Climbing rock. d, Facing left. e, Head pointed to UL.

Wmk. 352

1991, July 29 Litho. *Perf. 13*

751 A177 $1.10 Strip of 5, #a.-e. 6.00 6.00

Natural History Soc. of Jamaica, 50th anniv.

Indigenous Moths Type of 1989

1991, Aug. 12 *Perf. 14*

752 A168 50c Urania sloanus 1.50 .25
753 A168 $1.10 Phoenicoprocta jamaicensis 1.75 .70
754 A168 $1.40 Horama grotei 2.00 1.00
755 A168 $8 Amplypterus gannascus 5.75 5.75
Nos. 752-755 (4) 11.00 7.70

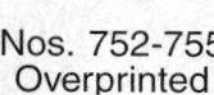
Nos. 752-755 Overprinted

1991, Sept. 23

756 A168 50c on No. 752 1.50 .25
757 A168 $1.10 on No. 753 2.00 .75
758 A168 $1.40 on No. 754 2.25 1.25
759 A168 $8 on No. 755 7.25 7.25
Nos. 756-759 (4) 13.00 9.50

Christmas Art Type of 1990

Children's drawings.

1991, Nov. 27 *Perf. 14x15*

760 A173 50c Doctor bird 1.00 .20
761 A173 $1.10 Road scene 1.75 .30
762 A173 $5 House, people 5.00 4.00
763 A173 $10 Cows grazing 8.25 8.25
Nos. 760-763 (4) 16.00 12.75

Christmas.

Discovery of America Type of 1990

Designs: 50c, Explorers did not land at Santa Gloria because of hostile Indians. $1.10, Fierce dog used to subdue the Indians. $1.40, Indians brought gifts of fruit. $25, Columbus describes Jamaica with crumpled paper.

1991, Dec. 16 *Perf. 13½x14*

764 A174 50c multicolored 1.00 .20
765 A174 $1.10 multicolored 1.25 .50
766 A174 $1.40 multicolored 1.25 .50
767 A174 $25 multicolored 10.00 10.00
a. Souvenir sheet of 4, #764-767 13.00 13.00
Nos. 764-767 (4) 13.50 11.20

Souvenir sheet also exists imperf. Same value as perf.

First Provincial Grand Master of English Freemasonry in Jamaica, 250th Anniv. — A178

Masonic symbols: 50c, Square and compass. $1.10, Stained glass window. $1.40, Square and compass on Bible. $25, Seeing eye.

1992, May 1 *Perf. 13½*

768 A178 50c multicolored 1.25 .40
769 A178 $1.10 multicolored 1.50 .55
770 A178 $1.40 multicolored 1.50 .55
771 A178 $25 multicolored 9.75 9.75
a. Souvenir sheet of 4, #768-771 16.00 16.00
Nos. 768-771 (4) 14.00 11.25

Destruction of Port Royal by Earthquake, 300th Anniv. — A179

Scenes of destruction: 50c, Ship in harbor. $1.10, Homes, church. $1.40, Homes toppling. $5, Port Royal from contemporary broadsheet. $25, Fissure in street.

1992, June 7 *Perf. 14x13½*

772 A179 50c multicolored .80 .45
773 A179 $1.10 multicolored 1.00 .55
774 A179 $1.40 multicolored 1.00 .55
775 A179 $25 multicolored 11.00 11.00
Nos. 772-775 (4) 13.80 12.55

Souvenir Sheet

Perf. 13x12

776 A179 $5 multicolored 8.25 8.25

No. 776 inscribed on reverse.

Independence, 30th Anniv. — A180

1992, Aug. 6 *Perf. 13½*

777 A180 50c black & multi .30 .25
778 A180 $1.10 green & multi .35 .30
779 A180 $25 yellow & multi 4.75 4.75
Nos. 777-779 (3) 5.40 5.30

Credit Union Movement in Jamaica, 50th Anniv. — A181

1992, Aug. 24 *Perf. 14x15*

780 A181 50c Emblem 1.50 .60
781 A181 $1.40 Emblem, O'Hare Hall 2.75 2.75

Pottery — A182

Designs: 50c, "Rainbow" vase, by Cecil Baugh O.D. $1.10, "Yabba Pot," by Louisa Jones (MaLou) O.D. $1.40, "Sculptured Vase," by Gene Pearson. $25, "Lidded Form," by Norma Rodney Harrack.

1993, Apr. 26 *Perf. 13½*

782 A182 50c multicolored .30 .20
783 A182 $1.10 multicolored .50 .25
784 A182 $1.40 multicolored .50 .25
785 A182 $25 multicolored 5.75 5.75
Nos. 782-785 (4) 7.05 6.45

Girls' Brigade, Cent. A183

1993, Aug. 9 *Perf. 14x13½*

786 A183 50c Parade 1.60 .60
787 A183 $1.10 Brigade members 1.75 1.75

Jamaica Combined Cadet Force, 50th Anniv. — A184

Designs: 50c, Tank, cadet, vert. $1.10, Airplane, female cadet. $1.40, Ships, female cadet, vert. $3, Cap badge, cadet.

1993, Nov. 8 *Perf. 14*

788 A184 50c multicolored .60 .25
789 A184 $1.10 multicolored .90 .45
790 A184 $1.40 multicolored .90 .45
791 A184 $3 multicolored 1.25 *1.75*
Nos. 788-791 (4) 3.65 2.90

Golf Courses A185

50c, $1.10, Constant Spring. $1.40, $2, Half Moon. $3, $10, Jamaica Jamaica. $25, Tryall, vert.

1993-94 Litho. Wmk. 352 *Perf. 14*

792 A185 50c yellow & multi .45 .20
793 A185 $1.10 blue & multi .50 .20
794 A185 $1.40 brn org & multi .70 .25
795 A185 $2 lilac & multi .85 .70
796 A185 $3 dark blue & multi 1.10 1.10
797 A185 $10 tan & multi 2.75 2.75
Nos. 792-797 (6) 6.35 5.20

Souvenir Sheets

798 A185 $25 green & multi 8.00 8.00
799 A185 $25 #798 inscribed with Hong Kong '94 emblem 8.00 8.00

Issued: #792-797, Dec. 21, 1993; #798, Dec. 16, 1993; #799, Feb. 18, 1994.

A186

A187

1994, Jan. 12 *Perf. 14x15*

800 A186 $25 Portrait 3.75 *4.00*
801 A186 $50 Portrait, diff. 4.75 *5.00*
a. Pair, #800-801 9.00 *10.00*

Norman Washington Manley, birth cent.

1994, Mar. 1 *Perf. 14*

Royal Visit: $1.10, Jamaican, United Kingdom flags. $1.40, Royal yacht Britannia. $25, Queen Elizabeth II. $50, Prince Philip, Queen.

802 A187 $1.10 multicolored .75 .20
803 A187 $1.40 multicolored 1.60 .40
804 A187 $25 multicolored 3.75 3.75
805 A187 $50 multicolored 7.00 *8.50*
Nos. 802-805 (4) 13.10 12.85

Air Jamaica, 25th Anniv. — A188

Wmk. 352

1994, Apr. 26 Litho. *Perf. 14*

806 A188 50c Douglas DC9 .55 .25
807 A188 $1.10 Douglas DC8 .60 .35
808 A188 $5 Boeing 727 1.10 1.10
809 A188 $50 Airbus A300 5.25 5.25
Nos. 806-809 (4) 7.50 6.95

Giant Swallowtail A189

Various views of the butterfly.

Perf. 14x13½

1994, Aug. 18 Litho. Wmk. 352

810 A189 50c multicolored .60 .30
811 A189 $1.10 multicolored .60 .30
812 A189 $10 multicolored 3.00 3.00
813 A189 $25 multicolored 4.75 4.75
Nos. 810-813 (4) 8.95 8.35

Souvenir Sheet

814 189 $50 multicolored 11.00 11.00

A190

Tourism A191

Designs: 50c, Royal Botanical Gardens, by Sidney McClaren. $1.10, Blue Mountains, coffee beans, leaves. $5, Woman in hammock, waterfalls.

Tourist poster: No. 818a, Flowers, birds (c). b, Diver (d). c, Vegetation, coastline (a, d). d, Guide, tourists on raft.

Wmk. 352

1994, Sept. 7 Litho. *Perf. 14*

815 A190 50c multicolored .75 .25
816 A190 $1.10 multicolored 1.25 .40
817 A190 $5 multicolored 4.00 4.00
Nos. 815-817 (3) 6.00 4.65

Souvenir Sheet

818 A191 $25 Sheet of 4, #a.-d. 10.50 10.50

Caribbean Tourism Conf. (#818).

Red Poll Cattle A192

1994, Nov. 16 *Perf. 14x13½*

819 A192 50c Calf .20 .20
820 A192 $1.10 Heifer .20 .20
821 A192 $25 Cow 2.00 2.00
822 A192 $50 Bull 4.50 4.50
Nos. 819-822 (4) 6.90 6.90

Christmas — A193

Paintings by Children: 50c, Clean-up crew. 90c, Hospital Room. $1.10, House. $50, Meadow.

1994, Dec. 1 *Perf. 14x14½*

823 A193 50c multicolored .20 .20
824 A193 90c multicolored .20 .20
825 A193 $1.10 multicolored .20 .20
826 A193 $50 multicolored 4.50 4.50
Nos. 823-826 (4) 5.10 5.10

Birds — A194

Wmk. 384

1995, Apr. 24 Litho. *Perf. 14*

827 A194 50c Ring-tailed pigeon .85 .35
828 A194 90c Yellow-billed parrot 1.10 .35
829 A194 $1.10 Black-billed parrot 1.10 .35
830 A194 $50 Brown owl 7.00 *8.00*
Nos. 827-830 (4) 10.05 9.05

Souvenir Sheet

831 A194 $50 Streamertail 9.00 9.00
a. Ovptd. in sheet margin 7.25 7.25

No. 831 is a continuous design.
No. 831a ovptd. with Singapore '95 emblem. Issued: 9/1/95.

Caribbean Development Bank, 25th Anniv. — A195

Anniversary emblem and: 50c, $1, Jamaican flag, graph, vert. $1.10, Industries, agriculture. $50, Bank notes, coins.

Wmk. 352

1995, May 11 Litho. *Perf. 13½*

832 A195 50c green & multi .20 .20
833 A195 $1 black & multi .20 .20
834 A195 $1.10 multicolored .20 .20
835 A195 $50 multicolored 5.50 5.50
Nos. 832-835 (4) 6.10 6.10

Bob Marley (1945-81), Reggae Musician — A196

Marley performing songs: 50c, Songs of Freedom, by Adrian Boot. $1.10, Fire, by Neville Garrick. $1.40, Time Will Tell, by Peter Murphy. $3, Natural Mystic, by Boot. $10, Live at Lyceum, by Boot.
$100, Legend, by Boot.

Wmk. 352

1995, July 31 Litho. *Perf. 14*

836 A196 50c multicolored .45 .20
837 A196 $1.10 multicolored .65 .25
838 A196 $1.40 multicolored .70 .35
839 A196 $3 multicolored 1.10 .90
840 A196 $10 multicolored 2.00 2.00
Nos. 836-840 (5) 4.90 3.70

Souvenir Sheet

841 A196 $100 multicolored 11.50 11.50

Souvenir Sheet

Queen Mother, 95th Birthday — A197

1995, Aug. 4 *Perf. 14x13½*

842 A197 $75 multicolored 7.00 7.00

Order of the Caribbean Community — A198

Designs: 50c, Michael Manley, former prime minister, Jamaica. $1.10, Sir Alister McIntyre, Vice Chancellor, UWI, Jamaica. $1.40, P. Telford Georges, former Chief Justice, Bahamas. $50, Dame Nita Barrow, Governor General, Barbados.

1995, Aug. 23 *Perf. 14x14½*

843 A198 50c multicolored .25 .25
844 A198 $1.10 multicolored .35 .20
845 A198 $1.40 multicolored .35 .20
846 A198 $50 multicolored 5.50 5.50
Nos. 843-846 (4) 6.45 6.15

UN, 50th Anniv.

Common Design Type

Designs: 50c, Signals Land Rover. $1.10, Antonov AN-32. $3, Bedford Articulated Tanker. $5, Fairchild DC-119 Flying Boxcar. $50, Observation vehicles.

Wmk. 352

1995, Oct. 24 Litho. *Perf. 14*

847 CD353 50c multicolored .35 .25
848 CD353 $1.10 multicolored .65 .30
849 CD353 $3 multicolored .85 .85
850 CD353 $5 multicolored .95 .95
Nos. 847-850 (4) 2.80 2.35

Souvenir Sheet

851 CD353 $50 multicolored 4.00 4.00

No. 851 has continuous design.

Arrival of East Indians in Jamaica, 150th Anniv. A199

Wmk. 352

1996, May 22 Litho. *Perf. 14*

852 A199 $2.50 Coming ashore .25 .20
853 A199 $10 Musicians, dancers 1.25 1.25

UNICEF, 50th Anniv. — A200

1996, Sept. 2 *Perf. 14½x14*

854 A200 $2.50 multicolored .80 .20
855 A200 $8 multicolored 1.75 1.75
856 A200 $10 multicolored 1.75 1.75
Nos. 854-856 (3) 4.30 3.70

Jamaican Hutia (Indian Coney) A201

$2.50, Two in den. $10, One on ledge. $12.50, Mother, young. $25, One up close.

1996, Sept. 23 *Perf. 13½x14*

857 A201 $2.50 multicolored .30 .20
858 A201 $10 multicolored 1.10 1.10
859 A201 $12.50 multicolored 1.25 1.25
860 A201 $25 multicolored 2.50 *3.00*
Nos. 857-860 (4) 5.15 5.55

World Wildlife Fund.

Kingston Parish Church of St. Thomas the Apostle, 300th Anniv. A202

$2, High altar. $8, Exterior view. $12.50, Carving, "The Angel," by Edna Manley, vert. $60, Exterior view at sunset.

Unwmk.

1997, Feb. 7 Litho. *Perf. 14*

861 A202 $2 multicolored .60 .20
862 A202 $8 multicolored 1.50 .90
863 A202 $12.50 multicolored 2.40 2.40
Nos. 861-863 (3) 4.50 3.50

Souvenir Sheet

864 A202 $60 multicolored 5.00 5.00

No. 864 contains one 42x56mm stamp.

Chernobyl's Children — A203

Perf. 13½x14

1997, Apr. 7 Litho. Unwmk.

865 A203 $55 multicolored 5.50 5.50

Caribbean Integration, 50th Anniv. — A203a

$2.50, Map of Caribbean. $8, $10, View of coastline.

Wmk. 352

1997, June 30 Litho. *Perf. 14*

865A A203a $2.50 multi *7.00 7.00*
865B A203a $8 multi *8.00 3.50*
865C A203a $10 multi *9.00 3.50*
Nos. 865A-865C (3) 24.00 14.00

Orchids A204

$1, Coelia triptera. $2, Oncidium pulchellum. $2.50, Oncidium triquetrum. $3, Broughtonia negrilensis. $5, Enclyclia frangrans.

Wmk. 352

1997, Oct. 6 Litho. *Perf. 14*

866 A204 $1 multi, vert. .40 .20
867 A204 $2 multi .50 .25
868 A204 $2.50 multi, vert. .55 .25
869 A204 $3 multi, vert. .60 .30
870 A204 $5 multi .60 .45
Nos. 866-870 (5) 2.65 1.45

See Nos. 873-877.

Diana, Princess of Wales (1961-97) — A205

Unwmk.

1998, Feb. 24 Litho. *Perf. 14*

871 A205 $20 Portrait 1.60 1.60

Souvenir Sheet

872 A205 $80 With Mother Teresa 9.00 9.00

No. 871 was issued in sheets of 6. No. 872 contains one 42x56mm stamp.

Orchid Type of 1997

Designs: $4.50, Oncidium gauntlettii. $8, Broughtonia sanguinea. $12, Phaius tankervilleae, vert. $25, Cochleanthes flabelliformis. $50, Broughtonia sanguinea (3 varieties).

Wmk. 352

1997, Dec. 1 Litho. *Perf. 14*

873 A204 $4.50 multicolored .75 .55
874 A204 $8 multicolored 1.00 .85
875 A204 $12 multicolored 1.25 1.00
876 A204 $25 multicolored 2.50 2.25
a. Inscribed "1999" *10.00 10.00*
877 A204 $50 multicolored 5.00 5.00
Nos. 873-877 (5) 10.50 9.65

No. 876 exists inscribed "1999." Value $3.

CARICOM, 25th Anniv. — A206

Perf. 13½

1998, Sept. 17 Litho. Unwmk.

878 A206 $30 multicolored 4.00 4.00

University of the West Indies, Mona, 50th Anniv. A207

$8, Chapel. $10, Philip Sherlock Centre for the Creative Arts. $50, University arms.

1998, July 31 Wmk. 352

879 A207 $8 multi .55 .50
880 A207 $10 multi .65 .60
881 A207 $50 multi, vert. 3.75 3.75
Nos. 879-881 (3) 4.95 4.85

1998 World Cup Soccer Championships, France, Jamaica's Debut in Tournament — A208

Wmk. 373

1998, Sept. 28 Litho. *Perf. 13½*

882 A208 $10 Player, vert. .65 .55
883 A208 $25 Team picture 1.60 1.60
884 A208 $100 Team picture, diff. 5.75 *6.50*
Nos. 882-884 (3) 8.00 8.65

Intl. Year of the Ocean A209

Designs: $10, Underwater scene. $30, Fishermen, Negril. $50, Long spiny black urchin. $100, Design elements from #885-887, vert.

Wmk. 352

1998, Dec. 23 Litho. *Perf. 14*

885 A209 $10 multicolored 1.25 .60
886 A209 $30 multicolored 3.00 1.75
887 A209 $50 multicolored 4.50 4.50

Size: 28x42mm

888 A209 $100 multicolored 8.75 *10.00*
Nos. 885-888 (4) 17.50 16.85

Christmas.

1st Manned Moon Landing, 30th Anniv.

Common Design Type

Designs: $7, Michael Collins. $10, Service module reverses to dock with lunar module. $25, Aldrin walks on lunar surface. $30, Command module back in earth orbit.
$100, Looking at earth from moon.

Perf. 14x13¾

1999, July 20 Litho. Wmk. 352

889 CD357 $7 multicolored .50 .35
890 CD357 $10 multicolored .65 .55
891 CD357 $25 multicolored 1.75 1.75
892 CD357 $30 multicolored 2.00 2.00
Nos. 889-892 (4) 4.90 4.65

Souvenir Sheet

Perf. 14

893 CD357 $100 multicolored 6.75 6.75

#893 contains one 40mm circular stamp.

Athletes A210

Designs: $5, Polo player Lesley Ann Masterton Fong-Yee. $10, Men's cricketers Collie Smith, Lawrence Rowe and Alfred Valentine. $20, Women's cricketer Vivalyn Latty-Scott, vert. $25, Soccer player Lindy Delapenha, vert. $30, Netball player Joy Grant-Charles, vert. $50, Boxers Percy Hayles, Gerald Gray and Bunny Grant.
$100, Delapenha and Grant-Charles.

Perf. 13¼x13¾, 13¾x13¼

1999, Aug. 3 Litho. Wmk. 352

894 A210 $5 multicolored .65 .30
895 A210 $10 multicolored 1.10 .55
896 A210 $20 multicolored 1.60 1.25
897 A210 $25 multicolored 1.75 1.50
898 A210 $30 multicolored 2.00 2.00
899 A210 $50 multicolored 3.25 3.25
Nos. 894-899 (6) 10.35 8.85

Souvenir Sheet

900 A210 $100 multicolored 8.00 8.00

No. 900 contains one 52x38mm stamp.

UPU, 125th Anniv. A211

Designs: $7, Mail ship "Spey." $10, Mail ship "Jamaica Planter." $25, Lockheed Constellation. $30, Airbus A-310.

Wmk. 352

1999, Oct. 8 Litho. *Perf. 14*

901 A211 $7 multicolored 1.50 .40
902 A211 $10 multicolored 1.75 .60
903 A211 $25 multicolored 3.00 3.00
904 A211 $30 multicolored 3.00 3.00
Nos. 901-904 (4) 9.25 7.00

Air Jamaica, 30th Anniv. — A212

Wmk. 352

1999, Nov. 1 Litho. *Perf. 14*

905 A212 $10 A-310 1.00 .45
906 A212 $25 A-320 2.00 2.00
907 A212 $30 A-340 3.00 *3.50*
Nos. 905-907 (3) 6.00 5.95

Dogs — A213

1999, Nov. 25 *Perf. 14¼*

908 A213 $7 Shih tzu 1.50 .60
909 A213 $10 German shepherd 2.00 .80
910 A213 $30 Doberman pinscher 3.50 3.50
Nos. 908-910 (3) 7.00 4.90

Parks A214

Designs: $7, Nelson Mandela Park. $10, St. William Grant Park. $25, Seaview Park. $30, Holruth Park.

1999, Dec. 15 *Perf. 14*

911 A214 $7 multi .65 .45
912 A214 $10 multi .75 .50
913 A214 $25 multi 1.75 1.75
914 A214 $30 multi 2.00 2.00
Nos. 911-914 (4) 5.15 4.70

Edna Manley (1900-87), Sculptor A215

Designs: $10, The Prophet, 1935. $25, Horse of the Morning, 1943. $30, The Angel, 1970. $100, Portrait of Manley.

2000, Mar. 1 Litho. *Perf. 13¾*

915 A215 $10 multi .60 .60
916 A215 $25 multi 1.50 1.50
917 A215 $30 multi 2.00 2.00
918 A215 $100 multi 5.75 5.75
a. Souvenir sheet, #915-918 10.50 10.50
Nos. 915-918 (4) 9.85 9.85

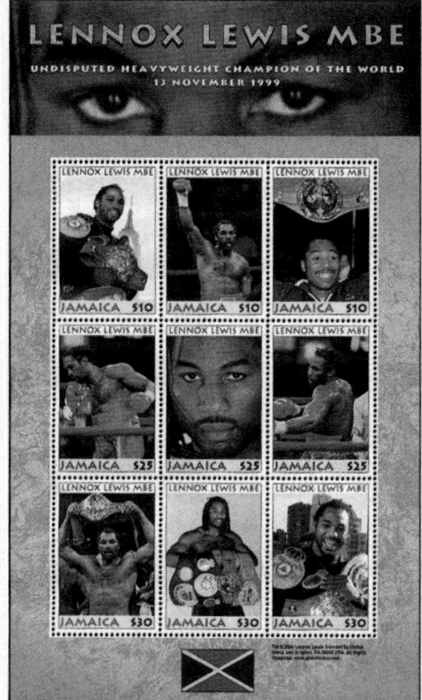

Lennox Lewis, Heavyweight Boxing Champion of the World — A216

a, $10, With belt & Empire State Building. b, $10, Holding up arm. c, $10, Holding up belt. d, $25, In ring with opponent. e, $25, Close-up. f, $25, In ring with referee. g, $30, Holding up belt, diff. h, $30, Holding 4 belts. i, $30, Holding belts in front of buildings.

Wmk. 352

2000, Mar. 24 Litho. *Perf. 14*

919 A216 Sheet of 9, #a.-i. 11.00 11.00

Ferrari Automobiles — A217

Unwmk.

2000, May 26 Litho. *Perf. 14*

920 A217 $10 1947 125S 1.00 1.00
921 A217 $10 1950 375F1 1.00 1.00
922 A217 $10 1966 312F1 1.00 1.00
923 A217 $25 1965 Dino 166P 1.75 1.75
924 A217 $25 1971 312P 1.75 1.75
925 A217 $25 1990 F190 1.75 1.75
Nos. 920-925 (6) 8.25 8.25

Queen Mother, 100th Birthday — A218

Various photos.

2000, Aug. 4 Wmk. 352

926 A218 $10 multi 1.00 .55
927 A218 $25 multi 1.50 1.50
928 A218 $30 multi 2.00 1.75
929 A218 $50 multi 4.25 4.25
Nos. 926-929 (4) 8.75 8.05

2000 Summer Olympics, Sydney — A219

Jamaican flag and various views of sculpture, "The Runner," by Alvin Marriott. Denominations, $10, $25, $30, vert., $50, vert.

Wmk. 352

2000, Sept. 1 Litho. *Perf. 14*

930-933 A219 Set of 4 8.00 8.00

Trees — A220

Designs: $10, Bull thatch palm. $25, Blue mahoe. $30, Silk cotton. $50, Yellow pout.

2000, Oct. 6

934-937 A220 Set of 4 8.50 8.50

Souvenir Sheet

938 A220 $100 Lignum vitae, horiz. 9.50 9.50

Christmas — A221

Designs: $10, Madonna and Child, by Osmond Watson, vert. $20, Boy in the Temple, by Carl Abrahams. $25, Ascension, by Abrahams, vert. $30, Jah Lives, by Watson.

Wmk. 352

2000, Dec. 6 Litho. *Perf. 13¾*
939-942 A221 Set of 4 5.50 5.50

Commonwealth Day, 25th Anniv. — A222

Wmk. 352

2001, Mar. 12 Litho. *Perf. 12½*
943 A222 $30 multi 2.00 2.00

Father Andrew Duffus Mowatt, Founder of Jamaica Burial Scheme Society A223

Wmk. 352

2001, Oct. 12 Litho. *Perf. 13¼*
944 A223 $15 multi 1.50 1.50

Lithographs of Daguerrotypes by Adolphe Duperly (1801-64) — A224

Designs: $15, The Market, Falmouth. $40, Ferry Inn, Spanish Town Road. $45, Coke Chapel. $60, King Street, Kingston.

2001, Nov. 14 *Perf. 13*
945-948 A224 Set of 4 10.00 10.00
a. Souvenir sheet, #945-948 10.00 10.00

Christmas — A225

Poinsettias with background colors of: $15, Light blue. $30, Pink. $40, Pale orange.

2001, Dec. 10 *Perf. 13¼*
949-951 A225 Set of 3 6.50 6.50

Reign Of Queen Elizabeth II, 50th Anniv. Issue

Common Design Type

Designs: Nos. 952, 956a, $15, Princess Elizabeth. Nos. 953, 953b, $40, Wearing striped dress. Nos. 954, 956c, $45, In 1953. Nos. 955, 956d, $60, In 1995. No. 956e, $30, 1955 portrait by Annigoni (38x50mm).

Perf. 14¼x14½, 13¾ (#956e)

2002, Feb. 6 Litho. Wmk. 373

With Gold Frames

952-955 CD360 Set of 4 10.00 10.00

Souvenir Sheet

Without Gold Frames

956 CD360 Sheet of 5, #a-e 10.00 10.00

Visit of Queen Elizabeth II and Prince Philip, Feb. 18-20 A226

Designs: $15, Queen and Prince in 1983, flag of the Royal Standard. $45, Queen in 1983, Jamaican arms.

Perf. 13¼x13¾

2002, Feb. 18 Litho. Wmk. 352
957-958 A226 Set of 2 5.75 5.75

Sir Philip Sherlock (1902-2000), Educator — A227

2002, Mar. 11 *Perf. 13¾*
959 A227 $40 multi 2.25 2.25

Pan-American Health Organization, Cent. — A228

Wmk. 352

2002, Dec. 2 Litho. *Perf. 13¾*
960 A228 $40 multi 2.75 2.75

Christmas — A229

Art: $15, Masquerade, by Osmond Watson, vert. $40, John Canoe in Guanaboa Vale, by Gaston Tabois. $45, Mother and Child, sculpture, by Kapo, vert. $60, Hills of Papine, sculpture by Edna Manley.

2002, Dec. 6
961-964 A229 Set of 4 8.50 8.50

Natl. Dance Theater Company, 40th Anniv. — A230

2002, Dec. 27 *Perf. 14*
965 A230 $15 multi 2.00 2.00

Independence, 40th Anniv. — A231

Flag and: $15, Natl. Dance Theater Company performers. $40, Sir Alexander Bustamante, Michael Manley. $60, Factory workers.

2002, Dec. 27
966-968 A231 Set of 3 9.00 9.00

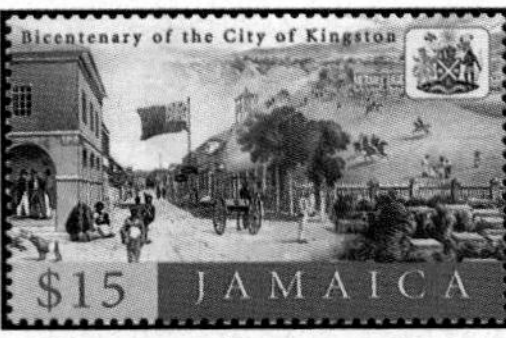
Kingston, Bicent. — A232

Historical views of Kingston and panel colors of: a, Brown. b, Olive green. c, Indigo.

2002, Dec. 31 *Perf. 13¾*
969 Horiz. strip of 3 4.50 4.50
a.-c. A232 $15 Any single 1.25 1.25

Coronation of Queen Elizabeth II, 50th Anniv.

Common Design Type

Designs: Nos. 970, $15, 972b, $100, Queen in chair awaiting crown. Nos. 971, $45, 972a, $50, Queen and Prince Philip in carriage.

Perf. 14¼x14½

2003, June 2 Litho. Wmk. 352

Vignettes Framed, Red Background

970-971 CD363 Set of 2 5.75 5.75

Souvenir Sheet

Vignettes Without Frame, Purple Panel

972 CD363 Sheet of 2, #a-b 8.00 8.00

Caribbean Community (CARICOM), 30th Anniv. — A233

Wmk. 352

2003, July 4 Litho. *Perf. 14*
973 A233 $40 multi 4.00 4.00

Bird Life International — A234

Designs: $15, Jamaican stripe-headed tanager, vert. $40, Crested quail dove. $45, Jamaican tody. $60, Blue Mountain vireo.

No. 978 — Jamaican blackbird: a, With beak open (35x30mm). b, Chicks in nest (35x30mm). c, In palm fronds, vert. (30x35mm). d, With beak open, vert. (30x35mm) e, With insect in beak (35x30mm).

2003, Sept. 19 *Perf. 14*
974-977 A234 Set of 4 11.00 11.00

Souvenir Sheet

Perf. 14¼x14½, 14½x14¼

978 A234 $30 Sheet of 5, #a-e 11.00 11.00

Maritime Heritage — A235

No. 979: a, Map, sailing ships. b, Sailing ships, ship with passengers. c, The Sugar Refiner and barges.

2003, Sept. 25 *Perf. 14x14¾*
979 Horiz. strip of 3 10.00 10.00
a.-c. A235 $40 Any single 3.00 3.00

Christmas — A236

Flowers and: $15, Adoration of the Magi. $30, Christ child. $60, Holy Family.

2003, Dec. *Perf. 13¼*
980-982 A236 Set of 3 8.00 8.00

Haitian Revolution, Bicent. — A237

Wmk. 352

2004, Jan. 30 Litho. *Perf. 13½*
983 A237 $40 multi 4.00 4.00

Caribbean Bird Festival A238

No. 984: a, Yellow-billed amazon. b, Jamaican oriole. c, Orangequit. d, Yellow-shouldered grassquit. e, Jamaican woodpecker. f, Red-billed streamertail. g, Jamaican mango. h, White-eyed thrush. i, Jamaican lizard cuckoo. j, Arrow-headed warbler.

Wmk. 352

2004, May 17 Litho. *Perf. 13¾*
984 Block of 10 10.00 10.00
a.-j. A238 $10 Any single .85 .85

Miniature Sheet

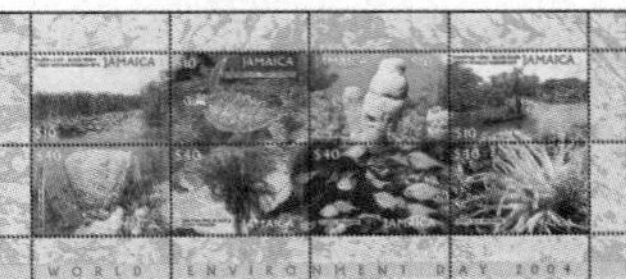
World Environment Day — A239

No. 985: a, $10, Water lilies. b, $10, Hawksbill turtle. c, $10, Tube sponge. d, $10, Boater on Parattee Pond. e, $40, Vase sponge, star coral. f, $40, Sea fan, black and white crinoid. g, $40, Glassy sweepers. h, $40, Giant sea anemone.

Unwmk.

2004, June 4 Litho. *Perf. 14*
985 A239 Sheet of 8, #a-h 9.00 9.00

2004 Summer Olympics, Athens — A240

Jamaican athletes: $30, Women's hurdles. $60, Running. $70, Swimming. $90, Rifle shooting, women's badminton.

Wmk. 352

2004, Aug. 10 Litho. *Perf. 14*
986-989 A240 Set of 4 10.00 10.00

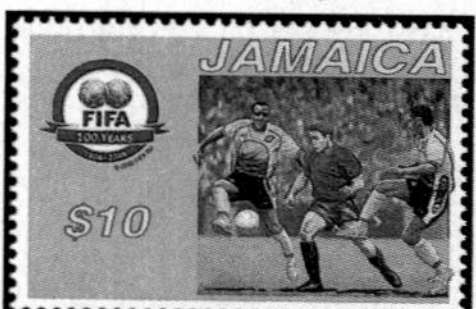

FIFA (Fédération Internationale de Football Association), Cent. — A241

FIFA emblem and various soccer players: $10, $30, $45, $50.

Wmk. 352

2004, Oct. 13 Litho. *Perf. 14*
990-993 A241 Set of 4 8.00 8.00

Jamaica Hotels Law, Cent. A242

Designs: No. 994, Ralph Lauren, Doctors Cave Beach, Montego Bay.
No. 995 — Ambassador John Pringle, Round Hill Hotel and: a, Pink panel. b, Lilac panel.
No. 996 — Tower Isle Hotel and: a, Abe Issa, yellow green panels. b, John Issa, green panels. c, Abe Issa, red panels. d, John Issa, yellow green panels. e, Abe Issa, green panels. f, John Issa, red panels.

2004 Unwmk. *Perf. 13¼x13½*
994 A242 $40 multi 2.50 2.50
995 A242 $40 Pair, #a-b 5.00 5.00
996 A242 $40 Sheet of 6, #a-f 14.00 14.00
Nos. 994-996 (3) 21.50 21.50

Issued: No. 994, 11/19; Nos. 995-996, 11/12. No. 994 printed in sheets of six; No. 995 printed in sheets containing three pairs.

Christmas — A243

White sorrel stalks: $10, $20, $50, $60. $50 and $60 are horiz.

Wmk. 352

2004, Nov. 22 Litho. *Perf. 14¼*
997-1000 A243 Set of 4 7.50 7.50

Founding of Moravian Church in Jamaica, 250th Anniv. A244

Designs: 90c, Mary Morris Knibb, Mizpah Moravian Church. $10, Rev. W. O'Meally, Mizpah Moravian Church. $50, Bishop S. U. Hastings, Redeemer Moravian Church.

2004, Dec. 14
1001-1003 A244 Set of 3 4.00 4.00

Buildings — A245

Designs: 90c, Rose Hall Great House, St. James. $5, Holy Trinity Cathedral. $30, National Commercial Bank, New Kingston. $60, Court House, Falmouth.

2005, Jan. 13 Wmk. 352 *Perf. 13¼*
1004 A245 90c multi .20 .20
1004A A245 $5 multi .25 .20
1005 A245 $30 multi 1.40 1.10
a. Dated 2006 at bottom .90 .90
b. Dated 2008 at bottom .75 .75
1006 A245 $60 multi 2.75 2.75
a. Dated 2008 at bottom 1.50 1.50
Nos. 1004-1006 (4) 4.60 4.25

Self-Adhesive

Serpentine Die Cut 12¼x12½

Unwmk.
1008 A245 $5 multi .30 .20
1008A A245 $30 multi 1.25 1.10
b. Booklet pane of 10 12.50
Complete booklet, #1008Ab 12.50
c. Dated 2006 at right .90 .90
1009 A245 $60 multi 2.75 2.75

Nos. 1005 and 1006 exist dated "2008."
See Nos. 1038-1053.

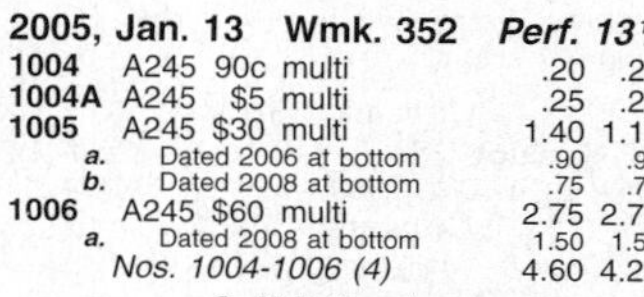

Chinese in Jamaica, 150th Anniv. A246

Flags of People's Republic of China and Jamaica and: $30, Food and fruits from China and Jamaica. $60, Chinatown. $90, Chinese Benevolent Association Building.

2005, Feb. 5 Wmk. 352 *Perf. 14¼*
1010-1012 A246 Set of 3 10.00 10.00

European Philatelic Cooperation, 50th Anniv. (in 2006) — A247

Designs: $60, Green square. $70, Yellow diamond. $100 Blue square.

Perf. 13½

2005, June 1 Litho. Unwmk.
1013-1015 A247 Set of 3 10.00 10.00
1015a Souvenir sheet, #1013-1015 10.00 10.00

Europa stamps, 50th anniv. (in 2006).

Battle of Trafalgar, Bicent. — A248

Designs: $20, Gun captain holding powder cartridge. $30, Admiral Horatio Nelson, vert. $50, British 12-pounder cannon. $60, HMS Africa, vert. $70, HMS Leviathan being attacked by the Intrepide, vert. $90, HMS Victory.
$200, HMS Africa at Port Royal, Jamaica.

Wmk. 352, Unwmkd. ($90)

2005, June 23 Litho. *Perf. 13¼*
1016-1021 A248 Set of 6 15.50 15.50

Souvenir Sheet

Perf. 13½
1022 A248 $200 multi 10.00 10.00

No. 1021 has particles of wood from the HMS Victory embedded in areas covered by a thermographic process that produces a raised, shiny effect. No. 1022 contains one 44x44mm stamp.

Rotary International, Cent. — A249

2005, June 30 Wmk. 352 *Perf. 13¾*
1023 A249 $30 multi 2.00 2.00

Pope John Paul II (1920-2005) A250

Unwmk.

2005, Aug. 18 Litho. *Perf. 14*
1024 A250 $30 multi 2.00 2.00

Battle of Trafalgar, Bicent. — A251

Designs: $50, HMS Victory. $90, Ships in battle, horiz. $100, Admiral Horatio Nelson.

Perf. 13¼

2005, Oct. 18 Litho. Unwmk.
1025-1027 A251 Set of 3 11.50 11.50

Mary Seacole (1805-81), Nurse — A252

Seacole and: $30, Herbal remedies and medicines. $50, Seacole Hall, University of the West Indies. $60, Crimean War soldiers. $70, Medals.

Wmk. 352

2005, Nov. 21 Litho. *Perf. 13½*
1028-1031 A252 Set of 4 7.00 7.00

World AIDS Day — A253

2005, Dec. 1 *Perf. 14¾x14*
1032 A253 $30 multi 1.25 1.25

Christmas A254

Star of Bethlehem and poinsettia with various frame designs: $20, $30, $50, $80.

2005, Dec. 1
1033-1036 A254 Set of 4 6.00 6.00

Jessie Ripoll (Sister Mary Peter Claver), Founder of Alpha Schools — A255

2005, Dec. 12 *Perf. 13½*
1037 A255 $30 multi 1.10 1.10

Alpha Schools, 125th anniv.

Buildings Type of 2005

Designs: $10, Court House, Morant Bay. $15, Spanish Town Square, St. Catherine. $20, Mico College. $25, Simms Building, Jamaica College. $50, Devon House, St. Andrew. $70, Ward Theater, Kingston. $90, Vale Royal, St. Andrew. $100, Falmouth Post Office.

Perf. 14x13¼

2006, May 12 Litho. Wmk. 352

No date inscription below design
1038 A245 $10 multi .30 .30
a. Inscribed "2008" .30 .30
1039 A245 $15 multi .50 .50
1040 A245 $20 multi .65 .65
a. Inscribed "2008" .65 .65
1041 A245 $25 multi .80 .80
1042 A245 $50 multi 1.60 1.60
a. Inscribed "2008" 1.60 1.60
1043 A245 $70 multi 2.25 2.25
a. Inscribed "2008" 2.25 2.25
1044 A245 $90 multi 3.00 3.00
a. Inscribed "2008" 3.00 3.00
1045 A245 $100 multi 3.25 3.25
Nos. 1038-1045 (8) 12.35 12.35

Self-Adhesive

Unwmk.

Serpentine Die Cut 13¼x14
1046 A245 $10 multi .30 .30
1047 A245 $15 multi .50 .50
1048 A245 $20 multi .65 .65
1049 A245 $25 multi .80 .80
1050 A245 $50 multi 1.60 1.60
1051 A245 $70 multi 2.25 2.25
1052 A245 $90 multi 3.00 3.00
1053 A245 $100 multi 3.25 3.25
Nos. 1046-1053 (8) 12.35 12.35

Worldwide Fund for Nature (WWF) A256

Black-billed Amazon parrot: $5, Chicks. $10, Head of adult bird. $30, Bird on branch. $50, Two birds.

Perf. 13¼x13½

2006, Nov. 30 Litho. Wmk. 352
1054-1057 A256 Set of 4 4.00 4.00
1057a Sheet, 4 each #1054-1057 16.00 16.00

Christmas A257

Flowers: $20, Cup and saucer. $30, Lignum vitae. $50, Neocogniauxia monophylla, vert. $60, Ghost orchid, vert.

Perf. 13¼x13¾, 13¾x13¼

2006, Nov. 30
1058-1061 A257 Set of 4 7.50 7.50

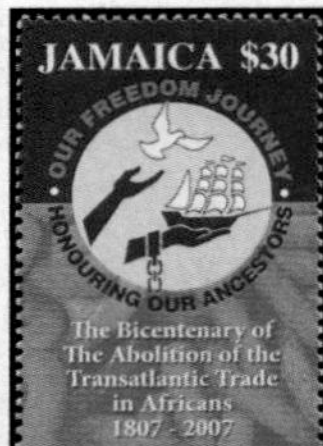

2007 ICC Cricket World Cup, West Indies — A258

Designs: No. 1062, $30, Courtney Walsh. No. 1063, $30, Collie Smith. $40, New Sabrina Park, horiz. $50, Like #1062. $60, Trelawney Multi-purpose Sports Complex, horiz.
$200, ICC Cricket World Cup.

Wmk. 352

2007, Feb. 28 Litho. *Perf. 14*
1062-1066 A258 Set of 5 10.00 10.00

Souvenir Sheet

1067 A258 $200 multi 9.00 9.00

British Abolition of the Slave Trade, Bicent. — A259

Wmk. 352

2007, June 7 Litho. *Perf. 14*
1068 A259 $30 multi 1.25 1.25

Scouting, Cent. A260

Designs: $5, Boy scout, Jamaican flag, Scout salute. $10, Scouts, compass. $30, Scouts, lashed poles. $70, Scouts handling Jamaican flag, Scout making craft.
No. 1073, vert.: a, $50, Scouts on parade. b, $100, Lord Robert Baden-Powell blowing kudu horn.

2007, July 9 *Perf. 13¾*
1069-1072 A260 Set of 4 4.25 4.25

Souvenir Sheet

1073 A260 Sheet of 2, #a-b 5.00 5.00

Christmas — A261

Flowers: $20, Tolumnia triquetra. $30, Broughtonia negrilensis, horiz. $50, Broughtonia sanguinea, horiz. $60, Spathelia sorbifolia.

Wmk. 352

2007, Nov. 9 Litho. *Perf. 14*
1074-1077 A261 Set of 4 6.00 6.00

2008 Summer Olympics, Beijing A262

Designs: $20, Fish, Asafa Powell. $60, Lanterns, Veronica Campbell-Brown.
No. 1079: a, Bamboo, Aleen Bailey, Veronica Campbell-Brown. b, Sherone Simpson, Tayna Lawrence, dragon.

Wmk. 352

2008, Apr. 30 Litho. *Perf. 13¼*
1078 A262 $20 multi .75 .75
1079 A262 $30 Horiz. pair, #a-b 2.50 2.50
1080 A262 $60 multi 2.50 2.50
Nos. 1078-1080 (3) 5.75 5.75

University of Technology, 50th Anniv. — A263

2008, May 26 Litho. *Perf. 14*
1081 A263 $30 multi 1.00 1.00
a. Souvenir sheet of 1 1.25 1.25

Associated Board of the Royal Schools of Music in Jamaica, Cent. — A264

Map of Jamaica and: $30, Piano keyboard. $70, Violin.

Wmk. 352

2008, Oct. 30 Litho. *Perf. 14*
1082-1083 A264 Set of 2 4.00 4.00

Christmas A265

Various ferns: $20, $30, $50, $60.

Wmk. 352

2008, Nov. 21 Litho. *Perf. 13¾*
1084-1087 A265 Set of 4 6.50 6.50

George Headley (1909-83), Cricket Player — A266

Designs: $10, Head of Headley. $30, Headley in front of wickets. $200, Statue of Headley.
$250, Statue of Headley, Sabina Park, Kingston.

Wmk. 352

2009, Sept. 25 Litho. *Perf. 14*
1088-1090 A266 Set of 3 6.00 6.00

Souvenir Sheet

Perf. 14¼x14

1091 A266 $250 multi 6.25 6.25

No. 1091 contains one 43x57mm stamp.

Christmas — A267

Paintings by Juanita Isabel Ramos: $20, Guardian Angel. $30, Madonna and Child. $50, Madonna and Flowers, horiz.

Wmk. 352

2009, Nov. 20 Litho. *Perf. 13½*
1092-1094 A267 Set of 3 3.00 3.00

Christmas A268

Musical groups: $40, NDTC Singers. $60, Kingston College Chapel Choir. $120, The University Singers. $160, The Jamaican Folk Singers.

Wmk. 352

2010, Dec. 13 Litho. *Perf. 13¾*
1095-1098 A268 Set of 4 9.00 9.00

SEMI-POSTAL STAMPS

Native Girl — SP1

Native Boy — SP2

Native Boy and Girl — SP3

1923, Nov. 1 Engr. *Perf. 12*
B1 SP1 ½p green & black .70 *6.25*
B2 SP2 1p car & black 2.00 *11.50*
B3 SP3 2½p blue & black 9.75 *20.00*
Nos. B1-B3 (3) 12.45 *37.75*

Each stamp was sold for ½p over face value. The surtax benefited the Child Saving League of Jamaica.

Catalogue values for unused stamps in this section, from this point to the end of the section, are for Never Hinged items.

Nos. 694-697 Surcharged "HURRICANE GILBERT RELIEF FUND" and New Value in Black

Wmk. 352

1988, Nov. 11 Litho. *Perf. 14*
B4 A164 25c +25c multi .20 .20
B5 A164 45c +45c multi .30 .25
B6 A164 $4 +$4 multi 3.00 *3.25*
B7 A164 $5 +$5 multi 3.00 *3.25*
Nos. B4-B7 (4) 6.50 6.95

Red Surcharge

B4a A164 25c + 25c .20 .20
B5a A164 45c + 45c .30 .25
B6a A164 $4 + $4 3.00 *3.25*
B7a A164 $5 + $5 3.00 *3.25*
Nos. B4a-B7a (4) 6.50 6.95

WAR TAX STAMPS

Regular Issues of 1906-19 Overprinted WAR STAMP.

1916 Wmk. 3 *Perf. 14*
MR1 A14 ½p green .20 .40
a. Without period 13.00 *27.50*
b. Double overprint 120.00 *140.00*
c. Inverted overprint 100.00 *130.00*
d. As "c," without period 350.00
MR2 A17 3p violet, *yel* 1.10 *20.00*
a. Without period 29.00 *90.00*

Surface-colored Paper

MR3 A17 3p violet, *yel* 17.50 *32.50*
Nos. MR1-MR3 (3) 18.80 *52.90*

Regular Issues of 1906-18 Overprinted

MR4 A14 ½p green .20 .30
a. Without period 15.00 *40.00*
b. Pair, one without ovpt. 4,500. 4,000.
c. "R" inserted by hand 1,500. 1,100.
d. "WAR" only 125.00
MR5 A17 1½p orange .20 .20
a. Without period 5.75 *8.50*
b. "TAMP" 160.00 *170.00*
c. "S" inserted by hand 425.00
d. "R" omitted 2,500. 2,250.
e. "R" inserted by hand 1,500. 1,200.
MR6 A17 3p violet, *yel* 3.75 1.10
a. Without period 45.00 *62.50*
b. "TAMP" 650.00 650.00
c. "S" inserted by hand 225.00 225.00
d. Inverted overprint 325.00 175.00
e. As "a," inverted
Nos. MR4-MR6 (3) 4.15 1.60

Regular Issues of 1906-19 Overprinted

1917, Mar.
MR7 A14 ½p green 1.00 .35
a. Without period 12.00 *24.00*
b. Overprinted on back instead of face 225.00
c. Inverted overprint 19.00 50.00
MR8 A17 1½p orange .20 .20
a. Without period 4.00 *20.00*
b. Double overprint 92.50 *100.00*
c. Inverted overprint 92.50 85.00
d. As "a," inverted
MR9 A17 3p violet, *yel* 1.00 *1.60*
a. Without period 20.00 *45.00*
b. Vertical overprint 375.00 375.00
c. Inverted overprint 160.00
d. As "a," inverted
Nos. MR7-MR9 (3) 2.20 2.15

There are many minor varieties of Nos. MR1-MR9.

Regular Issues of 1906-19 Overprinted in Red

1919, Oct. 4
MR10 A14 ½p green .20 .20
MR11 A17 3p violet, *yel* 4.50 3.50

OFFICIAL STAMPS

No. 16 Overprinted in Black

Type I — Word 15 to 16mm long.
Type II — Word 17 to 17½mm long.

1890 **Wmk. 2** ***Perf. 14***

O1	A7	½p green (II)	15.00	2.25
a.		Type I	35.00	29.00
b.		Inverted overprint (II)	90.00	*95.00*
c.		Double overprint (II)	90.00	*95.00*
d.		Dbl. ovpt., one invtd. (II)	450.00	450.00
e.		Dbl. ovpt., one vert. (II)	1,100.	
f.		Double overprint (I)	650.00	

Missing "O," "L" or one or both "I's" known.

No. 16 and Type of 1889 Overprinted

1890-91

O2	A7	½p green	11.00	1.75
O3	A10	1p carmine rose	7.25	1.50
O4	A10	2p slate	16.00	1.50
		Nos. O2-O4 (3)	34.25	4.75

JAPAN

jə-'pan

LOCATION — North Pacific Ocean, east of China
GOVT. — Constitutional monarchy
AREA — 142,726 sq. mi.
POP. — 126,182,077 (1999 est.)
CAPITAL — Tokyo

1000 Mon = 10 Sen
100 Sen = 1 Yen (or En)
10 Rin = 1 Sen

Catalogue values for unused stamps in this country are for Never Hinged items, beginning with Scott 375 in the regular postage section, Scott B8 in the semi-postal section, and Scott C9 in the airpost section.

Watermarks

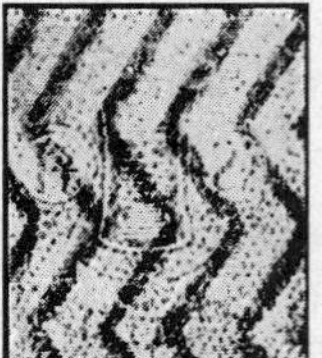

Wmk. 141 — Zigzag Lines

Wmk. 142 — Parallel Lines

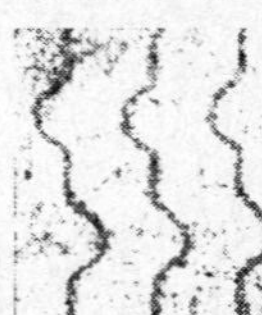

Wmk. 257 — Curved Wavy Lines

After 1945, Wmk. 257 exists also in a narrow spacing on a small number of issues.

Counterfeits of Nos. 1-71 are plentiful. Some are excellent and deceive many collectors.

Nos. 1-54A were printed from plates of 40 with individually engraved subjects. Each stamp in the sheet is slightly different.

Pair of Dragons Facing Characters of Value — A1

Plate I

Plate II

48 mon:
Plate I — Solid dots in inner border.
Plate II — Tiny circles replace dots.

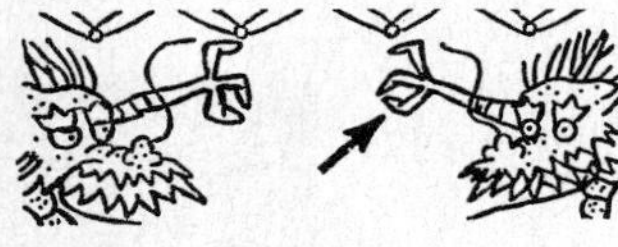
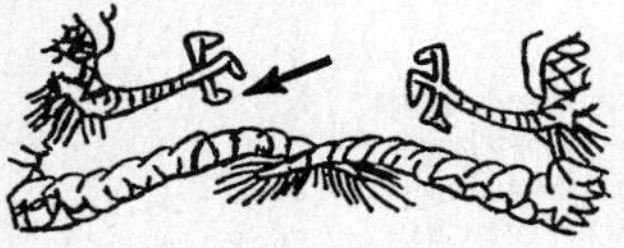

Plate I

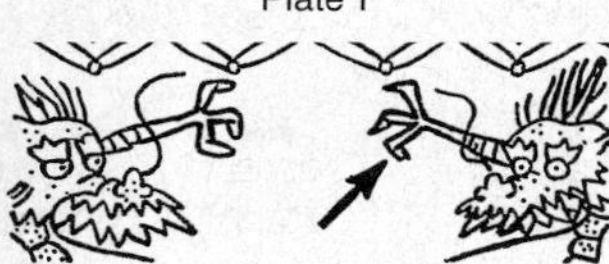
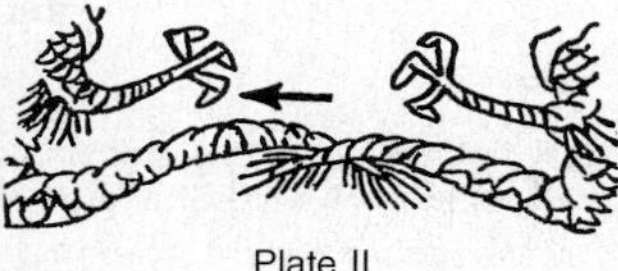

Plate II

100 mon:
Plate I — Lowest dragon claw at upper right and at lower left point upward.
Plate II — Same two claws point downward.

Plate I

Plate II

200 mon:
Plate I — Dot in upper left corner.
Plate II — No dot. (Some Plate I copies show dot faintly; these can be mistaken for Plate II.)

Plate I

Plate II

500 mon:
Plate I — Lower right corner of Greek-type border incomplete
Plate II — Short horizontal line completes corner border pattern.

Unwmk.

1871, Apr. 20 Engr. *Imperf.*

Native Laid Paper Without Gum
Denomination in Black

No.	Type	Description	Unused	Used
1	A1	48m brown (I)	300.	300.
a.		48m red brown (I)	375.	375.
b.		Wove paper (I)	325.	325.
c.		48m brown (II)	350.	350.
d.		Wove paper (II)	375.	375.
2	A1	100m blue (I)	275.	275.
a.		Wove paper (I)	350.	350.
b.		Plate II	550.	550.
c.		Wove paper (II)	800.	800.
3	A1	200m vermilion (I)	475.	400.
a.		Wove paper (I)	525.	450.
b.		Plate II	2,500.	2,000.
c.		Wove paper (II)		*4,000.*
4	A1	500m blue green (I)	650.	625.
a.		500m greenish blue (I)	700.	650.
b.		500m green (I)	2,000.	1,400.
c.		500m yellow green (I)	2,250.	1,500.
d.		Wove paper (I)	750.	625.
e.		500m blue green (II)	750.	*4,000.*
f.		500m greenish blue (II)	750.	*4,000.*
g.		Wove paper (II)	2,750.	*5,000.*
h.		Denomination inverted (I)		*175,000.*

Perforations, Nos. 5-8

Perforations on Nos. 5-8 generally are rough and irregular due to the perforating equipment used and the quality of the paper. Values are for stamps with rough perfs that touch the frameline on one or more sides.

Dragons and Denomination — A1a

½ sen:
Plate I — Same as 48m Plate II. Measures not less than 19.8x19.8mm. Some subjects on this plate measure 20.3x20.2mm.
Plate II — Same as 48m Plate II. Measures not more than 19.7x19.3mm. Some subjects measure 19.3x18.7mm.

Plate I & II

Plate III

1 sen:
Plate I — Same as 100m Plate I. Narrow space between frameline and Greek-type border.
Plate II — Same as 100m Plate II. Same narrow space between frameline and border.
Plate III — Space between frameline and border is much wider. Frameline thinner. Shading on dragon heads heavier than on Plates I and II.

Native Laid Paper
With or Without Gum

1872 *Perf. 9-12 & compound*

Denomination in Black

No.	Type	Description	Unused	Used
5	A1a	½s brown (II)	140.00	140.00
a.		½s red brown (II)	140.00	140.00
b.		½s gray brown (II)	140.00	140.00
c.		Wove paper (II)	725.00	675.00
d.		½s brown (I)	200.00	200.00
e.		½s red brown (I)	200.00	200.00
f.		½s gray brown (I)	200.00	200.00
g.		Wove paper (I)	275.00	275.00
6	A1a	1s blue (II)	400.00	400.00
a.		Wove paper (II)	675.00	675.00
b.		Plate I	1,400.	*3,000.*
c.		Wove paper (I)	*7,000.*	
d.		Plate III	*10,000.*	2,500.
e.		Wove paper (III)		*7,500.*
7	A1a	2s vermilion	550.00	550.00
a.		Wove paper	625.00	600.00
8	A1a	5s blue green	850.00	850.00
a.		5s yellow green	850.00	850.00
b.		Wove paper	900.00	900.00

In 1896 the government made imperforate imitations of Nos. 6-7 to include in a presentation book.

Beginning with No. 9, Japanese stamps intended for distribution outside the Postal Ministry were overprinted with three characters, as shown above, reading "Mihon" (specimen). These specimens were included in ministry announcements detailing forthcoming issues and were in presentation booklets given to government officials, foreign governments, etc.

Expect perforations on Nos. 9-71 to be rough and irregular.

Imperial Crest and Branches of Kiri Tree — A2

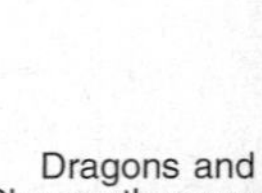

Dragons and Chrysanthemum Crest — A3

Imperial Chrysanthemum Crest — A4

Imperial Crest and Branches of Kiri Tree — A5

Perf. 9 to 13 and Compound

1872-73

Native Wove or Laid Paper of Varying Thickness

No.	Type	Description	Unused	Used
9	A2	½s brown, *hard wove*	25.00	18.00
a.		Upper character in left label has 2 diagonal top strokes missing	2,100.	1,250.
b.		Laid paper	80.00	—
c.		As "a," laid paper	2,200.	—
d.		½s gray brown, *soft porous native wove*	80.00	—

Nos. 9, 9a are on stiff, brittle wove paper. Nos. 9b, 9c and 9d on a soft, fibrous paper. Nos. 9b, 9c and 9d probably were never put in use, though genuine used examples do exist.

No.	Type	Description	Unused	Used
10	A2	1s blue, *wove*	50.00	26.00
a.		Laid paper	52.50	29.00
11	A2	2s ver, *wove*	100.00	50.00
12	A2	2s dull rose, *laid*	75.00	35.00
a.		Wove paper	100.00	50.00
13	A2	2s yel, *laid* ('73)	75.00	21.00
a.		Wove paper ('73)	175.00	26.00
14	A2	4s rose, *laid* ('73)	67.50	26.00
a.		Wove paper ('73)	210.00	32.00
15	A3	10s blue grn, *wove*	260.00	160.00
16	A3	10s yel grn, *laid*	475.00	325.00
a.		Wove paper ('73)	1,150.	500.00
17	A4	20s lilac, *wove*	650.00	400.00
a.		20s violet, *wove*	650.00	400.00
b.		20s red violet, *laid*		—
18	A5	30s gray, *wove*	450.00	350.00

See Nos. 24-25, 30-31, 37-39, 51-52.

1874

Foreign Wove Paper

No.	Type	Description	Unused	Used
24	A2	4s rose	600.	200.
25	A5	30s gray	—	*5,500.*

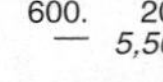

A6

A7

A8

Design A6 differs from A2 by the addition of a syllabic character in a box covering crossed kiri branches above SEN. Stamps of design A6 differ for each value in border and spandrel designs.

In design A7, the syllabic character appears just below the buckle. In design A8, it appears in an oval frame at bottom center below SE of SEN.

With Syllabic Characters

イロハニホヘトチ
i ro ha ni ho he to chi
1 2 3 4 5 6 7 8

リヌルチワカヨタ
ri nu ru wo wa ka yo ta
9 10 11 12 13 14 15 16

レソツ子ナラム
re so tsu ne na ra mu
17 18 19 20 21 22 23

Perf. 9½ to 12½ and Compound

1874

Native Laid or Wove Paper

28	A6	2s yellow (syll. 1)	*27,000.*	400.00
		Syllabic 16	425.00	
29	A7	6s vio brn (Syll. 1)	1,600.	450.00
		Syllabic 2	1,800.	475.00
		Syllabic 3	20,000.	1,100.
		Syllabic 4	20,000.	600.00
		Syllabic 5	20,000.	600.00
		Syllabic 6	20,000.	700.00
		Syllabic 7	25,000.	550.00
		Syllabic 8	25,000.	550.00
		Syllabic 9	20,000.	700.00
		Syllabic 10		3,500.
		Syllabic 11		3,000.
		Syllabic 12	20,000.	1,900.
30	A4	20s red vio (Syll. 3)	*10,000.*	
		Syllabic 1	150,000.	
		Syllabic 2	*10,000.*	
31	A5	30s gray (Syll. 1)	2,750.	3,000.
a.		Very thin laid paper	2,750.	3,000.

No. 30, syll. 1, comes only with small, elliptical specimen dot (*Sumiten*, "secret mark").

Perf. 11 to 12½ and Compound

1874

Foreign Wove Paper

32	A6	½s brown (Syll. 1)	25.00	20.00
		Syllabic 2	40.00	40.00
33	A6	1s blue (Syll. 4)	160.00	40.00
		Syllabic 1	150.00	35.00
		Syllabic 2	225.00	40.00
		Syllabic 3	200.00	40.00
		Syllabic 5	650.00	150.00
		Syllabic 6, 9	150.00	40.00
		Syllabic 7	350.00	45.00
		Syllabic 8	150.00	40.00
		Syllabic 10	225.00	70.00
		Syllabic 11	215.00	60.00
		Syllabic 12	250.00	65.00

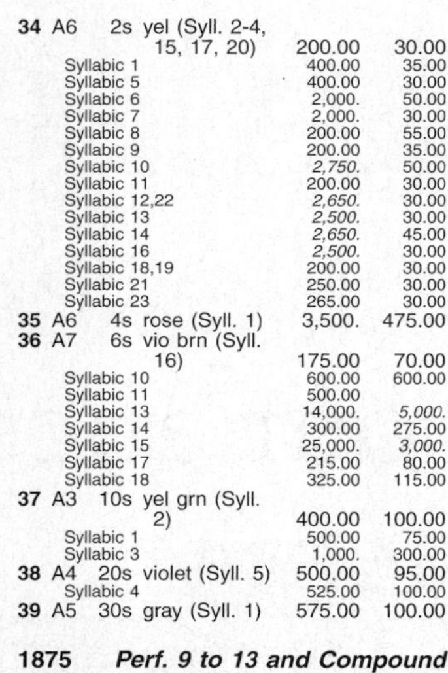

34	A6	2s yel (Syll. 2-4, 15, 17, 20)	200.00	30.00
		Syllabic 1	400.00	35.00
		Syllabic 5	400.00	30.00
		Syllabic 6	2,000.	50.00
		Syllabic 7	2,000.	30.00
		Syllabic 8	200.00	55.00
		Syllabic 9	200.00	35.00
		Syllabic 10	*2,750.*	50.00
		Syllabic 11	200.00	30.00
		Syllabic 12,22	*2,650.*	30.00
		Syllabic 13	*2,500.*	30.00
		Syllabic 14	*2,650.*	45.00
		Syllabic 16	*2,500.*	30.00
		Syllabic 18,19	200.00	30.00
		Syllabic 21	250.00	30.00
		Syllabic 23	265.00	30.00
35	A6	4s rose (Syll. 1)	3,500.	475.00
36	A7	6s vio brn (Syll. 16)	175.00	70.00
		Syllabic 10	600.00	600.00
		Syllabic 11	500.00	
		Syllabic 13	14,000.	*5,000.*
		Syllabic 14	300.00	275.00
		Syllabic 15	25,000.	*3,000.*
		Syllabic 17	215.00	80.00
		Syllabic 18	325.00	115.00
37	A3	10s yel grn (Syll. 2)	400.00	100.00
		Syllabic 1	500.00	75.00
		Syllabic 3	1,000.	300.00
38	A4	20s violet (Syll. 5)	500.00	95.00
		Syllabic 4	525.00	100.00
39	A5	30s gray (Syll. 1)	575.00	100.00

1875 ***Perf. 9 to 13 and Compound***

40	A6	½s gray (Syll. 2, 3)	22.50	20.00
		Syllabic 4	30.00	1,000.
41	A6	1s brn (Syll. 15)	35.00	22.50
		Syllabic 5	375.00	50.00
		Syllabic 7	2,250.	275.00
		Syllabic 8	*32,500.*	275.00
		Syllabic 12	900.00	225.00
		Syllabic 13	50.00	22.50
		Syllabic 14	50.00	22.50
		Syllabic 16-17	40.00	22.50
42	A6	4s green (Syll. 1)	125.00	27.50
		Syllabic 2	200.00	27.50
		Syllabic 3	125.00	27.50
43	A7	6s orange (Syll. 16,17)	100.00	25.00
		Syllabic 10	175.00	50.00
		Syllabic 11	150.00	40.00
		Syllabic 13	225.00	40.00
		Syllabic 14	160.00	32.50
		Syllabic 15		150,000.
44	A8	6s orange (Syll. 20)	100.00	25.00
		Syllabic 19	100.00	25.00
		Syllabic 21	100.00	25.00
		Syllabic 22	4,250.	1,750.

Dragons A9

Wild Goose A10

Wagtail — A11

Imperial Crest — A11a

Kiri Branches — A11b

Goshawk — A12

45	A9	10s ultra (Syll. 4)	175.00	27.50
		Syllabic 5	*4,150.*	350.00
46	A10	12s rose (Syll. 1)	450.00	150.00
		Syllabic 2	500.00	175.00
		Syllabic 3	*3,500.*	500.00
47	A11	15s lilac (Syll. 1)	350.00	150.00
		Syllabic 2	400.00	165.00
		Syllabic 3	350.00	175.00
48	A11a	20s rose (Syll. 8)	140.00	20.00
49	A11b	30s vio (Syll. 2-4)	175.00	65.00
50	A12	45s lake (Syll. 1)	600.00	275.00
		Syllabic 2	1,250.	450.00
		Syllabic 3	1,200.	425.00

Issued: #46, syll. 2, 1882; #46, syll. 3, 1883; others, 1875.

The 1s brown on laid paper, type A6, formerly listed as No. 50A, is one of several stamps of the preceding issue which exist on a laid type paper. They are difficult to identify and mainly of interest to specialists.

Without Syllabic Characters

1875

51	A2	1s brown	*6,500.*	675.00
52	A2	4s green	525.00	90.00

Branches of Kiri Tree Tied with Ribbon A13

Imperial Crest and Kiri Branches A14

1875-76

53	A13	1s brown	80.00	10.00
54	A13	2s yellow	100.00	16.00
54A	A14	5s green ('76)	200.00	100.00
		Nos. 53-54A (3)	380.00	126.00

A15

A16

Imperial Crest, Star and Kiri Branches A17

Sun, Kikumon and Kiri Branches A18

Imperial Crest and Kiri Branches A19

Kikumon A20

Perf. 8 to 14 and Compound

1876-77 **Typo.**

55	A15	5r slate	16.00	10.00
56	A16	1s black	37.50	4.25
a.		Horiz. pair, imperf. btwn.		
57	A16	2s brown ol	52.50	3.00
58	A16	4s blue grn	42.50	4.00
a.		4s green	42.50	4.00

59	A17	5s brown	65.00	22.50
60	A17	6s orange ('77)	160.00	65.00
61	A17	8s vio brn ('77)	67.50	6.00
62	A17	10s blue ('77)	55.00	2.50
63	A17	12s rose ('77)	210.00	150.00
64	A18	15s yel grn ('77)	150.00	2.50
65	A18	20s dk blue ('77)	160.00	12.00
66	A18	30s violet ('77)	210.00	110.00
a.		30s red violet	210.00	110.00
67	A18	45s carmine ('77)	625.00	525.00

1879

68	A16	1s maroon	15.00	1.25
69	A16	2s dk violet	40.00	2.00
70	A16	3s orange	60.00	24.00
71	A18	50s carmine	210.00	12.50
		Nos. 68-71 (4)	325.00	39.75

1883

72	A16	1s green	11.50	.60
73	A16	2s car rose	15.00	.25
74	A17	5s ultra	22.50	.50
		Nos. 72-74 (3)	49.00	1.35

1888-92

75	A15	5r gray blk ('89)	5.00	.45
76	A16	3s lilac rose ('92)	15.00	.45
77	A16	4s olive bis	13.00	.45
78	A17	8s blue lilac	19.00	1.60
79	A17	10s brown org	17.00	.45
80	A18	15s purple	57.50	.50
81	A18	20s orange	75.00	1.50
a.		20s yellow	75.00	1.50
82	A19	25s blue green	150.00	1.50
83	A18	50s brown	100.00	3.25
84	A20	1y carmine	160.00	4.25
		Nos. 75-84 (10)	611.50	14.40

Stamps of types A16-A18 differ for each value, in backgrounds and ornaments.

Nos. 58, 61-62, 64-65, 71-84 are found with telegraph or telephone office cancellations. These sell at considerably lower prices than postally used examples.

Cranes and Imperial Crest — A21

Perf. 11½ to 13 and Compound

1894, Mar. 9

85	A21	2s carmine	24.00	3.00
86	A21	5s ultra	37.50	11.00

25th wedding anniv. of Emperor Meiji (Mutsuhito) and Empress Haru.

Gen. Yoshihisa Kitashirakawa A22 A23

Field Marshal Akihito Arisugawa A24 A25

1896, Aug. 1 **Engr.**

87	A22	2s rose	26.00	2.75
88	A23	5s deep ultra	52.50	2.75
89	A24	2s rose	26.00	2.75
90	A25	5s deep ultra	52.50	2.75
		Nos. 87-90 (4)	157.00	11.00

Victory in Chinese-Japanese War (1894-95).

A26

A27

A28

A29

Perf. 11½ to 14 and Compound

1899-1907 **Typo.**

91 A26 5r gray 5.50 1.00
92 A26 ½s gray ('01) 3.00 .20
93 A26 1s lt red brn 3.50 .20
94 A26 1½s ultra ('00) 12.00 .85
95 A26 1½s violet ('06) 9.00 .25
96 A26 2s lt green 9.00 .20
97 A26 3s violet brn 8.50 .25
a. Double impression
98 A26 3s rose ('06) 5.00 .25
99 A26 4s rose 6.00 1.25
a. 4s pink ('06) 7.00 1.75
100 A26 5s orange yel 17.00 .25
101 A27 6s maroon ('07) 29.00 3.50
102 A27 8s olive grn 30.00 5.00
103 A27 10s deep blue 11.00 .20
104 A27 15s purple 40.00 2.00
105 A27 20s red orange 21.00 .25
106 A28 25s blue green 62.50 1.00
107 A28 50s red brown 62.50 2.00
108 A29 1y carmine 72.50 3.00
Nos. 91-108 (18) 407.00 21.65

For overprints see Nos. M1, Offices in China, 1-18, Offices in Korea, 1-14.

Boxes for Rice Cakes and Marriage Certificates A30

Symbols of Korea and Japan A31

Perf. 11½ to 12½ and Compound

1900, May 10

109 A30 3s carmine 28.00 2.50

Wedding of the Crown Prince Yoshihito and Princess Sadako.
For overprints see Offices in China No. 19, Offices in Korea No. 15.

1905, July 1

110 A31 3s rose red 80.00 19.00

Issued to commemorate the amalgamation of the postal services of Japan and Korea. Korean stamps were withdrawn from sale June 30, 1905, but remained valid until Aug. 31. No. 110 was used in the Korea and China Offices of Japan, as well as in Japan proper.

Field-piece and Japanese Flag — A32

Empress Jingo — A33

1906, Apr. 29

111 A32 1½s blue 26.00 4.00
112 A32 3s carmine rose 55.00 16.00

Triumphal military review following the Russo-Japanese War.

1908 **Engr.**

113 A33 5y green 750.00 5.00
114 A33 10y dark violet 1,000. 7.50

The frame of No. 114 differs slightly from the illustration.
See Nos. 146-147.
For overprints see Offices in China Nos. 20-21, 48-49.

A34

A35

A36

Perf. 12, 12x13, 13x13½

1913 **Typo.** **Unwmk.**

115 A34 ½s brown 7.00 .85
116 A34 1s orange 14.00 .85
117 A34 1½s lt blue 18.00 1.25
a. Booklet pane of 6 175.00
118 A34 2s green 19.00 .85
119 A34 3s rose 26.00 .45
a. Booklet pane of 6 175.00
120 A35 4s red 27.50 12.00
121 A35 5s violet 35.00 1.25
122 A35 10s deep blue 110.00 .60
123 A35 20s claret 110.00 1.25
124 A35 25s olive green 110.00 2.60
125 A36 1y yel grn & mar 750.00 26.00
Nos. 115-125 (11) 1,226. 47.95

1914-25 **Wmk. 141** **Granite Paper**

Size: 19x22½mm ("Old Die")

127 A34 ½s brown 2.10 .20
128 A34 1s orange 2.10 .20
129 A34 1½s blue 2.10 .20
a. Booklet pane of 6 72.50
d. As "a," imperf.
130 A34 2s green 4.25 .20
a. Booklet pane of 6 72.50
131 A34 3s rose 1.60 .20
a. Booklet pane of 6 60.00
132 A35 4s red 14.00 1.00
a. Booklet pane of 6 72.50
133 A35 5s violet 13.00 .45
134 A35 6s brown ('19) 18.00 2.40
136 A35 8s gray ('19) 15.00 9.00
137 A35 10s deep blue 15.00 .20
a. Booklet pane of 6 72.50
138 A35 13s olive brn ('25) 35.00 1.90
139 A35 20s claret 72.50 .60
140 A35 25s olive grn 12.00 .85
141 A36 30s orange brn ('19) 18.00 .50
143 A36 50s dk brown ('19) 26.00 1.00
145 A36 1y yel grn & mar 140.00 1.50
b. Imperf., pair
146 A33 5y green 425.00 4.00
147 A33 10y violet 625.00 6.00
Nos. 127-147 (18) 1,440. 30.40

1924-33

"New Die" Size: 18½x22mm (Flat Plate)

or 18½x22½mm (Rotary)

127a A34 ½s brown 1.75 .95
128a A34 1s orange 1.75 .95
129b A34 1½s blue 2.75 .30
c. Bklt. pane of 6 ('30) 19.00
131b A34 3s rose 1.10 .20
c. Bklt. pane of 6 ('28) 45.00
133a A35 5s violet 15.00 .20
135 A35 7s red org ('30) 7.75 .20
138a A35 13s bister brn ('25) 6.00 .20
140a A35 25s olive green 45.00 .20
142 A36 30s org & grn ('29) 17.00 .30
144 A36 50s yel brn & dk bl ('29) 12.00 .50
145a A36 1y yel grn & mar 67.50 1.00
Nos. 127a-145a (11) 177.60 5.00

See Nos. 212-213, 239-241, 243, 245, 249-252, 255. For overprints see Nos. C1-C2, M2-M5, Offices in China, 22-47.

Ceremonial Cap — A37

Imperial Throne — A38

Enthronement Hall, Kyoto — A39

Perf. 12½

1915, Nov. 10 **Typo.** **Unwmk.**

148 A37 1½s red & blk 2.00 .55
149 A38 3s orange & vio 2.50 .80

Engr.

Perf. 12x12½

150 A39 4s carmine rose 12.00 10.00
151 A39 10s ultra 24.00 16.00
Nos. 148-151 (4) 40.50 27.35

Enthronement of Emperor Yoshihito.

Mandarin Duck — A40

Ceremonial Cap — A41

1916, Nov. 3 **Typo.** ***Perf. 12½***

152 A40 1½s green, red & yel 4.00 1.75
153 A40 3s red & yellow 7.00 2.00
154 A41 10s ultra & dk blue 800.00 250.00

Nomination of the Prince Heir Apparent, later Emperor Hirohito.

A42

Dove and Olive Branch — A43

Perf. 12, 12½, 13½x13

1919, July 1 **Engr.**

155 A42 1½s dark brown 2.00 .60
156 A43 3s gray green 2.50 1.00
157 A42 4s rose 5.50 3.75
158 A43 10s dark blue 23.00 12.00
Nos. 155-158 (4) 33.00 17.35

Restoration of peace after World War I.

Census Officer, A.D. 652 — A44

Meiji Shrine, Tokyo — A45

Perf. 12½

1920, Sept. 25 **Typo.** **Unwmk.**

159 A44 1½s red violet 6.50 2.60
160 A44 3s vermilion 7.00 2.60

Taking of the 1st modern census in Japan. Not available for foreign postage except to China.

1920, Nov. 1 **Engr.**

161 A45 1½s dull violet 2.50 1.10
162 A45 3s rose 2.50 1.10

Dedication of the Meiji Shrine. Not available for foreign postage except to China.

National and Postal Flags — A46

Ministry of Communications Building, Tokyo — A47

Typographed (A46), Engraved (A47)

1921, Apr. 20 ***Perf. 12½, 13x13½***

163 A46 1½s gray grn & red 1.60 .90
164 A47 3s violet brn 2.10 1.00
165 A46 4s rose & red 40.00 17.00
166 A47 10s dark blue 200.00 125.00
Nos. 163-166 (4) 243.70 143.90

50th anniv. of the establishment of postal service and Japanese postage stamps.

Battleships "Katori" and "Kashima" — A48

1921, Sept. 3 **Litho.** ***Perf. 12½***

167 A48 1½s violet 2.00 1.00
168 A48 3s olive green 2.25 1.00
169 A48 4s rose red 30.00 15.00
170 A48 10s deep blue 35.00 18.00
Nos. 167-170 (4) 69.25 35.00

Return of Crown Prince Hirohito from his European visit.

Mount Fuji — A49

Mt. Niitaka, Taiwan — A50

Perf. 13x13½

1930-37 **Typo.** **Wmk. 141**

Granite Paper

Size: 18½x22mm ("New Die")

171 A49 4s green ('37) 2.40 .35
172 A49 4s orange 5.50 .25
174 A49 8s olive green 8.50 .20
175a A49 20s blue ('37) 19.00 26.00
176 A49 20s brown violet 26.00 .20
Nos. 171-176 (5) 61.40 27.00

1922-29

Size: 19x22½mm ("Old Die")

171a A49 4s green 7.50 2.60
172a A49 4s orange ('29) 75.00 7.50
173 A49 8s rose 15.00 5.25
174a A49 8s olive green ('29) 210.00 67.50
175 A49 20s deep blue 17.00 .50
176a A49 20s brown vio ('29) 75.00 1.25
Nos. 171a-176a (6) 399.50 84.60

See Nos. 242, 246, 248.

Perf. 12½

1923, Apr. 16 **Unwmk.** **Engr.**

177 A50 1½s orange 8.50 6.75
178 A50 3s dark violet 13.00 5.75

1st visit of Crown Prince Hirohito to Taiwan. The stamps were sold only in Taiwan, but were valid throughout the empire.

Cherry Blossoms A51

Sun and Dragonflies A52

Empress Jingo — A53

1923 **Wmk. 142** **Litho.** ***Imperf.***

Without Gum; Granite Paper

179 A51 ½s gray 4.50 2.25
180 A51 1½s lt blue 5.00 1.00
181 A51 2s red brown 4.50 1.00
182 A51 3s brt rose 3.25 .80
183 A51 4s gray green 40.00 12.00
184 A51 5s dull violet 15.00 1.00
185 A51 8s red orange 65.00 21.00
186 A52 10s deep brown 27.50 1.00
187 A52 20s deep blue 30.00 1.25
Nos. 179-187 (9) 194.75 41.30

#179-187 exist rouletted and with various perforations. These were made privately.

Perf. 12, 13x13½

1924 **Engr.** **Wmk. 141**

Granite Paper

188 A53 5y gray green 240.00 3.00
189 A53 10y dull violet 350.00 2.00

See Nos. 253-254.

Cranes — A54

Phoenix — A55

Perf. 10½ to 13½ and Compound

1925, May 10 **Litho.** **Unwmk.**

190 A54 1½s gray violet 2.00 1.00
191 A55 3s silver & brn org 2.60 1.50
a. Vert. pair, imperf. btwn. 425.00
192 A54 8s light red 20.00 11.00
193 A55 20s silver & gray grn 45.00 35.00
Nos. 190-193 (4) 69.60 48.50

25th wedding anniv. of the Emperor Yoshihito (Taisho) and Empress Sadako.

Mt. Fuji — A56

Yomei Gate, Nikko — A57

Nagoya Castle — A58

Perf. 13½x13

1926-37 **Typo.** **Wmk. 141**

Granite Paper

194 A56 2s green 1.60 .20
195 A57 6s carmine 6.00 .20
196 A58 10s dark blue 7.00 .20
197 A58 10s carmine ('37) 8.00 7.00
Nos. 194-197 (4) 22.60 7.60

See Nos. 244, 247. For surcharges see People's Republic of China No. 2L5-2L6.

Baron Hisoka Maeshima — A59

Map of World on Mollweide's Projection — A60

Perf. 12½, 13x13½

1927, June 20 **Unwmk.**

198 A59 1½s lilac 2.50 1.00
199 A59 3s olive green 2.50 1.00
200 A60 6s carmine rose 50.00 45.00
201 A60 10s blue 62.50 45.00
Nos. 198-201 (4) 117.50 92.00

50th anniv. of Japan's joining the UPU. Baron Maeshima (1835-1919) organized Japan's modern postal system and was postmaster general.

Phoenix — A61

Enthronement Hall, Kyoto — A62

1928, Nov. 10 **Engr.** ***Perf. 12½***

Yellow Paper

202 A61 1½s deep green 1.00 .50
203 A62 3s red violet 1.00 .50
204 A61 6s carmine rose 2.10 1.60
205 A62 10s deep blue 3.00 2.10
Nos. 202-205 (4) 7.10 4.70

Enthronement of Emperor Hirohito.

Great Shrines of Ise — A63

Map of Japanese Empire — A64

1929, Oct. 2 ***Perf. 12½***

206 A63 1½s gray violet 1.00 1.00
207 A63 3s carmine 1.50 1.10

58th rebuilding of the Ise Shrines.

1930, Sept. 25 **Unwmk.**

208 A64 1½s deep violet 2.00 1.25
209 A64 3s deep red 2.25 1.50

2nd census in the Japanese Empire.

Meiji Shrine — A65

1930, Nov. 1 **Litho.**

210 A65 1½s green 1.50 .85
211 A65 3s brown org 2.00 1.00

10th anniv. of dedication of Meiji Shrine.

Coil Stamps

Wmk. Zigzag Lines (141)

1933 **Typo.** ***Perf. 13 Horiz.***

212 A34 1½s light blue 13.00 17.00
213 A34 3s rose 14.00 21.00

Japanese Red Cross Badge — A66

Red Cross Building, Tokyo — A67

Perf. 12½

1934, Oct. 1 **Engr.** **Unwmk.**

214 A66 1½s green & red 1.50 1.00
215 A67 3s dull vio & red 1.75 1.25
216 A66 6s dk car & red 8.00 5.00
217 A67 10s blue & red 12.00 8.00
Nos. 214-217 (4) 23.25 15.25

15th International Red Cross Congress. Sheets of 20 with commemorative marginal inscription. One side of sheet is perf. 13.

White Tower of Liaoyang and Warship "Hiei" — A68

Akasaka Detached Palace, Tokyo — A69

1935, Apr. 2

218 A68 1½s olive green 1.00 .60
219 A69 3s red brown 1.50 1.00
220 A68 6s carmine 6.25 3.00
221 A69 10s blue 9.00 6.00
Nos. 218-221 (4) 17.75 10.60

Visit of Emperor Kang Teh of Manchukuo (Henry Pu-yi) to Tokyo, April 6, 1935. Sheets of 20 with commemorative marginal inscription. One side of sheet is perf. 13.

Mt. Fuji — A70

1935 **Typo.** ***Perf. 13x13½***

Granite Paper

222 A70 1½s rose carmine 10.00 .75
a. Miniature sheet of 20 700.00 500.00

Issued to pay postage on New Year's cards from Dec. 1-31, 1935. After Jan. 1, 1936, used for ordinary letter postage. No. 222 was issued in sheets of 100.

Mt. Fuji A71

Fuji from Lake Ashi A72

Fuji from Lake Kawaguchi — A73

Fuji from Mishima A74

1936, July 10 Photo. Wmk. 141

Granite Paper

No.	Type	Description	Unused	Used
223	A71	1½s red brown	3.00	2.00
224	A72	3s dark green	4.50	3.00
225	A73	6s carmine rose	10.00	8.00
226	A74	10s dark blue	12.00	10.00
		Nos. 223-226 (4)	29.50	23.00

Fuji-Hakone National Park.

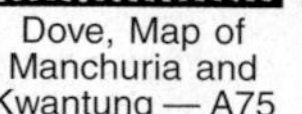

Dove, Map of Manchuria and Kwantung — A75

Shinto Shrine, Port Arthur — A76

Headquarters of Kwantung Government A77

1936, Sept. 1 Litho. *Perf. 12½*

Granite Paper

No.	Type	Description	Unused	Used
227	A75	1½s gray violet	18.00	10.00
228	A76	3s red brown	14.00	12.00
229	A77	10s dull green	200.00	130.00
		Nos. 227-229 (3)	232.00	152.00

30th anniv. of Japanese administration of Kwangtung Leased Territory and the South Manchuria Railway Zone.

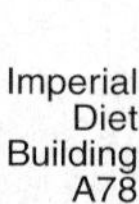

Imperial Diet Building A78

Grand Staircase A79

1936, Nov. 7 Engr. *Perf. 13*

No.	Type	Description	Unused	Used
230	A78	1½s green	2.00	1.00
231	A79	3s brown vio	3.00	1.50
232	A79	6s carmine	6.00	4.00
233	A78	10s blue	10.00	5.75
		Nos. 230-233 (4)	21.00	12.25

Opening of the new Diet Building, Tokyo.

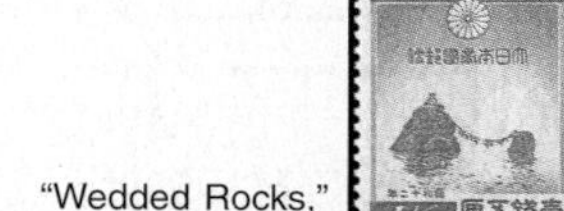

"Wedded Rocks," Futamigaura — A80

1936, Dec. 10 Photo.

No.	Type	Description	Unused	Used
234	A80	1½s rose carmine	3.50	.20

Issued to pay postage on New Year's greeting cards.

Types of 1913-26

Perf. 13½x13, 13x13½

1937 Typo. Wmk. 257

No.	Type	Description	Unused	Used
239	A34	½s brown	1.90	1.00
240	A34	1s orange yel	2.75	1.25
241	A34	3s rose	1.00	.20
242	A49	4s green	3.75	.20
243	A35	5s violet	5.00	.20
244	A57	6s crimson	8.00	.95
245	A35	7s red org	8.00	.25
246	A49	8s olive bister	8.50	.50
247	A58	10s carmine	6.75	.25
248	A49	20s blue	12.00	.50
249	A35	25s olive grn	35.00	2.00
250	A36	30s org & grn	25.00	.50
251	A36	50s brn org & dk bl	100.00	2.00
252	A36	1y yel grn & mar	55.00	1.50
		Nos. 239-252 (14)	272.65	11.30

Engr.

No.	Type	Description	Unused	Used
253	A53	5y gray green	275.00	3.25
254	A53	10y dull violet	425.00	3.00

For overprint see People's Republic of China No. 2L6.

Coil Stamp

1938 Typo. *Perf. 13 Horiz.*

No.	Type	Description	Unused	Used
255	A34	3s rose	4.00	4.00

New Year's Decoration — A81

1937, Dec. 15 Photo. *Perf. 13*

No.	Type	Description	Unused	Used
256	A81	2s scarlet	6.75	.20

Issued to pay postage on New Year's cards, later for ordinary use.

Trading Ship A82

Harvesting A83

Gen. Maresuke Nogi — A84

Power Plant — A85

Admiral Heihachiro Togo A86

Mount Hodaka A87

Garambi Lighthouse, Taiwan — A88

Diamond Mountains, Korea — A89

Meiji Shrine, Tokyo — A90

Yomei Gate, Nikko — A91

Plane and Map of Japan — A92

Kasuga Shrine, Nara — A93

Mount Fuji and Cherry Blossoms A94

Horyu Temple, Nara A95

Miyajima Torii, Itsukushima Shrine — A96

Golden Pavilion, Kyoto — A97

Great Buddha, Kamakura A98

Kamatari Fujiwara A99

Plum Blossoms — A100

Typographed or Engraved

1937-45 Wmk. 257 *Perf. 13*

No.	Type	Description	Unused	Used
257	A82	½s purple	.50	.30
258	A83	1s fawn	1.50	.25
259	A84	2s crimson	.35	.20
a.		Booklet pane of 20	50.00	
b.		2s pink, perf. 12 ('45)	1.25	.85
c.		2s vermilion ('44)	2.10	1.60
260	A85	3s green ('39)	.35	.20
261	A86	4s dark green	.75	.20
a.		Booklet pane of 20	13.00	
262	A87	5s dark ultra ('39)	.75	.20
263	A88	6s orange ('39)	1.50	.60
264	A89	7s deep green ('39)	.50	.20
265	A90	8s dk pur & pale vio ('39)	.45	.20
266	A91	10s lake ('38)	2.50	.20
267	A92	12s indigo ('39)	.50	.30
268	A93	14s rose lake & pale rose ('38)	.50	.25
269	A94	20s ultra ('40)	.50	.20
270	A95	25s dk brn & pale brn ('38)	.50	.20
271	A96	30s pck blue ('39)	1.25	.20
a.		Imperf., pair	400.00	

272	A97	50s ol & pale ol ('39)	.60	.20
a.		Pale olive (forest) omitted		
273	A98	1y brn & pale brn ('39)	3.50	1.00
274	A99	5y dp gray grn ('39)	25.00	2.00
275	A100	10y dk brn vio ('39)	16.50	1.50
		Nos. 257-275 (19)	58.00	8.40

Nos. 257-261, 265, 268, 270, 272- 273 are typographed; the others are engraved.

Coil Stamps

1938-39 Typo. *Perf. 13 Horiz.*

276	A82	½s purple ('39)	2.75	*4.50*
277	A84	2s crimson	3.25	*4.25*
278	A86	4s dark green	3.75	*4.25*
279	A93	14s rose lake & pale rose	140.00	75.00
		Nos. 276-279 (4)	149.75	88.00

See Nos. 329, 331, 333, 341, 351, 360 and 361. For surcharges see Nos. B4-B5, Burma 2N4-2N27, China-Taiwan, 8-9, People's Republic of China 2L3, 2L7, 2L9-2L10, 2L39, Korea 55-56. For overprints see Ryukyu Islands (Scott US Specialized catalogue) Nos. 2X1-2X2, 2X4-2X7, 2X10, 2X13-2X14, 2X17, 2X20, 2X23, 2X27, 2X29, 2X33-2X34, 3X2-3X7, 3X10-3X11, 3X14, 3X17, 3X19, 3X21, 3X23, 3X26-3X30, 5X1-5X3, 5X5-5X8, 5X10.

Mount Nantai — A101

Kegon Falls — A102

Sacred Bridge, Nikko A103

Mount Hiuchi A104

Unwmk.

1938, Dec. 25 Photo. *Perf. 13*

280	A101	2s brown orange	1.00	.50
281	A102	4s olive green	1.00	.50
282	A103	10s deep rose	6.00	3.75
283	A104	20s dark blue	6.00	3.75
a.		Souvenir sheet of 4, #280-283	70.00	75.00
		Never hinged	100.00	
		Nos. 280-283 (4)	14.00	8.50
		Set, never hinged	35.00	

Nikko National Park.
No. 283a sold for 50s.

Many souvenir sheets were sold in folders. Values are for sheets without folders.

Mount Daisen A106

Yashima Plateau, Inland Sea A107

Abuto Kwannon Temple A108

Tomo Bay, Inland Sea A109

1939, Apr. 20

285	A106	2s lt brown	1.00	.50
286	A107	4s yellow grn	1.60	1.00
287	A108	10s dull rose	7.00	4.00
288	A109	20s blue	7.00	4.00
a.		Souvenir sheet of 4, #285-288	27.50	40.00
		Never hinged	60.00	
		Nos. 285-288 (4)	16.60	9.50
		Set, never hinged	35.00	

Daisen and Inland Sea National Parks. No. 288a sold for 50s.

View from Kuju Village, Kyushu A111

Mount Naka A112

Crater of Mount Naka A113

Volcanic Cones of Mt. Aso A114

1939, Aug. 15

290	A111	2s olive brown	1.00	.50
291	A112	4s yellow green	3.00	2.00
292	A113	10s carmine	17.50	9.00
293	A114	20s sapphire	24.00	10.00
a.		Souvenir sheet of 4, #290-293	85.00	100.00
		Never hinged	140.00	
		Nos. 290-293 (4)	45.50	21.50
		Set, never hinged	90.00	

Aso National Park. No. 293a sold for 50s.

Globe — A116

Tsunetami Sano — A117

1939, Nov. 15 *Perf. 12½*

Cross in Carmine

295	A116	2s brown	1.50	.90
296	A117	4s yellow green	1.60	1.00
297	A116	10s crimson	8.00	7.00
298	A117	20s sapphire	8.00	7.00
		Nos. 295-298 (4)	19.10	15.90
		Set, never hinged	35.00	

Intl. Red Cross Society founding, 75th anniv.

Sacred Golden Kite — A118

Mount Takachiho — A119

Five Ayu Fish and Sake Jar — A120

Kashiwara Shrine — A121

1940 Engr. *Perf. 12*

299	A118	2s brown orange	1.00	1.00
300	A119	4s dark green	.75	.65
301	A120	10s dark carmine	3.75	3.25
302	A121	20s dark ultra	1.00	1.00
		Nos. 299-302 (4)	6.50	5.90
		Set, never hinged	7.50	

2,600th anniv. of the legendary date of the founding of Japan.

Mt. Hokuchin, Hokkaido A122

Mt. Asahi, Hokkaido A123

Sounkyo Gorge — A124

Tokachi Mountain Range A125

1940, Apr. 20 Photo. *Perf. 13*

303	A122	2s brown	1.00	1.00
304	A123	4s yellow green	3.00	2.00
305	A124	10s carmine	7.00	6.00
306	A125	20s sapphire	7.00	6.25
a.		Souvenir sheet of 4, #303-306	190.00	200.00
		Never hinged	350.00	
		Nos. 303-306 (4)	18.00	15.25
		Set, never hinged	35.00	

Daisetsuzan National Park. No. 306a sold for 50s.

Mt. Karakuni, Kyushu A127

Mt. Takachiho A128

Torii of Kirishima Shrine A129

Lake of the Six Kwannon A130

1940, Aug. 21

308	A127	2s brown	1.00	.75
309	A128	4s green	2.00	1.50
310	A129	10s carmine	7.00	5.00
311	A130	20s deep ultra	8.00	6.00
a.		Souvenir sheet of 4, #308-311	190.00	210.00
		Never hinged	350.00	
		Nos. 308-311 (4)	18.00	13.25
		Set, never hinged	40.00	

Kirishima National Park.
No. 311a sold for 50s.

Education Minister with Rescript on Education A132

Characters Signifying Loyalty and Filial Piety A133

1940, Oct. 25 Engr. *Perf. 12½*

313	A132	2s purple	1.00	1.00
314	A133	4s green	1.25	1.25
		Set, never hinged	2.25	

50th anniv. of the imperial rescript on education, given by Emperor Meiji to clarify Japan's educational policy.

Mt. Daiton, Taiwan A134

Central Peak of Mt. Niitaka A135

Buddhist Temple on Mt. Kwannon A136

View from Mt. Niitaka A137

1941, Mar. 10 Photo. *Perf. 13*

315	A134	2s brown	1.00	.80
316	A135	4s brt green	2.00	1.50
317	A136	10s rose red	6.00	3.75

318 A137 20s brilliant ultra 8.00 5.75
a. Souv. sheet of 4, #315-318 80.00 125.00
Never hinged 175.00
Nos. 315-318 (4) 17.00 11.80
Set, never hinged 45.00

Daiton and Niitaka-Arisan National Parks.
#318a sold with #323a in same folder for 90s.

Seisui Precipice, East Taiwan Coast — A139

Taroko Gorge — A141

Mt. Tsugitaka A140

Upper River Takkiri District A142

1941, Mar. 10

320 A139 2s brown 1.00 .80
321 A140 4s brt green 2.00 1.00
322 A141 10s rose red 6.00 2.00
323 A142 20s bril ultra 8.00 4.50
a. Souv. sheet of 4, #320-323 80.00 100.00
Never hinged 175.00
Nos. 320-323 (4) 17.00 8.30
Set, never hinged 30.00

Tsugitaka-Taroko National Park.
See note after No. 318.

War Factory Girl — A144

Building of Wooden Ship — A145

Hyuga Monument and Mt. Fuji A146

War Worker and Planes A147

Palms and Map of "Greater East Asia" A148

"Enemy Country Surrender" A149

Aviator Saluting and Japanese Flag A150

Torii of Yasukuni Shrine A151

Mt. Fuji and Cherry Blossoms A152

Torii of Miyajima A153

Garambi Lighthouse, Taiwan — A154

Typographed; Engraved

1942-45 Wmk. 257 *Perf. 13*

325 A144 1s orange brn ('43) .20 .20
328 A145 2s green .35 .25
329 A84 3s brown ('44) .45 .20
330 A146 4s emerald .20 .20
331 A86 5s brown lake .20 .20
332 A147 6s lt ultra ('44) .35 .25
a. Imperf., pair
333 A86 7s org ver ('44) .20 .20
334 A148 10s crim & dl rose .35 .20
a. Dull rose (map) omitted 300.00 300.00
335 A149 10s lt gray ('45) 1.90 1.90
336 A150 15s dull blue 1.25 .80
337 A151 17s gray vio ('43) .45 .35
338 A152 20s blue ('44) .45 .20
339 A151 27s rose brn ('45) .45 .35
340 A153 30s bluish grn ('44) 1.25 .50
341 A88 40s dull violet .35 .20
342 A154 40s dk violet ('44) .95 .80
Nos. 325,328-342 (16) 9.35 6.80

Nos. 325-335, 337-340 and 342 are typo. Nos. 336 and 341 are engr.
Nos. 329, 331, 333-334, 342 issued with and without gum. No. 335 issued only without gum. These are valued without gum.
#328, 342 exist with watermark sideways. #328 exists printed on gummed side.
Most stamps of the above series exist in numerous shades.
For overprints and surcharges see North Borneo Nos. N34, N37, N41-N42, People's Republic of China 2L4, 2L8, Korea 57-60, Ryukyu Islands (US Specialized) Nos. 2X3, 2X9, 2X12, 2X15-2X16, 2X18-2X19, 2X21-2X22, 2X24-2X26, 2X28, 3X1, 3X8-3X9, 3X12-3X13, 3X15-3X16, 3X18, 3X20, 3X25, 3X31, 4X1-4X2, 5X4.

Kenkoku Shrine, Hsinking — A155

Boys of Japan and Manchukuo A156

Orchid Crest of Manchukuo A157

1942 Unwmk. Engr. *Perf. 12*

343 A155 2s brown 1.00 1.00
344 A156 5s olive .65 .65
345 A155 10s red .75 .75
346 A157 20s dark blue 2.00 2.00
Nos. 343-346 (4) 4.40 4.40
Set, never hinged 7.50

The 2s and 10s were issued Mar. 1 for the 10th anniv. of the creation of Manchukuo; 5s and 20s on Sept. 15 for the 10th anniv. of Japanese diplomatic recognition of Manchukuo.

C-59 Locomotive A158

Yasukuni Shrine, Tokyo A159

1942, Oct. 14 Photo.

347 A158 5s Prus green 3.50 3.50
Never hinged 5.00

70th anniv. of Japan's 1st railway.

1944, June 29 *Perf. 13*

348 A159 7s Prus green .55 .55
Never hinged .85

75th anniversary of Yasukuni Shrine.

Kwantung Shrine and Map of Kwantung Peninsula — A160

1944, Oct. 1

349 A160 3s red brown 4.75 *9.00*
350 A160 7s gray violet 5.25 *9.50*
Set, never hinged 17.50

Dedication of Kwantung Shrine, Port Arthur.

Sun and Cherry Blossoms A161

Sunrise at Sea and Plane A162

Coal Miners A163

Yasukuni Shrine A164

Lithographed, Typographed

1945-47 Wmk. 257 *Imperf.*

Without Gum

351 A84 2s rose red .30 .30
352 A161 3s rose carmine .20 .30
353 A162 5s green .20 .20
a. 5s blue 9.00 6.75
354 A149 10s lt gray 10.00 7.50
354A A149 10s blue 22.50
355 A152 10s red orange .20 .20
356 A152 20s ultra ('46) .35 .20
357 A153 30s brt blue ('46) 1.50 .75
358 A163 50s dark brown ('46) .30 .20
a. Souvenir sheet of 5 ('47) 10.50 12.50
359 A164 1y dp ol grn ('46) 1.00 .75
360 A99 5y dp gray grn 5.00 .65
361 A100 10y dk brown vio 32.50 .75
Nos. 351-361 (12) 74.05
Nos. 351-354,355-361 (11) 11.80

Nos. 351 and 354 are typographed. The other stamps in this set are printed by offset lithography.
No. 358a was issued with marginal inscriptions to commemorate the Sapporo (Hokkaido) Philatelic Exhibition, Nov., 1947.
Nos. 351 to 361 are on grayish paper, and Nos. 355 to 361 also exist on white paper.
Most stamps of the above series exist in numerous shades and with private perforation or roulette.
Beware of forgeries of Nos. 352, 353, 355-357 and 360 on unwatermarked paper.

See No. 404. For overprints see Ryukyu Islands (US Specialized) Nos. 2X8, 2X11, 2X30, 3X22, 4X3, 5X9.

Baron Hisoka Maeshima A165

Horyu Temple Pagoda A166

"Thunderstorm below Fuji," by Hokusai A167

"First Geese," Print by Hokusai A168

Kintai Bridge, Iwakuni A169

Kiyomizu Temple, Kyoto A170

Goldfish A171

Noh Mask A172

Plum Blossoms — A173

Characters Read Right to Left

1946-47 Wmk. 257 Litho. *Imperf.*

Without Gum

362 A165 15s dark green .35 .25
363 A166 30s dull lilac .45 .20
364 A167 1y ultra .55 .20
a. 1y deep ultramarine 1.60 .20
b. 1y light blue .60 .20
365 A168 1.30y olive bister 1.90 .50
366 A169 1.50y dark gray 1.90 .35
367 A170 2y vermilion ('47) 1.60 .20
a. Souvenir sheet of 5 ('47) 21.00 20.00
368 A171 5y lilac rose 6.00 .45
Nos. 362-368 (7) 12.75 2.15

Engr.

369 A172 50y bister brn 62.50 .60
370 A173 100y brn car ('47) 62.50 .60

Perf. 13

371 A172 50y bis brn, with gum ('47) 62.50 .60
372 A173 100y brn car, with gum ('47) 62.50 .35

Litho.

Perf. 13x13½, 12, 12x12½

373 A166 30s dull lilac 3.00 2.75

Rouletted in Colored Lines

Typo. Unwmk.

With Gum

374 A166 30s deep lilac .95 1.40

Nos. 363, 368, 373 exist with and without gum, valued without gum, as are Nos. 371-372, 374.
No. 367a for the "Know Your Stamps" exhibition, Kyoto, Aug. 19-24, 1947. Size: 113x71mm
#362, 369 exist with watermark horizontal.
Beware of Nos. 362-364, 364a, 364b, 365 and 367 on unwatermarked paper.

See Nos. 384-387, 512A. For overprints see Ryukyu Islands (US Specialized) Nos. 2X32, 3X24, 4X4.

Catalogue values for unused stamps in this section, from this point to the end of the section, are for Never Hinged items.

Medieval Postman's Bell A175

Baron Hisoka Maeshima A176

Design of First Japanese Stamp — A177

Communication Symbols — A178

Perf. 12½, 13½x13

1946, Dec. 12 Engr. Unwmk.

375 A175 15s orange 5.00 3.00
376 A176 30s deep green 6.00 4.00
377 A177 50s carmine 3.00 2.00
378 A178 1y deep blue 3.00 2.00
a. Souvenir sheet of 4, #375-378, imperf. 160.00 140.00
Hinged 75.00
Nos. 375-378 (4) 17.00 11.00

Government postal service in Japan, 75th anniv.

No. 378a measures 180-183x125-127mm and is ungummed. There were 2 printings: I — The 4 colors were printed simultaneously. Arched top inscription and other inscriptions in high relief (no more than 2,000 sheets). II — Stamps were printed in one step, sheet inscriptions and 15s orange stamp in another. Lines of top inscription and inscriptions at lower left and lower right (flanking the 1y blue stamp) are much flatter (less raised) than the lines of the green, carmine and blue stamps, almost level with paper's surface (about 49,000 sheets). 1st printing value $800.

Mother and Child, Diet Building — A180

Bouquet of Japanese May Flowers — A181

Wmk. 257

1947, May 3 Litho. *Perf. 12½*
Without Gum

380 A180 50s rose brown .25 .30
381 A181 1y brt ultra .50 .40
a. Souv. sheet of 2, #380-381, imperf, without gum 9.50 5.00
b. As "a," 50s stamp omitted 800.00
c. As "a," 1y stamp omitted 800.00

Inauguration of the constitution of May 3, 1947.

A182

1947, Aug. 15 Photo. *Perf. 12½*

382 A182 1.20y brown 2.10 1.00
383 A182 4y brt ultra 4.25 1.40

Reopening of foreign trade on a private basis.

The ornaments on No. 383 differ from those shown in the illustration.

Types of 1946 Redrawn Characters Read Left to Right

1947-48 Wmk. 257 Typo. *Perf. 13*

384 A166 30s deep lilac 1.50 1.25
385 A166 1.20y lt olive grn 1.00 .35
a. Souvenir sheet of 15 160.00 110.00
386 A170 2y vermilion ('48) 4.00 .20
387 A168 4y lt ultra 2.60 .25
Nos. 384-387 (4) 9.10 2.05

No. 385a was issued with marginal inscriptions to commemorate the "Know Your Stamps" Exhibition, Tokyo, May, 1947.

On No. 386, the chrysanthemum crest has been eliminated and the top inscription centered.

Plum Blossoms — A183

1947 Typo. *Imperf.*
Without Gum

388 A183 10y dk brown vio 40.00 .65

This stamp is similar to type A100 but with new inscription "Nippon Yubin" (Japan Post), reading from left to right. The characters for the denomination are likewise transposed.

A184

A185

Baron Hisoka Maejima A186

Whaling A187

National Art, Imperial Treasure House, Nara — A188

1947 Typo. *Perf. 13x13½*

389 A184 35s green .40 .30

Litho.

390 A185 45s lilac rose .55 .50
a. Imperf., pair 700.00
b. Perf. 11x13½ 3.75 3.75
391 A186 1y dull brown 2.40 .35

Typo.

392 A187 5y blue 5.50 .20
a. Imperf., pair 500.00
b. Perf. 11x13½ 19.00 2.40

Engr.

Perf. 13½x13

393 A188 10y lilac 15.00 .20
a. Imperf., pair —
Nos. 389-393 (5) 23.85 1.55

No. 389 was produced on both rotary and flat press. Sheets of the rotary press printing have a border. Those of the flat press printing have none.

Lily of the Valley — A188a

1947, Sept. 13 Unwmk. *Perf. 12½*

394 A188a 2y dk Prus green 3.00 1.25

Relief of Ex-convicts Day, Sept. 13, 1947.

Souvenir Sheet

A189

1947 Wmk. 257 Litho. *Imperf.*
Without Gum

395 A189 Sheet of 5, ultra 3.50 2.60

Stamp Hobby Week, Nov. 1-7, 1947. Sheet size: 113½x71½mm, on white or grayish paper.

For overprint, see No. 408.

"Benkei," 1880 Locomotive — A190

1947, Oct. 14 Unwmk. Engr.
Without Gum

396 A190 4y deep ultra 17.50 16.50

75th anniv. of railway service in Japan.

Hurdling — A191

Diving — A192

Discus Throwing A193

Volleyball A194

1947, Oct. 25 Photo. *Perf. 12½*

397 A191 1.20y red violet 9.00 6.00
398 A192 1.20y red violet 9.00 6.00
399 A193 1.20y red violet 9.00 6.00
400 A194 1.20y red violet 9.00 6.00
a. Block of 4, #397-400 52.50 30.00

2nd Natl. Athletic Meet, held in Kanazawa, Oct. 30-Nov. 3.

Souvenir Sheets

A195

1948 Wmk. 257 Litho. *Imperf.*
Without Gum

401 A195 Sheet of 2, As #368, rose carmine 13.50 *15.00*

Same, Inscribed with Three instead of Two Japanese Characters at Bottom Center

402 A195 Sheet of 2, #368 15.00 *17.00*

Philatelic exhibitions at Osaka (No. 401) and Nagoya (No. 402).

For Nos. 401-402 overprinted in green, see Nos. 407, 407b.

Stylized Tree — A196

National Art Treasure, Nara — A197

Perf. 12½

1948, Apr. 1 Unwmk. Photo.

403 A196 1.20y dp yellow grn .90 .90

Forestation movement. Sheets of 30, marginal inscription.

Coal Miners Type of 1946, and Type A197

1948 Wmk. 257 Litho. *Perf. 13*

404 A163 50s dark brown 1.50 .95

Typo.

Perf. 13x13½

405 A197 10y rose violet 13.50 .20
a. Imperf., pair

See No. 515A.

School Children — A198

Perf. 12½

1948, May 3 Unwmk. Photo.

406 A198 1.20y dark carmine .90 .80

Reorganization of Japan's educational system. Sheets of 30, marginal inscription.

Souvenir Sheets

No. 402 Overprinted at Top, Bottom and Sides with Japanese Characters and Flowers in Green

1948, Apr. 3

407 A195 Sheet of 2 60.00 37.50
a. Overprint inverted 125.00 125.00
b. Overprint on No. 401 100.00 95.00

Mishima Philatelic Exhibition, Apr. 3-9.

No. 395 Overprinted at Top and Bottom With Japanese Characters in Plum

1948, Apr. 18

408 A189 Sheet of 5, ultra 22.50 19.00

Centenary of the death of Katsushika Hokusai, painter.

Sampans on Inland Sea, Near Suma — A199

Engr. & Litho.
1948, Apr. 22 Unwmk. *Imperf.*
Without Gum

409 A199 Sheet of 2, grn & rose car 12.00 7.50

Communications Exhib., Tokyo, Apr. 27-May 3, 1948. Sheet contains two 2y deep carmine stamps.
Sheet exists with green border omitted.

1948, May 20
Without Gum

410 A199 Sheet of 2, ultra & rose car 14.50 13.50

Aomori Newspaper and Stamp Exhibition. Border design of apples and apple blossoms.

Type A199 With Altered Border and Inscriptions

1948, May 23
Without Gum

411 A199 Sheet of 2, blue & rose car 14.50 13.50

Fukushima Stamp Exhibition. Border design of cherries and crossed lines.

Horse Race — A200

1948, June 6 Photo. *Perf. 12½*

412 A200 5y brown 2.50 .95

25th anniv. of the enforcement of Japan's horse racing laws. Each sheet contains 30 stamps and 2 labels, with marginal inscription.

A201 A202

Wmk. 257
1948, Sept. 10 Litho. *Perf. 13*

413 A201 1.50y blue 2.25 .45
414 A202 3.80y lt brown 6.50 5.25

Souvenir Sheet
Without Gum
Imperf

415 Sheet of 4 32.50 30.00

Kumamoto Stamp Exhibition, Sept. 20. Souvenir sheet, issued Sept. 20, contains two each of 1.50y deep blue (A201) and 3.80y brown (A202).

Rectifying Tower — A203

Perf. 12½
1948, Sept. 14 Photo. Unwmk.

416 A203 5y dark olive bister 2.75 1.50

Government alcohol monopoly.

Swimmer — A204

Runner — A205

Designs: No. 419, High jumper. No. 420, Baseball players. No. 421, Bicycle racers.

1948

417 A204 5y blue 3.50 1.60
418 A205 5y green 8.25 3.50
419 A205 5y green 8.25 3.50
420 A205 5y green 8.25 3.50
421 A205 5y green 8.25 3.50
a. Block of 4, #418-421 42.50 42.50
Nos. 417-421 (5) 36.50 15.60

3rd Natl. Athletic Meet. Swimming matches held at Yawata, Sept. 16-19, field events, Fukuoka, Oct. 29-Nov. 3.

"Beauty Looking Back," Print by Moronobu A206

1948, Nov. 29 *Perf. 13*

422 A206 5y brown 55.00 37.50
a. Sheet of 5 350.00 250.00
Hinged 275.00

Philatelic Week, Nov. 29-Dec. 5.
See Nos. 2418-2419.

Souvenir Sheet

1948, Dec. 3 *Imperf.*
Without Gum

423 A206 5y brown, sheet of 1 40.00 27.50

Kanazawa and Takaoka stamp exhibitions.

Child Playing Hane-tsuki — A207

1948, Dec. 13 Litho. *Perf. 13*

424 A207 2y scarlet 3.75 3.00

Issued to pay postage on New Year's cards, later for ordinary use.

Farm Woman A208

Whaling A209

Miner A210

Tea Picking A211

Girl Printer A212

Factory Girl with Cotton Bobbin A213

Mt. Hodaka A214

Planting A215

Postman A216

Blast Furnace A217

Locomotive Assembly A218

Typographed, Engraved
1948-49 Wmk. 257 *Perf. 13x13½*

425 A208 2y green 1.50 .20
a. Overprinted with 4 characters in frame .55 .75
b. As "a," overprint inverted 57.50
426 A209 3y lt grnsh bl ('49) 4.25 .20
427 A210 5y olive bis 15.00 .20
a. Booklet pane of 20 — 110.00
Hinged 110.00
428 A211 5y blue grn ('49) 30.00 4.75
429 A212 6y red org ('49) 6.75 .20
430 A210 8y brown org ('49) 6.75 .20
a. Booklet pane of 20 — 190.00
Hinged 175.00
431 A213 15y blue 3.00 .20
432 A214 16y ultra ('49) 8.00 3.50
433 A215 20y dk green ('49) 27.50 .20
434 A216 30y violet bl ('49) 45.00 .20
435 A217 100y car lake ('49) 600.00 1.10
436 A218 500y deep blue ('49) 475.00 1.75
Nos. 425-436 (12) 1,222. 12.70
Set, hinged 625.00

No. 425a has a red control overprint of four characters ("Senkyo Jimu," or "Election Business") arranged vertically in a rectangular frame. Each candidate received 1,000 copies.
Nos. 432, 435-436 are engraved.
See #442, 511-512, 514-515, 518, 520, 521A-521B.

Souvenir Sheets
Typo. and Litho.
1948, Oct. 16 *Imperf.*

437 A213 15y blue, sheet of 1 30.00 30.00

Nagano Stamp Exhibition, Oct. 16.

1948, Nov. 2 *Imperf.*

438 A210 5y ol bis, sheet of 2 40.00 35.00

Shikoku Traveling Stamp Exhib., Nov. 1948.

Sampans on Inland Sea A219

Perf. 13x13½
1949 Wmk. 257 Engr.

439 A219 10y rose lake 40.00 15.00
440 A219 10y car rose 25.00 14.00
441 A219 10y orange ver 27.50 13.50
442 A214 16y brt blue 12.00 4.50
Nos. 439-442 (4) 104.50 47.00
Set, hinged 57.50

Issued in sheets of 20 stamps with marginal inscription publicizing expositions at Takamatsu (#439), Okayama (#440) and Matsuyama (#441), Nagano Peace Exposition, Apr. 1-May 31, 1949 (#442).

Ice Skater — A221

Ski Jumper — A222

1949 Unwmk. Photo. *Perf. 12*

444 A221 5y violet 2.75 1.25
445 A222 5y ultra 3.00 1.25

Winter events of the 4th Natl. Athletic Meet: skating at Suwa Jan. 27-30, skiing at Sapporo Mar. 3-6. Issued: #444, 1/27; #445, 3/3.

Steamer in Beppu Bay — A223

1949, Mar. 10 Engr. *Perf. 13x13½*

446 A223 2y carmine & ultra 1.00 .65
447 A223 5y green & ultra 3.25 1.00

Scene at Fair — A224

Stylized Trees — A225

1949, Mar. 15 Photo. *Imperf.*

448 A224 5y brt rose 2.00 1.60
a. Perf. 13 3.00 1.50
b. Sheet of 20, imperf. 65.00 45.00

Issued to publicize the Japan Foreign Trade Fair, Yokohama, 1949.
No. 448a was printed in sheets of 50 (10x5); No. 448 in sheets of 20 (4x5) with marginal inscriptions (No. 448b).

1949, Apr. 1 Unwmk. *Perf. 12*

449 A225 5y bright green 8.00 1.50

Issued to publicize the forestation movement.

Lion Rock A226

Daiho-zan (Mt. Ohmine) — A227

Doro Gorge A228

Bridge Pier Rocks A229

1949, Apr. 10 Photo. *Perf. 13*

450 A226 2y brown 1.10 .75
451 A227 5y yellow grn 3.50 1.10
452 A228 10y scarlet 14.50 8.25
453 A229 16y blue 7.25 3.75
a. Souv. sheet of 4, #450-453, no gum 27.50 24.00
b. As "a," 10y stamp omitted
Nos. 450-453 (4) 26.35 13.85

Yoshino-Kumano National Park.
No. 453a sold for 40y.

Boy — A230

Radio Tower and Star — A231

1949, May 5 *Perf. 12*

455 A230 5y rose brn & org 4.25 1.40
a. Orange omitted 250.00

Children's Day, May 5, 1949.

Souvenir Sheets

1949, May 5 *Imperf.*

456 A230 5y rose brn & org, sheet of 10 375.00 275.00
Hinged 160.00

Children's Exhib., Inuyama, Apr. 1-May 31.

1949, May 11 *Perf. 13*

457 A231 20y dp bl, sheet of 1 120.00 85.00
Hinged 60.00

Electrical Communication Week, May 11-18.

Symbols of Communication A232

Central Meteorological Observatory, Tokyo — A233

Wmk. 257

1949, June 1 Engr. *Perf. 12*

458 A232 8y brt ultra 3.00 1.50

Establishment of the Post Ministry and the Ministry of Electricity and Communication.

1949, June 1 Unwmk. *Perf. 12½*

459 A233 8y deep green 3.00 1.50

75th anniv. of the establishment of the Central Meteorological Observatory.

Mt. Fuji in Autumn A234

Lake Kawaguchi — A235

Fiji from Mt. Shichimen — A236

Shinobuno Village and Mt. Fuji — A237

1949, July 15 Photo. *Perf. 13*

460 A234 2y yellow brown 3.00 .75
461 A235 8y yellow green 3.50 1.10
462 A236 14y carmine lake 1.50 .45
463 A237 24y blue 5.00 .60
a. Souv. sheet of 4, #460-463 50.00 35.00
Nos. 460-463 (4) 13.00 2.90

Fuji-Hakone National Park.
No. 463a sold for 55y.

Allegory of Peace A238

Doves over Nagasaki — A239

Perf. 13x13½, 13½x13

1949 Photo. Unwmk.

465 A238 8y yellow brown 6.50 1.75
466 A239 8y green 4.25 1.75

Establishment of Hiroshima as the City of Eternal Peace and of Nagasaki as the International City of Culture. Issued: #465, Aug. 6; #466, Aug. 9.

Boy Scout — A240

Pen Nib of Newspaper Stereotype Matrix — A241

1949, Sept. 22 *Perf. 13x13½*

467 A240 8y brown 5.75 1.90

Natl. Boy Scout Jamboree.

1949, Oct. 1 *Perf. 13½x13*

468 A241 8y deep blue 4.75 1.90

Natl. Newspaper Week.

Racing Swimmer Poised for Dive — A242

Javelin Thrower — A243

1949 *Perf. 13½*

469 A242 8y dull blue 3.00 1.10

Perf. 12

470 A243 8y shown 5.50 2.10
471 A243 8y Yacht Racing 5.50 2.10
472 A243 8y Relay Race 5.50 2.10
473 A243 8y Tennis 5.50 2.10
a. Block of 4, #470-473 25.00 32.50
Nos. 469-473 (5) 25.00 9.50

4th Natl. Athletic Meet. The swimming matches were held at Yokohama, Sept. 15-18 and the fall events at Tokyo, Oct. 30.
Issued: #469, Sept. 15; #470-473, Oct. 30.
Nos. 470-473 exist perf 12½. Values 50 percent above those of perf 12 copies.

Map and Envelopes Forming "75" — A244

Symbols of UPU — A245

1949, Oct. 10 Engr. *Perf. 12, 13½*

474 A244 2y dull green 2.25 1.00
475 A245 8y maroon 3.00 1.00
a. Souv. sheet of 2, #474-475, imperf. 4.00 4.75
476 A244 14y carmine 7.50 4.00
477 A245 24y aqua 11.50 4.50
a. Imperf., pair
Nos. 474-477 (4) 24.25 10.50

75th anniv. of the UPU.
No 745a was issued without gum.

Floating Zenith Telescope A246

"Moon and Geese," Print by Hiroshige A247

1949, Oct. 30 Photo. *Perf. 12*

478 A246 8y dk blue grn 3.00 1.25

50th anniv. of the Mizusawa Latitudinal Observatory.

1949, Nov. 1 *Perf. 13x13½*

479 A247 8y purple 90.00 40.00
a. Sheet of 5 500.00 350.00
Sheet, hinged 325.00

Postal Week, Nov. 1-7. See #2420-2421.

Dr. Hideyo Noguchi A248

Yukichi Fukuzawa A249

Soseki Natsume A250

Shoyo Tsubouchi A251

Danjuro Ichikawa — A252

Joseph Hardy Niijima — A253

Hogai Kano A254

Kanzo Uchimura A255

Ichiyo Higuchi — A256

Ogai Mori — A257

Shiki Masaoka — A258

Shunso Hishida — A259

Amane Nishi — A260

Kenjiro Ume — A261

Hisashi Kimura — A262

Inazo Nitobe — A263

Torahiko Terada — A264

Tenshin Okakura — A265

1949-52 Unwmk. Engr. *Perf. 12½*

480 A248 8y green 8.00 .95
a. Imperf., pair
481 A249 8y deep olive ('50) 3.25 .95
a. Imperf., pair
482 A250 8y dk Prus grn ('50) 3.25 .95
483 A251 8y Prus grn ('50) 3.00 .95
a. Imperf., pair
484 A252 8y dk violet ('50) 8.75 3.00
485 A253 8y vio brn ('50) 3.00 .95
486 A254 8y dk green ('51) 9.00 1.90
487 A255 8y dp purple ('51) 10.00 1.90
488 A256 8y carmine ('51) 15.00 1.90
489 A257 8y vio brn ('51) 25.00 2.10
490 A258 8y choc ('51) 15.00 2.10
491 A259 8y dk blue ('51) 12.50 2.10
492 A260 10y dk green ('52) 60.00 3.75
493 A261 10y brn vio ('52) 10.00 1.25
494 A262 10y carmine ('52) 3.00 1.10
495 A263 10y dk grn ('52) 5.25 1.10
496 A264 10y choc ('52) 4.25 1.10
497 A265 10y dk blue ('52) 4.25 1.10
Nos. 480-497 (18) 202.50 29.15
Set, hinged 110.00

Tiger — A266

Microphones of 1925 and 1950 — A267

1950, Feb. 1 Photo. *Perf. 12*

498 A266 2y dark red 5.25 1.50

6th prize (lottery), sheet of 5, value $175.

1950, Mar. 21 *Perf. 13*

499 A267 8y ultra 3.25 1.25

25th anniversary of broadcasting in Japan. Sheets of 20 with marginal inscription.

Dove and Olive Twig on Letter Box — A268

1950, Apr. 20 *Perf. 12*

500 A268 8y dp yellow grn 3.00 1.10

Day of Posts, Apr. 20.

Lake Akan and Mt. Akan A269

Lake Kutcharo, Hokkaido A270

Mt. Akan-Fuji A271

Lake Mashu A272

1950, July 15 Unwmk. *Perf. 13*

501 A269 2y yellow brn 1.50 .75
502 A270 8y dp yellow grn 2.25 1.10
503 A271 14y rose car 10.50 3.75
504 A272 24y brt blue 11.50 4.50
a. Souv. sheet of 4, #501-504 45.00 32.50
Nos. 501-504 (4) 25.75 10.10

Akan National Park.
No. 504a sold for 55y.

Gymnast on Rings — A273

Designs: No. 506, Pole vault. No. 507, Soccer. No. 508, Equestrian.

1950, Oct. 28 *Perf. 13½x13*

505 A273 8y rose brown 35.00 8.25
506 A273 8y rose brown 35.00 8.25
507 A273 8y rose brown 35.00 8.25
508 A273 8y rose brown 35.00 8.25
a. Strip of 4, #505-508 160.00 110.00
b. Block of 4, #505-508 160.00 125.00
As "b," hinged 90.00

5th National Athletic Meet. Sheets of 20 stamps in which each horizontal row contains all four designs. Value, sheet $850.

Types of 1947-49 and

Ishiyama-dera Pagoda A274

Hisoka Maeshima A275

Long-tailed Cock of Tosa A276

Goddess Kannon A277

Himeji Castle A278

Nyoirin Kannon of Chuguji A280

Phoenix Hall, Byodoin Temple A279

Perf. 13x13½, 13½x13 (14y)
1950-52 Typo. Unwmk.

509 A274 80s carmine ('51) 2.50 1.25
a. Sheet of 1 7.25 *9.50*

Photo.

510 A275 1y dk brown ('51) 4.00 .55
a. Souvenir sheet of 4 15.00 15.00

Typo.

511 A208 2y green ('51) 2.00 .20
512 A209 3y lt grnsh bl ('51) 50.00 .95
512A A168 4y lt ultra ('52) 40.00 1.10
513 A276 5y dp grn & org brn ('51) 6.00 .20
a. Orange brown omitted 210.00
514 A212 6y red org ('51) 7.00 .45
515 A210 8y dk org brn ('51) 35.00 .55
515A A197 10y rose vio ('51) 75.00 4.75
516 A277 10y red brn & lil ('51) 25.00 .20

Engr.

517 A278 14y brn & car ('51) 55.00 25.00
a. Sheet of 1 67.50 55.00

Typo.

518 A215 20y dk green ('51) 65.00 .95

Engr.

519 A279 24y dp ultra 40.00 12.50
a. Sheet of 1 50.00 35.00

Typo.

520 A216 30y vio bl ('52) 200.00 1.10

Photo.

521 A280 50y dk brown ('51) 150.00 .75
Hinged 95.00
c. Sheet of 1 225.00 210.00
Hinged 150.00

Engr.

521A A217 100y car lake ('52) 475.00 1.00
521B A218 500y dp blue ('52) 450.00 1.25
Nos. 509-521B (17) 1,681. 52.75

No. 510a for the 80th anniv. of Japan's postal service. On No. 512A, characters read from left to right.

Compare designs: A274 with A314c; A275 with A314a, A447, A563a; A277 with A332a; A278 with A373a; A279 with A385a; A280 with A314b and A565f.

Girl and Rabbit — A281

1951, Jan. 1 Photo. *Perf. 12*

522 A281 2y rose pink 5.00 .75

9th prize (lottery), sheet of 5, value $42.50. See No. 2655a.

Scenic Spots Issue

Skiers on Mt. Zao
A282 A283

1951, Feb. 15 *Perf. 13*

523 A282 8y olive 13.50 2.00
524 A283 24y blue 17.50 4.50

Tea Picking — A284

Mt. Fuji Seen from Nihon Plateau A285

Nihon-daira Plateau.

1951, Apr. 2

525 A284 8y olive green 14.00 2.75
526 A285 24y bright blue 82.50 20.00

Hot Springs, Hakone — A286

Lake Ashi, Hakone A287

1951, May 25

527 A286 8y chestnut brown 9.00 2.10
528 A287 24y deep blue 7.50 2.50

Senju Waterfall — A288

Ninai Waterfall A289

Akame 48 Waterfalls.

1951, June 1

529 A288 8y deep green 10.00 2.10
530 A289 24y deep blue 9.75 2.50

Pavilion, Wakanoura Bay — A290

Wakanoura Bay — A291

Wakanoura & Tomogashima.

1951, June 25

531 A290 8y brown 7.50 2.10
532 A291 24y brt blue 7.00 2.50

Uji River — A292

View from Uji Bridge A293

Perf. 13x13½, 13½x13

1951, Aug. 1 **Engr.**

533 A292 8y brown 7.50 2.10
534 A293 24y deep blue 7.00 2.50

Oura Catholic Church, Nagasaki — A294

Sofuku Temple A295

1951, Sept. 15 **Photo.** ***Perf. 13½***

535 A294 8y carmine rose 10.00 2.10
536 A295 24y dull blue 8.75 2.50

Marunuma — A296

Sugenuma A297

1951, Oct. 1

537 A296 8y rose violet 11.50 2.10
a. Imperf., pair
538 A297 24y dull blue grn 6.25 2.50

Kakuenpo (peak) — A298

Nagatoro Bridge A299

Shosenkyo Gorge.

1951, Oct. 15

539 A298 8y brown red 10.00 2.10
540 A299 24y dp Prus grn 10.50 2.50
Nos. 523-540 (18) 249.75 61.45

Boy's Head and Seedling — A300

1951, May 5 ***Perf. 13½***

541 A300 8y orange brown 22.50 2.25

Issued to publicize Children's Day, May 5, 1951.

Oirase River A301

Lake Towada A302

View from Kankodai A303

Mt. Hakkoda from Mt. Yokodake A304

1951, July 20 **Photo.** ***Perf. 13x13½***

542 A301 2y brown 2.10 .75
543 A302 8y green 7.50 1.10
544 A303 14y dark red 8.25 3.25
545 A304 24y blue 9.50 4.00
a. Souv. sheet of 4, #542-545 45.00 29.00
Nos. 542-545 (4) 27.35 9.10

Towada Natl. Park. No. 545a sold for 55y.

Chrysanthemum A305

National Flag A306

1951, Sept. 9 ***Perf. 13½***

546 A305 2y orange brown 1.90 .95
547 A306 8y slate blue & red 5.75 2.25
548 A305 24y blue green 17.00 6.00
Nos. 546-548 (3) 24.65 9.20

Signing of the peace treaty of 1951.

Putting the Shot — A307

Hockey — A308

1951, Oct. 27

549 A307 2y orange brown 3.25 1.60
550 A308 2y gray blue 3.25 1.60
a. Pair, #549-550 8.75 8.75

6th Natl. Athletic Meet, Hiroshima, 10/27-31.

Okina Mask — A309

1952, Jan. 16 **Photo.** ***Perf. 13½x13***

551 A309 5y crimson rose 9.50 .75

Sheets reproducing four of these stamps with Japanese inscriptions and floral ornament at left were awarded as sixth prize in the national lottery. Value $120.

Southern Cross from Ship — A310

Earth and Big Dipper — A311

1952, Feb. 19

552 A310 5y purple 5.25 .80
553 A311 10y dark green 13.50 2.00

75th anniv. of Japan's admission to the UPU.

Red Cross and Lilies — A312

Red Cross Nurse — A313

1952, May 1

554 A312 5y rose red & dk red 4.25 .95
555 A313 10y dk green & red 10.00 2.00
a. Red cross omitted
b. Imperf., pair

75th anniv. of the formation of the Japanese Red Cross Society.

Goldfish — A314

A314a

A314b

A314c

Japanese Serow — A315

1952 ***Perf. 13x13½***

556 A314 35y red orange 10.00 .20
a. Imperf., pair

Types of 1951
Redrawn; Zeros Omitted
Unwmk.

557 A314a 1y dark brown .40 .20
558 A314b 50y dark brown 4.50 .20

Typo.

559 A314c 4y dp cl & pale rose 1.50 .20
a. Background (pale rose) omitted

Ornamental frame and background added, denomination at upper left, Japanese characters at upper right.

Photo.

560 A315 8y brown .20 .20
Nos. 556-560 (5) 16.60 1.00

Mt. Yari — A316

Kurobe Valley — A317

Mt. Shirouma A318

Mt. Norikura A319

1952, July 5 ***Perf. 13½x13, 13x13½***

561 A316 5y brown 4.50 .50
562 A317 10y blue green 22.50 1.75
563 A318 14y bright red 5.75 3.00
564 A319 24y bright blue 9.50 3.00
a. Souv. sheet of 4, #561-564, imperf. 80.00 60.00
Nos. 561-564 (4) 42.25 8.25

Japan Alps (Chubu-Sangaku) National Park. No. 564a sold for 60y.

Yasuda Hall, Tokyo University A320

Yomei Gate, Nikko A321

1952, Oct. 1 **Engr.** ***Perf. 13***

565 A320 10y dull green 14.50 1.75

75th anniversary of the founding of Tokyo University.

1952, Oct. 15 **Photo.** ***Perf. 13x13½***

566 A321 45y blue 3.50 .20

Mountain Climber — A322

1952, Oct. 18
Dated "1952"

567 A322 5y shown 6.00 1.50
568 A322 5y Wrestlers 6.00 1.50
a. Pair, #567-568 15.00 7.50

7th Nat.l Athletic Meet, Fukushima, 10/18-22.

Mt. Azuma A323

Mt. Asahi A324

Mt. Bandai A325

Mt. Gatsun A326

Unwmk.
1952, Oct. 18 Photo. *Perf. 13*

569 A323 5y brown 3.75 .60
570 A324 10y olive grn 11.50 1.50
571 A325 14y rose red 4.50 2.25
572 A326 24y blue 10.00 4.00
a. Souv. sheet of 4, #569-572, imperf. 80.00 60.00
Nos. 569-572 (4) 29.75 8.35

Bandai-Asahi National Park.
No. 572a sold for 60y.

Kirin — A327

Flag of Crown Prince — A328

Engr. and Photo.
1952, Nov. 10 *Perf. 13½*

573 A327 5y red org & pur 1.90 .55
574 A327 10y red org & dk grn 2.25 .80
575 A328 24y deep blue 12.00 4.50
a. Souv. sheet of 3, #573-575, imperf. 90.00 175.00
Nos. 573-575 (3) 16.15 5.85

Issued to commemorate the nomination of Crown Prince Akihito as Heir Apparent.

No. 575a measures 130x129mm, and has a background design of phoenix and clouds in violet brown and blue. Sold for 50y.

Sambaso Doll — A329

First Electric Lamp in Japan — A330

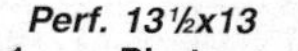

Perf. 13½x13
1953, Jan. 1 Photo. Unwmk.

576 A329 5y carmine 6.75 .75

For postage on New Year's cards, later for ordinary use.

Sheets of 4 were awarded as 6th prize in the natl. lottery. Value $80.

1953, Mar. 25

577 A330 10y brown 6.25 1.90

75th anniv. of electric lighting in Japan.

"Kintai Bridge," Print by Hiroshige — A331

Kintai Bridge as Rebuilt in 1953 # — A332

1953, May 3 *Perf. 13*

578 A331 10y chestnut 6.50 2.10
579 A332 24y blue 6.00 3.00

Kannon Type of 1951
Redrawn; Zeros Omitted

A332a

1953-54 Typo.

580 A332a 10y red brn & lilac 4.00 .20
a. Booklet pane 10 + 2 labels (souvenir) ('54) 175.00 125.00
b. Bklt. pane 10 + 2 labels ('54) 67.50 60.00

No. 580a was issued in honor of Philatelic Week 1954. The inscriptions on the two labels are arranged in two columns of boldface characters.

On No. 580b, the left-hand label inscriptions are arranged in three columns of mixed heavy and thin characters.

See Nos. 611a-611b and 672.

Lake Shikotsu, Hokkaido A333

Mt. Yotei A334

1953, July 25 Photo. *Perf. 13*

581 A333 5y ultra 2.10 .55
582 A334 10y green 6.00 1.10
a. Souv. sheet of 2, #581-582, imperf., no gum 37.50 32.50

Shikotsu-Toya National Park.
No. 582a sold for 20 yen.

Akita Dog A335

Cormorant Fishing A336

1953 Unwmk.

583 A335 2y gray .20 .20

Engr.

584 A336 100y dark red 25.00 .20
a. Imperf., pair 525.00

See No. 1622.

Futamigaura Beach — A337

Namikiri Coast A338

1953, Oct. 2 Photo.

585 A337 5y red 1.90 .55
586 A338 10y blue 3.75 1.10
a. Souv. sheet of 2, #585-586, imperf., no gum 21.00 17.50

Ise-Shima National Park.

Phoenix — A339

Design: 10y, Japanese crane in flight.

1953, Oct. 12 Engr. *Perf. 12½*

587 A339 5y brown carmine 2.75 1.10

Photo.

588 A339 10y dark blue 5.50 1.90

Nos. 587-588 were issued on the occasion of the return of Crown Prince Akihito from his visit to Europe and America. Issued in sheets of 20 with marginal inscription.

Rugby Match — A340

Judo — A341

1953, Oct. 22 *Perf. 13½*

589 A340 5y black 5.75 1.25
590 A341 5y blue green 5.75 1.25
a. Pair, #589-590 13.50 7.50

8th Natl. Athletic Meet, Matsuyama, Oct. 22-26.

Sky and Top of Observatory A342

1953, Oct. 29

591 A342 10y dk gray blue 9.00 1.50

75th anniversary of the Tokyo Astronomical Observatory.

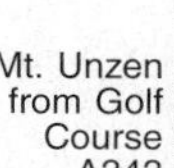

Mt. Unzen from Golf Course A343

Mt. Unzen from Chijiwa Beach A344

1953, Nov. 20 *Perf. 13*

592 A343 5y red 1.75 .55
593 A344 10y blue 4.50 1.10
a. Souv. sheet of 2, #592-593, imperf., no gum 20.00 17.50

Unzen National Park.

Toy Horse — A345

Racing Skaters — A346

1953, Dec. 25 *Perf. 13½x13*

594 A345 5y rose 5.25 .55

Issued to pay postage on New Year's cards, later for ordinary use. A sheet reproducing four of these stamps was awarded as sixth prize in the national lottery. Value $37.50.

1954, Jan. 16

595 A346 10y blue 4.50 1.40

World Speed Skating Matches for Men, Sapporo City, Jan. 16-17, 1954.

Golden Hall, Chusonji Temple A347

Thread, Pearls, Gears, Buttons and Globe A348

1954, Jan. 20

596 A347 20y olive green .95 .20

1954, Apr. 10

597 A348 10y dark red 3.25 1.00

International Trade Fair, Osaka, Apr. 10-23.

Little Cuckoo A349

Wrestlers A350

1954, May 10 *Perf. 13x13½*

598 A349 3y blue green .20 .20
a. Imperf., pair 300.00

For stamp inscribed "NIPPON," see No. 1067.

1954, May 22 Engr.

599 A350 10y deep green 2.75 1.00

World Free Style Wrestling Championship Matches, Tokyo, 1954.

Mt. Asama A351

Mt. Tanikawa A352

1954, June 25 ***Perf. 13***

600 A351 5y dk gray brn 2.00 .55
601 A352 10y dk blue grn 3.50 1.10
a. Souvenir sheet of 2, #600-601, no gum 19.00 15.00

Jo-Shin-etsu National Park.

Table Tennis — A353

Archery — A354

1954, Aug. 22 **Engr.** ***Perf. 12***

602 A353 5y dull brown 4.50 1.00
603 A354 5y gray green 4.50 1.00
a. Pair, #602-603 9.50 5.75

9th Natl. Athletic Meet, Sapporo, Aug. 22-26.

Morse Telegraph Instrument A355

ITU Monument A356

1954, Oct. 13 ***Perf. 13x13½, 13½x13***

604 A355 5y dark purple brown 1.90 .55
605 A356 10y deep blue 5.00 1.10

75th anniv. of Japanese membership in the ITU.

Daruma Doll — A357

1954, Dec. 20 **Photo.** ***Perf. 13½x13***

606 A357 5y black & red 5.25 .55

Sheets reproducing four of these stamps with Japanese inscriptions and ornaments were awarded as fifth prize in the national lottery. Value $37.50.

Mountain Stream, Tama Gorge — A358

Chichibu Mountains — A359

1955, Mar. 1 **Engr.** ***Perf. 13***

607 A358 5y blue 1.50 .55
608 A359 10y red brown 1.90 .75
a. Souv. sheet of 2, #607-608, imperf., no gum 21.00 17.50

Chichibu-Tama National Park.

Bridge and Iris — A360

1955, Mar. 15 ***Perf. 13x13½***

609 A360 500y deep plum 65.00 .40

Paper Carp as Flown on Boys' Day A361

Mandarin Ducks A362

Unwmk.

1955, May 16 **Photo.** ***Perf. 13***

610 A361 10y multicolored 4.25 1.10

15th congress of the International Chamber of Commerce, Tokyo, May 16-21, 1955.

1955-64

611 A362 5y lt bl & red brn .25 .20
a. Bklt. pane, 4 #611, 8 #580 ('59) 25.00
b. Bklt. pane, 4 #611, 8 #725 ('63) 27.50 17.00
c. Bklt. pane of 4 ('64) 4.25 2.75
d. Imperf., pair 700.00

See Nos. 738, 881d, 914b.

Benten Cape — A363

Jodo Beach A364

1955, Sept. 30

612 A363 5y deep green 1.40 .45
613 A364 10y rose lake 1.90 .75
a. Souv. sheet of 2, #612-613, imperf., no gum 22.50 17.50

Rikuchu-Kaigan National Park.
No. 613a sold for 20y.

Gymnastics A365

Runners A366

1955, Oct. 30 **Engr.**

614 A365 5y brown lake 2.00 .75
615 A366 5y bluish black 2.00 .75
a. Pair, #614-615 6.00 5.00

10th National Athletic Meet, Kanagawa Prefecture.
See Nos. 639-640, 657.

"A Girl Blowing Glass Toy," by Utamaro A367

1955, Nov. 1 **Photo.**

616 A367 10y multicolored 10.00 5.75

150th anniv. of the death of Utamaro, woodcut artist, and to publicize Philatelic Week, Nov. 1955. Issued in sheets of 10.

Kokeshi Dolls — A368

Table Tennis — A369

1955, Dec. 30 **Unwmk.** ***Perf. 13***

617 A368 5y olive grn & red 1.90 .25

Sheets reproducing four of these stamps, were awarded as fifth prize in the New Year's lottery. Value $27.50.

1956, Apr. 2 ***Perf. 13x13½***

618 A369 10y red brown 1.25 .75

Intl. Table Tennis Championship, Tokyo, 4/2-11.

Judo — A370

1956, May 2 ***Perf. 13***

619 A370 10y green & lilac 1.50 .75

Issued to publicize the first World Judo Championship Meet, Tokyo, May 3, 1956.

Boy and Girl with Paper Carp A371

1956, May 5

620 A371 5y lt blue & blk 1.10 .55

Establishment of World Children's Day, 5/5/56.

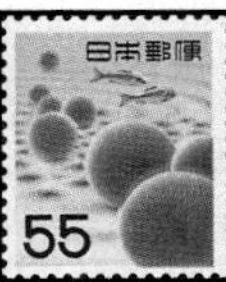

Water Plants, Lake Akan A372

Big Purple Butterfly A373

1956 **Unwmk.** ***Perf. 13***

621 A372 55y lt blue, grn & blk 12.50 .55
622 A373 75y multicolored 7.00 .55

See Nos. 887A, 917.

Castle Type of 1951
Redrawn; Zeros Omitted

A373a

1956 **Engr.** ***Perf. 13½x13***

623 A373a 14y gray olive 5.00 1.75

Osezaki Promontory — A374

Kujuku Island A375

1956, Oct. 1 **Photo.**

624 A374 5y red brown .95 .45

Engr. & Photo.

625 A375 10y lt blue & indigo 1.40 .75

Saikai National Park.
No. 625a sold for 20y.

Palace Moat and Modern Tokyo A376

1956, Oct. 1 **Engr.**

626 A376 10y dull purple 1.90 .75

500th anniv. of the founding of Tokyo.

Sakuma Dam — A377

1956, Oct. 15 **Unwmk.** ***Perf. 13***

627 A377 10y dark blue 1.90 .75

Completion of Sakuma Dam.

Long Jump A378

Basketball A379

1956, Oct. 28 *Perf. 13½x13*
628 A378 5y brown violet 1.10 .55
629 A379 5y steel blue 1.10 .55
a. Pair, #628-629 2.25 2.50

11th Natl. Athletic Meet, Hyogo Prefecture. See No. 658.

Kabuki Actor Ebizo Ichikawa by Sharaku A380

1956, Nov. 1 **Photo.** *Perf. 13*
630 A380 10y multicolored 8.50 5.50

Stamp Week. Sheets of 10.

Mount Manaslu A381

1956, Nov. 3
631 A381 10y multicolored 3.00 1.60

Japanese expedition which climbed Mount Manaslu in the Himalayas on May 9 and 11, 1956.

Electric Locomotive and Hiroshige's "Yui Stage" — A382

1956, Nov. 19 **Unwmk.** *Perf. 13*
632 A382 10y dk ol bis, blk & grn 4.00 1.60

Electrification of Tokaido Line.

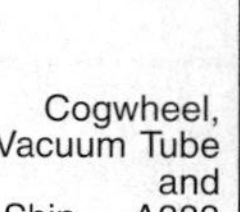

Cogwheel, Vacuum Tube and Ship — A383

1956, Dec. 18 **Engr.**
633 A383 10y ultra .90 .75

Japanese Machinery Floating Fair.

Toy Whale — A384

United Nations Emblem A385

1956, Dec. 20 **Photo.**
634 A384 5y multicolored 1.25 .20
a. Imperf., pair

Sheets reproducing four of these stamps, with inscriptions and ornaments, were awarded as sixth prize in the national lottery. Value $13.50.

Photogravure and Engraved
1957, Mar. 8 **Unwmk.** *Perf. 13½x13*
635 A385 10y lt blue & dk car .70 .55

Japan's admission to the UN, Dec. 18, 1956.

Temple Type of 1950 Redrawn; Zeros Omitted

A385a

1957-59 **Engr.** *Perf. 13x13½*
636 A385a 24y violet 14.00 2.25
636A A385a 30y rose lilac ('59) 50.00 .40
b. Imperf., pair —

IGY Emblem, Penguin and "Soya" — A386

Atomic Reactor — A387

1957, July 1 **Photo.** *Perf. 13*
637 A386 10y blue, yel & blk .75 .45

International Geophysical Year.

1957, Sept. 18 **Engr.** *Perf. 13*
638 A387 10y dark purple .45 .25

Completion of Japan's atomic reactor at Tokai-Mura, Ibaraki Prefecture.

Sports Type of 1955

No. 639, Girl on parallel bars. No. 640, Boxers.

1957, Oct. 26 **Unwmk.** *Perf. 13*
639 A366 5y ultra .35 .20
640 A366 5y dark red .35 .20
a. Pair, #639-640 .90 .75

12th Natl. Athletic Meet, Shizuoka Prefecture.

"Girl Bouncing Ball," by Suzuki Harunobu A388

1957, Nov. 1 **Photo.**
641 A388 10y multicolored 1.50 1.25

1957 Stamp Week. Issued in sheets of 10. See Nos. 646, 671, 728, 757.

Lake Okutama and Ogochi Dam — A389

1957, Nov. 26 **Engr.** *Perf. 13½*
642 A389 10y ultra .30 .20

Completion of Ogochi Dam, part of the Tokyo water supply system.

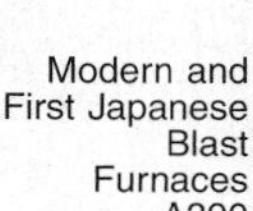

Modern and First Japanese Blast Furnaces A390

Toy Dog (Inu-hariko) — A391

1957, Dec. 1 **Photo.** **Unwmk.**
643 A390 10y orange & dk pur .25 .20

Centenary of Japan's iron industry.

1957, Dec. 20 *Perf. 13½x13*
644 A391 5y multicolored .25 .20

New Year 1958. Sheets reproducing 4 #644, with inscriptions and ornaments, were awarded as 5th prize in the New Year lottery. Value $5.

Shimonoseki-Moji Tunnel — A392

1958, Mar. 9 *Perf. 13x13½*
645 A392 10y multicolored .25 .20

Completion of the Kan-Mon Underwater Highway connecting Honshu and Kyushu Islands.

Stamp Week Type of 1957

Design: 10y, Woman with Umbrella, woodcut by Kiyonaga.

1958, Apr. 20 **Unwmk.** *Perf. 13*
646 A388 10y multicolored .50 .20

Stamp Week, 1958. Sheets of 10.

Statue of Ii Naosuke and Harbor A393

Unwmk.
1958, May 10 **Engr.** *Perf. 13*
647 A393 10y gray blue & car .25 .20

Cent. of the opening of the ports of Yokohama, Nagasaki and Hakodate to foreign powers.

National Stadium — A394

3rd Asian Games, Tokyo: 10y, Torch and emblem. 14y, Runner. 24y, Woman diver.

1958, May 24 **Photo.**
648 A394 5y bl grn, bis & pink .20 .20
649 A394 10y multicolored .25 .30
650 A394 14y multicolored .30 .25
651 A394 24y multicolored .35 .30
Nos. 648-651 (4) 1.10 1.05

Kasato Maru, Map and Brazilian Flag A395

1958, June 18
652 A395 10y multicolored .25 .20

50 years of Japanese emigration to Brazil.

Sado Island and Local Dancer A396

Mt. Yahiko and Echigo Plain — A397

1958, Aug. 20 **Unwmk.** *Perf. 13*
653 A396 10y multicolored .50 .20
654 A397 10y multicolored .45 .20

Sado-Yahiko Quasi-National Park.

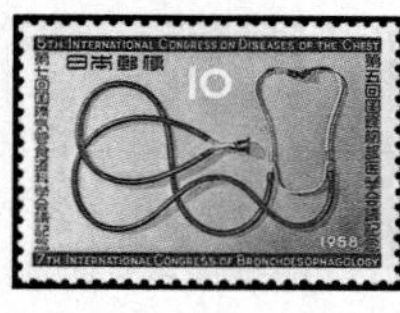

Stethoscope A398

1958, Sept. 7 **Photo.** *Perf. 13*
655 A398 10y Prussian green .25 .20

5th Intl. Cong. on Diseases of the Chest and the 7th Intl. Cong. of Bronchoesophagology.

"Kyoto" (Sanjo Bridge), Print by Hiroshige A399

1958, Oct. 5
656 A399 24y multicolored 2.00 .70

Issued for International Letter Writing Week, Oct. 5-11. See No. 679.

Sports Types of 1955-56

Designs: No. 657, Weight lifter. No. 658, Girl badminton player.

1958, Oct. 19 **Engr.**
657 A365 5y gray blue .25 .20
658 A379 5y claret .25 .20
a. Pair, #657-658 .75 .75

13th Natl. Athletic Meet, Toyama Prefecture.

Keio University and Yukichi Fukuzawa — A400

1958, Nov. 8 **Engr.** *Perf. 13½*
659 A400 10y magenta .25 .20

Centenary of Keio University.

Globe and Playing Children A401

1958, Nov. 23 **Photo.** *Perf. 13*
660 A401 10y deep green .25 .25

9th Intl. Conf. of Social Work and the 2nd Intl. Study Conf. on Child Welfare.

Flame: Symbol of Human Rights — A402

1958, Dec. 10 Unwmk. *Perf. 13*
661 A402 10y multicolored .25 .25

10th anniv. of the signing of the Universal Declaration of Human Rights.

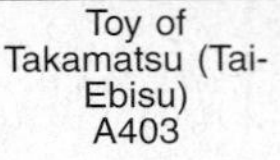

Toy of Takamatsu (Tai-Ebisu) A403

Tractor and Map of Kojima Bay A404

1958, Dec. 20 *Perf. 13½*
662 A403 5y multicolored .45 .20

New Year 1959. Sheets reproducing 4 #662, with inscriptions and ornaments, were awarded as prizes in the New Year lottery. Size: 103x89mm. Value $5.

1959, Feb. 1 *Perf. 12½*
663 A404 10y claret & bister brn .25 .25

Completion of the embankment closing Kojima Bay for reclamation.

Karst Plateau A405

Akiyoshi Cave — A406

1959, Mar. 16 Photo. *Perf. 13½*
664 A405 10y green, bl & ocher .80 .20
665 A406 10y multicolored 1.40 .20

Akiyoshidai Quasi-National Park.

Map of Southeast Asia — A407

1959, Mar. 27
666 A407 10y deep carmine .25 .25

Asian Cultural Cong., Tokyo, Mar. 27-31, marking the 2,500th anniv. of the death of Buddha.

Ceremonial Fan — A408

Prince Akihito and Princess Michiko — A409

Photogravure; Portraits Engraved

1959, Apr. 10
667 A408 5y magenta & violet .25 .20
668 A409 10y red brn & dull pur .50 .25
a. Souv. sheet of 2, #667-668, imperf. 4.50 4.50
669 A408 20y org brn & brn .75 .25
670 A409 30y yel grn & dk grn 2.25 .30
Nos. 667-670 (4) 3.75 1.00

Wedding of Crown Prince Akihito and Princess Michiko, Apr. 10, 1959.

Type of 1957

Women Reading Poetry, print by Eishi Fujiwara.

1959, May 20 Photo. *Perf. 13*
671 A388 10y multicolored 2.10 .90

Stamp Week. Issued in sheets of 10.

Redrawn Kannon Type of 1953
Coil Stamp
Perf. 13 Horiz.

1959, Jan. 20 Typo. Unwmk.
672 A332a 10y red brn & lilac 18.00 *20.00*

Measuring Glass, Tape Measure and Scales — A410

Nurses Carrying Stretcher A411

1959, June 5 Photo. *Perf. 13*
673 A410 10y lt blue & blk .25 .25

Adoption of the metric system.

1959, June 24
674 A411 10y olive grn & red .25 .25

Centenary of the Red Cross idea.

Mt. Fuji and Lake Motosu A412

1959, July 21 Engr. *Perf. 13*
675 A412 10y green, bl & sepia .45 .25

Establishment of Natural Park Day and 1st Natural Park Convention, Yumoto, Nikko, July 21, 1959.

Ao Cave Area of Yabakei A413

Hita, Mt. Hiko and Great Cormorant A414

1959, Sept. 25 Photo. *Perf. 13*
676 A413 10y multicolored .90 .25
677 A414 10y multicolored 1.00 .25

Yaba-Hita-Hiko Quasi National Park.

Golden Dolphin, Nagoya Castle — A415

Japanese Crane, IATA Emblem — A416

1959, Oct. 1
678 A415 10y brt bl, gold & blk .50 .25

350th anniversary of Nagoya.

Hiroshige Type of 1958

Design: 30y, "Kuwana," the 7-ri Crossing Point, print by Hiroshige.

1959, Oct. 4 Unwmk.
679 A399 30y multicolored 6.75 1.10

Intl. Letter Writing Week, Oct. 4-10.

1959, Oct. 12 Engr.
680 A416 10y brt grnsh blue .35 .25

15th General Meeting of the International Air Transport Association.

Shoin Yoshida and PTA Symbol — A417

Throwing the Hammer — A418

1959, Oct. 27 Photo. *Perf. 13*
681 A417 10y brown .25 .20

Centenary of the death of Shoin Yoshida, educator, and in connection with the Parent-Teachers Association convention.

1959, Oct. 25 Engr.

Design: No. 683, Woman Fencer.

682 A418 5y gray blue .35 .20
683 A418 5y olive bister .35 .20
a. Pair, #682-683 .75 .75

14th National Athletic Meet, Tokyo.

Globes A419

1959, Nov. 2 Photo.
684 A419 5y brown red .25 .20

15th session of GATT (General Agreement on Tariffs & Trade), Tokyo, Oct. 12-Nov. 21.

Toy Mouse of Kanazawa — A420

1959, Dec. 19 Unwmk. *Perf. 13½*
685 A420 5y gold, red, grn & blk .50 .20

New Year 1960. Sheets reproducing 4 #685, with marginal inscription and ornaments, were awarded as prizes in natl. lottery. Value $5.50.

Yukio Ozaki and Clock Tower, Ozaki Memorial Hall — A421

Nara Period Artwork, Shosoin Treasure House — A422

1960, Feb. 25 Photo. *Perf. 13½*
686 A421 10y red brn & dk brn .25 .20

Completion of Ozaki Memorial Hall, erected in memory of Yukio Ozaki (1858-1954), statesman.

1960, Mar. 10
687 A422 10y olive gray .25 .20

Transfer of the capital to Nara, 1250th anniv.

Scenic Trio Issue

Bay of Matsushima A423

Ama-no-hashidate (Heavenly Bridge) — A424

Miyajima from the Sea — A425

1960 Engr.
688 A423 10y maroon & bl grn 1.25 .45
689 A424 10y green & lt bl 1.60 .45
690 A425 10y vio blk & bl grn 1.60 .45
Nos. 688-690 (3) 4.45 1.35

Issued: #688, 3/15; #689, 7/15; #690, 11/15.

Takeshima, off Gamagori A426

1960, Mar. 20 Photo. *Perf. 13½*
691 A426 10y multicolored .75 .25

Mikawa Bay Quasi-National Park.

Poetess Isé, 13th Century Painting — A427

1960, Apr. 20 Unwmk. *Perf. 13*
692 A427 10y multicolored 1.60 1.60

Stamp Week, 1960.

Kanrin Maru — A428

Design: 30y, Pres. Buchanan receiving first Japanese diplomatic mission.

1960, May 17 **Engr.**
693 A428 10y bl grn & brn .50 .25
694 A428 30y car & indigo 1.10 .40

Cent. of the Japan-US Treaty of Amity and Commerce. Nos. 694 and 693 form pages of an open book when placed next to each other. Souvenir sheet is No. 703.

Crested Ibis (Toki) — A429

Radio Waves Encircling Globe — A430

1960, May 24 **Photo.** ***Perf. 13½***
695 A429 10y gray, pink & red .45 .30

12th Intl. Congress for Bird Preservation.

1960, June 1 **Engr.**
696 A430 10y carmine rose .30 .20

25th anniv. of the Intl. Radio Program by the Japanese Broadcasting Corporation.

Flower Garden (Gensei Kaen) — A431

1960, June 15 **Photo.**
697 A431 10y multicolored .90 .30

Abashiri Quasi-National Park.

Cape Ashizuri A432

1960, Aug. 1 **Unwmk.**
698 A432 10y multicolored .80 .30

Ashizuri Quasi-National Park.

Rainbow Spanning Pacific, Cherry Blossoms and Pineapples A433

Henri Farman's Biplane and Jet A434

1960, Aug. 20 ***Perf. 13½***
699 A433 10y multicolored .55 .25

75th anniversary of Japanese contract emigration to Hawaii.

1960, Sept. 20 ***Perf. 13***
700 A434 10y brn & chlky bl .45 .20

50th anniversary of Japanese aviation.

Seat Plan of Diet — A435

"Red Fuji" by Hokusai and Diet Building — A436

1960, Sept. 27
701 A435 5y indigo & org .25 .20
702 A436 10y blue & red brn .60 .25

49th Inter-Parliamentary Conference.

Souvenir Sheet

1960, Sept. 27 **Engr.**
703 A428 Sheet of 2, #693-694 22.50 22.50

Visit of Prince Akihito and Princess Michiko to the US.

"Night Snow at Kambara," by Hiroshige A437

1960, Oct. 9 **Photo.**
704 A437 30y multicolored 14.00 3.75

Issued for International Letter Writing Week, Oct. 9-15. See Nos. 735, 769.

Japanese Fencing (Kendo) — A438

Okayama Astrophysical Observatory A439

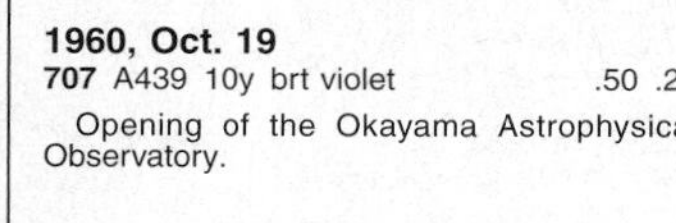

No. 706, Girl gymnast and vaulting horse.

1960, Oct. 23 **Engr.** ***Perf. 13½***
705 A438 5y dull blue .35 .20
706 A438 5y rose violet .35 .20
a. Pair, #705-706 .90 .90

15th National Athletic Meet, Kumamoto.

1960, Oct. 19
707 A439 10y brt violet .50 .20

Opening of the Okayama Astrophysical Observatory.

Lt. Naoshi Shirase and Map of Antarctica — A440

Little Red Calf of Aizu, Gold Calf of Iwate — A441

1960, Nov. 29 **Photo.**
708 A440 10y fawn & black .45 .20

50th anniv. of the 1st Japanese Antarctic expedition.

1960, Dec. 20 **Unwmk.** ***Perf. 13½***
709 A441 5y multicolored .50 .20

New Year 1961. Sheets reproducing 4 #709 were awarded as prizes in the New Year lottery. Size: 102x89mm. Value $6.

Diet Building at Night — A442

Opening of First Session — A443

1960, Dec. 24 **Photo.; Engr. (10y)**
710 A442 5y gray & dk bl .35 .20
711 A443 10y carmine .45 .20

70th anniversary of the Japanese Diet.

Narcissus — A444

Nojima Cape Lighthouse and Fisherwomen A445

#713, Plum blossoms. #714, Camellia japonica. #715, Cherry blossoms. #716, Peony. #717, Iris. #718, Lily. #719, Morning glory. #720, Bellflower. #721, Gentian. #722, Chrysanthemum. #723, Camellia sasanqua.

1961 **Photo.** ***Perf. 13½***
712 A444 10y lilac, yel & grn 3.00 .70
713 A444 10y brown, grn & yel 1.40 .70
714 A444 10y lem, grn, pink & yel 1.00 .70
715 A444 10y gray, brn, pink, yel & blk 1.00 .70
716 A444 10y blk, grn, pink & yel .90 .65
717 A444 10y gray, pur, grn & yel .55 .35
718 A444 10y gray grn, yel & brn .40 .30
719 A444 10y lt bl, grn & lil .40 .30
720 A444 10y lt yel grn, vio & grn .40 .30
721 A444 10y org, vio bl & grn .40 .30
722 A444 10y blue, yel & grn .40 .30
723 A444 10y sl, pink, yel & grn .40 .30
Nos. 712-723 (12) 10.25 5.60

1961, Mar. 15
724 A445 10y multicolored .50 .25

South Boso Quasi-National Park.

Cherry Blossoms A446

Hisoka Maeshima A447

Unwmk.

1961, Apr. 1 **Photo.** ***Perf. 13***
725 A446 10y lilac rose & gray .30 .20
a. Lilac rose omitted 300.00
b. Imperf., pair 500.00
c. Booklet pane of 4 5.50 2.25
d. Gray omitted 350.00

See No. 611b.

Coil Stamp

1961, Apr. 25 ***Perf. 13 Horiz.***
726 A446 10y lil rose & gray 5.00 1.90

1961, Apr. 20 ***Perf. 13***
727 A447 10y olive & black 1.10 .20

90th anniv. of Japan's modern postal service from Tokyo to Osaka, inaugurated by Deputy Postmaster General Hisoka Maeshima.

Type of 1957

"Dancing Girl" from a "Screen of Dancers."

1961, Apr. 20 ***Perf. 13½***
728 A388 10y multicolored .90 .60

Stamp Week, 1961. Sheets of 10 (5x2).

Lake Biwa — A448

1961, Apr. 25
729 A448 10y blk, dk bl & yel grn .50 .25

Lake Biwa Quasi-National Park.

Rotary Emblem and People of Various Races — A449

1961, May 29 **Engr.** ***Perf. 13***
730 A449 10y gray & orange .25 .20

52nd convention of Rotary Intl., Tokyo, May 29-June 1, 1961.

Faucet, Wheat, Insulator & Cogwheel A450

Sun, Earth and Meridian A451

1961, July 7 **Photo.** ***Perf. 13½***
731 A450 10y violet & aqua .30 .20

Aichi irrigation system, Kiso river.

1961, July 12
732 A451 10y yellow, red & blk .30 .20

75th anniv. of Japanese standard time.

Parasol Dance on Dunes of Tottori
A452

1961, Aug. 15
733 A452 10y multicolored .55 .25

San'in Kaigan Quasi-National Park.

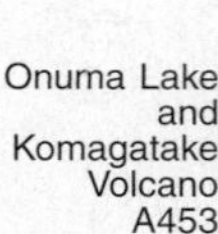

Onuma Lake and Komagatake Volcano
A453

Gymnast on Horizontal Bar — A454

1961, Sept. 15
734 A453 10y grn, red brn & bl .60 .25

Onuma Quasi-National Park.

Hiroshige Type of 1960

1961, Oct. 8 ***Perf. 13***

Design: 30y, "Hakone," print by Hiroshige from the 53 Stages of the Tokaido.

735 A437 30y multicolored 5.75 4.50

Intl. Letter Writing Week, Oct. 8-14.

1961, Oct. 8 Engr. ***Perf. 13½***

Design: No. 737, Women rowing.

736 A454 5y blue green .30 .20
737 A454 5y ultra .30 .20
a. Pair, #736-737 .75 .75

16th National Athletic Meet, Akita.
See Nos. 770-771, 816-817, 852-853.

Duck Type of 1955
Coil Stamp

1961, Oct. 2 Photo. ***Perf. 13 Horiz.***
738 A362 5y lt bl & red brn 2.50 2.00

National Diet Library and Book — A455

Papier Maché Tiger — A456

1961, Nov. 1 ***Perf. 13½***
739 A455 10y dp ultra & gold .25 .20

Opening of the new Natl. Diet Library, Tokyo.

1961, Dec. 15 ***Perf. 13½***
740 A456 5y multicolored .40 .20

New Year 1962. Sheets reproducing 4 #740 were awarded as 5th prize in the New Year lottery. Size: 102x90, Value $6.

Mt. Fuji from Lake Ashi — A457

Minokake-Iwa at Irozaki
A458

Mt. Fuji from Mitsu Pass — A459

Mt. Fuji from Cape of Ose — A460

1962, Jan. 16 Unwmk. Photo.
741 A457 5y deep green .40 .20
742 A458 5y dark blue .40 .20
743 A459 10y red brown 1.10 .25
744 A460 10y black 1.10 .30
Nos. 741-744 (4) 3.00 .95

Fuji-Hakone-Izu National Park.

Omishima
A461

1962, Feb. 15 ***Perf. 13½***
745 A461 10y ultra, red & yel .40 .25

Kitanagato-Kaigan Quasi-National Park.

Perotrochus Hirasei
A462

Sacred Bamboo
A463

Shari-den of Engakuji
A464

Yomei Gate, Nikko
A465

Noh Mask — A466

Copper Pheasant
A466a

Wind God, Fujin, by Sotatsu
A467

Japanese Crane
A468

Mythical Winged Woman, Chusonji
A469

1962-65 Unwmk. ***Perf. 13***
746 A462 4y dk brn & red ('63) .20 .20
747 A463 6y gray grn & car .20 .20
748 A464 30y violet black 3.50 .20
749 A465 40y rose red 4.00 .20
750 A466 70y yel brn & blk ('65) 1.75 .20
751 A466a 80y crim & brn ('65) .95 .20
752 A467 90y brt blue grn 24.00 .25
753 A468 100y pink & blk ('63) 7.50 .20
754 A469 120y purple 7.25 .55
Nos. 746-754 (9) 49.35 2.20

See Nos. 888, 888A, 1076, 1079, 1257.

Coil Stamp
Perf. 13 Horiz.
755 A464 30y dull violet ('63) 3.50 2.10

Hinamatsuri, Doll Festival — A470

1962, Mar. 3 ***Perf. 13½***
756 A470 10y brn, blk, bl & car .85 .40

The Doll Festival is celebrated Mar. 3 in honor of young girls.

Type of 1957

Design: Dancer from "Flower Viewing Party" by Naganobu Kano.

1962, Apr. 20 Photo. ***Perf. 13½***
757 A388 10y multicolored .90 .75

Stamp Week, 1962. Sheets of 10.

Sakurajima Volcano and Kagoshima Bay — A471

1962, Apr. 30
758 A471 10y multicolored .30 .25

Kinkowan Quasi-National Park.

Mount Kongo
A472

1962, May 15 ***Perf. 13½***
759 A472 10y gray bl, dk grn & sal .30 .25

Kongo-Ikoma Quasi-National Park.

Suigo Park Scene and Iris — A473

1962, June 1 ***Perf. 13½***
760 A473 10y multicolored .30 .25

Suigo Quasi-National Park.

Train Emerging from Hokuriku Tunnel — A474

1962, June 10 Photo.
761 A474 10y olive gray .65 .30

Opening of Hokuriku Tunnel between Tsuruga and Imajo, Fukui Prefecture.

Star Festival (Tanabata Matsuri) — A475

Boy Scout Hat on Map of Southeast Asia — A476

1962, July 7 Unwmk. ***Perf. 13½***
762 A475 10y multicolored .25 .20

The Tanabata festival is celebrated on the evening of July 7.

1962, Aug. 3
763 A476 10y red org, blk & bis .25 .20

Asian Boy Scout Jamboree, Mt. Fuji, Aug. 3-7.

Ozegahara Swampland and Mt. Shibutsu
A477

Fumes on Mt. Chausu, Nasu — A478

Lake Chuzenji and Mt. Nantai
A479

Senryu-kyo Narrows, Shiobara
A480

1962, Sept. 1
764 A477 5y greenish blue .25 .20
765 A478 5y maroon .25 .20
766 A479 10y purple .35 .20
767 A480 10y olive .35 .20
Nos. 764-767 (4) 1.20 .80

Nikko National Park.

Wakato Suspension Bridge — A481

Perf. 13½x13

1962, Sept. 26 Engr. Unwmk.
768 A481 10y rose red .55 .25

Opening of Wakato Bridge over Dokai Bay in North Kyushu.

Hiroshige Type of 1960

Design: 40y, "Nihonbashi," print by Hiroshige from the 53 Stages of the Tokaido.

1962, Oct. 7 Photo. ***Perf. 13***
769 A437 40y multicolored 4.50 3.75

Intl. Letter Writing Week, Oct. 7-13.

Sports Type of 1961

Design: No. 770, Woman softball pitcher. No. 771, Rifle shooting.

1962, Oct. 21 Engr. *Perf. 13½*

770 A454 5y bluish black .25 .20
771 A454 5y brown violet .25 .20
a. Pair, #770-771 .50 .50

17th National Athletic Meeting, Okayama.

Shichi-go-san Festival — A482

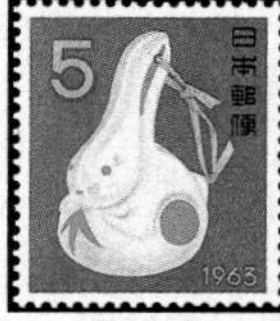

Rabbit Bell — A483

1962, Nov. 15 Photo. *Perf. 13½*

772 A482 10y multicolored .25 .20

This festival for 7 and 3-year-old girls and 5-year-old boys is celebrated on Nov. 15.

1962, Dec. 15

773 A483 5y multicolored .35 .20

New Year 1963. Sheets reproducing 4 #773 were awarded as prizes in the New Year lottery. Value $6.
See No. 2655b.

Mt. Ishizuchi A484

1963, Jan. 11 Unwmk. *Perf. 13½*

774 A484 10y multicolored .25 .20

Ishizuchi Quasi-National Park.

Setsubun, Spring Festival, Bean Scattering Ceremony A485

Map of City, Birds, Ship and Factory A486

1963, Feb. 3 Photo.

775 A485 10y multicolored .25 .20

1963, Feb. 10

776 A486 10y chocolate .25 .20

Consolidation of the communities of Moji, Kokura, Wakamatsu, Yawata and Tobata into Kita-Kyushu City.

"Frost Flowers" on Mt. Fugen A487

Amakusa Island and Mt. Unzen A488

1963, Feb. 15

777 A487 5y gray blue .20 .20
778 A488 10y carmine rose .25 .20

Unzen-Amakusa National Park.

Green Pond, Midorigaike A489

Hakusan Range A490

Perf. 13½

1963, Mar. 1 Unwmk. Photo.

779 A489 5y violet brown .20 .20
780 A490 10y dark green .25 .20

Hakusan National Park.

Keya-no-Oto Rock — A491

1963, Mar. 15

781 A491 10y multicolored .25 .20

Genkai Quasi-National Park.

Wheat Emblem and Globe — A492

1963, Mar. 21

782 A492 10y dark green .20 .20

FAO "Freedom from Hunger" campaign.

"Girl Reading Letter," Yedo Screen A493

1963, Apr. 20 *Perf. 13½*

783 A493 10y multicolored .45 .45

Issued to publicize Stamp Week, 1963.

World Map and Centenary Emblem A494

1963, May 8

784 A494 10y multicolored .20 .20

Centenary of the International Red Cross.

Globe and Leaf with Symbolic River System — A495

1963, May 15 Photo.

785 A495 10y blue .20 .20

5th Congress of the Intl. Commission on Irrigation and Drainage.

Ito-dake, Asahi Range A496

Lake Hibara and Mt. Bandai A497

1963, May 25 Unwmk. *Perf. 13½*

786 A496 5y green .20 .20
787 A497 10y red brown .20 .20

Bandai-Asahi National Park.

Lidth's Jay — A498

#789, Rock ptarmigan. #790, Eastern turtle dove. #791, Japanese white stork. #792, Bush warbler. #792A, Meadow bunting.

1963-64 *Perf. 13½*

Design and Inscription

788	A498	10y	lt green	.60	.40
789	A498	10y	blue	.25	.20
790	A498	10y	pale yellow	.25	.20
791	A498	10y	grnsh blue ('64)	.25	.20
792	A498	10y	green ('64)	.25	.20
792A	A498	10y	lt rose brn ('64)	.25	.20
	Nos. 788-792A (6)			1.85	1.40

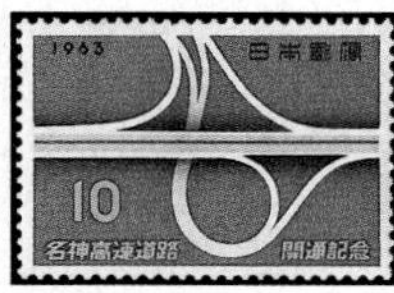

Intersection at Ritto, Shiga — A499

Girl Scout and Flag — A500

1963, July 15 Unwmk. *Perf. 13½*

793 A499 10y bl grn, blk & org .20 .20

Opening of the Nagoya-Kobe expressway, linking Nagoya with Kyoto, Osaka and Kobe.

1963, Aug. 1 Photo.

794 A500 10y multicolored .20 .20

Asian Girl Scout and Girl Guides Camp, Togakushi Heights, Nagano, Aug. 1-7.

View of Nashu A501

Whirlpool at Naruto A502

1963, Aug. 20

795 A501 5y olive bister .20 .20
796 A502 10y dark green .20 .20

Inland Sea National Park.

Lake Shikaribetsu, Hokkaido A503

Mt. Kurodake from Sounkyo Valley — A504

1963, Sept. 1 Unwmk. *Perf. 13½*

797 A503 5y deep Prus blue .20 .20
798 A504 10y rose violet .20 .20

Daisetsuzan National Park.

Parabolic Antenna for Space Communications A505

1963, Sept. 9 Photo.

799 A505 10y multicolored .20 .20

14th General Assembly of the International Scientific Radio Union, Tokyo.

"Great Wave off Kanagawa," by Hokusai A506

1963, Oct. 10 *Perf. 13*

800 A506 40y gray, dk bl & yel 3.00 1.25

Issued for International Letter Writing Week, Oct. 6-12. Design from Hokusai's "36 Views of Fuji." Printed in sheets of 10 (5x2).

Diver, Pole Vaulter and Relay Runner — A507

Woman Gymnast — A508

1963, Oct. 11 *Perf. 13½*

801 A507 10y bl, ocher, blk & red .20 .20

Tokyo Intl. (Pre-Olympic) Sports Meet, Tokyo, Oct. 11-16.

Perf. 13½

1963, Oct. 27 Unwmk. Engr.

Design: #803, Japanese wrestling (sumo).

802 A508 5y slate green .20 .20
803 A508 5y brown .20 .20
a. Pair, #802-803 .40 .45

18th National Athletic Meet, Yamaguchi.

Phoenix Tree and Hachijo Island — A509

Toy Dragons of Tottori and Yamanashi — A510

1963, Dec. 10 Photo.

804 A509 10y multicolored .20 .20

Izu Islands Quasi-National Park.

1963, Dec. 16

805 A510 5y gold, pink, aqua, ind & red .20 .20
a. Aqua omitted

New Year 1964. Sheets containing 4 #805 were awarded as 5th prize in the New Year lottery. Value $4.25.

Wakasa-Fuji from Takahama A511

1964, Jan 25 ***Perf. 13½***

806 A511 10y multicolored .25 .20

Wakasa Bay Quasi-National Park.

Agave and View from Horikiri Pass — A512

1964, Feb. 20 **Unwmk.**

807 A512 10y multicolored .25 .20

Nichinan-Kaigan Quasi-National Park.

Uji Bridge A513

View of Toba — A514

1964, Mar. 15 **Photo.**

808 A513 5y sepia .20 .20
809 A514 10y red lilac .25 .20

Ise-Shima National Park.

Takayama Festival Float and Mt. Norikura — A515

#811, Yamaboko floats & Gion Shrine, Kyoto.

1964 **Photo.** ***Perf. 13½***

810 A515 10y lt green & multi .20 .20
811 A515 10y grnsh blue & multi .20 .20

No. 810 issued for the annual Takayama spring and autumn festivals, Takayama City, Gifu Prefecture. No. 811 for the annual Gion festival of Kyoto, July 10-30.
Issue dates: #810, Apr. 15. #811, July 15.

Yadorigi Scene from Genji Monogatari Scroll — A516

1964, Apr. 20

814 A516 10y multicolored .25 .20

Stamp Week, 1964. Sheets of 10 (2x5).

Himeji Castle — A517

1964, June 1 ***Perf. 13½***

815 A517 10y dark brown .20 .20

Restoration of Himeji Castle.

Sports Type of 1961

1964, June 6 ***Perf. 13½***

816 A454 5y Handball .20 .20
817 A454 5y Woman on beam .20 .20
a. Pair, #816-817 .40 .45

19th National Athletic Meeting, Niigata.

Cable Cross Section, Map of Pacific Ocean A518

Tokyo Expressway Crossing Nihonbashi — A519

1964, June 19

818 A518 10y gray grn, dp mag & yel .20 .20

Opening of the transpacific cable.

1964, Aug. 1 **Photo.**

819 A519 10y green, silver & blk .20 .20

Opening of the Tokyo Expressway.

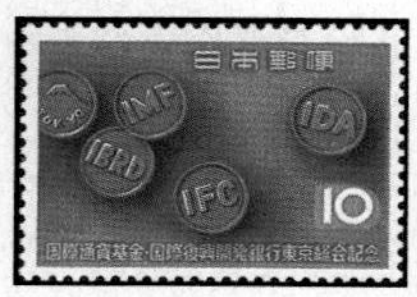

Coin-like Emblems A520

1964, Sept. 7 **Unwmk.** ***Perf. 13½***

820 A520 10y scarlet, gold & blk .20 .20

Annual general meeting of the Intl. Monetary Fund, Intl. Bank for Reconstruction and Development, Intl. Financial Corporation and the Intl. Development Assoc., Tokyo, Sept. 7-11.

Athletes, Olympic Flame and Rings — A521

National Stadium, Tokyo — A522

30y, Nippon Bodokan (fencing hall). 40y, Natl. Gymnasium. 50y, Komazawa Gymnasium.

1964

821 A521 5y multicolored .20 .20
822 A522 10y multicolored .20 .20
823 A522 30y multicolored .35 .20
824 A522 40y multicolored .45 .20
825 A522 50y multicolored .50 .20
a. Souvenir sheet of 5, #821-825 3.25 4.00
Nos. 821-825 (5) 1.70 1.00

18th Olympic Games, Tokyo, Oct. 10-25.
Issue dates: 5y, Sept. 9. Others, Oct. 10.

Hand with Grain, Cow and Fruit — A523

Express Train — A524

1964, Sept. 15 ***Perf. 13½***

826 A523 10y violet brn & gold .20 .20

Draining of Hachirogata Lagoon, providing new farmland for the future.

1964, Oct. 1

827 A524 10y blue & black .25 .20

Opening of the new Tokaido railroad line.

Mt. Fuji Seen from Tokaido, by Hokusai A525

1964, Oct. 4 ***Perf. 13***

828 A525 40y multicolored 1.00 .45

Issued for International Letter Writing Week, Oct. 4-10. Issued in sheets of 10 (5x2). See Nos. 850, 896, 932, 971, 1016.

"Straw Snake" Mascot — A526

1964, Dec. 15 **Photo.** ***Perf. 13½***

829 A526 5y crimson, blk & yel .20 .20

New Year 1965. Sheets containing 4 #829 were awarded as prizes in the New Year lottery (issued Jan. 20, 1965). Value $1.75.

Mt. Daisen A527

Paradise Cove, Oki Islands A528

1965, Jan. 20 **Unwmk.** ***Perf. 13½***

830 A527 5y dark blue .20 .20
831 A528 10y brown orange .20 .20

Daisen-Oki National Park.

Niseko-Annupuri — A529

1965, Feb. 15 **Photo.**

832 A529 10y multicolored .20 .20

Niseko-Shakotan-Otarukaigan Quasi-Natl. Park.

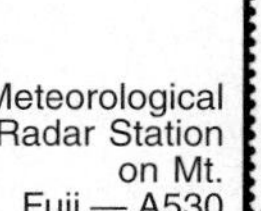

Meteorological Radar Station on Mt. Fuji — A530

1965, Mar. 10 **Photo.** ***Perf. 13½***

833 A530 10y multicolored .20 .20

Completion of the Meteorological Radar Station on Kengamine Heights of Mt. Fuji.

Kiyotsu Gorge — A531

Lake Nojiri and Mt. Myoko A532

1965, Mar. 15

834 A531 5y brown .20 .20
835 A532 10y magenta .20 .20

Jo-Shin-etsu Kogen National Park.

Communications Museum, Tokyo — A533

1965, Mar. 25 **Unwmk.** ***Perf. 13½***

836 A533 10y green .20 .20

Philatelic Exhibition celebrating the completion of the Communications Museum.

"The Prelude" by Shoen Uemura A534

1965, Apr. 20 **Photo.**

837 A534 10y gray & multi .30 .20

Issued for Stamp Week, 1965.

Playing Children, Cows and Swan — A535

Stylized Tree and Sun — A536

1965, May 5 Unwmk. *Perf. 13½*
838 A535 10y pink & multi .20 .20

Opening of the National Garden for Children, Tokyo-Yokohama.

1965, May 9
839 A536 10y multicolored .20 .20

Issued to publicize the forestation movement and the forestation ceremony, Tottori Prefecture.

Globe, Old and New Communication Equipment — A537

1965, May 17
840 A537 10y brt blue, yel & blk .20 .20

Cent. of the ITU.

Crater of Mt. Naka, Kyushu A538

Five Central Peaks of Aso and Mountain Road — A539

1965, June 15 Photo. *Perf. 13½*
841 A538 5y carmine rose .20 .20
842 A539 10y deep green .20 .20

Aso National Park.

ICY Emblem and Doves A540

1965, June 26 Unwmk.
843 A540 40y multicolored .45 .20

Intl. Cooperation Year, 1965, and 20th anniv. of the UN.

Horse Chase, Soma A541

Chichibu Festival Scene A542

1965 Photo. *Perf. 13x13½*
844 A541 10y multicolored .20 .20
845 A542 10y multicolored .20 .20

No. 844 issued to publicize the ancient Soma Nomaoi Festival, Fukushima Prefecture; No. 845, to publicize the festival dedicated to the Chichibu Myoken Shrine (built 1584).

Issue dates: #844, July 16; #845, Dec. 3.

Meiji Maru, Black-tailed Gulls — A543

1965, July 20 *Perf. 13½*
846 A543 10y grn, gray, blk & yel .20 .20

25th Maritime Day, July 20.

Drop of Blood, Girl's Face and Bloodmobile A544

1965, Sept. 1 *Perf. 13½*
847 A544 10y yel, grn, blk & red .20 .20

Issued to publicize the national campaign for blood donations, Sept. 1-30.

Tokai Atomic Power Station and Structure of Alpha Uranium — A545

1965, Sept. 21 Photo.
848 A545 10y multicolored .20 .20

9th General Conf. of the Intl. Atomic Energy Agency, IAEA, Tokyo, Sept. 21-30.

People and Flag — A546

1965, Oct. 1
849 A546 10y multicolored .20 .20

Tenth national census.

Hokusai Type of 1964

Design: No. 850, "Waters at Misaka" by Hokusai (Mt. Fuji seen across Lake Kawaguchi).

1965, Oct. 6 Unwmk. *Perf. 13*
850 A525 40y multicolored .65 .40

Issued for International Letter Writing Week, Oct. 6-12. Issued in sheets of 10 (5x2).

Emblems and Diagram of Seats in National Diet — A547

1965, Oct. 15 *Perf. 13½*
851 A547 10y multicolored .20 .20

75th anniv. of natl. suffrage, 40th anniv. of universal suffrage and 20th anniv. of women's suffrage.

Sports Type of 1961

Designs: No. 852, Gymnast on vaulting horse. No. 853, Walking race.

1965, Oct. 24 Engr. *Perf. 13½*
852 A454 5y red brown .20 .20
853 A454 5y yellow green .20 .20
a. Pair, #852-853 .35 .45

20th National Athletic Meeting, Gifu.

Profile and Infant A548

1965, Oct. 30 Photo. *Perf. 13*
854 A548 30y car lake, yel & lt bl .30 .20

8th Intl. Conf. of Otorhinolaryngology and the 11th Intl. Conf. of Pediatrics.

Mt. Iwo from Shari Coast, Hokkaido — A549

Rausu Lake and Mt. Rausu A550

1965, Nov. 15 *Perf. 13½*
855 A549 5y Prus green .20 .20
856 A550 10y bright blue .20 .20

Shiretoko National Park.

Aurora Australis, Map of Antarctica and "Fuji" — A551

1965, Nov. 20
857 A551 10y bl, yel & dk bl .20 .20

Issued to publicize the Antarctic expedition, which left on the observation ship "Fuji," Nov. 20, 1965.

"Secret Horse" Straw Toy, Iwate Prefecture A552

Telephone Dial and 1890 Switchboard A553

1965, Dec. 10
858 A552 5y lt blue & multi .20 .20

Issued for New Year 1966. Sheets containing four of No. 858 were awarded as prizes in the New Year lottery (issued Jan. 20, 1966). Value $1.50.

1965, Dec. 16
859 A553 10y multicolored .20 .20

75th anniversary of telephone service in Japan.

Japanese Spiny Lobster A554

Carp — A555

Bream A555a

Skipjack Tuna A555b

Three Ayu A555c

Eel A555d

Jack Mackeral A555e

Chum Salmon A555f

Yellowtail A555g

Tiger Puffer A555h

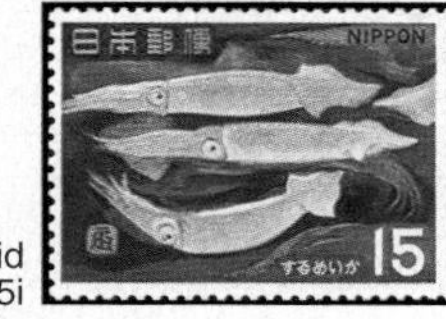

Squid A555i

Turbo Cornutus A555j

1966-67 Photo. *Perf. 13*
Multicolored; Background in Colors Indicated

860 A554 10y green & ultra .20 .20
861 A555 10y blue green .20 .20
862 A555a 10y dk blue .20 .20
863 A555b 10y dk ultra .20 .20
864 A555c 10y bis & dk grn .20 .20
865 A555d 15y grnsh bl & yel .30 .20
866 A555e 15y brt grn .30 .20
867 A555f 15y brt grn & bl .30 .20

868	A555g	15y lt bl grn ('67)	.30	.20
869	A555h	15y brt grn ('67)	.30	.20
870	A555i	15y ultra & grn ('67)	.30	.25
871	A555j	15y chlky bl ('67)	.55	.25
		Nos. 860-871 (12)	3.35	2.50

Famous Gardens Issue

A556

A557

A558

10y, Kobuntei Pavilion and plum blossoms, Kairakuen Garden, Ibaraki. #873, Japanese cranes and Okayama Castle, Korakuen Garden, Okayama. #874, Kenrokuen Garden in the snow.

1966-67 *Perf. 13½*

872	A556	10y gold, blk & grn	.20	.20
873	A557	15y blue, blk & mag	.30	.20
874	A558	15y silver, grn & dk brn	.30	.20
		Nos. 872-874 (3)	.80	.60

Issued: 10y, 2/25; #873, 11/3; #874, 1/25/67.

Crater Lake, Zao — A559

1966, Mar. 15

875 A559 10y multicolored .20 .20

Zao Quasi-National Park.

Muroto Cape — A560

Senba Cliffs, Anan Coast — A561

1966, Mar. 22 *Perf. 13½*

876	A560	10y multicolored	.20	.20
877	A561	10y multicolored	.20	.20

Muroto-Anan Coast Quasi-National Park.

AIPPI Emblem A562

1966, Apr. 11 *Perf. 13*

878 A562 40y multicolored .75 .20

26th General Assembly of the Intl. Association for the Protection of Industrial Properties, Tokyo, Apr. 11-16.

"Butterflies" by Takeji Fujishima — A563

Photogravure and Engraved

1966, Apr. 20 *Perf. 13½*

879 A563 10y gray & multi .25 .25

Stamp Week, 1966. Sheets of 10 (2x5). See No. 907.

Hisoka Maeshima A563a

Goldfish A564

Chrysanthemums — A565

Wisteria A565a

Hydrangea A565b

Golden Hall, Chusonji A565c

Yomei Gate, Nikko A565d

Nyoirin Kannon of Chuguji — A565f

Central Hall, Enryakuji Temple — A566

Ancient Clay Horse (Haniwa) — A567

A567a

A567b

A567c

Katsura Palace Garden — A568

A569

Bodhisattva Playing Flute (from Todaiji Lantern) — A570

Designs: 20y, Wisteria. 25y, Hydrangea. 35y, Luminescent squid. 45y, Lysichiton camtschatsense (white flowers). 500y, Deva King statue, South Gate, Todaiji.

1966-69 **Photo.** *Perf. 13*

879A	A563a	1y olive bis ('68)	.20	.20
880	A564	7y ol & dp org	1.10	.20
881	A565	15y bl & yel (bl "15")	.95	.20
b.		Bklt. pane of 2 + label ('67)	3.25	
c.		Bklt. pane of 4 ('67)	2.25	
d.		Bklt. pane of 4 (2 #881 + 2 #611) ('67)	6.00	
e.		Imperf., pair	300.00	
881A	A565a	20y vio & multi ('67)	1.90	*2.25*
882	A565b	25y grn & lt ultra	.50	.20
882A	A565c	30y dp ultra & gold ('68)	.55	.20
883	A564	35y blue, gray & blk	1.10	.20
883A	A565d	40y bl grn & brn ('68)	.75	.20
884	A565	45y blue & multi ('67)	.85	.20
885	A565f	50y dk car rose	6.50	.20
		Engr.		
886	A566	60y slate green	3.25	.20
		Photo.		
887	A567	65y orange brown	8.50	.20
887A	A567a	75y rose, blk, yel & pur	1.40	.20
888	A567b	90y gold & brn	1.75	.20
888A	A567c	100y ver & blk ('68)	1.90	.20
		Engr.		
889	A568	110y brown	2.10	.20
890	A569	120y red	2.25	.20
891	A570	200y Prus grn (22x33mm)	3.75	.20
891A	A570	500y dull pur ('69)	9.50	.20
		Nos. 879A-891A (19)	48.80	5.85

Nos. 880-881 were also issued with fluorescent frame on July 18, 1966.

See Nos. 913-916, 918, 926, 1072, 1079, 1081, 1244, 1256.

UNESCO Emblem — A571

Map of Pacific Ocean — A572

1966, July 2 **Photo.** *Perf. 13*

892 A571 15y multicolored .30 .20

20th anniv. of UNESCO.

1966, Aug. 22 *Perf. 13*

893 A572 15y bis brn, dl bl & rose .30 .20

11th Pacific Science Congress, Tokyo, Aug. 22-Sept. 10.

Amakusa Bridges, Kyushu — A573

Emblem of Post Office Life Insurance and Family — A574

1966, Sept. 24 **Photo.** *Perf. 13*

894 A573 15y multicolored .30 .20

Completion of five bridges linking Misumi Harbor, Kyushu, with Amakusa islands.

1966, Oct. 1

895 A574 15y yellow grn & multi .30 .20

Post office life insurance service, 50th anniv.

Hokusai Type of 1964

50y, "Sekiya on the Sumida" (horseback riders and Mt. Fuji) from Hokusai's "36 Views of Fuji."

1966, Oct. 6

896 A525 50y multicolored .95 .70

Intl. Letter Writing Week, Oct. 6-12. Printed in sheets of 10 (5x2).

Sharpshooter A575

Design: No. 898, Hop, skip and jump.

1966, Oct. 23 **Engr.** *Perf. 13½*

897	A575	7y ultra	.20	.20
898	A575	7y carmine rose	.20	.20
a.		Pair, #897-898	.45	.40

21st Natl. Athletic Meet, Oita, Oct. 23-28.

National Theater A576

Kabuki Scene — A577

Bunraku Puppet Show — A578

1966, Nov. 1 *Perf. 13, 13½*

899 A576 15y multicolored .20 .20
900 A577 25y multicolored .50 .25
901 A578 50y multicolored .95 .40
Nos. 899-901 (3) 1.65 .85

Inauguration of first National Theater in Japan. Nos. 900-901 issued in sheets of 10.

Rice Year Emblem A579

Ittobori Carved Sheep, Nara Prefecture A580

1966, Nov. 21 *Perf. 13½*

902 A579 15y red, blk & ocher .30 .20

FAO International Rice Year.

1966, Dec. 10 Photo. *Perf. 13½*

903 A580 7y bl, gold, blk & pink .20 .20

New Year 1967. Sheets containing 4 #903 were awarded as prizes in the New Year lottery. Value $1.25.

International Communications Satellite, Lani Bird 2 — A581

1967, Jan. 27 *Perf. 13½*

904 A581 15y dk Prus bl & sepia .30 .20

Inauguration in Japan of Intl. commercial communications service via satellite.

Around the World Air Route and Jet Plane — A582

1967, Mar. 6 Photo. *Perf. 13½*

905 A582 15y multicolored .30 .20

Issued to publicize the inauguration of Japan Air Lines Tokyo-London service via New York, which completes the around the world air route.

Library of Modern Japanese Literature A583

1967, Apr. 11

906 A583 15y grnsh bl, lt & dk brn .30 .20

Opening of the Library of Modern Japanese Literature, Komaba Park, Meguro-ku, Tokyo.

Painting Type of 1966

Design: 15y, Lakeside (seated woman), by Seiki (Kiyoteru) Kuroda.

1967, Apr. 20

907 A563 15y multicolored .30 .20

Stamp Week, 1967. Sheets of 10 (2x5).

Kobe Harbor A584

1967, May 8 Photo. *Perf. 13x13½*

908 A584 50y multicolored .95 .20

5th Cong. of the Intl. Association of Ports and Harbors, Tokyo, May 8-13.

Welfare Commissioner's Emblem A585

Traffic Light, Automobile and Children A586

1967, May 12 *Perf. 13½*

909 A585 15y dk brown & gold .30 .20

50th anniversary of the Welfare Commissioner System.

1967, May 22 *Perf. 13x13½*

910 A586 15y emer, red, blk & yel .30 .20

Issued to publicize traffic safety.

Kita and Kai-Koma Mountains A587

Akaishi and Hijiri Mountains A588

1967, July 10

911 A587 7y Prus blue .20 .20
912 A588 15y rose lilac .30 .20

South Japan Alps National Park.

Types of 1966-69 Redrawn and

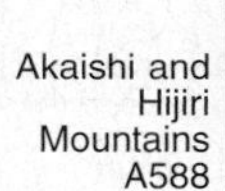

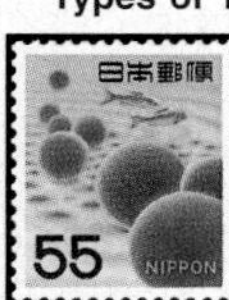

A588a

Original 20y No. 881A

Redrawn 20y No. 915

1967-69 Photo. *Perf. 13*

913 A564 7y brt yel grn & dp org .20 .20
914 A565 15y bl & yel (white "15") .30 .20
a. Pane of 10 (5x2) ('68) 2.75
b. Bklt. panes of 4 with gutter (6 #914 + 2 #611) ('68) 7.00
c. Imperf., pair 200.00
d. Blue shading omitted
e. Bklt. panes of 2 & 4 with gutter ('68) 45.00 45.00
915 A565a 20y vio & multi ('69) 1.10 .20
916 A565f 50y brt carmine .95 .20
917 A588a 55y lt bl, grn & blk ('69) 1.10 .20
918 A567 65y deep orange 1.25 .20
Nos. 913-918 (6) 4.90 1.20

Issued for use in facer-canceling machines. Issue dates: 7y, Aug. 1; 15y, 50y, July 1; 65y, July 20, 1967; 20y, Apr. 1, 1969; 55y, Sept. 1, 1969.

On No. 913 the background has been lightened and a frame line of shading added at top and right side.

No. 914a is imperf. on four sides.

The two panes of Nos. 914b and 914e are connected by a vertical creased gutter 21mm wide. The left pane of No. 914b consists of 2 No. 914 and 2 No. 611; the right pane, 4 of No. 914. The left pane of 2 of No. 914e includes a 4-line inscription.

On No. 915 the wisteria leaves do not touch frame at left and top. On No. 881A they do.

Coil Stamp

1968, Jan. 9 *Perf. 13 Horiz.*

926 A565 15y bl & yel (white "15") .60 .45

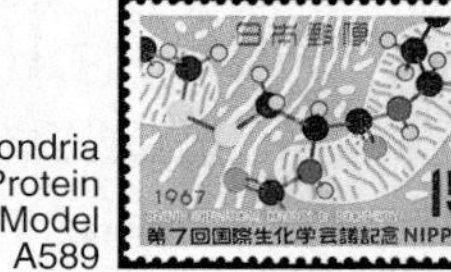

Mitochondria and Protein Model A589

1967, Aug. 19 Photo. *Perf. 13*

927 A589 15y gray & multi .30 .20

7th Intl. Biochemistry Cong., Tokyo, Aug. 19-25.

Gymnast on Horizontal Bar — A590

Universiade Emblem — A591

1967, Aug. 26

928 A590 15y red & multi .30 .20
929 A591 50y yellow & multi .95 .25

World University Games, Universiade 1967, Tokyo, Aug. 26-Sept. 4.

Paper Lantern, ITY Emblem — A592

"Sacred Mt. Fuji" by Taikan Yokoyama — A593

1967, Oct. 2 Photo. *Perf. 13*

930 A592 15y ultra & multi .20 .20
931 A593 50y multicolored 1.25 1.00

International Tourist Year, 1967. No. 931 issued in sheets of 10.

Hokusai Type of 1964

50y, "Kajikazawa, Koshu" (fisherman and waves) from Hokusai's "36 Views of Fuji."

1967, Oct. 6

932 A525 50y multicolored 1.25 .55

Issued for International Letter Writing Week, Oct. 6-12. Sheets of 10 (5x2).

Athlete, Wild Primrose and Chichibu Mountains — A594

1967, Oct. 22 Photo. *Perf. 13*

933 A594 15y gold & multi .30 .20

22nd Natl. Athletic Meet, Saitama, 10/22-27.

Miroku Bosatsu, Koryuji Temple, Kyoto — A595

Kudara Kannon, Horyuji Temple, Nara — A596

Golden Hall and Pagoda, Horyuji Temple, Nara — A597

1967, Nov. 1 Photo.

934 A595 15y multicolored .30 .25

Engr.

935 A596 15y pale grn, blk & red .30 .25

Photo. & Engr.

936 A597 50y multicolored 1.25 .75
Nos. 934-936 (3) 1.85 1.25

National treasures of Asuka Period (6th-7th centuries). No. 936 issued in sheets of 10.

Highway and Congress Emblem A598

1967, Nov. 5 Photo. *Perf. 13*

937 A598 50y multicolored .95 .20

13th World Road Cong., Tokyo, Nov. 5-11.

Mt. Kumotori A599

Lake Chichibu A600

1967, Nov. 27

938	A599	7y olive	.20	.20
939	A600	15y red lilac	.30	.20

Chichibu-Tama National Park

Climbing Monkey Toy (Noborizaru), Miyazaki Prefecture — A601

1967, Dec. 11 **Photo.** ***Perf. 13***

940	A601	7y multicolored	.20	.20

New Year 1968. Sheets containing 4 #940 were awarded as prizes in the New Year lottery. Value $1.25.

Mt. Sobo — A602

Takachiho Gorge — A603

1967, Dec. 20

941	A602	15y multicolored	.30	.20
942	A603	15y multicolored	.30	.20

Sobo Katamuki Quasi-National Park.

Girl, Boy and Sakura Maru — A604

1968, Jan. 19 **Photo.** ***Perf. 13***

943	A604	15y ultra, ocher & blk	.30	.20

Cent. of the Meiji Era, and 1st Japanese Youth Good Will Cruise in celebration of the centenary.

Ashura, Kofukuji Temple, Nara — A605

Gakko Bosatsu, Todaiji Temple, Nara — A606

Kichijo Ten, Yakushiji Temple, Nara — A607

1968, Feb. 1 **Engr.** ***Perf. 13***

944	A605	15y sepia & car	.30	.25

Engr. & Photo.

945	A606	15y dk brn, pale grn & org	.30	.25

Photo.

946	A607	50y multicolored	.95	.95
		Nos. 944-946 (3)	1.55	1.45

Issued to show National Treasures of the Nara Period (710-784).

Grazing Cows and Mt. Yatsugatake A608

Mt. Tateshina A609

1968, Mar. 21 **Photo.** ***Perf. 13***

947	A608	15y multicolored	.30	.20
948	A609	15y multicolored	.30	.20

Yatsugatake-Chushin-Kogen Quasi-Natl. Park.

Young Dancer (Maiko) in Tenjuan Garden, by Bakusen Tsuchida A610

1968, Apr. 20 **Photo.** ***Perf. 13***

949	A610	15y multicolored	.30	.20

Stamp Week, 1968. Sheets of 10 (5x2).

Rishiri Isl. Seen from Rebun Isl. — A611

1968, May 10 **Photo.** ***Perf. 13***

950	A611	15y multicolored	.30	.20

Rishiri-Rebun Quasi-National Park.

Gold Lacquer and Mother-of-Pearl Box — A612

"The Origin of Shigisan" Painting from Chogo-sonshiji, Nara — A613

Bodhisattva Samantabhadra — A614

1968, June 1 **Engr. & Photo.**

951	A612	15y lt blue & multi	.30	.25

Photo.

952	A613	15y tan & multi	.30	.25
953	A614	50y sepia & multi	2.00	1.50
		Nos. 951-953 (3)	2.60	2.00

Issued to show national treasures of the Heian Period (8-12th centuries).

Memorial Tower and Badge of Hokkaido — A615

1968, June 14

954	A615	15y grn, vio bl, bis & red	.30	.20

Centenary of development of Hokkaido.

Sunrise over Pacific and Fan Palms — A616

1968, June 26 **Photo.** ***Perf. 13***

955	A616	15y blk, org & red org	.30	.20

Return of Bonin Islands to Japan by US.

Map of Japan Showing Postal Codes — A617

Two types of inscription:
Type I (enlarged)

"Postal code also on your address"

Type II (enlarged)

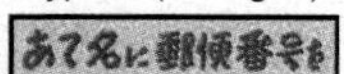

"Don't omit postal code on the address"

1968, July 1

956	A617	7y yel grn & red (I)	1.90	.50
957	A617	7y yel grn & red (II)	1.90	.50
a.		Pair, #956-957	4.00	4.00
958	A617	15y sky bl & car (I)	.75	.50
a.		Bklt. panes of 4 with gutter (4 #958 + 2 #959 + 2 #611)	60.00	60.00
959	A617	15y sky bl & car (II)	.75	.50
d.		Pair, #958-959	3.00	3.00
		Nos. 956-959 (4)	5.30	2.00

Introduction of the postal code system.

The double booklet pane, No. 958a, comes in two forms, the positions of the Postal Code types being transposed.

Coil Stamps
Perf. 13 Horiz.

959A	A617	15y sky blue & car (I)	.90	.75
959B	A617	15y sky blue & car (II)	.90	.75
c.		Pair, #959A-959B	3.75	3.75

Kiso River — A618

Inuyama Castle A619

1968, July 20 ***Perf. 13½***

960	A618	15y multicolored	.30	.20
961	A619	15y multicolored	.30	.20

Hida-Kisogawa Quasi-National Park.

Youth Hostel Emblem, Trees and Sun — A620

1968, Aug. 6 **Photo.** ***Perf. 13***

962	A620	15y citron & multi	.30	.20

27th Intl. Youth Hostel Cong., Tokyo, 8/6-20.

Boys Forming Tournament Emblem A621

Pitcher and Tournament Flag — A622

1968, Aug. 9

963	A621	15y yel grn, yel, blk & red	.30	.20
964	A622	15y red, yellow & blk	.30	.20
a.		Pair, #963-964	.65	.60

50th All-Japan High School Baseball Championship Tournament, Koshi-en Baseball Grounds, Aug. 9. Nos. 963-964 printed checkerwise.

Minamoto Yoritomo, Jingoji, Kyoto — A623

Heiji Monogatari Scroll Painting — A624

Red-threaded Armor, Kasuga Shrine, Nara — A625

1968, Sept. 16 **Photo.** ***Perf. 13***

965 A623 15y black & multi .40 .25
966 A624 15y tan & multi .40 .25

Photo. & Engr.

967 A625 50y multicolored 1.25 1.25
Nos. 965-967 (3) 2.05 1.75

National treasures of Kamakura period (1180-1192 to 1333).

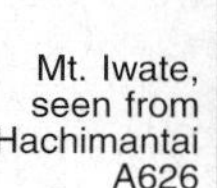

Mt. Iwate, seen from Hachimantai A626

Lake Towada, seen from Mt. Ohanabe A627

1968, Sept. 16 **Photo.**

968 A626 7y red brown .20 .20
969 A627 15y green .30 .20

Towada-Hachimantai National Park.

Gymnast, Tojimbo Cliff and Narcissus — A628

1968, Oct. 1 **Photo.** ***Perf. 13***

970 A628 15y multicolored .30 .20

23rd National Athletic Meet, Fukui Prefecture, Oct. 1-6.

Hokusai Type of 1964

Design: 50y, "Fujimihara in Owari Province" (cooper working on a barrel) from Hokusai's "36 Views of Fuji."

1968, Oct. 7

971 A525 50y multicolored 1.00 .60

Issued for International Letter Writing Week, Oct. 7-13. Sheets of 10 (5x2).

Centenary Emblem, Sun and First Western Style Warship — A629

Imperial Carriage Arriving in Tokyo (1868), by Tomote Kobori A630

1968, Oct. 23

972 A629 15y vio bl, red, gold & gray .30 .20
973 A630 15y multicolored .30 .20
a. Imperf., pair

Meiji Centenary Festival.

Old and New Lighthouses A631

1968, Nov. 1 **Photo.** ***Perf. 13***

974 A631 15y multicolored .30 .20

Centenary of the first western style lighthouse in Japan.

Ryo'o Court Dance and State Hall, Imperial Palace — A632

1968, Nov. 14

975 A632 15y multicolored .30 .20

Completion of the new Imperial Palace.

Mt. Takachiho A633

Mt. Motobu, Yaku Island A634

1968, Nov. 20

976 A633 7y purple .20 .20
977 A634 15y orange .30 .20

Kirishima-Yaku National Park.

Carved Toy Cock of Yonezawa, Yamagata Prefecture A635

Human Rights Flame, Dancing Children and Globe A636

1968, Dec. 5 **Photo.** ***Perf. 13***

978 A635 7y lt blue & multi .20 .20

New Year 1969. Sheets containing 4 #978 were awarded as prizes in the New Year lottery. Value $1.50.

1968, Dec. 10

979 A636 50y orange & multi .95 .25

International Human Rights Year.

Striped Squirrel A637

Kochomon Cave and Road A638

1968, Dec. 14

980 A637 15y emerald & blk .30 .20

Issued to promote saving.

1969, Jan. 27 **Photo.**

981 A638 15y multicolored .30 .20

Echizen-Kaga-Kaigan Quasi-National Park.

Silver Pavilion, Jishoji Temple, Kyoto — A639

Pagoda, Anrakuji Temple, Nagano — A640

Winter Landscape by Sesshu A641

1969, Feb. 10 **Photo.** ***Perf. 13***

982 A639 15y multicolored .30 .20

Photo. & Engr.

983 A640 15y lt green & multi .30 .20

Photo.

984 A641 50y tan, blk & ver 1.10 .75
Nos. 982-984 (3) 1.70 1.15

Issued to show national treasures of the Muromachi Period (1333-1572).

Mt. Chokai, seen from Tobishima Island — A642

1969, Feb. 25 **Photo.**

985 A642 15y brt blue & multi .30 .20

Chokai Quasi-National Park.

Mt. Koya Seen from Jinnogamine A643

Mt. Gomadan and Rhododendron — A644

1969, Mar. 25 **Photo.** ***Perf. 13***

986 A643 15y multicolored .30 .20
987 A644 15y multicolored .30 .20

Koya-Ryujin Quasi-National Park.

Hair (Kami), by Kokei Kobayashi A645

1969, Apr. 20 **Photo.** ***Perf. 13***

988 A645 15y multicolored .30 .20

Issued for Philatelic Week.

Mother, Son Crossing Street A646

Tokyo-Nagoya Expressway and Sakawagawa Bridge A647

1969, May 10 **Photo.** ***Perf. 13***

989 A646 15y lt blue, red & grn .30 .20

National traffic safety campaign.

1969, May 26

990 A647 15y multicolored .30 .20

Completion of Tokyo-Nagoya Expressway.

Nuclear Ship Mutsu and Atom Diagram A648

1969, June 12

991 A648 15y gray, blk, pink & bl .30 .20

Issued to publicize the launching of the first Japanese nuclear ship, Mutsu.

Museum of Modern Art and Palette A649

1969, June 11 **Photo.** ***Perf. 13½***

992 A649 15y lt bl, brn, yel & blk .30 .20

Opening of the new National Museum of Modern Art, Tokyo.

Cable Ship KKD Maru and Map of Japan Sea — A650

1969, June 25

993 A650 15y lt bl, blk & ocher .30 .20

Completion of the Japan sea cable between Naoetsu, Japan, and Nakhodka, Russia.

Postcards, Postal Code Symbol A651

Mailbox, Postal Code Symbol A652

1969, July 1 **Photo.** ***Perf. 13***

997 A651 7y yellow grn & car .20 .20
998 A652 15y sky blue & car .30 .20

1st anniv. of the postal code system and to promote its use.

Lions Emblem and Rose — A653

1969, July 2

999 A653 15y bl, blk, rose & gold .30 .20

52nd Convention of Lions Intl., Tokyo, July 2-5.

Hotoke-ga-ura on Shimokita Peninsula, Northern Honshu A654

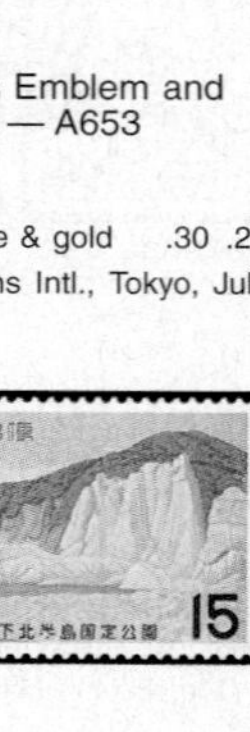

1969, July 15

1000 A654 15y multicolored .30 .20

Shimokita Hanto Quasi-National Park.

Himeji Castle, Hyogo Prefecture A655

"Pine Forest" (Detail), by Tohaku Hasegawa A656

"Cypresses," Attributed to Eitoku Kano — A657

1969, July 21 **Photo. & Engr.**

1001 A655 15y lt blue & multi .30 .25

Photo.

1002 A656 15y pale brown & blk .30 .25
1003 A657 50y gold & multi 1.10 .60
Nos. 1001-1003 (3) 1.70 1.10

Issued to show national treasures of the Momoyama period (1573-1614). The 50y is in sheets of 10 (2x5); Nos. 1001-1002 in sheets of 20 (5x4).

Harano-fudo Waterfall — A658

Mt. Nagisan A659

1969, Aug. 20

1004 A658 15y multicolored .30 .20
1005 A659 15y multicolored .30 .20

Hyobosen-Ushiroyama-Nagisan Quasi-Natl. Park.

Mt. O-akan, Hokkaido — A660

Mt. Iwo — A661

1969, Aug. 25 **Photo.** ***Perf. 13***

1006 A660 7y bright blue .20 .20
1007 A661 15y sepia .30 .20

Akan National Park.

Angling, by Taiga Ikeno — A662

The Red Plum, by Korin Ogata — A663

Pheasant-shaped Incense Burner — A664

No. 1010, The White Plum, by Korin Ogata.

1969, Sept. 25 **Photo.** ***Perf. 13x13½***

1008 A662 15y multicolored .30 .20

Perf. 13

1009 A663 15y gold & multi .30 .20
1010 A663 15y gold & multi .30 .20
a. Pair, #1009-1010 .75 .75

Photo. & Engr.

1011 A664 50y multicolored 1.00 .65
Nos. 1008-1011 (4) 1.90 1.25

Natl. treasures, Edo Period (1615-1867).

Birds Circling Globe and UPU Congress Emblem A665

Woman Reading Letter, by Utamaro A666

Designs (UPU Congress Emblem and): 50y, Two Women Reading a Letter, by Harunobu. 60y, Man Reading a Letter (Miyako Dennai), by Sharaku.

1969, Oct. 1 **Photo.** ***Perf. 13***

1012 A665 15y red & multi .30 .20
1013 A666 30y multicolored .60 .40
1014 A666 50y multicolored .95 .50
1015 A666 60y multicolored 1.10 .65
Nos. 1012-1015 (4) 2.95 1.75

16th UPU Congress, Tokyo, 10/1-11/16. 15y issued in sheets of 20, others in sheets of 10.

Hokusai Type of 1964

Design: 50y, "Passing through Koshu down to Mishima" from Hokusai's 36 Views of Fuji.

1969, Oct. 7 **Photo.** ***Perf. 13***

1016 A525 50y multicolored 1.00 .55

Issued for International Letter Writing Week Oct. 7-13. Sheets of 10 (5x2).

Rugby Player, Camellia and Oura Catholic Church — A667

1969, Oct. 26

1017 A667 15y lt ultra & multi .30 .20

24th Natl. Athletic Meet, Nagasaki, 10/26-31.

Cape Kitayama — A668

Goishi Coast — A669

1969, Nov. 20 **Photo.** ***Perf. 13***

1018 A668 7y gray & dk blue .20 .20
1019 A669 15y salmon & dk red .30 .20

Rikuchu Coast National Park.

Worker in Hard Hat — A670

Dog Amulet, Hokkeji, Nara — A671

1969, Nov. 26

1020 A670 15y ultra, blk yel & brn .30 .20

50th anniv. of the ILO.

1969, Dec. 10

1021 A671 7y orange & multi .20 .20

New Year 1970. Sheets containing 4 #1021 were awarded as prizes in the New Year lottery. Value $1.50.

Aso Bay and Tsutsu Women with Horse — A672

1970, Feb. 25 **Photo.** ***Perf. 13***

1022 A672 15y multicolored .30 .20

Iki-Tsushima Quasi-National Park.

Fireworks over EXPO '70 — A673

Cherry Blossoms Around Globe — A674

Irises, by Korin Ogata (1658-1716) — A675

1970, Mar. 14 **Photo.** ***Perf. 13***

1023 A673 7y red & multi .20 .20
1024 A674 15y gold & multi .30 .20
1025 A675 50y gold & multi .95 .65
a. Souv. sheet of 3, #1023-1025 1.75 1.75
b. Bklt. pane of 4 & 3 with gutter 3.00
Nos. 1023-1025 (3) 1.45 1.05

EXPO '70 Intl. Exposition, Senri, Osaka, Mar. 15-Sept. 13.

No. 1025b contains a pane of 4 No. 1023 and a pane with Nos. 1023-1025. A 35mm gutter separates the panes.

Woman with Hand Drum, by Saburosuke Okada A676

1970, Apr. 20 Photo. *Perf. 13*

1026 A676 15y multicolored .45 .20

Issued for Stamp Week, Apr. 20-26.

Mt. Yoshino — A677

Nachi Waterfall A678

1970, Apr. 30 Photo. *Perf. 13*

1027 A677 7y gray & pink .20 .20
1028 A678 15y pale blue & grn .30 .20

Yoshino-Kumano National Park.

Pole Lanterns at EXPO — A679

View of EXPO Within Globe — A680

Grass in Autumn Wind, by Hoitsu Sakai (1761-1828) — A681

1970, June 15 Photo. *Perf. 13*

1029 A679 7y red & multi .20 .20
1030 A680 15y blue & multi .30 .20
1031 A681 50y silver & multi .95 .20
a. Souv. sheet of 3, #1029-1031 1.75
b. Bklt. panes of 4 & 3 with gutter 3.00
Nos. 1029-1031 (3) 1.45 .60

EXPO '70, 2nd issue.

No. 1031b contains a pane of 4 No. 1029 and a pane with Nos. 1029-1031. A 35mm gutter separates the panes.

Buildings and Postal Code Symbol — A682

1970, July 1 Photo. *Perf. 13*

1032 A682 7y emerald & vio .35 .20
1033 A682 15y brt blue & choc .50 .20

Postal code system.

"Maiden at Dojo Temple" A683

Scene from "Sukeroku" A684

"The Subscription List" (Kanjincho) — A685

1970, July 10

1034 A683 15y multicolored .30 .20
1035 A684 15y multicolored .30 .20
1036 A685 50y multicolored .95 .40
Nos. 1034-1036 (3) 1.55 .80

Issued to publicize the Kabuki Theater.

Girl Scout — A686

1970, July 26

1037 A686 15y multicolored .30 .20

50th anniversary of Japanese Girl Scouts.

Kinoura Coast and Festival Drum — A687

Tate Mountains Seen from Himi Coast — A688

1970, Aug. 1

1038 A687 15y multicolored .30 .20
1039 A688 15y multicolored .30 .20

Noto Hanto Quasi-National Park.

Sunflower and UN Emblem — A689

1970, Aug. 17

1040 A689 15y lt blue & multi .30 .20

Issued to publicize the 4th United Nations Congress on the Prevention of Crime and the Treatment of Offenders, Kyoto, Aug. 17-26.

Mt. Myogi — A690

Mt. Arafune A691

1970, Sept. 11 Photo. *Perf. 13*

1041 A690 15y multicolored .30 .20
1042 A691 15y multicolored .30 .20

Myogi-Arafune-Sakukogen Quasi-Natl. Park.

G.P.O., Tokyo, by Hiroshige III A692

Equestrian, Mt. Iwate and Paulownia A693

1970, Oct. 6

1043 A692 50y multicolored .95 .30

Intl. Letter Writing Week, Oct. 6-12. Sheets of 10 (5x2). Design from wood block series, "Noted Places in Tokyo."

1970, Oct. 10 Photo. *Perf. 13*

1044 A693 15y silver & multi .30 .20

25th Natl. Athletic Meet, Morioka, 10/10-16.

Hodogaya Stage, by Hiroshige III — A694

Tree and UN Emblem A695

1970, Oct. 20

1045 A694 15y silver & multi .30 .20

Centenary of telegraph service in Japan.

1970, Oct. 24

50y, UN emblem and Headquarters with flags.

1046 A695 15y olive, ap grn & gold .30 .20
1047 A695 50y multicolored .95 .20

25th anniversary of United Nations.

Vocational Training Competition Emblem — A696

Diet Building and Doves A697

1970, Nov. 10 Photo. *Perf. 13*

1048 A696 15y multicolored .30 .20

The 19th International Vocational Training Competition, Chiba City, Nov. 10-19.

1970, Nov. 29

1049 A697 15y multicolored .30 .20

80th anniversary of Japanese Diet.

Wild Boar, Folk Art, Arai City, Niigata Prefecture — A698

1970, Dec. 10

1050 A698 7y multicolored .20 .20

New Year 1971. Sheets containing 4 #1050 were awarded as prizes in the New Year lottery. Value $1.50.

Gen-jo-raku A699

Ko-cho A700

Tai-hei-raku — A701

1971, Apr. 1 Photo. *Perf. 13*

1051 A699 15y multicolored .30 .20
1052 A700 15y multicolored .30 .20
1053 A701 50y multicolored .95 .20
Nos. 1051-1053 (3) 1.55 .60

Gagaku, classical Japanese court entertainment.

Woman Voter and Parliament A702

Pines and Maple Leaves A703

1971, Apr. 10 Photo. *Perf. 13*

1054 A702 15y orange & multi .30 .20

25th anniversary of woman suffrage.

1971, Apr. 18

1055 A703 7y emerald & violet .20 .20

National forestation campaign.

Woman of Tokyo, by Kiyokata Kaburagi — A704

1971, Apr. 19

1056	A704	15y gray & multi	.35	.20

Philatelic Week, Apr. 19-25.

Mailman A705

Mailbox A706

Railroad Post Office — A707

1971, Apr. 20

1057	A705	15y blk & org brn	.30	.20
1058	A706	15y multicolored	.30	.20
1059	A707	15y multicolored	.30	.20
		Nos. 1057-1059 (3)	.90	.60

Centenary of Japanese postage stamps.

Titmouse A708

Penguins A709

1971, May 10 Photo. *Perf. 13*

1060	A708	15y emer, blk & bis	.30	.20

25th Bird Week.

1971, June 23 Photo. *Perf. 13*

1061	A709	15y dk blue, yel & grn	.30	.20

Antarctic Treaty pledging peaceful uses of and scientific co-operation in Antarctica, 10th anniv.

Goto Wakamatsu Seto Region — A710

Kujukushima ("99 Islands"), Kyushu A711

1971, June 26 Photo. *Perf. 13*

1062	A710	7y dark green	.20	.20
1063	A711	15y deep brown	.30	.20

Saikai National Park.

Arabic Numerals and Postal Code Symbol — A712

1971, July 1

1064	A712	7y emerald & red	.20	.20
1065	A712	15y blue & carmine	.30	.20

Promotion for postal code system.

Inscribed "NIPPON" Types of 1962-67 and

Little Cuckoo A713

Mute Swan A714

Sika Deer A715

Beetle A716

Pine — A717

Noh Mask A717a

Pheasant A717b

Golden Eagle — A717c

Bronze Phoenix, Uji — A718

Burial Statue of Warrior, Ota — A718a

Buddha, Sculpture, 685 A718b

Tentoki Sculpture, 11th Century A718c

Bazara-Taisho, c. 710-794 A718d

Goddess Kissho A718e

Photo., Engr. (No. 1087)

1971-75 *Perf. 13*

1067	A713	3y emerald	.20	.20
a.		Bklt. pane of 20 ('72)	2.00	
1068	A714	5y bright blue	.20	.20
1069	A715	10y yel grn & sep ('72)	.20	.20
a.		Bklt. pane of 6 (2 #1069, 4 #1071 with gutter btwn.) ('72)	1.40	
1070	A716	12y deep brown	.20	.20
1071	A717	20y grn & sep ('72)	.25	.20
a.		Pane of 10 (5x2) ('72)	2.75	
1072	A565b	25y emer & lt ultra ('72)	.40	.20
1074	A717a	70y dp org & blk	1.00	.20
1075	A717b	80y crimson & brn	1.25	.20
1076	A467	90y org & dk brn	1.50	.20
1077	A717c	90y org & brn ('73)	1.50	.20
1079	A569	120y dk brn & lt grn ('72)	2.00	.20
1080	A718	150y lt & dk green	2.50	.20
1081	A570	200y dp car (18x22mm; '72)	3.50	.20
1082	A718a	200y red brn ('74)	3.50	.30
1083	A718b	300y dk blue ('74)	5.50	.25
1084	A718c	400y car rose ('74)	7.00	.25
1085	A718d	500y green ('74)	9.00	.20
1087	A718e	1000y multi ('75)	17.50	.50
a.		Miniature sheet of 1	15.00	15.00
		Nos. 1067-1087 (18)	57.20	4.10

No. 1071a is imperf. on four sides.

See #1249-1250, 1254, 1629.

Coil Stamp

Perf. 13 Horiz.

1088	A717	20y green & sep ('72)	.45	.30

Boy Scout Bugler — A719

Rose and Rings — A720

1971, Aug. 2

1090	A719	15y lt blue & multi	.30	.20

13th World Boy Scout Jamboree, Asagiri Plain, Aug. 2-10.

1971, Oct. 1

1091	A720	15y ultra & multi	.30	.20

50th anniv. of Japanese Conciliation System.

Tokyo Horsedrawn Streetcar, by Yoshimura A721

1971, Oct. 6

1092	A721	50y multicolored	.95	.30

Intl. Letter Writing Week. Sheets of 10 (5x2).

Emperor's Flag, Chrysanthemums and Phoenix — A722

"Beyond the Sea," by Empress Nagako A723

1971, Oct. 14

1093	A722	15y gold, vio, red & bl	.30	.20
1094	A723	15y gold, vio, red & bl	.30	.20
a.		Souv. sheet of 2, #1093-1094, imperf.	.85	.85
b.		Pair, #1093-1094	.60	.25

European trip of Emperor Hirohito and Empress Nagako, Sept. 28-Oct. 15. No. 1094a has violet map of Asia, Africa and Europe in background.

Tennis, Cape Shiono-misaki, Plum Blossoms — A724

Child's Face and "100" — A725

1971, Oct. 24 Photo. *Perf. 13*

1095	A724	15y orange & multi	.30	.20

26th National Athletic Meet, Wakayama Prefecture, Oct. 24-29.

1971, Oct. 27

1096	A725	15y pink, car & blk	.30	.20

Centenary of Japanese Family Registration System.

Tiger, by Gaho Hashimoto A726

Design: No. 1098, Dragon, from "Dragon and Tiger," by Gaho Hashimoto.

1971, Nov. 1 Engr. *Perf. 13*

1097	A726	15y olive & multi	.30	.20
1098	A726	15y olive & multi	.30	.20
a.		Pair, #1097-1098	.75	.30

Centenary of Government Printing Works. Nos. 1097-1098 printed checkerwise.

Mt. Yotei from Lake Toya — A727

Mt. Showa-Shinzan A728

Treasure Ship A729

1971, Dec. 6
1099 A727 7y slate grn & yel .20 .20
1100 A728 15y pink & vio bl .30 .20

Shikotsu-Toya National Park.

1971-72
1101 A729 7y emerald, gold & org .20 .20
1102 A729 10y lt blue, org & gold .20 .20

New Year 1972. Sheets containing 3 #1102 were awarded as prizes in the New Year lottery. Value $1.75.
Issued: 7y, Dec. 10; 10y, Jan. 11, 1972.

Downhill Skiing — A730

#1104, Bobsledding. 50y, Figure skating, pairs.

1972, Feb. 3 Photo. *Perf. 13*
Size: 24x34mm
1103 A730 20y ultra & multi .45 .20
1104 A730 20y ultra & multi .45 .20
Size: 49x34mm
1105 A730 50y ultra & multi .95 .25
a. Souv. sheet of 3, #1103-1105 1.75 1.75
Nos. 1103-1105 (3) 1.85 .65

11th Winter Olympic Games, Sapporo, Feb. 3-13. No. 1105a has continuous design extending into margin.

Bunraku, Ningyo Jyoruri Puppet Theater
A731 A732

A733

1972, Mar. 1 Photo. *Perf. 13½*
1106 A731 20y gray & multi .40 .20
Perf. 12½x13
1107 A732 20y multicolored .40 .20
Lithographed and Engraved
Perf. 13½x13
1108 A733 50y multicolored .95 .20
Nos. 1106-1108 (3) 1.75 .60

Japanese classical entertainment.

Express Train on New Sanyo Line — A734

Taishaku-kyo Valley — A735

Hiba Mountains Seen from Mt. Dogo — A736

1972, Mar. 15 Photo. *Perf. 13*
1109 A734 20y multicolored .40 .20

Centenary of first Japanese railroad.

1972, Mar. 24
1110 A735 20y gray & multi .40 .20
1111 A736 20y green & multi .40 .20

Hiba-Dogo-Taishaku Quasi-National Park.

Heart and UN Emblem A737

1972, Apr. 15
1112 A737 20y gray, red & black .40 .20

"Your heart is your health," World Health Day.

"A Balloon Rising," by Gakuryo Nakamura A738

1972, Apr. 20
1113 A738 20y violet bl & multi .40 .20

Philatelic Week, Apr. 20-26.

Shurei Gate, Okinawa A739

Camellia A740

1972, May 15
1114 A739 20y ultra & multi .40 .20

Ratification of the Reversion Agreement with US under which the Ryukyu Islands were returned to Japan.

1972, May 20
1115 A740 20y brt grn, vio bl & yel .40 .20

National forestation campaign and 23rd Arbor Day, May 21.

Mt. Kurikoma and Kijiyama Kokeshi Doll — A741

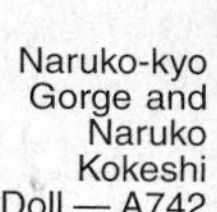

Naruko-kyo Gorge and Naruko Kokeshi Doll — A742

1972, June 20 Photo. *Perf. 13*
1116 A741 20y blue & multi .40 .20
1117 A742 20y red & multi .40 .20

Kurikoma Quasi-National Park.

Envelope, Postal Code Symbol A743

Mailbox, Postal Code Symbol A744

1972, July 1
1118 A743 10y blue, blk & gray .25 .20
1119 A744 20y emerald & org .40 .20

Publicity for the postal code system.

Mt. Hodaka A745

Mt. Tate — A746

1972, Aug. 10 Photo. *Perf. 13*
1120 A745 10y rose & violet .20 .20
1121 A746 20y blue & buff .40 .20

Chubu Sangaku National Park.

Ghost in "Tamura" A747

Lady Rokujo in "Lady Hollyhock" A748

"Hagoromo" (Feather Robe) — A749

1972, Sept. 20 Engr.
1122 A747 20y multicolored .40 .20
Photo.
1123 A748 20y multicolored .40 .20
Perf. 13½x13
1124 A749 50y multicolored .95 .20
Nos. 1122-1124 (3) 1.75 .60

Noh, classical public entertainment.

School Children — A750

Eitai Bridge, Tokyo, by Hiroshige III — A751

1972, Oct. 5 Photo. *Perf. 13*
1125 A750 20y lt ultra, vio bl & car .40 .20

Centenary of modern education system.

1972, Oct. 9
1126 A751 50y multicolored .95 .20

Intl. Letter Writing Week, Oct. 9-15.

Inauguration of Railway Service, by Hiroshige III — A752

Locomotive, Class C62 — A753

1972, Oct. 14
1127 A752 20y multicolored .40 .20
1128 A753 20y multicolored .40 .20

Centenary of Japanese railroad system.

Kendo (Fencing) and Sakurajima Volcano — A754

1972, Oct. 22
1129 A754 10y yellow & multi .20 .20

27th National Athletic Meet, Kagoshima Prefecture, Oct. 22-27.

Boy Scout Shaking Hand of Cub Scout — A755

1972, Nov. 4
1130 A755 20y yellow & multi .40 .20

50th anniversary of the Boy Scouts of Japan.

US Ship, Yokohama Harbor A756

"Clay Plate with Plum Blossoms" A757

1972, Nov. 28 Photo. *Perf. 13*
1131 A756 20y multicolored .40 .20

Centenary of Japanese customs. Wood block by Hiroshige III (d. 1896).

1972, Dec. 11
1132 A757 10y blue & multi .20 .20

New Year 1973. Art work by Kenzan Ogata (1663-1743). Sheets containing 3 #1132 were awarded as prizes in the New Year lottery. Value $1.75.

Mt. Tsurugi A758

Oboke Valley — A759

1973, Feb. 20 Photo. *Perf. 13*
1133 A758 20y multicolored .25 .20
1134 A759 20y multicolored .25 .20

Mt. Tsurugi Quasi-National Park.

Mt. Takao — A760

Minoo Falls — A761

1973, Mar. 12 Photo. *Perf. 13*
1135 A760 20y multicolored .25 .20
1136 A761 20y multicolored .25 .20

Meiji Forests Quasi-National Park.

Phoenix Tree — A762

Sumiyoshi Shrine Visitor — A763

1973, Apr. 7 Photo. *Perf. 13*
1137 A762 20y brt grn, yel & dk bl .30 .20

National forestation campaign.

1973, Apr. 20
1138 A763 20y multicolored .30 .20

Philatelic Week, Apr. 20-26. Design from painting by Ryusei Kishida (1891-1929) of his daughter, "A Portrait of Reiko Visiting Sumiyoshi Shrine."

Mt. Kamagatake A764

Mt. Haguro A765

1973, May 25 Photo. *Perf. 13*
1139 A764 20y multicolored .25 .20
1140 A765 20y multicolored .25 .20

Suzuka Quasi-National Park.

Chichijima Beach A766

Coral Reef on Minami Island — A767

1973, June 26
1141 A766 10y grnsh bl & Prus bl .20 .20
1142 A767 20y lilac & dk pur .25 .20

Ogasawara National Park.
5th anniversary of the return of the Bonin (Ogasawara Islands) to Japan.

Tree, Postal Code Symbol A768

Mailman, Postal Code Symbol A769

1973, July 1 Photo. *Perf. 13*
1143 A768 10y brt green & gold .20 .20
1144 A769 20y blue, purple & car .40 .20

Postal code system, 5th anniversary.

Sandan Gorge — A770

Mt. Shinnyu A771

1973, Aug. 28 Photo. *Perf. 13*
1145 A770 20y multicolored .40 .20
1146 A771 20y multicolored .40 .20

Nishi-Chugoku-Sanchi Quasi-National Park.

Tenryu Valley — A772

Mt. Horaiji — A773

1973, Sept. 18 Photo. *Perf. 13*
1147 A772 20y lilac & multi .40 .20
1148 A773 20y vio bl, lt bl & sil .40 .20

Tenryu-Okumikawa Quasi-National Park.

Cock, by Jakuchu Ito (1716-1800) A774

Woman Runner at Start A775

1973, Oct. 6
1149 A774 50y gold & multi .95 .25

International Letter Writing Week, Oct. 7-13. Sheets of 10.

1973, Oct. 14
1150 A775 10y silver & multi .20 .20

28th National Athletic Meet, Chiba Prefecture, Oct. 14-19.

Kan Mon Bridge A776

1973, Nov. 14 Engr. *Perf. 13*
1151 A776 20y black, rose & yel .40 .20

Opening of Kan Mon Bridge connecting Honshu and Kyushu.

Old Man and Dog — A777

Designs: No. 1153, Old man and wife pounding rice mortar, which yields gold. No. 1154, Old man sitting in tree and landlord admiring tree.

1973, Nov. 20 Photo.
1152 A777 20y multicolored .40 .20
1153 A777 20y multicolored .40 .20
1154 A777 20y multicolored .40 .20
Nos. 1152-1154 (3) 1.20 .60

Folk tale "Hanasaka-jiiji" (The Old Man Who Made Trees Bloom).

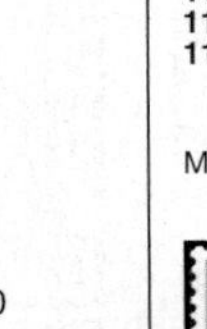
Bronze Lantern, Muromachi Period — A778

1973, Dec. 10
1155 A778 10y emerald, blk & org .20 .20

New Year 1974. Sheets containing 3 #1155 were awarded as prizes in the New Year lottery. Value $1.50.

Nijubashi, Tokyo A779

Imperial Palace, Tokyo A780

1974, Jan. 26 Photo. *Perf. 13*
1156 A779 20y gold & multi .40 .20
1157 A780 20y gold & multi .40 .20
a. Souv. sheet of 2, #1156-1157 .90 .40

50th anniversary of the wedding of Emperor Hirohito and Empress Nagako.

Young Wife A781

Crane Weaving A782

Cranes in Flight A783

1974, Feb. 20 Photo. *Perf. 13*
1158 A781 20y multicolored .40 .20
1159 A782 20y multicolored .40 .20
1160 A783 20y multicolored .40 .20
Nos. 1158-1160 (3) 1.20 .60

Folk tale "Tsuru-nyobo" (Crane becomes wife of peasant).

Marudu Falls — A784

Marine Scene — A785

1974, Mar. 15

1161 A784 20y multicolored .40 .20
1162 A785 20y multicolored .40 .20

Iriomote National Park.

"Finger," by Ito Shinsui — A786

Nambu Red Pine Sapling & Mt. Iwate — A787

1974, Apr. 20 Photo. *Perf. 13*

1163 A786 20y multicolored .40 .20

Philatelic Week, Apr. 20-27.

1974, May 18

1164 A787 20y multicolored .40 .20

National forestation campaign.

Supreme Court Building A788

1974, May 23 Engr.

1165 A788 20y redsh brown .40 .20

Completion of Supreme Court Building, Tokyo.

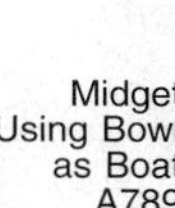

Midget Using Bowl as Boat A789

Designs: No. 1167, Midget fighting demon. No. 1168, Princess and midget changed into prince with magic hammer.

1974, June 10 Photo. *Perf. 13*

1166 A789 20y yellow & multi .40 .20
1167 A789 20y bister & multi .40 .20
1168 A789 20y bister & multi .40 .20
Nos. 1166-1168 (3) 1.20 .60

Folk tale "Issun Hoschi" (The Story of the Mini-mini Boy).

"Police," by Kunimasa Baido — A790

1974, June 17 *Perf. 13*

1169 A790 20y multicolored .40 .20

Centenary of the Tokyo Metropolitan Police Department.

Japanese Otter A791

Litho. and Engr.; Photo. and Engr. (Nos. 1172-1173)

1974

1170 A791 20y Mayailurus iriomotensis .40 .20
1171 A791 20y shown .40 .20
1172 A791 20y Pentalagus furnessi .40 .20
1173 A791 20y Pteropus pselaphon .40 .20
Nos. 1170-1173 (4) 1.60 .80

Nature conservation.
Issue dates: #1170, Mar. 25; #1171, June 25; #1172, Aug. 30; #1173, Nov. 15.

Transfusion Bottle, Globe, Doves — A794

1974, July 1 Photo.

1174 A794 20y brt blue & multi .40 .20

Intl. Red Cross Blood Donations Year.

Discovery of Kaguya Hime in Shining Bamboo A795

Kaguya Hime as Grown-up Beauty A796

Kaguya Hime and Escorts Returning to Moon A797

1974, July 29 Photo. *Perf. 13*

1175 A795 20y multicolored .40 .20
1176 A796 20y multicolored .40 .20
1177 A797 20y multicolored .40 .20
Nos. 1175-1177 (3) 1.20 .60

Folk tale "Kaguya Hime" or "Tale of the Bamboo Cutter."

Rich and Poor Men with Wens A798

Poor Man Dancing With Spirits A798a

Design: No. 1180, Rich man with two wens, poor man without wen, spirits.

1974, Sept. 9 Photo. *Perf. 13*

1178 A798 20y multicolored .40 .20
1179 A798a 20y multicolored .40 .20
1180 A798 20y multicolored .40 .20
Nos. 1178-1180 (3) 1.20 .60

Folk tale "Kobutori Jiisan," or "The Old Man who had his Wen Taken by Spirits."

Goode's Projection and Diet — A799

"Aizen" by Ryushi Kawabata — A800

1974, Oct. 1 Photo. *Perf. 13*

1181 A799 20y multicolored .40 .20
1182 A800 50y multicolored .95 .20

Interparliamentary Union, 61st Meeting, Tokyo, Nov. 2-11.

Pine and Hawk, by Sesson — A801

UPU Emblem — A802

Tending Cow, Fan by Sotatsu Tawaraya — A803

1974, Oct. 7

1183 A801 50y sepia, blk & dk brn .95 .20

Intl. Letter Writing Week, Oct. 6-12.

1974, Oct. 9

1184 A802 20y multicolored .40 .20
1185 A803 50y multicolored .95 .20

Centenary of Universal Postal Union.

Soccer Players and Sailboat A804

Various Mushrooms A805

1974, Oct. 20 Photo.

1186 A804 10y multicolored .20 .20

29th National Athletic Meet, Ibaraki Prefecture, Oct. 20-25.

1974, Nov. 2

1187 A805 20y multicolored .40 .20

9th International Congress on the Cultivation of Edible Fungi, Japan, Nov. 4-13.

Steam Locomotive Class D51 — A806

Class C57 — A807

Class 8620 — A808

Class C11 — A809

Designs: Steam locomotives.

1974, Nov. 26 Photo. *Perf. 13*

1188 A806 20y shown .40 .20
1189 A807 20y shown .40 .20
a. Pair, #1188-1189 .80 .20

1975, Feb. 25

1190 A806 20y Class D52 .40 .20
1191 A807 20y Class C58 .40 .20
a. Pair, #1190-1191 .80 .20

1975, Apr. 3

1192 A808 20y shown .40 .20
1193 A809 20y shown .40 .20
a. Pair, #1192-1193 .80 .20

1975, May 15

1194 A806 20y Class 9600 .40 .20
1195 A807 20y Class C51 .40 .20
a. Pair, #1194-1195 .80 .20

1975, June 10 Photo. & Engr.

1196 A806 20y Class 7100 .40 .20
1197 A806 20y Class 150 .40 .20
a. Pair, #1196-1197 .80 .20
Nos. 1188-1197 (10) 4.00 2.00

Japanese National Railways.

Ornamental Nail Cover, Katsura Palace — A810

1974, Dec. 10

1198 A810 10y blue & multi .20 .20

New Year 1975. Sheets containing 3 #1198 were awarded as prizes in the New Year Lottery. Value $1.50.

Short-tailed Albatrosses A811

Bonin Island Honey-eater A812

Temminck's Robin A813

Ryukyu-Yamagame Tortoise — A814

Design: No. 1200, Japanese cranes.

1975-76 Photo. & Engr. *Perf. 13*
1199 A811 20y multicolored .40 .20
1200 A811 20y multicolored .40 .20
1201 A812 20y multicolored .40 .20
1202 A813 50y multicolored .95 .20
1203 A814 50y multicolored .95 .20
Nos. 1199-1203 (5) 3.10 1.00

Nature conservation.
Issued: #1199, 1/16; #1200, 2/13; #1201, 8/8; #1202, 2/27/76; #1203, 3/25/76.

Taro Urashima Releasing Turtle A815

Palace of the Sea God and Fish A816

Smoke from Casket Making Taro an Old Man A817

1975, Jan. 28 Photo. *Perf. 13*
1204 A815 20y multicolored .40 .20
1205 A816 20y multicolored .40 .20
1206 A817 20y multicolored .40 .20
Nos. 1204-1206 (3) 1.20 .60

Folk tale "Legend of Taro Urashima."

Kan-mon-sho (Seeing and Hearing), by Shiko Munakata — A818

1975, Mar. 20 Photo. *Perf. 13*
1207 A818 20y brown & multi .40 .20

Japan Broadcasting Corp., 50th anniv.

Old Man Feeding Mouse A819

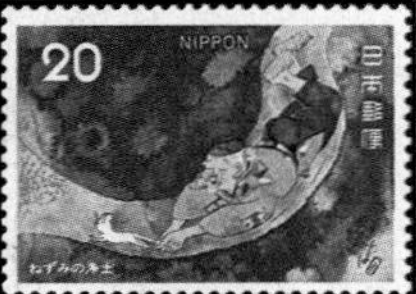

Man Following Mouse Underground — A820

Mice Entertaining and Bringing Gifts A821

1975, Apr. 15 Photo. *Perf. 13*
1208 A819 20y multicolored .40 .20
1209 A820 20y multicolored .40 .20
1210 A821 20y multicolored .40 .20
Nos. 1208-1210 (3) 1.20 .60

Folk tale "Paradise for the Mice."

Matsuura Screen (detail), 16th Century — A822

1975, Apr. 21
1211 20y denomination at lower left .40 .20
1212 20y denomination at lower right .40 .20
a. A822 Pair, #1211-1212 .80 .20

Philatelic Week, Apr. 21-27.

Oil Derricks, Congress Emblem — A824

1975, May 10 Photo. *Perf. 13*
1213 A824 20y multicolored .40 .20

9th World Petroleum Cong., Tokyo, May 11-16.

Trees and River — A825

IWY Emblem, Sun and Woman — A826

1975, May 24
1214 A825 20y green & multi .40 .20

National forestation campaign.

1975, June 23
1215 A826 20y orange & multi .40 .20

International Women's Year 1975.

Okinawan Dancer, EXPO 75 Emblem A827

Birds in Flight (Bingata) A828

Aquapolis and Globe — A829

1975, July 19 Photo. *Perf. 13*
1216 A827 20y ultra & multi .40 .20
1217 A828 30y blue grn & multi .60 .20
1218 A829 50y ultra & multi .95 .20
a. Souv. sheet of 3, #1216-1218 1.90 1.90
Nos. 1216-1218 (3) 1.95 .60

Oceanexpo 75, 1st Intl. Ocean Exposition, Okinawa, July 20, 1975-Jan. 18, 1976.

Historic Ship Issue

Kentoshi-sen 7th-9th Centuries — A830

Ships: #1220, Kenmin-sen, 7th-9th cent. #1221, Goshuin-sen, merchant ship, 16th-17th cent. #1222, Tenchi-maru, state barge, built 1630. #1223, Sengoku-bune (cargo ship) and fishing vessel. #1224, Shoheimaru, 1852, European-type sailing ship. #1225, Taisei-maru, four-mast bark training ship, 1903. #1226, Tenyomaru, first Japanese passenger liner, 1907. #1227, Asama-maru, passenger liner. #1228, Kinai-maru, transpacific freighter and Statue of Liberty. #1229, Container ship. #1230, Tanker.

1975-76 Engr. *Perf. 13*
1219 A830 20y rose red .40 .20
1220 A830 20y sepia .40 .20
a. Pair, #1219-1220 .80 .20
1221 A830 20y lt olive .40 .20
1222 A830 20y dark blue .40 .20
a. Pair, #1221-1222 .80 .20
1223 A830 50y violet blue .95 .20
1224 A830 50y lilac .95 .20
a. Pair, #1223-1224 1.90 .25
1225 A830 50y gray .95 .20
1226 A830 50y dark brown .95 .20
a. Pair, #1225-1226 1.90 .25
1227 A830 50y olive green .95 .20
1228 A830 50y olive brown .95 .20
a. Pair, #1227-1228 1.90 .25
1229 A830 50y ultra .95 .20
1230 A830 50y violet blue .95 .20
a. Pair, #1229-1230 1.90 .25
Nos. 1219-1230 (12) 9.20 2.40

Printed checkerwise in sheets of 20.
Issued: #1219-1220, 8/30; #1221-1222, 9/25; #1223-1224, 3/11/76; #1225-1226, 4/12/76; #1227-1228, 6/1/76; #1229-1230, 8/18/76.

Apple and Apple Tree — A831

Peacock, by Korin Ogata — A832

1975, Sept. 17 Photo. *Perf. 13*
1231 A831 20y gray, black & red .40 .20

Centenary of apple cultivation in Japan.

1975, Oct. 6 Photo. *Perf. 13*
1232 A832 50y gold & multi .95 .20

Intl. Letter Writing Week, Oct. 6-12.

American Flag and Cherry Blossoms A833

Japanese Flag and Dogwood A834

1975, Oct. 14
1233 A833 20y ultra & multi .40 .20
1234 A834 20y green & multi .40 .20
a. Souv. sheet of 2, #1233-1234 .90 .60

Visit of Emperor Hirohito and Empress Nagako to the United States, Oct. 1-14.

Savings Box and Coins — A835

Weight Lifter — A836

1975, Oct. 24
1235 A835 20y multicolored .40 .20

Japan's Postal Savings System, centenary.

1975, Oct. 25
1236 A836 10y multicolored .20 .20

30th National Athletic Meet, Mie Prefecture, Oct. 26-31.

Papier-mache Dragon, Fukushima Prefecture — A837

1975, Dec. 13 Photo. *Perf. 13*
1237 A837 10y multicolored .20 .20

New Year 1976. Sheets containing 3 #1237 were awarded as prizes in the New Year Lottery. Value $1.50.

Inscribed "NIPPON"
Types of 1963-74 and

Japanese Narcissus A841

Noh Mask, Old Man A843

Guardian Dog, Katori Shrine A845

Sho-Kannon, Yakushiji Temple A846

Designs: 50y, Nyoirin Kannon, Chuguji Temple. 150y, Bronze phoenix, Uji. 200y, Clay burial figure of warrior, Ota.

1976-79 Photo. *Perf. 13*
1244 A565f 50y emerald .95 .20
a. Bklt. panes of 2 & 4 with gutter 6.00
1245 A841 60y multicolored 1.10 .20
1248 A843 140y lil rose & lil 2.50 .20
1249 A718 150y red org & brn 2.75 .20
1250 A718a 200y red orange 3.75 .20

1251 A845 250y blue 4.75 .20
1253 A846 350y dk violet brn 6.50 .20
Nos. 1244-1253 (7) 22.30 1.40

Coil Stamps

Perf. 13 Horiz.

1254 A715 10y yel grn & sep ('79) .20 .20
1256 A565f 50y emerald 1.25 .20
1257 A468 100y ver & blk ('79) 1.90 .30
Nos. 1254-1257 (3) 3.35 .70

See No. 1631.

Hikone Folding Screen (detail), 17th Century — A850

1976, Apr. 20 Photo. *Perf. 13*

1258 50y denomination at lower right .95 .20
1259 50y denomination at upper right .95 .20
a. A850 Pair, #1258-1259 1.90 1.90

Philatelic Week, Apr. 20-26.

Plum Blossoms, Cedars, Mt. Tsukuba — A852

1976, May 22

1260 A852 50y multicolored .95 .20

National forestation campaign.

Green Tree Frog — A853

Bitterlings A854

Sticklebacks A855

1976 Photo. & Engr. *Perf. 13*

1261 A853 50y multicolored .95 .20
1262 A854 50y multicolored .95 .20
1263 A855 50y multicolored .95 .20
Nos. 1261-1263 (3) 2.85 .60

Nature conservation.

Issued: #1261, 7/20; #1262, 8/26; #1263, 9/16.

Crows, by Yosa Buson — A856

Gymnasts and Stadium — A857

1976, Oct. 6 Photo. *Perf. 13*

1264 A856 100y gray, blk & buff 1.90 .20

Intl. Letter Writing Week, Oct. 6-12.

1976, Oct. 23 Photo. *Perf. 13*

1265 A857 20y multicolored .40 .20

31st National Athletic Meet, Saga Prefecture, Oct. 24-29.

Cable, Cable Ship, Map of East China Sea — A858

1976, Oct. 25

1266 A858 50y blue, blk & silver .95 .20

Opening of Sino-Japanese cable between Shanghai and Reihoku-cho, Kumamoto Prefecture.

Classical Court Dance A859

Imperial Coach A860

1976, Nov. 10 Photo. *Perf. 13*

1267 A859 50y multicolored .95 .20
1268 A860 50y multicolored .95 .20
a. Souv. sheet of 2, #1267-1268 1.90 1.90

Emperor Hirohito's accession to the throne, 50th anniversary.

Kindergarten Class — A861

1976, Nov. 16

1269 A861 50y multicolored .95 .20

Centenary of first kindergarten in Japan.

Healthy Family A862

Bamboo Toy Snake A863

1976, Nov. 24

1270 A862 50y multicolored .95 .20

Natl. Health Insurance, 50th anniv.

1976, Dec. 1 Photo. *Perf. 13*

1271 A863 20y multicolored .40 .20

New Year 1977. Sheets containing 2 #1271 were awarded as prizes in the New Year lottery. Value $1.65.

National Treasures

East Pagoda, Yakushiji Temple, c. 730 — A864

Deva King in Armor Holding Spear, Nara Period A865

1976, Dec. 9 Photo. *Perf. 13*

1272 A864 50y multicolored .95 .20

Engr.

1273 A865 100y green & multi 1.90 .20

Golden Pavilion, Toshodai-ji Temple, 8th Century — A866

Praying Women, from Heike Nokyo Sutra, 12th Century A867

Photogravure and Engraved

1977, Jan. 20 *Perf. 13*

1274 A866 50y multicolored .95 .20

Photo.

1275 A867 100y multicolored 1.90 .20

Comic Picture Scroll, Attributed to Toba Sojo Kakuyu (1053-1140) — A868

Saint on Cloud, 11th Century Wood Carving, Byodoin Temple A869

1977, Mar. 25 Photo. *Perf. 13*

1276 A868 50y multicolored .95 .20

Engr.

1277 A869 100y multicolored 1.90 .20

Noblemen on Way to Court, from Picture Scroll, Heian Period — A870

Statue of Seitaka-doji, Messenger, Kamakura Period A871

1977, June 27 Photo. *Perf. 13*

1278 A870 50y multicolored .95 .20

Engr.

1279 A871 100y multicolored 1.90 .20

The Recluse Han Shan, 14th Century Painting — A872

Tower, Matsumoto Castle, 16th Century — A873

1977, Aug. 25 Photo. *Perf. 13*

1280 A872 50y multicolored .95 .20

Photogravure and Engraved

1281 A873 100y black & multi 1.90 .20

Pine and Flowers, Chishakuin Temple, Kyoto, 1591 — A874

Main Hall, Kiyomizu Temple, 1633 — A875

1977, Nov. 16 Photo. *Perf. 13*

1282 A874 50y multicolored .95 .20

Engr.

1283 A875 100y multicolored 1.90 .20

Scene from Tale of Genji, by Sotatsu Tawaraya — A876

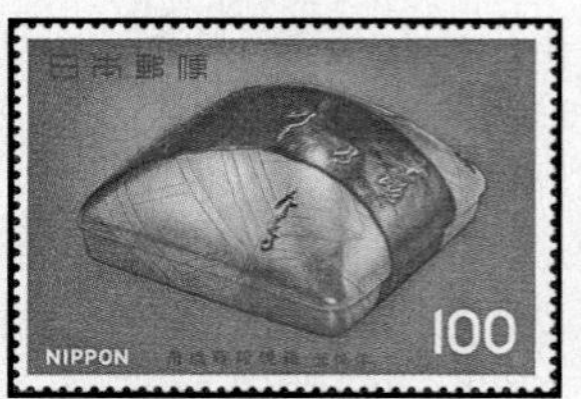

Inkstone Case, by Koetsu Honami — A877

1978, Jan. 26 Photo. *Perf. 13*

1284 A876 50y multicolored .95 .20

Photogravure and Engraved

1285 A877 100y black & multi 1.90 .25

Family Enjoying Cool Evening, by Morikage Kusumi — A878

Yomeimon, Toshogu Shrine, 1636 — A879

1978, Mar. 3 Photo. *Perf. 13*

1286 A878 50y gray & multi .95 .20

Photogravure and Engraved

1287 A879 100y multicolored 1.90 .25

Horseshoe Crabs A884

Graphium Doson Albidum — A885

Firefly A886

Cicada — A887

Dragonfly — A888

1977 Photo. *Perf. 13*

1292 A884 50y multicolored .95 .20

Photogravure and Engraved

1293 A885 50y multicolored .95 .20

1294 A886 50y multicolored .95 .20

1295 A887 50y multicolored .95 .20

Photo.

1296 A888 50y multicolored .95 .20

Nos. 1292-1296 (5) 4.75 1.00

Issued: #1292, 2/18; #1293, 5/18; #1294, 7/22; #1295, 8/15; #1296, 9/14.

Figure Skating — A889

Figure Skating Pair — A890

1977, Mar. 1

1297 A889 50y silver & multi .95 .20

1298 A890 50y silver & multi .95 .20

World Figure Skating Championships, National Yoyogi Stadium, March 1-6.

Sun Shining on Forest — A891

1977, Apr. 16 Photo. *Perf. 13*

1299 A891 50y green & multi .95 .20

National forestation campaign.

Weavers and Dyers (Detail from Folding Screen) — A892

1977, Apr. 20

1300 50y denomination at lower left .95 .20

1301 50y denomination at upper left .95 .20

a. A892 Pair, #1300-1301 1.90 .50

Philatelic Week, Apr. 20-26.

Nurses A894

1977, May 30 Photo. *Perf. 13*

1302 A894 50y multicolored .95 .20

16th Quadrennial Congress of the Intl. Council of Nurses, Tokyo, May 30-June 3.

Fast Breeder Reactor, Central Part — A895

1977, June 6

1303 A895 50y multicolored .95 .20

Experimental fast breeder reactor "Joyo," which began operating Apr. 24, 1977.

Workers and Safety Emblems A896

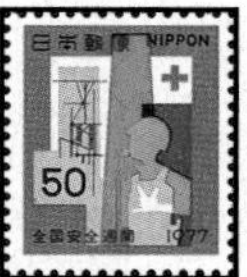

Work on High-rise Buildings A897

Cargo Unloading A898

Machinery Work A899

1977, July 1

1304 A896 50y multicolored .95 .20

1305 A897 50y multicolored .95 .20

1306 A898 50y multicolored .95 .20

1307 A899 50y multicolored .95 .20

a. Block or strip of 4, #1304-1307 4.00 .75

National Safety Week, July 1-July 7.

Carrier Pigeons, Mail Box, UPU Emblem A900

UPU Emblem, Postal Service Flag of Meiji Era, world Map A900a

1977, June 20 Photo. *Perf. 13*

1308 A900 50y multicolored .95 .20

1309 A900a 100y multicolored 1.90 .20

a. Souv. sheet of 2, #1308-1309 3.00 1.00

Cent. of Japan's admission to the UPU.

Surgeon in Operating Room — A901

1977, Sept. 3 Photo. *Perf. 13*

1310 A901 50y multicolored .95 .20

27th Cong. of the Intl. Surgeon's Society on the 75th anniv. of its founding, Kyoto, 9/3-8.

Child Using Telephone, Map of New Cable Route — A902

1977, Aug. 26

1311 A902 50y multicolored .95 .20

Inauguration of underwater telephone cable linking Okinawa, Luzon and Hong Kong.

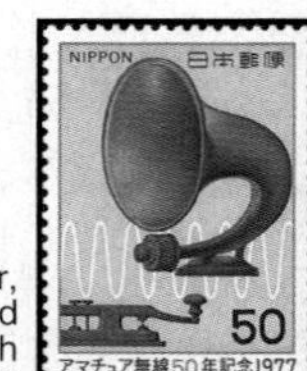

Early Speaker, Waves and Telegraph Key — A903

1977, Sept. 24 Photo. *Perf. 13*

1312 A903 50y multicolored .95 .20

50th anniversary of amateur radio in Japan.

Bicyclist, Mt. Iwaki and Iwaki River — A904

Flowers and Ducks, Attributed to Hasegawa Tohaku — A905

1977, Oct. 1

1313 A904 20y multicolored .40 .20

32nd National Athletic Meet, Aomori Prefecture, Oct. 2-7.

1977, Oct. 6

1314 A905 100y multicolored 1.90 .20

Intl. Letter Writing Week, Oct. 6-12.

Dinosaur, Stars, Museum A906

1977, Nov. 2 Photo. *Perf. 13*

1315 A906 50y multicolored .95 .20

Centenary of National Science Museum.

Decorated Horse, Fushimi Toy — A907

Tokyo Subway, 1927 A908

1977, Dec. 1 Photo. *Perf. 13*
1316 A907 20y multicolored .40 .20

New Year 1978. Sheets containing 2 #1316 were awarded as prizes in the New Year lottery. Value $1.50.

1977, Dec. 6
1317 A908 50y shown .95 .20
1318 A908 50y Subway, 1977 .95 .20
a. Pair, #1317-1318 1.50 .35

Tokyo Subway, 50th anniversary.

Primrose — A909

Pinguicula Ramosa — A910

Dicentra — A911

1978 Photo. & Engr. *Perf. 13*
1319 A909 50y multicolored .95 .20
1320 A910 50y multicolored .95 .20
1321 A911 50y multicolored .95 .20
Nos. 1319-1321 (3) 2.85 .60

Nature protection.
Issued: #1319, 4/12; #1320, 6/8; #1321, 7/25.

Kanbun Bijinzu Folding Screen, Edo Period — A912

1978, Apr. 20 Photo. *Perf. 13*
1322 50y inscribed at left .95 .20
1323 50y inscribed at right .95 .20
a. A912 Pair, #1322-1323 1.90 .35

Philatelic Week, Apr. 16-22.

Rotary Emblem, Mt. Fuji A914

Congress Emblem, by Taro Okamoto A915

1978, May 13 Photo. *Perf. 13*
1324 A914 50y multicolored .95 .20

69th Rotary International Convention, Tokyo, May 14-18.

1978, May 15
1325 A915 50y multicolored .95 .20

23rd International Ophthalmological Congress, Kyoto, May 14-20.

Narita International Airport, Tokyo — A916

1978, May 20
1326 A916 50y multicolored .95 .20

Opening of Tokyo International Airport.

Rainbow, Japanese Cedars, Cape Ashizuri A917

Lion, by Sotatsu Tawaraya, Lions Emblem A918

1978, May 20
1327 A917 50y multicolored .95 .20

National forestation campaign.

1978, June 21 Photo. *Perf. 13*
1328 A918 50y multicolored .95 .20

61st Lions Intl. Convention, Tokyo, 6/21-24.

Sumo Print Issues

Grand Champion Hidenoyama with Sword Bearer and Herald, by Kunisada I (Toyokuni III) — A919

Ekoin Drum Tower, Ryogoku, by Hiroshige — A921

Photogravure and Engraved

1978, July 1 *Perf. 13*
1329 50y multicolored .95 .20
1330 50y multicolored .95 .20
a. A919 Pair, #1329-1330 1.90 .30

Photo.

1331 A921 50y multicolored .95 .20
Nos. 1329-1331 (3) 2.85 .60

Champions Tanikaze and Onogawa in Ring-entry Ceremony, 1782, by Shunsho — A922

Jimmaku, Raiden and Referee Shonosuke, 1791 Bout, by Shun'ei — A924

Photogravure and Engraved

1978, Sept. 9 *Perf. 13*
1332 50y multicolored .95 .20
1333 50y multicolored .95 .20
a. A922 Pair, #1332-1333 1.90 .30
1334 A924 50y multicolored .95 .20
Nos. 1332-1334 (3) 2.85 .60

Referee Shonosuke and Champion Onomatsu, by Kunisada I — A925

Children's Sumo Play, by Utamaro — A927

1978, Nov. 11 *Perf. 13*
1335 50y multicolored .95 .20
1336 50y multicolored .95 .20
a. A925 Pair, #1335-1336 1.90 .30
1337 A927 50y multicolored .95 .20
Nos. 1335-1337 (3) 2.85 .60

Wrestlers on Ryogoku Bridge, by Kunisada I — A928

Bow-receiving Ceremony at Tournament, by Kunisada II — A930

1979, Jan. 13 *Perf. 13*
1338 50y multicolored .95 .20
1339 50y multicolored .95 .20
a. A928 Pair, #1338-1339 1.90 .30
1340 A930 50y multicolored .95 .20
Nos. 1338-1340 (3) 2.85 .60

Takekuma and Iwamigata (Hidenoyama) Wrestling, by Kuniyoshi — A931

Daidozan (Great Child Mountain) in Ring-entry Ceremony, by Sharaku — A933

1979, Mar. 10 *Perf. 13*
1341 50y multicolored .95 .20
1342 50y multicolored .95 .20
a. A931 Pair, #1341-1342 1.90 .30
1343 A933 50y multicolored .95 .20
Nos. 1341-1343 (3) 2.85 .60

Radio Gymnastics Emblem — A934

1978, Aug. 1 Photo. *Perf. 13*
1344 A934 50y multicolored .95 .20

Radio gymnastics program exercises, 50th anniversary.

Chamber of Commerce and Industry A935

1978, Aug. 28 Photo. *Perf. 13*
1345 A935 50y multicolored .95 .20

Tokyo Chamber of Commerce, centenary.

Symbolic Sculptures, Tokyo Stock Exchange — A936

Flowering Plum with Pheasant, from Screen, Tenkyuin Temple — A937

1978, Sept. 14 **Engr.** ***Perf. 13***
1346 A936 50y lilac, grn & brn .95 .20

Centenary of the Tokyo and Osaka Stock Exchanges.

1978, Oct. 6 **Photo.** ***Perf. 13***
1347 A937 100y multicolored 1.90 .25

Intl. Letter Writing Week, Oct. 6-12.

Softball and Mt. Yarigatake A938

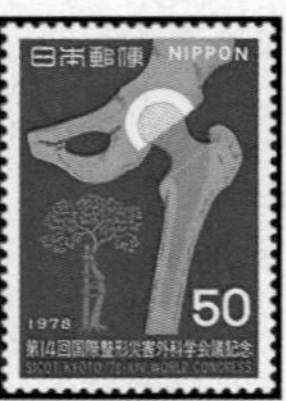
Artificial Hip, Orthopedists' Emblem A939

1978, Oct. 14
1348 A938 20y multicolored .40 .20

33rd National Athletic Meet, Nagano Prefecture, Oct. 15-20.

1978, Oct. 16
1349 A939 50y multicolored .95 .20

14th World Cong. of Intl. Soc. of Orthopedic Surgeons (50th anniv.), Kyoto, Oct. 15-20.

Telescope and Stars — A940

Sheep Bell, Nakayama Toy — A941

1978, Dec. 1 **Photo.**
1350 A940 50y multicolored .95 .20

Tokyo Astronomical Observatory, cent.

1978, Dec. 4
1351 A941 20y multicolored .40 .20

New Year 1979. Sheets containing 2 #1351 were awarded as prizes in the New Year Lottery. Value $1.50.

Family, Human Rights Emblem — A942

Hands Shielding Children — A943

1978, Dec. 4
1352 A942 50y multicolored .95 .20

Human Rights Week, Dec. 4-10.

1979, Feb. 16 **Photo.** ***Perf. 13***
1353 A943 50y multicolored .95 .20

Education of the handicapped, centenary.

Telephone Dials — A944

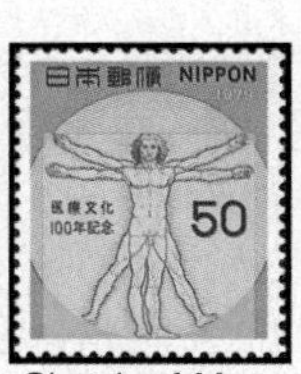
Sketch of Man, by Leonardo da Vinci — A945

1979, Mar. 14 **Photo.** ***Perf. 13***
1354 A944 50y multicolored .95 .20

Nation-wide telephone automatization completion.

Photogravure and Engraved

1979, Apr. 7 ***Perf. 13***
1355 A945 50y multicolored .95 .20

Centenary of promulgation of State Medical Act, initiating modern medicine.

Standing Beauties, Middle Edo Period — A946

1979, Apr. 20 **Photo.**
1356 50y multicolored .95 .20
1357 50y multicolored .95 .20
a. A946 Pair, #1356-1357 1.90 .35

Philatelic Week, Apr. 16-22.

Mt. Horaiji and Maple — A948

1979, May 26 **Photo.** ***Perf. 13***
1358 A948 50y multicolored .95 .20

National forestation campaign.

Modern Japanese Art Issue

Merciful Mother Goddess, by Kano Hogai — A949

Sea God's Princess, by Aoki Shigeru — A950

1979, May 30 **Photo.** ***Perf. 13***
1359 A949 50y multicolored .95 .20
1360 A950 50y multicolored .95 .20

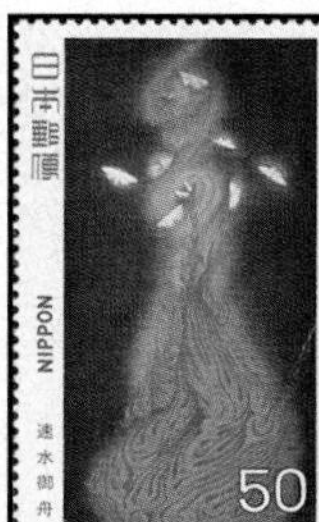
Fire Dance, by Gyoshu Hayami — A951

Leaning Figure, by Tetsugoro Yorozu — A952

1979, June 25 **Photo.** ***Perf. 13***
1361 A951 50y red & multi .95 .20

Photogravure and Engraved

1362 A952 50y red & multi .95 .20

The Black Cat, by Shunso Hishida — A953

Kinyo, by Sotaro Yasui — A954

1979, Sept. 21 **Photo.** ***Perf. 13***
1363 A953 50y multicolored .95 .20
1364 A954 50y multicolored .95 .20

Nude, by Kagaku Murakami A955

Harvest, by Asai Chu — A956

Photogravure and Engraved

1979, Nov. 22 ***Perf. 13***
1365 A955 50y multicolored .65 .20
1366 A956 50y multicolored .65 .20

Salmon, by Yuichi Takahashi A956a

Hall of the Supreme Buddha, by Kokei Kabayashi A956b

Photogravure and Engraved

1980, Feb. 22 ***Perf. 13½***
1367 A956a 50y multicolored .95 .20

Photo.

1368 A956b 50y multicolored .95 .20

Quarantine Officers, Ships, Plane, Microscope A957

1979, July 14 **Photo.**

1369 A957 50y multicolored .95 .20

Centenary of Japanese Quarantine system.

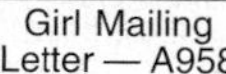

Girl Mailing Letter — A958

Hakata Doll with Letter-paper Roll — A959

1979, July 23

1370 A958 20y multicolored .40 .20
1371 A959 50y multicolored .95 .20

Letter Writing Day.

Pitcher, Baseball with Black Lion Emblem — A960

1979, July 27

1372 A960 50y multicolored .95 .20

50th National Inter-city Amateur Baseball Tournament, Tokyo, August.

Girl Floating in Space A961

Design: No. 1374, Boy floating in space.

1979, Aug. 1

1373 A961 50y magenta & multi .95 .20
1374 A961 50y blue & multi .95 .20
a. Souv. sheet of 2, #1373-1374 1.90 1.90

International Year of the Child.

Japanese Song Issue

Moon over Castle, by Rentaro Taki A962

Evening Glow, by Shin Kusakawa A963

Maple Leaves, by Teiichi Okano A964

The Birthplace, by Teiichi Okano — A965

Winter Landscape A966

Mt. Fuji — A967

Spring Brook A968

Cherry Blossoms A969

1979, Aug. 24 **Photo. & Engr.**

1375 A962 50y multicolored .95 .20
1376 A963 50y multicolored .95 .20

1979, Nov. 26

1377 A964 50y multicolored .95 .20
1378 A965 50y multicolored .95 .20

1980, Jan. 28 ***Perf. 13***

1379 A966 50y multicolored .95 .20
1380 A967 50y multicolored .95 .20

1980, Mar. 21

1381 A968 50y multicolored .95 .20
1382 A969 50y multicolored .95 .20
Nos. 1375-1382 (8) 7.60 1.60

Great Owl, by Okyo Maruyama — A970

1979, Oct. 8 **Photo.** ***Perf. 13***

1383 A970 100y multicolored 1.90 .25

Intl. Letter Writing Week, Oct. 8-14.

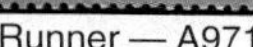

Runner — A971

"ITU," Globe — A972

1979, Oct. 13

1384 A971 20y multicolored .40 .20

34th National Athletic Meet, Miyazaki, Oct. 4-19.

1979, Oct. 13 **Litho.** ***Perf. 13½***

1385 A972 50y multicolored .95 .20

Admission to ITU, cent.

Woman and Fetus — A973

1979, Nov. 12 **Photo.**

1386 A973 50y multicolored .95 .20

9th World Congress of Gynecology and Obstetrics, Tokyo, Oct. 25-31.

Happy Monkeys, Osaka Toy — A974

Government Auditing Centenary A975

1979, Dec. 1 **Photo.** ***Perf. 13x13½***

1387 A974 20y multicolored .40 .20

New Year 1980. Sheets of 2 #1387 were New Year Lottery prizes. Value $1.50.

1980, Mar. 5 **Photo.** ***Perf. 13½***

1388 A975 50y multicolored .95 .20

Scenes of Outdoor Play in Spring, by Sukenobu Nishikawa — A976

1980, Apr. 21 **Photo.** ***Perf. 13½***

1389 50y multicolored .95 .20
1390 50y multicolored .95 .20
a. A976 Pair, #1389-1390 1.90 .50

Philatelic Week, Apr. 21-27. Sheets of 10.

Japanese Song Issue

The Sea — A978

The Night of the Hazy Moon — A979

Memories of Summer — A981

The Sun Flag — A980

1980 **Photo. & Engr.** ***Perf. 13***

1391 A978 50y multicolored .95 .20
1392 A979 50y multicolored .95 .20
1393 A980 50y multicolored .95 .20
1394 A981 50y multicolored .95 .20
Nos. 1391-1394 (4) 3.80 .80

Issued: #1391-1392, 4/28; #1393-1394, 6/16.

The Red Dragonfly A982

Song by the Sea — A983

1980, Sept. 18 ***Perf. 13***

1395 A982 50y multicolored .95 .20
1396 A983 50y multicolored .95 .20

Lullaby A984

Coconut, by Toraji Ohnaka — A985

1981, Feb. 9 ***Perf. 13***

1397 A984 60y multicolored 1.10 .20
1398 A985 60y multicolored 1.10 .20

Spring Has Come, by Tatsuyuki Takano — A986

Cherry Blossoms, by Hagoromo Takeshima A987

1981, Mar. 10 ***Perf. 13***

1399 A986 60y multicolored 1.10 .20
1400 A987 60y multicolored 1.10 .20

Modern Japanese Art Issue

Dancers, by Seiki Kuroda — A988

Mother and Child, by Shoen Uemura A989

1980, May 12 **Photo.** ***Perf. 13½***

1401 A988 50y multicolored .95 .20
1402 A989 50y multicolored .95 .20

The Black Fan, by Takeji Fujishima — A990

Dear Me . . . It's a Shower, by Seiho Takeuchi A991

1980, July 7 **Photo.** ***Perf. 13½***

1403 A990 50y multicolored .95 .20
1404 A991 50y multicolored .95 .20

Woman, by Morie Ogiwara — A992

Kurofuneya, by Yumeji Takehisa — A993

1980, Oct. 27 **Photo.** ***Perf. 13½***

1405 A992 50y multicolored .95 .20
1406 A993 50y multicolored .95 .20

Nippon Maru, Institute Emblem — A994

1980, May 17

1407 A994 50y multicolored .95 .20

Institute for Nautical Training, training ships Nippon Maru and Kaio Maru, 50th anniversary.

Mt. Gozaisho-dake, Cedars, Flowers — A995

1980, May 24 ***Perf. 13x13½***

1408 A995 50y multicolored .95 .20

National forestation campaign.

Yayosu Fire Brigade Review, by Hiroshige III — A996

1980, May 31

1409 A996 50y multicolored .95 .20

Fire fighting centenary.

A997

A997a

Letter Writing Day: 20y, Teddy Bear holding letter. 50y, Folded and tied letter of good wishes, horiz.

1980, July 23 ***Perf. 13x13½, 13½x13***

1410 A997 20y multicolored .40 .20
1411 A997a 50y multicolored .95 .20

Lühdorfla Japonica A998

1980, Aug. 2 ***Perf. 13½***

1412 A998 50y multicolored .95 .20

16th Intl. Cong. of Entomology, Kyoto, Aug. 3-9.

Three-dimensional World Map — A999

1980, Aug. 25 **Photo.**

1413 A999 50y multicolored .95 .20

24th Intl. Geographic Cong. and 10th Intl. Cartographic Conf., Tokyo, August.

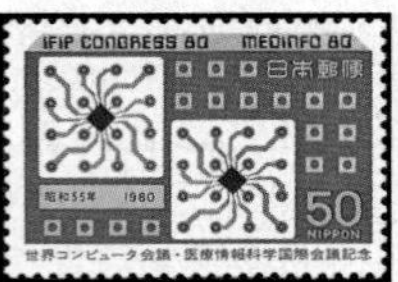

Integrated Circuit A1000

Camellia A1001

1980, Sept. 29

1414 A1000 50y multicolored .95 .20

Intl. Federation for Information Processing Cong. '80, Tokyo, Oct. 6-9 and World Conf. on Medical Informatics '80, Tokyo, 9/29-10/4.

1980, Oct. 1

1415 A1001 30y shown .60 .20
1416 A1001 40y Rape flower, cabbage butterflies .75 .20
1417 A1001 50y Cherry blossoms .95 .20
Nos. 1415-1417 (3) 2.30 .60

See No. 1437.

Cranes, by Motooki Watanabe A1002

Archery, Mt. Nantai A1003

1980, Oct. 6 ***Perf. 13***

1418 A1002 100y multicolored 1.90 .25

24th Intl. Letter Writing Week, Oct. 6-12.

1980, Oct. 11

1419 A1003 20y multicolored .40 .20

35th Natonal Athletic Meet, Tochigi, Oct.

Globe, Jaycee Emblem — A1004

Diet Building and Doves — A1005

1980, Nov. 8 ***Perf. 13***

1420 A1004 50y multicolored .95 .25

35th Jaycee (Intl. Junior Chamber of Commerce) World Congress, Osaka, Nov. 9-15.

1980, Nov. 29 ***Perf. 13½***

1421 A1005 50y multicolored .95 .20

90th anniversary of Japanese Diet.

Type of 1980 and:

Amur Adonis A1006

White Trumpet Lily A1007

Hanging Bell, Byodoin Temple A1008

Bronze Buddhist Ornament, 7th Century A1009

Writing Box Cover A1010

Mirror with Figures A1011

Heart-shaped Figurine A1012

Silver Crane A1013

Maitreya, Horyuji Temple A1014

Ichiji Kinrin, Chusonji Temple A1015

Komokuten, Todaiji Temple A1016

Lady Maya A1017

Enamel Jar, by Ninsei Nonomura A1018

Miroku Bosatsu, Koryuji Temple A1019

1980-82 **Photo.** ***Perf. 13x13½***

1422 A1006 10y multicolored .25 .20
1423 A1007 20y multicolored .30 .20
1424 A1008 60y multicolored 1.10 .20
a. Bklt. pane (#1424, 4 #1424 with gutter btwn.) ('81) 5.50
1425 A1009 70y multicolored 1.25 .30
1426 A1010 70y multicolored 1.25 .20
1427 A1011 80y multicolored 1.50 .20
1428 A1012 90y multicolored 1.75 .20
1429 A1013 100y multicolored 1.90 .20
1430 A1014 170y multicolored 3.25 .25
1431 A1015 260y multicolored 5.00 .40
1432 A1016 310y multicolored 6.00 .50
1433 A1017 410y multicolored 8.00 .75

1434 A1018 410y multicolored 8.00 .75
1435 A1019 600y multicolored 11.50 1.00
Nos. 1422-1435 (14) 51.05 5.35

Coil Stamps

Perf. 13 Horiz.

1436 A1006 10y multi ('82) .25 .20
1437 A1001 40y as #1416 .75 .30
1438 A1008 60y multi ('82) 1.10 .30
1439 A1013 100y multi ('82) 1.90 .50
Nos. 1436-1439 (4) 4.00 1.30

See Nos. 1627-1628.

Clay Chicken, Folk Toy — A1026

1980, Dec. 1 ***Perf. 13 Horiz.***
1442 A1026 20y multicolored .40 .20

New Year 1981.

Sheets of two were New Year Lottery Prizes. Value $1.50.

Modern Japanese Art Issue

Snow-Covered Power Station, by Shikanosuke Oka — A1027

NuKada-no-Ohkimi and Nara in Spring, by Yukihiko Yasuda — A1028

1981, Feb. 26 ***Perf. 13½***
1443 A1027 60y multicolored 1.10 .20

Photo.

1444 A1028 60y multicolored 1.10 .20

Artist's Family, by Narashige Koide — A1029

Bamboo Shoots, by Heihachiro Fukuda A1030

Photo. & Engr., Photo.

1981, June 18 ***Perf. 13½***
1445 A1029 60y multicolored 1.10 .20
1446 A1030 60y multicolored 1.10 .20

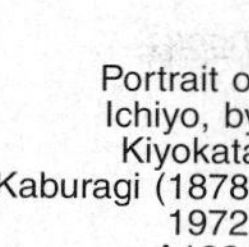

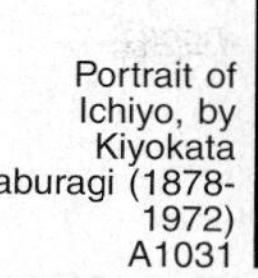

Portrait of Ichiyo, by Kiyokata Kaburagi (1878-1972) A1031

Portrait of Reiko, by Ryusei Kishida (1891-1929) A1032

Photo., Photo. and Engr.

1981, Nov. 27 **Engr.** ***Perf. 13½***
1447 A1031 60y multicolored 1.10 .20
1448 A1032 60y multicolored 1.10 .20

Yoritomo in a Cave, by Seison Maeda — A1033

Advertisement of a Terrace, by Yuzo Saeki — A1034

1982, Feb. 25 **Photo.** ***Perf. 13½***
1449 A1033 60y multicolored 1.10 .20
1450 A1034 60y multicolored 1.10 .20

Emblem, Port Island A1035

1981, Mar. 20 ***Perf. 13***
1451 A1035 60y multicolored 1.10 .20

Portopia '81, Kobe Port Island Exhibition, Mar. 20-Sept. 15.

Agriculture, Forestry and Fishery Promotion Centenary A1036

1981, Apr. 7
1452 60y multicolored 1.10 .20

Moonflower, by Harunobu Suzuki — A1037

1981, Apr. 20 **Photo.** ***Perf. 13½***
1453 60y multicolored 1.10 .20
1454 60y multicolored 1.10 .20
a. A1037 Pair, #1453-1454 2.20 .30

Philatelic Week, Apr. 21-27.

Cherry Blossoms — A1039

Cargo Ship and Crane A1040

1981, May 23 **Photo.** ***Perf. 13x13½***
1455 A1039 60y multicolored 1.10 .20

1981, May 25 ***Perf. 13***
1456 A1040 60y multicolored 1.10 .20

International Port and Harbor Association, 12th Convention, Nagoya, May 23-30.

Land Erosion Control Cent. — A1041

Stylized Man and Spinal Cord Dose Response Curve A1042

1981, June 27 ***Perf. 13½***
1457 A1041 60y multicolored 1.10 .20

1981, July 18 **Photo.** ***Perf. 13***
1458 A1042 60y multicolored 1.10 .20

8th Intl. Pharmacology Cong., Tokyo, July 19-24.

Girl Writing Letter A1043

Japanese Crested Ibis A1044

1981, July 23
1459 A1043 40y shown .75 .20
1460 A1043 60y Boy, stamp 1.10 .20

Letter Writing Day (23rd of each month).

1981, July 27 **Litho.**
1461 A1044 60y multicolored 1.10 .20

Plug, faucet A1044a

Plugs A1045

1981, Aug. 1 **Photo.**
1462 A1044a 40y multicolored .75 .20
1463 A1045 60y multicolored 1.10 .20

Energy conservation.

Western Architecture Issue

Oura Cathedral — A1046

Hyokei Hall, Tokyo A1047

Photogravure and Engraved

1981, Aug. 22
1464 A1046 60y multicolored 1.10 .20
1465 A1047 60y multicolored 1.10 .20

Old Kaichi School, Nagano A1048

Doshisha University Chapel, Kyoto A1049

1981, Nov. 9 ***Perf. 13***
1466 A1048 60y multicolored 1.10 .20
1467 A1049 60y multicolored 1.10 .20

St. John's Church, Meiji-mura A1050

Military Exercise Hall (Former Sapporo Agricultural School), Sapporo A1051

1982, Jan. 29 ***Perf. 13***
1468 A1050 60y multicolored 1.10 .20
1469 A1051 60y multicolored 1.10 .20

Former Kyoto Branch of Bank of Japan A1052

Main Building, Former Saiseikan Hospital — A1053

1982, Mar. 10 ***Perf. 13***
1470 A1052 60y multicolored 1.10 .20
1471 A1053 60y multicolored 1.10 .20

Oyama Shrine Gate, Kanazawa A1054

Former Iwasaki Family Residence, Tokyo A1055

1982, June 12 ***Perf. 13***
1472 A1054 60y multicolored 1.10 .20
1473 A1055 60y multicolored 1.10 .20

Hokkaido Prefectural Govt. Building, Sapporo A1056

Former Residence of Tsugumichi Saigo A1057

1982, Sept. 10 ***Perf. 13***
1474 A1056 60y multicolored 1.10 .20
1475 A1057 60y multicolored 1.10 .20

Old Mutsuzawa School — A1058

Sakuranomiya Public Hall — A1059

1983, Feb. 15
1476 A1058 60y multicolored 1.10 .20
1477 A1059 60y multicolored 1.10 .20

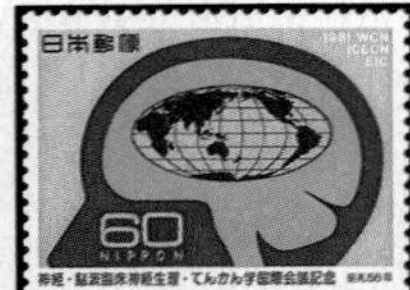
Globe on Brain A1060

1981, Sept. 12 **Photo.**
1478 A1060 60y multicolored 1.10 .20

Intl. medical conferences, Kyoto: 12th Neurology, Sept. 20-25; 10th Brainwaves and Clinical Neurophysiology, Sept. 13-17; 1981 Intl. Epilepsy Conference, Sept. 17-21.

Congress Emblem — A1061

Plum Trees and Fowl, by Sanraku Kano — A1062

1981, Sept. 16
1479 A1061 60y multicolored 1.10 .20

24th World PTTI (Post, Telegraph and Telephone Intl. Labor Federation) Cong., Tokyo, Sept. 16-22.

1981, Oct. 6 **Photo.**
1480 A1062 130y multicolored 2.50 .20

25th Intl. Letter Writing Week, Oct. 6-12.

A1063

A1064

1981, Oct. 9 **Photo. & Engr.**
1481 A1063 60y No. 1 1.10 .20
1482 A1063 60y No. 2 1.10 .20
1483 A1063 60y No. 3 1.10 .20
1484 A1063 60y No. 4 1.10 .20
a. Strip or block of 4, #1481-1484 4.50 4.50

Philatokyo '81 Intl. Stamp Exhibition,Tokyo, Oct. 9-18.

1981, Oct. 13 **Photo.**
1485 A1064 40y multicolored .75 .20

36th Natl. Athletic Meet, Oct. 13-18.

A1065

A1066

1981, Dec. 1 **Photo.** ***Perf. 13x13½***
1486 A1065 40y multicolored .75 .20

New Year of 1982 (Year of the Dog). Sheets of 2 were lottery prizes. Value $1.50.

1982, Mar. 20 **Photo.**

Ueno Zoo Centenary: a, Gorilla, flamingo. b, Penguins, lion. c, Panda, elephants. d, Zebras, giraffe.

1487 Strip of 4 4.50 1.40
a.-d. A1066 60y any single 1.10 .35

Views of the Snow on Matsuchiyama, by Kiyonaga Torii — A1067

1982, Apr. 20 **Photo.** ***Perf. 13½***
1488 60y multicolored 1.10 .30
1489 60y multicolored 1.10 .30
a. A1067 Pair, #1488-1489 2.25 .70

Philatelic Week.

Shisa (Lion-shaped Guard Dog) A1069

Natl. Forestation Campaign A1070

1982, May 15 **Photo.**
1490 A1069 60y multicolored 1.10 .30

10th anniv. of Reversion Agreement returning Ryukyu Islands.

1982, May 22 ***Perf. 13x13½***
1491 A1070 60y multicolored 1.10 .30

16th Intl. Dermatology Conference Tokyo, May 23-28 — A1071

1982, May 24 ***Perf. 13***
1492 A1071 60y Noh mask 1.10 .30

Tohoku-Shinkansen Railroad Line Opening — A1072

1982, June 23
1493 A1072 60y Diesel locomotive 1.10 .30
1494 A1072 60y Steam model 1290 1.10 .30
a. Pair, #1493-1494 2.25 .75

Letter Writing Day — A1073

1982, July 23 ***Perf. 13x13½, 13½x13***
1495 A1073 40y Sea gull, letter .75 .20
1496 A1073 60y Fairy, letter, horiz. 1.10 .30

Modern Japanese Art Issue

Kimono Patterned with Irises, by Saburosuke Okada (1869-1939) A1074

Bodhisattva Kuan-yin on Potalaka Island, by Tessai Tomioka (1837-1924) A1075

1982, Aug. 5 **Photo.** ***Perf. 13½***
1497 A1074 60y multicolored 1.10 .30
1498 A1075 60y multicolored 1.10 .30

The Sarasvati, by Shiko Munakata (1903-1975) A1076

Saltim-banque, by Seiji Togo (1897-1978) A1077

1982, Nov. 24
1499 A1076 60y multicolored 1.10 .30
1500 A1077 60y multicolored 1.10 .30

Snowstorm, by Shinsui Ito — A1078

Spiraeas and Callas with Persian Pot, by Zenzaburo Kojima A1079

1983, Jan. 24 **Photo.**

1501 A1078 60y multicolored 1.10 .30
1502 A1079 60y multicolored 1.10 .30

Innocence, by Taikan Yokoyama (1868-1958) A1080

Roen, by Koun Takamura (1852-1934) A1081

Photo., Photo. and Engr.

1983, Mar. 10 ***Perf. 13½***

1503 A1080 60y multicolored 1.10 .30
1504 A1081 60y multicolored 1.10 .30

A1082

A1083

A1084

1982, Aug. 23 ***Perf. 13x13½***

1505 A1082 60y Wreath 1.10 .35
1506 A1083 60y Crane 1.10 .35
1507 A1084 70y Tortoise 1.25 .35
Nos. 1505-1507 (3) 3.45 1.05

For use on greeting (Nos. 1506-1507) and condolence (No. 1505) cards.

See Nos. 1555-1556, 1836-1839, 2227-2230 and footnotes after Nos. 1708, 1765.

400th Anniv. of Boys' Delegation to Europe, Tensho Era — A1085

1982, Sept. 20 **Photo.** ***Perf. 13***

1508 A1085 60y 16th cent. ship, map 1.10 .30

10th Anniv. of Japanese-Chinese Relations Normalization — A1086

Design: Hall of Prayer for Good Harvests, Temple of Heaven, Peking, by Ryuzaburo Umehara.

1982, Sept. 29

1509 A1086 60y multicolored 1.10 .30

Table Tennis — A1087

"Amusement," Doll by Goyo Hirata — A1088

1982, Oct. 2

1510 A1087 40y multicolored .75 .25

37th Natl. Athletic Meet, Matsue, Oct. 3-8.

1982, Oct. 6

1511 A1088 130y multicolored 2.50 .60

Intl. Letter Writing Week, Oct. 6-12.

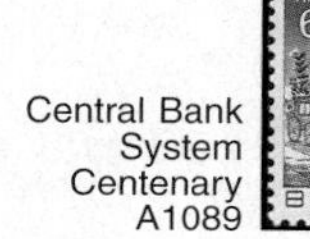

Central Bank System Centenary A1089

Design: The Bank of Japan near Eitaibashi in Snow, by Yasuji Inoue.

Photogravure and Engraved

1982, Oct. 12 ***Perf. 13½***

1512 A1089 60y multicolored 1.10 .30

Opening of Joetsu Shinkansen Railroad Line — A1090

1982, Nov. 15

1513 60y Locomotive, 1982 1.10 .30
1514 60y Locomotive, 1931 1.10 .30
a. A1090 Pair, #1513-1514 2.25 .70

New Year 1983 — A1092

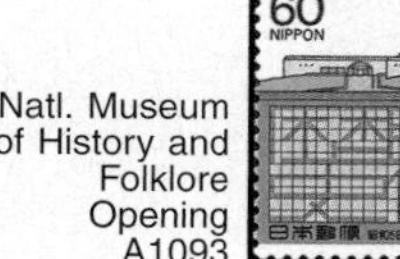

Natl. Museum of History and Folklore Opening A1093

1982, Dec. 1 ***Perf. 13x13½***

1515 A1092 40y Kintaro on Wild Boar .75 .20

Sheets of 2 were lottery prizes. Value, $1.50.

1983, Mar. 16 **Photo.** ***Perf. 13½x13***

1516 A1093 60y multicolored 1.10 .30

Women Working in the Kitchen, by Utamaro Kitagawa (1753-1806) — A1094

1983, Apr. 20 **Photo.** ***Perf. 13***

1517 60y multicolored 1.10 .30
1518 60y multicolored 1.10 .30
a. A1094 Pair, #1517-1518 2.25 .70

Philatelic Week.

Natl. Forestation Campaign A1096

50th Nippon Derby A1097

1983, May 21 ***Perf. 13***

1519 A1096 60y Hakusan Mountains, black lily, forest 1.10 .30

1983, May 28

1520 A1097 60y Colt, racing horse 1.10 .30

Islands Cleanup Campaign — A1098

1983, June 13 **Photo.** ***Perf. 13½***

1521 A1098 60y multicolored 1.10 .30

Western Architecture Series

Hohei Hall Sapporo A1099

Old Glover House, Nagasaki A1100

Gojyuku Bank, Hirosaki A1101

Gakushuin Elementary School, Tokyo A1102

Bank of Japan, Tokyo A1103

Old Hunter House, Kobe A1104

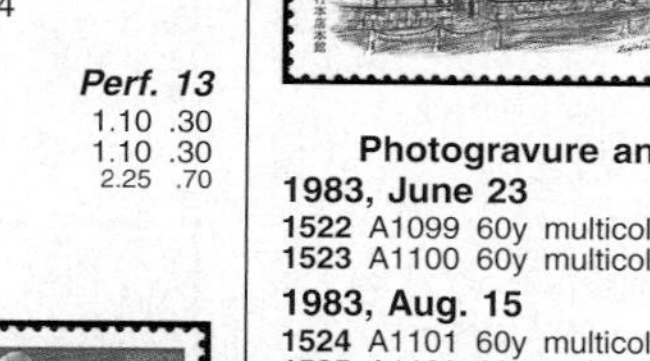

Photogravure and Engraved

1983, June 23 ***Perf. 13***

1522 A1099 60y multicolored 1.10 .30
1523 A1100 60y multicolored 1.10 .30

1983, Aug. 15

1524 A1101 60y multicolored 1.10 .30
1525 A1102 60y multicolored 1.10 .30

1984, Feb. 16

1526 A1103 60y multicolored 1.10 .30
1527 A1104 60y multicolored 1.10 .30
Nos. 1522-1527 (6) 6.60 1.80

Official Gazette Centenary A1107

Letter Writing Day A1108

Design: First issue, Drawing of the Government Bulletin Board at Nihonbashi, by Hiroshige Ando III.

1983, July 2 **Photo.**

1530 A1107 60y multicolored 1.10 .30

1983, July 23 ***Perf. 13x13½, 13½x13***

1531 A1108 40y Boy writing letter .75 .25
1532 A1108 60y Fairy bringing letter, horiz. 1.10 .30

Opening of Natl. Noh Theater, Tokyo A1109

1983, Sept. 14 **Photo.** ***Perf. 13***

1533 A1109 60y Masked actor, theater 1.10 .30

Endangered Birds Issue

Rallus Okinawae A1110

Ketupa Blakistoni
A1111

Photo. and Engr., Photo.

1983, Sept. 22 *Perf. 13*
1534 A1110 60y multicolored 1.10 .30
1535 A1111 60y multicolored 1.10 .30

Photo., Photo. & Engr.

1983, Nov. 25
1536 A1110 60y Sapheopipo noguchii 1.10 .30
1537 A1111 60y Branta canadensis leucopareia 1.10 .30

Photo., Photo. and Engr.

1984, Jan. 26
1538 A1111 60y Megalurus pryeri pryeri 1.10 .30
1539 A1110 60y Spilornis cheela perplexus 1.10 .30

1984, Mar. 15 **Photo.**
1540 A1110 60y Columba janthina nitens 1.10 .30
1541 A1111 60y Tringa guttifer 1.10 .30

1984, June 22
1542 A1110 60y Falco peregrinus frutti 1.10 .30

Photo. and Engr.

1543 A1111 60y Dendrocopus leucutus austoni 1.10 .30
Nos. 1534-1543 (10) 11.00 3.00

Souvenir Sheet

1984, Dec. 10 **Photo. & Engr.**
1544 Sheet of 3 3.50 3.50
a. A1111 60y Prus grn, engr., #1535 1.10 .30
b. A1110 60y vio brn, engr., #1539 1.10 .30
c. A1110 60y ol blk, engr., #1542 1.10 .30

Intl. Letter Writing Week — A1124

38th Natl. Athletic Meet — A1125

Chikyu Doll by Juzo Kagoshima (1898-1982).

1983, Oct. 6 **Photo.** *Perf. 13*
1548 A1124 130y multicolored 2.50 .70

1983, Oct. 15 *Perf. 13*
1549 A1125 40y Naginata event .75 .25

A1126

World Communications Year — A1127

1983, Oct. 17 **Photo.** *Perf. 13*
1550 A1126 60y multicolored 1.10 .30
1551 A1127 60y multicolored 1.10 .30

Showa Memorial National Park Opening
A1128

1983, Oct. 26 **Photo.** *Perf. 13*
1552 A1128 60y multicolored 1.10 .30

A1129 A1130

1983, Nov. 14 **Photo.**
1553 A1129 60y multicolored 1.10 .30

71st World Dentistry Congress.

1983, Nov. 14 **Photo.** *Perf. 13*
1554 A1130 60y multicolored 1.10 .30

Shirase, Antarctic observation ship, maiden voyage.

Type of 1982

1983, Nov. 22 **Photo.** *Perf. 12½*
1555 A1082 40y Wreath .75 .25
1556 A1083 40y Crane .75 .25

For use on condolence and greeting cards.

A1131

A1132

1983, Dec. 1 **Photo.** *Perf. 13x13½*
1557 A1131 40y Rat riding hammer .75 .25

New Year 1984. Sheets of 2 were lottery prizes. Value, $1.50.

1983, Dec. 5 **Photo.** *Perf. 13½*
1558 A1132 60y Emblem 1.10 .30

Universal Declaration of Human Rights, 35th anniv.

20th Grand Confectionery Fair, Tokyo, Feb. 24-Mar. 12 — A1133

1984, Feb. 24 **Photo.**
1559 A1133 60y Confection, tea whisk 1.10 .30

Natl. Bunraku Theater Opening, Osaka
A1134

1984, Apr. 6 **Photo.** *Perf. 13*
1560 A1134 60y Bunraku puppet 1.10 .30

A1135

Philatelic Week (Sharaku Prints): No. 1561, Hanshiro Iwai IV (facing right) Playing Shigenoi. No. 1562, Oniji Otani (facing left) Playing Edobe.

Photogravure and Engraved

1984, Apr. 20 *Perf. 13½*
1561 60y multicolored 1.10 .30
1562 60y multicolored 1.10 .30
a. A1135 Pair, #1561-1562 2.25 .70

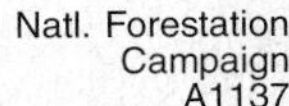

Natl. Forestation Campaign
A1137

Weather Forecasting Centenary
A1138

1984, May 19 **Photo.**
1563 A1137 60y Cedar Forest, Sakurajima 1.10 .30

1984, June 1 *Perf. 13x13½*
1564 A1138 60y Himawari satellite, map 1.10 .30

UNESCO Emblem, Doves — A1139

Letter Writing Day — A1140

1984, July 16 **Photo.**
1565 A1139 60y multicolored 1.10 .30

UNESCO Clubs and Associations World Congress, July 16-24.

1984, July 23 *Perf. 13x13½, 13½x13*
1566 A1140 40y Birds in tree .75 .20
1567 A1140 60y Bird holding letter, horiz. 1.10 .30

Disaster Relief
A1141

Perf. 13x12½, 12½x13

1984, Aug. 23 **Photo.**
1568 A1141 40y Fire, wind .75 .20
1569 A1141 60y Mother, child, vert. 1.10 .30

Alpine Plant Series

Leontopodium Fauriei — A1142

Lagotis Glauca
A1143

Photogravure and Engraved
Perf. 12½x13, 13x12½

1984, Aug. 27
1570 A1142 60y multicolored 1.10 .30
1571 A1143 60y multicolored 1.10 .30

Trollius Riederianus
A1144

Primula Cuneifolia
A1145

1984, Sept. 21 *Perf. 13*
1572 A1144 60y multicolored 1.10 .30
1573 A1145 60y multicolored 1.10 .30

Rhododendron Aureum — A1146

Oxytropis Nigrescens Var. Japonica
A1147

1985, Jan. 25 *Perf. 13*
1574 A1146 60y multicolored 1.10 .30
1575 A1147 60y multicolored 1.10 .30

Draba Japonica — A1148

Dryas Octopetala
A1149

1985, Feb. 28
1576 A1148 60y multicolored 1.10 .30
1577 A1149 60y multicolored 1.10 .30

Callianthemum Insigne Var. Miyabeanum
A1150

Gentiana Nipponica
A1151

1985, July 31 *Perf. 13*
1578 A1150 60y multicolored 1.10 .30
1579 A1151 60y multicolored 1.10 .30

Campanula Chamissonis
A1152

Viola Crassa A1153

1985, Sept. 27
1580 A1152 60y multicolored 1.10 .30
1581 A1153 60y multicolored 1.10 .30

Deapensia Lapponica A1154
Pedicularis Apodochila A1155

1986, Feb. 13 ***Perf. 13***
1582 A1154 60y multicolored 1.10 .30
1583 A1155 60y multicolored 1.10 .30

Basho's Street, Sendai — A1156

1984, Sept. 1 **Photo.** ***Perf. 13***
1584 A1156 60y multicolored 1.10 .30

Intl. Microbiological Association's 6th Intl. Congress of Virology, Sendai, Sept. 1-7.

Electronic Mail — A1157

28th Intl. Letter Writing Week, Oct. 6-12 — A1158

1984, Oct. 1 **Photo.**
1585 A1157 500y multicolored 9.50 4.50

1984, Oct. 6
1586 A1158 130y Wooden doll 2.50 .60

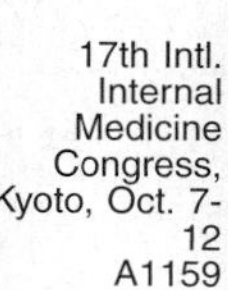

17th Intl. Internal Medicine Congress, Kyoto, Oct. 7-12
A1159

1984, Oct. 8
1587 A1159 60y Ginkakuji Temple 1.10 .30

39th Natl. Athletic Meet, Nara City, Oct. 12-17 — A1160

1984, Oct. 12
1588 A1160 40y Field hockey .75 .25

Traditional Crafts Series

Kutaniyaki Plates — A1161

Nishijinori Weavings — A1163

1984, Nov. 2 **Photo.** ***Perf. 12½x13***
1589 60y Birds 1.10 .30
1590 60y Flowers 1.10 .30
a. A1161 Pair, #1589-1590 2.25 .75
1591 60y Flowers 1.10 .30
1592 60y Leaves 1.10 .30
a. A1163 Pair, #1591-1592 2.25 .75

Edokimekomi Dolls — A1165

Ryukyubingata Cloth — A1167

1985, Feb. 15 **Photo.** ***Perf. 13***
1593 60y Adult figures 1.10 .30
1594 60y Child and pet 1.10 .30
a. A1165 Pair, #1593-1594 2.25 .75
1595 60y Bird and branch 1.10 .30
1596 60y Birds 1.10 .30
a. A1167 Pair, #1595-1596 2.25 .75

Ichii-ittobori Carved Birds — A1169

Imariyaki & Aritayaki Ceramic Ware — A1171

Kamakurabori Wood Carvings — A1173

Ojiyachijimi Weavings — A1175

Hakata Ningyo Clay Figures — A1177

Nanbu Tekki Iron Ware — A1179

1985, May 23 **Photo.** ***Perf. 13***
1597 60y Bird 1.10 .30
1598 60y Birds 1.10 .30
a. A1169 Pair, #1597-1598 2.25 .75
1599 60y Bowl 1.10 .30
1600 60y Plate 1.10 .30
a. A1171 Pair, #1599-1600 2.25 .75

1985, June 24 **Photo. & Engr.**
1601 60y Bird and flower panel 1.10 .30
1602 60y Round flower panel 1.10 .30
a. A1173 Pair, #1601-1602 2.25 .75

Litho.
1603 60y Hemp star pattern 1.10 .30
1604 60y Hemp linear pattern 1.10 .30
a. A1175 Pair, #1603-1604 2.25 .75

1985, Aug. 8 **Photo.**
1605 60y Man 1.10 .30
1606 60y Woman and child 1.10 .30
a. A1177 Pair, #1605-1606 2.25 .75

Photogravure and Engraved
1607 60y Silver kettle 1.10 .30
1608 60y Black kettle 1.10 .30
a. A1179 Pair, #1607-1608 2.25 .75

Wajimanuri Lacquerware — A1181

Izumo-ishidoro Sandstone Sculptures — A1183

Photo., Photo. & Engr. (#1611-1612)
1985, Nov. 15
1609 60y Bowl on table 1.10 .30
1610 60y Bowl 1.10 .30
a. A1181 Pair, #1609-1610 2.25 .75
1611 60y Columnar lantern 1.10 .30
1612 60y Lantern on four legs 1.10 .30
a. A1183 Pair, #1611-1612 2.25 .75

Kyo-sensu Silk Fans — A1185

Tobeyaki Porcelain — A1187

1986, Mar. 13 **Photo.** ***Perf. 13***
1613 60y Flower bouquets 1.10 .30
1614 60y Sun and trees 1.10 .30
a. A1185 Pair, #1613-1614 2.25 .75
1615 60y Jug 1.10 .30
1616 60y Jar 1.10 .30
a. A1187 Pair, #1615-1616 2.25 .75
Nos. 1613-1616 (4) 4.40 1.20

Japanese Professional Baseball, 50th Anniv. — A1189

1984, Nov. 15 ***Perf. 13½***
1617 60y Pitcher 1.10 .30
1618 60y Batter 1.10 .30
a. A1189 Pair, #1617-1618 2.25 .80
1619 A1189 60y Matsutaro Shoriki 1.10 .30
Nos. 1617-1619 (3) 3.30 .90

Industrial Education Centenary A1190

New Year 1984 — A1191

1984, Nov. 20 ***Perf. 13x12½***
1620 A1190 60y Workers, symbols 1.10 .30

1984, Dec. 1 Photo. *Perf. 13½x13*
1621 A1191 40y Sakushu Cattle Folk Toy .75 .25

Sheets of 2 were lottery prizes. Value, $1.50.

A1200 Akita

A1201 Ivory Shell

A1202 Hiougi-gai (Bivalve)

A1203 Rinbo Shell

A1204

A1205

A1206

A1207

A1208 A1209

Photo., Engr. (300y)

1984-89 *Perf. 13x13½*
1622 A1200 2y turq blue ('89) .20 .20
1623 A1201 40y multi ('88) .90 .20
1624 A1202 41y multi ('89) .80 .20
1624B A1202 41y Imperf., self-adhesive .80 .20
1625 A1203 60y multi ('88) 1.10 .20
a. Bklt. pane, 5 each #1623, 1625 9.25
1626 A1204 62y multi ('89) 1.10 .20
a. Bklt. pane, 2 #1624, 4 #1626 6.00
1626B A1204 62y Imperf., self-adhesive 1.10 .20
c. Bklt. pane, 2 #1624B, 4 #1626B ('89) 6.00
1627 A1205 72y dark vio, blk & org yel ('89) 1.40 .20
1628 A1206 175y multi ('89) 3.25 .25
1629 A1207 210y multi ('89) 4.00 .30
1630 A1208 300y dk red brown 5.75 .35
1631 A1209 360y dull pink & brn ('89) 6.75 .35
Nos. 1622-1631 (12) 27.15 2.85

Coil Stamps
Perf. 13 Horiz.

1636 A1202 41y multi ('89) .80 .20
1637 A1204 62y multi ('89) 1.10 .20

No. 1622 inscribed "Nippon," unlike No. 583.

No. 1626Bc is adhered to the booklet cover, made of peelable paper, folded in half and rouletted down the center fold.

Issued: 40y, 60y, 4/1; 300y, 4/3; 2y, 72y, 4/1; 42y, #1626, 1626a, 41y, #1637, 3/24; 175y, 210y, 360y, 6/1; #1626d, 7/3.

A1210

EXPO '85 — A1211

1985, Mar. 16 Photo. *Perf. 13*
1640 A1210 40y multicolored .75 .20
1641 A1211 60y multicolored 1.10 .30
a. Souv. sheet of 2, #1640-1641 1.60

University of the Air — A1212

1985, Apr. 1 Photo. *Perf. 13½*
1642 A1212 60y University broadcast tower 1.10 .35

Inauguration of adult education through broadcasting.

Nippon Telegraph & Telephone Co. — A1213

1985, Apr. 1
1643 A1213 60y Satellite receiver 1.10 .30

Inauguration of Japan's new telecommunications system.

World Import Fair, Nagoya A1214

1985, Apr. 5 Photo. *Perf. 13*
1644 A1214 60y 16th century map of Japan 1.10 .30

Industrial Proprietary System Cent. — A1215

Design: Portrait of Korekiyo Takashashi, system promulgator, inscriptions in English.

1985, Apr. 18 Photo. *Perf. 13½*
1645 A1215 60y multicolored 1.10 .30

Winter in the North — A1216

To the Morning Light — A1217

Paintings by Yumeji Takehisa (1884-1934).

1985, Apr. 20 *Perf. 13*
1646 A1216 60y multicolored 1.10 .30
1647 A1217 60y multicolored 1.10 .30
a. Pair, #1646-1647 2.25 .75

Philatelic Week. Printed in sheets of 10.

Natl. Land Forestation Project — A1218

Intl. Year of the Forest: Autumn bellflower, camphor tree, cattle and Mt. Aso.

1985, May 10 *Perf. 13½*
1648 A1218 60y multicolored 1.10 .30

Radio Japan, 50th Anniv. — A1219

Painting: Cherry Blossoms at Night, by Taikan Yokoyama.

1985, June 1 Photo. *Perf. 13*
1649 60y multi (Left) 1.10 .30
1650 60y multi (Right) 1.10 .30
a. A1219 Pair, #1649-1650 2.25 .70

Hisoka Maejima, 1st Postmaster General — A1220

1985, June 5 Photo. *Perf. 13*
1651 A1220 60y Portrait, former P.O. building 1.10 .30

Oonaruto Bridge Opening A1221

1985, June 7 *Perf. 13½*
1652 A1221 60y multicolored 1.10 .30

Intl. Youth Year A1222

Owl Carrying Letter — A1223

1985, July 20 Photo. *Perf. 13*
1653 A1222 60y Emblem, silhouette 1.10 .30

Perf. 13½x13, 13x13½
1985, July 23 Photo.
1654 A1223 40y shown .75 .25
1655 A1223 60y Girl, cat, bird, letter 1.10 .30

Letter Writing Day (23rd of each month).

Electronic Mail — A1224

Meson Theory, 50th Anniv. A1225

1985, Aug. 1 Photo. *Perf. 13x13½*
1656 A1224 500y multicolored 9.50 2.00

1985, Aug. 15 Photo. *Perf. 13*
1657 A1225 60y Portrait, nuclear particles 1.10 .30

Dr. Hideki Yukawa was presented the Nobel Prize for Physics for the Meson Theory in 1949, which is the foundation for high-energy physics.

A1226

A1227

1985, Aug. 24 Photo. *Perf. 13½*
1658 A1226 60y Gymnast, horse 1.10 .30

Universiade 1985, Kobe.

1985, Sept. 13 Photo.
1659 A1227 40y Emblem, competitor .75 .25

28th Intl. Vocational Training Competition, Oct. 21-27.

Normalization of Diplomatic Relations Between Japan and the Republic of Korea, 20th Anniv. — A1228

1985, Sept. 18
1660 A1228 60y Rose of Sharon 1.10 .30

Kan-Etsu Tunnel Opening A1229

1985, Oct. 2 *Perf. 13*
1661 A1229 60y Mountains, diagram, cross sections 1.10 .30

Seisen Doll by Goyo Hirata (1903-1981) A1230

1985, Oct. 7
1662 A1230 130y multicolored 2.50 .75

Intl. Letter Writing Week, Oct. 6-12.

30th Intl. Apicultural Congress, Oct. 10-16, Nagoya
A1231

1985, Oct. 9
1663 A1231 60y Honeybee, strawberry plants 1.10 .30

Japanese Overseas Cooperation Volunteers, 20th Anniv.
A1232

1985, Oct. 9 **Litho.**
1664 A1232 60y Planting crop 1.10 .30

40th Natl. Athletic Meet, Oct. 20-25, Tottori City Sports Arena — A1233

1985, Oct. 19 **Photo.**
1665 A1233 40y Handball player, Mt. Daisen .75 .25

New Year 1986 — A1234

Natl. Ministerial System of Government, Cent.
A1235

1985, Dec. 2 **Photo.** ***Perf. 13x13½***
1666 A1234 40y Shinno papier-mache tiger .75 .25

Sheets of 2 were lottery prizes. Value, $1.40.

1985, Dec. 20 **Litho.** ***Perf. 13½***
1667 A1235 60y Official seal, Cabinet emblem 1.10 .30

Building Institute, Cent. — A1236

Philately Week — A1237

1986, Apr. 9 **Photo.** ***Perf. 13***
1668 A1236 60y multicolored 1.10 .30

1986, Apr. 15

Southern Hateroma (details), by Keigetsu Kikuchi.

1669 A1237 60y Woman standing 1.10 .30
1670 A1237 60y Seated woman 1.10 .30
a. Pair, #1669-1670 2.25 .85

Kyoto Imperial Palace, Phoenix
A1238

#1672, Imperial chrysanthemum crest & partridges.

1986, Apr. 28
1671 A1238 60y multicolored 1.10 .30
1672 A1238 60y multicolored 1.10 .30
a. Souv. sheet of 2, #1671-1672 2.25 1.25

Reign of Emperor Hirohito, 60th anniv.

6th Intl. Summit, Tokyo
A1239

1986, May 2
1673 A1239 60y Mt. Fuji 1.10 .30

Shrike on Reed, Emperor Nintoku's Mausoleum
A1240

1986, May 9 ***Perf. 13½***
1674 A1240 60y multicolored 1.10 .30

Natl. Land Afforestation Campaign.

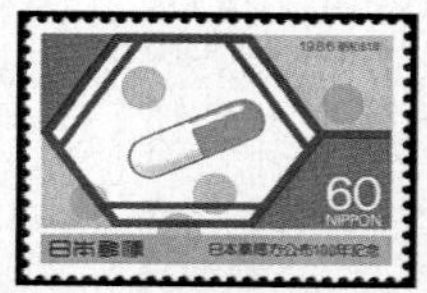

Japanese Pharmaceutical Regulatory Syst., Cent. — A1241

1986, June 25 **Photo.** ***Perf. 13½***
1675 A1241 60y multicolored 1.10 .30

Japanese Standard Time, Cent. — A1242

Letter Writing Day — A1243

1986, July 11 **Litho.** ***Perf. 13***
1676 A1242 60y Meridian, clock 1.10 .30

1986, July 23 **Photo.** ***Perf. 13x13½***
1677 A1243 40y Bird .75 .25
1678 A1243 60y Girl, rabbit, birds 1.10 .35
a. Bklt. pane, 5 each #1677-1678 9.25

Sheets of 2 were lottery prizes. Value, *$60.*

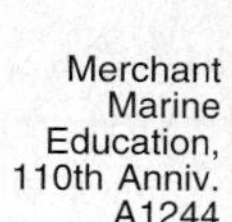

Merchant Marine Education, 110th Anniv.
A1244

Training ship Nihonmaru & navigation training institute founders Makoto Kondo, Yataro Iwasaki.

1986, July 26 ***Perf. 13***
1679 A1244 60y multicolored 1.10 .35

CTO's exist for Nos. 1680-1681, 1684-1685, 1688-1689, 1694-1695, 1696-1697. They read "Japan" between two arcs in a corner.

Insects

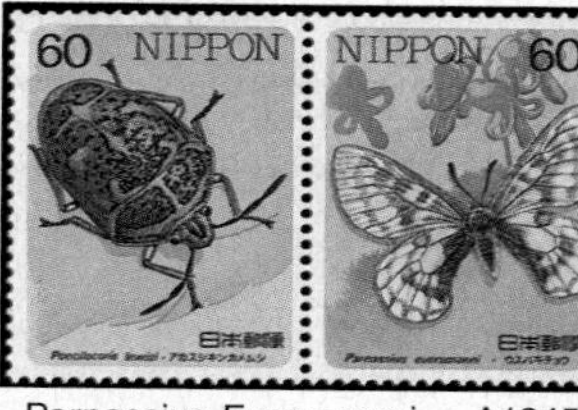

Parnassius Eversmanni — A1245

Photogravure and Engraved

1986, July 30 ***Perf. 13***
1680 60y shown 1.10 .35
1681 60y Poecilocoris lewisi 1.10 .35
a. A1245 Pair, #1680-1681 2.25 1.00
1682 60y Rasalia batesi 1.10 .35
1683 60y Epiophlebia superstes 1.10 .35
a. A1245 Pair, #1682-1683 2.25 1.00

1986, Sept. 26
1684 60y Dorcus hopei 1.10 .35
1685 60y Thermo- zephyrus ataxus 1.10 .35
a. A1245 Pair, #1684-1685 2.25 1.00
1686 60y Sympetrum pedemontanum 1.10 .35
1687 60y Damaster blaptoides 1.10 .35
a. A1245 Pair, #1686-1687 2.25 1.00

1986, Nov. 21
1688 60y Elcysma westwoodii 1.10 .35
1689 60y Rhyothemis variegata 1.10 .35
a. A1245 Pair, #1688-1689 2.25 1.00
1690 60y Tibicen japonicus 1.10 .35
1691 60y Chrysochroa holstii 1.10 .35
a. A1245 Pair, #1690-1691 2.25 1.00

1987, Jan. 23
1692 60y Parantica sita 1.10 .35
1693 60y Cheirotonus jambar 1.10 .35
a. A1245 Pair, #1692-1693 2.25 1.00
1694 60y Lucanus maculifemoratus 1.10 .35
1695 60y Anotogaster sieboldii 1.10 .35
a. A1245 Pair, #1694-1695 2.25 1.00

1987, Mar. 12
1696 60y Ascaraphus ramburi 1.10 .35
1697 60y Polyphylla laticollis 1.10 .35
a. A1245 Pair, #1696-1697 2.25 1.00
1698 60y Kallima inachus 1.10 .35
1699 60y Calopteryx cornelia 1.10 .35
f. A1245 Pair, #1698-1699 2.25 1.00
Nos. 1680-1699 (20) 22.00 7.00

Miniature Sheet

1699A Sheet of 4 (#1680, 1692, 1699b-1699c) 3.75 3.75
b. 40y Anthocaris cardamines .75 .35
c. 40y Sasakia charonda .75 .35
d. Bklt. pane, 5 #1680, 5 #1699b 9.25
e. Bklt. pane, 5 #1692, 5 #1699c 9.25
g. A1245 Pair, #1699b, 1680 1.90
h. A1245 Pair, #1699c, 1692 1.90

Booklet panes are perf. 13x13½ on 2 or 3 sides.

Folkways in Twelve Months (Detail), by Shunsho Katsukawa
A1265

Electron Microscope
A1266

1986, Aug. 23 **Photo.** ***Perf. 13***
1700 A1265 60y multicolored 1.10 .35

52nd conference of the Intl. Federation of Library Associations, Tokyo, Aug. 24-29.

1986, Aug. 30
1701 A1266 60y multicolored 1.10 .35

11th Int. Congress of Electron Microscopy, Kyoto, Aug. 31-Sept. 7.

23rd Intl. Conference on Social Welfare, Tokyo, Aug. 31-Sept. 5 — A1267

1986, Aug. 30 **Litho.**
1702 A1267 60y multicolored 1.10 .35

Ohmorimiyage Doll, by Juzoh Kagoshima
A1268

41st Natl. Athletic Meet, Oct. 12-17, Kofu
A1269

1986, Oct. 6 **Photo.**
1703 A1268 130y multicolored 2.50 .75

Intl. Letter Writing Week.

1986, Oct. 9
1704 A1269 40y multicolored .75 .25

5th World Ikebana Convention
A1270

Painting: Flower in Autumn and a Girl in Rakuhoku.

1986, Oct. 17 **Photo.** ***Perf. 13½x13***
1705 A1270 60y multicolored 1.10 .35

A1271

Intl. Peace Year
A1272

Lithographed, Photogravure (#1707)

1986, Nov. 28
1706 A1271 40y multicolored .75 .25
1707 A1272 60y multicolored 1.10 .35

New Year 1987 (Year of the Hare) — A1273

Design: A Couple of Rabbits Making Rice Cake, Nagoya clay figurine.

1986, Dec. 1 **Photo.** ***Perf. 13x13½***
1708 A1273 40y multicolored .75 .25

Sheets of two containing Nos. 1506 and 1708 were lottery prizes. Value, $1.75.

See No. 2655c.

Real Estate Registry System, Cent. A1274

1987, Jan. 30 Photo. ***Perf. 13½***

1709 A1274 60y multicolored 1.10 .35

Basho Series, Part I

A1275

A1277

A1279

A1281

A1283

A1285

A1287

A1289

A1291

A1293

#1710, Basho. #1711, Basho's haiku. #1712, Kegon Falls. #1713, Haiku. #1714, Cuckoo. #1715, Horse and haiku. #1716, Willow Tree. #1717, Rice Paddy and haiku. #1718, Chestnut Tree in Bloom. #1719, Chestnut Leaves and haiku. #1720, Planting Rice Paddy. #1721, Fern Leaves and haiku. #1722, Sweetflags. #1723, Sweetflags and haiku. #1724, Prosperous Man, 17th Cent. #1725, Summer Grass and haiku. #1726, Safflowers in Bloom. #1727, Haiku. #1728, Yamadera (Temple). #1729, Forest and haiku.

1987-89 Photo. ***Perf. 13x13½***

1710 60y multicolored 1.10 .35
1711 60y multicolored 1.10 .35
a. Sheet of 2, #1710-1711, imperf. ('89) 2.50
b. A1275 Pair, #1710-1711 2.25 1.00
1712 60y multicolored 1.10 .35
1713 60y multicolored 1.10 .35
a. Sheet of 2, #1712-1713, imperf. ('89) 2.50
b. A1277 Pair, #1712-1713 2.25 1.00
1714 60y multicolored 1.10 .35
1715 60y multicolored 1.10 .35
a. Sheet of 2, #1714-1715, imperf. ('89) 2.50
b. A1279 Pair, #1714-1715 2.25 1.00
1716 60y multicolored 1.10 .35
1717 60y multicolored 1.10 .35
a. Sheet of 2, #1716-1717, imperf. ('89) 2.50
b. A1281 Pair, #1716-1717 2.25 1.00
1718 60y multicolored 1.10 .35
1719 60y multicolored 1.10 .35
a. Sheet of 2, #1718-1719, imperf. ('89) 2.50
b. A1283 Pair, #1718-1719 1.10 1.00
1720 60y multicolored 1.10 .35
1721 60y multicolored 1.10 .35
a. Sheet of 2, #1720-1721, imperf. ('89) 2.50
b. A1285 Pair, #1720-1721 2.25 1.00
1722 60y multi ('88) 1.10 .35
1723 60y multi ('88) 1.10 .35
a. Sheet of 2, #1722-1723, imperf. ('89) 2.50
b. A1287 Pair, #1722-1723 2.25 1.00
1724 60y multi ('88) 1.10 .35
1725 60y multi ('88) 1.10 .35
a. Sheet of 2, #1724-1725, imperf. ('89) 2.50
b. A1289 Pair, #1724-1725 1.10 1.00
1726 60y multi ('88) 1.10 .35
1727 60y multi ('88) 1.10 .35
a. Sheet of 2, #1726-1727, imperf. ('89) 2.50
b. A1291 Pair, #1726-1727 2.25 1.00
1728 60y multi ('88) 1.10 .35
1729 60y multi ('88) 1.00 .35
a. Sheet of 2, #1728-1729, imperf. ('89) 2.50
b. A1293 Pair, #1728-1729 2.25 1.00
Nos. 1710-1729 (20) 21.90 7.00

Issued to commemorate the 300th anniversary of a trip from Edo (now Tokyo) to northern Japan by the famous haiku poet Matsuo Munefusa "Basho" (1644-1694). His prose account of the journey, *Oku no hosomichi* (*Narrow Road to a Far Province*), contains numerous 17-syllable poems (*haiku*), which are shown on the stamps.

In each setenant pair, a complete *haiku* by Basho is inscribed vertically at right on the left stamp and in the center of the right stamp. The same poem appears on both stamps in each pair.

Issued: #1710-1713, 2/26; #1714-1717, 6/23; #1718-1721, 8/25; #1722-1725, 1/3; #1726-1729, 3/26.

See Nos. 1775-1794.

12th World Orchid Congress, Tokyo
A1295 A1296

1987, Mar. 19 Photo. ***Perf. 13***

1730 A1295 60y multicolored 1.10 .35
1731 A1296 60y multicolored 1.10 .35

Railway Post Office Termination, Oct. 1, 1986 A1297

1987, Mar. 26 Litho. ***Perf. 13½***

1732 A1297 60y Mail car 1.10 .35
1733 A1297 60y Loading mail on car 1.10 .35
a. Pair, #1732-1733 2.25 1.00

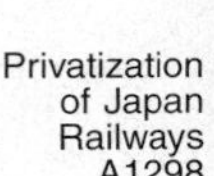

Privatization of Japan Railways A1298

1987, Apr. 1 Photo. ***Perf. 13½***

1734 A1298 60y Locomotive No. 137, c. 1900 1.10 .35
1735 A1298 60y Linear induction train, 1987 1.10 .35

Natl. Marine Biology Research, Cent. A1299

1987, Apr. 2 ***Perf. 13***

1736 A1299 60y Sea slugs 1.10 .35

Philately Week — A1300

1987, Apr. 14

1737 60y denomination at upper right 1.10 .35
1738 60y denomination at lower left 1.10 .35
a. A1300 Pair, #1737-1738 2.25 1.00

Map of Asia and Oceania A1302

1987, Apr. 27 Photo. ***Perf. 13½***

1739 A1302 60y multicolored 1.10 .35

20th annual meeting of the Asian Development Bank.

Nat'l. Land Afforestation Campaign A1303

1987, May 23

1740 A1303 60y Magpie, seashore 1.10 .35

National Treasures Series

A1304

A1305

Golden Turtle Sharito — A1306

Imuyama Castle Donjon, 1469 — A1307

Kongo Sanmai in Tahotoh Temple, Kamakura Era — A1308

Wood Ekoh-Dohji Statue in the Likeness of Kongobuji Fudodo, Kamakura Era, by Unkei — A1309

Itsukushima Shrine, Heian Period A1310

Kozakura-gawa, Braided Armor Worn by Minamoto-no-Yoshimitsu, Heian Period War Lord, Kai Province — A1311

Statue of *Nakatsu-hime-no-mikoto,* a Hachiman Goddess, Heian Period, Yakushiji Temple — A1312

Murou-ji Temple Pagoda, 9th Cent. — A1313

Designs: No. 1741, Yatsuhashi gold inkstone box, by Kohrin Ogata. No. 1742, Donjon of Hikone Castle, c. 1573-1592.

1987, May 26 Photo. *Perf. 13*
1741 A1304 60y multicolored 1.10 .35

Photo. & Engr.
Perf. 13½
1742 A1305 110y multicolored 2.10 .75

1987, July 17 Photo. *Perf. 13*
1743 A1306 60y multicolored 1.10 .35

Photo. & Engr.
Perf. 13½
1744 A1307 110y multicolored 2.10 .75

1988, Feb. 12 Photo. *Perf. 13*
1745 A1308 60y multicolored 1.10 .35

Photo. & Engr.
Perf. 13½
1746 A1309 110y multicolored 2.10 .75

1988, June 23 Photo. *Perf. 13*
1747 A1310 60y multicolored 1.10 .35

Photo. & Engr.
Perf. 13½
1748 A1311 100y multicolored 1.90 .75

1988, Sept. 26 Photo. *Perf. 13*
1749 A1312 60y multicolored 1.10 .35

Photo. & Engr.
Perf. 13½
1750 A1313 100y multicolored 1.90 .75
Nos. 1741-1750 (10) 15.60 5.50

Letter Writing Day — A1314

1987, July 23 Photo. *Perf. 13x13½*
1751 A1314 40y Flowers, envelope .75 .40
1752 A1314 60y Elephant 1.10 .35
a. Bklt. pane, 5 ea #1751-1752 7.00

Sheets of 2, Nos. 1751-1752, were lottery prizes. Value, *$4.25.*

Kiso Three Rivers Flood Control, Cent. A1315

1987, Aug. 7 Photo. *Perf. 13½*
1753 A1315 60y Kiso, Nagara and Ibi Rivers 1.10 .35

Japan — Thailand Diplomatic Relations, Cent. A1316

Design: Temple of the Emerald Buddha and cherry blossoms.

1987, Sept. 26 *Perf. 13*
1754 A1316 60y multicolored 1.10 .35

Intl. Letter Writing Week — A1317

13th World Congress of Certified Public Accountants, Tokyo, Oct. 11-15 — A1318

Dolls by Goyo Hirata: 130y, Gensho Kanto, by Royojo Hori (1898-1984). 150y, Utage-no-Hana (Fair Woman at the Party).

1987, Oct. 6 Photo. *Perf. 13*
1755 A1317 130y multicolored 2.50 1.00
1756 A1317 150y multicolored 2.75 1.10

1987, Oct. 9 *Perf. 13*

Design: Three Beauties (adaptation), by Toyokuni Utagawa (1769-1825).

1757 A1318 60y multicolored 1.10 .35

Modern Waterworks, Cent. — A1319

Shurei Gate, Okinawa, Basketball Players — A1320

Design: Lion's head public fountain, 1887, Waterworks Museum, Yokohama.

1987, Oct. 16 Engr.
1758 A1319 60y multicolored 1.10 .35

1987, Oct. 24 Photo.
1759 A1320 40y multicolored .75 .35

42nd Natl. Athletic Meet, Okinawa.

6th World Cong. on Smoking & Health, Nov. 9-12, Tokyo — A1321

World Telecommunications Conf., Nov. 15-18, Tokyo — A1322

1987, Nov. 9
1760 A1321 60y multicolored 1.10 .35

1987, Nov. 13 *Perf. 13½*

Design: Microwave dish antenna at Kashima Station Radio Research Laboratory.

1761 A1322 60y multicolored 1.10 .35

World Conference on Large Historic Cities, Nov. 18-21, Kyoto A1323

Design: Nijo Castle guardhouse roof and Ninomaru Hall, 17th cent.

1987, Nov. 18 *Perf. 13*
1762 A1323 60y multicolored 1.10 .35

Intl. Year of Shelter for the Homeless A1324

Prize-winning illustrations by: 40y, Takahiro Nahahama. 60y, Yoko Sasaki.

1987, Nov. 25
1763 A1324 40y multicolored .75 .35
1764 A1324 60y multicolored 1.10 .35

New Year 1988 (Year of the Dragon) — A1325

Design: Kurashiki papier-mache dragon, 1869, by Tajuro Omizu.

1987, Dec. 1 *Perf. 13x13½*
1765 A1325 40y multicolored .75 .35

Sheets of 2, Nos. 1506, 1765, were lottery prizes. Value, $2.25.

Seikan Tunnel Opening A1326

1988, Mar. 11 Photo. *Perf. 13¼*
1766 A1326 60y ED 79 locomotive, map 1.10 .35
a. Booklet pane of 10 11.00

Opening of Seto-Oohashi Bridge

Kagawa Side
A1327 A1328

Okayama Side
A1329 A1330

1988, Apr. 8 Engr. *Perf. 13½*
1767 A1327 60y multicolored 1.10 .35
1768 A1328 60y multicolored 1.10 .35
1769 A1329 60y multicolored 1.10 .35
1770 A1330 60y multicolored 1.10 .35
a. Strip of 4, #1767-1770 4.50 4.50

Nos. 1767-1768 and 1769-1770 have continuous designs.

Philately Week — A1331

Prints by Kotondo Torii (1900-76): No. 1771, Long Undergarment. No. 1772, Kimono Sash.

1988, Apr. 19 Photo. *Perf. 13*
1771 60y denomination at lower right 1.10 .35
1772 60y denomination at upper left 1.10 .35
a. A1331 Pair, #1771-1772 2.25

Souv. sheet of 2 exists. Value $6.

Silk Road Exposition, Apr. 24-Oct. 23, Nara — A1333

Design: Plectrum guard playing the biwa, detail of Raden-Shitan-no-Gogen-Biwa, a five-panel work of gold lacquer nacre on sandalwood preserved at Shosoin.

1988, Apr. 23 Photo. & Engr.
1773 A1333 60y multicolored 1.10 .35

Natl. Afforestation Campaign A1334

Design: Yahsima, site of the Genji-Heike war, and cuckoo on olive tree branch.

1988, May 20 Photo. *Perf. 13½*
1774 A1334 60y multicolored 1.10 .35

Basho Series, Part II

A1335

A1337

A1339

A1341

A1343

A1345

A1347

A1349

A1351

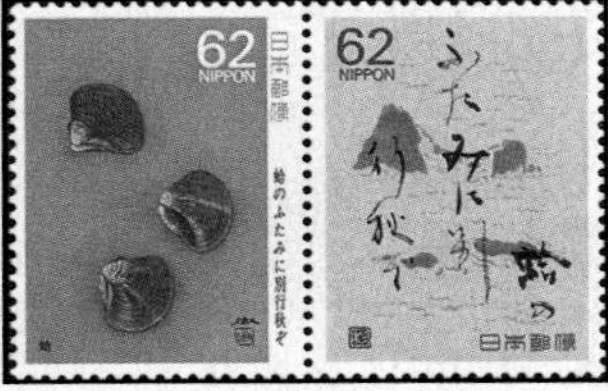
A1353

#1775, Mogami River. #1776, Haiku and flower. #1777, Mt. Gassan. #1778, Haiku and mountain.

1988, May 30 Photo. *Perf. 13x13½*

1775	60y multicolored	1.10	.35
1776	60y multicolored	1.10	.35
a.	Souv. sheet of 2, #1775-1776, imperf. ('89)	2.40	
b.	A1335 Pair, #1775-1776	2.25	1.00
1777	60y multicolored	1.10	.35
1778	60y multicolored	1.10	.35
a.	Souv. sheet of 2, #1777-1778, imperf. ('89)	2.40	
b.	A1337 Pair, #1777-1778	2.25	1.00

1988, Aug. 23

#1779, Mimosa in bloom. #1780, Verse, birds, Kisagata Inlet. #1781, Ocean waves. #1782, Verse and current.

1779	60y multicolored	1.10	.35
1780	60y multicolored	1.10	.35
a.	Souv. sheet of 2, #1779-1780, imperf ('89)	2.40	
b.	A1339 Pair, #1779-1780	2.25	1.00
1781	60y multicolored	1.10	.35
1782	60y multicolored	1.10	.35
a.	Souv. sheet of 2, #1781-1782, imperf. ('89)	2.40	
b.	A1341 Pair, #1781-1782	2.25	1.00

1988, Nov. 11

#1783, Rice. #1784, Birds in flight, haiku. #1785, Sun glow. #1786, Rice, haiku.

1783	60y multicolored	1.10	.35
1784	60y multicolored	1.10	.35
a.	Souv. sheet of 2, #1783-1784, imperf. ('89)	2.40	
b.	A1343 Pair, #1783-1784	2.25	1.00
1785	60y multicolored	1.10	.35
1786	60y multicolored	1.10	.35
a.	Souv. sheet of 2, #1785-1786, imperf. ('89)	2.40	
b.	A1345 Pair, #1785-1786	2.25	1.00

1989, Feb. 13

#1787, Nata-dera Temple. #1788, Haiku, white grass. #1789, Trees. #1790, Haiku, moonlit forest.

1787	60y multicolored	1.10	.35
1788	60y multicolored	1.10	.35
a.	Souv. sheet of 2, #1787-1788, imperf.	2.40	
b.	A1347 Pair, #1787-1788	2.25	1.00
1789	60y multicolored	1.10	.35
1790	60y multicolored	1.10	.35
a.	Souv. sheet of 2, #1789-1790, imperf.	2.40	
b.	A1349 Pair, #1789-1790	2.25	1.00

1989, May 12

#1791, Autumn on the beach. #1792, Haiku. #1793, Clams. #1794, Haiku.

1791	62y multicolored	1.10	.35
1792	62y multicolored	1.10	.35
a.	Souv. sheet of 2, #1791-1792, imperf.	2.40	
b.	A1351 Pair, #1791-1792	2.25	1.00
1793	62y multicolored	1.10	.35
1794	62y multicolored	1.10	.35
a.	Souv. sheet of 2, #1793-1794, imperf.	2.40	
b.	A1353 Pair, #1793-1794	2.25	1.00

Haiku from *Oku-no-hosomichi,* "*Narrow Road to a Far Province,*" 1694, a travel description written in by Matsuo Munefusa (1644-94), a haiku poet best known by his pen-name Basho.

In each setenant pair, a complete *haiku* by Basho is inscribed vertically at right on the left stamp and in the center of the right stamp. The same poem appears on both stamps in each pair.

Issued: Nos. 1776a-1794a, Aug. 1, 1989.

Intl. Conference on Volcanoes, Kagoshima A1355

1988, July 19 Photo. *Perf. 14*

1795	A1355 60y multicolored	1.10	.35

A1356

A1357

A1358

Letter Writing Day, 10th Anniv. — A1359

Designs and contest-winning children's drawings: No. 1796, Cat and letter. No. 1797, *Crab and Letter,* by Katsuyuki Yamada. No. 1798, Fairy and letter. No. 1799, *Girl and Letter,* by Takashi Ukai.

Photo., Litho. (Nos. 1797, 1799)

1988, July 23 *Perf. 13x13½*

1796	A1356 40y multicolored	.75	.50
1796A	A1356 40y Imperf., self-adhesive	.75	.35
1797	A1357 40y multicolored	.75	.35
1798	A1358 60y multicolored	1.10	.70
a.	Bklt. pane, 5 each #1796, 1798	9.25	
1798B	A1358 60y Imperf., self-adhesive	1.10	.35
c.	Bklt. pane, 3 each #1796A, 1798B	6.00	
1799	A1359 60y multicolored	1.10	.35
	Nos. 1796-1799 (6)	5.55	2.60

No. 1798c is adhered to the booklet cover, made of peelable paper, folded in half and rouletted down the center fold, with No. 1796a at left and No. 1798b at right of the roulette.

Sheets of 2 containing Nos. 1796, 1798 were lottery prizes. Value, $5.

15th World Puppetry Festival, July 27-Aug. 11 — A1360

Puppets: No. 1800, *Ohana,* string puppet from the film *Spring and Fall in the Meiji Era,* by Kinosuke Takeda (1923-1979), Japan. No. 1801, Girl, stick puppet from the Natl. Radost Puppet Theater, Brno, Czechoslovakia. No. 1802, Woman, shadow puppet from China. No. 1803, Knight, a marionette from Sicily.

1988, July 27 Photo. *Perf. 13*

1800	60y multicolored	1.10	.35
1801	60y multicolored	1.10	.35
1802	60y multicolored	1.10	.35
1803	60y multicolored	1.10	.35
a.	A1360 Block or strip of 4, #1800-1803	3.75	2.50

Japan-China Treaty, 10th Anniv. — A1364

1988, Aug. 12 Photo.

1804	60y Peony	1.10	.35
1805	60y Panda	1.10	.35
a.	A1364 Pair, #1804-1805	2.25	1.00

18th World Poultry Congress, Nagoya, Sept. 4-9 — A1366

1988, Sept. 3 *Perf. 13½*

1806	A1366 60y multicolored	1.10	.35

Rehabilitation Intl. 16th World Congress, Tokyo, Sept. 5-9 — A1367

Photo. & Embossed

1988, Sept. 5 *Perf. 13*

1807	A1367 60y multicolored	1.10	.35

A1368 A1369

Prints: 80y, *Kumesaburo Iwai as Chiyo,* by Kunimasa Utagawa (1773-1810), late Edo

Period. 120y, *Komazo Ichikawa III as Ganryu Sasaki,* by Toyokuni Utagawa (1769-1825).

1988, Oct. 6 **Photo.**
1808 A1368 80y multicolored 1.50 .60
1809 A1368 120y multicolored 2.25 1.00

Intl. Letter-Writing Week.

1988, Oct. 14

Design: Gymnast on parallel bars and "Kinkakuji," Temple of the Golden Pavilion.

1810 A1369 40y multicolored .75 .35

43rd Natl. Athletic Meet, Kyoto.

Japan-Mexico Trade Agreement, Cent. A1370

New Year 1989 (Year of the Snake) A1371

1988, Nov. 30 **Photo.**
1811 A1370 60y multicolored 1.10 .35

1988, Dec. 1

Clay bell snake by Masanobu Ogawa.

1812 A1371 40y multicolored .75 .35

Sheets of two containing Nos. 1506, 1812 were lottery prizes. Value, $2.50.

UN Declaration of Human Rights, 40th Anniv. — A1372

1988, Dec. 5 **Litho.** ***Perf. 13½***
1813 A1372 60y multicolored 1.10 .35

National Treasures Series

Votive Silver Lidded Bowl Used in Todai-ji Temple Ground-Breaking Ceremony, 8th Cent. — A1373

Bronze Yakushi-nyorai Buddha, Asuka Period, 7th Cent. — A1374

Kondo-Sukashibori-Kurakanagu, Bronze Saddle from Ohjin Imperial Mausoleum — A1375

Tamamushi-no-Zushi, Buddhist Altar in Lacquered Cypress from the Asuka Era — A1376

Kin-in, a Gokan Era Gold Seal Given to the King of Na by Emperor Kobutei — A1377

Shinninshaba-gazokyo, a 5th Cent. European Bronze Mirror Back — A1378

Photo., Photo & Engr. (100y)

1989, Jan. 20 ***Perf. 13, 13½ (100y)***
1814 A1373 60y multicolored 1.10 .35
1815 A1374 100y multicolored 1.90 .75

1989, June 30
1816 A1375 62y multicolored 1.10 .35
1817 A1376 100y multicolored 1.90 .75

1989, Aug. 15
1818 A1377 62y multicolored 1.10 .35
1819 A1378 100y multicolored 1.90 .75
Nos. 1814-1819 (6) 9.00 3.30

Asian-Pacific Expo, Fukuoka, Mar. 17-Sept. 3 — A1383

1989 **Photo.** ***Perf. 13***
1822 A1383 60y multicolored 1.10 .35
1823 A1383 62y multicolored 1.10 .65

Issue dates: 60y, Mar. 16; 62y, Apr. 18.

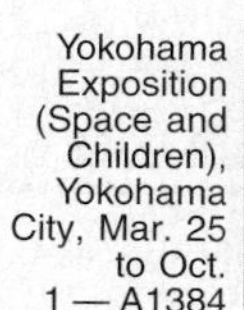

Yokohama Exposition (Space and Children), Yokohama City, Mar. 25 to Oct. 1 — A1384

Design: Detail of *Russian Lady Sight-seeing at the Port,* by Yoshitora, and entrance to the Yokohama City Art Museum.

1989, Mar. 24 **Litho.**
1824 A1384 60y multicolored 1.10 .35
1825 A1384 62y multicolored 1.10 .35

World Bonsai Convention, Omiya, Apr. 6-9 — A1385

1989, Apr. 6 **Photo.** ***Perf. 13***
1826 A1385 62y multicolored 1.10 .35

Awa-odori, by Tsunetomi Kitano (b. 1880) — A1386

1989, Apr. 18 ***Perf. 13***
1827 62y multicolored 1.10 .35
1828 62y multicolored 1.10 .35
a. A1386 Pair, #1827-1828 2.25

Philately Week. Sheets of 2 containing #1827-1828 were lottery prizes. Value, $5.

Holland Festival 1989 — A1388

1989, Apr. 19 ***Perf. 13½***
1829 A1388 62y Ship 1.10 .35

Fiber-optic Cable, the 3rd Transpacific Line Relay Linking Japan and the US — A1389

1989, May 10 ***Perf. 13½x13***
1830 A1389 62y Station tower, map 1.10 .35

Natl. Afforestation Campaign — A1390

1989, May 19 ***Perf. 13½***
1831 A1390 62y Bayberry, lime, Mt. Tsurugi 1.10 .35

World Design Exposition, Nagoya, July 15-Nov. 26
A1391 A1392

1989, July 14
1832 A1391 41y multicolored .80 .35
1833 A1392 62y multicolored 1.10 .35

Letter Writing Day
A1393 A1394

1989, July 21 ***Perf. 13x13½***
1834 A1393 41y multicolored .80 .35
1835 A1394 62y multicolored 1.10 .35
a. Bklt. pane, 5 each #1834-1835 9.50

Sheets of 2 containing Nos. 1834-1835 were lottery prizes. Value, $3.

Congratulations and Condolences Types of 1982

1989, Aug. 10 **Photo.** ***Perf. 13x13½***
1836 A1082 41y Wreath .80 .35
1837 A1083 41y Crane .80 .35
1838 A1083 62y Crane 1.10 .35
1839 A1084 72y Tortoise 1.40 .50
Nos. 1836-1839 (4) 4.10 1.55

6th Interflora World Congress, Tokyo, Aug. 27-30 — A1395

1989, Aug. 25 **Photo.** ***Perf. 13½***
1840 A1395 62y multicolored 1.10 .35

Prefecture Issues

Nos. 1841-1990 have been changed to Nos. Z1-Z150. The listings can be found in a new section immediately following the postage section and preceding the semi-postal listings.

Far East and South Pacific Games for the Disabled (FESPIC), Kobe, Sept. 15-20
A1546

1989, Sept. 14 **Photo.** ***Perf. 13½***
1991 A1546 62y multicolored 1.10 .35

Okuni Kabuki Screen
A1547 A1548

1989, Sept. 18 ***Perf. 13***
1992 A1547 62y multicolored 1.10 .35
1993 A1548 70y multicolored 1.25 .50

EUROPALIA '89, Japan.

A1549

A1550

Scenes from the Yadorigi and Takekawa Chapters of the Tales of the Genji picture scroll, attributed to Fujiwara-no-Takeyoshi, late Heian Period (897-1185).

1989, Oct. 6 Photo. *Perf. 13½*

1994	A1549	80y	multicolored	1.50	.60
1995	A1550	120y	multicolored	2.25	.75

Intl. Letter Writing Day.

Intl. Conference on Irrigation and Drainage A1551

100th Tenno Sho Horse Race A1552

1989, Oct. 13

1996	A1551	62y	Rice	1.10	.35

1989, Oct. 27 *Perf. 13*

1997	A1552	62y	Jockey riding Shinzan	1.10	.35

9th Hot Air Balloon World Championships, Saga — A1553

1989, Nov. 17 Photo. *Perf. 13x13½*

1998	A1553	62y	multicolored	1.10	.35

Copyright Control System, 50th Anniv. A1554

1989, Nov. 17 *Perf. 13*

1999	A1554	62y	Conductor	1.10	.35

New Year 1990 (Year of the Horse)

A1555 A1556

1989, Dec. 1 *Perf. 13x13½, 13½*

2000	A1555	41y	*Yawata-Uma* festival horse	.80	.35
2001	A1556	62y	*Kazari-Uma,* Meiji Period	1.10	.35

No. 2001 was sold through Jan. 10, 1990, serving as a lottery ticket.

Sheets of two containing Nos. 1838, 2000 were lottery prizes. Value, $2.

Electric Locomotives

10,000 A1557

Photo. & Engr., Photo.

1990 *Perf. 13*

2002	A1557	62y	shown	1.40	.40
2003	A1557	62y	EF58	1.40	.40
2004	A1557	62y	ED40	1.40	.40
2005	A1557	62y	EH10	1.40	.40
2006	A1557	62y	EF53	1.40	.40
2007	A1557	62y	ED70	1.40	.40
2008	A1557	62y	EF55	1.40	.40
2009	A1557	62y	ED61	1.40	.40
2010	A1557	62y	EF57	1.40	.40
2011	A1557	62y	EF30	1.40	.40
	Nos. 2002-2011 (10)			14.00	4.00

Issued two stamps at a time, the first photo. & engr., the second photo.

Issued: #2002-2003, Jan. 31; #2004-2005, Feb. 28; #2006-2007, Apr. 23; #2008-2009, May 23; #2010-2011, July 18.

Intl. Garden and Greenery Exposition, Osaka A1558

1990, Mar. 30 Photo. *Perf. 13*

2021	A1558	62y	multicolored	1.10	.35

See No. B45.

A1559

A1560

Painting: *Women Gazing at the Stars,* by Chou Ohta.

1990, Apr. 20 Photo. *Perf. 13*

2022	A1559	62y	multicolored	1.10	.35
a.			Souvenir sheet of 1	1.10	.65

Philately Week.

1990, May 18 Photo. *Perf. 13½*

2023	A1560	62y	Azalea, Mt. Unzen	1.10	.35

Natl. Land Afforestation Campaign.

Flower, Butterfly A1561

Abstract Art — A1561a

1990, June 1 Photo. *Perf. 13*

2024	A1561	62y	multicolored	1.10	.35
2025	A1561a	70y	multicolored	1.25	.35

Japan-Turkey Relations, Cent. — A1562

1990, June 13

2026	A1562	62y	multicolored	1.40	.35

Horses Series

Horse at Stable from Umaya-zu Byobu — A1563

Foals A1564

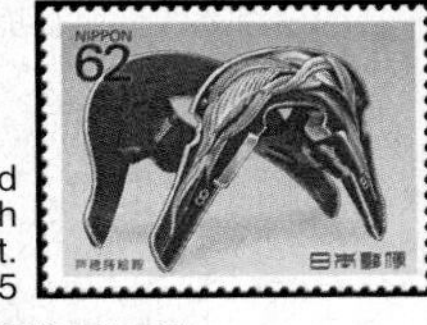

Lacquered Saddle, 16th Cent. A1565

Lacquered Stirrups, 16th Cent. A1566

Horse by S. Nishiyama A1567

Kettei A1568

"Kamo-Kurabeuma-Monyo-Kosode" A1569

Postal Carriages — A1569a

Inkstone Case "Sano-no-Watashi" — A1570

"Bushu-Senju-zu" by Hokusai — A1571

"Shudan" by Kogetsu Saigo A1571a

#2027-2031 each show a panel of folding screen with a different horse tied up at a stable.

Perf. 13x13½, 13

1990 Litho. & Engr.

Color of Horse

2027	A1563	62y	red brown	1.35	.35
2028	A1563	62y	gray	1.35	.35
2029	A1563	62y	beige	1.35	.35
2030	A1563	62y	tan	1.35	.35
2031	A1563	62y	mottled	1.35	.35
a.			Strip of 5, #2027-2031	6.75	

Photo.

2032	A1564	62y	shown	1.35	.35

Photo. & Engr.

2033	A1565	62y	shown	1.35	.35
2034	A1566	62y	shown	1.35	.35
a.			Pair, #2033-2034	2.75	1.00

Photo.

2035	A1567	62y	multicolored	1.35	.35
2036	A1568	62y	multicolored	1.35	.35
2037	A1569	62y	multicolored	1.35	.35

Photo. & Engr., Photo. (#2040, 2042)

1991 *Perf. 12½x13*

2038		62y	one horse	1.35	.35
2039		62y	two horses	1.35	.35
a.	A1569a		Pair, #2038-2039	2.75	1.00

Perf. 13½x13

2040	A1570	62y	multicolored	1.35	.35
2041	A1571	62y	multicolored	1.35	.35
2042	A1571a	62y	multicolored	1.35	.35
	Nos. 2027-2042 (16)			21.60	5.60

Issued: #2027-2032, 6/20; #2033-2035, 7/31; #2036-2037, 9/27; #2038-2040, Jan. 31. Nos. 2041-2042, Feb. 28.

38th Intl. Youth Hostel Fed. Conference A1573

1990, June 25 Litho. *Perf. 13*

2057	A1573	62y	multicolored	1.10	.35

Letter Writing Day

A1574 A1575

1990, July 23 Photo. *Perf. 13½*

2058	A1574	41y	multicolored	.80	.35
2059	A1575	62y	multicolored	1.10	.35
a.			Souv. sheet of 1	1.10	.35
b.			Bklt. pane, 5 ea #2058-2059	9.50	

See No. 2117.

21st Intl. Congress of Mathematicians — A1576

1990, Aug. 17 Photo. *Perf. 13*
2060 A1576 62y multicolored 1.10 .35

World Cycling Championships A1577

1990, Aug. 20 Litho. *Perf. 13½*
2061 A1577 62y multicolored 1.10 .35

Ogai Mori, Educator A1578

1990, Aug. 27 Photo.
2062 A1578 62y multicolored 1.10 .35

Intl. Assoc. for Germanic Studies (IVG), 8th Congress.

Character "Ji" in Shape of Rosetta Stone — A1579

1990, Sept. 7 *Perf. 13*
2063 A1579 62y multicolored 1.10 .35

Intl. Literacy Year.

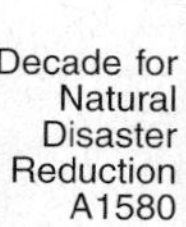

Decade for Natural Disaster Reduction A1580

1990, Sept. 27 Photo.
2064 A1580 62y multicolored 1.10 .35

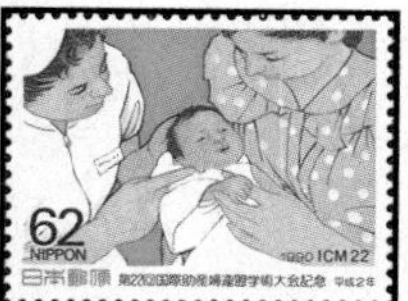

Intl. Confederation of Midwives, 22nd Congress A1581

1990, Oct. 5 Photo.
2065 A1581 62y multicolored 1.10 .35

A1582

"Choju-Jinbutsu-Giga" — A1583

Photo. & Engr.
1990, Oct. 5 *Perf. 13½*
2066 A1582 80y multicolored 1.50 .60
2067 A1583 120y multicolored 2.25 .75

Intl. Letter Writing Week.

"Fumizukai-zu" by Harunobu Suiendo A1584

1990, Oct. 16 Photo.
2068 A1584 100y multicolored 1.90 .75
a. Souv. sheet of 1 1.90 1.00

No. 2068a exists with surcharge which paid admission to PHILANIPPON '91. These were not sold by the post office.

Court System, Cent. — A1585

1990, Nov. 1 Photo. *Perf. 13x13½*
2069 A1585 62y "Justice" 1.10 .35

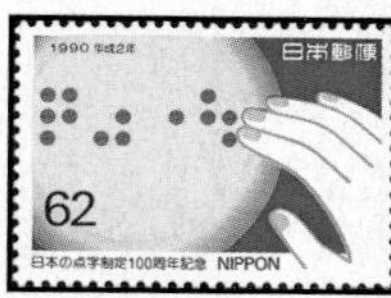

Japanese Braille, Cent. A1586

Photo & Embossed
1990, Nov. 1 *Perf. 13½*
2070 A1586 62y multicolored 1.10 .35

Enthronement of Akihito — A1587

#2071, Chinese phoenix depicted on Emperor's chair. #2072, Diamond pattern for costume worn at banquet ceremony.

1990, Nov. 9 Photo. *Perf. 13*
2071 A1587 62y multicolored 1.10 .35
2072 A1587 62y multicolored 1.10 .35
a. Souv. sheet of 2, #2071-2072 2.25 1.10

Japanese Diet, Cent. — A1588

1990, Nov. 29 Litho.
2073 A1588 62y multicolored 1.10 .35

New Year 1991 (Year of the Sheep)
A1589 A1590

1990, Dec. 3 Photo. *Perf. 13x13½*
2074 A1589 41y multicolored .80 .35

Photo. & Engr.
Perf. 13½
2075 A1590 41y multicolored .80 .45
2076 A1590 62y multi, diff. 1.10 .45
Nos. 2074-2076 (3) 2.70 1.25

Sheets of 2 No. 2074 were lottery prizes. Value, $1.50.

Dr. Yoshio Nishina, Physicist — A1591

Telephone Service, Cent. — A1592

1990, Dec. 6 Photo. *Perf. 13*
2077 A1591 62y multicolored 1.10 .35

Use of radio isotopes in Japan, 50th anniv.

1990, Dec. 14
2078 A1592 62y multicolored 1.10 .35

A1593

A1594

1991, Mar. 1 Photo. *Perf. 13½*
2079 A1593 41y Figure skating .80 .35
Perf. 13½x13
2080 A1593 62y Speed skating, horiz. 1.10 .35

1991 Winter Universiade.

1991, Apr. 1 Photo. *Perf. 13*
2081 A1594 62y multicolored 1.10 .35

Postal Life Insurance System.

Philately Week
A1595 A1596

#2082, Beauty Looking Back by Moronobu. #2083, Opening Dance by Shuho Yamakawa.

1991, Apr. 19
2082 A1595 62y multicolored 1.10 .35
2083 A1596 62y multicolored 1.10 .35
a. Souv. sheet of 2, #2082-2083 1.90 1.10
b. Pair, #2082-2083 1.90 1.10

Postal Service, 120th anniv.

Pairs of Nos. 2082-2083 with label between are available from sheets of 20.

A1597

A1598

1991, Apr. 19 *Perf. 13½*
2084 A1597 62y multicolored 1.10 .35

Ceramic World Shigaraki '91.

1991, May 24 Photo. *Perf. 13½*
2085 A1598 41y multicolored .80 .35

Natl. Land Afforestation Campaign.

Standard Datum of Leveling, Cent. — A1599

1991, May 30 Photo. *Perf. 13*
2086 A1599m 62y mutlicolored 1.10 .35

Int'l Stamp Design Contest Winning Entries

A1600

A1601

A1601a

A1601b

1991, May 31 Photo. *Perf. 13*

2087 A1600 41y Flowers .80 .35
2088 A1601 62y Couple in Ethnic Dress 1.10 .35
2089 A1601a 70y World peace 1.25 .50
2090 A1601b 100y Butterfly 1.90 .70
Nos. 2087-2090 (4) 5.05 1.90

Int'l. Stamp Design Contest winning entries.

Kabuki Series

Kagamijishi A1602

Yaegakihime A1603

Koshiro Matsumoto VII A1604

Danjuro Ichikawa XI A1605

Baigyoku Nakamura III A1606

Ganjiro Nakamura II A1607

Kichiemon Nakamura I — A1608

Nizaemon Kataoka XIII — A1609

Enjaku Jitsukawa II A1610

Hakuo Matsumoto I A1611

Fuji-Musume A1612

Kotobuki-Soganotaimen — A1613

Perf. 13 (62y), 13½ (100y)

1991-92 Photo.

2091 A1602 62y dp bl grn & gold 1.10 .35
2092 A1603 100y multicolored 1.90 .70
2093 A1604 62y multicolored 1.10 .35
2094 A1605 100y multicolored 1.90 .70
2095 A1606 62y multicolored 1.10 .35
2096 A1607 100y multicolored 1.90 .70
2097 A1608 62y multicolored 1.10 .35
2098 A1609 100y multicolored 1.90 .70
2099 A1610 62y multicolored 1.10 .35
2100 A1611 100y multicolored 1.90 .70
2101 A1612 62y multicolored 1.10 .35
2102 A1613 100y multicolored 1.90 .70
Nos. 2091-2102 (12) 18.00 6.30

Issued: #2091-2092, 6/28; #2093-2094, 9/27; #2095-2096, 11/20; #2097-2098, 2/20/92; #2099-2100, 4/10/92; #2101-2102, 6/30/92.

Waterbird Series

Gallinago Hardwickii (Latham's Snipe) A1614

1991-93 Photo. *Perf. 13½*

2103 A1614 62y shown 1.10 .35
2104 A1614 62y Sula leucogaster 1.10 .35
2105 A1614 62y Larus crassirostris 1.10 .35
2106 A1614 62y Podiceps ruficollis 1.10 .35
2107 A1614 62y Lunda cirrhata 1.10 .35
2108 A1614 62y Grus monacha 1.10 .35
2109 A1614 62y Cygnus cygnus 1.10 .35
2110 A1614 62y Rostratula benghalensis 1.10 .35
2111 A1614 62y Calonectris leucomelas 1.10 .35
2112 A1614 62y Halcyon coromanda 1.10 .35
2113 A1614 62y Alcedo atthis 1.10 .35
2114 A1614 62y Bubulcus ibis 1.10 .35
Nos. 2103-2114 (12) 13.20 4.20

#2103-2104 printed in blocks of 12 with gutter between in sheet of 24.

Issued: #2103-2104, 6/28; #2105-2106, 9/27; #2107-2108, 1/30/92; #2109-2110, 3/25/92; #2111-2112, 8/31/92; #2113-2114, 1/29/93.

See Nos. 2192-2195.

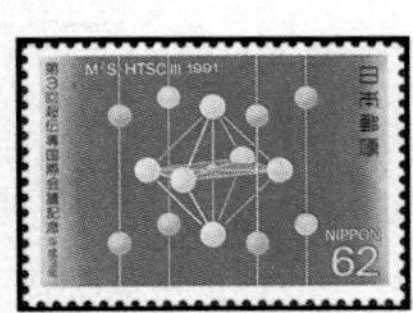
Intl. Conf. on Superconductivity — A1620

1991, July 19 Litho. *Perf. 13½*

2115 A1620 62y multicolored 1.10 .35

Type of Letter Writing Day of 1990 and

A1621

1991, July 23 Photo. *Perf. 13x13½*

2116 A1621 41y multicolored .80 .35
2117 A1575 62y multicolored 1.10 .35
a. Souvenir sheet of 1 1.10 .70
b. Bklt. pane, 5 each #2116-2117 9.50

Nos. 2117, 2117a have light blue frameline and inscription and violet denomination.

3rd IAAF World Track & Field Championships, Tokyo — A1622

1991, Aug. 23 *Perf. 13*

2118 A1622 41y High jump .80 .35
2119 A1622 62y Shot put 1.10 .35

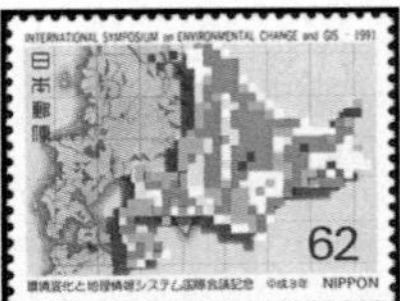
Intl. Symposium on Environmental Change and Geographical Information Systems — A1623

1991, Aug. 23

2120 A1623 62y multicolored 1.10 .35

Intl. Letter Writing Week A1624

Bandainagon-emaki picture scroll probably by Mitsunaga Tokiwa: 80y, Crowd of people. 120y, People, house.

Photo. & Engr.

1991, Oct. 7 *Perf. 13½*

2121 A1624 80y multicolored 1.50 .60
2122 A1624 120y multicolored 2.25 1.00

A1625

A1626

62y, Breezy Fine Weather by Hokusai.

1991, Oct. 8 Photo. *Perf. 13*

2123 A1625 62y multicolored 1.10 .35

Summit Conf. on Earthquake and Natural Disasters Countermeasures.

1991, Oct. 31 Litho. *Perf. 13*

2124 A1626 62y multicolored 1.10 .35

Japanese Green Tea, 800th anniv.

A1627

A1628

Koshaku-Musume by Kunisada Utagawa.

Photo. & Engr.

1991, Nov. 15 *Perf. 13*

2125 A1627 62y multicolored 1.10 .35
a. Sheet of 2 2.25 1.60

World Stamp Exhibition, Nippon '91.

1991, Nov. 20 Photo.

2126 A1628 62y multicolored 1.10 .35

Administrative Counselors System, 30th anniv.

A1629

A1630

New Year 1992 (Year of the Monkey)
A1631 A1632

1991, Dec. 2 Photo. *Perf. 13½*
2127 A1629 41y multicolored .80 .45
2128 A1630 62y multicolored 1.10 .45
2129 A1631 41y +3y, multi .85 .55
2130 A1632 62y +3y, multi 1.25 .55
Nos. 2127-2130 (4) 4.00 2.00

Sheets of 2 #2127 were lottery prizes.

8th Conference on Intl. Trade in Endangered Species (CITES) A1633

1992, Mar. 2 Photo. *Perf. 13*
2131 A1633 62y multicolored 1.10 .35

A1634 A1635

Flowers on the Chair, by Hoshun Yamaguchi.

1992, Apr. 20
2132 A1634 62y multicolored 1.10 .35

Philately Week.

1992, May 15
2133 A1635 62y multicolored 1.10 .35

Return of Ryukyu Islands to Japan, 20th anniv.

Intl. Space Year — A1636

1992, July 7 Photo. *Perf. 13*
2134 62y satellite at left 1.10 .35
2135 62y space station upper right 1.10 .35
a. A1636 Pair, #2134-2135 2.25 1.56

Letter Writing Day
A1638 A1639

1992, July 23 *Perf. 13x13½*
2136 A1638 41y multicolored .80 .35

Perf. 13½
2137 A1639 62y multicolored 1.10 .35
a. Souvenir sheet of 1 1.10 .75
b. Bklt. pane, 5 each #2136-2137 9.50

29th Intl. Geological Congress, Kyoto A1640

1992, Aug. 24 Photo. *Perf. 13½x13*
2138 A1640 62y multicolored 1.10 .35

47th Natl. Athletic Meet, Yamagata Prefecture — A1641

1992, Sept. 4 *Perf. 13½*
2139 A1641 41y multicolored .80 .35

Normalization of Japanese-Chinese Relations, 20th Anniv. — A1642

Photo. & Engr.

1992, Sept. 29 *Perf. 13*
2140 62y jug 1.10 .35
2141 62y long-neck jar 1.10 .35
a. A1642 Pair, #2140-2141 2.25 1.00

Intl. Letter Writing Week — A1644

Heiji picture scroll: 80y, Nobles, servants in carriages by Taikenmon gate. 120y, Fujiwara-no Nobuyori seated before samurai.

Photo. & Engr.

1992, Oct. 6 *Perf. 13½*
2142 A1644 80y multicolored 1.50 .75
2143 A1644 120y multicolored 2.25 1.00

Cat and Birds A1644a

Design: 70y, Santa Claus, snow scene.

Perf. 13½x13, 13x13½

1992, Oct. 9 Photo.
2144 A1644a 62y multicolored 1.10 .35
2145 A1644a 70y multicolored 1.25 .50

Winners of Third Postage Stamp Design contest.

30th Congress of Intl. Cooperative Alliance, Tokyo — A1644b

1992, Oct. 27 *Perf. 13x13½*
2146 A1644b 62y multicolored 1.10 .35

A1645 A1646

Cultural Pioneers: No. 2147, Takakazu Seki (1642?-1708), mathematician. No. 2148, Akiko Yosano (1878-1942), poet.

Photo. & Engr.

1992, Nov. 4 *Perf. 13*
2147 A1645 62y multicolored 1.10 .35
2148 A1645 62y multicolored 1.10 .35

See Nos. 2217-2219, 2642, 2717-2718.

1992, Nov. 9 Photo. *Perf. 13x13½*
2149 A1646 62y multicolored 1.10 .35

Certified Public Tax Accountant System, 50th anniv.

A1647 A1648

New Year 1993 (Year of the Rooster)
A1649 A1650

1992, Nov. 16 *Perf. 13x13½*
2150 A1647 41y multicolored .80 .35
2151 A1648 62y multicolored 1.10 .35
a. Souvenir sheet of 2, #2150-2151 2.00 1.10

Perf. 13½
2152 A1649 41y +3y multi .85 .45
2153 A1650 62y +3y multi 1.25 .45
Nos. 2150-2153 (4) 4.00 1.60

Surtax on Nos. 2152-2153 for lottery.

Flora and Fauna — A1651

1992-94 Photo. *Perf. 13x13½*
2154 A1651 9y Dragonfly .20 .20
2155 A1651 15y Swallowtail .30 .20
2156 A1651 18y Ladybug .35 .20
2157 A1651 41y Mandarin duck .80 .35
2158 A1651 50y Japanese white-eye .95 .45
2159 A1651 62y Rufous turtle dove 1.10 .20
a. Bklt. pane, 5 ea #2157, 2159 9.50
b. Booklet pane of 10 11.00
2160 A1651 72y Varied tit 1.40 .60
2161 A1651 80y Pied kingfisher 1.50 .20
a. Miniature sheet, 5 #2158, 10 #2161 + 3 labels *40.00*
2162 A1651 90y Spotbill duck 1.75 .80
2163 A1651 130y Bullfinch 2.50 1.25
2164 A1651 190y Fringed orchid 3.75 1.90
2165 A1651 270y Wild pink 5.00 2.25
2166 A1651 350y Adder's tongue lily 6.50 3.00
2167 A1651 420y Japanese iris 8.00 3.75
2167A A1651 430y Violet 8.25 4.00
Nos. 2154-2167A (15) 42.35 19.35

Coil Stamps

Perf. 13 Horiz.
2168 A1651 50y like #2156 .95 .45
2169 A1651 80y like #2161 1.50 .70

Booklet Stamps

Self-Adhesive

Die Cut
2170 A1651 41y like #2157 .80 .35
2171 A1651 50y like #2158 .95 .45
2172 A1651 62y like #2159 1.10 .50
a. Bklt. pane, 2 #2170, 4 #2172 5.50
2173 A1651 80y like #2161 1.50 .70
a. Bklt. pane, 4 #2171, 4 #2173 10.00

Issued: 41y, 62y, 72y, 11/30/92; 9y, 18y, #2158, 2161, 90y, 1/13/94; 270y, 350y, 420y, 1/24/94; 15y, 130y, 190y, 430y, 4/25/94.

Nos. 2172a, 2173a are adhered to the booklet cover, made of peelable paper, folded in half and rouletted down the center fold.

See Nos. 2475-2482, 2488B.

World Alpine Skiing Championships, Morioka-Shizukuishi — A1657

1993, Feb. 3 Photo. *Perf. 13*
2174 A1657 41y shown .80 .40
2175 A1657 62y Skier, diff. 1.10 .55

Seasonal Flowers Series

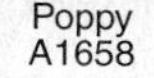

Poppy
A1658

Cherry Blossoms
A1659

Lily — A1660

Thistle — A1661

Chinese Bellflowers
A1662

Chrysanthemums
A1663

Plum Blossom A1664 — Winter Camellia A1665

Perf. 13½ (41y, 50y), 13 (62y, 80y)

1993-94 Photo.
2176 A1658 41y multicolored .80 .35

Perf. 13

2177 A1659 62y multicolored 1.10 .35
2178 A1660 41y multicolored .80 .35

Perf. 13

2179 A1661 62y multicolored 1.10 .35
2180 A1662 41y multicolored .80 .35
2181 A1663 62y multicolored 1.10 .35
2182 A1664 50y multicolored .95 .35
2183 A1665 80y multicolored 1.50 .70
Nos. 2176-2183 (8) 8.15 3.15

Issued: #2176-2177, 3/12; #2178-2179, 6/18; #2180-2181, 9/16; #2182-2183, 1/28/94.

Waterbird Type

1993 Photo. *Perf. 13½*
2192 A1614 62y Grus vipio 1.10 .35
2193 A1614 62y Ansner albifrons 1.10 .35
2194 A1614 62y Anas formosa 1.25 .35
2195 A1614 62y Haliaeetus albicilla 1.25 .35
Nos. 2192-2195 (4) 4.70 1.40

Issued: #2192-2193, 3/31; #2194-2195, 5/25.

Philately Week A1674 — Natl. Land Afforestation Campaign A1675

Painting: In the Studio, by Nampu Katayama.

1993, Apr. 20 Photo. *Perf. 13*
2196 A1674 62y multicolored 1.10 .35

1993, Apr. 23 *Perf. 13½*
2197 A1675 41y multicolored .80 .35

Mandarin Duck in the Nest — A1676 — Gardenia in the Nest — A1677

Design: 70y, Mandarin Duck and Gardenia emblems, horiz.

1993, June 8 Photo. *Perf. 13*
2198 A1676 62y multicolored 1.25 .35
2199 A1677 62y multicolored 1.25 .35
a. Pair, #2198-2199 2.50 1.25
2200 A1676 70y multicolored 1.25 .50
Nos. 2198-2200 (3) 3.75 1.20

Royal Wedding of Crown Prince Naruhito and Masako Owada.

5th Meeting of Signatories to Ramsar, Iran Convention on Wetlands and Waterfowl Habitats A1678

1993, June 10 Photo. *Perf. 13½*
2201 A1678 62y Crane with young 1.25 .35
2202 A1678 62y Crane's head 1.25 .35
a. Pair, #2201-2202 2.50 1.25

Commercial Registration System, Cent. — A1679

1993, July 1 Photo. *Perf. 13x13½*
2203 A1679 62y multicolored 1.25 .35

Letter Writing Day — A1680 — A1681

1993, July 23 *Perf. 13x13½*
2204 A1680 41y multicolored .80 .35

Perf. 13½x13

2205 A1681 62y multicolored 1.25 .35
a. Souvenir sheet of 1 1.25 .75
b. Booklet pane, 5 each #2204-2205 10.00

15th Intl. Botanical Congress, Tokyo A1682

Designs: No. 2206, Glaucidium palmatum. No. 2207, Sciadopitys verticillata.

1993, Aug. 23 Photo. *Perf. 13½x13*
2206 A1682 62y multicolored 1.25 .35
2207 A1682 62y multicolored 1.25 .35
a. Pair, #2206-2207 2.50 1.25

World Federation for Mental Health Congress, Chiba City — A1683

1993, Aug. 23 *Perf. 13½x13*
2208 A1683 62y multicolored 1.25 .35

A1684 — A1685

1993, Sept. 3 Photo. *Perf. 13½*
2209 A1684 41y Swimming .80 .35
2210 A1684 41y Karate .80 .35
a. Pair, #2209-2210 1.60 .80

48th natl. athletic meet, Kagawa Prefecture.

1993, Sept. 22 Photo. *Perf. 13*

Japanese-Portuguese Relations, 450th Anniv.: No. 2211, Arrival of Portuguese, folding screen, c. 1560-1630. No. 2212, Mother-of-Pearl Host Box, Jesuit symbols and grape motif.

2211 A1685 62y multicolored 1.25 .35
2212 A1685 62y multicolored 1.25 .35
a. Pair, #2211-2212 2.50 1.25

Intl. Letter Writing Week A1686

Portraits from Picture Scrolls of the Thirty-Six Immortal Poets: 80y, Ki no Tsurayuki. 120y, Kodai no Kimi.

1993, Oct. 6 *Perf. 13½*
2213 A1686 80y multicolored 1.50 .75
2214 A1686 120y multicolored 2.50 1.00

10th World Veterans' Track and Field Championships, Miyazaki Prefecture A1687

1993, Oct. 7 *Perf. 14*
2215 A1687 62y multicolored 1.25 .35

Souvenir Sheet

Wedding of Crown Prince Naruhito and Princess Masako — A1688

1993, Oct. 13 Photo. *Perf. 13½*
2216 A1688 62y multicolored 1.25 .35

Cultural Pioneers Type of 1992

#2217, Kazan Watanabe (1793-1841), artist. #2218, Umetaro Suzuki (1874-1943), chemist. #2219, Toson Shimazaki (1872-1943), poet.

1993, Nov. 4 Photo. *Perf. 13*
2217 A1645 62y multicolored 1.10 .35

Photo. & Engr.

2218 A1645 62y multicolored 1.10 .35
2219 A1645 62y multicolored 1.10 .35
Nos. 2217-2219 (3) 3.30 1.05

Agricultural Research Center, Cent. — A1689

1993, Nov. 17 *Perf. 13½*
2220 A1689 62y multicolored 1.10 .35

A1690 — A1691

New Year 1994 (Year of the Dog) A1692 — A1693

1993, Nov. 17 *Perf. 13x13½*
2221 A1690 41y multicolored .80 .35
2222 A1691 62y multicolored 1.10 .35

Perf. 13½

2223 A1692 41y +3y multi .80 .40
2224 A1693 62y +3y multi 1.25 .40
Nos. 2221-2224 (4) 3.95 1.50

Sheets of 2, Nos. 2221-2222, were lottery prizes. Value, $2.25.

Declaration of Human Rights, 45th Anniv. — A1694

Designs: 62y, Man with bird perched on head. 70y, Globe, dove, person breaking chains, peace symbol.

1993, Dec. 10 Photo. *Perf. 13*
2225 A1694 62y multicolored 1.25 .35
2226 A1694 70y multicolored 1.40 .70

Congratulations and Condolences Types of 1982

1994, Mar. 10 Photo. *Perf. 13x13½*
2227 A1082 50y Wreath .95 .35
2228 A1083 50y Crane .95 .35
2229 A1083 80y Crane 1.50 .40
2230 A1084 90y Tortoise 1.75 .50
Nos. 2227-2230 (4) 5.15 1.60

For use on condolence and greeting cards.

1994 World Figure Skating Championships, Tokyo — A1695

1994, Mar. 17 Photo. *Perf. 13*
2231 A1695 50y Ice dancing .95 .35
2232 A1695 50y Women's singles .95 .35
a. Pair, #2231-2232 2.00 1.00
2233 A1695 80y Men's singles, vert. 1.50 .40
2234 A1695 80y Pairs, vert. 1.50 .40
a. Pair, #2233-2234 3.00 1.50
Nos. 2231-2234 (4) 4.90 1.50

Philately Week — A1696

1994, Apr. 20 Photo. *Perf. 13*
2235 A1696 80y Irises 1.50 .40

Intl. Year of the Family — A1697

Natl. Land Afforestation Campaign A1698

Designs: No. 2236, "Love" spelled by people. No. 2237, Faces in flowers. No. 2238, Sun shining on people, homes. No. 2239, Family flying inside bird.

1994, May 13 Photo. *Perf. 13*
2236 A1697 50y multicolored 1.00 .35
2237 A1697 50y multicolored 1.00 .35
2238 A1697 80y multicolored 1.50 .40
a. Pair, #2236, 2238 2.50 1.25
2239 A1697 80y multicolored 1.50 .40
a. Pair, #2237, 2239 2.50 1.25
Nos. 2236-2239 (4) 5.00 1.50

1994, May 20
2240 A1698 50y multicolored 1.00 .35

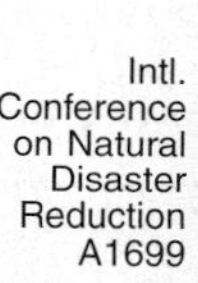

Intl. Conference on Natural Disaster Reduction A1699

1994, May 23
2241 A1699 80y multicolored 1.50 .40

No. 2241 printed in sheets of 16 with 4 labels.

A1700 A1701

1994, May 24
2242 A1700 80y multicolored 1.50 .40

Prototype Fast Breeder Reactor, Monju.

1994, June 3 Photo. *Perf. 13*
2243 A1701 80y multicolored 1.50 .40

Environment day.

Letter Writing Day
A1702 A1703

1994, July 22
2244 A1702 50y multicolored 1.00 .35
2245 A1703 80y multicolored 1.50 .40
a. Souvenir sheet of 1 1.50 .75
b. Bklt. pane, 5 each #2244-2245 12.50

Prefecture Issues

Nos. 2246-2400B have been changed to #Z151-Z307. The listings can be found in a new section immediately following the postage section and preceding the semi-postal listings.

10th Intl. Conference on AIDS, Yokohama — A1859

1994, Aug. 5 Photo. *Perf. 13*
2401 A1859 80y multicolored 1.50 .40

Postal History Series

A1860 A1861

A1862

A1863

A1864

First Japanese stamps (Baron Hisoka Maeshima and): No. 2402, #1. No. 2403, #2. No. 2404, #3. No. 2405, #4.

CTO's exist for Nos. 2402-2405. They read "Japan" between two arcs in a corner.

Photo. & Engr.

1994, Aug. 10 *Perf. 13*
2402 A1860 80y brown & black 1.50 .40
2403 A1860 80y blue & black 1.50 .40
2404 A1860 80y ver & black 1.50 .40
2405 A1860 80y olive grn & blk 1.50 .40
a. Strip of 4, #2402-2405 6.00 6.00

1994, Nov. 18 *Perf. 13½*

Early Japanese stamps (Edoardo Chiossone and): No. 2406, #55. No. 2407, Type A16. No. 2408, #63. No. 2409, #65.

2406 A1861 80y buff, slate & blk 1.50 .40
2407 A1861 80y gray & dk brown 1.50 .40
2408 A1861 80y gray lilac & rose 1.50 .40
2409 A1861 80y lt blue & dk blue 1.50 .40
a. Strip of 4, #2406-2409 6.00 6.00

1995, Jan. 25

Designs: No. 2410, #85, transporting mail by ricksha. No. 2411, #86, transporting mail by horse-drawn carriage.

2410 A1862 80y multicolored 1.50 .40
2411 A1862 80y multicolored 1.50 .40
Nos. 2402-2411 (10) 15.00 4.00

Photo. & Engr.

1995, May 25 *Perf. 13½*

Designs: No. 2412, #C3, First Osaka-Tokyo airmail flight. No. 2413, #C6, Workers loading freight onto airplane.

2412 A1863 110y multicolored 2.50 .60
2413 A1863 110y multicolored 2.50 .60

Nos. 2412-2413 printed in blocks of 10 with gutter between in sheets of 20.

Photo. & Engr.

1995, Sept. 19 *Perf. 13½*

#2414, Light mail van, #436. #2415, Cherub commemorative mail box, #428. #2416, Mail box, #435. #2417, Van, #433.

2414 A1864 80y multicolored 1.50 .40
2415 A1864 80y multicolored 1.50 .40
2416 A1864 80y multicolored 1.50 .40
2417 A1864 80y multicolored 1.50 .40
a. Block of 4, #2414-2417 6.00 6.00

Postal History Series Types of 1948-49 With "NIPPON" Inscribed at Bottom

Photo. & Engr.

1996, June 3 *Perf. 13½*

Size: 22x47mm

2418 A206 80y like #422, brown 1.50 .40
2419 A206 80y like #422, multi 1.50 .40
2420 A247 80y like #479, purple 1.50 .40
2421 A247 80y like #479, multi 1.50 .40
a. Strip of 4, #2418-2421 6.00 6.00

Opening of Kansai Intl. Airport — A1877

Designs: No. 2422, Airport, part of plane's vertical stabilizer. No. 2423, Aft section of airplane. No. 2424, Airport, jet.

1994, Sept. 2 Photo. *Perf. 13*
2422 A1877 80y multicolored 1.50 .40
2423 A1877 80y multicolored 1.50 .40
a. Vert. pair, #2422-2423 3.00 3.00
b. Vert. strip of 3, #2422-2424 4.50 4.50
2424 A1877 80y multicolored 1.50 .40
Nos. 2422-2424 (3) 4.50 1.20

A1878 A1879

1994, Sept. 19
2425 A1878 80y multicolored 1.40 .40

ITU Plenipotentiary Conference, Kyoto.

1994, Sept. 30
2426 A1879 50y Kick volleyball 1.00 .35
2427 A1879 80y Steeplechase 1.50 .40
2428 A1879 80y Synchronized swimming 1.50 .40
a. Pair, #2427-2428 3.00 1.75
Nos. 2426-2428 (3) 4.00 1.15

12th Asian Games, Hiroshima.

Intl. Letter Writing Week A1880

Screen paintings of popular indoor games, Momoyama, Edo periods: 90y, Sugoroku. 110y, Japanese chess. 130y, Go.

1994, Oct. 6 Photo. *Perf. 13x13½*
2429 A1880 90y multicolored 1.75 .75
2430 A1880 110y multicolored 2.10 .75
2431 A1880 130y multicolored 2.50 .75
Nos. 2429-2431 (3) 6.35 2.25

49th Natl. Athletic Meet, Aichi Prefecture — A1881

1994, Oct. 28 *Perf. 13½*
2432 A1881 50y multicolored 1.00 .35

A1882

1994, Nov. 4 Photo. *Perf. 13*
2433 A1882 80y multicolored 1.50 .40

Intl. Diabetes Federation, 15th Congress, Kobe.

Cultural Pioneers Type of 1992

Photo. & Engr.

1994, Nov. 4

Cultural pioneers: No. 2434, Michio Miyagi (1894-1956), Musician.
No. 2435, Gyoshu Hayami (1894-1935), artist.

2434 A1645 80y multicolored 1.50 .40
2435 A1645 80y multicolored 1.50 .40

Heiankyo (Kyoto), 1200th Anniv.
A1884 A1885

Kanpuzu, by Hideyori Kano, Momoyama period depicts autumn scene on Kiyotakigawa River: No. 2436, People seated, white birds. No. 2437, Bridge, people. No. 2438, Bridge, birds flying. No. 2439, People, Jingoji Temple, Atago-Jinja Shrine. No. 2440, People seated, tree.

No. 2441, Painting of Dry Garden (Sekitei), Ryoanji Temple, by Eizo Kato. No. 2442, Painting of artificial pond, Shugakuin Rikyu, by Kanji Kawai, horiz.

1994, Nov. 8 Photo. *Perf. 13x13½*

2436 A1884 80y multicolored 1.50 .40
2437 A1884 80y multicolored 1.50 .40
2438 A1884 80y multicolored 1.50 .40
2439 A1884 80y multicolored 1.50 .40
2440 A1884 80y multicolored 1.50 .40
a. Strip of 5, #2436-2440 7.50 7.50
2441 A1885 80y multicolored 1.50 .40

Perf. 13½x13

2442 A1885 80y multicolored 1.50 .40
Nos. 2436-2442 (7) 10.50 2.80

A1886

A1887

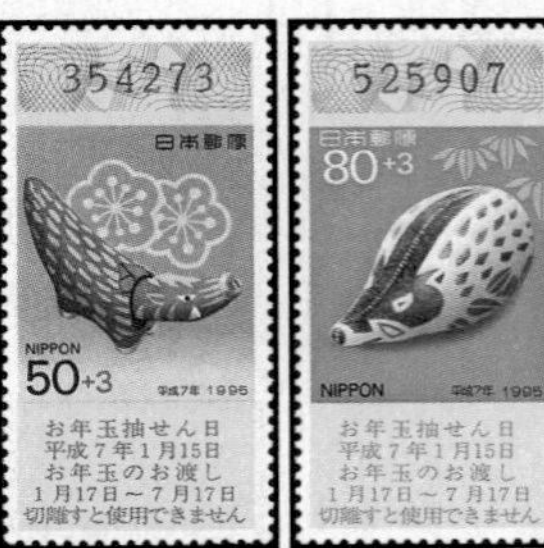

New Year 1995 (Year of the Boar)
A1888 A1889

1994, Nov. 15 *Perf. 13x13½*

2443 A1886 50y multicolored 1.00 .35
2444 A1887 80y multicolored 1.50 .40

Perf. 13½

2445 A1888 50y +3y multi 1.10 .40
2446 A1889 80y +3y multi 1.60 .50
Nos. 2443-2446 (4) 5.20 1.65

Sheets of two containing Nos. 2443-2444 were lottery prizes. Value $2.50.

World Heritage Series

Himeji Castle
A1890 A1891

A1892

Horyuji Temple
A1893

Cryptomeria Japonica
A1894

Cervus Nippon Yakushimae
A1895

Virgin Beech Forest
A1896

Black Woodpecker
A1897

1994, Dec. 14 Photo. *Perf. 13*

2447 A1890 80y multicolored 1.50 .40
2448 A1891 80y multicolored 1.50 .40

1995, Feb. 22

Designs: 80y, Goddess Kannon from inner temple wall. 110y, Temple exterior.

2449 A1892 80y multicolored 1.50 .40
2450 A1893 110y multicolored 2.25 .75

1995, July 28

2451 A1894 80y multicolored 1.50 .40
2452 A1895 80y multicolored 1.50 .40

1995, Nov. 21

2453 A1896 80y multicolored 1.50 .40
2454 A1897 80y multicolored 1.50 .40
Nos. 2447-2454 (8) 12.75 3.55

Japan-Brazil Friendship, Cent.
A1898

Designs: No. 2455, Natl. emblems, flowers. No. 2456, Soccer players.

1995, Mar. 3 Photo. *Perf. 13½*

2455 A1898 80y multicolored 1.50 .40
2456 A1898 80y multicolored 1.50 .40

A1899

Fujiwara-Kyo Palace, 1300th Anniv. — A1900

Designs: 50y, Unebiyama, Nijozan Mountains, roofing tile from palace. 80y, Portrait of a Woman, in Asuka and Hakuho era style, by Okada, 1925.

1995, Mar. 28

2457 A1899 50y multicolored 1.00 .35
2458 A1900 80y multicolored 1.50 .40

Modern Anatomical Education
A1901

1995, Mar. 31 *Perf. 13*

2459 A1901 80y multicolored 1.50 .40

A1902

A1903

1995, Apr. 12 Photo. *Perf. 13*

2460 A1902 80y multicolored 1.50 .40

1995 Census.

1995, Apr. 20

2461 A1903 80y multicolored 1.50 .40

Japanese Overseas Cooperation Volunteers, 30th anniv.

A1904

A1905

A1906

A1907

A1908

1995, Apr. 25 *Perf. 13x13½*

2462 A1904 50y multicolored 1.00 .35
2463 A1905 50y multicolored 1.00 .35
2464 A1906 80y multicolored 1.50 .40
2465 A1907 80y multicolored 1.50 .40
2466 A1908 90y multicolored 2.00 .75
Nos. 2462-2466 (5) 7.00 2.25

For use on condolence and greeting cards.

A1909

A1910

1995, May 19 Photo. *Perf. 13½x13*

2467 A1909 50y multicolored 1.00 .35

Natl. land afforestation campaign.

1995, June 1 *Die Cut Perf. 13½*

Greetings: No. 2468, Rainbow, hearts. No. 2469, Girl holding heart-shaped balloon. No. 2470, Flower holding pencil, sign. No. 2471, Star, sun, moon as flowers, fauna. No. 2472, Person, dog with flowers, butterfly in hair.

Self-Adhesive

2468 A1910 80y multicolored 1.50 .40
2469 A1910 80y multicolored 1.50 .40
2470 A1910 80y multicolored 1.50 .40
2471 A1910 80y multicolored 1.50 .40
2472 A1910 80y multicolored 1.50 .40
a. Miniature sheet, #2468-2472 + 5 labels 7.50

Letter Writing Day
A1911 A1912

1995, July 21 Photo. *Perf. 13½*

2473 A1911 50y multicolored 1.00 .35
2474 A1912 80y multicolored 1.50 .40
a. Souvenir sheet of 1 1.50 .75
b. Bklt. pane, 5 ea #2473-2474 12.50
Complete booklet, #2474b 12.50

Flora & Fauna Type of 1992 and

Shikikacho-zu
A1926

Matsutaka-Zu
A1926a

10y, Scarab, dandelions. 20y, Honey bee, flower. 30y, Hairstreak, flowers. 70y, Great tit. 110y, Plover. 120y, Shrike. 140y, Japanese grosbeak. 160y, Jay. 390y, Dayflower.

1995-98 Photo. *Perf. 13½*

2475 A1651 10y multi .20 .20
2476 A1651 20y multi .40 .25
2477 A1651 30y multi .60 .35
2478 A1651 70y multi 1.25 .90
2479 A1651 110y multi 2.10 1.40
2480 A1651 120y multi 2.25 1.40
2481 A1651 140y multi 2.50 1.60
2482 A1651 160y multi 3.00 1.90

Perf. 13x13½

2483 A1651 390y multi 7.50 5.25

Perf. 13½

2484 A1926 700y multi 15.00 11.50

Photo. & Engr.

2485 A1926a 1000y multi 19.00 14.50

Self-Adhesive

Die Cut Perf. 13x13½

2486	A1651	50y Like #2158	.75	.60
2487	A1651	80y Like #2161	1.25	.35

Coil Stamp

Perf. 13 Horiz.

2488	A1651	10y like #2475	.20	.20
		Nos. 2475-2488 (14)	56.00	40.40

Issued: 700y, 7/4/95; 390y, 1000y, 3/28/96; 70y, 110y, 7/22/97; #2475, 20y, 30y, 11/28/97; 120y, 140y, 2/16/98 160y, 2/23/98; #2488, 9/11/98. Nos. 2486-2487, 3/25/02.

Nos. 2486 and 2487 were issued in panes of 10.

End of World War II, 50th Anniv.
A1937 A1938

Design: No. 2491, Children holding hands behind stained glass window, peace dove, earth from space.

1995, Aug. 1 Photo. *Perf. 13*

2489	A1937	50y multicolored	1.00	.35
2490	A1938	80y multicolored	1.50	.40
2491	A1938	80y multicolored	1.50	.40
		Nos. 2489-2491 (3)	4.00	1.15

A1939 A1940

1995, Aug. 23

2492	A1939	80y multicolored	1.50	.40

18th Universiade, Fukuoka.

1995, Aug. 25

50y, Radio controlled plane, transmitter. 80y, Radio controlled helicopter, competitor, assistant.

2493	A1940	50y multicolored	1.00	.35
2494	A1940	80y multicolored	1.50	.40

1995 Aeromodel World Championships, Okayama Prefecture.

World Veterinary Congress, Yokohama A1941

World Sports Championships A1942

1995, Sept. 1 Photo. *Perf. 13*

2495	A1941	80y Dog, cow & horse	1.50	.40

1995, Sept. 28

#2496, 1995 World Judo Championships, Chiba Prefecture. #2497, 1995 World Gymnastics Championships, Sabae, Fukui Prefecture.

1995, Sept. 28

2496	A1942	80y multicolored	1.50	.40
2497	A1942	80y multicolored	1.50	.40

Letter Writing Week A1943

Screen paintings: 90y, Shell-matching game. 110y, Battledore and shuttlecock. 130y, Playing cards.

1995, Oct. 6 *Perf. 13½*

2498	A1943	90y multicolored	1.75	.75
2499	A1943	110y multicolored	2.10	.75
2500	A1943	130y multicolored	2.50	.75
		Nos. 2498-2500 (3)	6.35	2.25

A1944 A1945

1995, Oct. 13 *Perf. 13x13½*

2501	A1944	50y multicolored	1.00	.35

50th Natl. athletic meet, Fukushima prefecture.

1995, Oct. 24 *Perf. 13*

2502	A1945	80y UN, hearts	1.50	.40
2503	A1945	80y UNESCO, children	1.50	.40

UN, UNESCO, 50th anniv.

Cultural Pioneers Type of 1992

#2504, Tadataka Ino (1745-1818), cartographer. #2505, Kitaro Nishida (1870-1945), philosopher.

Photo. & Engr.

1995, Nov. 6 *Perf. 13*

2504	A1645	80y multicolored	1.50	.40
2505	A1645	80y multicolored	1.50	.40

A1947 A1948

New Year 1996 (Year of the Rat)
A1949 A1950

1995, Oct. 15 Photo. *Perf. 13x13½*

2506	A1947	50y multicolored	1.00	.35
2507	A1948	80y multicolored	1.50	.40

Perf. 13½

2508	A1949	50y +3y multi	1.10	.40
2509	A1950	80y +3y multi	1.60	.45
		Nos. 2506-2509 (4)	5.20	1.60

Sheets of two containing Nos. 2506-2507 were lottery prizes. Value $2.50.

Japanese-Korean Diplomatic Relations, 30th Anniv. — A1951

1995, Dec. 18 *Perf. 13*

2510	A1951	80y multicolored	1.50	.40

Nos. 2511-2512 are unassigned.

A1952 A1953

1996, Feb. 16 Photo. *Perf. 13*

2513	A1952	80y multicolored	1.50	.40

Philipp Franz von Siebold (1796-1866), naturalist.

1996, Mar. 1

2514	A1953	80y multicolored	1.50	.40

Labor Relations Commissions, 50th anniv.

Senior Citizens — A1954

1996, Mar. 21 *Perf. 13½*

2515	A1954	80y multicolored	1.50	.40

No. 2515 issued in sheets of 5.

50th Postwar Memorial Year
A1955 A1956

#2516, Crowd, Emperor's limosine approaching Diet. #2517, Prime Minister Yoshida signing Peace Treaty, San Francisco, 9/8/51. #2518, Women performing traditional Okinawan dance.

1996, Apr. 1 Photo. *Perf. 13*

2516	A1955	80y multicolored	1.50	.40
2517	A1955	80y multicolored	1.50	.40
a.		Pair, Nos. 2516-2517	3.00	1.50
2518	A1956	80y multicolored	1.50	.40
		Nos. 2516-2518 (3)	4.50	1.20

Promulgation of the the Constitution, 11/7/46 (#2517a). Return of Okinawa, 5/15/72 (#2518).

Woman Suffrage, 50th Anniv. — A1957

Philately Week — A1958

1996, Apr. 10 *Perf. 13½*

2519	A1957	80y multicolored	1.50	.40

1996, Apr. 19 *Perf. 13*

2520	A1958	80y multicolored	1.50	.40

UNICEF, 50th Anniv. — A1959

Child Welfare Week, 50th Anniv. — A1960

1996, May 1 Photo. *Perf. 13*

2521	A1959	80y multicolored	1.50	.40

1996, May 1

2522	A1960	80y multicolored	1.50	.40

Bird Week, 50th Anniv. — A1961

1996, May 10

2523		80y Birds	1.50	.40
2524		80y Field Glasses	1.50	.40
a.	A1961	Pair, #2523-2524	3.00	1.75

Natl. Afforestation Campaign — A1963

1996, May 17

2525	A1963	50y multicolored	.95	.35

50th Postwar Memorial Year
A1964 A1965

1996, June 24 Photo. *Perf. 13*

2526	A1964	80y multicolored	1.50	.40
2527	A1965	80y multicolored	1.50	.40

River Administration System, Cent. — A1966

1996, July 5 Photo. *Perf. 13½*

2528 80y denomination lower right 1.50 .40
2529 80y denomination lower left 1.50 .40
a. A1966 Pair, #2528-2529 3.00 1.75

A1968

Marine Day's Establishment A1969

1996, July 19

2530 A1968 50y multicolored .95 .35
2531 A1969 80y multicolored 1.50 .40

Letter Writing Day
A1970 A1971

1996, July 23

2532 A1970 50y multicolored .95 .35
2533 A1971 80y multicolored 1.50 .40
a. Souvenir sheet of 1 1.50 .75
b. Bklt. pane, 5 ea #2532-2533 11.50
Complete booklet 11.50

Cultural Pioneers Type of 1992

No. 2534, Kenji Miyazaw (1896-1933). No. 2535, Hokiichi Hanawa (1746-1821).

Photo. & Engr.

1996, Aug. 27 *Perf. 13*

2534 A1645 80y multicolored 1.50 .40
2535 A1645 80y multicolored 1.50 .40

A1974 A1975

Designs: No. 2536, Advances of women in society, diffusion of home electrical products. No. 2537, Modern highway, railway systems.

1996, Aug. 27 Photo. *Perf. 13*

2536 A1974 80y multicolored 1.50 .40
2537 A1975 80y multicolored 1.50 .40

51st Natl. Athletic Meet — A1976

Community Chest, 50th Anniv. — A1977

1996, Sept. 6 Photo. *Perf. 13½*

2538 A1976 50y Archery .95 .35

1996, Sept. 30

2539 A1977 80y multicolored 1.50 .40

Intl. Music Day — A1978

1996, Oct. 1 *Perf. 13*

2540 A1978 80y multicolored 1.50 .40

A1979

Intl. Letter Writing Week A1980

Paintings: #2541, Water wheel, Mt. Fuji. #2542, Flowers. #2543, Mt. Fuji in Clear Weather (Red Fuji), by Hokusai. #2544, Flowers, diff. #2545, Mt. Fuji, lake. #2546, Flowers, diff.

1996, Oct. 7 *Perf. 13½*

2541 A1979 90y multicolored 1.75 .75
2542 A1980 90y multicolored 1.75 .75
a. Pair, #2541-2542 3.50 1.75
2543 A1979 110y multicolored 2.10 .75
2544 A1980 110y multicolored 2.10 .75
a. Pair, #2543-2544 4.25 2.00
2545 A1979 130y multicolored 2.50 .75
2546 A1980 130y multicolored 2.50 .75
a. Pair, #2545-2546 5.00 2.25
Nos. 2541-2546 (6) 12.70 4.50

18th World Congress of Savings Banks — A1981

1996, Oct. 23 *Perf. 13*

2547 A1981 80y multicolored 1.50 .40

50th Postwar Memorial Year
A1982 A1983

#2548, Earth from space. #2549, Cellular telephone, fiber optic cable, satellite in orbit.

1996, Nov. 8 Photo. *Perf. 13*

2548 A1982 80y multicolored 1.50 .40
2549 A1983 80y multicolored 1.50 .40

A1984 A1985

New Year 1997 (Year of the Ox)
A1986 A1987

1996, Nov. 15 Photo. *Perf. 13x13½*

2550 A1984 50y multicolored .95 .35
2551 A1985 80y multicolored 1.50 .40

Perf. 13½

2552 A1986 50y +3y multi 1.00 .40
2553 A1987 80y +3y multi 1.60 .50
Nos. 2550-2553 (4) 5.05 1.65

Sheets of 2 containing Nos. 2550-2551 were lottery prizes. Value $3.

Yujiro Ishihara, Actor — A1988

Hibari Misora, Entertainer — A1990

Osamu Tezuka, Cartoonist — A1992

1997, Jan. 28 Photo. *Perf. 13*

2554 80y multicolored 1.50 .40
2555 80y multicolored 1.50 .40
a. A1988 Pair, #2554-2555 3.00 1.75
2556 80y multicolored 1.50 .40
2557 80y multicolored 1.50 .40
a. A1990 Pair, #2556-2557 3.00 1.75
2558 80y multicolored 1.50 .40
2559 80y multicolored 1.50 .40
a. A1992 Pair, #2558-2559 3.00 1.75
Nos. 2554-2559 (6) 9.00 2.40

Sparrow, Rice Plant, Camellia A1994

Sparrow, Maple, Camellia A1995

Perf. 14 Horiz. Syncopated Type A

1997, Apr. 10 Photo.

2560 A1994 50y multi 1.00 .35
2560A A1994 80y multi 1.50 .40
2560B A1994 90y multi 1.75 .50
2560C A1994 120y multi 2.25 .60
2560D A1994 130y multi *25.00 12.50*
2561 A1995 270y multi 5.00 2.00
Nos. 2560-2561 (6) 36.50 16.35

Denominations of Nos. 2560-2561 were printed by machine at point of sale, and were limited to the denominations listed.

Daigo, by Okumura Dogyu (1889-1990) A1996

1997, Apr. 18 Litho. *Perf. 13½*

2562 A1996 80y multicolored 1.50 .40

Philately Week.

Supreme Court, 50th Anniv. A1997

Doraemon A1998

1997, May 2 Photo. *Perf. 13*

2563 A1997 80y Main court room 1.50 .40

Serpentine Die Cut 13½

1997, May 2

Designs: No. 2564, Shown. No. 2565, With envelope. No. 2566, Standing on hand. No. 2567, With propeller. No. 2568, In love.

Self-Adhesive
Booklet Stamps

2564 A1998 80y multicolored 1.50 .40
2565 A1998 80y multicolored 1.50 .40
2566 A1998 80y multicolored 1.50 .40
2567 A1998 80y multicolored 1.50 .40
2568 A1998 80y multicolored 1.50 .40
a. Pane of 5, #2564-2568 7.50

Japanese Migration to Mexico, Cent. — A1999

1997, May 12 *Perf. 13*

2569 A1999 80y multicolored 1.50 .40

See Mexico No. 2035.

A2000

A2001

1997, May 16 ***Perf. 13½***

2570 A2000 50y Miyagi bush clover .95 .35

Natl. afforestation campaign.

1997, May 20 ***Perf. 13***

2571 A2001 80y Natl. Diet 1.50 .40

Natl. House of Councilors, 50th anniv.

A2002 A2003

A2004 A2005

Letter Writing Day

1997, July 23 **Photo.** ***Perf. 13***

2572	A2002	50y multicolored	.95	.35
2573	A2003	70y multicolored	1.25	.45
2574	A2004	80y multicolored	1.50	.40
a.		Souvenir sheet of 1	1.50	.40
b.		Bklt. pane, 5 ea #2572, 2574	12.50	
		Complete booklet, #2574b	12.50	
2575	A2005	90y multicolored	1.75	.50
		Nos. 2572-2575 (4)	5.45	1.70

A2006

A2007

1997, Aug. 11 **Photo.** ***Perf. 13***

2576 A2006 50y multicolored .95 .35

Part-time and correspondence education at upper secondary schools, 50th anniv.

1997, Sept. 1

2577 A2007 80y multicolored 1.50 .40

Labor Standards Law, 50th anniv.

Friendship Between Japan and Chile, Cent.
A2008

52nd Natl. Sports Festival
A2009

1997, Sept. 1 ***Perf. 13½***

2578 A2008 80y multicolored 1.50 .40

See Chile No. 1217.

1997, Sept. 12

2579 A2009 50y multicolored .95 .35

Intl. Letter Writing Week
A2010

Paintings of Tokaido's 53 Stations by Hiroshige: No. 2580, Hodogaya (bridge over waterway). No. 2582, Kameyama snow-covered mountain slope).

No. 2584, Sumida Riverbank Snowscape (woman in traditional attire beside river), by Hiroshige

From Scrolls of Flowers and Birds of the Four Seasons by Hoitsu Sakai: No. 2581, Bird on tree. No. 2583, Leaves and berries. No. 2585, Bird on tree branch of blossoms.

1997, Oct. 6 **Photo.** ***Perf. 13½***

2580	A2010	90y multicolored	1.75	.50
2581	A2010	90y multicolored	1.75	.50
a.		Pair, #2580-2581	3.50	1.75
2582	A2010	110y multicolored	2.10	.60
2583	A2010	110y multicolored	2.10	.60
a.		Pair, #2582-2583	4.25	1.75
2584	A2010	130y multicolored	2.50	.70
2585	A2010	130y multicolored	2.50	.70
a.		Pair, #2584-2585	5.00	1.75
		Nos. 2580-2585 (6)	12.70	3.60

Grand Opening of the Natl. Theater of Tokyo — A2011

1997, Oct. 9 ***Perf. 13***

2586 A2011 80y multicolored 1.50 .40

Favorite Songs

A2012 A2013

50y Departure on a Fine Day, by Tanimura Shinji. 80y, Desert Under the Moon, by Kato Masao & Sakasi Suguru.

1997, Oct. 24

2587 A2012 50y multicolored .95 .35

2588 A2013 80y multicolored 1.50 .40

Cultural Pioneers Type of 1992

#2589, Rohan Kouda (1867-1947), writer. #2590, Ando Hiroshige (1797-1858), artist.

1997, Nov. 4

2589 A1645 80y multicolored 1.50 .40

2590 A1645 80y multicolored 1.50 .40

A2016

A2017

New Year 1997 (Year of the Tiger)

A2018 A2019

1997, Nov. 14 ***Perf. 13x13½***

2591 A2016 50y multicolored .95 .35

2592 A2017 80y multicolored 1.50 .40

Perf. 13½

2593 A2018 50y +3y multi .95 .40

2594 A2019 80y +3y multi 1.50 .50

Sheets of two containing Nos. 2591-2592 were lottery prizes. Value $2.50.

Return of Okinawa to Japan, 25th Anniv. — A2020

1997, Nov. 21 ***Perf. 13***

2595 A2020 80y multicolored 1.50 .40

Shibuya Family's House
A2021

Tomizawa Family's House
A2022

Photo. & Engr.

1997, Nov. 28 ***Perf. 13½***

2596 A2021 80y multicolored 1.50 .40

2597 A2022 80y multicolored 1.50 .40

A2023 A2024

Woodprints: No. 2598, Mother Sea. No. 2599, Mother Earth.

1997, Dec. 1 **Photo.** ***Perf. 13***

2598 A2023 80y multicolored 1.50 .40

2599 A2023 80y multicolored 1.50 .40

a. Pair, #2598-2599 3.00 1.90

3rd Conference of the Parties to the UN Framework Convention on Climate Change, Kyoto.

1997, Dec. 2

2600 A2024 80y multicolored 1.50 .40

Agricultural Insurance System, 50th anniv.

Favorite Songs

A2025

A2026

A2027

A2028

1997, Dec. 8

2601 A2025 50y Sunayama .95 .35

2602 A2026 80y Jingle Bells 1.50 .40

1998, Jan. 26 **Photo.** ***Perf. 13***

2603 A2027 50y Shabondama .95 .35

2604 A2028 80y Kitaguni no Haru 1.50 .40

1998 Winter Olympic & Paralympic Games, Nagano

A2029 A2030

Paralympic logo and: No. 2605, Glaucidium palmatum. No. 2606, Ice hockey.

Olympic rings and: No. 2607: a, Gentiana nipponica. b, Caltha palustris. c, Fritillaria camtschatcensis. d, Paeonia japonica. e, Erythronium japonicum. f, Snowboarding. g, Curling. h, Speed skating. i, Cross-country skiing. j, Downhill skiing.

1998, Feb. 5

2605	A2029	50y multicolored	.95	.35
2606	A2030	80y multicolored	1.50	.40
a.		Pair, #2605-2606	2.50	1.00
2607		Sheet of 10	12.50	12.50
a.-e.		A2029 50y Any single	.95	.35
f.-j.		A2030 80y Any single	1.50	.40

Historic Houses

A2031

A2032

Photo. & Engr.

1998, Feb. 23 *Perf. 13½*

2608 A2031 80y multicolored 1.50 .40
2609 A2032 80y multicolored 1.50 .40

Japanese Fire Service, 50th Anniv. — A2033

1998, Mar. 6 **Photo.** *Perf. 13*

2610 80y multicolored 1.50 .40
2611 80y multicolored 1.50 .40
a. A2033 Pair, #2610-2611 3.00 1.25

Favorite Songs
A2035 A2036

1998 **Photo.** *Perf. 13*

2612 A2035 50y Medaka-no-Gak-ko .95 .35
2613 A2036 80y Aoi Sanmyaku 1.50 .40

Issued: 50y, 3/23; 80y, 3/16.

Greetings Stamps — A2037

Designs: a, Puppy. b, Kitten. c, Parakeets. d, Pansies. e, Bunny.

1998, Mar. 13 **Photo.** *Die Cut*
Self-Adhesive

2614 Sheet of 5 7.50
a.-e. A2037 80y any single 1.50 .40

Philately Week — A2038

"Poppies," by Kokei Kobayashi (1883-1957).

1998, Apr. 17 *Perf. 13½*

2615 A2038 80y multicolored 1.50 .40

1998 Year of France in Japan A2039

"Liberty Leading the People," by Delacroix.

1998, Apr. 28 *Perf. 13½*

2616 A2039 110y multicolored 2.10 .75

Natl. Afforestation Campaign — A2040

1998, May 8

2617 A2040 50y Trout, Renge azalea .95 .35

Favorite Songs

A2041 A2042

Designs: 50y, "Wild Roses," by Franz Schubert. 80y, "Hill Abloom with Tangerine Flowers," by Minoru Uminuma and Shogo Kato.

1998, May 25 *Perf. 13*

2618 A2041 50y multicolored .95 .35
2619 A2042 80y multicolored 1.50 .40

Historic Houses

Kowata Residence A2043

Kamihaga Residence A2044

Photo. & Engr.

1998, June 22 *Perf. 13½*

2620 A2043 80y multicolored 1.50 .40
2621 A2044 80y multicolored 1.50 .40

Favorite Songs

A2045 A2046

50y, Kono Michi, "This Road." 80y, Ware Wa Umino Ko, "I'm a Boy of the Sea."

1998, July 6 **Photo.** *Perf. 13*

2622 A2045 50y multicolored .95 .35
2623 A2046 80y multicolored 1.50 .40

Letter Writing Day — A2047

Stylized drawings of children: #2624, Child writing letter. #2625, Child wearing glasses, letter on table. #2626, Child with ink pen, flowers overhead. #2627, Child with ink pen, dove overhead. #2628, Children holding letters, envelopes.

1998, July 23 *Perf. 13*

2624 A2047 50y multi .95 .35
2625 A2047 50y multi .95 .35
a. Pair, #2624-2625 1.90 .75
2626 A2047 80y multi 1.50 .40
2627 A2047 80y multi 1.50 .40
2628 A2047 80y multi, horiz. 1.50 .40
a. Souvenir sheet of 1 1.50 .40
b. Sheet, 4 each #2626-2627, 2 #2628 15.00 15.00
c. Bklt. pane, 2 ea #2624-2628 13.00 13.00
Complete booklet, #2628c 13.00

See Nos. 2682-2686, 2738-2742, 2779-2783, 2824-2828. See Nos. 2733h-2733j for self-adhesive stamps.

Historic Houses

Kamio Residence A2048

Nakamura Residence A2049

Photo. & Engr.

1998, Aug. 24 *Perf. 13½*

2629 A2048 80y multicolored 1.50 .40
2630 A2049 80y multicolored 1.50 .40

53rd Natl. Sports Festival, Kanagawa — A2050

1998, Sept. 11 **Photo.** *Perf. 13½*

2631 A2050 50y multicolored .95 .35

Intl. Letter Writing Week, Greetings — A2051

Details or complete paintings by Jakuchu Ito: #2632, "Birds & Autumn Maple." #2633, "Parakeet in Oak Tree." #2634, "Mandarin Ducks in the Snow." #2635, "Golden Pheasant & Bamboo in Snow." #2636, "Leafy Peonies & Butterflies." #2637, "Parakeet in Rose Bush."

1998, Oct. 6 **Photo.** *Perf. 13½*

2632 A2051 90y multicolored 1.75 .50
2633 A2051 90y multicolored 1.75 .50
a. Pair, #2632-2633 3.50 1.75
2634 A2051 110y multicolored 2.10 .60
2635 A2051 110y multicolored 2.10 .60
a. Pair, #2634-2635 4.25 1.75
2636 A2051 130y multicolored 2.50 .70
2637 A2051 130y multicolored 2.50 .70
a. Pair, #2636-2637 5.00 1.75
Nos. 2632-2637 (6) 12.70 3.60

Nos. 2632, 2634, 2636 are from "Plants and Animals" and are inscribed for Intl. Letter Writing Week. Nos. 2633, 2635, 2637 are from "Painted Woodcuts of Flowers and Birds."

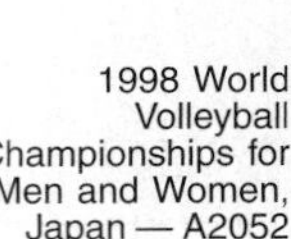

1998 World Volleyball Championships for Men and Women, Japan — A2052

1998, Nov. 2 *Perf. 13*

2638 A2052 80y Serve 1.50 .40
2639 A2052 80y Receive 1.50 .40
2640 A2052 80y Set & spike 1.50 .40
2641 A2052 80y Block 1.50 .40
a. Strip of 4, #2638-2641 6.00 6.00

Cultural Pioneer Type of 1992 and

Yoshie Fujiwara(1898-1976) — A2053

No. 2642, Bakin Takizawa (1767-1848).

Photo. & Engr.

1998, Nov. 4 *Perf. 13*

2642 A1645 80y multicolored 1.50 .40
2643 A2053 80y multicolored 1.50 .40

See #2719, 2747-2748, 2839-2840.

A2054 A2055

New Year 1999 (Year of the Rabbit)
A2056 A2057

1998, Nov. 13 **Photo.** *Perf. 13x13½*

2644 A2054 50y multicolored .95 .35
2645 A2055 80y multicolored 1.50 .40

Perf. 13½x13

2646 A2056 50y +3y multi 1.10 .40
2647 A2057 80y +3y multi 1.60 .50
Nos. 2644-2647 (4) 5.15 1.65

Sheets of two containing Nos. 2644-2645 were lottery prizes. Value $2.50.
See No. 2655.

Favorite Songs

A2058 A2059

50y, The Apple Song. 80y, Toys Cha-Cha-Cha at Night.

1998, Nov. 24 *Perf. 13x13½*

2648 A2058 50y multicolored .95 .35
2649 A2059 80y multicolored 1.50 .40

Japan-Argentina Friendship Treaty, Cent. — A2060

1998, Dec. 2 **Photo.** ***Perf. 13***

2650 A2060 80y multicolored 1.50 .40

A2061 A2062

Universal Declaration of Human Rights, 50th Anniv.

A2063 A2064

1998, Dec. 10

2651 A2061 50y multicolored .95 .35
2652 A2062 70y multicolored 1.25 .45
2653 A2063 80y multicolored 1.50 .40
2654 A2064 90y multicolored 1.75 .75
Nos. 2651-2654 (4) 5.45 1.95

Greetings Types of 1951, 1962, 1986 and 1998

1998, Dec. 15 **Photo.** ***Perf. 13x13½***

2655 50y Sheet of 8, 2 each #a.-c., 2644 7.75 7.75
a. A281 rose pink, like #522 .95 .70
b. A483 multi, like #773 .95 .70
c. A1273 multi, like #1708 .95 .70

Favorite Songs

A2065 A2066

50y, Flowing Like a River. 80y, Song of the Four Seasons.

1999, Jan. 26 **Photo.** ***Perf. 13***

2656 A2065 50y multicolored .95 .35
2657 A2066 80y multicolored 1.50 .40

Traditional Houses

Iwase Family House, Gokayama District A2067

Gassho-Zukuri Houses, Shirakawa-mura District — A2068

Gassho-Zukuri House — A2069

Photo. & Engr.

1999, Feb. 16 ***Perf. 13½***

2658 A2067 80y multicolored 1.50 .40
2659 A2068 80y multicolored 1.50 .40
2660 A2069 80y multicolored 1.50 .40
a. Pair, #2659-2660 3.00 1.50
Nos. 2658-2660 (3) 4.50 1.20

Rakugo (Comic Storytellers) Stamps

Kokontei Shinshou V — A2070

Katsura Bunraku VIII — A2071

Sanyutei Enshou VI — A2072

Yanagiya Kosan V — A2073

Katsura Beichou III — A2074

1999, Mar. 12 **Photo.** ***Perf. 13***

2661 A2070 80y multicolored 1.50 .40
2662 A2071 80y multicolored 1.50 .40
2663 A2072 80y multicolored 1.50 .40
2664 A2073 80y multicolored 1.50 .40
2665 A2074 80y multicolored 1.50 .40
a. Sheet, 2 each #2661-2665 15.00 15.00

Favorite Songs

Sukiyaki Song A2075

Soushunfu A2076

1999, Mar. 16

2666 A2075 50y multicolored .95 .35
2667 A2076 80y multicolored 1.50 .40

Greetings Stamps — A2077

a, Kitten, daisies. b, Checks, flowers, roses. c, Tartan, puppy. d, Flowers, brown rabbit. e, Gray and white rabbit, moon and stars.

1999, Mar. 23 ***Die Cut***

Self-Adhesive

2668 Sheet of 5 7.50
a.-e. A2077 80y Any single 1.50 .40

25th General Assembly of Japan Medical Congress A2078

1999, Apr. 2 ***Perf. 13***

2669 A2078 80y multicolored 1.50 .40

Philately Week — A2079

Rabbits Playing in the Field in Spring, by Doumoto Inshou (1891-1975): No. 2670, Three rabbits. No. 2671, Two rabbits.

1999, Apr. 20 ***Perf. 13½***

2670 80y three rabbits 1.50 .40
2671 80y Two rabbits 1.50 .40
a. A2079 Pair, #2670-2671 3.00 1.50

No. 2671a is a continuous design.

A2080 A2081

1999, May 18 **Photo.** ***Perf. 13***

2672 A2080 80y multicolored 1.50 .40

Japanese migration to Peru, cent.

1999, May 28 ***Perf. 13¼***

2673 A2081 50y multicolored .95 .35

Natl. afforestation campaign.

A2082 A2083

Painting: Ruins of Tholos, by Masayuki Murai.

1999, June 1 **Photo.** ***Perf. 13***

2674 A2082 80y multicolored 1.50 .40

Japanese-Greek Treaty of Commerce & Navigation, cent.

1999, June 3

2675 A2083 80y multicolored 1.50 .40

Japanese emigration to Bolivia, cent.

Land Improvement System, 50th Anniv. — A2084

Family Court, 50th Anniv. — A2085

1999, June 4

2676 A2084 80y multicolored 1.50 .40

1999, June 16

2677 A2085 80y multicolored 1.50 .40

Patent Attorney System in Japan, Cent. — A2086

1999, July 1 **Photo.** ***Perf. 13***

2678 A2086 80y multicolored 1.50 .40

A2087 A2088

1999, July 1

2679 A2087 80y multicolored 1.50 .40

Japanese Community-Based Treatment of Offenders System, 50th anniv.

1999, July 19

Enforcement of Civil and Commercial Codes, Cent.: Masaakira Tomii (1858-1935), Kenjiro Ume (1860-1910) and Nobushige Hozumi (1856-1926), drafters of Civil and Commerical Codes.

2680 A2088 80y multicolored 1.50 .40

Copyright System in Japan, Cent. — A2089

1999, July 22

2681 A2089 80y multicolored 1.50 .40

Letter Writing Day Type of 1998

Stylized drawings of children and toys: No. 2682, Boy and clown, letter. No. 2683, Teddy bear seated on pencil. No. 2684, Girl, ink pen. No. 2685, Clown with yellow hat, jumping up out of envelope.

No. 2686: a, Giraffes. b, Kite, bird, horiz. c, Boy holding kite string. d, Girl with pencil and paper. e, Bunny and bear. f, Boy blowing trumpet. g, Girl playing cello. h, Girl in red. i, Girl in yellow holding envelope. j, Three ducks.

1999, July 23 Photo. *Perf. 13*

2682	A2047 50y multicolored		.95	.35
2683	A2047 50y multicolored		.95	.35
2684	A2047 50y multicolored		.95	.35
2685	A2047 50y multicolored		.95	.35
a.	Strip of 4, #2682-2685		4.00	1.75
2686	Sheet of 10		15.00	15.00
a.-j.	A2047 80y any single		1.50	.40
k.	Booklet pane, #2682-2685, 2 each #2686c, 2686g, 2686i		13.00	
	Complete booklet, #2686k		13.00	
l.	Sheet of 2, #2682, 2686g		2.50	1.75

Nos. 2686a is 53x27mm. Nos. 2686d, 2685h, 2686j are 30mm in diameter. No. 2686f is 38x39mm. Sheet numbers are in center of rectangles at top of sheets.

The 20th Century — A2090

1900-10 (Sheet 1) — #2687: a, 50y, 1905-06 Serialized novel "Wagahai wa Neko de aru," by Soseki Natsume (stamp 7). b, 50y, 1906 Novel "Bochan," by Natsume (stamp 8). c, 80y, 1901 Collection of poems "Midaregami," by Akiko Yosano (stamp 1). d, 80y, Opening of Denkikan movie theater in Asakusa, 1903 (stamp 2). e, 80y, Electrification of streetcars, 1903 (stamp 3). f, 80y, Otojirou Kawakami & Sadayakko, actors (stamp 4). g, 80y, Westernization of fashion (stamp 9). h, 80y, Completion of Ryogoku Kokugikan sumo arena, 1909 (stamp 10). i, 80y, Russo-Japanese War soldiers on horseback (stamp 5). j, 80y, Russo-Japanese War soldiers in tent (stamp 6).

A2090a

1910-13 (Sheet 2) — #2688: a, 50y, 1st Japanese-produced airship, tail of 1st Japanese airplane (stamp 3). b, 50y, Front of 1st Japanese airplane (stamp 4). c, 80y, Elementary school song book published by Education ministry, 1910 (stamp 1). d, 80y, Antarctic expedition led by Nobu Shirase, 1910 (stamp 2). e, 80y, Dr. Hideyo Noguchi (stamp 5). f, 80y, Extinction of Japanese wolves (stamp 6). g, 80y, Runner Shizo Kanaguri at 1st participation in Olympic Games, 1912 (stamp 7). h, Takarazuka Musical Review founded, 1913 (stamp 8). i, 80y, "Song of Kachusha," by Sumako Matsui & Hogetsu Shimamura (stamp 9). j, 80y, 1st sale of caramels, 1913 (stamp 10).

A2090b

1914-20 (Sheet 3) — #2689: a, 50y, Painting of couple in boat by Yumeji Takehisa (stamp 9). b, 50y, Takehisa, painting of flowers (stamp 10). c, 80y, 1914 Opening of Tokyo train station (blimp in sky) (stamp 1). d, 80y, Tokyo train station main entrance (stamp 2). e, 80y, Japanese WWI seamen (stamp 3). f, 80y, Western-style women's hair styles (stamp 4). g, 80y, 1915 Poetry book "Rashomon," by Ryunosuke Akutagawa (stamp 5). h, 80y, 1916 Start of postal life insurance (goddess in clouds) (stamp 6). i, 80y, Sakuzo Yoshino, political scientist & democracy advocate, & tree (stamp 7). j, 80y, 1918 Rice riots (painting, photo of crowds) (stamp 8).

A2090c

1920-25 (Sheet 4) — #2690: a, 50y, Silent film star Matsunosuke Onoe (denomination at UR) (stamp 8). b, 50y, Silent film star Tsumasaburo Bandoh (denomination at UL) (stamp 9). c, 80y, 1st Hakone Relay Marathon, 1920 (stamp 1). d, 80y, Popularity of "Gondola Song" recording, spread of phonographs (stamp 2). e, 80y, Ruins from 1923 Kanto earthquake (stamp 3). f, "Nonki na Tosan" comic strip (man with dog) (stamp 4). g, 80y, "Adventures of Sho-chan" comic strip (man with vulture). h, 80y, Japanese crane nears extinction (stamp 6). i, 80y, 1924 Opening of Koshien Stadium (stamp 7). j, 80y, Man, woman in Western-style clothing (stamp 10).

A2090d

1927-28 (Sheet 5) — #2691: a, 50y, 1927 Opening of Tokyo subway (close-up of car) (stamp 2). b, 50y, Subway car approaching station (stamp 3). c, 80y, Movie "Kurama Tengu" (Samurai) (stamp 1). d, 80y, Radio broadcast of "National Health Gymnastics" exercise program (stamp 4). e, 80y, Yoshiyuki Tsuruta, 1928 Olympic swimming champion (stamp 5). f, 80y, Mikio Oda, 1928 Olympic triple jump champion (stamp 6). g, 80y, Olympic Games program (stamp 7). h, 80y, Runner Kinue Hitomi, 1st female Japanese Olympic medalist (stamp 8). i, 80y, Man in Western clothing, cafe (stamp 9). j, 1928 Publishing of "Horoki," by Fumiko Hayashi (stamp 10).

A2090e

1929-32 (Sheet 6) — #2692: a, 50y, Mass production of Japanese automobiles (green 1932 Datsun Model 10) (stamp 4). b, 50y, Black 1936 Toyota Model AA (stamp 5). c, 80y, Volcano, Mt. Asama (stamp 1). d, 80y, Takiji Kobayashi, writer of "Kani-kosen," crane, smokestacks (stamp 2). e, 80y, Man with shirt with open collar, woman with handbag (stamp 3). f, 80y, "Norakuro" comic strip (cat, brick wall) (stamp 6). g, 80y, 1932 Nippon Derby winner Wakataka & jockey (stamp 7). h, 80y, Nippon Derby winner Kabutoyama (stamp 8). i, 80y, Song "Longing for Your Shadow" (woman with closed eyes) (stamp 9). j, 80y, 1932, 1936 Political assassinations (soldiers, truck, building) (stamp 10).

A2090f

1932-36 (Sheet 7) — #2693: a, 50y, Front of D51 steam locomotive (stamp 8). b, 50y, Rear of D51 (stamp 9). c, 80y, Fumihiko Otsuki, lexicographer (Otsuki, geometric design) (stamp 1). d, 80y, Song "Tokyo Ondo" (woman, buildings) (stamp 2). e, 80y, Keinichi Enomoto, comic actor, with feather (stamp 3). f, 80y, Formation of Japanese Baseball League (catcher, umpire) (stamp 4). g, 80y, Batter (stamp 5). h, 80y, Hachiko, dog that waited for dead owner, statue of Hachiko (stamp 6). i, 80y, Eiji Yoshikawa, author of "Miyamoto Musashi." (stamp 7). j, Extinct species Okinawan pigeon (stamp 10).

A2090g

1937-40 (Sheet 8) — #2694: a, 50y, Nose of Kamikaze plane, tail of Nippon cargo plane (stamp 2). b, 50y, Nose of Nippon cargo plain, tail of Kamikaze plane (stamp 3). c, 80y, Helen Keller's 1st trip to Japan (stamp 1). d, 80y, Women with senninbari cloths, monpe work pants, man with kokumin-fuku uniform (stamp 4). e, 80y, Yuzo Yamamoto, author of "Robo No Ishi" (stamp 5). f, 80y, Woman & man embracing in movie, "Aizenkatsura" (stamp 6). g, 80y, Sumo wrestler Yokozuna Futabayama, winner of 69 consecutive matches (stamp 7). h, 80y, Baseball pitcher Eiji Sawamura (stamp 8). i, 80y, Song, "Dareka Kokyo" (ducks in flight) (stamp 9). j, 80y, Woodblock art of Shiko Munakata (stamp 10).

A2090h

1940-45 (Sheet 9) — #2695: a, 50y, "Ohgon Bat," cartoon by Ichiro Suzuki (character without hat) (stamp 9). b, 50y, "Ohgon Bat" character wearing hat (stamp 10). c, 80y, Chiune Sugihara, vice-consul in Lithuania who saved Jews from Holocaust (stamp 1). d, 80y, Start of Kokumin Gakko school system (children exercising) (stamp 2). e, 80y, Airplane in attack on Pearl Harbor (stamp 3). f, 80y, Kotaro Takamura, poet, winner of 1st Imperial Art Academy prize, & Japanese characters (stamp 4). g, 80y, Eruption of Mt. Showashinzan (stamp 5). h, 80y, Atomic Bomb Memorial Dome (stamp 6). i, 80y, Statue at Nagasaki Atomic Bomb Museum (stamp 7). j, Signing of World War II surrender documents on USS Missouri (stamp 8).

A2090i

1945-52 (Sheet 10) — #2696: a, 50y, "Captain Atom" cartoon by Osamu Tezuka (stamp 7). b, 50y, "Astro Boy," cartoon by Tezuka (stamp 8). c, 80y, Song, "Ringo No Uta" (Apple Song) (stamp 1). d, 80y, "Sazae San," cartoon by Machiko Hasegawa (stamp 2). e, 80y, Promulgation of Japanese Constitution (woman, child, buildings) (stamp 3). f, 80y, Swimming records by Hironoshin Furuhashi (stamp 4). g, 80y, Dr. Hideki Yukawa, Nobel laurate for Physics (stamp 5). h, 80y, New Year's Eve radio program "Kohaku Uta Gassen" on NHK (stamp 6). i, 80y, Radio soap opera "Kimino Na Wa" (woman and man) (stamp 9). j, 80y, Novel "Nijyu-Yon No Hitomi," by Sakae Tsuboi (stamp 10).

A2090j

1953-58 (Sheet 11) — #2697: a, 50y, Tokyo Tower (olive green panel) (stamp 9). b, 50y, Tokyo Tower from ground (stamp 10). c, 80y, Popularity of radio and television (stamp 1). d, 80y, Director Akira Kurosawa, camera, two Samurai from "Shinchinin No Samurai." (stamp 2). e, 80y, Five Samurai from "Shinchinin No Samurai." (stamp 3). f, 80y, Sumo wrestler Rikidozan and championship belt (stamp 4). g, 80y, Rikidozan in action (stamp 5). h, 80y, Movie "Godzilla" (stamp 6). i, 80y, Taiyozoku fashions (man, woman at seaside) (stamp 7), j, 80y, Portrait of Shotokutaishi from 10,000-yen bank note (stamp 8, 31x42mm oval stamp).

A2090k

1959-64 (Sheet 12) — #2698: a, 50y, Dog Taro, survivor of abandonment in Antarctica, ship's stern (stamp 1). b, 50y, Dog Giro, survivor of abandonment in Antarctic, ship's bow (stamp 2). c, 80y, Commemorative cake box from Wedding of Crown Prince Akihito (stamp 3). d, 80y, Weather map of Isewan Typhoon (stamp 4). e, 80y, "Sukiyaki Song," by Rokusuke Ei (stamp 5). f, 80y, Novelist Ryotaro Shiba and cover from "Ryomaga Yuku," depicting Ryoma Sakamoto (stamp 6). g, 80y, Baby doll, and song "Konnichiwa Akachan," by Ei (stamp 7). h, 80y, Inauguration of Bullet Train (stamp 8). i, 80y, Poster depicting swimmer from Tokyo Olympics (stamp 9). j, 80y, Poster depicting torchbearer from Tokyo Olympics (stamp 10).

A2090l

1964-71 (Sheet 13) — #2699: a, 50y, TV show puppets Don Gabacho and Torahige (stamp 1, 31x30mm semi-oval stamp with straight side at right). b, 50y, TV show puppets Hakase and Lion (stamp 2, 31x30mm semi-oval stamp with straight side at left). c, 80y, Color television, automobile and air conditioner (stamp 3). d, 80y, TV character, Ultraman (stamp 4). e, 80y, Baltan Seijin, character from Ultraman TV series (stamp 5). f, 80y, Electric guitars (stamp 6). g, 80y, Yasunari Kawabata and Kenzaburo Oe, Nobel laureates for Literature (stamp 7). h, 80y, Scene from movie "Otokowa Tsuraiyo" (man holding basket) (stamp 8). i, 80y, Tower from Expo '70, Osaka (stamp 9). j, 80y, Youth fashions and song "Senso O Shiranai Kodomotachi" (stamp 10).

A2090m

1972-74 (Sheet 14) — #2700: a, 50y, Baseball player Sadaharu Oh (leg in air) (stamp 7). b, 50y, Baseball player Shigeo Nagashima (Tokyo uniform) (stamp 8). c, 80y, Two men from Takamatsu Zuka wall paintings, Asuka (stamp 1). d, 80y, Four women from Takamatsu Zuka wall paintings (stamp 2). e, 80y, Pandas Kankan and Ranran, gift from China (stamp 3). f, Shureimon, Return of Okinawa to Japanese control (stamp 4). g, 80y, Oscar, from cartoon "Roses of Versailles," by Riyoko Ikeda (stamp 5). h, 80y, Conductor Seiji Ozawa (stamp 6). i, 80y, Erimo Cape, and song "Erimo Misaki" (stamp 9). j, 80y, Space battleship Yamato from cartoon "Uchu Senkan Yamato," by Reiji Matsumoto (stamp 10).

A2090n

1975-83 (Sheet 15) — #2701: a, 50y, Gundam and Zaku, from TV cartoon series "Kidosenshi Gundam" (blue background) (stamp 7). b, 50y, Amuro and Gundam, from "Kidonsenshi Gundam" (orange background) (stamp 8). c, 80y, Guitar, and song "Jidai" (stamp 1). d, 80y, Fish character Taiyaki Kun, from children's song "Oyoge! Taiyaki Kun" (stamp 2). e, 80y, Musical notes and microphones (popularity of karaoke) (stamp 3). f, 80y, Flower, and song "Cosmos" (stamp 4). g, 80y, UFO, and song "UFO" (stamp 5). h, 80y, Students from TV series, "San Nen B Gumi Kinpachi Sensei" (stamp 6). i, 80y, Musical notes and electronic synthesizer (stamp 9). j, 80y, Oshin, from TV series "Oshin" (stamp 10).

A2090o

1986-93 (Sheet 16) — #2702: a, 50y, Character from cartoon show "Soreike! Anpanman" (stamp 3). b, 50y, Four characters from "Soreike! Anpanman" (stamp 4). c, 80y, Return of Halley's Comet (stamp 1, pentagonal). d, 80y, Opening of Seikan Railroad Tunnel (stamp 2). e, 80y, Watchtower excavated at Yoshinogari Iseki ruins (stamp 5). f, 80y, Singer Hibari Misora, National Medal of Honor recipient (stamp 6). g, 80y, Mascot of J-League Soccer Games (stamp 7, 34x28mm semi-oval stamp with straight side at bottom). h, 80y, Soccer ball (stamp 8, 34x28mm stamp with straight side at top). i, 80y, Selection of Dunjuang as World Heritage Site (Cliffside, stamp 9). j, 80y, Selection of Horyuji Temple as World Heritage Site (Temple and sun, stamp 10).

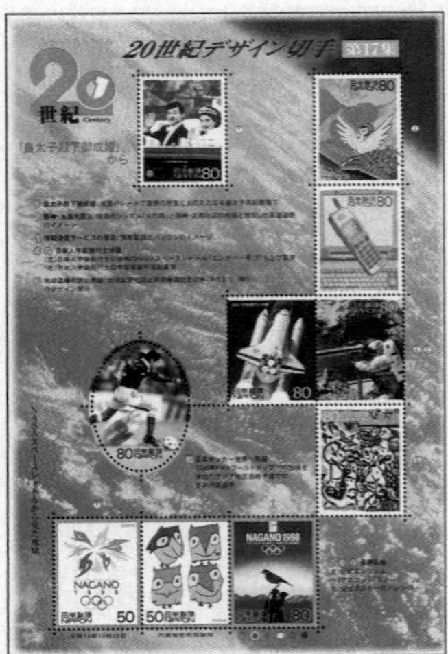

A2090p

1993-98 (Sheet 17) — #2703: a, 50y, Nagano Winter Olympics emblem (stamp 7). b, 50y, Four owl mascots of Nagano Winter Olympics (stamp 8). c, 80y, Wedding of Crown Prince Naruhito and Masako Owada (stamp 1). d, 80y, Phoenix and damage from Hanshin-Awaji earthquake (stamp 2). e, 80y, Cellular phone and computer (stamp 3). f, 80y, Launch of Japanese astronaut aboard Space Shuttle Endeavor (stamp 4). g, 80y, Astronaut Mamoru Mohri in space (stamp 5). h, 80y, Details from Kyoto Climate Change Conf. stamps, #2598-2599 (stamp 6). i, 80y, Poster for Nagano Winter Olympics (stamp 9). j, Soccer player at 1998 World Cup Championships (stamp 10, 42x31mm elliptical stamp).

Illustrations reduced.

1999-2000 Photo. *Perf. 13x13¼*

Sheets of 10

2687	A2090	#a.-j.	16.50	16.50
a.-b.		50y any single	1.10	.35
c.-j.		80y any single	1.75	.40
2688	A2090a	#a.-j.	16.50	16.50
a.-b.		50y any single	1.10	.35
c.-j.		80y any single	1.75	.40
2689	A2090b	#a.-j.	16.50	16.50
a.-b.		50y any single	1.10	.35
c.-j.		80y any single	1.75	.40
2690	A2090c	#a.-j.	16.50	16.50
a.-b.		50y any single	1.10	.35
c.-j.		80y any single	1.75	.40
2691	A2090d	#a.-j.	16.50	16.50
a.-b.		50y any single	1.10	.35
c.-j.		80y any single	1.75	.40
2692	A2090e	#a.-j.	16.50	16.50
a.-b.		50y any single	1.10	.93
c.-j.		80y any single	1.75	.40
2693	A2090f	#a.-j.	16.50	16.50
a.-b.		50y any single	1.10	.35
c.-j.		80y any single	1.75	.40
2694	A2090g	#a-j	16.50	16.50
a.-b.		50y Any single	1.10	.35
c.-j.		80y Any single	1.75	.40
2695	A2090h	#a-j	16.50	16.50
a.-b.		50y Any single	1.10	.35
c.-j.		80y Any single	1.75	.40
2696	A2090i	#a-j	16.50	16.50
a.-b.		50y Any single	1.10	.35
c.-j.		80y Any single	1.75	.40
2697	A2090j	#a-j	16.50	16.50
a.-b.		50y Any single	1.10	.35
c.-j.		80y Any single	1.75	.40
2698	A2090k	#a-j	16.50	16.50
a.-b.		50y Any single	1.10	.35
c.-j.		80y Any single	1.75	.40
2699	A2090l	#a-j	16.50	16.50
a.-b.		50y Any single	1.10	.35
c.-j.		80y Any single	1.75	.40
2700	A2090m	#a-j	16.50	16.50
a.-b.		50y Any single	1.10	.35
c.-j.		80y Any single	1.75	.40
2701	A2090n	#a-j	16.50	16.50
a.-b.		50y Any single	1.10	.35
c.-j.		80y Any single	1.75	.40
2702	A2090o	#a-j	16.50	16.50
a.-b.		50y Any single	1.10	.35
c.-j.		80y Any single	1.75	.40
2703	A2090p	#a-j	16.50	16.50
a.-b.		50y Any single	1.10	.35
c.-j.		80y Any single	1.75	.40

Sheet numbers are in UR corner of sheets or in center of rectangles at top of sheet. Stamp numbers are in sheet margin.

Issued: #2687, 8/23; #2688, 9/22; #2689, 10/22; #2690, 12/22; #2691, 1/21/00; #2692, 2/9/00; #2693, 2/23/00; #2694, 3/23/00; #2695, 4/21/00; #2696, 5/23/00; #2697, 6/23/00; #2698, 7/21/00; #2699, 8/23/00; #2700, 9/22/00; #2701, 10/23/00; #2702, 11/22; #2703, 12/22.

Hearts and Doves A2092

Celebration A2093

Red-crowned Crane — A2094

1999, Aug. 16 Photo. *Perf. 13¼*

2704	A2092 50y multi		.95	.35
2705	A2093 80y multi		1.50	.40
2706	A2094 90y multi		1.75	.50
	Nos. 2704-2706 (3)		4.20	1.25

A2095

A2096

1999, Sept. 10

2707	A2095 50y multi	.95	.35

54th Natl. Sports Festival.

1999, Oct. 1 *Perf. 12¾x13*

2708	A2096 80y multi	1.50	.40

Intl. Year of Older Persons.

A2097

A2098

A2099

Intl. Letter Writing Week A2100

Hokusai Paintings: #2709, Sea Route in Kazusa Area. #2710, Roses & a Sparrow. #2711, Rain Beneath the Mountaintop. #2712, Chrysanthemums & a Horsefly. #2713, Under the Fukagawa Bridge. #2714, Peonies & a Butterfly.

1999, Oct. 6 *Perf. 13¼*

2709	A2097 90y multi	1.75	.50
2710	A2098 90y multi	1.75	.50
a.	Pair, #2709-2710	3.50	1.75
2711	A2097 110y multi	2.10	.60
2712	A2099 110y multi	2.10	.60
a.	Pair, #2711-2712	4.25	1.75
2713	A2097 130y multi	2.50	.70
2714	A2100 130y multi	2.50	.70
a.	Pair, #2713-2714	5.00	1.75
	Nos. 2709-2714 (6)	12.70	3.60

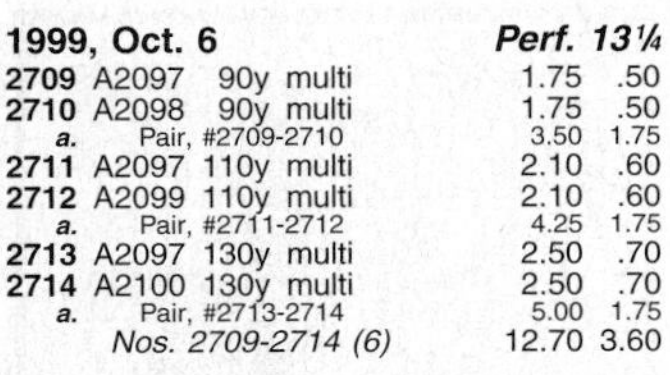

Central and Pacific Baseball Leagues, 50th Anniv. — A2101

Mascots wearing uniforms of: a, Yokohama Bay Stars. b, Chunichi Dragons. c, Seibu Lions. d, Nippon Ham Fighters. e, Yomiuri Giants. f, Yakult Swallows g, Orix Blue Wave. h, Fukuoka Daiei Hawks. i, Hiroshima Toyo Carp. j, Hanshin Tigers. k, Kintetsu Buffaloes. l, Chiba Lotte Marines.

1999, Oct. 22 *Die Cut*

Self-Adhesive

2715	A2101 Sheet of 12	18.00	
a.-l.	80y any single	1.50	.40

Natl. Science Council, 50th Anniv. — A2102

1999, Oct. 28 *Perf. 13x13¼*

2716	A2102 80y multi	1.40	.40

Cultural Pioneers Types of 1992-98

#2717, Hokusai (1760-1849), painter. #2718: Yasunari Kawabata (1899-1972), writer. #2719, Shoen Uemura (1875-1949), painter.

1999, Nov. 4 Photo. *Perf. 12¾x13*

2717	A1645 80y multi	1.50	.40

Photo. & Engr.

Perf. 13

2718	A1645 80y multi	1.50	.40
2719	A2053 80y multi	1.50	.40
	Nos. 2717-2719 (3)	4.50	1.20

Reign of Emperor Akihito, 10th Anniv. A2103

Designs: No. 2720, Paulownia and bamboo crest. No. 2721, Phoenix crest.

1999, Nov. 12 Photo. *Perf. 12¼*

2720	A2103 80y red & multi	1.50	.40
2721	A2103 80y yel & multi	1.50	.40
a.	Souvenir sheet, #2720-2721	3.00	3.00

A2104

A2105

New Year 2000 (Year of the Dragon)

A2106 A2107

1999, Nov. 15 *Perf. 13x13¼*

2722	A2104 50y multi	.95	.35
2723	A2105 80y multi	1.50	.40

Perf. 13¼

2724	A2106 50y +3y multi	1.00	.40
2725	A2107 80y +3y multi	1.60	.50

Sheets of 2 containing Nos. 2722-2723 were lottery prizes. Value $2.50.

Children's Book Day — A2108

a, Flower with child reading, bird in flight. b, Flower with child reading, bird perched. c, Child, left half of new Intl. Library of Children's Literature. d, Child, right half of library. e, Butterfly with child's head. f, Two children, library.

Perf. 12¾x13¼

2000, Mar. 31 Photo.

2726	A2108 Sheet of 10, #e-f, 2 each #a-d	15.00	15.00
a.-f.	80y any single	1.50	.40

Seishu Hanaoka (1760-1835), Physician, and Flower — A2109

2000, Apr. 11 *Perf. 12¾x13*

2727	A2109 80y multi	1.50	.40

Japan Surgical Society, 100th congress.

Japan-Netherlands Relations, 400th Anniv. — A2110

2000, Apr. 19 ***Perf. 13***

2728 80y multi 1.50 .40
2729 80y multi 1.50 .40
a. A2110 Pair, #2728-2729 3.00 1.50

Dragon and Tiger by Gaho Hashimoto — A2112

2000, Apr. 20 ***Perf. 13¼***
2730 80y multi 1.50 .40
2731 80y multi 1.50 .40
a. A2112 Pair, #2730-2731 3.00 1.50

Philately week.

Natl. Land Afforestation Campaign — A2114

2000, Apr. 21 ***Perf. 13¼***
2732 A2114 50y multi .95 .65

Phila Nippon 2001, Tokyo — A2115

Designs: a, Wild goose (dull green frame background). b, Wagtail (dull violet frame background). c, Goshawk (dull rose frame background). d, A Girl Blowing Glass Toy, by Utamaro. e, Kabuki Actor Ebizo Ichikawa, by Sharaku. f, Flowers. g, Dog and cat. h, Children with pen and envelope (blue background). i, Child with clown. j, Children with pen and envelope (red background).

2000, May 19 **Photo.** ***Die Cut***
Self-Adhesive
2733 A2115 Sheet of 10, #a-j 16.00
a.-j. 80y any single 1.60 .40

Kyushu-Okinawa Summit — A2116

2000, June 21 **Photo.** ***Perf. 12¾x13***
2734 80y multi 1.50 .40
2735 80y multi 1.50 .40
a. A2116 Pair, #2734-2735 3.00 1.50

A2117

2000, June 30
2736 80y Three flowers 1.50 .40
2737 80y Two flowers 1.50 .40
a. A2117 Pair, #2736-2737 3.00 1.50

Crime Prevention Campaign, 50th anniv.

Letter Writing Day Type of 1998

Designs: No. 2738, Girl with bows in hair, pen. No. 2739, Birds, house, letter. No. 2740, Clown with red hat, open envelope. No. 2741, Boy reading letter, puppy.

No. 2742: a, Child, dog, in basket. b, Apple tree, flower (circular stamp). c, Parrots holding envelope (elliptical stamp). d, Bicycle, rabbit, flower (oval stamp). e, Boy, girl, dove. f, Girl, letter, snail, porcupine (oval stamp). g, Child playing harp. h, Child playing recorder. i, Child playing bass (semicircular stamp). j, Girl with blue hat, pen, birds holding envelope.

2000, July 21 ***Perf. 12¾x13¼***
2738 A2047 50y multi .95 .35
2739 A2047 50y multi .95 .35
2740 A2047 50y multi .95 .35
2741 A2047 50y multi .95 .35
a. Strip of 4, #2738-2741 4.00 4.00
2742 Sheet of 10 15.00 15.00
a.-j. A2047 80y Any single 1.50 .40
k. Booklet pane, #2738-2741, 2742g, 2742h, 2 #2742e, 2742j 13.00
Booklet, #2742k 13.00
l. Souvenir sheet, #2739, 2742e 2.50 2.50

No. 2742b is 30mm in diameter, No. 2742c is 23x34mm, Nos. 2742d, 2742f are 28x40mm, and No. 2742i is 24x40mm.

Women's Private Higher Education, Cent. — A2118

2000, Sept. 22 **Photo.** ***Perf. 13***
2743 A2118 80y multi 1.50 .40

Intl. Letter Writing Week A2119

Artwork by Hiroshige: 90y, Okabe. 110y, Maisaka. 130y, Okazaki.

2000, Oct. 6 ***Perf. 13¼***
2744 A2119 90y multi 2.00 .75
2745 A2119 110y multi 2.40 .75
2746 A2119 130y multi 2.75 .75
Nos. 2744-2746 (3) 7.15 2.25

See Nos. 2791-2793, 2835-2837, 2865-2867, 2904-2906, 2938-2940, 2999-3001, 3064-3066.

Cultural Pioneers Type of 1998 and

Ukichiro Nakaya (1900-62), Snow Crystal Researcher A2120

Designs: No. 2747, Hantaro Nagaoka (1865-1950), physicist. No. 2748, Teijo Nakamura (1900-88), poet.

Photo. & Engr.

2000, Nov. 6 ***Perf. 13***
2747 A2053 80y multi 1.50 .40
2748 A2053 80y multi 1.50 .40
2749 A2120 80y multi 1.50 .40
Nos. 2747-2749 (3) 4.50 1.20

See No. 2841.

A2121

A2122

New Year 2001 (Year of the Snake)
A2123 A2124

2000, Nov. 15 **Photo.** ***Perf. 13x13¼***
2750 A2121 50y multi .95 .35
2751 A2122 80y multi 1.50 .40

Perf. 13¼x13½
2752 A2123 50y +3y multi 1.00 .40
2753 A2124 80y +3y multi 1.60 .50
Nos. 2750-2753 (4) 5.05 1.65

Sheets of 2, Nos. 2750-2751, were lottery prizes.

Diet, 110th Anniv. — A2125

2000, Nov. 29 ***Perf. 13***
2754 A2125 80y multi 1.50 .40

Internet Expo 2001 — A2126

2001, Jan. 5 ***Perf. 13x13¼***
2755 80y Denom. at L 1.50 .40
2756 80y Denom. at R 1.50 .40
a. A2126 Pair, #2755-2756 3.00 1.50

Intl. Volunteers Year — A2127

2001, Jan. 17 ***Perf. 13½x13¼***
2757 A2127 80y multi 1.50 .40

Administrative Scriveners System, 50th Anniv. — A2128

2001, Feb. 22 **Photo.** ***Perf. 13¼***
2758 A2128 80y multi 1.75 .40

World Heritage Sites

Sheet 1 — A2129

Sheet 2 — A2130

Sheet 3 — A2131

Sheet 4 — A2132

Sheet 5 — A2133

Sheet 6 — A2134

No. 2759 — Nikko: a, Bridge (stamp 1). b, Shrine with pillars in foreground (stamp 2). c, Temple gate (stamp 3). d, Dragon (stamp 4). e, Peacock (stamp 5). f, Cat (stamp 6). g, Statue of blue green figure (stamp 7). h, Statue of red figure (stamp 8). i, Shrine (stamp 9). j, Shrine and walkways (stamp 10).

No. 2760 — Itsukushima: a, Marodo Jinjya and pillar in water (stamp 1). b, Marodo Jinjya (stamp 2). c, Honsha (shrine entrance with steps, stamp 3). d, Koma-inu (lion statue, stamp 4). e, Marodo Jinjya and Gojyuno-tou (stamp 5). f, Bugakumen (sculpture with blue water background, stamp 6). g, Kazari-uma (horse statue, stamp 7). h, Noubutai (building with brown eaves, stamp 8). i, Tahoutou (building with cherry blossoms, stamp 9). j, Oomoto Jinjya (building with red fence, stamp 10).

No. 2761 — Kyoto: a, Hosodono Hall, Maidono Hall and Tsuchinoya Hall, Kamowakeikazuchi Shrine (buildings with cones in foreground, stamp 1). b, Romon Gate, Kamowakeikazuchi Shrine (building with stream, stamp 2). c, East Main Hall, Kamomioya Shrine (building with guardian dog statue on landing, stamp 3). d, Guardian dog statue, Kamomioya Shrine (stamp 4). e, South Great Gate and 5-Story Pagoda (deep blue sky, stamp 5). f, Fukuu Joju Nyorai Statue, Toji Temple (gold statue, stamp 6). g, Nyoirin Kannon, Toji Temple (painting, stamp 7). h, Daiitoku Myoo Statue, Toji Temple (stone statue, stamp 8). i, West Gate, 3-Story Pagoda, Kiyomizudera Temple (red gate and temple, stamp 9). j, Main Hall, Kiyomizudera Temple (building with cherry bloosoms, stamp 10).

No. 2762 — Kyoto: a, Konpon Chudo Hall, Enryakuji Temple (roof, stamp 1). b, Eternal Flame, Enryaluji Temple (stamp 2). c, Ninai-do Hall, Enryakuji Temple (building with large trees in foreground, stamp 3). d, Sanbo-in Temple Garden, Daigoji Temple (building, one end of small bridge, stamp 4). e, Sanbo-in Temple Garden (end of bridge, trees, stamp 5). f, 5-Story Pagoda, Daigoji Temple (white sky, stamp 6). g, Goten, Ninnaji Temple (buildings with walkways, stamp 7). h, 5-Story Pagoda (cherry trees in foreground, stamp 8). i, Phoenix Hall, Byodoin Temple (black sky, stamp 9). j, Wooden carving of Bodhisattvas Floating on Clouds, Byodoin Temple (stamp 10).

No. 2763 — Kyoto: a, Ujikami Shrine (low fence around shrine with denomination at UL, stamp 1). b, Kaeru Mata, Ujikami Shrine (thin, crossing diagonal strips, stamp 2). c, Front approach to Kozanji Temple (walkway of square panels, stamp 3). d, Sekisuiin, Kozanji Temple (yellow tree blossoms in front of temple, stamp 4). e, Kasumijima Garden, Saihoji Temple (moss-covered bridge, stamp 5) f, Kojokan Garden, Saihoji Temple (Stone stairs and rocks, stamp 6). g, View of garden and pond from under roof, Tenryuji Temple (denomination at left, stamp 7). h, View of garden and pond from under roof, Tenryuji Temple (denomination at right, stamp 8). i, Rokuonji Temple in autumn (Building on lake, green leaves on trees, stamp 9). j, Rokuonji Temple in winter (snow covered roofs and trees, stamp 10).

No. 2764 — Kyoto: a, Snow-covered Silver Pavilion, Jishoji Temple (stamp 1). b, Silver Pavilion without snow (stamp 2). c, Moss-covered rock, Hojo Garden, Ryoanji Temple (stamp 3). d, Rock and snow, Hojo Garden (stamp 4). e, Karamon, Honganji Temple (gate with curved roof, stamp 5). f, Hiunkaku, Honganji Temple (building near pond, stamp 6). g, Shoin, Honganji Temple (wall with landscape, stamp 7). h, Ninomaur Palace, Nijo Castle (roof with chrysanthemum crest at peak, stamp 8). i, Detail from "Hawks on Pine," Nijo Castle (hawk looking left, stamp 9). j, Detail from "Hawks on Pine," Nijo Castle (hawk looking down, stamp 10).

2001 Photo. *Perf. 13x13¼*

2759	A2129	Sheet of 10	17.50	17.50
a.-j.		80y Any single	1.75	.40
2760	A2130	Sheet of 10	17.50	17.50
a.-j.		80y Any single	1.75	.40
2761	A2131	Sheet of 10	17.50	17.50
a.-j.		80y Any single	1.75	.40
2762	A2132	Sheet of 10	17.50	17.50
a.-j.		80y Any single	1.75	.40
2763	A2133	Sheet of 10	17.50	17.50
a.-j.		80y Any single	1.75	.40
2764	A2134	Sheet of 10	17.50	17.50
a.-j.		80y Any single	1.75	.40

Issued: No. 2759, 2/23; No. 2760, 3/23; No. 2761, 6/22; No. 2762, 8/23. No. 2763, 12/21. No. 2764, 2/22/02.

Sheet numbers are in center of colored rectangles at top of sheet. Stamp numbers are in sheet margins.

Exhibit of Italian Art at Museum of Western Art, Tokyo — A2135

Designs: 80y, Show emblem. No. 2766, Angel, from The Annunciation, by Botticelli. No. 2767, Virgin Mary, from The Annunciation.

2001, Mar. 19 Photo. *Perf. 13*

2765	A2135	80y multi	1.75	.40

Size: 33x44mm

Perf. 13¼

2766	A2135	110y multi	2.40	.75
2767	A2135	110y multi	2.40	.75
a.		Pair, #2766-2767	5.00	3.00
		Nos. 2765-2767 (3)	6.55	1.90

Japanese Dermatological Association, 100th Annual Meeting — A2136

2001, Apr. 6 *Perf. 13¼*

Color of Triangle Behind "0" in Denomination

2768	A2136	80y pink	1.50	.40
2769	A2136	80y orange	1.50	.40
2770	A2136	80y yellow	1.50	.40
2771	A2136	80y green	1.50	.40
2772	A2136	80y blue	1.50	.40
a.		Vert. strip of 5, #2768-2772	7.50	7.50

Depositing Mail, by Senseki Nakamura A2137

2001, Apr. 20 *Perf. 13x13¼*

2773	A2137	80y multi	1.50	.40

Philately Week, Cent. of red cylindrical mailboxes.

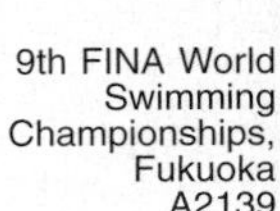

Membership in UNESCO, 50th Anniv. — A2138

2001, July 2 *Perf. 13¼*

2774	A2138	80y multi	1.25	.40

9th FINA World Swimming Championships, Fukuoka A2139

Designs: No. 2775, Swimming race. No. 2776, Synchronized swimming. No. 2777, Diving. No. 2778, Water polo.

2001, July 16 *Perf. 13x13¼*

2775	A2139	80y multi	1.50	.40
2776	A2139	80y multi	1.50	.40
2777	A2139	80y multi	1.50	.40
2778	A2139	80y multi	1.50	.40
a.		Horiz. strip of 4, #2775-2778	6.00	6.00

Letter Writing Day Type of 1998

Designs: No. 2779, Three rabbits, tulip background. No. 2780, Girl with pencil, pencil background. No. 2781, Boy with envelope, bird background. No. 2782, Girl, flower background.

No. 2783: a, Girl with rabbit, bird, flower (oval stamp). b, Bird in tree (circular stamp). c, Boy with pen behind back. d, Girl with envelope and dog. e, Girl on bicycle, flowers (semicircular stamp). f, Flowers, bird with envelope, insect (circular stamp). g, Bird flying, bird on roof. h, Chicken, chicks, pig (oval stamp). i, Rabbit, flowers (elliptical stamp). j, Boy with hat, rabbit (oval stamp).

2001, July 23 *Perf. 13x13¼*

2779	A2047	50y multi	.95	.35
2780	A2047	50y multi	.95	.35
2781	A2047	50y multi	.95	.35
2782	A2047	50y multi	.95	.35
a.		Horiz. strip of 4, #a-d	4.00	4.00
2783		Sheet of 10	15.00	15.00
a.-j.	A2047	80y Any single	1.50	.40
k.		Booklet pane, #2779-2782, 2 each #2783c, 2783d, 2783g	13.00	
		Booklet, #2783k	13.00	
l.		Souvenir sheet, #2780, 2783g	2.50	2.50

Phila Nippon '01 (Nos. 2783, 2783l). Nos. 2783a and 2783e are 35x29mm; Nos. 2783b and 2783f are 29mm in diameter; No. 2783h is 40x28mm; No. 2783i is 35x23mm; No. 2783j is 34x28mm.

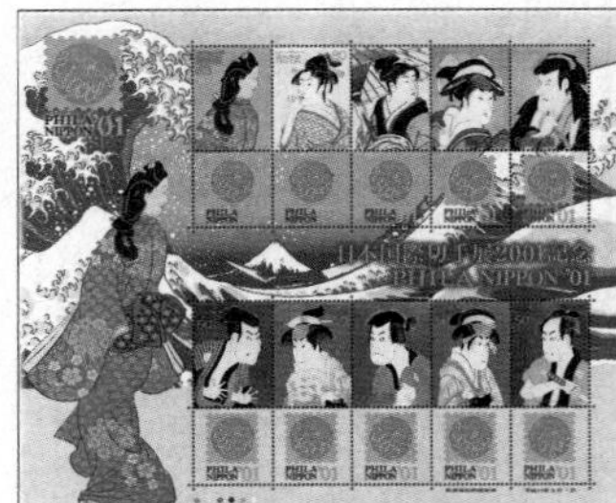

Phila Nippon '01 — A2140

Art: a, Oniji Otani as Edobei (striped kimono), by Sharaku. b, Hanshiro Iwai as Shigenoi (flowered kimono, facing left), by Sharaku. c, Hangoro Sakata as Mizuemon Fujikawa (brown kimono), by Sharaku. d, Kikunojo Segawa as Oshizu, Bunzo Tanabe's Wife (kimono with stars), by Sharaku. e, Omezo Ichikawa as Ippei Yakko (with sword), by Sharaku. f, Beauty Looking Back (flowered kimono), by Moronobu Hishikawa. g, A Girl Whistling a Vidro (checkered kimono), by Utamaro. h, Nishiki Fuzoku Higashino Returning From a Bathhouse in the Rain (with umbrella), by Kiyonaga Torii. i, Kumesaburo

Iwai as Chiyo (blue background), by Kunimasa Utagawa. j, Komazo Ichikawa as Ganryu Sasaki (with sword), by Toyokuni Utagawa.

2001, Aug. 1 *Perf. 13*

2784 A2140 Sheet of 10+10 labels 12.50 12.50
a.-e. 50y Any single .95 .35
f.-j. 80y Any single 1.50 .40

Labels could be personalized by customers at Phila Nippon stamp exhibition.

2001 World Games, Akita — A2141

Designs: No. 2785, Fishing, Frisbee throwing. No. 2786, Aerobics, billiards. No. 2787, Life saving, water skiing. No. 2788, Body building, tug-of-war.

2001, Aug. 16 *Perf. 13*

2785 A2141 50y multi .95 .35
2786 A2141 50y multi .95 .35
a. Pair, #2785-2786 1.90 1.00
2787 A2141 80y multi 1.50 .40
2788 A2141 80y multi 1.50 .40
a. Pair, #2787-2788 3.00 1.50
Nos. 2785-2788 (4) 4.90 1.50

Phila Nippon '01 — A2142

Designs: a, Hanshiro Iwai as Shigenoi (figure with stick in hair), by Sharaku. b, Oniji Otani as Edobei (figure with fingers splayed), by Sharaku. c, Mandarin duck in water. d, White-eye on branch. e, Children with letters. f, Kumesaburo Iwai as Chiyo (lilac background), by Kunimasa Utagawa. g, Komazo Ichikawa as Ganryu Sasaki (brown background), by Toyokuni Utagawa. h, Turtledove (blue background). i, Greater pied kingfisher (green background). j, Japan #1.

2001, Aug. 1 **Photo.** *Die Cut*
Self-Adhesive

2789 A2142 Sheet of 10 12.00
a.-e. 50y Any single .95 .35
f.-j. 80y Any single 1.50 .40

San Francisco Peace Treaty, 50th Anniv. — A2143

2001, Sept. 7 *Perf. 13*

2790 A2143 80y multi 1.60 .40

Intl. Letter Writing Week Type of 2000

Hiroshige paintings from 53 Stations of the Tokaido: 90y, Hara. 110y, Oiso. 130y, Sakanoshita.

2001, Oct. 5 *Perf. 13¼*

2791 A2119 90y multi 1.75 .75
2792 A2119 110y multi 2.10 .75
2793 A2119 130y multi 2.50 .75
Nos. 2791-2793 (3) 6.35 2.25

Town Safety Campaign — A2144

Designs: No. 2794, Boy, duck chicks, owl, frogs, insects. No. 2795, Girl, dogs, cats, birds, insects.

2001, Oct. 11 *Perf. 13x13¼*

2794 80y multi 1.50 .40
2795 80y multi 1.50 .40
a. A2144 Horiz. pair, #2794-2795 3.00 1.50

1st National Games for the Disabled — A2145

Designs: No. 2796, Disc throwing. No. 2797, Wheelchair race.

2001, Oct. 26 *Perf. 12¾x13*

2796 80y multi 1.50 .40
2797 80y multi 1.50 .40
a. A2145 Horiz. pair, #2796-2797 3.00 1.50

Norinaga Motoori (1730-1801), Physician, Scholar — A2146

Gidayu Takemoto (1651-1714), Joruri Chanter — A2147

Photo. & Engr.

2001, Nov. 5 *Perf. 12¾x13*

2798 A2146 80y multi 1.50 .40
2799 A2147 80y multi 1.50 .40

Commercial Broadcasting, 50th Anniv. — A2148

2001, Nov. 15 **Photo.**

2800 A2148 80y multi 1.50 .40

A2149

A2150

New Year 2002 (Year of the Horse)

A2151 A2152

2001, Nov. 15 *Perf. 13x13¼*

2801 A2149 50y multi .95 .35
2802 A2150 80y multi 1.50 .40

Perf. 13¼x13½

2803 A2151 50y +3y multi 1.00 .40
2804 A2152 80y +3y multi 1.60 .50
Nos. 2801-2804 (4) 5.05 1.65

Sheets of two containing Nos. 2801-2802 were lottery prizes.

Legal Aid System, 50th Anniv. — A2153

2002, Jan. 24 *Perf. 12¾x13*

2805 A2153 80y multi 1.50 .40

Japan — Mongolia Diplomatic Relations, 30th Anniv. — A2154

2002, Feb. 15

2806 A2154 80y multi 1.50 .40

Lions Clubs in Japan, 50th Anniv. — A2155

2002, Mar. 1 **Photo.** *Perf. 13x13¼*

2807 A2155 80y multi 1.50 .95

2002 World Figure Skating Championships, Nagano — A2156

2002, Mar. 8

2808 80y Men's Singles 1.50 .95
2809 80y Pairs 1.50 .95
a. A2156 Horiz. pair, #2808-2809 3.00 1.90

Diplomatic Relations Anniversaries A2157

Designs: No. 2810, Taj Mahal, India. No. 2811, Sculpture of "Priest King," Mohenjo Daro excavations, Pakistan. No. 2812, Sigiriya goddess, Lion's Rock, Sri Lanka. No. 2813, Carving from Buddhist Vihara, Paharpur, Bangladesh.

2002, Apr. 12

2810 A2157 80y multi 1.50 .95
2811 A2157 80y multi 1.50 .95
2812 A2157 80y multi 1.50 .95
2813 A2157 80y multi 1.50 .95
Nos. 2810-2813 (4) 6.00 3.80

Japanese diplomatic relations with India, 50th anniv. (#2810); Pakistan, 50th anniv. (#2811). Sri Lanka, 50th anniv. (#2812), and Bangladesh, 30th anniv. (#2813).

Philately Week — A2158

Folding screen panels depicting horse racing scenes: No. 2814, Denomination at bottom. No. 2815, Denomination at top.

2002, Apr. 19 *Perf. 13¼*

2814 80y multi 1.50 .95
2815 80y multi 1.50 .95
a. A2158 Horiz. pair, #2814-2815 3.00 1.90

Fulbright Exchange Program, 50th Anniv. — A2159

Return of Okinawa, 30th Anniv. — A2160

2002, May 8 *Perf. 12¾x13*

2816 A2159 80y multi 1.50 .95

2002, May 15 *Perf. 13x13¼*

2817 A2160 80y multi 1.50 .95

2002 World Cup Soccer Championships, Japan and Korea — A2161

2002, May 24

2818 80y Soccer field 1.50 .95
2819 80y World Cup 1.50 .95
a. A2161 Horiz. pair, #2818-2819 3.00 1.90

Nos. 2818-2819 were issued in sheets of 10 stamps, containing five of each. Thirteen different sheet margins exist.

World Heritage Sites

Sheet 7 — A2162

No. 2820 — Todaiji and Koufukuji Temples, Nara: a, Great Buddha Hall, Todaiji Temple (stamp 1). b, Underside of roof of Nandaimon Gate, Todaiji Temple (stamp 2). c, Engraving on lotus petal, Todaiji Temple (stamp 3). d, Head of Koumokuten, Todaiji Temple (stamp 4). e, Hokkedo Hall and steps, Todaiji Temple (stamp 5). f, Five-story pagoda, Koufukuji Temple (stamp 6). g, Hokuendo Hall (with roof ornament), Koufukuji Temple (stamp 7). h, Ashura (statue with four arms), Koufukuji Temple (stamp 8). i, Head of Buddha, Koufukuji Temple (stamp 9). j, Ogre under dragon lantern, Koufukuji Temple (stamp 10).

2002 Photo. *Perf. 13x13¼*
2820 A2162 Sheet of 10 15.00 15.00
a.-j. 80y Any single 1.50 1.40

Issued: No. 2820, 6/21.

Numbers have been reserved for additional sheets. Sheet numbers are in center of colored rectangle at top of sheet. Stamp numbers are in sheet margins.

World Heritage Series

Sheet 8 — A2163

Sheet 9 — A2164

Sheet 10 — A2165

No. 2821 — Nara: a, Covered passageway, Kasuga Taisha Shrine (stamp 1). b, Chumon, Kasuga Taisha Shrine (stamp 2). c, Deer in Kasuga-yama Primeval Forest (stamp 3). d, Gokurakubo Zenshitsu and Gokurakubo Hondo, Gango-ji Temple (stamp 4). e, Gokurakubo Five-story Pagoda, Gango-ji Temple (stamp 5). f, East and West Pagodas, Yakushi-ji Temple (stamp 6). g, Yakushi Nyorai (seated Buddha), Yakushi-ji Temple (stamp 7). h, Golden Hall, Toshodai-ji Temple (stamp 8). i, Senju Kannon Ryu-zo (standing image with hands together of Thousand-handed Goddess of Mercy), Toshodai-ji Temple (stamp 9). j, Suzakumon Gate, Heijo Imperial Palace (stamp 10).

No. 2822 — Villages of Shirakawa-go and Gokayama: a, House with large tree at left, Ogimachi (stamp 1). b, Two houses, trees in fall colors Ogimachi (stamp 2). c, House with flowers, Ogimachi (stamp 3). d, Myozen-ji Temple and house, Ogimachi (stamp 4). e, Two houses covered in snow at night, Ogimachi (stamp 5). f, Neighborhood of houses, Ainokura (stamp 6). g, Sonen-ji Temple with stone wall, Ainokura (stamp 7). h, Two houses, Ainokura (stamp 8). i, House with shrub in front, Suganuma (stamp 9). j, House covered in snow, Suganuma (stamp 10).

No. 2823 — Gusuku Sites of the Ryukyu Kingdom: a, Stone lion at royal mausoleum (stamp 1). b, Three steps and stone gate to Sonohyan'utaki Sanctuary (stamp 2). c, Cherry blossoms and ruins of Nakijinjou Castle (stamp 3). d, Steps and stone gate at ruins of Zakimijou Castle (stamp 4). e, Ruins of Katsurenjou Castle walls (stamp 5). f, Ruins of Nakagusukujou Castle citadel (walls with gate, stamp 6). g Kankaimon, main gate of Shurijou Castle (stamp 7). h, Main hall of Shurijou Castle (red building, stamp 8). i, Shikina'en, royal garden (stamp 9). j, Seifautaki Sanctuary (niche in rocks, stamp 10).

2002 Photo. *Perf. 13x13¼*
2821 A2163 Sheet of 10 15.00 15.00
a.-j. 80y Any single 1.50 1.40
2822 A2164 Sheet of 10 15.00 15.00
a.-j. 80y Any single 1.50 1.25
2823 A2165 Sheet of 10 15.00 15.00
a.-j. 80y Any single 1.50 1.40

Issued: No. 2821, 7/23; No. 2822, 9/20; No. 2823, 12/20. Sheet numbers are in center of colored rectangle at top of sheet. Stamp numbers are in sheet margins.

Letter Writing Day Type of 1998

Designs: No. 2824, Girl with bows in hair holding envelope. No. 2825, Monkey in tree holding envelope. No. 2826, House and flowers. No. 2827, Boy with arms raised, fence.

No. 2828: a, Cow and bird (triangular stamp). b, Boy and sheep (elliptical stamp). c, Caterpillar and ladybug under magnifying glass (round stamp). d, Girl with bows in hair, flowers (oval stamp). e, Boy with soccer ball. f, Girl with tennis racquet and ball. g, Man on bicycle. h, Girl with flower in vase (round stamp). i, Truck and automobile. j, Woman holding gift and coat, boy holding envelope

Perf. 13x13¼, 13 (#2828a)

2002, July 23 Photo.
2824 A2047 50y multi .95 .65
2825 A2047 50y multi .95 .65
2826 A2047 50y multi .95 .65
2827 A2047 50y multi .95 .65
a. Strip of 4, #2824-2827 4.00 2.60
2828 Sheet of 10 15.00 15.00
a.-j. A2047 80y Any single 1.50 1.00
k. Booklet pane, #2824-2827, 3 each #2828g, 2828j 13.00 —
Booklet, #2828k 13.00
l. Souvenir sheet, #2825, 2828j 2.50 2.50

No. 2828a is 34x28mm; No. 2828b is 29x26mm; No. 2828c is 29mm in diameter; No. 2828d is 28x40mm; Nos. 2828e and 2828f are 22x36mm; No. 2828h is 28mm in diameter; No. 2828i is 25x25mm.

12th World Congress of Psychiatry, Yokohama — A2166

2002, Aug. 1 Photo. *Perf. 12¾x13*
2829 A2166 80y multi 1.50 1.00

World Wheelchair Basketball Championships, Kitakyushu A2167

2002, Aug. 9
2830 A2167 80y multi 1.50 1.00

Civil Aviation, 50th Anniv. — A2168

2002, Sept. 6
2831 A2168 80y multi 1.50 1.00

Normalization of Diplomatic Relations Between Japan and People's Republic of China, 30th Anniv. — A2169

Designs: No. 2832, Purple wisteria flowers. No. 2833, Goldfish and cherry blossoms.

2002, Sept. 13 *Perf. 13x13¼*
2832 80y multi 1.50 1.00
2833 80y multi 1.50 1.00
a. A2169 Horiz. pair, #2832-2833 3.00 2.00

Intl. Fleet Review, Tokyo Bay — A2170

2002, Oct. 1
2834 A2170 80y multi 1.50 1.00

Letter Writing Week Type of 2000

Hiroshige paintings from 53 Stations of the Tokaido Highway: 90y, Yui. 110y, Shono. 130y, Tozuka.

2002, Oct. 7 *Perf. 13¼*
2835 A2119 90y multi 1.75 1.10
2836 A2119 110y multi 2.10 1.25
2837 A2119 130y multi 2.50 1.60
Nos. 2835-2837 (3) 6.35 3.95

Asian and Pacific Decade of Disabled Persons — A2171

2002, Oct. 10 *Perf. 12¾x13*
2838 A2171 80y multi 1.50 1.00

Cultural Pioneers Types of 1998-2000

Designs: No. 2839, Shiki Masaoka (1867-1902), poet. No. 2840, Ookawabata Yusuzumi-zu, by Kiyonaga Torii (1752-1815), artist. No. 2841, Aikitu Tanakadate (1856-1952), physicist.

Photo. & Engr., Photo. (#2840)

2002, Nov. 5 *Perf. 13*
2839 A2053 80y multi 1.50 1.00
2840 A2053 80y multi 1.50 1.00
2841 A2120 80y multi 1.50 1.00
Nos. 2839-2841 (3) 4.50 3.00

A2172

A2173

New Year 2003 (Year of the Ram)

A2174 A2175

2002, Nov. 15 Photo. *Perf. 13x13¼*
2842 A2172 50y multi .95 .60
2843 A2173 80y multi 1.50 1.00

Perf. 13½x13¼
2844 A2174 50y +3y multi 1.00 .65
2845 A2175 80y +3y multi 1.60 1.00
Nos. 2842-2845 (4) 5.05 3.25

Sheets of two containing Nos. 2842-2843 were lottery prizes.

Kabuki, 400th Anniv. — A2176

Designs: No. 2846, Shibaraku and Tsuchigumo. No. 2847, Okuni Kabuki-zu, detail from painted screen.

2003, Jan. 15 Photo. *Perf. 13x13¼*

2846	80y multi	1.75	1.00
2847	80y multi	1.75	1.00
a.	A2176 Horiz. pair, #2846-2847	3.50	2.00

Japanese Television, 50th Anniv.
A2177 A2178

2003, Jan. 31

2848	A2177 80y multi	1.75	1.00
2849	A2178 80y multi	1.75	1.00

A2179

Greetings — A2180

No. 2850: a, Roses. b, Reindeer. c, Cat and butterfly. d, Rabbits in automobile. e, White flowers.

No. 2851: a, Heart and flower. b, Dog with noisemaker. c, Bird and snowman. d, Bird and strawberries. e, Cranes and turtle.

2003, Feb. 10 *Die Cut Perf. 13½*
Self-Adhesive

2850	A2179 Pane of 5 + 5 labels	8.00	
a.-e.	80y Any single	1.60	1.00
2851	A2180 Pane of 5 + 5 labels	8.00	
a.-e.	80y Any single	1.60	1.00

World Heritage Series

Sheet 11 — A2181

No. 2852 — Hiroshima buildings and stamps on theme of "Peace": a, Atomic Bomb Dome (stamp 1). b, Hiroshima Prefectural Commercial Exhibit Hall (stamp 2). c, Dove over Atomic Bomb Dome, yellow denomination (stamp 3). d, Child's drawing of person with flower (stamp 4). e, Dove over Atomic Bomb Dome, blue denomination (stamp 5). f, Dove over Atomic Bomb Dome, red denomination (stamp 6). g, Doves, stylized person holding child (stamp 7). h, People on hill (stamp 8). i, Bird (stamp 9). j, Rabbit, butterflies and flowers (stamp 10).

2003, Mar. 20 Photo. *Perf. 13x13¼*

2852	A2181 Sheet of 10	14.00	14.00
a.-j.	80y Any single	1.40	1.00

Sheet numbers are in center of colored rectangle at top of sheet. Stamp numbers are in sheet margin.

Inauguration of Japan Post — A2182

No. 2853 — Flowers: a, Adonis (yellow flowers). b, Primrose (pink flowers). c, Violets and Japanese quince (violet and red flowers). d, Field horsetail (flowerless). e, Japanese wisteria (white hanging flowers). f, Weeping cherry tree (pink buds and flowers) and swallow. g, Hydrangea (lilac flowers). h, Japanese magnolia (white and pink flowers). i, Candock (yellow flower) and moorhen. j, Peony (pink flower and bud) and butterfly.

2003, Apr. 1 *Die Cut Perf. 13¼*
Self-Adhesive

2853	A2182 Sheet of 10	14.00	
a.-j.	80y Any single	1.40	1.00

Japan Post Mascots — A2183

Designs: a, Aichan (squirrel with pink bow). b, Male Kanchan (with heart on shorts). c, Posuton (with hands extended). d, Yuchan (squirrel with cap). e, Female Kanchan (with flower). f, Posuton (with letter). g, Posuton (with letter). h, Aichan (with pink bow), diff. i, Female Kanchan (with flower), diff. j, Posuton (with hands extended), diff. k, Yuchan (with cap), diff. l, Male Kanchan (waving).

2003, Apr. 1 *Die Cut Perf. 13¼*
Self-Adhesive

2854	A2183 Sheet of 12	13.00	
a.-f.	50y Any single	.85	.60
g.-l.	80y Any single	1.25	1.00

Ram and Tree Batik Screen Design — A2184

2003, Apr. 18 *Perf. 13¼*

2855	A2184 80y multi	1.40	1.00

Philately Week.

Edo Shogunate, 400th Anniv.

Screen Depicting Edo — A2185

Wall Decoration, Edo Castle — A2186

Armor of Ieyasu Tokugawa
A2187

Detail from Writing Box
A2188

Noh Mask and Costume — A2189

Sheet 2 — A2190

A2191

No. 2857 — Sheet 2: a, Nihonbashi, from 53 Stations of the Tokaido Road, by Hiroshige (stamp 1). b, Fireman's coat (stamp 2). c, Screen depicting Kabuki theater (stamp 3). d, Hina-matsuri fesitval doll of empress (no number). e, Hina-matsuri festival doll of emperor (stamp 4). f, Danjurou Ichikawa playing role of Goro Takenuki (stamp 5).

No. 2858 — Sheet 3: a, Stern of USS Powhatan (stamp 1). b, Bow of USS Powhatan (no number). c, Screen art depicting return of Commodore Perry's fleet to Japan (stamp 2). d, Ceramic platter for export to Europe (stamp 3). e, Portrait of a European Woman, probably by Gennai Hiraga (stamp 4). f, Perpetual clock (stamp 5).

2003 *Perf. 13x13¼*

2856	Vert. strip of 5	7.00	7.00
a.	A2185 80y multi	1.40	1.00
b.	A2186 80y multi	1.40	1.00
c.	A2187 80y multi	1.40	1.00
d.	A2188 80y multi	1.40	1.00
e.	A2189 80y multi	1.40	1.00
	Sheet, 2 #2856 (Sheet 1)	14.00	14.00
2857	A2190 Sheet of 10, #2857d-2857e, 2 each #2857a-2857c, 2857f	14.00	14.00
a.-f.	80y Any single	1.40	1.00
2858	A2191 Sheet of 10, #2858a-2858b, 2 each #2858c-2858f	14.00	14.00
a.-f.	80y Any single	1.40	1.40

Issued: No. 2856, 5/23; No. 2857, 6/12; No. 2858, 7/1. Sheet numbers are in center of arrows at top of sheet. Stamp numbers are in sheet margins.

ASEAN — Japan Exchange Year — A2192

No. 2859: a, Omar Ali Saifuddien Mosque, Brunei (stamp 1). b, Angkor Wat, Cambodia (stamp 2). c, Borobudur Temple, Indonesia (stamp 3). d, That Luang, Laos (stamp 4). e, Sultan Abdul Samad Building, Malaysia (stamp 5). f, Shwedagon Pagoda, Myanmar (stamp 6). g, Rice terraces, Philippines (stamp 7). h, Merlion Statue, Singapore (stamp 8). i, Wat Phra Kaeo, Thailand (stamp 9). j, Van Mieu, Viet Nam (stamp 10).

2003, June 16 Photo. *Perf. 13x13¼*

2859	A2192	Sheet of 10	14.00	14.00
a.-j.		80y Any single	1.40	1.00

Letter Writing Day — A2193

Designs: No. 2860, Bear with guitar, bird. No. 2861, Monkey with letter. No. 2862, Crocodile with accordion, bird. No. 2863, Cat with camera, letter.

No. 2864: a, Hippopotamus with umbrella, flowers, birds (oval stamp). b, Parakeet with letter. c, Owl (round stamp). d, Bear with letter, bird (oval stamp). e, Elephant with flowers. f, Giraffe with letter (oval stamp). g, Rabbit with letter, flowers (semi-circular stamp). h, Lion with letter, lantern. i, Goat with letter. j, Gorilla with koala, bird and owl.

2003, July 23 Photo. *Perf. 13x13¼*

2860	A2193	50y multi	.85	.65
2861	A2193	50y multi	.85	.65
2862	A2193	50y multi	.85	.65
2863	A2193	50y multi	.85	.65
a.		Horiz. strip of 4, #2860-2863	3.40	2.60
2864		Sheet of 10	14.00	14.00
a.-j.		A2193 80y Any single	1.40	1.00
k.		Booklet pane of 10, #2860-2863, 2 each #2864b, 2864h, 2864i	12.00	—
		Complete booklet, #2864k	12.00	
l.		Souvenir sheet, #2860, #2864b	2.25	1.75

Nos. 2864a, 2864d and 2864f are 28x40mm; No. 2864c is 30mm in diameter; No. 2864g is 40x24mm.

Intl. Letter Writing Week Type of 2000

Hiroshige paintings from 53 Stations of the Tokaido Highway: 90y, Kawasaki. 110y, Miya. 130y, Otsu.

2003, Oct. 6 *Perf. 13¼*

2865	A2119	90y multi	1.75	1.25
2866	A2119	110y multi	2.00	1.40
2867	A2119	130y multi	2.40	1.75
		Nos. 2865-2867 (3)	6.15	4.40

Cultural Pioneers — A2194

Designs: No. 2868, Mokichi Saito (1882-1953), poet. No. 2869, Shibasaburo Kitasato (1853-1931), bacteriologist.

Photo. & Engr.

2003, Nov. 4 *Perf. 13*

2868	A2194	80y multi	1.50	1.10
2869	A2194	80y multi	1.50	1.10

See Nos. 2907-2909.

Reversion of the Amami Islands to Japanese Control, 50th Anniv. — A2195

2003, Nov. 7 Photo.

2870	A2195	80y multi	1.50	1.10

A2196

A2197

New Year 2004 (Year of the Monkey)
A2198 A2199

2003, Nov. 14 *Perf. 13x13¼*

2871	A2196	50y multi	.95	.65
2872	A2197	80y multi	1.50	1.10

Photo. & Litho.

Perf. 13½x13¼

2873	A2198	50y +3y multi	1.00	.70
2874	A2199	80y +3y multi	1.60	1.10
		Nos. 2871-2874 (4)	5.05	3.55

Sheets of two containing Nos. 2871-2872 were lottery prizes.

Happy Face — A2199a

Sky — A2199b

Serpentine Die Cut 9¼x9

2003, Dec. 1 Photo.

Self-Adhesive

2874A	A2199a	80y multi + label	1.90	1.90

Serpentine Die Cut 6½x5½

Stamp + Label

Color of Japanese Inscription

2874B	A2199b	80y blue	1.90	1.90
2874C	A2199b	80y red orange	1.90	1.90
		Nos. 2874A-2874C (3)	5.70	5.70

Stamps and labels are separated by a line of rouletting on Nos. 2874B-2874C. Labels could be personalized. No. 2874A was printed in sheets of 4 stamps and 4 labels that sold for 500y, and sheets of 10 stamps and 10 labels that sold for 1000y. Nos. 2874B-2874C were printed in sheets containing five of each stamp and 10 labels that sold for 1000y.

Bubbles — A2199c

Bubbles — A2199d

Rose — A2199e

Serpentine Die Cut 6

2004, Jan. 23 Photo.

Self-Adhesive

2874D	A2199c	50y multi + label	1.25	1.25
2874E	A2199d	50y multi + label	1.25	1.25
2874F	A2199e	90y multi + label	1.90	1.90
		Nos. 2874D-2874F (3)	4.40	4.40

Stamps and labels are separated by a line of rouletting. Labels could be personalized. Nos. 2874D-2874E were printed in sheets containing ten of each stamp and 20 labels that sold for 1200y. No. 2874F was printed in a sheet of 20 stamps and 20 labels that sold for 2000y.

Science, Technology and Animation

Astro Boy — A2200

Bowman Doll — A2201

Hantaro Nagaoka A2202

H-II Rocket A2203

Morph 3 — A2204

Astro Boy — A2205

Astro Boy — A2206

Astro Boy — A2207

Super Jetter — A2208

Japanese Clock — A2209

Otomo — A2210

KAZ — A2211

Stratospheric Platform Airship — A2212

Super Jetter — A2213

Super Jetter — A2214

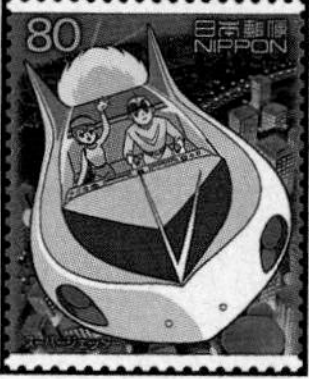

Super Jetter — A2215

2003-2004 Photo. *Perf. 13x13¼*

No.		Description	Unused	Used
2875		Vert. strip of 5	7.50	7.50
a.	A2200	80y multi	1.50	1.10
b.	A2201	80y multi	1.50	1.10
c.	A2202	80y multi	1.50	1.10
d.	A2203	80y multi	1.50	1.10
e.	A2204	80y multi	1.50	1.10
		Sheet, 2 #2875	15.00	15.00
2876		Sheet, #2875b-2875e, 2 each #2876a-2876c	15.00	15.00
a.	A2205	80y multi	1.50	1.10
b.	A2206	80y multi	1.50	1.10
c.	A2207	80y multi	1.50	1.10
2877		Vert. strip of 5	7.50	7.50
a.	A2208	80y multi	1.50	1.10
b.	A2209	80y multi	1.50	1.10
c.	A2210	80y multi	1.50	1.10
d.	A2211	80y multi	1.50	1.10
e.	A2212	80y multi	1.50	1.10
		Sheet, 2 #2875	15.00	15.00
2878		Sheet, #2877b-2877e, 2 each #2878a-2878c	15.00	15.00
a.	A2213	80y multi	1.50	1.10
b.	A2214	80y multi	1.50	1.10
c.	A2215	80y multi	1.50	1.10

Issued: Nos. 2875-2876, 12/16/03; Nos. 2877-2878, 1/23/04.

Science, Technology and Animation

Marvelous Melmo and Baby — A2216

Seishu Hanaoka (1760-1835), Surgeon — A2217

Wooden Microscope A2218

Jokichi Takamine (1854-1922), Chemist A2219

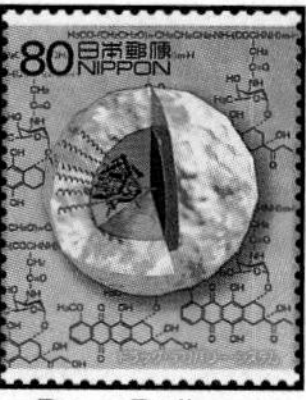

Drug Delivery System — A2220

Marvelous Melmo with Mother — A2221

Marvelous Melmo with Man — A2222

Marvelous Melmo and Others in Bottle — A2223

Science Ninja Team Gatchaman A2224

Proposed Perpetual Motion Machine of Michitaka Kume A2225

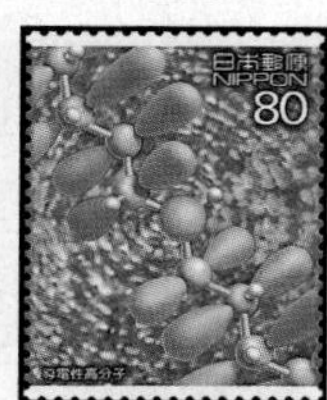

OHSUMI Satellite — A2226

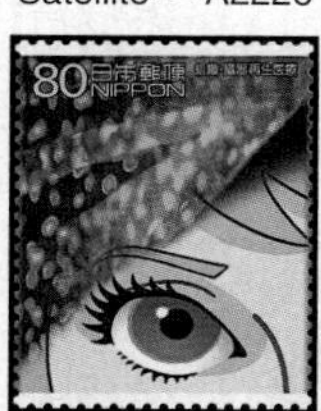

Conducting Polymer — A2227

Tissue and Organ Reproduction A2228

Science Ninja Team Gatchaman A2229

Science Ninja Team Gatchaman A2230

Science Ninja Team Gatchaman A2231

2004 Photo. *Perf. 13x13¼*

No.		Description	Unused	Used
2879		Vert. strip of 5	10.00	10.00
a.	A2216	80y multi	1.75	1.00
b.	A2217	80y multi	1.75	1.00
c.	A2218	80y multi	1.75	1.00
d.	A2219	80y multi	1.75	1.00
e.	A2220	80y multi	1.75	1.00
		Sheet, 2 #2879	19.00	19.00
2880		Sheet, #2879b-2879e, 2 each #2880a-2880c	19.00	19.00
a.	A2221	80y multi	1.75	1.00
b.	A2222	80y multi	1.75	1.00
c.	A2223	80y multi	1.75	1.00
2881		Vert. strip of 5	10.00	10.00
a.	A2224	80y multi	1.75	1.10
b.	A2225	80y multi	1.75	1.10
c.	A2226	80y multi	1.75	1.10
d.	A2227	80y multi	1.75	1.10
e.	A2228	80y multi	1.75	1.10
		Sheet, 2 #2881	19.00	19.00
2882		Sheet, #2881b-2881e, 2 each #2882a-2882c	19.00	19.00
a.	A2229	80y multi	1.75	1.10
b.	A2230	80y multi	1.75	1.10
c.	A2231	80y multi	1.75	1.10

Issued: Nos. 2879-2880, 2/23/04. Nos. 2881-2882, 3/23/04.

A2232

Hello Kitty — A2233

No. 2883: a, Red, white and blue flowers under chin. b, Red flower under chin, beige background. c, No flower under chin. d, Blue and red flowers under chin. e, Red flower under chin. f, Two blue flowers under chin. g, White flowers with green leaves under chin. h, Two pink flowers under chin. i, One blue flower under chin. j, Pink, yellow and green flower under chin.

No. 2884 — Head of Kitty with: a, Cherries. b, Bow. c, Strawberries. d, Blue flower. e, Spray of flowers.

Die Cut Perf. 13¼

2004, Feb. 6 Litho.

Self-Adhesive

No.		Description	Unused	Used
2883	A2232	Sheet of 10	9.50	
a.-j.		50y Any single	.95	.65
2884	A2233	Sheet of 5	7.75	
a.-e.		80y Any single	1.50	1.10

Uchu-no Sakura Gohiki-no Saru-zu, by Sosen Mori — A2234

Perf. 12½x12¾ Syncopated

2004, Apr. 20 Photo.

No.		Description	Unused	Used
2885	A2234	80y multi	1.40	1.00

Philatelic Week.

Japanese Racing Association, 50th Anniv. — A2235

Designs: No. 2886, Ten Point and Tosho Boy, 22nd Armia Memorial Stakes. No. 2887, Narita Brian, 61st Tolyo Yushun.

2004, May 28 *Perf. 13x13¼*

No.		Description	Unused	Used
2886		80y green & multi	1.50	1.10
2887		80y blue & multi	1.50	1.10
a.	A2235	Horiz. pair, #2886-2887	3.00	2.20

Police Law, 50th Anniv. — A2236

2004, June 21 *Perf. 13*

No.		Description	Unused	Used
2888		80y Police car	1.50	1.10
2889		80y Police motorcycle	1.50	1.10
a.	A2236	Horiz. pair, #2888-2889	3.00	2.20

Letter Writing Day — A2237

Designs: No. 2890, Donkichi with pencil. No. 2891, Hime (woman with letter). No. 2892, Shouchan (man with ski cap). No. 2893, Owl with letter.

No. 2894: a, Dove with letter, rainbow. b, Squirrel with wings, rainbow. c, Stork (round stamp). d, Hime with wings (oval stamp). e, Donkichi with wings, letter. f, Kuriko (elf in pink) with wings. g, Megami (woman in white) (oval stamp). h, Shouchan with wings. i, Squirrel with flowers, letter. j, Rabbit (round stamp).

2004, July 23 Photo. ***Perf. 13x13¼***

2890 A2237 50y multi .90 .65
2891 A2237 50y multi .90 .65
2892 A2237 50y multi .90 .65
2893 A2237 50y multi .90 .65
a. Horiz. strip of 4, #2890-2893 3.60 2.60
2894 Sheet of 10 14.50 14.50
a.-j. A2237 80y Any single 1.40 1.00
k. Booklet pane of 10, #2890-2893, 2 each #2894b, 2894e, 2894f 12.00 —
Complete booklet, #2894k 12.00
l. Souvenir sheet, #2890, #2894f 2.40 1.75

Nos. 2894c, 2894j are 30mm in diameter; No. 2894d is 28x37mm; No. 2894g is 28x40mm; No. 2894i is 28x29mm.

2004 Summer Olympics, Athens — A2238

Olympic rings and: No. 2895, Olympic Flame, Olympia. No. 2896, 2004 Athens Olympics emblem.

2004, Aug. 6 ***Perf. 13***

2895 80y multi 1.50 1.10
2896 80y multi 1.50 1.10
a. A2238 Horiz. pair, #2895-2896 3.00 2.20

Science, Technology and Animation

Mazinger-Z A2239

Steam Locomotive A2240

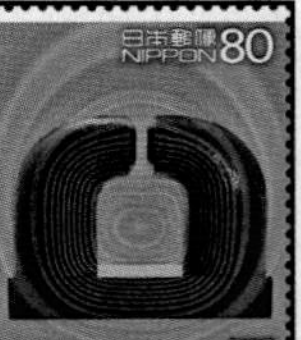

New KS Steel A2241

Shinkai 6500 Research Submarine A2242

Fuel Cell A2243

Mazinger-Z A2244

Mazinger-Z A2245

Mazinger-Z A2246

2004, Aug. 23 Photo. ***Perf. 13x13¼***

2897 Vert. strip of 5 7.50 7.50
a. A2239 80y multi 1.50 1.10
b. A2240 80y multi 1.50 1.10
c. A2241 80y multi 1.50 1.10
d. A2242 80y multi 1.50 1.10
e. A2243 80y multi 1.50 1.10
Sheet, 2 #2897 15.00 15.00
2898 Sheet, #2897b-2897e, 2 each #2898a-2898c 15.00 15.00
a. A2244 80y multi 1.50 1.10
b. A2245 80y multi 1.50 1.10
c. A2246 80y multi 1.50 1.10

Science, Technology and Animation

Doraemon A2247

Gennai Hiraga A2248

Mechanical Netsuke A2249

Television A2250

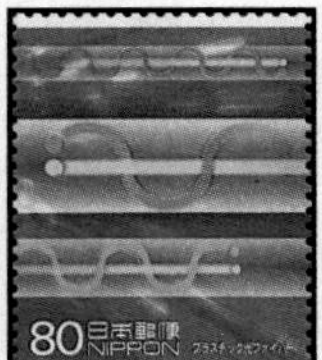

Optical Fiber A2251

Doraemon A2252

Doraemon A2253

Doraemon A2254

2004, Nov. 22 Photo. ***Perf. 13x13¼***

2899 Vert. strip of 5 8.00 8.00
a. A2247 80y multi 1.60 1.10
b. A2248 80y multi 1.60 1.10
c. A2249 80y multi 1.60 1.10
d. A2250 80y multi 1.60 1.10
e. A2251 80y multi 1.60 1.10
Sheet, 2, #2899 16.00 16.00
2900 Sheet, #2899b-2899e, 2 each #2900a-2900c 16.00 16.00
a. A2252 80y multi 1.60 1.10
b. A2253 80y multi 1.60 1.10
c. A2254 80y multi 1.60 1.10

Japan — United States Relationships, 150th Anniv. — A2255

Designs: No. 2901, Mt. Fuji, by Frederick Harris. No. 2902, Cafe, by Yasuo Kuniyoshi.

2004, Sept. 22 ***Perf. 13***

2901 80y multi 1.50 1.10
2902 80y multi 1.50 1.10
a. A2255 Horiz. pair, #2901-2902 3.00 2.20

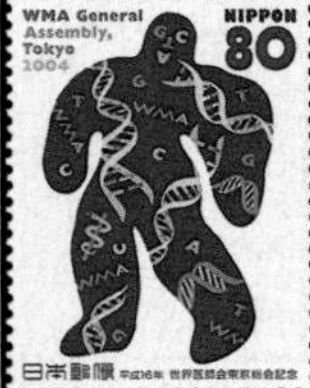

World Medical Association General Assembly, Tokyo — A2256

2004, Oct. 6 ***Perf. 12¾x13***

2903 A2256 80y multi 1.50 1.10

International Letter Writing Week Type of 2000

Hiroshige paintings from 53 Stations of the Tokaido Highway: 90y, Hiratsuka. 110y, Yokkaichi. 130y, Tsuchiyama.

2004, Oct. 8 ***Perf. 13¼***

2904 A2119 90y multi 1.75 1.25
2905 A2119 110y multi 2.00 1.40
2906 A2119 130y multi 2.40 1.60
Nos. 2904-2906 (3) 6.15 4.25

Cultural Pioneers Type of 2003

Designs: No. 2907, Lafcadio Hearn (1850-1904), writer. No. 2908, Isamu Noguchi (1904-88), sculptor. No. 2909, Masao Koga (1904-78), composer.

Litho. & Engr.

2004, Nov. 4 ***Perf. 12¾x13***

2907 A2194 80y multi 1.50 1.10
2908 A2194 80y multi 1.50 1.10
2909 A2194 80y multi 1.50 1.10
Nos. 2907-2909 (3) 4.50 3.30

A2257

A2258

New Year 2005 (Year of the Cock) A2259 A2260

2004, Nov. 15 Photo. ***Perf. 13x13¼***

2910 A2257 50y multi 1.00 .65
2911 A2258 80y multi 1.60 1.10

Photo. & Typo.

Perf. 13½x13¼

2912 A2259 50y +3y multi 1.10 .70
2913 A2260 80y +3y multi 1.75 1.10
Nos. 2910-2913 (4) 5.45 3.55

Miniature Sheet

Eto Calligraphy — A2261

Word "tori" in: a, Tensho style. b, Kinbun style (red). c, Kinbun style (black). d, Pictographic tensho style. e, Kana style. f, Sousho style. g, Kobun style (denomination at UR). h, Reisho style. i, Koukotsumoji style. j, Kobun style (denomination at LR).

Photo. & Embossed

2004, Dec. 1 ***Perf. 13***

2914 A2261 Sheet of 10 16.00 16.00
a.-j. 80y Any single 1.60 1.10

"Japan Post" — A2261a

A2261b

A2261c

Rose — A2261d

A2261e

A2261f

Die Cut Perf. 12½

2004, Dec. 15 **Photo.**

Stamp + Label

Denomination Color

2914K	A2261a	80y	rose	2.00	2.00
2914L	A2261a	80y	blue	2.00	2.00
2914M	A2261b	80y	lilac	2.00	2.00
2914N	A2261c	80y	green	2.00	2.00
2914O	A2261d	80y	rose	2.00	2.00
2914P	A2261e	80y	gray	2.00	2.00
2914Q	A2261f	80y	rose	2.00	2.00
	Nos. 2914K-2914Q (7)			14.00	14.00

Stamps and labels are separated by a line of rouletting. Labels could be personalized. Nos. 2914K-2914L were printed in sheets containing five of each stamp and 10 labels that sold for 1000y. Nos. 2914M-2914Q were printed in sheets of two of each stamps and 10 labels that sold for 1000y.

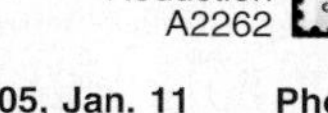

World Conference on Disaster Reduction A2262

2005, Jan. 11 **Photo.** ***Perf. 13***

2915 A2262 80y multi 1.60 1.10

Opening of Chubu Natl. Airport — A2263

2005, Feb. 1

2916 A2263 80y multi 1.60 1.10

Science, Technology and Animation

Time Bokan — A2264

Circular Loom — A2265

Bullet Train — A2266

Micromachines A2267

International Space Station — A2268

Time Bokan — A2269

Time Bokan — A2270

Time Bokan — A2271

2005, Mar. 23 **Photo.** ***Perf. 13x13¼***

2917	Vert. strip of 5	7.50	7.50
a.	A2264 80y multi	1.50	1.10
b.	A2265 80y multi	1.50	1.10
c.	A2266 80y multi	1.50	1.10
d.	A2267 80y multi	1.50	1.10
e.	A2268 80y multi	1.50	1.10
	Sheet, 2 #2917	15.00	15.00
2918	Sheet, #2917b-2917e, 2 each #2918a-2918c	15.00	15.00
a.	A2269 80y multi	1.50	1.10
b.	A2270 80y multi	1.50	1.10
c.	A2271 80y multi	1.50	1.10

Pokémon

Gonbe — A2272

Rayquaza A2273

Mew — A2274

Rizadon — A2275

Pikachu — A2276

2005, June 23 **Litho.** ***Perf. 13x13¼***

2919	Vert. strip of 5	6.25	6.25
a.	A2272 50y multi	.85	.85
b.	A2273 50y multi	.85	.85
c.	A2274 80y multi	1.50	1.50
d.	A2275 80y multi	1.50	1.50
e.	A2276 80y multi	1.50	1.50
	Sheet, 2 #2919	12.50	12.50

Self-Adhesive

Booklet Stamps

2919F	A2272 50y multi	1.40	1.40
i.	Booklet pane of 2	2.80	
2919G	A2276 80y multi	2.25	2.25
2919H	A2274 80y multi	2.25	2.25
j.	Booklet pane, #2919G-2919H	4.50	
	Complete booklet, #2919Fi, 2919Hj + 8 postal cards	18.00	

Complete booklet sold for 1000y.

Mobile Suit Gundam

Freedom Gundam and Kira Yamato — A2277

Justice Gundam and Athrun Zala — A2278

Gundam W — A2279

Hiiro — A2280

Kamille Bidan — A2281

Z Gundam
A2282

Zaku — A2283

Char
Aznable — A2284

Amuro
Ray — A2285

Gundam
A2286

2005, Aug. 1

2920	Sheet of 10	15.00	15.00
a.	A2277 50y multi	1.10	1.00
b.	A2278 50y multi	1.10	1.00
c.	A2279 50y multi	1.10	1.00
d.	A2280 50y multi	1.10	1.00
e.	A2281 80y multi	1.75	1.60
f.	A2282 80y multi	1.75	1.60
g.	A2283 80y multi	1.75	1.60
h.	A2284 80y multi	1.75	1.60
i.	A2285 80y multi	1.75	1.60
j.	A2286 80y multi	1.75	1.60

Expo 2005, Aichi — A2287

Designs: No. 2921, Earth and mammoth skull and tusks. No. 2922, Earth and mammoth.

2005, Mar. 25 Photo. *Perf. 13x13¼*

2921	80y multi	1.50	1.10
2922	80y multi	1.50	1.10
a.	A2287 Horiz. pair, #2921-2922	3.00	2.20

Daikei-shiyu-zu, by Jakuchu Itou — A2288

Perf. 12½x12¾ Syncopated

2005, Apr. 20

2923	A2288	80y multi	1.60	1.10

Philately Week.

Rotary International, Cent. — A2289

2005, Apr. 28 Litho. *Perf. 12¾x13*

2924	A2289	80y multi	1.60	1.10

Hodakadake
A2290

Hakusan-ichige
A2291

Yarigatake
A2292

Miyama-odamaki
A2293

2005, May 2 *Perf. 13¼*

2925	A2290	50y multi	1.10	.65
2926	A2291	50y multi	1.10	.65
2927	A2292	50y multi	1.10	.65
2928	A2293	50y multi	1.10	.65
a.		Horiz. strip of 4, #2925-2928	5.00	2.60

Japanese Alpine Club, cent.

Letter Writing Day — A2294

Designs: No. 2929, Owl on branch with envelope. No. 2930, Kuriko with letter. No. 2931, Squirrel with acorn. No. 2932, Rabbit and flowers.

No. 2933: a, Pigeon with pink letter. b, Donkichi in tree (round stamp). c, Castle and rainbow (oval stamp). d, Shochan with blue ski cap. e, Rabbit with pink letter (round stamp). f, Kuriko with flute on horse. g, Hime with bows in hair. h, Squirrel. i, Fox with letter (round stamp). j, Violets (oval stamp).

2005, July 22 Photo. *Perf. 13x13¼*

2929	A2294	50y multi	1.10	.65
2930	A2294	50y multi	1.10	.65
2931	A2294	50y multi	1.10	.65
2932	A2294	50y multi	1.10	.65
a.		Horiz. strip of 4, #2929-2932	4.75	2.60

2933	Sheet of 10	17.50	14.50
a.-j.	A2294 80y Any single	1.60	1.00
k.	Booklet pane of 10, #2929-2932, 2 each #2933d, 2933f, 2933g	15.00	—
	Complete booklet, #2933k	15.00	
l.	Souvenir sheet, #2932, #2933d	3.00	2.25

Nos. 2933a, 2933h are 28x29mm, Nos. 2933b, 2933e, 2933i are 30mm in diameter; No. 2933c, 2933j are 28x40mm.

Poetry Collections — A2295

Poets: No. 2934, Ono no Komachi. No. 2935, Fujiwara no Teika.

2005, Sept. 1 Litho. *Perf. 12¾x13*

2934		80y multi	1.50	1.10
2935		80y multi	1.50	1.10
a.	A2295	Horiz. pair, #2934-2935	3.00	2.25

Kokin Wakashu, 1100th anniv. (No. 2934), Shinkokin Wakashu, 800th anniv. (No. 2935).

Intl Astronautics Congress, Fukuoka — A2296

Designs: No. 2936, Himawari-6 satellite. No. 2937, H-IIA rocket launch.

2005, Oct. 3

2936		80y multi	1.40	1.00
2937		80y multi	1.40	1.00
a.	A2296	Horiz. pair, #2934-2935	2.80	2.00

Intl. Letter Writing Week Type of 2000

Hiroshige paintings from 53 Stations of the Tokaido Highway: 90y, Mariko. 110y, Minakuchi. 130y, Shinagawa.

2005, Oct. 7 Photo. *Perf. 13¼*

2938	A2119	90y multi	1.60	1.10
2939	A2119	110y multi	2.00	1.40
2940	A2119	130y multi	2.40	1.60
		Nos. 2938-2940 (3)	6.00	4.10

Souvenir Sheets

A2297

Greetings Stamps — A2298

No. 2941: a, Cyclamen. b, Elf and flower. c, Bear and bird. d, Owl, gorilla playing banjo. e, Snowman.

No. 2942: a, Santa Claus. b, Poinsettias and candle. c, Angel with gift. d, Hamster and strawberries. e, Owl, cat playing drums.

Litho. With Foil Application

Serpentine Die Cut 13¼

2005, Oct. 21

Self-Adhesive

2941	A2297 Sheet of 5	5.50	
a.-e.	50y Any single	1.10	.65

Serpentine Die Cut 13¼x13½

2942	A2298 Sheet of 5	8.50	
a.-e.	80y Any single	1.75	1.00

A2299

A2300

New Year 2006 (Year of the Dog)
A2301 A2302

2005, Nov. 15 Photo. *Perf. 13x13¼*

2943	A2299	50y multi	1.10	.60
2944	A2300	80y multi	1.75	1.00

Photo. & Typo.

Perf. 13¼

2945	A2301	50y +3y multi	1.20	.60
2946	A2302	80y +3y multi	1.90	1.00
		Nos. 2943-2946 (4)	5.95	3.20

Miniature Sheet

Germany — Japan Exchange Year — A2303

No. 2947: a, Ludwig van Beethoven. b, Benz automobile. c, Meissen porcelain figurine of Japanese man playing drum. d, Meissen porcelain figurine of female musician. e, Meissen porcelain figurine of woman on circus horse. f, Meissen porcelain figurine of a harlequin.

2005, Dec. 1 Photo. *Perf. 13*

2947	A2303 Sheet of 10, #a-b, 2 each #c-f	17.50	17.50
a.-f.	80y Any single	1.75	1.00

Miniature Sheet

Eto Calligraphy — A2304

Word "inu" in: a, Tensho style (connected lines). b, Kinbun style (on brown red panel). c, Pictograph (denomination at UL). d, Phonetic letters (2 lines unconnected, denomination at LR). e, Tensho style (2 red chops). f, Tensho style (blue half-circle). g, Symbolic characters (red). h, Semi-cursive style (red chop at L, denomination at LL). i, Semi-cursive style (oval chop in red at L). j, Koukotsumoji style (denomination at L, red chop at R).

Photo. & Embossed

2005, Dec. 1 ***Perf. 13x13¼***

2948 A2304 Sheet of 10 14.00 14.00
a.-j. 80y Any single 1.40 1.00

Animation

Galaxy Express 999 — A2305

No. 2949: a, Tetsuro and Galaxy Express 999 in flight. b, Matael and passenger cars. c, Claire holding book. d, The Conductor. e, Freija and Matael. f, Tetsuro and Moriki Yutaka. g, Emeraldas and Count Mecha. h, Herlock. i, Matael and galaxy. j, Galaxy Express 999.

2006, Feb. 1 Litho. ***Perf. 13x13¼***

2949 A2305 Sheet of 10 17.50 17.50
a.-j. 80y Any single 1.75 1.00

Detective Conan — A2306

No. 2950: a, Conan in green jacket. b, Conan wearing glasses, with woman in light blue jacket. c, With Shinichi, scratching chins. d, Ran holding letter. e, Dr. Agasa, Ayumi, front of car. f, Mitushiko, Genta, rear of car. g, Haibara Ai. h, Conan with backpack. i, Mysterious Thief Kid. j, Shinichi and Conan, city in background.

2006, Apr. 3 Litho. ***Perf. 13x13¼***

2950 A2306 Sheet of 10 17.50 17.50
a.-j. 80y Any single 1.75 1.00

International Exchanges and Friendships A2307

Designs: No. 2951, Rabbit and flowers. No. 2952, Children kissing. No. 2953, Bears and caught fish. No. 2954, Children's drawing of two animals. No. 2955, Chick, cat, dog, rabbit, squirrel and rocket.

2006, Mar. 1 Photo. ***Perf. 13***

2951 A2307 80y multi 1.60 1.00
2952 A2307 80y multi 1.60 1.00
2953 A2307 80y multi 1.60 1.00
2954 A2307 80y multi 1.60 1.00
2955 A2307 80y multi 1.60 1.00
a. Vert. strip of 5, #2951-2955 8.00 5.00
Sheet, 2 each #2951-2955 16.00 10.00

Morning Glories and Puppies, Door Painting by Okyu Maruyama — A2308

Designs: No. 2956, Morning glories. No. 2957, Puppies.

Perf. 13½x13 Syncopated

2006, Apr. 20 Photo.

2956 80y multi 1.75 1.10
2957 80y multi 1.75 1.10
a. A2308 Horiz. pair, #2956-2957 5.00 3.00

Philately Week.

Miniature Sheet

Australia-Japan Year of Exchange — A2309

No. 2958: a, Australian flag, Ayers Rock. b, Kangaroo and Ayers Rock. c, Sydney Opera House. d, Australian flag and Sydney Opera House. e, Fish of Great Barrier Reef. f, Heart Reef. g, Golden wattle flowers. h, Bottlebrush flowers. i, Koalas. j, Kookaburra.

2006, May 23 Photo. ***Perf. 13***

2958 A2309 Sheet of 10 17.50 17.50
a.-j. 80y Any single 1.75 1.10

Miniature Sheet

Sacred Sites and Pilgrimage Routes of the Kii Mountains World Heritage Site — A2310

No. 2959: a, Kumano Hongu-Taisha Shrine Building 3 (brown roof, part of stairs seen at bottom). b, Kumano Hongu-Taisha Shrine Building 4 (brown roof, full set of stairs at LR). c, Great Waterfall of Nachi. d, Overhead view of Kumano Nachi-Taisha Shrine (denomination at LL). e, Nachi Fire Festival. f, Seigantoji Temple (dark blue roof). g, Kongobuji Temple (blue green roof). h, Wooden Kongara-Doji-Ryuzo (statue, denomination at UL). i, Kinpusenji Temple (gray roof). j, Wooden Zao-Gongen-Ryuzo (statue, denomination at LL).

2006, June 23 ***Perf. 13x13¼***

2959 A2310 Sheet of 10 17.50 17.50
a.-j. 80y Any single 1.75 1.00

Miniature Sheets

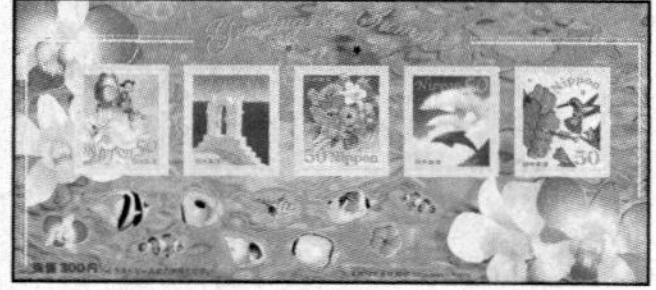

A2311

Greetings Stamps — A2312

No. 2960: a, Fairy and flower. b, Church bell. c, Flower bouquet and ribbons. d, Dolphin. e, Hibiscus and hummingbird.

No. 2961: a, Pink cattleya orchid. b, Fairy, flowers and trees. c, Flower and oranges. d, Parrot and flowers. e, Fairy with pail and orange flowers.

Litho. With Foil Application

Serpentine Die Cut 13¼

2006, June 30

Self-Adhesive

2960 A2311 Sheet of 5 5.25
a.-e. 50y Any single 1.00 .70

Serpentine Die Cut 13½

2961 A2312 Sheet of 5 8.75
a.-e. 80y Any single 1.75 1.25

No. 2960 sold for 300y; No. 2961 for 500y.

Taifu Iseno, Poet — A2313

Sadaijin Gotokudaijino, Poet — A2314

Mitsune Ooshikochino, Poet — A2315

Akahito Yamabeno, Poet — A2316

Naishi Suono, Poet — A2317

Poets and Poetry — A2318

No. 2963: a, Double Cherry Blossoms, by Yasuko Koyama. b, Iseno and poetry. c, Pale Morning Moon, by Keiso Mitsuoka. d, Gotokudaijino and poetry. e, White Chrysanthemum, by Shiko Miyazaki. f, Ooshikochino and poetry. g, Mt. Fuji, by Eiko Matsumoto. h, Yamabeno and poetry. i, Spring Night, by Soshu Miyake. j, Suono and poetry.

2006, July 21 Photo. *Perf. 13¼*

2962	Vert. strip of 5	5.75	5.75
a.	A2313 50y multi	1.10	.65
b.	A2314 50y multi	1.10	.65
c.	A2315 50y multi	1.10	.65
d.	A2316 50y multi	1.10	.65
e.	A2317 50y multi	1.10	.65
	Sheet, 2 #2962	11.50	11.50

Perf. 13

2963	A2318 Sheet of 10	16.00	16.00
a.-j.	80y Any single	1.60	1.00

Letter Writing Day.

Horizontal Lines and Colored Circles — A2318a

Die Cut Perf. 13¼

2006, Sept. 1 Litho.

Self-Adhesive

2963K	A2318a 80y multi	2.50	2.50

Printed in sheets of 10 that sold for 1000y. The image portion could be personalized. The image shown is a generic image.

Blue Flowers — A2318b

Pink Flowers — A2318c

Die Cut Perf. 13¼

2006, Sept. 1 Litho.

Self-Adhesive

2963L	A2318b 80y multi	2.50	2.50
2963M	A2318c 80y multi	2.50	2.50

Nos. 2963L-2963M were printed in sheets of 10, containing five of each stamp, that sold for 1000y. The image portions could be personalized. The images shown are generic images.

Accession to the United Nations, 50th Anniv. — A2319

Paintings by Toshiro Sawanuki: 90y, Glorious World To Come. 110y, Eternity.

2006, Sept. 29 Litho. *Perf. 13¾x14*

2964	A2319 90y multi	1.50	1.10
2965	A2319 110y multi	1.90	1.40

Miniature Sheet

Greetings — A2320

No. 2966: a, Mokara Lion's Gold orchid. b, Renanthera Singaporean orchid. c, Vanda Miss Joaquim orchid. d, Vanda Mimi Palmer orchid. e, Hollyhocks and Egret, by Hoitsu Sakai, horiz. f, Irises and Moorhens, by Sakai, horiz.

Litho. With Foil Application

2006, Oct. 3 *Die Cut Perf. 13½x13¾*

Self-Adhesive

2966	A2320 Sheet of 6	8.50	
a.-b.	50y Either single	.95	.65
c.-d.	80y Either single	1.50	1.10
e.	90y multi	1.60	1.10
f.	110y multi	2.00	1.40

Roulettes separate adjacent 50y and 80y stamps. No. 2966 sold for 500y. See Singapore Nos. 1225-1231.

Miniature Sheets

A2321

Scenes From Japanese Movies — A2322

No. 2967: a, Tange Sazen (scarred samurai, green). b, Carmen Kokyo-Ni-Kaeru (women waving, lilac). c, Ugetsu Monogatari (man and woman, maroon). d, Tokyo Monogatari (man and woman, brown). e, Shichinin-No-Samurai (helmeted samurai, deep green). f, Hawaii-No-Yoru (man and woman, olive green). g, Nemuri Kyoshiro (samurai, blue green). h, Guitar-Wo-Motta-Wataridori (man with guitar, blue). i, Miyamoto Musashi (swordsman, blue gray). j, Cupola-No-Aru-Machi (girl, brown).

No. 2968: a, Sailor-Fuku-To-Kikanju (woman with gun). b, Otoko-Ha-Tsuraiyo (man in light blue kimono). c, Kamata Koshin Kyoku (Three people). d, Yomigaeru Kinro (man in chair). e, Setouchi-Shonen-Yakyu-Dan (woman with baseball glove). f, HANA-BI (man standing). g, Shitsurakuen (Woman hugging man). h, Gamera (monster, denomination at UL). i, Tasogare Seibei (woman grooming man). j, Godzilla (monster, denomination at UR).

2006, Oct. 10 Photo. *Perf. 13*

2967	A2321 Sheet of 10	17.50	17.50
a.-j.	80y Any single	1.75	1.25
2968	A2322 Sheet of 10	17.50	17.50
a.-j.	80y Any single	1.75	1.25

Ikebana International Ninth World Convention — A2323

2006, Oct. 23 Litho. *Perf. 13x13¼*

Background Colors

2969	80y grn & lt grn	1.40	1.00
2970	80y red & yel	1.40	1.00
a.	A2323 Horiz. pair, #2969-2970	2.80	2.00

A2324

A2325

New Year 2007 (Year of the Pig)
A2326 A2327

2006, Nov. 1 Photo. *Perf. 13x13¼*

2971	A2324 50y multi	.85	.60
2972	A2325 80y multi	1.40	1.00

Photo. & Typo.

Perf. 13¼

2973	A2326 50y +3y multi	.90	.65
2974	A2327 80y +3y multi	1.40	1.00
	Nos. 2971-2974 (4)	4.55	3.25

New Year Greetings — A2327a

2006, Nov. 1 Photo. *Perf. 13¼*

Inscribed "'07 New Year"

Stamp + Label

Panel Color

2974A	A2327a 50y blue	1.10	1.10
2974B	A2327a 50y red violet	1.10	1.10
c.	Pair, #2974A-2974B + 2 labels	2.25	2.25

Labels could be personalized.
See Nos. 3010P-3010Q, 3074-3075.

Miniature Sheets

A2328

Greetings Stamps — A2329

No. 2975: a, Squirrel in mug. b, Bell with flowers. c, Clown with flower. d, Skating polar bear. e, Bear in Santa Claus suit, guitar, birds.

No. 2976: a, Cat in Santa Claus suit ringing bell. b, Fairy and cyclamen. c, Snowman with gift. d, Reindeer and star. e, Floral wreath.

Litho. with Foil Application

Die Cut Perf. 13½x13¼

2006, Nov. 24

Self-Adhesive

2975 A2328 Sheet of 5 5.25
a.-e. 50y Any single 1.00 .70

Die Cut Perf. 13

2976 A2329 Sheet of 5 8.75
a.-e. 80y Any single 1.75 1.25

No. 2975 sold for 300y; No. 2976 for 500y.

Miniature Sheet

Eto Calligraphy — A2330

No. 2977: a, Semicursive style (white background, red chop at lower left). b, Kinbun style (blue background). c, Reisho style (red background). d, Japanese cursive syllabary (white background, red chop at lower right, character with small arc at top). e, Kinbun style (white background, red chop at lower right, character with funnel-shaped line at top). f, Kinbun style (red character). g, Kinbun style (white background, red chop at lower left, character with flat line at top. h, Kinbun style (white background. red chop at lower right, character with large blotch at top). i, Tensho style (white background, red chop at lower left, character with long curved arc and circle at top) j, Reisho style (white background, red chop at lower right, character with dot and straight line at top).

Litho. & Embossed

2006, Dec. 1 ***Perf. 13x13¼***

2977 A2330 Sheet of 10 17.50 17.50
a.-j. 80y Any single 1.75 1.25

Miniature Sheet

A2331

Japanese Antarctic Research Expeditions, 50th Anniv. — A2332

No. 2978: a, Observation ship Fuji. b, Spotter plane. c, Adult emperor penguin and chick. d, Adult emperor penguins and five chicks. e, Observation ship Soya and Adelie penguins. f, Adult Adelie penguins and chick. g, Dog, Jiro, in snow, dog team. h, Dog, Taro, standing, dog sled. i, Scientist, observation ship Shirase. j, Snowmobile with cabin.

No. 2979: a, Snowmobile with cabin (26x28mm). b, Spotter plane (28mm diameter). c, Soya and dog sled (34x26mm). d, Weddell seal (28x23mm ellipse). e, Head of emperor penguin (26x37mm oval). f, Two Adelie penguins (26x28mm). g, Dog, Taro, standing with mouth open (28mm diameter). h, Emperor penguin chicks (28mm diameter). i, Adult emperor penguin and chick (26x28mm). j, Dog, Jiro, in snow (26x37mm oval).

2007, Jan. 23 Litho. ***Perf. 13***

2978 A2331 Sheet of 10 14.00 14.00
a.-j. 80y Any single 1.40 1.00

Self-Adhesive

Die Cut Perf. 13¾x13½

2979 A2332 Sheet of 10 14.00
a.-j. 80y Any single 1.40 1.00

Animation

Miniature Sheet

Neon Genesis Evangelion — A2333

No. 2980: a, Evangelion Unit 01. b, Shinji Ikari. c, Rei Ayanami. d, Evangelion Unit 00. e, Soryu Asuka Langley. f, Evangelion Unit 02. g, Rei Ayanami and Soryu Asuka Langley. h, Misato Katsuragi. i, Kawora Nagisa. j, Sachiel, the third angel.

2007, Feb. 23 ***Perf. 13x13¼***

2980 A2333 Sheet of 10 17.50 17.50
a.-j. 80y Any single 1.75 1.25

Animation

Miniature Sheet

Future Boy Conan — A2334

No. 2981: a, Conan (with name). b, Lana (with name). c, Lana (without name). d, Conan (without name). e, Monsley and airplane. f, Lepka. g, Jimsy and Umaso. h, Dyce on running robot. i, Dr. Lao and hovering craft. j, Grandpa.

2007, June 22 Litho. ***Perf. 13x13¼***

2981 A2334 Sheet of 10 17.50 17.50
a.-j. 80y Any single 1.75 1.25

World Heritage Sites

Miniature Sheet

Sacred Sites and Pilgrimage Routes of the Kii Mountains World Heritage Site — A2335

No. 2982: a, Yoshino Mikumari Shrine, cherry blossoms at left. b, Pictoral and rope decoration at Yoshino Mikumari shrine. c, Omine-Okugake-Michi trail. d, Kumano Hayatama-Taisha Shrine (black-roofed building with red trim). e, Kumano Hayatama-Taisha Shrine, diff. f, Wooden icon of Kumano-Fusumino-Okami-Zazo. g, Cherry trees in bloom at Kumano Sankei-Michi Nakahechi. h, Stone sculpture of Emperor Kazan riding ox and horse. i, Kongo-Sanmaiin Temple. j, Steps to Kong-Sanmain Temple.

2007, Mar. 23 Photo. ***Perf. 13x13¼***

2982 A2335 Sheet of 10 17.50 17.50
a.-j. 80y Any single 1.75 1.25

World Heritage Sites

Miniature Sheet

Shiretoko World Heritage Site — A2336

No. 2983: a, Lake and mountain, cloudless sky. b, Lake and mountain, cloud in sky. c, Blakiston's fish owl. d, Sea ice, Mt. Rausu. e, Cherry blossoms. f, Brown bear. g, Harbor seal. h, Ezo deer. i, Sea eagle. j, Shiretoko violets (white and yellow flowers).

2007, July 6 Photo. ***Perf. 13x13¼***

2983 A2336 Sheet of 10 17.50 17.50
a.-j. 80y Any single 1.75 1.25

Sleeping Boar, by Ippo Mori — A2337

Boar Loping Across Fields, by Mori — A2338

Sparrow, by Mori — A2339

Cherry Blossoms, by Mori — A2340

Bird Flock, by Mori — A2341

Great Tits Sitting In a Japanese Bush Clover, by Mori — A2342

Perf. 13¼x13 Syncopated

2007, Apr. 20			**Photo.**
2984 A2337 80y multi		1.40	1.00
2985 A2338 80y multi		1.40	1.00
a.	Horiz. pair, #2984-2985	2.80	2.00
	Sheet, 5 #2985a	14.00	14.00
2986 A2339 80y multi		1.40	1.00
2987 A2340 80y multi		1.40	1.00
2988 A2341 80y multi		1.40	1.00
2989 A2342 80y multi		1.40	1.00
a.	Vert. strip of 4, #2986-2989	5.60	4.00
	Sheet, 2 each #2985-2989	14.00	14.00
	Nos. 2984-2989 (6)	8.40	6.00

Miniature Sheet

Japan - India Friendship Year — A2343

No. 2990: a, Taj Mahal. b, Taj Mahal and camels. c, Bengal tiger. d, Peacock. e, Buddhist monastery, Sanchi, India. f, Statue of goddess, Sanchi. g, Painting of Indian woman facing left. h, Calico print of Indian facing right. i, Indian folk dancer. j, Character from Kathakali, Indian dance drama.

2007, May 23			***Perf. 13***
2990 A2343	Sheet of 10	14.00	14.00
a.-j.	80y Any single	1.40	1.00

Tsurayuki Kino, Poet — A2344

Empress Jito, Poet — A2345

Dayu Sarumaru, Poet — A2346

Kanemasa Minamotono, Poet — A2347

Sanuki Nijoinno, Poet — A2348

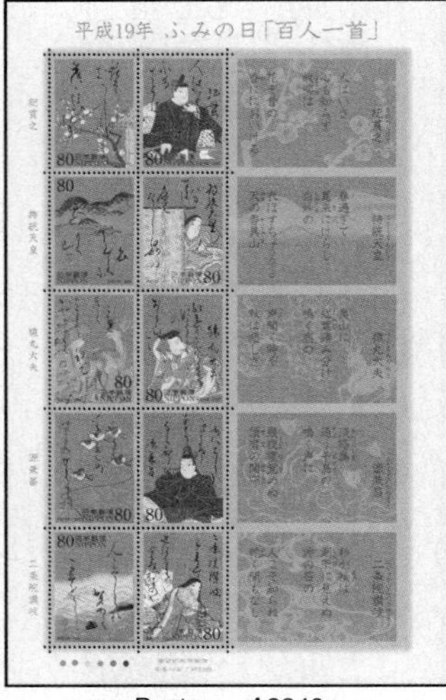

Poetry — A2349

No. 2996 — Poetry in Japanese calligraphy and: a, Plum blossoms. b, Tsurayuki Kino. c, Mount Kagu. d, Empress Jito. e, Deer. f, Dayu Sarumaru. g, Plovers. h, Kanemasa Minamotono. i, Stone in sea. j, Sanuki Nijoinno.

2007, July 23	**Photo.**		***Perf. 13½***
2991 A2344 50y multi		1.10	.70
2992 A2345 50y multi		1.10	.70
2993 A2346 50y multi		1.10	.70
2994 A2347 50y multi		1.10	.70
2995 A2348 50y multi		1.10	.70
a.	Vert. strip of 5, #2991-2995	5.75	4.00

Perf. 13

2996 A2349	Sheet of 10	17.50	17.50
a.-j.	80y Any single	1.75	1.25

Letter Writing Day.

Miniature Sheet

11th World Track and Field Championships, Osaka — A2350

No. 2997: a, Dai Tamesue (athlete 545), hurdler. b, Kumiko Ikeda (athlete 426), sprinter. c, Yuzo Kanemaru (athlete 300), runner. d, Shingo Suetsugu (athlete 526), runner. e, Kayoko Fukushi (athlete 422), runner. f, Masato Naito running over hurdle. g, Naoyuki Daigo high jumping. h, Kenji Narisako (athlete 531), hurdler. i, Daichi Sawano pole vaulting. j, Koji Murofushi (athlete 774), hammer throw.

2007, Aug. 23	**Litho.**		***Perf. 13x13¼***
2997 A2350	Sheet of 10	17.50	17.50
a.-j.	80y Any single	1.75	1.25

Miniature Sheet

Diplomatic Relations Between Japan and Thailand, 120th Anniv. — A2351

No. 2998: a, Maple leaves, bamboo. b, Cherry blossoms. c, Ratchaphruek (yellow flower) blossom. d, Rhynchostylis gigantea (purple and white orchids). e, Mother-of-pearl elephant. f, Mother-of-pearl flower. g, Thai dancer. h, Statue, Wat Phra Keo. i, Elephant with head at left, from Toshogu Shrine, Japan, horiz. j, Elephant with head at right, from Toshogu Shrine, horiz.

Die Cut Perf. and Serpentine Die Cut

2007, Sept. 26			**Litho.**

Self-Adhesive

2998 A2351	Sheet of 10	14.00	14.00
a.-j.	80y Any single	1.40	1.00

Vertical stamps are die cut perf. 13 at top and bottom, serpentine die cut 10¼ on side adjacent to another stamp, and die cut perf. 12½ on remaining side. Horizontal stamps are die cut perf. 13 at top and bottom, serpentine die cut 10¼ on side adjacent to another stamp, and die cut perf. 12¾ on remaining side.

See Thailand No. 2316.

International Letter Writing Week Type of 2000

Hiroshige paintings from 53 Stations of the Tokaido Highway: 90y, Hodogaya. 110y, Arai. 130y, Kusatsu.

2007, Sept. 28	**Litho.**		***Perf. 14***
2999 A2119 90y multi		1.60	1.10
3000 A2119 110y multi		1.90	1.40
3001 A2119 130y multi		2.25	1.60
	Nos. 2999-3001 (3)	5.75	4.10

Mandarin Duck A2352

Eastern Turtle Dove A2353

2007, Oct. 1	**Photo.**		***Perf. 13x13½***
3002 A2352 50y multi		.85	.60
3003 A2353 80y multi		1.40	1.00

Miniature Sheets

A2354

Establishment of Japan Post Corporation — A2355

No. 3004: a, Baron Hisoka Maejima (red panels). b, Japan #2 (red panels). c, Post office counter (orange panels). d, Postal workers loading mail coach (dark red panels). e, Postal saving counter (green panels). f, People at post office counters (blue panels).

No. 3005 — Paintings of flowers: a, Sunflower, by Hoitsu Sakai. b, Confederate Roses, by Sakai. c, Chrysanthemums, by Sakai. d, Maple Leaves, by Kiitsu Suzuki (showing branch). e, Maple Leaves, by Suzuki (no branch). f, Camellia, by Sakai. g, Cherry Tree, by Sakai (bird in tree). h, Tree Peony, by Sakai. i, Iris, by Sakai, j, Hydrangeas, by Sakai.

2007, Oct. 1 Photo. *Perf. 13¼*

3004	A2354	Sheet of 10, #a-b, 2 each #c-f	14.00	14.00
a.-f.		80y Any single	1.40	1.00
3005	A2355	Sheet of 10	14.00	14.00
a.-j.		80y Any single	1.40	1.00

Miniature Sheet

Intl. Skills Festival For All — A2356

No. 3006: a, Computer operator and robot. b, Computer operator. c, Plasterer and Geisha. d, Plasterer and pillar. e, Pastry chef and cake. f, Pastry chef and bowls. g, Flower arranger and flowers. h, Flower arranger holding scissors. i, Sheet metal worker and automobile. j, Sheet metal worker hammering metal.

2007, Oct. 23 Litho. *Perf. 13*

3006	A2356	Sheet of 10	17.50	17.50
a.-j.		80y Any single	1.75	1.25

A2357 A2358

New Year 2008 (Year of the Rat)
A2359 A2360

2007, Nov. 1 Photo. *Perf. 13x13½*

3007	A2357	50y multi	.90	.60
3008	A2358	80y multi	1.40	1.00

Photo. & Typo.

Perf. 13¼

3009	A2359	50y +3y multi	.95	.65
3010	A2360	80y +3y multi	1.50	1.10
		Nos. 3007-3010 (4)	4.75	3.35

Diamonds — A2360a

Die Cut Perf. 13¼

2007, Nov. 1 Litho.

Self-Adhesive

Green Diamonds

Color of Country Name

3010A	A2360a	50y blue	4.00	4.00
3010B	A2360a	50y green	4.00	4.00
3010C	A2360a	50y red	4.00	4.00
3010D	A2360a	50y purple	4.00	4.00
3010E	A2360a	50y black	4.00	4.00

Blue Diamonds

3010F	A2360a	80y blue	3.50	3.50
3010G	A2360a	80y green	3.50	3.50
3010H	A2360a	80y red	3.50	3.50
3010I	A2360a	80y purple	3.50	3.50
3010J	A2360a	80y black	3.50	3.50

Nos. 3010A-3010E were printed in sheets of 10, containing two of each stamp, that sold for 900y. Nos. 3010F-3010J were printed in sheets of 10, containing two of each stamp, that sold for 1200y. The image portion could be personalized. The image shown is a generic image.

New Year Greetings Type of 2006

2007, Nov. 1 Photo. *Perf. 13¼*

Inscribed "'08 New Year"

Stamp + Label

Panel Color

3010P	A2327a	50y red violet	2.00	2.00
3010Q	A2327a	50y orange	2.00	2.00
r.		Pair, #3010P-3010Q + 2 labels	4.00	4.00

Labels could be personalized.

Miniature Sheets

A2361

Greetings Stamps — A2362

No. 3011: a, White buildings. b, Fairies on flying swans. c, Santa Claus. d, Flowers and snow-covered trees. e, Cat and candy cane.

No. 3012: a, Santa Claus and reindeer. b, Fairy and flowers. c, Snowman with green cap. d, Strawberries. e, Snowman and flying reindeer.

2007, Nov. 26 Litho. *Die Cut Perf.*

Self-Adhesive

3011	A2361	Sheet of 5	4.50	
a.-e.		50y Any single	.90	.60

Die Cut Perf. 13

3012	A2362	Sheet of 5	7.50	
a.-e.		80y Any single	1.50	1.10

Miniature Sheet

Edo Calligraphy — A2363

No. 3013 — Charcters for "rat": a, In Kinbun style (red character). b, Black character with three long vertical lines at top, with red chop at LR. c, In Tensho style (gold character on red and brown background). d, In Reisho style (black character resembling a "3" with line through it, with red chop at LR). e, In Shoden style (gold character on blue and pink background). f, In Kana style (black characters resembling "12" with a check mark, with red chop at LR). g, In Reisho style (black characters, with red chop at LL). h, In Sosho style (black character with pink lines, with red chop at LL). i, Black character resembling stick figure with raised arms, with red chop at LR. j, In Kinbun style (black character with five short vertical lines at top, red chop at LL).

Litho. & Embossed

2007, Dec. 3 *Perf. 13*

3013	A2363	Sheet of 10	17.50	17.50
a.-j.		80y Any single	1.75	1.25

Mt. Fuji A2364

Mt. Fuji A2365

Mt. Fuji A2366

Mt. Fuji A2367

Mt. Fuji A2368

Bamboo — A2369

Someiyoshino Blossoms — A2370

Hydrangea Blossoms — A2371

Maple Leaves A2372

Narcissuses — A2373

2008, Jan. 23 Litho. *Perf. 13¾x14*

3014	Sheet of 10	17.50	17.50
a.	A2364 80y multi	1.75	1.10
b.	A2365 80y multi	1.75	1.10
c.	A2366 80y multi	1.75	1.10
d.	A2367 80y multi	1.75	1.10
e.	A2368 80y multi	1.75	1.10
f.	A2369 80y multi	1.75	1.10
g.	A2370 80y multi	1.75	1.10
h.	A2371 80y multi	1.75	1.10
i.	A2372 80y multi	1.75	1.10
j.	A2373 80y multi	1.75	1.10

Yokoso! Japan Weeks.

Souvenir Sheet

New Year 2008 (Year of the Rat) — A2374

No. 3015: a, Two rats. b, One rat.

2008, Jan. 28 Photo. *Perf. 13*

3015 A2374 Sheet of 2 2.50 2.50
a. 50y multi 1.00 .50
b. 80y multi 1.50 .75

Miniature Sheet

Animated Folktales — A2375

No. 3016: a, Man on horse, cherry trees, pagoda. b, Man in cherry tree. c, Moon Princess in bamboo stump, woodsman with ax. d, Moon Princess, flying horse and wagon, archers. e, Four statues in snow. f, Two statues in snow, man with basket. g, Boy in ship. h, Demons. i, Woman carrying roll of cloth. j, Man, woman, crane.

2008, Feb. 22 Litho. *Perf. 13*

3016 A2375 Sheet of 10 17.50 17.50
a.-j. 80y Any single 1.75 1.25

Folktales "The Old Man Who Made Cherry Trees Blossom" (#3016a-3016b), "The Moon Princess" (#3016c-3016d), "Six Little Statues" (#3016e-3016f), "The Peach Boy" (#3016g-3016h), "The Grateful Crane" (#3016i-3016j).

Miniature Sheet

Astronomical Society of Japan, Cent. — A2376

No. 3017: a, Jupiter. b, Saturn. c, Spiral galaxy. d, Suzaku X-ray satellite. e, Hayabusa probe. f, Asteroids and Earth. g, Subaru Telescope. h, Stars. i, Mars. j, Nobeyama Radio Telescope.

2008, Mar. 21

3017 A2376 Sheet of 10 17.50 17.50
a.-j. 80y Any single 1.75 1.25

Miniature Sheet

Diplomatic Relations Between Japan and Indonesia, 50th Anniv. — A2377

No. 3018: a, Kelimutu Volcano, Indonesia. b, Mt. Fuji, Japan, and cherry blossoms. c, Borobudur, Indonesia. d, Toji Temple, Kyoto. e, Rafflesia arnoldii. f, Cherry blossoms. g, Angklung (Indonesian musical instrument). h, Gaku biwa (Japanese musical instrument). i, Red arowana fish, horiz. j, Three koi, horiz.

2008, June 23 Photo. *Perf. 13*

3018 A2377 Sheet of 10 15.00 15.00
a.-j. 80y Any single 1.50 1.10

See Indonesia Nos. 2135-2139.

Small Bird in Cherry Blossom, by Seitei Watanabe A2378

Butterfly in Peony Branch, by Watanabe A2379

Egrets in the Rain Beneath Willow Trees, by Watanabe A2380

Grapes, by Watanabe A2381

Sea Birds on a Rocky Crag, by Watanabe A2382

Perf. 13½x13 Syncopated

2008, Apr. 18 Photo.

3019 A2378 80y multi 1.75 1.25
3020 A2379 80y multi 1.75 1.25
3021 A2380 80y multi 1.75 1.25
3022 A2381 80y multi 1.75 1.25
3023 A2382 80y multi 1.75 1.25
a. Vert. strip of 5, #3019-3023 8.75 8.75
Sheet, 2 #3023a 17.50 17.50

Philately Week.

See note after No. Z827 in the Prefecture Stamp listings.

Miniature Sheet

Home Towns — A2383

No. 3024 — Paintings by Taiji Harada of views of towns: a, Water Shield (Yamamoto District, Akita prefecture). b, Bell of Time (Kawago, Saitama prefecture). c, Enjoying the Evening Cool (Gujo, Gifu prefecture). d, The Little Electric Train (Choshi, Chiba prefecture). e, Sea of the Heart (Shozu District, Kagawa prefecture). f, Lake in the Evening Sun (Gamo District, Shiga prefecture). g, Tanabata Dolls (Matsumoto, Nagano prefecture). h, Town of Outdoor Warehouses (Ise, Mie prefecture). i, The Farm Clock (Aki, Kochi prefecture). j, Late Summer Heat in the Street (Hakusan, Ishikawa prefecture).

2008, May 2 Photo. *Perf. 13*

3024 A2383 Sheet of 10 16.00 16.00
a.-j. 80y Any single 1.60 1.25

Hideyo Noguchi Africa Prize — A2384

2008, May 23 Litho. *Perf. 13*

3025 80y Noguchi 1.60 1.25
3026 80y Map of Africa 1.60 1.25
a. A2384 Horiz. pair, #3025-3026 3.25 2.50

Miniature Sheet

National Afforestation Campaign — A2385

No. 3027 — Scenes from Akita prefecture: a, Aleutian avens and Mt. Moriyoshi, denomination at UL. b, Aleutian avens and Mt. Moriyoshi, denomination at UR. c, Fringed galax flowers, denomination at LL. d, Fringed galax flowers, denomination at LR. e, Autumn leaves, denomination at LL. f, Autumn leaves, denomination at UR. g, Beech forest in autumn, denomination in UL. h, Beech forest in autumn, denomination in UR. i, Weigela. j, Waterfall.

2008, June 13 Photo. *Perf. 13*

3027 A2385 Sheet of 10 9.25 9.25
a.-j. 50y Any single .90 .65

Miniature Sheet

Year of Exchange Between Japan and Brazil — A2386

No. 3028: a, Roasted coffee beans, seal of Brazilian vice-consulate in Kobe. b, Coffee cherries, ship. c, Christ the Redeemer Statue, Rio de Janeiro. d, Sugarloaf Mountain, Rio de Janeiro. e, Iguaçu Falls, denomination at UL. f, Iguaçu Falls, denomination at UR. g, Houses, denomination at LL. h, Houses, denomination at LR. i, Butterflies. j, Toucan.

2008, June 18 Litho. *Perf. 13*

3028	A2386	Sheet of 10	16.00	16.00
a.-j.		80y Any single	1.60	1.25

See Brazil No. 3051.

Miniature Sheet

Publication of *Anne of Green Gables,* by Lucy Maud Montgomery, Cent. — A2387

No. 3029: a, Anne holding buttercups. b, Green Gables House. c, Matthew Cuthbert, wearing hat, vert. d, Marilla Cuthbert, wearing hat, vert. e, Anne, Diana Barry holding hands, vert. f, Diana, vert. g, Anne in black dress, vert. h, Anne and Gilbert Blythe, vert. i, Matthew Cuthbert, without hat, vert. j, Anne, Marilla Cuthbert, vert.

Perf. 13¼x13 (#3029a-3029b), 13x13¼

2008, June 20

3029	A2387	Sheet of 10	16.00	16.00
a.-j.		80y Any single	1.60	1.25

See Canada Nos. 2276-2278.

Lily — A2388

Rugosa Rose — A2389

Rhododendron A2390

Safflower A2391

Gentian — A2392

Lily — A2393

Rugosa Rose A2394

Rhododendron A2395

Safflower A2396

Gentian A2397

2008, July 1 Photo. *Perf. 13¼*

3030	A2388	50y multi	1.10	.70
3031	A2389	50y multi	1.10	.70
3032	A2390	50y multi	1.10	.70
3033	A2391	50y multi	1.10	.70
3034	A2392	50y multi	1.10	.70
a.		Vert. strip of 5, #3030-3034	5.50	5.00
3035	A2393	80y multi	1.75	1.25
3036	A2394	80y multi	1.75	1.25
3037	A2395	80y multi	1.75	1.25
3038	A2396	80y multi	1.75	1.25
3039	A2397	80y multi	1.75	1.25
a.		Vert. strip of 5, #3035-3039	8.75	8.00
		Nos. 3030-3039 (10)	14.25	9.75

Flowers of Kanagawa, Hokkaido, Fukushima, Yamagata and Nagano prefectures.

Miniature Sheet

Hokkaido Local Autonomy Law, 60th Anniv. — A2398

No. 3040: a, Lake Toya, cranes (32x39mm). b, Goryokaku Fortress (28x33mm). c, Hills around Biei (28x33mm). d, Sea angel (28x33mm). e, Otaru Canal (28x33mm).

2008, July 1 *Perf. 13¼ (#3040a), 13*

3040	A2398	Sheet of 5	7.50	7.50
a.-e.		80y Any single	1.50	1.10

Miniature Sheet

G8 Summit, Toyako — A2399

No. 3041: a, Mt. Yotei (stamp #1). b, Showa Shinzan (stamp #2). c, Mt. Yotei and Lake Toya (stamp #3). d, Mt. Yotei and Fukidashi Park (stamp #4). e, Mt. Eniwa and Lake Shikotsu (stamp #5). f, Pink Japanese wood poppies (stamp #6). g, Squirrel (stamp #7). h, Beardtongue flowers (stamp #8). i, Mountain ash leaves and berries (stamp #9). j, Northern fox (stamp #10).

2008, July 7 Litho. *Perf. 13¾x14*

3041	A2399	Sheet of 10	15.00	15.00
a.-j.		80y Any single	1.50	1.10

Lady Shikibu Murasaki, Poet — A2400

Sanekata Fujiwara, Poet — A2401

Lady Shonagon Sei, Poet — A2402

Kinto Dainagon, Poet — A2403

Lady Shikibu Izumi, Poet — A2404

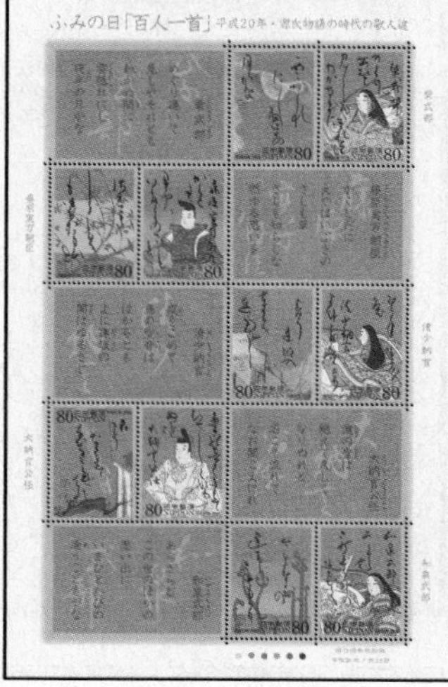

Poetry — A2405

No. 3047 — Poetry in Japanese calligraphy and: a, Moon behind cloud. b, Lady Shikibu Murasaki. c, Mugwort. d, Sanekata Fujiwara. e, Waterfall. f, Lady Shonagon Sei. g, Barrier. h, Kinto Dainagon. i, Bare branches. j, Lady Shikibu Izumi.

2008, July 23 Photo. *Perf. 13¼*

3042	A2400	50y multi	1.10	.65
3043	A2401	50y multi	1.10	.65
3044	A2402	50y multi	1.10	.65
3045	A2403	50y multi	1.10	.65
3046	A2404	50y multi	1.10	.65
a.		Vert. strip of 5, #3042-3046	5.50	3.75

Perf. 12¾x13

3047	A2405	Sheet of 10	17.50	17.50
a.-j.		80y Any single	1.75	1.10

Letter Writing Day.

Miniature Sheets

A2406

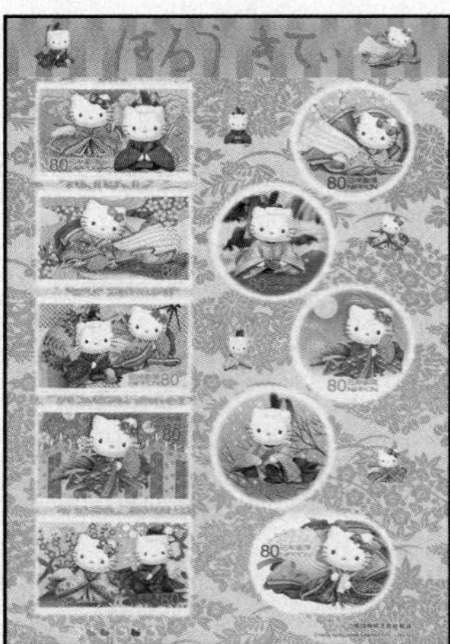

Hello Kitty — A2407

No. 3048 — Hello Kitty characters with: a, Gold denomination at UR. b, Green denomination at UR. c, Yellow denomination at UL, Kitty with pink flowers on head. d, Yellow denomination at UR, Kitty wearing green patterned kimono. e, Green denomination at UL, Kitty wearing black kimono. f, Green denomination at UL, Kitty with pink and blue flowers on head. g, Green denomination at UL, Kitty with bow and flowers on head. h, Yellow denomination at UL, Kitty wearing dark green kimono. i, Green denomination at UL, Kitty wearing brown kimono. j, Green denomination at UL, Kitty with purple and green flowers on head.

No. 3049 — Hello Kitty characters with: a, Green denomination at LL (41x27mm). b, Gold denomination at LR, one Kitty with two pink flowers on head (41x27mm). c, Gold denomination at LR, Kitty at right with purple and green flowers on head (41x27mm). d, Green denomination at UR (41x27mm). e, Gold denomination at LR, Kitty at left with bow and flower on head (41x27mm). f, Blue denomination (34mm diameter). g, Gold denomination, Kitty wearing gray kimono (34mm diameter). h, Gold denomination, Kitty holding fan (34mm diameter). i, Gold denomination, Kitty with snowflakes in background (34mm diameter). j, Blue denomination (40x28mm oval stamp).

Die Cut Perf. and Serpentine Die Cut (see note)

2008, July 23 — Litho.

Self-Adhesive

3048 A2406	Sheet of 10	9.50	
a.-j.	50y Any single	.95	.65

Die Cut Perf. 13x13¼ (#3049a-3049e), Die Cut Perf.

3049 A2407 Sheet of 10	15.00	15.00
a.-j. 80y Any single	1.50	1.10

Stamps on No. 3048 are arranged in five rows of se-tenant pairs. Each pair is die cut perf. 13¾ at top and bottom, die cut perf. 13½ on the outer sides, and serpentine die cut 11¼ between the stamps in the pair.

Love That Meets the Night, by Utamaro
A2408

Yatsumi Bridge, by Hiroshige
A2409

Mannen Bridge, Fukagawa, by Hiroshige
A2410

Koshiro Matsumoto IV as Gorobe Sakanaya of San'ya, by Sharaku
A2411

Hanazuma From Hyogoya, by Utamaro
A2412

Ayase River at Kanegafuchi, by Hiroshige
A2413

Tsukiji Hongan-ji Temple, Teppozu, by Hiroshige
A2414

Hikosaburo Bando III as Sanai Sagisaka, by Sharaku
A2415

Roko of Tatsumi, by Utamaro
A2416

Kameido Plum Gardens, by Hiroshige
A2417

2008, Aug. 1 — Litho. — *Perf. 13¼*

3050	Sheet of 10	17.50	17.50
a.	A2408 80y multi	1.75	1.25
b.	A2409 80y multi	1.75	1.25
c.	A2410 80y multi	1.75	1.25
d.	A2411 80y multi	1.75	1.25
e.	A2412 80y multi	1.75	1.25
f.	A2413 80y multi	1.75	1.25
g.	A2414 80y multi	1.75	1.25
h.	A2415 80y multi	1.75	1.25
i.	A2416 80y multi	1.75	1.25
j.	A2417 80y multi	1.75	1.25

Life in Edo (Tokyo).

Miniature Sheet

Hometown Festivals — A2418

No. 3051: a, Streamers for Sendai Tanabata Festival, Miyagi prefecture (light green background, denomination at UR). b, Streamers for Sendai Tanabata Festival (light green background, denomination at UL). c, Portable shrine for Kanda Festival, Tokyo prefecture (yellow background, denomination in red at LL). d, Portable shrine for Kanda Festival (yellow background, denomination in blue at UR). e, Dancers from Awa Dance Festival, Tokushima prefecture (pink background, denomination at LR). f, Dancers from Awa Dance Festival (pink background, denomination at UR). g, Participants and lanterns for Hakata Gion Yamakasa Festival, Fukuoka prefecture (light blue background, denomination at UL). h, Participants and float for Hakata Gion Yamakasa Festival (light blue background, denomination at UR). i, Drummers for Eisa Festival, Okinawa prefecture (yellow background, denomination in red at LR). j, Drummers for Eisa Festival (yellow background, denomination in blue at UR).

2008, Aug. 1 — Photo. — *Perf. 13½x13¼*

3051 A2418 Sheet of 10	9.50	9.50
a.-j. 50y Any single	.95	.65

Miniature Sheet

Treaty of Peace and Friendship Between Japan and People's Republic of China, 30th Anniv. — A2419

No. 3052: a, Temple of Heaven, Beijing. b, Huangshan Mountains, China. c, Mogao Cave Shrines, China. d, Temple of the Flourishing Law, Ikaruga, Japan. e, Female mandarin duck. f, Male mandarin duck. g, Panel from painting by Wang Chuanfeng depicting three stylized fish and red Japanese apricot flower. h, Panel from painting by Wang Chuanfeng depicting two stylized fish and water lily. i, Panel from painting by Wang Chuanfeng depicting one stylized fish and autumn leaves. j, Panel from painting by Wang Chuanfeng depicting two staylized fish and white and red narcissi. Nos. 3052a-3052d, 3052g-3052j are 28x49mm; Nos. 3052e-3052f, 32x49mm.

2008, Aug. 12 — Photo. — *Perf. 13*

3052 A2419 Sheet of 10	15.00	15.00
a.-j. 80y Any single	1.50	1.10

Animation

Miniature Sheet

Patlabor — A2420

No. 3053: a, Ingfram Model 1 robot. b, Noa Izumimn, with "2" on sleeve patch. c, Isao Ota, with crossed arms. d, Ingram Model 2 robot. e, Shinobu Nagumo, with long hair. f, Ingram Model 3 robot. g, Robot, diff. h, Asumo Shinohara, with hand on head. i, Ingram Model 1 robot and eight characters. j, Ingram Model 2 robot and three characters.

2008, Aug. 22 — Litho. — *Perf. 13x13¼*

3053 A2420 Sheet of 10	15.00	15.00
a.-j. 80y Any single	1.50	1.10

Miniature Sheet

Home Towns — A2421

No. 3054 — Paintings by Taiji Harada of views of towns: a, Idyllic Village (Farmhouses, Tonami, Toyama prefecture). b, Blessing (Wedding at Yamate Catholic Church, Yokohama, Kanagawa prefecture). c, Approaching Winter (Lake Nojiri, Kamiminochi District, Nagano prefecture). d, Konjac Field (Farmers planting, Numata, Gunma prefecture). e, Vespers (Family in garden near houses, Nara, Nara prefecture). f, Cosmos (Flowers, boats and boathouses, Mikatakaminaka District, Fukui prefecture). g, Voices of Excited Children (Farmhouse and hill, Haga District, Tochigi prefecture). h, Autumn Colors Everywhere (Farmhouse and train car, Namegata, Ibaraki prefecture). i, Small Market (Family at roadside market, Asakura District, Fukuoka prefecture). j, Lullaby Village (Village and bridge, Kuma District, Kumamoto prefecture).

2008, Sept. 1 Photo. *Perf. 13*

3054 A2421 Sheet of 10 15.00 15.00
a.-j. 80y Any single 1.50 1.10

Miniature Sheet

Kyoto Travel Scenes — A2422

No. 3055: a, Otagi Nebutsu Temple and stone sculptures (stamp #1). b, Toriimoto (stamp #2). c, Adashino Nenbutsu Temple (stamp #3). d, Gio Temple (stamp #4). e, Buddha sculptures, Nison Temple (stamp #5). f, Hut of Fallen Persimmons, persimmons on tree (stamp #6). g, Jojakko Temple (stamp #7). h, Sagano Scenic Railway bridge and trains (stamp #8). i, Rowboats on Hozu River (stamp #9). j, Togetsu Bridge (stamp #10).

2008, Sept. 1 Litho. *Perf. 13x13¼*

3055 A2422 Sheet of 10 15.00 15.00
a.-j. 80y Any single 1.50 1.10

Personalized Stamp — A2423

Die Cut Perf. 12¾ Syncopated

2008, Aug. 7 Litho.

Self-Adhesive

Color of Denomination

3056 A2423 80y blue 1.90 1.90
3057 A2423 80y red 1.90 1.90
3058 A2423 80y orange 1.90 1.90
3059 A2423 80y green 1.90 1.90
3060 A2423 80y black 1.90 1.90
Nos. 3056-3060 (5) 9.50 9.50

Nos. 3056-3060 were printed in sheets of 10 containing 2 of each stamp that sold for 1200y. The image portion could be personalized. The image shown is a generic image.

A2424

A2425

A2426

A2427

A2428

A2429

A2430

A2431

A2432

The Tale of Genji, by Shikibu Murasaki — A2433

2008, Sept. 22 Photo. *Perf. 13¼*

3061 Sheet of 10 16.00 16.00
a. A2424 80y multi 1.60 1.25
b. A2425 80y multi 1.60 1.25
c. A2426 80y multi 1.60 1.25
d. A2427 80y multi 1.60 1.25
e. A2428 80y multi 1.60 1.25
f. A2429 80y multi 1.60 1.25
g. A2430 80y multi 1.60 1.25
h. A2431 80y multi 1.60 1.25
i. A2432 80y multi 1.60 1.25
j. A2433 80y multi 1.60 1.25

Kyushu Oil Dome, Oita Sports Park — A2435

Fencing — A2436

Hurdler — A2437

Kayaker — A2438

2008, Sept. 26 *Perf. 13x13¼*

3062 Sheet of 10, 2 each #3062a, 3062b, 3062d, 4 #3062c 9.50 9.50
a. A2435 50y multi .95 .65
b. A2436 50y multi .95 .65
c. A2437 50y multi .95 .65
d. A2438 50y multi .95 .65

Miniature Sheet

Travel Scenes — A2439

No. 3063: a, Sanjunoto Pagoda (stamp #1). b, Kiyomizudera Temple (stamp #2). c, Detail from painted sliding partition showing flowers from Chishaku Temple, denomination at LL (stamp #3). d, Like "c," denomination at LR (stamp #4). e, Kodai Temple (stamp #5). f, Temple garden (stamp #6). g, Sannei Hill (stamp #7). h, Yasaka Pagoda (stamp #8). i, Apprentice geisha (stamp #9). j, Kamo River and waterfront (stamp #10).

2008, Oct. 1 Litho. *Perf. 13x13¼*

3063 A2439 Sheet of 10 16.00 16.00
a.-j. 80y Any single 1.60 1.25

International Letter Writing Week Type of 2000

Hiroshige paintings from 53 Stations of the Tokaido Highway: 90y, Kanagawa. 110y, Mishima. 130y, Ishibe.

2008, Oct. 9 Photo. *Perf. 13¼x13½*

3064 A2119 90y multi 1.90 1.40
3065 A2119 110y multi 2.25 1.75
3066 A2119 130y multi 2.60 2.00
Nos. 3064-3066 (3) 6.75 5.15

World Heritage Sites
Miniature Sheet

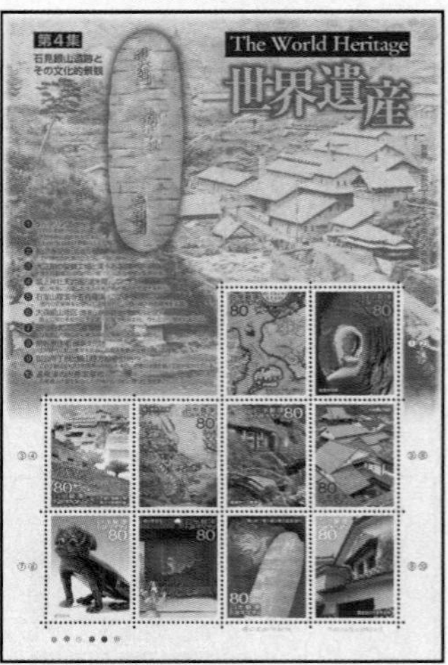

Iwami Silver Mine World Heritage Site — A2440

No. 3067: a, Map of Tartary by Abraham Ortelius (stamp #1). b, Ryugenji mine shaft (stamp #2). c, Smelting plant and ruins of Shimizudani smelting works (stamp #3). d, Painting of dragon, ceiling of Kigami Shinto shrine (stamp #4). e, Rakanji Temple (stamp #5). f, Omori silver mine district (stamp #6). g, Silver guardian dog (stamp #7). h, Interior of Kumagai family residence (stamp #8). i, Silver coin for official use and picture scroll (stamp #9). j, Naito Mansion, Yunotsu (stamp #10).

2008, Oct. 23 ***Perf. 13x13¼***

3067	A2440	Sheet of 10	16.00	16.00
a.-j.		80y Any single	1.60	1.25

Miniature Sheet

Kyoto Prefecture Local Autonomy Law, 60th Anniv. — A2441

No. 3068: a, Scene from The Tale of Genji, by Shikibu Murasaki (33x39mm). b, Cherry blossoms, Kyoto Prefectural Botanical Garden (28x33mm). c, Thatched-roof house, Nantan (28x33mm). d, Kaijusen Pagoda, Wazuka tea plantation (28x33mm). e, Amanohashidate Sandbar (28x33mm).

Perf. 13¼ (#3068a), 13x13¼

2008, Oct. 27 **Photo.**

3068	A2441	Sheet of 5	8.00	8.00
a.-e.		80y Any single	1.60	1.25

Miniature Sheet

Home Towns — A2442

No. 3069 — Paintings by Taiji Harada of views of towns: a, Stove Train (train, Kitatsugaru District, Aomori prefecture). b, New Year (buildings with snow-covered roofs, man shoveling snow, Nishimurayama District, Yamagata prefecture). c, Seaside Station (train station and telephone pole, Abashiri, Hokkaido prefecture). d, Incense Waterwheel (mill with waterwheel, Tsuyama, Okayama prefecture). e, Harness Straps (horse dragging log, Kurayoshi, Tottori prefecture). f, Life in the Snow Country (postman delivering mail to people at snow-covered house, Waga District, Iwate prefecture). g, Good Friends (people on town street in snowfall, Aizu Wakamatsu, Fukushima prefecture). h, Community of Stone Walls (people walking by stone wall, Minamiuwa District, Ehime prefecture). i, Village on Steep Slope (houses on mountainside, Miyoshi, Toskushima prefecture). j, Sedge-woven Hat (woman standing outside of building in snowstorm, Nakauonuma District, Niigata prefecture).

2008, Nov. 4 ***Perf. 13***

3069	A2442	Sheet of 10	16.00	16.00
a.-j.		80y Any single	1.60	1.25

A2443 A2444

New Year 2009 (Year of the Ox)
A2445 A2446

2008, Nov. 4 **Photo.** ***Perf. 13x13¼***

3070	A2443	50y multi	1.00	.75
3071	A2444	80y multi	1.60	1.25

Perf. 13¼

3072	A2445	50y +3y multi	1.10	.80
3073	A2446	80y +3y multi	1.75	1.40
		Nos. 3070-3073 (4)	5.45	4.20

New Year Greetings Type of 2006

2008, Nov. 4 **Photo.** ***Perf. 13¼***

Inscribed "'09 New Year"

Stamp + Label

Panel Color

3074	A2327a	50y blue green	1.75	1.75
3075	A2327a	50y red	1.75	1.75
a.		Pair, #3074-3075 + 2 labels	3.50	3.50

Labels could be personalized.

Miniature Sheet

Keio University, 150th Anniv. — A2447

No. 3076: a, Yukichi Fukuzawa (1835-1901), founder (stamp #1). b, University emblem (stamp #2). c, Old Library, denomination at LL (stamp #3). d, Old Library, denomination at LR (stamp #4). e, Keio and Waseda University rugby players (stamp #5). f, Keio and Waseda University baseball players (stamp #6). g, Stained-glass window depicting horse's head (stamp #7). h, Stained-glass window depicting goddess with upraised arm (stamp #8). i, Stained-glass window depicting feudal warrior (stamp #9). j, Stained-glass window with Latin inscription "Calamus Gladio Fortior" (stamp #10).

2008, Nov. 7 ***Perf. 13***

3076	A2447	Sheet of 10	16.00	16.00
a.-j.		80y Any single	1.60	1.25

Miniature Sheet

Edo Calligraphy — A2448

No. 3077 — Characters for "ox": a, Depiction of ox head (Kinbun style) with red chop at LL. b, Blue character on lilac background, in Kokotsubun style. c, Character with three horizontal lines and two vertical lines, in standard script, with red chop at LR. d, Red character in Kinbun style. e, Character with two horizontal lines and one vertical line, in standard script, with red chop at left center. f, Character in Tensho style with red chop at right center. g, Character with arc and crossed lines in Tensho style, with red chop at LR. h, Character with two crossing curves in Kokotsubun style, with red chop in center. i, Character with two components in Reisho style, with red chop at left. j, Character with dot above sinuous line in Hiragana style, with red chop at LR.

Litho. & Embossed

2008, Nov. 21 ***Perf. 13x13¼***

3077	A2448	Sheet of 10	17.50	17.50
a.-j.		80y Any single	1.75	1.40

A2449

A2450

A2451

A2452

A2453

Iron and Steel Industry, 150th Anniv. — A2454

2008, Dec. 1 **Photo.** ***Perf. 12¾x13***

3078		Sheet of 10, #3078a, 3078b, 2 each #3078c-3078f	17.50	17.50
a.	A2449	80y multi	1.75	1.40
b.	A2450	80y multi	1.75	1.40
c.	A2451	80y multi	1.75	1.40
d.	A2452	80y multi	1.75	1.40
e.	A2453	80y multi	1.75	1.40
f.	A2454	80y multi	1.75	1.40

Daffodils
A2455

Plum Blossoms
A2456

Fuki
A2457

Plum Blossoms
A2458

Weeping Cherry Blossoms
A2459

Daffodils
A2460

Plum Blossoms
A2461

Fuki
A2462

Plum Blossoms
A2463

Weeping Cherry Blossoms
A2464

2008, Dec. 1 Photo. *Perf. 13¼*

3079	A2455 50y multi		1.10	.85
3080	A2456 50y multi		1.10	.85
3081	A2457 50y multi		1.10	.85
3082	A2458 50y multi		1.10	.85
3083	A2459 50y multi		1.10	.85
a.	Vert. strip of 5, #3079-3083		5.50	4.25
3084	A2460 80y multi		1.75	1.40
3085	A2461 80y multi		1.75	1.40
3086	A2462 80y multi		1.75	1.40
3087	A2463 80y multi		1.75	1.40
3088	A2464 80y multi		1.75	1.40
a.	Vert. strip of 5, #3084-3088		8.75	7.00
	Nos. 3079-3088 (10)		14.25	11.25

Flowers of Fukui, Wakayama, Akita, Fukuoka and Kyoto prefectures.

Miniature Sheets

A2465

Greetings Stamps — A2466

No. 3089: a, Santa Claus holding star (26x30mm). b, Stylized man, woman as bell (26x30mm). c, Kittens (26x30mm). d, Teddy bears and gift box (26x30mm). e, Chick, flowers (29mm diameter).

No. 3090: a, Kittens (34x28mm oval). b, Elf with bag of toys (25x34mm). c, Bluebirds in bouquet of roses (25x34mm). d, Santa Claus with horn (25x34mm). e, Fruit and flowers (25x34mm).

Die Cut Perf. 13¼

2008, Dec. 8 Litho.

3089	A2465	Sheet of 5	5.50	5.50
a.-e.	50y Any single		1.10	.85

Die Cut Perf. 13

3090	A2466	Sheet of 5	8.75	8.75
a.-e.	80y Any single		1.75	1.40

Miniature Sheet

Shimane Prefecture Local Autonomy Law, 60th Anniv. — A2467

No. 3091: a, Tree peony, silver coin for official use (33x39mm). b, Kuniga Coast (28x33mm). c, Matsue Castle (28x33mm). d, Tsuwano (28x33mm). e, Bronze bell (28x33mm).

Perf. 13¼ (#3091a), 13x13¼

2008, Dec. 8 Photo.

3091	A2467	Sheet of 5	8.75	8.75
a.-e.	80y Any single		1.75	1.40

Miniature Sheet

Travel Scenes — A2468

No. 3092: a, Dragon from Shuri Castle Main Hall (stamp #1). b, Shuri Castle Main Hall (stamp #2). c, Ryukyuan dancer with arm raised at left (stamp #3). d, Ryukuan dancer with arm raised at right (stamp #4). e, Shurei Gate (stamp #5). f, Zuisen Gate and Rokoku Gate, Shuri Castle (stamp #6). g, Shikina Garden (stamp #7). h, Stone pavement, Kinjo (stamp #8). i, Guardian lion, International Street, Naha (stamp #9). j, Yui Monorail, Naha (stamp #10).

2009, Jan. 23 Litho. *Perf. 13x13¼*

3092	A2468	Sheet of 10	18.00	18.00
a.-j.	80y Any single		1.75	1.40

Miniature Sheet

Travel Scenes — A2469

No. 3093: a, Guardian Lion (stamp #1). b, Indian coral tree, Iejima (stamp #2). c, Fish in Okinawa Churaumi Aquarium, denomination at UR (stamp #3). d, As "c," denomination at LL (stamp #4). e, People watching fish in Okinawa Churaumi Aquarium, denomination at LL (stamp #5). f, As "e," denomination at LR (stamp #6). g, Nakijin Castle ruins (stamp #7). h, Okinawa rail (stamp #8). i, Cape Hedo, Okinawa (stamp #9). j, Mangroves, Gesashi Inlet (stamp #10).

2009, Feb. 2

3093	A2469	Sheet of 10	16.00	16.00
a.-j.	80y Any single		1.60	1.25

Yoshino Cherry Blossoms
A2470

Azaleas
A2471

Tulips
A2472

Rhododendron
A2473

Nara Cherry Blossoms
A2474

Yoshino Cherry Blossoms
A2475

Azaleas
A2476

Tulips
A2477

Rhododendrons
A2478

Nara Cherry Blossoms
A2479

2009, Feb. 2 Photo. *Perf. 13¼*

3094	A2470 50y multi		1.00	.75
3095	A2471 50y multi		1.00	.75
3096	A2472 50y multi		1.00	.75
3097	A2473 50y multi		1.00	.75
3098	A2474 50y multi		1.00	.75
a.	Vert. strip of 5, #3094-3098		5.00	3.75
3099	A2475 80y multi		1.60	1.25
3100	A2476 80y multi		1.60	1.25
3101	A2477 80y multi		1.60	1.25
3102	A2478 80y multi		1.60	1.25
3103	A2479 80y multi		1.60	1.25
a.	Vert. strip of 5, #3099-3103		8.00	6.25
	Nos. 3094-3103 (10)		13.00	10.00

Flowers of Tokyo, Tochigi, Niigata, Shiga and Nara prefectures.

Animation

Miniature Sheet

GeGeGe no Kitaro — A2480

No. 3104: a, Kitaro and Otoko Nezumi. b, Daddy Eyeball in bowl. c, Kitaro kicking. d, Kitaro in fire. e, Villain with elongated head, villain with blades for arms. f, Villains with red face, villain with snake. g, Kitaro and mermaid. h, Musume Neko. i, Otoko Nezumi, Musume Neko, Babaa Sunakake and Nurikabe. j, Kitaro, Daddy Eyeball, Jijii Konaki, Momen Ittan.

2009, Feb. 23 Litho. *Perf. 13x13¼*

3104	A2480	Sheet of 10	16.00	16.00
a.-j.	80y Any single		1.60	1.25

Miniature Sheet

Travel Scenes — A2481

No. 3105: a, Todai Temple (stamp #1). b, Buddha, Todai Temple (stamp #2). c, Asura, Kofuku Temple (stamp #3). d, Nara National Museum (stamp #4). e, Kasuga Taisha Shrine (stamp #5). f, Roof of Kasuga Taisha Shrine and overhanging roof (stamp #6). g, Japanese deer, Wakakusa Hill (stamp #7). h, Inanuishi family residence (stamp #8). i, Gazebo, Nara Park (stamp #9). j, Bridge to gazebo, Nara Park (stamp #10).

2009, Mar. 2

3105 A2481 Sheet of 10 16.00 16.00
a.-j. 80y Any single 1.60 1.25

Miniature Sheet

Home Towns — A2482

No. 3106 — Paintings by Taiji Harada of views of towns: a, Cultivating (farmer in field, Nishitama District, Tokyo prefecture). b, Children Planting Rice (children in rice paddy, Katta District, Miyagi prefecture). c, I'm Home (child running up hill to farmhouse, Yamagata District, Hiroshima prefecture). d, Northern Springtime (farmer and wheelbarrow in field of yellow flowers, Iwanai District, Hokkaido prefecture). e, Chinese Milk Vetch Field (people near farmhouse, Kyoto, Kyoto prefecture). f, Water Mortar (farmer near water mortar, Hita, Oita prefecture). g, Short Rest (woman resting on bench in front of building, Numazu, Shizuoka prefecture). h, Red Train (street scene with train in background, Izumo, Shimane prefecture). i, Oven-shaped Thatch Roofs (woman, children with toy car in front of farm house, Kishima District, Saga prefecture). j, Little Post Office (people outside of post office, Hosu District, Ishikawa prefecture).

2009, Mar. 2 Photo. *Perf. 13*

3106 A2482 Sheet of 10 16.00 16.00
a.-j. 80y Any single 1.60 1.25

Miniature Sheets

A2483

Weekly Comic Books For Boys, 50th Anniv — A2484

No. 3107: a, Osomatsu-kun (boy's face, green panel at top). b, Makoto Chan (boy with broom). c, Kamui Gaiden (swordsman with black hair). d, Gambare Genki (boxer, dark blue background). e, Paman (three characters with masks and capes). f, Urusei Yatsura (boy in cap, girl in bikini). g, Dame Oyaji (man holding radish and knife). h, Saibogu 009 (characters with galaxy in background). i, Purogorufa Saru (golfer). j, Tacchi (boy and girl looking over their shoulders).

No. 3108: a, Eitoman (android with "8" on chest). b, Taiga Masuku (caped man with tiger mask). c, Kyojin no Hoshi (Yomiuri Giants pitcher). d, Karate Baka Ichidai (karate master with green hair). e, GeGeGe no Kitaro (Kitaro, Daddy Eyeball and Otoko Nezumi). f, Ai to Makoto (girl with orange hair, boy with green hair). g, Tensai Bakabon (woman with yellow hair bow, screaming man). h, Tsurikichi Sanpei (boy holding fish). i, Ashita no Jo (boxer, pale blue background). j, Tonda Kappuru (boy, girl with green dress and orange bow).

2009, Mar. 17 Litho. *Perf. 13*

3107 A2483 Sheet of 10 16.00 16.00
a.-j. 80y Any single 1.60 1.25
3108 A2484 Sheet of 10 16.00 16.00
a.-j. 80y Any single 1.60 1.25

Wedding of Emperor Akihito and Empress Michiko, 50th Anniv. — A2485

Designs: No. 3109, Confectionery box. No. 3110, Fan.

2009, Apr. 10 Photo. *Perf. 13¼*

3109 80y multi 1.60 1.25
3110 80y multi 1.60 1.25
a. A2485 Pair, #3109-3110 3.20 2.50
b. Souvenir sheet, #3109-3110 3.20 2.50

Animation

Miniature Sheet

Detective Conan — A2486

No. 3111: a, Ai Haibara and Conan and brick wall. b, Mitsuhiko Tsuburaya, Ayumi Yoshida, and Genta Kojima and brick wall. c, Heiji Hattori and cherry blossoms. d, Kazuha Toyama and cherry blossoms. e, Conan and night sky. f, Gin and night sky. g, Conan and fence. h, Ran Mori and fence. i, Kiddo Kaito holding Christmas gift. j, Conan, Moon and hang-glider.

2009, Apr. 17 Litho. *Perf. 13x13¼*

3111 A2486 Sheet of 10 17.50 17.50
a.-j. 80y Any single 1.75 1.25

Peonies, by Yu Fei'an A2487

Peonies, by Ren Bonian A2488

Peonies, by Keika Kanashima A2489

Peonies, by Keika Kanashima A2490

Peonies, by Keika Kanashima A2491

Peonies, by Keika Kanashima A2492

2009, Apr. 20 Photo. *Perf. 13¼*

3112 Sheet of 10, #3112c-3112f, 3 each, #3112a-3112b 17.50 17.50
a. A2487 80y multi 1.75 1.25
b. A2488 80y multi 1.75 1.25
c. A2489 80y multi 1.75 1.25
d. A2490 80y multi 1.75 1.25
e. A2491 80y multi 1.75 1.25
f. A2492 80y multi 1.75 1.25

Philately Week.

Red Cross, 150th Anniv. — A2493

Designs: No. 3113, Henri Dunant (1828-1910), founder of Red Cross. No. 3114, Japanese Red Cross Day poster, 1933.

2009, May 8 Litho. *Perf. 13*

3113 80y multi 1.75 1.25
3114 80y multi 1.75 1.25
a. A2493 Pair, #3113-3114 3.50 2.50

Miniature Sheet

Nagano Prefecture Local Autonomy Law, 60th Anniv. — A2494

No. 3115: a, Kappa Bridge, Azusa River, Mt. Hodaka (33x39mm). b, Nanohana Park and Chikuma River, Iiyama City (28x33mm). c, Anraku Temple (28x33mm). d, Matsumoto Castle (28x33mm). e, Manji Buddha statue (28x33mm).

Perf. 13¼ (#3115a), 13x13¼

2009, May 14 Photo.

3115 A2494 Sheet of 5 8.75 8.75
a.-e. 80y Any single 1.75 1.40

Inauguration of Lay Judge System — A2495

Designs: No. 3116, Lay Judge System emblem. No. 3117, Birds on scale.

2009, May 21 Litho. *Perf. 13x13¼*

3116 80y multi 1.75 1.25
3117 80y multi 1.75 1.25
a. A2495 Pair, #3116-3117 3.50 2.50

Miniature Sheets

A2496

Weekly Comic Books For Boys, 50th Anniv — A2497

No. 3118: a, Gu-Gu Ganmo (child and chicken-like alien). b, Major (baseball player with bat, ball and glove). c, Patlabor Mobile Police (man standing on robot). d, Rekka no Hono (boy with gloved hand raised). e, Ushio to Tora (monster and boy holding torch). f, ARMS (boy with extended hand and slash marks in background). g, GS Mikami Gakuraku Daisakusen (woman with long red hair). h, Kekkaishi (magician pointing finger forward). i, Detective Conan (boy pointing forward wearing glasses and bow tie). j, Hayate no Gotoku (girl, boy and tower).

No. 3119: a, 1, 2 no Sanshiro (judo fighter with flame in background). b, Hajime no Ippo (boxer). c, Kabocha Wain (boy and tall girl). d, Kindaichi Shonen no Jikenbo (two boys and girl). e, Kotaro Makari Tooru (boy and girl in white clothes). f, GTO (boy with GTO tattoo). g, Bari Bari Densetsu (motorcyclist). h, RAVE (swordsman and other characters). i, Misuta Ajikko (chef). j, Daiya no A (baseball pitcher).

2009, May 22 Litho. *Perf. 13*

3118 A2496 Sheet of 10 17.50 17.50
a.-j. 80y Any single 1.75 1.25
3119 A2497 Sheet of 10 17.50 17.50
a.-j. 80y Any single 1.75 1.25

Opening of Japanese Ports, 150th Anniv.

Miniature Sheets

Nagasaki — A2498

Yokohama — A2499

Hakodate — A2500

No. 3120: a, 19th century woodblock print of Nagasaki Port (denomination at left in black). b, 19th century woodblock print of Nagasaki Port (denomination at right in black). c, Nagasaki Port at night (denomination at UL in white). d, Nagasaki Port at night (denomination at UR in black). e, Drawing of boats and ships (denomination at UL in black). f, Drawing of boats and ships (denomination at LR in white). g, Nagasaki Port at night (denomination at LL in white). h, Oura Catholic Church. i, Goddess Great Bridge, Nippon Maru cruise ship. j, Glover Garden, Nagasaki Port (lamppost in foreground).

No. 3121: a, Woodblock print of Yokohama Port, 1871 (denomination at LL in black). b, Woodblock print of Yokohama Port, 1871 (denomination at LR in black). c, Yokohama Port at night (denomination at UL in white, tall building at right). d, Yokohama Port at night (denomination at LR in white). e, Yokohama Bay Bridge. f, Yokohama City Port Opening Memorial Hall. g, Sailing ship Nippon Maru. h, Yokohama International Passenger Boat Terminal and cruise ship.

No. 3122: a, Woodblock print of Hakodate Port, 1882 (denomination at LL in black). b, Woodblock print of Hakodate Port, 1882 (denomination at UL in black). c, Hakodate Port at night (denomination at UR in white). d, Hakodate Port at night (denomination at UL in white). e, Street on Hachiman Slope, Hakodate Port at night. f, Hakodate Orthodox Christian Church. g, Ship, lamppost at Old Pier at night. h, Hakodate Park, Hakodate Port (denomination at UL in black).

2009, June 2 Litho. *Perf. 13*

3120 A2498 Sheet of 10 17.50 17.50
a.-j. 80y Any single 1.75 1.25
3121 A2499 Sheet of 10, #3120e-3120f, 3121a-3121h 17.50 17.50
a.-h. 80y Any single 1.75 1.25
3122 A2500 Sheet of 10, #3120e-3120f, 3122a-3122h 17.50 17.50
a.-h. 80y Any single 1.75 1.25
Nos. 3120-3122 (3) 52.50 52.50

Miniature Sheet

National Afforestation Campaign — A2501

No. 3123 — Flora from Fukui Prefecture: a, Weeping cherry blossoms. b, Japanese zelkova tree. c, Japanese red pine tree. d, Japanese bird cherry tree. e, Magnolia blossoms. f, Camellia. g, Japanese horse chestnut tree. h, Kousa dogwood blossoms. i, Narcissi (denomination at UL). j, Narcissi (denomination at UR).

2009, June 5 Litho. *Perf. 13*

3123 A2501 Sheet of 10 11.00 11.00
a.-j. 50y Any single 1.10 .80

Miniature Sheet

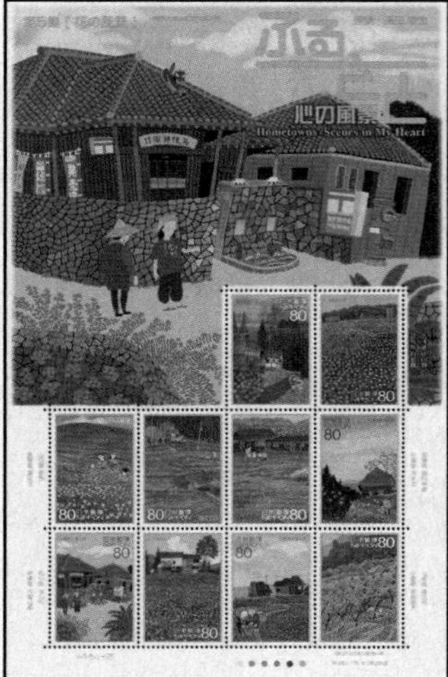

Home Towns — A2502

No. 3124 — Paintings by Taiji Harada of views of towns: a, Flowers Blooming in the Rain (mother and daughter under umbrellas on path by flower field, Tone District, Gumma prefecture). b, Potato Blossoms (train car near potato field, Nakagawa District, Hokkaido prefecture). c, High Country Flowers (people in flower field, Suwa, Nagano prefecture). d, Memories on the Wind (farmer with wheelbarrow on path near farmhouse, Hagi, Yamaguchi prefecture). e, Tranquility (people near stone wall in front of house, Sumoto, Hyogo prefecture). f, Sunset Skies (adult and child on hillside path near house, Nishiusuki District, Miyazaki prefecture). g, Island Post Office (people standing in front of post office, Yaeyama District, Okinawa prefecture). h, Lotus Blossoms (field of lotus with house and large tree in background, Hakusan, Ishikawa prefecture). i, Flower Garden (two women picking flowers with house and telephone pole in background, Minamiboso, Chiba prefecture). j, Peach Blossoms (adult and child picnicking under trees, Fuefuki, Yamanashi prefecture).

2009, June 23 Photo. *Perf. 13*

3124 A2502 Sheet of 10 17.50 17.50
a.-j. 80y Any single 1.75 1.25

Miniature Sheet

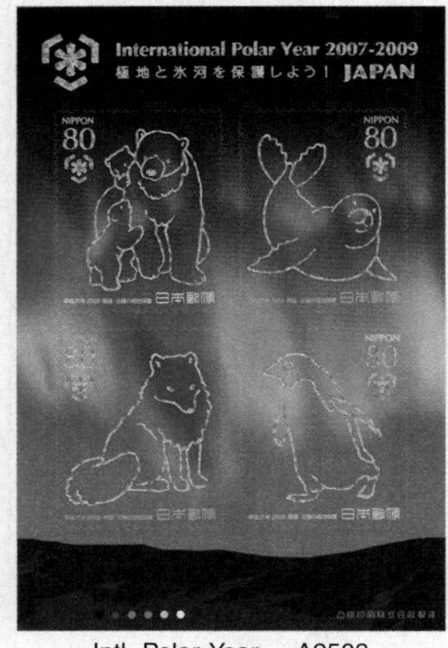

Intl. Polar Year — A2503

No. 3125: a, Polar bears. b, Weddell seal. c, Arctic fox. d, Adélie penguin.

Litho. With Hologram Affixed
2009, June 30 *Die Cut Perf. 13*
Self-Adhesive

3125 A2503 Sheet of 4 7.00
a.-d. 80y Any single 1.75 1.25

Gentian A2504 — Chrysanthemums A2505

Miyagi Bush Clover — A2506 — Black Lilies — A2507

Japanese Maple — A2508 — Gentian — A2509

Chrysanthemums A2510 — Miyagi Bush Clover A2511

Black Lilies — A2512 — Japanese Maple — A2513

2009, July 1 Photo. *Perf. 13¼*

3126 A2504 50y multi 1.10 .80
3127 A2505 50y multi 1.10 .80
3128 A2506 50y multi 1.10 .80
3129 A2507 50y multi 1.10 .80
3130 A2508 50y multi 1.10 .80
a. Vert. strip of 5, #3126-3130 5.50 4.00
3131 A2509 80y multi 1.75 1.25
3132 A2510 80y multi 1.75 1.25
3133 A2511 80y multi 1.75 1.25
3134 A2512 80y multi 1.75 1.25
3135 A2513 80y multi 1.75 1.25
a. Vert. strip of 5, #3131-3135 8.75 6.25
Nos. 3126-3135 (10) 14.25 10.25

Flora of Kumamoto, Hyogo, Miyagi, Ishikawa and Hiroshima prefectures.

Miniature Sheet

Niigata Prefecture Local Autonomy Law, 60th Anniv. — A2514

No. 3136: a, Japanese crested ibis over Sado Island (33x39mm). b, Cherry blossoms, Takada Castle (28x33mm). c, Fireworks over Nagaoka (28x33mm). d, Imori Pons, Mt. Myoko (28x33mm). e, Fireworks at Tokamichi Snow Festival (28x33mm).

Perf. 13¼ (#3136a), 13x13¼
2009, July 8 Photo.

3136 A2514 Sheet of 5 8.75 8.75
a.-e. 80y Any single 1.75 1.25

Statue of Eki Doji — A2515

2009, July 23 Photo. *Perf. 13x13½*

3137 A2515 300y multi 6.25 4.75

Ono no Komachi, Poet — A2516 — Ietaka Junii, Poet — A2517

Hoshi Jakuren, Poet — A2518 — Sakanoue no Korenori, Poet — A2519

Daini no Sanmi, Poet — A2520

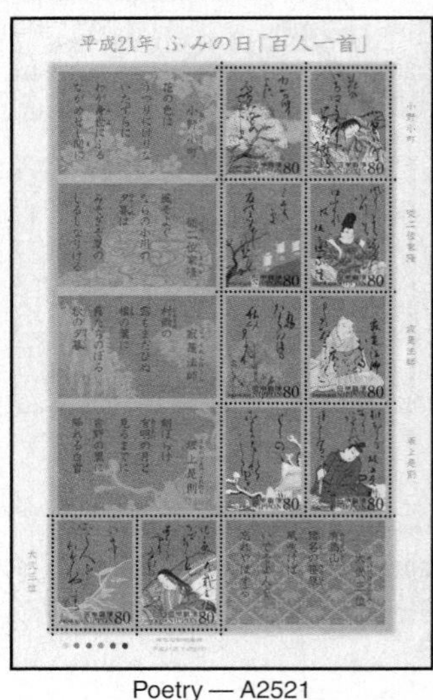

Poetry — A2521

No. 3143 — Poetry in Japanese calligraphy and: a, Tree with white blossoms. b, Ono no Komachi. c, Tree near pond. d, Ietaka Junii. e, Tree with green leaves. f, Hoshi Jakuren. g, House. h, Sakanoue no Korenori. i, Leaves. j, Daini no Sanmi.

2009, July 23 Photo. *Perf. 13¼*

3138 A2516 50y multi 1.10 .80
3139 A2517 50y multi 1.10 .80
3140 A2518 50y multi 1.10 .80
3141 A2519 50y multi 1.10 .80
3142 A2520 50y multi 1.10 .80
a. Vert. strip of 5, #3138-3142 5.50 4.00

Perf. 12¾x13

3143 A2521 Sheet of 10 17.50 17.50
a.-j. 80y Any single 1.75 1.25

Letter Writing Day.

Miniature Sheets

A2522

Hello Kitty and Dear Daniel — A2523

No. 3144: a, Hello Kitty with envelope. b, Hello Kitty, Dear Daniel, birds in pond. c, Hello Kitty, Dear Daniel, two trees. d, Hello Kitty and Dear Daniel with envelopes. e, Hello Kitty, Dear Daniel, three trees.

No. 3145: a, Hello Kitty with envelope (35mm diameter). b, Hello Kitty, two birds (35x28mm, heart-shaped). c, Hello Kitty, tree, three birds. d, Bird carrying envelope flying over Hello Kitty. e, Hello Kitty, bird, two trees. f, Hello Kitty, Dear Daniel, bird, squirrel and rabbit.

Die Cut Perf. 13½

2009, July 23 **Litho.**

3144	A2522	Sheet of 10, 2 each #a-e	11.00	
a.-e.		50y Any single	1.10	.80

Die Cut Perf. (#3145a-3145b), Die Cut Perf. 13½

3145	A2523	Sheet of 10, #a-b, 2 each #c-f	17.50	
a.-f.		80y Any single	1.75	1.25

Suwa Bluff, Nippori, by Hiroshige A2524

Pensive Love, by Utamaro A2525

Tokuji Otani as Yakko Sodesuke, by Sharaku A2526

Kumao Junisha Shrine, by Hiroshige A2527

Moon Promontory, by Hiroshige A2528

Woman Reading a Letter, by Utamaro A2529

Wadaemon Nakajima as Bodara Chozaemon and Konozo Nakamura as Funayado Kanagaway no Gon, by Sharaku A2530

Pagoda at Zojo Temple, by Hiroshige A2531

Clear Weather After Snowfall at Japan Bridge, by Hiroshige A2532

Kameikichi of Sodegaura, by Utamaro A2533

2009, Aug. 3 **Litho.** ***Perf. 13¼***

3146	Sheet of 10	17.50	17.50
a.	A2524 80y multi	1.75	1.25
b.	A2525 80y multi	1.75	1.25
c.	A2526 80y multi	1.75	1.25
d.	A2527 80y multi	1.75	1.25
e.	A2528 80y multi	1.75	1.25
f.	A2529 80y multi	1.75	1.25
g.	A2530 80y multi	1.75	1.25
h.	A2531 80y multi	1.75	1.25
i.	A2532 80y multi	1.75	1.25
j.	A2533 80y multi	1.75	1.25

Life in Edo (Tokyo).

Gujo Dance (Gifu) — A2534

Fukagawa Hachiman Festival (Tokyo) — A2535

Denomination at: No. 3147, Right. No. 3148, Left. No. 3149, Right. No. 3150, Left.

2009, Aug. 10

3147		50y multi	1.10	.80
3148		50y multi	1.10	.80
a.	A2534	Horiz. pair, #3147-3148	2.20	1.60
3149		50y multi	1.10	.80
3150		50y multi	1.10	.80
a.	A2535	Horiz. pair, #3149-3150	2.20	1.60
		Nos. 3147-3150 (4)	4.40	3.20

Miniature Sheet

Travel Scenes — A2536

No. 3151: a, Asuka, denomination at LL (stamp #1). b, Asuka, denomination at LR (stamp #2). c, Tachibana Temple, denomination at LL (stamp #3). d, Tachibana Temple, denomination at LR (stamp #4). e, Sculpture, Asuka Historical Museum (stamp #5). f, Stone burial mound (stamp #6). g, Tanzan Shrine, denomination at UR (stamp #7). h, Tanzan Shrine, denomination at UL (stamp #8). i, Picture scroll, denomination at UL (stamp #9). j, Picture scroll, denomination at LL (stamp #10).

2009, Aug. 21 ***Perf. 13x13¼***

3151	A2536	Sheet of 10	17.50	17.50
a.-j.		80y Any single	1.75	1.25

Persimmons and Haiku by Shiki Masaoka — A2537

Roofs of Dogo Onsen and Haiku by Shiki Masaoka — A2538

Mountain, Field and Haiku by Kyoshi Takahama A2539

House and Haiku by Soseki Natsume — A2540

Cherry Blossoms and Haiku by Hekigoto Kawahigashi A2541

2009, Sept. 1 **Litho.**

3152	A2537 80y multi		1.75	1.25
3153	A2538 80y multi		1.75	1.25
3154	A2539 80y multi		1.75	1.25
3155	A2540 80y multi		1.75	1.25
3156	A2541 80y multi		1.75	1.25
a.		Vert. strip of 5, #3152-3156	8.75	8.75

Miniature Sheet

National Athletic Meet (Niigata) — A2542

No. 3157: a, Tohoku Electric Power Big Swan Stadium. b, Soccer player. c, Boxer. d, Basketball player.

2009, Sept. 25 ***Perf. 13x13¼***

3157	A2542	Sheet of 10, 2 each #3157a-3157c, 4 #3157d	11.00	11.00
a.-d.		50y Any single	1.10	.80

Takayama Festival (Gifu) — A2543

Hakone Feudal Lord's Procession (Kanagawa) — A2544

Designs: No. 3158, Crowd at Night Festival. No. 3159, Shakkyo float puppet. No. 3160, Three men and box. No. 3161, Three men.

2009, Aug. 10 ***Perf. 13¼***

3158	50y multi	1.10	.80
3159	50y multi	1.10	.80
a.	A2543 Pair, #3158-3159	2.20	1.60
3160	50y multi	1.10	.80
3161	50y multi	1.10	.80
a.	A2544 Horiz. pair, #3160-3161	2.20	1.60
	Nos. 3158-3161 (4)	4.40	3.20

Miniature Sheet

Home Towns — A2545

No. 3162 — Paintings by Taiji Harada of views of towns: a, Nagasaki Kunchi (palanquin in parade, Nagasaki, Nagasaki prefecture). b, Rice Paddy Spirit Festival (people in rice paddy, Satsumasendai, Kagoshima prefecture). c, Carp Streamers (people making carp streamers, Iwakura, Aichi prefecture). d, Doll Send-off (winter parade, Waga District, Iwate prefecture). e, Deer Dance (musicians, people in blue, white, red and yellow costumes holding poles with banners, Kitauwa District, Ehime prefecture). f, Business Success Festival (crowd in front of Ebisu Shrine, Naniwa Ward, Osaka prefecture). g, Amahage Festival (masked man visiting children and parents, Akumi District, Yamagata prefecture). h, Lion Dance (large crowd surrounding float with dancers on tower, Wakayama, Wakayama prefecture). i, Floating Doll Festival (women dropping dolls into Sendai River, Tottori, Tottori prefecture). j, Gruel Doll Festival (children at table near Kama River, Tano District, Gumma prefecture).

2009, Oct. 8 **Photo.** ***Perf. 13***

3162	A2545	Sheet of 10	17.50	17.50
a.-j.		80y Any single	1.75	1.25

International Letter Writing Week Type of 2000

Hiroshige paintings from 53 Stations of the Tokaido Highway: 90y, Fujisawa. 110y, Okitsu. 130y, Chiryu.

2008, Oct. 9 **Photo.** ***Perf. 13¼***

3163	A2119	90y multi	2.00	1.50
3164	A2119	110y multi	2.50	1.90
3165	A2119	130y multi	3.00	2.25
		Nos. 3163-3165 (3)	7.50	5.65

Miniature Sheet

Diplomatic Relations Between Japan and Austria, 140th Anniv. — A2546

No. 3166: a, Portrait of Emilie Flöge, by Gustav Klimt (45x30mm). b, Autumn Clothing, by Shoen Uemura (45x30mm). c, Vienna Art History Museum and fountain (39x30mm). d, Empress Elizabeth of Austria, by Franz Winterhalter (39x30mm). e, Melk Abbey (steeple at right), Austria (39x30mm). f, Melk Abbey (steeple at left, 39x30mm). g, Wolfgang Amadeus Mozart and Salzburg (39x30mm). h, Salzburg (39x30mm). i, Hallstatt waterfront (39x30mm). j, Mountainside buildings, Hallstatt (39x30mm).

2009, Oct. 16 **Litho.** ***Perf. 13¼x13***

3166	A2546	Sheet of 10	17.50	17.50
a.-j.		80y Any single	1.75	1.25

See Austria No. 2227.

Miniature Sheet

Diplomatic Relations Between Japan and Hungary, 140th Anniv. — A2547

No. 3167: a, Hungarian flask. b, Mount Fuji, horiz. c, Jar from Japanese tea service. d, Hungarian Parliament (flag above building). e, Hungarian Parliament (building with dome). f, Matyo folk embroidery, Hungary. g, Elizabeth Bridge, Hungary, horiz. h, Crane and leaves fabric pattern from Japanese kimono. i, Herend porcelain figurine (Hussar examining sword blade). j, Herend porcelain vase.

Perf. 13x13¼, 13¼x13

2009, Oct. 16 **Litho.**

3167	A2547	Sheet of 10	17.50	17.50
a.-j.		80y Any single	1.75	1.25

See Hungary No. 4141.

Animation

Miniature Sheet

Naruto: Hurricane Chronicles — A2548

No. 3168: a, Naruto Uzumaki (yellow hair, black and orange shirt). b, Sasuke Uchiha (with open shirt). c, Sakura Haruno (girl with pink hair). d, Kakashi Hatake (with red spiral on sleeve). e, Sai (with sword). f, Shikamaru Nara (clasping hands). g, Deidara (girl with yellow hair and raised hand). h, Itachi Uchiha (with black hair and black and red robe). i, Jiraiya (with white hair). j, Fourth Hokage (yellow hair, white, gray and red robe).

2009, Oct. 23 **Litho.** ***Perf. 13x13¼***

3168	A2548	Sheet of 10	17.50	17.50
a.-j.		80y Any single	1.75	1.25

Miniature Sheet

Ibaraki Prefecture Local Autonomy Law, 60th Anniv. — A2549

No. 3169: a, H-2 rocket, Mt. Tsukuba (33x39mm). b, Fukuroda Falls (28x33mm). c, Mitsukuni Tokugawa (1628-1700), Mito daimyo (28x33mm). d, Boat on Kasumigaura (28x33mm). e, Fireworks over Tsuchiura (28x33mm).

Perf. 13¼ (#3169a), 13x13¼

2009, Nov. 4 **Photo.**

3169	A2549	Sheet of 5	9.00	9.00
a.-e.		80y Any single	1.75	1.25

A2550 A2551

New Year 2010 (Year of the Tiger)

A2552 A2553

2009, Nov. 11 **Photo.** ***Perf. 13x13½***

3170	A2550	50y multi	1.10	.80
3171	A2551	80y multi	1.75	1.25

Perf. 13¼

3172	A2552	50y +3y multi	1.25	.95
3173	A2553	80y +3y multi	1.90	1.40
		Nos. 3170-3173 (4)	6.00	4.40

Phoenix — A2554

Kirin Facing Right A2555

Kirin Facing Left A2556

2009, Nov. 12 **Photo.** ***Perf. 13¼***

3174	A2554	80y multi	1.75	1.40
3175	A2555	80y multi	1.75	1.40
3176	A2556	80y multi	1.75	1.40
a.		Souvenir sheet, #3175-3176	3.50	2.80
		Nos. 3174-3176 (3)	5.25	4.20

Enthronement of Emperor Akihito, 20th anniv. Nos. 3174-3176 were printed in sheets containing two each of Nos. 3175 and 3176 and six of No. 3174.

Miniature Sheet

Calligraphy — A2557

No. 3177 — Characters for "tiger" by calligraphers: a, Chikusei Hayashi (character in running script with red background). b, Chosho Kneko (character in clerical style, with denomination at LR, and large red chop at LL). c, Gakufu Toriyama (character in kinbun style in gold with blue green background). d, Hosen Takeuchi (character in kinbun style with denomination at LL, red chop at LR). e, Shiko Miyazaki (character in hiragana script with denomination above Japanese characters and "Nippon" at LL). f, Setsuzan Kitano (character in kokotsubun style with denomination and red chop at LL). g, Masato Seki (character in kinbun style in red). h, Junichi Yanagida (characters in running script with denomination at LL above Japanese characters and "Nippon" at LR). i, Kukoku Tamura (character in clerical script in blue with light blue and white background). j, Bokushun Kito (character in kinbun style with denomination at LR and small red chop at LL).

Litho. & Embossed

2009, Nov. 20 ***Perf. 13x13¼***

3177 A2557 Sheet of 10 17.50 17.50
a.-j. 80y Any single 1.75 1.40

Miniature Sheets

A2558

Greetings Stamps — A2559

No. 3178: a, Girl and apples. b, Snowman and stars. c, Angel holding toy rabbit. d, Apple, ribbon, ring of roses. e, Figures with blue and pink faces, horiz.

No. 3179: a, Christmas wreath. b, Santa Claus playing violin on chimney. c, Oil lamp and flowers. d, Angel with gift. e, Figure made of fir branches, candle.

Die Cut Perf. 12¾x13, 13x12¾

2009, Nov. 24 **Litho.**

Self-Adhesive

3178 A2558 Sheet of 5 5.50 5.50
a.-e. 50y Any single 1.10 .85

Die Cut Perf. 12¾x13

3179 A2559 Sheet of 5 9.00 9.00
a.-e. 80y Any single 1.75 1.40

Peach Blossoms A2560

Rape Blossoms A2561

Plum Blossoms and Primrose A2562

Bayberry A2563

Bungo Plum Blossoms A2564

Peach Blossoms A2565

Rape Blossoms A2566

Plum Blossoms and Primrose A2567

Bayberry A2568

Bungo Plum Blossoms A2569

2009, Dec. 1 **Photo.** ***Perf. 13¼***

3180 A2560 50y multi 1.10 .85
3181 A2561 50y multi 1.10 .85
3182 A2562 50y multi 1.10 .85
3183 A2563 50y multi 1.10 .85
3184 A2564 50y multi 1.10 .85
a. Vert. strip of 5, #3180-3184 5.50 4.25
3185 A2565 80y multi 1.75 1.40
3186 A2566 80y multi 1.75 1.40
3187 A2567 80y multi 1.75 1.40
3188 A2568 80y multi 1.75 1.40
3189 A2569 80y multi 1.75 1.40
a. Vert. strip of 5, #3185-3189 8.75 7.00
Nos. 3180-3189 (10) 14.25 11.25

Flowers of Okayama, Chiba, Osaka, Kochi and Oita prefectures.

Animation

Miniature Sheet

Sergeant Keroro — A2570

No. 3190: a, Sergeant Keroro, wearing helmet, holding post card. b, Fuyuki Hinata holding post card. c, Natsumi Hinata holding gift. d, Corporal Giroro, wearing helmet, with arms crossed. e, Private Tamama holding gift above head. f, Momoka Nishizawa holding letter. g, Saburo holding stamps. h, Sergeant Major Kururu with stamp on forehead. i, Lance Corporal Dororo, with white helmet, holding scroll. j, Koyuki Azumaya, holding scroll.

2010, Jan. 22 **Litho.** ***Perf. 13***

3190 A2570 Sheet of 10 17.50 17.50
a.-j. 80y Any single 1.75 1.40

Miniature Sheets

A2571

Greetings Stamps — A2572

No. 3191: a, Fairy with watering can. b, Fairy giving letter to bird. c, Fairies holding flower basket. d, Fairy with horn on back of flying bird. e, Fairy with violin on flower leaf.

No. 3192: a, Flower bouquet in red wrapping paper, butterflies. b, Woman with flute. c, Flower bouquet in white wrapping paper, butterflies. d, Flowers, G clef. e, Flowers, rabbit.

Die Cut Perf. 12¾x13

2010, Jan. 25 **Litho.**

Self-Adhesive

3191 A2571 Sheet of 5 5.50 5.50
a.-e. 50y Any single 1.10 .85
3192 A2572 Sheet of 5 9.00 9.00
a.-e. 80y Any single 1.75 1.40

Miniature Sheet

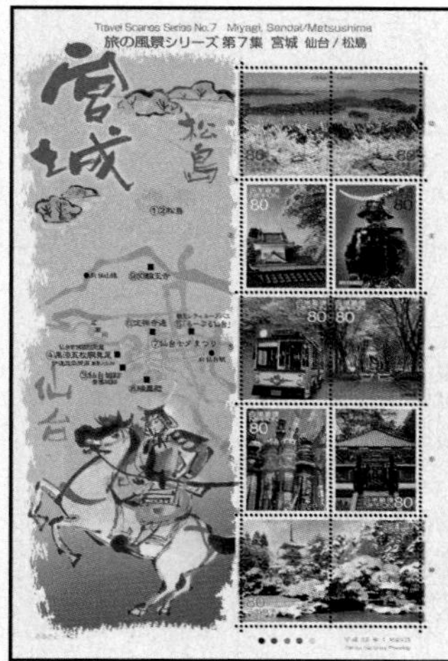

Travel Scenes — A2573

No. 3193: a, Matsushima, denomination at LL (stamp #1). b, Matsushima, denomination at LR (stamp #2). c, Sendai Castle ruins (stamp #3). d, Suit of armor and crested helmet (stamp #4). e, Sendai tourist bus (stamp #5). f, A Bathing Woman, sculpture by Venanzo Crocetti, Sendai (stamp #6). g, Tanabata Festival, Sendai (stamp #7). h, Zuihoden Mausoleum (stamp #8). i, Rinno Temple, denomination at LL (stamp #9). j, Garden and pond at Rinno Temple (stamp #10).

2010, Jan. 29 **Litho.** ***Perf. 13***

3193 A2573 Sheet of 10 17.50 17.50
a.-j. 80y Any single 1.75 1.40

Tulips — A2574

Chinese Milk Vetch — A2575

Nijisseiki Pear Blossoms A2576

Coral Tree Blossoms A2577

Fuji Cherry Blossoms A2578

Tulips A2579

Chinese Milk Vetch A2580

Nijisseiki Pear Blossoms A2581

Coral Tree Blossoms
A2582

Fuji Cherry Blossoms
A2583

2010, Feb. 1 Photo. *Perf. 13¼*

3194	A2574	50y multi		1.10	.85
3195	A2575	50y multi		1.10	.85
3196	A2576	50y multi		1.10	.85
3197	A2577	50y multi		1.10	.85
3198	A2578	50y multi		1.10	.85
a.		Vert. strip of 5, #3194-3198		5.50	4.25
3199	A2579	80y multi		1.75	1.40
3200	A2580	80y multi		1.75	1.40
3201	A2581	80y multi		1.75	1.40
3202	A2582	80y multi		1.75	1.40
3203	A2583	80y multi		1.75	1.40
a.		Vert. strip of 5, #3199-3203		8.75	7.00
		Nos. 3194-3203 (10)		14.25	11.25

Flowers of Toyama, Gifu, Tottori, Okinawa and Yamanashi prefectures.

Miniature Sheet

Nara Prefecture Local Autonomy Law, 60th Anniv. — A2584

No. 3204: a, Great Hall of State, cherry blossoms, kemari players (33x39mm). b, Hase Temple, peonies (28x33mm). c, Ukimodo during Nara Candlelight Festival (28x33mm). d, Muro Temple pagoda (28x33mm). e, Mt. Yoshino and cherry blossoms (28x33mm).

Perf. 13¼ (#3204a), 13x13¼

2010, Feb. 8 Photo.

3204	A2584	Sheet of 5	9.00	9.00
a.-e.		80y Any single	1.75	1.40

Miniature Sheet

Travel Scenes — A2585

No. 3205: a, Kurashiki District buildings, denomination at LL (stamp #1). b, Kurashiki District buildings, swans, denomination at UR (stamp #2). c, Ohara Museum of Art (stamp #3). d, Belgian Girl in Kimono, painting by Torajiro Kojima (stamp #4). e, Seto Great Bridge, from distance (stamp #5). f, Arches and roadway of Seto Great Bridge (stamp #6). g, Kotohira Shrine (stamp #7). h, Mt. Iino (stamp #8). i, Bridge, Ritsurin Park, Takamatsu, denomination at LL (stamp #9). j, Bridge, Ritsurin Park, and cherry blossoms, denomination at UR (stamp #10).

2010, Mar. 1 Litho. *Perf. 13*

3205	A2585	Sheet of 10	17.50	17.50
a.-j.		80y Any single	1.75	1.40

Miniature Sheet

Characters From Peanuts Comic Strip — A2586

No. 3206: a, Snoopy reading letter (33x32mm). b, Woodstock reading letter under lamp (33x32mm). c, Peppermint Patty reading letter (33x32mm). d, Snoopy hugging Woodstock (35mm diameter). e, Sally reading letter (33x32mm). f, Snoopy and Woodstock on doghouse (35x29mm heart-shaped). g, Snoopy giving letter to Woodstock (33x32mm). h, Charlie Brown writing letter (33x32mm).

Die Cut Perf. 13½

2010, Mar. 3 Litho.

Self-Adhesive

3206	A2586	Sheet of 10, #3206c-3206h, 2 each #3206a-3206b	17.50	17.50
a.-h.		80y Any single	1.75	1.40

Peony
A2587

Sudachi Flowers
A2588

Unzen Azalea Flowers
A2589

Kakitsubata Irises
A2590

Camphor Blossoms
A2591

Peonies
A2592

Sudachi Flowers
A2593

Unzen Azalea Flowers
A2594

Kakitsubata Irises
A2595

Camphor Blossoms
A2596

2010, Mar. 8 Photo. *Perf. 13¼*

3207	A2587	50y multi	1.10	.85
3208	A2588	50y multi	1.10	.85
3209	A2589	50y multi	1.10	.85
3210	A2590	50y multi	1.10	.85
3211	A2591	50y multi	1.10	.85
a.		Vert. strip of 5, #3207-3211	5.50	4.25
3212	A2592	80y multi	1.75	1.40
3213	A2593	80y multi	1.75	1.40
3214	A2594	80y multi	1.75	1.40
3215	A2595	80y multi	1.75	1.40
3216	A2596	80y multi	1.75	1.40
a.		Vert. strip of 5, #3212-3216	8.75	7.00
		Nos. 3207-3216 (10)	14.25	11.25

Flowers of Shimane, Tokushima, Nagasaki, Aichi and Saga prefectures.

Miniature Sheet

Friendship With San Marino — A2597

No. 3217: a, La Repubblica, statue by Vittorio Pocchini, San Marino (stamp #1). b, First Tower, San Marino (stamp #2). c, Saint Marinus, angel and crowd from Appearance of Saint Marinus to His People, mural by Emilio Retrosi (stamp #3). d, Angel and crowd from Appearance of Saint Marinus to His People (stamp #4). e, Statue of Liberty, San Marino Government Building (stamp #5). f, Basilica of Saint Marinus (stamp #6). g, Second Tower, San Marino (stamp #7). h, Bell tower, First Tower (stamp #8). i, St. Mary Magdalene, painting by Francesco Menzocchi (stamp #9). j, St. Marinus, painting by unknown artist (stamp #10).

2010, Mar. 23 Litho. *Perf. 13*

3217	A2597	Sheet of 10	17.50	17.50
a.-j.		80y Any single	1.75	1.40

See San Marino No. 1818.

Miniature Sheet

Hometown Festival — A2598

No. 3218 — Suwa Grand Shrine Sacred Pillar Festival, Nagano Prefecture: a, Honmiya Shrine, denomination in yellow. b, Maemiya Shrine, denomination in pink. c, Akimiya Shrine, denomination in greenish black. d, Harumiya Shrine, denomination in light blue. e, Men dragging logs to Miya River, denomination in pink. f, Nagamochi, denomination in black. g, Men dragging log down hill, denomination in blue.

2010, Apr. 1 Litho. *Perf. 13¼*
Self-Adhesive

3218	A2598	Sheet of 10, #3218a-3218d, 2 each #3218e-3218g	11.00	11.00
a.-g.		50y Any single	1.10	.85

Philately Week — A2599

No. 3219: a, Tiger from screen painting by Gaho Hashimoto, denomination at UL. b, Peonies from screen painting by Hashimoto, denomination at LL. c, Peonies and birds from screen painting by Hashimoto, denomination at UL. d, Tiger, by Zhang Shanzi, denomination at LR.

Perf. 12¾x12½ Syncopated
2010, Apr. 20 Photo.

3219	A2599	Block of 4	7.00	5.75
a.-d.		80y Any single	1.75	1.40

Miniature Sheet

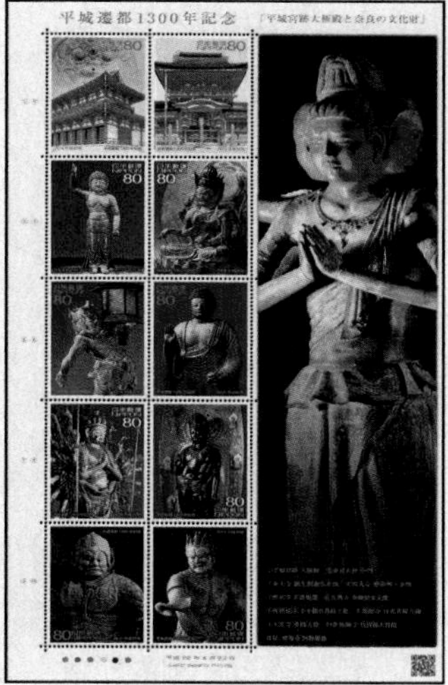

Treasures of Nara — A2600

No. 3220: a, Restored Heijo Palace (stamp #1). b, Inner gate, Kasuga Grand Shrine (stamp #2). c, Tanjo Shaka statue, denomination in white at UR (stamp #3). d, Aizen Myo-o statue, denomination in white at UL (stamp #4). e, Tentoki holding lantern, denomination in gold at UL (stamp #5). f, Buddha Yakushi, denomination in gold at UL (stamp #6). g, Thousand-armed Kannon statue, denomination in white at UR (stamp #7). h, Standing Bodhisattva statue, denomination in white at LR (stamp #8). i, Tamonten statue, denomination in gold at LL (stamp #9). j, Basara Taisho statue, denomination in gold at LR (stamp #10).

2010, Apr. 23 Litho. *Perf. 14x13¾*

3220	A2600	Sheet of 10	17.50	17.50
a.-j.		80y Any single	1.75	1.40

Move of Imperial capital to Nara, 1300th anniv.

Hanashobu Iris
A2601

Olive Blossoms
A2602

Azalea Flowers
A2603

Paulownia Blossoms
A2604

Crinum Flowers
A2605

Hanashobu Irises
A2606

Olive Blossoms
A2607

Azalea Flowers
A2608

Paulownia Blossoms
A2609

Crinum Flowers
A2610

2010, Mar. 8 Photo. *Perf. 13¼*

3221	A2601 50y multi		1.10	.85
3222	A2602 50y multi		1.10	.85
3223	A2603 50y multi		1.10	.85
3224	A2604 50y multi		1.10	.85
3225	A2605 50y multi		1.10	.85
a.	Vert. strip of 5, #3221-3225		5.50	4.25
3226	A2606 80y multi		1.75	1.40
3227	A2607 80y multi		1.75	1.40
3228	A2608 80y multi		1.75	1.40
3229	A2609 80y multi		1.75	1.40
3230	A2610 80y multi		1.75	1.40
a.	Vert. strip of 5, #3226-3230		8.75	7.00
	Nos. 3221-3230 (10)		14.25	11.25

Flowers of Mie, Kagawa, Gumma, Iwate and Miyazaki prefectures.

Miniature Sheet

A2611

Hello Kitty — A2612

No. 3231 — Hello Kitty: a, With butterflies and flowers (28x31mm heart-shaped). b, In kimono, flowers (28x31mm heart-shaped). c, With dragon (28x28mm). d, With mountain (28x28mm). e, With peonies (28x28mm). f, With origami cranes (28x28mm).

No. 3232 — Hello Kitty: a, And Shanghai skyline (30x32mm). b, And pagoda in Shanghai (30x32mm). c, And Tiger (30x32mm). d, With peonies (31x28mm heart-shaped). e, Holding fan (31mm diameter).

Die Cut Perf. 13½
2010, May 6 Litho.
Self-Adhesive

3231	A2611	Sheet of 10, #3231a-3231b, 2 each #3231c-3231f	11.00	11.00
a.-f.		50y Any single	1.10	.85

Die Cut Perf. 12½

3232	A2612	Sheet of 10, 2 each #3232a-3232e	17.50	17.50
a.-e.		80y Any single	1.75	1.40

Miniature Sheet

Kochi Prefecture Local Autonomy Law, 60th Anniv. — A2613

No. 3233: a, Ryoma Sakamoto (1836-67), samurai, and Katsura Beach (33x39mm). b, Farmhouse clock, Aki (28x33mm). c, Harimaya Bridge, streetcar (28x33mm). d, Paper carp streamers (28x33mm). e, Cape Ashizuri Lighthouse (28x33mm).

Perf. 13¼ (#3233a), 13x13¼
2010, May 14 Photo.

3233	A2613	Sheet of 5	8.75	8.75
a.-e.		80y Any single	1.75	1.40

Miniature Sheet

Kanagawa Prefecture Afforestation — A2614

No. 3234: a, Pinks. b, Japanese cedar. c, Sawtooth oak. d, Japanese maple. e, Golden-rayed lilies. f, Evergreen oak. g, Japanese chinquapin. h, Ginkgo. i, Beech. j, Gentians.

2010, May 21 Litho. *Perf. 13*

3234	A2614	Sheet of 10	11.00	11.00
a.-j.		50y Any single	1.10	.85

Miniature Sheets

A2615

2010 World Cup Soccer Championships, South Africa — A2616

No. 3235: a, Soccer ball, African animals (33x39mm). b, World Cup trophy (29x38mm). c, Poster for 2010 World Cup tournament (29x38mm). d, Emblem of 2010 World Cup (29x38mm). e, Emblem of Japan Soccer Association (29x38mm).

No. 3236 - Posters for World Cup tournaments of: a, 1930. b, 1934. c, 1938. d, 1950. e, 1954. f, 1958. g, 1962. h, 1970. i, 1978. j, 1986. k, 1990. l, 1994. m, 1998. n, 2002. o, 2006. p, Jules Rimet Cup. q, Jules Rimet Cup and hand.

Litho., Litho. & Embossed (#3235a)

Perf. 13, 14x13½ (#3235a)

2010, May 31

3235 A2615 Sheet of 5 8.75 8.75
a.-e. 80y Any single 1.75 1.40

Litho.

Perf. 13

3236 A2616 Sheet of 20, #3236a-3236o, 3 #3236p, 2 #3236q 35.00 35.00
a.-q. 80y Any single 1.75 1.40

Miniature Sheet

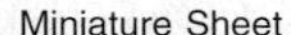

Asia-Pacific Economic Cooperation Economic Leader's Meeting, Yokohama — A2617

No. 3237: a, Flowers at top and left, denomination at LR. b, Flowers at top and right, denomination at LL. c, Purple flower at center right, denomination at UR. d, Purple flower at center left, denomination at UL. e, Pink rose at center right, denomination at LL. f, Pink rose at center left, denomination at LR. g, White flowers at center right, denomination at UR. h, White flowers at center left, denomination at UL. i, Flowers at bottom and left, red flowers at LR, denomination at UR. j, Flowers at bottom and right, red flowers at LL, denomination at UL.

2010, June 4 Litho. *Perf. 13*

3237 A2617 Sheet of 10 17.50 17.50
a.-j. 80y Any single 1.75 1.40

Emblem of Japan Academy A2618

Certificate and Photograph of First Awards Ceremony A2619

Venue of First Awards Ceremony A2620

Former Japan Academy Hall A2621

Rooster — A2622

2010, June 7 Litho. *Perf. 13*

3238 A2618 80y multi	1.75	1.40
3239 A2619 80y multi	1.75	1.40
3240 A2620 80y multi	1.75	1.40
3241 A2621 80y multi	1.75	1.40
3242 A2622 80y multi	1.75	1.40
a. Vert. strip of 5, #3238-3242	8.75	7.00
Nos. 3238-3242 (5)	8.75	7.00

Japan Academy Prizes, cent.

Animation

Miniature Sheet

Full Metal Alchemist — A2623

No. 3243: a, Edward Elric (with yellow hair and hand on his shoulder). b, Alphonse Elric (in black armor). c, Riza Hawkeye (holding gun). d, Roy Mustang with symbol on back of hand. e, Xiao Mei (panda). f, May Chang (with braided hair). g, Ling Yao holding sword. h, Lan Fan holding dagger. i, Winry Rockbell (girl in tank top). j, Edward Elric with dog, Den.

2010, June 14 Litho. *Perf. 13x13¼*

3243 A2623 Sheet of 10 19.00 19.00
a.-j. 80y Any single 1.90 1.40

Miniature Sheet

Gifu Local Autonomy Law, 60th Anniv. — A2624

No. 3244: a, Cormorant fishing on Nagara River (32x39mm). b, Gifu Castle (28x33mm). c, Yokokura Temple (28x33mm). d, Art exhibition, Mino (28x33mm). e, Restored buildings, Magome (28x33mm).

Perf. 13¼ (#3244a), 13x13¼

2010, June 18 Photo.

3244 A2624 Sheet of 5 9.50 9.50
a.-e. 80y Any single 1.90 1.40

Revision of Japan-United States Security Treaty, 50th Anniv. — A2625

Designs: No. 3245, Flags of U.S. and Japan, Japanese Prime Minister Nobusuke Kishi and U.S. President Dwight D. Eisenhower. No. 3246, Japanese Diet and U.S. Capitol.

2010, June 23 Litho. *Perf. 13*

3245 80y multi 1.90 1.40
3246 80y multi 1.90 1.40
a. A2625 Pair, #3245-3246 3.80 2.80

Miniature Sheet

National Fireworks Competition, Omagari, Akita Prefecture — A2626

No. 3247 — Various fireworks with denomination in: a, Yellow green at UL, country name in Japanese characters at LL. b, Yellow green at UR. c, Pale orange at LL. d, Blue at LL. e, Rose at UL. f, Rose at LR, country name in Japanese characters at LR. g, Rose at LR, country name in Japanese characters at LL. h, Blue green at LR. i, Yellow green at UL, country name in Japanese characters at LR. j, Yellow green at LR.

2010, July 1 Litho. *Perf. 13¼*

3247 A2626 Sheet of 10 11.50 11.50
a.-j. 50y Any single 1.10 .85

Miniature Sheet

Travel Scenes — A2627

No. 3248: a, Kurushima-Kaikyo Great Bridge, denomination at LL (stamp #1). b, Kurushima-Kaikyo Great Bridge, denomination at LR (stamp #2). c, Jodo Temple, denomination at UR (stamp #3). d, Jodo Temple, denomination at UL (stamp #4). e, Bridge, sculptures on Mt. Shirataki (stamp #5). f, Kojoji three-story pagoda (stamp #6). g, Oyamazumi Shrine (stamp #7). h, Omishima Bridge, boat (stamp #8). i, Building with red window shutters at Imabari Castle (stamp #9). j, Six-story donjon at Imabari Castle (stamp #10).

2010, July 8 Litho. *Perf. 13x13¼*

3248 A2627 Sheet of 10 19.00 19.00
a.-j. 80y Any single 1.90 1.40

Emperor Koko, Poet — A2628

Lady Ise, Poet — A2629

Saki no Daisojo Gyoson, Poet — A2630

Yushi Naishinno-ke no Kii, Poet — A2631

Sutoku In, Poet — A2632

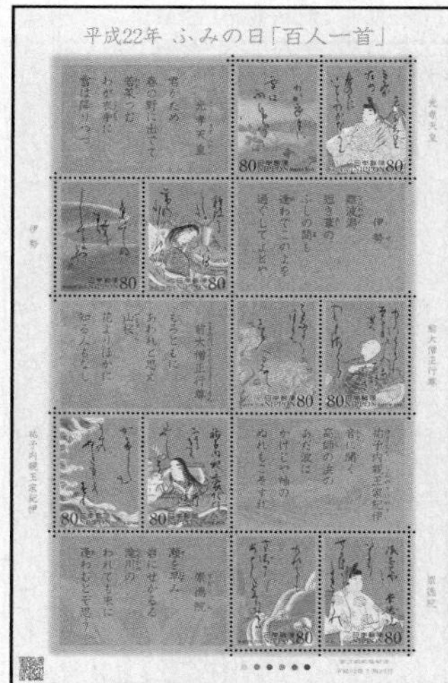

Poetry — A2633

No. 3254 — Poetry in Japanese calligraphy and: a, Purple flowers. b, Emperor Koko. c, Pond. d, Lady Ise. e, Hill and flowering trees. f, Saki no Daisojo Gyoson. g, Ocean waves. h, Yushi Naishinno-ke no Kii. i, Waterfall. j, Sutoku In.

2010, July 23 Photo. *Perf. 13¼*

3249 A2628 50y multi 1.25 .95
3250 A2629 50y multi 1.25 .95
3251 A2630 50y multi 1.25 .95
3252 A2631 50y multi 1.25 .95
3253 A2632 50y multi 1.25 .95
a. Vert. strip of 5, #3249-3253 6.25 6.25

Perf. 12¾x13

3254 A2633 Sheet of 10 19.00 19.00
a.-j. 80y Any single 1.90 1.40

Letter Writing Day.

Suruga Street, by Hiroshige A2634

Woman Reading a Letter, by Utamaro A2635

Dyer's Quarters, Kanda, by Hiroshige A2636

Sojuro Sawamura II as Kurando Ogishi, by Sharaku A2637

Asakusa Ricefields and Torinomachi Festival, by Hiroshige A2638

White Uchikake, by Utamaro A2639

Takinogawa, Oji, by Hiroshige A2640

Torazo Tanimura as Yaheiji Washizuka, by Sharaku A2641

Yamashita Park, Ueno, by Hiroshige A2642

Glass Goblet, by Utamaro A2643

2010, Aug. 2 Litho. *Perf. 13¼*

3255 Sheet of 10 19.00 19.00
a. A2634 80y multi 1.90 1.40
b. A2635 80y multi 1.90 1.40
c. A2636 80y multi 1.90 1.40
d. A2637 80y multi 1.90 1.40
e. A2638 80y multi 1.90 1.40
f. A2639 80y multi 1.90 1.40
g. A2640 80y multi 1.90 1.40
h. A2641 80y multi 1.90 1.40
i. A2642 80y multi 1.90 1.40
j. A2643 80y multi 1.90 1.40

Life in Edo (Tokyo).

Miniature Sheet

Fukui Local Autonomy Law, 60th Anniv. — A2644

No. 3256: a, Dinosaur at Tojimbo (32x39mm). b, Narcissus (28x33mm). c, Lake and flowers (28x33mm). d, Ichijodani ruins, cherry tree (28x33mm). e, Crab, Echizen-Kaga Kaigan Quasi-National Park (28x33mm).

Perf. 13¼ (#3256a), 13x13¼

2010, Aug. 9 Photo.

3256 A2644 Sheet of 5 9.50 9.50
a.-e. 80y Any single 1.90 1.40

Miniature Sheet

Home Towns — A2645

No. 3257 — Paintings by Taiji Harada of views of Hokkaido prefecture towns: a, Shiranuka Line (Farmhouses, haystack, two cows, Shiranuka). b, Shiranuka Line (Train, three cows, Shiranuka). c, Red-crowned Cranes (Building near forest in snow, Tsurui). d, Red-crowned Cranes (Woman feeding cranes, Tsurui). e, Flowers of the Land (Houses, trees hills, Biei). f, Flowers of the Land (Tractor, hills, trees, Biei). g, Farm (Farm buildings, mail box cows, Ishikari). h, Farm (Farm buildings, silo, farmer tending cow, Ishikari). i, Hibernation (Building in snow, fishing boats, Wakkanai). j, Canal in Spring (Boats in canal, Otaru).

2010, Sept. 10 Photo. *Perf. 13*

3257 A2645 Sheet of 10 19.00 19.00
a.-j. 80y Any single 1.90 1.40

Biplane of Henri Farman A2646

Aeronautical Research Plane A2647

Asuka A2648

Boeing 747-400 A2649

Mitsubishi Regional Jet — A2650

Monoplane of Hans Grade A2651

YS-11 A2652

Kawasaki T-4 A2653

US-2 A2654

Supersonic Plane A2655

2010, Sept. 21 Litho. ***Perf. 13***

3258	Sheet of 10	20.00	20.00
a.	A2646 80y multi	2.00	1.50
b.	A2647 80y multi	2.00	1.50
c.	A2648 80y multi	2.00	1.50
d.	A2649 80y multi	2.00	1.50
e.	A2650 80y multi	2.00	1.50
f.	A2651 80y multi	2.00	1.50
g.	A2652 80y multi	2.00	1.50
h.	A2653 80y multi	2.00	1.50
i.	A2654 80y multi	2.00	1.50
j.	A2655 80y multi	2.00	1.50

Aviation in Japan, cent.

Animation
Miniature Sheet

Chibi Maruko-chan — A2656

No. 3259: a, Sakura family members, Maruko, Sakiko, and mother Sumire (denomination in red at UL). b, Sakura family members father Hiroshi, grandfather Tomozo, and grandmother Kotake (denomination in white at LL). c, Maruko blowing bubbles (holding gun). d, Tomozo and bubbles. e, Hiroshi and Maruko with glow worm. f, Sakiko with glow worm. g, Sumire preparing food. h, Maruko and Kotake preparing food. i, Hamaji and Butaro (boys and snowflakes). j, Maruko and Tama-chan (and snowflakes).

2010, Sept. 22 Litho. ***Perf. 13x13¼***

3259	A2656 Sheet of 10	20.00	20.00
a.-j.	80y Any single	2.00	1.50

Chiba Central Sports Center and Chiba Marine Stadium — A2657

Hammer Throw — A2658

Equestrian A2659

Rock Climbing A2660

Pole Vault — A2661

2010, Sept. 24 Litho. ***Perf. 13x13¼***

3260	Sheet of 10, 2 each #a-e	12.50	12.50
a.	A2657 50y multi	1.25	.95
b.	A2658 50y multi	1.25	.95
c.	A2659 50y multi	1.25	.95
d.	A2660 50y multi	1.25	.95
e.	A2661 50y multi	1.25	.95

65th National Athletics Meet, Chiba.

Miniature Sheet

Travel Scenes — A2662

No. 3261: a, Akashi Strait Great Bridge, denomination in blue at UL (stamp #1). b, Akashi Strait Great Bridge, Sun Yat-sen Memorial Hall, Kobe, denomination at UR (stamp #2). c, Flowers, Awaji Island, denomination at UR to right of "Nippon" (stamp #3). d, Flowers, Awaji Island, denomination at UR below "Nippon" (stamp #4). e, Awaji puppet theater, denomination at UR (stamp #5). f, Awaji puppet theater, denomination at UL (stamp #6). g, Onaruto Bridge, denomination in white at LL (stamp #7). h, Onaruto Bridge, denomination in white at UR(stamp #8). i, Bridge, Naruto Whirlpools (stamp #9). j, Esaki Lighthouse (stamp #10).

2010, Oct. 1 Litho. ***Perf. 13x13¼***

3261	A2662 Sheet of 10	20.00	20.00
a.-j.	80y Any single	2.00	1.50

Miniature Sheet

Aichi Local Autonomy Law, 60th Anniv. — A2663

No. 3262: a, Golden dolphin sculpture at Nagoya Castle, irises, Atsumi Peninsula (32x39mm). b, Eurasian scops owl (28x33mm). c, Ginkgo leaves (28x33mm). d, Seto ceramic jar (28x33mm). e, Cherry blossoms (28x33mm).

Perf. 13¼ (#3262a), 13x13¼

2010, Oct. 4 Photo.

3262	A2663 Sheet of 5	10.00	10.00
a.-e.	80y Any single	2.00	1.50

Intl. Letter Writing Week — A2664

Painting details: 90y, Michitose, by Shinsui Ito. 110y, Nozaki Village, by Kiyokata Kaburagi. 130y, Botanyuki, by Shoen Uemura, horiz.

2010, Oct. 8 Photo. ***Perf. 13¼***

3263	A2664 90y multi	2.25	1.75
3264	A2664 110y multi	2.75	2.10
3265	A2664 130y multi	3.25	2.40
	Nos. 3263-3265 (3)	8.25	6.25

Miniature Sheet

Tenth Conference of Parties to the Convention on Biological Diversity, Nagoya — A2665

No. 3266: a, Lake Mashu, frost-covered trees. b, Spotted seal. c, Mt. Tsurugi. d, Japanese antelope. e, Buildings in mountains. f, Common tree frog and flowers. g, Banks of Shimanto River. h, Common kingfisher. i, Flowers at Cape Tamatori. j, False clownfish and sea anemone.

2010, Oct. 18 Litho. ***Perf. 13x13¼***

3266	A2665 Sheet of 10	20.00	20.00
a.-j.	80y Any single	2.00	1.50

Miniature Sheet

Friendship Between Japan and Portugal, 150th Anniv. — A2666

No. 3267: a, Japanese screen painting depicting bow of Portuguese ship, denomination at LL (30x45mm, stamp #1). b, Japanese screen painting depicting stern of Portuguese ship, denomination at LR (30x45mm, stamp #2). c, Belém Tower, Lisbon (30x43mm, stamp #3). d, Statue of St. Vincent (30x43mm, stamp #4). e, Monastery of the Hieronymites, Lisbon (30x43mm, stamp #5). f, Ruins of Roman Temple of Evora, Portugal (30x43mm, stamp #6). g, Oporto, Portugal, and boat (30x43mm, stamp #7). h, Batalha Monastery, Batalha, Portugal (30x43mm, stamp #8). i, Portuguese decorative tiles (30x43mm, stamp #9). j, Puppet of St. Isabel of Portugal (30x43mm, stamp #10).

2010, Oct. 22 Litho. ***Perf. 13¼x13***

3267	A2666 Sheet of 10	20.00	20.00
a.-j.	80y Any single	2.00	1.50

See Portugal No. 3271.

Seven People — A2667

Eight People — A2668

Congress Emblem A2669

Peace Statute, Nagasaki A2670

2010, Nov. 5 Photo. *Perf. 13*

3268	Sheet of 10, 2 each #3268a-3268c, 4 #3268d	20.00	20.00
a.	A2667 80y multi	2.00	1.50
b.	A2668 80y multi	2.00	1.50
c.	A2669 80y multi	2.00	1.50
d.	A2670 80y multi	2.00	1.50

Third UNI Global Union World Congress, Nagasaki.

Miniature Sheets

A2671

A2672

Greetings — A2673

No. 3269: a, Star and Santa Claus with sack. b, Poinsettias, ribbon and bell. c, Sleigh of Santa Claus over church, horiz. d, Heart-shaped wreath. e, Reindeer and Aurora Borealis.

No. 3270: a, Santa Claus. b, Christmas tree. c, Sleigh of Santa Claus over mountain, horiz. d, Wreath with pine cones. e, Reindeer and Aurora Borealis, diff.

No. 3271: a, Fairy with horn flying above town. b, Snowman juggling snowballs. c, Children singing, horiz. d, Rose in box. e, Cakes.

Die Cut Perf. 13

2010, Nov. 8 Litho.

Self-Adhesive

3269	A2671 Sheet of 5	6.25	
a.-j.	50y Any single	1.25	.95
3270	A2672 Sheet of 10	10.00	
a.-j.	80y Any single	2.00	1.50
3271	A2673 Sheet of 10	11.50	
a.-j.	90y Any single	2.25	1.75

A2674 A2675

New Year 2011 (Year of the Rabbit)

A2676 A2677

2010, Nov. 10 Photo. *Perf. 13x13½*

3272	A2674 50y multi	1.25	.95
3273	A2675 80y multi	2.00	1.50

Photo. & Typo.

Perf. 13¼

3274	A2676 50y +3y multi	1.40	1.10
3275	A2677 80y +3y multi	2.10	1.60
	Nos. 3272-3275 (4)	6.75	5.15

Miniature Sheet

Aomori Local Autonomy Law, 60th Anniv. — A2678

No. 3276: a, Apples, Nebuta Festival floats (32x39mm). b, Hirosaki Castle and cherry blossoms (28x33mm). c, Three Shrines Festival, Hachinohe (28x33mm). d, Lake Towada (28x33mm). e, Horse and Shiriyazaki Lighthouse (28x33mm).

Perf. 13¼ (#3276a), 13x13¼

2010, Nov. 15 Photo.

3276	A2678 Sheet of 5	10.00	10.00
a.-e.	80y Any single	2.00	1.50

Miniature Sheet

Edo Calligraphy — A2679

No. 3277 — Charcters for "rabbit": a, In Kinbun style (red character). b, In Six Dynasties style standard script (heavy black characters with red chop at LL, denomination at UR. c, In oracle bone script (single black character resembling animal with legs and tail, denomination at LR). d, In oracle bone script (three characters having horizontal line at UL, with red chop at LR, denomination at LR). e, In clerical script (silver character on green background). f, In small seal script (denomination at UL, "Nippon" at LR). g, In seal script (two black characters, with red chop, denomination and "Nippon" at LR). h, In Hirigana style (black character with denomination and "Nippon" at UL, red chop near center). i, In running script (black character with small dot at top, with denomination at LR and "Nippon" at LL). j, In standard script (two black characters with red chop and denomination at LR, "Nippon" at LL).

Litho. & Embossed

2010, Dec. 3 *Perf. 13x13¼*

3277	A2679 Sheet of 10	20.00	20.00
a.-j.	80y Any single	2.00	1.50

Miniature Sheet

Home Towns — A2681

No. 3280 — Paintings by Taiji Harada of views of Tohuku region towns: a, Paulownia Village (Cyclist near house, Mishima, Fukushima prefecture). b, Paulownia Village (Farmers and tree near water, Mishima). c, Bonnet Bus (White bus, Hiraizumi, Iwate prefecture). d, Bonnet Bus (Houses, people under umbrella, Hiraizumi). e, Bent House by the Sea (Mother with children near sea, Yurihonjo, Akita prefecture). f, After the Snowfall (Person and houses in snow, Akita, Akita prefecture). g, Railbus (Railbus and station, Kamikita District, Aomori prefecture). h, Railbus (People at station, Kamikita District). i, Dear Home (People on path near house, Tsuruoka, Yamagata prefecture). j, Kokeshi Doll (Children and adults near doll vendor's stall, Shiroishi, Miyagi prefecture).

2010, Dec. 1 Photo. *Perf. 13*

3280	A2681 Sheet of 10	20.00	20.00
a.-j.	80y Any single	2.00	1.50

PREFECTURE ISSUES

Japan has 47 prefectures (political subdivisions) and 13 postal regions (12 until 2004). Since 1989, the national postal ministry has issued stamps to publicize each prefecture. These prefectural stamps are valid throughout Japan and were issued not only in the prefecture named on the stamp but in all other prefectures in the postal region, and in one or more post offices in the other 11 or 12 postal regions. Prefectural stamps are distinguishable from other Japanese stamps by the style of the ideographic characters of "Nippon yubin" on each stamp:

Inscr. on National Stamps since 1948

Inscr. on Prefectural Stamps

Monkeys (Nagano) — ZA1

Cherries on Tree (Yamagata) — ZA2

Shurei-mon, Gate of Courtesy (Okinawa) — ZA3

Dogo Hot Spa (Ehime) — ZA4

Blue-eyed Doll (Kanagawa) ZA5

Seto Inland Sea (Hiroshima) — ZA6

Memorial Hall and Mandai Bridge (Niigata) — ZA8

Nagoya Castle and *Shachihoko* (Aichi) — ZA9

Mt. Takasaki Monkey Holding Perilla Leaf, Fruit (Oita) — ZA10

City Hall, 1888 (Hokkaido) ZA11

Runner, Flower (Hokkaido) ZA12

Kumamoto Castle (Kumamoto) ZA13

Stone Lantern, Kenroku-en Park (Ishikawa) — ZA14

Bunraku Puppets and Theater (Osaka) — ZA15

Shigaraki Ware Raccoon Dog and Lake Biwa (Shiga) ZA16

Apples and Blossoms (Aomori) — ZA17

Raccoon Dogs Dancing (Chiba) — ZA18

Blowfish Lanterns (Yamaguchi) ZA19

Tokyo Station (Tokyo) — ZA20

2nd Asian Winter Olympics (Hokkaido) ZA21

Waterfalls (Toyama) ZA22

Perf. 13, 13½ (#Z4, Z11, Z20), 13x13½ (#Z12-Z19)

1989-90 Photo., Litho. (#Z16-Z17)

Z1	ZA1	62y	multicolored	1.10	.65
Z2	ZA2	62y	multicolored	1.10	.65
Z3	ZA3	62y	multicolored	1.10	.65
Z4	ZA4	62y	multicolored	1.10	.65
Z5	ZA5	62y	multicolored	1.10	.65
Z6		62y	sampan, bridge	1.10	.65
Z7		62y	islands, stairs, starbursts	1.10	.65
a.	ZA6		Pair, #Z6-Z7	2.25	1.50
Z8	ZA8	62y	multicolored	1.10	.65
Z9	ZA9	62y	multicolored	1.10	.65
Z10	ZA10	62y	multicolored	1.10	.65
Z11	ZA11	62y	multicolored	1.10	.65
Z12	ZA12	62y	multicolored	1.10	.65
Z13	ZA13	62y	multicolored	1.10	.65
Z14	ZA14	62y	multicolored	1.10	.65
Z15	ZA15	62y	multicolored	1.10	.65
Z16	ZA16	62y	multicolored	1.10	.65
Z17	ZA17	62y	multicolored	1.10	.65
Z18	ZA18	62y	multicolored	1.10	.65
Z19	ZA19	62y	multicolored	1.10	.65
Z20	ZA20	62y	multicolored	1.10	.65
Z21	ZA21	62y	multicolored	1.10	.65
Z22	ZA22	62y	multicolored	1.10	.60
			Nos. Z1-Z22 (22)	24.20	14.25

Sheets containing 4 #Z1, Z2, Z4, Z11 or 3 #Z14 + label, 3 #Z19 + label were lottery prizes.

Issued: #Z1-Z2, 4/1; #Z3, 5/15; #Z4, 6/1; #Z5, 6/2; #Z6-Z7, 7/7; #Z8, 7/14; #Z9, 8/1; #Z10-Z11, 8/15; #Z12, 9/1; #Z13, 9/29; #Z14-Z17, 10/2; #Z18, 10/27; #Z19-Z20, 11/1; #Z21, 3/1/90; #Z22, 4/18/90.

See Nos. Z263, Z285, Z363.

Nos. Z23-Z69 were issued as one set. It is broken into sections for ease of reference. See No. Z69a for sheet containing all 47 stamps.

Hokkaido ZA23

Aomori ZA24

Iwate — ZA25

Miyagi — ZA26

Akita ZA27

Yamagata ZA28

Fukushima ZA29

Ibaraki ZA30

Flowers of the Prefectures.

1990, Apr. 27 Litho. *Perf. 13½*

Z23	ZA23	62y	Sweet briar	3.50	.75
Z24	ZA24	62y	Apple blossom	1.25	.75
Z25	ZA25	62y	Paulowina	1.25	.75
Z26	ZA26	62y	Japanese bush clover	1.25	.75
Z27	ZA27	62y	Butterbur flower	1.25	.75
Z28	ZA28	62y	Safflower	1.25	.75
Z29	ZA29	62y	Alpine rose	1.25	.75
Z30	ZA30	62y	Rose	1.25	.75
			Nos. Z23-Z30 (8)	12.25	6.00

See No. Z190.

Tochigi — ZA31

Gunma — ZA32

Saitama — ZA33

Chiba — ZA34

Tokyo ZA35

Kanagawa ZA36

Yamanashi ZA37

Nagano ZA38

Niigata — ZA39

Toyama — ZA40

Z31	ZA31	62y	Yashio azalea	1.25	.75
Z32	ZA32	62y	Japanese azalea	1.25	.75
Z33	ZA33	62y	Primrose	1.25	.75
Z34	ZA34	62y	Rape blossom	1.25	.75
Z35	ZA35	62y	Cherry blossom	1.25	.75
Z36	ZA36	62y	Gold-banded lily	1.25	.75
Z37	ZA37	62y	Cherry blossom	1.25	.75
Z38	ZA38	62y	Autumn bellflower	3.50	.75
Z39	ZA39	62y	Tulip	1.25	.75
Z40	ZA40	62y	Tulip	1.25	.75
			Nos. Z31-Z40 (10)	14.75	7.50

See No. Z197.

Ishikawa ZA41

Fukui ZA42

Gifu ZA43

Shizuoka ZA44

Aichi — ZA45

Mie — ZA46

Shiga — ZA47

Kyoto — ZA48

Osaka — ZA49

Hyogo — ZA50

Z41	ZA41	62y	Black lily	1.25	.75
Z42	ZA42	62y	Daffodil	1.25	.75
Z43	ZA43	62y	Chinese milk vetch	1.50	.75
Z44	ZA44	62y	Azalea	2.00	.75
Z45	ZA45	62y	Rabbit-ear iris	1.25	.75
Z46	ZA46	62y	Iris	1.25	.75
Z47	ZA47	62y	Alpine rose	3.00	.75
Z48	ZA48	62y	Drooping cherry blossom	3.00	.75
Z49	ZA49	62y	Japanese apricot and primrose	1.25	.75
Z50	ZA50	62y	Chrysanthemum	1.25	.75
			Nos. Z41-Z50 (10)	17.00	7.50

Nara
ZA51

Wakayama
ZA52

Tottori
ZA53

Shimane
ZA54

Okayama
ZA55

Hiroshima
ZA56

Yamaguchi
ZA57

Tokushima
ZA58

Kagawa — ZA59

Ehime — ZA60

Z51	ZA51	62y	Double cherry blossom	2.00	.75
Z52	ZA52	62y	Japanese apricot	1.50	.75
Z53	ZA53	62y	Pear blossom	1.25	.75
Z54	ZA54	62y	Peony	1.25	.75
Z55	ZA55	62y	Peach blossom	1.25	.75
Z56	ZA56	62y	Japanese Maple	1.25	.75
Z57	ZA57	62y	Summer orange blossom	1.25	.75
Z58	ZA58	62y	Sudachi orange blossom	1.50	.75
Z59	ZA59	62y	Olive blossom	5.00	.75
Z60	ZA60	62y	Mandarin orange blossom	2.50	.75
			Nos. Z51-Z60 (10)	18.75	7.50

Kochi
ZA61

Fukuoka
ZA62

Saga
ZA63

Nagasaki
ZA64

Kumamoto
ZA65

Oita
ZA66

Miyazaki
ZA67

Kagoshima
ZA68

Okinawa — ZA69

Z61	ZA61	62y	Myrica	2.00	.75
Z62	ZA62	62y	Japanese apricot	1.25	.75
Z63	ZA63	62y	Laurel	1.25	.75
Z64	ZA64	62y	Unzen azalea	1.25	.75
Z65	ZA65	62y	Autumn bellflower	1.25	.75
Z66	ZA66	62y	Japanese apricot of bungo	1.25	.75
Z67	ZA67	62y	Crinum	1.25	.75
Z68	ZA68	62y	Rosebay	1.25	.75
Z69	ZA69	62y	Coral tree	1.25	.75
a.			Sheet of 47 + 3 labels, #Z23-Z69	110.00	
			Nos. Z61-Z69 (9)	12.00	6.75

Nos. Z23-Z69 were issued in sheets of 20. No. Z69a was released in all prefectures.

Seven Baby Crows (Ibaraki) — ZA70

Inns of Tsumago & Magome (Nagano)
ZA71 ZA72

Mt. Fuji and Tea Picking (Shizuoka)
ZA73

Two Peaches (Fukushima)
ZA74

Mt. Sakurajima (Kagoshima)
ZA75

Fireworks Festival of Omagari (Akita)
ZA76

Travel Expo '90, Nagasaki (Nagasaki) — ZA77

Tokyo Shin Post Office (Tokyo)
ZA78

Yasukibushi Folk Song (Shimane)
ZA79

Ryukyu Dancer (Okinawa)
ZA80

Litho., Litho. & Engr. (#Z70-Z71)

1990 ***Perf. 13***

Z70	ZA70	62y	multicolored	1.10	.75
Z71	ZA71	62y	blk & buff	1.10	.75
Z72	ZA72	62y	blk & pale grn	1.10	.75
a.			Pair, #Z71-Z72	2.25	1.75
Z73	ZA73	62y	multicolored	1.10	.70
Z74	ZA74	62y	multicolored	1.10	.70
Z75	ZA75	62y	multicolored	1.10	.70
Z76	ZA76	62y	multicolored	1.10	.70
Z77	ZA77	62y	multicolored	1.10	.70
Z78	ZA78	62y	multicolored	1.10	.70
Z79	ZA79	62y	multicolored	1.10	.70
Z80	ZA80	62y	multicolored	1.10	.70
			Nos. Z70-Z80 (11)	12.10	7.85

Issued: #Z70-Z72, 5/1; #Z73, 5/2; #Z74, 6/1; #Z75-Z76, 7/2; #Z77, 8/1; #Z78, 8/6; #Z79-Z80, 8/15.

Sheets of 3 + label of #Z70, Z73, Z80 were lottery prizes. Value, each $3.25.

See Nos. Z332-Z333.

Dancing Girl (Kyoto)
ZA81

Old Path of Kumano (Wakayama)
ZA82

45th Natl. Athletic Meet (Fukuoka)
ZA83

Izu Swamp, Swans (Miyagi)
ZA84

Spring (Gifu) — ZA85

Summer (Gifu) — ZA86

Autumn (Gifu) — ZA87

Winter (Gifu) — ZA88

Nursery Rhyme, Toryanse (Saitama) — ZA89

Japanese Cranes (Hokkaido)
ZA90

1990

Z81	ZA81 62y multicolored		1.10	.75
Z82	ZA82 62y multicolored		1.10	.75
Z83	ZA83 62y multicolored		1.10	.75
Z84	ZA84 62y multicolored		1.10	.75
Z85	ZA85 62y multicolored		1.10	.75
Z86	ZA86 62y multicolored		1.10	.75
Z87	ZA87 62y multicolored		1.10	.75
Z88	ZA88 62y multicolored		1.10	.75
a.	Strip of 4, #Z85-Z88		4.50	4.50
Z89	ZA89 62y multicolored		1.10	.75
Z90	ZA90 62y multicolored		1.10	.75
	Nos. Z81-Z90 (10)		11.00	7.50

Issued: #Z81-Z83, 9/3; #Z84, 10/1; #Z85-Z88, 10/9; #Z89, 10/12; #Z90, 10/30.

Sheets of 3 #Z82 + label were lottery prizes. Value, $3.25.

See Nos. Z171-Z174.

Bizen Ware (Okayama) — ZA92

Battle of Yashima (Kagawa) — ZA91

Yoshinogari Ruins (Saga) — ZA94

Bride Under Cherry Blossoms (Yamanashi) ZA95

Carp (Niigata) ZA96

Lily Bell (Hokkaido) ZA97

Lilac (Hokkaido) ZA98

Day Lily (Hokkaido) ZA99

Rowanberry (Hokkaido) ZA100

Litho., Photo. (#Z94-Z95)

1991 ***Perf. 13***

Z91	ZA91	62y multicolored	1.10	.70
Z92		62y pedestal	1.10	.70
Z93		62y bowl	1.10	.70
a.	ZA92	Pair, #Z92-Z93	2.25	1.50
Z94	ZA94	62y multicolored	1.10	.70
Z95	ZA95	62y multicolored	1.10	.70
Z96	ZA96	62y multicolored	1.10	.70
Z97	ZA97	62y multicolored	1.10	.70
Z98	ZA98	62y multicolored	1.10	.70
Z99	ZA99	62y multicolored	1.10	.70

Z100	ZA100 62y multicolored	1.10	.70
a.	Strip of 4, #Z97-Z100	4.50	4.50
	Nos. Z91-Z100 (10)	11.00	7.00

Issued: #Z91, 2/19; #Z92-Z93, 4/5; #Z94, 4/12; #Z95, 4/18; #Z96, 5/1; #Z97-Z100, 5/31.

See Nos. Z304-Z307.

Nikkou Mountains (Tochigi) — ZA101

Mt. Iwate by Yaoji Hashimoto (Iwate) — ZA102

Wooden Puppet (Tokushima) ZA103

Whales (Kochi) ZA104

Fringed Orchids (Tokyo) ZA105

Cape Toi, Horses (Miyazaki) ZA106

Black Pearls of Kabira Bay (Okinawa) ZA107

Japanese Pears (Tottori) ZA108

Tsujun-kyo Bridge (Kumamoto) ZA109

1991 **Photo.**

Z101	ZA101 62y multicolored	1.10	.70
Z102	ZA102 62y multicolored	1.10	.70
a.	Booklet pane of 10	11.00	
	Complete booklet, #Z102a	11.00	
Z103	ZA103 62y multicolored	1.10	.70
a.	Pane of 10	11.00	
Z104	ZA104 62y multicolored	1.10	.70
a.	Pane of 10	11.00	
Z105	ZA105 41y multicolored	2.50	1.00
a.	Booklet pane of 10	15.00	
	Complete booklet, #Z105a	15.00	
Z106	ZA106 62y multicolored	1.10	.70
a.	Booklet pane of 10	15.00	
	Complete booklet, #Z106a	15.00	
Z107	ZA107 41y multicolored	.80	.50
Z108	ZA108 62y multicolored	1.10	.70
Z109	ZA109 62y multicolored	1.10	.70
a.	Booklet pane of 10	15.00	
	Complete booklet, #Z108a	15.00	
	Nos. Z101-Z109 (9)	11.00	6.40

Issued: #Z101, 5/29; #Z102, 6/10; #Z103-Z104, 6/26; #Z105-Z106, 7/1; #Z107-Z108, 8/1; #Z109, 8/26.

Sheets of 3 #Z106 + label were lottery prizes. Value, $3.

Ninja, Iga Ueno Castle (Mie) ZA111

46th Natl. Athletic Meet (Ishikawa) ZA110

Eyeglass Industry (Fukui) ZA112

Nursery Rhyme, Tortoise and the Hare — ZA113

Kobe City Weathervane (Hyogo) — ZA114

Spring (Nara) — ZA115

Autumn (Nara, Gunma) — ZA116

Litho., Photo. (#Z110, Z112)

1991 ***Perf. 13, 13½ (#Z110)***

Z110	ZA110 41y multicolored	.80	.50
a.	Pane of 10	8.00	
Z111	ZA111 62y multicolored	1.10	.75
a.	Booklet pane of 10	14.00	
	Complete booklet, #Z111a	14.00	
Z112	ZA112 62y multicolored	1.10	.75
a.	Booklet pane of 10	14.00	
	Complete booklet, #Z112a	14.00	
Z113	ZA113 62y multicolored	1.10	.75
a.	Booklet pane of 10	14.00	
	Complete booklet, #Z113a	14.00	
Z114	ZA114 62y multicolored	1.10	.75
a.	Booklet pane of 10	14.00	
	Complete booklet, #Z114a	14.00	
Z115	ZA115 62y multicolored	1.10	.75
Z116	ZA116 62y multicolored	1.10	.75
a.	Pair, #Z115-Z116	2.25	1.50
b.	Booklet pane, 5 #Z116a	14.00	
	Complete booklet, #Z116b	14.00	
	Nos. Z110-Z116 (7)	7.40	5.00

Issued: #Z110, 9/2; #Z111, 9/10; #Z112, 10/1; #Z113, 10/23; #Z114-Z116, 10/25.

See Nos. Z177-Z178.

Gogo-An Temple, Sea of Japan (Niigata) ZA117

Natl. Land Afforestation Campaign (Fukuoka) ZA118

Arctic Fox (Hokkaido) ZA119

Tateyama Mountain Range (Toyama) ZA120

Rikuchu Coast (Iwate) — ZA121

Kurushima Strait (Ehime) ZA122

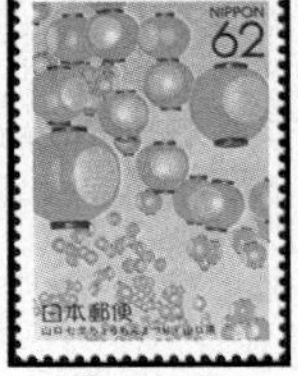

Tsurusaki Dance (Oita) ZA123

Tanabata Lantern Festival (Yamaguchi) ZA124

Shasui-no-taki Waterfall (Kanagawa) ZA125

Kurodabushi Dance (Fukuoka) ZA126

Boat Race (Okinawa) ZA127

Osaka Castle, Business Park (Osaka) ZA128

Owl, Mt. Horaiji (Aichi) — ZA129

1992 **Litho.** ***Perf. 13½***

Z117	ZA117 41y multicolored	.80	.50
a.	Pane of 10	8.00	

Photo.

Z118	ZA118 41y multicolored	.80	.50
Z119	ZA119 62y multicolored	1.10	.75
a.	Souvenir sheet of 3	3.50	3.50

Litho.

Z120	ZA120 62y multicolored	1.10	.75
a.	Pane of 10	11.00	

Photo.

Z121	ZA121 62y multicolored	1.10	.75
a.	Pane of 10	11.00	
Z122	ZA122 62y multicolored	1.10	.75
a.	Pane of 10	11.00	
Z123	ZA123 62y multicolored	1.10	.75
Z124	ZA124 62y multicolored	1.10	.75
Z125	ZA125 62y multicolored	1.10	.75
a.	Pane of 10	11.00	
b.	Souvenir sheet of 3	3.50	3.50

Litho.

Z126	ZA126 62y multicolored	1.10	.90
Z127	ZA127 62y multicolored	1.10	.90
Z128	ZA128 41y multicolored	.80	.60

Photo.

Z129	ZA129 62y multicolored	1.10	.75
a.	Souvenir sheet of 3	3.50	2.25
b.	Pane of 10	11.00	
	Nos. Z117-Z129 (13)	13.40	9.40

Issued: #Z117, 5/1; #Z118, 5/8; #Z119, 5/29; #Z121-Z122, 6/23; #Z124, 7/7; #Z123, 7/23; #Z125, 7/24; #Z126, 8/3; #Z127, 8/17; #Z129, 10/15.

See also No. Z320.

Oga Peninsula (Akita) ZA130

Fukuroda Waterfall (Ibaraki) ZA131

Notojima Bridge, Nanao Bay (Ishikawa) ZA132

Tama District Mountains (Metropolitan Tokyo) ZA133

Harbor Seal (Hokkaido) — ZA134

Peace Statue (Kagawa) ZA135

Hana Ta'ue Rice Planting Festival (Hiroshima) ZA136

Paradise Flycatcher and Mt. Fuji (Shizuoka) ZA137

Sailboats on Lake Biwa (Shiga) ZA138

Matumoto Castle & Japan Alps (Nagano) ZA139

Ohara Festival (Kagoshima) ZA140

Oirase Mountain Stream (Aomori) ZA141

Yourou Valley (Chiba) — ZA142

1993 Litho. *Perf. 13½*

Z130	ZA130 41y multicolored	.80	.50
a.	Pane of 10	8.00	
Z131	ZA131 62y multicolored	1.10	.75
a.	Pane of 10	11.00	

Photo.

Z132	ZA132 62y multicolored	1.10	.75
a.	Pane of 10	11.50	
Z133	ZA133 62y multicolored	1.10	.75
a.	Booklet pane of 10	11.50	
	Complete booklet, #Z133a	11.50	
Z134	ZA134 62y multicolored	1.10	.75
Z135	ZA135 62y multicolored	1.10	.75
a.	Pane of 10	11.50	
Z136	ZA136 62y multicolored	1.25	.75
Z137	ZA137 41y multicolored	.80	.50
a.	Pane of 10	12.00	
Z138	ZA138 62y multicolored	1.25	.75
a.	Pane of 10	12.00	
Z139	ZA139 62y multicolored	1.25	.75
a.	Pane of 10	12.00	
Z140	ZA140 41y multicolored	.80	.50
a.	Pane of 10	8.00	

Perf. 13x13½

Z141	ZA141 62y multicolored	1.10	.75
a.	Pane of 10	11.00	

Perf. 13½

Z142	ZA142 41y multicolored	.80	.50
a.	Pane of 10	8.00	
	Nos. Z130-Z142 (13)	13.55	8.75

Issued: #Z130, 2/12; #Z131, 3/26; #Z132, 4/2; #Z133, 4/23; #Z134, 5/17; #Z135, 5/21; #Z136, 6/4; #Z137, 6/23; #Z138, 7/1; #Z139, 7/16; #Z140, 9/1; #Z141, 9/22; #Z142, 10/1.

See also No. Z321.

Dream Bridge (Metropolitan Tokyo) ZA143

Kurobe Canyon & Dam (Toyama) ZA144

Haiku, Storehouse of Poet Issa (1763-1827) (Nagano) ZA145

Okuni, Izumo Great Shrine, Taisha (Shimane) ZA146

Fukiwari Falls (Gunma) ZA147

Ezoshika (Hokkaido) ZA148

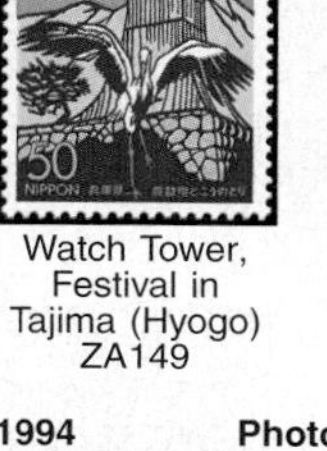

Watch Tower, Festival in Tajima (Hyogo) ZA149

Wakura Coast (Wakayama) ZA150

1994 Photo. *Perf. 13*

Z143	ZA143 50y multicolored	.95	.50
a.	Pane of 10	9.50	
Z144	ZA144 80y multicolored	1.50	.75
a.	Pane of 10	15.00	
Z145	ZA145 80y multicolored	1.50	.75
a.	Pane of 10	15.00	
Z146	ZA146 80y multicolored	1.50	.75
a.	Pane of 10	15.00	

Litho.

Z147	ZA147 80y multicolored	1.50	.75
a.	Pane of 10	15.00	
Z148	ZA148 50y multicolored	1.00	.75
a.	Pane of 10	10.00	
Z149	ZA149 50y multicolored	1.00	.65
a.	Pane of 10	10.00	
Z150	ZA150 80y multicolored	1.50	.75
a.	Pane of 10	15.00	
	Nos. Z143-Z150 (8)	10.45	5.65

Issued: #Z143, 3/23; #Z144, 4/25; #Z145-Z146, 5/2; #Z147, 6/6; #Z148, 6/7; #Z149, 6/23; #Z150, 7/15.

Kentish Plovers (Mie) ZA151

Awaodori Dance (Tokushima) ZA152

Tug-of-War (Okinawa) ZA153

Kehi Pine Wood (Fukui) ZA154

Matsushima (Miyagi) ZA155

Kunchi Festival (Nagasaki) ZA156

1994 Photo. *Perf. 13*

Z151	ZA151 80y multicolored	1.50	.75
a.	Pane of 10	15.00	
Z152	ZA152 50y multicolored	1.00	.50
a.	Pane of 10	10.00	
Z153	ZA153 50y multicolored	1.00	.50
Z154	ZA154 50y multicolored	1.00	.50
a.	Pane of 10	10.00	
Z155	ZA155 80y multicolored	1.60	.75
a.	Pane of 10	16.50	
Z156	ZA156 80y multicolored	1.60	.75
a.	Pane of 10	16.50	
	Nos. Z151-Z156 (6)	7.70	3.75

Issued: #Z151, 7/22; #Z152-Z153, 8/1; #Z154, 9/1; #Z155, 9/20; #Z156, 10/3.

Hokkaido Chipmunks (Hokkaido) — ZA157

Ushiwakamaru and Benkei (Kyoto) — ZA158

Utopia Flower (Gifu) ZA159

Jade Bead, Gyofu Soma (1883-1950), Lyricist (Niigata) ZA160

Cape Ashizuri-Misaki Lighthouse (Kochi) ZA161

Ishikawamon Gate, Kanazawa Castle (Ishikawa) ZA162

Akamon Gate, University of Tokyo (Tokyo) ZA163

Three Waterfalls, Kuroyama (Saitama) ZA164

Lady's Slipper, Rebun Island (Hokkaido) ZA165

Street with Zelkova Trees (Miyagi) ZA166

Eisa Festival (Okinawa) — ZA167

1995 Photo. *Perf. 13*

Z157 ZA157 80y multicolored 1.90 .75
a. Pane of 10 19.00

Perf. 13½

Z158 ZA158 80y multicolored 1.90 .75
a. Pane of 10 19.00
Z159 ZA159 80y multicolored 1.90 .75
a. Pane of 10 19.00
Z160 ZA160 80y multicolored 1.90 .75
a. Pane of 10 19.00
Z161 ZA161 80y multicolored 1.90 .75
a. Pane of 10 19.00
Z162 ZA162 80y multicolored 1.90 .75
a. Pane of 10 19.00
Z163 ZA163 50y multicolored 1.10 .50
a. Pane of 10 11.00
Z164 ZA164 80y multicolored 1.75 .75
a. Pane of 10 17.50
Z165 ZA165 80y multicolored 1.75 .75
a. Pane of 10 17.50
Z166 ZA166 50y multicolored 1.00 .50
a. Pane of 10 10.00
Z167 ZA167 80y multicolored 1.60 .75
Nos. Z157-Z167 (11) 18.60 7.75

Issued: #Z157, 3/3; #Z158, 4/3; #Z159, 4/26; #Z160, 5/1; #Z161-Z162, 6/1; #Z163-Z165, 7/7; #Z166-Z167, 8/1.

Seasons Types of 1990-91 and

Kishiwada Danjiri Festival (Osaka) ZA168

Yamadera Temple (Yamagata) ZA169

Karatsu Kunchi Festival (Saga) ZA170

Niimi-No-Shou Festival (Okayama) ZA171

Kirifuri Waterfall (Tochigi) ZA172

10th All-Japan Holstein Show (Chiba) ZA173

Nos. Z171-Z174: (Gifu).
No. Z177, (Nara). No. Z178, (Nara, Gunma).

1995 Photo. *Perf. 13½*

Z168 ZA168 80y multicolored 1.60 .75
a. Pane of 10 16.00
Z169 ZA169 80y multicolored 1.60 .75
a. Pane of 10 16.00
Z170 ZA170 80y multicolored 1.60 .75
a. Pane of 10 16.00

Perf. 13

Z171 ZA85 80y Spring 1.60 .75
Z172 ZA86 80y Summer 1.60 .75
Z173 ZA87 80y Autumn 1.60 .75
Z174 ZA88 80y Winter 1.60 .75
a. Strip of 4, #Z171-Z174 6.50 4.50

Perf. 13½

Z175 ZA171 80y multicolored 1.60 .75
Z176 ZA172 50y multicolored 1.00 .50
a. Pane of 10 10.00
Z177 ZA115 80y Spring 1.50 .75
Z178 ZA116 80y Autumn 1.50 .75
a. Pair, #Z177-Z178 3.00 1.75
Z179 ZA173 80y multicolored 1.60 .75
a. Pane of 10 15.00
Nos. Z168-Z179 (12) 18.40 8.75

Issued: #Z168, 9/1; #Z169, 9/15; #Z170-Z174, 10/2; #Z175, 10/13; #Z176, 10/27; #Z177-Z178, 11/6; #Z179, 11/21.

Clione Limancia (Hokkaido) ZA174

Ushibuka Haiya Festival (Kumamoto) ZA175

Peony of Sukagawa (Fukushima) ZA176

Hamayu (Mie) ZA177

Ama Divers (Mie) — ZA178

World Ceramics Expo '96 (Saga) — ZA179

Shosenkyo Gorge (Yamanashi) ZA180

Murasaki Shikibu of Takefu (Fukui) ZA181

1996 Litho. *Perf. 13½x13*

Z180 ZA174 80y multicolored 1.50 .75
a. Pane of 10 11.50

Photo.

Z181 ZA175 80y multicolored 1.50 .75
a. Pane of 10 15.00
Z182 ZA176 80y multicolored 1.50 .75
a. Pane of 10 15.00
Z183 ZA177 80y multicolored 1.50 .75
Z184 ZA178 80y multicolored 1.50 .75
a. Pair, #Z183-Z184 3.00 1.75
b. Pane, 5 #Z184a 15.00
Z185 ZA179 80y multicolored 1.50 .75

Perf. 13½

Z186 ZA180 50y multicolored .95 .50
a. Pane of 10 9.50
Z187 ZA181 80y multicolored 1.50 .75
a. Pane of 10 15.00
Nos. Z180-Z187 (8) 11.45 5.75

Issued: #Z180, 2/6; #Z181, 4/1; #Z182, 4/26; #Z183-Z184, 5/1; #Z185, 5/17; #Z186, 6/3; #Z187, 6/24.

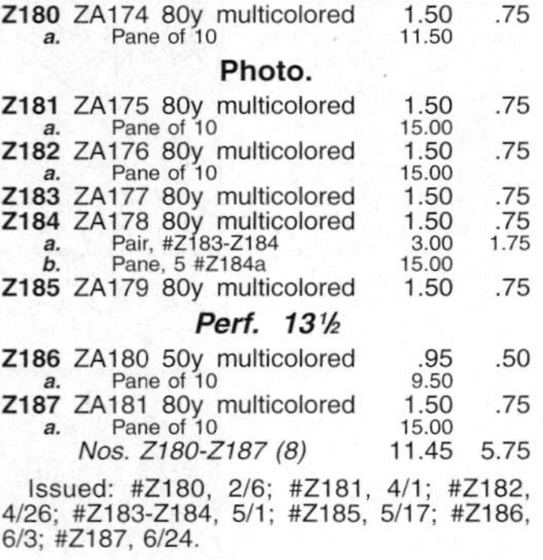
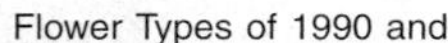
Flower Types of 1990 and

Ancient Trees, Kompon-chudo of Mt. Hiei (Shiga) ZA182

Nishiumi Marine Park (Ehime) ZA183

Nebuta Festival (Aomori) ZA184

Main Palace, Shuri Castle (Okinawa) ZA186

Shimozuru Usudaiko Odori Folk Dance (Miyazaki) ZA185

Asakusa Kaminarimon Gate (Metropolitan Tokyo) ZA187

Tottori Shanshan Festival (Tottori) ZA188

Saito Kinen Festival Matsumoto (Nagano) ZA189

#Z190, (Hokkaido). #Z197, (Nagano).

1996 Photo. *Perf. 13½*

Z188 ZA182 80y multicolored 1.50 .75
a. Pane of 10 15.00
Z189 ZA183 80y multicolored 1.50 .75
a. Pane of 10 15.00
Z190 ZA23 80y Sweetbriar 1.50 .75
Z191 ZA184 80y multicolored 1.50 .75
a. Pane of 10 15.00
Z192 ZA185 80y multicolored 1.50 .75
a. Pane of 10 15.00
Z193 ZA186 80y multicolored 1.50 .75
Z194 ZA187 80y multicolored 1.50 .75
a. Pane of 10 15.00
Z195 ZA188 80y multicolored 1.50 .75
Z196 ZA189 80y multicolored 1.50 .75
a. Pane of 10 15.00
Z197 ZA38 80y Autumn bell-flower 1.50 .75
Nos. Z188-Z197 (10) 15.00 7.50

Issued: #Z188-Z189, 7/1; #Z190, 7/5; #Z191, 7/23; #Z192-Z193, 8/1; #Z194, 8/8; #Z195, 8/16; #Z196-Z197, 8/22.

Sengokubara Marsh (Kanagawa) ZA190

Nagoya Festival (Aichi) — ZA191

Grass-burning Rite on Mt. Wakakusa (Nara) ZA193

1997 Men's Handball World Championships (Kumamoto) ZA194

Tea Picking (Shizuoka) ZA195

Dahurian Rhododendron (Hokkaido) ZA196

Mt. Fuji (Shizuoka) — ZA197

1996-97 **Photo.** ***Perf. 13½***

No.	Type	Description	Unused	Used
Z198	ZA190	80y multicolored	1.50	.75
a.		Pane of 10	15.00	
Z199		80y horse, rider	1.50	.75
Z200		80y two floats	1.50	.75
a.	ZA191	Pair, #Z199-Z200	3.00	1.75
b.		Pane, 5 #Z200a	15.00	
Z201	ZA193	50y multicolored	.95	.50
a.		Pane of 10	9.50	
Z202	ZA194	80y multicolored	1.50	.75
a.		Pane of 10	15.00	
Z203	ZA195	50y multicolored	.95	.50
a.		Pane of 10	9.50	
Z204	ZA196	80y multicolored	1.50	.75
a.		Pane of 10	15.00	
Z205		80y cattle	1.50	.75
Z206		80y orange grasses	1.50	.75
a.	ZA197	Pair, #Z205-Z206	2.50	1.75
b.		Pane, 5 #Z206a	12.50	
		Nos. Z198-Z206 (9)	12.40	6.25

Issued: #Z198, 9/6; #Z199-Z200, 10/1; #Z201, 11/15; #Z202, 4/17/97; #Z203-Z206, 4/25/97.

Marugame Castle (Kagawa) ZA199

Hokkaido Ermine (Hokkaido) ZA200

Okayama Castle (Okayama) ZA201

Okinawan Fruits (Okinawa) ZA202

ZA204 ZA205

ZA206 ZA207

Nagasaki Kaido Highway (Nagasaki, Saga, Fukuoka)

Fukiya Koji's Hanayome Ningyo, Doll of Bride (Niigata) ZA208

The Clock Tower of Kyoto University (Kyoto) ZA209

1997 **Photo.** ***Perf. 13½***

No.	Type	Description	Unused	Used
Z207	ZA199	80y multicolored	1.50	.75
a.		Pane of 10	15.00	
Z208	ZA200	50y multicolored	.95	.50
a.		Pane of 10	9.50	
Z209	ZA201	80y multicolored	1.50	.75
a.		Pane of 10	15.00	
Z210		50y pineapple	.95	.60
Z211		50y mango	.95	.60
a.	ZA202	Pair, #Z210-Z211	1.90	1.40
Z212	ZA204	80y multicolored	1.50	.75
Z213	ZA205	80y multicolored	1.50	.75
Z214	ZA206	80y multicolored	1.50	.75
Z215	ZA207	80y multicolored	1.50	.75
a.		Strip of 4, #Z212-Z215	6.00	6.00
Z216	ZA208	50y multicolored	.95	.50
a.		Pane of 10	9.50	
Z217	ZA209	80y multicolored	1.50	.75
a.		Pane of 10	15.00	
		Nos. Z207-Z217 (11)	14.30	7.45

Issued: #Z207, 5/15; #Z208-Z209, 5/30; #Z210-Z211, 6/2; #Z212-Z215, 6/3; #Z216-Z217, 6/18.

Kanto Festival (Akita) ZA210

San-in Yume Minato Exposition (Tottori) ZA211

Waterwheel Plant, Hozoji-numa Pond (Saitama) ZA212

Lake Kasumigaura (Ibaraki) ZA215

Bon Wind Festival, Owara (Toyama) — ZA213

Tokyo Big Site (Tokyo) ZA216

Telecom Center (Tokyo) ZA217

Rainbow Bridge (Tokyo) ZA218

Intl. Forum (Tokyo) ZA219

Tokyo Museum (Tokyo) ZA220

First World Walking Festival (Saitama) ZA221

1997 **Photo.** ***Perf. 13½***

No.	Type	Description	Unused	Used
Z218	ZA210	80y multicolored	1.50	.75
a.		Pane of 10	15.00	
Z219	ZA211	80y multicolored	1.50	.75
a.		Pane of 10	15.00	
Z220	ZA212	50y multicolored	.95	.50
a.		Pane of 10	9.50	
Z221		80y woman	1.50	.75
Z222		80y man	1.50	.75
a.	ZA213	Pair, #Z221-Z222	3.00	1.75
b.		Pane, 5 #Z222a	15.00	
Z223	ZA215	80y multicolored	1.50	.75
a.		Pane of 10	15.00	
Z224	ZA216	80y multicolored	1.50	.75
Z225	ZA217	80y multicolored	1.50	.75
Z226	ZA218	80y multicolored	1.50	.75
Z227	ZA219	80y multicolored	1.50	.75
Z228	ZA220	80y multicolored	1.50	.75
a.		Strip of 5, #Z224-Z228	7.50	5.00
b.		Pane, 2 #Z228a	15.00	
Z229	ZA221	80y multicolored	1.50	.75
a.		Pane of 10	15.00	
		Nos. Z218-Z229 (12)	17.45	8.75

Issued: #Z218, 7/7; #Z219, 7/11; #Z220, 8/1; #Z221-Z222, 8/20; #Z223, 9/1; #Z224-Z228, 10/1; #Z229, 10/28.

Kanagawa-Chiba Bridge Tunnel (Chiba, Kanagawa) — ZA222

Snow-Covered Tree (Hokkaido) ZA224

Flower in a Dream (Hokkaido) ZA225

Hiyoshi Dam (Kyoto) ZA226

Sanshin (Okinawa) ZA227

Okoshi Daiko (Gifu) ZA228

Kobe-Awaji Expressway (Tokushima, Hyogo) — ZA229

1997-98 **Litho.** ***Perf. 13½***

No.	Type	Description	Unused	Used
Z230		80y denomination upper right	1.50	.75
Z231		80y denomination lower left	1.50	.75
a.	ZA222	Pair, #Z230-Z231	3.00	1.75
b.		Pane, 5 #Z231a	15.00	
Z232	ZA224	80y multicolored	1.50	.75
Z233	ZA225	80y multicolored	1.50	.75
a.		Pair, #Z232-Z233	3.00	1.75
b.		Pane, 5 #Z233a	15.00	

Photo.

Perf. 13

No.	Type	Description	Unused	Used
Z234	ZA226	80y multicolored	1.50	.75
a.		Pane of 10	15.00	

Perf. 13½

No.	Type	Description	Unused	Used
Z235	ZA227	80y multicolored	1.50	.75
a.		Pane of 10	15.00	
Z236	ZA228	80y multicolored	1.50	.75
a.		Pane of 10	15.00	
Z237		80y bridge, whirlpool	1.50	.75
Z238		80y bridge, flowers	1.50	.75
a.	ZA229	Pair, #Z237-Z238	3.00	1.75
b.		Pane, 5 #Z238a	15.00	

Issued: #Z230-Z231, 12/18; #Z232-Z233, 2/5/98; #Z234, 3/2/98; #Z235, 3/4/98; #Z236, 3/19/98; #Z237-Z238, 3/20/98.

Jomon Figurine (Nagano) ZA231

Chaguchagu Umakko, Mt. Iwate (Iwate) ZA232

Tokyo '98 Business Show (Tokyo) ZA233

Mt. Heisei Shinzan (Nagasaki) ZA234

Oze (Gunma) — ZA235

Hanagasa Matsuri (Yamagata) ZA237

9th Women's World Softball Championships (Shizuoka) ZA238

1998	Photo.	*Perf. 13½*	
Z239 ZA231 80y multicolored		1.50	.75
a. Pane of 10		15.00	
Z240 ZA232 80y multicolored		1.50	.75
a. Pane of 10		15.00	
Z241 ZA233 80y multicolored		1.50	.75
a. Pane of 10		15.00	
Z242 ZA234 80y multicolored		1.50	.75
a. Pane of 10		15.00	
Z243 80y blue & multi		1.50	.75
Z244 80y brown & multi		1.50	.75
a. ZA235 Pair, #Z243-Z244		3.00	1.75
b. Pane, 5 #Z244a		15.00	
Z245 ZA237 50y multicolored		.95	.50
a. Pane of 10		9.50	
Z246 ZA238 80y multicolored		1.50	.75
a. Pane of 10		15.00	
Nos. Z239-Z246 (8)		11.45	5.75

Issued: #Z239, 4/1; #Z240, 4/24; #Z241, 5/19; #Z242, 5/20/98; #Z243-Z244, 5/21; #Z245, 6/5; #Z246, 6/22.

Mt. Hakusan (Ishikawa) ZA239

Hita Gion (Ohita) ZA240

World Puppetry Festival (Nagano) — ZA241

Views of Seto (Hiroshima) — ZA243

First Postage Stamps of Ryukyu Islands, 50th Anniv. (Ryukyu Islands) — ZA245

1998	Photo.	*Perf. 13½*	
Z247 ZA239 50y multicolored		.95	.70
a. Pane of 10		9.50	
Z248 ZA240 50y multicolored		.95	.50
a. Pane of 10		9.50	
Z249 50y stage left		.95	.50
Z250 50y stage right		.95	.50
a. ZA241 Pair, #Z249-Z250		1.90	1.00
b. Pane, 5 #Z250a		9.50	
Z251 80y harbor		1.50	.75
Z252 80y highway		1.50	.75
a. ZA243 Pair, #Z251-Z252		3.00	1.75
b. Pane, 5 #Z252a		15.00	

Z253 80y Ryukyu Islands #1		1.50	.75
Z254 80y Ryukyu Islands #228		1.50	.75
a. ZA245 Pair, #Z253-Z254		3.00	1.75
Nos. Z247-Z254 (8)		9.80	5.20

Issued: #Z247-Z248, 7/1; #Z249-Z252, 7/17; #Z253-Z254, 7/23.

Satsuma Pottery, 400th Anniv. (Kogoshima) — ZA247

Seto Ohashi Bridge (Kagawa) ZA249

Kobe Luminaries (Hyogo) ZA250

Apples (Aomori) ZA251

Kumano Path (Wakayama) ZA252

Tama Monorail (Tokyo) — ZA253

1998	Photo.	*Perf. 13½*	
Z255 80y bowl		1.50	.75
Z256 80y vase		1.50	.75
a. ZA247 Pair, #Z255-Z256		3.00	1.75
b. Pane, 5 #Z256a		15.00	
Z257 ZA249 80y multicolored		1.50	.75
a. Pane of 10		15.00	
Z258 ZA250 80y multicolored		1.50	.75
a. Pane of 10		15.00	
	Perf. 13		
Z259 ZA251 80y multicolored		1.50	.75
a. Pane of 10		15.00	
Z260 ZA252 80y multicolored		1.50	.75
	Perf. 13½		
Z261 ZA253 80y multicolored		1.50	.75
a. Pane of 10		15.00	
Nos. Z255-Z261 (7)		10.50	5.25

Issued: #Z255-Z256, 10/1; #Z257-Z258, 11/9; #Z259-Z260, 11/13; #Z261, 11/26.

Dogo Hot Spa (Ehime) Type of 1989 and

Ibara Line (Okayama, Hiroshima) — ZA254

ZA255

Ao-no-Domon (Oita) — ZA256

ZA257

ZA258

Snow World (Hokkaido) ZA259 ZA260

Tokamachi Snow Festival (Niigata) — ZA261

Orchids (Tokyo) — ZA262

Dinosaurs (Fukui) — ZA264

1999	Photo.	*Perf. 13½*	
Z262 ZA254 80y multicolored		1.50	.75
a. Pane of 10		15.00	
Z263 ZA4 80y multicolored		1.50	.75
Z264 ZA255 80y multicolored		1.50	.75
Z265 ZA256 80y multicolored		1.50	.75
a. Vert. pair, #Z264-Z265		3.00	1.75
b. Pane, 5 #Z265a		15.00	
Z266 ZA257 50y multicolored		.95	.50
Z267 ZA258 50y multicolored		.95	.50
Z268 ZA259 80y multicolored		1.50	.75
Z269 ZA260 80y multicolored		1.50	.75
a. Strip of 4, #Z266-Z269		5.00	3.50
Z270 ZA261 80y multicolored		1.50	.75
a. Pane of 10		15.00	
Z271 80y white flowers		1.50	.75
Z272 80y purple flowers		1.50	.75
a. ZA262 Pair, #Z271-Z272		3.00	1.75
b. Pane, 5 #Z272a		15.00	
Z273 80y denomination upper left		1.50	.75
Z274 80y denomination lower left		1.50	.75
a. ZA264 Pair, #Z273-Z274		3.00	1.75
b. Pane, 5 #Z274a		15.00	
Nos. Z262-Z274 (13)		18.40	9.25

Issued: #Z262, 1/1; #Z263-Z265, 2/1; #Z266-Z269, 2/5; #Z270-Z272, 2/12; #Z273-Z274, 2/22.

Lake Chuzenji (Tochigi) — ZA266

Renowned Cherry Tree (Gifu) ZA268

Kiso Observatory, Mt. Ontake (Nagano) ZA271

Postal Service in Okinawa, 125th Anniv. (Okinawa) — ZA269

ZA272

ZA273

ZA274

The Old Path for Kumano (Mie) — ZA275

1999	Photo.	*Perf. 13½*	
Z275 80y Spring		1.50	.75
Z276 80y Fall		1.50	.75
a. ZA266 Pair, #Z275-Z276		3.00	1.75
b. Pane, 5 #Z276a		15.00	
Z277 ZA268 80y multicolored		1.50	.75
a. Pane of 10		15.00	
Z278 80y Traditional costume		1.50	.75
Z279 80y Laughing lions		1.50	.75
a. ZA269 Pair, #Z278-Z279		3.00	1.75
b. Pane, 5 #Z279a		15.00	
Z280 ZA271 80y multicolored		1.50	.75
a. Pane of 10		15.00	
Z281 ZA272 80y Tsuzurato Pass		1.50	.75
Z282 ZA273 80y Matsumoto Pass		1.50	.75
Z283 ZA274 80y Umagoshi Pass		1.50	.75
Z284 ZA275 80y Touri Pass		1.50	.75
a. Strip of 4, #Z281-Z284		6.00	6.00
Nos. Z275-Z284 (10)		15.00	7.50

Issued: #Z275-Z276, 3/1. #Z277, 3/16. #Z278-Z279, 3/23. #Z280, 4/9. #Z281-Z284, 4/16.

Cherries (Yamagata) Type of 1989 and

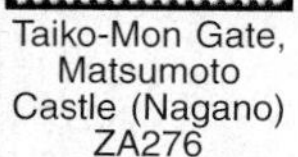

Taiko-Mon Gate, Matsumoto Castle (Nagano) ZA276

Firefly Squid (Toyama) ZA277

ZA278

ZA279

Four Seasons, Kenrokuen Garden (Ishikawa)
ZA280 ZA281

No. Z288, Kaisekitou Pagoda, Spring. No. Z289, Fountain, Summer. No. Z290, Kinjou-reitaku spring, Autumn. No. Z291, Kotoji stone lantern and yukitsuri, Winter.

1999, Apr. 26 Photo. *Perf. 13*

Z285 ZA2 80y like #Z2 1.50 .75

Perf. 13½

Z286 ZA276 80y multicolored 1.50 .75
a. Pane of 10 15.00
Z287 ZA277 80y multicolored 1.50 .75
a. Pane of 10 15.00
Z288 ZA278 80y multicolored 1.50 .75
Z289 ZA279 80y multicolored 1.50 .75
Z290 ZA280 80y multicolored 1.50 .75
Z291 ZA281 80y multicolored 1.50 .75
a. Strip of 4, #Z288-Z291 6.00 6.00
b. Souvenir sheet, #Z288-Z291 6.00 6.00
Nos. Z285-Z291 (7) 10.50 5.25

ZA282 ZA283

ZA284 ZA285

ZA286 ZA287

ZA288 ZA289

Opening of Shimanami Seaside Highway (Hiroshima & Ehime)
ZA290 ZA291

Designs: No. Z292, Onomichi-suido Channel. No. Z293, Kurushima-kaikyo Straits. No. Z294, Old, new Onomichi-oohashi Bridges. No. Z295, Kurushima-kaikyo-oohashi Bridge. No. Z296, Innoshima-oohashi Bridge. No. Z297, Kurushima-kaikyo-oohashi Bridge, diff. No. Z298, Ikuchibashi Bridge. No. Z299, Hakatabashi, Ooshima-oohashi Bridges. No. Z300, Tatara-oohashi Bridge. No. Z301, Oomishimabashi Bridge.

1999, Apr. 26 Photo. *Perf. 13½*

Z292 ZA282 80y multicolored 1.50 .75
Z293 ZA283 80y multicolored 1.50 .75
Z294 ZA284 80y multicolored 1.50 .75
Z295 ZA285 80y multicolored 1.50 .75
Z296 ZA286 80y multicolored 1.50 .75
Z297 ZA287 80y multicolored 1.50 .75
Z298 ZA288 80y multicolored 1.50 .75
Z299 ZA289 80y multicolored 1.50 .75
Z300 ZA290 80y multicolored 1.50 .75
Z301 ZA291 80y multicolored 1.50 .75
a. Block of 10, #Z292-Z301 15.00 15.00
b. Sheet of 8, # Z294-Z301 12.00 12.00

Flora (Hokkaido) Type of 1991 and

Southern Kii Peninsula (Wakayama) — ZA292

Designs: No. Z302, Nachi-no-taki Falls. No. Z303, Engetsutou Island.

1999, Apr. 28 Photo. *Perf. 13½*

Z302 80y multicolored 1.50 .75
Z303 80y multicolored 1.50 .75
a. ZA292 Pair, #Z302-Z303 3.00 1.75
b. Pane, 5 #Z303a 15.00

Perf. 13

Z304 ZA97 80y Lily bell 1.50 .75
Z305 ZA98 80y Lilac 1.50 .75
Z306 ZA99 80y Daylily 1.50 .75
Z307 ZA100 80y Rowanberry 1.50 .75
a. Strip of 4, #Z304-Z307 6.00 6.00

Sendai Tanabata Festival (Miyagi) ZA294

Souma Nomaoi Festival (Fukushima) ZA295

1999, May 14 Photo. *Perf. 13½*

Z310 ZA294 80y multicolored 1.50 .75
Z311 ZA295 80y multicolored 1.50 .75
a. Pair, #Z310-Z311 3.00 1.75
b. Pane, 5 #Z311a 15.00

Ryukyu Dance (Okinawa) — ZA296

1999, May 14

Z312 ZA296 80y multicolored 1.50 .75
a. Pane of 10 15.00

ZA297

Northern Paradise (Hokkaido) ZA298

1999, May 25

Z313 ZA297 50y Lavender field .95 .50
Z314 ZA298 80y Wheat field 1.50 .75

Kurashiki Sightseeing District (Okayama) — ZA299

1999, May 25 Photo. *Perf. 13½*

Z316 ZA299 80y multicolored 1.50 .75
a. Pane of 10 15.00

Shirone Big Kite Battle (Niigata)
ZA300 ZA301

1999, June 1 Litho. *Perf. 13½*

Z317 ZA300 80y multicolored 1.50 .75
Z318 ZA301 80y multicolored 1.50 .75
a. Pair, #Z317-Z318 3.00 1.75
b. Pane, 5 #Z318a 15.00

Noto Kiriko Festival (Ishikawa) — ZA302

1999, June 11

Z319 ZA302 80y multicolored 1.50 .75
a. Pane of 10 15.00

Hokkaido Types of 1992-93

1999, June 25 Photo. *Perf. 13½*

Z320 ZA119 80y Arctic fox 1.50 .75

Litho.

Z321 ZA134 80y Largha seals 1.50 .75

ZA303

Tokyo: #Z323, morning glories. #Z324, starburst fireworks over Sumida River. #Z325, flower burst fireworks.

1999, July 1 Photo. *Perf. 13½*

Z323 80y multicolored 1.50 .75
Z324 80y multicolored 1.50 .75
Z325 80y multicolored 1.50 .75
a. ZA303 Block of 3, #Z323-Z325 4.50 4.50
b. Souv. sheet of 2, #Z324-Z325 3.00 3.00

Hakata Gion Yamagasa Festival (Fukuoka) — ZA306

1999, July 1 Litho.

Z326 ZA306 80y multicolored 1.50 .75
a. Pane of 10 15.00

ZA307

ZA308

ZA309

ZA310

Five Fuji Lakes (Yamanashi) ZA311

1999, July 1

Z327	ZA307	80y	Yamanakako	1.50	.75
Z328	ZA308	80y	Kawaguchiko	1.50	.75
Z329	ZA309	80y	Saiko	1.50	.75
Z330	ZA310	80y	Shoujiko	1.50	.75
Z331	ZA311	80y	Motosuko	1.50	.75
a.			Strip of 5, #Z327-Z331	7.70	7.50
b.			Pane, 2 #Z331a	15.00	

Inns of Tsumago, Magome Types of 1990

Photo. & Engr.

1999, July 16 ***Perf. 13***

Z332	ZA71	80y	like #Z71	1.50	.75
Z333	ZA72	80y	like #Z72	1.50	.75
a.			Pair, #Z332-Z333	3.00	2.25

ZA312

Toki (Japanese Crested Ibis) (Niigata) ZA313

1999, July 16 **Litho.** ***Perf. 13½***

Z334	ZA312	80y	Youyou, Yangyang	1.50	.75
Z335	ZA313	80y	Kin	1.50	.75
a.			Pair, #Z334-Z335	3.00	1.75
b.			Pane, 5 #Z335a	15.00	

ZA314

ZA315

Design: Amanohashidate sandbar, Miyatsu Bay (Kyoto).

1999, July 16

Z336	ZA314	80y	multicolored	1.50	.75

1999, July 16

Design: Ooga lotus (Chiba).

Z337	ZA315	80y	multicolored	1.50	.75
a.			Pane of 10	15.00	

ZA316

ZA317

ZA318

ZA319

Designs: Birds (Hokkaido).

1999, July 23 **Photo.** ***Perf. 13½***

Z338	ZA316	50y	Steller's sea-eagle	.95	.50
Z339	ZA317	50y	Tufted puffin	.95	.50
Z340	ZA318	50y	Blakiston's fish owl	.95	.50
Z341	ZA319	50y	Red-crowned crane	.95	.50
a.			Strip of 4, #Z337-Z340	4.00	4.00

Hill on Ie Island, Sabani Boat (Okinawa) — ZA320

1999, July 23 **Litho.** ***Perf. 13¼***

Z343	ZA320	80y	multicolored	1.50	.75
a.			Pane of 10	15.00	

National Treasures (Wakayama) — ZA321

#Z344, Kouyasan, Buddhist monastic complex. #Z345, Natl. treasure, Kongara-douji.

1999, July 26 ***Perf. 13½***

Z344		80y	multicolored	1.50	.75
Z345		80y	multicolored	1.50	.75
a.			ZA321 Pair, #Z344-Z345	3.00	1.75
b.			Pane, 5 #Z345a	15.00	

Autumn Bellflowers (Iwate) — ZA323

1999, July 30

Z346	ZA323	50y	multicolored	.95	.50
a.			Pane of 10	9.50	

Shimizu Port, Cent. (Shizuoka) ZA324

Fishing Boat (Kumamoto) ZA325

1999, Aug. 2 **Litho.** ***Perf. 13¼***

Z347	ZA324	80y	multi	1.50	.75
a.			Pane of 10	15.00	
Z348	ZA325	80y	multi	1.50	.75
a.			Pane of 10	15.00	

Ritsurin Park (Kagawa) ZA326

Artificial Island, Dejima (Nagasaki) ZA327

1999, Aug. 2 ***Perf. 13¼***

Z349	ZA326	80y	multi	1.50	.75
a.			Pane of 10	15.00	

1999, Sept. 1 **Photo.**

Z350	ZA327	80y	multi	1.50	.75
a.			Pane of 10	15.00	

Yoritomo Minamotono (1174-99), Shogun (Kanagawa) ZA328

Shirakami Mountains (Aomori) ZA329

1999, Sept. 2 **Litho.**

Z351	ZA328	80y	multi	1.50	.75
a.			Pane of 10	15.00	

1999, Sept. 6

Z352	ZA329	80y	multi	1.50	.75
a.			Pane of 10	15.00	

Gassho-zukuri Farmhouses and Kokiriko Dance (Toyama) — ZA330

1999, Sept. 14 **Photo.**

Z353	ZA330	80y	multi	1.50	.75
a.			Pane of 10	15.00	

Corn (Hokkaido) ZA331

Potatoes (Hokkaido) ZA332

Asparagus (Hokkaido) ZA333

Muskmelon (Hokkaido) ZA334

1999, Sept. 17 **Litho.**

Z354	ZA331	50y	multi	.95	.50
Z355	ZA332	50y	multi	.95	.50
Z356	ZA333	50y	multi	.95	.50
Z357	ZA334	50y	multi	.95	.50
a.			Strip, #Z354-Z357	4.00	4.00

(Gumma) ZA335

(Osaka) ZA336

1999, Sept. 17 ***Perf. 13¼***

Z358	ZA335	80y	multi	1.50	.75
a.			Pane of 10	15.00	

Iwajuku Paleolithic Site Excavations, 50th anniv.

1999, Sept. 27

Z359	ZA336	80y	multi	1.50	.75

23rd Rhythmic Gymnastics World Championships.

Nihonmatsu Chrysanthemum Exhibition (Fukushima) ZA337

1999, Oct. 1

Z360	ZA337	80y	multi	1.50	.75

Town of Obi (Miyazaki) — ZA338

Designs: No. Z361, Taihei dance, front gate of Obi Castle. No. Z362, Shintokudou School, Komura Jutarou (1855-1911).

1999, Oct. 1 ***Perf. 13¼***

Z361		80y	multi	1.50	.75
Z362		80y	multi	1.50	.75
a.			ZA338 Pair, #Z361-Z362	3.00	1.75
b.			Pane, 5 #Z362a	15.00	

Nagano Monkey Type of 1989

1999, Oct. 13 **Photo.** ***Perf. 12¾x13***

Z363	ZA1	80y	multi	1.50	.75

(Aichi) — ZA340

#Z364, Ichiei Sato. #Z365, "Beautiful Yamato."

1999, Oct. 13 **Photo.** ***Perf. 13¼***

Z364		80y	multi	1.50	.75
Z365		80y	multi	1.50	.75
a.			ZA340 Pair, #Z364-Z365	3.00	1.75
b.			Pane, 5 #Z365a	15.00	

ZA342

#Z366, Hagi (Yamaguchi). #Z367, Tsuwano (Shimane).

1999, Oct. 13

Z366		80y	multi	1.50	.75
Z367		80y	multi	1.50	.75
a.			ZA342 Vert. pair, #Z366-Z367	3.00	1.75
b.			Pane, 5 #Z367a	15.00	

(Nara) — ZA344

#Z368, Yamato Three Mountains. #Z369, Ishibutai Tomb.

1999, Oct. 28 Litho. *Perf. 13¼*
Z368 80y multi 1.50 .75
Z369 80y multi 1.50 .75
a. ZA344 Pair, #Z368-Z369 3.00 1.75
b. Pane, 5 #Z369a 15.00

Shikina-en Garden (Okinawa) — ZA346

1999, Oct. 28
Z370 50y multi .95 .50
Z371 50y multi .95 .50
a. ZA346 Pair, #Z370-Z371 1.90 1.25
b. Pane, 5 #Z371a 9.50

(Fukui) — ZA348

#Z372, Echizen Crab. #Z373, Tojinbou Cliff.

1999, Nov. 4
Z372 80y multi 1.50 .75
Z373 80y multi 1.50 .75
a. ZA348 Pair, #Z372-Z373 3.00 1.75
b. Pane, 5 #Z373a 15.00

Children in Santa's Sleigh (Hokkaido) ZA350

Yoshinogari Dig Site (Saga) ZA351

1999, Nov. 11 *Perf. 13¼*
Z374 ZA350 80y multi 1.50 .75
a. Pane of 10 15.00
Z375 ZA351 80y multi 1.50 .75
a. Pane of 10 15.00

(Kochi) — ZA352

#Z376, Katsura Beach. #Z377, Sakamoto Ryoma.

1999, Nov. 15 Photo.
Z376 80y multi 1.50 .75
Z377 80y multi 1.50 .75
a. ZA352 Pair, #Z376-Z377 3.00 1.75
b. Pane, 5 #Z377a 15.00

Samurai House, Kakunodate (Akita) — ZA354

1999, Dec. 17 Litho. *Perf. 13¼*
Z378 ZA354 80y multi 1.50 .75
a. Pane of 10 15.00

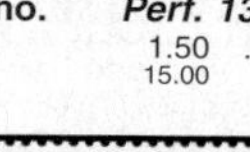

ZA355

ZA356

ZA357

ZA358

Tokyo Scenes (Tokyo) — ZA359

2000, Jan. 12 Litho. *Perf. 13¼*
Z379 ZA355 50y multi .95 .50
Z380 ZA356 50y multi .95 .50
Z381 ZA357 50y multi .95 .50
Z382 ZA358 50y multi .95 .50
Z383 ZA359 50y multi .95 .50
a. Horiz. strip, #Z379-Z383 4.75 4.75
b. Pane, 2 each #Z379-Z383 9.50

ZA360 ZA361

ZA362 ZA363
Snow World (Hokkaido)

2000, Feb. 7 Photo.
Z384 ZA360 80y multi 1.50 .75
Z385 ZA361 80y multi 1.50 .75
Z386 ZA362 80y multi 1.50 .75
Z387 ZA363 80y multi 1.50 .75
a. Strip, #Z384-Z387 6.00 6.00

ZA364

Japan Flora 2000 (Hyogo) — ZA365

2000, Mar. 1 Litho. *Perf. 13¼*
Z388 ZA364 50y multi .95 .50
Z389 ZA365 80y multi 1.50 .75
a. Pane, 5 each #Z388-Z389 12.50

ZA366 ZA367

ZA368 ZA369
Korakuen Gardens, 300th Anniv. (Okayama)

2000, Mar. 2 Photo.
Z390 ZA366 80y multi 1.50 .75
Z391 ZA367 80y multi 1.50 .75
Z392 ZA368 80y multi 1.50 .75
Z393 ZA369 80y multi 1.50 .75
a. Strip, #Z390-Z393 6.00 6.00
b. Souvenir sheet, #Z390-Z393 6.00 6.00

Cherry Blossoms in Takato (Nagano) ZA370

Dyed Fabrics (Okinawa) ZA371

Azumino (Nagano) — ZA372

2000, Mar. 3
Z394 ZA370 80y multi 1.50 .75
a. Pane of 10 15.00

2000, Mar. 17 Litho.
Z395 ZA371 50y multi .95 .50
a. Pane of 10 9.50

2000, Mar. 23 Photo.
Z396 ZA372 80y multi 1.50 .75
a. Pane of 10 15.00

Cherry Blossoms (Aomori) ZA373

Cherry Blossoms (Fukushima) ZA374

Cherry Blossoms (Iwate) — ZA375

Cherry Blossoms (Miyagi) — ZA376

Cherry Blossoms (Akita) — ZA377

Cherry Blossoms (Yamagata) ZA378

2000, Apr. 3 Litho.
Z397 ZA373 80y multi 1.50 .75
a. Pair, #Z397, Z399 3.00 1.75
b. Pair, #Z397, Z400 3.00 1.75
c. Pair, #Z397, Z401 3.00 1.75
d. Pair, #Z397, Z402 3.00 1.75
Z398 ZA374 80y multi 1.50 .75
a. Pair, #Z398, Z399 3.00 1.75
b. Pair, #Z398, Z400 3.00 1.75
c. Pair, #Z398, Z401 3.00 1.75
d. Pair, #Z398, Z402 3.00 1.75
Z399 ZA375 80y multi 1.50 .75
Z400 ZA376 80y multi 1.50 .75
Z401 ZA377 80y multi 1.50 .75
Z402 ZA378 80y multi 1.50 .75
a. Vert. strip, #Z399-Z402 6.00 6.00
Nos. Z397-Z402 (6) 9.00 4.50

Printed in sheets containing one column of four stamps of Nos. Z397 and Z398 at left and right respectively with 3 No. Z402a between.

Tulips (Toyama) — ZA379

2000, Apr. 28 Photo. *Perf. 13¼*
Z403 50y multi .95 .50
Z404 80y multi 1.50 .75
a. ZA379 Pair, #Z403-Z404 2.50 1.50
b. Pane, 5 #Z404a 12.50

Uwajima Castle (Ehime) — ZA381

2000, Apr. 28 *Perf. 13½x13¼*
Z405 ZA381 80y multi 1.50 .75

New Urban Center (Saitama) — ZA382

2000, May 1 *Perf. 13¼*

Z406 50y multi .95 .50
Z407 50y multi .95 .50
a. ZA382 Pair, #Z406-Z407 1.90 1.25
b. Pane, 5 #Z407a 9.50

Flowers of the Chugoku Region

(Tottori) ZA384

(Shimane) ZA385

(Okayama) ZA386

(Hiroshima) ZA387

(Yamaguchi) ZA388

2000, May 1 **Litho.** *Perf. 13¼*

Z408 ZA384 50y multi .95 .50
Z409 ZA385 50y multi .95 .50
Z410 ZA386 50y multi .95 .50
Z411 ZA387 50y multi .95 .50
Z412 ZA388 50y multi .95 .50
a. Vert. strip, #Z408-Z412 4.75 4.75
b. Pane, 2# Z412a 9.50

Cosmos (Tokyo) ZA389

Roses (Tokyo) ZA390

Bird of Paradise Flowers (Tokyo) ZA391

Sasanquas (Tokyo) ZA392

Freesias (Tokyo) — ZA393

2000, June 1 **Photo.** *Perf. 13¼*

Z413 ZA389 50y multi .95 .50
Z414 ZA390 50y multi .95 .50
Z415 ZA391 50y multi .95 .50
Z416 ZA392 50y multi .95 .50

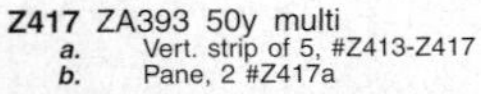

Z417 ZA393 50y multi .95 .50
a. Vert. strip of 5, #Z413-Z417 4.75 4.75
b. Pane, 2 #Z417a 9.50

Shonan Hiratsuka Tanabata Festival (Kanagawa) — ZA394

2000, June 2 **Litho.**

Z418 50y multi .95 .50
Z419 50y multi .95 .50
a. ZA394 Pair, #Z418-Z419 1.90 1.25
b. Pane, 5 #Z419a 9.50

Bankoku Shinryokan (Okinawa) — ZA396

2000, June 21 **Photo.** *Perf. 13¼*

Z420 ZA396 80y multi 1.50 .75
a. Pane of 10 15.00

World Performing Arts Festival (Osaka) — ZA397

Kujuku Islands (Akita) — ZA398

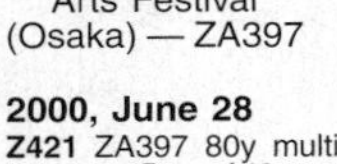

2000, June 28 **Litho.**

Z421 ZA397 80y multi 1.50 .75
a. Pane of 10 15.00

2000, July 7 **Photo.**

Z422 ZA398 80y multi 1.50 .75
a. Pane of 10 15.00

Potato Field (Hokkaido) — ZA399

Hillside and Hay Rolls (Hokkaido) — ZA400

2000, July 19

Z423 50y Flowers, barn .95 .50
Z424 50y Barn, silo .95 .50
a. ZA399 Pair, #Z423-Z424 1.90 1.10
Z425 80y + 20y Hayrolls, houses 1.90 1.00
Z426 80y + 20y Hayrolls, barns 1.90 1.00
a. ZA400 Pair, #Z425-Z426 3.80 2.50
Nos. Z423-Z426 (4) 5.70 3.00

Surtax on Nos. Z425-Z426 for refugees of eruption of Mt. Usu.

Awa-odori (Tokushima) ZA401

Golden Hall of Chusonji Temple (Iwate) ZA402

2000, July 31 **Litho.**

Z427 ZA401 80y multi 1.50 .75
a. Pane of 10 15.00

2000, Aug. 1

Z428 ZA402 80y multi 1.50 .75
a. Pane of 10 15.00

Hakata Doll (Fukuoka) ZA403

55th Natl. Athletic Meet (Toyama) ZA404

2000, Aug. 2

Z429 ZA403 80y multi 1.50 .75
a. Pane of 10 15.00

2000, Sept. 1 **Photo.**

Z430 ZA404 50y multi .95 .50
a. Pane of 10 9.50

25th World Parachuting Championships (Mie) — ZA405

2000, Sept. 13

Z431 80y 2 skydivers 1.50 .75
Z432 80y 3 skydivers 1.50 .75
a. ZA405 Pair, #Z431-Z432 3.00 1.75
b. Pane, 5 #Z432a 15.00

Friendly Tokyo (Tokyo) ZA406

Iwakuni Kintaikyo Bridge (Yamaguchi) ZA407

2000, Sept. 29 **Litho.**

Z433 ZA406 80y multi 1.50 .75
a. Pane of 10 15.00

2000, Oct. 10

Z434 ZA407 80y multi 1.50 .75
a. Pane of 10 15.00

Intl. Wheelchair Marathon (Oita) — ZA408

Willow and Frog (Aichi) — ZA409

2000, Oct. 11

Z435 ZA408 80y multi 1.50 .75
a. Pane of 10 15.00

2000, Oct. 20 **Photo.**

Z436 ZA409 80y multi 1.50 .75
a. Pane of 10 15.00

ZA410 ZA411

ZA412 ZA413

Four Seasons (Kyoto)

2000, Oct. 20 **Litho.**

Z437 ZA410 80y multi 1.50 .75
Z438 ZA411 80y multi 1.50 .75
a. Pane, 5 each #Z437-Z438 15.00
Z439 ZA412 80y multi 1.50 .75
Z440 ZA413 80y multi 1.50 .75
a. Horiz. strip, #Z437-Z440 6.00 3.50
b. Pane, 5 each #Z439-Z440 15.00

Odawarajo Castle (Kanagawa) — ZA414

2000, Oct. 27 *Perf. 13¼*

Z441 50y multi .95 .50
Z442 50y multi .95 .50
a. ZA414 Pair, #Z441-Z442 1.90 1.25
b. Pane, 5 #Z442a 9.50

Intl. Balloon Festival (Saga) — ZA415

2000, Nov. 1 **Litho.** *Perf. 13¼*

Z443 ZA415 80y multi 1.50 .75
a. Pane of 10 15.00

Miniature Sheet

Be Kind to Animals Week — SP26

No. B57: a, Dog, flower background. b, White cat, red background. c, White Yorkshire terrier, green curtain. d, Cat, bubbles in background. e, Black Labrador retriever puppy sitting. f, Cat, brown striped background. g, Shiba puppy standing. h, Scottish Fold cat, dots and stripes in background. i, Dog in doorway. j, Cat, crescent moon.

2009, Sept. 18 Litho. *Perf. 13¼*

B57	SP26	Sheet of 10	12.50	12.50
a.-j.		50y+5y Any single	1.25	1.25

Surtax for animal welfare organizations.

AIR POST STAMPS

Regular Issue of 1914 Overprinted in Red or Blue

Wmk. Zigzag Lines (141)

1919, Oct. 3 *Perf. 13x13½*

Granite Paper

C1	A34	1½s blue (R)	260.00	72.50
C2	A34	3s rose (Bl)	450.00	210.00

Excellent counterfeits exist.

Passenger Plane over Lake Ashi — AP1

1929-34 Engr. *Perf. 13½x13*

Granite Paper

C3	AP1	8½s orange brn	27.50	14.00
C4	AP1	9½s rose	9.00	3.75
C5	AP1	16½s yellow grn	9.00	4.00
C6	AP1	18s ultra	10.00	3.75
C7	AP1	33s gray	20.00	3.25
		Nos. C3-C7 (5)	75.50	28.75
		Set, never hinged	190.00	

Souvenir Sheet

C8	AP1	Sheet of 4, #C4-C7	1,250.	1,250.
		Never hinged	2,000.	

Issued: 9½s, 3/1/34; #C8, 4/20/34; others, 10/6/29. #C8 for Communications Commemoration Day (1st observance of establishment of the postal service and issuance of #1-4). Sold only at Phil. Exhib. p.o., Tokyo, 4/20-27. Size: 110x100mm.

Catalogue values for unused stamps in this section, from this point to the end of the section, are for Never Hinged items.

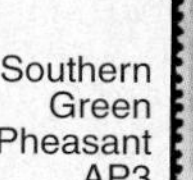

Southern Green Pheasant AP3

Perf. 13x13½

1950, Jan. 10 Engr. Unwmk.

C9	AP3	16y gray	40.00	10.00
C10	AP3	34y brown violet	55.00	12.00
C11	AP3	59y carmine	75.00	7.00
C12	AP3	103y orange yellow	50.00	20.00
C13	AP3	144y olive	60.00	22.50
		Nos. C9-C13 (5)	280.00	71.50
		Set, hinged	150.00	

Pagoda and Plane — AP4

Plane and Mt. Tsurugi-dake — AP5

1951-52 Photo.

C14	AP4	15y purple	3.50	2.75
C15	AP4	20y blue	30.00	1.25
C16	AP4	25y yellow grn	27.50	.45
C17	AP4	30y brown red	20.00	.45
C18	AP4	40y gray blk	8.00	.55
C19	AP5	55y brt blue	250.00	60.00
C20	AP5	75y brnsh red	160.00	35.00
C21	AP5	80y magenta	22.50	3.00
C22	AP5	85y black	27.50	7.25
C23	AP5	125y olive bis	14.00	3.25
C24	AP5	160y Prus green	30.00	3.75
		Nos. C14-C24 (11)	593.00	117.70
		Set, hinged	350.00	

Issue dates: 25y, 30y, Dec. 20; 15y, 20y, 40y, Sept. 1; 55y-160y, Feb. 11, 1952.

Redrawn; Underlined Zeros Omitted

1952-62

C25	AP4	15y purple ('62)	1.75	.60
C26	AP4	20y blue	60.00	1.00
C27	AP4	25y yel grn ('53)	1.25	.35
C28	AP4	30y brown red	8.00	.45
C29	AP4	40y gray blk ('53)	5.50	.45
C30	AP5	55y brt blue	75.00	4.00
C32	AP5	75y brnsh red	160.00	9.00
C33	AP5	80y magenta	110.00	3.00
C34	AP5	85y black	6.50	1.50
C36	AP5	125y olive bis	10.00	1.75
C38	AP5	160y Prus green	40.00	2.00
		Nos. C25-C38 (11)	478.00	24.10
		Set, hinged	225.00	

See No. C43.

Great Buddha of Kamakura — AP6

1953, Aug. 15 *Perf. 13½*

C39	AP6	70y red brown	5.25	.25
C40	AP6	80y blue	7.50	.25
C41	AP6	115y olive green	3.75	.50
C42	AP6	145y Prus green	25.00	3.00
		Nos. C39-C42 (4)	41.50	4.00

Coil Stamp

Redrawn Type of 1952-62

1961, Oct. 2 *Perf. 13 Horiz.*

C43	AP4	30y brown red	37.50	27.50

MILITARY STAMPS

Nos. 98, 119, 131 Overprinted

1910-14 Unwmk. *Perf. 11½ to 13½*

M1	A26	3s rose	225.00	35.00
M2	A34	3s rose ('13)	350.00	140.00

Wmk. 141

M3	A34	3s rose ('14)	35.00	16.00
		Nos. M1-M3 (3)	610.00	191.00

Nos. M1-M3 overprint type I has 3.85mm between characters; type II, 4-4.5mm (movable type).

1921 On Offices in China No. 37

M4	A34	3s rose	*5,750.*	*4,750.*

No. M4 is a provisional military stamp issued at the Japanese Post Office, Tsingtao, China. The overprint differs from the illustration, being 12mm high with thicker characters. Counterfeits are plentiful.

Overprint 16mm High

1924 On No. 131

M5	A34	3s rose	100.00	72.50
a.		3s rose (#131b)	100.00	75.00

Excellent forgeries exist of Nos. M1-M5.

JAPANESE OFFICES ABROAD

Offices in China

Regular Issues of Japan Overprinted in Red or Black

Perf. 11½, 12, 12½, 13½, 13x13½

1900-06 Unwmk.

1	A26	5r gray (R)	3.50	2.75
2	A26	½s gray (R) ('01)	2.10	.70
3	A26	1s lt red brn (R)	2.10	.70
4	A26	1½s ultra	9.50	2.10
5	A26	1½s vio ('06)	5.25	.95
6	A26	2s lt grn (R)	5.25	.70
7	A26	3s violet brn	5.75	.70
8	A26	3s rose ('06)	4.25	.50
9	A26	4s rose	4.75	1.25
10	A26	5s org yel (R)	9.50	1.25
11	A27	6s maroon ('06)	18.00	12.00
12	A27	8s ol grn (R)	9.50	6.00
13	A27	10s deep blue	9.50	1.00
14	A27	15s purple	20.00	1.75
15	A27	20s red org	18.00	1.00
16	A28	25s blue grn (R)	37.50	4.00
17	A28	50s red brown	40.00	3.00
18	A29	1y carmine	60.00	3.00
		Nos. 1-18 (18)	264.45	43.35

No. 6 with black overprint is bogus.

Nos. 5, 6, 8, 9 and 13 exist as booklet panes of 6, made from sheet stamps. They are rare.

1900

19	A30	3s carmine	27.50	15.00

Wedding of Crown Prince Yoshihito and Princess Sadako.

1908

20	A33	5y green	375.00	47.50
21	A33	10y dark violet	650.00	110.00

On #20-21 the space between characters of the overprint is 6½mm instead of 1½mm.

1913 *Perf. 12, 12x13, 13x13½*

22	A34	½s brown	15.00	15.00
23	A34	1s orange	16.00	16.00
24	A34	1½s lt blue	42.50	19.00
25	A34	2s green	50.00	21.00
26	A34	3s rose	24.00	8.00
27	A35	4s red	70.00	70.00
28	A35	5s violet	70.00	55.00
29	A35	10s deep blue	70.00	22.50
30	A35	20s claret	275.00	150.00
31	A35	25s olive green	100.00	22.50
32	A36	1y yel grn & mar	825.00	550.00
		Nos. 22-32 (11)	1,557.	949.00

Nos. 24, 25, 26, 27 and 29 exist in booklet panes of 6, made from sheet stamps. The No. 26 pane is very rare.

1914-21 Wmk. 141

Granite Paper

33	A34	½s brown	3.25	.80
34	A34	1s orange	3.75	.80
35	A34	1½s blue	4.25	.80
36	A34	2s green	2.75	.95
37	A34	3s rose	2.40	.80
38	A35	4s red	10.50	4.75
39	A35	5s violet	19.00	1.75
40	A35	6s brown ('20)	32.50	19.00
41	A35	8s gray ('20)	40.00	21.00
42	A35	10s dp blue	13.50	1.25
43	A35	20s claret	45.00	3.25
44	A35	25s olive grn	55.00	3.50
45	A36	30s org brn ('20)	80.00	29.00
46	A36	50s dk brn ('20)	95.00	32.50
47	A36	1y yel grn & mar ('18)	140.00	6.75
48	A33	5y green	1,900.	550.00
49	A33	10y violet ('21)	2,700.	1,700.
		Nos. 33-49 (17)	5,146.	2,376.

On Nos. 48-49 the space between characters of overprint is 4½mm, instead of 6½mm on Nos. 20-21 and 1½mm on all lower values. See No. M4.

No. 42 exists as a booklet pane of 6, made from sheet stamps. It is very rare.

Counterfeit overprints exist of Nos. 1-49.

Offices in Korea

Regular Issue of Japan Overprinted in Red or Black

1900 Unwmk. *Perf. 11½, 12, 12½*

1	A26	5r gray (R)	19.00	8.75
2	A26	1s lt red brn (R)	20.00	5.00
3	A26	1½s ultra	250.00	130.00
4	A26	2s lt green (R)	19.00	10.00
5	A26	3s violet brn	17.00	4.75
6	A26	4s rose	65.00	27.50
7	A26	5s org yel (R)	67.50	27.50
8	A27	8s ol grn (R)	250.00	120.00
9	A27	10s deep blue	35.00	9.00
10	A27	15s purple	62.50	6.00
11	A27	20s red orange	62.50	5.00
12	A28	25s blue grn (R)	220.00	55.00
13	A28	50s red brown	175.00	18.00
14	A29	1y carmine	475.00	14.00
		Nos. 1-14 (14)	1,737.	440.50

1900

15	A30	3s carmine	100.00	55.00

Wedding of Crown Prince Yoshihito and Princess Sadako.

Counterfeit overprints exist of Nos. 1-15.

Taiwan (Formosa)

Numeral of Value and Imperial Crest — A1

1945 Unwmk. Litho. *Imperf.*
Without Gum

1	A1	3s carmine	30.00	30.00
2	A1	5s blue green	22.50	22.50
3	A1	10s pale blue	35.00	35.00
		Nos. 1-3 (3)	87.50	87.50

Additional values, prepared, but not issued, were: 30s, 40s, 50s, 1y, 5y and 10y. The entire set of nine was overprinted by Chinese authorities after World War II and issued for use in Taiwan.

For overprints see China-Taiwan Nos. 1-7.

JORDAN

'jor-dən

Trans-Jordan

LOCATION — In the Near East, separated from the Mediterranean Sea by Israel
GOVT. — Kingdom
AREA — 38,400 sq. mi.
POP. — 4,561,147 (1999 est.)
CAPITAL — Amman

The former Turkish territory was mandated to Great Britain following World War I. It became an independent state in 1946.

10 Milliemes = 1 Piaster
1000 Mils = 1 Palestine Pound (1930)
1000 Fils = 100 piasters = 1 Jordan Dinar (1951)

Catalogue values for unused stamps in this country are for Never Hinged items, beginning with Scott 221 in the regular postage section, Scott B13 in the semi-postal section, Scott C1 in the air post section, Scott J47 in the postage due section, Scott RA1 in the postal tax section, Scott N1 in the occupation section, Scott NJ1 in the occupation postage due section, and Scott NRA1 in the occupation postal tax section.

Watermarks

Wmk. 305 — Roman and Arabic Initials

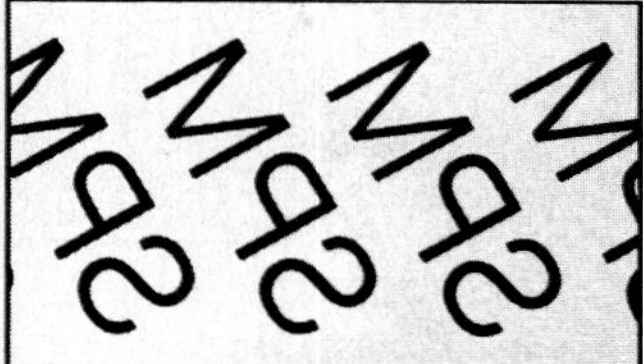

Wmk. 328 — UAR

Wmk. 388 — Multiple "SPM"

British Mandate

Stamps and Type of Palestine 1918 Overprinted in Black or Silver

Perf. 14, 15x14

1920, Nov. Wmk. 33

1 A1 1m dark brown 2.00 *2.00*
a. Inverted overprint 140.00 250.00
b. Perf. 14 2.25 2.25
c. As "b," inverted overprint 160.00
2 A1 2m blue green 3.00 .80
a. Perf. 15x14 9.50 *10.00*
3 A1 3m light brown 2.50 1.25
a. Perf. 14 19.50 17.50
4 A1 4m scarlet 2.75 1.25
a. Perf. 14 19.00 *21.00*
5 A1 5m orange 5.00 .90
a. Perf. 15x14 5.00 1.25
6 A1 1pi dark blue (S) 4.25 *1.90*
a. Perf. 15x14 *2,250.*
7 A1 2pi olive green 6.00 3.25
a. Perf. 15x14 6.75 *7.00*
8 A1 5pi plum 5.50 *6.50*
a. Perf. 15x14 29.00 *35.00*
9 A1 9pi bister 7.25 *25.00*
a. Perf. 15x14 1,000. *1,500.*
10 A1 10pi ultramarine 8.25 *25.00*
11 A1 20pi gray 15.00 *40.00*
Nos. 1-11 (11) *61.50* *107.85*

The overprint reads "Sharqi al-ardan" (East of Jordan).
For overprints see Nos. 12-63, 83A.

Stamps of 1920 Issue Handstamp Surcharged "Ashir el qirsh" (tenth of piaster) and numeral in Black, Red or Violet

1922

12 A1 1/10pi on 1m dk brn 35.00 *32.50*
13 A1 1/10pi on 1m dk brn (R) 90.00 67.50
13A A1 1/10pi on 1m dk brn (V) 77.50 70.00
14 A1 2/10pi on 2m bl grn 40.00 29.00
a. 3/10pi on 2m bl grn (error) 125.00 100.00
15 A1 2/10pi on 2m bl grn (R) 100.00 80.00
16 A1 2/10pi on 2m bl grn (V) 135.00 100.00
17 A1 3/10pi on 3m lt brn 17.50 10.00
17A A1 3/10pi on 3m lt brn (V) 175.00 150.00
18 A1 4/10pi on 4m scar 70.00 50.00
19 A1 5/10pi on 5m org 225.00 100.00
c. Perf. 15x14 200.00 100.00
19A A1 5/10pi on 5m dp org (R) 250.00
19B A1 5/10pi on 5m org (V) 325.00

For overprint see No. 83B.

Handstamp Surcharged "El qirsh" (piaster) and numeral in Black, Red or Violet

20 A1 1pi dk bl (R) 210.00 60.00
20A A1 1pi dk bl (V) 425.00
21 A1 2pi ol grn (Bk) 300.00 75.00
22 A1 2pi ol grn (R) 350.00 80.00
22A A1 2pi ol grn (V) 325.00 90.00
23 A1 5pi plum (Bk) 65.00 *70.00*
23A A1 5pi plum (V) *325.00*
24 A1 9pi bister (Bk) 350.00 *350.00*
25 A1 9pi bister (R) 175.00 140.00
a. Perf. 14 600.00 600.00
26 A1 10pi ultra (Bk) 975.00 *1,000.*
27 A1 20pi gray (Bk) 800.00 *850.00*
27A A1 20pi gray (V) 1,000. 950.00

Same Surcharge in Black on Palestine Nos. 13-14

28 A1 10pi on 10pi ultra *2,000.* *2,500.*
29 A1 20pi on 20pi gray *2,600.* *3,000.*

For overprints see Nos. 86, 88, 94, 97, 98.

Stamps of 1920 Handstamped in Violet, Black or Red

1922, Dec. ***Perf. 15x14, 14***

30 A1 1m dk brn (V) 32.50 20.00
31 A1 1m dk brn (Bk) 27.50 18.00
32 A1 1m dk brn (R) 17.50 *15.00*
33 A1 2m bl grn (V) 12.50 8.00
34 A1 2m bl grn (Bk) 15.00 10.00
35 A1 2m bl grn (R) 32.50 25.00
36 A1 3m lt brn (V) 12.50 7.00
37 A1 3m lt brn (Bk) 14.00 8.00
38 A1 3m lt brn (R) 55.00 40.00
39 A1 4m scar (V) 65.00 50.00
39A A1 4m scar (Bk) 50.00 50.00
40 A1 4m scar (R) 60.00 50.00
41 A1 5m orange (V) 22.50 10.00
42 A1 5m orange (R) 45.00 *10.00*
a. Perf. 14 325.00 75.00
43 A1 1pi dk blue (V) 22.50 9.00
44 A1 1pi dk blue (R) 32.50 15.00
45 A1 2pi ol grn (V) 30.00 15.00
a. Perf. 14 82.50 80.00
46 A1 2pi ol grn (Bk) 17.50 10.00
47 A1 2pi ol grn (R) 75.00 40.00
48 A1 5pi plum (V) 80.00 *80.00*
a. Perf. 14 110.00 *110.00*
49 A1 5pi plum (R) 100.00 *100.00*
50 A1 9pi bister (V) 250.00 *250.00*
50A A1 9pi bister (Bk) 72.50 *80.00*
50B A1 9pi bister (R) 450.00 *450.00*
51 A1 10pi ultra (V) 1,250. *1,600.*
51A A1 10pi ultra (R) *2,000.* *1,900.*
52 A1 20pi gray (V) 1,250. *1,800.*
52A A1 20pi gray (R) *1,750.* *2,000.*

The overprint reads "Hukumat al Sharqi al Arabia" (Arab Government of the East) and date, 1923. The surcharges or overprints on Nos. 12 to 52A inclusive are handstamped and, as usual, are found inverted and double.
Ink pads of several colors were in use at the same time and the surcharges and overprints frequently show a mixture of two colors.
For overprints see #84, 87, 89, 92-93, 95-96.

Stamps of 1920 Overprinted in Gold or Black

1923, Mar. 1 ***Perf. 14, 15x14***

53 A1 1m dark brn (G) 22.50 *24.00*
a. Perf. 15x14 1,600. *1,800.*
54 A1 2m blue grn (G) 20.00 18.00
a. Double overprint 300.00
b. Inverted overprint 375.00 350.00
55 A1 3m lt brn (G) 17.50 *15.00*
a. Black overprint 82.50 *85.00*
56 A1 4m scarlet (Bk) 15.00 12.00
57 A1 5m orange (Bk) 17.50 12.00
a. Perf. 15x14 55.00 45.00
58 A1 1pi dk blue (G) 17.50 14.00
a. Double overprint 500.00 *475.00*
b. Black overprint *875.00* *850.00*
59 A1 2pi ol grn (G) 22.00 *15.00*
a. Black overprint 275.00 250.00
b. Overprint on back 175.00
60 A1 5pi plum (G) 75.00 *80.00*
a. Inverted overprint 250.00
b. "922" for "921"
61 A1 9pi bister (Bk) 95.00 *100.00*
a. Perf. 15x14 *200.00* *200.00*
62 A1 10pi ultra (G) 82.50 *100.00*
63 A1 20pi gray (G) 85.00 *100.00*
a. Inverted overprint 400.00
b. Double overprint 475.00
c. Double ovpt., one inverted 475.00

The overprint reads "Hukumat al Sharqi al Arabia, Nissan Sanat 921" (Arab Government of the East, April, 1921).
For overprints see Nos. 85, 99, 100, 102.

Stamps of Hejaz, 1922, Overprinted in Black

Coat of Arms (Hejaz A7)

1923, Apr. Unwmk. ***Perf. 11½***

64 A7 1/8pi orange brn 3.25 *1.75*
a. Double overprint 225.00
65 A7 ½pi red 3.25 1.75
a. Inverted overprint 125.00
66 A7 1pi dark blue 1.60 1.00
a. Inverted overprint 140.00 140.00
67 A7 1½pi violet 2.50 *1.75*
a. Double overprint 160.00
68 A7 2pi orange 3.25 *6.00*
a. Inverted overprint
b. Pair, one without overprint
69 A7 3pi olive brn 4.50 *8.50*
a. Inverted overprint 250.00
b. Double overprint 250.00 250.00
c. Pair, one without overprint *400.00*
70 A7 5pi olive green 6.75 *9.50*
Nos. 64-70 (7) *25.10* *30.25*

The overprint is similar to that on the preceding group but is differently arranged. There are numerous varieties in the Arabic letters.
For overprints see Nos. 71-72, 91, J1-J5.

With Additional Surcharge of New Value in Arabic:

a

b

71 A7(a) ¼pi on 1/8pi 10.00 *11.00*
a. Inverted surcharge 175.00
72 A7(b) 10pi on 5pi 32.50 *32.50*

Independence Issue

Palestine Stamps and Type of 1918 Overprinted Vertically in Black or Gold

1923, May Wmk. 33 ***Perf. 15x14***

73 A1 1m dark brn (Bk) 22.50 *17.00*
a. Double ovpt., one reversed 725.00 650.00
73B A1 1m dark brn (G) 175.00 175.00
c. Double ovpt., one reversed 1,000.
74 A1 2m blue grn 35.00 *35.00*
75 A1 3m lt brown 12.50 *12.00*
76 A1 4m scarlet 12.50 *12.00*
77 A1 5m orange 60.00 *60.00*
78 A1 1pi dk blue (G) 60.00 *60.00*
a. Double overprint *650.00* *650.00*
79 A1 2pi olive grn 65.00 *70.00*
80 A1 5pi plum (G) 75.00 *70.00*
a. Double overprint *725.00*
81 A1 9pi bis, perf. 14 65.00 *60.00*
82 A1 10pi ultra, perf. 14 75.00 *80.00*
83 A1 20pi gray 85.00 *90.00*
Nos. 73-83 (12) 742.50 741.00

The overprint reads, "Arab Government of the East (abbreviated), Souvenir of Independence, 25th, May, 1923 ('923')."
There were printed 480 complete sets and a larger number of the 1, 2, 3 and 4m. A large number of these sets were distributed to high officials. The overprint was in a setting of twenty-four and the error "933" instead of "923" occurs once in the setting.
The overprint exists reading downward on all values, as illustrated, and reading upward on all except the 5m and 2pi.
Forged overprints exist.
For overprint see No. 101.

Stamps of Preceding Issues, Handstamp Surcharged

83A A1 2½ 10pi on 5m dp org 175.00 *175.00*
83B A1 5/10pi on 3m (#17) —
84 A1 5/10pi on 3m (#36) 25.00 20.00
85 A1 5/10pi on 3m (#55) 10.00 8.75
86 A1 5/10pi on 5pi (#23) 50.00 42.50
87 A1 5/10pi on 5pi (#48) 5.00 4.00
88 A1 1pi on 5pi (#23) 50.00 42.50
89 A1 1pi on 5pi (#48) *2,500.*

Same Surcharge on Palestine Stamp of 1918

90 A1 5/10pi on 3m lt brn *17,000.*

No. 90 is valued in the grade of fine-very fine. Very fine examples are not known.
As is usual with handstamped surcharges these are found double, inverted, etc.

No. 67 Surcharged by Handstamp

Unwmk. ***Perf. 11½***

91 A7 ½pi on 1½pi vio 4.00 *4.25*
a. Surcharge typographed 30.00 *32.50*

The surcharge reads: "Nusf el qirsh" (half piastre). See note after No. 90.

Stamps of Preceding Issues Surcharged by Handstamp

No. 92

Perf. 14, 15x14

1923, Nov. Wmk. 33

92 A1 ½pi on 2pi (#45) 50.00 45.00
93 A1 ½pi on 2pi (#47) 95.00 87.50
94 A1 ½pi on 5pi (#23) 30.00 27.50
95 A1 ½pi on 5pi (#48) 2,750. 2,000.
96 A1 ½pi on 5pi (#49) 1,800. 2,750.

No.	Type	Description	Unused	Used
97	A1	½pi on 9pi (#24)	*6,500.*	
98	A1	½pi on 9pi (#25)	95.00	87.50
99	A1	½pi on 9pi (#61)	200.00	160.00

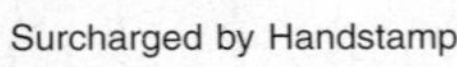

Surcharged by Handstamp

No. 102

No.	Type	Description	Unused	Used
100	A1	1pi on 10pi (#62)	*2,250.*	*2,000.*
101	A1	1pi on 10pi (#82)	*3,000.*	*3,000.*
102	A1	2pi on 20pi (#63)	30.00	*24.00*

Of the 25 examples of No. 100, a few were handstamped in violet.

Stamp of Hejaz, 1922, Overprinted by Handstamp

1923, Dec. Unwmk. *Perf. 11½*

No.	Type	Description	Unused	Used
103	A7	½pi red	4.00	*4.25*

Stamp of Hejaz, 1922, Overprinted

1924

No.	Type	Description	Unused	Used
104	A7	½pi red	4.50	*4.75*

King Hussein Issue

Stamps of Hejaz, 1922, Overprinted

1924

Gold Overprint

No.	Type	Description	Unused	Used
105	A7	½pi red	1.75	1.25
106	A7	1pi dark blue	2.50	1.75
107	A7	1½pi violet	2.25	1.50
108	A7	2pi orange	3.00	2.00

Black Overprint

No.	Type	Description	Unused	Used
109	A7	½pi red	1.00	.65
110	A7	1pi dark blue	1.10	.75
111	A7	1½pi violet	1.25	.90
112	A7	2pi orange	1.50	1.00
		Nos. 105-112 (8)	14.35	9.80

The overprint reads: "Arab Government of the East. In commemoration of the visit of H. M. the King of the Arabs, 11 Jemad el Than i 1342 (17th Jan. 1924)." The overprint was in a setting of thirty-six and the error "432" instead of "342" occurs once in the setting and is found on all values.

Stamps of Hejaz, 1922-24, Overprinted in Black or Red

Coat of Arms (Hejaz A8)

1924

No.	Type	Description	Unused	Used
113	A7	⅛pi red brown	.75	.20
a.		Inverted overprint	130.00	—
114	A7	¼pi yellow green	.30	.20
a.		Tête bêche pair	2.00	2.00
b.		Inverted overprint	85.00	—
115	A7	½pi red	.30	.20
116	A7	1pi dark blue	5.00	4.25
a.		Inverted overprint	—	—
117	A7	1½pi violet	4.50	3.75
118	A7	2pi orange	4.00	3.25
a.		Double overprint	—	—
119	A7	3pi red brown	3.00	2.40
a.		Double overprint	100.00	—
b.		Inverted overprint	100.00	—
120	A7	5pi olive green	3.50	*3.75*
121	A8	10pi vio & dk brn (R)	7.75	*7.50*
a.		Pair, one without overprint		
b.		Black overprint	200.00	—
		Nos. 113-121 (9)	29.10	25.50

The overprint reads: "Hukumat al Sharqi al Arabia, 1342." (Arab Government of the East, 1924).

Stamps of Hejaz, 1925, Overprinted in Black or Red

(Hejaz A9)

(Hejaz A10)

(Hejaz A11)

1925, Aug.

No.	Type	Description	Unused	Used
122	A9	⅛pi chocolate	.75	.60
a.		Inverted overprint	60.00	—
123	A9	¼pi ultramarine	.75	.60
a.		Inverted overprint	60.00	—
124	A9	½pi carmine rose	.75	.20
a.		Inverted overprint	60.00	—
125	A10	1pi yellow green	.75	.20
126	A10	1½pi orange	2.00	*2.50*
a.		Inverted overprint	60.00	—
127	A10	2pi deep blue	2.75	*3.00*
128	A11	3pi dark green (R)	3.25	*4.50*
a.		Inverted overprint	80.00	—
129	A11	5pi orange brn	5.00	*8.00*
a.		Inverted overprint	80.00	—
		Nos. 122-129 (8)	16.00	*19.60*

The overprint reads: "Hukumat al Sharqi al Arabi. 1343 Sanat." (Arab Government of the East, 1925). Nos. 122-129 exist imperforate, and with overprint double.

Type of Palestine, 1918

1925, Nov. 1 Wmk. 4 *Perf. 14*

No.	Type	Description	Unused	Used
130	A1	1m dark brown	.30	.20
131	A1	2m yellow	.30	.20
132	A1	3m Prussian bl	.30	.20
133	A1	4m rose	.30	.20
134	A1	5m orange	.30	.20
135	A1	6m blue green	.30	.20
136	A1	7m yel brown	.30	.20
137	A1	8m red	.30	.20
138	A1	1pi gray	.50	.35
139	A1	13m ultramarine	.60	*.75*
140	A1	2pi olive green	1.00	*1.25*
141	A1	5pi plum	4.50	*4.50*
142	A1	9pi bister	8.50	*9.00*
143	A1	10pi light blue	14.00	*15.00*
144	A1	20pi violet	27.50	*27.50*
		Nos. 130-144 (15)	59.00	*59.95*

This overprint reads: "Sharqi al-ardan" (East of Jordan).

For overprints see Nos. J12-J23.

No.	Type	Description	Unused	Used
142a	A1	9pi	860.	*1,425.*
143a	A1	10pi	100.	*110.*
144a	A1	20pi	1,375.	*1,275.*
		Nos. 142a-144a (3)	2,335.	*2,810.*

Amir Abdullah ibn Hussein
A1 A2

1927-29 Engr. *Perf. 14*

No.	Type	Description	Unused	Used
145	A1	2(m) Prus blue	.20	*.35*
146	A1	3(m) rose	.55	1.40
147	A1	4(m) green	1.10	*2.75*
148	A1	5(m) orange	.55	*.35*
149	A1	10(m) red	1.10	*1.40*
150	A1	15(m) ultra	1.10	.35
151	A1	20(m) olive grn	1.40	1.40
152	A2	50(m) claret	3.75	*5.50*
153	A2	90(m) bister	9.75	*15.00*
154	A2	100(m) lt blue	10.50	16.00
155	A2	200(m) violet	24.50	*35.00*
156	A2	500(m) dp brn ('29)	87.50	*110.00*
157	A2	1000(m) gray ('29)	175.00	*210.00*
		Nos. 145-157 (13)	317.00	*399.50*

For overprints see Nos. 158-168, B1-B12, J24-J29.

Stamps of 1927 Overprinted in Black

1928, Sept. 1

No.	Type	Description	Unused	Used
158	A1	2(m) Prus blue	1.00	*1.90*
159	A1	3(m) rose	1.15	*2.50*
160	A1	4(m) green	1.25	*2.50*
161	A1	5(m) orange	1.25	*1.60*
162	A1	10(m) red	1.90	*4.50*
163	A1	15(m) ultra	1.90	1.90
164	A1	20(m) olive grn	5.00	*10.00*
165	A2	50(m) claret	7.75	*11.50*
166	A2	90(m) bister	17.00	*32.50*
167	A2	100(m) lt blue	32.50	*50.00*
168	A2	200(m) violet	85.00	*125.00*
		Nos. 158-168 (11)	155.70	*243.90*

The overprint is the Arabic word "Dastour," meaning "Constitution." The stamps were in commemoration of the enactment of the law setting forth the Constitution.

A3

"MILS" or "L. P." at lower right and Arabic equivalents at upper left.

1930-36 Engr. *Perf. 14*

Size: 17¼x21mm

No.	Type	Description	Unused	Used
169	A3	1m red brn ('34)	.20	*.95*
170	A3	2m Prus blue	.20	*.55*
171	A3	3m rose	.55	*.80*
172	A3	3m green ('34)	1.40	*1.25*
173	A3	4m green	.90	*2.10*
174	A3	4m rose ('34)	2.25	1.75
175	A3	5m orange	.50	.20
a.		Perf. 13½x14 (coil) ('36)	16.00	10.00
176	A3	10m red	.95	.20
177	A3	15m ultra	.95	.20
a.		Perf. 13½x14 (coil) ('36)	16.00	10.00
178	A3	20m olive grn	1.75	.55

Size: 19¼x23½mm

No.	Type	Description	Unused	Used
179	A3	50m red violet	2.50	2.10
180	A3	90m bister	4.50	*5.75*
181	A3	100m light blue	5.75	*5.75*
182	A3	200m violet	14.00	*17.00*
183	A3	500m deep brown	26.00	*52.50*
184	A3	£1 gray	82.50	*125.00*
		Nos. 169-184 (16)	144.90	*216.65*

See Nos. 199-220, 230-235. For overprint see No. N15a.

1939 *Perf. 13½x13*

Size: 17¼x21mm

No.	Type	Description	Unused	Used
169a	A3	1m red brown	4.00	3.00
170a	A3	2m Prussian blue	10.25	3.00
172a	A3	3m green	17.00	6.25
174a	A3	4m rose	75.00	20.00
175b	A3	5m orange	80.00	4.75
176a	A3	10m red	110.00	6.25
177b	A3	15m ultramarine	42.50	5.50
178a	A3	20m olive green	65.00	19.00
		Nos. 169a-178a (8)	403.75	67.75

For overprint see No. N3a.

Mushetta — A4

Nymphaeum, Jerash — A5

Kasr Kharana — A6

Kerak Castle — A7

Temple of Artemis, Jerash — A8

Aijalon Castle — A9

Khazneh, Rock-hewn Temple, Petra — A10

Allenby Bridge, River Jordan — A11

Amir Abdullah ibn Hussein — A13

Ancient Threshing Floor — A12

1933, Feb. 1 *Perf. 12*

No.	Type	Description	Unused	Used
185	A4	1m dk brn & blk	1.00	*.95*
186	A5	2m claret & blk	1.10	*.75*
187	A6	3m blue green	1.25	*1.25*
188	A7	4m bister & blk	2.00	*1.90*
189	A8	5m orange & blk	2.25	*1.60*
190	A9	10m brown red	2.75	*2.75*
191	A10	15m dull blue	3.75	1.60
192	A11	20m ol grn & blk	5.50	*5.50*
193	A12	50m brn vio & blk	12.00	*12.50*
194	A6	90m yel & black	17.50	*22.50*
195	A8	100m blue & blk	20.00	*22.50*
196	A9	200m dk vio & blk	57.50	*70.00*
197	A10	500m brn & ver	175.00	*225.00*
198	A13	£1 green & blk	600.00	*825.00*
		Nos. 185-198 (14)	901.60	*1,193.*

Nos. 194-197 are larger than the lower values in the same designs.

Amir Abdullah ibn Hussein — A14

Perf. 13x13½

1942, May 18 Litho. Unwmk.

199 A14 1m dull red brn 1.00 *4.00*
200 A14 2m dull green 2.10 1.75
201 A14 3m dp yel green 2.10 *3.00*
202 A14 4m rose pink 2.10 *3.00*
203 A14 5m orange yel 2.40 1.40
204 A14 10m dull ver 2.75 2.75
205 A14 15m deep blue 3.50 3.50
206 A14 20m dull ol grn 10.50 10.50
Nos. 199-206 (8) 26.45 29.90

Type A14 differs from A3 in the redrawn inscription above the head and in the form of the "millieme" character at upper left.

For overprint see No. N1.

Abdullah Type of 1930-39
White Paper

1943-44 Engr. Wmk. 4 *Perf. 12*

Size: 17¾x21½mm

207 A3 1m red brown .20 .60
208 A3 2m Prussian grn .60 .60
209 A3 3m blue green 1.25 .75
210 A3 4m deep rose 1.25 .75
211 A3 5m orange 1.25 .20
212 A3 10m scarlet 3.00 1.00
213 A3 15m blue 3.00 .20
214 A3 20m olive ('44) 3.00 .90

Size: 20x24mm

215 A3 50m red lil ('44) 3.00 1.10
216 A3 90m ocher 5.50 4.50
217 A3 100m dp bl ('44) 7.50 1.60
218 A3 200m dk vio ('44) 12.00 6.75
219 A3 500m dk brn ('44) 18.00 15.00
220 A3 £1 black ('44) 37.50 30.00
Nos. 207-220 (14) 97.05 63.95

See Nos. 230-235. For overprints see Nos. 255-256, 259, 264-269, RA23, N2-N4, N7, N12-N17.

Catalogue values for unused stamps in this section, from this point to the end of the section, are for Never Hinged items.

Independent Kingdom

Symbols of Peace and Liberty — A15

Perf. 11½

1946, May 25 Unwmk. Litho.

221 A15 1m sepia .30 .20
222 A15 2m yel orange .30 .20
223 A15 3m dl ol grn .30 .20
224 A15 4m lt violet .30 .20
225 A15 10m orange brn .30 .20
226 A15 12m rose red .30 .20
227 A15 20m dark blue .35 .20
228 A15 50m ultra .75 .60
229 A15 200m green 2.25 2.25
Nos. 221-229 (9) 5.15 4.25

Independence of the Kingdom of Trans-Jordan.

Nos. 221-229 exist imperforate.

Abdullah Type of 1930-39

1947 Wmk. 4 Engr. *Perf. 12*

230 A3 3m rose carmine .40 .30
231 A3 4m deep yel green .40 .30
232 A3 10m violet .45 .30
233 A3 12m deep rose 1.10 .80
234 A3 15m dull olive grn 1.00 .90
235 A3 20m deep blue 1.25 1.00
Nos. 230-235 (6) 4.60 3.60

For overprints see Nos. 257-258, 260-263, RA24-RA25, N5-N6, N8-N11.

Parliament Building, Amman A16

1947, Nov. 1 Engr. Unwmk.

236 A16 1m purple .45 .20
237 A16 3m red orange .45 .20
238 A16 4m yel green .45 .20
239 A16 10m dk vio brn .45 .20
240 A16 12m carmine .45 .20
241 A16 20m deep blue .55 .20
242 A16 50m red vio .80 .35
243 A16 100m rose 1.00 .65
244 A16 200m dark green 1.75 1.50
Nos. 236-244 (9) 6.35 3.70

Founding of the new Trans-Jordan parliament, 1947.

Nos. 236-244 exist imperforate.

Symbols of the UPU A17

King Abdullah ibn Hussein A18

1949, Aug. 1 Wmk. 4 *Perf. 13*

245 A17 1m brown .45 .40
246 A17 4m green .80 .75
247 A17 10m red 1.00 .90
248 A17 20m ultramarine 1.75 1.25
249 A18 50m dull green 2.50 1.75
Nos. 245-249 (5) 6.50 5.05

UPU, 75th anniv. For overprints see #N18-N22.

Nos. 207-208, 211, 215-220, 230-235 Surcharged in Carmine, Black or Green

1952 Wmk. 4 *Perf. 12*

Size: 17¾x21½mm

255 A3 1f on 1m red brn (Bk) .40 .35
256 A3 2f on 2m Prus grn .40 .35
257 A3 3f on 3m rose car (Bk) .40 .35
258 A3 4f on 4m dp yel grn .40 .35
259 A3 5f on 5m org (G) 1.25 .45
260 A3 10f on 10m vio 1.00 .60
261 A3 12f on 12m dp rose (Bk) 1.00 .60
262 A3 15f on 15m dl ol grn 1.00 .40
263 A3 20f on 20m dp bl 1.40 .70

Size: 20x24mm

264 A3 50f on 50m red lil (G) 1.60 1.10
265 A3 90f on 90m ocher (G) 11.00 6.50
266 A3 100f on 100m dp bl 6.75 2.10
267 A3 200f on 200m dk vio 9.50 3.25
268 A3 500f on 500m dk brn 21.00 9.50
269 A3 1d on £1 black 47.50 12.00
Nos. 255-269 (15) 104.60 38.60

This surcharge also exists on Nos. 199-203, 205, 209-210, 212-214. Numerous inverted, double and wrong color surcharges exist.

Relief Map A19

Amir Abdullah ibn Hussein A20

Perf. 13½x13

1952, Apr. 1 Engr. Wmk. 4

270 A19 1f red brn & yel grn .35 .20
271 A19 2f dk bl grn & red .35 .20
272 A19 3f car & gray blk .35 .30
273 A19 4f green & orange .45 .30
274 A19 5f choc & rose vio .45 .30
275 A19 10f violet & brown .45 .45
276 A19 20f dark bl & blk .95 .50
277 A19 100f dp blue & brn 3.25 1.90
278 A19 200f purple & orange 6.75 3.25
Nos. 270-278 (9) 13.35 7.40

Unity of Jordan, Apr. 24, 1950.

For overprints see Nos. 297-305.

1952 Wmk. 4 *Perf. 11½*

279 A20 5f orange .40 .30
280 A20 10f violet .40 .30
281 A20 12f carmine 1.25 .95
282 A20 15f olive .75 .30
283 A20 20f deep blue .75 .40

Size: 20x24½mm

Perf. 12x12½

284 A20 50f plum 1.60 .75
285 A20 90f brn orange 4.50 2.50
286 A20 100f deep blue 5.00 1.60
Nos. 279-286 (8) 14.65 7.10

No. 288

Nos. RA5-RA7 Overprinted in Black or Carmine

Perf. 11½x12½

1953 Unwmk. Engr.

286A PT1 10m carmine 32.50 25.00
286B PT1 15m gray (C) 30.00 1.25
286C PT1 20m dark brown 70.00 47.50

Same Overprint on Nos. NRA4-NRA7

286D PT1 5m plum 45.00 25.00
286E PT1 10m carmine 45.00 25.00
286F PT1 15m gray (C) 45.00 25.00
286G PT1 20m dk brn (C) 45.00 25.00
Nos. 286A-286G (7) 285.50 173.75

In addition a few sheets of Nos. RA9, NRA1, NRA3, NRA8-NRA9 and RA37-RA41 have been reported with this overprint.It is doubtful whether they were regularly issued. See Nos. 344-347.

Same Overprint on Nos. RA28-RA31 in Black or Carmine

1953 Wmk. 4 *Perf. 11½x12½*

287 PT1 5f plum .30 .20
288 PT1 10f carmine .35 .25
289 PT1 15f gray (C) .70 .70
290 PT1 20f dark brown (C) 1.25 1.10
Nos. 287-290 (4) 2.60 2.25

King Hussein A21

Unwmk.

1953, Oct. 1 Engr. *Perf. 12*

Portrait in Black

291 A21 1f dark green .35 .20
292 A21 4f deep plum .35 .20
293 A21 15f deep ultra 1.10 .30
294 A21 20f dark purple 2.10 .30
295 A21 50f dark blue grn 4.75 2.25
296 A21 100f dark blue 9.25 6.50
Nos. 291-296 (6) 17.90 9.75

Accession of King Hussein, May 2, 1953.

Nos. 270-278 Overprinted in Black with Two Bars Through Center Inscription

1953 Wmk. 4 *Perf. 13½x13*

297 A19 1f red brn & yel grn .40 .20
298 A19 2f dk bl grn & red .40 .20
299 A19 3f car & gray blk .40 .20
300 A19 4f green & orange .40 .25
301 A19 5f choc & rose vio .40 .25
302 A19 10f violet & brown 1.00 .45
303 A19 20f dark bl & blk 1.00 .60
304 A19 100f dp blue & brn 5.25 1.50
305 A19 200f purple & org 7.00 4.50
Nos. 297-305 (9) 16.25 8.15

Two main settings of the bars exist on Nos. 297-300 and 304 — the "normal" 1½mm spacing, and the "narrow" ½mm spacing. Values above are for normal spacing. Value of set with narrow spacing, $150.

El Deir Temple, Petra — A22

Dome of the Rock — A23

Designs: 2f, 4f, 500f, 1d, King Hussein. 3f, 5f, Treasury Bldg., Petra. 12f, 50f, 100f, 200f, Al Aqsa Mosque. 20f, as 10f.

1954 Unwmk. Engr. *Perf. 12½*

306 A22 1f dk bl grn & red brn .35 .20
307 A22 2f red & black .35 .20
308 A22 3f dp plum & vio bl .35 .20
309 A22 4f org brn & dk grn .40 .30
310 A22 5f vio & dk grn .40 .30
311 A23 10f pur & dk grn .50 .35
312 A23 12f car rose & sep 1.25 .70
313 A23 20f dp bl & dk grn 1.25 .35
314 A23 50f dk bl & dp rose 3.75 3.50
315 A23 100f dk grn & dp bl 2.75 .75
316 A23 200f dp cl & pck bl 11.00 1.50
317 A22 500f choc & purple 27.50 8.25
318 A22 1d dk ol grn & rose brn 40.00 17.00
Nos. 306-318 (13) 89.85 33.60

See Nos. 324-337. For overprint see No. 425.

Globe — A23a

Perf. 13½x13

1955, Jan. 1 Photo. Wmk. 195

319 A23a 15f green .45 .30
320 A23a 20f violet .45 .30
321 A23a 25f yellow brown .60 .40
Nos. 319-321 (3) 1.50 1.00

Founding of the APU, July 1, 1954.

Princess Dina Abdul Hamid and King Hussein — A24

1955, Apr. 19 *Perf. 11x11½*

322 A24 15f ultramarine 1.50 .65
323 A24 100f rose brown 5.75 2.50

Marriage of King Hussein and Princess Dina Abdul Hamid.

Types of 1954

Design: 15f, Dome of the Rock.

Wmk. 305

1955-64 Engr. *Perf. 12½*

324 A22 1f dk bl grn & red brn ('57) .40 .20
325 A22 2f red & blk ('57) .40 .20

326 A22 3f dp plum & vio bl ('56) .40 .20
327 A22 4f org brn & dk grn ('56) .40 .20
328 A22 5f vio & dk grn ('56) .40 .20
329 A23 10f pur & grn ('57) .50 .20
330 A23 12f car rose & sep 1.25 .20
331 A23 15f dp brn & rose red .75 .20
332 A23 20f dp bl & dk grn ('57) .60 .20
333 A23 50f dk bl & dp rose 1.50 .35
334 A23 100f dk grn & dp bl ('62) 2.75 .90
335 A23 200f dp cl & pck bl ('65) 7.50 1.75
336 A22 500f choc & pur ('65) 24.00 9.00
337 A22 1d dk ol grn & rose brn ('65) 40.00 15.00
Nos. 324-337 (14) 80.85 28.80

Envelope A25

Wmk. 305

1956, Jan. 15 Engr. *Perf. 14*

"Postmarks" in Black

338 A25 1f light brown .30 .20
339 A25 4f dark car rose .30 .20
340 A25 15f blue .30 .20
341 A25 20f yellow olive .35 .25
342 A25 50f slate blue .55 .25
343 A25 100f vermilion .85 .50
Nos. 338-343 (6) 2.65 1.60

1st Arab Postal Congress in Amman.

Nos. RA1, RA3, RA8 and RA33 Overprinted in Carmine or Black

Perf. 11½x12½

1956, Jan. 5 Unwmk.

344 PT1 1m ultramarine .30 .25
345 PT1 3m emerald .35 .25
346 PT1 50m purple .60 .50

Wmk. 4

347 PT1 100f orange (Bk) 3.25 1.90
Nos. 344-347 (4) 4.50 2.90

Numerous inverted, double and wrong color surcharges exist.

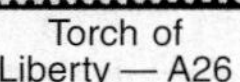

Torch of Liberty — A26

King Hussein — A27

1958 Wmk. 305 Engr. *Perf. 12½*

348 A26 5f blue & red brown .45 .40
349 A26 15f bister brn & blk .45 .40
350 A26 35f blue grn & plum 1.10 1.00
351 A26 45f car & olive grn 10.00 8.50
Nos. 348-351 (4) 12.00 10.30

10th anniv. of the Universal Declaration of Human Rights.

Perf. 12x11½

1959 Wmk. 305 Engr.

Centers in Black

352 A27 1f deep green .35 .20
353 A27 2f violet .35 .20
354 A27 3f deep carmine .35 .20
355 A27 4f brown black .40 .20
356 A27 7f dark green .40 .20
357 A27 12f deep carmine .50 .20
358 A27 15f dark red .50 .20
359 A27 21f green .50 .20
360 A27 25f ocher .70 .20
361 A27 35f dark blue 1.00 .30
362 A27 40f olive green 1.50 .30
363 A27 50f red 2.25 .30
364 A27 100f blue green 3.00 .50
365 A27 200f rose lake 7.00 3.00
366 A27 500f gray blue 17.50 7.50
367 A27 1d dark purple 35.00 19.00
Nos. 352-367 (16) 71.30 32.70

For overprints see Nos. 423-424, 425a, 426-427.

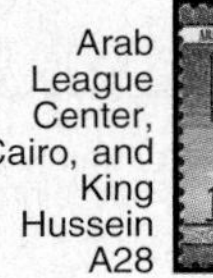

Arab League Center, Cairo, and King Hussein A28

Perf. 13x13½

1960, Mar. 22 Photo. Wmk. 328

368 A28 15f dull green & blk .35 .25

Opening of the Arab League Center and the Arab Postal Museum in Cairo.

World Refugee Year Emblem A29

Wmk. 305

1960, Apr. 7 Litho. *Perf. 13½*

369 A29 15f pale blue & red .35 .25
370 A29 35f bister & blue .50 .45

World Refugee Year, 7/1/59-6/30/60.
For overprints see Nos. 377-378.

Shah of Iran, King Hussein and Flags A30

Perf. 13x13½

1960, May 15 Wmk. 305

Flags in Green, Red & Black

371 A30 15f yellow & black .45 .20
372 A30 35f blue & black .60 .35
373 A30 50f salmon & black .95 .70
Nos. 371-373 (3) 2.00 1.25

Visit of Mohammed Riza Pahlavi, Shah of Iran, to Jordan, Nov. 2, 1959.

Oil Refinery, Zarka A31

1961, May 1 Engr. *Perf. 14x13*

374 A31 15f dull vio & blue .30 .20
375 A31 35f dl vio & brick red .30 .20

Opening of oil refinery at Zarka.

Urban and Nomad Families and Chart A32

Perf. 13x13½

1961, Oct. 15 Photo. Unwmk.

376 A32 15f orange brown .30 .20

First Jordanian census, 1961.

Nos. 369-370 Overprinted in English and Arabic, "In Memorial of Dag Hammarskjoeld 1904-1961," and Laurel Leaf Border

1961 Wmk. 305 Litho. *Perf. 13½*

377 A29 15f pale blue & red 3.75 3.50
378 A29 35f bister & blue 4.25 3.75

Dag Hammarskjold, Secretary General of the UN, 1953-1961.

Malaria Eradication Emblem — A33

Perf. 11x11½

1962, Apr. 15 Unwmk.

379 A33 15f bright pink .35 .20
380 A33 35f blue .45 .30

WHO drive to eradicate malaria. A souvenir sheet exists with one each of #379-380. Value $5.50.

Dial and Exchange Building, Amman A34

1962, Dec. 11 Engr. Wmk. 305

381 A34 15f blue & lilac .30 .20
382 A34 35f lilac & emer .35 .25

Telephone automation in Amman (in 1960).

Opening of the Port of 'Aqaba A35

1962, Dec. 11

383 A35 15f lilac & blk .40 .20
384 A35 35f violet bl & blk .60 .30
a. Souvenir sheet of 2, #383-384 3.75 3.75

No. 384a imperf., same value.

Dag Hammarskjold and UN Headquarters, NY — A36

Perf. 14x14½

1963, Jan. 24 Photo. Unwmk.

385 A36 15f ultra, ol grn & brn red .45 .20
386 A36 35f ol, brn red & ultra .80 .45
387 A36 50f brn red, ol & ultra 1.25 .80
Nos. 385-387 (3) 2.50 1.45

17th anniv. of the UN and in memory of Dag Hammarskjold, Secretary General of the UN, 1953-61. An imperf. souvenir sheet contains one each of #385-387 with simulated perforations. Value $9.

Imperforates

Starting with No. 385, imperforates exist of many Jordanian stamps.

Church of St. Virgin's Tomb, Jerusalem — A37

Arab League Building, Cairo — A38

Designs: No. 389, Basilica of the Agony, Gethsemane. No. 390, Church of the Holy Sepulcher, Jerusalem. No. 391, Church of the Nativity, Bethlehem. No. 392, Haram el-Khalil (tomb of Abraham), Hebron. No. 393, Dome of the Rock, Jerusalem. No. 394, Mosque of Omar el-Khatab, Jerusalem. No. 395, Al Aqsa Mosque, Jerusalem.

1963, Feb. 5 *Perf. 14½x14*

Center Multicolored

388 A37 50f blue 1.50 1.00
389 A37 50f dull red 1.50 1.00
390 A37 50f bright blue 1.50 1.00
391 A37 50f olive green 1.50 1.00
a. Vert. strip of 4, #388-391 15.00
392 A37 50f gray 1.50 1.00
393 A37 50f purple 1.50 1.00
394 A37 50f dull red 1.50 1.00
395 A37 50f light purple 1.50 1.00
a. Vert. strip of 4, #392-395 15.00
Nos. 388-395 (8) 12.00 8.00

1963, July 16 Photo. *Perf. 13½x13*

396 A38 15f slate blue .45 .20
397 A38 35f orange red .65 .20

Arab League.

Wheat and UN Emblem — A39

Perf. 11½x12½

1963, Sept. 15 Litho. Wmk. 305

398 A39 15f lt bl, grn & black .30 .20
399 A39 35f lt grn, grn & blk .30 .20
a. Souvenir sheet of 2, #398-399 1.50 1.50

FAO "Freedom from Hunger" campaign. No. 399a imperf., same value.

East Ghor Canal, Pylon, Gear Wheel and Wheat A40

1963, Sept. 20 *Perf. 14½x14*

400 A40 1f dull yel & black .35 .20
401 A40 4f blue & black .35 .20
402 A40 5f lilac & black .35 .20
403 A40 10f brt yel grn & blk .40 .20
404 A40 35f orange & black 1.25 .50
Nos. 400-404 (5) 2.70 1.30

East Ghor Canal Project.

UNESCO Emblem, Scales and Globe A41

Perf. 13½x13

1963, Dec. 10 Unwmk.

405 A41 50f pale vio bl & red .70 .60
406 A41 50f rose red & blue .70 .60

15th anniv. of the Universal Declaration of Human Rights.

Red Crescent and King Hussein — A42

1963, Dec. 24 Photo. *Perf. 14x14½*

407	A42	1f red & red lilac	.30	.20
408	A42	2f red & bl green	.30	.20
409	A42	3f red & dk blue	.30	.20
410	A42	4f red & dk green	.30	.20
411	A42	5f red & dk brown	.30	.20
412	A42	85f red & dp green	1.10	.95

Design: Red Cross at right, no portrait

413	A42	1f red lilac & red	.30	.20
414	A42	2f blue grn & red	.30	.20
415	A42	3f dk blue & red	.30	.20
416	A42	4f dk green & red	.30	.20
417	A42	5f dk brown & red	.30	.20
418	A42	85f dp green & red	4.00	1.50
		Nos. 407-418 (12)	8.10	4.45

Centenary of the Intl. Red Cross. Two 100f imperf. souvenir sheets, red and red lilac, exist in the Red Crescent and Red Cross designs. Value, pair of sheets $50.

Hussein ibn Ali and King Hussein A43

Perf. 11x11½

1963, Dec. 25 Litho. Unwmk.

419	A43	15f yellow & multi	.50	.20
420	A43	25f multicolored	.75	.35
421	A43	35f brt pink & multi	1.75	.85
422	A43	50f lt blue & multi	2.75	2.00
		Nos. 419-422 (4)	5.75	3.40

Arab Renaissance Day, June 10, 1916. Perf. and imperf. souvenir sheets exist containing one each of Nos. 419-422. Value: perf, $6.50; imperf, $9.

Nos. 359, 312, 357 and 361 Surcharged

Wmk. 305, Unwmk.
Perf. 12x11½, 12½

1963, Dec. 16 Engr.

423	A27	1f on 21f grn & blk	.35	.20
424	A27	2f on 21f grn & blk	.35	.20
425	A23	4f on 12f car rose & sepia	.40	.30
a.		4f on 12f dp car & blk (#357)	16.00	14.50
426	A27	5f on 21f grn & blk	.60	.40
427	A27	25f on 35f dk bl & blk	2.40	.90
		Nos. 423-427 (5)	4.10	*2.00*

Pope Paul VI, King Hussein and Al Aqsa Mosque, Jerusalem — A44

Portraits and: 35f, Dome of the Rock. 50f, Church of the Holy Sepulcher. 80f, Church of the Nativity, Bethlehem.

1964, Jan. 4 Litho. *Perf. 13x13½*

428	A44	15f emerald & blk	.80	.30
429	A44	35f car rose & blk	1.00	.40
430	A44	50f brown & black	1.75	.90
431	A44	80f vio bl & blk	3.00	1.50
		Nos. 428-431 (4)	6.55	3.10

Visit of Pope Paul VI to the Holy Land, Jan. 4-6. An imperf. souvenir sheet contains 4 stamps similar to Nos. 428-431. Value $27.50

A45

Crown Prince Abdullah ben Al-Hussein — A46

Design: 5f, Crown Prince standing, vert.

1964, Mar. 30 Photo. *Perf. 14*

432	A46	5f multicolored	.50	.20
433	A45	10f multicolored	.50	.20
434	A46	35f multicolored	.75	.45
		Nos. 432-434 (3)	1.75	.85

2nd birthday of Crown Prince Abdullah ben Al-Hussein (b. Jan. 30, 1962).

A47

Mercury Astronauts, Spacecraft — A48

Designs: b, M. Scott Carpenter. c, Entering space. d, Alan Shepard. e, At launch pad. f, Virgil Grissom. g, After separation. h, Walter Schirra. i, Lift-off. j, John Glenn. Stamp has point down on b, d, f, h, j.

1964, Mar. 25 Photo. *Perf. 14*

435	A47	20f Block of 10, #a.-j.	9.00	8.25

Imperf

Size: 111x80mm

436	A48	100f multicolored	17.50	15.00

Table Tennis A49

Designs: 1f, 2f, 3f, 5f vertical.

Perf. 14½x14, 14x14½

1964, June 1 Litho. Unwmk.

446	A49	1f Basketball	.50	.20
447	A49	2f Volleyball	.50	.20
448	A49	3f Soccer	.50	.20
449	A49	4f shown	.50	.20
450	A49	5f Running	.50	.20
451	A49	35f Bicycling	1.75	1.10
452	A49	50f Fencing	2.50	1.50
453	A49	100f Pole vault	4.50	2.75
		Nos. 446-453 (8)	11.25	6.35

1964 Olympic Games, Tokyo, Oct. 10-25. An imperf. 200f greenish blue souvenir sheet in design of 100f exists. Value $35.

Mother and Child — A50

1964, June 1 Wmk. 305 *Perf. 14*

454	A50	5f multicolored	.30	.20
455	A50	10f multicolored	.30	.20
456	A50	25f multicolored	.30	.20
		Nos. 454-456 (3)	.90	.60

Social Studies Seminar, fourth session.

Pres. John F. Kennedy — A51

1964, July 15 Unwmk.

457	A51	1f brt violet	.50	.40
458	A51	2f carmine rose	.50	.40
459	A51	3f ultramarine	.50	.40
460	A51	4f orange brown	.50	.40
461	A51	5f bright green	.50	.40
462	A51	85f rose red	18.50	11.00
		Nos. 457-462 (6)	21.00	13.00

President John F. Kennedy (1917-1963). An imperf. 100f brown souvenir sheet exists. Size of stamp: 58x83mm. Value $18.50.

Ramses II A52

Perf. 14½x14

1964, July Litho. Wmk. 305

463	A52	4f lt blue & dark brn	.30	.20
464	A52	15f yellow & violet	.30	.20
465	A52	25f lt yel grn & dk red	.30	.20
		Nos. 463-465 (3)	.90	.60

UNESCO world campaign to save historic monuments in Nubia.

King Hussein and Map of Jordan and Israel — A53

1964, Sept. 5 Unwmk. *Perf. 12*

466	A53	10f multicolored	.40	.20
467	A53	15f multicolored	.40	.20
468	A53	25f multicolored	.40	.20
469	A53	50f multicolored	.70	.25
470	A53	80f multicolored	1.00	.45
		Nos. 466-470 (5)	2.90	1.30

Council of the Heads of State of the Arab League (Arab Summit Conference), Cairo, Jan. 13, 1964. An imperf. souvenir sheet contains Nos. 466-470 with simulated perforations. Value $4.

Pope Paul VI, King Hussein and Patriarch Athenagoras; Church of St. Savior, Church of the Holy Sepulcher and Dome of the Rock — A54

1964, Aug. 17 Litho.

471	A54	10f dk grn, sep & org	.50	.20
472	A54	15f claret, sep & org	.50	.20
473	A54	25f choc, sepia & org	.50	.20
474	A54	50f blue, sepia & org	1.00	.70
475	A54	80f brt grn, sep & org	2.25	.60
		Nos. 471-475 (5)	4.75	1.90

Meeting between Pope Paul VI and Patriarch Athenagoras of the Greek Orthodox Church in Jerusalem, Jan. 5, 1964. An imperf. souvenir sheet contains Nos. 471-475 with simulated perforations. Value $11.

A two-line bilingual overprint, "Papa Paulus VI World Peace Visit to United Nations 1965", was applied to Nos. 471-475 and the souvenir sheet. These overprints were issued Apr. 27, 1966. Value, unused: set, $5; souvenir sheet, $10.

Pagoda, Olympic Torch and Emblem — A55

1964, Nov. 21 Litho. *Perf. 14*

476	A55	1f dark red	.45	.20
477	A55	2f bright violet	.55	.20
478	A55	3f blue green	.65	.20
479	A55	4f brown	.75	.30
480	A55	5f henna brown	.85	.35
481	A55	35f indigo	1.25	1.00
482	A55	50f olive	2.00	1.50
483	A55	100f violet blue	4.25	3.00
		Nos. 476-483 (8)	10.75	6.75

18th Olympic Games, Tokyo, Oct. 10-25. An imperf. 100f carmine rose souvenir sheet exists. Size of stamp: 82mm at the base. Value $20.

Scouts Crossing Stream on Log Bridge — A56

Designs: 2f, First aid. 3f, Calisthenics. 4f, Instruction in knot tying. 5f, Outdoor cooking. 35f, Sailing. 50f, Campfire.

1964, Dec. 7 Unwmk.

484	A56	1f brown	.70	.20
485	A56	2f bright violet	.70	.20
486	A56	3f ocher	.70	.20
487	A56	4f maroon	.70	.20
488	A56	5f yellow green	.70	.20
489	A56	35f bright blue	2.00	1.25
490	A56	50f dk slate green	3.50	1.75
		Nos. 484-490 (7)	9.00	4.00

Jordanian Boy Scouts. An imperf. 100f dark blue souvenir sheet in campfire design exists. Size of stamp: 104mm at the base. Value $22.50.

Yuri A. Gagarin — A57

Russian Cosmonauts: No. 492, Gherman Titov. No. 493, Andrian G. Nikolayev. No. 494, Pavel R. Popovich. No. 495, Valeri Bykovski. No. 496, Valentina Tereshkova.

1965, Jan. 20 Litho. *Perf. 14*

491	A57	40f	sepia & vio bl	1.25	.75
492	A57	40f	pink & dk grn	1.25	.75
493	A57	40f	lt bl & vio blk	1.25	.75
494	A57	40f	olive & dk vio	1.25	.75
495	A57	40f	lt grn & red brn	1.25	.75
496	A57	40f	chlky bl & blk	1.25	.75
			Nos. 491-496 (6)	7.50	4.50

Russian cosmonauts. A blue 100f souvenir sheet exists showing portraits of the 6 astronauts and space-ship circling globe. This sheet received later an additional overprint honoring the space flight of Komarov, Feoktistov and Yegorov. Value $20, each.

For overprints see Nos. 527-527E.

UN Headquarters and Emblem — A58

1965, Feb. 15 *Perf. 14x15*

497	A58	30f	yel brn, pur & lt bl	.60	.20
498	A58	70f	vio, lt bl & yel brn	1.00	.70

19th anniv. of the UN (in 1964). A souvenir sheet contains Nos. 497-498, imperf. Value $14.

Dagger in Map of Palestine — A59

Volleyball Player and Cup — A60

1965, Apr. 9 Photo. *Perf. 11x11½*

499	A59	25f	red & olive	4.50	1.25

Deir Yassin massacre, Apr. 9, 1948.

See Iraq Nos. 372-373 and Kuwait Nos. 281-282.

1965, June Litho. *Perf. 14½x14*

500	A60	15f	lemon	1.25	.20
501	A60	35f	rose brown	1.50	.20
502	A60	50f	greenish blue	2.25	.75
			Nos. 500-502 (3)	5.00	1.15

Arab Volleyball Championships. An imperf. 100f orange brown souvenir sheet exists. Size of stamp: 33x57mm. Value $22.50.

Cavalry Horsemanship A61

Army Day: 10f, Tank. 35f, King Hussein and aides standing in army car.

1965, May 24

503	A61	5f	green	.50	.20
504	A61	10f	violet blue	.55	.20
505	A61	35f	brown red	1.50	.55
			Nos. 503-505 (3)	2.55	.95

John F. Kennedy — A62

1965, June 1 Wmk. 305 *Perf. 14*

506	A62	10f	black & brt green	.30	.20
507	A62	15f	violet & orange	.50	.20
508	A62	25f	brown & lt blue	.50	.30
509	A62	50f	deep claret & emer	1.50	.60
			Nos. 506-509 (4)	2.80	1.30

John F. Kennedy (1917-63). An imperf. 50f salmon and dark blue souv. sheet exists. Value $17.50.

Pope Paul VI, King Hussein and Dome of the Rock — A63

Perf. 13½x14

1965, June 15 Litho. Wmk. 305

510	A63	5f	brown & rose lil	.50	.20
511	A63	10f	vio brn & lt yel grn	.90	.40
512	A63	15f	ultra & salmon	1.10	.50
513	A63	50f	black & rose	3.25	1.60
			Nos. 510-513 (4)	5.75	2.70

1st anniversary of the visit of Pope Paul VI to the Holy Land. An imperf. 50f violet and light blue souvenir sheet exists with simulated perforations. Value $25.

Jordan's Pavilion and Unisphere — A64

Perf. 14x13½

1965, Aug. Unwmk. Photo.

514	A64	15f	silver & multi	.45	.20
515	A64	25f	bronze & multi	.45	.20
516	A64	50f	gold & multi	.85	.40
a.			Souvenir sheet of 1, 100f	3.25	3.00
			Nos. 514-516 (3)	1.75	.80

New York World's Fair, 1964-65.

No. 516a contains a 100f gold and multicolored stamp, type A64, imperf.

Library Aflame and Lamp A64a

1965, Aug. Wmk. 305 *Perf. 11½x11*

517	A64a	25f	black, grn & red	.50	.20

Burning of the Library of Algiers, 6/7/62.

ITU Emblem, Old and New Telecommunication Equipment — A65

1965, Aug. Litho. *Perf. 14x13½*

518	A65	25f	lt blue & dk bl	.40	.20
519	A65	45f	grnsh gray & blk	.60	.35

ITU, centenary. An imperf. 100f salmon and carmine rose souvenir sheet exists with carmine rose border. Size of stamp: 39x32mm. Value $3.

Syncom Satellite over Pagoda — A66

Designs: 10f, 20f, Rocket in space. 15f, Astronauts in cabin.

1965, Sept. *Perf. 14*

521	A66	5f	multicolored	.30	.20
521A	A66	10f	multicolored	.30	.20
521B	A66	15f	multicolored	.50	.25
521C	A66	20f	multicolored	.60	.30
521D	A66	50f	multicolored	1.50	.75
			Nos. 521-521D (5)	3.20	1.70

Achievements in space research. A 50f multicolored imperf. souvenir sheet shows earth and Syncom satellite. Value $17.50.

Dead Sea A66a

Designs: b, Qumran Caves. c, Dead Sea. d, Dead Sea Scrolls.

1965, Sept. 23 Photo. *Perf. 14*

522	A66a	35f	Strip of 4, #a.-d.	6.00	6.00

Visit of King Hussein to France and U.S. — A66b

Wmk. 305

1965, Oct. 5 Litho. *Perf. 14*

523	A66b	5f	shown	.30	.20
523A	A66b	10f	With Charles DeGaulle	.30	.20
523B	A66b	20f	With Lyndon Johnson	.65	.50
523C	A66b	50f	like #523	1.50	1.10
			Nos. 523-523C (4)	2.75	2.00

No. 523C exists in a 50f imperf. souvenir sheet. Value $12.

Intl. Cooperation Year — A66c

1965, Oct. 24 *Perf. 14x13½*

524	A66c	5f	brt org & dk org	.40	.20
524A	A66c	10f	brt bl & dk bl	.75	.35
524B	A66c	45f	brt grn & dk violet	2.10	1.40
			Nos. 524-524B (3)	3.25	1.95

Arab Postal Union, 10th Anniv. — A66d

1965, Nov. 5 *Perf. 15x14*

525	A66d	15f	violet bl & blk	.30	.20
525A	A66d	25f	brt yel grn & blk	.50	.35

Dome of the Rock A66e

1965, Nov. 20 *Perf. 14x15*

526	A66e	15f	multicolored	1.10	1.10
526A	A66e	25f	multicolored	1.60	1.60

Nos. 491-496 with Spaceship and Bilingual Ovpt. in Blue "Alexei Leonov / Pavel Belyaev / 18-3-65"

1966, Jan. 15 Litho. *Perf. 14*

527	A57	40f	on No. 491	3.75	3.50
527A	A57	40f	on No. 492	3.75	3.50
527B	A57	40f	on No. 493	3.75	3.50
527C	A57	40f	on No. 494	3.75	3.50
527D	A57	40f	on No. 495	3.75	3.50
527E	A57	40f	on No. 496	3.75	3.50
			Nos. 527-527E (6)	22.50	21.00

Both souvenir sheets mentioned after No. 496 exist overprinted in red violet. Value, $50 each.

King Hussein A67

Perf. 14½x14

1966, Jan. 15 Photo. Unwmk.

Portrait in Slate Blue

528	A67	1f	orange	.40	.20
528A	A67	2f	ultramarine	.40	.20
528B	A67	3f	dk purple	.40	.20
528C	A67	4f	plum	.40	.20
528D	A67	7f	brn orange	.40	.20
528E	A67	12f	cerise	.40	.20
528F	A67	15f	olive brn	.40	.20

Portrait in Violet Brown

528G A67 21f green .55 .20
528H A67 25f greenish bl .55 .20
528I A67 35f yel bister .80 .35
528J A67 40f orange yel 1.00 .35
528K A67 50f olive grn 1.10 .20
528L A67 100f lt yel grn 2.10 .40
528M A67 150f violet 3.00 1.00
Nos. 528-528M,C43-C45 (17) 44.65 19.35

Anti-tuberculosis Campaign — A67a

1966, May 17 Photo. *Perf. 14x15*
Blue Overprint

529 A67a 15f multicolored .65 .50
529A A67a 35f multicolored 1.10 .95
529B A67a 50f multicolored 1.50 1.25
Nos. 529-529B (3) 3.25 2.70

Unissued Freedom from Hunger stamps overprinted. Two imperf. souvenir sheets exist, one with simulated perforations. Value, each $10.

Nos. 529-529B with Added Surcharge Obliterated with Black Bars

1966, May 17 Photo. *Perf. 14x15*

530 A67a 15f on 15f + 15f .75 .30
530A A67a 35f on 35f + 35f 1.50 .75
530B A67a 50f on 50f + 50f 2.75 1.25
Nos. 530-530B (3) 5.00 2.30

A67b

A67c

Designs: Stations on Jesus' walk to Calvary along Via Dolorosa (Stations of the Cross). Denominations expressed in Roman numerals.

1966, Sept. 14 Photo. *Perf. 15x14*
Design A67b

531 1f Condemned to death .40 .20
531A 2f Takes up cross .40 .20
531B 3f Falls the 1st time .40 .20
531C 4f Meets His mother .50 .25
531D 5f Simon helps carry cross .60 .30
531E 6f Woman wipes Jesus' brow .60 .30
531F 7f Falls 2nd time .80 .40
531G 8f Tells women not to weep .90 .45
531H 9f Falls 3rd time 1.00 .50
531I 10f Stripped of His garment 1.10 .55
531J 11f Nailed to cross 1.25 .60
531K 12f Death on cross 1.40 .65
531L 13f Removal from cross 1.50 .70
531M 14f Burial 1.60 .75
Nos. 531-531M (14) 12.45 6.05

Souvenir Sheet
Imperf

531N 100f like #531 *30.00 27.50*

1966, Nov. 15 Photo. *Perf. 15x14*

Astronauts and spacecraft from Gemini Missions 6-8.

Design A67c

532 1f Walter M. Schirra .35 .20
532A 2f Thomas P. Stafford .35 .20
532B 3f Frank Borman .35 .20
532C 4f James A. Lovell .35 .20
532D 30f Neil Armstrong 1.50 .70
532E 60f David R. Scott 2.10 1.50
Nos. 532-532E (6) 5.00 3.00

Imperf
Size: 119x89mm

532F 100f Gemini 6-8 astronauts *22.50 20.00*

Christmas — A67d

Perf. 14x15, 15x14
1966, Dec. 21 Photo.

533 5f Magi following star .35 .20
533A 10f Adoration of the Magi .35 .20
533B 35f Flight to Egypt, vert. 3.25 1.10
Nos. 533-533B (3) 3.95 1.50

Souvenir Sheet
Imperf

533C 50f like #533A *22.50 20.00*

King Hussein — A67e

Builders of World Peace: No. 534, Dag Hammarskjold. No. 534A, U Thant. No. 534B, Jawaharlal Nehru. No. 534C, Charles DeGaulle. No. 534D, John F. Kennedy. No. 534E, Lyndon B. Johnson. No. 534F, Pope John XXIII. No. 534G, Pope Paul VI. No. 534H, King Abdullah of Jordan.

1967, Jan. 5 Photo. *Perf. 15x14*
Background Color

534 A67e 5f gray .35 .20
534A A67e 5f brt yel grn .35 .20
534B A67e 10f rose lilac .35 .20
534C A67e 10f red brown .35 .20
534D A67e 35f olive green .95 .70
534E A67e 35f orange .95 .70
534F A67e 50f rose claret 1.10 1.00
534G A67e 50f yel bister 1.10 1.00
534H A67e 100f brt blue 2.50 2.10
534I A67e 100f dull blue 2.50 2.10
Nos. 534-534I (10) 10.50 8.40

Imperf
Size: 99x64mm

534J A67e 100f Kennedy, etc. *22.50 22.50*
534K A67e 100f DeGaulle, etc. *22.50 22.50*

King Hussein A67f

Photo. & Embossed
1967, Feb. 7 *Imperf.*
Gold Portrait and Border
Diameter: 50f, 100f, 48mm; 200f, 54mm
Portrait of King Hussein

535 A67f 5f dk bl & salmon .75 .75
535A A67f 10f purple & salmon .75 .75
535B A67f 50f blk brn & vio 4.25 4.25
535C A67f 100f dk ol grn & pink 5.00 5.00
535D A67f 200f dp bl & bl 7.75 7.75

Portrait of Crown Prince Hassan

536 A67f 5f brt yel grn & blk .75 .75
536A A67f 10f vio & blk .75 .75
536B A67f 50f bl & blk 4.25 4.25
536C A67f 100f bister & blk 5.00 5.00
536D A67f 200f brt pink & blk 7.75 7.75

Portrait of John F. Kennedy

537 A67f 5f brt bl & lt grn .75 .75
537A A67f 10f dp grn & pink .75 .75
537B A67f 50f brt rose & org yel 3.25 3.25
537C A67f 100f brn & apple grn 4.25 4.25
537D A67f 200f dk purple & pale grn 5.00 5.00
Nos. 535-537D (15) 51.00 51.00

1968 Summer Olympic Games, Mexico — A67g

Olympic torch and: 1f, Natl. University Library with O'Gormans mosaics, statue, Mexico City. 2f, Fishermen on Lake Patzcuaro. 3f, Natl. University buildings. 4f, Paseo de la Reforma, Mexico City. 30f, Guadalajara Cathedral. 60f, 100f, Palace of Fine Arts, Mexico City.

Perf. 14x15
1967, Mar. Photo. Unwmk.

538 A67g 1f lake, dk bl vio & blk .30 .25
538A A67g 2f blk, lake & dk bl vio .30 .25
538B A67g 3f dark bl vio, blk & lake .30 .25
538C A67g 4f bl, grn & brn .30 .25
538D A67g 30f grn, brn & bl .60 .60
538E A67g 60f brn, bl & grn 1.10 1.10
Nos. 538-538E (6) 2.90 2.70

Souvenir Sheet
Imperf

538F A67g 100f brn, dark bl & grn 22.50 22.50

Symbolic Water Cycle A68

Perf. 14½x14
1967, Mar. 1 Litho. Wmk. 305

539 A68 10f dp org, blk & gray .50 .20
540 A68 15f grnsh bl, blk & gray .50 .35
541 A68 25f brt rose lil, blk & gray .75 .50
Nos. 539-541 (3) 1.75 1.05

Hydrological Decade (UNESCO), 1965-74.

UNESCO Emblem — A69

1967, Mar. 16

542 A69 100f multicolored 1.10 1.10

20th anniv. of UNESCO.

Dromedary — A70

Animals: 2f, Karakul. 3f, Angora goat.

Perf. 14x15
1967, Feb. 11 Photo. Unwmk.

543 A70 1f dark brn & multi 1.10 .20
544 A70 2f yellow & multi 1.10 .20
545 A70 3f lt blue & multi 1.10 .20
Nos. 543-545,C46-C48 (6) 11.30 2.25

A souvenir sheet exists with a 100f in design and colors of No. C47, simulated perforation and marginal animal design. Value $35.

Inauguration of WHO Headquarters, Geneva — A71

1967, Apr. 7 Wmk. 305

546 A71 5f emerald & blk .40 .20
547 A71 45f dl orange & blk .50 .30

Arab League Emblem and Hands Reaching for Knowledge — A72

1968, May 5 Unwmk. *Perf. 11*

548 A72 20f org & slate grn .45 .20
549 A72 20f brt pink & dk bl .45 .20

Issued to publicize the literacy campaign.

"20" and WHO Emblem A73

Perf. 14½x14
1968, Aug. 10 Wmk. 305

550 A73 30f multicolored .60 .20
551 A73 100f multicolored 1.75 1.10

20th anniv. of the WHO.

European Goldfinch — A74

Protected Game: 10f, Rock partridge, vert. 15f, Ostriches, vert. 20f, Sand partridge. 30f, Dorcas gazelle. 40f, Oryxes. 50f, Houbara bustard.

1968, Oct. 5 Unwmk. *Perf. 13½*

552 A74 5f multicolored 3.25 1.25
553 A74 10f multicolored 6.50 1.25
554 A74 15f multicolored 8.50 1.50
555 A74 20f multicolored 8.50 1.75
556 A74 30f multicolored 5.25 1.25
557 A74 40f multicolored 8.00 1.50
558 A74 50f multicolored 12.50 3.00
Nos. 552-558,C49-C50 (9) 77.50 23.00

Human Rights Flame — A75

1968, Dec. 10 **Litho.** ***Perf. 13***

559 A75 20f dp org, lt org & blk .40 .20
560 A75 60f grn, lt blue & blk .75 .45

International Human Rights Year.

Dome of the Rock, Jerusalem A76

5f, 45f, Holy Kaaba, Mecca, & Dome of the Rock.

1969, Oct. 8 **Photo.** ***Perf. 12***

Size: 56x25mm

561 A76 5f dull vio & multi .80 .20

Size: 36x25mm

562 A76 10f vio blue & multi .80 .50
563 A76 20f Prus bl & multi 1.25 .60

Size: 56x25mm

564 A76 45f Prus bl & multi 2.10 .70
Nos. 561-564 (4) 4.95 2.00

ILO Emblem A77

1969, June 10 ***Perf. 13½x14***

565 A77 10f blue & black .35 .20
566 A77 20f bister brn & blk .35 .20
567 A77 25f lt olive & black .35 .20
568 A77 45f lil rose & black .50 .30
569 A77 60f orange & black .75 .35
Nos. 565-569 (5) 2.30 1.25

ILO, 50th anniversary.

Horses A78

20f, White stallion. 45f, Mare and foal.

1969, July 6 **Unwmk.** ***Perf. 13½***

570 A78 10f dark bl & multi 1.50 .25
571 A78 20f dl green & multi 3.50 .60
572 A78 45f red & multi 6.50 1.75
Nos. 570-572 (3) 11.50 2.60

Prince Hassan and Princess Tharwat A79

Designs: 60f, 100f, Prince Hassan and bride in western bridal gown.

1969, Dec. 2 **Photo.** ***Perf. 12½***

573 A79 20f gold & multi .50 .20
573A A79 60f gold & multi 1.00 .65
573B A79 100f gold & multi 1.50 1.25
c. Strip of 3, #573-573B 3.25 3.25

Wedding of Crown Prince Hassan, 11/14/68.

The Tragedy and the Flight of the Refugees A79a

Different design on each stamp. Each strip of 5 has five consecutive denominations.

Perf. 14½x13½

1969, Dec. 10 **Photo.**

574 A79a 1f-5f Strip of 5 11.00 11.00
f.-j. A79a 1f-5f Any single
574A A79a 6f-10f Strip of 5 11.00 11.00
a.-e. A79a 6f-10f Any single
574B A79a 11f-15f Strip of 5 11.00 11.00
a.-e. A79a 11f-15f Any single
574C A79a 16f-20f Strip of 5 11.00 11.00
a.-e. A79a 16f-20f Any single
574D A79a 21f-25f Strip of 5 11.00 11.00
a.-e. A79a 21f-25f Any single
574E A79a 26f-30f Strip of 5 11.00 11.00
a.-e. A79a 26f-30f Any single

For surcharges see Nos. 870-875.

Inscribed: Tragedy in the Holy Lands

Different design on each stamp. Each strip of 5 has five consecutive denominations.

Perf. 14½x13½

1969, Dec. 10 **Photo.**

575 A79a 1f-5f Strip of 5 5.00 5.00
f.-j. A79a 1f-5f Any single
575A A79a 6f-10f Strip of 5 5.00 5.00
a.-e. A79a 6f-10f Any single
575B A79a 11f-15f Strip of 5 5.00 5.00
a.-e. A79a 11f-15f Any single
575C A79a 16f-20f Strip of 5 5.00 5.00
a.-e. A79a 16f-20f Any single
575D A79a 21f-25f Strip of 5 5.00 5.00
a.-e. A79a 21f-25f Any single
575E A79a 26f-30f Strip of 5 5.00 5.00
a.-e. A79a 26f-30f Any single

For surcharges see Nos. 876-881.

Pomegranate Flower (inscribed "Desert Scabius") — A80

Oranges — A81

Black Bush Robin — A82

Designs: 15f, Wattle flower ("Caper"). 20f, Melon. 25f, Caper flower ("Pomegranate"). 30f, Lemons. 35f, Morning glory. 40f, Grapes. 45f, Desert scabius ("Wattle"). 50f, Olive-laden branch. 75f, Black iris. 100f, Apples. 180f, Masked shrike. 200f, Palestine sunbird. (Inscriptions incorrect on 5f, 15f, 25f and 45f.)

Perf. 14x13½ (flowers), 12 (fruit), 13½x14 (birds)

1969-70 **Photo.**

576 A80 5f yel & multi ('70) .40 .20
577 A81 10f blue & multi .40 .20
578 A80 15f tan & multi ('70) .70 .20
579 A81 20f sepia & multi .60 .20
580 A80 25f multi ('70) 1.00 .20
581 A81 30f vio bl & multi 1.00 .20
582 A80 35f multi ('70) 1.50 .20
583 A81 40f dull yel & multi 1.50 .20
584 A80 45f gray & multi ('70) 2.00 .25
585 A81 50f car rose & multi 2.00 .40
586 A80 75f multi ('70) 3.00 1.00
587 A81 100f dk gray & multi 3.25 1.25
588 A82 120f org & multi ('70) 10.00 2.00
589 A82 180f multi ('70) 17.50 4.75
590 A82 200f multi ('70) 20.00 7.00
Nos. 576-590 (15) 64.85 18.25

Issued: Fruits, 11/22; flowers, 3/21; birds, 9/1.

Soccer A83

Designs: 10f, Diver. 15f, Boxers. 50f, Runner. 100f, Bicyclist, vert. 150f, Basketball, vert.

1970, Aug. ***Perf. 13½x14, 14x13½***

651 A83 5f green & multi 1.00 .20
652 A83 10f lt bl & multi 1.00 .20
653 A83 15f gray & multi 1.00 .20
654 A83 50f gray & multi 1.50 .65
655 A83 100f yellow & multi 2.25 1.25
656 A83 150f multicolored 3.25 2.25
Nos. 651-656 (6) 10.00 4.75

Refugee Children A84

Emblems and: 10F, Boy Fetching Water, UNICEF and Refugee Emblems. 15f, Girl and tents. 20f, Boy in front of tent.

1970, Aug.

657 A84 5f multicolored .30 .20
658 A84 10f multicolored .40 .20
659 A84 15f multicolored .50 .20
660 A84 20f multicolored .70 .20
Nos. 657-660 (4) 1.90 .80

Issued for Childhood Day.

Nativity Grotto, Bethlehem A85

Church of the Nativity, Bethlehem: 10f, Manger. 20f, Altar. 25f, Interior.

1970, Dec. 25 **Photo.** ***Perf. 13½***

661 A85 5f blue & multi .45 .20
662 A85 10f scarlet & multi .45 .20
663 A85 20f rose lilac & multi .80 .30
664 A85 25f green & multi 1.00 .35
Nos. 661-664 (4) 2.70 1.05

Christmas.

Flag and Map of Arab League Countries A85a

1971, May 10 **Photo.** ***Perf. 11½x11***

665 A85a 10f orange & multi .40 .20
666 A85a 20f lt blue & multi .40 .20
667 A85a 30f olive & multi .40 .20
Nos. 665-667 (3) 1.20 .60

25th anniversary of the Arab League.

Emblem and Doves — A86

Designs: 5f, Emblem and 4 races, vert. 10f, Emblem as flower, vert.

1971, July

668 A86 5f green & multi .35 .30
669 A86 10f brick red & multi .40 .30
670 A86 15f dk blue & multi .50 .30
Nos. 668-670 (3) 1.25 .90

Intl. Year Against Racial Discrimination.

Dead Sea A87

Views of the Holy Land: 30f, Excavated building, Petra. 45f, Via Dolorosa, Jerusalem, vert. 60f, Jordan River. 100f, Christmas bell, Bethlehem, vert.

1971, Aug. ***Perf. 14x13½, 13½x14***

671 A87 5f blue & multi .90 .30
672 A87 30f pink & multi 1.75 .60
673 A87 45f blue & multi 2.25 .90
674 A87 60f gray & multi 3.75 1.50
675 A87 100f gray & multi 5.50 3.00
Nos. 671-675 (5) 14.15 6.30

Tourist publicity.

Opening of UPU Headquarters, Bern in 1970 — A88

1971, Oct. ***Perf. 11***

676 A88 10f brn, brn & yel grn .40 .20
677 A88 20f dk vio, grn & yel grn .70 .20

Averroes (1126-1198) A89

Child Learning to Write — A90

Arab Scholars: 5f, Avicenna (980-1037). 20f, ibn-Khaldun (1332-1406). 25f, ibn-Tufail (?-1185). 30f, Alhazen (965?-1039?).

1971, Sept. ***Perf. 12***

678 A89 5f gold & multi .35 .20
679 A89 10f gold & multi .35 .20
680 A89 20f gold & multi .65 .20
681 A89 25f gold & multi 1.00 .35
682 A89 30f gold & multi 1.50 .75
Nos. 678-682 (5) 3.85 1.70

1972, Feb. 9 Photo. *Perf. 11*

683 A90 5f ultra, brn & grn .35 .20
684 A90 15f mag, brn & blue .35 .20
685 A90 20f grn, brn & blue .35 .20
686 A90 30f org, brn & blue .75 .30
Nos. 683-686 (4) 1.80 .90

International Education Year.

Arab Mother and Child — A91

Pope Paul VI and Holy Sepulcher — A92

Mother's Day: 10f, Mothers and children, horiz. 20f, Mother and child.

1972, Mar. *Perf. 14x13½*

687 A91 10f lt grn & multi .50 .20
688 A91 20f red brown & blk .50 .20
689 A91 30f blue, brn & blk .75 .20
Nos. 687-689 (3) 1.75 .60

1972, Apr. Photo. *Perf. 14x13½*

690 A92 30f black & multi .90 .20

Easter. See Nos. C51-C52.

UNICEF Emblem, Children A93

UNICEF Emblem and: 20f, Child playing with blocks spelling "UNICEF," vert. 30f, Mother and child.

1972, May *Perf. 11½x11, 11x11½*

691 A93 10f bl, vio bl & blk .40 .20
692 A93 20f multicolored .40 .20
693 A93 30f blue & multi .50 .20
Nos. 691-693 (3) 1.30 .60

25th anniv. (in 1971) of UNICEF.

UN Emblem, Dove and Grain — A94

1972, July *Perf. 11x11½*

694 A94 5f vio & multi .50 .20
695 A94 10f multicolored .50 .20
696 A94 15f black & multi .50 .20
697 A94 20f green & multi .50 .20
698 A94 30f multicolored .85 .50
Nos. 694-698 (5) 2.85 1.30

25th anniv. (in 1970) of the UN.

Al Aqsa Mosque, Jerusalem — A95

Designs: 60f, Al Aqsa Mosque on fire. 100f, Al Aqsa Mosque, interior.

1972, Aug. 21 Litho. *Perf. 14½*

699 A95 30f green & multi 1.60 .20
700 A95 60f blue & multi 3.50 .85
701 A95 100f ocher & multi 5.50 1.50
Nos. 699-701 (3) 10.60 2.55

3rd anniversary of the burning of Al Aqsa Mosque, Jerusalem.

House in Desert A96

1972, Nov. *Perf. 14x13½, 13½x14*

702 A96 5f Falconer, vert .55 .20
703 A96 10f shown .55 .20
704 A96 15f Man on camel .55 .20
705 A96 20f Pipe line construction .95 .20
706 A96 25f Shepherd .95 .20
707 A96 30f Camels at water trough 1.25 .45
708 A96 35f Chicken farm 1.50 .65
709 A96 45f Irrigation canal 2.00 1.10
Nos. 702-709 (8) 8.30 3.20

Life in the Arab desert.

Wasfi el Tell and Dome of the Rock A97

Wasfi el Tell, Map of Palestine and Jordan — A98

Perf. 13x13½, 13½x13

1972, Dec. Photo.

710 A97 5f citron & multi .45 .20
711 A98 10f red & multi .50 .20
712 A97 20f dl blue & multi 1.00 .25
713 A98 30f green & multi 1.10 .85
Nos. 710-713 (4) 3.05 1.50

In memory of Prime Minister Wasfi el Tell, who was assassinated in Cairo by Black September terrorists.

Trapshooting A99

Designs: 75f, Trapshooter facing right, horiz. 120f, Trapshooter facing left, horiz.

1972, Dec. *Perf. 14x13½, 13½x14*

714 A99 25f multicolored .80 .20
715 A99 75f multicolored 1.10 .80
716 A99 120f multicolored 2.10 1.00
Nos. 714-716 (3) 4.00 2.00

World Trapshooting Championships.

Aero Club Emblem A100

1973, Jan. Photo. *Perf. 13½x14*

717 A100 5f blue, blk & yel .50 .20
718 A100 10f blue, blk & yel .50 .20
Nos. 717-718,C53-C55 (5) 4.00 1.25

Royal Jordanian Aero Club.

Peace Dove and Jordanian Flag A101

10f, Emblem. 15f, King Hussein. 30f, Map of Jordan.

1973, Mar. *Perf. 11½*

719 A101 5f blue & multi .45 .20
720 A101 10f pale grn & multi .45 .20
721 A101 15f olive & multi .45 .20
722 A101 30f yel grn & multi .90 .45
Nos. 719-722 (4) 2.25 1.05

Hashemite Kingdom of Jordan, 50th anniv.

Battle, Flag and Map of Palestine — A102

10f, 2 soldiers in combat, map of Palestine. 15f, Map of Palestine, olive branch, soldier on tank.

1973, Apr. 10 Photo. *Perf. 11*

723 A102 5f crimson & multi 1.00 .40
724 A102 10f crimson & multi 1.50 .60
725 A102 15f grn, blue & brn 2.25 1.25
Nos. 723-725 (3) 4.75 2.25

5th anniversary of Karama Battle.

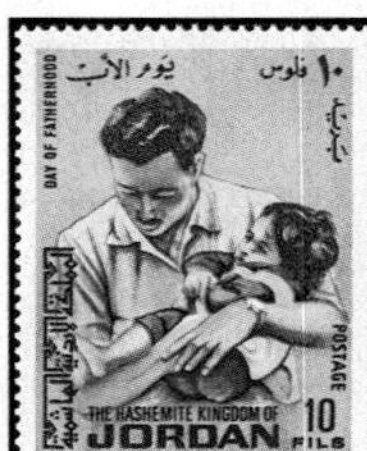

Father and Child — A103

Father's Day: 20f, Father & infant. 30f, Family.

1973, Apr. 20 *Perf. 13½*

726 A103 10f citron & multi .50 .20
727 A103 20f lt blue & multi .75 .25
728 A103 30f multicolored 1.25 .55
Nos. 726-728 (3) 2.50 1.00

Phosphate Mine A104

1973, June 25 Litho. *Perf. 13½x14*

729 A104 5f shown .40 .20
730 A104 10f Cement factory .40 .20
731 A104 15f Sharmasil Dam .50 .20
732 A104 20f Kafrein Dam .70 .25
Nos. 729-732 (4) 2.00 .85

Development projects.

Camel Racer A105

Designs: Camel racing.

1973, July 21

733 A105 5f multicolored .80 .20
734 A105 10f multicolored .80 .20
735 A105 15f multicolored .80 .20
736 A105 20f multicolored .80 .20
Nos. 733-736 (4) 3.20 .80

Book Year Emblem — A106

1973, Aug. 25 Photo. *Perf. 13x13½*

737 A106 30f dk grn & multi .75 .20
738 A106 60f purple & multi 1.00 .35

Intl. Book Year. For overprints see #781-782.

Family A107

Family Day: 30f, Family around fire. 60f, Large family outdoors.

1973, Sept. 18 Litho. *Perf. 13½*

739 A107 20f multicolored .50 .20
740 A107 30f multicolored .50 .20
741 A107 60f multicolored 1.00 .35
Nos. 739-741 (3) 2.00 .75

Kings of Iran and Jordan, Tomb of Cyrus the Great and Mosque of Omar — A108

1973, Oct. Litho. *Perf. 13*

742 A108 5f ver & multi .50 .20
743 A108 10f brown & multi .50 .20
744 A108 15f gray & multi .75 .20
745 A108 30f blue & multi 1.00 .40
Nos. 742-745 (4) 2.75 1.00

2500th anniversary of the founding of the Persian Empire by Cyrus the Great.

Palestine Week Emblem A109

Palestine Week: 10f, Torch and laurel. 15f, Refugee family behind barbed wire, vert. 30f, Children, Map of Palestine, globe. Sizes: 5f, 10f, 30f; 38½x22mm. 15f, 25x46mm.

1973, Nov. 17 Photo. *Perf. 11*

746 A109 5f multicolored .50 .20
747 A109 10f dl bl & multi .65 .20
748 A109 15f yel grn & multi .85 .20
749 A109 30f brt grn & multi 1.50 .40
Nos. 746-749 (4) 3.50 1.00

Traditional Harvest A110

Traditional and modern agricultural methods.

1973, Dec. 25 *Perf. 13½*

750 A110 5f shown .65 .20
751 A110 10f Harvesting machine .65 .20
752 A110 15f Traditional seeding .65 .20
753 A110 20f Seeding machine .65 .20
754 A110 30f Ox plow 1.00 .20
755 A110 35f Plowing machine 1.10 .20
756 A110 45f Pest control 1.25 .20
757 A110 60f Horticulture 1.75 1.10
Nos. 750-757,C56 (9) 9.95 3.50

Red Sea Fish A111

Designs: Various Red Sea fishes.

1974, Feb. 15 **Photo.** *Perf. 14*

758 A111 5f multicolored .50 .20
759 A111 10f multicolored .60 .20
760 A111 15f multicolored .75 .20
761 A111 20f multicolored .90 .35
762 A111 25f multicolored 1.25 .40
763 A111 30f multicolored 2.00 .50
764 A111 35f multicolored 2.25 .80
765 A111 40f multicolored 2.75 1.00
766 A111 45f multicolored 3.00 1.10
767 A111 50f multicolored 5.00 1.25
768 A111 60f multicolored 6.25 1.75
Nos. 758-768 (11) 25.25 7.75

Battle of Muta, 1250 A112

1974, Mar. 15 **Photo.** *Perf. 13½*

769 A112 10f shown .65 .20
770 A112 20f Yarmouk Battle, 636 1.25 .40
771 A112 30f Hitteen Battle, 1187 1.60 .65
Nos. 769-771 (3) 3.50 1.25

Clubfooted Boy, by Murillo — A113

Paintings: 10f, Praying Hands, by Dürer. 15f, St. George and the Dragon, by Paolo Uccello. 20f, Mona Lisa, by Da Vinci. 30f, Hope, by Frederic Watts. 40f, Angelus, by Jean F. Millet, horiz. 50f, The Artist and her Daughter, by Angelica Kauffmann. 60f, Portrait of my Mother, by James Whistler, horiz. 100f, Master Hare, by Reynolds.

Perf. 14x13½, 13½x14

1974, Apr. 15 **Litho.**

772 A113 5f black & multi 1.50 .20
773 A113 10f black & gray 1.50 .20
774 A113 15f black & multi 1.50 .20
775 A113 20f black & multi 1.50 .20
776 A113 30f black & multi 1.50 .20
777 A113 40f black & multi 1.75 .20
778 A113 50f black & multi 2.00 .95
779 A113 60f black & multi 2.50 1.00
780 A113 100f black & multi 3.50 1.75
Nos. 772-780 (9) 17.25 4.90

Nos. 737-738 Overprinted

1974, Apr. 20 **Photo.** *Perf. 13x13½*

781 A106 30f dk grn & multi .70 .20
782 A106 60f purple & multi 1.00 .50

Intl. Conf. for Damascus History, Apr. 20-25.

UPU Emblem — A114

1974 *Perf. 13x12½*

783 A114 10f yel grn & multi .40 .20
784 A114 30f blue & multi .50 .20
785 A114 60f multicolored .85 .30
Nos. 783-785 (3) 1.75 .70

Centenary of Universal Postal Union.

Camel Caravan at Sunset A115

3f, 30f, Palm at shore of Dead Sea. 4f, 40f, Hotel at shore. 5f, 50f, Jars from Qumran Caves. 6f, 60f, Copper scrolls, vert. 10f, 100f, Cracked cistern steps, vert. 20f, like 2f.

1974, June 25 **Photo.** *Perf. 14*

786 A115 2f multicolored .50 .20
787 A115 3f multicolored .50 .20
788 A115 4f multicolored .50 .20
789 A115 5f multicolored .75 .20
790 A115 6f multicolored .75 .20
791 A115 10f multicolored .75 .20
792 A115 20f multicolored .50 .20
793 A115 30f multicolored .65 .20
794 A115 40f multicolored .75 .50
795 A115 50f multicolored 1.75 .40
796 A115 60f multicolored 2.25 .50
797 A115 100f multicolored 3.50 .85
Nos. 786-797 (12) 13.15 3.85

WPY Emblem — A116

Water Skiing — A117

1974, Aug. 20 **Photo.** *Perf. 11*

798 A116 5f lt green, blk & pur .30 .20
799 A116 10f lt green, blk & car .30 .20
800 A116 20f lt green, blk & org .40 .20
Nos. 798-800 (3) 1.00 .60

World Population Year.

Perf. 14x13½, 13½x14

1974, Sept. 20

Water Skiing: 10f, 100f, Side view, horiz. 20f, 200f, Turning, horiz. 50f, like 5f.

801 A117 5f multicolored .50 .20
802 A117 10f multicolored .50 .20
803 A117 20f multicolored .50 .20
804 A117 50f multicolored .65 .20
805 A117 100f multicolored 1.25 .50
806 A117 200f multicolored 2.10 .95
Nos. 801-806 (6) 5.50 2.25

Holy Kaaba, Mecca, and Pilgrims — A118

1974, Nov. **Photo.** *Perf. 11*

807 A118 10f blue & multi .75 .20
808 A118 20f yellow & multi .80 .25

Pilgrimage season.

Amrah Palace A119

Ruins: 20f, Hisham Palace. 30f, Kharraneh Castle.

1974, Nov. 25 **Photo.** *Perf. 14x13½*

809 A119 10f black & multi .50 .20
810 A119 20f black & multi .75 .30
811 A119 30f black & multi 1.25 .50
Nos. 809-811 (3) 2.50 1.00

Jordanian Woman — A120

Designs: Various women's costumes.

1975, Feb. 1 **Photo.** *Perf. 12*

812 A120 5f lt green & multi .45 .20
813 A120 10f yellow & multi .50 .20
814 A120 15f lt blue & multi .65 .25
815 A120 20f ultra & multi 1.00 .35
816 A120 25f green & multi 1.40 .60
Nos. 812-816 (5) 4.00 1.60

Treasury, Petra — A121

Ommayyad Palace, Amman A122

Designs: 30f, Dome of the Rock, Jerusalem. 40f, Columns, Forum of Jerash.

Perf. 14x13½, 13½x14

1975, Mar. 1 **Photo.**

824 A121 15f lt blue & multi 1.00 .20
825 A122 20f pink & multi 1.00 .20
826 A122 30f yellow & multi 1.25 .20
827 A122 40f lt blue & multi 1.60 .20
Nos. 824-827,C59-C61 (7) 9.70 3.05

King Hussein — A123

1975, Apr. 8 **Photo.** *Perf. 14*
Size: 19x23mm

831 A123 5f green & ind .50 .20
832 A123 10f vio & indigo .50 .20
833 A123 15f car & indigo .50 .20
834 A123 20f brn ol & ind .50 .20
835 A123 25f vio bl & ind .50 .20
836 A123 30f brown & ind .50 .20
837 A123 35f vio & indigo .50 .20
838 A123 40f orange & ind .50 .20
839 A123 45f red lil & ind .50 .20
840 A123 50f bl green & ind .65 .20
Nos. 831-840,C62-C68 (17) 19.15 10.90

Globe, "alia" and Plane — A125

Designs: 30f, Boeing 727 connecting Jordan with world, horiz. 60f, Globe and "alia."

1975, June 15 **Photo.** *Perf. 11*

853 A125 10f multicolored .70 .20
854 A125 30f multicolored .75 .20
855 A125 60f multicolored 1.40 .85
Nos. 853-855 (3) 2.85 1.25

Royal Jordanian Airline, 30th anniversary.

Satellite Transmission System, Map of Mediterranean — A126

1975, Aug. 1 **Photo.** *Perf. 11*

856 A126 20f vio bl & multi .90 .20
857 A126 30f green & multi 1.10 .75

Opening of satellite earth station.

Chamber of Commerce Emblem — A127

1975, Oct. 15 **Photo.** *Perf. 11*

858 A127 10f yellow & blue .35 .20
859 A127 15f yel, red & blue .35 .20
860 A127 20f yel, grn & blue .35 .20
Nos. 858-860 (3) 1.05 .60

Amman Chamber of Commerce, 50th anniv.

Hand Holding Wrench, Wall and Emblem — A128

1975, Nov. Photo. *Perf. 11½*

861 A128 5f green, car & blk .35 .20
862 A128 10f car, green & blk .35 .20
863 A128 20f blk, green & car .35 .20
Nos. 861-863 (3) 1.05 .60

Three-year development plan.

Family and IWY Emblem A129

Salt Industry — A130

IWY Emblem and: 25f, Woman scientist with microscope. 60f, Woman graduate.

1976, Apr. 27 Litho. *Perf. 14x13½*

864 A129 5f multicolored .50 .20
865 A129 25f multicolored .50 .20
866 A129 60f multicolored 1.00 .40
Nos. 864-866 (3) 2.00 .80

International Women's Year.

1976, June 1 Litho. *Perf. 13½x14*

Arab Labor Organization Emblem and: 30f, Welders. 60f, Ship at 'Aqaba.

867 A130 10f gray & multi .50 .20
868 A130 30f bister & multi .50 .20
869 A130 60f brown & multi .75 .40
Nos. 867-869 (3) 1.75 .80

Arab Labor Organization.

Nos. 574-574E Surcharged

Perf. 14½x13½

1976, July 18 Photo.

Strips of 5

870 A79a 25f on 1f-5f 32.50 32.50
a.-e. Any single, 1f-5f
871 A79a 25f on 6f-10f 32.50 32.50
a.-e. Any single, 6f-10f
872 A79a 40f on 11f-15f 32.50 32.50
a.-e. Any single, 11f-15f
873 A79a 50f on 16f-20f 32.50 32.50
a.-e. Any single, 16f-20f
874 A79a 75f on 21f-25f 32.50 32.50
a.-e. Any single, 21f-25f
875 A79a 125f on 26f-30f 32.50 32.50
a.-e. Any single, 26f-30f

Nos. 575-575E Surcharged

876 A79a 25f on 1f-5f 32.50 32.50
a.-e. Any single, 1f-5f
877 A79a 25f on 6f-10f 32.50 32.50
a.-e. Any single, 6f-10f
878 A79a 40f on 11f-15f 32.50 32.50
a.-e. Any single, 11f-15f
879 A79a 50f on 16f-20f 32.50 32.50
a.-e. Any single, 16f-20f
880 A79a 75f on 21f-25f 32.50 32.50
a.-e. Any single, 21f-25f
881 A79a 125f on 26f-30f 32.50 32.50
a.-e. Any single, 26f-30f

Tennis — A132

Designs: 10f, Athlete and wreath. 15f, Soccer. 20f, Equestrian and Jordanian flag. 30f, Weight lifting. 100f, Stadium, Amman.

1976, Nov. 1 Litho. *Perf. 14x13½*

990 A132 5f buff & multi .75 .20
991 A132 10f lt bl & multi .75 .20
992 A132 15f green & multi .75 .20
993 A132 20f green & multi .75 .20
994 A132 30f green & multi 1.00 .20
995 A132 100f multicolored 2.00 1.25
Nos. 990-995 (6) 6.00 2.25

Sports and youth.

Dam — A133

Telephones, 1876 and 1976 — A134

Designs: Various dams.

1976, Dec. 7 Litho. *Perf. 14x13½*

996 A133 30f multicolored 1.00 .20
997 A133 60f multicolored 1.25 .70
998 A133 100f multicolored 2.25 1.10
Nos. 996-998 (3) 4.50 2.00

1977, Feb. 17 Litho. *Perf. 11½x12*

125f, 1876 telephone and 1976 receiver.

999 A134 75f rose & multi 1.50 .95
1000 A134 125f blue & multi 2.00 1.25

Centenary of first telephone call by Alexander Graham Bell, Mar. 10, 1876.

Street Crossing, Traffic Light — A135

Designs: 75f, Traffic circle and light. 125f, Traffic light and signs, motorcycle policeman.

1977, May 4 Litho. *Perf. 11x12*

1001 A135 5f rose & multi .55 .20
1002 A135 75f black & multi 1.50 .85
1003 A135 125f yellow & multi 2.25 1.40
Nos. 1001-1003 (3) 4.30 2.45

International Traffic Day.

Plane over Ship — A136

Child with Toy Bank — A137

Coat of Arms and: 25f, Factories and power lines. 40f, Fertilizer plant and trucks. 50f, Ground to air missile. 75f, Mosque and worshippers. 125f, Radar station and TV emblem.

1977, Aug. 11 Photo. *Perf. 11½x12*

1004 A136 10f sil & multi .40 .20
1005 A136 25f sil & multi .40 .20
1006 A136 40f sil & multi .70 .35
1007 A136 50f sil & multi .80 .40
1008 A136 75f sil & multi .95 .60
1009 A136 125f sil & multi 1.75 1.00
Nos. 1004-1009 (6) 5.00 2.75

Imperf

Size: 100x70mm

1009A A136 100f multicolored 8.50 8.50

25th anniv. of the reign of King Hussein.

1977, Sept. 1 Litho. *Perf. 11½x12*

Postal Savings Bank: 25f, Boy with piggy bank. 50f, Postal Savings Bank emblem. 75f, Boy talking to teller.

1010 A137 10f multicolored .40 .20
1011 A137 25f multicolored .60 .20
1012 A137 50f multicolored .75 .40
1013 A137 75f multicolored 1.10 .65
Nos. 1010-1013 (4) 2.85 1.45

King Hussein and Queen Alia — A138

Queen Alia — A139

1977, Nov. 1 Litho. *Perf. 11½x12*

1014 A138 10f lt grn & multi .40 .20
1015 A138 25f rose & multi .40 .20
1016 A138 40f yellow & multi .50 .20
1017 A138 50f blue & multi .70 .20
Nos. 1014-1017 (4) 2.00 .80

1977, Dec. 1 Litho. *Perf. 11½x12*

1018 A139 10f green & multi .50 .20
1019 A139 25f brown & multi .50 .20
1020 A139 40f blue & multi .70 .20
1021 A139 50f yellow & multi .95 .25
Nos. 1018-1021 (4) 2.65 .85

Queen Alia, died in 1977 air crash.

Jinnah, Flags of Pakistan and Jordan — A140

APU Emblem, Members' Flags — A141

1977, Dec. 20 *Perf. 11½*

1022 A140 25f multicolored .30 .20
1023 A140 75f multicolored .70 .40

Mohammed Ali Jinnah (1876-1948), 1st Governor General of Pakistan.

1978, Apr. 12 Litho. *Perf. 12x11½*

1024 A141 25f yellow & multi .75 .50
1025 A141 40f buff & multi 1.25 .75

25th anniv. (in 1977), of Arab Postal Union.

Copper Coffee Set — A142

Roman Amphitheater, Jerash A143

Handicraft: 40f, Porcelain plate and ashtray. 75f, Vase and jewelry. 125f, Pipe holder.

1978, May 30 Photo. *Perf. 11½x12*

1026 A142 25f olive & multi .50 .20
1027 A142 40f lilac & multi .65 .20
1028 A142 75f ultra & multi 1.10 .65
1029 A142 125f orange & multi 1.75 1.00
Nos. 1026-1029 (4) 4.00 2.05

1978, July 30 Litho. *Perf. 12*

Tourist Views: 20f, Roman Columns, Jerash. 40f, Goat, grapes and man, Roman mosaic, Madaba. 75f, Rock formations, Rum, and camel rider.

1030 A143 5f multicolored .55 .20
1031 A143 20f multicolored .55 .20
1032 A143 40f multicolored 1.00 .20
1033 A143 75f multicolored 1.40 .75
Nos. 1030-1033 (4) 3.50 1.35

King Hussein and Pres. Sadat — A144

Designs: No. 1035, King Hussein and Pres. Assad, Jordanian and Syrian flags, horiz. No. 1036, King Hussein, King Khalid, Jordanian and Saudi Arabian flags, horiz.

1978, Aug. 20 *Perf. 11½x12*

1034 A144 40f multicolored .90 .50
1035 A144 40f multicolored .90 .50
1036 A144 40f multicolored .90 .50
Nos. 1034-1036 (3) 2.70 1.50

Visits of Arab leaders to Jordan.

Cement Factory A145

Designs: 10f, Science laboratory. 25f, Printing press. 75f, Artificial fertilizer plant.

1978, Sept. 25 Litho. *Perf. 12*

1037 A145 5f multicolored .60 .20
1038 A145 10f multicolored .60 .20
1039 A145 25f multicolored .80 .20
1040 A145 75f multicolored 1.60 .90
Nos. 1037-1040 (4) 3.60 1.50

Industrial development.

"UNESCO" Scales and Globe — A146

1978, Dec. 5 Litho. *Perf. 12x11½*

1041 A146 40f multicolored .75 .35
1042 A146 75f multicolored 1.25 .70

30th anniversary of UNESCO.

1976-1980 Development Plan — A147

1979, Oct. 25 Litho. *Perf. 12½x12*

1043 A147 25f multicolored .30 .20
1044 A147 40f multicolored .70 .25
1045 A147 50f multicolored .95 .25
Nos. 1043-1045 (3) 1.95 .70

IYC Emblem, Flag of Jordan — A148

1979, Nov. 15 Litho. *Perf. 12x12½*

1046 A148 25f multicolored .50 .20
1047 A148 40f multicolored .75 .20
1048 A148 50f multicolored 1.25 .35
Nos. 1046-1048 (3) 2.50 .75

International Year of the Child.

1979 Population and Housing Census A149

1979, Dec. 25 Litho. *Perf. 12½x12*

1049 A149 25f multicolored .50 .20
1050 A149 40f multicolored .70 .25
1051 A149 50f multicolored .80 .30
Nos. 1049-1051 (3) 2.00 .75

King Hussein — A150

1980 Litho. *Perf. 13½x13*

1052 A150 5f multicolored .30 .20
b. Inscribed 1981 .30 .20
1053 A150 10f multicolored .30 .20
b. Inscribed 1981 .30 .20
1055 A150 20f multicolored .30 .20
b. Inscribed 1981 .30 .20
1056 A150 25f multicolored .30 .20
a. Inscribed 1979 .30 .20
b. Inscribed 1981 .30 .20
1058 A150 40f multicolored .60 .20
a. Inscribed 1979 .50 .20
b. Inscribed 1981 .60 .20
1059 A150 50f multicolored .80 .25
1060 A150 75f multicolored 1.00 .30
1061 A150 125f multicolored 1.50 .35
a. Complete booklet, 4 each #1056, 1058-1061 17.50
Nos. 1052-1061 (8) 5.10 1.90

International Nursing Day — A151

El Deir Temple, Petra — A152

1980, May 12 Litho. *Perf. 12x12½*

1062 A151 25f multicolored .50 .20
1063 A151 40f multicolored .70 .25
1064 A151 50f multicolored .85 .25
Nos. 1062-1064 (3) 2.05 .70

1980 Litho. *Perf. 14½*

1065 A152 25f multicolored .60 .20
1066 A152 40f multicolored .90 .50
1067 A152 50f multicolored 1.25 .60
Nos. 1065-1067 (3) 2.75 1.30

World Tourism Conf., Manila, Sept. 27.

Hegira (Pilgrimage Year) — A153

1980, Nov. 11 Litho. *Perf. 14½*

1068 A153 25f multicolored .30 .20
1069 A153 40f multicolored .45 .25
1070 A153 50f multicolored .75 .30
1071 A153 75f multicolored 1.50 .40
1072 A153 100f multicolored 1.50 .70
Nos. 1068-1072 (5) 4.50 1.85

Souvenir Sheet

Imperf

1073 A153 290f multicolored 6.50 6.50

#1073 contains designs of #1068-1071.

11th Arab Summit Conference, Amman — A153a

1980, Nov. 25 Litho. *Perf. 14½*

1073A A153a 25f multi .40 .20
1073B A153a 40f multi .60 .25
1073C A153a 50f multi .80 .30
1073D A153a 75f multi 1.00 .45
1073E A153a 100f multi 1.10 .65
f. Souv. sheet of 5, #1073A-1073E, imperf. 6.50 6.50
Nos. 1073A-1073E (5) 3.90 1.85

A154

A155

1981, May 8 Litho. *Perf. 14½*

1074 A154 25f multicolored .50 .20
1075 A154 40f multicolored .80 .60
1076 A154 50f multicolored .95 .70
Nos. 1074-1076 (3) 2.25 1.50

Red Crescent Society.

1981, June 17 Litho. *Perf. 14x14½*

1077 A155 25f multicolored .75 .20
1078 A155 40f multicolored .90 .90
1079 A155 50f multicolored 1.25 .90
Nos. 1077-1079 (3) 2.90 2.00

13th World Telecommunications Day.

Nos. 174 and 832 — A156

Perf. 13½x14½, 14½x13½

1981, July 1 Litho.

1080 A156 25f shown .55 .20
1081 A156 40f Nos. 313, 189, vert. 1.00 .65
1082 A156 50f Nos. 272, 222 1.10 .90
Nos. 1080-1082 (3) 2.65 1.75

Postal Museum opening.

A157

A158

Arab Women: 25f, Khawla Bint El-Azwar, Ancient Warrior. 40f, El-Khansa (d.645), writer. 50f, Rabia El-Adawiyeh, religious leader.

1981, Aug. 25 Litho. *Perf. 14½x14*

1083 A157 25f multicolored .20 .20
1084 A157 40f multicolored 2.00 1.25
1085 A157 50f multicolored 3.00 1.50
Nos. 1083-1085 (3) 5.20 2.95

1981, Oct. 16 Litho. *Perf. 14x14½*

1086 A158 25f multicolored .20 .20
1087 A158 40f multicolored .80 .55
1088 A158 50f multicolored 1.00 .65
Nos. 1086-1088 (3) 2.00 1.40

World Food Day.

Intl. Year of the Disabled A159

Hands Reading Braille — A160

1981, Nov. 14 Litho. *Perf. 14½x14*

1089 A159 25f multicolored .20 .20
1090 A159 40f multicolored 1.00 .70
1091 A159 50f multicolored 1.40 .90
Nos. 1089-1091 (3) 2.60 1.80

1981, Nov. 14 *Perf. 14x14½*

1092 A160 25f multicolored .20 .20
1093 A160 40f multicolored 1.00 .70
1094 A160 50f multicolored 1.40 .90
Nos. 1092-1094 (3) 2.60 1.80

A161 A162

Design: Hand holding jug and stone tablet.

1982, Mar. 10 Litho. *Perf. 14x14½*

1095 A161 25f multicolored .50 .20
1096 A161 40f multicolored 1.10 .60
1097 A161 50f multicolored 1.25 .80
Nos. 1095-1097 (3) 2.85 1.60

Nos. 1095-1097 inscribed 1981.

1982, Apr. 12 Litho. *Perf. 14x14½*

1098 A162 10f multicolored .20 .20
1099 A162 25f multicolored .65 .20
1100 A162 40f multicolored .90 .65
1101 A162 50f multicolored 1.10 .80
1102 A162 100f multicolored 2.40 1.60
Nos. 1098-1102 (5) 5.25 3.45

30th anniv. of Arab Postal Union.

King Hussein and Rockets A163

1982, May 25 Litho. *Perf. 14½x14*

1103 A163 10f shown .20 .20
1104 A163 25f Tanks crossing bridge .65 .20
1105 A163 40f Jet .90 .65
1106 A163 50f Tanks, diff. 1.25 .75
1107 A163 100f Raising flag 2.25 1.50
Nos. 1103-1107 (5) 5.25 3.30

Independence and Army Day; 30th anniv. of King Hussein's accession to the throne.

Salt Secondary School A164

1982, Sept. 12 Litho. *Perf. 14½x14*

1108 A164 10f multicolored .20 .20
1109 A164 25f multicolored .60 .20
1110 A164 40f multicolored .85 .60
1111 A164 50f multicolored 1.10 .65
1112 A164 100f multicolored 2.25 1.25
Nos. 1108-1112 (5) 5.00 2.90

International Heritage of Jerusalem — A165

1982, Nov. 14 Litho. *Perf. 14x14½*

1113 A165 10f Gate to Old City .20 .20
1114 A165 25f Minaret 1.00 .45
1115 A165 40f Al Aqsa 1.25 .80
1116 A165 50f Dome of the Rock 1.60 .90
1117 A165 100f Dome of the Rock, diff. 3.25 1.75
Nos. 1113-1117 (5) 7.30 4.10

Yarmouk Forces A166

1982, Nov. 14 *Perf. 14½x14*

1118 A166 10f multicolored .20 .20
1119 A166 25f multicolored .45 .20
1120 A166 40f multicolored .80 .45
1121 A166 50f multicolored .95 .60
1122 A166 100f multicolored 2.10 1.40
Nos. 1118-1122 (5) 4.50 2.85

Size: 71x51mm

Imperf

1123 A166 100f Armed Forces emblem 15.00 15.00

2nd UN Conf. on Peaceful Uses of Outer Space, Vienna, Aug. 9-21 — A167

1982, Dec. 1 *Perf. 14½x14*

1124 A167 10f multicolored .20 .20
1125 A167 25f multicolored .50 .20
1126 A167 40f multicolored .75 .50
1127 A167 50f multicolored .95 .60
1128 A167 100f multicolored 2.00 1.25
Nos. 1124-1128 (5) 4.40 2.75

Birth Centenary of Amir Abdullah ibn Hussein — A168

1982, Dec. 13 Litho. *Perf. 14½*

1129 A168 10f multicolored .20 .20
1130 A168 25f multicolored .40 .20
1131 A168 40f multicolored .60 .45
1132 A168 50f multicolored .95 .80
1133 A168 100f multicolored 2.25 1.40
Nos. 1129-1133 (5) 4.40 3.05

Roman Ruins of Jerash A169

1982, Dec. 29 Litho. *Perf. 15*

1134 A169 10f Temple colonnade .20 .20
1135 A169 25f Arch .90 .20
1136 A169 40f Columns 1.40 .90
1137 A169 50f Ampitheater 1.75 1.00
1138 A169 100f Hippodrome 3.25 2.10
Nos. 1134-1138 (5) 7.50 4.40

King Hussein — A170

1983 Litho. *Perf. 14½x14*

1139 A170 10f multicolored .20 .20
1140 A170 25f multicolored .25 .20
1141 A170 40f multicolored .40 .30
1142 A170 60f multicolored .60 .40

1143 A170 100f multicolored 1.00 .65
1144 A170 125f multicolored 1.25 .70
Nos. 1139-1144 (6) 3.70 2.45

Issue dates: 10f, 60f, Feb. 1; 40f, Feb. 8; 25f, 100f, 125f, Mar. 3. Inscribed 1982.

Massacre at Shatilla and Sabra Palestinian Refugee Camps A171

10f, 25f, 50f, No. 1149, Various victims. 40f, Children. No. 1150, Wounded child.

1983, Apr. 9 Litho. *Perf. 14½*

1145 A171 10f multicolored *.45 .20*
1146 A171 25f multicolored *.80 .70*
1147 A171 40f multicolored *1.25 .90*
1148 A171 50f multicolored *1.50 1.25*
1149 A171 100f multicolored *2.25 1.75*
Nos. 1145-1149 (5) *6.25 4.80*

Souvenir Sheet

Imperf

1150 A171 100f multicolored *18.00*

Opening of Queen Alia Intl. Airport A172

1983, May 25 Litho. *Perf. 12½*

1151 A172 10f Aerial view .20 .20
1152 A172 25f Terminal buildings .80 .20
1153 A172 40f Hangar 1.10 .80
1154 A172 50f Terminal buildings, diff. 1.40 .90
1155 A172 100f Embarkation Bridge 2.75 1.75
Nos. 1151-1155 (5) 6.25 3.85

Royal Jordanian Radio Amateurs' Society A173

1983, Aug. 11 Litho. *Perf. 12*

1156 A173 10f multicolored .20 .20
1157 A173 25f multicolored .65 .20
1158 A173 40f multicolored .90 .65
1159 A173 50f multicolored 1.25 .75
1160 A173 100f multicolored 2.40 1.50
Nos. 1156-1160 (5) 5.40 3.30

Royal Academy for Islamic Cultural Research A174

1983, Sept. 16 Litho. *Perf. 12*

1161 A174 10f Academy Bldg. .20 .20
1162 A174 25f Silk carpet .70 .50
1163 A174 40f Mosque, Amman 1.10 .70
1164 A174 50f Dome of the Rock 1.50 .90
1165 A174 100f Islamic city views 2.75 1.75
Nos. 1161-1165 (5) 6.25 4.05

A 100f souvenir sheet shows letter from Mohammed. Value $15.

World Food Day A175

1983, Oct. 16 Litho. *Perf. 12*

1166 A175 10f Irrigation canal .20 .20
1167 A175 25f Greenhouses .60 .20
1168 A175 40f Light-grown crops 1.00 .60
1169 A175 50f Harvest 1.25 .70
1170 A175 100f Sheep farm 2.50 1.40
Nos. 1166-1170 (5) 5.55 3.10

World Communications Year — A176

1983, Nov. 14

1171 A176 10f Radio switchboard operators .20 .20
1172 A176 25f Earth satellite station 1.00 .20
1173 A176 40f Symbols of communication 1.25 1.00
1174 A176 50f Emblems 1.50 1.00
1175 A176 100f Airmail letter 3.25 1.75
Nos. 1171-1175 (5) 7.20 4.15

Intl. Palestinian Solidarity Day A177

Dome of the Rock, Jerusalem.

1983, Nov. 29 *Perf. 12*

1176 A177 5f multicolored .85 .45
1177 A177 10f multicolored 1.40 .65

35th Anniv. of UN Declaration of Human Rights A178

1983, Dec. 10

1178 A178 10f multicolored .20 .20
1179 A178 25f multicolored .65 .20
1180 A178 40f multicolored .75 .65
1181 A178 50f multicolored 1.25 .75
1182 A178 100f multicolored 2.50 1.50
Nos. 1178-1182 (5) 5.35 3.30

Anti-Paralysis — A179

1984, Apr. 7 *Perf. 13½x11½*

1183 A179 40f multicolored 1.10 .70
1184 A179 60f multicolored 1.60 .95
1185 A179 100f multicolored 2.75 1.60
Nos. 1183-1185 (3) 5.45 3.25

Anti-Polio Campaign.

Israeli Bombing of Iraq Nuclear Reactor — A180

Various designs.

1984, June 7 Litho. *Perf. 13½x11½*

1186 A180 40f multicolored 1.25 .55
1187 A180 60f multicolored 1.75 .70
1188 A180 100f multicolored 2.75 1.25
Nos. 1186-1188 (3) 5.75 2.50

Independence and Army Day — A181

King Hussein and various armed forces.

1984, June 10

1189 A181 10f multicolored .20 .20
1190 A181 25f multicolored .65 .20
1191 A181 40f multicolored 1.00 .65
1192 A181 60f multicolored 1.60 .90
1193 A181 100f multicolored 2.75 1.60
Nos. 1189-1193 (5) 6.20 3.55

1984 Summer Olympics, Los Angeles — A182

1984, July 28

1194 A182 25f shown .30 .20
1195 A182 40f Swimming .50 .30
1196 A182 60f Shooting, archery 1.10 .45
1197 A182 100f Gymnastics 1.60 .75
Nos. 1194-1197 (4) 3.50 1.70

An imperf. 100f souvenir sheet exists picturing pole vaulting. Value $14.

Water and Electricity Year — A183

1984, Aug. 11

1198 A183 25f Power lines, factory .45 .20
1199 A183 40f Amman Power Station .70 .45
1200 A183 60f Irrigation 1.10 .60
1201 A183 100f Hydro-electric dam 1.75 1.10
Nos. 1198-1201 (4) 4.00 2.35

Coins A184

1984, Sept. 26 Photo. *Perf. 13*

1202 A184 40f Omayyad gold dinar 1.10 .60
1203 A184 60f Abbasid gold dinar 1.40 .80
1204 A184 125f Hashemite silver dinar 3.00 1.75
Nos. 1202-1204 (3) 5.50 3.15

Royal Society for the Conservation of Nature — A185

1984, Oct. 18

1205 A185 25f Four antelopes .70 .20
1206 A185 40f Grazing 1.10 .70
1207 A185 60f Three antelopes 1.60 .95
1208 A185 100f King Hussein, Queen Alia, Duke of Edinburgh 2.75 1.60
Nos. 1205-1208 (4) 6.15 3.45

Natl. Universities — A186

Designs: 40f, Mu'ta Military University, Karak. 60f, Yarmouk University, Irbid. 125f, Jordan University, Amman.

1984, Nov. 14 *Perf. 13x13½*

1209 A186 40f multicolored .55 .40
1210 A186 60f multicolored .95 .55
1211 A186 125f multicolored 2.00 1.10
Nos. 1209-1211 (3) 3.50 2.05

Al Sahaba Tombs A187

Designs: 10f, El Harath bin Omier el-Azdi and Derer bin El-Azwar. 25f, Sharhabil bin Hasna and Abu Obaidah Amer bin el-Jarrah. 40f, Muath bin Jabal. 50f, Zaid bin Haretha and Abdullah bin Rawaha. 60f, Amer bin Abi Waqqas. 100f, Jafar bin Abi Taleb.

1984, Dec. 5 Litho. *Perf. 13½x11½*

1212 A187 10f multicolored .20 .20
1213 A187 25f multicolored .50 .20
1214 A187 40f multicolored .75 .50
1215 A187 50f multicolored .95 .55
1216 A187 60f multicolored 1.25 .65
1217 A187 100f multicolored 2.00 1.25
Nos. 1212-1217 (6) 5.65 3.35

Independence and Army Day — A188

Designs: 25f, King Hussein, soldier descending mountain. 40f, Hussein, Arab revolt flag, globe, King Abdullah. 60f, Flag, natl. arms, equestrian. 100f, Natl. flag, arms, King Abdullah.

1985, June 10 *Perf. 13x13½*

1218 A188 25f multicolored .45 .20
1219 A188 40f multicolored .90 .45
1220 A188 60f multicolored 1.40 .75
1221 A188 100f multicolored 2.25 1.40
Nos. 1218-1221 (4) 5.00 2.80

Men in Postal History A189

1985, July 1

1222	A189	40f	Sir Rowland Hill	.75	.45
1223	A189	60f	Heinrich von Stephan	1.10	.65
1224	A189	125f	Yacoub al-Sukkar	2.40	1.40
			Nos. 1222-1224 (3)	4.25	2.50

1st Convention of Jordanian Expatriates A190

Various designs.

1985, July 20 **Photo.**

1225	A190	40f	multicolored	.75	.45
1226	A190	60f	multicolored	1.10	.65
1227	A190	125f	multicolored	2.40	1.40
			Nos. 1225-1227 (3)	4.25	2.50

Intl. Youth Year — A191

Various designs.

1985, Aug. 11 **Litho.** ***Perf. 13½x13***

1228	A191	10f	multicolored	.20	.20
1229	A191	25f	multicolored	.50	.20
1230	A191	40f	multicolored	.80	.50
1231	A191	60f	multicolored	1.25	.70
1232	A191	125f	multicolored	2.50	1.50
			Nos. 1228-1232 (5)	5.25	3.10

World Tourism Organization, 10th Anniv. — A192

1985, Sept. 13 ***Perf. 13½x13***

1233	A192	10f	Ruins of the Treasury, Petra	.20	.20
1234	A192	25f	Jerash Temple	.50	.20
1235	A192	40f	Roman baths	.80	.50
1236	A192	50f	Jordanian valley town	1.00	.60
1237	A192	60f	Aqaba Bay	1.25	.70
1238	A192	125f	Roman amphitheater	2.50	1.40
			Nos. 1233-1238 (6)	6.25	3.60

An imperf. 100f souvenir sheet exists picturing flower, 10 and natl. flag. Value $6.50.

UN Child Survival Campaign A193

Various designs.

1985, Oct. 7

1239	A193	25f	multicolored	.50	.20
1240	A193	40f	multicolored	.75	.50
1241	A193	60f	multicolored	1.25	.70
1242	A193	125f	multicolored	2.50	1.50
			Nos. 1239-1242 (4)	5.00	2.90

An imperf. 100f souvenir sheet exists picturing campaign emblem and the faces of healthy children. Value $12.

5th Jerash Festival A194

1985, Oct. 21

1243	A194	10f	Opening ceremony, 1980	.20	.20
1244	A194	25f	Folk dancers	.45	.20
1245	A194	40f	Dancers	.90	.45
1246	A194	60f	Choir, Roman theater	1.50	.75
1247	A194	100f	King and Queen	2.40	1.50
			Nos. 1243-1247 (5)	5.45	3.10

UN, 40th Anniv. A195

1985, Oct. 25 **Photo.** ***Perf. 13x13½***

1248	A195	60f	multicolored	1.25	1.00
1249	A195	125f	multicolored	2.50	2.00

King Hussein, 50th Birthday A196

Various photos of King.

1985, Nov. 14 **Litho.** ***Perf. 14½***

1250	A196	10f	multicolored	.20	.20
1251	A196	25f	multicolored	.50	.20
1252	A196	40f	multicolored	.90	.50
1253	A196	60f	multicolored	1.50	.75
1254	A196	100f	multicolored	2.40	1.50
			Nos. 1250-1254 (5)	5.50	3.15

An imperf. 200f souvenir sheet exists picturing flags, King Hussein and Dome of the Rock. Value $15.

Restoration of Al Aqsa Mosque, Jerusalem A196a

1985, Nov. 25 **Litho.** ***Perf. 13x13½***

1254A	A196a	5f	multicolored	*1.10*	*1.10*
1254B	A196a	10f	multicolored	*2.40*	*2.25*

Police A197

1985, Dec. 18

1255	A197	40f	Patrol car	1.10	.20
1256	A197	60f	Crossing guard	1.40	1.10
1257	A197	125f	Police academy	3.00	2.00
			Nos. 1255-1257 (3)	5.50	3.30

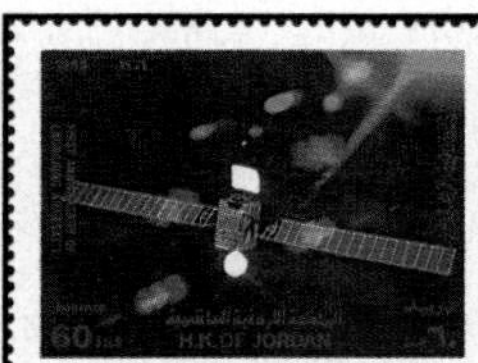

Launch of ARABSAT-1, 1st Anniv. — A198

1986, Feb. 8 **Litho.** ***Perf. 13½x13***

1258	A198	60f	Satellite in orbit	.85	.20
1259	A198	100f	Over map of Arab countries	1.40	.85

Arabization of the Army, 30th Anniv. A199

40f, King Hussein presenting flag. 60f, Greeting army sergeant. 100f, Hussein addressing army.

1986, Mar. 1 ***Perf. 11½x12½***

1260	A199	40f	multicolored	.75	.20
1261	A199	60f	multicolored	.90	.20
1262	A199	100f	multicolored	1.60	.90
			Nos. 1260-1262 (3)	3.25	1.30

An imperf. souvenir sheet exists with design of 100f. Value $10.

Natl. Independence, 40th Anniv. — A200

Design: King Abdullah decorating soldier.

1986, May 25 ***Perf. 12½x11½***

1263	A200	160f	multicolored	2.75	2.10

Arab Revolt against Turkey, 70th Anniv. — A201

Unattributed paintings (details): 40f, The four sons of King Hussein, Prince of Mecca, vert. 60f, Abdullah, retainers and bodyguard. 160f, Abdullah and followers on horseback.

Perf. 12½x11½, 11½x12½

1986, June 10

1264	A201	40f	multicolored	.65	.20
1265	A201	60f	multicolored	.85	.20
1266	A201	160f	multicolored	2.50	1.25
			Nos. 1264-1266 (3)	4.00	1.65

An imperf. 200f souvenir sheet exists picturing the Arab Revolt flag, King Abdullah and text from independence declaration. Value $9.

Intl. Peace Year A202

1986, July 1 **Litho.** ***Perf. 13½x13***

1267	A202	160f	multicolored	2.25	1.25
1268	A202	240f	multicolored	3.25	1.90

King Hussein Medical City Cardiac Center A203

1986, Aug. 11

1269	A203	40f	Cardiac Center	.90	.20
1270	A203	60f	Surgery	1.10	.90
1271	A203	100f	Surgery, diff.	1.75	.95
			Nos. 1269-1271 (3)	3.75	2.05

UN, 40th Anniv. — A204

Excerpts from King Hussein's speech: 40f, In Arabic. 80f, Arabic, diff. 100f, English.

1986, Sept. 27 ***Perf. 12½x11½***

1272	A204	40f	multicolored	.75	.20
1273	A204	80f	multicolored	1.25	.85
1274	A204	100f	multicolored	1.60	.85
			Nos. 1272-1274 (3)	3.60	1.90

An imperf. 200f stamp 90x70mm exists picturing speech in Arabic and English, King Hussein at podium. Value $8.50.

Arab Postal Union, 35th Anniv. A205

1987, Apr. 12 **Litho.** ***Perf. 13½x13***

1275	A205	80f	Old post office	.85	.60
1276	A205	160f	New post office	1.90	1.10

Chemical Soc. Emblem and Chemists — A206

Designs: 60f, Jaber ibn Hayyan al-Azdi (720-813). 80f, Abu-al-Qasem al-Majreeti (950-1007). 240f, Abu-Bakr al-Razi (864-932).

1987, Apr. 24

1277	A206	60f	multicolored	.75	.50
1278	A206	80f	multicolored	1.00	.60
1279	A206	240f	multicolored	2.75	1.60
			Nos. 1277-1279 (3)	4.50	2.70

SOS Children's Village — A207

1987, May 7

1280 A207 80f Village in Amman 1.25 .70
1281 A207 240f Child, bird mural 3.25 1.90

4th Brigade, 40th Anniv. A208

1987, June 10

1282 A208 60f shown 1.40 .95
1283 A208 80f Soldiers in armored vehicle 1.60 1.10

Size: 70x91mm

Imperf

1284 A208 160f Four veterans 8.00 7.50
Nos. 1282-1284 (3) 11.00 9.55

Indigenous Birds — A209

1987, June 24

1285 A209 10f Hoopoe 1.60 .55
1286 A209 40f Palestine sunbird 1.60 .55
1287 A209 50f Black-headed bunting 2.00 .60
1288 A209 60f Spur-winged plover 2.50 .90
1289 A209 80f Greenfinch 3.00 1.25
1290 A209 100f Black-winged stilt 4.00 1.75
Nos. 1285-1290 (6) 14.70 5.60

King Hussein — A210

1987, June 24 Litho. *Perf. 13x13½*

1291 A210 60f multicolored .40 .30
1292 A210 80f multicolored .85 .40
1293 A210 160f multicolored 1.75 1.10
1294 A210 240f multicolored 2.50 1.75
Nos. 1291-1294 (4) 5.50 3.55

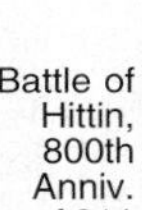

Battle of Hittin, 800th Anniv. A211

Dome of the Rock and Saladin (1137-1193), Conqueror of Jerusalem — A212

1987, July 4

1295 A211 60f Battle, Jerusalem .75 .70
1296 A211 80f Horseman, Jerusalem, Dome of the Rock 1.50 .85
1297 A211 100f Saladin 2.25 1.50
Nos. 1295-1297 (3) 4.50 3.05

Souvenir Sheet

Perf. 12x12½

1298 A212 100f shown 8.00 7.75

No. 1298 exists imperf.

Natl. Coat of Arms — A213

Perf. 11½x12½

1987, Aug. 11 Litho.

1299 A213 80f multicolored 1.00 .65
1300 A213 160f multicolored 2.00 1.25

Amman Industrial Park at Sahab — A214

1987, Aug. 11 *Perf. 13½x13*

1301 A214 80f multicolored 1.00 .80

University Crest A215

University Entrance — A216

Perf. 11½x11, 12½x11½

1987, Sept. 2

1302 A215 60f multicolored .80 .50
1303 A216 80f multicolored .95 .65

University of Jordan, 25th anniv.

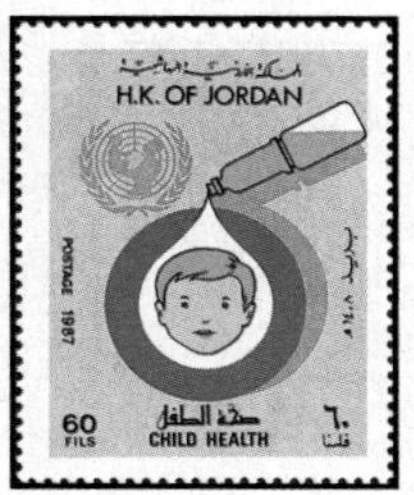

UN Child Survival Campaign A217

1987, Oct. 5 Litho. *Perf. 13x13½*

1304 A217 60f Oral vaccine .75 .60
1305 A217 80f Natl. flag, child 1.25 .80
1306 A217 160f Growth monitoring 2.50 1.60
Nos. 1304-1306 (3) 4.50 3.00

Parliament, 40th Anniv. — A218

1987, Oct. 20 *Perf. 13½x13*

1307 A218 60f Opening ceremony, 1947 1.00 .60
1308 A218 80f In session, 1987 1.25 .80

A219

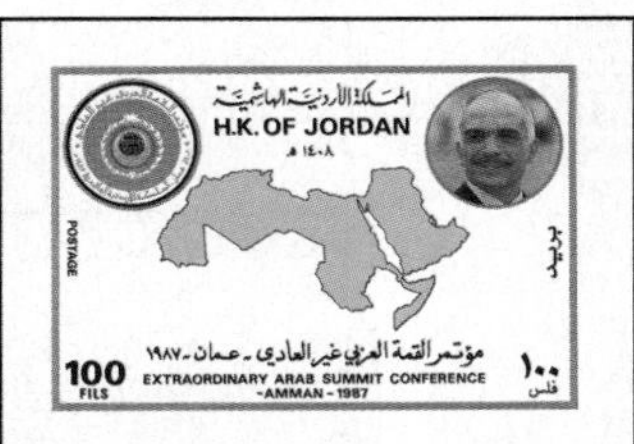

Special Arab Summit Conference, Amman — A220

1987, Nov. 8

1309 A219 60f multicolored .55 .50
1310 A219 80f multicolored .90 .55
1311 A219 160f multicolored 2.00 1.25
1312 A219 240f multicolored 2.75 2.00
Nos. 1309-1312 (4) 6.20 4.30

Size: 90x66mm

Imperf

1313 A220 100f multicolored 7.50 7.50

King Hussein, Dag Hammarskjold Peace Prize Winner for 1987 — A221

1988, Feb. 6 Litho. *Perf. 12½*

1314 A221 80f Hussein, woman, vert. .95 .75
1315 A221 160f shown 1.90 1.25

Natl. Victory at the 1987 Arab Military Basketball Championships — A222

1988, Mar. 1 *Perf. 13½x13*

1316 A222 60f Golden Sword Award .80 .50
1317 A222 80f Hussein congratulating team 1.10 .65
1318 A222 160f Jump ball 2.10 1.25
Nos. 1316-1318 (3) 4.00 2.40

WHO, 40th Anniv. — A223

1988, Apr. 7 Photo. *Perf. 13x13½*

1319 A223 60f multicolored 1.00 .70
1320 A223 80f multicolored 1.25 .90

Arab Scouts, 75th Anniv. — A224

1988, July 2 Litho. *Perf. 13x13½*

1321 A224 60f multicolored 1.00 .90
1322 A224 80f multicolored 1.25 1.10

Birds A225

1988, July 21 Litho. *Perf. 11½x12*

1323 A225 10f Crested lark 2.25 .70
1324 A225 20f Stone curlew 2.25 .80
1325 A225 30f Redstart 2.25 .90
1326 A225 40f Blackbird 3.25 1.00
1327 A225 50f Rock dove 4.00 1.10
1328 A225 160f Smyrna kingfisher 11.00 1.75
Nos. 1323-1328 (6) 25.00 6.25

Size: 71x90mm

Imperf

1328A A225 310f Six species 17.50 15.00

Restoration of San'a, Yemen Arab Republic A226

1988, Aug. 11 Litho. *Perf. 12x11½*
1329 A226 80f multicolored .95 .70
1330 A226 160f multicolored 1.90 1.50

Historic Natl. Sites A227

1988, Aug. 11 *Perf. 13½x13*
1331 A227 60f Umm Al-rasas .70 .50
1332 A227 80f Umm Qais .90 .70
1333 A227 160f Iraq Al-amir 1.90 1.50
Nos. 1331-1333 (3) 3.50 2.70

An imperf. souvenir sheet of 3 exists containing one each Nos. 1331-1333. Value $5.

1988 Summer Olympics, Seoul — A228

1988, Sept. 17 Litho. *Perf. 13x13½*
1334 A228 10f Tennis .20 .20
1335 A228 60f Character trademark .90 .70
1336 A228 80f Running, swimming 1.40 .90
1337 A228 120f Basketball 1.75 1.50
1338 A228 160f Soccer 2.50 1.75
Nos. 1334-1338 (5) 6.75 5.05

Size: 70x91mm

Imperf

1339 A228 100f Emblems 17.50 17.50

Royal Jordanian Airlines, 25th Anniv. — A229

1988, Dec. 15 Litho. *Perf. 11½x12*
1340 A229 60f Ruins of Petra 1.00 .75
1341 A229 80f Aircraft, world map 1.25 1.00

UN Declaration of Human Rights, 40th Anniv. — A230

1988, Dec. 10
1342 A230 80f multicolored .75 .60
1343 A230 160f multicolored 1.75 1.10

Arab Cooperation Council, Feb. 16 — A231

1989 Litho. *Perf. 13½x13*
1344 A231 10f shown .20 .20
1345 A231 30f multi, diff. .20 .20
1346 A231 40f multi, diff. .20 .20
1347 A231 60f multi, diff. 1.00 .95
Nos. 1344-1347 (4) 1.60 1.55

Martyrs of Palestine and Their Families — A232

1989 *Perf. 14½*
1348 A232 5f multi .90 .30
1349 A232 10f multi .90 .30

Interparliamentary Union, Cent. — A233

1989 Litho. *Perf. 12*
1350 A233 40f multicolored .35 .20
1351 A233 60f multicolored .55 .35

Arab Housing Day and World Refuge Day A234

Designs: 5f, Housing complex, emblems, vert. 60f, Housing complex, emblem.

1989
1352 A234 5f multicolored .20 .20
1353 A234 40f shown .55 .20
1354 A234 60f multicolored .75 .55
Nos. 1352-1354 (3) 1.50 .95

Ministry of Agriculture, 50th Anniv. — A235

1989 Litho. *Perf. 12*
1355 A235 5f shown .20 .20
1356 A235 40f Tree, anniv. emblem .20 .20
1357 A235 60f Fruit tree, emblem, apiary 2.25 .20
Nos. 1355-1357 (3) 2.65 .60

Arabian Horse Festival A236

1989 *Perf. 12*
1358 A236 5f shown .40 .20
1359 A236 40f Horse, building facade .85 .20
1360 A236 60f Horse's head, vert. 2.40 .20
Nos. 1358-1360 (3) 3.65 .60

Size: 90x70mm

Imperf

1361 A236 100f Mare and foal0 *25.00 22.50*

Natl. Library Assoc. A237

1989 *Perf. 12*
1362 A237 40f multicolored .20 .20
1363 A237 60f multicolored 1.00 .20

Mosque of the Martyr King Abdullah — A238

1989 *Perf. 12*
1364 A238 40f multicolored .20 .20
1365 A238 60f multicolored 1.00 .20

Size: 90x70mm

Imperf

1366 A238 100f multicolored *6.75 6.75*

Mosaics A239

1989, Dec. 23 Litho. *Perf. 12*
1367 A239 5f Man with Basket .60 .30
1368 A239 10f Building .60 .30
1369 A239 40f Deer 1.50 .50
1370 A239 60f Man with stick 2.00 .65
1371 A239 80f Town, horiz. 2.50 .90
Nos. 1367-1371 (5) 7.20 2.65

Size: 90x70mm

Imperf

1372 A239 100f like #1371, horiz. *17.50 17.50*

Arab Cooperation Council, 1st Anniv. — A240

1990, Feb. 16 *Perf. 13*
1373 A240 5f multicolored .20 .20
1374 A240 20f multicolored .20 .20
1375 A240 60f multicolored .75 .45
1376 A240 80f multicolored 1.00 .65
Nos. 1373-1376 (4) 2.15 1.50

Nature Conservation — A241

1990, Apr. 22
1377 A241 40f Horses .20 .20
1378 A241 60f Mountain .50 .20
1379 A241 80f Oasis .65 .35
Nos. 1377-1379 (3) 1.35 .75

Prince Abdullah's Arrival in Ma'an, 70th Anniv. — A243

1990 Litho. *Perf. 13½x13*
1382 A243 40f org & multi .20 .20
1383 A243 60f grn & multi .40 .20

Size: 90x70mm

Imperf

1384 A243 200f multicolored *7.00 7.00*

UN Development Program, 40th Anniv. — A244

1990 *Perf. 13*
1385 A244 60f multicolored .25 .20
1386 A244 80f multicolored .55 .20

King Hussein — A245

1990-92 Litho. *Perf. 12x13½*
1387 A245 5f yel org & multi .25 .25
a. Slightly larger vignette, inscr. 1991 .25 .25
1390 A245 20f blue green & multi .25 .25
1391 A245 40f orange & multi .25 .25
1393 A245 60f blue & multi .45 .45
1395 A245 80f pink & multi .70 .70
a. Slightly larger vignette, inscr. 1991 .70 .70
1397 A245 240f brown & multi 1.25 .90
1398 A245 320f red lilac & multi 1.75 1.25
1399 A245 1d yel green & multi 2.75 2.40
Nos. 1387-1399 (8) 7.65 6.45

#1390 dated 1991.

Issued: 20f, 1992; 5f, 60f, 80f 1990; others 1991.

Nos. 1387, 1395 exist dated "1991," with slightly larger vignette.

Endangered Animals A246

1991, Sept. 1 Litho. ***Perf. 13x13½***

No.	Type	Description	Unused	Used
1401	A246	5f Nubian ibex	.20	.20
1402	A246	40f Onager	.50	.25
1403	A246	80f Arabian gazelle	2.25	.40
1404	A246	160f Arabian oryx	1.60	1.10
		Nos. 1401-1404 (4)	4.55	1.95

Energy Rationalization Program — A247

Designs: 5f, Light bulbs. 40f, Solar panels, sun, vert. 80f, Electric table lamp, vert.

Perf. 13½x13, 13x13½

1991, Oct. 3 Litho.

No.	Type	Description	Unused	Used
1405	A247	5f multicolored	.20	.20
1406	A247	40f multicolored	.20	.20
1407	A247	80f multicolored	.70	.20
		Nos. 1405-1407 (3)	1.10	.60

Grain Production for Food Security — A248

1991, Oct. 16 ***Perf. 13½x13***

No.	Type	Description	Unused	Used
1408	A248	5f Different grains	.20	.20
1409	A248	40f shown	.20	.20
1410	A248	80f Wheat stalk, kernels	.70	.20
		Nos. 1408-1410 (3)	1.10	.60

Palestinian Uprising — A249

1991, Nov. 29 Litho. ***Perf. 11***

No.	Type	Description	Unused	Used
1411	A249	20f multicolored	2.00	.75

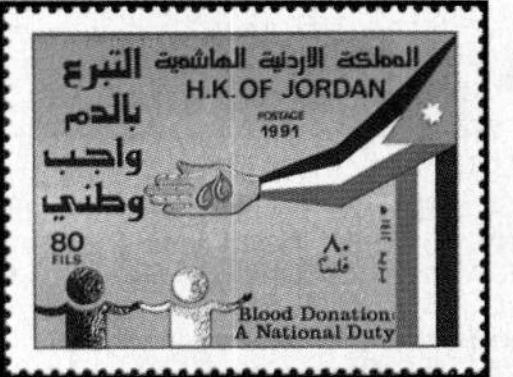

Blood Donation Campaign — A250

1991, Nov. 14 Litho. ***Perf. 13½x13***

No.	Type	Description	Unused	Used
1412	A250	80f multicolored	.75	.20
1413	A250	160f multicolored	1.50	.75

Expo '92, Seville A251

1992, Feb. 20

No.	Type	Description	Unused	Used
1414	A251	80f multicolored	.65	.20
1415	A251	320f multicolored	1.60	.95

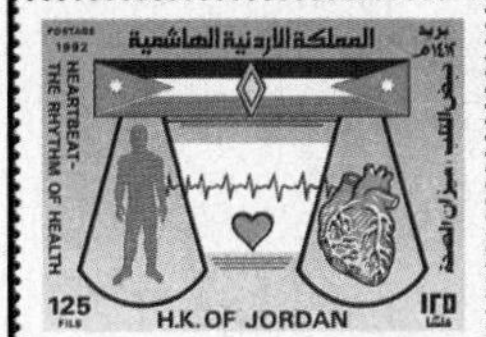

Healthy Hearts A252

80f, Man & woman, heart at center of scale, vert.

Perf. 13x13½, 13½x13

1992, Apr. 7 Litho.

No.	Type	Description	Unused	Used
1416	A252	80f multicolored	.70	.20
1417	A252	125f multicolored	.80	.50

SOS Children's Village, 'Aqaba — A253

1992, Apr. 30 Litho. ***Perf. 13½x13***

No.	Type	Description	Unused	Used
1418	A253	80f shown	.70	.20
1419	A253	125f Village	.80	.50

1992 Summer Olympics, Barcelona — A254

Stylized designs with Barcelona Olympic emblem: 5fr, Judo, 40f, Runner, vert. 80f, Diver. 125f, Flag, Cobi, map, vert. 160f, Table tennis.

100f, Incorporates all designs of set.

Perf. 13½x13, 13x13½

1992, July 25 Litho.

No.	Type	Description	Unused	Used
1420	A254	5f multicolored	.20	.20
1421	A254	40f multicolored	.20	.20
1422	A254	80f multicolored	.50	.20
1423	A254	125f multicolored	.75	.35
1424	A254	160f multicolored	1.10	.50
		Nos. 1420-1424 (5)	2.75	1.45

Size: 70x90mm

Imperf

No.	Type	Description	Unused	Used
1425	A254	100f multicolored	*15.00*	*12.00*

King Hussein, 40th Anniv. of Accession — A255

Designs: 40f, Flags, King in full dress uniform, vert. 125f, King wearing headdress, flags. 160f, King in business suit, crown. 200f, Portrait.

1992, Aug. 11 ***Perf. 13x13½***

No.	Type	Description	Unused	Used
1426	A255	40f multicolored	.20	.20

Perf. 13½x13

No.	Type	Description	Unused	Used
1427	A255	80f shown	.45	.20
1428	A255	125f multicolored	.75	.35
1429	A255	160f multicolored	1.10	.50
		Nos. 1426-1429 (4)	2.50	1.25

Size: 90x70mm

Imperf

No.	Type	Description	Unused	Used
1430	A255	200f multicolored	*7.25*	*7.25*

Butterflies — A256

5f, Danaus chrysippus. 40f, Aporia cartaegi. 80f, Papilio machaon. 160f, Pseudochazara telephassa. 200f, Same as #1431-1434.

1992, Dec. 20 Litho. ***Perf. 13½x13***

No.	Type	Description	Unused	Used
1431	A256	5f multicolored	.50	.20
1432	A256	40f multicolored	1.00	.25
1433	A256	80f multicolored	2.00	.50
1434	A256	160f multicolored	4.50	1.25
		Nos. 1431-1434 (4)	8.00	2.20

Imperf

Size: 90x70mm

No.	Type	Description	Unused	Used
1435	A256	200f multicolored	*17.50*	*17.50*

See Nos. 1448-1452.

Intl. Customs Day — A257

1993, Jan. 26 Litho. ***Perf. 13½x13***

No.	Type	Description	Unused	Used
1436	A257	80f green & multi	.60	.20
1437	A257	125f pale orange & multi	.90	.45

Royal Scientific Society — A258

1993, June 10 Litho. ***Perf. 12½x13***

No.	Type	Description	Unused	Used
1438	A258	80f multicolored	.50	.20

Es Salt Municipality, Cent. — A259

1993, Sept. 1 Litho. ***Perf. 12***

No.	Type	Description	Unused	Used
1439	A259	80f pink & multi	.60	.20
1440	A259	125f green & multi	.90	.45
a.		Souvenir sheet of 2, #1439-1440, imperf.	*6.25*	*6.25*

No. 1440a sold for 200f.

Great Arab Revolt and Army Day A260

Designs: 5f, Rockets, planes, tank, King Hussein, 40f, King Hussein, military activities. 80f, Amir Abdullah ibn Hussein, Dome of the Rock, map, flags. 125f, Amir Abdullah ibn Hussein, Dome of the Rock, riders. 100f, King Hussein, flags.

1993, June 10

No.	Type	Description	Unused	Used
1441	A260	5f multicolored	.20	.20
1442	A260	40f multicolored	.20	.20
1443	A260	80f multicolored	.50	.20
1444	A260	125f multicolored	.85	.35
		Nos. 1441-1444 (4)	1.75	.95

Size: 90x70mm

Imperf

No.	Type	Description	Unused	Used
1445	A260	100f multicolored	*6.00*	*6.00*

White Cane Day A261

Design: 125f, Lighted world, cane, eye, vert.

1993, Oct. 23 Litho. ***Perf. 12***

No.	Type	Description	Unused	Used
1446	A261	80f shown	.60	.20
1447	A261	125f multicolored	.90	.45

Butterfly Type of 1992

Designs: 5f, Lampides boeticus. 40f, Melanargria titea. 80f, Allancastria deyrollei. 160f, Gonepteryx cleopatra. 100f, Same designs as Nos. 1448-1451.

1993, Oct. 10 Litho. ***Perf. 12***

No.	Type	Description	Unused	Used
1448	A256	5f multicolored	.40	.20
1449	A256	40f multicolored	.75	.30
1450	A256	80f multicolored	1.00	.40
1451	A256	160f multicolored	2.50	1.00
		Nos. 1448-1451 (4)	4.65	1.90

Size: 83x65mm

Imperf

No.	Type	Description	Unused	Used
1452	A256	100f multicolored	*25.00*	*25.00*

UN Declaration of Human Rights, 45th Anniv. — A262

1993, Dec. 10 ***Perf. 12***

No.	Type	Description	Unused	Used
1453	A262	40f yellow & multi	.20	.20
1454	A262	160f red & multi	1.10	.75

Recovery & Homecoming, 1st Anniv. — A263

King Hussein: 80f, Crowd. 125f, Waving to people. 160f, Embracing woman. 100f, Standing on airplane ramp.

1993, Nov. 25

No.	Type	Description	Unused	Used
1455	A263	80f multicolored	.50	.20
1456	A263	125f multicolored	.85	.40
1457	A263	160f multicolored	1.00	.50
		Nos. 1455-1457 (3)	2.35	1.10

Size: 85x65

Imperf

No.	Type	Description	Unused	Used
1458	A263	100f multicolored	*5.50*	*3.75*

World AIDS Day — A264

1993, Dec. 1 ***Perf. 12***
1459 A264 80f red & multi .50 .20
1460 A264 125f green & multi .85 .45

Size: 83x70mm

Imperf

1461 A264 200f like #1459-1460 *6.25 4.50*

King Hussein
A265

King Hussein wearing: 40f, Military uniform. 80f, Traditional costume. 125f, Business suit. 160f, 100f, Dress uniform in portrait with Queen Noor, horiz.

1993, Nov. 14 ***Perf. 12***
1462 A265 40f multi, horiz. .20 .20
1463 A265 80f multi, horiz. .50 .20
1464 A265 125f multi, horiz. .80 .35
1465 A265 160f multicolored 1.25 .50
Nos. 1462-1465 (4) 2.75 1.25

Size: 82x68mm

Imperf

1466 A265 100f multicolored *8.00 5.75*

Assumption of Constitutional Powers by King Hussein, 40th anniv.

Saladin (1138-1193), Dome of the Rock — A266

1993, Nov. 25 ***Perf. 12***
1467 A266 40f blue & multi .20 .20
1468 A266 80f gray & multi .55 .20
1469 A266 125f yellow & multi .75 .40
Nos. 1467-1469 (3) 1.50 .80

Triumphal Arch, Jerash — A267

Perf. 12x13½ (5f, No. 80f, 1473A, 1475, 160f, 320f, 1d), 12 (25f, 40f, 50f, #1474C, 240f, No. 1478C, No. 1479), 14x13½ (75f, No. 1474, 150f, 200f, 300f, 400f), 13½x14 (#120f), 12¾x13¼ (#1479B)

1993-2003 **Litho.**
1470 A267 5f blue & multi .20 .20
1471 A267 25f pale violet & multi .20 .20
b. Perf 12¾x13¼, inscr. "2003" .20 .20
1471A A267 40f green & multi .20 .20
1472 A267 50f yellow & multi .25 .25
a. Perf 12, inscr. "1996" .25 .25
b. Perf 12¾x13¼ .25 .25
c. Perf 13½x14 .25 .25
d. As "b," inscr. "2003" .25 .25
1472E A267 75f buff & multi .40 .40
1473 A267 80f green & multi .35 .20
1473A A267 100f red & multi .40 .20
b. Perf. 12 .40 .20
c. As "b," inscribed "1996" .40 .20
1474 A267 100f apple green & multi .50 .50
a. Perf. 12 .50 .50
d. As "a," inscr. "1996" .50 .50
1474B A267 120f bl grn & multi .65 .65
1474C A267 125f lt bl & multi .60 .60
1475 A267 125f buff & multi .50 .20
a. Perf. 12 .50 .20
1475B A267 150f salmon pink & multi .90 .90
1476 A267 160f yellow & multi .65 .25
b. Perf. 12 .75 .25
c. As "b," inscribed "1994" .75 .25
1476A A267 200f gray & multi 1.10 1.10
d. Perf. 12 1.10 1.10
1477 A267 240f pink & multi 1.00 .25
b. Perf. 12x13½ .90 .25
c. perf 12, inscribed "1994" 1.25 1.25
1477A A267 300f pink & multi 1.75 1.75
d. Perf. 12 1.75 1.75
1478 A267 320f brown & multi 1.25 .35
1478A A267 320f sal & multi 1.25 .35
1478C A267 400f bright blue & multi 2.50 2.50
b. Perf. 13x13¼ 2.50 2.50
1479 A267 500f bister & multi 2.00 .85
a. Perf. 12x13½ 2.00 .85
1479B A267 500f yel & multi 2.50 2.50
1480 A267 1d olive & multi 4.00 1.25
a. Perf. 12¾x13¼ 5.00 1.25
Nos. 1470-1480 (22) 23.15 15.65

#Nos. 1472E, 1473, 1473A , 1477b, 1479a are dated 1992; Nos. #1471A, 1473Ab, 1476b, 1993; No. 1474, 1994; No. 1477Ac, 1995; Nos. 1478Ab, 1479B, 1480a, 1997.

Issued: 5f, 320f, 1/13/93 (dated 1992); 25f, 1/18/96 (dated 1995); 40f, 1994; 100f, 200f, 300f, 5/15/96; 1d, 1/13/93; 125f, 160f, 1/13/93; 240f, 3/23/94; 50f, 1995; 150f, 400f, 5/15/96; 500f, 10/25/96; 75f, 5/15/96; #1478Ab, 5/10/98. 80f, Nos. 1473A, 1477b, 1479a, 1/13/93; Nos. 1473Ab, 1476b, 3/23/94; 120f, 5/15/96; No. 1474C, 2/13/95; Nos. 1476Ad, 1477Ad, 1/18/96; No. 1478C, 1993; Nos. 1479B, 1480a, 5/10/98.

Hashemite Charity Organization — A268

Designs: 80f, Loading supplies into plane. 125f, People gathering at plane.

1994, Mar. 20 **Litho.** ***Perf. 12***
1481 A268 80f multicolored .55 .20
1482 A268 125f multicolored .80 .50

Third Hashemite Restoration of Al Aqsa Mosque, Dome of the Rock — A269

King Hussein with various scenes of restoration.

1994, Apr. 18 **Litho.** ***Perf. 12x12½***
1483 A269 80f yellow & multi .40 .20
1484 A269 125f lt orange & multi .70 .35
1485 A269 240f lilac & multi 1.25 .60
Nos. 1483-1485 (3) 2.35 1.15

Imperf

Size: 90x70mm

1486 A269 100f green & multi *8.00 5.50*

ILO, 75th Anniv. A270

1994, June 13 **Litho.** ***Perf. 12***
1487 A270 80f yellow & multi .45 .20
1488 A270 125f brt pink & multi .70 .35

Intl. Red Cross and Red Crescent Societies, 75th Anniv. — A271

1994, May 8 ***Perf. 12***
1489 A271 80f shown .45 .20
1490 A271 160f Doves, emblems, vert .80 .45

Size: 61x78mm

Imperf

1491 A271 200f #1489-1490 *11.00 8.25*

Intl. Year of the Family A272

1994, Aug. 11 **Litho.** ***Perf. 12***
1492 A272 80f green & multi .45 .20
1493 A272 125f pink & multi .80 .40
1494 A272 160f yellow & multi 1.00 .45
Nos. 1492-1494 (3) 2.25 1.05

Intl. Olympic Committee, Cent. — A273

Olympic rings and: 80f, Globe, venue symbols, vert. 100f, Jordanian colors. 125f, Venue symbols, diff., vert. 160f, shown. 240f, Torch.

1994, June 23
1495 A273 80f blue & multi .40 .20
1496 A273 125f multicolored .65 .30
1497 A273 160f multicolored 1.10 .40
1498 A273 240f multicolored 1.60 .65
Nos. 1495-1498 (4) 3.75 1.55

Size: 90x70mm

Imperf

1499 A273 100f multicolored *8.50 8.50*

Jordanian Participation in UN Peacekeeping Forces — A274

Designs: 80f, King Hussein greeting troops. 125f, King inspecting troops. 160f, Checkpoint.

1994, Aug. 11 **Litho.** ***Perf. 12***
1500 A274 80f multicolored .45 .20
1501 A274 125f multicolored .70 .35
1502 A274 160f multicolored .85 .45
Nos. 1500-1502 (3) 2.00 1.00

Water Conservation Day — A275

80f, Hands, water droplet. 125f, Water faucet, foods, factory. 160f, Child, rain drops.

1994, Nov. 14 **Litho.** ***Perf. 14***
1503 A275 80f multicolored .60 .20
1504 A275 125f multicolored 1.00 .55
1505 A275 160f multicolored 1.25 .60
Nos. 1503-1505 (3) 2.85 1.35

ICAO, 50th Anniv. A276

1994, Oct. 25 ***Perf. 12***
1506 A276 80f green & multi .45 .20
1507 A276 125f red & multi .70 .35
1508 A276 160f blue & multi .85 .45
Nos. 1506-1508 (3) 2.00 1.00

Crown Prince's Award, 10th Anniv. A277

1994, Dec. 11 **Litho.** ***Perf. 12***
1509 A277 80f yel grn & multi .70 .20
1510 A277 125f org brn & multi .90 .55
1511 A277 160f vio bl & multi 1.25 .70
Nos. 1509-1511 (3) 2.85 1.45

UN, 50th Anniv. A278

1995, Apr. 1 **Litho.** ***Perf. 14***
1512 A278 80f green & multi .65 .20
1513 A278 125f pink & multi .95 .55

May Day A279

80f, Emblem, workers, flag. 125f, Emblem, world map, worker. 160f, Hands holding wrench, torch, Jordanian map, emblem.

1995, May 1
1514 A279 80f multicolored .45 .20
1515 A279 125f multicolored .65 .40
1516 A279 160f multicolored .90 .45
Nos. 1514-1516 (3) 2.00 1.05

Jordan Week in Japan A280

Globe in two hemispheres with olive branches and: 125f, Japanese, Jordanian flags. 160f, Flags above wall.

1995, May 22 **Litho.** ***Perf. 14***

1517 A280 80f green & multi .45 .20
1518 A280 125f pink & multi .70 .30
1519 A280 160f gray & multi .85 .45
Nos. 1517-1519 (3) 2.00 .95

Opening of Al al-Bayt University A281

1995, Feb. 8 **Litho.** ***Perf. 12***

1520 A281 80f green blue & multi .50 .20
1521 A281 125f olive green & multi .75 .40
a. Souvenir sheet, #1520-1521, imperf. 3.75 3.25

No. 1521a sold for 200f. Nos. 1520-1521 are dated 1994.

Petra, the Rose City A282

Archaeological discoveries: 50f, Amphitheater. 75f, Facial carvings, bowl, pitcher. 80f, Columns of building, vert. 160f, Front of building with columns, vert. 200f, Building in side of mountain.

1995, Aug. 11 **Litho.** ***Perf. 14***

1524 A282 50f multicolored .20 .20
1525 A282 75f multicolored .85 .20
1526 A282 80f multicolored .95 .20
1527 A282 160f multicolored 1.75 .95
Nos. 1524-1527 (4) 3.75 1.55

Size: 90x70mm

Imperf

1528 A282 200f multicolored *20.00 20.00*

Arab League, 50th Anniv. A283

1995, Sept. 20 **Litho.** ***Perf. 14***

1529 A283 80f green & multi .45 .20
1530 A283 125f pink & multi .70 .20
1531 A283 160f gray & multi .85 .45
Nos. 1529-1531 (3) 2.00 .85

FAO, 50th Anniv. A284

Designs: 125f, "50," FAO emblem, shafts of grain. 160f, UN, FAO emblems, "50."

1995, Oct. 16 **Litho.** ***Perf. 14***

1532 A284 80f shown .50 .20
1533 A284 125f multicolored .85 .40
1534 A284 160f multicolored 1.00 .50
Nos. 1532-1534 (3) 2.35 1.10

Middle East and North Africa Economic Summit, Amman — A285

1995, Oct. 29 ***Perf. 12***

1535 A285 80f brt pink & multi .50 .20
1536 A285 125f org yel & multi .75 .40

The Deaf A286

1995, Nov. 30 ***Perf. 14***

1537 A286 80f shown .50 .20
1538 A286 125f Emblems, hand sign .75 .35

King Hussein, 60th Birthday A287

Designs: 40f, Crown over King's picture in business suit. 80f, Crown, flag, dove, ruins of Petra, King in traditional head wear, military uniform. 100f, King dress uniform, crown, "60." 125f, King in traditional head wear, business suit, crown, flag, olive branch. 160f, Flag, King in business suit. 200f, "60," Dome of the Rock, King in dress uniform, olive branch.

1995, Nov. 14

1539 A287 25f multicolored .20 .20
1540 A287 40f multicolored .20 .20
1541 A287 80f multicolored .45 .20
1542 A287 100f multicolored .50 .20
1543 A287 125f multicolored 1.00 .35
1544 A287 160f multicolored 1.25 .45
Nos. 1539-1544 (6) 3.60 1.60

Size: 83x63mm

Imperf

1545 A287 200f multicolored *6.25 6.25*

Independence, 50th Anniv. — A288

King Hussein and: No. 1547, Outline map of Jordan, crown, dove of peace, Amir Abdullah ibn Hussein. 300f, Jordanian monuments, flag.
No. 1549, Map of Jordan surrounded by wreath, dove, national flags.

1996, May 25 **Litho.** ***Perf. 12***

1546 A288 100f multicolored .55 .20
1547 A288 200f multicolored 1.10 .40
1548 A288 300f multicolored 1.75 .65
Nos. 1546-1548 (3) 3.40 1.25

Size: 86x66mm

1549 A288 200f multicolored *7.50 7.50*

1996 Summer Olympic Games, Atlanta A289

1996 Olympic Games Emblem and: 50f, Natl. flag, Olympic rings, sports pictograms. 100f, Sports pictograms. 200f, Hands. 300f, Torch, Olympic rings, natl. flag.

1996, July 19 **Litho.** ***Perf. 12***

1550 A289 50f multicolored .20 .20
1551 A289 100f multicolored .70 .20
1552 A289 200f multicolored 1.60 .70
1553 A289 300f multicolored 2.50 1.10
Nos. 1550-1553 (4) 5.00 2.20

Protection of the Ozone Layer — A290

1996, Sept. 16

1554 A290 100f multicolored 1.25 .20

UNICEF, 50th Anniv. — A291

1996, Dec. 11 **Litho.** ***Perf. 12***

1555 A291 100f green & multi .60 .20
1556 A291 200f gray lilac & multi 1.00 .60

Crown Prince El-Hassan, 50th Birthday — A292

Designs: 50f, On horseback. 100f, Wearing suit & tie, vert. No. 1559, Natl. flag, wearing traditional attire.
No. 1560, Wearing graduation cap.

1997, Mar. 20 **Litho.** ***Perf. 12***

1557 A292 50f multicolored .20 .20
1558 A292 100f multicolored .70 .20
1559 A292 200f multicolored 1.10 .70
Nos. 1557-1559 (3) 2.00 1.10

Size: 84x64mm

Imperf

1560 A292 200f multicolored *8.25 8.25*

Heinrich von Stephan (1831-97) A293

1997, Apr. 8 **Litho.** ***Perf. 12***

1561 A293 100f multicolored .90 .20
1562 A293 200f multicolored 1.60 .80

Discovery of the Madeba Mosaic Map, Cent. — A294

1997, Apr. 7

1563 A294 100f Karak, vert. .75 .35
1564 A294 200f River Jordan 1.50 .50
1565 A294 300f Jerusalem, vert. 2.50 .90
Nos. 1563-1565 (3) 4.75 1.75

Size: 86x67mm

Imperf

1566 A294 100f Entire map *15.00 15.00*

Jordanian Rosefinch — A295

1997, May 25 **Litho.** ***Perf. 12***

1567 A295 50f multicolored .20 .20
1568 A295 100f multi, diff. .65 .20
1569 A295 150f multi, diff. 1.00 .45
1570 A295 200f multi, diff. 1.50 .65
Nos. 1567-1570 (4) 3.35 1.50

Jerash Festival, 15th Anniv. A296

Designs: 50f, Couples in traditional costumes, ruins. 100f, Symphony orchestra, silhouettes of buildings. 150f, Pillars, parade of dignitaries. 200f, Women in traditional costumes, crowd, ruins.
15d, Queen Noor lighting torch.

1997, July 23 **Litho.** ***Perf. 12***

1571 A296 50f multicolored .20 .20
1572 A296 100f multicolored .60 .20
1573 A296 150f multicolored .95 .45
1574 A296 200f multicolored 1.50 .65
Nos. 1571-1574 (4) 3.25 1.50

Size: 90x70mm

Imperf

1575 A296 15d multicolored 8.50 8.50

Natl. Forum for Women A297

Emblem and: 50f, Women in tradtional and modern dress, vert. 100f, Natl. flag, flame, book. 150fr, Natl. flag, women seated at conference table.

1997, Dec. 20 **Litho.** ***Perf. 12***

1576 A297 50f multicolored .20 .20
1577 A297 100f multicolored .50 .20
1578 A297 150f multicolored .80 .35
Nos. 1576-1578 (3) 1.50 .75

Jordanian Team, 1997 Arab Soccer Champions — A298

Designs: 50f, Team parading in stadium. 75f, Team in red uniforms. 100f, Team in white uniforms, ceremony.
200f, Formal presentation to King Hussein, motorcade.

1997, Dec. 15

1579	A298	50f multicolored	.20	.20
1580	A298	75f multicolored	.40	.20
1581	A298	100f multicolored	.55	.20
		Nos. 1579-1581 (3)	1.15	.60

Size: 91x70mm

Imperf

1582	A298	200f multicolored	*9.00*	*7.50*

House of Parliament, 50th Anniv. — A299

100f, Outside view of building, drawing. 200f, Speaker, members assembled in chamber.

1997, Nov. 1 ***Perf. 12½***

1583	A299	100f multicolored	.60	.20
1584	A299	200f multicolored	.90	.60

53rd General Meeting of Intl. Air Transport Association A300

1997, Nov. 3 **Litho.** ***Perf. 13x13½***

1585	A300	100f lt blue & multi	1.00	1.00
1586	A300	200f red & multi	1.00	1.00
1587	A300	300f gray & multi	1.00	1.00

Two additional stamps were issued in this set. The editors would like to examine them.

King Hussein II, 62nd Birthday A301

1997, Nov. 14 **Litho.** ***Perf. 13x13½***

Frame Color

1588	A301	100f red	1.00	1.00
1589	A301	200f gold	1.00	1.00
1590	A301	300f blue	1.00	1.00

Souvenir Sheet

Perf. 12

1590A	A301	200f gold	8.50	8.50

No. 1590A contains one 44x60mm stamp.

Earth Day A302

Children's drawings: 50f, Various ways of polluting air and water. 100f, Pollution from factory smoke, automobiles. 150f, Earth chained to various methods of pollution, vert.

1998, Apr. 29 **Litho.** ***Perf. 14***

1591	A302	50f multicolored	.20	.20
1592	A302	100f multicolored	.50	.20
1593	A302	150f multicolored	.80	.50
		Nos. 1591-1593 (3)	1.50	.90

Trans-Jordan Emirate, 75th Anniv. — A303

Designs: 100f, Camel rider holding flag, Amir Abdullah ibn Hussein. 200f, Camel rider holding flag, King Hussein. 300f, King Hussein, arms, #81, Amir Abdullah ibn Hussein.

1998, May 25 ***Perf. 12***

1594	A303	100f multicolored	.50	.50
1595	A303	200f multicolored	1.00	1.00
1596	A303	300f multicolored	1.75	1.75
		Nos. 1594-1596 (3)	3.25	3.25

Size: 80x70mm

Imperf

1597	A303	300f like #1596	*8.50*	*8.50*

Mosaics, Um Ar-Rasas A304

1998, July 22 **Litho.** ***Perf. 14***

1598	A304	100f multicolored	.50	.50
1599	A304	200f multi, diff.	1.00	1.00
1600	A304	300f multi, diff.	1.75	1.75
		Nos. 1598-1600 (3)	3.25	3.25

Flowers A305

1998, July 7

1601	A305	50f purple & white, thorns	.30	.25
1602	A305	100f Poppies	.60	.55
1603	A305	150f shown	1.00	.75
		Nos. 1601-1603 (3)	1.90	1.55

Size: 60x80mm

Imperf

1604	A305	200f Flower, map of Jordan	*8.50*	*8.50*

2nd Arab Beekeepers Conference — A306

Various pictures of bees, flowers, honeycomb.

1998, Aug. 3 **Litho.** ***Perf. 14***

1605	A306	50f multicolored	.50	.40
1606	A306	100f multi, vert.	.85	.50
1607	A306	150f multicolored	1.25	.60
		Nos. 1605-1607 (3)	2.60	1.50

Size: 80x60mm

Imperf

1608	A306	200f Bees, flowers, emblem	*9.00*	*9.00*

World Stamp Day A307

1998, Oct. 9 **Litho.** ***Perf. 14***

1609	A307	50f shown	.20	.20
1610	A307	100f World map, emblems	.90	.90
1611	A307	150f Globe, stamps	1.75	1.75
		Nos. 1609-1611 (3)	2.85	2.85

Universal Declaration of Human Rights, 50th Anniv. — A308

1998, Dec. 10

1612	A308	100f shown	.60	.60
1613	A308	200f Emblems, people	1.00	1.00

King Hussein, 63rd Birthday A309

1998, Nov. 14 **Litho.** ***Perf. 14x14½***

1614	A309	100f green & multi	.65	.45
1615	A309	200f violet & multi	1.25	1.00
1616	A309	300f violet blue & multi	2.25	1.50
		Nos. 1614-1616 (3)	4.15	2.95

Size: 90x70mm

Imperf

1617	A309	300f gold & multi	*8.50*	*8.50*

Arab Police and Security Chiefs Meeting, 25th Anniv. (in 1997) A310

Map of Arab world and: 100f, King Hussein, emblem. 200f, Flags of Arab countries, emblem, flame, vert. 300f, Beret.

1998, Nov. 18 ***Perf. 14***

1618	A310	100f multicolored	.65	.65
1619	A310	200f multicolored	1.10	1.10
1620	A310	300f multicolored	2.00	1.75
		Nos. 1618-1620 (3)	3.75	3.50

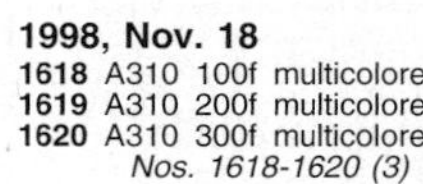

Mustafa Wahbi (1899-1949), Poet — A311

1999, May 25 **Litho.** ***Perf. 14¼***

1621	A311	100f multicolored	.90	.90

Environmental Protection — A312

Designs: 100f, Children, bandaged Earth. 200f, Earth as fruit in hands.

1999, Oct. 14 **Litho.** ***Perf. 13¼x13¾***

1622	A312	100f multi	.50	.50
1623	A312	200f multi	1.00	1.00

Hijazi Railway Museum A313

Train and: 100f, 200f, Map of Jordan, museum building. 300f, Museum building.

1999, Sept. 7 **Litho.** ***Perf. 13½x13¾***

1624-1626	A313	Set of 3	6.00	6.00

9th Arab Sports Tournament — A314

Bird mascot, emblem and: 50f, Weight lifting, tennis, wrestling, soccer. 100f, Torch. No. 1629, Shooting, fencing, swimming, track & field, vert. 300f, Flag, map, discus thrower, tennis player.
No. 1631, Basketball, volleyball, boxing, swimming.

Perf. 13¼x13¾, 13¾x13¼

1999, Aug. 15 **Litho.**

1627	A314	50f multi	.20	.20
1628	A314	100f multi	.65	.65
1629	A314	200f multi	1.40	1.40
1630	A314	300f multi	2.25	2.25
		Nos. 1627-1630 (4)	4.50	4.50

Imperf

Size: 90x70mm

1631	A314	200f multi	3.25	3.25

UPU, 125th Anniv. A315

Designs: 100f, "125," UPU emblems, stripes of airmail envelope. No. 1633, Airmail envelope with UPU emblem.

No. 1634, Like No. 1633, yellow background.

1999, Oct. 9 ***Perf. 13¼x13¾***

1632 A315 100f multi .65 .65
1633 A315 200f multi 1.10 1.10

Imperf

Size: 90x70mm

1634 A315 200f multi 2.50 2.50

Gulf of Aqaba Corals A316

Designs: 50f, Pachyseris speciosa. 100f, Acropora digitifera. No. 1637, 200f, Oxypora lacera. 300f, Fungia echinata.

No. 1639, 200f, Gorgonia.

1999, Oct. 2 Litho. ***Perf. 13½x13¾***

1635-1638 A316 Set of 4 4.00 4.00

Imperf

Size: 90x70mm

1639 A316 200f multi *12.00 12.00*

Cradle of Civilizations — A317

Archaeological sites — Petra: No. 1640, 100f, Al-Deir. No. 1641, 200f, Khazneh. No. 1642, 300f, Obelisk tomb.

Jerash: No. 1643, 100f, Cardo Maximus. No. 1644, 200f, Temple of Artemis. No. 1645, 300f, Nymphaeum.

Amman: No. 1646, 100f, Roman Theater. No. 1647, 200f, Citadel. No. 1648, 300f, Ain Ghazal statues.

Wadi Rum and Aqaba: No. 1649, 100f, Camel riders, Wadi Rum. No. 1650, 200f, House, Aqaba. No. 1651, Ruins, Aqaba.

Madaba: No. 1652, 100f, Mosaic. No. 1653, 200f, Church. No. 1654, 300f, Mosaic map of Jerusalem.

Baptism Site (Bethany): No. 1655, Plant life near water. No. 1656, 200f, Aerial view. No. 1657, 300f, Excavation site.

Aljoun: No. 1658, 100f, Ruins. No. 1659, 200f, Ruins diff. No. 1660, 300f, Ruins, diff.

Pella: No. 1661, 100f, Ruins of Byzantine cathedral. No. 1662, 200f, Three large pillars. No. 1663, 300f, Ruins.

1999-2000 Litho. ***Perf. 13½x14***

1640-1663 A317 Set of 12 23.00 23.00

Issued: #1640-1645, 10/24; #1646-1651, 10/31; #1652-1654, 12/22; #1655-1657, 12/23; #1658-1663, 3/7/00.

See Nos. 1688-1693.

Museum of Political History — A318

100f, Building interior. 200f, Museum entrance and plaza. 300f, Museum entrance.

1999, Nov. 14 Litho. ***Perf. 13½x14***

1664-1666 A318 Set of 3 3.75 3.75

Jordan Philatelic Club, 20th Anniv. — A318a

Designs: 100f, #534H and other stamps. 200f, #284 and other stamps.

1999, Nov. 14 ***Perf. 14¼***

1666A-1666B A318a Set of 2 1.50 1.50

SOS Children's Village, Irbid — A318b

100f, SOS Children's Village 50th anniv. emblem, Jordanian flag. 200f, Woman, children.

1999, Nov. 23

1666C-1666D A318b Set of 2 1.50 1.50

Coronation of King Abdullah II — A319

1999, Dec. 27 Litho. ***Perf. 11¾***

Frame Color

1667 A319 100f red .90 .90
1668 A319 200f green .90 .90
1669 A319 300f blue .90 .90

Souvenir Sheet

1670 A319 200f gold 1.00 1.00

King Abdullah II and Queen Rania A319a

1999, Dec. 27 Litho. ***Perf. 11¾***

1670A A319a 100f red .95 .95
1670B A319a 200f green .95 .95
1670C A319a 300f blue .95 .95

Souvenir Sheet

1670D A319a 200f gold *5.25 5.25*

Issued: 1670D, 12/27/99.

Numbers have been reserved for three additional stamps in this set. The editors would like to examine any examples of them.

King Abdullah II, 38th Birthday A320

King, crown and: 100f, Olive branches. 200f, Nos. #1672 #1674, Flag, "38," horiz. 300f, Flag, "38," eagle, olive branch, horiz.

Perf 12, Imperf (#1674)

2000, Jan. 30 Litho.

1671-1673 A320 Set of 3 3.00 3.00

Size: 90x74mm

1674 A320 200f multi *3.50 3.50*

Geneva Convention, 50th Anniv. — A321

Perf. 13½x13¾

2000, Feb. 15 Litho.

1675 Horiz. strip of 3 3.50 3.50
a. A321 100f lt bl & multi .50 .50
b. A321 200f ocher & multi 1.00 1.00
c. A321 300f gray & multi 1.50 1.50

Dated 1999.

Millennium A322

No. 1678: a, Jordanian flag, "Jordan, The River & The Land of the Baptism" in English. b, Fish in river. c, As "a," with Arabic inscription.

Perf. 13¼x13¾

2000, Feb. 22 Litho.

1678 Strip of 3 3.25 3.25
a. A322 100f multi .45 .45
b. A322 200f multi .90 .90
c. A322 300f multi 1.25 1.25

King Abdullah II, Houses of Worship and Pope John Paul II — A323

Color of lower panel: 100f, Dull blue green. 200f, Lilac. 300f, Bright yellow green.

2000, Mar. 20 Litho. ***Perf. 12***

1679-1681 A323 Set of 3 3.25 3.25

Visit of Pope Paul VI to Jordan, 36th anniv.

Visit of Pope John Paul II to Jordan A324

Pope John Paul II, King Abdullah II and: 100f, "2000." 200f, River. 300f, Vatican and Jordanian flags, map of Jordan. No. 1685, Pope, baptism of Christ, vert.

Perf 12, Imperf (#1685)

2000, Mar. 20

1682-1684 A324 Set of 3 3.25 3.25

Size: 70x90mm

1685 A324 200f multi *17.50 17.50*

World Meteorological Organization, 50th Anniv. — A325

Designs: 100f, Globe, emblem, anniversary emblem. 200f, Globe with arrows, emblem, anniversary emblem.

2000, Mar. 23 Litho. ***Perf. 12***

1686 A325 100f multi .75 .75
1687 A325 200f multi 1.25 1.25

Cradle of Civilizations Type of 1999

Archaeological sites — Palaces: No. 1688, 100f, Mushatta. No. 1689, 200f, Kharaneh. No. 1690, 300f, Amra.

Um Qais: No. 1691, 100f, Decumanus. No. 1692, 200f, Amphitheater. No. 1693, 300f, Ruins.

2000, Apr. 7 Litho. ***Perf. 13½x14***

Palaces

1688-1690 A317 Set of 3 4.00 4.00

Um Qais

1691-1693 A317 Set of 3 4.00 4.00
a. Sheet, #1640-1663, 1688-1693 40.00 —

Scouting in Jordan, 90th Anniv. A326

"90" and: 100f, Emblem, Jordanian flag. 200f, Tents. 300f, Tents, Jordanian flag. No. 1697, Like No. 1694.

Perf 12, Imperf (#1697)

2000, May 11 Litho.

1694-1696 A326 Set of 3 5.00 5.00

Size: 90x70mm

1697 A326 200f multi *7.50 7.50*

Expo 2000, Hanover — A327

Designs: No. 1698, 200f, Inscribed clay tablet. 300f, Artifact with two heads.

No. 1700, 200f, King, Queen, Jordan pavilion interior.

2000, June 1 Litho. ***Perf. 11¾***

Granite Paper

1698-1699 A327 Set of 2 3.50 3.50

Imperf

Size: 90x70mm

1700 A327 200f multi 3.00 3.00

Palace of Justice A328

Palace and: 100f, Scales of justice. 200f, Scales, Jordanian flag.

2000, June 25 Unwmk. ***Perf. 12***

1701 A328 100f multi .75 .75

Wmk. 388

1702 A328 200f multi 1.25 1.25

A number has been reserved for an additional stamp in this set. The editors would like to examine it.

Al-Amal Cancer Center — A329

Emblem and: 200f, Building. 300f, Family.

Perf. 11¾

2000, July 17 Litho. Unwmk.

Granite Paper

1704-1705 A329 Set of 2 3.75 3.75

Flora and Fauna — A330

Designs: 50f, Dove. 100f, Arabian oryx. 150f, Caracal. 200f, Red fox. 300f, Jal'ad iris. 400f, White broom.

2000, Sept. 28 ***Perf. 14¼***

Booklet Stamps

1706 A330 50f multi .35 .30
1707 A330 100f multi .75 .50
a. Booklet pane, 2 each #1706-1707 4.00 —
1708 A330 150f multi 1.25 .60
1709 A330 200f multi 1.50 .80
a. Booklet pane, 2 each #1708-1709 7.00 —
1710 A330 300f multi 2.50 1.75
1711 A330 400f multi 3.00 1.90
a. Booklet pane, 2 each #1710-1711 13.00 —
Booklet, #1707a, 1709a, 1711a 30.00

World Conservation Union — A331

Background color: 200f, Green. 300f, Blue.

2000, Oct. 4 ***Perf. 11¾***

Granite Paper

1712-1713 A331 Set of 2 3.50 3.50

Tourist Sites A332

Designs: 50f, Petra. 100f, Jerash. 150f, Mount Nebo. 200f, Dead Sea. 300f, Aqaba. 400f, Wadi Rum.

2000, Oct. 9 ***Perf. 14¼***

Booklet Stamps

1714 A332 50f multi .35 .35
1715 A332 100f multi .75 .60
a. Booklet pane, 2 each #1714-1715 2.25 —
1716 A332 150f multi 1.25 .90
1717 A332 200f multi 1.75 1.10
a. Booklet pane, 2 each #1716-1717 6.00 —
1718 A332 300f multi 2.25 1.50
1719 A332 400f multi 2.75 2.25
a. Booklet pane, 2 each #1718-1719 10.00 —
Booklet, #1715a, 1717a, 1719a 22.50

King Hussein (1935-99) A333

Designs: 50f, King, vert. No. 1721, 150f, No. 1723, 200f, King and wreath. No. 1722, 200f, King, symbols of industry and agriculture.

2000, Nov. 14 Litho. ***Perf. 11¾***

Granite Paper

1720-1722 A333 Set of 3 *2.75 2.75*

Size: 90x70mm

Imperf

1723 A333 200f multi *4.50 4.50*

UN High Commissioner for Refugees, 50th Anniv. — A334

Designs: 200f, Man, women, child. 300f, Emblem.

2000, Dec. 3 Litho. ***Perf. 11¾***

Granite Paper

1724-1725 A334 Set of 2 3.50 3.50

13th Arab Summit Conference A335

Emblem, map of Middle East and: 50f, Jordanian flag. 200f, Jordanian flags. 250f, King Abdullah II.

2001, Aug. 1 ***Perf. 14***

1726-1728 A335 Set of 3 3.00 3.00

Palestinian Intifada A336

Dome of the Rock and: 200f, Rock throwers, man carrying flag. 300f, Rock throwers, Israeli troops.

2001, Aug. 5

1729-1730 A336 Set of 2 3.00 3.00

Mohammed Al-Dorra, Boy Killed in Intifada Crossfire A337

Designs: 200f, Al-Dorra and father, Dome of the Rock. 300f, Close-up of Al-Dorra, Al-Dorra dead on father's lap.

2001, Aug. 5

1731-1732 A337 Set of 2 3.00 3.00

Healthy Non-smoking Students — A338

Designs: 200f, Students. 300f, Cartoon character, vert.

2001, Sept. 1

1733-1734 A338 Set of 2 3.00 3.00

Sports For People With Special Needs — A339

Stylized figures and: 200f, Man in wheelchair. 300f, Woman.

2001, Sept. 15

1735-1736 A339 Set of 2 3.00 3.00

Olive Trees A340

Designs: 200f, Olives on branch, tree, map of Jordan. 300f, Woman picking olives, vert.

2001, Oct. 1

1737-1738 A340 Set of 2 3.00 3.00

Year of Dialogue Among Civilizations A341

Emblem and: 200f, Family, handshake, world map. 300f, Other stylized drawings.

2001, Oct. 21

1739-1740 A341 Set of 2 3.00 3.00

Cooperation Between Jordan and Japan — A342

Designs: 200f, Sheikh Hussein Bridge, flags. 300f, King Hussein Bridge, handshake.

2001, Nov. 12 Litho. ***Perf. 14¼***

1741-1742 A342 Set of 2 3.00 3.00

Jordan - People's Republic of China Diplomatic Relations, 25th Anniv. A343

Designs: 200f, Dove with envelope. 300f, King Abdullah II and Chinese Pres. Jiang Zemin.

2002 ***Perf. 12***

1743-1744 A343 Set of 2 2.25 2.25

Amman, 2002 Arab Cultural Capital A344

Designs: 100f, Arabic script, star. 200f, Pen, torch. 300f, Amphitheater.

2002 ***Perf. 14¼***

1745-1747 A344 Set of 3 3.00 3.00

Paintings A345

Paintings by, 100f, Rafiq Laham. 150f, Mahmoud Taha, horiz. 200f, Mohanna Durra. 300f, Wijdan, horiz.

2002, July 2 ***Perf. 13¼***

1748-1751 A345 Set of 4 4.50 4.50

Vision 2020 — A346

Designs: 200f, Symbols of business and technology. 300f, Fingers, electronic device.

2002 Litho. ***Perf. 13¼***

1752-1753 A346 Set of 2 2.25 2.25

Migratory Birds A347

Designs: 100f, Goldfinch. No. 1755, 200f, Rufous bush robin. 300f, White stork.
No. 1757, 200f, Golden oriole, goshawk, ortolan bunting, hoopoe.

2002 ***Perf. 13¼***
1754-1756 A347 Set of 3 4.00 4.00

Imperf

Size: 70x90mm

1757 A347 200f multi *8.50 8.50*

Hashemite Rulers A348

No. 1758: a, Sherif Hussein bin Ali. b, King Abdullah. c, King Talal bin Abdullah. d, King Hussein bin Talal. e, King Abdullah II.

2003, July 2 **Litho.** ***Perf. 14***
1758 Miniature sheet of 5 4.50 4.50
a.-e. A348 200f Any single .75 .75

Salt Museum A349

Views of building exterior: 150f, 250f.

2003, July 2
1759-1760 A349 Set of 2 1.75 1.75

Trees A350

Designs: 50f, Cupressus sempervirens. 100f, Pistacia atlantica. 200f, Quercus aegilops.

2003, Aug. 7
1761-1763 A350 Set of 3 2.25 2.25

Flowers A351

Designs: 50f, Cistanche tubulosa. 100f, Ophioglossum polyphyllum, vert. 150f, Narcissus tazetta. 200f, Gynandriris sisyrinchium, vert.

2003, Aug. 7
1764-1767 A351 Set of 4 3.00 3.00

Birds of Prey — A352

Designs: 100f, Ciraetus gallicus. No. 1769, 200f, Falco peregrinus. 300f, Accipiter nisus.
No. 1771, 200f, Ciraetus gallicus, diff.

2003, Dec. 9 **Litho.** ***Perf. 14***
1768-1770 A352 Set of 3 3.50 3.50

Size: 70x90mm

Imperf

1771 A352 200f multi 6.00 6.00

Royal Cars Museum A353

Designs: 100f, Red sports car. 150f, Black limousine. 300f, White limousine.
200f, Three automobiles.

2003, Dec. 23 **Litho.** ***Perf. 14***
1772-1774 A353 Set of 3 3.50 3.50

Size: 90x70mm

Imperf

1775 A353 200f multi 4.50 4.50

Jordan Post Company A354

Emblem and: 50f, Arch. 100f, Pillars, vert.

2003, Dec. 23 **Litho.** ***Perf. 14***
1776-1777 A354 Set of 2 1.00 1.00

Triumphal Arch Type of 1993-98

2003 **Litho.** ***Perf. 12¾x13¼***

Granite Paper

1777A A267 25f gray & multi — —

Arabian Horses A355

Various horses: 5pi, 7.50pi, 12.50pi, 15pi, 25pi.
10pi, Two horses, horiz.

2004, Dec. 27 **Litho.** ***Perf. 14¼***

Granite Paper

1778-1782 A355 Set of 5 3.25 3.25

Imperf

Size: 90x70mm

1783 A355 10pi multi *8.50 8.50*

Ain Ghazal Statues A356

Various statues: 5pi, 7.50pi, 12.50pi, 15pi, 25pi.
10pi, Two statues.

2004, Dec. 29

Granite Paper

1784-1788 A356 Set of 5 3.00 3.00

Imperf

Size: 70x90mm

1789 A356 10pi multi *5.00 5.00*

Children's Paintings — A357

Various paintings: 5pi, 7.50pi, 12.50pi, 15pi, 25pi.
10pi, Parts of various paintings.

2004, Dec. 27

Granite Paper

1790-1794 A357 Set of 5 2.75 2.75

Imperf

Size: 90x70mm

1795 A357 10pi multi *5.50 5.50*

Miniature Sheet

Nazareth Iris — A358

No. 1796 — Various photographs of Nazareth Iris: a, 5pi. b, 7.50pi. c, 10pi (70x90mm). d, 12.50pi. e, 15pi. f, 25pi.

2004, Dec. 29 ***Perf. 14¼***

Granite Paper

1796 A358 Sheet of 6, #a-f *6.00 6.00*

Miniature Sheet

Details From Mosaic Floor of Church of the Holy Martyrs Lot and Procopius, Mount Nebo — A359

No. 1797: a, 10pi, Man with scythe (68x90mm). b, 10pi, Man with flute, grapes. c, 15pi, Building. d, 25pi, Man with Basket.

2004, Dec. 27 **Litho.**

Granite Paper

1797 A359 Sheet of 4, #a-d *6.00 6.00*

Expo 2005, Aichi, Japan A360

No. 1798: a, Dead Sea salt crystal. b, Dead Sea salt crystal, diff. c, Dead Sea salt crystal, diff. d, Dead Sea (70x70mm).

2005, Aug. 7 **Litho.** ***Perf. 13¾***
1798 Sheet of 4 3.25 3.25
a. A360 5pi multi .30 .30
b. A360 7.50pi multi .45 .45
c. A360 12.50pi multi .75 .75
d. A360 20pi multi .90 .90

Fish — A361

Various Red Sea fish: 5f, 5pi, 7.50pi, 12.50pi.

Perf. 13½x13¾

2005, Dec. 27 **Litho.**
1799-1802 A361 Set of 4 2.50 2.50

Souvenir Sheet

1803 A361 20pi Lionfish *5.00 5.00*

Intl. Sports Year — A362

Children's drawings of: 1pi, Tennis player. 10pi, Medal winner. 15pi, Soccer game, horiz. No. 1807, 20pi, Swimmer, horiz.
No. 1808, Basketball player.

Perf. 13½x13¾, 13¾x13½

2005, Dec. 27
1804-1807 A362 Set of 4 3.50 3.50

Size: 71x90mm

Imperf

1808 A362 20pi multi *6.00 6.00*

Worldwide Fund for Nature — A363

Arabian oryx: 1.50pi, Grazing. 5pi, Three oryx. 7.50pi, Adults and juvenile. 12.50pi, Two adults.
20pi, Adult, three oryx in background.

2005, Dec. 27 ***Perf. 13¾x13½***
1809-1812 A363 Set of 4 *7.25 7.25*

Souvenir Sheet

1813 A363 20pi multi *22.50 22.50*

Child Protection — A364

Designs: 7.50pi, Hands of adult and child. 10pi, Mother holding infant. 12.50pi, Adult hugging child.
20pi, Child.

2005, Dec. 27 ***Perf. 13¾***
1814-1816 A364 Set of 3 3.00 3.00

Size: 70x90mm

Imperf

1817 A364 20pi multi *6.50 6.50*

Friendship of Jordan and Japan — A365

Design: 7.50pi, Gallery of Japanese calligraphy. 12.50pi, Building. 15pi, Building at night.
20pi, Pottery in museum gallery.

2005, Dec. 27 ***Perf. 13¾x13½***
1818-1820 A365 Set of 3 2.75 2.75

Size: 70x90mm

Imperf

1821 A365 20pi multi *5.75 5.75*

Islamic Art Revival A366

Designs: 5pi, Woodworker. 7.50pi, Engraver. 10pi, Calligrapher. 15pi, Woodworker, diff.
20pi, Calligrapher, diff.

2005, Dec. 27 ***Perf. 13¾x13½***
1822-1825 A366 Set of 4 3.00 3.00

Size: 90x71mm

Imperf

1826 A366 20pi multi *6.00 6.00*

Modern Architecture A367

Various buildings with panel color of: 7.50pi, Green. 10pi, Lemon, horiz. 12.50pi, Red brown.
20pi, Brown, horiz.

2006, Jan. 1 **Litho.** ***Perf. 14***
1827-1829 A367 Set of 3 3.50 3.50

Imperf

Size: 90x70mm

1830 A367 20pi multi *4.50 4.50*

Government Vehicles — A368

Designs: 10pi, Police car. 12.50pi, Fire truck. 17.50pi, Garbage truck. No. 1834, 20pi, Mail vans.
No. 1835, 20pi, Ambulance.

2006, Jan. 1 ***Perf. 14***
1831-1834 A368 Set of 4 3.75 3.75

Imperf

Size: 90x70mm

1835 A368 20pi multi *4.50 4.50*

Ancient Coins — A369

Various coins with background color of: 5pi, Purple. 7.50pi, Yellow brown. 10pi, Gray. 12.50pi, Blue. 15pi, Dark red.
30pi, Dark blue, horiz.

2006, Jan. 1 ***Perf. 13¾***
1836-1840 A369 Set of 5 4.50 4.50

Imperf

Size: 90x70mm

1841 A369 30pi multi *6.50 6.50*

2006 World Cup Soccer Championships, Germany A370

Background color: 5pi, Light blue. 7.50pi, Yellow. 10pi, Tan. 12.50pi, Green. 15pi, Blue.
30pi, Yellow green, horiz.

2006, Jan. 1 ***Perf. 14***
1842-1846 A370 Set of 5 4.50 4.50

Imperf

Size: 90x70mm

1847 A370 30pi multi *5.50 5.50*

Art — A371

Various works of art by unnamed artists: 5pi, 10pi, 15pi. 20pi.
No. 1852, Four works of art, horiz.

2006, Oct. 21 **Litho.** ***Perf. 14¼***

Granite Paper

1848-1851 A371 Set of 4 3.50 3.50

Imperf

Size: 90x70mm

1852 A371 20pi multi *6.00 6.00*

Desert Reptiles A372

Designs: 5pi, Lizard. 7.50pi, Snake. 10pi, Lizards. 12.50pi, Lizard, diff. 15pi, Lizard, horiz. 20pi, Snake, diff.
No. 1859, Lizard, diff., horiz.

2006, Oct. 21 ***Perf. 14¼***

Granite Paper

1853-1858 A372 Set of 6 3.25 3.25

Imperf

Size: 90x70mm

1859 A372 20pi multi *5.25 5.25*

Information and Communications Technology in Education — A373

Design: 7.50pi, Man at computer. 12.50pi, Woman punching keys on keypad. 15pi, Man and computer screen. 20pi, Man using cellular phone.
No. 1864, Circuit board, design of unissued 50f stamp showing finger punching keypad.

2006, Nov. 11 ***Perf. 14¼***

Granite Paper

1860-1863 A373 Set of 4 2.75 2.75

Imperf

Size: 70x90mm

1864 A373 20pi multi *5.50 5.50*

National Symbols A374

Designs: 5pi, King Abdullah II in dress uniform. 7.50pi, King Abdullah II in suit and tie. 10pi, Jordanian soldiers, horiz. 12.50pi, King Abdullah II in camouflage uniform. 15pi, Flag, horiz. 20pi, Men in army uniforms and native garb, horiz. 25pi, Parade of tanks, horiz. 30pi, Flag and rose, horiz.

2006, Nov. 11 ***Perf. 14¼***

Granite Paper

1865-1872 A374 Set of 8 6.25 6.25

Pitchers and Spouted Pots — A375

Designs: 10pi, Spouted pot. 20pi, Spouted pot with legs. 30pi, Pitcher.
25pi, Spouted pot, horiz.

Perf. 13½x13¾

2007, Dec. 31 **Litho.**
1873-1875 A375 Set of 3 1.75 1.75

Imperf

Size: 90x70mm

1876 A375 25pi multi *2.25 2.25*

Culture and Identity A376

Designs: 10pi, Books. No. 1878, 20pi, Lute. 25pi, Bottle. 30pi, Arabic text.
No. 1881, 20pi, Arabic text, paint brushes, bottle, lute, books.

2007, Dec. 31 ***Perf. 13½x13¾***
1877-1880 A376 Set of 4 2.40 2.40

Imperf

Size: 70x90mm

1881 A376 20pi multi *1.50 1.50*

Butterflies A377

Various butterflies with denomination color of: 10pi, Orange. 15pi, Yellow green. 20pi, Gray. 25pi, Olive gray, horiz. 30pi, Orange, horiz.
40pi, Olive green, horiz.

Perf. 13½x13¾, 13¼x13½

2007, Dec. 31
1882-1886 A377 Set of 5 3.00 3.00

Imperf

Size: 90x70mm

1887 A377 40pi multi *4.50 4.50*

Aqaba A378

Designs: 10pi, Arch and beach. 15pi, Scuba diver. 20pi, Motor boats. 30pi, Double-masted ship.

2008, July 16 **Litho.** ***Perf. 14¼***

Granite Paper

1888-1891 A378 Set of 4 2.10 2.10

Traditional Women's Clothing A379

Designs: 10pi, Mafraq. 15pi, Ma'an. 20pi, Amman. 25pi, Jerash. 30pi, Salt.

2008, July 16
Granite Paper
1892-1896 A379 Set of 5 3.00 3.00

Fruit — A380

Designs: 10pi, Oranges. 15pi, Cherries. 20pi, Figs. 25pi, Pomegranates. 30pi, Grapes.

2008, July 16
Granite Paper
1897-1901 A380 Set of 5 3.00 3.00

Petra — A381

Designs: 10pi, Sculpture of face. 15pi, Ceramic plate. 20pi, Sculpture of grapevine. 25pi, Siq al Barid fresco. 30pi, Rock formations. 40pi, Treasury.

2008, July 16 Litho. *Perf. 14¼*
Granite Paper
1902-1906 A381 Set of 5 3.00 3.00
Size: 66x86mm
1907 A381 40pi multi 1.25 1.25
Imperf
1908 A381 40pi multi 1.25 1.25

Bridge A382

50th Anniversary Emblem of Engineer's Association A383

2008, Sept. 22 Litho. *Perf. 14¼*
Granite Paper
1909 A382 15pi shown .45 .45
1910 A383 20pi shown .60 .60
1911 A382 25pi Power station .70 .70
Nos. 1909-1911 (3) 1.75 1.75

2008 Summer Olympics, Beijing A384

Desings: 20pi, Taekwondo. 30pi, Equestrian. 40pi, Table tennis. 50pi, Running.

2008, Sept. 22 Litho.
Granite Paper
1912-1915 A384 Set of 4 4.00 4.00

Musical Instruments A385

Designs: 20pi, Oud. 40pi, Rebab. 60pi, Zither. 80pi, Flutes. 100pi, Tambourine and drum.
50pi, Oud, rebab, zither, flutes, tambourine and drum, horiz.

2008, Sept. 22 *Perf. 14¼*
Granite Paper
1916-1920 A385 Set of 5 8.50 8.50
Imperf
Size: 90x70mm
1921 A385 50pi multi 1.40 1.40

Flowers A386

Designs: 5pi, Egyptian catchfly. 10pi, Lupine. 15pi, Judean viper's bugloss. 20pi, Pimpernel. 30pi, Asiatic crowfoot. 40pi, Grape hyacinth. No. 1928, 50pi, Large flowered sage. 60pi, Star of Bethlehem. 80pi, Pyramidalis. 100pi, Calotropis.
No. 1932, 50pi, Cyclamen, horiz.

2008, Nov. 25 Litho. *Perf. 14¼*
Granite Paper
1922-1931 A386 Set of 10 12.00 12.00
Imperf
Size: 90x70mm
1932 A386 50pi multi 1.40 1.40

Art From Quseir Amra UNESCO World Heritage Site — A387

Designs: 40pi, Woman with arm raised. 60pi, Grapes. 80pi, Hunters on horseback, bath. 100pi, Face of woman.
50pi, Quseir Amra Palace.

2008, Nov. 25 *Perf. 14¼x14*
Granite Paper
1933-1936 A387 Set of 4 8.00 8.00
Imperf
Size: 90x69mm
1937 A387 50pi multi 1.40 1.40

Hejaz Railway, Cent. A388

Designs: 20pi, Train on bridge. 30pi, Locomotive and tender. 50pi, Station and road.

2009, Feb. 1 Litho. *Perf. 14¼*
Granite Paper
1938-1940 A388 Set of 3 3.00 3.00
Dated 2008.

Birds A389

Designs: 10pi, Mallard duck. 15pi, Saker. 20pi, Crouser cream. 30pi, Palestine sunbird. 40pi, Hoopoe. No. 1946, 50pi, Black francolin. 60pi, Little green bee-eater. 80pi, Sinai rosefinch.
No. 1949, 50pi, Kingfisher.

2009, Feb. 1 *Perf. 14¼*
Granite Paper
1941-1948 A389 Set of 8 8.75 8.75
Imperf
Size: 90x70mm
1949 A389 50pi multi *4.75 4.75*
Dated 2008.

Arabian Coffee Tools — A390

Designs: 40pi, Mortar and pestle. 60pi, Coffee pots and roasting pan. 80pi, Coffee pot and cups. 100pi, Bowl, roasting pan and shovel.
50pi, Mortar, pestle, coffee pot, bowl, roasting pan and shovel.

2009, Mar. 1 *Perf. 14¼*
Granite Paper
1950-1953 A390 Set of 4 8.00 8.00
Imperf
Size: 70x90mm
1954 A390 50pi multi *4.25 4.25*
Dated 2008.

Traditional Costumes A391

Close-ups of costumes and: 40pi, Woman. 60pi, Woman, diff. 80pi, Woman, diff. 100pi, Man and woman.
50pi, Woman only.

2009, Mar. 1 *Perf. 14¼*
Granite Paper
1955-1958 A391 Set of 4 8.00 8.00
Imperf
Size: 70x90mm
1959 A391 50pi multi *4.25 4.25*

Visit of Pope Benedict XVI to Jordan A392

Designs: 20pi, Pope Benedict XVI, King Abdullah II, walkway to river. 30pi, Pope Benedict XVI. 40pi, Pope and King shaking hands.
50pi, Pope and King shaking hands, walkway to river, crucifix.

2009, May 8 *Perf. 14¼*
Granite Paper
1960-1962 A392 Set of 3 2.60 2.60
Imperf
Size: 90x70mm
1963 A392 50pi multi *4.75 4.75*

King Abdullah II, 10th Anniv. of Accession to Throne — A393

2009, June 9 *Perf. 13¾*
Granite Paper
Background Color

1964	A393	10pi	maroon	.30	.30
1965	A393	15pi	dark blue	.45	.45
1966	A393	20pi	bright blue	.60	.60
1967	A393	25pi	tan	.70	.70
1968	A393	30pi	dark green	.85	.85
1969	A393	35pi	blue	1.00	1.00
1970	A393	40pi	purple	1.10	1.10
1971	A393	45pi	black	1.25	1.25
1972	A393	50pi	brown	1.40	1.40
1973	A393	1d	blue gray	3.00	3.00
	Nos. 1964-1973 (10)			10.65	10.65

E-Government A394

Designs: 20pi, Computer cables. 30pi, Spiral emblem. 40pi, Internet address of Jordanian government. 50pi, Letter, compass, Earth.

2009, Aug. 25 Litho. *Perf. 13¼*
Granite Paper
1974-1977 A394 Set of 4 4.00 4.00

A395 A396

A397 A398

A399

University emblems: No. 1983, Al-Hussein Bin Jalal University. No. 1984, Tafila Technical University. No. 1985, German-Jordanian University. No. 1986, Al-Balqa Applied University. No. 1987, Yarmouk University.

2009, Aug. 25 ***Perf. 13¼***
Granite Paper

1978 A395 20pi multi .60 .60
1979 A396 20pi multi .60 .60
1980 A397 20pi multi .60 .60
1981 A398 20pi multi .60 .60
1982 A399 20pi multi .60 .60
1983 A399 20pi multi .60 .60
1984 A399 20pi multi .60 .60
1985 A399 20pi multi .60 .60
1986 A399 20pi multi .60 .60
1987 A399 20pi multi .60 .60
Nos. 1978-1987 (10) 6.00 6.00

Waterfalls, Ma'een — A400

Designs: 10pi, Waterfall, orange brown panel. 20pi, Building and mountain, fawn panel. 30pi, Waterfall, black panel. 40pi, Waterfall, gray green panel. 50pi, Waterfall, olive brown panel.
60pi, Waterfall, blue panel.

2009, Aug. 25 **Litho.**
Granite Paper

1988-1992 A400 Set of 5 4.25 4.25

Size: 70x91mm
Imperf

1993 A400 60pi multi 1.75 1.75

Animals A401

Designs: 10pi, Horse. 20pi, Rabbits. 30pi, Fox. 40pi, Maha gazelle. 50pi, Gazelle.
60pi, Camel.

2009, Aug. 25 **Litho.**
Granite Paper

1994-1998 A401 Set of 5 4.25 4.25

Size: 70x91mm
Imperf

1999 A401 60pi multi 1.75 1.75

Vegetables A402

No. 2000: a, Corn. b, Onions, garlic. c, Beans, peas, okra. d, Cabbages. e, Eggplants. f, Pumpkins. g, Bell peppers. h, Hot peppers. i, Radishes, turnips, beets. j, Tomatoes, zucchini.

2009, Aug. 25 ***Perf. 13¼***
Granite Paper

2000 Sheet of 10 6.00 6.00
a.-j. A402 20pi Any single .60 .60

Environmental Protection — A403

Designs: 20pi, Tree, shrub, flower. 30pi, Man and fire. 40pi, Animals grazing. 50pi, Litter in stream.

2009 **Litho.**
Granite Paper

2001-2004 A403 Set of 4 4.00 4.00

Insects — A404

Designs: 10pi, Beetle. 15pi, Butterfly. 20pi, Ladybug. 25pi, Bee. 30pi, Mantis. 40pi, Moth. 50pi, Dragonfly. 60pi, Fly. 80pi, Grasshopper. 100pi, Dragonflies.

2009, Dec. 13 **Litho.** ***Perf. 13¼***
Granite Paper

2005-2014 A404 Set of 10 12.50 12.50

Nos. 588-590 Surcharged

Methods and Perfs As Before
2009, Dec. 20

2015 A82 80pi on 120f #588 2.25 2.25
2016 A82 80pi on 180f #589 2.25 2.25
2017 A82 80pi on 200f #590 2.25 2.25
Nos. 2015-2017 (3) 6.75 6.75

No. 1471b Surcharged

Tourism A405

Perf. 12¾x13¼
2009, Dec. 20 **Litho.**

2018 A267 80pi on 25f multi 2.25 2.25

Sites in: 10pi, Ajlun. 20pi, Amman. 30pi, Karak. 40pi, Showbak.
50pi, Jerash.

2010, Oct. 3 ***Perf. 14***

2019-2022 A405 Set of 4 3.00 3.00

Size: 90x70mm
Imperf

2023 A405 50pi multi 1.50 1.50

Miniature Sheet

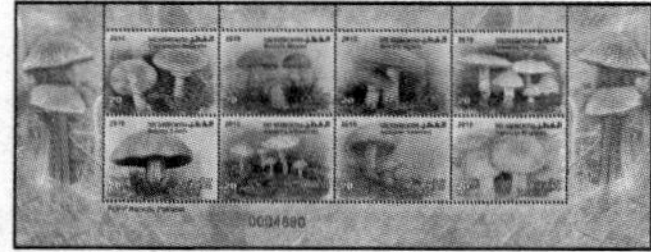
Mushrooms — A406

No. 2024: a, Cortinarius balteatus. b, Russula bicolor. c, Red fly agaric. d, Amanita muscaria. e, Boletus edulis. f, Amanita albocreata. g, Agaricus anderwij. h, Agaricus bisporus.

2010, Oct. 3 ***Perf. 14***

2024 A406 20pi Sheet of 8, #a-h 4.50 4.50

Mosques in Jordan A407

Designs: 10pi, Jordan University Mosque. 20pi, Abu-Darwiesh Mosque. 30pi, Al Hussainy Mosque. 40pi, King Abdullah Mosque. 50pi, King Hussein bin Talal Mosque.

2010, Nov. 30

2025-2029 A407 Set of 5 4.25 4.25

Sports — A408

Designs: 10pi, Skydiving. 20pi, Swimming. 30pi, Hot-air ballooning. 40pi, Racing boats.
50pi, Jordan Rally.

2010, Nov. 30 ***Perf. 14***

2030-2033 A408 Set of 4 3.00 3.00

Size: 70x90mm
Imperf

2034 A408 50pi multi 1.50 1.50

SEMI-POSTAL STAMPS

Locust Campaign Issue

Nos. 145-156 Overprinted

1930, Apr. 1 **Wmk. 4** ***Perf. 14***

B1 A1 2(m) Prus blue 1.60 *3.50*
a. Inverted overprint 200.00
B2 A1 3(m) rose 1.60 *3.50*
B3 A1 4(m) green 1.75 *4.75*
B4 A1 5(m) orange 18.00 16.75
a. Double overprint 300.00
B5 A1 10(m) red 1.90 *3.50*
B6 A1 15(m) ultra 1.90 *3.50*
a. Inverted overprint 200.00
B7 A1 20(m) olive grn 1.90 *5.00*
B8 A2 50(m) claret 6.75 *11.50*
B9 A2 90(m) bister 15.00 *45.00*
B10 A2 100(m) lt blue 18.00 *47.50*
B11 A2 200(m) violet 42.50 *110.00*
B12 A2 500(m) brown 125.00 *160.00*
a. "C" of "Locust" omitted 750.00
Nos. B1-B12 (12) 235.90 *414.50*

These stamps were issued to raise funds to help combat a plague of locusts.

Catalogue values for unused stamps in this section, from this point to the end of the section, are for Never Hinged items.

Jerusalem — SP1

1997, Nov. 29 **Litho.** ***Perf. 13½x13***

B13 SP1 100f +10f bl & multi .75 .75
B14 SP1 200f +20f yel & multi 1.50 1.50
B15 SP1 300f +30f bl grn & multi 2.25 2.25
Nos. B13-B15 (3) 4.50 4.50

Breast Cancer Prevention — SP2

2009, Aug. 25 **Litho.** ***Perf. 13¼***
Granite Paper

B16 SP2 30pi +50pi multi 2.25 2.25

Jerusalem, Capital of Arab Culture — SP3

Panel color: 20pi+25pi, Orange. 30pi+25pi, Purple. 40pi+25pi, Red. 50pi+25pi, Gray green.

2009, Dec. 13 ***Perf. 13¼***
Granite Paper

B17-B20 SP3 Set of 4 6.75 6.75

AIR POST STAMPS

Catalogue values for unused stamps in this section are for Never Hinged items.

Plane and Globe — AP1

Temple of Artemis, Jerash — AP2

Perf. 13½x13
1950, Sept. 16 **Engr.** **Wmk. 4**

C1 AP1 5f org & red vio 1.25 .20
C2 AP1 10f pur & brown 1.25 .20
C3 AP1 15f ol grn & rose car 1.25 .20
C4 AP1 20f deep blue & blk 1.50 .60
C5 AP1 50f rose pink & dl grn 1.75 .75
C6 AP1 100f blue & brown 3.00 1.50
C7 AP1 150f blk & red org 4.50 2.25
Nos. C1-C7 (7) 14.50 5.70

1954 **Unwmk.** ***Perf. 12***

C8 AP2 5f blue blk & org .70 .20
C9 AP2 10f vio brn & ver .70 .20
C10 AP2 25f bl grn & ultra .85 .20
C11 AP2 35f dp plum & grnsh bl 1.00 .20
C12 AP2 40f car rose & blk 1.25 .20
C13 AP2 50f dp ultra & org yel 1.40 .40
C14 AP2 100f dk bl & vio brn 1.60 .75
C15 AP2 150f stl bl & red brn 2.50 1.00
Nos. C8-C15 (8) 10.00 3.15

1958-59 Wmk. 305 *Perf. 12*
C16 AP2 5f blue blk & org .80 .20
C17 AP2 10f vio brn & ver .80 .20
C18 AP2 25f bl grn & ultra .80 .20
C19 AP2 35f dp plum grnsh bl .80 .20
C20 AP2 40f car rose & blk 1.00 .50
C21 AP2 50f dp ultra & org yel ('59) 1.50 1.00
Nos. C16-C21 (6) 5.70 2.30

Stadium and Torch AP3

Perf. 11x11½
1964, July 12 Litho. Wmk. 305
C22 AP3 1f yellow & multi .40 .20
C23 AP3 4f red & multi .40 .20
C24 AP3 10f blue & multi .40 .20
C25 AP3 35f yel grn & multi .75 .40
a. Souvenir sheet of 4, #C22-C25 2.00 1.25
Nos. C22-C25 (4) 1.95 1.00

Opening of Hussein Sports City. No. C25a also exists imperf.

Gorgeous Bush-Shrike — AP4

Birds: 500f, Ornate hawk-eagle, vert. 1d, Gray-headed kingfisher, vert.

Perf. 14x14½
1964, Dec. 18 Photo. Unwmk.
Birds in Natural Colors
C26 AP4 150f lt grn, blk & car 27.50 11.00
C27 AP4 500f brt bl, blk & grn 70.00 30.00
C28 AP4 1d lt ol grn & blk 125.00 50.00
Nos. C26-C28 (3) 222.50 91.00

Pagoda, Olympic Torch and Emblem — AP5

1965, Mar. 5 Litho. *Perf. 14*
C29 AP5 10f deep rose .50 .20
C30 AP5 15f violet .60 .20
C31 AP5 20f blue .75 .20
C32 AP5 30f green .90 .20
C33 AP5 40f brown 1.40 .25
C34 AP5 60f carmine rose 2.00 .40
Nos. C29-C34 (6) 6.15 1.45

18th Olympic Games, Tokyo, Oct. 10-25, 1964. An imperf. 100f violet blue souvenir sheet exists. Size of stamp: 60x60mm. Value $12.50.

For overprints see Nos. C42A-C42F.

Forum, Jerash — AP6

Antiquities of Jerash: No. C36, South Theater. No. C37, Triumphal arch. No. C38, Temple of Artemis. No. C39, Cathedral steps. No. C40, Artemis Temple, gate. No. C41, Columns. No. C42, Columns and niche, South Theater. Nos. C39-C42 are vertical.

1965, June 22 Photo. *Perf. 14x15*
Center Multicolored
C35 AP6 55f bright pink 1.50 1.00
C36 AP6 55f light blue 1.50 1.00
C37 AP6 55f green 1.50 1.00
C38 AP6 55f black 1.50 1.00
C39 AP6 55f light green 1.50 1.00
C40 AP6 55f carmine rose 1.50 1.00
C41 AP6 55f gray 1.50 1.00
C42 AP6 55f blue 1.50 1.00
Nos. C35-C42 (8) 12.00 8.00

#C35-C38 are printed in horizontal rows of 4; #C39-C42 in vertical rows of 4; sheets of 16.

Nos. C29-C34 with Bilingual Ovpt. "James McDivitt / Edward White / 2-6-1965" and Rocket

1965, Sept. 25 Litho. *Perf. 14*
C42A AP5 10f deep rose 1.50 .95
C42B AP5 15f violet 2.00 1.40
C42C AP5 20f blue 2.50 2.00
C42D AP5 30f green 4.00 3.00
C42E AP5 40f brown 5.00 4.00
C42F AP5 60f carmine rose 6.50 5.75
Nos. C42A-C42F (6) 21.50 17.10

The imperf. 100f blue souvenir sheet exists overprinted. Value $21.50.

King Hussein Type of Regular Issue

1966, Jan. 15 Photo. *Perf. 14½x14*
Portrait in Brown
C43 A67 200f brt blue grn 5.75 1.25
C44 A67 500f light green 10.00 5.00
C45 A67 1d light ultra 17.00 9.00
Nos. C43-C45 (3) 32.75 15.25

Animal Type of Regular Issue, 1967

Animals: 4f, Striped hyena. 30f, Arabian stallion. 60f, Persian gazelle.

1967, Feb. 11 Photo. *Perf. 14x15*
C46 A70 4f dk brn & multi 1.75 .20
C47 A70 30f lt bl & multi 2.25 .45
C48 A70 60f yellow & multi 4.00 1.00
Nos. C46-C48 (3) 8.00 1.65

Game Type of Regular Issue, 1968

Protected Game: 60f, Nubian ibex, vert. 100f, Wild ducks.

1968, Oct. 5 Litho. *Perf. 13½*
C49 A74 60f multicolored 10.00 4.50
C50 A74 100f multicolored 15.00 7.00

Easter Type of Regular Issue

Designs: 60f, Altar, Holy Sepulcher. 100f, Feet Washing, Holy Gate, Jerusalem.

1972, Apr. Photo. *Perf. 14x13½*
C51 A92 60f dk bl & multi 1.40 .70
C52 A92 100f multicolored 1.75 1.10

Aero Club Type of Regular Issue

15f, Two Piper 140s. 20f, R.J.A.C. Beechcraft. 40f, Aero Club emblem with winged horse.

1973, Jan. Photo. *Perf. 13½x14*
C53 A100 15f blue, blk & red .75 .20
C54 A100 20f blue, blk & red .75 .20
C55 A100 40f mag, blk & yel 1.50 .45
Nos. C53-C55 (3) 3.00 .85

Agriculture Type of Regular Issue

Design: 100f, Soil conservation.

1973, Dec. 25 *Perf. 13½*
C56 A110 100f multicolored 2.25 1.00

King Hussein Driving Car — AP7

1974, Dec. 20 *Perf. 12*
C57 AP7 30f multicolored .70 .20
C58 AP7 60f multicolored 1.40 .75

Royal Jordanian Automobile Club.

Building Type of Regular Issue

Designs: 50f, Palms, Aqaba. 60f, Obelisk tomb. 80f, Fort of Wadi Rum.

1975, Mar. 1 Photo. *Perf. 13½x14*
C59 A121 50f pink & multi 1.25 .65
C60 A121 60f lt bl & multi 1.60 .80
C61 A121 80f yellow & multi 2.00 .80
Nos. C59-C61 (3) 4.85 2.25

Hussein Type of Regular Issue

1975, Apr. 8 Photo. *Perf. 14x13½*
Size: 22x27mm
C62 A123 60f dk grn & brn 1.00 .35
C63 A123 100f org brn & brn 1.75 .40
C64 A123 120f dp bl & brn 1.25 .65
C65 A123 180f brt mag & brn 1.60 1.00
C66 A123 200f grnsh bl & brn 1.90 1.25
C67 A123 400f pur & brown 2.75 2.00
C68 A123 500f orange & brn 3.75 3.25
Nos. C62-C68 (7) 14.00 8.90

POSTAGE DUE STAMPS

Stamps of Regular Issue (Nos. 69, 66-68 Surcharged with New Value like No. 91) Overprinted

This overprint reads: "Mustahaq" (Tax or Due)

1923 Unwmk. *Perf. 11½*
Typo. Ovpt. "Mustahaq" 10mm long
J1 A7 ½pi on 3pi ol brn 45.00 *55.00*
a. Inverted overprint 175.00 175.00
b. Double overprint 175.00 175.00

Handstamped Overprint 12mm long
J2 A7 ½pi on 3pi ol brn 12.50 *15.00*
a. Inverted overprint 50.00 —
b. Double overprint 50.00 —
J3 A7 1pi dark blue 8.00 *9.00*
a. Inverted overprint 45.00 —
b. Double overprint 50.00 —
J4 A7 1½pi violet 8.00 *9.00*
a. Inverted overprint 45.00 —
b. Double overprint 50.00 —
J5 A7 2pi orange 9.00 *10.00*
a. Inverted overprint 60.00 —
b. Double overprint 65.00 —
Nos. J1-J5 (5) 82.50 *98.00*

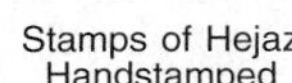

Stamps of Hejaz Handstamped

J6 A7 ½pi red 1.00 *1.25*
J7 A7 1pi dark blue 1.10 *1.75*
J8 A7 1½pi violet 1.40 *2.25*
J9 A7 2pi orange 2.00 *3.00*
J10 A7 3pi olive brown 3.00 *5.50*
J11 A7 5pi olive green 5.50 *8.00*
Nos. J6-J11 (6) 14.00 *21.75*

Type of Palestine, 1918, Overprinted

1925 Wmk. 4 *Perf. 14*
J12 A1 1m dark brown 1.75 *5.00*
J13 A1 2m yellow 2.50 *3.25*
J14 A1 4m rose 4.25 *5.00*
J15 A1 8m red 5.00 *8.50*
J16 A1 13m ultramarine 6.75 *8.50*
J17 A1 5pi plum 7.75 *11.50*
a. Perf. 15x14 67.50 *77.50*
Nos. J12-J17 (6) 28.00 *41.75*

The overprint reads: "Mustahaq. Sharqi al'Ardan." (Tax. Eastern Jordan).

Stamps of Palestine, 1918, Surcharged

1926
J18 A1 1m on 1m dk brn 3.50 *5.00*
J19 A1 2m on 1m dk brn 3.50 *5.00*
J20 A1 4m on 3m Prus bl 3.50 *6.75*
J21 A1 8m on 3m Prus bl 3.75 *7.50*
J22 A1 13m on 13m ultra 3.75 *8.50*
J23 A1 5pi on 13m ultra 5.00 *10.50*
Nos. J18-J23 (6) 23.00 *43.25*

The surcharge reads "Tax—Eastern Jordan" and New Value.

Stamps of Regular Issue, 1927, Overprinted

1929
J24 A1 2m Prussian bl 1.25 *3.75*
J25 A1 10m red 2.00 *3.75*
J26 A2 50m claret 7.75 *16.00*
Nos. J24-J26 (3) 11.00 *23.50*

With Additional Surcharge
J27 A1 1(m) on 3(m) rose 1.25 *4.25*
J28 A1 4(m) on 15(m) ultra 2.00 *4.25*
a. Inverted surch. and ovpt. 95.00
J29 A2 20(m) on 100(m) lt bl 5.75 *13.00*
Nos. J27-J29 (3) 9.00 *21.50*

D1

1929 Engr. *Perf. 14*
Size: 17¼x21mm
J30 D1 1m brown .75 *3.25*
a. Perf. 13½x13 90.00 45.00
J31 D1 2m orange .75 *3.75*
J32 D1 4m green .75 *4.25*
J33 D1 10m carmine 2.00 *4.75*
J34 D1 20m olive green 7.75 *15.00*
J35 D1 50m blue 9.50 *19.00*
Nos. J30-J35 (6) 21.50 *50.00*

See Nos. J39-J43 design with larger type. For surcharge see No. J52. For overprints see Nos. NJ1a, NJ3, NJ5a, NJ6-NJ7.

D2

1942 Unwmk. Litho. *Perf. 13x13½*
J36 D2 1m dull red brn .20 .20
J37 D2 2m dl orange yel 3.00 3.00
J38 D2 10m dark carmine 4.00 4.00
Nos. J36-J38 (3) 7.20 7.20

For overprints see Nos. NJ8-NJ10.

Type of 1929

1943-44 Engr. Wmk. 4 *Perf. 12*
Size: 17¾x21¼mm
J39 D1 1m orange brn .20 .20
J40 D1 2m yel orange .20 .20
J41 D1 4m yel green .20 .20
J42 D1 10m rose carmine .20 .20
J43 D1 20m olive green 10.00 10.00
Nos. J39-J43 (5) 10.80 10.80

For overprints see Nos. J47-J51, NJ1-NJ2, NJ3a, NJ5, NJ6a.

Catalogue values for unused stamps in this section, from this point to the end of the section, are for Never Hinged items.

Nos. J39-J43, J35 Surcharged "FILS" and its Arabic Equivalent in Black, Green or Carmine

1952 Wmk. 4 Perf. 12
J47 D1 1f on 1m org brn (Bk) 2.00 .20
J48 D1 2f on 2m yel org (G) 2.00 .20
J49 D1 4f on 4m yel grn 2.00 .20
J50 D1 10f on 10m rose car (Bk) 2.50 1.75
J51 D1 20f on 20m ol grn 4.50 2.50

Perf. 14
J52 D1 50f on 50m blue 5.00 3.25
Nos. J47-J52 (6) 18.00 8.10

This overprint exists on Nos. J34, J36-J38. Exists inverted, double and in wrong color.

D3

Inscribed: "The Hashemite Kingdom of the Jordan"

1952 Engr. Perf. 11½
J53 D3 1f orange brown .65 *.45*
J54 D3 2f yel orange .65 *.45*
J55 D3 4f yel green .65 *.45*
J56 D3 10f rose carmine 1.00 *.80*
J57 D3 20f yel brown 1.00 *.95*
J58 D3 50f blue 2.75 *2.25*
Nos. J53-J58 (6) 6.70 *5.35*

Type of 1952 Redrawn

Inscribed: "The Hashemite Kingdom of Jordan"

1957 Wmk. 305 Perf. 11½
J59 D3 1f orange brown .70 *.40*
J60 D3 2f yel orange .70 *.40*
J61 D3 4f yel green .70 *.60*
J62 D3 10f rose carmine 1.00 *.55*
J63 D3 20f yel brown 1.40 *1.25*
Nos. J59-J63 (5) 4.50 *3.20*

OFFICIAL STAMP

Saudi Arabia No. L34 Overprinted

1924, Jan. Typo. Perf. 11½
O1 A7 ½pi red 100.00 —

Overprint reads: "(Government) the Arabian East 1342."

POSTAL TAX STAMPS

Catalogue values for unused stamps in this section are for Never Hinged items.

Mosque at Hebron — PT1

Designs: 10m, 15m, 20m, 50m, Dome of the Rock. 100m, 200m, 500m, £1, Acre.

Perf. 11½x12½
1947 Unwmk. Engr.
RA1 PT1 1m ultra .35 .20
RA2 PT1 2m carmine .35 .20
RA3 PT1 3m emerald .50 .25
RA4 PT1 5m plum .60 .20
RA5 PT1 10m carmine .75 .30
RA6 PT1 15m gray 1.00 .30
RA7 PT1 20m dk brown 3.50 1.40
RA8 PT1 50m purple 8.00 3.50
RA9 PT1 100m orange red 15.00 8.00
RA10 PT1 200m dp blue 35.00 24.00
RA11 PT1 500m green 55.00 40.00
RA12 PT1 £1 dk brown 95.00 90.00
Nos. RA1-RA12 (12) 215.05 168.35

Issued to help the Welfare Fund for Arabs in Palestine. Required on foreign-bound letters to the amount of half the regular postage.

For overprints and surcharges see #286A-286C, 344-346, RA37-RA46, NRA1-NRA12.

Nos. 211, 232 and 234 Overprinted in Black

1950 Wmk. 4 Perf. 12
RA23 A3 5m orange 12.50
RA24 A3 10m violet 20.00
RA25 A3 15m dull olive grn 22.50
Nos. RA23-RA25 (3) 55.00

Arch and Colonnade, Palmyra, Syria — PT2

Two types of 5m:
Type I — "A" with serifs. Arabic ovpt. 8mm wide.
Type II — "A" without serifs. Arabic ovpt. 5mm wide.

Black or Carmine Overprint

1950-51 Engr. Perf. 13½x13
RA26 PT2 5m orange (I) 20.00
a. Type II ('51) 27.50
RA27 PT2 10m violet (C) 20.00

The overprint on No. RA27 is similar to that on RA23-RA25 but slightly bolder.

Type of 1947

Designs: 5f, Hebron Mosque. 10f, 15f, 20f, Dome of the Rock. 100f, Acre.

1951 Wmk. 4 Perf. 11½x12½
RA28 PT1 5f plum .20 .20
RA29 PT1 10f carmine .20 .20
RA30 PT1 15f gray .20 .20
RA31 PT1 20f dk brown .90 .90
RA33 PT1 100f orange 5.75 5.75
Nos. RA28-RA33 (5) 7.25 7.25

The tax on Nos. RA1-RA33 was for Arab aid in Palestine.
For overprints see Nos. 287-290.

Postal Tax Stamps of 1947 Surcharged "FILS" or "J.D." and Their Arabic Equivalents and Bars in Carmine or Black

1952 Unwmk.
RA37 PT1 1f on 1m ultra .75 .20
RA38 PT1 3f on 3m emer .75 .20
RA39 PT1 10f on 10m car 1.25 .75
RA40 PT1 15f on 15m gray 1.60 1.25
RA41 PT1 20f on 20m dk brown 2.40 1.60
RA42 PT1 50f on 50m pur 5.75 3.75
RA43 PT1 100f on 100m org red 15.00 9.50
RA44 PT1 200f on 200m dp blue 40.00 12.00
RA45 PT1 500f on 500m grn 67.50 24.00
RA46 PT1 1d on £1 dk brn 100.00 60.00
Nos. RA37-RA46 (10) 235.00 113.25

"J.D." stands for Jordanian Dinar.

OCCUPATION STAMPS

Catalogue values for unused stamps in this section are for Never Hinged items.

For Use in Palestine

Stamps of Jordan Overprinted in Red, Black, Dark Green, Green or Orange Red

On No. 200

1948 Unwmk. Perf. 13x13½
N1 A14 2m dull green (R) 2.50 2.00

On #207-209, 211, 230-235, 215-220

1948 Wmk. 4 Perf. 12, 13½x13, 14
N2 A3 1m red brown .75 .60
N3 A3 2m Prus green (R) .75 .60
a. 2m Prussian blue, perf. 13½x13 (R) (#170a) 1.00 *1.25*
N4 A3 3m blue green (R) .90 .75
N5 A3 3m rose carmine .50 .35
N6 A3 4m dp yel grn (R) .50 .35
N7 A3 5m orange (G) .50 .35
N8 A3 10m violet (OR) 1.25 1.00
N9 A3 12m deep rose 1.25 .80
N10 A3 15m dl ol grn (R) 1.75 1.00
N11 A3 20m dp blue (R) 2.25 1.40
N12 A3 50m red lil (Dk G) 2.75 1.75
N13 A3 90m ocher (Dk G) 10.75 4.75
N14 A3 100m dp blue (R) 12.50 5.50
N15 A3 200m dk vio (R) 8.00 7.00
a. 200m vio, perf. 14 (R) (#182) 35.00 25.00
N16 A3 500m dk brn (R) 45.00 14.00
N17 A3 £1 black (R) 80.00 42.50
Nos. N2-N17 (16) 169.40 82.70

The first overprinting of these stamps include Nos. N1-N6, N9-N17. The second overprinting includes Nos. N1, N3, N5-N17, in inks differing in shade from the originals.

Many values exist with inverted or double overprint.

Jordan Nos. 245-249 Overprinted in Black or Red

1949, Aug. Wmk. 4 Perf. 13
N18 A17 1m brown (Bk) 1.10 .35
N19 A17 4m green 1.10 .35
a. "PLAESTINE" 25.00
N20 A17 10m red 1.50 .65
N21 A17 20m ultra 1.50 .65
N22 A18 50m dull green 2.25 1.60
a. "PLAESTINE" 25.00
Nos. N18-N22 (5) 7.45 3.60

The overprint is in one line on No. N22.
UPU, 75th anniversary.

OCCUPATION POSTAGE DUE STAMPS

Catalogue values for unused stamps in this section are for Never Hinged items.

Jordan Nos. J39, J30a, J40, J32, J41-J43, J34 and J35 Overprinted in Black, Red or Carmine

1948-49 Wmk. 4 Perf. 12, 14
NJ1 D1 1m org brn, perf. 12 1.50 1.25
a. Perf. 13½x13 (#J30a) 50.00 45.00
NJ2 D1 2m yel orange 1.50 1.25
NJ3 D1 4m grn (R) (#J32) 2.75 2.50
a. 4m yel grn (C) (#J41) 5.00
NJ5 D1 10m rose car (#J42) ('49) 4.50 3.75
a. Perf. 14 (#J33) 80.00
NJ6 D1 20m ol grn (R), perf. 14 2.75 2.50
a. Perf. 12 (R) (#J43) 62.50
NJ7 D1 50m blue (R) 4.25 2.50
Nos. NJ1-NJ3,NJ5-NJ7 (6) 17.25 13.75

The second overprinting of these stamps includes Nos. NJ1-NJ3, NJ3a and NJ5-NJ7, in inks differing in shade from the originals.
Double and inverted overprints exist.

Same Overprint in Black on Jordan Nos. J36-J38

1948-49 Unwmk. Perf. 13x13½
NJ8 D2 1m dl red brn *115.00 115.00*
NJ9 D2 2m dl org yel ('49) 12.00 11.00
NJ10 D2 10m dark car 10.00 9.00

OCCUPATION POSTAL TAX STAMPS

Catalogue values for unused stamps in this section are for Never Hinged items.

Postal Tax Stamps of 1947 Overprinted in Red or Black

1950
NRA1 PT1 1m ultra (R) .40 .35
NRA2 PT1 2m carmine .45 .35
NRA3 PT1 3m emerald (R) .60 .35
NRA4 PT1 5m plum 1.00 .35
NRA5 PT1 10m carmine 1.75 .50
NRA6 PT1 15m gray (R) 2.75 .90
NRA7 PT1 20m dk brown (R) 4.00 1.10
NRA8 PT1 50m purple (R) 4.75 1.75
NRA9 PT1 100m org red 7.00 2.40
NRA10 PT1 200m dp blue (R) 19.00 6.00
NRA11 PT1 500m green (R) 50.00 18.00
NRA12 PT1 £1 dk brown (R) 105.00 35.00
Nos. NRA1-NRA12 (12) 196.70 67.05

For overprints see Nos. 286D-286G.

KARELIA

kə-'rē-lə-ə

LOCATION — In northwestern Soviet Russia
GOVT. — An autonomous republic of the Soviet Union
AREA — 55,198 sq. mi. (approx.)
POP. — 270,000 (approx.)
CAPITAL — Petrozavodsk (Kalininsk)

In 1921 the Karelians rebelled and for a short period a form of sovereignty independent of Russia was maintained.

100 Pennia = 1 Markka

Bear — A1

1922 Unwmk. Litho. *Perf. 11½, 12*

No.	Type	Description	Unused	Used
1	A1	5p dark gray	15.00	*40.00*
2	A1	10p light blue	15.00	*40.00*
3	A1	20p rose red	15.00	*40.00*
4	A1	25p yellow brown	15.00	*40.00*
5	A1	40p magenta	15.00	*40.00*
6	A1	50p gray green	15.00	*40.00*
7	A1	75p orange yellow	25.00	*40.00*
8	A1	1m pink & gray	25.00	*40.00*
9	A1	2m yel grn & gray	27.50	*90.00*
10	A1	3m lt blue & gray	27.50	*110.00*
11	A1	5m red lil & gray	27.50	*140.00*
12	A1	10m lt brn & gray	27.50	*200.00*
13	A1	15m green & car	27.50	*200.00*
14	A1	20m rose & green	27.50	*200.00*
15	A1	25m yellow & blue	27.50	*200.00*
		Nos. 1-15 (15)	332.50	*1,460.*
		Set, never hinged	400.00	

Nos. 1-15 were valid Jan. 31-Feb. 16, 1922. Use probably ended Feb. 3, although cancellations of the 4th and 5th exist.
Counterfeits abound.

OCCUPATION STAMPS

Issued under Finnish Occupation

Issued in the Russian territory of Eastern Karelia under Finnish military administration.

Types of Finland Stamps, 1930 Overprinted in Black:

On A26

On A27-A28

1941 Unwmk. *Perf. 14*

No.	Type	Description	Unused	Used
N1	A26	50p brt yel grn	.30	*.60*
N2	A26	1.75m dk gray	.70	*1.25*
N3	A26	2m dp org	2.25	*4.00*
N4	A26	2.75m yel org	.50	*1.00*
N5	A26	3½m lt ultra	3.00	*5.00*
N6	A27	5m rose vio	3.75	*7.75*
N7	A28	10m pale brn	4.50	*7.75*
		Nos. N1-N7 (7)	15.00	*27.35*
		Set, never hinged	30.00	

Types of Finland Stamps, 1930 Overprinted in Green:

On A26

On A27-A29

No.	Type	Description	Unused	Used
N8	A26	50p brt yel grn	.30	*.55*
N9	A26	1.75m dk gray	.35	*.65*
N10	A26	2m dp org	.70	*1.25*
N11	A26	2.75m yel org	.50	*.75*
N12	A26	3½m lt ultra	.70	*1.25*
N13	A27	5m rose vio	1.60	*4.00*
N14	A28	10m pale brown	3.25	*6.75*
N15	A29	25m green	3.50	*7.25*
		Nos. N8-N15 (8)	10.90	*22.45*
		Set, never hinged	50.00	

Mannerheim Type of Finland Overprinted

1942

No.	Type	Description	Unused	Used
N16	A48	50p dk yel grn	.65	*1.50*
N17	A48	1.75m slate bl	.65	*1.50*
N18	A48	2m red org	.65	*1.50*
N19	A48	2.75m brn org	.55	*1.50*
N20	A48	3.50m brt ultra	.55	*1.50*
N21	A48	5m brn vio	.55	*1.50*
		Nos. N16-N21 (6)	3.60	*9.00*
		Set, never hinged	10.00	

Same Overprint on Ryti Type of Finland

No.	Type	Description	Unused	Used
N22	A49	50p dk yel grn	.55	*1.50*
N23	A49	1.75m slate bl	.55	*1.50*
N24	A49	2m red org	.55	*1.50*
N25	A49	2.75m brn org	.60	*1.50*
N26	A49	3.50m brt ultra	.60	*1.50*
N27	A49	5m brn vio	.60	*1.50*
		Nos. N22-N27 (6)	3.45	*9.00*
		Set, never hinged	10.00	

The overprint translates, "East Karelia Military Administration."

OCCUPATION SEMI-POSTAL STAMP

Arms of East Karelia — SP1

1943 Unwmk. Engr. *Perf. 14*

No.	Type	Description	Unused	Used
NB1	SP1	3.50m + 1.50m dk ol	.75	*2.25*
		Never hinged	3.00	

This surtax aided war victims in East Karelia.

KATANGA

kə-'täŋ-gə

LOCATION — Central Africa
GOVT. — Republic
CAPITAL — Elisabethville

Katanga province seceded from the Congo (ex-Belgian) Republic in July, 1960, but established nations did not recognize it as an independent state. The UN declared the secession ended in Sept, 1961. The last troops surrendered Sept. 1963.

During the secession Katanga stamps were tolerated in the international mails, but the government authorizing them was not recognized.

100 Centimes = 1 Franc

Catalogue values for all unused stamps in this country are for Never Hinged items.

Belgian Congo Nos. 318-322 Overprinted "KATANGA"

Perf. 11½

1960, Sept. 12 Photo. Unwmk.

No.	Type	Description	Unused	Used
1	A94	50c golden brn, ocher & red brn		
2	A94	1fr dk bl, pur & red brn		
3	A94	2fr gray, brt bl & red brn		
		Nos. 1-3 (3)	1.00	1.00

Inscription in French

No.	Type	Description	Unused	Used
4	A95	3fr gray & red	10.00	10.00

Inscription in Flemish

No.	Type	Description	Unused	Used
5	A95	3fr gray & red	10.00	10.00

Inverted overprints exist on No. 1-5. Values: 1-3 $4 each; 4-5 $10 each.

For surcharges see Nos. 50-51.

Animal Type of Belgian Congo, Nos. 306-317, Overprinted "KATANGA"

1960, Sept. 19

Granite Paper

No.	Type	Description	Unused	Used
6	A92	10c bl & brn		
7	A93	20c red org & slate		
8	A92	40c brn & bl		
9	A93	50c brt ultra, red & sep		
10	A92	1fr brn, grn & blk		
11	A93	1.50fr blk & org yel		
12	A92	2fr crim, blk & brn		
13	A93	3fr blk, gray & lil rose		
14	A92	5fr brn, dk brn & brt grn		
15	A93	6.50fr bl, brn & org yel		
16	A92	8fr org brn, ol bis & lil		
17	A93	10fr multi		
		Nos. 6-17 (12)	62.50	32.50

Inverted overprints exist. Value $10 each.

Flower Type of Belgian Congo, Nos. 263-271, 274-281, Overprinted "KATANGA"

1960, Sept. 22

Granite Paper

Flowers in Natural Colors

No.	Type	Description	Unused	Used
18	A86	10c dp plum & ocher		
19	A86	15c red & yel grn		
20	A86	20c grn & gray		
21	A86	25c dk grn & dl org		
22	A86	40c grn & sal		
23	A86	50c dk car & aqua		
24	A86	60c bl grn & pink		
25	A86	75c dp plum & gray		
26	A86	1fr car & yel		
27	A86	2fr ol grn & buff		
28	A86	3fr ol grn & pink		
29	A86	4fr choc & lil		
30	A86	5fr dp plum & lt bl grn		
31	A86	6.50fr dk car & lil		
32	A86	7fr dk grn & fawn		
33	A86	8fr grn & lt yel		
34	A86	10fr dp plum & pale ol		
		Nos. 18-34 (17)	70.00	35.00

Inverted overprints exist. Value $12 each.

Carving and Mask Type of Belgian Congo, Nos. 241, 246, 254-256, Surcharged or Overprinted "KATANGA"

1960, Sept. 22 *Perf. 12½*

No.	Type	Description	Unused	Used
35	A82	1.50fr on 1.25fr	1.50	.50
36	A82	3.50fr on 2.50fr	1.75	.60
37	A82	20fr red org & vio brn	9.00	4.25
38	A82	50fr dp org & blk	18.50	7.50
39	A82	100fr crim & blk brn	75.00	30.00
		Nos. 35-39 (5)	105.75	42.85

Inverted surcharges and overprints exist. Values, No. 37 $42.50, No. 38 $50, No. 39 $80.

Map Type of Congo Democratic Republic, Nos. 356-365, Overprinted "11 / JUILLET / DE / L'ETAT DU KATANGA"

1960, Oct. 26 *Perf. 11½*

Granite Paper

No.	Type	Description	Unused	Used
40	A93a	20c brown	.20	.20
41	A93a	50c rose red	.20	.20
42	A93a	1fr green	.20	.20
43	A93a	1.50fr red brn	.20	.20
44	A93a	2fr rose car	.20	.20
45	A93a	3.50fr lilac	.25	.20
46	A93a	5fr brt bl	.25	.20
47	A93a	6.50fr gray	.25	.20
48	A93a	10fr orange	.30	.20
49	A93a	20fr ultra	.40	.20
		Nos. 40-49 (10)	2.45	2.00

Inverted and double surcharges exist.

Belgian Congo Nos. 321-322 Surcharged

1961, Jan. 16

No.	Type	Description	Unused	Used
50	A95	3.50fr on 3fr #321	4.00	4.00
51	A95	3.50fr on 3fr #322	4.00	4.00

Inverted surcharges exist. Value $5.50 each.

A1

A2

Katangan Wood Carvings: 3.50fr-8fr, Preparing meal. 10fr-100fr, Family group.

1961, Mar. 1 *Perf. 11½*

Granite Paper

No.	Type	Description	Unused	Used
52	A1	10c grn & lt grn	.20	.20
53	A1	20c purple & lil	.20	.20
54	A1	50c blue & lt bl	.20	.20
55	A1	1.50fr ol grn & lt ol grn	.20	.20
56	A1	2fr red brn & lt brn	.20	.20
57	A1	3.50fr dk blue & lt bl	.25	.20
58	A1	5fr bl grn & lt bl grn	.25	.20
59	A1	6fr org brn & tan	.25	.25
60	A1	6.50fr bl vio & gray vio	.25	.25
61	A1	8fr claret & pink	.25	.25
62	A1	10fr dk brn & lt brn	.25	.25
63	A1	20fr dk ol & lt grn	.35	.25
64	A1	50fr brn & lt brn	.75	.45
65	A1	100fr Prus bl & lt bl	1.25	.75
		Nos. 52-65 (14)	4.85	3.85

1961, July 8 *Perf. 11½*

1fr, 5fr, Abstract vehicle. 2.50fr, 6.50fr, Gear.

Granite Paper

No.	Type	Description	Unused	Used
66	A2	50c blk, grn & red	.20	.20
67	A2	1fr blk & blue	.20	.20
68	A2	2.50fr blk & yellow	.25	.20
69	A2	3.50fr blk, brn & scar	.25	.20
70	A2	5fr blk & purple	.40	.40
71	A2	6.50fr blk & orange	.75	.65
		Nos. 66-71 (6)	2.05	1.85

Katanga International Fair.
Imperfs exist. Value, set $45.

Air Katanga A3

Design: 6.50fr, 10fr, Plane on ground.

1961, Aug. 1 *Perf. 11½*

Granite Paper

No.	Type	Description	Unused	Used
72	A3	3.50fr multicolored		
73	A3	6.50fr multicolored		
74	A3	8fr multicolored		
75	A3	10fr multicolored		
		Nos. 72-75 (4)	8.50	7.50

Imperfs exist. Value, set $60.

Katanga Gendarmerie — A4

1962, Oct. 1 *Perf. 11½*

Granite Paper

No.	Type	Description	Unused	Used
76	A4	6fr multicolored		
77	A4	8fr multicolored		
78	A4	10fr multicolored		
		Nos. 76-78 (3)	6.00	5.00

Imperfs exist.Value, set $40.

SEMI-POSTAL STAMPS

Pres. Moise Tshombe — SP1

1961, July 11 *Perf. 11½*

Granite Paper

B1 SP1 6.50fr + 5fr multi
B2 SP1 8fr + 5fr multi
B3 SP1 10fr + 5fr multi
Nos. B1-B3 (3) 9.50 6.00

Imperf exist. Value, set $65.

POSTAGE DUE STAMPS

Belgian Congo Nos. J8a-J10a, J16-J19 Handstamped "KATANGA" in Blue

1960, Dec. 30 Unwmk. *Perf. 12½*

J1 D2 10c olive green
J2 D2 20c dark ultra
J3 D2 50c green

Perf. 11½

J4 D3 1fr light blue
J5 D3 2fr vermilion
J6 D3 4fr purple
J7 D3 6fr violet blue
Nos. J1-J7 (7) 35.00 35.00

This overprint also exists on Belgian Congo Nos. J11a-J12a, J13-J15. Value, set $180.

KAZAKHSTAN

ˌka-ˌzak-ˈstan

(Kazakstan)

LOCATION — Bounded by southern Russia, Uzbekistan, Kyrgyzstan, and China.
GOVT. — Independent republic, member of the Commonwealth of Independent States.
AREA — 1,049,155 sq. mi.
POP. — 16,824,825 (1999 est.)
CAPITAL — Astana

With the breakup of the Soviet Union on Dec. 26, 1991, Kazakhstan and ten former Soviet republics established the Commonwealth of Independent States.

100 Kopecks = 1 Ruble
100 Tijn = 1 Tenge

Catalogue values for all unused stamps in this country are for Never Hinged items.

Overprinted Stamps

The Philatelic Club of Alma Ata, Kazakhstan, has announced that various overprinted stamps of the USSR were not generally available nor were they in values reflecting actual postal rates.

A1

Perf. 12x12½

1992, Mar. 23 Litho. Unwmk.

1 A1 50k multicolored .30 .20

Saiga Tatarica A2

1992, Sept. 11 Litho. *Perf. 12*

2 A2 75k multicolored .30 .20

Camels and Train, by K. Kasteev — A3

1992, Sept. 11 Litho. *Perf. 12½x12*

3 A3 1r multicolored .30 .30

Day of the Republic A3a

1992, Dec. 16 Litho. *Perf. 12*

4 A3a 5r multicolored .50 .50

Space Ship and Yurt — A4

Natl. Flag — A5

1993, Jan. 24 Litho. *Perf. 13x12½*

22 A4 1r green .20 .20
23 A4 3r red .20 .20
24 A4 10r golden brown .20 .20
25 A4 25r purple .90 .90

Perf. 14

26 A5 50r multicolored 1.75 1.75
Nos. 22-26 (5) 3.25 3.25

See Nos. 64, 69, 108-115.

Space Mail A6

1993, Mar. 5 Litho. *Perf. 13½*

35 A6 100r multicolored 2.00 1.40

New Year 1993 (Year of the Rooster) — A7

1993, Mar. 22 Litho. *Perf. 13x13½*

36 A7 60r yellow, black & red 1.40 1.40

See Nos. 54, 98, 141, 187A, 220, 268.

Cosmonauts' Day — A8

1993, Apr. 12 *Perf. 13½x13*

37 A8 90r multicolored 1.90 1.40

Pres. Nursultan Nasarbajev — A9

1993, Aug. 2 Litho. *Perf. 14*

38 A9 50r multicolored 1.00 .70

Bukar Zhirav Kalkaman (1668-1781), Poet — A10

1993, Aug. 18 *Perf. 13½x13*

39 A10 15r multicolored .50 .20

Map, Pres. Nasarbajev — A11

1993, Sept. 24 Litho. *Perf. 13*

40 A11 100r multicolored 1.75 1.10

Wildlife A12

Designs: 5r, Selevinia betpakdalensis. 10r, Hystrix leucura. 15r, Vormela peregusna. 20r, Equis hemionus onager. 25r, Ovis orientalis. 30r, Acinonyx jubatus venaticus.

1993, Nov. 11 *Perf. 12x12½*

41 A12 5r multicolored .45 .30
42 A12 10r multicolored .50 .35
43 A12 15r multicolored .50 .35
44 A12 20r multicolored .60 .45
45 A12 25r multicolored .70 .50
46 A12 30r multicolored .80 .65
Nos. 41-46 (6) 3.55 2.60

Nos. 1-46 were sold after the currency changeover as stamps denominated in one or both of the new currency units. Nos. 47-50, 54, 64 and 69 were sold as stamps denominated in tijn, and later as tenge.

1994 Winter Olympics, Lillehammer A13

1994, Jan. 24 Litho. *Perf. 13½x13*

47 A13 15te Ice hockey .35 .35
48 A13 25te Slalom skiing .50 .50
49 A13 90te Ski jumping 1.75 1.75
50 A13 150te Speed skating 2.75 2.75
Nos. 47-50 (4) 5.35 5.35

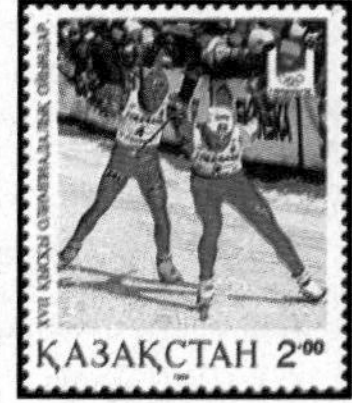

1994 Winter Olympics, Lillehammer A14

Designs: 2te, Skiers Vladimir Smirnov, Kazakhstan; Bjorn Daehlie, Norway. 6.80te, 12te, Smirnov.

1994, Feb. 19 Litho. *Perf. 13x13½*

51 A14 2te multicolored .35 .25
52 A14 6.80te multicolored 1.10 1.10
a. Pair, #51-52 1.60 1.60
53 A14 12te like No. 52 1.25 1.25
Nos. 51-53 (3) 2.70 2.60

No. 53 has an additional two line Cyrillic inscription.

New Year Type of 1993

Size: 26x38mm

1994, Mar. 22 *Perf. 12*

54 A7 30te green, black & blue .70 .25

New Year 1994 (Year of the Dog).

Space Program A15

1994, Apr. 12 *Perf. 13½x13*

55 A15 2te multicolored .70 .70

Souvenir Sheet

Russian Space Shuttle, Cosmonaut — A16

1994, July 12 *Perf. 13*

56 A16 6.80te Sheet of 4 3.50 3.50

Space Ship and Yurt Type of 1993

1994, July 12 Litho. *Perf. 11½*

64 A4 15ti blue .95 .80
69 A4 80ti lake 2.10 1.60

For surcharges see Nos. 70-76, 122.

This is an expanding set. Numbers may change.

Nos. 64, 69 Surcharged in Lake or Purple

1995-2004 Litho. *Perf. 11½*

70 A4 1te on 15te #64 .35 .35
71 A4 2te on 15te #64 .35 .35
72 A4 3te on 80te #69 (P) .35 .35
73 A4 4te on 80te #69 (P) .45 .45
74 A4 6te on 80te #69 (P) .50 .50
75 A4 8te on 80ti .80 .80
76 A4 12te on 80te #69 (P) .85 .85
77 A4 20te on 80te #69 (P) .95 .95
78 A4 200te on 80ti #69 (P) 4.75 4.75
Nos. 70-78 (9) 9.35 9.35

Issued: 1te, 2te, 12te, 2/2/95. 3te, 4te, 6te, 20te, 2/10/95. 8te, 9/25/95. 200te, 1/29/04.

Music Competition Festival
A18

Designs: 10te, Snow-covered mountain top. 15te, Aerial view of stadium at night.

1994, Aug. 1 *Perf. 13½*

81 A18 10te multicolored .55 .55
82 A18 15te multicolored .75 .75

For surcharges see Nos. 119A-119B.

Reptiles
A19

Designs: 1te, Agrionemys horsfieldi. 1.20te, Phrynocephalus mystaceus. 2te, Agkistrodon halys. 3te, Teratoscincus scincus. 5te, Trapelus sanguinolenta. 7te, Ophisaurus apodus. 10te, Varanus griseus.

1994, Oct. 10 *Perf. 12½x12*

83 A19 1te multicolored .20 .20
84 A19 1.20te multicolored .25 .25
85 A19 2te multicolored .30 .30
86 A19 3te multicolored .35 .35
87 A19 5te multicolored .45 .45
88 A19 7te multicolored .50 .50
Nos. 83-88 (6) 2.05 2.05

Souvenir Sheet

89 A19 10te multicolored 1.50 1.50

Prehistoric Animals
A20

1994, Nov. 24 **Litho.** *Perf. 12½x12*

90 A20 1te Entelodon .20 .20
91 A20 1.20te Saurolophus .25 .25
92 A20 2te Plesiosaurus .30 .30
93 A20 3te Sordes pilosus .35 .35
94 A20 5te Mosasaurus .45 .45
95 A20 7te Megaloceros giganteum .50 .50
Nos. 90-95 (6) 2.05 2.05

Souvenir Sheet

96 A20 10te Koelodonta antiquitatis 2.00 2.00

Day of the Republic
A21

1994, Oct. 25 *Perf. 11½*

97 A21 2te multicolored .60 .60

For surcharge see No. 160B.

New Year Type of 1993

1995, Mar. 22 **Litho.** *Perf. 14*

Size: 27x32mm

98 A7 10te blue, black & ultra .85 .85

New Year 1995 (Year of the Boar).

Abai (Ibraghim) Kynanbaev (1845-1904), Poet — A22

1995, Mar. 31

99 A22 4te Portrait .30 .30
100 A22 9te Portrait, diff. .60 .60

Space Day — A23

Designs: 10te, Cosmonauts Malenchenko, Musabaev and Merbold.

1995, Apr. 12 **Litho.** *Perf. 14*

101 A23 2te multicolored 3.75 3.75
102 A23 10te multicolored 16.00 16.00

Mahatma Gandhi (1869-1948) — A24

1995, Oct. 2

103 A24 9te multicolored 2.40 2.40
104 A24 22te multicolored 5.50 5.50

End of World War II, 50th Anniv.
A25

Designs: 1te, Hero, battle scene. 3te, Heroine, tank. 5te, Dove, monument.

1995, May 9 **Litho.** *Perf. 14*

105 A25 1te multicolored 1.00 1.00
106 A25 3te multicolored 3.00 3.00
107 A25 5te multicolored 5.00 5.00
Nos. 105-107 (3) 9.00 9.00

Spaceship and Yurt Type of 1993

1995, Mar. 24 **Litho.** *Perf. 14x14½*

108 A4 20ti orange .45 .45
109 A4 25ti yellow brown .45 .45
110 A4 50ti gray .45 .45
111 A4 1te green .65 .65
112 A4 2te blue .85 .85
113 A4 4te bright pink 1.10 1.10
114 A4 6te gray green 1.40 1.40
115 A4 12te lilac 2.75 2.75
Nos. 108-115 (8) 8.10 8.10

Nos. 108-115 are inscribed "1995."

Paintings — A26

Designs: 4te, "Springtime," by S. Mambeev. 9te, "Mountains," by Z. Shchardenov. 15te, "Kulash Baiseitova in role of Kyz Zhibek," by G. Ismailova, vert. 28te, "Kokpar," by K. Telzhanov.

1995, June 23 **Litho.** *Perf. 14*

116 A26 4te multicolored .75 .75
117 A26 9te multicolored 1.60 1.60
118 A26 15te multicolored 2.75 2.75
119 A26 28te multicolored 4.75 4.75
Nos. 116-119 (4) 9.85 9.85

Nos. 81-82 Ovptd.

1995, July 25 **Litho.** *Perf. 13½*

119A A18 10te multicolored 1.10 1.10
119B A18 15te multicolored 1.50 1.50

Dauletkerey (1820-87), Composer — A27

1995, Sept. 1 **Litho.** *Perf. 14*

120 A27 2te yellow & multi .90 .85
121 A27 28te lake & multi 6.50 6.50

UN, 50th Anniv. — A28

1995, Nov. 24 **Litho.** *Perf. 14*

123 A28 10te multicolored 1.50 1.50
124 A28 36te gold & lt blue 5.00 5.00

Resurrection Cathedral
A29

Circus
A29a

Buildings in Alma-Ata: 2te, Culture Palace. 3te, Opera and Ballet House. 6te, Kazakh Science Academy. 48te, Dramatics Theatre.

Perf. 14, 13x12 (#126, 129)

1995-96 **Litho.**

125 A29 1te green .30 .30
126 A29a 1te green .30 .30
127 A29 2te blue .55 .55
128 A29 3te red .75 .75
129 A29a 6te olive .90 .90
130 A29 48te brown 8.00 8.00
Nos. 125-130 (6) 10.80 10.80

Issued: Nos. 125, 127-128, 130, 10/25/95; Nos. 126, 129, 7/5/96.

Raptors
A30

1te, Haliaeetus albicilla. 3te, Pandion haliaetus. 5te, Gypaetus barbatus. 6te, Gyps himalayensis. 30te, Falco cherrug. 50te, Aquila chrysaetus.

1995, Dec. 20 **Litho.** *Perf. 14*

131 A30 1te multicolored .25 .25
132 A30 3te multicolored .25 .25
133 A30 5te multicolored .50 .50
134 A30 6te multicolored .65 .65
135 A30 30te multicolored 2.75 2.75
136 A30 50te multicolored 4.75 4.75
Nos. 131-136 (6) 9.15 9.15

New Year Type of 1993

Size: 27x32mm

1996, Mar. 21 **Litho.** *Perf. 14*

141 A7 25te lil, blk & red 2.40 2.40

New Year 1996 (Year of the Rat).

Space Day — A32

1996, Apr. 12

142 A32 6te Earth 2.25 2.25
143 A32 15te Cosmonaut 2.75 2.75
144 A32 20te Space station Mir 5.00 5.00
Nos. 142-144 (3) 10.00 10.00

Souvenir Sheet

Save the Aral Sea — A33

Designs: a, Felis caracal. b, Salmo trutta aralensis. c, Hyaena hyaena. d, Pseudoscaphirhynchus kaufmanni. e, Aspiolucius esocinus.

1996, Apr. 20 **Litho.** *Perf. 14*

145 A33 20te Sheet of 5, #a.-e. 5.00 5.00

See Kyrgyzstan No. 107, Tadjikistan No. 91, Turkmenistan No. 52, Uzbekistan No. 113.

1996 Summer Olympic Games, Atlanta — A34

1996, June 19 **Litho.** *Perf. 14*

146 A34 4te Cycling .50 .50
147 A34 6te Wrestling 1.25 1.25
148 A34 30te Boxing 6.25 6.25
Nos. 146-148 (3) 8.00 8.00

Souvenir Sheet

149 A34 50te Hurdles 4.00 4.00

Issued: #146-148, 6/19/96; #149, 7/19/96.

Architectural Sites — A35

1te, Tomb, 8-9th cent. 3te, Mausoleum, 11-12th cent. 6te, Mausoleum, 13th cent. 30te, Hadji Ahmet Yassauy's Mausoleum, 14th cent.

1996, Sept. 27 **Litho.** *Perf. 14*

150 A35 1te multicolored .50 .50
151 A35 3te multicolored 1.40 1.40
152 A35 6te multicolored 3.00 3.00
Nos. 150-152 (3) 4.90 4.90

Souvenir Sheet

153 A35 30te multicolored 3.00 3.00

World Post Day — A37

1996, Oct. 9 Litho. *Perf. 14*

156 A37 9te shown .90 .90
157 A37 40te UPU emblem 3.50 3.50

A38

A39

1996, Aug. 21

158 A38 12te multicolored 1.25 1.25

Schambyl Schabaev (1846-1945).

1996, Oct. 2

159 A39 46te Space station Mir 3.50 3.50
160 A39 46te T. Aubakirov 3.50 3.50
a. Pair, #159-160 8.00 8.00

T. Aubakirov, 1st Kazak cosmonaut.

No. 97 Surcharged

1997, Oct. 25 Litho. *Perf. 11½*

160B A21 21te on 2te multi 1.50 1.50

Surcharge adds numeral 1 to existing value to appear as 21, obliterates original date and adds new date.

Butterflies A40

4te, Saturnia schenki. 6te, Parnassius patricius. 12te, Parnassius ariadne. 46te, Colias draconis.

1996, Nov. 21 Litho. *Perf. 14*

161 A40 4te multicolored .30 .30
162 A40 6te multicolored .30 .30
163 A40 12te multicolored .65 .65
164 A40 46te multicolored 2.75 2.75
Nos. 161-164 (4) 4.00 4.00

Hunting Dogs A41

1996, Nov. 29

165 A41 5te multicolored .50 .50

Souvenir Sheet

166 A41 100te like #165 5.25 5.25

No. 166 is a continuous design.

A42

A43

Traditional Costumes, Furnishings: a, 10te, Woman outside tent. b, 16te, Man outside tent. c, 45te, Interior view of furnishings.

1996, Dec. 5

167 A42 Strip of 3, #a.-c. 6.50 6.50

Nos. 167a-167b have continuous design.

1996, Dec. 24

Archives, Bicent.: 4te, Quill pen, candle, documents. 68te, Scroll, papers, book.

168 A43 4te brown .30 .30
169 A43 68te purple 3.50 3.50

Motion Pictures, Cent. — A44

Film scenes: a, Man in hat holding up fingers. b, Horse, woman, man. c, Two men, from "His Time Arrives." d, Woman holding paper, boy holding hat.

1996, Dec. 25 Litho. *Perf. 14*

170 A44 24te Sheet of 4, #a.-d. 10.00 10.00

Vormela Peregusna — A45

1997, Feb. 12 Litho. *Perf. 14*

171 A45 6te shown .80 .80
172 A45 10te Adult .95 .95
173 A45 32te Two young 2.10 2.10
174 A45 46te Adult, tail up 3.50 3.50
Nos. 171-174 (4) 7.35 7.35

World Wildlife Fund.

Zodiac Constellations A47

1997, Mar. 26 Litho. *Perf. 14*

176 A47 1te Aries .20 .20
177 A47 2te Taurus .20 .20
178 A47 3te Gemini .20 .20
179 A47 4te Cancer .20 .20
180 A47 5te Leo .20 .20
181 A47 6te Virgo .20 .20
182 A47 7te Libra .20 .20
183 A47 8te Scorpio .30 .30
184 A47 9te Sagittarius .35 .35
185 A47 10te Capricorn .35 .35
186 A47 12te Aquarius .50 .50
187 A47 20te Pisces .65 .65
b. Sheet of 12, #176-187 7.50 7.50

New Year Type of 1993 With Kazakhstan Inscribed in Both Cyrillic & Roman Letters

1997, Mar. 22 Litho. *Perf. 14*

187A A7 40te multicolored 1.75 1.75

New Year 1997 (Year of the Ox).

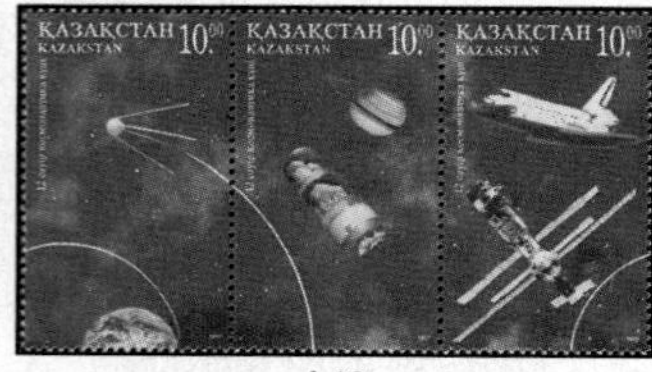
A48

A49

Cosmonauts' Day: a, Earth, Sputnik. b, Space vehicle, Saturn. c, Space shuttle, space station.

1997, Apr. 12

188 A48 10te Strip of 3, #a.-c. 3.25 3.25

No. 188 has continuous design.

1997, Apr. 23

189 A49 15te org yel & grn .75 .75
190 A49 60te org yel & grn 2.50 2.50

UNESCO World Book Day.

Mukhtar Auezov (1897-1961), Writer — A50

1997, May

191 A50 25te House 1.00 1.00
192 A50 40te Auezov at his desk 1.75 1.75

Orders and Medals — A51

Various medals.

1997, June 30 Litho. *Perf. 14*

193 A51 15te grn & yel ribbon .60 .60
194 A51 15te grn, red & pink ribbon .60 .60
195 A51 20te grn bl & multi .85 .85
196 A51 30te grn yel & multi 1.10 1.10
Nos. 193-196 (4) 3.15 3.15

Tulips — A52

15te, Tulipa regelii. No. 198, Tulipa greigii. No. 199, Tulipa alberti.

1997, Aug. 7 Litho. *Perf. 13½*

197 A52 15te multicolored .60 .60
198 A52 35te multicolored 1.40 1.40
199 A52 35te multicolored 1.40 1.40
Nos. 197-199 (3) 3.40 3.40

Paintings — A53

Designs: No. 200, Roping of a Wild Horse, by Moldakhmet S. Kenbaev. No. 201, Shepherd, by Sh. T. Sariev, vert. No. 202, Fantastic Still Life, by Sergei I. Kalmykov, vert.

1997, Sept. 10 Litho. *Perf. 14*

200 A53 25te multicolored 1.25 1.25
201 A53 25te multicolored 1.25 1.25
202 A53 25te multicolored 1.25 1.25
Nos. 200-202 (3) 3.75 3.75

Agate — A54

Azurite — A55

1997, Oct. 15 Litho. *Perf. 14*

203 A54 15te shown .65 .65
204 A54 15te Chalcedony .65 .65
205 A55 20te shown .90 .90
206 A55 20te Malachite .90 .90
a. Souvenir sheet, #203-206 3.25 3.25
Nos. 203-206 (4) 3.10 3.10

Desert Fauna — A56

Designs: No. 207, Gylippus rickmersi. No. 208, Anemelobathus rickmersi. No. 209, Latrodectus pallidus. No. 210, Oculicosa supermirabilis.

1997, Nov. 26 Litho. *Perf. 14*

207 A56 30te multicolored 1.25 1.25
208 A56 30te multicolored 1.25 1.25
209 A56 30te multicolored 1.25 1.25
210 A56 30te multicolored 1.25 1.25
Nos. 207-210 (4) 5.00 5.00

Souvenir Sheet

Nature Park — A57

Designs: a, Mountain goat. b, Trees on side of mountain. c, Rock formations, wildflowers.

1997, Dec. 22

211 A57 30te Sheet of 3, #a.-c. 3.50 3.50

See No. 257A.

A58

Sports A59

Designs: No. 212, Woman, man riding horses. No. 213, Wrestling match. No. 214, Group of men on galloping horses.

1997, Dec. 30 Litho. *Perf. 14*

212 A58 20te multicolored 1.25 1.25
213 A58 20te multicolored 1.25 1.25
214 A58 20te multicolored 1.25 1.25
215 A59 20te multicolored 1.25 1.25
Nos. 212-215 (4) 5.00 5.00

1998 Winter Olympic Games, Nagano — A60

Children's Paintings — A61

1998, Mar. 13 Litho. *Perf. 14*

216 A60 15te Figure skating .70 .70
217 A60 30te Biathlon 1.40 1.40

1998, Mar. 20

218 A61 15te shown .50 .50
219 A61 15te Outdoor scene, horiz. .50 .50

New Year Type of 1993 with "Kazakhstan" inscribed in both Cyrillis and Roman letters

1998, Mar. 22 Litho. *Perf. 14*

220 A7 30te yellow, black & brown 1.50 1.50

New Year 1998 (Year of the Tiger).

Kurmangazy (1823-96), Composer — A62

#222, Ahmet Baitursynov (1873-1937), poet.

1998 Litho. *Perf. 14*

221 A62 30te multicolored 1.00 1.00
222 A62 30te multicolored 1.00 1.00

Issued: No. 221, 4/10/98. No. 222, 4/28/98.

Ancient Gold Folk Art A63

15te, Ram's heads. 30te, Jeweled pendants, vert. 40te, Animal filigree diadem fragment.

1998, Apr. 30

223 A63 15te multicolored .55 .55
224 A63 30te multicolored .95 .95
225 A63 40te multicolored 2.00 2.00
Nos. 223-225 (3) 3.50 3.50

Cosmonaut's Day — A64

#226, Apollo 8, moon, sun. #227, Apollo 8, moon, Earth. 50te, Vostok 6, Earth.

1998, May 4

226 A64 30te multi, vert. 1.25 1.25
227 A64 30te multi, vert. 1.25 1.25
a. Pair, #226-227 2.50 2.50
228 A64 50te multi 2.00 2.00
Nos. 226-228 (3) 4.50 4.50

Astana, New Capital City — A64a

A65

Buildings: 10te, Mosque. 15te, Govt., vert. 20te, Parliament, vert. 25te, Office. 100te, Presidential office.

1998 Litho. *Perf. 13½*

229 A64a 10te brown .50 .50
230 A64a 15te dark blue .80 .80
231 A64a 15te blue .80 .80
232 A64a 20te green blue 1.00 1.00
232A A64a 25te purple 1.25 1.25
Nos. 229-232A (5) 4.35 4.35

Souvenir Sheet

233 A65 100te multicolored 5.00 5.00

Issued: Nos. 229-232, 233, 6/10; 25te, 12/98. No. 230 is inscribed "AKMOLA" in Cyrillic. No. 231 is inscribed "ACTANA."

Souvenir Sheet

Climbing Mt. Everest — A67

1998, July 29 Litho. *Perf. 14*

239 A67 100te multicolored 4.25 4.25

Fauna — A68

Birds: No. 240, Ciconia nigra. No. 241, Phoenicopterus roseus. No. 242, Grus leucogeranus.

Wild cats: No. 243, Lynx lynx isabellinus. No. 244, Felis margarita. No. 245, Uncia uncia.

1998, July 31

240 A68 15te multicolored .70 .70
241 A68 30te multicolored 1.25 1.25
242 A68 50te multicolored 2.10 2.10
Nos. 240-242 (3) 4.05 4.05

1998, Aug. 8

243 A68 15te multicolored .70 .70
244 A68 30te multicolored 1.25 1.25
245 A68 50te multicolored 2.10 2.10
Nos. 243-245 (3) 4.05 4.05

Souvenir Sheet

Admission of Kazakhstan to UPU — A69

1998, Oct. 9 Litho. *Perf. 14*

246 A69 50te multicolored 3.00 3.00

Natl. Arms A70

World Stamp Day A71

Republic, 5th Anniv. — A72

1998 Litho. *Perf. 13½*

Inscribed "1998"

247 A70 1te green .20 .20
a. Inscribed "1999" .20 .20
248 A70 2te blue .20 .20
a. Inscribed "1999" .20 .20
249 A70 3te red .20 .20
250 A70 4te bright pink .20 .20
251 A70 5te orange yellow .20 .20
a. Inscribed "1999" .20 .20
252 A70 8te orange .50 .50
253 A71 30te olive 1.60 1.60
254 A72 40te orange 2.25 2.25
Nos. 247-254 (8) 5.35 5.35

Issued; 1te-5te, 6/29; 8te-40te, 11/12. "1999" varieties issued: 1te, 1/28/00; 2te, 9/7/99; 5te, 11/12/99.

See Nos. 296, 299. Compare with Nos. 444-455.

Natl. Epic A73

Horseman: 20te, Holding sword. 30te, Shooting bow and arrow. 40te, Charging with spear.

1998, Dec. *Perf. 14*

255 A73 20te multicolored 1.25 1.25
256 A73 30te multicolored 1.90 1.90
257 A73 40te multicolored 2.40 2.40
Nos. 255-257 (3) 5.55 5.55

Souvenir Sheet

Nature Park Type of 1997

Designs: a, Island in middle of lake, mountains. b, Lake, mountain peaks.

1998, Dec. Litho. *Perf. 14*

257A A57 30te Sheet of 2, #a.-b. 3.50 3.50

1999 Census A74

Space Communications A77

K. Satpayev (1899-1964)
A75 A76

1999 Litho. *Perf. 13½*

258 A74 1te green .20 .20
259 A75 15te rose lake .85 .85
260 A76 20te brown 1.10 1.10
261 A77 30te olive 1.60 1.60
Nos. 258-261 (4) 3.75 3.75

Issued: 1te, 2/5/99; 30te, 3/19/99.

See Nos. 270, 272.

Trains — A78

Map showing Orenburg-Tashkent Rail Line, 1890-1906, and: 40te, Steam train. 50te, Diesel locomotive. 60te, Bullet train. 80te, Interurban train.

1999 *Perf. 14*

262 A78 40te yel & multi 1.75 1.75
263 A78 50te pink & multi 2.25 2.25
264 A78 60te grn & multi 3.00 3.00
265 A78 80te blue & multi 4.00 4.00
Nos. 262-265 (4) 11.00 11.00

Space Achievements — A79

1999

266 A79 50te Soviet space-craft, vert. 6.00 6.00
267 A79 90te Apollo 11 mission 11.50 11.50

Cosmonaut Day (#266), first manned lunar landing, 30th anniv. (#267).

New Year Type of 1993 with "Kazakhstan" inscribed in both Cyrillis and Roman letters

1999, Mar. 19 Litho. *Perf. 14*

268 A7 40te multicolored 2.75 2.75

New Year 1999 (Year of the Rabbit).

Space Communications Type of 1999 and:

A79a

A79b

1999 Litho. *Perf. 13½*

270 A77 3te red .30 .30
271 A79a 4te bright pink .30 .30
272 A77 9te bright green .70 .70
273 A79b 10te purple .75 .75
274 A79a 30te olive green 2.10 2.10
Nos. 270-274 (5) 4.15 4.15

No. 273 is for the UPU, 125th Anniv.

Flowers — A80

Movies — A81

Designs: 20te, Pseudoeremostachys severzowii. 30te, Rhaphidophyton regelii. 90te, Niedzwedkia semiretscenskia.

1999, June 28 Litho. *Perf. 14¼x14*

276	A80 20te multicolored		1.60	1.60
277	A80 30te multicolored		2.25	2.25
278	A80 90te multicolored		6.50	6.50
	Nos. 276-278 (3)		10.35	10.35

1999 Litho. *Perf. 14*

No. 279: a, 15te, Film scene from 1929. b, 20te, Scenes from 1988, 1997, M. Berkovich. c, 30te, Scenes from 1935, 1938, 1957. d, 35te, Scenes from 1989, 1994, 1997. e, 50te, Alfred Hitchcock. f, 60te, Sergei Eisenstein.

279 A81 Sheet of 10, #e.-f., 2 each #a.-d. 12.00 12.00

Foxes A82

Designs: 20te, Vulpes vulpes. 30te, Cuon alpinus. 90te, Vulpes corsac.

1999 Litho. *Perf. 14x 14¼*

280	A82 20te multicolored	1.50	1.50
281	A82 30te multicolored	2.50	2.50
282	A82 90te multicolored	6.50	6.50
	Nos. 280-282 (3)	10.50	10.50

Souvenir Sheet

Environmental Protection — A83

Designs: a, 15te, Cessation of nuclear tests at Semipalatinsk, 10th anniv. b, 45te, Save the ozone layer. c, 60te, Save nature.

1999 Litho. *Perf. 14x13¾*

283 A83 Sheet of 3, #a.-c. 4.50 4.50

Kazakhstan Hockey Team — A84

1999 Litho. *Perf. 14*

284	A84 20te Face-off	1.10	1.10
285	A84 30te Team photo	1.75	1.75

10th Gusman Kosanov Memorial Track & Field Meet — A85

1999

286 A85 40te multi 1.75 1.75

Cosmonauts — A86

1999 *Perf. 14*

287	A86 40te Talgat Musabayev	1.60	1.60
288	A86 50te Toktar Aubakirov, vert.	1.90	1.90

Souvenir Sheet

UPU, 125th Anniv. — A87

1999, Dec. 20 Litho. *Perf. 14x13¾*

289 A87 20te multi 1.75 1.75

Arms Type of 1998 and

Spireanthus Schrenhianus A88

Echo Satellite A89

Oil Rig A90

Mukhammed Khaidar Dulati (1499-1551), Historian A91

Sabit Mukanov (1900-73), Writer — A92

2000 Litho. *Perf. 13½*

290	A88	1te green		.25	.25
291	A88	2te bright blue		.25	.25
291A	A89	5te orange yellow		.25	.25
292	A90	7te red		.40	.40
293	A91	8te dark blue		.40	.40
294	A92	10te olive green		.40	.40
295	A89	15te violet blue		.50	.50
296	A70	20te orange		1.00	1.00
297	A89	20te indigo		.70	.70
299	A70	50te blue		2.25	2.25
300	A88	50te blue		2.10	2.10
		Nos. 290-300 (11)		8.50	8.50

Issued: 7te, 20te, 50te, 1/18/00; 1te, 2te, No. 300, 11/24; 5te, 15te, No. 297, 9/28; 8te, 8/25; 10te, 6/30. 20te and 50te are dated 1999.

Navruz Bayram — A93

2000, Mar. 21 Litho. *Imperf.*

301 A93 20te multi 1.75 1.75

Millennium — A94

2000, Mar. 24 Litho. *Perf. 13½*

302 A94 30te org & blue green 2.25 2.25

Victory in World War II, 55th Anniv. — A95

2000, May 8 Litho. *Perf. 13½*

303 A95 3te brown & red .25 .25

Souvenir Sheet

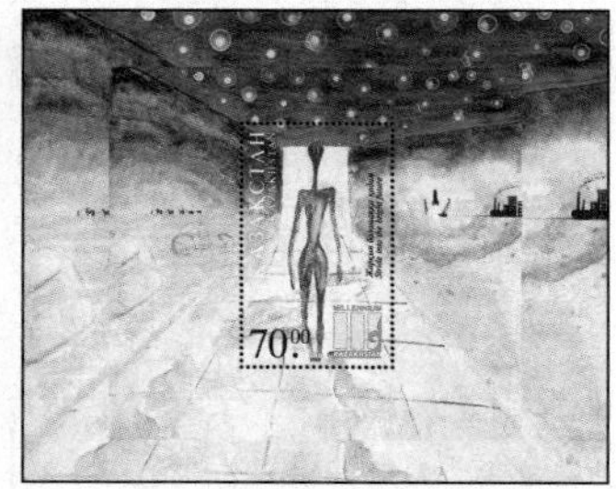
Millennium — A96

2000, June 1 *Perf. 14x13¾*

304 A96 70te multi 3.50 3.50

Containers — A97

No. 305: a, 15te, Leather vessel for koumiss, Kazakhstan. b, 50te, Teapot, China.

2000, June 28 *Perf. 12½x12*

305 A97 Horiz. pair, #a-b 5.00 5.00

See China (PRC) Nos. 3042-3043.

2000 Summer Olympics, Sydney — A98

Designs: 35te, Rowing. No. 307, 40te, Taekwondo. No. 308, 40te, Men's gymnastics. 50te, Triathlon.

2000, Sept. 15 *Perf. 12*

306-309 A98 Set of 4 7.75 7.75

Souvenir Sheet

Turkistan, 1500th Anniv. — A99

Mausoleums of: a, 50te, Arystan Bab, 12th-20th cents. b, 50te, Karashash Ana, 12th-18th cents. c, 70te, Hadji Ahmet Yassauy, 14th cent.

2000, Oct. 19 *Perf. 13½*

310 A99 Sheet of 3, #a-c 10.00 10.00
Complete booklet, #310 *24.00*

Bourzhan Momush-Uly (1910-82), Hero of the Soviet Union — A100

2000, Dec. 22 *Perf. 13½*

311 A100 4te black & brown .50 .50

No. B1Surcharged in Dark Blue

Method and Perf. as Before

2001, Jan. 26

Block of 3, #a-c, + Label

312 SP1 10te on 1te+30ti multi 1.25 1.25

New Year Type of 1993 with "Kazakhstan" Inscribed in Both Cyrillic and Roman Letters

2001, Mar. 2 Litho. *Perf. 13¾x14*

313 A7 40te org, blk & blue 2.10 2.10

Dated 2000. New Year 2000 (Year of the Snail).

Cosmonaut's Day — A101

Designs: 40te, Dogs Belka and Strelka. 70te, Rocket launch, vert.

2001, Mar. 6 *Perf. 14*

314-315 A101 Set of 2 7.75 7.75

Dated 2000. Spaceflight of Belka and Strelka, 40th anniv., Baikonur Cosmodrome, 45th anniv.

New Year Type of 1993 with "Kazakhstan" Inscribed in Both Cyrillic and Roman Letters

2001, Mar. 21 Litho. *Perf. 13¾x14*

316 A7 40te grn, blk & brn 1.40 1.40

New Year 2001 (Year of the Snake).

Souvenir Sheet

Ministry of Communications, 10th Anniv. — A102

2001, Apr. 4 *Perf. 11½*
317 A102 100te multi 9.00 9.00

Cosmonaut's Day — A103

Designs: 45te, Soyuz 11 and Salyut. 60te, Yuri Gagarin, Earth.

2001, Apr. 12 *Perf. 14*
318-319 A103 Set of 2 5.00 5.00

Aquilegia Karatavica A104

School, Almaty A105

Phodopus Roborovskii — A106

Perf. 13½, 14 (#321, 326)

2001			**Litho.**	
320	A104	3te olive green	.20	.20
321	A105	7te red violet	.20	.20
322	A106	8te orange	.30	.30
323	A104	10te yellow green	.35	.35
324	A106	15te dark blue	.50	.50
325	A106	20te deep blue	.60	.60
326	A105	30te greenish gray	.75	.75
327	A106	50te brown	1.25	1.25
		Nos. 320-327 (8)	4.15	4.15

Issued: 7te, 30te, 10/19/01.

Kazakh State Khans — A107

Designs: 50te, Abulkhair Khan (1693-1748). 60te, Abylai Khan (1711-81).

2001, May 24 **Litho.** *Perf. 13¾x14*
328-329 A107 Set of 2 4.00 4.00

Dated 2000.

Owls A108

Designs: 30te, Bubo bubo. 40te, Asio otus. 50te, Surnia ulula.

2001, June 7 *Perf. 14*
330-332 A108 Set of 3 7.00 7.00

Dated 2000.

Communications Program 2030 — A109

2001, June 21 *Perf. 14x13¾*
333 A109 40te multi 1.90 1.90

Dated 2000.

Souvenir Sheet

Lake Markakol — A110

No. 334: a, Cervus elaphus. b, Ursus arctos. c, Brachymystax lenok.

2001, July 5 *Perf. 13¾x14*
334 A110 30te Sheet of 3, #a-c 5.00 5.00

Souvenir Sheet

Flora & Fauna — A111

No. 335: a, 9te, Marmota bobac. b, 12te, Otis tarda. c, 25te, Larus relictus. d, 60te, Felis libyca. e, 90te, Nymphaea alba. f, 100te, Pelecanus crispus.

2001, July 19 *Perf. 14x14¼*
335 A111 Sheet of 6, #a-f 9.00 9.00

Souvenir Sheet

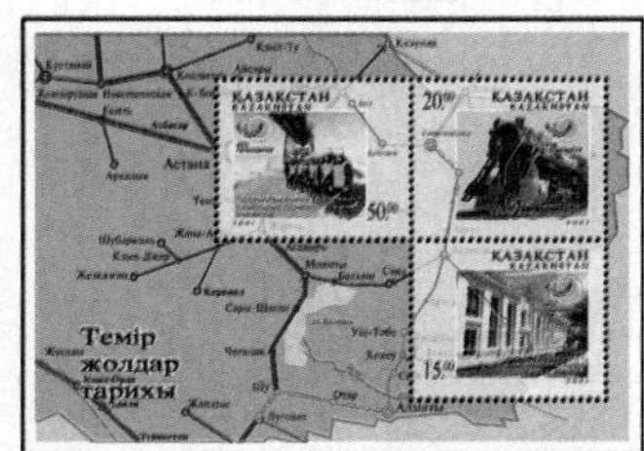

Kazakh Railways, 10th Anniv. — A112

No. 336: a, 15te, Building. b, 20te, Turkestan-Siberia locomotive. c, 50te, Railroad workers.

2001, Aug. 4 *Perf. 14x13¾*
336 A112 Sheet of 3, #a-c *17.50 17.50*

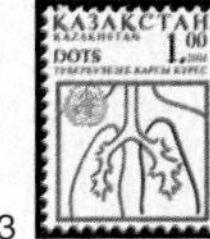

Medicine — A113

Designs: 1te, WHO emblem, lungs (tuberculosis prevention). 5te, Ribbon, book (AIDS prevention).

2001, Aug. 9 *Perf. 13½*
337-338 A113 Set of 2 .40 .40

Intl. Year of Mountains (in 2002) — A114

Various mountains: 35te, 60te.

2001, Sept. 26 *Perf. 14*
339-340 A114 Set of 2 3.25 3.25

Space Achievements — A115

Designs: 50te, Alexei Leonov's walk in space, 1965, vert. 70te, Apollo-Soyuz mission, 1975.

2001, Oct. 2
341-342 A115 Set of 2 10.00 10.00

Dated 2000.

Year of Dialogue Among Civilizations A116

2001, Oct. 9 *Perf. 13¾x14*
343 A116 45te multi 1.50 1.50

Worldwide Fund for Nature (WWF) — A117

Various views of Equus hemionus kulan: 9te, 12te, 25te, 50te.

2001, Nov. 1 *Perf. 14*
344-347 A117 Set of 4 4.00 4.00

Commonwealth of Independent States, 10th Anniv. — A118

2001, Dec. 12 **Litho.** *Perf. 14*
348 A118 40te multi 2.10 2.10

Visit of Pope John Paul II — A119

No. 349: a, 20te, Pres. Nazarbayev, Pope. b, 50te, Pope, Pres. Nazarbayev.

2001, Dec. 14 *Perf. 11½*
349 A119 Horiz. pair, #a-b 4.00 4.00

A120

Independence, 10th Anniv. — A121

No. 351: a, 9te, Monument of Independence, Almaty. b, 25te, Parliament, Astana. c, 35te, Pres. Nazarbayev.

2001 *Perf. 13½*
350 A120 40te multi 1.75 1.75

Souvenir Sheet

Perf. 13¾x14

351 A121 Sheet of 3, #a-c 5.50 5.50

Issued: 40te, 12/18; No. 351, 12/16.

Native Attire — A122

No. 352: a, 25te, Male attire. b, 35te, Female attire.

2001, Dec. 25 *Perf. 14x13¾*
352 A122 Horiz. pair, #a-b 2.40 2.40

2002 Winter Olympics, Salt Lake City A123

Designs: 50te, Women's ice hockey. 150te, Freestyle skiing.

2002, Feb. 14 *Perf. 14*
353-354 A123 Set of 2 8.50 8.50

New Year Type of 1993 With "Kazakhstan" Inscribed in Both Cyrillic and Roman Letters

2002, Mar. 21 *Perf. 11½*
355 A7 50te multi 1.75 1.75

New Year 2002 (Year of the Horse).

Horses A124

Horses: 9te, English. 25te, Kustenai. 60te, Akhalteka.

2002, Mar. 28
356-358 A124 Set of 3 5.75 5.75

Pterygostemon Spathulatus A125

Gani Muratbaev (1902-25), Political Leader A126

Salpingotus Pallidus
A127

Trade House, Petropavlovsk
A128

Monument, Petro-pavlovsk
A129

Gabiden Mustafin (1902-85), Writer
A130

2002 Litho. *Perf. 13½*

No.	Type	Value	Color	Unused	Used
359	A125	1te	blue green	.25	.25
360	A125	2te	blue	.25	.25
361	A125	3te	green	.25	.25
362	A126	3te	brown	.25	.25
363	A127	5te	rose lilac	.25	.25
364	A128	6te	red	.25	.25
365	A128	7te	lilac	.25	.25
366	A129	8te	orange	.25	.25
367	A125	10te	violet	.25	.25
368	A130	10te	blue	.25	.25
369	A125	12te	pink	.40	.40
370	A127	15te	dark blue	.40	.40
371	A129	23te	gray blue	.70	.70
372	A125	25te	purple	.70	.70
373	A125	35te	olive green	.95	.95
374	A127	40te	bister brown	1.10	1.10
375	A127	50te	brown	1.60	1.60
			Nos. 359-375 (17)	8.35	8.35

Petropavlovsk, 250th anniv. (#364-366, 371). Issued: 1te, 2te, 5/7; Nos. 361, 367, 35te, 4/30; 5te, 15te, 40te, 50te, 4/4; 6te, 7te, 8te, 23te, 7/9; 12te, 25te, 5/14; No. 362, 12/19; No. 368, 12/18.

Cosmonauts Day — A131

Designs: 30te, Cosmonauts Yuri Baturin, Talgat Musabaev and first space tourist Dennis Tito. 70te, Globe, rocket, flags of US, Kazakhstan and Russia.

2002, Apr. 10 Litho. *Perf. 11¾*
376-377 A131 Set of 2 3.75 3.75

2002 World Cup Soccer Championships, Japan and Korea — A132

Two players, one with: No. 378, 10te, Jersey No. 8. No. 379, 10te, Jersey No. 7.

2002, May 31
378-379 A132 Set of 2 1.50 1.50

Transeurasia 2002 Conference — A133

2002, June 6 *Perf. 13½*
380 A133 30te multi 1.00 1.00

Souvenir Sheet

Flora and Fauna — A134

No. 381: a, Leontopodium fedtschenkoanum. b, Mustela erminea. c, Aport Alexander apples.

2002, June 6 *Perf. 11¾x11½*
381 A134 30te Sheet of 3, #a-c 3.25 3.25

Art — A135

Designs: 8te, Kazakh Folk Epos, by E. Sidorkin, 1961. 9te, Makhambet, by M. Kisamedinov, 1973. 60te, Batyr, by Sidorkin, 1979.

2002, July 19 *Perf. 11¾*
382-384 A135 Set of 3 3.00 3.00

Birds — A136

No. 385: a, 10te, Larus ichthyaetus pallas. b, 15te, Anthropoides virgo.

2002, Aug. 29 *Perf. 12*
385 A136 Horiz. pair, #a-b 1.75 1.75

See Russia No. 6709.

Marine Life — A137

No. 386: a, 20te, Huso huso ponticus. b, 35te, Phoca caspica.

2002, Sept. 6
386 A137 Horiz. pair, #a-b 2.75 2.75

See Ukraine No. 483.

Souvenir Sheet

Taraz, 2000th Anniv. — A138

2002, Sept. 25
387 A138 70te multi 2.90 2.90

Souvenir Sheet

International Year of Mountains — A139

2002, Oct. 4 *Perf. 11½x11¾*
388 A139 50te multi 1.90 1.90

Gabit Musrepov (1902-85)
A140

2002, Dec. 30 Litho. *Perf. 11½*
389 A140 20te multi .65 .65

Airplanes
A141

Designs: 20te, Ilyushin-86. 40te, Tupolev-144 and map.

Perf. 11½x11¾
2002, Dec. 23 Litho.
390-391 A141 Set of 2 2.40 2.40

First Moscow to Alma Ata flight of Tupolev-144, 25th anniv. (No. 391).

Type of 1999, Types of 2000-01 Redrawn and

Monument to Victims of Political Reprisals
A142

Selevinia Betpak-dalensis
A143

2003 Litho. *Perf. 13½*

No.	Type	Value	Color	Unused	Used
392	A88	1te	green	.20	.20
393	A142	1te	red violet	.20	.20
394	A88	2te	bright blue	.20	.20
394A	A77	3te	red	.20	.20
395	A143	4te	brown	.20	.20
396	A143	5te	bister	.20	.20
397	A143	6te	gray green	.20	.20
398	A143	7te	dull green	.20	.20
399	A106	8te	orange	.20	.20
400	A142	8te	red brown	.20	.20
401	A77	9te	dark blue	.20	.20
402	A143	10te	blue	.20	.20
403	A106	15te	deep blue	.45	.45
404	A106	20te	gray blue	.55	.55
405	A106	35te	dark green	1.00	1.00
406	A143	63te	fawn	1.90	1.90
407	A77	84te	purple	2.40	2.40
408	A77	100te	orange	2.75	2.75
409	A143	150te	claret	4.00	4.00
			Nos. 392-409 (19)	15.45	15.45

Issued: No. 392, 2te, 2/24; Nos. 393, 400, 4/17; 4te, 5te, 6te, 7te, 10te, 63te, 150te, 1/31; No. 399, 15te, 20te, 35te, 3/28; 84te, 100te, 5/30; 3te, 9te, 9/12.

Nos. 392 and 394 are dated "2003" and have smaller Cyrillic inscription of country name, and longer Roman inscription of country name than Nos. 290-291.

Nos. 394A is dated "2003" and has a smaller denomination with thinner zeroes than No. 270.

Nos. 399, 403 and 404 are dated "2003" and have taller Cyrillic inscription of country name than Nos. 322, 324-325.

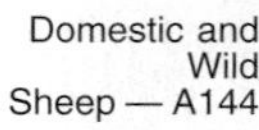

Domestic and Wild Sheep — A144

Various rams, ewes and lambs: 20te, 40te, 50te.

2003, Feb. 26 *Perf. 11½x11¾*
410-412 A144 Set of 3 3.25 3.25

New Year Type of 1993 With "Kazakhstan" Inscribed in Both Cyrillic and Roman Letters

2003, Mar. 21 *Perf. 11½*
413 A7 40te lt bl, blk & dk bl 1.60 1.60

New Year 2003 (Year of the Ram).

Cosmonaut's Day — A145

Designs: 40te, Pioneer 10 and Jupiter. 70te, Mir Space Station, vert.

2003, Apr. 12 *Perf. 11¾*
414-415 A145 Set of 2 3.75 3.75

Intl. Association of Academies of Science, 10th Anniv. — A146

2003, Apr. 23 Litho. *Perf. 11½*
416 A146 50te multi 1.60 1.60

Souvenir Sheet

Ethnic Groups in Kazakhstan — A147

No. 417: a, Kazakhs (woman with red vest). b, Russians (woman with yellow blouse). c, Ukrainians (woman with blue vest).

2003, Apr. 29 Litho. *Perf. 11¾x11½*
417 A147 35te Sheet of 3, #a-c 3.25 3.25

Musical Instruments
A148

Designs: 25te, Dombra. 50te, Kobyz.

2003, May 26
418-419 A148 Set of 2 2.25 2.25

Fairy Tales
A149

Designs: 30te, Aldar Kose and Alasha Khan. 40te, Aldar Kose and Karynbaj.

2003, June 27 ***Perf. 11½***
420-421 A149 Set of 2 3.00 3.00

Art — A150

Designs: 20te, Chess Match, by Arturo Ricci (1854-1919). 35te, Portrait of the Shepherd, sculpture by H. Nauryzbaev. 45te, Bowls of Koumiss, by Aisha Galimbaeva (1917-).

2003, July 7 ***Perf. 11¾***
422-424 A150 Set of 3 3.75 3.75

Famous
Men — A151

Designs: No. 425, 60te, Tole Bey (1663-1756). No. 426, 60te, Kazybek Bey (1667-1763). No. 427, 60te, Aiteke Bey (1689-1766).

2003, Aug. 11 ***Perf. 11¾x11½***
425-427 A151 Set of 3 5.00 5.00

Halyk Bank, 80th Anniv.
A152

2003, Aug. 15 ***Perf. 11½x11¾***
428 A152 23te multi .95 .95

International Transit Conference, Almaty — A153

2003, Aug. 28
429 A153 40te multi 1.25 1.25

World Post
Day — A154

2003, Oct. 9 ***Perf. 13½***
430 A154 23te pur & blue .80 .80

Houses of Worship, Almaty — A155

Designs: No. 431, 50te, Cathedral. No. 432, 50te, Mosque.

2003, Oct. 10 ***Perf. 11¾x11½***
431-432 A155 Set of 2 3.00 3.00

Tenge Currency, 10th Anniv. — A156

2003, Nov. 15 ***Perf. 13½***
433 A156 25te blue & yel org .70 .70

Paintings — A157

No. 434: a, Baxt, by S. Ayitbaev, 1966. b, Tong. Onalik, by R. Ahmedov, 1962.

2003, Nov. 25 ***Perf. 12***
434 A157 100te Horiz. pair, #a-b 7.50 7.50

See Uzbekistan No. 385.

Populus Diversifolia
A158

2003, Dec. 10 ***Perf. 11½***
435 A158 100te multi 3.00 3.00

Petroglyphs, Tamgaly — A159

Designs. 25te, Cows. 30te, Man as sun on bull, vert.

Perf. 11½x11¾, 11¾x11½
2003, Dec. 19
436-437 A159 Set of 2 1.90 1.90

Abylkhan Kasteev (1904-73), Artist — A160

2004, Feb. 28 **Litho.** ***Perf. 11¾***
439 A160 115te multi 3.50 3.50

New Year Type of 1993 With "Kazakhstan" Inscribed in Both Cyrillic and Roman Letters

2004, Mar. 23 ***Perf. 11½***
440 A7 35te lt bl, dk bl & org .90 .90

New Year 2004 (Year of the Monkey).

Cosmonaut's Day — A161

Designs: 40te, Mariner 10, vert. 50te, Luna 3.

Perf. 11¾x11½, 11½x11¾
2004, Apr. 12
441-442 A161 Set of 2 2.75 2.75

Kazakhstan
Flag — A162

2004, Apr. 19 ***Perf. 13½***
443 A162 25te yel & brt blue .70 .70

Arms Type of 1998 Redrawn

2004		**Litho.**		***Perf. 13½***
444 A70	1te	green	.20	.20
445 A70	2te	bright blue	.20	.20
446 A70	4te	bright pink	.20	.20
447 A70	5te	orange yellow	.20	.20
448 A70	10te	olive green	.20	.20
449 A70	16te	brt purple	.40	.40
450 A70	20te	purple	.50	.50
451 A70	35te	bright yellow	.85	.85
452 A70	50te	brt green	1.25	1.25
453 A70	72te	orange	1.75	1.75
454 A70	100te	greenish blue	2.50	2.50
455 A70	200te	vermilion	4.75	4.75
		Nos. 444-455 (12)	13.00	13.00

Issued: 1te, 2te, 4te, 4/19; 20te, 35te, 72te, 100te, 200te, 5/11; 5te, 10te, 16te, 50te, 6/10.

Nos. 444-455 are dated "2004," arms and "Kazakhstan" in Roman letters are larger and denominations are smaller than those features on Nos. 247-254.

No. 447 is dated "2004," arms and "Kazakhstan" in Roman letters are larger and denomination is smaller than those features on No. 251.

Souvenir Sheet

Kazakhstan Railways, Cent. — A163

2004, Apr. 22 **Litho.** ***Perf. 11¾x11½***
456 A163 150te multi 3.25 3.25

Souvenir Sheet

Ethnic Groups in Kazakhstan — A164

No. 457: a, Uzbeks (denomination at left). b, Germans (denomination at right).

2004, May 12
457 A164 65te Sheet of 2, #a-b 4.75 4.75

FIFA (Fédération Internationale de Football Association), Cent. — A165

FIFA emblem, soccer player and soccer ball at: No. 458, 100te, Left. No. 459, 100te, Center.

2004, May 21 **Litho. & Embossed**
458-459 A165 Set of 2 6.00 6.00

Children's
Art — A166

Designs: No. 460, 45te, Yurts and sheep, by A. Sadykov. No. 461, 45te, Woman, by D. Iskhanova, vert.

2004, June 20 **Litho.** ***Perf. 11½***
460-461 A166 Set of 2 2.40 2.40

Souvenir Sheet

2004 Summer Olympics, Athens — A167

No. 462: a, 70te, Boxing. b, 115te, Shooting.

Litho., Margin Embossed

2004, June 28
462 A167 Sheet of 2, #a-b 4.00 4.00

Souvenir Sheet

Fauna in Altyn Emel Reserve — A168

No. 463: a, Acgypius monacus. b, Capra sibirica. c, Gazella subgutturosa.

2004, Aug. 11 ***Perf. 11½x11¾***
463 A168 50te Sheet of 3, #a-c 4.50 4.50

Souvenir Sheet

Kazaktelecom, 10th Anniv. — A169

Perf. 11½x11¾

2004, Aug. 18 **Litho.**
464 A169 70te multi 1.75 1.75

Alkei Khakan Margulan (1904-85), Archaeologist A170

2004, Sept. 23
465 A170 115te multi 2.50 2.50

Flowers — A171

2004, Oct. 4 ***Perf. 12¼x11½***
466 A171 25te multi + label .60 .60

Printed in sheets of 12 + 12 labels.

World Post Day Type of 2003

2004, Oct. 9 ***Perf. 13½***
467 A154 3te red vio & blue .30 .30
468 A154 30te yel org & blue .90 .90

New Year 2005 — A172

2004, Nov. 23 ***Perf. 13¼***
469 A172 65te multi 1.50 1.50

Musical Instruments — A173

No. 470: a, Adyma. b, Gizhak and bow.

2004, Nov. 29 ***Perf. 11½x11¾***
470 A173 100te Horiz. pair, #a-b 4.25 4.25

See Tajikistan No. 248.

Saken Seifullin (1894-1939), Writer — A174

2004, Dec. 28
471 A174 35te multi .80 .80

Women's Headdresses — A175

No. 472: a, Kazakh headdress, denomination at left. b, Mongol headdress, denomination at right.

2004, Dec. 30
472 A175 72te Horiz. pair, #a-b 4.25 4.25

See Mongolia No. 2590.

Veterinary Research Institute, Cent. — A176

2005, Jan. 14 ***Perf. 13½***
473 A176 7te multi .30 .30

Constitution, 10th Anniv. — A177

2005, Apr. 8 **Litho.** ***Perf. 13½***
474 A177 1te blue & brn .25 .25
475 A177 2te vio & brn .25 .25
476 A177 3te brt grn & brn .25 .25
477 A177 8te brt bl & brn .25 .25
478 A177 10te red & brn .25 .25
479 A177 A red vio & brn .70 .70
480 A177 50te olive & brn 1.25 1.25
481 A177 65te bl grn & brn 1.50 1.50
Nos. 474-481 (8) 4.70 4.70

No. 479 sold for 25te on day of issue.

Europa — A178

2005, Apr. 14 **Litho.** ***Perf. 11½x12¼***
482 A178 90te multi 4.25 4.25

End of World War II, 60th Anniv. — A179

2005, Apr. 28 **Litho.** ***Perf. 13¼x13***
483 A179 72te multi 1.90 1.90

Souvenir Sheet

Baikonur Space Complex, 50th Anniv. — A180

No. 484: a, Rocket. b, Buran space shuttle. c, Capsule and parachute.

2005, June 2 ***Perf. 11½x11¾***
484 A180 72te Sheet of 3, #a-c 5.50 5.50

Peace and Harmony Palace — A181

Litho. & Embossed

2005, July 6 ***Perf. 13¼***
485 A181 65te multi 1.75 1.75

Minerals — A182

Designs: 50te, Azurite. 70te, Agate.

2005, July 12 **Litho.** ***Perf. 11¾x11½***
486-487 A182 Set of 2 3.00 3.00

Fairy Tales Type of 2003

Designs: 35te, Aldar Kose and the Musician. 45te, Aldar Kose and the Raiser of Asses.

2005, Aug. 11
488-489 A149 Set of 2 2.10 2.10

Constitution, 10th Anniv. — A183

2005, Aug. 26
490 A183 72te multi 1.75 1.75

Souvenir Sheet

Olympic Gold Medalists — A184

No. 491: a, Zaksylik Ushkempirov, 1980, 48kg Greco-Roman wrestling. b, Vitaly Savin, 1988, 4x100m relay. c, Vasily Zhirov, 1996, light heavyweight boxing. d, Bekzat Sattarkhanov, 2000, featherweight boxing.

2005, Sept. 22 **Litho.** ***Perf. 11¾***
491 A184 100te Sheet of 4, #a-d 9.50 9.50

Akhmet Baitursynov (1873-1937), Writer — A185

Litho. with Foil Application

2005, Oct. 6 ***Perf. 13¾x14***
492 A185 30te multi .70 .70

No. 492 not issued without gold overprint.

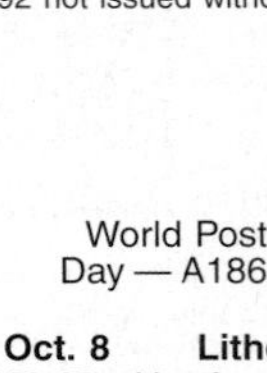

World Post Day — A186

2005, Oct. 8 **Litho.** ***Perf. 13½***
493 A186 35te blue & pur .80 .80
494 A186 40te pur & red .95 .95

Dogs — A187

No. 495: a, Kazakh hound (dog with curled tail). b, Estonian hound (white, black and brown dog).

2005, Oct. 19 ***Perf. 11½x11¾***
495 A187 138te Horiz. pair, #a-b 7.50 7.50

See Estonia No. 523.

United Nations, 60th Anniv. — A188

2005, Oct. 31 ***Perf. 13½***
496 A188 150te multi 4.00 4.00

New Year 2006 — A189

2005, Nov. 10 **Litho.** ***Perf. 13¼***
497 A189 65te multi 1.75 1.75

Evgeny Brusilovsky (1905-81), Composer — A190

2005, Nov. 18 ***Perf. 11½x11¾***
498 A190 150te multi 3.75 3.75

Assembly of Peoples of Kazakhstan, 10th Anniv. — A191

2005, Nov. 24 ***Perf. 13½***
499 A191 80te multi 2.00 2.00

Souvenir Sheet

National Symbols — A192

No. 500: a, 70te, Flag and eagle. b, 70te, National anthem. c, 300te, Arms.

Litho. & Embossed

2005, Dec. 22 ***Perf. 13¼***
500 A192 Sheet of 3, #a-c 10.50 10.50

Turgen Waterfall A193

Mountain Lake A194

2005, Dec. 23 **Litho.** ***Perf. 13½***
501 A193 12te multi .30 .30
502 A194 100te multi 2.40 2.40

Hans Christian Andersen (1805-75), Author — A195

2005, Dec. 30 ***Perf. 11¾x11½***
503 A195 200te multi 4.75 4.75

Parliament, 10th Anniv. — A196

2006, Jan. 17 **Litho.** ***Perf. 11½x11¾***
504 A196 50te multi 1.40 1.40

Abylai Khan, by Aubakir Ismailov A197

Litho. With Foil Application

2006, Jan. 27 ***Perf. 13x13¼***
505 A197 94te multi 2.25 2.25

2006 Winter Olympics, Turin — A198

Perf. 11½x11¾

2006, Feb. 20 **Litho.**
506 A198 138te multi 3.25 3.25

Cosmonaut's Day — A199

Paintings of cosmonauts by: 100te, P. M. Popov. 120te, A. M. Stepanov.

2006, Apr. 12 ***Perf. 11¾x11½***
507-508 A199 Set of 2 5.00 5.00

Traditional Jewelry — A200

No. 509: a, Bracelet, Kazakhstan. b, Brooch, Latvia.

2006, Apr. 19 ***Perf. 11½x11¾***
509 A200 110te Horiz. pair, #a-b 5.00 5.00

See Latvia No. 650.

Saksaul Tree — A201

2006, Apr. 27 ***Perf. 11¾x11½***
510 A201 25te multi .60 .60

Europa — A202

2006, May 3
511 A202 210te multi 3.75 3.75
a. Tete-beche pair 7.50 7.50

Turkestan-Siberia Railway, 75th Anniv. — A203

2006, May 31 ***Perf. 13x13¼***
512 A203 200te multi 4.50 4.50

2006 World Cup Soccer Championships, Germany — A204

2006, June 2 ***Perf. 11½x11¾***
513 A204 150te multi 3.50 3.50

Intl. Year of Deserts and Desertification — A205

2006, July 7 ***Perf. 13¼***
514 A205 110te multi 2.75 2.75

Mosque, Astana — A206

2006 **Litho.** ***Perf. 13½x13¾***

515	A206	5te emerald	.20	.20
516	A206	8te Prus blue	.20	.20
517	A206	10te olive grn	.25	.25
518	A206	A purple	.55	.55
518A	A206	100te dark blue	2.25	2.25
519	A206	110te brown	2.50	2.50
520	A206	120te green	2.75	2.75
521	A206	200te red violet	4.75	4.75
		Nos. 515-521 (8)	13.45	13.45

No. 518 sold for 25te on day of issue.
Issued: 100te, 10/10/06; rest, 7/20/06.

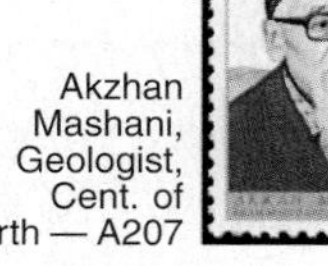

Akzhan Mashani, Geologist, Cent. of Birth — A207

2006, July 21 **Litho.** ***Perf. 11½x11¾***
522 A207 85te multi 2.00 2.00

Houses of Worship in Almaty — A208

Designs: No. 523, 25te, Catholic Church (denomination in orange). No. 524, 25te, Synagogue (denomination in white).

2006, Aug. 17 ***Perf. 11¾x11½***
523-524 A208 Set of 2 1.25 1.25

Souvenir Sheet

Famous Men — A209

No. 525: a, Chokan Valikhanov (1835-65), diplomat. b, Saken Sejfullin (1894-1938), poet. c, Nazir Tjurjakulov (1893-1937). d, Kanysh Satpaev (1899-1964), geologist.

2006, Aug. 20 ***Perf. 11½***
525 A209 90te Sheet of 4, #a-d 8.25 8.25

Third Meeting of Economic Cooperation Organization Postal Authorities, Turkey — A210

2006, Sept. 15 ***Perf. 12***
526 A210 210te multi 4.50 4.50

No. 526 Overprinted in Gold

2006, Sept. 22
527 A210 210te multi 4.50 4.50

Overprint corrects site of meeting from Istanbul to Ankara.

Ahmet Zhubanov (1906-68), Composer A211

2006, Oct. 13 ***Perf. 11½***
528 A211 85te multi 1.90 1.90

Coats of Arms — A212

Arms of: 17te, Almaty. 80te, Astana.

2006, Oct. 20 **Litho.** ***Perf. 13½x13¾***
529-530 A212 Set of 2 2.10 2.10

New Year 2007 — A213

2006, Nov. 1 **Litho.** ***Perf. 13¼***
531 A213 25te multi .60 .60

Latif Khamidi (1906-83), Composer A214

2006, Nov. 9 ***Perf. 11½x11¾***
532 A214 110te multi 2.25 2.25

Mukagali Makataev (1931-76), Writer — A215

2006, Nov. 29 ***Perf. 13½x13¾***
533 A215 1te dark blue .20 .20
534 A215 4te olive grn .20 .20
535 A215 7te rose claret .20 .20
536 A215 15te red brown .30 .30
Nos. 533-536 (4) .90 .90

Manash Kozybaev (1931-2002), Historian — A216

2006, Nov. 29
537 A216 20te brown .45 .45
538 A216 30te brn lake .65 .65

Character From Opera *Silk Girl* — A217

2006, Dec. 15 ***Perf. 13¼***
539 A217 80te multi 1.75 1.75

Values are for stamps with surrounding selvage.

18th Century Helmet — A218

2006, Dec. 15 ***Perf. 13x12¾***
540 A218 85te multi 1.90 1.90

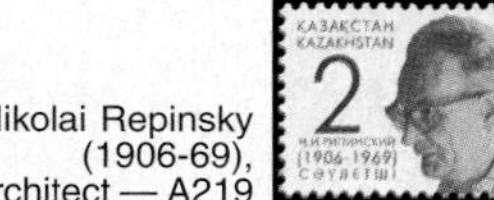

Nikolai Repinsky (1906-69), Architect — A219

2006, Dec. 20 ***Perf. 13½x13¾***
541 A219 2te brown .20 .20
542 A219 3te yel brn .20 .20
543 A219 105te gray grn 2.25 2.25
544 A219 150te blue 3.25 3.25
545 A219 500te rose claret 10.00 10.00
Nos. 541-545 (5) 15.90 15.90

Miniature Sheet

Kurgalzhinsky Nature Reserve — A220

No. 546: a, 25te, Phoenicopterus roseus. b, 100te, Cygnus cygnus. c, 120te, Meles meles.

2006, Dec. 29 ***Perf. 11½x11¾***
546 A220 Sheet of 3, #a-c 5.50 5.50

KazTransOil, 10th Anniv. — A221

2007, Apr. 12 **Litho.** ***Perf. 12¾***
547 A221 25te multi .70 .70

Cosmonaut's Day — A222

Designs: 80te, Konstantin E. Tsiolkovsky (1857-1935), rocket pioneer. 110te, Sergei P. Korolev (1906-66), aeronautical engineer.

2007, Apr. 12 ***Perf. 12¼x11¾***
548-549 A222 Set of 2 4.25 4.25

Europa — A223

No. 550 — Children's art: a, 25te, Scout bugler and tents. b, 65te, Scouts with backpacks, dog.

2007, May 8 ***Perf. 11½x11¾***
550 A223 Pair, #a-b 2.00 2.00

Scouting, cent.

63rd Session of UN Economic and Social Commission for Asia and the Pacific, Almaty — A224

2007, May 17 ***Perf. 12¾***
551 A224 25te multi .65 .65

Gali Ormanov (1907-78), Poet — A225

2007, Sept. 28 **Litho.** ***Perf. 11½***
552 A225 25te multi .60 .60

Conference on Interaction and Confidence-Building Measures in Asia, 15th Anniv. — A226

2007, Oct. 17 ***Perf. 13½***
553 A226 80te multi 1.75 1.75

Maulen Balakaev (1907-95), Philologist — A227

2007, Oct. 29 **Litho.** ***Perf. 13½***
554 A227 1te red brown .20 .20
555 A227 4te green .20 .20
556 A227 5te dk brown .20 .20
Nos. 554-556 (3) .60 .60

Almaty Zoo Animals — A228

No. 557: a, 25te, Zebras. b, 110te, Elephant.

2007, Oct. 31 **Litho.** ***Perf. 11½***
557 A228 Pair, #a-b 3.25 3.25

Printed in sheets containing 4 each of Nos. 557a and 557b, with a central label.

Hirundo Rustica — A229

2007, Nov. 15 ***Perf. 13½***
558 A229 20te multi .50 .50
559 A229 25te multi .70 .70
560 A229 50te multi 1.40 1.40
561 A229 100te multi 2.90 2.90
Nos. 558-561 (4) 5.50 5.50

Saddle A230

2007, Nov. 27 ***Perf. 12***
562 A230 80te multi 2.00 2.00

Launch of Sputnik 1, 50th Anniv. — A231

2007, Nov. 27 ***Perf. 12½x12¾***
563 A231 500te multi 9.00 9.00

Karagand Arms — A232

Pavlodar Arms — A233

2007, Dec. 10 ***Perf. 13½x13¼***
564 A232 10te multi .40 .40
565 A233 10te multi .40 .40

Miniature Sheet

Olympic Gold Medalists — A234

No. 566: a, Vladimir Smirnov, 1994, 50-kilometer skiing. b, Yuri Melinichenko, 1996, Greco-Roman wrestling. c, Olga Shishigina, 2000, 100-meter hurdles. d, Ermahan Ibraimov, 2000, boxing.

2007, Dec. 28 ***Perf. 12x11½***
566 A234 150te Sheet of 4, #a-d 12.00 12.00

Souvenir Sheet

Peoples of Kazakhstan — A235

No. 567: a, Uighur man and woman (denomination at left). b, Tatar man and woman (denomination at right).

2007, Dec. 28 ***Perf. 11½***
567 A235 105te Sheet of 2, #a-b 5.25 5.25

New Year — A236

2008, Jan. 23 **Litho.** ***Perf. 13¼***
568 A236 25te multi .65 .65

Printed in sheets of 8 + central label.

Miniature Sheet

Women's Day — A237

No. 569 — Various flowers with: a, Denomination at LL. b, Denomination at LR. c, Denomination and country name at UL. d, Denomination and country name at UR, Kazakh text in lower panel justified at right. e, Denomination at L, country name at LL. f, Denomination and country name at UR, Kazakh text in lower panel justified at left.

2008, Mar. 14 *Perf. 13¼*
569 A237 25te Sheet of 6, #a-f, + 3 labels 7.00 7.00

Navruz Bayram — A238

2008, Mar. 21 *Perf. 12¾*
570 A238 25te multi .65 .65

2008 Summer Olympics, Beijing — A239

2008, Apr. 2 *Perf. 14x14¼*
571 A239 25te multi .65 .65

Kazakhstan Postal Service, 15th Anniv. — A240

2008, Apr. 4 *Perf. 12¾*
572 A240 25te multi .65 .65

Cosmonaut's Day — A241

Designs: 100te, Space Station Mir. 150te, International Space Station.

2008, Apr. 10 *Perf. 14x14¼*
573-574 A241 Set of 2 5.00 5.00

Europa — A242

No. 575 — Color of dove: a, Blue. b, Red.

2008, May 6 *Perf. 14x14¼*
575 A242 150te Horiz. pair, #a-b 6.00 6.00

2008 Summer Olympics, Beijing — A243

No. 576: a, Judo. b, Handball.

2008, Aug. 10 Litho. *Perf. 14x14¼*
576 A243 100te Horiz. pair, #a-b 4.00 4.00

Deer — A244

No. 577: a, Cervus elaphus sibiricus. b, Cervus nippon.

2008, Sept. 18
577 A244 110te Horiz. pair, #a-b 4.50 4.50

See Moldova No. 596.

Ancient Jewelry From Iran and Kazakhstan — A245

No. 578: a, Buckle depicting snow leopard and mountains, 4th-5th cent. B.C., Kazakhstan. b, Gold medal depicting lions, 7th cent. B.C., Iran.

2008, Oct. 3 *Perf. 14x14¼*
578 Horiz. pair + flanking label 4.00 4.00
a. A245 25te multi .60 .60
b. A245 150te multi 3.50 3.50

See Iran No. 2965.

Universal Declaration of Human Rights, 60th Anniv. — A246

Perf. 11¾x11½
2008, Dec. 10 **Litho.**
579 A246 25te multi .60 .60

Taiyr Zharakov (1908-65), Poet — A247

2008, Dec. 12 *Perf. 11½*
580 A247 25te multi .60 .60

Shakarim Kudaiberdyuly (1859-1931), Poet — A248

2008, Dec. 12
581 A248 25te multi .60 .60

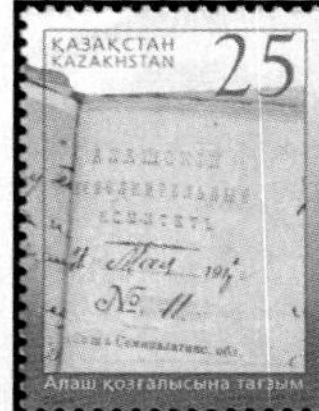

Alash Movement, 90th Anniv. — A249

2008, Dec. 18
582 A249 25te multi .60 .60

Musical Instruments — A250

No. 583: a, 25te, Zhelbuaz. b, 100te, Dauylpaz.

2008, Dec. 19
583 A250 Pair, #a-b 2.60 2.60

Paintings — A251

No. 584: a, 25te, Portrait of Kenesary, by A. Kasteev. b, 100te, Guest, by S. Aitbayev.

2008, Dec. 19
584 A251 Pair, #a-b 2.60 2.60

Insects — A252

No. 585: a, 25te, Callisthenes semenovi. b, 100te, Dorcadion acharlense.

2008, Dec. 22
585 A252 Pair, #a-b 2.60 2.60

Peter Aravin (1908-79), Musicologist A253

Perf. 13¾x13½
2008, Dec. 25 **Litho.**
586 A253 10te multi .25 .25

Eagle — A254

2008, Dec. 25
587 A254 20te multi .50 .50

Arms of Atyrau — A255

Arms of Taraz — A256

2008, Dec. 25 Litho. *Perf. 14x13½*
588 A255 A multi .70 .70
589 A256 A multi .70 .70

On day of issue, Nos. 588-589 each sold for 25te.

Preservation of Polar Regions and Glaciers — A257

2009, Mar. 12 Litho. *Perf. 12¾*
590 A257 230te multi 4.00 4.00

Navruz Bayram — A258

2009, Mar. 20
591 A258 25te multi .50 .50

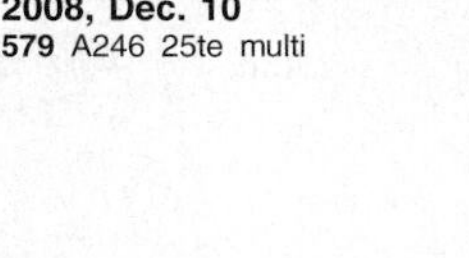

Louis Braille (1809-52), Educator of the Blind — A259

2009, Mar. 26 ***Perf. 11½***
592 A259 230te multi 4.00 4.00

Europa — A260

Telescopes and: No. 593, 230te, Galileo Galilei, Moon. No. 594, 230te, Taurus constellation, Kazakhs looking at sky.

2009, Apr. 3
593-594 A260 Set of 2 8.75 8.75

Intl. Year of Astronomy.

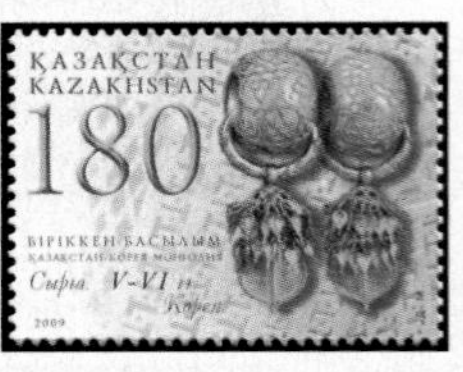

Earrings A261

No. 595 — Earring from: a, Korea, 5th-6th cent. b, Mongolia, 18th-19th cent. c, Kazakhstan, 2nd-1st cent, B.C.

2009, June 12 Litho. ***Perf. 13x12¾***
595 Horiz. strip of 3 9.00 9.00
a.-c. A261 180te Any single 3.00 3.00

See South Korea No. 2313, Mongolia No. 2674.

Astronomy A262

Designs: 180te, Telescope. 230te, Observatories.

2009, June 25 ***Perf. 13***
596-597 A262 Set of 2 6.75 6.75

Horsemen and Shield — A263

2009, July 9 ***Perf. 12¾x12½***
598 A263 190te multi 3.75 3.75

Maria Lizogub (1909-98), Painter — A264

2009, Aug. 25 ***Perf. 11½***
599 A264 180te multi 3.00 3.00

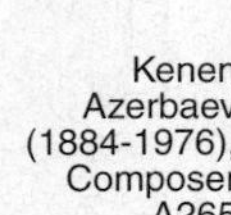

Kenen Azerbaev (1884-1976), Composer A265

2009, Sept. 2
600 A265 180te multi 3.00 3.00

Garifolla Kurmangaliev (1909-93), Singer — A266

2009, Sept. 8
601 A266 180te multi 3.00 3.00

18th Session of World Tourism Organization, Astana — A267

2009, Oct. 5
602 A267 140te multi 2.40 2.40

Miniature Sheet

Ballet — A268

No. 603: a, 180te, Dancers from Giselle (woman in white, man in black). b, 180te, Dancers from Don Quixote (woman in red, man in black and white). c, 180te, Dancers from Swan Lake (man and woman in white). d, 180te, Dancer from Tilep and Sarykyz. e, 230te, Dancer in red from Legend About Love. f, 230te, Dancer in blue from Bahchisarayski Fountain.

2009, Oct. 8 ***Perf. 13¼***
603 A268 Sheet of 6, #a-f 19.00 19.00

National Games — A269

No. 604: a, 140te, Blindfolded man on horseback. b, 180te, Horsemen in competition.

2009, Nov. 16 ***Perf. 12***
604 A269 Pair, #a-b 5.50 5.50

Abdilda Tazhibaev (1909-98), Writer — A270

2009, Nov. 16 ***Perf. 11½***
605 A270 180te multi 3.50 3.50

Flora and Fauna A271

Designs: No. 606, 180te, Crataegus ambigua. No. 607, 180te, Mellivora capensis.

2009, Dec. 3 Litho. ***Perf. 13***
606-607 A271 Set of 2 6.00 6.00

Iskander Tynyshpaev (1909-95), Cinematographer — A272

2009, Dec. 9 ***Perf. 11½x11¾***
608 A272 25te multi .50 .50

Tuleu Basenov (1909-76), Architect A273

2009, Dec. 30
609 A273 25te multi .50 .50

Birzhan Sal Kozhagululy (1834-97), Composer A274

2009, Dec. 30
610 A274 25te multi .50 .50

Construction of Central Asian Gas Pipeline — A275

Perf. 12½x12¾
2009, Dec. 30 Litho.
611 A275 25te multi .50 .50

Kazakhstan Chairmanship of Organization for Security and Cooperation in Europe — A276

2010, Jan. 6 Litho. ***Perf. 12***
612 A276 230te multi 4.00 4.00

Navruz Bayram — A277

2010, Apr. 15 ***Perf. 12¾***
613 A277 32te multi .60 .60

Victory in World War II, 65th Anniv. A278

2010, Apr. 15 ***Perf. 12***
614 A278 32te multi .60 .60

2010 Winter Olympics, Vancouver A279

Designs: 32te, Ski jumper. 190te, Alpine skier.

2010, Apr. 29 Litho. ***Perf. 12***
615-616 A279 Set of 2 4.00 4.00

Europa — A280

2010, May 5 ***Perf. 12¾***
617 A280 240te multi 4.50 4.50

Temirtau, 50th Anniv. A281

2010, June 1 Litho. ***Perf. 14x14¼***
618 A281 32te multi .65 .65

Khan Shatyr Entertainment Center, Astana — A282

2010, July 1
619 A282 32te multi .65 .65

2010 World Cup Soccer Championships, South Africa — A283

2010, July 12
620 A283 240te multi 4.50 4.50

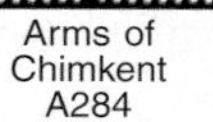
Arms of Chimkent A284

Arms of Aktyubinsk A285

2010 *Perf. 14¼ Syncopated*

621 A284 5te multi .20 .20
622 A285 10te multi .25 .25

Issued: 5te, 8/17; 10te, 7/27.

Constitution, 15th Anniv. — A286

2010, Aug. 20 *Perf. 14x14¼*

623 A286 32te multi .65 .65

Baikonur Cosmodrome, 55th Anniv. — A288

2010, Aug. 27 Litho. *Perf. 13x13¼*

625 A288 190te multi 3.50 3.50

Souvenir Sheet

Baurjan Momasuhly (1910-82), World War II Hero — A290

2010, Sept. 24 Litho. *Perf. 14x14¼*

627 A290 140te multi 2.60 2.60

Shokan Valikhanov (1835-65), Historian — A291

2010, Oct. 21 *Perf. 14¼x14*

628 A291 140te multi 2.60 2.60

SEMI-POSTAL STAMP

Cartoons SP1

a, Mother and child. b, Cow, rabbit. c, Horses.

1994, Nov. 3 Litho. *Perf. 12½x12*

B1 SP1 1te +30ti Block of 3 + label .75 .75

KENYA

'ke-nyə

LOCATION — East Africa, bordering on the Indian Ocean
GOVT. — Republic
AREA — 224,960 sq. mi.
POP. — 28,808,658 (1999 est.)
CAPITAL — Nairobi

Formerly a part of the British colony of Kenya, Uganda, Tanganyika, Kenya gained independence Dec. 12, 1963.

100 Cents = 1 Shilling

Catalogue values for all unused stamps in this country are for Never Hinged items.

Treetop Hotel and Elephants — A1

Designs: 5c, Cattle ranching. 10c, Wood carving. 15c, Riveter. 20c, Timber industry. 30c, Jomo Kenyatta facing Mt. Kenya. 40c, Fishing industry. 50c, Flag and emblem. 65c, Pyrethrum industry (daisies). 1sh, National Assembly bldg. 2sh, Harvesting coffee. 5sh, Harvesting tea. 10sh, Mombasa port. 20sh, Royal College, Nairobi.

Perf. 14x14½

1963, Dec. 12 Photo. Unwmk.

Size: 21x17½mm

1 A1 5c bl, buff & dk brn .20 *.60*
2 A1 10c brown .20 .20
a. Booklet pane of 4 .30
3 A1 15c deep magenta .75 .20
a. Booklet pane of 4 .30
4 A1 20c yel grn & dk brn .20 .20
a. Booklet pane of 4 .40
5 A1 30c yel & black .20 .20
a. Booklet pane of 4 .55
6 A1 40c blue & brown .20 .45
7 A1 50c grn, blk & dp car .25 .20
a. Booklet pane of 4 1.25
8 A1 65c steel blue & yel .50 .90

Perf. 14½

Size: 41½x25½mm

9 A1 1sh multicolored .25 .20
10 A1 1.30sh grn, brn & blk 6.00 .30
11 A1 2sh multicolored 1.25 .45
12 A1 5sh ultra, yel grn & brn 1.50 .90
13 A1 10sh brn & dark brn 8.50 3.25
14 A1 20sh pink & grnsh blk 7.50 *8.50*
Nos. 1-14 (14) 27.50 16.55

President Jomo Kenyatta and Flag of Kenya — A2

Flag and: 15c, Cockerel. 50c, African lion. 1.30sh, Hartlaub's touraco. 2.50sh, Nandi flame flower.

1964, Dec. 12 Photo. *Perf. 13x12½*

15 A2 15c lt violet & multi .25 .20
16 A2 30c dk blue & multi .25 .20
17 A2 50c dk brown & multi .25 .20
18 A2 1.30sh multicolored 2.75 .50
19 A2 2.50sh multicolored .85 *3.75*
Nos. 15-19 (5) 4.35 *4.85*

Establishment of the Republic of Kenya, Dec. 12, 1964.

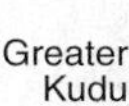
Greater Kudu A3

Animals: 5c, Thomson's gazelle. 10c, Sable antelope. 15c, Aardvark. 20c, Senegal bush baby. 30c, Warthog. 40c, Zebra. 50c, Buffalo. 65c, Black rhinoceros. 70c, Ostrich. 1.30sh, Elephant. 1.50sh, Bat-eared fox. 2.50sh, Cheetah. 5sh, Vervet monkey. 10sh, Giant pangolin. 20sh, Lion.

1966-69 Unwmk. *Perf. 14x14½*

Size: 21x17mm

20 A3 5c gray, black & org .30 .20
21 A3 10c black & yel green .20 .20
22 A3 15c dp orange & black .20 .20
23 A3 20c ultra, lt brn & black .20 .20
24 A3 30c lt ultra & blk .25 .25
25 A3 40c ocher & blk .20 .20
26 A3 50c dp orange & blk .25 .20
27 A3 65c dp yel green & blk 2.00 *2.00*
28 A3 70c rose lake & black 5.00 1.75

Perf. 14½

Size: 41x25mm

29 A3 1sh gray bl, ol & blk .70 .20
30 A3 1.30sh yel grn & blk 4.00 .35
31 A3 1.50sh brn org, brn & black 3.00 *2.50*
32 A3 2.50sh ol bis, yel & blk 3.50 1.75
33 A3 5sh brt grn, ultra & black 2.00 1.00
34 A3 10sh red brn, bis & black 5.50 3.75
35 A3 20sh ocher, bis, gold & black 12.50 *12.50*
Nos. 20-35 (16) 39.80 27.25

Issued: #28, 31, 9/15/69; others, 12/12/66.

Branched Murex — A4

Sea shells: 5c, Morning pink. 10c, Episcopal miter. 15c, Strawberry-top shell. 20c, Humpback cowrie. 30c, variable abalone. 40c, Flame-top shell. 50c, Violet sailor. 60c, Bull's-mouth helmet. 70c, Pearly nautilus. 1.50sh, Neptune's trumpet. 2.50sh, Mediterranean tulip shell. 5sh, Fluctuating turban. 10sh, Textile cone. 20sh, Scorpion shell.

1971 Dec. 13 Photo. *Perf. 14½x14*

Size: 17x21mm

36 A4 5c bister & multi .20 *.45*
37 A4 10c dull grn & multi .20 .20
a. Booklet pane of 4 .60
38 A4 15c tan & multi .20 .20
a. Booklet pane of 4 .60
39 A4 20c tan & multi .20 .20
a. Booklet pane of 4 .75
40 A4 30c yellow & multi .25 .20
a. Booklet pane of 4 2.25
41 A4 40c gray & multi .25 .20
a. Booklet pane of 4 2.25
42 A4 50c buff & multi *(Janthina globosa)* .40 .30
a. Booklet pane of 4 3.50
43 A4 60c lilac & multi .35 *1.75*
44 A4 70c gray grn & multi *(Nautilus pompileus)* .50 *1.50*
a. Booklet pane of 4 5.00

Perf. 14½

Size: 25x41mm

45 A4 1sh ocher & multi .40 .35
46 A4 1.50sh pale grn & multi 1.00 .30
47 A4 2.50sh vio gray & multi 1.75 .50
48 A4 5sh lemon & multi 2.50 *.20*
49 A4 10sh multicolored 4.00 *.20*
50 A4 20sh gray & multi 8.00 *.25*
Nos. 36-50 (15) 20.20 *6.80*

Used values of Nos. 48-50 are for stamps with printed cancellations.
For surcharges see Nos. 53-55.

Nos. 42, 44 with Revised Inscription

1974, Jan. 20 *Perf. 14½x14*

51 A4 50c *(Janthina janthina)* 14.50 2.50
52 A4 70c *(Nautilus pompilius)* 11.00 6.00

Nos. 46-47, 50 Surcharged with New Value and 2 Bars

1975, Nov. 17 Photo. *Perf. 14½*

53 A4 2sh on 1.50sh multi 6.00 *5.00*
54 A4 3sh on 2.50sh multi 10.00 *22.00*
55 A4 40sh on 20sh multi 6.00 *18.00*
Nos. 53-55 (3) 22.00 *45.00*

Microwave Tower — A5

Designs: 1sh, Cordless switchboard and operators, horiz. 2sh, Telephones of 1880, 1930 and 1976. 3sh, Message switching center, horiz.

1976, Apr. 15 Litho. *Perf. 14½*

56 A5 50c blue & multi .20 .20
57 A5 1sh red & multi .20 .20
58 A5 2sh yellow & multi .20 .35
59 A5 3sh multicolored .45 .45
a. Souvenir sheet of 4 2.75 *2.75*
Nos. 56-59 (4) 1.05 1.20

Telecommunication development in East Africa. No. 59a contains 4 stamps similar to Nos. 56-59 with simulated perforations.

Akii Bua, Ugandan Hurdler — A6

Designs: 1sh, Filbert Bayi, Tanzanian runner. 2sh, Steve Muchoki, Kenyan boxer. 3sh, Olympic torch, flags of Kenya, Tanzania and Uganda.

1976, July 5 Litho. *Perf. 14½*

60 A6 50c blue & multi .20 .20
61 A6 1sh red & multi .20 .20
62 A6 2sh yellow & multi .50 .40
63 A6 3sh blue & multi 1.00 .75
a. Souv. sheet of 4, #60-63, perf. 13 9.50 9.50
Nos. 60-63 (4) 1.90 1.55

21st Olympic Games, Montreal, Canada, July 17-Aug. 1.

Tanzania-Zambia Railway — A7

Designs: 1sh, Nile Bridge, Uganda. 2sh, Nakuru Station, Kenya. 3sh, Class A locomotive, 1896.

1976, Oct. 4 Litho. *Perf. 14½*

64 A7 50c lilac & multi .50 .20
65 A7 1sh emerald & multi .60 .20
66 A7 2sh brt rose & multi 1.75 1.00
67 A7 3sh yellow & multi 1.90 1.75
a. Souv. sheet of 4, #64-67, perf. 13 11.00 11.00
Nos. 64-67 (4) 4.75 3.15

Rail transport in East Africa.

Nile Perch — A8

Game Fish: 1sh, Tilapia. 3sh, Sailfish. 5sh, Black marlin.

1977, Jan. 10 Litho. *Perf. 14½*

68	A8 50c multicolored	.20	.20
69	A8 1sh multicolored	.55	.20
70	A8 3sh multicolored	1.50	.75
71	A8 5sh multicolored	1.50	1.00
a.	Souvenir sheet of 4, #68-71	11.00	11.00
	Nos. 68-71 (4)	3.75	2.15

Festival Emblem and Masai Tribesmen Bleeding Cow — A9

Festival Emblem and: 1sh, Dancers from Uganda. 2sh, Makonde sculpture, Tanzania. 3sh, Tribesmen skinning hippopotamus.

1977, Jan. 15 *Perf. 13½x14*

72	A9 50c multicolored	.20	.20
73	A9 1sh multicolored	.40	.20
74	A9 2sh multicolored	1.25	1.25
75	A9 3sh multicolored	1.50	1.50
a.	Souvenir sheet of 4, #72-75	6.00	6.00
	Nos. 72-75 (4)	3.35	3.15

2nd World Black and African Festival, Lagos, Nigeria, Jan. 15-Feb. 12.

Automobile Passing through Village — A10

Safari Rally Emblem and: 1sh, Winner at finish line. 2sh, Car going through washout. 5sh, Car, elephants and Mt. Kenya.

1977, Apr. 5 Litho. *Perf. 14*

76	A10 50c multicolored	.25	.20
77	A10 1sh multicolored	.40	.25
78	A10 2sh multicolored	.75	.75
79	A10 5sh multicolored	2.25	2.25
a.	Souvenir sheet of 4, #76-79	5.00	5.00
	Nos. 76-79 (4)	3.65	3.45

25th Safari Rally, Apr. 7-11.

Rev. Canon Apolo Kivebulaya — A11

1sh, Uganda Cathedral. 2sh, Early grass-topped Cathedral. 5sh, Early tent congregation, Kigezi.

1977, June 20 Litho. *Perf. 14*

80	A11 50c multicolored	.20	.20
81	A11 1sh multicolored	.25	.25
82	A11 2sh multicolored	.40	.40
83	A11 5sh multicolored	1.75	1.75
a.	Souvenir sheet of 4, #80-83	3.50	3.50
	Nos. 80-83 (4)	2.60	2.60

Church of Uganda, centenary.

Elizabeth II and Prince Philip at Sagana Lodge — A12

Designs: 5sh, "Treetops" observation hut, Aberdare Forest, and elephants, vert. 10sh, Pres. Jomo Kenyatta, Elizabeth II, crossed spears and shield. 15sh, Elizabeth II and Pres. Kenyatta in open automobile. 50sh, Elizabeth II and Prince Philip at window in Treetops.

1977, July 20 Litho. *Perf. 14*

84	A12 2sh multicolored	.20	.20
85	A12 5sh multicolored	.25	*.25*
86	A12 10sh multicolored	.60	*.60*
87	A12 15sh multicolored	.75	*.75*
a.	Souvenir sheet of 1	1.50	1.50
	Nos. 84-87 (4)	1.80	*1.80*

Souvenir Sheet

88	A12 50sh multicolored	5.00	5.00

Reign of Queen Elizabeth II, 25th anniv.

Pancake Tortoise — A13

Wildlife Fund Emblem and; 1sh, Nile crocodile. 2sh, Hunter's hartebeest. 3sh, Red colobus monkey. 5sh, Dugong.

1977, Sept. 26 Litho. *Perf. 14x13½*

89	A13 50c multicolored	.55	.25
90	A13 1sh multicolored	.75	.30
91	A13 2sh multicolored	2.50	1.50
92	A13 3sh multicolored	3.00	2.50
93	A13 5sh multicolored	3.50	3.50
a.	Souvenir sheet of 4, #90-93	10.00	10.00
	Nos. 89-93 (5)	10.30	8.05

Endangered species.

Kenya-Ethiopia Border Point — A14

Designs: 1sh, Station wagon at Archer's Post. 2sh, Thika overpass. 5sh, Marsabit Game Lodge and elephant.

1977, Nov. 10 Litho. *Perf. 14*

94	A14 50c multicolored	.20	.20
95	A14 1sh multicolored	.20	.20
96	A14 2sh multicolored	.35	.35
97	A14 5sh multicolored	.75	.75
a.	Souvenir sheet of 4, #94-97	3.00	3.00
	Nos. 94-97 (4)	1.50	1.50

Opening of Nairobi-Addis Ababa highway.

Minerals Found in Kenya — A15

A16

Perf. 14½x14, 14½ (A16)

1977, Dec. 13 Photo.

98	A15	10c Gypsum	1.60	.20
99	A15	20c Trona	2.40	.20
100	A15	30c Kyanite	2.40	.20
101	A15	40c Amazonite	1.90	.20
102	A15	50c Galena	1.90	.20
103	A15	70c Silicified wood	9.00	1.00
104	A15	80c Fluorite	9.00	1.00
105	A16	1sh Amethyst	1.90	.20
106	A16	1.50sh Agate	1.90	.40
107	A16	2sh Tourmaline	1.90	.45
108	A16	3sh Aquamarine	2.40	.95
109	A16	5sh Rhodolite garnet	2.40	1.50
110	A16	10sh Sapphire	2.40	2.50
111	A16	20sh Ruby	6.00	5.25
112	A16	40sh Green grossular garnet	25.00	24.00
		Nos. 98-112 (15)	72.10	38.25

The 10c, 20c, 40c, 50c and 80c were also issued in booklet panes of 4. The 50c was also issued in a booklet pane of 2.

For surcharge see No. 242.

Soccer, Joe Kadenge and World Cup — A17

World Cup and: 1sh, Mohammed Chuma receiving trophy, and his portrait. 2sh, Shot on goal and Omari S. Kidevu. 3sh, Backfield defense and Polly Ouma.

1978, Apr. 10 Litho. *Perf. 14x13½*

113	A17 50c green & multi	.20	.20
114	A17 1sh lt brown & multi	.20	.20
115	A17 2sh lilac & multi	.40	*.40*
116	A17 3sh dk blue & multi	.75	*.75*
a.	Souvenir sheet of 4, #113-116	4.00	4.00
	Nos. 113-116 (4)	1.55	1.55

World Soccer Cup Championships, Argentina 78, June 1-25.

Boxing and Games' Emblem A18

Games Emblem and: 1sh, Pres. Kenyatta welcoming 1968 Olympic team. 3sh, Javelin. 5sh, Pres. Kenyatta, boxing team and trophy.

1978, July 15 Photo. *Perf. 13x14*

117	A18 50c multicolored	.20	.20
118	A18 1sh multicolored	.20	.20
119	A18 3sh multicolored	.60	.60
120	A18 5sh multicolored	.75	.75
	Nos. 117-120 (4)	1.75	1.75

Commonwealth Games, Edmonton, Canada, Aug. 3-12.

Overloaded Truck — A19

Road Safety: 1sh, Observe speed limit. 1.50sh, Observe traffic lights. 2sh, School crossing. 3sh, Passing. 5sh, Railroad crossing.

1978, Sept. 18 Litho. *Perf. 13½x14*

121	A19	50c multicolored	.65	.20
122	A19	1sh multicolored	.90	.45
123	A19	1.50sh multicolored	1.10	.90
124	A19	2sh multicolored	1.60	1.00
125	A19	3sh multicolored	1.90	*1.90*
126	A19	5sh multicolored	2.75	*3.00*
		Nos. 121-126 (6)	8.90	7.45

Pres. Kenyatta at Harambee Water Project Opening — A20

Kenyatta Day: 1sh, Prince Philip handing over symbol of independence, 1963. 2sh, Pres. Jomo Kenyatta addressing independence rally. 3sh, Stage at 15th independence anniversary celebration. 5sh, Handcuffed Kenyatta led by soldiers, 1952.

1978, Oct. 16 Litho. *Perf. 14*

127	A20 50c multicolored	.20	.20
128	A20 1sh multicolored	.20	.20
129	A20 2sh multicolored	.35	.35
130	A20 3sh multicolored	.75	.75
131	A20 5sh multicolored	1.00	1.00
	Nos. 127-131 (5)	2.50	2.50

Soldiers and Emblem A21

Anti-Apartheid Emblem and: 1sh, Anti-Apartheid Conference. 2sh, Stephen Biko, South African Anti-Apartheid leader. 3sh, Nelson Mandela, jailed since 1961. 5sh, Bishop Lamont, expelled from Rhodesia in 1977.

1978, Dec. 11 Litho. *Perf. 14x14½*

132	A21 50c multicolored	.20	.20
133	A21 1sh multicolored	.20	.20
134	A21 2sh multicolored	.40	.40
135	A21 3sh multicolored	.60	.60
136	A21 5sh multicolored	.75	.75
	Nos. 132-136 (5)	2.15	2.15

Anti-Apartheid Year and Namibia's struggle for independence.

Children on School Playground — A22

Children's Year Emblem and: 2sh, Boy catching fish. 3sh, Children dancing and singing. 5sh, Children and camel caravan.

1979, Feb. 5 Litho. *Perf. 14*

137	A22 50c multicolored	.35	.35
138	A22 2sh multicolored	.75	.75
139	A22 3sh multicolored	.80	.80
140	A22 5sh multicolored	1.50	1.50
	Nos. 137-140 (4)	3.40	3.40

International Year of the Child.

"The Lion and the Jewel" A23

National Theater: 1sh, Dancers and drummers. 2sh, Programs of various productions. 3sh, View of National Theater. 5sh, "Genesis," performed by Nairobi City Players.

1979, Apr. 6 Litho. *Perf. 13½x14*

141	A23 50c multicolored	.20	.20
142	A23 1sh multicolored	.40	.40
143	A23 2sh multicolored	.60	.60
144	A23 3sh multicolored	.90	.90
145	A23 5sh multicolored	1.50	1.50
	Nos. 141-145 (5)	3.60	3.60

Village Workshop — A24

Salvation Army Emblem and: 50c, Blind telephone operator, vert. 1sh, Care for the aged, vert. 5sh, Vocational training (nurse).

1979, June 4 ***Perf. 13½x13, 13x13½***

146	A24	50c multicolored	.20	.20
147	A24	1sh multicolored	.40	.40
148	A24	3sh multicolored	1.00	1.00
149	A24	5sh multicolored	2.00	2.00
		Nos. 146-149 (4)	3.60	3.60

Salvation Army Social Services, 50th anniv.

Funeral Procession — A25

British East Africa No. 2, Hill, Signature — A26

Kenyatta: 1sh, Taking oath of office. 3sh, Addressing crowd. 5sh, As young man with wooden trying plane.

1979, Aug. 22 **Litho.** ***Perf. 13½x14***

150	A25	50c multicolored	.20	.20
151	A25	1sh multicolored	.35	.35
152	A25	3sh multicolored	.60	.60
153	A25	5sh multicolored	1.00	1.00
		Nos. 150-153 (4)	2.15	2.15

Jomo Kenyatta (1893-1978), first president of Kenya.

1979, Nov. 27 **Litho.** ***Perf. 14***

Hill, Signature and: 1sh, Kenya, Uganda and Tanzania #54. 2sh, Penny Black. 5sh, Kenya #19.

154	A26	50c multicolored	.20	.20
155	A26	1sh multicolored	.20	.20
156	A26	2sh multicolored	.35	.35
157	A26	5sh multicolored	.75	.75
		Nos. 154-157 (4)	1.50	1.50

Sir Rowland Hill (1795-1879), originator of penny postage.

Highways, Globe, Conference Emblem — A27

Conference Emblem and: 1sh, Truck at Athi River, New Weighbridge. 3sh, New Nyali Bridge, Mombasa. 5sh, Jomo Kenyatta Airport Highway.

1980, Jan. 10 **Litho.** ***Perf. 14***

158	A27	50c multicolored	.20	.20
159	A27	1sh multicolored	.25	.20
160	A27	3sh multicolored	.60	.60
161	A27	5sh multicolored	1.00	1.00
		Nos. 158-161 (4)	2.05	2.00

4th IRF African Highway Conference, Nairobi, Jan. 20-25.

Patient Airlift A28

1980, Mar. 20 **Litho.** ***Perf. 14½***

162	A28	50c Outdoor clinic	.20	.20
163	A28	1sh Mule transport of patient, vert.	.40	.35
164	A28	3sh Surgery, vert.	.85	.85
165	A28	5sh shown	1.25	1.25
a.		Souvenir sheet of 4, #162-165	3.25	3.25
		Nos. 162-165 (4)	2.70	2.65

Flying doctor service.

Hill Statue, Kidderminster and Mt. Kenya — A29

1980, May 6 **Litho.** ***Perf. 14***

166	A29	25sh multicolored	2.00	2.00
a.		Souvenir sheet	2.25	2.25

London 1980 International Stamp Exhibition, May 6-14.

Pope John Paul II and Crowd A30

Visit of Pope John Paul II to Kenya: 1sh, Pope, Nairobi Cathedral, papal flag and arms, vert. 5sh, Pope, papal and Kenya flags, dove, vert. 10sh, Pres. arap Moi of Kenya, Pope, flag of Kenya on map of Africa.

1980, May 8 ***Perf. 13½***

167	A30	50c multicolored	.30	.20
168	A30	1sh multicolored	.50	.30
169	A30	5sh multicolored	1.25	1.25
170	A30	10sh multicolored	2.75	2.75
		Nos. 167-170 (4)	4.80	4.50

Sting Ray — A31

1980, June 27 **Litho.** ***Perf. 14½***

171	A31	50c shown	.55	.55
172	A31	2sh Alkit snapper	1.25	.80
173	A31	3sh Sea slug	1.75	1.75
174	A31	5sh Hawksbill turtle	2.00	2.00
		Nos. 171-174 (4)	5.55	5.10

National Archives, 1904 A32

1980, Oct. 9 **Litho.** ***Perf. 14***

175	A32	50c shown	.20	.20
176	A32	1sh Commissioner's Office, Nairobi, 1913	.20	.20
177	A32	1.50sh Nairobi House, 1913	.25	.25
178	A32	2sh Norfolk Hotel, 1904	.40	.40
179	A32	3sh McMillan Library, 1929	.50	.50
180	A32	5sh Kipande House, 1913	.75	.75
		Nos. 175-180 (6)	2.30	2.30

Woman in Wheelchair and Child — A33

1981, Feb. 10 **Litho.** ***Perf. 14x13½***

181	A33	50c shown	.20	.20
182	A33	1sh Pres. arap Moi, team captain	.20	.20
183	A33	3sh Blind mountain climbers, Mt. Kenya, 1965	.75	.75
184	A33	5sh Disabled artist	1.25	1.25
		Nos. 181-184 (4)	2.40	2.40

International Year of the Disabled.

Longonot Earth Station Complex — A34

1981, Apr. 4 **Litho.** ***Perf. 14x14½***

185	A34	50c shown	.20	.20
186	A34	2sh Intelsat V	.45	.45
187	A34	3sh Longonot I	.60	.60
188	A34	5sh Longonot II	.75	.75
		Nos. 185-188 (4)	2.00	2.00

Conference Center, OAU Flag — A35

18th Organization for African Unity Conference, Nairobi: 1sh, Map of Africa showing Panaftel earth stations. 3sh, Parliament Building, Nairobi. 5sh, Jomo Kenyatta Intl. Airport. 10sh, OAU flag.

1981, June 24 **Wmk. 373** ***Perf. 13½***

189	A35	50c multicolored	.20	.20
190	A35	1sh multicolored	.20	.20
191	A35	3sh multicolored	.60	.60
192	A35	5sh multicolored	.75	.75
193	A35	10sh multicolored	1.75	1.75
a.		Souvenir sheet of 1, perf. 14½	2.00	2.00
		Nos. 189-193 (5)	3.50	3.50

St. Paul's Cathedral — A36

Reticulated Giraffe — A37

1981, July 29 **Litho.** ***Perf. 14, 12***

194	A36	50c Charles, Pres. arap Moi	.20	.20
195	A36	3sh shown	.20	.20
196	A36	5sh Britannia	.30	.30
197	A36	10sh Charles	.40	*.60*
		Nos. 194-197 (4)	1.10	1.30

Souvenir Sheet

198	A36	25sh Couple	1.50	1.50

Royal Wedding.

1981, Aug. 31 **Litho.** ***Perf. 14½***

199	A37	50c shown	.30	.30
200	A37	2sh Bongo	.60	.60
201	A37	5sh Roan antelope	1.40	1.40
202	A37	10sh Mangabey	3.00	3.00
		Nos. 199-202 (4)	5.30	5.30

World Food Day — A38

Ceremonial Tribal Costumes A39

1981, Oct. 16 **Litho.** ***Perf. 14***

203	A38	50c Plowing	.20	.20
204	A38	1sh Rice field	.20	.20
205	A38	2sh Irrigation	.50	.50
206	A38	5sh Cattle	1.25	1.25
		Nos. 203-206 (4)	2.15	2.15

Perf. 14½x13½

1981, Dec. 18 **Litho.**

207	A39	50c Kamba	.55	.20
208	A39	1sh Turkana	.65	.55
209	A39	2sh Giriama	1.50	1.10
210	A39	3sh Masai	2.00	2.00
211	A39	5sh Luo	3.00	*4.00*
		Nos. 207-211 (5)	7.70	7.85

Australopithecus Boisei — A40

1982, Jan. 16 **Litho.** ***Perf. 14***

212	A40	50c shown	2.00	1.00
213	A40	2sh Homo erectus	4.00	2.10
214	A40	3sh Homo habilis	4.00	3.75
215	A40	5sh Proconsul africanus	4.75	4.75
		Nos. 212-215 (4)	14.75	11.60

Scouting Year A41

1982, June 2 **Litho.** ***Perf. 14½***

216	A41	70c Tree planting	.50	.50
217	A41	70c Paying homage	.50	.50
a.		Pair, #216-217	1.25	1.25
218	A41	3.50sh Be Prepared	1.25	1.25
219	A41	3.50sh Intl. friendship	1.25	1.25
a.		Pair, #218-219	3.00	3.00
220	A41	5sh Helping disabled	2.00	2.00
221	A41	5sh Community service	2.00	2.00
a.		Pair, #220-221	4.50	4.50
222	A41	6.50sh Paxtu Cottage	2.75	2.75
223	A41	6.50sh Lady Baden-Powell	2.75	2.75
a.		Pair, #222-223	6.25	6.25
		Nos. 216-223 (8)	13.00	13.00

Souvenir Sheet

224		Sheet of 4	6.00	6.00
a.	A41	70c like #216	.20	.20
b.	A41	3.50sh like #218	1.25	.45
c.	A41	5sh like #220	1.90	.70
d.	A41	6.50sh like #222	2.40	.85

1982 World Cup — A42

Various soccer players on world map.

1982, July 5 **Litho.** ***Perf. 12½***

225	A42	70c multicolored	1.50	.50
226	A42	3.50sh multicolored	3.25	2.50
227	A42	5sh multicolored	4.50	4.25
228	A42	10sh multicolored	6.50	*6.50*
		Nos. 225-228 (4)	15.75	13.75

Souvenir Sheet
Perf. 13½x14

229 A42 20sh multicolored 7.75 7.75

A43

A44

1982, Sept. 28 Litho. *Perf. 14½*

230 A43 70c Cattle judging .90 .45
231 A43 2.50sh Farm machinery 1.50 1.25
232 A43 3.50sh Musical ride 2.00 2.00
233 A43 6.50sh Emblem 3.00 3.00
Nos. 230-233 (4) 7.40 6.70

Agricultural Society, 80th anniv.

1982, Oct. 27 Photo. *Perf. 11½*
Granite Paper

234 A44 70c Microwave radio system .20 .20
235 A44 3.50sh Ship-to-shore communication 2.00 1.75
236 A44 5sh Rural telecommunication 2.75 2.50
237 A44 6.50sh Emblem 4.00 3.75
Nos. 234-237 (4) 8.95 8.20

ITU Plenipoteniaries Conf., Nairobi, Sept.

5th Anniv. of Kenya Ports Authority A45

1983, Jan. 20 Litho. *Perf. 14*

238 A45 70c Container cranes 1.00 1.00
239 A45 2sh Cranes, diff. 1.80 1.80
240 A45 3.50sh Cranes, diff. 3.00 3.00
241 A45 5sh Mombasa Harbor map 4.50 4.50
a. Souvenir sheet of 4, #238-241 10.00 10.00
Nos. 238-241 (4) 10.30 10.30

No. 104 Surcharged

1983, Jan. Photo. *Perf. 14½x14*

242 A15 70c on 80c multicolored 1.50 1.50

A45a

1983, Mar. 14 Litho. *Perf. 14½*

243 A45a 70c Coffee picking, vert. .20 .20
244 A45a 2sh Pres. arap Moi, vert. .30 .25
245 A45a 5sh Globe .50 .50
246 A45a 10sh Masai dance 1.00 1.00
Nos. 243-246 (4) 2.00 1.95

Commonwealth Day.

Dichrostachys Cinerea A46

Dombeya Burgessiae A47

Perf. 14½x14, 14x14½

1983, Feb. 15 Photo.

247 A46 10c shown .45 .20
248 A46 20c Rhamphicarpa montana .65 .20
249 A46 30c Barleria eranthemoides .65 .20
250 A46 40c Commelina .65 .20
251 A46 50c Canarina abyssinica .65 .20
252 A46 70c Aspilia mossambicensis .70 .20
253 A47 1sh Dombeya burgessiae .75 .20
254 A47 1.50sh Lantana trifolia 2.25 .60
255 A47 2sh Adenium obesum 2.50 .85
256 A47 2.50sh Terminalia orbicularis 3.00 1.00
257 A47 3.50sh Ceropegia ballyana 2.75 1.50
258 A47 5sh Ruttya fruticosa 2.75 1.90
259 A47 10sh Pentanisia ouranogyne 3.00 5.25
260 A47 20sh Brillantaisia nyanzarum 3.50 *6.25*
261 A47 40sh Crotalaria axillaris 5.75 *10.00*
Nos. 247-261 (15) 30.00 *28.75*

See Nos. 350-354.

30th Anniv. of Customs Cooperation Council — A48

1983, May 11 Litho. *Perf. 14½*

262 A48 70c Parcel check .30 .20
263 A48 2.50sh Headquarters, Mombasa .70 .30
264 A48 3.50sh Headquarters, Brussels .80 .50
265 A48 10sh Patrol boat 2.50 2.50
Nos. 262-265 (4) 4.30 3.50

World Communications Year — A49

1983, July 4 Litho. *Perf. 14½*

266 A49 70c Satellite, dish antenna, vert. .65 .20
267 A49 2.50sh Mailbox, birthday card, telephone, vert. 1.70 1.25
268 A49 3.50sh Jet, ship 2.25 2.25
269 A49 5sh Railroad bridge, highway 3.50 3.50
Nos. 266-269 (4) 8.10 7.20

Intl. Maritime Organization, 25th Anniv. — A50

1983, Sept. 22 Litho. *Perf. 14½*

270 A50 70c Kilindini Harbor 1.25 .20
271 A50 2.50sh Life preserver 2.25 1.75
272 A50 3.50sh Mombasa Container Terminal 3.00 3.00
273 A50 10sh Marine Park 4.00 4.00
Nos. 270-273 (4) 10.50 8.95

29th Commonwealth Parliamentary Conference — A51

1983, Oct. 31 Litho. *Perf. 14*

274 A51 70c shown .30 .20
275 A51 2.50sh Parliament Bldg., vert. 1.10 1.10
276 A51 5sh State Opening, vert. 2.00 2.00
a. Souv. sheet of 3, #274-276 + label 4.00 4.00
Nos. 274-276 (3) 3.40 3.30

Royal Visit A52

1983, Nov. 10 Litho. *Perf. 14*

277 A52 70c Flags .60 .20
278 A52 3.50sh Sagana State Lodge 2.00 1.50
279 A52 5sh Tree Tops Hotel 2.25 2.25
280 A52 10sh Elizabeth II and Daniel arap Moi 3.50 3.50
Nos. 277-280 (4) 8.35 7.45

Souvenir Sheet

281 A52 25sh multicolored 5.00 5.00

No. 281 contains Nos. 277-280 without denominations showing simulated perforations.

President Daniel arap Moi, Monument — A53

1983, Dec. 9 Litho. *Perf. 14½*

282 A53 70c shown .20 .20
283 A53 2sh Tree planting .20 .20
284 A53 3.50sh Map, flag, emblem .35 .35
285 A53 5sh School, milk program .60 .60
286 A53 10sh People, flag, banner 1.00 1.00
Nos. 282-286 (5) 2.35 2.35

Souvenir Sheet
Imperf

287 A53 25sh multicolored 2.50 2.50

Independence, 20th Anniv. No. 287 contains Nos. 282, 284-286 without denominations.

Rare Local Birds — A54

1984, Feb. 6 Litho. *Perf. 14½x13½*

288 A54 70c White-backed night heron 2.75 2.75
289 A54 2.50sh Quail plover 4.00 3.50
290 A54 3.50sh Heller's ground thrush 5.00 5.00
291 A54 5sh Papyrus gonolek 5.75 5.75
292 A54 10sh White-winged Apalis 7.25 7.25
Nos. 288-292 (5) 24.75 24.25

Intl. Civil Aviation Org., 40th Anniv. A55

1984, Apr. 2 Litho. *Perf. 14*

293 A55 70c Radar, vert. .20 .20
294 A55 2.50sh Kenya School of Aviation .65 .65
295 A55 3.50sh Jet, Moi Intl. Airport 1.00 1.00
296 A55 5sh Air traffic control center, vert. 1.50 1.50
Nos. 293-296 (4) 3.35 3.35

1984 Summer Olympics — A56

1984, May 21 *Perf. 14½*

297 A56 70c Running .20 .20
298 A56 2.50sh Hurdles 1.00 1.00
299 A56 5sh Boxing 2.50 2.40
300 A56 10sh Field Hockey 4.75 4.75
Nos. 297-300 (4) 8.45 8.35

Souvenir Sheet
Imperf

301 A56 25sh Torch bearers 6.00 6.00

No. 301 contains designs of Nos. 297-300.

Bookmobile — A57

1984, Aug. 10 Litho. *Perf. 14½*

302 A57 70c Emblem .20 .20
303 A57 3.50sh shown .70 .70
304 A57 5sh Adult library 1.10 1.10
305 A57 10sh Children's library 2.00 2.00
Nos. 302-305 (4) 4.00 4.00

Intl. Fed. of Library Associations, 50th Conf.

Kenya Export Year (KEY) A58

1984, Oct. 1 Litho. *Perf. 14*

306 A58 70c Emblem, vert. .20 .20
307 A58 3.50sh Airport 1.90 1.90
308 A58 5sh Harbor, vert. 3.50 3.50
309 A58 10sh Exports 5.50 5.50
Nos. 306-309 (4) 11.10 11.10

A59

Tribal Costumes A60

1984, Aug. 23 Litho. *Perf. 14x14½*

310 A59 70c Doves, cross .20 .20
311 A59 2.50sh Doves, Hinduism symbol 1.50 1.50
312 A59 3.50sh Doves, Sikhism symbol 2.25 2.25
313 A59 6.50sh Doves, Islam symbol 4.00 4.00
Nos. 310-313 (4) 7.95 7.95

World Conference on Religion and Peace, Nairobi, Aug. 23-31, 1984.

1984, Nov. 5 Litho. *Perf. 14½x13½*

314 A60 70c Luhya .90 .90
315 A60 2sh Kikuyu 2.25 2.25
316 A60 3.50sh Pokomo 3.25 3.25
317 A60 5sh Nandi 3.50 3.50
318 A60 10sh Rendile 5.75 5.75
Nos. 314-318 (5) 15.65 15.65

60th Anniv., World Chess Federation — A61

1984, Dec. 21 Litho. *Perf. 14½*

319 A61 70c Nyayo Stadium, knight 2.25 .40
320 A61 2.50sh Fort Jesus, rook 3.25 2.10
321 A61 3.50sh National Monument, bishop 4.00 4.50
322 A61 5sh Parliament, queen 4.50 4.50
323 A61 10sh Nyayo Fountain, king 7.25 7.25
Nos. 319-323 (5) 21.25 18.75

Energy Conservation — A62

1985, Jan. 22 Litho. *Perf. 13½*

324 A62 70c Stove, fire pit .40 .40
325 A62 2sh Solar panel .50 .50
326 A62 3.50sh Biogas tank .75 .75
327 A62 10sh Plowing field 2.50 2.50
328 A62 20sh Energy conservation 4.50 4.50
Nos. 324-328 (5) 8.65 8.65

No. 328 contains Nos. 324-327 without denominations.

Girl Guides, 75th Anniv. A63

1985, Mar. 27 Litho. *Perf. 13½*

329 A63 1sh Girl Guide, handicrafts .90 .90
330 A63 3sh Community service 2.00 1.50
331 A63 5sh Lady Baden-Powell, Kenyan leader 2.50 2.50
332 A63 7sh Food project 4.00 4.00
Nos. 329-332 (4) 9.40 8.90

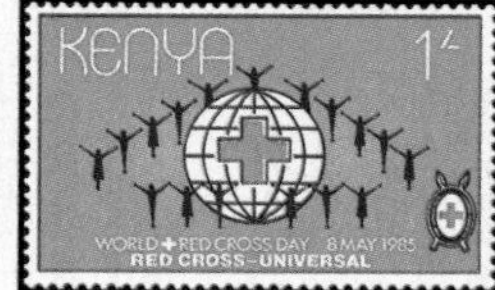

Intl. Red Cross Day A64

1985, May 8 *Perf. 14½*

333 A64 1sh Emblem 1.00 .90
334 A64 4sh First Aid 3.00 3.00
335 A64 5sh Blood donation 3.50 3.50
336 A64 7sh Famine relief, cornucopia 4.50 4.50
Nos. 333-336 (4) 12.00 11.90

A65

A66

Diseases caused by microorganisms carried by insects.

1985, June 25

337 A65 1sh Malaria 2.25 .30
338 A65 3sh Leishmaniasis 4.00 2.75
339 A65 5sh Trypanosomiasis 4.75 4.25
340 A65 7sh Babesiosis 7.50 *7.50*
Nos. 337-340 (4) 18.50 14.80

7th Intl. Congress on Protozoology, Nairobi, June 22-29.

1985, July 15

341 A66 1sh Repairing water pipes .20 .20
342 A66 3sh Traditional food processing .75 .75
343 A66 5sh Basket weaving 1.50 1.50
344 A66 7sh Dress making 2.00 2.00
Nos. 341-344 (4) 4.45 4.45

UN Decade for Women.

43rd Intl. Eucharistic Congress, Nairobi, Aug. 11-18 — A67

1985, Aug. 15 *Perf. 13½*

345 A67 1sh The Last Supper 1.00 1.00
346 A67 3sh Afro-Christian family 2.10 2.10
347 A67 5sh Congress altar, Uhuru Park 3.00 3.00
348 A67 7sh St. Peter Claver's Church 3.75 3.25
Nos. 345-348 (4) 9.85 9.35

Souvenir Sheet

349 A67 25sh Pope John Paul II 7.75 7.75

Flower Types of 1983

1985 Photo. *Perf. 14½x14, 14½*

350 A46 80c like #250 4.50 2.50
351 A46 1sh Dombeya burgessiae 4.50 1.60
352 A47 3sh Calotropis procera 8.50 5.00
353 A47 4sh Momordica foetida 5.25 *6.75*
354 A47 7sh Oncoba spinosa 7.00 *7.00*
Nos. 350-354 (5) 29.75 *22.85*

Endangered Wildlife — A68

1985, Dec. 10 Litho. *Perf. 14½*

355 A68 1sh Diceros bicornis 2.75 1.50
356 A68 3sh Acinonyx jubatus 3.75 3.25
357 A68 5sh Cercopithecus neglectus 4.00 4.00
358 A68 10sh Equus greyvi 7.00 7.00
Nos. 355-358 (4) 17.50 15.75

Size: 130x122mm

Imperf

359 A68 25sh Hunter pursuing game 12.00 12.00

Trees A69

1986, Jan. 24 *Perf. 14½*

360 A69 1sh Borassus aethiopum 1.40 .20
361 A69 3sh Acacia xanthophloea 3.50 2.75
362 A69 5sh Ficus natalensis 4.75 4.75
363 A69 7sh Spathodea nilotica 6.75 6.75
Nos. 360-363 (4) 16.40 14.45

Size: 117x97mm

Imperf

364 A69 25sh Glade 6.00 6.00

Intl. Peace Year — A70

1986 World Cup Soccer Championships, Mexico — A71

1986, Apr. 17 *Perf. 14½*

365 A70 1sh Dove, UN emblem .55 .55
366 A70 3sh UN General Assembly, horiz. 1.25 1.25
367 A70 7sh Mushroom cloud 2.40 2.40
368 A70 10sh Isaiah 2:4, horiz. 3.75 3.75
Nos. 365-368 (4) 7.95 7.95

1986, May 9

369 A71 1sh Dribbling 1.10 .55
370 A71 3sh Penalty shot 2.25 1.10
371 A71 5sh Tackling 3.50 2.25
372 A71 7sh Champions 4.50 4.50
373 A71 10sh Heading the ball 5.75 5.75
Nos. 369-373 (5) 17.10 14.15

Size: 110x86mm

Imperf

374 A71 30sh Harambee Stars 6.50 6.50

EXPO '86, Vancouver — A72

1986, June 11 *Perf. 13½x13*

375 A72 1sh Rural post office 1.25 .60
376 A72 3sh Container depot, Embakasi 2.40 1.25
377 A72 5sh Plane landing 3.75 2.40
378 A72 7sh Shipping exports 4.75 4.75
379 A72 10sh Goods transport 6.25 6.25
Nos. 375-379 (5) 18.40 15.25

TELECOM '86, Nairobi, Sept. 16-23 — A73

1986, Sept. 16 Litho. *Perf. 14½*

380 A73 1sh Telephone-computer links .30 .30
381 A73 3sh Telephones, 1876-1986 1.25 1.25
382 A73 5sh Satellite communications 2.10 2.10
383 A73 7sh Switchboards 3.50 3.50
Nos. 380-383 (4) 7.15 7.15

A74

Dhows (Ships) — A75

1986, Oct. 30 Litho. *Perf. 14½*

384 A74 1sh Mashua 1.00 .20
385 A74 3sh Mtepe 2.50 1.50
386 A74 5sh Dau La Mwao 3.50 3.00
387 A74 10sh Jahazi 7.00 7.00
Nos. 384-387 (4) 14.00 11.70

Souvenir Sheet

388 A75 25sh Lamu, map 8.00 8.00

Christmas A76

1986, Dec. 5 *Perf. 12*

389 A76 1sh Nativity, vert. .40 .20
390 A76 3sh Shepherd boy, vert. 2.00 2.00
391 A76 5sh Angel, map 2.75 2.75
392 A76 7sh Magi 4.00 4.00
Nos. 389-392 (4) 9.15 8.95

UNICEF, 40th Anniv. — A77

Child Survival Campaign: 1sh, Universal immunization by 1990. 3sh, Food and nutrition. 4sh, Oral rehydration. 5sh, Family planning. 10sh, Literacy of women.

1987, Jan. 6 Litho. *Perf. 14½*

393 A77 1sh multicolored .70 .70
394 A77 3sh multicolored 1.40 1.40
395 A77 4sh multicolored 1.90 1.90
396 A77 5sh multicolored 2.40 2.40
397 A77 10sh multicolored 3.75 3.75
Nos. 393-397 (5) 10.15 10.15

A78

Tourism — A79

1987, Mar. 25 Litho. *Perf. 14½*

398 A78 1sh Akamba carvers .60 .20
399 A78 3sh Beach 3.25 2.00
400 A78 5sh Escarpment 4.00 4.00
401 A78 7sh Pride of lions 6.00 6.00
Nos. 398-401 (4) 13.85 12.20

Souvenir Sheet

402 A79 30sh Kenya geysers 14.00 14.00

Ceremonial Costumes A80

1987, May 20 *Perf. 14½x13½*

403 A80 1sh Embu 1.25 .60
404 A80 3sh Kisii 2.75 1.40
405 A80 5sh Samburu 4.25 2.40
406 A80 7sh Taita 4.75 4.75
407 A80 10sh Boran 5.00 5.00
Nos. 403-407 (5) 18.00 14.15

See Nos. 505-509.

Posts & Telecommunications Corp., 10th Anniv. — A81

1987, July 1 Litho. *Perf. 13½*

408 A81 1sh Telecommunications satellite .75 .30
409 A81 3sh Rural post office, Kajiado 1.75 1.75
410 A81 4sh Athletics 2.25 2.25
411 A81 5sh Rural communication 2.50 2.50
412 A81 7sh Speedpost 3.50 3.50
Nos. 408-412 (5) 10.75 10.30

Souvenir Sheet

413 A81 25sh Natl. Flag 4.50 4.50

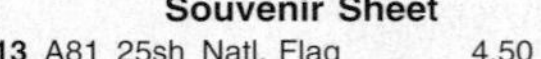

A82

A83

1987, Aug. 5 *Perf. 14½x14*

414 A82 1sh Volleyball .20 .20
415 A82 3sh Cycling .55 .55
416 A82 4sh Boxing .75 .75
417 A82 5sh Swimming .90 .90
418 A82 7sh Steeple chase 1.25 1.25
Nos. 414-418 (5) 3.65 3.65

Souvenir Sheet

Perf. 14x14½

419 A82 30sh Kasarani Sports Complex 4.75 4.75

4th All Africa Games, Nairobi, Aug. 1-12. Nos. 414-418, vert.

1987, Oct. 27 Litho. *Perf. 13½x14*

Medicinal herbs.

420 A83 1sh Aloe volkensii 1.10 .65
421 A83 3sh Cassia didymobotrya 2.25 1.50
422 A83 5sh Erythrina abyssinica 3.00 2.40
423 A83 7sh Adenium obesum 3.75 3.75
424 A83 10sh Herbalist's clinic 5.00 5.00
Nos. 420-424 (5) 15.10 13.30

Butterflies — A84

1988-90 Photo. *Perf. 15x14*

424A A84 10c Cyrestis camillus 1.00 1.00
425 A84 20c Iolaus sidus .30 .30
426 A84 40c Vanessa cardui .40 .30
427 A84 50c Colotis euippe omphale .40 .30
428 A84 70c Precis westermanni .40 .30
429 A84 80c Colias electo .40 .30
430 A84 1sh Eronia leda .40 .20
430A A84 1.50sh Papilio dardanus planemoides 5.00 1.00

Size: 25x41mm

Perf. 14½

431 A84 2sh Papilio rex .75 .75
432 A84 2.50sh Colotis phisadia .80 .75
433 A84 3sh Papilio desmondi teita .80 .75
434 A84 3.50sh Papilio demodocus .85 .75
435 A84 4sh Papilio phorcas .90 .80
436 A84 5sh Charaxes druceanus teita 1.00 1.00
437 A84 7sh Cymothoe teita 1.25 1.25
438 A84 10sh Charaxes zoolina 1.75 1.75
439 A84 20sh Papilio dardanus 3.50 3.50
440 A84 40sh Charaxes cithaeron kennethi 7.25 7.25
Nos. 424A-440 (18) 27.15 22.25

Issued: 10c, 9/1/89; 1.50sh, 5/18/90; others, 2/14/88.

Game Lodges A85

1988, May 31 Litho. *Perf. 14½*

441 A85 1sh Samburu .75 .35
442 A85 3sh Naro Moru River 1.10 1.10
443 A85 4sh Mara Serena 1.75 1.75
444 A85 5sh Voi Safari 1.90 1.90
445 A85 7sh Kilimanjaro Buffalo Lodge 2.25 2.25
446 A85 10sh Meru Mulika 2.75 2.75
Nos. 441-446 (6) 10.50 10.10

World Expo '88, Brisbane A86

EXPO '88 and Australia bicentennial emblems plus: 1sh, Stadium, site of the 1982 Commonwealth Games, and runners. 3sh, Flying Doctor Service aircraft. 4sh, HMS Sirius, a 19th cent. immigrant ship. 5sh, Ostrich and emu. 7sh, Pres. Daniel arap Moi, Queen Elizabeth II and Robert Hawke, prime minister of Australia. 30sh, Kenya Pavilion at EXPO '88.

1988, June 10

447 A86 1sh multicolored .70 .60
448 A86 3sh multicolored 2.50 1.75
449 A86 4sh multicolored 3.00 3.00
450 A86 5sh multicolored 4.00 4.00
451 A86 7sh multicolored 5.00 5.00
Nos. 447-451 (5) 15.20 14.35

Souvenir Sheet

452 A86 30sh multicolored 4.25 4.25

World Health Organization, 40th Anniv. — A87

1988, July 1 Litho. *Perf. 14½*

453 A87 1sh shown .35 .35
454 A87 3sh Nutrition 1.40 1.40
455 A87 5sh Immunization 2.50 2.50
456 A87 7sh Water supply 3.75 3.75
Nos. 453-456 (4) 8.00 8.00

1988 Summer Olympics, Seoul — A88

1988, Aug. 1 Litho. *Perf. 14½x14*

457 A88 1sh Handball .50 .20
458 A88 3sh Judo 1.00 .80
459 A88 5sh Weight lifting 1.50 1.50
460 A88 7sh Javelin 2.00 2.00
461 A88 10sh 400-meter relay 2.50 2.50
Nos. 457-461 (5) 7.50 7.00

Souvenir Sheet

462 A88 30sh Tennis 5.00 5.00

Utensils A89

Perf. 14½x14, 14x14½

1988, Sept. 20 Litho.

463 A89 1sh Calabashes, vert. .45 .20
464 A89 3sh Milk gourds, vert. .90 .55
465 A89 5sh Cooking pots 1.25 .90
466 A89 7sh Winnowing trays 1.50 1.50
467 A89 10sh Reed baskets 2.00 2.00
Nos. 463-467 (5) 6.10 5.15

Souvenir Sheet

468 A89 25sh Gourds, calabash, horn 4.50 4.50

10-Year Presidency of Daniel arap Moi — A90

Designs: 1sh, Swearing-in ceremony, 1978. 3sh, Promoting soil conservation. 3.50sh, Public transportation (bus), Nairobi. 4sh, Jua Kali artisans at market. 5sh, Moi University, Eldoret, established in 1985. 7sh, Hospital ward expansion. 10sh, British Prime Minister Margaret Thatcher and Pres. Moi inaugurating the Kapsabet Telephone Exchange, Jan. 6, 1988.

1988, Oct. 13 Litho. *Perf. 13½x14½*

469 A90 1sh multicolored .70 .70
470 A90 3sh multicolored 1.75 1.75
471 A90 3.50sh multicolored 2.00 2.00
472 A90 4sh multicolored 2.25 2.25
473 A90 5sh multicolored 2.75 2.75
474 A90 7sh multicolored 3.50 3.50
475 A90 10sh multicolored 5.50 5.50
Nos. 469-475 (7) 18.45 18.45

Independence, 25th Anniv. — A91

1988, Dec. 9 Litho. *Perf. 11½*

476 A91 1sh Natl. flag .40 .40
477 A91 3sh Coffee picking 2.10 2.10
478 A91 5sh Model of postal hq. 3.50 3.50
479 A91 7sh Harambee Star Airbus A310-300 5.00 5.00
480 A91 10sh Locomotive 9401 7.00 7.00
Nos. 476-480 (5) 18.00 18.00

Natl. Monuments — A92

1989, Mar. 15 Litho. *Perf. 14½*

481 A92 1.20sh Gedi Ruins, Malindi .40 .40
482 A92 3.40sh Vasco Da Gama Pillar, Malindi, vert. 1.00 1.00
483 A92 4.40sh Ishiakani Monument, Kiunga 2.00 2.00
484 A92 5.50sh Ft. Jesus, Mombasa 2.50 2.50
485 A92 7.70sh She Burnan Omwe, Lamu, vert. 3.00 3.00
Nos. 481-485 (5) 8.90 8.90

Red Cross, 125th Anniv. A93

1989, May 8 Litho. *Perf. 14x13½*

486 A93 1.20sh Anniv. and natl. soc. emblems .35 .35
487 A93 3.40sh First aid 1.25 1.25
488 A93 4.40sh Disaster relief 1.75 1.75
489 A93 5.50sh Jean-Henri Dunant 2.40 2.40
490 A93 7.70sh Blood donation 3.75 3.75
Nos. 486-490 (5) 9.50 9.50

World Wildlife Fund A94

Mushrooms A95

Giraffes, Giraffa Camelopardalis Reticulata.

1989, July 12 Litho. *Perf. 14½*

491 A94 1.20sh multicolored 2.50 2.25
492 A94 3.40sh multicolored 5.25 5.00
493 A94 4.40sh multicolored 6.00 6.00
494 A94 5.50sh multicolored 7.25 *8.00*
Nos. 491-494 (4) 21.00 21.25

Size: 80x110mm

Imperf

495 A94 30sh multicolored 12.00 *12.00*

No. 495 contains four labels like Nos. 491-494, perf. 14½, without denominations or WWF emblem.

1989, Sept. 6 Litho. *Perf. 14½*

496 A95 1.20sh Oyster 2.40 .65
497 A95 3.40sh Chestnut 3.50 2.40
498 A95 4.40sh White button 4.00 3.25
499 A95 5.50sh Termite 4.75 3.75
500 A95 7.70sh Shiitake 6.50 6.50
Nos. 496-500 (5) 21.15 16.55

Jawaharlal Nehru, 1st Prime Minister of Independent India — A96

1989, Nov. 9 Litho. *Perf. 13½x14*

501 A96 1.20sh Independence struggle 2.00 1.50
502 A96 3.40sh Education 2.50 2.00
503 A96 5.50sh Portrait 4.50 4.50
504 A96 7.70sh Industry 7.50 7.50
Nos. 501-504 (4) 16.50 15.50

Costume Type of 1980

1989, Dec. 8 Litho. *Perf. 14½x13½*

505 A80 1.20sh Kipsigis 1.25 .45
506 A80 3.40sh Rabai 2.50 2.50
507 A80 5.50sh Duruma 3.25 2.40
508 A80 7.70sh Kuria 4.50 3.75
509 A80 10sh Bajuni 5.50 5.50
Nos. 505-509 (5) 17.00 14.60

Pan-African Postal Union, 10th Anniv. — A97

Perf. 14x13½, 13½x14

1990, Jan. 31 Litho.

510 A97 1.20sh EMS Speedpost .25 .25
511 A97 3.40sh Mail runner .80 .80
512 A97 5.50sh Mandera P.O. 1.00 1.00
513 A97 7.70sh EMS, diff., vert. 1.25 1.25
514 A97 10sh PAPU emblem, vert. 1.60 1.60
Nos. 510-514 (5) 4.90 4.90

Soccer Trophies — A98

Designs:1.50sh, Moi Golden Cup. 4.50sh, East & Central Africa Challenge Cup. 6.50sh, East & Central Africa Club Championship Cup. 9sh, World Cup.

1990, May 21 Litho. *Perf. 14½*

515 A98 1.50sh multicolored .50 .50
516 A98 4.50sh multicolored 3.00 3.00
517 A98 6.50sh multicolored 4.00 4.00
518 A98 9sh multicolored 5.00 5.00
Nos. 515-518 (4) 12.50 12.50

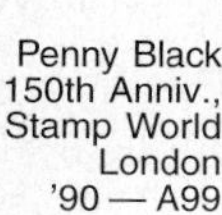

Penny Black 150th Anniv., Stamp World London '90 — A99

1990, Apr. 27 Litho. *Perf. 11½*

519 A99 1.50sh shown .40 .30
520 A99 4.50sh Great Britain No. 1 1.50 1.50
521 A99 6.50sh Early British cancellations 2.25 2.25
522 A99 9sh Main P.O. 3.25 3.25
a. Souvenir sheet of 4, #519-522 8.50 8.50
Nos. 519-522 (4) 7.40 7.30

No. 522a sold for 30 shillings.

ITU, 125th Anniv. A100

Designs: 4.50sh, Telephone assembly. 6.50sh, ITU Anniv. emblem. 9sh, Telecommunications development.

1990, July 12

523 A100 1.50sh multicolored .45 .20
524 A100 4.50sh multicolored .90 .65
525 A100 6.50sh multicolored 1.25 1.10
526 A100 9sh multicolored 1.60 1.60
Nos. 523-526 (4) 4.20 3.55

Common Design Types pictured following the introduction.

Queen Mother, 90th Birthday

Common Design Types

Perf. 14x15

1990, Aug. 4 Litho. Wmk. 384

527 CD343 10sh Queen Mother 1.50 1.50

Perf. 14½

528 CD344 40sh At garden party, 1947 5.50 5.50

Kenya African National Union (KANU), 50th Anniv. A101

1990, June 11

529 A101 1.50sh KANU flag .35 .20
530 A101 2.50sh Nyayo Monument .40 .35
531 A101 4.50sh KICC Party Headquarters .85 .85
532 A101 5sh Jomo Kenyatta 1.00 1.00
533 A101 6.50sh Daniel T. arap Moi 1.10 1.10
534 A101 9sh KANU mass meeting 1.75 1.75
535 A101 10sh Voters 1.75 1.75
Nos. 529-535 (7) 7.20 7.00

Kenya Postage Stamps, Cent. — A102

Intl. Literacy Year — A103

Designs: 1.50sh, Kenya #431. 4.50sh, East Africa and Uganda Protectorates #2. 6.50sh, British East Africa #1. 9sh, Kenya and Uganda #25. 20sh, Kenya, Uganda, Tanzania #232.

1990, Sept. 5 Litho. *Perf. 14x14½*

536 A102 1.50sh multicolored 1.50 .45
537 A102 4.50sh multicolored 3.00 2.50
538 A102 6.50sh multicolored 4.00 3.75
539 A102 9sh multicolored 5.25 4.75
540 A102 20sh multicolored 8.50 8.50
Nos. 536-540 (5) 22.25 19.95

1990, Nov. 30 Litho. *Perf. 13½x14*

541 A103 1.50sh Adult literacy class .65 .65
542 A103 4.50sh Radio teaching program 1.60 1.60
543 A103 6.50sh Technical training 2.25 2.25
544 A103 9sh Literacy year emblem 3.50 3.50
Nos. 541-544 (4) 8.00 8.00

1992 Summer Olympics, Barcelona — A106

1991, Nov. 29 Litho. *Perf. 14x13½*

554 A106 2sh National flag .45 .45
555 A106 6sh Basketball 1.90 1.90
556 A106 7sh Field hockey 2.50 2.50
557 A106 8.50sh Table tennis 3.00 3.00
558 A106 11sh Boxing 4.50 4.50
Nos. 554-558 (5) 12.35 12.35

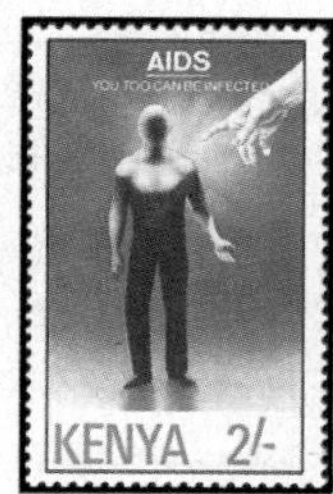

Fight AIDS — A107

Wildlife — A108

1991, Oct. 31 Litho. *Perf. 13½x14*

559 A107 2sh You too can be infected 1.25 .20
560 A107 6sh Has no cure 2.50 2.25
561 A107 8.50sh Casual sex is unsafe 3.50 3.00
562 A107 11sh Sterilize syringe before use 4.75 4.75
Nos. 559-562 (4) 12.00 10.20

Queen Elizabeth II's Accession to the Throne, 40th Anniv.

Common Design Type

1992, Feb. 6 Litho. *Perf. 14x13½*

563 CD349 3sh multicolored .20 .20
564 CD349 8sh multicolored 1.00 1.00
565 CD349 11sh multicolored 1.25 1.25
566 CD349 14sh multicolored 1.50 1.50
567 CD349 40sh multicolored 4.75 4.75
Nos. 563-567 (5) 8.70 8.70

1992, May 8 *Perf. 14½*

568 A108 3sh Leopard 2.25 .35
569 A108 8sh Lion 3.00 2.00
570 A108 10sh Elephant 6.25 3.00
571 A108 11sh Buffalo 3.75 3.00
572 A108 14sh Rhinoceros 10.50 5.00
Nos. 568-572 (5) 25.75 13.35

Vintage Cars A109

Designs: 3sh, Intl. Harvester S.S. motor truck, 1926. 8sh, Fiat 509, 1924. 10sh, "R" Hupmobile, 1923. 11sh, Chevrolet Box Body, 1928. 14sh, Bentley Parkward, 1934.

1992, June 24 *Perf. 14½*

573 A109 3sh multicolored 2.25 .70
574 A109 8sh multicolored 3.00 1.90
575 A109 10sh multicolored 3.50 2.50
576 A109 11sh multicolored 4.00 3.50
577 A109 14sh multicolored 5.50 5.50
Nos. 573-577 (5) 18.25 14.10

1992 Summer Olympics, Barcelona — A110

1992, July 24 Litho. *Perf. 14½*

578 A110 3sh Runners .55 .55
579 A110 8sh Judo 2.00 2.00
580 A110 10sh Women's volleyball 3.25 3.25
581 A110 11sh 4x100-meter relay 3.25 3.25
582 A110 14sh 10,000-meter run 4.25 4.25
Nos. 578-582 (5) 13.30 13.30

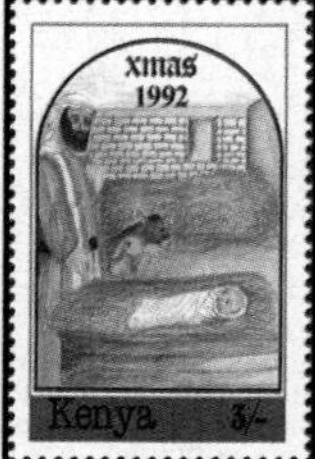

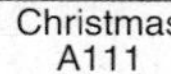

Christmas A111

Lighthouses A112

Designs: 3sh, Joseph, Jesus & animals in stable. 8sh, Mary holding Jesus in stable. 11sh, Map of Kenya, Christmas tree. 14sh, Adoration of the Magi.

1992, Dec. 14 Litho. *Perf. 13½x14*

583 A111 3sh multicolored .45 .45
584 A111 8sh multicolored 1.10 1.10
585 A111 11sh multicolored 1.60 1.60
586 A111 14sh multicolored 1.75 1.75
Nos. 583-586 (4) 4.90 4.90

1993, Jan. 25 *Perf. 14½*

Designs: 3sh, Asembo Bay, Lake Victoria. 8sh, Ras Serani, Mombasa. 11sh, Ras Serani, Mombasa, diff. 14sh, Gingira, Lake Victoria.

587 A112 3sh multicolored 2.25 .90
588 A112 8sh multicolored 4.00 2.75
589 A112 11sh multicolored 5.00 4.50
590 A112 14sh multicolored 6.75 6.75
Nos. 587-590 (4) 18.00 14.90

Birds — A113

Designs: 50c, Superb starling. 1sh, Red and yellow barbet. 1.50sh, Ross's turaco. 3sh, Greater honeyguide. 5sh, African fish eagle. 6sh, Vulturine guineafowl. 7sh, Malachite kingfisher. 8sh, Speckled pigeon. 10sh, Cinnamon-chested bee-eater. 11sh, Scarlet-chested sunbird. 14sh, Reichenow's weaver. 50sh, Yellow-billed hornbill. 80sh, Lesser flamingo. 100sh, Hadada ibis.

1993-99 Photo. *Perf. 15x14*

Granite Paper

594 A113 50c multi .20 .20
597 A113 1sh multi .20 .20
598 A113 1.50sh multi .20 .20
600 A113 3sh multi .20 .20
601 A113 5sh multi .25 .25
601A A113 6sh multi *5.00* 1.00
602 A113 7sh multi .45 .45
603 A113 8sh multi .55 .55
604 A113 10sh multi .65 .65
605 A113 11sh multi .70 .70
606 A113 14sh multi .90 .90

Size: 25x42mm

Perf. 14½

608 A113 50sh multi 3.25 3.25
609 A113 80sh multi 5.00 5.00
610 A113 100sh multi 6.50 6.50
Nos. 594-610 (14) 24.05 20.05

Issued: 1.50sh, 5sh, 2/14/94; 6sh, 1999; others, 2/22/93.

This is an expanding set. Numbers may change.

17th World Congress of Rehabilatation Intl. — A114

1993, July 1 Litho. *Perf. 14½*

611 A114 3sh Health care, vert. .90 .20
612 A114 8sh Recreation 1.40 .75
613 A114 10sh Vocational training 1.60 1.60
614 A114 11sh Recreation & sports 1.60 1.60
615 A114 14sh Emblem, vert. 2.00 2.00
Nos. 611-615 (5) 7.50 6.15

Maendeleo ya Wanawake Organization, 42th Anniv. — A115

Designs: 3.50sh, Maendeleo House. 9sh, Planting trees. 11sh, Rural family planning services, vert. 12.50sh, Water nearer the people. 15.50sh, Maendeleo improved wood cookstove, vert.

Perf. 14x13½, 13½x14

1994, Mar. 17 Litho.

616 A115 3.50sh multicolored 1.10 .20
617 A115 9sh multicolored 1.60 .60
618 A115 11sh multicolored 1.25 1.25
619 A115 12.50sh multicolored 2.25 2.25
620 A115 15.50sh multicolored 2.50 2.50
Nos. 616-620 (5) 8.70 6.80

Orchids — A116

Designs: 3.50sh, Ansellia africana. 9sh, Aerangis lutecalba. 12.50sh, Polystachya bella. 15.50sh, Brachycorythis kalbreyeri. 20sh, Eulophia guineensis.

1994, June 27 Litho. *Perf. 13½x14*

621 A116 3.50sh multicolored 2.40 .20
622 A116 9sh multicolored 3.25 1.00
623 A116 12.50sh multicolored 3.50 2.50
624 A116 15.50sh multicolored 4.25 4.25
625 A116 20sh multicolored 5.50 5.50
Nos. 621-625 (5) 18.90 13.45

African Development Bank, 30th Anniv. — A117

1994, Nov. 21 Litho. *Perf. 14½*

626 A117 6sh KICC, Nairobi 1.10 .25
627 A117 25sh Isinya, Kajiado 4.25 4.25

Intl. Year of the Family — A118

Rotary, 50th Anniv. — A119

1994, Dec. 22

628 A118 6sh Family planning 1.00 .20
629 A118 14.50sh Health 3.50 1.50
630 A118 20sh Education, horiz. 4.00 4.00
631 A118 25sh Emblem, horiz. 4.00 4.00
Nos. 628-631 (4) 12.50 9.70

1994, Dec. 29 *Perf. 13½x14*

Designs: 6sh, Paul P. Harris, founder. 14.50sh, Rotary Club of Mombasa. 17.50sh, Polio plus vaccine. 20sh, Water projects. 25sh, Emblem, motto.

632 A119 6sh multicolored .60 .20
633 A119 14.50sh multicolored 1.60 .75
634 A119 17.50sh multicolored 2.00 2.00
635 A119 20sh multicolored 2.25 2.25
636 A119 25sh multicolored 2.75 2.75
Nos. 632-636 (5) 9.20 7.95

SPCA — A120

Golf — A121

1995, Jan. 13 Litho. *Perf. 14½*

637 A120 6sh Donkey .50 .20
638 A120 14.50sh Cattle 1.40 .50
639 A120 17.50sh Sheep 1.75 1.00
640 A120 20sh Dog 1.90 1.90
641 A120 25sh Cat 2.40 2.40
Nos. 637-641 (5) 7.95 6.00

Kenya Society for Prevention of Cruelty to Animals.

1995, Feb. 28 Litho. *Perf. 14½*

642 A121 6sh Man in vest 1.00 .20
643 A121 17.50sh Woman 3.25 1.00
644 A121 20sh Man in red shirt 3.50 1.25
645 A121 25sh Golf club 4.50 1.50
Nos. 642-645 (4) 12.25 3.95

Traditional Crafts — A122

1995, Mar. 24 Litho. *Perf. 14x13½*

646 A122 6sh Perfume containers .50 .20
647 A122 14.50sh Basketry 1.00 .95
648 A122 17.50sh Preservation pots 1.40 1.40
649 A122 20sh Gourds 1.75 1.75
650 A122 25sh Wooden containers 2.40 2.40
Nos. 646-650 (5) 7.05 6.70

UN, 50th Anniv. A123

Designs: 23sh, UN Headquarters, Nairobi. 26sh, People holding UN emblem. 32sh, UN Peacekeeper's helmet. 40sh, UN emblem.

1995, Oct. 24 Litho. *Perf. 13½*

651 A123 23sh multicolored 1.50 .75
652 A123 26sh multicolored 1.60 1.00
653 A123 32sh multicolored 2.25 2.10
654 A123 40sh multicolored 2.50 2.50
Nos. 651-654 (4) 7.85 6.35

A124 A125

1995, Sept. 29 Litho. *Perf. 13½*

655 A124 14sh Tse-tse fly .70 .35
656 A124 26sh Tick 1.25 .90
657 A124 32sh Wild silk moth 1.60 1.25
658 A124 33sh Maize borer 1.75 1.75
659 A124 40sh Locust 2.10 2.10
Nos. 655-659 (5) 7.40 6.35

ICIPE, 25th anniv.

1995, Oct. 16

660 A125 14sh Maize production 1.00 .35
661 A125 28sh Cattle rearing 2.25 1.00
662 A125 32sh Poultry keeping 2.50 2.00
663 A125 33sh Fishing 2.50 2.50
664 A125 40sh Fruits 3.25 3.25
Nos. 660-664 (5) 11.50 9.10

FAO, 50th anniv.

Miniature Sheets

1996 Summer Olympics, Atlanta — A126

No. 665: a, 14sh, Swimming. b, 20sh, Archery. c, 32sh, Javelin. d, 40sh, Fencing. e, 50sh, Discus. f, 20sh, Weight lifting.

No. 666: a, Pole vault. b, Equestrian. c, Diving. d, Track e, Torch bearer. f, Hurdles. g, Kayak. h, Boxing. i, Gymnastics.

No. 667- Medal winners: a, Greg Louganis, diving. b, Muhammed Ali, boxing. c, Nadia Comaneci, gymnastics. d, Daley Thompson, decathlon. e, Kipchoge "Kip" Keino, track and field. f, Kornelia Enders, swimming. g, Jackie Joyner-Kersee, track and field. h, Michael Jordan, basketball. i, Shun Fujimoto, gymnastics.

No. 668, 100sh, Torch bearer. No. 669, 100sh, Gold medalist.

1996, Jan. 5 Litho. *Perf. 14*

665 A126 Sheet of 6, #a.-f. 12.00 12.00
666 A126 20sh Sheet of 9, #a.-i. 13.00 13.00
667 A126 25sh Sheet of 9, #a.-i. 14.00 14.00

Souvenir Sheets

668-669 A126 Set of 2 12.00 12.00

World Tourism Organization, 20th Anniv. — A127

1996, Jan. 31 Litho. *Perf. 13½*

670 A127 6sh Lions .50 .20
671 A127 14sh Mount Kenya 1.00 .35
672 A127 20sh Water sports 1.50 .80
673 A127 25sh Hippopotomus 2.00 2.00
674 A127 40sh Culture 3.00 3.00
Nos. 670-674 (5) 8.00 6.35

Perf. 13x13½

675 A127 50sh Giraffes, vert. 5.00 5.00

Wild Animals A128

1996 *Perf. 13x13½*

Booklet Stamps

676 A128 20sh Water buck 1.25 1.00
677 A128 20sh Rhinoceros 1.25 1.00
678 A128 20sh Cheetah 1.25 1.00
679 A128 20sh Oryx 1.25 1.00
680 A128 20sh Reticulated giraffe 1.25 1.00
681 A128 20sh Bongo 1.25 1.00
a. Booklet pane of 6, #676-681 10.00
Complete booklet, 4 #681a 40.00

Nos. 676-681 appear in No. 681a in two different orders. Complete booklet contains 2 of each type of pane.

1996 Summer Olympic Games, Atlanta — A129

Red Cross — A130

1996, July 18 Litho. *Perf. 13½x14*

682 A129 6sh Woman running .30 .30
683 A129 14sh Steeple chase .60 .60
684 A129 20sh Victory lap .90 .90
685 A129 25sh Boxing 1.10 1.10
686 A129 40sh Man running 1.90 1.90
Nos. 682-686 (5) 4.80 4.80

1996, Aug. 30 Litho. *Perf. 14*

687 A130 6sh Emblem .40 .40
688 A130 14sh Blood donation .80 .80
689 A130 20sh Immunization 1.25 1.25
690 A130 25sh Refugees 1.50 1.50
691 A130 40sh Clean environment 2.50 2.50
Nos. 687-691 (5) 6.45 6.45

A131 A132

1996, Sept. 10 Litho. *Perf. 14½*

693 A131 6sh Impala .40 .40
694 A131 20sh Colobus monkey 1.50 1.50
695 A131 25sh Elephant 1.75 1.75
696 A131 40sh Black rhino 3.25 3.25
Nos. 693-696 (4) 6.90 6.90

East African Wildlife Society.

1996, Oct. 31 Litho. *Perf. 13½*

697 A132 6sh Logo .30 .30
698 A132 14sh Eye camps .95 .95
699 A132 20sh Wheel chair 1.50 1.50
700 A132 25sh Ambulance 1.75 1.75
Nos. 697-700 (4) 4.50 4.50

Lions Club Intl.

COMESA (Common Market for Eastern and Southern Africa — A133

1997, Jan. 15 **Litho.** ***Perf. 13½x14***
701 A133 6sh COMESA logo .20 .20
702 A133 20sh Natl. flag 1.40 1.40

Fish of Lake Victoria A134

Haplochromis: #703, Orange rock hunter. #704, Chilotes. #705, Cinctus. #706, Nigricans.

1997, Jan. 31 ***Perf. 14x13½***
703 A134 25sh multicolored *3.50 1.75*
704 A134 25sh multicolored *3.50 1.75*
705 A134 25sh multicolored *3.50 1.75*
706 A134 25sh multicolored *3.50 1.75*
Nos. 703-706 (4) 14.00 7.00

World Wildlife Fund.

Locomotives — A135

1997, Feb. 20 **Litho.** ***Perf. 14x13½***
707 A135 6sh Class 94, 1981 .75 .20
708 A135 14sh Class 87, 1964 1.10 .40
709 A135 20sh Class 59, 1955 1.50 .65
710 A135 25sh Class 57, 1939 1.50 1.10
711 A135 30sh Class 23, 1923 1.75 1.75
712 A135 40sh Class 10, 1914 2.00 2.00
Nos. 707-712 (6) 8.60 6.10

Dated 1996.

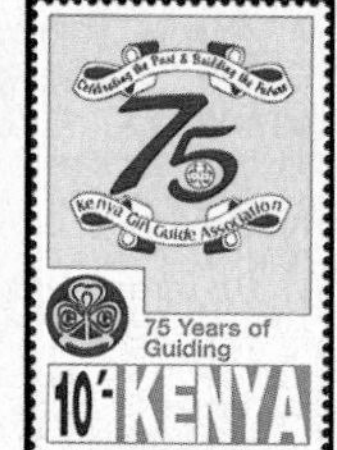

Fruits — A136 A137

1997, Feb. 28 ***Perf. 14½***
713 A136 6sh Orange .20 .20
714 A136 14sh Pineapple 2.10 .50
715 A136 20sh Mango 3.00 2.00
716 A136 25sh Papaya 3.75 2.50
Nos. 713-716 (4) 9.05 5.20

1997, Sept. 1 **Litho.** ***Perf. 14½***

Scouting Organizations: No. 717, Girl Guides, 75th anniv. No. 718, Lord Baden Powell. No. 719, Girl scouts hiking. No. 720, Rangers camping. No. 721, Girl Guides planting trees. No. 722, Boy Scouts first aid. No. 723, Boy Scouts camping. No. 724, Brownies.

717 A137 10sh multicolored .35 .35
718 A137 10sh multicolored .35 .35
a. Pair, #717-718 .75 .75
719 A137 27sh multicolored .90 .90
720 A137 27sh multicolored .90 .90
a. Pair, #719-720 2.25 2.25
721 A137 33sh multicolored 1.25 1.25
722 A137 33sh multicolored 1.25 1.25
a. Pair, #721-722 3.00 3.00
723 A137 42sh multicolored 1.50 1.50
724 A137 42sh multicolored 1.50 1.50
a. Pair, #723-724 3.50 3.50
Nos. 717-724 (8) 8.00 8.00

Tourist Attractions — A138

Designs: 10sh, Crocodile. 27sh, Hot Springs, Lake Bogoria. 30sh, Warthogs. 33sh, Wind surfing. 42sh, Traditional huts.

1997, Oct. 9 ***Perf. 13½***
725 A138 10sh multicolored 1.25 .25
726 A138 27sh multicolored 2.00 1.60
727 A138 30sh multicolored 2.00 1.90
728 A138 33sh multicolored 2.25 2.25
729 A138 42sh multicolored 2.50 2.50
Nos. 725-729 (5) 10.00 8.50

Vasco da Gama's Stop in Malindi, 500th Anniv. A139

Designs: 10sh, Residents greeting ships as they arrive. 24sh, Three ships. 33sh, Map of voyage. 42sh, Ships in bay, monument.

1998, Apr. 4 **Litho.** ***Perf. 13***
730 A139 10sh multicolored .60 .30
731 A139 24sh multicolored 1.40 .75
732 A139 33sh multicolored 2.00 2.00
733 A139 42sh multicolored 2.50 2.50
Nos. 730-733 (4) 6.50 5.55

Pan African Postal Union (PAPU) A140

1998, June 10 **Litho.** ***Perf. 14½***
734 A140 10sh Lion 1.90 .25
735 A140 24sh Buffalo 2.40 .75
736 A140 33sh Grant's gazelle 3.25 3.25
737 A140 42sh Cheetah 4.25 4.25
Nos. 734-737 (4) 11.80 8.50

Souvenir Sheet

738 A140 50sh Hirola gazelle 3.75 3.75

Pres. Daniel arap Moi Taking Oath of Office, 1998 A141

1998, Dec. 8 **Litho.** ***Perf. 13½***
739 A141 14sh multicolored 1.60 .90

Turtles A142

Designs: 17sh, Leatherback. 20sh, Green sea. 30sh, Hawksbill. 47sh, Olive Ridley. 59sh, Loggerhead.

2000, Apr. 13 **Litho.** ***Perf. 13½x13¾***
740 A142 17sh multi 1.00 .35
741 A142 20sh multi 1.25 .40
742 A142 30sh multi 1.75 1.00
743 A142 47sh multi 2.50 2.50
744 A142 59sh multi 3.00 3.00
Nos. 740-744 (5) 9.50 7.25

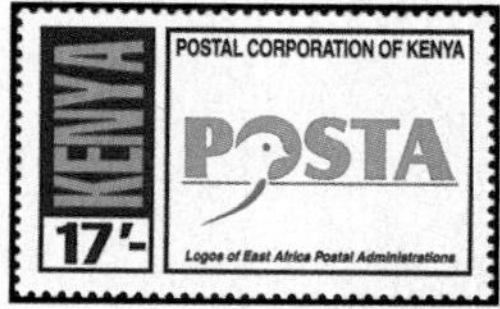

Emblems of East African Postal Administrations — A143

Designs: 17sh, Postal Corporation of Kenya. 35sh, Uganda Posta Limited. 50sh, Tanzania Posts Corporation. 70sh, Postal Corporation of Kenya.

2000, May 31 ***Perf. 13¾x13½***
745 A143 17sh multi .85 .35
746 A143 35sh multi 1.60 1.25
747 A143 50sh multi 2.25 2.25
Nos. 745-747 (3) 4.70 3.85

Souvenir Sheet

Perf. 13¼x13

748 A143 70sh multi 4.50 4.50

Crops — A144

2001, Feb. 28 **Photo.** ***Perf. 14½x14***
749 A144 2sh Cotton .20 .20
750 A144 4sh Bananas .20 .20
751 A144 5sh Avocados .20 .20
752 A144 6sh Cassava .20 .20
753 A144 8sh Arrowroot .20 .20
754 A144 10sh Papayas .25 .20
755 A144 19sh Oranges .50 .35
756 A144 20sh Pyrethrum .50 .35
757 A144 30sh Peanuts .75 .60
758 A144 35sh Coconuts .90 .60
759 A144 40sh Sisal 1.00 .75
760 A144 50sh Cashews 1.25 .90

Size: 25x42mm

Perf. 14¼

761 A144 60sh Tea 1.50 1.00
762 A144 80sh Corn 2.00 1.50
763 A144 100sh Coffee 2.50 1.75
764 A144 200sh Finger millet 5.00 3.50
765 A144 400sh Sorghum 10.00 7.00
766 A144 500sh Sugar cane 12.50 8.50
Nos. 749-766 (18) 39.65 28.00

2001 **Photo.** ***Perf. 14¾ Horiz.***

Coil Stamps

766A A144 5sh Avocados — —
766B A144 10sh Papayas — —

Historic Sites of East Africa A145

Designs: 19sh, Source of Nile River, Jinja, Uganda. 35sh, Lamu Fort, Kenya (28x28mm). 40sh, Olduvai Gorge, Tanzania. 50sh, Thimlich Ohinga, Kenya (28x28mm).

Perf. 14¼, 13½ (35sh, 50sh)

2002 **Litho.**
767-770 A145 Set of 4 9.50 9.50

Kenya - People's Republic of China Diplomatic Relations, 40th Anniv. — A146

Flags of Kenya and People's Republic of China and: 21sh, Section of Mombasa Road. 66sh, Kasarani Stadium.

2003, Dec. 14 **Litho.** ***Perf. 12***
771-772 A146 Set of 2 6.00 6.00

Mammals — A147

Designs: 21sh, Lioness and baby oryx. 60sh, Leopard and cub. 66sh, Zebra and calf. 88sh, Bongo and calf.

2004, Nov. 19 **Litho.** ***Perf. 14½***
773-776 A147 Set of 4 10.00 10.00

Easter — A148

Designs: 25sh, Jesus with hand raised. 65sh, Jesus condemned to death. 75sh, Crucifixion. 95sh, Jesus praying.

2005, Apr. 1 **Litho.** ***Perf. 13½***
777-780 A148 Set of 4 8.00 8.00

Rotary International, Cent. — A149

Rotary emblem and: 25sh, Polio vaccination. 65sh, Donation of Jaipur feet. 75sh, Don Bosco Center, Nairobi. 95sh, Donation of sewing machine.

2005, May 26
781-784 A149 Set of 4 12.00 12.00

Native Costumes A150

Designs: 21sh, Gabbra. 60sh, Pokot. 66sh, Meru. 88sh, Digo.

2005, Dec. 6 **Litho.** ***Perf. 14½***
785-788 A150 Set of 4 8.00 8.00

Fish A151

Design: 25sh, Elephant snout fish. 95sh, Redbreast tilapia.

2006, May 4 **Litho.** ***Perf. 13½x13***
789 A151 25sh multi —
792 A151 95sh multi —

Two additional stamps were issued in this set. The editors would like to examine any examples.

24th Universal Postal Union Congress, Nairobi — A152

2006, Oct. 11 Litho. *Perf. 13½*
793 A152 25sh multi 1.25 1.25

Values are for stamps with surrounding selvage. Due to political unrest in Kenya, the UPU Congress was moved to Geneva, Switzerland.

Hippopotamus and Tortoise — A153

2006, Dec. 15 Litho. *Perf. 12½x13*
794 A153 25sh multi 2.00 2.00

Tourism A155

2006, Dec. 15 *Perf. 13*
Booklet Stamps
795 A155 25sh Roan antelope *2.60 2.60*
796 A155 25sh Weaver bird *2.60 2.60*
797 A155 25sh Monkey *2.60 2.60*
a. Booklet pane of 3, #795-797 *8.00 —*
798 A155 25sh Turkana hut *2.60 2.60*
799 A155 25sh Sports *2.60 2.60*
800 A155 25sh Golf course *2.60 2.60*
a. Booklet pane of 3, #798-800 *8.00 —*
801 A155 25sh Abadares Waterfall *2.60 2.60*
802 A155 25sh Balloon safari *2.60 2.60*
803 A155 25sh Bull fighting *2.60 2.60*
a. Booklet pane of 3, #801-803 *8.00 —*
804 A155 25sh Chimpanzee *2.60 2.60*
805 A155 25sh Maasai *2.60 2.60*
806 A155 25sh Kit Mikaye *2.60 2.60*
a. Booklet pane of 3, #804-806 *8.00 —*
Complete booklet, #797a, 800a, 803a, 806a *32.00*
Nos. 795-806 (12) *31.20 31.20*

Mountains — A156

Designs: 25sh, Mt. Kenya, Kenya. 75sh, Mt. Ruwenzori, Uganda. 95sh, Mt. Kilimanjaro, Tanzania.

2007, Feb. 28 Litho. *Perf. 13½*
807-809 A156 Set of 3 6.25 6.25

Breast Cancer Awareness A157

2007, Oct. 28 *Perf. 13¼*
810 A157 25sh multi 1.25 1.25

Ceremonial Costumes — A158

Men's and women's costumes: 25sh, Ogiek. 65sh, Sabaot. 75sh, Ribe. 95sh, Elmolo.

2007, Nov. 21 *Perf. 14½*
811-814 A158 Set f 4 8.25 8.25

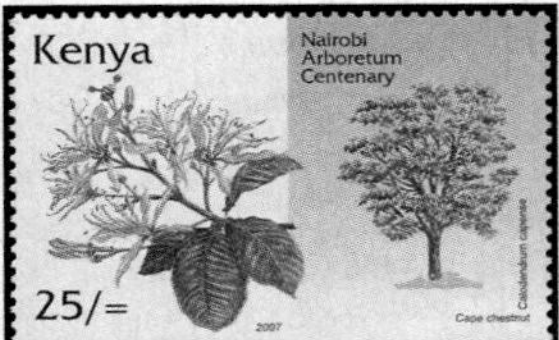

National Arboretum, Cent. — A159

Designs: 25sh, Cape chestnut tree and blossom. 65sh, Bhutan cypress tree, Tree Center. 75sh, Nandi flame tree and blossom. 95sh, Calabash nutmeg tree and blossom.

2007, Dec. 13 Litho. *Perf. 13¾*
815-818 A159 Set of 4 8.25 8.25

24th UPU Congress — A160

Design: 25sh, Sitalunga gazelle in Saiwa Swamp. 65sh, Jackson's hartebeest at Ruma Park. 75sh, Steeplechase runner. 95sh, Kenyatta Intl. Conference Center, Nairobi.

2008, Feb. 7 Litho. *Perf. 14½*
819 A160 25sh multi *1.00 .50*
820 A160 65sh multi *2.50 1.50*
821 A160 75sh multi *3.00 2.25*
822 A160 95sh multi *3.75 3.75*
Nos. 819-822 (4) *10.25 8.00*

Because of political turmoil in Kenya, the 24th UPU Congress was moved from Nairobi to Geneva, Switzerland.

2008 Summer Olympics, Beijing — A161

Designs: 25sh, Kenyan athletes holding Kenyan flag. 65sh, Women's volleyball, vert. 75sh, Women runners. 95sh, Boxing.

2008, Aug. 21 Litho. *Perf. 14½*
823-826 A161 Set of 4 7.50 7.50

Heroes of Kenya — A162

Designs: 25sh, Vice-president Oginga Odinga (c. 1911-94), Pio Gama Pinto (1927-65), politician, Tom Mboya (1930-69), politician, Ronald Ngala (1923-72), politician. 65sh, The Kapenguria Six. 75sh, Dedan Kimathi (1920-57), rebel leader, Elijah Masinde (c. 1910-87), Bukusu tribal leader, Mekatilili Wa Menza, female leader of 1914 rebellion, Koitalel Samoei (1860-1905), Nandi chief. 95sh, Kenya Army Peacekeeping Force.

2008, Oct. 17 *Perf. 12¾x13¼*
827-830 A162 Set of 4 8.50 8.50

Theosophical Order of Service, Cent. — A163

2008, Nov. 17 Litho. *Perf. 14x13¾*
831 A163 25sh multi 1.25 1.25

Aga Khan, 50th Anniv.of Reign A164

Designs: 25sh, Madrasa program (40x40mm). 65sh, Coastal rural support program (40x40mm). 75sh, Aga Khan Academy, Mombasa (44x30mm). 95sh, Aga Khan University Hospital, Nairobi (44x30mm).

Perf. 13, 14½ (75sh, 95sh)
2008, Dec. 13
832-835 A164 Set of 4 7.50 7.50

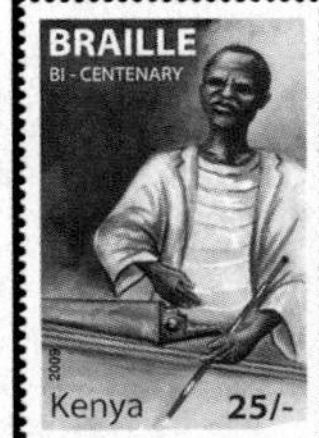

Blind Man — A165

2009, July 20 *Perf. 14½*
836 A165 25sh multi .65 .65

Louis Braille (1809-52), educator of the blind.

East Africa Natural History Society, Cent. A167

Bird on branch and: 25sh, Taita African violet, Amegilla bee. 65sh, Reed frog. 75sh, Great blue turaco. 95sh, Golden-rumped sengi.

2010, Mar. 25 Litho. *Perf. 13*
Granite Paper
849-852 A167 Set of 4 6.75 6.75

POSTAGE DUE STAMPS

D1

Perf. 14x13½
1967-85 Litho. Unwmk.
"POSTAGE DUE" 12½mm long
J1 D1 5c dark red .25 2.75
J2 D1 10c green .35 2.75
J3 D1 20c dark blue .70 3.25
J4 D1 30c reddish brown 1.00 4.00
J5 D1 40c brt red lilac 1.25 6.75
Perf. 14
J6 D1 80c brick red 1.00 6.25
Perf. 14x13½
J7 D1 1sh orange 3.00 *9.00*
"POSTAGE DUE" 11½mm long
Perf. 14¾x14
J8 D1 2sh pale violet .90 .90
Nos. J1-J8 (8) 8.45 *35.65*

Issued: 80c, 1978. 2sh, 1985; others, 1/3/67.
See Nos. J9-J14.

1969-70 *Perf. 14*
J1a D1 5c .20 5.25
J2a D1 10c .25 5.25
J3a D1 20c .45 5.75
J4a D1 30c .70 6.75
J5a D1 40c .90 10.50
J7a D1 1sh 2.00 *13.50*
Nos. J1a-J7a (6) 4.50 *47.00*

Issued: 1sh, 2/18/70; others, 12/16/69.

1971-73 *Perf. 14x15*
J1b D1 5c 1.75 5.25
J2b D1 10c 1.75 5.25
J3b D1 20c 1.50 5.75
J4b D1 30c 10.50 13.50
J5b D1 40c 1.25 9.00
J7b D1 1sh 2.50 *13.50*
Nos. J1b-J7b (6) 19.25 52.25

Issued: 30c, 7/13/71; others, 2/20/73. The 10c, 20c, 1sh on chalky paper were issued 7/13/71.

1973, Dec. 12 *Perf. 15*
J1c D1 5c .45 4.00
J2c D1 10c .45 4.00
J3c D1 20c .45 5.00
J4c D1 30c .45 5.75
J5c D1 40c 5.25 10.00
J7c D1 1sh 1.75 *12.50*
Nos. J1c-J7c (6) 8.80 41.25

1983 Wmk. 373 *Perf. 14x14¼*
J2d D1 10c .45 *2.00*
J3d D1 20c .45 *2.00*
J5d D1 40c 8.50 *10.00*

Nos. J5, J7-J8 Redrawn
Perf. 14¾x14
1987-98 Litho. Unwmk.
J8A D1 30c brown .20 .20
J9 D1 40c bright red lilac .20 .20
J10 D1 50c dark green .20 .20
J10A D1 80c red brown .20 .20
J11 D1 1sh light orange .80 .80
a. light orange .20 .20
J12 D1 2sh pale violet .20 .20
J13 D1 3sh dark blue .45 .45
J14 D1 5sh red brown .45 .45
J15 D1 10sh brown .45 .45
J16 D1 20sh red lilac .80 .80
Nos. J8A-J16 (10) 3.95 3.95

"KENYA" is 9mm wide on Nos. J9, J11. "CENTS" is 4½mm wide and "SHILLING" has cross bar on "G"; both are in a new font.

"KENYA" is 8½mm wide on No. J12. "POSTAGE DUE" is 11mm wide on Nos. J10, J11a, J15, J16.

Issued: 40c, 1sh, 1987; 10sh, 20sh, 1998; others, Dec. 6, 1993.

OFFICIAL STAMPS

Nos. 1-5 and 7 Overprinted

Perf. 14x14½

1964, Oct. 1 Photo. Unwmk.

Size: 21x17½mm

No.	Type	Description	Unused	Used
O1	A1	5c blue, buff & dk brn	.20	.20
O2	A1	10c brown	.20	.20
O3	A1	15c dp magenta	1.50	.30
O4	A1	20c yel green & dk brn	.30	.45
O5	A1	30c yellow & black	.40	.65
O6	A1	50c green, blk & dp car	2.50	1.10
		Nos. O1-O6 (6)	5.10	2.90

KENYA, UGANDA, & TANZANIA

'ke-nyə, ü-'gan-də, ˌtan-zə-'nē-ə

LOCATION — East Africa, bordering on the Indian Ocean
GOVT. — States in British Commonwealth
AREA — 679,802 sq. mi.
POP. — 42,760,000 (est. 1977)
CAPITAL — Nairobi (Kenya), Kampala (Uganda), Dar es Salaam (Tanzania)

Kenya became a crown colony in 1906, including the former East Africa Protectorate leased from the Sultan of Zanzibar and known as the Kenya Protectorate. In 1963 the colony became independent. Its stamps are listed under "Kenya."

The inland Uganda Protectorate, lying west of Kenya Colony, was declared a British Protectorate in 1894. Uganda became independent in 1962.

Tanganyika, a trust territory larger than Kenya or Uganda, was grouped with them postally from 1935 under the East African Posts & Telecommunications Administration. Tanganyika became independent in 1961. When it merged with Zanzibar in 1964, "Zanzibar" was added to the inscriptions on stamps issued under the E.A.P. & T. Administration. In 1965 the multiple inscription was changed to "Kenya, Uganda, Tanzania," variously arranged.

Zanzibar withdrew its own stamps in 1968, and K., U. & T. stamps became valid Jan. 1, 1968.

100 Cents = 1 Rupee
100 Cents = 1 Shilling (1922)
20 Shillings = 1 Pound

Catalogue values for unused stamps in this country are for Never Hinged items, beginning with Scott 90.

East Africa and Uganda Protectorates

King George V
A1 A2

1921 Typo. Wmk. 4 *Perf. 14*

Ordinary Paper

No.	Type	Description	Unused	Used
1	A1	1c black	.90	*1.90*
2	A1	3c green	6.75	*10.00*
3	A1	6c rose red	8.50	*12.00*
4	A1	10c orange	9.75	1.40
5	A1	12c gray	8.50	*140.00*
6	A1	15c ultramarine	12.50	*18.50*

Chalky Paper

No.	Type	Description	Unused	Used
7	A1	50c gray lilac & blk	16.50	*120.00*
8	A2	2r blk & red, *blue*	82.50	*190.00*
9	A2	3r green & violet	150.00	*325.00*
10	A2	5r gray lil & ultra	175.00	*275.00*
11	A2	50r gray grn & red	3,250.	*6,000.*
		Nos. 1-10 (10)	470.90	*1,093.*

The name of the colony was changed to Kenya in August, 1920, but stamps of the East Africa and Uganda types were continued in use. Stamps of types A1 and A2 watermarked Multiple Crown and C A (3) are listed under East Africa and Uganda Protectorates.

For stamps of Kenya and Uganda overprinted "G. E. A." used in parts of former German East Africa occupied by British forces, see Tanganyika Nos. 1-9.

Kenya and Uganda

King George V
A3 A4

1922-27 Wmk. 4

No.	Type	Description	Unused	Used
18	A3	1c brown	1.10	*3.50*
19	A3	5c violet	4.00	1.00
20	A3	5c green ('27)	2.40	.55
21	A3	10c green	1.75	.35
22	A3	10c black ('27)	4.50	.25
23	A3	12c black	8.00	*29.00*
24	A3	15c car rose	1.40	.20
25	A3	20c orange	3.75	.20
26	A3	30c ultra	3.50	.60
27	A3	50c gray	2.75	.20
28	A3	75c ol bister	6.50	*15.00*
29	A4	1sh green	4.75	3.00
30	A4	2sh gray lilac	10.00	*14.00*
31	A4	2sh50c brown ('25)	24.00	*100.00*
32	A4	3sh gray black	20.00	7.50
33	A4	4sh gray ('25)	29.00	*100.00*
34	A4	5sh carmine	27.50	27.50
35	A4	7sh50c org ('25)	100.00	*200.00*
36	A4	10sh ultra	60.00	*60.00*
37	A4	£1 org & blk	225.00	*300.00*
		Revenue cancel		20.00
38	A4	£2 brn vio & grn ('25)	800.00	*1,400.*
		Revenue cancel		110.00
39	A4	£3 yel & dl vio ('25)	1,650.	—
		Revenue cancel		150.00
40	A4	£4 rose lil & blk ('25)	2,200.	—
		Revenue cancel		200.00
41	A4	£5 blue & blk	6,000.	—
		Revenue cancel		100.00
41A	A4	£10 grn & blk	*14,000.*	
		Revenue cancel		225.00
41B	A4	£20 grn & red ('25)	*21,000.*	
		Revenue cancel		550.00
41C	A4	£25 red & blk	*28,750.*	
		Revenue cancel		375.00
41D	A4	£50 brn & blk	*32,500.*	
		Revenue cancel		400.00
41E	A4	£75 gray & purple	*90,000.*	
		Revenue cancel		1,000.
41F	A4	£100 blk & red	*100,000.*	
		Revenue cancel		1,100.
		Nos. 18-37 (20)	539.90	*862.85*

Nos. 37 and 38 are commonly found with court or fiscal cancellations. Values are much lower than those shown, which are for postally used stamps.

Nos. 39-41F are likely to bear court or fiscal cancels only.

High face value stamps are known with revenue cancellations removed and forged postal cancellations added.

Common Design Types pictured following the introduction.

Kenya, Uganda, Tanganyika Silver Jubilee Issue

Common Design Type

1935, May Engr. *Perf. 13½x14*

No.	Type	Description	Unused	Used
42	CD301	20c ol grn & lt bl	1.50	.20
43	CD301	30c blue & brown	2.50	*3.50*
44	CD301	65c indigo & green	2.00	*3.25*
45	CD301	1sh brt vio & indigo	2.25	*3.75*
		Nos. 42-45 (4)	8.25	*10.70*
		Set, never hinged	15.00	

Kavirondo Cranes — A5

Dhow on Lake Victoria — A6

Lion — A7

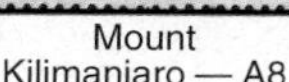
Mount Kilimanjaro — A8

Jinja Bridge by Ripon Falls — A9

Mount Kenya — A10

Lake Naivasha A11

FIVE CENTS
Type I — Left rope does not touch sail.
Type II — Left rope touches sail.

Perf. 13, 14, 11½x13, 13x11½

Engr.; Typo. (10c, £1)

1935, May 1

No.	Type	Description	Unused	Used
46	A5	1c red brn & blk	1.00	*1.50*
47	A6	5c grn & blk (I)	2.00	.50
a.		Type II	*24.00*	6.00
b.		Perf. 13x11½ (I)	*7,000.*	*650.00*
c.		Perf. 13x11½ (II)	*700.00*	*200.00*
48	A7	10c black & yel	4.50	.65
49	A8	15c red & black	2.75	.20
50	A5	20c red org & blk	3.50	.20
51	A9	30c dk ultra & blk	2.75	1.00
52	A6	50c blk & red vio	3.75	.20
53	A10	65c yel brn & blk	4.75	*2.00*
54	A11	1sh grn & black	3.50	.80
a.		Perf. 13x11½ ('36)	*1,350.*	125.00
55	A8	2sh red vio & rose brn	8.50	4.50
56	A11	3sh blk & ultra	12.00	*17.50*
a.		Perf. 13x11½	*2,250.*	
57	A9	5sh car & black	20.00	*35.00*
58	A5	10sh ultra & red vio	82.50	*100.00*
59	A7	£1 blk & scar	210.00	*275.00*
		Nos. 46-59 (14)	361.50	439.05
		Set, never hinged	725.00	

Coronation Issue

Common Design Type

1937, May 12 Engr. *Perf. 13½x14*

No.	Type	Description	Unused	Used
60	CD302	5c deep green	.20	.20
61	CD302	20c deep orange	.30	.35
62	CD302	30c brt ultra	.50	*1.00*
		Nos. 60-62 (3)	1.00	1.55
		Set, never hinged	2.00	

Kavirondo Cranes — A12

Dhow on Lake Victoria — A13

Lake Naivasha — A14

Jinja Bridge, Ripon Falls — A16

Mt. Kilimanjaro A15

Lion — A17

FIFTY CENTS:
Type I — Left rope does not touch sail.
Type II — Left rope touches sail.

1938-54 Engr. *Perf. 13x13½*

No.	Type	Description	Unused	Used
66	A12	1c vio brn & blk ('42)	.25	*.50*
a.		1c red brown & gray black, perf. 13	2.00	.85

Perf. 13x11½

No.	Type	Description	Unused	Used
67	A13	5c grn & blk	3.00	.50
68	A13	5c red org & brn ('49)	.40	*5.00*
a.		Perf. 13x12½ ('50)	1.60	*4.00*
69	A14	10c org & brn	2.00	.20
a.		Perf. 14 ('41)	90.00	10.00
70	A14	10c grn & blk ('49)	.25	*1.25*
a.		Perf. 13x12½ ('50)	1.75	.20

Perf. 13x12½

No.	Type	Description	Unused	Used
71	A14	10c gray & red brn ('52)	.80	.55

Perf. 13½x13, 13x13½

No.	Type	Description	Unused	Used
72	A15	15c car & gray blk ('43)	3.25	*3.75*
a.		Booklet pane of 4	14.00	
b.		Perf. 13	25.00	.55
73	A15	15c grn & blk ('52)	1.60	*6.00*
74	A12	20c org & gray blk ('42)	5.75	.20
a.		Booklet pane of 4	24.00	
b.		Imperf., pair		
c.		Perf. 13	*35.00*	.30
d.		Perf. 14 ('41)	*50.00*	3.00

Perf. 13x12½

No.	Type	Description	Unused	Used
75	A13	25c car & blk ('52)	1.25	*2.25*

Perf. 13x13½

No.	Type	Description	Unused	Used
76	A16	30c dp bl & gray blk ('42)	2.00	.35
a.		Perf. 14 ('41)	*130.00*	12.50
b.		Perf. 13	*40.00*	.40
77	A16	30c brn & pur ('52)	1.25	.40
78	A12	40c brt bl & gray blk ('52)	1.50	*5.00*

Perf. 13x12½

No.	Type	Description	Unused	Used
79	A13	50c gray blk & red vio (II) ('49)	5.75	.60
a.		Perf. 13x11½ (II)	14.00	1.10
b.		Perf. 13x11½ (I)	175.00	*250.00*

Perf. 13x11½

No.	Type	Description	Unused	Used
80	A14	1sh yel brn & gray blk	18.00	.25
a.		Perf. 13x12½ ('49)	10.00	.60

Perf. 13½x13

No.	Type	Description	Unused	Used
81	A15	2sh red vio & org brn ('44)	22.50	.30
a.		Perf. 13	*100.00*	2.50
b.		Perf. 14 ('41)	*62.50*	13.00

Perf. 13x12½

No.	Type	Description	Unused	Used
82	A14	3sh gray blk & ultra ('50)	27.50	5.50
a.		Perf. 13x11½	35.00	6.00

Perf. 13x13½

No.	Type	Description	Unused	Used
83	A16	5sh car rose & gray blk ('44)	27.50	1.50
a.		Perf. 13	*125.00*	17.50
b.		Perf. 14 ('41)	*35.00*	2.75
84	A12	10sh ultra & red vio ('44)	40.00	5.50
a.		Perf. 13	110.00	22.00
b.		Perf. 14 ('41)	32.50	25.00

Typo.
Perf. 14

85 A17 £1 blk & scar ('41) 22.50 *20.00*
a. Perf. 11½x13 275.00 135.00
b. Perf. 12½ ('54) 12.00 *35.00*
Nos. 66-85 (20) 187.05 *59.60*
Set, never hinged 275.00

Nos. 85-85b were printed on chalky paper. No. 85 also exists on ordinary paper, from a 1944 printing. Values are the same.

See Nos. 98-99.

South Africa Nos. 48, 57, 60 and 62 Surcharged

Basic stamps of Nos. 86-89 are inscribed alternately in English and Afrikaans.

1941-42 Wmk. 201 ***Perf. 15x14, 14***
86 A6 5c on 1p car & gray, pair 1.00 *2.00*
a. Single, English .20 .20
b. Single, Afrikaans .20 .20
87 A17 10c on 3p ultra, pair 2.50 *10.00*
a. Single, English .30 .35
b. Single, Afrikaans .30 .35
88 A7 20c on 6p org & grn, pair 2.25 *3.75*
a. Single, English .20 .25
b. Single, Afrikaans .20 .25
89 A11 70c on 1sh lt bl & ol brn, pair 15.00 *7.00*
a. Single, English .50 .45
b. Single, Afrikaans .50 .45
Nos. 86-89 (4) 20.75 22.75
Set, never hinged 30.00

Issued: #86-88, 7/1/41; #89, 4/20/42.

Values are for horizontal pairs. Vertical pairs are worth substantially less.

Catalogue values for unused stamps in this section, from this point to the end of the section, are for Never Hinged items.

Peace Issue
Common Design Type
Perf. 13½x14
1946, Nov. 11 Engr. Wmk. 4
90 CD303 20c red orange .25 .20
91 CD303 30c deep blue .40 .40

Silver Wedding Issue
Common Design Types
1948, Dec. 1 Photo. ***Perf. 14x14½***
92 CD304 20c orange .20 .20

Engr.; Name Typo.
Perf. 11½x11
93 CD305 £1 red 45.00 *70.00*

UPU Issue
Common Design Types
Engr.; Typo. on Nos. 95 and 96
1949, Oct. 10 ***Perf. 13, 11x11½***
94 CD306 20c red orange .20 .20
95 CD307 30c indigo 1.75 *2.25*
96 CD308 50c gray .40 .40
97 CD309 1sh red brown .50 .50
Nos. 94-97 (4) 2.85 3.35

Type of 1949 with Added Inscription: "Royal Visit 1952"

1952, Feb. 1 Engr. ***Perf. 13x12½***
98 A14 10c green & black .30 *1.60*
99 A14 1sh yel brn & gray blk 1.25 *2.25*

Visit of Princess Elizabeth, Duchess of Edinburgh, and the Duke of Edinburgh, 1952.

Coronation Issue
Common Design Type
1953, June 2 ***Perf. 13½x13***
101 CD312 20c red orange & blk .25 .20

Owen Falls Dam — A18

Giraffe — A19

Elizabeth II — A21

Mt. Kilimanjaro A20

1954, Apr. 28 ***Perf. 12½x13***
102 A18 30c dp ultra & black .50 .20

Visit of Queen Elizabeth II and the Duke of Edinburgh, 1954.

1954-59 ***Perf. 12½x13, 13x12½***

5c, 30c, Owen Falls Dam (without "Royal Visit 1954"). 20c, 40c, 1sh, Lion. 15c, 1.30sh, 5sh, Elephants. 10sh, Royal Lodge, Sagana.

103 A18 5c choc & blk 1.75 .65
a. Booklet pane of 4 7.00
b. Vignette (dam) inverted *67,500.*
104 A19 10c carmine 1.75 .20
a. Booklet pane of 4 7.00
105 A20 15c lt blue & blk (no period below "c") ('58) .75 1.60
a. Booklet pane of 4 3.50
106 A20 15c lt blue & blk (period below "c") ('59) 1.00 1.60
a. Booklet pane of 4 4.00
107 A19 20c org & black 2.00 .20
a. Booklet pane of 4 8.00
b. Imperf., pair *1,300.* 1,500.
108 A18 30c ultra & black 1.50 .20
a. Booklet pane of 4 6.00
b. Vignette (dam) inverted *32,500.*
109 A19 40c brown ('58) 1.50 1.00
110 A19 50c dp red lilac 3.50 .20
a. Booklet pane of 4 14.00
111 A20 65c brn car & grn ('55) 3.50 2.00
112 A19 1sh dp mag & blk 3.50 .20
113 A20 1.30sh pur & red org ('55) 15.00 .20
114 A20 2sh dp grn & gray 14.00 1.50
115 A20 5sh black & org 27.50 3.50
116 A20 10sh ultra & black 30.00 4.50
117 A21 £1 black & ver 21.00 18.00
Nos. 103-117 (15) 128.25 35.55

No. 103b is unique.

For "Official" overprints see Tanganyika Nos. O1-O12.

Map Showing Lakes Victoria and Tanganyika A22

Perf. 12½x13
1958, July 30 Engr. Wmk. 314
118 A22 40c green & blue .70 .40
119 A22 1.30sh violet & green .75 *1.00*

Cent. of the discovery of Lakes Victoria and Tanganyika by Sir Richard F. Burton and Capt. J. H. Speke.

Sisal — A23

A25

Mount Kenya and Giant Plants A24

10c, Cotton. 15c, Coffee. 20c, Gnu. 25c, Ostriches. 30c, Thompson's gazelles. 40c, Manta ray. 50c, Zebras. 65c, Cheetah. 1.30sh, Murchison Falls & hippopotamuses. 2sh, Mt. Kilimanjaro & giraffes. 2.50sh, Candelabra tree & black rhinoceroses. 5sh, Crater Lake & Mountains of the Moon. 10sh, Ngorongoro Crater & buffaloes.

Perf. 14½x14
1960, Oct. 1 Photo. Wmk. 314
120 A23 5c dull blue .20 .20
121 A23 10c lt olive green .20 .20
a. Booklet pane of 4 .60
122 A23 15c dull purple .40 .20
a. Booklet pane of 4 1.75
123 A23 20c brt lilac rose .25 .20
a. Booklet pane of 4 1.20
124 A23 25c olive gray 4.00 1.25
125 A23 30c brt vermilion .20 .20
a. Booklet pane of 4 .90
126 A23 40c bright blue .30 .20
127 A23 50c dull violet .45 .20
a. Booklet pane of 4 1.90
128 A23 65c lemon .65 *1.70*

Engr.
Perf. 14
129 A24 1sh vio & red lilac .90 .20
130 A24 1.30sh choc & dk car 5.00 .20
131 A24 2sh dk bl & dull bl 6.50 .55
132 A24 2.50sh ol grn & dull bl 9.00 2.75
133 A24 5sh rose red & lilac 4.50 .60
134 A24 10sh sl bl & ol grn 11.00 8.75

Perf. 13½x13
135 A25 20sh lake & bluish violet 22.50 27.50
Nos. 120-135 (16) 66.05 44.90

Booklets issued in 1961.

On Nos. 120-134, positions of "Kenya," "Uganda" and "Tanganyika" are rotated.

For "Official" overprints see Tanganyika Nos. O13-O20.

Agricultural Development — A26

Design: 30c, 1.30sh, Farmer picking corn.

Unwmk.
1963, Mar. 21 Photo. ***Perf. 14***
136 A26 15c lt ol grn & ultra .25 .20
137 A26 30c yel & red brown .40 .20
138 A26 50c dp org & ultra .50 .20
139 A26 1.30sh lt blue & red brn 1.00 1.00
Nos. 136-139 (4) 2.15 1.60

FAO "Freedom from Hunger" campaign.

Scholars and Open Book A27

1963, June 28 Unwmk. ***Perf. 14***
140 A27 30c multicolored .20 .20
141 A27 1.30sh multicolored .35 .35

Inauguration of University of East Africa.

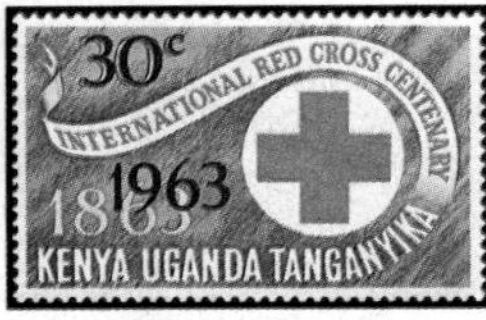

Red Cross A28

1963, Sept. 2
142 A28 30c blue & red 1.50 .30
143 A28 50c bister brown & red 2.00 1.25

Centenary of International Red Cross.

Kenya, Uganda, Tanganyika and Zanzibar

Issued by the East African Common Services Organization. Not used in Zanzibar.

Japanese Crest and Olympic Rings — A29

Olympic Rings and Banners A30

Unwmk.
1964, Oct. 25 Photo. ***Perf. 14***
144 A29 30c org & dk purple .20 .20
145 A29 50c dk purple & org .20 .20
146 A30 1.30sh blue, grn & org .40 .30
147 A30 2.50sh blue, vio & lil rose .60 .60
Nos. 144-147 (4) 1.40 1.30

18th Olympic Games, Tokyo, Oct. 10-25.

Kenya, Uganda, Tanzania

Issued by the East African Common Services Organization.

Safari Rally Emblem and Leopard — A31

1.30sh, 2.50sh, Car on road through national park & emblem of the East African Safari Rally.

1965, Apr. 15 Unwmk. ***Perf. 14***
148 A31 30c blue grn, yel & blk .20 .20
149 A31 50c brown, yel & blk .20 .20
150 A31 1.30sh lt ultra, ocher & green .35 .30
151 A31 2.50sh blue, dk grn & dull red .65 .65
Nos. 148-151 (4) 1.40 1.35

13th East African Safari Rally, 4/15-19/65.

ITU Emblem, Old and Modern Communication Equipment — A32

1965, May 17 Photo.
152 A32 30c lilac rose, gold & brn .25 .20
153 A32 50c gray, gold & brown .25 .20
154 A32 1.30sh lt vio bl, gold & brn .65 .30
155 A32 2.50sh brt bl grn, gold & brn 1.50 1.50
Nos. 152-155 (4) 2.65 2.20

Cent. of the ITU.

ICY Emblem — A33

1965, Aug. 4 Unwmk. *Perf. 14*
156 A33 30c green & gold .20 .20
157 A33 50c slate blk & gold .25 .20
158 A33 1.30sh ultra & gold .50 .30
159 A33 2.50sh car & gold 1.25 1.25
Nos. 156-159 (4) 2.20 1.95

International Cooperation Year.

Game Park Lodge A34

Tourist Publicity: 50c, Murchison Falls, Uganda. 1.30sh, Lake Nakuru, Kenya. 2.50sh, Deep-sea fishing, Tanzania.

1966, Apr. 4 Photo. *Perf. 14*
160 A34 30c ocher & multi .20 .20
161 A34 50c green & multi .50 .20
a. Blue omitted
162 A34 1.30sh multicolored 3.25 .35
163 A34 2.50sh gray & multi 2.50 3.50
Nos. 160-163 (4) 6.45 4.25

Javelin Thrower and Games' Emblem A35

1966, Aug. 2 Unwmk. *Perf. 14*
164 A35 30c multicolored .20 .20
165 A35 50c multicolored .20 .20
166 A35 1.30sh multicolored .25 .20
167 A35 2.50sh multicolored .35 *1.25*
Nos. 164-167 (4) 1.00 1.85

8th British Commonwealth and Empire Games, Jamaica, Aug. 4-13, 1966.

UNESCO Emblem — A36

1966, Oct. 3 Photo. *Perf. 14*
168 A36 30c rose red, brt grn & blk .40 .20
169 A36 50c lt brn, brt grn & blk .55 .20
170 A36 1.30sh gray, brt grn & blk 1.50 .25
171 A36 2.50sh yel, brt grn & blk 2.40 4.50
Nos. 168-171 (4) 4.85 5.15

20th anniv. of UNESCO.

Dragon Rapide A37

Planes: 50c, Super VC10. 1.30sh, Comet 4. 2.50sh, F.27 Friendship.

1967, Jan. 23 Unwmk.
172 A37 30c multicolored .35 .20
173 A37 50c multicolored .45 .20
174 A37 1.30sh multicolored .95 .40
175 A37 2.50sh multicolored 2.10 3.50
Nos. 172-175 (4) 3.85 4.30

21st anniversary of East African Airways.

Pillar Tomb, East African Coast — A38

Designs: 50c, Man hunting elephant, petroglyph, Tanzania. 1.30sh, Clay head, Luzira, Uganda. 2.50sh, Proconsul skull, Rusinga Island, Kenya.

1967, May 2 Photo. *Perf. 14*
176 A38 30c rose lake, blk & yel .20 .20
177 A38 50c gray, black & ver .60 .20
178 A38 1.30sh green, yel & blk 1.00 .30
179 A38 2.50sh cop red, yel & blk 2.00 3.50
Nos. 176-179 (4) 3.80 4.20

Archaeological relics of East Africa.

Emblems of Kenya, Tanzania and Tanganyika — A39

Photo.; Gold Impressed
1967, Dec. 1 *Perf. 14½x14*
180 A39 5sh gray, black & gold .60 *1.00*

Establishment of East African Community.

Mount Kenya A40

30c Mountain climber. 1.30sh, Mount Kilimanjaro. 2.50sh, Ruwenzori Mountains.

1968, Mar. 4 Photo. *Perf. 14½*
181 A40 30c multicolored .20 .20
182 A40 50c multicolored .40 .20
183 A40 1.30sh multicolored .70 .35
184 A40 2.50sh multicolored 1.50 *2.25*
Nos. 181-184 (4) 2.80 3.00

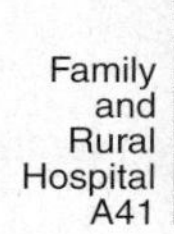

Family and Rural Hospital A41

Family and: 50c, Student nurse. 1.30sh, Microscope. 2.50sh, Mosquito and hand holding hypodermic.

1968, May 13 Photo. *Perf. 13½*
185 A41 30c multicolored .20 .20
186 A41 50c rose vio, blk & brt pink .20 .20
187 A41 1.30sh brn org, blk & brt pink .20 .20
188 A41 2.50sh gray, blk & brt pink .30 *1.25*
Nos. 185-188 (4) .90 1.85

20th anniv. of the WHO.

Stadium A42

Designs: 50c, Diving tower. 1.30sh, Pylons and tracks. 2.50sh, Boxing ring, vert.

Perf. 14½x14, 14x14½
1968, Oct. 14 Photo.
189 A42 30c dull pur & gray grn .20 .20
190 A42 50c brt grn, blk & gray .20 .20
191 A42 1.30sh gray grn, blk & dk car .30 .20
192 A42 2.50sh buff, brn org & brn blk .50 *1.25*
Nos. 189-192 (4) 1.20 1.85

19th Olympic Games, Mexico City, 10/12-27.

Railroad Ferry MV Umoja A43

Water Transport: 50c, Transatlantic liner S.S. Harambee. 1.30sh, Lake motor vessel Victoria. 2.50sh, Ferry St. Michael.

1969, Jan. 20 Photo. *Perf. 14*
193 A43 30c blue, gray & dk bl .40 .20
194 A43 50c blue, gray & scar .45 .20
195 A43 1.30sh bl, dk bl & dk green .90 .25
196 A43 2.50sh bl, dk bl & org 2.00 *3.25*
Nos. 193-196 (4) 3.75 3.90

Farm Workers and ILO Emblem A44

ILO Emblem and: 50c, Construction. 1.30sh, Industry. 2.50sh, Shipping.

1969, Apr. 14 Photo. *Perf. 14*
197 A44 30c green, blk & yel .20 .20
198 A44 50c car rose, blk & car .20 .20
199 A44 1.30sh dp org, blk & org .20 .20
200 A44 2.50sh grnsh bl, blk & ultra .30 *.75*
Nos. 197-200 (4) .90 1.35

50th anniv. of the ILO.

Pope Paul VI, Mountains of the Moon, Papal Arms, Crested Crane — A45

Euphorbia Tree in Shape of Africa, Development Bank Emblem — A46

1969, July 31 Photo. *Perf. 14*
201 A45 30c dk blue, blk & gold .20 .20
202 A45 70c plum, blk & gold .25 .20
203 A45 1.50sh gray bl, blk & gold .30 .25
204 A45 2.50sh dp vio, blk & gold .35 *1.25*
Nos. 201-204 (4) 1.10 1.90

Visit of Pope Paul VI to Uganda, 7/31-8/2.

Perf. 14x13½
1969, Dec. 8 Litho. Unwmk.
205 A46 30c brt grn, dk grn & gold .20 .20
206 A46 70c plum, dk grn & gold .20 .20
207 A46 1.50sh grnsh bl, dk grn & gold .25 .20
208 A46 2.50sh brn org, dk grn & gold .50 .50
Nos. 205-208 (4) 1.15 1.10

African Development Bank, 5th anniv.

Amadinda, Uganda — A47

Musical Instruments: 30c, Marimba, Tanzania. 1.50sh, Nzomari (trumpet), Kenya. 2.50sh, Adeudeu, Kenya.

1970, Feb. 16 Litho. *Perf. 11x12*
209 A47 30c multicolored .20 .20
210 A47 70c multicolored .30 .20
211 A47 1.50sh dk rose brn & org .65 .20
212 A47 2.50sh multicolored 1.25 1.25
Nos. 209-212 (4) 2.40 1.85

Satellite Earth Station A48

Designs: 70c, Radar station by day. 1.50sh, Radar station by night. 2.50sh, Satellite transmitting communications to and from earth.

1970, May 18 Litho. *Perf. 14½*
213 A48 30c multicolored .20 .20
214 A48 70c multicolored .20 .20
215 A48 1.50sh org, blk & vio .30 .20
216 A48 2.50sh dull bl & multi .60 *2.00*
Nos. 213-216 (4) 1.30 2.60

Opening of the East African Satellite Earth Station, Mt. Margaret, Kenya.

Runner — A49

1970, July 16 Litho. *Perf. 14½*
217 A49 30c org brn, dk brn & blk .20 .20
218 A49 70c grn, dk brn & blk .20 .20
219 A49 1.50sh dull pur, dk brn & blk .20 .20
220 A49 2.50sh grnsh bl, dk brn & blk .30 *1.00*
Nos. 217-220 (4) .90 1.60

9th British Commonwealth Games, Edinburgh, July 16-25.

UN Emblem and People A50

1970, Oct. 19 Photo. *Perf. 14½*
221 A50 30c org brn, gold & black .20 .20
222 A50 70c bl grn, gold & black .20 .20
223 A50 1.50sh dull red brn, gold & blk .25 .20
224 A50 2.50sh olive, gold & blk .45 *1.75*
Nos. 221-224 (4) 1.10 2.35

25th anniversary of the United Nations.

Conversion from Pounds to Kilograms — A51

Designs: 70c, Conversion from Fahrenheit to centigrade. 1.50sh, Conversion from gallons to liters. 2.50sh, Conversion from miles to kilometers.

1971, Jan. 4 Photo. *Perf. 14½*

225	A51	30c silver & multi	.20	.20
226	A51	70c silver & multi	.20	.20
227	A51	1.50sh silver & multi	.25	.20
228	A51	2.50sh silver & multi	.35	.80
		Nos. 225-228 (4)	1.00	1.40

Conversion to metric system of weights and measures.

Locomotive — A52

Designs: Various locomotives.

1971, Apr. 19 Photo. *Perf. 14½*

229	A52	30c gold & multi	.35	.20
230	A52	70c gold & multi	.55	.25
231	A52	1.50sh gold & multi	1.25	.25
232	A52	2.50sh gold & multi	2.00	*2.25*
a.		Souvenir sheet of 4, #229-232	11.00	11.00
		Nos. 229-232 (4)	4.15	2.95

70th anniversary of the completion of the Mombasa to Kisumu line.

Campaign Emblem and Cow — A53

Designs: 1.50sh, Like 30c. 70c, 2.50sh, Bull and Campaign Emblem.

1971, July 5 Photo. *Perf. 14½*

233	A53	30c yel grn, blk & bis	.20	.20
234	A53	70c gray bl, blk & bis	.20	.20
235	A53	1.50sh mag, blk & bis	.20	.20
236	A53	2.50sh red org, blk & bis	.30	*.65*
		Nos. 233-236 (4)	.90	1.25

Rinderpest campaign by the Organization for African Unity.

Meeting of Stanley and Livingstone — A54

1971, Oct. 28 Litho. *Perf. 14*

237	A54	5sh multicolored	.50	.50

Centenary of the meeting at Ujiji of Dr. David Livingstone, missionary, and Henry M. Stanley, journalist, who had been sent to find Livingstone.

Modern Farming Village — A55

Designs: 30c, Pres. Julius K. Nyerere carried in triumph, 1961, vert. 1.50sh, University of Dar es Salaam. 2.50sh, Kilimanjaro International Airport.

1971, Dec. 9 *Perf. 14*

238	A55	30c bister & multi	.20	.20
239	A55	70c lt blue & multi	.20	.20
240	A55	1.50sh lt green & multi	.25	.25
241	A55	2.50sh yel & multi	1.00	1.00
		Nos. 238-241 (4)	1.65	1.65

10th anniv. of independence of Tanzania.

Flags of African Nations and Fair Emblem — A56

1972, Feb. 23 *Perf. 13½x14*

242	A56	30c lt bl & multi	.20	.20
243	A56	70c gray & multi	.20	.20
244	A56	1.50sh yel & multi	.25	.25
245	A56	2.50sh multicolored	.35	*.75*
		Nos. 242-245 (4)	1.00	1.40

First All-Africa Trade Fair, Nairobi, Kenya, Feb. 23-Mar. 5.

Child Drinking Milk, UNICEF Emblem A57

25th Anniv. (in 1971) of UNICEF: 70c, Children playing ball. 1.50sh, Child writing on blackboard. 2.50sh, Boy playing with tractor.

1972, Apr. 24 Litho. *Perf. 14½x14*

246	A57	30c brn org & multi	.20	.20
247	A57	70c lt ultra & multi	.20	.20
248	A57	1.50sh yel & multi	.20	.20
249	A57	2.50sh green & multi	.25	*.75*
		Nos. 246-249 (4)	.85	1.35

Hurdles, Olympic and Motion Emblems — A58

1972, Aug. 28

250	A58	40c shown	.20	.20
251	A58	70c Running	.20	.20
252	A58	1.50sh Boxing	.25	.20
253	A58	2.50sh Hockey	.60	*1.75*
a.		Souvenir sheet of 4, #250-253	8.00	8.00
		Nos. 250-253 (4)	1.25	2.35

20th Olympic Games, Munich, 8/26-9/11.

Uganda Kob, Semliki Game Reserve — A59

1972, Oct. 9 Litho. *Perf. 14*

254	A59	40c shown	.25	.20
255	A59	70c Intl. Conf. Center	.25	.20
256	A59	1.50sh Makerere Univ., Kampala	.65	.30
257	A59	2.50sh Uganda arms	1.40	*2.25*
a.		Souvenir sheet of 4, #254-257, perf. 13x14	5.50	5.50
		Nos. 254-257 (4)	2.55	2.95

Uganda's independence, 10th anniv. #256 also for 50th anniv. of Makerere University, Kampala.

Flag of East Africa — A60

1972, Dec. 1 Litho. *Perf. 14½x14*

258	A60	5sh multicolored	1.25	1.25

5th anniv. of the East African Community.

Anemometer, Lake Victoria Station — A61

WMO Emblem and: 70c, Release of weather balloon, vert. 1.50sh, Hail suppression by meteorological rocket. 2.50sh, Meteorological satellite receiving antenna.

1973, Mar. 5 Litho. *Perf. 14*

259	A61	40c multicolored	.20	.20
260	A61	70c ultra & multi	.20	.20
261	A61	1.50sh emer & multi	.35	.30
262	A61	2.50sh multicolored	.65	.65
		Nos. 259-262 (4)	1.40	1.35

Cent. of intl. meteorological cooperation.

Scouts Laying Bricks — A62

Designs: 70c, Baden-Powell's gravestone, Nyeri, Kenya. 1.50sh, World Scout emblem. 2.50sh, Lord Baden-Powell.

1973, July 16 Litho. *Perf. 14*

263	A62	40c ocher & multi	.20	.20
264	A62	70c multicolored	.30	.30
265	A62	1.50sh multicolored	.60	.60
266	A62	2.50sh grn & ultra	1.60	1.60
		Nos. 263-266 (4)	2.70	2.70

24th Boy Scout World Conference (1st in Africa), Nairobi, Kenya, July 16-21.

International Bank for Reconstruction and Development and Affiliates' Emblems — A63

Designs: 40c, Arrows dividing 4 bank affiliate emblems. 70c, Vert. lines dividing 4 emblems. 1.50sh, Kenyatta Conference Center, Nairobi, vert.

1973, Sept. 24 Litho. *Perf. 14x13½*

267	A63	40c gray, blk & grn	.20	.20
268	A63	70c brn, gray & blk	.20	.20
269	A63	1.50sh lem, gray & blk	.50	.50
270	A63	2.50sh blk, org & gray	.95	1.75
a.		Souvenir sheet of 4	6.00	6.00
		Nos. 267-270 (4)	1.85	2.65

Intl. Bank for Reconstruction and Development and Affiliate Intl. Monetary Fund Meetings, Nairobi.

No. 270a contains stamps similar to Nos. 267-270 with simulated perforations.

INTERPOL Emblem, Policeman and Dog — A64

Designs: 70c, East African policemen and emblem. 1.50sh, INTERPOL emblem. 2.50sh, INTERPOL Headquarters, St. Cloud, France.

1973-74 Litho. *Perf. 14x14½*

271	A64	40c yellow & multi	.65	.20
272	A64	70c multicolored	1.25	.20
273	A64	1.50sh violet & multi	2.00	.90
274	A64	2.50sh lemon & multi *(St. Clans)*	5.00	6.00
275	A64	2.50sh lemon & multi *(St. Cloud)* ('74)	5.00	6.00
		Nos. 271-275 (5)	13.90	13.30

50th anniv. of Intl. Criminal Police Org. Issued: Nos. 271-274, Oct. 24, 1973.

Tea Factory, Nandi Hills — A65

1973, Dec. 12 Photo. *Perf. 13x14*

276	A65	40c shown	.20	.20
277	A65	70c Kenyatta Hospital	.20	.20
278	A65	1.50sh Nairobi Airport	.70	.25
279	A65	2.50sh Kindaruma hydroelectric plant	1.25	*1.75*
		Nos. 276-279 (4)	2.35	2.40

10th anniversary of independence.

Afro-Shirazi Party Headquarters — A66

Designs: 70c, Michenzani housing development. 1.50sh, Map of East Africa and television screen with flower. 2.50sh, Amaan Stadium.

1974, Jan. 12 Litho. *Perf. 13½x14*

280	A66	40c multicolored	.20	.20
281	A66	70c multicolored	.20	.20
282	A66	1.50sh black & multi	.60	.35
283	A66	2.50sh black & multi	1.25	*3.50*
		Nos. 280-283 (4)	2.25	4.25

10th anniversary of Zanzibar revolution.

Symbol of Union A67

Designs: 70c, Map of Tanganyika and Zanzibar, and handshake. 1.50sh, Map of Tanganyika and Zanzibar, and communications symbols. 2.50sh, Flags of Tanu, Tanzania and Afro-Shirazi Party.

1974, Apr. 24 Litho. *Perf. 14½*

284	A67	40c sepia & multi	.20	.20
285	A67	70c blue grn & multi	.25	.20
286	A67	1.50sh ultra & multi	.55	.30
287	A67	2.50sh multicolored	1.50	*2.75*
		Nos. 284-287 (4)	2.50	3.45

Union of Tanganyika and Zanzibar, 10th anniv.

Family and Home A68

Designs: 70c, Drummer at dawn. 1.50sh, Family hoeing, and livestock. 2.50sh, Telephonist, train, plane, telegraph lines.

1974, July 15 Litho. *Perf. 14½*

288	A68	40c multicolored	.20	.20
289	A68	70c multicolored	.20	.20
290	A68	1.50sh multicolored	.45	.45
291	A68	2.50sh multicolored	1.00	1.00
		Nos. 288-291 (4)	1.85	1.85

17th Intl. Conf. on Social Welfare, 7/14-20.

Post and Telegraph Headquarters, Kampala — A69

Cent. of the UPU: 70c, Mail train and truck. 1.50sh, UPU Headquarters, Bern. 2.50sh, Loading mail on East African Airways VC-10.

1974, Oct. 9 Litho. *Perf. 14*

292	A69	40c lt green & multi	.20	.20
293	A69	70c gray & multi	.20	.20
294	A69	1.50sh yel & multi	.25	.25
295	A69	2.50sh lt blue & multi	.75	*1.25*
		Nos. 292-295 (4)	1.40	1.90

Family Planning Clinic A70

World Population Year: 70c, "Tug of War." 1.50sh, Scales and world population figures. 2.50sh, World Population Year emblem.

1974, Dec. 16 Litho. *Perf. 14½*

296	A70	40c multicolored	.20	.20
297	A70	70c purple & multi	.20	.20
298	A70	1.50sh multicolored	.20	.25
299	A70	2.50sh blue blk & multi	.30	*1.50*
		Nos. 296-299 (4)	.90	2.15

Seronera Wild Life Lodge, Tanzania — A71

Game lodges of East Africa: 70c, Mweya Safari Lodge, Uganda. 1.50sh, Ark-Aberdare Forest Lodge, Kenya. 2.50sh, Paraa Safari Lodge, Uganda.

1975, Feb. 24 Litho. *Perf. 14½*

300	A71	40c multicolored	.20	.20
301	A71	70c multicolored	.20	.20
302	A71	1.50sh multicolored	.55	.35
303	A71	2.50sh multicolored	1.10	*3.00*
		Nos. 300-303 (4)	2.05	3.75

Wooden Comb, Bajun, Kenya — A72

African Artifacts: 1sh, Earring, Chaga, Tanzania. 2sh, Armlet, Acholi, Uganda. 3sh, Kamba gourd, Kenya.

1975, May 5 Litho. *Perf. 13½*

304	A72	50c gray & multi	.20	.20
305	A72	1sh gray & multi	.20	.20
306	A72	2sh multicolored	.35	.45
307	A72	3sh multicolored	.85	*1.50*
		Nos. 304-307 (4)	1.60	2.35

Map Showing OAU Members, Ugandan Flag — A73

Elephant, Kenya — A74

OAU Emblem and: 50c, Entebbe Airport, horiz. 2sh, Nile Hotel, Kampala, horiz. 3sh, Ugandan Martyrs' Shrine, Namugongo.

Perf. 11½x11, 11x11½

1975, July 28 Litho.

308	A73	50c multicolored	.35	.20
309	A73	1sh multicolored	.35	.20
310	A73	2sh multicolored	.50	.50
311	A73	3sh multicolored	1.00	*1.50*
		Nos. 308-311 (4)	2.20	2.40

Organization for African Unity (OAU), Summit Conf., Kampala, July 28 - Aug. 1.

1975, Sept. 11 Litho. *Perf. 11x11½*

Protected animals: 1sh, Albino buffalo, Uganda. 2sh, Elephant, exhibit in National Museum, Kenya. 3sh, Abbott's duiker, Tanzania.

312	A74	50c multicolored	.75	.20
313	A74	1sh brown & multi	.90	.20
314	A74	2sh yel green & multi	3.00	2.25
315	A74	3sh blue grn & multi	3.50	3.00
		Nos. 312-315 (4)	8.15	5.65

Masai Villagers Bleeding Cow, Masai, Kenya — A75

Festival Emblem and: 1sh, Ugandan dancers. 2sh, Family, Makonde sculpture, Tanzania. 3sh, Skinning hippopotamus, East Africa.

1975, Nov. 3 Litho. *Perf. 13½x14*

316	A75	50c org brown & multi	.25	.20
317	A75	1sh brt green & multi	.25	.20
318	A75	2sh dk blue & multi	.80	.80
319	A75	3sh lilac & multi	1.50	1.40
		Nos. 316-319 (4)	2.80	2.60

2nd World Black and African Festival of Arts and Culture, Lagos, Nigeria, Jan. 5 - Feb. 12.

Fokker Friendship, Nairobi Airport — A76

East African Airways, 30th anniv.: 1sh, DC-9 Kilimanjaro Airport. 2sh, Super VC10, Entebbe Airport. 3sh, East African Airways emblem.

1976, Jan. 2 Litho. *Perf. 11½*

320	A76	50c ultra & multi	1.50	.75
321	A76	1sh rose & multi	1.75	.75
322	A76	2sh orange & multi	5.25	3.50
323	A76	3sh black & multi	6.00	4.25
		Nos. 320-323 (4)	14.50	9.25

POSTAGE DUE STAMPS

Kenya and Uganda

D1

D2

Perf. 14½x14

1928-33 Typo. Wmk. 4

J1	D1	5c deep violet	3.00	1.00
J2	D1	10c orange red	3.00	1.00
J3	D1	20c yel green	3.00	4.00
J4	D1	30c ol brn ('31)	22.50	16.00
J5	D1	40c dull blue	8.50	*16.00*
J6	D1	1sh grnsh gray ('33)	77.50	*140.00*
		Nos. J1-J6 (6)	117.50	*178.00*
		Set, never hinged	200.00	

Kenya, Uganda, Tanganyika

1935, May 1 *Perf. 13½x14*

J7	D2	5c violet	3.50	2.25
J8	D2	10c red	.35	.65
J9	D2	20c green	.55	.65
J10	D2	30c brown	1.25	*.90*
J11	D2	40c ultramarine	2.00	*4.00*
J12	D2	1sh gray	25.00	*25.00*
		Nos. J7-J12 (6)	32.65	*33.45*
		Set, never hinged	50.00	

OFFICIAL STAMPS

The 1959-60 "OFFICIAL" overprints on Nos. 103-104, 106-108, 110, 112-117, 120-123, 125, 127, 129, 133 are listed under Tanganyika, as they were used by the Tanganyika government.

KIAUCHAU

(Kiautschou)

LOCATION — A district of China on the south side of the Shantung peninsula.
GOVT. — German colony
AREA — 200 sq. mi.
POP. — 192,000 (approx. 1914).

The area was seized by Germany in 1897 and through negotiations that followed was leased to Germany by China.

100 Pfennig = 1 Mark
100 Cents = 1 Dollar (1905)

TSINGTAU ISSUES

Stamps of Germany, Offices in China 1898, with Additional Surcharge:

a

b

c

On Nos. 1-9, a blue or violet line is drawn through "PF. 10 PF." All exist without this line. All examples of Nos. 1b, 2b and 3b lack the colored line.

The three surcharge types can most easily be distinguished by the differences in the lower loop of the "5."

1900

"China" Overprint at 56 degree Angle

1	A10(a)	5pfg on 10pf car	45.00	*55.00*
c.		Dbl. surch., one inverted	675.00	
2	A10(b)	5pfg on 10pf car	45.00	*55.00*
c.		Dbl. surch., one inverted	675.00	
3	A10(c)	5pfg on 10pf car	45.00	*55.00*
c.		Dbl. surch., one inverted	675.00	
		Nos. 1-3 (3)	135.00	165.00

"China" Overprint at 45 degree Angle

1a	A10(a)	5pfg on 10pf car	145.00	*135.00*
b.		Double surcharge	450.00	*550.00*
2a	A10(b)	5pfg on 10pf car	145.00	
b.		Double surcharge	450.00	*550.00*
3a	A10(c)	5pfg on 10pf car	145.00	*135.00*
b.		Double surcharge	450.00	*550.00*
		Nos. 1a-3a (3)	435.00	270.00

Surcharged:

d

e

5 Pf.

f

"China" Overprint at 48 degree Angle on Nos. 4-9

4	A10(d)	5pf on 10pf car	3,250.	4,000.
a.		Double surcharge	*7,500.*	*16,500.*
5	A10(e)	5pf on 10pf car	*3,250.*	*4,000.*
a.		Double surcharge	*7,500.*	*16,500.*
6	A10(f)	5pf on 10pf car	*3,250.*	*4,000.*
a.		Double surcharge	*7,500.*	*16,500.*
b.		5fP		*16,500.*
c.		As "b," double surcharge	—	—

5

With Additional Handstamp

7	A10(d)	5pf on 10pf car	*37,500.*	*45,000.*
8	A10(f)	5pf on 10pf car	*37,500.*	*45,000.*
a.		On No. 6b	—	—

With Additional Handstamp

9	A10(f)	5pf on 10pf car	*7,500.*	*11,000.*
a.		Double surcharge	—	
b.		On No. 6a		
c.		On No. 6b		
d.		On No. 6c		

Kaiser's Yacht "Hohenzollern"
A1 A2

1901, Jan. Unwmk. Typo. *Perf. 14*

10	A1	3pf brown	2.00	2.00
11	A1	5pf green	2.00	1.75
12	A1	10pf carmine	2.50	2.10
13	A1	20pf ultra	7.50	8.50
14	A1	25pf org & blk, *yel*	13.50	*17.00*
15	A1	30pf org & blk, *sal*	13.50	*16.00*
16	A1	40pf lake & blk	16.00	*21.00*
17	A1	50pf pur & blk, *sal*	16.00	*23.50*
18	A1	80pf lake & blk, *rose*	30.00	*55.00*

Engr. *Perf. 14½x14*

19	A2	1m carmine	50.00	*92.50*
20	A2	2m blue	75.00	*110.00*
21	A2	3m blk vio	75.00	*200.00*
22	A2	5m slate & car	210.00	*675.00*
		Nos. 10-22 (13)	513.00	*1,224.*
		Set, never hinged	1,450.	

A3

A4

1905 **Typo.**

23	A3	1c brown	1.25	1.75
24	A3	2c green	2.00	1.75
25	A3	4c carmine	4.25	1.75
26	A3	10c ultra	8.50	5.50
27	A3	20c lake & blk	34.00	20.00
28	A3	40c lake & blk, *rose*	100.00	*100.00*
		Engr.		
29	A4	$½ carmine	72.50	*85.00*
30a	A4	$1 blue	150.00	125.00
31	A4	$1½ blk vio	1,200.	*1,700.*
32	A4	$2½ slate & car, 26x17 holes	1,500.	*4,400.*
a.		$2½ slate & car, 25x16 holes	2,100.	*3,500.*
		Nos. 23-32 (10)	3,072.	*6,440.*
		Set, never hinged	7,750.	

1905-16 **Wmk. 125** **Typo.**

33	A3	1c brown ('06)	1.25	1.75
a.		1c yellow brown ('16)	.50	—
34	A3	2c green ('09)	1.10	*1.10*
a.		2c dark green ('14)	.50	*2.10*
35	A3	4c carmine ('09)	.85	*1.25*
36	A3	10c ultra ('09)	1.10	*3.75*
a.		10c blue	12.00	5.00
37	A3	20c lake & blk ('08)	2.50	*17.50*
38	A3	40c lake & blk, *rose*	3.25	*55.00*
		Engr.		
39	A4	$½ carmine, 26x17 holes ('07)	10.00	*67.50*
40	A4	$1 blue, 26x17 holes ('06)	12.50	*72.50*
41	A4	$1½ blk violet	20.00	*225.00*
42	A4	$2½ slate & car	50.00	*500.00*
		Nos. 33-42 (10)	102.55	945.35
		Set, never hinged	525.00	

Four values of the design A3 and A4 stamps in recognizably different shades were printed and released in 1918, but by then Germany had lost control of Kiauchau, and these stamps are not known used. The four stamps and their unused values are: 20c red & black, $1.75; $½ pale rose, $5.50; $1 bright blue, $6.75; $1½ gray violet, $20.

KIONGA

'kyoŋ-gə

LOCATION — Southeast Africa and northeast Mozambique, on Indian Ocean south of Rovuma River
GOVT. — Part of German East Africa
AREA — 400 sq. mi.

This territory, occupied by Portuguese troops during World War I, was allotted to Portugal by the Treaty of Versailles. Later it became part of Mozambique.

100 Centavos = 1 Escudo

Lourenco Marques No. 149 Surcharged in Red

1916, May 29 **Unwmk.** ***Perf. 11½***

1	A2	½c on 100r bl, *bl*	30.00	20.00
2	A2	1c on 100r bl, *bl*	22.50	17.00
3	A2	2½c on 100r bl, *bl*	22.50	17.00
4	A2	5c on 100r bl, *bl*	22.50	17.00
		Nos. 1-4 (4)	97.50	71.00

Most of the stock of Lourenço Marques #149 used for these surcharges lacked gum. Unused examples with original gum are worth approximately 50% more than the values shown.

KIRIBATI

'kir-ə-,bas

LOCATION — A group of islands in the Pacific Ocean northeast of Australia
GOVT. — Republic
AREA — 277 sq. mi.
POP. — 85,501 (1999 est.)
CAPITAL — Tarawa

100 Cents = 1 Australian Dollar

Kiribati, former Gilbert Islands, consists of the Gilbert, Phoenix, Ocean and Line Islands.

Catalogue values for all unused stamps in this country are for Never Hinged items.

Watermark

Wmk. 380 — "POST OFFICE"

Kiribati Flag A50

Parliament, London, Assembly, Tarawa — A51

Wmk. 373

1979, July 12 **Litho.** ***Perf. 14***

325	A50	10c multicolored	.20	.20
326	A51	45c multicolored	.40	.40

Independence.

Training Ship Teraaka A52

Designs: 3c, Passenger launch Tautunu. 5c, Hibiscus. 7c, Cathedral, Tarawa. 10c, House of Assembly, Bikenibeu Island. 12c, Betio harbor. 15c, Reef egret. 20c, Flamboyant tree. 25c, Moorish idol (fish). 30c, Frangipani blossoms. 35c, Chapel, Tangintebu Island. 50c, Hypolimnas bolina elliciana (butterfly). $1, Tarawa Lagoon ferry, Tabakea. $2, Sunset over lagoon. $5, Natl. flag.

1979-80 **Wmk. 373**

327	A52	1c multicolored	.20	.60
328	A52	3c multicolored	.25	.35
329	A52	5c multicolored	.20	.20
330	A52	7c multicolored	.20	.20
331	A52	10c multicolored	.20	.20
332	A52	12c multicolored	.20	*.25*
333	A52	15c multicolored	.45	.30
334	A52	20c multicolored	.25	*.30*
335	A52	25c multicolored	.40	.30
336	A52	30c multicolored	.30	.30
337	A52	35c multicolored	.30	.30
338	A52	50c multicolored	.80	.55
339	A52	$1 multicolored	.70	.70
340	A52	$2 multicolored	.90	.70
340A	A52	$5 multicolored	2.00	*4.00*
		Nos. 327-340A (15)	7.35	9.25

Issued: $5, 8/27/80; others, 7/12/79.

1980-81 **Unwmk.**

327a	A52	1c multi ('81)	.20	.20
328a	A52	3c multi ('81)	.20	.20
329a	A52	5c multi	.20	.20
330a	A52	7c multi	.20	.20
331a	A52	10c multi	.20	.20
332a	A52	12c multi	.20	.20
333a	A52	15c multi	.65	.20
334a	A52	20c multi ('81)	.20	.20
335a	A52	25c multi	.35	.20
336a	A52	30c multi ('81)	.20	.50
337a	A52	35c multi ('81)	.20	.50
338a	A52	50c multi ('81)	.90	.75
339a	A52	$1 multi	.75	.50
340b	A52	$2 multi	1.40	.70
340c	A52	$5 multi ('80)	2.25	2.50
		Nos. 327a-340c (15)	8.10	7.25

For overprints see Nos. O1-O15.

Gilbert and Ellice Islands No. 1 — A53

Simulated Cancel and: 20c, Gilbert and Ellice No. 70. 25c, Great Britain No. 139. 45c, Gilbert and Ellice No. 31.

Wmk. 373

1979, Oct. 4 **Litho.** ***Perf. 14***

341	A53	10c multicolored	.20	.20
342	A53	20c multicolored	.20	.20
343	A53	25c multicolored	.25	.25
344	A53	45c multicolored	.25	.25
a.		Souvenir sheet of 4, #341-344	1.25	1.25
		Nos. 341-344 (4)	.90	.90

Sir Rowland Hill (1795-1879), originator of penny postage.

Boy Climbing Coconut Palm, IYC Emblem — A54

IYC Emblem, Coat of Arms and: 10c, Boy and giant clam shell. 45c, Girl reading book. $1, Boy wearing garlands. All vert.

Perf. 14x13½, 13½x14

1979, Nov. 28 **Litho.**

345	A54	10c multicolored	.20	.20
346	A54	20c multicolored	.20	.20
347	A54	45c multicolored	.20	.20
348	A54	$1 multicolored	.30	.30
		Nos. 345-348 (4)	.90	.90

International Year of the Child.

Downrange Station — A55

National Space Development Agency of Japan (NASDA) Satellite Tracking: 45c, Experimental satellite trajectory (map). $1, Rocket launch, Tanegashima, Japan, vert.

1980, Feb. 20 **Litho.** ***Perf. 14½***

349	A55	25c multicolored	.20	.20
350	A55	45c multicolored	.20	.20
351	A55	$1 multicolored	.40	.40
		Nos. 349-351 (3)	.80	.80

T.S. Teraaka, London 1980 Emblem A56

1980, Apr. 30 **Litho.** **Unwmk.**

352	A56	12c shown	.20	.20
353	A56	25c Air Tungaru plane, Bonriki Airport	.20	.20
354	A56	30c Radio operator	.20	.20
355	A56	$1 Bairiki post office	.30	.30
a.		Souvenir sheet of 4, #352-355	1.00	1.00
		Nos. 352-355 (4)	.90	.90

London 1980 Intl. Stamp Exhib., May 6-14.

Achaea Janata A57

1980, Aug. 27 **Litho.** ***Perf. 14***

356	A57	12c shown	.25	.25
357	A57	25c Ethmia nigroapicella	.30	.30
358	A57	30c Utetheisa pulchelloides	.35	.35
359	A57	50c Anua coronata	.70	.70
		Nos. 356-359 (4)	1.60	1.60

Capt. Cook Hotel A58

1980, Nov. 19 **Wmk. 373** ***Perf. 13½***

360	A58	10c shown	.20	.20
361	A58	20c Stadium	.20	.20
362	A58	25c Intl. Airport, Bonriki	.20	.20
363	A58	35c National Library	.20	.20
364	A58	$1 Otintai Hotel	.30	.30
		Nos. 360-364 (5)	1.10	1.10

Acalypha Godseffiana A59

Perf. 14x13½

1981, Feb. 18 **Litho.** **Wmk. 373**

365	A59	12c shown	.20	.20
366	A59	30c Hibiscus schizopetalus	.20	.20
367	A59	35c Calotropis gigantea	.20	.20
368	A59	50c Euphorbia pulcherrima	.30	.30
		Nos. 365-368 (4)	.90	.90

Abaiang and Marakei Islands, String Figures — A60

Wmk. 380

1981, May 6 **Litho.** ***Perf. 14***

369	A60	12c shown	.20	.20
370	A60	30c Butaritari, Little Makin, house	.20	.20
371	A60	35c Maiana, Coral Road	.25	.25
372	A60	$1 Christmas Isld., Resolution	.60	.60
		Nos. 369-372 (4)	1.25	1.25

Prince Charles, Lady Diana, Royal Yacht Charlotte A60a

Prince Charles and Lady Diana — A60b

Wmk. 380

1981, July 29 Litho. *Perf. 14*

373 A60a 12c Couple, The Katherine .20 .20
a. Bklt. pane of 4, perf. 12, unwmkd. .60
374 A60b 12c Couple .30 .20
375 A60a 50c The Osborne .85 .50
376 A60b 50c like #374 .90 .50
a. Bklt. pane of 2, perf. 12, unwmkd. 1.75
377 A60a $2 Britannia 2.50 1.60
378 A60b $2 like #374 2.50 1.60
Nos. 373-378 (6) 7.25 4.60

Souvenir Sheet

Perf. 12

379 A60b $1.20 like #374 3.50 3.50

Royal wedding.

Stamps of the same denomination issued in sheets of 7 (6 type A60a and 1 type A60b).

Bonriki Tuna Fish Bait Breeding Center A61

1981, Nov. 19

380 A61 12c shown .20 .20
381 A61 30c Fishing boat .20 .20
382 A61 35c Cold storage, Betio .25 .25
383 A61 50c Nei Manganibuka .35 .35
a. Souvenir sheet of 4, #380-383 1.25 1.25
Nos. 380-383 (4) 1.00 1.00

Pomarine Jaegers A62

1982-85 Litho. *Perf. 14*

384 A62 1c shown .20 .20
385 A62 2c Mallards .20 .20
386 A62 4c Collared petrels .20 .20
387 A62 5c Blue-faced boobies .25 .20
388 A62 7c Friendly quail dove .30 .20
389 A62 8c Shovelers .30 .20
390 A62 12c Christmas Isld. warblers .35 .25
391 A62 15c Pacific plovers .45 .35
392 A62 20c Reef herons .50 .50
392A A62 25c Brown noddies ('83) 3.50 1.75
393 A62 30c Brown boobies .65 .60
394 A62 35c Audubon's shearwaters .95 .70
395 A62 40c White-throated storm petrels, vert. .85 .80
396 A62 50c Bristle-thighed curlews, vert. .95 .65
396A A62 55c Fairy tern ('85) 15.50 *17.00*
397 A62 $1 Scarlet-breasted lorikeets, vert. 2.00 .85
398 A62 $2 Long-tailed cuckoo, vert. 2.75 1.10
399 A62 $5 Great frigate birds, vert. 5.50 4.00
Nos. 384-399 (18) 35.40 29.75

Issued: 25c, 1/31/83; 55c, 11/19/85; others, 2/18/82.

For overprints see Nos. O16-O20.

Air Tungaru A63

1982, Feb. 18 Wmk. 380

400 A63 12c De Havilland DH114 Heron .20 .20
401 A63 30c Britten-Norman Trislander .25 .25
402 A63 35c Casa 212 Aviocar .25 .25
403 A63 50c Boeing 727 .60 .60
Nos. 400-403 (4) 1.30 1.30

21st Birthday of Princess Diana, July 1 — A64

1982, May 19

404 A64 12c Mary of Teck, 1893 .30 .30
405 A64 50c Teck arms .60 .60
406 A64 $1 Diana .85 .85
Nos. 404-406 (3) 1.75 1.75

Overprinted: "ROYAL BABY"

1982, July 14

407 A64 12c multicolored .30 .30
408 A64 50c multicolored .60 .60
409 A64 $1 multicolored .85 .85
Nos. 407-409 (3) 1.75 1.75

Birth of Prince William of Wales, June 21.

Scouting Year — A65

1982, Aug. 12

410 A65 12c First aid .25 .25
411 A65 25c Repairing boat .25 .25
412 A65 30c Saluting .30 .30
413 A65 50c Gilbert Islds. #304 .50 .50
Nos. 410-413 (4) 1.30 1.30

Visit of Queen Elizabeth II and Prince Philip A66

Wmk. 380

1982, Oct. 23 Litho. *Perf. 14*

414 A66 12c Couple, dancer .20 .20
415 A66 25c Couple, boat .30 .30
416 A66 35c Philatelic Bureau .50 .50
Nos. 414-416 (3) 1.00 1.00

Souvenir Sheet

417 A66 50c Queen Elizabeth II, vert. 1.40 1.40

Nos. 414-416 also issued in sheets of 6.

A67

1983, Mar. 14 Wmk. 380 *Perf. 14*

418 A67 12c Obaia the Feathered legend .20 .20
419 A67 30c Robert Louis Stevenson Hotel, Abemama .20 .20
420 A67 50c Betio Harbor .30 .30
421 A67 $1 Map .70 .70
Nos. 418-421 (4) 1.40 1.40

Commonwealth day.

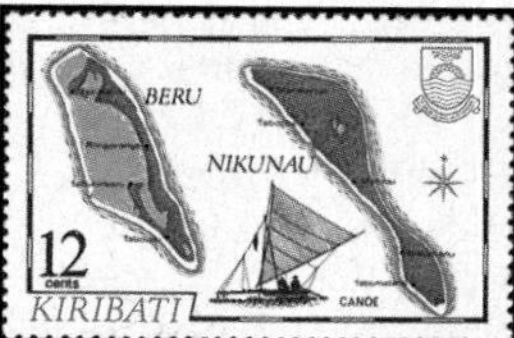

Map of Beru and Nikunau Islds., Canoe — A68

1983, May 19 Litho. *Perf. 14*

422 A68 12c shown .20 .20
423 A68 25c Abemama, Kuria, Aranuka .20 .20
424 A68 35c Nonouti, vert. .30 .30
425 A68 50c Tarawa, vert. .45 .45
Nos. 422-425 (4) 1.15 1.15

See #436-439, 456-459, 475-479, 487-490.

Copra Industry A69

Designs: 12c, Collecting fallen Coconuts. 25c, Selecting Coconuts for Copra. 30c, Removing Husk from Coconuts. 35c, Drying Copra in the Sun. 50c, Loading Copra, Betio Harbor.

1983, Aug. 8 Litho. *Perf. 14*

426 A69 12c multicolored .30 .25
427 A69 25c multicolored .50 .40
428 A69 30c multicolored .65 .60
429 A69 35c multicolored .70 .70
430 A69 50c multicolored .95 .95
Nos. 426-430 (5) 3.10 2.90

Battle of Tarawa, 40th Anniv. A70

1983, Nov. 17 Litho. Wmk. 380

431 A70 12c War memorials .20 .20
432 A70 30c Battle map .20 .20
433 A70 35c Defense gun .20 .20
434 A70 50c Scenes, 1943, 1983 .35 .35
435 A70 $1 Amphibious Assault Ship USS Tarawa .75 .75
Nos. 431-435 (5) 1.70 1.70

Map Type of 1983

1984, Feb. 14 Wmk. 380 *Perf. 14*

436 A68 12c Teraina .20 .20
437 A68 30c Nikumaroro .35 .35
438 A68 35c Kanton .40 .40
439 A68 50c Banaba .60 .60
Nos. 436-439 (4) 1.55 1.55

Local Ships A71

1984, May 9 Litho. Wmk. 380

440 A71 12c Tug boat .55 .20
441 A71 35c Ferry landing craft 1.00 .60
442 A71 50c Ferry 1.25 .85
443 A71 $1 Cargo and passanger boat 2.00 2.00
a. Souvenir sheet of 4, #440-443, perf. 13½ 6.00 6.00
Nos. 440-443 (4) 4.80 3.65

Ausipex '84 — A72

1984, Aug. 21 Litho. *Perf. 14*

444 A72 12c South Tarawa sewer & water system .20 .20
445 A72 30c Fishing boat Nouamake .30 .30
446 A72 35c Overseas communications training .35 .35
447 A72 50c Intl. telecommunications link .50 .50
Nos. 444-447 (4) 1.35 1.35

Legends A73

Designs: 12c, Tabakea supporting Banaba on his back. 30c, Nakaa, Judge of the Dead. 35c, Naareau and Tiku-Tiku-Tamoamoa. 50c, Whistling Ghosts.

1984, Nov. 21 Wmk. 380 *Perf. 14*

448 A73 12c multicolored .20 .20
449 A73 30c multicolored .25 .25
450 A73 35c multicolored .30 .30
451 A73 50c multicolored .45 .45
Nos. 448-451 (4) 1.20 1.20

See Nos. 464-467.

Reef Fish A74

1985, Feb. 19 Litho. *Perf. 14*

452 A74 12c Tang .85 .35
453 A74 25c White-barred triggerfish 1.50 .80
454 A74 35c Surgeon fish 1.75 1.25
455 A74 80c Squirrel fish 3.50 3.50
a. Souvenir sheet of 4, #452-455 8.50 8.50
Nos. 452-455 (4) 7.60 5.90

See Nos. 540-554, 567.

Map Type of 1983

1985, May 9 Litho. *Perf. 13½*

456 A68 12c Tabuaeran, frigate bird 1.50 .45
457 A68 35c Rawaki, coconuts 2.00 .70
458 A68 50c Arorae, xanthid crab 2.25 1.10
459 A68 $1 Tamana, fish hook 2.75 *2.75*
Nos. 456-459 (4) 8.50 5.00

Intl. Youth Year A76

1985, Aug. 5

460 A76 15c Boys playing soccer .85 .50
461 A76 35c Emblems 1.25 1.25
462 A76 40c Girl processing fruit, vert. 1.50 1.50
463 A76 55c Intl. youth exchange 2.00 2.00
Nos. 460-463 (4) 5.60 5.25

Legends Type of 1984

15c, Nang Kineia & the Tickling Ghosts. 35c, Myth of Auriaria & Tituabine. 40c, First Coming of Babai at Arorae. 55c, Riiki & the Milky Way.

1985, Nov. 19 Wmk. 380 *Perf. 14*

464 A73 15c multicolored .70 .70
465 A73 35c multicolored .95 .95
466 A73 40c multicolored 1.10 1.10
467 A73 55c multicolored 1.60 1.60
Nos. 464-467 (4) 4.35 4.35

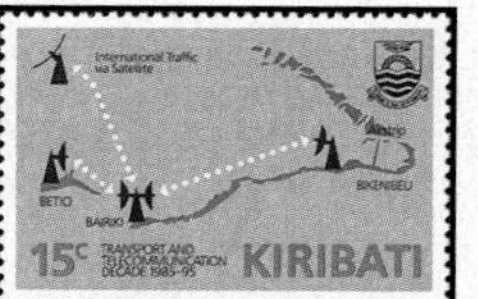

Transport and Telecommunications Decade 1985-95 — A77

1985, Dec. 9 Litho. *Perf. 14*

468 A77 15c Satellite network 3.25 3.00
469 A77 40c Tarawa-Suva feeder service 4.25 3.75

Common Design Types pictured following the introduction.

Queen Elizabeth II 60th Birthday
Common Design Type

15c, Review of Girl Guides, Windsor Castle, 1938. 35c, Birthday parade, Buckingham Palace, 1980. 40c, With Prince Philip during royal tour, 1982. 55c, Banquet, Austrian embassy in London, 1966. $1, Visiting Crown Agents' offices, 1983.

1986, Apr. 21 *Perf. 14½x14*

470 CD337 15c scar, black & sil .20 .20
471 CD337 35c ultra & multi .30 .30
472 CD337 40c green & multi .35 .35
473 CD337 55c violet & multi .50 .50
474 CD337 $1 rose vio & multi 1.25 1.25
Nos. 470-474 (5) 2.60 2.60

For overprints see Nos. 495-499.

Map Type of 1983

1986, June 17 Wmk. 380 *Perf. 14*

475 A68 15c Manra 3.25 1.50
476 A68 30c Birnie, McKean 4.25 2.00
477 A68 35c Orona 5.00 2.50
478 A68 40c Malden 5.25 3.00
479 A68 55c Vostok, Caroline, Flint 5.50 3.50
Nos. 475-479 (5) 23.25 12.50

Lizards A79

1986, Aug. 26 Unwmk. *Perf. 14*

480 A79 15c Lepidodactylus lugubris 2.25 1.00
481 A79 35c Gehyra mutilata 3.00 1.75
482 A79 40c Hemidactylus frenatus 3.50 2.25
483 A79 55c Gehyra oceanica 5.00 4.50
Nos. 480-483 (4) 13.75 9.50

See Nos. 491-494.

America's Cup — A80

Perf. 14x14½

1986, Dec. 29 Unwmk.

484 Strip of 3 2.50 2.50
a. A80 15c Map of Australia .25 .25
b. A80 55c Course, trophy .60 .60
c. A80 $1.50 Australia II 1.50 1.50

No. 484 has a continuous design.

Transport and Telecommunications Decade (1985-1995) — A81

Designs: 30c, Nei Moamoa, flagship of Kiribati overseas shipping line. 55c, Manual and electronic telephone switching systems.

1987, Mar. 31 Litho. *Perf. 14*

485 A81 30c multicolored 4.00 4.00
486 A81 55c multicolored 5.50 5.50

Map Type of 1983

1987, Sept. 22 Litho. Unwmk.

487 A68 15c Starbuck, red-tailed tropicbird .75 .55
488 A68 30c Enderbury, white tern .80 .55
489 A68 55c Tabiteuea, pandanus 1.10 .65
490 A68 $1 Onotoa, Okai house 1.75 *1.75*
Nos. 487-490 (4) 4.40 3.50

Nos. 487-490 vert.

Lizard Type of 1986

1987, Oct. 27 *Perf. 15*

491 A79 15c Emoia nigra .50 .40
492 A79 35c Cryptoblepharus .70 .60
493 A79 40c Emoia cyanura .70 .75
494 A79 $1 Lipinia noctua 1.50 *1.75*
a. Souvenir sheet of 4, #491-494 3.75 3.75
Nos. 491-494 (4) 3.40 3.50

Nos. 470-474 Overprinted in Silver

Perf. 14½x14

1987, Nov. 30 Litho. Unwmk.

495 CD337 15c scar, black & sil .20 .35
496 CD337 35c ultra & multi .40 .35
497 CD337 40c green & multi .55 .40
498 CD337 55c violet & multi .75 .50
499 CD337 $1 rose vio & multi 1.50 *1.75*
Nos. 495-499 (5) 3.40 3.35

Intl. Red Cross and Red Crescent Organizations, 125th Annivs. — A83

15c, Jean Henri Dunant (1828-1910), founder. 35c, Red Cross volunteers on parade. 40c, Stretcher bearers. 55c, Gilbert and Ellice Islands #159.

Perf. 14½x14

1988, May 8 Litho. Unwmk.

500 A83 15c multicolored 1.00 .60
501 A83 35c multicolored 1.25 *1.50*
502 A83 40c multicolored 1.50 *1.50*
503 A83 55c multicolored 3.00 *3.50*
Nos. 500-503 (4) 6.75 *7.10*

A84

SYDPEX '88, Australia Bicentennial — A85

Emblem and: 15c, Australia-assisted causeway construction. 35c, Capt. Cook, map of Australia and Kiribati. No. 506, Australia bicentennial banknote obverse. No. 507, Bank note reverse. $2, "Logistic Ace."

1988, July 30 Litho. *Perf. 14½*

504 A84 15c multicolored .35 .35
505 A84 35c multicolored .70 .70
506 A84 $1 multicolored 2.00 2.00
507 A84 $1 multicolored 2.00 2.00
a. Pair, #506-507 4.25 4.25
Nos. 504-507 (4) 5.05 5.05

Souvenir Sheet

Perf. 13½x14

508 A85 $2 multicolored 7.00 7.00

Robert F. Stockton, 1st propeller-driven steamship, 150th anniv.

Transport and Telecommunications Decade (1985-1995) — A86

Wmk. 373

1988, Dec. 28 Litho. *Perf. 14*

509 A86 35c Telephone operator, map 1.25 1.25
510 A86 45c Betio-Bairiki Causeway 1.75 1.75

Ships A87

Wmk. 384

1989, May 26 Litho. *Perf. 14½*

511 A87 15c Brigantine Hound, 1835 1.50 .90
512 A87 30c Brig Phantom, 1854 2.25 1.50
513 A87 40c HMS Alacrity, 1873 2.75 2.75
514 A87 $1 Whaler Charles W. Morgan, 1851 4.25 4.25
Nos. 511-514 (4) 10.75 9.40

See Nos. 557-561, 687-690.

A88

Birds — A89

Perf. 13½x14

1989, July 12 Litho. Wmk. 384

515 A88 15c House of Assembly .50 .50
516 A88 $1 Constitution 3.00 3.00

Natl. Independence, 10th anniv.

Moon Landing, 20th Anniv.
Common Design Type

Apollo 10: 20c, Service and command modules, launch escape system. 50c, Eugene A. Cernan, Thomas P. Stafford and John W. Young. 60c, Mission emblem. 75c, Splashdown, Honolulu. $2.50, Apollo 11 command module in space.

1989, July 20 *Perf. 14*

Size of Nos. 518-519: 29x29mm

517 CD342 20c multicolored .55 .55
518 CD342 50c multicolored 1.00 1.00
519 CD342 60c multicolored 1.25 1.25
520 CD342 75c multicolored 1.50 1.50
Nos. 517-520 (4) 4.30 4.30

Souvenir Sheet

521 CD342 $2.50 multicolored 10.00 10.00

Perf. 14½x14

1989, June 28 Litho. Wmk. 384

522 A89 15c Eastern reef heron 1.75 1.75
523 A89 15c Brood in nest 1.75 1.75
a. Pair, #522-523 4.00 4.00
524 A89 $1 White-tailed tropicbird in flight 3.25 3.25
525 A89 $1 Seated tropicbird 3.25 3.25
a. Pair, #524-525 7.00 7.00
Nos. 522-525 (4) 10.00 10.00

Nos. 523a, 525a have continuous designs.
For overprints see Nos. 534-535.

Souvenir Sheets

A90

A91

Perf. 14x13½

1989, Aug. 7 Litho. Wmk. 384

526 A90 $2 Gilbert & Ellice Isls. #58 7.00 7.00

Perf. 14x13½

1989, Sept. 25 Litho. Unwmk.

Workmen renovating the Statue of Liberty: a, Torch. b, Drilling copper sheeting. c, Glancing at a sketch of the statue.

527 Sheet of 3 5.50 5.50
a.-c. A91 35c any single 1.60 1.60

World Stamp Expo '89, Washington, DC, PHILEXFRANCE '89, Paris. No. 526 margin pictures #435, France #634 and US #2224.

Transport and Telecommunications Decade, 1985-95 — A92

1989, Oct. 16 Wmk. 384 *Perf. 14*

528 A92 30c shown 3.00 3.00
529 A92 75c MV *Mataburo* 4.50 4.50

Christmas — A93

Paintings: 10c, *Adoration of the Holy Child* (detail), by Denys Calvert. 15c, *Adoration of the Holy Child* (entire painting). 55c, *The Holy Family and St. Elizabeth*, by Rubens. $1, *Madonna with Child and Mary Magdalene*, School of Corregio.

1989, Dec. 1
530 A93 10c multicolored 1.25 .70
531 A93 15c multicolored 1.60 .85
532 A93 55c multicolored 4.00 2.25
533 A93 $1 multicolored 5.75 *7.50*
Nos. 530-533 (4) 12.60 11.30

Nos. 524-525 Ovptd.

1989, Oct. 21 Litho. *Perf. 14½x14*
534 A89 $1 on No. 524 5.25 5.25
535 A89 $1 on No. 525 5.25 5.25
a. Pair, #534-535 11.00 11.00

STAMPSHOW '89, Melbourne.

Penny Black 150th Anniv., Stamp World London '90 — A94

Stamps on stamps: 15c, Gilbert & Ellice #15, Great Britain #2. 50c, Gilbert & Ellice #8, Great Britain #1 canceled. 60c, Kiribati #384, Great Britain #58. $1, Gilbert Islands #269, Great Britain #3.

1990, May 1 Litho. *Perf. 14*
536 A94 15c multicolored 1.75 1.75
537 A94 50c multicolored 3.50 3.50
538 A94 60c multicolored 3.50 3.50
539 A94 $1 multicolored 5.50 5.50
Nos. 536-539 (4) 14.25 14.25

Fish Type of 1985

Fish: 1c, Blue-barred orange parrotfish. 5c, Honeycomb rock cod. 10c, Bluefin jack. 15c, Paddle tail snapper. 20c, Variegated emperor. 25c, Rainbow runner. 30c, Black saddled coral trout. 35c, Great barracuda. 40c, Convict surgeonfish. 50c, Violet squirrelfish. 60c, Freckled hawkfish. 75c, Pennant coral fish. $1, Yellow and blue sea perch. $2, Pacific sailfish. $5, Whitetip reef shark.

Wmk. 373
1990, July 12 Litho. *Perf. 14*
540 A74 1c multicolored .40 .40
541 A74 5c multicolored .50 .50
542 A74 10c multicolored .65 .65
543 A74 15c multicolored .75 .75
544 A74 20c multicolored .90 .90
545 A74 25c multicolored 1.00 1.00
546 A74 30c multicolored 1.10 1.10
547 A74 35c multicolored 1.25 1.25
548 A74 40c multicolored 1.50 1.50
549 A74 50c multicolored 2.00 2.00
550 A74 60c multicolored 2.25 2.25
551 A74 75c multicolored 2.50 2.50
552 A74 $1 multicolored 3.50 3.50
553 A74 $2 multicolored 5.00 5.00
554 A74 $5 multicolored 9.50 9.50
Nos. 540-554 (15) 32.80 32.80

Dated 1990. See No. 567. For overprints see Nos. 587-590.

Queen Mother 90th Birthday
Common Design Types

1990, Aug. 4 Wmk. 384 *Perf. 14x15*
555 CD343 75c Queen Mother 1.75 1.75

Perf. 14½
556 CD344 $2 King, Queen & WWII bombing victim, 1940 4.25 4.25

Ships Type of 1989

1990, Nov. 5 Litho. *Perf. 14½*
557 A87 15c Whaling ship Herald, 1851 1.10 .70
558 A87 50c Bark Belle, 1849 2.25 1.75
559 A87 60c Schooner Supply, 1851 2.75 2.75
560 A87 75c Whaling ship Triton, 1848 3.25 3.25
Nos. 557-560 (4) 9.35 8.45

Souvenir Sheet
561 A87 $2 Convict transport Charlotte, 1789 12.00 12.00

Manta Ray A95

1991, Jan. 17 Wmk. 373 *Perf. 14*
562 A95 15c shown 2.00 1.25
563 A95 20c Manta ray, diff. 2.25 1.75
564 A95 30c Whale shark 3.00 2.75
565 A95 35c Whale shark, diff. 3.50 3.25
Nos. 562-565 (4) 10.75 9.00

World Wildlife Fund.

Fish Type of 1985

Design: 23c, Bennett's pufferfish.

1991, Apr. 30 Wmk. 384
567 A74 23c multicolored 2.00 2.00

For overprint see No. 587.

Elizabeth & Philip, Birthdays
Common Design Types

1991, June 17 *Perf. 14½*
571 CD345 65c multicolored 2.00 2.00
572 CD346 70c multicolored 2.00 2.00
a. Pair, #571-572 + label 4.50 4.50

Phila Nippon '91 — A96

Opening of new Tungaru Central Hospital: 23c, Aerial view. 50c, Traditional dancers. 60c, Main entrance. 75c, Foundation stone, plaque. $5, Ambulance, nursing staff.

1991, Nov. 16 *Perf. 13½x14*
573 A96 23c multicolored .65 .65
574 A96 50c multicolored 1.25 1.25
575 A96 60c multicolored 1.75 1.75
576 A96 75c multicolored 2.10 2.10
Nos. 573-576 (4) 5.75 5.75

Souvenir Sheet
577 A96 $5 multicolored 10.50 10.50

Christmas A97

Designs: 23c, Island mother and child. 50c, Family in island hut. 60c, Nativity Scene. 75c, Adoration of the Shepherds.

1991, Dec. 2 Wmk. 373
578 A97 23c multicolored .90 .60
579 A97 50c multicolored 1.50 1.50
580 A97 60c multicolored 2.00 2.00
581 A97 75c multicolored 2.50 2.50
Nos. 578-581 (4) 6.90 6.60

Queen Elizabeth II's Accession to the Throne, 40th Anniv.
Common Design Type

Wmk. 373
1992, Feb. 6 Litho. *Perf. 14*
582 CD349 23c multicolored .40 .40
583 CD349 30c multicolored .60 .60
584 CD349 50c multicolored .90 .90
585 CD349 60c multicolored 1.10 1.10
586 CD349 75c multicolored 1.40 1.40
Nos. 582-586 (5) 4.40 4.40

Nos. 550-551, 553, & 567 Ovptd.

Wmk. 384, 373
1992, June 1 Litho. *Perf. 14*
587 A74 23c on No. 567 1.10 .85
588 A74 60c on No. 550 2.25 2.25
589 A74 75c on No. 551 3.00 3.00
590 A74 $2 on No. 553 3.25 3.50
Nos. 587-590 (4) 9.60 9.60

Marine Training Center, 25th Anniv. A98

1992, Aug. 28 *Perf. 14*
591 A98 23c Entrance .70 .70
592 A98 50c Cadets at morning parade 1.10 1.10
593 A98 60c Fire school 1.40 1.40
594 A98 75c Lifeboat training 1.75 1.75
Nos. 591-594 (4) 4.95 4.95

FAO, WHO A99

Wmk. 373
1992, Dec. 1 Litho. *Perf. 14*
595 A99 23c Children running 1.25 1.25
596 A99 50c Night fishing 1.50 1.50
597 A99 60c Fruit 2.00 2.00
598 A99 75c Ship 3.25 3.25
Nos. 595-598 (4) 8.00 8.00

Water Birds — A100

Wmk. 373
1993, May 28 Litho. *Perf. 14½*
599 A100 23c Phoenix petrel .75 .75
600 A100 23c Cooks petrel .75 .75
a. Pair, #599-600 1.60 1.60
601 A100 60c Northern pintail 1.40 1.40
602 A100 60c Eurasian widgeon 1.40 1.40
a. Pair, #601-602 3.00 3.00
603 A100 75c Spectacled tern 1.75 1.75
604 A100 75c Black naped tern 1.75 1.75
a. Pair, #603-604 3.75 3.75
605 A100 $1 Stilt wader 2.00 2.00
606 A100 $1 Wandering tattler 2.00 2.00
a. Pair, #605-606 4.50 4.50
Nos. 599-606 (8) 11.80 11.80

Insects — A101

Perf. 14½x14
1993, Aug. 23 Litho. Wmk. 373
607 A101 23c Chilocorus nigritus 1.50 1.25
608 A101 60c Rodolia pumila 2.50 2.50
609 A101 75c Rodolia cardinalis 3.00 3.00
610 A101 $1 Cryptolaemus montrouzieri 3.50 *3.75*
Nos. 607-610 (4) 10.50 10.50

Liberation of Kiribati, 50th Anniv. — A102

No. 611: a, Air reconnaissance of Tarawa Atoll. b, USS Nautilus surveys Tarawa. c, USS Indianapolis. d, USS Pursuit leads seaborne assault. e, Kingfisher spotter plane. f, Destroyers USS Ringgold and USS Dashiell. g, Sherman tank on seabed. h, Fighter plane in lagoon. i, Naval gun on seabed. j, First US aircraft to land on Betio Island.

No. 612: a, Transports disembark landing craft. b, Marines assault Betio Island. c, Sea and air assault of Betio. d, Marines pinned down in surf. e, USS Maryland firing broadside. f, Betio from the air. g, Memorial to US Navy dead. h, Memorial to expatriates. i, Memorial to Japanese dead. j, Battle map of Betio.

Wmk. 373
1993, Nov. 1 Litho. *Perf. 14*
Sheets of 10
611 A102 23c #a.-j. + label 8.50 8.50
612 A102 75c #a.-j. + label 22.50 22.50

Christmas — A103

Perf. 13½x14
1993, Dec. 1 Litho. Wmk. 373
613 A103 23c Shepherds .75 .40
614 A103 40c Three kings 1.10 1.00
615 A103 60c Holy Family 1.50 *1.75*
616 A103 75c Mother, children 1.90 *2.10*
Nos. 613-616 (4) 5.25 5.25

Souvenir Sheet
617 A103 $3 Madonna and Child 7.00 7.00

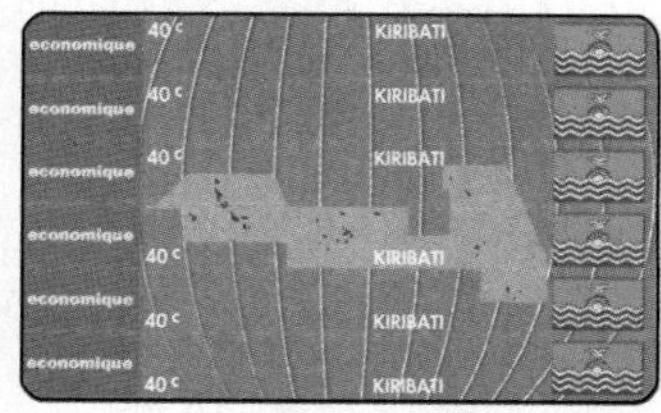

Stampcards — A104

Rouletted 6 on 2 or 3 Sides
1993, Nov. 1 Litho.
Self-Adhesive
Cards of 6 + 6 labels
618 A104 40c #a.-f. *5.00*
619 A104 $1 #a.-f. *12.00*
620 A104 $1.20 #a.-f. *15.00*
621 A104 $1.60 #a.-f. *22.50*
Nos. 618-621 (4) *54.50*

Nos. 619-621 are airmail. Individual stamps measure 70x9mm and have a card backing. Se-tenant labels on No. 618 inscribed "economique." Se-tenant labels on Nos. 619-621 inscribed "prioritaire AIR MAIL."

It has been stated that these stamps were available only from the Philatelic Bureau and were not accepted by local post offices as valid for postage, though this is contradicted by the Controller of Postal Services.

Souvenir Sheet

New Year 1994 (Year of the Dog) — A105

Wmk. 373

1994, Feb. 18 Litho. *Perf. 14*

622 A105 $3 multicolored 7.50 7.50

Hong Kong '94.

Whales A106

Designs: 23c, Bryde's whale. 40c, Blue whale. 60c, Humpback whale. 75c, Killer whale.

1994, May 2

623 A106 23c multicolored 1.50 1.50
624 A106 23c multicolored 1.50 1.50
a. Pair, #623-624 3.25 3.25
625 A106 40c multicolored 1.75 1.75
626 A106 40c multicolored 1.75 1.75
a. Pair, #625-626 3.75 3.75
627 A106 60c multicolored 2.75 2.75
628 A106 60c multicolored 2.75 2.75
a. Pair, #627-628 6.00 6.00
629 A106 75c multicolored 3.00 3.00
630 A106 75c multicolored 3.00 3.00
a. Pair #629-630 6.50 6.50
Nos. 623-630 (8) 18.00 18.00

Value at UL on Nos. 623, 625, 627, 629; at UR on others.
Nos. 624a-630a have continuous designs.

Environmental Protection — A107

Designs: 40c, Family on beach at sunset. 60c, Fish. 75c, Frigate birds.

1994, July 12

631 A107 40c multicolored 1.10 .90
632 A107 60c multicolored 1.25 1.10
633 A107 75c multicolored 1.75 1.75
Nos. 631-633 (3) 4.10 3.75

Independence, 15th anniv.

Butterflies A108

Flowers — A109

Designs: 1c, Diaphania indica. 5c, Herpetogamma licarsisalis. 10c, Parotis suralis. 12c, Sufetula sunidesalis. 20c, Aedia sericea. 23c, Anomis vitiensis. 30c, Anticarsia irrorata. 35c, Spodoptera litura. 40c, Mocis frugalis. 45c, Agrius convolvuli. 50c, Cephonodes picus. 55c, Gnathothlibus erotus. 60c, Macroglossum hirundo. 75c, Badamia exclamationis. $1, Precis villida. $2, Danaus plexippus. $3, Hypolimnas bolina (male). $5, Hypolimnas bolina (female).

1994, Aug. 19 *Perf. 14½x14*

634 A108 1c multicolored .20 .20
635 A108 5c multicolored .20 .20
636 A108 10c multicolored .25 .20
637 A108 12c multicolored .30 .25
638 A108 20c multicolored .40 .35
639 A108 23c multicolored .50 .45
640 A108 30c multicolored .65 .55
641 A108 35c multicolored .75 .65
642 A108 40c multicolored .85 .70
643 A108 45c multicolored .90 .80
644 A108 50c multicolored 1.00 .85
645 A108 55c multicolored 1.20 .95
646 A108 60c multicolored 1.25 1.00
647 A108 75c multicolored 1.50 1.25
648 A108 $1 multicolored 2.00 2.00
a. Souvenir sheet of 1 2.75 2.75
649 A108 $2 multicolored 3.75 *4.00*
650 A108 $3 multicolored 5.75 *6.00*
651 A108 $5 multicolored 9.50 *10.00*
Nos. 634-651 (18) 30.95 30.40

No. 648a issued 2/12/97 for Hong Kong '97.
For overprints see #763-767.

1994, Oct. 31

652 A109 23c Nerium oleander .75 .75
653 A109 60c Catharanthus roseus 1.25 1.25
654 A109 75c Ipomea pes-caprae 1.75 1.75
655 A109 $1 Calophyllum mophyllum 2.25 2.25
Nos. 652-655 (4) 6.00 6.00

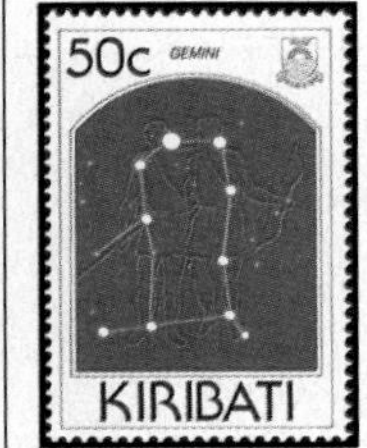

A110

Constellations.

1995, Jan. 31

656 A110 50c Gemini 1.25 1.25
657 A110 60c Cancer 1.40 1.40
658 A110 75c Cassiopeia 1.75 1.75
659 A110 $1 Southern cross 2.50 2.50
Nos. 656-659 (4) 6.90 6.90

A111

Wmk. 384

1995, Apr. 3 Litho. *Perf. 14½*

Scenes of Kiribati: No. 660: a, Architecture. b, Men, canoe, sailboat. c, Gun emplacement, Tarawa. d, Children, shells. e, Outdoor sports.
No. 661: a, Women traditionally attired. b, Windsurfing. c, Filleting fish. d, Snorkeling, scuba diving. e, Weaving.

660 A111 30c Strip of 5, #a.-e. 4.50 4.50
661 A111 40c Strip of 5, #a.-e. 6.50 6.50
f. Booklet pane, #660, #661 + 5 labels 12.00 *12.00*
Complete booklet, #661f 13.00

Visit South Pacific Year.

End of World War II, 50th Anniv.
Common Design Type

Designs: 23c, Grumman TBM-3E Avenger. 40c, Curtiss SOC. 3-1 seagull. 50c, Consolidated B-24J Liberator. 60c, Grumman Goose. 75c, Martin B-26 Marauder. $1, Northrop P-61B Black Widow. $2, Reverse of War Medal 1939-45.

Perf. 14x13½

1995, May 8 Wmk. 373

662 CD351 23c multicolored 1.25 1.25
663 CD351 40c multicolored 1.50 1.50
664 CD351 50c multicolored 1.75 1.75
665 CD351 60c multicolored 2.00 2.00
666 CD351 75c multicolored 2.75 2.75
667 CD351 $1 multicolored 3.75 3.75
Nos. 662-667 (6) 13.00 13.00

Souvenir Sheet

Perf. 14

668 CD352 $2 multicolored 5.25 5.25

For overprints see Nos. 691-697.

Souvenir Sheet of 4

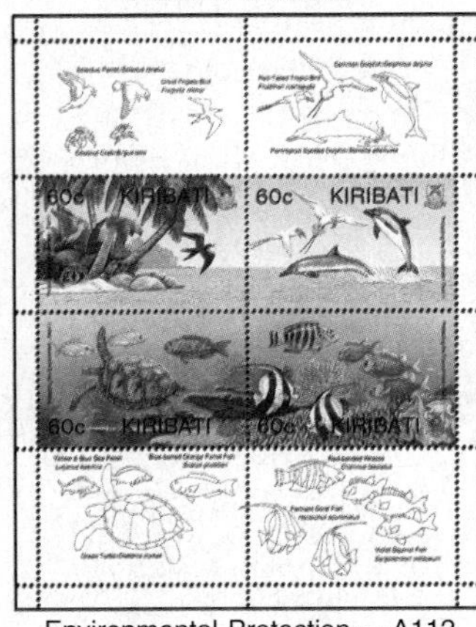

Environmental Protection — A112

Marine life: a, Electus parrot, great frigate bird, coconut crab. b, Red-tailed tropic bird, common dolphin, pantropical spotted dolphin. c, Yellow & blue sea perch, green turtle, blue-barred orange parrot fish. d, Pennant coral fish, red-banded wrasse, violet squirrel fish.

Wmk. 373

1995, July 12 Litho. *Perf. 14*

669 A112 60c #a.-d. + 4 labels 5.50 5.50

For overprint see No. 672.

Souvenir Sheet

New Year 1995 (Year of the Boar) — A113

$2, Sow, piglets.

1995, Sept. 1 Litho. *Perf. 13*

670 A113 $2 multicolored 4.50 4.50

Singapore '95.

Souvenir Sheet

Beijing '95 — A114

Design: $2, like #670.

1995, Sept. 14

671 A114 $2 multicolored 4.50 4.50

No. 669 Overprinted for Jakarta '95

Wmk. 373

1995, Aug. 19 Litho. *Perf. 14*

672 A112 60c #a.-d. + 4 labels 9.00 9.00

Police Maritime Unit — A115

Patrol boat RKS Teanoai: No. 673, In harbor. No. 674, Under way.

Wmk. 373

1995, Nov. 30 Litho. *Perf. 13*

673 75c multicolored 2.50 2.50
674 75c multicolored 2.50 2.50
a. A115 Pair, #673-674 5.25 5.25

Dolphins A116

Designs: 23c, Pantropical spotted. 60c, Spinner. 75c, Fraser's. $1, Rough-toothed.

Wmk. 384

1996, Jan. 15 Litho. *Perf. 14*

675 A116 23c multicolored 1.75 1.00
676 A116 60c multicolored 2.50 1.50
677 A116 75c multicolored 3.25 2.50
678 A116 $1 multicolored 4.00 *4.25*
Nos. 675-678 (4) 11.50 9.25

UNICEF, 50th Anniv. — A117

Portion of UNICEF emblem and: a, Water faucet, clean water. b, Documents, chilren's rights. c, Hypodermic, health care. d, Open book, education.

Wmk. 373

1996, Apr. 22 Litho. *Perf. 13*

679 A117 30c Block of 4, #a.-d. 3.00 3.00

No. 679 is a continuous design.

Souvenir Sheet

CHINA '96, 9th Intl. Philatelic Exhibition — A118

1996, Apr. 30 Wmk. 384 *Perf. 13½*

680 A118 50c multicolored 2.00 2.00

New Year 1996, Year of the Rat.

Souvenir Sheet

No. 5609 Gilbert and Ellice Islands LMS Jubilee Class 4-6-0 Locomotive — A119

Wmk. 373

1996, June 8 Litho. *Perf. 12*

681 A119 $2 multicolored 4.25 4.25

CAPEX '96.

Sea Crabs A120

Wmk. 373

1996, Aug. 6 Litho. *Perf. 14*

682	A120 23c Rathbun red	.75	.55
683	A120 60c Red & white painted	1.75	1.25
684	A120 75c Red spotted	2.00	2.00
685	A120 $1 Red spotted white	2.50	*2.75*
	Nos. 682-685 (4)	7.00	6.55

Souvenir Sheet

Taipei '96 — A121

Wmk. 384

1996, Oct. 21 Litho. *Perf. 14½*

686 A121 $1.50 Outrigger canoe 4.50 4.50

Ships Type of 1989

23c, Whaling ship, "Potomac," 1843. 50c, Barkentine "Southern Cross IV," 1891. 60c, Bark "John Williams III," 1890. $1, HMS Dolphin, 1765.

Wmk. 384

1996, Dec. 2 Litho. *Perf. 14½*

687	A87 23c multicolored	.80	.55
688	A87 50c multicolored	1.25	1.25
689	A87 60c multicolored	1.50	1.50
690	A87 $1 multicolored	2.50	2.50
	Nos. 687-690 (4)	6.05	5.80

Nos. 662-668 Ovptd.

Perf. 14x13½

1997, May 29 Litho. Wmk. 373

691	CD351 23c multicolored	.70	.50
692	CD351 40c multicolored	.95	.80
693	CD351 50c multicolored	1.25	1.10
694	CD351 60c multicolored	1.50	1.50
695	CD351 75c multicolored	1.75	1.75
696	CD351 $1 multicolored	2.25	2.25
	Nos. 691-696 (6)	8.40	7.90

Souvenir Sheet

697 CD351 $2 multicolored 5.00 5.00

Queen Elizabeth II and Prince Philip, 50th Wedding Anniv. — A122

No. 698, Queen Elizabeth II. No. 699, Horse team going down river bank. No. 700, Queen in open carriage. No. 701, Prince Philip. No. 702, Prince, Queen. No. 703, Riding horse.
$2, Queen, Prince in open carriage, horiz.

Perf. 14½x14

1997, July 10 Litho. Wmk. 373

698	50c multicolored	1.50	1.50
699	50c multicolored	1.50	1.50
a.	A122 Pair, #698-699	3.25	3.25
700	60c multicolored	1.75	1.75
701	60c multicolored	1.75	1.75
a.	A122 Pair, #700-701	3.75	3.75
702	75c multicolored	2.75	2.75
703	75c multicolored	2.75	2.75
a.	A122 Pair, #702-703	6.00	6.00
	Nos. 698-703 (6)	12.00	12.00

Souvenir Sheet

704 A122 $2 multicolored 7.00 7.00

Birds — A123

#705-706, Rock dove. #707-708, Pacific pigeon. #709-710, Micronesian pigeon.

Wmk. 373

1997, Dec. 1 Litho. *Perf. 14*

705	50c Immature	1.10	1.10
706	50c Adult	1.10	1.10
a.	A123 Pair, #705-706	2.40	2.40
707	60c Adult	1.50	1.50
708	60c Immature	1.50	1.50
a.	A123 Pair, #707-708	3.25	3.25
709	75c Adult	1.75	1.75
710	75c Immature	1.75	1.75
a.	A123 Pair, #709-710	3.75	3.75
	Nos. 705-710 (6)	8.70	8.70

Nos. 705-706, 709-710 With Added Inscription

Wmk. 373

1997, Dec. 5 Litho. *Perf. 14*

711	50c on #705	1.25	1.25
712	50c on #706	1.25	1.25
a.	A123 Pair, #711-712	2.75	2.75
713	75c on #709	2.00	2.00
714	75c on #710	2.00	2.00
a.	A123 Pair, #713-714	4.25	4.25

Asia '97.

Spiny Lobster A124

Wmk. 373

1998, Feb. 2 Litho. *Perf. 14*

715	A124 25c shown	.80	.80
716	A124 25c Crawling right	.80	.80
717	A124 25c Crawling left	.80	.80
718	A124 25c Looking upward	.80	.80
a.	Strip of 4, #715-718	3.50	3.50

Souvenir Sheet

719 A124 $1.50 Looking straight forward 3.75 3.75

World Wildlife Fund.

Diana, Princess of Wales (1961-97)

Common Design Type

Various portraits — #720: a, 50c. b, 60c. c, 75c.

Perf. 14½x14

1998, Mar. 31 Litho. Wmk. 373

719A CD355 25c multicolored .60 .60

Sheet of 4

720 CD355 #a.-c., 719A 4.75 4.75

No. 720 sold for $2.10 + 50c, with surtax from international sales being donated to the Princess Diana Memorial Fund, and surtax from national sales being donated to designated local charity.

Intl. Year of the Ocean — A125

Whales and dolphins: No. 721, Indo-Pacific humpbacked dolphin. No. 722, Bottlenose dolphin. No. 723, Short-snouted spinner dolphin. No. 724, Risso's dolphin. No. 725, Striped dolphin. No. 726, Sei whale. No. 727, Fin whale. No. 728, Minke whale.

Wmk. 373

1998, Oct. 1 Litho. *Perf. 14*

721	25c multicolored	.60	.60
722	25c multicolored	.60	.60
a.	A125 Pair, #721-722	1.50	1.50
723	60c multicolored	1.25	1.25
724	60c multicolored	1.25	1.25
a.	A125 Pair, #723-724	2.75	2.75
725	75c multicolored	1.75	1.75
726	75c multicolored	1.75	1.75
a.	A125 Pair, #725-726	3.75	3.75
727	$1 multicolored	2.00	2.00
728	$1 multicolored	2.00	2.00
a.	A125 Pair, #727-728	4.50	4.50
	Nos. 721-728 (8)	11.20	11.20

Souvenir Sheet

Children of Kiribati — A125a

1998, Sept. 15

729 A125a $1 multicolored 2.25 2.25

Souvenir Sheet

Reuben K. Uatioa Stadium — A126

Wmk. 373

1998, Oct. 23 Litho. *Perf. 14*

730 A126 $2 multicolored 4.00 4.00

Italia '98 World Philatelic Exhibition.

Greenhouse Effect — A127

Designs: 25c, Contributors to Greenhouse gases. 50c, Explanation of the Greenhouse Effect. 60c, Greenhouse Effect on Tarawa Atoll. 75c, Greenhouse Effect on Kiritimati Island.
$1.50, People in sailboat, "Kiribati way of life."

Wmk. 373

1998, Dec. 1 Litho. *Perf. 13½*

731	A127 25c multicolored	.60	.60
732	A127 50c multicolored	.90	.90
733	A127 60c multicolored	1.25	1.25
734	A127 75c multicolored	1.75	1.75
	Nos. 731-734 (4)	4.50	4.50

Souvenir Sheet

735 A127 $1.50 multicolored 3.75 3.75

Souvenir Sheet

HMS Resolution at Christmas Island — A128

Wmk. 373

1999, Mar. 19 Litho. *Perf. 14*

736 A128 $2 multicolored 4.25 4.25

Australia '99 World Stamp Expo.

IBRA '99, Philatelic Exhibition, Nuremberg — A129

Ducks: 25c, Northern shoveller, male. 50c, Northern shoveller, female. 60c, Green-winged teal, male. 75c, Green-winged teal, female and ducklings.
$3, Green winged teal, male, duckling.

Wmk. 373

1999, Apr. 27 Litho. *Perf. 14*

737	A129 25c multicolored	.65	.50
738	A129 50c multicolored	1.25	.80
739	A129 60c multicolored	1.40	1.40
740	A129 75c multicolored	1.75	*2.00*
	Nos. 737-740 (4)	5.05	4.70

Souvenir Sheet

741 A129 $3 multicolored 6.00 6.00

Independence, 20th Anniv. — A130

Designs: 25c, Millennium Island. 60c, Map of Kiribati. 75c, Map of Nikumaroro. $1, Amelia Earhart, Lockheed 10E Electra airplane.

Wmk. 373

1999, July 12 Litho. *Perf. 13½*

742	A130	25c multicolored	.60	.60
743	A130	60c multicolored	1.10	1.10
744	A130	75c multicolored	1.40	1.40
745	A130	$1 multicolored	3.00	3.00
a.		Souvenir sheet, #744-745	4.25	4.25
		Nos. 742-745 (4)	6.10	6.10

1st Manned Moon Landing, 30th Anniv.

Common Design Type

Designs: 25c, Edwin Aldrin. 60c, Service module docks with lander. 75c, Apollo 11 on lunar surface. $1, Command module separates from service module.

$2, Earth as seen from moon.

Perf. 14x13¾

1999, July 20 Litho. Wmk. 384

746	CD357	25c multicolored	.60	.60
747	CD357	60c multicolored	1.10	1.10
748	CD357	75c multicolored	1.40	1.40
749	CD357	$1 multicolored	1.75	1.75
		Nos. 746-749 (4)	4.85	4.85

Souvenir Sheet

Perf. 14

750	CD357	$2 multicolored	4.00	4.00

No. 750 contains one 40mm circular stamp 40mm.

UPU, 125th Anniv., Christmas A131

Wmk. 373

1999, Oct. 9 Litho. *Perf. 13½*

751	A131	25c Santa in canoe	.55	.45
752	A131	60c Santa on dock	1.00	.85
753	A131	75c Santa in sleigh	1.25	1.25
754	A131	$1 Santa at computer	1.50	1.50
		Nos. 751-754 (4)	4.30	4.05

Millennium A132

Perf. 13¼x13

2000, Jan. 1 Litho. Wmk. 373

755	A132	25c Faith	.55	.45
756	A132	40c Harmony	.80	.70
757	A132	60c Hope	1.10	1.10
758	A132	75c Enlightenment	1.75	1.75
759	A132	$1 Peace	2.00	2.00
		Nos. 755-759 (5)	6.20	6.00

Sesame Street Characters — A133

No. 760: a, Bert. b, Baby Bear. c, Grover. d, Elmo, Cookie Monster. e, Telly Monster. f. Zoe. g, Ernie. h, Big Bird, Rosita. i, Oscar the Grouch.

No. 761, Grover as mailman.

Perf. 14½x14¾

2000, Mar. 22 Litho. Wmk. 373

760	A133	20c Sheet of 9, #a-i	4.00	4.00

Souvenir Sheet

761	A133	$1.50 multi	2.75	2.75

Souvenir Sheet

The Stamp Show 2000, London — A134

2000, May 8 Wmk. 373 *Perf. 13¾*

762	A134	$5 Queen Elizabeth II	8.00	8.00

Nos. 635, 636, 638, 648 and 650 Ovptd.

Perf. 14½x14

2000, June 1 Wmk. 373

763	A108	5c multi	.45	.45
764	A108	10c multi	.45	.45
765	A108	20c multi	.55	.55
766	A108	$1 multi	1.75	1.75
767	A108	$3 multi	4.50	4.50
		Nos. 763-767 (5)	7.70	7.70

Prince William, 18th Birthday A135

Various views of Prince William with Prince Charles.

Wmk. 373

2000, July 24 Litho. *Perf. 12¾*

768	A135	25c multi	.40	.40
769	A135	60c multi	.90	.90
770	A135	75c multi	1.25	1.25
771	A135	$1 multi	1.50	1.50
		Nos. 768-771 (4)	4.05	4.05

Ducks A136

Designs: No. 772, 25c, Blue duck. No. 773, 25c, Green-winged teal. No. 774, 25c, Mallard. No. 775, 25c, Northern shoveler. No. 776, 25c, Pacific black duck. No. 777, 25c, Wandering whistling duck.

Wmk. 373

2001, Jan. 22 Litho. *Perf. 14*

772-777	A136	Set of 6	4.50	4.50

Souvenir Sheet

778	A136	$1 Gray teal	5.00	5.00

Water Conservation A137

Children's art by: 25c, Tiare Hongkai. 50c, Gilbert Z. Tluanga. 60c, Mantokataake Tebaiuea, vert. 75c, Tokaman Karanebo, vert. $2, Taom Simon.

2001, July 12 Litho. *Perf. 13¼*

779-783	A137	Set of 5	6.25	6.25

Phila Nippon '01 A138

Development projects: 75c, Betio Port. $2, New Parliament House.

2001, Aug. 1

784-785	A138	Set of 2	5.00	5.00

Tourism — A139

Designs: 75c, Norwegian Cruise Line ship, map of cruise to Fanning Island. $3, The Betsey, map of Fanning Island.

Perf. 13¼

2001, Nov. 14 Litho. Unwmk.

786-787	A139	Set of 2	5.75	5.75

Fish — A140

Designs: 5c, Paracanthurus hepatus. 10c, Centropyge flavissimus. 15c, Anthias squamipinnis. 20c, Centropyge loriculus. 25c, Acanthurus lineatus. 30c, Oxycirrhites typus. 40c, Dascyllus trimaculatus. 50c, Acanthurus achilles. 60c, Pomacentrus coeruleus. 75c, Acanthurus glaucopareus. 80c, Thalassoma lunare. 90c, Arothron meleagris. $1, Odonus niger. $2, Cephalopholis miniatus. $5, Pomacanthus imperator. $10, Balistoides conspicillum.

2002, Feb. 28 Unwmk. *Perf. 13*

788	A140	5c multi	.25	.25
789	A140	10c multi	.30	.30
790	A140	15c multi	.35	.35
791	A140	20c multi	.40	.40
792	A140	25c multi	.45	.45
793	A140	30c multi	.50	.50
794	A140	40c multi	.70	.70
795	A140	50c multi	.80	.80
796	A140	60c multi	.90	.90
797	A140	75c multi	1.10	1.10
798	A140	80c multi	1.40	1.40
799	A140	90c multi	1.75	1.75
800	A140	$1 multi	2.00	2.00
801	A140	$2 multi	4.00	4.00
802	A140	$5 multi	9.00	9.00
803	A140	$10 multi	16.50	16.50
		Nos. 788-803 (16)	40.40	40.40

Pacific Explorers A141

Designs: 25c, Adm. Fabian von Bellingshausen and the Vostok, 1820. 40c, Capt. Charles Wilkes and the Vincennes, 1838-42. 60c, Capt. Edmund Fanning and the Betsey, 1798. 75c, Capt. Coffin and the Transit, 1823. $1, Commodore John Byron and the Dolphin, 1765. $2, Capt. Broughton and HMS Providence, 1795.

$5, Capt. James Cook, 1777, vert.

2002, Mar. 25 Wmk. 373 *Perf. 14*

804-809	A141	Set of 6	8.00	8.00

Souvenir Sheet

810	A141	$5 multi	8.00	8.00

In Remembrance of Sept. 11, 2001 Terrorist Attacks — A142

No. 811: a, 25c. b, $2.

2002, May 3 Wmk. 373 *Perf. 13¾*

811	A142	Vert. pair, #a-b	5.00	5.00

Issued in sheets of 2 pairs.

Reign of Queen Elizabeth II, 50th Anniv. — A143

Various photographs by Dorothy Wilding. Panel colors: 25c, Purple.

No. 812: a, Maroon. b, Purple.

2002, June 3 Wmk. 373 *Perf. 14*

812	A143	25c multi	.80	.80

Souvenir Sheet

813	A143	$2 Sheet of 2, #a-b	10.00	10.00

Christmas A144

Ribbons and bow with various basketry weaves: 25c, 60c, 75c, $1, $2.50.

2002, Dec. 2 Litho. *Perf. 13x13¼*
814-818 A144 Set of 5 5.75 5.75

Cowrie Shells — A145

Designs: 25c, Cypraea mappa. 50c, Cypraea eglantina. 60c, Cypraea mauritiana. 75c, Cypraea cribaria. $1, Cypraea talpa. $2.50, Cypraea depressa.

Perf. 14½x14¼
2003, May 12 Litho. Unwmk.
819-824 A145 Set of 6 8.00 8.00
824a Souvenir sheet, #819-824 8.00 8.00

Coronation of Queen Elizabeth II, 50th Anniv.
Common Design Type

Designs: Nos. 825, 25c, 827a, $2, Queen and Prince Philip waving. Nos. 826, $3, 827b, $5, Prince Philip paying homage to Queen at coronation.

Perf. 14¼x14½
2003, June 2 Litho. Wmk. 373
Vignettes Framed, Red Background
825-826 CD363 Set of 2 4.25 4.25
Souvenir Sheet
Vignettes Without Frame, Purple Panel
827 CD363 Sheet of 2, #a-b 9.25 9.25

Powered Flight, Cent. — A146

Designs: 25c, Sopwith Camel. 50c, Northrop Alpha. No. 830, 60c, DeHavilland Comet. 75c, Boeing 727. $1, English Electric Canberra. $2.50, Lockheed Martin F-22.
No. 834: a, 40c, Mitsubishi A6M-5 Zero. b, 60c, Grumman F6F Hellcat.

Wmk. 373
2003, Aug. 29 Litho. *Perf. 14*
Stamp + Label
828-833 A146 Set of 6 10.00 10.00
Souvenir Sheet
834 A146 Sheet of 2, #a-b 3.50 3.50

Christmas — A147

Christmas Island scenes: 25c, Teareba Taomeka, Tabwakea. 40c, Seventh Day Adventist Church, London. 50c, St. Teresa Catholic Church, Tabakea Village. 60c, Betaera Fou, London. 75c, Children, church bells, London. $1.50, Emanuira Church, London. $2.50, Church of Christ (60x24mm).

2003, Dec. 20 Unwmk. *Perf. 13¼*
835-841 A147 Set of 7 12.00 12.00
841a Souvenir sheet, #835-841 12.00 12.00

Road Safety — A148

No. 842: a, Accident. b, Automobile. c, Beverage can, drink, cigarette. d, Children.

2004, Apr. 7 Litho. *Perf. 13x13¼*
842 Horiz. strip of 4 5.00 5.00
a. A148 30c multi .60 .50
b. A148 40c multi .90 .70
c. A148 50c multi 1.00 .90
d. A148 60c multi 1.25 1.10
e. Souvenir sheet, #842 5.25 5.25

World Health Day.

Bird Life International A149

Designs: 25c, Pacific golden plover. 40c, Whimbrel. 50c, Wandering tattler. 60c, Sanderling. 75c, Bar-tailed godwit. $2.50, Ruddy turnstone.
No. 849 — Bristle-thighed curlew: a, One in tree, one at water's edge. b, Head of bird. c, Front of bird, head facing right, vert. d, Back of bird, head facing left, vert. e, Two birds at water's edge.

Perf. 14¼x13¾
2004, Apr. 29 Litho. Unwmk.
843-848 A149 Set of 6 13.00 13.00
Souvenir Sheet
Perf. 14¼x14½
849 A149 $1 Sheet of 5, #a-e 14.00 14.00

2004 Summer Olympics, Athens — A150

Designs: 25c, Runners. 50c, Taekwondo. 60c, Weight lifting. 75c, Women's running.

2004, July 12 Wmk. 373 *Perf. 14*
850-853 A150 Set of 4 4.50 4.50

Souvenir Sheet

Celebration Games — A151

No. 854: a, Runners on track. b, Athletes, dancer, building.

2004, July 12
854 A151 $2.50 Sheet of 2, #a-b 11.00 11.00

Orchids A152

No. 855: a, Dendrobium anosmum. b, Dendrobium chrysotoxum. c, Dendrobium laevifolium. d, Dendrobium mohlianum. e, Dendrobium pseudoglomeratum. f, Dendrobium purpureum. g, Grammatophyllum speciosum. h, Dendrobium williamsianum. i, Spathoglottis plicata. j, Vanda hindsii.

2004, Aug. 28 Unwmk. *Perf. 13½*
855 Block of 10 18.00 18.00
a.-j. A152 $1 Any single 1.60 1.50

Merchant Ships A153

Designs: 50c, MV Montelucia. 75c, MS Pacific Princess. $2.50 MS Prinsendam. $5, MS Norwegian Wind.

2004, Oct. 25 Litho. *Perf. 13¼*
856-859 A153 Set of 4 17.50 17.50

Battle of Trafalgar, Bicent. — A154

Designs: 25c, French 16-pounder cannon. 50c, San Ildefonso in action against HMS Defence. 75c, HMS Victory lashed to the Redoubtable. $1, Emperor Napoleon Bonaparte, vert. $1.50, HMS Victory. No. 865, $2.50, Vice-admiral Sir Horatio Nelson, vert.
No. 866: a, Admiral Federico Gravina. b, Santissima Trinidad.

2005, Mar. 29 Litho. *Perf. 13¼*
860-865 A154 Set of 6 15.00 15.00
Souvenir Sheet
866 A154 $2.50 Sheet of 2, #a-b 10.00 10.00

No. 864 has particles of wood from the HMS Victory embedded in the areas covered by a thermographic process that produces a raised, shiny effect.

End of World War II, 60th Anniv. — A155

No. 867: a, Japanese Type 95 Ha-Go tank invading Gilbert Islands. b, Japanese A6M Zero fighter on Gilbert Islands. c, USS Argonaut and Nautilus land Marines at Butaritari in Carlson Raid. d, Pacific Fleet Admiral Chester W. Nimitz. e, USS Liscome Bay sunk by Japanese submarine. f, US Higgins landing craft approaching Tarawa Red Beach. g, F6F-3 Hellcats provide air cover over Tarawa Red Beach. h, LVTs hit the shore at Tarawa Red Beach. i, Sherman tank at Tarawa Red Beach. j, US Marines take cover on Tarawa Red Beach.
$5, Australian Prime Minister John Curtin, British Prime Minister Winston Churchill.

2005, Apr. 21 *Perf. 13¾*
867 A155 75c Sheet of 10, #a-j 20.00 20.00
Souvenir Sheet
868 A155 $5 multi 15.00 15.00

Pacific Explorer 2005 World Stamp Expo, Sydney (No. 868).

BirdLife International — A156

No. 869, 25c — Birds of Christmas Island: a, Lesser frigatebird. b, Red-tailed tropicbird. c, Blue noddy. d, Christmas shearwater. e, Sooty tern. f, Masked booby.
No. 870, $2 — Birds of Kiribati: a, White-tailed tropicbird. b, Black noddy. c, Red-footed booby. d, Wedge-tailed shearwater. e, White tern. f, Great frigatebird.

2005, Aug. 15 *Perf. 13¼x13*
Sheets of 6, #a-f
869-870 A156 Set of 2 32.50 32.50

Pope John Paul II (1920-2005) A157

2005, Aug. 18 Litho. *Perf. 14*
871 A157 $1 multi 2.25 2.25

Battle of Trafalgar, Bicent. — A158

Designs: 25c, HMS Victory. 50c, Ships, horiz. $5, Admiral Horatio Nelson

2005, Oct. 18 Litho. *Perf. 13½*
872-874 A158 Set of 3 15.00 15.00

Worldwide Fund for Nature (WWF) — A159

Various depictions of harlequin shrimp: 50c, 60c, 75c, $5.

2005, Dec. 1 *Perf. 14*
875-878 A159 Set of 4 16.50 16.50
878a Miniature sheet, 2 each #875-878 34.00 34.00

Queen Elizabeth II, 80th Birthday A160

Queen: 50c, As young woman. 75c, Wearing tiara, sepia photograph. $1, Wearing tiara, color photograph. $2, Wearing pink hat.
No. 883: a, $1.50, Like $1. b, $2.50, Like 75c.

2006, Apr. 21 Litho. *Perf. 14*
Stamps With White Frames

879-882 A160 Set of 4 10.00 10.00

Souvenir Sheet
Stamps Without White Frames

883 A160 Sheet of 2, #a-b 14.00 14.00

Europa Stamps, 50th Anniv. — A161

Flags of European Union and Kiribati with gradiating background colors of: $2, Gray green. $2.50, Purple. $3, Yellowish brown. $5, Blue.

2006, May 4 *Perf. 13¼*

884-887 A161 Set of 4 22.00 22.00
887a Souvenir sheet, #884-887 22.00 22.00

Anniversaries — A162

No. 888, 25c: a, Charles Darwin and marine life. b, Fish and marine life.
No. 889, 50c: a, Isambard Kingdom Brunel. b, Glowing rivet.
No. 890, 75c: a, Christopher Columbus. b, Ship.
No. 891, $1: a, Thomas Alva Edison. b, Tin foil phonograph.
No. 892, $1.25: a, Wolfgang Amadeus Mozart. b, Violin and quill pen.
No. 893, $1.50: a, Concorde. b, Wing of Concorde, Concorde in flight.

2006, May 27 *Perf. 13x12½*
Horiz. Pairs, #a-b

888-893 A162 Set of 6 22.50 22.50

Darwin's voyage on the Beagle, 250th anniv., Birth of Brunel, bicent., Death of Columbus, 500th anniv., Death of Edison, 75th anniv., Birth of Mozart, 250th anniv., Inaugural Concorde flights, 30th anniv.

Dinosaurs A163

Designs: 25c, Ultrasaurus. 50c, Rhamphorhynchus. 60c, Dilophosaurus. 75c, Brachiosaurus. No. 898, $1, Minmi paravertebra. No. 899, $1, Eoraptor. $1.25, Stegosaurus. $1.50, Gigantosaurus.

2006, Sept. 15 *Perf. 13¼x13½*

894-901 A163 Set of 8 12.50 12.50

Miniature Sheet

Victoria Cross, 150th Anniv. — A164

No. 902: a. Troop Sergeant Major John Berryman with Captain Webb at Balaclava. b, Private W. Norman bringing in two Russian prisoners. c, Sergeant Major John Greive saving officer's life at Balaclava. d, Private Thomas Beach rescuing Colonel Carpenter at Inkerman. e, Brevet Major C. H. Lumley engaged with Russian gunners in the Redan. f, Major F. C. Elton working in trenches.

2006, Oct. 20 Litho. *Perf. 13¼x12½*

902 A164 $1.50 Sheet of 6, #a-f, + 6 labels 19.00 19.00

60th Wedding Anniversary of Queen Elizabeth II and Prince Philip — A165

Designs: 50c, Portrait of Elizabeth and Philip. 75c, Wedding procession. $1, Bride and groom waving. $1.50, Queen reading.
$5, Wedding portrait.

2007, Jan. 31 Litho. *Perf. 13¾*

903-906 A165 Set of 4 6.00 6.00

Souvenir Sheet
Perf. 14

907 A165 $5 multi 7.75 7.75

No. 907 contains one 42x56mm stamp

Scouting, Cent. A166

Designs: 25c, Scouts with Kiribati flag, hands tying neckerchief. 50c, Scouts learning about AIDS, Scout saluting. 75c, Scout leaders, hand with compass. $2, 1962 Scout shelter, hands lashing rope.
No. 912, vert.: a, $1, Emblem of Kiribati Scouts. b, $1.50, Lord Robert Baden-Powell.

Perf. 13x13¼
2007, Sept. 21 Litho. Wmk. 373

908-911 A166 Set of 4 7.50 7.50

Souvenir Sheet
Perf. 13¼x13

912 A166 Sheet of 2, #a-b 5.25 5.25

Princess Diana (1961-97) A167

Designs: No. 913, 25c, Wearing white dress, facing right. No. 914, 25c, Wearing pink dress, facing left. 50c, Wearing pink dress, diff. No. 916, 75c, Wearing emerald necklace. No. 917, 75c, Wearing black and white dress. $1, Wearing red dress.

Perf. 13¼x12½
2007, Nov. 1 Litho. Unwmk.

913-918 A167 Set of 6 7.00 7.00

Military Uniforms — A168

Uniforms of: 25c, Royal Engineers. 40c, 95th Rifles. 50c, 24th Regiment of Foot. 60c, New Zealand soldiers. 75c, 93rd Sutherland Highlanders. 90c, Irish Guard. $1, Japanese soldiers. $1.50, United States Marine Corps.

2007, Nov. 20 Wmk. 373 *Perf. 14*

919-926 A168 Set of 8 12.00 12.00

Birds — A169

Designs: 5c, Great crested tern. 10c Eurasian teal. 15c, Laughing gull. 20c, Black-tailed godwit. 25c, Pectoral sandpiper. 50c, Band-rumped storm petrel. 60c, Sharp-tailed sandpiper. 75c, Gray-tailed tattler. 90c, Red phalarope. $1, Pink-footed shearwater. $2, Ring-billed gull. $5, Bonin petrel.

Wmk. 373
2008, Feb. 9 Litho. *Perf. 13¾*

927	A169	5c multi	.20	.20
928	A169	10c multi	.20	.20
929	A169	15c multi	.30	.30
930	A169	20c multi	.40	.40
931	A169	25c multi	.45	.45
932	A169	50c multi	.95	.95
933	A169	60c multi	1.10	1.10
934	A169	75c multi	1.40	1.40
935	A169	90c multi	1.75	1.75
936	A169	$1 multi	2.00	2.00
937	A169	$2 multi	4.25	4.25
a.		Souvenir sheet, #929, 933-937	10.50	10.50
938	A169	$5 multi	10.50	10.50
a.		Souvenir sheet, #927-928, 930-932, 938	13.00	13.00
		Nos. 927-938 (12)	23.50	23.50

A170

Royal Air Force, 90th Anniv. — A171

Designs: 25c, Avro Shackleton. 50c, Harrier GR3. 75c, Eurofighter Typhoon. $1, Vickers Valiant.
$2.50, Dambusters Raid.

Wmk. 373
2008, Apr. 1 Litho. *Perf. 14*

939-942 A170 Set of 4 5.50 5.50

Souvenir Sheet

943 A171 $2.50 multi 5.50 5.50

Phoenix Island Protected Area A172

Designs: 40c, Huts. 75c, Map of Kanton Island. 80c, Map of various islands. 85c, Phoenix petrel. $1.25, Acropora nobilis and reef fish. $1.75, Blacktip reef shark.

2008, July 12 *Perf. 13¾*

944-949 A172 Set of 6 11.50 11.50
949a Souvenir sheet of 6, #944-949 11.50 11.50

2008 Summer Olympics, Beijing A173

Designs: 25c, Bamboo, weight lifting. 50c, Dragon, running. 60c, Lanterns, cycling. 75c, Fish, javelin.

Wmk. 373
2008, Aug. 8 Litho. *Perf. 13½*

950-953 A173 Set of 4 3.75 3.75

Christmas — A174

No. 954, 25c: a, Lady Sacred Heart Church, Bairiki. b, Kiribati Protestant Church, Bikenibeu.
No. 955, 40c: a, Kaotitaeka Roman Catholic Church, Betio. b, Mormon Church, Iesu Kristo.
No. 956, 50c: a, Moaningaina Church, Eita. b, Sacred Heart Cathedral, Tarawa.
No. 957, 75c: a, St. Paul's Millennium Church, Betio. b, Kainkatikun Kristo Church, Naninimo.

Wmk. 406
2008, Dec. 8 Litho. *Perf. 13*
Pairs, #a-b

954-957 A174 Set of 4 5.00 5.00
957c Souvenir sheet, #954a-954b, 955a-955b, 956a-956b, 957a-957b 5.00 5.00

Explorers — A175

Designs: 25c, Sir Ernest Shackleton (1874-1922). 40c, Robert Falcon Scott (1868-1912). 50c, Captain James Cook (1728-79). 75c, Marco Polo (1254-1324). $1.50, Matthew Flinders (1774-1814). $1.75, John Cabot (c. 1450-99).

Wmk. 406

2009, Mar. 9 Litho. *Perf. 14*

958-963	A175	Set of 6	7.50	7.50

Naval Aviation, Cent. A176

Aircraft: 40c, Grumman Avenger. 50c, Chance Vought Corsair. 75c, Westland Whirlwind helicopter. $1.25, McDonnell Douglas Phantom.
$3, Helicopter on deck of HMS Ark Royal.

Wmk. 406

2009, May 12 Litho. *Perf. 14*

964-967	A176	Set of 4	4.75	4.75

Souvenir Sheet

968	A176	$3 multi	4.75	4.75

Nos. 964-968 each were printed in sheets of 8 + central label.

Space Exploration A177

Designs: 40c, Mars Science Laboratory. 50c, International Space Station. 75c, Space Shuttle Endeavour and Boeing transporter plane. $1.25, Launch of Apollo 12. No. 973, $3, Luna 16.
No. 974, $3, Astronaut on Moon, painting by Capt. Alan Bean, vert.

Wmk. 406

2009, July 20 Litho. *Perf. 13¼*

969-973	A177	Set of 5	9.25	9.25

Souvenir Sheet

Perf. 13x13½

974	A177	$3 multi	4.75	4.75

First man on the Moon, 40th anniv. No. 974 contains one 40x60mm stamp.

Battle of Britain, 70th Anniv. — A178

Stained-glass windows of Biggin Hill Memorial Chapel depicting: 25c, Aircraft servicing. 40c, Knight, English flag, airplanes. 50c, Parachute packing. 75c, Ground control. $1, Rescue services. $1.50, Royal Air Force emblem.
$3, Photograph of Sir Douglas Bader.

Wmk. 406

2010, Apr. 14 Litho. *Perf. 13*

975-980	A178	Set of 6	8.25	8.25

Souvenir Sheet

981	A178	$3 multi	5.75	5.75

POSTAGE DUE STAMPS

Natl. Arms — D1

1981, Aug. 27 Litho. *Perf. 14*

J1	D1	1c brt pink & black	.20	.20
J2	D1	2c greenish blue & blk	.20	.20
J3	D1	5c brt yel grn & black	.20	.20
J4	D1	10c lt red brown & blk	.20	.20
J5	D1	20c ultra & black	.20	.20
J6	D1	30c yel bister & black	.20	.25
J7	D1	40c brt pur & black	.30	.35
J8	D1	50c green & black	.40	.50
J9	D1	$1 red orange & blk	.75	.90
		Nos. J1-J9 (9)	2.65	3.00

Imperfs exist from the liquidation of Format International. They are not errors.

OFFICIAL STAMPS

Nos. 327a-340c Overprinted "O.K.G.S."

1981, May Litho. Unwmk. *Perf. 14*

O1	A52	1c multicolored	.20	.20
O2	A52	3c multicolored	.20	.20
O3	A52	5c multicolored	.20	.20
O4	A52	7c multicolored	.20	.20
O5	A52	10c multicolored	.20	.20
O6	A52	12c multicolored	.20	.20
O7	A52	15c multicolored	.20	.20
O8	A52	20c multicolored	.20	.20
O9	A52	25c multicolored	.20	.20
O10	A52	30c multicolored	.25	.25
O11	A52	35c multicolored	.30	.30
O12	A52	50c multicolored	.45	.45
O13	A52	$1 multicolored	.80	.80
O14	A52	$2 multicolored	1.60	1.60
O15	A52	$5 multicolored	4.25	4.25
		Nos. O1-O15 (15)	9.45	9.45

Nos. O1-O15 have thick overprint.

1981 Wmk. 373

O1a	A52	1c multi	4.00	4.25
O5a	A52	10c multi	20.00	21.00
O6a	A52	12c multi	6.00	6.00
O7a	A52	15c multi	20.00	20.00
O8a	A52	20c multi	13.00	13.00
O10a	A52	30c multi	8.00	9.00
O12a	A52	50c multi	7.50	7.50
O13a	A52	$1 multi	14.00	14.00
O14a	A52	$2 multi	16.00	17.00
O15a	A52	$5 multi	4.50	4.50
		Nos. O1a-O15a (10)	113.00	116.25

Nos. 390, 393-394, 396, 398 Overprinted "O.K.G.S."

1983, June 28 Litho. *Perf. 14*

O16	A62	12c multicolored	.45	.45
O17	A62	30c multicolored	.80	.80
O18	A62	35c multicolored	.90	.90
O19	A62	50c multicolored	1.25	1.25
O20	A62	$2 multicolored	3.75	3.75
		Nos. O16-O20 (5)	7.15	7.15

This overprint has shorter, thinner letters than the one used for Nos. O1-O15. It also exists on Nos. 327, 331-334, 336-340. These have been questioned.

KOREA

kə-'rē-ə

(Corea)

(Chosen, Tyosen, Tae Han)

LOCATION — Peninsula extending from Manchuria between the Yellow Sea and the Sea of Japan (East Sea)
GOVT. — Republic
AREA — 38,221 sq. mi.
POP. — 47,904,370 (2001 est.)
CAPITAL — Seoul

Korea (or Corea) an independent monarchy for centuries under Chinese influence, came under Japanese influence in 1876. Chinese and Japanese stamps were used there as early as 1877. Administrative control was assumed by Japan in 1905 and annexation followed in 1910. Postage stamps of Japan were used in Korea from 1905 to early 1946.

At the end of World War II, American forces occupied South Korea and Russian forces occupied North Korea, with the 38th parallel of latitude as the dividing line. A republic was established in 1948 following an election in South Korea. North Korea issues its own stamps.

100 Mon = 1 Poon
5 Poon = 1 Cheun
1000 Re = 100 Cheun = Weun
100 Weun = 1 Hwan (1953)
100 Chun = 1 Won (1962)

Catalogue values for unused stamps in this country are for Never Hinged items, beginning with Scott 283 in the regular postage section, Scott B5 in the semipostal section, and Scott C23 in the airpost section.

Watermarks

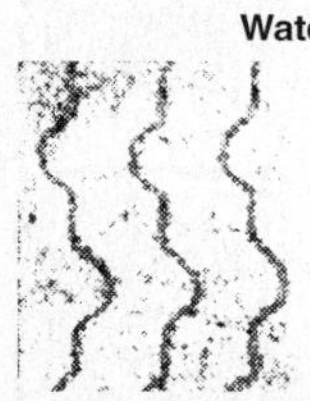

Wmk. 257 — Curved Wavy Lines

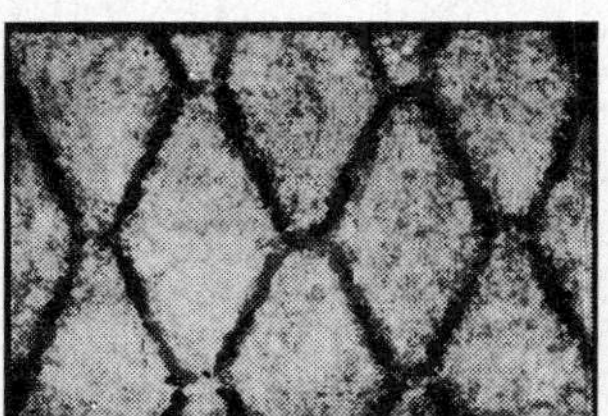

Wmk. 312 — Zigzag Lines

Wmk. 317 — Communications Department Emblem

Souvenir Sheets of 2

Stylized Yin Yang
A1 A2

Perf. 8½ to 11½

1884 Typo. Unwmk.

1	A1	5m rose	55.00
2	A2	10m blue	12.00

Reprints and counterfeits of Nos. 1-2 exist.

These stamps were never placed in use. Values: 25 and 50 mon, each $4; 100 mon $8.
Counterfeits exist.

Yin Yang — A6

Two types of 50p:
I — No period after "50."
II — Period after "50."

Perf. 11½, 12, 12½, 13 and Compound

1895 Litho.

6	A6	5p green	21.00	15.00
	a.	5p pale yellow green	29.00	18.00
	b.	Vert. pair, imperf horiz.	50.00	50.00
	c.	Horiz. pair, imperf. vert.	50.00	50.00
	d.	Vertical pair, imperf. between	55.00	55.00
	e.	Horiz. pair, imperf. btwn.	55.00	55.00

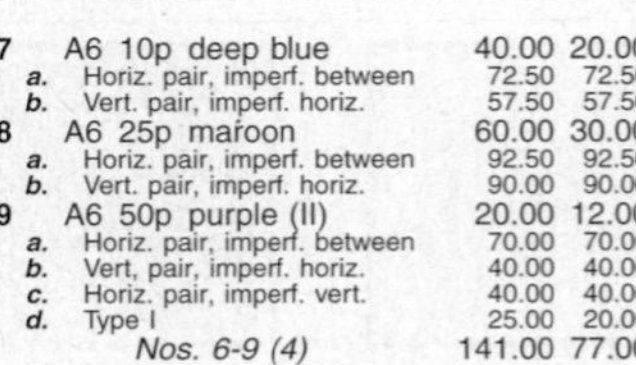

7 A6 10p deep blue 40.00 20.00
a. Horiz. pair, imperf. between 72.50 72.50
b. Vert. pair, imperf. horiz. 57.50 57.50
8 A6 25p maroon 60.00 30.00
a. Horiz. pair, imperf. between 92.50 92.50
b. Vert. pair, imperf. horiz. 90.00 90.00
9 A6 50p purple (II) 20.00 12.00
a. Horiz. pair, imperf. between 70.00 70.00
b. Vert. pair, imperf. horiz. 40.00 40.00
c. Horiz. pair, imperf. vert. 40.00 40.00
d. Type I 25.00 20.00
Nos. 6-9 (4) 141.00 77.00

For overprints and surcharges see Nos. 10-17C, 35-38.

Counterfeits exist of Nos. 6-9 and all surcharges and overprints.

Overprinted "Tae Han" in Korean and Chinese Characters

1897

Red Overprint

10 A6 5p green 90.00 10.00
a. 5p pale yellow green 200.00 150.00
b. Inverted overprint 150.00 150.00
c. Without ovpt. at bottom 150.00 130.00
d. Without overprint at top 150.00 130.00
f. Double overprint at top 140.00 140.00
g. Overprint at bottom in blk 160.00 160.00
h. Pair, one without overprint 450.00 450.00
i. Double overprint at top, inverted at bottom 550.00
11 A6 10p deep blue 100.00 15.00
a. Without ovpt. at bottom 150.00 150.00
b. Without overprint at top 150.00 150.00
c. Double overprint at top 150.00 150.00
d. Bottom overprint inverted 140.00 140.00
e. Top ovpt. dbl., one in blk 210.00 210.00
f. Top overprint omitted, bottom overprint inverted 450.00
12 A6 25p maroon 110.00 17.00
a. Overprint at bottom invtd. 150.00 150.00
b. Overprint at bottom in blk 210.00 210.00
c. Bottom overprint omitted 150.00 150.00
e. Top ovpt. dbl., one in blk 225.00 225.00
f. Top and bottom overprints double, one of each in blk 250.00 250.00
g. Pair, one without overprint 425.00 425.00
13 A6 50p purple 90.00 12.00
a. Without ovpt. at bottom 110.00 110.00
b. Without overprint at top 110.00 110.00
c. Bottom overprint double 110.00 110.00
e. Pair, one without overprint 275.00 275.00
Nos. 10-13 (4) 390.00 54.00

1897

Black Overprint

13F A6 5p green 300.00 85.00
13G A6 10p deep blue 300.00 100.00
h. Without ovpt. at bottom 350.00
14 A6 25p maroon 300.00 100.00
a. Without ovpt. at bottom 350.00
b. Without overprint at top 350.00
c. Double overprint at bottom 350.00
15 A6 50p purple 300.00 80.00
a. Without ovpt. at bottom 350.00
Nos. 13F-15 (4) 1,200.

These stamps with black overprint, also No. 16A, are said not to have been officially authorized.

Nos. 6, 6a and 8 Surcharged in Red or Black

1900

15B A6 1p on 5p grn (R) *3,500. 750.00*
c. Yellow green
16 A6 1p on 25p mar 100.00 60.00

Same Surcharge in Red or Black on Nos. 10, 10a, 12, 12c and 14

16A A6 1p on 5p grn (R) 1,000.
b. 1p on 5p pale yellow green 1,000.
17 A6 1p on 25p (#12) 50.00 22.50
a. Figure "1" omitted 90.00
b. On #12c 80.00 70.00
17C A6 1p on 25p (#14) 775.00 175.00

Counterfeit overprints and surcharges of Nos. 10-17C exist. See note after No. 15.

A8

A9

A10

A11

A12

A13

A14

A15

A16

A17

A18

A19

A20

A21

1900-01 **Typo.** ***Perf. 11***

18 A8 2re gray 5.00 3.50
19 A9 1ch yellow grn 12.00 4.50
20B A11 2ch pale blue 27.50 12.00
21 A12 3ch orange red 12.00 5.25
a. Vert. pair, imperf. horiz. 200.00 200.00
22 A13 4ch carmine 35.00 16.00
23 A14 5ch pink 32.50 8.00
24 A15 6ch dp blue 40.00 7.25
25 A16 10ch purple ('01) 47.50 27.50
26 A17 15ch gray vio 72.50 45.00
27 A18 20ch red brown 140.00 47.50
31 A19 50ch ol grn & pink 600.00 240.00
32 A20 1wn rose, blk & bl 1,200. 525.00
33 A21 2wn pur & yel grn 1,750. 800.00
Nos. 18-33 (13) 3,974. 1,741.

Nos. 22, 23, 25, 26, 33 exist imperf.

Some examples of Nos. 18-27 exist with forged Tae Han overprints in red. It is believed that Nos. 18 and 21 exist with genuine Tae Han overprints.

Reprints of No. 24 were made in light blue, perf. 12x13, in 1905 for a souvenir booklet. See note after No. 54.

See Nos. 52-54.

Perf. 10

18a A8 2re 17.50 5.25
19a A9 1ch 10.00 4.50
20 A10 2ch blue 37.50 18.00
a. Horiz. pair, imperf. btwn. *725.00*
20Ba A11 2ch pale blue 50.00 45.00
21b A12 3ch 16.00 5.25
22a A13 4ch 45.00 20.00
23a A14 5ch 40.00 10.00
24a A15 6ch 47.50 12.00
26a A17 15ch 160.00 140.00
27a A18 20ch 225.00 225.00
Nos. 18a-27a (10) 648.50 485.00

Emperor's Crown — A22

1902, Oct. 18 ***Perf. 11½***

34 A22 3ch orange 67.50 35.00

40th year of the reign of Emperor Kojong. An imperf. single was part of the 1905 souvenir booklet. See note following No. 54.

Counterfeits exist.

Nos. 8 and 9 Handstamp Surcharged in Black

1ch

2ch

3ch

Perf. 11½, 12, 12½, 13 and Compound

1902

35 A6 1ch on 25p maroon 25.00 6.00
b. Horiz. pair, imperf. btwn. 80.00
c. Imperf. 50.00
d. Vert. pair, imperf. horiz. 50.00
e. On No. 12 90.00 90.00
36 A6 2ch on 25p maroon 29.00 7.00
b. Imperf. 45.00
d. On No. 12 90.00 90.00
36E A6 2ch on 50p purple 175.00 175.00
f. Character "cheun" unabbreviated (in two rows instead of one) 250.00 175.00
37 A6 3ch on 50p purple 25.00 7.00
b. With character "cheun" unabbreviated (in two rows instead of one) 2,100. 800.00
d. Horiz. pair, imperf. btwn. 60.00
e. Vert. pair, imperf. btwn. 75.00
g. On No. 13 75.00 75.00
38 A6 3ch on 25p maroon 65.00 65.00
Nos. 35-38 (5) 319.00 260.00

There are several sizes of these surcharges. Being handstamped, inverted and double surcharges exist.

Counterfeit surcharges exist.

Falcon — A23

1903 ***Perf. 13½x14***

39 A23 2re slate 10.00 6.25
40 A23 1ch violet brn 11.00 7.50
41 A23 2ch green 15.00 7.50
42 A23 3ch orange 13.00 7.50
43 A23 4ch rose 22.50 9.50
44 A23 5ch yellow brn 22.50 11.00
45 A23 6ch lilac 26.00 12.50
46 A23 10ch blue 32.50 16.00
47 A23 15ch red, *straw* 45.00 22.50
48 A23 20ch vio brn, *straw* 67.50 32.50
49 A23 50ch red, *grn* 210.00 120.00
50 A23 1wn vio, *lav* 550.00 300.00
51 A23 2wn vio, *org* 550.00 300.00
Nos. 39-51 (13) 1,575. 852.75

Values are for stamps with perfs touching the design.

Types of 1901

1903 ***Perf. 12½***

Thin, Semi-Transparent Paper

52 A19 50ch pale ol grn & pale pink *400.00 160.00*
53 A20 1wn rose, blk & bl *600.00 200.00*
54 A21 2wn lt vio & lt grn *875.00 250.00*
Nos. 52-54 (3) *1,875.* 610.00

No. 24, perf. 12x13, No. 34 imperf. and most examples of Nos. 52-54 unused are from souvenir booklets made up in 1905 when the Japanese withdrew all Korean stamps from circulation.

WARNING

In 1957 the Ministry of Communications issued 4000 presentation booklets containing Nos. 1-54 reproduced on watermark 312 paper.

Other presentation booklets included full-color reproductions of Nos. 1-54 and Japan No. 110 printed on the pages. Beware of wide-margined imperfs cut from these booklets.

Issued under US Military Rule

Stamps of Japan Nos. 331, 268, 342, 332, 339 and 337 Surcharged in Black

1946, Feb. 1 **Wmk. 257** ***Perf. 13***

55 A86 5ch on 5s brn lake 5.50 *12.00*
56 A93 5ch on 14s rose lake & pale rose 1.25 *3.00*
a. 5ch on 40s dark violet (error) 175.00
57 A154 10ch on 40s dk vio 1.25 *3.00*
58 A147 20ch on 6s lt ultra 1.25 *3.00*
a. 20ch on 27s rose brown (error) 175.00
b. Double surcharge 30.00
59 A151 30ch on 27s rose brn 1.25 *3.00*
a. 30ch on 6s light ultra (error) 100.00
b. Double surcharge 25.00
60 A151 5wn on 17s gray vio 6.00 *12.50*
Nos. 55-60 (6) 16.50 *36.50*
Set, never hinged 30.00

Five essays for this provisional issue exist both with and without additional overprint of two Chinese characters ("specimen") in vermilion. The essays are: 20ch on Japan No. 269; 50ch on No. 272; 1wn on No. 336; 1wn on No. 273; 10wn on No. 265. Other denominations have been reported.

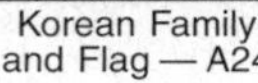

Korean Family and Flag — A24

Arms of Korea — A25

Wmk. 257

1946, May 1 **Litho.** ***Perf. 10½***

61 A24 3ch orange yellow .60 1.00
62 A24 5ch green .60 1.00
63 A24 10ch carmine .60 1.00
64 A24 20ch dark blue .60 1.00
65 A25 50ch brown violet 1.50 *1.50*
66 A25 1wn lt brown 2.50 *1.75*
Nos. 61-66 (6) 6.40 *7.25*
Set, never hinged 10.00

Liberation from Japan.

Imperfs., Part Perfs.

Imperforate and part-perforate examples of a great many Korean stamps from No. 61 onward exist.

The imperfs. include Nos. 61-90, 93-97, 116-117, 119-126, 132-173, 182-186, 195, 197-199, 202A, 203, 204-205, 217, etc.

The part-perfs. include Nos. 62-65, 69, 72-73, 109, 111-113, 132, etc.

Printers waste includes printed on both sides, etc.

As the field is so extensive, the editors believe that they belong more properly in a specialized catalogue.

Dove — A26

1946, Aug. 15 **Unwmk.**

67 A26 50ch deep violet 4.00 *3.00*
Never hinged 6.00

First anniversary of liberation.

Perforations often are rough on stamps issued between Aug. 1946 and the end of 1954. This is not considered a defect.

Flags of US and Korea A27

1946, Sept. 9 ***Perf. 11***

68 A27 10wn carmine 6.00 *4.75*
Never hinged 12.00

Resumption of postal communication with the US.

Astronomical Observatory, Kyongju — A28

Hibiscus with Rice — A29

Map of Korea — A30

Gold Crown of Silla Dynasty — A31

Admiral Li Sun-sin — A32

1946 ***Rouletted 12***

69 A28 50ch dark blue .75 *1.50*
70 A29 1wn buff .95 *2.00*
71 A30 2wn indigo 1.10 2.00
72 A31 5wn magenta 9.00 *12.50*
73 A32 10wn emerald 10.00 *12.50*
Nos. 69-73 (5) 21.80 *30.50*
Set, never hinged 40.00

Perf. 11

70a A29 1wn 1.50 *2.00*
71a A30 2wn 75.00 *90.00*
72a A31 5wn 55.00 120.00
Nos. 70a-72a (3) 131.50 212.00
Set, never hinged 160.00

Korean Phonetic Alphabet — A33

1946, Oct. 9 ***Perf. 11***

74 A33 50ch deep blue 2.00 1.50
Never hinged 5.00

500th anniv. of the introduction of the Korean phonetic alphabet (Hangul).

Li Jun — A34

Admiral Li Sun-sin — A35

Perf. 11½x11, 11½

1947, Aug. 1 **Litho.** **Wmk. 257**

75 A34 5wn lt blue green 7.00 *9.00*
76 A35 10wn light blue 7.00 *9.00*
Set, never hinged 28.00

Presentation Sheets

Starting in 1947 with No. 75, nearly 100 Korean stamps were printed in miniature or souvenir sheets and given to government officials and others. These sheets were released in quantities of 300 to 4,000. In 1957 the Ministry of Communications began to sell the souvenir sheets at post offices at face value to be used for postage. They are listed from No. 264a onward.

Letter-encircled Globe — A36

1947, Aug. 1 ***Perf. 11½x11***

77 A36 10wn light blue 10.00 *9.50*
Never hinged 21.00

Resumption of international mail service between Korea and all countries of the world.

Granite Paper

Starting with No. 77, most Korean stamps through No. 751, except those on Laid Paper, are on Granite Paper. Granite Paper is noted above listing if the issue was printed on both ordinary and Granite Paper, such as Nos. 360a-374A.

Arch of Independence, Seoul — A37

Tortoise Ship, First Ironclad War Vessel — A38

1948, Apr.

78 A37 20wn rose 3.00 *4.00*
79 A38 50wn dull red brown 57.50 40.00
Set, never hinged 120.00

Republic

Flag and Ballot — A39

Woman and Man Casting Ballots — A40

Perf. 11x11½

1948, May 10 **Litho.** **Wmk. 257**

80 A39 2wn orange 12.00 8.50
81 A39 5wn lilac rose 20.00 12.00
82 A39 10wn lt violet 27.50 20.00
83 A40 20wn carmine 40.00 27.50
84 A40 50wn blue 27.50 22.50
Nos. 80-84 (5) 127.00 90.50
Set, never hinged 250.00

South Korea election of May 10, 1948.

Korean Flag and Olive Branches — A41

Olympic Torchbearer and Map of Korea — A42

1948, June 1 ***Perf. 11x11½, 11½x11***

85 A41 5wn green 100.00 65.00
86 A42 10wn purple 40.00 24.00
Set, never hinged 280.00

Korea's participation in the 1948 Olympic Games.

National Assembly — A43

1948, July 1 **Wmk. 257** ***Perf. 11½***

87 A43 4wn orange brown 16.00 *12.00*
Never hinged 32.50

Opening of the Assembly July 1, 1948. Exists without period between "5" and "31."

Korean Family and Capitol — A44

Flag of Korea A45

1948, Aug. 1 **Litho.**

88 A44 4wn emerald 35.00 35.00
89 A45 10wn orange brown 15.00 *20.00*
Set, never hinged 125.00

Signing of the new constitution, 7/17/48.

Pres. Syngman Rhee — A46

1948, Aug. 5

90 A46 5wn deep blue 150.00 140.00
Never hinged 300.00

Inauguration of Korea's first president, Syngman Rhee.

Dove — A47

Hibiscus — A48

Two types of 5wn:

I — "1948" 3mm wide; top inscription 9mm wide; periods in "8.15." barely visible.

II — "1948" 4mm wide; top inscription 9½mm; periods in "8.15." bold and strong.

1948 ***Perf. 11, 11x11½***

91 A47 4wn blue 32.50 *32.50*
92 A48 5wn rose lilac (II) 55.00 40.00
a. Type I 120.00 100.00
Set, never hinged 175.00

Issued to commemorate the establishment of Korea's republican government.

Li Jun — A49

Observatory, Kyongju — A50

1948, Oct. 1 ***Perf. 11½x11***

93 A49 4wn rose carmine .75 1.25
94 A50 14wn deep blue .75 1.25
a. 14wn light blue 200.00 80.00
Set, never hinged 3.50

For surcharges see Nos. 127, 174, 176.

Doves over UN Emblem — A51

1949, Feb. 12 Wmk. 257 *Perf. 11*

95 A51 10wn blue *20.00 20.00*
Never hinged *40.00*

Arrival of the UN Commission on Korea, Feb. 12, 1949.

Korean Citizen and Census Date — A52

1949, Apr. 25

96 A52 15wn purple 25.00 22.50
Never hinged 52.50

Census of May 1, 1949.

Korean Boy and Girl A53

1949, May 5

97 A53 15wn purple 12.50 12.00
Never hinged 25.00

20th anniv. of Children's Day, May 5, 1949.

Postman — A54

Worker and Factory — A55

Rice Harvesting A56

Japanese Cranes A57

Diamond Mountains A58

Ginseng Plant A59

South Gate, Seoul — A60

Tabo Pagoda, Kyongju — A61

1949 Litho. *Perf. 11*

98	A54	1wn rose	2.50	3.00
99	A55	2wn dk blue gray	2.00	3.00
100	A56	5wn yellow green	8.00	8.00
101	A57	10wn blue green	.90	1.20
102	A58	20wn orange brown	.60	1.00
103	A59	30wn blue green	.60	1.00
104	A60	50wn violet blue	.60	1.00
105	A61	100wn dull yellow grn	.60	1.00
		Nos. 98-105 (8)	15.80	19.20
		Set, never hinged	42.50	

For surcharges see Nos. 129-131, 175, 177B-179, 181.

Phoenix and Yin Yang — A62

1949, Aug. 25

106 A62 15wn deep blue 17.50 14.00
Never hinged 35.00

1st anniv. of Korea's independence.

Express Train "Sam Chun Li" A63

1949, Sept. 18 *Perf. 11½x12*

107 A63 15wn violet blue 110.00 40.00
Never hinged 220.00

50th anniversary of Korean railroads.

Korean Flag — A64

Perf. 11½x11

1949, Oct. 15 Wmk. 257

108 A64 15wn red org, yel & dk bl 12.00 12.00
Never hinged 27.50

75th anniv. of the UPU.

No. 108 exists unwatermarked. These are counterfeit.

Hibiscus — A65

Magpies and Map of Korea — A66

Stylized Bird and Globe — A67

Diamond Mountains A68

Admiral Li Sun-sin A69

1949 Wmk. 257 Litho. *Perf. 11*

109	A65	15wn vermilion	.45	*1.20*
110	A66	65wn deep blue	1.00	*2.00*
111	A67	200wn green	.45	*1.20*
112	A68	400wn brown	.45	*1.20*
113	A69	500wn deep blue	.45	*1.20*
		Nos. 109-113 (5)	2.80	*6.80*
		Set, never hinged	8.00	

For surcharges see Nos. 128, 177, 180.

Canceled to Order

More than 100 Korean stamps and souvenir sheets were canceled to order, the cancellation incorporating the date "67.9.20." These include 81 stamps between Nos. 111 and 327, 18 airmail stamps between Nos. C6 and C26, and 5 souvenir sheets between Nos. 313 and 332, etc.

Also exists with later dates and on other stamps.

These c-t-o stamps and souvenir sheets are sold for much less than the values shown below, which are for postally used examples.

A70

A71

Ancient postal medal (Ma-Pae).

1950, Jan. 1

114	A70	15wn yellow green	7.50	*16.00*
115	A70	65wn red brown	5.00	*8.00*
		Set, never hinged	50.00	

50th anniv. of Korea's entrance into the UPU.

1950, Mar. 10 *Perf. 11½*

Revolutionists.

116	A71	15wn olive	12.00	*15.00*
117	A71	65wn light violet	9.00	6.50
		Set, never hinged	65.00	

41st anniversary of Korea's declaration of Independence.

Korean Emblem and National Assembly — A72

1950, May 30

118 A72 30wn bl, red, brn & grn 7.50 7.00
Never hinged 17.50

2nd natl. election of the Korean Republic.

Syngman Rhee — A73

Korean Flag and White Mountains — A74

Flags of UN and Korea, Map of Korea A75

1950, Nov. 20 Wmk. 257 *Perf. 11*

119	A73	100wn blue	2.00	*3.00*
120	A74	100wn green	1.75	*3.00*
121	A75	200wn dark green	1.75	*2.00*
		Nos. 119-121 (3)	5.50	8.00
		Set, never hinged	16.00	

Crane — A76

Tiger Mural — A77

Dove and Flag — A78

Postal Medal — A79

Mural from Ancient Tomb — A80

1951 Unwmk. *Perf. 11*

Ordinary Paper

122	A76	5wn orange brown	1.00	*2.25*
123	A77	20wn purple	1.25	*3.00*
124	A78	50wn green	9.00	*17.50*
125	A79	100wn deep blue	15.00	17.50
126	A80	1000wn green	17.50	16.00
		Nos. 122-126 (5)	43.75	56.25
		Set, never hinged	105.00	

Rouletted 12

122a	A76	5wn orange brown	.80	*2.00*
123a	A77	20wn purple	.80	*2.00*
124a	A78	50wn green	2.00	*5.00*
125a	A79	100wn blue	2.00	*5.00*
		Nos. 122a-125a (4)	5.60	*14.00*
		Set, never hinged	16.00	

No. 126 also exists perforated 12½. See Nos. 187-189.

No. 93 Surcharged with New Value and Wavy Lines in Blue

1951 Wmk. 257 *Perf. 11½x11*

127 A49 100wn on 4wn rose car		.85	.60
a.	Inverted surcharge	24.00	*35.00*
	Never hinged	40.00	

Nos. 109, 101, 102 and 104 Surcharged in Blue or Brown

Perf. 11

128 A65 200wn on 15wn 2.75 6.00
a. Inverted surcharge 30.00
Never hinged 50.00
129 A57 300wn on 10wn (Br) 5.75 4.50
a. Inverted surcharge 30.00
Never hinged 50.00
130 A58 300wn on 20wn 4.50 4.50
a. Inverted surcharge 35.00
Never hinged 75.00
131 A60 300wn on 50wn (Br) 7.00 3.50
Nos. 127-131 (5) 20.85 19.10
Set, never hinged 100.00

Size and details of surcharge varies. Numeral upright on Nos. 129 and 131; numeral slanted on Nos. 175 and 179. See Nos. 174-181.

On No. 130, the zeros in "300" are octagonal; on No. 177B they are oval.

Flags of US and Korea and Statue of Liberty — A81

Design (blue stamps): Flag of same country as preceding green stamp, UN emblem and doves.

1951-52 Wmk. 257 *Perf. 11*

Flags in Natural Colors, Participating Country at Left

132 A81 500wn green 8.25 4.50
133 A81 500wn blue 8.25 4.50
134 A81 500wn grn *(Australia)* 7.00 4.50
135 A81 500wn blue 8.25 4.50
136 A81 500wn grn *(Belgium)* 7.00 4.00
137 A81 500wn blue 7.00 4.00
138 A81 500wn grn *(Britain)* 7.25 5.00
139 A81 500wn blue 7.25 5.00
140 A81 500wn grn *(Canada)* 7.25 5.00
141 A81 500wn blue 7.00 4.00
142 A81 500wn grn *(Colombia)* 7.00 4.00
143 A81 500wn blue 8.25 5.00
144 A81 500wn grn *(Denmark)* 12.00 *10.00*
145 A81 500wn blue 12.50 *10.00*
146 A81 500wn grn *(Ethiopia)* 7.00 4.00
147 A81 500wn blue 8.25 5.00
148 A81 500wn grn *(France)* 7.00 4.00
149 A81 500wn blue 8.25 5.00
150 A81 500wn grn *(Greece)* 8.25 5.00
151 A81 500wn blue 8.25 5.00
152 A81 500wn grn *(India)* 10.00 5.75
153 A81 500wn blue 11.00 6.50
154 A81 500wn grn *(Italy)* 10.00 5.75
a. Flag without crown ('52) 12.00
155 A81 500wn blue 10.00 5.75
a. Flag without crown ('52) 12.00
156 A81 500wn grn *(Luxembourg)* 10.00 5.75
157 A81 500wn blue 8.25 5.00
158 A81 500wn grn *(Netherlands)* 7.00 4.00
159 A81 500wn blue 7.00 4.00
160 A81 500wn grn *(New Zealand)* 8.25 5.00
161 A81 500wn blue 8.25 5.00
162 A81 500wn grn *(Norway)* 10.00 5.75
163 A81 500wn blue 10.00 5.75
164 A81 500wn grn *(Philippines)* 8.25 5.00
165 A81 500wn blue 8.25 5.00
166 A81 500wn grn *(Sweden)* 7.00 4.00
167 A81 500wn blue 8.25 5.00
168 A81 500wn grn *(Thailand)* 7.00 4.00
169 A81 500wn blue 8.25 5.00
170 A81 500wn grn*(Turkey)* 8.25 5.00
171 A81 500wn blue 8.25 5.00
172 A81 500wn grn *(Union of So. Africa)* 8.25 5.00
173 A81 500wn blue 8.25 5.00
Nos. 132-173 (42) 351.00 214.00
Set, never hinged 600.00

Twenty-two imperf. souvenir sheets of two, containing the green and the blue stamps for each participating country (including both types of Italy) were issued. Size: 140x90mm. Value, set $800.

Nos. 93-94, 101-105, 109-110 Surcharged Like Nos. 128-131 in Blue or Brown

1951 Wmk. 257 *Perf. 11½x11, 11*

174 A49 300wn on 4wn 2.75 *4.00*
a. Inverted surcharge 30.00 —
Never hinged 50.00
175 A57 300wn on 10wn (Br) 1.75 *5.00*
a. Inverted surcharge 30.00 —
Never hinged 50.00
176 A50 300wn on 14wn (Br) 3.25 *4.00*
a. 300wn on 14wn lt bl 3,750. 1,200.
b. Inverted surcharge 30.00 —
Never hinged 50.00
177 A65 300wn on 15wn 2.75 *4.00*
a. Inverted surcharge 30.00 —
Never hinged 50.00
177B A58 300wn on 20wn 7.00 5.00
178 A59 300wn on 30wn (Br) 2.75 *4.00*
a. Inverted surcharge 30.00 —
Never hinged 50.00
179 A60 300wn on 50wn (Br) 2.75 3.50
180 A66 300wn on 65wn (Br) 1.75 *4.00*
a. Inverted monad 90.00 —
181 A61 300wn on 100wn 3.25 3.25
a. Inverted surcharge 45.00 —
Never hinged 75.00
Nos. 174-181 (9) 28.00 36.75
Set, never hinged 75.00

"300" slanted on Nos. 175, 177B and 179; "300" upright on Nos. 129 and 131. The surcharge exists double on several of these stamps.

No. 177B differs from No. 130 in detail noted after No. 131.

Syngman Rhee and "Happiness" — A82

1952, Sept. 10 Litho. *Perf. 12½*

182 A82 1000wn dark green 3.00 *8.00*
Never hinged 8.00

Second inauguration of President Syngman Rhee, Aug. 15, 1952.

Sok Kul Am, Near Kyongju — A83

Bool Gook Temple, Kyongju — A84

Tombstone of Mu Yal Wang — A85

Choong Yul Sa Shrine, Tongyung — A86

1952 Wmk. 257 Typo. *Perf. 12½*

183 A83 200wn henna brown .55 *1.25*
184 A84 300wn green 1.00 1.25
185 A85 500wn carmine 1.10 *1.60*
186 A86 2000wn deep blue .85 .85

Rough Perf. 10-11, 11½x11 and Compound

Litho.

186A A83 200wn henna brown .80 *1.60*
186B A84 300wn green .65 *.85*
Nos. 183-186B (6) 4.95 7.40
Set, never hinged 15.00

Types of 1951

Designs slightly smaller

1952-53 *Rough Perf. 10-11*

187 A77 20wn purple 1.00 *3.00*
187A A78 50wn green 14.00 *22.50*
187B A79 100wn deep blue 1.60 1.60
187C A80 1000wn green 82.50 30.00
Nos. 187-187C (4) 99.10 57.10
Set, never hinged 225.00

Designs slightly larger

Perf. 12½

187D A78 50wn green 1.75 2.75
188 A79 100wn deep blue 1.00 *2.00*
189 A80 1000wn green ('53) 3.50 .85
Nos. 187D-189 (3) 6.25 5.60
Set, never hinged 13.00

Type of 1952

1953

189A A85 500wn deep blue 35.00 *160.00*

All examples of No. 189A were affixed to postal cards before sale. Values are for stamps removed from the cards.

See Nos. 191-192, 203B, 248.

Types of 1952 and

Planting Trees — A87

Wmk. 257

1953, Apr. 5 Litho. *Perf. 12½*

190 A87 1h aqua .35 *.65*
191 A85 2h aqua .45 .45
192 A85 5h bright green .55 .45
193 A87 10h bright green 1.60 1.50
194 A86 20h brown 1.90 *1.60*
Nos. 190-194 (5) 4.85 4.65
Set, never hinged 12.00

See Nos. 203A, 247.

Map and YMCA Emblem — A88

1953, Oct. 25 *Perf. 13½*

195 A88 10h dk slate bl & red 2.25 *4.00*
Never hinged 6.50

50th anniv. of the Korean YMCA.

Tombstone of Mu Yal Wang — A88a

A89

Sika Deer — A90

1954, Apr. *Perf. 12½*

196 A88a 5h dark green 1.10 *1.25*
197 A89 100h brown carmine 7.00 3.00
198 A90 500h brown orange 35.00 6.00
199 A90 1000h bister brown 80.00 7.00
Nos. 196-199 (4) 123.10 17.25
Set, never hinged 250.00

See Nos. 203C, 203D, 238-239, 248A, 250-251, 259, 261-262, 269-270, 279, 281-282.

Dok Do (Dok Island) — A91

Design: 10h, Dok Do, lateral view.

1954, Sept. 15

200 A91 2h claret .60 *2.50*
201 A91 5h blue 1.25 *2.50*
202 A91 10h blue green 2.00 *2.50*
Nos. 200-202 (3) 3.85 7.50
Set, never hinged 10.00

Moth and Flag — A92

Pagoda Park, Seoul — A92a

1954, Apr. 16 Wmk. 257 *Perf. 12½*

202A A92 10h brown 2.50 2.00
203 A92a 30h dark blue .55 1.50
Set, never hinged 5.00

See Nos. 203E, 260, 280.

Types of 1952-54

1955-56 Unwmk. *Perf. 12½*

Laid Paper

203A A87 1h aqua ('56) .30 *.50*
203B A85 2h aqua ('56) .30 *.50*
203C A88a 5h brt green ('56) .30 *.40*
203D A89 100h brown carmine 8.00 4.50
203E A92a 200h violet 6.00 2.50
Nos. 203A-203E (5) 14.90 8.40
Set, never hinged 55.00

On No. 203C the right hand character is redrawn as in illustration above No. 212D.

Nos. 203A and 203C are found on horizontally and vertically laid paper.

Erosion Control on Mountainside A93

1954, Dec. 12 Wmk. 257

204 A93 10h dk grn & yel grn 1.50 1.25
205 A93 19h dk grn & yel grn 1.50 *2.00*
Set, never hinged 12.50

Issued to publicize the 1954 forestation campaign.

Presidents Rhee and Eisenhower Shaking Hands — A94

1954, Dec. 25 *Perf. 13½*

206 A94 10h violet blue 1.40 *1.60*
207 A94 19h brown 1.40 *1.60*
208 A94 71h dull green 2.50 2.50
Nos. 206-208 (3) 5.30 5.70
Set, never hinged 15.00

Adoption of the US-Korea mutual defense treaty.

"Reconstruction"
A95

Wmk. 257

1955, Feb. 10 Litho. *Perf. 12½*

209 A95 10h brown 1.75 3.00
210 A95 15h violet 1.75 3.00
211 A95 20h blue 500.00 20.00
Never hinged 1,250.
212 A95 50h plum 5.00 1.60
Nos. 209-210,212 (3) 8.50
Set, #209-210, 212, never hinged 20.00
Nos. 209-212 (4) 27.60

Korea's industrial reconstruction.

1955, Oct. 19 Unwmk. *Perf. 12½*
Laid Paper

212A A95 15h violet 1.75 1.00
212B A95 20h blue 1.75 1.00
212C A95 50h plum 3.00 1.40
Nos. 212A-212C (3) 6.50 3.40
Set, never hinged 18.00

No. 212B is found on horizontally and vertically laid paper.

Same with Right Character at Top Redrawn

Original

Redrawn

1956, June 5 Unwmk. *Perf. 12½*
Laid Paper

212D A95 10h brown 2.00 *2.50*
212E A95 15h violet 2.00 *2.50*
212F A95 20h blue 2.00 .85
a. Booklet pane of 6 175.00
Nos. 212D-212F (3) 6.00 5.85
Set, never hinged 16.00

Nos. 212D-212F are found on horizontally and vertically laid paper. See Nos. 248B, 256, 272, 276.

Rotary Emblem — A96

1955, Feb. 23 Wmk. 257 *Perf. 13½*

213 A96 20h violet 4.00 3.00
214 A96 25h dull green 2.00 1.50
215 A96 71h magenta 2.00 1.50
Nos. 213-215 (3) 8.00 6.00
Set, never hinged 15.00

Rotary International, 50th anniversary.

Syngman Rhee, 80th Birthday, Apr. 26 — A98

1955, Mar. 26

217 A98 20h deep blue 8.00 8.00
Never hinged 20.00

Flag and Arch of Independence
A99

1955, Aug. 15 Litho. *Perf. 13½*

218 A99 40h Prus green 3.00 2.00
219 A99 100h lake 3.00 3.00
Set, never hinged 18.00

Tenth anniversary of independence.

UN Emblem in Circle of Clasped Hands — A100

1955, Oct. 24

221 A100 20h bluish green 1.75 1.50
222 A100 55h aqua 1.75 1.50
Set, never hinged 9.00

United Nations, 10th anniversary.

Olympic Torch and Runners — A101

1955, Oct. 23

223 A101 20h claret 2.00 2.00
224 A101 55h dark green 2.00 2.00
Set, never hinged 10.00

36th National Athletic Meet.

Adm. Li Sun-sin, Navy Flag and Tortoise Ship
A102

Perf. 13x13½

1955, Nov. 11 Unwmk.
Laid Paper

225 A102 20h violet blue 2.00 2.00
Never hinged 9.00

Korean Navy, 10th anniversary.

Rhee Monument near Seoul — A103

1956, Mar. 26 *Perf. 13½x13*

226 A103 20h dull green 2.50 2.50
Never hinged 7.50

81st birthday of Pres. Syngman Rhee.
No. 226 is found on horizontally and vertically laid paper.

Third Inauguration of Pres. Syngman Rhee — A104

1956, Aug. 15 *Perf. 13x13½*

227 A104 20h brown 35.00 25.00
228 A104 55h violet blue 15.00 12.00
Set, never hinged 150.00

Olympic Rings and Torch — A105

1956, Nov. 1 Litho. *Perf. 12½*
Laid Paper

229 A105 20h red orange 2.00 *2.50*
230 A105 55h brt green 2.00 *2.50*
Set, never hinged 10.00

16th Olympic Games in Melbourne, 11/22-12/8.

Central Post Office, Seoul
A107

Stamp of 1884 — A108

Mail Delivered by Donkey
A109

1956, Dec. 4 Laid Paper Unwmk.

232 A107 20h lt blue green 4.00 3.00
233 A108 50h lt carmine 6.00 5.00
234 A109 55h green 3.00 2.00
Nos. 232-234 (3) 13.00 10.00
Set, never hinged 40.00

Issued to commemorate Postal Day.

Types of 1954 Redrawn and

Hibiscus — A110

King Sejong — A111

Kyongju Observatory
A112

No Hwan Symbol; Redrawn Character

1956, Dec. 4 Unwmk. *Perf. 12½*
Laid Paper

235 A110 10h lilac rose .80 .75
236 A111 20h lilac 1.40 .75
237 A112 50h violet 1.75 .75
238 A89 100h brown carmine 10.50 4.50
239 A90 500h brown orange 26.00 5.00
Nos. 235-239 (5) 40.45 11.75
Set, never hinged 100.00

On Nos. 238-239, the character after numeral has been omitted and the last character of the inscription has been redrawn as illustrated above No. 212D.

Nos. 235-236 are found on horizontally and vertically laid paper.

See Nos. 240-242, 253, 255, 258, 273, 275, 278, 291Bd, 291Bf, B3-B4.

Types of 1956

1957, Jan. 21 Wmk. 312 *Perf. 12½*

240 A110 10h lilac rose .90 .65
241 A111 20h red lilac 2.10 1.25
242 A112 50h violet 3.00 .65
Nos. 240-242 (3) 6.00 2.55
Set, never hinged 15.00

Telecommunication Symbols — A117

1957, Jan. 31 *Perf. 13½*

243 A117 40h lt ultra 1.50 1.40
244 A117 55h brt green 1.50 1.40
Set, never hinged 6.00

5th anniv. of Korea's joining the ITU.

Boy Scout and Emblem
A118

1957, Feb. 27 Wmk. 312

245 A118 40h pale purple 1.00 *1.40*
246 A118 55h lt magenta 1.00 *1.40*
Set, never hinged 5.00

50th anniversary of Boy Scout movement.

Types of 1953-56
Top Right Character Redrawn; Hwan Symbol Retained

1957 Wmk. 312 *Perf. 12½*

247 A87 1h aqua .35 *.55*
248 A85 2h aqua .45 *.55*
248A A88a 5h brt green .45 *.55*
248B A95 15h violet 3.50 2.00
Nos. 247-248B (4) 4.75 3.65
Set, never hinged 12.00

Redrawn Types of 1954, 1956 and

Planting Trees — A119

South Gate, Seoul — A120

Tiger
A121

Diamond Mountains
A122

No Hwan Symbol; Redrawn Character

1957 Wmk. 312 Litho. *Perf. 12½*

249 A119 2h aqua .30 *.40*
250 A88a 4h aqua .45 .40
251 A88a 5h emerald .45 .40
252 A120 10h green .45 .20
253 A110 20h lilac rose .55 .40
254 A121 30h pale lilac .55 .40
255 A111 40h red lilac .75 .35
a. Booklet pane of 6 80.00
256 A95 50h lake 3.25 .65
257 A122 55h violet brn 1.10 1.00
258 A112 100h violet 1.50 .50
259 A89 200h brown car 1.75 .50
260 A92a 400h brt violet 27.50 5.00
261 A90 500h ocher 27.50 6.50
262 A90 1000h dk ol bis 55.00 12.50
Nos. 249-262 (14) 121.10 29.20
Set, never hinged 300.00

The "redrawn character" is illustrated above No. 212D.
See Nos. 268, 271, 274, 277, 291c, 291e.

Mercury and Flags of Korea and US
A123

1957, Nov. 7 Wmk. 312 *Perf. 13½*

263 A123 40h dp orange .75 *.90*
264 A123 205h emerald 1.60 *1.90*
a. Souv. sheet of 2, #263-264, imperf. 750.00
Never hinged 1,500.
Set, never hinged 6.00

Treaty of friendship, commerce and navigation between Korea and the US.

Star of Bethlehem and Pine Cone — A124

Designs: 25h, Christmas tree and tassel. 30h, Christmas tree, window and dog.

1957, Dec. 11 Litho. *Perf. 12½*

265 A124 15h org, brn & grn 3.75 *2.00*
a. Souv. sheet of 1, imperf. 600.00
Never hinged 1,000.
266 A124 25h lt grn, yel & red 3.75 *2.00*
a. Souv. sheet of 1, imperf. 600.00
Never hinged 1,000.
267 A124 30h bl, lt grn & yel 7.50 3.00
a. Souv. sheet of 1, imperf. 600.00
Never hinged 1,000.
Nos. 265-267 (3) 15.00 7.00
Set, never hinged 35.00

Issued for Christmas and the New Year.

Redrawn Types of 1954-57

Wmk. 317

1957-59 Litho. *Perf. 12½*

268 A119 2h aqua .30 *.45*
269 A88a 4h aqua .45 .45
270 A88a 5h emerald ('58) .45 .45
271 A120 10h green .55 .45
272 A95 15h violet ('58) 2.25 2.25
273 A110 20h lilac rose .75 .35
274 A121 30h pale lilac ('58) .85 .35
275 A111 40h red lilac .85 .35
276 A95 50h lake ('58) 4.00 .80
277 A122 55h vio brn ('59) 1.25 .85
278 A112 100h violet 1.50 .45
279 A89 200h brn car ('59) 1.75 .45
280 A92a 400h brt vio ('59) 40.00 3.50
281 A90 500h ocher ('58) 35.00 3.50
282 A90 1000h dk ol bis ('58) 60.00 8.50
Nos. 268-282 (15) 149.95 23.15
Set, never hinged 375.00

Nos. 268-282 have no hwan symbol, and final character of inscription is the redrawn one illustrated above No. 212D.
See No. 291B.

Catalogue values for unused stamps in this section, from this point to the end of the section, are for Never Hinged items.

Winged Envelope — A125

1958, May 20 Wmk. 317

283 A125 40h dk blue & red 2.00 .75
a. Souv. sheet of 1, imperf. *1,900.*

Issued for the Second Postal Week.

Children Looking at Industrial Growth
A126

Design: 40h, Hibiscus forming "10".

1958, Aug. 15 *Perf. 13½*

284 A126 20h gray 1.60 .65
285 A126 40h dk carmine 2.40 .90
a. Souv. sheet of 2, # 284-285, imperf. 550.00

10th anniversary of Republic of Korea.

UNESCO Building, Paris
A127

1958, Nov. 3 Wmk. 317

286 A127 40h orange & green 1.25 .60
a. Souv. sheet of 1, imperf. 210.00

Opening of UNESCO. headquarters in Paris, Nov. 3.

Children Flying Kites — A128

Christmas Tree and Fortune Screen — A129

Children in Costume — A130

1958, Dec. 11 Litho. *Perf. 12½*

287 A128 15h yellow green 2.00 .75
a. Souv. sheet of 1, imperf. 75.00
288 A129 25h blue, red & yel 2.00 .75
a. Souv. sheet of 1, imperf. 75.00
289 A130 30h yellow, ultra & red 3.50 1.25
a. Souv. sheet of 1, imperf. 75.00
Nos. 287-289 (3) 7.50 2.75
Nos. 287a-289a (2) 5.50

Issued for Christmas and the New Year.

Flag and Pagoda Park
A131

1959, Mar. 1 *Perf. 13½*

290 A131 40h rose lilac & brn 1.25 .60
a. Souv. sheet of 1, imperf. 125.00 125.00

40th anniv. of Independence Movement Day.

Korean Marines Landing
A132

1959, Apr. 15

291 A132 40h olive grn 1.25 .60
a. Souv. sheet of 1, imperf. 12.50 12.50

Korean Marine Corps, 10th anniversary.

Types of 1956-57

Souvenir Sheet

Wmk. 317

1959, May 20 Litho. *Imperf.*

291B Sheet of 4 10.00 *12.00*
c. A120 10h green 1.40 1.00
d. A110 20h lilac rose 1.40 1.00
e. A121 30h pale lilac 1.40 1.00
f. A111 40h red lilac 1.40 1.00

3rd Postal Week, May 20-26.

WHO Emblem and Family
A133

1959, Aug. 17 Wmk. 317 *Perf. 13½*

292 A133 40h pink & rose vio 1.25 .65
a. Souv. sheet of 1, imperf. 12.50 12.50

10th anniv. of Korea's joining the WHO.

Diesel Train
A134

1959, Sept. 18 Litho.

293 A134 40h brown & bister 2.00 1.00
a. Souv. sheet of 1, imperf. 32.50 32.50

60th anniversary of Korean railroads.

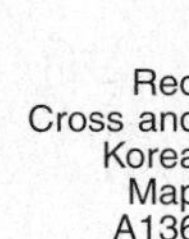

Relay Race and Emblem
A135

1959, Oct. 3

294 A135 40h lt bl & red brn 1.50 .70
a. Souv. sheet of 1, imperf. 15.00 15.00

40th National Athletic Meet.

Red Cross and Korea Map
A136

55h, Red Cross superimposed on globe.

1959, Oct. 27 *Perf. 13½*

295 A136 40h red & bl grn 1.00 .50
296 A136 55h pale lilac & red 1.50 .50
a. Souv. sheet of 2, #295-296, imperf. 35.00 35.00

Centenary of the Red Cross idea.

Old Postal Flag and New Communications Flag — A137

1959, Dec. 4

297 A137 40h blue & red 1.25 .60
a. Souv. sheet of 1, imperf. 20.00 20.00

75th anniv. of the Korean postal system.

Mice and Chinese Happy New Year Character — A138

Designs: 25h, Children singing Christmas hymns. 30h, Red-crested crane.

1959, Dec. 15 *Perf. 12½*

298 A138 15h gray, vio bl & pink 1.25 .35
a. Souv. sheet of 1, imperf. 30.00
299 A138 25h blue, red & emer 1.25 .40
a. Souv. sheet of 1, imperf. 30.00 30.00
300 A138 30h lt lilac, blk & red 2.50 .60
a. Souv. sheet of 1, imperf. 30.00 30.00
Nos. 298-300 (3) 5.00 1.35
Nos. 298a-300a (3) 90.00

Issued for Christmas and the New Year.

UPU Monument and Means of Transportation — A139

Wmk. 317

1960, Jan. 1 Litho. *Perf. 13½*

301 A139 40h grnsh bl & brn 1.50 .75
a. Souv. sheet of 1, imperf. 25.00 25.00

60th anniv. of Korean membership in the UPU.

Bee, Honeycomb and Clover — A140

Snail and Money Bag — A141

1960, Apr. 1 Wmk. 317 *Perf. 12½*

302 A140 10h emer, brn & org 1.25 .75
303 A141 20h pink, bl & brn 1.50 .75

Issued to encourage systematic saving by children. See No. 313, souvenir sheet.
See Nos. 377-380.

Uprooted Oak Emblem and Yin Yang — A142

1960, Apr. 7 Wmk. 312 *Perf. 13½*

304 A142 40h emer, car & ultra 1.25 .60
a. Souv. sheet of 1, imperf. 50.00 50.00

Issued to publicize World Refugee Year, July 1, 1959-June 30, 1960.

Dwight D. Eisenhower A143

1960, June 19 Litho. Wmk. 317

305 A143 40h bl, red & bluish grn 4.00 2.00
a. Souv. sheet of 1, imperf. 35.00 35.00

Pres. Eisenhower's visit to Korea, June 19.

Children in School and Ancient Home Teaching A144

1960, Aug. 3 Wmk. 317 *Perf. 13½*

306 A144 40h multicolored 1.25 .50
a. Souv. sheet of 1, imperf. 7.50 7.50

75th anniv. of the modern educational system.

Hibiscus and House of Councilors A145

1960, Aug. 8

307 A145 40h blue 1.25 .50
a. Souv. sheet of 1, imperf. 7.50 7.50

Inaugural session, House of Councilors.

Woman Holding Torch and Man with Flag — A146

1960, Aug. 15

308 A146 40h bis, lt bl & brn 1.25 .60
a. Souv. sheet of 1, imperf. 7.50 7.50

15th anniversary of liberation.

Weight Lifter A147

40h, South Gate, Seoul, & Olympic emblem.

1960, Aug. 25 Litho.

309 A147 20h brn, lt bl & sal 1.50 .75
310 A147 40h brn, lt bl & dk bl 1.50 .75
a. Souv. sheet of 2, #309-310, imperf. 25.00 25.00

17th Olympic Games, Rome, 8/25-9/11.

Swallow and Telegraph Pole — A148

1960, Sept. 28 *Perf. 13½*

311 A148 40h lt bl, lil & gray 1.50 .75
a. Souv. sheet of 1, imperf. 7.50 7.50

Establishment of telegraph service, 75th anniv.

Students and Sprout A149

1960, Oct. 1 Wmk. 317

312 A149 40h bl, sal pink & emer 1.25 .50
a. Souv. sheet of 1, imperf. 6.50 6.50

Rebirth of the Republic.

Savings Types of 1960
Souvenir Sheet

1960, Oct. 7 *Imperf.*

313 Sheet of two 4.50 4.50
a. A140 10h emer, brn & org 2.00 2.00
b. A141 20h pink, blue & brown 2.00 2.00

4th Postal Week, Oct. 7-13, and Intl. Letter Writing Week, Oct. 3-9.

Torch — A150

1960, Oct. 15 *Perf. 13½*

314 A150 40h dk bl, lt bl & yel 1.25 .50
a. Souv. sheet of 1, imperf. 6.50

Cultural Month (October).

UN Flag, Globe and Laurel — A151

1960, Oct. 24 Litho.

315 A151 40h rose lil, bl & grn 1.25 .50
a. Souv. sheet of 1, imperf. 6.50

15th anniversary of United Nations.

UN Emblem and Grave Markers — A152

1960, Nov. 1 Wmk. 317

316 A152 40h salmon & brn 1.25 .50
a. Souv. sheet of 1, imperf. 6.50

Establishment of the UN Memorial Cemetery, Tanggok, Pusan, Korea.

"Housing, Agriculture, Population" — A153

1960, Nov. 15 *Perf. 13½*

317 A153 40h multicolored 1.25 .50
a. Souv. sheet of 1, imperf. 6.50

Issued to publicize the 1960 census.

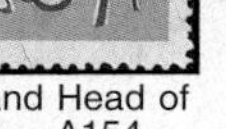

Boy and Head of Ox — A154

Star of Bethlehem and Korean Sock — A155

Girl Giving New Year's Greeting — A156

1960, Dec. 15 Litho. *Perf. 12½*

318 A154 15h gray, brn & org yel 1.75 .40
a. Souv. sheet of 1, imperf. 10.00 10.00
319 A155 25h vio bl, red & grn 2.25 .40
a. Souv. sheet of 1, imperf. 10.00 10.00
320 A156 30h red, vio bl & yel 3.00 .75
a. Souv. sheet of 1, imperf. 10.00 10.00
Nos. 318-320 (3) 7.00 1.55
Nos. 318a-320a (3) 30.00

Issued for Christmas and the New Year.

UN Emblem, Windsock and Ancient Rain Gauge A157

1961, Mar. 23 *Perf. 13½*

321 A157 40h lt blue & ultra 1.25 .50
a. Souv. sheet of 1, imperf. 4.00 4.00

1st World Meteorological Day.

Children, Globe and UN Emblem A158

1961, Apr. 7 Wmk. 317

322 A158 40h salmon & brown 1.25 .50
a. Souv. sheet of 1, imperf. 4.00 4.00

10th World Health Day.

Students Demonstrating — A159

1961, Apr. 19 Litho.

323 A159 40h red, grn & ultra 1.50 .60
a. Souv. sheet of 1, imperf. 10.00 10.00

1st anniv. of the Korean April revolution.

Workers — A160

1961, May 6

324 A160 40h brt green 1.25 .60
a. Souv. sheet of 1, imperf. 6.00 6.00

International Conference on Community Development, Seoul.

Girl Scout A161

1961, May 10

325 A161 40h brt green 1.25 .60
a. Souv. sheet of 1, imperf. 12.50 12.50

15th anniversary of Korea's Girl Scouts.

Soldier's Grave — A162

Wmk. 317

1961, June 6 Litho. *Perf. 13½*

326 A162 40h blk & ol gray 2.50 1.25
a. Souv. sheet of 1, imperf. 10.00 10.00

6th National Mourning Day.

Soldier with Torch — A163

1961, June 16

327 A163 40h brown & yellow 2.50 1.25
a. Souv. sheet of 1, imperf. 10.00 10.00

Military Revolution of May 16, 1961.

Map of Korea, Torch and Broken Chain — A164

1961, Aug. 15 Wmk. 317 *Perf. 13½*

328 A164 40h dk bl, ver & aqua 2.50 1.25
a. Souv. sheet of 1, imperf. 5.00 5.00

16th anniv. of liberation.

Flag and Servicemen — A165

1961, Oct. 1 **Litho.**
329 A165 40h vio bl, red & brn 3.00 1.25
a. Souv. sheet of 1, imperf. 5.00 5.00

Issued for Armed Forces Day.

Kyongbok Palace Art Museum — A166

1961, Nov. 1 **Wmk. 317** ***Perf. 13½***
330 A166 40h beige & dk brn 1.50 .60
a. Souv. sheet of 1, imperf. 4.00 4.00

10th Natl. Exhibition of Fine Arts.

"UNESCO," Candle and Laurel — A167

1961, Nov. 4
331 A167 40h lt grn & dk bl 1.50 .60
a. Souv. sheet of 1, imperf. 4.00 4.00

15th anniv. of UNESCO.

Mobile X-Ray Unit A168

1961, Nov. 16
332 A168 40h rose beige & red brn 1.25 .60
a. Souv. sheet of 1, imperf. 4.00 4.00

Tuberculosis Prevention Week.

Ginseng — A169

King Sejong and Hangul Alphabet — A170

Tristram's Woodpecker A171

Rice Farmer A172

Ancient Drums — A173

1961-62 **Unwmk.** **Litho.** ***Perf. 12½***
338 A169 20h rose brn ('62) 1.90 .60
339 A170 30h pale purple 5.25 .60
340 A171 40h dk blue & red 4.50 .60
341 A172 40h dk green ('62) 7.75 .75
342 A173 100h red brown 10.50 1.50
Nos. 338-342 (5) 29.90 4.05

See #363-366, 368, 388-392, 517-519, B5-B7.

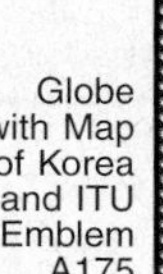

Globe with Map of Korea and ITU Emblem A175

1962, Jan. 31 **Unwmk.** ***Perf. 13½***
348 A175 40h ver & dk blue 1.75 1.00
a. Souv. sheet of 1, imperf. 12.00 12.00

10th anniv. of Korea's joining the ITU.

Atomic Reactor and Atom Symbol A176

1962, Mar. 30 **Litho.** ***Perf. 13½***
349 A176 40h lt bl, sl grn & ol gray 1.75 .50

Inauguration of the Triga Mark II atomic reactor.

Malaria Eradication Emblem and Mosquito — A177

1962, Apr. 7 **Unwmk.**
350 A177 40h green & red org 1.25 .75
a. Souv. sheet of 1, imperf. 3.50 3.50

WHO drive to eradicate malaria.

YWCA Emblem and Girl A178

1962, Apr. 20 ***Perf. 13½***
351 A178 40h pink & dk blue 3.25 .60

40th anniv. of the Korean Young Women's Christian Association.

South Gate and FPA Emblem A179

1962, May 12 **Wmk. 317**
352 A179 40h lt bl, dk vio & red 3.00 .75

Meeting of the Federation of Motion Picture Producers in Asia, May 12-16.

Men Pushing Cogwheel A180

Soldiers on Hang Kang Bridge — A181

Yin Yang and Factory A182

Wmk. 317

1962, May 16 **Litho.** ***Perf. 13½***
353 A180 30h brn & pale olive 3.00 1.00
a. Souv. sheet of 1, Korean text 20.00 20.00
b. Souv. sheet of 1, English text 35.00 35.00
354 A181 40h brn, lt bl & citron 3.00 1.00
a. Souv. sheet of 1, Korean text 20.00 20.00
b. Souv. sheet of 1, English text 35.00 35.00
355 A182 200h ultra, yel & red 22.50 9.00
a. Souv. sheet of 1, Korean text 35.00 35.00
b. Souv. sheet of 1, English text 75.00 75.00
Nos. 353-355 (3) 28.50 11.00

1st anniv. of the May 16th Revolution.
The souvenir sheets are imperf.
The sheets with English text also exist with "E" in "POSTAGE" omitted. The English-text sheets are not watermarked except those with "E" omitted. Value, each $75.

Tortoise Warship, 16th Century A183

Design: 4w, Tortoise ship, heading right.

1962, Aug. 14 **Unwmk.** ***Perf. 13½***
356 A183 2w dk bl & pale bl 10.00 1.50
357 A183 4w blk, bluish grn & lil 15.00 2.50

370th anniv. of Korea's victory in the naval battle with the Japanese off Hansan Island.

Flag, Scout Emblem and Tents — A184

Wmk. 312

1962, Oct. 5 **Litho.** ***Perf. 13½***
358 A184 4w brown, bl & red 1.90 .75
a. Souv. sheet of 1, imperf., unwmkd. 7.00 7.00

Wmk. 317

359 A184 4w green, bl & red 1.90 .75
a. Souv. sheet of 1, imperf., unwmkd. 7.00 7.00

40th anniv. of Korean Boy Scouts.

Types of 1961-62 and

Hanabusaya Asiatica — A185

Miruk Bosal — A186

Long-horned Beetle — A186a

Symbols of Thrift and Development A186b

Meesun Blossoms and Fruit A186c

Library of Early Buddhist Scriptures A186d

Sika Deer A186e

King Songdok Bell, 8th Cent. — A186f

Bodhisattva in Cavern Temple, Silla Dynasty — A187

Tile of Silla Dynasty — A187a

Designs: 20ch, Jin-Do dog. 1w, Folk dancers. 1.50w, Miruk Bosal. 2w, Ginseng. 3w, King Sejong. 4w, Rice farmer. 5w, Dragon waterpot. 10w, Ancient drums. 500w, Blue dragon fresco, Koguryo dynasty.

1962-63 **Unwmk.** **Litho.** ***Perf. 12½***

Ordinary Paper

Size: 22x25mm, 25x22mm

360 A186 20ch gldn brown 1.40 .40
361 A185 40ch blue 1.40 .40
362 A186 50ch claret brn 1.40 .40
363 A169 1w brt blue ('63) 2.75 .40
364 A169 2w red brown 4.25 .40
365 A170 3w violet brown 4.50 .40
366 A172 4w green 5.00 .40
367 A186 5w grnsh blue 5.50 .90
368 A173 10w red brown 85.00 4.00
369 A186c 20w lil rose ('63) 15.00 2.00
370 A186d 40w dl pur ('63) 125.00 5.00
Nos. 360-370 (11) 251.20 14.70

1964-66

Granite Paper

360a A186 20ch org brn .90 .25
361a A185 40ch blue .95 .25
362a A186 50ch claret brn .95 .25
362B A186a 60ch black ('66) .90 .30
363a A169 1w bright blue 3.00 .25
363B A186 1.50w dk sl grn ('66) .70 .30

364a A169 2w red brown 4.50 .40
365a A170 3w vio brown 13.00 .30
366a A172 4w green 5.75 .30
367a A186 5w grnsh blue 30.00 1.50
367B A186b 7w lilac rose ('66) 2.50 .75
368a A173 10w red brown 5.00 .40
369a A186c 20w lilac rose 10.00 1.50
370a A186d 40w vio brown 50.00 2.25
371 A186e 50w red brn 62.50 1.50
372 A186f 100w slate grn 100.00 3.00
373 A187 200w dk & lt grn ('65) 25.00 3.00
374 A187a 300w sl grn & buff ('65) 50.00 4.00
374A A187a 500w dk & lt bl ('65) 25.00 4.00
Nos. 360a-374A (19) 390.65 24.50

The paper of Nos. 360a to 374A contains a few colored fibers; the paper of Nos. 385-396 contains many fibers.

Postal counterfeits exist of Nos. 369a, 370a, 371 and 372.

See Nos. 385-396, 516, 521-522, 582-584, 1076-1079, B8.

Map, Mackerel and Trawler A188

1962, Oct. 10 ***Perf. 13½***
375 A188 4w dk bl & grnsh bl 3.50 .75

10th anniv. of the Pacific Fishery Council.

ICAO Emblem and Plane A189

1962, Dec. 11 ***Perf. 13½***
376 A189 4w blue & brown 1.75 .75
a. Souv. sheet of 1, imperf. 9.50 9.50

10th anniv. of Korea's joining the ICAO.

Savings Types of 1960

1962-64 **Unwmk.** ***Perf. 12½***
377 A140 1w emer, brn & org ('63) 5.50 1.25
a. Granite paper 20.00 9.00
378 A141 2w pink, bl & brn 9.50 1.50
a. Granite paper 12.50 2.50

Wmk. 317

379 A140 1w emer, brn & org ('64) 30.00 10.00
380 A141 2w pink, bl & brn ('64) 12.50 1.75
Nos. 377-380 (4) 57.50 14.50

Wheat Emblem A190

Wmk. 317

1963, Mar. 21 **Litho.** ***Perf. 13½***
381 A190 4w emer, dk bl & ocher 1.50 .75
a. Souv. sheet of 1, imperf. 4.25 4.25

FAO "Freedom from Hunger" campaign.

Globe and Letters A191

1963, Apr. 1
382 A191 4w rose lil, ol & dk bl 1.75 .60
a. Souv. sheet of 1, imperf. 4.00 4.00

1st anniv. of the formation of the Asian-Oceanic Postal Union, AOPU.

Centenary Emblem and World Map A192

1963, May 8 **Litho.**
383 A192 4w org, red & gray 1.25 .60
384 A192 4w lt bl, red & gray 1.25 .60
a. Souv. sheet of 2, #383-384, imperf. 10.00 10.00

Cent. of the Intl. Red Cross.

Types of 1961-63

Designs as before.

1963-64 **Wmk. 317** ***Perf. 12½***

Granite Paper

Size: 22x25mm, 25x22mm

385 A186 20ch gldn brn ('64) .85 .25
386 A185 40ch blue .85 .25
387 A186 50ch cl brn ('64) .85 .25
388 A169 1w brt blue 3.00 .35
389 A169 2w red brown 4.50 .40
390 A170 3w vio brown 13.00 .35
391 A172 4w green 6.00 .60
392 A173 10w red brown 5.00 .60
393 A186c 20w lil rose ('64) 10.00 1.75
394 A186d 40w dull purple 50.00 2.50
395 A186e 50w brown 62.50 2.00
396 A186f 100w slate grn 100.00 4.00
Nos. 385-396 (12) 256.55 13.30

Hibiscus and "15" A193

1963, Aug. 15 **Wmk. 317** ***Perf. 13½***
398 A193 4w vio bl, pale bl & red 2.50 1.25

15th anniversary of the Republic.

Army Nurse and Corps Emblem A194

1963, Aug. 26 **Litho.**
399 A194 4w citron, grn & blk 2.00 .85

Army Nurses Corps, 15th anniversary.

First Five-Year Plan Issue

Transformer and Power Transmission Tower A195

Irrigated Rice Fields A196

#402, Cement factory. #403, Coal Miner. #404, Oil refinery. #405, Fishing industry (ships). #406, Cargo ship and cargo. #407, Fertilizer plant and grain. #408, Radar and telephone. #409, Transportation (plane, train, ship and map).

1962-66 **Unwmk.** ***Perf. 12½***
400 A195 4w org & dk vio 15.00 1.50
401 A196 4w lt bl & vio bl 15.00 1.50

Wmk. 317

402 A195 4w dk bl & gray 5.00 1.25
403 A196 4w buff & brn 5.00 1.25
404 A195 4w yel & ultra 2.00 1.00
405 A196 4w lt bl & blk 2.00 1.00

Unwmk.

406 A195 4w pale pink & vio bl 2.00 1.00
407 A196 4w bis brn & blk 2.00 1.00
408 A195 7w yel bis & blk 3.75 1.00
409 A196 7w vio bl & lt bl 3.75 1.00
Nos. 400-409 (10) 55.50 11.50

Economic Development Five-Year Plan. Issued: #400-401, 12/28/62; #402-403, 9/1/63; #404-405, 6/15/64; #406-407, 6/1/65; #408-409, 6/1/66.

Ramses Temple, Abu Simbel — A197

Wmk. 317

1963, Oct. 1 **Litho.** ***Perf. 13½***
410 3w gray & ol gray 5.00 2.00
411 4w gray & ol gray 5.00 2.00
a. Souv. sheet of 2, #410-411, imperf. 10.00 10.00
b. A197 Pair, #410-411 12.00 10.00

UNESCO world campaign to save historic monuments in Nubia.

Rugby and Torch Bearer A199

1963, Oct. 4 **Wmk. 317** ***Perf. 13½***
412 A199 4w pale bl, red brn & dk grn 3.25 1.00

44th National Athletic Games.

Nurse & Mobile X-Ray Unit — A200

1963, Nov. 6 ***Perf. 13½***
413 A200 4w org & bluish blk 2.00 .75

10h anniv. of the Korean Natl. Tuberculosis Association.

Eleanor Roosevelt A201

1963, Dec. 10 **Litho.** **Wmk. 317**

Design: 4w, Hands holding torch and globe.

414 A201 3w lt red brn & dk bl 1.25 .50
415 A201 4w dl org, ol & dk bl 1.75 .75
a. Souv. sheet of 2, 414-415, imperf. 6.00 6.00

Eleanor Roosevelt; 15th anniv. of the Universal Declaration of Human Rights.

Korean Flag and UN Headquarters A202

1963, Dec. 12 **Wmk. 317** ***Perf. 13½***
416 A202 4w grnsh bl, ol & blk 1.25 .50
a. Souv. sheet of 1, imperf. 4.50 4.50

15th anniv. of Korea's recognition by the UN.

Tang-piri (Recorder) A203

Musical Instruments: No. 418, Pyen-kyeng (chimes). No. 419, Chang-ko (drums). No. 420, Tai-keum (large flute). No. 421, Taipyeng-so (Chinese oboe). No. 422, Na-bal (brass trumpet). No. 423, Hyang-pipa (Chinese short lute). No. 424, Wul-keum (banjo). No. 425, Kaya-ko (zither), horiz. No. 426, Wa-kong-hu (harp), horiz.

1963, Dec. 17 **Unwmk.**
417 A203 4w pink, blk & car 4.75 .75
418 A203 4w bl, bl grn & blk 4.75 .75
419 A203 4w rose, vio bl & brn 4.75 .75
420 A203 4w tan, dk grn & brn 4.75 .75
421 A203 4w yel, vio bl & brn 4.75 .75
422 A203 4w gray, brn & vio 4.75 .75
423 A203 4w pink, vio bl & red brn 4.75 .75
424 A203 4w grnsh bl, blk & bl 4.75 .75
425 A203 4w rose, red brn & blk 4.75 .75
426 A203 4w lil, blk & bl 4.75 .75
Nos. 417-426 (10) 47.50 7.50

Pres. Park and Capitol A204

1963, Dec. 17 **Wmk. 317**
427 A204 4w black & brt grn 47.50 12.50

Inauguration of Pres. Park Chung Hee.

Symbols of Metric System A205

1964, Jan. 1 **Litho.**
428 A205 4w multicolored 1.25 .50
a. Imperf., pair *75.00*

Introduction of the metric system.

UNESCO Emblem and Yin Yang — A206

1964, Jan. 30 Wmk. 317 *Perf. 13½*
429 A206 4w red, lt bl & ultra 1.50 .75

Korean Natl. Commission for UNESCO, 10th anniv.

Industrial Census A207

1964, Mar. 23 Wmk. 317 *Perf. 13½*
430 A207 4w gray, blk & red brn 1.50 .75

National Mining and Industrial Census.

YMCA Emblem and Head A208

1964, Apr. 12 Litho.
431 A208 4w ap grn, dk bl & red 1.25 .50

50th anniv. of the Korean YMCA.

Unisphere, Ginseng and Cargo Ship — A209

Design: 100w, Korean pavilion and globe.

1964, Apr. 22 Wmk. 317 *Perf. 13½*
432 A209 40w buff, red brn & grn 6.00 1.00
433 A209 100w bl red brn & ultra 20.00 5.00
a. Souv. sheet of 2, imperf. 47.50 47.50

New York World's Fair, 1964-65.

Secret Garden, Changdok Palace, Seoul A210

Views: 2w, Whahong Gate, Suwon. 3w, Uisang Pavilion, Yangyang-gun. 4w, Maitreya Buddha, Bopju Temple at Mt. Songni. 5w, Paekma River and Rock of Falling Flowers. 6w, Anab Pond, Kyongju. 7w, Choksok Pavilion, Chinju. 8w, Kwanghan Pavilion. 9w, Whaom Temple, Mt. Chiri. 10w, Chonjeyon Falls, Soguipo.

1964, May 25 Wmk. 317 *Perf. 13½*
Light Blue Background
434 A210 1w green 1.10 .50
435 A210 2w gray 1.10 .50
436 A210 3w dk green 1.10 .50
437 A210 4w emerald 2.25 1.00
438 A210 5w violet 4.00 1.50
439 A210 6w vio blue 5.25 2.00
a. Souv. sheet of 2 (5w, 6w) 17.50 17.50
440 A210 7w dk brown 7.50 2.50
a. Souv. sheet of 2 (4w, 7w) 17.50 17.50
441 A210 8w brown 8.00 2.50
a. Souv. sheet of 2 (3w, 8w) 17.50 17.50
442 A210 9w lt violet 8.00 2.50
a. Souv. sheet of 2 (2w, 9w) 17.50 17.50
443 A210 10w slate grn 11.00 3.00
a. Souv. sheet of 2 (1w, 10w) 17.50 17.50
Nos. 434-443 (10) 49.30 16.50
Nos. 439a-443a (5) 87.50

The five souvenir sheets are imperf.

Globe and Wheel A211

1964, July 1 Litho. *Perf. 13½*
444 A211 4w lt ol grn, dl brn & ocher 1.25 .60
a. Souv. sheet of 1, imperf. 4.00 4.00

Colombo Plan for co-operative economic development of south and southeast Asia.

Hands and World Health Organization Emblem — A212

1964, Aug. 17 Wmk. 317 *Perf. 13½*
445 A212 4w brt yel grn, yel grn & blk 1.25 .60
a. Souv. sheet of 1, imperf. 4.00 4.00

15th anniv. of Korea's joining the UN.

Runner A213

1964, Sept. 3
446 A213 4w red lil, grn & pink 3.50 1.25

45th Natl. Athletic Meet, Inchon, Sept. 3-8.

UPU Monument, Bern — A214

1964, Sept. 15
447 A214 4w pink, red brn & bl 1.25 .60
a. Souv. sheet of 1, imperf. 4.00 4.00

1st Intl. Cong. for establishing the UPU, 90th anniv.

Crane Hook and Emblem — A215

1964, Sept. 29 Wmk. 317 *Perf. 13½*
448 A215 4w red brn & dull grn 1.25 .60

5th Convention of the Intl. Federation of Asian and Western Pacific Contractors' Assoc. (IFAWPCA), Seoul, Sept. 29-Oct. 7.

Marathon Runners A216

#453, "V," Olympic rings, laurel & track, vert.

1964, Oct. 10 Litho.
449 A216 4w shown 2.50 .90
450 A216 4w Equestrian 2.50 .90
451 A216 4w Gymnast 2.50 .90
452 A216 4w Rowing 2.50 .90
453 A216 4w multicolored 2.50 .90
Nos. 449-453 (5) 12.50 4.50

18th Olympic Games, Tokyo, Oct. 10-25.

Souvenir Sheets of 1, Imperf., Unwmk.
449a A216 4w 3.50 3.50
450a A216 4w 3.50 3.50
451a A216 4w 3.50 3.50
452a A216 4w 3.50 3.50
453a A216 4w 3.50 3.50
Nos. 449a-453a (5) 17.50 17.50

Stamp of 1885 — A217

Yong Sik Hong — A218

1964, Dec. 4 Unwmk. *Perf. 13½*
454 A217 3w lilac, vio & dl bl grn 3.00 1.00
455 A218 4w gray, vio bl & blk 5.00 1.25

80th anniv. of the Korean postal system. Hong Yong-Sik (1855-84) was Korea's 1st general postmaster.

Pine Branch and Cones — A219

#457, Plum Blossoms. #458, Forsythia. #459, Azalea. #460, Lilac. #461, Sweetbrier. #462, Garden balsam. #463, Hibiscus. #464, Crape myrtle. #465, Chrysanthemum lucidum. #466, Paulownia coreana. #467, Bamboo.

1965 Litho. *Perf. 13½*
456 A219 4w pale grn, dp grn & brn 2.00 .75
457 A219 4w gray, blk, rose & yel 2.00 .75
458 A219 4w lt bl, yel & brn 2.00 .75
459 A219 4w brt grn, lil rose & sal 2.00 .75
460 A219 4w red lil & brt grn 2.00 .75
461 A219 4w yel grn, grn, car & brn 2.00 .75
462 A219 4w bl, grn & red 2.00 .75
463 A219 4w bluish gray, rose red & grn 2.00 .75
464 A219 4w multicolored 2.00 .75
465 A219 4w pale grn, dk brn, grn & car rose 2.00 .75
466 A219 4w buff, ol grn & brn 2.00 .75
467 A219 4w ultra & emer 2.00 .75
Nos. 456-467 (12) 24.00 9.00

Souvenir Sheets of 1, Imperf.
456a A219 4w 3.00 3.00
457a A219 4w 3.00 3.00
458a A219 4w 3.00 3.00
459a A219 4w 3.00 3.00
460a A219 4w 3.00 3.00
461a A219 4w 3.00 3.00
462a A219 4w 3.00 3.00
463a A219 4w 3.00 3.00
464a A219 4w 3.00 3.00
465a A219 4w 3.00 3.00
466a A219 4w 3.00 3.00
467a A219 4w 3.00 3.00
Nos. 456a-467a (12) 36.00 36.00

Dancing Women, PATA Emblem and Tabo Tower A220

1965, Mar. 26
468 A220 4w lt bl grn, dk brn & dk vio bl 1.00 .50
a. Souv. sheet of 1, imperf. 3.00 3.00

14th conf. of the Pacific Travel Association, Seoul, Mar. 26-Apr. 2.

Map of Viet Nam and Flag of Korean Assistance Group — A221

1965, Apr. 20 *Perf. 13½*
469 A221 4w blk, lt yel grn & grnsh bl 1.25 .50
a. Souv. sheet of 1, imperf. 3.50 3.50

Issued to honor the Korean military assistance group in Viet Nam.

Symbols of 7-Year Plan — A222

1965, May 1 Litho.
470 A222 4w emer, dk grn & dk brn 1.25 .50

Issued to publicize the 7-year plan for increased food production.

Scales with Families and Homes A223

1965, May 8
471 A223 4w lt & dk grn & gray 1.25 .50
a. Souv. sheet of 1, imperf. 3.00 3.00

May as Month of Family Planning.

ITU Emblem, Old and New Communication Equipment — A224

1965, May 17
472 A224 4w lt bl, car & blk 1.25 .50
a. Souv. sheet of 1, imperf. 3.00 3.00

Cent. of the ITU.

UN Emblem and Flags of Australia, Belgium, Great Britain, Canada and Colombia
A225

Gen. Douglas MacArthur and Flags of Korea, UN and US
A226

UN Emblem and Flags: No. 474, Denmark, Ethiopia, France, Greece and India. No. 475, Italy, Luxembourg, Netherlands, New Zealand and Norway. No. 476, Philippines, Sweden, Thailand, Turkey and South Africa.

1965, June 25

Flags in Original Colors

473	A225	4w	gray & vio bl	1.25	.75
474	A225	4w	grnsh bl & vio bl	1.25	.75
475	A225	4w	grnsh bl & vio bl	1.25	.75
476	A225	4w	grnsh bl & vio bl	1.25	.75
477	A226	10w	lt bl, blk, vio bl & red	4.00	1.50
			Nos. 473-477 (5)	9.00	4.50

15th anniv. of the participation of UN Forces in the Korean war.

Souvenir Sheets of 1, Imperf.

473a	A225	4w	1.75	1.75
474a	A225	4w	1.75	1.75
475a	A225	4w	1.75	1.75
476a	A225	4w	1.75	1.75
477a	A226	10w	3.00	3.00
	Nos. 473a-477a (5)		10.00	10.00

Flag, Factories and "20" — A227

South Gate, Seoul, Fireworks and Yin Yang — A228

1965, Aug. 15 **Litho.**

478 A227 4w lt bl, vio bl & red 2.25 .60
479 A228 10w vio bl, lt bl & red 2.75 .80

20th anniv. of liberation from the Japanese.

Factory, Leaf and Ants — A229

1965, Sept. 20 ***Perf. 13½***

480 A229 4w brt yel grn, brn & bister 1.25 .50

Issued to publicize the importance of saving.

Parabolic Antenna, Telephone Dial and Punched Tape
A230

Telegraph Operator, 1885
A231

1965, Sept. 28

481 A230 3w lt bl, blk & ol 2.00 .50
482 A231 10w citron, Prus bl & blk 4.00 .75

80th anniv. of telegraph service between Seoul and Inchon.

Korean Flag and Capitol, Seoul — A232

1965, Sept. 28

483 A232 3w org, slate grn & bl grn 2.50 1.25

15th anniversary of recapture of Seoul.

Pole Vault
A233

1965, Oct. 5

484 A233 3w black, lilac & salmon 2.00 1.00

46th Natl. Athletic Meet, Kwangju, Oct. 5-10.

ICY Emblem
A234

UN Flag and Headquarters, NY — A235

1965, Oct. 24 **Litho.**

485 A234 3w lt & dk grn & org brn 1.00 .50
a. Souv. sheet of 1, imperf. 3.50 3.50
486 A235 10w lt bl, vio bl & grn 2.00 .75
a. Souv. sheet of 1, imperf. 3.50 3.50

ICY, 1965, and 20th anniv. of the UN.

Child Posting Letter
A236

Design: 10w, Airmail envelope, telephone.

1965, Dec. 4 ***Perf. 13½***

487 A236 3w bl grn, blk, grn & red 2.50 1.00
488 A236 10w ol, dk bl & red 5.00 1.75

Tenth Communications Day.

Children with Sled — A237

Children and South Gate — A238

1965, Dec. 11 **Litho.** ***Perf. 12½***

489 A237 3w pale grn, vio bl & red 1.75 .60
490 A238 4w lt bl, grn, vio bl & red 2.75 1.75
a. Souv. sheet of 2, #489-490, imperf. 4.00 4.00

Issued for Christmas and the New Year.

Freedom House
A239

1966, Feb. 15 **Unwmk.** ***Perf. 12½***

491 A239 7w brt grn, blk & cit 1.75 .75
492 A239 39w lil, blk & pale grn 10.00 3.00
a. Souv. sheet of 2, #491-492, imperf. 17.50 17.50

Opening of "Freedom House" at Panmunjom.

Wildlife Issue

Mandarin Ducks
A240

Alaska Pollack
A241

Firefly
A242

Badger
A243

Birds: 5w, Japanese cranes. 7w, Ring-necked pheasants.

1966, Mar. 15 **Litho.** ***Perf. 12½***

493 A240 3w multicolored 2.00 1.25
494 A240 5w multicolored 2.10 1.25
495 A240 7w multicolored 3.25 1.25

1966, June 15

Fish: 5w, Manchurian trout. 7w, Yellow corvina.

496 A241 3w bl, dk brn & yel 2.50 .90
497 A241 5w grnsh bl, blk & mag 3.00 .90
498 A241 7w brt grnsh bl, blk & yel 4.00 1.00

1966, Sept. 15

Insects: 5w, Grasshopper. 7w, Silk butterfly (sericinus telamon).

499 A242 3w multicolored 2.00 .90
500 A242 5w dp yellow & multi 2.00 .90
501 A242 7w lt blue & multi 2.50 1.00

1966, Dec. 15

Animals: 5w, Asiatic black bear. 7w, Tiger.

502	A243	3w	multicolored	2.50	1.00
503	A243	5w	multicolored	2.50	1.00
504	A243	7w	multicolored	3.25	1.00
			Nos. 493-504 (12)	31.60	12.35

Souvenir Sheets of 1, Imperf.

493a	A240	3w	3.00	3.00
494a	A240	5w	3.00	3.00
495a	A240	7w	5.00	5.00
496a	A241	3w	3.00	3.00
497a	A241	5w	3.50	3.50
498a	A241	7w	4.00	4.00
499a	A242	3w	3.00	3.00
500a	A242	5w	3.00	3.00
501a	A242	7w	4.00	4.00
502a	A243	3w	4.00	4.00
503a	A243	5w	4.00	4.00
504a	A243	7w	5.00	5.00
	Nos. 493a-504a (12)		44.50	44.50

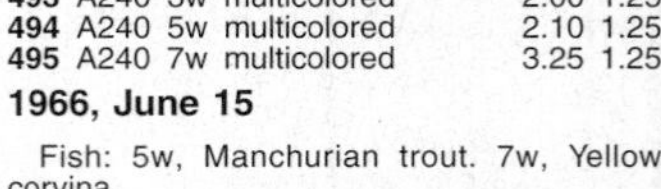

Hwansung-gun and Kwangnung Forests — A244

1966, Apr. 5 **Unwmk.** ***Perf. 12½***

505 A244 7w green & brown 1.25 .60

Forestation Movement.

Symbolic Newspaper Printing and Pen — A245

1966, Apr. 7 **Litho.**

506 A245 7w lt bl, vio brn & yel 1.00 .60

Tenth Newspaper Day.

Proper Guidance of Young People — A246

1966, May 1 **Unwmk.** ***Perf. 12½***

507 A246 7w Children & bell 1.00 .60

Opening of WHO Headquarters, Geneva — A247

1966, May 3 **Litho.**

508 A247 7w lt bl, blk & yel 1.25 .60
a. Souv. sheet of 1, imperf. 3.50 3.50
509 A247 39w bluish gray, yel & red 9.75 3.50

Girl Scout and Flag — A248

1966, May 10
510 A248 7w yel, emer & dk bl 2.00 .80

Girl Scouts of Korea, 20th anniversary.

Pres. Park and Flags of Korea, Malaysia, Thailand and Republic of China A249

1966, May 10
511 A249 7w multicolored 7.00 2.50

State visits of President Chung Hee Park.

Women's Ewha University, Seoul, and Student A250

1966, May 31
512 A250 7w lt bl, vio bl & dp org 1.00 .50

80th anniv. of modern education for women.

Types of 1961-66 Inscribed "Republic of Korea," and

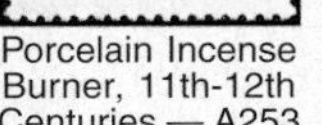

Porcelain Incense Burner, 11th-12th Centuries — A253

Celadon Vessel, 12th Century — A254

Unjin Miruk Buddha, Kwanchok Temple — A255

60ch, Long-horned beetle. 1w, Folk dancers. 2w, Ginseng. 3w, King Sejong. 5w, Dragon waterpot. 7w, Symbols of thrift & development.

Perf. 12½
1966, Aug. 20 **Unwmk.** **Litho.**
Size: 22x19mm, 19x22mm
Granite Paper

516 A186a 60ch gray green .40 .20
517 A169 1w green 3.00 4.00
518 A169 2w blue green .50 .20
519 A170 3w dull red brn .50 .20
521 A186 5w gray green 3.50 .70
522 A186b 7w grnsh blue 4.00 .30

Size: 22x25mm

523 A253 13w vio blue 4.00 .75
524 A254 60w green 22.50 1.50
525 A255 80w slate grn 8.50 1.50
Nos. 516-525 (9) 46.90 9.35

Souvenir Sheet

Carrier Pigeons — A258

1966, July 13 **Wmk. 317** ***Imperf.***
Red Brown Surcharge
534 A258 7w on 40h emer & dk grn 3.00 3.00

6th Intl. Letter Writing Week, June 13-19. No. 534 was not issued without surcharge.

Children and World Map Projection A259

1966, July 28 **Unwmk.** ***Perf. 12½***
535 A259 7w lt & dk vio bl & gray 1.25 .50
a. Souv. sheet of 1, imperf. 3.00 3.00

15th annual assembly of WCOTP (World Conf. of Teaching Profession), Seoul, July 28-Aug. 9.

Factory, Money Bag and Honeycomb A260

1966, Sept. 1 **Unwmk.** ***Perf. 12½***
536 A260 7w multicolored 1.00 .50

Issued to publicize systematic saving.

Map of Korea, and People A261

1966, Sept. 1 **Litho.**
537 A261 7w multicolored 1.00 .50

Ninth national census.

CISM Emblem and Round-Table Conference A262

1966, Sept. 29 **Unwmk.** ***Perf. 12½***
538 A262 7w multicolored 1.00 .50
a. Souv. sheet of 1, imperf. 3.00 3.00

21st General Assembly of the Intl. Military Sports Council (CISM), Seoul, 9/29-10/9.

Flags of Korea and Viet Nam and Korean Soldiers A263

1966, Oct. 1
539 A263 7w multicolored 8.00 2.25

1st anniv. of Korean combat troops in Viet Nam.

Wrestlers A264

1966, Oct. 10
540 A264 7w red brn, buff & blk 2.00 1.00

47th Natl. Athletic Meet, Seoul, Oct. 10-15.

Lions Emblem and Map of Southeast Asia — A265

1966, Oct. 15
541 A265 7w multicolored 1.00 .50
a. Souv. sheet of 1, imperf. 3.00 3.00

5th East and Southeast Asia Lions Convention, Seoul, Oct. 15-17.

Seoul University Emblem A266

1966, Oct. 15 **Litho.**
542 A266 7w multicolored 1.00 .50

20th anniversary of Seoul University.

Anticommunist League Emblem — A267

1966, Oct. 31 **Unwmk.** ***Perf. 12½***
543 A267 7w multicolored 1.00 .50
a. Souv. sheet of 1, imperf. 3.00 3.00

12th Conf. of the Asian Anticommunist League, Seoul, Oct. 31-Nov. 7.

Presidents Park and Johnson, Flags of US and Korea A268

1966, Oct. 31 **Litho.** ***Perf. 12½***
544 A268 7w multicolored 2.00 .75
545 A268 83w multicolored 12.00 3.50
a. Souv. sheet of 2, #544-545, imperf. 12.00 12.00

Visit of Pres. Lyndon B. Johnson to Korea.

UNESCO Emblem and Symbols of Learning — A269

1966, Nov. 4
546 A269 7w multicolored 1.00 .40
a. Souvenir sheets 3.00 3.00

20th anniv. of UNESCO.

Good Luck Bag and "Joy" A270

Ram and "Completion" A271

1966, Dec. 10 ***Perf. 12½x13, 13x12½***
547 A270 5w multicolored 1.75 .35
a. Souv. sheet of 1, imperf. 3.50 3.50
548 A271 7w multicolored 2.75 .35
a. Souv. sheet of 1, imperf. 3.50 3.50

Issued for Christmas and the New Year.

Syncom Satellite over Globe — A272

1967, Jan. 31 **Litho.** ***Perf. 12½***
549 A272 7w dk blue & multi 1.25 .60
a. Souv. sheet of 1, imperf. 3.50 3.50

15th anniv. of Korea's membership in the ITU.

Presidents Park and Lübke A273

Perf. 12½
1967, Mar. 2 **Litho.** **Unwmk.**
550 A273 7w multicolored 2.00 1.25
a. Souv. sheet of 1, imperf. 4.00 4.00

Visit of Pres. Heinrich Lübke of Germany, Mar. 2-6.

Hand Holding Coin, Industrial and Private Buildings A274

1967, Mar. 3
551 A274 7w lt green & blk brn 1.25 .50

1st anniv. of the Natl. Taxation Office.

Folklore Series

Okwangdae Clown — A275

5w, Sandi mask & dance, horiz. 7w, Hafoe mask.

1967, Mar. 15 **Litho.** ***Perf. 12½***
552 A275 4w gray, blk & yel 1.75 .60
553 A275 5w multicolored 1.75 .70
554 A275 7w multicolored 2.50 1.00

Perfect Peace Dance — A276

Designs: 4w, Sword dance, horiz. 7w, Buddhist Monk dance.

1967, June 15

555	A276 4w multicolored		1.75	.60
556	A276 5w multicolored		1.75	.70
557	A276 7w multicolored		2.50	1.00

Girls on Seesaw — A277

Designs: 4w, Girls on swing, horiz. 7w, Girls dancing in the moonlight.

1967, Sept. 15

558	A277 4w multicolored	3.50	.75
559	A277 5w multicolored	3.50	1.00
560	A277 7w multicolored	6.00	1.20

Korean Shuttlecock — A278

Designs: 5w, Girls celebrating full moon, horiz. 7w, Archery.

1967, Dec. 15

561	A278 4w multicolored	.75	.20
562	A278 5w multicolored	1.00	.20
563	A278 7w multicolored	1.50	.30
	Nos. 552-563 (12)	28.25	8.25

Souvenir Sheets of 1, Imperf.

552a	A275	4w	3.00	3.00
553a	A275	5w	3.00	3.00
554a	A275	7w	4.50	4.50
555a	A276	4w	3.00	3.00
556a	A276	5w	3.00	3.00
557a	A276	7w	4.50	4.50
558a	A277	4w	5.50	5.50
559a	A277	5w	5.50	5.50
560a	A277	7w	7.00	7.00
561a	A278	4w	3.50	3.50
562a	A278	5w	3.50	3.50
563a	A278	7w	4.00	4.00
	Nos. 552a-563a (12)		50.00	50.00

JCI Emblem and Kyunghoe Pavilion A279

1967, Apr. 13 Litho. *Perf. 12½*

564	A279 7w dk brn, brt grn, bl & red	1.25	.40
a.	Souv. sheet of 1, imperf.	3.00	3.00

Intl. Junior Chamber of Commerce Conf., Seoul, Apr. 13-16.

Emblem, Map of Far East — A280

1967, Apr. 24 Unwmk. *Perf. 12½*

565	A280 7w vio bl & multi	1.25	.40
a.	Souv. sheet of 1, imperf.	3.00	3.00

Issued to publicize the 5th Asian Pacific Dental Congress, Seoul, Apr. 24-28.

EXPO '67 Korean Pavilion A281

1967, Apr. 28

566	A281 7w yel, blk & red	3.00	.75
567	A281 83w lt bl, blk & red	19.50	5.00
a.	Souv. sheet of 2, #566-567, imperf.	16.00	16.00

EXPO '67, Intl. Exhibition, Montreal, Apr. 28-Oct. 27, 1967.

Worker, Soldier, Emblem and Buildings — A282

1967, May 1

568	A282 7w multicolored	1.50	.40

Veterans' Day, May 1.

Second Five-Year Plan Issue

Nut and Arrows A283

#570, Iron wheel and rail. #571, Express highway. #572, Cloverleaf intersection. #573, Rising income for fishermen and farmers (oysters, silk worm, mushrooms and bull's head). #574, Machine industry (cogwheels, automobile, wrench and motor). #575, Harbor. #576, Housing projects plans. #577, Atomic power plant. #578, Four Great River Valley development.

1967-71 Litho. *Perf. 12½*

569	A283 7w blk, red brn & dl org	6.00	1.00
570	A283 7w dl org, yel & blk	6.00	1.00
571	A283 7w grn, bl & ol	10.00	1.00
572	A283 7w dk brn, yel & grn	7.00	1.00

Perf. 13x12½

573	A283 7w brn, grn, yel & org	1.25	.40
574	A283 7w dk bl, lil rose & buff	1.25	.40
575	A283 10w dk bl, bl, yel & grn	1.25	.40
576	A283 10w lt bl, bl, grn & red	1.25	.40

Photo. *Perf. 13*

577	A283 10w blk, car & bl	1.25	.40
578	A283 10w blk, grn & brn	1.25	.40
	Nos. 569-578 (10)	36.50	6.40

Second Economic Development Five-Year Plan.

Issued: #569-570, 6/1/67; #571-572, 12/5/68; #573-574, 12/5/69; #575-576, 12/5/70; #577-578, 12/5/71.

President Park and Phoenix A284

1967, July 1 Unwmk. *Perf. 12½*

579	A284 7w multicolored	20.00	3.50
a.	Souv. sheet of 1, imperf.	60.00	60.00

Inauguration of President Park Chung Hee for a 2nd term, July 1, 1967.

Korean Boy Scout, Emblem and Tents — A285

20w, Korean Boy Scout emblem, bridge & tents.

1967, Aug. 10 Litho. *Perf. 12½*

580	A285 7w multicolored	1.00	.60
a.	Souv. sheet of 1, imperf.	5.00	5.00
581	A285 20w multicolored	5.00	2.25
a.	Souv. sheet of 1, imperf.	5.00	5.00

3rd Korean Boy Scout Jamboree, Hwarangdae, Seoul, Aug. 10-15.

Types of 1962-66 Redrawn (Inscribed "Republic of Korea")

Designs: 20w, Meesun blossoms and fruit. 40w, Library of early Buddhist scriptures. 50w, Deer.

1967, Aug. 25

Granite Paper

582	A186c 20w green & lt bl grn	70.00	1.50
583	A186d 40w dk grn & lt ol	42.50	1.50
584	A186e 50w dk brn & bister	9.00	1.50
	Nos. 582-584 (3)	121.50	4.50

The printing of redrawn designs of the regular issue of 1962-66 became necessary upon discovery of large quantities of counterfeits, made to defraud the post. The position of the denominations was changed and elaborate fine background tracings were added.

Freedom Center and Emblem A286

Hand Breaking Chain — A287

1967, Sept. 25 Litho. *Perf. 12½*

586	A286 5w multicolored	1.25	.40
a.	Souv. sheet of 1, imperf.	5.00	5.00
587	A287 7w multicolored	1.25	.40
a.	Souv. sheet of 1, imperf.	5.00	5.00

1st Conf. of the World Anti-Communist League, WACL, Taipei, China, Sept. 25-29.

Boxing — A288

1967, Oct. 5

Design: 7w, Women's basketball.

588	A288 5w tan & multi	1.75	.75
589	A288 7w pale rose & multi	2.75	.75

48th Natl. Athletic Meet, Seoul, Oct. 5-10.

Students' Memorial, Kwangjoo — A289

1967, Nov. 3 Litho. *Perf. 12½*

590	A289 7w lt green & multi	1.25	.40

Issued for Student Day commemorating 1929 students' uprising against Japan.

Symbolic Water Cycle — A290

1967, Nov. 20

591	A290 7w multicolored	1.25	.40

Hydrological Decade (UNESCO), 1965-74.

Children Spinning Top — A291

Monkey and Oriental Zodiac — A292

1967, Dec. 10

592	A291 5w sal, org & vio bl	2.50	.35
a.	Souv. sheet of 1, imperf.	3.50	3.50
593	A292 7w yel bis, brn & vio bl	3.00	.35
a.	Souv. sheet of 1, imperf.	3.50	3.50

Issued for Christmas and New Year.

Parabolic Antenna and Electric Waves — A293

1967, Dec. 21

594	A293 7w lt bl, blk & yel	1.25	.50
a.	Souv. sheet of 1, imperf.	3.00	3.00

Opening of the natl. microwave communications network, Dec. 21.

Carving from King Songdok Bell — A294

Earrings, 6th Cent. — A295

Flag — A296

Perf. 13x12½

1968, Feb. 1 Litho. Unwmk.

Granite Paper

595	A294 1w yellow & brown	.35	.20
596	A295 5w dk green & yellow	2.75	.40
597	A296 7w dark blue & red	1.25	.25
	Nos. 595-597 (3)	4.35	.85

WHO, 20th Anniv. — A297

1968, Apr. 7 Unwmk. *Perf. 12½*

598	A297 7w multicolored	1.25	.40
a.	Souv. sheet of 1, imperf.	3.00	3.00

EATA Emblem and Korean Buildings — A298

1968, Apr. 9 **Litho.**

599 A298 7w multicolored 1.25 .40
a. Souv. sheet of 1, imperf. 4.00 4.00

2nd General Meeting of the East Asia Travel Association (EATA), Seoul, Apr. 9-13.

Door Knocker, Factories and Emblem A299

1968, May 6 **Unwmk.** ***Perf. 12½***

600 A299 7w multicolored 1.25 .40
a. Souv. sheet of 1, imperf. 3.50 3.50

2nd Conf. of the Confederation of Asian Chambers of Commerce and Industry, Seoul.

Pres. Park and Emperor Haile Selassie A300

1968, May 18 **Litho.**

601 A300 7w multicolored 3.50 1.50
a. Souv. sheet of 1, imperf. 7.00 7.00

Visit of Haile Selassie I, May 18-20.

Mailman's Pouch A301

Mailman A302

1968, May 31 **Unwmk.** ***Perf. 12½***

602 A301 5w multicolored 1.25 .60
603 A302 7w multicolored 1.25 .60

First Postman's Day, May 31, 1968.

Atom Diagram and Symbols of Development A303

1968, June 1 **Litho.**

604 A303 7w dk bl, citron & ver 1.25 .40

Issued to promote science and technology.

Kyung Hee University and Conference Emblem A304

1968, June 18 **Unwmk.**

605 A304 7w bl, pink & blk 1.25 .40
a. Souv. sheet of 1, imperf. 5.00 5.00

2nd Conf. of the Intl. Association of University Presidents.

Liberated People A305

1968, July 1 **Litho.** ***Perf. 12½***

606 A305 7w multicolored 1.25 .40

Issued to publicize the movement to liberate people under communist rule.

Peacock and Industrial Plant — A306

1968, Aug. 15 **Unwmk.** ***Perf. 12½***

607 A306 7w multicolored 1.50 .40

Republic of Korea, 20th anniversary.

Fair Entrance A307

1968, Sept. 9 **Unwmk.** ***Perf. 12½***

608 A307 7w lilac & multi 1.50 .40

Issued to publicize the first Korean Trade Fair, Seoul, Sept. 9-Oct. 18.

Assembly Emblem and Pills — A308

1968, Sept. 16 **Litho.**

609 A308 7w multicolored 1.50 .40

3rd General Assembly of the Federation of Asian Pharmaceutical Associations, Seoul, Sept. 16-21.

Soldier, Insigne and Battle Scene — A309

#611, Sailor, insigne & ship's guns. #612, Servicemen & flags. #613, Aviator, insigne & planes. #614, Marine, insigne & landing group.

1968, Oct. 1

610 A309 7w green & org 6.00 2.00
611 A309 7w lt & dk blue 6.00 2.00
612 A309 7w dk blue & org 6.00 2.00
613 A309 7w dk & lt blue 6.00 2.00
614 A309 7w orange & grn 6.00 2.00
a. Vert. strip of 5, #610-614 32.50 10.00

20th anniv. of the Korean armed forces.

Colombo Plan Emblem and Globe — A310

1968, Oct. 8 **Litho.** ***Perf. 12½***

615 A310 7w dk brn, pale sal & grn 1.50 .35

19th meeting of the Consultative Committee of the Colombo Plan, Seoul, Oct. 8-28.

Bicycling (Type I) — A311

Type II — (2nd line flush left)

#617, Bicycling, Type II. #618-619, Wrestling. #620-621, Boxing. #622-623, Olympic flame, "68" & symbols of various sports events.

1968, Oct. 12 **Unwmk.** ***Perf. 12½***

616 A311 7w pink & multi (I) 12.50 4.50
617 A311 7w pink & multi (II) 12.50 4.50
a. Souv. sheet of 2, #616-617, imperf. 10.00 10.00
b. Pair, #616-617 30.00 10.00
618 A311 7w olive & multi (I) 12.50 4.50
619 A311 7w olive & multi (II) 12.50 4.50
a. Souv. sheet of 2, #618-619, imperf. 10.00 10.00
b. Pair, #618-619 30.00 10.00
620 A311 7w orange & multi (I) 12.50 4.50
621 A311 7w orange & multi (II) 12.50 4.50
a. Souv. sheet of 2, #620-621, imperf. 10.00 10.00
b. Pair, #620-621 30.00 10.00
622 A311 7w bluish grn & multi (I) 12.50 4.50
623 A311 7w bluish grn & multi (II) 12.50 4.50
a. Souv. sheet of 2, #622-623, imperf. 10.00 10.00
b. Pair, #622-623 30.00 10.00
Nos. 616-623 (8) 100.00 36.00

19th Olympic Games, Mexico City, 10/12-27.

The position of the "7" is reversed on Nos. 619, 621, 623 as are the designs of Nos. 619, 621.

"Search for Knowledge" and School Girls — A312

1968, Oct. 15

624 A312 7w multicolored 1.50 .40

60th anniv. of public secondary education for women.

Coin and Statistics A313

1968, Nov. 1

625 A313 7w multicolored 1.50 .40

National Wealth Survey.

Memorial to Students' Uprising — A314

1968, Nov. 23

626 A314 7w gray & multi 1.50 .40

Issued to commemorate the anti-communist students' uprising, Nov. 23, 1945.

Men With Banners Declaring Human Rights A315

1968, Dec. 10

627 A315 7w multicolored 1.50 .40

Declaration of Human Rights, 20th anniv.

Christmas Decorations A316

Cock and Good Luck Characters A317

1968, Dec. 11

628 A316 5w salmon & multi 9.00 .50
a. Souv. sheet of 1, imperf. 7.50 7.50
629 A317 7w multicolored 9.00 .50
a. Souv. sheet of 1, imperf. 7.50 7.50

Issued for Christmas and the New Year.

UN Emblems and Korean House A318

1968, Dec. 12

630 A318 7w lt blue & multi 1.25 .35

20th anniv. of the recognition of the Republic of Korea by the UN.

Regional Boy Scout Conf. — A319

Design: Boy Scout Emblem.

1968, Sept. 30 **Litho.** ***Perf. 12½***

631 A319 7w black & multi 2.00 .75

Sam-il Movement, 50th Anniv. — A320

1969, Mar. 1 **Unwmk.** ***Perf. 12½***

Design: Torch, map and students Demonstrating against Japan, 1919.

632 A320 7w multicolored 1.25 .40

Hyun Choong Sa Shrine and Tortoise Ships A321

1969, Apr. 28 Unwmk. *Perf. 12½*
633 A321 7w deep bl, grn & brn 1.25 .40

Completion of the Hyun Choong Sa Shrine at Onyang, dedicated to the memory of Adm. Li Sun-sin.

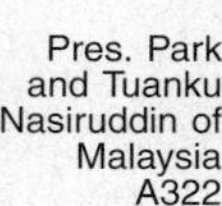

Pres. Park and Tuanku Nasiruddin of Malaysia A322

1969, Apr. 29 Litho.
634 A322 7w yellow & multi 1.50 .50
a. Souv. sheet of 1, imperf. *25.00*

Visit of Tuanku Ismail Nasiruddin, ruler of Malaysia, Apr. 29, 1969.

Hanabusaya Asiatica A323

Flag of Korea A324

Ancient Drums A325

Red-crested Cranes A326

Highway and Farm A327

Pitcher (12-13th Centuries) A328

Ceramic Duck (Water Jar) A329

Library of Early Buddhist Scriptures A330

Miruk Bosal — A333

1w, Old man's mask. #637, Stone lamp, 8th cent. #638, Chipmunk. #644, Tiger lily. #649, Bee. #651, Vase, Yi dynasty, 17th-18th centuries. #653, Gold crown, Silla Dynasty.

Zeros Omitted except 7w, No. 639

Perf. 13x12, 12x13 (Litho.); 13½x12½, 12½x13½ (Photo.)
Litho. (40ch, Nos. 641, 650); Photo.
1969-74 Unwmk.
Granite Paper (Lithographed); Ordinary Paper (Photogravure)

635 A323 40ch green 1.25 .30
636 A326 1w dk rose brn ('74) .40 .20
637 A328 5w brt plum .95 .25
638 A326 5w maroon ('74) .35 .20
639 A324 7w blue ("7.00") 3.25 .40
640 A324 7w blue ("7") 1.25 .30
641 A325 10w ultra 25.00 .70
642 A324 10w ultra ("10") ('70) 1.25 .25
643 A326 10w bl & dk bl ('73) 1.25 .40
644 A323 10w grn & multi ('73) .95 .20
645 A327 10w grn, red & gray ('73) .35 .20
647 A328 20w green 2.00 .40
648 A329 30w dull grn ('70) 3.25 .75
649 A326 30w yel & dk brn ('74) .75 .20
650 A330 40w vio bl & pink 40.00 2.25
651 A328 40w ultra & lilac 2.40 .75
652 A333 100w dp claret & yel 80.00 2.25
653 A333 100w brn & yel ('74) 35.00 2.25
Nos. 635-653 (18) 199.65 12.25

See No. 1090. For surcharge see No. B18. Counterfeits exist of No. 653.

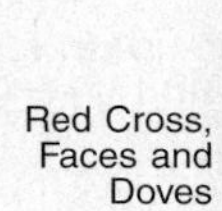

Red Cross, Faces and Doves A336

1969, May 5 Litho. *Perf. 12½*
654 A336 7w multicolored 1.50 .40
a. Souv. sheet of 1, imperf. 5.00 5.00

50th anniv. of the League of Red Cross Societies.

Savings Bank, Factories and Highway — A337

1969, May 20 Unwmk. *Perf. 12½*
655 A337 7w yellow grn & multi 1.25 .40

Second Economy Drive.

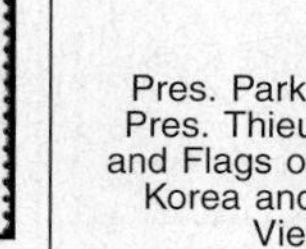
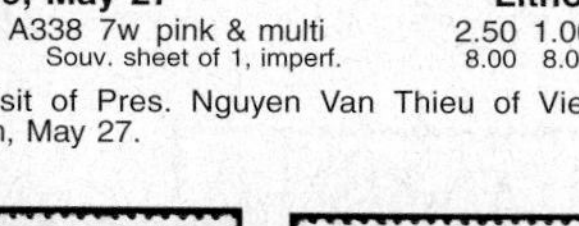
Pres. Park, Pres. Thieu and Flags of Korea and Viet Nam — A338

1969, May 27 Litho.
656 A338 7w pink & multi 2.50 1.00
a. Souv. sheet of 1, imperf. 8.00 8.00

Visit of Pres. Nguyen Van Thieu of Viet Nam, May 27.

"Reforestation and Parched Fields" — A339

Growing and Withering Plants — A340

1969, June 10
657 A339 7w multicolored 1.25 .35
658 A340 7w multicolored 1.25 .35

Issued to publicize the need for prevention of damages from floods and droughts.

Apollo 11, Separation of Second Stage A341

#660, Apollo 11, separation of 3rd Stage. #661, Orbits of command & landing modules around moon. #662, Astronauts gathering rock samples on moon. 40w, Spacecraft splashdown.

1969, Aug. 15 Unwmk. *Perf. 12½*
659 A341 10w indigo, bl & red 3.50 1.00
660 A341 10w indigo, bl & red 3.50 1.00
661 A341 20w indigo, bl, red & lem 3.50 1.00
662 A341 20w indigo, bl, red & lem 3.50 1.00
663 A341 40w indigo, bl & red 3.50 1.00
a. Souv. sheet of 5, #659-663, imperf. 35.00 35.00
b. Strip of 5, #659-663 17.50 9.00

Man's 1st landing on the moon, July 20, 1969. US astronauts Neil A. Armstrong and Col. Edwin E. Aldrin, Jr., with Lieut. Col. Michael Collins piloting Apollo 11.

Fable Issue

Girl and Stepmother A342

Kongji and Patji (Cinderella): 7w, Sparrows help Kongji separate rice. 10w, Ox helps Kongji to weed a field. 20w, Kongji in a sedan chair on the way to the palace.

1969, Sept. 1 Litho. *Perf. 12½*
664 A342 5w apple grn & multi 3.75 .75
665 A342 7w yellow & multi 3.75 .75
666 A342 10w lt violet & multi 5.50 1.25
667 A342 20w lt green & multi 5.50 1.25

The Sick Princess A343

1969, Nov. 1 *Perf. 13x12½*

"The Hare's Liver": 7w, Hare riding to the palace on back of turtle. 10w, Hare telling a lie to the King to save his life. 20w, Hare mocking the turtle.

668 A343 5w yellow & multi 2.25 .65
669 A343 7w lt vio & multi 2.25 .65
670 A343 10w lt grnsh bl & multi 2.25 .90
671 A343 20w lt yel grn & multi 3.50 .90

Mother Meeting Tiger — A344

1970, Jan. 5

"The Sun and the Moon": 7w, Tiger disguised as mother at children's house. 10w, Tiger, and children on tree. 20w, Children safe on cloud, and tiger falling to his death.

672 A344 5w orange & multi 2.25 .65
673 A344 7w gray grn & multi 2.25 .65
674 A344 10w lt green & multi 2.25 .90
675 A344 20w gray & multi 3.50 .90

Woodcutter Stealing Fairy's Clothes A345

1970, Mar. 5

Designs: No. 677, Woodcutter with wife and children. No. 678, Wife taking children to heaven. No. 679, Husband joining family in heaven.

676 A345 10w dull bl grn & multi 2.50 .90
677 A345 10w buff & multi 2.50 .90
678 A345 10w lt grnsh bl & multi 2.50 .90
679 A345 10w pink & multi 2.50 .90

Heungbu and Wife Release Healed Swallow A346

1970, May 5 *Perf. 12½*

Designs: No. 681, Heungbu and wife finding gold treasure in gourd. No. 682, Nolbu and wife with large gourd. No. 683, Demon emerging from gourd punishing evil Nolbu and wife.

680 A346 10w lt grnsh bl & multi 5.50 1.00
681 A346 10w orange & multi 5.50 1.00
682 A346 10w apple grn & multi 5.50 1.00
683 A346 10w tan & multi 5.50 1.00
Nos. 664-683 (20) 71.00 17.80

Souvenir Sheets of 1, Imperf.

664a A342 5w 5.50 5.50
665a A342 7w 5.50 5.50
666a A342 10w 5.50 5.50
667a A342 20w 5.50 5.50
668a A343 5w 5.00 5.00
669a A343 7w 5.00 5.00
670a A343 10w 5.00 5.00
671a A343 20w 5.00 5.00
672a A344 5w 5.00 5.00
673a A344 7w 5.00 5.00
674a A344 10w 5.00 5.00
675a A344 20w 5.00 5.00
676a A345 10w 5.00 5.00
677a A345 10w 5.00 5.00
678a A345 10w 5.00 5.00
679a A345 10w 5.00 5.00
680a A346 10w 10.00 10.00
681a A346 10w 10.00 10.00
682a A346 10w 10.00 10.00
683a A346 10w 10.00 10.00
Nos. 664a-683a (20) 122.00 122.00

1869 Locomotive and Diesel Train — A347

Design: No. 685, Early locomotive.

Perf. 12½
1969, Sept. 18 Litho. Unwmk.
684 A347 7w yellow & multi 1.50 .60
685 A347 7w green & multi 1.50 .60

70th anniversary of Korean Railroads.

Formation of F-5A Planes A348

Design: No. 687, F-4D Phantom.

1969, Oct. 1 Photo. *Perf. 13½x13*
686 A348 10w blue, blk & car 5.00 .75

Litho. *Perf. 13x12½*
687 A348 10w multicolored 6.00 .75

20th anniversary of Korean Air Force.

Cha-jun Game A349

1969, Oct. 3
688 A349 7w ap grn, dk bl & blk 1.00 .35

10th National Festival of Traditional Skills.

"Telecommunication" — A394

1971, May 17

755 A394 10w blue & multi 1.10 .45

3rd World Telecommunications Day.

UN Organizations A395

Korean Flag — A396

No. 756, ILO. No. 757, FAO. No. 758, General Assembly (UN Headquarters). No. 759, UNESCO. No. 760, WHO. No. 761, World Bank. No. 762, Intl. Development Association (IDA). No. 763, Security Council. No. 764, Intl. Finance Corp. (IFC). No. 765, Intl. Monetary Fund. No. 766, ICAO. No. 767, Economic and Social Council. No. 768, Korean Flag. No. 769, Trusteeship Council. No. 770, UPU. No. 771, ITU. No. 772, World Meteorological Org. (WMO). No. 773, Intl. Court of Justice. No. 774, Intl. Maritime Consultative Org. No. 775, UNICEF. No. 776, Intl. Atomic Energy Agency. No. 777, UN Industrial Development Org. No. 778, UN Commission for the Unification and Rehabilitation of Korea. No. 779, UN Development Program. No. 780, UN Conf. on Trade and Development.

1971, May 30 ***Perf. 13½x13***

756 A395 10w green, blk & pink 3.00 1.20
757 A395 10w pink, blk & bl 3.00 1.20
758 A395 10w bl, blk, grn & pink 3.00 1.20
759 A395 10w pink, blk & bl 3.00 1.20
760 A395 10w green, blk & pink 3.00 1.20
761 A395 10w pink, blk & bl 3.00 1.20
762 A395 10w blue, blk & pink 3.00 1.20
763 A395 10w green, blk & pink 3.00 1.20
764 A395 10w blue, blk & pink 3.00 1.20
765 A395 10w pink, blk & bl 3.00 1.20
766 A395 10w blue, blk & pink 3.00 1.20
767 A395 10w green, blk & pink 3.00 1.20
768 A396 10w blue, blk & pink 3.00 1.20
769 A395 10w green, blk & pink 3.00 1.20
770 A395 10w blue, blk & pink 3.00 1.20
771 A395 10w pink, blk & bl 3.00 1.20
772 A395 10w blue, blk & pink 3.00 1.20
773 A395 10w green, blk & pink 3.00 1.20
774 A395 10w blue, blk & pink 3.00 1.20
775 A395 10w pink, blk & bl 3.00 1.20
776 A395 10w green, blk & pink 3.00 1.20
777 A395 10w pink, blk & bl 3.00 1.20
778 A395 10w blue, blk & pink 3.00 1.20
779 A395 10w pink, blk & bl 3.00 1.20
780 A395 10w green, blk & pink 3.00 1.20
Nos. 756-780 (25) 75.00 30.00

Sheet of 50 incorporates 2 each of #756-780.

Boat Ride, by Shin Yun-bok — A397

Man and Boy under Pine Tree — A398

Paintings by Shin Yun-bok: No. 782, Greeting travelers. No. 783, Sword dance. No. 784, Lady traveling with servants. No. 785, Man and woman on the road.

Perf. 13x13½, 13½x13

1971, June 20 **Photo.**

781 A397 10w multicolored 6.00 1.75
782 A397 10w multicolored 6.00 1.75
783 A397 10w multicolored 6.00 1.75
784 A397 10w multicolored 6.00 1.75
785 A397 10w multicolored 6.00 1.75
b. Vert. strip of 5, #781-785 36.00 36.00
786 A398 10w multicolored 6.00 1.75
Nos. 781-786 (6) 36.00 10.50

Souvenir Sheets of 2

781a A397 10w 12.00 12.00
782a A397 10w 12.00 12.00
783a A397 10w 12.00 12.00
784a A397 10w 12.00 12.00
785a A397 10w 12.00 12.00
786a A398 10w 12.00 12.00
Nos. 781a-786a (6) 72.00 72.00

Types A397-A398 with Inscription at Left

1971, July 20

Paintings: No. 787, Farmyard scene, by Kim Deuk-shin. No. 788, Family living in valley, by Lee Chae-kwan. No. 789, Man reading book under pine tree, by Lee Chae-kwan.

787 A397 10w pale grn & multi 3.00 1.25
788 A398 10w pale grn & multi 3.00 1.25
789 A398 10w lt yel grn & multi 3.00 1.25
Nos. 787-789 (3) 9.00 3.75

Souvenir Sheets of 2

787a A397 10w 8.00 8.00
788a A398 10w 8.00 8.00
789a A398 10w 8.00 8.00
Nos. 787a-789a (3) 24.00 24.00

Teacher and Students, by Kim Hong-do A399

Paintings by Kim Hong-do (Yi Dynasty): No. 791, Wrestlers. No. 792, Dancer and musicians. No. 793, Weavers. No. 794, At the Well.

1971, Aug. 20 ***Perf. 13½x13***

790 A399 10w blk, lt grn & rose 5.00 2.50
791 A399 10w blk, lt grn & rose 5.00 2.50
792 A399 10w blk, lt grn & rose 5.00 2.50
793 A399 10w blk, lt grn & rose 5.00 2.50
794 A399 10w blk, lt grn & rose 5.00 2.50
b. Horiz. strip of 5, #790-794 27.50 27.50

Souvenir Sheets of 2

790a A399 10w 12.00 12.00
791a A399 10w 12.00 12.00
792a A399 10w 12.00 12.00
793a A399 10w 12.00 12.00
794a A399 10w 12.00 12.00
Nos. 790a-794a (5) 60.00 60.00

Pres. Park, Highway and Phoenix A400

1971, July 1 ***Perf. 13½x13***

795 A400 10w grn, blk & org 20.00 2.00
a. Souvenir sheet of 2 70.00 70.00

Inauguration of President Park Chung Hee for a third term, July 1.

Campfire and Tents — A401

1971, Aug. 2 **Photo.** ***Perf. 13x13½***

796 A401 10w blue grn & multi 1.25 .35

13th Boy Scout World Jamboree, Asagiri Plain, Japan, Aug. 2-10.

Symbol of Conference A402

1971, Sept. 27 ***Perf. 13***

797 A402 10w multicolored 1.25 .45
a. Souvenir sheet of 2 50.00 50.00

Asian Labor Ministers' Conference, Seoul, Sept. 27-30.

Archers — A403

1971, Oct. 8 **Photo.** ***Perf. 13x13½***

798 A403 10w shown 2.00 .75
a. Souvenir sheet of 3 35.00 35.00
799 A403 10w Judo 2.00 .75
a. Souvenir sheet of 3 35.00 35.00

52nd National Athletic Meet.

Taeguk on Palette A404

1971, Oct. 11 ***Perf. 13½x13***

800 A404 10w yellow & multi 1.25 .25

20th National Fine Arts Exhibition.

Physician, Globe and Emblem A405

1971, Oct. 13

801 A405 10w multicolored 1.25 .25

7th Congress of the Confederation of Medical Associations in Asia and Oceania.

Symbols of Contest Events — A406

1971, Oct. 20 **Photo.** ***Perf. 13x13½***

802 A406 10w multicolored 1.25 .25
a. Souvenir sheet of 2 40.00 40.00

2nd National Skill Contest for High School Students.

Slide Caliper and KS Emblem A407

1971, Nov. 11 ***Perf. 13x13½***

803 A407 10w multicolored 1.25 .25

10th anniversary of industrial standardization in Korea.

Rats — A408

Japanese Crane — A409

1971, Dec. 1

804 A408 10w multicolored 1.50 .35
a. Souvenir sheet of 3 25.00 25.00
805 A409 10w multicolored 1.50 .35
a. Souvenir sheet of 3 25.00 25.00

New Year 1972.

Emblem of Hangul Hakhoe and Hangul Letters — A410

1971, Dec. 3 **Photo.**

806 A410 10w dk blue & multi 1.00 .25

50th anniversary of Korean Language Research Society (Hangul Hakhoe).

Red Cross Headquarters and Map of Korea A411

1971, Dec. 31 ***Perf. 13½x13***

807 A411 10w multicolored 1.25 .60
a. Souvenir sheet of 2 12.50 12.50

First South and North Korean Red Cross Conference, Panmunjom, Aug. 20, 1971.

Globe and Book — A412

1972, Jan. 5 ***Perf. 13x13½***

808 A412 10w multicolored 1.00 .30

a. Souvenir sheet of 2 12.50 12.50

International Book Year 1972.

Intelsat 4 Sending Signals to Korea — A413

1972, Jan. 31 ***Perf. 13½x13***

809 A413 10w dk blue & multi 1.00 .30

Korea's entry into ITU, 20th anniv.

Figure Skating, Sapporo '72 Emblem — A414

Design: No. 811, Speed skating.

1972, Feb. 3 ***Perf. 13x13½***

810 A414 10w lt & dk bl & car 1.25 .60

811 A414 10w lt & dk bl & car 1.25 .60

a. Souvenir sheet of 2, #810-811 12.50 12.50

11th Winter Olympic Games, Sapporo, Japan, Feb. 3-13.

Map of Korea with Forest Sites — A415

1972, Mar. 10 **Photo.** ***Perf. 13x13***

812 A415 10w buff, bl grn & red 1.25 .30

Publicity for forests planted to mark hope for re-unification of Korea.

Junior Chamber of Commerce Emblem and Beetles A416

1972, Mar. 19 ***Perf. 13½x13***

813 A416 10w pink & multi 1.25 .30

Junior Chamber of Commerce, 20th anniversary.

UN Emblem, Agriculture and Industry — A417

1972, Mar. 28 ***Perf. 13x13½***

814 A417 10w violet, grn & car 1.25 .30

Economic Commission for Asia and the Far East (ECAFE), 25th anniversary.

Flags — A418

1972, Apr. 1 ***Perf. 13½x13***

815 A418 10w blue & multi 1.25 .30

Asian-Oceanic Postal Union, 10th anniv.

Homeland Reserve Forces Flag — A419

1972, Apr. 1 **Photo.** ***Perf. 13x13½***

816 A419 10w yellow & multi 1.50 .40

Homeland Reserve Forces Day, Apr. 1.

YWCA Emblem, Butterflies — A420

1972, Apr. 20

817 A420 10w violet & multi 1.25 .40

50th anniv. of the YWCA of Korea.

Community Projects — A421

1972, May 1 ***Perf. 13x13½***

818 A421 10w pink & multi 1.25 .40

Rural rehabilitation and construction movement.

Korean Flag & Inscription — A422

1972, May 1

819 A422 10w green & multi 1.25 .40

Anti-espionage and victory over communism month.

Children with Balloons A423

1972, May 5 ***Perf. 13½x13***

820 A423 10w yellow & multi 1.25 .40

Children's Day, May 5.

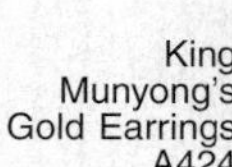

King Munyong's Gold Earrings A424

Design: No. 822, Gold ornament from King's crown, vert.

1972, May 10 ***Perf. 13½x13, 13x13½***

821 A424 10w green & multi 1.25 .40

822 A424 10w green & multi 1.25 .40

National treasures from tomb of King Munyong of Paekche, who reigned 501-523.

Kojo Island — A425

National parks: No. 823, Crater Lake.

1972, May 30 ***Perf. 13½x13***

823 A425 10w blue grn & multi 3.25 .40

824 A425 10w green & multi 3.25 .40

UN Conference on Human Environment, Stockholm, June 5-16 — A426

1972, May 30 **Litho.** ***Perf. 13x13½***

825 A426 10w Daisy, environment emblem 1.25 .35

a. Souvenir sheet of 2 8.50 8.50

7th Meeting of Asian-Pacific Council (ASPAC) — A427

1972, June 14

826 A427 10w Gwanghwa Gate, flags of participants 1.25 .35

Farm and Fish Hatchery A428

Third Five-Year Plan Issue

1972, July 1 **Photo.** ***Perf. 13½x13***

827 A428 10w shown 2.00 .50

828 A428 10w Steel industry and products 2.00 .50

829 A428 10w Globe and cargo 2.00 .50

Nos. 827-829 (3) 6.00 1.50

3rd Economic Development Five-Year Plan.

Weight Lifting — A429

1972, Aug. 26 **Photo.** ***Perf. 13x13½***

830 A429 20w shown 1.25 .50

831 A429 20w Judo 1.25 .50

a. Souvenir sheet of 2, #830-831 6.00 6.00

b. Pair, #830-831 5.00 2.50

832 A429 20w Boxing 1.25 .50

833 A429 20w Wrestling 1.25 .50

a. Souvenir sheet of 2, #832-833 6.00 6.00

b. Pair, #832-833 5.00 2.50

Nos. 830-833 (4) 5.00 2.00

20th Olympic Games, Munich, Aug. 26-Sept. 11. Nos. 831b, 833b each printed checkerwise.

Families Reunited by Red Cross A430

1972, Aug. 30 **Photo.** ***Perf. 13½x13***

834 A430 10w lt blue & multi 1.75 .60

a. Souvenir sheet of 2 27.50 27.50

Plenary meeting of the South-North Red Cross Conference, Pyongyang, Aug. 30, 1972.

Bulkuk-sa Temple, Kyongju Park — A431

Bopju-sa Temple, Mt. Sokri Park — A432

1972, Sept. 20 **Photo.** ***Perf. 13½x13***

835 A431 10w brown & multi 1.25 .40

836 A432 10w blue & multi 1.25 .40

National parks.

"5" and Conference Emblem — A433

1972, Sept. 25 ***Perf. 13x13½***

837 A433 10w vio blue & multi 1.20 .35

Fifth Asian Judicial Conf., Seoul, 9/25-29.

Lions Emblem, Taeguk Fan — A434

1972, Sept. 28 ***Perf. 13½x13***

838 A434 10w multicolored 1.20 .35

11th Orient and Southeast Asian Lions Convention, Seoul, Sept. 28-30.

Scout Taking Oath, Korean Flag and Scout Emblem A435

1972, Oct. 5

839 A435 10w yellow & multi 1.50 .45

Boy Scouts of Korea, 50th anniversary.

Children and Ox — A436

Children in Balloon — A437

1972, Dec. 1 Photo. *Perf. 13x13½*

840 A436 10w green & multi	1.25	.30
a. Souvenir sheet of 2	4.00	4.00
841 A437 10w blue & multi	1.25	.30
a. Souvenir sheet of 2	4.00	4.00

New Year 1973.

Mt. Naejang Park and Temple — A438

Mt. Sorang and Madeungryong Pass — A439

1972, Dec. 10 *Perf. 13x13½, 13½x13*

842 A438 10w multicolored	1.25	.30
843 A439 10w multicolored	1.25	.30

National parks.

Pres. Park, Korean Flag and Modern Landscape — A440

1972, Dec. 27 *Perf. 13x13½*

844 A440 10w multicolored	7.50	1.50
a. Souvenir sheet of 2	67.50	67.50

Inauguration of Park Chung Hee for a 4th term as president of Korea.

Tourism Issue

Kyongbok Palace (National Museum) A441

Mt. Sorak and Kejo-am Temple A442

Palmi Island and Beach — A443

Sain-am Rock, Mt. Dokjol — A444

Shrine for Adm. Li Sun-sin — A445

Limestone Cavern, Kusan-ni — A446

Namhae Bridge A447

Hongdo Island — A448

Mt. Mai — A449

Tangerine Orchard, Cheju Island A450

1973, Feb. 20 Photo. *Perf. 13½x13*

845 A441 10w multicolored	1.25	.30
846 A442 10w multicolored	1.25	.30

1973, Apr. 20 *Perf. 13x13½*

847 A443 10w multicolored	1.25	.30
848 A444 10w multicolored	1.25	.30

1973, June 20

849 A445 10w multicolored	1.50	.30
850 A446 10w multicolored	1.50	.30

1973, Aug. 20 *Perf. 13½x13*

851 A447 10w multicolored	1.25	.30
852 A448 10w multicolored	1.25	.30

1973, Oct. 20

853 A449 10w multicolored	.85	.25
854 A450 10w multicolored	.85	.25
Nos. 845-854 (10)	12.20	2.90

Praying Family — A451

1973, Mar. 1 *Perf. 13x13½*

855 A451 10w yellow & multi	1.00	.30

Prayer for national unification.

Flags of Korea and South Viet Nam, Victory Sign — A452

1973, Mar. 1

856 A452 10w violet & multi	1.00	.30

Return of Korean Expeditionary Force from South Viet Nam.

Workers, Factory, Cogwheel A453

Satellite, WMO Emblem A454

1973, Mar. 10 Unwmk.

857 A453 10w blue & multi	.80	.30

10th Labor Day.

1973, Mar. 23

858 A454 10w blue & multi	.80	.30
a. Souvenir sheet of 2	5.00	5.00

Cent. of Intl. Meteorological Cooperation.

King's Ceremonial Robe — A455

Traditional Korean Costumes (Yi dynasty): No. 860, Queen's ceremonial dress. No. 861, King's robe. No. 862, Queen's robe. No. 863, Crown Prince. No. 864, Princess. No. 865, Courtier. No. 866, Royal bridal gown. No. 867, Official's wife. No. 868, Military official.

1973 Photo. *Perf. 13½x13*

859 A455 10w ocher & multi	3.50	.70
860 A455 10w salmon & multi	3.50	.70
861 A455 10w rose lilac & multi	3.25	.60
862 A455 10w apple grn & multi	3.25	.60
863 A455 10w lt blue & multi	3.00	.60
864 A455 10w lilac rose & multi	3.00	.60
865 A455 10w yellow & multi	1.50	.50
866 A455 10w lt blue & multi	1.50	.50
867 A455 10w ocher & multi	1.25	.35
868 A455 10w lil rose & multi	1.25	.35
Nos. 859-868 (10)	25.00	5.50

Issued: #859-860, 3/30; #861-862, 5/30; #863-864, 7/30; #865-866, 9/30; #867-868, 11/30.

Souvenir Sheets of 2

859a A455 10w (#1)	7.50	7.50
860a A455 10w (#2)	7.50	7.50
861a A455 10w (#3)	7.50	7.50
862a A455 10w (#4)	7.50	7.50
863a A455 10w (#5)	7.50	7.50
864a A455 10w (#6)	7.50	7.50
865a A455 10w (#7)	4.00	4.00
866a A455 10w (#8)	4.00	4.00
867a A455 10w (#9)	4.00	4.00
868a A455 10w (#10)	4.00	4.00
Nos. 859a-868a (10)	61.00	61.00

Parenthetical numbers after souvenir sheet listings appear in top marginal inscriptions.

Nurse Holding Lamp — A456

1973, Apr. 1 *Perf. 13½x13*

869 A456 10w rose & multi	1.00	.20

50th anniv. of Korean Nurses Association.

Homeland Reservists and Flag — A457

1973, Apr. 7 *Perf. 13x13½*

870 A457 10w yellow & multi	1.25	.30

Homeland Reserve Forces Day on 5th anniversary of their establishment.

Table Tennis Player, and Globe — A458

1973, May 23 *Perf. 13x13½*

871 A458 10w pink & multi	1.50	.70

Victory of Korean women's table tennis team, 32nd Intl. Table Tennis Championships, Sarajevo, Yugoslavia, Apr. 5-15.

World Vision Children's Choir — A459

1973, June 25 *Perf. 13x13½*

872 A459 10w multicolored	1.00	.30

20th anniversary of World Vision International, a Christian service organization.

Converter, Pohang Steel Works — A460

1973, July 3 *Perf. 13x13½*

873 A460 10w blue & multi	1.00	.45

Inauguration of Pohang iron and steel plant.

INTERPOL Emblem A461

1973, Sept. 3 *Perf. 13½x13*

874 A461 10w lt violet & multi	1.00	.20

50th anniversary of the International Criminal Police Organization (INTERPOL).

Children with Stamp Albums A462

1973, Oct. 12 *Perf. 13½x13*

875 A462 10w dp green & multi	.80	.30
a. Souvenir sheet of 2	15.00	15.00

Philatelic Week, Oct. 12-18.

Woman Hurdler — A463

1973, Oct. 12 *Perf. 12½x13½*

876 A463 10w shown	.90	.30
877 A463 10w Tennis player	.90	.30

54th Natl. Athletic Meet, Pusan, Oct. 12-17.

Soyang River Dam, Map Showing Location A464

1973, Oct. 15 *Perf. 13½x13*

878 A464 10w blue & multi	.50	.20

Inauguration of Soyang River Dam and hydroelectric plant.

Fire from Match and Cigarette — A465

1973, Nov. 1 *Perf. 13x13½*

879 A465 10w multicolored	.50	.20

10th Fire Prevention Day.

Tiger and Candles — A466

Toys — A467

1973, Dec. 1 Photo. *Perf. 13x13½*

880 A466 10w emerald & multi	1.00	.30
a. Souvenir sheet of 2	4.50	4.50
881 A467 10w blue & multi	1.00	.30
a. Souvenir sheet of 2	4.50	4.50

New Year 1974.

Human Rights Flame, and Head — A468

1973, Dec. 10 *Perf. 13½x13*

882 A468 10w orange & multi	.50	.20

25th anniversary of Universal Declaration of Human Rights.

Musical Instruments Issue

Komunko, Six-stringed Zither — A469

Design: 30w, Nagak, shell trumpet.

1974, Feb. 20 Photo. *Perf. 13x13½*

883 A469 10w lt bl, blk & brn	1.10	.30
884 A469 30w orange & multi	3.00	.60

1974, Apr. 20

Designs: 10w, Tchouk; wooden hammer in slanted box, used to start orchestra. 30w, Eu; crouching tiger, used to stop orchestra.

885 A469 10w brt blue & multi	1.00	.25
886 A469 30w lt green & multi	2.00	.35

1974, June 20

Designs: 10w, A-chaing, 7-stringed instrument. 30w, Kyobang-ko, drum.

887 A469 10w dull yel & multi	.90	.25
888 A469 30w salmon pink & multi	1.90	.35

1974, Aug. 20

Designs: 10w, So, 16-pipe ritual instrument. 30w, Kaikeum, 2-stringed fiddle.

889 A469 10w lt blue & multi	.90	.30
890 A469 30w brt pink & multi	1.90	.45

1974, Oct. 20

10w, Pak (clappers). 30w, Pyenchong (bell chimes).

891 A469 10w lt lilac & multi	.90	.30
892 A469 30w lemon & multi	1.90	.45
Nos. 883-892 (10)	15.50	3.60

Souvenir Sheets of 2

883a	A469	10w	(#1)	5.00	5.00
884a	A469	30w	(#2)	7.50	7.50
885a	A469	10w	(#3)	3.50	3.50
886a	A469	30w	(#4)	5.50	5.50
887a	A469	10w	(#5)	3.50	3.50
888a	A469	30w	(#6)	5.00	5.00
889a	A469	10w	(#7)	2.75	2.75
890a	A469	30w	(#8)	4.50	4.50
891a	A469	10w	(#9)	2.75	2.75
892a	A469	30w	(#10)	4.50	4.50
Nos. 883a-892a (10)				44.50	

Fruit Issue

Apricots — A470

1974, Mar. 30 Photo. *Perf. 13x13½*

893 A470 10w shown	.75	.30
894 A470 30w Strawberries	2.25	.45

1974, May 30

895 A470 10w Peaches	.75	.30
896 A470 30w Grapes	2.25	.45

1974, July 30

897 A470 10w Pears	.60	.30
898 A470 30w Apples	2.25	.45

1974, Sept. 30

899 A470 10w Cherries	.65	.30
900 A470 30w Persimmons	1.40	.45

1974, Nov. 30

901 A470 10w Tangerines	.50	.30
902 A470 30w Chestnuts	1.25	.35
Nos. 893-902 (10)	12.65	3.65

Souvenir Sheets of 2

893a	A470	10w	(#1)	3.50	3.50
894a	A470	30w	(#2)	7.50	7.50
895a	A470	10w	(#3)	3.50	3.50
896a	A470	30w	(#4)	7.00	7.00
897a	A470	10w	(#5)	3.00	3.00
898a	A470	30w	(#6)	7.50	7.50
899a	A470	10w	(#7)	2.00	2.00
900a	A470	30w	(#8)	3.00	3.00
901a	A470	10w	(#9)	2.50	2.50
902a	A470	30w	(#10)	3.00	3.00
Nos. 893a-902a (10)				42.50	42.50

Reservist and Factory A471

1974, Apr. 6 Photo. *Perf. 13½x13*

903 A471 10w yellow & multi	.50	.20

Homeland Reserve Forces Day.

WPY Emblem and Scales — A472

1974, Apr. 10 *Perf. 13x13½*

904 A472 10w salmon & multi	.50	.20
a. Souvenir sheet of 2	4.00	4.00

World Population Year 1974.

Train and Communications Emblem — A473

1974, Apr. 22 *Perf. 13½x13*

905 A473 10w multicolored	.50	.25

19th Communications Day.

Emblem and Stylized Globe — A474

1974, May 6 Photo. *Perf. 13*

906 A474 10w red lilac & multi	.50	.20

22nd Session of Intl. Chamber of Commerce (Eastern Division), Seoul, May 6-8.

New Dock at Inchon A475

1974, May 10

907 A475 10w yellow & multi	.50	.20

Dedication of dock, Inchon.

UNESCO Emblem, "20" and Yin Yang — A476

1974, June 14 Photo. *Perf. 13*

908 A476 10w org yel & multi	.50	.20

20th anniversary of the Korean National Commission for UNESCO.

EXPLO '74 Emblems — A477

Design: No. 910, EXPLO emblem rising from map of Korea.

1974, Aug. 13 Photo. *Perf. 13*

909 A477 10w orange & multi	.45	.20
910 A477 10w blue & multi	.45	.20

EXPLO '74, International Christian Congress, Yoido Islet, Seoul, Aug. 13-18.

Subway, Bus and Plane — A478

1974, Aug. 15

911 A478 10w green & multi	1.00	.25

Inauguration of Seoul subway (first in Korea), Aug. 15, 1974.

Target Shooting — A479

1974, Oct. 8 Photo. *Perf. 13x13½*

912 A479 10w shown	.40	.20
913 A479 30w Rowing	1.25	.40

55th National Athletic Meet.

UPU Emblem A480

1974, Oct. 9 *Perf. 13*

914 A480 10w yellow & multi	.50	.20
a. Souvenir sheet of 2	5.50	5.50

Cent. of UPU. See No. C43.

International Landmarks — A481

1974, Oct. 11

915 A481 10w multicolored	.50	.20

Intl. People to People Conf., Seoul, 10/11-14.

Korea Nos. 1-2 — A482

1974, Oct. 17

916 A482 10w lilac & multi	.50	.50
a. Souvenir sheet of 2	8.00	8.00

Philatelic Week, Oct. 17-23 and 90th anniversary of first Korean postage stamps.

Taekwondo and Kukkiwon Center
A483

1974, Oct. 18

917 A483 10w yellow grn & multi .50 .20

First Asian Taekwondo (self-defense) Games, Seoul, Oct. 18-20.

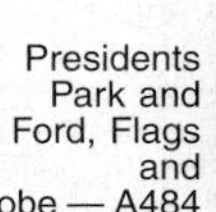

Presidents Park and Ford, Flags and Globe — A484

1974, Nov. 22 Photo. *Perf. 13*

918 A484 10y multicolored 1.00 .30
a. Souvenir sheet of 2 7.50 7.50

Visit of Pres. Gerald R. Ford to South Korea.

Yook Young Soo — A485

1974, Nov. 29

919 A485 10w green .85 .30
920 A485 10w orange .85 .30
921 A485 10w lilac .85 .30
922 A485 10w blue .85 .30
a. Souvenir sheet of 4, #919-922 35.00 35.00
b. Block of 4, #919-922 3.00 2.00

Yook Young Soo (1925-1974), wife of Pres. Park.

Rabbits — A486

Good-luck Purse — A487

1974, Dec. 1 Litho. *Perf. 12½x13*

923 A486 10w multicolored .60 .20
a. Souvenir sheet of 2 3.75 3.75
924 A487 10w multicolored .60 .20
a. Souvenir sheet of 2 3.75 3.75

New Year 1975.

Good-luck Key and Pigeon
A488

1975, Jan. 1 Photo. *Perf. 13*

925 A488 10w lt blue & multi .50 .20

Introduction of Natl. Welfare Insurance System.

UPU Emblem and "75" — A489

UPU Emblem and Paper Plane — A490

1975, Jan. 1

926 A489 10w yellow & multi .50 .20
927 A490 10w lt blue & multi .50 .20

75th anniv. of Korea's membership in UPU.

Dr. Albert Schweitzer, Map of Africa, Hypodermic Needle
A491

1975, Jan. 14

928 A491 10w olive .90 .35
929 A491 10w brt rose .90 .35
930 A491 10w orange .90 .35
931 A491 10w brt green .90 .35
a. Block of 4, #928-931 5.00 3.00

Folk Dance Issue

Dancer — A492

Bupo Nori — A492a

#933, Dancer with fan. #934, Woman with butterfly sleeves. #935, Group of Women. #936, Pongsan mask dance. #937, Pusan mask dance. #938, Buddhist drum dance. #939, Bara (cymbals) dance. #940, Sogo dance.

1975, Feb. 20 Photo. *Perf. 13*

932 A492 10w emerald & multi .70 .25
933 A492 10w brt blue & multi .70 .25

1975, Apr. 20

934 A492 10w yel grn & multi .70 .25
935 A492 10w yellow & multi .70 .25

1975, June 20

936 A492 10w pink & multi .70 .25
937 A492 10w blue & multi .70 .25

1975, Aug. 20

938 A492 20w yellow & multi 1.00 .45
939 A492 20w salmon & multi 1.00 .45

1975, Oct. 20

940 A492 20w blue & multi 1.00 .45
941 A492a 20w yellow & multi 1.00 .45
Nos. 932-941 (10) 8.20 3.30

Souvenir Sheets of 2

932a	A492	10w	(#1)	2.00	2.00
933a	A492	10w	(#2)	2.00	2.00
934a	A492	10w	(#3)	1.60	1.60
935a	A492	10w	(#4)	1.60	1.60
936a	A492	10w	(#5)	1.60	1.60
937a	A492	10w	(#6)	1.60	1.60
938a	A492	20w	(#7)	2.50	2.50
939a	A492	20w	(#8)	2.50	2.50
940a	A492	20w	(#9)	2.10	2.10
941a	A492	20w	(#10)	2.10	2.10
	Nos. 932a-941a (10)			19.60	19.60

Globe and Rotary Emblem
A493

1975, Feb. 23

942 A493 10w multicolored .50 .20

Rotary International, 70th anniversary.

Women and IWY Emblem
A494

1975, Mar. 8

943 A494 10w multicolored .50 .20

International Women's Year 1975.

Flower Issue

Violets
A495

Anemones
A496

Clematis Patens — A496a

Broad-bell Flowers — A496b

Designs: No. 946, Rhododendron. No. 948, Thistle. No. 949, Iris. No. 951, Bush clover. No. 952, Camellia. No. 953, Gentian.

1975, Mar. 15

944 A495 10w orange & multi .60 .25
945 A496 10w yellow & multi .60 .25

1975, May 15

946 A495 10w dk green & multi .75 .25
947 A496a 10w yellow grn & multi .75 .25

1975, July 15

948 A495 10w emerald & multi .75 .25
949 A495 10w blue & multi .75 .25

1975, Sept. 15

950 A496b 20w yellow & multi 1.10 .30
951 A495 20w blue grn & multi 1.10 .30

1975, Nov. 15

952 A495 20w yellow & multi 1.60 .50
953 A496 20w salmon & multi 1.60 .50
Nos. 944-953 (10) 9.60 3.10

Forest and Water Resources — A497

1975, Mar. 20

954 A497 Strip of 4 5.00 3.00
a. 10w Saemaeul forest .75 .30
b. 10w Dam and reservoir .75 .30
c. 10w Green forest .75 .30
d. 10w Timber industry .75 .30

Natl. Tree Planting Month, Mar. 21-Apr. 20.

Map of Korea, HRF Emblem — A498

1975, Apr. 12 Photo. *Perf. 13*

955 A498 10w blue & multi .60 .20

Homeland Reserve Forces Day.

Lily — A499

Ceramic Jar — A500

Ceramic Vase
A501

Adm. Li Sun-sin
A502

1975 Photo. *Perf. 13½x13*

963 A499 6w green & bl grn .40 .20
964 A500 50w gray grn & brn .75 .25
965 A501 60w brown & yellow .75 .25
966 A502 100w carmine 1.75 .25
Nos. 963-966 (4) 3.65 .95

Issued: Nos. 964-965, 3/15/75; Nos. 963, 966, 10/10/75.

Metric System Symbols
A507

1975, May 20 *Perf. 13*

975 A507 10w salmon & multi .50 .20

Centenary of International Meter Convention, Paris, 1875.

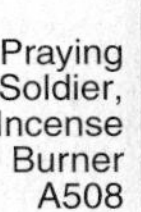

Praying Soldier, Incense Burner
A508

1975, June 6 Photo. *Perf. 13*

976 A508 10w multicolored .50 .20

20th Memorial Day.

Flags of Korea, UN and US — A509

Designs (Flags of): No. 978, Ethiopia, France, Greece, Canada, South Africa. No. 979, Luxembourg, Australia, Great Britain, Colombia, Turkey. No. 980, Netherlands, Belgium, Philippines, New Zealand, Thailand.

1975, June 25 Photo. *Perf. 13*

977 A509 10w dk blue & multi .75 .30
978 A509 10w dk blue & multi .75 .30
979 A509 10w dk blue & multi .75 .30
980 A509 10w dk blue & multi .75 .30
a. Strip of 4, #977-980 5.00 3.00

25th anniv. of beginning of Korean War.

Presidents Park and Bongo, Flags of Korea and Gabon
A510

1975, July 5

981 A510 10w blue & multi .50 .20
a. Souvenir sheet of 2 3.00 3.00

Visit of Pres. Albert Bongo of Gabon, 7/5-8.

Scout Emblem, Tents and Neckerchief — A511

1975, July 29 Photo. *Perf. 13*

982 A511 10w shown .75 .30
983 A511 10w Pick and oath .75 .30
984 A511 10w Tents .75 .30
985 A511 10w Ax, rope and tree .75 .30
986 A511 10w Campfire .75 .30
a. Strip of 5, #982-986 5.00 3.50

Nordjamb 75, 14th Boy Scout Jamboree, Lillehammer, Norway, July 29-Aug. 7.

Flame and Broken Chain A512

Balloons with Symbols of Development over Map — A513

1975, Aug. 15 *Perf. 13½x13*

987 A512 20w gold & multi .70 .25
988 A513 20w silver & multi .70 .25

30th anniversary of liberation.

Taekwondo — A514

1975, Aug. 26 *Perf. 13*

989 A514 20w multicolored .50 .20

2nd World Taekwondo Championships, Seoul, Aug. 25-Sept. 1.

National Assembly and Emblem A515

1975, Sept. 1 Photo. *Perf. 13½x13*

990 A515 20w multicolored .50 .20

Completion of National Assembly Building.

Convention Emblem and Dump Truck — A516

1975, Sept. 7 Photo. *Perf. 13½x13*

991 A516 20w ultra & multi .50 .20

14th Convention of the Intl. Fed. of Asian and Western Pacific Contractors.

Cassegrainian Telescope and Morse Key — A517

1975, Sept. 28

992 A517 20w red lil, org & blk .50 .20

90th anniversary of Korean telecommunications system.

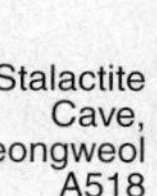

Stalactite Cave, Yeongweol A518

View of Mt. Sorak A519

1975, Sept. 28

993 A518 20w multicolored .50 .20
994 A519 20w multicolored .50 .20

International Tourism Day.

Armed Forces Flag and Missiles — A519a

1975, Oct. 1 Photo. *Perf. 13*

994A A519a 20w multicolored .50 .20

Armed Forces Day.

Gymnastics A520

Handball A521

1975, Oct. 7 Photo. *Perf. 13*

995 A520 20w yellow & multi .50 .20
996 A521 20w multicolored .50 .20

56th Natl. Athletic Meet, Taegu, Oct. 7-12.

Stamp Collecting Kangaroo A522

Hands and UN Emblem A523

1975, Oct. 8

997 A522 20w multicolored .50 .20

Philatelic Week, Oct. 8-14.

1975, Oct. 24

998 A523 20w multicolored .50 .20

United Nations, 30th anniversary.

Red Cross and Activities — A524

Emblem and Dove — A525

1975, Oct. 30

999 A524 20w orange, red & brn .50 .20

Korean Red Cross, 70th anniversary.

1975, Nov. 30 Photo. *Perf. 13*

1000 A525 20w multicolored .50 .20

Asian Parliamentary Union, 10th anniv.

Children Playing — A526

Dragon — A527

1975, Dec. 1

1001 A526 20w multicolored .50 .20
a. Souvenir sheet of 2 2.00 2.00
1002 A527 20w multicolored .50 .20
a. Souvenir sheet of 2 2.00 2.00

New Year 1976.

Inchong-Bukpyong Railroad — A528

1975, Dec. 5 Photo. *Perf. 13*

1003 A528 20w multicolored .75 .20

Opening of electric cross-country railroad.

Butterfly Issue

Dilipa Fenestra A529

Byasa Alcinous Klug — A529a

Graphium Sarpedon A529b

Fabriciana Nerippe A529c

Nymphalis Xanthomelas A529d

Butterflies: No. 1005, Luehdorfia puziloi. No. 1006, Papilio xuthus linne. No. 1007, Parnassius bremeri. No. 1008, Colias erate esper. No. 1010, Hestina assimilis.

1976, Jan. 20 Photo. *Perf. 13*

1004 A529 20w dp rose & multi 1.50 .30
1005 A529 20w dp blue & multi 1.50 .30

1976, Mar. 20

1006 A529 20w yellow & multi 1.50 .30
1007 A529 20w yel grn & multi 1.50 .30

1976, June 20

1008 A529 20w lt violet & multi 1.50 .30
1009 A529a 20w citron & multi 1.50 .30

1976, Aug. 20

1010 A529 20w tan & multi 2.10 .75
1011 A529b 20w lt gray & multi 2.10 .75

1976, Oct. 20

1012 A529c 20w lt green & multi 2.00 .90
1013 A529d 20w lilac & multi 2.00 .90
Nos. 1004-1013 (10) 17.20 5.10

Emblems of Science, Industry and KIST — A530

1976, Feb. 10 Photo. *Perf. 13*

1014 A530 20w multicolored .50 .20

Korean Institute of Science and Technology (KIST), 10th anniversary.

Birds Issue

A531

A532

A532a

A532b

A532c

A532d

A532e A532f

A532g

A532h

1976, Feb. 20 Photo. ***Perf. 13x13½***

1015 A531 20w Siberian Bustard 1.50 .35
1016 A532 20w White-naped Crane 1.50 .35

1976, May 20

1017 A532a 20w Blue-winged pitta 1.50 .35
1018 A532b 20w Tristam's woodpecker 1.50 .35

1976, July 20

1019 A532c 20w Wood pigeon 1.50 .35
1020 A532d 20w Oyster catcher 1.50 .35

1976, Sept. 20

1021 A532e 20w Black-faced spoonbill 1.50 .35
1022 A532f 20w Black stork 1.50 .35

1976, Nov. 20

1023 A532g 20w Whooper swan 3.50 1.40
1024 A532h 20w Black vulture 3.50 1.40
Nos. 1015-1024 (10) 19.00 5.60

1876 and 1976 Telephones, Globe — A533

1976, Mar. 10

1025 A533 20w multicolored .50 .20

Centenary of first telephone call by Alexander Graham Bell, Mar. 10, 1876.

Homeland Reserves A534

1976, Apr. 3 Photo. ***Perf. 13½x13***

1026 A534 20w multicolored .50 .20

8th Homeland Reserve Forces Day.

"People and Eye" — A535

1976, Apr. 7 ***Perf. 13x13½***

1027 A535 20w multicolored .50 .20

World Health Day; "Foresight prevents blindness."

Pres. Park, New Village Movement Flag — A536

Intellectual Pursuits — A537

1976, Apr. 22

1028 A536 20w shown 1.50 .45
1029 A537 20w shown 1.50 .45
1030 A537 20w Village improvement 1.50 .45
1031 A537 20w Agriculture 1.50 .45
1032 A537 20w Income from production 1.50 .45
a. Strip of 5, #1028-1032 10.00 6.00

6th anniv. of Pres. Park's New Village Movement for National Prosperity.

Mohenjo-Daro A538

1976, May 1 ***Perf. 13½x13***

1033 A538 20w multicolored .50 .20

UNESCO campaign to save the Mohenjo-Daro excavations in Pakistan.

13-Star and 50-Star Flags — A539

American Bicentennial (Bicentennial Emblem and): No. 1035, Statue of Liberty. No. 1036, Map of US and Mt. Rushmore monument. No. 1037, Liberty Bell. No. 1038, First astronaut on moon.

1976, May 8 ***Perf. 13x13½***

1034 A539 100w blk, dp bl & red 3.00 1.00
a. Souvenir sheet of 1 6.00 6.00
1035 A539 100w blk, dp bl & red 3.00 1.00
1036 A539 100w blk, dp bl & red 3.00 1.00
1037 A539 100w blk, dp bl & red 3.00 1.00
1038 A539 100w blk, dp bl & red 3.00 1.00
Nos. 1034-1038 (5) 15.00 5.00

Girl Scouts, Campfire and Emblem — A540

1976, May 10

1039 A540 20w orange & multi .50 .20

Korean Federation of Girl Scouts, 30th anniv.

Stupas, Buddha of Borobudur A541

"Life Insurance" A542

1976, June 10

1040 A541 20w multicolored .50 .20

UNESCO campaign to save the Borobudur Temple, Java.

1976, July 1 Photo. ***Perf. 13x13½***

1041 A542 20w multicolored .50 .20

National Life Insurance policies: "Over 100 billion-won," Apr. 30, 1976.

Volleyball — A543

1976, July 17

1042 A543 20w shown .50 .20
1043 A543 20w Boxing .50 .20

21st Olympic Games, Montreal, Canada, July 17-Aug. 1.

Children and Books A544

1976, Aug. 10 ***Perf. 13½x13***

1044 A544 20w brown & multi .50 .20

Books for children.

Civil Defense Corps, Flag and Members — A545

1976, Sept. 15 ***Perf. 13x13½***

1045 A545 20w multicolored .50 .20

Civil Defense Corps, first anniversary.

Chamsungdan, Mani Mountain — A546

Front Gate, Tongdosa Temple A547

1976, Sept. 28 ***Perf. 13½x13***

1046 A546 20w multicolored .75 .25
1047 A547 20w multicolored .75 .25

International Tourism Day.

Cadets and Academy A548

1976, Oct. 1

1048 A548 20w multicolored .50 .20

Korean Military Academy, 30th anniversary.

Leaves and Stones, by Cheong Ju — A549

1976, Oct. 5 ***Perf. 13x13½***

1049 A549 20w blk, gray & red .50 .20
a. Souvenir sheet of 2 5.00 5.00

Philatelic Week, Oct. 5-11.

Snake-headed Figure, Bas-relief A550

Door-pull and Cranes A551

1976, Dec. 1 Photo. ***Perf. 13x13½***

1050 A550 20w multicolored .50 .25
a. Souvenir sheet of 2 2.50 2.50
1051 A551 20w multicolored .50 .25
a. Souvenir sheet of 2 2.50 2.50

New Year 1977.

Arrows, Cogwheels, Worker at Lathe — A552

No. 1053, Arrows, Cogwheels, ship in dock.

1977, Jan. 20 Photo. ***Perf. 13½x13***

1052 A552 20w multicolored .50 .20
1053 A552 20w multicolored .50 .20

4th Economic Development Five-Year Plan.

Satellite Antenna and Microwaves — A553

1977, Jan. 31 *Perf. 13x13½*

1054 A553 20w multicolored .50 .20

Membership in ITU, 25th anniv.

Korean Broadcasting Center A554

1977, Feb. 16 *Perf. 13½x13*

1055 A554 20w multicolored .50 .20

50th anniversary of broadcasting in Korea.

Parents and Two Children — A555

1977, Apr. 1 Photo. *Perf. 13½x13*

1056 A555 20w brt grn & orange 2.00 .25

Family planning.

Reservist on Duty — A556

Head with Symbols — A557

1977, Apr. 2 *Perf. 13x13½*

1057 A556 20w multicolored .50 .20

9th Homeland Reserve Forces Day.

1977, Apr. 21 Photo. *Perf. 13x13½*

1058 A557 20w dp lilac & multi .50 .20

10th anniversary of Science Day.

Book, Map, Syringe A558

1977, Apr. 25

1059 A558 20w blue & multi .50 .20

35th Intl. Meeting on Military Medicine.

Boy with Flowers and Dog — A559

Veteran's Emblem and Flag — A560

1977, May 5

1060 A559 20w multicolored .50 .20

Proclamation of Children's Charter, 20th anniversary.

1977, May 8

1061 A560 20w multicolored .50 .20

25th anniversary of Korean Veterans' Day.

Buddha, 8th Century, Sokkulam Grotto — A561

1977, May 25 Photo. *Perf. 13x13½*

1062 A561 20w sepia & olive .50 .20

a. Souvenir sheet of 2 5.00 5.00

"2600th" anniversary of birth of Buddha.

Ceramic Issues

Jar with Grape Design, 17th Century — A562

Celadon Vase, Bamboo Design, 12th Century — A563

Celadon Jar with Peonies A564

Vase with Willow Reed Peony Pattern — A565

Celadon Manshaped Wine Jug — A566

Celadon Melon-shaped Vase — A567

Punch'ong Jar — A568

Celadon Cylindrical Vase — A569

1977, Mar. 15 Photo. *Perf. 13x13½*

1063 A562 20w vio brn & multi 2.00 .30

1064 A563 20w gray, grn & bis 2.00 .30

Perf. 13x13½, 13½x13

1977, June 15 Photo.

1065 A564 20w multicolored .75 .30

1066 A565 20w multicolored .75 .30

1977, July 15

1067 A566 20w multicolored .75 .25

1068 A567 20w multicolored .75 .25

1977, Aug. 15

Designs: No. 1069, White porcelain bowl with inlaid lotus vine design. No. 1070, Black Koryo ware vase with plum blossom vine.

1069 A564 20w multicolored .75 .25

1070 A565 20w multicolored .75 .25

1977, Nov. 15

1071 A568 20w multicolored .75 .25

1072 A569 20w multicolored .75 .25

Nos. 1063-1072 (10) 10.00 2.70

Types of 1962-66 Designs as Before

1976-77 Litho. *Perf. 12½*

Granite Paper

1076 A187 200w brown & lt grn 25.00 7.00

1077 A187a 300w sl grn & sal ('76) 50.00 8.00

1078 A187a 300w brown & salmon 50.00 8.00

1079 A187a 500w purple & lt grn 100.00 10.00

Magpie A570

Nature Protection A571

"Family Planning" A572

Children on Swing A573

Ceramic Horseman A574

Muryangsu Hall, Busok Temple A575

Pagoda, Pobjusa Temple A576

Gold Crown, from Chonmachong Mound A577

Monster Mask Tile, 6th or 7th Century — A578

Flying Angels from Bronze Bell from Sangwon-sa, 725 A.D. — A579

Perf. 12½x13½, 13½x12½

1977-79 Photo.

1088 A570 3w lt blue & blk .75 .25

1090 A326 10w emer & blk .70 .25

1091 A571 20w multicolored .50 .20

1092 A572 20w emer & blk ('78) .50 .20

1093 A573 20w grn & org ('79) .50 .20

1097 A574 80w lt brn & sep 1.50 .40

1099 A575 200w salmon & brn 2.00 .50

1100 A576 300w brn purple 2.75 .60

1101 A577 500w multicolored 22.50 1.50

Perf. 13½x13

1102 A578 500w brown & pur 11.00 1.00

Perf. 13

1103 A579 1000w slate grn ('78) 10.00 1.50

Nos. 1088-1103 (11) 52.70 6.60

Ulleung Island — A580

Design: No. 1105, Haeundae Beach.

1977, Sept. 28 Photo. *Perf. 13*

1104 A580 20w multicolored .50 .20

1105 A580 20w multicolored .50 .20

World Tourism Day.

Armed Forces Day — A581

1977, Oct. 1 Photo. *Perf. 13*

1106 A581 20w green & multi .50 .20

Mt. Inwang after the Rain, by Chung Seon (1676-1759) — A582

1977, Oct. 4

1107 20w mountain, clouds .90 .25

1108 20w mountain, house .90 .25

a. Souvenir sheet of 2 8.50 8.50

b. A582 Pair, #1107-1108 2.25 1.50

Philatelic Week, Oct. 4-10.

Rotary Emblem on Bronze Bell, Koryo Dynasty — A584

1977, Nov. 10 Photo. *Perf. 13*

1109 A584 20w multicolored .65 .20

Korean Rotary Club, 50th anniversary.

Korean Flag on Mt. Everest A585

1977, Nov. 11

1110 A585 20w multicolored .65 .20

Korean Mt. Everest Expedition, reached peak, Sept. 15, 1977.

Children and Kites A586

Horse-headed Figure, Bas-relief A587

1977, Dec. 1 Photo. *Perf. 13*

1111 A586 20w multicolored .45 .25
 a. Souvenir sheet of 2 2.25 2.25
1112 A587 20w multicolored .45 .25
 a. Souvenir sheet of 2 2.25 2.25

New Year 1978.

Clay Pigeon Shooting A588

Designs: No. 1114, Air pistol shooting. No. 1115, Air rifle shooting and target.

1977, Dec. 3

1113 A588 20w multicolored .50 .20
 a. Souvenir sheet of 2 ('78) 3.50 3.50
1114 A588 20w multicolored .50 .20
 a. Souvenir sheet of 2 ('78) 3.50 3.50
1115 A588 20w multicolored .50 .20
 a. Souvenir sheet of 2 ('78) 3.50 3.50
 Nos. 1113-1115 (3) 1.50 .60
 Nos. 1113a-1115a (3) 10.50

42nd World Shooting Championships, Seoul, 1978.

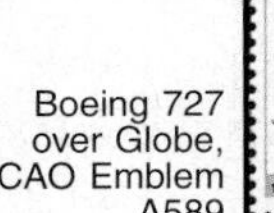

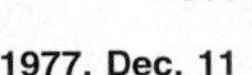

Boeing 727 over Globe, ICAO Emblem A589

1977, Dec. 11

1116 A589 20w multicolored .50 .20

25th anniv. of Korea's membership in the ICAO.

Plane, Cargo, Freighter and Globe A590

1977, Dec. 22 Photo. *Perf. 13*

1117 A590 20w multicolored .60 .20

Korean exports.

Ships and World Map — A591

1978, Mar. 13 Photo. *Perf. 13*

1118 A591 20w multicolored .50 .20

Maritime Day.

Stone Pagoda Issue

Four Lions Pagoda, Hwaom-sa A592

Kyongch'on sa Temple A594

Punhwang-sa Temple A593

#1120, Seven-storied pagoda, T'appyongri.

1978, Mar. 20 Photo. *Perf. 13*

1119 A592 20w lt green & multi 1.25 .30
1120 A592 20w ocher & multi 1.25 .30

1978, May 20

Design: No. 1122, Miruk-sa Temple.

1121 A593 20w lt green & blk 1.25 .30
1122 A593 20w grn, brn & yel 1.25 .30

1978, June 20

Designs: #1123, Tabo Pagoda, Pulguk-sa. #1124, Three-storied pagoda, Pulguk-sa.

1123 A592 20w gray, lt grn & blk .75 .25
1124 A592 20w lilac & black .75 .25

1978, July 20 *Perf. 13½x12½*

Design: No. 1126, Octagonal Pagoda, Wolchong-sa Temple.

1125 A594 20w gray & brn 1.25 .30
1126 A594 20w lt green & blk 1.25 .30

1978, Nov. 20 *Perf. 13x13½*

Designs: No. 1127, 13-storied pagoda, Jeonghye-sa. No. 1128, Three-storied pagoda, Jinjeon-sa.

1127 A592 20w pale grn & multi .50 .20
1128 A592 20w lilac & multi .50 .20
 Nos. 1119-1128 (10) 10.00 2.70

Ants and Coins — A595

Reservist with Flag — A596

1978, Apr. 1

1129 A595 20w multicolored .50 .20

Importance of saving.

1978, Apr. 1

1130 A596 20w multicolored .50 .20

10th Homeland Reserve Forces Day.

Seoul Cultural Center A597

1978, Apr. 1

1131 A597 20w multicolored .50 .20

Opening of Seoul Cultural Center.

National Assembly in Plenary Session A598

1978, May 31

1132 A598 20w multicolored .50 .20

30th anniversary of National Assembly.

Hands Holding Tools, Competition Emblem — A599

Bell of Joy and Crater Lake, Mt. Baegdu — A600

1978, Aug. 5 Photo. *Perf. 13*

1133 A599 20w multicolored .50 .20
 a. Souvenir sheet of 2 3.00 3.00

24th World Youth Skill Olympics, Busan, Aug. 30-Sept. 15.

1978, Aug. 15

1134 A600 20w multicolored .50 .20

Founding of republic, 30th anniversary.

Nurse, Badge and Flowers A601

Sobaeksan Observatory A602

1978, Aug. 26

1135 A601 20w multicolored .50 .20

Army Nurse Corps, 30th anniversary.

1978, Sept. 13 Photo. *Perf. 13*

1136 A602 20w multicolored .50 .20

Opening of Sobaeksan Natl. Observatory.

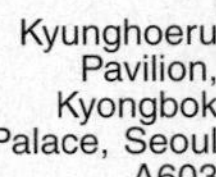

Kyunghoeru Pavilion, Kyongbok Palace, Seoul A603

Design: No. 1138, Baeg Do (island).

1978, Sept. 28

1137 A603 20w multicolored .40 .20
1138 A603 20w multicolored .40 .20

Tourist publicity.

Customs Flag and Officers A604

1978, Sept. 28

1139 A604 20w multicolored .40 .20

Cent. of 1st Korean Custom House, Busan.

Armed Forces A605

1978, Oct. 1 Photo. *Perf. 13*

1140 A605 20w multicolored .40 .20

Armed Forces, 30th anniversary.

Clay Figurines, Silla Dynasty A606

Portrait of a Lady, by Shin Yoon-bok A607

1978, Oct. 1

1141 A606 20w lt green & blk .40 .20

Culture Month, October 1978.

1978, Oct. 24

1142 A607 20w multicolored .40 .20
 a. Souvenir sheet of 2 4.00 4.00

Philatelic Week, Oct. 24-29.

Young Men, YMCA Emblem A608

1978, Oct. 28

1143 A608 20w multicolored .40 .20

75th anniv. of founding of Korean YMCA.

Hand Protecting Against Fire — A609

1978, Nov. 1 Photo. *Perf. 13*

1144 A609 20w multicolored .40 .20

Fire Prevention Day, Nov. 1.

Winter Landscape A610

Ram-headed Figure, Bas-relief A611

1978, Dec. 1 Photo. ***Perf. 13x13½***

1145 A610 20w multicolored .45 .20
a. Souvenir sheet of 2 1.75 1.75
1146 A611 20w multicolored .45 .20
a. Souvenir sheet of 2 1.75 1.75

New Year 1979.

Hibiscus, Students, Globe — A612

President Park — A613

1978, Dec. 5

1147 A612 20w multicolored .40 .20

Proclamation of National Education Charter, 10th anniversary.

1978, Dec. 27

1148 A613 20w multicolored .80 .20
a. Souvenir sheet of 2 12.50 12.50

Inauguration of Park Chung Hee for fifth term as president.

Nature Conservation Issue

Golden Mandarinfish A614

Lace-bark Pines A615

Mandarin Ducks — A616

Neofinettia Orchid — A617

Goral — A618

Lilies of the Valley — A619

Rain Frog A620

Asian Polypody A621

Firefly — A622

Meesun Tree — A623

1979, Feb. 20 Photo. ***Perf. 13x13½***

1149 A614 20w multicolored 1.50 .20
1150 A615 20w multicolored 1.50 .20

1979, May 20

1151 A616 20w multicolored 1.50 .25
1152 A617 20w multicolored 1.50 .25

1979, June 20

1153 A618 20w multicolored 1.50 .20
1154 A619 20w multicolored 1.50 .20

1979, Nov. 25

1155 A620 20w multicolored 1.50 .20
1156 A621 20w multicolored 1.50 .20

1980, Jan. 20

1157 A622 30w multicolored 1.50 .20
1158 A623 30w multicolored 1.50 .20
Nos. 1149-1158 (10) 15.00 2.10

Samil Monument — A624

1979, Mar. 1 Photo. ***Perf. 13x13½***

1159 A624 20w multicolored .40 .20

Samil independence movement, 60th anniv.

Worker and Bulldozer A625

1979, Mar. 10 ***Perf. 13½x13***

1160 A625 20w multicolored .40 .20

Labor Day.

Hand Holding Tools, Gun and Grain — A626

1979, Apr. 1 ***Perf. 13x13½***

1161 A626 20w multicolored .40 .20

Strengthening national security.

Tabo Pagoda, Pulguk-sa Temple — A627

Women, Silk Screen — A628

Art Treasures: No. 1163, Statue. No. 1164, Crown. No. 1165, Celadon Vase.

1979, Apr. 1

1162 A627 20w gray bl & multi .45 .20
1163 A627 20w bister & multi .45 .20
1164 A627 20w violet & multi .45 .20
1165 A627 20w brt grn & multi .45 .20
1166 A628 60w multicolored .90 .30
a. Souvenir sheet of 2 3.25 3.25
Nos. 1162-1166 (5) 2.70 1.10

5000 years of Korean art.
See Nos. 1175-1179, 1190.

Pulguk-sa Temple and PATA Emblem A629

1979, Apr. 16 ***Perf. 13½x13***

1167 A629 20w multicolored .40 .20

28th Pacific Area Travel Association (PATA) Conf., Seoul, Apr. 16-18, and Gyeongju, Apr. 20-21.

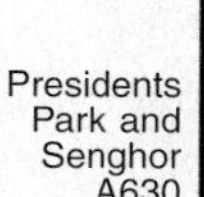

Presidents Park and Senghor A630

1979, Apr. 22 ***Perf. 13½x13***

1168 A630 20w multicolored .40 .20
a. Souvenir sheet of 2 1.50 1.50

Visit of Pres. Leopold Sedar Senghor of Senegal.

Basketball — A631

1979, Apr. 29 ***Perf. 13x13½***

1169 A631 20w multicolored .50 .20

8th World Women's Basketball Championship, Seoul, Apr. 29-May 13.

Children and IYC Emblem A632

1979, May 5 Photo. ***Perf. 13½x13***

1170 A632 20w multicolored .40 .20
a. Souvenir sheet of 2 1.50 1.50

International Year of the Child.

Traffic Pollution — A633

1979, June 5 Photo. ***Perf. 13x13½***

1171 A633 20w green & dk brn .75 .25

Pollution control.

Flags, Presidents Park and Carter A634

1979, June 29 ***Perf. 13½x13***

1172 A634 20w multicolored .40 .20
a. Souvenir sheet of 2 1.50 1.50

Visit of Pres. Jimmy Carter.

Korean Exhibition Center A635

1979, July 3

1173 A635 20w multicolored .30 .20

Opening of Korean Exhibition Center.

Jet, Globe, South Gate — A636

1979, Aug. 1 Photo. ***Perf. 13½x13***

1174 A636 20w multicolored .40 .20

10th anniversary of Korean airlines.

Art Treasure Types

Designs: No. 1175, Porcelain jar, 17th century. No. 1176, Man on horseback, ceremonial pitcher, horiz. No. 1177, Sword Dance, by Shin Yun-bok. No. 1178, Golden Amitabha with halo, 8th century. No. 1179, Hahoe ritual mask.

1979 Photo. ***Perf. 13x13½, 13½x13***

1175 A627 20w lilac & multi .60 .25
1176 A627 20w multicolored .60 .25
1177 A628 60w multicolored .85 .30
a. Souvenir sheet of 2 4.00 4.00
Nos. 1175-1177 (3) 2.05 .80

Issued: #1177, Sept. 1; #1175-1176, Oct. 15.

1979, Nov. 15

1178 A627 20w dp green & multi .50 .25
1179 A627 20w multicolored .50 .25

Yongdu Rock — A637

1979, Sept. 28

1180 A637 20w shown .40 .20
1181 A637 20w Mt. Mai, vert. .40 .20

World Tourism Day.

People, Blood and Heart — A637a

1979, Oct. 1 ***Perf. 13½x13***

1182 A637a 20w multicolored .75 .20

Blood Banks, 4th anniversary.

"My Life in the Year 2000" — A638

1979, Oct. 30 ***Perf. 13½x13***

1183 A638 20w multicolored .30 .20
a. Souvenir sheet of 2 1.40 1.40

Philatelic Week, Oct. 30-Nov. 4.

Monkey-headed Figure, Bas-relief A639

Children Playing Yut A640

1979, Dec. 1

1184 A639 20w multicolored .40 .20
a. Souvenir sheet of 2 1.25 1.25
1185 A640 20w multicolored .40 .20
a. Souvenir sheet of 2 1.25 1.25

New Year 1980.

Inauguration of Pres. Choi Kyu-hah A641

1979, Dec. 21

1186 A641 20w multicolored .45 .20
a. Souvenir sheet of 2 5.00 5.00

President Park — A642

1980, Feb. 2 **Photo.** ***Perf. 13x13½***

1187 A642 30w orange brn .45 .20
1188 A642 30w dull purple .45 .20
a. Souvenir sheet of 2 4.00 4.00
b. Pair, #1187-1188 2.25 2.25

President Park Chung Hee (1917-1979) memorial.

Art Treasure Type of 1979 and

Dragon-shaped Kettle — A643

Design: 60w, Landscape, by Kim Hong-do.

Perf. 13½x13, 13x13½

1980, Feb. 20 **Photo.**

1189 A643 30w multicolored .60 .20
1190 A628 60w multicolored 1.00 .30
a. Souvenir sheet of 2 3.50 3.50

Art Treasure Issue

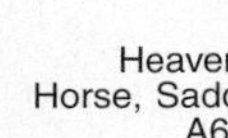

Heavenly Horse, Saddle A644

Dragon Head, Banner Staff A645

Tiger, Granite Sculpture A647

Mounted Nobleman Mural — A646

Human Face, Roof Tile — A648

Deva King Sculpture — A650

White Tiger Mural — A649

Earthenware Ducks — A651

Tiger, Folk Painting — A653

Perf. 13½x13, 13x13½

1980-83 **Photo.**

1191 A644 30w multicolored .60 .20
1192 A645 30w multicolored .60 .20
1193 A646 30w multicolored .60 .20
1194 A647 30w multicolored .60 .20
1195 A648 30w multicolored .50 .20
1196 A649 30w multicolored .50 .20

Engr. ***Perf. 12½x13***

1197 A650 30w black .55 .20
1198 A650 30w red .55 .20

1983 **Litho.** ***Perf. 13***

1199 1000w bis brn & red brn 5.00 .80
1200 1000w bis brn & red brn 5.00 .80
a. A651 Pair, #1199-1200 10.00 5.00
1201 A653 5000w multicolored 25.00 5.00
a. Souvenir sheet, perf. 13½x13 30.00
Nos. 1191-1201 (11) 39.50 8.20

Issued: #1191-1192, 4/20; #1193-1194, 5/20; #1195-1196, 8/20; #1197-1198, 11/20. #1199-1200, 11/25/83. #1201, 12/1/83.

No. 1201a for PHILAKOREA '84. No. 1201a exists imperf. Value $150.

Lotus Blossoms and Ducks — A656

Tiger and Magpie A657

1980, Mar. 10 ***Perf. 13x13½, 13½x13***

1203 A656 30w multicolored .55 .20
1204 A657 60w multicolored 1.00 .50

Red Phoenix (in Form of Rooster) — A658

Moon Over Mt. Konryun — A659

No. 1207, Sun over Mt. Konryun. No. 1207a has continuous design.

1980, May 10 ***Perf. 13x13½***

1205 A658 30w multicolored .50 .20
1206 A659 60w multicolored 1.50 .45
1207 A659 60w multicolored 1.50 .45
a. Souvenir sheet of 2, #1206-1207 5.00 5.00
b. Pair, #1206-1207 3.75 3.00
Nos. 1205-1207 (3) 3.50 1.10

Rabbits Pounding Grain in a Mortar — A660

Dragon in the Clouds — A661

1980, July 10 **Photo.** ***Perf. 13x13½***

1208 A660 30w multicolored .60 .25
1209 A661 30w multicolored .60 .25

Pine Tree, Pavilion, Mountain A662

Flowers and Birds, Bridal Room Screen A663

1980, Aug. 9 **Photo.** ***Perf. 13x13½***

1210 A662 30w multicolored .55 .25
1211 A663 30w multicolored 1.10 .30

Tortoises and Cranes A664

Symbols of longevity: a, cranes, tortoises. b, buck. c, doe. d, waterfall.

1980, Nov. 10 **Photo.** ***Perf. 13½x13***

1212 Strip of 4 6.50 4.50
a.-d. A664 30w any single 1.40 .20

New Community Movement, 10th Anniv. — A668

Freighters at Sea — A669

1980, Apr. 22 ***Perf. 13x13½***

1216 A668 30w multicolored .40 .20

1980, Mar. 13

1217 A669 30w multicolored .40 .20

Increase of Korea's shipping tonnage to 5 million tons.

Soccer — A670

1980, Aug. 23 ***Perf. 13x13½***

1218 A670 30w multicolored .40 .20

10th President's Cup Soccer Tournament, Aug. 23-Sept. 5.

Mt. Sorak — A671

Paikryung Island — A672

Perf. 12½x13½

1980, Apr. 10 **Photo.**

1219 A671 15w multicolored .35 .20
1220 A672 90w multicolored 1.00 .20

Flag — A673

1980 ***Perf. 13½x13***

1221 A673 30w multicolored .45 .20

Coil Stamp

Perf. Vert.

1221A A673 30w multicolored 1.40 .20

UN Intervention, 30th Anniv. — A674

Election of Miss World in Seoul — A675

1980, June 25 ***Perf. 13x13½***

1222 A674 30w multicolored .40 .20

1980, July 8

1223 A675 30w multicolored .40 .20

Women's Army Corps, 30th Anniversary A676

1980, Sept. 6 ***Perf. 13½x13***

1224 A676 30w multicolored .40 .20

Baegma River — A677

Three Peaks of Dodam A678

1980, Sept. 28

1225 A677 30w multicolored .40 .20

1226 A678 30w multicolored .40 .20

Inauguration of Pres. Chun Doo-hwan A679

1980, Sept. 1

1227 A679 30w multicolored .45 .20

a. Souvenir sheet of 2 3.00 3.00

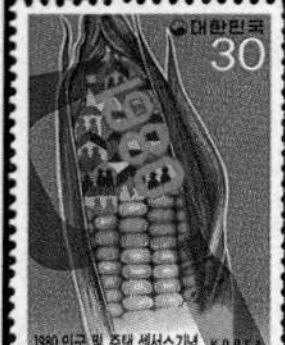

Ear of Corn — A680

Symbolic Tree — A681

1980, Oct. 20 ***Perf. 13x13½***

1228 A680 30w multicolored .40 .20

12th population and housing census.

1980, Oct. 27

1229 A681 30w multicolored .40 .20

National Red Cross, 75th anniversary.

"Mail-Delivering Angels" — A682

1980, Nov. 6 ***Perf. 13½x13***

1230 A682 30w multicolored .40 .20

a. Souvenir sheet of 2 1.40 1.40

Philatelic Week, Nov. 6-11.

Korea-Japan Submarine Cable System Inauguration A683

1980, Nov. 28 ***Perf. 13x13½***

1231 A683 30w multicolored .40 .20

Rooster — A684

Cranes — A685

1980, Dec. 1

1232 A684 30w multicolored .45 .20

a. Souvenir sheet of 2 1.40 1.40

1233 A685 30w multicolored .45 .20

a. Souvenir sheet of 2 1.40 1.40

New Year 1981.

Second Inauguration of Pres. Chun Doo-hwan A686

1981, Mar. 3 Photo. ***Perf. 13½x13***

1234 A686 30w multicolored .40 .20

a. Souvenir sheet of 2 1.25 1.25

Ship Issue

Oil Tanker A687

Cargo Ship — A688

Oil Tanker A689

Cargo Ship — A690

Tug Boat — A691

Stern Trawler A692

Log Carrier A693

Auto Carrier A694

Chemical Carrier A695

Passenger Boat A696

1981, Mar. 13 ***Perf. 13½x13, 13x13½***

1235 A687 30w multicolored .50 .20

1236 A688 90w multicolored .80 .25

5th Maritime Day.

1981, May 10 Photo. ***Perf. 13½x13***

1237 A689 30w multicolored .50 .20

1238 A690 90w multicolored .90 .30

1981, July 10 ***Perf. 13½x13***

1239 A691 40w multicolored .65 .20

1240 A692 100w multicolored 1.10 .30

1981, Aug. 10

1241 A693 40w multicolored .65 .20

1242 A694 100w multicolored 1.10 .30

1981, Nov. 10 Engr. ***Perf. 13x12½***

1243 A695 40w black .55 .20

1244 A696 100w dk blue 1.00 .30

Nos. 1235-1244 (10) 7.75 2.45

11th Natl. Assembly Opening Session A697

1981, Apr. 17 Photo. ***Perf. 13½x13***

1245 A697 30w gold & dk brn .40 .20

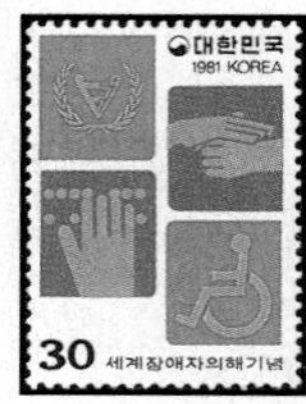

Hand Reading Braille, Helping Hands — A698

1981, Apr. 20 Photo. ***Perf. 13x13½***

1246 A698 30w shown .40 .20

1247 A698 90w Man in wheel-chair .75 .20

International Year of the Disabled.

Ribbon and Council Emblem A699

Clena River and Mountains A700

1981, June 5 Photo. ***Perf. 13x13½***

1248 A699 40w multicolored .40 .20

Advisory Council on Peaceful Unification Policy (North and South Korea) anniv.

1981, June 5

1249 A700 30w shown .40 .20

1250 A700 90w Seagulls .85 .25

10th World Environment Day.

Pres. Chun and Pres. Suharto of Indonesia A701

Pres. Chun Visit to Asia: b, King of Malaysia. c, Korean, Singapore flags. d, King Bhumibol Adulyadej of Thailand. e, Pres. Marcos of Philippines.

1981, June 25 ***Perf. 13½x13***

1251 Strip of 5 4.50 3.75

a.-e. A701 40w, any single .55 .20

f. Souvenir sheet of 5, imperf. 2.50 2.50

Size: 49x33mm

Perf. 13x13½

1252 A701 40w multicolored .55 .20

a. Souvenir sheet of 2, imperf. 2.25 2.25

36th Anniv. of Liberation — A702

1981, Aug. 15 Photo. ***Perf. 13x13½***

1253 A702 40w multicolored .40 .20

Tolharubang, "Stone Grandfather" A704

Rose of Sharon A705

Porcelain Jar, 17th Cent. — A706

Chomsongdae Observatory, 7th Cent. — A707

Mounted Warrior, Earthenware Jug, 5th Cent. A708

Family Planning A709

Walking Stick A710

Ryu Kwan-soon (1904-20), Martyr A711

"Tasan" Chung Yak-yong, Lee Dynasty Scholar A712

Ahn Joong-geun (1879-1910), Martyr A713

Ahn Chang-ho (1878-1938), Independence Fighter A714

Koryo Celadon Incense Burner A715

Kim Ku (1876-1949), Statesman A716

Mountain Landscape Brick Bas-relief A717

Mandarin Duck, Celadon Incense Burner — A718

Perf. 13½x12½ (Nos. 1256, 1257, 1266), 13, 13½x13, 13x13½

1981-89 **Photo., Engr.**

1255	A704	20w	multi ('86)	.40	.20
1256	A705	40w	multi	.50	.20
1257	A706	60w	multi	.50	.20
1258	A707	70w	multi	.75	.20
1259	A708	80w	multi ('83)	.85	.20
1260	A709	80w	multi ('86)	1.00	.25
1261	A710	80w	multi ('89)	2.50	.25
1262	A711	100w	lilac	1.00	.20
1263	A712	100w	gray blk ('86)	2.50	.20
1264	A713	200w	lt ol grn & ol	1.50	.25
1265	A714	300w	dl lil ('83)	2.25	.25
1266	A715	400w	multi	5.00	.50
1267	A715	400w	pale grn & multi ('83)	3.50	.40
1268	A716	450w	dk vio brn ('86)	2.75	.40
1269	A717	500w	multi	3.50	.75
1270	A718	700w	multi ('83)	5.00	.80
	Nos. 1255-1270 (16)			33.50	5.25

Inscription and denomination of No. 1266, colorless, No. 1267, dark brown.

See Nos. 1449, 1449C, 1594F.

Coil Stamp

Photo. ***Perf. 13 Horiz.***

1271 A707 70w multicolored 2.00 .50

Girl Flying Model Plane — A721

Air Force Chief of Staff Cup, 3rd Aeronautic Competition: Various model planes.

1981, Sept. 20 ***Perf. 13½x13***

1272	Strip of 5	4.50	3.75
a.	A721 10w multi	.50	.20
b.	A721 20w multi	.50	.20
c.	A721 40w multi	.50	.20
d.	A721 50w multi	.65	.30
e.	A721 80w multi	.90	.40

WHO Emblem, Citizens — A722

World Tourism Day — A723

1981, Sept. 22 ***Perf. 13x13½***

1273 A722 40w multicolored .40 .20

WHO, 32nd Western Pacific Regional Committee Meeting, Seoul, Sept. 22-28.

1981, Sept. 28

1274	A723 40w Seoul Tower	.40	.20
1275	A723 40w Ulreung Isld.	.40	.20

Bicycle Racing A724

1981, Oct. 10 ***Perf. 13½x13***

1276	A724 40w shown	.45	.20
1277	A724 40w Swimming	.45	.20

62nd Natl. Sports Festival, Seoul, 10/10-15.

Flags, Presidents Chun and Carazo A725

1981, Oct. 12 ***Perf. 13½x13***

1278 A725 40w multicolored .45 .20

Visit of Pres. Rodrigo Carazo Odio of Costa Rica, Oct. 12-14.

World Food Day — A726

1981, Oct. 16 ***Perf. 13x13½***

1279 A726 40w multicolored .40 .20

First Natl. Aviation Day — A727

1981, Oct. 30 ***Perf. 13½x13***

1280 A727 40w multicolored .45 .20

1988 Olympic Games, Seoul — A728

1981, Oct. 30 ***Perf. 13x13½***

1281 A728 40w multicolored .60 .20

9th Philatelic Week, Nov. 18-24 — A729

1981, Nov. 18 ***Perf. 13½x13***

1282	A729 40w multicolored	.40	.20
a.	Souvenir sheet of 2	1.60	1.60

Camellia and Dog — A730

Children Flying Kite — A731

1981, Dec. 1 ***Perf. 13x13½***

1283	A730 40w multicolored	.40	.20
a.	Souvenir sheet of 2	1.60	1.60
1284	A731 40w multicolored	.40	.20
a.	Souvenir sheet of 2	1.60	1.60

New Year 1982 (Year of the Dog).

Hangul Hakhoe Language Society, 60th Anniv. A732

1981, Dec. 3 ***Perf. 13½x13***

1285 A732 40w multicolored .45 .20

Telecommunications Authority Inauguration A733

1982, Jan. 4 **Photo.** ***Perf. 13x13½***

1286 A733 60w multicolored .50 .20

Scouting Year — A734

1982, Feb. 22

1287 A734 60w multicolored .50 .20

60th Anniv. of YWCA in Korea — A735

1982, Apr. 20 **Photo.** ***Perf. 13x13½***

1288 A735 60w multicolored .45 .20

Intl. Polar Year Centenary A736

1982, Apr. 21 ***Perf. 13½x13***

1289 A736 60w multicolored .50 .20

60th Children's Day — A737

1982, May 5 ***Perf. 13½x13***

1290 A737 60w multicolored .45 .20

Visit of Liberian Pres. Samuel K. Doe, May 9-13 A738

1982, May 9 **Litho.** ***Perf. 13x12½***

1291	A738 60w multicolored	.50	.20
a.	Souvenir sheet of 2, imperf.	1.60	1.60

Centenary of US-Korea Treaty of Amity — A739

1982, May 18 **Photo.** ***Perf. 13½x13***

1292	A739 60w Statue of Liberty, pagoda	.45	.20
1293	A739 60w Emblem	.45	.20
a.	Souvenir sheet of 2	3.50	3.50
b.	Pair, #1292-1293	1.50	1.50

Visit of Zaire Pres. Mobutu Sese Seko, June 7-10 A740

1982, June 7 Litho. ***Perf. 13x12½***

1294	A740 60w multicolored		.45	.20
	a.	Souvenir sheet of 2, imperf.	1.60	1.60

Historical Painting Issue

Gen. Kwon Yul's Victory at Haengju, by Oh Seung-woo — A747

Designs: No. 1295, Territorial Expansion by Kwanggaeto the Great, by Lee Chong-sang, 1975. No. 1296, Gen. Euljimunduck's Victory at Salsoo, by Park Kak-soon, 1975. No. 1297, Shilla's Repulse of Tang's Army, by Oh Seung-woo. No. 1298, Gen. Kang Kam-chan's Victory at Kyiju, by Lee Yong-hwan. No. 1299, Admiral Yi Sun-sin's Victory at Hansan, 1592, by Kim Hyung-ku. No. 1300, Gen. Kim Chwa-jin's Battle at Chungsanri, by Sohn Soo-kwang. No. 1302, Kim Chong-suh's Exploitation of Yukjin, 1434, by Kim Tae.

1982 Photo. ***Perf. 13x13½***

1295	A747 60w multicolored	.75	.40
1296	A747 60w multicolored	1.40	.60
1297	A747 60w multicolored	.65	.30
1298	A747 60w multicolored	.65	.30
1299	A747 60w multicolored	1.00	.40
1300	A747 60w multicolored	1.00	.40
1301	A747 60w shown	1.10	.40
1302	A747 60w multicolored	1.10	.40
	Nos. 1295-1302 (8)	7.65	3.20

Issued: #1295-1296, 6/15; #1297-1298, 7/15; #1299-1300, 10/15; #1301-1302, 12/15.

55th Intl. YMCA Convention, Seoul, July 20-23 — A749

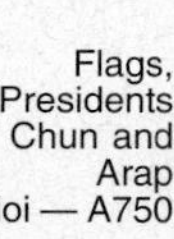

Flags, Presidents Chun and Arap Moi — A750

1982, July 20

1303	A749 60w multicolored	.40	.20

1982, Aug. 17 ***Perf. 13½x13***

Pres. Chun's Visit to Africa & Canada: #1304, Kenya (Pres. Daniel T. Arap Moi), Aug. 17-19. #1305, Nigeria (Pres. Alhaji Shehe Shagari), Aug. 19-22. #1306, Gabon (Pres. El Hadj Omar Bongo), Aug. 22-24. #1307, Senegal (Pres. Abdou Diouf), Aug. 24-26. #1308, Canada, Aug. 28-31.

1304	A750 60w multicolored	.45	.20
1305	A750 60w multicolored	.45	.20
1306	A750 60w multicolored	.45	.20
1307	A750 60w multicolored	.45	.20
1308	A750 60w multicolored	.45	.20
	Nos. 1304-1308 (5)	2.25	1.00

Souvenir Sheets of 2

1304a	A750 60w	2.25	2.25
1305a	A750 60w	2.25	2.25
1306a	A750 60w	2.25	2.25
1307a	A750 60w	2.25	2.25
1308a	A750 60w	2.25	2.25
	Nos. 1304a-1308a (5)	11.25	11.25

Natl. Flag Centenary A751

1982, Aug. 22

1309	A751 60w multicolored		.45	.20
	a.	Souvenir sheet of 2	2.25	2.25

2nd Seoul Open Intl. Table Tennis Championship, Aug. 25-31 — A752

1982, Aug. 25

1310	A752 60w multicolored	.50	.20

27th World Amateur Baseball Championship Series, Seoul, Sept. 4-18 — A753

1982, Sept. 4 Engr. ***Perf. 13***

1311	A753 60w red brn	.50	.20

Seoul Intl. Trade Fair (SITRA '82), Sept. 24-Oct. 18 — A754

1982, Sept. 17 Photo. ***Perf. 13½x13***

1312	A754 60w multicolored	.45	.20

Philatelic Week, Oct. 15-21 — A755

Design: Miners reading consolatory letters.

1982, Oct. 15

1313	A755 60w multicolored		.45	.20
	a.	Souvenir sheet of 2	1.50	1.50

Visit of Indonesian Pres. Suharto, Oct. 16-19 — A756

1982, Oct. 16 Litho. ***Perf. 13x12½***

1314	A756 60w multicolored		.40	.20
	a.	Souvenir sheet of 2, imperf.	1.40	1.40

37th Jaycee (Intl. Junior Chamber of Commerce) World Congress, Seoul, Nov. 3-18 — A757

1982, Nov. 3 ***Perf. 13½x13***

1315	A757 60w multicolored	.40	.20

2nd UN Conference on Peaceful Uses of Outer Space, Vienna, Aug. 9-21 — A758

1982, Nov. 20 ***Perf. 13x13½***

1316	A758 60w multicolored	.45	.20

New Year 1983 (Year of the Boar) — A759

1982, Dec. 1

1317	A759 60w Magpies, money bag		.45	.20
	a.	Souvenir sheet of 2	2.00	2.00
1318	A759 60w Boar, bas-relief		.45	.20
	a.	Souvenir sheet of 2	2.00	2.00

Flags of Korea and Turkey — A760

1982, Dec. 20 ***Perf. 13***

1319	A760 60w multicolored		.45	.20
	a.	Souvenir sheet of 2, imperf.	1.50	1.50

Visit of Pres. Kenan Evren of Turkey, Dec. 20-23.

Letter Writing Campaign — A761

1982, Dec. 31 Photo. ***Perf. 13x13½***

1320	A761 60w multicolored	.40	.20

First Intl. Customs Day — A762

1983, Jan. 26 ***Perf. 13½x13***

1321	A762 60w multicolored	.50	.20

Korean-made Vehicle Issue

Hyundai Pony-2 A764

Daewoo Maepsy A765

Super Titan Truck — A768

Flat-bed Truck — A770

1983 Photo. ***Perf. 13½x13***

1322	A764 60w Keohwa Jeep		.75	.25
1323	A764 60w shown		.75	.25
	a.	Pair, #1322-1323	2.25	2.25
1324	A765 60w shown		.75	.25
1325	A764 60w Kia minibus		.75	.25
	a.	Pair, #1324-1325	2.25	2.25
1326	A764 60w Highway bus		.75	.25
1327	A768 60w shown		.75	.25
1328	A764 70w Dump truck		.90	.25
1329	A770 70w shown		.90	.25
1330	A764 70w Cement mixer		.90	.25
1331	A764 70w Oil truck		.90	.25
	Nos. 1322-1331 (10)		8.10	2.50

Issued: #1322-1323, Feb. 25; #1324-1325, Mar. 25; #1326-1327, May 25; #1328-1329, July 25; #1330-1331, Aug. 25.

Visit of Malaysian Seri Paduka Baginda, Mar. 22-26 — A773

1983, Mar. 22

1332	A773 60w multicolored		.40	.20
	a.	Souvenir sheet of 2	1.40	1.40

Postal Service Issue

General Bureau of Postal Administration Building A774

Mailman, 1884 — A776

Ancient Mail Carrier A778

Nos. 1-2 — A780

Pre-modern Period Postal Symbol, Mailbox A782

Designs: #1334, Seoul Central PO. #1336, Mailman on motorcycle, 1983. #1338, Modern mail transport. #1340, No. 1201. #1342, Current postal symbol, mailbox.

1983-84 Photo. *Perf. 13½x13*

1333 A774 60w multicolored .60 .25
1334 A774 60w multicolored .60 .25
1335 A776 70w multicolored .70 .25
1336 A776 70w multicolored .70 .25
1337 A778 70w multicolored .90 .25
1338 A778 70w multicolored .90 .25
1339 A780 70w multicolored .60 .20
1340 A780 70w multicolored .60 .20
1341 A782 70w multicolored .60 .20
1342 A782 70w multicolored .60 .20
Nos. 1333-1342 (10) 6.80 2.30

PHILAKOREA '84, Seoul, Oct. 22-31, 1984.
Issued: #1333-1334, Apr. 22; #1335-1336, June 10; #1337-1338, Aug. 10; #1339-1340, Feb. 10, 1984; #1341-1342, Mar. 10, 1984.

Teachers' Day — A784

1983, May 15 Photo. *Perf. 13x13½*

1343 A784 60w Village school-house, score .50 .20
a. Souvenir sheet of 2 2.00 2.00

World Communications Year — A785

1983, June 20

1344 A785 70w multicolored .50 .20
a. Souvenir sheet of 2 1.50 1.50

Communications Life Insurance Inauguration — A786

1983, July 1 Photo. *Perf. 13½x13*

1345 A786 70w multicolored .70 .20

Science and Technology Symposium, Seoul, July 4-8 — A787

1983, July 4

1346 A787 70w multicolored .50 .20

Visit of Jordan's King Hussein, Sept. 10-13 A788

1983, Sept. 10 Litho. *Perf. 13x12½*

1347 A788 70w Pres. Hwan, King Hussein, flags .50 .20
a. Souvenir sheet of 2, imperf. 1.50 1.50

ASTA, 53rd World Travel Congress, Seoul — A789

1983, Sept. 25 Photo. *Perf. 13*

1348 A789 70w multicolored .50 .20

A790

A791

1983, Oct. 4 Photo. *Perf. 13*

1349 A790 70w multicolored .50 .20
a. Souvenir sheet of 2 1.50 1.50

70th Inter-Parliamentary Union Conference.

1983, Oct. 6 Photo. *Perf. 13*

1350 A791 70w Gymnastics .65 .20
1351 A791 70w Soccer .65 .20

64th National Sports Festival.

Pres. Chun and Pres. U San Yu of Burma A791a

Pres. Chun's Curtailed Visit to Southwest Asia: No. 1351B, India. No. 1351C, Pres. Junius R. Jayawardene, Sri Lanka. No. 1351D, Australia, flag. No. 1351E, New Zealand, flag. Withdrawn after one day due to political assassination.

1983, Oct. 8 Photo. *Perf. 13½x13*

1351A A791a 70w multicolored 1.50 .75
1351B A791a 70w multicolored 1.50 .75
1351C A791a 70w multicolored 1.50 .75
1351D A791a 70w multicolored 1.50 .75
1351E A791a 70w multicolored 1.50 .75
Nos. 1351A-1351E (5) 7.50 3.75

Souvenir Sheets of 2

1351f A791a 70w 5.00 5.00
1351g A791a 70w 5.00 5.00
1351h A791a 70w 5.00 5.00
1351i A791a 70w 5.00 5.00
1351j A791a 70w 5.00 5.00
Nos. 1351f-1351j (5) 25.00 25.00

Water Resource Development A792

1983, Oct. 15 Litho. *Perf. 13*

1352 A792 70w multicolored .50 .20

Newspaper Publication Cent. — A793

1983, Oct. 31 Litho. *Perf. 13*

1353 A793 70w multicolored .50 .20

Natl. Tuberculosis Assoc., 30th Anniv. — A794

1983, Nov. 6 Photo. *Perf. 13*

1354 A794 70w multicolored .50 .20

Presidents Chun and Reagan, Natl. Flags — A795

1983, Nov. 12 Photo. *Perf. 13*

1355 A795 70w multicolored .50 .20
a. Souvenir sheet of 2 3.00 3.00

Visit of Pres. Ronald Reagan, Nov. 12-14.

11th Philatelic Week — A796

1983, Nov. 18 Photo. *Perf. 13*

1356 A796 70w multicolored .50 .20
a. Souvenir sheet of 2 2.75 2.75

New Year 1984
A797 A798

1983, Dec. 1 Photo. *Perf. 13*

1357 A797 70w Mouse, stone wall relief .50 .20
a. Souvenir sheet of 2 2.50 2.50
1358 A798 70w Cranes, pine tree .50 .20
a. Souvenir sheet of 2 2.50 2.50

Bicentenary of Catholic Church in Korea — A799

1984, Jan. 4 Photo. *Perf. 13x13½*

1359 A799 70w Cross .40 .20
a. Souvenir sheet of 2 3.25 3.25

Visit of Brunei's Sultan Bolkiah-Apr. 7-9 — A800

1984, Apr. 7 Litho. *Perf. 13x12½*

1360 A800 70w multicolored .50 .20
a. Souvenir sheet of 2, imperf. 1.50 1.50

Visit of Qatar's Sheik Khalifa, Apr. 20-22 A801

1984, Apr. 20

1361 A801 70w multicolored .50 .20
a. Souvenir sheet of 2, imperf. 1.50 1.50

Girl Mailing Letter — A802

Mailman in City — A803

1984, Apr. 22 Photo. *Perf. 13½x13*

1362 A802 70w multicolored .40 .20
a. Souvenir sheet of 2 1.75 1.75
1363 A803 70w multicolored .40 .20
a. Souvenir sheet of 2 1.75 1.75

Korean postal service.

Visit of Pope John Paul II, May 3-7 — A808

1984, May 3 Engr. *Perf. 12½*

1368 A808 70w dk brn .60 .20

Photogravure & Engraved

1369 A808 70w multicolored .60 .20
a. Souvenir sheet of 2, #1368-1369, perf. 13½ 2.50 2.50

A809

A810

1984, May 11 Photo. *Perf. 13x13½*
1370 A809 70w Tools, brushes, flower .50 .20

Workers' Cultural Festival.

1984, May 21 Photo. *Perf. 13x13½*
1371 A810 70w Jet, ship, Asia map .50 .20

Customs Cooperation Council 63rd-64th Sessions, Seoul, May 21-25.

Visit of Sri Lanka's Pres. Jayewardene, May 27-30 — A811

1984, May 27 *Perf. 13½x13*
1372 A811 70w Asia map, flags, flowers .50 .20
a. Souvenir sheet of 2 1.50 1.50

Advertising Congress Emblem — A812

'88 Olympic Expressway Opening — A813

1984, June 18 Photo. *Perf. 13x13½*
1373 A812 70w ADASIA '84 emblem .50 .20

14th Asian Advertising Cong., Seoul, June 18-21.

1984, June 22
1374 A813 70w multicolored .65 .20

Intl. Olympic Committee, 90th Anniv. — A814

1984, June 23
1375 A814 70w multicolored .50 .20

Asia-Pacific Broadcasting Union, 20th Anniv. A815

1984, June 30 *Perf. 13½x13*
1376 A815 70w Emblem, microphone .50 .20

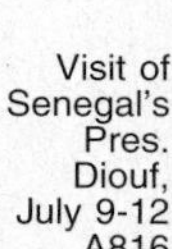

Visit of Senegal's Pres. Diouf, July 9-12 A816

1984, July 9 Litho. *Perf. 13x12½*
1377 A816 70w Flags of Korea & Senegal .50 .20
a. Souvenir sheet of 2, imperf. 2.00 2.00

1984 Summer Olympics A817

Lithographed and Engraved

1984, July 28 *Perf. 12½*
1378 A817 70w Archery .75 .25
1379 A817 440w Fencing 3.00 .75

Korean Protestant Church Cent. A818

Groom on Horseback A819

Stained glass windows.

1984, Aug. 16 *Perf. 13*
1380 A818 70w Crucifixion .75 .20
1381 A818 70w Cross, dove .75 .20
a. Souvenir sheet of 2 6.00 6.00
b. Pair, #1380-1381 2.00 2.00

1984, Sept. 1 Photo. *Perf. 13x13½*

Wedding Procession: a, Lantern carrier. b, Groom. c, Musician. d, Bride in sedan chair (52x33mm).

1382 Strip of 4 3.00 1.50
a.-d. A819 70w any single .70 .25
e. Souvenir sheet 2.50 2.50

No. 1382e contains No. 1382d.

Pres. Chun's Visit to Japan, Sept. 6-8 A820

1984, Sept. 6 Litho. *Perf. 13x12½*
1383 A820 70w Chun, flag, Mt. Fuji .50 .20
a. Souvenir sheet of 2, imperf. 2.00 2.00

Visit of Gambia's Pres. Jawara, Sept. 12-17 A821

1984, Sept. 12
1384 A821 70w Flags of Korea & Gambia .50 .20
a. Souvenir sheet of 2, imperf. 2.00 2.00

Visit of Gabon's Pres. Bongo, Sept. 21-23 — A822

1984, Sept. 21 *Perf. 13*
1385 A822 70w Flags of Korea & Gabon .50 .20
a. Souvenir sheet of 2, imperf. 1.75 1.75

Seoul Intl. Trade Fair — A823

1984, Sept. 18 Photo. *Perf. 13x13½*
1386 A823 70w Products .50 .20

65th Natl. Sports Festival, Taegu, Oct. 11-16 — A824

1984, Oct. 11 Photo. *Perf. 13½x13*
1387 A824 70w Badminton .50 .20
1388 A824 70w Wrestling .50 .20

Philakorea '84 Stamp Show, Seoul, Oct. 22-31 A825

1984, Oct. 22 *Perf. 13½x13, 13x13½*
1389 A825 70w South Gate, stamps .50 .20
a. Souvenir sheet of 4 3.50 3.50
1390 A825 70w Emblem under magnifier, vert. .50 .20
a. Souvenir sheet of 4 3.50 3.50

Visit of Maldives Pres. Maumoon Abdul Gayoom, Oct. 29-Nov. 1 A826

1984, Oct. 29 Litho. *Perf. 13x12½*
1392 A826 70w multicolored .50 .20
a. Souvenir sheet of 2, imperf. 2.00 2.00

Chamber of Commerce and Industry Cent. A827

Children Playing Jaegi-chagi A828

1984, Oct. 31 Photo. *Perf. 13x13½*
1393 A827 70w "100" .50 .20

1984, Dec. 1 Photo. *Perf. 13x13½*

New Year 1985 (Year of the ox).

1394 A828 70w Ox, bas-relief .50 .20
a. Souvenir sheet of 2 1.75 1.75
1395 A828 70w shown .50 .20
a. Souvenir sheet of 2 1.75 1.75

Intl. Youth Year — A829

1985, Jan. 25 Photo. *Perf. 13½x13*
1396 A829 70w IYY emblem .50 .20

Folkways — A830

1985, Feb. 19 Photo. *Perf. 13x13½*
1397 A830 70w Pounding rice .50 .20
1398 A830 70w Welcoming full moon .50 .20

1985, Aug. 20
1399 A830 70w Wrestling .75 .20
1400 A830 70w Janggi, Korean chess .75 .20

Modern Art Series

Rocky Mountain in the Early Spring, 1915, by Shimjoen, (Ahn Jung-shik) A831

Still-life with a Doll, 1927, by Suhlcho, (Lee Chong-woo) A832

Spring Day on a Farm, 1961, by Eijai, (Huh Paik-ryun, 1903-1977) A833

The Exorcist, 1941, by Chulma, (Kim Chung-hyun, 1901-1953) — A834

Chunhyang-do, by Kim Un-ho — A835

Flowers, by Lee Sang-bum A836

Image of A Friend, by Ku Bon-wung A837

Woman in a Ski Suit, by Son Ung-seng A838

Valley of the Peach Blossoms, 1964, by Pyen Kwan-Sik (1899-1976) A839

Rural Landscape, 1940, by Lee Yong-Wu (1904-1952) A840

Male, 1932, by Lee Ma-Dong A841

Woman with a Water Jar on Her Head, 1944, by Yun Hyo-Chung (1917-1967) A842

Photo.; Litho. & Engr. (#1411-1412)

1985-87 ***Perf. 13½x13, 13x13½***

1401	A831 70w multicolored	.75	.25
1402	A832 70w multicolored	.75	.25
1403	A833 70w multicolored	.75	.25
1404	A834 70w multicolored	.75	.25
1405	A835 80w multi ('86)	1.25	.40
1406	A836 80w multi ('86)	1.25	.40
1407	A837 80w multi ('86)	1.25	.40
1408	A838 80w multi ('86)	1.25	.40
1409	A839 80w multi ('87)	*3.50*	.90
1410	A840 80w multi ('87)	*3.50*	.90
1411	A841 80w multi ('87)	*3.50*	.90
1412	A842 80w multi ('87)	*3.50*	.90
	Nos. 1401-1412 (12)	*22.00*	6.20

Issued: #1401-1402, 4/10; #1403-1404, 7/5; #1405-1408, 12/1; #1409-1412, 6/12.

State Visit of Pres. Chun to the US — A843

Photo. & Engr.

1985, Apr. 24 ***Perf. 13***

1413	A843 70w multicolored	.50	.20
a.	Souvenir sheet of 2	2.00	2.00

Coastal and Inland Fish Series

Gak-si- Bung-eo (silver carp) — A844

Dot-sac-chi (sword fish) — A845

Eoreumchi A846

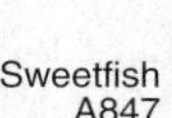

Sweetfish A847

Sardine A848

Hammerhead Shark A849

Cham-jung-go-ji — A850

Swi-ri — A851

Oar Fish — A852

Devil-ray A853

1985-87 **Photo.** ***Perf. 13½x13***

1414	A844 70w multicolored	.75	.25
1415	A845 70w multicolored	.75	.25
1416	A846 70w multi ('86)	2.00	.55
1417	A847 70w multi ('86)	2.00	.55
1418	A848 70w multi ('86)	2.00	.55
1419	A849 70w multi ('86)	2.00	.55
1420	A850 80w multi ('87)	2.50	1.00
1421	A851 80w multi ('87)	2.50	1.00
1422	A852 80w multi ('87)	2.50	1.00
1423	A853 80w multi ('87)	2.50	1.00
	Nos. 1414-1423 (10)	19.50	6.70

Issued: #1414-1415, 5/30; #1416-1423, 7/25.

Yonsei University and Medical School, Cent. A854

Photogravure and Engraved

1985, May 6 ***Perf. 13***

1424	A854 70w Underwood Hall	.50	.20

State Visit of Pres. Mohammad Zia-Ul-Haq of Pakistan, May 6-10 — A855

1985, May 6 **Photo.** ***Perf. 13x13½***

1425	A855 70w multicolored	.50	.20
a.	Souvenir sheet of 2	1.50	1.50

State Visit of Pres. Luis Alberto Monge of Costa Rica, May 19-23 — A856

1985, May 18 ***Perf. 13½x13***

1426	A856 70w multicolored	.50	.20
a.	Souvenir sheet of 2	1.50	1.50

State Visit of Pres. Hussain Muhammad Ershad of Bangladesh, June 15-19 A857

1985, June 15

1427	A857 70w multicolored	.50	.20
a.	Souvenir sheet of 2, imperf.	1.50	1.50

State Visit of Pres. Joao Bernardo Vieira of Guinea-Bissau, June 25-28 — A858

1985, June 25

1428	A858 70w multicolored	.50	.20
a.	Souvenir sheet of 2, imperf.	1.50	1.50

Liberation from Japanese Occupation Forces, 40th Anniv. — A859

Heavenly Lake, Mt. Paektu, natl. flower.

1985, Aug. 14 **Litho.** ***Perf. 13x12½***

1429	A859 70w multicolored	.50	.20

Folk Music Series

The Spring of My Home, Music by Hong Nan-pa and Lyrics by Lee Won-su A860

A Leaf Boat, Music by Yun Yong-ha and Lyrics by Park Hong-Keun A861

Half Moon, 1924, by Yun Keuk-Young A862

Let's Go and Pick the Moon, by Yun Seok-Jung and Park Tae Hyun A863

Korean Farm Music A864

Barley Field, by Park Wha-mok and Yun Yong-ha — A865

Magnolia, by Cho Young-Shik and Kim Dong-jin — A866

Chusok, Harvest Moon Festival — A867

1985, Sept. 10 Photo. *Perf. 13x13½*

1430	A860 70w multicolored		.75	.25
1431	A861 70w multicolored		.75	.25

1986, June 25 Photo. *Perf. 13x13½*

1432	A862 70w multicolored	1.00	.30
1433	A863 70w multicolored	1.50	.60

1986, Aug. 26 Photo. *Perf. 13½x13*

Musicians with: a, Flag, hand gong. b, Drum flute. c, Drum, hand gong. d, Taborets, ribbons. e, Taboret, sun, woman, child. Has continuous design.

1434	Strip of 5	7.50	7.50
a.-e.	A864 70w, any single	1.25	.25

1987, Mar. 25 Photo. *Perf. 13x13½*

1435	A865 80w multicolored	3.00	1.00
1436	A866 80w multicolored	3.00	1.00

1987, Sept. 10 Photo. *Perf. 13x13½*

Harvest moon dance: No. 1437a, Eight dancers, harvest moon. No. 1437b, Four dancers, festival wheels, balloons. No. 1437c, Three dancers, children on see-saw. No. 1437d, Four dancers, women preparing meal.

1437	A867 Strip of 4	16.00	16.00
a.-d.	80w any single	3.00	1.00

Folklore Series

Tano, Spring Harvest Festival — A868

Sick for Home, by Lee Eun-sang and Kim Kong-jin A869

Pioneer, by Yoon Hae-young and Cho Doo-nam A870

Mask Dance (Talchum) — A871

Designs: a, Woman on shore, riding a swing. b, Sweet flag coiffures. c, Boy picking flowers, girl on swing. d, Boys wrestling.

1988, Aug. 25 Photo. *Perf. 13x13½*

1438	A868 Strip of 4	6.00	6.00
a.-d.	80w multicolored	1.25	.40

1988, Nov. 15

1439	A869 80w multicolored	.75	.25
1440	A870 80w multicolored	.75	.25

1989, Feb. 25

Designs: a, Two mask dancers with scarves. b, Dancers with fans. c, Dancers with scarf and laurel or fan. d, Three dancers, first as an animal and two more carrying fan and bells or torch.

1441	A871 Strip of 4	5.00	5.00
a.-d.	80w any single	1.25	.40

Korean Telecommunications, Cent. — A872

1985, Sept. 28 *Perf. 13½x13*

1442	A872 70w Satellite, emblem, dish receiver	.50	.20

World Bank Conference, Seoul, Oct. 8-11 — A873

1985, Oct. 8 *Perf. 13x13½*

1443	A873 70w Emblem	.50	.20

Intl. Bank for Reconstruction & Development, 40th Anniv.

UN, 40th Anniv. A874

1985, Oct. 24 *Perf. 13½x13*

1444	A874 70w Emblem, doves	.50	.20

Natl. Red Cross, 80th Anniv. A875

1985, Oct. 26

1445	A875 70w red, blk & bl	.50	.20

Segment of Canceled Cover — A876

1985, Nov. 18 Photo. *Perf. 13½x13*

1446	A876 70w multicolored	.50	.20

12th Philatelic Week, Nov. 18-23.

New Year 1986 — A877

Lithographed and Engraved

1985, Dec. 2 *Perf. 13x13½*

1447	A877 70w multicolored	.50	.20

Mt. Fuji, Korean Airlines Jet — A878

1985, Dec. 18 Photo.

1448	A878 70w brt bl, blk & red	.75	.30

Normalization of diplomatic relations between Korea and Japan, 20th anniv.

See No. C44.

Statesman Type of 1986 and Types of 1981-86

Engr., Photo. (40w)

1986-87 *Perf. 13*

1449	A716	550w indigo	3.00	.40

Coil Stamps

Perf. 13 Vert.

1449A	A704	20w multicolored	1.00	.40
1449B	A705	40w multicolored	1.25	.30
1449C	A708	80w multicolored	1.75	.60
	Nos. 1449A-1449C (3)		4.00	1.30

Issue dates: 550w, Dec. 10; others, 1987.

Intl. Peace Year — A879

1986, Jan. 15 Photo. *Perf. 13x13½*

1450	A879 70w multicolored	.50	.20

See No. C45.

State Visits of Pres. Chun — A880

Portrait, natl. flags and: No. 1452, Parliament, Brussels. No. 1453, Eiffel Tower, Paris. No. 1454, Cathedral, Cologne. No. 1455, Big Ben, London.

1986, Apr. 4 Litho. *Perf. 12½x13*

1452	A880	70w multicolored	.75	.30
1453	A880	70w multicolored	.75	.30
1454	A880	70w multicolored	.75	.30
1455	A880	70w multicolored	.75	.30
	Nos. 1452-1455 (4)		3.00	1.20

Souvenir Sheets of 2

Perf. 13½

1452a	A880	70w	3.50	3.50
1453a	A880	70w	3.50	3.50
1454a	A880	70w	3.50	3.50
1455a	A880	70w	3.50	3.50
	Nos. 1452a-1455a (4)		14.00	14.00

Science Series

Observatories — A881

Weather — A883

Clocks — A885

Early Printing Methods — A887

A889

Designs: No. 1456, Chomsongdae Observatory, Satellites. No. 1457, Kwanchondae Observatory, Halley's Comet.

1986, Apr. 21 *Perf. 13½x13*

1456	70w multicolored	2.50	.85
1457	70w multicolored	2.50	.85
a.	A881 Pair, #1456-1457	7.50	2.75

1987, Apr. 21 Photo. *Perf. 13½*

Designs: No. 1458, Wind observatory stone foundation, Chosun Dynasty. No. 1459, Rain gauge, Sejong Period to Chosun Dynasty.

1458	80w multicolored	2.75	1.00
1459	80w multicolored	2.75	1.00
a.	A883 Pair, #1458-1459	7.50	4.00

1988, Apr. 21 Photo. *Perf. 13½x13*

Designs: No. 1460, *Chagyokru,* water clock invented by Chang Yongshil and Kim Bin in 1434. No. 1461, *Angbuilgu,* sundial completed during King Sejong's reign (1418-1450).

1460	80w multicolored	.75	.30
1461	80w multicolored	.75	.30
a.	A885 Pair, #1460-1461	2.00	2.00

1989, Apr. 21

Designs: No. 1462, Sutra manuscript (detail) printed from wood type, Shila Dynasty, c.704-751. No. 1463, Two characters from a manuscript printed from metal type, Koryo, c.1237.

1462	80w buff & sepia	1.60	.40
1463	80w buff & sepia	1.60	.40
a.	A887 Pair, #1462-1463	3.25	3.25

1990, Apr. 21

Designs: No. 1464, 7th century gilt bronze Buddha. No. 1465, Bronze Age dagger, spear molds.

1464 100w multicolored .60 .25
1465 100w multicolored .60 .25
a. A889 Pair, #1464-1465 1.50 1.50
Complete bklt., 2 each #1464-1465 2.50
Nos. 1456-1465 (10) 16.40 5.60

Pairs have continuous designs.

Souvenir Booklets

Booklets containing the stamps listed below have a stamp, pair or strip of stamps, tied to the booklet cover with a first day cancel.

1464-1465, 1523-1524, 1529-1532, 1535-1536, 1539-1540, 1553, 1559-1566, 1572-1576, 1583-1584, 1595-1608, 1613-1621, 1622-1623B, 1624, 1635-1650, 1655-1656, 1657-1668, 1669-1676, 1678-1690, 1693-1699, 1700-1702, 1713-1714, 1745-1748, 1751-1758, 1763-1764, 1767-1768, 1770-1773, 1776-1787, 1797, 1799-1802, 1803-1806, 1810-1811.

Assoc. of Natl. Olympic Committees, 5th General Assembly, Seoul, Apr. 21-25 — A891

1986, Apr. 21 ***Perf. 13x13½***
1466 A891 70w multicolored .50 .20

Souvenir Sheet

Butterflies A892

1986, May 22 **Litho.** ***Perf. 13½***
1467 Sheet of 6 25.00 25.00
a. A892 70w multicolored 3.00 1.50
b. A892 370w multicolored 3.00 1.50
c. A892 400w multicolored 3.00 1.50
d. A892 440w multicolored 3.00 1.50
e. A892 450w multicolored 3.00 1.50
f. A892 470w multicolored 3.00 1.50

AMERIPEX '86, Chicago, May 22-June 1. No. 1467 contains stamps of different sizes (370w, 42x41mm; 400w, 42x33mm; 440w, 39x45mm; 450w, 32x42mm; 470w, 33x44mm); margin continues the designs.

Women's Education, Cent. A893

1986, May 31 ***Perf. 13x12½***
1468 A893 70w multicolored .50 .20

State Visit of Pres. Andre Kolingba, Central Africa A894

1986, June 10 ***Perf. 13***
1469 A894 70w multicolored .50 .20
a. Souvenir sheet of 2, imperf. 1.50 1.50

Completion of Han River Development Project — A895

1986, Sept. 10 **Litho.** ***Perf. 13***
1470 Strip of 3 4.50 4.50
a. A895 30w Bridge 1.20 .30
b. A895 60w Buildings 1.20 .30
c. A895 80w Seoul Tower, buildings 1.20 .30

Printed in a continuous design.

Fireworks, Seoul Tower — A896

Games Emblem — A897

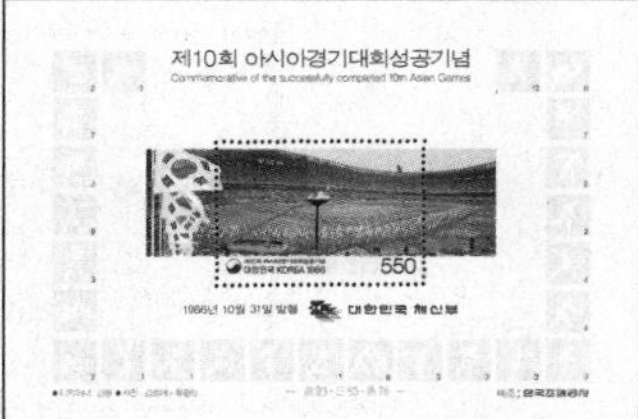

10th Asian Games, Seoul, Sept. 20-Oct. 5 — A898

1986, Sept. 20 **Photo.** ***Perf. 13x13½***
1471 A896 80w multicolored .70 .30
a. Souvenir sheet of 2 7.50 7.50
1472 A897 80w multicolored .70 .30
a. Souvenir sheet of 2 7.50 7.50

Souvenir Sheet

1986, Oct. 31
1473 A898 550w multicolored 21.00 21.00

Juan Antonio Samaranch, Korean IOC Delegation, 1981 — A899

1986, Sept. 30
1474 A899 80w multicolored 1.10 .40

Intl. Olympic Committee decision to hold 24th Olympic Games in Seoul, 5th anniv.

Philatelic Week — A900

1986, Nov. 18 **Photo.** ***Perf. 13½x13***
1475 A900 80w Boy fishing for stamp .70 .25

New Year 1987 (Year of the Hare) — A901

Birds — A902

1986, Dec. 1 **Photo.** ***Perf. 13x13½***
1476 A901 80w multicolored .75 .30

1986, Dec. 20 ***Perf. 13x14***
1477 A902 80w Waxwing 1.25 .40
1478 A902 80w Oriole 1.25 .40
1479 A902 80w Kingfisher 1.25 .40
1480 A902 80w Hoopoe 1.25 .40
1481 A902 80w Roller 1.25 .40
a. Strip of 5, #1477-1481 7.50 7.50

Coil Stamps
Perf. 14 Horiz.

1481B A902 80w like No. 1479 3.00 .75
1481C A902 80w like No. 1480 3.00 .75
1481D A902 80w like No. 1481 3.00 .75
1481E A902 80w like No. 1477 3.00 .75
1481F A902 80w like No. 1478 3.00 .75
g. Strip of 5, #1481B-1481F 25.00 25.00

Wildlife Conservation A903

Endangered species: No. 1482, Panthera tigris altaica. No. 1483, Felis bengalensis. No. 1484, Vulpes vulpes. No. 1485, Sus scrofa.

1987, Feb. 25 **Photo.** ***Perf. 13½x13***
1482 A903 80w multicolored 2.50 .70
1483 A903 80w multicolored 2.50 .70
1484 A903 80w multicolored 2.50 .70
1485 A903 80w multicolored 2.50 .70
a. Strip of 4, #1482-1485 12.00 12.00

Flowers — A904

1987, Mar. 20 **Photo.** ***Perf. 14x13***
1486 A904 550w Dicentra spectabilis 2.25 .60
1487 A904 550w Hanabusaya asiatica 2.25 .60
1488 A904 550w Erythronium japonicum 2.25 .60
1489 A904 550w Dianthus chinensis 2.25 .60
1490 A904 550w Chrysanthemum zawadskii coreanum 2.25 .60
a. Strip of 5, #1486-1490 12.50 12.50

Coil Stamps
Perf. 13 Vert.

1490B A904 550w like No. 1486 3.00 1.00
1490C A904 550w like No. 1487 3.00 1.00
1490D A904 550w like No. 1488 3.00 1.00
1490E A904 550w like No. 1489 3.00 1.00
1490F A904 550w like No. 1490 3.00 1.00
g. Strip of 5, #1490B-1490F 17.50 17.50

State Visit of Pres. Ahmed Abdallah Abderemane of the Comoro Isls., Apr. 6-9 — A905

1987, Apr. 6 **Litho.** ***Perf. 13½x13***
1491 A905 80w multicolored .50 .20
a. Souvenir sheet of 2 2.00 2.00

Electrification of Korea, Cent. — A906

1987, Apr. 10 **Photo.**
1492 A906 80w multicolored .50 .20

Int'l. Assoc. of Ports and Harbors, 15th General Session, Seoul — A907

1987, Apr. 25 **Photo.** ***Perf. 13½x13***
1493 A907 80w multicolored .50 .20

State Visit of Pres. U San Yu of Burma A908

1987, June 8 **Litho.** ***Perf. 13½x13***
1494 A908 80w multicolored .50 .20
a. Souvenir sheet of 2 2.00 2.00

Year of The Communications for Information Society — A909

1987, June 30 ***Perf. 13x13½***
1495 A909 80w Map, digital telephone .60 .25
1496 A909 80w Emblem .60 .25

Introduction of automatic switching telephone system.

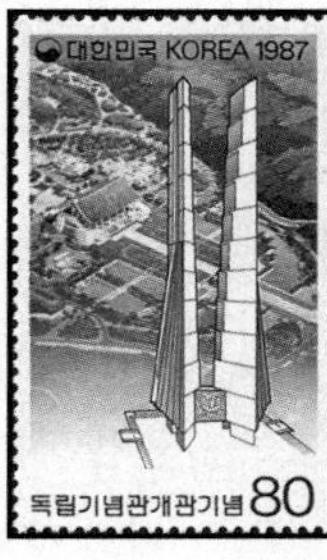

Independence Hall, Monument to the Nation — A910

Statue of Indomitable Koreans, Nat'l. Flag — A911

1987, Aug. 14 **Photo.** ***Perf. 13½x13***
1497 A910 80w multicolored 1.00 .30
a. Souvenir sheet of 2 12.50 12.50
1498 A911 80w multicolored 1.00 .30
a. Souvenir sheet of 2 12.50 12.50

Opening of Independence Hall, Aug. 15.

16th Pacific Science Congress, Seoul, Aug. 20-30 — A912

1987, Aug. 20 ***Perf. 13x13½***
1499 A912 80w multicolored .60 .20
a. Souvenir sheet of 2 3.50 3.50

State Visit of Pres. Virgilio Barco of Colombia A913

1987, Sept. 8 **Litho.** ***Perf. 13½x13***
1500 A913 80w multicolored .50 .20
a. Souvenir sheet of 2 2.25 2.25

Installation of 10-millionth Telephone A914

1987, Sept. 28 ***Perf. 13½x13***
1501 A914 80w multicolored .50 .20

Armed Forces, 39th Anniv. — A915

Armed Forces Day: Servicemen, flags of three military services.

1987, Sept. 30 **Litho.** ***Perf. 13***
1502 A915 80w multicolored .60 .25

14th Philatelic Week, Nov. 18-24 — A916

1987, Nov. 18 **Photo.** ***Perf. 13½***
1503 A916 80w Boy playing the nalrali .60 .25

A917

A918

1987, Nov. 28 **Litho.**
1504 A917 80w multicolored .75 .40

Signing of the Antarctic Treaty by Korea, 1st anniv.

1987, Dec. 1 **Photo.**
1505 A918 80w multicolored 1.00 .30

New Year 1988 (Year of the Dragon).

Natl. Social Security Program A919

1988, Jan. 4 **Litho.** ***Perf. 13½x13***
1506 A919 80w multicolored .60 .25

Completion of the Korean Antarctic Base — A919a

1988, Feb. **Photo.** ***Perf. 13x13½***
1506A A919a 80w multicolored 1.00 .30

Inauguration of Roh Tae-Woo, 13th President A920

1988, Feb. 24 **Photo.** ***Perf. 13½x13***
1507 A920 80w multicolored 1.25 .40
a. Souvenir sheet of 2 22.50 22.50

World Wildlife Fund — A921

White-naped crane *(Grus vipio)* displaying various behaviors: a, Calling (1). b, Running (2). c, Spreading wings (3). d, Flying (4).

1988, Apr. 1 ***Perf. 13x13½***
1508 Strip of 4 9.00 9.00
a.-d. A921 80w any single 1.40 .80

Intl. Red Cross & Red Crescent Organizations, 125th Annivs. — A922

Telepress Medium, 1st Anniv. — A923

1988, May 7 **Photo.** ***Perf. 13x13½***
1509 A922 80w multicolored .60 .25

1988, June 1 **Litho.**
1510 A923 80w multicolored .60 .25

Pierre de Coubertin, Olympic Flag — A924

Olympic Temple A925

View of Seoul — A926

Folk Dancers — A927

Litho. & Engr.

1988, Sept. 16 ***Perf. 13½x13***
1511 A924 80w multicolored .75 .30
1512 A925 80w multicolored .75 .30

Photo.

Perf. 13x13½
1513 A926 80w multicolored .75 .30
1514 A927 80w multicolored .75 .30
Nos. 1511-1514 (4) 3.00 1.20

1988 Summer Olympics, Seoul.

Souvenir Sheets of 2

1511a A924 80w 2.25 2.25
1512a A925 80w 2.25 2.25
1513a A926 80w 2.25 2.25
1514a A927 80w 2.25 2.25
Nos. 1511a-1514a (4) 9.00 9.00

Margin inscriptions on #1511a-1512a are photo.

OLYMPHILEX '88, Sept. 19-28, Seoul — A928

1988, Sept. 19 **Photo.** ***Perf. 13x13½***
1515 A928 80w multicolored .50 .20
a. Souvenir sheet of 2 2.00 2.00

22nd Congress of the Intl. Iron and Steel Institute, Seoul A929

1988, Oct. 8 ***Perf. 13½x13***
1516 A929 80w multicolored .50 .20

A930

A931

1988, Oct. 15 ***Perf. 13x13½***
1517 A930 80w shown 1.00 .60
1518 A930 80w Archer seated in wheelchair .75 .30

1988 Natl. Special Olympics (Paralympics), Seoul.

1988, Dec. 1 **Photo.** ***Perf. 13x13½***
1519 A931 80w multicolored .70 .25

New Year 1989 (Year of the Snake).

Souvenir Sheet

Successful Completion of the 1988 Summer Olympics, Seoul — A932

1988, Dec. 20 **Litho.** ***Perf. 13x12½***
1520 A932 550w Opening ceremony 16.00 16.00

Folklore Series

Arirang — A933

Doraji — A934

Pakyon Falls A935

Chonan-Samkori A936

Willowing Bow — A937

Spinning Wheel A938

Treating Threads A939

Weaving Fabric A940

Orchard Avenue — A941

In Flower Garden — A942

Opening of Bohyunsan Optical Astronomical Observatory
A1183

1995, Sept. 13 Litho. ***Perf. 13x13½***

1816 A1183 130w multicolored .50 .20
Complete booklet, 6 #1816 5.00

Literature Series

Kuji-ga Song (The Turtle's Back Song) — A1184

Chongeop-sa Song
A1185

A1186

A1187

Record of Travel to Five Indian Kingdoms — A1188

A Poem to the Sui General Yu Zhong Wen — A1189

A1190

A1191

A1192

A1193

A1194  A1195

Perf. 13x13½, 13½x13

1995-99 **Photo.**

1817 A1184 130w multi .45 .20
a. Souvenir sheet of 2 1.25 1.25
Complete booklet, 6 #1817 5.00
1818 A1185 130w multi .45 .20
a. Souvenir sheet of 2 1.25 1.25
Complete booklet, 6 #1818 5.00
1819 A1186 150w multi .50 .25
a. Souvenir sheet of 2 1.25 1.25
Complete booklet, 10 #1819 *10.00*
1820 A1187 150w multi .50 .25
a. Souvenir sheet of 2 1.25 1.25
Complete booklet, 10 #1820 *10.00*
1821 A1188 170w multi .50 .25
a. Souvenir sheet of 2 1.25 1.25
Complete booklet, 10 #1821 7.50
1822 A1189 170w multi .50 .25
a. Sheet of 2 1.25 1.25
Complete booklet, 10 #1822 7.50

Photo. & Engr.

1823 A1190 170w multi .50 .25
Complete booklet, 10 #1823 7.50
a. Souvenir sheet of 1 .75 .75
1824 A1191 170w multi .50 .25
Complete booklet, 10 #1824 7.50
a. Souvenir sheet of 1 .75 .75
1825 A1192 170w multi .50 .30
Complete booklet, 10 #1825 7.50
1826 A1193 170w multi .50 .30
Complete booklet, 10 #1826 7.50
1827 A1194 170w multi .50 .30
Complete booklet, 10 #1827 7.50
1828 A1195 170w multi .50 .30
Complete booklet, 10 #1828 7.50
Nos. 1817-1828 (12) 5.90 3.10

Souvenir Sheets

1828A A1192 340w multi 1.25 .60
1828B A1193 340w multi 1.25 .60
1828C A1194 340w multi 1.25 .60
1828D A1195 340w multi 1.25 .60

Issued: #1817-1818, 9/25/95; #1819-1820, 9/16/96; #1821-1822, 12/12/97; #1823-1824, 9/14/98; #1825-1828D, 10/20/99

FAO, 50th Anniv.
A1196

Litho. & Engr.

1995, Oct. 16 ***Perf. 13***

1829 A1196 150w dp vio & blk .50 .25
Complete booklet, 10 #1829 *7.50*

Korean Bible Society, Cent.
A1197

1995, Oct. 18 **Litho.**

1830 A1197 150w multicolored .50 .25
Complete booklet, 10 #1830 *7.50*

Population and Housing Census — A1198

1995, Oct. 20

1831 A1198 150w multicolored .50 .25
Complete booklet, 10 #1831 *7.50*

UN, 50th Anniv.
A1199

1995, Oct. 24 **Photo.**

1832 A1199 150w multicolored .50 .25
Complete booklet, 10 #1832 *7.50*

Wilhelm Röntgen (1845-1923), Discovery of the X-Ray, Cent.
A1200

1995, Nov. 8 ***Perf. 13½x13***

1833 A1200 150w multicolored .50 .25
Complete booklet, 10 #1833 7.50

Philatelic Week — A1201

1995, Nov. 18 Photo. ***Perf. 13x13½***

1834 A1201 150w multicolored .50 .25
a. Souvenir sheet of 2 1.25 1.25
Complete booklet, 10 #1834 *7.50*

A1202

New Year 1996 (Year of the Rat) — A1203

1995, Dec. 1 ***Perf. 13x13½, 13½x13***

1835 A1202 150w multicolored .50 .25
a. Souvenir sheet of 2 1.25 1.25
Complete booklet, 10 #1835 7.50
1836 A1203 150w multicolored .50 .25
a. Souvenir sheet of 2 1.25 1.25
Complete booklet, 10 #1836 7.50

Normalization of Korea-Japan Relations, 30th Anniv. — A1204

1995, Dec. 18 Litho. ***Perf. 13x13½***

1837 A1204 420w multicolored 1.50 .70
Complete booklet, 4 #1837 *7.50*

Types of 1993-97 and

Gallicrex Cinerea
A1206

Zosterops Japonica
A1208

Luffa Cylindrica
A1209

Numenius Madagascariensis
A1210

Cambaroides Similis — A1211

747 Airplane
A1215

Mare and Colt — A1221

Soksu Stone Carving
A1223

Bronze Incense Burner in Shape of Lotus Flowers — A1224

Photo., Photo. & Embossed (#1844)

1996-98 ***Perf. 13x13½, 13½x13***

1839 A1206 50w multi .30 .20
1840 A1208 80w multi .30 .20
1841 A1209 100w multi .45 .20
1842 A1118 140w multi .45 .25

Perf. 13

1843 A1210 170w multi .45 .25
1844 A1210 170w like #1843, braille inscription 1.50 .45

Perf. 13x13½, 13½x13

1845 A1211 170w multi 1.00 .30
1846 A997c 190w multi 1.00 .30
1847 A1119 260w multi 1.50 .40

Perf. 13x14

1848 A1119 300w Alauda arvensis 1.00 .40

Perf. 13½x13, 13x13½, 13 (#1855)

1849 A1215 340w green blue & multi 1.60 .45
1850 A1215 380w lt lilac & multi 1.75 .50
1851 A1001 420w like #1593 2.40 .45
1852 A1002 480w like #1594 2.50 .50
1854 A1221 800w multi 2.25 .60
1855 A1223 1000w multi 3.75 1.25
1856 A1224 1170w multi 4.00 2.00
1857 A1128 1190w multi 4.00 2.00
1858 A1215 1340w brt green & multi 4.50 1.60

1859 A1215 1380w pink & multi 5.00 1.90
Nos. 1839-1859 (20) 39.70 14.20

Coil Stamps
Perf. 13 Horiz., 13 Vert. (#1860, 1862)

1996-97 **Photo.**
1860 A998 150w like #1591 1.25 .75
1861 A1211 170w like No. 1845 1.00 .30
1862 A997c 190w like No. 1846 1.00 .30
Nos. 1860-1862 (3) 3.25 1.35

Issued: 300w, 1/22/96; #1860, 2/1/96; 420w, 480w, 3/20/96; 1000w, 12/16/96; 100w, 3/5/97; 80w, 7/1/97; #1845-1846, 9/1/97; 340w, 380w, 1340w, 1380w, 9/12/97; #1842, 1847, 1856, 1857, 11/1/97; #1861, 1862, 11/18/97; #1843, 12/15/97; 50w, 2/19/98; 800w, 4/4/98; #1844, 10/15/98.

Opening of China-Korea Submarine Fiber Optic Cable System A1229

1996, Feb. 8 **Litho.** ***Perf. 13½x13***
1863 A1229 420w multicolored 1.75 .50
Complete booklet, 4 #1863 *10.00*

See People's Republic of China No. 2647.

Korea Institute of Science and Technology, 30th Anniv. A1230

1996, Feb. 10 **Photo.** ***Perf. 13½x13***
1864 A1230 150w multicolored .50 .25
Complete booklet, 10 #1864 *7.50*

Protection of Nature A1231

1996, Mar. 5 **Photo.** ***Perf. 13½x13***
1865 A1231 150w Geoclemys reevesii .50 .25
a. Souvenir sheet of 2 1.25 1.25
Complete booklet, 10 #1865 *8.50*
1866 A1231 150w Scincella laterale .50 .25
a. Souvenir sheet of 2 1.25 1.25
Complete booklet, 10 #1866 *8.50*

Successful Launches of Mugunghwa Satellites A1232

1996, Mar. 18 **Photo.** ***Perf. 13***
1867 A1232 150w multicolored .50 .25
Complete booklet, 10 #1867 *7.50*

Tongnip Shinmum, First Privately Published Newspaper, Cent. A1233

So Chae-p'il, lead article of first issue.

Litho. & Engr.

1996, Apr. 6 ***Perf. 13***
1868 A1233 150w multicolored .50 .25
Complete booklet, 10 #1868 *8.50*

Wildflower Type of 1992

#1869, Cypripedium macranthum. #1870, Trillium tschonoskii. #1871, Viola variegata. #1872, Hypericum ascyron.

1996, Apr. 22 **Photo.** ***Perf. 13***
1869 A1013 150w multicolored .50 .25
Complete booklet, 10 #1869 *10.00*
1870 A1013 150w multicolored .50 .25
Complete booklet, 10 #1870 *10.00*
1871 A1013 150w multicolored .50 .25
Complete booklet, 10 #1871 *10.00*
1872 A1013 150w multicolored .50 .25
Complete booklet, 10 #1872 *10.00*
Nos. 1869-1872 (4) 2.00 1.00

Korea Military Academy, 50th Anniv. A1234

1996, May 1 **Litho.** ***Perf. 13½x13***
1873 A1234 150w multicolored .50 .25
Complete booklet, 10 #1873 *10.00*

Cartoons A1235

1996, May 4 **Photo.**
1874 A1235 150w Gobau running .50 .25
a. Souvenir sheet of 1 1.25 1.25
Complete booklet, 10 #1874 *10.00*
1875 A1235 150w Kkach'i in swordfight .50 .25
a. Souvenir sheet of 1 1.25 1.25
Complete booklet, 10 #1875 *10.00*

Girl Scouts of Korea, 50th Anniv. A1236

1996, May 10 **Litho.**
1876 A1236 150w multicolored .50 .25
Complete booklet, 10 #1876 *12.00*

35th IAA World Advertising Congress — A1237

1996, June 8 **Litho.** ***Perf. 13***
1877 A1237 150w multicolored .50 .25
Complete booklet, 10 #1877 *9.50*

Campaign Against Illegal Drugs A1238

1996, June 26 **Photo.** ***Perf. 13½x13***
1878 A1238 150w multicolored .60 .25
Complete booklet, 10 #1878 *12.00*

Winter Universiade '97, Muju-Chonju A1239

1996, July 1 ***Perf. 13½x13, 13x13½***
1879 A1239 150w shown .50 .25
Complete booklet, 10 #1879 *10.00*
1880 A1239 150w Emblem, vert. .50 .25
Complete booklet, 10 #1880 *10.00*

1996 Summer Olympic Games, Atlanta
A1240 A1241

1996, July 20 ***Perf. 13x13½***
1881 A1240 150w multicolored .50 .25
Complete booklet, 10 #1881 *10.00*
1882 A1241 150w multicolored .50 .25
Complete booklet, 10 #1882 *10.00*

Mushroom Type of 1993

Designs: No. 1883, Paxillus atrotomentosus. No. 1884, Sarcodon imbricatum. No. 1885, Rhodophyllus crassipes. No. 1886, Amanita inaurata.

1996, Aug. 19 **Photo.** ***Perf. 13x13½***
1883 A1098 150w multicolored .50 .25
a. Souvenir sheet of 2 1.25 1.25
Complete booklet, 10 #1883 *10.00*
1884 A1098 150w multicolored .50 .25
a. Souvenir sheet of 2 1.25 1.25
Complete booklet, 10 #1884 *10.00*
1885 A1098 150w multicolored .50 .25
a. Souvenir sheet o 2 1.25 1.25
Complete booklet, 10 #1885 *10.00*
1886 A1098 150w multicolored .50 .25
a. Souvenir sheet of 2 1.25 1.25
Complete booklet, 10 #1886 *10.00*
Nos. 1883-1886 (4) 2.00 1.00

Souvenir Sheets

2002 World Cup Soccer Championships, Korea — A1242

#1887, Players, Korean flag. #1888, 2 players.

1996, Aug. 1 **Photo.** ***Perf. 13½***
1887 A1242 400w Sheet of 4 7.50 7.50
1888 A1242 400w Sheet of 4 7.50 7.50

Korean Alphabet, 550th Anniv. — A1243

Litho. & Engr.

1996, Oct. 9 ***Perf. 13x13½***
1889 A1243 150w multicolored .50 .25
a. Souvenir sheet of 2 1.25 1.25
Complete booklet, 10 #1889 *10.00*

Suwon Castle, Bicent. A1244

Photo. & Engr.

1996, Oct. 10 ***Perf. 13½x13***
1890 A1244 400w multicolored 1.50 .60
Complete booklet, 10 #1890 *20.00*

Seoul Natl. University, 50th Anniv. A1245

1996, Oct. 15 **Photo.** ***Perf. 13½x13***
1891 A1245 150w multicolored .50 .25
Complete booklet, 10 #1891 *10.00*

Philatelic Week — A1246

Painting: Poppy and a Lizard, by Shin Saimdang.

1996, Nov. 18 **Photo.** ***Perf. 13x13½***
1892 A1246 150w multicolored .50 .25
a. Souvenir sheet of 2 1.25 1.25
Complete booklet, 10 #1892 *10.00*

A1247

New Year 1997 (Year of the Ox) — A1248

1996, Dec. 2 ***Perf. 13***
1893 A1247 150w multicolored .50 .25
a. Souvenir sheet of 2 1.25 1.25
Complete booklet, 10 #1893 *10.00*
1894 A1248 150w multicolored .50 .25
a. Souvenir sheet of 2 1.25 1.25
Complete booklet, 10 #1894 *10.00*

Winter Universiade '97, Muju-Chonju A1249

1997, Jan. 24 **Photo.** ***Perf. 13***
1895 A1249 150w Skier .45 .25
Complete booklet, 10 #1895 *10.00*
1896 A1249 150w Ice skater .45 .25
Complete booklet, 10 #1896 *10.00*

Modern Banking System in Korea, Cent. A1250

1997, Feb. 19 **Litho.** ***Perf. 13½x13***
1897 A1250 150w multicolored .45 .25
Complete booklet, 10 #1897 *9.00*

A1251 A1252

1997, Apr. 10 ***Perf. 13x13½***
1898 A1251 150w multicolored .45 .20
Complete booklet, 10 #1898 *9.00*

97th Inter-Parliamentary Conference, 160th Inter-Parliamentary Council.

1997, Apr. 23 **Litho.**
1899 A1252 150w multicolored .45 .20
Complete booklet, 10 #1899 *9.00*

World Book & Copyright Day.

Cartoons A1253

#1900, Mother holding child from "A Long, Long Journey in Search of Mommy." #1901, Girl in air holding medal from "Run, Run, Hannie."

1997, May 3 Photo. *Perf. 13½x13*

1900	A1253 150w multicolored	.70	.25
a.	Souvenir sheet of 1	1.00	1.00
	Complete booklet, 10 #1900	*11.00*	
1901	A1253 150w multicolored	.70	.25
a.	Souvenir sheet of 1	1.00	1.00
	Complete booklet, 10 #1901	*11.00*	

Nos. 1900a, 1901a are continuous designs.

2nd Pusan East Asian Games — A1254

1997, May 10 Litho. *Perf. 13x13½*

1902	A1254 150w multicolored	.50	.25
	Complete booklet, 10 #1900	*9.00*	

2002 World Cup Soccer, Korea/Japan
A1255 A1256

No. 1903, Jules Rimet, founder of World Cup. No. 1904, Painting of Ch'ukkuk match.

1997, May 31 Photo. *Perf. 13x13½*

1903	A1255 150w multicolored	.60	.25
a.	Souvenir sheet of 2	1.50	1.50
	Complete booklet, 10 #1903	*10.00*	
1904	A1256 150w multicolored	.60	.25
a.	Souvenir sheet of 3	2.00	2.00
	Complete booklet, 10 #1904	*10.00*	

Wildlife Protection A1257

Fish: No. 1905, Pungitius sinensis. No. 1906, Coreoperca kawamebari.

1997, June 5 *Perf. 13*

1905	A1257 150w multicolored	.45	.25
a.	Souvenir sheet of 2	1.00	1.00
	Complete booklet, 10 #1905	*10.00*	
1906	A1257 150w multicolored	.45	.25
a.	Souvenir sheet of 2	1.00	1.00
	Complete booklet, 10 #1906	*10.00*	

Wildflower Type of 1992

#1907, Belamcanda chinensis. #1908, Hylomecon ernale. #1909, Campanula takesimana. #1910, Magnolia sieboldii.

1997, June 19 Photo. *Perf. 13*

1907	A1013 150w multicolored	.45	.25
	Complete booklet, 10 #1907	*12.00*	
1908	A1013 150w multicolored	.45	.25
	Complete booklet, 10 #1908	*12.00*	
1909	A1013 150w multicolored	.45	.25
	Complete booklet, 10 #1909	*12.00*	
1910	A1013 150w multicolored	.45	.25
	Complete booklet, 10 #1910	*12.00*	
	Nos. 1907-1910 (4)	1.80	1.00

1997 Kwangju Biennale — A1258

1997, July 1

1911	A1258 150w multicolored	.45	.25
	Complete booklet, 10 #1911	*8.00*	

Mushroom Type of 1993

Designs: No. 1912, Inocybe fastigiata. No. 1913, Panaeolus papilionaceus. No. 1914, Ramaria flava. No. 1915, Amanita muscaria.

1997, July 21 Photo. *Perf. 13x13½*

1912	A1098 150w multicolored	.45	.25
a.	Souvenir sheet of 2	1.00	1.00
1913	A1098 150w multicolored	.45	.25
a.	Souvenir sheet of 2	1.00	1.00
1914	A1098 150w multicolored	.45	.25
a.	Souvenir sheet of 2	1.00	1.00
1915	A1098 150w multicolored	.45	.25
a.	Souvenir sheet of 2	1.00	1.00
	Nos. 1912-1915 (4)	1.80	1.00

85th World Dental Congress, Seoul A1259

1997, Sept. 5 Photo. *Perf. 13½x13*

1916	A1259 170w multicolored	.45	.25

Opening of Port of Mokpo, Cent. A1260

Litho. & Engr.

1997, Oct. 1 *Perf. 13½x13*

1917	A1260 170w multicolored	.45	.25

Soongsil Academy, Cent. A1261

1997, Oct. 10 Photo. & Engr.

1918	A1261 170w multicolored	.45	.25

Beauty Series

Wrapping Cloths — A1262

1997, Nov. 3 Photo. *Perf. 13x13½*

1919	170w multicolored	.60	.25
1920	170w multicolored	.60	.25
1921	170w multicolored	.60	.25
1922	170w multicolored	.60	.25
a.	A1262 Strip of 4, #1919-1922	2.25	2.25

Philatelic Week — A1266

1997, Nov. 18

1923	A1266 170w multicolored	.50	.25
a.	Souvenir sheet of 2	1.00	1.00

New Year 1998 (Year of the Tiger)
A1267 A1268

1997, Dec. 1 Photo. *Perf. 13x13½*

1924	A1267 170w multicolored	.60	.25
a.	Souvenir sheet of 2	1.25	1.25
1925	A1268 170w multicolored	.60	.25
a.	Souvenir sheet of 2	1.25	1.25

Pulguksa Temple — A1269

Litho. & Engr.

1997, Dec. 9 *Perf. 13x13½*

1926	A1269 Sheet of 14	25.00	25.00
a.	170w Buddha, Sokkuram Grotto	.85	.85
b.	380w Temple	3.50	3.50

Top part of No. 1926 contains one each #1926a-1926b and is separated from the bottom portion of the sheet by a row of perforations. The lower part of No. 1926 contains 9 #1926a and 3 #1926b.

Electric Power in Korea, Cent. A1271

1998, Jan. 26 Photo. *Perf. 13½x13*

1927	A1271 170w multicolored	.50	.20

Inauguration of the 15th President, Kim Dae-jung A1272

1998, Feb. 25 Litho. *Perf. 13½x13*

1928	A1272 170w multicolored	.80	.40
a.	Souvenir sheet of 1	*5.50*	*5.50*

Protection of Wild Animals and Plants — A1273

Designs: a, Panthera pardus orientalis. b, Selenarctos thibetanus ussuricus. c, Lutra lutra. d, Moschus moschiferus.

1998, Mar. 21 *Perf. 13x13½*

1929	Sheet of 12	20.00	20.00
a.-d.	A1273 340w Any single	1.25	.30

Top part of #1929 contains one each #1929a-1929d and is separated from the bottom portion of the sheet by a row of perforations. The lower part of #1929 contains 2 each #1929a-1929d.

Cartoons A1274

Designs: 170w, Boy daydreaming while holding flower, from "Aktong-i," by Lee Hi-jae. 340w, Mother on motorcycle, son making fists from "Challenger," by Park Ki-jong.

1998, May 4 Photo. *Perf. 13½x13*

1930	A1274 170w multicolored	.50	.25
a.	Souvenir sheet of 1	.75	.75
b.	Booklet pane of 10	20.00	
	Complete booklet, #1930b	20.00	

Photo. & Engr.

1931	A1274 340w multicolored	1.10	1.10
a.	Souvenir sheet of 1	1.50	1.50
b.	Booklet pane of 10	26.00	
	Complete booklet, #1931b	26.00	

Natl. Assembly, 50th Anniv. A1275

1998, May 30 Litho. *Perf. 13½x13*

1932	A1275 170w multicolored	.50	.20

2002 World Cup Soccer Championships, Korea/Japan — A1276

Designs: a, Player. b, Two players. c, Player heading ball. d, Player performing bicycle kick.

1998, May 30 *Perf. 13x13½*

1933	Strip of 4, #a.-d.	3.00	3.00
a.-d.	A1276 170w any single	.60	.25
e.	Souvenir sheet, #1933	3.25	3.25

Information Culture Special A1277

Communication through the ages: a, Rock drawings. b, Horseback messenger, beacon fire. c, Telephone, mailbox. d, Computers.

1998, June 1 Litho. *Perf. 13½x13*

1934	Strip of 4	3.50	3.50
a.-c.	A1277 170w any single	.50	.25
d.	A1277 340w multicolored	1.00	.45

No. 1934d is 68x70mm.

Mushroom Type of 1993

Designs: a, Pseudocolus schellenbergiae. b, Cyptotrama asprata. c, Laccaria vinaceoavellanea. d, Phallus rugulosus.

1998, July 4

1935 Sheet of 16 12.00 12.00
a.-d. A1098 170w Any single .75 .30

Left part of #1935 contains 3 each #1935a-1935d, with each strip in a different order. This is separated from the right portion of the sheet by a row of perforations. The right part of #1935 contains 1 each #1935a-1935d.

Republic of Korea, 50th Anniv. A1278

1998, Aug. 14 Photo. *Perf. 13½x13*

1937 A1278 170w multicolored .50 .25

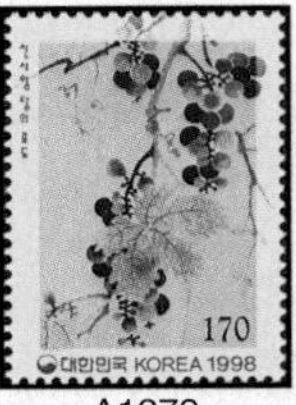

A1279

A1280

1998, Aug. 19 *Perf. 13x13½*

1938 A1279 170w multicolored .50 .25
a. Souvenir sheet of 2 1.10 1.10

Philatelic Week.

1998, Sept. 24 Photo. *Perf. 13x13½*

1939 A1280 170w multicolored .50 .25
Complete booklet, 10 #1939 12.00

1998 Pusan Intl. Film Festival.

Founding of Songkyunkwan, 600th Anniv. — A1281

Photo. & Engr.

1998, Sept. 25 *Perf. 13*

1940 A1281 170w multicolored .50 .25
Complete booklet, 5 #1940 5.00

A1282

A1283

1998, Oct. 1

1941 A1282 170w multicolored .50 .25
Complete booklet, 10 #1941 7.50

Korean Armed Forces, 50th anniv.

1998, Oct. 9

1942 A1283 170w multicolored .50 .25
Complete booklet, 10 #1942 6.50

World Stamp Day.

Beauty Series

Ceramics — A1284

#1944, Box with cranes on lid. #1945, Fish. #1946, Red, white blossom with blue leaf. #1947, Frog. #1948, Dragon. #1949, Monkeys. #1950, Pagoda.

1998, Nov. 20 Photo. *Perf. 13*

1943 A1284 170w multicolored .75 .40
1944 A1284 170w multicolored .75 .40
1945 A1284 170w multicolored .75 .40
1946 A1284 170w multicolored .75 .40
1947 A1284 170w multicolored .75 .40
1948 A1284 170w multicolored .75 .40
1949 A1284 170w multicolored .75 .40
1950 A1284 170w multicolored .75 .40
a. Block of 8, #1243-1250 7.50 7.50

New Year 1999 (Year of the Rabbit) — A1286

1998, Dec. 1 *Perf. 13x13½*

1952 A1286 170w multicolored .50 .25
Complete booklet, 10 #1952 7.50

Woodblock of Buddhist Tripitaka Koreana, Haeinsa Temple A1287

Haeinsa Temple Changgyong P'anjon Complex — A1288

Litho. & Engr.

1998, Dec. 9 *Perf. 13½*

1953 Sheet of 12 20.00 20.00
a. A1287 170w multicolored .75 .50
b. A1288 380w multicolored 2.25 1.50

Top part of #1953 contains one each #1953a-1953b and is separated from the bottom portion of the sheet by a row of perforations. The lower part of #1953 contains 6 #1953a and 4 #1953b.

Opening of Kunsan Port, Cent. A1289

1999, May 1 Litho. *Perf. 13¼*

1954 A1289 170w multicolored .50 .25

Opening of Masan Port, Cent. — A1290

1999, May 1

1955 A1290 170w multicolored .50 .25

Cartoons A1291

No. 1956, Boy and dog, "Tokgo T'ak," by Lee Sang-mu. No. 1957, Choson Dynasty robber, "Im Kkuk-jung," by Lee Du-ho. No. 1958, Fighter against alien invaders, "Rai-Fi," by Kim San-ho, vert.

1999, May 3 Photo. *Perf. 13½*

1956 A1291 170w multicolored .50 .25
1957 A1291 170w multicolored .50 .25
1958 A1291 170w multicolored .50 .25
Nos. 1956-1958 (3) 1.50 .75

Souvenir Sheets

1959 A1291 340w like #1956 1.40 1.25
1960 A1291 340w like #1957 1.40 1.25
1961 A1291 340w like #1958 1.40 1.25
Nos. 1959-1961 (3) 4.20 3.75

Nos. 1959-1961 are continuous designs.

A1292

A1293

Raptors: a, Falco peregrinus. b, Accipiter soloensis. c, Bubo bubo. d, Haliaeetus pelagicus.

1999, June 5 Litho. *Perf. 13x13¼*

1962 Sheet of 12 24.00 24.00
a.-b. A1292 170w each 1.00 .30
c.-d. A1292 340w each 1.75 .60

Top part of #1962 contains one each #1962a-1962d and is separated from the bottom portion of the sheet by a row of perforations. The lower part of #1962 contains 2 blocks of #1962a-1962d.

1999, June 12 Photo. *Perf. 13x13¼*

1963 A1293 170w multicolored .50 .25
Complete booklet, 10 #1963 12.00

1999 Intl. Olympic Committee Congress, Seoul.

Johann Wolfgang von Goethe, German Poet (1749-1832) A1294

Litho. & Engr.

1999, Aug. 12 *Perf. 13x13½*

1964 A1294 170w multicolored .70 .30

Souvenir Sheet

1965 A1294 480w multicolored 2.00 2.00

Kumgang Mountain by Kyomjae (1676-1759) — A1295

1999, Aug. 13 Litho.

1966 A1295 170w multicolored .50 .30

Souvenir Sheet

1967 A1295 340w multicolored 1.25 1.25

Korean National Railroad, Cent. — A1296

Litho. & Engr.

1999, Sept. 18 *Perf. 13x13¼*

1968 A1296 170w multicolored .70 .30
Complete booklet, 10 #1968 12.00

Millennium — A1297

Prehistoric sites and artifacts — No. 1969: a, Paleolithic ruins, Chungok-ri (black denomination at LL). b, Neolithic sites, Amsa-dong (white denomination at UR). c, Neolithic shell mound ruins, Tongsam-dong (black denomination at LR). d, Dolmen, Pukon-ri (black denomination at UR). e, Bronze Age artifacts and ruins, Songguk-ri. f, Rock carvings, Ulsan.

Three Countries Era artifacts — No. 1970: a, Tiger-shpaed belt buckle from tomb of Sarari, duck-shaped earthenware container, Kyongsang. b, Gold crown, silver cup from Hwangnamdae tomb. c, Wall painting of hunting scene from Tomb of the Dancers, Chibanri. d, Gold diadem ornaments, curved jade pieces from tomb of King Muryong. e, Gold crown from Koryong, armor from Kimhae. f, Decorative tiles, Anapji Pond.

Ancient Choson to Unified Shilla periods — No. 1971: a, Writing, site of Asadal, ancient capital of Choson. b, Korean wrestlers. c, King Kwanggaet'o, stone stele, and circular artifact with writing. d, Archers on horseback. e, Admiral Chang Po-go, ship.

Koryo dynasty — No. 1972: a, Writing and buildings (civil service examinations). b, Monk and Tripitaka Koreana wood blocks. c, Jade and movable metal type. d, Scholar An-hyang, writing and buildings. e, Mun Ik-jom, cotton plants and spinning wheel.

Early Choson dynasty — No. 1973: a, King Sejong and Korean alphabet. b, Korean script and Lady Shin Saimdang, calligrapher and painter. c, Yi Hwang and Yi I and Confucian academy building. d, Admiral Yi Sun-shin and turtle boat. e, Sandae-nori mask dance dramas.

Late Choson Dynasty — No. 1974: a, Tongui Pogam, medical treatises by Huh Joon (anatomic diagram, mortar and pestle) b, Dancer and Musicians, by Kim Hong-do. c, Plum Blossoms and Bird, by Chong Yak-yong and building. d, Map of Korea, by Kim Chong-ho and compass. e, Carved stone monument at Tongchak Peasant Uprsing Memorial Hall.

Historic relics of Koryo and Choson Dynasties — No. 1975: a, Container, pitcher, Kangjin kiln site. b, Fenced-off monument and Nirvana Hall, Pongjungsa Temple (yellow building). c, Hahoe and Pyongsan wooden masks. d, Kunjong Hall, Kyongbok Palace. e, Dream Journey to the Peach Blossom land, by An Kyon. f, Water clock of King Sejong.

Joseon Dynasty — No. 1976: a, Spring Outing, by Sin Yun-bok. b, Chusa-style calligraphy, birthplace of Kim Jeong-hui. c, Beacon Lighthouse, book of technical drawings. d, Myeongdong Cathedral. e, Wongaksa Theater, performers. f, KITSAT-1 satellite.

Vision of the Future — No. 1977: a, Bicycle with wheels represening the two Koreas. b, Rainbow (environmental protection). c, Human genome project. d, IMT 2000 and satellites. e, Children's drawing of space travel. f, Solar-powered vehicle, windmills.

Pre-independence historic events and personalities — No. 1978: a, Kim Ku. b, March 1 Independence Movement, Declaration of Independence. c, Establishment of Korean interim government. d, Ahn Ik-tae, composer of national anthem. e, Yun Dong-ju, poet.

Historic events since independence — No. 1979: a, Liberation after World War II (People with flag). b, Korean War (soldiers, barbed wire). c, Construction of Seoul-Busan Expressway. d, Saemaul Undong movement (workers and flag). e, 1988 Summer Olympics, Seoul.

1999-2001 Litho. *Perf. 13x13½*

1969 Sheet of 6 5.00 5.00
a.-f. A1297 170w any single .60 .30
1970 Sheet of 6 5.00 5.00
a.-f. A1297 170w any single .60 .30

Perf. 13½

1971 Sheet of 5 + label 4.75 4.75
a.-e. A1297 170w any single .60 .30

Photo.

1972 Sheet of 5 + label 4.75 4.75
a.-e. A1297 170w any single .60 .30
1973 Sheet of 5 + label 4.75 4.75
a.-e. A1297 170w any single .60 .30
1974 Sheet of 5 + label 4.75 4.75
a.-e. A1297 170w Any single .60 .30

Perf. 13

1975 Sheet of 6 5.25 5.25
a.-f. A1297 170w Any single .60 .30
1976 Sheet of 6 5.00 5.00
a.-f. A1297 170w Any single .60 .30

1977 Sheet of 6 5.00 5.00
a.-f. A1297 170w Any single .60 .30

Perf. 13½

1978 Sheet of 5 + label 4.50 4.50
a.-e. A1297 170w Any single .60 .30
1979 Sheet of 5 + label 4.50 4.50
a.-e. A1297 170w Any single .60 .30
Nos. 1969-1979 (11) 53.25 53.25

Size of stamps on Nos. 1971-1972, 1974, 1978-1979: 35x36mm.

Issued: #1969, 10/2; #1970, 11/16; #1971, 1/3/00; #1972, 3/2/00; #1973, 5/1/00; #1974, 7/1/00; #1975, 9/1/00; #1976, 11/1/00; #1977, 1/2/01; #1978, 4/2/01; #1979, 7/2/01.

UPU, 125th Anniv. — A1298

1999, Oct. 9 Litho. ***Perf. 13x13½***
1980 A1298 170w multi .50 .25

Beauty Series

A1299

a, Purple panel, 4 orange flowers in purple and blue vase, rabbit, duck. b, Blue green panel, red jar, rooster. c, Orange panel, 4 orange flowers in yellow vase. d, Purple panel, fish, purple vase with flower decoration. e, Blue green panel, fish in net. f, Red panel, crab. g, Purple panel, birds, red flowers. h, Orange panel, deer, 3 orange flowers.

1999, Nov. 3 Litho. ***Perf. 13x13¼***
1981 A1299 Sheet of 8, #a.-h. 12.00 12.00
a.-h. 340w any single 1.50 .60

New Year 2000 (Year of the Dragon) — A1300

1999, Dec. 1 **Photo.**
1982 A1300 170w multi .60 .30
a. Souvenir sheet of 2 1.25 1.25

A1301

Registration of Korean Sites on World Heritage List — A1302

Litho. & Engr.

1999, Dec. 9 ***Perf. 13x13¼***
1983 Sheet of 10 12.50 12.50
a. A1301 170w multicolored .55 .30
b. A1302 340w multicolored 1.50 .70

Top part of #1983 contains one each #1983a-1983b. The lower part of #1983 contains 4 each #1983a-1983b.

Flag
A1303

Nycticorax Nycticorax
A1304

Vitis Amurensis
A1305

Purpuricenus Lituratus
A1306

Eophona Migratoria
A1307

Limenitis Populi
A1310

Plow
A1311

Sseore
A1311a

Sowing Basket, Namtae
A1311b

Hoes
A1311c

Namu-janngun, Jaetbak
A1311d

Yongdurei
A1311e

Winnower, Thresher
A1311f

Meongseok, Wicker Tray
A1311g

Mortar, Pestle, Grindstone
A1311h

Carrier, Rice Chest
A1311i

Hibiscus Syriacus
A1312

Chionectes Opilio
A1313

Falco Tinnunculus — A1314

Hibiscus Syriacus
A1314a

Hibiscus Syriacus
A1314b

Ficedula Zanthopygia — A1315

Hibiscus Syriacus
A1315a

Celadon Pitcher
A1316

Porcelain Container
A1316a

Hong Yong-Sik, 1st General Postmaster
A1317

Koryo Jade Ornament — A1319

Kylin Roof-End Tile — A1320

Ridge-End Tile — A1321

Porcelain Vase With Bamboo Design — A1322

Crown From Tombs of Shinch'on-ni
A1323

Malus Asiatica
A1326

Aquilegia Flabeliata — A1327

Perf. 13¼x13 (#2000, 2002, 2004, 2005), 13x13¼ (#2001, 2003, 2006, 2007), 12¾x13¾ (#1984-1990, 1996), 13¾x12¾ (#1986, 1991, 1993, 1994, 1995, 1997, 1998)

1999-2003 **Photo.**

1984	A1303	10w multi	.20	.20
1985	A1304	20w multi	.30	.30
1986	A1305	30w multi	.50	.35
1987	A1306	40w multi	.30	.30
1988	A1307	60w multi	.55	.35
1989	A1310	160w multi	.55	.30
1990		Horiz. strip of 10	20.00	12.50
a.		A1311 170w multi	1.25	.30
b.		A1311a 170w multi	1.25	.30
c.		A1311b 170w multi	1.25	.30
d.		A1311c 170w multi	1.25	.30
e.		A1311d 170w multi	1.25	.30
f.		A1311e 170w multi	1.25	.30
g.		A1311f 170w multi	1.25	.30
h.		A1311g 170w multi	1.25	.30
i.		A1311h 170w multi	1.25	.30
j.		A1311i 170w multi	1.25	.30
1991	A1312	190w multi	.50	.30
1992	A1313	200w multi	.75	.35
1993	A1314	210w multi	.75	.30
1994	A1314a	220w multi	.75	.30
1995	A1314b	240w multi	.85	.45
1996	A1315	280w multi	1.10	.45
1997	A1315a	310w multi	1.00	.60
1998	A1316	400w multi	1.25	.90
1999	A1316a	500w multi	1.60	1.00
2000	A1317	600w multi	2.50	1.00
2001	A1319	700w multi	3.00	1.00
2002	A1320	1290w multi	4.00	2.50
2003	A1321	1310w multi	4.50	2.50
2004	A1320	1490w buff & multi	5.00	3.50
2005	A1321	1510w brn & multi	5.00	3.50
2006	A1322	1520w multi	5.00	3.50
2007	A1323	2000w multi	6.00	1.50

Booklet Stamps

Self-Adhesive

Serpentine Die Cut 11¼x11½, 11½x11¼

2008	A1326	190w multi	1.00	.35
a.		Booklet pane of 20	20.00	
2008A	A1327	190w multi	1.00	.35
a.		Booklet pane of 20	20.00	
		Nos. 1984-2008A (26)	67.95	38.65

Issued: 600w, 11/15; 2000w, 11/1; 20w, 700w, 1/17/00; 40w, 6/10/00; No. 1992, 1/20/01; 200w, 3/5/01. 160w, 210w, 280w, 1290w, 1310w, 1/15/02; 10w, 3/6/03; 30w, 9/10/01; 60w, 3/15/02; 400w, 4/11/03; 1490w, 1510w, 1/1/03; Nos. 2008-2008A, 7/1/03; 500w, 7/11/03; No. 1991, 220w, 240w, 310w, 1520w, 11/1/04.

2002 World Cup Soccer Championships, Korea & Japan — A1328

Various players in action.

1999, Dec. 31 Photo. *Perf. 13x13½*
Denomination Color

2009	170w orange	.50	.35
2010	170w green	.50	.35
2011	170w red	.50	.35
2012	170w blue	.50	.35
a.	A1328 Strip of 4, #2009-2012	2.75	2.75
b.	Souvenir sheet, #2009-2012	3.50	3.50

Korea's Entry into UPU, Cent. A1329

2000, Jan. 3 Photo. *Perf. 13¼x13*

2013	A1329 170w multi	.50	.30
	Booklet, 10 #2013	12.00	

Steam Locomotives — A1330

Designs: No. 2014, Pashi. No. 2015, Teho. No. 2016, Mika. No. 2017, Hyouki.

2000, Feb. 1 Photo. *Perf. 13¾x12¾*

2014	A1330 170w tan, blk & vio	.60	.30
2015	A1330 170w pink, blk & vio	.60	.30
2016	A1330 170w gray, blk & vio	.60	.30
2017	A1330 170w cit, blk & vio	.60	.30
a.	Block of 4, #2014-2017	2.75	2.75
	Booklet, 2 #2017a	—	

Endangered Flowers — A1331

a, Lilium cernuum. b, Hibiscus hamabo. c, Sedirea japonica. d, Cypripedium japonicum.

2000, Feb. 25 *Perf. 13x13¼*

2018	Sheet of 12	12.00	12.00
a.-d.	A1331 170w any single	.75	.30

Top part of No. 2018 contains one each of Nos. 2018a-2018d and the lower part contains two each. No. 2018 is impregnated with floral scent.

World Water Day — A1332

2000, Mar. 22 Photo. *Perf. 13¼x13*

2019	A1332 170w multi	.50	.30
	Booklet, 10 #2019	10.00	

World Meteorological Organization, 50th Anniv. — A1333

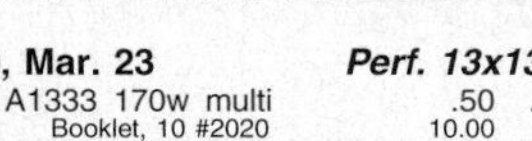

2000, Mar. 23 *Perf. 13x13¼*

2020	A1333 170w multi	.50	.30
	Booklet, 10 #2020	10.00	

Love A1334

2000, Apr. 20 Photo. *Perf. 13¼*

2021	A1334 170w multi	1.00	.30

No. 2021 has floral scent. Value is for copy with surrounding selvage.

Cyber Korea 21 Technology Plan — A1335

2000, Apr. 22 Litho. *Perf. 13¼x13*

2022	A1335 170w multi	.50	.30
	Booklet, 10 #2022	10.00	

Cartoons — A1336

Designs: No. 2023: Goindol, by Park Soo-dong (cavemen). No. 2024, Youngsim-i, by Bae Gum-taek (girl with lipstick).

2000, May 4 Photo. *Perf. 13x13¼*

2023	A1336 170w multi	.50	.40
a.	Souvenir sheet of 1	.75	.75
	Booklet, 10 #2023	10.00	
2024	A1336 170w multi	.50	.40
a.	Souvenir sheet of 1	.75	.75
	Booklet, 10 #2024	10.00	

Summit Meeting Between North and South Korea A1337

2000, June 12 Photo. *Perf. 13¼x13*

2025	A1337 170w multi	.60	.50

41st Intl. Mathematical Olympiad — A1338

2000, July 13 Photo. *Perf. 13x13¼*

2026	A1338 170w multi	.50	.35
	Booklet, 10 #2026	7.50	

Literature Series

The Nine Cloud Dream, by Kim Man-jung A1339

From the Sea to a Child, by Chun Nam-seon A1340

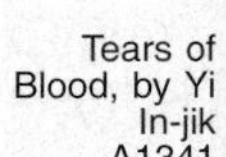

Tears of Blood, by Yi In-jik A1341

Yolha Diary, by Park Ji-won A1342

The Fisherman's Calendar, by Yun Seon-do A1343

2000, Aug. 1 *Perf. 13¼x13, 13x13¼*

2027	A1339 170w multi	.60	.35
a.	Souvenir sheet of 1	.75	.75
2028	A1340 170w multi	.60	.35
a.	Souvenir sheet of 1	.75	.75
2029	A1341 170w multi	.60	.35
a.	Souvenir sheet of 1	.75	.75
2030	A1342 170w multi	.60	.35
a.	Souvenir sheet of 1	.75	.75
2031	A1343 170w multi	.60	.35
a.	Souvenir sheet of 1	.75	.75
	Nos. 2027-2031 (5)	3.00	1.75

The Puljongdae Cliff of Mt. Kumgang, by Chong Son — A1344

2000, Aug. 2 Litho. *Perf. 13¼x13*

2032	A1344 340w multi	1.00	.70
a.	Souvenir sheet of 1	1.40	1.40

Philately Week.

2000 Summer Olympics, Sydney — A1345

2000, Sept. 15 Photo. *Perf. 13x13¼*

2033	A1345 170w multi	.60	.45

Public Secondary Schools, Cent. — A1346

2000, Oct. 2 Litho. & Engr. *Perf. 13*

2034	A1346 170w multi	.60	.45

Third Asia-Europe Summit Meeting, Seoul A1347

2000, Oct. 20 Photo. *Perf. 13¼x13*

2035	A1347 170w multi	.50	.35

Intl. Council of Graphic Design Associations Millennium Congress — A1348

2000, Oct. 25 *Perf. 13x13¼*

2036	A1348 170w org & blk	.50	.35

Cartoon Character Gobau. 50th Anniv. — A1349

2000, Nov. 1 Litho. *Perf. 13¼*

2037	A1349 170w multi	.60	.35

Beauty Series

Tortoise-shell Comb A1350

Woman's Ceremonial Headdress A1351

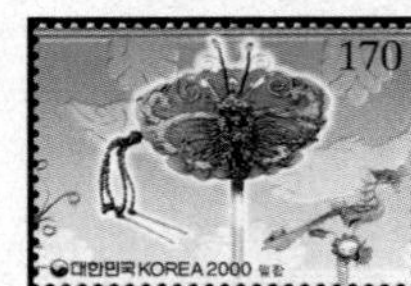

Butterfly-shaped Hair Pin — A1352

Dragon and Phoenix Hair Pins — A1353

2000, Nov. 16 Photo. *Perf. 13¼x13*

2038	Horiz. strip of 4	2.75	2.50
a.	A1350 170w multi	.50	.35
b.	A1351 170w multi	.50	.35
c.	A1352 170w multi	.50	.35
d.	A1353 170w multi	.50	.35

Seoul World Cup Stadium A1354

Busan Sports Complex Main Stadium A1355

Daegu Sports Complex Stadium A1356

Incheon Munhak Stadium A1357

Gwangju World Cup Stadium A1358

Daejeon World Cup Stadium A1359

Ulsan Munsu Soccer Stadium A1360

Suwon World Cup Stadium A1361

Jeonju World Cup Stadium A1362

Jeju World Cup Stadium A1363

2000, Nov. 24 Photo. *Perf. 13¼x13*

2039	Block of 10	12.00	10.00
a.	A1354 170w multi	1.20	.35
b.	A1355 170w multi	1.20	.35
c.	A1356 170w multi	1.20	.35
d.	A1357 170w multi	1.20	.35
e.	A1358 170w multi	1.20	.35
f.	A1359 170w multi	1.20	.35
g.	A1360 170w multi	1.20	.35
h.	A1361 170w multi	1.20	.35
i.	A1362 170w multi	1.20	.35
j.	A1363 170w multi	1.20	.35
k.	Souvenir sheet, #2039a-2039b	2.50	2.50
l.	Souvenir sheet, #2039c-2039d	2.50	2.50
m.	Souvenir sheet, #2039e-2039f	2.50	2.50
n.	Souvenir sheet, #2039g-2039h	2.50	2.50
o.	Souvenir sheet, #2039i-2039j	2.50	2.50

New Year 2001 (Year of the Snake) A1364

2000, Dec. 1 Photo. *Perf. 13¼*

2040	A1364 170w multi	.60	.35
a.	Souvenir sheet of 2	1.25	1.25

Self-Adhesive

Serpentine Die Cut 10¼

2041	A1364 170w multi	1.00	.35

No. 2041 issued in sheets of 10.

King Sejong and Hunmin Chongun Manuscript — A1365

Annals of the Choson Dynasty and Repository — A1365a

Litho. & Engr.

2000, Dec. 9 *Perf. 13x13¼*

2042	Sheet of 8	17.00	17.00
a.	A1365 340w multi	1.50	1.10
b.	A1365a 340w multi	1.50	1.10

Addition of Hunmin Chongun manuscript and Annals of the Choson Dynasty to UNESCO Memory of the World Register. Top part of No. 2042 contains one each Nos. 2042a-2042b the lower part contains three each Nos. 2042a-2042b.

Awarding of Nobel Peace Prize to Pres. Kim Dae-jung A1366

2000, Dec. 9 Photo.

2043	A1366 170w multi	.60	.35
a.	Souvenir sheet of 1	2.50	2.50

Oksun Peaks, by Kim Hong-do A1367

2001, Jan. 10 Photo. *Perf. 13¼*

2044	A1367 170w multi	.50	.35

Visit Korea Year.

A1368

A1369

A1370

Diesel and Electric Trains A1371

2001, Feb. 1 Photo. *Perf. 13¾x12¾*

2045	Block of 4	3.50	3.50
a.	A1368 170w multi	.75	.45
b.	A1369 170w multi	.75	.45
c.	A1370 170w multi	.75	.45
d.	A1371 170w multi	.75	.45

Endangered Flowers — A1372

Designs: a, Diapensia lapponica. b, Rhododendron aureum. c, Jeffersonia dubia. d, Sedum orbiculatum.

2001, Feb. 26 *Perf. 13x13¼*

2046	Sheet of 12	15.00	15.00
a.-d.	A1372 170w Any single	.75	.40

Top part of No. 2046 contains one each Nos. 2046a-2046d, the lower part contains two each Nos. 2046a-2046d.

Opening of Inchon Intl. Airport A1373

2001, Mar. 29

2047	A1373 170w multi	.60	.40

Intl. Olympic Fair, Seoul A1374

2001, Apr. 27 *Perf. 13¼x13*

2048	A1374 170w multi	.60	.40
a.	Souvenir sheet of 2	1.75	1.75

Personalized Greetings — A1375

Designs: No. 2049, 170w, Hugging bears. No. 2050, 170w, Carnation. No. 2051, 170w, Congratulations. No. 2052, 170w, Birthday cake.

2001 Photo. *Perf. 13¼*

Stamps + Labels

2049-2052	A1375 Set of 4	6.00	6.00

Issued: Nos. 2049-2050, 4/30; No. 2051, 6/1; No. 2052, 7/2. Each stamp was issued in sheets of 20+20 labels that could be personalized. Each sheet sold for 700w.

Cartoons — A1376

Designs: No. 2053, Iljimae, by Ko Woo-young (shown). No. 2054, Kkeobeongi, by Kil Chang-duk (student at desk).

2001, May 4 Photo. *Perf. 13x13¼*

2053	A1376 170w multi	.60	.40
a.	Souvenir sheet of 1	1.00	1.00
2054	A1376 170w multi	.60	.40
a.	Souvenir sheet of 1	1.00	1.00

2002 World Cup Soccer Championships, Japan and Korea — A1377

Years of previous championships, soccer players, flags and scenes from host countries: a, 1954, Switzerland, mountains. b, 1986, Mexico, Chichen Itza. c, 1990, Italy, Colosseum. d, 1994, US, World Trade Center and Statue of Liberty. e, 1998, France, Eiffel Tower.

2001, May 31 *Perf. 13¼x13*

2055	Horiz. strip of 5	5.00	5.00
a.-e.	A1377 170w Any single	.75	.40
f.	Souvenir sheet, 2 #2055a	2.00	2.00
g.	Souvenir sheet, 2 #2055b	2.00	2.00
h.	Souvenir sheet, 2 #2055c	2.00	2.00
i.	Souvenir sheet, 2 #2055d	2.00	2.00
j.	Souvenir sheet, 2 #2055e	2.00	2.00

Kkakdugi A1378

Bossam Kimchi A1379

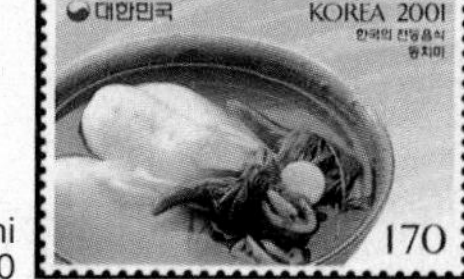

Dongchimi A1380

Baechu Kimchi A1381

2001, June 15 *Perf. 13x13¼*

2056	Vert. strip of 4	3.00	3.00
a.	A1378 170w multi	.60	.40
b.	A1379 170w multi	.60	.40
c.	A1380 170w multi	.60	.40
d.	A1381 170w multi	.60	.40

Roses A1382

2001, July 18 Photo. *Perf. 13¼*

2057	A1382 170w Red Queen	.60	.40
a.	Souvenir sheet of 2	1.50	1.50
2058	A1382 170w Pink Lady	.60	.40
a.	Souvenir sheet of 2	1.50	1.50

Phila Korea 2002, (#2057a, 2058a).

Love — A1383

2001, Aug. 2
2059 A1383 170w multi .70 .40
a. Souvenir sheet of 2 1.75 1.75

World Ceramics Exhibition — A1384

2001, Oct. 10 ***Perf. 13x13¼***
2060 A1384 170w multi .50 .40

53rd Session of the Intl. Statistical Institute A1385

2001, Aug. 22 Litho. ***Perf. 13¼x13***
2061 A1385 170w multi .50 .40

Korea Minting and Security Printing Corp., 50th Anniv. A1386

Litho. & Engr.
2001, Sept. 28 ***Perf. 13¼***
2062 A1386 170w multi .50 .40

Intl. Council of Industrial Design Societies Congress, Seoul — A1387

2001, Oct. 8 Photo. ***Perf. 13x13¼***
2063 A1387 170w multi .50 .40

Year of Dialogue Among Civilizations A1388

2001, Oct. 9 **Litho.**
2064 A1388 170w multi .50 .40

Intl. Organization of Supreme Audit Institutions, 17th Congress A1389

2001, Oct. 19 ***Perf. 13¼x13***
2065 A1389 170w blue & red .50 .40

Orchids — A1390

New Year 2002 (Year of the Horse) — A1391

No. 2066: a, Habenaria radiata. b, Orchis cyclochila. c, Dendrobium moniliforme. d, Gymnadenia camschatica.

2001, Nov. 12 Photo. ***Perf. 13¼x13***
2066 Horiz. strip of 4 3.00 3.00
a.-d. A1390 170w Any single .60 .40

No. 2066 is impregnated with orchid scent.

2001, Dec. 3 ***Perf. 13x13¼***
2067 A1391 170w multi .60 .40
a. Souvenir sheet of 2 1.40 1.40

Seonjeongjeon Hall, Changdeok Palace — A1392

Injeongjeon Hall, Changdeok Palace — A1393

Litho. & Engr.
2001, Dec. 10 ***Perf. 13x13¼***
2068 Sheet of 10 15.00 12.00
a. A1392 170w multi .75 .40
b. A1393 340w multi 1.50 .75

Top part of #2068 contains one each #2068a-2068b. The lower part of #2068 contains 4 each #2068a-2068b.

Priority Mail — A1394

2002, Jan. 15 Photo. ***Perf. 13¼x13***
Background Color
2069 A1394 280w orange 1.10 .40
2070 A1394 310w blue 1.20 .50
2071 A1394 1380w green 3.50 2.40
2072 A1394 1410w red 3.50 2.50
Nos. 2069-2072 (4) 9.30 5.80

See Nos. 2113-2114.

Lily — A1395

Roses — A1395a

Fish — A1396

Chick — A1396a

2002, Jan. 15 Photo. ***Perf. 13¼***
Stamp + Label
2073 A1395 190w multi 2.00 1.00
2073A A1395a 190w multi 2.00 1.00
2074 A1396 190w multi 2.00 1.00
2074A A1396a 190w multi 2.00 1.00
Nos. 2073-2074A (4) 8.00 4.00

Nos. 2073, 2073A and 2074 are impregnated with scents of items depicted. Labels could be personalized.

Korea's Entrance in Intl. Telecommunications Union, 50th Anniv. — A1397

2002, Jan. 31 Photo. ***Perf. 13x13¼***
2075 A1397 190w multi .60 .40

Trains — A1398

No. 2076: a, Blue and white locomotive. b, Green, yellow and white locomotive. c, Green, yellow and white locomotive pulling cars. d, Red, yellow and white locomotive pulling cars.

2002, Feb. 4 Photo. ***Perf. 13¾x12¾***
2076 A1398 190w Block of 4, #a-d 3.00 3.00

Dye Plants — A1399

No. 2077: a, Carthamus tinctorius. b, Lithospermum erythrorhizon. c, Fraxinus rhynchophylla. d, Persicaria tinctoria.

2002, Feb. 25 Photo. ***Perf. 13¼x13***
2077 A1399 190w Block of 4, #a-d 3.00 3.00

See No. 2117, 2140, 2170.

Intl. Flower Exhibition, Anmyeon Island A1400

2002, Apr. 26 ***Perf. 13¼***
2078 A1400 190w multi .40 .40

Cartoons A1401

Designs: No. 2079, Girl from "Wogdoggle Dugdoggle," by Mi-Na Hwang. No. 2080, Schoolmaster and children from "Mengkkong-i Seodang Village School," by Seung-woon Yoon.

2002, May 4 ***Perf. 13¼x13***
2079 A1401 190w multi .60 .40
a. Souvenir sheet of 1 1.25 1.25
2080 A1401 190w multi .60 .40
a. Souvenir sheet of 1 1.25 1.25

64th Rally of Intl. Federation of Camping and Caravanning, Donghae A1402

2002, May 16
2081 A1402 190w multi *10.00* —

2002 World Cup Soccer Championships, Japan and Korea — A1403

No. 2082: a, Player with pink feet, part of map of Europe. b, Player with blue green feet, part of map of North and Central America. c, Player with blue violet feet, part of map of southeast Asia. d, Player with purple feet, part of map of southern Africa. e, Player with brown orange feet, part of map of South America.

2002, May 31 ***Perf.***
2082 A1403 190w Sheet, 2 each #a-e, + label 7.50 7.50
f. Souvenir sheet, 2 #2082a .70 .40
g. Souvenir sheet, 2 #2082b .70 .40
h. Souvenir sheet, 2 #2082c .70 .40
i. Souvenir sheet, 2 #2082d .70 .40
j. Souvenir sheet, 2 #2082e .70 .40

Korean Cuisine — A1404

No. 2083: a, Jeolpyeon (blue background). b, Shirutteok (red background). c, Injeolmi (tan background). d, Songpyeon (green background).

2002, June 15 ***Perf. 13x13¼***

2083 A1404 190w Block of 4, #a-d 3.00 3.00

Women's Week — A1405

2002, July 1 Litho. ***Perf. 13x13¼***

2084 A1405 190w multi .70 .40

Philakorea 2002 World Stamp Exhibition, Seoul A1406

Designs: No. 2085, Children, globe. No. 2086, Child, stamps showing flags of the world.

2002, July 1 Photo. ***Perf. 13¼***

2085 A1406 190w multi .55 .40
a. Souvenir sheet of 2 1.50 1.50
2086 A1406 190w multi .55 .40
a. Souvenir sheet of 2 1.50 1.50

Regions of Korea

Busan — A1407

Chungbuk — A1408

Chungnam — A1409

Daegu — A1410

Daejeon — A1411

Gangwon — A1412

Gwangju — A1413

Gyeongbuk — A1414

Gyeonggi — A1415

Gyeongnam — A1416

Incheon — A1417

Jeju — A1418

Jeonbuk — A1419

Jeonnam — A1420

Seoul — A1421

Ulsan — A1422

No. 2087: a, Dongnaeyaryu Festival. b, Cliffs.
No. 2088: a, Martial arts. b, Beopju Temple.
No. 2089: a, Weaver. b, Men in sailboat.
No. 2090: a, Forest and river. b, Gwanbong Seokjoyeorae statue.
No. 2091: a, Daeok Science Town, scientist at work. b, Expo Science Park.
No. 2092: a, Gangneung mask drama. b, Ulsanbawi Rock.
No. 2093: a, Men playing tug-of-war game. b, Statues and tower at May 18th Cemetery.
No. 2094: a, Men playing game with tied logs. b, Dokdo Island.
No. 2095: a, Yangjubyeol Sandaenori mask dance. b, Panmunjom Freedom House.
No. 2096: a, Goseong Ogwangdae clowns performing. b, Rock formations in Hallyeo Haesang Natl. Maritime Park.
No. 2097: a, Chamseongdam dancers. b, Cliffs.
No. 2098: a, Traditional house and gate. b, Mt. Halla.
No. 2099: a, Iri folk band. b, Mt. Mai.
No. 2100: a, Ganggang Sullae circle dance. b, Odong Island.
No. 2101: a, Songpa Sandaenori mask dance. b, Heung-injimun Fortress.
No. 2102: a, Cheoyongmu mask dance. b, Cheonjeonnigakseok prehistoric inscriptions.

2002, Aug. 1 ***Perf. 13x13¼***

2087 A1407 190w Horiz. pair, #a-b 1.40 .75
2088 A1408 190w Horiz. pair, #a-b 1.40 .75
2089 A1409 190w Horiz. pair, #a-b 1.40 .75
2090 A1410 190w Horiz. pair, #a-b 1.40 .75
2091 A1411 190w Horiz. pair, #a-b 1.40 .75
2092 A1412 190w Horiz. pair, #a-b 1.40 .75
2093 A1413 190w Horiz. pair, #a-b 1.40 .75
2094 A1414 190w Horiz. pair, #a-b 1.40 .75
2095 A1415 190w Horiz. pair, #a-b 1.40 .75
2096 A1416 190w Horiz. pair, #a-b 1.40 .75
2097 A1417 190w Horiz. pair, #a-b 1.40 .75
2098 A1418 190w Horiz. pair, #a-b 1.40 .75
2099 A1419 190w Horiz. pair, #a-b 1.40 .75
2100 A1420 190w Horiz. pair, #a-b 1.40 .75
2101 A1421 190w Horiz. pair, #a-b 1.40 .75
2102 A1422 190w Horiz. pair, #a-b 1.40 .75
Nos. 2087-2102 (16) 22.40 12.00

Philakorea 2002 World Stamp Exhibition, Seoul A1423

2002, Aug. 2 ***Perf. 13¼x13***

2103 A1423 190w multi .60 .40
a. Sheet of 2, imperf. 1.50 1.50

Philately Week A1424

2002, Aug. 2 ***Perf. 13¼***

2104 A1424 190w multi .60 .40
a. Souvenir sheet of 2 1.50 1.50

South Korean Soccer Team's Fourth Place Finish at World Cup Championships — A1425

No. 2105: a, Coach Guus Hiddink. b, Goalie (jersey #1). c, Player with red shirt with white accents. d, Player with red shirt with white accents, with white sock. e, Player with white shirt with red accents, ball near shoulder. f, Player (jersey #5). g, Player (jersey #6). h, Player (jersey #7). i, Player (jersey #8.) j, Player (jersey #9). k, Player (jersey #10). l, Player with ball hiding part of head. m, Goalie with red hair, white gloves with dark trim. n, Player (jersey #13). o, Player (jersey #14). p, Player (jersey #15). q, Player with white shirt with red accents, with white sock. r, Player (jersey #17). s, Player (jersey #18). t, Player (jersey #19). u, Player (jersey #20). v, Player (jersey #21). w, Player (jersey #22). x, Goalie with brown hair, black gloves with red trim.

2002, Aug. 7 ***Perf. 13¼x13***

2105 A1425 190w Sheet of 24, #a-x 15.00 15.00

14th Asian Games, Busan — A1426

2002, Sept. 28 Litho. ***Perf. 13***

2106 A1426 190w multi .60 .40
a. Souvenir sheet of 2 1.50 1.50

8th Far East and South Pacific Games for the Disabled, Busan — A1427

2002, Oct. 26 Photo. ***Perf. 13x13¼***

2107 A1427 190w multi .60 .40

Orchids — A1428

No. 2108: a, Cymbidium kanran. b, Gastrodia elata. c, Pogonia japonica. d, Cephalanthera falcata.

2002, Nov. 12 ***Perf. 13¼x13***

2108 A1428 190w Block of 4, #a-d 3.00 3.00

No. 2108 is impregnated with orchid scent.

Martial Arts — A1429

No. 2109: a, Taekwondo (white clothes). b, Kung Fu (red clothes).

2002, Nov. 20 ***Perf. 13x13¼***

2109 A1429 190w Horiz. pair, #a-b 1.50 1.50

See People's Republic of China No. 3248.

New Year 2003 (Year of the Ram) — A1430

2002, Dec. 2

2110 A1430 190w multi .60 .40
a. Souvenir sheet of 2 1.40 1.40

Gongsimdon Observation Tower, Hwaseong Fortress — A1431

Banghwasuryu Pavilion, Hwaseong Fortress — A1432

2002, Dec. 9 **Litho. & Engr.**

2111 Sheet of 10 10.00 10.00
a. A1431 190w multi .60 .40
b. A1432 280w multi .90 .55

Top part of No. 2111 contains one each of #2111a-2111b. The lower part contains 4 each #2111a-2111b.

South Korea — Viet Nam Diplomatic Relations, 10th Anniv. — A1433

No. 2112: a, Dabo Pagoda, Gyeongju (denomination at right). b, Mot Cot Pagoda, Hanoi, Viet Nam (denomination at left).

2002, Dec. 21 Photo. ***Perf. 13¼x13***

2112 A1433 190w Horiz. pair, #a-b 1.40 1.10

See Viet Nam Nos. 3167-3168.

Priority Mail Type of 2002

2003, Jan. 1 Photo. ***Perf. 13¼x13***

Background Color

2113 A1394 1580w lilac 3.75 3.75
2114 A1394 1610w brown 3.75 3.75

Korean Immigration to the US, Cent. — A1434

2003, Jan. 13 Photo. ***Perf. 13¼x13***

2115 A1434 190w multi .60 .40

Gondola Car A1435

Box Car A1436

Tanker Car A1437

Hopper Car A1438

2003, Feb. 4 ***Perf. 13¾x13***

2116 Block of 4 3.00 2.25
a. A1435 190w multi .60 .40
b. A1436 190w multi .60 .40
c. A1437 190w multi .60 .40
d. A1438 190w multi .60 .40

Dye Plants Type of 2002

No. 2117: a, Rubia akane. b, Rhus javanica. c, Sophora japonica. d, Isatis tinctoria.

2003, Feb. 22 Photo. ***Perf. 13¼x13***

2117 A1399 190w Horiz. strip of 4, #a-d 3.00 2.25

Inauguration of Pres. Roh Moo-hyun A1439

2003, Feb. 25 ***Perf. 13x13¼***

2118 A1439 190w multi .60 .40
a. Souvenir sheet of 1 1.50 1.50

Traditional Culture

Footwear — A1440

Sedan Chairs — A1441

Lighting Implements — A1442

Tables — A1443

No. 2119: a, Unhye (denomination at LL, date at LR). b, Mokhwa (denomination at UR, date at L). c, Jipsin (denomination at UL, date at LR). d, Namaksin (denomination at LR, date at LL).

No. 2120: a, Eoyeon (no handles). b, Choheon (wheeled). c, Saingyo (with handles and roof). d, Nanyeo (with handles only).

No. 2121: a, Jojokdeung (round lantern). b, Deungjan (lamp oil container). c, Juchilmokje Yukgakjedeung (hexagonal lantern). d, Brass candlestick holder with butterfly design.

No. 2122: a, Gujok-ban (round table with legs connected at base. b, Punghyeol-ban (12-sided table, denomination at top). c, Iljuban (12-sided table, denomination at top). d, Haeju-ban (octagonal table).

2003 Engr. ***Perf. 12½***

2119 A1440 190w Horiz. strip of 4, #a-d 3.00 2.25
2120 A1441 190w Horiz. strip of 4, #a-d 3.00 2.25
2121 A1442 190w Horiz. strip of 4, #a-d 3.00 2.25
2122 A1443 190w Horiz. strip of 4, #a-d 3.00 2.25
Nos. 2119-2122 (4) 12.00 9.00

Issued: No. 2119, 3/19; No. 2120, 5/19; No. 2121, 7/25; No. 2122, 9/25.

Cartoons — A1444

Designs: No. 2123, The Goblin's Cap, by Shin Moon-soo (shown). No. 2124, The Sword of Fire, by Kim Hye-rin (woman with sword).

2003, May 2 Photo. ***Perf. 13x13¼***

2123 A1444 190w multi .60 .40
a. Souvenir sheet of 1 1.10 1.10
2124 A1444 190w multi .60 .40
a. Souvenir sheet of 1 1.10 1.10

Lighthouse Construction in Korea, Cent. — A1445

2003, May 30 ***Perf. 13¼x13***

2125 A1445 190w multi .60 .40

Dasik A1446

Yeot Gangjeong A1447

Yakgwa A1448

Yugwa A1449

2003, June 13 ***Perf. 13x13¼***

2126 Vert. strip of 4 2.75 2.25
a. A1446 190w multi .55 .40
b. A1447 190w multi .55 .40
c. A1448 190w multi .55 .40
d. A1449 190w multi .55 .40

Priority Mail Type of 2002

2003, July 1 Photo. ***Perf. 13¼x13***

Background Color

2127 A1394 420w blue green 1.25 .90

Philately Week A1450

2003, Aug. 1 ***Perf. 13¼***

2128 A1450 190w multi .60 .40
a. Souvenir sheet of 2, imperf. 1.50 1.50

2003 Summer Universiade, Daegu — A1451

2003, Aug. 21 ***Perf. 13x13¼***

2129 A1451 190w multi .60 .40
a. Souvenir sheet of 2 1.40 1.40

YMCA in Korea, Cent. — A1452

Soong Eui School, Cent. — A1453

2003, Oct. 28 Photo. ***Perf. 13¼x13***

2130 A1452 190w multi .60 .40

2003, Oct. 31 ***Perf. 13x13¼***

2131 A1453 190w multi .60 .40

Natl. Tuberculosis Association, 50th Anniv. — A1454

2003, Nov. 6 **Litho.**

2132 A1454 190w black & red .60 .40

Orchids — A1455

No. 2133: a, Cremastra appendiculata. b, Cymbidium lancifolium. c, Orchis graminifolia. d, Bulbophyllum drymoglossum.

2003, Nov. 12 Photo. *Perf. 13¼x13*
2133 A1455 190w Block of 4, #a-d 3.00 2.25

No. 2133 is impregnated with a floral scent.

New Year 2004 (Year of the Monkey) — A1456

2003, Dec. 1 *Perf. 13x13¼*
2134 A1456 190w multi .60 .40
a. Souvenir sheet of 2 1.40 1.40

A1457

Dolmens — A1458

Litho. & Engr.

2003, Dec. 9 *Perf. 13x13¼*
2135 Sheet of 10 12.00 12.00
a. A1457 190w multi .70 .40
b. A1458 280w multi .90 .50

Top part of No. 2135 contains one each of Nos. 2135a-2135b. The lower part contains 4 each Nos. 2135a-2135b.

South Korea — India Diplomatic Relations, 30th Anniv. — A1459

No. 2136: a, Cheomsongdae Astronomical Observatory, Gyeongju, South Korea. b, Jantar Mantar, Jaipur, India.

2003, Dec. 10 Photo. *Perf. 13¼x13*
2136 A1459 190w Horiz. pair, #a-b 1.40 1.10

Dokdo Island Flora and Fauna A1460

No. 2137: a, Calystegia soldanella. b, Aster spathulifolius, butterfly. c, Calonectris laucomelas. d, Larus crassirostris.

2004, Jan. 16 *Perf. 13x13¼*
2137 Horiz. strip of 4 *15.00* —
a.-d. A1460 190w Any single *3.50 3.50*

Korean National Commission for UNESCO, 50th Anniv. — A1461

2004, Jan. 30
2138 A1461 190w multi .35 .20

Multiple Tie Tamper A1462

Ballast Regulator A1463

Track Inspection Car — A1464

Ballast Cleaner A1465

2004, Feb. 4 *Perf. 13¾x12¾*
2139 Block of 4 2.75 2.75
a. A1462 190w brown & multi .60 .40
b. A1463 190w lilac & multi .60 .40
c. A1464 190w blue green & multi .60 .40
d. A1465 190w blue & multi .60 .40

Dye Plants Type of 2002

No. 2140: a, Juglans regia. b, Acer ginnala. c, Pinus densiflora. d, Punica granatum.

2004, Feb. 25 *Perf. 13¼x13*
2140 A1399 190w Block of 4, #a-d 2.75 2.75

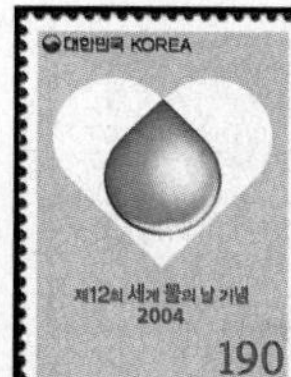
A1466

A1467

2004, Mar. 22 Litho. *Perf. 13x13¼*
2141 A1466 190w multi .50 .40

12th World Water Day.

2004, Mar. 25 Photo.
2142 A1467 190w multi .50 .40

Korean Meteorological Service, cent.

Inauguration of High Speed Railroads A1468

2004, Apr. 1 *Perf. 13¼x13*
2143 A1468 190w multi .50 .40

A1469

Winners of Future of Science Stamp Design Contest — A1470

Perf. 13¼x13, 13x13¼

2004, Apr. 21 Photo.
2144 A1469 190w multi .50 .40
2145 A1470 190w multi .50 .40

A1471

A1472

Cartoons: No. 2146, Wicked Boy Simsultong, by Lee Jeong-moon (shown). No. 2147, Nation of Winds, by Kim Jin.

2004, May 4 Photo. *Perf. 13x13¼*
2146 A1471 190w multi .50 .40
a. Souvenir sheet of 1 1.00 1.00
2147 A1471 190w multi .50 .40
a. Souvenir sheet of 1 1.00 1.00

2004, May 21
2148 A1472 190w multi .50 .40

FIFA (Fédération Internationale de Football Association), cent.

Korean Cuisine — A1473

No. 2149: a, Sinseollo (blue background). b, Hwayangjeok (green background). c, Bibimbap (pink background). d, Gujeolpan (orange background).

2004, June 15
2149 A1473 190w Block of 4, #a-d 2.50 2.50

Traditional Culture

Needlework Equipment — A1474

Head Coverings — A1475

No. 2150: a, Octagonal storage basket. b, Thimbles with flower decorations. c, Cylindrical bobbin, bobbin and thread. d, Needle cases.

No. 2151: a, Gold crown with tassels. b, Bamboo hat with untied neck band. c, Gauze hat. d, Horsehair hat with tied neck band.

2004 Engr. *Perf. 12½*
2150 A1474 190w Horiz. strip of 4, #a-d 2.50 2.50
2151 A1475 190w Horiz. strip of 4, #a-d 2.50 2.50

National Academies, 50th Anniv. — A1476

No. 2152: a, National Academy of Science. b, National Academy of Arts.

2004, July 16 Litho. *Perf. 13x13¼*
2152 A1476 190w Horiz. pair, #a-b 1.25 1.25

Congratulations — A1477

2004, July 22 Photo. *Perf. 13¼*
2153 A1477 190w multi .60 .40
a. Souvenir sheet of 2 1.00 1.00

2004 Summer Olympics, Athens — A1478

2004, Aug. 13 *Perf. 13x13¼*
2154 A1478 190w multi .60 .40

Bridges — A1479

No. 2155: a, Geumcheongyo Bridge (two arches). b, Jeongotgyo Bridge (pillars and flat slabs). c, Jincheon Nongdari Bridge (loose rocks). d, Seungseongyo Bridge (single arch).

Perf. 13¼ Syncopated

2004, Sept. 24
2155 A1479 190w Block fo 4, #a-d 2.50 2.50

Intl. Council of Museums, 20th General Conference, Seoul — A1480

2004, Oct. 1 *Perf. 13x13¼*
2156 A1480 190w multi .60 .40

Obaegnahan — A1481

Seonjakjiwat — A1482

Baengnokdam — A1483

Oreum A1484

2004, Oct. 18

2157	Block of 4	2.50	2.50
a.	A1481 190w multi	.60	.40
b.	A1482 190w multi	.60	.40
c.	A1483 190w multi	.60	.40
d.	A1484 190w multi	.60	.40

Flag — A1485

Flowers — A1486

Flower and Bee — A1487

Lamb, Church and Bible — A1488

Children and Lotus Flower — A1489

Stylized Animals — A1490

Teddy Bear — A1491

Dinosaur — A1492

Flower and Envelope — A1493

2004, Nov. 1 **Photo.** *Perf. 13¼*

2158	A1485 220w multi + label	1.50	1.50
2159	A1486 220w multi + label	1.50	1.50
2160	A1487 220w multi + label	1.50	1.50
2161	A1488 220w multi + label	1.50	1.50
2162	A1489 220w multi + label	1.50	1.50
2163	Strip of 4 + 4 alternating labels	6.00	6.00
a.	A1490 220w multi + label	1.50	1.50
b.	A1491 220w multi + label	1.50	1.50
c.	A1492 220w multi + label	1.50	1.50
d.	A1493 220w multi + label	1.50	1.50
	Nos. 2158-2163 (6)	13.50	13.50

Labels attached to Nos. 2158-2163 could be personalized.

Orchids — A1494

No. 2164: a, Goodyera maximowicziana. b, Sarcanthus scolopendrifolius. c, Calanthe sieboldii. d, Bletilla striata.

2004, Nov. 12 *Perf. 13¼x13*
2164 A1494 220w Block of 4, #a-d 2.75 2.75

No. 2164 is impregnated with orchid scent.

New Year 2005 (Year of the Chicken) — A1495

2004, Dec. 1 *Perf. 13x13¼*

2165	A1495 220w multi	.75	.45
a.	Souvenir sheet of 2	1.25	1.25

Daenungwon Tumuli Park, Seosuhyeong Ceramics, Royal Crown of Geumgwanchong — A1496

Anapji Pond, Scissors, Buddha, Lion Incense Burner — A1497

2004, Dec. 9 **Litho. & Engr.**

2166	Sheet of 10	9.00	9.00
a.	A1496 310w multi	.75	.45
b.	A1497 310w multi	.75	.45

Top part of No. 2166 contains one each of Nos. 2166a-2166b. The lower part contains 4 each of Nos. 2166a-2166b.

Fish of Marado Island A1498

No. 2167: a, Girella punctata. b, Epinephelus septemfasciatus. c, Chromis notata. d, Sebastiscus marmoratus.

2005, Jan. 18 **Photo.**

2167	Horiz. strip of 4	3.50	3.50
a.-d.	A1498 220w Any single	.60	.45

Cloning of Human Embryonic Stem Cells, 1st Anniv. — A1499

2005, Feb. 12 *Perf. 12¾x13½*
2168 A1499 220w multi .70 .40

Rotary International, Cent. A1500

2005, Feb. 23 *Perf. 13¼x13*
2169 A1500 220w multi .50 .40

Dye Plants Type of 2002

No. 2170: a, Taxus cuspidata. b, Smilax china. c, Clerodendron trichotomum. d, Gardenia jasminoides.

2005, Feb. 25
2170 A1399 220w Block of 4, #a-d 2.50 2.50

Gyeonggi Province Tourism — A1501

2005, Mar. 10 **Litho.** *Perf. 13x13¼*
2171 A1501 220w multi .50 .40

A1502

Information and Communication of the Future — A1503

2005, Apr. 22 **Photo.** *Perf. 13¼x13*
2172 A1502 220w multi .50 .40

Perf. 13x13¼

2173 A1503 220w multi .50 .40

Korea University, Cent.
A1504

2005, May 4 Litho. *Perf. 13x13¼*

2174 A1504 220w multi .50 .40

57th Intl. Whaling Commission Meeting, Ulsan
A1505

2005, May 27 Photo. *Perf. 13¼x13*

2175 A1505 220w multi .50 .40

Neobani (Broiled Beef)
A1506

Bindaetteok (Fried Ground Mung Beans)
A1507

Jeongol (Stew)
A1508

Hwajeon (Fried Rice Cakes and Flower Petals)
A1509

2005, June 15 *Perf. 13x13¼*

2176 Block of 4 3.00 3.00
- *a.* A1506 220w multi .60 .40
- *b.* A1507 220w multi .60 .40
- *c.* A1508 220w multi .60 .40
- *d.* A1509 220w multi .60 .40

Goguryeo Kingdom — A1510

No. 2177: a, Sword, armored soldier on horse. b, Armored soldiers on horses, Onyeo Fortress, Baek-am Castle.

Perf. 13x13¼ Syncopated

2005, July 1

2177 A1510 310w Vert. pair, #a-b 2.00 2.00

Strix Aluco
A1513

Arctous Ruber
A1514

Parus Major
A1516

Crinum Asiaticum
A1517

Planned City — A1521

Brown Hawk Owl — A1522

Rose of Sharon — A1523

Whistling Swans
A1525

Celadon Incense Burner
A1527

Buncheong Jar — A1529

Gilt Bronze Pagoda — A1531

Euryale Ferox — A1532

2005-09 Photo. *Perf. 13¾x12¾*

2180 A1513 50w multi .75 .25

2181 A1514 70w multi .20 .20

Perf. 12¾x13¾

2183 A1516 90w multi .50 .25

Perf. 13¾x12¾

2184 A1517 100w multi .50 .25

Perf. 13x13¼

2188 A1521 220w multi .50 .25

2189 A1522 250w multi .75 .40

Perf. 13½

2190 A1523 250w multi + label .75 .40

Perf. 13¾x13

2192 A1525 340w multi .75 .40

Perf. 13x13¼

2194 A1527 1000w multi 1.75 .85

2196 A1529 1720w multi 3.50 1.75

Perf. 13x13½

2197 A1530 1750w multi 3.75 1.90

Perf. 13x13¼

2198 A1531 2000w multi 3.25 1.60

Serpentine Die Cut 11¾x11½

2199 A1532 250w multi .50 .25

Nos. 2180-2199 (13) 17.45 8.75

Issued: 50w, 9/1; 1720w, 8/1; 90w, 6/5/06; 100w, 3/2/06; 220w, 12/27/05. Nos. 2189, 2190, 2192, 2197, 11/1/06. 70w, 7/10/07. No. 2199, 6/30/08. No. 2194, 11/17/09; No. 2198, 5/25/09.

No. 2190 was printed in sheets of 20 stamps and 20 labels that could be personalized.

Happy Birthday
A1536

2005, Aug. 3 Photo. *Perf. 13¼*

2203 A1536 220w multi .50 .35
- *a.* Souvenir sheet of 2 1.25 1.25

Philately Week. Portions of the design were printed with a thermochromic ink that changes color when warmed.

Liberation of Korea, 60th Anniv.
A1537

No. 2204: a, Charter and headquarters of provisional government. b, Proclamation of Korean Independence. c, Soldiers taking oath. d, Emblem of 60th anniv. of Korean liberation.

2005, Aug. 12 *Perf. 13¼x13*

2204 Horiz. strip of 4 6.50 6.50
- *a.* A1537 480w multi 1.00 .75
- *b.* A1537 520w multi 1.25 1.00
- *c.* A1537 580w multi 1.40 1.10
- *d.* A1537 600w multi 1.50 1.25

Fusion of Eastern and Western Cultures — A1538

2005, Aug. 18 Litho. *Perf. 13x13¼*

2205 A1538 220w multi .70 .45

Hangang Bridge — A1539

Expogyo — A1540

Banghwa Bridge — A1541

Tongyeong Bridge — A1542

Perf. 13¼ Syncopated

2005, Sept. 23 Photo.

2206 Block of 4 2.50 2.50
- *a.* A1539 220w multi .50 .40
- *b.* A1540 220w multi .50 .40
- *c.* A1541 220w multi .50 .40
- *d.* A1542 220w multi .50 .40

Ikki Falls
A1543

Piagol Valley
A1544

Cheonwangbong Peak — A1545

Baraebong Peak
A1546

2005, Oct. 18 *Perf. 13x13¼*

2207 Horiz. strip of 4 2.50 2.50
- *a.* A1543 220w multi .50 .40
- *b.* A1544 220w multi .50 .40
- *c.* A1545 220w multi .50 .40
- *d.* A1546 220w multi .50 .40

Korean Red Cross, Cent. — A1547

2005, Oct. 27

2208 A1547 220w multi .60 .50

Relocation and Reopening of National Museum A1548

2005, Oct. 28 *Perf. 13¼x13*

2209 A1548 220w multi .75 .50

Orchids — A1549

No. 2210: a, Epipactis thunbergii. b, Cymbidium goeringii. c, Cephalanthera erecta. d, Spiranthes sinensis.

2005, Nov. 11

2210 A1549 220w Block of 4, #a-d 2.50 2.50

2005 Asian-Pacific Economic Cooperation Economic Leaders' Meeting, Busan — A1550

No. 2211: a, The Sun, the Moon and Five Peaks. b, Murimaru APEC House, Dongbaek Island.

2005, Nov. 18 Photo. *Perf. 13x13¼*

2211 A1550 220w Horiz. pair, #a-b 1.00 1.00

New Year 2006 (Year of the Dog) — A1551

2005, Dec. 1

2212 A1551 220w multi .75 .50
- *a.* Souvenir sheet of 2 1.50 1.50

Jikjisimcheyojeol, Book Produced in 1377 by Movable Type — A1552

Seungjeongwon Ilgi, Diaries of the Joseon Dynasty — A1553

2005, Dec. 9 **Litho. & Engr.**

2213 Sheet of 10 10.00 10.00
- *a.* A1552 310w multi .75 .50
- *b.* A1553 310w multi .75 .50

Top part of No. 2213 contains one each of Nos. 2213a-2213b. The lower part contains 4 each of Nos, 2213a-2213b.

Wildlife of Baengnyeongdo — A1554

Designs: No. 2214, Phoca vitulina largha. No. 2215, Phalacrocorax pelagicus. No. 2216, Orithyia sinica. No. 2217, Ammodytes personatus.

2006, Jan. 18 **Photo.**

2214 A1554 220w multi .75 .50
2215 A1554 220w multi .75 .50
2216 A1554 220w multi .75 .50
2217 A1554 220w multi .75 .50
- *a.* Horiz. strip of 4, #2214-2217 3.00 2.00

Nos. 2214-2217 (4) 3.00 2.00

Designation of Cheju Island as Island of World Peace — A1555

2006, Jan. 27 *Perf. 13¾x12¾*

2218 A1555 220w multi .75 .50

Exports

Automobiles — A1556

Semiconductors — A1557

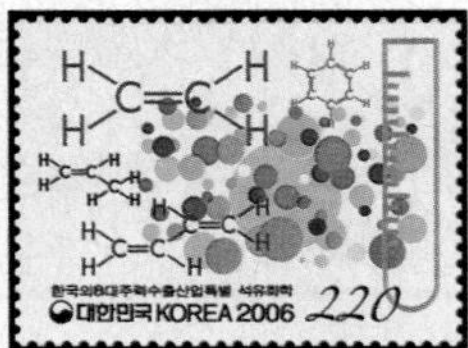

Petrochemicals — A1558

Electronics — A1559

Machinery A1560

Ships A1561

Steel A1562

Textiles A1563

2006, Mar. 15 *Perf. 13x13¼*

2219 Block of 8 6.50 6.50
- *a.* A1556 220w multi .75 .50
- *b.* A1557 220w multi .75 .50
- *c.* A1558 220w multi .75 .50
- *d.* A1559 220w multi .75 .50
- *e.* A1560 220w multi .75 .50
- *f.* A1561 220w multi .75 .50
- *g.* A1562 220w black .75 .50
- *h.* A1563 220w multi .75 .50

Gyeongnam Goseong Dinosaur World Expo — A1564

Serpentine Die Cut 11¼x11

2006, Apr. 14

2220 A1564 Horiz. pair 1.50 1.50
- *a.* 220w Iguanodon .75 .50
- *b.* 220w Megaraptor .75 .50

A1565

Children's Drawings on Automated World A1566

2006, Apr. 21 *Perf. 13x13¼, 13¼x13*

2221 A1565 220w multi .75 .50
2222 A1566 220w multi .75 .50

Dongguk University, Cent. — A1567

2006, May 8 **Litho.** *Perf. 13x13¼*

2223 A1567 220w multi .60 .40

Sookmyung Women's University, Cent. — A1568

Perf. 12¾x13¾

2006, May 22 **Photo.**

2224 A1568 220w multi .50 .40

2006 World Cup Soccer Championships, Germany — A1569

2006, June 2 **Photo.** *Perf. 13¼*

2225 A1569 220w multi + label 1.50 1.50

No. 2225 was printed in sheets of 14 stamps + 14 labels picturing members of South Korean World Cup soccer team + one large label picturing entire team. Sheets sold for 6000w.

A1570

2006 World Cup Soccer Championships, Germany — A1571

Perf. 12¾x13¾

2006, June 9 **Photo.**

2226 Pair 1.50 1.50
- *a.* A1570 220w multi .75 .50
- *b.* A1571 220w multi .75 .50

Goguryeo Kingdom A1572

No. 2227: a, Janggun Tomb and Sanseongha Tombs. b, Sun and Moon Gods from Ohoebun Tomb No. 4.

Perf. 13x13¼ Syncopated

2006, July 3 **Photo.**

2227 A1572 480w Vert. pair, #a-b 3.00 3.00

No. 2227 was printed in sheets containing seven of each stamp.

Philately Week A1573

No. 2228: a, Denomination below heart. b, Denomination above heart.

2006, Aug. 3 **Photo.** ***Perf. 13¼***

2228 A1573 220w Pair, #a-b 1.00 1.00

c. Souvenir sheet, #2228a-2228b 1.50 1.50

Skateboarding — A1574

No. 2229: a, Tail stole. b, Drop in. c, Backside spin. d, Backside grab.

Serpentine Die Cut 11¾x11¼

2006, Sept. 5

Self-Adhesive

2229 A1574 220w Block of 4, #a-d 2.00 2.00

World Ginseng Expo, Geumsan — A1575

2006, Sept. 22 ***Perf. 13x13¼***

2230 A1575 220w multi .50 .40

Jindo Bridge — A1576

Changseon-Samcheonpo Bridge — A1577

Olympic Bridge — A1578

Seohae Bridge — A1579

Perf. 13¼ Syncopated

2006, Sept. 26

2231	Block of 4	2.00	2.00
a.	A1576 220w multi	.50	.40
b.	A1577 220w multi	.50	.40
c.	A1578 220w multi	.50	.40
d.	A1579 220w multi	.50	.40

Hangeul Day — A1580

2006, Oct. 9 ***Perf. 13x13¼***

2232 A1580 (220w) multi .60 .40

Use of Hangeul as official Korean writing system, 560th anniv.

Sahmyook University, Cent. — A1581

2006, Oct. 10

2233 A1581 220w multi .60 .40

Lineage — A1582

Maple Story — A1583

Ragnarok A1584

Gersang A1585

Legend of Mir III — A1586

Kartrider A1587

Mu — A1588

Pangya — A1589

Fortress 2 Forever Blue — A1590

Mabinogi A1591

Serpentine Die Cut 11¾

2006, Nov. 9

2234	Block of 10	10.00	10.00
a.	A1582 250w multi	.90	.60
b.	A1583 250w multi	.90	.60
c.	A1584 250w multi	.90	.60
d.	A1585 250w multi	.90	.60
e.	A1586 250w multi	.90	.60
f.	A1587 250w multi	.90	.60
g.	A1588 250w multi	.90	.60
h.	A1589 250w multi	.90	.60
i.	A1590 250w multi	.90	.60
j.	A1591 250w multi	.90	.60

Internet games.

Janggunbong Peak — A1592

Ulsanbawi Rock A1593

Daecheongbong Peak — A1594

Sibiseonnyeotang Valley — A1595

2006, Nov. 16 ***Perf. 13x13¼***

2235	Block of 4	3.00	3.00
a.	A1592 250w multi	.75	.60
b.	A1593 250w multi	.75	.60
c.	A1594 250w multi	.75	.60
d.	A1595 250w multi	.75	.60

New Year 2007 (Year of the Pig) — A1596

2006, Dec. 1 **Photo.** ***Perf. 13x13¼***

2236 A1596 250w multi .60 .40

a. Souvenir sheet of 2 1.50 1.50

Text of Heungboga and Pansori Singer — A1597

Mo Heung-gap, Pansori Singer — A1598

Litho. & Engr.

2006, Dec. 8 ***Perf. 13x13¼***

2237	Sheet of 10	20.00	20.00
a.	A1597 480w multi	2.00	1.60
b.	A1598 480w multi	2.00	1.60

Top part of No. 2237 contains one each of Nos. 2237a-2237b. The lower part contains 4 each of Nos. 2237a-2237b.

A1599

Sharing and Caring A1600

2006, Dec. 14 Photo. ***Perf. 13x13¼***
2238 A1599 250w multi .55 .25

Perf. 13¼x13

2239 A1600 250w multi .55 .25

No. 2238 is impregnated with a pine scent; No. 2239 with a chocolate scent.

Nakdong River in Autumn — A1601

Nakdong River in Winter — A1602

Nakdong River in Spring — A1603

Nakdong River in Summer — A1604

Perf. 13¼ Syncopated

2007, Jan. 18 **Photo.**

2240	Block of 4	2.25	1.10
a.	A1601 250w multi	.55	.25
b.	A1602 250w multi	.55	.25
c.	A1603 250w multi	.55	.25
d.	A1604 250w multi	.55	.25

Megatron/Matrix — A1605

TV Buddha A1606

The More the Better A1607

Oh-Mah (Mother) A1608

2007, Jan. 29 ***Perf. 13¼***

2241	Sheet of 12, 3 each #a-d	6.75	6.75
a.	A1605 250w multi	.55	.25
b.	A1606 250w multi	.55	.25
c.	A1607 250w multi	.55	.25
d.	A1608 250w multi	.55	.25

Art by Nam June Paik (1932-2006).

National Debt Repayment Movement, Cent. — A1609

2007, Feb. 21 Photo. ***Perf. 13x13¼***
2242 A1609 250w multi .55 .25

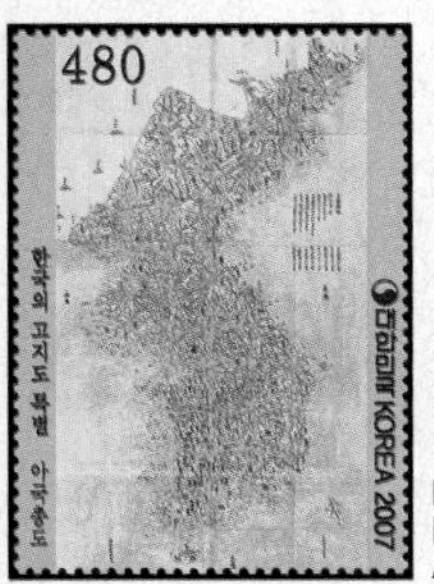

Maps of Korea A1610

No. 2243: a, Map from Atlas of Korea, 1780. b, Complete Territorial Map of the Great East, 19th cent. c, Map of the Eight Provinces, 1531. d, Comprehensive Map of the World and Nation's Successive Capitals, 1402.

2007, Feb. 28 Photo. ***Perf. 13½x13***

2243	Sheet of 8, 2 each #a-d	9.25	9.25
a.	A1610 480w multi	1.00	.50
b.	A1610 520w multi	1.10	.55
c.	A1610 580w multi	1.25	.60
d.	A1610 600w multi	1.25	.65

Daehan Hospital, Seoul, Cent. — A1611

2007, Mar. 15 Litho. ***Perf. 13x13¼***
2244 A1611 250w multi .55 .25

Ninth Asia Pacific Orchid Conference, Goyang — A1612

2007, Mar. 16 **Photo.**
2245 A1612 250w multi .55 .25

Biology Year — A1613

2007, Mar. 19 ***Perf. 13¼x13***

2246	A1613 250w multi	.55	.25
a.	Souvenir sheet of 2	1.10	.50

Sunflower — A1614

2007, Mar. 21 Litho. ***Perf. 13¼***
2247 A1614 250w multi + label .80 .40

Printed in sheets of 20 stamps + 20 labels and 14 stamps + 14 labels that sold for 7500w. Labels could be personalized.

Clover — A1615

Pig — A1616

2007, Mar. 21 Photo. ***Perf. 13¼***

2248	A1615 250w multi + label	1.00	.50
2249	A1616 250w multi + label	1.00	.50

Nos. 2248-2249 were each printed in sheets of 9 stamps + 9 labels. Each sheet sold for 4300w. Labels could be personalized.

Chinese Bride and Groom — A1617

Indian Bride and Groom — A1618

Malaysian Bride and Groom — A1619

Eurasian Bride and Groom — A1620

No. 2250 — Korean brides and grooms with: e, Mountains in background. f, Flowers on orange background. g, Flowers and foliage in background. h, Ducks in background.

2007, Mar. 30 ***Perf. 13¼x13***

2250	Block of 8	7.00	7.00
a.	A1617 250w multi	.55	.25
b.	A1618 250w multi	.55	.25
c.	A1619 250w multi	.55	.25
d.	A1620 250w multi	.55	.25
e.	A1620 480w multi	1.00	.50
f.	A1620 520w multi	1.10	.55
g.	A1620 580w multi	1.25	.60
h.	A1620 600w multi	1.25	.65

See Singapore No. 1241.

Opening of Fortress Wall in Mt. Bugaksan — A1621

2007, Apr. 5 Photo. ***Perf. 13¾x12¾***
2251 A1621 250w multi .55 .25

A1622

Internet Culture A1623

2007, Apr. 20 Litho. ***Perf. 13¼x13***
2252 A1622 250w multi .55 .25

Photo.

2253 A1623 250w multi .55 .25

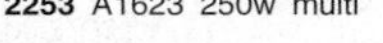

Children's Charter, 50th Anniv. — A1624

Serpentine Die Cut

2007, May 4 **Photo.**

Self-Adhesive

2254 A1624 250w multi .55 .25

No. 2254 is impregnated with a strawberry scent.

Dispatch of Special Envoys to Second Hague Peace Conference, Cent. — A1625

Litho. & Engr.

2007, June 27 ***Perf. 13x13¼***
2255 A1625 250w multi .55 .25

A1626

Goguryeo Kingdom A1627

No. 2256: a, Cooks preparing food. b, Host welcoming guest.

Perf. 13 Syncopated

2007, July 2 **Photo.**

2256	Sheet of 14, 7 each #a-b	14.00	14.00
a.	A1626 480w multi	1.00	.50
b.	A1627 480w multi	1.00	.50

Philately Week — A1628

No. 2257: a, Korea #1. b, Korea #2.

2007, Aug. 2 **Photo.** ***Perf. 13x13¼***

2257	Horiz. pair	1.10	.55
a.-b.	A1628 250w Either single	.55	.25
c.	Souvenir sheet, #2257	1.10	.55

Rollerblading — A1629

No. 2258: a, Drop-in. b, Flip. c, Spin. d, Grind.

Serpentine Die Cut 11¾x11¼

2007, Sept. 5 **Photo.**

Self-Adhesive

2258	A1629 250w Block of 4, #a-d	2.25	1.10

Korean Bar Association, Cent. — A1630

2007, Sept. 21 **Litho.** ***Perf. 13x13¼***

2259	A1630 250w multi	.55	.25

Gwangan Bridge — A1631

Seongsu Bridge — A1632

Seongsan Bridge — A1633

Yeongjong Bridge — A1634

Perf. 13¼x13½ Syncopated

2007, Sept. 28 **Photo.**

2260	Block of 4	2.25	1.10
a.	A1631 250w multi	.55	.25
b.	A1632 250w multi	.55	.25
c.	A1633 250w multi	.55	.25
d.	A1634 250w multi	.55	.25

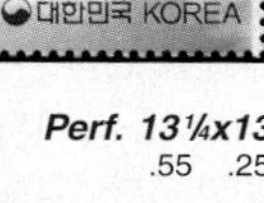
Inter-Korean Summit, Pyongyang, North Korea — A1635

2007, Oct. 2 ***Perf. 13¼x13***

2261	A1635 250w multi	.55	.25

Hyeongje Falls A1636

Rimyeongsu Falls — A1637

Lake Samjiyeon A1638

Lake Chonji A1639

2007, Oct. 18 **Photo.** ***Perf. 13x13½***

2262	Block of 4	2.25	1.10
a.	A1636 250w multi	.55	.25
b.	A1637 250w multi	.55	.25
c.	A1638 250w multi	.55	.25
d.	A1639 250w multi	.55	.25

A1640

A1641

A1642

Korean Films A1643

No. 2263: a, Arirang, 1926. b, The Ownerless Ferryboat, 1932. c, Looking for Love, 1928. d, Chunhyangjeon, 1935.

2007, Oct. 26 ***Perf. 13x13¼***

2263	Sheet of 16, 4 each #a-d	9.00	9.00
a.	A1640 250w multi	.55	.25
b.	A1641 250w multi	.55	.25
c.	A1642 250w multi	.55	.25
d.	A1643 250w multi	.55	.25

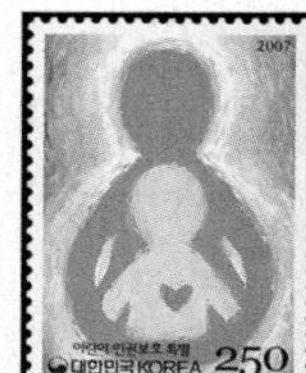

A1644

Protection of Children's Rights A1645

2007, Nov. 20 **Photo.** ***Perf. 13x13¼***

2264	A1644 250w multi	.55	.25

Litho.

Perf. 13¼x13

2265	A1645 250w multi	.55	.25

Opening of New Central Post Office, Seoul — A1646

No. 2266: a, Hanseong Post Office, 1915, and new building. b, New building.

2007, Nov. 22 **Photo.** ***Perf. 13x13¼***

2266	A1646 250w Horiz. pair, #a-b	1.10	.55

No. 2266 printed in sheet containing 7 pairs.

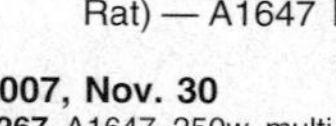
New Year 2008 (Year of the Rat) — A1647

2007, Nov. 30

2267	A1647 250w multi	.55	.25
a.	Souvenir sheet of 2	1.10	.50

Tapdeunggut Exorcism, Dano Festival, Gangneung — A1648

Gwanno Mask Drama, Dano Festival — A1649

2007, Dec. 7 **Litho. & Engr.**

2268	Sheet of 10, 5 each #a-b	10.50	10.50
a.	A1648 480w multi	1.00	.50
b.	A1649 480w multi	1.00	.50

Top part of No. 2268 contains one each of Nos. 2268a-2268b. The lower part contains 4 each of Nos. 2268a-2268b.

Seomjin River in Autumn — A1650

Seomjin River in Winter — A1651

Seomjin River in Spring — A1652

Seomjin River in Summer — A1653

Perf. 13½x13¼ Syncopated

2008, Jan. 18 **Photo.**

2269 Block of 4 2.25 1.10
a. A1650 250w multi .55 .25
b. A1651 250w multi .55 .25
c. A1652 250w multi .55 .25
d. A1653 250w multi .55 .25

Miniature Sheet

King Sejong Antarctic Station — A1654

No. 2270 — Penguins and: a, Scientists on snowmobiles. b, Station.

2008, Feb. 15 **Photo.** ***Perf. 13¼***

2270 A1654 250w Sheet of 10, 5 each #a-b 5.50 2.75

Inauguration of Pres. Lee Myung-Bak — A1655

2008, Feb. 25 **Photo.** ***Perf. 13x13¼***

2271 A1655 250w multi .55 .25
a. Souvenir sheet of 1 .55 .25

African Savanna — A1656

No. 2272: a, African child and mask. b, Leopard. c, Elephant. d, Zebra.

Die Cut Perf. (outer edge) x Serpentine Die Cut 11 (radial sides) x Die Cut (inner edge)

2008, Mar. 26

Self-Adhesive

2272 A1656 250w Block of 4, #a-d, + central label 2.10 1.10

Philakorea 2009 Intl. Stamp Exhibition, Seoul — A1657

No. 2273 — Dancers: a, Buchaechum (orange background). b, Salpurichum (pink background). c, Seungmu (blue background). d, Taepyeongmu (green background).

2008, Apr. 10 ***Perf. 13¼x13***

2273 Horiz. strip or block of 4 2.10 1.10
a.-d. A1657 250w Any single .55 .25
e. Souvenir sheet, #2273a-2273d, + label 2.10 1.10

A1658

Winning Designs in "Mailboxes of the Future" Children's Stamp Design Contest — A1659

2008, Apr. 22 **Photo.** ***Perf. 13¼x13***

2274 A1658 250w multi .50 .25

Litho.

Perf. 13x13¼

2275 A1659 250w multi .50 .25

Nurturing of Children
A1660 A1661

Litho., Engr. & Embossed

2008, May 8 ***Perf. 13x13¼***

2276 A1660 250w multi .50 .25

Litho.

2277 A1661 250w multi .50 .25

Sun and Moon — A1662

Hands Making Heart — A1663

Tree-lined Path — A1664

Roses — A1665

2008, May 19 **Photo.** ***Perf. 13¼***

2278 A1662 250w multi + label .50 .25
2279 A1663 250w multi + label .50 .25
2280 A1664 250w multi + label .50 .25
2281 A1665 250w multi + label .50 .25
Nos. 2278-2281 (4) 2.00 1.00

Nos. 2278-2279 each were printed in sheets of 3 stamps + 3 labels, No. 2280 was printed in sheets of 14 stamps + 15 labels, and No. 2281 was printed in sheets of 20 stamps + 20 labels. Labels could be personalized.

Organization for Economic Cooperation and Development Ministerial Meeting, Seoul — A1666

2008, June 17 ***Perf. 13¼***

2282 A1666 250w multi .50 .25

Yun Bong-Gil (1908-32), Assassin of Japanese Colonial Generals A1667

2008, June 20

2283 A1667 250w multi .50 .25

Miniature Sheet

Dangun Wanggeom — A1668

No. 2284: a, Hwanung descending from heavens at Taebaek Mountain. b, Bear and tiger who prayed to become human. c, Birth of Dangun Wanggeom. d, Dangun Wanggeom as adult.

2008, July 10 **Photo.** ***Perf. 13¼x13***

2284 A1668 250w Sheet of 12, 3 each #a-d 6.00 6.00

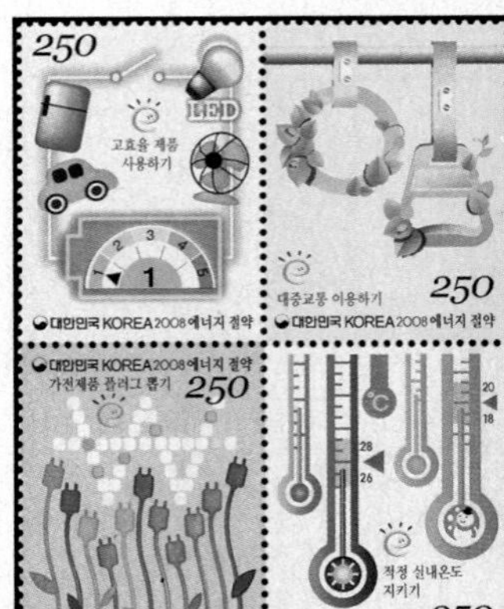

Energy Conservation — A1669

No. 2285: a, Open electrical circuit, car, refrigerator, light bulb, fan, meter. b, Handstraps for public transportation. c, Electrical plugs on flower stems. d, Thermometers.

2008, Aug. 1 **Photo.** ***Perf. 13¼x13***

2285 A1669 250w Block or horiz. strip of 4, #a-d 2.00 1.00

Philately Week — A1670

No. 2286: a, South Korea #34. b, South Korea #176.

2008, Aug. 7 **Photo.** ***Perf. 13¼x13***

2286 A1670 250w Pair, #a-b 1.00 .50
c. Souvenir sheet, #2286a-2286b 1.00 .50

2008 Summer Olympics, Beijing A1671

2008, Aug. 8 **Photo.** ***Perf. 13¼x13***

2287 A1671 250w multi .50 .25

Republic of Korea, 60th Anniv. — A1672

2008, Aug. 14

2288 A1672 250w multi .50 .25

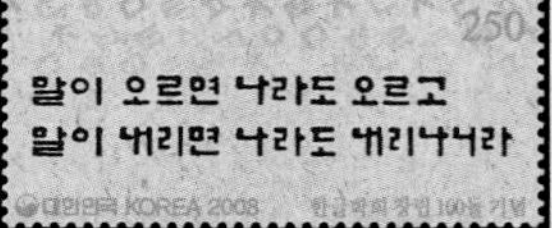

Korean Language Society, Cent. — A1673

2008, Aug. 29 ***Perf. 12¾x13½***

2289 A1673 250w multi .50 .25

Seoul Water Works, Cent. — A1674

2008, Sept. 1 Litho. *Perf. 13x13¼*
2290 A1674 250w multi .45 .25

Amateur Radio Direction Finding Championships, Hwaseong A1675

2008, Sept. 2
2291 A1675 250w multi .45 .25

Snowboarding — A1676

No. 2292: a, Carving turn. b, Indy grab. c, Nose grab. d, Air.

Serpentine Die Cut 11¾x11¼
2008, Sept. 5 Photo.
Self-Adhesive
2292 A1676 250w Block of 4, #a-d 1.90 1.00

Salvation Army in Korea, Cent. — A1677

2008, Oct. 1 Photo. *Perf. 13x13¼*
2293 A1677 250w multi .40 .20

Republic of Korea Armed Forces, 60th Anniv. A1678

2008, Oct. 1
2294 A1678 250w multi .40 .20

Diplomatic Relations Between South Korea and Thailand, 50th Anniv. — A1679

No. 2295: a, Chakri Mahaprasat Hall, Thailand (denomination at left). b, Juhamnu Pavilion, South Korea (denomination at right).

2008, Oct. 1 Litho. *Perf. 13¼*
2295 A1679 250w Pair, #a-b .80 .40

Manmulsang — A1680

Gwimyeonam Rock — A1681

Outer Geumgangsan — A1682

Sangpaldam Pools — A1683

2008, Oct. 17 Photo. *Perf. 13x13½*

2296	Block of 4	1.60	.80
a.	A1680 250w multi	.40	.20
b.	A1681 250w multi	.40	.20
c.	A1682 250w multi	.40	.20
d.	A1683 250w multi	.40	.20

Korean Films — A1684

No. 2297: a, A Coachman, 1961 (blue background). b, Wedding Day, 1956 (dull lilac background). c, The Seashore Village, 1965 (dull green background). d, Mother and a Guest, 1961 (gray olive background).

2008, Oct. 27 Litho. *Perf. 13x13½*
2297 A1684 250w Block of 4, #a-d 1.60 .80

Upo Wetlands — A1685

2008, Oct. 28 Photo. *Perf. 13¼*
2298 A1685 250w multi .40 .20

Tenth Ramsar Convention Meeting, Changwon.

Masks — A1686

No. 2299: a, Chwibari Mask, Korea (denomination at LL). b, Big head Buddha mask, Hong Kong (denomination at LR).

2008, Nov. 6 *Perf. 13¼x13*
2299 A1686 250w Horiz. pair, #a-b .75 .40

See Hong Kong Nos. 1337-1338.

New Year 2009 (Year of the Ox) — A1687

2008, Dec. 1 *Perf. 13x13¼*
2300 A1687 250w multi .35 .20
a. Souvenir sheet of 2 .70 .35

Louis Braille (1809-52), Educator of the Blind — A1688

2009, Jan. 2 *Perf. 12¾x13½*
2301 A1688 250w multi .40 .20

Intl. Year of Astronomy — A1689

No. 2302: a, Whirlpool Galaxy M51. b, Planetary Nebula NGC 3132.

2009, Jan. 15 Photo. *Perf. 13x13¼*
2302 A1689 250w Horiz. pair, #a-b .75 .40

Geum River in Autumn — A1690

Geum River in Winter — A1691

Geum River in Spring — A1692

Geum River in Summer — A1693

Perf. 13¼ Syncopated
2009, Feb. 10

2303	Block or horiz. strip of 4	1.40	.70
a.	A1690 250w multi	.35	.20
b.	A1691 250w multi	.35	.20
c.	A1692 250w multi	.35	.20
d.	A1693 250w multi	.35	.20

Diplomatic Relations Between South Korea and the Philippines, 60th Anniv. A1694

Designs: No. 2304, 250w, Panagbenga Flower Festival, Baguio, Philippines. No. 2305, 250w, Cow Play, Hangawi, South Korea.

2009, Mar. 3 Photo. *Perf. 13x13¼*
2304-2305 A1694 Set of 2 .65 .30

Historic Trees — A1695

No. 2306: a, Fir tree (Natural monument No. 495). b, Zelkova tree (Natural monument No. 478), horiz. c, Ginkgo tree (Natural monument No. 30). d, Seosongnyeong tree (Natural monument No. 294), horiz.

2009, Apr. 3 Litho. *Perf. 12¾*
2306 A1695 250w Block of 4, #a-d 1.50 .75

Republic of Korea Marine Corps, 60th Anniv. A1696

2009, Apr. 15 *Perf. 12½*
2307 A1696 250w multi .40 .20

A1697

Asia Becoming One — A1698

2009, Apr. 22 Photo. *Perf. 13¼x13*
2308 A1697 250w multi .40 .20

Litho.
Perf. 13x13¼
2309 A1698 250w multi .40 .20

A1699

Love For the Earth — A1700

2009, Apr. 22 Litho. *Perf. 13¼x13*

2310 A1699 250w multi .40 .20

Photo.

Perf. 13x13¼

2311 A1700 250w multi .40 .20

Cartooning in Korea, Cent. A1701

2009, June 2 Litho. *Perf. 13x13¼*

2312 A1701 250w multi .40 .20

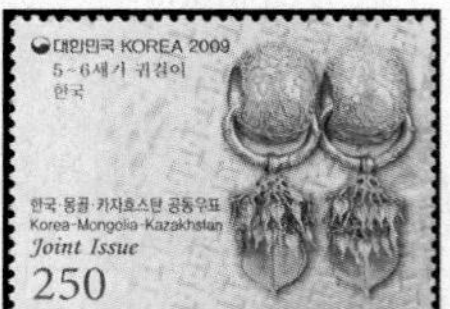

Earrings From Korea, 5th-6th Cent. A1702

Earrings From Mongolia, 18th-19th Cent. A1703

Earrings From Kazakhstan, 2nd-1st Cent. B.C. — A1704

2009, June 12 Photo. *Perf. 13x13¼*

2313 Strip of 3 1.25 .60
- *a.* A1702 250w multi .40 .20
- *b.* A1703 250w multi .40 .20
- *c.* A1704 250w multi .40 .20

See Kazakhstan No. 595, Mongolia No. 2674.

Philately Week — A1707

No. 2315: a, Korea #19. b, South Korea #639.

2009, July 30 Photo. *Perf. 13¼x13*

2315 Pair .85 .40
- *a.-b.* A1707 250w Either single .40 .20
- *c.* Souvenir sheet, #2315 .85 .40

A1708

A1709

A1710

A1711

A1712

A1713

A1714

Bird Drawings A1715

2009, July 30 Litho. *Perf. 13¼x13*

2316 Block of 8 3.25 1.60
- *a.* A1708 250w multi .40 .20
- *b.* A1709 250w multi .40 .20
- *c.* A1710 250w multi .40 .20
- *d.* A1711 250w multi .40 .20
- *e.* A1712 250w multi .40 .20
- *f.* A1713 250w multi .40 .20
- *g.* A1714 250w multi .40 .20
- *h.* A1715 250w multi .40 .20
- *i.* Souvenir sheet of 2, #2316a, 2316e .80 .40
- *j.* Souvenir sheet of 2, #2316b, 2316f .80 .40
- *k.* Souvenir sheet of 2, #2316c, 2316g .80 .40
- *l.* Souvenir sheet of 2, #2316d, 2316h .80 .40

Philakorea 2009, Seoul.

Command From God To Move Country's Capital A1716

Establishment of East Buyeo — A1717

Birth of King Geumwawang — A1718

King Geumwawang on Throne — A1719

2009, Aug. 18 Photo. *Perf. 13x13¼*

2317 Sheet of 12, 3 each #a-d 5.00 5.00
- *a.* A1716 250w multi .40 .20
- *b.* A1717 250w multi .40 .20
- *c.* A1718 250w multi .40 .20
- *d.* A1719 250w multi .40 .20

Legend of King Geumwawang of the Buyeo Kingdom.

Green Energy — A1720

No. 2318: a, House with solar panels, bicycle. b, Automobile with solar panels. c, Wind turbines. d, Dam.

2009, Aug. 21 Photo. *Perf. 13¼*

2318 A1720 250w Block of 4, #a-d 1.60 .80

Groundbreaking for Taekwondo Park, Muju-gun — A1721

2009, Sept. 4 *Perf. 13¾x12¾*

2319 A1721 250w multi .40 .20

BMX Bicycling — A1722

No. 2320: a, X-up. b, No hand jump. c, One foot can can. d, Superman seat grab.

Serpentine Die Cut 11¾x11¼

2009, Sept. 8 Photo.

2320 A1722 250w Block of 4, #a-d 1.90 .95

Rice — A1723

No. 2321: a, Rice flowers and plants. b, Red, black and white rice grains.

2009, Sept. 25 Litho. *Perf. 13¼*

2321 Pair .90 .45
- *a.-b.* A1723 250w Either single .45 .20

Third Organization for Economic Cooperation and Development World Forum, Busan — A1724

2009, Oct. 27 Litho. *Perf. 13¼*

2322 A1724 250w multi .45 .20

A1725

A1726

A1727

Korean Films A1728

No. 2323: a, Chilsu and Mansu, 1988. b, Never, Never Forget Me, 1976. c, A Road to Sampo, 1975. d, Yalkae, A Joker in High School, 1976.

2009, Oct. 27 ***Perf. 13x13¼***

2323 Block or strip of 4 1.80 .90
- *a.* A1725 250w multi .45 .20
- *b.* A1726 250w multi .45 .20
- *c.* A1727 250w multi .45 .20
- *d.* A1728 250w multi .45 .20

Diplomatic Relations Between South Korea and Brazil, 50th Anniv. — A1729

No. 2324: a, Octavio Frias de Oliveira Bridge, Brazil (denomination at UL). b, Incheon Bridge, South Korea (denomination at UR).

2009, Oct. 30 ***Perf. 13¼***

2324 A1729 250w Pair, #a-b .85 .45

See Brazil No. 3113.

New Year 2010 (Year of the Tiger) — A1730

2009, Dec. 1 Photo. ***Perf. 13x13¼***

2325 A1730 250w multi .45 .20
- *a.* Souvenir sheet of 2 .90 .45

Visit Korea Year — A1731

No. 2326: a, Stylized face, denomination in blue. b, People as Korean flag, denomination in white.

2010, Jan. 4 Photo. ***Perf. 13¼x13***

2326 A1731 250w Pair, #a-b .90 .45

2010 Winter Olympics, Vancouver — A1732

No. 2327: a, Figure skater. b, Speed skater.

2010, Feb. 12 ***Perf. 12¾x13½***

2327 A1732 250w Pair, #a-b .90 .45

Diplomatic Relations Between South Korea and Malaysia, 50th Anniv. — A1733

No. 2328: a, Panthera tigris altaica. b, Panthera tigris jacksoni.

2010, Feb. 23 Litho. ***Perf. 13¼***

2328 A1733 250w Pair, #a-b .90 .45

Ahn Jung-geun (1879-1910), Assassin of Ito Hirobumi, Japanese Resident-General of Korea — A1734

No. 2329 — Ahn Jung-geun and: a, Hand-print. b, Characters written on Korean flag with blood from his severed finger.

Litho. & Engr.

2010, Mar. 26 ***Perf. 13¼***

2329 A1734 250w Pair, #a-b .90 .45

Seoul National University of Technology, Cent. — A1735

Jinju National University, Cent. — A1736

2010, Apr. 1 Photo. ***Perf. 12¾x13½***

2330 A1735 250w multi .45 .20

2331 A1736 250w multi .45 .20

Historic Trees — A1737

No. 2332: a, Old Buddha's plum tree (Natural Monument No. 486). b, Pine tree (Natural Monument No. 290), horiz. c, Entwined Chinese junipers (Natural Monument No. 88). d, Three Thunbergii camphor trees (Natural Monument No. 481), horiz.

2010, Apr. 5 Litho. ***Perf. 12¾***

2332 A1737 250w Block of 4, #a-d 1.90 .95

Mo Tae Bum A1738

Le Sang Hwa A1739

Lee Seung Hoon A1740

Kim Yu Na A1741

Kwak Yoon Gy A1742

Kim Seoung Il A1743

Park Seung Hi A1744

Sung Si Bak A1745

Lee Eun Byul A1746

Lee Jung Su A1747

Lee Ho Suk A1748

2010, May 6 Photo. ***Perf. 13½x12¾***

2333 Sheet of 11 + label 5.00 5.00
- *a.* A1738 250w multi .45 .20
- *b.* A1739 250w multi .45 .20
- *c.* A1740 250w multi .45 .20
- *d.* A1741 250w multi .45 .20
- *e.* A1742 250w multi .45 .20
- *f.* A1743 250w multi .45 .20
- *g.* A1744 250w multi .45 .20
- *h.* A1745 250w multi .45 .20
- *i.* A1746 250w multi .45 .20
- *j.* A1747 250w multi .45 .20
- *k.* A1748 250w multi .45 .20

Medalists at 2010 Winter Olympics, Vancouver.

Han River in Spring — A1749

Han River in Summer — A1750

Han River in Autumn — A1751

Han River in Winter — A1752

2010, May 11 ***Perf. 13½ Syncopated***

2334 Block or strip of 4 1.90 1.90
- *a.* A1749 250w multi .45 .20
- *b.* A1750 250w multi .45 .20
- *c.* A1751 250w multi .45 .20
- *d.* A1752 250w multi .45 .20

Bird Drawings Type of 2009

2009, July 30 Litho. ***Perf. 13¼x13***

2010 World Cup Soccer Championships, South Africa — A1753

Perf. 13¼x13½

2010, June 11 **Photo.**

2335 A1753 250w multi .40 .20

World Refugee Day, 10th Anniv. — A1754

2010, June 18 ***Perf. 13¼***
2336 A1754 250w multi .40 .20

Diplomatic Relations Between South Korea and United Arab Emirates, 30th Anniv. — A1755

No. 2337: a, Flag of United Arab Emirates and air-conditioning tower. b, Flag of South Korea and Mt. Amisan Chimney, Gyeongbokgung Palace.

2010, June 18 Photo. ***Perf. 13x13¼***
2337 A1755 250w Pair, #a-b .85 .40

Start of Korean War, 60th Anniv. A1756

2010, June 25 ***Perf. 13½x13***
2338 A1756 250w multi .40 .20

Philately Week — A1757

No. 2339: a, South Korea #1197. b, South Korea #1198.

2010, July 29 ***Perf. 13¼x13¼x13***
2339 Pair, #a-b .85 .40
a.-b. A1757 250w Either single .40 .20
c. Souvenir sheet, #2339a-2339b .85 .40

23rd Intl. Union of Forest Research Organizations World Congress, Seoul A1759

Litho. & Embossed

2010, Aug. 23 ***Perf. 12½***
2341 A1759 340w multi .60 .30

Legend of Goguryeo Jumong — A1760

No. 2342: a, King Geumwa and soldiers meet woman. b, Baby Jumong, birds and animals. c, Jumong and others fleeing King Geumwa on horseback. d, Jumong on horse and followers at Jolboncheon.

2010, Sept. 14 Photo. ***Perf. 13x13½***
2342 A1760 250w Block of 4, #a-d 1.75 .85

A1761

A1762

A1763

Korean Films A1764

No. 2343: a, Seopyeonje, 1993. b, Shiri, 1999. c, Tae Guk Gi: The Brotherhood of War, 2004. d, Take Off, 2009.

2010, Oct. 27 Litho. ***Perf. 13x13¼***
2343 Block of 4 1.80 .90
a. A1761 250w multi .45 .20
b. A1762 250w multi .45 .20
c. A1763 250w multi .45 .20
d. A1764 250w multi .45 .20

Recycling A1765

No. 2344: a, Flowers in pot. b, Recycling robot.

2010, Nov. 11 Photo. ***Perf. 13¼x13***
2344 A1765 250w Pair, #a-b .90 .45

New Year 2011 (Year of the Rabbit) — A1767

2010, Dec. 1 Photo. ***Perf. 13x13¼***
2346 A1767 250w multi .45 .20
a. Souvenir sheet of 2 .90 .40

SEMI-POSTAL STAMPS

Catalogue values for unused stamps in this section are for Never Hinged items.

Field Hospital SP1

Nurses Supporting Patient — SP2

Perf. 13½x14, 14x13½

1953, Aug. 1 Litho. Wmk. 257

Crosses in Red

B1 SP1 10h + 5h bl grn 16.00 4.50
B2 SP2 10h + 5h blue 16.00 4.50

The surtax was for the Red Cross. Nos. B1-B2 exist imperf.

Type of Regular Issue, 1956, with Added inscription at Upper Left

1957, Sept. 1 Wmk. 312 ***Perf. 12½***

Granite Paper

B3 A111 40h + 10h lt bl grn 11.00 2.25

Wmk. 317

B4 A111 40h + 10h lt bl grn 11.00 2.25

The surtax was for flood relief.

Rice Farmer Type of Regular Issue, 1961-62

1963, July 10 Wmk. 317 ***Perf. 12½***
B5 A172 4w + 1w dk bl 9.00 1.25

The surtax was for flood victims in southern Korea.

1965, Oct. 1 Unwmk. ***Perf. 12½***
B6 A172 4w + 2w indigo 4.50 1.25

The surtax was for flood relief.

1965, Oct. 11
B7 A172 4w + 2w magenta 4.50 1.25

The surtax was for a scholarship fund.

Type of Regular Issue 1964-66

1966, Nov. 10 Litho. ***Perf. 12½***

Granite Paper

B8 A186b 7w + 2w car rose 6.00 1.75

The surtax was to help the needy.

Soldier with Wife and Child SP3

Reservist SP4

1967, June 20 ***Perf. 12½x13***
B9 SP3 7w + 3w rose lil & blk 7.50 1.25

The surtax was for veterans of the war in Viet Nam and their families.

1968, Aug. 1 Litho. ***Perf. 13x12½***
B10 SP4 7w + 3w grn & blk 12.50 1.75

Issued for the fund-raising drive to arm reservists.

Flag — SP5

1968, Nov. 1 Litho. Unwmk.
B11 SP5 7w + 3w dk bl & red 40.00 7.50

The surtax was for disaster relief.

1969, Feb. 15
B12 SP5 7w + 3w lt grn, dk bl & red 11.00 1.25

Surtax for military helicopter fund.

Flag Type of 1968 Redrawn Zeros Omitted

1969, Nov. 1 Litho. ***Perf. 13x12½***
B13 SP5 7w + 3w dk bl & red 37.50 1.60

The surtax was for the searchlight fund.

"Pin of Love" — SP6

1972, Aug. 1 Photo. ***Perf. 13½x12½***
B14 SP6 10w + 5w blue & car 1.90 .75

Disaster relief.

"Pin of Love" — SP7

Paddle and Ball — SP8

1973, July 1 Photo. ***Perf. 12½x13½***
B15 SP7 10w + 5w multicolored 1.10 .45

Disaster relief.

1973, Aug. 1 Photo. ***Perf. 13½x12½***
B16 SP8 10w + 5w multicolored 1.25 .30

Surtax was for gymnasium to be built to commemorate the victory of the Korean women's table tennis team at the 32nd World Table Tennis Championships.

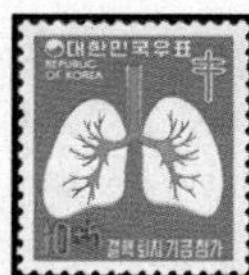

Lungs — SP9

1974, Nov. 1 ***Perf. 13½x12½***
B17 SP9 10w + 5w green & red .90 .25

Surtax was for tuberculosis control.

No. 647 Surcharged

Perf. 13½x12½

1977, July 25 Photo.
B18 A328 20w + 10w green *12.00 12.00*

Surtax was for flood relief.

Seoul 1988 Olympic Games Series

'88 Seoul Games Emblem — SP10

Korean Tiger, Mascot — SP11

Track and Field SP12

Equestrian SP18

1985, Mar. 20 Photo. *Perf. 13x13½*

B19 SP10 70w + 30w blk & multi .50 .30
B20 SP11 70w + 30w blk & multi .50 .30
a. Souvenir sheet of 2, #B19-20 1.75 1.75

1985, June 10

B21 SP12 70w + 30w shown .50 .30
B22 SP12 70w + 30w Rowing .50 .30
a. Souvenir sheet of 2, #B21-B22 1.75 1.75

1985, Sept. 16

B23 SP12 70w + 30w Boxing .50 .30
B24 SP12 70w + 30w Women's basketball .50 .30
a. Souvenir sheet of 2, #B23-B24 1.75 1.75

1985, Nov. 1

B25 SP12 70w + 30w Canoeing .50 .30
B26 SP12 70w + 30w Cycling .50 .30
a. Souvenir sheet of 2, #B25-B26 1.75 1.75

Surtax for the 24th Summer Olympic Games, Sept. 17-Oct. 2, 1988.

1986, Mar. 25 Photo. *Perf. 13x13½*

Designs: No. B28, Fencing. No. B29, Soccer. No. B30, Gymnastic rings.

B27 SP18 70w + 30w multi .50 .30
B28 SP18 70w + 30w multi .50 .30
B29 SP18 70w + 30w multi .50 .30
B30 SP18 70w + 30w multi .50 .30

Souvenir Sheets

B31 Sheet of 4 9.00 9.00
a. SP18 370w + 100w like #B27 2.25 2.25
B32 Sheet of 4 10.00 10.00
a. SP18 400w + 100w like #B28 2.50 2.50
B33 Sheet of 4 12.00 12.00
a. SP18 440w + 100w like #B29 3.00 3.00
B34 Sheet of 4 13.50 13.50
a. SP18 470w + 100w like #B30 3.50 3.50

1986 Photo. *Perf. 13x13½*

B35 SP18 80w +50w Weight lifting 1.50 .75
B36 SP18 80w +50w Team handball 1.50 .75
B37 SP18 80w +50w Judo 1.50 .75
B38 SP18 80w +50w Field hockey 1.50 .75

Souvenir Sheets

B39 Sheet of 4 10.00 10.00
a. SP18 370w + 100w like #B35 2.50 2.50
B40 Sheet of 4 10.00 10.00
a. SP18 400w + 100w like #B36 2.50 2.50
B41 Sheet of 4 12.00 12.00
a. SP18 440w + 100w like #B37 3.00 3.00
B42 Sheet of 4 13.50 13.50
a. SP18 470w + 100w like #B38 3.50 3.50

Issue dates: Nos. B35-B36, B39-B40, Oct. 10; others, Nov. 1.

1987, May 25 Photo. *Perf. 13x13½*

B43 SP18 80w +50w Women's tennis 1.00 .50
B44 SP18 80w +50w Wrestling 1.00 .50
B45 SP18 80w +50w Show jumping 1.00 .50
B46 SP18 80w +50w Diving 1.00 .50

1987, Oct. 10

B47 SP18 80w +50w Table Tennis 1.00 .40
B48 SP18 80w +50w Men's shooting 1.00 .40
B49 SP18 80w +50w Women's archery 1.00 .40
B50 SP18 80w +50w Women's volleyball 1.00 .40

1988, Mar. 5 Photo. *Perf. 13x13½*

B51 SP18 80w +20w Sailing .75 .35
B52 SP18 80w +20w Taekwondo .75 .35

1988, May 6 Photo. *Perf. 13½x13*

B53 SP18 80w +20w Torch relay, horiz. .75 .35

Litho. & Engr.

B54 SP18 80w +20w Olympic Stadium, horiz. .75 .35

See Greece No. 1627.

Souvenir Sheets of 2

B43a	SP18	80w +50w	2.25	2.25
B44a	SP18	80w +50w	2.25	2.25
B45a	SP18	80w +50w	2.25	2.25
B46a	SP18	80w +50w	2.25	2.25
B47a	SP18	80w +50w	2.25	2.25
B48a	SP18	80w +50w	2.25	2.25
B49a	SP18	80w +50w	2.25	2.25
B50a	SP18	80w +50w	2.25	2.25
B51a	SP18	80w +20w	3.75	3.75
B52a	SP18	80w +20w	3.75	3.75
B53a	SP18	80w +20w	2.25	2.25
B54a	SP18	80w +20w	2.25	2.25

AIR POST STAMPS

Four-motor Plane and Globe — AP1

Perf. 11½x11

1947-50 Litho. Wmk. 257

C1 AP1 50wn carmine rose 3.00 3.50
a. Horiz. pair, imperf. btwn. *100.00*

Perf. 11

C2 AP1 150wn blue ('49) 1.50 1.50
a. "KORFA" 15.00 *30.00*
C3 AP1 150wn green ('50) 5.00 12.50
Nos. C1-C3 (3) 9.50
Set, never hinged 35.00

#C2-C3 are redrawn and designs differ slightly from type AP1.

Issued: 50wn, 10/1.

For surcharge see No. C5.

Plane and Korea Map — AP2

1950, Jan. 1

C4 AP2 60wn light blue 10.00 7.50
Never hinged 37.50

No. C2 Surcharged with New Value and Wavy Lines in Black

1951, Oct. 10

C5 AP1 500wn on 150wn bl 7.00 3.50
Never hinged 10.50
a. "KORFA" 30.00 *60.00*
b. Surcharge inverted 125.00

Douglas C-47 and Ship — AP3

Perf. 13x12½

1952, Oct. 15 Litho. Wmk. 257

C6 AP3 1200wn red brown 1.50 .75
C7 AP3 1800wn lt blue 1.50 .75
C8 AP3 4200wn purple 5.00 1.50
Nos. C6-C8 (3) 8.00 3.00
Set, never hinged 12.50

Nos. C6-C8 exist imperf.

1953, Apr. 5

C9 AP3 12h dp blue 2.50 .75
C10 AP3 18h purple 3.00 .75
C11 AP3 42h Prus green 4.00 1.50
Nos. C9-C11 (3) 9.50 3.00
Set, never hinged 12.50

Douglas DC-7 over East Gate, Seoul — AP4

1954, June 15 *Perf. 12½*

C12 AP4 25h brown 3.00 1.40
C13 AP4 35h deep pink 3.00 1.60
C14 AP4 38h dark green 3.00 1.60
C15 AP4 58h ultra 3.00 2.00
C16 AP4 71h deep blue 7.50 2.50
Nos. C12-C16 (5) 19.50 9.10
Set, never hinged 37.50

Nos. C12-C16 exist imperf.

Type of 1954 Redrawn

1956, July 20 Unwmk.

Laid Paper

C17 AP4 70h brt bluish grn 4.00 3.50
C18 AP4 110h brown 4.00 3.50
C19 AP4 205h magenta 8.00 3.50
Nos. C17-C19 (3) 16.00 10.50
Set, never hinged 40.00

Nos. C18-C19 are found on horizontally and vertically laid paper.

1957, July Wmk. 312 *Perf. 12½*

Granite Paper

C20 AP4 70h brt bluish grn 6.00 3.50
C21 AP4 110h brown 6.00 3.50
C22 AP4 205h magenta 9.00 3.50
Nos. C20-C22 (3) 21.00 10.50
Set, never hinged 45.00

On the redrawn stamps, Nos. C17-C22, the lines of the entire design are lighter, and the colorless character at right end of bottom row has been redrawn as in illustration above No. 212D.

Catalogue values for unused stamps in this section, from this point to the end of the section, are for Never Hinged items.

Girl on Palace Balcony AP5

Designs: 100h, Suwon Castle. 200h, Songnyu Gate, Tuksu Palace. 400h, Kyunghoeru Pavilion.

Perf. 12½

1961, Dec. 1 Unwmk. Litho.

C23 AP5 50h lt blue & violet 22.50 6.00
C24 AP5 100h pale grn & sepia 30.00 10.00
C25 AP5 200h pale grn & brn 45.00 12.00
C26 AP5 400h grn & pale bl 52.50 12.50
Nos. C23-C26 (4) 150.00 40.50

Values in Won; Same Designs; Underlined Zeros Added

1962-63

C27 AP5 5w lt bl & vio ('63) 90.00 16.00
C28 AP5 10w pale grn & sepia 82.50 16.00
C29 AP5 20w pale grn & brn ('63) 260.00 30.00
C30 AP5 40w grn & pale bl ('63) 90.00 30.00
Nos. C27-C30 (4) 522.50 92.00

1964, May 10 Wmk. 317 *Perf. 12½*

Granite Paper

C32 AP5 10w pale grn & sepia 15.00 4.50
C33 AP5 20w pale grn & brn 52.50 7.50
C34 AP5 40w pale bl & grn 29.00 6.00
Nos. C32-C34 (3) 96.50 18.00

1964, Oct. Unwmk. *Perf. 12½*

Designs: 39w, Girl on palace balcony. 64w, Suwon Castle. 78w, Songnyu Gate, Tuksu Palace. 112w, Kyunghoeru Pavilion.

Granite Paper

C35 AP5 39w vio bl & gray olive 11.00 2.25
C36 AP5 64w bl & grnsh gray 10.00 2.50
C37 AP5 78w grnsh bl & ultra 26.00 4.50
C38 AP5 112w blue & green 12.50 2.50
Nos. C35-C38 (4) 59.50 11.75

World Map and Plane — AP6

Designs: 135w, Plane over eastern hemisphere. 145w, Plane over world map. 180w, Plane over world map.

1973, Dec. 30 Photo. *Perf. 13x12½*

C39 AP6 110w pink & multi 9.00 3.50
C40 AP6 135w yel grn & red 10.00 3.50
C41 AP6 145w lt bl & rose 13.50 4.50
C42 AP6 180w lilac & yellow 32.50 6.50
Nos. C39-C42 (4) 65.00 18.00

UPU Type of 1974

1974, Oct. 9 Photo. *Perf. 13*

C43 A480 110w blue & multi 2.25 1.00
a. Souvenir sheet of 2 20.00 20.00

Mt. Fuji, Korean Airlines Jet Type

1985, Dec. 18 Photo. *Perf. 13x13½*

C44 A878 370w brt bl, blk & red 3.00 1.00

Int'l Year of Peace Type

1986, Jan. 15 Photo. *Perf. 13x13½*

C45 A879 400w multicolored 4.00 1.50

Issued in sheets with two blocks of four.

KOREA, DEMOCRATIC PEOPLE'S REPUBLIC

kə-'rē-ə

LOCATION — Peninsula extending from Manchuria between the Yellow Sea and the Sea of Japan (East Sea)
GOVT. — Republic
AREA — 47,398 sq. mi.
POP. — 22,170,000 (2000 est.)
CAPITAL — Pyongyang

At the end of World War II, American forces occupied South Korea and Russian forces occupied North Korea, with the 38th parallel of latitude as the dividing line. North Korea was administered by a Provisional People's Committee after Feb. 9, 1946. Unoverprinted Japanese stamps continued to be used until the first North Korean issue of March 12, 1946. On Sept. 9, 1948, the Democratic People's Republic of Korea was established, and the last Soviet troops left Korea by the end of the year.

100 Chon = 1 Won (1962)

Catalogue values for unused stamps in this country are for Never Hinged items.

Souvenir Sheet

North Korean stamps were issued without gum, unless otherwise noted.
Early issues typically exist in a variety of color shades.
Used values are for cancelled-to-order stamps from 1957-on. Postally used stamps are worth more. Examples on non-philatelic covers are scarce, especially for 1946-1960 issues.

REPRINTS

During 1955-57 the North Korean Postal Administration created "reprints," actually imitations, of most 1946-56 issues for sale to collectors. These reprints were postally valid, and in some cases may have served real postal needs, but most were created for and sold to overseas collectors.
The reprints are more finely printed than the original stamps and are normally printed on a higher quality white wove paper. They often differ from the original printings in both size and design details. Specific distinguishing characteristics are provided below, with the descriptions of each issue.
Value of reprints, $2-$5 each, unused or cto, unless otherwise noted.

SOVIET OCCUPATION

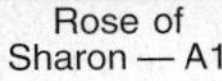

Rose of Sharon — A1

Diamond Mountains (small "50") — A2

Diamond Mountains (large "50") — A3

Perf 11, rouletted 12(#3), 11x Imperf or Imperf x11 (#4,5)

1946, Mar. 12-1955 Litho.

1 A1 20ch red 85.00 *300.00*
2 A2 50ch apple grn ('46) 55.00 *82.50*
a. 50ch yel green, *buff* 55.00 *82.50*
3 A2 50ch car rose 2,800. *2,300.*
4 A3 50ch rose red 165.00 125.00
a. Perf 12 ('48) 165.00 125.00
c. Perf 10 ('55) — —
5 A3 50ch violet 18.00 —
a. Perf 11 ('50) 300.00 —
b. Imperf ('50) 55.00 —
c. Perf 10 ('55) — —
d. ImperfxPerf 11, soft paper, vert. lines 1,200.
e. Vert. pair, *tete-beche* 1,250.
Nos. 1-5 (5) 3,123. 2,807.

No. 4 has lines of colored dots along the horizontal rouletting.
Design sizes: No. 1, 18x21.5-22mm; No. 4, 17.5-18x22-23mm.
Reprints of No. 1 are in yellow green, perf 8½, 8½x9½, 10 or imperf, and measure 18-18.5x23mm. Denomination panel is 4mm high, rather than 3mm. Value $10.
Reprints of No. 4 are perf 10, 10x10½, 11 or imperf, on gummed paper, and measure 17.5-18x22-22.5mm. The double frame lines are clearly separated, and the figures of value are thin and well-formed. Value $6.

Gen. Kim Il Sung (1912-1994) — A4

1946, Aug. 15 Litho. *Pin-Perf*

6 A4 50ch brown 700.00 700.00

First anniversary of liberation from Japan.
No. 6 has lines of colored dots along the horizontal pin perforations.
No. 6 is inscribed in Korean, Chinese and Russian.
No. 6 in chocolate and a 50ch red, similar in design, were printed for presentation to officials and privileged people. Value, $1,900 and $2,250, respectively.

Peasants — A5

Pin-Perf 12, Imperf (#10)

1947, Apr. 22-1955 Litho.

7 A5 1w turquoise 450.00 55.00
8 A5 1w violet ('49) 800.00 175.00
9 A5 1w dark blue, *buff* ('50) 110.00 55.00
10 A5 1w dark blue ('50) 60.00 60.00
a. Perf 11ximperf ('50) 6.00 *60.00*
b. Perf 10 ('55) — —

1st anniversary of agrarian reform.
Nos. 7-9 have lines of colored dots along the horizontal pin perforations.
Reprints of type A5 measure 21x24mm, versus the originals' 21-21.5x24-25mm, are finely printed in light blue and are perf 9, 10½, 11 or imperf. Value $10.

Worker and Factory — A6

1948, June 5 Litho. *Perf. 11*

11 A6 50ch dark blue 3,200. 1,000.

Second anniversary of the Labor Law.
Design size: 20-20.5x31mm.
Reprints measure 20x30-30.5mm and are perf 9, 10½, 11 or imperf. Value, $8 perf, $10 imperf.

Workers and Flag — A7

1948, Aug. 15

12 A7 50ch red brown *4,000.* 1,500.

Third anniversary of liberation from Japan.

Flag and Map — A8

1948, Aug. 20

13 A8 50ch indigo & red *2,500.* 450.00

Adoption of the Constitution of the Democratic People's Republic of Korea, July 10, 1948.

DEMOCRATIC PEOPLE'S REPUBLIC

North Korean Flag — A9

1948, Sept. 19 *Rouletted 12*

14 A9 25ch reddish violet 15.00 *100.00*
15 A9 50ch gray blue 20.00 *50.00*
a. Perf 10½ 40.00 *75.00*

Establishment of the People's Republic, 9/9/48.
Design size: 23x30mm.
Reprints of No. 14 are in blue, on gummed paper, perf 9, 10½ or imperf. Size 20.5x28mm. Value, $6.50.
No. 15a is perforated over rouletting.

North Korean Flag — A10

1949, Feb. 9

16 A10 6w red & blue 4.00 *12.00*
a. Perf 10¼ 35.00 *35.00*

No. 16 exists on both brownish wove and white wove papers.
Design size: 24x32.5-33mm.
Reprints are perf 10¼, 11 or imperf. Size 19x26.5mm. On the originals, the top and bottom panels are blue, with the center field red. On the reprints, these colors are reversed.
For surcharge see No. 42. For overprint see No. 76.

A11

A12

Kim Il Sung University, Pyongyang

1949

17 A11 1w violet 400.00 200.00
18 A12 1w blue 1,200. 125.00

Issue dates: No. 17, 8/9; No. 18, Sept.
Design size: 34x21mm.
Reprints of No. 17 are in slate lilac to reddish lilac, perf 8½, 9, 9x9½, 10 or imperf, on gummed paper. Size 31.5-32x20-20.5mm. Value, $3.50 perf, $10 imperf.

North Korean Flags
A13 A14

Perf 11 or Rouletted 12 (#19)

1949, Aug. 15

With or Without Gum

19 A13 1w red, grn & blue 850.00 175.00
a. Imperfx11 850.00 175.00
20 A14 1w red, grn & turq 2,000. *1,800.*

4th anniversary of Liberation from Japan.
Design sizes: No. 19, 20.5x31mm; No. 20, 20x29.5mm

Order of the National Flag — A15

#21c Control overprint

Rouletted 12, Imperf (#23)

1950, Apr. 4-1956

Lithographed

21 A15 1w pale sage green 7.00 *12.00*
a. 1w olive green 7.00 *12.00*
b. 1w yellow green 7.00 *12.00*
c. With control overprint ('51) — —
22 A15 1w red orange 20.00 *125.00*

Typographed

23 A15 1w brown orange *3,250.* *1,000.*
24 A15 1w dark green ('51) 60.00 *25.00*
a. Perf 10¼ ('56) 90.00 —
25 A15 1w light green 150.00 60.00

Design sizes: No. 21, 23-23.5x35mm; No. 22, 20x32mm; No. 23, 22.5-23x36-37mm; No. 24, 22x35.5mm; No. 25, 22.5x36mm.
No. 21c bears the seal of the DPRK MInistry of Posts and Telecommunications, which was applied to validate various stamps during the chaotic months following the landing of United Nations' forces at Inchon in mid-September, 1950, the retreat of North Korean forces to the far north by October, and their renewed advance, after the entry of the Chinese Volunteer Army into the war.
Reprints of type A15 are in dull blue green on white paper, perf 10¼ or imperf, size 22x35mm, or in red orange on white paper, perf 8½, 9, 10½, 10ximperf or imperf, size 20-20.5x32.5mm. Value (orange), $5 perf.

Flags, Liberation Monument A16

Flags, Soldier A17

Peasant and Worker — A18

Tractor — A19

1950, June 20-1956
Lithographed, Thin Paper
Roul. 12xImperf, Roul. 12 (#28, 29)

26 A16 1w indigo, lt blue & red 3.50 *17.50*
a. Perf 10¼ ('55) 12.00 *24.50*
27 A16 1w brown orange 9.00 *60.00*
28 A17 2w red, steel blue & black 5.00 *17.50*
a. Perf 10¼ ('55) 12.00 *24.00*
29 A18 6w green 6.50 —
30 A19 10w brown 9.50 —

Typographed, Thin Paper, Roul. 12

31 A18 6w red 3.50 *17.50*
a. Perf 10¼ ('55) 29.00 *24.00*
b. Thick brownish paper, imperf x roul. 12 29.00 *24.00*
32 A19 10w brown 3.50 —
a. Thick brownish paper, imperf x roul. 12 36.00 *32.50*
Nos. 26-32 (7) 40.50 112.50

Fifth anniversary of liberation from Japan.

Design sizes: No. 30, 20x27.5mm; No. 31, 22x33mm; No. 32, 22x30mm.

Reprints of No. 26 are on medium white paper, distinguishable by numerous design differences, among which are: characters in top inscription are 1½mm high, rather than 1mm, with 3 short lines at either side, rather than 2; top corner ornaments have a dark center, rather than white; 4 ray beams at left of monument, rather than 3; no dots on right face of spire, while originals have 3 small dots; value numerals within well-formed circles.

Reprints of Nos. 28 and 29 are on medium white paper, perf 10¼, 11 or imperf. No. 28 reprints are in light green, No. 29 in rose red, dull blue and black.

Reprints of type A19 are 22x31mm in size, on medium white paper and are perf 10¼ or imperf.

Capitol, Seoul — A20

1950, July 10 Litho. *Roul. 12*

33 A20 1w bl grn, red & blue 45.00 —

Capture of Seoul.

Order of Ri Sun Sin — A21

1951, Apr. 5 Typo. *Imperf*

34 A21 6w orange 15.00 15.00
a. Perf 10¼ 30.00 —

No. 34 also exists perf 9x10½.

No. 34 is on brownish laid paper. Design size: 21.5-22x29.5-30mm.

Reprints are on white paper, perf 10¼ or imperf. Size 21.5x30mm. On the reprints, the center of the lower left point of the star is open; on the originals, it is hatched.

For surcharge see No. 43.

Hero Kim Ki Ok — A22

1951, Apr. 17

35 A22 1w blue 19.50 19.50
a. Perf 10¼ *180.00* —

No. 35 was printed on unbleached and off-white wood-pulp laid papers, with wood chips visible. The laid lines are often difficult or impossible to detect.

Design size: 23-23.5x35.5-36mm.

Reprints are on white wove paper, perf 10¼, 10½ or imperf. Size 22.5x33.5mm.

Soviet and North Korean Flags A23

Hero Kim Ki U A24

N. Korean, Chinese & Russian Soldiers — A25

1951, Aug. 15-1955 Litho. *Roul. 12*

36 A23 1w dark blue 105.00 *105.00*
37 A23 1w red 275.00 *275.00*
38 A24 1w dark blue 170.00 *170.00*
39 A24 1w red 170.00 *170.00*
40 A25 2w dark blue 65.00 *65.00*
41 A25 2w red 65.00 *65.00*
Nos. 36-41 (6) 850.00 *850.00*
Nos. 36-41 (6) 850.00 *850.00*

Perf 10¼ Over Roulette (1955)

36a A23 1w dark blue) 75.00 *75.00*
37a A23 1w red 275.00 *275.00*
38a A24 1w dark blue 275.00 *275.00*
39a A24 1w red 170.00 *170.00*
40a A25 2w dark blue 75.00 *75.00*
41a A25 2w red 40.00 *40.00*
Nos. 36a-41a (6) 910.00 *910.00*
Nos. 36a-41a (6) 910.00 *910.00*

Nos. 36-41 and 36a-41a exist on both coarse buff and white wove papers. Values are the same. Various perfs and roulettes and roulettes exists; not all combinations are known.

Design sizes: Nos. 36 and 37, 17x23.5mm; Nos. 38 and 39, 16x23mm; Nos. 40 and 41, 23x16.5mm.

Reprints of No. 36 are perf 9, 10½x10 or imperf. Size 15.5-16x22.5mm.

Reprints of No. 38 are perf 9, 10 or imperf. They have no lines of shading between the characters in the top inscription.

Reprints of No. 40 are perf 9, 10 or imperf. Size 22-22.5x16.5mm. The Korean "Won" character at lower right is in 4 parts, rather than 3.

Reprints are all light ultramarine.

#16 Surcharged #34 Surcharged

1951, Nov. 1 *Imperf*

42 A10 5w on 6w red & blue (#16) 150.00 60.00
43 A21 5w on 6w orange (#34) 725.00 725.00

Order of Soldier's Honor — A26

1951, Nov. 15-1956

44 A26 40w scarlet (16.5x25mm) 22.50 4.50
a. Perf 10¼ ('56) 22.50 7.75
45 A26 40w scarlet (17x24mm) 12.00 4.50
a. Perf 10¼ ('56) 12.00 7.75

Victory Propaganda — A27

1951, Nov. 15-1956

46 A27 10w dark blue 15.00 7.75
47 A27 10w dark blue 15.00 7.75
a. Perf 10¼ ('56) 22.50 22.50

No. 47 also exists perf 8½.

Design sizes: No. 46, 17x25.5mm; No. 47, 16.5-17x25mm.

Reprints are in light blue, perf 10¼, 11 or imperf. Size 16.5-17x25mm. Value and inscription at bottom are outlined and clear against cross-hatched background.

Ri Su Dok, Guerilla Hero — A28

1952, Jan. 10-1955

48 A28 70w brown 15.00 3.50
a. Perf 10¼ ('55) 25.00 12.00
b. 70w black brown 120.00
c. As "b," perf 10¼ 60.00

Dove, Flag & Globe — A29

1952, Jan. 20-1957

49 A29 20w scarlet, deep blue & lt blue 24.00 6.00
a. Perf 10¼ ('55) 24.00 12.00
b. Perf 9 ('57) — —
c. Perf 9½x8½ ('57) — —

Peace Propaganda.

No. 49 also exists perf 8½, 11 and rouletted 11½.

No. 49 was printed on off-white or buff paper, with broken lines between stamps. Design size: 22x31-31.5mm.

Reprints are perf 10¼ or imperf, in red, slate blue and pale turquoise blue on white paper. Size 22x31mm. They lack the broken lines between stamps. Value, each $20.

Gen. Pang Ho-san — A30

1952, Apr.

50 A30 10w dull purple 60.00 24.00

Honoring Chinese People's Volunteers.

No. 50 is also known with locally-applied rough perforation.

Labor Day — A31

1952, Apr. 20-1955 *Imperf*

51 A31 10w rose red 210.00 *210.00*
a. Perf 10¼ ('55) 210.00 —

Enforcement of the Labor Law, 6th Anniv. — A32

1952, June 1-1955

52 A32 10w light blue 360.00 *325.00*
a. Perf 10¼ ('55) — —

Design size: 18x26mm. Broken lines between stamps.

Reprints are in dull or slate blue, on thick, gummed paper, with no broken lines between stamps. Size 17.5x25.5-26mm.

Day of Anti-U.S. Imperialist Struggle — A33

1952, June 4-1956

53 A33 10w rose red 180.00 150.00
a. Perf 10¼ ('56) 180.00 —

Design size: 17.5x25.5-26mm. Broken lines between stamps.

Reprints are in bright rose red, perf 10, 10¼, 11 or imperf. on thick, gummed paper, with no broken lines between stamps. Size 17.5x26mm.

North Korean-Chinese Friendship — A34

1952, July 25-1956

54 A34 20w deep blue 50.00 24.00
a. Perf 10¼ ('56) 50.00 —

Design size: 18x21.5mm. Printed on thin white wove paper, with clearly discernible mesh pattern.

Reprints are perf 10¼, 11 or imperf, on thick white wove paper, with no pattern visible. Size 18.5-19x21.5-22mm.

Flags & Monument A35 Soldier & Monument A36

1952-55

55 A35 10w carmine 120.00 —
a. Perf 10¼ ('55) — —
56 A36 10w scarlet 240.00 —
a. Perf 10¼ ('55) — —

Seventh Anniversary of Liberation from Japan.

Issue dates: No. 55, 7/25/52; No. 56, 8/1/52.

Design sizes: No. 55, 20.5-21x27.5-28mm; No. 56, 29.5-30x18.5mm.

Reprints of No. 55 are in vermilion, on thick paper, perf 10½, 11 or imperf. Size 20.5x27-27.5mm.

Reprints of No. 56 are in rose red, perf 10, 10¼, 11 or imperf. Size 30.5-31x18.5-19mm.

Note: original are typographed; reprints are lithographed on thin white paper.

International Youth Day — A37

1952, Oct. 20-1955

57 A37 10w deep green 72.50 —
a. Perf 10¼ ('55) 72.50

No. 57 is on thick paper, with very thin gum. Design size: 20.5-21x28mm.

Reprints are on thin to medium paper, without gum, perf 10¼, 11 or imperf. Size 20x27mm.

Soldiers in Battle — A38

Soldier and Flag — A39

1953, Jan. 20-1955

58 A38 10w rose carmine 130.00 —
a. Perf 10¼ ('55) 130.00 —
59 A39 40w red brown 60.00 —
a. Perf 10¼ ('55) 75.00 —

Fifth Anniversary of the Founding of the Korean People's Army.

Design sizes: No. 58, 21.5-22x26-26.5mm; No. 59, 21.5x27mm.

Reprints of No. 58 are on thick, gummed paper, perf 10¼, 11 or imperf. Size: 21.5-22x26.5mm.

Reprints of No. 59 are on thick, gummed paper, perf 10, 10½, 11 or imperf. Size: 21.5x26.5mm.

Woman with Flag — A40

Women and Globe — A41

1953, Mar. 1-1955

60 A40 10w carmine 60.00 —
a. Perf 10¼ ('55) 60.00 —
61 A41 40w yellow green 72.50 —
a. Perf 10¼ ('55) 72.50 —

International Women's Day.

Design sizes: No. 60, 20x29.5mm; No. 61, 21x29mm.

Reprints of No. 60 are in rose carmine, on thin paper, perf 10¼, 11 or imperf. Size 20.5x30mm.

Reprints of No. 61 may be distinguished from the originals by design differences: the dove's wing consists of many small feathers (3 large feathers on original), the women's mouths are all open (closed on original), and 3 thin connected lines on center woman's shirt (3 thick separate lines on original).

Worker — A42

Workers Marching — A43

1953, Apr. 15-1955

62 A42 10w yellow green 60.00 —
a. Perf 10¼ ('55) 72.50 —
63 A43 40w orange brown 60.00 —
a. Perf 10¼ ('55) 72.50 —

May Day

Reprints of No. 62 are in green or emerald green, perf 9½x8½, 10¼, 11 or imperf. Among many design differences, they have 4 horizontal lines between flag and frame line at upper left, many short hatching lines between frame line and top inscription, many horizontal lines between flag and flag pole at upper right, and won letter clear. On originals, there are one or no lines at upper left, no lines between frame line and top inscription, no lines between flag and flag pole, and the won character is not clearly defined.

Reprints of No. 63 are perf 10, 10¼ or imperf. On the reprints, the right flag pole touches the frame line, and the left center element of the won character resembles a "T." On the originals, the right flag pole does not touch the frame line, and the center element of the won character resembles an inverted "L."

Soldier — A44

Battle — A45

1953, June 1-1955

64 A44 10w greenish blue 110.00 —
a. Perf 10¼ ('55) 110.00 —
65 A45 40w scarlet 110.00 —
a. Perf 10¼ ('55) 110.00 —

Day of Anti-U.S. Imperialist Struggle.

Nos. 64 and 65 were issued with gum. Design sizes: 10w, 24x33mm; 40w, 24-24.5x33mm.

Reprints of No. 64 and 65 are on thick paper, perf 10¼, 11 or imperf. Design sizes: 10w, 23.5-24x32mm; 40w, 24x32-32.5mm. No. 64 is in turquoise blue, No. 65 in vermilion or orange vermilion.

4th World Festival of Youth & Students
A46 A47

1953, June 10-1955
With Gum

66 A46 10w dp dull blue & pale turq. blue 72.50 —
a. Perf 10¼ ('55) 85.00 —
67 A47 20w gray grn &pink 60.00 36.00
a. Perf 10¼ ('55) 72.50 —

Two types of reprints of No. 66 exist. On the reprints, the forelocks of the center and right heads have detailed hairlines, and the right head shows eye and eyebrow. On the originals, both features are solid.

Victory Issue — A48

1953, June 1-1955
With Gum

68 A48 10w brn & yel 360.00 —
a. Perf 10¼ ('55) 325.00 —

8th Anniversary of Liberation from Japan — A49

1953, Aug. 5-1955

69 A49 10w red orange *3,600.* *3,000.*

Design size: 25x35.5mm.

Reprints are perf 10¼ or imperf. Size: 24.5-25x34.5-35mm. Left side of monument is shaded, and windows are fully drawn and shaded. On the originals, the monument is unshaded, and the windows are only partially drawn and half shaded.

5th Anniv. Founding of D.P.R.K. — A50

1953, Aug. 25-1955

70 A50 10w dp blue & red 72.50 72.50
a. Perf 10¼ ('55) 95.00 —

Design size: 21.5-22x29.5-30mm. Inscribed "1948-1953."

Reprints are in blue and vermilion, perf 9x9½ or imperf and are inscribed "1948-1955." Size: 22.5x30mm. Value, each $30.

Liberation Monument — A51

1953, Dec. 25-1955
With Gum

71 A51 10w deep slate 72.50 47.50
a. Perf 10¼ ('55) 72.50 —

Design size: 20x31mm.

Reprints are in deep gray. Size: 19-19.5x30.5-31mm.

Worker & Crane — A52

1954, Jan. 25-1955
With Gum

72 A52 10w light blue 85.00 55.00
a. Perf 10¼ ('55) 110.00 —

Reconstruction and Economic Development.

Design size: 22x31.5mm.

Reprints are in greenish blue or dull blue, without gum. Size: 21.5x31mm. The horizontal lines defining the sky and clouds are clear and even, and the details of the crane are distinct.

Korean People's Army, 6th Anniv. — A53

1954, Jan. 25-1955
With Gum

73 A53 10w dp car red 725.00 —
a. Perf 10¼ ('55) 725.00 —
b. Rouletted 725.00

Design size: 23.5-24x38mm.

Reprints are in vermilion or orange vermilion. Size: 23-23.5x37.5-38mm. The design is much clearer than in the originals, with thin distinct characters in top inscription and complete unbroken frame line at right.

International Women's Day — A54

1954, Feb. 25-1955
With Gum

74 A54 10w carmine 220.00 —
a. Perf 10¼ ('55) — —

Design size: 19.5-20x29-29.5mm.

Reprints are in vermilion. Size: 20-20.5x29.5-30mm. The USSR and PRC flags at top right are legible, and the shading under the center and right women's chins is represented by several fine lines (solid on originals).

Labor Day — A55

1954, Apr. 15-1955
With Gum

75 A55 10w vermilion 72.50 —
a. Perf 10¼ ('55) 72.50 —

Design size: 20x27-27.5mm.

Reprints are in orange vermilion, perf 8½x9, 9, 10¼ or imperf. Size: 19-19.5x26-26.5.

#16 overprinted "Fee Collected" in Korean

1954, May (?)

76 A10 6w red & blue 2,500. 2,250.

Day of Anti-U.S. Imperialist Struggle — A56

1954, June 10-1955
With Gum

77 A56 10w red brown 210.00 *210.00*
a. Perf 10¼ ('55) 210.00 *210.00*

National Congress of Young Activists — A57

1954, July 20-1955
With Gum

78 A57 10w blue, red & slate 600.00 300.00
a. Perf 10¼ ('55) — —

Design size: 20x30mm.

Reprints are in blue, scarlet vermilion & deep slate. Size: 19.5-20x29-29.5mm. On the originals, the worker's hand is beneath the tassel of the flag and is less than 1mm from the frame line. On the reprints, hand is to the right of the tassel and 2mm from frame line.

Liberation from Japan, 9th Anniv. — A58

1954, Aug. 1-1955
With Gum

79 A58 10w chestnut 50.00 50.00
a. Perf 10¼ ('55) 50.00 —

Design size: 20-20.5x30mm.

Reprints of No. 79 are perf 10¼, 11 or imperf. Size: 20x29-29.5mm. Soldier's nose line straight and strong, 3 lines of cooling holes in gun barrel (2 on originals).

North Korean Flag — A59

1954, Aug. 25-1955

With Gum

80 A59 10w blue & dp red 60.00 *60.00*
a. Perf 10¼ ('55) — —

Design size: 24x31.5-32mm.
Reprints are in dull blue and bright rose red. Size: 25-25.5x30.5-31mm.

Taedong Gate, Pyongyang A60

1954, Sept. 1-1956

With Gum

81 A60 5w reddish brown 15.00 3.75
a. Perf 10¼ ('56) 22.50 —
82 A60 5w lilac brown 15.00 3.75
a. Perf 10¼ ('56) 22.50 —

Hwanghae Iron Works — A61

Hwanghae Iron Works & Workers — A61a

#84, Hwanghae Iron Works & workers, horiz.

1954, Nov. 1-1956

83 A61 10w light blue 22.50 3.00
a. Perf 10¼ ('55) 45.00 —
84 A61a 10w chocolate 22.50 3.00
a. Perf 10¼ ('55) 45.00 —
b. Perf 9x8½ ('56) — —

Korean People's Army, 7th Anniversary — A62

1955, Jan. 25

With Gum

85 A62 10w rose red 36.00 36.00
a. Perf 10¼ 36.00 —

International Women's Day — A63

1955, Feb. 25

With Gum

86 A63 10w deep blue 36.00 36.00
a. Perf 10¼ 45.00 —

Reprints are in blue, perf 10¼, imperf and imperf x 10¼. Corners of design are clearly and uniformly indented.

— A63A

— A63A Labor Day

1955, Apr. 16

With Gum

86A A63A 10w green 60.00 30.00
a. Perf 10¼ — —
86B A63B 10w violet brown 60.00 30.00
a. Perf 10¼ 60.00 —

Design sizes: No. 86A, 19.5-20x30mm. No. 86B, 19x30mm.
Reprints of No. 86A measure 19.5x29mm. Reprints of 86B measure 19x29.5mm and are without gum.

Admiral Ri Sun-Sin — A64

1955, May 14-1956

87 A64 1w blue, *pale green* 15.00 15.00
a. Perf 10¼ ('56) 18.00 —
88 A64 2w rose, *buff* 15.00 1.50
a. Perf 10¼ ('56) 22.00 —
89 A64 2w rose red ('56) 30.00 2.75
a. Perf 10¼ ('56) 30.00 —
Nos. 87-89 (3) 60.00 19.25

No. 89 is redrawn, with a larger "2."
Design sizes: Nos. 87, 88, 20x29-30mm.
Reprints of No. 87 are in dull blue, on pale apple green, perf 10¼, 11½x10½, imperf, or roul. 8½. Size 19x28-28.5mm. Reprints of No. 88 are 19-19.5x28.-28.5mm in size.

Labor Law, 9th Anniv. — A65

1955, May 30

90 A65 10w rose 90.00 90.00
a. Perf 10¼ — —

No. 90 was issued with a very thin yellow gum. Design size: 18.5-19x27.5-28mm.
Reprints exist perf 10¼, 11 or imperf. Size 18-18.5x27-27.5mm. Value unused, $5.

Korea-U.S.S.R. Friendship Month

A66 A67

1955, July ***Perf. 10***

91 A66 10w rose red 30.00 —
a. Imperf 30.00 21.00
92 A66 10w org red & vio blue 30.00 —
a. Imperf 30.00 21.00
93 A67 20w red & lt blue 30.00 —
a. Imperf 30.00 24.00
b. Inscription below flag in two colors — —
c. As "b," imperf — —
94 A67 20w verm & lt blue 24.00 —
a. Imperf 24.00 21.00
Nos. 91-94 (4) 114.00

Issue dates: Nos. 91, 93, 7/16; Nos. 92, 94, 7/20.
Design sizes: No. 91, 22x32.5mm; No. 92, 29.5x43mm; No. 93, 18.5x32mm; No. 94, 24.5-25x42.5x43mm.
Reprints of No. 94 are in light vermilion and light blue, perf 10¼, 11 or imperf, with a very thin gum. Size: 24-24.5x42-43mm. The two blue bands of the flag are solidly colored, with many white spots. On the originals, this area consists of fine lines with few or no white areas.

Liberation from Japan, 10th Anniv. — A68

1955, July 20 ***Perf. 10¼***

95 A68 10w dull green 24.00 —
a. Imperf 24.00 18.00
96 A68 10w ver, dull blue & chestnut 24.00 —
a. Imperf 24.00 18.00

Design sizes: No. 95, 21.5-22x31.5-32mm; No. 96, 29-29.5-42-43mm.
Reprints of No. 95 are in dull blue green, perf 10¼, 11 or imperf, on gummed paper. Size: 21-21.5x31mm. Reprints of No. 96 are in rose red, dull to greenish blue and yellow brown, perf 10¼ or imperf. Size: 28-28.5x42.5-43mm.

Standing Rock in Sea-Kumgang Maritime Park — A69

1956, Jan. 20

97 A69 10w blue, *bluish* 20.00 —
a. Imperf 20.00 8.00

People's Army, 8th Anniv. — A70

1956, Jan. 20

98 A70 10w lt brn, *pale yel grn* 90.00 *90.00*
a. Imperf *72.50 72.50*

Design size: 20x27-27.5mm.
Reprints are in chestnut on pale sage green paper, perf 10¼, 11 or imperf. Size: 19.5-20x27mm. Creases in the soldier's shirt are distinct, and nose and eyes are strongly shaded.

May Day — A71

1956, Apr. 29

99 A71 10w blue *55.00 55.00*
a. Imperf *55.00 55.00*

Design size: 23.5-24x35-35.5mm.
Reprints are perf 10¼, 11 or imperf, on gummed paper. Size: 23.5x35mm. Clear hatching lines at right of top inscription; many feathers in dove's wing.

Ryongwang Pavilion and Taedong Gate, Pyongyang — A72

1956, May 8

100 A72 2w light blue *55.00 55.00*
a. Imperf *55.00 55.00*

Reprints of No. 100 are on thicker, gummed paper. The tail of the central left element in the "won" inscription at lower right extends beyond the left edge of the L-shaped character beneath it.

Moranbong Theater, Pyongyang A73

1956, May 8

101 A73 40w light green 30.00 12.00
a. Imperf 85.00 72.50

Labor Law, 10th Anniv. — A74

1956, June 7

102 A74 10w dark brown 8.00 2.50
a. Perf 9 *80.00 60.00*
b. Imperf 150.00 90.00

Korean Children's Union, 10th Anniv. A75

1956, June 7

103 A75 10w dk brown 15.00 6.50
a. Imperf *135.00 30.00*

Law on Equality of the Sexes, 10th Anniv. A76

1956, July 10

104 A76 10w dark brown 10.00 3.75
a. Perf 9 *25.00 15.00*
b. Imperf 30.00 14.00

Nationalization of Major Industries, 10th Anniv. — A77

1956, July 10

105 A77 10w dark brown 90.00 —
a. Imperf *180.00* —

Liberation from Japan, 11th Anniv. — A78

1956, July 24

106 A78 10w rose red 14.00 3.25
a. Imperf *130.00* *25.00*

Machinist
A79

1956, July 28

107 A79 1w dark brown 3.75 2.00
a. Perf 9 *12.50* *8.00*
b. Imperf 27.50 12.00

Kim Il Sung University, 10th Anniv. — A80

1956, Sept. 30

108 A80 10w dark brown 10.00 9.00
a. Imperf *27.50* *12.00*

4th Congress, Korean Democratic Youth League — A81

1956, Nov. 3

109 A81 10w dark brown 14.00 3.25
a. Imperf 27.50 15.00

Model Peasant — A82

1956, Nov. 14

110 A82 10w rose 7.50 2.25
a. Imperf 18.00 9.50
b. Rouletted — —

220th Anniv. Birth of Pak Ji Won (1737-1805)
A83

1957, Mar. 4

111 A83 10w blue 5.00 1.25
a. Imperf 16.00 8.50

Tabo Pagoda in Pulguk Temple
A84

Ulmil Pavilion, Pyongyang
A85

1957, Mar. 20

112 A84 5w light blue 6.00 2.50
a. Rouletted — —
b. Perf 11 (with gum) — —
c. Imperf 72.50 18.00
113 A85 40w gray green 7.50 3.25
a. Perf 11 — —
b. Imperf 19.00 9.50

No. 113b was issued both with and without gum.

Productivity Campaign — A86

1957, July 4

With or Without Gum

114 A86 10w ultramarine 6.75 4.50
a. Perf 11 — —
b. Imperf 27.50 13.00

Steelworker — A87

Voters Marching — A88

1957, Aug.

115 A87 1w orange 3.50 .75
a. Imperf 8.00 3.50
116 A87 2w brown 3.50 .75
a. Imperf 8.00 3.50
117 A88 10w vermilion 17.50 3.25
a. Imperf 55.00 29.00
Nos. 115-117 (3) 24.50 4.75

Second General Election.

There are two types of the 1w. On type 1, the won character is approx. 2½mm in diameter and is distinct. On type 2, the character is approx. 1½mm in diameter and is virtually illegible.

Issued: 10w, 8/10; 1w, 2w, 8/13.

Founding of Pyongyang, 1530th Anniv. — A89

1957, Sept. 28 ***Perf. 10***

118 A89 10w blue green 3.00 .65
a. Imperf 25.00 7.50

Lenin — A90

Lenin & Flags — A91

Kim Il Sung at Pochonbo
A92

Pouring Steel
A93

1957

119 A90 10w gray blue 2.00 .95
a. Imperf 25.00 7.50
120 A91 10w blue green 2.00 .95
a. Imperf 25.00 7.50
b. Rouletted 13 — —
121 A92 10w red 2.00 .95
a. Imperf 25.00 7.50
b. Rouletted 13 — —
122 A93 10w red orange 4.50 .95
a. Imperf 100.00 11.00
b. Rouletted 13 — —
Nos. 119-122 (4) 10.50 3.80

40th Anniversary of the Russian October Revolution.

Issued: Nos. 119, 120, 9/30; No. 121, 10/3; 122, 10/16.

No. 120 exists with gum.

4th Congress World Federation of Trade Unions — A94

1957, Oct. 3

123 A94 10w ultra & lt grn 2.50 1.10
a. Imperf 25.00 9.50

No. 123a exists with or without gum.

Russian Friendship Month — A95

1957, Oct. 16

124 A95 10w green 4.50 1.10
a. Imperf *180.00* *120.00*

Doctor Weighing Baby — A96

Bandaging Hand — A97

1957, Nov. 1

125 A96 1w red 9.00 1.25
a. Imperf 55.00 11.00
126 A96 2w red 9.00 1.25
a. Imperf 55.00 11.00
b. Rouletted — —
127 A97 10w red 35.00 3.75
a. Imperf 110.00 29.00
Nos. 125-127 (3) 53.00 6.25

Red Cross.

No. 126 exists without or without gum. No. 126a was issued with gum.

Flying Dragon Kettle — A98

Flying Dragon Incense Burner — A99

1958, Jan. 14

128 A98 10w blue 12.00 1.60
a. Imperf 72.50 17.00
129 A99 10w gray green 12.00 1.60
a. Imperf 72.50 17.00

Nos. 128a and 129a exist with or without gum.

Woljong Temple Pagoda — A100

1958, Feb. 21 ***10 (#130), 10½ (#131)***

130 A100 5w lt green 1.90 .75
a. Imperf 22.00 11.00
b. Rouletted — —
131 A100 10w lt blue 5.50 2.50
a. Imperf 27.50 15.00
b. Rouletted — —

No. 130 was issued with gum.

Soldier — A101

Soldier, Flag & Hwanghae Iron Works — A102

Photo (#132), Litho (#133)

1958, Feb. ***Perf. 10***

132 A101 10w blue 8.00 1.10
a. Imperf 44.00 18.00
b. Rouletted — —
c. Perf 11 — —
133 A102 10w rose 11.00 1.25
a. Imperf 44.00 18.00

10th Anniversary of the Korean People's Army.

No. 133 was issued with or without gum.

Rocket Launch, Sputnik — A103

Sputnik in Orbit — A104

1958, Mar. 26 **Photo.**

Designs: 40w, Sputnik over observatory.

134 A103 10w dull blue green 8.50 5.00
a. Imperf 55.00 18.00
135 A104 20w dull blue green 8.50 5.00
a. Imperf 55.00 18.00
b. Rouletted — —
136 A104 40w dull blue green 8.50 5.00
a. Imperf 55.00 18.00
137 A103 70w dull blue green 10.00 9.00
a. Imperf 85.00 29.00
Nos. 134-137 (4) 35.50 24.00

International Geophysical Year.
Nos. 134-137 exist with or without gum.

Young Socialist Constructors Congress — A105

1958, May 12 **Litho.**

138 A105 10w blue 4.50 1.25
a. Imperf 25.00 9.50

Opening of Hwanghae Iron Works — A106

1958, May 22

139 A106 10w lt blue 8.50 1.25
a. Imperf 35.00 12.00

Commemorative Badge — A107

1958, May 27

140 A107 10w multicolored 7.00 1.50
a. Imperf 23.00 5.50
b. Perf 11 — —
c. Rouletted — —

Departure of Chinese People's Volunteers. See No. 150.

4th International Democratic Women's Congress — A108

1958, June 5

141 A108 10w blue 1.90 .75
a. Imperf 35.00 9.50

Congress Emblem A109

1958, July 4

142 A109 10w grn & red brn 3.75 2.50
a. Imperf 25.00 5.50
b. Perf 11 12.50 —

First Congress of the Young Workers of the World Federation of Trade Unions.

Apartment House, East Pyongyang A110

1958, July 24

143 A110 10w lt blue 5.00 1.25
a. Imperf 22.00 7.50
b. Perf 11 — —

Workers' Apartment House, Pyongyang A111

1958, Aug. 21

144 A111 10w blue green 5.00 1.25
a. Imperf 22.00 7.50

Hungnam Fertilizer Plant — A112

Pyongyang Railway Station A113

DPRK Arms — A114

Weaver — A115

Dam, Pyongyang A116

1958 **Litho, Photo (#148, 149)**

145 A112 10w blue green 6.00 .95
a. Imperf *110.00* *15.00*
b. Perf 11 — —
146 A113 10w dp blue green *22.50* 3.25
a. Imperf *130.00* *36.00*
b. Perf 11 — —
147 A114 10w rd brn & yel grn 4.50 .95
a. Imperf *275.00* *90.00*
148 A115 10w sepia 18.00 3.75
a. Imperf *180.00* *47.50*
149 A116 10w sepia 30.00 12.50
a. Imperf *130.00* *30.00*
Nos. 145-149 (5) 81.00 21.40

10th Anniversary Korean People's Republic.
Issued: Nos. 145, 146, 8/21; No. 147, 9/7; Nos. 148, 149, 9/10.

Soldier and Troop Train — A117

1958, Sept. 10 **Photo.** ***Perf. 10***

150 A117 10w sepia 45.00 12.50
a. Imperf *300.00* *65.00*

Departure of Chinese People's Volunteers.

Transplanting Rice Seedlings A118

1958, Sept. 10 **Litho.**

With or Without Gum

151 A118 10w sepia 2.00 .65
a. Imperf 12.50 5.50

Winged Horse of Chollima — A119

1958, Sept. 16

152 A119 10w brick red 3.50 .60
a. Imperf 27.50 3.50

National Congress of the Innovators in Production.

North Korea-China Friendship Month — A120

1958, Oct. 8

With or Without Gum

153 A120 10w multicolored 2.25 .55
a. Imperf 15.00 3.50
b. Rouletted — —

National Congress of Agricultural Cooperatives A121

1959, Jan. 5

With or Without Gum

154 A121 10w dk grnish blue 2.50 .60
a. Imperf 15.00 3.25

Gen. Ulji Mundok — A122

1959, Feb. 11

With Gum

155 A122 10w lilac brn & yel 5.50 1.10
a. Imperf *27.50* *12.00*

See Nos. 157-159 and 209-212.

National Women's Workers Congress — A123

1959, Mar. 29

With or Without Gum

156 A123 10ch brown & red 3.75 1.25
a. Imperf *45.00* —

Jon Pong Jun — A124

Kang Kam Chan — A125

Ulji Mundok — A126

1959, Apr. 1

157 A124 2ch blue, *lt green* 2.50 .45
a. Imperf *90.00* —
158 A125 5ch lilac brn, *buff* 2.90 .50
a. Imperf *130.00* —
159 A126 10ch red brn, *cream* 5.75 .65
a. Imperf *130.00* —
Nos. 157-159 (3) 11.15 1.60

Nos. 157-159 were issued with gum. Nos. 157a-159a were issued with or without gum.

Soviet Luna 1 Moon Rocket Launch A127

1959, May 4 ***Perf. 10, 10½***

160 A127 2ch dk violet, *pale buff* 12.50 6.50
a. Imperf 220.00 47.50
161 A127 10ch blue, *pale green* 25.00 9.50
a. Imperf 220.00 47.50

Issued with gum (perf 10) or without gum (perf 10½). Nos. 160a and 161a were issued with gum.

Land Irrigation Program — A128

1959, May 27 ***Perf. 10***

162 A128 10ch multicolored 10.00 2.75
a. Imperf 36.00 9.50

Slogan-inscribed Tree, Chongbong Bivouac — A129

Statue of Kim Il Sung — A130

Mt. Paektu A131

1959, June 4 ***10, 10¾ (#164)***

163 A129 5ch multicolored 3.25 1.25
a. Imperf *72.50* 15.00
b. Perf 10¾ — —
c. Rouletted — —
164 A130 10ch blue & grnsh bl 3.75 1.25
a. Imperf *55.00* 15.00

165 A131 10ch violet blue		5.00	—
a.	Imperf	*55.00*	—
	Nos. 163-165 (3)	12.00	2.50

22nd Anniversary of the Battle of Pochondo.
No. 163 also exists perf 10¾.
No. 164 was issued with gum.

Chollima Tractor A132

Jongihwa-58 Electric Locomotive — A133

Red Star-58 Bulldozer A134

Chollima Excavator A135

SU-50 Universal Lathe A136

Sungri-58 Truck A137

With or without gum

1959, June 12 ***Perf. 10¾***

166 A132 1ch multicolored		1.50	.50
a.	Imperf	*55.00*	*30.00*
b.	Rouletted	—	—
167 A133 2ch multicolored		11.00	3.25
a.	Imperf	*110.00*	*45.00*
b.	Rouletted	—	—
168 A134 2ch multicolored		2.50	.65
a.	Imperf	*72.50*	*15.00*
b.	Rouletted	—	—
169 A135 5ch multicolored		2.50	1.25
a.	Imperf	*180.00*	—
b.	Rouletted	—	—
170 A136 10ch multicolored		2.50	.95
a.	Imperf	*180.00*	—
b.	Rouletted	—	—
171 A137 10ch multicolored		4.50	.65
a.	Imperf	*180.00*	—
	Nos. 166-171 (6)	24.50	7.25

Machine-building Industry.

Armistice Building, Panmunjom — A138

Anti-U.S. Protester A139

Anti-South Korean Emigration Campaign A140

Peaceful Reunification of Korea — A141

1959, June 25

With Gum

172 A138 10ch dk blue & blue		5.00	.30
a.	Imperf	*145.00*	—
b.	Perf 10¼	—	—
173 A139 20ch dk blue & lt blue		1.50	.50
174 A140 20ch sepia & brown		7.00	1.90
175 A141 70ch dk brn & lt brn		45.00	12.50
a.	Imperf	*145.00*	—
b.	Perf 10¼xRoul	—	—
	Nos. 172-175 (4)	58.50	15.20

Day of Struggle for the withdrawal of U.S. troops from South Korea.

Metal Type A142

Samil Wolgan Monthly Breaking Chains — A143

Flag with Symbols of Peace and Literature A144

Korean Alphabet of 1443 — A145

1959, Aug. 1

176 A142 5ch sepia		25.00	9.50
177 A143 5ch green & red		7.50	2.90
178 A144 10ch bright blue		7.50	2.90
179 A145 10ch dp bl & pale bl		11.50	4.75
a.	Souvenir sheet of 4, #176-179 imperf	110.00	55.00
	Nos. 176-179 (4)	51.50	20.05

International Book and Fine Arts Exhibition, Leipzig.

Nos. 176 and 178 were issued with gum. Nos. 177, 179 and 179a were issued without gum.

Milk Cow Farm A146

Pig Farm — A147

1959, Sept. 20

180 A146 2ch multicolored	4.00	.95
181 A147 5ch multicolored	5.50	1.25

No. 180 was issued without gum, No. 181 with gum.

Economic Development

Cement Making A148

Hydroelectrical Dam — A149

Salt Making — A150

Construction A151

Grain A152

Sugar A153

Steel-Making A154

Fishing A155

Iron-Making A156

Coal Mining A157

Textile Production A158

Fruit — A159

Perf. 10½ (#182), 11

1959, Sept. 20-1960

182 A148 1ch multicolored		.75	.55
a.	Imperf	*145.00*	—
183 A149 2ch multicolored		1.90	.55
a.	Imperf	*145.00*	—
184 A150 5ch multicolored		3.00	.70
a.	Imperf	*145.00*	—
185 A151 10ch multicolored		3.50	1.00
a.	Imperf	*145.00*	—
186 A152 10ch multicolored		1.50	.55
a.	Imperf	*145.00*	—

187	A153 10ch multicolored		2.75	.55
a.	Imperf		*145.00*	—
188	A154 10ch multicolored		2.50	.55
a.	Imperf		*145.00*	—
189	A155 10ch multicolored		2.25	.55
a.	Imperf		*145.00*	—
190	A156 10ch multicolored		1.50	.55
191	A157 10ch multicolored		2.75	.55
192	A158 10ch multicolored		1.50	.55
a.	Imperf		*145.00*	—
193	A159 10ch multicolored ('60)		4.00	.55
	Nos. 182-193 (12)		27.90	7.20

No. 193 issued August 1960.

Nos. 183 and 185 were issued with gum, the other values without gum.

Musk Deer A160

Sable A161

Marten A162

Otter A163

Sika Deer — A164

Pheasant A165

1959-62 ***Perf. 11***

194	A160 5ch multicolored	6.50	.75
195	A161 5ch multicolored	6.50	.75
196	A162 5ch multicolored	6.50	.75
197	A163 5ch multicolored	6.50	.75
198	A164 10ch multicolored	6.50	.75
199	A165 10ch multicolored	30.00	2.50
	Nos. 194-199 (6)	62.50	6.25

Game Preservation.

Issued: No. 198, 10/24/59; No. 199, 3/25/60; No. 194, 11/11/60; Nos. 195-197, 1/24/62.

Nos. 198 and 199 were issued with gum, Nos. 194-197 without gum.

3rd Korean Trade Unions Congress A166

1959, Nov. 4

With Gum

200	A166 5ch multicolored	1.40	.35

Electric Locomotive — A167

Freighter A168

1959, Nov. 5

With Gum

201	A167 5ch brnish purple	20.00	2.90
202	A168 10ch slate green	8.25	2.25

Korean People's Army, 12th Anniv. A169

1960, Feb. 8

With Gum

203	A169 5ch blue	225.00	125.00

Sword Dance — A170

Janggo Dance — A171

Peasant Dance — A172

1960, Feb. 25

204	A170 5ch multicolored	5.00	.45
205	A171 5ch multicolored	5.00	.45
206	A172 10ch multicolored	5.00	.45
	Nos. 204-206 (3)	15.00	1.35

Women of 3 Races, Dove — A173

Woman Worker — A174

1960, Mar. 8

With Gum

207	A173 5ch grnish blue & red vio	2.75	.20
208	A174 10ch grn & org	2.75	.50

50th Anniv. of International Women's Day.

Kim Jong Ho, Geographer A175

Kim Hong Do, Painter A176

Pak Yon, Musician A177

Jong Ta San, Scholar A178

1960

With Gum

209	A175 1ch gray & pale grn	2.75	.20
210	A176 2ch dp blue & yel buff	3.50	.20
211	A177 5ch grnish blue & grnish yel	12.75	.20
212	A178 10ch brn & yel	3.50	.20
	Nos. 209-212 (4)	22.50	.80

Issued: 1ch-5ch, 3/16/60; 10ch 6/60.

Grapes — A179

Wild fruits: No. 214, Fruit of Actinidia arguta planch. No. 215, Pine-cone. No. 216, Hawthorn berries. No. 217, Chestnuts.

1960, Apr. 8

With Gum

213	A179 5ch multicolored	3.25	1.00
214	A179 5ch multicolored	3.25	1.00
215	A179 5ch multicolored	3.25	1.00
216	A179 10ch multicolored	3.75	1.25
217	A179 10ch multicolored	3.75	1.25
	Nos. 213-217 (5)	17.25	5.50

Nos. 214-215 also exist imperf.

Lenin, 90th Birthday — A180

1960, Apr. 22

With Gum

218	A180 10ch violet brown	1.75	.30

Koreans and Caricature of U.S. Soldier — A181

1960, June 20

With Gum

219	A181 10ch dark blue	7.75	.75

Day of Struggle for Withdrawal of U.S. Troops from South Korea.

Mao Tse-Tung Plaza — A182

Taedong River Promenade A183

Youth Street — A184

People's Army Street — A185

Stalin Street — A186

1960, June 29

With Gum

220	A182 10ch gray green	1.25	.20
221	A183 20ch dk bl green	2.50	.30
222	A184 40ch blackish green	4.00	.75
223	A185 70ch emerald	7.25	1.75
224	A186 1w blue	10.00	2.75
	Nos. 220-224 (5)	25.00	5.75

Views of rebuilt Pyongyang.

Luna 3 — A187

Luna 2 — A188

1960, July 15

No.	Type	Denomination	Unused	Used
225	A187	5ch multicolored	7.75	6.00
226	A188	10ch multicolored	11.00	3.00

Soviet space flights.

The 5ch was issued with gum, the 10ch without gum.

Mirror Rock — A189

Devil-faced Rock — A190

Dancing Dragon Bridge A191

Nine Dragon Falls — A192

Mt. Diamond on the Sea A193

1960, July 15-1961

No.	Type	Denomination	Unused	Used
227	A189	5ch multicolored	1.75	.25
228	A190	5ch multicolored	1.75	.25
229	A191	10ch multicolored ('61)	6.25	.35
230	A192	10ch multicolored	5.50	.35
231	A193	10ch multicolored	2.10	.20
		Nos. 227-231 (5)	17.35	1.40

Diamond Mountains scenery.

No. 229 issued 2/8/61.

See Nos. 761-764.

Lily A194

Rhododendron A195

Hibiscus A196

Blue Campanula A197

Mauve Campanula A198

1960, July 15-1961

With Gum

No.	Type	Denomination	Unused	Used
232	A194	5ch multicolored	1.90	.30
233	A195	5ch multicolored	1.90	.30
234	A196	10ch multicolored	2.75	.50
235	A197	10ch multicolored	2.75	.50
236	A198	10ch multicolored ('61)	2.75	.50
		Nos. 232-236 (5)	12.05	2.10

No. 236 issued 6/1/61.

Nos. 232-234 and 236 also exist without gum.

"The Arduous March" A199

Crossing the Amnok River A200

Young Communist League Meeting — A201

Showing the Way at Pochonbo A202

Return to Pyongyang — A203

1960, July 26

No.	Type	Denomination	Unused	Used
237	A199	5ch carmine red	.85	.20
238	A200	10ch deep blue	1.50	.20
239	A201	10ch deep blue	1.50	.20
240	A202	10ch carmine red	1.50	.20
241	A203	10ch carmine red	1.50	.20
		Nos. 237-242 (5)	6.85	1.00

Revolutionary activities of Kim Il Sung.

15th Anniv. Liberation from Japan A204

1960, Aug. 6

No.	Type	Denomination	Unused	Used
242	A204	10ch multicolored	5.50	.25

North Korean-Soviet Friendship Month — A205

1960, Aug. 6

No.	Type	Denomination	Unused	Used
243	A205	10ch lake, *cream*	1.40	.25

Okryu Bridge A206

Grand Theater A207

Okryu Restaurant A208

1960, Aug. 11

No.	Type	Denomination	Unused	Used
244	A206	10ch gray blue	4.00	.35
245	A207	10ch dull violet	3.50	.20
246	A208	10ch turquoise	1.40	.20
		Nos. 244-246 (3)	8.90	.75

Pyongyang buildings.

Tokro River Dam — A209

1960, Sept. 9

With Gum

No.	Type	Denomination	Unused	Used
247	A209	5ch slate blue	2.50	.25

Inauguration of Tokro River Hydroelectric Power Station.

World Federation of Trade Unions, 15th Anniv. — A210

1960, Sept. 16

No.	Type	Denomination	Unused	Used
248	A210	10ch blue & lt blue	1.60	.25

Repatriation of Korean Nationals from Japan — A211

1960, Sept. 26

No.	Type	Denomination	Unused	Used
249	A211	10ch brnish violet	5.50	.30

Korean-Soviet Friendship — A212

1960, Oct. 5

With Gum

No.	Type	Denomination	Unused	Used
250	A212	10ch brn & org	1.75	.25

Liberation Day Sports Festival, Pyongyang A213

Designs: 5ch (#251), Runner. 5ch (#252), Weight-lifter. 5ch (#253), Cyclist. 5ch (# 254), Gymnast. 5ch (# 255), Soccer players, horiz. 10ch (#256), Swimmer, horiz. 10ch (#257), Moranbong Stadium, horiz.

1960, Oct. 5

No.	Type	Denomination	Unused	Used
251-257	A213	Set of 7	13.50	2.25

Chinese & North Korean Soldiers A214

Friendship Monument — A215

1960, Oct. 20

With Gum

No.	Type	Denomination	Unused	Used
258	A214	5ch rose	1.40	.20
259	A215	10ch dp blue	1.40	.20

10th Anniversary of Chinese People's Volunteers' Entry into Korean War.

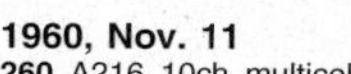

World Federation of Democratic Youth, 15th Anniv. — A216

1960, Nov. 11

No.	Type	Denomination	Unused	Used
260	A216	10ch multicolored	1.40	.25

Woodpecker
A217

Mandarin Ducks
A218

Scops Owl — A219

Oriole — A220

1960-61

261	A217	2ch	yel grn & multi	7.25	.40
262	A218	5ch	blue & multi	7.75	.50
263	A219	5ch	lt blue & multi	12.50	1.00
264	A220	10ch	lt bl grn & multi	7.75	1.00
			Nos. 261-264 (4)	35.25	2.90

Issued: No. 262, 12/15/60; No. 264, 3/15/61; No. 261, 4/22/61; No. 263, 6/1/61.

Wrestling
A221

Swinging — A222

Archery
A223

Seesaw — A224

1960, Dec. 15-1961

265	A221	5ch	dull grn & multi	1.00	.20
266	A222	5ch	yel & multi ('61)	1.00	.20
267	A223	5ch	yel gold & multi	4.50	.45
268	A224	10ch	lt bl grn & multi	1.00	.20
			Nos. 265-268 (4)	7.50	1.05

No. 266 issued 1/6/61.

Agriculture
A225

Light Industry
A226

Korean Workers' Party Flag — A227

Power Station
A228

Steel-Making — A229

1960, Dec. 15-1961

269	A225	5ch	multicolored	1.90	.20
270	A226	5ch	multicolored	3.50	.20
271	A227	10ch	multicolored	.95	.20
272	A228	10ch	multicolored	1.90	.20
273	A229	10ch	multicolored	1.40	.20
			Nos. 269-273 (5)	9.65	1.00

Wild Ginseng — A230

Design: 10ch, cultivated ginseng

1961

274	A230	5ch	multicolored	5.00	.25
275	A230	10ch	multicolored	5.00	.25

Issued: 10ch, 1/5; 5ch, 3/15.

A231

A232

A233

Factories
A234

1961, Feb. 8

With Gum

276	A231	5ch	red & pale yel	1.40	.20
277	A232	10ch	bl grn & pale yel	3.00	.25
278	A233	10ch	dp vio blue & pale yel	3.00	.25
279	A234	20ch	vio & pale yel	3.75	.55
			Nos. 276-279 (4)	11.15	1.25

Construction of Vinalon Factory.
See Nos. 350-353.

Pyongyang Students' and Children's Palace
A235

1961, Feb. 8

With Gum

280	A235	2ch	red, *yellow*	1.00	.25

Korean Revolution Museum
A236

1961, Feb. 8

With Gum

281	A236	10ch	red	.85	.25

Soviet Venus Rocket
A237

1961, Feb. 8

282	A237	10ch	turq bl & multi	6.25	.30

Tractor-Plow
A238

Disk-Harrow
A239

Wheat Harvester
A240

Corn Harvester
A241

Tractors
A242

1961, Feb. 21

With Gum

283	A238	5ch	violet	.95	.20
284	A239	5ch	blue green	.95	.20
285	A240	5ch	dp gray green	.95	.20
286	A241	10ch	violet blue	1.40	.20
287	A242	10ch	purple	1.40	.20
			Nos. 283-287 (5)	5.65	1.00

Opening of Industrial College — A243

1961, Mar. 1

With Gum

288	A243	10ch	red brn, *buff*	3.00	.25

Agrarian Reform Law, 15th Anniv.
A244

1961, Mar. 1

With Gum

289	A244	10ch	dull green, *yel*	2.10	.25

20-Point Political Program, 20th Anniv.
A245

1961, Mar. 15

With Gum

290	A245	10ch	dull vio, *pale yel*	1.00	.25

Mackerel
A246

Dolphin
A247

Whale
A248

Tunny — A249

Walleye Pollack A250

1961, Apr. 3

291	A246	5ch yel grn & multi	5.00	.50
292	A247	5ch lt blue & multi	12.00	1.50
293	A248	10ch lt grnish blue & multi	13.50	.50
294	A249	10ch gray & multi	5.00	.50
295	A250	10ch dk grn & multi	5.00	.50
		Nos. 291-295 (5)	40.50	3.50

Crane-Mounted Tractor — A251

"Sungri-1010" Truck A252

Vertical Milling Machine A253

Victory April-15 Automobile A254

8-Meter Turning Lathe A255

Radial Boring Lathe — A256

Hydraulic Press — A257

750-Kg Air Hammer A258

200mm Boring Lathe A259

3,000-Ton Press A260

3-Ton Air Hammer A261

Ssangma-15 Excavator A262

Jangbaek Excavator A263

400-HP Diesel Engine — A264

Honing Lathe — A265

Trolley — A266

8-Meter Planer — A267

Boring Lathe — A268

Hobbing Lathe — A269

Tunnel Drill — A270

1961-65

296	A251	1ch red brown	2.75	.20
297	A252	2ch dk brown	2.75	.20
298	A253	2ch dk green	1.00	.20
299	A253	2ch grayish brn	50.00	12.50
300	A254	4ch dk blue	7.00	.20
301	A255	5ch dk green	4.00	.20
302	A256	5ch dk bl gray	2.10	.20
a.		5ch dark gray green	50.00	12.50
303	A257	5ch bl green	2.10	.20
304	A258	5ch red brown	1.75	.20
305	A259	5ch sl violet	2.50	.20
306	A260	10ch gray violet	3.75	.20
a.		10ch dark blue	50.00	.20
307	A261	10ch blue	3.50	.20
308	A261	10ch brown	*200.00*	*50.00*
309	A262	10ch dk vio gray	1.75	.20
310	A263	10ch dk green	3.75	.20
311	A264	10ch dk sl blue	3.75	.20
312	A265	10ch dk blue	3.25	.20
313	A266	40ch dk blue	13.50	.20
314	A267	90ch dk bl green	6.00	.30
315	A268	1w dk vio brown	17.50	.50
316	A269	5w dk brown	37.50	3.75
317	A270	10w vio brown	50.00	7.50
		Nos. 296-317 (22)	420.20	77.75

Issued: 1ch, 4/22/61; 2ch, 4/27/61; Nos. 301, 306, 5/20/61; Nos. 307, 308, 3/13/62; Nos. 302, 317, 7/30/62; 5w, 9/5/62; No. 302a, 9/15/62; No. 308, 12/26/62; Nos. 297, 298, 2/11/63; No. 303, 4/9/63; 90ch, 5/15/63; 4ch, 6/15/63; 40ch, 9/13/63; 1w, 10/16/63; No. 310, 3/20/64; No. 305, 4/28/64; No. 311, 6/25/64; No. 312, 1/1/65.

Nos. 296, 297, 301, 303, 306 and 316 are perf 10¾. Other values are perf 12½.

Nos. 296-302, 304-307 and 309-315 were issued with gum. Nos. 303, 308, 316 and 317 were issued without gum.

Nos. 296-297, 301, 303, 306-308 and 316 are lithographed. Other values are engraved.

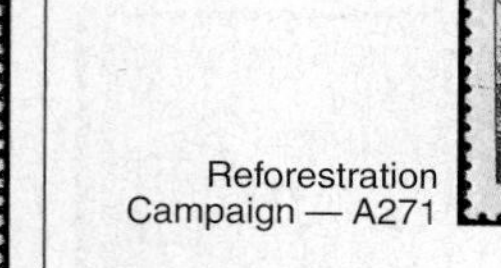

Reforestation Campaign — A271

1961, Apr. 27

With Gum

318	A271	10ch green	2.50	.35

Peaceful Reunification of Korea — A272

1961, May 9

319	A272	10ch multicolored	30.00	2.50

Young Pioneers (Children's Union) of Korea, 15th Anniv. — A273

Designs: 5ch, Pioneers swimming. 10ch (#321), Pioneer bugler. 10ch (#322) Pioneer visiting battlefield.

1961, June 1

320-322	A273	Set of 3	6.50	1.00

Labor Law, 15th Anniv. A274

1961, June 21

With Gum

323	A274	10ch dp blue, *pale yel*	1.75	.30

Plums — A275

Peaches A276

Apples A277

Persimmons A278

Pears — A279

1961, July 11

324	A275	5ch multicolored	1.60	.20
325	A276	5ch multicolored	1.60	.20
326	A277	5ch multicolored	1.60	.20
327	A278	10ch multicolored	1.60	.20
328	A279	10ch multicolored	1.60	.20
		Nos. 324-328 (5)	8.00	1.00

Yuri Gagarin & Vostok I — A280

1961, July 11

329	A280	10ch dp bl & pale bl	2.50	.50
330	A280	10ch red vio & pale bl	2.50	.50

First manned space flight, April 12.

Nationalization of Industry, 15th Anniv. — A281

1961, July 11

With Gum

331	A281	10ch lt red brown	20.00	.90

Sex Equality Law, 15th Anniv. A282

1961, July 27

With Gum

332	A282	10ch brn red & rose	1.25	.25

Children Planting Tree — A283

Children: 5ch (#334), Reading book. 10ch (#335), Playing with ball. 10ch (#336), Building a toy house. 10ch (#337), Waving banner.

1961, Aug. 29

333-337	A283	Set of 5	6.50	.90

Livestock Breeding — A284

Fishing Industry A285

Farming A286

Kwanum Waterfalls A512

1965, June 20 — Litho.
With Gum

594 A510	2ch	multicolored	.95	.20
595 A511	5ch	multicolored	1.60	.20
596 A512	10ch	multicolored	4.50	.25
	Nos. 594-596 (3)		7.05	.65

Diamond Mountain Scenery.

Nos. 594-596 exist imperf. Value, unused $100.

Kusimuldong — A513

Lake Samji A514

Photo.
With Gum

597 A513	5ch	slate blue	.85	.20
598 A514	10ch	grnsh blue	1.10	.20

Revolutionary battle sites.

Soccer Player — A515

Emblem & Stadium — A516

1965, Aug. 1 — Litho.
With Gum

599 A515	10ch	multicolored	1.60	.20
600 A516	10ch	multicolored	1.60	.20

GANEFO Games, Pyongyang.

Nos. 599-600 exist imperf, with gum. Value, $20 unused.

Liberation from Japan, 20th Anniv. — A517

1965, Aug. 15
With Gum

601 A517	10ch	multicolored	1.10	.20

Friedrich Engels, 145th Anniv. Birth — A518

1965, Sept. 10 — Engr. — *Perf. 12½*
With Gum

602 A518	10ch	brown	.55	.20

Sports — A519

Designs: 2ch, Pole vault. 4ch, Javelin. 10ch (#605), Discus. 10ch (#606), High jump. 10ch (#607), Shot put.

1965, Sept. 24 — Litho. — *Perf. 11*
With Gum

603-607 A519	Set of 5	4.50	1.00

Nos. 603-607 exist imperf, without gum. Value. $18 unused.

Korean Workers' Party, 20th Anniv. — A520

Designs: #608, 10ch, Korean fighters. #609, 10ch, Party emblem. #610, 10ch, Lenin & Marx. #611, 10ch, Workers marching. #612, 10ch, Soldiers & armed workers. #613, 40ch, Workers.

1965, Oct. 10 — Photo. — *Perf. 13X13½*
With Gum

608-613 A520	Set of 6	11.00	5.00
613a A520	Block of 6, #608-613	55.00	25.00
613b	Souvenir sheet of 6, #608-613	600.00	*400.00*

Chongjin Steel Mill A521

Kim Chaek Iron Works A522

1965, Nov. 25 — Engr. — *Perf. 12½*
With Gum

614 A521	10ch	deep violet	5.50	.20
615 A522	10ch	sepia	5.50	.20

Rainbow Trout — A523

Dolly Trout — A524

Grass Carp — A525

Carp — A526

Manchurian Trout — A527

Crucian Carp — A528

1965, Dec. 10 — Photo. — *Perf. 13½*
With Gum

616 A523	2ch	multicolored	.85	.20
617 A524	4ch	multicolored	1.00	.20
618 A525	10ch	multicolored	2.25	.20
619 A526	10ch	multicolored	2.25	.20
620 A527	10ch	multicolored	2.25	.20
621 A528	40ch	multicolored	3.75	.50
	Nos. 616-621 (6)		12.35	1.50

Freshwater fishes.

Nos. 616-621 exist imperf, without gum. Value $20 unused.

House Building — A529

Hemp Weaving — A530

Blacksmith A531

Wrestling A532

School — A533

Dance — A534

1965, Dec. 15 — Engr. — *Perf. 12½*
With Gum

622 A529	2ch	green	.70	.20
623 A530	4ch	maroon	1.40	.20
624 A531	10ch	violet	1.75	.20
625 A532	10ch	carmine red	2.00	.20
626 A533	10ch	blue	1.25	.20
627 A534	10ch	brown	1.10	.20
	Nos. 622-627 (6)		8.20	1.20

Paintings by Kim Hong Do, 18th century Korean artist.

Students' Extracurricular Activities A535

Designs: 2ch, Children in workshop. 4ch, Boxing. 10ch (#630), Playing violin. 10ch (#631), Chemistry lab.

1965, Dec. 15 — Litho. — *Perf. 13¼*
With Gum

628-631 A535	Set of 4	3.00	.50

Nos. 628-631 exist imperf. Value, unused $75.

Whaler A536

Service Vessel A537

1965, Dec. 15 — Engr. — *Perf. 12½*
With Gum

632 A536	10ch	deep blue	1.90	.25
633 A537	10ch	slate green	1.90	.25

Korean fishing boats.

Black-capped Kingfisher — A538

Korean Great Tit — A539

Blue Magpie A540

White-faced Wagtail A541

Migratory Korean Grosbeak A542

Perf. 11, 13½ (#640)

1965, Dec. 30 **Litho.**

With Gum

634	A538	4ch pale yel & multi	2.50	.20
635	A539	10ch pale salmon & multi	3.25	.25
636	A540	10ch pale grnsh blue & multi	3.25	.25
637	A541	10ch yel & multi	3.25	.25
638	A542	40ch pale yel grn & multi	9.50	.85
		Nos. 634-638 (5)	21.75	1.80

Korean birds.

Nos. 634-638 exist imperf, without gum. Value $27.50 unused.

Korean sericulture — A543

Designs: 2ch, Silkworm moth & cocoon. No. 640, 10ch, Ailanthus silk moth. No. 641, 10ch, Chinese Oak silk moth.

1965, Dec. 30 **Engr.** ***Perf. 12½***

With Gum

639-641 A543 Set of 3 100.00 3.00

Hooded Crane — A544

Japanese White-necked Crane — A545

Manchurian Crane — A546

Gray Heron — A547

1965, Dec. 30

With Gum

642	A544	2ch olive brown	3.25	.20
643	A545	10ch dp vio blue	3.75	.40
644	A546	10ch slate purple	3.75	.40
645	A547	40ch slate green	6.50	.70
		Nos. 642-645 (4)	17.25	1.70

Wading birds.

Mollusks A548

Designs: 5ch, Japanese common squid. 10ch, Giant Pacific octopus.

1965, Dec. 31 **Litho.** ***Perf. 11***

With Gum

646-647 A548 Set of 2 5.50 .40

Nos. 646-647 exist imperf, without gum. Value $8 unused.

Korean Ducks — A549

Designs: 2ch, Spotbill. 4ch, Ruddy shelduck. 10ch, Mallard. 40ch, Baikal teal.

1965, Dec. 31 **Litho.** ***Perf. 11***

With Gum

648-651 A549 Set of 4 16.50 2.00

Nos. 648-651 exist imperf. Value $30 unused.

Circus, Pyongyang — A550

Trapeze Performers A551

Balancing Act — A552

Seesawing A553

Tightrope Walker — A554

1965, Dec. 31 **Photo.**

652	A550	2ch multicolored	.85	.20
653	A551	10ch multicolored	2.25	.20
654	A552	10ch multicolored	2.25	.20
655	A553	10ch multicolored	2.25	.20
656	A554	10ch multicolored	2.25	.20
		Nos. 652-656 (5)	9.85	1.00

Korean acrobatics.

Nos. 652-655 were issued with gum, No. 656 without gum.

Korean Flowers — A555

Designs: No. 657, 4ch, Marvel-of-Peru. No. 658, 10ch, Peony (violet background). No. 659, 10ch, Moss rose (yellow background). No. 660, 10ch, Magnolia (light blue background).

1965, Dec. 31 **Litho.**

657-660 A555 Set of 4 13.00 1.00

No. 657 was issued without gum, Nos. 658-660 with gum.

Nos. 657-660 exist imperf, without gum. Value $20 unused.

Yachts — A556

Designs: No. 661, 2ch, Finn Class. No. 662, 10ch, Dragon Class (blue background). No. 663, 10ch, 5.5 Class (violet background). No. 664, 40ch, Star Class.

1965, Dec. 31 ***Perf. 13½***

With Gum

661-664 A556 Set of 4 6.50 2.00

Nos. 661-664 exist imperf, without gum. Value $10 unused.

10ch depicting Netherlands class yacht, with blue background, not issued. Value $750.

1st Congress of the Org. of Solidarity of Asia, Africa and Latin America — A557

1966, Jan. 3 ***Perf. 11***

With Gum

665 A557 10ch multicolored .55 .20

Hosta — A558

Dandelion — A559

Lily of the Valley — A560

Pink Convolvulus A561

Catalpa Blossom — A562

1966, Jan. 15

With Gum

666	A558	2ch multicolored	1.40	.25
667	A559	4ch multicolored	1.40	.25
668	A560	10ch multicolored	1.90	.25
669	A561	10ch multicolored	1.90	.25
670	A562	40ch multicolored	6.00	.75
		Nos. 666-670 (5)	12.60	1.75

Korean wildflowers.

Imperfs exist, without gum. Value, $25 unused.

Primrose — A563

Brillian Campion — A564

Amur Pheasant's Eye — A565

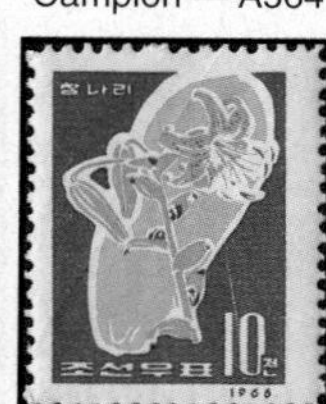
Orange Lily — A566

Rhododendron A567

1966, Feb. 10

With Gum

671	A563	2ch multicolored	1.10	.20
672	A564	4ch multicolored	1.10	.20
673	A565	10ch multicolored	1.60	.20
674	A566	10ch multicolored	1.60	.20
675	A567	90ch multicolored	7.75	1.00
		Nos. 671-675 (5)	13.15	1.80

Korean wildflowers.

A568

Land Reform Law, 20th Anniv.

1966, Mar. 5
With Gum

676 A568 10ch multicolored 1.00 .20

Battle of Jiansanfen A569

Battle of Taehongdan — A570

Battle of Dashahe A571

1966, Mar. 25 **Engr.** ***Perf. 12½***

677	A569	10ch violet brown	.65	.20
678	A570	10ch dp blue green	.65	.20
679	A571	10ch brown carmine	.65	.20
		Nos. 677-679 (3)	1.95	.60

Battles of the anti-Japanese revolution.
No. 678 was issued without gum, the other values with gum.

Art Treasures of the Silla Dynasty — A572

Designs: 2ch, Covered bowl. 5ch, Jar. 10ch, Censer.

1966, Apr. 30
With Gum

680-682 A572 Set of 3 5.00 .60

Labor Day, 80th Anniv. — A573

1966, May 1 **Litho.** ***Perf. 11***
With Gum

683 A573 10ch multicolored .85 .20

Assoc. for the Restoration of the Fatherland, 30th Anniv. — A574

1966, May 5 **Photo.**
With Gum

684 A574 10ch brn red & yel .85 .20

Farmer A575

Worker A576

1966, May 30 **Litho.**
With Gum

685	A575	5ch multicolored	.55	.20
686	A576	10ch multicolored	.85	.20

Young Pioneers, 20th Anniv. A577

1966, June 6
With Gum

687 A577 10ch multicolored .85 .20

Kangson Steel Works A578

Pongung Chemical Works A579

1966, June 10 **Engr.** ***Perf. 12½***
With Gum

688	A578	10ch gray	5.50	.20
689	A579	10ch deep red	5.50	.20

Korean Factories.

Fish — A580

Designs: 2ch, Saury. 5ch, Pacific cod. No. 692, Chum salmon. No. 693, Mackerel. 40ch, Pink salmon.

1966, June 10 **Photo.** ***Perf. 11***

690-694 A583 Set of 5 16.50 5.00

Nos. 690-692 were issued with gum, Nos. 693-694 without gum.
Nos. 690-694 exist imperf, without gum. Value, $22, either unused or cancelled.

Prof. Kim Bong Han & Kyongrak Biological System — A581

1966, June 30 **Photo.**
With Gum

695-702		Set of 8	6.50	1.60
702a	A581	Block of 8, #695-702	12.00	9.00
702b	A581	Souvenir sheet of 8, #695-702	125.00	100.00

Voshkod 2 A582

Luna 9 A583

Luna 10 A584

1966, June 30

703	A582	5ch multicolored	.35	.20
704	A583	10ch multicolored	1.10	.30
705	A584	40ch multicolored	1.90	.40
		Nos. 703-705 (3)	3.35	.90

Space Flight Day.
Nos. 703-705 exist imperf. Value, $8 unused.

Jules Rimet Cup A585

Dribbling A586

Goal-keeper A587

1966, July 11 **Litho.**

706	A585	10ch multicolored	1.90	.25
707	A586	10ch multicolored	1.90	.25
708	A587	10ch multicolored	1.90	.25
		Nos. 706-708 (3)	5.70	.75

World Cup Championship.
Nos. 706-708 exist imperf. Value, $20 unused.

Battle of Naphalsan A588

Battle of Seoul A589

Battle of Height 1211 A590

1966, July 27 **Engr.** ***Perf. 12½***
With Gum

709	A588	10ch red violet	.85	.20
710	A589	10ch deep green	.85	.20
711	A590	10ch violet	.85	.20
		Nos. 709-711 (3)	2.55	.60

Korean War of 1950-53.

Sex Equality Law, 20th Anniv. A591

1966, July 30 **Litho.** ***Perf. 11***
With Gum

712 A591 10ch multicolored .85 .20

Nationalization of Industry, 20th Anniv. — A592

1966, Aug. 10
With Gum

713 A592 10ch multicolored 1.10 .20

Water Jar Dance — A593

Bell Dance — A594

Dancer in Mural Painting — A595

Sword Dance — A596

Golden Cymbal Dance — A597

1966, Aug. 10

714	A593	5ch multicolored	1.60	.20
715	A594	10ch multicolored	2.75	.20
716	A595	10ch multicolored	2.75	.20
717	A596	15ch multicolored	2.75	.20
718	A597	40ch multicolored	5.00	.30
		Nos. 714-718 (5)	14.85	1.10

Korean Folk Dances.

5ch and 10ch issued with or without gum. Other values issued without gum.

Nos. 714-718 exist imperf, without gum. Value, $20 unused.

Attacking U.S. Soldier — A598

Worker with Child — A599

Industrialization A600

1966, Aug. 15 Engr. *Perf. 12½*
With Gum

719	A598	10ch deep green	1.40	.20
720	A599	10ch red violet	1.40	.20
721	A600	10ch violet	6.50	.45
		Nos. 719-721 (3)	9.30	.85

Korean Reunification Campaign.

Crop-spraying — A601

Observing Forest Fire — A602

Geological Survey — A603

Fish Shoal Detection A604

1966, Sept. 30 Photo. *Perf. 11*

722	A601	2ch multicolored	.55	.20
723	A602	5ch multicolored	7.75	.20
724	A603	10ch multicolored	1.90	.20
725	A604	40ch multicolored	1.90	.20
		Nos. 722-725 (4)	12.10	.80

Industrial uses of aircraft.

2ch, 5ch issued without gum. 10ch, 40ch issued with gum.

Nos. 722-725 exist imperf, without gum. Value, $20 unused.

A three-value set honoring revolutionary fighters, with designs similar to types A334-A339, was prepared but not issued. Value $3,500.

Kim Il Sung University, 20th Anniv. — A605

1966, Oct. 1 Engr. *Perf. 12½*
With Gum

726	A605	10ch slate violet	.90	.20

Imperforate Stamps

Imperforate varieties are without gum, unless otherwise noted.

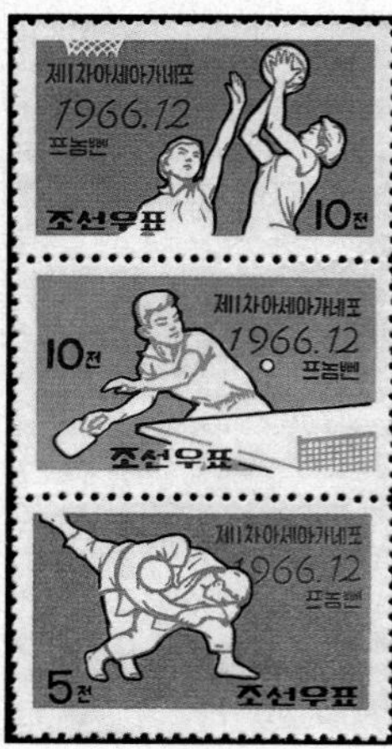
1st Asian GANEFO Games A606

Designs: a, 5ch, Judo. b, 10ch, Basketball. c, 10ch, Table tennis.

1966, Oct. 30 Litho. *Perf. 11*

727	A606	Strip of 3, #a-c	2.25	.60
		Strip of 3, #a-c imperf	50.00	—

Scarlet Finch — A607

Hoopoe — A608

Korean Crested Lark — A609

Brown Thrush A610

White-bellied Black Woodpecker A611

1966, Oct. 30

730	A607	2ch multicolored	2.50	.20
731	A608	5ch multicolored	2.75	.20
732	A609	10ch multicolored	3.25	.30
733	A610	10ch multicolored	3.25	.30
734	A611	40ch multicolored	6.50	.80
		Nos. 730-734 (5)	18.25	1.80
		Set of 5, imperf	35.00	—

Korean birds.

Construction — A612

Machine-Tool Production — A613

Worker & Graph A614

Miners A615

1966, Nov. 20

735	A612	5ch multicolored	.35	.20
736	A613	10ch multicolored	.60	.20
737	A614	10ch multicolored	.60	.20
738	A615	40ch multicolored	1.90	.40
		Nos. 735-738 (4)	3.45	1.00

Propaganda for increased production.

Nos. 735-737 issued with gum. No. 738 issued without gum.

Parachuting — A616

Show Jumping A617

Motorcycling — A618

Telegraphists' Competition — A619

1966, Nov. 30 Engr. *Perf. 12½*
With Gum

739	A616	2ch dark brown	.95	.20
740	A617	5ch org vermilion	.70	.20
741	A618	10ch dp violet blue	3.25	.30
742	A619	40ch deep green	2.25	.25
		Nos. 739-742 (4)	7.15	.95

National Defense sports.

Samil Wolgan Magazine, 30th Anniv. — A620

1966, Dec. 1 **Photo.** ***Perf. 11***

743 A620 10ch multicolored — —

Korean Deer — A621

Designs: 2ch, Red deer. 5ch, Sika deer. 10ch (#746), Reindeer (grazing). 10ch (#747), Japanese sambar (erect). 70ch, Fallow deer.

1966, Dec. 20 **Litho.**

744-748 A627 Set of 5 20.00 5.00
Imperf, #744-748 — —

No. 747 was issued with gum. Other values issued without gum.

Wild Fruit — A622

Designs: 2ch, Blueberries. 5ch, Pears. 10ch (#751), Plums. 10ch (#752), Schizandra. 10ch (#753), Raspberries. 40ch, Jujube.

1966, Dec. 30

749-754 A622 Set of 6 6.50 1.00
Imperf, #749-754 14.00 —

Samson Rocks — A623

Ryonju Pond — A624

Jinju Pond — A625

The Ten Thousand Rocks, Manmulsang A626

1966, Dec. 30 **Litho.** ***Perf. 11***

755	A623	2ch multicolored	1.10	.20
756	A624	4ch multicolored	4.50	.20
757	A625	10ch multicolored	1.10	.20
758	A626	10ch multicolored	4.50	.20
		Nos. 755-758 (4)	11.20	.80

Diamond Mountains scenery.

Nos. 755-758 are inscribed "1964" but were actually issued in 1966.

2ch and 4ch issued without gum. 10ch values issued with gum.

Onpo A627

Myohyang — A628

Songdowon — A629

Hongwon A630

1966, Dec. 30 **Engr.** ***Perf. 12½***

With Gum

759	A627	2ch blue violet	.50	.20
760	A628	4ch turquoise green	.55	.20
761	A629	10ch dp blue green	.90	.20
762	A630	40ch black	1.60	.35
		Nos. 759-762 (4)	3.55	.95

Korean rest homes.

Korean People's Army, 19th Anniv. A631

1967, Feb. 8 **Photo.** ***Perf. 11***

763 A631 10ch multicolored .85 .20

Livestock Farming A632

Designs: 5ch, Sow. 10ch, Goat. 40ch, Bull.

1967, Feb. 28 **Litho.**

764-766 A632 Set of 3 7.50 1.75
Imperf, #764-766 55.00 —

5ch, 10ch issued without gum. 40ch issued both with and without gum.

Battle of Pochonbo, 30th Anniv. — A633

1967, Feb. 28 **Photo.**

With Gum

767 A633 10ch multicolored .85 .20

Universal Compulsory Technical Education A634

1967, Apr. 1

768 A634 10ch multicolored .85 .20

29th World Table Tennis Championships, Pyongyang — A635

10ch, 40ch designs similar to 5ch.

1967, Apr. 11 **Litho.**

769-771 A635 Set of 3 3.50 .60
Imperf, #769-771 100.00 —

5ch issued with or without gum. 10ch, 40ch issued without gum.

People Helping Guerrillas, Wangyugou — A636

Blowing Up Railway Bridge A637

Shooting Down Japanese Plane A638

1967, Apr. 25 **Engr.**

With Gum

772	A636	10ch deep violet	.55	.20
773	A637	10ch dk vio brown	4.50	.25
774	A638	10ch slate	.55	.20
		Nos. 772-774 (3)	5.60	.65

Paintings of the guerrilla war against Japan.

Ri Tae Hun A639

Choe Jong Un A640

Kim Hwa Ryong A641

1967, Apr. 25

With Gum

775	A639	10ch slate	1.10	.20
776	A640	10ch reddish violet	3.25	.20
777	A641	10ch ultramarine	1.10	.20
		Nos. 775-777 (3)	5.45	.60

Heroes of the Republic.

Labor Day A642

1967, May 1 **Litho.**

778 A642 10ch multicolored .80 .20

Pre-School Education — A643

Designs of children: 5ch, Learning to count. 10ch, Making model tractor. 40ch, Playing with ball.

1967, June 1

779-781 A643 Set of 3 4.00 .60

Victory Monument, Battle of Pochonbo — A644

1967, June 4

782 A644 10ch multicolored 1.10 .20

Military Sculpture A645

Designs: 2ch, Soldier attacking tank. 5ch, Soldiers with musical instruments. 10ch, Soldier in heroic pose. 40ch, Soldier and child.

1967, June 25 **Photo.**
783-786 A645 Set of 4 3.25 .80

2ch issued with or without gum. Other values issued without gum.

Medicinal Plants — A646

Designs: 2ch, Polygonatum japonicum. 5ch, Abelmoschus manihat. 10ch (#789), Rehmannia glutinosa (olive yellow). 10ch (#790), Scutellaria baicalensis (turquoise blue background). 10ch (#791), Pulsatilla koreana (violet blue). 40ch, Tanacetum boreale.

1967, July 20 **Photo.**
787-792 A646 Set of 6 12.50 1.20

Nos. 787-789, 791 issued with or without gum. Nos. 790, 792 issued without gum.

Korean People's Army — A647

Designs: 5ch, Aviator, sailor, soldier. 10ch (#794), Officer decorating soldier. 10ch (#795), Soldier and farmer.

1967, July 25
793-795 A647 Set of 3 1.60 .50

5ch issued with or without gum. 10ch values issued without gum.

Freighter "Chollima" A648

1967, July 30 **Engr.**
With Gum
796 A648 10ch deep green 1.90 .20

Drilling Rock — A649

Felling Trees — A650

Reclaiming Tideland — A651

1967, Aug. 5
797 A649 5ch black brown .65 .20
798 A650 10ch blue green .90 .20
799 A651 10ch slate 1.25 .20
Nos. 797-799 (3) 2.80 .60

Revolutionary paintings.
5ch issued without gum. 10ch values issued with gum.

Crabs A652

Designs: 2ch, Erimaculus isenbeckii. 5ch, Neptunus trituberculatus. 10ch, Paralithodes camtschatica. 40ch, Chionoecetes opilio.

1967, Aug. 10 **Photo.**
800-803 A652 Set of 4 8.75 1.00

Reunification of Korea Propaganda — A653

1967, Aug. 15 **Litho.**
804 A653 10ch Multicolored 4.00 .40

A five-value set, featuring details from famous Korean paintings of the 15th-16th centuries, was prepared for release in August, 1967, but was not issued. Value $2,500.

A 10ch stamp celebrating the 10th anniversary of the launch of the first USSR space satellite was prepared for release on Sept. 10 but was not issued. Value $1,500.

Waterfalls A654

Designs: 2ch, Tongrim waterfalls 10ch, Sanju waterfall, Mt. Myohyang. 40ch, Sambang waterfall, Mt. Chonak.

1967, Oct. 10
805-807 A654 Set of 3 13.00 .80

2ch issued with or without gum. 10ch, 40ch issued without gum.

"For Fresh Great Revolutionary Upsurge" — A655

Designs: 5ch, Ship, train and truck. 10ch (#809), Machine industry. 10ch (#810), Truck, bulldozer, tractor and farmers. 10ch (#811), Construction machinery, buildings. 10ch (#812), Chollima flying horse and banners.

1967, Nov. 1 **Engr.**
808-812 A655 Set of 5 11.00 1.00

Russian Revolution, 50th Anniv. — A656

1967, Nov. 7 **Photo.**
813 A656 10ch Multicolored 1.10 .20

Korean Elections — A657

Designs: 10ch (#814), Voters and flags. 10ch (#815), Woman casting ballot (vert.)

1967, Nov. 23 **Litho.**
814-815 A657 Set of 2 1.40 .40

Raptors A658

Designs: 2ch, Black vulture. 10ch, Rough-legged buzzard. 40ch, White-tailed eagle.

1967, Dec. 1 **Photo.**
816-818 A658 Set of 3 16.00 2.00

2ch issued with or without gum. 10ch, 40ch issued without gum.

Chongjin — A659

Hamhung — A660

Sinuiju A661

1967, Dec. 20 **Engr.**
With Gum
819 A659 5ch bronze green 1.10 .20
820 A660 10ch violet 1.10 .20
821 A661 10ch red violet 1.10 .20
Nos. 819-821 (3) 3.30 .60

Korean cities.

Whaler Firing Harpoon A662

1967, Dec. 30
With or Without Gum
822 A662 10ch ultramarine 2.50 .30

Soldier with Red Book A663

Soldier Mounting Bayonet — A664

Worker and Bayoneted Rifle — A665

Litho or Photo (#829)
1967, Dec. 30
823 A663 10ch multicolored .55 .20
824 A664 10ch multicolored .55 .20
825 A665 10ch multicolored .55 .20
Nos. 823-825 (3) 1.65 .60

Korean People's Army, 20th Anniv. — A666

Designs: a, Airman, soldier and sailor. b, Soldier, battle in background. c, Soldier & KDPR arms. d, Soldier & flag. e, Soldier with Red Book. f, Three soldiers, North Korean flag. g, Soldier & worker. h, Soldier saluting. i, Soldier attacking. j, Soldier, sailor & airman beneath flag.

1968, Feb. 3 **Litho.**
826 A666 Sheet of 10 80.00 *30.00*
a.-j. 10ch, any single .45 .20

Ri Su Bok (1934-51) — A667

Han Kye Ryol (1926-51) — A668

1968, Feb. 10 **Engr.**
With Gum

827 A667 10ch dark rose *550.00*
828 A667 10ch light violet .55 .20
829 A668 10ch dark green 550.00
830 A668 10ch lt blue violet .55 .20
Nos. 827-830 (4) 1,101. .40

War heroes.
Nos. 827 and 829 were prepared but not issued.

Apartment Building, Pyongyang — A669

1968, Mar. 5 **Litho.**
With Gum

831 A669 10ch bright blue .85 .20

Kim Il Sung, 56th Birthday A670

1968, Apr. 15
With Gum

832 A670 40ch multicolored 1.10 .40

Printed in sheets of four stamps.
Exists in a miniature sheet of one, which is rare (2 examples reported),

Kim Il Sung's Family Home in Mangyongdae — A671

Leaving Home at Age 13 — A672

Mangyong Hill — A673

Kim Il Sung with Father — A674

Kim Il Sung with Mother — A675

1968, Apr. 15

833 A671 10ch multicolored .65 .20
834 A672 10ch multicolored .65 .20
835 A673 10ch multicolored .65 .20
836 A674 10ch multicolored .65 .20
837 A675 10ch multicolored .65 .20
Nos. 833-837 (5) 3.25 1.00

Childhood of Kim Il Sung.
See Nos. 883-887, 927-930.

Dredger *2 September* A676

1968, June 5

838 A676 5ch green 1.60 .20
839 A676 5ch blue *850.00 600.00*

Matsutake Mushroom A677

Shiitake Mushroom — A678

Meadow Mushroom A679

1968, Aug. 10 **Photo.**
With Gum

840 A677 5ch multicolored 22.50 .60
841 A678 10ch multicolored 45.00 1.00
842 A679 10ch multicolored 45.00 1.00
Nos. 840-842 (3) 112.50 2.60

Founding of the Korean Democratic People's Republic, 20th Anniv. — A680

Designs: a, Statue of national arms. b, North Korean flag. c, Worker, peasant & flag. d, Soldier & flag. e, Flying Horse of Chollima. f, Soldiers & tanks. g, Battle scene. h, Workers, banner & monument.

1968, Sept. 2 **Litho.**
With Gum

843 A680 Block of 8, #a.-h. 45.00 *40.00*
a.-h. 10ch, any single 1.40 .20

Kaesong Students' and Children's Palace A681

1968, Oct. 5
With Gum

844 A681 10ch greenish blue .55 .20

Domestic Goods — A682

Designs: 2ch, Shopper with domestic items. 5ch, Textile manufacturing. 10ch, Cannery.

1968, Nov. 5 **Photo.**
With Gum

845-847 A682 Set of 3 2.75 .60

Kim Il Sung's 10-Point Program A683

Design: 10ch, Two soldiers, Red Book, horiz.

1968, Dec. 5 **Litho.**

848-849 A683 Set of 2 1.10 .20

Increasing Agricultural Production — A684

Designs: 5ch, Woman carrying eggs. 10ch (#851), Woman harvesting wheat. 10ch (#852), Woman holding basket of fruit.

1968, Dec. 10 **Photo.**
With Gum

850-852 A684 Set of 3 1.40 .50

Shellfish A685

Designs: 5ch (#853), Scallop. 5ch (#854), Clam. 10ch, Mussel.

1968, Dec. 20
With Gum

853-855 A685 Set of 3 6.50 .50

Details of Battle of Pochonbo Victory Monument — A686

Designs (all 10ch): #856, Kim Il Sung at head of columns, vert. #857, shown. #858, Figures marching to right, green sky at right (42.75x28mm). #859, Figures marching to left (55.5x28mm). #860, Figures marching to right (55.5x28mm). #861, Figures marching to left, sky at right (42.75x28mm). #862, Figures marching to left, sky at left (42.75x28mm).

1968, Dec. 30

856-862 A686 Set of 7 3.75 1.40

Grand Theater, Pyongyang — A687

1968, Dec. 30

863 A687 10ch dark brown 1.10 .20

Revolutionary Museum, Pochonbo — A688

1968, Dec. 30

864 A688 2ch dark green .55 .20

Rural Technical Development — A689

Designs: 2ch, Irrigation. 5ch, Mechanization of agriculture. 10ch, Electrification. 40ch, Mechanical fertilization and spraying.

1969, Feb. 25

865-868 A689 Set of 4 2.50 .80

Rabbits
A690

Designs: 2ch, Gray rabbits. 10ch (#870), White rabbits. 10ch (#871), Black rabbits. 10ch (#872), Brown rabbits. 40ch, White rabbits.

1969, Mar. 10
869-873 A690 Set of 5 11.00 1.25

Nos. 869-873 were issued both with and without gum.

Public Health
A691

Designs: 2ch, Old man & girl. 10ch, Nurse with syringe. 40ch, Doctor with woman & child.

1969, Apr. 1
874-876 A691 Set of 3 4.50 .60

Farm Machines — A692

Designs: 10ch (#877), Rice sower. 10ch (#878), Rice harvester. 10ch (#879), Herbicide sprayer. 10ch (#880), Wheat & barley thresher.

1969, Apr. 10 **Engr.**
877-880 A692 Set of 4 3.50 .80

Mangyongdae — A693

Ponghwa — A694

1969, Apr. 15 **Litho.**
881 A693 10ch multicolored 1.90 .20
882 A694 10ch multicolored 1.90 .20

Revolutionary historical sites.

Early Revolutionary Years of Kim Il Sung — A695

Designs (all 10ch): #883, Kim crossing into Manchuria 1926, aged 13. #884, Kim talking to four students around table (blue green frame). #885, Kim speaking outdoors to Young Communist League meeting (apple green frame). #886, Kim speaking to Young Communist League meeting indoors (lilac frame). #887, Kim leading demonstration against teachers (peach frame).

1969, Apr. 15
883-887 A695 Set of 5 3.25 1.00

No. 884 was issued with gum. The other values were issued without gum.

Kang Pan Sok (1892-1932), Mother of Kim Il Sung — A696

Designs (all 10ch): #888, Birthplace at Chilgol. #889, Resisting Japanese police in home. #890, Meeting with women's revolutionary association.

1969, Apr. 21 **Photo.**
888-890 A696 Set of 3 4.50 .60

A697

Bivouac Sites in War against Japan

Designs: 5ch, Pegaebong. 10ch (#892), Mupho, horiz. 10ch (#893), Chongbong. 40ch, Konchang, horiz.

1969, Apr. 21
891-894 A697 Set of 4 3.00 .80

Chollima Statue — A698

1969, May 1
895 A698 10ch blue .85 .20

Poultry
A699

Designs: 10ch (#896), Mangyong chickens. 10ch (#897), Kwangpho ducks.

1969, June 1 **Engr.**
896-897 A699 Set of 2 5.75 .50

Socialist Education System — A700

Designs: 2ch, Kim Il Sung & children. 10ch, Student & worker with books. 40ch, Male & female students, figure "9."

1969, June 1 **Photo.**
898-900 A700 Set of 3 2.25 .60

Pochonbo Battlefield Memorials — A701

Designs: 5ch, Machine gun platform on mountainside. 10ch (#902), Statue of Kim Il Sung, vert. 10ch (#903), Aspen Tree monument (stele & enclosed tree trunk). 10ch (#904), Konjang Hill monument (within forest).

1969, June 4
901-904 A701 Set of 4 2.25 .80

Kim Hyong Jik (1894-1926), Father of Kim Il Sung — A702

Designs: 10ch (#905), Teaching at Myongsin School. 10ch (#906), Outdoor meeting with five other members of Korean National Association.

1969, July 10
905-906 A702 Set of 2 1.90 .40

A 10ch stamp honoring the Juvenile Chess Game of Socialist Countries was prepared for release Aug. 5, 1969, but was not issued. Value $1,000.

Sports Day, 20th Anniv. — A703

1969, Sept. 10
907 A703 10ch multicolored 1.10 .20

Korean Revolution Museum, Pyongyang
A704

1969, Sept. 10 **Litho.**
908 A704 10ch dk blue green .85 .20

Pres. Nixon Attacked by Pens — A705

1969, Sept. 18 **Litho.**
909 A705 10ch multi 3.25 .20

Anti-U.S. Imperialism Journalists' Conference, Pyongyang.

Implementation of the 10-Point Program — A706

Designs: 5ch, Soldiers, battle. 10ch (#911), Globe, bayonets attacking dismembered U.S. soldier. 10ch (#912), Workers holding Red Books & slogan, vert.

1969, Oct. 1 **Photo.**
910-912 A706 Set of 3 3.25 .60

Reunification of Korea — A707

Designs: 10ch (#913), Kim Il Sung, marching workers. 10ch (#914), Worker & soldier bayoneting U.S. soldier. 50ch, Armed workers in battle, horiz.

1969, Oct. 1 **Litho.**
913-915 A707 Set of 3 1.60 .60

Refrigerator-Transport Ship "Taesongsan" — A708

1969, Dec. 20 **Engr.**
916 A708 10ch slate purple 1.40 .20

Korean Fishes
A709

Designs: 5ch, Yellowtail. 10ch, Dace. 40ch, Mullet.

1969, Dec. 20 **Photo.**
917-919 A709 Set of 3 6.00 .60

Guerrilla Conference Sites
A710

Designs: 2ch, Dahuangwai, 1935. 5ch, Yaoyinggou, 1935 (log cabin). 10ch, Xiaohaerbaling, 1940 (tent).

1970, Feb. 10
920-922 A710 Set of 3 1.40 .45

Mt. Paektu, Birthplace of the Revolution — A711

Views of Mt. Paektu (all 10ch): #923, Lake Chon (dull green, tan, black). #924, Janggun Peak (pale peach, dull blue, black). #925, Piryu Peak (dull yellow, blue green, black). #926, Pyongsa Peak (brown orange, blue, red violet).

1970, Mar. 10
923-926 A711 Set of 4 2.75 .60

See Nos. 959-961.

Support for North Vietnam — A712

1970, Mar. 10
927 A712 10ch multicolored .65 .20

Revolutionary Activities of Kim Il Sung — A713

Designs (all 10ch): #928, Receiving his father's pistols from his mother. #929, Receiving smuggled pistols from his mother (other young revolutionaries present). #930, Kim speaking with four farmers in field. #931, Kim speaking at Kalun meeting.

1970, Apr. 15 **Litho.**
928-931 A713 Set of 4 5.50 .90

Lenin Birth Centenary A714

Design: 10ch (#933), Lenin with cap, in three-quarter profile.

1970, Apr. 22 **Photo.**
932-933 A714 Set of 2 1.60 .40

Assoc. of Koreans in Japan, 15th Anniv. — A715

Designs (both 10ch): #934, Red. #935, Maroon.

1970, Apr. 27 **Engr.**
934-935 A715 Set of 2 1.40 .40

Worker-Peasant Red Guard — A716

Design: 10ch (#936), Factory worker in uniform, vert.

1970, May 5 **Photo.**
936-937 A716 Set of 2 1.10 .40

Peasant Education — A717

Designs: 2ch, Students & newspapers. 5ch, Peasant reading book. 10ch, Students in class.

1970, June 25
938-940 A717 Set of 3 1.60 .45

Army Electrical Engineer A718

1970, June 25
941 A718 10ch purple brown .85 .20

Month of the Campaign for Withdrawal of U.S. Troops from South Korea — A719

Design: 10ch, Soldier & partisan.

1970, June 25
942-943 A719 Set of 2 1.50 .20

Anti-U.S., South Korea Propaganda — A720

1970, June 25 **Engr.**
944 A720 10ch deep violet .65 .20

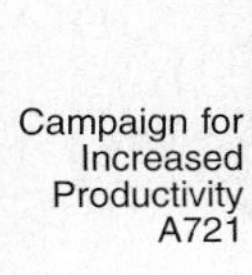

Campaign for Increased Productivity A721

Designs (all 10ch): #945, Quarryman. #946, Steelworker. #947, Machinist. #948, Worker with bag. #949, Construction worker. #950, Railway flagman.

1970, Sept. 10 **Photo.**
945-950 A721 Set of 6 4.50 1.20

Workers' Party Program A722

Designs: 5ch, Peasant, farm scene. 10ch, Steelworker. 40ch, Soldiers.

1970, Oct. 5 **Engr.**
951-953 A722 Set of 3 4.00 .50

Korean Workers' Party, 25th Anniv. — A723

1970, Oct. 10 **Photo.**
954 A723 10ch multicolored .85 .20

5th Korean Workers' Party Congress — A724

Issued in miniature sheet of 10, with one 40ch value (#955a) and nine 10ch values. Designs: a, Kim Il Sung, marchers. b, Family & apartment buildings. c, Soldier with Red Book. d, Soldier with binoculars, various weapons. e, Steelworker. f, Workers killing U.S. soldier. g, Farmers. h, Students. i, Schoolgirl with Red Book, atomic energy symbol. j, Cooperation with South Korean guerillas.

1970, Nov. 2 **Litho.**
955 Sheet of 10, #a.-j. 900.00
a.-i. A724 Any single 1.40 .50
j. A724 10ch 600.00

Soon after release, a design error was discovered on No. 955j, and this stamp was removed from souvenir sheets remaining in stock, usually with the bottom selvage. This is the form in which this set is commonly offered. Value, $25. The full sheet of 10 is scarce.

League of Socialist Working Youth of Korea, 25th Anniv. — A725

1971, Jan. 17 **Photo.**
956 A725 10ch multicolored .55 .20

Nanhutou Conference, 35th Anniv. — A726

1971, Feb. 28
957 A726 10ch multicolored .55 .20

Land Reform Law, 25th Anniv. A727

1971, Mar. 5
958 A727 2ch multicolored .55 .20

Mt. Paektu, Second Issue — A728

Designs: 2ch, Mountainscape. 5ch, Paektu Waterfalls, vert. 10ch, Western Peak.

1971, Mar. 10
959-961 A728 Set of 3 5.00 .60

Revolutionary Museums — A729

Designs (all 10ch): #962, Mangyongdae (red orange & ultramarine). #963, Phophyong (yellow & brown). #964, Junggang (salmon & green).

1971, Apr. 1
962-964 A729 Set of 3 1.60 .60

Coal Production 6-Year Plan — A730

1971, Apr. 1
965 A730 10ch multicolored .85 .20

Revolutionary Activities of Kim Il Sung — A731

Designs (all 10ch): #966, Portrait, vert. #967, Kim addressing crowd at guerrilla base camp. #968, Kim speaking with children on hillside. #969, Kim reviewing Anti-Japanese Guerrilla Army 1932.

1971, Apr. 15 **Litho.**
966-969 A731 Set of 4 3.25 .80

May Day — A732

1971, May 1 **Photo.**
970 A732 1w multicolored 3.75 .40

Association for the Restoration of the Fatherland, 35th Anniv. — A733

1971, May 5
971 A733 10ch multicolored .85 .20

Battles in the Musan Area Command (1939) — A734

Designs: 5ch, Sinsadong Monument. 10ch, Taehongdan Monument, with encased machine guns, horiz. 40ch, Musan headquarters (log cabins in forest), horiz.

1971, May 23
972-974 A734 Set of 3 2.25 .60

Koreans in Japan A735

1971, May 25
975 A735 10ch chocolate .65 .20

A 10ch stamp commemorating the Asia-Africa Invitational Table Tennis Game for Friendship was prepared for release on May 27, 1971, but was not issued. Value $750.

Korean Children's Union, 25th Anniv. — A736

1971, June 6
976 A736 10ch multicolored .55 .20

6th Congress, League of Socialist Working Youth of Korea — A737

Designs: 5ch, Marchers & banners. 10ch, Marchers, banners & globe with map of Korea.

1971, June 21
977-978 A737 Set of 2 1.10 .25

Labor Law, 25th Anniv. A738

1971, June 24
979 A738 5ch multicolored .60 .20

Sex Equality Law, 25th Anniv. A739

1971, July 30
980 A739 5ch multicolored .60 .20

A740

Universal Compulsory Primary Education, 15th Anniv.

1971, Aug. 1
981 A740 10ch multicolored .70 .20

South Korean Revolutionaries — A741

Designs: 5ch, Choe Yong Do (1923-69). 10ch (#983), Kim Jong Thae (1926-69), portrait with rioters killing U.S. soldier. 10ch (#984), Guerrilla fighter with machine gun & Red Book, battle scene.

1971, Aug. 1
982-984 A741 Set of 3 1.40 .45

Nationalization of Industry, 25th Anniv. — A742

1971, Aug. 10
985 A742 5ch multicolored 2.75 .20

Anti-Imperialist, Anti-U.S. Struggle — A743

Designs: 10ch (#986), N. Korean soldier, U.S. prisoners. 10ch (#987), S. Korean guerrilla fighter. 10ch (#988), N. Vietnamese soldiers, map. 10ch (#989), Cuban soldier, map. 10ch (#990), African guerrilla fighters, map. 40ch, six soldiers of various nationalities bayoneting dismembered U.S. soldier.

1971, Aug. 12
986-991 A743 Set of 6 5.00 1.00

Kim Il Sung University, 25th Anniv. A744

1971, Oct. 1
992 A744 10ch multicolored .55 .20

Large Machines — A745

Designs: 2ch, 6,000-ton press. 5ch, Refrigerated cargo ship "Ponghwasan." 10ch (#995), Sungrisan heavy truck. 10ch (#996), Bulldozer.

1971, Nov. 2 **Litho.**
993-996 A745 Set of 4 6.50 .50

Tasks of the 6-Year Plan — A746

Designs (all 10ch): #997, Workers & text on red field. #998, Mining. #999, Consumer goods. #1000, Lathe. #1001, Construction equipment. #1002, Consumer electronic products. #1003, Grains, farming. #1004, Railway track, transportation. #1005, Freighter. #1006, Hand with wrench, manufacturing scenes. #1007, Crate & export goods on dock.

1971, Nov. 2 **Photo.**
997-1007 A746 Set of 11 14.50 1.75

Cultural Revolution — A747

Designs: 2ch, Technical students, university. 5ch, Mechanic. 10ch (#1010), Chemist. 10ch (#1011), Composer at piano. 10ch (#1012), Schoolchildren.

1971, Nov. 2
1008-1012 A747 Set of 5 4.50 .40

Ideological Revolution — A748

Designs (all 10ch): #1013, Workers with Red Books, banners. #1014, Worker with hydraulic drill. #1015, Two workers reading Red Book. #1016, Workers' lecture.

1971, Nov. 2
1013-1016 A748 Set of 4 2.50 .40

Improvement in Living Standards — A749

1971, Nov. 2
1017 A749 10ch multicolored .60 .20

Solidarity with International Revolutionary Forces — A750

Designs (all 10ch): #1018, Revolutionary placards being driven into U.S. soldier. #1019, Japanese militarists being hammered by mallet. #1020, Bayoneted rifles held aloft. #1021, Armed international revolutionaries advancing, horiz.

1971, Nov. 2
1018-1021 A750 Set of 4 3.25 .50

6-Year Plan — A751

1971, Nov. 2
1022 A751 10ch multicolored 1.75 .20

Three sets were prepared for release on Nov. 2, 1971, but were not issued: Butterflies (3 stamps), value $2,500; Korean Reunification (2 10ch stamps), value $750; Cultural Revolution/Improvement of the People's Living Standards (7 10ch stamps), value $5,000.

Samil Wolgan Monthly, 35th Anniv. — A752

1971, Dec. 1
1023 A752 10ch multicolored 1.10 .20

Domestic Printings

Sometime in the early 1970s, the DPRK post office begin to produce separate printings of some issues for domestic use. These stamps were generally printed on poorer quality white or brownish unsurfaced papers and demonstrated poorer overall production values. Serious students of the period are now working to identify just which stamps exist in this form and how to easily distinguish them from the higher-quality printings intended for sale to foreign collectors. At this time, these domestic-use printings are generally sold for $5-$20 per stamp.

Poultry Breeding — A753

Designs: 5ch, Chicks. 10ch, Chickens & automated henhouse. 40ch, Eggs, canned chicken, dead chickens hanging on hooks.

1972, Feb. 1

1024-1026 A753 Set of 3 2.25 .60

War Films A754

Designs (all 10ch): #1027, Man & woman, from *Vintage Shrine.* #1028, Guerrilla bayoneting soldier in back, from *The Fate of a Self-Defense Corps Member.* #1029, Young woman with a pistol, from *Sea of Blood.*

1972, Apr. 1

1027-1029 A754 Set of 3 3.75 .30

A 10ch value picturing *The Flower Girl* was prepared but not issued. Value $2,000.

Kim Il Sung A755

Kim at Military Conference — A756

Kim by Lake Chon — A757

Various portraits of Kim Il Sung: #1030, shown. #1031, In heroic pose. #1032, shown. #1033, In wheatfield. #1034, In factory. #1035, With foundry workers. #1036, Aboard whaling ship. #1037, Visiting hospital. #1038, Visiting fruit farm. #1039, With railroad surveyors. #1040, With women workers. #1041, Sitting with villagers. #1042, Touring chicken plant. #1043, On park bench with children. #1044, Portrait with marchers.

1972, Apr. 15 **Litho.**

1030	A755 5ch multicolored	.20	.20
a.	Strip of 3, #1030-1031, 1044	2.25	
1031	A755 5ch multicolored	.20	.20
1032	A756 5ch multicolored	.20	.20
a.	Pair, #1032, 1043	1.10	
1033	A756 10ch multicolored	.50	.20
a.	Block of 10, #1033-1042	10.00	
1034	A756 10ch multicolored	2.25	.40
1035	A756 10ch multicolored	.20	.20
1036	A756 10ch multicolored	.65	.20
1037	A756 10ch multicolored	1.00	.20
1038	A756 10ch multicolored	.20	.20
1039	A756 10ch multicolored	2.25	.20
1040	A756 10ch multicolored	1.40	.20
1041	A756 10ch multicolored	.20	.20
1042	A756 10ch multicolored	.45	.20
1043	A755 40ch multicolored	.60	.20
1044	A756 1wn multicolored	.90	.40
	Nos. 1030-1044 (15)	11.20	3.40

Souvenir Sheet

1045 A757 3wn multicolored 10.00 6.00

60th birthday of Kim Il Sung.

Nos. 1030-1031 and 1044, 1032 and 1043, and 1033-1042, respectively, were printed setenant within their sheets.

A 4-stamp set (2ch, 5ch, 10ch and 15ch values) honoring the 20th Olympic Games were prepared but not issued. Value $3,000.

Guerrilla Army, 40th Anniv. — A758

1972, Apr. 25 **Photo.**

1046 A758 10ch multicolored .95 .20

Revolutionary Sites — A759

Designs: 2ch, Ryongpho. 5ch, Onjong. 10ch, Kosanjin. 40ch, Jonsung.

1972, July 27 **Litho.**

1047-1050 A759 Set of 4 2.25 .50

Olympic Games, Munich A760

Designs: 2ch, Volleyball. 5ch, Boxing, horiz. 10ch (#1053), Judo. 10ch (#1054), Wrestling, horiz. 40ch, Rifle-shooting.

1972, Oct. 1

1051-1055 A760 Set of 5 3.75 1.00

Chollima Street, Pyongyang — A761

Designs (street scenes): 5ch, salmon & black. 10ch (#1057), dull yellow & black. 10ch (#1058), green & black.

1972, Nov. 1

1056-1058 A766 Set of 3 5.50 .85

Resource Management — A762

Designs: 5ch, Dredging river. 10ch, Forest conservation. 40ch, Tideland reclamation.

1972, Nov. 1 **Photo.**

1059-1061 A762 Set of 3 2.75 .35

6-Year Plan - Metallurgical — A763

Designs (all 10ch): #1062, Sheet metal, ingots, smelters. #1063, Pipes, foundry.

1972, Nov. 1

1062-1063 A763 Set of 2 3.75 .35

6-Year Plan — Mining Industry — A764

Designs (all 10ch): #1064, Iron ore. #1065, Coal.

1972, Nov. 1 **Litho.**

1064-1065 A764 Set of 2 4.50 .45

Three Major Goals of the Technical Revolution — A765

Designs (all 10ch): #1066, Agricultural mechanization. #1067, Industrial automation. #1068, Lightening of women's household chores.

1972, Nov. 2 **Photo.**

1066-1068 A765 Set of 3 3.25 .45

6-Year Plan - Machine-Building — A766

Designs (all 10ch): #1069, Machine tools. #1070, Electronics & automation tools. #1071, Single-purpose machines.

1972, Nov. 2 **Photo.**

1069-1071 A766 Set of 3 2.75 .45

6-Year Plan — Chemical Industry — A767

Designs (all 10ch): #1072, Chemical fertilizers, herbicides, insecticides. #1073, Tire, tubing, various chemical products.

1972, Nov. 2

1072-1073 A767 Set of 2 2.25 .35

6-Year Plan — Light Industry — A768

Designs (all 10ch): #1074, Clothing, textiles. #1075, Clothing, kitchenware. #1076, Household Goods.

1972, Nov. 2

1074-1076 A768 Set of 3 2.75 .45

6-Year Plan - Rural Economy — A769

Designs (all 10ch): #1077, Irrigating field. #1078, Bulldozers levelling field. #1079, Applying chemical fertilizer.

1972, Nov. 2 **Litho.**

1077-1079 A769 Set of 3 2.50 .45

6-Year Plan - Transportation — A770

Designs (all 10ch): #1080, Electric train. #1081, New railway construction. #1082, Coastal & river transport.

1972, Nov. 2

1080-1082 A770 Set of 3 6.50 .45

6-Year Plan - Military — A771

Designs (all 10ch): #1083, Soldier with artillery shell. #1084, Navy gunner. #1085, Air Force pilot in cockpit.

1972, Nov. 2

1083-1085 A771 Set of 3 4.50 .45

6-Year Plan - Food Storage — A772

Designs (all 10ch): #1086, Food Processing. #1087, Packing foodstuffs. #1088, Food storage (radishes, fruit, fish).

1972, Nov. 2 **Photo.**
1086-1088 A772 Set of 3 8.25 .45

Struggle for Reunification of Korea — A773

Designs (all 10ch): #1089, South Koreans with banners praising Kim Il Sung. #1090, S. Korean guerrillas killing U.S. & S. Korean soldiers. #1091, March of armed S. Korean workers. #1092, S. Koreans rioting, rioters on top of U.S. tank. #1093, N. Koreans demonstrating in support of S. Korean revolutionaries. #1094, International revolutionaries condemning U.S. soldier. #1095, S. Korean marchers carrying banner & Red Book.

1972, Nov. 2
1089-1095 A773 Set of 7 11.00 1.00

A 10ch anti-United States propaganda stamp was prepared for release Nov. 2, 1972, but not issued. Value $750.

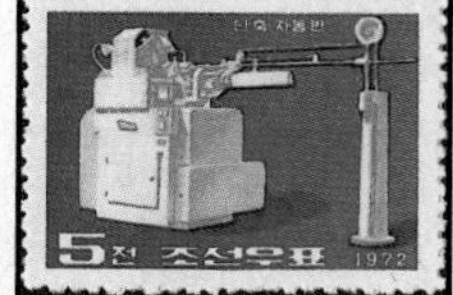

Machine Tools A774

Designs: 5ch, Single-axis automatic lathe. 10ch, *Kusong-3* lathe. 40ch, 2,000-ton crank press.

1972, Dec. 1 **Litho.**
1096-1098 A774 Set of 3 2.75 .45

National Elections A775

Designs (both 10ch): #1099, Voter with registration card. #1100, Voter casting ballot.

1972, Dec. 12 **Photo.**
1099-1100 A775 Set of 2 1.90 .30

Korean People's Army, 25th Anniv. — A776

Designs: 5ch, Soldier. 10ch, Sailor. 40ch, Pilot.

1973, Feb. 8
1101-1103 A781 Set of 3 3.75 .75

Mangyongdae Historic Sites — A777

Scenes from Kim Il Sung's childhood: 2ch, Wrestling site. 5ch, "Warship" rock. 10ch (#1106), Swinging tree, vert. 10ch (#1107), Sliding rock. 40ch, Fishing spot on riverside.

1973, Apr. 15
1104-1108 A777 Set of 5 4.50 1.00

Mansu Hill Monument A778

Designs: 10ch (#1109), Anti-Japanese revolutionary monument. 10ch (#1110), Socialist Revolution & Construction monument. 40ch, Statue of Kim Il Sung. 3w, Korean Revolution Museum, hrz.

1973, Apr. 15 **Litho.**
1109-1112 A778 Set of 4 13.00 2.25

Secret Revolutionary Camps in the 1932 Guerrilla War — A780

Designs: 10ch (#1113), Karajibong Camp. 10ch (#1114), Soksaegoi Camp.

1973, Apr. 26
1113-1114 A780 Set of 2 1.40 .20

Anti-Japanese Propaganda — A781

1973, June 1
1115 A781 10ch multicolored .55 .20

Reunification of Korea — A782

Designs: 2ch, Finger pointing down at destroyed U.S. tanks. 5ch, Electric train, crane lifting tractor. 10ch (#1118), Hand holding declaration, map of Korea. 10ch (#1119), Leaflets falling on happy crowd. 40ch, Flag & globe.

1973, June 23
1116-1120 A782 Set of 5 6.50 .75

Trucks & Tractors A783

Designs: 10ch (#1121), Trucks. 10ch (#1122), Bulldozer, tractors.

1973, July 1 **Photo.**
1121-1122 A783 Set of 2 1.60 .30

Socialist Countries' Junior Women's Volleyball Games — A784

1973, July 27 **Litho.**
1123 A784 10ch multicolored 1.10 .20

North Korean Victory in the Korean War A785

Designs: 10ch (#1124), Triumphant N. Koreans & battlefield scene. 10ch (#1125), N. Koreans & symbols of military & industrial power.

1973, July 27 **Photo.**
1124-1125 A785 Set of 2 3.25 .30

Mansudae Art Troupe — A786

Dances: 10ch, *Snow Falls,* dancers with red streamers. 25ch, *Bumper Harvest of Apples.* 40ch, *Azalea of the Fatherland.*

1973, Aug. 1 **Litho.**
1126-1128 A786 Set of 3 4.50 .75

Compulsory Secondary Education, 10th Anniv. A787

1973, Sept. 1
1129 A787 10ch multicolored .85 .20

Writings of Kim Il Sung — A788

Designs (all 10ch): #1130, *On Juche in Our Revolution* (claret scene). #1131, *Kim Il Sung Selected Works,* crowd holding glowing book aloft. #1132, *Let Us Further Strengthen Our Socialist System,* four figures holding open book aloft.

1973, Sept. 1
1130-1132 A788 Set of 3 1.90 .30

See Nos. 1180-1181.

DPRK, 25th Anniv. A789

Designs: 5ch, Foundation of the republic ("1948-1973"). 10ch, Korean War ("1950-1953"). 40ch, Farmer, worker & soldier with scenes of economic development in background ("1948-1973").

1973, Sept. 9
1133-1135 A789 Set of 3 2.75 .60

Mt. Myohyang Scenes — A790

Designs: 2ch, Popwang Peak. 5ch, Inhodae Rock. 10ch, Taeha Falls, vert. 40ch, Ryongyon Falls, vert.

1973, Oct. 1 **Photo.**
1136-1139 A790 Set of 4 8.25 .75

Party Founding Museum — A791

1973, Oct. 10
1140 A791 1w multicolored 2.25 .45

People's Athletic Meeting A792

Designs: 2ch, Soccer player, basketball players. 5ch, High jumper, women sprinters. 10ch (#1143), Wrestlers, skier. 10ch (#1144), Speed skaters, skier. 40ch, Parachutist, motorcyclists.

1973, Nov. 1 **Litho.**
1141-1145 A792 Set of 5 6.50 .75

Socialist Countries' Junior Weightlifting Competition A793

1973, Nov. 21
1146 A793 10ch multicolored 1.40 .20

Moran Hill Scenery — A794

Designs: 2ch, Chongryu Cliff. 5ch, Moran Waterfalls. 10ch, Pubyok Pavilion. 40ch, Ulmil Pavilion.

1973, Nov. 1
1147-1150 A794 Set of 4 9.25 1.00

Mt. Kumgang Scenery A795

Designs: 2ch, Mujigae (Rainbow) Bridge. 5ch, Suspension bridge, Okryu Valley, horiz. 10ch (#1153), Chonnyo Peak. 10ch (#1154), Chilchung Rock & Sonji Peak, horiz. 40ch, Sujong & Pari Peaks, horiz.

1973, Nov. 1
1151-1155 A795 Set of 5 8.25 1.00

Magnolia A796

1973, Nov. 1
1156 A796 10ch multicolored 2.25 .40

South Korean Revolutionary Struggle — A797

Designs (both 10ch): #1157, Mob beating U.S. soldier. #1158, Armed demonstrators killing U.S. soldier.

1973, Nov. 2 **Photo.**
1157-1158 A797 Set of 2 5.25 .30

Scenes from *Butterflies and Cock* Fairy Tale — A798

Designs: 2ch, Cock appearing in the village of butterflies. 5ch, Butterflies discussing how to repel cock. 10ch (#1161), Cock chasing butterflies with basket. 10ch (#1162), Butterflies luring cock up cliff. 40ch, Cock chasing butterflies off cliff edge. 90ch, Cock drowning.

1973, Dec. 1 **Litho.**
1159-1164 A798 Set of 6 17.50 1.20

Revolutionary Sites — A799

Designs: 2ch, Buildings, Yonphung. 5ch, Buildings, iron-rail fence, Hyangha. 10ch, Three buildings surrounding courtyard, Changgol. 40ch, Monuments in park-like setting, Paeksong.

1973, Dec. 1
1165-1168 A799 Set of 4 3.25 .60

Modern Buildings in Pyongyang — A800

Designs: 2ch, Science Library, Kim Il Sung University. 5ch, Building No. 2, Kim Il Sung University, vert. 10ch, War Museum. 40ch, People's Palace of Culture. 90ch, Pyongyang Indoor Stadium.

1973, Dec. 1 **Photo.**
1169-1173 A800 Set of 5 4.00 1.00

Socialist Constitution of North Korea — A801

Designs (all 10ch): #1174, Socialist Constitution, national scenes. #1175, Marchers with Red Book & national arms. #1176, Marchers with Red Books, national flag, banners.

1973, Dec. 27 **Litho.**
1174-1176 A801 Set of 3 1.60 .60

Korean Songbirds A802

Designs: 5ch, Great reed warbler. 10ch (#1178), Gray starling (green background). 10ch (#1179), Daurian starling (pink background).

1973, Dec. 28 **Photo.**
1177-1179 A802 Set of 3 14.50 2.00

Writings of Kim Il Sung A803

Designs (both 10ch): #1180, *Let Us Intensify the Anti-Imperialist, Anti-U.S. Struggle,* bayonets threatening U.S. soldier. #1181, *On the Chollima Movement and the Great Upsurge of Socialist Construction,*, Chollima statue.

1974, Jan. 10 **Litho.**
1180-1181 A803 Set of 2 1.60 .30

Opening of Pyongyang Metro — A804

Designs (all 10ch): #1182, Train at platform. #1183, Escalators. #1184, Underground station hall.

1974, Jan. 20
1182-1184 A804 Set of 3 2.75 .45

Socialist Construction — A805

Designs (all 10ch): #1185, Capital construction. #1186, Industry (foundry), vert. #1187, Agriculture. #1188, Transport. #1189, Fishing industry.

1974, Feb. 20
1185-1189 A805 Set of 5 6.50 1.00

Theses on the Socialist Rural Question in Our Country, 10th Anniv. of Publication — A806

1974, Feb. 25
1190 A806 10ch Strip of 3, #a-c 2.75 .50

Farm Machines A807

Designs: 2ch, Compost sprayer. 5ch, *Jonjin* tractor. 10ch, *Taedoksan* tractor (with flat bed).

1974, Feb. 25 **Photo.**
1193-1195 A807 Set of 3 3.25 .45

N. Korean Victories at 1973 Sports Contests A808

Designs: 2ch, Archery (Grenoble). 5ch, Gymnastics (Varna). 10ch, Boxing (Bucharest). 20ch, Volleyball (Pyongyang). 30ch, Rifle-shooting (Sofia). 40ch, Judo (Tbilisi). 60ch, Model aircraft flying (Vienna), horiz. 1.50w, Table tennis (Beijing), horiz.

Perf. 11, 12 (#1200, 1206)

1974, Mar. 10 **Litho.**
1196-1203 A808 Set of 8 11.00 2.00

D.P.R.K.: World's First Tax-Free Country — A809

1974, Apr. 1 ***Perf. 11***
1204 A809 10ch multicolored 1.10 .20

Revolutionary Activities of Kim Il Sung — A810

Designs (all 10ch): #1205, Kim at Nanhutou Meeting (in log room). #1206, Kim writing the 10-Point Program in forest. #1207, Kim instructing revolutionary (sitting on bench, outdoor winter scene). #1208, Kim at Battle of Laoheishan.

1974, Apr. 15 ***Perf. 12***
1205-1208 A810 Set of 4 3.00 .60

Scenes from the Revolutionary Opera *The Flower Girl* — A811

Designs: 2ch, Kkot Pun's blind younger sister. 5ch, Death of Kkot Pun's mother. 10ch, Kkot Pun resists landlord. 40ch, Kkot Pun setting out on the road of revolution.

1974, Apr. 30
1209-1212 A811 Set of 4 12.00 .60

Souvenir Sheet

1213 A811 50ch multicolored 16.50 1.50

No. 1213 contains one larger 50ch value, depicting Kroi Pun (The Flower Girl) and the flowers of Revolution, imperf.

Pyongyang Zoo, 15th Anniv. — A812

A813

Designs: 2ch, Wildcat. 5ch, Lynx. 10ch (#1216), Fox. 10ch (#1217), Wild boar. 20ch, Wolf. 40ch, Bear. 60ch, Leopard. 70ch, Korean tiger. 90ch, Lion.

1974, May 10 ***Perf. 11***
1214-1222 A812 Set of 9 14.50 2.50

Souvenir Sheet

1223 A813 Sheet of 4, imperf 60.00 —

Wild Roses — A814

Designs: 2ch, Prickly wild rose. 5ch, Yellow sweet briar. 10ch (#1226), Pink aromatic rose. 10ch (#1227), Aronia sweet briar (yellow centers). 40ch, Rosa rugosa.

1974, May 20
1224-1228 A814 Set of 5 8.25 1.00

Kim Il Sung with Children — A815

1974, June 1 ***Imperf***
1229 A815 1.20w Souv. Sheet 8.25 7.50

Wild Flowering Plants — A816

Designs: 2ch, Chinese trumpet vine. 5ch, Day lily. 10ch, Shooting star lily. 20ch, Tiger lily. 40ch, Azalea. 60ch, Yellow day lily.

1974, May 20 ***Perf. 11***
1230-1235 A816 Set of 6 8.25 1.00

U.P.U. Centenary — A817

Designs, U.P.U. emblem and: 10ch, Postwoman & construction site. 25ch, Chollima statue. 40ch, World map & airplanes.

1974, June 30 ***Perf. 12***
1236-1238 A817 Set of 3 6.00 .50

A 60ch souvenir sheet was prepared but not issued. Value $750.

Amphibians — A818

Designs: 2ch, Black spotted frog. 5ch, Oriental fire belly toad. 10ch, North American bull frog. 40ch, Common toad.

1974, July 10 ***Perf. 11***
1239-1242 A818 Set of 4 15.50 1.50

Soviet Space Flights — A819

Designs: 10ch, Electron 1 & 2. 20ch, Proton 1. 30ch, Venera 3. 40ch, Venera 5 & 6. 50ch, Launch of Chinese satellite Chicomsat 1. 1w, Space flight of dogs "Bjelka" and "Strjelka."

1974, July 10
1243-1246 A819 Set of 4 3.75 .60

Souvenir Sheets

Imperf

1247 A819 50ch multicolored 8.25 1.00
1248 A819 1w multicolored 18.50 3.00

Nos. 1247-1248 each contain one 47x72mm stamp.

Korean Paintings — A820

Designs: 2ch, *Woman in Namgang Village.* 5ch, *Old Man on the Raktong River.* 10ch, *Inner Kumgang in the Morning.* 20ch, *Mt. Kumgang.* 1.50w, *Evening Glow Over Kangson.*

1974, July 10
1249-1252 A820 Set of 4 5.75 .75

Souvenir Sheet

Imperf

1253 A820 1.50w multicolored 11.00 10.00

Korean Civil Aviation A821

Designs: 2ch, Antonov AN-2. 5ch, Lisunov LI-2. 10ch, Ilyushin IL-14P. 40ch, Antonov AN-24. 60ch, Ilyushin IL-18. 90ch, Antonov AN-24.

1974, Aug. 1
1254-1258 A821 Set of 5 9.25 1.75

Souvenir Sheet

Imperf

1259 A821 90ch multicolored 13.00 6.50

No. 1264 contains one 49x30mm stamp.

Alpine Plants — A822

Designs: 2ch, Rhododendron. 5ch, White mountain-avens. 10ch, Shrubby cinquefoil. 20ch, Poppies. 40ch, Purple mountain heather. 60ch, Oxytropis anertii.

1974, Aug. 10 ***Perf. 12***
1260-1265 A822 Set of 6 7.00 1.75

Korean Paintings — A823

Designs: 10ch, *Sobaek Stream in the Morning.* 20ch, *Combatants of Mt. Laohei.*. 30ch, *Spring on the Terraced Field.* 40ch, *Night of Tideland.* 60ch, *Daughter.*

1974, Aug. 15 ***Perf. 11***
1266-1270 A823 Set of 5 12.00 2.00

Italian Communist Newspaper L'Unita, 50th Anniv. — A824

1974, Sept. 1 ***Imperf***
1271 A824 1.50w multicolored 24.50 5.00

Revolutionary Sites — A825

Designs: 5ch, Munmyong. 10ch, Unha (log cabin).

1974, Sept. 9 ***Perf. 11***
1272-1273 A825 Set of 2 1.40 .20

Oil-producing Crops — A826

Designs: 2ch, Sesame. 5ch, Perilla-oil plant. 10ch, Sunflower. 40ch, Castor bean.

1974, Sept. 30
1274-1277 A826 Set of 4 5.50 1.00

Revolutionary Activities of Kim Il Sung — A827

Designs (all 10ch): #1278, Portrait in guerrilla uniform, vert. #1279, On horseback. #1280, Helping a farm family. #1281, Negotiating anti-Japanese united front with Chinese commander.

1974, Oct. 10 ***Perf. 12***
1278-1281 A827 Set of 4 3.25 .60

No. 1278 is 42x65mm. Nos. 1279-1281 are 52x34.5mm.

Grand Monument on Mansu Hill — A828

Designs (all 10ch): #1282, Soldiers marching right, lead figure holding rifle aloft. #1283, Soldiers marching left, lead figure holding rifle aloft. #1284, Workers marching right, lead figure holding torch aloft. #1285, Workers marching left, lead figure holding torch aloft.

1974, Oct. 10 ***Perf. 11***
1282-1285 A828 Set of 4 2.75 .60

Deep-Sea Fishing — A829

Designs: a, 2ch, Factory ship *Chilbosan.* b, 5ch, Factory ship *Paektusan.* c, 10ch, Cargo ship *Moranbong.* d, 20ch, All-purpose ship. e, 30ch, Trawler. f, 40ch, Stern trawler.

1974, Nov. 20
1286 A829 Block of 6 7.75 2.00
a.-f. Any single 1.25 .30

A830

Kim Il Sung's Crossing of the Amnok River, 50th Anniv.

1975, Feb. 3 ***Perf. 12***
1287 A830 10ch multicolored .65 .20

Pak Yong Sun — A831

33rd World Table Tennis Championships — A832

1975, Feb. 16 ***Perf. 11x12***
1288 A831 10ch multicolored 1.90 .20

Souvenir Sheet

Imperf

1289 A832 80ch multicolored 3.25 1.50

Honoring Pak Yong Sun, winner of the 33rd World Table Tennis Championship, Calcutta.

Pyongyang Zoo — A833

Designs: 10ch (#1290), Zebra. 10ch (#1291), African buffalo. 20ch, Giant panda, horiz. 25ch, Bactrian camel. 30ch, Indian elephant, horiz.

Perf. 12¼, 10¾ (#1291, 1294)

1975, Feb. 20
1290-1294 A833 Set of 5 6.25 1.00

Koguryo Period Tomb Paintings, 7th Century — A834

Designs: 10ch, Blue dragon. 15ch, White tiger. 25ch, Red phoenix, vert. 40ch, Turtle and snake.

1975, Mar. 20 ***Perf. 12***
1295-1298 A834 Set of 4 6.50 1.00

The Guerrilla Base in Spring (1968) — A835

Guerrilla Army Landing at Unggi (1969) — A836

The Sewing Team Members (1961) — A837

North Manchuria of China in Spring (1969) — A838

Comrade Kim Jong Suk Giving Guidance to the Children's Corps Members (1970) — A839

1975, Mar. 30
1299 A835 10ch multicolored .55 .20
1300 A836 10ch multicolored .55 .20
1301 A837 15ch multicolored .85 .20
1302 A838 20ch multicolored 1.75 .20
1303 A839 30ch multicolored 1.40 .20
Nos. 1299-1303 (5) 5.10 1.00

Korean Paintings, Anti-Japanese Struggle. Compare with Nos. 1325-1329, 1330-1335.

Cosmonauts' Day — A840

Designs: 10ch, Cosmonaut. 30ch, Lunokhod-2 on Moon, horiz. 40ch, Soyuz and Saiyut coupling, horiz.

1975, Apr. 12 ***Perf. 11¾***
1304-1306 A840 Set of 3 3.25 .50

Revolutionary Activities of Kim Il Sung — A841

Multicolor portraits of Kim Il Sung: 10ch (#1307), Speaking with troops in tent (aqua frame). 10ch (#1308), Greeting peasants bringing supplies (tan frame). 10ch (#1309), Speaking to crowd, arm upraised (light blue frame). 10ch (#1310), With soldiers around winter campfire (pale tan frame). 10ch (#1311), Lecturing to troops (pink frame). 15ch, At head of troop column in forest. 25ch, Standing by lake. 30ch, Speaking with peasants, child in lap. 40ch, Presiding over staff meeting, in tent.

1975, Apr. 15 ***Perf. 12***
1307-1315 A841 Set of 9 8.25 2.00

Souvenir Sheet

Victory Monument — A842

1975, Apr. 15 ***Imperf***
1316 A842 1w multicolored 16.50 4.00

Battle of Pochonbo, 38th Anniversary.

Flower Basket & Kim Il Sung's Birthplace A843

Kim Il Sung's Birthplace, Mangyongdae — A844

1975, Apr. 15 ***Perf. 12***
1317 A843 10ch multicolored .35 .20
1318 A844 40ch multicolored 1.60 .20

63rd Birthday of Kim Il Sung.

April 19 South Korean Popular Uprising, 15th Anniv. — A845

1975, Apr. 19 ***Perf. 11***
1319 A845 10ch multicolored .65 .20

Ri Dynasty Paintings A846

Designs: 5ch, *Kingfisher at Lotus Pond.* 10ch, *Crabs.* 15ch, *Rose of Sharon.* 25ch, *Lotus and Water Bird.* 30ch, *Tree Peony and Cock and Hen.*

1975, May 10
1320-1324 A846 Set of 5 13.00 1.25

On the Road of Advance Southward (1966) A847

The Assigned Post (1968) A848

For the Sake of the Fatherland (1965) — A849

Retaliation (1970) — A850

The Awaited Ranks (1970) — A851

1975, May 10

1325	A847	5ch multicolored	2.25	.20
1326	A848	10ch multicolored	1.25	.20
1327	A849	15ch multicolored	1.90	.20
1328	A850	25ch multicolored	2.75	.25
1329	A851	30ch multicolored	4.50	.25
		Nos. 1325-1329 (5)	12.65	1.10

Korean Paintings, Anti-Japanese Struggle.

Blue Signal Lamp (1960) A852

Pine Tree (1966) A853

Night with Snowfall (1963) — A854

Smelters (1968) — A855

Reclamation of Tideland (1961) — A856

Mt. Paekgum (1966) — A857

1975, May 20

1330	A852	10ch multicolored	1.10	.20
1331	A853	10ch multicolored	3.75	.20
1332	A854	15ch multicolored	1.10	.20
1333	A855	20ch multicolored	1.25	.20
1334	A856	25ch multicolored	1.25	.20
1335	A857	30ch multicolored	1.25	.20
		Nos. 1330-1335 (6)	9.70	1.20

Korean Paintings.

Chongryon Assoc. of Koreans in Japan, 20th Anniv. — A858

1975, May 25 ***Perf. 11¾***

1336	A858	10ch multicolored	1.10	—
1337	A858	3w multicolored	40.00	—

Marathon Race of Socialist Countries — A859

1975, June 8 ***Imperf***

1338 A859 1w multicolored 22.50 4.00

Diving — A860

Divers: 10ch, Man entering water feet-first. 25ch, Man performing somersalt pike. 40ch, Woman entering water head-first.

1975, June 20 ***Perf. 10¾***

1339-1341 A860 Set of 3 3.25 .75

Month of Anti-U.S. Joint Struggle — A861

1975, June 25 ***Perf. 12¼***

1342 A861 10ch multicolored 1.40 .20

Fresh-Water Fish — A862

Fish: 10ch (#1343), Memorial fish, swimming to left. 10ch (#1344), White fish, swimming to right. 15ch, Notch-jowl. 25ch, Amur catfish. 30ch (#1347), Catfish, swimming to right. 30ch (#1348), Snakehead, swimming to left.

1975, June 25 ***Perf. 10¾***

1343-1348 A862 Set of 6 9.25 1.25

10th International Socialist Countries' Junior Friendship Soccer Tournament

A863

A864

Soccer players, with diff. stadiums in background: 5ch, Green border. 10ch, Tan border. 15ch, Lilac border. 20ch, Pale violet border. 50ch, Dull gold border.

Perf. 10¾, Imperf (#1354)

1975, July 10

1349-1353 A863 Set of 5 4.50 1.00

Souvenir Sheet

1354 A864 1w multicolored 9.25 3.50

Parrots — A865

Parrots: 10ch, Blue & yellow macaw. 15ch, Sulphur-crested cockatoo. 20ch, Blyth's parakeet. 25ch, Rainbow lory. 30ch, Budgerigar.

1975, July 10 ***Perf. 12***

1355-1359 A865 Set of 5 19.50 1.50

Saesallim Street A866

Apartment House — A867

Pothonggang Hotel — A868

1975, July 20 ***Perf. 11, 12 (#1360)***

1360	A866	90ch multicolored	20.00	20.00
1361	A867	1w multicolored	25.00	25.00
1362	A868	2w multicolored	35.00	35.00
		Nos. 1360-1362 (3)	80.00	80.00

New street, buildings in Pyongyang.

Blossoms A869

Blossoms of Flowering Trees: 10ch, White peach. 15ch, Red peach. 20ch, Red plum. 25ch, Apricot. 30ch, Cherry.

1975, Aug. 20 ***Perf. 10¾***

1363-1367 A869 Set of 5 7.75 1.50

Diamond Mts. Landscapes A870

Designs: 5ch, Sejon Peak. 10ch, Chonson Rock. 15ch, Pisa Gate. 25ch, Manmulsang. 30ch, Chaeha Peak.

1975, Aug. 20 ***Perf. 11¾***

1368-1372 A870 Set of 5 7.75 1.00

Flowers A871

Designs: 5ch, Azalea. 10ch, White azalea. 15ch, Mountain rhododendron. 20ch, White rhododendron. 25ch, Rhododendron. 30ch, Yellow rhododendron.

1975, Aug. 30 ***Perf. 10¾***
1373-1378 A871 Set of 6 6.50 1.50

Aerial Sports for National Defence

A872

A873

Designs: 5ch (#1379), Gliders. 5ch (#1380), Remote-controlled model airplane. 10ch (#1381), Parachutist in free fall, vert. 10ch (#1382), Parachutists landing, vert. 20ch, Parachutist with bouquet of flowers.
50ch, Formation skydiving.

Perf. 12x11¾, Imperf (#1384)

1975, Sept. 9
1379-1383 A872 Set of 5 5.00 .75

Souvenir Sheet

1384 A873 50ch multicolored 6.00 .50

Flowers — A874

Fruit tree blossoms: 10ch, Wild apple. 15ch, Wild pear. 20ch, Hawthorn. 25ch, Chinese quince. 30ch, Flowering quince.

1975, Sept. 30 ***Perf. 12¼x12***
1385-1389 A874 Set of 5 5.00 1.25

Korean Workers' Party, 30th Anniv. A875

Designs: 2ch (#1390), Symbolic creation of the Juche Idea. 2ch (#1391), Korean soldiers above American graves. 5ch (#1392), Hand holding torch with Juche inscription. 5ch (#1393), Monument of Chollima, idealized city. 10ch (#1394), Chollima winged horse and rider with banner. 10ch (#1395), Worker with Red Book. 25ch, South Koreans rioting. 70ch, Map of Korea, Red Book, flowers.
90ch (#1398), Kim Il Sung addressing workers, horiz. stamp, vert. souvenir sheet. 90ch (#1399), Kim with crowd of workers, city skyline in background, horiz. stamp, horiz. souvenir sheet.

Perf. 12, Imperf (#1398-1399)

1975, Oct. 10
1390-1397 A875 Set of 8 4.50 1.00
1398-1399 A875 Set of 2 sheets 8.25 4.00

Return of Kim Il Sung to Pyongyang, 30th Anniv. — A876

1975, Oct. 14 ***Perf. 12***
1400 A876 20ch multicolored 1.00 .20

Redong Sinmun, 30th Anniv. — A877

1975, Nov. 1 ***Perf. 11***
1401 A877 10ch multicolored .85 .20
a. 1w, souvenir sheet, imperf 5.50 5.00

Hyonmu Gate A878

Taedong Gate A879

Pothong Gate A880

Jongum Gate A881

Chilsong Gate — A882

Perf. 12x12¼, 12¼x12 (#1406)

1975, Nov. 20
1402 A878 10ch multicolored 1.40 .20
1403 A879 10ch multicolored 1.40 .20
1404 A880 15ch multicolored 1.90 .20
1405 A881 20ch multicolored 3.50 .20
1406 A882 30ch multicolored 5.00 .40
Nos. 1402-1406 (5) 13.20 1.20

Ancient gates of Pyongyang.

Mt. Chilbo Views — A883

Designs: 10ch (#1407), Mae Rock (pale green border). 10ch (#1408), Jangsu Peak (pale yellow border). 15ch, Suri Peak. 20ch, Jangsu Peak, diff. view. 30ch, Rojok Peak.

1975, Nov. 30 ***Perf. 12x11¾***
1407-1411 A883 Set of 5 10.00 1.25

Wangjaesan Monument — A884

Designs: 10ch, Workers marching. 15ch, Soldiers marching. 25ch, Monument beacon tower, vert. 30ch, Base of tower, statues of Kim Il Sung, workers and soldiers.

Perf. 11¾, 10¾ (#1413)

1975, Dec. 20
1412-1415 A884 Set of 4 2.75 .75

Banners, Slogan — A885

Banners, Workers — A886

1976, Jan. 17 ***Perf. 12***
1416 A885 2ch multicolored .30 .20
1417 A886 70ch multicolored 1.60 .75

League of Socialist Working Youth, 30th Anniv.

Ducks & Geese A887

Designs: 10ch, Geese. 20ch, Domesticated ducks. 40ch, Kwangpo ducks.

Perf. 12, 12x12¼ (#1418)

1976, Feb. 5
1418-1420 A887 Set of 3 8.25 .50

Korean People's Army, Sculpture A888

Designs: 5ch, *Oath.* 10ch (#1422), *Unity Between Men and Officers*, horiz. 10ch (#1423), *This Flag to the Height.*

Perf. 12, 12¼x12 (#1421)

1976, Feb. 8
1421-1423 A888 Set of 3 2.75 .50

Rural Road at Evening (1965) A889

Passing-on Technique (1970) — A890

Mother (1965) A891

Medical Examination in Kindergarten (1970) — A892

Doctress of the Village (1970) — A893

1976, Feb. 10 ***Perf. 12***

1424 A889 10ch multicolored	.65	.20
1425 A890 15ch multicolored	.70	.20
1426 A891 25ch multicolored	1.10	.20
1427 A892 30ch multicolored	1.90	.20
1428 A893 40ch multicolored	2.25	.35
Nos. 1424-1428 (5)	6.60	1.15

Modern Korean paintings.

Agrarian Reform Law, 30th Anniv. — A894

1976, Mar. 5 ***Perf. 12***
1429 A894 10ch multicolored .65 .20

Telephone Communication Centenary — A895

Designs: 2ch, Telephones and communication satellite. 5ch, Satellite and antenna. 10ch, Satellite and telecommunications systems. 15ch, Telephone and lineman. 25ch, Satellite and map of receiving stations. 40ch, Satellite and cable-laying barge.
50ch, Satellite and antique telephone.

Surface Coated Paper

1976, Mar. 12 ***Perf. 13¼***
1430-1435 A895 Set of 6 8.75 1.00
1435a Sheet of 8, as #1430-1436 + label, ordinary paper 10.00 —

Souvenir Sheet

Imperf, Without Gum

1436 A895 50ch multicolored 3.25 .50

Flowers A896

Designs: 5ch, Cosmos. 10ch, Dahlia. 20ch, Zinnia. 40ch, China aster.

1976, Mar. 20 ***Perf. 12***
1437-1440 A896 Set of 4 3.00 1.00

Pukchong Conference, 15th Anniv. — A897

Designs: 5ch, Fruit processing industry. 10ch, Fruit and orchards.

1976, Apr. 7 ***Perf. 11½x12***
1441-1442 A897 Set of 2 2.25 .25

Locomotives — A898

Designs: 5ch, *Pulgungi* electric train. 10ch, *Jaju* underground electric train. 15ch, *Saeppyol* diesel locomotive.

1976, Apr. 10 ***Perf. 11¾***
1443-1445 A898 Set of 3 3.25 .50

Many North Korean issues from 1976-on were also issued imperforate. These imperfs were issued for sale for hard currency, mostly to overseas collectors, and were not valid for postage.

Limited quantities of many sets from Scott No. 1446-on were issued without gum.

Day of Space Flight — A899

Designs: 2ch, Satellite. 5ch, Space station. 10ch, Communications satellite. 15ch, Future space station. 25ch, Satellite. 40ch, Communications satellite.
50ch, Lunar surface vehicle.

1976, Apr. 12 ***Perf. 13¼***
1446-1451 A899 Set of 6 3.25 1.00

Souvenir Sheet

Imperf

1452 A899 50ch multicolored 1.60 .50

A900

Kim Il Sung, 64th Birthday — A901

1976, Apr. 15 ***Perf. 12***
1453 A900 10ch multicolored .85 .20

Souvenir Sheet

Imperf

1454 A901 40ch multicolored 5.00 .75

A902

3rd Asian Table Tennis Championships — A903

Designs: 5ch, Paddle and ribbon. 10ch, Three female players with bouquet. 20ch, Female player. 25ch, Male player.

Without Gum

1976, Apr. 25 ***Perf. 12***
1455-1458 A902 Set of 4 2.50 1.00

Souvenir Sheet

Imperf

1459 A903 50ch multicolored 2.50 .75

Association for the Restoration of the Fatherland, 40th Anniv. — A904

1976, May 5 ***Perf. 12***
1460 A904 10ch multicolored .50 .20

Pheasants — A905

Designs: 2ch, Golden pheasant. 5ch, Lady Amherst's pheasant. 10ch, Silver pheasant. 15ch, Reeves' pheasant. 25ch, Copper pheasant. 40ch, Albino ring-necked pheasant.
50ch, Ring-necked pheasant.

Surface Coated Paper

1976, May 5 ***Perf. 11¾***
1461-1466 A905 Set of 6 5.00 1.50
1466a Sheet of 8, as #1461-1467 + label, perf 12, ordinary paper 7.50 7.50

Souvenir Sheet

Imperf

1467 A905 50ch multicolored 3.50 1.50

Potong River Monument A906

1976, May 21 ***Perf. 11½***
1468 A906 10ch multicolored 75.00 —

21st Olympic Games, Montreal — A907

Stadium, Olympic rings, and: 2ch, Runners. 5ch, Diver. 10ch, Judo. 15ch, Gymnast. 25ch, Gymnast. 40ch, Fencers.
50ch, Runner with Olympic Torch.

Surface Coated Paper

1976, July 17 ***Perf. 13¾***
1469-1474 A907 Set of 6 5.00 1.00
1474a Sheet of 8, as #1469-1475 + label, perf 12, ordinary paper 9.00 —

Souvenir Sheet

Imperf

1475 A907 50ch multicolored 3.50 1.50

For overprints, see Nos. 1632-1638.

Winners, 21st Olympic Games, Montreal A908

Designs: 2ch, Bronze Medal, Hockey — Pakistan. 5ch, Bronze Medal, Free Pistol — Rudolf Dollinger (Austria). 10ch, Silver Medal, Boxing — Li Byong Uk (DPRK). 15ch, Silver Medal, Cycling — Daniel Morelon (France). 25ch, Gold Medal, Marathon — Waldemar Cierpinski (DDR). 40ch, Gold Medal, Boxing — Ku Yong Jo (DPRK).
50ch, Gold, Silver, Bronze Medals.

Multicolored, with Winners' Inscriptions in Silver

Surface Coated Paper

1976, Aug. 2 ***Perf. 13¼***

1476-1481 A908 Set of 6 6.00 1.00

1481a Sheet of 8, as #1476-1482 + label 9.00 —

Souvenir Sheet

Imperf

1482 A908 50ch multicolored 4.00 2.00

Same, with Different Winners' Names

Designs: 2ch, Swimming — David Wilkie (UK). 5ch, Running — Lass Viren (Finland). 10ch, Weight Lifting — Vasili Alexeev (USSR). 15ch Swimming — Kornelia Ender (DDR). 25ch, Platform Diving — Klaus Dibiasi (Italy). 40ch, Boxing — Ku Yong Jo (DPRK). 50ch, Gymnastics — Nadia Comaneci (Romania),

Ordinary Paper

Perf. 13¼

1483-1489 A908 Sheet of 7 + label 10.00 4.00

Souvenir Sheet

Imperf

1490 A908 50ch ovptd. "Kornelia Ender" 4.00 2.00

For overprints, see Nos. 1639-1645.

Winners, 21st Olympic Games, Montreal A909

Designs: 2ch, Boxing — Ku Yong Jo (DPRK). 5ch, Gymastics — Nadie Comaneci (Romania). 10ch, Pole Vault — Tadeusz Slusarski (Poland). 15ch, Hurdling — Guy Drut (France). 25ch, Cycling — Bernt Johansson (Sweden). 40ch, Soccer (DDR).
50ch, Boxing — Ko Yong Do (DPRK).

Surface Coated Paper

1976, Aug. 2 ***Perf. 13¼***

1491-1496 A909 Set of 6 4.50 1.00

1496a Sheet of 12, as #1491-1497 + 5 labels, ordinary paper 8.00 —

Souvenir Sheet

Imperf

1497 A909 50ch multicolored 3.00 .50

International Activities — A910

Designs: 2ch, UPU Headquarters, Bern. 5ch, World Cup. 10ch, Montreal Olympics Stadium. 15ch, Runner with Olympic Torch. 25ch, Satellite, junk. 40ch, Satellites.
50ch, World map.

Surface Coated Paper

1976, Aug. 5 ***Perf. 13¼***

1506-1511 A910 Set of 6 5.00 1.50

1511a Sheet of 8, as #1505-1512 + label, ordinary paper 7.00 —

Souvenir Sheet

Imperf

1512 A910 50ch multicolored 2.50 2.50

For overprints, see Nos. 1646-1652.

Embroidery — A911

Designs: 2ch, "Marsh Magpies." 5ch, "Golden Bird." 10ch, "Deer." 15ch, "Golden Bird." 25ch, "Fairy." 40ch, "Tiger."
50ch, "Tiger."

Surface Coated Paper

1976, Aug. 8 ***Perf. 12***

1513-1518 A911 Set of 6 7.50 1.50

1518a Sheet of 8, as #1513-1519 + label, perf 13¾, ordinary paper 18.00 —

Souvenir Sheet

Imperf

1519 A911 50ch multicolored 4.00 .50

Model Airplane Championships (1975) — A912

Designs: 5ch, Trophy, certificate and medal. 10ch, Trophy and medals. 20ch, Model airplane and emblem. 40ch, Model glider and medals.

Without Gum

1976, Aug. 15 ***Perf. 12***

1520-1523 A912 Set of 4 4.75 1.00

5th Summit Conference of Non-Aligned States — A913

Without Gum

1976, Aug. 16

1524 A913 10ch multicolored .50 .20

Locomotives — A914

Designs: 2ch, "Pulgungi" diesel locomotive. 5ch, "Saeppyol" diesel locomotive. 10ch, "Saeppyol" diesel locomotive (diff.). 15ch, Electric train. 25ch, "Kumsong" diesel locomotive. 40ch, "Pulgungi" electric locomotive.
50ch, "Kumsong" diesel locomotive.

Surface Coated Paper

1976, Sept. 14 ***Perf. 12x11¾***

1525-1530 A914 Set of 6 5.50 1.00

1530a Sheet of 8, as #1525-1531 + label, perf 10½ 15.00 —

Souvenir Sheet

Imperf

1531 A914 50ch multicolored 6.00 3.50

House of Culture A915

Without Gum

1976, Oct. 7 ***Perf. 12***

1532 A915 10ch black & brown 75.00 —

Revolutionary Activities of Kim Il Sung — A916

Kim Il Sung: 2ch, Visiting the Tosongrang. 5ch, With peasants on hillside. 10ch, With boy and man at seashore. 15ch, Giving house to farm-hand. 25ch, On muddy road at front, with driver and girl. 40ch, Walking in rain with umbrella.
50ch, Watching boy draw picture by roadside.

1976, Oct. 10 ***Perf. 13¼***

1533-1538 A916 Set of 6 3.00 .75

Souvenir Sheet

Imperf

1539 A916 50ch multicolored 2.00 1.50

Down-With-Imperialism Union, 50th Anniv. — A917

Without Gum

1976, Oct. 17 ***Perf. 12***

1540 A917 20ch black & brown 1.00 .20

21st Olympic Games, Montreal A918

Olympic Rings, stadium and: 5ch, Fencer. 10ch, Weightlifter. 15ch, Horse racer. 20ch, Runner. 25ch, Shot putter. 40ch, Basketball player.
60ch, Yacht race.

Simulated 3-D Printing Using Plastic Overlays

1976, Dec. 21 ***Imperf.***

1541-1546 A918 Set of 6 25.00 25.00

Souvenir Sheet

1547 A918 60ch multicolored 45.00 45.00

No. 1547 Overprinted with Gold Medal Winners' Names, Events

1548 A918 60ch multicolored — —

New Year — A919

Without Gum

1977, Jan. 1 ***Perf. 12¼x12***

1549 A919 20ch black & brown .50 .20

21st Olympic Games, Montreal (1976) — A920

Designs: 5ch, Reverse of Bronze Medal, Montreal skyline. 10ch, Obverse of Bronze Medal, diff. Montreal skyline. 15ch, Obverse of Silver Medal, stadium. 20ch, Reverse of Silver Medal, stadium. 25ch, Reverse of Gold Medal, Olympic Flame. 40ch, Obverse of Gold Medal, Olympic Flame.
60ch, Gold, Silver and Bronze Medals.

Simulated 3-D Printing Using Plastic Overlays

1977, Jan. 23 ***Imperf.***

1550-1555 A920 Set of 6 25.00 25.00

Souvenir Sheet

1556 A920 60ch multicolored 55.00 55.00

No. 1556 Overprinted with Gold Medal Winners' Names, Events

1557 A920 60ch multicolored — —

National Costumes of Li Dynasty A921

Seasonal costumes: 10ch, Spring. 15ch, Summer. 20ch, Autumn. 40ch, Winter.

1977, Feb. 10 ***Perf. 11¾x12***

1558-1561 A921 Set of 4 3.50 .75

1561a Sheet of 4, #1558-1561 5.00 —

No. 1561 is airmail.

Korean Cultural Relics (5th-12th Centuries) A922

Designs: 2ch, Two Deva kings, Koguryo Dynasty. 5ch, Gold-copper ornament, Koguryo Dynasty. 10ch, Bronze Buddha, Koguryo Dynasty. 15ch, Gold-copper Buddha, Paekje Dynasty. 25ch, Gold crown, Koguryo Dynasty, horiz. 40ch, Gold-copper ornament, Koguryo Dynasty, horiz. 50ch, Gold crown, Silla Dynasty.

1977, Feb. 26 ***Perf. 13¼***

1562-1568 A922 Set of 7 5.00 1.50
1568a Sheet of 8, #1562-1568 + label 6.00 —

No. 1568 is airmail.

Five-Point Program for Land Development — A923

Without Gum

1977, Mar. 5 ***Perf. 12***

1569 A923 10ch multicolored .50 .20

21st Olympic Games, Montreal (1976) A924

Events, winner's name, nationality, and: 5ch, Cycling. 10ch, Weightlifting. 15ch, Judo. 20ch, Wrestling. 25ch, Football (soccer). 40ch, Boxing.
60ch, Boxing.

Simulated 3-D Printing Using Plastic Overlays

1977, Mar.8 ***Imperf.***

1570-1575 A924 Set of 6 45.00 45.00

Souvenir Sheet

1576 A924 60ch multicolored — —

Korean National Association, 60th Anniv. — A925

Without Gum

1977, Mar. 23 ***Perf. 11¾***

1577 A925 10ch multicolored .65 .20

34th World Table-Tennis Championships — A926

Designs: 10ch, Emblem and trophy. 15ch, Pak Yong Sun. 20ch, Pak Yong Sun with trophy. 40ch, Pak Yong Ok and Yang Ying with trophy.

1977, Apr. 5 ***Perf. 12***

1578-1581 A926 Set of 4 3.25 .75

No. 1581 is airmail.

Kim Il Sung, 65th Birthday — A927

Painting of Kim Il Sung: 2ch, Leading Mingyuehkou Meeting. 5ch, Commanding encirclement operation. 10ch, Visiting workers in Kangson. 15ch, Before battle. 25ch, Visiting school. 40ch, Looking over grain fields.

1977, Apr. 15 ***Perf. 12***

1582-1587 A927 Set of 6 2.25 .50

Souvenir Sheet

Imperf

1588 A927 50ch multicolored 1.50 .90

Trolley Buses A928

Designs: 5ch, "Chollima 72." 10ch, "Chollima 74."

Without Gum

1977, Apr. 20 ***Perf. 12***

1589-1590 A928 Set of 2 3.00 .20

Korean People's Revolutionary Army, 45th Anniv. — A929

Without Gum

1977, Apr. 25 ***Perf. 12***

1591 A929 40ch multicolored 1.50 .20

Battle of Pochonbo, 40th Anniv. — A930

Without Gum

1977, June 4 ***Perf. 13¼***

1592 A930 10ch multicolored .50 .20

Porcelain A931

Designs: 10ch, White ceramic teapot, Koryo dynasty. 15ch, White ceramic vase, Ri dynasty. 20ch, Celadon vase, Koryo dynasty. 40ch, Celadon vase, Koryo dynasty, diff.

1977, June 10 ***Perf. 13¼***

1593-1596 A931 Set of 4 3.50 .75
1596a Sheet of 4, #1593-1596 7.00 .95

No. 1596 is airmail.

Postal Service A932

Designs: 2ch, Railway, ship and trucks. 10ch, Postwoman delivering mail. 30ch, Mil Mi-8 helicopter. 40ch, Airliner and world map.

Without Gum

1977, June 28 ***Perf. 13¼***

1597-1600 A932 Set of 4 4.00 1.00

A 3-stamp set and souvenir sheet commemorating the Second Conference of Third World Youth was prepared for release July 1, 1977, but was not issued. Value $3,500.

Butterflies — A933

Designs: 2ch, Rapala arata. 5ch, Colias aurora. 10ch, Limenitis populi. 15ch, Anax partherope julius. 25ch, Sympetrum pedemontanum elatum.
50ch, Papilio maackii.

1977, July 25 ***Perf. 12x12¼***

1601-1606 A933 Set of 6 7.00 1.00
1606a Sheet of 6, #1601-1606 15.00 —

No. 1606 is airmail.

Cats and Dogs

A934

A935

Cats: 2ch, Gray cat. 10ch, Black and white cat. 25ch, Ginger cat.
Dogs: 5ch, Brindled dog. 15ch, Chow. 50ch, Pungsang.

1977, Aug. 10 ***Perf. 11¾x12***

1607-1609 A934 Set of 3 6.00 .50
1609a Sheet of 3, #1607-1609 8.00 —
1610-1612 A935 Set of 3 4.00 .50
1612a Sheet of 3, #1610-1612 6.00 —

No. 1612 is airmail.

Visit of Pres. Tito of Yugoslavia A936

1977, Aug. 25 ***Perf. 12***

1613-1616 A936 Set of 4 40.00 8.00

11-Year Compulsory Education, 5th Anniv. — A937

Without Gum

1977, Sept. 1 ***Perf. 13¼x13½***

1617 A937 10ch multicolored .50 .20

Shell-Fish and Fish — A938

Designs: 2ch, Mactra sulcataria. 5ch, Natica fortunel. 10ch, Arca inflata. 25ch, Rapana thomasiana. 50ch, Sphoeroides porphyreus.

1977, Sept. 5 ***Perf. 11¾x12***

1618-1622 A938 Set of 5 5.00 1.00
1622a Sheet of 6, #1618-1622 + label 9.00 —

No. 1622 is airmail.

Publication of Kim Il Sung's *Theses on Socialist Education* A939

Designs: 10ch, Students, banners and *Theses.* 20ch, Students, crowd and *Theses.*

1977, Sept. 5

1623-1624 A939 Set of 2 1.00 .20

Int'l Seminar on the Juche Idea — A940

Designs: 2ch, Juche Torch. 5ch, Interracial crowd holding copies of Kim's Red Book. 10ch, Chollima statue, flags. 15ch, Joined hands of different races, banner and globe. 25ch, Map of Korea. 40ch, Crowd and slogan. 50ch, Seminar emblem.

1977, Sept. 14 ***Perf. 11¾x12***

1625-1630 A940 Set of 6 3.50 .60

Souvenir Sheet

Imperf

1631 A940 50ch multicolored 3.00 1.00

Stamps of 1976 Overprinted

Methods & Perfs as Before

1977, Nov. 8

On Montreal Olympics, #1469-1474

1632-1637 A907 Set of 6 9.00 —
1637a On #1474a, sheet of 8 10.00 —

Souvenir Sheet

Imperf

1638 A907 50ch multicolored 5.00 —

On Montreal Olympics Medal Winners, #1476-1482

1639-1644 A908 Set of 6 13.00 —
1644a On #1481a, sheet of 8 15.00 —

Souvenir Sheet

Imperf

1645 A908 50ch multicolored 5.00 —

On International Activities, #1506-1512

1646-1651 A910 Set of 6 10.00 —
1651a On #1511a, sheet of 8 15.00 —

Souvenir Sheet

Imperf

1652 A910 50ch multicolored 5.00 —

Amphilex '77 International Stamp Exhibition, Amsterdam.

Election of Deputies, Supreme People's Assembly A941

1977, Nov. 11 ***Perf. 12¼x12***

1653 A941 10ch multicolored .50 .20

Argentina '78, World Soccer Championship — A942

Designs: 10ch, Defense. 15ch, Attack. 40ch, Tackle. 50ch, Shot.

1977, Dec. 10 ***Perf. 13½***

1654-1656 A942 Set of 3 3.50 .75
1656a Sheet of 4, as #1654-1657 10.00 —

Souvenir Sheet

Imperf

1657 A942 50ch multicolored 2.50 —

Reelection of Kim Il Sung — A943

1977, Dec. 15 ***Perf. 12***

1658 A943 10ch multicolored .60 .20

Org. for Communication Cooperation of Socialist Countries, 20th Anniv. — A944

Without Gum

1977, Dec. 16 ***Perf. 11¾x12***

1659 A944 10ch multicolored .50 .20

New Year — A945

1978, Jan. 1 ***Perf. 13¼***

1660 A945 10ch multicolored .60 .20

Winter Olympic Games, Sapporo-Innsbruck — A946

Designs: 2ch, 19th century skater. 5ch, Skier. 10ch, Ice ballet. 15ch, Hunter on skis. 20ch, 18th century woman skiier. 25ch, Medieval Scandinavian hunter. 40ch, Skiier. 50ch, Landscape. 60ch, Speed skater.

1978, Feb. 18 ***Perf. 13¼***

1661-1667 A946 Set of 7 6.00 1.00
1667a Sheet of 10, as #1661-1669 + label 9.00 —

Souvenir Sheets

1668 A946 50ch multicolored 5.00 .50
1669 A946 60ch multicolored 4.00 .50

No. 1667 is airmail.
For overprints, see Nos. 1821-1829.

Postal History A947

Designs: 2ch, Post rider and horse token. 5ch, Postman on motorcycle. 10ch, Electric train and postal van. 15ch, Mail steamer and Mi-8 helicopter. 25ch, Tupolev Tu-154 jetliner and satellite. 40ch, Dove and UPU headquarters.
50ch, Dove and UPU emblem. 60ch, Dove and UPU headquarters.

1978, Mar. 2 ***Perf. 13¼***

1670-1675 A947 Set of 6 6.00 1.00
1675a Sheet of 8, as #1670-1677 8.00 —

Souvenir Sheets

1676-1677 A947 Set of 2 6.00 —

No. 1675 is airmail.

Rubens, 400th Anniv. Birth — A948

2ch, 5ch, 40ch, 50ch, Self-portrait, same design.

1978, Mar. 20

1678-1680 A948 Set of 3 2.50 .50
1680a Sheet of 4, as #1678-1681 6.00 —

Souvenir Sheet

1681 A948 50ch multicolored 3.00 1.50

Farm Machines A949

Designs: 10ch (#1682), *Chungsong* tractor. 10ch (#1683), Sprayer.

1978, Apr. 1 ***Perf. 11¾x12***

1682-1683 A949 Set of 2 2.50 .20

Pre-Olympics, Moscow 1980 — A950

Equestrian events: 2ch, Show jumping. 5ch, Jumping bar. 10ch, Cross Country. 15ch, Dressage. 25ch, Water splash. 40ch, Dressage (diff.).
50ch, 3-Step bar jump.

1978, Apr. 1 ***Perf. 13¼***

1684-1689 A950 Set of 6 3.50 1.50
1689a Sheet of 8, as #1684-1690 + label 7.00 —

Souvenir Sheet

1690 A950 50ch multicolored 2.50 —

Korean People's Army Day — A951

Designs: 5ch, Soldier, battle scene. 10ch, Pilot, soldier, sailor saluting.

1978, Apr. 1 ***Perf. 11¾x12***

1691-1692 A951 Set of 2 1.00 .20

Ships — A952

Korean ships: 2ch, Cargo ship *Mangyongbong.* 5ch, Freighter *Hyoksin.* 10ch, Freighter *Chongchongang.* 30ch, Tanker *Sonbang.* 50ch, Freighter *Taedonggang.*

1978, May 5 ***Perf. 13¼***

1693-1697 A952 Set of 5 6.00 1.25
1697a Sheet of 6, as #1693-1697+ label 8.00 —

No. 1697 is airmail.

History of the World Cup — A953

World Cup Winners (all 20ch, except Nos. 1709, 1710): #1698, Uruguay 1930. #1699, Italy 1934. #1700, France 1938. #1701, Brazil 1950. #1702, Switzerland 1954. #1703, Sweden 1958. #1704, Chile 1962. #1705, England 1966. #1706, Mexico 1970. #1707, West Germany 1974. #1708, Argentina 1978. 50ch (#1709), Soccer players and emblem, horiz.
50ch (#1710), World Cup and championship emblem.

1978, June 1

1698-1709 A953 Set of 12 10.00 3.00
1709a Sheet of 12, as #1698-1708, 1710 12.00 —

Souvenir Sheet

1710 A953 50ch multicolored 6.00 .60

No. 1709 is airmail.
For overprints, see Nos. 2051-2063.

World Cup Winners — A954

Designs: 5ch, Uruguay, 1930, 1950. 10ch, Italy, 1934, 1938. 15ch, West Germany, 1954, 1974. 25ch, Brazil, 1958, 1962, 1970. 40ch, England, 1966. 50ch, World Cup, vert.
50ch, World Cup.

1978, June 1

1711-1716 A954 Set of 6 5.00 1.25
1716a Sheet of 6, as #1711-15, 1717 6.00 —

Souvenir Sheet

1717 A954 50ch multicolored 4.00 .75

No. 1716 is airmail.

Art of the Revolution — A955

Designs: 10ch, Opera, *Sea of Love.* 15ch, Embroidered kerchief with floral design in the form of map of Korea. 20ch, *Tansimjul* dance. 40ch, *Song of Korea.*

1978, June 2

1718-1720 A955 Set of 3 2.50 .50

Souvenir Sheet

1721 A955 40ch multicolored 2.50 .50

Domestic Printings

Beginning in the 1970s, a number of North Korean stamps have been reprinted for sale and use within the country. Typically, these printings were on unsurfaced paper, with poorer production qualities, and without gum.

Second Seven-Year Plan — A956

Designs: 5ch, Electricity and Coal. 10ch, Steel and nonferrous metals. 15ch, Machine products and chemical fertilizers. 30ch, Cement and fishing. 50ch, Grain and tideland reclamation.

1978, June 15 ***Perf. 11½x12***

1722-1726 A956 Set of 5 3.25 .90
1722a 5ch Unsurfaced white paper, without gum 8.00 —
1723a 10ch Unsurfaced white paper, without gum 8.00 —
1724a 15ch Unsurfaced white paper, without gum 8.00 —
1725a 30ch Unsurfaced white paper, without gum 5.00 —

History of Olympic Games & Winners — A957

Games emblems / medal winners (all 20ch): #1727, Athens 1896 / Alfred Flatow. #1728, Paris 1900 / Michel Theato. #1729, London 1908 / Wyndham Halswelle. #1730, Stockholm 1912 / William Kinnear. #1731, Antwerp 1920 / Paul Anspach. #1732, Paris 1924 / Ugo Frigerio. #1733, Amsterdam 1928 / Ahmed El Quafi. #1734, Berlin 1936 / Robert Charpentier. #1735, London 1948 / Josef Stalder. #1736, Helsinki 1952 / Laszlo Papp. #1737, Melbourne 1956 / Ronald Delany. #1738, Rome 1960 / Jolanda Balas. #1739, Tokyo 1964 / Valery Brumel. #1740, Mexico 1968 / Vera Caslavska. #1741, Munich 1972 / Li Ho Jun.
50ch, Montreal 1976 / Ku Yong Jo.

1978, June 16 ***Perf. 13¼***

1727-1741 A957 Set of 15 12.00 4.50
1741a Sheet of 16, as #1727-1741 14.00 —

Souvenir Sheet

1742 A957 50ch multicolored 2.00 .75

Passenger Aircraft — A958

Designs: 2ch, Douglas CD-8-63 jetliner and Comte AC-4 Gentleman. 10ch, Ilyushin Il-62M jetliner and Avia BH-25. 15ch, Douglas DC-8-63 jetliner and Savola Marchetti S-71. 20ch, Tupolev Tu-144 jetliner and Kalinin K-5. 25ch, Tupolev Tu-154 jetliner and Antonov An-2 biplane. 30ch, Ilyushin Il-18 airliner and '30s-era airplane. 40ch, Concorde supersonic jetliner and Wibault 283 trimotor.
50ch, Airbus.

1978, July 25

1743-1749 A958 Set of 7 7.00 1.20
1749a Sheet of 8, as #1743-1750 10.00 —

Souvenir Sheet

1750 A958 50ch multicolored 2.50 .50

White-Bellied Black Woodpecker Preservation A959

Designs: 5ch, White-bellied black woodpecker (Tristam's *Dryocopus javensis richardsi*), map of habitat, inset map of Korea. 10ch, Woodpecker and eggs. 15ch, Woodpecker feeding young. 25ch, Woodpecker feeding young (diff.). 50ch, Woodpecker on tree trunk.

1978, Aug. 5 ***Perf. 11¾x12***

1751-1755 A959 Set of 5 7.50 2.00
1755a Sheet of 6, #1751-1755 + label 9.00 —

Democratic People's Republic of Korea, 30th Anniv. A960

Designs (all 10ch): #1756, Building and flag. #1757, Flag with silhouetttes of workers and peasants. #1758, Flag with aviator and two soldiers. #1759, Chollima statue and city. #1760, Workers demonstrating, map of Korea in background. #1761, Asian, European and African clasping hands, with torch and "Solidarity" in background.

Without Gum

1978, Sep. 9 ***Perf. 13½x13¼***

1756-1761 A960 Set of 6 2.75 .50
1758a 10ch Unsurfaced toned paper 10.00 —
1759a 10ch Unsurfaced toned paper 15.00 —
1760a 10ch Unsurfaced toned paper 15.00 —

Paintings by Ri Am (16th Century) A961

Designs: 10ch, *Cat and Pup.* 15ch, *Cat on a Tree.* 40ch, *A Pair of Wild Geese.*

1978, Oct. 16 ***Perf. 13¼***

1762-1764 A961 Set of 3 7.50 1.10
1764a Sheet of 4, #1762-1764 + label 11.00 —

World Cup Winners, Argentina '78 — A962

Soccer players: 10ch, Argentina, Champion. 15ch, Holland, Sub-Champion. 25ch, Brazil, Third Place.
50ch, Argentina, Champion.

1978, Dec. 15

1765-1767 A962 Set of 3 3.00 .50
1767a Sheet of 4, as #1765-1768 12.00 —

Souvenir Sheet

1768 A962 50ch multicolored 2.50 1.50

New Year — A963

Without Gum

1979, Jan. 1 ***Perf. 12***

1769 A963 10ch Multicolored .50 .20

A964

International Year of the Child — A965

Kim Il Sung and children: 5ch, With Children's Corps members in Maanshan. 10ch, Children's Corps members in classroom. 15ch, "The New Year Gathering." 20ch, by roadside, with snowman, kite. 30ch, Looking at children's school work.
Children: 10ch, Tug of war. 15ch, Ballerinas. 20ch, Children of different races holding hands in circle around globe. 25ch, Singing at piano. 30ch, Playing on toy airplane ride.
50ch (#1780), Kim visiting a kindergarten. 50ch (#1781): As #1776.

1979, Jan. 1 ***Perf. 13¼x13½***

1770-1774 A964 Set of 5 4.00 1.00
1775-1779 A965 Set of 5 3.00 1.00

Souvenir Sheets

Imperf

1780 A964 50ch multicolored 2.50 1.75
1781 A965 50ch multicolored 2.50 1.75

Nos. 1770-1779 were issued with setenant labels.

A set of four stamps depicting roses, similar to Type A970, was prepared for release on Jan. 5, 1979, but was not issued.

Story of Two Generals A966

Designs: 5ch, Two warriors on horseback. 10ch (#1783), Man blowing feather. 10ch (#1784), Two generals fighting Japanese invaders. 10ch (#1785), Two generals on horseback.

Without Gum

1979, Jan. 10 *Perf. 11¾x12*
1782-1785 A966 Set of 4 3.00 .50

Worker-Peasant Red Guards, 20th Anniv. — A967

Without Gum

1979, Jan. 14 *Perf. 12x11¾*
1786 A967 10ch multicolored .50 .20

Airships — A968

Designs: 10ch, Clement-Bayard Airship *Fleurus*. 20ch, NI *Norge*. 50ch, *Graf Zeppelin*.

1979, Feb. 27 *Perf. 13¼*
1787-1788 A968 Set of 2 2.00 .40
1788a Sheet of 3, as #1787-1789 5.00 —

Souvenir Sheet

1789 A968 50ch multicolored 3.00 1.75

March 1 Popular Uprising, 60th Anniv. A969

Without Gum

1979, Mar. 1 *Perf. 11¾x12*
1790 A969 10ch multicolored .60 .20

Roses A970

Designs: 5ch, Rose. 10ch, Red star rose. 15ch, Flamerose. 20ch, Yellow rose. 30ch, White rose. 50ch, Deep pink rose.

1979, Apr. 18 *Perf. 13¼*
1791-1796 A970 Set of 6 3.50 1.00
1796a Sheet of 6, #1791-1796 4.00 —

No. 1796 is airmail.

35th World Table Tennis Championships, Pyongyang — A971

Designs: 5ch, Championship Cup. 10ch, Female doubles. 15ch, Female singles. 20ch, Male doubles. 30ch, Male singles. 50ch, Chollima statue. "Welcome."

1979, Apr. 25
1797-1801 A971 Set of 5 3.00 .75
1801a Sheet of 6, as #1797-1802 4.00 —

Souvenir Sheet

1802 A971 50ch multicolored 3.00 .45

"Let Us Step Up Socialist Construction Under the Banner of the Juche Idea" — A972

Designs: 5ch, Marchers, banner. 10ch (#1804), Map of Korea. 10ch (#1805), Hand holding torch.

Without Gum

1979, Apr. 28 *Perf. 12*
1803-1805 A972 Set of 3 3.00 .25
1803a 5ch Unsurfaced dull white paper 15.00 —
1804a 10ch Unsurfaced dull white paper 15.00 —
1805a 10ch Unsurfaced dull white paper 15.00 —

Order of Honor of the Three Revolutions — A973

Without Gum

1979, May 2
1806 A973 10ch dp blue & lt blue 1.50 .20
a. Unsurfaced dull white paper 15.00 —

World Telecommunications Day — A974

Without Gum

1979, May 17
1807 A974 10ch multicolored 1.00 .20

Battle in Musan Area, 40th Anniv. A975

Without Gum

1979, May 23
1808 A975 10ch multicolored .60 .20

Int'l Friendship Exhibition A976

Without Gum

1979, May 29
1809 A976 10ch multicolored .60 .20

Albrecht Dürer, 450th Anniv. Death A977

Details from Dürer paintings: 15ch, "Peonies." 20ch, "Akeley." 25ch, "A Big Tuft of Grass." 30ch, 50ch, "Wing of a Bird."

1979, June 8 *Perf. 13¼*
1810-1813 A977 Set of 4 5.50 .75
1813a Sheet of 4, as #1810-1813 9.00 —

Souvenir Sheet

1814 A977 50ch multicolored 3.50 .60

Olympic Games, Moscow 1980 — A978

Olympic Torch, Moscow 1980 emblem and: 5ch, Fencers. 10ch, Gymnast. 20ch, Yacht race. 30ch, Runner. 40ch, Weightlifter. 50ch, Horse jump.

1979, July 1
1815-1819 A978 Set of 5 3.50 1.25
1819a Sheet of 6, as #1815-1820 5.00 —

Souvenir Sheet

1820 A978 50ch multicolored 3.00 1.50

Nos. 1661-1669 Overprinted

1979, July 17
1821-1827 A946 Set of 7 10.00 3.50
1827a Sheet of 10, as #1821-1829 + label 18.00 —

Souvenir Sheets

1828 A946 50ch multicolored 4.25 1.50
1829 A946 60ch Multicolored 8.50 —

No. 1827 is airmail.

Koguryo Dynasty Horsemen — A979

Designs: 5ch, Hunting. 10ch, Archery contest. 15ch, Drummer. 20ch, Rider blowing horn. 30ch, Horse and rider in chain mail. 50ch, Hawk hunting.

1979, Aug. 1
1830-1835 A979 Set of 6 6.00 .75
1835a Sheet of 6, as #1830-1835 9.00 —

Olympic Games, Moscow 1980 — A980

Designs: 5ch, Judo. 10ch, Volleyball. 15ch, Cycling. 20ch, Basketball. 25ch, One-oared boat. 30ch, Boxing. 40ch, Shooting. 50ch, Gymnastics.

1979, Aug. 5 *Perf. 11¾x12*
1836-1842 A980 Set of 7 5.00 1.25
1842a Sheet of 8, as #1836-1843 + label 9.00 —

Souvenir Sheet

1843 A980 50ch Multicolored 3.00 1.00

Ri Dynasty Knights' Costumes A981

Designs: 5ch, Knight in armor. 10ch, Knight in ceremonial dress. 15ch, Knight in armor (diff.) 20ch, Soldier in uniform. 30ch, Knight in armor (diff.) 50ch, Knight in armor (diff.)

1979, Aug. 6 *Perf. 11¾*
1844-1849 A981 Set of 6 3.75 .75
1849a Sheet of 6, #1844-1849 6.00 —

No. 1849 is airmail.

Olympic Games, Moscow 1980 — A982

Designs: 10ch, Judo. 15ch, Handball. 20ch, Archery. 25ch, Ground hockey. 30ch, Boat race. 40ch, Soccer. 50ch, Horse race.

1979, Sep. 5 *Perf. 11¾x11½*
1850-1855 A982 Set of 6 5.25 1.25
1855a Sheet of 8, as #1850-1856 + label 8.00 —

Souvenir Sheet

1856 A982 50ch Multicolored 3.00 1.25

Chongbong Monument A983

Without Gum

1979, Sep. 10 *Perf. 12*
1857 A983 10ch multicolored .60 .20

Sika Deer A984

Designs: 5ch, Breeder feeding fawn from bottle. 10ch, Doe and suckling fawn. 15ch, Deer drinking from stream. 20ch, Buck walking. 30ch, Deer running.
50ch, Antlers.

1979, Oct. 5 ***Perf. 13½***
1858-1863 A984 Set of 6 4.00 1.25
1863a Sheet of 6, #1858-1863 6.00 —

Central Zoo, Pyongyang A985

Designs: 5ch, Moscovy ducks. 10ch, Ostrich. 15ch, Turkey. 20ch, Pelican. 30ch, Guinea fowl. 50ch, Mandarin ducks.

1979, Oct. 9 ***Perf. 12***
1864-1869 A985 Set of 6 5.00 1.50
1869a Sheet of 6, #1864-1869 6.00 —

No. 1869 is airmail.

Int'l Year of the Child — A986

Designs: 20ch (#1870), Girl with toy sail boat. 20ch (#1871), Boy with toy train. 20ch (#1872), Boy with model biplane. 20ch (#1873), Boy with model spaceman. 30ch (#1874), Boy with toy motor boat. 30ch (#1875), Boy sitting on toy train. 30ch (#1876), Boy with model airplane. 30ch (#1877), Boy with model spaceman.
Souvenir Sheets (all 80ch): #1878, Boy and model ocean liner. #1879, Boy and girl with model train. #1880, Boy and Concorde. #1881, Girl and satellite.
Miniature sheets of 4: #1882, Nos. 1870, 1874, 1878 + label. #1883, Nos. 1871, 1875, 1879 + label. #1884, Nos. 1872, 1876, 1880 + label. #1885, Nos. 1873, 1877, 1881 + label.

1979, Oct. 13 ***Perf. 12x11¾***
1870-1877 A986 Set of 8 12.00 2.50

Souvenir Sheets

1878-1881 A986 Set of 4 25.00 2.50

Miniature Sheets

1882-1885 A986 Set of 4 25.00 2.50

Int'l Year of the Child — A987

Children playing soccer: 20ch, Kicking. 30ch, Dribbling.
80ch, Tackling.

1979, Nov. 15 ***Perf. 12x11¾***
1886-1887 A987 Set of 2 5.00 .75
1887a Sheet of 3, as #1886-1888 10.00 —

Souvenir Sheet

1888 A987 80ch Multicolored 5.00 .75

Marine Life — A988

Designs: 20ch, Devil stinger fish (*Inimicas japonicus*). 30ch, Black rockfish (*Sebastes schlegeli*). 50ch, Northern sea lion (*Eumetopias jubatus*).

1889-1891 A988 Set of 3 3.50 .75
1891a Sheet of 3, #1889-1891 5.00 —

Winter Olympics Games, Lake Placid — A989

Designs: 10ch, Figure skating (Irina Rodnina and Aleksandr Zaitsev). 20ch, Ice hockey (Soviet team). 30ch, Ladies' ski relay team. 40ch, Cross-country skiing (Sergei Saveliev, USSR), vert. 50ch, Ladies' speed skating (Tatiana Averina), vert.
60ch, Ice dancing (Ludmila Pakhomova and Aleksandr Gorshkov), stamp vert.

1979, Dec. 9
1892-1896 A989 Set of 5 6.00 1.50
1892a Sheet of 3, #1892-1894 5.00 —
1895a Sheet of 3, as #1895-1897 10.00 —

Souvenir Sheet

1897 A989 60ch Multicolored 5.50 4.50

Honey Bees — A990

Designs: 20ch, Bee gathering nectar. 30ch, Bee and blossoms. 50ch, Bee over flower.

1979, Dec. 22
1898-1900 A990 Set of 3 6.00 .60
1900a Sheet of 3, #1898-1900 7.50 —

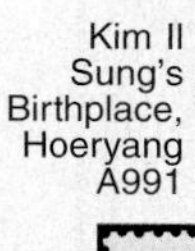

Kim Il Sung's Birthplace, Hoeryang A991

Sinpha Revolutionary Museum — A992

1979, Dec. 24
1901 A991 10ch multicolored .75 .20
1902 A992 10ch multicolored .75 .20

Revolutionary historical sites.

New Year A993

1980, Jan. 1
1903 A993 10ch multicolored 1.00 .20

Studying — A994

1980, Jan. 10 ***Perf. 12x11¾***
1904 A994 10ch multicolored .50 .20

Unryul Mine Conveyor Belt — A995

1980, Jan. 20 ***Perf. 11¾x12***
1905 A995 10ch multicolored 1.00 .20

Kim Il Sung, Soldiers and Children — A996

Children Playing — A997

Kim Visiting Kindergarten — A998

International Day of the Child

Type A997 (all 10ch): #1907, Black, Asian and White children with "6" and "1." #1908, Children playing accordion. #1909, Children on airplane ride. #1910, Children on rocket ride. #1911, Children riding tricycles. #1912, Children playing with model train.

1980, Jan. 28 ***Perf. 12x11¾***
1906 A996 10ch multicolored .35 .20
1907 A997 10ch multicolored 1.50 .35
1908 A997 10ch multicolored .35 .20
1909 A997 10ch multicolored .60 .20
1910 A997 10ch multicolored 2.25 .50
1911 A997 10ch multicolored .50 .20
1912 A997 10ch multicolored .35 .20
Nos. 1906-1912 (7) 5.90 1.85

Souvenir Sheet

Perf. 13¼

1913 A998 50ch multicolored 3.00 1.25

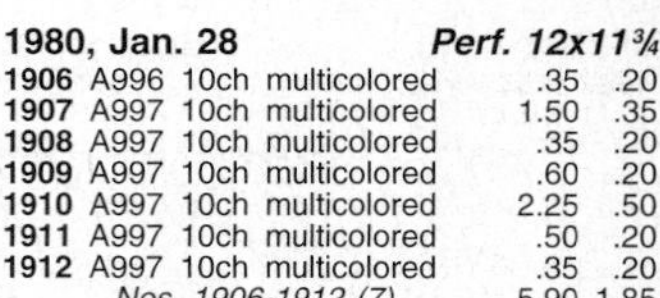

Chongsan-ri Monument — A999

Chongsan-ri Party Headquarters — A1000

1980, Feb. 5 ***Perf. 11¾x12***
1914 A999 10ch multicolored .50 .20
1915 A1000 10ch multicolored .50 .20

Monument in Honor of Kim Jong Suk's Return A1001

1980, Feb. 16
1916 A1001 10ch multicolored .50 .20

Explorers A1002

Designs: 10ch, Vasco Nunez be Balboa (Spain). 20ch, Francisco de Orellana (Spain). 30ch, Haroun Tazieff (France). 40ch, Sir Edmund Hillary (New Zealand) and Shri Tenzing (Nepal).
70ch, Ibn Battuta (Morocco).

1980, Feb. 18 ***Perf. 13¼***
1917-1920 A1002 Set of 4 4.50 1.00
1920a Sheet of 6, as #1917-1921 + label 10.00 —

Souvenir Sheet

1921 A1002 70ch multicolored 4.50 1.50

Ryongpo Revolutionary Museum — A1003

1980, Feb. 23 ***Perf. 11¾***
1922 A1003 10ch lt blue & black .50 .20

Rowland Hill (1795-1879), Centenary of Death — A1004

Rowland Hill and stamps of: 30ch, Germany, Great Britain (#1), Russia, Switzerland, DPRK and Wurttemberg. 50ch, Great Britain (#1, pair), France, Roman States, Canada, Two Sicilies and India.

1980, Mar. 1

1923-1924 A1004 Set of 2 7.00 1.00
1924a Sheet of 2, #1923-1924 10.00 —

World Red Cross Day — A1005

Designs (all 10ch): #1925, Emblem of DPRK Red Cross. #1926, J.H. Dunant. #1927, Nurse and infant. #1928, Red Cross ship. #1929, Red Cross helicopter. #1930, Nurse with child and doll. #1931, Map, Red Cross, transports.
50ch, Nurse with syringe.

1980, Apr. 17 ***Perf. 11¾x11½***

1925-1931 A1005 Set of 7 8.00 1.50
1931a Sheet of 8, as #1925-1932 15.00 —

Souvenir Sheet

1932 A1005 50ch multicolored 5.50 1.75

For overprints, see Nos. 2043-2050.

Conquerors of the Sea A1006

Designs: 10ch, Fernando Magellan (Portugal). 20ch, Fridtjof Nansen (Norway). 30ch, Auguste and Jacques Piccard (Sweden). 40ch, Jacques Cousteau (France).
70ch, Capt. James Cook (UK).

1980, Apr. 30 ***Perf. 13¼***

1933-1936 A1006 Set of 4 8.00 1.50
1936a Sheet of 6, as #1933-1937 + label 15.00 —

Souvenir Sheet

1937 A1006 70ch multicolored 6.50 1.50

London 1980 Int'l Philatelic Exhibition — A1007

Designs: 10ch, Great Britain #1 and Korean stamps. 20ch, British Guiana One-Cent Magenta and Korean cover. 30ch, Korea #1 (in blue) and modern Korean First Day Cover. 40ch, DPRK Nos. 1 (in green) and 1494. 50ch, DPRK Nos. 470-471.

1980, May 6

1938-1942 A1007 Set of 5 10.00 1.50

Souvenir Sheet

1943 A1007 Sheet of 3, #1939, 1941, 1942 15.00 1.50

No. 1941 is airmail.

Conquerors of Sky and Space A1008

Designs: 10ch, Wright Brothers (USA). 20ch, Louis Bleriot (France). 30ch, Anthony Fokker (USA). 40ch, Secondo Campini (Italy) and Sir Frank Whittle (UK).
70ch, Count Ferdinand von Zeppelin (Germany).

1980, May 10

1944-1947 A1008 Set of 4 6.00 1.25
1947a Sheet of 6, as #1944-1948 + label 13.00 —

Souvenir Sheet

1948 A1008 70ch multicolored 5.00 1.25

Conquerors of the Universe A1009

Designs: 10ch, Spaceships. 20ch, Spaceship landing on another planet. 30ch, Spaceships landing on another planet, greeted by dinosaurs. 40ch, Spaceship, dinosaurs.
70ch, Spaceman and dragons.

1980, May 20 ***Perf. 11¾x12***

1949-1952 A1009 Set of 4 3.50 1.25
1952a Sheet of 6, as #1949-1953 + label 12.00 —

Souvenir Sheet

1953 A1009 70ch multicolored 3.50 1.25

Chongryon, 25th Anniv. — A1010

1980, May 25 ***Perf. 12¼x12***

1954 A1010 10ch multicolored .50 .20

Chongryon is the General Association of Korean Residents in Japan.

Pyongyang Maternity Hospital — A1011

1980, May 30 ***Perf. 12***

1955 A1011 10ch multicolored 1.10 .20

Changgwang Health Complex — A1012

1980, June 2 ***Perf. 11¾x12***

1956 A1012 2ch black & lt blue .60 .20

Korean Revolutionary Army, 50th Anniv. — A1013

1980, July 6 ***Perf. 12***

1957 A1013 10ch multicolored .60 .20

Regular Issue — A1014

Designs (all 10ch): #1958, Workers' hostel, Samjiyon. #1959, *Chongsanri* rice harvester. #1960, *Taedonggang* rice transplanter. #1961, corn harvester. #1962, Samhwa Democratic Propaganda Hall. #1963, Songmun-ri revolutionary historic building (with trees). #1964, Sundial. #1965, Turtle ship. #1966, Phungsan dog. #1967, Quail.

Perf. 11¾, 11½ (#1960, 1965), 12x11¾ (#1964)

1980

1958-1967 A1014 Set of 10 25.00 3.00

Issued: Nos. 1958-1961, 7/25. Nos. 1962-1967, 8/1.

6th Congress, Workers' Party of Korea A1015

"Leading the van in the Arduous March" — A1016

"The great leader inspires and encourages colliers on the spot." — A1017

Designs (all 10ch): #1968, Party emblem, fireworks. #1969, Students, Red Book. #1970, Workers, banner, Red Book. #1971, Young workers, one with accordion. #1972, Worker holding wrench aloft. #1973, Four young workers, one with streamer, building in background. #1974, Map, propaganda slogans. #1975, Workers marching with three banners, smoke stacks in background.

1980, July 30 ***Perf. 12¼x12***

1968-1975 A1015 Set of 8 6.00 1.25

Souvenir Sheets

1976 A1016 50ch multicolored 3.00 .75
1977 A1017 50ch multicolored 2.00 .75

World Cup Soccer Championship 1978-1982 A1018

Designs: 20ch, Two soccer players dribbling ball. 30ch, Tackling.
40ch, Tackling (diff.). 60ch, Moving in to tackle.

1980, Aug. 5 ***Perf. 12***

1978-1979 A1018 Set of 2 7.50 2.00
1979a Sheet of 4, as #1978-1980 — —

Souvenir Sheet

1980 A1018 Sheet of 2 + label 16.00 2.00
a. 40ch multicolored 3.00 1.00
b. 60ch multicolored 4.00 1.00

Winter Olympic Games 1980, Gold Medal Winners — A1019

Designs: 20ch, Irina Rodnina and Aleksandr Zaitsev.
1w, Natalia Linitschnuk and Gennadi Karponosov.

1980, Aug. 10 ***Perf. 13¼***

1981 A1019 20ch multicolored 6.00 1.50
a. Sheet of 2, as #1981-1982 15.00 —

Souvenir Sheet

1982 A1019 1w multicolored 6.50 2.00

Albrecht Dürer, 450th Anniv. Death — A1020

Designs: 20ch, *Soldier with Horse.*
1w, *Horse and Rider.*

1980, Aug. 18 ***Perf. 11¾x12***

1983 A1020 20ch multicolored 6.00 1.50
a. Sheet of 2 as #1983-1984 20.00 —

Souvenir Sheet

1984 A1020 1w multicolored 9.00 2.50

Johannes Kepler, 350th Anniv. Death — A1021

Designs: 20ch, Kepler, astrolabe and satellites.
1w, Kepler, astrolabe and satellites (diff.).

1980, Aug. 25
1985 A1021 20ch multicolored 2.75 1.25
a. Sheet of 2, as #1985-1986 12.00 —
Souvenir Sheet
1986 A1021 1w multicolored 6.00 2.00

3rd Int'l Stamp Fair Essen 1980 — A1022

Designs, Stamps from German and Russian Zeppelin sets, respectively: 10ch, 1m and 30k. 20ch, 2m and 35k. 30ch, 4m and 1r.
50ch, Russian 2r Polar Flight stamp and DPRK No. 1780 stamp.

1980, Sep. 25 ***Perf. 13¼***
1987-1989 A1022 Set of 3 6.50 1.25
1989a Sheet of 4, as #1987-1990 30.00 —
Souvenir Sheet
1990 A1022 50ch multicolored 9.00 2.50

A1023

Moscow Olympic Games Winners — A1024

Designs: 10ch, Free pistol shooting — Aleksandr Melentiev (USSR). 20ch, 4000m Individual pursuit bicycle race — Robert Dill-Bundi (Switzerland). 25ch, Gymnastics — Stoyan Deltchev (Bulgaria). 30ch, Free style wrestling — K). 35ch, Weight-lifting — Ho Bong Choi (DPRK). 40ch, Running — Marita Koch (DDR). 50ch, Modern pentathlon — Anatoly Starostin (USSR).

No. 1998, Boxing — Teofilo Stevenson (Cuba). No. 1999, Ancient Greek rider on horse.

1980, Oct. 20 ***Perf. 12x11¾***
1991-1997 A1023 Set of 7 7.00 2.25
1997a Sheet of 8, as #1991-1998 12.00 —
Souvenir Sheet
1998 A1023 70ch multicolored 2.75 2.00
1999 A1024 70ch multicolored 4.50 2.00

Josip Broz Tito (1892-1980) A1025

1980, Dec. 4 ***Perf. 12¼x12***
2000 A1025 20ch multicolored 1.00 .20

First Post-WWII Lufthansa Flight, 25th Anniv. A1026

Designs: 20ch, Convair CV 340 airliner.
1w, Airbus A 300.

1980, Dec. 10 ***Perf. 13¼***
2001 A1026 20ch multicolored 5.50 2.00
a. Sheet of 2, as #2001-2002 15.00 —
Souvenir Sheet
2002 A1026 1w multicolored 7.00 3.00

Liverpool-Manchester Railway, 150th Anniv. — A1027

Designs: 20ch, *The Rocket.*
1w, Locomotive pulling passenger car and horse car.

1980, Dec. 16 ***Perf. 11¾***
2003 A1027 20ch multicolored 6.00 3.00
a. Sheet of 2, as #2003-2004 15.00 —
Souvenir Sheet
2004 A1027 1w multicolored 6.00 2.50

Electric Train Centenary — A1028

Designs: 20ch, First E-type electric and steam locomotives.
1w, Electric locomotive exhibited in Berlin, 1879.

1980, Dec. 24 ***Perf. 13¼***
2005 A1028 20ch multicolored 6.00 2.00
a. Sheet of 2, as #2005-2006 20.00 —
Souvenir Sheet
2006 A1028 1w multicolored 12.00 2.50

Dag Hammarskjold (1905-61), 75th Anniv. of Birth — A1029

Designs: 20ch, Hammarskjold and UN Building.
1w, Hammarskjold (diff.).

1980, Dec. 26 ***Perf. 11¾***
2007 A1029 20ch multicolored 3.25 2.25
a. Sheet of 2, as #2007-2008 10.00 —
Souvenir Sheet
2008 A1029 1w multicolored 4.50 2.75

World Chess Championship, Merano — A1030

Designs: 20ch, Bobby Fischer-Boris Spassky chess match.
1w, Viktor Korchnoi-Anatoly Karpov chess match.

1980, Dec. 28 ***Perf. 13¼***
2009 A1030 20ch multicolored 7.00 2.00
a. Sheet of 2, as #2009-2010 17.00 —
Souvenir Sheet
2010 A1030 1w multicolored 9.00 2.00

Robert Stolz (1880-1975), Composer, Birth Cent. — A1031

Designs: 20ch, Stoltz with music from *At the Flower Bed.*
1w, Stoltz working with stamp collection.

1980, Dec. 30
2011 A1031 20ch multicolored 3.00 1.00
a. Sheet of 2, as #2011-2012 12.00 —
Souvenir Sheet
2012 A1031 1w multicolored 5.00 1.00

New Year — A1032

1981, Jan. 1 ***Perf. 12***
2013 A1032 10ch multicolored .90 .20

Fairy Tales A1033

Designs (all 10ch): #2014 Russian fairy tale. #2015 Icelandic. #2016, Swedish. #2017, Irish. #2018, Italian. #2019, Japanese. #2020, German.
70ch (#2021): Korean fairy tale, *A Gold Nugget and Maize Cake.*

1981, Jan. 30 ***Perf. 13¼***
2014-2020 A1033 Set of 7 10.00 3.50
2020a Sheet of 8, as #2014-2021 15.00 —
Souvenir Sheet
2021 A1033 70ch multicolored 5.75 3.00

International Year of the Child, 1979.

Changgwang Street, Pyongyang — A1034

1981, Feb. 16 ***Perf. 11¾x12***
2022 A1034 10ch multicolored .70 .20

World Soccer Cup Championship ESPAÑA '82 — A1035

Designs: 10ch, Tackling. 20ch, Kicking. 30ch, Feinting.
70ch, Three players.

1981, Feb. 20 ***Perf. 13¼***
2023-2025 A1035 Set of 3 9.00 2.75
2025a Sheet of 4, as #2023-2026 17.00 —
Souvenir Sheet
2026 A1035 70ch multicolored 8.00 3.25

For overprints, see Nos. 2216.

World Soccer Cup Championship ESPAÑA '82 (2nd issue) — A1036

Designs: 10ch, Emblem, map and cup. 20ch, Dribbling. 25ch, Tackling. 30ch, Pass.
70ch, Sliding tackle.

1981, Feb. 28
2027-2031 A1036 Set of 5 9.00 3.75
2031a Sheet of 6, as #2027-2032 18.00 —
Souvenir Sheet
2032 A1036 70ch multicolored 9.00 3.00

Implementations of Decisions of 6th Korean Workers' Party Congress A1037

Designs: 2ch, Marchers with book, banners. 10ch (#2034), Worker with book. 10ch (#2035), Workers and factory. 10ch (#2036), Electricity generation (horiz.). 10ch (#2037), Factory, construction scene (horiz.). 10ch (#2038), Cement factory, fertilizer (horiz.). 30ch, Fishing, fabrics (horiz.). 40ch, Grain, port facilities (horiz.). 70ch, Clasped hands, map of Korea. 1w, Hand holding torch, "peace" and "solidarity" slogans.

1981, Mar. 15 ***Perf. 12¼***

2033-2042 A1037 Set of 10 6.00 2.50

2033a 2ch Unsurfaced white paper, without gum 10.00 —

2034a 10ch Unsurfaced white paper, without gum 10.00 —

2035a 10ch Unsurfaced white paper, without gum 10.00 —

2039a 30ch Unsurfaced white paper, without gum 10.00 —

2040a 40ch Unsurfaced white paper, without gum 10.00 —

2041a 70ch Unsurfaced white paper, without gum 10.00 —

2042a 1w Unsurfaced white paper, without gum 10.00 —

Nos. 1925-1932 Overprinted

For Nobel Prize Winners in Medicine

1981, Mar. 20 ***Perf. 11¾x11½***

2043-2049 A1005 Set of 7 9.00 3.00

2049a Sheet of 8, as #2043-2050 12.00 —

Souvenir Sheet

2050 A1005 50ch multicolored 9.00 —

Nos. 1698-1710 Overprinted

History of the World Cup

1981, Mar. 20 ***Perf. 13¼***

2051-2062 A953 Set of 12 24.00 —

2062a Sheet of 12, #2051-2062 25.00 —

Souvenir Sheet

2063 A953 50ch multicolored 12.00 —

Copa de Oro Mini-World Cup Championships — A1038

Designs: 20ch, Uruguayan and Brazilian soccer players.
1w, Goalkeeper blocking ball.

1981, Mar. 27

2064 A1038 20ch multicolored 4.00 1.25

Souvenir Sheet

2065 A1038 1w multicolored 8.00 1.00

España '82 — A1039

Nos. 2066-2068 depict different designs incorporating bleachers and crowds, with images of soccer players and trophy that appear or disappear, depending upon the angle from which the stamps are viewed. This effect is created by printing on multiple layers of thin plastic, with gummed paper backing.

1981, Apr. 10 ***Imperf.***

2066-2067 A1039 Set of 2, 20ch, 30ch 25.00 9.00

Souvenir Sheet

2068 A1039 1w multicolored 25.00 25.00

Nos. 2066-2068 are airmail.

Naposta '81 Int'l Stamp Exhibition, Stuttgart — A1040

Designs: 10ch, Dornier Do-X flying boat. 20ch, Count von Zeppelin and airship LZ-120. 30ch, Goetz von Berlichingen (1480-1562), German knight and subject of poem by Johann von Goethe (1749-1832), also pictured.
70ch, Mercedes-Benz W 196, 1954 automobile.

1981, Apr. 28 ***Perf. 12x11¾***

2069-2071 A1040 Set of 3 8.00 1.60

Souvenir Sheet

Perf. 11½x11¾

2072 A1040 70ch multicolored 5.50 2.75

World Telecommunications Day — A1041

1981, May 17 ***Perf. 11¾x11½***

2073 A1041 10ch multicolored 2.75 .25

Flowers — A1042

Designs: 10ch, Iris pseudodacorus. 20ch, Iris pallasii. 30ch, Gladiolus gandavensis.

1981, May 20 ***Perf. 12x11¾***

2074-2076 A1042 Set of 3 3.50 1.60

2076a Sheet of 3, #2074-2076 3.75 —

WIPA 1981 Stamp Exhibition, Vienna — A1043

Designs: 20ch, Austrian WIPA 1981 and Rudolf Kirchschlager stamps. 30ch, Austrian Maria Theresa and Franz Josef stamps.
50ch, Kim Il Sung and Korean Children's Union choir, vert.

1981, May 22 ***Perf. 13¼***

2077-2078 A1043 Set of 2 6.00 1.60

Souvenir Sheet

Perf. 11½

2079 A1043 50ch multicolored 6.00 2.75

International Gymnastc Federation, Centen. A1044

Gymnastic events: 10ch, Rings. 15ch, Pommel horse. 20ch, Long horse. 25ch, Floor. 30ch, Hoop.
70ch, Ribbon, horiz.

1981, May 25 ***Perf. 11¾x12***

2080-2084 A1044 Set of 5 3.75 1.40

2084a Sheet of 6, as #2080-2085 15.00 —

Souvenir Sheet

Perf. 11½x11¾

2085 A1044 70ch multicolored 3.00 1.00

For surcharges, see Nos. 2270-2275

Mingyuehgou Meeting, 50th Anniv. — A1045

1981, June 15 ***Perf. 12¼x12***

2086 A1045 10ch multicolored .50 .20

Taen Work System, 20th Anniv. A1046

1981, June 25 ***Perf. 12x12¼***

2087 A1046 10ch multicolored .50 .20

New System of Agricultural Guidance, 20th Anniv. — A1047

1981, June 25

2088 A1047 10ch multicolored .50 .20

Anti-Japanese Women's Assoc., 55th Anniv. — A1048

1981, July 5 ***Perf. 12¼***

2089 A1048 5w multicolored 12.00 1.00

Opera *Sea of Blood,* 10th Anniv. A1049

1981, July 17 ***Perf. 12***

2090 A1049 10w multicolored 30.00 10.00

Joan of Arc, 550th Anniv. Death A1050

Designs: 10ch (#2091), Joan of Arc. 10ch (#2092a), Archangel Michael. 70ch, Joan of Arc in armor.
No. 2094, as #2093.

1981, July 20

2091 A1050 Set of 3 3.50 .75

2092 Sheet of 2, #2092a-2092b 9.00 —

a. 10ch multicolored — —

b. 70ch multicolored — —

Souvenir Sheet

Perf. 11½

2094 A1050 70ch multicolored 7.00 1.90

Down-with-Imperialism Union, 55th Anniv. — A1051

1981, July 25 ***Perf. 12¼***

2095 A1051 1w multicolored 6.00 2.00

Rembrandt, 375th Birth Anniv. A1052

Designs: 10ch, *Young Girl by the Window.* 20ch, *Rembrandt's Mother.* 30ch, *Saskia van Uylenburgh.* 40ch, *Pallas Athenae.*
70ch, *Self-portrait.*

1981, July 25 ***Perf. 13¼***

2096-2099 A1052 Set of 4 7.00 2.75

Souvenir Sheet

2100 A1052 70ch multicolored 5.50 3.00

Symposium of the Non-Aligned Countries on Increasing Agricultural Production — A1053

Designs: 10ch, Emblem, banners over Pyongyang. 50ch, Harvesting grain. 90ch, Marchers with banners, tractors, fields, factories.

1981, Aug. 26 ***Perf. 12***

2101-2103 A1053 Set of 3 2.00 1.00

Royal Wedding A1054

Designs: 10ch, St. Paul's Cathedral. 20ch, Prince Charles on Great Britain stamp, Scott #599. 30ch, Princess Diana. 40ch, Prince Charles in military uniform.

70ch, Prince Charles and Princess Diana.

1981, Sept. 18 ***Perf. 13¼***

2104-2107 A1054 Set of 4 10.00 3.00

Souvenir Sheet

2108 A1054 70ch multicolored 15.00 5.00

For overprints, see Nos. 2205-2209.

Reubens Paintings — A1055

Designs: 10ch, *The Four Philosophers.* 15ch, *Portrait of Helena Fourment.* 20ch, *Portrait of Isabella Brandt.* 25ch, *The Education of Maria de Medici.* 30ch, *Helena Fourment and Her Child.* 40ch, *Helena Fourment in Her Wedding Dress.*

70ch, *Portrait of Nikolaas Rubens.*

1981, Sept. 20 ***Perf. 11¾x12***

2109-2114 A1055 Set of 6 9.00 2.75

Souvenir Sheet

Perf 11½

2115 A1055 70ch multicolored 5.50 2.75

Royal Wedding — A1056

Designs: 10ch, Prince Charles and Princess Diana wedding portrait. 20ch, Charles and Diana with Flower Girl. 30ch, Charles and Diana leaving St. Paul's Cathedral. 40ch, Wedding portrait (diff.)

70ch, Charles and Diana with Queen Elizabeth on balcony.

1981, Sept. 29 ***Perf. 13¼***

2116-2119 A1056 Sheet of 4 20.00 4.50

Souvenir Sheet

2120 A1056 70ch multicolored 25.00 6.00

Philatokyo '81 International Stamp Exhibition, Tokyo — A1057

Design: 10ch, Rowland Hill and first stamps of Great Britain, Japan and DPRK. 20ch, DPRK World Fairy Tale stamps. 30ch, Three Japanese stamps.

70ch, Exhibition Hall.

1981, Oct. 9 ***Perf. 11¾x11x½***

2121-2123 A1057 Set of 3 9.00 2.50

2123a Sheet of 4, as #2121-2124, perf 12x11½ 27.50 —

Souvenir Sheet

2124 A1057 70ch multicolored 7.00 2.00

Philatokyo '81 — A1058

Designs (both 10ch): #2125, Two DPRK stamps. #2126, DPRK stamp featuring Juche torch.

1981, Oct. 9 ***Perf. 12x12¼***

2125-2126 A1058 Set of 2 4.00 1.40

League of Socialist Working Youth of Korea, 7th Congress — A1059

1981, Oct. 20 ***Perf. 12x11¾***

2127 A1059 10ch multicolored .20 .20

2128 A1059 80ch multicolored 1.00 .35

Bulgarian State, 1300th Anniv. A1060

1981, Oct. 20 ***Perf. 12x12¼***

2129 A1060 10ch multicolored .50 .20

Georgi Dimitrov (1882-1949), Birth Centenary A1061

1981, Nov. 5 ***Perf. 12***

2130 A1061 10ch multicolored .50 .20

Philatelia '81 Int'l Stamp Fair, Frankfurt-am-Main — A1062

1981, Nov. 14 ***Perf. 13¼***

2131 A1062 20ch multicolored 3.00 .45

A1063

Philexfrance '82 International Stamp Exhibition, Paris A1064

Designs: 10ch, Count Ferdinand von Zeppelin, *Graf Zeppelin*, Concorde. 20ch, Aircraft — Santos-Dumont 1905, Brequet 1930, Brequet Provence 1950, Concorde 1970. 30ch, Mona Lisa, six French stamps.

No. 2135: 10ch, Hotel des Invalides, Paris. 20ch, Pres. Mitterand of France. 30ch, International Friendship Building. 70ch, Kim Il Sung.

No. 2136: 60ch, Two French stamps picturing Rembrandt portrait and Picasso painting.

1981, Nov. 14 ***Perf. 13¼***

2132-2134 A1063 Set of 3 10.00 2.00

2135 Sheet of 4, #a.-d. 7.50 2.50

a. A1064 10ch multicolored 1.25 .50

b. A1064 20ch multicolored 1.25 .50

c. A1064 30ch multicolored 1.25 .50

d. A1064 70ch multicolored 1.25 .50

Souvenir Sheet

2136 A1063 60ch multicolored 7.50 2.25

New Year — A1065

1982, Jan. 1 ***Perf. 12***

2137 A1065 10ch multicolored .90 .20

"Korea Prospering Under the Wise Leadership of the Party" — A1066

Party emblem and: 2ch, banners. 10ch (#2139), Iron industry. 10ch (#2140), Produce, city, countryside. 10ch (#2141), Film industry. 10ch (#2142), Mining. 10ch (#2143), Lighthouse, helicopter. 40ch, Idealized cityscape.

1982, Feb. 1

2138-2144 A1066 Set of 7 7.00 1.50

A1067

Pablo Picasso (1881-1973), Painter, Birth Centenary — A1068

Designs (#2145-2148): 10ch, *La Coiffure.* 20ch, *Woman Leaning on Arm.* 25ch, *Child with Pigeon.* 35ch, *Portrait of Gertrude Stein.*

No. 2149: 10ch, *Paulo on a Donkey.* 20ch, *Harlequin.* 25ch, *Reading a Letter.* 35ch, *Harlequin* (diff.) 80ch, *Minotaur.* 90ch, *Mother and Child.*

Nos. 2150-2151: 80ch, *Minotaur.* 90ch, *Mother and Child.*

1982, Mar. 30 ***Perf. 11¾***

2145-2148 A1067 Set of 4 6.00 1.50

2149 Sheet of 6, #a.-f. 14.00 2.75

a. A1067 10ch multicolored 2.25 .45

b. A1067 20ch multicolored 2.25 .45

c.	A1067 25ch multicolored	2.25	.45
d.	A1067 35ch multicolored	2.25	.45
e.	A1067 80ch multicolored	2.25	.45
f.	A1067 90ch multicolored	2.25	.45

Souvenir Sheets

2150-2151 A1068 Set of 2 8.00 4.00

A1069

A1070

Kim Il Sung, 70th Birthday — A1071

Type A1069 (both 10ch): #2152, Kim Il Sung's Birthplace. #2153, Fireworks over Pyongyang.

Type A1070 (10ch), paintings of Kim Il Sung: #2154, "The Day Will Dawn." #2155, Signaling the start of the Pochonbo battle. #2156, Groundbreaking of Potong River Project. #2157, Embracing bereaved children. #2158, Directing operations at front. #2159, "On the Road of Advance." #2160, Speaking with workers at Kangson Steel Plant. #2161, Talking with peasants. #2162, Choosing site for reservoir.

Type A1070 (20ch): #2163, Visiting Komdok Valley. #2164, With Red Flag Company. #2165, With farmers. #2166, Opening metallurgical plant. #2167, Talking with smelters. #2168, At chemical plant. #2169, With fishermen.

No. 2170, Kim surrounded by adoring Koreans. #2171, Kim as a boy.

Perf. 11¾x12 (#2151-2152), 12x11¾

1982, Apr. 15

2152-2169 Set of 18 8.00 2.25

Souvenir Sheets

Perf. 13¼

2170-2171 A1071 60ch Set of 2 5.00 1.75

All type A1070 stamps were issued with setenant labels bearing inscriptions relating to theme of stamp. Values are for stamps with labels attached.

Korean People's Army, 50th Anniv. A1072

1982, Apr. 25 ***Perf. 12***

2172 A1072 10ch multicolored .50 .20

ESSEN '82 Int'l Stamp Fair — A1073

1982, Apr. 28 ***Perf. 11¾x12***

2173 A1073 30ch multicolored 4.50 .50

Four Nature-Remaking Tasks — A1074

1982, Apr. 30 ***Perf. 12***

2174 A1074 10ch multicolored .60 .20

Issued to publicize the program for nature transformation contained in the Second Seven-Year Plan, which included irrigation, land reclamation, terracing, afforestation and water conservation, and reclamation of tidal lands.

Princess Diana, 21st Birthday A1075

Princess Diana (#2175-2178): 10ch, As a baby. 20ch, As little girl on swing. 30ch, As little girl wearing red parka.

No. 2179: 50ch, As girl, wearing blue turtleneck sweater. 60ch, With long hair, wearing gray hat. 70ch, Wearing white hat. 80ch, Wearing white blouse and sweater.

Nos. 2180-2181: 40ch, Diana pushing her brother on swing. 80ch, As #2178d.

1982, May 1 ***Perf. 13¼***

2175-2177	A1075 Set of 3	4.00	1.00
2178	Sheet of 4, #a.-d.	18.00	5.50
a.	A1075 50ch multicolored	3.50	1.25
b.	A1075 60ch multicolored	3.50	1.25
c.	A1075 70ch multicolored	3.50	1.25
d.	A1075 80ch multicolored	3.50	1.25

Souvenir Sheets

2179-2180 A1075 Set of 2 10.00 5.00

For overprints, see Nos. 2210-2215.

Tower of the Juche Idea — A1076

1982, May 21 ***Perf. 12***

2182 A1076 2w multicolored 7.50 2.00

Arch of Triumph — A1077

1982, May 22

2183 A1074 3w multicolored 8.50 2.00

Tigers A1078

(#2184-2185): 20ch, Tiger cubs. 30ch, Tiger cubs (diff.)

No. 2186 (designs horizontal): 30ch, Tiger cub with mother. 40ch, Two cubs playing. 80ch, Two cubs playing, diff.

Nos. 2187: 80ch, Two cubs, horiz.

Perf. 11¾x12 (#2185-2186), 12x11¾

1982, May 30

2184-2185	A1078 Set of 2	7.00	1.00
2186	Sheet of 3, #a.-c.	16.00	3.00
a.	A1078 30ch multicolored	3.00	.50
b.	A1078 40ch multicolored	3.00	.50
c.	A1078 80ch multicolored	3.00	.50

Souvenir Sheet

2187 A1078 80ch Multicolored 6.00 1.50

ESPANA '82 World Cup Championship — A1079

Flags and players of: 10ch, Group 1 countries — Italy, Peru, Poland, Cameroun. 20ch, Group 2 countries — Germany, Chile, Algeria, Austria. 30ch, Group 3 countries — Argentina, Hungary, Belgium, El Salvador. 40ch, Group 4 countries — Great Britain, Czechoslovakia, France, Kuwait. 50ch, Group 5 countries — Spain, Yugoslavia, Honduras, Northern Ireland. 60ch, Group 6 countries — Brazil, Scotland, USSR, New Zealand.

1w, Soccer players, flags, trophy and ESPANA '82 emblem.

1982, June 12 ***Perf. 13¼***

2188-2193 A1079 Set of 6 13.00 4.00

Souvenir Sheet

2194 A1079 1w multicolored 11.00 4.00

For overprints, see Nos. 2217-2223.

Space Exploration A1080

Designs: 10ch, Rocket launch. 20ch, Spaceship over planet. 80ch, Spaceship between planets.

80ch, Spaceship exploring desert area of other planet.

1982, June 20 ***Perf. 11¾x11½***

2195-2196	A1080 Set of 2	3.50	1.50
2197	Sheet of 3, #2196-2197, 2197c + label	6.00	2.50
c.	A1080 80ch multicolored	2.00	.75

Souvenir Sheet

2198 A1079 80ch multicolored 3.75 1.50

Nos. 2195, 2196, and 2197c were issued setenant within No. 2197. Nos. 2195 and 2196 were also issued in large sheet format.

Johann von Goethe (1749-1832), Writer, 150th Death Anniv. A1081

Silhouettes: 10ch, Charlotte von Stein, 20ch, Goethe's sister. 25ch, Charlotte Buff. 35ch, Lili Schönemann.

No. 2203: 10ch, Goethe's mother. 20ch, Angelika Kauffman. 25ch, Anna Amalia. 35ch, Charlotte von Lengefeld. 80ch, Goethe.

No. 2204: 80ch, Goethe.

1982, July 25 ***Perf. 11¾x12***

2199-2202	A1081 Set of 4	3.75	1.50
2203	Sheet of 5, #a.-e. + label	9.00	2.00
a.	A1081 10ch multicolored	1.75	.50
b.	A1081 20ch multicolored	1.75	.50
c.	A1081 25ch multicolored	1.75	.50
d.	A1081 35ch multicolored	1.75	.50
e.	A1081 80ch multicolored	1.75	.50

Souvenir Sheet

2204 A1081 80ch multicolored 4.00 1.75

Nos. 2104-2108 Overprinted in Blue

1982, Aug. 20

2205-2208 A1054 Set of 4 15.00 —

Souvenir Sheet

2209 A1054 70ch multicolored 15.00 —

Nos. 2175-2179 Overprinted in Blue

1982, Aug. 20

2210-2212	A1075	Set of 3	15.00	—
2213		Sheet of 4	30.00	—

Souvenir Sheet

2214-2215	A1075	Set of 2	25.00	—

Nos. 2025a, 2188-2194 Overprinted in Blue

1982, Aug. 25

2216	A1035	Sheet of 4, #a.-d.	14.00	—
a.		10ch multicolored	1.00	—
b.		20ch multicolored	2.00	—
c.		30ch multicolored	3.00	—
d.		70ch multicolored	6.00	—
2217-2222	A1079	Set of 6	15.00	—

Souvenir Sheet

2223	A1079	1w multicolored	12.50	—

ESPANA '82 World Soccer Cup Winners — A1082

Designs: 20ch, Player holding World Cup aloft. 30ch, Three players with World Cup.

No. 2226: 30ch, as No. 2222. 40ch, As No. 2223. 80ch, King Juan Carlos of Spain and two players with World Cup.

No. 2227: 80ch, as No. 2226c.

1982, Aug. 30 ***Perf. 13¼***

2224-2225	A1082	Set of 2	4.00	1.00
2226		Sheet of 4, #a.-c. + label	8.00	—
a.		A1082 30ch multicolored	—	—
b.		A1082 40ch multicolored	—	—
c.		A1082 80ch multicolored	—	—

Souvenir Sheet

2227	A1082	80ch multicolored	9.00	2.00

A1083

1st Wedding Anniv. of Prince and Princess of Wales — A1084

1982, Sept. 21

2228	A1083	30ch multicolored	10.00	4.00

Souvenir Sheet

2229	A1084	80ch multicolored	15.00	5.00

No. 2228 was issued in sheets of four stamps and two labels.

Birth of Prince William of Wales A1085

Designs: 10ch, Charles and Diana with Prince William (Charles in suit, Diana in pink hat and dress). 20ch, Couple with William. 30ch, Couple with William (diff.). 40ch, Diana with William. 50ch, Diana with William (diff.).

No. 2235: 10ch, Diana holding bouquet. 20ch, Charles carrying William, with Diana. 30ch, Charles carrying William, with Diana (diff.). 80ch, Couple with William (diff.).

No. 2236 (horiz.): 40ch, Charles and Diana. 50ch, Charles and Diana in evening dress. 80ch, Charles holding William, with Diana.

Nos. 2237-2238 (both 50ch): Diana holding William, with Royal Family; Diana holding William, with godparents.

1982, Sept. 29

2230-2234	A1085	Set of 5	16.00	5.00
2235		Sheet of 4, #a.-d.	15.00	6.00
a.		A1085 10ch multicolored	3.25	1.25
b.		A1085 20ch multicolored	3.25	1.25
c.		A1085 30ch multicolored	3.25	1.25
d.		A1085 80ch multicolored	3.25	1.25
2236		Sheet of 3, #a.-c.	15.00	6.00
a.		A1085 40ch multicolored	4.00	1.75
b.		A1085 50ch multicolored	4.00	1.75
c.		A1085 80ch multicolored	4.00	1.75

Souvenir Sheets

2237-2238	A1085	Set of 2	20.00	8.00

A1086

Birth of Prince William of Wales — A1087

Nos. 2239-2244 are composed of layered plastic, on gummed paper, which creates two different images on each stamp, depending on the angle at which it is viewed.

Designs Nos. 2239-2241 (all 30ch): #2239, Charles, Diana and William/Diana holding William. #2240, Charles, Diana and William (diff.)/Couple with William (Charles in suit, Diana in pink hat and dress). #2241, Diana and William/Charles and Diana with William (Charles in suit, Diana in blue dress).

Designs Nos. 2242-2244 (all 80ch): #2242, Diana and William, Portrait of Diana/Charles. #2243, Diana and William, St. Paul's Church/Wedding portrait of Royal Couple. #2244, Charles and Diana with William/Diana holding bouquet.

1982, Oct. 1 ***Imperf.***

2239-2241	A1086	Set of 3	35.00	—

Souvenir Sheets

2242-2244	A1087	Set of 3	60.00	—

Bicentenary of Manned Flight — A1088

Designs: 10ch, Baldwin's airship *Nulli Secundus II*, 1908. 20ch, Tissandier Brothers' airship, 1883. 30ch, Parseval *PL VIII*, 1912. 40ch, Count Lennox's balloon *Eagle*, 1834.

No. 2249: 10ch, Pauley and Durs Egg's airship, *The Dolphin*, 1818. 20ch, Guyton de Morveau's balloon, 1784. 30ch, Sir George Cayley's airship, 1837. 40ch, Camille Vert's balloon *Poisson Volant*, 1859. 80ch, Dupuy de Lôme's airship, 1872.

No. 2250: Masse's oar-powered balloon, 1784, vert.

1982, Nov. 21 ***Perf. 13¼***

2245-2248	A1088	Set of 4	7.00	2.00
2249		Sheet of 5, #a.-e. + label	13.00	6.00
a.		A1088 10ch multicolored	2.25	1.00
b.		A1088 20ch multicolored	2.25	1.00
c.		A1088 30ch multicolored	2.25	1.00
d.		A1088 40ch multicolored	2.25	1.00
e.		A1088 80ch multicolored	2.25	1.00

Souvenir Sheet

2250	A1085	80ch multicolored	4.50	2.00

Bicentenary of Manned Flight A1089

Designs: 10ch, Balthasar Antoine Dunker's *Utopic Balloon Post*, 1784-90. 20ch, "and they fly into heaven and have no wings." 30ch, Pierre Testu-Brissy's balloon flight with horse, 1796. 40ch, Test flight of Gaston Tissandier's balloon *Zenith*, 1875.

No. 2255: 10ch, Montgolfier balloon at Versailles, 1783. 20ch, Montgolfier Brothers' balloon, 1783. 30ch, Charles' hydrogen balloon landing at Nesle. 40ch, Blanchard and Jeffries' flight over the English Channel, 1785. 80ch, Henri Giffard's balloon *Le Grand Ballon Captif* at World's Fair, 1878.

No. 2256: "Ballons Monte" balloon mail service from besieged Paris, 1870-1871.

1982, Dec. 10

2251-2254	A1089	Set of 4	11.00	4.00
2255		Sheet of 5, #a.-e. + label	25.00	6.50
a.		A1089 10ch multicolored	4.50	1.25
b.		A1089 20ch multicolored	4.50	1.25
c.		A1089 30ch multicolored	4.50	1.25
d.		A1089 40ch multicolored	4.50	1.25
e.		A1089 80ch multicolored	4.50	1.25

Souvenir Sheet

2256	A1089	80ch multicolored	5.00	2.00

Tale of the Hare — A1090

Designs: 10ch, Turtle searching for hare. 20ch, Turtle and hare going to Dragon King Palace. 30ch, Hare swindling Dragon King, demanding her liver. 40ch, Hare cheating turtle.

1982, Dec. 25 ***Perf. 12***

2257-2260	A1090	Set of 4	8.00	1.25

Socialist Constitution, 10th Anniv. — A1091

1982, Dec. 27

2261	A1091	10ch multicolored	.50	.20

New Year — A1092

1983, Jan. 1 ***Perf. 12¼x12***

2262	A1092	10ch multicolored	.50	.20

Saenal Newspaper, 55th Anniv. — A1093

1983, Jan. 15 ***Perf. 11½x11¾***

2263 A1093 10ch multicolored .90 .20

Rembrandt Paintings A1094

Designs: 10ch, *Man in Oriental Costume.* 20ch, *The Noble Slav.* 30ch, *Dr. Tulp's Anatomy Lesson* (detail). 40ch, *Two Scholars Disputing.*

No. 2268: 10ch, *Child with Dead Peacocks.* 20ch, *Old Man in Fur Hat.* 30ch, *Portrait of a Fashionable Couple.* 40ch, *Woman with Child.* 80ch, *Woman Holding an Ostrich Feather Fan.*

No. 2269: 80ch, *Self-Portrait.*

1983, Jan. 25 ***Perf. 11¾x11½***

2264-2267 A1094 Set of 4 7.50 1.50
2268 Sheet of 5, #a.-e. + label 15.00 7.50
a. A1094 10ch multicolored 2.00 1.00
b. A1094 20ch multicolored 2.00 1.00
c. A1094 30ch multicolored 2.00 1.00
d. A1094 40ch multicolored 2.00 1.00
e. A1094 80ch multicolored 2.00 1.00

Souvenir Sheet

Perf. 11¾x12

2269 A1094 80ch multicolored 4.00 1.25

Nos. 2080-2085 Overprinted "XXIII Summer Olympic Games 1984" and Olympic Rings

1983, Feb. 10

2270-2274 A1044 Set of 5 20.00 —

Souvenir Sheet

2275 A1044 70ch multicolored 25.00 —

Luposta Int'l Air Mail Exhib., Köln — A1095

1983, Jan. 25 ***Perf. 11¾x11½***

2276 30ch multicolored 3.00 1.00
2277 40ch multicolored 3.00 1.00
a. Pair, #2276-2277 7.00 3.00

Virgin and Child, by Stephan Lochner — A1096

Souvenir Sheet

Perf. 13¼

2278 A1096 80ch multicolored 3.50 1.75

Wangjaesen Meeting, 50th Anniv. A1097

1983, Mar. 11 ***Perf. 11½x11¾***

2279 A1097 10ch multicolored .50 .20

Karl Marx, Centenary of Death — A1098

1983, Mar. 14 ***Perf. 11¾x12***

2280 A1098 10ch multicolored 2.25 .25

Thousand-ri Journey for Learning, 60th Anniv. — A1099

1983, Mar. 16 ***Perf. 12***

2281 A1099 10ch multicolored 1.00 .20

A1100

Raphael (1483-1520), 500th Birth Anniv. — A1101

Designs: 10ch, *Madonna of the Goldfinch.* 30ch, *Madonna of the Grand Duke.* 50ch (#2284), *Madonna of the Chair.*

No. 2285: 20ch, *The School of Athens* (detail). 50ch (#2285b), *Madonna of the Lamb.* 80ch, *The Beautiful Gardener.*

No. 2286: 80ch, *Madonna of St. Sixte.*

1983, Mar. 20 ***Perf. 13½***

2282-2284 A1100 Set of 3 6.00 1.00
2285 Sheet of 3, #a.-c. + label 15.00 3.50
a. A1100 20ch multicolored 4.00 .75
b. A1100 50ch multicolored 4.00 .75
c. A1100 80ch multicolored 4.00 .75

Souvenir Sheet

2286 A1101 80ch multicolored 4.50 1.25

Pyongyang Buildings — A1102

Designs: 2ch, Chongryu Restaurant. 10ch (#2288), Munsu Street. 10ch (#2289), Ice Rink. 40ch, Department Store No. 1. 70ch, Grand People's Study House.

1983, Apr. 7 ***Perf. 12¼***

2287-2291 A1102 Set of 5 6.00 .75
2287a 2ch Unsurfaced white paper, without gum 10.00 —
2288a 10ch Unsurfaced white paper, without gum 10.00 —
2289a 10ch Unsurfaced white paper, without gum 10.00 —
2290a 40ch Unsurfaced white paper, without gum 10.00 —
2291a 40ch Unsurfaced white paper, without gum 10.00 —

Int'l Institute of the Juche Idea, 5th Anniv. — A1103

1983, Apr. 9 ***Perf. 12¼x12***

2292 A1103 10ch multicolored .50 .20

Pre-Olympic Games, Los Angeles '84 — A1104

Designs (values in gold): 20ch (#2293), Judo. 30ch (#2294), Judo (diff.). 40ch (#2295), Boxing. 50ch (#2296), Weightlifting.

No. 2297 (values in black): 20ch, Wrestling. 30ch, Judo (diff.). 40ch, Shooting. 50ch, Wrestling. (diff.) 80ch, Boxing (diff.).

No. 2298: 80ch, Judo (diff.)

1983, Apr. 20 ***Perf. 11¼***

2293-2296 A1104 Set of 4 13.00 1.50
2297 Sheet of 5, #a.-e. + label 25.00 1.00
a. A1104 20ch multicolored 4.00 .20
b. A1104 30ch multicolored 4.00 .20
c. A1104 40ch multicolored 4.00 .20
d. A1104 50ch multicolored 4.00 .20
e. A1104 80ch multicolored 4.00 .20

Souvenir Sheet

Perf. 13½

2298 A1104 80ch multicolored 10.00 1.00

World Communications Year — A1105

1983, Apr. 30 ***Perf. 11¾x12***

2299 A1105 10ch multicolored 2.00 .20

TEMBAL '83 Int'l Topical Stamp Exhib., Basel — A1106

Designs: 20ch, Emblem, giant panda and stamp. 30ch, Emblem, DPRK flag and "Basel Dove" stamp (Switzerland No. 3L1).

1983, May 21 ***Perf. 12***

2300-2301 A1106 Set of 2 7.50 .75

Old Ships — A1107

Designs: 20ch, *Colourful Cow* (Hamburg, 1402). 35ch, *Great Harry* (England, 1555). 50ch, *Eagle of Lübeck* (Lübeck, 1567).

No. 2305: 20ch, Turtle Boat (Korea, 1592). 35ch, Admiral Li Sun Sin (1545-98), inventor of the Turtle Boat. 50ch, *Merkur* (Prussia, 1847). 80ch, *Duchess Elisabeth* (West Germany).

No. 2306: 80ch, *Christoforo Colombo* (Italy).

1983, May 30 ***Perf. 11x11¼***

2302-2304 A1107 Set of 3 5.00 1.50
2305 Sheet of 4, #a.-d. + 2 labels 12.00 2.50
a. A1107 20ch multicolored 3.00 .50
b. A1107 35ch multicolored 3.00 .50
c. A1107 50ch multicolored 3.00 .50
d. A1107 80ch multicolored 3.00 .50

Souvenir Sheet

Perf. 13½x13¼

2306 A1107 80ch multicolored 6.00 3.00

Steam Locomotives — A1108

Designs: 20ch, *Locomotion* (Great Britain, 1825). 35ch, *De Adler* (Germany, 1835). 50ch, *Austria* (1837).

No. 2310: 20ch, *Drache* (Germany, 1848. 35ch, Korean Train. 50ch, Bristal and Exeter Railway locomotive (Great Britain, 1853). 80ch, Caledonian Railway locomotive (Great Britain, 1859).

No. 2311: 80ch, *Ilmarinen* (Finland, 1860).

1983, June 20 ***Perf. 12x11¾***

2307-2309 A1108 Set of 3 13.00 2.50
2310 Sheet of 4, #a.-d. + 2 labels 40.00 3.50
a. A1108 20ch multicolored 3.00 .75
b. A1108 35ch multicolored 3.00 .75

c. A1108 50ch multicolored 3.00 .75
d. A1108 80ch multicolored 3.00 .75

Souvenir Sheet

Perf. 12

2311 A1108 80ch multicolored 30.00 1.50

Publication of the Five-Point Policy for Korean Reunification, 10th Anniv. — A1109

1983, June 23 ***Perf. 12¼***
2312 A1109 10ch multicolored 1.40 .20

World Conference of Journalists Against Imperialism and for Friendship and Peace — A1110

Designs: 10ch, Emblem, Tower of Juche Idea, fireworks, "Welcome." 40ch, Emblem, clasped hands, rainbow, "Friendship." Emblem, map, hand with raised forefinger, "Korea Is One."

1983, July 2 ***Perf. 12x11¾***
2313-2315 A1110 Set of 3 1.75 .30

"Let's Create the Speed of the 80s" A1111

1983, July 10 ***Perf. 12x12¼***
2316 A1111 10ch multicolored .50 .20

Korean War, 30th Anniv. A1112

1983, July 27
2317 A1112 10ch multicolored .50 .20

Bangkok 1983 Int'l Stamp Exhib. — A1113

Designs: 40ch, *Gorch Foch* and 1978 DPRK 2ch stamp depicting the *Mangyongbong* (Scott #1693). 80ch, Bangkok temple, Great Britain Penny Black (Scott #1) and DPRK IYC stamp

1983, Aug. 4 ***Perf. 12x11¾***
2318 A1113 40ch multicolored 3.50 1.00

Souvenir Sheet

Perf. 11½x11¾

2319 A1113 80ch multicolored 7.00 3.50

A1114

Winter Olympic Games, Sarajevo 1984 — A1115

Designs: 10ch, Skiier. 30ch, Figure skaters. 50ch, Ski jumper.
No. 2323 (all vert.): 20ch, Woman figure skater. 50ch, Hockey player. 80ch, Speed skater.
No. 2324, 80ch, Skier shooting rifle (biathlon).

1983, Aug. 20
2320-2322 A1114 Set of 3 8.00 1.50
2323 Sheet of 3, #a.-c., perf 11¾x12 17.00 2.75
a. A1114 20ch multicolored 4.00 .75
b. A1114 50ch multicolored 4.00 .75
c. A1114 80ch multicolored 4.00 .75

Souvenir Sheet

2324 A1115 80ch multicolored 7.50 1.25

Democratic People's Republic of Korea, 35th Anniv. — A1116

1983, Sept. 9 ***Perf. 13¼x13½***
2325 A1116 10ch multicolored .65 .20

Folk Games — A1117

Designs: 10ch (#2326), Archery. 40ch (#2327), Seesaw. No. 2328: 10ch, Flying kites. 40ch, Swinging.

1983, Sept. 20 ***Perf. 11¾x12***
2326-2327 A1117 Set of 2 5.00 .50
2328 Sheet of 2, #a.-b. 2.50 .40
a. A1117 10ch multicolored .75 .20
b. A1117 40ch multicolored .75 .20

Korean-Chinese Friendship A1118

1983, Oct. 25 ***Perf. 12***
2329 A1118 10ch multicolored .75 .20

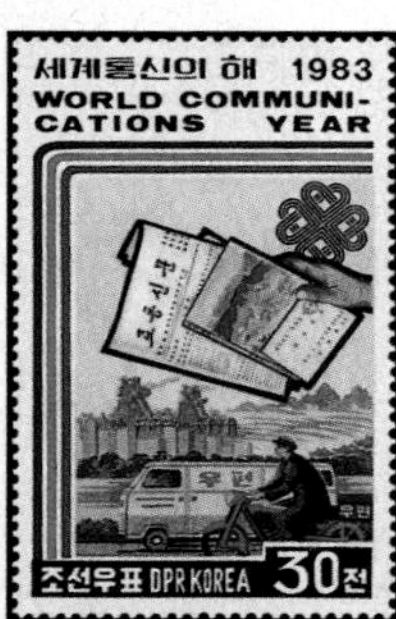

A1119

World Communications Year — A1120

Designs: 30ch (#2330), *Redong Sinmun* and magazine. 40ch (#2331), Letters and forms of postal transport.
No. 2332: 30ch, Communications satellite, satellite dish. 40ch, TV camera and relay tower. 80ch, Telephone and satellite dishes.
No. 2333, 80ch, Emblem, communications satellite.

1983, Oct. 30 ***Perf. 13½***
2330-2331 A1119 Set of 2 9.00 1.75
2332 Sheet of 3, #a.-c. 5.50 1.00
a. A1119 30ch multicolored 1.00 .25
b. A1119 40ch multicolored 1.00 .25
c. A1119 80ch multicolored 1.00 .25

Souvenir Sheet

2333 A1120 80ch multicolored 6.00 1.25

A1121

Paintings by Peter Paul Rubens — A1122

Designs: 40ch (#2334), *Portrait of Helene Fourmet.*
No. 2335 (both horiz.): 40ch, Detail from *Portrait of a Young Lady.* 80ch, *Diana Returning from Hunt.*
No. 2336, 80ch, *The Bear Hunt.*

1983, Nov. 10
2334 A1121 40ch multicolored 1.75 .45
2335 Sheet of 2, #a.-b. 4.50 1.25
a. A1121 40ch multicolored 1.75 .45
b. A1121 80ch multicolored 1.75 .45

Souvenir Sheet

2336 A1122 80ch multicolored 3.25 .75

Olympic Games, Los Angeles 1984 A1123

Designs: 10ch, Sprinter. 30ch, Cyclists. 50ch, Volleyball.
No. 2340: 20ch, Show jumping. 50ch, Fencing. 80ch, Gymnastics.
No. 2341: 80ch, Judo.

1983, Nov. 30 ***Perf. 11½***
2337-2339 A1123 Set of 3 10.50 1.25
2340 Sheet of 3, #a.-c. 30.00 2.00
a. A1123 20ch multicolored 7.00 .50
b. A1123 50ch multicolored 7.00 .50
c. A1123 80ch multicolored 7.00 .50

Souvenir Sheet

2341 A1123 80ch multicolored 3.50 1.00

Six deluxe souvenir sheets of one, each denominated 1w, exist. Value, set of 6 sheets, $100.

A1124

Antonio Correggio (1489-1534), 450th Death Anniv. — A1125

Designs: 20ch, *St. Catherine.* 35ch, *Madonna.* 50ch, *Madonna with St. John.*
No. 2345: 20ch, *Morning* (detail). 35ch, *Morning* (diff. detail). 50ch, *St. Catherine* (diff.). 80ch, *Madonna and Child.*
No. 2346: 80ch, *Madonna and Child with Music-Making Angels.*

1983, Dec. 12 ***Perf. 13¼***
2342-2344 A1124 Set of 3 5.00 1.25
2345 Sheet of 4, #a.-d. 12.00 3.50
a. A1124 20ch multicolored 2.50 .75
b. A1124 35ch multicolored 2.50 .75
c. A1124 50ch multicolored 2.50 .75
d. A1124 80ch multicolored 2.50 .75

Souvenir Sheet

2346 A1125 80ch multicolored 4.50 1.25

Cats A1126

Domestic cats, each different, denominated 10ch. Frame color: #2347, green. #2348, gray. #2349, gold. #2350, red. #2351, blue.

1983, Dec. 20
2347-2351 A1126 Set of 5 12.00 .50

Six souvenir sheets inscribed Sarajevo '84, each containing one 1w stamp, were issued on Dec. 31, 1983. Value $80.

New Year — A1127

1984, Jan. 1 ***Perf. 12***
2352 A1127 10ch multicolored 1.00 .20

Korean Workers Party A1128

Designs (both 10ch): No. 2353, Komdok General Mining Enterprise, Ore-dressing Plant No. 3, and Party flag. No. 2354, Worker holding books, and Party flag.

1984, Feb. 16
2353-2354 A1128 Set of 2 1.00 .20
2353a 10ch, unsurfaced white paper, without gum 20.00 —
2354a 10ch, unsurfaced white paper, without gum 20.00 —

Farm Worker, Grain A1129

1984, Feb. 25
2355 A1129 10ch multicolored .60 .20

Publication of the *Theses on the Socialist Rural Question in Our Country*, 20th anniv.

Changdok School, Chilgol A1130

Kim's Birthplace, Rejoicing Crowd A1131

1984, Apr. 15
2356 A1130 5ch multicolored .50 .20
a. Unsurfaced white paper, without gum 15.00 —

2357 A1131 10ch multicolored .50 .20
a. Unsurfaced white paper, without gum 20.00 —

Kim Il Sung, 72nd birthday.

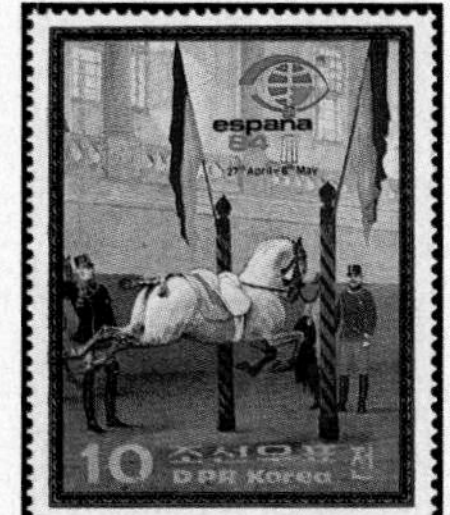
A1132

España '84 Int'l Stamp Exhib. — A1133

Designs: 10ch, *Spanish Riding School of Vienna*, by Julius von Blaas. 20ch, *Ferdinand of Austria*, by Rubens.
No. 2360: 80ch, *Spanish Riding School*, by von Blaas.

1984, Apr. 27 ***Perf. 13½***
2358-2359 A1132 Set of 2 3.50 .75

Souvenir Sheet

2360 A1133 80ch multicolored 6.50 1.25

Kiyang Irrigation System, 25th Anniv. — A1134

1984, Apr. 30
2361 A1134 10ch multicolored .65 .20

Raphael, 500th Anniv. of Birth (in 1983) — A1135

Designs: 10ch, *Portrait of Angolo Doni.* 20ch, *Portrait of La Donna Velata.* 30ch, *Portrait of Jeanne d'Aragon.*
80ch, *St. Sebastian.*

1984, Apr. 30 ***Perf. 11¾x12***
2362-2364 A1135 Set of 3 4.00 1.00

Souvenir Sheet
Perf. 11¾x11½

2365 A1135 80ch multicolored 3.50 1.25

Socialist Construction A1136

1984, May 20 ***Perf. 12***
2366 A1136 10ch multicolored .65 .20

1984 Winter Olympics Games Medal Winners — A1137

Designs: 20ch (#2367), Speed skating (Karin Enke, DDR). 30ch (#2368), Bobsledding (DDR).
No. 2369: 10ch, Ski jumping (Matti Nykaenen, Finland). 20ch (#2369b), Slalom (Max Julen, Switzerland). 30ch (#2369c), Downhill skiing (Maria Walliser, Switzerland).
No. 2370 (both vert.): 40ch, Cross-country skiing (Thomas Wassberg, Sweden). 80ch, Cross-country skiing (Maria Liisa Hamalainen).
No. 2371 (vert.): 80ch, Biathlon (Peter Angerer, West Germany).

1984, May 20 ***Perf. 13½***
2367-2368 A1137 Set of 2 3.00 .75
2369 Sheet of 3, #a.-c. 25.00 1.25
a. A1137 10ch multicolored 6.00 .35
b. A1137 20ch multicolored 6.00 .35
c. A1137 30ch multicolored 6.00 .35
2370 Sheet of 2, #a.-b. 5.00 1.00
a. A1137 40ch multicolored 2.00 .40
b. A1137 80ch multicolored 2.00 .40

Souvenir Sheet

2371 A1137 80ch multicolored 3.50 1.00

Essen '84 Int'l Stamp Exhib. — A1138

Designs: 20ch, Type "202" express locomotive (1939). 30ch, Type "E" freight locomotive (1919).
No. 2375: 80ch, Type "D" locomotive in Germany.

1984, May 26 ***Perf. 12x11¾***
2372-2373 A1138 Set of 2 10.00 1.00

Souvenir Sheet

2374 A1138 80ch multicolored 9.00 1.25

Edgar Degas, 150th Birth Anniv. — A1139

Designs: 10ch, *Mlle. Fiocre in the Ballet 'La Source.'* 20ch, *The Dance Foyer at the Rue le Peletier Opera.* 30ch, *Race Meeting.*
No. 2378: 80ch, *Dancers at the Bars.*

1984, June 10 ***Perf. 12***
2375-2377 A1138 Set of 3 8.00 1.25

Souvenir Sheet
Perf. 11½

2378 A1139 80ch multicolored 4.50 1.25

Irrigation Experts Meeting — A1140

1984, June 16 ***Perf. 11¾x12***
2379 A1140 2ch multicolored .80 .20

UPU Congress/Hamburg 1984 Stamp Exhib. — A1141

No. 2381: 80ch, *Gorch Fock*, DPRK stamp depicting Turtle Boat..

1984, June 19
2380 A1141 20ch multicolored 3.50 .35

Souvenir Sheet
Perf. 11¾x11½

2381 A1141 80ch multicolored 6.00 2.00

Tripartite Talks Proposal — A1142

1984, June 25 ***Perf. 12¼***
2382 A1142 10ch multicolored .65 .20

Alfred Bernhard Nobel, 150th Birth Anniv. (in 1983) A1143

Designs: 20ch, Nobel in laboratory. 30ch, Nobel portrait.
No. 2385: 80ch, Nobel portrait, diff.

1984, June 30 ***Perf. 13½***
2383-2384 A1143 Set of 2 8.00 .75

Souvenir Sheet

2385 A1143 80ch multicolored 7.00 2.00

Nos. 2383 and 2384 were issued se-tenant with labels depicting Nobel's laboratory and home, respectively.

Improvement of Korean Living Standards — A1144

1984, July 10 *Perf. 11¾x12*
2386 A1144 10ch multicolored .70 .20

Kuandian Conf., 65th Anniv. A1145

1984, Aug. 17 *Perf. 12x12¼*
2387 A1145 10ch multicolored 1.25 .20

Sunhwa School, Mangyongdae — A1146

1984, Aug. 17 *Perf. 12*
2388 A1146 10ch multicolored 1.10 .20

School of Kim Il Sung's father, Kim Hyong Jik.

A1147

A1148

Flowers: 10ch, *Cattleya loddigesii*. 20ch, *Thunia bracteata*. 30ch, *Phalaenopsis amabilis*.
No. 2392: 80ch, *Kimilsungia*.

1984, Aug. 20
2389-2391 A1147 Set of 3 4.00 .60

Souvenir Sheet

2392 A1148 80ch multicolored 5.00 1.00

Fishing Industry A1149

Designs: 5ch, Swordfish and trawler. 10ch, Marlin and trawler. 40ch, *Histiophorus orientalis*.

1984, Aug. 25
2393-2395 A1149 Set of 3 4.50 1.00

Revolutionary Museum, Chilgol — A1150

1984, Aug. 29
2396 A1150 10ch multicolored .90 .20

"Let's All Become the Kim Hyoks and Cha Gwang Sus of the '80s!" — A1151

1984, Aug. 31
2397 A1151 10ch multicolored .90 .20

Orient Express, Centenary — A1152

Designs: 10ch, Inauguration of a French railway line in 1860. 20ch, Opening of a British railway line in 1821. 30ch, Inauguration of Paris-Rouen line, 1843.
No. 2401: 80ch, Interior views of passenger cars, 1905.

1984, Sept. 7 *Perf. 13½x13¼*
2398-2400 A1152 Set of 3 8.00 1.25

Souvenir Sheet

2401 A1152 80ch multicolored 7.00 1.75

Greenwich Meridian Time, Centenary A1153

Designs: 10ch, Clockface, astronomical observatory.
No. 2403: 80ch, Clock face, buildings, Chollima statue.

1984, Sept. 15 *Perf. 12*
2402 A1153 10ch multicolored 4.00 —

Souvenir Sheet
Perf. 11¾x11½

2403 A1153 80ch multicolored 6.00 1.25

Hamhung Grand Theater A1154

1984, Sept. 21
2404 A1154 10ch multicolored .90 .20

Automation of Industry — A1155

1984, Sept. 25 *Perf. 12¼*
2405 A1155 10ch multicolored .90 .25
a. Unsurfaced white paper, without gum 8.00 —

A1156

18th Century Korean Paintings — A1157

Designs: 10ch, *Dragon Angler*. 20ch, *Ox Driver*, horiz. 30ch, *Bamboo*, horiz.
80ch, *Autumn Night*.

1984, Sept. 30 *Perf. 12 (#2406), 13¼*
2406-2408 A1156 Set of 3 4.00 .60

Souvenir Sheet
Perf. 13¼

2409 A1157 80ch multicolored 3.50 1.25

K.E. Tsiolkovski (1857-1935), Russian Space Scientist A1158

Designs: 20ch, Portrait. 30ch, Earth, sputnik.
No. 2412: 80ch, Rocket launch.

1984, Oct. 5 *Perf. 11¾*
2410-2411 A1158 Set of 2 2.00 .45

Souvenir Sheet
Perf. 11¾x11½

2412 A1158 80ch multicolored 4.00 .75

Container Ships — A1159

Designs: 10ch, *Pongdaesan*. 20ch, *Ryongnamsan*. 30ch, *Rungrado*.
No. 2416: 80ch, *Kumgangsan*

1984, Oct. 6 *Perf. 12x11¾*
2413-2415 A1158 Set of 3 3.50 .75

Souvenir Sheet
Perf. 12

2416 A1159 80ch multicolored 5.00 1.25

A1160

A1161

Wild Animals: 10ch, Spotted hyenas. 20ch, Caracal. 30ch, Black-backed jackals. 40ch, Foxes.
80ch, Falcon.

1984, Oct. 13 *Perf. 13¼*
2417-2420 A1160 Set of 4 4.50 1.00

Souvenir Sheet

2421 A1161 80ch multicolored 6.50 1.25

Marie Curie (1867-1934), Physicist, 50th Death Anniv. A1162

No. 2423: 80ch, Portrait of Mme. Curie.

1984, Oct. 21 *Perf. 12*
2422 A1162 10ch multicolored 4.00 .20

Souvenir Sheet
Perf. 11¾x11½

2423 A1162 80ch multicolored 6.00 1.25

A1163

Birds: 10ch, Hoopoe. 20ch, South African crowned cranes. 30ch, Saddle-bill stork. 40ch, Chestnut-eared Aracari.
No. 2428: 80ch, Black kite.

1984, Nov. 5 ***Perf. 11½***
2424-2427 A1163 Set of 4 8.50 1.25

Souvenir Sheet

2428 A1163 80ch multicolored 8.50 1.25

Space Exploration — A1164

Designs: 10ch, Cosmonaut. 20ch, Cosmonaut on space-walk. 30ch, Cosmonaut (diff.)
No. 2432: 80ch, Moon vehicle.

1984, Nov. 15 ***Perf. 12***
2429-2431 A1164 Set of 3 2.50 .50

Souvenir Sheet

2432 A1164 80ch multicolored 4.00 1.00

Russian Icebreakers — A1165

Designs: 20ch, *Arktika.* 30ch, *Ermak.*
No. 2435: 80ch, *Lenin.*

1984, Nov. 26 ***Perf. 13¼***
2433-2434 A1165 Set of 2 3.25 .60

Souvenir Sheet

2435 A1165 80ch multicolored 5.00 1.25

A1166

Dmitri Mendeleev (1834-1907), Chemist, 150th Birth Anniv. — A1167

1984, Dec. 1 ***Perf. 13¼***
2436 A1166 10ch multicolored 1.75 .20

Souvenir Sheet

2437 A1167 80ch multicolored 4.00 1.25

Historic European Royalty, Scenes — A1168

British Monarchs — A1169

Queen Elizabeth II — A1170

No. 2438 (all 10ch): a, Konrad III, 1149 (Germany). b, Henry VIII (England). c, Henry VI (England). d, King John (England). e, Fleet of Elizabeth I (England). f, Philip II Augustus (France). g, Thames and London Bridge, 1616. h, Elizabeth I (England). i, Charles VII, parade (England).
No. 2439 (all 10ch): a, Prince Eugene, 1706 (Savoy). b, Kaiser Wilhelm II (Germany). c, Philip V (Spain). d, Ludwig II (Bavaria). e, Alfonso XIII (Spain). f, Mary Stuart (Scotland). g, Charles Edward Stuart, 1745 (Scotland). h, Marie-Louise (Austria). i, Charles V, 1547 (Spain).
No. 2440 (Horiz., all 10ch): a, Maria Theresa (Austria). b, Francis I, 1814 (Austria). c, Leopold II, 1844 (Austria). d, Louis XVIII (France). e, Versailles, 1688. f, Louis XIV (France). g, Prince Wilhelm (Germany). h, Franz Joseph I (Austria). i, Ludwig II (Bavaria).
No. 2441 (Horiz., all 10ch): a, Napoleon III (France. b, Rudolph of Habsburg, Basel 1273. c, Henry IV (France). d, Louis XII (France). e, Maximilian I (Holy Roman Empire). f, Peter the Great, Amsterdam Harbor (Russia). g, Louis VIII (France). h, Don Juan/Battle of Lepanto, 1571. i, Neuschwaustein Castle.
No. 2442 (all 10ch): a, William I. b, Richard II. c, Henry V. d, Henry VI. e, Richard III. f, Edward IV. g, Henry VII. h, Henry VIII, full length portrait. i, Henry VIII, ¾-face portrait, as young man.
No. 2443 (all 10ch): a, Henry VIII, ¾-face portrait, as middle-aged man. b, Mary I. c, Elizabeth I, facing left. d, Edward VI. e, Elizabeth I, facing right. f, Lady Jane Grey. g, Mary, Queen of Scots. h, James I. i, Charles I.
No. 2444 (all 10ch): a, Charles I. b, Henrietta Marie. c, Charles II. d, James II. e, George I, seated. f, William IV. g, Queen Anne, full-length portrait. h, George I, in profile. i. Queen Mary II.
No. 2445 (all 10ch): a, Queen Anne, with her son, William, Duke of Gloucester. b, George II, facing forward. c, George II, in profile. d, George IV. e, George III. f, William III. g, William IV. h, Queen Victoria. i, Prince Albert.
No. 2446 (all 10ch): a, Edward VII. b, Queen Alexandra. c, George V and Royal Family. d, George VI. e, George VI and Royal Family. f, Queen Elizabeth II. g, Prince Charles. h, Prince William of Wales, with Prince Charles and Princess Diana. i, Princess Diana.

1984, Dec. 20 ***Perf. 12¼x12***

Sheets of 9

2438-2446 Set of 9 125.00 —

Souvenir Sheet

Perf. 11½

2447 A1170 80ch multicolored 20.00 12.00

Kim Il Sung's Visits to Eastern Europe — A1171

No. 2448 (all 10ch): a, USSR. b, Poland. c, DDR. d, Czechoslovakia.
No. 2249 (all 10ch): a, Hungary. b, Bulgaria. c, Romania.
No. 2450: 10ch, China.

1984, Dec. 30 ***Perf. 12***
2448 A1171 Sheet of 4, #a.-d. 4.50 1.25
2449 A1171 Sheet of 3, #a.-c. 3.50 1.00

Souvenir Sheet

Perf. 11½

2450 A1171 10ch multicolored 2.75 1.00

New Year — A1172

1985, Jan. 1 ***Perf. 12***
2451 A1172 10ch multicolored 1.90 .20

Kim Il Sung's 1,000-ri Journey, 60th Anniv. — A1173

1985, Jan. 22 ***Perf. 12¼***
2452 A1173 Pair, #a.-b. 2.25 .20
a. 5ch multicolored .75 .20
b. 10ch multicolored .75 .20

A1174

History of the Motorcar — A1175

Designs: 10ch, Gugnot's Steam Car, 1769. 15ch, Goldsworthy Steam Omnibus, 1825. 20ch, Gottlieb Daimler diesel car, 1885. 25ch, Benx three-wheeled diesel car, 1886. 30ch, Peugot diesel car, 1891.
80ch, Wind-power car.

1985, Jan. 25 ***Perf. 11½***
2453-2457 A1165 Set of 5 7.00 .85

Souvenir Sheet

2458 A1175 80ch multicolored 4.50 1.25

Secret Camp, Mt. Paektu — A1176

1985, Feb. 16 ***Perf. 12***
2459 A1176 10ch multicolored .65 .20
Korean Revolution Headquarters

Lighthouses — A1177

10ch, Taechodo. 20ch, Sodo. 30ch, Pido. 40ch, Suundo.

1985, Feb. 23 ***Perf. 12¼x11¾***
2460-2463 A1177 Set of 4 9.00 1.25

The Hedgehog Defeats the Tiger, Fairy Tale A1178

Designs: 10ch, Tiger bragging about his strength. 20ch, Tiger going to stamp on rolled-up hedgehog. 30ch, Hedgehog clinging to tiger's nose. 35ch, Fleeing tiger. 40ch, Tiger crawling before hedgehog.

1985, Mar. 6 ***Perf. 11½***
2464-2468 A1178 Set of 5 6.50 1.25

A1179

Mushrooms: 10ch, *Pieurotus cornucopiae.* 20ch, *Pluerotus ostreatus.* 30ch, *Catathelasma ventricosum.*

1985, Mar. 16
2469-2471 A1179 Set of 3 6.00 .65

A1180

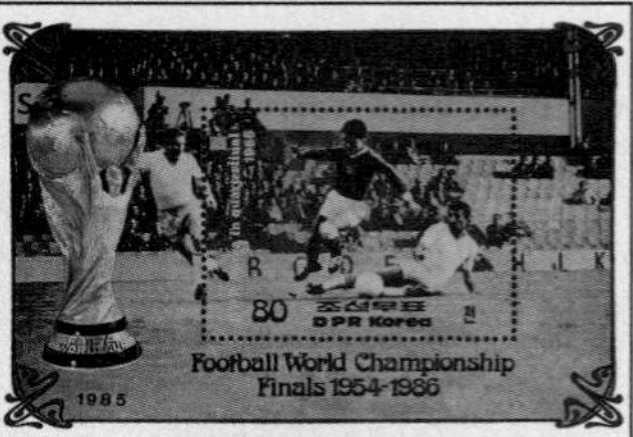

World Cup Soccer 1954-1966 — A1181

Designs: 10ch, W. Germany vs. Hungary, 1954. 20ch, Brazil vs. Sweden, 1958. 30ch, Brazil vs. Czechoslovakia, 1962. 40ch, England vs. W. Germany, 1966.
80ch, DPRK team in quarter final, 1966.

1985, Mar. 20 ***Perf. 13¼***
2472-2475 A1180 Set of 4 4.50 1.00

Souvenir Sheet

2476 A1181 80ch multicolored 4.00 1.25

A1182

World Cup Soccer 1970-1986 — A1183

Designs: 10ch, Brazil vs. Italy, 1970. 20ch, W. Germany vs. Netherlands, 1974. 30ch, Argentina vs. Netherlands, 1978. 40ch, Italy vs. W. Germany, 1982.
80ch, Aztec Stadium, Mexico City.

1985, Mar. 20 ***Perf. 13¼***
2477-2480 A1182 Set of 4 4.00 1.00

Souvenir Sheet

2481 A1183 80ch multicolored 4.00 1.25

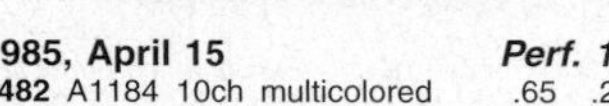

Kim Il Sung, 73rd Birthday A1184

1985, April 15 ***Perf. 12***
2482 A1184 10ch multicolored .65 .20

4th Century Musical Instruments A1185

Designs: 10ch, Horn player. 20ch So (pan-pipes) player.

1985, May 7 ***Perf. 11½***
2483-2484 A1185 Set of 2 3.50 .25

Chongryon Hall, Tokyo — A1186

1985, May 25
2485 A1186 10ch deep brown .65 .20

30th anniv. of Chongryon, the General Association of Korean Residents in Japan.

A1187

Mammals: 5ch, Common marmoset (*callithrix jacchus*). 10ch, Ring-tailed lemur (*Lemur catta*).

1985, June 7
2486-2487 A1187 Set of 2 2.50 .20

National Emblem — A1188

1985, June 20
2488 A1188 80ch multicolored 3.00 .70

A1189

Argentina '85 Int'l Stamp Exhib. — A1190

Designs: 10ch, Buenos Aires and Argentina stamp. 20ch, Iguaçu Falls and Argentine, DPRK stamps, horiz.
80ch, Gaucho.

1985, July 5 ***Perf. 11¾***
2489-2490 A1189 Set of 2 3.50 .25

Souvenir Sheet

2491 A1190 80ch multicolored 4.00 4.00

12th World Youth and Students' Festival, Moscow — A1191

Designs: 10ch, Korean dancer with streamer, gymnast. 20ch, Spassky Tower, Festival emblem. 30ch, Youths of different races.

1985, July 27 ***Perf. 12¼***
2492-2494 A1191 Set of 3 3.50 .75

Pyongyang Buildings — A1192

Designs: 2ch, Phyonghwa Pavilion. 40ch, Skyscraper apartments, Chollima Street.

1985, Aug. 1 ***Perf. 12***
2495-2496 A1192 Set of 2 .90 .20
2495a 2cg Thick toned unsurfaced paper, without gum 10.00 —
2496a 40ch Thick toned unsurfaced paper, without gum 5.00 —

A1193

Liberation, 40th Anniv. — A1194

Designs: 5ch, Soldiers, battle scene. 10ch (#2498), Korean and Russian soldier with raised arms. 10ch (#2499), Japanese soldiers surrendering. 10ch (#2500), Crowd with banners, Flame of Juche. 10ch (#2501), Student marchers with banners. 10ch (#2502), Liberation monument, vert. 40ch, Students bearing banners.
80ch, Monument.

1985, Aug. 15 ***Perf. 11½***
2497-2503 A1193 Set of 7 2.50 1.00
2497a 5ch Toned unsurfaced paper, without gum 8.00 —
2498a 10ch Toned unsurfaced paper, without gum 8.00 —
2499a 10ch Toned unsurfaced paper, without gum 8.00 —
2500a 10ch Toned unsurfaced paper, without gum 8.00 —
2501a 10ch Toned unsurfaced paper, without gum 8.00 —
2502a 10ch Toned unsurfaced paper, without gum 8.00 —
2503a 40ch Toned unsurfaced paper, without gum 8.00 —

Souvenir Sheet

2504 A1194 80ch multicolored 2.00 2.00

A1195

Halley's Comet — A1196

Designs: 10ch, Halley and Comet. 20ch, Comet, diagram of course, space probe.
80ch, Comet's trajectory.

1985, Aug. 25 ***Perf. 13½***
2505-2506 A1195 Set of 2 2.00 .25

Souvenir Sheet

2507 A1196 80ch multicolored 4.00 1.25

Flowers — A1197

Designs: 10ch, *Hippeastrum hybridum*. 20ch, *Camellia japonica*. 30ch, *Cyclamen persicum*.

1985, Sept. 10 ***Perf. 12***
2508-2510 A1197 Set of 3 7.00 .65

A1198

Koguryo Culture, 4th-6th Centuries A.D. — A1199

Designs: 10ch, Hero. 15ch, Heroine. 20ch, Flying fairy. 25ch, Hunting.
50ch, Pine tree.

1985, Sep. 30 ***Perf. 13¼***
2511-2514 A1198 Set of 4 3.50 .65
2514a Sheet of 4, #2511-2514 4.00 1.00

Souvenir Sheet
Perf. 12

2515 A1199 50ch multicolored 3.00 .75

Nos. 2511-2514 were issued both in separate sheets and in setenant sheets of four stamps (#2514a).

Korean Worker's Party, 40th Anniv. — A1200

Designs: 5ch, Party Founding Museum. 10ch (#2517), Soldier, workers. 10ch (#2518), Miner, workers. 40ch, Worker, peasant, professional worker holding up Party emblem.
No. 2520: 90ch, People holding bouquets of flowers.

1985, Oct. 10 ***Perf. 11½***
2516-2519 A1200 Set of 4 1.40 .75
2516a 5ch Thick toned unsurfaced paper, without gum 5.00 —
2517a 10ch Thick toned unsurfaced paper, without gum 10.00 —
2518a 10ch Thick toned unsurfaced paper, without gum 5.00 —
2519a 40ch Thick toned unsurfaced paper, without gum 10.00 —

Souvenir Sheet

2520 A1200 90ch multicolored 1.60 .50

Kim Il Sung's Return, 40th Anniv. — A1201

1985, Oct. 14 ***Perf. 12***
2521 A1201 10ch red brn & lt grn 1.00 .20
a. Dull white unsurfaced paper, without gum 8.00 —

Italia '85, Int'l Stamp Exhib., Rome A1202

Designs: 10ch, Colosseum, Rome, and DPRK stamp. 20ch, *The Holy Family*, by Raphael. 30ch. Head of Michelangelo's *David*, vert.
No. 2525: 80ch, Pantheon, Rome.

1985, Oct. 25 ***Perf. 11½***
2522-2524 A1200 Set of 3 2.75 .65

Souvenir Sheet

2525 A1202 80ch multicolored 4.00 1.25

South-West German Stamp Bourse, Sindelfingen — A1203

Designs, Mercedes Benz: 10ch, Type 300, 1960. 15ch, Type 770. 20ch, Type W150, 1937. 30ch, Type 600, 1966.
No. 2530: 80ch, Mercedes Benz, Type W31, 1938.

1985, Oct. 25
2526-2529 A1203 Set of 4 6.50 .65

Souvenir Sheet
Perf. 11¾

2530 A1203 80ch multicolored 5.25 .75

A1204

13th World Cup Championship, Mexico City — A1205

Designs: 20ch, Dribbling and sliding tackle. 30ch, Jumping kick.
80ch, Goalkeeper and Mexican monuments.

1985, Nov. 1 ***Perf. 13¼***
2531-2532 A1204 Set of 2 3.25 .50

Souvenir Sheet

2533 A1205 80ch multicolored 4.50 1.10

Int'l Youth Year A1206

Designs: 10ch, Traditional dance. 20ch, Sculpture depicting gymnasts. 30ch, Scientific research.
No. 2537: 80ch, Young people of different races.

1985, Nov. 9 ***Perf. 11½***
2534-2536 A1206 Set of 3 3.50 .50

Souvenir Sheet

2537 A1206 80ch multicolored 4.50 1.10

A1207

13th World Cup Championship, Mexico City — A1208

Designs: 20ch, Dribbling. 30ch, Tackling.
80ch, Goalkeeper, bullfighter.

1985, Nov. 20 ***Perf. 12***
2538-2539 A1207 Set of 2 3.50 .50

Souvenir Sheet

2540 A1208 80ch multicolored 5.00 1.10

Juche Torch — A1209

New Year

1986, Jan. 1 ***Perf. 12x12¼***
2541 A1209 10ch multicolored 1.25 .20

History of the Motor Car A1210

Designs: 10ch, Amédée Bollée and Limousine, 1901. 20ch, Stewart Rolls, Henry Royce and Silver Ghost, 1906. 25ch, Giovanni Agnelli and Fiat car, 1912. 30ch, Ettore Bugatti and Royal coupe, 1928. 40ch, Louis Renault and fiacre, 1906.
No. 2547: 80ch, Gottlieb Daimler, Karl Benz and Mercedes S, 1927.

1986, Jan. 20 ***Perf. 11½***
2542-2546 A1210 Set of 5 9.50 1.25

Souvenir Sheet

2547 A1210 80ch multicolored 7.50 .75

World Chess Championship, Moscow A1211

Designs: 20ch, Gary Kasparov.
No. 2549: 80ch, Kasparov-Karpov chess match.

1986, Feb. 5 ***Perf. 11¾x12***
2548 A1211 20ch multicolored 2.25 .20

Souvenir Sheet
Perf. 12

2549 A1211 80ch multicolored 5.00 1.25

Revolutionary Martyrs' Cemetery, Pyongyang — A1212

Designs: 5ch, Cemetery Gate. 10ch, Bronze sculpture of draped flag, soldier, workers (detail).

1986, Feb. 10 ***Perf. 12***
2550-2551 A1212 Set of 2 1.50 .20

Songgan Revolutionary Site, 37th Anniv. of Kim Il Sung's Visit — A1213

1986, Feb. 16
2552 A1213 10ch multicolored .90 .20

Mt. Myohyang Historic Buildings — A1214

Designs: 10ch, Buddhist Scriptures Museum. 20ch, Taeung Hall of the Pohyon Temple.

1986, Feb. 20 ***Perf. 12¼***
2553-2554 A1214 Set of 2 2.00 .20

Tropical Fish A1215

Designs: 10ch, *Heniochus acuminatus*. 20ch, *Amphiprion frenatus*.

1986, Mar. 12 ***Perf. 11½***
2555-2556 A1215 Set of 2 2.50 .30

World Cup Championship, Mexico City — A1216

Designs, soccer players and flags of: 5ch, Italy, Bulgaria, Argentina. 20ch, Mexico, Belgium, Paraguay, Iraq. 25ch, France, Canada, USSR, Hungary. 30ch, Brazil, Spain, Algeria, Northern Ireland. 35ch, W. Germany, Uruguay, Scotland, Denmark. 40ch, Poland, Portugal, Morocco, England.
No. 2563: 80ch, Soccer players, World Cup, gold soccer ball, boots.

1986, Mar. 21 ***Perf. 12***
2557-2562 A1216 Set of 6 10.00 1.60

Souvenir Sheet

2563 A1216 80ch multicolored 6.50 .65

For overprints see Nos. 2599-2605.

4th Spring Friendship Art Festival, Pyongyang — A1217

1986, Apr. 5
2564 A1217 1w multicolored 3.00 .65

Mercedes-Benz, 60th Anniv. — A1218

Designs: 10ch (#2565), Dailmer No. 1 ("Motorwagen"), 1886. 10ch (#2566), Benz-Velo, 1894. 20ch (#2567), Mercedes, 1901. 20ch (#2568), Benz limousine, 1909. 30ch (#2569), Mercedes Tourenwagen, 1914. 30ch (#2570), Mercedes Benz 170/6 cylinder, 1931. 40ch (#2571), Mercedes Benz 380, 1933. 40ch (#2572), Mercedes Benz 540K, 1936.
No. 2573: 80ch, Mercedes-Simplex Phaeton, 1904.

1986, Apr. 8 ***Perf. 11½***
2565-2572 A1218 Set of 8 9.00 2.00

Souvenir Sheet

2573 A1218 80ch multicolored 5.00 1.25

Kim Il Sung, 74th Birthday — A1219

1986, Apr. 15 ***Perf. 12***
2574 A1219 10ch multicolored .65 .20

Association for the Restoration of the Fatherland, 50th Anniv. — A1220

1986, May 5 ***Perf. 11¾x12***
2575 A1220 10ch multicolored .65 .20

Intl. Year of Peace A1221

Designs: 10ch, Dove carrying letter. 20ch, Dove, UN Headquarters. 30ch, Dove, globe, broken missiles.
No. 2579: 80ch, Sculpture of children and dove.

1986, June 18 ***Perf. 11¾x12***
2576-2578 A1221 Set of 3 4.00 1.25

Souvenir Sheet

Perf. 11¾x11½

2579 A1221 80ch multicolored 5.00 .75

Mona Lisa, by da Vinci — A1222

1986, July 9 ***Perf. 13½x13¼***
2580 A1222 20ch multicolored 3.00 .20

Irises — A1223

Designs: 20ch, Pink iris. 30ch, Violet iris.
No. 2583: 80ch, Magenta iris.

1986, July 20 ***Perf. 11½***
2581-2582 A1223 Set of 2 5.00 .50

Souvenir Sheet

2583 A1223 80ch multicolored 6.50 1.10

Tennis Players — A1224

Designs: 10ch, Kim Un Suk. 20ch, Ivan Lendi. 30ch, Steffi Craf. 50ch, Boris Becker.

1986, July 30 ***Perf. 13½***
2584 A1224 Block of 4, #a.-d. 7.00 1.00
a. 10ch multicolored 1.50 .20
b. 20ch multicolored 1.50 .20
c. 30ch multicolored 1.50 .20
d. 50ch multicolored 1.50 .20
e. 10ch Toned unsurfaced paper, without gum 10.00 —

No. 2584 was printed in sheets containing two setenant blocks.
No. 2584d is airmail.

Stampex '86 Stamp Exhib., Adelaide A1225

Designs: 10ch, Cockatoo; 80ch, Kangaroo, map of Australia, emblems.

1986, Aug. 4 ***Perf. 11½***
2585 A1225 10ch multicolored 5.50 .20

Souvenir Sheet

2586 A1226 80ch multicolored 5.50 1.10

L'Unita Festival, Milan A1227

Designs: 10ch, First issue of *L'Unita*. 20ch, Milan Cathedral. 30ch, Michelangelo's *Pieta*, vert.
No. 2590: 80ch, Enrico Berlinguer, Italian Communist Party leader.

1986, Aug. 26
2587-2589 A1227 Set of 3 5.50 2.50

Souvenir Sheet

2590 A1227 80ch multicolored 4.50 .75

National Festival of *L'Unita*, the Italian Communist Party newspaper.

A1228

Stockholmia '86 Int'l Stamp Exhib., Stockholm — A1229

Design: 10ch, Icebreaker *Express II* and Swedish stamp.
80ch, UPU emblem, mail coach and Swedish stamps.

1986, Aug. 28
2591 A1228 10ch multicolored 2.00 .20

Souvenir Sheet

2592 A1229 80ch multicolored 7.00 1.50

DPRK Postage Stamps, 40th Anniv. — A1230

Designs: 10ch, Perf green reprint of Scott No. 1. 15ch, Imperf green reprint of Scott No. 1. 50ch, Scott No. 5.

1986, Sep. 12 ***Perf. 12¼x12***
2593-2595 A1230 Set of 3 6.00 1.50

No. 2595 is airmail.

DPRK Postage Stamps, 40th Anniv. — A1231

Designs: 10ch, Postal emblems, DPRK stamps (#387, 2505). 15ch, Postal emblems, General Post Office, Pyongyang, DPRK stamps (#1529, 1749). 50ch, Postal emblems, Kim Il Jung. DPRK stamps (#1, #1 reprint in green), vert.

1986, Oct. 5 ***Perf. 12***
2596-2598 A1231 Set of 3 8.00 1.00

No. 2598 is airmail.

Nos. 2557-2563 Overprinted with World Cup Soccer Championship Results

1986, Oct. 14
2599-2604 A1216 Set of 6 16.00 2.50

Souvenir Sheet

2605 A1216 80ch multicolored 10.00 1.40

Down-with-Imperialism Union, 60th Anniv. — A1232

1986, Oct. 17 ***Perf. 11½***
2606 A1232 10ch multicolored .70 .25

Gift Animals House, 1st Anniv. — A1233

1986, Oct. 18 ***Perf. 12x11¾***
2607 A1233 2w multicolored 8.50 .90
a. On toned unsurfaced paper, without gum 10.00 —

United Nations Educational, Scientific and Cultural Organization (UNESCO), 40th anniv. — A1234

Designs: 10ch, Schoolchildren. 50ch, UNESCO emblem, Grand People's Study House, televion, communications satellite and dish, horiz.

1986, Nov. 4 ***Perf. 12***
2608-2609 A1234 Set of 2 4.50 1.25

Inter-Sputnik, 15th Anniv. — A1235

1986, Nov. 15
2610 A1235 5w multicolored 10.00 2.25
a. On toned unsurfaced paper, without gum 10.00 —

West Sea Barrage — A1236

Designs: 10ch, Oil tanker, lock. 40ch, Aerial view of dam. 1.20w, Aerial view of dam (diff.)

1986, Nov. 20 ***Perf. 12x11¾***

2611-2613	A1236	Set of 3	8.50	1.00
2611a	10ch	Toned unsurfaced paper, without gum	5.00	—
2612a	40ch	Toned unsurfaced paper, without gum	8.00	—
2613a	1.20w	Toned unsurfaced paper, without gum	8.00	—

Mushrooms and Minerals — A1237

Designs: a, 10ch Lengenbachite. b, 10ch Clitocybe infundibuliformis. c, 15ch Rhodocrosite. d, 15ch Morchella esculenta. e, 50ch Annabergite. f, 50ch Russula.

1986, Nov. 23 ***Perf. 13¼***

2614	A1237	Block of 6, #a.-f.	16.50	1.25
a.		10ch multicolored	2.50	.20
b.		10ch multicolored	2.50	.20
c.		15ch multicolored	2.50	.20
d.		15ch multicolored	2.50	.20
e.		50ch multicolored	2.50	.20
f.		50ch multicolored	2.50	.20

Printed in setenant blocks within the sheet.
Nos. 2614e and 2614f are airmail.

A1238

Exhib. of North Korean 3-D Photos and Stamps, Lima — A1239

Design: 10ch, Machu Picchu and DPRK Stamp (Scott #1402).
80ch, Korean and Peruvian children.

1986, Nov. 25 ***Perf. 13¼x13½***

2615	A1238	10ch multicolored	2.00	.20

Souvenir Sheet

2616	A1239	80ch multicolored	9.00	2.00

New Year — A1240

Designs: 10ch, Sun, pine tree; 40ch, Hare.

1987, Jan. 1 ***Perf. 12***

2617-2618	A1240	Set of 2	3.50	.50

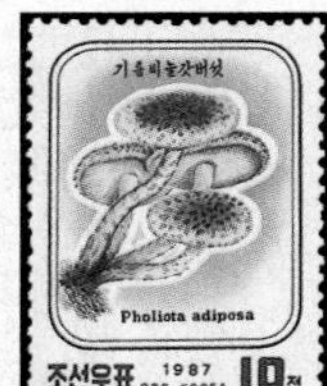

A1241

Fungi — A1242

Designs: 10ch, *Pholiota adiposa*; 20ch, *Cantharellus cibarius*; 30ch, *Boletus impolitus*. 80ch, *Gomphidius rutilus*.

1987, Jan. 5 ***Perf. 11½***

2619-2621	A1241	Set of 3	5.75	.75

Souvenir Sheet

2622	A1242	80ch multicolored	7.00	1.50

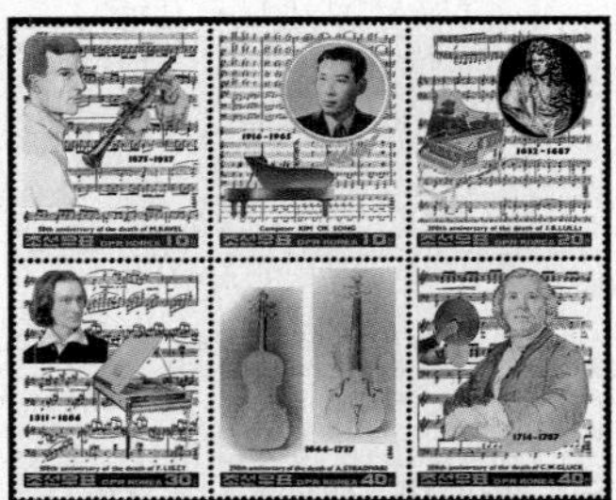
Famous Composers, Death Anniv. — A1243

Designs: 10ch (#2623a), Maurice Ravel (1875-1937); 10ch (#2623b), Kim Ok Song (1916-65); 20ch, Giovanni Lully (1632-67); 30ch, Franz Liszt (1811-86); 40ch (#2623e), Stradivarius violins (Antonio Stradivari, 1644-1737); 40ch (#2623f), Christoph Gluck (1714-87).

1987, Jan. 29 ***Perf. 13¼***

2623	A1243	Block of 6, #a.-f.	12.00	1.10
a.		10ch multicolored	1.50	.20
b.		10ch multicolored	1.50	.20
c.		20ch multicolored	1.50	.20
d.		30ch multicolored	1.50	.20
e.		40ch multicolored	1.50	.20
f.		40ch multicolored	1.50	.20

No. 2623 was printed in se-tenant blocks of six within the sheet.

Kim Jong Il, 45th Birthday — A1244

1987, Feb. 16

2624	A1244	80ch multicolored	2.50	.40

Buildings — A1245

Designs: 5ch, East Pyongyang Grand Theater; 10ch, Pyongyang Koryo Hotel (vert.); 3w, Rungnado Stadium.

1987, Feb. 23 ***Perf. 12***

2625-2627	A1245	Set of 3	7.50	1.20
2625a	5ch	Stiff paper, without gum	10.00	—
2626a	10ch	Stiff paper, without gum	5.00	—
2627a	3w	Stiff paper, without gum	5.00	—

Sailing Ships — A1246

Designs: 20ch, *Gorch Fock*; 30ch, *Tovarisch* (vert.); 50ch (#2630), *Belle Poule* (vert.); 50ch (#2631), *Sagres II* (vert.); 1w (#2632), Merchantman, Koryo Period (918-1392); 1w (#2633), *Dar Mlodziezy* (vert.).

1987, Feb. 25 ***Perf. 13¼***

2628-2633	A1246	Set of 6	11.50	2.75

Nos. 2630-2633 are airmail.

Fire Engines — A1247

Designs: 10ch, German fire engine; 20ch, Benz fire engine; 30ch, Chemical fire engine; 50ch, Soviet fire engine.

1987, Feb. 27 ***Perf. 12***

2634-2637	A1247	Set of 4	10.00	1.20

No. 2637 is airmail.

Road Safety — A1248

Designs (multiple traffic signs): 10ch (#2638), Blue sign lower center; 10ch (#2639), Red sign lower center; 20ch, Various signs; 50ch, Various signs (diff.)

1987, Feb. 27

2638-2641	A1248	Set of 4	7.50	.90

Nos. 2641 is airmail.

Butterflies and Flowers — A1249

Designs: 10ch (#2642), *Apatura ilia* and spiraea; 10ch (#2643), *Ypthinia argus* and fuchsia; 20ch (#2644), *Neptis philyra* and aguilegia; 20ch (#2645), *Papilio protenorand* and chrysanthemum; 40ch (#2646), *Parantica sita* and celosia; 40ch (#2847), *Vanessa indica* and hibiscus.

1987, Mar. 12

2642-2647	A1249	Set of 6	11.00	1.50

Korean National Assoc., 70th Anniv. — A1250

Design: 10ch, Association Monument, Pyongyang.

1987, Mar. 23 ***Perf. 11½***

2648	A1250	10ch multicolored	.60	.20

5th Spring Friendship Art Festival — A1251

1987, Apr. 6

2649	A1251	10ch multicolored	.70	.20

A1252

Kim Il Sung, 75th Birthday — A1253

Designs: No. 2650, Mangyong Hill; No. 2651, Kim Il Sung's birthplace, Mangyongdae (horiz.); No 2652, Painting, *Profound Affection for the Working Class*; No. 2653, Painting, *A Bumper Crop of Pumpkins*.

1987, Apr. 15 ***Perf. 12***

2650 A1252 10ch multicolored .50 .20
2651 A1252 10ch multicolored .50 .20
2652 A1253 10ch multicolored .50 .20
2653 A1253 10ch multicolored .50 .20
Nos. 2650-2653 (4) 2.00 .80

Horses — A1254

Designs: 10ch (#2654a), Bay. 10ch (#2654b), Bay (diff.); 40ch (#2654c), Gray, rearing; 40ch (#2654d), White horse on beach.

1987, Apr. 20 ***Perf. 13¼***

2654 A1254 Block of 4, #a.-d. 7.00 2.10
a. 10ch multicolored .50 .20
b. 10ch multicolored .50 .20
c. 40ch multicolored 2.50 .70
d. 40ch multicolored 2.50 .70

No. 2654 was printed in se-tenant blocks of four within the sheet.

Transport — A1255

Designs: 10ch (#2655), Electric train *Juche*; 10ch (#2656), Electric train *Mangyongdae*; 10ch (#2657), *Sputnik I* (vert.); 20ch (#2658), Laika, first animal in space (vert.); 20ch (#2659), Tupolev Tu-144 jetliner; 20ch (#2660), Concorde jetliner; 30ch, Count Ferdinand von Zeppelin and LZ-4; 80ch, Zeppelin and diagrams of airships.

1987, Apr. 30

2655 A1255 10ch multicolored .60 .20
2656 A1255 10ch multicolored .60 .20
a. Pair, #2655-2656 .75 .40
2657 A1255 10ch multicolored .60 .20
2658 A1255 20ch multicolored 1.10 .20
a. Pair, #2657-2658 2.00 .40
2659 A1255 20ch multicolored 1.10 .20
2660 A1255 20ch multicolored 1.10 .20
a. Pair, #2659-2660 2.50 .40
2661 A1255 30ch multicolored 1.50 .25
2662 A1255 80ch multicolored 4.50 1.00
a. Pair, #2661-2662 7.00 1.25
Nos. 2655-2662 (8) 11.10 2.45

Nos. 2655/2656, 2657/2658, 2659/2660, 2661/2662 were printed se-tenant within their sheets.

No. 2662 is airmail.

CAPEX '87 Int'l Stamp Exhibition, Toronto — A1256

Designs: 10ch, Musk ox; 40ch, Jacques Cartier, *Grand Hermine* and modern ice-breaker (horiz.); 60ch, Ice hockey, Calgary '88 (horiz.)

1987, May 30 ***Perf. 11***

2663-2665 A1256 Set of 3 6.00 1.25

Int'l Circus Festival, Monaco — A1257

Designs: 10ch (#2666), Trapeze artists; 10ch (#2667), "Brave Sailors" (N. Korean acrobatic troupe) (vert.); 20ch (#2668), Korean performers receiving prize; 20ch (#2669), Clown and elephant (vert.); 40ch, Performing cat, horses; 50ch, Prince Rainier and family applauding.

1987, May 31 ***Perf. 12***

2666-2671 A1257 Set of 6 9.50 1.50

No. 2871 is airmail.

Battle of Pochonbo, 50th Anniv. — A1258

1987, June 4 ***Perf. 11½***

2672 A1258 10ch multicolored .75 .25

Chongchun Street Sports Complex — A1259

Designs: 5ch, Various sports; 10ch, Indoor swimming pool; 40ch, Weightlifting gymnasium; 70ch, Table-tennis gymnasium; 1w, Angol football stadium; 1.20w, Handball gymnasium.

1987, June 18 ***Perf. 12***

2673-2678 A1259 Set of 6 10.00 2.25
2675a 40ch Toned unsurfaced paper, without gum 8.00 —
2676a 70ch Toned unsurfaced paper, without gum 8.00 —
2677a 1w Toned unsurfaced paper, without gum 8.00 —
2678a 1.20w Toned unsurfaced paper, without gum 8.00 —

Mandarin Ducks (WWF) — A1260

Designs (ducks): 20ch (#2679), On branch; 20ch (#2680), On shore; 20ch (#2681), In water and on shore; 40ch, In water.

1987, Aug. 4 ***Perf. 13¼***

2679-2682 A1260 Set of 4 11.50 2.00

A1261

OLYMPHILEX '87 Stamp Exhibition, Rome — A1262

1987, Aug. 29 ***Perf. 13¼***

2683 A1261 10ch multicolored 1.50 .20

Souvenir Sheet

2684 A1262 80ch multicolored 7.00 1.25

Railway Uniforms — A1263

Designs: 10ch (#2685), Electric train and Metro dispatcher; 10ch (#2686), Underground station and conductress; 20ch, Train and conductress; 30ch, Train and railway dispatcher; 40ch (#2689), Orient Express and conductor; 40ch (#2690), Express train and ticket inspector.

1987, Sep. 23

2685-2690 A1263 Set of 6 7.50 1.25

HAFNIA '87 Int'l Stamp Exhibition, Copenhagen — A1264

Designs: 40ch, White stork; 60ch, The Little Mermaid and sailing ship *Danmark*.

1987, Sep. 26

2691-2692 A1264 Set of 2 5.25 .70

A1265

Winter Olympic Games, Calgary — A1266

Designs (all 40ch): #2693, Figure skating; #2694, Ski jump; #2695, Downhill skiing; #2696, Cross-country skiing.

1987, Oct. 16

2693-2696 A1265 Set of 4 8.00 1.00

Souvenir Sheet

2697 A1266 80ch multicolored 5.25 1.00

920 Victory Column

PHILATELIA '87 (Koln) and 750th Anniv. Berlin — A1267

Designs: 10ch, Victory Column; 20ch, Reichstag (horiz.); 30ch, Pfaueninsel Castle; 40ch, Charlottenburg Castle (horiz.).

No. 2706: 80ch, Olympic Stadium.

1987, Nov. 5 ***Perf. 12***

2698-2701 A1267 Set of 4 150.00

Souvenir Sheet

Perf. 11½x12

2702 A1267 80ch multicolored 100.00

Roland Garros Birth Centenary and Tennis as an Olympic Sport — A1268

Designs: 20ch (#2703), Roland Garros (1888-1918), aviator; 20ch (#2704), Ivan Lendl and trophy; 40ch, Steffi Graf.
No. 2706: 80ch, Steffi Graf and trophy.

1987, Nov. 10 ***Perf. 13¼***
2703-2705 A1268 Set of 3 7.50 .75

Souvenir Sheet
Perf. 11½x12
2706 A1268 80ch multicolored 10.00 3.00

Kim Jong Suk (1917-49), Revolutionary Hero — A1269

1987, Dec. 24
2707 A1269 80ch multicolored 2.50 .50

Pyongyang Buildings — A1270

Dragon — A1271

1988, Jan. 1 ***Perf. 12***
2708 A1270 10ch multicolored .60 .20
2709 A1271 40ch multicolored 1.50 .20

New Year.

Saenal Newspaper, 60th Anniv. — A1272

1988, Jan. 15 ***Perf. 11½***
2710 A1272 10ch multicolored .90 .20

A1273

Kim Jong Il, 46th Birthday — A1274

Designs: 10ch, Kim Jong Il's birthplace, Mt. Paektu. 80ch, Kim Jong Il.

1988, Feb. 16 ***Perf. 12x11¾***
2711 A1273 10ch multicolored .50 .20

Souvenir Sheet
2712 A1274 80ch multicolored 2.50 .50

Int'l Red Cross, 125th Anniv. — A1275

Designs: 10ch, Henry Dunant; 20ch (#2714), N. Korean Red Cross emblem, map; 20ch (#2715), International Committee Headquarters, Geneva; 40ch, Doctor examining child, Pyongyang Maternity Hospital.
80ch: Red Cross and Red Crescent, flags, globe.

1988, Feb. 17 ***Perf. 12***
2713-2716 Set of 4 6.75 .90
2716a A1275 Sheet of 4, #2717-2720 7.00 .90

Souvenir Sheet
2717 A1275 80ch multicolored 4.50 .75

Nos. 2713-2716 were printed in sheets of 4 (#2716a).

A1276

Columbus' Discovery of America, 500th Anniv. — A1277

Designs: 10ch, *Santa Maria*; 20ch, *Pinta*; 30ch, *Nina*.
80ch, Columbus.

1988, Mar. 10 ***Perf. 13¼***
2718 A1276 Strip of 3 5.25 .75
a. 10ch multicolored 1.25 .20
b. 20ch multicolored 1.25 .20
c. 30ch multicolored 1.25 .25

Souvenir Sheet
2719 A1277 80ch multicolored 5.25 .75

Nos. 2718a-2718c were printed together in the sheet in se-tenant strips of three.

JUVALUX '88 — A1278

Designs: 40ch, Hot air balloons; 60ch, Steam engine, railroad map of Luxembourg 1900.

1988, Mar. 29
2720-2721 A1278 Set of 2 5.25 .75

JUVALUX '88 International Youth Stamp Exhibition, Luxembourg.

6th Spring Friendship Art Festival — A1279

Designs: 10ch, Singer. 1.20w, Dancers.

1988, Apr. 7 ***Perf. 12***
2722-2723 A1279 Set of 2 4.25 1.25
2722a 10ch, on toned unsurfaced paper, without gum 8.00 —

Int'l Institute of the Juche Idea, 10th Anniv. — A1280

1988, Apr. 9
2724 A1280 10ch multicolored .50 .20

A1281

Kim Il Sung, 76th Birthday — A1282

Designs: 10ch, Kim Il Sung's Birthplace, Mangyongdae.
80ch, Kim Il Sung and schoolchildren.

1988, Apr. 15
2725 A1281 10ch multicolored .50 .20

Souvenir Sheet
2726 A1282 80ch multicolored 2.50 .40

FINLANDIA '88 Int'l Stamp Exhibition, Helsinki — A1283

Designs: 40ch, *Urho* ice-breaker; 60ch, Matti Nykänen, Finnish Olympic ski-jumping gold and silver medallist.

1988, May 2 ***Perf. 13¼***
2727-2728 A1283 Set of 2 5.00 .60

ITALIA '90, 14th World Soccer Championships — A1284

Designs: 10ch, Soccer match; 20ch, Postcard for 1934 Championship; 30ch, Player tackling (horiz.)
80ch: Italian team, 1982 winners (horiz.)

1988, May 19
2729-2731 A1284 Set of 3 5.25 .50

Souvenir Sheet
2732 A1284 80ch multicolored 4.50 .60

13th World Festival of Youth and Students — A1285

Designs: 10ch, Festival emblem; 10ch (#2735), Woman dancer; 10ch (#2736), Woman, gymnast, Angol Sports Village; 10ch (#2737), Map of Korea, globe and doves; 10ch (#2738), Finger pointing at broken rockets ("Let's build a new world without nuclear weapons"); 1.20w, Three hands of different races releasing dove.

1988, May 27 ***Perf. 12***
2734-2739 A1285 Set of 6 7.50 1.25
2734a 10ch Thick toned unsurfaced paper, without gum 8.00 —
2735a 10ch Thick toned unsurfaced paper, without gum 8.00 —
2736a 10ch Thick toned unsurfaced paper, without gum 8.00 —
2739a 1.20w Thick toned unsurfaced paper, without gum 8.00 —

Eight Fairies of Mt. Kumgang, Folk-Tale — A1286

Designs: 10ch, Fairy playing the *haegum*; 15ch, Fairies with rainbow; 20ch, Fairy and herdsman husband; 25ch, Couple with infant; 30ch, Couple with son and daughter; 35ch, Family on rainbow, returning to Mt. Kumgang.

1988, June 20
2740-2745 A1286 Set of 6 5.00 1.10

PRAGA '88 Int'l Stamp Exhibition, Prague — A1287

Designs: 20ch, Mallard ducks; 40ch, Vladimir Remek, Czechoslovak cosmonaut.

1988, June 26 ***Perf. 13¼***
2746-2747 A1287 Set of 2 4.00 .45

Birds — A1288

Designs: 10ch, Red crossbill (*Loxia curvirostra japonica*); 15ch, Stonechat (*Saxicola torquata stejnegeri*); 20ch, European nuthatch (*Sitta eoropaea hondoensis*); 25ch, Great spotted woodpecker (*Dendrocopos major japonicus*); 30ch, Common kingfisher (*Alcedo atthis bengalensis*); 35ch, Bohemian waxwing (*Bombycilla garrula centralasiae*).

1988, July 9 ***Perf. 12***
2748-2753 A1288 Set of 6 10.00 1.75

A1289

RICCIONE '88 Int'l Stamp Fair — A1290

1988, July 25
2754 A1289 20ch multicolored .90 .20

Souvenir Sheet

2755 A1290 80ch multicolored 3.75 .50

A1291

Australia Bicentenary — A1292

Designs: 10ch, Emu; 15ch, Statin bower birds; 25ch, Kookaberra (vert.).
80ch, H.M.S. *Resolution*.

1988, July 30 ***Perf. 13¼***
2756-2758 A1291 Set of 3 4.00 .60

Souvenir Sheet

2759 A1292 80ch multicolored 5.00 .65

Ships — A1293

Designs: 10ch, Floating crane *5-28*; 20ch, Cargo ship *Hwanggumsan*; 30ch, Cargo ship *Jangjasan Chongnyon-ho*; 40ch, Passenger ship *Samjiyon*.

1988, Aug. 12 ***Perf. 12***
2760-2763 A1293 Set of 4 5.50 .85

A1294

Count Ferdinand von Zeppelin, 150th Birth Anniv. — A1295

Designs: 10ch, LZ 13 *Hansa*; 20ch, LZ 10 *Schwaben*; 30ch, LZ 11 *Viktoria Luise*; 40ch, LZ 3.
1w, Count von Zeppelin.

1988, Aug. 21 ***Perf. 11¼***
2764-2767 A1294 Set of 4 5.50 .85

Souvenir Sheet

Perf. 13¼

2768 A1295 1w multicolored 5.00 1.00

Kim Il Sung and Jambyn Batmunkh — A1296

1988, Aug. 30 ***Perf. 12***
2769 A1296 10ch multicolored .75 .20

Kim Il Sung's visit to Mongolia.

National Heroes Congress — A1297

1988, Sep. 1 ***Perf. 11¾***
2770 A1297 10ch multicolored 4.50 .20

A1298

Independence, 40th Anniversary — A1299

Designs: 5ch, Tower of Juche Idea. 10ch (#2772), Worker, factory. 10ch (#2773), Soldier and Mt. Paektu. 10ch (#2774), Map, broken U.S. missile. 10ch (#2775), Hand holding sign, peace march, globe, doves.
1.20w, Kim Il Sung presiding over design of DPRK flag and emblem.

1988, Sept. 9 ***Perf. 12***
2771-2775 A1298 Set of 5 1.75 .55
2771a 5ch Toned unsurfaced paper, without gum 20.00 —

Souvenir Sheet

Perf. 11½

2776 A1299 1.20w multicolored 2.50 .75

FILACEPT '88 Philatelic Exhib., The Hague A1300

Designs: 40ch, *Sunflowers*, by Vincent Van Gogh. 60ch, *The Chess Game*, by Lucas van Leyden.

1988, Sept. 18 ***Perf. 13½***
2777-2778 A1300 Set of 2 7.50 1.40

Emblem — A1301

1988, Sep. 23 ***Perf. 11½***
2779 A1301 10ch multicolored .60 .20

16th Conference of the Ministers of Communications of Socialist Countries.

Dump Trucks A1302

Designs: 10ch, *Jaju 82* 10-ton truck. 40ch, *Kumsusan* 40-ton truck.

1988, Sept. 18 ***Perf. 13½***
2780-2781 A1302 Set of 2 2.00 .75

Paintings by O Un Byol — A1303

Designs: 10ch, *Owl*. 15ch, *Dawn*. 20ch, *The Beautiful Rose Received by the Respected Marshall*. 25ch, *The Sun and Bamboo*. 30ch, *Autumn*.

1988, Oct. 5 ***Perf. 11½***
2782-2786 A1303 Set of 5 6.00 .90

Historic Locomotives — A1304

Designs: 10ch, *Junggi No. 35.* 20ch, *Junggi No. 22.* 30ch, *Jongihwa No. 3.* 40ch, *Junggi No. 307.*

1988, Oct. 28 ***Perf. 12***
2787-2790 A1304 Set of 4 5.00 .75

A1305

Calgary '88 Winter Olympic Games Winners — A1306

Designs: 10ch, Pirmin Zurbriggen (Switzerland). 20ch, Yvonne Van Gennip (Netherlands). 30ch, Marjo Matikainen (Finland). 40ch, USSR hockey team.
80ch, Katarina Witt (DDR).

1988, Nov. 1 ***Perf. 13¼***
2791-2794 A1305 Set of 4 3.50 1.25

Souvenir Sheet

2795 A1306 80ch multicolored 2.50 .50
a. Overprinted with names of winners in selvage 2.50 .50

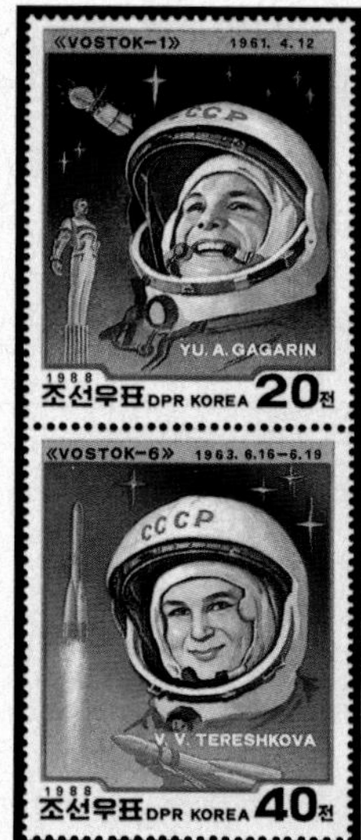

First Man and Woman in Space — A1307

Designs: 20ch, Yuri Gagarin. 40ch, Valentina Tereshkova.

1988, Nov. 12 ***Perf. 13¼***
2796 A1307 Pair, #a.-b. 1.75 .60
a. 20ch multicolored .40 .20
b. 40ch multicolored 1.10 .45

A1308

INDIA '89 Int'l Philatelic Exhib., New Delhi — A1309

Design: 20ch, Jawaharlal Nehru (1889-1964), 100th anniversary of birth.
60ch, *Fan Dance*, Korean Folk Dance.

1988, Dec. 15 ***Perf. 11¾x12***
2797 A1308 20ch multicolored 1.20 .20

Souvenir Sheet

Perf. 11¾x11½

2798 A1309 60ch multicolored 3.50 .40

New Year — A1310

Designs: 10ch, Chollima Statue. 20ch, Painting, *Dragon Angler.* 40ch, *Tortoise Serpent*, Kangso tomb mural painting (horiz.)

1989, Jan. 1 ***Perf. 13¼***
2799-2801 A1310 Set of 3 3.50 .50

Archery — A1311

Designs: 10ch, Archery. 15ch, Rifle shooting. 20ch, Pistol shooting. 25ch, Parachuting. 30ch, Launching model glider.

1989, Jan. 10 ***Perf. 12***
2802-2806 A1311 Set of 5 4.50 .75

National defense training.

A1312

Pets Presented to Kim Il Sung — A1313

Designs: 10ch, Dobermann pinscher. 20ch, Labrador. 25ch, German shepherd. 30ch, Border collies (horiz.). 35ch, Serval (horiz.).
80ch, *Felix libica.*

1989, Jan. 23 ***Perf. 13½***
2807-2811 A1312 Set of 5 5.00 .90

Souvenir Sheet

2812 A1313 80ch multicolored 4.00 .60

Kim Jong Il, 47th Birthday — A1314

1989, Feb. 16 ***Perf. 11¾x12***
2813 A1314 80ch multicolored 2.00 .45

Agriculture A1315

1989, Feb. 25 ***Perf. 12***
2814 A1315 10ch multicolored .70 .20
a. Toned unsurfaced paper, without gum 5.00 —

25th anniversary of publication of Kim Il Sung's *Theses on the Socialist Rural Question in Our Country.*

Mushrooms and Wild Fruits — A1316

Designs: 10ch, *Rozites caperata* and *Vitisamurensis.* 20ch, *Amanita caesarea* and *Schizandra chinensis.* 25ch, *Lactarius hygrophoides* and *Eleagnus crispa.* 30ch, *Agaricus placomyces* and *Actinidia arguta.* 35ch, *Agaricus arvensis* and *Lycium chinense.* 40ch, *Suillus grevillei* and *Juglans cordiformis.*
1w, *Gomphidius roseus* and *Diospyros lotus.*

1989, Feb. 27 ***Perf. 12***
2815-2820 A1316 Set of 6 8.00 1.25

Souvenir Sheet

Perf. 11½x11¾

2821 A1316 1w multicolored 4.50 .90

13th World Youth and Students' Festival — A1317

Designs: 10ch, Girl. 20ch, Children of different races. 30ch, Fairy, rainbow. 40ch, Young people and Tower of Juche Idea.

1989, Mar. 18 ***Perf. 12¼***
2822-2825 A1317 Set of 4 2.75 1.00
2822a 10ch Soft toned unsurfaced paper, without gum 15.00 —
2823a 20ch Soft toned unsurfaced paper, without gum 8.00 —
2824a 30ch Soft toned unsurfaced paper, without gum 8.00 —
2825a 40ch Soft toned unsurfaced paper, without gum 8.00 —
2825b 40ch Stiff dull white unsurfaced paper, without gum 8.00 —

A1318

Butterflies and Insects — A1319

Designs: 10ch, *Parnassius eversmanni.* 15ch, *Colias heos.* 20ch, *Dilipa fenestra.* 25ch, *Buthus martensis.* 30ch, *Trichogramma ostriniae.* 40ch, *Damaster constricticollis.*
80ch, *Parnassius nomion.*

1989, Mar. 23 ***Perf. 12***
2826 A1318 Sheet of 6, #a.-f. 6.00 1.00

Souvenir Sheet

2827 A1319 80ch multicolored 3.75 .75

Spring Friendship Art Festival — A1320

1989, Apr. 6
2828 A1320 10ch multicolored .80 .20

Kim Il Sung, 77th Birthday — A1321

1989, Apr. 15 ***Perf. 11½***
2829 A1321 10ch multicolored .50 .20
a. Toned unsurfaced paper, without gum 10.00 —

Battle of the Musan Area, 50th Anniv. A1322

1989, May 19 ***Perf. 12***
2830 A1322 10ch multicolored 1.10 .20

Jamo System of Dance Notation — A1323

Designs: 10ch, Mexican dance. 20ch, Ballet duet in *Don Quixote*. 25ch, Dance of Guinea. 30ch, Cambodian folk dance.
80ch, Korean folk dance.

1989, May 30
2831-2834 A1323 Set of 4 3.75 .65

Souvenir Sheet

2835 A1323 80ch multicolored 3.25 .50

13th World Festival of Youth and Students

A1324 A1325

1989, June 8 ***Perf. 11½***
2836 A1324 5ch Deep blue .25 .20
a. Soft toned unsurfaced paper, without gum 15.00 —
2837 A1325 10ch Red brown .30 .20

Cartoon, *Badger Measures the Height* — A1326

Designs: 10ch, Badger racing cat and bear to flag pole. 40ch, Cat and bear climbing pole, while badger measures shadow. 50ch, Badger winning the prize.

1989, June 21
2838-2840 A1326 Set of 3 4.00 .65

Astronomy A1327

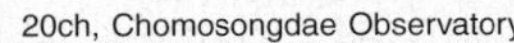

20ch, Chomosongdae Observatory.
80ch, Saturn (horiz.)

1989, June 29 ***Perf. 12***
2841 A1327 20ch multicolored 1.40 .20

Souvenir Sheet

2842 A1327 80ch multicolored 3.00 .50

Eugène Delacroix's *Liberty Guiding the People* — A1328

PHILEXFRANCE '89, Int'l Philatelic Exhib., Paris

1989, July 7 ***Perf. 12x11½***
2843 A1328 70ch multicolored 3.00 2.00

BRASILIANA '89, Int'l Philatelic Exhib., Rio de Janeiro — A1329

1989, July 28 ***Perf. 12***
2844 A1329 40ch Pele, #1714 1.40 .30

Fire Brigade and Emergency Medical Services — A1330

Designs: 10ch, Nurse and ambulance. 20ch, Surgeon and ambulance. 30ch, Fireman and fire engine. 40ch, Fireman and fire engine (diff.)

1989, Aug. 12
2845-2848 A1330 Set of 4 6.00 .65

Plants Presented as Gifts to Kim Il Sung — A1331

Designs: 10ch, Kafir lily (*Clivia miniata*). 15ch, Tulips (*Tulipa gesneriana*). 20ch, Flamingo lily (*Anthurium andreanum*). 25ch, *Rhododendron obtusum*. 30ch, Daffodils (*Narcissus pseudonarcissus*).
80ch, (*Gerbera hybrida*).

1989, Aug. 19
2849-2853 A1331 Set of 5 5.50 1.00

Souvenir Sheet

2854 A1331 80ch multicolored 4.50 .50

150th Anniv. of Postage Stamps / STAMP WORLD LONDON '90 Int'l Philatelic Exhib. — A1332

Designs: 5ch, Letter, ship, plane, map. 10ch, Letters and mail box. 20ch, Stamps, magnifying glass, tongs. 30ch, Fiirst stamps pf DPRK. 40ch, UPU emblem, headquarters, Berne. 50ch, Sir Rowland Hill and Penny Black.

1989, Aug. 27
2855-2860 A1332 Set of 6 7.50 1.25

A1333

Alpine Flowers — A1334

Designs: 10ch, *Iris setosa*. 15ch, *Aquilegia japonica*. 20ch, *Bistorta incana*. 25ch *Rhodiola elongata*. 30ch, *Sanguisorba sitchensis*.
80ch, (*Trollius japonicus*).

1989, Sept. 8 ***Perf. 11½***
2861-2865 A1333 Set of 5 5.25 1.00

Souvenir Sheet

2866 A1334 80ch multicolored 3.50 .55

Trees bearing Anti-Japanese Patriotic Slogans — A1335

Designs: 10ch, "20 million compatriots, an anti-Japanese heroine of Korea rose on Mt. Paektu," inscribed on tree, Mt. Paektu. 3w, "The future of Korea is bright with the Luminous Star of Mt. Paektu," inscribed on tree, Qun-dong, Pyongyang. 5w, "The General Star of Mt. Paektu shines three thousand-ri expanse of land," inscribed on tree, Mt. Kanbaek.

1989, Sept. 21 ***Perf. 12¼***
2867-2869 A1335 Set of 3 18.00 11.00

Compare with No. 2885.

Children's Games — A1336

Designs: 10ch, Girl skipping rope. 20ch, Boy with whirligig. 30ch, Boy flying kite. 40ch, Girl spinning top.

1989, Sept. 30 ***Perf. 12***
2870 A1336 Block of 4, #a.-d. 4.00 .80
a. 10ch multicolored .25 .20
b. 20ch multicolored 1.75 .20
c. 30ch multicolored .50 .20
d. 40ch multicolored .60 .20

Int'l March for Peace and Reunification of Korea — A1337

1989, Oct. 1 ***Perf. 11½x12***
2871 A1337 80ch multicolored 3.00 1.75

Locomotives — A1338

Designs: 10ch, Electric train entering station yard. 20ch, Electric train crossing bridge. 25ch, Diesel locomotive. 30ch, Diesel locomotive (diff.). 40ch, Steam locomotive. 50ch, Steam locomotive (diff.).

1989, Oct. 19 ***Perf. 11¾x12¼***
2872-2877 A1338 Set of 6 6.00 1.25

14th World Soccer Championship, *Italia '90* — A1339

Designs: 10ch, Players and map of Italy. 20ch, Free kick. 30ch, Goal scrimmage. 40ch, Goalkeeper blocking ball.

1989, Oct. 28 ***Perf. 12x11¾***
2878-2881 A1339 Set of 4 4.00 .60

Magellan A1340

1989, Nov. 25 ***Perf. 12***
2882 A1340 30ch multicolored 1.25 .20

Descobrex '89 International Philatelic Exhibition, Portugal.

A1341

A1342

10ch, Mangyong Hill and snow-covered pine branches. 20ch, Koguryo warriors.

Perf. 11½ (#2883), 12 (#2884)

1990, Jan. 1

2883 A1341 10ch multicolored .25 .20
a. Toned unsurfaced paper, without gum 15.00 —
2884 A1342 20ch multicolored 1.20 .20
a. Toned unsurfaced paper, without gum 5.00 —

New Year.

Tree, Mt. Paektu, Bearing Anti-Japanese Patriotic Slogan — A1343

1990, Jan. 12 ***Perf. 11½***

2885 A1343 5ch multicolored .50 .20
a. Toned unsurfaced paper, without gum 5.00 —

Dogs — A1344

Designs: 20ch, Ryukwoli. 30ch, Phalryuki. 40ch, Komdungi. 50ch, Olruki.

1990, Jan. 17

2886 A1344 Block of 4, #a.-d. 5.50 1.50
a. 20ch multicolored .90 .20
b. 30ch multicolored .90 .20
c. 40ch multicolored .90 .20
d. 50ch multicolored .90 .20

Birthplace, Mt. Paektu — A1345

1990, Feb. 16

2887 A1345 10ch deep red brown .50 .20
a. Toned unsurfaced paper, without gum 5.00 —

Kim Jong Il's 48th birthday.

Stone Age Man A1346

Designs: 10ch, Primitive man, stone tools. 20ch, Paleolithic and Neolithic men, camp scene.

1990, Feb. 21

2888-2889 A1346 Set of 2 3.00 .30

Bridges — A1347

Designs: 10ch, Rungra Bridge, Pyongyang. 20ch, Pothong Bridge, Pyongyang. 30ch, Suspension bridge between Sinuiju-Ryucho Island. 40ch, Chungsongui Bridge, Pyongyang.

1990, Feb. 27 ***Perf. 11½***

2890-2893 A1347 Set of 4 4.50 .60
2890a 10ch Thin, coarse brownish paper, without gum 5.00 —

Traditional Warriors' Costumes A1348

Designs: 20ch, Infantryman (3rd century BC-7th century AD). 30ch, Archer. 50ch, Commander in armor (3rd century BC-7th century AD). 70ch, Koguryo Period officer (10th-14th centuries).

1989, Mar. 18

2894-2897 A1348 Set of 4 6.25 2.00
2897a 70ch Dull white unsurfaced paper, without gum 5.00 —

Crabs A1349

Designs: 20ch, *Atergatis subdentatus.* 30ch, *Platylambrus validus.* 50ch, *Uca arcuata.*

1990, Mar. 25

2898-2900 A1349 Set of 3 3.00 .60

Dancers — A1350

1990, Apr. 7

2901 A1350 10ch multicolored .50 .20

Spring Friendship Art Festival, Pyongyang.

A1351

Kim Il Sung's 78th Birthday A1352

Designs: 10ch, 'Fork in the Road' Monument, Mangyongdae Revolutionary Site. 80ch, Kim Il Sung.

1990, Apr. 15 ***Perf. 11½x11¾***

2902 A1351 10ch multicolored .50 .20

Souvenir Sheet

2903 A1352 80ch multicolored 2.50 .50

Cacti — A1353

Designs: 10ch, *Gynmocalycium sp.* 30ch, *Phyllocactus hybridus.* 50ch, *Epiphyllum truncatum.*

1990, Apr. 21 ***Perf. 12¼***

2904-2906 A1353 Set of 3 4.00 .60

A1354

Stamp World London '90 — A1355

Designs: 20ch, Exhibition emblem. 70ch, Sir Rowland Hill.

1990, May 3 ***Perf. 11½***

2907 A1354 20ch multicolored .90 .20

Souvenir Sheet

2908 A1355 70ch multicolored 2.75 1.20

A1356

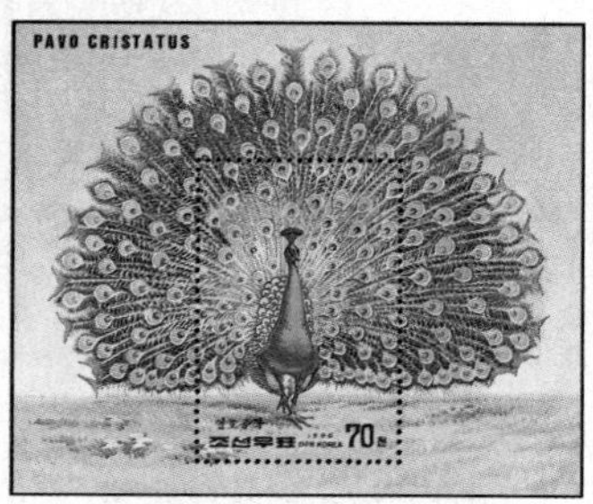
Peafowl — A1357

Designs: 10ch, Congo peafowl *Afropavo congensis.* 20ch, Common peafowl *Pavo cristatus.*
70ch, Common peafowl with tail displayed.

1990, May 10 ***Perf. 11¾x12***

2909-2910 A1356 Set of 2 3.00 .60

Souvenir Sheet

2911 A1357 70ch multicolored 3.00 .60

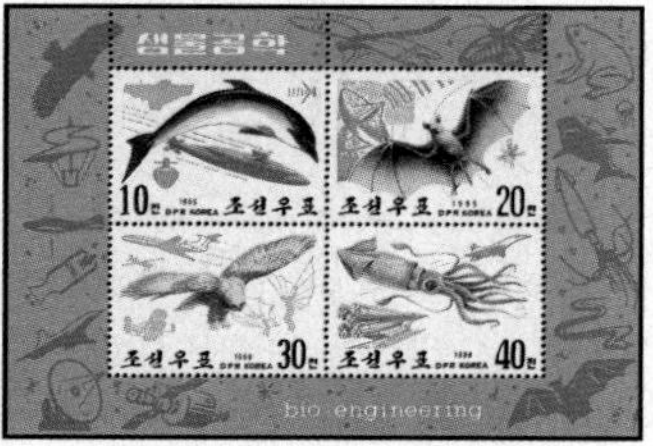
Bio-engineering — A1358

Designs: 10ch, Dolphin and submarine. 20ch, Bat and sonar dish, satellite. 30ch, Eagle and airplanes. 40ch, Squid and jets.

1990, May 24

2912 A1358 Sheet of 4, #a.-d. 7.00 1.25
a. 10ch multicolored 1.25 .25
b. 20ch multicolored 1.25 .25
c. 30ch multicolored 1.25 .25
d. 40ch multicolored 1.25 .25

BELGICA '90 Int'l Philatelic Exhib., Brussels A1359

Designs: 10ch, Rembrandt, *Self Portrait.* 20ch, Raphael, *Self Portrait.* 30ch, Rubens, *Self Portrait.*

1990, June 2 ***Perf. 12¼x12***

2913-2915 A1359 Set of 3 2.25 .40

Düsseldorf '90, 10th Int'l Youth Philatelic Exhib. — A1360

Designs: 20ch, Steffi Graf, tennis player, with bouquet. 30ch, Exhibition emblem. 70ch, K.H. Rummenigge, German soccer player.

1990, June 20
2916-2918 A1360 Set of 3 7.00 .75

A1361

Designs: 10ch, Games mascot, Workers' Stadium, Beijing. 30ch, Chollina Statue and Korean athletes. 40ch, Games emblem, athletes.

1990, July 14
2919-2921 A1361 Set of 3 2.00 .60

11th Asian Games, Beijing (#3021, 3022). Third Asian Winter Games, Samjiyon (#3023).

14th World Cup Soccer Championship — A1362

Designs: 15ch, Emblem of F.I.F.A. (Federation of Football Associations). 20ch, Jules Rimet. 25ch, Soccer ball. 30ch, Olympic Stadium, Rome. 35ch, Goalkeeper. 40ch, Emblem of the German Football Association.
80ch, Emblem of German Football Association and trophy.

1990, Aug. 8 ***Perf. 13½***
2922-2927 A1362 Set of 6 6.00 1.00

Souvenir Sheet

2928 A1362 80ch multicolored 3.00 1.50

New Zealand '90 Int'l Philatelic Exhib., Auckland A1363

1990, Aug. 24 ***Perf. 12***
2929 A1363 30ch multicolored 1.75 .40

Summer at Chipson Peak — A1364

1990, Aug. 24 ***Perf. 11½***
2930 A1364 80ch multicolored 3.00 .50

Europa '90 International Stamp Fair, Riccione.

Koguryo Wedding Procession — A1365

Designs: 10ch, Man on horse blowing bugle. 30ch, Bridegroom on horse. 50ch, Bride in carriage. 1w, Man on horse beating drum.

1990, Sept. 3 ***Perf. 12***
2931 Strip of 4, #a.-d. 6.00 .80
a. A1365 10ch multicolored 1.25 .20
b. A1365 30ch multicolored 1.25 .20
c. A1365 50ch multicolored 1.25 .20
d. A1365 1w multicolored 1.25 .20

Printed in setenant strips of four within the sheet.

A1366

Pan-National Rally for Peace and Reunification of Korea — A1367

Designs: 10ch, Rally emblem, crowd descending Mt. Paektu.
1w, Crowd watching dancers.

1990, Sept. 15
2932 A1366 10ch multicolored .50 .20

Souvenir Sheet

2933 A1367 1w multicolored 2.75 .55

Insects A1368

Designs: 20ch, Praying mantis (*Mantis religiosa*). 30ch, Lady bug (*Coccinella septempunctata*). 40ch, *Pheropsophus jussoensis*. 70ch, *Phyllium siccifolium*.

1990, Sept. 20
2934-2936A A1368 Set of 4 6.00 1.10

Soccer Players — A1369

1990, Oct. 11
2937 A1369 Pair, #a.-b. 2.75 .40
a. 10ch multicolored 1.25 .20
b. 20ch multicolored 1.25 .20

Souvenir Sheet

Design: 1w, North and South Korean players entering May Day Stadium.

2938 A1369 1w multicolored 4.50 .75

North-South Reunification Soccer Games, Pyongyang.

National Reunification Concert — A1370

1990, Oct. 17
2939 A1370 10ch multicolored .50 .20

Farm Animals — A1371

Designs: 10ch, Ox. 20ch, Pig. 30ch, Goat. 40ch, Sheep. 50ch, Horse.

1990, Oct. 18
2940-2944 A1371 Set of 5 5.75 .85
2944a Sheet of 10, 2 ea #2940-2944 13.00 1.75

A1372

A1373

Chinese Entry Into Korean War, 40th Anniv. — A1374

Designs: 10ch, N. Korean and Communist Chinese soldiers. 20ch, Korean civilians welcoming Chinese soldiers. 30ch, Battle scene, victorious soldiers. 40ch, Postwar reconstruction.
80ch, Friendship Monument.

1990, Oct. 23
2945 A1372 10ch multicolored .20 .20
2946 A1373 20ch multicolored .75 .20
2947 A1373 30ch multicolored 1.00 .20
2948 A1373 40ch multicolored 1.50 .20
Nos. 2945-2948 (4) 3.45 .80

Souvenir Sheet

Perf. 11¾x11½

2949 A1374 80ch multicolored 3.00 .50

For overprint see No. 3282.

UN Development Program, 40th Anniv. A1375

1990, Oct. 24 ***Perf. 13¼***
2950 A1375 1w multicolored 4.00 1.20

Fish — A1376

Designs: 10ch, Sturgeon (*Acipenser mikadoi*). 20ch, Sea bream (*Sparus macrocephalus*). 40ch, Fat greenling (*Hergrammos otakii*). 50ch, Ray (*Myliobatus tobeijei*).

1990, Nov. 20 ***Perf. 12***
2951-2955 A1376 Set of 5 5.75 2.00
2955a Sheet of 10, 2 ea #2951-2955 12.00 4.00

New Year — A1377

1990, Dec. 1
2956 A1377 40ch multicolored 1.75 .20

Birds — A1378

Designs: 10ch, Moorhen (*Gallinula chloropus*). 20ch, Jay (*Garrulus glandarius*). 30ch, Three-toed woodpecker (*Picodes

tridactylus). 40ch, Whimbrel (*Numenius phaeopus*). 50ch, Water rail (*Rallus aquaticus*)

1990, Dec. 18 ***Perf. 12***

2957-2961 A1378 Set of 5 6.50 2.00
2961a Sheet of 10, 2 ea #2957-2961 13.00 5.00

A1379

Pandas — A1380

Designs: 10ch, Giant panda. 20ch, Two giant pandas feeding. 30ch, Giant panda on limb. 40ch, Giant panda on rock. 50ch, Pair of giant pandas. 60ch, Giant panda in tree.

1991, Jan. 10 ***Perf. 11¾x12***

2962-2967 A1379 Set of 6 7.00 1.75
2967a Sheet of 6, #2962-2967 7.00 1.75

Souvenir Sheet

Perf. 11½

2968 A1380 1w multicolored 3.25 .60

A1381

Revolutionary Sites — A1382

1991, Jan. 10 ***Perf. 12***

2969 A1381 5ch Changsan .25 .20
2970 A1382 10ch Oun .30 .20

Endangered Birds — A1383

Designs: 10ch, Black-faced spoonbills (*Platalea minor*). 20ch, Gray herons (*Ardea cinerea*). 30ch, Great egrets (*Egretta alba*). 40ch, Manchurian cranes (*Grus japonensis*). 50ch, Japanese white-necked cranes (*Grus vipio*). 70ch, White storks (*Ciconia boyciana*).

1991, Feb. 5

2971-2976 A1383 Set of 6 6.00 1.40
2976a Sheet of 6, #2971-2976 7.50 1.75

Alpine Butterflies — A1384

Designs: 10ch, *Clossiana angarensis*. 20ch, *Erebia embla*. 30ch, *Nymphalis antiopa*. 40ch, *Polygonia c-album*). 50ch, *Colias erate*. 60ch, *Thecla betulae*).

1991, Feb. 20 ***Perf. 13¼***

2977-2982 A1384 Set of 6 7.50 2.50
2982a Sheet of 6, #2977-2982 7.50 2.50

Fungi — A1385

Designs: 10ch, *Hydnum repandum*. 20ch, *Phylloporus rhodoxanthus*. 30ch, *Calvatia craniformis*. 40ch, *Ramaria botrytis*. 50ch, *Russula integra*.

1991, Feb. 26 ***Perf. 12x12¼***

2983-2987 A1385 Set of 5 5.00 1.25
2987a Sheet of 10, 2 ea #2983-2987 10.00 2.50

A1386

Revolutionary Sites — A1387

1991, Mar. 15 ***Perf. 12***

2988 A1386 10ch Kumchon .30 .20
2989 A1387 40ch Samdung 1.20 .30

A1388

Silkworm Research A1389

Designs: 10ch, Dr. Kye Ung (1893-1967), silkworm researcher. 20ch, Chinese oak silk moth, *Antheraea pernyi*. 30ch, *Attacus ricini*. 40ch, *Antheraea yamamai*). 50ch, *Bombyx mori*. 60ch, *Aetias artemis*).

1991, Mar. 27

2990 A1388 10ch multicolored .20 .20
2991 A1389 20ch multicolored .60 .30
2992 A1389 30ch multicolored .80 .40
2993 A1389 40ch multicolored 1.20 .50
2994 A1389 50ch multicolored 1.60 .75
2995 A1389 60ch multicolored 2.00 .80
a. Sheet of 6, #2990-2995 6.50 3.50
Nos. 2990-2995 (6) 6.40 2.95

9th Spring Friendship Art Festival, Pyongyang A1390

1991, Apr. 3

2996 A1390 10ch multicolored .50 .20

Antarctic Exploration A1391

Designs: 10ch, Penguins. 20ch, Research station. 30ch, Elephant seals. 40ch, Research ship. 50ch, Black-backed gulls.
80ch, DPRK flag and map of Antarctica.

1991, Apr. 20 ***Perf. 11¾x12***

2997-3001 A1391 Set of 5 6.00 1.25

Souvenir Sheet

Perf. 11¾

3002 A1391 80ch multicolored 3.00 .55

85th Interparliamentary Union Conference, Pyongyang — A1392

Designs: 10ch, Peoples Palace of Culture. 1.50w, Conference emblem and azalea.

1991, Apr. 29 ***Perf. 12***

3003-3004 A1392 Set of 2 5.00 1.40

Map and Kim Jong Ho — A1393

1991, May 8 ***Perf. 11¾x12***

3005 A1393 90ch multicolored 2.50 .80

Dinosaurs — A1394

Designs: 10ch, Cynognathus. 20ch, Brontosaurus. 30ch, Stegosaurus and allosaurus. 40ch, Pterosauria. 50ch, Ichthyosaurus.

1991, May 21 ***Perf. 12x11¾***

3006-3010 A1394 Strip of 5 + label 7.50 1.75
3010a Sheet of 5 + label 17.00 2.00

Barcelona '92 Olympic Games — A1395

Designs: #3011, 10ch, 100-Meter dash. #3012, 10ch, Hurdle race. #3013 20ch, Broad jump. #3014, 20ch, Throwing discus. #3015, 30ch, Shot-put. #3016, 30ch, Pole vault. #3017, 40ch, High jump. #3018, 40ch, Javelin throw.
#3019, 80ch, 400-meter race. #3020, 80ch, 1500-meter race.

1991, June 18

3011-3018 A1395 Set of 8 4.00 1.40
3018a Sheet of 10, #3011-3020 12.50 2.75

Souvenir Sheets

Perf. 11½x11¾

3019-3020 A1395 Set of 2 3.50 1.25

No. 3018a contains single stamps from #3019-3020 in addition to Nos. 3011-3018.

Cats — A1396

Designs: 10ch, Cats and birds. 20ch, Cat and rat. 30ch, Cat and butterfly. 40ch, Cats and ball. 50ch, Cat and frog.

1991, July 21 ***Perf. 13¼***

3021-3025 A1396 Set of 5 5.25 2.25

Riccione '91 Int'l Stamp Fair — A1397

1991, Aug. 27 ***Perf. 11¾x12***

3026 A1397 80ch multicolored 2.75 .60

Horses
A1398

Designs: 10ch, Wild horse (*Equus caballus*). 20ch, Hybrid of wild ass and wild horse (*Equus asinus* and *Equus caballus*). 30ch, Przewalski's horse (*Equus przewalskii*). 40ch, Wild ass (*Equus asinus*). 50ch, Wild horse (*Equus caballus*), diff.

1991, Sept. 2 ***Perf. 13½***
3027-3031 A1398 Set of 5 5.00 1.25
3031a Sheet of 5, #3027-3031 5.00 1.40

A1399

Phila Nippon '91 International Stamp Exhibition — A1400

Fish: 10ch, Pennant coral fish (*Heniochus acuminatus*). 20ch, Big-spotted trigger fish (*Balistoides conspicillum*). 30ch, Anemone fish (*Amphiprion frenatus*). 40ch, Blue surgeon fish (*Paracanthurus hepatus*). 50ch, Angel fish (*Pterophyllum eimekei*).
80ch, Tetras (*Hyphessobrycon innesi*).

1991, Sept. 20 ***Perf. 12x12¼***
3032-3036 A1399 Set of 5 5.00 1.25
3036a Sheet of 5, #3032-3036 5.00 1.25

Souvenir Sheet
Perf. 11¾

3037 A1400 80ch multicolored 5.00 .60

No. 3036 is airmail.

Flowers
A1401

Designs: 10ch, Begonia. 20ch, Gerbera. 30ch, Rhododendrons. 40ch, Phalaenopsis. 50ch, *Impatiens sultani*. 60ch, Streptocarpus.

1991, Oct. 16 ***Perf. 12¼x12***
3038-3043 A1401 Set of 6 6.50 1.75
3043a Sheet of 6, #3038-3043 6.50 2.00

Nos. 3041-3043 commemorate Canada '92 International Youth Stamp Exhibition, Montreal, and include the exhibition emblem.

Panmunjon — A1402

1991, Oct. 12 ***Perf. 12***
3044 A1402 10ch multicolored .60 .20

Magnolia — A1403

1991, Nov. 1 ***Perf. 11½***
3045 A1403 10ch multicolored .60 .20

DPRK National Flower.

Women's World Soccer Championship, China — A1404

Designs: 10ch, Dribbling. 20ch, Dribbling, diff. 30ch, Heading the ball. 40ch, Overhead kick. 50ch, Tackling. 60ch, Goalkeeper.

1991, Nov. 3 ***Perf. 12***
3046-3051 A1404 Set of 6 6.50 1.75
3051a Sheet of 6, #3046-3051 6.50 2.00

A1405

Monkeys — A1406

Designs: 10ch, Squirrel monkeys (*Samiri sciureus*). 20ch, Pygmy marmosets (*Cebuella pygmaea*). 30ch, Red-handed tamarins (*Saquinas midas*).
80ch, Monkey leaping.

1992, Jan. 1
3052-3054 A1405 Set of 3 2.25 .70
3054a Sheet of 3, #3052-3054 2.50 .80

Souvenir Sheet
Perf. 11¾x11½

3055 A1406 80ch multicolored 2.50 1.00

A1407

Birds of Prey — A1408

Designs: 10ch, Great horned owl (*Bubo bubo*). 20ch, Hawk (*Buteo buteo*). 30ch, African fish eagle (*Haliaeetus vocifer*). 40ch, Stellar's sea eagle (*Haliaeetus pelagicus*). 50ch, Golden eagle (*Aquila chrysaetos*).
80ch, Common kestrel (*Falco tinnunculus*).

1992, Jan. 5 ***Perf. 13¼***
3056-3060 A1407 Set of 5 4.75 1.75
3060a Sheet of 12, 2 #3056-3060 + 2 labels 10.00 3.50

Souvenir Sheet
Perf. 11½

3061 A1408 80ch multicolored 2.50 .60

No. 3060a, Granada '92 International Stamp Exhibition.

A1409

50th Birthday of Kim Jong Il — A1410

Designs: 10ch, Birthplace, Mt. Paektu. 20ch, Mt. Paektu. 30ch, Lake Chon on top of Mt. Paektu. 40ch, Lake Samji.
80ch, *Snowstorm in Mt. Paektu.*

1992, Feb. 16 ***Perf. 12x11¾***
3062-3065 A1409 Set of 4 3.25 .75

Souvenir Sheet
Perf. 11¾x11½

3066 A1410 80ch multicolored 3.00 .60

Transport
A1411

Designs: 10ch, Bus, "Jipsam 88." 20ch, Bus, "Pyongyang 86." 30ch, Trolley bus, "Chollima 84." 40ch, Bus, "Kwangbok Sonyon." 50ch, Tram. 60ch, July 17 Tram.

1992, Feb. 20 ***Perf. 12¼***
3067-3072 A1411 Set of 6 6.50 1.75
3072a Sheet of 6, #3067-3072 6.50 1.90

No. 3072a, Essen '92 International Stamp Fair.

Spring Fellowship Art Festival, Pyongyang
A1412

1992, Apr. 7
3073 A1412 10ch multicolored .50 .20

A1413

80th Birthday of Kim Il Sung — A1414

Revolutionary Sites: 10ch (#3074), Birthplace, Mangyongdao. 10ch (#3075), Party emblem, Turubong. 10ch (#3076), Map, Ssuksom. 10ch (#3077), Statue of soldier, Tongchang. 40ch (#3078), Chollima Statue, Kangson. 40ch (#3079), Cogwheels, Taean. 1.20w, Monument, West Sea Barrage.
80ch, Kim Il Sung among participants in the April Spring Friendship Art Festival.

1992, Apr. 15
3074-3080 A1413 Set of 7 7.50 2.25

Souvenir Sheet
Perf. 11½

3081 A1414 80ch multicolored 3.00 .60

No. 2080 is airmail.

Kang Ban Sok, Mother of Kim Il Sung, Birth Centenary — A1415

1992, Apr. 21 ***Perf. 13¼***
3082 A1415 80ch multicolored 2.25 .60

Korean People's Army, 60th Anniv.
A1416

Designs (all 10ch): #3083, Soldier, troops on parade. #3084, Pilot, soldiers. #3085, Soldier with two civilian women.

1992, Apr. 25 *Perf. 12¼*
3083-3085 A1416 Set of 3 1.10 .25
3085a Sheet of 9, 4 #3085, 2 ea. #3083-3084 + label 3.00 1.00

25th Olympic Games, Barcelona '92 — A1417

Women's events: 10ch, Hurdle race. 20ch, High jump. 30ch, Shot-put. 40ch, 200-meter race. 50ch, Broad jump. 60ch, Javelin throw.
80ch, 800-meter race.

1992, May 10 *Perf. 12x11¾*
3086-3091 A1417 Set of 6 6.50 1.75
3091a Sheet of 8, #3086-3092 + label 9.50 2.50

Souvenir Sheet

3092 A1416 80ch multicolored 2.75 .60

Prehistoric Man — A1418

Designs: 10ch, Planting crops. 20ch, Family in shelter, with cooking pot. 30ch, Plowing. 40ch, Indoor life. 50ch, Laying a dolmen.

1992, June 1 *Perf. 12x11¾*
3093-3097 A1418 Set of 5 5.00 1.25
3097a Sheet of 5, #3093-3097 + label 6.00 1.40

Birds — A1419

Designs: 10ch, White-bellied woodpecker (*Dryocopus javensis*). 20ch, Ring-necked pheasant (*Phasianis colchicus*). 30ch, White stork (*Ciconia boyciana*). 40ch, Blue-winged pitta (*Pitta brachyura*). 50ch, Pallas's sand-grouse (*Syrrhaptes paradoxus*). 60ch, Black grouse (*Lyrurus tetrix*).
80ch, European starling (*Sturnus sturnus*).

1992, June 28 *Perf. 11½*
3098-3103 A1419 Set of 6 7.00 1.75
3103a Sheet of 7, #3098-3104 + label 15.00 —

Souvenir Sheet

3104 A1418 80ch multicolored 3.50 1.40

No. 3103a contains a single stamp from #3104 in addtion to #3098-3103.

North-South Joint Statement, 20th Anniv. — A1420

1992, July 4
3105 A1420 1.50w multicolored 4.50 1.40

Souvenir Sheet

3106 A1420 3w multicolored 9.00 2.75

No. 3106 contains two copies of No. 3105 and label.

Flowers — A1421

Designs: 10ch, *Bougainvillea spectabilis.* 20ch, *Ixora chinensis.* 30ch, *Dendrobium taysuwie.* 40ch, *Columnea gloriosa.* 50ch, *Crinum.* 60ch, *Ranunculus asiaticus.*

1992, July 15 *Perf. 12¼*
3107-3112 A1421 Set of 6 6.50 1.75
3112a Sheet of 8, #3107-3112 + 2 labels 7.00 2.00

No. 3112a, Genova '92 International Stamp Exhibition.

The Solar System — A1422

No. 3113: a, Satellite, Venus, Earth, Mars. b, Jupiter. c, Saturn. d, Uranus. e, Neptune, Pluto.

1992, Aug. 10 *Perf. 11½*
3113 A1422 50ch Strip of 5, #a-e 8.00 2.50
3113f Sheet of 10, 2 #3113 + 5 labels 9.00 2.75

Souvenir Sheet

3114 A1422 80ch multicolored 2.50 1.50

Riccione '92 Int'l Stamp Fair — A1423

Designs: 10ch, C-class yacht. 20ch, Sailboard. 30ch, Rager-class yacht. 40ch, Pinclass yacht. 50ch, 470-class yacht. 60ch, Fair emblem.

1992, Aug. 27 *Perf. 12¼*
3119-3124 A1423 Set of 6 6.50 2.25
3119a Sheet of 6 stamps, 2 ea. #3119, 3121, 3123 6.50 2.50
3120a Sheet of 6 stamps, 2 ea. #3120, 3122, 3124 6.50 2.50

A1424

U.C. Sampdoria, Italian Soccer Champion 1991 — A1425

Designs: 20ch, Moreno Mannini, defender. 30ch, Gianluca Vialli, forward. 40ch, Pietro Vierchowod, back. 50ch, Fausto Pari, center-half. 60ch, Roberto Mancini, forward. 1w, club president.
1w, Vialli and Riccardo Garrone, president of club sponsor, ERG.

1992, Aug. 31 *Perf. 12*
3125-3130 A1424 Sheet of 6 9.00 3.00

Souvenir Sheet

Perf. 11½x12

3131 A1425 1w multicolored 3.00 1.50

A1426

8th World Taekwondo Championship, Pyongyang — A1427

Designs: 10ch, Team pattern. 30ch, Side kick. 50ch, Flying high kick. 70ch, Flying twisting kick. 90ch, Black-belt breaking tiles with fist.
1.20w, Flying twin foot side kick; Choe Hong Hin, president of International Taekwon-Do Federation, in margin.

1992, Sept. 1 *Perf. 12*
3132-3136 A1426 Set of 5 8.00 2.50
3136a Sheet of 5, #3132-3136 + label 8.00 2.50

Souvenir Sheet

3137 A1427 1.20w multicolored 4.00 1.75

No. 3137 is airmail.

Frogs and Toads A1428

Designs: 40ch (#3138), *Rana chosenica.* 40ch (#3139), Moor frog (*Rana arvalis*). 40ch (#3140), Common toad (*Bufo bufo*). 70ch (#3141), Common pond frog (*Rana nigromaculata*). 70ch (#3142), Japanese tree toad (*Hyla japonica*). 70ch (#3143), (*Rana coreana*).

1992, Sept. 10 *Perf. 12¼*
3138-3143 A1428 Set of 6 10.00 3.00
3139a Sheet of 7, 3 #3139, 2 ea. #3138, #3140 + label 15.00 5.00
3142a Sheet of 7, 3 #3142, 2 ea. #3141, #3143 + label 15.00 5.00

No. 3143 is airmail.

World Environment Day — A1429

Designs: 10ch, Flower (*Rhododendron mucronulatum*). 30ch, Barn swallow (*Hirundo rustica*). 40ch, Flower (*Stewartia koreana*). 50ch, Beetle (*Dictoptera aurora*). 70ch, Tree (*Metasequoia glyptostroboides*). 90ch, Chinese salamander (*Hynobius leechi*). 1.20w, Tree (*Gingko biloba*). 1.40w, Fish (*Cottus poecilopus*).

1992, Oct. 20 *Perf. 12*
3144-3151 A1429 Set of 8 19.00 4.75
3151a Sheet of 8 stamps, #3144-3151 20.00 5.25

Nos. 3150 and 3151 are airmail.

Whales and Dolphins A1430

Designs (all 50ch): #3152, Fin whale (*Balaenoptera physalus*). #3153, Common dolphin (*Delphinus delphis*). #3154, Killer whale (*Orcinus orca*). #3155, Hump-backed whale (*Megaptera nodosa*). #3156, Bottle-nosed whale (*Berardius bairdii*). #3157, Sperm whale (*Physeter catadon*).

1992, Oct. 20
3152-3157 A1430 Set of 6 12.00 2.75
3152a Sheet of 3, #3152-3154 5.50 1.25
3155a Sheet of 3, #3155-3157 5.50 1.25

No. 3157 is airmail.

New Year (Year of the Rooster) A1431

Chickens in various cartoon forms: 10ch, Hen and chicks. 20ch, Young hen. 30ch, Strong cock. 40ch, Prince cock. 50ch, Princess hen. 60ch, King cock.
1.20w, Cock.

1992, Dec. 7 *Perf. 11½*
3158-3163 A1431 Set of 6 6.50 1.75
3163a Sheet of 4, #3158-3160, 3163c 4.00 1.50
3163b Sheet of 4, #3161-3163, 3163c 5.00 2.00

Souvenir Sheet

3163C A1431 1.20w multicolored 5.00 1.00

A single stamp like that in No. 3163C is included in Nos. 3163a and 3163b.

N. Korean Gold Medal Winners at Barcelona Olympics A1432

Designs: 10ch, Choe Chol Su (boxing). 20ch, Pae Kil Su (gymnastics). 50ch, Ri Hak Son (Wrestling). 60ch, Kim Il (wrestling).

No. 3168: a, 30ch, Archer, flame, gold medal, flags of DPRK and Spain. b, 40ch, Emblem, game mascot and Church of the Holy Family, Barcelona.

1992, Dec. 20 *Perf. 12*
3164-3167 A1432 Set of 4 4.50 1.20

Sheet of 6

3168 #3164-3167, 3168a-3168b 7.00 .60
a. A1432 30ch multicolored .35 .25
b. A1432 40ch multicolored .50 .30

Fungi — A1433

Designs: 10ch, Golden mushroom (*Flammulina velutipes*). 20ch, Shaggy caps (*Coprinus comatus*). 30ch, *Ganoderma lucidum*. 40ch, Brown mushroom (*Lentinus edodes*). 50ch, (*Volvaria bombycina*). 60ch, (*Sarcodon aspratus*).
1w, Scarlet caterpillar (*Cordyceps militaris*).

1993, Jan. 10 ***Perf. 11½***
3169-3174 A1433 Set of 6 7.50 2.50
3169a Sheet of 4, #3169, 3172, 3174, 3175 7.00 2.25
3170a Sheet of 4, #3170, 3171, 3173, 3175 7.00 2.25

Souvenir Sheet

3175 A1433 1w multicolored 4.50 .80

A single stamp like that in No. 3175 is included in Nos. 3169a and 3170a.

A1434

Korean Plants — A1435

Designs: 10ch, (*Keumkangsania asiatica*). 20ch, (*Echinosophora koreensis*). 30ch, (*Abies koreana*). 40ch, (*Benzoin angustifolium*). 50ch, (*Abeliophyllum distichum*). 60ch, (*Abelia mosanensis*).
1w, *Pentactina rupicola*.

1993, Jan. 20 ***Perf. 12¼***
3176-3181 A1434 Set of 6 7.00 2.00
3181a Sheet of 6, #3176-3181 7.00 2.25

Souvenir Sheet

Perf. 11½

3182 A1435 1w multicolored 3.50 2.00

8th Congress of the League of Socialist Working Youth of Korea — A1436

Designs: 10ch, Youths, banner. 20ch, Flame, emblem, motto.

1993, Jan. 25 ***Perf. 12¼***
3183-3184 A1436 Set of 2 1.50 .40

Phophyong Revolutionary Site Tower & March Corps Emblem — A1437

1993, Jan. 29 ***Perf. 12x12¼***
3185 A1437 10ch multicolored .50 .20

70th anniv. of the 250-mile Journey for Learning.

Tower of the Juche Idea, Grand Monument, Mt. Wangjae A1438

1993, Feb. 11
3186 A1438 60ch multicolored .50 .20

60th anniv. of the Wangjaesan Meeting.

A1439

Kim Jong Il, 51st Birthday — A1440

Designs: 10ch, *Kimjongilia* (Begonia).
1w, Kim Il Sung writing poem praising Kim Jong Il. Illustration of stamp only. Shee measures 170mmx95mm, with marginal inscriptions that include reproductions of Kim Il Sung's poem.

1993, Feb. 16 ***Perf. 12***
3187 A1439 10ch multicolored 1.00 .20

Souvenir Sheet

Perf. 13¼

3188 A1440 1w multicolored 3.50 .75

Sea Fish A1441

Designs: 10ch, Pilot fish (*Naucrates ductor*). 20ch, Japanese stingray (*Dasyatis akajei*). 30ch, Moonfish (*Lampris guttatus*). 40ch, Coelacanth (*Latimeria chalumnae*). 50ch, Grouper (*Epinephelus moara*).
1.20w, Mako shark (*Isurus oxyrhynchus*).

1993, Feb. 25 ***Perf. 11½***
3189-3193 A1441 Set of 5 5.00 1.25
3189a Sheet of 2, #3189, #3194 3.25 .45
3190a Sheet of 2, #3190, #3193 3.25 .45
3191a Sheet of 2, #3191, #3192 3.25 .45

Souvenir Sheet

3194 A1441 1.20w multicolored 4.50 .80

A single stamp like that in No. 3194 is included in No. 3189a.
No. 3194, Naposta '93.

Spring on the Hill, 18th century Korean Painting — A1442

1993, Mar. 20 ***Perf. 12x11½***
3195 A1442 Sheet of 5 6.50 1.75
a.-e. 40ch, any single 1.00 .30

Spring Friendship Art Festival — A1443

1993, Apr. 5 ***Perf. 12x12¼***
3196 A1443 10ch multicolored .75 .20

A1444

Kim Il Sung, 80th Birthday, and Publication of *With the Century* — A1445

Designs: 10ch, *With the Century*, Kim Il Sung's Memoir.
1w, Kim Il Sung writing *With the Century*.

1993, Apr. 15
3197 A1444 10ch multicolored .50 .20

Souvenir Sheet

Perf. 11½

3198 A1445 1w multicolored 3.50 .75

A1446

Pyongyang Scenes — A1447

Designs: 10ch, Kwangbok Street. 20ch, Chollima Street. 30ch, Munsu Street. 40ch, Moranbong Street. 50ch, Thongil Street.
1w, Changgwang Street.

1993, Apr. 20 ***Perf. 12x11¾***
3199-3203 A1446 Set of 5 4.50 1.25

Souvenir Sheet

Perf. 11½

3204 A1447 1w multicolored 3.50 .75

Insects A1448

Designs: 10ch, Fly (*Trichogramma dendrolimi*). 20ch, Fly (*Brachymeria obscurata*). 30ch, Cricket (*Metrioptera brachyptera*). 50ch, Cricket (*Gryllus campestris*). 70ch, Beetle (*Geocoris pallidipennis*). 90ch, Wasp (*Cyphononyx dorsalis*).

1993, May 10 ***Perf. 12x12¼***
3205-3210 A1448 Set of 6 10.00 2.25
3205a Sheet of 3, #3205, 3207, 3210 5.00 1.25
3206a Sheet of 3, #3206, 3208, 3209 5.00 1.25

Nos. 3205-3210 were issued both in separate sheets and in sheets of 3.

A1449

A1450

1993, May 19 ***Perf. 11½***
3211 A1449 10ch multicolored .50 .20

Souvenir Sheet

Perf. 13¼

3212 A1450 1.20w multicolored 4.00 .80

Release of Ri In Mo, North Korean war correspondent, from South Korean prison.

World Cup Soccer Championship, U.S.A. — A1451

World Cup and soccer players: 10ch, Tackling. 20ch, Kicking. 30ch, Kicking (diff.). 50ch, Tackling (diff.). 70ch, Blocking. 90ch, Feinting.

1993, May 25 ***Perf. 11½***

3213-3218	A1451 Set of 6	8.50	2.25
3213a	Sheet of 3, #3213, 3215, 3218	4.25	1.25
3214a	Sheet of 3, #3214, 3216, 3217	4.25	1.25

Birds — A1452

Designs: 10ch, Gray-headed green woodpecker (*Picus canus*). 20ch, King of paradise (*Cicinnurus regius*0. 30ch, Lesser bird of paradise (*Paradisea minor*). 40ch, Paradise whydah (*Steganura paradisea*). 50ch, Magnificent bird of paradise (*Diphyllodes magnificus*). 60ch, Greater bird of paradise (*Paradisea apoda*).

1993, May 29 ***Perf. 12***

3219-3224	A1452 Set of 6	7.00	1.75
3219a	Sheet of 4, 2 ea. #3219, 3224	4.00	1.10
3220a	Sheet of 4, 2 ea. #3220, 3223	4.00	1.10
3221a	Sheet of 2, #3221, #3222	4.00	1.10

Nos. 3221, 3221a, 3222, Indopex '93 International Stamp Exhibition, Surabaya, Indonesia.

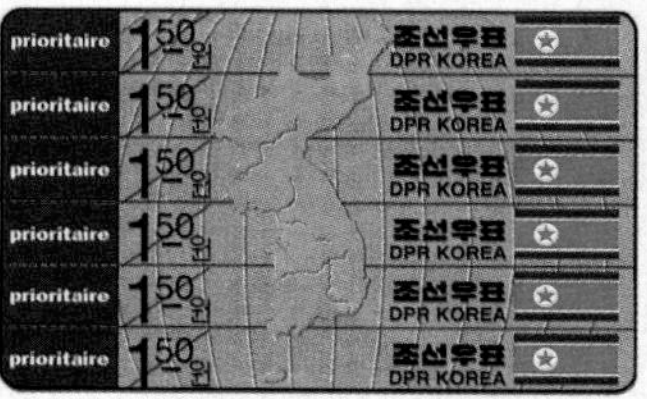

Stampcard — A1453

Map of Korean peninsula.

1993, May 29 ***Rouletted***

Self-adhesive

3225	A1453 Card of 6 stamps	20.00	20.00
a.-f.	1.50w, any single	3.00	3.00

For surcharges, see No. 3441.

Korean World Champions — A1454

Designs: 10ch, Kim Myong Nam (weight-lifting, 1990). 20ch, Kim Kwang Suk (gymnastics, 1991). 30ch, Pak Yong Sun (table tennis, 1975, 1977). 50ch, Kim Yong Ok (radio direction-finding, 1990). 70ch, Han Yun Ok (taekwondo, 1987, 1988, 1990). 90ch, Kim Yong Sik (free-style wrestling, 1986, 1989).

1993, June 15 ***Perf. 12x11¾***

3226-3231	A1454 Set of 6	9.00	2.25
3226a	Sheet of 6, 2 ea. #3226, 3228, 3231	9.00	2.50
3227a	Sheet of 6, 2 ea. #3227, 3229, 3230	9.00	2.50

Fruits and Vegetables A1455

Designs: 10ch, Cabbage and chili peppers. 20ch, Squirrel and horse chestnuts. 30ch, Peach and grapes. 40ch, Birds and persimmons. 50ch, Tomatoes, eggplant and cherries. 60ch, Onion, radishes, garlic bulbs.

1993, June 25 ***Perf. 11¾x12***

3232-3237	A1455 Set of 6	6.50	1.75
3232a	Sheet of 3, #3232, 3235, 3237	2.50	.90
3232b	As "a.," ovptd. "Polska '93"	5.00	1.25
3233c	Sheet of 3, #3233, 3234, 3236	2.50	.90

National Emblem — A1456

1993, July 5 ***Perf. 12***

3238	A1456 10ch vermilion	.60	.20

Korean War, 40th Anniv. A1457

A1458

A1459

A1460

Kim Leading Soldiers on the Front — A1461

Kim Surveying Battlefield — A1462

Kim Making 1953 Victory Speech — A1463

Designs: No. 3239, 10ch, Soldiers and civilian women; No. 3240, 10ch, Officer and enlisted man; No. 3241, 10ch, Anti-aircraft missiles on military trucks; No. 3242, 10ch, Guided missiles on carriers; No. 3243, 10ch, Self-propelled missile launchers.

No. 3244, 1w, Kim Il Jong taking salute of paraders.

No. 3245, 10ch, Victory statue (soldier with flag); No. 3246, 10ch, Machine-gunners and refugees; 40ch, Soldiers and flag.

No. 3248a, 10ch, Kim Il Sung conducting planning meeting; b, 20ch, Kim inspecting artillery unit. No. 3249a, 10ch, Kim directing battle for Height 1211; b, 20ch, Kim encouraging machine gun crew. No. 3250a, 10ch, Kim at munitions factory; b, 20ch, Kim directing units of the Second Front. No. 3251a, 10ch, Kim with tank commanders; b, 20ch, Kim directing airmen. No. 3252a, 10ch, Kim with victorious soldiers; b, 20ch, Musicians.

1993, July 27

3239-3243	A1457 Set of 5	2.50	.75

Souvenir Sheet

Perf. 13¼

3244	A1458 1w multicolored	4.00	.55

Perf. 11¾x12

3245-3247	A1459 Set of 3	2.25	.50
3247a	Sheet of 3, #3245-3247	2.50	.60

Souvenir Sheets of 2, #a-b

Perf. 11½

3248-3252	A1460 Set of 5	5.00	1.40

Souvenir Sheets

Perf. 13¼

3253	A1461 80ch multicolored	4.50	.60
3254	A1462 80ch multicolored	4.50	.60
3255	A1463 1w multicolored	6.00	.60

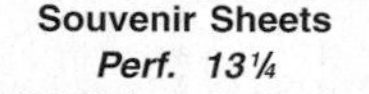

National Reunification Prize Winners — A1464

Designs: 10ch, Choe Yong Do (1923-69). 20ch, Kim Gu (1875-1949). 30ch, Hong Myong Hui (1888-1968). 40ch, Ryo Un Hyong (1886-1947). 50ch, Kim Jong Thae (1926-69). 60ch, Kim Chaek (1903-51).

1993, Aug. 1 ***Perf. 12***

3256-3261	A1464 Set of 6	6.50	1.75

A1465

Taipei '93 Int'l Philatelic Exhib. — A1466

Designs: 20ch, *Robina sp.* 30ch, *Hippeastrum cv.*

1w, Deer.

1993, Aug. 14

3262-3263	A1465 Set of 2	1.50	.45

Souvenir Sheet

3264	A1466 1w multicolored	3.50	1.50

350th Anniv. Birth of Sir Isaac Newton, Mathematician and Scientist A1467

Designs: 10ch, Portrait of Newton. 20ch, Apple tree and formula for Law of Gravitation. 30ch, Reflecting telescope invented by Newton. 50ch, Formula of Binomial Theorem. 70ch, Newton's works, statue.

1993, Sept. 1 ***Perf. 12¼x12***

3265-3269	A1467 Set of 5	7.50	1.50
3265a	Sheet of 3, #3265, 3266, 3269	3.75	3.75
3265b	Sheet of 3, #3265, 3267, 3268	3.75	3.75

A1468

Restoration of the Tomb of King Tongmyong, Founder of Koguryo — A1469

Designs: 10ch, King Tongmyong shooting arrow. 20ch, King Tongmyong. 30ch, Restoration monument. 40ch, Jongrung Temple of the Tomb of King Tongmyong. 50ch, Tomb.
80ch, Kim Il Sung visiting restored tomb.

1993, Sept. 10
3270-3274 A1468 Set of 5 4.50 1.25

Souvenir Sheet
Perf. 11½

3275 A1469 80ch multicolored 2.50 1.50

Bangkok '93 Int'l Philatelic Exhib. — A1470

1.20w, First stamps of North Korea and Thailand.

1993, Oct. 1
3276 A1470 1.20w multicolored 5.00 2.00

Orchids — A1471

Designs: 10ch, *Cyrtopodium andresoni.* 20ch, *Cattleya.* 30ch, *Cattleya intermedia* "Oculata." 40ch, *Potinaria* "Maysedo godonsia." 50ch, "Kimilsungia."

1993, Oct. 15 ***Perf. 12***
3277-3281 A1471 Set of 5 6.00 1.25
3281a Strip of 5, #3277-3281 6.00 6.00
3277b-3281b Set of 5 complete booklets, each containing 5 stamps 30.00

Nos. 3277b-3281b each contain horizontal strips of 5 of one value, taken from sheets.

No. 2949 Overprinted

1993, Nov. 16
3282 A1373 80ch vermilion 2.50 1.50

Mao Zedong, Birth Centennial.

A1472

A1473

Mao Zedong, Birth Centennial — A1474

Designs: 10ch, Mao in Yannan (1940). 20ch, Mao in Beijing (1960). 30ch, Mao voting (1953). 40ch, Mao with middle-school students (1959).
No. 3287: #3283-3286; a, Mao proclaiming People's Republic of China (1949); b, Mao and his son, Mao Anying, in Xiangshan, Beijing (1949); c, Mao and Kim Il Sung (1975).
No. 3288: As No. 3287c.

1993, Dec. 26 ***Perf. 11½***
3283-3286 A1472 Set of 4 3.25 .90

Souvenir Sheets

3287 A1473 Sheet of 7 6.00 6.00
a. 25ch multicolored .50 .30
b. 25ch multicolored .50 .30
c. 1w multicolored 2.00 .90
3288 A1474 1w multicolored 2.00 2.00

A1475

A1476

New Year, Year of the Dog — A1477

Designs: 10ch, Phungsan. 20ch, Yorkshire terriers. 30ch, Gordon setter. 40ch, Pomeranian. 50ch, Spaniel with pups.
No. 3294, Pointer.
No. 3295, 2 #3289, 1 #3294a; No. 3296, 2 #3290, 1 #3294a; No. 3297, 2 #3291, 1 #3294a; No. 3298, 2 #3292, 1 #3294a; No. 3299, 2 #3293, 1 #3294a.

1994, Jan. 1 ***Perf. 12***
3289-3293 A1475 Set of 5 5.00 1.00
3289a-3293a Set of 5 complete booklets, each containing 5 stamps 25.00

Souvenir Sheet

3294 A1476 1w multicolored 4.50 1.25

Sheets of 3
Perf. 12

3295-3299 A1477 Set of 5 30.00 30.00

Nos. 3289a-3293a each contain horizontal strips of 5 of one value, taken from sheets.

A1478

Kim Jong Il, 52nd Birthday — A1479

Designs: 10ch, Purple hyosong flower (*Prinula polyantha*). 40ch, Yellow hyosong flower (*Prinula polyantha*).
No. 3302, Kim Il Sung and Kim Jong Il, from embroidery *The Sun of Juche.*

1994, Feb. 16 ***Perf. 13¼***
3300-3301 A1478 Set of 2 1.50 .45
a. Pair, #3300-3301 1.75 1.75

Souvenir Sheet

3302 A1479 1w multicolored 3.50 1.25

Nos. 3300-3301 exist in a miniature sheet containing 4 of each value, with central label depicting Jong Il Peak and *Kimjongilia.*

Goldfish — A1480

Designs: 10ch, Red and black dragon-eye. 30ch, Red and white bubble-eye. 50ch, Red and white long-finned wenyu. 70ch, Red and white fringetail.

1994, Feb. 18 ***Perf. 12***
3303-3306 A1480 Sheet of 4 6.50 1.25

A1481

Publication of the *Program of Modeling the Whole Society on the Juche Idea,* 20th Anniv. — A1482

Kim Il Sung proclaiming the *Program,* 1974.

1994, Feb. 19
3307 A1481 20ch multicolored .50 .20

Souvenir Sheet
Perf. 11½

3308 A1482 1.20w multicolored 4.25 1.25

A1483

A1484

Publication of Kim Il Sung's *Theses on the Socialist Rural Question in Our Country,* 30th Anniv. — A1485

Designs: 10ch (#3309), Woman propagandist, sound truck. 10ch (#3310), Electrical generator, pylon. 10ch (#3311), Farm, farm equipment, piles of grain. 40ch (#3312), Lab technician with microscope. 40ch (#3313), Dancers celebrating bounty harvest.
No. 3314, Kim Il Sung in field. No. 3315, Kim Jong Il walking through field with peasants.

1994, Feb. 25 ***Perf. 12***
3309-3313 A1483 Set of 5 3.50 .90

Souvenir Sheets
Perf. 11½

3314 A1484 1w multicolored 2.50 1.25
3315 A1485 1w multicolored 2.50 1.25

Ships A1486

Designs: 20ch, Passenger ship, *Mangyongbong-92.* 30ch, Cargo ship, *Osandok.*

40ch, Processing stern trawler, *Ryongaksan*. 50ch, Stern trawler.
80ch, Passenger ship, *Maekjon No. 1*.

1994, Mar. 25 ***Perf. 12***

3316-3319 A1486 Set of 4 4.50 1.25
3320 Sheet of 6, #3316-3319 + 2 #3320a 10.00 2.50
a. A1486 80ch multicolored 2.50 .75

DPRK Flag — A1487

1994, Mar. 30 ***Perf. 13¼***

3321 A1487 10ch car & dp blue .50 .20

A1488

Kim Il Sung, 82nd Birthday — A1489

Designs: 10ch, Magnolia and Kim's home. 40ch, *Kimilsungia* and Kim's home.

No. 3324, Five 40ch stamps, together forming design of Lake Chon (crater lake of Mt. Paektu), with *Song of General Kim Il Sung* music within design, lyrics in sheet margin.

1994, Apr. 15 ***Perf. 12***

3322-3323 A1488 Set of 2 1.50 .50
3323a 10ch Sheet of 8 7.00 2.25
3323b 40ch Sheet of 8 7.00 2.25

Souvenir Sheet

3324 A1489 2w Sheet of 5 7.00 7.00
a.-e. 40ch any single 1.25 1.25

Alpine Plants of the Mt. Paektu Area — A1490

Designs: 10ch, *Chrysoplenium sphaerospermum*. 20ch, *Campanula cephalotes*. 40ch, *Trollius macropetafus*. 50ch, *Sedum kamtschaticum*.
1w, *Dianthus repens*.

1994, Apr. 25 ***Perf. 13¼***

3325-3329 A1490 Set of 5 4.50 1.25
3325a Sheet of 3, #3325, 3327, #3330 4.25 1.75
3326a Sheet of 3, #3326, 3328, 3329 4.25 1.75

Souvenir Sheet

3330 A1490 1w multicolored 3.50 1.50

A single stamp like that in No. 3330 is included in No. 3325a.

A1491

Int'l Olympic Committee Centenary — A1492

Designs: 10ch, Olympic rings, DPRK flag. 20ch, Pierre de Coubertin, founder. 30ch, Olympic flag, flame. 50ch, IOC Centenary Congress emblem.

No. 3335, Runner with Olympic Torch. No. 3336, Juan Antonio Samaranch, IOC President and new IOC headquarters.

1994, May 2 ***Perf. 12***

3331-3334 A1491 Set of 4 4.00 1.00

Souvenir Sheets

Perf. 13¼

3335-3336 A1492 Set of 2 6.50 2.00

International Federation of Red Cross and Red Crescent Societies, 75th Anniv. — A1493

Designs: 10ch, Train, pedestrians crossing on overpass ("Prevention of traffic accident"). 20ch, Medical personnel in Red Cross boat ("Relief on the Sea"). 30ch, Man and girl planting tree ("Protection of the environment"). 40ch, Dam, sailboat on lake ("Protection of drought damage").

1994, May 5

3337-3340 A1493 Strip of 4 3.50 2.50

No. 3225 Surcharged

1994, May 29 **Self-adhesive** ***Imperf***

3341 A1452 1.60w on 1.50w Card of 6 28.00 28.00
a.-f. 1.60w on 1.50w, any single 7.00 7.00

A1494

Seals — A1495

Designs: 10ch, Northern fur seal (*Callorhinus ursinus*). 40ch, Southern elephant seal (*Mirounga leonina*). 60ch, Southern sea lion (*Otaria byronia*).

No. 3345: 20ch, California sea lion (*Zalophus californianus*). 30ch, Ringed seal (*Phoca hispida*). 50ch, Walrus (*Odobenus rosmarus*).

No. 3346, Harp seal (*Pagophilus groenlandicus*).

1994, June 10 ***Perf. 11½***

3342-3344 A1494 Set of 3 4.00 .90
3345 A1494 Sheet of 3 4.50 1.00
a. 20ch multicolored .75 .20
b. 30ch multicolored 1.25 .25
c. 50ch multicolored 2.25 .50

Souvenir Sheet

3346 A1495 1w multicolored 3.50 1.00

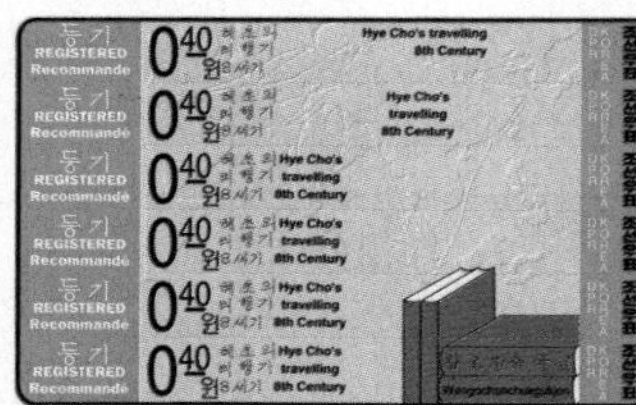

Stampcard — A1496

Map of Asia, books.

1994, June 17 ***Rouletted***

Self-adhesive

3347 A1496 Card of 6 stamps 10.00 10.00
a.-f. 40ch, any single 1.65 1.65

Hye Cho's 8th century travels in Central Asia and India.

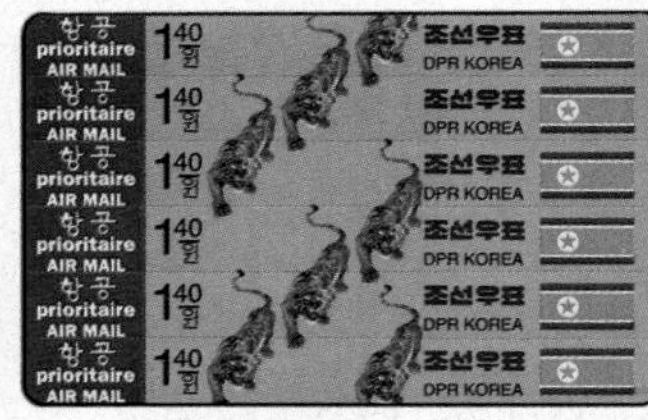

Stampcard — A1497

Korean Tigers.

1994, June 18 ***Rouletted***

Self-adhesive

3348 A1497 Card of 6 stamps 30.00 30.00
a.-f. 1.40w, any single 5.00 5.00

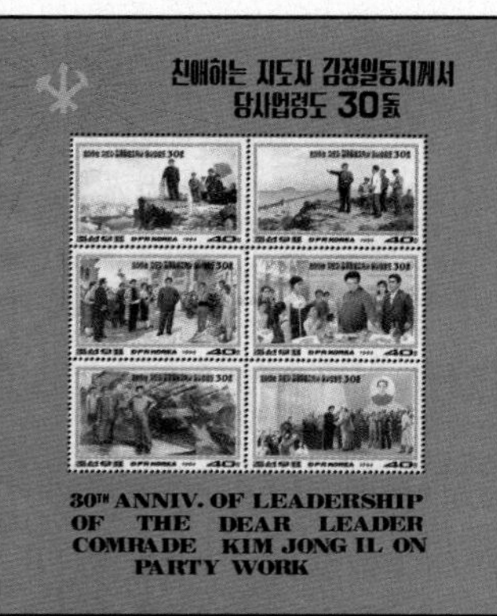

A1498

Kim Il Sung's Leadership of the Korean Workers' Party, 30th Anniv. — A1499

Designs (all 40ch): #3349, Kim and supporters on cliff ledge, overlooking lake. #3350, Kim on mountain top, pointing across lake to Mt. Paektu. #3351, Kim on film set. #3352, Kim visiting restaurant. #3353, Kim reviewing tank corps. #3354, Kim at conference, shaking hands onstage as audience applauds.

1994, June 19 ***Perf. 12***

3349-3354 A1498 Sheetlet of 6 8.00 2.50
3350a Booklet pane of 6, 3 ea. #3349-3350 8.00 —
Complete booklet, #3350a 8.50
3353a Booklet pane of 6, 3 ea. #3351, 3353 8.00 —
Complete booklet, #3353a 8.50
3354a Booklet pane of 6, 3 ea. #3352, 3354 8.00 —
Complete booklet, #3354a 8.50

Souvenir Sheet

Perf. 11½

3355 A1499 1w multicolored 3.00 1.00

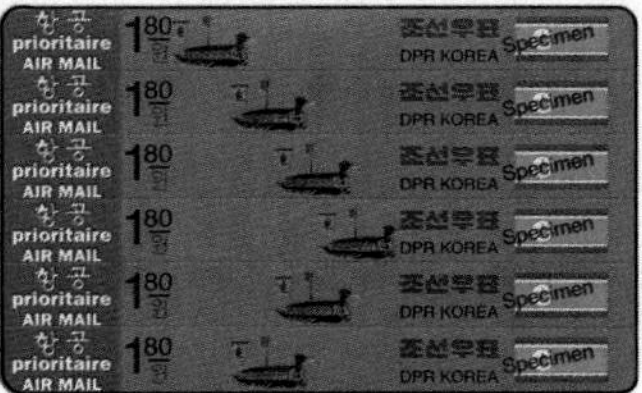

Stampcard — A1500

Turtle ship.

1994, June 20 ***Rouletted***

Self-adhesive

3356 A1500 Card of 6 stamps 33.00 33.00
a.-f. 1.80w, any single 5.50 5.50

A1501

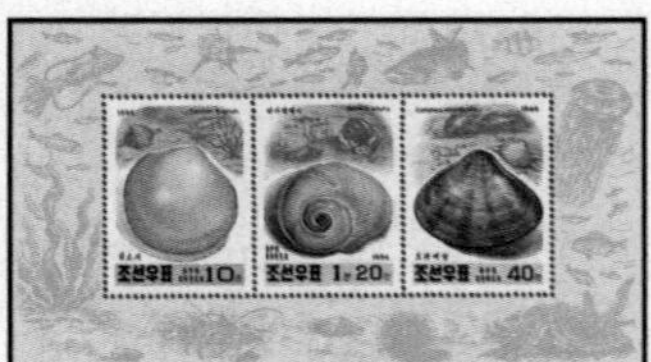

A1502

Mollusks — A1503

Designs: 30ch, Banded bonnet (*Phalium strigatum*). 40ch, Equilateral venus (*Gomphina veneriformis*).

No. 3359: a, 10ch, Cockle (*Cardium muticum*). b, 1.20w, Bladder moon (*Neverita didyma*). c, as No. 3358.

No. 3360: a, 20ch, Whelk (*Buccinum bayani*). b, 30ch, as No. 3357. The 1.20w value, identical to No. 3359b, is included in this sheet.

No. 3361, same as No. 3359b.

1994, June 25 ***Perf. 12***

3357-3358 A1501 Set of 2 2.50 .60

Sheets of 3

Perf. 13¼

3359-3360 A1502 Set of 2 14.00 10.00

Souvenir Sheet

3361 A1503 1.20w multicolored 5.00 1.40

Circus Acrobats — A1504

Designs: a, 10ch, Flying trapeze. b, 20ch, Rope dance. c, 30ch, Seesaw. d, 40ch, Unicycle show.

1994, July 7 ***Perf. 11½***

3362 A1504 Sheet of 4, #a.-d. 4.00 1.25

A1505

Centenary of Birth of Kim Hyong Jik (1894-1926), Father of Kim Il Sung — A1506

1994, July 10 ***Perf. 13¼***

3363 A1505 10ch multicolored .50 .20

Souvenir Sheet

Perf. 11¾x11½

3364 A1506 1w multicolored 3.50 1.25

Jon Pong Pun & Battle Scene — A1507

1994, July 15 ***Perf. 12***

3365 A1507 10ch multicolored .60 .20

Centenary of Kabo Peasant War.

Inoue Shuhachi — A1508

1994, July 30 ***Perf. 13¼***

3366 A1508 1.20w multicolored 4.00 1.25

Award of the First International Kim Il Sung Prize to Inoue Shuhachi, Director General of the International Institute of the Juche Idea (Japan).

Workers Marching A1509

1994, Aug. 1 ***Perf. 11½***

3367 A1509 10ch multicolored .50 .20

Workers' Party Economic Strategy.

Fossils A1510

Designs: 40ch (#3368), Onsong fish. 40ch (#3369), Metasequoia. 40ch (#3370), Mammoth teeth. 80ch, Archaeopteryx.

No. 3372 contains 2 #3368 and 2 #3371. No. 3373 contains 2 #3369 and 2 #3371. No. 3374 contains 2 #3370 and 2 #3371.

1994, Aug. 10 ***Perf. 12***

3368-3371 A1510 Set of 4 13.00 1.75
Complete booklet, 7 #3368 16.00
Complete booklet, 7 #3369 16.00
Complete booklet, 7 #3370 16.00
Complete booklet, 7 #3371 32.00

Souvenir Sheets

3372-3374 A1510 Set of 3 sheets 26.00 20.00

Medicinal Plants — A1511

Designs: 20ch, *Acorus calamus*. 30ch, *Arctium lappa*.

No. 3377 (133x86mm): a, 80ch, *Lilium lancifolium*. b, 80ch, *Codonopsis lanceolata*.

No. 3378 (56x83mm): 1w, Ginseng (*Panax schinseng*), vert.

1994, Aug. 25

3375-3376 A1511 Set of 2 1.75 .50
Complete booklet, 10 #3375 7.00
Complete booklet, 10 #3376 10.50

Souvenir Sheets

Perf. 13¼

3377-3378 A1511 Set of 2 sheets 8.00 2.00

Calisthenics — A1512

Gymnastic routines: a, 10ch, Ribbon twirling. b, 20ch, Ball. c, 30ch, Hoop. d, 40ch, Ribbon twirling (diff.). e, 50ch, Clubs.

1994, Sept. 7 ***Perf. 12***

3379 A1512 Strip of 5 + label 5.50 1.50

No. 3379 was printed in sheets of 18, containing three #3379 in horizontal rows, with a different label in each row.

A1513

A1514

Zhou Enlai (1898-1976), Birth Centenary — A1515

Portraits of Zhou Enlai: 10ch, As student revolutionary (1919). 20ch, Arrival in Northern Shansi after Long March (1936). 30ch, At Conference of Asian and African Countries, Bandung, Indonesia (1955). 40ch, Speaking with children.

No. 3384: 80ch, Zhou Enlai and Kim Il Sung (1970).

No. 3385: 10ch, as #3380. a, 20ch, Zhou leading Nanchang Uprising (1927). 40ch, as #3383. b, 80ch, as #3384.

No. 3386: 20ch, as #3381. a, 20ch, Zhou and Mao Tzedong at airport, horiz. 30ch, as #3383. 80ch, as #3385b.

1994, Oct. 1 ***Perf. 11½***

3380-3383 A1513 Set of 4, with labels 3.25 1.00

Souvenir Sheets

Perf. 13¼

3384 A1514 80ch multicolored 2.75 1.00

Perf 11½ (Vert. stamps), 11¾x12¼ (Horiz. stamps)

3385-3386 A1515 Set of 2 sheets 9.50 4.00

Nos. 3380-3383 were issued in sheets of 30 (6x5), with a label beneath each stamp.

World Environment Day — A1516

Each sheetlet contains two 50ch stamps with designs reflecting environmental issues. Themes: No. 3387, Prevention of air pollution. No. 3388, Preventation of water pollution. No. 3389, Protection of animal resources. No. 3390, Protection of forest resources.

1994, Oct. 5 ***Perf. 12***

3387-3390 A1516 Set of 4 sheets 12.50 12.50

A1517

A1518

Kim Il Sung (1912-94) — A1519

Photos of Kim Il Sung (all 40ch).

No. 3391: a, As young man (1927). b, With Kim Jong Suk, his first wife and mother of Kim Jong Il. c, As captain in Soviet army (1944).

No. 3392: Speaking at lectern upon return to Pyongyang (1945). b, Sitting at desk in office of People's Committee of North Korea. c, Speaking at microphone.

1994, Oct. 8

3391 A1517 Sheet of 3, #a.-c. 4.00 2.00
3392 A1518 Sheet of 3, #a.-c. 4.00 2.00

Souvenir Sheet

Perf. 12¼x11¾

3393 A1519 1w multicolored 3.75 1.25

Compare with Nos. 3401-3403.

A1520

World Cup '94, 15th World Soccer Championship — A1521

Soccer Players Dribbling: 10ch, Player No. 4. 20ch, Player No. 5. 30ch, Player No. 6. 40ch, Player No. 7. 1w, Player No. 8. 1.50w, Player No. 9.

1994, Oct. 13 ***Perf. 13½***

3394-3399 A1520 Set of 6 12.00 6.00
3399a Sheet of 6, #3394-3399 18.00 10.00

Souvenir Sheet

3400 A1521 2.50w multicolored 7.50 4.00

Nos. 3394-3400 were also issued imperf. Value: set, $24; souvenir sheet, $15.

Nos. 3394-3399 exist in sheetlets on one, perf and imperf. Value: perf, $24; imperf, $47.50.

A1522

Kim Il Sung (1912-94) — A1523

Photos of Kim Il Sung (all 40ch).

No. 3401: a, Making radio broadcast (1950). b, With soldiers (1951). c, Clapping hands, crowd of soldiers in background (1953).

No. 3402: a, Talking with workers at Chongjin Steel Plant (1959). b, Standing in field, Onchon Plain. c, Talking on telephone.

No. 3403, Kim Il Sung and Kim Jong Il.

1994, Oct. 15 ***Perf. 12***

3401-3402 A1522 Set of 2 sheets 8.00 4.00

Perf. 12¼x11¾

3403 A1523 1w multicolored 3.50 1.50

Compare with Nos. 3391-3393.

A1524

North Korean-Chinese Friendship — A1525

1w, Kim Il Sung with Mao Zedong.

1994, Oct. 25 ***Perf. 11½***

3404 A1524 40ch multicolored 1.50 .50

Souvenir Sheet

Perf. 13¼

3405 A1525 1.20w multicolored 4.25 2.00

Composers A1526

Designs: #3406, Ri Myon Sang (1908-89), score from *It Snows.* #3407, Pak Han Gyu (1919-92), score from *Nobody Knows.* #3408, Ludwig van Beethoven (1770-1827), score of *Piano Sonata No. 14.* #3409, Wolfgang Mozart (1756-91), score of *Symphony No. 39.*

1994, Nov. 25 ***Perf. 11½***

3406-3409 A1526 50ch Set of 4 6.50 2.25

National Emblem — A1527

1994, Dec. 10 ***Perf. 12***

3410 A1527 1w dp bl green 4.00 1.00
3411 A1527 3w deep brown 8.00 2.50

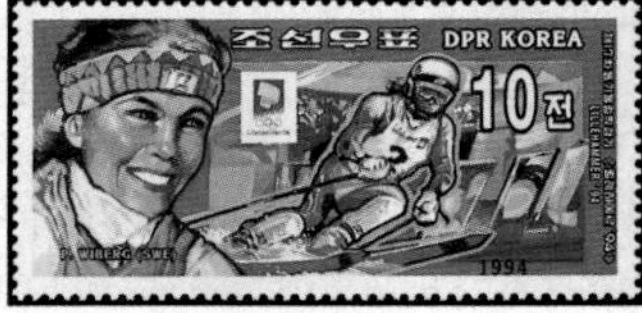

A1528

A1529

Gold Medal Winners, Winter Olympic Games, Lillehammer — A1530

Designs: 10ch, Pernilla Wiberg (Sweden), Alpine combined skiing. 20ch, Deborah Compagnoni (Italy), Slalom. 30ch, Oksana Baiul (Ukraine), Figure skating. 40ch, Dan Jansen (USA), Speed skating. 1w (#3416), Yubow Jegorowa (Russia), Cross-country skiing. 1w (#3417), Bonnie Blair (USA), Speed skating.

#3418, Bjorn Däehlie and Norwegian skiing team, Alpine combined skiing. #3419, Jekaterina Gordejewa and Serge Grinkow (Russia), Pairs figure skating. #3420, Vreni Schneider (Switzerland), Alpine combined skiing. #3421, Georg Hackl (Germany), Luge. #3422, Jens Weissflog (Germany), Ski jumping. #3423, Masashi Abe, Takanori Kono, Kenji Ogiwara (Japan), Cross-country skiing.

#3424, Tommy Moe (USA), Downhill skiing.

1994, Dec. 20 ***Perf. 13¼***

3412-3417 A1528 Set of 6 11.00 3.00
3417a Sheet of 6, #3412-3417 12.00 5.00

Souvenir Sheets

3418-3423 A1529 1w Set of 6 18.00 6.00
3424 A1530 2.50w multicolored 8.00 1.50

New Year — Year of the Pig A1531

Designs: 20ch, Pigs relaxing. 40ch, Pigs going to work.

Each 1w: No. 3427, Pigs carrying pumpkin. No. 3428, Piglets bowing to adult pig.

1995, Jan. 1 ***Perf. 11½***

3425-3426 A1531 Set of 2 1.10 .65
3426a Sheet of 4, 2 ea #3425-3426 3.50 3.50

Souvenir Sheets

3427-3428 A1531 Set of 2 6.00 5.00

No. 3426a inscribed in margins for Singapore '95 Intl. Stamp Exhibition. Issued, 9/1.

World Tourism Org., 20th Anniv. — A1532

Designs, each 30ch: a, Tower of the Juche Idea, Pyongyang. b, Pison Falls on Mt. Myohyang. c, Myogilsang (relief carving of Buddha), Mt. Kumgang.

1995, Jan. 2 ***Perf. 12¼***

3429 A1532 Sheet of 3, #a.-c. 3.50 .90

Mangyondae, Badasgou, Emblem — A1533

1995, Jan. 22 ***Perf. 11½***

3430 A1533 40ch multicolored 1.50 .90

70th anniversary of 250-Mile Journey for the Restoration of the Fatherland.

A1534

A1535

A1536

Kim Jong Il, 53rd Birthday — A1537

Designs: 10ch, Jong Il Peak (Mt. Paekdu) and 50th Birthday Ode Monument.

No. 3432 (horiz.): a, 20ch Kim Il Sung and Kim Jong Il; b, 80ch Kim Jong Il inspecting the West Sea Barrage. No. 3433 (vert.): a, 40ch Kim Jong Il in business suit; b, Kim Jong Il in uniform in Taesongsan Martyrs' Cemetary. No. 3434: 1w, Kim Jong Il inspecting the Ryongsong Machine Complex.

1995, Feb. 16 ***Perf. 12¼***

3431 A1534 10ch multicolored .20 .20

Souvenir Sheets

3432 A1535 Sheet of 2, #a.-b. 2.00 1.50
3433 A1536 Sheet of 2, #a.-b. 1.75 1.25
3434 A1537 1w multicolored 2.00 2.00

Mausoleum of King Tangun —A1537a

King Tangun and Mausoleum —A1537b

Designs: 10ch, Monument. 30ch, Straight bronze dagger tower. 50ch, Monument inscribed with King Tangun's exploits. 70ch, Gate of mausoleum.

50ch, King Tangun and Mausoleum.

1995, Feb. 25 ***Perf. 12¼***

3434A-3434D A1537a Set of 4 3.00 3.00

Souvenir Sheet

Perf. 11½

3434E A1537b 1.40w multi 3.00 3.00

Lighthouses A1538

Designs: 20ch, Tamaedo Lighthouse. 1.20w, Phido Lighthouse, West Sea Barrage.

1995, Mar. 10 ***Perf. 13½***

3435-3436 A1538 Set of 2 5.00 1.75

Mushrooms A1539

Designs: 20ch, *Russula virescens*. 30ch, *Russula atropurpurea*.

1w, Caesar's Mushroom (*Amanita caesarea*.

1995, Mar. 25

3437-3438 A1539 Set of 2 2.00 .60
3437a Booklet pane of 10 #3437 3.50 —
Complete booklet, #3437a 4.00
3438a Booklet pane of 10 #3438 17.00 —
Complete booklet, #3438a 17.50

Souvenir Sheet

3439 A1539 1w multicolored 4.50 2.50

Tree Planting Day — A1540

1995, Apr. 6 ***Perf. 11½***

3440 A1540 10ch multicolored .60 .20
a. Sheet of 6 3.50 3.50

Finlandia '95

No. 3225 Surcharged with New Values

1995, Apr. 8 ***Rouletted***

3441 Card of 6 stamps 8.00 8.00
a.-f. 30ch on 1.50w, any single 1.30 1.30

A1541

A1542

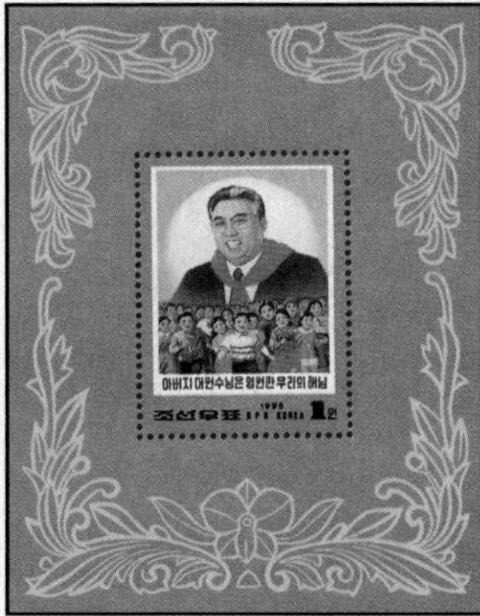

Kim Il Sung, 82nd Birthday — A1543

Designs: 10ch, Kim's birthplace, Mangyongdae. 40ch, Tower of the Juche Idea, and *Kimilsungia*.

1w, Kim and children.

1995, Apr. 15 ***Perf. 11½***

3442 A1541 10ch multicolored .25 .20
a. Sheet of 6 1.50 1.50
3443 A1542 40ch multicolored 1.25 1.00
a. Sheet of 6 7.50 7.50

Souvenir Sheet

Perf. 13½

3444 A1543 1w multicolored 3.50 3.50

A1544

Kim Il Sung's Visit to China, 20th Anniv. — A1545

Designs: 10ch, Deng Xiaoping waving. 20ch, Deng sitting in armchair, vert.

50ch, Kim and Deng sitting in armchairs.

1995, Apr. 17 ***Perf. 13½***

3445-3446 A1544 Set of 2 1.25 1.25

Souvenir Sheet

Perf. 11½

3447 A1545 50ch multicolored 2.00 2.00

A1546

A1547

Asian-African Conf., Bandung, 40th Anniv. — A1548

Designs: 10ch, Site of Bendung Conference. 50ch, Kim Il Sung receiving honorary doctorate from Indonesia University.

1w, Kim Il Sung and Kim Jong Il at Conference 40th Anniversary ceremony.

1995, Apr. 18 ***Perf. 11½***

3448 A1546 10ch multicolored .25 .20
3449 A1547 50ch multicolored 1.75 .70

Souvenir Sheet

3450 A1548 1w multicolored 3.50 3.50

A1549

Int'l Sports and Cultural Festival for Peace, Pyongyang — A1550

Designs: 20ch, Emblem. 40ch (#3452), Dancer. 40ch (#3453), Inoki Kanji, leader of Sports Peace Party of Japan.

1w, Nikidozan, wrestling champion.

1995, Apr. 28

3451-3453 A1549 Set of 3 3.00 2.00
3451a Sheet of 3, 1 #3451 + 2 #3452 3.00 2.00

3453a	Sheet of 3, 2 #3453 + 1 as #3454	7.00	4.00

Souvenir Sheet

3454	A1550 1w multicolored	3.50	3.50

Amethyst — A1551

1995, May 2

3455	A1551 20ch multicolored	1.00	.40
a.	Sheet of 6	7.50	7.50
b.	Booklet pane of 10	10.00	—
	Complete booklet, #3455b	11.00	

Finlandia '95. No. 3455a marginal selvage contains a mountain valley scene and is inscribed "Finlandia 95." No. 3455b has selvage around the block of 10 stamps.

White Animals — A1552

Each 40ch: No. 3456, Tree sparrow (*Passer montanus*). No. 3457, Sea slug (*Stichopus japonicus*).

1995, May 12 ***Perf. 13½***

3456-3457	A1552 Set of 2	2.50	1.50
3457a	Sheet of 6, 3 #3456 + 3 #3457	9.00	

Fossils — A1553

Designs: a, 50ch, Ostrea. b, 1w, Cladophiebis (fern).

1995, May 15 ***Perf. 12***

3458	A1553 Pair, #a.-b.	4.00	1.75

Traditional Games A1554

Designs: 30ch, Chess. 60ch, Taekwondo. 70ch, Yut.

1995, May 20 ***Perf. 11½***

3459-3461	A1554 Set of 3	5.25	2.00
3459a	Sheet of 2 #3459 + label	1.75	1.75
3460a	Sheet of 2 #3460 + label	4.00	4.00
3461a	Sheet of 2 #3461 + label	6.00	6.00
3461b	Booklet pane of 6, 2 ea. #3459-3461	10.50	—
	Complete booklet, #3461b	11.00	

General Assoc. of Koreans in Japan, 40th Anniv. — A1555

1995, May 25

3462	A1555 1w multicolored	3.50	.90

Atlanta '96 — A1556

Designs, each 50ch: No. 3463, Weight lifter. No. 3464, Boxing.
1w, Marksman shooting clay pigeon.

1995, June 2

3463-3464	A1556 Set of 2	3.25	1.25
3464a	Sheet of 2 #3463 + 2 #3464	7.50	7.50

Souvenir Sheet

3465	A1556 1w multicolored	5.00	5.00

Fungi — A1557

Designs: 40ch, *Russula citrina*. 60ch, *Craterellus cornucopioides*. 80ch, *Coprinus comatus*.

1995, July 1 ***Perf. 13¼***

3466-3468	A1557 Set of 3	6.50	2.00
3466a	Booklet pane of 10 #3466	14.00	—
	Complete booklet, #3466a	14.50	
3467a	Booklet pane of 10 #3467	21.00	—
	Complete booklet, #3467a	22.00	
3468a	Booklet pane of 10 #3468	29.00	—
	Complete booklet, #3468a	30.00	

A1558

A1559

A1560

Kim Il Sung, 1st Death Anniv. — A1561

No. 3469, 1w, Kim addressing conference for development of agriculture in African countries, 1981.
No. 3470: a, 10ch, Kim greeting Robert Mugabe, President of Zimbabwe. b, 70ch, Kim with King Norodom Sihanouk of Cambodia.
No. 3471: a, 20ch, Kim receiving honorary doctorate, Algeria University, 1975. b, 50ch, Kim with Fidel Castro, 1986.
No. 3472: a, 30ch, Kim talking with Ho Chi Minh, 1958. b, 40ch, Kim greeting Che Guevara, 1960.

1995, July 8

3469	A1558 1w multicolored	2.75	2.75
3470	A1559 Sheet of 2, #a.-b.	2.25	2.25
3471	A1560 Sheet of 2, #a.-b.	2.50	2.50
3472	A1561 Sheet of 2, #a.-b.	2.00	2.00

Liberation, 50th Anniv. — A1562

Designs: 10ch, Korean army officer. 30ch, Map of Korea, family. 60ch, Hero of the DPRK medal.
No. 3476, a, 20ch revolutionary soldier, #3414, 2 each.
No. 3477, a, 40ch demonstrators, #3474, 2 each.

1995, Aug. 15 ***Perf. 11½***

3473-3475	A1562 Set of 3	2.75	1.25
3475a	Booklet pane of 5, #3473-3475, 3476a, 3477a	4.50	—
	Complete booklet, #3475a	5.00	

Souvenir Sheets

3476	Sheetl of 4	2.50	2.50
a.	A1562 20ch multicolored	.50	.20
3477	Sheet of 4	4.50	4.50
a.	A1562 40ch multicolored	1.00	.45

1st Military World Games — A1564

1995, Sept. 4

3479	A1564 40ch multicolored	1.00	.45

A1565

A1566

Korea-China Friendship — A1567

Designs: No. 3480, 80ch, Kim Il Sung and Mao Zedong. No. 3481, 80ch, Kim and Zhou Enlai.
No. 3482: a, 50ch, Kim and Zhou Enlai. b, 50ch, Kim receiving gift from Deng Ying-Chao, Premier of the State Council of the People's Republic of China.

1995, Oct. 1 ***Perf. 12¼***

3480	A1565 80ch multicolored	1.50	1.50
3481	A1566 80ch multicolored	1.50	1.50
3482	A1567 Sheet of 2, #a.-b.	2.25	2.25

A1568

Korean Workers' Party, 50th Anniv. — A1569

Designs: 10ch, Korean Workers' Party Emblem and Banner. 20ch, Statue of three workers holding party symbols. 40ch, Monument to founding of Party.
No. 3486, Kim Il Sung.

1995, Oct. 10 ***Perf. 11½***

3483-3485	A1568 Set of 3	1.60	.75

Souvenir Sheet

Perf. 13½

3486	A1569 1w multicolored	2.75	2.75

Kim Il Sung's Return to Korea, 50th Anniv. A1570

Design: 50ch, Arch of Triumph, Pyongyang.

1995, Oct. 14 *Perf. 11½*

3487 A1570 10ch multicolored .60 .20

Great Tunny — A1571

Nos. 3488-3512 are printed in chocolate and black.

1995 *Perf. 13¼*

Fish

3488	40ch	Great tunny	1.25	.35
3489	50ch	Pennant coralfish	1.50	.40
3490	50ch	Needlefish	1.50	.40
3491	60ch	Bullrout	1.75	.45
3492	5w	Imperial butterfly fish	15.00	3.50
a.		Horiz. strip of 5, #3488-3492	22.50	5.00

Machines

3493	10ch	40-ton truck *Kum-susan*	.35	.20
3494	20ch	Large bulldozer	.75	.20
3495	30ch	Hydraulic excavator	1.00	.25
3496	40ch	Wheel loader, vert.	1.60	.30
3497	10w	Tractor *Chollima-80*, vert.	27.50	7.50
a.		Horiz. strip of 5, #3493-3497	32.50	10.00

Animals

3498	30ch	Giraffe, vert.	.85	.20
3499	40ch	Ostrich, vert.	1.10	.35
3500	60ch	Bluebuck, vert.	1.60	.50
3501	70ch	Bactrian camel	2.00	.55
3502	3w	Indian rhinoceros	8.00	2.25
a.		Horiz. strip of 5, #3498-3502	16.00	4.00

Sculptures of Children

3503	30ch	Boy and pigeon, vert.	.85	.20
3504	40ch	Boy and goose, vert.	1.10	.35
3505	60ch	Girl and geese vert.	1.60	.50
3506	70ch	Boy and girl comparing heights, vert.	2.00	.50
3507	2w	Boy and girl with soccer ball, vert.	5.75	1.60
a.		Vert. strip of 5, #3503-3507	13.00	4.00

Buildings

3508	60ch	Pyongyang Circus	1.75	.50
3509	70ch	Country apartment bldg.	2.00	.55
3510	80ch	Pyongyang Hotel	2.25	.65
3511	90ch	Urban apt. towers	2.50	.75
3512	1w	Sosan Hotel	2.75	.85
a.		Horiz. strip of 5, #3508-3512	13.00	4.00

Issued: Nos. 3488-3492, 10/20; Nos. 3493-3497, 11/2; Nos. 3498-3502, 11/20; Nos. 3503-3507, 12/5; Nos. 3508-3512, 12/15.

Nos. 3488-3492, 3493-3497, 3498-3502, 3503-3507, and 3508-3512 were printed in vertical (#3503-3507) or horizontal se-tenant strips within their sheets.

No. 3512B

No. 3512D

1995, Oct. 20 *Rouletted x Imperf*

Stampcards

Self-Adhesive

3512B	black, *gold*, card of 8	6.00	6.00
a.	20ch single stamp	.75	.75
3512D	card of 2	50.00	50.00
e.	20ch red, *gold*	—	—
f.	17.80w On 20ch, red, *gold*	—	—

50th anniversary of the first North Korean stamps.

Kim Hyong Gwon, Kim Il Sung's Uncle, 90th Birth Anniv. — A1572

1995, Nov. 4 *Perf. 12½x12*

3513 A1572 1w multicolored 2.75 1.50

New Year — A1573

Rodents: 20ch (#3514), Guinea pig. 20ch (#3515), Squirrel. 30ch, White mouse.

1996, Jan. 1 *Perf. 11½*

3514-3516 A1573 Strip of 3 3.00 .75

Nos. 3514-3516 were issued together in sheetlets of eight stamps, two each #3514 and #3515 and four #3516, plus one center label picturing an idyllic landscape, inscribed "1996."

League of Socialist Working Youth, 50th Anniv. — A1574

1996, Jan. 17

3517 A1574 10ch multicolored .50 .20

Reconstruction of Tomb of King Wanggon of Koryo — A1575

Designs: 30ch, Restoration monument, horiz. 40ch, Entrance gate to royal cemetery. 50ch, King Wanggon's tomb, horiz.

1996, Jan. 30

3518-3520 A1575 Set of 3 3.50 1.00

Teng Li-Chuang (Chinese Singer) — A1576

1996, Feb. 1 *Perf. 13¼*

3521 A1576 40ch multicolored 1.50 .50

3rd Asian Winter Games, Harbin, China — A1577

Designs, each 30ch: a, Kim Song Sun, Korean speed skater. b, Ye Qiaobo, Chinese sprint skater.

1996, Feb 4 *Perf. 11½*

3522 A1577 Sheet of 2, #a.-b. 3.50 .50

See No. 3556.

A1578

Kim Jong Il, 54th Birthday — A1579

10ch, Jong Il Peak and *Kimjongilia.*
80ch, Kim Jong Il and soldiers.

1996, Feb. 16

3523 A1578 10ch multicolored .50 .20

Souvenir Sheet

Perf. 13¼

3524 A1579 80ch multicolored 2.75 .75

5th Paektusan Prize International Figure Skating Championship. A1580

Various pairs figure skaters: 10ch, 20ch, 30ch.
50ch, Women's individual skating.

1996, Feb. 17 *Perf. 11½*

3525-3527	A1580 Set of 3	2.00	.60
3527a	Booklet pane of 4, #3525-3527, 3528a	5.50	—
	Complete booklet, #3527a	6.00	

Souvenir Sheet

3528	Sheet of 4	3.50	1.00
a.	A1580 50ch multi	3.25	

Folk Tales — A1581

Screen painting by Ryu Suk: 8 stamps in continuous design, within 206mmx84mm skeetlet.

1996, Mar. 2

3529	Sheet of 8	5.00	2.25
a.-h.	A1581 any single	.60	.20

Agrarian Reform Law, 50th Anniv. A1582

1996, Mar. 5

3530 A1582 10ch multicolored .50 .20

No. 3530 was issued in sheetlets of six, containing 5 #3530 and a label depicting a music score, *Song of Plowing.*

First North Korean Stamps, 50th Anniv. — A1583

1996, Mar. 12

3531 A1583 1w multicolored 3.25 .85

Yangzhou, China — A1584

Taihou Lake, China — A1585

1996, Mar. 20

3532	A1584	50ch multicolored	1.75	.50
3533	A1585	50ch multicolored	1.75	.50

Chinese Imperial Post, Centennial.

A1586

Kim Il Sung, 83rd Birthday — A1587

Designs: 10ch, Birthplace, Mangyondae.
1w, Portrait of Kim Il Sung.

1996, Apr. 15
3534 A1586 10ch multicolored .50 .20

Souvenir Sheet

3535 A1587 1w multicolored 3.25 .85

China '96 Int'l Stamp Exhib., Beijing — A1588

Designs: No. 3536, Seacoast gateway. No. 3537, Haiyin Pool.
60ch. Pantuo Stone.

1996, Apr. 22 ***Perf. 13½***
3536-3537 A1588 10ch Set of 2 .50 .25

Souvenir Sheet
Perf. 11½

3538 A1588 60ch multicolored 1.60 .60

Folk Games A1589

Designs: 20ch, Kicking stone handmill. 40ch, Shuttlecock. 50ch, Sledding.

1996, May 2
3539-3541 A1589 Set of 3 3.50 1.00
3539a-3541a Set of 3 sheets of 2 + label 7.00 7.00

Assoc. for the Restoration of the Fatherland, 60th Anniv. — A1590

1996, May 5
3542 A1590 10ch multicolored .50 .20
a. Sheet of 5 #3542 + label 2.50 1.50

Ri Po Ik — A1591

1996, May 31 ***Perf. 13½***
3543 A1591 1w multicolored 3.00 .80

Ri Po Ik, Kim Il Sung's grandmother, 125th birth anniv.

Polar Animals — A1592

Designs, each 50ch: #3544a, Arctic fox. #3544b, Polar bear. #3545a, Emperor penguins. #3546b, Leopard seals.

1996, June 2 ***Perf. 11½***
3544-3545 A1592 Set of 2 sheets 6.50 4.00

A1593

Korea Children's Union, 50th Anniv. — A1594

Designs: 10ch, Boy saluting.
1w, Painting of Kim Il Sung with Children's Union members, *There's Nothing to Envy in the World.*

1996, June 6
3546 A1593 10ch multicolored .50 .20

Souvenir Sheet
Perf. 11½x12

3547 A1594 1w multicolored 3.00 .85

Locomotives A1595

Designs, all 50ch: No. 3548, Steam locomotive, facing left. No. 3549, Electric locomotive, facing right. No. 3550, Steam locomotive, facing right. No. 3551, Electric locomotive, facing left.

1996, June 6 ***Perf. 11½***
3548-3551 A1595 Set of 4 3.50 1.25

Capex '96 World Philatelic Exhibition.

Kim Chol Ju, Kim Il Sung's Brother, 80th Birth Anniv. — A1596

1996, June 12 ***Perf. 13¼***
3552 A1596 1.50w multicolored 4.25 2.00

Open Book — A1597

1996, June 15 ***Perf. 13½***
3553 A1597 40ch multicolored 1.10 .50

760th anniversary of publication of the *Complete Collection of Buddhist Scriptures Printed from 80,000 Wooden Blocks.*

Labor Law, 50th Anniv. A1598

1996, June 24 ***Perf. 11½***
3554 A1598 50ch multicolored .50 .40

Seasonal Birds — A1599

Designs: 10ch, Broad-billed roller. 40ch, Tri-color flycatcher. 50ch, Cuckoo.

1996, July 5
3555 A1599 Sheet of 3, #a.-c. 4.00 2.00

See No. 3569.

3rd Asian Winter Games, Harbin, China (2nd issue) — A1600

Design same as No. 3522, but with a new 30ch value picturing Ye Qiaobo replacing No. 3522b

1996, July 5
3556 A1600 Sheet of 2 1.75 1.00
a. 30ch multi .85 .40

Kumsusan Memorial Palace — A1601

Outdoor Crowd, Statue of Kim Il Sung — A1602

Hymn, *The Leader will be with us forever* — A1603

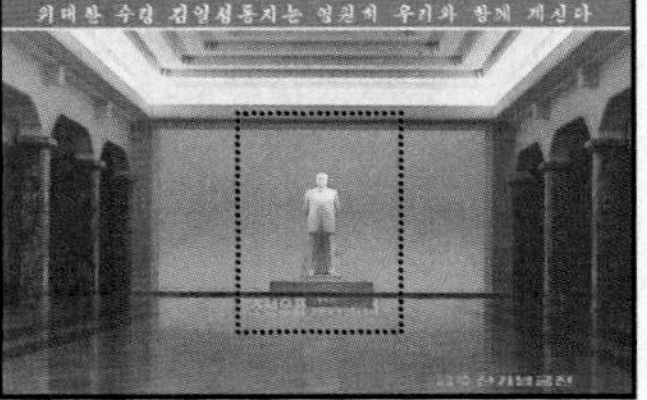
Statue of Kim Il Sung in hall of the Kumsusan Memorial Palace — A1604

1996, July 8 ***Perf. 12***
3557 A1601 10ch multicolored .25 .20

Souvenir Sheets

***Perf.* 13¼, 12 (#3558)**

3558 A1602 1w multicolored 3.00 1.00
3559 A1603 1w multicolored 3.00 1.00
3560 A1604 1w multicolored 3.00 1.00

Kim Il Sung, 2nd Death Anniv.

A1605

Designs, both 10ch: #3561, Kim Il Sung meeting Mao Zedong of China, 1954. #3562, Kim Il Sung meeting Jiang Zemin of China, 1991.

80ch, Kim shaking hands with Deng Xiaoping of China, horiz.

1996, July 11 ***Perf. 11½***
3561-3562 A1605 Set of 2 .50 .25

Souvenir Sheet

3563 A1605 80ch multicolored 2.25 1.00

26th Olympic Games, Atlanta — A1606

Designs, each 50ch: #3564, Soccer. #3565, Tennis. #3566, Hammer throw. #3567, Baseball.

1996, July 19 ***Perf. 12¼***
3564-3567 A1606 Set of 4 5.50 2.00

Sexual Equality Law, 50th Anniv. — A1607

1996, July 30 ***Perf. 11½***
3568 A1607 10ch multicolored .25 .20

Seasonal Bird Type

Designs: 10ch, Crested shelduck. 40ch, Demoiselle crane. 50ch, White swan.

1996, Aug. 5
3569 A1600 Sheet of 3, #a.-c. 2.75 1.25

Industrial Nationalization, 50th Anniv. — A1608

1996, Aug. 10 ***Perf. 11½***
3570 A1608 50ch multicolored .90 .40

UNICEF, 50th Anniv. — A1609

Designs: 10ch, Boy with ball, net. 20ch, Boy playing with building blocks. 50ch, Boy eating meal, holding watermelon slice. 60ch, Girl playing accordion.

1996, Aug. 20
3571-3574 A1609 Set of 4 2.75 1.10

Nos. 3571-3574 were issued in sheets of four, one containing 2 #3571, 1 #3574 and a label, the other containing 2 #3572, 1 #3573 and a different label.

1st Asian Gymnastics Championship, Changsha, China — A1610

Designs, each 15ch: #3575, Pae Kil Sun (N. Korea), men's pommel. #3576, Chen Cui Ting (China), rings. #3577, Li Jing (China). #3578, Kim Kwang Suk (N. Korea), asymmetrical bars.

1996, Sept. 24
3575-3578 A1610 Sheet of 4 1.50 .60

Kim Il Sung University, 50th Anniv. A1611

1996, Oct. 1
3579 A1611 10ch multicolored .50 .20

Tiger — A1612

Designs, each 50ch: #3580, Tiger. #3581, Royal spoonbill.

80ch: Stylized dove/hand nurturing sapling, growing out of planet Earth.

1996, Oct. 13
3580-3581 A1612 Set of 2 3.00 .70

Souvenir Sheet

3582 A1612 80ch multicolored 6.50 1.50

Nos. 3580-3581 were each printed in sheets of four, containing three stamps and a label.

Down-with-Imperialism Union, 70th Anniv. — A1613

1996, Oct. 17
3583 A1613 10ch multicolored .25 .20

A1614

Designs: a, 30ch Huang Ji Gwang. b, 10ch, Score of theme song of film *Red Mountain Ridge*. c, 30ch Huang Ji Gwang heroically dying in battle.

1996, Oct. 25
3584 A1614 Sheet of 3, #a.-c. 2.00 1.00

Hwang Ji Gwang, Chinese Volunteer, hero of Korean War, 44th death anniv.

History of the Earth — A1615

Each 50ch: a, Earth 7.5 billion years ago. b, 4.5-5 billion years ago. c, 450 million-4.5 billion years ago. d, 100-450 million years ago. e, 100 million years ago to the present.

1996, Nov. 1 ***Perf. 13½***
3585 A1615 Sheet of 5, #a.-e. 8.00 4.00

Freshwater Fish A1616

Designs, each 20ch: #3586, Japanese eel. #3587, Menada gray mullet.

80ch, Silver carp.

1996, Nov. 20 ***Perf. 11½***
3586-3587 A1616 Set of 2 1.50 .35

Souvenir Sheet

3588 A1616 80ch multicolored 3.00 .75

Kim Jong Il' Appointment as Supreme Commander of the People's Army, 5th Anniv. — A1617

1996, Dec. 24 ***Perf. 12***
3589 A1617 20ch multicolored .60 .20

New Year — Year of the Ox A1618

Designs, each 70ch: #3590, *Ox Driver*, by Kim Tu Ryang. #3591, Bronze ritual plate decorated with a tiger and two bulls. #3592, Cowboy and bull. #3593, Cowboy playing flute, sitting on bull.

80ch, *Kosong People's Support to the Front.*

1997, Jan. 1 ***Perf. 11¾***
3590-3593 A1618 Set of 4 8.00 2.00
3591a, 3593a Set of 2 sheets 8.00 2.00

Souvenir Sheet

3594 A1618 80ch multicolored 3.00 .75

No. 3591a contains Nos. 3590 and 3591, with a central label depicting a bull's head surrounded by zodiacal signs. No. 3593a contains Nos. 3592 and 3593, with the same label.

Flowers and Butterflies, by Nam Kye-u (1811-88) — A1619

Designs, each 50ch: a, Three butterflies, flower. b, One small butterfly, flower. c, Large butterfly, leaves.

1997, Jan. 5 ***Perf. 12¼x11¾***
3595 A1618 Sheetlet of 3, #a.-c. 4.50 1.00
b. Complete booklet, pane of 6, 2 ea. #3595a-3595b 9.00

Paintings of Cats and Dogs — A1620

Designs, both 50ch: #3598, Puppy in basket, touching noses with kitten. #3599, Two dogs in basket, kitten.

Both 50ch: #3600a, Cat in basket, with dog and skein of yarn alongside. #3600b, Kitten in basket with fruit and flowers, puppy alongside.

1997, Jan. 25 ***Perf. 11¾x12¼***
3598-3599 A1620 Set of 2 3.25 1.00

Sheets of 4

3600 Sheet of 4, #3698, 3600b, 2 #3600a 3.50 1.50
3600a A1620 50ch multicolored 1.50
3600b A1620 50ch multicolored 1.50
3601 Sheet of 4, #3599, #3600a, 2 #3600b 3.50 1.50

Return of Hong Kong to China — A1621

Hong Kong nightscape, each 20ch: a, Skyscraper with double antennae. b, Skyscraper with single spire. c, Round skyscraper, high-rise apartment buildings.

1997, Feb. 1 *Perf. 13½*
3602 A1621 Sheet of 3, #a.-c. 2.50 .65

A1622

Kim Jong Il, 55th Birthday — A1623

Designs: 10ch, Birthplace, Mt. Paekdu.
#3604, Kim Il Sung and Kim Jong Il with farm machine. #3605, Kim Jong Il inspecting a Korean People's Army unit.

1997, Feb. 16 *Perf. 12*
3603 A1622 10ch multicolored .50 .20

Souvenir Sheets

3604-3605 A1623 1w Set of 2 5.50 1.75

6th Paektusan Prize Int'l Figure Skating Championships, Pyongyang — A1624

Pairs skating, different routines, each 50ch: #3606, pale reddish brown. #3607, blue. #3608, green.

1997, Feb. 17 *Perf. 11½*
3606-3608 A1624 Set of 3 4.00 1.00
3607a Sheet of 4, 2 ea #3606, 3607 5.50 1.50
3608a Booklet pane of 6, 2 ea. #3606-3608 8.00 —
Complete booklet, #3608a 8.50
3608b Sheet of 4, 2 ea #3607, 3608 5.50 1.50

Kye Sun Hui, Women's Judo Gold Medalist, 1996 Summer Olympic Games, Atlanta — A1625

1997, Feb. 20
3611 A1625 80ch multicolored 2.50 .60

Choe Un A — A1626

1997, Feb. 25
3612 A1626 80ch multicolored 3.00 .60
a. Booklet pane of 5
Complete booklet, #3612a

Issued to honor Choe Un A, a seven-year-old entrant in the World Go Championships.

Apricots — A1627

Various types of apricots, each 50ch: #3613, *Prunus ansu.* #3614, *Prunus mandshurica.* #3615, *Prunus armeniaca.* #3616, *Prunus sibirica*

1997, Mar. 4 *Perf. 11¼*
3613-3616 A1627 Set of 4 6.00 1.50
3613a Sheet of 8, 2 ea#3613-3614 12.00 3.00

Foundation of Korean National Assoc., 80th Anniv. — A1628

1997, Mar. 23 *Perf. 12¼*
3617 A1628 10ch lt brn & dk grn .50 .20
a. Sheet of 8 4.00 1.00

A1629

Reforestation Day, 50th Anniv. — A1630

Designs: 10ch, Pine sapling.
No. 3619, Kim Il Sung planting sapling on Munsu Hill.

1997, Apr. 6 *Perf. 11½*
3618 A1629 10ch multicolored .50 .20
a. Complete booklet, 8 #3618

Souvenir Sheet

Perf. 13¼

3619 A1630 1w multicolored 3.00 .90

A1631

A1632

Kim Il Sung, 85th Birth Anniv. — A1633

Designs: 10ch, Kim's birthplace, Mangyongdae. 20ch, Sliding rock, horiz. 40ch, Warship Rock, horiz.
Each 1w: #3623, Painting of Kim among crowd symbolic of the Korean people. #3624, Kim in business suit, surrounded by flowers.

1997, Apr. 15 *Perf. 12¼*
3620-3622 A1631 Set of 3 2.00 .55

Souvenir Sheets

Perf. 13¼ (#3623), 11¾x12¼ (#3624)

3623 A1632 1w multicolored 2.75 .90
3624 A1633 1w multicolored 2.75 .90

A1634

Korean People's Army, 65th Anniv. — A1635

Designs: 10ch, KPA cap badge, rockets and jet fighters.
1w, Kim Il Sung and Kim Jong Il at military review.

1997, Apr. 25 *Perf. 11½*
3625 A1634 10ch multicolored .50 .20

Souvenir Sheet

Perf. 12¼x11¾

3626 A1635 1w multicolored 3.00 .90

A1636

North-South Agreement, 25th Anniv. — A1637

Designs: 10ch, Map of Korea.
1w, Monument to Kim Il Sung's Autograph, Phanmunjom.

1997, May 4 *Perf. 11½*
3627 A1636 10ch multicolored 1.00 .20

Souvenir Sheet

Perf. 12x11½

3628 A1637 1w multicolored 4.00 .90

A1638

Each 10ch: #3629, Tower of Juche Idea, flag. #3630, Man with flag. #3631, Soldier, miner, farmer, scientist.

1997, May 25 ***Perf. 12¼x12***

3629-3631 A1638 Set of 3 .90 .40

Int'l Friendship Exhib., Myohyang Mountains — A1639

Each 70ch: #3632, Exhibition Center. #3633, Statue of Kim Il Sung in exhibition entrance hall. #3634, Ivory sculpture *Native House in Mangyongdae* . #3635, Stuffed crocodile holding wooden cups, with ashtray.

1997, May 30 ***Perf. 11¾***

3632-3635 A1639 Set of 4 sheets 7.50 5.00

Battle of Poconbo, 60th Anniv. — A1640

1997, June 4 ***Perf. 11½***

3636 A1640 40ch multicolored 1.25 .35
a. Sheet of 6 7.50 7.50
b. Booklet pane of 6 #3636 7.50 —
Complete booklet, #3636b 8.00

No. 3636b contains six stamps in a horizontal strip, within decorative selvage.

Rice Transplantation, Mirin Plain, 50th Anniv. — A1641

Each 1w: #3637, Kim Il Sung transplanting rice. #3638, Kim Il Sung inspecting a rice-transplanting machine.

1997, June 7 ***Perf. 13¼***

3637-3638 A1641 Set of 2 sheets 5.75 1.75

A1642

Return of Hong Kong to China — A1643

No. 3639, each 20ch: a, Signing the Nanjing Treaty, 1842. b, Signing the China-Britain Joint Statement, 1984. c, Deng Xiaoping and Margaret Thatcher. d, Jiang Zenin and Tong Jianhua.

97ch, Deng Xiaoping.

1997, July 1 ***Perf. 11¾***

3639 A1642 Sheet of 4, #a.-d. 3.00 .75

Souvenir Sheet

Perf. 13¼

3640 A1643 97ch multicolored 3.00 1.00

Fossils — A1644

Designs: 50ch, *Redlichia chinensis*. 1w, *Ptychoparia coreanica*.

1997, July 5 ***Perf. 11½***

3641-3642 A1644 Pair 5.00 1.25
3641a Booklet pane, 5 #3641 8.75 —
Complete booklet #3641a 9.00
3642a Booklet pane, 5 #3642 17.50 —
Complete booklet #3642a 18.00

Nos. 3641a-3642a contain horizontal strips of five stamps.

Kim Il Sung, 3rd Death Anniv. A1645

Each 50ch, Portrait of Kim Il Sung and: #3643, Kim speaking at party conference, 1985. #3644, Kim inspecting Kim Chaek Ironworks, 1985. #3645, Kim at Songsin Cooperative Farm, Sadong District, 1993. #3646, Kim being cheered by performing artists, 1986. #3647, Kim visiting Jonchon Factory, Jagang Province, 1991. #3648, Kim receiving bouquet from soldiers.

1997, July 8 ***Perf. 11¾x12***

3643-3648 A1645 Set of 6 9.00 2.25
3645a Sheet of 3, #3643-3645 4.50 2.00
3648a Sheet of 3, #3646-3648 4.50 2.00

Folk Games A1646

Designs: 30ch, Blindman's Bluff. 60ch, Jackstones. 70ch, Arm wrestling.

1997, July 26 ***Perf. 11½***

3649-3651 A1646 Set of 3 4.50 1.25
3649a-3651a Set of 3 sheets 9.00 4.00
3651b Booklet pane of 6, 2 ea. #3649-3651 9.00 —
Complete booklet, #3651b 9.50

Nos. 3649a-3651a each contain 2 stamps + a central label.

No. 3281b contains two each of #3649-3651, printed in a se-tenant block (3x2), with decorative selvage.

Traditional Korean Women's Clothing — A1647

Designs: 10ch, Spring costume. 40ch, Summer. 50ch, Autumn. 60ch, Winter.

1997, Aug. 10

3652-3655 A1647 Set of 4 4.50 2.00
3652a-3654a Set of 3 sheets 18.00 12.00

No. 3652a contains 2 #3652 and 2 #3653; No. 3653a contains 2 #3652a contains 2 #3653 and 2 #3654; No. 3654a contains 2 #3654 and 2 #3655.

Chongryu Bridge A1648

Both 50ch: #3656, Night view of Chongryu Bridge. #3657, Panoramic view.

1997, Aug. 25

3656-3657 A1648 Set of 2 3.00 1.00
3657a Sheet of 2, #3656-3657 3.50 1.50
3657b Booklet pane of 6, 3 ea. #3656-3657 9.00 —
Complete booklet, #3657b 9.50

A1649

Juche Era and Sun Day, 85th Anniv. — A1650

10ch, Sun, magnolias, banner, balloons.

Each 1w: #3659, Kim Il Sung, slogan, doves. #3660, Kim, birthplace Mongyangdae. #3661, Kim, Lake Chon, Mt. Paekdu. #3662, Kim, Kumsusan Memorial Palace.

1997, Sept. 3 ***Perf. 13¼***

3658 A1649 10ch multicolored .50 .20

Souvenir Sheets

3659-3662 A1650 Set of 4 sheets 11.00 6.00

Theses on Socialist Education, 20th Anniv. of Publication A1651

1997, Sept. 5 ***Perf. 11½***

3663 A1651 10ch multicolored .50 .20

No. 3663 was issued in sheetlets of 6.

Air Koryo — A1652

Sheets of 2 stamps and central label: 20ch, TU-134. 30ch, TU-154. 50ch, IL-62.

1997, Sept. 14 ***Perf. 13¼***

3664-3666 A1652 Set of 3 sheets 5.00 1.50
3665a Complete booklet, pane of 8, 4 ea. #3664, 3666 7.00
3666a Complete booklet, pane of 8, 4 ea. #3665, 3666 8.00

Korean Membership in World Tourism Org., 10th Anniv. — A1653

Views of Mt. Chilbo, each 50ch: #3667, Kim Chol Ung. #3668, Rojok Beach. #3669, Chonbul Peak.

1997, Sept. 22 ***Perf. 12***

3667-3669 A1653 Set of 3 4.50 1.25
3669a Sheet, #3667-3669 + label 5.00 1.40

Kumgang Mountains A1654

Each 50ch: #3670, Kumgang Gate. #3671, Podok Hermitage.

1997, Oct. 2

3670-3671 A1654 Set of 2 3.00 .75
3670a Booklet pane of 5 #3670 7.50 —
Complete booklet, #3670a 8.00
3671a Sheet of 6, 3 each #3670-3671 10.00 4.00
3671b Booklet pane of 5 #3671 7.50 —
Complete booklet, #3671b 8.00

Mangyongdae Revolutionary School, 50th Anniv. — A1655

Perf. 11½

3672 A1655 40ch multicolored 1.25 .30
a. Booklet pane of 6 7.50 —
Complete booklet, #3672a 8.00

Gift Animals A1656

Animals presented to Kim Il Sung as gifts from foreign governments: 20ch, Lion (from Ethiopia, 1987). 30ch, Jaguar (Japan, 1992). 50ch, Barbary sheep (Czechoslovakia, 1992). 80ch, Scarlet macaw (Austria, 1979).

1997, Oct. 15

3673-3676 A1656 Set of 4 5.50 1.25
3673a Sheet of 8, 2 each #3673-3676 11.00 5.00
3673b Booklet pane of 8, 2ea. #3673-3676 11.00 —
Complete booklet, #3673b 12.00

Qu Shao Yun, Chinese Volunteer Hero — A1657

Designs: a, 30ch, Bust of Qu Shao Yun. b, 10ch, Monument to Qu Shao Yun. c, 30ch, Qu Shao Yun burning to death in battle.

1997, Oct. 18

3677 A1657 Sheet of 3, #a.-c. 2.25 .75

Sports — A1658

Each 50ch: #3678, Bowling. #3679, Fencing. #3680, Golf.

1997, Nov. 10 ***Perf. 13¼***

3678-3680 A1658 Set of 3 5.25 1.25
3680a Sheet, 2 each #3678-380 + 2 labels 11.00 5.00

Snails — A1659

Each 50ch: #3681, Two snails copulating. #3682, Snail laying eggs. #3683, Snail.

1997, Nov. 15 ***Perf. 12¼***

3681-3683 A1659 Strip of 3 4.75 2.00
3683a Sheet of 6, 2 each #3681-3683 9.50 4.00
3683b Booklet pane of 6, 2 ea. #3681-3683 9.50 —
Complete booklet, #3683b 10.00

Shanghai Int'l Stamp & Coin Exhib. — A1660

1997, Nov. 19 ***Perf. 11½***

3684 A1660 Sheet of 2, #a.-b. 2.50 1.00
a. 30ch multicolored 1.00 .30
b. 50ch multicolored 1.50 .60

New Year — Year of the Tiger
A1661 A1662

Designs: 10ch, "Juche 87," pine boughs, temple. 50ch (#3686), Tiger in rocket. 50ch (#3687), Tiger in ship.
80ch, Tiger in train.

Perf. 13¼, 11½ (#3686-3687)

1997, Dec. 15

3685 A1661 10ch multicolored .20 .20
3686 A1662 50ch multicolored .90 .25
3687 A1662 50ch multicolored .90 .25
a. Sheet of 4, 1 ea #3686-#3687, 2 #3688 4.50 2.00
Nos. 3685-3687 (3) 2.00 .70

Souvenir Sheet

3688 A1662 80ch multicolored 2.00 .75

A single stamp like that in No. 3688 is included in No. 3687a.

Birthplace, Hoeryong A1663

Kim Jong Suk, 80th Birth Anniv. — A1664

1997, Dec. 24 ***Perf. 13¼***

3689 A1663 10ch multicolored .50 .20

Souvenir Sheet

3690 A1664 1w multicolored 3.00 .75

Winter Olympic Games, Nagano, Japan — A1665

Designs: 20ch, Skiing. 40ch, Speed skating.

1998, Feb. 7 ***Perf. 11½***

3691-3692 A1665 Set of 2 1.25 .65
3692a Sheet of 4, 2 ea #3691-#3692 2.50 1.25
3692b Booklet pane of 8, 4 ea. #3691-3692 5.00 —
Complete booklet, #3692b 5.50

A1666

Kim Jong Il, 56th Birthday — A1667

Designs: 10ch, Birth date ("2.16").
3w, Birthplace, log cabin on Mt. Paekdu.

1998, Feb. 16

3693 A1666 10ch multicolored .50 .20

Souvenir Sheet

3694 A1667 3w multicolored 4.50 2.00

A1668

Paintings of Mt. Paekdu Wildlife — A1669

Designs, each 50ch: #3695, Korean tigers. #3696, White crane.
No. 3697, each 50ch: a, Bears. b, Racoons.

1998, Mar. 6 ***Perf. 11¾x12***

3695-3696 A1668 Set of 2 2.00 1.00
3696a Booklet pane of 8, 2 ea. #3695-3696, 3697a-3697b 8.00 —
Complete booklet, #3696a 8.50

Souvenir Sheet

3697 A1669 Sheet of 4, #3695-3696, 3697a-3697b 4.00 2.00
a. A1668 50ch multicolored 1.00 .50
b. A1668 50ch multicolored 1.00 .50

Kim Il Sung's 1000-ri Journey, 75th Anniv. A1670

1998, Mar. 16 ***Perf. 11½***

3698 A1670 10ch multicolored .50 .20
a. Sheet of 10 5.00 1.50

Appt. of Kim Jong Il as Chairman of the Nat'l Defense Commission, 5th Anniv. A1671

1998, Apr. 9

3699 A1671 10ch multicolored .50 .20

A1672

Kim Il Sung, 86th Birth Anniv. — A1673

Designs: 10ch, Birthplace, flags, flowers.

Circular stamps, each 80ch, within 84x155mm sheetlets, depicting portraits of Kim Il Sung at different stages in his life: #3701, As child. #3702, As middle school student. #3703, As young revolutionary. #3704, In suit and tie, ca. 1946. #3705, In military uniform during Korean War. #3706, As middle-aged man, in uniform. #3707, As middle-aged man, in suit and tie. #3708, As old man in suit and tie.

1998, Apr. 15

3700 A1672 10ch multicolored .50 .20

Souvenir Sheets

3701-3708 A1673 Set of 8 9.00 4.00

North-South Joint Conference, 50th Anniv. — A1674

1998, Apr. 21 ***Perf. 13¼***

3709 A1674 10ch multicolored .50 .20

16th World Cup Soccer Championship, France — A1675

Designs: 30ch, Dribbling. 50ch, Kicking.

1998, May 5 ***Perf. 11½***

3710-3711 A1675 Set of 2 1.60 .80

3711a Sheet of 6, 2 ea #3710-3711, #3712 6.00 3.00

3711b Booklet pane of 10, 5 ea. #3710-3711 8.00 —

Complete booklet, #3711b 8.50

Souvenir Sheet

3712 A1675 80ch multicolored 1.60 .80

A single stamp like that in No. 3712 is included in No. 3711a.

A1676

Int'l Friendship Art Exhib., Mt. Myohyang — A1677

Designs, each 1w: #3713, *Diagram of Automatic Space Station* (USSR). #3714, Ceramic flower vase (Egypt). #3715, *Crane* (USA).

1w, Kim Il Sung receiving a gift from Deng Xiaoping.

1998, May 20 ***Perf. 11¾***

3713-3715 A1676 Set of 3 4.50 2.25

3714a Sheet of 2, #3712 & #3714 2.75 1.40

3715a Sheet of 2, #3712 & #3715 2.75 1.40

Souvenir Sheet

Perf. 13¼

3716 A1677 1w multicolored 2.00 1.00

A1678

Korean Art Gallery — A1679

Designs: 60ch, *A Countryside in May.* 1.40w, *Dance.*

3w, *Heart-to-heart Talk with a Peasant.*

1998, May 20

3717-3718 A1678 Set of 2 3.00 1.50

Souvenir Sheet

3719 A1679 3w multicolored 4.50 2.25

Vegetables — A1680

Designs: 10ch, Cabbage. 40ch, Radish. 50ch, Green onion. 60ch, Cucumber. 70ch, Pumpkin. 80ch, Carrot. 90ch, Garlic. 1w, Red pepper.

1998, May 20 ***Perf. 13¼***

3720-3727 A1680 Sheet of 8 9.00 4.50

A1681

Int'l Year of the Ocean — A1682

Designs: 10ch, Hydro-Meteorological Headquarters building, ship, oceanographic floating balloons, dolphins, emblem. 80ch, Woman holding child, yachts, emblem.

5w, Vasco da Gama (1460-1524), Portuguese explorer.

1998, May 22

3730-3731 A1681 Set of 2 2.00 .90

3731a Sheet of 4, 2 ea. #3730-3731 2.00 .90

Souvenir Sheet

3732 A1682 5w multicolored 7.50 3.75

A1683

Korean Central History Museum, Pyongyang — A1684

Designs: 10ch, Stone Age tool. 2.50w, Fossil monkey skull.

4w, Kim Il Sung visiting the museum.

1998, June 15

3733-3734 A1683 Set of 2 4.00 2.00

Souvenir Sheet

3735 A1684 4w multicolored 6.00 3.00

A1685

Dr. Ri Sung Gi (1905-96), Inventor of Vinalon — A1686

Designs: 40ch, Dr. Ri Sung Gi and diagram of vinalon nuclear structure.

80ch, Gi working in laboratory.

1998, June 15 ***Perf. 11½***

3736 A1685 40ch multicolored .60 .20

a. Booklet pane of 10

Complete booklet, #3736a

Souvenir Sheet

3737 A1686 80ch multicolored 1.60 1.00

Squirrels and Hedgehogs Cartoon — A1687

Designs: 20ch, Squirrel and Commander of Hedgehog Unit. 30ch, Commander of Hedgehog Unit receiving invitation to banquet celebrating bumper crop. 60ch, Weasel Commander and mouse. 1.20w, Bear falling dead-drunk. 2w, Weasel Commander and mice invading the flower village. 2.50w, Hedgehog scout saving the squirrel.

1998, June 15

3738-3743 A1687 Set of 6 12.00 6.00

3743a Sheet of 6, #3737-3743 12.00 6.00

A1688

Return of Hong Kong to China, 1st Anniv. — A1689

Designs, each 10w: #3744, Deng Xiaoping (1904-97), Chinese Prime Minister. #3745, Mao Zedong. #3746, Kim Il Sung.

#3747, Deng Xiaoping, Mao Zedong and Kim Il Sung, horiz.

1998, July 1

Embossed with gold foil application

3744-3746 A1688 Set of 3 30.00 10.00

Souvenir Sheet

3747 A1689 10w Gold & multi 10.00 10.00

Orchids — A1834

Designs: 10ch, *Eria pannea.* 40ch, *Cymbidium.* 90ch, *Sophrolaeliocattleya.* 1.60w, *Cattleya trianae.*

No. 4159: 2w, *Cypripedium macranthum.*

2001, Aug. 1

4155-58 A1834 Set of 4 6.00 3.00
4158a Booklet pane of 6, #4155-4156, 4158, #4159a, 2 #4157 11.00 —
Complete booklet, #4158a 11.50

Souvenir Sheet

4159 A1834 2w multicolored 4.00 2.00

No. 4158a contains the six stamps in a se-tenant horizontal strip of 6, with decorative selvage on left and right sides.

Lighthouses — A1835

Designs: 40ch, Pibaldo Lighthouse. 70ch, Soho Lighthouse. 90ch, Komalsan Lighthouse.

No. 4163: 1.50w, Alsom Lighthouse.

2001, Aug. 18

4160-4162 A1835 Set of 3 4.00 2.00
4162a Booklet pane of 6, #4160-4161, 2 #4162, 2 #4163a 12.50 —
Complete booklet, #4162a 13.00
4162b Sheet of 4, #4160-4162, 4163a 7.00 3.50

Souvenir Sheet

4163 A1835 1.50w multicolored 3.00 1.50

Nos. 4160-4162 were issued both separately in large sheets and together, with the 1.50w value from No. 4163, in a sheet of 5 (#4162b). No. 4162a contains the six stamps in a horizontal strip of 6, with thin plain selvage.

Kim Po Hyon (1871-1955), Grandfather of Kim Il Sung — A1836

2001, Aug. 19

4164 A1836 1w multicolored 1.50 .75

Protected Animals — A1837

Designs: 10ch, Black stork (*Ciconia nigra*). 40ch, Cinereous vulture (*Aegypius monachus*). 70ch, Chinese water deer (*Hydropotes inermis*). 90ch, Goral (*Nemorhaedus goral*).

No. 4169: 1.30w, Northern eagle owl (*Bubo bubo*).

2001, Sept. 2

4165-4168 A1837 Set of 4 4.00 2.00
4168a Sheet of 5, #4165-4168, 4169a 6.50 —
4168b Booklet pane of 6, #4165-1467, 1469a, 2 x 1468 7.50 —
Complete booklet, #4168b 8.00

Souvenir Sheet

4169 A1837 1.30w multicolored 2.50 1.25

Nos. 4165-4168 were issued both separately in large sheets and together, with the 1.30w value from No. #4169, in a sheet of 5 (#4168a).

No. 4168b contains the six stamps in a se-tenant vertical strip, within narrow decorated selvage.

Olympic Games 2008, Beijing — A1838

Designs, each 56ch: a, Deng Ya Ping, Gold medalist ('96), Women's Singles, Table Tennis. b, Jiang Zemin, PRC president. c, Wang Jun Xia, Chinese athlete. d, Li Ning, Chinese gymnast. e, Fu Ming Xia, Chinese diver.

2001, Sept. 10 ***Perf. 12½***

4170 A1838 Sheet of 5, #a.-e. 5.00 2.50

Cycle Sports — A1839

Designs: 10ch, Cycle soccer. 40ch, Road racing. 1.50w, Mountainbike racing. 2w, Indoor race.

2001, Sept. 20 ***Perf. 12***

4171 A1839 Sheet of 4, #a.-d. 7.00 3.50

Space Exploration — A1840

Designs: 10ch, Yuri Gagarin (1934-68), Soviet Cosmonaut. 40ch, Apollo 11 Moon Landing. 1.50w, *Kwangmyongsong*, North Korean satellite (1998). 2w, Edmund Hailey (1656-1742), Halley's Comet and *Giotto* satellite.

2001, Sept. 25

4172 A1840 Sheet of 4, #a.-d. 6.50 3.25
e. Booklet pane of 5, #4172a-4172c, 2 #1472d 10.00 —
Complete booklet, #4172e 11.00

No. 4172e contains five stamps in a se-tenant horizontal strip.

Vladimir Putin and Kim Jong Il — A1841

2001, Oct. 12 ***Perf. 12½x12***

4173 A1841 1.50w multicolored 2.25 1.10

Visit of Kim Jong Il to Russia.

Kim Jong Il and Jiang Zemin — A1842

2001, Oct. 25 ***Perf. 11½x12***

4174 A1842 1.50w multicolored 2.25 1.10

Meeting between Kim Jong Il and Jiang Zemin, president of the People's Republic of China.

Kim Jong Suk in Battle — A1843

2001, Nov. 24 ***Perf. 12½x12***

4175 A1843 1.60w multicolored 3.00 1.50

Kim Jong Suk, anti-Japanese revolutionary hero, 84th birth anniv.

Kim Jong Il Inspecting Troops — A1844

2001, Dec. 1 ***Perf. 13½***

4176 A1844 1w multicolored 1.50 .75

10th anniv. of appointment of Kim Jong Il as Supreme Commander of the Korean People's Army.

Chollima Statue — A1845

2002, Jan. 1

4177 A1845 10ch multicolored .30 .20

New Year.

A1846

A1847

Horses from painting *Ten Horses*, by Wang Zhi Cheng (1702-68): 10ch, White horse. 40ch, Bay. 60ch, Pinto. 1.30w, Piebald.
1.60w, Black stallion, from painting *Horse Master Jiu Fang Gao*, by Xu Bei Hong (1895-1953).

2002, Jan. 1

4178-4181 A1846 Set of 4 3.75 1.75
4181a Sheet of 5, #4178-4181, 4182a 6.25 3.00

Souvenir Sheet

4182 A1847 1.60w multicolored 2.50 1.25

Traditional New Year — Year of the Horse.
Nos. 4178-4181 were issued both separately in large sheets and together, with the 1.60w value from No. 4182, in a sheet of 5 (#4181a).

Flower Basket — A1848

Kim Jong Il with Soldiers — A1849

Kim Jong Il — A1850

Kim Il Sung, Kim Jong Il, Kim Jong Suk — A1851

2002, Feb. 1 ***Perf. 13½***

4183 A1848 10ch multicolored .30 .20

Souvenir Sheets

4184 A1849 1.50w multicolored 2.50 1.25

Perf. 11½x12

4185 A1850 2w multicolored 3.00 1.50

Perf. 12x12½

4186 A1851 Sheet of 3, #a.-c. 6.00 3.00

Kim Jong Il, 60th Birthday.
No. 4185 bears a metallic gold application.

Centenary of First Zeppelin Flight — A1852

Designs: 40ch, LZ-1. 80ch, LZ-120. 1.20w, Zeppelin NT.
2.40w, Zeppelin NT (different view).

2002, Feb. 5 ***Perf. 12***

4187-4189 A1852 Set of 3 3.75 1.75
4189a Sheet of 4, #4187-4189, 4190a 7.50 3.75

Souvenir Sheet

4190 A1852 2.40w multicolored 3.75 1.75

Nos. 4187-4187 were issued both separately in large sheets and together, with the 2.40w value from No. 4190, in a sheet of 4 (#4189a).

Banner, Torch, Soldiers — A1853

2002, Feb. 25 ***Perf. 13½***

4191 A1853 10ch multicolored .30 .20

Annual joint editorial of the three state newspapers, *Rodong Sinmun, Josoninmingum* and *Chongnyonjonwi.*

Mushrooms — A1854

Designs: a, 10ch, *Collybia confluons.* b, 40ch, *Sparassis laminosa.* c, 80ch, *Amanita vaginata.* d, 1.20w, *Russia integra.* e, 1.50w, *Pholiota squarrosa.*

2002, Feb. 25 ***Perf. 13½***

4192 A1854 Block of 5, #a-e + label 6.50 3.25

A1855

A1856

Kim Il Sung (1912-1994) — A1857

Designs: 10ch, Kim Il Sung's birthplace, *Kimsungilia.*
Nos. 4198-4200 (each 1.50w): No. 4198, Kim Il Sung with Kim Jong Suk (1941). No. 4199, Kim Il Sung as student, with black cap (1927). No. 4200, Kim Il Sung and Kim Chaek, political commissar.
No. 4201: 2w, Portrait of Kim Il Sung.

2002, Mar. 15 ***Perf. 13½***

4197 A1855 10ch multicolored .30 .20

Souvenir Sheets

4198-4200 A1856 1.50w Set of 3 6.00 3.00

With Gold Metallic Application

Perf. 11½x12

4201 A1857 2w multicolored 3.00 1.50

Kang Pan Suk — A1858

2002, Mar. 21 ***Perf. 11½x11¾***

4202 A1858 1w multicolored 1.50 .75

Kang Pan Sok, mother of Kim Il Sung, 110th birth anniv.

20th April Spring Friendship Art Festival — A1859

2002, Mar. 25 ***Perf. 13¼***

4203 A1859 10ch multicolored .50 .25

Locomotives A1860

Designs: 10ch, *Kanghaenggun 1.5-01* electric train. 40ch, *Samjiyon 1001* electric train. 1.50w, Steam locomotive. 2w, Steam locomotive (diff.).

No. 4208, 2w, *Pulgungi 5112* diesel locomotive.

2002, Apr. 10 ***Perf. 11½***
4204-4207 A1860 Set of 4 6.00 3.00

Souvenir Sheet

4208 A1860 2w multicolored 3.00 1.50

He Baozhen, 100th Anniv. Birth — A1861

Designs: a, 1w, He Baozhen and Liu Shaoqi in 1923. b, 40ch, He Baozhen's family. c, 30ch, Family home in Dao xian County, Henan Province. d, 10ch, Letter in Chinese, from Liu Ying, a wife of Zhang Wentian, Chinese Communist Party official. e, 20ch, Monument at He Baozhen's birthplace.

2002, Apr. 20 ***Perf. 13¼***
4209 A1861 Sheet of 5, #a.-e. 3.00 1.50

He Baozhen, first wife of Liu Shaoqi, Chairman of the People's Republic of China 1959-68.

Shellfish A1862

Designs: 10ch, *Cristaria plicata*. 40ch, *Lanceolaria cospidata kuroda*. 1w, *Schistodesmus lampreyanus*. 1.50w, *Lamprotula coreana*.

2002, Apr. 21
4210-4213 A1862 Set of 4 5.00 2.50

A1863

Korean People's Army, 70th Anniv. — A1864

Designs: 10ch, Soldier, sailor, pilot, symbolizing the three branches of the armed forces.

1.60w, Kim Il Sung and Kim Jong Il walking with army officers and political functionaries.

2002, Apr. 25 ***Perf. 12¼x11¾***
4214 A1863 10ch multicolored .30 .20

Souvenir Sheet

4215 A1864 1.60w multicolored 2.50 1.25

Legend 'Arirang' — A1865

Designs: a, 10ch, Ri Rang and Song Bu as children. b, 40ch, As young adults. c, 50ch, Ri Rang killing the landlord. d, 1.50w, Song Bu.

2002, Apr. 28 ***Perf. 13¼***
4216 A1865 Sheet of 4, #a.-d. 3.75 1.75

A1866

Mass Gymnastics and Artistic Performance of 'Arirang' — A1867

Designs: 10ch, Actors. 20ch, Cartoon characters. 30ch, Dancer holding fan. 40ch, Dancer, gymnasts with hoops.

1w, Dancer with tambourine.

2002, Apr. 28 ***Perf. 12¼***
4217-4220 A1866 Set of 4 1.50 .75

Souvenir Sheet

4221 A1867 1w multicolored 1.75 .90

Nos. 4217-4220 were each issued in sheets of 6, with pictorial margins and Arirang logo.

Symbols of Modern Science & Industry A1868

2002, May 2 ***Perf. 13¼***
4222 A1868 10ch multicolored .30 .20

Science and Technology promotion: "Science and Technology are the Driving Force of Building a Great Prosperous Powerful Nation."

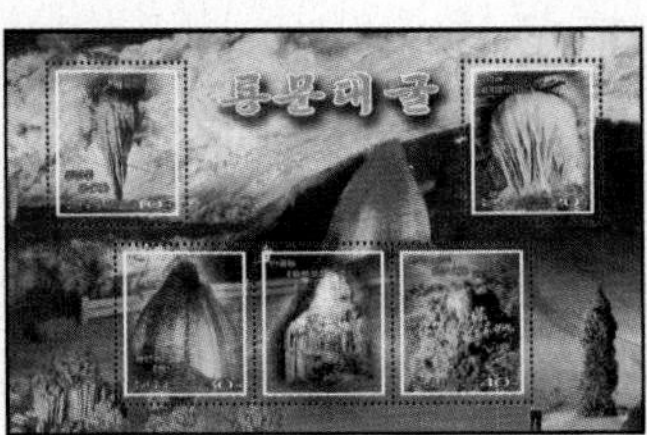
Ryongmun Cavern — A1869

Designs: a, 10ch, Pink stalactite. b, 20ch, Green stalactite. c, 30ch, Golden stalagmite. d, 40ch, Rough-surfaced orange stalagmite.

2002, May 25 ***Perf. 11½***
4223 A1869 Sheet of 4, #a.-d. 2.50 1.25

Monument — A1870

2002, May 2 ***Perf. 13¼***
4224 A1870 10ch multicolored .30 .20

30th Anniv. of the Elucidation of the Three Principles for National Reunification.

Butterflies — A1871

Designs: a, 10ch, *Stauropus fagi*. b, 40ch, *Agrias claudina*. c, 1.50w, *Catocala nupta*. d, 2w, *Morpho rhetenor*.

2002, June 30 ***Perf. 11¾***
4225 A1871 Block of 4, #a.-d. 7.50 3.75

Nos. 4147-4149 with Added Flags in Margins

A1872

2002, June 30 ***Perf. 11½***
4226-4228 A1872 Set of 3 sheets 4.00 2.00

16th National Congress of the Communist Party of China, Beijing, Nov. 8-14.

Compare with Nos. 4147-4149.

Elderly Man, Child, Hospital A1873

2002, July 5 ***Perf. 12¼***
4229 A1873 10ch multicolored .30 .20

50th Anniv. of Universal Free Medical System.

Kim Jong Suk (1917-49) — A1874

Designs: a, 10ch, As child. b, 40ch, As young woman in Children's Corps. c, 1w, In army uniform. d, 1.50w, With long hair, in civilian clothing.

2002, July 20 ***Perf. 13¼***
4230 A1874 Sheet of 4, #a.-d. 2.25 1.10

Kim Jong Suk, first wife of Kim Il Sung and mother of Kim Jong Il.

Soldier, Worker, Farmer — A1875

2002, July 29 ***Perf. 11½***
4231 A1875 10ch multicolored .30 .20

30th anniv. of the DPRK Constitution.

A1876

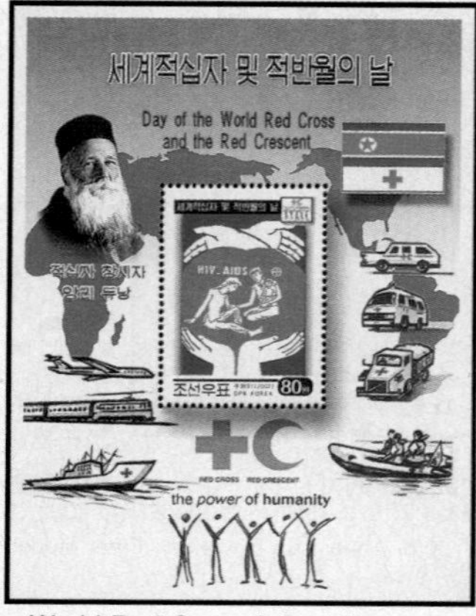

World Red Cross & Red Crescent Day — A1877

No. 4232: a, 3w, Korean returnees. b, 12w, Red Cross medics administering first aid. c, 150w, N. Korean truck delivering aid to South Korean flood victims.
No. 4233: 80w, AIDs victim, family.

2002, Sept. 20 ***Perf. 13¼***

Sheet of 6

4232 A1876 Sheet, 2 each #a.-c. 5.00 2.50

Souvenir Sheet

4233 A1877 80w multicolored 1.50 .75

Hong Chang Su, 2000 World Super-Flyweight Boxing Champion — A1878

2002, Sept. 25 ***Perf. 11½***

4234 A1878 75w multicolored 1.50 .75

Kim Jong Il with Pres. Putin — A1879

Kim Jong Il Shaking Hands with Pres. Putin — A1880

No. 4235 measures 85x70mm, No. 4236 120x100mm.

2002, Oct. 15 ***Perf. 13¼***

Souvenir Sheets

4235 A1879 70w multicolored 1.50 .75
4236 A1880 120w multicolored 2.00 1.00

Kim Jong Il's Visit to Russia

Siamese Cat — A1881

Cavalier King Charles Spaniel — A1882

Designs:12w, Phungsan dog. 100w, White shorthair cat. 150w, Black and white shorthair cat.

2002, Oct. 20 ***Perf. 12***

4237-4240 A1881 Set of 4 5.00 2.50

Souvenir Sheet

4241 A1882 150w multicolored 3.00 1.50
a. Inscr. "World Philatelic Exhibition Bangkok 2003" and emblem in margin 3.00 1.50

No. 4241a issued 10/4/2003.

Minerals — A1883

Designs: a, 3w, Pyrite. b, 12w, Magnetite. c, 130w, Calcite. d, 150w, Galena.

2002, Oct. 25 ***Perf. 13¼***

4242 A1883 Block of 4, #a-d 5.50 2.75

Kim Jong Il and PM Junichiro Signing Declaration — A1884

Kim Jong Il with Japanese Prime Minister Koizumi Junichiro — A1885

Japan-Korea Bilateral Declaration

No. 4246 measures 90x80mm, No. 4247 75x65mm.

2002, Oct. 25

Souvenir Sheets

4246 A1884 120w multicolored 2.00 1.00
4247 A1885 150w multicolored 3.00 1.50

Kim Il Sung's Birthplace, Mangyongdae — A1886

Kim Jong Il's Birthplace, Mt. Paektu — A1887

Kim Jong Suk's Birthplace, Hoeryong A1888

Kimilsungia A1889

Torch, Tower of Juche Idea A1890

DPRK Flag A1891

Kimjongilia A1892

Magnolia Blossom A1893

DPRK Coat of Arms A1894

Chollima Statue A1895

Victory Monument A1896

Party Founding Monument — A1897

Perf. 11½, 13¼x13½ (#4252-4253, 4256-4259)

2002, Nov. 20

4248	A1886	1w violet brn	.20	.20
4249	A1887	3w blue green	.20	.20
4250	A1888	5w olive brn	.20	.20
4251	A1889	10w dk lilac rose	.25	.20
4252	A1890	12w dk reddish brn	.25	.20
4253	A1891	20w dp blue & red	.35	.20
4254	A1892	30w brnsh red	.50	.25
4255	A1893	40w dp grnsh blue	.65	.35
4256	A1894	50w dk brown	.75	.40
4257	A1895	70w dk olive grn	1.00	.50
4258	A1896	100w brown	1.50	.75
4259	A1897	200w dk lilac rose	3.00	1.50
	Nos. 4248-4259 (12)		8.85	4.95

See No. 4877.

New Year — A1898

2003, Jan. 1 ***Perf. 13¼***

4260 A1898 3w multicolored .30 .20

A1899

Animated Film, *Antelopes Defeat Bald Eagles* — A1900

Designs: 3w, Mother antelope pleading with bald eagle stealing her baby. 50w, Antelopes uniting to defeat bald eagle. 70w, Bald eagle eating fish poisoned by antelopes. 100w, Mother antelope reunited with her child.
150w, Antelopes carrying litter full of fruit.

2003, Jan. 1
4261-4264 A1899 Set of 4 2.50 1.25

Souvenir Sheet

4265 A1900 150w multicolored 1.50 .75

Folk Festivals A1901

Designs: 3w, Mother and children greeting Full Moon (Lunar New Year, Jan. 15). 12w, Dancers with Full Moon (Lunar New Year). 40w, Two girls on swing (Spring Festival). 70w, Mother and daughter laying flowers on anti-Japanese martyrs' monument (Hangawi - Harvest Moon Festival). 140w, Peasant dance (Hangawi - Harvest Moon Festival).
112w, Wresting (Spring Festival).

2003, Jan. 20 ***Perf. 11¾***
4266-4270 A1901 Set of 5 2.75 1.50

Souvenir Sheet

4271 A1901 112w multicolored 1.50 .75

Soldier A1902

2003, Feb. 14 ***Perf. 13¼***
4272 A1902 12w multicolored .40 .20

Annual joint editorial of the three state newspapers, *Rodong Sinmun, Josoninmingum* and *Chongnyonjonwi.*

Weapons, Proclamation A1903

2003, Feb. 15
4273 A1903 30w multicolored .50 .25

North Korean withdrawal from the Nuclear Non-Proliferation Treaty.

Ode Monument — A1904

Sunrise at Mt. Paektu — A1905

2003, Feb. 16 ***Perf. 12¼x11¼***
4274 A1904 3w multicolored .30 .20

Souvenir Sheet

4275 A1905 75w multicolored 1.00 .50

Kim Jong Il, 61st Birthday.

A1906

Ships — A1907

Designs: 15w, Cargo ship *Paekmagang.* 50w, Dredger *Konsol.* 70w, Passenger ship *Undok No. 2.* 112w, Cargo ship *Piryugang.*
150w, Excursion ship *Pyongyang No. 1.*

2003, Feb. 18 ***Perf. 11¾***
4276-4279 A1906 Set of 4 3.00 1.50

Souvenir Sheet

4280 A1907 150w multicolored 1.75 .90

A1908

Cars Used by Kim Il Sung — A1909

Designs: 3w, *Zis.* 14w, *Gaz.* 70w, *Pobeda.* 90w, *Mercedes Benz.*
150w, Painting by Kim San Gon *Delaying His Urgent Journey.*

2003, Feb. 20
4281-4284 A1908 Set of 4 2.25 1.10

Souvenir Sheet

4285 A1909 150w multicolored 2.00 1.00

Book — A1910

Souvenir Sheet

2003, Mar. 15
4286 A1910 120w multicolored 1.75 .90

On the Art of Cinema, by Kim Jong Il, 30th anniv. of publication.

Army Trumpeter, Map, Soldiers Marching — A1911

2003, Mar. 16
4287 A1911 15w multicolored .30 .20

80th anniv. of Kim Il Sung's "250-mile Journey for Learning."

Soldier & Workers — A1912

2003, Mar. 29
4288 A1912 3w multicolored .20 .20

Propaganda issue: "Let us meet the requirements of Songun in ideological viewpoint, fighting spirit and way of life!"

A1913

Election of Kim Jong Il as Chairman of the DPRK National Defense Commission, 10th Anniv. — A1914

Designs: 3w, Flags, "10."
No. 4290: a, 12w, Kim Jong Il with computer. b, 70w, Kim with military officers, pointing. c, 112w, Kim, with military officers, hand raised.

2003, Apr. 9
4289 A1913 3w multicolored .20 .20

Souvenir Sheet

4290 A1914 Sheet of 3, #a.-c. 3.50 1.75

Kim Il Sung's Birthplace, Mangyongdae, *Kimsungilia* — A1915

2003, Apr. 15
4291 A1915 3w multicolored .20 .20

Day of the Sun—Kim Il Sung, 91st birth anniv.

A1916

Medals and Orders Presented to Kim Il Sung — A1917

Designs: 12w, Order of Suhbaatar (Mongolia, 1953). 35w, National Order of Grand Cross (Madagascar, 1985). 70w, Order of Lenin (USSR, 1987). 140w, Order of Playa Giron (Cuba, 1987).
120w, Kim Il Sung being presented with medal by Fidel Castro (1986).

2003, Apr. 15 ***Perf. 13¼***
4292-4295 A1916 Set of 4 3.50 1.75

Souvenir Sheet
Perf. 13¼

4296 A1917 120w multicolored 1.50 .75

Insects — A1918

Designs: a, 15w, *Pantala flavescens.* b, 70w, *Tibicen japonicus.* c, 220w, Xylotrupes dichotomus. d, 300w, *Lycaena dispar.*

2003, Apr. 20 ***Perf. 13¼***
4297 A1918 Sheet of 4, #a.-d. 9.00 4.50

Korean National Dishes — A1919

Designs: 3w, Glutinous rice cake. 30w, Thongkimchi. 70w, Sinsollo.
120w, Pyongyang cold noodles.

2003, May 1 ***Perf. 11¾***

4298-4300 A1919 Set of 3 1.50 .75

Souvenir Sheet

4301 A1919 120w multicolored 1.50 .75

Victory Monument, Battle in Musan Area — A1920

2003, May 19 ***Perf. 12¾***

4302 A1920 90w multicolored 1.25 .60

Ryangchon Temple — A1921

Designs: 3w, Manse Pavilion. 12w, Buddhist statues. 40w, Painting of Buddha with two saints. 50w, Painting of Buddha with four saints.
120w, Taeung Hall, main shrine of temple.

2003, May 30 ***Perf. 13¼***

4303-4306 A1921 Set of 4 1.75 .90

Souvenir Sheet

4307 A1921 120w multicolored 1.75 .90

Map, Song "We Are One" — A1922

2003, June 1

4308 A1922 60w multicolored 1.00 .50

Wild Animals — A1923

Designs: a, 3w, Tigers. b, 70w, Bears. c, 150w, Wild boars. d, 230w, Roe deer.

2003, June 10

4309 A1923 Sheet of 4, #a.-d. 2.25 1.10

Public Bonds of 1950, 2003 — A1924

2003, July 25 ***Perf. 13½***

4310 A1924 140w multicolored 2.25 1.10

Campaign to promote purchase of public bonds.

A1925

A1926

DPRK "Victory" in Korean War, 50th Anniv. — A1927

Designs: 3w, Distinguished Service Medal.
No. 4312: Kim Il Sung in commander's uniform.
No. 4313: a, 12w, Kim delivering radio address. 35w, Kim talking to soldiers. c, 70w, Kim ratifying armistace agreement. d, 140w, Kim in uniform.
No. 4314: a, 12w, Kim smiling, surrounded by soldiers. 35w, Kim inspecting soldier. c, 70w, Kim Il Sung, Kim Jong Il inspecting army training. d, 140w, Middle-aged Kim Il Sung in suit and tie.
No. 4315: a, 12w, Kim Jong Il receiving bouquet from female soldier. 35w, Kim Jong Il being applauded by soldiers. c, 70w, Kim Jong Il on military inspection. d, 140w, Smiling Kim Jong Il.

2003, July 27 ***Perf. 13¼***

4311 A1925 3w multicolored .20 .20

Souvenir Sheet

4312 A1926 120w multicolored 1.75 .90

Sheets of 4

Perf. 11½

4313-4315 A1927 Set of 3 12.00 6.00

Orchids — A1928

Designs: a, 3w, *Minicattleya coerulea.* b, 100w, *Phalanopsis aphrodite.* c, 150w, *Calanthe discolor.* d, 200w, *Dendrobium snowflake.*

2003, July 29 ***Perf. 13¼***

4316 A1928 Sheet of 4, #a.-d. 7.00 3.50

e. Booklet pane of 4, #4316a-4316d 7.00 —

Complete booklet, #4316e 7.50

No. 4316e contains Nos. 4316a-4316d in a horizontal strip of four, with selvage similar to that of No. 4316.

A1929

Birds — A1930

Designs: 12w, *Grus vipio.* 70w, *Nycticorax nycticorax.* 100w, *Columba livia var doestricus.* 120w, *Nymphicus hollandicus.* 150w, *Strix aluco.*
225w, *Pseudogyps africanus.*

2003, Aug. 4 ***Perf. 13¼***

4317-4321 A1929 Set of 5 6.00 3.00

Souvenir Sheet

Perf. 11¾

4322 A1930 225w multicolored 3.00 1.50

Arctic & Antarctic Animals — A1931

Designs: a, 15w, Adelie penguins *(Pygoscelis adeliae).* b, 70w, Walrus *(Odobenus rosmarus).* c, 140w, Polar bear and cubs *(Thalarctos maritimus).* d, 150w, Bowhead whale *(Balaena mysticetus).* e, 220w, Spotted seals *(Phoca largha).*

2003, Aug. 20 ***Perf. 11½***

4323 A1931 Sheet of 5, #a.-e. + label 9.00 4.50

a. Booklet pane of 5 + label —

Complete booklet 13.00

No. 4323a contains one pane, with stamps and label in same arrangement as in No. 4323, surrounded by selvage containing a distinctive arrangement of Polar animals on a primarily yellowish background.

Mushrooms — A1932

Designs: a, 3w, *Pholiota flammans.* b, 12w, *Geastrum fimbriatum.* c, 70w, *Coprinus atramentarius.* d, 130w, *Pleuotus cornucopiae.*
250w, *Elfvingia applanata.*

2003, Sep. 5 ***Perf. 13¼***

4324 A1932 Block of 4, #a-d 3.50 1.75

Souvenir Sheet

4328 A1932 250w multicolored 4.00 2.00

Korean Stamp Exhibition Hall — A1933

Korean Stamps, Interior of Hall — A1934

2003, Sep. 5

4329 A1933 3w multicolored .20 .20

4330 A1934 60w multicolored 1.00 .50

Korean Stamp Exhibition celebrating the 55th anniversary of the DPRK and the inauguration of the Korean Stamp Exhibition Hall.

A1935

A1936

55th Anniv. Founding of DPRK — A1937

Designs: 3w, DPRK Arms, Flag.
No. 4332: Kim Il Sung.
Sheets of 2 with central label: No. 4333: a, 60w, "The Birth of a New Korea" (Kim saluting marchers carrying DPRK flag). b, 60w, "In the Period of Building a New Korea" (Kim Jong Suk and factory workers). No. 4334: a, 60w, "Braving Through a Rain of Bullets Personally" (Kim in jeep in war zone). b, 60w, "Comrade Kim Il Sung, Ever-Victorious Iron-Willed Commander, Personally Commanding the Battle at Height 1211" (Kim on bluff, pointing to battlefield.) No. 4335: a, 60w, "We Trust and Follow Only You, the Leader" (Kim being greeted by villagers). b, 60w, "The Great Leader Kim Il Sung Giving On-the-Spot Guidance to the Pukchang Thermal Power Station" (Kim and factory workers). No. 4336: a, 60w, "The Victory of Korean Revolution Will Be Ensured by the Arms in Our Hand" (Kim speaking to soldiers, Kim Jong Il standing behind). b, 60w, "Keeping Up Songun Politics as All-Powerful Means" (Smiling Kim walking with soldiers symbolizing modern arms).

2003, Sep. 9 ***Perf. 11½***
4331 A1935 3w multicolored .20 .20

Souvenir Sheet
Perf. 13¼
4332 A1936 120w multicolored 2.00 1.00

Sheets of 2, #a.-b. + label
Perf. 12¼x12
4333-4336 A1937 Set of 4 6.00 3.00

Mao Zedong, 110th Birth Anniv. — A1938

No. 4337: a, 20w, Young Mao speaking at political meeting; b, 30w, Mao walking on shore with woman carrying manuscript. No. 4338: a, 30w, Mao addressing Red partisans; b, 30w, Mao (wearing trenchcoat) leading partisans in field. No. 4339: a, 20w, Mao talking with workers, soldiers; b, 30w, Mao in casual setting, leading discussion with soldiers. No. 4340: a, 30w, Mao addressing crowd in Beijing; b, 30w, Mao with people of various races and nationalities.
No. 4341: Sheet containing Nos. 4337-4338, with attached large label depicting 110 stamps picturing Mao and denominated 140w, the price for which the sheet was sold. No. 4342: Same, but containing Nos. 4339-4340.

2003, Dec. 26 ***Perf. 13¼***
Se-Tenant Pairs with Label Between
4337-4340 A1938 Set of 4 3.50 1.75

Souvenir Sheets
4341-4342 A1938 Set of 2 4.00 2.00

New Year — A1939

Design: 2w, Soldier, workers, tower.

2004, Jan. 1 ***Perf. 11½***
4343 A1939 3w multicolored .20 .20

A1940

Monkeys — A1941

Designs: 3w, *Cebus apella.* 60w, *Papio doguera.* 70w, *Cercopithecus aethiops.* 100w, *Saguinus oedipus.*
150w, *Macaca mulatta.*

2004, Jan. 1
4344-4347 A1940 Set of 4 4.00 2.00

Souvenir Sheet
4348 A1941 155w multicolored 2.50 2.00

See Nos. 4351-4355.

Lunar New Year's Day — A1942

2004, Jan. 1
4349 A1942 3w multicolored .20 .20

Souvenir Sheet

First Chinese Manned Space Flight — A1943

Designs: a, 91w, Yong Liwei, first Chinese cosmonaut (46mm diameter). b, 98w, Landing capsule, parachute, helicopter (54x45mm).

Perf. 13¼, Perf. (#4350a)
2004, Jan. 30
4350 A1943 Sheet of 2, #a.-b. 3.00 1.50
c. Booklet pane, 2 each #4350a-4350b — —
Complete booklet, #4350c —
d. #4350 with Hong Kong 2004 emblem opvt. in sheet margin 3.00 1.50

Nos. 4344-4348 with Hong Kong 2004 Emblem

2004, Jan. 30
4351-4354 A1940 Set of 4 4.00 2.00

Souvenir Sheet
4355 A1941 155w multicolored 2.50 1.25

Joint Editorial *Rodong Sinmun, Josoninmingun* and *Chongnyonjonwi* Newspapers — A1944

2004, Feb. 15 ***Perf. 13¼***
4357 A1944 3w multicolored .20 .20

A1945

Kim Jong Il, 62nd Birthday — A1946

No. 4358: 3w, Kim Jong Il's birthplace, Mt. Paektu.
No. 4359 (each 30w): a, "The Thaw of Sobaek Stream" (Spring). b, "The Thunderclap of Jong Il Peak" (Summer). c, "The Secret Camp in Autumn" (Autumn). d, "Hoarfrost in February" (Winter).

2004, Feb. 16 ***Perf. 11½***
4358 A1945 3w multicolored .20 .20

Souvenir Sheet
Perf. 13¼
4359 A1946 Sheet of 4, #a.-d. 2.00 1.00

Kim Jong Il — A1947

2004, Feb. 19 ***Perf. 13¼***
4360 A1947 120w multicolored 2.00 1.00

30th anniv, of publication of the *Program of Modelling the Whole Society on the Juche Idea.*

Rural Village A1948

Kim Il Sung and Farmers — A1949

2004, Feb. 25 ***Perf. 11½***
4361 A1948 3w multicolored .20 .20

Souvenir Sheet
Perf. 12½ x11¾
4362 A1949 120w multicolored 1.75 1.75

40th anniv. of publication of the "Theses on the Socialist Rural Question in Our Country."

Lighthouses — A1950

Designs: a, 3w, Sokgundo Lighthouse. b, 12w, Yubundo Lighthouse. c, 100w, Jangdokdo Lighthouse. d, 195w, Amryongdan Lighthouse.

2004, Mar. 20 ***Perf. 11¾x12½***
4363 A1950 Sheet of 4, #a.-d. 5.00 2.50
e. Booklet pane of 4, #4363a-4363d 5.00 —
Complete booklet, #4363e 5.50

No. 4363e contains Nos. 4363a-4363d in a horizontal strip of 4, surrounded by a seashore selvage.

A1951

Board Games — A1952

Designs: a, 3w, Korean Chess. b, 12w, Goe. c, 90w, Yut. d, 120w, Kknoni (Chinese Checkers).
98w, Playing Korean Chess.

2004, Mar. 20 ***Perf. 13¼***
4364 A1951 Sheet of 4, #a.-d. 4.00 2.00
e. Booklet pane of 5, #4364a-4364b, 4364d, 2 x 4364c 5.00 —
Complete booklet, #4363e 5.50

Souvenir Sheet

4365 A1952 98w multicolored 2.00 1.00

No. 4364e contains Nos. 4364a-4364d in a horizontal strip of 5, which includes a second copy of the 90w value, with a distinctive printed selvage.

Kim Il Sung's Birthplace, Mangyongdae — A1953

Kim Il Sung — A1954

2004, Apr. 15 ***Perf. 13¼***
4366 A1953 3w multicolored .20 .20

Souvenir Sheet
Perf. 11¾

4367 A1954 120w multicolored 1.75 .90

Kim Il Sung, 92nd birth anniv.

A1955

Tok Islands — A1956

No. 4368: a, 3w, 19th century map of Korea. b, 12w, Western island. c, 106w, Eastern island.
No. 4369: 116w, Both islands, sea gulls.

2004, Apr. 20 ***Perf. 11½***
4368 A1955 Sheet, #a.-c. + label 2.50 1.25

Souvenir Sheet
Perf.

4369 A1956 116w multicolored 2.00 1.00
a. Booklet pane of 4, #4368a-4368c, 4369 — —
Complete booklet, #4369a —

Fossils — A1957

No. 4370: a, 3w, *Calcinoplax antiqua*. b, 12w, *Podozamites lanceolatus*. c, 70w, *Comptonia naumannii*. d, 140w, *Clinocardium asagaiense*.
No. 4371: 120w, *Tingia carbonica*

2004, May 20 ***Perf. 13¼***
4370 A1957 Sheet of 4, #a.-d. 4.00 2.00
e. Booklet pane of 5, #4370a-4370d, #4371a 5.00 —
Complete booklet, #4370e 5.50 —

Souvenir Sheet
Perf. 12½

4371 A1957 120w multicolored 2.00 1.00
a. single stamp 2.00 1.00

Cacti — A1958

No. 4372: a, 70w, *Notocactus leninghausii*. b, 90w, *Echinocactus grusonii*. c, 100w, *Gymnocalycium baldianum*. d, 140w, *Mammillaria insularis*.

2004, June 2 ***Perf. 11¾x12¼***
4372 A1958 Sheet of 4, #a.-d. 5.00 2.50
a. Ovptd. "World Stamp Championship 2004" and Singapore 2004 emblem in margin 5.00 2.50

No. 4372a issued Aug. 28.

Unofficial Visit of Kim Jong Il to China

A1959

Unofficial Visit of Kim Jong Il to China — A1960

No. 4373: a, 74w, Kim Jong Il with Hu Jintao, President of the People's Republic of China.
No. 4374: a, 3w, Kim shaking hands with Hu Jintao. b, 12w, Kim with Jiang Zemin, President of China 1997-2003. c, 40w, Kim with Wu Bangguo, Chinese Communist Party leader. d, 60w, Kim clapping hands at outdoor reception.
No. 4375: a, 3w, Kim with Wen Jiabao, Premier of the State Council of the PRC. b, 12w, Kim with Jia Qinglin, Chinese Communist Party leader. c, 40w, Kim with Zeng Qinghong, Vice-President of the PRC. d, 60w, Kim visiting Tianjin.

2004, June 18 ***Perf. 13¼***

Souvenir Sheet

4373 A1959 74w multicolored 1.25 .60
a. As No. 4373, diff. (horiz.) selvage 1.25 .60

Sheets of 4, #a-d

4374-4375 A1960 Set of 2 3.50 1.75
4375e Booklet pane of 9, #4373a, 4374a-d, 4375a-d 5.00 —
Complete booklet, #4375e 5.50

No. 4373a is from the booklet No. 4375e.

WPK Flag A1961

A1962

Kim Jong Il's Appointment to the Central Committe of the Workers' Party of Korea, 40th Anniv. — A1963

No. 4377: a, 12w, Kim reading at desk. b, 100w, Kim standing in front of renderings of proposed Samjiyon Battle Site memorial.
No. 4378: a, 12w, Kim inspecting power station in Jagang Province. b, 100w, Kim with army officers.
No. 4379: a, 12w, Kim visiting the Komdok mine. b, 100w, Kim, outdoor photo portrait.
No. 4380: 130w, Kim Jong Il and Kim Il Sung.

2004, June 19
4376 A1961 3w multicolored .20 .20

Sheets of 4

4377-4379 A1962 3 Sheets, 2 ea. #a.-b. 5.00 2.50

Souvenir Sheet

4380 A1963 130w multicolored 1.25 .60

A1964

A1965

Kim Il Sung, 10th Death Anniv. — A1966

48th World Table Tennis Championships, Shanghai — A2000

Designs: 3w, Pak Young Sun, Korea. b, 5w, Mao Zedong playing table tennis at the Communist base in Yanan. c, 12w, Wang Liqin, China. d, 20w, J.O. Waldner, Sweden. e, Zhang Yining, China. f, 102w, Werner Schlager, Austria.

2005, Apr. 23 ***Perf. 11½***

4426 A2000 Sheet of 6, #a.-f. 3.00 1.50
g. Booklet pane of 6, #4426a-4426f 3.00 —
Complete booklet, #4426g 3.50

No. 4426g contains Nos. 4426a-4426f in a se-tenant horizontal strip of six, surrounded by blue selvage depicting the Shanghai 2005 emblem, stylized athletes and Korean inscription.

Pandas A2001

Designs: 15w, Panda on tree limb. 45w, Panda walking. 70w, Two pandas. 140w, Panda standing
120w, Panda with cub.

2005, May 3 ***Perf. 13¼***

4427-4430 A2001 Set of 4 4.00 .20
4430a Booklet pane of 5, #4427-4430, 4432a 4.00 —
Complete booklet, #4430a 4.50

Sheet of 5

4431 A2001 Sheet, #4427-4430, 4432a 6.00 3.00

Souvenir Sheet

4432 A2001 120w multicolored 3.00 —
a. single stamp

Nos. 4427-4430 were each issued in separate large panes. No. 4430a contains #4427-30, 4432a in a se-tenant horizontal strip of 5, with plain white marginal selvage.
For overprints, see Nos. 4451-4455.

Ecosystem of Tok Island — A2002

Designs: a, 3w, *Dianthus superbus.* b, 3w, *Eumetopia jubata.* c, 12w, Seagull. d, 50w, *Lysimachia mauritania Lam.*
e, 97w: Eastern and Western islands, Tok Island.

Perf. 11¼, Perf. (#4433e)

2005, May 5

4433 A2002 Sheet of 9, #4433e, 2 each #4433a-4433d + 2 labels 12.00 6.00
f. Booklet pane, #4433e —
g. Booklet pane of 8, 2 each #4433a-4433d, perf. 11¼ on 3 sides — —
Complete booklet, # 4433f, 4433g —

A2003

General Association of Korean Residents in Japan, 50th Anniv. — A2004

Designs: 3w, Korean family waving flag.
130w: Kim Il Sung shaking hands with man in suit.

2005, May 25 ***Perf. 13¼***

4434 A2003 3w multicolored .20 .20

Souvenir Sheet

4435 A2004 130w multicolored 1.50 .75

Fauna — A2005

Designs, each 40w: No. 4436, Korean Tiger. No. 4437, Sable.

2005, June 1

4436 40w multicolored .75 .40
4437 40w multicolored .75 .40
a. A2005 Pair, #4436-4437 with label between 2.00 1.00
b. Booklet pane, 2 #4437a 2.00 —
Complete booklet, #4437b 2.50

See Russia No. 6911.

A2006

Koguryo Historic Site — A2007

Designs: a, Tomb of a general of Koguryo. b, 70w, Tomb mural depicting hunting scene. c, 100w, Mt. Songsan fortress. d, 130w, Gilded arrowheads.
97w: Monument at Mausoleum of King Kwanggaetho.

2005, June 14

4438 A2006 Sheet of 4, #a.-d. 4.00 2.00
a. Booklet pane, #4438a-4438d, 4439a 6.00 —
Complete booklet, #4438a 6.50

Souvenir Sheet

4439 A2007 97w multicolored 2.00 1.00
a. 97w, single from souvenir sheet 2.00 1.00

No. 4438a contains #4438a-4438d in a horizontal strip of 4, with #4439a placed separately, within a 69mmx279mm sheetlet with selvage depicting hunting scene, artifacts and inscription.

Kim Chol Ju (1919-35), Brother of Kim Il Sung. — A2008

Souvenir Sheet

2005, June 14 ***Perf. 11½***

4440 A2008 170w multicolored 1.50 .75

A2009

North-South Joint Declaration, 5th Anniv. — A2010

Designs, all 112w: a, Kim Jong Il and S. Korean President Kim Dae Jung shaking hands. b, Kim Jong Il and Kim Dae Jung standing side-by-side. c, Kim Il Jong and Kim Dae Jung sitting together at table with large flower arrangement. d, Kim Dae Jong and Kim Il Jong at conference table.
167w, Kim Dae Jung and Kim Jong Il smiling, shaking hands, with representatives in background.

2005, June 15

4441 A2009 Sheet of 4, #a.-d. 6.00 3.00

Souvenir Sheet

4442 A2010 167w multicolored 2.50 1.25

A2011

Amur Tiger — A2012

Designs: a, 3w, Tiger looking left. b, 12w, Tiger growling. c, 130w, Tiger looking forward. d, 200w, Tiger growling, turned to right.
150w: Tiger with cubs.

2005, July 10 ***Perf. 11¾***

4443 A2011 Sheet of 4, #a.-d. 4.00 2.00
e. Booklet pane, #4443a-4443d 4.00 —
Complete booklet, #4443e 4.50

Souvenir Sheet

Perf. 11½

4444 A2012 150w multicolored 2.00 1.00

No. 4443e contains #4443a-4443d in a horizontal strip of 4, within selvage depicting forest skyline and inscription "Panthera tigris altaika."

Map of Korea — A2013

Souvenir Sheet

2005, July 25 *Perf. 11½*
4445 A2013 130w multicolored 1.50 .75

"June 25-July 27 - Period of Joint Anti-US Struggle" A2014

Design: 3w, Korean soldier, U.S. POWs, military cemetary, military vehicles.

2005, July 27 *Perf. 12*
4446 A2014 3w multicolored .20 .20

A2015

A2016

A2017

National Liberation, 60th Anniv. — A2018

Design: 3w, Arch of Triumph, magnolia.

No. 4448: a, 60w, Kim Il Sung receiving his father's pistol from his mother. b, 60w, Kim Il Sung founding the Juche-oriented revolutionary armed force. c, 60w, Kim Il Sung commanding the battle at Taehongdan. 60w, Kim Il Sung addressing staff on eve of final offensive against the Japanese. 102w, Kim Il Sung, WWII-era photo.

No. 4449: a, Kim Il Sung on ship en route to Wonsan Port landing. b, 60w, Kim Il Sung visiting Kangson Steel Works. c, 60w, Kim Il Sung delivering speech. d, 60w, Kim Il Sung meeting his grandparents, upon his return to Korea. e, 102w, Kim Il Sung with microphone.

No. 4450: 128w, Kim Il Sung.

2005, Aug. 15 *Perf. 13¼*
4447 A2015 3w multicolored .20 .20

Sheets of 5

4448 A2016 Sheet, #a.-e. 4.00 2.00
4449 A2017 Sheet, #a.-e. 4.00 2.00

Souvenir Sheet

4450 A2018 128w multicolored 1.50 .75

Nos. 4427-4430, 4432 Overprinted "Taipei 2000" and Emblem in Red and Blue

2005, Aug. 19 *Perf. 13¼*
4451-4454 A2001 Set of 4 4.00 2.00

Souvenir Sheet

4455 A2001 120w multicolored 2.25 1.10

18th Asian International Stamp Exhibition, Taipei.

A2019

National Costumes — A2020

Designs: a, 3w, Woman in red dress. b, 80w, Woman in blue dress. c, 100w, Woman in green dress. d, 120w, Woman in white dress with fur collar.

140w, Children.

2005, Aug. 30 *Perf. 11½*
4456 A2019 Sheet of 4, #a.-d. 3.50 1.75
4456e Booklet pane of 4, #4456a-d 3.50 —
Complete booklet, #4456e 4.00

Souvenir Sheet
Perf. 11¾

4457 A2020 140w multicolored 1.75 .90

No. 4456e contains Nos. 4456a-d in a horizontal strip of 4, without the small decorative labels that are printed below the stamps in No. 4456. The stamps are surrounded by a narrow selvage similar to that of the sheet of 4.

Korean Workers' Party, 60th Anniv. — A2021

Design: 3w, Korean soldier and workers, banners, proclamation of Joint Slogan.

2005, Sept. 8 *Perf. 13¼*
4458 A2021 3w multicolored .20 .20

A2022

A2023

A2024

A2025

Korean Workers' Party, 60th Anniv. — A2026

Design: 3w, Monument to founding of Party.

No. 4460: a, 12w, Kim Il Sung organizing Down-with-Imperialism Union. b, 30w, Kim Il Sung forming the first Juche-oriented Party organization. c, 60w, Kim Il Sung discussing a draft resolution to Communist Party leaders. d, 90w, Kim Il Sung addressing Central Committee of the Communist Party.

No. 4461: a, 12w, Kim Il Sung at bank of microphones, addressing 6th Congress of the WPK. b, 30w, Kim Il Sung and Kim Jong Il with military officers. c, 60w, Kim Jong Il inspecting Tabaksol Company, a camouflaged army unit. d, 90w, Kim Jong Il addressing crowd in stadium.

No. 4462: 120w, Kim Il Sung. No. 4463: 120w, Kim Jong Il.

2005, Oct. 10 *Perf. 13¼*
4459 A2022 3w multicolored .20 .20

Sheets of 4
Perf. 11¾

4460 A2023 Sheet, #a.-d. 2.00 1.00
4461 A2024 Sheet, #a.-d. 2.00 1.00

Souvenir Sheets
Perf. 13¼

4462 A2025 120w multicolored 1.25 .60
4463 A2026 120w multicolored 1.25 .60

Bees — A2027

Designs: a, 3w, Four bees surrounding queen. 12w, Two bees attending to larva. 128w, Bee filling comb cell with honey. 200w, Bee flying.

2005, Oct. 20 *Perf. 11½*

4464 A2027 Sheet of 4, #a.-d. 4.00 2.00
e. Booklet pane, as #4464a-4464d 4.00 —
Complete booklet, #4443e 4.50

No. 4464e contains four stamps like Nos. 4464a-4464d, but with slightly less yellow in the comb background and a slightly paler blue on the blue design elements. It bears a marginal selvage, with Korean inscription at left and three bees at right.

United Nations, 60th Anniv. A2028

2005, Oct. 24 *Perf. 13¼*

4465 A2028 15w multicolored .30 .20

A2029

Kaesong Historic Site — A2030

No 4466: a, 35w, Pogwang Hall. b, 35w, Monument to Taegakguksa. c, 35w, Pojo Hall. d, 75w, Ryongthong Temple.

No. 4467: a, 35w, Taesong Shrine. b, 35w, Myongryun Hall. c, 35w, Metal type (round). d, 75w, Sam Gate.

2005, Oct. 31 *Perf. 12*

Sheets of 4, #a.-d.

4466 A2029 multicolored 2.00 1.00
4467 A2030 multicolored 2.00 1.00

Nos. 4466-4467 each contain three non-denominated labels.

Kim Hyong Gwon Monument — A2031

Souvenir Sheet

2005, Nov. 4 *Perf. 11½*

4468 A2031 120w multicolored 1.50 .75

Kim Hyong Gwon (1905-36), uncle of Kim Il Sung.

Ulsa Treaty, Centennial A2032

2005, Nov. 17 *Perf. 11¾*

4469 A2032 12w multicolored .30 .20

Ulsa Treaty, under which Korea became a Japanese protectorate.

A2033

A2034

Kaesong Historic Site — A2035

No 4470: a, 35w, Kaesong Namdaemun. b, 35w, Mausoleum of King Kongmin. c, 35w, Sonjuk Bridge. d, 35w, Sungyang Private School. e, 35w, Anhwa Temple (Five Hundred Rahan). f, 35w, Tomb of Pak Ji Won (Yonam).

No. 4471: a, 35w, King Wanggon, founder of Kingdom of Koryo, 935 A.D., round. b, 35w, Front Gate at Mausoleum of King Wanggon. c, 75w, Mausoleum of King Wanggon.

No. 4472: a, 35w, Fortress on Mt. Taehung (North Gate). b, 35w, Marble statue of Kwanumbosal, Kwanum Temple. c, 75w, Pakyon Falls.

2005, Nov. 18

Sheet of 6, #a.-f. + 6 labels

Perf. 11½

4470 A2033 multicolored 1.50 .75

Sheet of 3, #a.-c. + 2 labels

Perf. 13¼

4471 A2034 multicolored 1.50 .75

Sheet of 3, #a.-c. + 4 labels

Perf. 12¼ (a, b); 11½ (c)

4472 A2035 multicolored 1.50 .75

Visit to DPRK by Hu Jintao, President of the People's Republic of China — A2036

Design: a, 35w, Kim Jong Il meeting with Hu Jintao. b, 35w, Kim Jong Il and Hu Jintao visiting the Taean Friendship Glass Factory. c, 35w, Kim Jong Il and Hu Jintao at state banquet. d, 102w, Kim Jong Il shaking hands with Hu Jintao.

Perf. 11½, 13¼ (#4473d)

2005, Dec. 15

Sheet of 4, #a.-d.

4473 A2036 multicolored 2.50 1.25

New Year 2006 — A2037

2006, Jan. 1 **Litho.** *Perf. 11½*

4474 A2037 3w multi .20 .20

New Year 2006 (Year of the Dog) — A2038

Various dogs: 3w, 70w.

No. 4477 — Various dogs: a, 15w. b, 100w. c, 130w.

2006, Jan. 1 *Perf. 13¼*

4475-4476 A2038 Set of 2 1.50 .55
4477 A2038 Sheet of 5, #4475-4476, 4477a-4477c 4.50 2.25
d. Souvenir sheet of 1 #4477c 2.60 1.25

A2039

League of Socialist Working Youth, 60th Anniv. — A2040

No. 4478: a, 3w, Kim Il Sung and microphone. b, 111w, Kim Il Sung and crowd. c, 150w, Kim Jong Il receiving torch.

2006, Jan. 17 *Perf. 13¼*

4478 A2039 Sheet of 3, #a-c 5.25 2.00

Souvenir Sheet

Perf. 11½x12

4479 A2040 128w multi 2.60 1.25

A2041

New Year 2006 (Year of the Dog) — A2042

Photo. & Engr.

2006, Jan. 29 *Perf. 11x11¼*

4480 A2041 12w multi .20 .20

Souvenir Sheet

Perf. 11½x11¼

4481 A2042 70w multi 1.00 .50

Down With Imperialism Union, 80th Anniv. — A2043

2006, Feb. 9 **Litho.** *Perf. 13½*

4482 A2043 3w multi .20 .20

Miniature Sheet

2006 Winter Olymics, Turin — A2044

No. 4483: a, 15w, Ice dancing. b, 85w, Ice hockey. c, 110w, Ski jumping. d, 135w, Speed skating.

2006, Feb. 10 ***Perf. 13¼***

4483 A2044 Sheet of 4, #a-d 5.00 2.50
4483e Booklet pane of 4, #4483a-4483d 5.25 —
Complete booklet, #4483e 5.25

Complete booklet sold for 362w.

A2045

Kim Jong Il, 64th Birthday — A2046

No. 4485: a, 12w, Polemonium racemosum. b, 45w, Day lily. c, 100w, Dandelion. d, 140w, Parnassia palustris.

2006, Feb. 16 ***Perf. 13½***

4484 A2045 3w multi .20 .20

Souvenir Sheet

4485 A2046 Sheet of 4, #a-d 4.25 2.10

A2047

Visit of Kim Jong Il to People's Republic of China — A2048

No. 4486 — Kim Jong Il: a, 3w, At Crop Research Institute. b, 12w, At optical fiber factory. c, 35w, At Three Gorges Dam. d, 70w, At Guangzhou Intl. Conference and Exhibition Center. e, 100w, At air conditioner factory. f, 120w, At port of Yandian.
102w, Kim Jong Il and Hu Jintao.

2006, Mar. 4 ***Perf. 12x12¼***

4486 A2047 Sheet of 6, #a-f 4.75 2.40

Souvenir Sheet

Perf. 11¾

4487 A2048 102w multi 1.50 .75

A2049

Agrarian Reform Law, 60th Anniv. — A2050

2006, Mar. 5 ***Perf. 11½***

4488 A2049 12w multi + label .20 .20

Souvenir Sheet

4489 A2050 150w multi 2.10 1.10

Souvenir Sheet

First North Korean Postage Stamps, 60th Anniv. — A2051

2006, Mar. 12 ***Perf. 11¾***

4490 A2051 158w multi 2.25 1.10

Mt. Kumgang Scenery A2052

Designs: 3w, Pibong Falls. 12w, Podok Hermitage. 35w, Sokka Peak. 50w, Jipson Peak. 70w, Chongsok Rocks, horiz. 100w, Sejon Peak, horiz. 120w, Chonhwa Rock, horiz. 140w, Piro Peak, horiz.

2006, Mar. 15 ***Perf. 11¾x12¼***

4491-4498 A2052 Set of 8 7.50 3.75

Belgica 2006 World Youth Philatelic Exhibition, Brussels A2053

Designs: No. 4499, 140w, Jules Verne (1828-1905), writer. No. 4500, 140w, Tyto alba, Volvariella speciosa, Scouting emblem. No. 4501, 140w, Disa grandiflora, Nymphalidae. No. 4502, 140w, Australopithecus afarensis, rocks. No. 4503, 140w, Alaskan malamute, Birman cat, Scouting emblem. No. 4504, 140w, Sunflowers, by Vincent Van Gogh. No. 4505, 140w, Soccer ball, chess knight, table tennis paddle and ball. No. 4506, 140w, Tursiops truncatus, Scouting emblem. No. 4507, 140w, Maglev train, horiz. No. 4508, 140w, 1962 Ernst Grube Type S 4000-1 fire truck, horiz.

2006, Apr. 13 ***Perf. 11¾***

4499-4508 A2053 Set of 10 20.00 10.00

Kim Il Sung, 94th Anniv. of Birth — A2054

2006, Apr. 15 ***Perf. 11½***

4509 A2054 3w multi + label .20 .20

Association for the Restoration of the Fatherland, 70th Anniv. A2055

2006, May 5 ***Perf. 13½***

4510 A2055 3w multi .20 .20

Pothong River Improvement Project, 60th Anniv. — A2056

2006, May 21 ***Perf. 12***

4511 A2056 12w multi .20 .20

During May-Oct. 2006 North Korean authorities surcharged approximately 100 older issues with new values to pay current postal rates. The editors are holding Nos. 4512-4611 for these issues, pending review. They would welcome any information, as well as the opportunity to examine actual stamps.

Korean Children's Union, 60th Anniv. A2057

2006, June 6 **Litho.** ***Perf. 13½***

4612 A2057 3w multi .20 .20

2006 World Cup Soccer Championships, Germany A2058

Various soccer players in action: 3w, 130w, 160w, 210w.

2006, June 9 ***Perf. 13½***

4613-4616 A2058 Set of 4 7.00 3.50
4616a Souvenir sheet, #4616 + label 3.00 1.50
4616b Booklet pane of 4, #4613-4616 7.25 —
Complete booklet, #4616b 7.25

Issued: No. 4616a, 10/21/09. Italia 2009 Intl. Philatelic Exhibition (#4616a).
Complete booklet sold for 520w.

Souvenir Sheet

Kim Chol Ju (1919-35) — A2059

2006, June 12 ***Perf. 11½x12***

4617 A2059 170w multi 2.40 1.25

Souvenir Sheet

Ri Su Bok (1933-51), War Hero and Poet — A2060

2006, July 27 ***Perf. 11¾***

4618 A2060 120w multi 1.75 .85

Miniature Sheet

Circus Performers — A2061

Designs: a, 3w, Trapeze artists (42x35mm). b, 12w, Aerial acrobatic troupe (42x35mm). c, 130w, Seesaw jumper (42x35mm). d, 200w, Juggler (42x64mm).

Perf. 11½, 11½x12 (200w)

2006, Aug. 10 **Litho.**

4619 A2061 Sheet of 4, #a-d 5.00 2.50

Korean Cuisine A2062

Designs: 3w, Kimchi. 12w, Umegi. 130w, Rice cake dumplings with bean paste. 200w, Sweet rice.

2006, Aug. 12 *Perf. 13½*

4620-4623 A2062 Set of 4 5.00 2.50
4623a Booklet pane of 4, #4620-4623 5.00 —
Complete booklet, #4623a 5.00

Sea Mammals — A2063

Designs: 3w, Megaptera nodosa. 70w, Balaenoptera musculus. 160w, Physeter catodon. 240w, Inia geoffrensis.

2006, Aug. 20 *Perf. 11¾*

4624-4627 A2063 Set of 4 6.75 3.25
4627a Booklet pane of 4, #4624-4627 6.75 —
Complete booklet, #4627a 6.75

Motorcycles A2064

Various motorcycles.

2006, Sept. 1 *Perf. 11½*

4628 Horiz. strip of 4 7.00 3.50
a. A2064 3w multi .20 .20
b. A2064 102w multi 1.40 .70
c. A2064 150w multi 2.10 1.00
d. A2064 240w multi 3.25 1.60
e. Booklet pane of 4, #4628a-4628d 7.00 —
Complete booklet, #4628e 7.00

Sinking of the General Sherman, 140th Anniv. A2065

2006, Sept. 2 Litho. *Perf. 13¼*

4629 A2065 130w multi 1.90 .95

Owls A2066

Designs: 12w, Tyto alba. 111w, Strix uralensis. 130w, Strix aluco. 160w, Nyctea scandiaca.

2006, Sept. 10 *Perf. 11¾*

4630-4633 A2066 Set of 4 5.75 3.00
4633a Booklet pane of 4, #4630-4633 5.75 —
Complete booklet, #4633a 5.75

For overprints see Nos. 4648-4651.

Souvenir Sheet

Kim Il Sung University, 60th Anniv. — A2067

2006, Oct. 1 *Perf. 11½x12*

4634 A2067 70w multi 1.00 .50

Famous Koreans A2068

Designs: 3w, Ulgi Mundok, general. 12w, So Hui (942-998), diplomat and general. 35w, Kim Ung So (1564-1624), general. 70w, Kang Kam Chan (948-1031), general. 102w, Yongae Somun, general. 130w, Ri Kyu Bo (1168-1241), poet. 160w, Mun Ik Jom (1329-98), civil official.

2006, Oct. 2 *Perf. 13½*

4635-4641 A2068 Set of 7 7.25 3.75

A2069

Down With Imperialism Union, 80th Anniv. — A2070

No. 4643: a, 70w, Kim Il Sung and followers (50x38mm). b, 102w, Kim Il Sung (46mm diameter). c, 120w, Kim Il Sung and followers on railroad track (50x38mm).

2006, Oct. 17 Litho. *Perf. 13¼*

4642 A2069 3w multi —

Souvenir Sheet

Perf. 11¾ (#4643a, 4643c), Perf.

4643 A2070 Sheet of 3, #a-c 4.25 2.10

Red Cross Society of North Korea, 60th Anniv. — A2071

2006, Oct. 18 Litho. *Perf. 13½*

4644 A2071 30w multi .45 .20

Souvenir Sheet

Secondary Education for Koreans in Japan, 60th Anniv. — A2072

2006, Oct. 21 *Perf. 13¼*

4645 A2072 110w multi 1.60 .80

Miniature Sheet

Koguryo Tombs UNESCO World Heritage Site — A2073

No. 4646 — Murals: a, 3w, King (30x42mm). b, 70w, Queen (30x42mm). c, 130w, Subak (52x34mm). d, 135w, Procession (52x34mm). e, 160w, Kitchen (52x34mm).

Perf. 13¼ (3w, 70w), 12¼x11¾

2006, Nov. 4 Litho.

4646 A2073 Sheet of 5, #a-e —

Souvenir Sheet

Joson University, 50th Anniv. — A2074

2006, Nov. 4 *Perf. 11½*

4647 A2074 110w multi + label 1.60 .80

Nos. 4630-4633 Overprinted in Gold

Methods and Perfs As Before

2006, Nov. 16

4648 A2066 12w on #4630 .20 .20
4649 A2066 111w on #4631 1.50 .75
4650 A2066 130w on #4632 1.90 .95
4651 A2066 160w on #4633 2.25 1.10
Nos. 4648-4651 (4) 5.85 3.00

Belgica 2006 World Youth Stamp Exhibition. Location of the overprint varies.

Souvenir Sheet

Wooden Sculpture Presented by People's Army Soldiers to Kim Jong Il — A2075

2006, Dec. 24 Litho. *Perf. 11½x12*

4652 A2075 130w multi 1.90 .95

New Year 2007 A2076

2007, Jan. 1 Litho. *Perf. 13½*

4653 A2076 3w multi .20 .20

New Year 2007 (Year of the Pig) A2077

Various pigs: 3w, 45w.
No. 4656 — Various pigs: a, 70w. b, 130w.

2007, Jan. 1 *Perf. 11½*

4654-4655 A2077 Set of 2 .70 .35
4656 A2077 Sheet, #4654-4655, 4656a, 4656b 3.50 1.75
c. Booklet pane, #4654-4655, 4656a, 4656b 3.50 —
Complete booklet, #4656c 3.50
d. Souvenir sheet of 1 #4656a 1.00 .50

A2078

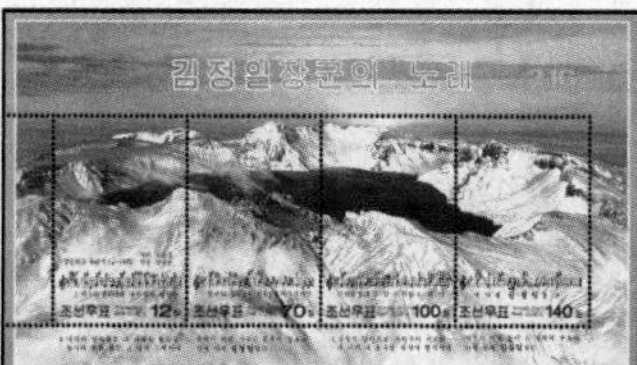
Kim Jong Il, 65th Birthday — A2079

Designs: 3w, Kimiljonghwa begonia and butterfly.
No. 4658 — Mountain, lake and musical score: a, 12w. b, 70w. c, 100w. d, 140w.

2007, Feb. 16 ***Perf. 13¼***
4657 A2078 3w multi .20 .20
4658 A2079 Sheet of 4, #a-d 4.50 2.25

Symbols of Progress A2080

2007, Feb. 28 ***Perf. 13¼***
4659 A2080 3w multi .20 .20
Annual joint editorial of state newspapers.

Butterflies — A2081

Designs: 15w, Callicore selima. 85w, Morpho rhetenor. 110w, Atrophaneura alcinous. 160w, Parnassius bremeri.

2007, Mar. 5
4660-4663 A2081 Set of 4 5.25 2.60
4663a Booklet pane of 4, #4660-4663 5.25 —
Complete booklet, #4663a 5.25

Miniature Sheet

Koguryo Tombs UNESCO World Heritage Site — A2082

No. 4664 — Anak Tomb No. 3 paintings: a, 3w, Stable (60x42mm). b, 70w, Well (60x42mm). c, 130w, Milling area (30x42mm). d, 160w, Man blowing horn (30x42mm).

2007, Mar. 10
4664 A2082 Sheet of 4, #a-d 5.25 2.60
e. Booklet pane of 4, #4664a-4664d 5.25 —
Complete booklet, #4664e 5.25

Korean National Association, 90th Anniv. — A2083

2007, Mar. 23
4665 A2083 12w multi .20 .20

Ludwig van Beethoven (1770-1827), Composer — A2084

2007, Mar. 26
4666 A2084 80w multi 1.10 .55

Mangyongdae, Birthplace of Kim Il Sung — A2085

Paintings of Kim Il Sung — A2086

Kim Il Sung and Family — A2087

No. 4668: a, 45w, The Great Leader Kim Il Sung on the 250-Mile Journey for Learning. b, 70w, The Great Leader Kim Il Sung Who Braved Through the Arduous Road of the Anti-Japanese War. c, 100w, Ever Victorious Road. d, 160w, At the Field Predicting the Rich Harvest.

2007, Apr. 15 ***Perf. 13¼***
4667 A2085 3w multi .20 .20

Perf. 11¾

4668 A2086 Sheet of 4, #a-d 5.25 2.60

Souvenir Sheet

Perf. 11¾x11½

4669 A2087 130w multi 1.90 .95
Kim Il Sung (1912-94).

Miniature Sheet

Rodents — A2088

No. 2088: a, 3w, Sciururs vulgaris. b, 12w, Muscardinus avellanarius. c, 20w, Hypogeomys antimena. d, 30w, Lemniscomys striatus. e, 40w, Pedetes capensis. f, 50w, Rattus norvegicus. g, 80w, Eliomys quercinus. h, 102w, Micromys minutus.

2007, Apr. 20 ***Perf. 13x13x12¼***
4670 A2088 Sheet of 8, #a-h, + 2 labels 4.75 2.40

Korean People's Army Soldiers and Mt. Paektu A2089

Leaders Reviewing Troops — A2090

Kim Il Sung and Kim Jong Il Reviewing Troops — A2091

No. 4672: a, 80w, Kim Il Sung and Kim Jong Il reviewing troops. b, 100w, Kim Jong Il and soldiers.

2007, Apr. 25 ***Perf. 13¼***
4671 A2089 12w multi .20 .20

Perf. 11¾

4672 A2090 Sheet of 2, #a-b 2.50 1.25

Souvenir Sheet

Perf. 12x11½

4673 A2091 120w multi 1.75 .85
Korean People's Army, 75th anniv.

Prevention of Bird Flu — A2092

2007, May 10 ***Perf. 13¼***
4674 A2092 85w multi 1.25 .60

Miniature Sheet

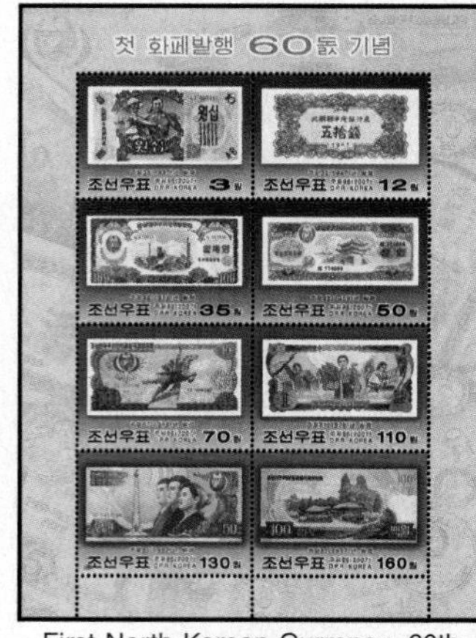
First North Korean Currency, 60th Anniv. — A2093

No. 4675 — Banknotes: a, 3w, 10-won note of 1947. b, 12w, 50-chon note of 1947. c, 35w, 100-won note of 1959. d, 50w, 10-won note of 1959. e, 70w, 10-won note of 1978. f, 110w, 1-won note of 1978. g, 130w, 50-won note of 1992. h, 160w, 100-won note of 1992.

2007, May 20 **Litho.**
4675 A2093 Sheet of 8, #a-h 8.00 4.00

Souvenir Sheet

Battle of Pochonbo, 70th Anniv. — A2094

2007, June 4 ***Perf. 11½x12***
4676 A2094 120w multi 1.75 .85

Fish A2095

Designs: 15w, Naso lituratus. 50w, Carassius auratus. 110w, A. citrinellus. 200w, Symphysodon discus.

2007, July 1 ***Perf. 13¼***
4677-4680 A2095 Set of 4 5.25 2.60
4680a Booklet pane of 4, #4677-4680 5.25 —
Complete booklet, #4680a 5.25

Self-disembowelment of Ri Jun at Hague Intl. Peace Conference, Cent. — A2096

2007, July 14
4681 A2096 110w brn & grn 1.60 .80

Fossils
A2097

Designs: 15w, Tetracorallia. 70w, Neuropteridium. 130w, Yoldia. 200w, Rhinoceros mandible.

2007, July 20

4682-4685 A2097 Set of 4 6.00 3.00
4685a Booklet pane of 4, #4682-4685 6.00 —
Complete booklet, #4685a 6.00

Miniature Sheet

Orchids — A2098

No. 4686: a, 3w, Oncidium wyattianum. b, 70w, Cymbidium Red Beauty "Carmen." c, 127w, Dendrobium thyrsifolium. d, 140w, Dendrobium Candy Stripe "Kodama."

2007, Aug. 3 ***Perf. 12¾***

4686 A2098 Sheet of 4, #a-d 4.75 2.40
e. Booklet pane of 4, #4686a-4686d 4.75 —
Complete booklet, #4686e 4.75

Women's Soccer — A2099

No. 4687 — Various women soccer players making plays: a, 12w. b, 40w. c, 70w. d, 110w. e, 140w.

2007, Sept. 10 ***Perf.***

4687 A2099 Sheet of 5, #a-e 5.25 2.60

Souvenir Sheet

4688 A2099 130w shown 1.90 .95

Miniature Sheet

Flowers — A2100

No. 4689: a, Gladiolus gandavensis. b, Iris ensata. c, Rosa hybrida. d, Nelumbo nucifera.

2007, Sept. 26 ***Perf. 13¼***

4689 A2100 30w Sheet of 4, #a-d 1.75 .85
e. Booklet pane of 4, #4689a-4689d 1.75 —
Complete booklet, #4689e 1.75

See Russia No. 7045.

Furniture and Household Furnishings — A2103

Designs: 3w, Seal box. 12w, Ornamental chest. 40w, Collapsible dressing table. 70w, Wardrobe. 110w, Chest of drawers. 130w, Chest of drawers, diff.

2007, Nov. 1 **Litho.** ***Perf. 13¼***

4694-4699 A2103 Set of 6 7.00 5.00
4699a Booklet pane of 6, #4694-4699 7.00 —
Complete booklet, #4699a 7.00

Food
A2104

Designs: 12w, Potato and rice cakes. 50w, Yongchae kimchi. 70w, Fermented flatfish. 110w, Potato cakes.

2007, Nov. 5

4700-4703 A2104 Set of 4 4.50 3.25
4703a Booklet pane of 4, #4700-4703 4.50 —
Complete booklet, #4703a 4.50

Souvenir Sheet

Summit Meeting of Pres. Kim Jong Il and South Korean Pres. Roh Moo Hyun — A2105

2007, Nov. 10 ***Perf. 11½x12***

4704 A2105 170w multi 3.00 2.50

Miniature Sheets

Scenes From Arirang Gymnastics Performance — A2106

No. 4705 — Various scenes: a, 12w. b, 50w. No. 4706 — Various scenes: a, 120w. b, 155w.

2007, Nov. 15 ***Perf. 11½***
Sheets of 2, #a-b, + Label

4705-4706 A2106 Set of 2 5.00 3.50

Paintings of Kim Dong Ho — A2107

Designs: 3w, Plowing. 12w, Weaving a Straw Mat. 70w, Thrashing. 130w, Archery.

2007, Nov. 18 ***Perf. 13¼***

4707-4710 A2107 Set of 4 4.00 2.50
4710a Booklet pane of 4, #4707-4710 4.00 —
Complete booklet, #4710a 4.00

Souvenir Sheet

Visit of Viet Nam Communist Party Secretary General Nong Duc Manh — A2108

2007, Dec. 16 ***Perf. 12x11½***

4711 A2108 120w multi 2.25 1.50

Home of Kim Jong Suk — A2109

Paintings Depicting Kim Jong Suk — A2110

No. 4713: a, 30w, Kim Jong Suk and Kim Il Sung (54x45mm). b, 70w, Kim Jong Suk (45mm diameter). c, 110w, Kim Jong Suk in battle (54x45mm).

2007, Dec. 24 ***Perf. 12x11½***

4712 A2109 3w multi .30 .20

Souvenir Sheet
Perf. 13¼, Perf. (#4713b)

4713 A2110 Sheet of 3, #a-c 4.00 3.00

New Year 2008 — A2111

2008, Jan. 1 **Litho.** ***Perf. 13¼***

4714 A2111 3w multi .20 .20

Publication of Saenal Sinmun, 80th Anniv. — A2112

2008, Jan. 15

4715 A2112 85w multi 1.25 .60

Joint Editorials of State Newspapers — A2113

Red flag in upper left corner and: No. 4716, 3w, Arms and flag of North Korea, tower. No. 4717, 3w, Soldiers. No. 4718, 12w, Soldier and flag. No. 4719, 12w, Soldiers, factories and electrical tower, horiz. 30w, Woman and food, horiz. 120w, Musicians, children playing soccer, building. 130w, Men and woman, doves, map of Korea.

2008, Jan. 30 ***Perf. 11¾***

4716-4722 A2113 Set of 7 5.75 4.00

Parrots
A2114

Designs: 15w, Melopsittacus undulatus. 85w, Agapornis roseicollis. 155w, Agapornis personata, horiz. 170w, Two Melopsittacus undulatus, horiz.

2008, Feb. 5 ***Perf. 13¼***

4723-4726 A2114 Set of 4 8.00 6.00
4726a Booklet pane of 4, #4723-4726 8.00 —
Complete booklet, #4726a 8.00

Souvenir Sheet

Naming of Kimjongilhwa Begonia, 20th Anniv. — A2115

2008, Feb. 13 ***Perf. 11½x12***

4727 A2115 85w multi 1.75 1.25

A2116

Flowers — A2117

Designs: 3w, Pyrethrum hybridum.
No. 4729: a, 12w, Tulipa gesneriana (30x42mm). b, 70w, Adonis amurensis (30x42mm). c, 120w, Mathiola incana (30x42mm). d, 155w, Kimjongilhwa begonia (44mm diameter)

2008, Feb. 16 ***Perf. 13¼***
4728 A2116 3w multi .40 .20
4729 A2117 Sheet of 4, #a-d 6.50 4.50

Kim Jong Il, 66th birthday.

Kim Il Sung Birthplace Type of 2002

2008, Mar. 15 **Litho.** ***Perf. 11½***
4730 A1886 3w red .40 .20

Miniature Sheet

Publication of "On the Art of Cinema," by Kim Jong Il, 35th Anniv. — A2118

No. 4731 — Various actors and actresses: a, 3w, Musician. b, 85w, Man holding gun. c, 135w, Martial artist. d, 170w, Man, woman and children.

2008, Mar. 15 ***Perf. 13¼***
4731 A2118 Sheet of 4, #a-d 5.50 2.75

250-Mile Journey for Learning, 85th Anniv. — A2119

2008, Mar. 16 ***Perf. 12***
4732 A2119 15w multi .40 .20

2008 Summer Olympics, Beijing — A2120

No. 4733: a, 3w, Soccer. b, 12w, Basketball. c, 30w, Tennis. d, 70w, Table tennis.

2008, Mar. 28 ***Perf. 13¼***
4733 A2120 Block or horiz. strip of 4, #a-d 2.25 1.10

Famous Men — A2121

Designs: 85w, Choe Yong (1316-88), military leader. 160w, Ho Jun (1546-1615), doctor.

2008, Mar. 29 ***Perf. 12***
4734-4735 A2121 Set of 2 3.50 1.75

Election of Kim Jong Il as Chairman of National Defense Commission, 15th Anniv. — A2122

2008, Apr. 9 ***Perf. 13¼***
4736 A2122 12w multi .40 .20

International Friendship Exhibition A2124

Gifts to Kim Il Sung: 3w, Pitcher and oil lamp. 85w, Painting of rooster. 155w, Throne. 135w, Vase with two handles.

2008, Apr. 15 **Litho.** ***Perf. 11½***
4738-4740 A2124 Set of 3 3.50 1.75

Souvenir Sheet

4741 A2124 135w multi 2.25 1.25

North-South Joint Conference, 60th Anniv. — A2125

2008, Apr. 21 ***Perf. 12***
4742 A2125 12w gray green .40 .20

Mushrooms A2126

Designs: 12w, Amanita muscaria. 50w, Armillariella mellea. 135w, Macrolepota procera. 155w, Tricholoma terreum.

2008, May 8 ***Perf. 11½***
4743-4746 A2126 Set of 4 5.50 3.25
4746a Booklet pane of 4, #4743-4746 5.50 —
Complete booklet, #4746a 5.50

Buildings on Mt. Ryongak A2127

Designs: 35w, Two buildings. 155w, Building and wall.

2008, May 25 ***Perf. 13¼***
4747-4748 A2127 Set of 2 3.00 1.75

Musical Instruments — A2128

Designs: 15w, Hyangbipha (stringed instrument). 50w, Phiri (contrabassoon). 120w, Jangsaenap (oboe). 160w, Kayagum (zither), horiz.

2008, June 1 ***Perf. 13¼***
4749-4752 A2128 Set of 4 5.50 3.25
4752a Booklet pane of 4, #4749-4752 5.50 —
Complete booklet, #4752a 5.50

Opera Scenes and Scores — A2129

Designs: 3w, Sea of Blood. 12w, The Flower Girl. 85w, The True Daughter of the Party. 120w, Tell Oh Forest. 155w, The Song of Mt. Kumgang.

2008, June 5 ***Perf. 12x11½***
4753-4757 A2129 Set of 5 5.75 4.00

North Korea No. 1 and Romania No. 1 — A2130

2008, June 20 ***Perf. 12¼x11¾***
4758 A2130 85w multi 1.50 .80

EFIRO 2008 Intl. Stamp Exhibition, Bucharest, Romania.

Capture of the USS Pueblo, 40th Anniv. — A2131

2008, June 25 ***Perf. 12¼x11¾***
4759 A2131 12w multi .40 .20

Souvenir Sheet

Olympic Torch Relay in Pyongyang — A2132

2008, June 26 ***Perf. 11¾x12¼***
4760 A2132 120w multi 2.25 1.10

Minerals — A2133

Designs: 12w, Serpentine. 75s, Copper pyrite. 135w, Sphalerite. 155w, Molybdenite.

2008, July 5 ***Perf. 12¼x11¾***
4761-4764 A2133 Set of 4 6.00 3.50
4764a Booklet pane of 4, #4761-4764 6.00 —
Complete booklet, #4764a 6.00

Souvenir Sheets

A2134

A2135

Korean War Ceasefire, 55th Anniv. — A2136

No. 4765: a, 3w, Kim Il Sung leading troop crossing of Han River. b, 120w, Kim Il Sung with troops.

No. 4766: a, 35w, Kim Il Sung and seated troops. b, 155w, Celebration.

85w, Kim Il Sung at battleground.

2008, July 27 ***Perf. 12x11½***

4765 A2134 Sheet of 2, #a-b 2.00 1.25
4766 A2135 Sheet of 2, #a-b 3.00 1.75

Perf. 11½

4767 A2136 85w multi 1.50 .85

Souvenir Sheet

Jong Il Peak, 20th Anniv. of Renaming — A2137

2008, Aug. 9 ***Perf. 13¼***

4768 A2137 120w multi 2.25 1.25

Food A2138

Designs: 3w, Rice and wormwood cakes. 70w, Rice cakes. 135w, Pancakes. 155w, Garlic in soy sauce.

2008, Aug. 20 **Litho.** ***Perf. 13¼***

4769-4772 A2138 Set of 4 5.50 3.25
4772a Booklet pane of 4, #4769-4772 5.50 —
Complete booklet, #4772a 5.50

A2139

Songun Revolutionary Leadership — A2140

2008, Aug. 25

4773 A2139 12w multi .20 .20

Souvenir Sheet

4774 A2140 135w multi 2.25 1.25

Miniature Sheet

Koguryo Tombs UNESCO World Heritage Site — A2141

No. 4775 — Anak Tomb No. 3 paintings: a, 3w, Mask dance (60x42mm). b, 90w, Janghaedok, aide to King Kogukwon (30x42mm). c, 120w, Garage (60x42mm). d, 155w, Stable (60x42mm).

2008, Sept. 2 **Litho.** ***Perf. 13¼***

4775 A2141 Sheet of 4, #a-d, + label 5.50 3.25
e. Booklet pane of 4, #4775a-4775d 5.50 —
Complete booklet, #4775e 5.50

A2142

Flag A2143

2008, Sept. 9 ***Perf. 11½***

4776 A2142 3w multi .40 .20
4777 A2143 155w multi 2.50 1.50

See No. 4876.

A2144

Creation of North Korea, 60th Anniv. — A2145

Designs: 3w, Chollima Statue, flag of North Korea, city and flowers. 12w, Torch, flag of the Supreme Commander, people. 70w, Soldiers. 120w, People on horses. 160w, Handshake.

155w, Creation of National Flag and Arms.

2008, Sept. 9 ***Perf. 13¼***

4778-4782 A2144 Set of 5 5.50 3.50

Souvenir Sheet

4783 A2145 155w multi 2.50 1.25

Transportation — A2146

Designs: No. 4784, 680w, Niña, ship of Christopher Columbus. No. 4785, 680w, 1910 Russian steam engine. No. 4786, 680w, Hindenburg over Lake Constance. No. 4787, 680w, Siberian husky dog sled team. No. 4788, 680w, Ivan Basso, cyclist. No. 4789, 680w, Mercedes-Benz-Mets LF 16 fire truck. No. 4790, 680w, Two Ferrari Enzos. No. 4791, 680w, Eurostar train. No. 4792, 680w, Concorde. No. 4793, 680w, Laika the dog and Sputnik 2.

2008, Sept. 15 ***Perf.***

4784-4793 A2146 Set of 10 160.00 125.00

Nos. 4784-4793 each were printed in sheets of 2.

Souvenir Sheet

Salvelinus Malma — A2147

2008, Oct. 2 **Litho.** ***Perf. 13¼***

4794 A2147 135w multi 1.90 .95

Miniature Sheet

Moran Hill, Pyongyang — A2148

No. 4795: a, 3w, Small shelter and bridge. b, 45w, Large shelter and walkway. c, 100w, Flora with small shelter, bridges and Pyongyang in distance. d, 135w, Building with steps.

2008, Oct. 20

4795 A2148 Sheet of 4, #a-d 4.25 2.50

Introduction of Compulsory Secondary Education, 50th Anniv. — A2149

2008, Nov. 1

4796 A2149 12w multi .40 .20

Soldier and Flag A2150

Woman in Bean Field A2151

2008, Nov. 17

4797 A2150 12w multi .30 .20
4798 A2151 85w multi 1.25 .60

Furniture A2152

Designs: 50w, Haeju table. 70w, Inkstone table. 120w, Dressing table with drawer. 170w, Jewel box.

2008, Dec. 3

4799-4802 A2152 Set of 4 5.75 3.00
4802a Booklet pane of 4, #4799-4802 5.75 —
Complete booklet, #4802a 5.75

Souvenir Sheet

Ulmil Pavilion, Moran Hill, Pyongyang — A2153

Litho. With Three-Dimensional Plastic Affixed

2008, Dec. 15 ***Perf. 13¼***

Without Gum

4803 A2153 85w multi 2.00 1.00

New Year 2009 A2154

2009, Jan. 1 Litho. *Perf. 11½*

4804 A2154 3w multi .40 .20

A2155

Red Guards, 50th Anniv. — A2156

2009, Jan. 14 ***Perf. 11¾***

4805 A2155 12w multi .40 .20

Souvenir Sheet

4806 A2156 160w multi 2.50 1.60

Traditional Games — A2157

Designs: 3w, Tug-of-war. 120w, Knee fighting.

2009, Jan. 25 ***Perf. 13¼***

4807-4808 A2157 Set of 2 2.00 1.25

Kim Jong Il, 67th Birthday A2158

Unnamed butterfly and flowers: 3w, Crinum bracteatum. 12w, Begonia. 120w, Callistemon phoeniceus. 160w, Plumeria rubra.

2009, Feb. 16 ***Perf. 11¾***

4809-4812 A2158 Set of 4 4.50 2.50

Souvenir Sheet

Proclamation of Juche Model for Society, 50th Anniv. — A2159

2009, Feb. 19 ***Perf. 11½x12***

4813 A2159 170w multi 2.75 1.50

Souvenir Sheets

A2160

A2161

A2162

Joint Editorials of State Newspapers — A2163

No. 4814: a, 3w, Torch, Chollima statue. b, 170w, Symbols of industry and transportation.
No. 4815: a, 12w, Food crops, canned foods, city. b, 150w, Musical instruments, sheet music, orchestra, soccer players.
No. 4816: a, 30w, Soldiers, flag, ships, airplanes and missiles. b, 120w, Soldiers, flags, city.
No. 4817: a, 80w, Map of Korea, text. b, 100w, Hands crushing bomb.

2009, Feb. 22 ***Perf. 11½***

4814 A2160 Sheet of 2, #a-b, + 2 labels 2.75 1.75
4815 A2161 Sheet of 2, #a-b, + 2 labels 2.50 1.50
4816 A2162 Sheet of 2, #a-b, + 2 labels 2.25 1.50
4817 A2163 Sheet of 2, #a-b, + 2 labels 2.75 1.75
Nos. 4814-4817 (4) 10.25 6.50

Souvenir Sheets

China 2009 World Stamp Exhibition, Luoyang — A2164

No. 4818: a, 3w, Flowers. b, 100w, Flowers, diff.
No. 4819: a, 12w, Statue of horse. b, 90w, Building, steps, sculpture.

2009, Feb. 25 ***Perf. 11¾***

Sheets of 2, #a-b

4818-4819 A2164 Set of 2 4.50 2.00
4819c Booklet pane of 4, #4818a-4818b, 4819a-4819b 4.50 —
Complete booklet, #4819c 4.50

March 1 Uprising Against Japan, 90th Anniv. — A2165

2009, Mar. 1 ***Perf. 12¼x11¾***

4820 A2165 90w multi 1.50 1.00

Intl. Women's Day, Cent. — A2166

2009, Mar. 8 ***Perf. 13¼***

4821 A2166 35w multi .50 .30

Gifts to Kim Il Sung — A2167

Designs: 3w, Painting of horses. 12w, Fossil fish. 140w, Rifle. 150w, Bear skin.

2009, Apr. 15 ***Perf. 13¼***

4822-4825 A2167 Set of 4 4.75 3.00

Central Zoo, Pyongyang, 50th Anniv. A2168

Birds: 12w, Anthropoides paradisea. 70w, Accipiter gentilis. 120w, Larus argentatus. 140w, Balearica pavonina.

2009, Apr. 30 ***Perf. 11¾x12¼***

4826-4829 A2168 Set of 4 5.25 3.25
4829a Booklet pane of 4, #4826-4829 5.25 —
Complete booklet, #4829a 5.25

Central Botanical Garden, Pyongyang, 50th Anniv. A2169

Trees: 3w, Catalpa ovata. 50w, Betula platyphylla. 120w, Juglans cordiformis. 160w, Metasequoia glyptostroboides.

2009, Apr. 30 ***Perf. 13¼***

4830-4833 A2169 Set of 4 5.25 3.25
4833a Booklet pane of 4, #4830-4833 5.25 —
Complete booklet, #4833a 5.25

Sports A2170

Designs: 12w, Baseball. 90w, Bowling. 160w, Fencing. 200w, Golf.

2009, May 2

4834-4837 A2170 Set of 4 6.75 3.25
4837a Booklet pane of 4, #4834-4837 6.75 —
Complete booklet, #4837a 6.75

No. 4189a Surcharged in Gold

No. 4838: a, 20w on 40ch, LZ1. b, 40w on 80ch, LZ120. c, 1w+109w on 1.20w, Zeppelin NT. d, 2w+168w on 2.40w, Zeppelin NT, diff.

Method and Perf As Before

2009, May 5

4838 A1852 Sheet of 4, #a-d 5.25 3.25

Naposta '09 and IBRA '09, Essen, Germany. On Nos. 4838c and 4838d, the obliterator covers the part of the original denomination expressed in chon.

Children's Union Camp A2171

Children: 3w, Mountaineering. 80w, Collecting butterflies. 120w, At campfire. 170w, At beach.

2009 **Litho.** ***Perf. 11½***

4839-4842 A2171 Set of 4 5.75 3.25
4842a Booklet pane of 4, #4839-4842 5.75 —
Complete booklet, #4842a 5.75
4842b Souvenir sheet of 4, #4839-4842 5.75 3.25

Issued: Nos. 4839-4842, 4842a, 5/6; No. 4842b, 5/14. Hong Kong 2009 Intl. Stamp Exhibition (#4842b).

Souvenir Sheet

Battle of Musan, 70th Anniv. — A2172

2009, May 22 ***Perf. 13¼***

4843 A2172 120w multi 2.50 1.25

Miniature Sheet

Kim Jong Il as Member of Central Committee of Workers' Party, 45th Anniv. — A2173

No. 4844 — Kim Jong Il: a, 3w, At desk. b, 12w, At machine shop. c, 120w, Wearing white lab jacket. d, 170w, Looking inside cooking pot.

2009, June 19 ***Perf. 11¾***

4844 A2173 Sheet of 4, #a-d 5.00 3.00

Universal Postal Union, 135th Anniv. — A2174

2009, June 20 ***Perf. 13¼***

4845 A2174 50w multi .90 .50

Insects A2175

Designs: 50w, Vespa mandarinia, rose. 90w, Cicindela japonica, dandelion. 120w, Locusta migratoria, plant. 140w, Aphaenogaster famelica, mushroom.

2009, July 1 ***Perf. 11½***

4846-4849 A2175 Set of 4 6.00 4.00
4849a Booklet pane of 4, #4846-4849 6.00 —
Complete booklet, #4849a 6.00

Okryu Restaurant, Pyongyang — A2176

Renovated Pyongyang Buildings — A2177

No. 4851: a, 3w, Kim Chaek University Library (35x28mm). b, 70w, Taedongmun Theater (35x28mm). c, 90w, Chongryu Restaurant (70x28mm). d, 150w, Pyongyang Grand Theater (70x28mm).

2009, July 2 ***Perf. 13¼***

4850 A2176 12w multi .30 .20

Perf. 11½

4851 A2177 Sheet of 4, #a-d 4.75 2.75

Miniature Sheet

Eternal Sun of Juche — A2178

No. 4852 — Paintings: a, 12w, The Great Leader Kim Il Sung Drawing the Brush Into Our Party's Emblem. b, 50w, First Military Flag. c, 70w, Birth. d, 140w, Every Field With Bumper Harvest.

2009, July 8 ***Perf. 13¼***

4852 A2178 Sheet of 4, #a-d 4.50 2.75

Nurse and Child A2179

Ambulance and Hospital — A2180

2009, July 25

4853 A2179 12w multi .30 .20
4854 A2180 150w multi 2.25 1.50

Souvenir Sheet

Launch of Kwangmyongsong 2 Rocket — A2181

2009, July 27 ***Perf. 11½x12***

4855 A2181 120w multi 2.25 1.25

Souvenir Sheet

Northern Area Victory Monument, Hamgyong Province — A2182

2009, Aug. 3 ***Perf. 13¼***

4856 A2182 120w multi 2.25 1.25

Musical Instruments A2183

Designs: 12w, Saenap. 80w, Drum. 140w, Sogoghu. 170w, Flute.

2009, Aug. 5 **Litho.**

4857-4860 A2183 Set of 4 5.75 3.00

150-Day Innovation Campaign — A2184

2009, Aug. 10

4861 A2184 12w multi .30 .20

Fish A2185

Ships and: 15w, Theragra chalcogramma. 60w, Cyprinus carpio. 140w, Euthynnus pelamis. 160w, Mugil cephalus.

2009, Sept. 1

4862-4865 A2185 Set of 4 5.50 3.25
4865a Booklet pane of 4, #4862-4865 5.50 —
Complete booklet, #4865a 5.50

Miniature Sheets

Intl. Year of Astronomy — A2186

No. 4866, 95w: a, Chollima Statue, solar eclipse. b, Galileo Galilei, telescope, planets, satellite.
No. 4867, 95w: a, Rabbits, solar eclipse. b, Planets, galaxy.
No. 4868, 95w: a, Dogs, total solar eclipse. b, Chomsongdae Observatory.

2009, Aug. 29 **Litho.** ***Perf. 13½***

Sheets of 2, #a-b, + 2 Labels

4866-4868 A2186 Set of 3 8.00 6.00
4868c Souvenir sheet of 1, #4868a 1.25 .80
4868d Booklet pane of 6, #4866a-4866b, 4867a-4867b, 4868a-4868b 8.00 —
Complete booklet, #4868d 8.00

Souvenir Sheets

A2187

Year of Friendship With People's Republic of China — A2188

No. 4869: a, #3287c, 3384, 3716. b, #3563, 4374b, 4473c.
No. 4870: a, Five stamps. b, Six stamps.

2009, Sept. 2 ***Perf. 13½***

4869 A2187 60w Sheet of 2, #a-b 2.00 1.00
4870 A2188 60w Sheet of 2, #a-b 2.00 1.00

Miniature Sheet

Birdpex 2010, Antwerp, Belgium — A2189

No. 4871: a, 12w, Coturnicops exquisitus. b, 90w, Porzana pusilla. c, 170w, Porzana fusca.

2009, Sept. 12 ***Perf. 11½***

4871 A2189 Sheet of 5, #4871c, 2 each #4871a-4871b, + label 5.25 2.60
d. Booklet pane of 3, #4871a-4871c 4.00 —
Complete booklet, #4871d 4.00

Souvenir Sheet

Intl. Red Cross and Red Crescent Year — A2190

No. 4872 — Flags of Red Cross, North Korea and: a, 75w, Jean-Henri Dunant, founder of Red Cross. b, 95w, Disaster risk reduction. c, 95w, First aid.

2009, Sept. 21 *Perf. 13½*

4872 A2190 Sheet of 3, #a-c 3.75 1.90

Souvenir Sheet

Kim Jong Suk (1917-49), Mother of Kim Jong Il — A2191

No. 4873: a, 90w, Portrait (33x45mm). b, 100w, Kim Jong Suk with troops, horiz. (57x36mm).

2009, Sept. 22

4873 A2191 Sheet of 2, #a-b 2.75 1.40

Miniature Sheet

People's Republic of China, 60th Anniv. — A2192

No. 4874: a, 10w, Chinese President Hu Jintao. b, 67w, Chinese astronauts. c, 67w, National Stadium, Beijing. d, 84w, National Grand Theater, Beijing.

2009, Oct. 1

4874 A2192 Sheet of 4, #a-d 3.50 2.00

Worldwide Fund for Nature (WWF) — A2193

No. 4875 — Platalea minor and: a, Snail. b, Fish. c, Crab. d, Shrimp.

2009, Oct. 5 *Perf. 13½*

4875 Horiz. strip of 4 5.50 2.75
a. A2193 3w multi .20 .20
b. A2193 12w multi .20 .20
c. A2193 99w multi 1.40 .70
d. A2193 266w multi 3.75 1.90
e. Sheet of 8, 2 each #4875a-4875d, + label 11.00 5.50

Flag and Torch Types of 2002-08

2009, Oct. 15 Litho. *Perf. 11½*

4876 A2142 10w multi .20 .20

Perf. 13¼

4877 A1890 30w multi .45 .20

Reptiles — A2194

Designs: 15w, Chamaeleo jacksonii. 50w, Naja naja. 110w, Caretta caretta, horiz. 160w, Crocodylus niloticus, horiz.

2009, Oct. 20

4878-4881 A2194 Set of 4 4.75 2.40
4881a Booklet pane of 4, #4878-4881 4.75 —
Complete booklet, #4881a 4.75

Miniature Sheets

Lighthouses — A2195

No. 4882: a, Cape Palliser Lighthouse, New Zealand, and Sousa chinensis. b, Tater Du Lighthouse, United Kingdom, and Mary Rose. c, Hornby Lighthouse, Australia, and Passat, Germany. d, Rubjerg Knude Lighthouse, Denmark, and Wappen von Hamburg.

No. 4883: a, Bengtskär Lighthouse, Finland, and Phoebastria albatrus. b, Fanad Lighthouse, Ireland, and Bolma rugosa. c, Cordouan Lighthouse, France, and Sterna fuscata. d, Brandaris Lighthouse, Netherlands, and Pleurotomaria africana.

2009, Oct. 24 Litho. *Perf. 13x13½*

4882 A2195 760w Sheet of 4, #a-d 42.50 42.50
e. Souvenir sheet of 2 #4882a 21.00 21.00
f. Souvenir sheet of 2 #4882b 21.00 21.00
g. Souvenir sheet of 2 #4882c 21.00 21.00
h. Souvenir sheet of 2 #4882d 21.00 21.00
4883 A2195 760w Sheet of 4, #a-d 42.50 42.50
e. Souvenir sheet of 2 #4883a 21.00 21.00
f. Souvenir sheet of 2 #4883b 21.00 21.00
g. Souvenir sheet of 2 #4883c 21.00 21.00
h. Souvenir sheet of 2 #4883d 21.00 21.00

Lighthouses Type of 2009

Miniature Sheets

No. 4884: a, Cape St. Vincent Lighthouse, Portugal, and Sula bassana. b, Europa Point Lighthouse, Gibraltar, and Lambis scorpio. c, Vorontsov Lighthouse, Ukraine, and Grampus griseus. d, Gelendzhik Lighthouse, Russia, and Gibbula magus.

No. 4885: a, Hoy High Lighthouse, Scotland, and Delphinus delphis. b, Lindesnes Lighthouse, Norway, and Stenella coeruleoalba. c, Reykjanesviti Lighthouse, Iceland, and Chlamys varia. d, Seal Point Lighthouse, South Africa, and Chroicocephalus ridibundus.

2009, Oct. 24 Litho. *Perf. 13x13½*

4884 A2195 760w Sheet of 4, #a-d 42.50 42.50
e. Souvenir sheet of 2 #4884a 21.00 21.00
f. Souvenir sheet of 2 #4884b 21.00 21.00
g. Souvenir sheet of 2 #4884c 21.00 21.00
h. Souvenir sheet of 2 #4884d 21.00 21.00
4885 A2195 760w Sheet of 4, #a-d 42.50 42.50
e. Souvenir sheet of 2 #4885a 21.00 21.00
f. Souvenir sheet of 2 #4885b 21.00 21.00
g. Souvenir sheet of 2 #4885c 21.00 21.00
h. Souvenir sheet of 2 #4885d 21.00 21.00

Souvenir Sheet

Repatriation of Korean Nationals in Japan, 50th Anniv. — A2196

2009, Dec. 16 Litho. *Perf. 11½x12*

4887 A2196 160w multi 2.25 1.10

Souvenir Sheet

Kim Jong Il and Workers — A2198

2009, Dec. 31 Litho. *Perf. 13¼*

4889 A2198 100w multi 1.40 .70

End of Juche 98.

New Year 2010 A2199

2010, Jan. 1 *Perf. 13¼*

4890 A2199 10w multi .20 .20

Tigers A2200

Tiger and: 30w, Sun. 67w, Tree. 171w, Tiger and cubs, horiz.

2010, Jan. 5 Litho. *Perf. 11¾x12¼*

4891-4892 A2200 Set of 2 1.40 .70
4892a Booklet pane of 4, 2 each #4891-4892 3.00 —
Complete booklet, #4892a 3.00

Souvenir Sheet

Litho. with Three-Dimensional Plastic Affixed

Perf. 13¼

Without Gum

4893 A2200 171w multi 2.40 1.25

Complete booklet sold for 213w. No. 4893 contains one 60x42mm stamp.

Wildlife A2201

Designs: 35w, Ailuropoda melanoleuca. 60w, Aix galericulata. 80w, Lagenorhynchus obliquidens. 110w, Panthera pardus.

2010, Jan. 30 Litho. *Perf. 13¼*

4894-4897 A2201 Set of 4 4.00 2.00

Miniature Sheet

2010 Winter Olympics, Vancouver — A2202

No. 4898: a, 10w, Ice hockey. b, 40w, Figure skating. c, 50w, Speed skating. d, 70w, Skiing.

2010, Feb. 1 *Perf. 13*

4898 A2202 Sheet of 8, 2 each #a-d 4.75 4.75

See No. 4919.

Kim Jong Il, 68th Birthday — A2203

No. 4899: a, 10w, Impatiens sultanii Royal Rose. b, 50w, Gazania hybrida. c, 70w, Paeonia suffructicosa. d, 110w, Bougainvillea glabra Sanderiana.

2010, Feb. 16 *Perf. 11½*

4899 A2203 Vert. strip or block of 4, #a-d, + 8 labels 3.50 1.75
e. Booklet pane of 4, #4899a-4899d, + 8 labels 3.75 —
Complete booklet, #4899e 3.75

Complete booklet sold for 259w.

Miniature Sheet

Joint Editorials of State Newspapers — A2204

No. 4900: a, 10w, People, soldier, Party Founding Monument, flowers. b, 20w, Woman, city, manufactured items. c, 30w, Woman carrying crops, vegetables. d, 57w, Worker, factory, train, dam. e, 67w, Soldiers. f, 95w, People holding flag showing mpa of unified Korea. g, 125w, Doves, map showing unified Korea.

2010, Feb. 20 ***Perf. 13¼***

4900 A2204 Sheet of 7, #a-g, + 2 labels 5.75 3.00

A2205

Anti-Imperialism Posters A2206

2010, Mar. 5

4901 A2205 76w multi 1.10 .55
4902 A2206 95w multi 1.40 .70

Cats A2207

Designs: 10w, Cat, chicks. 70w, Cats, flower, butterfly. 133w, Cat, mouse. 170w, Cat, kittens, ball of yarn.

2010, Mar. 25 ***Perf. 11½***

4903-4906 A2207 Set of 4 5.50 2.75
4906a Booklet pane of 4, #4903-4906 5.75 —
Complete booklet, #4906a 5.75

Complete booklet sold for 402w.

Souvenir Sheet

Birds — A2208

No. 4907: a, 30w, Brachyramphus perdix. b, 125w, Gallinago solitaria. c, 133w, Porzana paykullii.

2010, Apr. 9

4907 A2208 Sheet of 3, #a-c, + 3 labels 4.00 2.00
d. Booklet pane of 3, #4907a-4907c 4.25 —
Complete booklet, #4907d 4.25

Antverpia 2010 International Philatelic Exhibition, Antwerp. Complete booklet sold for 307w.

Gifts to Kim Il Sung A2209

Designs: 10w, Eagle figurine. 30w, Crane figurine. 95w, Tiger painting. 152w, Sea turtle figurine, horiz.

2010, Apr. 15 ***Perf. 13¼***

4908-4911 A2209 Set of 4 4.00 2.00

Orchids and Insects A2210

Designs: 30w, Sophronitella brevipenduncu-lata, bee. 80w, Epidendrum radiatum, dragonfly. 120w, Cymbidium Lillian Stewart "Red Carpet," bee. 152w Dendrobium hybrid, butterfly.

2010, Apr. 20 ***Perf. 11½***

4912-4915 A2210 Set of 4 5.50 2.75
4915a Booklet pane of 4, #4912-4915 5.75 —
Complete booklet, #4915a 5.75

Nos. 4912-4915 each were printed in sheets of 5 + label. Complete booklet sold for 401w.

Souvenir Sheet

Expo 2010, Shanghai — A2211

No. 4916: a, 10w, Chollima statue, city, flowers. b, 80w, Children watering plant, wind turbines, wildlife.

2010, May 1 **Litho.**

4916 A2211 Sheet of 2, #a-b, + 2 labels 1.25 .65

Miniature Sheet

Table Tennis — A2212

No. 4917: a, 10w, Man with green shirt. b, 30w, Woman with red shirt. c, 95w, Woman with blue shirt. d, 152w, Man with pink shirt.

2010, May 10 ***Perf.***

4917 A2212 Sheet of 4, #a-d 4.00 2.00
e. Booklet pane of 4, #4917a-4917d 4.25 —
Complete booklet, #4917e 4.25

Complete booklet sold for 306w.

Joint Slogans — A2213

2010, May 12 ***Perf. 11½***

4918 A2213 10w multi .20 .20

Miniature Sheet
No. 4898 With Flags of Countries Winning Depicted Events Added at Left of Athlete

No. 4919: a, 10w, Ice hockey, flag of Canada. b, 40w, Figure skating, flag of People's Republic of China. c, 50w, Speed skating, flag of Netherlands. d, 50w, Speed skating, flag of Czech Republic. e, 70w, Skiing, flag of Italy. f, 70w, Skiing, flag of Germany.

2010, May 25 ***Perf. 13***

4919 A2202 Sheet of 8, #4919c-4919f, 2 each #4919a-4919b 4.75 4.75

Souvenir Sheet

Dinosaurs — A2214

No. 4920: a, 10w, Brontosaurus. b, 125w, Allosaurus. c, 152w, Pterodactylus.

2010, June 16 ***Perf. 12¾***

4920 A2214 Sheet of 3, #a-c, + label 4.00 2.00
d. Booklet pane of 3, #4920a-4920c 4.25 —
Complete booklet, #4920d 4.25

Complete booklet sold for 306w.

2010 World Cup Soccer Championships, South Africa — A2215

No. 4921 — Shirt colors of soccer players: a, 20w, Green, yellow. b, 57w, Yellow, blue. c, 190w, Red, white.
114w, Yellow, white.

2010, May 31 ***Perf. 13¼***

4921 A2215 Sheet of 3, #a-c, + 3 labels 3.75 1.90

Souvenir Sheet

4922 A2215 114w multi 1.60 .80
a. Booklet pane of 4, #4921a-4921c, 4922 5.75 —
Complete booklet, #4922a 5.75

Complete booklet sold for 400w.

Souvenir Sheet

Intl. Children's Day, 60th Anniv. — A2216

2010, June 1 ***Perf. 11¾***

4923 A2216 95w multi 1.40 .70
a. As #4923, with Bangkok 2010 emblem in sheet margin 1.40 .70

Issued: No. 4923a, 8/4.

Joint Declaration of June 15, 2000 on Reunification of Korea — A2217

2010, June 15 ***Perf. 13¼***

4924 A2217 190w multi 2.75 1.40

A2218

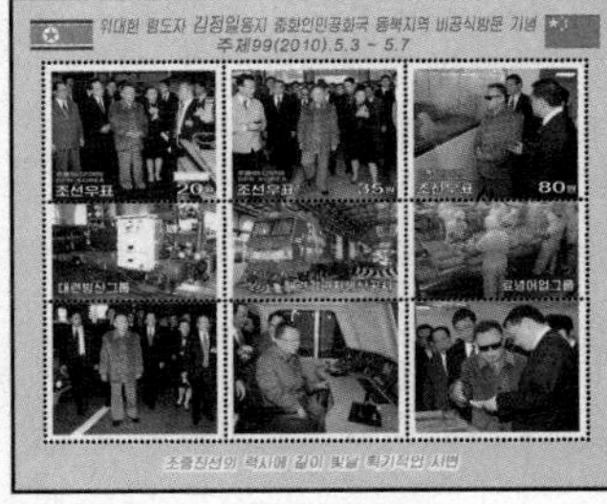

A2219

A2220

Visit of Kim Jong Il to People's Republic of China — A2221

No. 4925 — Kim Jong Il: a, 20w, And Chinese man pointing. b, 40w Pointing. c, 67w, Walking.

No. 4926 — Kim Jong Il: a, 20w, Standing next to woman. b, 35w, With leg raised. c, 80w, Looking through window.

No. 4927 — Kim Jong Il: a, 30w, Standing next to Chinese Pres. Hu Jintao. b, 40w, Seated at table with Pres. Hu. c, 70w, Shaking hands with Pres. Hu.

60w, Kim Jong Il and Pres. Hu.

2010, June 20 ***Perf. 13¼***

4925 A2218 Sheet of 3, #a-c, + 6 labels 1.75 .90
4926 A2219 Sheet of 3, #a-c, + 6 labels 1.90 .95
4927 A2220 Sheet of 3, #a-c, + 3 labels 2.00 1.00
Nos. 4925-4927 (3) 5.65 2.85

Souvenir Sheet

Perf. 11½x12

4928 A2221 60w multi .85 .40

Miniature Sheet

Children's Animated Films — A2222

No. 4929 — Scenes from children's animated films: a, 10w, Butterfly and Cock. b, 30w, A Clever Raccoon Dog. c, 95w, A Hedgehog Defeats a Tiger. d, 133w, Regret of Rabbit.

2010, June 30 ***Perf. 13¼***

4929 A2222 Sheet of 4, #a-d 3.75 1.90

Souvenir Sheet

Azaleas — A2223

2010, July 1 **Litho.**

4930 A2223 85w multi 1.25 .60

Souvenir Sheet

National Anthem — A2224

2010, July 5 ***Perf. 13½***

4931 A2224 50w black .70 .35

A2225

Liberation of Korea, 65th Anniv. — A2226

No. 4932 — Paintings: a, 10w, The Great Leader Forming the Korean Revolutionary Army. b, 15w, Bloody and Long Anti-Japanese War. c, 20w, The Azalea in the Fatherland. d, 40w, Pyongyang in New Spring. e, 100w, Historical That Night.

60w, February Festival on the Eve of Korea's Liberation.

2010, Aug. 15 ***Perf. 13¼***

4932 A2225 Sheet of 5, #a-e, + label 2.60 1.40

Souvenir Sheet

4933 A2226 60w multi .85 .40

A2227

A2228

Start of Songun Revolutionary Leadership, 50th Anniv. — A2229

No. 4935 — Paintings: a, 15w, General Kim Jong Il Instilling the Traditions of Mt. Paektu in the Soldiers (63x41mm). b, 30w, Military Song of Victory (50x38mm). c, 55w, General to the Frontline, Children to the Camp (50x38mm). d, 80w, Saying He Feels Happiest Among the Soldiers (50x38mm).

70w, Blizzard on Mt. Paektu.

2010, Aug. 25 ***Perf. 11½***

4934 A2227 10w multi .20 .20

Perf. 12x11½ (#4935a), 11¾

4935 A2228 Sheet of 4, #a-d 2.50 1.25

Souvenir Sheet

Perf. 11¾

4936 A2229 70w multi 1.00 .50

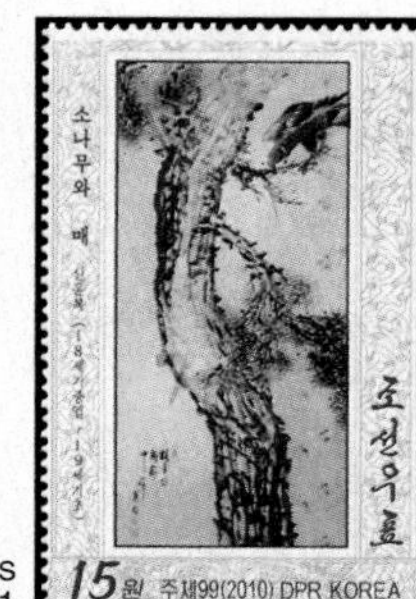

Paintings A2231

Designs: 15w, Pine Tree and Hawk, by Sin Yun Bok. 35w, Waves of Ongchon, by Jong Son. 70w, Reeds and Wild Geese, by Jo Sok Jin. 100w, After Picking Medicinal Herbs, by Kim Hong Do.

2010, Sept. 1 **Litho.** ***Perf. 13¼***

4938-4941 A2231 Set of 4 3.25 1.60
4941a Booklet pane of 4, #4938-4941 3.25 —
Complete booklet, #4941a 3.25

Expo 2010, Shanghai A2239

2010, Sept. 6 **Litho.** ***Perf. 11½***

4949 A2239 25w multi .35 .20

No. 4949 was printed in sheets of 6 + 9 labels.

A2242

A2243

Worker's Party of Korea, 65th Anniv. — A2244

Designs: 10w, Flag of Worker's Party.

No. 4953 — Kim Il Sung: a, 20w, On naval vessel. b, 25w, At rail yard. c, 50w, With farmers. d, 50w, At technology display. e, 60w, With fabric vendor.

70w, Kim Il Sung with party flag.

2010, Oct. 10 **Litho.** ***Perf. 11¾***

4952 A2242 10w multi .20 .20
4953 A2243 Sheet of 6, #4952, 4953a-4953e 3.25 1.60

Souvenir Sheet

Perf. 13½

4954 A2244 70w multi 1.00 .50

AIR POST STAMPS

Lisunov Li-2 Airliner over Pyongyang AP1

1958, Feb. 4 **Photo.** ***Perf. 10***

C1 AP1 20w blue 11.00 2.00
a. Imperf 22.50 10.00
b. Perf 11 12.00 2.50
c. Rouletted 15.00 10.00

Korean Civil Aviation.

REPUBLIC OF KOSOVO

'ko-sə-vō

LOCATION — North of Albania and Macedonia
GOVT. — REPUBLIC
AREA — 4,212 sq. mi.
POP. — 2,100,000 (2007 est.)
CAPITAL — Pristina

From 1974 to 1990, Kosovo was an autonomous province of Serbia, a republic within Yugoslavia. In 1990, the autonomy of Kosovo was revoked. A Separatist faction declared Kosovo independence that year, but only Albania recognized it. In 1999, the United Nations Security Council placed Kosovo under a transitional United Nations Administration, and the institutions created by the independent Kosovo were replaced with the United Nations Interim Administration. Starting in 2000, postage stamps were issued by the United Nations Interim Administration, and these can be found as part of the listings for United Nations. The Kosovo Assembly declared independence on Feb. 17, 2008. Kosovo was recognized as independent by numerous countries soon thereafter, and the United Nations Interim Administration ceased issuing stamps. Serbia maintains its claim to the territory.

100 pfennigs = 1 mark
100 cents = (€)1 (2002)

Catalogue values for all unused stamps in this country are for Never Hinged items.

Peace in Kosovo — A1

Designs: 20pf, Mosaic depicting Orpheus, c. 5th-6th cent., Podujeve. 30pf, Dardinian idol, Museum of Kosovo. 50pf, Silver coin of Damastion from 4th cent. B.C. 1m, Statue of Mother Teresa, Prizren. 2m, Map of Kosovo.

Perf. 13½x13, 13½x13¼ (30pf)

2000, Mar. 14 Litho. Unwmk.

1 A1 20pf multicolored 1.00 .75
2 A1 30pf multicolored 1.25 1.00
3 A1 50pf multicolored 1.75 1.25
4 A1 1m multicolored 3.00 2.00
5 A1 2m multicolored 6.00 4.00
Nos. 1-5 (5) 13.00 9.00

Beginning with No. 6, Kosovan stamps were not available to collectors through the United Nations Postal Administration.

Peace in Kosovo — A2

Designs: 20pf, Bird. 30pf, Street musician. 50pf, Butterfly and pear. 1m, Children and stars. 2m, Globe and handprints.

2001, Nov. 12 Litho. *Perf. 14*

6 A2 20pf multicolored 1.50 1.50
7 A2 30pf multicolored 2.00 2.00
8 A2 50pf multicolored 3.75 3.75
9 A2 1m multicolored 7.50 7.50
10 A2 2m multicolored 15.00 15.00
Nos. 6-10 (5) 29.75 29.75

Peace in Kosovo Type of 2001 With Denominations in Euros Only

2002, May 2 Litho. *Perf. 14*

11 A2 10c Like #6 1.50 1.50
12 A2 15c Like #7 2.00 2.00
13 A2 26c Like #8 3.75 3.75
14 A2 51c Like #9 7.50 7.50
15 A2 €1.02 Like #10 15.00 15.00
Nos. 11-15 (5) 29.75 29.75

Christmas — A3

Designs: 50c, Candles and garland. €1, Stylized men.

2003, Dec. 20 Litho. *Perf. 14*

16 A3 50c multicolored *15.00 14.00*
17 A3 €1 multicolored *30.00 20.00*

Return of Refugees — A4

Five Years of Peace — A5

2004, June 29 Litho. *Perf. 13¼x13*

18 A4 €1 multicolored *17.50 16.00*
19 A5 €2 multicolored *26.00 22.50*

Musical Instruments — A6

2004, Aug. 31 Litho. *Perf. 13¼x13*

20 A6 20c Flute *19.00 13.50*
21 A6 30c Ocarina *27.50 17.50*

Aprons A7

Vests — A8

Designs: 20c, Apron from Prizren. 30c, Apron from Rugova. 50c, Three vests. €1, Two vests.

2004, Oct. 28 Litho. *Perf. 13x13¼*

22 A7 20c multicolored *9.00 9.00*
23 A7 30c multicolored *14.00 14.00*
24 A8 50c multicolored *22.50 22.50*
25 A8 €1 multicolored *45.00 45.00*
Nos. 22-25 (4) 90.50 90.50

Mirusha Waterfall A9

2004, Nov. 26 Litho. *Perf. 13x13¼*

26 A9 €2 multicolored *15.00 15.00*

House A10

2004, Dec. 14 Litho. *Perf. 13x13¼*

27 A10 50c multicolored *7.00 7.00*

Flowers — A11

2005, June 29 Litho. *Perf. 13½*

28 A11 15c Peony *3.50 3.50*
29 A11 20c Poppies *4.50 4.50*
30 A11 30c Gentian *8.00 8.00*
Nos. 28-30 (3) 16.00 16.00

A12

Handicrafts A13

2005, July 20 *Perf. 13¼x13*

31 A12 20c shown *3.00 3.00*
32 A12 30c Cradle *4.00 4.00*
33 A13 50c shown *6.00 6.00*
34 A12 €1 Necklace *13.00 13.00*
Nos. 31-34 (4) 26.00 26.00

Village A14

Town A15

City — A16

2005, Sept. 15 *Perf. 13x13½*

35 A14 20c multicolored *3.50 3.50*
36 A15 50c multicolored *6.50 6.50*
37 A16 €1 multicolored *12.50 12.50*
Nos. 35-37 (3) 22.50 22.50

Archaeological Artifacts — A17

2005, Nov. 2 *Perf. 13½x13*

38 A17 20c shown *2.50 2.50*
39 A17 30c Statue *3.50 3.50*
40 A17 50c Sculpture *6.00 6.00*
41 A17 €1 Helmet *15.00 15.00*
Nos. 38-41 (4) 27.00 27.00

Minerals A18

2005, Dec. 10 *Perf. 13x13½*

42 A18 €2 multicolored *22.00 22.00*

A19

Europa — A20

2006, July 20 *Perf. 13¼x13*

43 A19 50c multicolored *3.50 3.50*
44 A20 €1 multicolored *8.50 8.50*

Fauna A21

2006, May 23 Litho. *Perf. 13*

45 A21 15c Wolf *1.00 1.00*
46 A21 20c Cow *1.25 1.25*
47 A21 30c Pigeon *1.75 1.75*
48 A21 50c Swan *2.50 2.50*
49 A21 €1 Dog *4.50 4.50*
a. Souvenir sheet, #45-49, + label *12.50 12.50*
Nos. 45-49 (5) 11.00 11.00

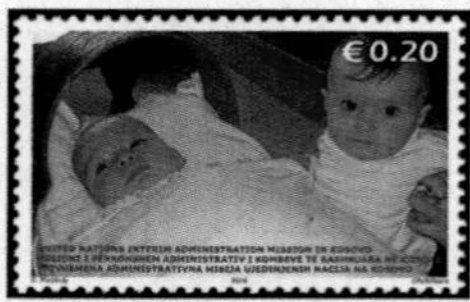

Children A22

Designs: 20c, Children in cradle. 30c, Children reading. 50c, Girls dancing. €1, Child in water.

2006, June 30 Litho. *Perf. 13*

50 A22 20c multicolored *1.00 1.00*
51 A22 30c multicolored *1.50 1.50*
52 A22 50c multicolored *2.00 2.00*
53 A22 €1 multicolored *4.50 4.50*
a. Souvenir sheet, #50-53 *10.50 10.50*
Nos. 50-53 (4) 9.00 9.00

A23

A24

A25

Tourist Attractions — A26

2006, Sept. 1 Litho. *Perf. 13*

54 A23 20c multicolored *1.25 1.25*
55 A24 30c multicolored *1.75 1.75*
56 A25 50c multicolored *2.75 2.75*
57 A26 €1 multicolored *5.50 5.50*
a. Souvenir sheet, #54-57 *11.00 11.00*
Nos. 54-57 (4) 11.25 11.25

Intl. Peace Day — A27

2006, Sept. 21 Litho. *Perf. 13*

58 A27 €2 multicolored *10.00 10.00*

Ancient Coins — A28

Various coins.

2006, Nov. 1 Litho. *Perf. 13*

59 A28 20c multicolored *1.25 1.25*
60 A28 30c multicolored *1.75 1.75*
61 A28 50c multicolored *2.50 2.50*

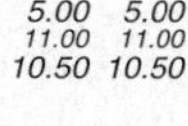

62 A28 €1 multicolored *5.00 5.00*
a. Souvenir sheet, #59-62 *11.00 11.00*
Nos. 59-62 (4) 10.50 10.50

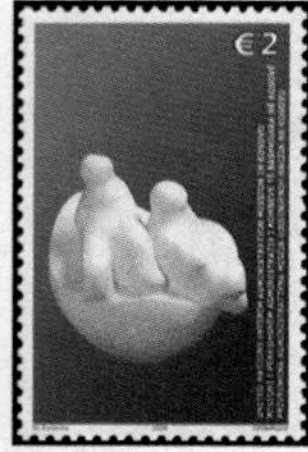

Sculpture — A29

2006, Dec. 1 Litho. *Perf. 13*

63 A29 €2 multicolored *9.50 9.50*
a. Miniature sheet, #45-57, 59-63, + 2 labels *85.00 85.00*

Convention on the Rights of Persons With Disabilities — A30

Emblems of handicaps and: 20c, Children and butterfly. 50c, Handicapped women. 70c, Map of Kosovo. €1, Stylized flower.

2007, Apr. 23 Litho. *Perf. 14x14¼*

64 A30 20c multicolored *1.25 1.25*
65 A30 50c multicolored *2.75 2.75*
66 A30 70c multicolored *4.00 4.00*
67 A30 €1 multicolored *5.50 5.50*
a. Souvenir sheet, #64-67 *12.50 12.50*
Nos. 64-67 (4) 13.50 13.50

Scouting, Cent. — A31

Europa — A32

2007, May 12 Litho. *Perf. 13¼*

68 A31 70c multicolored *5.00 5.00*
69 A32 €1 multicolored *9.00 9.00*
a. Souvenir sheet, #68-69 *40.00 40.00*

A33

A34

International Children's Day — A36

Native Costumes — A37

Masks — A38

Sports — A39

Architecture A40

A35

2007, June 1 Litho. *Perf. 13¼*

70 A33 20c multicolored *1.25 1.25*
71 A34 30c multicolored *1.75 1.75*
72 A35 70c multicolored *3.50 3.50*
73 A36 €1 multicolored *7.00 7.00*
Nos. 70-73 (4) 13.50 13.50

Designs: 20c, Serbian woman. 30c, Prizren Region woman. 50c, Sword dancer. 70c, Drenica Region woman. €1, Shepherd, Rugova.

2007, July 6 Litho. *Perf. 13½x13¼*

74 A37 20c multicolored *1.25 1.25*
75 A37 30c multicolored *1.75 1.75*
76 A37 50c multicolored *2.50 2.50*
77 A37 70c multicolored *4.00 4.00*
78 A37 €1 multicolored *5.00 5.00*
a. Souvenir sheet, #74-78, + label *15.00 15.00*
Nos. 74-78 (5) 14.50 14.50

Various masks.

Perf. 13½x13¼

2007, Sept. 11 Litho.

79 A38 15c multicolored *.75 .75*
80 A38 30c multicolored *1.00 1.00*
81 A38 50c multicolored *2.00 2.00*
82 A38 €1 multicolored *4.00 4.00*
Nos. 79-82 (4) 7.75 7.75

Designs: 20c, Soccer ball, basketball, two people standing, person in wheelchair. 50c, Wrestlers. €1, Symbols of 24 sports.

2007, Oct. 2 Litho. *Perf. 13¼x13½*

83 A39 20c multicolored *1.00 1.00*
84 A39 50c multicolored *2.50 2.50*
85 A39 €1 multicolored *5.00 5.00*
Nos. 83-85 (3) 8.50 8.50

Designs: 30c, Stone bridge, Vushtrri. 50c, Hamam, Prizren. 70c, Tower. €1, Tower, diff.

2007, Nov. 6 Litho. *Perf. 13¼*

86 A40 30c multicolored *1.10 1.10*
87 A40 50c multicolored *1.75 1.75*
88 A40 70c multicolored *2.75 2.75*
89 A40 €1 multicolored *3.75 3.75*
Nos. 86-89 (4) 9.35 9.35

Locomotives A41

Designs: €1, Diesel locomotive. €2, Steam locomotive

2007, Dec. 7 Litho. *Perf. 13¼*

90 A41 €1 multicolored *5.50 5.50*
91 A41 €2 multicolored *9.50 9.50*

Skanderbeg (1405-68), Albanian National Hero — A42

2008, Jan. 17 Litho. *Perf. 13¼*

92 A42 €2 multicolored *8.00 8.00*

Kosovo declared its independence from Serbia on Feb. 17, 2008, ending the United Nations Interim Administration.

Republic of Kosovo

A42

Teacher's Day — A43

2008, Mar. 7 Litho. *Perf. 13x13¼*

93 A42 70c multi 2.50 2.50
94 A43 €1 multi 3.50 3.50

Independence A44

2008, Mar. 19 *Perf. 13¼x13*

Stamps With White Frames

95 Vert. pair 7.00 7.00
a. A44 20c vio blue & multi 1.00 .65
b. A44 70c red & multi 3.50 2.25

Souvenir Sheet

Stamp With Colored Border

96 A44 70c red & multi *11.00 11.00*

Earth Day — A45

Designs: 30c, Globe, olive branch. 50c, Trees. 70c, Tree, parched land. €1, Man holding tree.

2008, Apr. 22 *Perf. 13x13¼*

97-100 A45 Set of 4 11.00 11.00

Europa — A46

Designs: Nos. 101, 103a, 70c, Handwritten letter, pen. Nos. 102, 103b, €1, Letter folded into paper airplane.

2008, May 9 **Litho.**

Stamps With White Frames

101-102 A46 Set of 2 *8.00 8.00*

Souvenir Sheet

Stamps With Colored Frames

103 A46 Sheet of 2, #a-b *25.00 25.00*

Filigree — A47

Designs: 10c, Chest. 15c, Earring. 20c, Figurine of woman. 50c, Necklace. €1, Necklace, diff.

2008, June 12 ***Perf. 13¼x13***

104-108 A47 Set of 5 6.75 6.75

A48 A49

Medicinal Herbs

A50 A51

2008, Sept. 9 **Litho.** ***Perf. 13¼x13***

109	Horiz. strip of 4	8.00	8.00
a.	A48 30c multi	1.00	1.00
b.	A49 50c multi	1.60	1.60
c.	A50 70c multi	2.40	2.40
d.	A51 €1 multi	3.00	3.00

Breast Cancer Prevention — A52

2008, Oct. 15 **Litho.** ***Perf. 13¼x13***

110 A52 €1 multi 7.00 7.00

Albanian Alphabet, Cent. — A53

No. 111: a, 70c, Alphabet. b, €1, Notebook page for handwriting practice.

2008, Nov. 14 ***Perf. 13x13¼***

111 A53 Vert. pair, #a-b 4.50 4.50

Adem Jashari (1955-98), Independence Leader — A54

2008, Nov. 28 ***Perf. 13¼x13***

112 A54 €2 multi 6.50 6.50

A55

A56

A57

Visual Arts — A58

2008, Dec. 2 **Litho.** ***Perf. 13¼***

113	Horiz. strip of 4	9.50	9.50
a.	A55 20c multi	.75	.75
b.	A56 50c multi	1.50	1.50
c.	A57 70c multi	2.25	2.25
d.	A58 €1 multi	3.00	3.00

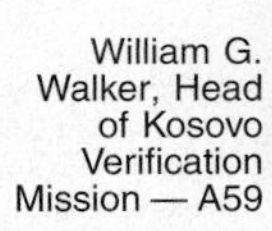

William G. Walker, Head of Kosovo Verification Mission — A59

Torn Page — A60

2009, Jan. 15

114 A59 50c multi 2.00 2.00

115 A60 70c multi 2.75 2.75

Reçak Massacre, 10th anniv.

Independence, 1st Anniv. — A61

No. 116: a, €1, Hand with pen, independence declaration. b, €2, Flag of Kosovo, date of independence.

Illustration reduced.

2009, Feb. 16 **Litho.** ***Perf. 13¼***

116 A61 Horiz. pair, #a-b 9.00 9.00

Edith Durham (1863-1944), Writer — A62

2009, Mar. 21

117 A62 €1 multi 3.25 3.25

A63

Decan Monastery — A64

Designs: No. 118, €1, Monastery. No. 119, €2, Monastery, diff.

No. 120: a, €1, Window. b, €2, Painting of Jesus.

2009, Apr. 22

118-119 A63 Set of 2 8.00 8.00

Souvenir Sheet

120 A64 Sheet of 2, #a-b 8.00 8.00

Europa — A65

Designs: €1, Map of Europe, ring of stars, man and girl at telescope. No. 122, €2, Boy and rocket on map of Europe (with white frame around stamp).

No. 123, Like #122, without white frame around stamp.

2009, May 9

121-122 A65 Set of 2 9.75 9.75

Souvenir Sheet

123 A65 €2 multi 10.00 10.00

Intl. Year of Astronomy.

A66 A67

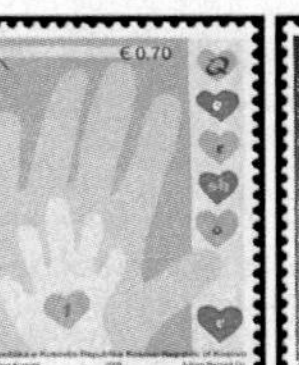

Declaration of the Rights of the Child, 20th Anniv.

A68 A69

2009, June 1

124	A66 20c multi	.75	.75
125	A67 50c multi	2.00	2.00
126	A68 70c multi	2.75	2.75
127	A69 €1 multi	4.00	4.00
	Nos. 124-127 (4)	9.50	9.50

Kosovo's Friendship With United States — A70

2009, Sept. 4

128 A70 €2 multi 7.25 7.25

Lorenc Antoni (1909-91), Composer — A71

2009, Sept. 23

129 A71 €1 multi 4.75 4.75

Germany Weeks in Kosovo — A72

2009, Oct. 3 **Litho.** ***Perf. 13¼***

130 A72 €1 multi 3.00 3.00

Pjeter Bogdani (c. 1630-89), Writer — A73

2009, Nov. 22

131 A73 €1 multi 3.00 3.00

Art — A74

Works by: 30c, M. Mulliqi. 50c, I. Kodra. 70c, G. Gjokaj. €1, M. Mulliqi, diff.

2009, Dec. 4

132-135	A74	Set of 4	7.50	7.50

A75

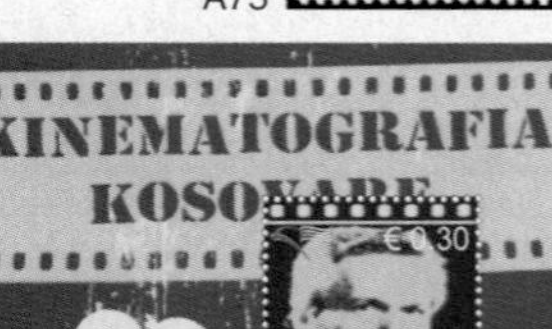

Film Personalities — A76

Designs: No. 136, 30c, Faruk Begolli (1944-2007), actor and director. No. 137, 70c, Melihate Qena (1939-2005), actress. €1, Abdurrahman Shala (1922-94), actor and producer.
No. 139: a, 30c, Unnamed person in yellow. b, 70c, Unnamed person in brown, diff.

2010, Jan. 26

136-138	A75	Set of 3	5.50	5.50

Souvenir Sheet

139	A76	Sheet of 2, #a-b	2.75	2.75

Emblems of Kosovo Police, Defense Forces and Security Forces — A77

Police and Emblem — A78

Security Forces — A79

2010, Feb. 16 **Litho.**

140	A77	30c multi	.85	.85
141	A78	50c multi	1.40	1.40
142	A79	70c multi	1.90	1.90
		Nos. 140-142 (3)	4.15	4.15

A80

Europa — A81

Designs: €1, Child reading book under tree. No. 144, €2, Child leaving open book.
No. 145, €2, Boy sitting on book.

2010, May 5 ***Perf. 13¼***

143-144	A80	Set of 2	7.75	7.75

Souvenir Sheet

Perf. 14x14¼

145	A81	€2 multi	5.25	5.25

2010 World Cup Soccer Championships, South Africa — A82

Designs: €1, Map of Kosovo and emblem of Kosovo Soccer Federation, map of Africa with soccer field. €2, Map of Kosovo and emblem of Kosovo Soccer Federation, map of Africa on soccer ball.
No. 148: a, Soccer ball as pendant on multicolored ribbon. b, Flag of South Africa on soccer ball.

2010, June 29 ***Perf. 13¼***

146-147	A82	Set of 2	7.50	7.50

Souvenir Sheet

Perf. 14¼x14

148	A82	50c Sheet of 2, #a-b	2.50	2.50

Azem (1889-1924) and Shota (1895-1927) Galica, Fighters for Albanian Independence A83

2010, July 14 ***Perf. 13¼***

149	A83	€2 multi	5.25	5.25

National Parks — A84

Scenery from: 20c, Mirusha National Park. 50c, Rugova National Park. 70c, Gjeravica National Park. €1, Sharri National Park.

2010, Aug. 2 **Litho.**

150-153	A84	Set of 4	6.50	6.50

Mother Teresa (1910-97), Humanitarian A85

2010, Aug. 26 ***Perf. 13***

154	A85	€1 multi	2.60	2.60

KUWAIT

ku-ˈwāt

LOCATION — Northwestern coast of the Persian Gulf
GOVT. — Sheikdom
AREA — 7,000 sq. mi.
POP. — 1,991,115 (1999 est.)
CAPITAL — Kuwait

Kuwait was under British protection until June 19, 1961, when it became a fully independent state.

16 Annas = 1 Rupee
100 Naye Paise = 1 Rupee (1957)
1000 Fils = 1 Kuwaiti Dinar (1961)

Catalogue values for unused stamps in this country are for Never Hinged items, beginning with Scott 72 in the regular postage section, Scott C5 in the air post section, and Scott J1 in the postage due section.

There was a first or trial setting of the overprint with the word "Koweit." Twenty-four sets of regular and official stamps were printed with this spelling. Value for set, $10,000.

Catalogue values for Nos. 1-71 used, are for postally used examples. Stamps with telegraph cancellations are worth less.

Iraqi Postal Administration

Stamps of India, 1911-23, Overprinted

a

b

1923-24 **Wmk. 39** ***Perf. 14***

1	A47(a)	½a	green	4.75	*6.50*
2	A48(a)	1a	dk brown	4.50	*3.00*
3	A58(a)	1½a	chocolate	3.75	*4.75*
4	A49(a)	2a	violet	6.00	*5.00*
5	A57(a)	2a6p	ultra	4.50	*10.00*
6	A51(a)	3a	brown org	6.75	*22.50*
7	A51(a)	3a	ultra ('24)	12.50	3.00
8	A52(a)	4a	ol green	11.50	*27.50*
9	A53(a)	6a	bister	13.00	*16.00*
10	A54(a)	8a	red violet	12.00	*38.00*
11	A55(a)	12a	claret	25.00	*47.50*
12	A56(b)	1r	grn & red brown	32.50	*30.00*
13	A56(b)	2r	brn & car rose	57.50	*100.00*
14	A56(b)	5r	vio & ultra	130.00	*240.00*
15	A56(b)	10r	car & green	190.00	*375.00*
			Nos. 1-15 (15)	514.25	*928.75*

Overprint "a" on India No. 102 is generally considered unofficial.

Nos. 1-4, 6-7 exist with inverted overprint. None of these are believed to have been sold at the Kuwait post office.
For overprints see Nos. O1-O13.

Stamps of India, 1926-35, Overprinted type "a"

1929-37 **Wmk. 196**

17	A47	½a	green	4.00	1.75
18	A71	½a	green ('34)	7.00	1.75
19	A48	1a	dark brown	11.00	1.90
20	A72	1a	dk brown ('34)	7.00	1.25
21	A60	2a	dk violet	5.50	1.25
22	A60	2a	vermilion	35.00	*95.00*
23	A49	2a	ver ('34)	32.50	6.75
a.			Small die	5.00	2.50
24	A51	3a	ultramarine	6.00	2.00
25	A51	3a	car rose ('34)	9.00	*4.50*
26	A61	4a	olive green	37.50	*82.50*
27	A52	4a	ol green ('34)	10.00	*14.50*
28	A53	6a	bister ('37)	27.50	*65.00*
29	A54	8a	red violet	12.00	17.50
30	A55	12a	claret	35.00	*47.50*

Overprinted

c

31	A56	1r	green & brown	22.50	*30.00*
32	A56	2r	buff & car rose	24.00	*72.50*
33	A56	5r	dk vio & ultra ('37)	115.00	*275.00*
34	A56	10r	car & grn ('34)	225.00	*450.00*
35	A56	15r	ol grn & ultra ('37)	700.00	*900.00*
			Nos. 17-35 (19)	1,325.	*2,070.*

For overprints see Nos. O15-O25.

Stamps of India, 1937, Overprinted type "a" (A80, A81) or "c" (A82)

1939 **Wmk. 196** ***Perf. 13½x14***

45	A80	½a	brown	1.50	*1.60*
46	A80	1a	carmine	1.50	*1.60*
47	A81	2a	scarlet	2.75	*2.75*
48	A81	3a	yel green	3.75	*2.75*
49	A81	4a	dark brown	5.50	*16.00*
50	A81	6a	peacock blue	5.50	*10.00*
51	A81	8a	blue violet	12.00	*37.50*
52	A81	12a	car lake	10.00	*55.00*
53	A82	1r	brown & slate	3.75	*4.25*
54	A82	2r	dk brown & dk violet	13.50	*15.00*
55	A82	5r	dp ultra & dk green	20.00	*24.50*
56	A82	10r	rose car & dk violet	85.00	100.00
a.			Double overprint	350.00	350.00
57	A82	15r	dk green & dk brown	105.00	*200.00*
			Nos. 45-57 (13)	269.75	*470.95*
			Set, never hinged	400.00	

Indian Postal Administration

From May 24, 1941, until August 1947, the Kuwaiti postal service was administered by India, and during 1941-45 unoverprinted Indian stamps were used in Kuwait.

Kuwait postal services were administered by Pakistan from August 1947 through March 1948. Control was transferred to Great Britain on April 1, 1948.

Stamps of India 1940-43, Overprinted in Black

1945 **Wmk. 196** ***Perf. 13½x14***

59	A83	3p	slate	2.75	*4.75*
60	A83	½a	rose violet	1.75	*3.50*
61	A83	9p	lt green	3.75	*11.50*
62	A83	1a	car rose	2.00	*2.50*
63	A84	1½a	dark purple	2.75	*11.00*
64	A84	2a	scarlet	3.00	*4.50*
65	A84	3a	violet	5.00	*6.50*
66	A84	3½a	ultramarine	5.50	*11.00*
67	A85	4a	chocolate	5.00	*4.75*
68	A85	6a	peacock blue	17.50	13.00
69	A85	8a	blue violet	9.50	5.00

70 A85 12a car lake 10.00 5.50
71 A81 14a rose violet 17.50 *25.00*
Nos. 59-71 (13) 86.00 *108.50*
Set, never hinged 110.00

Catalogue values for unused stamps in this section, from this point to the end of the section, are for Never Hinged items.

British Postal Administration

See Oman (Muscat) for similar stamps with surcharge of new value only.

Great Britain Nos. 258 to 263, 243 and 248 Surcharged in Black

1948-49 Wmk. 251 *Perf. 14½x14*
72 A101 ½a on ½p grn 2.50 *2.50*
73 A101 1a on 1p ver 2.50 *2.50*
74 A101 1½a on 1½p lt red brown 3.50 2.50
75 A101 2a on 2p lt org 2.75 *2.50*
76 A101 2½a on 2½p ultra 3.75 1.40
77 A101 3a on 3p violet 2.75 1.25
a. Pair, one without surcharge — —
78 A102 6a on 6p rose lil 2.75 1.00
79 A103 1r on 1sh brown 6.00 2.75

Great Britain Nos. 249A, 250 and 251A Surcharged in Black

Wmk. 259 *Perf. 14*
80 A104 2r on 2sh6p yel grn 7.00 *7.50*
81 A104 5r on 5sh dull red 11.00 7.50
81A A105 10r on 10sh ultra 50.00 10.00
Nos. 72-81A (11) 94.50 41.40

Issued: #72-81, Apr., 1948; 10r, July 4, 1949.
Bars of surcharge at bottom on No. 81A.

Silver Wedding Issue

Great Britain Nos. 267 and 268 Surcharged in Black

Perf. 14½x14, 14x14½
1948 Wmk. 251
82 A109 2½a on 2½p brt ultra 3.00 3.00
83 A110 15r on £1 deep chalky blue 42.50 42.50

Three bars obliterate the original denomination on No. 83.

Olympic Games Issue

Great Britain Nos. 271 to 274 Surcharged "KUWAIT" and New Value in Black

1948 *Perf. 14½x14*
84 A113 2½a on 2½p brt ultra 1.50 3.00
85 A114 3a on 3p dp violet 1.50 3.00
86 A115 6a on 6p red violet 1.75 3.50
87 A116 1r on 1sh dk brown 1.75 3.50
Nos. 84-87 (4) 6.50 13.00

A square of dots obliterates the original denomination on No. 87.

UPU Issue

Great Britain Nos. 276 to 279 Surcharged "KUWAIT", New Value and Square of Dots in Black

1949, Oct. 10 Photo.
89 A117 2½a on 2½p brt ultra 1.25 1.00
90 A118 3a on 3p brt vio 1.50 1.25
91 A119 6a on 6p red vio 2.00 *2.50*
92 A120 1r on 1sh brown 2.25 1.50
Nos. 89-92 (4) 7.00 6.25

Great Britain Nos. 280-285 Surcharged Like Nos. 72-79 in Black

1950-51 Wmk. 251 *Perf. 14½x14*
93 A101 ½a on ½p lt org 2.50 1.90
94 A101 1a on 1p ultra 2.50 1.90
95 A101 1½a on 1½p green 2.50 *2.75*
96 A101 2a on 2p lt red brown 2.75 1.90
97 A101 2½a on 2½p ver 2.75 *2.75*
98 A102 4a on 4p ultra ('50) 2.50 1.60

Great Britain Nos. 286-288 Surcharged in Black

Perf. 11x12
Wmk. 259
99 A121 2r on 2sh6p green 20.00 5.50
100 A121 5r on 5sh dl red 30.00 6.50
101 A122 10r on 10sh ultra 40.00 9.25
Nos. 93-101 (9) 105.50 34.05

Longer bars, at lower right, on No. 101.
Issued: 4a, 10/2/50; others, 5/3/51.

Stamps of Great Britain, 1952-54 Surcharged "KUWAIT" and New Value in Black or Dark Blue

1952-54 Wmk. 298 *Perf. 14½x14*
102 A126 ½a on ½p red org ('53) .30 .40
103 A126 1a on 1p ultra ('53) .30 .20
104 A126 1½a on 1½p green .30 .25
105 A126 2a on 2p red brn ('53) .30 .20
106 A127 2½a on 2½p scarlet .30 .25
107 A127 3a on 3p dk pur (Dk Bl) ('54) .75 .20
108 A128 4a on 4p ultra ('53) 2.25 .40
109 A129 6a on 6p lilac rose ('54) 2.25 .20
111 A132 12a on 1sh3p dk green ('53) 7.00 1.00
112 A131 1r on 1sh6p dk blue ('53) 6.00 .20
Nos. 102-112 (10) 19.75 3.30

Coronation Issue

Great Britain Nos. 313-316 Surcharged "KUWAIT" and New Value in Black

1953, June 3
113 A134 2½a on 2½p scarlet 4.00 1.25
114 A135 4a on 4p brt ultra 4.00 1.25
115 A136 12a on 1sh3p dk grn 6.00 2.00
116 A137 1r on 1sh6p dk blue 5.00 .50
Nos. 113-116 (4) 19.00 5.00

Squares of dots obliterate the original denominations on Nos. 115 and 116.

Great Britain Stamps of 1955-56 Surcharged "KUWAIT" and New Value in Black

1955 Wmk. 308 Engr. *Perf. 11x12*
117 A133 2r on 2sh6p dk brown 9.00 1.50
118 A133 5r on 5sh crimson 10.00 4.25
119 A133 10r on 10sh dp ultra 11.00 4.25
Nos. 117-119 (3) 30.00 10.00

The surcharge on #117-119 exists in two types.

1956 Photo. *Perf. 14½x14*
120 A126 ½a on ½p red org .35 *.40*
121 A126 1a on 1p ultra .75 *.80*
122 A126 1½a on 1½p green .40 *.30*
123 A126 2a on 2p red brown .40 *.30*
124 A127 2½a on 2½p scar .85 *.75*
125 A128 4a on 4p ultra 6.00 2.25
126 A129 6a on 6p lil rose 3.00 .25
127 A132 12a on 1sh3p dk grn 12.50 5.50
128 A131 1r on 1sh6p dk bl 6.25 .20
Nos. 120-128 (9) 30.50 *10.75*

Great Britain Nos. 317-325, 328 and 332 Surcharged "KUWAIT" and New Value in Black

1957-58 Wmk. 308 *Perf. 14½x14*
129 A129 1np on 5p lt brown .35 .35
130 A126 3np on ½p red org 1.00 1.25
131 A126 6np on 1p ultra 1.00 .60
132 A126 9np on 1½p green 1.00 1.00
133 A126 12np on 2p red brn 1.00 1.00
134 A127 15np on 2½p scar, type I 1.00 1.00
a. Type II ('58) 25.00 35.00
135 A127 20np on 3p dk pur 1.00 .20
136 A128 25np on 4p ultra 3.50 2.00
137 A129 40np on 6p lilac rose 1.75 .20
138 A130 50np on 9p dp ol grn 7.75 3.00
139 A132 75np on 1sh3p dk grn 8.00 2.50
Nos. 129-139 (11) 27.35 13.10

The arrangement of the surcharge varies on different values; there are three bars through value on No. 138.

Sheik Abdullah
A1

Dhow
A2

Oil Derrick
A3

Designs: 50np, Pipe lines. 75np, Main square, Kuwait. 2r, Dhow, derrick and Sheik. 5r, Mosque and Sheik. 10r, Oil plant at Burgan and Sheik.

Perf. 12½
1959, Feb. 1 Unwmk. Engr.
140 A1 5np green .60 .20
141 A1 10np rose brown .35 .20
142 A1 15np yellow brown .45 .20
143 A1 20np gray violet .35 .20
144 A1 25np vermilion .50 .20
145 A1 40np rose claret 3.25 .45

Perf. 13½x13
146 A2 40np dark blue .85 .20
147 A2 50np carmine .85 .20
148 A2 75np olive green 1.00 .25

Perf. 14x13½
149 A3 1r claret 3.00 .30
150 A3 2r red brn & dp bl 9.50 .60
151 A3 5r green 9.00 1.25
152 A3 10r purple 27.50 3.75
Nos. 140-152 (13) 57.20 8.00

No. 140-141 and 145 were issued in 1958 for local use. They became valid for international mail on Feb. 1, 1959, but No. 145 was withdrawn after two weeks.

Sheik Abdullah and Flag — A4

1960, Feb. 25 Engr. *Perf. 14*
153 A4 40np olive grn & red .65 .20
154 A4 60np blue & red .95 .30

10th anniv. of the accession of Sheik Sir Abdullah As-Salim As-Sabah.

Types of 1959, Redrawn

Designs: 20f, 3d, Mosque and Sheik. 25f, 100f, Vickers Viscount. 30f, 75f, Dhow, derrick and Sheik. 35f, 90f, Shuwaikh secondary school. 45f, 1d, Wara Hill, Burgan oil field.

1961 *Perf. 12½*
155 A1 1f green .35 .20
156 A1 2f rose brown .35 .20
157 A1 4f yellow brown .35 .20
158 A1 5f gray violet .35 .20
159 A1 8f salmon pink .35 .20
160 A1 15f rose claret .35 .20

Perf. 14x13½, 13½ (40f, 250f)
161 A3 20f green .35 .20
162 A3 25f blue .75 .20
163 A3 30f red brn & dp bl .75 .20
164 A3 35f ver & black .70 .30
165 A2 40f dark blue .55 .20
166 A3 45f violet brown .65 .20
167 A3 75f green & sepia 1.25 .60
168 A3 90f ultra & brown 1.00 .50
169 A3 100f rose red 4.50 .30
170 A2 250f olive green 11.00 1.40
171 A3 1d orange 20.00 4.25
172 A3 3d brick red 47.50 25.00
Nos. 155-172 (18) 91.10 34.55

Nos. 165 and 170 are 32x22mm.
Issued: 75f, 90f, 4/27; 35f, 5/8; others, 4/1.

Symbols of Telecommunications — A5

Perf. 11½
1962, Jan. 11 Unwmk. Photo.
Granite Paper
173 A5 8f blue & black .45 .20
174 A5 20f rose & black 1.00 .55

4th Arab Telecommunications Union Conference.

Mubarakiya School and Sheiks Abdullah and Mubarak — A6

1962, Apr. 15 Unwmk. *Perf. 11½*
175 A6 8f gldn brn, blk, org & gold .45 .20
176 A6 20f lt blue, blk, org & gold .90 .45

50th anniversary of Mubarakiya School.

Arab League Building, Cairo, and Emblem — A7

1962, Apr. 23 *Perf. 13½x13*
177 A7 20f purple .30 .20
178 A7 45f brown 1.00 .55

Arab Publicity Week, Mar. 22-28.

Flag of Kuwait — A8

Malaria Eradication Emblem — A9

1962, June 19 *Perf. 11½*
Flag in Green, Black & Red
179 A8 8f black & tan .30 .20
180 A8 20f black & yellow .45 .30
181 A8 45f black & lt blue .70 .45
182 A8 90f black & lilac 2.00 .90
Nos. 179-182 (4) 3.45 1.85

Issued for National Day, June 19.

1962, Aug. 1 *Perf. 13½x13*
183 A9 4f slate green & yel grn .30 .20
184 A9 25f green & gray .60 .30

WHO drive to eradicate malaria.
No. 184 has laurel leaves added and inscription rearranged.

Cogwheel, Oil Wells, Camels and Modern Building — A10

Perf. 11x13

1962, Dec. 8 Unwmk. Litho.

185 A10 8f multicolored .50 .20
186 A10 20f multicolored .65 .20
187 A10 45f multicolored 1.00 .35
188 A10 75f multicolored 2.10 .60
Nos. 185-188 (4) 4.25 1.35

Bicentenary of the Sabah dynasty.

Mother and Child — A11

1963, Mar. 21 Photo. *Perf. 14½x14*

189 A11 8f yel, red, blk & green .35 .20
190 A11 20f blue, red, blk & grn .50 .20
191 A11 45f lt ol, red, blk & grn .90 .30
192 A11 75f gray, red, blk & green 1.25 .35
Nos. 189-192 (4) 3.00 1.05

Issued for Mother's Day, Mar. 21, 1963.

Wheat Emblem, Date Palm, Cow and Sheep — A12

1963, Mar. 21 *Perf. 14x14½*

193 A12 4f red brn, lt blue & grn .50 .20
194 A12 8f brown, yel & green .80 .20
195 A12 20f red brn, pale vio & green 1.10 .40
196 A12 45f red brn, rose & green 2.10 .90
Nos. 193-196 (4) 4.50 1.70

FAO "Freedom from Hunger" campaign.

Test Tube, Oil Drops and Ship — A13

1963, Apr. 15 Photo. *Perf. 14½x14*

197 A13 4f brown, yel & blue .30 .20
198 A13 20f green, yel & blue .60 .20
199 A13 45f brt mag, yel & blue 1.25 .30
Nos. 197-199 (3) 2.15 .70

Issued for Education Day.

Sheik Abdullah, Flags and Map of Kuwait A14

1963, June 19 *Perf. 14x13*

Flags in Black, Bright Green & Red; Denominations in Black

200 A14 4f ultramarine 1.40 .35
201 A14 5f ocher 1.60 .65
202 A14 20f bright lilac 5.25 2.75
203 A14 50f olive 9.50 4.50
Nos. 200-203 (4) 17.75 8.25

Second anniversary of National Day.

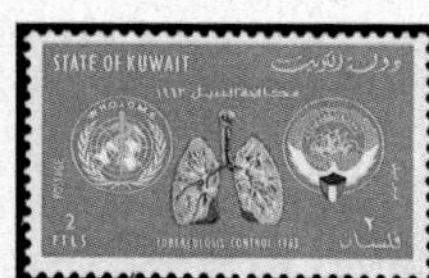

Lungs and Emblems of World Health Organization and Kuwait Tuberculosis Society A15

1963, July 27 *Perf. 13x13½*

Design in Yellow, Black, Emerald & Red

204 A15 2f ocher .35 .20
205 A15 4f dark green .55 .20
206 A15 8f lt violet blue .65 .20
207 A15 20f rose brown 1.10 .30
Nos. 204-207 (4) 2.65 .90

Issued to publicize tuberculosis control.

Sheik Abdullah, Scroll and Scales of Justice — A16

1963, Oct. 29 Photo. *Perf. 11x13*

Center in Gray

208 A16 4f dp red & red brn .60 .20
209 A16 8f dk green & red brn .75 .20
210 A16 20f vio brown & red brn .85 .30
211 A16 45f brown org & red brn 1.50 .65
212 A16 75f purple & red brown 2.00 1.25
213 A16 90f ultra & red brown 2.75 1.60
Nos. 208-213 (6) 8.45 4.20

Promulgation of the constitution.

Soccer — A17

Sports: 4f, Basketball. 5f, Swimming, horiz. 8f, Track. 15f, Javelin, horiz. 20f, Pole vault, horiz. 35f, Gymnast on rings, horiz. 45f, Gymnast on parallel bars.

1963, Nov. 8 Unwmk. *Perf. 14½x14*

214 A17 1f multicolored .45 .20
215 A17 4f multicolored .45 .20
216 A17 5f multicolored .45 .20
217 A17 8f multicolored .45 .20
218 A17 15f multicolored .75 .20
219 A17 20f multicolored 1.25 .40
220 A17 35f multicolored 2.10 .75
221 A17 45f multicolored 3.25 1.50
Nos. 214-221 (8) 9.15 3.65

Arab School Games of 1963.

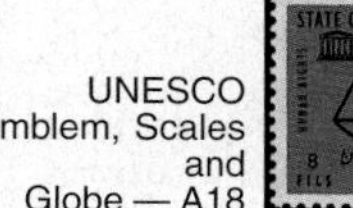

UNESCO Emblem, Scales and Globe — A18

1963, Dec. 10 Litho. *Perf. 13x12½*

222 A18 8f violet, blk & pale grn .50 .20
223 A18 20f gray, black & yel .65 .30
224 A18 25f blue, black & tan 1.25 .75
Nos. 222-224 (3) 2.40 1.25

15th anniv. of the Universal Declaration of Human Rights.

Sheik Abdullah — A19

Perf. 12½x13

1964, Feb. 1 Unwmk. Photo.

Portrait in Natural Colors

225 A19 1f gray & silver .30 .20
a. Booklet pane of 6 ('66) 1.90
226 A19 2f brt blue & silver .30 .20
227 A19 4f ocher & silver .30 .20
a. Booklet pane of 6 ('66) 1.90
228 A19 5f fawn & silver .30 .20
229 A19 8f dk brown & sil .30 .20
230 A19 10f citron & sil .45 .20
a. Booklet pane of 6 ('66) 1.90
231 A19 15f brt green & sil 1.00 .45
a. Booklet pane of 6 ('66) 6.00
232 A19 20f blue gray & sil .60 .20
a. Booklet pane of 6 ('66) 3.00
233 A19 25f green & silver .70 .30
234 A19 30f gray grn & sil 1.00 .30
235 A19 40f brt vio & sil 1.20 .45
236 A19 45f violet & silver 1.30 .55
237 A19 50f olive & silver 1.40 .55
238 A19 70f red lilac & sil 1.75 .65
239 A19 75f rose red & sil 2.25 .75
240 A19 90f ultra & silver 3.25 .75
241 A19 100f pale lilac & sil 3.75 .65

Perf. 14x14½

Size: 25x30mm

242 A19 250f brown & sil 10.00 2.75
243 A19 1d brown vio & sil 40.00 10.00
Nos. 225-243 (19) 70.15 19.55

Ramses II Battling the Hittites (from Abu Simbel) — A20

Engr. & Litho.

1964, Mar. 8 *Perf. 13x12½*

244 A20 8f buff, ind & maroon .35 .20
245 A20 20f lt blue, indigo & vio .95 .55
246 A20 30f bluish grn, ind & vio 1.50 .65
Nos. 244-246 (3) 2.80 1.40

UNESCO world campaign to save historic monuments in Nubia.

Mother and Child — A21

1964, Mar. 21 Litho. *Perf. 14x13*

247 A21 8f green, gray & vio blk .35 .20
248 A21 20f green, red & vio blk .45 .20
249 A21 30f green, ol bis & vio blk .65 .40
250 A21 45f green, saph & vio blk .75 .60
Nos. 247-250 (4) 2.20 1.40

Issued for Mother's Day, Mar. 21.

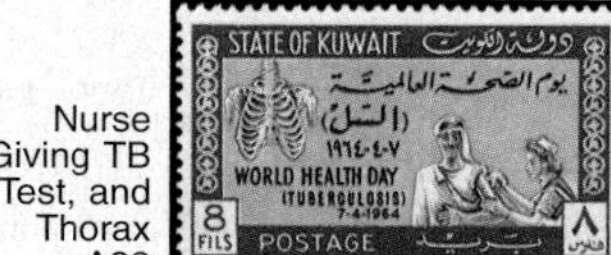

Nurse Giving TB Test, and Thorax A22

Perf. 13x13½

1964, Apr. 7 Photo. Unwmk.

251 A22 8f brown & green .60 .20
252 A22 20f green & rose red 1.60 .35

Issued for World Health Day (fight against tuberculosis), Apr. 7, 1964.

Microscope and Dhow — A23

1964, Apr. 15 *Perf. 12½x13*

253 A23 8f multicolored .30 .20
254 A23 15f multicolored .40 .20
255 A23 20f multicolored .60 .20
256 A23 30f multicolored .90 .45
Nos. 253-256 (4) 2.20 1.05

Issued for Education Day.

Doves and State Seal — A24

1964, June 19 Litho. *Perf. 13½*

Seal in Blue, Brown, Black, Red & Green

257 A24 8f black & bister brn .55 .20
258 A24 20f black & green .65 .20
259 A24 30f black & gray 1.10 .40
260 A24 45f black & blue 1.40 .65
Nos. 257-260 (4) 3.70 1.45

Third anniversary of National Day.

Arab Postal Union Emblem — A25

1964, Nov. 21 Photo. *Perf. 11x11½*

261 A25 8f lt blue & brown .40 .20
262 A25 20f yellow & ultra .90 .20
263 A25 45f olive & brown 1.50 .40
Nos. 261-263 (3) 2.80 .80

Permanent Office of the APU, 10th anniv.

Conference Emblem A26

1965, Feb. 8 Litho. *Perf. 14*

264 A26 8f black, org brn & yel .60 .20
265 A26 20f multicolored 1.10 .20

First Arab Journalists' Conference.

Oil Derrick, Dhow, Sun and Doves — A27

Mother and Children — A28

1965, Feb. 25 *Perf. 13½*

266 A27 10f lt green & multi .45 .20
267 A27 15f pink & multi .75 .20
268 A27 20f gray & multi 1.50 .35
Nos. 266-268 (3) 2.70 .75

Fourth anniversary of National Day.

1965, Mar. 21 Unwmk. *Perf. 13½*
269 A28 8f multicolored .40 .20
270 A28 15f multicolored .55 .20
271 A28 20f multicolored .85 .30
Nos. 269-271 (3) 1.80 .70

Mother's Day, Mar. 21.

Weather Balloon A29

1965, Mar. 23 Photo. *Perf. 11½x11*
272 A29 4f deep ultra & yellow .60 .20
273 A29 5f blue & dp orange 1.00 .20
274 A29 20f dk blue & emerald 1.25 .20
Nos. 272-274 (3) 2.85 .60

Fifth World Meteorological Day.

Census Chart, Map and Family A30

1965, Mar. 28 Litho. *Perf. 13½*
275 A30 8f multicolored .50 .20
276 A30 20f multicolored 1.10 .25
277 A30 50f multicolored 2.25 .55
Nos. 275-277 (3) 3.85 1.00

Issued to publicize the 1965 census.

ICY Emblem A31

1965, Mar. 7 Engr.
278 A31 8f red & black .30 .20
279 A31 20f lt ultra & black .75 .40
280 A31 30f emerald & black 1.50 .65
Nos. 278-280 (3) 2.55 1.25

International Cooperation Year.

Dagger in Map of Palestine — A31a

Perf. 11x11½
1965, Apr. 9 Photo. Unwmk.
281 A31a 4f red & ultra 2.00 .35
282 A31a 45f red & emerald 4.50 .70

Deir Yassin massacre, Apr. 9, 1948. See Iraq Nos. 372-373 and Jordan No. 499.

Tower of Shuwaikh School and Atom Symbol A32

1965, Apr. 15 Litho. *Perf. 14x13*
283 A32 4f multicolored .30 .20
284 A32 20f multicolored .75 .40
285 A32 45f multicolored 1.50 1.00
Nos. 283-285 (3) 2.55 1.60

Issued for Education Day.

ITU Emblem, Old and New Communication Equipment — A33

1965, May 17 *Perf. 13½x14*
286 A33 8f dk blue, lt bl & red .85 .30
287 A33 20f green, lt grn & red 1.60 .50
288 A33 45f red, pink & blue 3.00 1.00
Nos. 286-288 (3) 5.45 1.80

ITU, centenary.

Library Aflame and Lamp A33a

1965, June 7 Photo. *Perf. 11*
289 A33a 8f black, green & red 1.10 .20
290 A33a 15f black, red & green 1.40 .40

Burning of Library of Algiers, June 7, 1962.

Falcon — A34

Book and Wreath Emblem — A35

1965, Dec. 1 Engr. *Perf. 13*
Center in Sepia
291 A34 8f red lilac 2.50 .30
292 A34 15f olive green 2.10 .30
293 A34 20f dark blue 3.50 .45
294 A34 25f orange 4.00 .65
295 A34 30f emerald 5.00 .75
296 A34 45f blue 9.00 1.25
297 A34 50f claret 10.00 1.40
298 A34 90f carmine 17.50 2.75
Nos. 291-298 (8) 53.60 7.85

1966, Jan. 10 Photo. *Perf. 14x15*
299 A35 8f lt violet & multi .60 .20
300 A35 20f brown red & multi .90 .40
301 A35 30f blue & multi 1.25 .60
Nos. 299-301 (3) 2.75 1.20

Issued for Education Day.

Sheik Sabah as-Salim as-Sabah — A36

1966, Feb. 1 Photo. *Perf. 14x13*
302 A36 4f lt blue & multi .30 .20
303 A36 5f pale rose & multi .30 .20
304 A36 20f multicolored 1.00 .20
305 A36 30f lt violet & multi 1.10 .35
306 A36 40f salmon & multi 1.25 .50
307 A36 45f lt gray & multi 1.50 .60
308 A36 70f yellow & multi 2.75 .85
309 A36 90f pale green & multi 3.75 1.10
Nos. 302-309 (8) 11.95 4.00

Wheat and Fish — A37

1966, Feb. 15 *Perf. 11x11½*
310 A37 20f multicolored 2.50 .90
311 A37 45f multicolored 4.00 1.60

"Freedom from Hunger" campaign.

Eagle, Banner, Scales and Emblems — A38

1966, Feb. 25 Litho. *Perf. 12½x13*
312 A38 20f tan & multi 1.50 .40
313 A38 25f lt green & multi 1.90 .55
314 A38 45f gray & multi 3.50 1.25
Nos. 312-314 (3) 6.90 2.20

Fifth anniversary of National Day.

Wheel of Industry and Map of Arab Countries A39

1966, Mar. 1 *Perf. 14x13½*
315 A39 20f brt blue, brt grn & blk .80 .25
316 A39 50f lt red brn, brt grn & black 1.50 .75

Issued to publicize the conference on industrial development in Arab countries.

Mother and Children — A40

1966, Mar. 21 *Perf. 11½x11*
317 A40 20f pink & multi .85 .20
318 A40 45f multicolored 1.90 .75

Mother's Day, Mar. 21.

Medical Conference Emblem — A41

1966, Apr. 1 Photo. *Perf. 14½x14*
319 A41 15f blue & red .75 .75
320 A41 30f red & blue 1.25 .75

Fifth Arab Medical Conference, Kuwait.

Composite View of a City — A42

1966, Apr. 7 Litho. *Perf. 12½x13*
321 A42 8f multicolored .75 .20
322 A42 10f multicolored 1.10 .30

Issued for World Health Day, Apr. 7.

Inauguration of WHO Headquarters, Geneva — A43

1966, May 3 Litho. *Perf. 11x11½*
323 A43 5f dull sal, ol grn & vio bl .75 .20
324 A43 10f lt grn, ol grn & vio blue 1.50 .20

Traffic Signal at Night A44

"Blood Transfusion" A45

1966, May 4
325 A44 10f green, red & black 1.00 .20
326 A44 20f green, red & black 1.25 .40

Issued for Traffic Day.

1966, May 5 *Perf. 13½*
327 A45 4f multicolored .75 .20
328 A45 8f multicolored 1.25 .50

Blood Bank Day, May 5.

Sheik Ahmad and Ship Carrying First Crude Oil Shipment A46

1966, June 30 *Perf. 13½*
329 A46 20f multicolored 1.25 .50
330 A46 45f multicolored 2.50 1.00

20th anniv. of the first crude oil shipment, June 30, 1946.

Ministry of Guidance and Information — A47

1966, July 25 Photo. *Perf. 11½x11*
331 A47 4f rose & brown .35 .20
332 A47 5f yel brown & brt green .40 .20
333 A47 8f brt green & purple .55 .20
334 A47 20f salmon & ultra .85 .30
Nos. 331-334 (4) 2.15 .90

Opening of Ministry of Guidance and Information Building.

Fishing Boat, Lobster, Fish, Crab and FAO Emblem A48

1966, Oct. 10 Litho. *Perf. 13½*
335 A48 4f buff & multi 1.50 .25
336 A48 20f lt lilac & multi 2.25 .90

Fisheries' Conference of Near East Countries under the sponsorship of the FAO, Oct. 1966.

United Nations Flag — A49

UNESCO Emblem — A50

1966, Oct. 24 ***Perf. 13x14***

337 A49 20f blue, dk blue & pink 1.25 .30
338 A49 45f blue, dk bl & pale grn 2.75 1.00

Issued for United Nations Day.

1966, Nov. 4 **Litho.** ***Perf. 12½x13***

339 A50 20f multicolored 1.25 .30
340 A50 45f multicolored 2.75 1.25

20th anniversary of UNESCO.

Kuwait University Emblem — A51

1966, Nov. 27 **Photo.** ***Perf. 14½***

Emblem in Yellow, Bright Blue, Green and Gold

341 A51 8f lt ultra, vio & gold .50 .20
342 A51 10f red, brown & gold 1.00 .20
343 A51 20f lt yel grn, slate & gold 1.10 .30
344 A51 45f buff, green & gold 2.00 .90
Nos. 341-344 (4) 4.60 1.60

Opening of Kuwait University.

Jabir al-Ahmad al-Jabir and Sheik Sabah A52

1966, Dec. 11 ***Perf. 14x13***

345 A52 8f yel green & multi .80 .20
346 A52 20f yellow & multi 1.00 .40
347 A52 45f pink & multi 2.00 1.00
Nos. 345-347 (3) 3.80 1.60

Appointment of the heir apparent, Jabir al-Ahmad al-Jabir.

Scout Badge and Square Knot — A52a

1966, Dec. 21 **Litho.** ***Perf. 14x13***

347A A52a 4f lt ol green & fawn 1.50 .35
347B A52a 20f yel brn & blue grn 4.50 1.25

Kuwait Boy Scouts, 30th anniversary.

"Symbols of Science and Peace" — A53

1967, Jan. 15 **Litho.** ***Perf. 13x14***

348 A53 10f multicolored .50 .20
349 A53 45f multicolored 1.50 .50

Issued for Education Day.

Fertilizer Plant — A54

1967, Feb. 19 **Unwmk.** ***Perf. 13***

350 A54 8f lt blue & multi .90 .20
351 A54 20f cream & multi 1.75 .40

Opening of Chemical Fertilizer Plant.

Sun, Dove and Olive Branch — A55

1967, Feb. 25 **Litho.** ***Perf. 13***

352 A55 8f salmon & multi .50 .20
353 A55 20f yellow & multi 1.25 .45

Sixth anniversary of National Day.

Map of Arab States and Municipal Building A56

1967, Mar. 11 ***Perf. 14½x13***

354 A56 20f gray & multi 2.00 .50
355 A56 30f lt brown & multi 3.00 1.25

1st conf. of the Arab Cities Org., Kuwait.

Family — A57

1967, Mar. 21 **Litho.** ***Perf. 13x13½***

356 A57 20f pale rose & multi 1.50 .50
357 A57 45f pale green & multi 3.25 1.25

Issued for Family Day, Mar. 21.

Arab League Emblem — A58

1967, Mar. 27 ***Perf. 13x14***

358 A58 8f gray & dk blue .75 .20
359 A58 10f bister & green .85 .20

Issued for Arab Publicity Week.

Sabah Hospital and Physicians at Work — A59

1967, Apr. 7 ***Perf. 14x13***

360 A59 8f dull rose & multi 1.50 .20
361 A59 20f gray & multi 1.75 .60

Issued for World Health Day.

Two Heads of Ramses II — A60

1967, Apr. 17 ***Perf. 13½***

362 A60 15f citron, green & brn 1.00 .30
363 A60 20f chalky blue, grn & pur 1.75 .50

Arab Week to Save the Nubian Monuments.

Traffic Policeman A61

1967, May 4 **Litho.** ***Perf. 14x13***

364 A61 8f lt green & multi 1.25 .35
365 A61 20f rose lilac & multi 2.75 .95

Issued for Traffic Day.

ITY Emblem — A62

1967, June 4 **Photo.** ***Perf. 13***

366 A62 20f Prus blue, lt bl & blk 1.25 .65
367 A62 45f rose lilac, lt bl & blk 2.50 1.40

International Tourist Year.

Arab League Emblem and Hands Reaching for Knowledge — A63

Map of Palestine and UN Emblem — A64

1967, Sept. 8 **Litho.** ***Perf. 13x14***

368 A63 8f blue & multi 1.50 .20
369 A63 20f dull rose & multi 2.40 .60

Issued to publicize the literacy campaign.

1967, Oct. 24 **Litho.** ***Perf. 13***

370 A64 20f blue & pink 2.50 .30
371 A64 45f orange & pink 3.75 .75

Issued for United Nations Day.

Factory and Cogwheels — A65

1967, Nov. 25 **Photo.** ***Perf. 13***

372 A65 20f crimson & yellow 1.10 .30
373 A65 45f gray & yellow 2.50 1.00

3rd Conf. of Arab Labor Ministers, Kuwait.

Flag and Open Book — A66

Map of Kuwait and Oil Derrick — A67

1968, Jan. 15 **Litho.** ***Perf. 14***

374 A66 20f brt blue & multi .75 .30
375 A66 45f yel orange & multi 2.25 1.00

Issued for Education Day.

1968, Feb. 23 **Litho.** ***Perf. 12***

376 A67 10f multicolored 1.25 .50
377 A67 20f multicolored 2.50 1.00

30th anniv. of the discovery of oil in the Greater Burgan Field.

Sheik Sabah and Sun — A68

1968, Feb. 25 **Litho.** ***Perf. 14x15***

378 A68 8f red lilac & multi .50 .20
379 A68 10f lt blue & multi .60 .20
380 A68 15f violet & multi .75 .25
381 A68 20f vermilion & multi 1.00 .35
Nos. 378-381 (4) 2.85 1.00

Seventh anniversary of National Day.

Open Book and Emblem — A69

1968, Mar. 2 ***Perf. 14***

382 A69 8f yellow & multi .85 .20
383 A69 20f lilac rose & multi 1.00 .20
384 A69 45f orange & multi 1.75 1.00
Nos. 382-384 (3) 3.60 1.40

Issued for Teachers' Day.

Family Picnic A70

1968, Mar. 21 ***Perf. 13½x13***

385 A70 8f blue & multi .50 .20
386 A70 10f red & multi .50 .20
387 A70 15f lilac & multi .75 .20
388 A70 20f dk brown & multi 1.00 .20
Nos. 385-388 (4) 2.75 .80

Issued for Family Day.

Sheik Sabah, Arms of WHO and Kuwait — A71

1968, Apr. 7 **Photo.** ***Perf. 12***

389 A71 20f brt lilac & multi 1.00 .80
390 A71 45f multicolored 2.50 1.75

20th anniv. of WHO.

Dagger in Map of Palestine — A72

1968, Apr. 9 Litho. *Perf. 14*
391 A72 20f lt blue & vermilion 3.00 .50
392 A72 45f lilac & vermilion 5.00 1.00

Deir Yassin massacre, 20th anniv.

Street Crossing A74

1968, May 4 Photo. *Perf. 14x14½*
395 A74 10f dk brown & multi 1.60 1.00
396 A74 15f brt violet & multi 1.90 1.25
397 A74 20f green & multi 2.75 1.40
Nos. 395-397 (3) 6.25 3.65

Issued for Traffic Day.

Map of Palestine and Torch — A75

1968, May 15 Litho. *Perf. 13½x12½*
398 A75 10f lt ultra & multi 1.25 .40
399 A75 20f yellow & multi 2.75 .50
400 A75 45f aqua & multi 5.00 1.75
Nos. 398-400 (3) 9.00 2.65

Issued for Palestine Day.

Palestinian Refugees — A76

1968, June 5 Litho. *Perf. 13x13½*
401 A76 20f pink & multi .85 .20
402 A76 30f ultra & multi 1.00 .40
403 A76 45f green & multi 1.75 .50
404 A76 90f lilac & multi 3.00 1.50
Nos. 401-404 (4) 6.60 2.60

International Human Rights Year.

Museum of Kuwait — A77

Perf. 12½
1968, Aug. 25 Unwmk. Engr.
405 A77 1f dk brown & brt grn .30 .20
406 A77 2f dp claret & grn .30 .20
407 A77 5f black & orange .30 .20
408 A77 8f dk brown & grn .30 .20
409 A77 10f Prus blue & cl .45 .20
410 A77 20f org brown & blue .75 .20
411 A77 25f dk blue & orange .85 .25
412 A77 30f Prus blue & yel grn 1.10 .30
413 A77 45f plum & vio black 1.75 .60
414 A77 50f green & carmine 2.00 1.00
Nos. 405-414 (10) 8.10 3.35

Man Reading Book, Arab League, UN and UNESCO Emblems A78

1968, Sept. 8 Litho. *Perf. 12½x13*
415 A78 15f blue gray & multi .60 .20
416 A78 20f pink & multi 1.00 .30

Issued for International Literacy Day.

Map of Palestine on UN Building and Children with Tent — A79

1968, Oct. 25 Litho. *Perf. 13*
417 A79 20f multicolored .50 .20
418 A79 30f gray & multi .75 .40
419 A79 45f salmon pink & multi 1.10 .50
Nos. 417-419 (3) 2.35 1.10

Issued for United Nations Day.

Kuwait Chamber of Commerce A80

1968, Nov. 6 Litho. *Perf. 13½x12½*
420 A80 10f dp orange & dk brn .40 .20
421 A80 15f rose claret & vio bl .50 .20
422 A80 20f brown org & dk green .75 .40
Nos. 420-422 (3) 1.65 .80

Opening of the Kuwait Chamber of Commerce Building.

Conference Emblem — A81

1968, Nov. 10 Litho. *Perf. 13*
Emblem in Ocher, Blue, Red and Black
423 A81 10f dk brown & blue .50 .20
424 A81 15f dk brown & orange .60 .20
425 A81 20f dk brown & vio blue .75 .40
426 A81 30f dk brown & org brn 1.00 .50
Nos. 423-426 (4) 2.85 1.30

14th Conference of the Arab Chambers of Commerce, Industry and Agriculture.

Shuaiba Refinery — A82

1968, Nov. 18 *Perf. 13½*
Emblem in Red, Black and Blue
427 A82 10f black & lt blue grn .75 .20
428 A82 20f black & gray 1.50 .40
429 A82 30f black & salmon 1.60 .65
430 A82 45f black & emerald 3.00 1.00
Nos. 427-430 (4) 6.85 2.25

Opening of Shuaiba Refinery.

Koran, Scales and People A83

1968, Dec. 19 Photo. *Perf. 14x14½*
431 A83 8f multicolored .60 .20
432 A83 20f multicolored 1.25 .60
433 A83 30f multicolored 1.75 .85
434 A83 45f multicolored 2.50 1.25
Nos. 431-434 (4) 6.10 2.90

The 1400th anniversary of the Koran.

Boeing 707 — A84

1969, Jan. 1 Litho. *Perf. 13½x14*
435 A84 10f brt yellow & multi 1.00 .20
436 A84 20f green & multi 1.40 .50
437 A84 25f multicolored 1.50 .60
438 A84 45f lilac & multi 2.75 1.10
Nos. 435-438 (4) 6.65 2.40

Introduction of Boeing 707 service by Kuwait Airways.

Globe, Retort and Triangle — A85

1969, Jan. 15 *Perf. 13*
439 A85 15f gray & multi .85 .30
440 A85 20f multicolored 1.00 .50

Issued for Education Day.

Kuwait Hilton Hotel — A86

1969, Feb. 15 Litho. *Perf. 14x12½*
441 A86 10f brt blue & multi .60 .20
442 A86 20f pink & multi 1.25 .30

Opening of the Kuwait Hilton Hotel.

Teachers' Society Emblem, Father and Children — A87

1969, Feb. 15 *Perf. 13*
443 A87 10f violet & multi .50 .20
444 A87 20f rose & multi 1.00 .45

Issued for Education week.

Wreath, Flags and Dove — A88

1969, Feb. 25 Photo. *Perf. 14½x14*
445 A88 15f lilac & multi .60 .25
446 A88 20f blue & multi .70 .30
447 A88 30f ocher & multi 1.00 .55
Nos. 445-447 (3) 2.30 1.10

Eighth anniversary of National Day.

Emblem, Teacher and Students — A89

1969, Mar. 8 Litho. *Perf. 13x12½*
448 A89 10f multicolored .50 .20
449 A89 20f deep red & multi .90 .45

Issued for Teachers' Day.

Family A90

1969, Mar. 21 *Perf. 13½*
450 A90 10f dark blue & multi .90 .20
451 A90 20f deep car & multi 1.40 .30

Issued for Family Day.

Avicenna, WHO Emblem, Patient and Microscope — A91

1969, Apr. 7 Litho. *Perf. 13½*
452 A91 15f red brown & multi 1.00 .20
453 A91 20f lt green & multi 2.75 .30

Issued for World Health Day, Apr. 7.

Motorized Traffic Police A92

1969, May 4 Litho. *Perf. 12½x13*
454 A92 10f multicolored 1.75 .25
455 A92 20f multicolored 3.50 .60

Issued for Traffic Day.

ILO Emblem A93

1969, June 1 *Perf. 11½*

456 A93 10f red, black & gold .50 .20
457 A93 20f lt blue grn, blk & gold 1.00 .30

50th anniv. of the ILO.

S.S. Al Sabahiah A94

1969, June 10 **Litho.** *Perf. 13½*

458 A94 20f multicolored 1.25 .50
459 A94 45f multicolored 3.00 1.50

4th anniversary of Kuwait Shipping Co.

UNESCO Emblem, Woman, Globe and Book — A95

1969, Sept. 8 **Litho.** *Perf. 13½*

460 A95 10f blue & multi .35 .20
461 A95 20f rose red & multi .90 .40

International Literacy Day, Sept. 8.

Sheik Sabah — A96

UN Emblem and Scroll — A97

1969-74 **Litho.** *Perf. 14*

462 A96 8f lt blue & multi .40 .20
463 A96 10f pink & multi .45 .20
464 A96 15f gray & multi .50 .20
465 A96 20f yellow & multi .55 .20
466 A96 25f violet & multi .75 .30
467 A96 30f sal & multi 1.00 .35
468 A96 45f tan & multi 1.50 .50
469 A96 50f yel grn & multi 1.75 .50
470 A96 70f multicolored 2.00 .75
471 A96 75f ultra & multi 2.75 .90
472 A96 90f pale rose & multi 3.00 1.25
a. 90f brownish rose & multi 2.50 1.00
473 A96 250f lilac & multi 9.00 3.50
473A A96 500f gray green & multi 16.50 11.00
473B A96 1d lilac rose & multi 32.50 18.00
Nos. 462-473B (14) 72.65 37.85

Issued: #473A-473B, 1/12/74; others 10/5/69.

1969, Oct. 24 **Litho.** *Perf. 13*

474 A97 10f emer & multi .60 .20
475 A97 20f bister & multi 1.25 .20
476 A97 45f rose red & multi 2.50 .80
Nos. 474-476 (3) 4.35 1.20

Issued for United Nations Day.

Radar, Satellite Earth Station, Kuwait A98

Design: 45f, Globe and radar, vert.

1969, Dec. 15 **Photo.** *Perf. 14½*

477 A98 20f silver & multi 1.50 .35
478 A98 45f silver & multi 3.00 1.10

Inauguration of the Kuwait Earth Station for Satellite Communications.

Globe with Science Symbols, and Education Year Emblem — A99

1970, Jan. 15 **Photo.** *Perf. 13½x13*

479 A99 20f brt lilac & multi .85 .35
480 A99 45f blue & multi 1.50 .95

International Education Year.

Shoue A100

Old Kuwaiti Vessels: 10f, Sambook. 15f, Baghla. 20f, Batteel. 25f, Boom. 45f, Bakkara. 50f, Shipbuilding.

1970, Feb. 1 *Perf. 14½x14*

481 A100 8f multicolored .65 .30
482 A100 10f multicolored .75 .40
483 A100 15f multicolored 1.25 .50
484 A100 20f multicolored 1.75 .65
485 A100 25f multicolored 2.00 .75
486 A100 45f multicolored 3.25 1.25
487 A100 50f multicolored 3.75 1.50
Nos. 481-487 (7) 13.40 5.35

Refugee Father and Children A101

Kuwait Flag, Emblem and Sheik Sabah A102

1970 **Photo.** *Perf. 14x12½*

488 A101 20f red brown & multi 2.50 .65
489 A101 45f olive & multi 4.75 1.75

Issued for Universal Palestinian Refugees Week, Dec. 16-22, 1969.

1970, Feb. 25 *Perf. 13½x13*

490 A102 15f silver & multi .85 .20
491 A102 20f gold & multi 1.10 .25

Ninth anniversary of National Day.

Dome of the Rock, Jerusalem, and Boy Commando — A103

Designs: 20f, Dome and man commando. 45f, Dome and woman commando.

1970, Mar. 4 **Litho.** *Perf. 13*

492 A103 10f pale violet & multi 1.50 .75
493 A103 20f lt blue & multi 3.00 1.50
494 A103 45f multicolored 6.50 3.00
Nos. 492-494 (3) 11.00 5.25

Honoring Palestinian commandos.

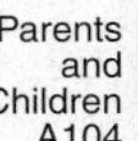

Parents and Children A104

1970, Mar. 21 *Perf. 14*

495 A104 20f multicolored .75 .20
496 A104 30f pink & multi 1.00 .35

Issued for Family Day.

Map of Arab League Countries, Flag and Emblem A104a

1970, Mar. 22 *Perf. 11½x11*

497 A104a 20f lt blue, grn & lt brn .75 .25
498 A104a 45f salmon, grn & dk pur 1.75 .60

25th anniversary of the Arab League.

Census Graph and Kuwait Arms A105

1970, Apr. 1 **Litho.** *Perf. 13½x13*

499 A105 15f dull orange & multi .50 .20
500 A105 20f yellow & multi .55 .20
501 A105 30f pink & multi .80 .30
Nos. 499-501 (3) 1.85 .70

Issued to publicize the 1970 census.

"Fight Cancer," Kuwait Arms, WHO Emblem — A106

1970, Apr. 7 *Perf. 13½x13*

502 A106 20f blue, vio bl & rose lil 1.25 .30
503 A106 30f dl yel, vio bl & lil rose 1.50 .40

World Health Organization Day, Apr. 7, and to publicize the fight against cancer.

Traffic Signs A107

1970, May 4 **Photo.** *Perf. 13½*

504 A107 20f multicolored 1.50 .75
505 A107 30f multicolored 2.50 1.25

Issued for Traffic Day.

Red Crescent A108

1970, May 8 **Litho.** *Perf. 12½x13½*

506 A108 10f yellow & multi .70 .20
507 A108 15f emerald & multi 1.25 .25
508 A108 30f tan & multi 2.25 .70
Nos. 506-508 (3) 4.20 1.15

Intl. Red Crescent and Red Cross Day.

Opening of UPU Headquarters, Bern — A109

1970, May 25 **Photo.** *Perf. 12x11½*

509 A109 20f multicolored 1.10 .35
510 A109 30f multicolored 1.40 .55

Sheik Sabah A110

1970, June 15 **Photo.** *Perf. 14*

511 A110 20f silver & multi 1.75 .20
512 A110 45f gold & multi 3.25 .50
a. Miniature sheet of 2 7.50 1.75

Nos. 511-512 have circular perforation around vignette set within a white square of paper, perforated on 4 sides. #512a contains 2 imperf. stamps similar to #511-512.

UN Emblem, Symbols of Peace, Progress, Justice — A111

1970, July 1 **Litho.** *Perf. 13½x12½*

513 A111 20f lt green & multi .75 .20
514 A111 45f multicolored 1.25 .40

25th anniversary of the United Nations.

Tanker Loading Crude Oil from Sea Island A112

1970, Aug. 1 *Perf. 13½x13*

515 A112 20f multicolored 1.75 .50
516 A112 45f multicolored 4.25 1.10

Issued to publicize the artificial "Sea Island" loading facilities in Kuwait.

"Writing," Kuwait and UN Emblems A113

1970, Sept. 8 **Photo.** *Perf. 13½*

517 A113 10f brt blue & multi 1.10 .20
518 A113 15f brt green & multi 1.75 .20

International Literacy Day, Sept. 8.

National Guard and Emblem A114

1970, Oct. 20 Photo. *Perf. 13x13½*

519 A114 10f gold & multi 1.10 .20
520 A114 20f silver & multi 2.00 .25

First National Guard graduation.

Flag of Kuwait, Symbols of Development A115

1971, Feb. 25 Litho. *Perf. 12*

521 A115 20f gray & multi 1.50 .40
522 A115 30f multicolored 1.90 .65

Tenth anniversary of National Day.

Charles H. Best, Frederick G. Banting A116

1971, Apr. 7 Litho. *Perf. 14*

523 A116 20f multicolored 1.75 .20
524 A116 45f multicolored 3.25 .70

World Health Day; discoverers of insulin.

Globe with Map of Palestine A117

1971, May 3 Litho. *Perf. 12½x13*

525 A117 20f yel green & multi 2.75 1.10
526 A117 45f lilac & multi 4.50 2.25

International Palestine Week.

ITU Emblem and Waves A118

1971, May 17 Photo. *Perf. 13x13½*

527 A118 20f silver, dk red & blk 1.50 .30
528 A118 45f gold, dk red & blk 3.00 .85

3rd World Telecommunications Day.

Men of 3 Races — A119

1971, June 5 Litho. *Perf. 11½x11*

529 A119 15f red brown & multi 1.00 .30
530 A119 30f ultra & multi 1.50 .70

Intl. Year against Racial Discrimination.

Arab Postal Union Emblem A120

1971, Aug. 30 *Perf. 13x12½*

531 A120 20f brown & multi 1.00 .40
532 A120 45f blue & multi 1.75 .55

25th anniv. of the Conf. of Sofar, Lebanon, establishing the Arab Postal Union.

Symbols of Learning, UNESCO and Kuwait Emblems A121

1971, Sept. 8 *Perf. 12*

533 A121 25f dull yellow & multi 1.25 .25
534 A121 60f lt blue & multi 2.50 .90

International Literacy Day, Sept. 8.

Soccer A122

Design: 30f, Soccer, different.

1971, Dec. 10 *Perf. 13*

535 A122 20f green & multi 2.25 .55
536 A122 30f ultra & multi 2.75 .75

Regional Sports Tournament, Kuwait, Dec.

UNICEF Emblem and Arms of Kuwait — A123

Litho. & Engr.

1971, Dec. 11 *Perf. 11x11½*

537 A123 25f gold & multi 1.00 .30
538 A123 60f silver & multi 1.75 .70

25th anniv. of UNICEF.

Book Year Emblem A124

1972, Jan. 2 Litho. *Perf. 14x13*

539 A124 20f black & buff 1.00 .40
540 A124 45f black & lt blue grn 1.75 .90

International Book Year.

Kuwait Emblem with 11 Rays, Olive Branch A125

1972, Feb. 25 Litho. *Perf. 13x13½*

541 A125 20f pink, gold & multi 1.50 .70
542 A125 45f lt blue, gold & multi 2.00 1.25

11th anniversary of National Day.

Telecommunications Center — A126

1972, Feb. 28 *Perf. 13½*

543 A126 20f lt blue & multi 1.75 .60
544 A126 45f multicolored 4.00 1.50

Opening of Kuwait Telecommunications Center.

"Your Heart is your Health" — A127

1972, Apr. 7 Photo. *Perf. 14½x14*

545 A127 20f red & multi 2.25 .60
546 A127 45f red & multi 5.00 1.40

World Health Day.

Nurse and Child — A128

1972, May 8 Litho. *Perf. 12½x13*

547 A128 8f vio blue, red & emer 1.50 .20
548 A128 40f pink & multi 4.00 1.00

Red Cross and Red Crescent Day.

Soccer, Olympic Emblems — A129

1972, Sept. 2 Litho. *Perf. 14½*

549 A129 2f shown .35 .20
550 A129 4f Running .35 .20
551 A129 5f Swimming .35 .20
552 A129 8f Gymnastics .35 .20
553 A129 10f Discus .35 .20
554 A129 15f Equestrian 1.25 .30
555 A129 20f Basketball 1.50 .35
556 A129 25f Volleyball 1.60 .40
Nos. 549-556 (8) 6.10 2.05

20th Olympic Games, Munich, 8/26-9/11.

FAO Emblem, Vegetables, Fish and Ship — A130

1972, Sept. 9 Litho. *Perf. 14x13½*

557 A130 5f blue & multi .60 .40
558 A130 10f emerald & multi 2.00 1.10
559 A130 20f orange & multi 3.50 2.00
Nos. 557-559 (3) 6.10 3.50

11th FAO Regional Conference in the Near East, Kuwait, Sept.

National Bank Emblem A131

1972, Nov. 15 Photo. *Perf. 13x14*

560 A131 10f green & multi .75 .25
561 A131 35f dull red & multi 2.00 1.00

20th anniversary of Kuwait National Bank.

Capitals A132

Relics of Failaka: 5f, View of excavations. 10f, Acanthus leaf capital. 15f, Excavations.

1972, Dec. 4 Litho. *Perf. 12*

562 A132 2f lilac rose & multi .40 .20
563 A132 5f bister & multi .40 .20
564 A132 10f lt blue & multi 1.50 .20
565 A132 15f green & multi 2.00 .40
Nos. 562-565 (4) 4.30 1.00

Flower and Kuwait Emblem — A133

INTERPOL Emblem A134

1973, Feb. 25 Litho. *Perf. 13½x13*

566 A133 10f lt olive & multi .75 .25
567 A133 20f multicolored 1.25 .65
568 A133 30f yellow & multi 1.75 .95
Nos. 566-568 (3) 3.75 1.85

12th anniversary of National Day.

1973, June 3 Litho. *Perf. 12*

569 A134 10f emerald & multi 1.25 .85
570 A134 15f red orange & multi 2.00 1.10
571 A134 20f blue & multi 3.25 1.60
Nos. 569-571 (3) 6.50 3.55

50th anniv. of Intl. Criminal Police Org. (INTERPOL).

I.C.M.S. Emblem and Flag of Kuwait — A135

Kuwait Airways Building — A136

1973, June 24 ***Perf. 13***

572 A135 30f gray & multi 1.25 .55
573 A135 40f brown & multi 2.00 .75

Intl. Council of Military Sports, 25th anniv.

1973, July 1 Litho. ***Perf. 12½x14***

574 A136 10f lt green & multi 1.00 .20
575 A136 15f lilac & multi 1.10 .30
576 A136 20f lt ultra & multi 1.50 .40
Nos. 574-576 (3) 3.60 .90

Opening of Kuwait Airways Corporation Building.

Weather Map of Suez Canal and Persian Gulf Region — A137

1973, Sept. 4 Photo. ***Perf. 14***

577 A137 5f red & multi .75 .20
578 A137 10f green & multi 1.00 .20
579 A137 15f multicolored 1.50 .25
Nos. 577-579 (3) 3.25 .65

Intl. meteorological cooperation, cent.

Sheiks Ahmad and Sabah — A138

1973, Nov. 12 Photo. ***Perf. 14***

580 A138 10f lt green & multi 1.00 .20
581 A138 20f yel orange & multi 1.50 .40
582 A138 70f lt blue & multi 4.00 1.40
Nos. 580-582 (3) 6.50 2.00

Stamps overprinted "Kuwait," 50th anniv.

Mourning Dove, Eurasian Hoopoe, Rock Dove, Stone Curlew — A139

Designs: Birds and traps.

1973, Dec. 1 Litho. ***Perf. 14***
Size (single stamp): 32x32mm

583 A139 Block of 4 5.50 5.50
a. 5f Mourning dove .70 .25
b. 5f Eurasian hoopoe .70 .25
c. 5f Rock dove .70 .25
d. 5f Stone curlew .70 .25
584 A139 Block of 4 7.25 7.25
a. 8f Great gray shrike .90 .35
b. 8f Red-backed shrike .90 .35
c. 8f Rufous-backed shrike .90 .35
d. 8f Black-naped oriole .90 .35
585 A139 Block of 4 8.00 8.00
a. 10f Willow warbler 1.00 .45
b. 10f Great reed warbler 1.00 .45
c. 10f Blackcap 1.00 .45
d. 10f Common (barn) swallow 1.00 .45
586 A139 Block of 4 12.50 12.50
a. 15f Common rock thrush 1.60 .75
b. 15f European redstart 1.60 .75
c. 15f Wheatear 1.60 .75
d. 15f Bluethroat 1.60 .75
587 A139 Block of 4 14.50 14.50
a. 20f Houbara bustard 1.75 .85
b. 20f Pin-tailed sandgrouse 1.75 .85
c. 20f Ypecaha wood rail 1.75 .85
d. 20f Spotted crake 1.75 .85

Size (single stamp): 35x35mm

588 A139 Block of 4 16.00 16.00
a. 25f American sparrow hawk 2.00 1.00
b. 25f Great black-backed gull 2.00 1.00
c. 25f Purple heron 2.00 1.00
d. 25f Wryneck 2.00 1.00
589 A139 Block of 4 24.00 24.00
a. 30f European bee-eater 3.00 1.40
b. 30f Goshawk 3.00 1.40
c. 30f Gray wagtail 3.00 1.40
d. 30f Pied wagtail 3.00 1.40
590 A139 Block of 4 32.50 32.50
a. 45f Crossbows 4.25 1.90
b. 45f Tent-shaped net 4.25 1.90
c. 45f Hand net 4.25 1.90
d. 45f Rooftop trap 4.25 1.90
Nos. 583-590 (8) 120.25 120.25

Human Rights Flame — A141

1973, Dec. 10 Litho. ***Perf. 12***

594 A141 10f red & multi 1.00 .20
595 A141 40f lt green & multi 2.00 .50
596 A141 75f lilac & multi 3.00 .85
Nos. 594-596 (3) 6.00 1.55

25th anniv. of the Universal Declaration of Human Rights.

Promoting Animal Resources A142

Stylized Wheat and Kuwaiti Flag — A143

1974, Feb. 16 Litho. ***Perf. 12½***

597 A142 30f violet blue & multi 1.10 .30
598 A142 40f rose & multi 1.50 .40

4th Congress of the Arab Veterinary Union, Kuwait.

1974, Feb. 25 ***Perf. 13½x13***

599 A143 20f lemon & multi .50 .20
600 A143 30f bister brn & multi 1.50 .40
601 A143 70f silver & multi 2.25 .90
Nos. 599-601 (3) 4.25 1.50

13th anniversary of National Day.

Conference Emblem and Sheik Sabah — A144

1974, Mar. 8 ***Perf. 12½***

602 A144 30f multicolored 2.50 .70
603 A144 40f yellow & multi 3.50 .90

12th Conf. of the Arab Medical Union and 1st Conf. of the Kuwait Medical Soc.

Tournament Emblem — A145

1974, Mar. 15

604 A145 25f multicolored 1.50 .50
605 A145 45f multicolored 2.50 .75

Third Soccer Tournament for the Arabian Gulf Trophy, Kuwait, Mar. 1974.

Scientific Research Institute — A146

1974, Apr. 3 Photo. ***Perf. 12½***

606 A146 15f magenta & multi 1.50 .25
607 A146 20f green & multi 2.50 .35

Opening of Kuwait Scientific Research Institute.

Arab Postal Union, Kuwait and UPU Emblems A147

1974, May 1 ***Perf. 13x14***

608 A147 20f gold & multi .75 .20
609 A147 30f gold & multi 1.00 .30
610 A147 60f gold & multi 1.50 .80
Nos. 608-610 (3) 3.25 1.30

Centenary of Universal Postal Union.

Telephone Dial with Communications Symbols and Globe — A148

1974, May 17 ***Perf. 14x13½***

611 A148 10f blue & multi .75 .20
612 A148 30f multicolored 2.00 .60
613 A148 40f black & multi 2.50 .80
Nos. 611-613 (3) 5.25 1.60

World Telecommunications Day, May 17.

Emblem of Unity Council and Flags of Member States — A149

1974, June 25 Litho. ***Perf. 13½***

614 A149 20f red, black & green 1.10 .40
615 A149 30f green, black & red 1.50 .55

17th anniversary of the signing of the Arab Economic Unity Agreement.

WPY Emblem, Embryo, "Growth" — A150

1974, Aug. 19 Litho. ***Perf. 14x14½***

616 A150 30f black & multi 1.50 .40
617 A150 70f violet blue & multi 2.50 .90

World Population Year.

Development Building and Emblem — A151

1974, Oct. 30 Litho. ***Perf. 13x13½***

618 A151 10f pink & multi 1.00 .20
619 A151 20f ultra & multi 1.50 .30

Kuwait Fund for Arab Economic Development.

Emblem of Shuaiba Industrial Area — A152

1974, Dec. 17 Litho. ***Perf. 12½x12***

620 A152 10f lt blue & multi 1.00 .20
621 A152 20f salmon & multi 2.00 .40
622 A152 30f lt green & multi 2.50 .80
Nos. 620-622 (3) 5.50 1.40

Shuaiba Industrial Area, 10th anniversary.

Arms of Kuwait and "14" — A153

1975, Feb. 25 Litho. ***Perf. 13x13½***

623 A153 20f multicolored 1.00 .30
624 A153 70f yel green & multi 2.00 .85
625 A153 75f rose & multi 2.75 1.00
Nos. 623-625 (3) 5.75 2.15

14th anniversary of National Day.

Male and Female Symbols — A154

1975, Apr. 14 Photo. *Perf. 11½x12*

626 A154 8f lt green & multi .50 .20
627 A154 20f rose & multi .55 .25
628 A154 30f blue & multi .75 .40
629 A154 70f yellow & multi 2.00 .85
630 A154 100f black & multi 3.00 1.40
Nos. 626-630 (5) 6.80 3.10

Kuwaiti census 1975.

IWY and Kuwaiti Women's Union Emblems — A155

1975, June 10 Litho. *Perf. 14½*

631 A155 15f brown org & multi 1.00 .25
632 A155 20f olive & multi 1.25 .40
633 A155 30f violet & multi 1.50 .65
Nos. 631-633 (3) 3.75 1.30

International Women's Year.

Classroom and UNESCO Emblem A156

1975, Sept. 8 Litho. *Perf. 12½x12*

634 A156 20f green & multi 1.00 .25
635 A156 30f multicolored 1.50 .65

International Literacy Day.

Symbols of Measurements A157

UN Flag, Rifle and Olive Branch — A158

1975, Oct. 14 Photo. *Perf. 14x13*

636 A157 10f green & multi .75 .20
637 A157 20f purple & multi 1.10 .40

World Standards Day.

1975, Oct. 24 Litho. *Perf. 12x12½*

638 A158 20f multicolored 1.00 .25
639 A158 45f orange & multi 1.75 .70

United Nations, 30th anniversary.

Sheik Sabah — A159

1975, Dec. 22 Litho. *Perf. 12½x12*

640 A159 8f yellow & multi .95 .20
641 A159 20f lilac & multi 1.25 .40
642 A159 30f buff & multi 1.60 .50
643 A159 50f salmon & multi 2.50 .90
644 A159 90f lt blue & multi 5.25 1.60
645 A159 100f multicolored 5.75 1.90
Nos. 640-645 (6) 17.30 5.50

"Progress" — A160

1976, Feb. 25 Litho. *Perf. 12*

646 A160 10f multicolored .75 .20
647 A160 20f multicolored 1.40 .20

15th anniversary of National Day.

Medical Equipment, Emblem and Surgery — A161

Telephones, 1876 and 1976 — A162

1976, Mar. 1 Litho. *Perf. 14½*

648 A161 5f dull green & multi .50 .20
649 A161 10f blue & multi 1.25 .30
650 A161 30f gray & multi 3.50 .80
Nos. 648-650 (3) 5.25 1.30

Kuwait Medical Assoc., 2nd annual conference.

1976, Mar. 10 Litho. *Perf. 12*

651 A162 5f orange & black .50 .20
652 A162 15f lt blue & black 1.25 .20

Centenary of first telephone call by Alexander Graham Bell, Mar. 10, 1876.

Human Eye — A163

Photo. & Engr.

1976, Apr. 7 *Perf. 11½*

653 A163 10f multicolored .75 .20
654 A163 20f black & multi 1.25 .30
655 A163 30f multicolored 2.00 .50
Nos. 653-655 (3) 4.00 1.00

World Health Day: "Foresight prevents blindness."

Red Crescent Emblem A164

1976, May 8 Litho. *Perf. 12x11½*

656 A164 20f brt green, blk & red .85 .30
657 A164 30f vio blue, blk & red 1.40 .35
658 A164 45f yellow, blk & red 2.00 .70
659 A164 75f lilac rose, blk & red 3.25 1.00
Nos. 656-659 (4) 7.50 2.35

Kuwait Red Crescent Society, 10th anniv.

Modern Suburb of Kuwait A165

1976, June 1 Photo. *Perf. 13x13½*

660 A165 10f light green & multi .75 .20
661 A165 20f salmon & multi 1.25 .25

Habitat, UN Conference on Human Settlements, Vancouver, Canada, May 31-June 11.

Basketball, Kuwait Olympic Emblem — A166

Various Races, Map of Sri Lanka — A167

Designs: 8f, Running. 10f, Judo. 15f, Fieldball. 20f, Gymnastics. 30f, Water polo. 45f, Soccer. 70f, Swimmers at start.

1976, July 17 Litho. *Perf. 14½*

662 A166 4f black & multi .40 .20
663 A166 8f red & multi .40 .20
664 A166 10f green & multi .40 .20
665 A166 15f lemon & multi .50 .20
666 A166 20f blue & multi .75 .20
667 A166 30f lilac & multi 1.00 .40
668 A166 45f multicolored 1.25 .55
669 A166 70f brown & multi 1.75 .85
Nos. 662-669 (8) 6.45 2.80

21st Olympic Games, Montreal, Canada, July 17-Aug. 1.

1976, Aug. 16 Photo. *Perf. 14*

670 A167 20f dk blue & multi .60 .20
671 A167 30f purple & multi .75 .45
672 A167 45f green & multi 1.50 .65
Nos. 670-672 (3) 2.85 1.30

5th Summit Conf. of Non-aligned Countries, Colombo, Sri Lanka, Aug. 9-19.

"UNESCO," Torch and Kuwait Arms — A168

1976, Nov. 4 Litho. *Perf. 12x11½*

673 A168 20f yel green & multi 1.00 .20
674 A168 45f scarlet & multi 1.75 .70

30th anniversary of UNESCO.

Blindman's Buff A169

Popular games. 5f, 15f, 30f, vertical.

Perf. 14½x14, 14x14½

1977, Jan. 10 Litho.

675 A169 5f Pot throwing .50 .20
676 A169 5f Kite flying .50 .20
677 A169 5f Balancing sticks .50 .20
678 A169 5f Spinning tops .50 .20
a. Block of 4, #675-678 2.00 2.00
679 A169 10f shown .75 .20
680 A169 10f Rowing .75 .20
681 A169 10f Hoops .75 .20
682 A169 10f Ropes .75 .20
a. Block of 4, #679-682 3.00 3.00
683 A169 15f Rope skipping 1.25 .35
684 A169 15f Marbles 1.25 .35
685 A169 15f Cart steering 1.25 .35
686 A169 15f Teetotum 1.25 .25
a. Block of 4, #683-686 5.00 5.00
687 A169 20f Halma 1.50 .55
688 A169 20f Model boats 1.50 .55
689 A169 20f Pot and candle 1.50 .55
690 A169 20f Hide and seek 1.50 .55
a. Block of 4, #687-690 6.00 6.00
691 A169 30f Throwing bones 1.75 .75
692 A169 30f Mystery gifts 1.75 .75
693 A169 30f Hopscotch 1.75 .75
694 A169 30f Catch as catch can 1.75 .75
a. Block of 4, #691-694 7.00 7.00
695 A169 40f Bowls 3.00 1.00
696 A169 40f Sword fighting 3.00 1.00
697 A169 40f Mother and child 3.00 1.00
698 A169 40f Fivestones 3.00 1.00
a. Block of 4, #695-698 12.00 12.00
699 A169 60f Hiding a cake 4.00 1.75
700 A169 60f Chess 4.00 1.75
701 A169 60f Dancing 4.00 1.75
702 A169 60f Treasure hunt 4.00 1.75
a. Block of 4, #699-702 16.00 16.00
703 A169 70f Hobby-horses 4.75 1.90
704 A169 70f Hide and seek 4.75 1.90
705 A169 70f Catch 4.75 1.90
706 A169 70f Storytelling 4.75 1.90
a. Block of 4, #703-706 19.00 19.00
Nos. 675-706 (32) 70.00 26.70

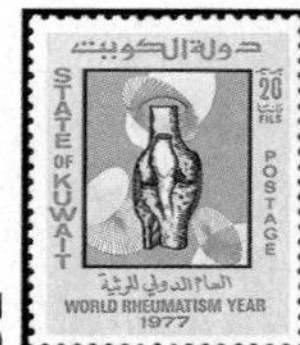

Diseased Knee — A170

1977, Feb. 15 *Perf. 13x13½*

707 A170 20f yellow & multi .75 .25
708 A170 30f multicolored 1.25 .45
709 A170 45f red & multi 1.50 .70
710 A170 75f black & multi 2.50 1.25
Nos. 707-710 (4) 6.00 2.65

World Rheumatism Year.

Sheik Sabah A171

1977, Feb. 25 Photo. *Perf. 13½x13*

711 A171 10f multicolored .50 .20
712 A171 15f multicolored .65 .30
713 A171 30f multicolored .85 .35
714 A171 80f multicolored 2.25 .95
Nos. 711-714 (4) 4.25 1.80

16th National Day.

Kuwait Tower — A172

APU Emblem — A173

1977, Feb. 26 *Perf. 14x13½*

715 A172 30f multicolored 1.00 .25
716 A172 80f multicolored 2.50 .80

Inauguration of Kuwait Tower.

1977, Apr. 12 Litho. *Perf. 13½x14*

717 A173 5f yellow & multi .55 .20
718 A173 15f pink & multi .60 .20
719 A173 30f lt blue & multi 1.00 .30
720 A173 80f lilac & multi 2.00 .90
Nos. 717-720 (4) 4.15 1.60

Arab Postal Union, 25th anniversary.

Electronic Tree — A174

1977, May 17 Litho. *Perf. 12x12½*

721 A174 30f brown & red 1.25 .40
722 A174 80f green & red 2.50 1.00

World Telecommunications Day.

Sheik Sabah — A175

Games Emblem — A176

1977, June 1 Photo. *Perf. 11½x12*

723 A175 15f blue & multi 1.40 1.10
724 A175 25f yellow & multi 2.25 1.10
725 A175 30f red & multi 2.75 1.60
726 A175 80f violet & multi 9.00 4.00
727 A175 100f dp org & multi 9.75 4.50
728 A175 150f ultra & multi 13.50 7.25
729 A175 200f olive & multi 18.00 10.00
Nos. 723-729 (7) 56.65 29.55

1977, Oct. 1 Litho. *Perf. 12*

730 A176 30f multicolored 1.00 .75
731 A176 80f multicolored 2.50 1.50

4th Asian Basketball Youth Championship, Oct. 1-15.

Dome of the Rock, Bishop Capucci, Fatima Bernawi, Sheik Abu Tair — A177

1977, Nov. 1 *Perf. 14*

732 A177 30f multicolored 3.00 1.25
733 A177 80f multicolored 6.50 3.00

Struggle for the liberation of Palestine.

Children and Houses A178

Children's Paintings: No. 735, Women musicians. No. 736, Boats. No. 737, Women preparing food, vert. No. 738, Women and children, vert. No. 739, Seated woman, vert.

1977, Nov. Photo. *Perf. 13½x13*

734 A178 15f lt green & multi .65 .30
735 A178 15f yellow & multi .65 .30
736 A178 30f brt yellow & multi 1.10 .60
737 A178 30f lt violet & multi 1.10 .60
738 A178 80f black & multi 2.10 1.60
739 A178 80f rose & multi 2.10 1.60
Nos. 734-739 (6) 7.70 5.00

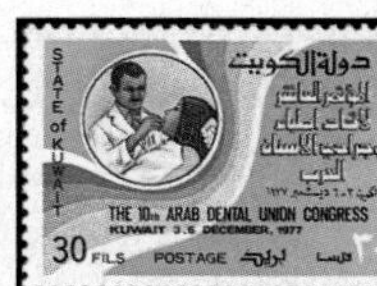
Dentist Treating Patient A179

1977, Dec. 3

740 A179 30f green & multi 1.50 1.00
741 A179 80f violet & multi 3.50 1.90

10th Arab Dental Union Congress, Kuwait, Dec. 3-6.

Ships Unloading Water A180

Kuwait water resources. 30f, 80f, 100f, vert.

Perf. 14x13½, 13½x14

1978, Jan. 25 Litho.

742 Block of 4 1.50 1.50
a. 5f shown .30 .20
b. 5f Home delivery by camel .30 .20
c. 5f Man with water bags .30 .20
d. 5f Man with wheelbarrow .30 .20
743 Block of 4 2.50 2.50
a. 10f Well .50 .20
b. 10f Trough .50 .20
c. 10f Water hole .50 .20
d. 10f Irrigation .50 .20
744 Block of 4 3.00 3.00
a. 15f Sheep drinking .60 .20
b. 15f Laundresses .60 .20
c. 15f Sheep and camels drinking .60 .20
d. 15f Water stored in skins .60 .20
745 Block of 4 3.50 3.50
a. 20f Animals at well .75 .20
b. 20f Water in home .75 .20
c. 20f Water pot .75 .20
d. 20f Communal fountain .75 .20
746 Block of 4 4.25 4.25
a. 25f Distillation plant .85 .30
b. 25f Motorized delivery .85 .30
c. 25f Water trucks .85 .30
d. 25f Water towers .85 .30
747 Block of 4 6.00 6.00
a. 30f Shower bath 1.25 .30
b. 30f Water tower 1.25 .30
c. 30f Gathering rain water 1.25 .30
d. 30f 2 water towers 1.25 .30
748 Block of 4 13.50 13.50
a. 80f Donkey with water bags 2.75 .90
b. 80f Woman with water can 2.75 .90
c. 80f Woman with water skin 2.75 .90
d. 80f Loading tank car 2.75 .90
749 Block of 4 17.50 17.50
a. 100f Truck delivering water 3.50 1.10
b. 100f Barnyard water supply 3.50 1.10
c. 100f Children at water basin 3.50 1.10
d. 100f Well in courtyard 3.50 1.10
Nos. 742-749 (8) 51.75 51.75

Radar, Torch, Minarets A181

1978, Feb. 25 Litho. *Perf. 14x14½*

750 A181 30f multicolored .60 .25
751 A181 80f multicolored 1.50 .75

17th National Day.

Man with Smallpox, Target — A182

1978, Apr. 17 Litho. *Perf. 12½*

752 A182 30f violet & multi 1.25 .50
753 A182 80f green & multi 2.75 1.40

Global eradication of smallpox.

Antenna and ITU Emblem A183

1978, May 17 *Perf. 14*

754 A183 30f silver & multi .75 .30
755 A183 80f silver & multi 2.00 .75

10th World Telecommunications Day.

Sheik Sabah — A184

1978, June 28 Litho. *Perf. 13x14*

Portrait in Brown

Size: 21½x27mm

756 A184 15f green & gold .40 .20
757 A184 30f orange & gold .65 .45
758 A184 80f rose lilac & gold 1.50 1.10
759 A184 100f lt green & gold 1.75 1.25
760 A184 130f lt brown & gold 2.00 1.75
761 A184 180f violet & gold 3.50 2.75

Size: 23½x29mm

762 A184 1d red & gold 15.00 12.50
763 A184 4d blue & gold 62.50 57.50
Nos. 756-763 (8) 87.30 77.50

Mt. Arafat, Pilgrims, Holy Kaaba A185

1978, Nov. 9 Photo. *Perf. 11½*

764 A185 30f multicolored 1.25 .65
765 A185 80f multicolored 3.00 1.60

Pilgrimage to Mecca.

UN and Anti-Apartheid Emblems — A186

1978, Nov. 27 Litho. *Perf. 12*

766 A186 30f multicolored .60 .30
767 A186 80f multicolored 1.25 .80
768 A186 180f multicolored 3.25 1.90
Nos. 766-768 (3) 5.10 3.00

Anti-Apartheid Year.

Refugees, Human Rights Emblems A187

1978, Dec. 10 Photo. *Perf. 13x13½*

769 A187 30f multicolored .75 .35
770 A187 80f multicolored 1.75 .90
771 A187 100f multicolored 2.50 1.10
Nos. 769-771 (3) 5.00 2.35

Declaration of Human Rights, 30th anniv.

Information Center — A188

1978, Dec. 26 Photo. *Perf. 13*

772 A188 5f multicolored .40 .20
773 A188 15f multicolored .50 .20
774 A188 30f multicolored .75 .35
775 A188 80f multicolored 1.75 .85
Nos. 772-775 (4) 3.40 1.60

New Kuwait Information Center.

Kindergarten A189

1979, Jan. 24 Photo. *Perf. 13½x14*

776 A189 30f multicolored 1.25 .50
777 A189 80f multicolored 2.25 1.25

International Year of the Child.

Flag and Peace Doves — A190

1979, Feb. 25 *Perf. 14½x14*

778 A190 30f multicolored .75 .35
779 A190 80f multicolored 1.50 .85

18th National Day.

Modern Agriculture in Kuwait — A191

1979, Mar. 13 Photo. *Perf. 14*

780 A191 30f multicolored .85 .45
781 A191 80f multicolored 2.00 1.10

4th Congress of Arab Agriculture Ministers of the Gulf and Arabian Peninsula.

World Map, Book, Symbols of Learning A192

1979, Mar. 22

782 A192 30f multicolored 1.00 .45
783 A192 80f multicolored 2.00 1.10

Cultural achievements of the Arabs.

Children with Balloons — A193

Children's Paintings: No. 785, Boys flying kites. No. 786, Girl and doves. No. 787, Children and houses, horiz. No. 788, Four children, horiz. No. 789, Children sitting in circle, horiz.

1979, Apr. 18 Photo. *Perf. 14*
784 A193 30f yellow & multi 1.00 .45
785 A193 30f buff & multi 1.00 .45
786 A193 30f pale yel & multi 1.00 .45
787 A193 80f lt blue & multi 2.25 1.25
788 A193 80f yel green & multi 2.25 1.25
789 A193 80f lilac & multi 2.25 1.25
Nos. 784-789 (6) 9.75 5.10

Cables, ITU Emblem, People A194

1979, May 17
790 A194 30f multicolored 1.00 .40
791 A194 80f multicolored 2.00 1.25

World Telecommunications Day.

Military Sports Council Emblem — A195

1979, June 1 Photo. *Perf. 14*
792 A195 30f multicolored 1.00 .40
793 A195 80f multicolored 2.00 1.25

29th Intl. Military Soccer Championship.

Child, Industrial Landscape, Environmental Emblems — A196

1979, June 5 *Perf. 12x11½*
794 A196 30f multicolored 1.25 .60
795 A196 80f multicolored 3.00 1.60

World Environment Day, June 5.

Children Holding Globe, UNESCO Emblem A197

1979, July 25 Litho. *Perf. 11½x12*
796 A197 30f multicolored 1.00 .40
797 A197 80f multicolored 2.00 1.10
798 A197 130f multicolored 2.75 1.75
Nos. 796-798 (3) 5.75 3.25

Intl. Bureau of Education, Geneva, 50th anniv.

Kuwait Kindergartens, 25th Anniversary A198

Children's Drawings: 80f, Children waving flags.

1979, Sept. 15 Litho. *Perf. 12½*
799 A198 30f multicolored 1.00 .40
800 A198 80f multicolored 2.00 1.10

Pilgrims at Holy Ka'aba, Mecca Mosque A199

1979, Oct. 29 *Perf. 14x14½*
801 A199 30f multicolored 1.25 .50
802 A199 80f multicolored 3.00 1.50

Hegira (Pilgrimage Year).

International Palestinian Solidarity Day — A200

1979, Nov. 29 Photo. *Perf. 11½x12*
803 A200 30f multicolored 3.00 .95
804 A200 80f multicolored 5.75 1.90

Kuwait Airways 25th Anniversary A201

1979, Dec. 24 Photo. *Perf. 13x13½*
805 A201 30f multicolored 1.25 .60
806 A201 80f multicolored 3.00 1.75

19th National Day A202

1980, Feb. 25 Litho. *Perf. 14x14½*
807 A202 30f multicolored 1.00 .40
808 A202 80f multicolored 2.00 1.10

1980 Population Census A203

1980, Mar. 18 *Perf. 13½x14*
809 A203 30f multicolored 1.00 .35
810 A203 80f multicolored 2.00 .85

World Health Day A204

1980, Apr. 7
811 A204 30f multicolored 1.25 .55
812 A204 80f multicolored 3.00 1.60

Kuwait Municipality, 50th Anniversary A205

1980, May 1 Photo. *Perf. 14*
813 A205 15f multicolored .60 .20
814 A205 30f multicolored 1.10 .50
815 A205 80f multicolored 2.50 1.25
Nos. 813-815 (3) 4.20 1.95

Citizens of Kuwait A206

Future Kuwait (Children's Drawings): 80f, Super highway.

1980, May 14 Litho. *Perf. 14x14½*
816 A206 30f multicolored 1.25 .50
817 A206 80f multicolored 3.00 1.60

World Environment Day — A207

1980, June 5 Litho. *Perf. 12x11½*
818 A207 30f multicolored 1.25 .35
819 A207 80f multicolored 2.75 .95

Swimming, Moscow '80 and Kuwait Olympic Committee Emblems — A208

1980, July 19 Litho. *Perf. 12x12½*
820 A208 15f Volleyball .40 .20
821 A208 15f Tennis .40 .20
a. Vert. pair, #820-821 .90 .90
822 A208 30f shown .70 .30
823 A208 30f Weight lifting .70 .30
824 A208 30f Basketball .70 .30
825 A208 30f Judo .70 .30
a. Block of 4, #822-825 3.25 3.25
826 A208 80f Gymnast 1.75 .80
827 A208 80f Badminton 1.75 .80
828 A208 80f Fencing 1.75 .80
829 A208 80f Soccer 1.75 .80
a. Block of 4, #826-829 7.75 7.75
Nos. 820-829 (10) 10.60 4.80

22nd Summer Olympic Games, Moscow, July 19-Aug. 3.

20th Anniversary of OPEC A209

1980, Sept. 16 Litho. *Perf. 14x14½*
830 A209 30f multicolored 1.25 .60
831 A209 80f multicolored 3.00 .90

Hegira (Pilgrimage Year) A210

1980, Nov. 9 Photo. *Perf. 12x11½*
832 A210 15f multicolored .50 .20
833 A210 30f multicolored 1.10 .45
834 A210 80f multicolored 3.00 1.25
Nos. 832-834 (3) 4.60 1.90

Dome of the Rock, Jerusalem — A211

1980, Nov. 29 *Perf. 12x11½*
835 A211 30f multicolored 3.00 .60
836 A211 80f multicolored 5.00 1.60

International Palestinian Solidarity Day.

Avicenna (980-1037), Philosopher and Physician A212

Conference Emblem — A213

1980, Dec. 7 *Perf. 12x12½*
837 A212 30f multicolored 1.50 .35
838 A212 80f multicolored 2.75 .95

1981, Jan. 12 Photo. *Perf. 13½x13*
839 A213 30f multicolored 1.00 .75
840 A213 80f multicolored 3.50 2.10

First Islamic Medical Conference.

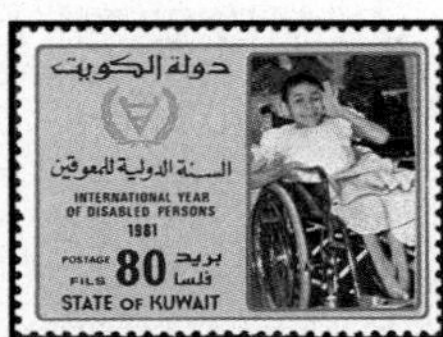

Girl in Wheelchair A214

International Year of the Disabled: 30f, Man in wheelchair playing billiards, vert.

Perf. 13½x13, 13x13½
1981, Jan. 26 Photo.
841 A214 30f multicolored 1.00 .55
842 A214 80f multicolored 2.50 1.60

20th National Day
A215

1981, Feb. 25 Litho. ***Perf. 13x13½***

843 A215 30f multicolored 1.00 .55
844 A215 80f multicolored 2.50 1.60

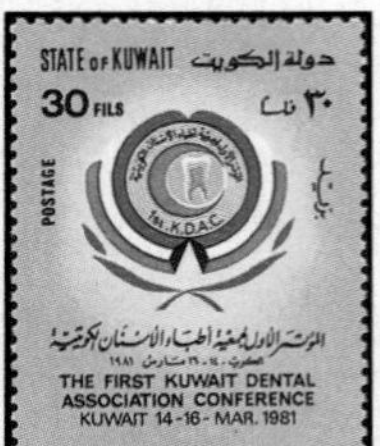

First Kuwait Dental Association Conference
A216

1981, Mar. 14 ***Perf. 11½x12***

845 A216 30f multicolored 2.00 1.10
846 A216 80f multicolored 6.00 2.75

A217

A218

1981, May 8 Photo. ***Perf. 14***

847 A217 30f multicolored 2.00 1.25
848 A217 80f multicolored 6.00 3.50

Intl. Red Cross day.

1981, May 17 Litho. ***Perf. 14½x14***

849 A218 30f multicolored 1.75 1.00
850 A218 80f multicolored 4.50 2.40

13th World Telecommunications day.

World Environment Day — A219

1981, June 5 Photo. ***Perf. 12***

851 A219 30f multicolored 1.10 .70
852 A219 80f multicolored 3.25 1.90

Sief Palace
A220

A221

1981, Sept. 16 Litho. ***Perf. 12***

853 A220 5f multicolored .20 .20
854 A220 10f multicolored .20 .20
855 A220 15f multicolored .20 .20
856 A220 25f multicolored .20 .20
857 A220 30f multicolored .25 .20
858 A220 40f multicolored .40 .20
859 A220 60f multicolored .65 .25
860 A220 80f multicolored .85 .45
861 A220 100f multicolored 1.10 .65
862 A220 115f multicolored 1.25 .80
863 A220 130f multicolored 1.40 1.00
864 A220 150f multicolored 1.75 1.00
865 A220 180f multicolored 2.10 1.10
866 A220 250f multicolored 3.00 1.25
867 A220 500f multicolored 6.00 1.75
868 A221 1d multicolored 11.00 2.50
869 A221 2d multicolored 24.00 3.50
870 A221 3d multicolored 35.00 11.00
871 A221 4d multicolored 45.00 14.00
Nos. 853-871 (19) 134.55 40.45

Islamic Pilgrimage
A222

1981, Oct. 7 Photo. ***Perf. 13x13½***

872 A222 30f multicolored .85 .70
873 A222 80f multicolored 3.00 1.75

World Food Day
A223

1981, Oct. 16 Litho. ***Perf. 13***

874 A223 30f multicolored .95 .65
875 A223 80f multicolored 3.00 1.75

A224

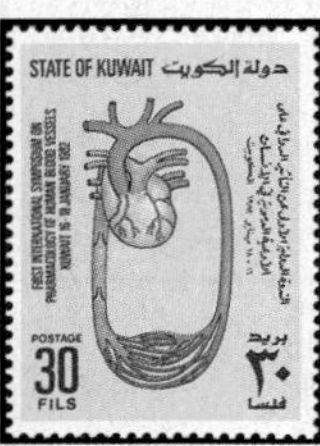

A225

1981, Dec. 30 Photo. ***Perf. 14***

876 A224 30f multicolored 1.00 .65
877 A224 80f multicolored 3.00 1.75

20th anniv. of national television.

1982, Jan. 16 Photo. ***Perf. 14***

878 A225 30f multicolored 1.10 1.10
879 A225 80f multicolored 3.50 1.75

First Intl. Pharmacology of Human Blood Vessels Symposium, Jan. 16-18.

21st Natl. Day — A226

1982, Feb. 25 ***Perf. 13½x13***

880 A226 30f multicolored .70 .45
881 A226 80f multicolored 2.00 1.25

Scouting Year
A227

1982, Mar. 22 Photo. ***Perf. 12x11½***

882 A227 30f multicolored .90 .55
883 A227 80f multicolored 2.50 1.50

Arab Pharmacists' Day — A228

1982, Apr. 2 Litho. ***Perf. 12x11½***

884 A228 30f lt green & multi 1.25 .90
885 A228 80f pink & multi 4.00 2.50

World Health Day — A229

Arab Postal Union, 30th Anniv. — A230

1982, Apr. 7 Litho. ***Perf. 13½x13***

886 A229 30f multicolored 1.40 .65
887 A229 80f multicolored 4.00 1.75

1982, Apr. 12 Photo. ***Perf. 13½x13***

888 A230 30f multicolored 1.25 .85
889 A230 80f multicolored 4.00 2.25

TB Bacillus Centenary
A231

1982, May 24 Litho. ***Perf. 11½x12***

890 A231 30f multicolored 2.00 .90
891 A231 80f multicolored 5.75 2.50

1982 World Cup
A232

1982, June 17 Photo. ***Perf. 14***

892 A232 30f multicolored 1.10 .65
893 A232 80f multicolored 3.50 1.75

10th Anniv. of Science and Natural History Museum
A233

1982, July 14 ***Perf. 14***

894 A233 30f multicolored 4.50 2.00
895 A233 80f multicolored 11.00 5.00

6th Anniv. of United Arab Shipping Co.
A234

Designs: Freighters.

1982, Sept. 1 ***Perf. 13***

896 A234 30f multicolored 1.25 .40
897 A234 80f multicolored 2.75 1.10

Arab Day of the Palm Tree — A235

1982, Sept. 15 ***Perf. 14***

898 A235 30f multicolored .75 .45
899 A235 80f multicolored 2.25 1.25

Islamic Pilgrimage
A236

1982, Sept. 26 **Litho.**

900 A236 15f multicolored .50 .30
901 A236 30f multicolored 1.25 .65
902 A236 80f multicolored 3.25 1.75
Nos. 900-902 (3) 5.00 2.70

Desert Flowers & Plants — A237

Frame colors: No. 903a, green. b, violet. c, deep salmon. d, rose red. e, pale brown. f, deep green. g, pale orange. h, brown red. i, tan. j, violet blue.

No. 904: a, yellow green. b, pink. c, pale blue. d, dark blue. e, pale gray green. f, lake.

g, pale orange. h, blue. i, red lilac. j, red orange.

No. 905: a, brown. b, pink. c, blue. d, olive green. e, orange red. f, dark blue. g, green. h, rose. i, bister. j, pale orange.

No. 906: a, yellow green. b, dark blue. c, pale orange. d, rose red. e, green. f, gray violet. g, gray blue. h, violet. i, yellow brown. j, orange red.

No. 907: a, lilac. b, blue green. c, pale orange. d, pale brown. e, violet blue. f, yellow. g, green blue. h, purple. i, pale brown. j, pale orange.

1983, Jan. 25 Litho. *Perf. 12*

903	Strip of 10	3.50	1.00
a.-j.	A237 10f any single	.30	.20
904	Strip of 10	4.50	1.25
a.-j.	A237 15f any single	.40	.20
905	Strip of 10	7.50	2.75
a.-j.	A237 30f any single	.65	.25
906	Strip of 10	9.00	3.25
a.-j	A237 40f any single, horiz.	.80	.30
907	Strip of 10	20.00	7.00
a.-j.	A237 80f any single, horiz.	1.75	.60
	Nos. 903-907 (5)	44.50	15.25

22nd Natl. Day A238

1983, Feb. 25 Litho. *Perf. 12½*

908	A238 30f multicolored	.80	.50
909	A238 80f multicolored	2.25	1.40

25th Anniv. of Intl. Maritime Org. A239

1983, Mar. 17 Photo. *Perf. 14*

910	A239 30f multicolored	.50	.30
911	A239 80f multicolored	1.40	.85

Map of Middle East and Africa, Conference Emblem — A240

1983, Mar. 19 *Perf. 13*

912	A240 15f multicolored	.40	.20
913	A240 30f multicolored	1.00	.50
914	A240 80f multicolored	3.00	1.40
	Nos. 912-914 (3)	4.40	2.10

3rd Intl. Conference on the Impact of Viral Diseases on the Development of the Middle East and Africa, Mar. 19-27.

World Health Day A241

1983, Apr. 7 *Perf. 12x11½*

915	A241 15f multicolored	.45	.30
916	A241 30f multicolored	.95	.70
917	A241 80f multicolored	2.75	1.90
	Nos. 915-917 (3)	4.15	2.90

World Communications Year — A242

1983, May 17 Photo. *Perf. 13x13½*

918	A242 15f multicolored	.55	.30
919	A242 30f multicolored	1.10	.70
920	A242 80f multicolored	3.25	1.90
	Nos. 918-920 (3)	4.90	2.90

World Environment Day — A243

1983, June 5 Litho. *Perf. 12½*

921	A243 15f multicolored	.65	.30
922	A243 30f multicolored	1.25	.70
923	A243 80f multicolored	3.75	1.90
	Nos. 921-923 (3)	5.65	2.90

Wall of Old Jerusalem A244

1983, July 25 Litho. *Perf. 12*

924	A244 15f multicolored	.75	.25
925	A244 30f multicolored	1.75	.55
926	A244 80f multicolored	5.00	1.60
	Nos. 924-926 (3)	7.50	2.40

World Heritage Year.

Islamic Pilgrimage A245

1983, Sept. 15 Photo. *Perf. 11½*

927	A245 15f multicolored	.40	.25
928	A245 30f multicolored	1.00	.55
929	A245 80f multicolored	2.75	1.60
	Nos. 927-929 (3)	4.15	2.40

Intl. Palestinian Solidarity Day — A246

1983, Nov. 29 Photo. *Perf. 14*

930	A246 15f multicolored	.50	.25
931	A246 30f multicolored	1.25	.55
932	A246 80f multicolored	3.50	1.60
	Nos. 930-932 (3)	5.25	2.40

21st Pan Arab Medical Congress, Jan. 30-Feb. 2 — A247

1984, Jan. 30 Litho. *Perf. 14½x14*

933	A247 15f purple & multi	.50	.25
934	A247 30f blue grn & multi	1.25	.55
935	A247 80f pink & multi	3.25	1.60
	Nos. 933-935 (3)	5.00	2.40

Key, Natl. Emblem, and Health Establishments Emblem A248

1984, Feb. 20 Photo. *Perf. 13x13½*

936	A248 15f multicolored	.45	.25
937	A248 30f multicolored	1.10	.55
938	A248 80f multicolored	3.00	1.60
	Nos. 936-938 (3)	4.55	2.40

Inauguration of Amiri and Al-Razi Hospitals, Allergy Center and Medical Stores Center.

23rd National Day — A249

1984, Feb. 25 Litho. *Perf. 13½*

939	A249 15f multicolored	.40	.25
940	A249 30f multicolored	1.00	.55
941	A249 80f multicolored	2.75	1.60
	Nos. 939-941 (3)	4.15	2.40

2nd Kuwait Intl. Medical Science Conf., Mar. 4-8 — A250

1984, Mar. 4 Photo. *Perf. 12*
Granite Paper

942	A250 15f multicolored	.50	.25
943	A250 30f multicolored	1.25	.55
944	A250 80f multicolored	3.25	1.60
	Nos. 942-944 (3)	5.00	2.40

30th Anniv. of Kuwait Airways Corp. A251

1984, Mar. 15 *Perf. 13½*

946	A251 30f multicolored	1.10	.90
947	A251 80f multicolored	2.75	1.60

Al-Arabi Magazine, 25th Anniv. — A252

1984, Mar. 20 *Perf. 14½x14*

948	A252 15f multicolored	.45	.25
949	A252 30f multicolored	.95	.50
950	A252 80f multicolored	2.50	1.40
	Nos. 948-950 (3)	3.90	2.15

World Health Day — A253

1984, Apr. 7 *Perf. 12*

951	A253 15f multicolored	.40	.25
952	A253 30f multicolored	1.00	.55
953	A253 80f multicolored	2.75	1.60
	Nos. 951-953 (3)	4.15	2.40

Hanan Kuwaiti Orphan Village, Sudan A254

1984, May 15 Litho. *Perf. 12*

954	A254 15f multicolored	.40	.25
955	A254 30f multicolored	1.00	.55
956	A254 80f multicolored	2.75	1.60
	Nos. 954-956 (3)	4.15	2.40

Intl. Civil Aviation Org., 40th Anniv. A255

1984, June 12

957	A255 15f multicolored	.40	.25
958	A255 30f multicolored	1.10	.55
959	A255 80f multicolored	3.00	1.60
	Nos. 957-959 (3)	4.50	2.40

Arab Youth Day — A256

1984, July 5 *Perf. 13½*

960	A256 30f multicolored	1.00	.55
961	A256 80f multicolored	2.75	1.60

1984 Summer Olympics A257

1984, July 28 *Perf. 15x14*

962	A257 30f Swimming	.55	.35
963	A257 30f Hurdles	.55	.35
a.	Pair, #962-963	1.10	1.10
964	A257 80f Judo	1.40	.90
965	A257 80f Equestrian	1.40	.90
a.	Pair, #964-965	3.00	3.00
	Nos. 962-965 (4)	3.90	2.50

10th Anniv. of the Science Club A258

1984, Aug. 11 Photo. *Perf. 13½x13*

966	A258 15f multicolored	.50	.25
967	A258 30f multicolored	1.25	.55
968	A258 80f multicolored	3.00	1.60
	Nos. 966-968 (3)	4.75	2.40

Islamic Pilgrimage — A259

1984, Sept. 4 Photo. ***Perf. 12x11½***

969 A259 30f multicolored 1.25 .55
970 A259 80f multicolored 3.25 1.60

INTELSAT '84, 20th Anniv. A260

1984, Oct. 1 Litho. ***Perf. 13½x14***

971 A260 30f multicolored 1.25 .55
972 A260 80f multicolored 3.00 1.60

G.C.C. Supreme Council, 5th Session A261

1984, Nov. 24 Litho. ***Perf. 15x14***

973 A261 30f multicolored 1.00 .55
974 A261 80f multicolored 2.50 1.60

Map of Israel, Fists, Shattered Star of David — A262

1984, Nov. 29 Photo. ***Perf. 12***

975 A262 30f multicolored 1.40 .55
976 A262 80f multicolored 3.25 1.60

Intl. Palestinian Solidarity Day.

Globe, Emblem A263

1984, Dec. 24 ***Perf. 12x11½***

Granite Paper

977 A263 30f multicolored 1.00 .25
978 A263 80f multicolored 2.75 1.10

Kuwait Oil Co., 50th anniv.

Intl. Youth Year — A264

24th Natl. Day — A265

1985, Jan. 15 ***Perf. 13½***

979 A264 30f multicolored .55 .25
980 A264 80f multicolored 1.60 1.10

1985, Feb. 25 Litho. ***Perf. 14x15***

981 A265 30f multicolored .75 .40
982 A265 80f multicolored 2.75 1.60

Intl. Program for the Development of Communications — A266

1985, Mar. 4 Photo. ***Perf. 11½***

Granite Paper

983 A266 30f multicolored 1.00 .55
984 A266 80f multicolored 2.50 1.60

1st Arab Gulf Week for Social Work — A267

1985, Mar. 13 Photo. ***Perf. 13½x13***

985 A267 30f multicolored 1.00 .55
986 A267 80f multicolored 2.50 1.60

Kuwait Dental Assoc. 3rd Conference A268

1985, Mar. 23 Litho. ***Perf. 13½***

987 A268 30f multicolored 1.00 .55
988 A268 80f multicolored 2.50 1.60

1985 Census — A269

World Health Day — A270

1985, Apr. 1 ***Perf. 14x13½***

989 A269 30f multicolored 1.25 .55
990 A269 80f multicolored 2.75 1.60

1985, Apr. 7 Photo. ***Perf. 13½x13***

991 A270 30f multicolored 1.25 .55
992 A270 80f multicolored 2.75 1.60

Names of Books, Authors and Poets in Arabic — A271

1985, May 20 ***Perf. 12***

Granite Paper

993 A271 Block of 4 6.75 2.00
a.-d. 30f any single 1.50 .45
994 A271 Block of 4 16.50 5.75
a.-d. 80f any single 3.75 1.25

Central Library, 50th anniv.

World Environment Day — A272

1985, June 5 ***Perf. 11½***

995 A272 30f multicolored 1.50 .55
996 A272 80f multicolored 3.50 1.60

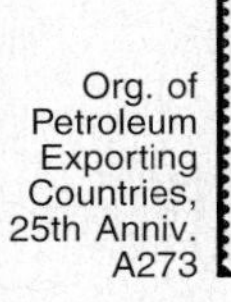

Org. of Petroleum Exporting Countries, 25th Anniv. A273

1985, Sept. 1 ***Perf. 13x13½***

997 A273 30f multicolored 1.25 .55
998 A273 80f multicolored 2.75 1.60

Inauguration of Civil Information System — A274

1985, Oct. 1 Photo. ***Perf. 12x11½***

999 A274 30f multicolored 1.10 .55
1000 A274 80f multicolored 2.75 1.60

Intl. Day of Solidarity with Palestinian People A275

1985, Nov. 29 Photo. ***Perf. 12***

1001 A275 15f multicolored 1.00 .45
1002 A275 30f multicolored 1.75 .90
1003 A275 80f multicolored 3.75 2.25
Nos. 1001-1003 (3) 6.50 3.60

25th Natl. Day A276

1986, Feb. 25 Litho. ***Perf. 15x14***

1004 A276 15f multicolored .25 .20
1005 A276 30f multicolored 1.25 .55
1006 A276 80f multicolored 3.25 1.25
Nos. 1004-1006 (3) 4.75 2.00

Natl. Red Crescent Soc., 20th Anniv. A277

1986, Mar. 26 Photo. ***Perf. 13½***

1007 A277 20f multicolored .60 .65
1008 A277 25f multicolored 1.00 1.00
1009 A277 70f multicolored 3.50 2.75
Nos. 1007-1009 (3) 5.10 4.40

World Health Day — A278

1986, Apr. 7 ***Perf. 13½x13***

1010 A278 20f multicolored .75 .65
1011 A278 25f multicolored 1.25 1.00
1012 A278 70f multicolored 4.00 2.75
Nos. 1010-1012 (3) 6.00 4.40

Intl. Peace Year A279

1986, June 5 Litho. ***Perf. 13½***

1013 A279 20f multicolored .50 .45
1014 A279 25f multicolored 1.25 .70
1015 A279 70f multicolored 3.25 2.00
Nos. 1013-1015 (3) 5.00 3.15

United Arab Shipping Co., 10th Anniv. A280

1986, July 1 Photo. ***Perf. 12x11½***

1016 A280 20f Al Mirqab .75 .60
1017 A280 70f Al Mubarakiah 4.00 2.40

Gulf Bank, 25th Anniv. A281

1986, Oct. 1 Photo. Perf. 12½
1018 A281 20f multicolored .65 .50
1019 A281 25f multicolored 1.10 .70
1020 A281 70f multicolored 3.25 2.25
Nos. 1018-1020 (3) 5.00 3.45

Sadu Art — A282

Various tapestry weavings.

1986, Nov. 5 Photo. Perf. 12x11½
Granite Paper
1021 A282 20f multicolored .75 .40
1022 A282 70f multicolored 2.75 1.50
1023 A282 200f multicolored 7.00 4.25
Nos. 1021-1023 (3) 10.50 6.15

Intl. Day of Solidarity with the Palestinian People — A283

1986, Nov. 29 Perf. 14
1024 A283 20f multicolored 1.50 .85
1025 A283 25f multicolored 2.00 1.10
1026 A283 70f multicolored 5.25 3.25
Nos. 1024-1026 (3) 8.75 5.20

5th Islamic Summit Conference — A284

1987, Jan. 26 Litho. Perf. 14½
1027 A284 25f multicolored .90 .45
1028 A284 50f multicolored 1.75 1.00
1029 A284 150f multicolored 5.25 3.00
Nos. 1027-1029 (3) 7.90 4.45

26th Natl. Day A285

1987, Feb. 25 Perf. 13½x14
1030 A285 50f multicolored 1.50 1.00
1031 A285 150f multicolored 4.50 3.00

Natl. Health Sciences Center A286

1987, Mar. 15 Photo. Perf. 12x11½
Granite Paper
1032 A286 25f multicolored .75 .35
1033 A286 150f multicolored 4.25 2.00

3rd Kuwait Intl. Medical Sciences Conference on Infectious Diseases in Developing Countries.

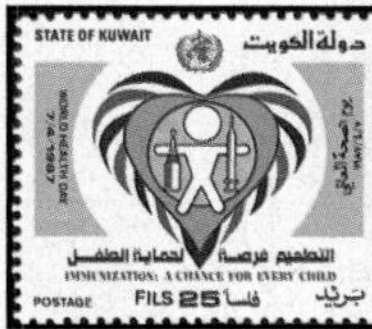

World Health Day — A287

1987, Apr. 7 Photo. Perf. 13x13½
1034 A287 25f multicolored .75 .50
1035 A287 50f multicolored 1.75 1.00
1036 A287 150f multicolored 5.25 2.75
Nos. 1034-1036 (3) 7.75 4.25

Day of Ghods (Jerusalem) — A288

1987, June 7 Photo. Perf. 12x11½
1037 A288 25f multicolored .85 .25
1038 A288 50f multicolored 1.75 .65
1039 A288 150f multicolored 5.00 1.90
Nos. 1037-1039 (3) 7.60 2.80

Islamic Pilgrimage to Miqat Wadi Mihrim — A289

1987, Aug. Photo. Perf. 13½x14½
1040 A289 25f multicolored .85 .55
1041 A289 50f multicolored 1.75 .90
1042 A289 150f multicolored 5.25 2.10
Nos. 1040-1042 (3) 7.85 3.55

Arab Telecommunications Day — A290

1987, Sept. 9 Litho. Perf. 14x13½
1043 A290 25f multicolored .65 .30
1044 A290 50f multicolored 1.25 .80
1045 A290 150f multicolored 4.00 1.25
Nos. 1043-1045 (3) 5.90 2.35

World Maritime Day A291

1987, Sept. 24 Perf. 12x11½
Granite Paper
1046 A291 25f multicolored 1.00 .35
1047 A291 50f multicolored 2.00 .90
1048 A291 150f multicolored 5.75 2.25
Nos. 1046-1048 (3) 8.75 3.50

Al Qurain Housing Project — A292

1987, Oct. 5 Perf. 13x13½
1049 A292 25f multicolored .55 .35
1050 A292 50f multicolored 1.25 .90
1051 A292 150f multicolored 4.75 2.25
Nos. 1049-1051 (3) 6.55 3.50

Port Authority, 10th Anniv. — A293

1987, Nov. 16 Litho. Perf. 14½
1052 A293 25f multicolored .75 .20
1053 A293 50f multicolored 1.50 .50
1054 A293 150f multicolored 5.50 1.75
Nos. 1052-1054 (3) 7.75 2.45

A294

A295

1987, Nov. 29 Perf. 14x13½
1055 A294 25f multicolored .65 .30
1056 A294 50f multicolored 1.25 .60
1057 A294 150f multicolored 4.00 2.00
Nos. 1055-1057 (3) 5.90 2.90

Intl. Day of Solidarity with the Palestinian People

1988, Feb. 3 Photo. Perf. 14
1058 A295 25f multicolored .65 .30
1059 A295 50f multicolored 1.00 .50
1060 A295 150f multicolored 3.25 1.25
Nos. 1058-1060 (3) 4.90 2.05

Women's Cultural and Social Soc., 25th anniv.

A296

A297

1988, Feb. 25
1061 A296 25f multicolored .65 .30
1062 A296 50f multicolored 1.00 .50
1063 A296 150f multicolored 3.25 1.25
Nos. 1061-1063 (3) 4.90 2.05

National Day, 27th anniv.

1988, Apr. 7 Litho. Perf. 14x15
1064 A297 25f multicolored .85 .20
1065 A297 50f multicolored 1.40 .40
1066 A297 150f multicolored 4.25 1.25
Nos. 1064-1066 (3) 6.50 1.85

World Health Day, WHO 40th anniv.

A298

A299

1988, Apr. 24 Photo. Perf. 12
Granite Paper
1067 A298 35f multicolored .90 .35
1068 A298 50f multicolored 1.40 .55
1069 A298 150f multicolored 4.50 1.50
Nos. 1067-1069 (3) 6.80 2.40

Regional Marine Environment Day. Kuwait Regional Convention on the Marine Environment, 10th anniv. See Iraq Nos. 1333-1336.

1988, July 10 Photo. Perf. 14
1070 A299 25f multicolored .85 .20
1071 A299 50f multicolored 1.40 .55
1072 A299 150f multicolored 4.75 1.50
Nos. 1070-1072 (3) 7.00 2.25

Kuwait Teachers Soc., 25th anniv.

Pilgrimage to Mecca A300

1988, Sept. 12 Litho. Perf. 13½x14
1073 A300 25f multicolored .85 .20
1074 A300 50f multicolored 1.40 .55
1075 A300 150f multicolored 4.75 1.75
Nos. 1073-1075 (3) 7.00 2.50

Palestinian "Children of Stone" Fighting Israelis — A301

1988, Sept. 15 Photo. Perf. 13x13½
1076 A301 50f multicolored 2.00 .70
1077 A301 150f multicolored 7.00 2.50

Palestinian Uprising. Dated 1987.

Arab Housing Day — A302

1988, Oct. 3

1078 A302 50f multicolored 1.25 .60
1079 A302 100f multicolored 2.25 1.00
1080 A302 150f multicolored 4.00 1.50
Nos. 1078-1080 (3) 7.50 3.10

Intl. Day for Solidarity with the Palestinian People A303

1988, Nov. 29 Litho. *Perf. 14x13*

1081 A303 50f multicolored 1.10 .60
1082 A303 100f multicolored 2.25 1.00
1083 A303 150f multicolored 4.00 1.75
Nos. 1081-1083 (3) 7.35 3.35

A304

A305

1988, Dec. 5 *Perf. 13x14*

1084 A304 50f multicolored .90 .50
1085 A304 100f multicolored 2.25 1.00
1086 A304 150f multicolored 3.75 1.25
Nos. 1084-1086 (3) 6.90 2.75

Intl. Volunteers Day.

1989, Feb. 18 Litho. *Perf. 14x13½*

1087 A305 50f multicolored 1.00 .30
1088 A305 100f multicolored 2.00 .55
1089 A305 150f multicolored 3.50 .90
Nos. 1087-1089 (3) 6.50 1.75

18th Arab Engineering Conference.

28th Natl. Day A306

1989, Feb. 25 *Perf. 13x13½*

1090 A306 50f multicolored 1.00 .30
1091 A306 100f multicolored 2.00 .55
1092 A306 150f multicolored 3.50 .90
Nos. 1090-1092 (3) 6.50 1.75

5th Natl. Dental Assoc. Conference A307

1989, Mar. 30 Litho. *Perf. 13½x13*

1093 A307 50f multicolored 1.50 .50
1094 A307 150f multicolored 3.00 1.25
1095 A307 250f multicolored 3.25 1.75
Nos. 1093-1095 (3) 7.75 3.50

World Health Day A308

1989, Apr. 7 *Perf. 13x13½*

1096 A308 50f multicolored .90 .40
1097 A308 150f multicolored 2.50 1.00
1098 A308 250f multicolored 4.00 1.60
Nos. 1096-1098 (3) 7.40 3.00

A309

A310

1989, May 10 *Perf. 13x14*

1099 A309 50f multicolored .90 .25
1100 A309 150f multicolored 2.50 .75
1101 A309 250f multicolored 4.00 1.25
Nos. 1099-1101 (3) 7.40 2.25

Arab Board for Medical Specializations, 10th anniv.

1989, June 10 Litho. *Perf. 14x15*

1102 A310 50f multicolored .90 .40
1103 A310 200f multicolored 3.50 1.50
1104 A310 250f multicolored 4.50 2.00
Nos. 1102-1104 (3) 8.90 3.90

Natl. Journalists Assoc., 25th anniv.

Al-Taneem Mosque — A311

1989, July 9 Litho. *Perf. 13½x14½*

1105 A311 50f multicolored 1.00 .30
1106 A311 150f multicolored 3.00 .50
1107 A311 200f multicolored 4.00 1.40
Nos. 1105-1107 (3) 8.00 2.20

Pilgrimage to Mecca.

Arab Housing Day — A312

1989, Oct. 2 *Perf. 13½*

1108 A312 25f multicolored .65 .20
1109 A312 50f multicolored 1.60 .25
1110 A312 150f multicolored 5.00 .75
Nos. 1108-1110 (3) 7.25 1.20

Annual Greenery Week Celebration — A313

Dhow — A314

1989, Oct. 15 *Perf. 13½x13*

1111 A313 25f multicolored .65 .20
1112 A313 50f multicolored 1.60 .25
1113 A313 150f multicolored 5.00 .75
Nos. 1111-1113 (3) 7.25 1.20

Numbers in Black, Moon and Dhow in Gold

1989, Nov. 1 *Perf. 14x15*

Coil Stamps

1114 A314 50f brt apple grn *2.25 2.25*
1115 A314 100f brt blue *4.00 4.00*
1116 A314 200f vermilion *8.50 8.50*
Nos. 1114-1116 (3) *14.75 14.75*

Nos. 1114-1116 available only at two post office locations, where they were dispensed from machines. Printed in rolls of 3000 consecutively numbered stamps. Stamps with overprinted asterisks but lacking printed numbers are from the ends of coil rolls.

Gulf Investment Corp., 5th Anniv. — A315

1989, Nov. 4 *Perf. 15x14*

1117 A315 25f multicolored .90 .20
1118 A315 50f multicolored 1.60 .25
1119 A315 150f multicolored 5.00 .75
Nos. 1117-1119 (3) 7.50 1.20

Declaration of Palestinian State, 1st Anniv. — A316

Zakat House, Orphan Sponsorship Program — A317

1989, Nov. 15 Litho. *Perf. 14x15*

1120 A316 50f multicolored 1.00 .25
1121 A316 150f multicolored 3.00 .85
1122 A316 200f multicolored 4.00 1.10
Nos. 1120-1122 (3) 8.00 2.20

1989, Dec. 10 *Perf. 13½x13*

1123 A317 25f multicolored .50 .20
1124 A317 50f multicolored 1.10 .35
1125 A317 150f multicolored 3.25 1.00
Nos. 1123-1125 (3) 4.85 1.55

Kuwait Police, 50th Anniv. — A318

1989, Dec. 30 Litho. *Perf. 15x14*

1126 A318 25f gray & multi .50 .20
1127 A318 50f lt ultra & multi 1.10 .35
1128 A318 150f lt violet & multi 3.25 1.00
Nos. 1126-1128 (3) 4.85 1.55

National Day, 29th Anniv. — A319

1990, Feb. 25 *Perf. 14x13½*

1129 A319 25f multicolored .55 .20
1130 A319 50f multicolored 1.00 .35
1131 A319 150f multicolored 3.25 1.00
Nos. 1129-1131 (3) 4.80 1.55

World Meteorological Day — A320

1990, Mar. 23 Litho. *Perf. 13½x14*

1132 A320 50f multicolored .90 .30
1133 A320 100f multicolored 2.10 .60
1134 A320 150f multicolored 3.00 .90
Nos. 1132-1134 (3) 6.00 1.80

World Health Day — A321

1990, Apr. 7 *Perf. 14x15*

1135 A321 50f multicolored 1.10 .25
1136 A321 100f multicolored 2.25 .60
1137 A321 150f multicolored 3.00 1.00
Nos. 1135-1137 (3) 6.35 1.85

Hawk — A322

Liberation of Kuwait — A323

1990, July 7 Litho. *Perf. 14½*

1138 A322 50f blue & gold 4.00 4.00
1139 A322 100f maroon & gold 8.00 8.00
1140 A322 150f green & gold 12.00 12.00
Nos. 1138-1140 (3) 24.00 24.00

1991 Litho. *Perf. 14½*

1141 A323 25f multicolored .75 .30
1142 A323 50f multicolored 1.50 .75
1143 A323 150f multicolored 4.00 2.00
Nos. 1141-1143 (3) 6.25 3.05

Peace
A324

Reconstruction
A325

1991, May ***Perf. 13½x14***

1144 A324 50f multicolored 1.25 .75
1145 A324 100f multicolored 2.50 1.50
1146 A324 150f multicolored 4.00 2.25
Nos. 1144-1146 (3) 7.75

1991, May

1147 A325 50f multicolored 1.50 .85
1148 A325 150f multicolored 3.75 2.25
1149 A325 200f multicolored 5.00 3.00
Nos. 1147-1149 (3) 10.25 6.10

Liberation of Kuwait — A326

Flags of forces joining international coalition for liberation of Kuwait: a, Sweden. b, USSR. c, U.S. d, Kuwait. e, Saudi Arabia. f, UN. g, Singapore. h, France. i, Italy. j, Egypt. k, Morocco. l, UK. m, Philippines. n, UAE. o, Syria. p, Poland. q, Australia. r, Japan. s, Hungary. t, Netherlands. u, Denmark. v, New Zealand. w, Czechoslovakia. x, Bahrain. y, Honduras. z, Turkey. aa, Greece. ab, Oman. ac, Qatar. ad, Belgium. ae, Sierra Leone. af, Argentina. ag, Norway. ah, Canada. ai, Germany. aj, South Korea. ak, Bangladesh. al, Bulgaria. am, Senegal. an, Spain. ao, Niger. ap, Pakistan.

No. 1151, Flags of all forces of coalition.

1991, July 25 **Litho.** ***Perf. 14½***

1150 A326 50f Sheet of 42 *75.00 75.00*
a.-ap. Any single 1.25 1.25

Size: 87x134mm

Imperf

1151 A326 1d multicolored *35.00 35.00*

Invasion of Kuwait, 1st Anniv. — A327

1991, Aug. 2 ***Perf. 14½***

1152 A327 50f Human terror *1.25* 1.00
1153 A327 100f Invasion of Kuwait *3.50* 1.50
1154 A327 150f Environmental terrorism, horiz. *5.00* 2.50

Size: 90x65mm

Imperf

1155 A327 250f Desert Storm 12.00 12.00
Nos. 1152-1155 (4) *21.75* 17.00

12th Gulf Cooperation Council Summit
A328

Design: 150f, Tree of flags.

1991, Dec. 23 **Litho.** ***Perf. 14½***

1156 A328 25f multicolored .75 .55
a. see footnote .80 .55
1157 A328 150f multicolored 4.25 3.25
a. Sheet, 2 ea #1156-1157 16.00 16.00
b. Sheet, 2 ea #1156a, 1157 16.00 16.00

No. 1156a has tree with inscriptions (country names in Arabic) in colors of flags shown on No. 1157.

Intl. Literacy Year — A329

OPEC, 30th Anniv. (in 1990) — A330

1992, Feb. 12 **Litho.** ***Perf. 13½x13***

1158 A329 50f dark blue & buff 1.50 .90
1159 A329 100f dark blue & cit 3.00 1.75
1160 A329 150f dk blue & pale lil 4.00 2.50
Nos. 1158-1160 (3) 8.50 5.15

Dated 1990.

1992, Oct. 29 ***Perf. 14½x13½***

1161 A330 25f red & multi 1.00 .50
1162 A330 50f yellow & multi 2.00 1.00
1163 A330 150f green & multi 5.00 3.25
Nos. 1161-1163 (3) 8.00 4.75

31st Natl. Day
A331

1992 ***Perf. 14½***

1164 A331 50f Flag, doves 1.00 .75
1165 A331 150f Flags 3.00 2.00
a. Min. sheet, 2 ea #1164-1165 9.50 9.50

Liberation Day (No. 1165). Issue dates, 50f, Feb. 25; 150f, Feb. 26.

Don't Forget Our P.O.W.'s — A332

1991, Nov. 16

1166 A332 50f Flag, chains 2.00 .75
1167 A332 150f Cell bars, chains 4.50 2.25
a. Min. sheet, 2 each #1166-1167 *14.00 14.00*

Dated 1991. Issued: 50f, 2/25; 150f, 2/26.

Camels
A333

1991, Nov. 16 ***Perf. 12½***

1168 A333 25f pink & multi .60 .60
1169 A333 50f beige & multi 1.25 1.25
1170 A333 150f lt violet & multi 3.25 3.25
1171 A333 200f blue & multi 4.00 4.00
1172 A333 350f orange & multi 7.00 7.00
Nos. 1168-1172 (5) 16.10

Environmental Terrorism, by Jafar Islah — A334

Designs: No. 1174, Snake, flag, map. No. 1175, Skull, dead fish. No. 1176, Dying camel.

1992, June ***Perf. 14½***

1173 A334 150f multicolored 3.00 1.75
1174 A334 150f multicolored 3.00 1.75
1175 A334 150f multicolored 3.00 1.75
1176 A334 150f multicolored 3.00 1.75
a. Block of 4, #1173-1176 13.00 10.00
b. Minature sheet of 4, #1173-1176 19.00 19.00

Earth Summit, Rio De Janeiro. No. 1176a printed in continuous design.

EXPO '92, Seville
A335

Designs: No. 1177, Kuwaiti Pavilion, La Giralda Tower, Seville. No. 1178, Dhows. No. 1179, Dhow. No. 1180, Pavilion, dhow.

Flags of Spain or Kuwait and: No. 1181, Pavilion. No. 1182, La Giralda Tower. No. 1183, La Giralda Tower, dhow. No. 1184, Pavilion, dhow.

1992, June 19

1177 A335 50f multicolored .75 .75
1178 A335 50f multicolored .75 .75
1179 A335 50f multicolored .75 .75
1180 A335 50f multicolored .75 .75
a. Block of 4, #1177-1180 3.25 3.25
1181 A335 150f multicolored 2.50 2.50
1182 A335 150f multicolored 2.50 2.50
1183 A335 150f multicolored 2.50 2.50
1184 A335 150f multicolored 2.50 2.50
a. Block of 4, #1181-1184 11.00 11.00
b. Miniature sheet of 8, #1177-1184 16.50 16.50
Nos. 1177-1184 (8) 13.00 13.00

Nos. 1180a, 1184a have continuous designs.

Palace of Justice
A336

1992, July 4 ***Perf. 12½***

1185 A336 25f lilac & multi .50 .40
1186 A336 50f lilac rose & multi 1.00 .60
1187 A336 100f yel green & multi 2.00 1.10
1188 A336 150f yel orange & multi 2.75 1.75
1189 A336 250f blue green & multi 4.00 3.00
Nos. 1185-1189 (5) 10.25 6.85

1992 Summer Olympics, Barcelona — A337

Olympic flag, Fahed Al Ahmed Al Sabah, member of the Intl. Olympic committee and: 50f, Swimmer, soccer player. 100f, Runner, basketball player. 150f, Judo, equestrian.

1992, July 25 ***Perf. 14½***

1190 A337 50f multicolored 1.25 .75
1191 A337 100f multicolored 2.50 1.50
1192 A337 150f multicolored 4.00 2.50
Nos. 1190-1192 (3) 7.75 4.75

Invasion by Iraq, 2nd Anniv.
A338

Children's paintings: No. 1193, Tanks, people holding signs, two people being tortured. No. 1194, Truck, Iraqi soldiers looting. No. 1195, Iraqi soldiers killing civilians, tanks. No. 1196, Houses ablaze. No. 1197, Tanks, civilians, soldiers. No. 1198, Planes bombing in attack on fort. No. 1199, Tank, civilians holding flags, signs. No. 1200, Battlefield.

1992, Aug. 2 **Litho.** ***Perf. 14x14½***

1193 A338 50f multicolored .75 .75
1194 A338 50f multicolored .75 .75
1195 A338 50f multicolored .75 .75
1196 A338 50f multicolored .75 .75
a. Block of 4, #1193-1196 3.50 3.50
1197 A338 150f multicolored 2.50 2.50
1198 A338 150f multicolored 2.50 2.50
1199 A338 150f multicolored 2.50 2.50
1200 A338 150f multicolored 2.50 2.50
a. Block of 4, #1197-1200 10.50 10.50
b. Min. sheet of 8, #1193-1200 15.00 15.00
Nos. 1193-1200 (8) 13.00 13.00

Extinguishing of Oil Well Fires, 1st Anniv. — A339

Various scenes showing oil well fire being extinguished.

1992 **Litho.** ***Perf. 14½***

1201 A339 25f multi, vert. .50 .50
1202 A339 50f multi, vert. .90 .90
1203 A339 150f multi, vert. 2.50 2.50
1204 A339 250f multicolored 4.50 4.50
Nos. 1201-1204 (4) 8.40 8.40

Kuwait Tower — A340

A341

1993, Jan. 16 **Litho.** ***Perf. 14x15***

Background Color

1205 A340 25f lilac .35 .20
1206 A340 100f blue 1.40 .70
1207 A340 150f salmon 2.00 1.25
Nos. 1205-1207 (3) 3.75 2.15

1993, Feb. 25 **Litho.** ***Perf. 13½x14***

1208 A341 25f green & multi .35 .20
1209 A341 50f blue & multi .75 .35
1210 A341 150f pink & multi 2.00 1.25
Nos. 1208-1210 (3) 3.10 1.80

National Day, 32nd anniv.

Liberation Day, 2nd Anniv. — A342

1993, Feb. 26 ***Perf. 15x14***

1211 A342 25f org yel & multi .25 .25
1212 A342 50f green & multi .55 .55
1213 A342 150f red lilac & multi 1.60 1.60
Nos. 1211-1213 (3) 2.40 2.40

Remembering Prisoners of War — A343

Designs: 50f, Prisoner shackled in cell, vert. 150f, Shackled hand pointing to cell window, bird. 200f, Cell, prisoner's face, vert.

Perf. 13½x14, 14x13½

1993, May 15 **Litho.**

1214 A343 50f multicolored .60 .60
1215 A343 150f multicolored 1.60 1.60
1216 A343 200f multicolored 2.25 2.25
Nos. 1214-1216 (3) 4.45 4.45

A344

A345

1993, Apr. 20 **Litho.** ***Perf. 11½x12***

Granite Paper

1217 A344 25f gray & multi .20 .20
1218 A344 50f green & multi .55 .35
1219 A344 150f yellow & multi 1.60 1.10
1220 A344 350f blue & multi 4.00 2.60
Nos. 1217-1220 (4) 6.35 4.25

18th Deaf Child Week.

1993, Aug. 2 **Litho.** ***Perf. 13½x14***

1221 A345 50f green & multi .50 .40
1222 A345 150f orange & multi 1.50 1.25

Invasion by Iraq, 3rd anniv.

Kuwait Airforce, 40th Anniv. A346

1993, Dec. 9 **Litho.** ***Perf. 13x13½***

1223 A346 50f blue & multi .50 .40
1224 A346 150f green & multi 1.40 1.10

Natl. Day, 33rd Anniv. — A347

Liberation Day, 3rd Anniv. — A348

1994, Feb. 25 **Litho.** ***Perf. 13½x14***

1225 A347 25f salmon & multi .20 .20
1226 A347 50f yellow & multi .50 .40
1227 A347 150f green & multi 1.75 1.40
Nos. 1225-1227 (3) 2.45 2.00

1994, Feb. 26

1228 A348 25f yellow & multi .20 .20
1229 A348 50f blue & multi .55 .40
1230 A348 150f gray green & multi 1.50 1.10
Nos. 1228-1230 (3) 2.25 1.70

Central Bank of Kuwait, 25th Anniv. — A349

1994, Apr. 20 **Litho.** ***Perf. 13½x13***

1231 A349 25f salmon & multi .20 .20
1232 A349 50f green & multi .60 .40
1233 A349 150f blue violet & multi 1.75 1.25
Nos. 1231-1233 (3) 2.55 1.85

A350

A351

Intl. Year of the Family A352

1994, May 15 **Litho.** ***Perf. 13***

1234 A350 50f multicolored .65 .40
1235 A351 150f multicolored 1.75 1.10
1236 A352 200f multicolored 2.40 1.50
Nos. 1234-1236 (3) 4.80 3.00

A353

A354

1994, June 5 **Litho.** ***Perf. 14***

1237 A353 50f yellow & multi .60 .40
1238 A353 100f blue & multi 1.10 .75
1239 A353 150f green & multi 1.60 1.10
Nos. 1237-1239 (3) 3.30 2.25

Industrial Bank of Kuwait, 20th anniv.

1994, June 15 **Litho.** ***Perf. 13***

1240 A354 50f Whirlpool .75 .50
1241 A354 100f Shifting sands 1.50 1.00
1242 A354 150f Finger print 2.50 1.50
1243 A354 250f Clouds 4.00 2.50
a. Min. sheet of 4, #1240-1243 9.00 9.00
Nos. 1240-1243 (4) 8.75 5.50

Martyr's Day.

A355

A356

1994, June 25 **Litho.** ***Perf. 14***

1244 A355 50f vio & multi .75 .50
1245 A355 150f pink & multi 2.25 1.25
1246 A355 350f blue & multi 5.25 2.75
Nos. 1244-1246 (3) 8.25 4.50

ILO, 75th anniv.

1994, Aug. 2 **Litho.** ***Perf. 12½x13½***

1247 A356 50f green blue & multi .75 .50
1248 A356 150f blue & multi 2.50 1.50
1249 A356 350f lilac & multi 5.75 3.00
Nos. 1247-1249 (3) 9.00 5.00

Invasion by Iraq, 4th anniv.

Port Authority — A357

Science Club, 20th Anniv. — A358

1994, Aug. 31 **Litho.** ***Perf. 12½x14***

1250 A357 50f pink & multi .75 .50
1251 A357 150f blue & multi 2.25 1.25
1252 A357 350f green & multi 5.25 2.75
Nos. 1250-1252 (3) 8.25 4.50

1994, Sept. 11 ***Perf. 14***

1253 A358 50f blue & multi .75 .50
1254 A358 100f green & multi 1.75 1.00
1255 A358 150f red & multi 2.00 1.50
Nos. 1253-1255 (3) 4.50 3.00

A359

A360

Designs showing emblem and: 50f, Map of Arab countries, building. 100f, Windows, building. 150f, Doors below portico.

1994, Nov. 12 ***Perf. 11½***

1256 A359 50f multicolored .75 .50
1257 A359 100f multicolored 1.50 1.00
1258 A359 150f multicolored 3.00 1.50
Nos. 1256-1258 (3) 5.25 3.00

Arab Towns Organization, opening of headquarters.

1994, Dec. 7 ***Perf. 14½***

Designs: 100f, Emblems, sailing ship. 150f, Emblems, co-operation, co-ordination. 350f, Emblem, airplane in flight.

1259 A360 100f silver, gold & multi 1.60 1.00
1260 A360 150f silver, gold & multi 2.50 1.50
1261 A360 350f gold & multi 5.50 3.50
Nos. 1259-1261 (3) 9.60 6.00

ICAO, 50th anniv.

A361

A362

1994, Dec. 20 ***Perf. 13x14***

1262 A361 50f lake & multi .75 .50
1263 A361 100f green & multi 1.50 .85
1264 A361 150f slate & multi 2.50 1.50
Nos. 1262-1264 (3) 4.75 2.85

Kuwait Airways, 40th anniv.

1995, Feb. 6 **Litho.** ***Perf. 14***

1265 A362 50f yellow & multi .75 .50
1266 A362 100f green & multi 1.50 .85
1267 A362 150f brown & multi 2.25 1.50
Nos. 1265-1267 (3) 4.50 2.85

1995 Census.

National Day, 34th Anniv. — A363

Liberation Day, 4th Anniv. — A364

1995, Feb. 25 *Perf. 13*

No.	Type	Description	Unused	Used
1268	A363	25f blue & multi	.35	.25
1269	A363	50f yellow & multi	.75	.45
1270	A363	150f lilac & multi	2.25	1.25
		Nos. 1268-1270 (3)	3.35	1.95

1995, Feb. 26

No.	Type	Description	Unused	Used
1271	A364	25f blue & multi	.35	.25
1272	A364	50f green & multi	.75	.45
1273	A364	150f rose lilac & multi	2.25	1.25
		Nos. 1271-1273 (3)	3.35	1.95

Medical Research A365

1995, Mar. 20 *Perf. 14*

No.	Type	Description	Unused	Used
1274	A365	50f Medical building	.70	.50
1275	A365	100f Classroom instruction	1.50	.85
1276	A365	150f Map of Kuwait	2.25	1.25
		Nos. 1274-1276 (3)	4.45	2.60

Arab League, 50th Anniv. A366

Designs: 50f, Kuwaiti, league flags over emblems, map, vert. 100f, Flags over "50," emblem. 150f, Flags as clasping hands, vert.

1995, Mar. 22 *Perf. 13*

No.	Type	Description	Unused	Used
1277	A366	50f multicolored	.70	.50
1278	A366	100f multicolored	1.50	.85
1279	A366	150f multicolored	2.25	1.25
		Nos. 1277-1279 (3)	4.45	2.60

A367

A368

1995, Apr. 7 **Litho.** *Perf. 13½x13*

No.	Type	Description	Unused	Used
1280	A367	50f blue & multi	.75	.50
1281	A367	150f pink & multi	2.50	1.50
1282	A367	200f yellow & multi	3.25	2.25
		Nos. 1280-1282 (3)	6.50	4.25

World Health Day.

1995, June 5 **Litho.** *Perf. 14*

Designs: 50f, One gold ball. 100f, Gold "1," one gold ball. 150f, "1," both balls in gold.

No.	Type	Description	Unused	Used
1283	A368	50f shown	.75	.50
1284	A368	100f multicolored	1.50	.75
1285	A368	150f multicolored	2.25	1.25
		Nos. 1283-1285 (3)	4.50	2.50

Volleyball, cent.

Invasion by Iraq, 5th Anniv. — A369

1995, Aug. 2 **Litho.** *Perf. 13*

No.	Type	Description	Unused	Used
1286	A369	50f purple & multi	.75	.50
1287	A369	100f red & multi	1.75	.85
1288	A369	150f green & multi	3.00	1.25
		Nos. 1286-1288 (3)	5.50	2.60

UN, 50th Anniv. A370

1995, Aug. 12 *Perf. 13x13½*

No.	Type	Description	Unused	Used
1289	A370	25f multi	.75	.30
1290	A370	50f orange & multi	1.50	.60
1291	A370	150f bl grn & multi	2.25	1.25
		Nos. 1289-1291 (3)	4.50	2.15

FAO, 50th Anniv. — A371

People in traditional dress with: 50f, Cattle, camels, sheep. 100f, Fish, boat. 150f, Poultry, fruits, vegetables.

1995, Sept. 21 *Perf. 13½x13*

No.	Type	Description	Unused	Used
1292	A371	50f multicolored	.75	.50
1293	A371	100f multicolored	1.60	1.00
1294	A371	150f multicolored	2.50	1.50
a.		Min. sheet of 3, #1292-1294	5.00	5.00
		Nos. 1292-1294 (3)	4.85	3.00

A372

World Standards Day — A373

1995, Oct. 14 *Perf. 13*

No.	Type	Description	Unused	Used
1295	A372	50f multicolored	.75	.50
1296	A373	100f green & multi	1.50	1.00
1297	A373	150f violet & multi	2.25	1.25
		Nos. 1295-1297 (3)	4.50	2.75

Flowers — A374

Natl. Day, 35th Anniv. — A375

Designs: 5f, Onobrychis ptolemaica. 15f, Convolvulus oxyphyllus. 25f, Papaver rhoeas. 50f, Moltkiopsis ciliata. 150f, Senecio desfontainei.

1995, Nov. 15 **Litho.** *Perf. 14½*

No.	Type	Description	Unused	Used
1298	A374	5f multicolored	.30	.20
1299	A374	15f multicolored	.50	.30
1300	A374	25f multicolored	.75	.50
1301	A374	50f multicolored	1.50	1.00
1302	A374	150f multicolored	4.00	2.75
		Nos. 1298-1302 (5)	7.05	4.75

1996, Feb. 25 *Perf. 14*

No.	Type	Description	Unused	Used
1303	A375	25f lil rose & multi	.50	.25
1304	A375	50f blue green & multi	.85	.50
1305	A375	150f salmon & multi	2.25	1.50
		Nos. 1303-1305 (3)	3.60	2.25

Liberation Day, 5th Anniv. A376

1996, Feb. 26

No.	Type	Description	Unused	Used
1306	A376	25f violet & multi	.50	.25
1307	A376	50f brown & multi	.85	.50
1308	A376	150f blue green & multi	2.50	1.50
		Nos. 1306-1308 (3)	3.85	2.25

Arab City Day — A377

A378

1996, Mar. 1 *Perf. 13½*

No.	Type	Description	Unused	Used
1309	A377	50f yel grn & multi	.85	.50
1310	A377	100f pink & multi	1.75	1.00
1311	A377	150f blue green & multi	2.50	1.50
		Nos. 1309-1311 (3)	5.10	3.00

1996, Jan. 27 *Perf. 14*

No.	Type	Description	Unused	Used
1312	A378	50f blue & multi	.55	.45
1313	A378	100f gray & multi	1.10	.85
1314	A378	150f rose lilac & multi	2.25	1.50
		Nos. 1312-1314 (3)	3.90	2.80

Scouting in Kuwait, 60th Anniv. — A379

50f, On top of watchtower. 100f, Drawing water from well. 150f, Planting seedling.

1996, Jan. 14 *Perf. 13½*

No.	Type	Description	Unused	Used
1315	A379	50f yellow & multi	1.10	.50
1316	A379	100f lilac & multi	2.50	1.00
1317	A379	150f blue green & multi	3.50	1.50
		Nos. 1315-1317 (3)	7.10	3.00

Kuwait Money Show — A380

1996, Jan. 2 *Perf. 14*

No.	Type	Description	Unused	Used
1318	A380	25f gold & multi	.50	.30
1319	A380	100f blue & multi	1.75	1.00
1320	A380	150f dk gray & multi	2.25	1.50
		Nos. 1318-1320 (3)	4.50	2.80

7th Kuwait Dental Assoc. Conference A381

UNESCO, 50th Anniv. A382

1996, Mar. 27 **Litho.** *Perf. 14x13½*

No.	Type	Description	Unused	Used
1321	A381	25f orange & multi	.45	.30
1322	A381	50f violet & multi	.85	.50
1323	A381	150f blue & multi	2.40	1.75
		Nos. 1321-1323 (3)	3.70	2.55

1996, Apr. 10 *Perf. 13½x14*

No.	Type	Description	Unused	Used
1324	A382	25f violet & multi	.40	.30
1325	A382	100f green & multi	1.75	1.00
1326	A382	150f orange & multi	2.25	1.50
		Nos. 1324-1326 (3)	4.40	2.80

1st Oil Exports, 50th Anniv. — A383

Rule of Al-Sabah Family, Cent. — A384

1996, June 30 **Litho.** *Perf. 13*

No.	Type	Description	Unused	Used
1327	A383	25f multicolored	.50	.30
1328	A383	100f gray & multi	1.75	1.25
1329	A383	150f bister & multi	2.50	1.75
		Nos. 1327-1329 (3)	4.75	3.30

1996, Aug. 12

No.	Type	Description	Unused	Used
1330	A384	25f shown	.50	.30
1331	A384	50f Shiek, flags	.85	.60
1332	A384	150f like #1330	2.50	1.75
		Nos. 1330-1332 (3)	3.85	2.65

1996 Summer Olympic Games, Atlanta — A385

1996, Oct. 5 *Perf. 13½*

No.	Type	Description	Unused	Used
1333	A385	25f Shooting	.50	.35
1334	A385	50f Running	1.00	.75
1335	A385	100f Weight lifting	1.75	1.25
1336	A385	150f Fencing	2.75	2.00
		Nos. 1333-1336 (4)	6.00	4.35

A 750f souvenir sheet exists. Value $100.

Kuwait University, 30th Anniv. — A386

1st Children's Cultural Festival — A387

1996, Nov. 27 Litho. *Perf. 13½x14*

1337 A386 25f green & multi .45 .25
1338 A386 100f blue & multi 1.75 1.00
1339 A386 150f yellow & multi 2.25 1.50
Nos. 1337-1339 (3) 4.45 2.75

1996, Nov. 20 *Perf. 14x13½*

1340 A387 25f brn gray & multi .45 .25
1341 A387 100f multicolored 1.75 1.00
1342 A387 150f yel grn & multi 2.25 1.50
Nos. 1340-1342 (3) 4.45 2.75

3rd Al-Qurain Cultrual Festival — A388

Liberation Tower — A389

1996, Nov. 20 *Perf. 14*

1343 A388 50f orange & multi .85 .50
1344 A388 100f blue & multi 1.75 1.25
1345 A388 150f green & multi 2.50 1.75
Nos. 1343-1345 (3) 5.10 3.50

1996, Dec. 10 *Perf. 13x13½*

1346 A389 5f red & multi .20 .20
1347 A389 10f yel bis & multi .25 .20
1348 A389 15f brt rose & multi .40 .30
1349 A389 25f pale pink & multi .50 .45
a. Booklet pane of 4 —
Complete booklet, #1349a —
1350 A389 50f violet & multi 1.25 .90
a. Booklet pane of 4 —
Complete booklet, #1350a —
1351 A389 100f brt yel & multi 2.25 1.25
1352 A389 150f blue & multi 3.50 2.00
a. Booklet pane of 4 —
Complete booklet, #1352a —
1353 A389 200f pink & multi 5.00 4.00
1354 A389 250f dp blue & multi 6.00 5.00
1355 A389 350f blue & multi 8.25 6.00
Nos. 1346-1355 (10) 27.60 20.30
Set of 3 booklets, #1349a-1350a, 1352a *31.00*

National Day, 36th Anniv. A390

1997, Feb. 25 Litho. *Perf. 14½*

1356 A390 25f blue & multi .45 .45
1357 A390 50f lilac & multi .85 .85
1358 A390 150f orange & multi 2.25 2.25
Nos. 1356-1358 (3) 3.55 3.55

Liberation Day, 6th Anniv. A391

1997, Feb. 26 *Perf. 13x13½*

1359 A391 25f tan & multi .45 .45
1360 A391 50f lilac & multi .85 .85
1361 A391 150f blue & multi 2.25 2.25
Nos. 1359-1361 (3) 3.55 3.55

Marine Life — A392

No. 1368: Various views of a school of shrimp: a, b, c, d, 25f. e, f, g, h, 50f. i, j, k, l, 100f. m, n, o, p, 150f.

1997, Jan. 15 *Perf. 14½*

1362 A392 25f Maid .50 .50
1363 A392 50f Sheim .85 .85
1364 A392 100f Hamoor 1.75 1.75
1365 A392 150f Sobaity 2.50 2.50
1366 A392 200f Nagroor 3.50 3.50
1367 A392 350f Zobaidy 6.00 6.00
Nos. 1362-1367 (6) 15.10 15.10

Sheet of 16

1368 A392 Sheet of 16, #a.-p. 22.50 22.50

Montreal Protocol on Substances that Deplete Ozone Layer, 10th Anniv. — A393

1997, Sept. 16 Litho. *Perf. 13½x13*

1369 A393 25f blue & multi .40 .40
1370 A393 50f violet & multi .75 .75
1371 A393 150f bl grn & multi 2.75 2.75
Nos. 1369-1371 (3) 3.90 3.90

Industries Exhibition A394

1997, Oct. 1

1372 A394 25f brt pink & multi .40 .40
1373 A394 50f green & multi .75 .75
1374 A394 150f blue & multi 2.75 2.75
Nos. 1372-1374 (3) 3.90 3.90

22nd Kuwait Arabic Book Exhibition A395

1997, Nov. 19 Litho. *Perf. 13½x13*

Border Color

1375 A395 25f pink .40 .40
1376 A395 50f blue .75 .75
1377 A395 150f blue green 2.75 2.75
Nos. 1375-1377 (3) 3.90 3.90

Cultural History A396

a, 50f, Qibliya Girls School, 1937. b, 50f, Scissors cutting ribbon, Fine Arts Exhibition, 1959. c, 150f, Folk Theatre Group, 1956. d, 25f, 1st Book Fair, 1975. e, 25f, Kuwait Magazine, 1928. f, 50f, Mubarakiya School, 1912. g, 50f, Kuwait Natl. Museum, 1958. h, 150f, Academy of Music, 1972. i, 25f, A'lam Al-Fikr (periodical), 1970. j, 25f, Al'Bitha Magazine, 1946. k, 50f, Building complex, 1953 (Al-Arabi Magazine). l, 50f, Building, 1959. m, 150f, Al-Sharqiya Cinema, 1955. n, 25f, Al'Lam Al Ma'rifa (periodical), 1978. o, 25f, Dalil Almohtar Fi Alaam al-Bihar (boat), 1923. p, 50f, Alma'had Aldini (arabesques), 1947. q, 50f, Folklore Center, 1956. r, 150f, Theatrical Academy, 1967. s, 25f, Al-Arabi Magazine, 1958. t, 25f, Public Library (book), 1923. u, 50f, Al Ma'Arif Printing Press (Arabic writing), 1947. v, 50f, Literary Club, 1924. w, 150f, Bas Ya Bahar (1st Kuwaitii feature film), 1970. x, 25f, Al Thaqafa Al-Alamiya (periodical), 1981. y, 25f, The World Theatre (periodical), 1969.

1997, Nov. 30

1378 A396 Sheet of 25, #a.-y. 27.50 27.50

Nos. 1378a-1378y each contain year date of event depicted.

Educational Science Museum, 25th Anniv. A397

Designs: 25f, Whale, quadrant, vert. 50f, Space exploration, whale, dinosaur. No. 1381, Astronaut, dinosaur, satellite dish, airplane, globe, skeleton encircling whale, vert.
No. 1382, Coelacanth.

Perf. 13½x13, 13x13½

1997, Nov. 1 Litho.

1379 A397 25f multicolored .45 .45
1380 A397 50f multicolored .85 .85
1381 A397 150f multicolored 2.75 2.75
Nos. 1379-1381 (3) 4.05 4.05

Souvenir Sheet

1382 A397 150f multicolored 17.50 17.50

No. 1382 is a continuous design and sold for 1d.

18th Summit of Gulf Cooperation Countries — A398

Designs: 25f, Flags of member countries, doves, vert. 50f, Map, birds with flag colors. 150f, Doves perched atop flags, vert.

1997, Dec. 20 *Perf. 13½x14*

1383 A398 25f multicolored .55 .55
1384 A398 50f multicolored 1.10 1.10
1385 A398 150f multicolored 3.50 3.50
a. Bklt. pane of 3, #1383-1385 *14.00*
Complete booklet, #1385a *14.00*
Nos. 1383-1385 (3) 5.15 5.15

National Day, 37th Anniv. A399

1998, Feb. 25 Litho. *Perf. 13x13½*

1386 A399 25f yellow & multi .55 .55
1387 A399 50f pink & multi 1.10 1.10
1388 A399 150f blue & multi 3.25 3.25
Nos. 1386-1388 (3) 4.90 4.90

Liberation Day, 7th Anniv. A400

1998, Feb. 26

1389 A400 25f yellow & multi .55 .55
1390 A400 50f orange & multi 1.10 1.10
1391 A400 150f green & multi 3.25 3.25
Nos. 1389-1391 (3) 4.90 4.90

A401

A402

1998, Mar. 16 Litho. *Perf. 13½x13*

1392 A401 25f tan & multi .55 .55
1393 A401 50f blue & multi 1.10 1.10
1394 A401 150f white & multi 3.25 3.25
Nos. 1392-1394 (3) 4.90 4.90

Say No to Drugs.

1997, May 2 Litho. *Perf. 13½x13*

1395 A402 25f orange & multi .55 .55
1396 A402 50f blue & multi 1.10 1.10
1397 A402 150f red & multi 3.25 3.25
Nos. 1395-1397 (3) 4.90 4.90

Chernobyl disaster, 10th anniv.

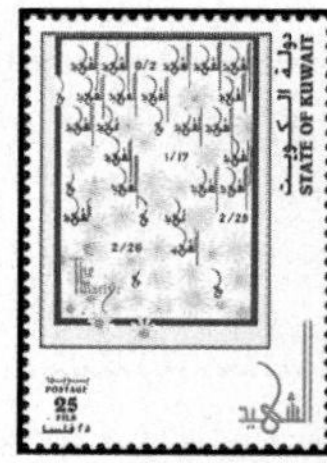

Martyrs — A403

25f, Dates, 1/17, 2/25, 2/26, flowers. 50f, Stylized tree. 150f, Lines, inscriptions.
No. 1401: a, Man with hands in dirt. b, Three boys emptying basket of dirt.

1998, Mar. 31 Litho. *Perf. 14*

1398 A403 25f multicolored .55 .55
1399 A403 50f multicolored 1.10 1.10
1400 A403 150f multicolored 3.50 3.50
a. Bklt. pane, 2 ea #1398-1400 16.00
Complete booklet, #1400a 16.00

Perf. 14½ Between

Size: 31x54mm

1401 A403 500f Pair, a.-b. 22.50 22.50
Nos. 1398-1401 (4) 27.65 27.65

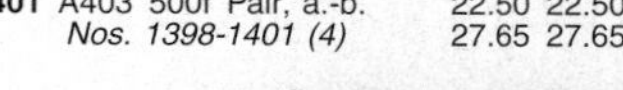

Ban Land Mines — A405

Stylized amputees using crutches for support: 25f, Two people. 50f, One person. 150f, Two people, nurse.
500f, Three people, nurse.

1998, Aug. 2 *Perf. 14½*

1402 A405 25f multicolored .55 .55
1403 A405 50f multicolored 1.10 1.10
1404 A405 150f multicolored 2.50 2.50

Size: 89x82mm

Imperf

1405 A405 500f multicolored 11.00 11.00
Nos. 1402-1405 (4) 15.15 15.15

Life in Pre-Oil Kuwait — A406

Designs: 25f, Seated at ceremonial meal. 50f, Building boat. 100f, Weaving. 150f, Loading boat. 250f, Pouring water from water skin into bowl. 350f, Man with pigeons.

1998, Apr. 14 Litho. *Perf. 14*

Booklet Stamps

1406	A406	25f multicolored	.60	.60
1407	A406	50d multicolored	1.25	1.25
1408	A406	100f multicolored	2.50	2.50
1409	A406	150f multicolored	3.50	3.50
1410	A406	250f multicolored	6.00	6.00
1411	A406	350f multicolored	8.00	8.00
a.		Booklet pane, #1406-1411	27.50	
		Complete booklet, #1411a	27.50	

1998, Sept. 1 Litho. *Perf. 14*

25f, Man shaving another man's head. 50f, Woman using grindstone. 100f, Man pulling thread through cloth. 150f, Man gluing artifacts together. 250f, Potter. 350f, Veiled woman holding rope.

Booklet Stamps

1412	A406	25f multicolored	.60	.60
1413	A406	50f multicolored	1.25	1.25
1414	A406	100f multicolored	2.50	2.50
1415	A406	150f multicolored	3.50	3.50
1416	A406	250f multicolored	6.00	6.00
1417	A406	350f multicolored	8.00	8.00
a.		Booklet pane, #1412-1417	27.50	
		Complete booklet, #1417a	27.50	

Emblem of Kuwait Post A407

1998, Oct. 3 Litho. *Perf. 13x13½*

1418	A407	25f green & multi	.50	.50
1419	A407	50f blue & multi	1.00	1.00
1420	A407	100f brt pink & multi	2.00	2.00
1421	A407	150f orange & multi	3.00	3.00
1422	A407	250f brick red & multi	5.50	5.50
		Nos. 1418-1422 (5)	12.00	12.00

Intl. Year of the Ocean — A408

1998, June 1 Litho. *Perf. 13½*

1423	A408	25f green & multi	.60	.60
1424	A408	50f blue & multi	1.25	1.25
1425	A408	150f lilac & multi	3.75	3.75
		Nos. 1423-1425 (3)	5.60	5.60

No. 1424 is 27x37mm.

Union of Consumer Co-operative Societies, 25th Anniv. — A409

1998, July 1 Litho. *Perf. 13½x13*

1426	A409	25f buff & multi	.50	.50
1427	A409	50f blue & multi	1.00	1.00
1428	A409	150f multicolored	3.50	3.50
		Nos. 1426-1428 (3)	5.00	5.00

Children's Cultural House — A410

1998, Nov. 28 Litho. *Perf. 13½x13*

1429	A410	25f yellow & multi	.60	.60
1430	A410	50f grn, yel & multi	1.25	1.25
1431	A410	150f green & multi	3.50	3.50
		Nos. 1429-1431 (3)	5.35	5.35

A411

A412

1998, Dec. 10 *Perf. 14x14½*

1432	A411	25f multicolored	.60	.60
1433	A411	50f multicolored	1.25	1.25
1434	A411	150f multicolored	3.75	3.75
		Nos. 1432-1434 (3)	5.60	5.60

Universal Declaration of Human Rights, 50th anniv.

1998 Litho. *Perf. 14x14½*

1435	A412	25f orange & multi	.50	.50
1436	A412	50f violet & multi	1.00	1.00
1437	A412	150f green & multi	3.00	3.00
		Nos. 1435-1437 (3)	4.50	4.50

The Public Authority for Applied Education and Training, 25th anniv.

Organ Transplantation in Kuwait, 20th Anniv. — A413

1999 Litho. *Perf. 13x13½*

1438	A413	50f Liver	.80	.80
1439	A413	150f Heart	2.50	2.50

Liberation Day, 8th Anniv. A414

1999, Feb. 26

1440	A414	50f Building	2.00	1.00
1441	A414	150f Building, diff.	4.00	3.00

Sief Palace Complex — A415

Various buildings in complex.

1999 *Perf. 15x14*

1442	A415	25f multicolored	.35	.35
1443	A415	50f multicolored	.75	.35
1444	A415	100f multicolored	1.50	1.50
1445	A415	150f multicolored	2.75	2.75
1446	A415	250f multicolored	4.50	4.50
1447	A415	350f multicolored	6.00	6.00
a.		Booklet pane, #1442-1447	16.00	
		Complete booklet, #1447a	16.00	
		Nos. 1442-1447 (6)	15.85	15.45

Al Arabi Magazine A416

1999 *Perf. 13½x13*

1448	A416	50f violet & multi	.75	.75
1449	A416	150f green & multi	2.50	2.50

Natl. Day, 38th Anniv. A417

1999 *Perf. 13x13½*

1450	A417	50f brown & multi	.75	.75
1451	A417	150f blue & multi	2.50	2.50

A418

A419

1999(?)-2003 Litho. *Perf. 14½x14*

1452	A418	25f Hawk	1.00	1.00
1453	A418	50f Camel	2.00	2.00

Coil Stamp

1453A	A419	100f multi	2.50	2.50
1454	A419	150f Sailing ship	5.00	5.00
		Nos. 1452-1454 (4)	10.50	10.50

Issued: 100f, Jan. 2003.

Science Club, 25th Anniv. A420

Background color: 50f, Blue. 150f, Green. 350f, Red.

1999, Oct. 20 Litho. *Perf. 13x13¼*

1455-1457	A420	Set of 3	8.00	8.00

Intl. Civil Aviation Day — A421

1999, Dec. 7 Litho. *Perf. 13x13¼*

1458	A421	50f multi	1.00	1.00
1459	A421	150f multi	3.00	3.00
1460	A421	250f multi	5.00	5.00
		Nos. 1458-1460 (3)	9.00	9.00

UPU, 125th Anniv. — A421a

Panel colors: 50f, Orange. 150f, Purple. 350f, Green.

1d, Two hemispheres.

1999 Litho. *Perf. 13¼x13*

1460A-1460C	A421a	Set of 3	8.50	8.50
1460Ce		Booklet pane, #1460A-1460C + label	8.50	
		Booklet, #1460Ce	8.50	

Size: 100x75mm

Imperf

1460D	A421a	1d multi	14.50	14.50

Kuwait Intl. Airport — A422

2000, Jan. 2 *Perf. 13¼x13*

1461	A422	50f multi	.60	.60
1462	A422	150f multi	1.75	1.75
1463	A422	250f multi	3.00	3.00
		Nos. 1461-1463 (3)	5.35	5.35

National Day, 39th Anniv. — A423

2000

1464	A423	25f multi	.50	.50
1465	A423	50f multi	1.25	1.25
1466	A423	150f multi	3.50	3.50
		Nos. 1464-1466 (3)	5.25	5.25

Liberation Day, 9th Anniv. — A424

2000

1467	A424	25f multi	1.00	1.00
1468	A424	50f multi	3.00	3.00
1469	A424	150f multi	7.00	7.00
		Nos. 1467-1469 (3)	11.00	11.00

Kuwait Conference for Autism and Communication Deficits — A425

Designs: 25f, Puzzle pieces, three children, Kuwait Tower. 50f, Puzzle pieces, children. 150f, Children, Kuwait Tower, flowers.

2000 ***Perf. 13x13¼***

1470 A425 25f multi	.60	.60
1471 A425 50f multi	1.25	1.25
1472 A425 150f multi	3.75	3.75
Nos. 1470-1472 (3)	5.60	5.60

Kuwait City — A425a

Background colors: 50f, Blue. 150f, Green. 350f, Red violet.

2000, Apr. 24 Litho. ***Perf. 14x14½***
1472A-1472C A425a Set of 3 8.50 8.50

Third Special Education Week — A425b

Background color: 50f, Yellow. 150f, Salmon. 350f, Blue.

2000, May 10 ***Perf. 13¼x13***
1472D-1472F A425b Set of 3 8.00 8.00

2000 Summer Olympics, Sydney A425c

Emblems of 2002 Olympics, Kuwait Olympic Committee and: 25f, Judo. 50f, Shooting. 150f, Swimming. 200f, Weight lifting. 250f, Hurdles. 350f, Soccer.

2000 Litho. ***Perf. 13x13¼***
1472G-1472L A425c Set of 6 16.00 16.00

Souvenir Sheet

Design: 1d, Emblems of 2002 Olympics, Kuwait Olympic Committee and judo, swimming, shooting, weight lifting, hurdles and soccer.

Size: 98x69mm

1472M A425c 1d multi *65.00 65.00*

Sixth Gulf Cooperation Council Countries Joint Stamp Exhibition, Kuwait A425d

Denomination color: 25f, Blue. 50f, Red. 150f, Green.
1d, Emblems of previous exhibitions.

2000 Litho. ***Perf. 14¼***
1472N-1472P A425d Set of 3 5.00 5.00

Size: 146x112mm

Imperf

1472Q A425d 1d multi 17.00 17.00

Intl. Investment Forum A426

Background colors: 25f, Gray. 50f, White. 150f, Black.

2000, Mar. 4 Litho. ***Perf. 13x13¼***
1473-1475 A426 Set of 3 5.00 5.00

National Committee for Missing and Prisoner of War Affairs A426a

Designs: 25f, Emblem. 50f, Emblem and chains. 150f, Emblem and years.

2000, Aug. 2 Litho. ***Perf. 13x13¼***
1475A-1475C A426a Set of 3 3.25 3.25

Kuwaiti Dental Association, 25th Anniv. — A426b

Frame color: 50f, Pink. 150f, Light blue. 350f, Lilac.

2000, Oct. 15 ***Perf. 13¼x13***
1475D-1475F A426b Set of 3 8.50 8.50

World Environment Day — A427

Denominations, 50f, 150f, 350f.

2000 Litho. ***Perf. 13x13¼***
1476-1478 A427 Set of 3 8.50 8.50

Gulf Investment Corporation, 15th Anniv. — A428

New Gulf Investment Corporation headquarters, emblem, "15" and frame color of: 25f, Green. 50f, Blue. 150f, Red.

2000, Oct. 31 Litho. ***Perf. 13x13¼***
1479-1481 A428 Set of 3 5.00 5.00

General Administration of Customs, Cent. — A429

Denominations: 50f, 150f, 350f.

2000 Litho. ***Perf. 13¼x14***
1482-1484 A429 Set of 3 8.50 8.50

Imperf

Size: 100x75mm

1485 A429 1d multi 15.00 15.00

No. 1485 contains one 47x28mm perf. 13¼x14 non-denominated label.

Hala Fibrayar — A430

Panel colors: 25f, Purple. 50f, Red violet. 150f, Blue.

2001 Litho. ***Perf. 13¼x13***
1486-1488 A430 Set of 3 5.00 5.00

Prisoners of War — A431

Background colors: 25f, White. 50f, Blue & blue green. 150f, Multicolored.

2001 ***Perf. 13x13¼***
1489-1491 A431 Set of 3 5.00 5.00

UN High Commissioner for Refugees, 50th Anniv. — A432

Various depictions of anniversary emblem: 25f, 50f, 150f.

2001
1492-1494 A432 Set of 3 5.00 5.00

Kuwait, 2001 Arab Cultural Capital A433

Background colors: 25f, Yellow. 50f, Green. 150f, Blue.

2001
1495-1497 A433 Set of 3 5.00 5.00

Liberation Day, 10th Anniv. — A434

Frame color: 25f, Lilac. 50f, Blue. 150f, Yellow.

2001 ***Perf. 13¼x13***
1498-1500 A434 Set of 3 5.00 5.00

National Day, 40th Anniv. — A435

Frame color: 25f, Orange. 50f, Yellow. 150f, Blue green.

2001
1501-1503 A435 Set of 3 5.00 5.00

Kuwait Diving Team, 10th Anniv. A436

"10" and: 25f, Fish. 50f, Divers. 150f, Shark, turtle, vert.

2001 ***Perf. 13x13¼, 13¼x13***
1504-1506 A436 Set of 3 5.00 5.00

Radio Kuwait, 50th Anniv. A437

Frame color: 25f, Yellow brown. 50f, Blue, vert. 150f, Red, vert.

2001 ***Perf. 13x13¼, 13¼x13***
1507-1509 A437 Set of 3 5.00 5.00

Intifada A438

Dome of the Rock, Jerusalem: 25f, 50f, 150f.

2001 ***Perf. 13x13¼***
1510-1512 A438 Set of 3 5.00 5.00

Year of Dialogue Among Civilizations A439

Background colors: 25f, Orange & yellow. 50f, Dark & light green. 150f, Rose & pink.

2001 ***Perf. 13¼x13***
1513-1515 A439 Set of 3 5.00 5.00

Human Rights A440

Designs: 25f, Hands covering man's face, vert. 50f, Barbed wire, clock, man's face. 150f, Chains, globe, child, woman.

2001 ***Perf. 13¼x13, 13x13¼***
1516-1518 A440 Set of 3 5.00 5.00

A441

A442

AWQAF Foundation A443

2001 *Perf. 14x13*

1519	A441	25f multi	.50	.50
1520	A442	50f multi	1.25	1.25
1521	A443	150f multi	3.50	3.50
	Nos. 1519-1521 (3)		5.25	5.25

Kuwait Fund for Arab Economic Development, 40th Anniv. — A444

Background colors: 25f, Yellow. 50f, Green & gray.

2001 *Perf. 13¼x13*
1522-1523 A444 Set of 2 1.50 1.50

Touristic Enterprises Company, 25th Anniv. — A445

Stylistic flora: 25f, 50f, 100f, 150f. 250f, Combined designs of four stamps.

2001 *Perf. 13¼x13*
1524-1527 A445 Set of 4 7.50 7.50

Size: 60x80mm

Imperf

1528 A445 250f multi 6.00 6.00

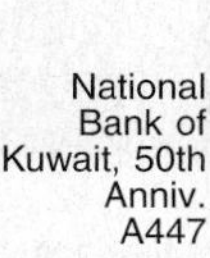

National Bank of Kuwait, 50th Anniv. A447

Emblem and: 25f, Facade of old building. 50f, Modern building. 150f, Camels.

2002, Jan. 16 Litho. *Perf. 13x13¼*
1532-1534 A447 Set of 3 5.00 5.00

Liberation Day, 11th Anniv. — A448

Background color: 25f, Light blue. 50f, Light yellow. 150f, White.

2002, Feb. 26 *Perf. 13¼x13*
1535-1537 A448 Set of 3 5.00 5.00

Social Development Office, 10th Anniv. — A449

Background color: 25f, Light yellow. 50f, Light blue.

2002, Apr. 21
1538-1539 A449 Set of 2 1.50 1.50

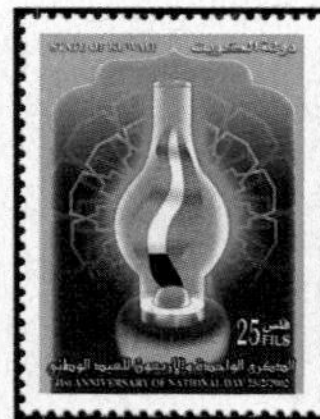

41st National Day — A450

Frame color: 25f, Orange. 50f, Green. 150f, Purple.

2002, Feb. 25 Litho. *Perf. 13¼x13*
1540-1542 A450 Set of 3 5.00 5.00

Nomadism From the Hejaz to Africa — A451

Top panel color: 25f, Pale orange. 50f, Blue. 150f, Purple.

2002, Mar. 11
1543-1545 A451 Set of 3 5.00 5.00

Rehabilitation of Al-Qurain Landfill Site — A452

Panel color: 25f, Blue. 50f, Purple. 150f, Green.

2002, Apr. 1
1546-1548 A452 Set of 3 5.00 5.00

Kuwait Scientific Center — A453

Designs; Nos. 1549a, 1550e, Lapwing. Nos. 1549b, 1550d, Spur-winged plover. Nos. 1549c, 1550c, Eurasian river otter. Nos. 1549d, 1550b, Saltwater crocodile. Nos. 1549e, 1550i, Fennec fox. Nos. 1549f, 1550h, Caracal. Nos. 1549g, 1550g, Cushion sister starfish. Nos. 1549h, 1550f, Cuttlefish. Nos. 1549i, 1550m, Sand tiger shark. Nos. 1549j, 1550l, Lionfish. Nos. 1549k, 1550k, Kestrel. Nos. 1549l, 1550j, Egyptian fruit bat. Nos. 1549m, 1550a, Science center.

Perf. 13¼x13¾, 14x13¼ (#1550k)

2002, Apr. 17

1549	Sheet of 13	24.00	24.00
a.-l.	A453 25f Any single	.20	.20
m.	A453 50f multi	.30	.30
1550	Booklet of 13 panes	40.00	
a.-m.	A453 50f Any single pane	.30	.30

Imperf

Size: 80x60mm

1551 A453 250f shown 12.00 12.00

Stamp sizes: Nos. 1549a-1549l, 30x25mm; No. 1549m, 45x27mm. Nos. 1550a-1550j, 1550l-1550m, 50x36mm; No. 1550k, 32x48mm.

Kuwait Foundation for the Advancement of Sciences, 25th Anniv. (in 2001) — A454

Foundation emblem and: 25f, 25th anniversary emblem. 50f, 25th anniversary emblem and building. 150f, Map of Kuwait, vert.

Perf. 13x13¼, 13¼x13

2002 ? Litho.
1552-1554 A454 Set of 3 5.00 5.00

Intl. Volunteers Year (in 2001) — A455

Background colors: 25f, White. 50f, Lilac. 150f, Yellow.

2002 ? *Perf. 13¼x13*
1555-1557 A455 Set of 3 5.00 5.00

National Council for Culture, Arts and Letters, 25th Anniv. — A456

Panel color: 25f, Lilac. 50f, Olive green. 150f, Bright blue. 500f, Lilac.

2002 ? *Perf. 13¼x13*
1558-1560 A456 Set of 3 5.00 5.00

Souvenir Sheet

Imperf

1561 A456 500f multi 10.00 10.00

No. 1561 contains one 42x58mm stamp.

Kuwait Society of Engineers, 40th Anniv. A457

Panel color at LR: 25f, Brown. 50f, Bright green. 150f, Yellow green.

2002 *Perf. 13x13¼*
1562-1564 A457 Set of 3 5.00 5.00

Public Authority for Applied Education and Training, 20th Anniv. — A458

"20," "1982-2002" and: 25f, Men at work. 50f, Surgeon. 100f, Man with machine. 150f, Building and Kuwait flag. 250f, Ironworkers.

2002 *Perf. 13¼x13*
1565-1569 A458 Set of 5 12.50 12.50

42nd National Day — A459

Frame color: 25f, Green. 50f, Red. 150f, Blue.

2003, Feb. 25 Litho. *Perf. 13x13¼*
1570-1572 A459 Set of 3 6.00 6.00

Martyr's Bureau A460

Emblem and: 25f, Ship. 50f, Flag on Qarow Island. 150f, Fingerprint. 350f, Map of Kuwait.

2003

1573-1576	A460 Set of 4	14.00	14.00
1576a	Booklet pane, #1573-1576	14.00	—
	Complete booklet, #1576a	14.00	

Intl. Day Against Desertification A461

Designs: 25f, Dead tree. 50f, Log. 150f, Palm trees.

2003 Litho. *Perf. 13¼x13*
1577-1579 A461 Set of 3 5.00 5.00

Commercial Bank of Kuwait, 43rd Anniv. — A462

"43" and: 25f, Geometric design. 50f, Old bank building. 150f, New bank building.

2003 *Perf. 13*
1580-1582 A462 Set of 3 5.00 5.00

Kuwait Awqaf Public Foundation, 10th Anniv. A463

Emblem, "10," and: 50f, Building, family. 100f, Fingers. 150f, Man, minaret.

2004, Jan. 19
1583-1585 A463 Set of 3 6.00 6.00

A464

A465

Ministry of Information, 50th Anniv. — A466

2003
1586 A464 25f multi .75 .75
1587 A465 100f multi 2.25 2.25
1588 A466 150f multi 3.50 3.50
Nos. 1586-1588 (3) 6.50 6.50

43rd National Day — A467

Designs: 25f, Palm tree. 50f, Pearl in shell. 150f, Fortress, flags. 350f, Buildings, dhow.

2004, Feb. 25 ***Perf. 13¼x13***
1589-1592 A467 Set of 4 13.00 13.00

Kuwait Airways, 50th Anniv. A468

Various airplanes: 25f, 50f, 75f, 100f, 125f, 150f.

2004, Dec. 18 Litho. ***Perf. 13x13¼***
1593-1598 A468 Set of 6 8.00 8.00

Kuwait Petroleum Corporation, 25th Anniv. — A469

Headquarters: 50f, In daytime. 75f, With sun on horizon. 125f, At night.

2005, Jan. 1 ***Perf. 14½***
1599-1601 A469 Set of 3 4.00 4.00

44th National Day — A470

Sheikhs, dhow, eagle and: 75f, Towers. 125f, Truck at port.

2005, Feb. 25 ***Perf. 14***
1602-1603 A470 Set of 2 2.10 2.10

Liberation Day, 14th Anniv. — A471

Sheikhs, flag and: 50f, Airplane, satellite dish. 150f, Tower.

2005, Feb. 26
1604-1605 A471 Set of 2 3.25 3.25

Technical Education, 50th Anniv. — A472

Background color: 25f, Purple. 50f, Red. 75f, Orange. 125f, Green.

2005, Mar. 15
1606-1609 A472 Set of 4 4.50 4.50

Flags and Emblems A473

Designs: No. 1610, Triangular 1961 ship and harbor flag. No. 1611, 1940 official flag. No. 1612, 1903 special event flag. No. 1613, 1940-50 ruling family flag. No. 1614, Two 1914 right triangle flags. No. 1615, 1921-40, 1956-62 and 1962 emblems.

No. 1616, 1962-56 emblem. No. 1617, 1921-40 emblem.

No. 1618, Right triangle flag of 1914 with Arabic script and emblem in center and script along short side like that on #1613. No. 1619, Right triangle flag of 1914 with Arabic script in center. No. 1620, Right triangle flag of 1914 with Arabic script in center and script along short side.

No. 1621, Triangular 1921 ship and harbor flag. No. 1622, Like #1610. No. 1623, Rectangular 1961 ship and harbor flag. No. 1624, Rectangular 1921 ship and harbor flag.

No. 1625, 1914-61 official flag. No. 1626, 1871-1914 official flag. No. 1627, 1746-1871 official flag. No. 1628, Like #1611. No. 1629, 1921-61 official flag.

No. 1630, 1903 special event flag. No. 1631, 1866 special event flag. No. 1632, 1921 special event flag.

No. 1633, 1921-40 ruling family flag with two white stripes. No. 1634, Like #1613, with colored background. No. 1635, 1921-40 ruling family flag with one white stripe.

2005, Oct. 15 Litho. ***Perf. 14x13¾***
1610 A473 200f multi 2.25 2.25
1611 A473 250f multi 3.25 3.25

Perf. 14

Size: 40x30mm

1612 A473 350f multi 4.00 4.00
1613 A473 500f multi 6.50 6.50

Perf. 14x13¾

Size: 60x30mm

1614 A473 1d multi 11.00 11.00
1615 A473 1d multi 11.00 11.00
Nos. 1610-1615 (6) 38.00 38.00

Booklet Stamps

Self-Adhesive

Die Cut Perf. 13

Size:40x34mm

1616 A473 100f multi 2.00 2.00
1617 A473 100f multi 2.00 2.00
a. Booklet pane, #1616-1617 4.00

Die Cut Perf. 13x13¼

Size: 40x30mm

1618 A473 175f multi 3.75 3.75
1619 A473 175f multi 3.75 3.75
1620 A473 175f multi 3.75 3.75
a. Booklet pane, #1618-1620 11.50

Die Cut Perf. 10x10¾

Size: 30x20mm

1621 A473 200f multi 3.75 3.75
1622 A473 200f multi 3.75 3.75
1623 A473 200f multi 3.75 3.75
1624 A473 200f multi 3.75 3.75
a. Booklet pane, #1621-1624 15.00
1625 A473 250f multi 3.75 3.75
1626 A473 250f multi 3.75 3.75
1627 A473 250f multi 3.75 3.75
1628 A473 250f multi 3.75 3.75
1629 A473 250f multi 3.75 3.75
a. Booklet pane #1625-1629 19.00

Die Cut Perf. 13x13¼

Size: 40x30mm

1630 A473 350f multi 5.75 5.75
1631 A473 350f multi 5.75 5.75
1632 A473 350f multi 5.75 5.75
a. Booklet pane, #1630-1632 17.50
1633 A473 500f multi 9.50 9.50
1634 A473 500f multi 9.50 9.50
1635 A473 500f multi 9.50 9.50
a. Booklet pane, #1633-1635 28.50
Complete booklet, #1617a, 1620a, 1624a, 1629a, 1632a, 1635a 97.50
Nos. 1616-1635 (20) 94.75 94.75

Civil Defense A474

Designs: 50f, Civil defense workers and emergency vehicles. 75f, Civil defense workers and children. 125f, Civil defene workers.

2005, Nov. 15 Litho. ***Perf. 14½***
1636-1638 A474 Set of 3 4.00 4.00

Al-Arabi Al-Saghir Children's Magazine, 20th Anniv. A475

Background colors: 100f, Blue. 200f, Yellow. 350f, Red.

2006, Feb. 1 Litho. ***Perf. 14¼x13¾***
1639-1641 A475 Set of 3 11.50 11.50

45th National Day — A476

Frame color: 75f, Purple. 200f, Green. 250f, Black. 350f, Red.

2006, Feb. 25 ***Perf. 13¼***
1642-1645 A476 Set of 4 13.00 13.00

A477

Gulf Cooperation Council, 25th Anniv. — A478

Illustration A478 reduced.

Litho. With Foil Application

2006, May 25 ***Perf. 14***
1646 A477 50f multi 4.00 4.00

Imperf

Size: 165x105mm

1647 A478 500f multi 14.00 14.00

See Bahrain Nos. 628-629, Oman Nos. 477-478, Qatar Nos. 1007-1008, Saudi Arabia No. 1378, and United Arab Emirates Nos. 831-832.

Emblem A479

A480

A481

A482

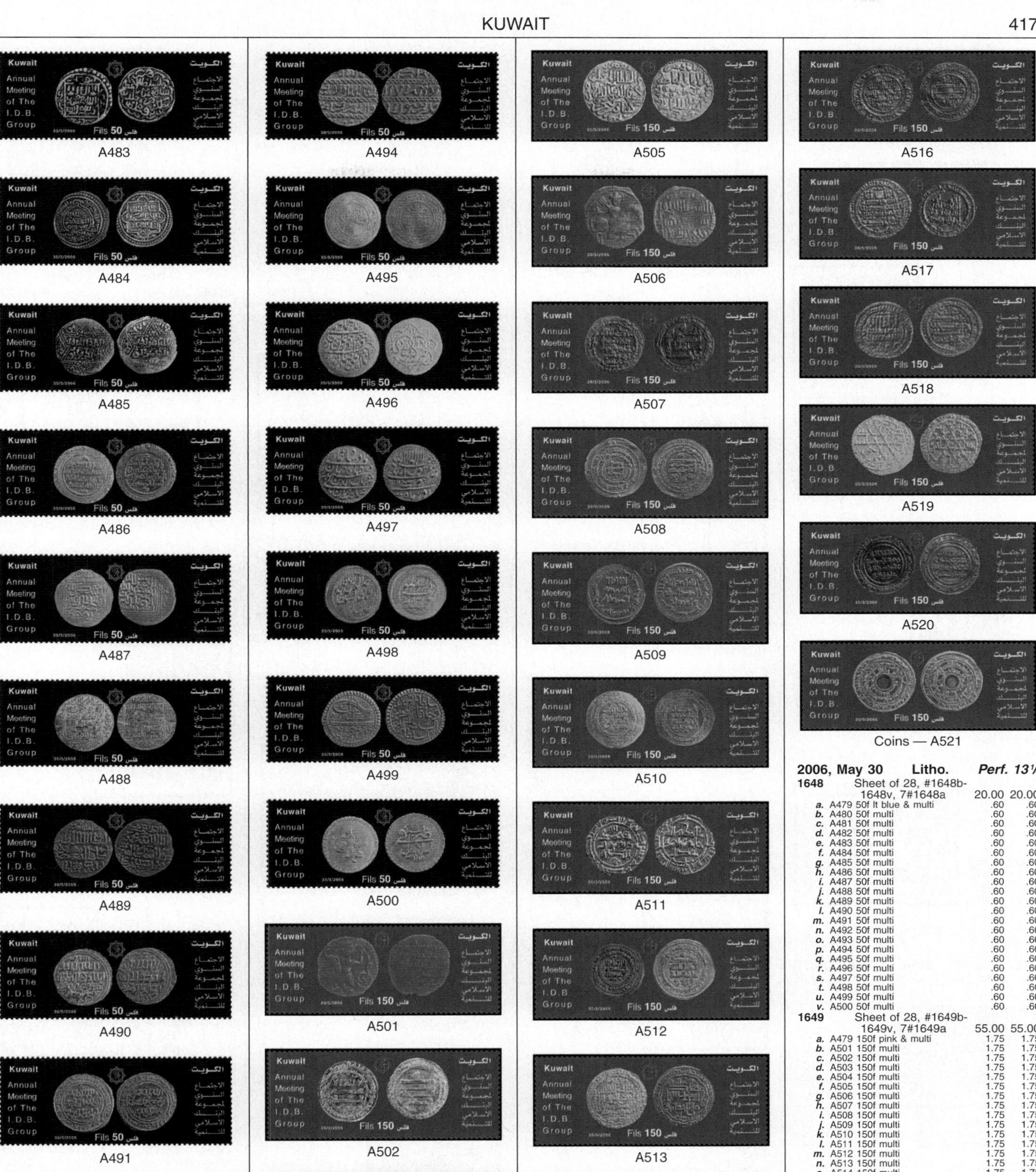

Coins — A521

2006, May 30 Litho. *Perf. 13¼*

1648	Sheet of 28, #1648b-1648v, 7#1648a	20.00	20.00
a.	A479 50f lt blue & multi	.60	.60
b.	A480 50f multi	.60	.60
c.	A481 50f multi	.60	.60
d.	A482 50f multi	.60	.60
e.	A483 50f multi	.60	.60
f.	A484 50f multi	.60	.60
g.	A485 50f multi	.60	.60
h.	A486 50f multi	.60	.60
i.	A487 50f multi	.60	.60
j.	A488 50f multi	.60	.60
k.	A489 50f multi	.60	.60
l.	A490 50f multi	.60	.60
m.	A491 50f multi	.60	.60
n.	A492 50f multi	.60	.60
o.	A493 50f multi	.60	.60
p.	A494 50f multi	.60	.60
q.	A495 50f multi	.60	.60
r.	A496 50f multi	.60	.60
s.	A497 50f multi	.60	.60
t.	A498 50f multi	.60	.60
u.	A499 50f multi	.60	.60
v.	A500 50f multi	.60	.60
1649	Sheet of 28, #1649b-1649v, 7#1649a	55.00	55.00
a.	A479 150f pink & multi	1.75	1.75
b.	A501 150f multi	1.75	1.75
c.	A502 150f multi	1.75	1.75
d.	A503 150f multi	1.75	1.75
e.	A504 150f multi	1.75	1.75
f.	A505 150f multi	1.75	1.75
g.	A506 150f multi	1.75	1.75
h.	A507 150f multi	1.75	1.75
i.	A508 150f multi	1.75	1.75
j.	A509 150f multi	1.75	1.75
k.	A510 150f multi	1.75	1.75
l.	A511 150f multi	1.75	1.75
m.	A512 150f multi	1.75	1.75
n.	A513 150f multi	1.75	1.75
o.	A514 150f multi	1.75	1.75
p.	A515 150f multi	1.75	1.75
q.	A516 150f multi	1.75	1.75
r.	A517 150f multi	1.75	1.75
s.	A518 150f multi	1.75	1.75
t.	A519 150f multi	1.75	1.75
u.	A520 150f multi	1.75	1.75
v.	A521 150f multi	1.75	1.75

Islamic Development Bank Group annual meeting.

15th Asian Games, Doha, Qatar A522

Designs: 25f, Tennis. 50f, Bowling. 150f, Shooting. 250f, Equestrian. 350f, Fencing.

2006 Litho. *Perf. 14½*
1650-1654 A522 Set of 5 13.00 13.00

Campaign Against Hypertension A523

Frame colors: 50f, Green. 150f, Red. 350f, Brown.

2007, Jan. 15 *Perf. 13¼x13*
1655-1657 A523 Set of 3 9.25 9.25

46th National Day — A524

Sky color: 25f, Dark blue. 50f, Blue. 150f, Orange brown.

2007, Feb. 25
1658-1660 A524 Set of 3 4.00 4.00

Liberation Day, 16th Anniv. A525

Frame color: 25f, Red. 50f, Dark blue. 150f, Purple.

2007, Feb. 26 Litho. *Perf. 13x13¼*
1661-1663 A525 Set of 3 4.00 4.00

Kuwait University, 40th Anniv. (in 2006) A526

Color behind emblem: 25f, Blue. 50f, Yellow. 150f, Green. 350f, Red.

2007, Mar. 20
1664-1667 A526 Set of 4 10.00 10.00

Kuwait Oil Tanker Company, 50th Anniv. A527

Background colors: 25f, Pale blue. 50f, Pale green. 150f, Gray.

Litho. & Embossed With Foil Application

2007, Nov. 25 *Perf. 13*
1668-1670 A527 Set of 3 5.25 5.25

Kuwait Philatelic & Numismatic Society, 1st Anniv. — A528

2007, Dec. 5 Litho. *Perf. 13¼*
1671 Horiz. strip of 3 5.00 5.00
a. A528 25f Coin .60 .60
b. A528 50f Kuwait #146 1.00 1.00
c. A528 150f Society emblem 2.75 2.75

No. 1671c is 60x35mm.

47th National Day — A529

Designs: 25f, Women voting. 150f, Stylized people, dhows, fish, towers, horiz.

Perf. 13¼x13, 13x13¼
2008, Feb. 25 Litho.
1672-1673 A529 Set of 2 3.25 3.25

Liberation Day, 17th Anniv. A530

Hand holding map of Kuwait with background color of: 25f, Dull rose. 50f, Purple.

2008, Feb. 26 Litho. *Perf. 13x13¼*
1674-1675 A530 Set of 2 .55 .55

First Gulf Cooperation Council Women's Sports Tournament A531

No. 1676 — Emblem and: a, Gymnastics. b, Running. c, Shooting. d, Basketball. e, Tennis.

No. 1677, horiz. — Emblem, five sports with background color of: a, Orange. b, Red. c, Purple. d, Olive green. e, Red violet.

2008, Mar. 5 Litho. *Perf. 13¼x13*
1676 Vert. strip of 5 2.50 2.50
a.-e. A531 25f Any single .40 .40

Perf. 13x13¼
1677 Horiz strip of 5 8.00 8.00
a.-e. A531 150f Any single 1.25 1.25

Diplomatic Relations Between Kuwait and Romania, 45th Anniv. — A532

No. 1678: a, Kuwaiti man building ship model. b, Romanian woman weaving.

500f, Flags of Romania and Kuwait, handshake, vert.

2008, June 21 *Perf. 13¼x13*
1678 Horiz. pair + 2 labels *10.00 10.00*
a.-b. A532 150f Either single + label *4.75 4.75*
c. Miniature sheet, 4 #1678 *40.00* —

Souvenir Sheet

Perf. 13x13¼
1679 A532 500f multi *20.00 20.00*

Labels of Nos. 1678a and 1678b are separated from stamps by a partial row of perforations. The labels, which have different designs, are to the left of No. 1678a and to the right of No. 1678b. The labels are adjacent to each other on half of the pairs on No. 1678c. No. 1678 was also printed in sheets containing 6 pairs, two of which have the labels adjacent. Value, $60.

See Romania Nos. 5053-5054.

Old Kuwait A533

Designs: 25f, Drummer and swordsmen. 50f, Drummers and boat painter. 100f, Street with thatched roof. 150f, Fair. 200f, Man and minarets. 250f, Donkey riders at town gate. 350f, Boats in harbor. 500f, People at town gate.

2008, Aug. 1 *Perf. 13*
1680 A533 25f multi .20 .20
1681 A533 50f multi .40 .40
1682 A533 100f multi .75 .75
1683 A533 150f multi 1.10 1.10
1684 A533 200f multi 1.50 1.50
1685 A533 250f multi 1.90 1.90
1686 A533 350f multi 2.75 2.75
1687 A533 500f multi 3.75 3.75
Nos. 1680-1687 (8) 12.35 12.35

48th National Day — A534

Frame color: 25f, Black. 50f, Green. 150f, Red.

250f, No frame.

2009, Feb. 25 Litho. *Perf. 13¼*
1688-1690 A534 Set of 3 1.60 1.60

Size: 100x66mm

Imperf
1691 A534 250f multi 1.75 1.75

Liberation Day, 18th Anniv. — A535

Denomination color: 25f, Green. 50f, Red. 150f, Black.

2009, Feb. 26 *Perf. 13¾*
1692-1694 A535 Set of 3 1.60 1.60

Kuwait Finance House A536

Denomination color: 25f, White. 50f, Silver. 150f, Gold.

Litho. & Embossed

2009, June 21 *Perf. 13¾*
1695-1697 A536 Set of 3 1.60 1.60

Kuwait Chamber of Commerce and Industry, 50th Anniv. — A537

Designs: 25f, Building. 50f, Dhow. 150f, Cogwheels.

2009 Litho.

Granite Paper
1698-1700 A537 Set of 3 1.60 1.60

49th National Day — A538

Designs: 25f, Buildings and falcon. 50f, Sheikhs and falcon. 150f, Sheikhs and buildings.

2010, Feb. 25 Litho. *Perf. 13¼x13*
1701-1703 A538 Set of 3 4.25 4.25

Liberation Day, 19th Anniv. A539

Designs: 25f, Children's drawing of people waving flags in car and on side of road. 50f, Child waving flags. 150f, Fabric art of girls wearing dresses in colors of Kuwait flag.

2010, Feb. 26 *Perf. 13x13¼*
1704-1706 A539 Set of 3 4.25 4.25

Jerusalem, Capital of Arab Culture — A540

Denomination color: 25f, Green. 50f, Red.

2010, Mar. 26 *Perf. 13¼x13*
1707-1708 A540 Set of 2 1.50 1.50

Kuwait E-Gate A541

Frame color: 25f, Pink. 50f, Yellow. 150f, Light green.

2010, Apr. 20 ***Perf. 14x13¼***

1709-1711	A541	Set of 3	3.75 3.75

Organization of the Petroleum Exporting Countries, 50th Anniv. A542

Background color: 25f, Gray. 50f, Light blue. 150f, White.

Litho. & Embossed With Foil Application

2010, May 23 ***Perf. 13¾***

1712-1714	A542	Set of 3	3.75 3.75

AIR POST STAMPS

Air Post Stamps of India, 1929-30, Overprinted type "c"

1933-34 **Wmk. 196** ***Perf. 14***

C1	AP1	2a dull green	12.00	*17.00*
C2	AP1	3a deep blue	2.25	*2.75*
C3	AP1	4a gray olive	110.00	*150.00*
C4	AP1	6a bister ('34)	4.50	*5.00*
		Nos. C1-C4 (4)	128.75	*174.75*

Counterfeits of Nos. C1-C4 exist.

Catalogue values for unused stamps in this section, from this point to the end of the section, are for Never Hinged items.

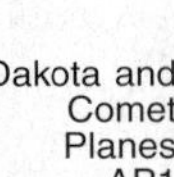

Dakota and Comet Planes AP1

Perf. 11x11½

1964, Nov. 29 **Litho.** **Unwmk.**

C5	AP1	20f multicolored	.90	.30
C6	AP1	25f multicolored	1.00	.40
C7	AP1	30f multicolored	1.25	.40
C8	AP1	45f multicolored	1.50	.60
		Nos. C5-C8 (4)	4.65	1.70

10th anniversary of Kuwait Airways.

POSTAGE DUE STAMPS

Catalogue values for unused stamps in this section are for Never Hinged items.

D1

Perf. 14x15

1963, Oct. 19 **Unwmk.** **Litho.**

Inscriptions in Black

J1	D1	1f ocher	.50	.30
J2	D1	2f lilac	.55	.45
J3	D1	5f blue	.85	.30
J4	D1	8f pale green	1.25	.55
J5	D1	10f yellow	1.50	1.00
J6	D1	25f brick red	2.75	*3.25*
		Nos. J1-J6 (6)	7.40	5.85

D2

1965, Apr. 1 ***Perf. 13***

J7	D2	4f rose & yellow	.35	.30
J8	D2	15f dp rose & blue	1.25	.55
J9	D2	40f blue & brt yel grn	2.25	1.25
J10	D2	50f green & pink	3.00	1.75
J11	D2	100f dk blue & yel	4.50	3.25
		Nos. J7-J11 (5)	11.35	7.10

OFFICIAL STAMPS

Stamps of India, 1911-23, Overprinted

Nos. O1-O9

Nos. O10-O14

1923-24 **Wmk. 39** ***Perf. 14***

O1	A47	½a green	3.00	*10.00*
O2	A48	1a brown	3.50	*9.00*
O3	A58	1½a chocolate	4.00	*20.00*
O4	A49	2a violet	6.00	*17.50*
O5	A57	2a6p ultra	6.00	*30.00*
O6	A51	3a brown org	6.50	*40.00*
O7	A51	3a ultra ('24)	6.75	*30.00*
O8	A52	4a olive grn	5.25	*45.00*
O9	A54	8a red violet	8.50	*55.00*
O10	A56	1r grn & brn	26.00	*80.00*
O11	A56	2r brn & car rose	27.50	*200.00*
O12	A56	5r vio & ultra	100.00	*400.00*
O13	A56	10r car & grn	180.00	*375.00*
O14	A56	15r ol grn & ultra	275.00	*550.00*
		Nos. O1-O14 (14)	658.00	*1,861.*

Stamps of India, 1926-30, Overprinted

Nos. O15-O20

Nos. O21-O25

1929-33 **Wmk. 196**

O15	A48	1a dk brown	5.00	*20.00*
O16	A60	2a violet	65.00	*175.00*
O17	A51	3a blue	5.50	*30.00*
O18	A61	4a ol green	6.25	*65.00*
O19	A54	8a red violet	7.00	*85.00*
O20	A55	12a claret	35.00	*150.00*
O21	A56	1r green & brn	7.00	*170.00*
O22	A56	2r buff & car rose	13.50	*300.00*
O23	A56	5r dk vio & ultra	37.50	*450.00*
O24	A56	10r car & green	72.50	*750.00*
O25	A56	15r olive grn & ultra	180.00	*1,250.*
		Nos. O15-O25 (11)	434.25	*3,445.*

KYRGYZSTAN

ˌkir-gi-ˈstan

(Kirghizia)

LOCATION — Bounded by Kazakhstan, Uzbekistan, Tadjikistan and China.
GOVT. — Independent republic, member of the Commonwealth of Independent States.
AREA — 77,180 sq. mi.
POP. — 4,546,055 (1999 est.)
CAPITAL — Bishkek

With the breakup of the Soviet Union on Dec. 26, 1991, Kyrgyzstan and ten former Soviet republics established the Commonwealth of Independent States.

100 Kopecks = 1 Ruble
100 Tyiyn = 1 Som

Catalogue values for all unused stamps in this country are for Never Hinged items.

Sary-Chelek Nature Preserve — A1

Unwmk.

1992, Feb. 4 **Litho.** ***Perf. 12***

1	A1	15k multicolored	.45	.45

Hawk — A2

1992, Aug. 31 **Litho.** ***Perf. 12½x12***

2	A2	50k multicolored	.80	.80

Man with Cattle, by G.A. Aytiev — A3

1992, Aug. 31

3	A3	1r multicolored	.35	.35

Handicrafts A4

1992, Dec. 1 **Litho.** ***Perf. 12x11½***

4	A4	1.50r multicolored	.40	.40

Sites and Landmarks A5

Designs: 10k, Petroglyphs. 50k, 11th Cent. tower, vert. 1r + 25k, Mausoleum, vert. 2r + 50k, 12th Cent. mausoleum. 3r, Yurt. 5r + 50k, Statue of epic hero Manas, Pishpek. 9r, Commercial complex, Pishpek. 10r, Native jewelry.

1993, Mar. 21 **Litho.** ***Perf. 12***

5	A5	10k multicolored	.20	.20
6	A5	50k multicolored	.20	.20
7	A5	1r +25k multi	.20	.20
8	A5	2r +50k multi	.20	.20
9	A5	3r multicolored	.20	.20
10	A5	5r +50k multi	.30	.30
11	A5	9r multi	.50	.50
		Nos. 5-11 (7)	1.80	1.80

Souvenir Sheet

12	A5	10r multicolored	1.00	1.00

Independence and Admission to UN, 2nd Anniv. — A6

#15a, 120t, like #13. #15b, 130t, like #14.

Perf. 13x12½, 12½x13

1993, Aug. 31 **Litho.**

13	A6	50t Map	.80	.80
14	A6	60t UN emblem, flag, building, vert.	.95	.95

Souvenir Sheet

Imperf

15	A6	Sheet of 2, #a.-b.	6.00	6.00

Nos. 15a-15b have simulated perforations.

Russia Nos. 4598, 5838, 5984 Surcharged in Violet Blue, Prussian Blue or Black

Methods and Perfs as Before

1993, Apr. 6

16	A2765	10r on 1k #5838 (VB)	.25	.20
17	A2765	20r on 2k #5984 (PB)	.30	.25
18	A2139	30r on 3k #4598 (Blk)	.35	.30
		Nos. 16-18 (3)	.90	.75

Russia Nos. 4599-4600 Surcharged in Blue or Red

Methods and Perfs as Before

1993, June 29

19	A2138	20t on 4k #4599 (Bl)	.70	.70
20	A2139	30t on 6k #4600 (R)	1.00	1.00

New Year 1994 (Year of the Dog) — A7

1994, Feb. 10 **Litho.** ***Perf. 12x12½***

26	A7	60t multicolored	.80	.80

Musical Instrument — A8

1993, Dec. 30 Litho. *Perf. 13x12½*

27 A8 30t Komuz .35 .35

Souvenir Sheet

Perf. 13

28 A8 140t multi 17.50 17.50

No. 28 exists imperf. Value $45.
Issued: #27, 12/30; #28, 4/4/94.

Panthera Uncia A9

1994, Mar. 21 Litho. *Perf. 12½x12*

29 A9 10t shown .40 .40
30 A9 20t Lying down .50 .50
31 A9 30t Seated .75 .75
32 A9 40t Up close .95 .95
Nos. 29-32 (4) 2.60 2.60

World Wildlife Fund.

Flowers — A10

Minerals — A11

Perf. 12x12½, 12½x12

1994, Aug. 31 Litho.

Color of Flower

33 A10 1t violet & white .20 .20
34 A10 3t white & yellow, horiz. .20 .20
a. Miniature sheet of 6 1.40 1.40
35 A10 10t red & yellow .30 .30
36 A10 16t white & yellow .30 .30
37 A10 20t pink & yellow .40 .40
38 A10 30t white & yellow .45 .45
39 A10 40t yellow & brown .55 .55
a. Miniature sheet of 6, #33, #35-39 5.75 5.75
b. Strip of 7, #33-39 4.00 4.00

Souvenir Sheet

40 A10 50t yellow & orange 1.40 1.40

For surcharge see No. 141.

1994, Dec. 1 Litho. *Perf. 13½x13*

41 A11 80t Fluorite-Cinnabar .60 .60
42 A11 90t Calcite .65 .65
43 A11 100t Getchellite .70 .70
44 A11 110t Barite .80 .80
45 A11 120t Orpiment .85 .85
46 A11 140t Stibnite 1.25 1.25
Nos. 41-46 (6) 4.85 4.85

Souvenir Sheet

47 A11 200t Cinnabar 4.25 4.25
a. Miniature sheet of 6 9.00 9.00

No. 47a contains #42-46 and single from #47.

Fish — A12

Designs: 110t, Glyptosternum reticulatum. 120t, Leuciscus schmidti. 130t, Piptychus dybowskii. 140t, Nemachilus strauchi. 200t, Cyprinus carpio.

1994, Dec. 1 *Perf. 13x13½*

48 A12 110t multicolored .50 .50
49 A12 120t multicolored .60 .60
50 A12 130t multicolored .65 .65
51 A12 140t multicolored .75 .75
a. Miniature sheet, #48-51 3.25 3.25
Nos. 48-51 (4) 2.50 2.50

Souvenir Sheet

52 A12 200t multicolored 2.25 2.25

Wild Animals — A13

#60a, 130t, Raptor, diff. b, 170t, Bighorn sheep.

Perf. 12x12½, 12½x12

1995, Apr. 21 Litho.

53 A13 110t Bear .30 .30
54 A13 120t Snow leopard, horiz. .30 .30
55 A13 130t Raptor .35 .35
56 A13 140t Woodchuck, horiz. .40 .40
57 A13 150t Raptor, horiz. .45 .45
58 A13 160t Vulture .50 .50
59 A13 190t Fox, horiz. .65 .65
Nos. 53-59 (7) 2.95 2.95

Souvenir Sheet

60 A13 Sheet of 2, #a.-b. 1.50 1.50

Nos. 53-60 exist imperf. Value $7.

Natl. Costumes — A14

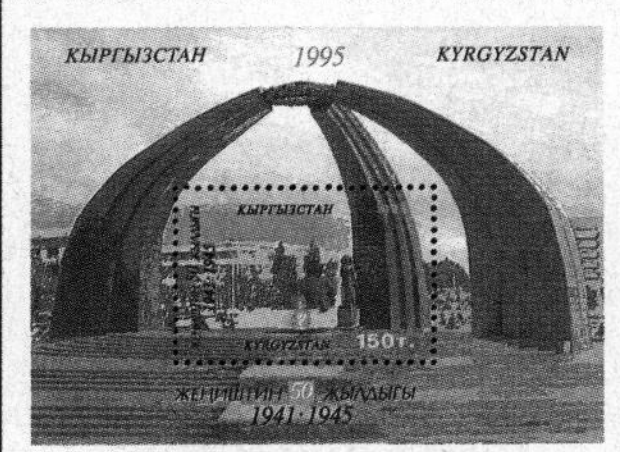

Traffic Safety — A15

1995, Mar. 24 *Perf. 12x12½*

61 A14 50t shown .30 .30
62 A14 50t Man with mandolin .30 .30
63 A14 100t Man with falcon .45 .45
64 A14 100t Woman seated .45 .45
Nos. 61-64 (4) 1.50 1.50

Nos. 61-64 exist imperf. Value, set $2.50.

1995, Mar. 24 *Perf. 12*

65 A15 200t multicolored 1.00 1.00

Souvenir Sheet

End of World War II, 50th Anniv. — A16

1995, May 4 Litho. *Perf. 12x12½*

66 A16 150t multicolored 1.40 1.40

UPU Intl. Letter Week A17

Natl. Arms — A18

1995, Oct. 3 Litho. *Perf. 12x12½*

67 A17 200t multicolored 1.10 1.10

1995, Oct. 13 *Perf. 12*

68 A18 20t purple .35 .35
69 A18 50t blue .35 .35
70 A18 100t brown .45 .45
71 A18 500t green 1.50 1.50
Nos. 68-71 (4) 2.65 2.65

Compare with design A37.

Horses A19

Various adult, juvenile horses.

1995, Oct. 16 *Perf. 12½x12, 12x12½*

Background Color

72 A19 10t olive brown .25 .25
73 A19 50t light brown, vert. .25 .25
74 A19 100t tan, vert. .25 .25
75 A19 140t yellow brown, vert. .30 .30
76 A19 150t lilac .40 .40
77 A19 200t gray .45 .45
78 A19 300t yellow green .65 .65
Nos. 72-78 (7) 2.55 2.55

Souvenir Sheet

79 A19 600t Herd of horses, vert. 2.50 2.50

Raptors — A20

1995, Sept. 12 *Perf. 12x12½*

80 A20 10t Pandion haliaetus .25 .25
81 A20 50t Aquila rapax .25 .25
82 A20 100t Gyps himalayensis .30 .30
83 A20 140t Falco cherrug .35 .35
84 A20 150t Circaetus gallicus .40 .40
85 A20 200t Gypaetus barbatus .45 .45
86 A20 300t Aquila chrysaetos .65 .65
Nos. 80-86 (7) 2.65 2.65

Souvenir Sheet

87 A20 600t Halliaeetus albicilla 2.50 2.50

"Aquila" spelled wrong on #86.

Nos. 80-87 exist imperf. Value: #80-86, $4.25; #87, $2.75.

Souvenir Sheet

UN, 50th Anniv. — A21

Designs: a, UN headquarters, NYC. b, Mountains, rainbow.

1995, Oct. 24 Litho. *Perf. 12½x12*

88 A21 100t Sheet of 2, #a.-b. 1.00 1.00

Natural Wonders of the World — A22

10t, Nile River. 50t, Kilimanjaro. 100t, Sahara Desert. 140t, Amazon River, vert. 150t, Grand Canyon, vert. 200t, Victoria Falls, vert. 350t, Mount Everest. 400t, Niagara Falls.

Issyk-Kul Lake, Kyrgyzstan: No. 97, Raptor, row boat, sail boats. No. 98, Water bird, motor boat, row boat.

1995, Dec. 29 *Perf. 11½*

89 A22 10t multicolored .30 .30
90 A22 50t multicolored .35 .35
91 A22 100t multicolored .45 .45
92 A22 140t multicolored .50 .50
93 A22 150t multicolored .55 .55
94 A22 200t multicolored .70 .70
95 A22 350t multicolored .90 .90
96 A22 400t multicolored 1.25 1.25
Nos. 89-96 (8) 5.00 5.00

Souvenir Sheets

97 A22 600t multicolored 1.75 1.75
98 A22 600t multicolored 1.75 1.75

Reptiles A23

Designs: 20t, Psammophis lineolatum. No. 100, Natrix tessellata. No. 101, Eublepharis macularius. 100t, Agkistrodon halys. 150t, Eremias arguta. 200t, Elaphe dione. 250t, Asymblepharus. 500t, Lacerta agilis.

1996, Feb. 2 *Perf. 12½x12*

99 A23 20t multicolored .25 .25
100 A23 50t multicolored .25 .25
101 A23 50t multicolored .25 .25
102 A23 100t multicolored .30 .30
103 A23 150t multicolored .40 .40
104 A23 200t multicolored .50 .50
105 A23 250t multicolored .65 .65
Nos. 99-105 (7) 2.60 2.60

Souvenir Sheet

106 A23 500t multicolored 2.25 2.25

Souvenir Sheet

Save the Aral Sea — A24

Designs: a, Felis caracal. b, Salmo trutta aralensis. c, Hyaena hyaena. d, Pseudoscaphirhynchus kaufmanni. e, Aspiolucius esocinus.

1996, Apr. 29 Litho. *Perf. 14*
107 A24 100t Sheet of 5, #a.-e. 4.00 4.00

See Kazakhstan No. 145. Tadjikistan No. 91, Turkmenistan No. 52, Uzbekistan No. 113.

Fauna — A27

a, Aquila chrysaetos. b, Capra falconeri. c, Ovis ammon. d, Gyps himalayensis. e, Equus hemionus. f, Canis lupus. g, Ursus arctor. h, Saiga tatarica.

1997, Aug. 29 Litho. *Perf. 12x12½*
114 A27 600t Sheet of 8, #a.-h. 7.00 7.00

See No. 117.

New Year 1998 (Year of the Tiger) A28

1998, June 5 Litho. *Perf. 13½x14*
115 A28 600t multicolored 1.40 1.40

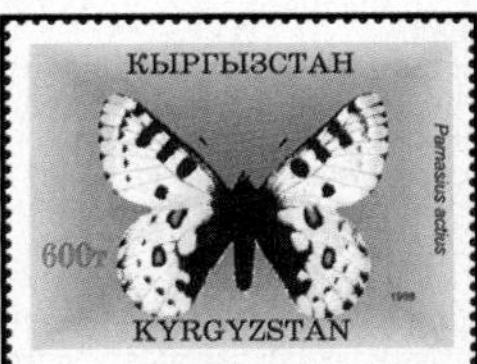

Butterflies — A29

Designs: a, Parnasius actius. b, Colias christophi. c, Papilio machaon. d, Colias thisoa. e, Parnassius delphius. f, Panassius tianschanicus.

1998, June 5
116 A29 600t Sheet of 6, #a.-f. 3.75 3.75

Fauna Type of 1997

a, 600t, Capreolus capreolus. b, 1000t, Oriolus oriolus. c, 600t, Pandion haliaetus. d, 1000t, Uncia uncia. e, 600t, Upupa epops. f, 600t, Ciconia ciconia. g, 1000t, Alcedo atthis. h, 1000t, Falco tinnunculus.

1998, June 5 Litho. *Perf. 12x12½*
117 A27 Sheet of 8, #a-h *9.00 9.00*

Dinosaurs — A31

Designs: a, Saurolophus, vert. b, Euoplocephalus. c, Velociraptor. d, Tyrannosaurus, vert. e, Gallimimus. f, Protoceratops.

Perf. 14x13½, 13½x14
1998, Dec. 4 Litho.
118 A31 10s Sheet of 6, #a.-f. 6.00 6.00

Universal Declaration of Human Rights, 50th Anniv. — A32

a, Andrei Sakharov (1921-89). b, Crowd of people raising their arms. c, Martin Luther King, Jr. d, Mahatma Gandhi. e, Eleanor Roosevelt.

1998, Dec. 4 *Perf. 14x13½*
119 A32 10s Sheet of 5, #a.-e. + label 5.00 5.00

No. 119 exists with 2 different inscriptions on label.

Constitution, 5th Anniv. — A33

1998, Dec. *Perf. 12*
120 A33 1000t multi 1.60 1.60

Imperf
Size: 120x90mm
120A A33 10,000t multi *65.00 65.00*

No. 120A, issued 2/5/99.

Fauna A34

Designs: a, 600t, Fish, denomination UR. b, 1000t, Duck standing beside rocks. c, 1000t, Two birds. d, 1000t, Duck standing beside water. e, 1000t, Duck swimming. f, 1000t, Rodent. g, 1000t, Bird. h, 600t, Fish, denomination UL.

1998, Dec. Litho. *Perf. 12*
121 A34 Sheet of 8, #a.-h. 9.00 9.00

Corsac Fox (Vulpes Corsac) A35

World Wildlife Fund: Nos. 122a, 123a, 10s, Adult sitting. Nos. 122b, 123b, 10s, Adult sleeping. Nos. 122c, 123c, 30s, Two standing. Nos. 122d, 123d, 50s, Adult with young.

1999, Apr. 27 Litho. *Perf. 12½x12*
122 A35 Block of 4, #a.-d. 5.50 5.50

Size: 48x34mm
Perf. 13½
123 A35 Block of 4, #a.-d. 7.00 7.00

Nos. 123a-123d each contain a holographic image. Soaking in water may affect the hologram. IBRA '99, World Philatelic Exhibition, Nuremberg (#123). No. 123 was issued in sheets of 8 stamps.

Aleksandr Pushkin (1799-1837), Poet — A36

No. 124: a, 36t, Knight, giant. b, 6s, Man, woman, fish. c, 10s, Archer, angel. d, 10s, King in carriage.
20s, Portrait of Pushkin.

1999, June Litho. *Perf. 12x12½*
124 A36 Strip of 4, #a.-d. 4.00 4.00

Souvenir Sheet
125 A36 20s multicolored 3.75 3.75

No. 124 printed in sheets of 8 stamps.

Natl. Arms — A37

1999, July Litho. *Perf. 11¼x11½*
126 A37 20t dark blue .95 .95

Souvenir Sheet

China 1999 World Philatelic Exhibition — A38

No. 131: a, 10s, Ailuropoda melanoleuca. b, 15s, Strix leptogrammica.

1999, Aug. 21 Litho. *Perf. 13x12½*
131 A38 Sheet of 2, #a.-b. 2.25 2.25

Exists imperf. Value $3.75.

12th World Kickboxing Championships, Bishkek — A39

Emblem, globe and: No. 132, White background. No. 133, Blue panel. c, No. 134, Green, red, and black panels.
No. 135: a, Black background. b, Yellow and brown panels.

1999, Oct. 7 Litho. *Perf. 13¼*
132 A39 3s multi .70 .70
133 A39 3s multi .70 .70
134 A39 3s multi .70 .70
Nos. 132-134 (3) 2.10 2.10

Souvenir Sheet
Perf. 12½
135 A39 6s Sheet of 2, #a.-b., + label *2.00 2.00*

No. 135 contains 37x26mm stamps.

UPU, 125th Anniv. A40

1999, Oct. *Perf. 14x14¼*
136 A40 3s shown *.50 .50*
137 A40 6s Airplane, man on horse *1.00 1.00*

Dogs — A41

No. 138: a, 3s, Taigan. b, 6s, Tasy. c, 6s, Afghan hound. d, 10s, Saluki. e, 15s, Mid-Asian shepherd. f, 15s, Akbash dog. g, 20s, Chow chow. h, 25s, Akita.

2000, Mar. 18 Litho. *Perf. 12¼x12*
138 A41 Sheet of 8, #a-h 6.75 6.75

Exists imperf. Value $10.

Kyrgyzstan postal officials have declared as "not authentic and not valid" stamps with a face value of 20s depicting the Beatles, Madonna, Pop music stars, Tiger Woods, 2000 French Olympic gold medal winners, Mushrooms, American Political Cartoons concerning the 2000 Presidential election, The Simpsons, Superman, and Warner Brothers cartoon characters.

Bulat Minzhilkiev(1940-98), Opera Singer — A42

2000, Apr. 20 Litho. *Perf. 14x14¼*
139 A42 5s multi *.60 .60*

Victory in World War II, 55th Anniv. A43

Heroes: a, Cholponbay Tuleberdiev (1922-42). b, I. V. Panfilov (1893-1941), vert. c, Duyshenkul Shopokov (1915-41).

Perf. 14x14¼ (#140a, 140c), 14¼x14 (#140b)

2000, May 20 **Litho.**
140 A43 6s Vert. strip of 3, #a-c *2.50 2.50*

Issued in sheets of 2 each #140a-140c.

No. 33 Surcharged

2000, Sept. 22 **Litho.** ***Perf. 12x12½***
141 A10 36t on 1t multi *.25 .25*

No. 141 exists with bar obliterators with smaller numerals and with thinner numerals and rosette obliterators in magenta. Value: each, $11.

2000 Summer Olympics, Sydney A44

Designs: 1s, Wrestling. 3s, Hurdles, vert. 6s, Boxing. 10s, Weight lifting, vert.

Perf. 14x14¼, 14¼x14

2000, Sept. 23
142-145 A44 Set of 4 *4.25 4.25*

Kyrgyzstan postal officials have declared as "not authentic and not valid" a sheet of nine 20s stamps depicting the History of Golf.

Atay Ogunbaev, Composer A45

2000, Oct. 28 **Litho.** ***Perf. 14x14¼***
146 A45 6s multi *.80 .80*

Butterflies — A46

Designs: No. 147, 3s, Aglais urticae. No. 148, 3s, Argynnis aglaja. No. 149, 3s, Colias thisoa. No. 150, 3s, Inachis io. No. 151, 3s, Papilio machaon. No. 152, 3s, Parnassius apollo.

2000, Nov. 18 ***Perf. 13½***
147-152 A46 Set of 6 *4.50 4.50*

Kyrgyzstan postal officials have declared as "not authentic and not valid" stamps with a face value of 20s in sheets of 6 depicting Jennifer Aniston and Tennis, and sheets of 9 depicting Backstreet Boys, Beverly Hills 90210, Minerals, Penguins, Tom and Jerry, Prince William, Babylon 5 and the End of Mir.

Intl. Year of Mountains (in 2002) — A47

Designs: No. 153, 10s, Khan-Tengri Mountain, 7,010 meters. No. 154, 10s, Victory Peak, 7,439 meters. No. 155, 10s, Lenin Peak, 7,134 meters.

2000, Dec. 23 **Litho.** ***Perf. 13½***
153-155 A47 Set of 3 *3.00 3.00*
a. Souvenir sheet, #153-155 + label *3.00 3.00*

Medals — A48

No. 156: a, 36t, Dank. b, 48t, Baatyr Jene. c, 1s, Manas (third class). d, 2s, Manas (second class). e, 3s, Manas (first class). f, 6s, Danaker. g, 10s, Ak Shumkar.

2001, Jan. 20 **Litho.** ***Perf. 14¼x14***
156 A48 Sheet of 7, #a-g, + label *3.00 3.00*

UN High Commissioner for Refugees — A49

2001, Mar. 10 **Litho.** ***Perf. 14x14¼***
157 A49 10s multi *.85 .85*

New Year 2002 (Year of the Snake) A50

2001, Mar. 17
158 A50 6s multi *.75 .75*

Exists imperf. Value $2.

Year of Dialogue Among Civilizations A51

2001, Apr. 14 ***Perf. 13½***
159 A51 10s multi *1.25 1.25*

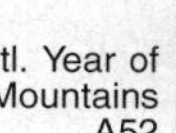

Intl. Year of Mountains A52

Mountains and: Nos. 160, 163a, 10s, Horses crossing stream. Nos. 161, 163b, 10s, Grazing animals, yurt. Nos. 162, 163c, 10s, Valley.

2001, July 7 ***Perf. 14x14¼***
With White Frame
160-162 A52 Set of 3 *3.00 3.00*

Souvenir Sheet
Without White Frame
163 A52 10s Sheet of 3, #a-c, + label *3.50 3.50*

Bishkek Buildings — A53

Designs: 48t, Communications Building. 1s, Town Hall. 3s, Opera House.

2001, July 7 ***Perf. 14x13¼***
164 A53 48t slate gray *.30 .20*
165 A53 1s olive gray *.30 .20*
166 A53 3s violet brown *.35 .30*
a. Horiz. strip, #164-166 *.95 .95*

Intl. Year of Ecotourism (in 2002) A54

Designs: No. 167, 10s, Mountains, lake. No. 168, 10s, Mountains, field of flowers. No. 169, 10s, Sailboat on lake.
No. 170, Mosque, vert.

2001, July 21 ***Perf. 14x14¼***
167-169 A54 Set of 3 *4.00 4.00*

Souvenir Sheet
Imperf (Simulated Perfs)
170 A54 10s multi *1.75 1.75*

Independence, 10th Anniv. — A55

Designs: 1.50s, Eagle, mountain. 7s, Pres. Askar Akaev, flag.
11.50s, Governmental building.

2001, Aug. 29 ***Perf. 14x14¼***
171-172 A55 Set of 2 *3.50 3.50*

Souvenir Sheet
173 A55 11.50s Sheet of 1 + 8 labels *4.25 4.25*

Kurmanbek Baatyr, 500th Anniv. of Birth — A56

2001, Sept. 8 ***Perf. 14¼x14***
174 A56 1.50s multi *.90 .90*

Nos. 123a-123b Surcharged

and Nos. 123c-123d Overprinted With Text Only

No. 175: a, 25s on 10s #123a. b, 25s on 10s, #123b. c, 30s #123c. d, 50s #123d.

Litho. With Hologram

2001 ***Perf. 13½***
175 A35 Block of 4, #a-d *8.25 8.25*

Regional Communications Accord, 10th Anniv. — A57

2001, Oct. 20 **Litho.** ***Perf. 14¼x14***
176 A57 7s multi *1.00 1.00*

Commonwealth of Independent States, 10th Anniv. — A58

2001, Dec. 8
177 A58 6s Prus bl & yel *1.10 1.10*

Kyrgyzstan postal officials have declared as "illegal:"

Stamps with a face value of 20s in sheets of nine depicting Shrek, Harry Potter, Concorde, Dogs, Tigers, Formula 1 racing, Mother Teresa, and The Beatles;

Stamps with various face values in sheets of nine depicting Defenders of Peace and Freedom, Superman, Green Lantern, Flash, Ironman, Legends of Baseball;

Stamps with various values in sheets of three depicting Princess Diana and Elvis Presley;

Stamps with a face value of 20s in sheets of six depicting Harley Davidson motorcycles;

Souvenir sheets of one 100s stamp depicting Harry Potter and Penguins.

2002 Winter Olympics, Salt Lake City — A59

Designs: 50t, Speed skating. 1.50s, Biathlon. 7s, Ice hockey. 10s, Ski jumping.
50s, Downhill skiing.

2002, Feb. 23 **Litho.** ***Perf. 14x14¼***
178-181 A59 Set of 4 *2.50 2.50*

Souvenir Sheet
182 A59 50s multi + label *6.50 6.50*

Campaign Against Drug Abuse — A129

2008, Dec. 6 ***Perf. 14¼x14***
330 A129 12s multi 1.25 1.25

New Year 2009 (Year of the Ox) A130

2009, Feb. 1 ***Perf. 14x14¼***
331 A130 25s multi 2.00 2.00

Ishembai Abdraimov (1914-2001), Soviet Pilot — A131

2009, Feb. 26 ***Perf. 14¼x14***
332 A131 10s multi .95 .95

Kok-boru (Buzkashi) A132

2009, Apr. 25 ***Perf. 14x14¼***
333 A132 25s multi 1.75 1.75

Miniature Sheet

Horses — A133

No. 334 — Various horses: a, 16s. b, 42s. c, 50s. d, 60s.

2009, May 30 ***Perf. 13x13½***
334 A133 Sheet of 4, #a-d 11.00 11.00

Worldwide Fund for Nature (WWF) A134

Saker falcon: 10s, Head. 15s, On nest. 25s, In flight. 50s, On nest, with chicks.

2009, June 20 ***Perf. 13½x14***
335-338 A134 Set of 4 5.50 5.50
338a Sheet, 4 each #335-338 22.00 22.00

Miniature Sheet

Scenes From Writings of Chynghyz Aitmatov (1928-2008) — A135

No. 339: a, 7s, Woman, horse, cart and farmer in field. b, 12s, Man and horse. c, 16s, Woman and truck. d, 21s, Women near train. e, 28s, Man carrying boy. f, 30s, Boy with binoculars, buck. g, 45s, Birds flying above horse and rider. h, 60s, Men in canoe.

2009, Aug. 13 Litho. ***Perf. 13x13¼***
339 A135 Sheet of 8, #a-h, + label 13.50 13.50

Barpy Alykulov (1884-1949), Poet — A136

2009, Aug. 22 Litho. ***Perf. 14x13½***
340 A136 16s multi 1.10 1.10

Horses Type of 2009

Designs: 16s, Like #334a. 42s, Like #334b. 50s, Like #334c. 60s, Like #334d.

2009, Sept. 19 Litho. ***Perf. 14x14¼***
341-344 A133 Set of 4 12.00 12.00

Nos. 341-344 were each printed in sheets of 6.

National Library, 75th Anniv. A137

2009, Sept. 30 ***Perf. 13½x14***
345 A137 12s multi .90 .90

Miniature Sheet

Glaciers — A138

No. 346: a, 12s, Ak-Sai Glacier. b, 16s, Kotur Glacier. c, 21s, Semenovsky Glacier. d, 28s, Zvezdochka Glacier. e, 45s, North Inylchek Glacier. f, 60s, South Inylchek Glacier.

2009, Dec. 12 ***Perf. 13x13¼***
346 A138 Sheet of 6, #a-f 12.50 12.50

Railways of Kyrgyzstan A139

Designs: 16s, Station. 42s, Train on bridge. 50s, Train leaving tunnel. 60s, Train on bridge over highway.

2009, Dec. 19 ***Perf. 14x14¼***
347-350 A139 Set of 4 12.00 12.00

United Nations Declaration of the Rights of the Child, 50th Anniv. (in 2009) A140

2010, Feb. 6
351 A140 21s multi 1.50 1.50

New Year 2010 (Year of the Tiger) A141

2010, Feb. 6
352 A141 25s multi 1.75 1.75

2010 Winter Olympics, Vancouver — A142

Designs: 21s, Cross-country skiing. 28s, Biathlon. 45s, Giant slalom. 60s, Snowboarding.

2010, Feb. 12 ***Perf. 14¼x14***
353-356 A142 Set of 4 10.50 10.50

Peonies — A143

No. 357: a, 25s, Flowers. b, 30s, Flower.

2010, Mar. 30 ***Perf. 12½***
357 A143 Horiz. pair, #a-b 3.75 3.75
c. Souvenir sheet, #357b 2.10 2.10

Victory in World War II, 65th Anniv. A144

2010, Apr. 10 ***Perf. 14x14¼***
358 A144 12s multi .75 .75

Miniature Sheet

Kyrgyz National Museum of Fine Arts, 75th Anniv. — A145

No. 359 — Paintings: a, 12s, Portrait of Y. M. Vengerov, by Ilya E. Repin, 1916. b, 16s, Cabbage Field, by Robert R. Falk, 1910. c, 21s, Dishes on a Red Cloth, by Pyotr P. Konchalovsky, 1916. d, 24s, Seascape in the Crimea, by Ivan K. Ayvazovsky, 1866. e, 28s, Autumn Djailoo, by Semen A. Chuykov, 1945. f, 30s, Evening in the South of Kyrgyzstan, by Gapar A. Aitiev, 1967. g, 42s, Autumn Garden, by A. Ignatev, 1989. h, 45s, By Night, by D. N. Deymant, 1971.

2010, Apr. 24 ***Perf. 13x13¼***
359 A145 Sheet of 8, #a-h, + central label 13.00 13.00

2010 World Cup Soccer Championships, South Africa — A146

Players and: 24s, Emblem. 30s, World Cup. 42s, Emblem, diff. 60s, World Cup, diff.

2010, June 26 Litho. ***Perf. 14x14¼***
360-363 A146 Set of 4 10.00 10.00

Ancient Silver Jewelry A147

Designs: 16s, Earrings. 24s, Buttons. 58s, Bangles. 66s, Hair ornaments.

2010, July 31 ***Perf. 13½***
364-367 A147 Set of 4 11.00 11.00

Souvenir Sheet

Kambar-Ata 2 Hydroelectric Station — A148

No. 368: a, 28s, Explosion. b, 42s, Station under construction. c, 60s, Station under construction, diff.

2010, Aug. 31 ***Perf. 13x13¼***
368 A148 Sheet of 3, #a-c 7.75 7.75

SEMI-POSTAL STAMPS

Natl. Epic Poem, Manas, Millennium
SP1

SP2

Designs: 10t+5t, Woman with bird in hand. 20t+10t, Bird on man's wrist. No. B3, Women watching as baby held up. No. B4, Woman with spear, leading horse. 40t+15t, Warrior looking at dead dragon. No. B6, Warrior on horse holding axe. No. B7, Man wearing tall hat on horseback. No. B8, Warrior with sword on horseback.

No. B9, Man in red cradling fallen warrior. No. B10, Man in black seated in desert, tornado.

Perf. 12, Imperf

1995, June 16 **Litho.**

B1	SP1	10t +5t blue & bis	.35	.35
B2	SP1	20t +10t blue & bis	.35	.35
B3	SP1	30t +10t blue & bis	.35	.35
B4	SP1	30t +10t blue & bis	.35	.35
B5	SP1	40t +15t blue & bis	.35	.35
B6	SP1	50t +15t blue & bis	.35	.35
B7	SP1	50t +15t blue & bis	.35	.35
B8	SP1	50t +15t blue & bis	.35	.35
a.		Sheet of 8, #B1-B8 + label	3.75	3.75

Souvenir Sheets

B9	SP2	2s +50t multi	2.00	2.00
B10	SP2	2s +50t multi	2.00	2.00

1996 Summer Olympic Games, Atlanta
SP3

Designs: 100t+20t, Equestrian events. 140t+30t, Boxing. 150t+30t, Archery. 300t+50t, Judo, hot air balloon, sailing, water skiing.

1996, July 10 **Litho.** ***Perf. 12½x12***

B11	SP3	100t +20t multi	.30	.30
B12	SP3	140t +30t multi	.60	.60
B13	SP3	150t +30t multi	.80	.80
B14	SP3	300t +50t multi	1.25	1.25
		Nos. B11-B14 (4)	2.95	2.95

Town of Osh, 3000th Anniv. — SP4

No. B15: a, Globe, mountains, mosque, "Osh" and "3000." b, Mosque with three arches, mountains (green panel at UR). c, Solomon's Throne (mosque on mountain). d, Mausoleum of Asaf ibn Burkiya (denomination at LL).

Illustration reduced.

2000, Feb. 19 **Litho.** ***Perf. 13½***

B15	SP4	6s +25t Sheet of 4, #a-d	*3.50*	*3.50*

Exists imperf. Value $5.

Kurmanzhan Datka, 190th Anniv. of Birth — SP5

2001, Oct. 13 **Litho.** ***Perf. 14x14¼***

B16	SP5	10s +70t ind & gray	*1.50*	*1.50*

LABUAN

lə-'bü-ən

LOCATION — An island in the East Indies, about six miles off the northwest coast of Borneo

GOVT. — A British possession, administered as a part of the North Borneo Colony

AREA — 35 sq. mi.

POP. — 8,963 (estimated)

CAPITAL — Victoria

The stamps of Labuan were replaced by those of Straits Settlements in 1906.

100 Cents = 1 Dollar

Watermark

Wmk. 46 — C A over Crown

Queen Victoria — A1

On Nos. 1, 2, 3, 4 and 11 the watermark is 32mm high. It is always placed sideways and extends over two stamps.

1879, May **Engr.** **Wmk. 46** ***Perf. 14***

1	A1	2c green	1,500.	975.00
2	A1	6c orange	240.00	215.00
3	A1	12c carmine	1,925.	850.00
4	A1	16c blue	77.50	*170.00*
		Nos. 1-4 (4)	3,742.	2,210.

See Nos. 5-10, 16-24, 33-39, 42-48. For surcharges see Nos. 12-15, 25, 31, 40-41.

1880-82 **Wmk. 1**

5	A1	2c green	27.50	*42.50*
6	A1	6c orange	135.00	*145.00*
7	A1	8c carmine ('82)	135.00	*135.00*
8	A1	10c yel brown	195.00	*100.00*
9	A1	12c carmine	330.00	*400.00*
10	A1	16c blue ('81)	100.00	100.00
		Nos. 5-10 (6)	922.50	*922.50*

A2

A3

A3a

A4

1880-83 **Wmk. 46**

11	A2	6c on 16c blue (with additional "6" across original value) R)	3,000.	1,200.

Wmk. 1

12	A2	8c on 12c carmine	1,725.	1,000.
a.		Original value not obliterated	3,500.	2,000.
b.		Additional surcharge "8" across original value	2,175.	1,450.
c.		"8" inverted	2,100.	1,200.
d.		As "a," "8" inverted	—	—
13	A3	8c on 12c car ('81)	425.00	475.00
14	A3a	8c on 12c car ('81)	145.00	155.00
a.		"Eighr"	*22,500.*	
b.		Inverted surcharge	*15,000.*	
c.		Double surcharge	2,100.	2,100.
15	A4	$1 on 16c blue (R) ('83)	*4,800.*	

On No. 12 the original value is obliterated by a pen mark in either black or red.

1883-86 **Wmk. 2**

16	A1	2c green	26.00	*40.00*
a.		Horiz. pair, imperf. btwn.	15,000.	
17	A1	2c rose red ('85)	4.25	*16.00*
18	A1	8c carmine	325.00	120.00
19	A1	8c dk violet ('85)	35.00	9.00
20	A1	10c yellow brn	50.00	*55.00*
21	A1	10c black brn ('86)	24.00	*60.00*
22	A1	16c blue	115.00	*215.00*
23	A1	16c gray blue ('86)	170.00	
24	A1	40c ocher	25.00	*130.00*
		Nos. 16-24 (9)	774.25	*645.00*

Nos. 1-10, 16-24 are in sheets of 10.
For surcharges see Nos. 26-30, 32.

A5 A6

A7

A8

1885 **Wmk. 1**

25	A5	2c on 16c blue	1,150.	*1,100.*

Wmk. 2

26	A5	2c on 8c car	275.00	*500.00*
a.		Double surcharge		—
27	A6	2c on 16c blue	135.00	*200.00*
a.		Double surcharge		*7,500.*
28	A7	2c on 8c car	80.00	*145.00*

1891

Black or Red Surcharge

29	A8	6c on 8c violet	15.00	13.00
a.		6c on 8c dark violet	170.00	145.00
b.		Double surcharge	390.00	—
c.		As "a," "Cents" omitted	550.00	550.00
d.		Inverted surcharge	90.00	*85.00*
e.		Dbl. surch., one inverted	1,100.	—
f.		Dbl. surch., both inverted	1,100.	—
g.		"6" omitted	600.00	
h.		Pair, one without surcharge	1,800.	1,800.
30	A8	6c on 8c dk vio (R)	1,325.	675.00
a.		Inverted surcharge	1,800.	850.00

Wmk. 46

31	A8	6c on 16c blue	2,750.	2,200.
a.		Inverted surcharge	12,000.	8,000.

Wmk. 2

32	A8	6c on 40c ocher	13,000.	5,750.
a.		Inverted surcharge	12,000.	9,000.

1892 **Engr.** **Unwmk.**

33	A1	2c rose	7.25	4.25
34	A1	6c yellow green	10.00	5.75
35	A1	8c violet	9.50	15.00
36	A1	10c brown	20.00	9.50
37	A1	12c deep ultra	11.00	*8.00*
38	A1	16c gray	22.00	*38.00*
39	A1	40c ocher	50.00	*42.50*
		Nos. 33-39 (7)	129.75	123.00

The 2c, 8c and 10c are in sheets of 30; others in sheets of 10.

Nos. 39 and 38 Surcharged

1893

40	A1	2c on 40c ocher	200.00	110.00
a.		Inverted surcharge	500.00	*675.00*
41	A1	6c on 16c gray	450.00	180.00
a.		Inverted surcharge	675.00	350.00
b.		Surcharge sideways	675.00	375.00
c.		"Six" omitted	—	—
d.		"Cents" omitted	—	—
e.		Handstamped "Six Cents"	*2,275.*	

Surcharges on Nos. 40-41 each exist in 10 types. Counterfeits exist.

No. 41e was handstamped on examples of No. 41 on which the surcharge failed to print or was printed partially or completely albino.

From Jan. 1, 1890, to Jan. 1, 1906, Labuan was administered by the British North Borneo Co. Late in that period, unused remainders of Nos. 42-83, 53a, 63a, 64a, 65a, 66a, 68a, 85-86, 96-118, 103a, 107a, J1-J9, J3a and J6a were canceled to order by bars forming an oval. Values for these stamps used are for those with this form of cancellation, unless described as postally used, which are for stamps with dated town cancellations. Nos. 63b, 64b, 65b, 104a, J6a, and possibly others, only exist c.t.o.

For detailed listings of Labuan, see the *Scott Classic Specialized Catalogue.*

1894, Apr. **Litho.**

42	A1	2c bright rose	2.00	.65
43	A1	6c yellow green	21.50	.65
a.		Horiz. pair, imperf. btwn.	*9,500.*	
44	A1	8c bright violet	22.00	.65
45	A1	10c brown	60.00	.65
46	A1	12c light ultra	30.00	.80
47	A1	16c gray	32.50	.65
48	A1	40c orange	60.00	.65
		Nos. 42-48 (7)	228.00	4.70

Counterfeits exist.

Dyak Chieftain — A9

Malayan Sambar — A10

Sago Palm
A11

Argus Pheasant
A12

Arms of North Borneo — A13

Dhow — A14

Saltwater Crocodile — A15

Mt. Kinabalu — A16

Arms of North Borneo — A17

Perf. 12 to 16 and Compound

1894 **Engr.**

No.	Type	Description	Unused	Used
49	A9	1c lilac & black	2.00	.65
a.		Vert. pair, imperf. between	1,300.	575.00
50	A10	2c blue & black	3.00	.65
a.		Imperf., pair	725.00	
51	A11	3c bister & black	4.50	.65
52	A12	5c green & black	38.50	1.10
a.		Horiz. pair, imperf. between	*1,800.*	
53	A13	6c brn red & blk	3.00	.65
a.		Imperf., pair	725.00	350.00
54	A14	8c rose & black	8.75	.65
55	A15	12c orange & black	27.50	.65
56	A16	18c ol brn & blk	26.50	.65
b.		Vert. pair, imperf. between		*2,500.*
57	A17	24c lilac & blue	18.00	.65
		Nos. 49-57 (9)	131.75	6.30

A18

A19

A20

A21

1895, June **Litho.** ***Perf. 14***

No.	Type	Description	Unused	Used
58	A18	4c on $1 red	1.60	.50
59	A18	10c on $1 red	7.50	.50
60	A18	20c on $1 red	40.00	.50
61	A18	30c on $1 red	42.50	1.10
62	A18	40c on $1 red	42.50	1.10
		Nos. 58-62 (5)	134.10	3.70

1896

No.	Type	Description	Unused	Used
63	A19	25c blue green	32.50	.80
a.		Imperf, pair		72.50
b.		Without overprint	29.00	2.00
c.		As "b," imperf, pair	55.00	
64	A20	50c claret	32.50	.80
a.		Imperf, pair		72.50
b.		Without overprint	26.50	2.00
c.		As "b," imperf, pair	52.50	
65	A21	$1 dark blue	80.00	.80
a.		Imperf, pair		72.50
b.		Without overprint	40.00	2.00
c.		As "b," imperf, pair	60.00	
		Nos. 63-65 (3)	145.00	2.40

For surcharges and overprint see #93-95, 116-118, 120.

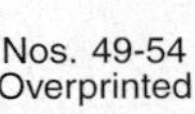

Nos. 49-54 Overprinted

1896 ***Perf. 12 to 15 and Compound***

No.	Type	Description	Unused	Used
66	A9	1c lilac & black	24.00	1.10
a.		"JEBILEE"	1,450.	360.00
b.		"JUBILE"	*3,000.*	
c.		Orange overprint	240.00	24.00
e.		Double overprint	450.00	—
67	A10	2c blue & black	52.50	1.35
a.		Vert. pair, imperf. btwn.	1,100.	
b.		"JEBILEE"	1,725.	
c.		"JUBILE"	*3,500.*	
d.		Vert. strip of 3, imperf between	*8,000.*	
68	A11	3c bister & black	50.00	1.10
a.		"JEBILEE"	2,250.	850.00
b.		"JUBILE"	—	—
g.		Double overprint	925.00	200.00
h.		Triple overprint		*975.00*
69	A12	5c green & black	72.50	1.35
a.		Double overprint	925.00	
70	A13	6c brown red & blk	37.50	1.00
a.		Double overprint	975.00	
b.		"JUBILE"	*3,500.*	
71	A14	8c rose & black	57.50	1.00
a.		Double overprint		
		Nos. 66-71 (6)	294.00	6.90

Cession of Labuan to Great Britain, 50th anniv.

Dyak Chieftain A22

Malayan Sambar A23

Sago Palm A24

Argus Pheasant A25

A26

Dhow — A27

Saltwater Crocodile — A28

Mt. Kinabalu "Postal Revenue" — A29

Coat of Arms — A30

Perf. 13½ to 16 and Compound

1897-1900 **Engr.**

No.	Type	Description	Unused	Used
72	A22	1c lilac & black	5.00	.60
72A	A22	1c red brn & blk	3.75	.80
73	A23	2c blue & black	30.00	.90
a.		Vert. pair, imperf between		925.00
b.		Horiz. pair, imperf between		975.00
74	A23	2c grn & blk ('00)	4.50	.35
a.		Horiz. pair, imperf between	*3,000.*	
75	A24	3c bister & blk	10.00	.60
a.		Vert. pair, imperf between	1,100.	675.00
76	A25	5c green & blk	60.00	.85
77	A25	5c lt bl & blk ('00)	27.50	.80
78	A26	6c brn red & blk	11.00	.60
a.		Vert. pair, imperf between		850.00
79	A27	8c red & black	21.50	
80	A28	12c red & black	40.00	1.20

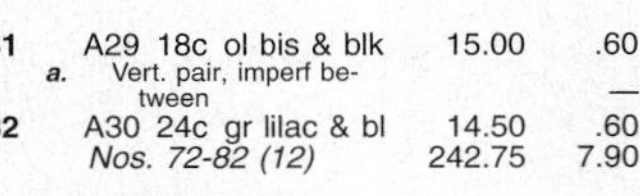

No.	Type	Description	Unused	Used
81	A29	18c ol bis & blk	15.00	.60
a.		Vert. pair, imperf between		—
82	A30	24c gr lilac & bl	14.50	.60
		Nos. 72-82 (12)	242.75	7.90

"Postage & Revenue" — A31

"Postage & Revenue" — A32

Perf. 13½ to 16 and Compound

1897

No.	Type	Description	Unused	Used
83	A31	18c bister & black	95.00	2.40
84a	A32	24c 24c ocher & blue	*37.50*	4.00

"Postage & Revenue" — A33

"Postage & Revenue" — A34

1898

No.	Type	Description	Unused	Used
85	A33	12c red & black	57.50	4.00
86a	A34	18c bister & black	38.50	3.25

No. 85a cto is always perf. 13½x14.

For surcharges see Nos. 90-91, 113-114.

Regular Issue Surcharged in Black

1899

No.	Type	Description	Unused	Used
87	A25	4c on 5c grn & blk	48.00	31.50
88	A26	4c on 6c brn red & blk	27.50	22.50
89	A27	4c on 8c red & blk	72.50	48.00
90	A33	4c on 12c red & blk	55.00	42.50
91	A34	4c on 18c bis & blk	32.50	21.50
a.		Double surcharge	500.00	*600.00*
92a	A32	4c on 24c lil & bl	32.50	*36.00*
93	A19	4c on 25c blue grn	7.25	*8.00*
94	A20	4c on 50c claret	8.00	*8.00*
95	A21	4c on $1 dk blue	8.00	*8.00*
		Nos. 87-95 (9)	282.75	*219.00*

Orangutan A35

Sun Bear A36

Railroad Train — A37

Crown — A38

Perf. 12 to 16 and Compound

1899-1901

No.	Type	Description	Unused	Used
96	A35	4c yel brown & blk	10.00	.75
a.		Vert. pair, imperf. btwn.	1,350.	
97a	A35	4c car & blk ('00)	6.00	.60
98	A36	10c gray vio & dk brn ('01)	60.00	.75
99	A37	16c org brn & grn (G) ('01)	60.00	3.00
		Nos. 96-99 (4)	136.00	5.10

Perf. 12½ to 16 and Compound

1902-03 **Engr.**

No.	Type	Description	Unused	Used
99A	A38	1c vio & black	5.50	.60
100	A38	2c green & blk	5.00	.35
100A	A38	3c sepia & blk	4.00	.35
101	A38	4c car & black	4.00	.35
102	A38	8c org & black	15.00	.60
103	A38	10c sl blue & brn	4.00	.35
a.		Vert. pair, imperf. between		850.00
104	A38	12c yel & black	11.00	.35
a.		Vert. strip of 3, imperf. horiz.		*4,000.*
105	A38	16c org brn & grn	5.75	.35
a.		Vert. pair, imperf. between	—	*2,300.*
106	A38	18c bis brn & blk	4.00	.35
107	A38	25c grnsh bl & grn	9.00	.60
a.		25c greenish blue & black		600.00
108	A38	50c gray lil & vio	12.00	2.25
109	A38	$1 org & red brn	10.00	2.00
		Nos. 99A-109 (12)	89.25	8.50

There are 3 known examples of No. 104a, all cto. A 16c vertical pair, imperf between has been reported. The editors would like to receive evidence of the existence of this item.

Regular Issue of 1896-97 Surcharged in Black

1904

No.	Type	Description	Unused	Used
110	A25	4c on 5c green & blk	55.00	17.00
111	A26	4c on 6c brown red & black	14.50	*17.00*
112	A27	4c on 8c red & blk	30.00	17.00
113	A33	4c on 12c red & blk	27.50	17.00
114	A34	4c on 18c bis & blk	30.00	17.00
115	A32	4c on 24c brn lil & bl	19.25	17.00
116	A19	4c on 25c blue green	10.00	*17.00*
117	A20	4c on 50c claret	10.00	*17.00*
a.		Double surcharge	400.00	
118	A21	4c on $1 dark blue	10.00	*17.00*
		Nos. 110-118 (9)	206.25	153.00

Stamps of North Borneo, 1893, and Labuan No. 65a Overprinted in Black:

a

b

c

1905

No.	Type	Denom.	Description	Unused	Used
119	A30(a)	25c	slate blue	1,325.	1,100.
120	A21(c)	$1	blue		1,050.
121	A33(b)	$2	gray green	*4,000.*	
122	A34(c)	$5	red violet	*7,250.*	*1,700.*
a.			$5 dull purple		—
123	A35(c)	$10	brown	*32,500.*	*11,500.*

POSTAGE DUE STAMPS

Regular Issues Overprinted

1901 Unwmk. *Perf. 14*

No.	Type	Denom.	Description	Unused	Used
J1	A23	2c	green & black	22.50	1.10
a.			Double overprint	425.00	
J2	A24	3c	bister & black	30.00	.90
J3b	A35	4c	car & black	52.50	2.50
a.			Double overprint		875.00
J4	A25	5c	lt blue & black	60.00	1.35
J5	A26	6c	brown red & blk	50.00	1.10
J6	A27	8c	red & black	92.50	2.25
a.			Center inverted, ovpt. reading down		*12,000.*
J7	A33	12c	red & black	140.00	5.50
a.			Overprint reading down		*1,000.*
J8	A34	18c	ol bister & blk	32.50	1.60
J9	A32	24c	brown lil & bl	70.00	6.75
			Nos. J1-J9 (9)	545.00	21.15

See note after No. 41.

The stamps of Labuan were superseded by those of Straits Settlements in 1906.

LAGOS

'lā-ˌgäs

LOCATION — West Africa, bordering on the former Southern Nigeria Colony
GOVT. — British Crown Colony and Protectorate
AREA — 3,460 sq. mi. (approx.)
POP. — 1,500,000 (1901)
CAPITAL — Lagos

This territory was purchased by the British in 1861 and placed under the Governor of Sierra Leone. In 1874 it was detached and formed part of the Gold Coast Colony until 1886 when the Protectorate of Lagos was established. In 1899 Lagos and the territories of the Royal Niger Company were surrendered to the Crown of Great Britain and formed into the Northern and Southern Nigeria Protectorates. In 1906 Lagos and Southern Nigeria were united to form the Colony and Protectorate of Southern Nigeria.

12 Pence = 1 Shilling

Queen Victoria — A1

1874-75 Typo. Wmk. 1 *Perf. 12½*

No.	Type	Denom.	Description	Unused	Used
1	A1	1p	lilac	70.00	40.00
2	A1	2p	blue	72.50	35.00
3	A1	3p	red brown ('75)	100.00	47.50
4	A1	4p	rose	110.00	45.00
5	A1	6p	blue green	120.00	17.50
6	A1	1sh	orange ('75)	350.00	70.00
a.			Value 15½mm instead of 16½mm long	550.00	160.00
			Nos. 1-6 (6)	822.50	255.00

1876 *Perf. 14*

No.	Type	Denom.	Description	Unused	Used
7	A1	1p	lilac	45.00	21.00
8	A1	2p	blue	65.00	15.00
9	A1	3p	red brown	115.00	21.00
10	A1	4p	rose	210.00	12.50
11	A1	6p	green	125.00	7.00
12	A1	1sh	orange	800.00	95.00
			Nos. 7-12 (6)	1,360.	171.50

The 4p exists with watermark sideways.

1882-1902 Wmk. 2

No.	Type	Denom.	Description	Unused	Used
13	A1	½p	green ('86)	2.25	.95
14	A1	1p	lilac	24.00	18.50
15	A1	1p	car rose	2.25	.95
16	A1	2p	blue	180.00	6.50
17	A1	2p	gray	85.00	8.00
18	A1	2p	lil & bl ('87)	5.50	3.25
19	A1	2½p	ultra ('91)	5.75	2.00
a.			2½p blue	90.00	57.50
20	A1	3p	orange brn	21.00	6.00
21	A1	3p	lilac & brn orange ('91)	3.00	*3.75*
22	A1	4p	rose	180.00	14.00
23	A1	4p	violet	140.00	9.50
24	A1	4p	lil & blk ('87)	2.50	2.00
25	A1	5p	lil & grn ('94)	3.00	*12.50*
26	A1	6p	olive green	9.00	*47.50*
27	A1	6p	lilac & red violet ('87)	5.50	3.50
28	A1	6p	lilac & car rose ('02)	5.75	*13.50*
29	A1	7½p	lilac & car rose ('94)	2.50	*35.00*
30	A1	10p	lil & yel ('94)	3.75	*15.00*
31	A1	1sh	orange ('85)	11.00	*22.50*
32	A1	1sh	yellow green & blk ('87)	6.50	*27.50*
33	A1	2sh6p	ol brn ('86)	375.00	325.00
34	A1	2sh6p	green & car rose ('87)	27.50	*92.50*
35	A1	5sh	blue ('86)	650.00	500.00
36	A1	5sh	green & ultra ('87)	47.50	*175.00*
37	A1	10sh	brn vio ('86)	1,700.	1,150.
38	A1	10sh	grn & brn ('87)	95.00	*225.00*

Excellent forgeries exist of Nos. 33, 35 and 37 on paper with genuine watermark.

No. 24 Surcharged in Black

1893

No.	Type	Denom.	Description	Unused	Used
39	A1	½p	on 4p lilac & blk	6.00	3.00
a.			Double surcharge	62.50	62.50
b.			Triple surcharge	140.00	
c.			½p on 2p lilac & blue (#18)	—	25,000.

Four settings of surcharge.

Only one used example is known of No. 39c. The two unused examples are in museums.

King Edward VII — A3

1904, Jan. 22

No.	Type	Denom.	Description	Unused	Used
40	A3	½p	grn & bl grn	1.75	*6.25*
41	A3	1p	vio & blk, *red*	1.10	.20
42	A3	2p	violet & ultra	6.75	7.00
43	A3	2½p	vio & ultra, *bl*	1.25	*1.75*
44	A3	3p	vio & org brn	3.25	2.00
45	A3	6p	vio & red vio	40.00	11.50
46	A3	1sh	green & blk	40.00	*47.50*
47	A3	2sh6p	grn & car rose	130.00	*275.00*
48	A3	5sh	grn & ultra	150.00	*325.00*
49	A3	10sh	green & brn	325.00	*850.00*
			Nos. 40-49 (10)	699.10	*1,526.*

1904-05 Wmk. 3

Ordinary Paper

No.	Type	Denom.	Description	Unused	Used
50	A3	½p	grn & bl grn	8.50	3.00
51	A3	1p	vio & blk, *red*	8.00	.20
52	A3	2p	violet & ultra	2.50	2.25
53	A3	2½p	vio & ultra, *bl*, smaller letters of value	62.50	*140.00*
54	A3	3p	vio & org brn	4.00	1.50
55	A3	6p	vio & red vio	7.50	3.75
56	A3	1sh	green & blk	15.00	21.00
57	A3	2sh6p	grn & car rose	20.00	*72.50*
58	A3	5sh	grn & ultra	25.00	*110.00*
59	A3	10sh	green & brn	80.00	*225.00*
			Nos. 50-59 (10)	233.00	*579.20*

The 2½p is on chalky paper, the other values are on both ordinary and chalky. See *Scott Classic Specialized Catalogue* for detailed listings.

The stamps of Lagos were superseded by those of Southern Nigeria.

LAOS

'laus

LOCATION — In northwestern Indo-China
GOVT. — Republic
AREA — 91,400 sq. mi.
POP. — 5,407,453 (1999 est.)
CAPITAL — Vientiane

Before 1949, Laos was part of the French colony of Indo-China and used its stamps until 1951. The kingdom was replaced by the Lao Peoples Democratic Republic Dec. 2, 1975.

100 Cents = 1 Piaster
100 Cents = 1 Kip (1955)

Imperforates

Most Laos stamps exist imperforate in issued and trial colors, and also in small presentation sheets in issued colors.

Catalogue values for all unused stamps in this country are for Never Hinged items.

Boat on Mekong River — A1

King Sisavang-Vong A2

Laotian Woman A3

Designs: 50c, 60c, 70c, Luang Prabang. 1pi, 2pi, 3pi, 5pi, 10pi, Temple at Vientiane.

1951-52 Unwmk. Engr. *Perf. 13*

No.	Type	Denom.	Description	Unused	Used
1	A1	10c	dk grn & emer	.40	.25
2	A1	20c	dk car & car	.40	.25
3	A1	30c	ind & dp ultra	1.75	1.25
4	A3	30c	ind & pur ('52)	1.00	.30
5	A1	50c	dark brown	.50	.50
6	A1	60c	red & red org	.50	.50
7	A1	70c	ultra & bl grn	1.00	.30
8	A3	80c	brt grn & dk bl green ('52)	1.00	.60
9	A1	1pi	dk pur & pur	1.00	.50
10	A3	1.10pi	dark plum & carmine ('52)	1.25	1.25
11	A2	1.50pi	blk brn & vio brown	1.50	1.25
12	A3	1.90pi	indigo & dp blue ('52)	1.50	1.25
13	A1	2pi	dk grn & gray green	20.00	9.00
14	A1	3pi	dk car & red	1.50	1.50
15	A3	3pi	choc & black brown ('52)	1.75	1.25
16	A1	5pi	ind & dp ultra	2.00	1.75
17	A1	10pi	blk brn & vio brown	4.25	2.00
			Nos. 1-17 (17)	41.30	23.70
			Set, hinged	25.00	

A booklet containing 26 souvenir sheets was issued in 1952 on the anniversary of the first issue of Laos stamps. Each sheet contains a single stamp in the center (Nos. 1-17, C2-C4, J1-J6). Value $225.

See No. 223.

UPU Monument and King Sisavang-Vong — A4

1952, Dec. 7

No.	Type	Denom.	Description	Unused	Used
18	A4	80c	ind, blue & pur	.60	.60
19	A4	1pi	dk car, car & org brown	.60	.60
20	A4	1.20pi	dk pur, purple & ultra	.65	.65
21	A4	1.50pi	dk grn, bl grn & dk brn	1.00	1.00
22	A4	1.90pi	blk brn, vio brn & dk Prus grn	1.25	1.25
			Nos. 18-22,C5-C6 (7)	13.85	13.85

Laos' admission to the UPU, May 13, 1952.

Court of Love — A5

1953, July 14

No.	Type	Denom.	Description	Unused	Used
23	A5	4.50pi	indigo & bl grn	.85	.55
24	A5	6pi	gray & dark brn	1.25	.55

Composite of Laotian Temples — A6

1954, Mar. 4

No.	Type	Denom.	Description	Unused	Used
25	A6	2pi	indigo & purple	35.00	22.50
26	A6	3pi	blk brn & dk red	35.00	22.50
			Nos. 25-26,C13 (3)	255.00	230.00

Accession of King Sisavang-Vong, 50th anniv.

Buddha Statue and Monks — A7

1956, May 24 Engr. *Perf. 13*

27	A7	2k reddish brown	3.00	2.00
28	A7	3k black	3.50	2.50
29	A7	5k chocolate	5.50	3.50
		Nos. 27-29,C20-C21 (5)	72.00	59.00

2500th anniversary of birth of Buddha.

UN Emblem — A8

1956, Dec. 14 *Perf. 13½x13*

30	A8	1k black	.65	.45
31	A8	2k blue	.90	.70
32	A8	4k bright red	1.25	.95
33	A8	6k purple	1.40	1.10
		Nos. 30-33,C22-C23 (6)	15.20	14.20

Admission of Laos to the UN, 1st anniv.

Khouy Player — A9

Khene Player — A10

Musical Instrument: 8k, Ranat.

1957, Mar. 25 Unwmk. *Perf. 13*

34	A9	2k multicolored	1.75	1.10
35	A10	4k multicolored	2.00	1.25
36	A9	8k org, bl & red brn	2.50	2.00
		Nos. 34-36,C24-C26 (6)	15.50	11.35

See No. 224.

Harvesting Rice — A11

Drying Rice — A12

1957, July 22 Engr. *Perf. 13*

37	A11	3k shown	.90	.60
38	A12	5k shown	1.25	.75
39	A12	16k Winnowing rice	2.00	1.50
40	A11	26k Polishing rice	4.00	2.00
		Nos. 37-40 (4)	8.15	4.85

Elephants — A13

Various Elephants: 30c, 5k, 10k, 13k, vert.

1958, Mar. 17

41	A13	10c multi	1.00	.50
42	A13	20c multi	1.00	.50
43	A13	30c multi	1.00	.50
44	A13	2k multi	1.50	.90
45	A13	5k multi	2.75	1.50
46	A13	10k multi	3.00	2.00
47	A13	13k multi	5.00	2.50
		Nos. 41-47 (7)	15.25	8.40

For surcharge see No. B5.

Globe and Goddess — A14

UNESCO Building and Mother with Children — A15

Designs: 70c, UNESCO building, globe and mother with children. 1k, UNESCO building and Eiffel tower.

1958, Nov. 3 Engr. *Perf. 13*

48	A14	50c multicolored	.45	.20
49	A15	60c emer, vio & maroon	.45	.20
50	A15	70c ultra, rose red & brn	.45	.20
51	A14	1k ol bis, cl & grnsh bl	1.00	.60
		Nos. 48-51 (4)	2.35	1.20

UNESCO Headquarters in Paris opening, Nov. 3.

King Sisavang-Vong — A16

1959, Sept. 16 Unwmk.

52	A16	4k rose claret	.35	.35
53	A16	6.50k orange red	.35	.35
54	A16	9k bright pink	.35	.35
55	A16	13k green	.75	.60
		Nos. 52-55 (4)	1.80	1.65

For surcharges see Nos. 112-113, B4.

Dancers A17

Student and Torch of Learning — A18

Portal of Wat Phou, Pakse — A19

Education and Fine Arts: 3k, Globe, key of knowledge and girl student. 5k, Dancers and temple.

1959, Oct. 1 Engr. *Perf. 13*

56	A17	1k vio blk, ol & bl	.40	.20
57	A18	2k maroon & black	.40	.20
58	A17	3k slate grn & vio	.60	.30
59	A18	5k rose vio, yel & brt grn	1.10	.60
		Nos. 56-59 (4)	2.50	1.30

1959, Nov. 2 Unwmk. *Perf. 13*

Historic Monuments: 1.50k, That Inghang, Savannakhet, horiz. 2.50k, Phou Temple, Pakse, horiz. 7k, That Luang, Vientiane. 11k, That Luang, Vientiane, horiz. 12.50k, Phousi, Luang Prabang.

60	A19	50c sepia, grn & org	.20	.20
61	A19	1.50k multi	.35	.20
62	A19	2.50k pur, vio bl & ol	.50	.40
63	A19	7k vio, olive & claret	.75	.50
64	A19	11k brn, car & grn	.90	.75
65	A19	12.50k bl, vio & bister	1.25	.80
		Nos. 60-65 (6)	3.95	2.85

Funeral Urn and Monks — A20

King Sisavang-Vong A21

Designs: 6.50k, Urn under canopy. 9k, Catafalque on 7-headed dragon carriage.

1961, Apr. 29 Engr. *Perf. 13*

66	A20	4k black, bis & org	.70	.50
67	A20	6.50k black & bister	.70	.50
68	A20	9k black & bister	.70	.50
69	A21	25k black	3.00	2.00
		Nos. 66-69 (4)	5.10	3.50

King Sisavang-Vong's (1885-1959) funeral, Apr. 23-29, 1961.

King Savang Vatthana — A22

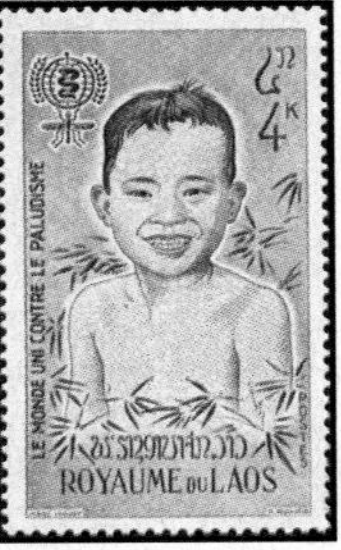

Boy and Malaria Eradication Emblem — A23

1962, Apr. 16 *Perf. 13*

Portrait in Brown and Carmine

70	A22	1k ultramarine	.25	.20
71	A22	2k lilac rose	.25	.20
72	A22	5k greenish blue	.35	.30
73	A22	10k olive	.90	.40
		Nos. 70-73 (4)	1.75	1.10

1962, July 19 Engr.

9k, Girl. 10k, Malaria eradication emblem.

74	A23	4k bluish grn, blk & buff	.30	.20
75	A23	9k lt bl, blk & lt brn	.70	.40
76	A23	10k ol, bis & rose red	1.25	.45
		Nos. 74-76 (3)	2.25	1.05

WHO drive to eradicate malaria. A souvenir sheet exists. Value, $200.

A24

A25

Designs: 50c, Modern mail service (truck, train, plane). 70c, Globe, stamps, dancer. 1k, Ancient mail service (messenger on elephant). 1.50k, Royal Messenger

1962, Nov. 15 Unwmk. *Perf. 13*

77	A24	50c multicolored	.60	.60
78	A24	70c multicolored	.60	.60
79	A25	1k dp claret, grn & blk	1.25	1.25
80	A25	1.50k multicolored	1.00	1.00
		Nos. 77-80 (4)	3.45	3.45

Souvenir sheets exist. One contains the 50c and 70c; the other, the 1k and 1.50k. The sheets exist both perf and imperf in a souvenir booklet of four sheets. Value intact booklet, $200.

Fishermen with Nets — A26

Threshing Rice — A27

Designs: 5k, Plowing and planting in rice paddy. 9k, Woman with infant harvesting rice.

1963, Mar. 21 *Perf. 13*

81	A26	1k grn, bister & pur	.35	.30
82	A27	4k bister, bl & grn	.45	.35
83	A26	5k grn, bis & indigo	.65	.45
84	A27	9k grn, vio bl & ocher	1.00	.50
a.		Min. sheet of 4, #81-84, imperf.	5.00	5.00
		Nos. 81-84 (4)	2.45	1.60

FAO "Freedom from Hunger" campaign.

Queen Khamphouy Handing out Gifts — A28

1963, Oct. 10 **Engr.**

85	A28	4k brn, dp car & blue	.40	.40
86	A28	6k grn, red, yel & bl	.55	.50
87	A28	10k bl, dp car & dk brn	.65	.65
a.		Miniature sheet of 3, #85-87	4.00	4.00
		Nos. 85-87 (3)	1.60	1.55

Centenary of the International Red Cross.

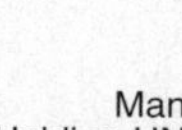

Man Holding UN Emblem A29

1963, Dec. 10 **Unwmk.** *Perf. 13*

88	A29	4k dk bl, dp org & vio brn	1.50	.80

15th anniv. of the Universal Declaration of Human Rights.

No. 88 exists imperf. Value, $15.

Temple of That Luang, Map of Nubia and Ramses II — A30

1964, Mar. 8 **Engr.**

89	A30	4k multicolored	.40	.40
90	A30	6k multicolored	.60	.60
91	A30	10k multicolored	.75	.75
a.		Miniature sheet of 3, #89-91	3.00	3.00
		Nos. 89-91 (3)	1.75	1.75

UNESCO world campaign to save historic monuments in Nubia. No. 91a sold for 25k.

Ceremonial Chalice A31

Designs: 15k, Buddha. 20k, Soldier leading people through Mekong River Valley. 40k, Royal Palace, Luang Prabang.

1964, July 30 **Unwmk.** *Perf. 13*

92	A31	10k multicolored	.40	.30
93	A31	15k multicolored	.60	.40
94	A31	20k multicolored	.80	.60
95	A31	40k multicolored	1.25	.75
a.		Miniature sheet of 4, #92-95	3.50	3.50
		Nos. 92-95 (4)	3.05	2.05

"Neutral and Constitutional Laos." When the stamps are arranged in a block of four with 40k and 15k in first row and 10k and 20k in second row, the map of Laos appears.

Prince Vet and Wife Mathie — A32

Lao Women — A33

Scenes from Buddhist Legend of Phra Vet Sandone: 32k, God of the Skies sending his son to earth. 45k, Phaune's daughter with beggar husband. 55k, Beggar cornered by guard and dogs.

1964, Nov. 17 **Photo.** *Perf. 13x12½*

96	A32	10k multicolored	.50	.50
97	A32	32k multicolored	.75	.75
98	A32	45k multicolored	1.00	1.00
99	A32	55k multicolored	1.25	1.25
a.		Miniature sheet of 4	5.00	3.75
		Nos. 96-99 (4)	3.50	3.50

#99a contains 4 imperf. stamps similar to #96-99.

1964, Dec. 15 **Engr.** *Perf. 13*

100	A33	25k blk, org brn & pale ol	.75	.75
		Nos. 100,C43-C45 (4)	3.45	2.35

Butterflies A34

1965, Mar. 13 **Unwmk.** *Perf. 13*

Size: 36x36mm

101	A34	10k Cethosia biblis	2.25	1.25
102	A34	25k Precis cebrene	4.50	1.75

Size: 48x27mm

103	A34	40k Dysphania militaris	11.50	2.50
		Nos. 101-103,C46 (4)	24.25	8.00

Teacher and School, American Aid — A35

Designs: 25k, Woman at Wattay Airport, French aid, horiz. 45k, Woman bathing child and food basket, Japanese aid. 55k, Musicians broadcasting, British aid, horiz.

1965, Mar. 30 **Engr.** *Perf. 13*

104	A35	25k bl grn, brn & car rose	.45	.30
105	A35	45k ol grn & brn	.95	.50
106	A35	55k brt bl & bister	1.25	.65
107	A35	75k multicolored	1.75	.80
		Nos. 104-107 (4)	4.40	2.25

Issued to publicize foreign aid to Laos.

Hophabang Temple A36

1965, Apr. 23 **Unwmk.** *Perf. 13*

108	A36	10k multicolored	.65	.25

Telewriter, Map of Laos and Globe A37

30k, Communication by satellite & map of Laos. 50k, Globe, map of Laos & radio.

1965, June 15 **Engr.** *Perf. 13*

109	A37	5k vio bl, brn & red lil	.20	.20
110	A37	30k bl, org brn & sl grn	.65	.50
111	A37	50k crim, lt bl & bis	1.25	.90
a.		Miniature sheet of 3, #109-111	4.25	4.25
		Nos. 109-111 (3)	2.10	1.60

ITU, centenary.

Nos. 52-53 Surcharged in Dark Blue with New Value and Bars

1965, July 5 **Unwmk.** *Perf. 13*

112	A16	1k on 4k rose claret	.50	.30
113	A16	5k on 6.50k org red	.55	.35

Mother and Child, UNICEF and WHO Emblems — A38

Map of Laos and UN Emblem — A39

1965, Sept. 1 **Engr.** *Perf. 13*

114	A38	35k lt ultra & dk red	.85	.70
a.		Miniature sheet	4.50	4.50

Mother and Child Protection movement, 6th anniv.

1965, Nov. 3 *Perf. 12½x13*

115	A39	5k emer, gray & vio bl	.30	.25
116	A39	25k lil rose, gray & vio bl	.45	.35
117	A39	40k bl, gray & vio bl	.70	.50
		Nos. 115-117 (3)	1.45	1.10

UN, 20th anniv. Although first day covers were canceled "Oct. 24," the actual day of issue is reported to have been Nov. 3.

Tikhy (Hockey) A40

Pastimes: 10k, Two bulls fighting. 25k, Canoe race. 50k, Rocket festival.

1965, Dec. 23 **Engr.** *Perf. 13*

118	A40	10k org, brn & gray	.30	.25
119	A40	20k grn, ver & dk bl	.40	.30
120	A40	25k brt blue & multi	.40	.35
121	A40	50k orange & multi	.80	.50
		Nos. 118-121 (4)	1.90	1.40

Slaty-headed Parakeet — A41

Birds: 15k, White-crested laughing thrush. 20k, Osprey. 45k, Bengal roller.

1966, Feb. 10 **Engr.** *Perf. 13*

122	A41	5k car rose, ol & brn	.85	.50
123	A41	15k bluish grn, brn & blk	1.10	.60
124	A41	20k dl bl, sep & bister	1.60	1.00
125	A41	45k vio, Prus bl & sepia	4.50	2.40
		Nos. 122-125 (4)	8.05	4.50

WHO Headquarters, Geneva — A42

1966, May 3 **Engr.** *Perf. 13*

126	A42	10k bl grn & indigo	.25	.20
127	A42	25k car & dk green	.40	.30
128	A42	50k ultra & black	.75	.70
a.		Miniature sheet of 3, #126-128	17.50	17.50
		Nos. 126-128 (3)	1.40	1.20

Inauguration of the WHO Headquarters, Geneva. No. 128a sold for 150k.

Ordination of Buddhist Monk — A43

Folklore: 25k, Women building ceremonial sand hills. 30k, Procession of the Wax Pagoda, vert. 40k, Wrist-tying ceremony (3 men, 3 women), vert.

1966, May 20 ***Perf. 13***

129 A43 10k multicolored .30 .25
130 A43 25k multicolored .45 .30
131 A43 30k multicolored .75 .50
132 A43 40k multicolored 1.00 .70
Nos. 129-132 (4) 2.50 1.75

UNESCO Emblem A44

1966, July 7 **Engr.** ***Perf. 13***

133 A44 20k ocher & gray .20 .20
134 A44 30k brt blue & gray .40 .30
135 A44 40k brt green & gray .55 .30
136 A44 60k crimson & gray .75 .35
a. Miniature sheet, #133-136 6.00 6.00
Nos. 133-136 (4) 1.90 1.15

UNESCO, 20th anniv. No. 136a sold for 250k.

Addressed Envelope Carrier Pigeon, Globe and Hand with Quill Pen — A45

1966, Sept. 7 **Engr.** ***Perf. 13***

137 A45 5k red, brn & bl .25 .20
138 A45 20k bl grn, blk & lil .45 .30
139 A45 40k bl, red brn & dk ol bister .55 .35
140 A45 45k brt rose lil, bl grn & black .75 .50
a. Min. sheet of 4, #137-140 6.00 6.00
Nos. 137-140 (4) 2.00 1.35

Intl. Letter Writing Week, Oct. 6-12. No. 140a sold for 250k.

Sculpture from Siprapouthbat Temple — A46

Sculptures: 20k, from Visoun Temple. 50k, from Xiengthong Temple. 70k, from Visoun Temple.

1967, Feb. 21 **Engr.** ***Perf. 12½x13***

141 A46 5k olive grn & grn .30 .25
142 A46 20k brn ol & gray bl .70 .40
143 A46 50k dk brn & dp claret 1.25 .50
144 A46 70k dk brn & dk magenta 1.50 .80
Nos. 141-144 (4) 3.75 1.95

General Post Office A47

1967, Apr. 6 **Engr.** ***Perf. 13***

145 A47 25k brn, grn & vio brn .35 .25
146 A47 50k ind, brt blue & grn .55 .40
147 A47 70k dk red, grn & brn 1.25 .75
Nos. 145-147 (3) 2.15 1.40

Inauguration of the new Post and Telegraph Headquarters.

Snakehead A48

Fish: 35k, Giant catfish. 45k, Spiny eel. 60k, Knifefish.

1967, June 8 **Engr.** ***Perf. 13x12½***

148 A48 20k dl bl, bis & blk 1.25 .50
149 A48 35k aqua, bis & gray 1.50 .60
150 A48 45k pale grn, bis & ol brn 2.50 .70
151 A48 60k sl grn, bis & blk 3.75 .80
Nos. 148-151 (4) 9.00 2.60

Drumstick Tree Flower — A49

Blossoms: 55k, Turmeric. 75k, Peacock flower. 80k, Pagoda tree.

1967, Aug. 10 **Engr.** ***Perf. 12½x13***

152 A49 30k red lil, yel & grn .60 .35
153 A49 55k org, mag & lt grn .90 .45
154 A49 75k bl, red & lt grn 1.25 .65
155 A49 80k brt grn, mag & yel 1.50 .75
Nos. 152-155 (4) 4.25 2.20

Banded Krait — A50

Reptiles: 40k, Marsh crocodile. 100k, Malayan moccasin. 200k, Water monitor.

1967, Dec. 7 **Engr.** ***Perf. 13***

156 A50 5k emer, ind & yel .60 .40
157 A50 40k sep, lt grn & yel 1.60 .80
158 A50 100k lt grn, brn & ocher 3.50 1.75
159 A50 200k grn, blk & bister 6.25 3.25
Nos. 156-159 (4) 11.95 6.20

Human Rights Flame — A51

1968, Feb. 8 **Engr.** ***Perf. 13***

160 A51 20k brt grn, red & grn .30 .25
161 A51 30k brn, red & grn .40 .30
162 A51 50k brt bl, red & grn .80 .60
a. Souv. sheet of 3, #160-162 5.00 5.00
Nos. 160-162 (3) 1.50 1.15

Intl. Human Rights Year. #162a sold for 250k.

WHO Emblem — A52

1968, July 5 **Engr.** ***Perf. 12½x13***

163 A52 15k rose vio, ver & ocher .25 .20
164 A52 30k brt bl, brt grn & ocher .25 .20
165 A52 70k ver, plum & ocher .55 .40
166 A52 110k brn, brt rose lil & ocher .90 .55
167 A52 250k brt grn, brt bl & ocher 2.40 1.50
a. Souv. sheet of 5, #163-167 6.50 6.50
Nos. 163-167 (5) 4.35 2.85

WHO, 20th anniv. No. 167a sold for 500k.

Parade and Memorial Arch — A53

Designs: 20k, Armored Corps with tanks. 60k, Three soldiers with Laotian flag.

1968, July 15 ***Perf. 13***

168 A53 15k multicolored .35 .25
169 A53 20k multicolored .45 .35
170 A53 60k multicolored .90 .45
Nos. 168-170,C52-C53 (5) 5.80 3.15

Laotian Army. For souvenir sheet see No. C53a.

Chrysochroa Mnizechi — A54

Mangoes — A55

Insects: 50k, Aristobia approximator. 90k, Eutaenia corbetti.

1968, Aug. 28 **Engr.** ***Perf. 13***

171 A54 30k vio bl, grn & yel .90 .35
172 A54 50k lil, blk & ocher 1.50 .50
173 A54 90k bis, blk & org 2.25 1.25
Nos. 171-173,C54-C55 (5) 8.40 4.20

1968, Oct. 3 **Engr.** ***Perf. 13***

Fruits: 50k, Tamarind. 180k, Jackfruit, horiz. 250k, Watermelon, horiz.

174 A55 20k ind, lt bl & emer .40 .25
175 A55 50k lt bl, emer & brn .70 .40
176 A55 180k sep, org & yel grn 2.00 1.10
177 A55 250k sep, bis & emer 2.75 1.60
Nos. 174-177 (4) 5.85 3.35

Hurdling — A56

1968, Nov. 15 **Engr.** ***Perf. 13***

178 A56 15k shown .50 .50
179 A56 80k Tennis 1.00 .50
180 A56 100k Soccer 1.00 .50
181 A56 110k High jump 1.50 1.00
Nos. 178-181 (4) 4.00 2.50

19th Olympic Games, Mexico City, 10/12-27.

Wedding of Kathanam and Nang Sida A57

Design: 200k, Thao Khathanam battling the serpent Ngou Xouang and the giant bird Phanga Houng. Design from panels of the central gate of Ongtu Temple, Vientiane. Design of 150k is from east gate.

1969, Feb. 28 **Photo.** ***Perf. 12x13***

182 A57 150k blk, gold & red 2.00 1.25
183 A57 200k blk, gold & red 2.75 1.75

Soukhib Ordered to Attack — A58

Scenes from Royal Ballet: 15k, Pharak pleading for Nang Sita. 20k, Thotsakan reviewing his troops. 30k, Nang Sita awaiting punishment. 40k, Pharam inspecting troops. 60k, Hanuman preparing to rescue Nang Sita.

1969 **Photo.** ***Perf. 14***

184 A58 10k multicolored .40 .25
185 A58 15k blue & multi .55 .40
186 A58 20k lt bl & multi .65 .50
187 A58 30k salmon & multi 1.00 .55
188 A58 40k salmon & multi 1.40 .70
189 A58 60k pink & multi 2.00 1.10
Nos. 184-189,C56-C57 (8) 14.25 8.50

For surcharges see #B12-B17, CB1-CB2.

ILO Emblem and Basket Weavers at Vientiane Vocational Center A59

1969, May 7 **Engr.** ***Perf. 13***

190 A59 30k claret & violet .45 .40
191 A59 60k slate grn & vio brn 1.00 .75
Nos. 190-191,C58 (3) 6.20 4.40

ILO, 50th anniv.

Chinese Pangolin — A60

1969, Nov. 6 **Photo.** ***Perf. 13x12***

192 A60 15k multicolored .60 .25
193 A60 30k multicolored 1.00 .50
Nos. 192-193,C59-C61 (5) 7.45 3.85

That Luang, Luang Prabang A61

King Sisavang-Vong — A62

1969, Nov. 19 Engr. *Perf. 13*

194	A61 50k dk brn, bl & bister	.80	.60
195	A62 70k maroon & buff	1.40	1.00
a.	Pair, #194-195 + label	3.00	3.00

Death of King Sisavang-Vong, 10th anniv.

Carved Capital from Wat Xiengthong A63

1970, Jan. 10 Photo. *Perf. 12x13*

196	A63 70k multicolored	1.75	1.25
	Nos. 196,C65-C66 (3)	5.15	2.90

Kongphene (Midday) Drum — A64

Designs: 55k, Kongthong (bronze) drum.

1970, Mar. 30 Engr. *Perf. 13*

197	A64 30k bl gray, ol & org	1.00	.60
198	A64 55k ocher, blk & yel grn	1.75	1.35
	Nos. 197-198,C67 (3)	5.75	3.45

Lenin Explaining Electrification Plan, by L. Shmatko — A65

1970, Apr. 22 Litho. *Perf. 12½x12*

199	A65 30k blue & multi	1.10	.55
200	A65 70k rose red & multi	1.40	.75

Lenin (1870-1924), Russian communist leader.

Silk Weaver and EXPO Emblem A66

1970, July 7 Engr. *Perf. 13*

201	A66 30k shown	.50	.30
202	A66 70k Woman winding thread	.90	.80
	Nos. 201-202,C69 (3)	2.80	2.35

Laotian silk industry; EXPO '70 Intl. Exposition, Osaka, Japan, Mar. 15-Sept. 13.

Wild Boar A67

1970, Sept. 7 Engr. *Perf. 13*

203	A67 20k green & dp brn	.45	.25
204	A67 60k dp brn & ol bis	.90	.45
	Nos. 203-204,C70-C71 (4)	7.35	4.45

Buddha, UN Headquarters and Emblem — A68

1970, Oct. 24

Size: 22x36mm

205	A68 30k ultra, brn & rose red	.60	.40
206	A68 70k brt grn, sep & vio	.90	.60
	Nos. 205-206,C75 (3)	3.25	2.10

UN, 25th anniv.

Nakhanet, Symbol of Arts and Culture — A69

1971, Feb. 5

207	A69 70k shown	.90	.60
208	A69 85k Rahu swallowing the moon	1.10	.85
	Nos. 207-208,C76 (3)	4.25	2.45

Silversmithing — A70

1971, Apr. 12 Engr. *Perf. 13*

Size: 36x36mm

209	A70 30k shown	.35	.25
210	A70 50k Pottery	.55	.35

Size: 47x36mm

211	A70 70k Boat building	1.10	.40
	Nos. 209-211 (3)	2.00	1.00

Laotian and African Children, UN Emblem — A71

60k, Women musicians, elephants, UN emblem.

1971, May 1 Engr. *Perf. 13*

212	A71 30k lt grn, brn & blk	.50	.30
213	A71 60k yel, pur & dull red	1.10	.50

Intl. year against racial discrimination.

Miss Rotary, Wat Ho Phrakeo — A72

Dendrobium Aggregatum A73

Design: 30k, Monk on roof of That Luang and Rotary emblem, horiz.

1971, June 28 Engr. *Perf. 13*

214	A72 30k purple & ocher	.60	.40
215	A72 70k gray ol, dk bl & rose	1.25	.55

Rotary International, 50th anniversary.

Perf. 12½x13, 13x12½

1971, July 7 Photo.

Size: 26x36, 36x26mm

216	A73 30k shown	.75	.40
217	A73 50k Asocentrum ampullaceum, horiz.	1.30	.95
218	A73 70k Trichoglottis fasciata, horiz.	2.00	1.25
	Nos. 216-218,C79 (4)	7.55	4.10

See Nos. 230-232, C89.

Palm Civet A74

Animals: 40k, like 25k. 50k, Lesser Malay chevrotain. 85k, Sika deer.

1971, Sept. 16 Engr. *Perf. 13*

219	A74 25k pur, dk bl & blk	.80	.45
220	A74 40k grn, ol bis & blk	1.00	.60
221	A74 50k brt grn & ocher	1.50	.70
222	A74 85k sl grn, grn & brn orange	2.50	1.25
	Nos. 219-222,C83 (5)	10.05	5.75

Types of 1952-57 with Ornamental Panels and Inscriptions

Designs: 30k, Laotian woman. 40k, So player (like #C25). 50k, Rama (like #C19).

1971, Nov. 2

223	A3 30k brn vio & brn	.45	.30
a.	Souvenir sheet of 3	5.00	5.00
224	A10 40k sepia, blk & ver	.55	.50
225	AP7 50k ultra, blk & salmon	1.00	.70
	Nos. 223-225,C84 (4)	3.40	2.90

20th anniv. of Laotian independent postal service. All stamps inscribed: "Vingtième Anniversaire de la Philatélie Lao," "Postes" and "1971." No. 223a contains No. 223 and 60k and 85k in design of 30k, sold for 250k.

Children Learning to Read A75

1972, Jan. 30 Engr. *Perf. 13*

Size: 36x22mm

226	A75 30k shown	.25	.25
227	A75 70k Scribe writing on palm leaves	.50	.50
	Nos. 226-227,C87 (3)	1.75	1.75

Intl. Book Year.

Nam Ngum Hydroelectric Dam, Monument and ECAFE Emblem — A76

1972, Mar. 28 Engr. *Perf. 13*

228	A76 40k grn, ultra & lt brn	.30	.25
229	A76 80k grn, brn ol & dk bl	.50	.40
	Nos. 228-229,C88 (3)	1.60	1.45

25th anniv. of the Economic Commission for Asia and the Far East (ECAFE), which helped build the Nam Ngum Hydroelectric Dam.

Orchid Type of 1971

Orchids: 40k, Rynchostylis giganterum. 60k, Paphiopedilum exul. 80k, Cattleya, horiz.

1972, May 1 Photo. *Perf. 13*

Size: 26x36mm, 36x26mm

230	A73 40k lt bl & multi	.80	.35
231	A73 60k multicolored	1.40	.45
232	A73 80k lt bl & multi	1.75	.50
	Nos. 230-232,C89 (4)	7.95	2.80

Woman Carrying Water, UNICEF Emblem — A77

Children's drawings: 80k, Child learning bamboo-weaving, UNICEF emblem.

1972, July 20 Engr. *Perf. 13*

233	A77 50k blue & multi	.60	.45
234	A77 80k brown & multi	.80	.65
	Nos. 233-234,C90 (3)	2.40	2.10

25th anniv. (in 1971) of UNICEF.

Attopeu Costume, Religious Ceremony — A78

Lion from Wat That Luang and Lions Emblem — A79

Design: 90k, Phongsaly festival costume.

1973, Feb. 16 Engr. *Perf. 13*

235 A78 40k maroon & multi .45 .25
236 A78 90k multicolored 1.00 .50
Nos. 235-236,C101-C102 (4) 3.25 2.55

1973, Mar. 30 Engr. *Perf. 13*

237 A79 40k vio bl, rose cl & lil .50 .25
238 A79 80k pur, org brn & yel .80 .40
Nos. 237-238,C103 (3) 2.55 1.40

Lions International of Laos.

Dr. Hansen, Map of Laos, "Dok Hak" Flowers — A80

1973, June 28 Engr. *Perf. 13*

239 A80 40k multicolored .55 .30
240 A80 80k multicolored 1.00 .45

Centenary of the discovery by Dr. Armauer G. Hansen of the Hansen bacillus, the cause of leprosy.

Wat Vixun, Monk Blessing Girl Scouts — A81

1973, Sept. 1 Engr. *Perf. 13*

241 A81 70k ocher & brown .60 .40
Nos. 241,C106-C107 (3) 2.15 1.10

25th anniv. of Laotian Scout Movement.

INTERPOL Headquarters — A82

1973, Dec. 22 Engr. *Perf. 13x12½*

242 A82 40k greenish bl .25 .25
243 A82 80k brown .65 .60
Nos. 242-243,C110 (3) 2.00 1.45

Intl. Criminal Police Org., 50th anniv.

Boy Mailing Letter — A83

Eranthemum Nervosum — A84

1974, Apr. 30 Engr. *Perf. 13*

244 A83 70k bl, lt grn & ocher .50 .25
245 A83 80k lt grn, bl & ocher .60 .35
Nos. 244-245,C114-C115 (4) 6.10 3.60

UPU, cent.

1974, May 31

Size: 26x36mm, 36x26mm

246 A84 30k grn & vio .55 .40
247 A84 50k Water lilies, horiz. .80 .50
248 A84 80k Scheffler's kapokier, horiz. 1.25 .75
Nos. 246-248,C116 (4) 7.60 4.65

Mekong River Ferry — A85

90k, Samlo (passenger tricycle), vert.

1974, July 31 Engr. *Perf. 13*

249 A85 25k red brn & choc .40 .40
250 A85 90k brown ol & lt ol 1.25 1.25
Nos. 249-250,C117 (3) 4.15 3.15

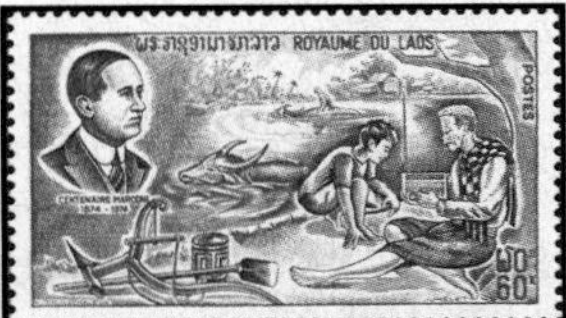

Marconi, Indigenous Transmission Methods, Transistor Radio — A86

1974, Aug. 28 Engr. *Perf. 13*

251 A86 60k multicolored .50 .50
252 A86 90k multicolored .75 .75
Nos. 251-252,C118 (3) 3.50 2.35

Guglielmo Marconi (1874-1937), Italian electrical engineer and inventor.

Diastocera Wallichi Tonkinensis A87

1974, Oct. 23 Engr. *Perf. 13*

253 A87 50k shown .90 .60
254 A87 90k Macrochenus isabellunus 1.40 .85
255 A87 100k Purpuricenus malaccensis 1.75 .90
Nos. 253-255,C119 (4) 5.80 3.35

Temple, Houeisai, and Sapphire A88

1975, Feb. 12 Engr. *Perf. 13x12½*

256 A88 100k bl, brn & grn .80 .50
257 A88 110k Sapphire panning at Attopeu 1.25 .75

King Sisavang-Vong, Princes Souvanna Phouma and Souphanou-Vong — A89

1975, Feb. 21 Engr. *Perf. 13*

258 A89 80k olive & multi .60 .40
259 A89 300k multicolored 1.25 .90
260 A89 420k multicolored 1.40 1.25
Nos. 258-260 (3) 3.25 2.55

1st anniv. of Peace Treaty of Vientiane.

A souvenir sheet exists, embossed on paper with a foil application. Value, $10.

Fortuneteller Working on Forecast for New Year (Size of pair: 100x27mm) — A90

New Year Riding Rabbit, and Tiger (Old Year) — A92

Designs: 40k, Chart of New Year symbols. 200k, Fortune teller. 350k, As shown.

1975, Apr. 14 Engr. *Perf. 13*

261 40k bister & red brn .50 .20
262 200k bis, red brn & sl 1.40 .80
a. A90 Pair, #261-262 2.25 1.75
263 A92 350k blue & multi 2.50 1.60
Nos. 261-263 (3) 4.40 2.60

New Year 1975, Year of the Rabbit.

UN Emblem, "Equality" — A93

200k, IWY emblem, man and woman.

1975, June 19 Engr.

264 A93 100k dl bl & vio bl .40 .40
265 A93 200k multi .85 .85
a. Miniature sheet of 2, #264-265 4.50 4.50

International Women's Year.

UPU, Cent. — A93a

Designs: 15k, Runner, rocket reaching orbit, vert. 30k, Docked Soyuz capsules, chariot, vert. 40k, Biplane, Concorde. 1000k, Apollo spacecraft in orbit. 1500k, Apollo spacecraft, astronaut, vert. No. 266G, Mail truck, Concorde. No. 266H, Wagon train, Lunar Rover. No. 266I, Zeppelin, locomotive.

Perf. 13x14, 14x13

1975, July 7 Litho.

266 A93a 10k multicolored .20 .20
266A A93a 15k multicolored .40 .20
266B A93a 30k multicolored .50 .20
266C A93a 40k multicolored .80 .25
266D A93a 1000k multicolored 2.50 1.00
266E A93a 1500k multicolored 4.00 1.50
Nos. 266-266E (6) 8.40 3.35

Litho. & Embossed

Perf. 13½

266G A93a 3000k gold & multi —

Souvenir Sheets

266H A93a 2500k gold & multi 8.00 2.50
266I A93a 3000k gold & multi 8.00 2.50

Nos. 266D-266E, 266G-266I are airmail.
Nos. 266-266I also exist imperf.

Apollo-Soyuz Mission — A93b

Designs: 125k, Astronauts, Thomas Stafford, Vance D. Brand, Donald Slayton. 150k, Cosmonauts Alexei Leonov, Valery Koubasov. 200k, Apollo-Soyuz link-up. 300k, Handshake in space. 450k, Preparation for re-entry. 700k, Apollo splashdown.

1975, July 7 Litho. *Perf. 14x13*

267 A93b 125k multicolored .40 .20
267A A93b 150k multicolored .60 .20
267B A93b 200k multicolored 1.00 .30
267C A93b 300k multicolored 2.00 .75
267D A93b 450k multicolored 2.75 .60
267E A93b 700k multicolored 3.75 1.50
Nos. 267-267E (6) 10.50 3.55

Nos. 267D-267E are airmail.
Nos. 267-267E also exist imperf.

Scene from Vet Sandone Legend — A94

Designs: Scenes from Buddhist legend of Prince Vet Sandone.

1975, July 22 Photo. *Perf. 13*

268 A94 80k multicolored .65 .30
268A A94 110k multicolored .70 .40
268B A94 120k multicolored .90 .50
268C A94 130k multicolored 1.50 .60
Nos. 268-268C (4) 3.75 1.80

American Revolution, Bicent. — A94a

Presidents: 10k, Washington, J. Adams, Jefferson, Madison. 15k, Monroe, J.Q. Adams,

Jackson, Van Buren. 40k, Harrison, Tyler, Polk, Taylor. 1000k, Truman, Eisenhower, Kennedy. 1500k, L. Johnson, Nixon, Ford.

1975, July 30 Litho. *Perf. 13½*

269 A94a 10k multicolored —
269A A94a 15k multicolored —
269B A94a 40k multicolored —
269C A94a 1000k multicolored —
269D A94a 1500k multicolored —

Nos. 269C-269D are airmail. Stamps of similar design in denominations of 50k, 100k, 125k, 150k, and 200k exist but were not available in Laotian post offices. Value for set of 10, $60.

Buddha, Stupas of Borobudur — A95

Design: 200k, Borobudur sculptures and UNESCO emblem.

1975, Aug. 20 Engr. *Perf. 13*

270 A95 100k indigo & multi .75 .40
271 A95 200k multicolored 1.40 .85
a. Miniature sheet of 2, #270-271 2.50 2.50

UNESCO campaign to save Borobudur Temple, Java.

Coat of Arms of Republic — A96

Thathiang Pagoda, Vientiane — A97

1976, Dec. 2 Litho. *Perf. 14*

272 A96 1k blue & multi .20 .20
273 A96 2k rose & multi .20 .20
274 A96 5k brt grn & multi .25 .20
275 A96 10k lilac & multi .45 .40
276 A96 200k orange & multi 3.00 2.25
a. Min. sheet of 5, #272-276 7.50 7.50
Nos. 272-276 (5) 4.10 3.25

Miniature sheets of 1 exist. Value $50.
For overprints, see Nos. 426A, 426V, 508C, 676H.

1976, Dec. 18 *Perf. 13½*

Designs: 2k, 80k, 100k, Phonsi Pagoda, Luang Prabang. 30k, 300k, like 1k.

277 A97 1k multicolored .20 .20
278 A97 2k multicolored .25 .20
279 A97 30k multicolored .75 .50
280 A97 80k multicolored 1.50 1.00
281 A97 100k multicolored 2.25 1.40
282 A97 300k multicolored 3.75 2.50
Nos. 277-282 (6) 8.70 5.80

Silversmith — A98

Perf. 13x12½, 12½x13

1977, Apr. 1 Litho.

283 A98 1k shown .20 .20
284 A98 2k Weaver .20 .20
285 A98 20k Potter .65 .25
286 A98 50k Basket weaver, vert. 1.25 .40
Nos. 283-286 (4) 2.30 1.05

Miniature sheets of 2 exist, perf. and imperf. Value $7.50, perf or imperf.
For overprints, see Nos. 426B, 426C, 426D, 426R, 676B.

Cosmonauts A.A. Gubarev, G.M. Grechko A99

Government Palace, Vientiane, Kremlin, Moscow — A100

20k, 50k, Lenin speaking on Red Square.

Perf. 12x12½, 12½x12

1977, Oct. 25 Litho.

287 A99 5k multicolored .20 .20
288 A99 20k multicolored .20 .20
289 A99 50k multicolored .50 .25
290 A99 60k multicolored .55 .40
291 A100 100k multicolored 1.00 .65
a. Souv. sheet of 3, #288, 290-291 4.50 4.50
292 A100 250k multicolored 2.25 1.50
a. Souv. sheet of 3, #287, 289, 292 5.00 5.00
Nos. 287-292 (6) 4.70 3.20

60th anniv. of Russian October Revolution.
For overprints, see Nos. 426F, 426N, 676C, 676F, 676I.

Natl. Arms — A101

A102

1978, May 26 Litho. *Perf. 12½*

293 A101 5k dull org & blk .20 .20
294 A101 10k tan & black .20 .20
295 A101 50k brt pink & blk .50 .20
296 A101 100k yel grn & blk 1.00 .45
297 A101 250k violet & blk 2.00 .85
Nos. 293-297 (5) 3.90 1.90

For overprints, see Nos. 426G, 676J.

Perf. 12½x12¼, 12½x12¾

1978, Sept. 15 Litho.

Army Day: 20k, Soldiers with flag. 40k, Fighters and burning house, horiz. 300k, Anti-aircraft battery.

298 A102 20k multicolored .20 .20
299 A102 40k multicolored .25 .20
300 A102 300k multicolored 1.75 1.00
Nos. 298-300 (3) 2.20 1.40

For overprints see No. 426O, 426Q, 676A, 676L.

Marchers with Banner A103

1978, Dec. 2 Litho. *Perf. 11½*

301 A103 20k shown .30 .20
302 A103 50k Women with flag .30 .20
303 A103 400k Dancer 2.25 1.40
a. Sheet of 3, #301-303, imperf. 4.25
Nos. 301-303 (3) 2.85 1.80

National Day. A second printing in slightly different colors and with rough perforation exists; values the same. Stamps in souvenir sheet are in reverse order.

Electronic Tree, Map of Laos, ITU Emblem — A104

Design: 250k, Electronic tree, map of Laos and broadcast tower.

1979, Jan. 18 Litho. *Perf. 12½*

304 A104 30k multicolored .20 .20
305 A104 250k multicolored 1.50 .75

World Telecommunications Day, 1978.
For overprints, see Nos. 426P, 426W, 676K.

Woman Mailing Letter A105

10k, 80k, Processing mail. 100k, like 5k.

1979, Jan. 18

306 A105 5k multicolored .20 .20
307 A105 10k multicolored .20 .20
308 A105 80k multicolored .75 .30
309 A105 100k multicolored 1.00 .40
Nos. 306-309 (4) 2.15 1.10

Asian-Oceanic Postal Union, 15th anniv.
For overprints, see Nos. 426H, 426J, 426K, 426T, 426U, 676E, 676G.

Intl. Year of the Child A106

1979 Litho. *Perf. 11*
Without Gum

310 A106 20k Playing with ball, vert. .25 .20
311 A106 50k Studying .40 .20
312 A106 100k Playing musical instruments .50 .35
313 A106 200k Breast-feeding, vert. 2.00 .65
314 A106 200k Map, globe, vert. 1.00 .65
315 A106 500k Immunization, vert. 5.25 1.50
316 A106 600k Girl dancing, vert. 3.00 1.50
Nos. 310-316 (7) 12.40 5.05

Issued: #310-311, 313, 315, 8/1; others, 12/25.
Imperf sheets of 4 containing #310-311, 313, 315 and of 3 containing #312, 314, 316 exist. Value for both sheets $25.

Traditional Modes of Transportation — A107

1979, Oct. 9 *Perf. 12½x13*

317 A107 5k Elephants, buffalo, pirogues .20 .20
318 A107 10k Buffalo, carts .20 *.35*
319 A107 70k like 10k .60 *1.50*
320 A107 500k like 5k 2.50 2.00
Nos. 317-320 (4) 3.50 *4.05*

For overprints, see Nos. 426I, 426L, 426S, 676D.

5th Anniv. of the Republic — A108

1980, May 30 *Perf. 11*

321 A108 30c Agriculture, vert. .20 .20
322 A108 50c Education, health services .20 .20
323 A108 1k Three women, vert. .60 .40
324 A108 2k Hydroelectric energy 1.25 1.10
Nos. 321-324 (4) 2.25 1.90

Imperf. souvenir sheet of 4 exists. Value $10.

Lenin, 110th Birth Anniv. A109

1980, July 5 *Perf. 12x12½, 12½x12*

325 A109 1k Lenin reading .25 .20
326 A109 2k Writing .45 .25
327 A109 3k Lenin, red flag, vert. .65 .40
328 A109 4k Orating, vert. 1.10 .55
Nos. 325-328 (4) 2.45 1.40

Imperf. souvenir sheet of 4 exists. Value $5.

From this point to No. 1365, used values are for CTO stamps. For Nos. 426A-426W, 676A-676L, 1318A-1318C, 1359, used values are for postally used stamps.

5th Anniv. of the Republic — A110

1980, Dec. 2 *Perf. 11*
Without Gum

329 A110 50c Threshing rice .20 .20
330 A110 1.60k Logging .35 .20
331 A110 4.60k Veterinary medicine .75 .50
332 A110 5.40k Rice paddy 1.10 .80
Nos. 329-332 (4) 2.40 1.70

Imperf. souvenir sheet of 4 exists. Value $10.

26th Communist Party (PCUS) Congress A111

1981, June 26 *Perf. 12x12½*

Without Gum

333 A111 60c shown .20 .20
334 A111 4.60k Globe, broken chains 1.50 .80
335 A111 5.40k Grain, cracked bomb 2.00 .85
a. Souv. sheet of 3, #333-335, imperf. 6.00 6.00
Nos. 333-335 (3) 3.70 1.85

No. 335a sold for 15k.

Souvenir Sheet

PHILATOKYO '81 — A112

1981, Sept. 20 *Perf. 13*

Without Gum

336 A112 10k Pandas 5.50 4.00

1982 World Cup Soccer Championships, Spain — A113

Intl. Year of the Disabled A114

1981, Oct. 15 *Perf. 12½*

Without Gum

337 A113 1k Heading ball .20 .20
338 A113 2k Dribble .40 .20
339 A113 3k Kick .55 .25
340 A113 4k Goal, horiz. .75 .25
341 A113 5k Dribble, diff. 1.00 1.00
342 A113 6k Kick, diff. 1.40 .80
Nos. 337-342 (6) 4.30 2.70

1981 *Perf. 13*

Without Gum

343 A114 3k Office worker 1.25 .40
344 A114 5k Teacher 1.40 .80
345 A114 12k Weaver, fishing net 3.50 2.00
Nos. 343-345 (3) 6.15 3.20

Wildcats — A115

1981 *Perf. 12½*

Without Gum

346 A115 10c Felis silvestris ornata .20 .20
347 A115 20c Felis viverrinus .20 .20
348 A115 30c Felis caracal .20 .20
349 A115 40c Neofelis nebulosa .20 .20
350 A115 50c Felis planiceps .20 .20
351 A115 9k Felis chaus 3.50 1.25
Nos. 346-351 (6) 4.50 2.25

6th Anniv. of the Republic A116

1981, Dec. *Perf. 13*

Without Gum

352 A116 3k Satellite dish, flag .60 .30
353 A116 4k Soldier, flag .75 .40
354 A116 5k Map, flag, women, soldier 1.00 .50
Nos. 352-354 (3) 2.35 1.20

Indian Elephants A117

1982, Jan. 23 *Perf. 12½x13*

Without Gum

355 A117 1k Head .20 .20
356 A117 2k Carrying log in trunk .50 .25
357 A117 3k Transporting people .65 .30
358 A117 4k In trap .90 .30
359 A117 5k Adult and young 1.25 .55
360 A117 5.50k Herd 1.60 .70
Nos. 355-360 (6) 5.10 2.30

Laotian Wrestling A118

Various moves.

1982, Jan. 30 *Perf. 13*

Without Gum

361 A118 50c multicolored .20 .20
362 A118 1.20k multi, diff. .20 .20
363 A118 2k multi, diff. .30 .20
364 A118 2.50k multi, diff. .35 .20
365 A118 4k multi, diff. .60 .35
366 A118 5k multi, diff. 1.00 .55
Nos. 361-366 (6) 2.65 1.70

Water Lilies A119

1982, Feb. 10 *Perf. 12½x13*

Without Gum

367 A119 30c Nymphaea zanzibariensis .20 .20
368 A119 40c Nelumbo nucifera gaertn rose .20 .20
369 A119 60c Nymphaea rosea .20 .20
370 A119 3k Nymphaea nouchali .65 .40
371 A119 4k Nymphaea white 1.00 .40
372 A119 7k Nelumbo nucifera gaertn white 1.75 .50
Nos. 367-372 (6) 4.00 1.90

Birds A120

1982, Mar. 9 *Perf. 13*

Without Gum

373 A120 50c Hirundo rustica, vert. .20 .20
374 A120 1k Upupa epops, vert. .20 .20
375 A120 2k Alcedo atthis, vert. .50 .20
376 A120 3k Hypothymis azurea .65 .25
377 A120 4k Motacilla cinerea 1.25 .25
378 A120 10k Orthotomus sutorius 2.75 .80
Nos. 373-378 (6) 5.55 1.90

A121

1982 World Cup Soccer Championships, Spain — A122

Various match scenes.

1982, Apr. 7

Without Gum

379 A121 1k multicolored .25 .20
380 A121 2k multicolored .40 .25
381 A121 3k multicolored .55 .30
382 A121 4k multicolored .70 .40
383 A121 5k multicolored 1.00 .45
384 A121 6k multicolored 1.25 .55
Nos. 379-384 (6) 4.15 2.15

Souvenir Sheet

385 A122 15k multicolored 4.00 4.00

Butterflies A123

1982, May 5 *Perf. 12½x13*

Without Gum

386 A123 1k Herona marathus .25 .20
387 A123 2k Neptis paraka .60 .25
388 A123 3k Euripus halitherses .75 .30
389 A123 4k Lebadea martha 1.25 .30

Size: 42x26mm

Perf. 12½

390 A123 5k Iton semamora 1.75 .70

Size: 54x36½mm

Perf. 13x12½

391 A123 6k Elymnias hypermnestra 2.25 .70
Nos. 386-391 (6) 6.85 2.45

Souvenir Sheet

PHILEXFRANCE '82 — A124

1982, June 9 *Perf. 13*

Without Gum

392 A124 10k Temple, Vientiane 2.75 2.75

River Vessels A125

1982, June 24

Without Gum

393 A125 50c Raft .20 .20
394 A125 60c River punt .20 .20
395 A125 1k Houseboat .20 .20
396 A125 2k Passenger steamer .35 .20
397 A125 3k Ferry .55 .40
398 A125 8k Self-propelled barge 1.50 .70
Nos. 393-398 (6) 3.00 1.90

Pagodas A126

1982, Aug. 2

Without Gum

399 A126 50c Chanh .20 .20
400 A126 60c Inpeng .20 .20
401 A126 1k Dong Mieng .20 .20
402 A126 2k Ho Tay .35 .25
403 A126 3k Ho Pha Keo .60 .30
404 A126 8k Sisaket 1.60 .65
Nos. 399-404 (6) 3.15 1.80

Dogs A127

1982, Oct. 13

Without Gum

405 A127 50c Poodle .20 .20
406 A127 60c Samoyed .20 .20
407 A127 1k Boston terrier .25 .20
408 A127 2k Cairn terrier .40 .20
409 A127 3k Chihuahua .75 .40
410 A127 8k Bulldog 2.50 .65
Nos. 405-410 (6) 4.30 1.85

World Food Day — A128

1982, Oct. 16

Without Gum

411 A128 7k Watering seedlings 1.75 .65
412 A128 8k Planting rice 2.00 .80

Classic Automobiles — A129

1982, Nov. 7

Without Gum

413 A129 50c 1925 Fiat .20 .20
414 A129 60c 1925 Peugeot .20 .20
415 A129 1k 1925 Berliet .20 .20
416 A129 2k 1925 Ballot .40 .20
417 A129 3k 1926 Renault .75 .40
418 A129 8k 1925 Ford 2.00 .65
Nos. 413-418 (6) 3.75 1.85

7th Anniv. of the Republic A130

1982, Dec. 2

Without Gum

419 A130 50c Kaysone Phomvihan, vert. .20 .20
420 A130 1k Tractors, field, industry .20 .20
421 A130 2k Cows, farm .45 .20
422 A130 3k Truck, microwave dish .65 .25
423 A130 4k Nurse, child, vert. .90 .40
424 A130 5k Education 1.10 .40
425 A130 6k Folk dancer, vert. 1.40 .50
Nos. 419-425 (7) 4.90 2.15

Bulgarian Flag, Coat of Arms and George Dimitrov (1882-1949), Bulgarian Statesman — A131

1982, Dec. 15 ***Perf. 12½***

Without Gum

426 A131 10k multicolored 1.90 1.10

Nos. 272, 276, 283, 284, 286-288, 293, 298, 299, 304-309, 317-319 Overprinted in Red or Black

Methods and Perfs as before

1982

426A A96 1k multi 30.00 30.00
426B A98 1k multi (Bk) 10.00 10.00
a. "I" instead of "1" in overprint —
b. "à" instead of "2" in overprint —
c. Inverted "8n overprint —
426C A98 1k multi — —
a. "I" instead of "1" in overprint —
b. "9" in overprint omitted —
c. Inverted "8n overprint —
426D A98 2k multi — —
426F A99 5k multi 10.00 10.00
a. Double overprint —
426G A101 5k dull org & blk 10.00 10.00
426H A105 5k multi 10.00 10.00
a. Inverted "8" in overprint — —
b. Inverted "1" in overprint —
426I A107 5k multi 10.00 10.00
426J A105 10k multi (Bk) — —
a. Inverted "8" in overprint — —
b. Double overprint, one inverted —
426K A105 10k multi 10.00 10.00
426L A107 10k multi (Bk) 10.00 10.00
a. Inverted "8" in overprint — —
426N A99 20k multi 20.00 20.00
426O A102 20k multi 20.00 20.00
a. Small "2" in overprint — —
426P A104 30k multi 25.00 25.00
a. Small "2" in overprint —
426Q A102 40k multi 30.00 30.00
a. Inverted "8" in overprint — —
426R A98 50k multi 40.00 40.00
a. Inverted "8" in overprint — —
426S A107 70k multi 50.00 50.00
a. Inverted "8" in overprint — —
426T A105 80k multi (Bk) 60.00 60.00
a. Inverted "8" in overprint — —
426U A105 100k multi 75.00 75.00
a. Inverted "8" in overprint — —
426V A96 200k org & multi (Bk) 125.00 125.00
426W A104 250k multi (Bk) 150.00 150.00
a. Inverted "8n overprint —
b. Double overprint, one inverted —
Nos. 426A-426W (21) 695.00 695.00

Five additional stamps were issued in this set. The editors would like to examine any examples.

Constitution of the USSR, 60th Anniv. — A132

1982, Dec. 30

Without Gum

427 A132 3k Kremlin .65 .40
428 A132 4k Maps .90 .55

Souvenir Sheet

Perf. 13½x13

428A Sheet of 2 3.75 2.00
b. A132 5k like 3k 1.25 .65
c. A132 10k like 4k 2.50 1.75

Nos. 428Ab-428Ac not inscribed in Laotian at top; buff and gold decorative margin contains the inscription.

1984 Summer Olympics, Los Angeles A133

1983, Jan. 25 ***Perf. 13***

Without Gum

429 A133 50c Hurdling .20 .20
430 A133 1k Women's javelin .20 .20
431 A133 2k Basketball .35 .20
432 A133 3k Diving .55 .20
433 A133 4k Gymnastics .75 .40
434 A133 10k Weight lifting 2.10 .80
Nos. 429-434 (6) 4.15 2.00

Souvenir Sheet

435 A133 15k Soccer 3.25 2.00

No. 435 contains one stamp 32x40mm.

Horses A134

Various breeds.

1983, Feb. 1

Without Gum

436 A134 50c multicolored .20 .20
437 A134 1k multi, diff. .25 .20
438 A134 2k multi, diff. .40 .20
439 A134 3k multi, diff. .65 .25
440 A134 4k multi, diff. .80 .30
441 A134 10k multi, diff. 2.75 .80
Nos. 436-441 (6) 5.05 1.95

A135

Raphael, 500th Birth Anniv. — A136

Paintings (details) by Raphael: 50c, St. Catherine of Alexandra, Natl. Gallery, London. 1k, Adoration of the Kings (spectators), Vatican. 2k, Granduca Madonna, Pitti Gallery, Florence. 3k, St. George and the Dragon, The Louvre, Paris. 4k, Vision of Ezekiel, Pitti Gallery. No. 447, Adoration of the Kings (Holy Family), Vatican. No. 448, Coronation of the Virgin, Vatican.

1983, Mar. 9 ***Perf. 12½x13***

Without Gum

442 A135 50c multicolored .20 .20
443 A135 1k multicolored .20 .20
444 A135 2k multicolored .35 .20
445 A135 3k multicolored .60 .25
446 A135 4k multicolored .75 .30
447 A135 10k multicolored 2.50 .80
Nos. 442-447 (6) 4.60 1.95

Souvenir Sheet

Perf. 13x13½

448 A136 10k multicolored 2.50 1.50

INTERCOSMOS Space Cooperation Program — A137

Cosmonaut and flags of USSR and participating nations.

1983, Apr. 12 ***Perf. 12½***

449 A137 50c Czechoslovakia .20 .20
450 A137 50c Poland .20 .20
451 A137 1k East Germany .25 .20
452 A137 1k Bulgaria .25 .20
453 A137 2k Hungary .40 .20
454 A137 3k Mongolia .65 .25
455 A137 4k Romania .80 .25
456 A137 6k Cuba 1.25 .40
457 A137 10k France 2.25 .80
Nos. 449-457 (9) 6.25 2.70

Souvenir Sheet

Perf. 13½x13

458 A137 10k Vietnam 2.75 1.50

No. 458 contains one stamp 32x40mm.

A138

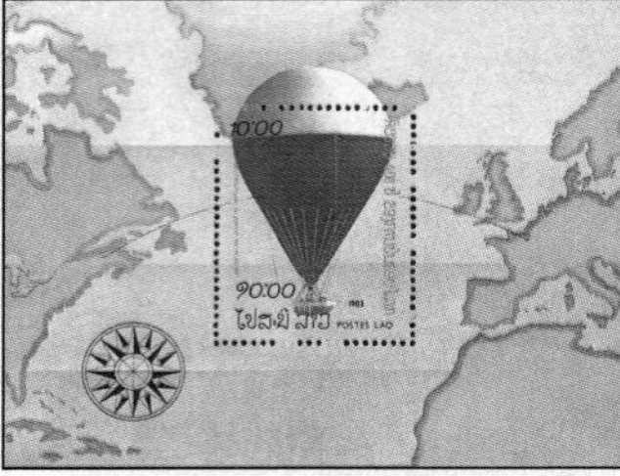

First Manned Balloon Flight, Bicent. — A139

Various balloons.

1983, May 4 ***Perf. 12½x13***

459 A138 50c shown .20 .20
460 A138 1k multi, diff. .20 .20
461 A138 2k multi, diff. .35 .20
462 A138 3k multi, diff. .50 .25
463 A138 4k multi, diff. .65 .40
464 A138 10k multi, diff. 2.25 .80
Nos. 459-464 (6) 4.15 2.05

Souvenir Sheet

Perf. 13½x13

465 A139 10k shown 2.40 1.50

Souvenir Sheet

TEMBAL '83, Basel — A140

1983, May 21 ***Perf. 13x13½***

Without Gum

466 A140 10k German Maybach 3.00 1.60

Flora A141

1983, June 10 ***Perf. 13***

Without Gum

467 A141 1k Dendrobium sp. .25 .20
468 A141 2k Aerides odoratum .40 .20
469 A141 3k Dendrobium aggregatum .60 .25
470 A141 4k Dendrobium .75 .25
471 A141 5k Moschatum 1.10 .30
472 A141 6k Dendrobium sp., diff. 1.40 .50
Nos. 467-472 (6) 4.50 1.70

1984 Winter Olympics, Sarajevo — A142

1983, July 2

Without Gum

473 A142 50c Downhill skiing .20 .20
474 A142 1k Slalom .25 .20
475 A142 2k Ice hockey .40 .20
476 A142 3k Speed skating .70 .25
477 A142 4k Ski jumping .85 .30
478 A142 10k Luge 2.25 .80
Nos. 473-478 (6) 4.65 1.95

Souvenir Sheet

Perf. 13x13½

479 A142 15k 2-Man bobsled 3.50 1.50

No. 479 contains one 40x32mm stamp.

Souvenir Sheet

BANGKOK '83 — A143

1983, Aug. 4 ***Perf. 13½x13***

480 A143 10k Boats on river 2.25 1.50

Mekong River Fish — A144

1983, Sept. 5 ***Perf. 12½***

Without Gum

481 A144 1k Notopterus chitala .25 .20
482 A144 2k Cyprinus carpio .40 .20
483 A144 3k Pangasius sp. .65 .25
484 A144 4k Catlocarpio siamensis .75 .25
485 A144 5k Morulius sp. 1.10 .30
486 A144 6k Tilapia nilotica 1.50 .50
Nos. 481-486 (6) 4.65 1.70

Explorers and Their Ships — A145

1983, Oct. 8 ***Perf. 13x12½***

Without Gum

487 A145 1k Victoria, Magellan .25 .20
488 A145 2k Grand Hermine, Cartier .40 .20
489 A145 3k Santa Maria, Columbus .65 .25
490 A145 4k Cabral and caravel .75 .25
491 A145 5k Endeavor, Capt. Cook 1.10 .30
492 A145 6k Pourquoi-Pas, Charcot 1.50 .50
Nos. 487-492 (6) 4.65 1.70

No. 492 incorrectly inscribed "CABOT."

Domestic Cats A146

1983, Nov. 9 ***Perf. 12½x13***

Without Gum

493 A146 1k Tabby .25 .20
494 A146 2k Long-haired Persian .60 .20
495 A146 3k Siamese .75 .25
496 A146 4k Burmese .85 .25
497 A146 5k Persian 1.25 .30
498 A146 6k Tortoiseshell 1.75 .50
Nos. 493-498 (6) 5.45 1.70

Karl Marx (1818-1883) — A147

1983, Nov. 30 ***Perf. 13***

Without Gum

499 A147 1k shown .25 .20
500 A147 4k Marx, 3 flags, diff., vert. 1.00 .20
501 A147 6k Marx, flag of Laos 1.60 .55
Nos. 499-501 (3) 2.85 .95

8th Anniv. of the Republic — A148

1983, Dec. 2 ***Perf. 12½x13, 13x12½***

Without Gum

502 A148 1k Elephant dragging log, vert. .25 .20
503 A148 4k Oxen, pig 1.00 .20
504 A148 6k Produce, vert. 1.60 .55
Nos. 502-504 (3) 2.85 .95

World Communications Year — A149

1983, Dec. 15 ***Perf. 13***

505 A149 50c Teletype .20 .20
506 A149 1k Telephone .20 .20
507 A149 4k Television .65 .30
508 A149 6k Satellite, dish receiver 1.00 .55
Nos. 505-508 (4) 2.05 1.25

Nos. 275, 306 Overprinted in Red

1983 **Method and Perf. As Before**

508B A105 5k multi — —
508C A96 10k lilac & multi

Additional stamps were issued in this set. The editors would like to examine any examples.

1984 Winter Olympics, Sarajevo — A150

1984, Jan. 16

509 A150 50c Women's figure skating .20 .20
510 A150 1k Speed skating .25 .20
511 A150 2k Biathlon .40 .20
512 A150 4k Luge .80 .30
513 A150 5k Downhill skiing 1.00 .30
514 A150 6k Ski jumping 1.25 .50
515 A150 7k Slalom 1.50 .55
Nos. 509-515 (7) 5.40 2.25

Souvenir Sheet

Perf. 13½x13

516 A150 10k Ice hockey 2.25 1.50

Nos. 509-511, 514-515 vert. No. 516 contains one stamp 32x40mm.

World Wildlife Fund A151

Panthera tigris.

1984, Feb. 1 ***Perf. 13***

517 A151 25c Adult, vert. *.50* .25
518 A151 25c shown *.50* .25
519 A151 3k Nursing cubs *5.00* 1.25
520 A151 4k Two cubs, vert. *8.00* 1.75
Nos. 517-520 (4) *14.00* 3.50

1984 Summer Olympics, Los Angeles A152

Gold medals awarded during previous games, and athletes. 50c, Athens 1896, women's diving. 1k, Paris 1900, women's volleyball. 2k, St. Louis 1904, running. 4k, London 1908, basketball. 5k, Stockholm 1912, judo. 6k, Antwerp 1920, soccer. 7k, Paris 1924, gymnastics. 10k, Moscow 1980, wrestling.

1984, Mar 26

521 A152 50c multicolored .20 .20
522 A152 1k multicolored .25 .20
523 A152 2k multicolored .60 .20
524 A152 4k multicolored 1.10 .20
525 A152 5k multicolored 1.25 .30
526 A152 6k multicolored 1.60 .40
527 A152 7k multicolored 1.90 .50
Nos. 521-527 (7) 6.90 2.00

Souvenir Sheet

Perf. 12½

528 A152 10k multicolored 2.75 1.50

No. 528 contains one stamp 32x40mm.

Musical Instruments — A153

1984, Mar. 27 ***Perf. 13***

529 A153 1k Tuned drums .25 .20
530 A153 2k Xylophone .40 .20
531 A153 3k Pair of drums .65 .25
532 A153 4k Hand drum .90 .30
533 A153 5k Barrel drum 1.10 .30
534 A153 6k Pipes, string instrument 1.25 .50
Nos. 529-534 (6) 4.55 1.75

Natl. Day — A154

Chess A155

1984, Mar. 30 ***Perf. 12½***

535 A154 60c Natl. flag .25 .20
536 A154 1k Natl. arms .40 .20
537 A154 2k like 1k .60 .25
Nos. 535-537 (3) 1.25 .65

1984, Apr. 14 ***Perf. 12½x13***

Illustrations of various medieval and Renaissance chess games.

538 A155 50c multi .20 .20
539 A155 1k multi, diff. .25 .20
540 A155 2k multi, red brn board, diff. .50 .20
541 A155 2k multi, blk board, diff. .50 .20
542 A155 3k multi, diff. .70 .30
543 A155 4k multi, diff. 1.25 .30
544 A155 8k multi, diff. 2.25 .50
a. Souv. sheet of 6, #538-540, 542-544, with gutter between 6.00 2.00
Nos. 538-544 (7) 5.65 1.90

Souvenir Sheet

Perf. 13½x13

545 A155 10k Royal game, human chessmen 2.75 1.50

World Chess Federation, 60th anniv. No. 545 contains one stamp 32x40mm.

ESPANA '84, Madrid — A156

Woodland Flowers — A157

Paintings: 50c, Cardinal Nino de Guevara, by El Greco. 1k, Gaspar de Guzman, Duke of Olivares, on Horseback, byVelazquez. No. 548, The Annunciation, by Murillo. No. 549, Portrait of a Lady, by Francisco de Zurburan (1598-1664). 3k, The Family of Charles IV, by Goya. 4k, Two Harlequins, by Picasso. 8k, Abstract, by Miro. 10k, Burial of the Count of Orgaz, by El Greco.

1984, Apr. 27 ***Perf. 12½***

546 A156 50c multicolored .20 .20
547 A156 1k multicolored .25 .20
548 A156 2k multicolored .45 .20
549 A156 2k multicolored .45 .20
550 A156 3k multicolored .65 .30
551 A156 4k multicolored .90 .30
552 A156 8k multicolored 1.75 .50
Nos. 546-552 (7) 4.65 1.90

Souvenir Sheet

Perf. 13½x13

553 A156 10k multicolored 2.75 1.50

No. 553 contains one stamp 32x40mm.

1984, May 11 ***Perf. 13***

554 A157 50c Adonis aestivalis .20 .20
555 A157 1k Alpinia speciosa .25 .20
556 A157 2k Aeschynanthus speciosus .45 .20
557 A157 2k Cassia lechenaultiana .45 .20
558 A157 3k Datura meteloides .65 .30
559 A157 4k Quamoclit pennata .90 .30
560 A157 8k Commelina benghalensis 1.75 .50
Nos. 554-560 (7) 4.65 1.90

A158

19th UPU Congress, Hamburg — A159

Classic sport and race cars.

1984, June 19

561 A158 50c Nazzaro .20 .20
562 A158 1k Daimler .20 .20
563 A158 2k Delage .35 .20
564 A158 2k Fiat S 57/14B .35 .20
565 A158 3k Bugatti .50 .30
566 A158 4k Itala .65 .30
567 A158 8k Blitzen Benz 1.40 .50
Nos. 561-567 (7) 3.65 1.90

Souvenir Sheet

Perf. 12½

568 A159 10k Winton Bullet 1.90 1.25

Paintings by Correggio (1494-1534) A160

Designs: 50c, Madonna and Child (Holy Family). 1k, Madonna and Child (spectators). No. 571, Madonna and Child (Holy Family, diff.). No. 572, Mystical Marriage of St. Catherine (Catherine, child, two women). 3k, The Four Saints. 4k, Noli Me Tangere. 8k, Christ Bids Farewell to the Virgin Mary. 10k, Madonna and Child, diff.

1984, June 26 ***Perf. 13***

569 A160 50c multicolored .20 .20
570 A160 1k multicolored .25 .20
571 A160 2k multicolored .45 .20
572 A160 2k multicolored .45 .20
573 A160 3k multicolored .65 .30
574 A160 4k multicolored .75 .30
575 A160 8k multicolored 1.40 .50
Nos. 569-575 (7) 4.15 1.90

Souvenir Sheet

Perf. 13½x13

576 A160 10k multicolored 3.25 1.75

No. 576 contains one stamp 32x40mm.

Space Exploration A161

1984, July 12 ***Perf. 13***

577 A161 50c Luna 1 .20 .20
578 A161 1k Luna 2 .20 .20
579 A161 2k Luna 3 .30 .20
580 A161 2k Sputnik 2, Kepler, horiz. .30 .20
581 A161 3k Lunokhod 2, Newton, horiz. .45 .25
582 A161 4k Luna 13, Jules Verne, horiz. .65 .40
583 A161 8k Space station, Copernicus, horiz. 1.10 .65
Nos. 577-583 (7) 3.20 2.10

Reptiles A162

1984, Aug. 20

584 A162 50c Malaclemys terrapin .20 .20
585 A162 1k Bungarus fasciatus .25 .20
586 A162 2k Python reticulatus .40 .20
587 A162 2k Python molurus, vert. .40 .20
588 A162 3k Gekko gecko .75 .25
589 A162 4k Natrix subminiata 1.00 .40
590 A162 8k Eublepharis macularius 1.90 .65
Nos. 584-590 (7) 4.90 2.10

Marsupials — A163

1984, Sept. 21

591 A163 50c Schoinobates volans .20 .20
592 A163 1k Ornithorhynchus anatinus .25 .20
593 A163 2k Sarcophilus harrisii .40 .20
594 A163 2k Lasiorhinus latifrons .40 .20
595 A163 3k Thylacinus cynocephalus .75 .25
596 A163 4k Dasyurops maculatus 1.00 .40
597 A163 8k Wallabia isabelinus 1.90 .65
Nos. 591-597 (7) 4.90 2.10

Souvenir Sheet

Perf. 12½

598 A163 10k Macropus rufus 2.75 1.50

AUSIPEX '84, Melbourne. No. 598 contains one stamp 32x40mm.

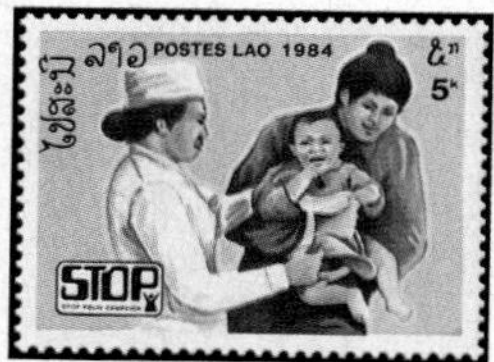

Stop Polio Campaign — A164

1984, Sept. 29 ***Perf. 13***

599 A164 5k shown .85 .55
600 A164 6k Vaccinating child 1.00 .55

Art A165

1984, Oct. 26

601 A165 50c Dragon (hand rail) .20 .20
602 A165 1k Capital .20 .20
603 A165 2k Oval panel .35 .20
604 A165 2k Deity .35 .20
605 A165 3k Leaves .55 .25
606 A165 4k Floral pattern .65 .40
607 A165 8k Lotus flower (round panel) 1.40 .65
Nos. 601-607 (7) 3.70 2.10

Nos. 601-604 and 607 vert.

9th Anniv. of the Republic — A166

1984, Dec. 17

608 A166 1k River boats .20 .20
609 A166 2k Aircraft .45 .25
610 A166 4k Bridge building .90 .65
611 A166 10k Surveying, construction 2.25 .95
Nos. 608-611 (4) 3.80 2.05

1986 World Cup Soccer Championships, Mexico — A167

Various match scenes and flag of Mexico.

1985, Jan. 18

612 A167 50c multicolored .20 .20
613 A167 1k multi, diff. .25 .20
614 A167 2k multi, diff. .50 .20
615 A167 3k multi, diff. .65 .20
616 A167 4k multi, diff. .85 .30
617 A167 5k multi, diff. 1.10 .40
618 A167 6k multi, diff. 1.40 .65
Nos. 612-618 (7) 4.95 2.15

Souvenir Sheet

Perf. 12½

619 A167 10k multi, diff. 2.25 1.50

No. 619 contains one stamp 32x40mm.

Motorcycle, Cent. — A168

1985, Feb. 25 ***Perf. 12½***

620 A168 50c shown .20 .20
621 A168 1k 1920 Gnome Rhone .20 .20
622 A168 2k 1928 F.N. M67C .35 .20
623 A168 3k 1930 Indian Chief .50 .20
624 A168 4k 1914 Rudge Multi .65 .30
625 A168 5k 1953 Honda Benly J .85 .40
626 A168 6k 1938 CZ 1.00 .65
Nos. 620-626 (7) 3.75 2.15

Mushrooms — A169

Lenin, 115th Birth Anniv. — A170

1985, Apr. 8 ***Perf. 13***

627 A169 50c Amanita muscaria .20 .20
628 A169 1k Boletus edulis .25 .20
629 A169 2k Coprinus comatus .50 .20
630 A169 2k Amanita rubescens .50 .20
631 A169 3k Xerocomus subtomentosus .75 .30
632 A169 4k Lepiota procera 1.00 .40
633 A169 8k Paxillus involutus 2.00 .60
Nos. 627-633 (7) 5.20 2.10

End of World War II, 40th Anniv. A169a

1k, Battle of Kursk. 2k, Red Army parade, Moscow. 4k, Battle of Stalingrad. 5k, Battle for Berlin. 6k, Victory parade through Brandenburg Gate.

1985, May **Litho.** ***Perf. 12½x12***

633A A169a 1k multicolored .30 .20
633B A169a 2k multicolored .65 .20
633C A169a 4k multicolored 1.10 .40
633D A169a 5k multicolored 1.50 .50
633E A169a 6k multicolored 2.00 .55
Nos. 633A-633E (5) 5.55 1.85

1985, June 28 ***Perf. 12½***

634 A170 1k Reading Pravda, horiz. .25 .20
635 A170 2k shown .55 .30
636 A170 10k Addressing revolutionaries 1.75 .30
Nos. 634-636 (3) 2.55 .80

Orchids — A171

Fauna — A172

1985, July 5 *Perf. 13*

637 A171 50c Cattleya percivaliana .20 .20
638 A171 1k Odontoglossum luteo-purpureum .25 .20
639 A171 2k Cattleya lueddemanniana .45 .20
640 A171 2k Maxillaria sanderiana .45 .20
641 A171 3k Miltonia vexillaria .70 .25
642 A171 4k Oncidium varicosum 1.00 .30
643 A171 8k Cattleya dowiana aurea 2.25 .65
Nos. 637-643 (7) 5.30 2.00

Souvenir Sheet

Perf. 13½x13

644 A171 10k Catasetum fimbriatum 2.75 1.50

ARGENTINA '85, Buenos Aires. No. 644 contains one stamp 32x40mm.

1985, Aug. 15 *Perf. 13*

645 A172 2k Macaca mulatta .35 .20
646 A172 3k Bos sauveli .55 .20
647 A172 4k Hystrix leucura, horiz. .80 .30
648 A172 5k Selenarctos thibotanus, horiz. 1.00 .30
649 A172 10k Manis pentadactyla 2.00 .65
Nos. 645-649 (5) 4.70 1.65

Apollo-Soyuz Flight, 10th Anniv. — A173

1985, Sept. 6

650 A173 50c Apollo launch pad, vert. .20 .20
651 A173 1k Soyuz launch pad, vert. .20 .20
652 A173 2k Apollo approaching Soyuz .40 .20
653 A173 2k Soyuz approaching Apollo .65 .20
654 A173 3k Apollo, astronauts .80 .25
655 A173 4k Soyuz, cosmonauts 1.00 .30
656 A173 8k Docked spacecrafts 1.60 .65
Nos. 650-656 (7) 4.85 2.00

Aircraft A174

1985, Oct. 25

657 A174 50c Fiat .20 .20
658 A174 1k Cant z.501 .20 .20
659 A174 2k MF-5 .40 .20
660 A174 3k Macchi Castoldi .65 .20
661 A174 4k Anzani .80 .25
662 A174 5k Ambrosini 1.00 .30
663 A174 6k Piaggio 1.10 .35
Nos. 657-663 (7) 4.35 1.70

Souvenir Sheet

Perf. 13x13½

664 A174 10k MF-4 4.50 2.40

ITALIA '85, Rome. No. 664 contains one stamp 40x32mm.

Miniature Sheet

Columbus's Fleet — A175

1985, Oct. 25 *Perf. 13*

665 Sheet of 5 + 4 labels 2.75 2.40
a. A175 1k Pinta .20 .20
b. A175 2k Nina .30 .20
c. A175 3k Santa Maria .50 .25
d. A175 4k Columbus .65 .30
e. A175 5k Map of 1st voyage .80 .40

ITALIA '85.

UN, 40th Anniv. — A176

Health — A177

1985, Oct.

666 A176 2k UN and natl. flag .55 .25
667 A176 3k Coats of arms .80 .30
668 A176 10k Map, globe 2.50 1.00
Nos. 666-668 (3) 3.85 1.55

1985, Nov. 15

669 A177 1k Mother feeding child .20 .20
670 A177 3k Immunization, horiz. .50 .20
671 A177 4k Hospital care, horiz. .65 .30
672 A177 10k Breast-feeding 1.75 .80
Nos. 669-672 (4) 3.10 1.50

10th Anniv. of the Republic A178

1985, Dec. 2

673 A178 3k shown .65 .25
674 A178 10k multi, diff. 2.00 1.00

People's Revolutionary Party, 30th Anniv. — A179

1985, Dec. 30

675 A179 2k shown .55 .20
676 A179 8k multi, diff. 1.90 .65

Nos. 276, 286, 289, 291-292, 297, 299-300, 305, 308-309, 319 Overprinted in Red

Methods and Perfs As Before

1985

676A A102 40k multi 10.00 10.00
m. Inverted "8n overprint —
676B A98 50k multi 10.00 10.00
n. Inverted overprint —
o. "1895" instead of "1985" —
676C A99 50k multi 10.00 10.00
676D A107 70k multi 10.00 10.00
676E A105 80k multi 20.00 20.00
676F A100 100k multi 20.00 20.00
676G A105 100k multi 20.00 20.00
676H A96 200k org & multi 40.00 40.00
676I A100 250k multi 50.00 50.00
676J A101 250k vio & blk
676K A104 250k multi 100.00 100.00
p. Inverted overprint —
676L A102 300k multi 100.00 100.00
Nos. 676A-676L (12) 390.00 390.00

1986 World Cup Soccer Championships, Mexico — A180

Various match scenes.

1986, Jan. 20

677 A180 50c multicolored .20 .20
678 A180 1k multi, diff. .25 .20
679 A180 2k multi, diff. .40 .20
680 A180 3k multi, diff. .50 .25
681 A180 4k multi, diff. .70 .25
682 A180 5k multi, diff. .80 .30
683 A180 6k multi, diff. 1.10 .40
Nos. 677-683 (7) 3.95 1.80

Souvenir Sheet

Perf. 13x13½

684 A180 10k multi, diff. 2.00 .90

No. 684 contains one stamp 40x32mm.

27th Congress of the Communist Party of the Soviet Union A180a

1986, Jan. **Litho.** *Perf. 12x12½*

684A A180a 4k Cosmonaut, spacecraft 1.00 .30
684B A180a 20k Lenin 4.25 1.00

Flowering Plants — A181

1986, Feb. 28 *Perf. 13*

685 A181 50c Pelargonium grandiflorum .20 .20
686 A181 1k Aquilegia vulgaris .25 .20
687 A181 2k Fuchsia globosa .45 .25
688 A181 3k Crocus aureus .65 .25
689 A181 4k Althaea rosea .80 .30
690 A181 5k Gladiolus purpureo 1.00 .40
691 A181 6k Hyacinthus orientalis 1.25 .55
Nos. 685-691 (7) 4.60 2.15

Butterflies A182

1986, Mar. 30

692 A182 50c Aporia hippia .20 .20
693 A182 1k Euthalia irrubescens .25 .20
694 A182 2k Japonica lutea .45 .25
695 A182 3k Pratapa ctesia .65 .25
696 A182 4k Kallina inachus .80 .30
697 A182 5k Ixias pyrene 1.00 .40
698 A182 6k Parantica sita 1.25 .55
Nos. 692-698 (7) 4.60 2.15

A183

First Man in Space, 25th Anniv. — A184

Designs: 50c, Launch, Baikonur Space Center, vert. 1k, Interkosmos communications satellite, vert. 2k, Salyut space station. 3k, Yuri Gagarin, Sputnik 1 disengaging stage. 4k, Luna 3, the Moon, vert. 5k, Komarov on first space walk, vert. 6k, Luna 16 lifting off Moon, vert. 10k, Spacecrafts docking.

1986, Apr. 12

699 A183 50c multicolored .20 .20
700 A183 1k multicolored .25 .20
701 A183 2k multicolored .40 .20
702 A183 3k multicolored .65 .20
703 A183 4k multicolored .80 .25
704 A183 5k multicolored 1.00 .40
705 A183 6k multicolored 1.10 .50
Nos. 699-705 (7) 4.40 1.95

Souvenir Sheet

Perf. 13x13½

706 A184 10k multicolored 2.50 1.00

Fauna — A185

1986, May 22 *Perf. 12½x13, 13x12½*

707 A185 50c Giraffa camelopardalis .20 .20
708 A185 1k Panthera leo .25 .20
709 A185 2k Loxodonta africana africana .40 .20
710 A185 3k Macropus rufus .70 .25

711 A185 4k Gymnobelideus leadbeateri 1.00 .25
712 A185 5k Phoenicopterus ruber 1.25 .30
713 A185 6k Ailuropoda melanoleucus 1.50 .55
Nos. 707-713 (7) 5.30 1.95

Souvenir Sheet

Perf. 13½x13

714 A185 10k Bison, vert. 3.00 1.50

Nos. 707-712 vert.

No. 714 has the Ameripex '86 stamp exhibition logo in the margin.

Pheasants — A187

1986, June 29 ***Perf. 12½x13***

715 A187 50c Argusianus argus .20 .20
716 A187 1k Cennaeus nycthemerus .25 .20
717 A187 2k Phasianus colchicus .45 .20
718 A187 3k Chrysolophus amherstiae .60 .25
719 A187 4k Symaticus reevesii .80 .25
720 A187 5k Chrysolophus pictus 1.00 .30
721 A187 6k Syrmaticus soemmerringii 1.25 .40
Nos. 715-721 (7) 4.55 1.80

Snakes — A188

1986, July 21 ***Perf. 12½x13, 13x12½***

722 A188 50c Elaphe guttata .20 .20
723 A188 1k Thalerophis richardi .30 .20
724 A188 1k Lampropeltis doliata annulata .35 .20
725 A188 2k Diadophis amabilis .40 .25
726 A188 4k Boiga dendrophila .70 .25
727 A188 5k Python molurus 1.00 .30
728 A188 8k Naja naja 1.25 .40
Nos. 722-728 (7) 4.20 1.80

Nos. 722-723 and 728 vert.

Halley's Comet — A189

50c, Acropolis, Athens. #730a, 1k, Bayeux Tapestry. #730b, 2k, Edmond Halley. #731a, 3k, Vega space probe. #731b, 4k, Galileo. #732a, 5k, Comet. #732b, 6k, Giotto probe.

1986, Aug. 22 ***Perf. 12½x13***

729 A189 50c multi .20 .20
730 A189 Pair, #a.-b. .75 .40
731 A189 Pair, #a.-b. 1.25 .50
732 A189 Pair, #a.-b. 2.25 .70
Nos. 729-732 (4) 4.45 1.80

Souvenir Sheet

Perf. 13x13½

733 A189 10k Comet, diff. 2.50 1.25

#730-732 printed in continuous designs. Sizes of #730a, 731a, 732a: 46x25mm; #730b, 731b, 732b; 23x25mm. #733 contains one 40x32mm stamp.

Dogs — A190

Cacti — A191

1986, Aug. 28 ***Perf. 13***

737 A190 50c Keeshond .20 .20
738 A190 1k Elkhound .25 .20
739 A190 2k Bernese .45 .20
740 A190 3k Pointing griffon .65 .25
741 A190 4k Sheep dog (border collie) .85 .25
742 A190 5k Irish water spaniel 1.00 .30
743 A190 6k Briard 1.25 .55
Nos. 737-743 (7) 4.65 1.95

Souvenir Sheet

Perf. 13x13½

744 A190 10k Brittany spaniels 2.10 1.10

STOCKHOLMIA '86. Nos. 738-743 horiz. No. 744 contains one 40x32mm stamp.

1986, Sept. 28 ***Perf. 13***

Designs: 50c, Mammillaria matudae. 1k, Mammillaria theresae. 2k, Ariocarpus trigonus. 3k, Notocactus crassigibbus. 4k, Astrophytum asterias hybridum. 5k, Melocactus manzanus. 6k, Astrophytum ornatum hybridum.

745 A191 50c multicolored .20 .20
746 A191 1k multicolored .25 .20
747 A191 2k multicolored .40 .20
748 A191 3k multicolored .65 .25
749 A191 4k multicolored .80 .25
750 A191 5k multicolored 1.00 .30
751 A191 6k multicolored 1.10 .40
Nos. 745-751 (7) 4.40 1.80

Intl. Peace Year — A192

UNESCO Programs in Laos — A193

1986, Oct. 24

752 A192 3k Natl, arms, dove, globe .75 .25
753 A192 5k Dove, shattered bomb 1.10 .40
754 A192 10k Emblem held aloft 2.25 1.00
Nos. 752-754 (3) 4.10 1.65

1986, Nov. 4

755 A193 3k Vat Phu Champasak ruins .60 .25
756 A193 4k Satellite dish, map, globe .85 .30
757 A193 9k Laotians learning to read, horiz. 1.60 .65
Nos. 755-757 (3) 3.05 1.20

1988 Winter Olympics, Calgary — A194

1987, Jan. 14

758 A194 50c Speed skating .20 .20
759 A194 1k Biathlon .25 .20
760 A194 2k Pairs figure skating .40 .20
761 A194 3k Luge .60 .25
762 A194 4k 4-Man bobsled .75 .25
763 A194 5k Ice hockey 1.00 .30
764 A194 6k Ski jumping 1.10 .40
Nos. 758-764 (7) 4.30 1.80

Souvenir Sheet

Perf. 13½x13

765 A194 10k Slalom 2.25 1.10

Nos. 758-760 vert. No. 765 contains one stamp 32x40mm.

1988 Summer Olympics, Seoul — A195

1987, Feb. 2 ***Perf. 12½x13, 13x13½***

766 A195 50c Women's gymnastics .20 .20
767 A195 1k Women's discus .25 .20
768 A195 2k Running .40 .20
769 A195 3k Equestrian .65 .25
770 A195 4k Women's javelin .75 .25
771 A195 5k High jump 1.00 .30
772 A195 6k Wrestling 1.10 .40
Nos. 766-772 (7) 4.35 1.80

Souvenir Sheet

Perf. 12½

773 A195 10k Runners leaving start 2.00 1.00

Nos. 766, 768, 770 and 772 vert. No. 773 contains one 40x32mm stamp.

Dogs A196

1987, Mar. 5 ***Perf. 12½x13***

774 A196 50c Great Dane .20 .20
775 A196 1k Labrador retriever .25 .20
776 A196 2k St. Bernard .40 .20
777 A196 3k Schippercke .65 .25
778 A196 4k Alsatian (German shepherd) .75 .25
779 A196 5k Beagle 1.00 .30
780 A196 6k Spaniel 1.25 .55
Nos. 774-780 (7) 4.50 1.95

Space Flight, 30th Anniv. A197

1987, Apr. 12 ***Perf. 13***

781 A197 50c Sputnik 1 .20 .20
782 A197 1k Sputnik 2 .25 .20
783 A197 2k Cosmos 87 .40 .20
784 A197 3k Cosmos .50 .25
785 A197 4k Mars .65 .25
786 A197 5k Luna 1 .80 .30
787 A197 9k Luna 3, vert. 1.25 .50
Nos. 781-787 (7) 4.05 1.90

Packet Ships and Stampless Packet Letters — A198

Canada No. 282 — A199

1987, May 12

788 A198 50c "Montreal" .20 .20
789 A198 1k "Paid Montreal" .25 .20
790 A198 2k "Paid" and "Montreal Nov 24" .35 .20
791 A198 3k "Williamsbvrg" and "Forwarded" .55 .25
792 A198 4k "Montreal Fe 18 1844" .75 .25
793 A198 5k "Paid" and "Montreal Jy 10 1848" .85 .30
794 A198 6k "Paid" and "Montreal Paid Ap 16 1861 Canada" 1.10 .40
Nos. 788-794 (7) 4.05 1.80

Souvenir Sheet

Perf. 12½

795 A199 10k multicolored 2.50 1.25

CAPEX '87.

Orchids — A200

1987, Aug. 10 **Litho.** ***Perf. 13***

796 A200 3k *Vanda teres* .20 .20
796A A200 7k *Laeliocattleya* .25 .20
796B A200 10k *Paphiopedilum hibrido* .40 .20
796C A200 39k *Sobralia* .75 .25
796D A200 44k *Paphiopedilum hibrido, diff.* .80 .30
796E A200 47k *Paphiopedilum hibrido, diff.* 1.00 .40
796F A200 50k *Cattleya trianaei* 1.10 .40
Nos. 796-796F (7) 4.50 1.95

Souvenir Sheet

Perf. 12½

796G A200 95k *Vanda tricolor* 2.25 1.10

No. 796G contains one 32x40mm stamp.

Automobiles — A201

1987, July 2 **Litho.** ***Perf. 12½***

797 A201 50c Toyota 480 .20 .20
798 A201 1k Alfa 33 .25 .20
799 A201 2k Ford Fiesta .40 .20
800 A201 3k Datsun .65 .25
801 A201 4k Vauxhall Cavalier .80 .25

802 A201 5k Renault 5 1.00 .30
803 A201 6k Rover-800 1.25 .55
Nos. 797-803 (7) 4.55 1.95

Miniature Sheet

Perf. 13

804 A201 10k Talbot 2.10 1.00

HAFNIA '87, Denmark A202

Various Indian elephants.

1987, Sept. 2 ***Perf. 13***

805 A202 50c Adult, calf .20 .20
806 A202 1k Two adults, calf .25 .20
807 A202 2k Adult eating grass .40 .20
808 A202 3k Adult, diff. .60 .25
809 A202 4k Adult, calf drinking .75 .25
810 A202 5k Adult, diff. .90 .30
811 A202 6k Adult, vert. 1.10 .40
Nos. 805-811 (7) 4.20 1.80

Souvenir Sheet

812 A202 10k Herd, diff. 2.25 1.10

No. 812 contains one stamp 40x32mm.

Horses — A203

Perf. 13x12½, 12½x13

1987, June 3 **Litho.**

813 A203 50c multicolored .20 .20
814 A203 1k multi, diff. .25 .20
815 A203 2k multi, diff. .40 .20
816 A203 3k multi, diff. .60 .25
817 A203 4k multi, diff. .75 .25
818 A203 5k multi, diff. 1.00 .30
819 A203 6k multi, diff. 1.10 .40
Nos. 813-819 (7) 4.30 1.80

Nos. 814-819 vert.

Fish A204

Designs: 3k, Botia macracantha. 7k, Oxymocanthus longirostris. 10k, Adioryx caudimaculatus. 39k, Synchiropus splendidus. 44k, Cephalopolis miniatus. 47k, Dendrochirus zebra. 50k, Pomacantus semicirculatus.

1987, Oct. 14 **Litho.** ***Perf. 13x12½***

820 A204 3k multicolored .20 .20
821 A204 7k multicolored .25 .20
822 A204 10k multicolored .40 .20
823 A204 39k multicolored .70 .25
824 A204 44k multicolored .80 .30
825 A204 47k multicolored 1.00 .40
826 A204 50k multicolored 1.10 .40
Nos. 820-826 (7) 4.45 1.95

World Food Day A205

1987, Oct. 16 ***Perf. 13***

827 A205 1k Tending crops .20 .20
828 A205 3k Harvesting corn, vert. .25 .20
829 A205 5k Harvesting wheat .30 .20
830 A205 63k Youths, fish, vert. 1.25 .50
831 A205 142k Tending pigs, chickens 2.40 1.00
Nos. 827-831 (5) 4.40 2.10

Cultivation of Rice in Mountainous Regions — A206

1987, Nov. 9 ***Perf. 13***

832 A206 64k Tilling soil 1.25 .30
833 A206 100k Rice paddy 1.90 .80

October Revolution, Russia, 70th Anniv. A207

Paintings: 1k, Wounded soldier on battlefield. 2k, Mother and child. 4k, Storming the Winter Palace. 8k, Lenin and revolutionaries. 10k, Rebuilding Red Square.

1987, Nov. ***Perf. 12x12½***

834 A207 1k multicolored .20 .20
835 A207 2k multicolored .40 .25
836 A207 4k multicolored .70 .25
837 A207 8k multicolored 1.25 .50
838 A207 10k multicolored 1.75 .65
Nos. 834-838 (5) 4.30 1.85

Women Wearing Regional Costumes A208

1987, Dec. 2

839 A208 7k Mountain .20 .20
840 A208 38k Urban .80 .25
841 A208 144k Mountain, diff. 2.75 1.10
Nos. 839-841 (3) 3.75 1.55

A209

1988 Winter Olympics, Calgary — A210

1988, Jan.10 ***Perf. 13x12½***

842 A209 1k Bobsled .20 .20
843 A209 4k Biathlon .25 .20
844 A209 20k Skiing .45 .20
845 A209 42k Ice hockey .75 .30
846 A209 63k Speed skating 1.10 .50
847 A209 70k Slalom 1.25 .55
Nos. 842-847 (6) 4.00 1.95

Souvenir Sheet

Perf. 13

848 A210 95k Slalom, diff. 2.25 1.10

No. 848 contains one stamp 40x32mm.

ESSEN '88 — A211

Locomotives: 6k, Nonpareil, vert. 15k, Rocket, vert. 20k, Royal George. 25k, Trevithick. 30k, Novelty. 100k, Tom Thumb. 95k, Locomotion.

1988 ***Perf. 12½x13, 13x12½***

849 A211 6k multicolored .20 .20
850 A211 15k multicolored .25 .20
851 A211 20k multicolored .45 .20
852 A211 25k multicolored .55 .25
853 A211 30k multicolored .65 .25
854 A211 100k multicolored 1.90 .80
Nos. 849-854 (6) 4.00 1.90

Souvenir Sheet

Perf. 13

855 A211 95k multicolored 2.25 1.10

No. 855 contains one stamp 40x32mm.

Intl. Year of Shelter for the Homeless — A212

1988 **Litho.** ***Perf. 13***

856 A212 1k Building frame of house .20 .20
857 A212 27k Cutting lumber .55 .25
858 A212 46k Completed house 1.00 .30
859 A212 70k Community 1.60 .65
Nos. 856-859 (4) 3.35 1.40

Dinosaurs — A213

Perf. 13x12½, 12½x13

1988, Mar. 3 **Litho.**

860 A213 3k Tyrannosaurus .20 .20
861 A213 7k Ceratosaurus nasicornis .25 .20
862 A213 39k Iguanodon bernissartensis .75 .25
863 A213 44k Scolosaurus .80 .40
864 A213 47k Phororhacus 1.00 .40
865 A213 50k Trachodon 1.10 .40
Nos. 860-865 (6) 4.10 1.85

Souvenir Sheet

Perf. 12½

866 A213 95k Pteranodon 2.25 1.10

JUVALUX '88. Nos. 861-864 vert.
Identifications on Nos. 860 and No. 865 are switched.
No. 866 contains one 40x32mm stamp.

WHO, 40th Anniv. A214

1988, Apr. 8 ***Perf. 12½***

867 A214 5k Students, teacher .20 .20
868 A214 27k Pest control .50 .20
869 A214 164k Public water supply, vert. 3.00 1.25
Nos. 867-869 (3) 3.70 1.65

Flowers — A215

Birds — A216

1988 ***Perf. 13x12½***

870 A215 8k *Plumieria rubra* .20 .20
871 A215 9k *Althaea rosea* .25 .20
872 A215 15k *Ixora coccinea* .40 .20
873 A215 33k *Cassia fistula* .75 .25
874 A215 64k *Dahlia coccinea* (pink) 1.25 .50
875 A215 69k *Dahlia coccinea* (yellow) 1.50 .55
Nos. 870-875 (6) 4.35 1.90

Souvenir Sheet

Perf. 13

876 A215 95k Plumieria, Althaea, Ixora 2.50 1.25

FINLANDIA '88. No. 876 contains one 32x40mm stamp.

1988 ***Perf. 13***

877 A216 6k *Pelargopsis capensis* .20 .20
878 A216 10k *Coturnix japonica* .25 .20
879 A216 13k *Psittacula roseata* .40 .20
880 A216 44k *Treron bicincta* .85 .25
881 A216 63k *Pycnonotus melanicterus* 1.10 .50
882 A216 64k *Ducula badia* 1.10 .55
Nos. 877-882 (6) 3.90 1.90

1988 Summer Olympics, Seoul — A217

1988 ***Perf. 12½x12***

883 A217 2k Javelin .20 .20
884 A217 5k Long jump .25 .20
885 A217 10k Horizontal bar .40 .20
886 A217 12k Canoeing .50 .20
887 A217 38k Balance beam .80 .25
888 A217 46k Fencing 1.00 .30
889 A217 100k Wrestling 2.00 .70
Nos. 883-889 (7) 5.15 2.05

Souvenir Sheet

Perf. 13

889A A217 95k Horizontal bar, diff. 2.10 1.00

No. 889A contains one 40x32mm stamp.

Decorative Stencils — A218

1988 ***Perf. 13***

890 A218 1k Scarf .20 .20
891 A218 2k Pagoda entrance, vert. .25 .20
892 A218 3k Pagoda wall, vert. .35 .20
893 A218 25k Pagoda pillar .50 .25
894 A218 163k Skirt 3.00 1.50
Nos. 890-894 (5) 4.30 2.35

Completion of the 5-Year Plan (1981-85) — A219

1988 **Litho.** ***Perf. 13***

895 A219 20k Health care .40 .25
896 A219 40k Literacy .80 .40
897 A219 50k Irrigation 1.00 .55
898 A219 100k Communication, transport 1.75 1.00
Nos. 895-898 (4) 3.95 2.20

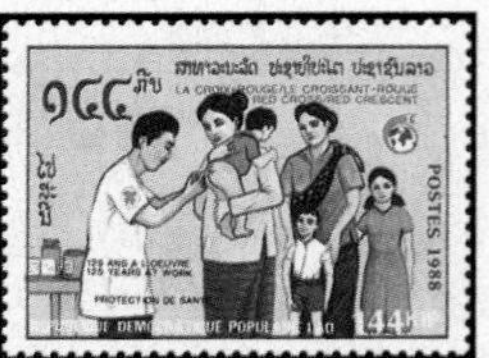

Intl. Red Cross and Red Crescent Organizations, 125th Annivs. — A220

Designs: 4k, Dove, 3 stylized figures representing mankind, vert. 52k, Giving aid to the handicapped, vert. 144k, Child immunization.

1988

899 A220 4k multi .20 .20
900 A220 52k multi 1.10 .55
901 A220 144k multi 2.75 1.50
Nos. 899-901 (3) 4.05 2.25

Chess Champions — A220a

1988 **Litho.** ***Perf. 13***

901A A220a 1k R. Segura .20 .20
901B A220a 2k Adolph Anderssen .20 .20
901C A220a 3k P. Morphy .20 .20
901D A220a 6k W. Steinitz .25 .20
901E A220a 7k E. Lasker .30 .20
901F A220a 12k J.R. Capablanca .40 .25
901G A220a 172k A. Alekhine 3.00 1.10
Nos. 901A-901G (7) 4.55 2.35

Nos. 901C is incorrectly inscribed "Murphy."

1990 World Cup Soccer Championships, Italy — A221

Various plays.

1989 ***Perf. 13x12½***

902 A221 10k multi .20 .20
903 A221 15k multi, diff. .25 .20
904 A221 20k multi, diff. .40 .20
905 A221 25k multi, diff. .55 .25
906 A221 45k multi, diff. .80 .30
907 A221 105k multi, diff. 2.00 .80
Nos. 902-907 (6) 4.20 1.95

Souvenir Sheet

Perf. 13

907A A221 95k multi, diff. 2.10 1.10

No. 907A contains one 40x32mm stamp.

INDIA '89 A222

Cats.

1989, Jan. 7 ***Perf. 12½***

908 A222 5k multi .20 .20
909 A222 6k multi, diff. .25 .20
910 A222 10k multi, diff. .40 .20
911 A222 20k multi, diff. .60 .20
912 A222 50k multi, diff. 1.10 .40
913 A222 172k multi, diff. 3.25 1.00
Nos. 908-913 (6) 5.80 2.20

Souvenir Sheet

Perf. 13

914 A222 95k multi, diff. 2.10 1.00

No. 914 contains one 32x40mm stamp.

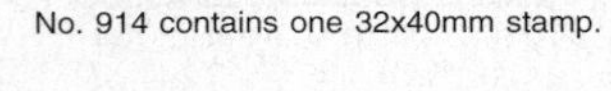

1992 Winter Olympics, Albertville — A223

Various figure skaters.

1989, May 1 ***Perf. 13***

915 A223 9k multi, vert. .20 .20
916 A223 10k shown .25 .20
917 A223 15k multi, diff., vert. .35 .20
918 A223 24k multi, diff., vert. .50 .25
919 A223 29k multi, diff., vert. .65 .25
920 A223 114k multi, diff., vert. 2.00 1.00
Nos. 915-920 (6) 3.95 2.10

Souvenir Sheet

Perf. 12½

921 A223 95k Pairs figure skating 2.10 1.10

No. 921 contains one 32x40mm stamp.

People's Army, 40th Anniv. A224

1989, Jan. 20 ***Perf. 13***

922 A224 1k shown .20 .20
923 A224 2k Military school, vert. .20 .20
924 A224 3k Health care .20 .20
925 A224 250k Ready for combat 6.00 1.00
Nos. 922-925 (4) 6.60 1.60

1992 Summer Olympics, Barcelona — A225

Perf. 12x12½, 12½x12

1989, June 1 **Litho.**

926 A225 5k Pole vault, vert. .20 .20
927 A225 15k Gymnastic rings, vert. .20 .20
928 A225 20k Cycling .30 .25
929 A225 25k Boxing .40 .30
930 A225 70k Archery, vert. 1.10 .55
931 A225 120k Swimming, vert. 1.75 .65
Nos. 926-931 (6) 3.95 2.15

Souvenir Sheet

Perf. 13

932 A225 95k Baseball 2.10 1.10

No. 932 contains one 32x40mm stamp.

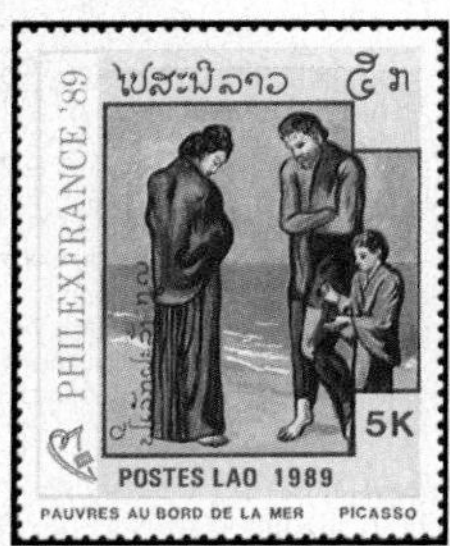

PHILEXFRANCE '89 — A226

Paintings by Picasso: 5k, *Beggars by the Edge of the Sea*. 7k, *Maternity*. 8k, *Portrait of Jaime S. Le Bock*. 9k, *Harlequins*.95k, *Spanish Woman from Majorca*. 105k, *Dog with Boy*. 114k, *Girl Balancing on Ball*.
95k *Woman in Hat*.

1989, July 17 ***Perf. 12½x13***

933 A226 5k multi .20 .20
934 A226 7k multi .25 .20
935 A226 8k multi .25 .20
936 A226 9k multi .35 .25
937 A226 105k multi 1.75 .65
938 A226 114k multi 2.00 .80
Nos. 933-938 (6) 4.80 2.30

Souvenir Sheet

Perf. 12½

939 A226 95k shown 2.10 1.10

No. 939 contains one 32x40mm stamp.

Cuban Revolution, 30th Anniv. — A227

1989, Apr. 20 **Litho.** ***Perf. 13***

940 A227 45k shown 1.10 .40
941 A227 50k Flags 1.25 .40

Fight the Destruction of Forests — A228

1989, Mar. 30 **Litho.** ***Perf. 13***

942 A228 4k Planting saplings .20 .20
943 A228 10k Fight forest fires .25 .20
944 A228 12k Do not chop down trees .25 .25
945 A228 200k Map of woodland 3.25 1.00
Nos. 942-945 (4) 3.95 1.65

Nos. 944-945 are vert.

Jawaharlal Nehru (1889-1964), Indian Statesman A229

1989, Nov. 9 **Litho.** ***Perf. 12½***

946 A229 1k multicolored .20 .20
947 A229 60k multi, horiz. 1.10 .50
948 A229 200k multi, diff. 3.50 1.10
Nos. 946-948 (3) 4.80 1.80

A231

Mani Ikara Zapota — A230

1989, Sept. 18 ***Perf. 12½x13***

949 A230 5k shown .20 .20
950 A230 20k Psidium guajava .40 .20
951 A230 20k Annona sguamosa .40 .20
952 A230 30k Durio zibethinus .55 .25
953 A230 50k Punica granatum .90 .50
954 A230 172k Moridica charautia 3.00 1.00
Nos. 949-954 (6) 5.45 2.35

1989, Oct. 19 **Litho.** ***Perf. 12½***

Historic Monuments: No. 955, That Sikhotabong, Khammouane. No. 956, That Dam, Vientiane. No. 957, That Ing Hang, Savannakhet. No. 958, Ho Vay Phra Thatluang, Vientiane.

955 A231 5k multicolored .20 .20
956 A231 15k multicolored .30 .20
957 A231 61k multicolored 1.10 .55
958 A231 161k multicolored 2.75 1.25
Nos. 955-958 (4) 4.35 2.20

1992 Summer Olympics, Barcelona A232

1990, Mar. 5 Litho. *Perf. 12½x13*

959 A232 10k Basketball .20 .20
960 A232 30k Hurdles .45 .20
961 A232 45k High jump .65 .25
962 A232 50k Cycling .75 .30
963 A232 60k Javelin .90 .50
964 A232 90k Tennis 1.40 .80
Nos. 959-964 (6) 4.35 2.25

Souvenir Sheet

965 A232 95k Rhythmic gymnastics 2.00 1.00

1992 Winter Olympics, Albertville — A233

1990, June 20 *Perf. 13*

966 A233 10k Speed skating .20 .20
967 A233 25k Cross country skiing, vert. .40 .20
968 A233 30k Slalom skiing .45 .25
969 A233 35k Luge .55 .25
970 A233 80k Ice dancing, vert. 1.25 .55
971 A233 90k Biathlon 1.40 .65
Nos. 966-971 (6) 4.25 2.10

Souvenir Sheet

972 A233 95k Hockey, vert. 2.00 1.00

New Zealand Birds A234

Designs: 10k, Prosthemadera novaeseelandie. 15k, Alauda arvensis. 20k, Haemotopus unicolor. 50k, Phalacrocorax carbo. 60k, Demigretta sacra. 100k Apteryx australis mantelli. 95k, Phalacrocorax corunculatus.

1990, Aug. 24 *Perf. 12½*

973 A234 10k multicolored .20 .20
974 A234 15k multicolored .35 .20
975 A234 20k multicolored .45 .25
976 A234 50k multicolored .90 .30
977 A234 60k multicolored 1.10 .50
978 A234 100k multicolored 1.90 .80
Nos. 973-978 (6) 4.90 2.25

Souvenir Sheet

979 A234 95k multicolored 2.25 1.10

World Stamp Expo, New Zealand '90. No. 979 contains one 32x40mm stamp.

That Luang Temple, 430th Anniv. A235

1990, July 25 *Perf. 13x12½, 12½x13*

980 A235 60k 1867 1.10 .50
981 A235 70k 1930 1.25 .65
982 A235 130k 1990, vert. 2.40 1.25
Nos. 980-982 (3) 4.75 2.40

Ho Chi Minh (1890-1969), Vietnamese Leader — A236

1990, May 11 *Perf. 13*

983 A236 40k Addressing people .60 .30
984 A236 60k With Laotian President .90 .45
985 A236 160k Waving, vert. 2.50 1.25
Nos. 983-985 (3) 4.00 2.00

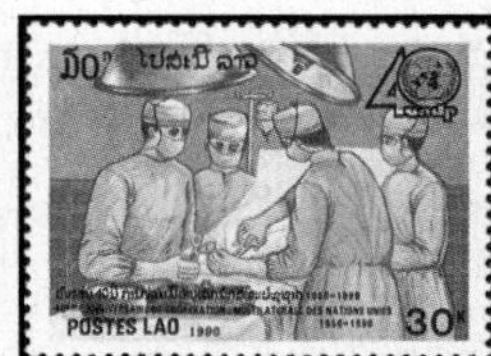

UN Development Program, 40th Anniv. — A237

1990, Oct. 24 Litho. *Perf. 13*

986 A237 30k Surgeons .50 .25
987 A237 45k Fishermen .70 .30
988 A237 80k Flight controller, vert. 1.40 .75
989 A237 90k Power plant 1.50 .90
Nos. 986-989 (4) 4.10 2.20

15th Anniv. of the Republic A238

Designs: 15k, Placing flowers at monument. 20k, Celebratory parade. 80k, Visiting sick. 120k, Women marching with banner.

1990, Dec. 2 Litho. *Perf. 13*

990 A238 15k multicolored .30 .20
991 A238 20k multicolored .40 .20
992 A238 80k multicolored 1.60 .90
993 A238 120k multicolored 2.50 1.25
Nos. 990-993 (4) 4.80 2.55

New Year's Day A239

1990, Nov. 20

994 A239 5k shown .20 .20
995 A239 10k Parade .30 .20
996 A239 50k Ceremony .90 .40

Size: 40x29mm

997 A239 150k Ceremomy, diff. 2.50 1.25
Nos. 994-997 (4) 3.90 2.05

World Cup Soccer Championships, Italy — A240

Designs: Various soccer players in action.

1990 Litho. *Perf. 13*

998 A240 10k multicolored .25 .20
999 A240 15k multicolored .30 .20
1000 A240 20k multicolored .45 .20
1001 A240 25k multicolored .55 .25
1002 A240 45k multicolored .85 .30
1003 A240 105k multicolored 1.90 .80
Nos. 998-1003 (6) 4.30 1.95

Souvenir Sheets

Perf. 12½

1004 A240 95k multi, horiz. 2.00 1.00

Perf. 13

1004A A240 95k multi 2.00 1.00

No. 1004 contains one 39x31mm stamp; No. 1004A one 32x40mm stamp.

Intl. Literacy Year A241

1990, Feb. 27 Litho. *Perf. 12½*

1005 A241 10k shown .35 .20
1006 A241 50k Woman with child, vert. 1.60 .75
1007 A241 60k Monk teaching class 2.00 .90
1008 A241 150k Two women, man reading 4.75 1.25
Nos. 1005-1008 (4) 8.70 3.10

Stamp World London '90 — A242

Stamps, modes of mail transport: 15k, Great Britain #1, stagecoach. 20k, US #1, train. 40k, France #3, balloons. 50k, Sardinia #1, post rider. 60k, Indo-China #3, elephant. 95k, Laos #272, jet. 100k, Spain #1, sailing ship.

1990, Apr. 26 Litho. *Perf. 13x12½*

1009 A242 15k multicolored .25 .20
1010 A242 20k multicolroed .40 .25
1011 A242 40k multicolored .70 .25
1012 A242 50k multicolored 1.00 .30
1013 A242 60k multicolored 1.10 .50
1014 A242 100k multicolored 1.90 .75
Nos. 1009-1014 (6) 5.35 2.25

Souvenir Sheet

Perf. 13

1015 A242 95k multicolored 2.00 1.00

No. 1015 contains one 40x32mm stamp.

Endangered Animals — A242a

1990, Sept. 15 Litho. *Perf. 12½*

1015A A242a 10k Brow-antlered deer .25 .20
1015B A242a 20k Gaur .40 .20
1015C A242a 40k Wild water buffalo .70 .25
1015D A242a 45k Kouprey .75 .30
1015E A242a 120k Javan rhinoceros 1.75 1.00
Nos. 1015A-1015E (5) 3.85 1.95

A243

1992 Olympics, Barcelona and Albertville — A244

Perf. 12½x12, 12x12½, 13 (A244)

1991, Jan. 25

1016 A243 22k 2-man canoe .20 .20
1017 A243 32k 1-man kayak .20 .20
1018 A244 32k Bobsled, vert. .20 .20
1019 A244 135k Cross country skiing .25 .20
1020 A244 250k Ski jumping .55 .25
1021 A244 275k Biathlon .60 .30
1022 A243 285k Diving, vert. .65 .30
1023 A243 330k Sailing, vert. .70 .35
1024 A244 900k Speed skating 1.90 1.00
1025 A243 1000k Swimming 2.00 1.00
Nos. 1016-1025 (10) 7.25 4.00

Souvenir Sheets

Perf. 12½, 13½x13

1026 A243 700k 2-man kayak 2.00 1.00
1027 A244 700k Slalom skiing, vert. 2.00 1.00

No. 1026 contains one 40x32mm stamp. No. 1027 contains one 32x40mm stamp.

Tourism — A245

Designs: 155k, Rapids, Champassak. 220k, Vangvieng. 235k, Waterfalls, Saravane, vert. 1000k Plain of Jars, Xieng Khouang, vert.

1991 *Perf. 13x12½, 12½x13*

1028 A245 155k multicolored .45 .25
1029 A245 220k multicolored .60 .30
1030 A245 235k multicolored .70 .35
1031 A245 1000k multicolored 2.25 1.10
Nos. 1028-1031 (4) 4.00 2.00

1994 World Cup Soccer Championships — A246

Designs: Various players in action.

1991 Litho. *Perf. 13*

1032 A246 32k multicolored .20 .20
1033 A246 330k multicolored .75 .35
1034 A246 340k multi, vert. .85 .40
1035 A246 400k multicolored 1.00 .45
1036 A246 500k multicolored 1.25 .65
Nos. 1032-1036 (5) 4.05 2.05

Souvenir Sheet

Perf. 13½x13

1037 A246 700k multi, vert. 2.00 1.00

No. 1037 contains one 32x40mm stamp.

Espamer '91, Buenos Aires — A247

Espamer '91 Type

1991, June 30 Litho. *Perf. 12½x12*

1038 A247 25k Mallard 4-4-2 .20 .20
1039 A247 32k Pacific 231 4-6-2 .25 .20
1040 A247 285k American style 4-8-4 .90 .35
1041 A247 650k Canadian Pacific 4-6-2 2.00 .75
1042 A247 750k Beyer-Garrant 4-8-2 2-8-4 2.25 1.10
Nos. 1038-1042 (5) 5.60 2.60

Souvenir Sheet

Perf. 12½

1043 A247 700k Inter-city diesel 2.00 1.00

Espamer '91, Buenos Aires. No. 1039 does not show denomination or country in Latin characters. Size of Nos. 1038, 1040-1042: 44x28mm.

Musical Celebrations — A248

Designs: 220k, Man playing mong, vert. 275k, Man, woman singing Siphandone, vert. 545k, Man, woman singing Khapngum. 690k, People dancing.

1991, July 10 Litho. *Perf. 13*

1044 A248 20k multicolored .20 .20
1045 A248 220k multicolored .55 .25
1046 A248 275k multicolored .75 .30
1047 A248 545k multicolored 1.25 .65
1048 A248 690k multicolored 1.75 1.00
Nos. 1044-1048 (5) 4.50 2.40

Butterflies — A248a

1991, Oct. 15 Litho. *Perf. 12½x12*

1048A A248a 55k Sasakia charonda .25 .20
1048B A248a 90k Luendorfia puziloi .30 .20
1048C A248a 255k Papilio bianor .90 .25
1048D A248a 285k Papilio machaon 1.00 .30
1048E A248a 900k Graphium doson 2.50 1.10
Nos. 1048A-1048E (5) 4.95 2.05

Souvenir Sheet

Perf. 13

1048F A248a 700k Cyrestis thyodamas 3.25 1.25

No. 1048F contains one 40x32mm stamp. Phila Nippon '91.

Arbor Day A249

700k, 6 people planting trees. 800k, Nursery.

1991, June 1 *Perf. 12½*

1049 A249 250k multicolored .70 .35
1050 A249 700k multicolored 1.60 .80
1051 A249 800k multicolored 2.00 1.10
Nos. 1049-1051 (3) 4.30 2.25

1992 Winter Olympics, Albertville A250

Perf. 12½x12, 12x12½

1992, Jan. 12 Litho.

1052 A250 200k Bobsled .50 .20
1053 A250 220k Skiing .60 .25
1054 A250 250k Skiing, horiz. .70 .25
1055 A250 500k Luge 1.25 .30
1056 A250 600k Figure skater 1.50 .80
Nos. 1052-1056 (5) 4.55 1.80

Souvenir Sheet

Perf. 12½

1057 A250 700k Speed skater 2.00 1.00

No. 1057 contains one 32x40mm stamp.

1992 Summer Olympics, Barcelona A251

1992, Feb. 21 Litho. *Perf. 12½*

1058 A251 32k Women's running .20 .20
1059 A251 245k Baseball .70 .25
1060 A251 275k Tennis .80 .25
1061 A251 285k Basketball .90 .30
1062 A251 900k Boxing, horiz. 2.25 1.00
Nos. 1058-1062 (5) 4.85 2.00

Souvenir Sheet

1062A A251 700k Diving 2.00 1.00

No. 1062A contains one 40x32mm stamp.

World Health Day A252

Designs: 200k, Spraying for mosquitoes. 255k, Campaign against smoking. 330k, Receiving blood donation. 1000k, Immunizing child, vert.

1992, Apr. 7

1063 A252 200k multicolored .50 .25
1064 A252 255k multicolored .70 .30
1065 A252 330k multicolored .90 .65
1066 A252 1000k multicolored 2.25 1.25
Nos. 1063-1066 (4) 4.35 2.45

A253

A254

Flags, ball and players: 260k, Argentina, Italy. 305k, Germany, Great Britain. 310k, US, World Cup trophy (no players). 350k, Italy, Great Britain. 800k, Germany, Argentina.

1992, May 1 Litho. *Perf. 13*

1067 A253 260k multicolored .60 .20
1068 A253 305k multicolored .65 .25
1069 A253 310k multicolored .70 .30
1070 A253 350k multicolored .80 .50
1071 A253 800k multicolored 1.90 1.00
Nos. 1067-1071 (5) 4.65 2.25

Souvenir Sheet

Perf. 12½

1072 A253 700k Goalie 3.25 1.65

1994 World Cup Soccer Championships, US.

1992, Nov. 8 Litho. *Perf. 13*

Children playing.

1073 A254 220k Playing drum .85 .25
1074 A254 285k Jumping rope, horiz. 1.10 .25
1075 A254 330k Walking on stilts 1.25 .30
1076 A254 400k Escape from line, horiz. 1.60 .65
Nos. 1073-1076 (4) 4.80 1.45

Poisonous Snakes — A255

Perf. 12½x13, 13x12½

1992, July 10 Litho.

1078 A255 280k Naja naja kaouthia .85 .25
1079 A255 295k Naja naja atra .85 .25
1080 A255 420k Trimeresurus wagleri 1.25 .35
1081 A255 700k Ophiophagus hannah, vert. 2.25 1.00
Nos. 1078-1081 (4) 5.20 1.85

Restoration of Wat Phou — A256

Different views of Wat Phou.

Perf. 13x12½, 12½x13

1992, Aug. 22 Litho.

1082 A256 185k multicolored .50 .30
1083 A256 220k multicolored .60 .30
1084 A256 1200k multi, horiz. 2.75 1.40
Nos. 1082-1084 (3) 3.85 2.00

Genoa '92 — A257

Sailing ships and maps by: 100k, Juan Martinez. 300k, Piri Reis, vert. 350k, Paolo del Pozo Toscanelli. 400k, Gabriel de Vallseca. 455k, Juan Martinez, diff. 700k, Juan de la Cosa.

Perf. 13x12½, 12½x13

1992, Sept. 12

1085 A257 100k multicolored .25 .20
1086 A257 300k multicolored .75 .25
1087 A257 350k multicolored .90 .25
1088 A257 400k multicolored 1.00 .50
1089 A257 455k multicolored 1.25 .65
Nos. 1085-1089 (5) 4.15 1.85

Souvenir Sheet

Perf. 13

1090 A257 700k multicolored 2.00 1.00

Traditional Costumes of the Montagnards A258

Various costumes.

1992, Oct. 2 Litho. *Perf. 13*

1091 A258 25k multicolored .20 .20
1092 A258 55k multicolored .25 .20
1093 A258 400k multicolored 1.00 .50
1094 A258 1200k multicolored 2.75 1.25
Nos. 1091-1094 (4) 4.20 2.15

A259

A260

UN, UNESCO emblems, stylized faces and: 330k, Drum. 1000k, Traditional flute.

1991, Nov. 1 Litho. *Perf. 13*

1095 A259 285k shown .80 .35
1096 A259 330k multicolored 1.00 .35
1097 A259 1000k multicolored 2.75 1.25
Nos. 1095-1097 (3) 4.55 1.95

Cultural Development Decade, 1988-1997.

1992, Dec. 22

Designs: Apes.

1098 A260 10k Black gibbon .20 .20
1099 A260 100k Douc langur .25 .20
1100 A260 250k Pileated gibbon .75 .35
1101 A260 430k Francois langur 1.10 .50
1102 A260 800k Pygmy loris 2.00 .80
Nos. 1098-1102 (5) 4.30 2.05

Natl. Customs A261

Designs: 100k, Woman praying before Buddha, vert. 160k, Procession. 1500k, People giving food to monks.

1992, Dec. 2 *Perf. 12½*

1103 A261 100k multicolored .30 .20
1104 A261 140k multicolored .40 .25
1105 A261 160k multicolored .45 .25
1106 A261 1500k multicolored 4.50 2.25
Nos. 1103-1106 (4) 5.65 2.95

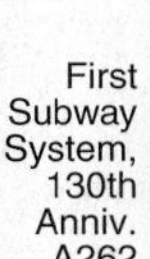

First Subway System, 130th Anniv. A262

1993, Jan. 9 **Litho.** *Perf. 13*

1107 A262 15k New York .20 .20
1108 A262 50k Berlin .25 .20
1109 A262 100k Paris .30 .20
1110 A262 200k London .75 .35
1111 A262 900k Moscow 2.75 1.40
Nos. 1107-1111 (5) 4.25 2.35

Souvenir Sheet

Perf. 13x13½

1112 A262 700k Antique engine, vert. 2.50 1.25

No. 1112 contains one 32x40mm stamp.

Frogs A263

1993, Feb. 1 **Litho.** *Perf. 12½*

1113 A263 55k Kaloula pulchra .25 .20
1114 A263 90k Xenopus muelleri .30 .20
1115 A263 100k Centrolenella vireovittata, vert. .35 .20
1116 A263 185k Bufo marinus .70 .35
1117 A263 1200k Hyla arborea, vert. 3.50 1.25
Nos. 1113-1117 (5) 5.10 2.20

Animals A264

1993, Mar. 13 **Litho.** *Perf. 13*

1118 A264 45k Tupaia glis .25 .20
1119 A264 60k Cynocephalus volans .25 .20
1120 A264 120k Loris grasilis .45 .25
1121 A264 500k Tarsium spectrum 1.60 .75
1122 A264 600k Symphalangus syndactylus 1.90 1.25
Nos. 1118-1122 (5) 4.45 2.65

Native Houses A265

Various houses.

1993, July 12 **Litho.** *Perf. 13*

1123 A265 32k multi, vert. .20 .20
1124 A265 200k multicolored .75 .25
1125 A265 650k multicolored 2.50 .75
1126 A265 750k multicolored 2.75 1.40
Nos. 1123-1126 (4) 6.20 2.60

Campaign Against Illegal Drugs — A266

Designs: 200k, Drugs, skull smoking cigarette. 430k, Burning confiscated drugs. 900k, Instructor showing danger of drugs to audience.

1993, June 26 *Perf. 12½*

1127 A266 200k multicolored .65 .35
1128 A266 430k multicolored 1.50 .75
1129 A266 900k multicolored 3.25 1.40
Nos. 1127-1129 (3) 5.40 2.50

A267

A268

Shells: 20k, Chlamys senatorius nobilis. 30k, Epitonium prestiosum. 70k, Lambis rugosa. 500k, Conus aulicus. 1000k, Lambis millepeda.

1993, May 29 **Litho.** *Perf. 12x12½*

1130 A267 20k multicolored .20 .20
1131 A267 30k multicolored .20 .20
1132 A267 70k multicolored .30 .20
1133 A267 500k multicolored 1.60 .75
1134 A267 1000k multicolored 3.00 1.40
Nos. 1130-1134 (5) 5.30 2.75

1993, Aug. 10 **Litho.** *Perf. 13*

Birds of prey.

1135 A268 10k Aquila clanga .20 .20
1136 A268 100k Athene brama .50 .25
1137 A268 330k Circus melanoleucos 1.50 .50
1138 A268 1000k Circaetus gallicus 4.00 1.40
Nos. 1135-1138 (4) 6.20 2.35

No. 1137 is horiz.

Environmental Protection — A269

Designs: 32k, Fighting forest fire. 40k, Animals around clean river. 260k, Rice paddies. 1100k, Water buffalo, people in water.

1993, Sept. 25 **Litho.** *Perf. 13*

1139 A269 32k multicolored .20 .20
1140 A269 40k multicolored .20 .20
1141 A269 260k multicolored 1.00 .35
1142 A269 1100k multicolored 4.25 1.40
Nos. 1139-1142 (4) 5.65 2.15

Bangkok '93 A270

Butterflies: 35k, Narathura atosia. 80k, Parides philoxenus. 150k, Euploea harrisi. 220k, Ixias pyrene. 500k, Elymnias hypermnestra. 700k, Stichopthalma louisa.

1993, Oct. 1 **Litho.** *Perf. 13*

1143 A270 35k multicolored .20 .20
1144 A270 80k multicolored .25 .20
1145 A270 150k multicolored .45 .25
1146 A270 220k multicolored .75 .35
1147 A270 500k multicolored 2.00 .85
Nos. 1143-1147 (5) 3.65 1.85

Souvenir Sheet

1148 A270 700k multicolored 3.00 1.50

No. 1148 contains one 40x32mm stamp.

1994 World Cup Soccer Championships, US — A271

Various soccer players.

1993, Nov. 3 *Perf. 13*

1149 A271 10k multicolored .20 .20
1150 A271 20k multicolored .20 .20
1151 A271 285k multicolored 1.10 .25
1152 A271 400k multicolored 1.60 .50
1153 A271 800k multicolored 3.25 1.25
Nos. 1149-1153 (5) 6.35 2.40

Souvenir Sheet

Perf. 12½

1154 A271 700k multicolored 2.75 1.40

Nos. 1154 contains one 32x40mm stamp.

Prehistoric Birds — A272

1994, Jan. 20 **Litho.** *Perf. 13*

1155 A272 10k Hesperornis .20 .20
1156 A272 20k Dronte .20 .20
1157 A272 150k Archaeopterix .60 .25
1158 A272 600k Phororhachos 2.00 .50
1159 A272 700k Dinornis maximus 2.25 1.00
Nos. 1155-1159 (5) 5.25 2.15

Souvenir Sheet

1160 A272 700k Teratornis, horiz. 2.50 1.25

Intl. Olympic Committee, Cent. — A273

100k, Flag, flame. 250k, Ancient Olympians. 1000k, Baron de Coubertin, Olympic runner.

Perf. 12x12½, 12½x12

1994, Mar. 15 **Litho.**

1161 A273 100k multi, vert. .25 .20
1162 A273 250k multi .75 .25
1163 A273 1000k multi, vert. 3.25 1.50
Nos. 1161-1163 (3) 4.25 1.95

1994 World Cup Soccer Championships, U.S. — A274

Various soccer plays.

1994, June 15 **Litho.** *Perf. 12½*

1164 A274 40k multicolored .20 .20
1165 A274 50k multicolored .25 .20
1166 A274 60k multicolored .30 .20
1167 A274 320k multicolored 1.75 .50
1168 A274 900k multicolored 5.00 1.25
Nos. 1164-1168 (5) 7.50 2.35

Souvenir Sheet

Perf. 13

1169 A274 700k multicolored 3.75 1.65

No. 1169 contains one 32x40mm stamp.

Pagodas A275

Various ornate gables.

1994, July 1 **Litho.** *Perf. 12½*

1170 A275 30k multicolored .20 .20
1171 A275 150k multicolored .65 .25
1172 A275 380k multicolored 1.60 .40
1173 A275 1100k multicolored 4.50 1.65
Nos. 1170-1173 (4) 6.95 2.50

Ursus Malayanus — A276

1994, July 23

1174 A276 50k shown .75 .20
1175 A276 90k Adult 1.00 .40
1176 A276 200k Cub, adult 2.25 1.00
1177 A276 220k Adult standing 3.25 1.25
Nos. 1174-1177 (4) 7.25 2.85

World Wildlife Fund.

Reptiles — A277

Intl. Year of the Family — A278

70k, Natrix natrix. 80k, Natrix tessellata. 90k, Salamandra salamandra. 600k, Triturus alpestris. 700k, Triturus cristatus. 800k, Lacerta viridis.

1994, Aug. 1 Litho. *Perf. 12½*

No.	Type	Description	Unused	Used
1178	A277	70k multi, horiz.	.30	.20
1179	A277	80k multi, horiz.	.35	.20
1180	A277	90k multi, horiz.	.40	.20
1181	A277	600k multi, horiz.	2.50	.50
1182	A277	800k multicolored	3.25	1.25
		Nos. 1178-1182 (5)	6.80	2.35

Souvenir Sheet

No.	Type	Description	Unused	Used
1183	A277	700k multi, horiz.	3.25	1.25

No. 1183 contains one 40x32mm stamp.

1994, Sept. 24

Designs: 500k, Mother taking child to school, horiz. No. 1186, Mother walking with children. No. 1187, Family.

No.	Type	Description	Unused	Used
1184	A278	200k multicolored	.85	.35
1185	A278	500k multicolored	2.10	.75
1186	A278	700k multicolored	3.25	1.25
		Nos. 1184-1186 (3)	6.20	2.35

Souvenir Sheet

No.	Type	Description	Unused	Used
1187	A278	700k multicolored	3.25	1.25

No. 1187 contains one 32x40mm stamp.

Drums A279

Designs: 440k, Two people with hanging drum. 450k, Barrel shaped drum. 600k, Hanging drum.

Perf. 12½, 13x12½ (#1189)

1994, Oct. 20 Litho.

No.	Type	Description	Unused	Used
1188	A279	370k multicolored	1.60	.40
1189	A279	440k multicolored	1.75	.50
1190	A279	450k multicolored	1.75	.50
1191	A279	600k multicolored	2.40	.75
		Nos. 1188-1191 (4)	7.50	2.15

No. 1189 is 40x29mm.

Elephants — A280

1994, Nov. 25

No.	Type	Description	Unused	Used
1192	A280	140k shown	.55	.25
1193	A280	400k Beside railing	1.60	.80
1194	A280	890k Being ridden, vert.	3.25	1.40
		Nos. 1192-1194 (3)	5.40	2.45

Peace Bridge Between Laos and Thailand — A281

1994, Apr. 8 Litho. *Perf. 14x14½*

No.	Type	Description	Unused	Used
1195	A281	500k multicolored	1.75	1.25

Buddha — A282

Dinosaurs A283

15k, Phra Xayavoraman 7. 280k, Phra Thong Souk. 390k, Phra Monolom. 800k, Phra Ongtu.

1994, Aug. 25 Litho. *Perf. 13*

No.	Type	Description	Unused	Used
1196	A282	15k multicolored	.20	.20
1197	A282	280k multicolored	1.25	.35
1198	A282	390k multicolored	1.60	.50
1199	A282	800k multicolored	3.50	1.40
		Nos. 1196-1199 (4)	6.55	2.45

1994, Dec. 8

No.	Type	Description	Unused	Used
1200	A283	50k Theropod	.25	.20
1201	A283	380k Iguanodon	1.75	.65
1202	A283	420k Sauropod	2.00	.75
		Nos. 1200-1202 (3)	4.00	1.60

World Tourism Organization, 20th Anniv. — A284

1995, Jan. 2 Litho. *Perf. 12½*

No.	Type	Description	Unused	Used
1203	A284	60k Traditional music	.25	.20
1204	A284	250k Traditional dance	1.00	.25
1205	A284	400k Traditional food	1.75	.50
1206	A284	650k Waterfalls, vert.	2.75	.90
		Nos. 1203-1206 (4)	5.75	1.85

Souvenir Sheet

Perf. 13

No.	Type	Description	Unused	Used
1207	A284	700k like #1206, vert.	4.00	2.40

No. 1207 contains one 32x44mm stamp.

Dinosaurs A285

1995, Feb. 20 *Perf. 12½*

No.	Type	Description	Unused	Used
1208	A285	50k Tracodon	.20	.20
1209	A285	70k Protoceratops	.30	.20
1210	A285	300k Brontosaurus	1.25	.35
1211	A285	400k Stegosaurus	1.75	.50
1212	A285	600k Tyranosaurus	2.50	.75
		Nos. 1208-1212 (5)	6.00	2.00

Birds A286

1995, Mar. 10

No.	Type	Description	Unused	Used
1213	A286	50k Acridotheres javanicus	.20	.20
1214	A286	150k Starnus burmannicus	.65	.20
1215	A286	300k Acridotheres tristis	1.25	.40
1216	A286	700k Gracula religiosa	3.00	.90
		Nos. 1213-1216 (4)	5.10	1.70

Francophonie, 25th Anniv. — 1216A

Designs: 50k, People with arms linked. 380k, Temple. 420k, Map of Laos.

1995, Mar. 20 Litho. *Perf. 13*

No.	Type	Description	Unused	Used
1216A	A286a	50k multi	.20	.20
1216B	A286a	380k multi	1.50	.65
1216C	A286a	420k multi	1.75	.75
		Nos. 1216A-1216C (3)	3.45	1.60

Antique Containers A287

1995, May 1 Litho. *Perf. 12½*

No.	Type	Description	Unused	Used
1217	A287	70k "Hanche" cup, vert.	.30	.20
1218	A287	200k Resin bowl	.85	.25
1219	A287	450k Button design bowl	1.90	.55
1220	A287	600k Loving cup	2.50	.75
		Nos. 1217-1220 (4)	5.55	1.75

1996 Atlanta Pre-Olympics A288

1995, Apr. 5

No.	Type	Description	Unused	Used
1221	A288	60k Pole vault	.25	.20
1222	A288	80k Javelin	.35	.20
1223	A288	200k Hammer throw	.85	.25
1224	A288	350k Long jump	1.60	.40
1225	A288	700k High jump	3.25	.90
		Nos. 1221-1225 (5)	6.30	1.95

Souvenir Sheet

No.	Type	Description	Unused	Used
1226	A288	700k Baseball	3.25	1.90

No. 1226 contains one 40x32mm stamp.

Rocket Festival A289

Designs: 80k, Launching rocket from scaffolding, vert. 160k, Carrying rocket in procession led by monk. 500k, Man carrying rocket on shoulder. 700k, People looking at rockets on tripods.

1995, June 1 Litho. *Perf. 13*

No.	Type	Description	Unused	Used
1227	A289	80k multicolored	.30	.20
1228	A289	160k multicolored	.65	.25
1229	A289	500k multicolored	1.90	.55
1230	A289	700k multicolored	2.50	.90
		Nos. 1227-1230 (4)	5.35	1.90

Domestic Cats A290

Designs: 40k, Red tabby longhair. 50k, Siamese seal point. 250k, Red tabby longhair. 400k, Tortoise-shell shorthair. 650k, Tortoise-shell shorthair, vert. 700k, Tortoise-shell shorthair.

1995, July 25 Litho. *Perf. 12½*

No.	Type	Description	Unused	Used
1231	A290	40k multicolored	.20	.20
1232	A290	50k multicolored	.20	.20
1233	A290	250k multicolored	1.00	.25
1234	A290	400k multicolored	1.75	.30
1235	A290	650k multicolored	3.00	.75
		Nos. 1231-1235 (5)	6.15	1.70

Souvenir Sheet

No.	Type	Description	Unused	Used
1236	A290	700k multicolored	3.25	1.90

No. 1236 contains one 40x32mm stamp.

Insect-Eating Plants — A291

Designs: 90k, Nepenthes villosa. 100k, Dionaea muscipula. 350k, Sarracenia flava. 450k, Sarracenia purpurea. 500k, Nepenthes ampullaria.
1000k, Nepenthes gracilis.

1995, Aug. 24

No.	Type	Description	Unused	Used
1237	A291	90k multicolored	.20	.20
1238	A291	100k multicolored	.20	.20
1239	A291	350k multicolored	.65	.35
1240	A291	450k multicolored	.85	.35
1241	A291	500k multicolored	2.75	.75
		Nos. 1237-1241 (5)	4.65	1.85

Souvenir Sheet

No.	Type	Description	Unused	Used
1242	A291	1000k multicolored	5.75	2.40

No. 1242 contains one 40x32mm stamp.

Insects A292

Designs: 40k, Lucanus cervus. 50k, Melolontha melolontha. 500k, Xylocopa violacea. 800k, Tettigonia viridissima.

1995, Sept. 20

No.	Type	Description	Unused	Used
1243	A292	40k multicolored	.20	.20
1244	A292	50k multicolored	.20	.20
1245	A292	500k multicolored	2.00	.50
1246	A292	800k multicolored	3.25	.90
		Nos. 1243-1246 (4)	5.65	1.80

FAO, 50th Anniv. A293

Designs: 80k, Cattle grazing. 300k, Farmer tilling rice paddy. 1000k, Planting, irrigating rice paddies, stocking pond with fish.

1995, Oct. 16 Litho. *Perf. 12½*

No.	Type	Description	Unused	Used
1247	A293	80k multicolored	.25	.20
1248	A293	300k multicolored	1.00	.50
1249	A293	1000k multicolored	3.50	1.70
		Nos. 1247-1249 (3)	4.75	2.40

Traditional Culture — A294

Designs: 50k, Man with musical instrument, two women. 280k, Dance. 380k, Playing game with bamboo poles. 420k, Woman, man with musical instruments.

1996, Jan. 10

1250 A294 50k multicolored .25 .20
1251 A294 280k multicolored 1.40 .35
1252 A294 380k multicolored 2.00 .50
1253 A294 420k multicolored 2.25 .50
Nos. 1250-1253 (4) 5.90 1.55

1996 Summer Olympics, Atlanta — A295

1996, Feb. 20

1254 A295 30k Cycling .20 .20
1255 A295 150k Soccer .75 .20
1256 A295 200k Basketball, vert. 1.00 .25
1257 A295 300k Running, vert. 1.50 .30
1258 A295 500k Shooting 2.50 .65
Nos. 1254-1258 (5) 5.95 1.60

Souvenir Sheet

1259 A295 1000k Pole vault 3.50 1.70

No. 1259 contains one 38x30mm stamp.

Fauna — A296

Designs: 40k, Helarctos malayanus. 60k, Pelecanus philippensis. 200k, Panthera pardus. 250k, Papilio machaon. 700k, Python molurus.

1996, Feb. 26 **Litho.** ***Perf. 13***

1260 A296 40k multicolored .25 .20
1261 A296 60k multicolored .35 .20
1262 A296 200k multicolored 1.10 .25
1263 A296 250k multicolored 1.25 .30
1264 A296 700k multicolored 3.00 .90
Nos. 1260-1264 (5) 5.95 1.85

Intl. Women's Day A297

20k, Weaving textile. 290k, Instructing calisthenics. 1000k, Feeding infant, vert.

1996, Mar. 8

1265 A297 20k multicolored .20 .20
1266 A297 290k multicolored 1.10 .30
1267 A297 1000k multicolored 3.50 1.70
Nos. 1265-1267 (3) 4.80 2.20

A298

A299

Various soccer plays.

1996, May 3 **Litho.** ***Perf. 13***

1268 A298 20k multicolored .20 .20
1269 A298 50k multicolored .25 .20
1270 A298 300k multicolored 1.25 .30
1271 A298 400k multicolored 1.50 .50
1272 A298 500k multicolored 2.00 .60
Nos. 1268-1272 (5) 5.20 1.80

Souvenir Sheet

1273 A298 1000k multicolored 3.50 1.70

1998 World Soccer Cup Championships, France.

No. 1273 contains one 32x40mm stamp.

1996, Apr. 15 **Litho.** ***Perf. 13½x13***

Various rats.

1274 A299 50k purple & multi .25 .20
1275 A299 340k blue & multi 1.25 .65
1276 A299 350k green & multi 1.25 .65
1277 A299 370k red & multi 1.25 .75
Nos. 1274-1277 (4) 4.00 2.25

New Year 1996 (Year of the Rat).

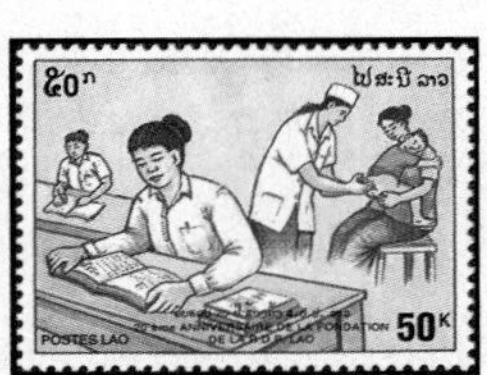

Laos Rural Development Program, 20th Anniv. — A300

50k, Instruction for giving medical care. 280k, Irrigation system. 600k, Bridge over waterway.

1995, Dec. 2 ***Perf. 13***

1278 A300 50k multicolored .20 .20
1279 A300 280k multicolored 1.00 .50
1280 A300 600k multicolored 2.10 1.00
Nos. 1278-1280 (3) 3.30 1.70

UN, 50th Anniv. A301

Designs: 290k, Men seated at round table. 310k, Men playing game, checkers. 440k, Boys in swing, playing ball.

1995, Oct. 24

1281 A301 290k multicolored 1.00 .40
1282 A301 310k multicolored 1.10 .50
1283 A301 440k multicolored 1.50 .75
Nos. 1281-1283 (3) 3.60 1.65

Antique Aircraft A302

1996, July 5 **Litho.** ***Perf. 13***

1284 A302 25k Morane .20 .20
1285 A302 60k Sopwith Camel .25 .20
1286 A302 150k De Haviland DH-4 .65 .20
1287 A302 250k Albatros 1.10 .35
1288 A302 800k Caudron 2.50 1.00
Nos. 1284-1288 (5) 4.70 1.95

Capex '96.

Carts A303

1996, Aug. 21

1289 A303 50k shown .25 .20
1290 A303 100k Cart, diff. .40 .25
1291 A303 440k Pulled by oxen 1.50 .65
Nos. 1289-1291 (3) 2.15 1.10

Flowers — A304

Designs: 50k, Dendrobium secundum. 200k, Ascocentrum miniatum. 500k, Aerides multiflorum. 520k, Dendrobium aggregatum.

1996, Oct. 25 **Litho.** ***Perf. 13***

1292 A304 50k multicolored .20 .20
1293 A304 200k multicolored .75 .25
1294 A304 500k multicolored 1.90 .65
1295 A304 520k multicolored 2.00 .65
Nos. 1292-1295 (4) 4.85 1.75

Draft Horses — A305

Various breeds.

1996, Nov. 5 **Litho.** ***Perf. 13***

1296 A305 50k yellow & multi .20 .20
1297 A305 80k green & multi .25 .20
1298 A305 200k pink & multi .55 .25
1299 A305 400k blue & multi 1.25 .50
1300 A305 600k yellow & multi 1.75 .75
Nos. 1296-1300 (5) 4.00 1.90

Souvenir Sheet

1301 A305 1000k pink & multi 3.00 1.50

No. 1301 contains one 32x40mm stamp.

UNICEF, 50th Anniv. A306

1996, Dec. 11 **Litho.**

1302 A306 200k Children in school .80 .30
1303 A306 500k Child breastfeeding, vert. 2.00 .90
1304 A306 600k Woman pumping water 2.40 1.25
Nos. 1302-1304 (3) 5.20 2.45

Greenpeace, 25th Anniv. — A306a

Turtles: 150k, Dermochelys coriacea on sand. 250k, Dermochelys coriacea in surf. 400k, Erethochelys imbricata. 450k, Chelonia agassizi.

1996, Dec. 27 **Litho.** ***Perf. 13***

1304A A306a 150k multicolored .80 .25
1304B A306a 250k multicolored 1.25 .50
1304C A306a 400k multicolored 2.00 .80
1304D A306a 450k multicolored 2.25 .90
e. Souvenir sheet, #1304A-1304D 6.50 4.75
Nos. 1304A-1304D (4) 6.30 2.45

Steam Locomotives — A307

Designs: 100k, Kinnaird, 1846. 200k, Pioneer, 1836, portrait of George Stephenson. 300k, Portrait of Robert Stephenson, Long Boiler Express, 1848. 400k, Adler, 1835. 500k, Lord of the Isles, 1851-84. 600k, The Columbine, 1845.

2000k, Best friend of Charleston, 1830.

Perf. 12½x12, 12x13 (#1306-1309)

1997 **Litho.**

1305 A307 100k multicolored .30 .20
1306 A307 200k multicolored .60 .25
1307 A307 300k multicolored .95 .35
1308 A307 400k multicolored 1.25 .50
1309 A307 500k multicolored 1.50 .65
1310 A307 600k multicolored 1.75 .75
Nos. 1305-1310 (6) 6.35 2.70

Souvenir Sheet

Perf. 12½

1311 A307 2000k multicolored 5.75 4.50

Nos. 1306-1309 are 42x21mm.

No. 1311 contains one 40x32mm stamp.

Parrots — A308

Designs: 50k, Agapornis personata. 150k, Agapornis cana. 200k, Agapornis lilianae. 400k, Agapornis fischeri. 500k, Agapornis nigregenis. 800k, Agapornis roseicollis.

2000k, Agapornis taranta.

1997 ***Perf. 12½***

1312 A308 50k multicolored .20 .20
1313 A308 150k multicolored .45 .20
1314 A308 200k multicolored .60 .25
1315 A308 400k multicolored 1.25 .50
1316 A308 500k multicolored 1.50 .65
1317 A308 800k multicolored 2.40 1.00
Nos. 1312-1317 (6) 6.40 2.80

Souvenir Sheet

1318 A308 2000k multicolored 6.50 4.75

No. 1318 contains one 32x40mm stamp.

Year of the Ox — A308a

Designs: 300k, Ox, rider with flag, vert. 440k, Ox, rider with umbrella.

1997 **Litho.** ***Perf. 13x13½, 13½x13***

1318A A308a 50k multi .20 .20
1318B A308a 300k multi 1.60 1.40
1318C A308a 440k multi 2.25 1.75
Nos. 1318A-1318C (3) 4.05 3.35

Cooking Utensils A309

50k, Cooking over open fire, vert. 340k, Traditional food containers. 370k, Traditional meal setting.

1997

1319	A309	50k multicolored	.20	.20
1320	A309	340k multicolored	1.00	.55
1321	A309	370k multicolored	1.00	.60
		Nos. 1319-1321 (3)	2.20	1.35

Orchids A310

Designs: 50k, Roeblingiana. 100k, Findlayanum. 150k, Crepidatum. 250k, Sarcanthus birmanicus. 400k, Cymbidium lowianum. 1000k, Dendrobium gratiossissimum. 2000k, Chamberlainianum.

1997 Litho. *Perf. 12½*

1322	A310	50k multicolored	.20	.20
1323	A310	100k multicolored	.30	.20
1324	A310	150k multicolored	.45	.20
1325	A310	250k multicolored	.80	.35
1326	A310	400k multicolored	1.25	.50
1327	A310	1000k multicolored	3.00	1.25
		Nos. 1322-1327 (6)	6.00	2.70

Souvenir Sheet

1328	A310	2000k multicolored	6.00	4.50

No. 1328 contains one 32x40mm stamp.

Elephants — A311

Elephas maximus: 100k, Adult, vert. 250k, Adult holding log. 300k, Adult, calf.

Loxodonta africana: 350k, Adult. 450k, Adult in water. 550k, Adult, vert. 2000k, Head of adult.

1997 Litho. *Perf. 12½*

1329	A311	100k multicolored	.30	.20
1330	A311	250k multicolored	.75	.35
1331	A311	300k multicolored	.85	.35
1332	A311	350k multicolored	1.10	.40
1333	A311	450k multicolored	1.25	.55
1334	A311	550k multicolored	1.60	.65
		Nos. 1329-1334 (6)	5.85	2.50

Souvenir Sheet

1335	A311	2000k multicolored	5.75	4.00

No. 1335 contains one 32x40mm stamp.

Head Pieces and Masks A312

Various designs.

1997 Litho. *Perf. 12½*

1336	A312	50k multi, vert.	.20	.20
1337	A312	100k multi, vert	.25	.20
1338	A312	150k multi	.40	.20
1339	A312	200k multi, vert.	.55	.25
1340	A312	350k multi, vert.	1.25	.40
		Nos. 1336-1340 (5)	2.65	1.25

1998 World Cup Soccer Championships, France — A313

Various soccer plays.

1997 Litho. *Perf. 12½*

1341	A313	100k multicolored	.25	.20
1342	A313	200k multicolored	.50	.25
1343	A313	250k multicolored	.65	.30
1344	A313	300k multicolored	.75	.30
1345	A313	350k multicolored	.90	.40
1346	A313	700k multicolored	1.75	.80
		Nos. 1341-1346 (6)	4.80	2.25

Souvenir Sheet

1347	A313	2000k multicolored	5.00	4.00

Sailing Ships A314

50k, Phoenician. 100k, 13th cent. ship. 150k, 15th cent. vessel. 200k, Portuguese caravel, 16th cent. 400k, Dutch, 17th cent. 900k, HMS Victory.

2000k, Grand Henry, 1514.

1997 *Perf. 13*

1348	A314	50k multicolored	.20	.20
1349	A314	100k multicolored	.25	.20
1350	A314	150k multicolored	.40	.20
1351	A314	200k multicolored	.55	.25
1352	A314	400k multicolored	1.10	.50
1353	A314	900k multicolored	2.50	1.10
		Nos. 1348-1353 (6)	5.00	2.45

Souvenir Sheet

1354	A314	2000k multicolored	5.00	4.00

No. 1354 contains one 40x28mm stamp.

Canoe Races A315

Designs: 50k, Team in red shirts, team in yellow shirts rowing upward. 100k, Crowd cheering on teams. 300k, Teams rowing left. 500k, People standing in canoe cheering on teams.

1997 Litho. *Perf. 12½*

1355	A315	50k multicolored	.20	.20
1356	A315	100k multicolored	.25	.20
1357	A315	300k multicolored	.75	.30
1358	A315	500k multicolored	1.25	.55
		Nos. 1355-1358 (4)	2.45	1.25

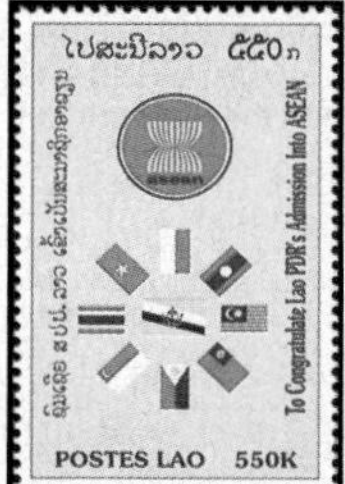

Admission of Laos to ASEAN — A316

Central flag: a, Brunei. b, Indonesia. c, Laos. d, Malaysia. e, Taiwan. f, Philippines. g, Singapore. h, Thailand. i, Viet Nam.

1997, July 23 Litho. *Perf. 14x14½*

1359	A316	550k Strip of 9, #a.-i.	9.50	9.50
j.		Sheet of 9, #1359a-1359i + label	9.50	9.50

Nos. 1359a-1359i also exist in souvenir sheets of 1. No. 1359 was not available in the philatelic market until 8/98.

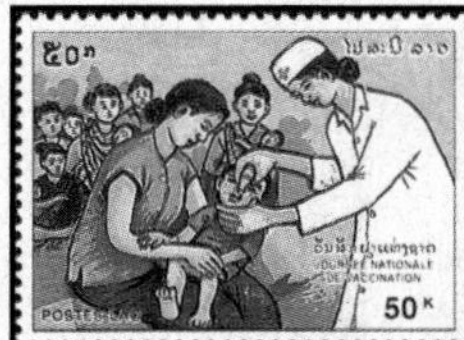

Vaccination Day — A317

Design: 50k, Child receiving oral vaccination. 340k, Child receiving shot. 370k, Child in wheelchair.

1997, Jan. 3 Litho. *Perf. 13x13¼*

1363	A317	50k multi	*.20*	.20
1364	A317	340k multi	*1.50*	.65
1365	A317	370k multi	*1.60*	.75
		Nos. 1363-1365 (3)	*3.30*	1.60

Beginning with No. 1366, used values are for postally used stamps.

Pseudoryx Saola — A319

Various views of Pseudoryx saola.

1997, Feb. 10 *Perf. 13x13¼, 13¼x13*

1366	A319	350k multi	*1.60*	*1.60*
1367	A319	380k multi, vert.	*1.75*	*1.75*
1368	A319	420k multi	*2.00*	*2.00*
		Nos. 1366-1368 (3)	*5.35*	*5.35*

ASEAN (Assoc. of South East Asian Nations), 30th Anniv. — A321

1997, Aug. 8 Litho. *Perf. 13*

1373	A321	150k Headquarters	.90	.65
1374	A321	600k Map of Laos	3.50	2.75

Fishing A322

Designs: 50k, Holding large net with a pole, vert. 100k, Casting net. 450k, Woman using small net, vert. 600k, Placing fish traps in water.

1997

1375	A322	50k multicolored	.30	.20
1376	A322	100k multicolored	.60	.30
1377	A322	450k multicolored	2.00	1.60
1378	A322	600k multicolored	2.75	2.00
		Nos. 1375-1378 (4)	5.65	4.10

New Year 1998 (Year of the Tiger) A323

1998

1379	A323	150k green & multi	.90	.70
1380	A323	350k gray & multi	1.75	1.60
1381	A323	400k pale lilac & multi	1.90	1.75
		Nos. 1379-1381 (3)	4.55	4.05

Canoes — A325

Designs: 1100k, Barque. 1200k, Covered pirogue. 2500k, Motorized pirogue.

1998 Litho. *Perf. 14½x14*

1387	A325	1100k multicolored	2.50	2.50
1388	A325	1200k multicolored	2.75	2.75
1389	A325	2500k multicolored	6.25	6.25
		Nos. 1387-1389 (3)	11.50	11.50

A326

A327

Various wind musical instruments.

1998 *Perf. 14x14½*

1390	A326	900k multicolored	2.25	2.25
1391	A326	1200k multicolored	3.25	3.25
1392	A326	1500k multicolored	4.00	4.00
		Nos. 1390-1392 (3)	9.50	9.50

1998

Buddha Luang, Phabang.

1393	A327	3000k multicolored	7.50	7.50

Orchids — A328

Designs: 900k, Paphiopedilum callosum. 950k, Paphiopedilum concolor. 1000k, Dendrobium thyrsiflorum, vert. 1050k, Dendrobium lindleyi, vert.

1998 *Perf. 14½x14, 14x14½*

1394	A328	900k multicolored	2.75	2.75
1395	A328	950k multicolored	3.00	3.00
1396	A328	1000k multicolored	3.00	3.00
1397	A328	1050k multicolored	3.25	3.25
		Nos. 1394-1397 (4)	12.00	12.00

Universal Declaration of Human Rights, 50th Anniv. — A329

Designs: 170k, Women voting. 300k, Children in classroom.

1998 ***Perf. 14½x14***
1398 A329 170k multicolored 2.25 2.25
1399 A329 300k multicolored 3.75 3.75

Historic Sites — A330

Designs: 10,000k, Hotay Vat Sisaket, vert. 25,000k, Vat Phou. 45,000k, That Luong.

1998 Litho. ***Perf. 14x14¼, 14¼x14***
1400-1402 A330 Set of 3 *35.00 35.00*

People's Army, 50th Anniv. — A331

Designs: 1300k, Soldiers, flag, flowers. 1500k, Soldiers, cave, jungle, vert.

1999 Litho. ***Perf. 13¼***
1403 A331 1300k multi *1.40 1.40*
1404 A331 1500k multi *1.50 1.50*

Souvenir Sheet

Visit Laos Year (in 2000) — A331a

Various temples: b, 2500k. c, 4000k, d, 5500k, e, 8000k.

1999 ? Typo. ***Perf. 13¼***
Gold Stamps
1404A A331a Sheet of 4, #b-e 5.25 5.25
f. As 1404A, with larger margins with Thaipex 99 and China Stamp Exhibition 99 emblems 5.25 5.25
g. As 1404A, with larger margins with China 1999 Philatelic Exhibition emblem 5.25 5.25

Luang Prabang World Heritage Site — A332

Designs: 400k, Commemorative marker, vert. 1150k, Building. 1250k, Vat Xiengthong (building with curved roof).

1999
1405 A332 400k multi *.40 .40*
1406 A332 1150k multi *1.10 1.10*
1407 A332 1250k multi *1.25 1.25*
Nos. 1405-1407 (3) 2.75 2.75

Tourism — A333

Designs: 200k, Yaos, Muong Sing. 500k, Phadeang, Vangvieng District. 1050k, That Makmo, Luang Prabang. 1300k, Patuxay, Vientiane, vert.

1999 Litho. ***Perf. 14¾x14, 14x14¾***
1408 A333 200k multi *.30*
1409 A333 500k multi *.60*
1410 A333 1050k multi *1.10*
1411 A333 1300k multi *1.50*
Nos. 1408-1411 (4) 3.50

Nocturnal Creatures A334

Designs: 900k, Glaucidium brodiei. 1600k, Otus lempiji. 2100k, Tyto alba. 2800k, Chironax melanocephalus.

1999 Litho. ***Perf. 14x14½***
1412 A334 900k multi *.70 .70*
1413 A334 1600k multi *1.50 1.50*
1414 A334 2100k multi *2.00 2.00*
1415 A334 2800k multi *2.75 2.75*
Nos. 1412-1415 (4) 6.95 6.95

New Year 1999 (Year of the Rabbit) — A335

1500k, Rabbit, other animals of calendar cycle. 1600k, Rabbit.

1999 Litho. ***Perf. 14x14¼***
1416 A335 1500k multi, vert. *4.00 5.00*
Perf. 14¾x14
1417 A335 1600k multi, horiz. *5.00 6.00*

Farming Implements — A336

1999 Litho. ***Perf. 14¾x14***
1418 A336 1500k Plow *1.00 1.00*
1419 A336 2000k Yoke *1.50 1.50*
1420 A336 3200k Plow, diff. *2.25 2.25*
Nos. 1418-1420 (3) 4.75 4.75

UPU, 125th Anniv. A337

1999
1421 A337 2600k shown *2.00 2.00*
1422 A337 3400k Postman *2.50 2.50*

Wildlife — A338

700k, Rhinoceros sondaicus. 900k, Bubalus bubalis. 1700k, Prionodon pardicolor. 1800k, Cervus unicolor. 1900k, Panthera leo.

1999 ***Perf. 14¾x14, 14x14¾***
1423 A338 700k multi *.60 .60*
1424 A338 900k multi, vert. *.80 .80*
1425 A338 1700k multi *1.50 1.50*
1426 A338 1800k multi *1.75 1.75*
1427 A338 1900k multi, vert. *1.90 1.90*
Nos. 1423-1427 (5) 6.55 6.55

Expo '99, Kunming, China — A339

Designs: 300k, Carved tree stump. 900k, China Hall. 2300k, Science and Technology Hall. 2500k, Laos traditional wooden house.

1999 ***Perf. 14¾x14***
1428 A339 300k multi *.25 .25*
1429 A339 900k multi *.75 .75*
1430 A339 2300k multi *1.90 1.90*
1431 A339 2500k multi *2.00 2.00*
Nos. 1428-1431 (4) 4.90 4.90

Millennium — A340

No. 1432, 2000k: a, Airport, bus, hospital. b, Temple, tractor, elephant. c, Building, truck. d, River, waterfalls.

2000, Jan. 1 Litho. ***Perf. 13½***
1432 A340 Block of 4, #a-d *5.50* 5.50
e. Souvenir sheet, #1432 *6.75 6.75*

No. 1432e sold for 10,000k.

New Year 2000 (Year of the Dragon) — A341

Dragons: 1800k, And other zodiac animals. 2300k, In water.

2000, Apr. 1 ***Perf. 14½x14***
1433-1434 A341 Set of 2 1.25 1.25

Wedding Costumes A342

Designs: 800k, Lao Theung. 2300k, Lao Lum. 3400k, Lao Sung.

2000, Oct. 30 ***Perf. 14x14½***
1435-1437 A342 Set of 3 2.60 2.60

Children's Drawings — A343

Designs: 300k, Waterfall. 400k, Forest fire. 2300k, Animals at river. 3200k, Animals at river, vert.

2000, June 1 ***Perf. 14½x14, 14x14½***
1438-1441 A343 Set of 4 3.00 3.00

Bangkok 2000 Stamp Exhibition — A344

Orchids: 500k, Dendrobium draconis. 900k, Paphiopedilum hirsutissimum. 3000k, Dendrobium sulcatum. 3400k, Rhynchostylis gigantea.

2000, Mar. 25 ***Perf. 14x14½***
1442-1445 A344 Set of 4 3.00 3.00
1445a Souv. sheet, #1442-1445, perf. 13½ 4.00 4.00

No. 1445a sold for 10,000k.

Peacocks A345

700k, Male with feathers down, vert., 1000k, Male with feathers up, vert., 1800k, Female. 3500k, Male and female.
10,000k, Male with feathers up, vert.

2000, July 10 ***Perf. 14x14½, 14½x14***
1446-1449 A345 Set of 4 2.50 2.50

Souvenir Sheet
Perf. 13½
Litho. With Foil Application
1450 A345 10,000k multi 4.00 4.00

2000 Summer Olympics, Sydney — A346

Designs: 500k, Cycling. 900k, Boxing. 2600k, Judo. 3600k, Kayaking.

2000, Sept. 15 Litho. ***Perf. 14½x14***
1451-1454 A346 Set of 4 3.00 3.00
1454a Souvenir sheet, #1451-1454, perf. 13½ 3.75 3.75

No. 1454a sold for 10,000k.

Laotian postal officials have declared as "illegal" a sheet of stamps for Great People of the 20th Century (Elvis Presley, Roberto Clemente, Marilyn Monroe, Dr. Martin Luther King, Jr., Pope John Paul II, Frank Sinatra, Albert Einstein, Princess Diana and Walt Disney) and stamps depicting Tiger Woods, Payne Stewart, Arnold Palmer, Elvis Presley, Marilyn Monroe, John Lennon and the Beatles.

Women's Costumes — A347

2000, Mar. 8 Litho. ***Perf. 14¼x14½***

1455	A347	100k Kor Loma	.20	.20
1456	A347	200k Kor Pchor	.20	.20
1457	A347	500k Nhuan Krom	.20	.20
1458	A347	900k Taidam	.40	.40
1459	A347	2300k Yao	1.00	1.00
1460	A347	2500k Meuy	1.10	1.10
1461	A347	2600k Sila	1.10	1.10
1462	A347	2700k Hmong	1.25	1.25
1463	A347	2800k Yao, diff.	1.25	1.25
1464	A347	3100k Kor Nukkuy	1.40	1.40
1465	A347	3200k Kor Pouxang	1.40	1.40
1466	A347	3300k Yao Lanten	1.40	1.40
1467	A347	3400k Khir	1.50	1.50
1468	A347	3500k Kor	1.50	1.50
1469	A347	3900k Hmong, diff.	1.75	1.75
		Nos. 1455-1469 (15)	15.65	15.65

Laotian-Japanese Bridge Project — A348

Flags, various views of bridge: 900k, 2700k, 3200k.

2000, Aug. 2 ***Perf. 14½x14***
1470-1472 A348 Set of 3 2.75 2.75

Souvenir Sheet

No. 1472A: b, 4000k, Similar to #1470. c, 7500k, Similar to #1471. d, 8500k, Similar to #1472.

2000 Typo. ***Perf. 13¼x13½***
1472A A348 Sheet of 3, #b-d 7.00 7.00

No. 1472A contains three 48x33mm stamps in gold.

Tourism — A349

Designs: 300k, Phousy Stupa, Luang Prabang. 600k, Than Chang Cave. 2800k, Inhang Stupa. 3300k, Buddha, Phiawat Temple.

2000, Nov. 20 ***Perf. 14x14½***
1473-1476 A349 Set of 4 3.00 3.00

Lao People's Democratic Republic, 25th Anniv. — A350

2000, Dec. 2 ***Perf. 13¼***
1477 A350 4000k multi 1.50 1.50

Mekong River at Twilight A351

Various views: 900k, 2700k, 3400k.

2000, June 20 ***Perf. 14½x14***
1478-1480 A351 Set of 3 2.50 2.50

Anti-Drug Campaign — A352

Designs: 100k, Poppy field. 4000k, Burning of seized drugs.

2000, June 26 **Litho.**
1481-1482 A352 Set of 2 1.50 1.50

Souvenir Sheet

Route 13 Bridge Reconstruction Project — A353

Bridge in: a, Savannakhet. b, Saravane. c, Pakse.

2000, Feb. 14 ***Perf. 13¼***
1483 A353 4000k Sheet of 3, #a-c 4.00 4.00

Souvenir Sheet

Anti-Polio Campaign — A354

No. 1484: a, 900k, People receiving vaccine. b, 2500k, Family, map of Laos.

2000, June 1
1484 A354 Sheet of 2, #a-b 1.25 1.25

Millennium A355

Designs: 3200k, Satellite, telecommunication dishes, map of Laos, student. 4000k, High tension lines, dam.

2001, Jan. 1 ***Perf. 14x14½***
1485-1486 A355 Set of 2 2.25 2.25

New Year 2001 (Year of the Snake) A356

Designs: 900k, Snake coiled around branch. 3500k, Snake, other zodiac animals.

2001, Apr. 15 ***Perf. 14½x14***
1487-1488 A356 Set of 2 1.50 1.50

Cockfighting — A357

Pair of cocks fighting: 500k, 900k, 3300k, 3500k.
10,000k, Single cock, vert.

2001, Mar. 10 ***Perf. 14½x14***
1489-1492 A357 Set of 4 3.25 3.25

Souvenir Sheet

Perf. 13¼

1493 A357 10,000k multi 4.00 4.00

No. 1493 contains one 36x50mm stamp.

Laos-People's Republic of China Diplomatic Relations, 40th Anniv. — A358

2001, Apr. 25 ***Perf. 14¼x14½***
1494 A358 1000k multi .40 .40

Phila Nippon '01 A359

Birds: Nos. 1495, 1499a, 700k, Egretta intermedia. Nos. 1496, 1499b, 800k, Bubulcus ibis (36x50mm). Nos. 1497, 1499c, 3100k, Ardea cinera (36x50mm). Nos. 1498, 1499d, 3400k, Egretta alba.

Perf. 14½x14, 13¼ (#1496-1497)

2001, Aug. 1

With White Frames

1495-1498 A359 Set of 4 2.75 2.75

Souvenir Sheet

Without White Frames

Perf. 13¼

1499 A359 Sheet of 4, #a-d 2.75 2.75

No. 1499 sold for 10,000k.

Mortars and Pestles — A360

Designs: 900k, Two women using large hand-held pestle, vert. 2600k, Water-driven mortar and pestle. 3500k, Woman operating mechanical mortar and pestle, vert.

Perf. 14x14½, 14½x14

2001, Nov. 15
1500-1502 A360 Set of 3 2.25 2.25

Ceremonies — A361

Designs: 300k, Pou Nyer and Nya Nyer, vert. 600k, Hae Nang Sangkhan, vert. 1000k, Sand Stupa. 2300k, Hae Prabang, vert. 4000k, Takbat, vert.

2001, Apr. 13 ***Perf. 14x14½, 14½x14***
1503-1507 A361 Set of 5 3.50 3.50

Buddhist Art — A362

Designs: 200k, Himavanta. 900k, Vanapavesa. 3200k, Kumarakanda. 3600k, Sakkapabba.

2001, Dec. 5 ***Perf. 13¼***
1508-1511 A362 Set of 4 3.25 3.25
1511a Souvenir sheet, #1508-1511 3.25 3.25

Men's Costumes — A363

Designs: 100k, Yao Mane. 200k, Gnaheun. 500k, Katou. 2300k, Hmong Dam. 2500k, Harlak. 2600k, Kui. 2700k, Krieng. 3100k, Khmu Nhuan. 3200k, Ta Oy. 3300k, Tai Theng. 3400k, Hmong Khao. 3500k, Gnor. 3600k, Phouthai Na Gnom. 4000k, Yao. 5000k, Hmong.

2001, Feb. 20 ***Perf. 14¼x14½***

1512	A363	100k multi	.20	.20
1513	A363	200k multi	.20	.20
1514	A363	500k multi	.20	.20
1515	A363	2300k multi	.80	.80
1516	A363	2500k multi	.85	.85
1517	A363	2600k multi	.85	.85
1518	A363	2700k multi	.90	.90
1519	A363	3100k multi	1.00	1.00
1520	A363	3200k multi	1.10	1.10
1521	A363	3300k multi	1.10	1.10
1522	A363	3400k multi	1.25	1.25
1523	A363	3500k multi	1.25	1.25

1524 A363 3600k multi 1.25 1.25
1525 A363 4000k multi 1.50 1.50
1526 A363 5000k multi 1.90 1.90
Nos. 1512-1526 (15) 14.35 14.35

Buddhist Temple Doors — A364

Various doors: 600k, 2300k, 2500k, 2600k.

2001, Sept. 17 Litho. ***Perf. 14x14½***
1527-1530 A364 Set of 4 2.50 2.50

Frangipani Flowers — A365

Designs: 1000k, White flowers. 2500k, Pink flowers, vert. 3500k, Red flowers.

2001, Oct. 2 ***Perf. 14½x14, 14x14½***
1531-1533 A365 Set of 3 2.25 2.25
a. Souvenir sheet, #1531-1533, perf. 13¼ 2.25 2.25

Intl. Volunteers Year — A366

2001, Dec. 29 ***Perf. 13¼***
1534 A366 1000k multi .40 .40

Women's Costumes — A367

Designs: 200k, Meuy. 300k, Leu. 500k, Tai Kouane. 700k, Tai Dam. 1000k, Tai Men. 1500k, Lanten. 2500k, Hmong. 3000k, Phouxang. 3500k, Taitheng. 4000k, Tai O. 5000k, Tai Dam, diff.

2002, Jan. 10 ***Perf. 14x14½***
1535 A367 200k multi .20 .20
1536 A367 300k multi .20 .20
1537 A367 500k multi .20 .20
1538 A367 700k multi .25 .25
1539 A367 1000k multi .30 .30
1540 A367 1500k multi .45 .45
1541 A367 2500k multi .75 .75
1542 A367 3000k multi .95 .95
1543 A367 3500k multi 1.10 1.10
1544 A367 4000k multi 1.25 1.25
1545 A367 5000k multi 1.60 1.60
Nos. 1535-1545 (11) 7.25 7.25

Intl. Year of Mountains — A368

Designs: No. 1546, 1500k, Pha Tang. No. 1547, 1500k, Phou Phamane.

2002, Mar. 30 ***Perf. 14½x14***
1546-1547 A368 Set of 2 1.10 1.10

New Year 2002 (Year of the Horse) A369

Designs: 1500k, Horse, zodiac animals. 3500k, Galloping horse.

2002, Apr. 14
1548-1549 A369 Set of 2 1.60 1.60

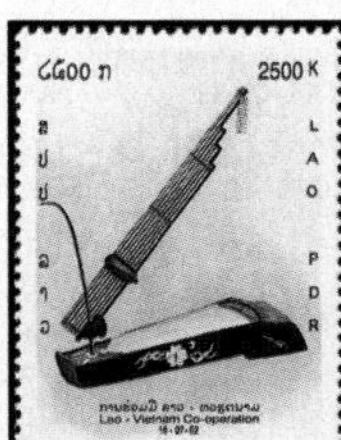

Laos - Viet Nam Cooperation A370

Designs: 2500k, Musical instruments. 3500k, Laotian leader with Ho Chi Minh, horiz.

2002, July 18 ***Perf. 13***
1550-1551 A370 Set of 2 1.90 1.90

Phila Korea 2002 World Stamp Exhibition, Seoul — A371

Insects: Nos. 1552a, 1553a, Sagra femorata. Nos. 1552b, 1552c, Cerambycidae. Nos. 1552c, 1552c, Chrysochroa mniszechii. Nos. 1552d, 1553d, Anoplophora sp. Nos. 1552e, 1553e, Chrysochroa sandersi. Nos. 1552f, 1553f, Mouhotia batesi. Nos. 1552g, 1553g, Megaloxantha assamensis. Nos. 1552h, 1553h, Eupatorus gracillicornis.

2002, Aug. 1 ***Perf. 14½x14***
Insects and Colored Backgrounds
1552 Vert. strip of 8 2.50 2.50
a.-h. A371 1000k Any single .30 .30

Souvenir Sheet
Insects On Vegetation
1553 A371 1000k Sheet of 8, #a-h 2.75 2.75

Admission to UPU, 50th Anniv. A372

2002, May 20 Litho. ***Perf. 13x13¼***
1554 A372 3000k black .95 .95

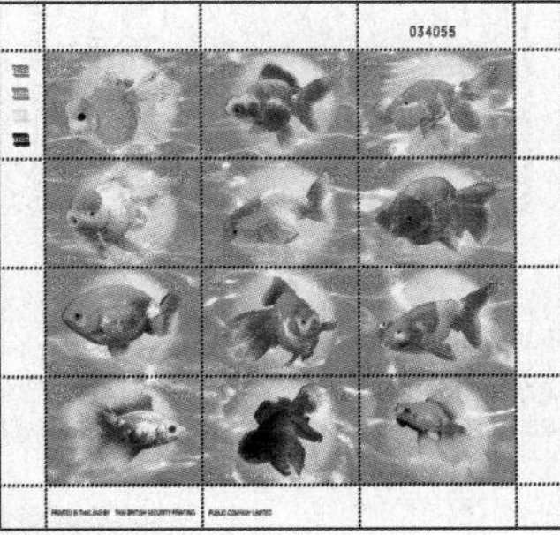

Goldfish — A373

No. 1555: a, Pearlscale goldfish. b, Moor. c, Bubble eyes goldfish. d, Red-capped oranda. e, Lionhead goldfish. f, Pom pom. g, Ranchu. h, Fantail goldfish. i, Celestial goldfish. j, Ryukin. k, Brown oranda. l, Veiltail goldfish.

2002, Oct. 2 ***Perf. 13¼***
1555 A373 1000k Sheet of 12, #a-l 4.00 4.00

Buffalo Fighting A374

Various buffalo: 200k, 300k, 3000k, 4000k.

2002, Dec. 15 ***Perf. 13x13¼***
1556-1559 A374 Set of 4 2.50 2.50

Souvenir Sheet

National Route 9 Improvement Project — A375

No. 1560: a, Curve. b, Interchange. c, Curve and building.

2002, Dec. 18 Litho. ***Perf. 13¼***
1560 A375 1500k Sheet of 3, #a-c 1.60 1.60

Vat Phou World Heritage Site — A376

Designs: 1500k, Temple, vert. 3000k, Temple, diff. 4000k, Statue of Buddha, vert. 10,000k, Stone carving.

2003, Feb. 14 ***Perf. 14x14½, 14½x14***
1561-1563 A376 Set of 3 2.60 2.60

Souvenir Sheet
Perf. 13¼
1564 A376 10,000k multi 3.50 3.50

No. 1564 contains one 93x27mm stamp.

Butterflies — A377

No. 1565: a, Hasora schoenherr. b, Spindasis lohita. c, Graphium sarpedon. d, Polyura schreiber. e, Castalius rosimon. f, Dalias pasithoe. g, Pachliopta aristolochiae. h, Papilio memnon.
10,000k, Danaus genutia.

2003, Mar. 8 ***Perf. 14½x14***
1565 Block of 8 3.50 3.50
a.-h. A377 1000k Any single .40 .35

Souvenir Sheet
Perf. 13¼
1566 A377 10,000k multi 4.25 4.25

No. 1566 exists imperf.

New Year 2003 (Year of the Goat) A378

Designs: 2500k, Two goats. 5000k, Goat, zodiac animals.

2003, Apr. 15 ***Perf. 14½x14***
1567-1568 A378 Set of 2 2.25 2.25

Orchids — A379

Designs: 200k, Phalaenopsis Paifang's Golden Lion. 300k, Coelogyne lentiginosa. 500k, Phalaenopsis sumatrana. 1000k, Phalaenopsis bellina. 1500k, Paphiopedilum appletonianum. 2000k, Vanda bensonii. 2500k, Dendrobium harveyanum. 3000k, Paphiopedilum glaucophyllum. 3500k, Paphiopedilum gratrixianum. 4000k, Vanda roeblingiana. 5000k, Phalaenopsis Lady Sakhara.

2003, Apr. 25 ***Perf. 14½x14¼***
1569 A379 200k multi .20 .20
1570 A379 300k multi .20 .20
1571 A379 500k multi .20 .20
1572 A379 1000k multi .30 .30
1573 A379 1500k multi .45 .45
1574 A379 2000k multi .60 .60
1575 A379 2500k multi .75 .75
1576 A379 3000k multi .90 .90
1577 A379 3500k multi 1.00 1.00
1578 A379 4000k multi 1.25 1.25
1579 A379 5000k multi 1.50 1.50
Nos. 1569-1579 (11) 7.35 7.35

Wood Handicrafts — A380

Designs: 500k, Bowl. 1500k, Pitcher and goblets. 2500k, Fluted bowl. 3500k, Bowl, vert.

2003, May 10 ***Perf. 13***
1580-1583 A380 Set of 4 2.40 2.40

Traditional Games A381

Designs: 1000k, Walking on stringed coconut shells. 3000k, Top spinning. 4000k, Field hockey.

2003, June 1
1584-1586 A381 Set of 3 2.40 2.40

Stop Hunting Campaign A382

Designs: 1500k, Deer. 2000k, Gun. 4500k, Wild animals.

2003, July 25 Litho. ***Perf. 13***
1587-1589 A382 Set of 3 2.50 2.50

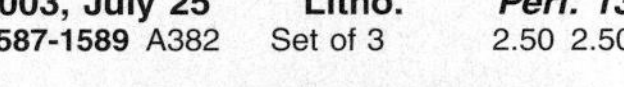

Fruit A383

Designs: 500k, Mango. 1500k, Watermelon. 2500k, Custard apple. 4000k, Pineapple.

2003, Aug. 8 ***Perf. 14½x14***
1590-1593 A383 Set of 4 2.60 2.60

Palm Leaf Manuscripts A384

Designs: 500k, Monk writing palm leaf manuscript. 1500k, Palm leaf manuscript. 2500k, Manuscript casket. 3000k, Ho Tai.

2003, Sept. 12 ***Perf. 14x14½***
1594-1597 A384 Set of 4 3.00 3.00

Bangkok 2003 Intl. Philatelic Exhibition — A385

Buddhas of Luang Prabang: 500k, Pha Sene Souk. 1500k, Pha Gnai. 3000k, Pha Ong Luang. 3500k, Pha Ong Sene.
10,000k, Pha Attharatsa.

2003, Oct. 4 ***Perf. 14x14½***
1598-1601 A385 Set of 4 3.25 3.25

Souvenir Sheet

Perf. 13½

1602 A385 10,000k multi 3.75 3.75

No. 1602 contains one 30x95mm stamp and exists imperf.

Textiles — A386

Various textiles with panel colors of: 500k, Blue. 1000k, Red brown. 3000k, Green. 4000k, Yellow brown.

2003, Dec. 1 ***Perf. 14x14½***
1603-1606 A386 Set of 4 3.00 3.00

Installed Emerald Buddha — A387

2004, Feb. 5 **Litho.** ***Perf. 14½x14***
1607 A387 5500k multi 1.90 1.90

Birds — A388

Designs: 2000k, Buceros bicornis. 2500k, Pycnonotus jocosus. 3000k, Ploceus hypoxanthus. 3500k, Alcedo atthis. 4000k, Magalaima incognita. 4500k, Serilophus lunatus. 5000k, Lacedo pulchella. 5500k, Eurylaimus ochromalus.

2004, Feb. 20 ***Perf. 14¼x14½***
1608-1615 A388 Set of 8 11.00 11.00

Dolphins — A389

Two dolphins: 1500k With heads above water. 2500k, Leaping out of water. 3500k, Underwater.

2004, Mar. 29 ***Perf. 14½x14***
1616-1618 A389 Set of 3 2.50 2.50

New Year 2004 (Year of the Monkey) — A390

Designs: 500k, Two monkeys. 4500k, Monkey, zodiac animals.

2004, Apr. 15
1619-1620 A390 Set of 2 1.75 1.75

FIFA (Fédération Internationale de Football Association), Cent. — A391

No. 1621 — FIFA emblem and: a, Flags of various countries. b, Soccer players.

2004, May 21 ***Perf. 13½***
1621 A391 12,000k Pair, #a-b 8.00 8.00

Values are for stamps with surrounding selvage,

Children's Day — A392

Designs: 3500k, Four children. 4500k, Children, globe, school.

2004, June 1 ***Perf. 14½x14***
1622-1623 A392 Set of 2 2.60 2.60

11th ASEAN Postal Business Meeting — A393

2004, July 5 **Litho.** ***Perf. 14x14½***
1624 A393 5000k multi 1.75 1.75

Worldwide Fund for Nature (WWF) — A394

No. 1625 — Cuora amboinensis: a, 5000k, In water. b, 5500k, On rock near water. c, 6000k, Pair. d, 7000k, Head, feet and shell.

2004, Aug. 16 **Litho.** ***Perf. 13½x14***
1625 A394 Block of 4, #a-d 5.00 5.00

Dances — A395

Designs: 1000k, Tangwai. 1500k, Khabthoume Luangprabang. 2000k, Lao Lamvong. 2500k, Salavan.

2004, Aug. 23 ***Perf. 14x14¾***
1626-1629 A395 Set of 4 2.10 2.10
1629a Souvenir sheet, #1626-1629, perf. 13¼ 3.00 3.00

No. 1629a sold for 10,000k and exists imperf.

Marigolds A396

Designs: 3500k, Yellow, orange marigolds. 5000k, Red and orange marigolds. 5500k, Decorations made with marigolds.

2004, Sept. 28 ***Perf. 13¼x13***
1630-1632 A396 Set of 3 4.75 4.75

Scenes From Ramakian — A397

Various scenes: 3500k, 4500k, 5500k, 6500k.

2004, Oct. 10 ***Perf. 13¼***
1633-1636 A397 Set of 4 6.75 6.75

Naga Fireball — A398

Designs: 2000k, Figure above river, serpent in river. 3000k, Buildings, serpent, horiz. 3500k, Fireball in serpent's mouth, horiz. 4000k, Fireballs above serpent.

2004, Oct. 28 ***Perf. 13 Syncopated***
1637-1640 A398 Set of 4 4.25 4.25

Betel Tray A399

Designs: 2000k, Betel nuts, bowls and containers. 4000k, Betel nut and leaf. 6000k, Betel tray.

2004, Nov. 11 **Litho.** ***Perf. 13***
1641-1643 A399 Set of 3 4.00 4.00

Laos — Sweden Diplomatic Relations, 40th Anniv. — A400

2004, Dec. 12 **Litho.** ***Perf. 13x13½***
1644 A400 8500k multi 2.75 2.75

Handicrafts — A401

Designs: 1000k, Short, round basket. 2000k, Paddle. 2500k, Basket with handle, vert. 5500k, Basket with handle and lid, vert.

Perf. 14½x14, 14x14½

2005, Mar. 10 **Litho.**
1645-1648 A401 Set of 4 3.25 3.25

New Year 2005 (Year of the Rooster) — A402

Rooster and: 2000k, Hen. 7500k, Zodiac animals.

2005, Apr. 13 ***Perf. 14½x14***
1649-1650 A402 Set of 2 3.50 3.50

Daily Buddhas — A403

Buddha for: 500k, Sunday. 1000k, Monday. 1500k, Tuesday, horiz. 2000k, Wednesday. 2500k, Thursday. 3000k, Friday. 3500k, Saturday.

Perf. 14x14½, 14½x14

2005, May 15 **Litho.**
1651-1657 A403 Set of 7 4.50 4.50

Rice — A404

Designs: 1500k, Rice plants. 3000k, Cooked rice on plate, horiz. 6500k, Bundles of rice plants, horiz.

Perf. 13 Syncopated

2005, June 1 **Litho.**
1658-1660 A404 Set of 3 3.25 3.25

Mekong River Giant Catfish — A405

Designs: 3500k, Shown. 6500k, Catfish, diff.

2005, July 13 **Litho.** ***Perf. 14½x14***
1661-1662 A405 Set of 2 3.25 3.25

Gold Panning — A406

Designs: 2000k, Pan. 7500k, Woman panning for gold, vert.

Perf. 13 Syncopated

2005, Aug. 1 **Litho.**
1663-1664 A406 Set of 2 3.00 3.00

Folk Songs — A407

Designs: 1000k, Two musicians standing. 3500k, Two musicians seated. 5500k, Four musicians, horiz.

2005, Sept. 2
1665-1667 A407 Set of 3 3.00 3.00

Europa Stamps, 50th Anniv. (in 2006) A408

Designs: 6000k, Stonehenge, England, and Plain of Jars, Laos. No. 1669, 7000k, Knossos Palace, Greece, and Patuxay, Laos. No. 1670, 7000k, Colosseum, Rome, and Wat Phu, Laos. No. 1671, 7500k, Stave Church, Lom, Norway, and Wat Xieng Thong, Laos. No. 1672, 7500k, Notre Dame Cathedral, Paris, and That Luang, Laos. 8000k, Trier Cathedral, Germany, and Wat Phra Keo, Laos.

2005, Oct. 24 **Litho.** ***Perf. 14¾x14***
1668-1673 A408 Set of 6 12.50 12.50
1673a Souvenir sheet, #1668-1673 12.50 12.50

No. 1673a exists imperf.

People's Democratic Republic, 30th Anniv. — A409

Designs: 500k, Flag and building. 1000k, Flag and people. 2000k, Flag and coat of arms. 5000k, People and coat of arms.

2005, Dec. 2 ***Perf. 13***
1674-1677 A409 Set of 4 2.50 2.50

Diplomatic Relations with Thailand, 55th Anniv. — A410

2005, Dec. 19
1678 A410 7500k multi 2.25 2.25

Laos-United Nations Cooperation, 50th Anniv. — A411

Designs: No. 1679, 3000k, Rice harvesters. No. 1679A, 3000k, Children at school gate. No. 1679B, 3000k, Infant health care.

2005, Oct. 24 **Litho.** ***Perf. 13x13¼***
1679-1679B A411 Set of 3 3.50 3.50
1679Bc Souvenir sheet, #1679-1679B 5.25 5.25

No. 1679Bc sold for 15,000k.

Lao People's Democratic Republic, 30th Anniv. — A411a

Designs: 500k, Buildings and flag. 1000k, Map, people and flag. 2000k, Flag, coat of arms. 5000k, Arms, people.

2005, Dec. 2 **Litho.** ***Perf. 13***
1679D-1679G A411a Set of 4 4.50 4.50

Lao People's Democratic Republic, 30th Anniv. — A411b

2005, Dec. 16 **Litho.** ***Perf. 13¼x13***
1679H A411b 15,500k multi 5.50 5.50

Souvenir Sheet

1679I A411b 20,000k multi 7.00 7.00

Diplomatic Relations Between Laos and Japan, 50th Anniv. — A411c

Designs: 7000k, Flowers. 20,000k, Temples.

2005, Dec. 30 ***Perf. 13***
1679J A411c 7000k multi 2.60 2.60

Size: 170x130mm

Imperf

1679K A411c 20,000k multi 7.00 7.00

Statue of King Phangum Lenglathorany A412

2006, Mar. 9 **Litho.** ***Perf. 14x14½***
1680 A412 8500k multi 2.60 2.60

A souvenir sheet containing one perf. 13½ example of No. 1680 sold for 20,000k.

New Year 2006 (Year of the Dog) A413

Designs: 2000k, Dog. 6500k, Dog, zodiac animals.

2006, Apr. 14 ***Perf. 14½x14***
1681-1682 A413 Set of 2 3.50 3.50

AGL Insurance in Laos, 15th Anniv. — A414

AGL Insurance emblem and: 8000k, Car, minivan and motorcycle. 8500k, Map of Laos. 9500k, Family.

2006, May 1 ***Perf. 13***
1683-1685 A414 Set of 3 7.75 7.75

Friendship Between Vientiane and Moscow — A415

Laotian and Russian: 7500k, Women. 8500k, Sculptures and houses of worship.

2006, May 1
1686-1687 A415 Set of 2 4.75 4.75
1687a Souvenir sheet, #1686-1687 6.00 6.00

No. 1687a sold for 20,000k.

Diplomatic Relations Between Laos and People's Republic of China, 45th Anniv. — A416

2006, May 24 ***Perf. 13x12¾***
1688 A416 8500k multi 2.60 2.60

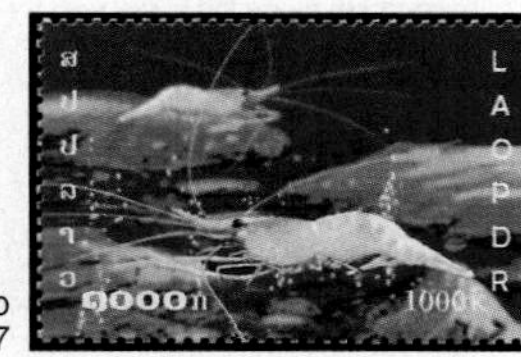
Shrimp A417

Various depictions of shrimp: 1000k, 2000k, 4000k, 6000k.

2006, July 10 ***Perf. 13***
1689-1692 A417 Set of 4 4.00 4.00
1692a Souvenir sheet, #1689-1692 4.50 4.50

No. 1692a sold for 15,000k.

Léopold Sédar Senghor (1906-2001), First President of Senegal — A418

2006, Sept. 4
1693 A418 8500k multi 2.60 2.60

Bronze Drums A419

Various drums with background colors of: 2000k, Red brown. 3500k, Blue. 7500k, Olive green.

2006, Oct. 9
1694-1696 A419 Set of 3 4.00 4.00
1696a Souvenir sheet, #1694-1696 5.50 5.50

No. 1696a sold for 15,000k.

Xieng Khouane Temple — A420

Various views of temple and sculptures: 1000k, 2500k, 3000k, 5000k.

2006, June 10 **Litho.** ***Perf. 13***
1697-1700 A420 Set of 4 4.00 4.00

Bananas A421

Designs: 1000k, Pisang Masak Hijau. 2000k, Pisang Mas. 4000k, Pisang Ambon. 8000k, Pisang Awak.

2006, Nov. 1
1701-1704 A421 Set of 4 5.00 5.00

Opening of Second Thai-Lao Friendship Bridge — A422

Designs: No. 1705, 7500k, Bridge in daylight. No. 1706, 7500k, Bridge at night.

2006, Dec. 20
1705-1706 A422 Set of 2 5.00 5.00

Jewelry — A423

Designs: 2000k, Pins. 5000k, Bracelet. 7000k, Earrings. 7500k, Necklace and pendant.

2007, Jan. 15 Litho. *Perf. 13¼x13*
1707-1710 A423 Set of 4 8.00 8.00
1710a Souvenir sheet, #1707-1710 9.50 9.50

No. 1710a sold for 25,000k.

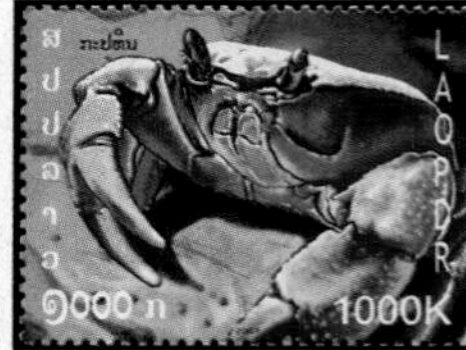
Crabs A424

Various crabs: 1000k, 2000k, 7000k, 7500k.

2007, Feb. 20 *Perf. 13x13¼*
1711-1714 A424 Set of 4 6.50 6.50
1714a Souvenir sheet, #1711-1714, perf. 13½x13¾ 7.50 7.50

No. 1714a sold for 20,000k.

New Year 2007 (Year of the Pig) A425

Designs: No. 1715, 7500k, Pig and piglets. No. 1716, 7500k, Pig, zodiac animals.

2007, Apr. 15 *Perf. 13x13¼*
1715-1716 A425 Set of 2 5.75 5.75

Takbat Festival — A425a

Designs: 2000k, Monks standing, women placing items on ground. 5000k, Woman reaching into monk's bowl. 7500k, Women holding bowls.

2007, July 10 Litho. *Perf. 13*
1716A-1716C A425a Set of 3 5.50 5.50

Association of South East Asian Nations (ASEAN), 40th Anniv. — A426

Designs: 7000k, Typical house, Laos.
No. 1718: a, Like 7000k. b, Secretariat Building, Bandar Seri Begawan, Brunei. c, National Museum of Cambodia. d, Fatahillah Museum, Jakarta, Indonesia. e, Malayan Railway Headquarters Building, Kuala Lumpur, Malaysia. f, Yangon Post Office, Myanmar. g, Malacañang Palace, Philippines. h, National Museum of Singapore. i, Vimanmek Mansion, Bangkok, Thailand. j, Presidential Palace, Hanoi, Viet Nam.

2007, Aug. 8 Litho. *Perf. 13*
1717 A426 7000k multi 3.00 3.00
1718 Sheet of 10 3.00 3.00
a.-j. A426 700k Any single .30 .30

See Brunei No. 607, Burma No. 370, Cambodia No. 2339, Indonesia Nos. 2120-2121, Malaysia No. 1170, Philippines Nos. 3103-3105, Singapore No. 1265, Thailand No. 2315, and Viet Nam Nos. 3302-3311.

Transportation — A426a

Designs: 2000k, Airplanes. 5000k, Ferry. 7500k, Trucks.

2007, Sept. 1 Litho. *Perf. 13*
1718K-1718M A426a Set of 3 6.00 6.00

That Luang Festival — A426b

Designs: 2000k, Monks leading procession. 5000k, Procession with temple in background. 8000k, Temple at night.

2007, Nov. 13
1718N-1718P A426b Set of 3 5.75 5.75

Traditional Foods — A426c

Designs: 2000k, Sticky rice cooked in bamboo tubes. 5500k, Green papaya salad. 7500k, Grilled chicken.

2007, Dec. 30
1718Q-1718S A426c Set of 3 5.75 5.75

Worldwide Fund for Nature (WWF) A427

Hylobates lar: 6000k, Head. 7000k, Adult and juvenile. 8000k, With open mouth. 9000k, Two adults.

2008 Litho. *Perf. 13½x14*
1719-1722 A427 Set of 4 7.25 7.25
1722a Miniature sheet, 4 each #1719-1722 29.00 29.00

Nos. 1719-1722, 1722a exist imperf.

2008 Summer Olympics, Beijing A428

Designs: No. 1723, 5000k, Taekwondo. No. 1724, 5000k, High jump. No. 1725, 5000k, Cycling. No. 1726, 5000k, Soccer.

2008 *Perf. 12½x13*
1723-1726 A428 Set of 4 4.75 4.75

Elephant Festival — A429

Designs: 1000k, Tuskless elephant and rider. 2000k, Two elephants and riders. 3000k, Man in crowd holding rope. 5000k, Tusked elephant with rider. 7500k, Woman decorating elephant. 8500k, Elephants moving logs. 20,000k, Elephants, riders and guides.

2008 Litho. *Perf. 13*
1727-1732 A429 Set of 6 11.00 11.00

Size: 146x110mm
Imperf
1733 A429 20,000k multi + label 8.50 8.50

Coffee — A430

Designs: Nos. 1734, 1737a, 3000k, Mug and roasted coffee beans. Nos. 1735, 1737b, 5000k, Coffee berries. Nos. 1736, 1737c, 6000k, Roasted coffee beans.

2008, Feb. 11 Litho. *Perf. 13*
Size: 30x45mm
1734-1736 A430 Set of 3 6.25 6.25

Souvenir Sheet
Perf. 13¼x13
1737 A430 Sheet of 3, #a-c 8.00 8.00

No. 1737 contains three 32x43mm stamps and sold for 18,000k.

Worldwide Fund for Nature (WWF) — A431

No. 1738 — Hylobates lar: a, 6000k, Head. b, 7000k, Adult and juvenile. c, 8000k, Adult with open mouth. d, 9000k, Two adults.

2008, Apr. 3 *Perf. 13½x13¾*
1738 A431 Block of 4, #a-d 7.50 7.50

Cotton A432

Designs: Nos. 1739, 1742a, 1000k, Woman at cotton gin. Nos. 1740, 1742b, 5000k, Cotton plant. Nos. 1741, 1742c, 5500k, Cotton plant, diff.

2008, Apr. 10 *Perf. 13*
Size: 45x30mm
1739-1741 A432 Set of 3 5.25 5.25

Souvenir Sheet
Perf. 13½x13¾
1742 A432 Sheet of 3, #a-c 6.75 6.75

No. 1742 contains three 42x32mm stamps and sold for 15,000k.

2008 Summer Olympics, Beijing A433

Designs: No. 1743, 5000k, Cycling. No. 1744, 5000k, High jump. No. 1745, 5000k, Judo. No. 1746, 5000k, Soccer.

2008, Apr. 17 *Perf. 12½x13*
1743-1746 A433 Set of 4 9.00 9.00

Bees A434

Designs: 1000k, Bees and honeycomb. 4000k, Bees on flower. 6000k, Beehive. 8500k, Bee in flight.

2008, June 23 *Perf. 13*
1747-1750 A434 Set of 4 8.75 8.75

Waterfalls A435

Designs: Nos. 1751, 1755a, 500k, Taat Fan Waterfall. Nos. 1752, 1755b, 2000k, Tad Sae Waterfall, horiz. Nos. 1753, 1755c, 5000k, Kuang Si Waterfall. Nos. 1754, 1755d, 6500k, Khonphapheng Waterfall, horiz.

2008, July 28 *Perf. 13*
Sizes: 30x45mm, 45x30mm (Horiz. Stamps)
1751-1754 A435 Set of 4 6.25 6.25

Souvenir Sheet
Perf. 13¾x13½, 13½x13¾
1755 A435 Sheet of 4, #a-d 7.25 7.25

No. 1755 contains two 32x42mm stamps and two 42x32mm stamps and sold for 16,000k.

Eggplants — A436

Designs: Nos. 1756, 1760a, 1000k, White eggplants. Nos. 1757, 1760b, 2000k, Green eggplants. Nos. 1758, 1760c, 4000k, Green, striped eggplants. Nos. 1759, 1760d, 5500k, Purple eggplants.

2008, Oct. 1 *Perf. 13*

Size: 45x30mm

1756-1759 A436 Set of 4 5.75 5.75

Souvenir Sheet

1760 A436 Sheet of 4, #a-d 6.75 6.75

No. 1760 contains four 42x32mm stamps and sold for 15,000k.

Hmong New Year — A437

Designs: Nos. 1761, 1765a, 1000k, Woman. Nos. 1762, 1765b, 5500k, Two oxen, horiz. Nos. 1763, 1765c, 6000k, Musician. Nos. 1764, 1765d, 7500k, Two women holding umbrellas, horiz.

2008, Dec. 1 *Perf. 13*

Size: 30x45mm, 45x30mm (Horiz. Stamps)

1761-1764 A437 Set of 4 9.00 9.00

Souvenir Sheet

Perf. 13¾x13½, 13½x13¾

1765 A437 Sheet of 4, #a-d 9.00 9.00

No. 1765 contains two 32x42mm stamps and two 42x32mm stamps.

Antiquities of Laos — A438

Designs: Nos. 1766, 1770a, 1000k, Haw Phra Kaew. Nos. 1767, 1770b, 2000k, Plain of Jars. Nos. 1768, 1770c, 4000k, Phat That Luang. Nos. 1769, 1770d, 7500k, Temple.

2009, Jan. 3 *Perf. 13*

Stamps With White Frames

1766-1769 A438 Set of 4 5.00 5.00

Souvenir Sheet

Stamps With Colored Frames

1770 A438 Sheet of 4, #a-d 5.25 5.25

No. 1770 sold for 15,000k.

A439

A440

A441

Army, 60th Anniv. A442

2009, Jan. 20

1771 A439 2000k multi .85 .85
1772 A440 2000k multi .85 .85
1773 A441 2000k multi .85 .85
1774 A442 2000k multi .85 .85
a. Souvenir sheet of 4, #1771-1774 4.00 4.00
Nos. 1771-1774 (4) 3.40 3.40

No, 1774a sold for 10,000k.

A443

A444

Opening of Laos-Thailand Rail Link — A445

2009, Mar. 5

1775 A443 3000k multi 1.10 1.10
1776 A444 3000k multi 1.10 1.10
1777 A445 3000k multi 1.10 1.10
a. Souvenir sheet of 3, #1775-1777 5.50 5.50
Nos. 1775-1777 (3) 3.30 3.30

No. 1777a sold for 15,000k.

China 2009 World Stamp Exhibition A446

Color of flower: No. 1778, 7500k, White. No. 1779, 7500k, Red.

2009, Mar. 20

1778-1779 A446 Set of 2 5.75 5.75
1779a Souvenir sheet of 2, #1778-1779 8.00 8.00

No. 1779a sold for 20,000k.

Flowers A447

Designs: 500k, Mari flower. 2000k, Ixora. 4000k, White Vuddish flowers (Calotropis gigantea). 7500k, Lilac Vuddish flowers (Calotropis gigantea).

2009, May 15

1780-1783 A447 Set of 4 4.75 4.75
1783a Souvenir sheet of 4, #1780-1783 5.25 5.25

No. 1783a sold for 15,000k.

Rice Alcohol — A448

Designs: 1000k, Pots with sticks. 2000k, Horn and pot. 5500k, Man and pot.

2009, Aug. 11

1784-1786 A448 Set of 3 3.75 3.75

A souvenir sheet containing Nos. 1784-1786 sold for 18,000k.

Postmarks A449

No. 1787 — Postmark of: a, R. P. Vientiane. b, Centre de Tri. c, Phongsaly. d, Luangnamtha. e, Oudomxay. f, Bokeo. g, Luangpabang. h, Huaphan. i, Sayaboury. j, Xiengkhouang. k, Vientiane. l, Bolikhamxay. m, Khammouane. n, Savannakhet. o, Saravan. p, Sekong. q, Champasack. r, Attapeu.

2009, Oct. 9 *Perf. 13½*

1787 Sheet of 18 12.50 12.50
a.-r. A449 2000r Any single .65 .65

25th South East Asian Games, Vientiane — A450

Mascots and: 5000k, Red background. 7000k, Flag, blue background.

2009, Nov. 16 *Perf. 14½x14*

1788-1789 A450 Set of 2 4.50 4.50
1789a Souvenir sheet of 2, #1788-1789 5.50 5.50

No. 1789a sold for 15,000k.

Wat Simuong A451

Designs: 4000k, Statue. 5000k, Stone temple. 6000k, Temple.

2009, Dec. 7 *Perf. 13*

1790-1792 A451 Set of 3 5.75 5.75
1792a Souvenir sheet of 3, #1790-1792 7.25 7.25

No. 1792a sold for 18,000k.

Flora A452

Designs: 1000k, Litsea cubeba. 3000k, Orthosiphon stamineus, vert. 4000k, Strychnos nux-vomica, vert. 5000k, Zingiber sp. 8000k, Styrax tonkinensis, vert. 9000k, Aquilaria crassna, vert.

2010 **Litho.**

1793-1798 A452 Set of 6 21.00 21.00

SEMI-POSTAL STAMPS

Laotian Children — SP1

Unwmk.

1953, July 14 **Engr.** *Perf. 13*

B1 SP1 1.50pi + 1pi multi 2.25 1.75
B2 SP1 3pi + 1.50pi multi 2.25 1.75
B3 SP1 3.90pi + 2.50pi multi 2.25 1.75
Nos. B1-B3 (3) 6.75 5.25

The surtax was for the Red Cross.

Nos. 52 and 46 Surcharged: "1k ANNEE MONDIALE DU REFUGIE 1959-1960"

1960, Apr. 7

B4 A16 4k + 1k rose claret 1.25 1.25
B5 A13 10k + 1k multicolored 1.25 1.25

World Refugee Year, July 1, 1959-June 30, 1960. The surcharge was for aid to refugees.

Flooded Village SP2

40k+10k, Flooded market place and truck. 60k+15k, Flooded airport and plane.

1967, Jan. 18 **Engr.** *Perf. 13*

B6 SP2 20k + 5k multi .50 .25
B7 SP2 40k + 10k multi .50 .25
B8 SP2 60k + 15k multi 1.25 1.00
a. Miniature sheet of 3 3.00 3.00
Nos. B6-B8 (3) 2.25 1.50

The surtax was for victims of the Mekong Delta flood. No. B8a contains one each of Nos. B6-B8. Size: 148x99mm. Sold for 250k.

Women Working in Tobacco Field — SP3

1967, Oct. 5 **Engr.** *Perf. 13*

B9 SP3 20k + 5k multi .50 .50
B10 SP3 50k + 10k multi .75 .75
B11 SP3 60k + 15k multi 1.00 1.00
a. Souv. sheet of 3, #B9-B11 3.00 3.00
Nos. B9-B11 (3) 2.25 2.25

Laotian Red Cross, 10th anniv. No. B11a sold for 250k+30k.

Nos. 184-189 Surcharged: "Soutien aux Victimes / de la Guerre / + 5k"

1970, May 1 **Photo.** *Perf. 14*

B12 A58 10k + 5k multi .50 .25
B13 A58 15k + 5k multi .50 .25
B14 A58 20k + 5k multi .50 .25
B15 A58 30k + 5k multi .50 .25
B16 A58 40k + 5k multi .75 .50
B17 A58 60k + 5k multi 1.00 .50
Nos. B12-B17,CB1-CB2 (8) 9.75 6.50

AIR POST STAMPS

Weaving — AP1

Design: 3.30pi, Wat Pra Keo.

Unwmk.

1952, Apr. 13 Engr. *Perf. 13*

C1 AP1 3.30pi dk pur & pur 1.10 .75
C2 AP1 10pi ultra & bl grn 2.25 1.50
C3 AP1 20pi deep cl & red 4.00 2.75
C4 AP1 30pi blk brn & dk brn violet 4.50 3.75
Nos. C1-C4 (4) 11.85 8.75

See note following No. 17.

UPU Monument and King Sisavang-Vong — AP2

1952, Dec. 7

C5 AP2 25pi vio bl & indigo 4.25 4.25
C6 AP2 50pi dk brn & vio brn 5.50 5.50

Laos' admission to the UPU, May 13, 1952.

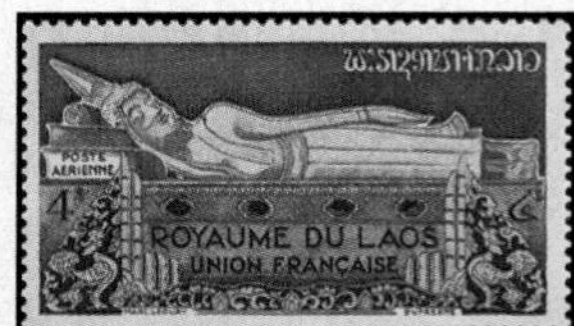

AP3

AP4

Designs: Various Buddha statues.

1953, Nov. 18

C7 AP3 4pi dark green 1.25 .60
C8 AP4 6.50pi dk bl green 1.25 .60
C9 AP4 9pi blue green 1.75 .90
C10 AP3 11.50pi red, yel & dk vio brn 2.75 1.25
C11 AP4 40pi purple 4.50 1.75
C12 AP4 100pi olive 8.00 4.50
Nos. C7-C12 (6) 19.50 9.60

Great Oath of Laos ceremony.

Accession Type of Regular Issue

1954, Mar. 4 Unwmk.

C13 A6 50pi indigo & bl grn 185.00 185.00
Hinged 100.00

Ravana — AP6

Sita and Rama — AP7

Scenes from the Ramayana: 4k, Hanuman, the white monkey. 5k, Ninh Laphath, the black monkey. 20k, Lucy with a friend of Ravana. 30k, Rama.

1955, Oct. 28 Engr. *Perf. 13*

C14 AP6 2k bl grn, emer & ind 1.00 .50
C15 AP6 4k red brn, dk red brn & ver 1.50 1.00
C16 AP6 5k scar, sep & olive 2.50 1.50
C17 AP7 10k blk, org & brn 5.00 1.75
C18 AP7 20k vio, dk grn & olive 6.00 2.50
C19 AP7 30k ultra, blk & salmon 8.00 4.00
Nos. C14-C19 (6) 24.00 11.25

See No. 225.

Buddha Type of Regular Issue, 1956

1956, May 24

C20 A7 20k carmine rose 30.00 23.50
C21 A7 30k olive & olive bister 30.00 27.50

2500th anniversary of birth of Buddha.

UN Emblem AP8

1956, Dec. 14

C22 AP8 15k light blue 4.50 4.50
C23 AP8 30k deep claret 6.50 6.50

Admission of Laos to the UN, 1st anniv.

Types of Regular Issue, 1957

Musical Instruments: 12k, Khong vong. 14k, So. 20k, Kong.

1957, Mar. 25 Unwmk. *Perf. 13*

C24 A9 12k multicolored 2.75 1.75
C25 A10 14k multicolored 3.00 2.25
C26 A10 20k bl grn, yel grn & pur 3.50 3.00
Nos. C24-C26 (3) 9.25 7.00

Monk Receiving Alms — AP9

Monks Meditating in Boat — AP10

18k, Smiling Buddha. 24k, Ancient temple painting (horse and mythological figures.)

1957, Nov. 5

C27 AP9 10k dk pur, pale brn & dk grn 1.25 1.25
C28 AP10 15k dk vio brn, brn org & yel 1.25 1.25
C29 AP9 18k slate grn & ol 1.50 1.50
C30 AP10 24k claret, org yel & blk 3.25 3.25
Nos. C27-C30 (4) 7.25 7.25

No. C28 measures 48x27mm. No. C30, 48x36mm. See No. C84.

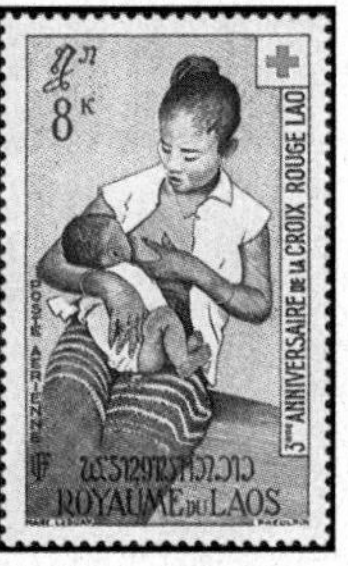

Mother Nursing Infant — AP11

1958, May 2

Cross in Red

C31 AP11 8k lil gray & dk gray 1.50 .75
C32 AP11 12k red brn & brn 1.75 1.00
C33 AP11 15k sl grn & bluish green 2.00 1.00
C34 AP11 20k bister & vio 2.50 1.50
Nos. C31-C34 (4) 7.75 4.25

3rd anniversary of Laotian Red Cross.

Plain of Stones, Xieng Khouang AP12

Papheng Falls, Champassak — AP13

Natl. Tourism Industry: 15k, Buffalo cart. 19k, Buddhist monk and village.

1960, July 1 Engr. *Perf. 13*

C35 AP12 9.50k bl, ol & claret .50 .50
C36 AP13 12k vio bl, red brn & gray .50 .50
C37 AP13 15k yel grn, ol gray & cl .75 .75
C38 AP12 19k multicolored 1.00 1.00
Nos. C35-C38 (4) 2.75 2.75

Pou Gneu Nha Gneu Legend — AP14

Garuda — AP15

Hanuman, the White Monkey — AP16

Nang Teng One Legend AP17

1962, Feb. 19 Unwmk. *Perf. 13*

C39 AP14 11k grn, car & ocher .60 .60
C40 AP15 14k ultra & org .60 .60
C41 AP16 20k multicolored .80 .80
C42 AP17 25k multicolored .90 .90
Nos. C39-C42 (4) 2.90 2.90

Makha Bousa festival.

Yao Hunter — AP18

Phayre's Flying Squirrel — AP19

1964, Dec. 15 Engr. *Perf. 13*

C43 AP18 5k shown .55 .25
C44 AP18 10k Kha hunter .55 .35
C45 AP18 50k Meo woman 1.60 1.00
a. Min. sheet of 4, #100, C43-C45 7.50 6.50
Nos. C43-C45 (3) 2.70 1.60

No. C45a exists imperf.

Butterfly Type of 1965

1965, Mar. 13
Size: 48x27mm

C46 A34 20k Atlas moth 6.00 2.50

1965, Oct. 7 Engr. *Perf. 13*

Designs: 25k, Leopard cat. 75k, Javan mongoose. 100k, Crestless porcupine. 200k, Binturong.

C47 AP19 25k dk brn, yel grn & ocher .50 .20
C48 AP19 55k brown & blue .75 .35
C49 AP19 75k brt grn & brn 1.00 .50
C50 AP19 100k ocher, brn & blk 1.75 1.10
C51 AP19 200k red & black 3.50 2.50
Nos. C47-C51 (5) 7.50 4.65

Army Type of Regular Issue

Design: 200k, 300k, Parading service flags before National Assembly Hall.

1968, July 15 Engr. *Perf. 13*

C52 A53 200k multicolored 1.60 .85
C53 A53 300k multicolored 2.50 1.25
a. Souv. sheet of 5, #168-170, C52-C53 5.00 5.00

No. C53a sold for 600k.

Insect Type of Regular Issue

Insects: 120k, Dorysthenes walkeri, horiz. 160k, Megaloxantha bicolor, horiz.

1968, Aug. 28 Engr. *Perf. 13*

C54 A54 120k brn, org & blk 1.50 .85
C55 A54 160k rose car, Prus bl & yel 2.25 1.25

Ballet Type of Regular Issue

Designs: 110k, Sudagnu battling Thotsakan. 300k, Pharam dancing with Thotsakan.

1969 Photo. *Perf. 14*

C56 A58 110k multicolored 2.75 1.75
a. Souv. sheet of 4, #187-189, C56, imperf. 20.00 20.00
C57 A58 300k multicolored 5.50 3.25
a. Souv. sheet of 4, #184-186, C57, imperf. 20.00 20.00

No. C56a sold for 480k; No. C57a for 650k.
For surcharges see Nos. CB1-CB2.

Timber Industry, Paksane
AP20

1969, May 7 Engr. *Perf. 13*

C58 AP20 300k olive bister & blk 4.75 3.25

ILO, 50th anniversary.

Animal Type of Regular Issue

Animals: 70k, Asiatic black bear. 120k, White-handed gibbon, vert. 150k, Tiger.

1969, Nov. 6 Photo. *Perf. 12x13*

C59 A60 70k multicolored 1.10 .60
C60 A60 120k multicolored 2.00 1.10
C61 A60 150k multicolored 2.75 1.40
Nos. C59-C61 (3) 5.85 3.10

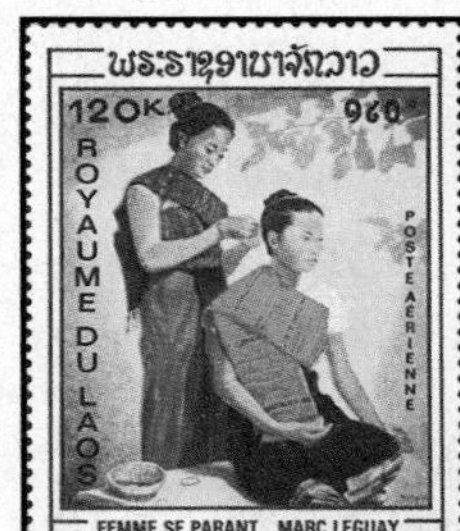

Hairdressing, by Marc Leguay — AP21

Paintings: No. C63, Village Market, by Marc Leguay, horiz. No. C64, Tree on the Bank of the Mekong, by Marc Leguay, horiz.

1969-70 Photo. *Perf. 12x13, 13x12*

C62 AP21 120k multicolored 1.00 .40
C63 AP21 150k multicolored 2.00 .65
C64 AP21 150k multi ('70) 2.00 .65
Nos. C62-C64 (3) 5.00 1.70

See Nos. C72-C74.

Wat Xiengthong, Luang Prabang — AP22

1970, Jan. 10 *Perf. 12x13, 13x12*

C65 AP22 100k Library, Wat Sisaket, vert. 1.40 .65
C66 AP22 120k shown 2.00 1.00

Drum Type of 1970

1970, Mar. 30 Engr. *Perf. 13*

C67 A64 125k Pong wooden drum, vert. 3.00 1.50

Franklin D. Roosevelt (1882-1945) — AP23

1970, Apr. 12

C68 AP23 120k olive & slate 1.60 1.10

EXPO '70 Type of Regular Issue

Design: 125k, Woman boiling cocoons in kettle, and spinning silk thread.

1970, July 7 Engr. *Perf. 13*

C69 A66 125k olive & multi 1.40 1.25

See note after No. 202.

Animal Type of Regular Issue

1970, Sept. 7 Engr. *Perf. 13*

C70 A67 210k Leopard 2.00 1.25
C71 A67 500k Gaur 4.00 2.50

Painting Type of 1969-70

Paintings by Marc Leguay: 100k, Village Foot Path. 120k, Rice Field in Rainy Season, horiz. 150k, Village Elder.

Perf. 11½x13, 13x11½
1970, Dec. 21 Photo.

C72 AP21 100k multicolored 1.10 1.10
C73 AP21 120k multicolored 1.40 1.40
C74 AP21 150k multicolored 1.60 1.60
Nos. C72-C74 (3) 4.10 4.10

UN Type of Regular Issue

125k, Earth Goddess Nang Thorani wringing her hair; UN Headquarters and emblem.

1970, Oct. 24
Size: 26x36mm

C75 A68 125k brt bl, pink & dk grn 1.75 1.10

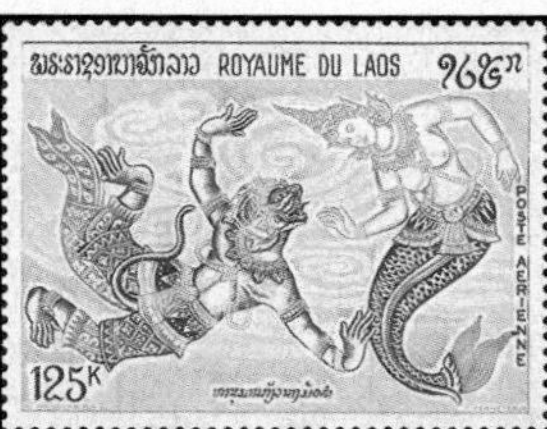

Hanuman and Nang Matsa — AP24

1971, Feb. 5

C76 AP24 125k multicolored 2.25 1.00

Orchid Type of Regular Issue

Design: 125k, Brasilian cattleya.

1971, July Photo. *Perf. 13x12½*
Size: 48x27mm

C79 A73 125k Brasilian cattleya 3.50 1.50

Laotian and French Women, That Luang Pagoda and Arms
AP25

1971, Aug. 6 Engr. *Perf. 13*

C80 AP25 30k brn & dull red .25 .20
C81 AP25 70k vio & lilac .50 .40
C82 AP25 100k slate grn & grn .70 .55
Nos. C80-C82 (3) 1.45 1.15

Kinship between the cities Keng Kok, Laos, and Saint Astier, France.

Animal Type of Regular Issue

1971, Sept. 16

C83 A74 300k Javan rhinoceros 4.25 2.75

Type of 1957 with Ornamental Panel and Inscription

Design: Monk receiving alms (like No. C27).

1971, Nov. 2 Engr. *Perf. 13*

C84 AP9 125k dk pur, pale brn & dk grn 1.40 1.40

20th anniv. of Laotian independent postal service. No. C84 inscribed: "Vingtième Anniversaire de la Philatélie Lao," "Poste Aerienne" and "1971."

Sunset Over the Mekong, by Chamnane Prisayane — AP26

Design: 150k, "Quiet Morning" (village scene), by Chamnane Prisayane.

1971, Dec. 20 Photo. *Perf. 13x12*

C85 AP26 125k black & multi 1.00 1.00
C86 AP26 150k black & multi 1.25 1.25

Book Year Type of Regular Issue

Design: 125k, Father teaching children to read palm leaf book.

1972, Jan. 30 Engr. *Perf. 13*
Size: 48x27mm

C87 A75 125k bright purple 1.00 1.00

Dam Type of Regular Issue

Design: 145k, Nam Ngum Hydroelectric Dam and ECAFE emblem.

1972, Mar. 28 Engr. *Perf. 13*

C88 A76 145k brown, bl & grn .80 .80

Orchid Type of Regular Issue

1972, May 1 Photo. *Perf. 13x12½*
Size: 48x27mm

C89 A73 150k Vanda teres, horiz. 4.00 1.50

UNICEF Type of Regular Issue

Design: 120k, Boy riding buffalo to water hole (child's drawing).

1972, July Engr. *Perf. 13*

C90 A77 120k multicolored 1.00 1.00

Nakharath, Daughter of the Dragon King
AP27

Wood carvings from Wat Sikhounvieng Dongmieng, Vientiane: 120k, Nang Kinnali, Goddess from Mt. Kailath. 150k, Norasing, Lion King from Himalayas.

1972, Sept. 15 Engr. *Perf. 13*

C91 AP27 100k blue green .70 .70
C92 AP27 120k violet .80 .80
C93 AP27 150k brn orange 1.10 1.10
Nos. C91-C93 (3) 2.60 2.60

That Luang Religious Festival — AP28

1972, Nov. 18 Engr. *Perf. 13*

C94 AP28 110k Presentation of wax castles .90 .90
C95 AP28 125k Procession 1.10 1.10

Workers in Rice Field, by Leguay
AP29

Paintings by Mark Leguay: No. C97, Women and water buffalo in rice field. Nos. C98, Rainy Season in Village (Water buffalo in water). No. C99, Rainy Season in Village (Water buffalo on land). 120k, Mother and Child.

1972, Dec. 23 Photo. *Perf. 13*

C96 AP29 50k multicolored .45 .45
C97 AP29 50k multicolored .45 .45
C98 AP29 70k multicolored .65 .65
C99 AP29 70k multicolored .65 .65
C100 AP29 120k yel & multi 1.25 1.25
Nos. C96-C100 (5) 3.45 3.45

Nos. C97, C99 have denomination and frame at right.

Costume Type of Regular Issue

Women's Costumes: 120k, Luang Prabang marriage costume. 150k, Vientiane evening costume.

1973, Feb. 16 Engr. *Perf. 13*

C101 A78 120k multicolored .80 .80
C102 A78 150k brown & multi 1.00 1.00

Lions Club Emblems, King Sayasettha-Thirath — AP30

1973, Mar. 30 Engr. *Perf. 13*

C103 AP30 150k rose & multi 1.25 .75

Lions Club of Vientiane.

Rahu with Rockets and Sputnik — AP31

Space achievements: 150k, Laotian festival rocket and US lunar excursion module.

1973, May 11 Engr. *Perf. 13*

C104 AP31 80k ultra & multi .55 .35
C105 AP31 150k buff & ultra 1.00 .45

Dancing Around Campfire — AP32

Design: 125k, Boy Scouts helping during Vientiane Flood, 1966.

1973, Sept. 1 Engr. *Perf. 13*

C106 AP32 110k vio & orange .65 .30
C107 AP32 125k Prus grn & bis .90 .40

Laotian Scout Movement, 25th anniv.

Sun Chariot and WMO Emblem — AP33

Design: 90k, Nang Mékhala, the weather goddess, and WMO emblem, vert.

1973, Oct. 24 Engr. *Perf. 13*

C108 AP33 90k vio, red & ocher .75 .35
C109 AP33 150k ocher, red & brn ol .85 .50

Intl. meteorological cooperation, cent.

Woman in Poppy Field, INTERPOL Emblem — AP34

1973, Dec. 22 Engr. *Perf. 13*

C110 AP34 150k vio, yel grn & red 1.10 .60

Intl. Criminal Police Org., 50th anniv.

Phra Sratsvady, Wife of Phra Phrom AP35

Designs: 110k, Phra Indra on 3-headed elephant Erawan. 150k, Phra Phrom, the Creator, on phoenix. Designs show giant sculptures in park at Thadeua.

1974, Mar. 23 Engr. *Perf. 13*

C111 AP35 100k lilac, red & blk .80 .40
C112 AP35 110k car, vio & brn 1.00 .50
C113 AP35 150k ocher, vio & sepia 1.25 .70
Nos. C111-C113 (3) 3.05 1.60

UPU Emblem, Women Reading Letter — AP36

1974 Engr. *Perf. 13*

C114 AP36 200k lt brn & car 1.25 1.00
C115 AP36 500k lilac & red 3.75 2.00
a. Souvenir sheet 5.50 5.50

Centenary of Universal Postal Union. Issue dates: 200k, Apr. 30; 500k, Oct. 9.

Flower Type of 1974

1974, May 31

Size: 36x36mm

C116 A84 500k Pitcher plant 5.00 3.00

Transportation Type of Regular Issue

1974, July 31 Engr. *Perf. 13*

C117 A85 250k Sampan 2.50 1.50

Marconi Type of 1974

Old & new means of communications.

1974, Aug. 28 Engr. *Perf. 13*

C118 A86 200k vio bl & brn 2.25 1.10

Insect Type of 1974

1974, Oct. 23 Engr. *Perf. 13*

C119 A87 110k Sternocera multipunctata 1.75 1.00

Boeing 747 — AP37

1986, June 2 Litho. *Perf. 12½*

C120 AP37 20k shown 3.50
C121 AP37 50k IL86 8.00

AIR POST SEMI-POSTAL STAMPS

Nos. C56-C57 Surcharged: "Soutien aux Victimes / de la Guerre / + 5k"

1970, May 1 Photo. *Perf. 13*

CB1 A58 110k + 5k multi 2.00 1.50
CB2 A58 300k + 5k multi 4.00 3.00

The surtax was for war victims.

POSTAGE DUE STAMPS

Vat-Sisaket Monument D1

Boat and Raft D2

Perf. 13½x13

1952-53 Unwmk. Engr.

J1 D1 10c dark brown .25 .25
J2 D1 20c purple .25 .25
J3 D1 50c carmine .25 .25
J4 D1 1pi dark green .25 .25
J5 D1 2pi deep ultra .25 .25
J6 D1 5pi rose violet 1.00 1.00
J7 D2 10pi indigo ('53) 1.25 1.25
Nos. J1-J7 (7) 3.50 3.50

Serpent — D3

1973, Oct. 31 Photo. *Perf. 13*

J8 D3 10k yellow & multi .25 .25
J9 D3 15k emerald & multi .25 .25
J10 D3 20k blue & multi .25 .25
J11 D3 50k scarlet & multi .50 .50
Nos. J8-J11 (4) 1.25 1.25

PARCEL POST STAMPS

Wat Ong Theu PP1

2000, June 7 Litho. *Die Cut*

Self-Adhesive

Serial Number in Black

Q1 PP1 5000k orange *5.00 5.00*
Q2 PP1 40,000k milky blue *25.00 25.00*
Q3 PP1 60,000k gray blue *32.50 32.50*
Q4 PP1 80,000k cerise *50.00 50.00*
Q5 PP1 100,000k carmine *60.00 60.00*
Q6 PP1 250,000k ultra *150.00 150.00*
Nos. Q1-Q6 (6) 322.50 322.50

Phra That Luang — PP2

2003, Aug. 14 *Die Cut*

Self-Adhesive

Serial Number in Black

Q7 PP2 5000k vio bl & bl 3.00 3.00
Q8 PP2 40,000k claret & red 15.00 15.00
Q9 PP2 60,000k grn & claret 25.00 25.00
Q10 PP2 90,000k red & blue 35.00 35.00
Nos. Q7-Q10 (4) 78.00 78.00

LATAKIA

ˌla-tə-ˈkē-ə

LOCATION — A division of Syria in Western Asia
GOVT. — French Mandate
AREA — 2,500 sq. mi.
POP. — 278,000 (approx. 1930)
CAPITAL — Latakia

This territory, included in the Syrian Mandate to France under the Versailles Treaty, was formerly known as Alaouites. The name Latakia was adopted in 1930. See Alaouites and Syria.

100 Centimes = 1 Piaster

Stamps of Syria Overprinted in Black or Red

Perf. 12x12½, 13½

1931-33 Unwmk.

1 A6 10c red violet 1.25 .25
2 A6 10c vio brn ('33) 1.60 1.60
3 A7 20c dk blue (R) 1.25 1.25
4 A7 20c brown org ('33) 1.60 1.60
5 A8 25c gray grn (R) 1.25 1.25
6 A8 25c dk bl gray (R) ('33) 1.60 1.60
7 A9 50c violet 2.00 2.00
8 A15 75c org red ('32) 3.25 3.25
9 A10 1p green (R) 2.40 2.40
10 A11 1.50p bis brn (R) 3.25 3.25
11 A11 1.50p dp grn ('33) 4.00 4.00
12 A12 2p dk vio (R) 3.25 3.25
13 A13 3p yel grn (R) 5.25 5.25
14 A14 4p orange 5.25 5.25
15 A15 4.50p rose car 5.50 5.50
16 A16 6p grnsh blk (R) 5.50 5.50
17 A17 7.50p dl blue (R) 4.50 4.50
a. Inverted overprint 650.00
18 A18 10p dp brown (R) 9.50 9.50
a. Inverted overprint 650.00
19 A19 15p dp green (R) 10.00 10.00
20 A20 25p violet brn 20.00 20.00
21 A21 50p dk brown (R) 20.00 20.00
a. Inverted overprint 650.00
22 A22 100p red orange 47.50 47.50
Nos. 1-22 (22) 159.70 158.70

AIR POST STAMPS

Air Post Stamps of Syria, 1931, Overprinted in Black or Red

1931-33 Unwmk. *Perf. 13½*

C1 AP2 50c ocher 1.25 1.25
a. Inverted overprint 1,200. 1,200.
C2 AP2 50c blk brn (R) ('33) 2.40 2.40
C3 AP2 1p chestnut brn 2.40 2.40
C4 AP2 2p Prus blue (R) 3.50 3.50
C5 AP2 3p blue grn (R) 4.75 4.75
C6 AP2 5p red violet 6.50 6.50
C7 AP2 10p slate grn (R) 8.00 8.00
C8 AP2 15p orange red 11.00 11.00
C9 AP2 25p orange brn 22.50 22.50
C10 AP2 50p black (R) 36.00 36.00
C11 AP2 100p magenta 40.00 40.00
Nos. C1-C11 (11) 138.30 138.30

POSTAGE DUE STAMPS

Postage Due Stamps of Syria, 1931, Overprinted like Regular Issue

1931 Unwmk. *Perf. 13½*

J1 D7 8p blk, *gray bl* (R) 24.00 24.00
J2 D8 15p blk, *dl rose* (R) 24.00 24.00

Stamps of Latakia were superseded in 1937 by those of Syria.

LATVIA

'lat-vē-ə

(Lettonia, Lettland)

LOCATION — Northern Europe, bordering on the Baltic Sea and the Gulf of Riga
GOVT. — Independent Republic
AREA — 25,395 sq. mi.
POP. — 2,353,874 (1999 est.)
CAPITAL — Riga

Latvia was created a sovereign state following World War I and was admitted to the League of Nations in 1922. In 1940 it became a republic in the Union of Soviet Socialist Republics. Latvian independence was recognized by the Soviet Union on Sept. 6, 1991.

100 Kapeikas = 1 Rublis
100 Santims = 1 Lat (1923, 1993)
100 Kopecks = 1 Ruble (1991)

Catalogue values for unused stamps in this country are for Never Hinged items, beginning with Scott 300 in the regular postage section, Scott B150 in the semi-postal section, and Scott 2N45 in the Russian Occupation section.

Watermarks

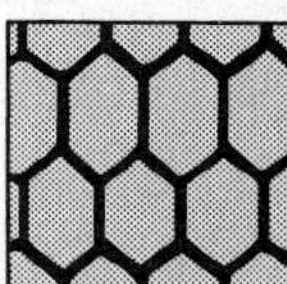

Wmk. 108 Honeycomb

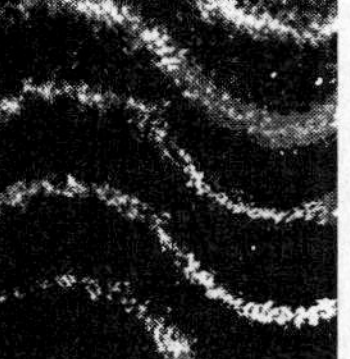

Wmk. 145 — Wavy Lines

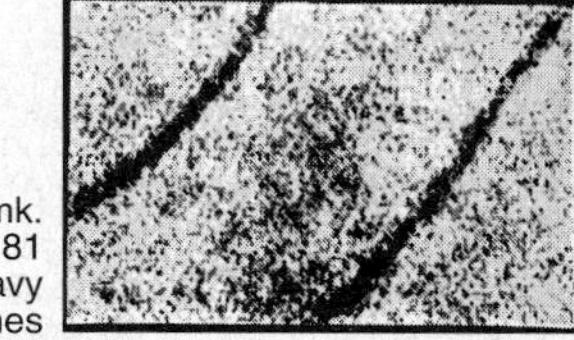

Wmk. 181 Wavy Lines

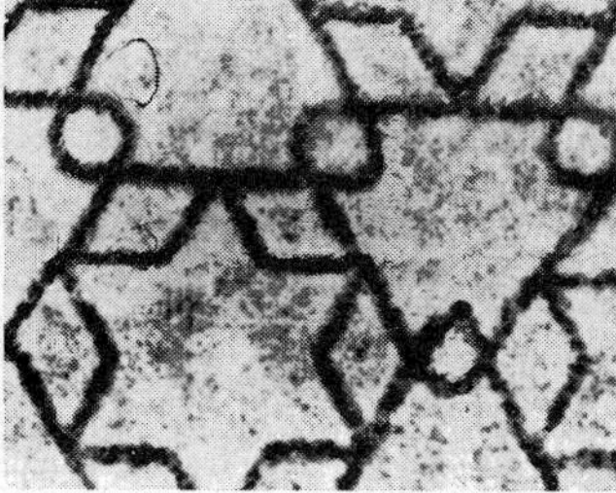

Wmk. 197 — Star and Triangles

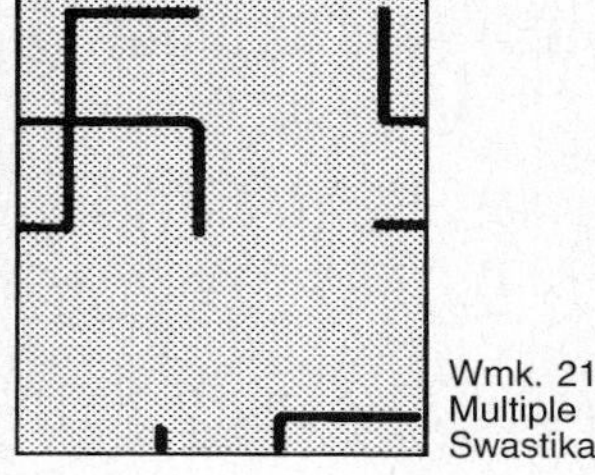

Wmk. 212 Multiple Swastikas

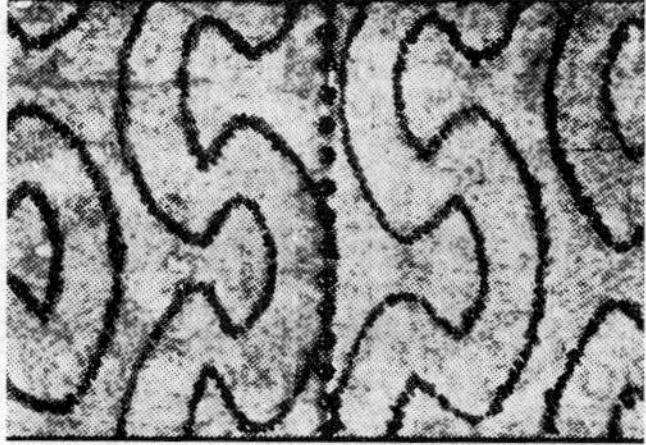

Wmk. 265 — Multiple Waves

Wmk. 387 — Squares and Rectangles

Arms — A1

Printed on the Backs of German Military Maps

Unwmk.

1918, Dec. 18 Litho. *Imperf.*

1 A1 5k carmine .30 .50

Perf. 11½

2 A1 5k carmine .30 .50

Values given are for stamps where the map on the back is printed in brown and black. Maps printed only in black are valued at: No. 1 unused $2.00; used $6; No. 2 unused $1.20, used $2.50. Stamps with no map at all valued: No. 1 unused $1.50, used $3.28; No. 2 unused $1.20, used $2.50. Stamps with no printing on the back are from the outer rows of some sheets.

Redrawn

Paper with Ruled Lines

1919 *Imperf.*

3 A1 5k carmine .20 .20
4 A1 10k dark blue .20 .20
5 A1 15k green .50 .50

Perf. 11½

6 A1 5k carmine 2.50 *4.00*
7 A1 10k dark blue 2.50 *4.00*
8 A1 15k deep green 7.75 *9.50*
Nos. 3-8 (6) 13.65 18.40

In the redrawn design the wheat heads are thicker, the ornament at lower left has five points instead of four, and there are minor changes in other parts of the design.

The sheets of this and subsequent issues were usually divided in half by a single line of perforation gauging 10. Thus stamps are found with this perforation on one side.

1919 Pelure Paper *Imperf.*

9 A1 3k lilac 5.00 4.50
10 A1 5k carmine .20 .20
11 A1 10k deep blue .20 .20
12 A1 15k dark green .20 .20
13 A1 20k orange .20 .20
13A A1 25k gray 40.00 40.00
14 A1 35k dark brown .20 .20
15 A1 50k purple .20 .20
16 A1 75k emerald 2.50 2.50
Nos. 9-16 (9) 48.70 48.20

Perf. 11½, 9½

17 A1 3k lilac 35.00 35.00
18 A1 5k carmine .80 .80
19 A1 10k deep blue 4.00 3.00
20 A1 15k dark green 3.00 3.00
21 A1 20k orange 3.75 3.75
22 A1 35k dark brown 4.50 4.50
23 A1 50k purple 6.00 6.00
24 A1 75k emerald 7.50 7.50
Nos. 17-24 (8) 64.55 63.55

Values are for perf 11½. Examples Perf 9½ sell for more.

Nos. 17-24 are said to be unofficially perforated varieties of Nos. 9-16.

1919 Wmk. 108 *Imperf.*

25 A1 3k lilac .30 .20
26 A1 5k carmine .30 .20
27 A1 10k deep blue .30 .20
28 A1 15k deep green .35 .20
29 A1 20k orange .40 .25
30 A1 25k gray .85 .50
31 A1 35k dark brown .45 .25
32 A1 50k purple .45 .25
33 A1 75k emerald .55 .25
Nos. 25-33 (9) 3.95 2.30

The variety "printed on both sides" exists for 3k, 10k, 15k, 20k and 35k. Value, $20 each.

See #57-58, 76-82. For surcharges and overprints see #86, 132-133, 2N1-2N8, 2N12-2N19.

Liberation of Riga — A2

Rising Sun — A4

1919 Wmk. 108

43 A2 5k carmine .25 .25
44 A2 15k deep green .25 .25
45 A2 35k brown .35 *.80*
Nos. 43-45 (3) .85 1.30

Unwmk.

Pelure Paper

49 A2 5k carmine 9.50 *15.00*
50 A2 15k deep green 9.50 *15.00*
51 A2 35k brown 20.00 15.00
Nos. 49-51 (3) 39.00 45.00

For surcharge and overprints see Nos. 87, 2N9-2N11, 2N20-2N22.

1919 *Imperf.*

55 A4 10k gray blue .85 .60

Perf. 11½

56 A4 10k gray blue 1.00 1.50

Type of 1918

1919 Laid Paper *Perf. 11½*

57 A1 3r slate & org 1.00 1.00
58 A1 5r gray brn & org 1.00 1.00

Independence Issue

Allegory of One Year of Independence A5

1919, Nov. 18 Unwmk.

Wove Paper

Size: 33x45mm

59 A5 10k brown & rose 1.25 1.00

Laid Paper

60 A5 10k brown & rose 1.25 1.00

Size: 28x38mm

61 A5 10k brown & rose .30 .30
a. Imperf. 50.00
62 A5 35k indigo & grn .30 .30
a. Vert. pair, imperf. btwn. 50.00 45.00

Wmk. 197

Thick Wove Paper

Blue Design on Back

63 A5 1r green & red .40 .40
Nos. 59-63 (5) 3.50 3.00

There are two types of Nos. 59 and 60. In type I the trunk of the tree is not outlined. In type II it has a distinct white outline.

No. 63 was printed on the backs of unfinished 5r bank notes of the Workers and Soldiers Council, Riga.

For surcharges see Nos. 83-85, 88, 94.

Warrior Slaying Dragon — A6

1919-20 Unwmk. *Perf. 11½*

Wove Paper

64 A6 10k brown & car .50 .50
a. Horiz. pair, imperf. btwn. 55.00 45.00
65 A6 25k ind & yel grn .50 .50
a. Pair, imperf. btwn. 55.00 45.00
66 A6 35k black & bl ('20) .50 .50
a. Horiz. pair, imperf. btwn. 55.00 45.00
67 A6 1r dk grn & brn ('20) .50 .50
a. Horiz. pair, imperf. vert. 50.00 40.00
b. Horiz. pair, imperf. btwn. 50.00 40.00
Nos. 64-67 (4) 2.00 2.00
Set, never hinged 5.75

Issued in honor of the liberation of Kurzeme (Kurland). The paper sometimes shows impressed quadrille lines.

For surcharges see Nos. 91-93.

Latgale Relief Issue

Latvia Welcoming Home Latgale Province — A7

1920, Mar.

Brown and Green Design on Back

68 A7 50k dk green & rose 1.00 .50
a. Horiz. pair, imperf. vert. 50.00
69 A7 1r slate grn & brn .50 .50
a. Horiz. pair, imperf. vert. 50.00
Set, never hinged 10.00

No. 68-69 were printed on the backs of unfinished bank notes of the government of Colonel Bermondt-Avalov and on the so-called German "Ober-Ost" money.

For surcharges see Nos. 95-99.

First National Assembly Issue

Latvia Hears Call to Assemble — A8

1920

70 A8 50k rose .50 .30
a. Imperf., pair 5.00 5.00
71 A8 1r blue .50 .30
a. Vert. pair, imperf. btwn. 45.00 45.00
b. Imperf., pair 20.00 15.00
72 A8 3r dk brn & grn .50 *.75*
73 A8 5r slate & vio brn .80 .80
Nos. 70-73 (4) 2.30 2.15
Set, never hinged 10.00

For surcharges see Nos. 90, 134.

Type of 1918 Issue

Wove Paper

1920-21 Unwmk. *Perf. 11½*

76 A1 5k carmine .20 .20
78 A1 20k orange .20 .20
79 A1 40k lilac ('21) .30 .20
80 A1 50k violet .35 .20
81 A1 75k emerald .35 .20
82 A1 5r gray brn & org ('21) 2.00 1.00
Nos. 76-82 (6) 3.40 2.00
Set, never hinged 8.00

No. 63 Surcharged in Black, Brown or Blue

1920, Sept. 1

83 A5 10r on 1r grn & red (Bk) 1.50 1.50
84 A5 20r on 1r grn & red (Br) 3.50 3.00
85 A5 30r on 1r grn & red (Bl) 5.00 5.00
Nos. 83-85 (3) 10.00 9.50
Set, never hinged 20.00

Types of 1919 Surcharged

1920-21 Wmk. 108 *Perf. 11½*

86 A1 2r on 10k dp blue 1.75 *4.00*
87 A2 2r on 35k brown .50 *3.75*
Set, never hinged 5.00

No. 62 Surcharged in Red

Unwmk.

88 A5 2r on 35k ind & grn .35 .50
Never hinged .75

No. 70 Surcharged in Blue

1921

90 A8 2r on 50k rose .50 .60
Never hinged 1.00

Nos. 64-66 Surcharged in Red or Blue

1920-21

91 A6 1r on 35k blk & bl (R) .30 .35
92 A6 2r on 10k brn & rose (Bl) .60 .75
93 A6 2r on 25k ind & grn (R) .35 .40
a. Imperf. —
Nos. 91-93 (3) 1.25 1.50
Set, never hinged 2.50

On Nos. 92 and 93 the surcharge reads "DIVI 2 RUBLI."

No. 83 with Added Surcharge

1921 Wmk. 197

94 A5 10r on 10r on 1r 1.25 1.00
Never hinged 5.00

Latgale Relief Issue of 1920 Surcharged in Black or Blue

1921, May 31 Unwmk.

95 A7 10r on 50k 1.25 1.25
a. Imperf. —
96 A7 20r on 50k 3.50 3.50
97 A7 30r on 50k 5.00 3.50
98 A7 50r on 50k 7.50 5.50
99 A7 100r on 50k (Bl) 17.50 15.00
Nos. 95-99 (5) 34.75 28.75
Set, never hinged 60.00

Excellent counterfeits exist.

Arms and Stars for Vidzeme, Kurzeme & Latgale — A10

Coat of Arms — A11

Type I, slanting cipher in value.
Type II, upright cipher in value.

Perf. 10, 11½ and Compound
Wmk. Similar to 181

1921-22 Typo.

101 A10 50k violet (II) .50 .30
102 A10 1r orange yel .50 .30
103 A10 2r deep green .20 .20
104 A10 3r brt green .65 .45
105 A10 5r rose 1.40 .40
106 A10 6r dp claret 2.10 .75
107 A10 9r orange 1.25 .50
108 A10 10r blue (I) 1.25 .20
109 A10 15r ultra 3.25 .60
a. Printed on both sides *50.00*
110 A10 20r dull lilac (II) 20.00 2.00

1922, Aug. 21 *Perf. 11½*

111 A11 50r dk brn & pale brn (I) 30.00 4.50
112 A11 100r dk bl & pale bl (I) 35.00 5.00
Nos. 101-112 (12) 96.10 15.20
Set, never hinged 200.00

#101-131 sometimes show letters of a paper maker's watermark "PACTIEN LIGAT MILLS."

See Nos. 126-131, 152-154.

A12

2 SANTIMS
Type A, tail of "2" ends in an upstroke.
Type B, tail of "2" is nearly horizontal.

1923-25 *Perf. 10, 11, 11½*

113 A12 1s violet .40 .20
114 A12 2s org yel (A) .60 .30
115 A12 4s dark green .60 .20
a. Horiz. pair, imperf. btwn. 55.00 50.00
116 A12 5s lt green ('25) 2.50 .60
117 A12 6s grn, *yel* ('25) 3.50 .25
118 A12 10s rose red (I) 1.50 .25
a. Horiz. pair, imperf. btwn. 55.00 50.00
119 A12 12s claret .25 .25
120 A12 15s brn, *sal* 3.50 .20
a. Horiz. pair, imperf. btwn. 55.00 50.00
121 A12 20s dp blue (II) 1.50 .20
122 A12 25s ultra ('25) .50 .20
123 A12 30s pink (I) ('25) 5.00 .25
124 A12 40s lilac (I) 2.00 .25
125 A12 50s lil gray (II) 3.75 .30
126 A11 1 l dk brn & pale brn 12.50 1.00
127 A11 2 l dk blue & blue 20.00 1.50
130 A11 5 l dp grn & pale grn 60.00 5.00
131 A11 10 l car rose & pale rose (I) 3.00 6.00
Nos. 113-131 (17) 121.10 16.95
Set, never hinged 250.00

Value in "Santims" (1s); "Santimi" (2s-6s) or "Santimu" (others).

See note after No. 110.

See Nos. 135-151, 155-157. For overprints and surcharges see Nos. 164-167, B21-B23.

Nos. 79-80 Surcharged

No. 72 Surcharged

1927 Unwmk. *Perf. 11½*

132 A1 15s on 40k lilac .30 .30
133 A1 15s on 50k violet 1.00 1.00
134 A8 1 l on 3r brn & grn 12.00 5.00
Nos. 132-134 (3) 13.30 6.30
Set, never hinged 27.50

Types of 1923-25 Issue

1927-33 Wmk. 212 *Perf. 10, 11½*

135 A12 1s dull violet .25 .20
136 A12 2s org yel (A) .40 .20
137 A12 2s org yel (B) ('33) .30 .20
138 A12 3s org red ('31) .20 .20
139 A12 4s dk green ('29) 4.75 2.00
140 A12 5s lt green ('31) .60 .20
141 A12 6s grn, *yel* .20 .20
142 A12 7s dk green ('31) .60 .20
143 A12 10s red (I) 2.75 .70
144 A12 10s grn, *yel* (I) ('32) 12.00 .20
145 A12 15s brn, *sal* 3.50 .45
146 A12 20s pink (I) 5.00 .20
147 A12 20s pink (II) 6.00 .20
148 A12 30s lt blue (I) 1.50 .20
149 A12 35s dk blue ('31) 1.50 .20
150 A12 40s dl lil (I) ('29) 2.50 .20
151 A12 50s gray (II) 2.75 .45
152 A11 1 l dk brn & pale brn 8.00 .30
153 A11 2 l dk bl & bl ('31) 32.50 2.25
154 A11 5 l grn & pale grn ('33) 140.00 35.00
Nos. 135-154 (20) 225.30 43.75
Set, never hinged 400.00

The paper of Nos. 141, 144 and 145 is colored on the surface only.

See note above No. 113 for types A and B, and note above No. 101 for types I and II.

Type of 1927-33 Issue
Paper Colored Through

1931-33 *Perf. 10*

155 A12 6s grn, *yel* .20 .20
156 A12 10s grn, *yel* (I) ('33) 15.00 .20
157 A12 15s brn, *salmon* 3.00 .20
Nos. 155-157 (3) 18.20 .60
Set, never hinged 37.50

View of Rezekne — A13

Designs (Views of Cities): 15s, Jelgava. 20s, Cesis (Wenden). 30s, Liepaja (Libau). 50s, Riga. 1 l, Riga Theater.

1928, Nov. 18 Litho. *Perf. 10, 11½*

158 A13 6s dp grn & vio 1.00 .40
159 A13 15s dk brn & ol grn 1.00 .40
160 A13 20s cerise & bl grn 1.25 .45
161 A13 30s ultra & vio brn 1.50 .40
162 A13 50s dk gray & plum 1.50 1.00
163 A13 1 l blk brn & brn 3.75 1.75
Nos. 158-163 (6) 10.00 4.40
Set, never hinged 20.00

10th anniv. of Latvian Independence.

Riga Exhibition Issue

Stamps of 1927-33 Overprinted

1932, Aug. 30 *Perf. 10, 11*

164 A12 3s orange 1.00 .50
165 A12 10s green, *yel* 1.00 .50
166 A12 20s pink (I) 2.00 1.00
167 A12 35s dark blue 5.00 2.00
Nos. 164-167 (4) 9.00 4.00
Set, never hinged 30.00

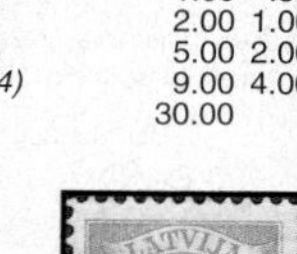

Riga Castle — A19

Arms and Shield — A20

Allegory of Latvia — A21

Ministry of Foreign Affairs — A22

1934, Dec. 15 Litho. *Perf. 10½, 10*

174 A19 3s red orange .25 .20
175 A20 5s yellow grn .25 .20
176 A20 10s gray grn 1.00 .20
177 A21 20s deep rose 1.00 .20
178 A22 35s dark blue .35 .20
179 A19 40s brown .35 .20
Nos. 174-179 (6) 3.20 1.20
Set, never hinged 6.00

Atis Kronvalds A23

A. Pumpurs A24

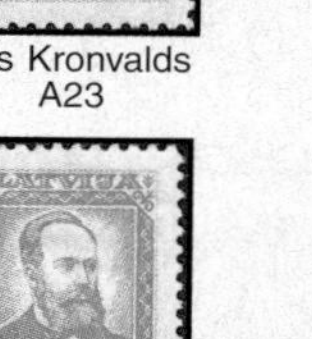

Juris Maters A25

Mikus Krogzemis (Auseklis) A26

1936, Jan. 4 Wmk. 212 *Perf. 11½*

180 A23 3s vermilion 3.50 *4.50*
181 A24 10s green 3.50 *4.50*
182 A25 20s rose pink 3.50 *6.00*
183 A26 35s dark blue 3.50 *6.00*
Nos. 180-183 (4) 14.00 21.00
Set, never hinged 50.00

President Karlis Ulmanis — A27

1937, Sept. 4 Litho. *Perf. 10, 11½*

No.	Type	Denom.	Color	Unused	Used
184	A27	3s	org red & brn org	.30	.25
185	A27	5s	yellow grn	.30	.25
186	A27	10s	dk sl grn	.75	.75
187	A27	20s	rose lake & brn lake	1.50	.75
188	A27	25s	black vio	2.50	1.25
189	A27	30s	dark blue	2.50	1.25
190	A27	35s	indigo	2.25	1.10
191	A27	40s	lt brown	2.25	1.25
192	A27	50s	olive blk	2.50	1.60
			Nos. 184-192 (9)	14.85	8.45
			Set, never hinged	30.00	

60th birthday of President Ulmanis.

Independence Monument, Rauna (Ronneburg) A28

Independence Monument, Jelgava — A30

Monument Entrance to Cemetery at Riga A29

War Memorial, Valka — A31

Independence Monument, Iecava — A32

Independence Monument, Riga — A33

Tomb of Col. Kalpaks — A34

Unwmk.

1937, July 12 Litho. *Perf. 10*

Thick Paper

No.	Type	Denom.	Color	Unused	Used
193	A28	3s	vermilion	.75	*.90*
194	A29	5s	yellow grn	.75	*.90*
195	A30	10s	deep grn	.75	*.90*
196	A31	20s	carmine	1.75	*1.10*
197	A32	30s	lt blue	2.25	2.25

Wmk. 212

Engr. *Perf. 11½*

Thin Paper

No.	Type	Denom.	Color	Unused	Used
198	A33	35s	dark blue	2.25	2.25
199	A34	40s	brown	3.50	3.25
			Nos. 193-199 (7)	12.00	11.55
			Set, never hinged	25.00	

View of Vidzeme — A35

General J. Balodis A37

President Karlis Ulmanis A38

Views: 5s, Latgale. 30s, Riga waterfront. 35s, Kurzeme. 40s, Zemgale.

1938, Nov. 17 *Perf. 10, 10½x10*

No.	Type	Denom.	Color	Unused	Used
200	A35	3s	brown org	.20	.20
a.			Booklet pane of 4	*40.00*	
201	A35	5s	yellow grn	.20	.20
a.			Booklet pane of 4	*40.00*	
202	A37	10s	dk green	.25	.20
a.			Booklet pane of 2	*40.00*	
203	A38	20s	red lilac	.20	.20
a.			Booklet pane of 2	*40.00*	
204	A35	30s	deep blue	1.20	.20
205	A35	35s	indigo	1.20	.20
a.			Booklet pane of 2	*40.00*	
206	A35	40s	rose violet	1.00	.25
			Nos. 200-206 (7)	4.25	1.45
			Set, never hinged	10.00	

The 20th anniversary of the Republic.

School, Riga — A42

Independence Monument, Riga — A45

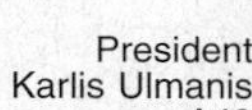

President Karlis Ulmanis A49

Designs: 5s, Castle of Jelgava. 10s, Riga Castle. 30s, Symbol of Freedom. 35s, Community House Daugavpils. 40s, Powder Tower and War Museum, Riga.

1939, May 13 Photo. *Perf. 10*

No.	Type	Denom.	Color	Unused	Used
207	A42	3s	brown orange	.25	.75
208	A42	5s	deep green	.50	.75
209	A42	10s	dk slate grn	.75	.75
210	A45	20s	dk car rose	1.50	1.25
211	A42	30s	brt ultra	1.00	.75
212	A42	35s	dark blue	1.50	1.75
213	A45	40s	brown violet	2.00	1.00
214	A49	50s	grnsh black	3.00	1.00
			Nos. 207-214 (8)	10.50	8.00
			Set, never hinged	20.00	

5th anniv. of National Unity Day.

Harvesting Wheat — A50

Apple — A51

1939, Oct. 8

No.	Type	Denom.	Color	Unused	Used
215	A50	10s	slate green	1.00	.60
216	A51	20s	rose lake	1.00	.65
			Set, never hinged	3.00	

8th Agricultural Exposition held near Riga.

Arms and Stars for Vidzeme, Kurzeme and Latgale — A52

1940

No.	Type	Denom.	Color	Unused	Used
217	A52	1s	dk vio brn	.25	.40
218	A52	2s	ocher	.35	.60
219	A52	3s	red orange	.20	.20
220	A52	5s	dk olive brn	.20	.20
221	A52	7s	dk green	.25	.40
222	A52	10s	dk blue grn	.75	.25
224	A52	20s	rose brown	.75	.25
225	A52	30s	dp red brn	1.00	.40
226	A52	35s	brt ultra	.20	.50
228	A52	50s	dk slate grn	1.50	.75
229	A52	1 l	olive green	3.00	2.25
			Nos. 217-229 (11)	8.45	6.20
			Set, never hinged	15.00	

Catalogue values for unused stamps in this section, from this point to the end of the section, are for Never Hinged items.

Natl. Arms — A70

1991, Oct. 19 Litho. *Perf. 13x12½*

No.	Type	Denom.	Color	Unused	Used
300	A70	5k	multicolored	*5.50*	*5.50*
301	A70	10k	multicolored	.40	.40
302	A70	15k	multicolored	.50	.50
303	A70	20k	multicolored	.65	.65
304	A70	40k	multicolored	1.40	1.40
305	A70	50k	multicolored	1.90	1.90

Size: 28x32mm

Perf. 13½x14

No.	Type	Denom.	Color	Unused	Used
306	A70	100k	silver & multi	3.00	3.00
307	A70	200k	gold & multi	5.50	5.50
			Nos. 300-307 (8)	18.85	18.85

Most issues, Nos. 300-342, have one blocked value that was not freely available at Latvian post offices.

Russia Nos. 5984, 5985a Ovptd. "LATVIJA" and Surcharged in Red Lilac, Orange, Green, Violet

1991, Dec. 23 Photo. *Perf. 12x11½*

No.	Type	Description	Unused	Used
308	A2765	100k on 7k (RL)	*.50*	.50
a.		Vert. pair, one without ovpt.	9.50	
b.		Litho., perf. 12x12½	*.50*	.50

Perf. 12x12½

Litho.

No.	Type	Description	Unused	Used
309	A2765	300k on 2k (O)	*.85*	.85
a.		Vert. pair, one without ovpt.	9.50	
310	A2765	500k on 2k (G)	*1.25*	1.25
a.		Vert. pair, one without ovpt.	9.50	
311	A2765	1000k on 2k (V)	*2.40*	2.40
a.		Vert. pair, one without ovpt.	9.50	
		Nos. 308-311 (4)	*5.00*	5.00

On Nos. 308-311 the sixth row of the sheet was not surcharged.

Forgeries exist.

Liberty Monument, Riga — A71

1991, Dec. 28 *Perf. 12½x13*

No.	Type	Denom.	Color	Unused	Used
312	A71	10k	ol brn & multi	.45	.45
313	A71	15k	violet & multi	*.85*	*.85*
314	A71	20k	bl grn & multi	.80	.80
315	A71	30k	ol grn & multi	1.00	1.00
316	A71	50k	choc & multi	1.60	1.60
317	A71	100k	dp blue & multi	2.25	1.25
			Nos. 312-317 (6)	6.95	5.95

A72

A73

Monuments — A74

1992, Feb. 29 *Perf. 14*

No.	Type	Denom.	Color	Unused	Used
318	A72	10k	black	.25	.20
319	A73	20k	violet black	.50	.20
320	A73	30k	brown	.70	.20
321	A72	30k	purple	.70	.20
322	A74	40k	violet blue	.95	.20
323	A74	50k	green	1.10	.20
324	A73	50k	olive green	1.10	.20
325	A74	100k	red brown	2.25	.60
326	A72	200k	blue	3.50	1.10
			Nos. 318-326 (9)	11.05	3.10

Russia Nos. 4599, 5984, 5985a Ovptd. "LATVIJA" and Surcharged in Red, Brown, Emerald and Violet

1992, Apr. 4 Photo. *Perf. 12x11½*

No.	Type	Description	Unused	Used
327	A2765	1r on 7k (R)	.20	.20

Perf. 12x12½

Litho.

No.	Type	Description	Unused	Used
328	A2765	3r on 2k (Br)	.40	.25
329	A2765	5r on 2k (E)	.65	.35
330	A2765	10r on 2k (V)	1.10	.75
331	A2138	25r on 4k	2.25	1.75
		Nos. 327-331 (5)	4.60	3.30

Surcharged denominations expressed in rubles (large numerals) and kopecks (small zeros).

Birds of the Baltic Shores — A75

Litho. & Engr.

1992, Oct. 3 *Perf. 12½x13*

Booklet Stamps

332 A75 5r Pandion haliaetus .30 .30
333 A75 5r Limosa limosa .30 .30
334 A75 5r Mergus merganser .30 .30
335 A75 5r Tadorna tadorna .30 .30
a. Booklet pane of 4, #332-335 2.25

See Estonia Nos. 231-234a, Lithuania Nos. 427-430a, and Sweden Nos. 1975-1978a.

Christmas A76

2r, 10r Angels with children around Christmas tree. 3r, Angels with musical instruments, Christmas tree. 15r, Nativity scene.

1992, Nov. 21 Litho. *Perf. 13½x13*

336 A76 2r silver & multi *1.00 1.00*
337 A76 3r multicolored *.30 .20*
338 A76 10r gold & multi *.85 .60*
339 A76 15r multicolored *1.10 1.00*
Nos. 336-339 (4) *3.25 2.80*

Russia Nos. 4728, 5107, 5109 Surcharged in Brown or Blue

Perfs. & Printing Methods as Before

1993, Feb. 26

340 A2229 50r on 6k #4728 (Br) *1.10 .55*
341 A2435 100r on 6k #5109 *2.25 1.00*
342 A2435 300r on 6k #5107 *6.00 3.00*
Nos. 340-342 (3) *9.35 4.55*

Traditional Costumes — A77

1993, Apr. 29 Litho. *Perf. 13x13½*

343 A77 5s Kuldiga *.20 .20*
344 A77 10s Alsunga *.30 .20*
345 A77 20s Lielvarde *.55 .30*
346 A77 50s Rucava *1.50 .80*
347 A77 100s Zemgale *3.00 1.50*
348 A77 500s Ziemellatgale *15.00 12.00*
a. Miniature sheet of 6, #343-348 *25.00 25.00*
Nos. 343-348 (6) *20.55 15.00*

See #400-401, 415-416, 440-441, 466-467.

21st Natl. Song Festival
A78 A79

1993, July 3 Litho. *Perf. 12½x13*

349 A78 3s rose brn, gold & black *1.40 .50*
350 A78 5s purple, gold & black *2.60 .80*
351 A79 15s multicolored *3.50 1.25*
Nos. 349-351 (3) *7.50 2.55*

A80 A81

1993, Aug. 28 Litho. *Perf. 14*

352 A80 15s Pope John Paul II *1.25 1.00*

1993, Nov. 11 Litho. *Perf. 12½x13*

353 A81 5s silver, black & red *.90 .30*
354 A81 15s gold, black & red *1.60 .45*

Independence, 75th anniv.

A82 A83

1994, Apr. 2 Litho. *Perf. 14*

355 A82 15s multicolored *1.40 .35*

Evalds Valters, actor, 100th birthday.

1994, Apr. 20 Litho. *Perf. 12½x13*

356 A83 5s Biathlon *.40 .40*
357 A83 10s 2-man bobsled *.85 .40*
358 A83 15s Luge *1.25 .65*
359 A83 100s Men's figure skating *7.50 3.75*
Nos. 356-359 (4) *10.00 5.20*

Souvenir Sheet

360 A83 200s like #357 *12.00 9.50*

1994 Winter Olympics, Lillehammer.

Ethnographical Open Air Museum — A84

1994, Apr. 30 Litho. *Perf. 13x12½*

361 A84 5s multicolored *1.60 .35*

1994 Basketball Festival, Riga — A85

1994, June 4 Litho. *Perf. 12½x13*

362 A85 15s multicolored *1.90 .45*

Provincial Municipal Arms — A86

Nos. 363-377A are inscribed with the year date of issue below the design. The year noted in each description is the date that appears on the stamp.

Perf. 13x12½, 14x14¼ (#373)

1994-2007

363 A86 1s Kurzeme, "1994" .25 .20
a. "1996" .25 .20
b. "1997" 1.00 .20
c. "1998" .25 .20
d. Perf 14x14¼, "1999" 2.00 2.00
e. As "d," "2002" .25 .20
f. Perf. 13¼x13¾, "2006" .25 .20
g. As "f," "2007" .20 .20
364 A86 2s Auce, "1996" .40 .20
a. "1997" .40 .20
b. "1998" .30 .20
c. Perf 14x14¼, "1999" 2.50 2.50
d. As "c," "2000" .40 .20
e. As "c," "2002" .20 .20
f. Perf 13¼x13¾, "2005" .20 .20
g. As "f," "2006" .20 .20
h. As "f," "2007" .20 .20
365 A86 3s Zemgale, 1994 .55 .35
a. Perf 14x14¼, "1999" .55 .35
b. As "a," "2000" .55 .35
c. As "a," "2002" .20 .20
d. Perf 13¼x13¾, "2005" .20 .20
e. As "d," "2006" .20 .20
f. As "d," "2007" .20 .20
g. Perf. 14x14¼, "2010" .20 .20
366 A86 5s Vidzeme, "1994" .55 .20
a. "1996" 1.50 .60
b. Perf 14x14¼, "1999" 3.00 1.00
c. As "b," "2000" 2.50 .85
367 A86 8s Livani, "1995" 1.20 .40
a. "1996" 1.50 .40
368 A86 10s Latgale, "1994" 1.00 1.00
a. "1997" 1.60 1.00
b. "1998" .50 .50
369 A86 13s Preili, "1996" .70 .70
a. Perf. 14x14¼, "2010" .50 .50
370 A86 16s Ainazi, "1995" .80 .80
a. "1996" 2.00 1.00
371 A86 20s Grobina, "1995" 1.00 1.00
a. "1996" 1.00 1.00
372 A86 24s Tukums, "1995" 1.10 1.10
a. "1996" 1.10 1.10
373 A86 28s Madona, "1996" 1.75 1.50
374 A86 30s Riga, "1994" 1.50 1.50
375 A86 36s Priekule, "1996" 2.25 1.50
376 A86 50s Natl. arms, "1994" 2.25 2.25

Size: 29x24mm

Perf. 14

377 A86 100s Riga *4.25 2.50*
377A A86 200s Natl. arms *8.75 4.75*
Nos. 363-377A (16) 28.30 19.95

Issued: #363, 6/21/94; #363a, 1/30/96; #363b, 2/5/97; #363c, 1/12/98; #363d, 1/20/99; #363e, 2/6/02; #363f, 9/9/06; #363g, 6/8/97. #364, 4/12/96; #364a, 2/5/97; #364b, 2/11/98; #364c, 1/20/99; #364d, 4/26/00; #364e, 2/6/02; #364f, 9/10/05; #364g, 9/9/06; #364h, 6/8/07. #365, 6/21/94; #365a, 3/16/99; #365b, 4/26/00; #365c, 2/6/02; #365d, 9/10/05; #365e, 9/9/06; #365f, 6/8/07; #365g, 2/15/10; .#366, 6/21/94; #366a, 1/30/96; #366b, 1/20/99; #366c, 4/26/00. #367, 6/1/95; #367a, 1/30/96. #368, 6/21/94; #368a, 8/28/97; #368b, 8/4/98. #369, 4/12/96; #369a, 3/12/10 #370, 6/1/95; #370a, 4/8/96. #371, 6/1/95; #371a, 9/6/96. #372, 6/1/95; #372a, 4/8/96. #373, 11/5/96. #374, 12/21/94. #375, 11/5/96. #376, 377, 378, 12/21/94.

See Nos. 450-451, 472-473, 482-483, 506-507, 525-526.

A87

A88

1994, Sept. 24 Litho. *Perf. 14*

378 A87 5s multicolored *.75 .30*

University of Latvia, 75th anniv.

1994, Oct. 29 Litho. *Perf. 14x13½*

Items balanced on scales (Europa): 10s, Latvian coins. 50s, Locked chest, money card.

379 A88 10s multicolored *.65 .25*
a. Tete-beche pair *1.40 .50*
380 A88 50s multicolored *3.50 1.50*
a. Tete-beche pair *7.00 3.00*

Doormouse A89

1994, Nov. 19 Litho. *Perf. 13½x13*

381 A89 5s shown *.55 .35*
382 A89 10s Among leaves *.85 .35*
383 A89 10s Eating berries *.85 .35*
384 A89 15s Berry, large mouse *1.75 .50*
Nos. 381-384 (4) *4.00 1.55*

World Wildlife Fund.

A90 A91

Christmas: 3s, Angel. 8s, Angels playing flute & violin. 13c, Angels singing. 100s, Candles.

1994, Dec. 3 *Perf. 14*

385 A90 3s multicolored *.30 .20*
386 A90 8s multicolored *.55 .20*
387 A90 13s multicolored *1.25 .30*
388 A90 100s multicolored *5.50 2.10*
Nos. 385-388 (4) *7.60 2.80*

Perf. 13x12½ on 3 Sides

1994, Dec. 17

Children's Fairy Tales, by Margarita Staraste: 5s, Elf with candle. No. 390, Small bear in snow. No. 391, Boy on sled.

Booklet Stamps

389 A91 5s multicolored *.25 .20*
390 A91 10s multicolored *.50 .20*
391 A91 10s multicolored *.50 .20*
a. Booklet pane, 2 each #389-391 *2.75*
Complete booklet, #391a + label *3.50*
Nos. 389-391 (3) *1.25 .60*

A92 A93

1995, Feb. 18 *Perf. 14*

392 A92 10s multicolored *1.00 .35*

European safe driving week.

1995, Mar. 4 Litho. *Perf. 14*

393 A93 15s silver, blue & red *1.50 .55*

UN, 50th anniv.

A94

A95

Via Baltica Highway Project: 8s, No. 395b, Castle, Bauska, Latvia. No. 395a, Beach Hotel, Parnu, Estonia. c, Kaunas, Lithuania.

1995, Apr. 20 Litho. *Perf. 14*
394 A94 8s multicolored *.40 .20*

Souvenir Sheet

395 A94 18s Sheet of 3, #a.-c. *3.25 2.00*

See Estonia #288-289, Lithuania #508-509.

1995, July 8 Litho. *Perf. 12½*
396 A95 8s Dendrocopos leucotos *.35 .20*
397 A95 20s Crex crex *.85 .40*
398 A95 24s Chlidonias leucopterus *1.10 .50*
Nos. 396-398 (3) 2.30 1.10

European nature conservation year.

Julian Cardinal Vaivods, Birth Cent. — A96

1995, Aug. 18 Litho. *Perf. 14*
399 A96 8s multicolored *.60 .25*

Traditional Costume Type of 1993

1995, Sept. 8 Litho. *Perf. 13x13½*
400 A77 8s Nica *.45 .20*

Souvenir Sheet

401 A77 100s Like #400 4.75 4.75

Friendly Appeal, by Karlis Ulmanis, 60th Anniv. — A97

1995, Sept. 8 *Perf. 14*
402 A97 8s multicolored *.60 .25*

Riga, 800th Anniv. — A98

1995, Sept. 23 *Perf. 13½*
403 A98 8s Natl. Opera *.40 .25*
404 A98 16s Natl. Theatre *.80 .40*

Size: 45x27mm

405 A98 24s Academy of Arts *1.10 .60*
406 A98 36s State Art Museum *1.75 .90*
Nos. 403-406 (4) 4.05 2.15

See Nos. 508-511, 529-531, 529-531.

Peace and Freedom — A99

Heroes from national epic, Lacplesis, dates of independence: 16s, Spidola with sword and shield, 1918. 50s, Lacplesis with leaves and banner, 1991.

1995, Nov. 15 Litho. *Perf. 13½*
407 A99 16s multicolored *.75 .30*
a. Tete beche pair 1.50 1.50
408 A99 50s multicolored *2.25 .95*
a. Tete beche pair 4.50 4.50

Europa.

Christmas A100

Designs: No. 409, Characters surrounding Christmas tree at night. No. 410, Santa gliding through sky holding candle. 15s, Characters outside snow-covered house. 24s, Santa standing between dog and cat.

1995, Dec. 2
409 A100 6s multicolored *.55 .25*
410 A100 6s multicolored *.55 .25*
411 A100 15s multicolored *.30 .60*
412 A100 24s multicolored *2.50 1.00*
Nos. 409-412 (4) 3.90 2.10

Pauls Stradins (1896-1958), Physician — A101

1996, Jan. 17 Litho. *Perf. 14*
413 A101 8s multicolored *.50 .25*

Zenta Maurina (1897-1978) A102

1996, May 10 Litho. *Perf. 13½x14*
414 A102 36s multicolored *1.60 .95*
a. Tete beche pair 3.25 3.25

Europa.

Traditional Costume Type of 1993

1996, May 18 Litho. *Perf. 13x13½*
415 A77 8s Barta *.50 .25*

Souvenir Sheet

416 A77 100s like No. 415 *4.50 3.00*

Souvenir Sheet

Children's Games — A103

1996, June 8 Litho. *Perf. 14x13½*
417 A103 48s Sheet of 1 *2.10 1.50*

1996 Summer Olympic Games, Atlanta A104

Perf. 14x13½, 13½x14

1996, June 19
418 A104 8s Cycling,vert. *.40 .20*
419 A104 16s Basketball, vert *.85 .40*
420 A104 24s Walking, vert. *1.00 .50*
421 A104 36s Canoeing *1.60 .80*
Nos. 418-421 (4) 3.85 1.90

Souvenir Sheet

422 A104 100s Javelin *4.00 2.25*

Nature Museum, 150th Anniv. A105

Butterflies: 8s, Papilio machaon. 24s, Catocala fraxini. 80s, Pericallia matronula.

1996, Aug. 30 *Perf. 13*
423 A105 8s multicolored *.35 .20*
424 A105 24s multicolored *.90 .45*
425 A105 80s multicolored *3.75 1.90*
Nos. 423-425 (3) 5.00 2.55

Car Production in Latvia — A106

Designs: 8s, 1912 Russo-Balt fire truck. 24s, 1899 Leutner-Russia. 36s, 1939 Ford-Vairogs.

1996, Oct. 25 Litho. *Perf. 13x12½*
426 A106 8s multicolored *.35 .20*
427 A106 24s multicolored *1.25 .55*
428 A106 36s multicolored *1.75 .85*
Nos. 426-428 (3) 3.35 1.60

City of Riga, 800th Anniv. — A107

1996, Dec. 5 Litho. *Perf. 13½*
429 A107 8s Building front *.40 .20*

Size: 30x26mm

430 A107 16s Stained glass window *.75 .40*

Size: 37x26mm

431 A107 24s Buildings *1.25 .55*
432 A107 30s Art figures *1.40 .70*
Nos. 429-432 (4) 3.80 1.85

Christmas A108

Designs: 6s, Santa's elves, presents. 14s, Santa on skis, dog, children in animal costumes. 20s, Child in front of Christmas tree, santa in chair, pets.

1996, Dec. 7 *Perf. 14*
433 A108 6s multicolored *.30 .20*
434 A108 14s multicolored *.70 .35*
435 A108 20s multicolored *1.00 .50*
Nos. 433-435 (3) 2.00 1.05

See Nos. 458-460.

Birds — A109

Designs: 10s, Caprimulgus eurpaeus. 20s, Aquila clanga. 30s, Acrocephalus paludicola.

1997, Feb. 8 *Perf. 13x12½*
436 A109 10s multicolored *.50 .25*
437 A109 20s multicolored *.90 .45*
438 A109 30s multicolored *1.40 .70*
Nos. 436-438 (3) 2.80 1.40

Turn of the Epochs — A110

Legend of Rozi Turaidas — A111

1997, Mar. 25 Litho. *Perf. 14*
439 A110 10s multicolored *.70 .35*

Traditional Costume Type of 1993

1997, Apr. 3 *Perf. 13x13½*
440 A77 10s Rietumvidzeme *1.75 .80*

Souvenir Sheet

441 A77 100s like #440 *4.50 2.50*

Stamp Day.

1997, Apr. 26 Litho. *Perf. 12½x13*
442 A111 32s multicolored *1.50 .70*
a. Tete beche pair 2.50 2.50

Europa.

Old Baltic Ships — A112

Designs: 10s, Linijkugis, 17th cent.
No. 444: a, Linijkugis, 17th cent., diff. b, Kurenas 16th cent. c, Maasilinn ship, 16th cent.

1997, May 10 *Perf. 14x14½*
443 A112 10s multicolored *.85 .40*

Souvenir Sheet

444 A112 20s Sheet of 3, #a.-c. *3.50 2.75*

See Estonia #322-323, Lithuania #571-572.

Port of Ventspils, Cent. — A113

1997, May 21 Litho. *Perf. 13½x14*
445 A113 20s Hermes, Poseidon *1.00 .50*

Children's Activities A114

Designs: 10s, Stamp collecting. 12s, Riding dirt bike, vert. 20s, Boy in hockey uniform, girl in skiwear, vert. 30s, Tennis, soccer, basketball.

1997, June 7 *Perf. 13½x13*
446 A114 10s multicolored *.45 .20*
447 A114 12s multicolored *.60 .30*
448 A114 20s multicolored *.95 .45*
449 A114 30s multicolored *1.50 .75*
Nos. 446-449 (4) 3.50 1.70

Municipal Arms Type of 1994

1997-2005 Litho. *Perf. 13x12½*

Date imprint below design

450 A86 10s Valmiera, "1997" .85 .40
a. "1998" .85 .40
b. Perf 14x14¼, "1999" .85 .40
c. "2000" .85 .40
d. Perf. 13¼x13¾, "2001" .85 .40
e. "2005" .65 .30
451 A86 20s Rezekne, "1997" 1.75 .85

Issued: #450, 9/6/97; #450a, 1/12/98; #450b, 1/20/99; #450c, 4/26/00; #450d, 9/12/01; #450e, 9/10/05. #451, 9/6/97.

Nature Preserves A115

1997, Oct. 18 Litho. *Perf. 13x12½*
452 A115 10s Moricsala, 1912 *.55 .25*
453 A115 30s Slitere, 1921 *1.60 .80*

See Nos. 464-465.

City of Riga, 800th Anniv. A116

10s, Woman, house, 12th cent. 20s, Monument to Bishop Albert, seal of the bishop, rosary, writing tool, 13th-16th cent. 30s, Riga castle, weapons used during Middle Ages. 32s, Houses, arms of Riga, statue of St. John.

1997, Nov. 27 Litho. *Perf. 13x14*
454 A116 10s multicolored *.45 .20*
455 A116 20s multicolored *.80 .40*
456 A116 30s multicolored *1.25 .60*

Size: 27x26mm
457 A116 32s multicolored *1.40 .70*
Nos. 454-457 (4) 3.90 1.90

See Nos. 468-471, 488-491, 508-511, 529-531.

Christmas Type of 1996

People dressed in masks, costumes for mummery: 8s, Santa, bear. 18s, Two goats. 28s, Horse.

1997, Nov. 29 *Perf. 14*
458 A108 8s multicolored *.40 .20*
459 A108 18s multicolored *.80 .40*
460 A108 28s multicolored *1.25 .60*
Nos. 458-460 (3) 2.45 1.20

A117

A118

1998, Jan. 31 Litho. *Perf. 14x13½*
461 A117 20s multicolored *1.00 .50*

1998 Winter Olympic Games, Nagano.

1998, Feb. 21 Litho. *Perf. 13½*

Statue at Spridisi, museum home of Anna Brigadere(1861-1933), writer.

462 A118 10s multicolored .60 .25

National Song Festival — A119

1998, Mar. 28 Litho. *Perf. 13x14*
463 A119 30s multicolored 2.75 1.25
a. Tete beche pair 4.00 4.00

Europa.

Nature Preserves Type of 1997

1998, Apr. 30 *Perf. 13x12½*
464 A115 10s Grini, 1936 .55 .25
465 A115 30s Teici, 1982 1.75 .85

Traditional Costume Type of 1993

#467, Krustpils, man wearing crown of leaves.

1998, May 9 *Perf. 13x13½*
466 A77 10s Krustpils region .75 .30

Souvenir Sheet
467 A77 100s multicolored 6.00 4.00

City of Riga, 800th Anniv., Type of 1997

10s, Dannenstern House, 16th and 17th cent. coins issued by kings of Poland and Sweden, 17th cent. wooden sculpture. 20s, City Library, monument to G. Herder, poet, philosopher, teacher. 30s, 18th cent. arsenal, column celebrating defeat of Napoleon's troops, octant, compass. 40s, Sculpture of Mother Latvia at Warriors' Cemetery, entrance to Cemetery, obv. & rev. of 5 lat coin, 1930.

1998, May 29 Litho. *Perf. 13x14*
468 A116 10s multicolored .50 .25
469 A116 20s multicolored 1.00 .45
470 A116 30s multicolored 1.40 .60
471 A116 40s multicolored 2.00 .85
Nos. 468-471 (4) 4.90 2.15

No. 468 is 30x26mm.

Municipal Arms Type of 1994

1998-2004 Litho. *Perf. 13¼x13¾*
Date imprint below design
472 A86 15s Bauska, "1998" .75 .35
473 A86 30s Liepaja, "1998" 1.50 .75
a. Perf 13½x14, "2004" 1.60 .85

Issued: #472, 473, 9/26/98; #473a, 9/7/04.

World Stamp Day — A120

1998, Oct. 20 Litho. *Perf. 14*
474 A120 30s #2, various stamps 1.25 .60

Dome Church, Riga, 1211 A121

Pres. Janis Cakste (1859-1927) A122

1998, Oct. 23
475 A121 10s multicolored .60 .30

1998, Nov. 11 *Perf. 14x13½*
476 A122 10s multicolored .60 .30

See No. 497, 515, 524.

Independence, 80th Anniv. — A123

1998, Nov. 14 *Perf. 13x12½*
477 A123 10s shown .45 .20
478 A123 30s Arms, flags 1.50 .75

Christmas A124

Christmas elves: 10s, Rolling snow balls. 20s, Decorating tree, preparing presents. 30s, Pulling sled over snow.

1998, Nov. 28 *Perf. 13½x14*
479 A124 10s multicolored .60 .30
480 A124 20s multicolored 1.40 .65
481 A124 30s multicolored 1.90 .85
Nos. 479-481 (3) 3.90 1.80

Municipal Arms Type of 1994

1999-2004 Litho. *Perf. 13¼x13¾*
Date imprint below design
482 A86 15s Ogre, "1999" .80 .40
a. "2000" .90 .50
483 A86 40s Jelgava, "1999" 2.00 1.00
a. "2004" 1.50 .75

Issued: #482, 2/12/99; #482a, 2/25/00. #483, 4/10/99; #483a, 9/7/04.

Nature Parks and Reserves A125

Europa: 30s, Krustkalnu Nature Reserve. 60s, Gauja Natl. Nature Park.

1999, Mar. 20 *Perf. 13x12½*
484 A125 30s multicolored 1.75 .85
485 A125 60s multicolored 4.00 1.75

Council of Europe, 50th Anniv. — A126

1999, Apr. 24
486 A126 30s multicolored 1.75 .80

Rudolfs Blaumanis (1863-1908), Writer — A127

1999, Apr. 24 *Perf. 14x13*
487 A127 110s multicolored 5.00 2.40

City of Riga, 800th Anniv. Type

10s, Streetcar. 30s, Schooner "Widwud." 40s, Airplane. 70s, TK-type locomotive.

Perf. 13¼x13¾
1999, June 26 Litho.
488 A116 10s multicolored .45 .20
489 A116 30s multicolored 1.40 .70
490 A116 40s multicolored 1.90 .95
491 A116 70s multicolored 3.25 1.60
Nos. 488-491 (4) 7.00 3.45

No. 488 is 30x27mm.

Aglona Basilica — A129

"Baltic Chain," 10th Anniv. — A130

1999, July 10 Litho. *Perf. 14x14½*
492 A129 15s multicolored .80 .35
Complete booklet, 6 #492 15.00

1999, Aug. 23 Litho. *Perf. 12½x13*

Families and flags: 15s, No. 494a, Latvian. No. 494: b, Lithuanian. c, Estonian.

493 A130 15s multicolored 1.25 .50

Souvenir Sheet
494 A130 30s Sheet of 3, #a.-c. 5.00 4.00

See Estonia Nos. 366-367, Lithuania Nos. 639-640.

Rundāle Palace — A131

1999, Sept. 25 Litho. *Perf. 14*
495 A131 20s multicolored 1.00 .50

See Nos. 512, 536, 578.

Landscape, by Julijs Feders (1838-1909) — A132

1999, Oct. 13 Litho. *Perf. 13½*
496 A132 15s multi 1.00 .45

Presidents Type of 1998

1999, Nov. 16 Litho. *Perf. 14x13½*
497 A122 15s Pres. Gustavs Zemgals (1871-1939) 1.00 .45

A134

A135

1999, Nov. 25 *Perf. 14x14½*
498 A134 40s multi 1.75 .85

UPU, 125th anniv.

1999, Nov. 27 *Perf. 14¼*

Christmas and Millennium: 12s, Santa, tree, candle. 15s, Santa, tree, children. 40s, Santa, tree with ornaments.

499 A135 12s multi .55 .25
500 A135 15s multi .70 .35
501 A135 40s multi 1.75 .85
Nos. 499-501 (3) 3.00 1.45

Nude, by J. Rozentals A136

Perf. 14½x14¼
2000, Feb. 26 Litho.
502 A136 40s multi 2.00 1.00

Aleksandrs Caks (1901-50), Poet — A137

2000, Apr. 8 Litho. *Perf. 14x13½*

503 A137 40s multi 2.00 .90
Booklet, 6 #503 12.00

Europa, 2000
Common Design Type

2000, May 9

504 CD17 60s multi 5.00 2.40
a. Tete beche pair 10.00 10.00

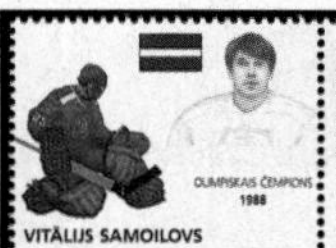

Ice Hockey — A138

Wmk. 387

2000, June 21 Litho. *Perf. 14*

505 A138 70s multi + label 3.50 1.40

Issued in sheets of 8 + 8 labels. Vertical columns of four labels, which depict players Helmut Balderis, Vitalijs Samoilovs, Sandis Ozolinsh and Arturs Irbe, flank a central block of eight stamps. Color photos of the players appear at left or right of the labels.

Municipal Arms Type of 1994

2000-05 Unwmk. *Perf. 13¼x13¾*

Date imprint below design

506 A86 15s Daugavpils, "2000" .85 .40
a. "2005" .75 .35
507 A86 15s Jūrmala, "2000" .85 .40
a. "2001" .85 .40
b. "2002" .85 .40
c. "2005" .75 .35

Issued: #506, 7/6/00; #506a, 8/5/05. #507, 7/6/00; #507a, 9/12/01; #507b, 1/12/02; #507c, 8/5/05.

City of Riga, 800th Anniv. Type of 1995

20s, Central Market. #509, Riga Zoo. #510, Riga Dome Organ. 70s, Powder Tower.

2000, July 22 *Perf. 13¼x14*

Size: 40x28mm

508 A98 20s multi 1.00 .50

Size: 47x28mm

509 A98 40s multi 2.00 1.00

Perf. 14x13¼

Size: 28x32mm

510 A98 40s multi 2.00 1.00
511 A98 70s multi 3.50 1.25
Nos. 508-511 (4) 8.50 3.75

Palace Type of 1999

2000, Aug. 12 *Perf. 13¼x14*

512 A131 40s Jelgava Palace 2.00 1.00
Booklet, 6 #512 15.00

2000 Summer Olympics, Sydney — A139

2000, Sept. 15 *Perf. 14¼x14*

513 A139 70s multi + label 3.25 2.00

See No. 518.

Millennium — A140

No. 514: a, 15s, Freedom Monument, Riga. b, House of Blackheads, Riga.

Perf. 14x13¼

2000, Sept. 28 Litho. Wmk. 387

514 A140 Pair + label 3.00 1.50
a. 15s multi .90 .40
b. 50s multi 2.10 1.10

President Type of 1998

Perf. 13¾x13¼

2000, Nov. 11 Unwmk.

515 A122 15s Alberts Kveisis (1881-1936) .80 .40

Orthodox Cathedral — A141

2000, Nov. 17 *Perf. 14*

516 A141 40s multi 2.00 1.00

See Nos. 537, 559, 573.

Red Cross — A142

2000, Nov. 22

517 A142 15s multi .80 .40

Olympics Type of 2000

2000, Nov. 22

518 A139 40s multi 1.75 .85

Issued in sheets of 4 + 2 different labels depicting gold medal winner Igors Vihrovs.

Christmas — A143

Designs: 12s, Watch. No. 520, 15s, Angels. No. 521, 15s, Madonna and child.

2000, Nov. 25

519-521 A143 Set of 3 2.00 1.00

International Recognition of Latvia, 80th Anniv. — A144

2001, Jan. 13 Litho. *Perf. 14*

522 A144 40s multi 2.00 1.00

Kad Silavas Mostas, by Vilhelmis Purvitis A145

Perf. 14¼x14½

2001, Feb. 1 Litho. Unwmk.

523 A145 40s multi 3.00 1.50
Booklet, 6 #523 18.00

President Type of 1998

2001, Feb. 17 *Perf. 13¾x13¼*

524 A122 15s Karlis Ulmanis (1877-1942) .75 .35

Municipal Arms Type of 1994

2001-06 *Perf. 13¼x13¾*

Date imprint below design

525 A86 5s Smiltene, "2001" .50 .25
a. "2002" .50 .25
b. "2005" .25 .20
c. "2006" .25 .20
526 A86 15s Kuldiga, "2001" .60 .30
a. "2002" .60 .30

Issued: #525, 3/5/01; #525a, 9/16/02; #525b, 9/10/05; #525c, 9/9/06. #526, 3/5/01; #526a, 9/16/02.

Narrow Gauge Locomotive A146

2001, Mar. 24 *Perf. 14*

527 A146 40s multi 2.10 1.00

Europa — A147

2001, Apr. 14

528 A147 60s multi 3.50 1.75
a. Tete beche pair 4.50 4.50

Riga, 800th Anniv. Type of 1995

Riga in: No. 529a, 20th cent. No. 529b, 21st cent. 60s, 16th cent. 70s, 17th cent.

2001, May 24 Litho. *Perf. 13¾x13½*

Size: 29x33mm (each stamp)

529 A98 15s Horiz. pair, #a-b 1.50 .75

Size: 47x28mm

Perf. 13½x13¾

530 A98 60s multi 2.50 1.25
531 A98 70s multi 2.75 1.40
Nos. 529-531 (3) 6.75 3.40

Kakisa Dzirnavas, by Karlis Skalbe — A148

2001, June 9 *Perf. 13¾*

532 A148 40s multi 2.00 1.00
Booklet, 6 #532 12.00

Souvenir Sheet

Mikhail Tal (1936-92), Chess Champion — A149

2001, Aug. 18 Litho. *Perf. 14*

533 A149 100s multi 4.75 2.25

Baltic Coast Landscapes A150

Designs: 15s, No. 535a, Vidzeme. No. 535b, Palanga. No. 535c, Lahemaa.

2001, Sept. 15 *Perf. 13½*

534 A150 15s multi 1.50 .75
Booklet, 6 #534 10.00

Souvenir Sheet

535 Sheet of 3 5.00 2.50
a.-c. A150 30s Any single 1.60 .80

See Estonia Nos. 423-424, Lithuania Nos. 698-699.

Palace Type of 1999

2001, Oct. 24 *Perf. 14½x14*

536 A131 40s Cesvaines Palace 2.00 1.00
a. Perf. 13¼x14 2.00 1.00
b. Booklet pane, 6 #536a 10.00 —
Booklet, #536b 10.00

House of Worship Type of 2000

2001, Nov. 3 *Perf. 13¾x14*

537 A141 70s Riga Synagogue 3.00 1.50
Booklet, 6 #537 24.00

Latvian Seamen — A151

Designs: 15s, Krisjanis Valdemars (1825-91), founder of Naval College. 70s, Duke Jekabs Ketlers (1610-82), shipbuilder.

2001, Nov. 14 *Perf. 13¼x14*

538-539 A151 Set of 2 3.00 1.50

Christmas A152

Designs: 12s, Rabbits. No. 541, 15s, Dog, rabbit. No. 542, 15s, Lambs.

2001, Nov. 22 *Perf. 13¼*

540-542 A152 Set of 3 2.00 1.00

Town Arms — A153

2002, Jan. 29 Litho. *Perf. 13¼x13¾*

543 A153 5s Ludza .35 .35
544 A153 10s Dobele .50 .35
545 A153 15s Sigulda .75 .40
Nos. 543-545 (3) 1.60 1.10

See Nos. 565-567, 585-587, 609-611, 638-640, 670-672, 696-698, 726-728, 753-755.

2002 Winter Olympics, Salt Lake City — A154

2002, Feb. 8 *Perf. 13¼x13¾*

546 A154 40s multi 1.75 .85
a. Booklet pane of 6, perf. 13¼x13¾ on 3 sides 15.00 —
Booklet, #546a 15.00

2002 Winter Paralympics, Salt Lake City — A155

2002, Mar. 5 *Perf. 14¼x13¾*
547 A155 15s multi .60 .30

Refugees, by Jekabs Kazaks — A156

2002, Apr. 20 Litho. *Perf. 14½x14¼*
548 A156 40s multi 1.75 .85

Europa — A157

2002, May 4 *Perf. 14*
549 A157 60s multi 3.00 1.50
a. Tete-beche pair 6.00 3.00

Endangered Plants — A158

Designs: 15s, Cypripedium calceolus. 40s, Trapa natans.

2002, May 25 *Perf. 13¾*
550-551 A158 Set of 2 2.75 1.40

See Nos. 568-569, 589-590, 612-613.

Latvian Armed Forces — A159

2002, June 15 *Perf. 13¾x13¼*
552 A159 40s multi 1.90 .95

Janis Jaunsudrabins (1877-1962), Writer — A160

2002, July 6 *Perf. 13¾x13½*
553 A160 40s multi 2.00 1.00
a. Booklet pane of 6, perf. 13¾x13½ on 3 sides 12.00
Booklet, #553a 12.00

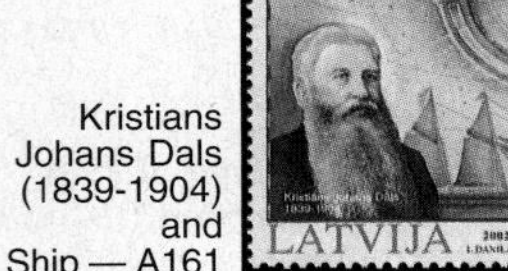

Kristians Johans Dals (1839-1904) and Ship — A161

2002, July 20 *Perf. 13¼x13¾*
554 A161 70s multi 3.00 1.50

Fish — A162

Designs: 15s, Gadus morhua callarias. 40s, Siluris glanis.

2002, Aug. 10 Litho. *Perf. 14*
555-556 A162 Set of 2 3.00 1.50
a. Booklet pane, perf. 14 on 3 sides 13.00
Booklet, #556a 13.00

Souvenir Sheet

Venta River Bridge — A163

2002, Aug. 24 *Perf. 12¾x12½*
557 A163 100s multi 4.50 2.25

Jaunmoku Palace — A164

2002, Sept. 14 *Perf. 14¼x13¾*
558 A164 40s multi 1.90 .95

House of Worship Type of 2000

2002, Oct. 12 *Perf. 13¾x14*
559 A141 70s Grebenschikov Old Belief Praying House 3.25 1.60
a. Booklet pane of 6, perf. 13¾x14 on 3 sides 20.00
Booklet, #559a 20.00

Mittens A165

2002, Nov. 2 *Perf. 13¼x13¾*
560 A165 15s multi .70 .35

See Nos. 579, 604, 629.

Christmas — A166

Designs: 12s, Elf on sack, Christmas tree. No. 562, 15s, Angel, Christmas tree. No. 563, 15s, Elves on gift.

2002, Nov. 23 *Perf. 13¾x13¼*
561-563 A166 Set of 3 2.00 1.00

A Man Entering a Room, by Niklavs Strunke (1894-1966) A167

2003, Jan. 25 Litho. *Perf. 13¼x14*
564 A167 40s multi 2.00 1.00

Town Arms Type of 2002

2003, Feb. 15 *Perf. 13¼x13¾*
565 A153 10s Balvi .50 .25
566 A153 15s Gulbene .75 .35
567 A153 20s Ventspils 1.00 .50
Nos. 565-567 (3) 2.25 1.10

Endangered Plants Type of 2002

Designs: 15s, Ophrys insectifera. 30s, Taxus baccata.

2003, Mar. 21 *Perf. 13¾*
568 A158 15s multi .60 .30
569 A158 30s multi 1.40 .70
a. Perf. 14½x14¼ on 3 sides 1.40 .70
b. Booklet pane, 6 #569a 8.50 —
Complete booklet, #569b 8.50

Straumeni, by Edvarts Virza (1883-1940) A168

2003, Apr. 12 *Perf. 13¾x13¼*
570 A168 40s multi 2.00 1.00

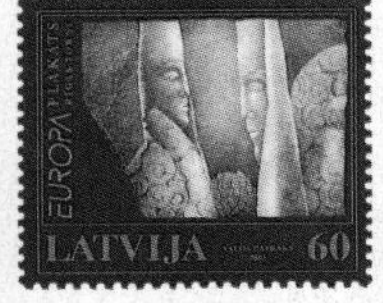

Europa — A169

2003, May 3 Litho. *Perf. 13¼x13¾*
571 A169 60s multi 3.00 1.50
a. Tete beche pair 5.00 5.00

Kolka Lighthouse — A170

2003, May 17 *Perf. 13¾x13¼*
572 A170 60s multi 3.00 1.50

See Nos. 602, 626, 662, 676, 709, 746.

House of Worship Type of 2000

2003, June 6 *Perf. 13¼x13¾*
573 A141 70s Salvation Temple, horiz. 3.25 1.60

Souvenir Sheet

Gauja River Bridge, Sigulda — A171

2003, July 19
574 A171 100s multi 5.00 2.50

Fish — A172

Designs: 15s, Thymallus thymallus. 30s, Salmo salar.

2003, Aug. 2 *Perf. 14x13¾*
575 A172 15s multi .90 .45
576 A172 30s multi 2.10 1.00
a. Booklet pane of 6, perf. 14x13¾ on 3 sides 13.00 —
Complete booklet, #576a 13.00

Motacilla Alba — A173

2003, Aug. 30 *Perf. 14¾x14*
577 A173 15s multi .70 .35

Palace Type of 1999

2003, Sept. 27 *Perf. 14¼x13¾*
578 A131 40s Birini Palace 1.75 .85
a. Booklet pane of 6 11.00
Complete booklet, #578a 11.00

Mittens Type of 2002

2003, Oct. 11 *Perf. 14x13¾*
579 A165 15s Libiesi mittens .75 .35

Motorcycle Racing A174

2003, Oct. 31 *Perf. 13¼x13¾*
580 A174 70s multi 3.25 1.60
a. Booklet pane of 6 20.00 —
Complete booklet, #580a 20.00

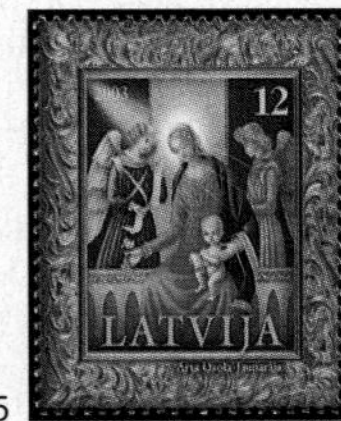

Christmas — A175

Designs: 12s, Madonna and Child with two angels. No. 582, 15s, The Annunciation (golden brown frame). No. 583, 15s, Nativity (gray frame).

2003, Nov. 22 *Perf. 13¾x14¼*
581-583 A175 Set of 3 2.00 1.00

Still Life with Triangle, by Romans Suta — A176

2004, Jan. 25 Litho. *Perf. 13¼x14*
584 A176 40s multi 1.75 .85

Town Arms Type of 2002

2004, Feb. 14 *Perf. 13¼x13¾*
585 A153 5s Valka .25 .20
586 A153 15s Cesis .65 .35
587 A153 20s Saldus .85 .45
Nos. 585-587 (3) 1.75 1.00

Reinis (1839-1920) and Matiss (1848-1926) Kaudzites, Writers — A177

2004, Mar. 20 *Perf. 13¾*
588 A177 40s multi 1.75 .85

Endangered Plants Type of 2002

Designs: 15s, Gentiana cruciata. 30s, Onobrychis arenaria.

2004, Apr. 3
589-590 A158 Set of 2 2.10 1.00

2006 World Ice Hockey Championships, Riga — A178

2004, Apr. 17 Litho. *Perf. 13¼x13¾*
591 A178 30s multi 1.25 .60
a. Booklet pane of 4, perf. 13¼x13¾ on 3 sides 5.00 —
Complete booklet, #591a 5.00

Admission to European Union — A179

Designs: No. 592, 30s, Stars, map of Europe, flags of newly-added countries. No. 593, 30s, Seven stars.

2004, May 1 *Perf. 13x13¼*
592-593 A179 Set of 2 2.50 1.25

Europa — A180

2004, May 8 Litho. *Perf. 13¼x13¾*
594 A180 60s multi 3.00 1.50
a. Tete beche pair 5.00 5.00

European Soccer Championships, Portugal — A181

2004, June 3 *Perf. 14x13½*
595 A181 30s multi 1.25 .60

Fish — A182

Designs: 15s, Oncorhynchus mykiss. 30s, Psetta maxima.

2004, June 26 *Perf. 13¼x14*
596 A182 15s multi .60 .30
597 A182 30s multi 1.40 .70
a. Booklet pane of 6, perf. 13¼x14 on 3 sides 8.50 —
Complete booklet, #597a 8.50

See Nos. 620-621.

Visit of Pres. Bill Clinton to Latvia, 10th Anniv. — A183

2004, July 6 *Perf. 13¾x13¼*
598 A183 40s multi 1.75 .85

Souvenir Sheet

Dzelzcela Bridge, Riga — A184

2004, July 24 *Perf. 13¼x13¾*
599 A184 100s multi 4.50 4.50

2004 Summer Olympics, Athens A185

2004, Aug. 14 Litho. *Perf. 14*
600 A185 30s multi 1.25 .60

St. Jacob's Cathedral — A186

Perf. 13¾x13¼
2004, Aug. 28 Litho.
601 A186 40s multi 1.75 .85

Lighthouse Type of 2003

2004, Sept. 18
602 A170 60s Mikelbaka 2.75 1.40
a. Booklet pane of 4, perf. 13¾x13¼ on 3 sides 11.00 —
Complete booklet, #602a 11.00

Jaunpils Palace — A187

2004, Oct. 15 *Perf. 14¼x13¾*
603 A187 40s multi 1.75 .85
a. Booklet pane of 6, perf. 14¼x13¾ on 3 sides 10.50 —
Complete booklet, #603a 10.50

See Nos. 628, 678.

Mittens Type of 2002

2004, Nov. 6 *Perf. 13¼x13¾*
604 A165 15s Piebalga mittens .70 .35

Christmas — A188

Designs: 12s, Children, rabbit, bird, heart. No. 606, 15s, Snowman, birds. No. 607, 15s, Angel.

2004, Dec. 4 *Perf. 13¾x13¼*
605-607 A188 Set of 3 1.90 .95

1905 Revolution, Cent. A189

2005, Jan. 13 Litho. *Perf. 13¾x13¼*
608 A189 15s multi 1.25 .60

Town Arms Type of 2002

2005, Feb. 11 *Perf. 13¼x13¾*
609 A153 15s Aluksne .65 .30
610 A153 15s Talsi .65 .30
611 A153 40s Jekabpils 1.75 .85
Nos. 609-611 (3) 3.05 1.45

Endangered Plants Type of 2002

Designs: 20s, Pulsatilla patens. 30s, Allium ursinum.

2005, Mar. 5 *Perf. 13¼*
612-613 A158 Set of 2 2.00 1.00
613a Booklet pane of 6 #613, perf. 13¼ on 3 sides 7.25 —
Complete booklet, #613a 7.25

Krimuldas Church, 800th Anniv. A190

2005, Mar. 19 *Perf. 13¼x13¾*
614 A190 40s multi 1.60 .80

The Adventures of Baron Munchausen, by Rudolph Erich Raspe A191

2005, Apr. 1 Litho. *Perf. 13¼x13¾*
615 A191 30s multi 1.40 .70

Europa — A192

2005, Apr. 23
616 A192 60s multi 2.75 1.40
a. Tete beche pair 5.50 2.75

Mother and Child, by Janis Rozentals A193

2005, May 8 *Perf. 14x13¼*
617 A193 40s multi 1.75 .85
a. Booklet pane of 4, perf. 14x13¼ on 3 sides 7.25 —
Complete booklet, #617a 7.25

Baumanu Karlis (1835-1905), Composer of National Anthem — A194

2005, May 21 *Perf. 13¾x13¼*
618 A194 20s multi .85 .40

Kaive Oak — A195

Serpentine Die Cut 14
2005, June 11
Self-Adhesive
619 A195 15s multi 1.25 .60

Printed in sheets of 8.

Fish Type of 2004

Designs: 15s, Lampetra fluviatilis. 40s, Clupea harengus membras.

2005, Aug. 13 Litho. *Perf. 13¼x14*
620-621 A182 Set of 2 2.50 1.25

Pope John Paul II (1920-2005) A196

2005, Aug. 14 *Perf. 14¼x13½*
622 A196 15s multi .80 .40

Souvenir Sheet

Latvian National Library — A197

2005, Aug. 27 *Perf. 13¼x12¾*
623 A197 100s multi 4.75 2.40

Janis Plieksans (Rainis), (1865-1929), Writer — A198

2005, Sept. 10 *Perf. 14¼*
624 A198 40s multi 1.60 .80
a. Booklet pane of 6, perf. 14¼ on 3 sides 9.75 —
Complete booklet, #624a 9.75

Souvenir Sheet

Bridge Over Railroad Tracks, Riga — A199

2005, Sept. 24 ***Perf. 13¼x13¾***
625 A199 100s multi 6.00 3.00

Lighthouse Type of 2003

2005, Oct. 8 Litho. ***Perf. 14x13¼***
626 A170 40s Daugavgrivas 1.75 .85
a. Booklet pane of 4, perf. 14x13¼ on 3 sides 7.25 —
Complete booklet, #626a 7.25

Gunars Astra (1931-88), Human Rights Activist in Soviet Union — A200

2005, Oct. 22 ***Perf. 13½x14¼***
627 A200 15s multi .65 .30

Palace Type of 2004

2005, Nov. 5 ***Perf. 13¼x14***
628 A187 40s Durbes Palace, horiz. 1.60 .80

Mittens Type of 2002

2005, Nov. 26 ***Perf. 13¼x13¾***
629 A165 20s Dienvidlatgale mittens .80 .40

Christmas A201

Designs: 12s, Goat riding on wolf's back. No. 631, 15s, Woman, dog near tree, vert. No. 632, 15s, Cat, woman carrying rooster, vert.

2005, Dec. 3 ***Serpentine Die Cut 15***
Self-Adhesive
630-632 A201 Set of 3 1.75 .85

Europa Stamps, 50th Anniv. A202

Latvian Europa stamps: Nos. 633, 637a, 10s, #414. Nos. 634, 637b, 15s, #463. Nos. 635, 637c, 15s, #442. Nos. 636, 637d, 20s, #484-485.

2006, Jan. 7 Litho. ***Perf. 13¾x13¼***
633-636 A202 Set of 4 2.50 1.25

Souvenir Sheet

Perf. 13½ Syncopated
637 A202 Sheet of 4, #a-d 2.50 1.25

No. 637 contains four 45x28mm stamps.

Town Arms Type of 2002

2006, Jan. 11 ***Perf. 13¼x13¾***
638 A153 7s Aizkraukle .30 .20
639 A153 22s Kraslava .85 .40
640 A153 31s Limbazi 1.25 .60
Nos. 638-640 (3) 2.40 1.20

2006 Winter Olympics, Turin — A203

2006, Feb. 4 ***Perf. 14***
641 A203 45s multi 1.75 .85

Stamerienas Palace — A204

2006, Feb. 25 ***Perf. 14¼x13¾***
642 A204 95s multi 3.75 1.90

Zvartes Iezis — A205

Serpentine Die Cut 14
2006, Mar. 11
Self-Adhesive
643 A205 22s multi .90 .45

Printed in sheets of 8.

Souvenir Sheet

Raunu Railroad Bridge — A206

2006, Mar. 25 ***Perf. 13½x14***
644 A206 100s multi 3.75 1.90

2006 World Ice Hockey Championships, Riga — A207

Perf. 13½x14¼
2006, Mar. 31 Litho.
645 A207 55s multi + label 2.00 1.00
a. Booklet pane of 4, perf. 13½x14¼ on 3 sides, without labels 8.00 —
Complete booklet, #645a 8.00

Cesis, 800th Anniv. — A208

Various sites in Cesis: 22s, 31s, 45s, 55s. 45s and 55s are horiz.

Perf. 13¼x13¾, 13¾x13¼
2006, Apr. 7
646-649 A208 Set of 4 6.00 3.00

Traditional Jewelry — A209

No. 650: a, Brooch, Latvia. b, Bracelet, Kazakhstan.

2006, Apr. 19 ***Perf. 14x13¾***
650 A209 22s Horiz. pair, #a-b 1.75 .85

See Kazakhstan No. 509.

Europa — A210

2006, May 3 ***Perf. 13½x14¼***
651 A210 85s multi 4.00 2.00
a. Tete beche pair 8.00 4.00

Ciganiete ar Tamburinu, by Karlis Huns — A211

2006, May 13 ***Perf. 13¼x14***
652 A211 40s multi 1.60 .80
a. Booklet pane of 4, perf. 13¼x14 on 3 sides 6.50 —
Complete booklet, #652a 6.50

A212

Personalizable Stamps A213

2006, June 9 ***Perf. 13¾***
653 A212 31s yel bister 1.25 .60
654 A213 31s yel bister 1.25 .60

Stamp vignettes could be personalized by customers, presumably for an extra fee.

"Big Christopher" Statue — A214

2006, June 16 ***Perf. 14x13½***
655 A214 36s multi 1.40 .70

Art by Anna Koshkina — A215

Die Cut Perf. 14½x13 on 3 Sides
2006, Aug. 11
Booklet Stamp
Self-Adhesive
656 A215 22s multi .90 .45
a. Booklet pane of 8 7.25

Volunteer Army, 15th Anniv. — A216

2006, Aug. 23 ***Perf. 13½x14***
657 A216 22s multi .90 .45

Staburags — A217

2006, Sept. 9 Litho. ***Perf. 14¼x13¾***
658 A217 58s multi 2.10 1.10
a. Tete beche pair 4.25 2.25

Wild Animals and Their Tracks — A218

Designs: 45s, Lynx lynx. 55s, Cervus elaphus.

2006, Sept. 23 ***Perf. 14¼x13½***
659-660 A218 Set of 2 3.75 1.90
659a Booklet pane of 4 #659, perf. 14¼x13½ on 3 sides 6.50 —
Complete booklet, #659a 6.50
659b Tete beche pair 3.50 3.50
660a Tete beche pair 4.00 4.00

See Nos. 691-692, 719-720, 744-745.

Pansija Pili, Novel by Anslavs Eglitis (1906-93) A219

2006, Oct. 14 Litho. ***Perf. 13¼x13½***
661 A219 67s multi 2.50 1.25

Lighthouse Type of 2003

2006, Oct. 27 ***Perf. 14¼x13½***
662 A170 40s Mersraga Lighthouse 1.50 .75
a. Booklet pane of 4, perf. 14¼x13½ on 3 sides 6.00 —
Complete booklet, #662a 6.00

NATO Summit, Riga A220

2006, Nov. 17 ***Perf. 13¾x13¼***
663 A220 55s multi 2.10 1.10

Christmas A221

Cookies in shape of: 18s, Christmas tree. 22s, Star. 31s, Crescent moon. 45s, Bell.

Serpentine Die Cut 14

2006, Nov. 17

Self-Adhesive

664-667 A221 Set of 4 4.50 2.25

Oskars Kalpaks (1882-1919), First Commander-in-chief of Latvian Army — A222

2007, Jan. 6 ***Perf. 14¼x14***

668 A222 22s multi 1.00 .50

Mobile Telecommunications in Latvia, 15th Anniv. — A223

2007, Jan. 19

669 A223 22s multi 1.00 .50
a. Tete beche pair 2.00 1.00

Town Arms Type of 2002

2007, Feb. 3 ***Perf. 13¼x13¾***

670 A153 5s Staicele .25 .20
a. Perf. 14x14¼, "2010" .20 .20
671 A153 10s Sabile .50 .25
672 A153 22s Vecumnieki 1.00 .50
Nos. 670-672 (3) 1.75 .95

Issued: No. 670a, 3/12/10.

Tilts Tornkalna, Painting by Ludolfs Liberts (1895-1959) A224

2007, Feb. 17 ***Perf. 14¼x14***

673 A224 58s multi 2.50 1.25

Pauls Stradins Museum of the History of Medicine, Riga, 50th Anniv. A225

2007, Mar. 9 ***Perf. 14x14¼***

674 A225 22s multi 1.00 .50

Baltic Coast — A226

Serpentine Die Cut 14

2007, Mar. 24

Self-Adhesive

675 A226 22s multi 1.00 .50

Lighthouse Type of 2003

2007, Apr. 14 ***Perf. 13¾x13½***

676 A170 67s Papes Lighthouse 3.00 1.50
a. Booklet pane of 4, perf. 13¾x13½ on 3 sides 12.00 —
Complete booklet, #676a 12.00

Europa — A227

2007, Apr. 28 Litho. ***Perf. 13½x14¼***

677 A227 85s multi 3.75 1.90
a. Tete beche pair 7.50 3.75

Scouting, cent.

Palace Type of 2004

2007, June 8 Litho. ***Perf. 13½x14¼***

678 A187 22s Krustpils, horiz. 1.00 .50

UNESCO World Heritage Sites — A228

Designs: 36s, Historic Center of Riga. 45s, Historic Centers of Straslund and Wismar, Germany.

2007, July 12 Litho. ***Perf. 14x13¾***

679-680 A228 Set of 2 3.75 1.90

See Germany Nos. 2449-2450.

Sigulda, 800th Anniv. — A229

Designs: 22s, New Sigulda Castle. 31s, Bobsled course. 40s, Sigulda Castle ruins.

Serpentine Die Cut 15¼

2007, Aug. 10

Self-Adhesive

681-683 A229 Set of 3 4.00 2.00

Berries and Mushrooms A230

Designs: 22s, Vaccinium vitis-idaea. 58s, Cantharellus cibarius.

2007, Aug. 25 ***Perf. 14x13½***

684 A230 22s multi 1.00 .45
a. Tete beche pair 2.00 2.00
685 A230 58s multi 2.50 1.25
a. Booklet pane of 4, perf. 14x13½ on 3 sides 10.00 —
Complete booklet, #685a 10.00
b. Tete beche pair 5.00 5.00

See Nos. 715-716, 742-743, 767-768.

Organized Soccer in Latvia, Cent. — A231

2007, Sept. 8 ***Perf. 13¾***

686 A231 45s multi 2.00 1.00

Values are for stamps with surrounding selvage.

Souvenir Sheet

Aivieksti Railroad Bridge — A232

2007, Oct. 13 ***Perf. 14***

687 A232 100s multi 4.50 2.25

Latvia Post, 375th Anniv. A233

Designs: 22s, Postrider. 31s, Postal worker and van.

Serpentine Die Cut 15

2007, Oct. 20 **Litho.**

Self-Adhesive

688-689 A233 Set of 2 2.50 1.25

13th Century Decorations A234

2007, Nov. 3 ***Perf. 13¼x14***

690 A234 60s multi 2.75 1.40

Wild Animals and Their Tracks Type of 2006

Designs: 45s, Vulpes vulpes. 55s, Alces alces.

2007, Nov. 16 ***Perf. 14¼x13½***

691 A218 45s multi 2.00 1.00
a. Tete beche pair 3.50 3.50
692 A218 55s multi 2.50 1.25
a. Tete beche pair 5.00 5.00

Christmas A235

Christmas tree and children with: 22s, Musical instruments. 31s, Cookies. 45s, Skis and sled.

Serpentine Die Cut 15

2007, Nov. 24

Self-Adhesive

693-695 A235 Set of 3 4.50 2.25

Town Arms Type of 2002 With Country Name at Top

2008, Feb. 9 ***Perf. 13¼x13¾***

696 A153 22s Salaspils .95 .50
697 A153 28s Plavinas 1.25 .60
698 A153 45s Saulkrasti 2.00 1.00
Nos. 696-698 (3) 4.20 2.10

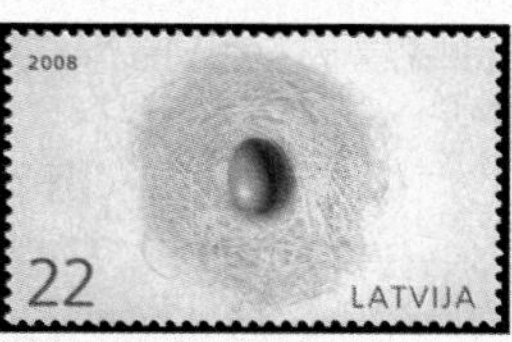

Easter A236

2008, Feb. 23 ***Perf. 13¼x13***

699 A236 22s multi 1.00 .50

Augli, by Leo Svemps A237

2008, Mar. 8 Litho. ***Perf. 13x13¼***

700 A237 63s multi 3.00 3.00

State Awards of the Baltic Countries — A238

Designs: Nos. 701, 702a, Order of Three Stars, Latvia. No. 702b, Order of Vytautas the Great, Lithuania. No. 702c, Order of the National Coat of Arms, Estonia.

2008, Mar. 15 ***Perf. 13½x13¾***

701 A238 31s multi 1.40 1.40

Souvenir Sheet

702 A238 31s Sheet of 3, #a-c 4.25 4.25

On No. 701, the second line of type above the medal is 18mm wide, while it is 15mm wide on No. 702a.

See Estonia Nos. 592-593, Lithuania Nos. 862-863.

Worldwide Fund for Nature (WWF) — A239

Bats: 22s, Barbastella barbastellus. 31s, Myotis dasycneme. 45s, Barbastella barbastellus, vert. 55s, Myotis dasycneme, vert.

Perf. 13½x14¼, 14¼x13½

2008, Apr. 12

703 A239 22s multi 1.00 1.00
a. Tete beche pair 2.00 2.00
704 A239 31s multi 1.40 1.40
a. Tete beche pair 2.80 2.80
705 A239 45s multi 2.00 2.00
a. Tete beche pair 4.00 4.00
706 A239 55s multi 2.40 2.40
a. Tete beche pair 4.80 4.80
Nos. 703-706 (4) 6.80 6.80

Europa — A240

Designs: 45s, Letters and postcards. 85s, Person writing letter.

2008, Apr. 22 *Perf. 13½*

707 A240 45s multi 2.00 2.00
a. Tete beche pair 4.00 4.00
708 A240 multi 3.75 3.75
a. Tete beche pair 7.50 7.50

Lighthouse Type of 2003

2008, May 5 *Perf. 14¼x13½*

709 A170 63s Akmenraga Lighthouse 3.00 3.00

European Orienteering Championships, Ventspils — A241

2008, May 23 Litho. *Perf. 13x13¼*

710 A241 45s multi 2.10 2.10
a. Tete beche pair 4.25 4.25

Nature Protection A242

Serpentine Die Cut 12½

2008, June 7

Self-Adhesive

711 A242 22s multi .95 .95

Riga Museum Foundations — A243

2008, June 26 *Perf. 13x13½*

712 A243 22s multi 1.00 1.00

2008 Summer Olympics, Beijing — A244

2008, Aug. 8 *Perf. 13½x13*

713 A244 63s multi 2.75 2.75

Sudraba Fairy Tale — A245

Perf. 14¼x13½

2008, Aug. 23 Litho.

714 A245 22s multi .95 .95
a. Tete beche pair 1.90 1.90

Berries and Mushrooms Type of 2007

Designs: 22s, Vaccinium myrtillus. 58s, Leccinum aurantiacum.

2008, Sept. 6 *Perf. 14x13½*

715 A230 22s multi .90 .90
a. Tete beche pair 1.90 1.90
716 A230 58s multi 2.25 2.25
a. Perf. 13½x14 on 3 sides 2.25 2.25
b. Booklet pane of 4 #716a 9.00 —
Complete booklet, #716b 9.00
c. Tete beche pair 4.50 4.50

Souvenir Sheet

Kandavas Bridge — A246

2008, Sept. 27 *Perf. 14*

717 A246 100s multi 4.00 4.00

Tautas Fronte Newspaper, 20th Anniv. — A247

2008, Oct. 8 *Perf. 13½*

718 A247 22s multi 1.00 1.00
a. Tete beche pair 1.75 1.75

Wild Animals and Their Tracks Type of 2006

Designs: 45s, Martes martes. 55s, Castor fiber.

2008, Oct. 10 *Perf. 14¼x13½*

719-720 A218 Set of 2 4.25 4.25

Maris Strombergs, 2008 BMX Cycling Olympic Gold Medalist — A248

2008, Oct. 24 *Perf. 13½*

721 A248 22s multi 1.00 1.00

Plate, Bow and Tablecloth A249

2008, Oct. 25 *Perf. 13½x13¾*

722 A249 28s multi 1.25 1.25

Latvian Republic, 90th Anniv. — A250

2008, Nov. 7 *Perf. 13¼x13*

723 A250 31s multi 1.40 1.40

Mezotnes Palace A251

2008, Nov. 8 *Perf. 13½x14¼*

724 A251 63s multi 2.75 2.75

Christmas — A252

2008, Nov. 28 *Perf. 14¼x13¾*

725 A252 25s multi 1.10 1.10

Town Arms Type of 2002 With Country Name at Top

2009, Jan. 10 Litho. *Perf. 14x14¼*

726 A153 33s Dagda 1.40 1.40
727 A153 35s Balozi 1.60 1.60
728 A153 60s Stende 2.50 2.50
Nos. 726-728 (3) 5.50 5.50

Brooch, 8th Cent. A. D. — A253

2009, Jan. 24 *Perf. 14*

729 A253 98s multi 4.25 4.25

Dancing Boy and Animals Folktale A254

2009, Feb. 21 *Perf. 13¼*

730 A254 40s multi 1.75 1.75

Souvenir Sheet

Preservation of Polar Regions and Glaciers — A255

No. 731: a, 35s, Polar bear. b, 55s, Penguins.

2009, Mar. 18 Litho. *Perf. 13¼*

731 A255 Sheet of 2, #a-b 3.50 3.50

Europa — A256

Designs: 50s, Janis Ikaunieks, astronomer, and Baldone Observatory telescope. 55s, Map of solar system, asteroid, University of Latvia Institute of Astronomy, radio telescope, five astronomers.

2009, Apr. 2 *Perf. 14x13¾*

732-733 A256 Set of 2 4.00 4.00

Intl. Year of Astronomy.

Natl. Museum of History A257

2009, May 14 *Perf. 13½*

734 A257 35s multi 1.40 1.40

Basketball A258

Player from opposing team and: 35s, Male Latvian team player, 1935. 40s, Female TTT Riga player. 60s, Male ASK Riga player.

120s, Latvian player in 2009 Women's European Basketball Championships.

2009, June 6

735-737 A258 Set of 3 5.50 5.50

Souvenir Sheet

738 A258 120s multi 5.00 5.00

Nos. 735-737 each were printed in sheets of 9 + label.

Bauska, 400th Anniv. A259

2009, July 10 Litho. *Perf. 13½x14*

739 A259 38s multi 1.50 1.50

Steam Locomotive — A260

2009, Aug. 5 Litho. *Perf. 13½*

740 A260 35s multi 1.40 1.40

Souvenir Sheet

Dienvidu Bridge, Riga — A261

2009, Aug. 22

741 A261 100s multi 4.25 4.25

Berries and Mushrooms Type of 2007

Designs: 55s, Fragaria vesca. 60s, Russula paludosa.

2009, Sept. 12

742-743 A230 Set of 2 4.75 4.75
743a Perf. 13½ on 3 sides 2.50 2.50
743b Booklet pane of 4 #743a 10.00 —
Complete booklet, #743b 10.00

Wild Animals and Their Tracks Type of 2006

Designs: 35s, Canis lupus. 98s, Lepus europaeus.

2009, Oct. 21 ***Perf. 13½x14¼***

744-745 A218 Set of 2 5.75 5.75

Lighthouse Type of 2003

2009, Nov. 5 Litho. *Perf. 13¼*

746 A170 63s Liepaja Lighthouse 2.75 2.75

Republic of Latvia, 91st Anniv. — A262

Designs: 35s, Formation of Latvian People's Council, Nov. 17, 1918. 40s, Proclamation of Latvian Republic, Nov. 18, 1918. 100s, First meeting of Constitutional Assembly, May 1, 1920.

2009, Nov. 14 Litho. *Perf. 14*

747-749 A262 Set of 3 7.50 7.50

Christmas A263

Designs: 35s, Horse Christmas ornament, building. 55s, Fish Christmas ornament, building. 60s, Snowflake Christmas ornament.

2009, Nov. 27 ***Perf. 13¼***

750-752 A263 Set of 3 6.25 6.25

Town Arms Type of 2002 With Country Name at Top

2010, Jan. 16 Litho. *Perf. 14x14¼*

753 A153 35s Viesite 1.40 1.40
754 A153 40s Ligatne 1.60 1.60
755 A153 55s Iecava 2.25 2.25
Nos. 753-755 (3) 5.25 5.25

2010 Winter Olympics, Vancouver — A264

2010, Feb. 5 ***Perf. 13¼x13¾***

756 A264 55s multi 2.25 2.25

Peonies A265

2010, Mar. 26 ***Perf. 13¼***

757 A265 35s multi 1.40 1.40

Europa A266

Designs: 55s, Girl holding books, characters from children's books. 120s, Boy reading book, ship, castle, mountain.

2010, Apr. 9 Litho. *Perf. 13½x13¼*

758-759 A266 Set of 2 6.75 6.75

Expo 2010, Shanghai A267

2010, Apr. 23 ***Perf. 13¼***

760 A267 150s multi 5.75 5.75

Declaration of May 4, 1990, 20th Anniv. A268

2010, May 4

761 A268 35s multi 1.25 1.25

Fire Fighting Museum A269

2010, May 21

762 A269 98s multi 3.50 3.50

Birds — A270

Designs: 35s, Coracias garrulus. 98s, Bubo bubo, vert.

Perf. 14x13¾, 13¾x14

2010, June 18

763-764 A270 Set of 2 4.75 4.75

Talsos Sports Hall — A271

2010, July 16 ***Perf. 13¼***

765 A271 150s multi 5.50 5.50

RP Series Locomotive — A272

2010, Aug. 5 ***Perf. 13¼x13½***

766 A272 40s multi 1.50 1.50

Berries and Mushrooms Type of 2007

Designs: 55s, Rubus ideus. 120s, Leccinum scabrum.

2010, Sept. 10 ***Perf. 13½x13¼***

767 A230 55s multi 2.00 2.00
768 A230 120s multi 4.50 4.50

Republic of Latvia, 92nd Anniv. — A273

National symbols: 35s, Flag. 38s, Arms. 98s, Anthem.

2010, Nov. 12 Litho. *Perf. 14*

770-772 A273 Set of 3 6.75 6.75

Christmas A274

Designs: 35s, Girl, cat, Christmas tree. 60s, Boy with gift, bird in tree.

2010, Dec. 3 ***Perf. 13½x13¼***

773 A274 35s multi 1.40 1.40
774 A274 60s multi 2.25 2.25

SEMI-POSTAL STAMPS

"Mercy" Assisting Wounded Soldier — SP1

1920 Unwmk. Typo. *Perf. 11½*

Brown and Green Design on Back

B1 SP1 20(30)k dk brn & red .50 *1.25*
B2 SP1 40(55)k dk bl & red .50 *1.25*
B3 SP1 50(70)k dk grn & red .50 *1.50*
B4 SP1 1(1.30)r dl sl & red .50 *2.50*

Wmk. 197

Blue Design on Back

B5 SP1 20(30)k dk brn & red .50 *1.25*
B6 SP1 40(55)k dk bl & red .50 *1.25*
a. Vert. pair, imperf. btwn. 40.00
B7 SP1 50(70)k dk grn & red .50 *1.50*
B8 SP1 1(1.30)r dk sl & red .50 *2.50*

Wmk. Similar to 145

Pink Paper *Imperf.*

Brown, Green and Red Design on Back

B9 SP1 20(30)k dk brn & red 1.00 *2.50*
B10 SP1 40(55)k dk bl & red 1.00 *2.50*
B11 SP1 50(70)k dk grn & red 1.00 *2.50*
B12 SP1 1(1.30)r dk sl & red 2.00 *4.25*
Nos. B1-B12 (12) 9.00 *24.75*
Set, never hinged 17.50

These semi-postal stamps were printed on the backs of unfinished bank notes of the Workers and Soldiers Council, Riga, and the Bermondt-Avalov Army. Blocks of stamps showing complete banknotes on reverse are worth approximately three times the catalogue value of the stamps.

Nos. B1-B8 Surcharged

1921 Unwmk. *Perf. 11½*

Brown and Green Design on Back

B13 SP1 20k + 2r dk brn & red 1.00 *4.00*
B14 SP1 40k + 2r dk bl & red 1.00 *4.00*
B15 SP1 50k + 2r dk grn & red 1.00 *4.00*
B16 SP1 1r + 2r dk sl & red 1.00 *4.00*

Wmk. 197

Blue Design on Back

B17 SP1 20k + 2r dk brn & red 10.00 *35.00*
B18 SP1 40k + 2r dk bl & red 10.00 *35.00*
B19 SP1 50k + 2r dk grn & red 10.00 *35.00*
B20 SP1 1r + 2r dk sl & red 10.00 *35.00*
Nos. B13-B20 (8) 44.00 *156.00*
Set, never hinged 140.00

Regular Issue of 1923-25 Surcharged in Blue

1923 Wmk. Similar to 181 *Perf. 10*

B21 A12 1s + 10s violet .75 1.75
B22 A12 2s + 10s yellow .75 1.75
B23 A12 4s + 10s dk green .75 1.75
Nos. B21-B23 (3) 2.25 5.25
Set, never hinged 5.00

The surtax benefited the Latvian War Invalids Society.

Lighthouse and Harbor, Liepaja (Libau) SP2

Church at Liepaja — SP5

Coat of Arms of Liepaja — SP6

Designs: 15s (25s), City Hall, Liepaja. 25s (35s), Public Bathing Pavilion, Liepaja.

1925, July 23 ***Perf. 11½***

B24 SP2 6s (12s) red brown & deep blue 2.50 *5.00*
B25 SP2 15s (25s) dk bl & brn 1.50 *4.00*
B26 SP2 25s (35s) violet & dark green 2.50 2.50
B27 SP5 30s (40s) dark blue & lake 4.50 *12.00*

B28	SP6	50s (60s) dark grn & violet	6.50	*15.00*
		Nos. B24-B28 (5)	17.50	*38.50*
		Set, never hinged	30.00	

Tercentenary of Liepaja (Libau). The surtax benefited that city. Exist imperf. Value, unused set $500.

President Janis Cakste — SP7

1928, Apr. 18 **Engr.**

B29	SP7	2s (12s) red orange	2.50	2.00
B30	SP7	6s (16s) deep green	2.50	2.00
B31	SP7	15s (25s) red brown	2.50	2.00
B32	SP7	25s (35s) deep blue	2.50	2.00
B33	SP7	30s (40s) claret	2.50	2.00
		Nos. B29-B33 (5)	12.50	10.00
		Set, never hinged	20.00	

The surtax helped erect a monument to Janis Cakste, 1st pres. of the Latvian Republic.

Venta River — SP8

Allegory, "Latvia" — SP9

View of Jelgava SP10

National Theater, Riga — SP11

View of Cesis (Wenden) SP12

Riga Bridge and Trenches SP13

Perf. 11½, Imperf.

1928, Nov. 18 **Wmk. 212** **Litho.**

B34	SP8	6s (16s) green	1.50	*2.00*
B35	SP9	10s (20s) scarlet	1.50	*2.00*
B36	SP10	15s (25s) maroon	2.00	2.00
B37	SP11	30s (40s) ultra	1.50	2.00
B38	SP12	50s (60s) dk gray	1.50	1.00
B39	SP13	1 l (1.10 l) choc	3.75	2.00
		Nos. B34-B39 (6)	11.75	11.00
		Set, never hinged	25.00	

The surtax was given to a committee for the erection of a Liberty Memorial.

Z. A. Meierovics SP14

1929, Aug. 22 ***Perf. 11½, Imperf.***

B46	SP14	2s (4s) orange	2.50	2.50
B47	SP14	6s (12s) dp grn	2.50	2.50
B48	SP14	15s (25s) red brown	2.50	2.50
B49	SP14	25s (35s) deep blue	2.50	2.50
B50	SP14	30s (40s) ultra	2.50	2.50
		Nos. B46-B50 (5)	12.50	12.50
		Set, never hinged	30.00	

The surtax was used to erect a monument to Z. A. Meierovics, Latvian statesman.

Tuberculosis Cross — SP15

Allegory of Hope for the Sick — SP16

Gustavs Zemgals — SP17

Riga Castle — SP18

Daisies and Double-barred Cross — SP20

Tuberculosis Sanatorium, near Riga — SP22

Cakste, Kviesis and Zemgals SP23

Designs: No. B61, Janis Cakste, 1st pres. of Latvia. No. B63, Pres. Alberts Kviesis.

1930, Dec. 4 **Typo.** ***Perf. 10, 11½***

B56	SP15	1s (2s) dk vio & red orange	.85	.85
B57	SP15	2s (4s) org & red orange	.85	.85
a.		Cliché of 1s (2s) in plate of 2s (4s)	*700.00*	*700.00*
B58	SP16	4s (8s) dk grn & red	.85	.85
B59	SP17	5s (10s) brt grn & dk brown	1.75	1.75
B60	SP18	6s (12s) ol grn & bister	1.75	1.75
B61	SP17	10s (20s) dp red & black	2.50	2.25
B62	SP20	15s (30s) mar & dl green	2.50	2.25
B63	SP17	20s (40s) rose lake & ind	2.50	2.25
B64	SP22	25s (50s) multi	3.50	3.50
B65	SP23	30s (60s) multi	4.25	5.00
		Nos. B56-B65 (10)	21.30	21.30
		Set, never hinged	50.00	

Surtax for the Latvian Anti-Tuberculosis Soc.

For surcharges see Nos. B72-B81.

J. Rainis and New Buildings, Riga SP24

Character from Play and Rainis SP25

Characters from Plays — SP26

Rainis and Lyre SP27

Flames, Flag and Rainis SP28

1930, May 23 **Wmk. 212** ***Perf. 11½***

B66	SP24	1s (2s) dull violet	.75	*3.00*
B67	SP25	2s (4s) yellow org	.75	*3.00*
B68	SP26	4s (8s) dp green	.75	*3.00*
B69	SP27	6s (12s) yel grn & red brown	.75	*3.00*
B70	SP28	10s (20s) dark red	20.00	*45.00*
B71	SP27	15s (30s) red brn & yellow green	20.00	*45.00*
		Nos. B66-B71 (6)	43.00	*102.00*
		Set, never hinged	80.00	

Sold at double face value, surtax going to memorial fund for J. Rainis (Jan Plieksans, 1865-1929), writer and politician.

Exist imperf. Value twice that of perf. stamps.

Nos. B56 to B65 Surcharged in Black

1931, Aug. 19 ***Perf. 10, 11½***

B72	SP18	9s on 6s (12s)	1.00	1.00
B73	SP15	16s on 1s (2s)	12.50	15.00
B74	SP15	17s on 2s (4s)	1.25	1.25
B75	SP16	19s on 4s (8s)	3.75	*6.00*
B76	SP17	20s on 5s (10s)	2.50	*6.00*
B77	SP20	23s on 15s (30s)	1.00	2.00
B78	SP17	25s on 10s (20s)	2.50	3.00
B79	SP17	35s on 20s (40s)	3.75	*4.50*
B80	SP22	45s on 25s (50s)	10.00	*12.50*
B81	SP23	55s on 30s (60s)	12.50	*20.00*
		Nos. B72-B81 (10)	50.75	71.25
		Set, never hinged	100.00	

The surcharge replaces the original total price, including surtax.

Nos. B73-B81 have no bars in the surcharge. The surtax aided the Latvian Anti-Tuberculosis Society.

Lacplesis, the Deliverer SP29

Designs: 1s, Kriva telling stories under Holy Oak. 2s, Enslaved Latvians building Riga under knight's supervision. 4s, Death of Black Knight. 5s, Spirit of Lacplesis over freed Riga.

Inscribed: "AIZSARGI" (Army Reserve)

1932, Feb. 10 ***Perf. 10½, Imperf.***

B82	SP29	1s (11s) vio brn & bluish	2.50	2.50
B83	SP29	2s (17s) ocher & ol green	2.50	2.50
B84	SP29	3s (23s) red brn & org brown	2.50	2.50
B85	SP29	4s (34s) dk green & green	2.50	2.50
B86	SP29	5s (45s) green & emerald	2.50	2.50
		Nos. B82-B86 (5)	12.50	12.50
		Set, never hinged	20.00	

Surtax aided the Militia Maintenance Fund.

Marching Troops SP30

Infantry in Action SP31

Nurse Binding Soldier's Wound — SP32

Army Soup Kitchen — SP33

Gen. J. Balodis — SP34

1932, May ***Perf. 10½, Imperf.***

B87	SP30	6s (25s) ol brn & red violet	4.50	6.00
B88	SP31	7s (35s) dk bl grn & dark blue	4.50	6.00
B89	SP32	10s (45s) ol green & black brown	4.50	6.00
B90	SP33	12s (55s) lake & ol green	4.50	6.00
B91	SP34	15s (75s) red org & brown violet	4.50	6.00
		Nos. B87-B91 (5)	22.50	30.00
		Set, never hinged	40.00	

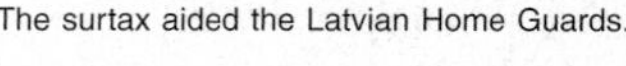

The surtax aided the Latvian Home Guards.

Symbolical of Unified Latvia — SP35

Aid to the Sick — SP37

Symbolical of the Strength of the Latvian Union
SP36

"Charity"
SP38

Wmk. 212

1936, Dec. 28 Litho. *Perf. 11½*

B92 SP35 3s orange red 1.50 *3.50*
B93 SP36 10s green 1.50 *3.50*
B94 SP37 20s rose pink 1.50 *4.50*
B95 SP38 35s blue 1.50 *4.50*
Nos. B92-B95 (4) 6.00 *16.00*
Set, never hinged 12.00

Souvenir Sheets

SP39

1938, May 12 Wmk. 212 *Perf. 11*

B96 SP39 Sheet of 2 7.50 *20.00*
Never hinged 15.00
a. 35s Justice Palace, Riga 2.00 *5.00*
b. 40s Power Station, Kegums 2.00 *5.00*

Sold for 2 l. The surtax of 1.25 l was for the National Reconstruction Fund.

No. B96 exists imperf.

Overprinted in Blue with Dates 1934 1939 and "15" over "V"

1939

B97 SP39 Sheet of 2 15.00 *40.00*
Never hinged 30.00

5th anniv. of Natl. Unity Day. Sold for 2 lats. Surtax for the Natl. Reconstruction Fund.

Natl. Olympic Committee
SP50

1992, Feb. 8 Litho. *Perf. 13½x13*

Background Color

B150 SP50 50k +25k gray .85 .85
B151 SP50 50k +25k buff 1.75 1.75
B152 SP50 100k +50k bister 1.25 1.25
Nos. B150-B152 (3) 3.85 3.85

No. B150 inscribed "Berlin 18.09.91."

AIR POST STAMPS

Blériot XI — AP1

Wmk. Wavy Lines Similar to 181

1921, July 30 Litho. *Perf. 11½*

C1 AP1 10r emerald 2.50 4.00
a. Imperf. 7.50 *13.00*
C2 AP1 20r dark blue 2.50 4.00
a. Imperf. 7.50 *13.00*
Set, perf, never hinged 10.00
Set, imperf, never hinged 25.00

1928, May 1

C3 AP1 10s deep green 2.50 1.50
C4 AP1 15s red 1.50 1.50
C5 AP1 25s ultra 3.50 2.50
a. Pair, imperf. btwn. 35.00
Nos. C3-C5 (3) 7.50 5.50
Set, never hinged 15.00

Nos. C1-C5 sometimes show letters of a paper maker's watermark "PACTIEN LIGAT MILLS."

1931-32 Wmk. 212 *Perf. 11, 11½*

C6 AP1 10s deep green 1.00 .90
C7 AP1 15s red 1.50 1.00
C8 AP1 25s deep blue ('32) 8.50 1.25
Nos. C6-C8 (3) 11.00 3.15
Set, never hinged 17.50

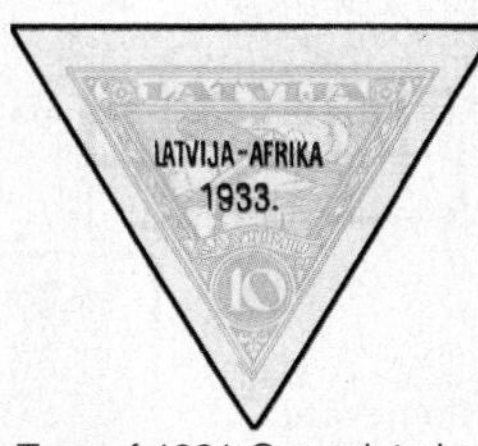

Type of 1921 Overprinted or Surcharged in Black

1933, May 26 Wmk. 212 *Imperf.*

C9 AP1 10s deep green 40.00 *75.00*
C10 AP1 15s red 40.00 *75.00*
C11 AP1 25s deep blue 40.00 *75.00*
C12 AP1 50s on 15s red 200.00 *500.00*
C13 AP1 100s on 25s dp blue 200.00 *500.00*
Nos. C9-C13 (5) 520.00 *1,225.*
Set, never hinged 800.00

Honoring and financing a flight from Riga to Bathurst, Gambia. The plane crashed at Neustettin, Germany.

Counterfeits exist of Nos. C1-C13.

AIR POST SEMI-POSTAL STAMPS

Durbes Castle, Rainis Birthplace — SPAP1

Wmk. 212

1930, May 26 Litho. *Perf. 11½*

CB1 SPAP1 10s (20s) red & olive green 5.00 *12.00*
CB2 SPAP1 15s (30s) dk yel green & copper red 5.00 *12.00*
Set, never hinged 20.00

Surtax for the Rainis Memorial Fund.

Imperf.

CB1a SPAP1 10s (20s) 7.50 *25.00*
CB2a SPAP1 15s (30s) 7.50 *25.00*
Set, never hinged 30.00

Nos. C6-C8 Surcharged in Magenta, Blue or Red

1931, Dec. 5

CB3 AP1 10s + 50s deep green (M) 5.00 *6.10*
CB4 AP1 15s + 1 l red (Bl) 5.00 *6.10*
CB5 AP1 25s + 1.50 l deep blue 5.00 *6.10*
Nos. CB3-CB5 (3) 15.00 *18.30*
Set, never hinged 30.00

Surtax for the Latvian Home Guards.

Imperf.

CB3a AP1 10s + 50s 8.00 *9.00*
CB4a AP1 15s + 1 l 8.00 *9.00*
CB5a AP1 25s + 1.50 l 8.00 *9.00*
Nos. CB3a-CB5a (3) 24.00 *27.00*
Set, never hinged 50.00

SPAP2

1932, June 17 *Perf. 10½*

CB6 SPAP2 10s (20s) dk sl grn & green 12.50 *22.50*
CB7 SPAP2 15s (30s) brt red & buff 12.50 *22.50*
CB8 SPAP2 25s (50s) dp bl & gray 12.50 *22.50*
Nos. CB6-CB8 (3) 37.50 *67.50*
Set, never hinged 75.00

Surtax for the Latvian Home Guards.

Imperf.

CB6a SPAP2 10s (20s) 12.50 22.50
CB7a SPAP2 15s (30s) 12.50 22.50
CB8a SPAP2 25s (50s) 12.50 22.50
Nos. CB6a-CB8a (3) 37.50 *67.50*
Set, never hinged 75.00

Icarus — SPAP3

Leonardo da Vinci — SPAP4

Charles Balloon — SPAP5

Wright Brothers Biplane
SPAP6

Bleriot Monoplane
SPAP7

1932, Dec. *Perf. 10, 11½*

CB9 SPAP3 5s (25s) ol bister & green 15.00 *20.00*
CB10 SPAP4 10s (50s) ol brn & gray grn 15.00 *20.00*
CB11 SPAP5 15s (75s) red brown & gray grn 15.00 *20.00*
CB12 SPAP6 20s (1 l) gray grn & lil rose 15.00 *20.00*
CB13 SPAP7 25s (1.25 l) brn & bl 15.00 *20.00*
Nos. CB9-CB13 (5) 75.00 100.00
Set, never hinged 125.00

Issued to honor pioneers of aviation. The surtax of four times the face value was for wounded Latvian aviators.

Imperf.

CB9a SPAP3 5s (25s) 15.00 *20.00*
CB10a SPAP4 10s (50s) 15.00 *20.00*
CB11a SPAP5 15s (75s) 15.00 *20.00*
CB12a SPAP6 20s (1 l) 15.00 *20.00*
CB13a SPAP7 25s (1.25 l) 15.00 *20.00*
Nos. CB9a-CB13a (5) 75.00 100.00
Set, never hinged 125.00

Icarus Falling
SPAP8

Monument to Aviators
SPAP9

Proposed Tombs for Aviators
SPAP10 SPAP11

1933, Mar. 15 *Perf. 11½*

CB14 SPAP8 2s (52s) blk & ocher 12.50 *20.00*
CB15 SPAP9 3s (53s) blk & red org 12.50 *20.00*
CB16 SPAP10 10s (60s) blk & dk yel green 12.50 *20.00*
CB17 SPAP11 20s (70s) blk & cerise 12.50 *20.00*
Nos. CB14-CB17 (4) 50.00 *80.00*
Set, never hinged 100.00

50s surtax for wounded Latvian aviators.

Imperf.

CB14a SPAP8 2s (52s) 13.00 *21.00*
CB15a SPAP9 3s (53s) 13.00 *21.00*
CB16a SPAP10 10s (60s) 13.00 *21.00*
CB17a SPAP11 20s (70s) 13.00 *21.00*
Nos. CB14a-CB17a (4) 52.00 84.00
Set, never hinged 110.00

Monoplane Taking Off
SPAP12

Designs: 7s (57s), Biplane under fire at Riga. 35s (1.35 l), Map and planes.

1933, June 15 Wmk. 212 *Perf. 11½*

CB18 SPAP12 3s (53s) org & sl blue 17.50 *40.00*
CB19 SPAP12 7s (57s) sl bl & dk brn 17.50 *40.00*
CB20 SPAP12 35s (1.35 l) dp ultra & ol black 17.50 *40.00*
Nos. CB18-CB20 (3) 52.50 *120.00*
Set, never hinged 110.00

Surtax for wounded Latvian aviators. Counterfeits exist.

Imperf.

CB18a SPAP12 3s (53s) 20.00 *42.50*
CB19a SPAP12 7s (57s) 20.00 *42.50*
CB20a SPAP12 35s (1.35 l) 20.00 *42.50*
Nos. CB18a-CB20a (3) 60.00 *127.50*
Set, never hinged 120.00

American Gee-Bee
SPAP13

English Seaplane S6B
SPAP14

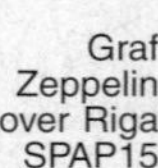

Graf Zeppelin over Riga
SPAP15

DO-X
SPAP16

1933, Sept. 5 *Perf. 11½*

CB21	SPAP13 8s (68s) brn & gray black		30.00	*85.00*
CB22	SPAP14 12s (1.12 l) brn car & ol green		30.00	*85.00*
CB23	SPAP15 30s (1.30 l) blue & gray black		35.00	*90.00*
CB24	SPAP16 40s (1.90 l) brn vio & indi-go		30.00	*85.00*
	Nos. CB21-CB24 (4)		125.00	345.00
	Set, never hinged		250.00	

Surtax for wounded Latvian aviators.

Imperf.

CB21a	SPAP13	8s (68s)	30.00	*85.00*
CB22a	SPAP14	12s (1.12 l)	30.00	*85.00*
CB23a	SPAP15	30s (1.30 l)	35.00	*95.00*
CB24a	SPAP16	40s (1.90 l)	30.00	*90.00*
	Nos. CB21a-CB24a (4)		125.00	*355.00*
	Set, never hinged		250.00	

OCCUPATION STAMPS

Issued under German Occupation

German Stamps of 1905-18 Handstamped

1919 **Wmk. 125** *Perf. 14, 14½*

Red Overprint

1N1	A22	2½pf gray	225.00	225.00
1N2	A16	5pf green	175.00	90.00
1N3	A22	15pf dk vio	275.00	90.00
1N4	A16	20pf blue vio	110.00	40.00
1N5	A16	25pf org & blk, *yel*	375.00	275.00
1N6	A16	50pf pur & blk, *buff*	375.00	275.00

Blue Overprint

1N7	A22	2½pf gray	225.00	225.00
1N8	A16	5pf green	110.00	60.00
1N9	A16	10pf carmine	92.50	35.00
1N10	A22	15pf dk vio	275.00	150.00
1N11	A16	20pf bl vio	110.00	35.00
1N12	A16	25pf org & blk, *yel*	375.00	275.00
1N13	A16	50pf pur & blk, *buff*	375.00	275.00
		Nos. 1N1-1N13 (13)	3,097.	2,050.

Inverted and double overprints exist, as well as counterfeit overprints.

Some experts believe that Nos. 1N1-1N7 were not officially issued. All used examples are canceled to order.

Russian Stamps Overprinted

1941, July

1N14	A331	5k red (#734)	.80	*4.25*
1N15	A109	10k blue (#616)	.80	*4.25*
1N16	A332	15k dark green (#735)	27.50	*67.50*
1N17	A97	20k dull green (#617)	.80	*4.25*
1N18	A333	30k deep blue (#736)	.80	*4.25*
1N19	A111	50k dp brn (#619A)	3.25	*10.00*
		Nos. 1N14-1N19 (6)	33.95	*94.50*
		Set, never hinged	50.00	

Issued: 20k, 30k, 7/17; 5k, 10k, 7/18; 15k, 7/19; 50k, 7/23.

Nos. 1N14-1N19 were replaced by German stamps in mid-October. On Nov. 4, 1941, German stamps overprinted "Ostland" (Russia Nos. N9-N28) were placed into use.

The overprint exists on imperf examples of the 10k and 50k stamps. Value, each $800.

Counterfeit overprints exist.

KURLAND

German Stamps Surcharged

1945, Apr. 20

1N20	A115	6pf on 5pf dp yellow grn (#509)	37.50	*62.50*
		Never hinged	65.00	
1N21	A115	6 pf 10pf dk brown (#511A)	15.00	*30.00*
		Never hinged	25.00	
a.		Inverted surcharge	100.00	*175.00*
		Never hinged	175.00	
b.		Double surcharge	85.00	*150.00*
		Never hinged	150.00	
1N22	A115	6 pf on 20pf blue	8.50	*13.50*
		Never hinged	15.00	
a.		Inverted surcharge	100.00	*175.00*
		Never hinged	175.00	
b.		Double surcharge	85.00	*150.00*
		Never hinged	150.00	

Perf 13½

1N23	MPP1	12pf on (-) red brown, (#MQ1)	42.50	*72.50*
		Never hinged	82.50	
a.		Inverted surcharge	150.00	*275.00*
		Never hinged	275.00	
b.		Double surcharge	150.00	*275.00*
		Never hinged	275.00	

Rouletted

1N24	MPP1	12pf on (-) red brown, (#MQ1a)	6.50	*10.00*
		Never hinged	12.50	
a.		Inverted surcharge	75.00	*135.00*
		Never hinged	135.00	
b.		Double surcharge	67.50	*120.00*
		Never hinged	120.00	
		Nos. 1N20-1N24 (5)	110.00	*188.50*
		Set, never hinged	200.00	

Nos. 1N20-1N24 were used in the German-held enclave of Kurland (Courland) from April 20-May 8, 1945.

Counterfeit surcharges are plentiful.

ISSUED UNDER RUSSIAN OCCUPATION

Fake overprints/surcharges exist on Nos. 2N1-2N36.

The following stamps were issued at Mitau during the occupation of Kurland by the West Russian Army under Colonel Bermondt-Avalov.

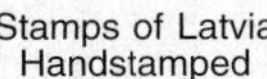

Stamps of Latvia Handstamped

1919 **Wmk. 108** ***Imperf.***

On Stamps of 1919

2N1	A1	3k lilac	40.00	*52.50*
2N2	A1	5k carmine	40.00	*52.50*
2N3	A1	10k dp blue	140.00	*240.00*
2N4	A1	20k orange	40.00	*52.50*
2N5	A1	25k gray	40.00	*52.50*
2N6	A1	35k dk brown	40.00	*52.50*
2N7	A1	50k purple	40.00	*52.50*
2N8	A1	75k emerald	40.00	*80.00*

On Riga Liberation Stamps

2N9	A2	5k carmine	40.00	*52.50*
2N10	A2	15k dp green	20.00	*40.00*
2N11	A2	35k brown	20.00	*40.00*

Stamps of Latvia Overprinted

On Stamps of 1919

2N12	A1	3k lilac	6.00	*9.50*
2N13	A1	5k carmine	6.00	*9.50*
2N14	A1	10k dp blue	120.00	*200.00*
2N15	A1	20k orange	12.00	*20.00*
2N16	A1	25k gray	27.50	*60.00*
2N17	A1	35k dk brown	20.00	*27.50*
2N18	A1	50k purple	20.00	*27.50*
2N19	A1	75k emerald	20.00	*27.50*

On Riga Liberation Stamps

2N20	A2	5k carmine	4.00	*8.00*
2N21	A2	15k dp green	4.00	*8.00*
2N22	A2	35k brown	4.00	*8.00*
a.		Inverted overprint	*200.00*	
		Nos. 2N1-2N22 (22)	743.50	*1,173.*

The letters "Z. A." are the initials of "Zapadnaya Armiya"-i.e. Western Army.

Russian Stamps of 1909-17 Surcharged

Perf. 14, 14½x15

Unwmk.

On Stamps of 1909-12

2N23	A14	10k on 2k grn	6.00	*8.00*
a.		Inverted surcharge	*30.00*	
2N24	A15	30k on 4k car	8.00	*8.00*
2N25	A14	40k on 5k cl	8.00	*9.50*
2N26	A15	50k pn 10k dk bl	6.00	*8.00*
2N27	A11	70k on 15k red brn & bl	6.00	*8.00*
a.		Inverted surcharge	*200.00*	
2N28	A8	90k on 20k bl & car	12.00	*16.00*
2N29	A11	1r on 25k grn & vio	6.00	8.00
2N30	A11	1½r on 35k red brn & grn	47.50	65.00
2N31	A8	2r on 50k vio & grn	12.00	16.00
a.		Inverted surcharge	*120.00*	
2N32	A11	4r on 70k brn & org	20.00	27.50

Perf. 13½

2N33	A9	6r on 1r pale brn, brn & org	27.50	40.00

On Stamps of 1917

Imperf

2N34	A14	20k on 3k red	6.00	*8.00*
2N35	A14	40k on 5k claret	95.00	*100.00*
2N36	A12	10r on 3.50r mar & lt grn	80.00	*80.00*
a.		Inverted surcharge	*300.00*	
		Nos. 2N23-2N36 (14)	340.00	*402.00*

Eight typographed stamps of this design were prepared in 1919, but never placed in use. They exist both perforated and imperforate. Value, set, imperf. $1, perf. $2.

Reprints and counterfeits exist.

Catalogue values for unused stamps in this section, from this point to the end of the section, are for Never Hinged items.

Arms of Soviet Latvia — OS1

1940 **Typo.** **Wmk. 265** ***Perf. 10***

2N45	OS1	1s dk violet	.20	.20
2N46	OS1	2s orange yel	.20	.20
2N47	OS1	3s orange ver	.20	.20
2N48	OS1	5s dk olive grn	.20	.20
2N49	OS1	7s turq green	.20	.80
2N50	OS1	10s slate green	2.00	.40
2N51	OS1	20s brown lake	1.20	.20
2N52	OS1	30s light blue	2.40	.40
2N53	OS1	35s brt ultra	.20	*.40*
2N54	OS1	40s chocolate	2.00	1.20
2N55	OS1	50s lt gray	1.75	1.20
2N56	OS1	1 l lt brown	3.25	1.50
2N57	OS1	5 l brt green	24.00	13.50
		Nos. 2N45-2N57 (13)	37.80	20.40

Used values of Nos. 2N45-2N57 are for CTOs. Commercially used examples are worth three times as much.

LEBANON

'le-bə-nən

(Grand Liban)

LOCATION — Asia Minor, bordering on the Mediterranean Sea
GOVT. — Republic
AREA — 4,036 sq. mi.
POP. — 3,562,699 (1999 est.)
CAPITAL — Beirut

Formerly a part of the Syrian province of Turkey, Lebanon was occupied by French forces after World War I. It was mandated to France after it had been declared a separate state. Limited autonomy was granted in 1927 and full independence achieved in 1941. The French issued two sets of occupation stamps (with T.E.O. overprint) for Lebanon in late 1919. The use of these and later occupation issues (of 1920-24, with overprints "O.M.F." and "Syrie-Grand Liban") was extended to Syria, Cilicia, Alaouites and Alexandretta. By custom, these are all listed under Syria.

100 Centimes = 1 Piaster
100 Piasters = 1 Pound

Watermark

Wmk. 400

Catalogue values for unused stamps in this country are for Never Hinged items, beginning with Scott 177 in the regular postage section, Scott B13 in the semi-postal section, Scott C97 in the airpost section, Scott CB5 in the airpost semi-postal section, Scott J37 in the postage due section, and Scott RA11 in the postal tax section.

Issued under French Mandate

Stamps of France 1900-21 Surcharged

1924 Unwmk. *Perf. 14x13½*

1 A16 10c on 2c vio brn 1.60 1.60
a. Inverted surcharge 45.00 45.00
2 A22 25c on 5c orange 1.60 1.60
3 A22 50c on 10c green 1.60 1.60
4 A20 75c on 15c sl grn 2.75 2.40
5 A22 1p on 20c red brn 1.60 1.60
a. Double surcharge 45.00 45.00
b. Inverted surcharge 45.00 45.00
6 A22 1.25p on 25c blue 4.50 2.40
a. Double surcharge 40.00 40.00
7 A22 1.50p on 30c org 2.75 2.00
8 A22 1.50p on 30c red 2.75 2.40
9 A20 2.50p on 50c dl bl 2.40 2.00
a. Inverted surcharge 35.00 35.00

Surcharged

10 A18 2p on 40c red & pale bl 5.50 3.75
a. Inverted surcharge 27.50 27.50
11 A18 3p on 60c violet & ultra 8.00 6.75
12 A18 5p on 1fr cl & ol green 10.00 7.50
13 A18 10p on 2fr org & pale bl 15.00 12.00
a. Inverted surcharge 50.00 50.00
14 A18 25p on 5fr dk bl & buff 22.50 19.00
a. Inverted surcharge 85.00 85.00
Nos. 1-14 (14) 82.55 66.60

Broken and missing letters and varieties of spacing are numerous in these surcharges.
For overprints see Nos. C1-C4.

Stamps of France, 1923, (Pasteur) Surcharged "GRAND LIBAN" and New Values

15 A23 50c on 10c green 3.50 1.10
a. Inverted surcharge 35.00 25.00
16 A23 1.50p on 30c red 4.50 2.25
17 A23 2.50p on 50c blue 3.75 1.10
a. Inverted surcharge 30.00 27.50
Nos. 15-17 (3) 11.75 4.45

Commemorative Stamps of France, 1924, (Olympic Games) Surcharged "GRAND LIBAN" and New Values

18 A24 50c on 10c gray grn & yel grn 32.50 *32.50*
a. Inverted surcharge 350.00
19 A25 1.25p on 25c rose & dk rose 32.50 *32.50*
a. Inverted surcharge 350.00
20 A26 1.50p on 30c brn red & blk 32.50 *32.50*
a. Inverted surcharge 350.00
21 A27 2.50p on 50c ultra & dk bl 32.50 *32.50*
a. Inverted surcharge 350.00
Nos. 18-21 (4) 130.00 130.00

Stamps of France, 1900-24, Surcharged

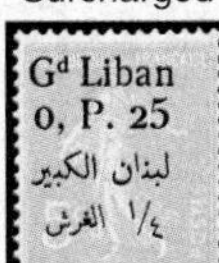

1924-25

22 A16 10c on 2c vio brn 1.00 .50
23 A22 25c on 5c orange 1.25 .75
24 A22 50c on 10c green 2.00 1.40
25 A20 75c on 15c gray grn 1.75 1.10
26 A22 1p on 20c red brn 1.50 .95
27 A22 1.25p on 25c blue 2.25 1.60
28 A22 1.50p on 30c red 2.00 1.25
29 A22 1.50p on 30c orange 62.50 57.50
30 A22 2p on 35c vio ('25) 2.25 1.60
31 A20 3p on 60c lt vio ('25) 3.00 2.10
32 A20 4p on 85c ver 3.50 2.50

Surcharged

33 A18 2p on 40c red & pale bl 2.25 1.60
a. 2nd line of Arabic reads "2 Piastre" (singular) 2.50 .50
34 A18 2p on 45c green & blue ('25) 27.50 22.50
35 A18 3p on 60c violet & ultra 3.50 2.50
36 A18 5p on 1fr cl & ol green 4.25 3.25
37 A18 10p on 2fr org & pale bl 9.75 8.50
38 A18 25p on 5fr dk bl & buff 15.00 13.50
Nos. 22-38 (17) 145.25 123.10

Last line of surcharge on No. 33 has four characters, with a 9-like character between the third and fourth in illustration. Last line on No. 33a is as illustrated.
The surcharge may be found inverted on most of Nos. 22-38, and double on some values.
For overprints see Nos. C5-C8.

Stamps of France 1923-24 (Pasteur) Surcharged as Nos. 22-32

39 A23 50c on 10c green 2.00 .85
a. Inverted surcharge 35.00 25.00
b. Double surcharge 40.00 21.00
40 A23 75c on 15c green 2.25 1.40
41 A23 1.50p on 30c red 2.75 1.40
a. Inverted surcharge 35.00 25.00
42 A23 2p on 45c red 5.00 3.50
a. Inverted surcharge 35.00 21.00
43 A23 2.50p on 50c blue 2.00 .95
a. Inverted surcharge 35.00 21.00
b. Double surcharge 40.00 21.00
44 A23 4p on 75c blue 5.00 3.50
Nos. 39-44 (6) 19.00 11.60

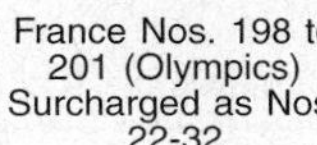

France Nos. 198 to 201 (Olympics) Surcharged as Nos. 22-32

45 A24 50c on 10c 32.50 *32.50*
46 A25 1.25p on 25c 32.50 *32.50*
47 A26 1.50p on 30c 32.50 *32.50*
48 A27 2.50p on 50c 32.50 *32.50*
Nos. 45-48 (4) 130.00 130.00

France No. 219 (Ronsard) Surcharged as Nos. 22-32

49 A28 4p on 75c bl, *bluish* 3.50 3.50
a. Inverted surcharge 65.00 50.00

Cedar of Lebanon — A1

Crusader Castle, Tripoli — A3

View of Beirut A2

Designs: 50c, Crusader Castle, Tripoli. 75c, Beit-ed-Din Palace. 1p, Temple of Jupiter, Baalbek. 1.25p, Mouktara Palace. 1.50p, Harbor of Tyre. 2p, View of Zahle. 2.50p, Ruins at Baalbek. 3p, Square at Deir-el-Kamar. 5p, Castle at Sidon. 25p, Square at Beirut.

1925 Litho. *Perf. 12½, 13½*

50 A1 10c dark violet .50 .20

Photo.

51 A2 25c olive black .95 .20
52 A2 50c yellow grn .75 .20
53 A2 75c brn orange .75 .20
54 A2 1p magenta 2.00 .80
55 A2 1.25p deep green 2.25 1.40
56 A2 1.50p rose red 1.00 .20
57 A2 2p dark brown 1.25 .20
58 A2 2.50p peacock bl 2.00 .80
59 A2 3p orange brn 2.75 1.10
60 A2 5p violet 3.00 1.40
61 A3 10p violet brn 7.50 2.10
62 A2 25p ultramarine 20.00 12.00
Nos. 50-62 (13) 44.70 20.80

For surcharges and overprints see Nos. 63-107, B1-B12, C9-C38, CB1-CB4.

Stamps of 1925 with Bars and Surcharged

1926

63 A2 3.50p on 75c brn org 1.50 1.50
64 A2 4p on 25c ol blk 2.50 2.50
65 A2 6p on 2.50p pck bl 2.00 2.00
66 A2 12p on 1.25p dp grn 1.40 1.40
67 A2 20p on 1.25p dp grn 6.75 6.75

Stamps of 1925 with Bars and Surcharged

68 A2 4.50p on 75c brn org 2.75 2.75
69 A2 7.50p on 2.50p pck bl 2.75 2.75
70 A2 15p on 25p ultra 2.75 2.75
Nos. 63-70 (8) 22.40 22.40

No. 51 with Bars and Surcharged

1927

71 A2 4p on 25c ol blk 2.50 2.50

Issues of Republic under French Mandate

Stamps of 1925 Issue Overprinted in Black or Red

1927

72 A1 10c dark vio (R) .55 .20
a. Black overprint 35.00
73 A2 50c yellow grn .55 .20
74 A2 1p magenta .55 .20
75 A2 1.50p rose red .80 .60
76 A2 2p dark brown 1.10 .90
77 A2 3p orange brn .90 .20
78 A2 5p violet 1.75 1.00
79 A3 10p violet brn 2.25 1.10
80 A2 25p ultramarine 19.00 8.00
Nos. 72-80 (9) 27.45 12.40

On Nos. 72 and 79 the overprint is set in two lines. On all stamps the double bar obliterates GRAND LIBAN.

Same Overprint on Provisional Issues of 1926-27

15 PIASTERS ON 25 PIASTERS
TYPE I — "République Libanaise" at foot of stamp.
TYPE II — "République Libanaise" near top of stamp.

81 A2 4p on 25c ol blk .75 .20
82 A2 4.50p on 75c brn org .85 .20
83 A2 7.50p on 2.50p pck bl 1.10 .20
84 A2 15p on 25p ultra (I) 7.50 5.25
a. Type II 11.50 8.00
Nos. 81-84 (4) 10.20 5.85

Most of Nos. 72-84 are known with overprint double, inverted or on back as well as face.

Stamps of 1927 Overprinted in Black or Red

1928

86 A1 10c dark vio (R) .80 .60
a. French overprint omitted, on #50
87 A2 50c yel grn (Bk) 2.00 1.50
a. Arabic overprint inverted 35.00 25.00
88 A2 1p magenta (Bk) 1.00 .70
a. Inverted overprint 35.00 25.00
89 A2 1.50p rose red (Bk) 2.00 1.50
90 A2 2p dark brown (R) 2.75 2.10
90A A2 2p dk brn (Bk+R) 110.00 110.00
91 A2 3p org brown (Bk) 1.90 1.40
92 A2 5p violet (Bk+R) 3.50 2.75
93 A2 5p violet (R) 3.00 2.40
a. French ovpt. below Arabic 30.00 14.00
94 A3 10p vio brn (Bk) 5.00 4.25
a. Double overprint 100.00 90.00
b. Double overprint inverted
c. Inverted overprint 100.00 70.00
95 A2 25p ultra (Bk+R) 11.50 10.50
95A A2 25p ultra (R) 13.00 13.00
Nos. 86-95A (12) 156.45 150.70

On all stamps the double bar with Arabic overprint obliterates Arabic inscription.

Same Overprint on Nos. 81-84

96 A2 4p on 25c (Bk+R) 2.00 1.50
97 A2 4.50p on 75c (Bk) 2.00 1.50
98 A2 7.50p on 2.50p (Bk+R) 4.50 3.50
99 A2 7.50p on 2.50p (R) 7.00 6.00
100 A2 15p on 25p (II) (Bk+R) 11.00 9.50
a. Arabic overprint inverted
101 A2 15p on 25p (I) (R) 14.00 12.00
Nos. 96-101 (6) 40.50 34.00

The new values are surcharged in black. The initials in ( ) refer to the colors of the overprints.

Stamps of 1925 Surcharged in Red or Black

1928-29 *Perf. 13½*

102	A2	50c on 75c brn org (Bk) ('29)	1.50	1.90
103	A2	2p on 1.25p dp grn	1.50	1.90
104	A2	4p on 25c ol blk	1.50	1.90
a.		Double surcharge	35.00	25.00
105	A2	7.50p on 2.50p pck bl	2.50	2.75
a.		Double surcharge	40.00	25.00
b.		Inverted surcharge	55.00	25.00
106	A2	15p on 25p ultra	22.50	10.00
		Nos. 102-106 (5)	29.50	18.45

On Nos. 103, 104 and 105 the surcharged numerals are 3¼mm high, and have thick strokes.

No. 86 Surcharged in Red

1928

107	A1	5c on 10c dk vio	1.75	.30

Silkworm, Cocoon and Moth — A4

1930, Feb. 11 **Typo.** *Perf. 11*

108	A4	4p black brown	15.00	15.00
109	A4	4½p vermilion	15.00	15.00
110	A4	7½p dark blue	15.00	15.00
111	A4	10p dk violet	15.00	15.00
112	A4	15p dark green	15.00	15.00
113	A4	25p claret	15.00	15.00
		Nos. 108-113 (6)	90.00	90.00

Sericultural Congress, Beirut. Presentation imperfs exist.

Pigeon Rocks, Ras Beirut — A5

View of Bickfaya A8

Beit-ed-Din Palace A10

Crusader Castle, Tripoli A11

Ruins of Venus Temple, Baalbek A12

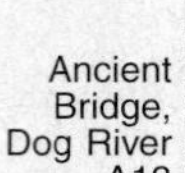

Ancient Bridge, Dog River A13

Belfort Castle A14

Afka Falls — A19

20c, Cedars of Lebanon. 25c, Ruins of Bacchus Temple, Baalbek. 1p, Crusader Castle, Sidon Harbor. 5p, Arcade of Beit-ed-Din Palace. 6p, Tyre Harbor. 7.50p, Ruins of Sun Temple, Baalbek. 10p, View of Hasbeya. 25p, Government House, Beirut. 50p, View of Deir-el-Kamar. 75c, 100p, Ruins at Baalbek.

1930-35 **Litho.** *Perf. 12½, 13½*

114	A5	10c brown orange	.60	.20
115	A5	20c yellow brn	.60	.20
116	A5	25c deep blue	.75	.45

Photo.

117	A8	50c orange brn	3.00	1.50
118	A11	75c ol brn ('32)	1.50	1.00
119	A8	1p deep green	1.75	1.25
120	A8	1p brn vio ('35)	3.00	1.00
121	A10	1.50p violet brn	3.25	1.90
122	A10	1.50p dp grn ('32)	3.50	1.50
123	A11	2p Prussian bl	4.50	1.60
124	A12	3p black brown	4.50	1.60
125	A13	4p orange brn	4.75	1.60
126	A14	4.50p carmine	5.00	1.60
127	A13	5p greenish blk	3.00	1.50
128	A13	6p brn violet	5.25	2.75
129	A10	7.50p deep blue	5.00	1.60
130	A10	10p dk ol grn	9.00	1.60
131	A19	15p blk violet	11.50	3.50
132	A19	25p blue green	20.00	6.00
133	A8	50p apple grn	60.00	15.00
134	A11	100p black	65.00	19.00
		Nos. 114-134 (21)	215.45	66.35

See Nos. 135, 144, 152-155. For surcharges see Nos. 147-149, 161, 173-174.

Pigeon Rocks Type of 1930-35 Redrawn

1934 **Litho.** *Perf. 12½x12*

135	A5	10c dull orange	6.75	4.00

Lines in rocks and water more distinct. Printer's name "Hélio Vaugirard, Paris," in larger letters.

Cedar of Lebanon A23

President Emile Eddé A24

Dog River Panorama A25

1937-40 **Typo.** *Perf. 14x13½*

137	A23	10c rose car	.50	.20
137A	A23	20c aqua ('40)	.50	.20
137B	A23	25c pale rose lilac ('40)	.50	.20
138	A23	50c magenta	.50	.20
138A	A23	75c brown ('40)	.50	.20

Engr.

Perf. 13

139	A24	3p dk violet	4.00	.75
140	A24	4p black brown	.75	.20
141	A24	4.50p carmine	1.00	.20
142	A25	10p brn carmine	2.25	.20
142A	A25	12½p dp ultra ('40)	1.00	.20
143	A25	15p dk grn ('38)	4.00	.75
143A	A25	20p chestnut ('40)	1.00	.20
143B	A25	25p crimson ('40)	1.50	.60
143C	A25	50p dk vio ('40)	5.00	1.60
143D	A25	100p sepia ('40)	3.50	2.25
		Nos. 137-143D (15)	26.50	7.95

Nos. 137A, 137B, 138A, 142A, 143A, 143B, 143C, and 143D exist imperforate.

For surcharges see Nos. 145-146A, 150-151, 160, 162, 175-176.

View of Bickfaya A26

Type A8 Redrawn

1935 (?) **Photo.** *Perf. 13½*

144	A26	50c orange brown	17.50	9.75

Arabic inscriptions more condensed.

Stamps of 1930-37 Surcharged in Black or Red

1937-42 *Perf. 13, 13½*

145	A24	2p on 3p dk vio	1.50	1.50
146	A24	2½p on 4p blk brn	1.50	1.50
146A	A24	2½p on 4p black brown (R) ('42)	1.50	1.50
147	A10	6p on 7.50p dp bl (R)	4.00	4.00

Stamps of 1930-35 and Type of 1937-40 Surcharged in Black or Red

Perf. 13½, 13

148	A8	7.50p on 50p ap grn	2.50	2.50
149	A11	7.50p on 100p blk (R)	2.50	2.50
150	A25	12.50p on 7.50p dk bl (R)	5.00	5.00

Type of 1937-40 Surcharged in Red with Bars and

1939 **Engr.** *Perf. 13*

151	A25	12½p on 7.50p dk bl	2.00	2.00
		Nos. 145-151 (8)	20.50	20.50

Type of 1930-35 Redrawn
Imprint: "Beiteddine-Imp.-Catholique-Beyrouth-Liban."

1939 **Litho.** *Perf. 11½*

152	A10	1p dk slate grn	2.25	.20
153	A10	1.50p brn violet	2.25	.75
154	A10	7.50p carmine lake	2.25	1.10
		Nos. 152-154 (3)	6.75	2.05

Bridge Type of 1930-35
Imprint: "Degorce" instead of "Hélio Vaugirard"

1940 **Engr.** *Perf. 13*

155	A13	5p grnsh blue	1.50	.20

Exists imperforate.

Independent Republic

Amir Beshir Shehab — A27

1942, Sept. 18 **Litho.** *Perf. 11½*

156	A27	50c emerald	3.75	3.75
157	A27	1.50p sepia	3.75	3.75
158	A27	6p rose pink	3.75	3.75
159	A27	15p dull blue	3.75	3.75
		Nos. 156-159 (4)	15.00	15.00

1st anniv. of the Proclamation of Independence, Nov. 26, 1941.

Nos. 156-159 exist imperforate.

Nos. 140, 154 and 142A Surcharged in Blue, Green or Black

1943 *Perf. 13, 11½*

160	A24	2p on 4p (Bl)	6.75	*7.25*
161	A10	6p on 7.50p (G)	3.00	1.00
162	A25	10p on 12½p (Bk)	3.00	1.00
		Nos. 160-162 (3)	12.75	9.25

The surcharge is arranged differently on each value.

Parliament Building A28

Government House, Beirut — A29

1943 **Litho.** *Perf. 11½*

163	A28	25p salmon rose	15.00	6.00
164	A29	50p bluish green	15.00	6.00
165	A28	150p light ultra	15.00	6.00
166	A29	200p dull vio brn	15.00	6.00
		Nos. 163-166 (4)	60.00	24.00
		Nos. 163-166,C82-C87 (10)	149.25	97.00

2nd anniv. of Proclamation of Independence. Nos. 163-166 exist imperforate. For overprints see Nos. 169-172.

Quarantine Station, Beirut A30

1943, July 8 **Photo.**

Black Overprint

167	A30	10p cerise	7.00	4.00
168	A30	20p light blue	7.00	4.00
		Nos. 167-168,C88-C90 (5)	28.00	18.75

Arab Medical Congress, Beirut.

Nos. 163 to 166 Overprinted in Blue, Violet, Red or Black

1944

169 A28 25p sal rose (Bl) 16.00 13.50
170 A29 50p bluish green (V) 16.00 13.50
171 A28 150p lt ultra (R) 16.00 13.50
172 A29 200p dull vio brn (Bk) 22.50 19.00
Nos. 169-172,C91-C96 (10) 226.25 207.75

Return to office of the president and his ministers, Nov. 22, 1943.

Type of 1930 and No. 142A Surcharged in Violet, Black or Carmine

1945 Unwmk. Engr. *Perf. 13*

173 A13 2p on 5p dk bl grn (V) 1.50 .20
174 A13 3p on 5p dk bl grn (Bk) 1.50 .20
175 A25 6p on 12½p deep ultra (Bk) 2.00 .35
176 A25 7½p on 12½p deep ultra (C) 3.00 .95
Nos. 173-176 (4) 8.00 1.70

Trees at bottom on Nos. 175 and 176.

Catalogue values for unused stamps in this section, from this point to the end of the section, are for Never Hinged items.

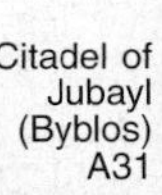

Citadel of Jubayl (Byblos) A31

Crusader Castle, Tripoli A32

1945 Litho. *Perf. 11½*

177 A31 15p violet brown 5.50 4.00
178 A31 20p deep green 5.50 4.00
179 A32 25p deep blue 5.50 4.00
180 A32 50p dp carmine 9.50 4.50
Nos. 177-180,C97-C100 (8) 77.00 37.10

See Nos. 229-233.

Soldiers and Flag of Lebanon A33

1946 Litho.

Stripes of Flag in Red Orange

181 A33 7.50p red & pale lil 1.75 .20
182 A33 10p lil & pale lilac 3.00 .20
183 A33 12.50p choc & yel grn 4.00 .20
184 A33 15p sepia & pink 5.00 .25
185 A33 20p ultra & pink 4.25 .30
186 A33 25p dk grn & yel green 7.00 .35
187 A33 50p dk bl & pale bl 15.00 1.50
188 A33 100p gray blk & pale bl 20.00 3.00
Nos. 181-188 (8) 60.00 6.00

Type of 1946 Overprinted in Red

1946, May 8

Stripes of Flag in Red

189 A33 7.50p choc & pink 1.50 .20
190 A33 10p dk vio & pink 1.75 .20
191 A33 12.50p brn red & pale lilac 2.00 .45
192 A33 15p lt grn & yel green 3.25 .65
193 A33 20p sl grn & yel green 3.00 .70
194 A33 25p sl bl & pale bl 5.00 .95
195 A33 50p ultra & gray 7.50 .90
196 A33 100p blk & pale bl 11.00 2.25
Nos. 189-196 (8) 35.00 6.30

See Nos. C101-C106, note after No. C106.

Cedar of Lebanon — A34

Night Herons over Mt. Sanin A35

1946-47 Unwmk. *Perf. 10½*

197 A34 50c red brn ('47) 1.50 .20
198 A34 1p purple ('47) 1.50 .20
199 A34 2.50p violet 2.75 .20
200 A34 5p red 4.00 .20
201 A34 6p gray ('47) 4.00 .20

Perf. 11½

202 A35 12.50p deep car 30.00 .20
Nos. 197-202,C107-C110 (10) 121.25 10.50

For surcharge see No. 246.

A36

Crusader Castle, Tripoli A37

1947 Litho. *Perf. 14x13½*

203 A36 50c dark brown 2.00 .20
204 A36 2.50p bright green 3.25 .20
205 A36 5p car rose 4.00 .20

Perf. 11½

206 A37 12.50p rose pink 10.50 .50
207 A37 25p ultramarine 12.50 .55
208 A37 50p turq green 32.50 1.10
209 A37 100p violet 45.00 5.75
Nos. 203-209 (7) 109.75 8.50

A38

Zubaida Aqueduct — A39

1948 *Perf. 14x13½*

210 A38 50c blue .75 .20
211 A38 1p yel brown .90 .20
212 A38 2.50p rose violet 1.10 .20
213 A38 3p emerald 2.75 .20
214 A38 5p crimson 3.25 .20

Perf. 11½

215 A39 7.50p rose red 7.00 .20
216 A39 10p dl violet 5.00 .20
217 A39 12.50p blue 10.50 .40
218 A39 25p blue vio 18.00 .90
219 A39 50p green 32.50 4.75
Nos. 210-219 (10) 81.75 7.45

See Nos. 227A-228A, 234-237. For surcharge see No. 245.

Europa A40

Avicenna — A41

1948 Litho.

220 A40 10p dk red & org red 6.00 1.40
221 A40 12.50p pur & rose 7.00 1.90
222 A40 25p ol grn & pale green 8.00 1.50
223 A41 30p org brn & buff 9.00 1.50
224 A41 40p Prus grn & buff 13.00 1.50
Nos. 220-224 (5) 43.00 7.80

UNESCO. Nos. 220 to 224 exist imperforate (see note after No. C145).

Camel Post Rider A42

1949, Aug. 16 Unwmk. *Perf. 11½*

225 A42 5p violet 2.00 .40
226 A42 7.50p red 3.00 .60
227 A42 12.50p blue 4.00 1.00
Nos. 225-227,C148-C149 (5) 29.00 10.50

UPU, 75th anniv. See note after No. C149.

Cedar Type of 1948 Redrawn and Jubayl Type of 1945

1949 Litho. *Perf. 14x13½*

227A A38 50c blue 2.75 .20
228 A38 1p red orange 2.75 .20
228A A38 2.50p rose lilac 13.00 .35

Perf. 11½

229 A31 7.50p rose red 4.00 .20
230 A31 10p violet brn 7.00 .20
231 A31 12.50p deep blue 14.00 .20
232 A31 25p violet 25.00 .40
233 A31 50p green 47.50 1.90
Nos. 227A-233 (8) 116.00 3.65

On No. 227A in left numeral tablet, top of "P" stands higher than flag of the 1¼mm high "5." On No. 210, tops of "P" and the 2mm "5" are on same line.

On No. 228, "1 P." is smaller than on No. 211, and has no line below "P."

On No. 228A, the "O" does not touch tablet frame; on No. 212, it does. No. 228A exists on gray paper.

Cedar Type of 1948 Redrawn and

Ancient Bridge across Dog River — A43

1950 Litho. *Perf. 14x13½*

234 A38 50c rose red 1.25 .20
235 A38 1p salmon 1.75 .20
236 A38 2.50p violet 2.50 .20
237 A38 5p claret 4.00 .20

Cedar slightly altered and mountains eliminated.

Perf. 11½

238 A43 7.50p rose red 5.50 .20
239 A43 10p rose vio 6.00 .20
240 A43 12.50p light blue 9.00 .20
241 A43 25p deep blue 2.25 1.25
242 A43 50p emerald 35.00 5.00
Nos. 234-242 (9) 67.25 7.65

See Nos. 251-255, 310-312.

Flags and Building A44

Cedar — A45

1950, Aug. 8 *Perf. 11½*

243 A44 7.50p gray 2.75 .20
244 A44 12.50p lilac rose 2.75 .20
Nos. 243-244,C150-C153 (6) 21.00 4.10

Conf. of Emigrants, 1950. See note after #C153.

Nos. 213 and 201 Surcharged with New Value and Bars in Carmine

1950 Unwmk. *Perf. 14x13½, 10½*

245 A38 1p on 3p emerald 1.50 .20
246 A34 2.50p on 6p gray 2.50 .20

1951 Litho. *Perf. 14x13½*

247 A45 50c rose red 1.75 .20
248 A45 1p light brown 2.50 .20
249 A45 2.50p slate gray 5.50 .20
250 A45 5p rose lake 5.50 .20

Bridge Type of 1950, Redrawn

Typo. *Perf. 11½*

251 A43 7.50p red 6.50 .20
252 A43 10p dl rose vio 9.00 .20
253 A43 12.50p blue 15.00 .20
254 A43 25p dull blue 19.00 .50
255 A43 50p green 40.00 3.75
Nos. 247-255 (9) 104.75 5.65

Nos. 238-242 are lithographed from a fine-screen halftone; "P" in the denomination has serifs. Nos. 251-255 are typographed and much coarser; "P" without serifs.

Cedar — A46

Ruins at Baalbek A47

Design: 50p, 100p, Beaufort Castle.

1952 Litho. *Perf. 14x13½*

256 A46 50c emerald 1.50 .20
257 A46 1p orange brn 1.75 .20
258 A46 2.50p grnsh blue 2.75 .20
259 A46 5p car rose 3.75 .20

Perf. 11½

260 A47 7.50p red 5.00 .20
261 A47 10p brt violet 7.00 .70
262 A47 12.50p blue 7.75 .70
263 A47 25p violet bl 8.50 1.40
264 A47 50p dk blue grn 24.00 2.75
265 A47 100p chocolate 47.50 7.50
Nos. 256-265 (10) 109.50 14.05

Cedar of Lebanon A48

Postal Administration Building A49

1953 ***Perf. 14x13½***
266 A48 50c blue 2.25 .20
267 A48 1p rose lake 2.25 .20
268 A48 2.50p lilac 2.50 .20
269 A48 5p emerald 2.50 .20

Perf. 11½
270 A49 7.50p car rose 5.00 .20
271 A49 10p dp yel grn 5.50 .65
272 A49 12.50p aquamarine 6.50 .75
273 A49 25p ultra 9.50 1.40
274 A49 50p violet brn 15.00 3.00
Nos. 266-274 (9) 51.00 6.80

See No. 306.

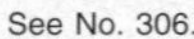

A50

Gallery, Beit-ed-Din Palace — A51

1954 ***Perf. 14x13½***
275 A50 50c blue 1.75 .20
276 A50 1p dp orange 2.00 .20
277 A50 2.50p purple 2.25 .20
278 A50 5p blue green 3.75 .20

Perf. 11½
279 A51 7.50p dp carmine 5.50 .20
280 A51 10p dl ol grn 6.50 .35
281 A51 12.50p blue 8.50 1.00
282 A51 25p vio blue 12.50 2.75
283 A51 50p aqua 20.00 5.00
284 A51 100p black brn 40.00 9.00
Nos. 275-284 (10) 102.75 19.10

Arab Postal Union Issue

Globe — A52

1955, Jan. 1 **Litho.** ***Perf. 13½x13***
285 A52 12.50p blue green 1.50 .20
286 A52 25p violet 1.75 .25
Nos. 285-286,C197 (3) 4.75 .65

Founding of the APU, July 1, 1954.

Cedar A53

Jeita Cave A54

1955 ***Perf. 14x13½***
287 A53 50c violet blue 2.00 .20
288 A53 1p vermilion 2.00 .20
289 A53 2.50p purple 2.00 .20
290 A53 5p emerald 2.50 .20

Perf. 11½
291 A54 7.50p deep orange 3.00 .20
292 A54 10p yellow grn 3.25 .20
293 A54 12.50p blue 3.50 .20
294 A54 25p dp vio blue 4.75 .25
295 A54 50p dk gray grn 6.25 .45
Nos. 287-295 (9) 29.25 2.10

See Nos. 308-309, 315-318, 341-343A. For overprint see No. 351.

Cedar of Lebanon A55

Globe and Columns A56

1955 **Unwmk.** ***Perf. 13x13½***
296 A55 50c dark blue 1.75 .20
297 A55 1p deep orange 1.75 .20
298 A55 2.50p deep violet 2.00 .20
299 A55 5p green 2.25 .20
300 A56 7.50p yel org & cop red 2.75 .20
301 A56 10p emer & sal 2.50 .20
302 A56 12.50p ultra & bl grn 3.00 .20
303 A56 25p dp ultra & brt pink 4.50 .20
304 A56 50p dk grn & lt bl 5.00 .25
305 A56 100p dk brn & sal 7.50 .50
Nos. 296-305 (10) 33.00 2.35

For surcharge see No. 333.

Cedar Type of 1953 Redrawn

1956 **Litho.** ***Perf. 13x13½***
306 A48 2.50p violet 10.00 1.75

No. 306 measures 17x20½mm. The "2p.50" is in Roman (upright) type face.

Cedar Type of 1955 Redrawn and Bridge Type of 1950, Second Redrawing

1957 **Litho.** ***Perf. 13x13½***
308 A53 50c light ultra 1.50 .20
309 A53 2.50p claret 2.00 .20

Perf. 11½
310 A43 7.50p vermilion 2.25 .40
311 A43 10p brn orange 3.00 .50
312 A43 12.50p blue 4.00 .75
Nos. 308-312 (5) 12.75 2.05

On Nos. 308 and 309 numerals are slanted and clouds slightly changed.

Nos. 310-312 inscribed "Liban" instead of "Republique Libanaise," and different Arabic characters.

Runners — A57

1957, Sept. 12 **Litho.** ***Perf. 13***
313 A57 2.50p shown 1.75 .20
314 A57 12.50p Soccer players 2.25 .35
Nos. 313-314,C243-C244 (4) 11.25 4.30

Second Pan-Arab Games, Beirut.

A souvenir sheet of 4 contains Nos. 313-314, C243-C244.

Cedar Type of 1955 Redrawn and

Workers — A58

Ancient Potter — A59

1957 **Unwmk.** ***Perf. 13x13½***
315 A53 50c light blue 1.75 .20
316 A53 1p light brown 1.75 .20
317 A53 2.50p bright vio 2.00 .20
318 A53 5p light green 2.50 .20

Perf. 11½, 13½x13 (A59)
319 A58 7.50p crim rose 2.50 .20
320 A58 10p dull red brn 2.50 .20
321 A58 12.50p bright blue 2.75 .20
322 A59 25p dull blue 2.75 .20
323 A59 50p yellow grn 4.50 .30
324 A59 100p sepia 5.50 .75
Nos. 315-324 (10) 28.50 2.65

The word "piaster" is omitted on No. 315; on Nos. 316 and 318 there is a line below "P"; on No. 317 there is a period between "2" and "50."

Nos. 315-318 are 16mm wide and have three shading lines above tip of cedar. See No. 343A and footnote.

For surcharges see Nos. 334-335, 339.

Cedar of Lebanon A60

Soldier and Flag A61

1958 **Litho.** ***Perf. 13***
325 A60 50c blue 1.75 .20
326 A60 1p dull orange 1.75 .20
327 A60 2.50p violet 1.75 .20
328 A60 5p yellow grn 2.00 .20
329 A61 12.50p bright blue 2.25 .20
330 A61 25p dark blue 2.50 .20
331 A61 50p orange brn 2.75 .25
332 A61 100p black brn 4.00 .40
Nos. 325-332 (8) 18.75 1.85

For surcharges see Nos. 336-338.

No. 304 Surcharged

1959, Sept. 1
333 A56 30p on 50p dk grn & lt bl 2.50 .25

Arab Lawyers Congress. See No. C265.

No. 323 Surcharged

1959 ***Perf. 13½x13***
334 A59 30p on 50p yel grn 2.25 .20
335 A59 40p on 50p yel grn 2.50 .35

Convention of the Assoc. of Arab Emigrants in the United States.

Nos. 329-330 and 323 Surcharged with New Value and Bars

1959 ***Perf. 13, 13½x13***
336 A61 7.50p on 12.50p brt bl 1.25 .20
337 A61 10p on 12.50p brt bl 1.50 .20
338 A61 15p on 25p dark blue 1.60 .20
339 A59 40p on 50p yel grn 2.25 .20
Nos. 336-339,C271 (5) 9.60 1.10

Arab League Center, Cairo A62

Perf. 13x13½
1960, May 23 **Unwmk.** **Litho.**
340 A62 15p lt blue green 1.75 .20

Opening of the Arab League Center and the Arab Postal Museum in Cairo.

For overprint see No. 352.

Cedar Type of 1955, Second Redrawing

1960 **Litho.** ***Perf. 13x13½***
341 A53 50c light violet 1.25 .20
342 A53 1p rose claret 1.25 .20
343 A53 2.50p ultramarine 1.50 .20
343A A53 5p light green 1.75 .20
Nos. 341-343A (4) 5.75 .80

Nos. 341-343A are 16½-17mm wide and have two shading lines above cedar. In other details they resemble the redrawn A53 type of 1957 (Nos. 315-318).

President Fuad Chehab
A63 A64

1960 **Photo.** ***Perf. 13½***
344 A63 50c deep green 1.25 .20
345 A63 2.50p olive 1.25 .20
346 A63 5p green 1.25 .20
347 A63 7.50p rose brown 1.50 .20
348 A63 15p bright blue 1.75 .20
349 A63 50p lilac 2.00 .20
350 A63 100p brown 2.50 .20
Nos. 344-350 (7) 11.50 1.40

Nos. 343A and 340 Overprinted in Red

1960, Nov. **Litho.** ***Perf. 13x13½***
351 A53 5p light green 1.25 .20
352 A62 15p lt blue green 1.75 .20

Arabian Oil Conference, Beirut.

1961, Feb. **Litho.** ***Perf. 13½x13***
353 A64 2.50p blue & light bl 1.25 .20
354 A64 7.50p dark vio & pink 1.25 .20
355 A64 10p red brn & yel 1.25 .20
Nos. 353-355 (3) 3.75 .60

Cedar — A65

Post Office, Beirut A66

1961 **Unwmk.** **Litho.** ***Perf. 13***
356 A65 2.50p green 2.50 .20

Redrawn
357 A65 2.50p orange 2.50 .25
358 A65 5p maroon 1.25 .20
359 A65 10p black 1.75 .20

Nos. 357-359 have no clouds.

Perf. 11½
361 A66 2.50p rose carmine 1.25 .20
362 A66 5p bright green 2.00 .20
363 A66 15p dark blue 2.75 .20
Nos. 356-363 (7) 14.00 1.45

Cedars — A67

10p, 15p, 50p, 100p, View of Zahle.

1961	**Litho.**	***Perf. 13***		
365 A67	50c	yellow green	1.50	.20
366 A67	1p	brown	1.50	.20
367 A67	2.50p	ultramarine	1.50	.20
368 A67	5p	carmine	1.75	.20
369 A67	7.50p	violet	2.00	.20
370 A67	10p	dark brown	2.25	.20
371 A67	15p	dark blue	2.50	.20
372 A67	50p	dark green	2.75	.25
373 A67	100p	black	3.25	.35
		Nos. 365-373 (9)	19.00	2.00

See Nos. 381-384.

Unknown Soldier Monument — A68

1961, Dec. 30	**Unwmk.**	***Perf. 12***		
374 A68	10p	shown	3.00	.20
375 A68	15p	Soldier & flag	3.75	.20

Anniv. of Lebanon's independence; evacuation of foreign troops, Dec. 31, 1946. See Nos. C329-C330.

Bugler — A69

Scout Carrying Flag and Scout Emblem A70

Designs: 2.50p, First aid. 6p, Lord Baden-Powell. 10p, Scouts building campfire.

1962, Mar. 1	**Litho.**	***Perf. 12***		
376 A69	50c	yel grn, blk & yel	1.50	.20
377 A70	1p	multicolored	1.50	.20
378 A70	2.50p	dk red, blk & grn	1.50	.20
379 A69	6p	multicolored	1.50	.20
380 A70	10p	dp bl, blk & yel	1.50	.20
		Nos. 376-380,C331-C333 (8)	10.75	1.80

50th anniversary of Lebanese Boy Scouts.

Type of 1961 Redrawn

Designs as before.

1962	**Unwmk.**	***Perf. 13***		
381 A67	50c	yellow green	1.50	.20
382 A67	1p	brown	1.50	.20
383 A67	2.50p	ultramarine	1.60	.20
384 A67	15p	dark blue	4.00	.20
		Nos. 381-384,C341-C342 (6)	15.95	1.40

Temple of Nefertari, Abu Simbel — A71

Cherries — A72

1962, Aug. 1	**Unwmk.**	***Perf. 13***		
390 A71	5p	light ultra	1.25	.20
391 A71	15p	brn lake & mar	1.75	.20

Campaign to save the historic monuments in Nubia. See Nos. C351-C352.

1962 **Litho.**

Designs: 50c, 2.50p, 7.50p, Cherries. 1p, 5p, Figs. 10p, 17.50p, 30p, Grapes. 50p, Oranges. 100p, Pomegranates.

Vignette Multicolored

392 A72	50c	violet blue	1.50	.20
393 A72	1p	gray blue	1.50	.20
394 A72	2.50p	brown	1.50	.20
395 A72	5p	bright blue	1.50	.20
396 A72	7.50p	lilac rose	1.50	.20
397 A72	10p	chocolate	1.75	.20
398 A72	17.50p	slate	2.50	.20
399 A72	30p	slate grn	2.75	.20
400 A72	50p	green	3.00	.20
401 A72	100p	brown blk	5.00	.50
		Nos. 392-401,C359-C366 (18)	31.65	4.30

Elementary Schoolboy — A73

1962, Oct. 1	**Litho.**	***Perf. 12***		
404 A73	30p	multicolored	1.50	.20

Students' Day, Oct. 1. See No. C355.

Cedar of Lebanon A74 A75

1963-64	**Unwmk.**	***Perf. 13x13½***		
405 A74	50c	green	7.00	.20
406 A75	50c	gray grn ('64)	1.50	.20
407 A75	2.50p	ultra ('64)	1.50	.20
408 A75	5p	brt pink ('64)	1.60	.20
409 A75	7.50p	orange ('64)	1.75	.20
410 A75	17.50p	rose lil ('64)	2.25	.20
		Nos. 405-410 (6)	15.60	1.20

Bicyclist — A76

Hyacinth — A77

1964, Feb. 11	**Litho.**	***Perf. 13***		
415 A76	2.50p	shown	1.50	.20
416 A76	5p	Basketball	1.50	.20
417 A76	10p	Track	1.50	.20
		Nos. 415-417,C385-C387 (6)	6.70	1.20

4th Mediterranean Games, Naples, Sept. 21-29, 1963.

1964	**Unwmk.**	***Perf. 13x13½***		
		Size: 26x27mm		
418 A77	50c	shown	1.50	.20
419 A77	1p	Hyacinth	1.50	.20
420 A77	2.50p	Hyacinth	1.50	.20
421 A77	5p	Cyclamen	1.50	.20
422 A77	7.50p	Cyclamen	1.50	.20
		Perf. 13		
		Size: 26x37mm		
423 A77	10p	Poinsettia	1.50	.20
424 A77	17.50p	Anemone	2.50	.20
425 A77	30p	Iris	3.50	.20
426 A77	50p	Poppy	7.00	.45
		Nos. 418-426,C391-C397 (16)	29.20	3.55

See Nos. C391-C397.

Temple of the Sun, Baalbek A78

1965, Jan. 11	**Litho.**	***Perf. 13x13½***		
429 A78	2.50p	blk & red org	2.00	.20
430 A78	7.50p	black & blue	2.75	.20
		Nos. 429-430,C420-C423 (6)	9.10	1.65

International Festival at Baalbek.

Swimmer A79

1965, Jan. 23	**Engr.**	***Perf. 13***		
431 A79	2.50p	shown	2.50	.20
432 A79	7.50p	Fencer	2.75	.20
433 A79	10p	Basketball, vert.	4.00	.20
		Nos. 431-433,C424-C426 (6)	11.10	1.20

18th Olympic Games, Tokyo, Oct. 10-25, 1964.

Golden Oriole A80

1965	**Engr.**	***Perf. 13***		
434 A80	5p	Bullfinch	8.00	.20
435 A80	10p	European goldfinch	13.00	.20
436 A80	15p	Hoopoe	10.00	.20
437 A80	17.50p	Rock partridge	12.00	.20
438 A80	20p	shown	15.00	.20
439 A80	32.50p	European bee-eater	20.00	.20
		Nos. 434-439 (6)	78.00	1.20

For surcharge see No. 459.

Cow and Calf — A81

1965	**Photo.**	***Perf. 11x12***		
440 A81	50c	shown	2.00	.20
441 A81	1p	Rabbit	2.25	.20
442 A81	2.50p	Ewe & lamb	2.50	.20
		Nos. 440-442 (3)	6.75	.60

Hippodrome, Beirut — A82

1p, Pigeon Rocks. 2.50p, Tabarja. 5p, Ruins, Beit-Méry. 7.50p, Statue and ruins, Anjar.

1966	**Unwmk.**	***Perf. 12x11½***		
443 A82	50c	gold & multi	1.75	.20
444 A82	1p	gold & multi	2.00	.20
445 A82	2.50p	gold & multi	2.25	.20
446 A82	5p	gold & multi	2.50	.20
447 A82	7.50p	gold & multi	2.75	.20
		Nos. 443-447 (5)	11.25	1.00

See #C486-C492. For surcharge see #460.

ITY Emblem and Cedars A83

1967	**Photo.**	***Perf. 11x12***		
448 A83	50c	lem, blk & brt bl	4.00	.20
449 A83	1p	sal, blk & brt bl	4.00	.20
450 A83	2.50p	gray, blk & brt bl	4.00	.20
451 A83	5p	lt rose lil, blk & brt bl	4.00	.20
452 A83	7.50p	yel, blk & brt bl	4.00	.20
		Nos. 448-452 (5)	20.00	1.00

Intl. Tourist Year; used as a regular issue. See #C515-C522. For surcharge see #461.

Goat and Kid A84

1968, Feb.	**Photo.**	***Perf. 12x11½***		
453 A84	50c	shown	3.00	.20
454 A84	1p	Cattle	4.00	.20
455 A84	2.50p	Sheep	5.00	.20
456 A84	5p	Camels	6.00	.20
457 A84	10p	Donkey	7.00	.20
458 A84	15p	Horses	9.00	.20
		Nos. 453-458 (6)	34.00	1.20

See Nos. C534-C539.

No. 439 Surcharged

1972, Apr.	**Engr.**	***Perf. 13***		
459 A80	25p	on 32.50p multi	22.50	.20

Nos. 447 and 452 Surcharged with New Value and Bars

Perf. 12x11½, 11x12

1972, May		**Photo.**		
460 A82	5p	on 7.50p multi	*4.50*	.20
461 A83	5p	on 7.50p multi	*4.50*	.20

Cedar — A85

Army Badge — A86

1974	**Litho.**	***Perf. 11***		
462 A85	50c	orange & olive	*.25*	.25

1980, Dec. 28	**Litho.**	***Perf. 11½***		
463 A86	25p	multicolored	2.50	.20

Army Day. See Nos. C792-C793.

Pres. Elias Sarkis — A87

World Communications Year — A89

World Food Day, Oct. 16, 1981 A88

1981, Sept. 23 Photo. *Perf. 14x13½*

464 A87	125p multicolored		2.75	.80
465 A87	300p multicolored		2.75	1.60
466 A87	500p multicolored		7.50	2.40
	Nos. 464-466 (3)		13.00	4.80

1982, Nov. 23 Photo. *Perf. 12x11½*

467 A88	50p Stork carrying food packages	1.75	.30
468 A88	75p Wheat, globe	2.00	.50
469 A88	100p Produce	2.25	.65
	Nos. 467-469 (3)	6.00	1.45

1983, Dec. 19 Photo. *Perf. 14*

470 A89	300p multicolored	6.00	1.75

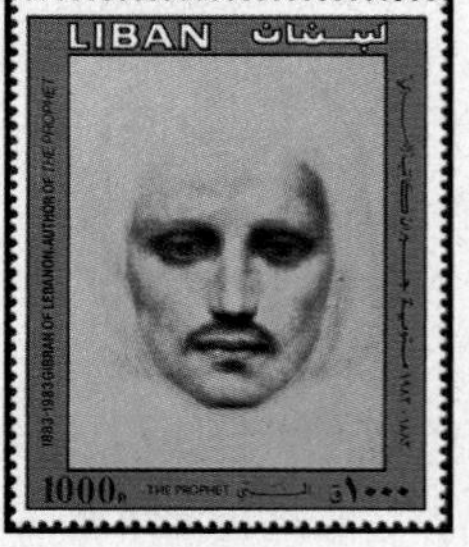
Illustrations from Khalil Gibran's The Prophet A90

1983, Dec. 19 *Perf. 13½x14*

471 A90	200p The Soul Is Back	2.75	1.00
472 A90	300p The Family	4.25	1.75
473 A90	500p Self-portrait	7.50	2.40
474 A90	1000p The Prophet	15.00	4.75
a.	Souvenir sheet, #471-474	37.50	37.50
	Nos. 471-474 (4)	29.50	9.90

No. 474a sold for £25.

Scouting Year — A91

Cedar of Lebanon — A93

1983, Dec. 19 *Perf. 14*

475 A91	200p Rowing	3.50	.65
476 A91	300p Signaling	4.00	.80
477 A91	500p Camp	7.25	1.25
	Nos. 475-477 (3)	14.75	2.70

1984, Dec. Photo. *Perf. 14½x13½*

481 A93	5p multicolored	2.00	.25

Flowers — A94

Defense — A95

1984, Dec. Photo. *Perf. 14½x13½*

482 A94	10p Iris of Sofar	2.00	.20
483 A94	25p Periwinkle	3.00	.30
484 A94	50p Flowering thorn	4.00	.40
	Nos. 482-484 (3)	9.00	.90

For surcharges see Nos. 531-532.

1984, Dec. Photo. *Perf. 14½x13½*

485 A95	75p Dove over city	3.50	.90
486 A95	150p Soldier, cedar	4.75	1.90
487 A95	300p Olive wreath, cedar	6.25	3.50
	Nos. 485-487 (3)	14.50	6.30

Temple Ruins A96

1985 Photo. *Perf. 13½x14½*

488 A96	100p Fakra	3.00	.55
489 A96	200p Bziza	3.50	1.10
490 A96	500p Tyre	6.50	2.75
	Nos. 488-490 (3)	13.00	4.40

Pres. Gemayel, Map of Lebanon, Dove, Text — A97

Pres. Gemayel, Military Academy Graduate — A98

1988, Feb. 1 Litho. *Perf. 14*

491 A97	£50 multicolored	5.00	2.00

1988, Mar. 9

492 A98	£25 multicolored	5.50	1.50

Arab Scouts, 75th Anniv. A99

1988, Mar. 9 *Perf. 13½x14½*

493 A99	£20 multicolored	5.50	1.25

UN Child Survival Campaign A100

1988, Mar. 9 *Perf. 14½x13½*

494 A100	£15 multicolored	3.50	.75

Prime Minister Rashid Karame (1921-1987), Satellite, Flags, Earth A101

1988, Mar. 9 *Perf. 13½x14½*

495 A101	£10 multicolored	2.50	.60

1st World Festival for Youths of Lebanese Descent in Uruguay A102

1988, Mar. 9

496 A102	£5 multicolored	3.25	.50

Cedar — A103

1989 Photo. *Perf. 13x13½*

497 A103	£50 dk grn & vio	3.00	.35
498 A103	£70 dk grn & brn	3.50	.50
499 A103	£100 dk grn & brt yel	4.00	.50
500 A103	£200 dk grn & bluish grn	6.00	1.25
501 A103	£500 dk grn & brt yel grn	11.00	3.00
	Nos. 497-501 (5)	27.50	5.60

Independence, 50th Anniv. — A104

Designs: £200, Al Muntazah Restaurant, Zahle, 1883. £300, Sea Castle, Sidon, vert. £500, Presidential Palace, Baabda. £1000, Army graduation ceremony, vert. £3000, Beirut 2000, architectural plan. £5000, Pres. Elias Harawi, Lebanese flag, vert.

1993 Litho. *Perf. 14*

502 A104	£200	multi	1.75	.20
503 A104	£300	multi	2.25	.55
504 A104	£500	multi	3.50	.85
505 A104	£1000	multi	5.00	1.75
506 A104	£3000	multi	9.25	3.00
507 A104	£5000	multi	17.50	8.25
	Nos. 502-507 (6)		39.25	14.60

For overprints, see Nos. 533B, 533C, 533G.

Size: 126x150mm

Imperf

508 A104	£10,000 multi	57.50	57.50

A105

A106

Environmental Protection: £100, Stop polluting atmosphere. £200, Stop fires. £500, Trees, building. £1000, Birds, trees in city. £2000, Mosaic of trees. £5000, Green tree in middle of polluted city.

1994, May 7 Litho. *Perf. 13½x13*

509 A105	£100	multicolored	1.75	.20
510 A105	£200	multicolored	2.00	.45
511 A105	£500	multicolored	3.25	.95
512 A105	£1000	multicolored	5.25	1.60
513 A105	£2000	multicolored	8.75	2.75
514 A105	£5000	multicolored	20.00	6.50
	Nos. 509-514 (6)		41.00	12.45

For overprints see Nos. 533D, 533H, 537.

1995, May 6 Litho. *Perf. 13½x13*

515 A106	£1500 Martyr's Day	7.00	3.00

For overprint see No. 534.

Anniversaries and Events — A107

Anniversaries and Events of 1995 — A108

£500, UNICEF, 50th anniv., horiz. £1000, Intl. Year of the Family (1994), horiz. £2000, ILO, 75th anniv. (in 1994), horiz. £3000, Bar Association (Berytus Nutrix Legum), 75th anniv.

1996, Feb. 21 Litho. *Perf. 14*

516	A107	£500 multi, horiz.	4.25	1.10
517	A107	£1000 multi, horiz.	6.75	2.25
518	A107	£2000 multi, horiz.	12.00	4.25
519	A107	£3000 multicolored	17.50	6.75
		Nos. 516-519 (4)	40.50	14.35

For overprints, see Nos. 533E, 534A, 535A.

1996, Feb. 21 *Perf. 13½x13*

£100, Opening of Museum of Arab Postage Stamps. £500, FAO, 50th anniv. £1000, UN, 50th anniv. £2000, Arab League, 50th anniv. £3000, Former Pres. René Moawad (1925-89).

520	A108	£100 multicolored	2.75	.20
521	A108	£500 multicolored	4.25	1.10
522	A108	£1000 multicolored	7.00	2.10
523	A108	£2000 multicolored	11.50	4.00
524	A108	£3000 multicolored	17.50	6.50
		Nos. 520-524 (5)	43.00	13.90

For overprints see Nos. 533A, 533F, 533I, 535-536.

Massacre at Cana A109

1997, Oct. 13 Litho. *Perf. 14*

525 A109 £1100 multicolored 11.00 2.75

For overprint, see No. 533J.

1997 Visit of Pope John Paul II to Lebanon A110

1997 Litho. *Perf. 13½x13*

526 A110 £10,000 multi 100.00 32.50

For overprint see Nos. 533O, 538.

Fakhr al-Din Palace, Deir-el-Kamar — A111

1999 Litho. *Perf. 12*

527	A111	£100 Chehab Palace, Hasbaya, vert.	1.50	.20
528	A111	£300 ESCWA Building, Beirut, vert.	2.50	.45
529	A111	£500 shown	3.00	.80
530	A111	£1100 Grand Seraglio, Beirut	6.00	1.75
		Nos. 527-530 (4)	13.00	3.20

Nos. 484, 485 and C775 Surcharged in Silver and Black

Methods and Perfs. as before

1999

531	A94	£100 on 50p (#484)	1.75	.20
532	A95	£300 on 75p (#485)	2.50	.45
533	AP154	£1100 on 70p (#C775)	6.00	1.75
		Nos. 531-533 (3)	10.25	2.40

Nos. 502, 504-505, 511-512, 516, 518-522, 525 Overprinted in Gold

Similar to Nos. 534-538 but with Symbol Oriented as a Cross

Methods and Perfs As Before

1999 (?)

533A	A108	£100 multi	15.00
533B	A104	£200 multi	15.00
533C	A104	£500 multi	25.00
533D	A105	£500 multi	25.00
533E	A107	£500 multi	25.00
533F	A108	£500 multi	25.00
533G	A104	£1000 multi	50.00
533H	A105	£1000 multi	47.50
533I	A108	£1000 multi	30.00
533J	A109	£1100 multi	300.00
533K	A106	£1500 multi	40.00
533L	A107	£2000 multi	75.00
533M	A107	£3000 multi	115.00
533N	A105	£5000 multi	225.00
533O	A110	£10,000 multi	425.00
		Nos. 533A-533O (15)	1,437.

Nos. 514, 515, 523, 524 and 526 Overprinted in Gold or Silver

Methods and Perfs As Before

2000 (?)

534	A106	£1500 multi	6.00	2.50
535	A108	£2000 multi	8.50	3.25
536	A108	£3000 multi (S)	13.00	5.25
537	A105	£5000 multi	19.00	8.50
538	A110	£10,000 multi	37.50	17.00
		Nos. 534-538 (5)	84.00	36.50

Cedar of Lebanon — A112

Perf. 13x13¼, 11x11¼ (£500, £1000, £1100)

2000 ? Litho. Unwmk.

539	A112	£100 dark red	.50	.20
540	A112	£300 Prus blue	1.00	.35

Wmk. 400

541	A112	£500 green	1.50	.65
a.		Perf. 13x13¼	1.50	.65
b.		Booklet pane, 10 #541a	15.00	
		Booklet, #541b	15.00	
542	A112	£1000 blue	3.50	1.25
543	A112	£1100 olive brn	3.75	1.40
a.		Perf. 13x13¼	3.75	1.40
b.		Booklet pane, 10 #543a	37.50	
		Booklet, #543b	37.50	
544	A112	£1500 vio blue	4.50	1.90
a.		Booklet pane, 10 #544	45.00	
		Booklet, #544a	45.00	
b.		Perf. 11x11¼	4.50	1.90
		Nos. 539-544 (6)	14.75	5.75

A113

2001 ? Litho. *Perf. 11¼x11*

545 A113 £1100 multi 4.00 1.50

Geneva Conventions, 50th Anniv. (in 1999) — A114

Red Cross/Red Crescent A115

2001 Litho. *Perf. 11x11½*

546	A114	£500 shown	2.00	.70
547	A114	£1100 "50," fist	4.00	1.50
548	A115	£1500 shown	5.00	2.10
		Nos. 546-548 (3)	11.00	4.30

SOS Children's Villages A116

2001

549 A116 £300 multi 1.25 .40

Prisoners in Israel A117

2001

550 A117 £500 multi 2.00 .70

Ibrahim Abd el Al (1908-59), Hydrologist A118

2001

551 A118 £1000 multi 3.50 1.40

Abdallah Zakher (1680-1748), Printer — A119

2001

552 A119 £1000 multi 3.50 1.40

Elias Abu Chabke (1904-49), Poet — A120

2001 *Perf. 11½x11*

553 A120 £1500 multi 5.00 2.10

Saint Joseph University, 125th Anniv. (in 2000) A121

2001 *Perf. 11x11½*

554 A121 £5000 multi 15.00 7.00

Economic & Social Commission for Western Asia, 25th Anniv. (in 1999) — A122

2001 *Perf. 11½x11*

555 A122 £10,000 multi 32.50 20.00

Arab Woman's Day — A123

2002, Feb. 1 Litho. *Perf. 13¼x13½*

556 A123 £1000 multi 3.25 2.60

Arab League Summit Conference, Beirut — A124

Arab League member flags and: £2000, Emblem. £3000, Cedar tree, Lebanese Pres. Emile Lahoud.

2002, Mar. 27

557-558 A124 Set of 2 11.00 9.25

Souvenir Sheet

Israeli Withdrawal From Southern Lebanon, 2nd Anniv. — A125

No. 559: a, Pres. Emile Lahoud, flag. b, Pres. Lahoud holding book. c, Pres. Lahoud and map. d, Pres. Lahoud receiving sword.

2002, Mar. 27 ***Perf. 13¼***

559 A125 £1100 Sheet of 4, #a-d 10.50 9.50

Souvenir Sheet

Martyrs of Justice — A126

2002, June 14 ***Perf. 13¼x13½***

560 A126 £3000 multi 7.00 5.75

UPU, 125th Anniv. (in 1999) A127

2002, Oct. 11 Litho. ***Perf. 13½x13¼***

561 A127 £2000 multi 7.00 5.75

City Views — A128

Ruins — A129

Paleontonlogy — A130

Designs: £100 Old souk, Zouk Mikael. £300, Old souk, Sidon. £500, Byblos. £1000, Souk, Tripoli. £1100, Bziza. £1500, Arqa. £2000, Niha. £3000, Mousailaha Citadel. £5000, Libanobythus milkii in amber. £10,000, Nematonotus longispinus fossil.

Perf. 13¼x13½, 13½x13¼

2002-03 **Litho.**

No.	Type	Value		Unused	Used
562	A128	£100	multi	.50	.20
563	A128	£300	multi	.90	.50
564	A128	£500	multi	1.75	.90
565	A128	£1000	multi	2.50	1.75
566	A129	£1100	multi	3.00	2.00
567	A129	£1500	multi	3.50	2.75
568	A129	£2000	multi	4.50	3.75
569	A129	£3000	multi	7.25	5.75
570	A130	£5000	multi	10.50	9.25
571	A130	£10,000	multi	21.00	18.00
		Nos. 562-571 (10)		55.40	44.85

Issued: £100, £300, 10/11; £1000, £1500, £2000, £3000, £10,000, 11/20; £500, £1100, 12/20; £5000, 1/8/03.

Ninth Francophone Summit, Beirut — A131

Summit emblem and: No. 572, £1500, Mountains. No. 573, £1500, Pres. Emile Lahoud.

2002, Oct. 23 ***Perf. 13¼x13½***

572-573 A131 Set of 2 7.00 5.50

Beirut, 1999 Arab Cultural Capital — A132

2002, Nov. 13

574 A132 £2000 multi 5.00 4.00

Independence, 60th Anniv. (in 2001) — A133

Stylized flag and: No. 575, £1250, Crowd viewing horse and rider. No. 576, £1250, Men and flag on staff. No. 577, £1750, Arabic text. No. 578, £1750, Soldier saluting group of men. £6000, Vignettes of Nos. 575-578.

2003, Dec. 5 Litho. ***Perf. 12¾x13***

575-578 A133 Set of 4 14.00 14.00

Imperf

Size: 160x110mm

579 A133 £6000 multi 14.00 14.00

Faqra Ski Resort A134

2004 Litho. ***Perf. 11x11¼***

580 A134 £500 multi 1.25 1.25

General Post Office, Beirut — A135

Post office in: £100, 1953. £300, 2002.

2004 ***Perf. 11¼x11***

581-582 A135 Set of 2 1.00 1.00

Al Bustan Festival A136

2004 Litho. ***Perf. 11x11¼***

583 A136 £1000 multi 2.50 2.50

St. George's Hospital, Beirut, 125th Anniv. (in 2003) — A137

2004, Oct. 28 Litho. ***Perf. 11x11¼***

584 A137 £3000 multi 4.00 4.00

Ski Resorts A138

2004 Litho. ***Perf. 11x11¼, 11¼x11***

No.	Type	Value	Design	Unused	Used
586	A138	£100	Aayoun Siman	.20	.20
587	A138	£250	Laklouk, vert.	.35	.35
589	A138	£300	Kanat Bakish	.40	.40
590	A138	£1000	Cedres	1.40	1.40
		Nos. 586-590 (4)		2.35	2.35

Issued: £250, 11/26; Nos. 586, 589, £1000, 12/10. Numbers have been reserved for two additional stamps in this set.

Baalbeck Intl. Festival A139

Tyre Festival — A140

Beiteddine Festival — A141

Byblos Intl. Festival — A142

Perf. 11x11¼, 11¼x11

2004, Nov. 26 **Litho.**

No.	Type	Value		Unused	Used
591	A139	£500	multi	.70	.70
592	A140	£1250	multi	1.75	1.75
593	A141	£1400	multi	1.90	1.90
594	A142	£1750	multi	2.40	2.40
		Nos. 591-594 (4)		6.75	6.75

Rotary International, Cent. — A143

2005, Feb. 23 ***Perf. 11¼x11***

595 A143 £3000 multi 4.00 4.00

Beirut Buildings A144

Designs: £100, Rafiq Hariri Intl. Airport. £250, Parliament. £300, Camille Chamoun Sports Center. £500, National Museum. £1000, Governmental Palace. £1250, Bank of Lebanon. £1400, St. Paul's Cathedral. £1750, Bahaeddine Hariri Mosque. £2000, Presidential Palace.

2005 Litho. ***Perf. 13x13½***

596-604 A144 Set of 9 15.00 15.00

Issued: £100, £300, £500, £1000, 10/11; others, 11/11.

Pres. Rafiq Hariri (1944-2005) — A145

Designs: No. 605, £1250, Pres. Hariri, flag. No. 606, £1250, Pres. Hariri, mosque, church and statues. No. 607, £1750, Pres. Hariri, mosque. No. 608, £1750, Child kissing picture of Pres. Hariri.

2006, Feb. 13 ***Perf. 13¼x13***
605-608 A145 Set of 4 10.50 10.50
608a Souvenir sheet, #605-608, imperf. 10.50 10.50

No. 608a has embossed margin and simulated perforations between stamps.

Arabic Book Exhibition A146

2007, Apr. 18 Litho. ***Perf. 13x13¼***
609 A146 £1000 multi 1.40 1.40

Basil Fuleihan (1963-2005), Economy Minister — A147

Fuleihan: £500, Wearing cap and gown, suit and tie. £1500, With flags of Lebanon and European Union. £2000, With flag of Lebanon. £4000, Vignettes of Nos. 610-612, map and flag of Lebanon.

2007, Apr. 18 ***Perf. 13¼x13***
610-612 A147 Set of 3 5.75 5.75

Size: 160x100mm

Imperf

613 A147 £4000 multi 5.75 5.75

Pres. Fouad Chehab (1902-73) — A148

2007, June 4 ***Perf. 13¼x13***
614 A148 £1400 multi 1.90 1.90

World Summit on the Information Society, Tunis (in 2005) A149

2007, July 2 ***Perf. 13x13¼***
615 A149 £100 multi .20 .20

Léopold Sédar Senghor (1906-2001), First President of Senegal — A150

2007, July 2 ***Perf. 13¼x13***
616 A150 £300 multi .45 .45

Intl. Year of Sports and Physical Education (in 2005) A151

2007, July 2 ***Perf. 13x13¼***
617 A151 £500 multi .70 .70

OPEC Development Fund, 30th Anniv. — A152

2007, July 2
618 A152 £1400 multi 1.90 1.90

Baalbeck Intl. Festival, 50th Anniv. — A153

50th anniv. emblem and: £1000, Names of performers. £5000, Female performers.

2007, July 2 ***Perf. 13¼x13***
619-620 A153 Set of 2 7.50 7.50

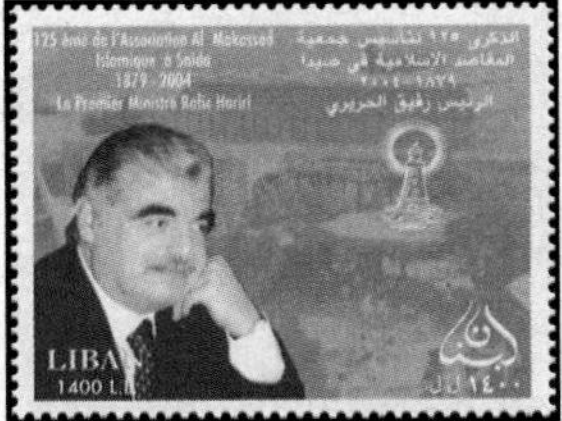

Islamic Makassed Association of Sidon, 125th Anniv. (in 2004) — A154

Emblem and: £1400, Pres. Rafiq Hariri. £1750, Prime Minister Riad El Solh.

2007, July 2
621-622 A154 Set of 2 4.00 4.00

Islamic Makassed Association of Beirut, 125th Anniv. (in 2003) — A155

Emblem and: £250, "125" in Arabian script. £500, Prime Minister Saeb Salam. £1400, Pres. Rafiq Hariri. £1750, Omar El Daouk.

2007, July 2
623-626 A155 Set of 4 5.00 5.00

Souvenir Sheet

2006 Ascent of Mt. Everest by Maxime Chaya — A156

2007, July 2
627 A156 £3000 multi 3.75 3.75

2004 Return of Freed Prisoners — A157

2007, July 2 ***Imperf.***
628 A157 £5000 multi 6.25 6.25

Souvenir Sheet

Hills, by Nizar Daher — A158

2007, July 2 Litho. ***Perf. 13¼x13***
629 A158 £5000 multi 6.25 6.25

Rotary International District 2450 Conference, Beirut — A159

2008, Apr. 30 Litho. ***Perf. 13¼x13***
630 A159 £2000 multi 3.00 3.00

Kahlil Gibran (1883-1931), Writer and Artist — A160

Designs: £100, Mother and Her Child. £500, Sultana. £1400, Gibran Museum, Bsharri. £2000, Gibran.
£4000, Gibran and vignettes of Nos. 631-634, horiz.

2008, Apr. 30 ***Perf. 13x13¼***
631-634 A160 Set of 4 5.75 5.75

Imperf

Size: 160x110mm

635 A160 £4000 multi 5.75 5.75

Army Day A161

Emblem and: £500, Soldier and flag of Lebanon. £1000, Stylized flag of Lebanon. £1250, Soldier holding wheat stalks. £1750, Eye.
£4500, Soldiers and vignettes of Nos. 636-639.

2008 Litho. ***Perf. 13¼x13***
636-639 A161 Set of 4 6.00 6.00

Size: 160x110mm

Imperf

640 A161 £4500 multi 6.00 6.00

Souvenir Sheet

Arab Postal Day — A162

No. 641 — Emblem and: a, World map and pigeon. b, Camel caravan.

Perf. 13¼ Vert. Through Center

2008
641 A162 £5000 Sheet of 2, #a-b 13.50 13.50

Stamps have simulated perforations on three sides.

Lebanon Post, 10th Anniv. — A163

Simulated postmarks, Lebanon Post emblem, streamers, airplane and: £1250, "10" in Arabian script. £1750, Open envelope and "10th anniversary."
£3000, Simulated postmarks, Lebanon Post emblem, streamers, airplane and vignettes of Nos. 642-643.

2008 ***Perf. 13¼x13***
642-643 A163 Set of 2 4.00 4.00

Size: 160x110mm
Imperf

644 A163 £3000 multi 4.00 4.00

Trees and Map of Mediterranean Area — A164

2008, Nov. 20 ***Perf. 13***
645 A164 £1750 multi 2.40 2.40

See France No. 3569.

Gen. François El Hajj (1953-2007) — A165

2009, Jan. 8 ***Perf. 13x13¼***
646 A165 £1750 multi 2.60 2.60

Universal Declaration of Human Rights, 60th Anniv. — A166

2009, Jan. 8 ***Perf. 13¼x13***
647 A166 £2000 multi 3.00 3.00

Dated 2008.

Beirut, World Book Capital A167

2009, Sept. 17 Litho. ***Perf. 13x13¼***
648 A167 £750 multi 1.25 1.25

Jerusalem, Capital of Arab Culture — A168

2009, Sept. 17 ***Perf. 13¼x13***
649 A168 £1000 multi 1.60 1.60

Pierre Deschamps (1873-1958), Founder of French Lay Mission — A169

2009, Sept. 17
650 A169 £500 blue & black .85 .85

Sixth Francophone Games, Beirut — A170

2009, Sept. 28
651 A170 £1000 multi 1.60 1.60

Fire Fighters A171

Fire fighters with panel color of: £100, Green. £250, Red.

2010, Aug. 2 Litho. ***Perf. 13x13¼***
652-653 A171 Set of 2 .50 .50

Nature Reserves A172

2010, Aug. 2
654 A172 £300 multi .45 .45

Architecture A173

Various buildings with frame color of: £500, Red. £1000, Blue. £1200, Red.

2010, Aug. 2 ***Perf. 13¼x13***
655-657 A173 Set of 3 3.75 3.75

Soap Production A174

2010, Aug. 2 ***Perf. 13x13¼***
658 A174 £1400 multi 1.90 1.90

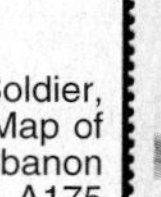

Soldier, Map of Lebanon A175

2010, Aug. 2
659 A175 £1750 multi 2.40 2.40

Lungs and Cigarette Butts A176

2010, Aug. 2
660 A176 £2000 multi 2.75 2.75

Syringe and Arrows — A177

2010, Aug. 2 ***Perf. 13¼x13***
661 A177 £5000 black & red 7.00 7.00

Imam Al Ouzaai (707-74) — A178

2010, Oct. 9
662 A178 £1000 multi 1.40 1.40

Grand Mufti Hassan Khaled (1921-89) — A179

Musa as-Sadr (1929-78), Religious Leader A180

2010, Oct. 9 ***Perf. 13¼x13***
663 A179 £1400 multi 2.00 2.00

Perf. 13x13¼
664 A180 £1400 multi 2.00 2.00

Assassinated Political Leaders — A181

Designs: No. 665, £1400, Kamal Jumblatt (1917-77). No. 666, £1400, Prime Minister Rashid Karami (1921-87). No. 667, £1400, President René Moawad (1925-89). No. 668, £1400, President Bachir Gemayel (1947-82), horiz.

2010, Oct. 9 ***Perf. 13x13¼, 13¼x13***
665-668 A181 Set of 4 8.00 8.00

World Tourism Day A182

2010, Oct. 9 ***Perf. 13x13¼***
669 A182 £2000 multi 3.00 3.00

Dove and Flowers A183

2010, Oct. 9
670 A183 £3000 multi 4.25 4.25

SEMI-POSTAL STAMPS

Regular Issue of 1925 Surcharged in Red or Black

1926 Unwmk. ***Perf. 14x13½***

No.	Type	Description	Unused	Used
B1	A2	25c + 25c ol blk	4.25	4.25
B2	A2	50c + 25c yellow green (B)	4.25	4.25
B3	A2	75c + 25c brown orange (B)	4.25	4.25
B4	A2	1p + 50c mag	4.25	4.25
B5	A2	1.25p + 50c dp grn	4.75	4.75
B6	A2	1.50p + 50c rose red (B)	4.75	4.75
a.		Double surcharge	40.00	30.00
B7	A2	2p + 75c dk brn	4.25	4.25
B8	A2	2.50p + 75c pck bl	4.75	4.75
B9	A2	3p + 1p org brn	4.75	4.75
B10	A2	5p + 1p vio (B)	4.75	4.75
B11	A3	10p + 2p violet brown (B)	4.75	4.75
B12	A2	25p + 5p ultra	4.75	4.75
		Nos. B1-B12 (12)	54.50	54.50

On No. B11 the surcharge is set in six lines to fit the shape of the stamp. All values of this series exist with inverted surcharge. Value each, $14.

See Nos. CB1-CB4.

Catalogue values for unused stamps in this section, from this point to the end of the section, are for Never Hinged items.

Boxing — SP1

1961, Jan. 12 Litho. *Perf. 13*
B13 SP1 2.50p + 2.50p shown .50 .20
B14 SP1 5p + 5p Wrestling .50 .20
B15 SP1 7.50p + 7.50p Shot put .50 .20
Nos. B13-B15,CB12-CB14 (6) 10.50 5.40

17th Olympic Games, Rome, Aug. 25-Sept. 11, 1960.

Nos. B13-B15 with Arabic and French Overprint in Black, Blue or Green and two Bars through Olympic Inscription: "CHAMPIONNAT D'EUROPE DE TIR, 2 JUIN 1962"

1962, June 2
B16 SP1 2.50p + 2.50p blue & brn (Bk) .50 .20
B17 SP1 5p + 5p org & brn (G) .90 .20
B18 SP1 7.50p + 7.50p vio & brn (Bl) 1.00 .40
Nos. B16-B18,CB15-CB17 (6) 8.65 4.25

European Marksmanship Championships held in Lebanon.

Red Cross SP2

1988, June 8 Litho. *Perf. 14*
B19 SP2 £10 + £1 shown 1.75
B20 SP2 £20 + £2 Stylized profile 2.75
B21 SP2 £30 + £3 Globe, emblems, dove 3.75
Nos. B19-B21 (3) 8.25

AIR POST STAMPS

Nos. 10-13 with Additional Overprint

1924 Unwmk. *Perf. 14x13½*
C1 A18 2p on 40c 13.00 *13.00*
a. Double surcharge 52.50 52.50
C2 A18 3p on 60c 13.00 *13.00*
a. Invtd. surch. and ovpt. 87.50 87.50
C3 A18 5p on 1fr 13.00 *13.00*
a. Dbl. surch. and ovpt. 72.50 72.50
b. "5" omitted 300.00
C4 A18 10p on 2fr 13.00 *13.00*
a. Invtd. surch. and ovpt. 110.00 110.00
b. Dbl. surch. and ovpt. 60.00 60.00
Nos. C1-C4 (4) 52.00 *52.00*

Nos. 33, 35-37 Overprinted

C5 A18 2p on 40c 13.00 13.00
a. Overprint reversed 45.00
C6 A18 3p on 60c 13.00 13.00
a. Overprint reversed 45.00
C7 A18 5p on 1fr 13.00 13.00
a. Overprint reversed 45.00
C8 A18 10p on 2fr 13.50 13.50
a. Overprint reversed 45.00
b. Double surcharge 45.00
Nos. C5-C8 (4) 52.50 52.50

Nos. 57, 59-61 Overprinted in Green

1925
C9 A2 2p dark brown 4.50 4.50
C10 A2 3p orange brown 4.50 4.50
C11 A2 5p violet 4.50 4.50
a. Inverted overprint
C12 A3 10p violet brown 4.50 4.50
Nos. C9-C12 (4) 18.00 18.00

Nos. 57, 59-61 Overprinted in Red

c

1926
C13 A2 2p dark brown 4.75 4.75
C14 A2 3p orange brown 4.75 4.75
C15 A2 5p violet 4.75 4.75
C16 A3 10p violet brown 4.75 4.75
Nos. C13-C16 (4) 19.00 19.00

Airplane pointed down on No. C16.
Exist with inverted overprint. Value, each $45.

Issues of Republic under French Mandate

Nos. C13-C16 Overprinted

d

1927
C17 A2 2p dark brown 5.50 5.50
C18 A2 3p orange brown 5.50 5.50
C19 A2 5p violet 5.50 5.50
C20 A3 10p violet brown 5.50 5.50
Nos. C17-C20 (4) 22.00 22.00

On No. C19 "Republique Libanaise" is above the bars. Overprint set in two lines on No. C20.

Nos. C17-C20 with Additional Overprint

e

1928

Black Overprint
C21 A2 2p brown 12.50 10.00
a. Double overprint 65.00 65.00
b. Inverted overprint 65.00 65.00
C22 A2 3p orange brown 12.50 10.00
a. Double overprint 65.00 65.00
C23 A2 5p violet 12.50 10.00
a. Double overprint 65.00 65.00
C24 A3 10p violet brown 12.50 10.00
a. Double overprint 65.00 65.00
Nos. C21-C24 (4) 50.00 40.00

On Nos. C21-C24 the airplane is always in red.

Nos. 52, 54, 57, 59-62 Overprinted in Red or Black (No. C34)

f

1928
C25 A2 2p dark brown 4.50 4.50
C26 A2 3p orange brown 3.00 3.00
C27 A2 5p violet 4.50 4.50
C28 A3 10p violet brown 4.50 4.50

1929
C33 A2 50c yellow green 1.25 1.25
a. Inverted overprint 45.00 45.00
C34 A2 1p magenta (Bk) 1.00 1.00
a. Inverted overprint 45.00 45.00
C35 A2 25p ultra 190.00 160.00
a. Inverted overprint 525.00 525.00
Nos. C25-C34 (6) 18.75 18.75
Nos. C25-C35 (7) 208.75 178.75

On Nos. C25-C28 the airplane is always in red.

On No. C28 the overprinted orientation is horizontal. The bars covering the old country names are at the left.

The red overprint of a silhouetted plane and "Republique Libanaise," as on Nos. C25-C27, was also applied to Nos. C9-C12. These are believed to have been essays, and were not regularly issued.

No. 62 with Surcharge Added in Red

Two types of surcharge:
I — The "5" of "15 P." is italic. The "15" is 4mm high. Arabic characters for "Lebanese Republic" and for "15 P." are on same line in that order.
II — The "5" is in Roman type (upright) and smaller; "15" is 3½mm high. Arabic for "Lebanese Republic" is centered on line by itself, with Arabic for "15 P." below right end of line.

C36 A2 15p on 25p ultra (I) 225.00 175.00
a. Type II (#106) *800.00 800.00*

Nos. 102 Overprinted Type "c" in Blue

C37 A2 50c on 75c 1.00 1.00
a. Airplane inverted 45.00
b. French and Arabic surch. invtd.
c. "P" omitted
d. Airplane double 50.00

No. 55 Surcharged in Red

1930
C38 A2 2p on 1.25p dp green 1.75 1.25
a. Inverted surcharge 72.50 45.00

Airplane over Racheya AP2

Designs: 1p, Plane over Broumana. 2p, Baalbek. 3p, Hasroun. 5p, Byblos. 10p, Kadicha River. 15p, Beirut. 25p, Tripoli. 50p, Kabeljas. 100p, Zahle.

1930-31 Photo. *Perf. 13½*
C39 AP2 50c dk violet ('31) .50 .50
C40 AP2 1p yellow grn ('31) .80 .80
C41 AP2 2p dp orange ('31) 2.50 2.50
C42 AP2 3p magenta ('31) 2.50 2.50
C43 AP2 5p indigo 2.50 2.50
C44 AP2 10p orange red 3.25 3.25
C45 AP2 15p orange brn 3.25 3.25
C46 AP2 25p gray vio ('31) 4.75 4.75
C47 AP2 50p dp claret 9.00 9.00
C48 AP2 100p olive brown 12.00 12.00
Nos. C39-C48 (10) 41.05 41.05

Nos. C39-C48 exist imperforate. Value, set $200.

Tourist Publicity Issue

Skiing in Lebanon AP12

Bay of Jounie AP13

1936, Oct. 12
C49 AP12 50c slate grn 3.00 3.00
C50 AP13 1p red orange 3.75 3.75
C51 AP12 2p black violet 3.75 3.75
C52 AP13 3p yellow grn 4.00 4.00
C53 AP12 5p brown car 4.00 4.00
C54 AP13 10p orange brn 4.00 4.00
C55 AP13 15p dk carmine 37.50 37.50
C56 AP12 25p green 125.00 125.00
Nos. C49-C56 (8) 185.00 185.00

Nos. C49-C56 exist imperforate. Value, set $650.

Lebanese Pavilion at Exposition AP14

1937, July 1 *Perf. 13½*
C57 AP14 50c olive black 1.50 1.50
C58 AP14 1p yellow green 1.50 1.50
C59 AP14 2p dk red orange 1.50 1.50
C60 AP14 3p dk olive grn 1.50 1.50
C61 AP14 5p deep green 2.00 2.00
C62 AP14 10p carmine lake 9.00 9.00
C63 AP14 15p rose lake 10.00 10.00
C64 AP14 25p orange brn 17.50 17.50
Nos. C57-C64 (8) 44.50 44.50

Paris International Exposition.

Arcade of Beit-ed-Din Palace AP15

Ruins of Baalbek AP16

1937-40 Engr. *Perf. 13*
C65 AP15 50c ultra ('38) .35 .20
C66 AP15 1p henna brn ('40) .35 .20
C67 AP15 2p sepia ('40) .35 .20
C68 AP15 3p rose ('40) 3.25 1.25
C69 AP15 5p lt green ('40) .35 .20
C70 AP16 10p dull violet .35 .20
C71 AP16 15p turq bl ('40) 2.75 1.75
C72 AP16 25p violet ('40) 6.00 5.00
C73 AP16 50p yellow grn ('40) 11.00 7.00
C74 AP16 100p brown ('40) 6.00 3.50
Nos. C65-C74 (10) 30.75 19.50

Nos. C65-C74 exist imperforate.

Medical College of Beirut AP17

1938, May 9 Photo. *Perf. 13*
C75 AP17 2p green 3.00 *3.50*
C76 AP17 3p orange 3.00 *3.50*
C77 AP17 5p lilac gray 5.50 *6.50*
C78 AP17 10p lake 10.50 *12.00*
Nos. C75-C78 (4) 22.00 *25.50*

Medical Congress.

Maurice Noguès and View of Beirut — AP18

1938, July 15 *Perf. 11*

C79	AP18	10p brown carmine	4.00	1.50
a.		Souv. sheet of 4, perf. 13½	35.00	20.00
b.		Perf. 13½	7.50	4.00

10th anniversary of first Marseille-Beirut flight, by Maurice Noguès.

No. C79a has marginal inscriptions in French and Arabic. Exists imperf.; value $250.

Independent Republic

Plane Over Mt. Lebanon AP19

1942, Sept. 18 **Litho.** *Perf. 11½*

C80	AP19	10p dk brown vio	7.00	*8.00*
C81	AP19	50p dk gray grn	7.00	*8.00*

1st anniv. of the Proclamation of Independence, Nov. 26, 1941.

Nos. C80 and C81 exist imperforate.

Bechamoun AP20

Rachaya Citadel AP21

Air View of Beirut AP22

1943, May 1 *Perf. 11½*

C82	AP20	25p yellow grn	4.75	4.75
C83	AP20	50p orange	6.50	5.50
C84	AP21	100p buff	6.50	5.50
C85	AP21	200p blue vio	8.00	7.25
C86	AP22	300p sage green	21.00	17.50
C87	AP22	500p sepia	42.50	32.50
		Nos. C82-C87 (6)	74.25	59.50

2nd anniv. of the Proclamation of Independence. Nos. C82-C87 exist imperforate.

See #163-166. For overprints see #C91-C96.

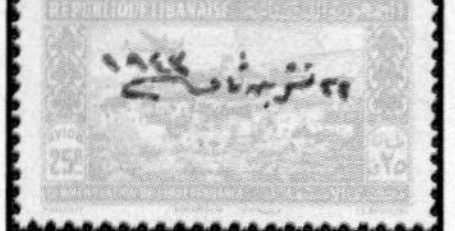

Bhannes Sanatorium AP23

1943, July 8 **Photo.**

Black Overprint

C88	AP23	20p orange	3.75	2.75
C89	AP23	50p steel blue	4.25	3.50
C90	AP23	100p rose violet	6.00	4.50
		Nos. C88-C90 (3)	14.00	8.25

Arab Medical Congress, Beirut.

Nos. C82 to C87 Overprinted in Red, Blue or Violet

1944, Nov. 23

C91	AP20	25p yel grn (R)	7.25	7.25
C92	AP20	50p orange (Bl)	12.00	12.00
C93	AP21	100p buff (V)	14.00	14.00
C94	AP21	200p blue vio (R)	25.00	25.00
C95	AP22	300p sage grn (R)	32.50	30.00
C96	AP22	500p sepia (Bl)	65.00	60.00
		Nos. C91-C96 (6)	155.75	148.25

Return to office of the President and his ministers, Nov. 22, 1943.

Catalogue values for unused stamps in this section, from this point to the end of the section, are for Never Hinged items.

Falls of Litani — AP24

The Cedars AP25

1945, July **Unwmk.** **Litho.**

C97	AP24	25p gray brown	3.50	2.10
C98	AP24	50p rose violet	5.00	2.75
C99	AP25	200p violet	15.00	5.25
C100	AP25	300p brown black	27.50	10.50
		Nos. C97-C100 (4)	51.00	20.60

Lebanese Soldiers at Bir Hacheim AP26

1946, May 8

C101	AP26	15p bl blk, org & red org	1.00	.25
C102	AP26	20p red, lil & bl	1.00	.60
C103	AP26	25p brt bl, org & red	1.25	.20
C104	AP26	50p gray blk, bl & red	1.75	.50
C105	AP26	100p pur, pink & red	5.00	1.25
C106	AP26	150p brn, pink & red	6.00	3.75
		Nos. C101-C106 (6)	16.00	6.55

Victory of the Allied Nations in WWII, 1st anniv.

Three imperf. souvenir sheets of 14 exist. They contain one each of Nos. C101-C106 and 189-196 in changed colors. One has sepia inscriptions, and one on thin white card has blue inscriptions. Value $30 each. The third, with blue inscriptions, is on thick honeycombed chamois card. Value $110.

Night Herons Type

1946, Sept. 11

C107	A35	10p orange	7.00	1.00
C108	A35	25p ultra	8.00	.20
C109	A35	50p blue green	25.00	1.60
C110	A35	100p dk vio brn	37.50	6.50
		Nos. C107-C110 (4)	77.50	9.30

Symbols of Communications — AP28

1946, Nov. 22

C111	AP28	25p deep blue	1.75	.70
C112	AP28	50p green	2.50	.80
C113	AP28	75p orange red	4.25	1.75
C114	AP28	150p brown black	6.00	2.75
		Nos. C111-C114 (4)	14.50	6.00

Arab Postal Congress, Sofar, 1946.

Stone Tablet, Dog River and Pres. Bechara el-Khoury AP29

1947, Feb. 11

C115	AP29	25p ultra	7.00	.35
C116	AP29	50p dull rose	9.00	.60
C117	AP29	75p gray black	11.00	.65
C118	AP29	150p blue green	17.50	1.40
		Nos. C115-C118 (4)	44.50	3.00

Evacuation of foreign troops from Lebanon, Dec. 31, 1946.

Bay of Jounie AP30

Government House, Beirut — AP31

1947, Feb. 11

Grayish Paper

C119	AP30	5p dp blue grn	.60	.20
C120	AP30	10p rose vio	.90	.20
C121	AP30	15p vermilion	2.25	.20
C122	AP30	20p orange	2.50	.20
a.		20p red orange, white paper	2.25	.20
C123	AP30	25p deep blue	3.00	.20
C124	AP30	50p henna brn	5.00	.20
C125	AP30	100p chocolate	10.50	.30
C126	AP31	150p dk vio brn	18.00	.50
C127	AP31	200p slate	27.50	2.40
C128	AP31	300p black	45.00	6.00
		Nos. C119-C128 (10)	115.25	10.40

See Nos. C145A-C147B.

Post Horn and Letter — AP32

Phoenician Galley AP33

1947, June 17 **Litho.**

C129	AP32	10p brt ultra	1.75	.50
C130	AP32	15p rose car	2.00	.50
C131	AP32	25p bright blue	2.50	.80
C132	AP33	50p dk slate grn	5.75	.90
C133	AP33	75p purple	7.00	1.90
C134	AP33	100p dark brown	9.00	2.50
		Nos. C129-C134 (6)	28.00	7.10

Lebanon's participation in the 12th UPU congress, Paris.

Lebanese Village AP34

1948, Sept. 1 *Perf. 11½*

C135	AP34	5p dp orange	.75	.20
C136	AP34	10p rose lilac	1.75	.20
C137	AP34	15p orange brn	3.50	.20
C138	AP34	20p slate	4.50	.20
C139	AP34	25p Prus blue	10.50	1.00
C140	AP34	50p gray black	17.50	1.40
		Nos. C135-C140 (6)	38.50	3.20

Apollo — AP35

Minerva AP36

1948, Nov. 23 **Unwmk.**

C141	AP35	7.50p blue & lt blue	4.00	1.00
C142	AP35	15p black & gray	5.00	1.25
C143	AP35	20p rose brn & rose	5.25	1.90
C144	AP36	35p car rose & rose	8.00	2.50
C145	AP36	75p bl grn & lt green	15.00	5.00
		Nos. C141-C145 (5)	37.25	11.65

UNESCO. Nos. C141-C145 exist imperforate, and combined with Nos. 220-224 in an imperforate souvenir sheet on thin buff cardboard, with black inscriptions in top margin in Arabic and at bottom in French. Value $275.

Bay Type of 1947 Redrawn

1949

White Paper

C145A	AP30	10p rose lilac	9.00	1.00
C146	AP30	15p dark green	11.00	1.25
C147	AP30	20p orange	25.00	9.00
C147A	AP30	25p dark blue	65.00	3.25
C147B	AP30	50p brick red	275.00	35.00
		Nos. C145A-C147B (5)	385.00	49.50

In the redrawn designs, Nos. C145A, C147 and C147B have zeros with broader centers than in the 1947 issue (Nos. C120, C122 and C124).

Helicopter Mail Delivery — AP37

1949, Aug. 16 **Unwmk.** *Perf. 11½*

C148	AP37	25p deep blue	8.00	4.00
C149	AP37	50p green	12.00	4.50
a.		Souvenir sheet of 5, #225-227, C148-C149	75.00	35.00

UPU, 75th anniv. No. 149a exists on thin cardboard. Value $250.

Homing Birds AP38

Pres. Bechara el-Khoury AP39

1950, Aug. 8 **Litho.**

C150	AP38	5p violet blue	3.75	.65
C151	AP38	15p rose vio	4.25	.70
C152	AP39	25p chocolate	3.00	.95
C153	AP39	35p gray green	4.50	1.40
a.		Souvenir sheet of 6, #243-244, C150-C153, chamois paper	70.00	55.00
		Nos. C150-C153 (4)	15.50	3.70

Conference of Emigrants, 1950.

Crusader Castle, Sidon Harbor AP40

1950, Sept. 7

C154	AP40	10p chocolate	1.00	.20
C155	AP40	15p dark green	2.00	.20
C156	AP40	20p crimson	4.00	.20
C157	AP40	25p ultra	7.00	.80
C158	AP40	50p gray black	10.00	2.25
		Nos. C154-C158 (5)	24.00	3.65

1951, June 9 Redrawn Typo.

C159	AP40	10p grnsh black	2.00	.20
C160	AP40	15p black brown	3.00	.20
C161	AP40	20p vermilion	3.00	.20
C162	AP40	25p deep blue	4.00	.20
C163	AP40	35p lilac rose	8.00	2.40
C164	AP40	50p indigo	11.00	2.40
		Nos. C159-C164 (6)	31.00	5.60

Nos. C154-C158 are lithographed from a fine-screen halftone; Nos. C159-C164 are typographed and much coarser, with larger plane and many other differences.

Khaldé International Airport, Beirut — AP41

Design: 50p to 300p, Amphitheater, Byblos.

1952 Litho. *Perf. 11½*

C165	AP41	5p crimson	1.50	.20
C166	AP41	10p dark gray	1.50	.20
C167	AP41	15p rose lilac	1.75	.20
C168	AP41	20p brown org	2.00	.20
C169	AP41	25p grnsh blue	2.00	.20
C170	AP41	35p violet bl	2.75	.20
C171	AP41	50p blue green	14.00	.60
C172	AP41	100p deep blue	55.00	2.40
C173	AP41	200p dk blue grn	35.00	3.50
C174	AP41	300p black brn	52.50	7.50
		Nos. C165-C174 (10)	168.00	15.20

Lockheed Constellation — AP42

1953, Oct. 1

C175	AP42	5p yellow green	.90	.20
C176	AP42	10p deep plum	1.25	.20
C177	AP42	15p scarlet	1.75	.20
C178	AP42	20p aqua	2.25	.20
C179	AP42	25p blue	4.00	.20
C180	AP42	35p orange brn	5.75	.20
C181	AP42	50p violet blue	11.00	.30
C182	AP42	100p black brown	16.00	2.40
		Nos. C175-C182 (8)	42.90	3.90

Ruins at Baalbek AP43

Irrigation Canal, Litani AP44

1954, Mar.

C183	AP43	5p yel green	.75	.20
C184	AP43	10p dull purple	.90	.20
C185	AP43	15p carmine	1.50	.20
C186	AP43	20p brown	2.00	.20
C187	AP43	25p dull blue	2.50	.20
C188	AP43	35p black brn	3.00	.20
C189	AP44	50p dk olive grn	10.00	.25
C190	AP44	100p deep carmine	19.00	.35
C191	AP44	200p dark brown	27.50	.70
C192	AP44	300p dk gray blue	50.00	1.50
		Nos. C183-C192 (10)	117.15	4.00

Khaldé International Airport, Beirut — AP45

1954, Apr. 23 *Perf. 11½*

C193	AP45	10p pink & rose red	1.25	.20
C194	AP45	25p dp bl & gray bl	2.75	.50
C195	AP45	35p dl brn & yel brn	4.25	.90
C196	AP45	65p dp grn & grn	6.25	1.60
		Nos. C193-C196 (4)	14.50	3.20

Opening of Beirut's Intl. Airport. Exist imperf.

Arab Postal Union Type of Regular Issue, 1955

1955, Jan. 1 *Perf. 13½x13*

C197	A52	2.50p yellow brn	1.50	.20

Rotary Emblem AP47

1955, Feb. 23 *Perf. 11½*

C198	AP47	35p dull green	1.50	.40
C199	AP47	65p dull blue	2.50	.55

Rotary International, 50th anniversary.

Skiing Among the Cedars AP48

1955, Feb. 24 Litho.

C200	AP48	5p blue green	2.00	.20
C201	AP48	15p crimson	2.25	.20
C202	AP48	20p lilac	2.75	.20
C203	AP48	25p blue	5.00	.20
C204	AP48	35p olive brn	6.50	.20
C205	AP48	50p chocolate	11.00	.70
C206	AP48	65p deep blue	17.50	2.10
		Nos. C200-C206 (7)	47.00	3.80

See #C233-C235. For surcharge see #C271.

Tourist — AP49

1955, Sept. 10 Unwmk. *Perf. 13*

C207	AP49	2.50p brn vio & lt bl	.50	.20
C208	AP49	12.50p ultra & lt bl	.65	.20
C209	AP49	25p indigo & lt bl	1.50	.20
C210	AP49	35p ol grn & lt bl	1.75	.20
a.		Sheet of 4, #C207-C210, imperf.	22.50	7.75
		Nos. C207-C210 (4)	4.40	.80

Tourist Year. No. C210a is printed on cardboard.

Oranges AP50

Designs: 25p, 35p, 50p, Grapes, vert. 65p, 100p, 200p, Apples.

1955, Oct. 15

C211	AP50	5p yel grn & yel	1.10	.20
C212	AP50	10p dk grn & dp orange	1.25	.20
C213	AP50	15p yel grn & red orange	1.40	.20
C214	AP50	20p olive & yel org	2.00	.20
C215	AP50	25p blue & vio bl	2.75	.20
C216	AP50	35p green & cl	3.25	.20
C217	AP50	50p blk brn & dl yellow	3.25	.20
C218	AP50	65p green & lemon	6.50	.20
C219	AP50	100p yel grn & dp orange	8.50	.85
C220	AP50	200p green & car	15.00	4.25
		Nos. C211-C220 (10)	45.00	6.70

For surcharge see No. C265.

United Nations Emblem AP52

1956, Jan. 23 *Perf. 11½*

C221	AP52	35p violet blue	5.25	1.90
C222	AP52	65p green	6.50	2.25

UN, 10th anniv. (in 1955).

An imperf. souvenir sheet contains one each of Nos. C221 and C222. Value $90.

Temple of the Sun Colonnade, Masks and Lion's Head — AP53

Temple of Bacchus, Baalbek AP54

Design: 35p, 65p, Temple of the Sun colonnade, masks and violincello.

1956, Dec. 10 Litho. *Perf. 13*

C223	AP53	2.50p dark brown	.85	.20
C224	AP53	10p green	1.10	.20
C225	AP54	12.50p light blue	1.10	.20
C226	AP54	25p brt vio bl	1.60	.35
C227	AP53	35p red lilac	3.00	.45
C228	AP53	65p slate blue	4.25	.90
		Nos. C223-C228 (6)	11.90	2.30

International Festival at Baalbek.

Skiing Type of 1955 Redrawn and

Irrigation Canal, Litani AP55

1957 Litho. *Perf. 11½*

C229	AP55	10p brt violet	.65	.20
C230	AP55	15p orange	.90	.20
C231	AP55	20p yel green	1.00	.20
C232	AP55	25p slate blue	1.10	.20
C233	AP48	35p gray green	2.50	.20
C234	AP48	65p dp claret	4.00	.20
C235	AP48	100p brown	6.00	.65
		Nos. C229-C235 (7)	16.15	1.85

Different Arabic characters used for the country name; letters in "Liban" larger.

For surcharge see No. C271.

Pres. Camille Chamoun and King Saud AP56

King Saud, Pres. Chamoun, King Hussein, Pres. Kouatly, King Faisal, Pres. Nasser — AP57

Pres. Chamoun and: No. C237, King Hussein. No. C238, Pres. Kouatly. No. C239, King Faisal. No. C240, Pres. Nasser. 25p, Map of Lebanon.

1957, July 15 Litho. *Perf. 13*

C236	AP56	15p green	.75	.20
C237	AP56	15p blue	.75	.20
C238	AP56	15p red lilac	.75	.20
C239	AP56	15p red orange	.75	.20
C240	AP56	15p claret	.75	.20
C241	AP56	25p blue	.75	.20
C242	AP57	100p dl red brn	6.00	1.50
		Nos. C236-C242 (7)	10.50	2.70

Congr. of Arab Leaders, Beirut, 11/12-15/56.

Fencing AP58

50p, Pres. Chamoun and stadium with flags.

1957, Sept. 12 Unwmk. *Perf. 13*

C243	AP58	35p claret	3.25	1.50
C244	AP58	50p lt green	4.00	2.25

2nd Pan-Arab Games, Beirut. See note on souvenir sheet below No. 314.

Symbols of Communications — AP59

Power Plant, Chamoun AP60

1957 *Perf. 13x13½, 11½ (AP60)*

C245	AP59	5p brt green	.55	.20
C246	AP59	10p yel orange	.60	.20
C247	AP59	15p brown	.60	.20
C248	AP59	20p maroon	.80	.20
C249	AP59	25p violet blue	1.10	.20
C250	AP60	35p violet brn	1.40	.20
C251	AP60	50p green	1.60	.20
C252	AP60	65p sepia	2.25	.20
C253	AP60	100p dark gray	3.00	.55
		Nos. C245-C253 (9)	11.90	2.15

Plane at Airport AP61

Cogwheel AP62

1958-59 Unwmk. *Perf. 13*

C254	AP61	5p green	.55	.20
C255	AP61	10p magenta	.75	.20
C256	AP61	15p dull violet	.90	.20

C257 AP61 20p orange ver 1.10 .20
C258 AP61 25p dk vio bl 1.40 .20
C259 AP62 35p grnsh gray 1.60 .20
C260 AP62 50p aquamarine 2.25 .20
C261 AP62 65p pale brown 3.75 .30
C262 AP62 100p brt ultra 4.25 .20
Nos. C254-C262 (9) 16.55 1.90

Nos. C259 and C261 Surcharged in Black or Dark Blue

1959 Unwmk. Litho. *Perf. 13*
C263 AP62 30p on 35p grnsh gray 1.00 .20
C264 AP62 40p on 65p pale brn (Bl) 1.40 .45

Arab Engineers Congress.

No. C217 Surcharged

1959, Sept. 1
C265 AP50 40p on 50p blk brn & dull yel 1.50 .50

Arab Lawyers Congress.

Myron's Discobolus — AP63

Wreath and Hand Holding Torch AP64

1959, Oct. 11 Litho. *Perf. 11½*
C266 AP63 15p shown 1.00 .20
C267 AP63 30p Weight lifter 1.25 .30
C268 AP64 40p shown 1.90 .40
Nos. C266-C268 (3) 4.15 .90

3rd Mediterranean Games, Beirut.
A souvenir sheet on white cardboard contains one each of Nos. C266-C268, imperf. Sold for 100p. Value *$67.50*

Soldiers and Flag — AP65

Hands Planting Tree — AP66

1959, Nov. 25 *Perf. 13½x13*
C269 AP65 40p sep, brick red & sl 1.50 .30
C270 AP65 60p sep, dk grn & brick red 2.00 .35

Lebanon's independence, 1941-1959.

No. C234 Surcharged with New Value and Bars

1959, Dec. 15 *Perf. 11½*
C271 AP48 40p on 65p dp claret 3.00 .30

1960, Jan. 18 Litho. *Perf. 11½*
C272 AP66 20p rose vio & grn 1.00 .20
C273 AP66 40p dk brn & green 1.25 .40

Friends of the Tree Society, 25th anniv.

Postal Administration Building — AP67

1960, Feb. Unwmk. *Perf. 13*
C274 AP67 20p green .90 .20

President Fuad Chehab AP68

Uprooted Oak Emblem AP69

1960, Mar. 12 Photo. *Perf. 13½*
C275 AP68 5p green .50 .20
C276 AP68 10p Prus blue .50 .20
C277 AP68 15p orange brn .50 .20
C278 AP68 20p brown .55 .20
C279 AP68 30p olive .80 .20
C280 AP68 40p dull red .90 .20
C281 AP68 50p blue 1.00 .20
C282 AP68 70p red lilac 1.10 .20
C283 AP68 100p dark green 2.00 .40
Nos. C275-C283 (9) 7.85 2.00

1960, Apr. 7 Litho. *Perf. 13½x13*
Size: 20½x36½mm
C284 AP69 25p yellow brn 1.00 .20
C285 AP69 40p green 1.25 .30
a. Souv. sheet of 2, #C284-C285, imperf. 45.00 19.00

Size: 20x36mm
C284b AP69 25p yellow brown 1.00 .40
C285b AP69 40p green 1.75 .65

World Refugee Year, 7/1/59-6/30/60.
No. C285a sold for 150p.
Nos. C284b-C285b appear fuzzy and pale when compared to the bolder, clear-cut printing of Nos. C284-C285. Issue date: July 18.
Nos. C284b-C285b exist with carmine surcharges of "30P.+15P." (on C284b) and "20P.+10P." (on C285b), repeated in Arabic, with ornaments covering original denominations.

Martyrs' Monument — AP70

Martyrs of May 6th: 70p, Statues from Martyrs' monument, vert.

1960, May 6 *Perf. 13x13½, 13½x13*
C286 AP70 20p rose lilac & grn .80 .20
C287 AP70 40p Prus grn & dk grn 1.00 .30
C288 AP70 70p gray olive & blk 2.00 .50
Nos. C286-C288 (3) 3.80 1.00

Pres. Chehab and King of Morocco AP71

1960, June 1 *Perf. 13x13½*
C289 AP71 30p choc & dk brn 1.00 .30
C290 AP71 70p blk, dk brn & buff 2.00 .35

Visit of King Mohammed V of Morocco.
A souvenir sheet of 2 on white cardboard contains Nos. C289-C290, imperf. Value $72.50.

Child Learning to Walk — AP72

Bird, Ribbon of Flags and Map of Beirut — AP73

1960, Aug. 16 Litho. *Perf. 13½x13*
C291 AP72 20p shown 1.00 .20
C292 AP72 60p Mother & child 2.00 .40
Nos. C291-C292,CB10-CB11 (4) 5.90 1.40

Day of Mother and Child, Mar. 21-22.

Perf. 13½x13, 13x13½
1960, Sept. 20 Unwmk.

40p, Cedar & birds. 70p, Globes & cedar, horiz.

C293 AP73 20p multicolored .50 .20
C294 AP73 40p vio, bl & grn .75 .20
C295 AP73 70p multicolored 1.00 .20
Nos. C293-C295 (3) 2.25 .60

Union of Lebanese Emigrants in the World.
A souvenir sheet of 3 contains Nos. C293-C295, imperf., printed on cardboard. Sold for 150p. Value $22.50.

Pres. Chehab and Map of Lebanon — AP74

Casino, Maameltein Lebanon AP75

1961, Feb. Litho. *Perf. 13½x13*
C296 AP74 5p bl grn & yel grn .50 .20
C297 AP74 10p brown & bister .50 .20
C298 AP74 70p vio & rose lilac 1.25 .35

1961 *Perf. 13x13½*
C299 AP75 15p rose claret .60 .20
C300 AP75 30p greenish blue 1.00 .20
C301 AP75 40p brown 1.25 .20
C302 AP75 200p bis brn & dl bl 5.25 1.40
Nos. C296-C302 (7) 10.35 2.75

On Nos. C299-C301, the denomination, inscription and trees differ from type AP75.

UN Headquarters, New York — AP76

20p, UN Emblem & map of Lebanon. 30p, UN Emblem & symbolic building. 20p, 30p are vert.

1961, May 5 *Perf. 13½x13, 13x13½*
C306 AP76 20p lake & lt blue .70 .20
C307 AP76 30p green & beige .85 .20
C308 AP76 50p vio bl & grnsh bl 1.40 .20
a. Souvenir sheet of 3 9.00 9.00
Nos. C306-C308 (3) 2.95 .60

UN, 15th anniv. (in 1960).
No. C308a contains one each of Nos. C306-C308, imperf., against a light blue background showing UN emblem. Sold for 125p.

Pottery Workers AP77

1961, July 11 Litho. *Perf. 13x13½*
C309 AP77 30p shown 2.75 .20
C310 AP77 70p Weaver 1.60 .20

Issued for Labor Day, 1961.

Fireworks AP78

Water Skiing AP79

70p, Tourists on boat ride through cave.

1961, Aug. 8 *Perf. 13½x13, 13x13½*
C311 AP78 15p lt pur & dk bl 1.50 1.00
C312 AP79 40p blue & pink 2.10 1.25
C313 AP79 70p dull brn & pink .90 .50
Nos. C311-C313 (3) 4.50 2.75

Issued to publicize tourist month.

Highway Circle at Dora, Beirut Suburb AP80

1961, Aug. *Perf. 11½*
C314 AP80 35p yellow green 1.00 .30
C315 AP80 50p orange brown 1.25 .45
C316 AP80 100p gray 1.25 .55
Nos. C314-C316 (3) 3.50 1.30

Beach at Tyre — AP81

Afka Falls — AP82

1961, Sept. Litho. *Perf. 13*
C317 AP81 5p carmine rose .50 .20
C318 AP81 10p brt violet .75 .20
C319 AP81 15p bright blue .80 .20
C320 AP81 20p orange 1.00 .20
C321 AP81 30p brt green 1.25 .20
C322 AP82 40p dp claret 1.00 .20
C323 AP82 50p ultramarine 1.10 .20
C324 AP82 70p yellow green 1.50 .25
C325 AP82 100p dark brown 2.00 .35
Nos. C317-C325 (9) 9.90 2.00

See Nos. C341-C342.

Entrance to UNESCO Building AP83

"UNESCO" and Cedar — AP84

Design: 50p, UNESCO headquarters, Paris.

1961, Nov. 20 Unwmk. *Perf. 12*

C326 AP83 20p bl, buff & blk .65 .20
C327 AP84 30p lt grn, blk & mag .80 .20
C328 AP83 50p multicolored 1.25 .20
Nos. C326-C328 (3) 2.70 .60

UNESCO, 15th anniv.

Emir Bechir and Fakhr-el-Din El Maani — AP85

Design: 25p, Cedar emblem.

1961, Dec. 30 Litho.

C329 AP85 25p Cedar emblem .65 .20
C330 AP85 50p shown 1.00 .30

See note after No. 375.

Scout Types of Regular Issue, 1962

15p, Trefoil & cedar emblem. 20p, Hand making Scout sign. 25p, Lebanese Scout emblem.

1962, Mar. 1 Unwmk. *Perf. 12*

C331 A70 15p grn, blk & red .80 .20
C332 A69 20p lil, blk & yel .95 .20
C333 A70 25p multicolored 1.50 .40
Nos. C331-C333 (3) 3.25 .80

Arab League Building, Cairo — AP86

1962, Mar. 20 *Perf. 13*

C334 AP86 20p ultra & lt bl .60 .20
C335 AP86 30p red brn & pink .75 .20
C336 AP86 50p grn & grnsh bl 1.00 .30
Nos. C334-C336 (3) 2.35 .70

Arab League Week, Mar. 22-28. See Nos. C372-C375.

Blacksmith AP87

Farm Tractor AP88

Perf. 13½x13, 13x13½

1962, May 1 Litho.

C337 AP87 5p green & lt blue .50 .20
C338 AP87 10p blue & pink .50 .20
C339 AP88 25p brt vio & pink .75 .20
C340 AP88 35p car rose & blue 1.00 .20
Nos. C337-C340 (4) 2.75 .80

Issued for Labor Day.

Types of 1961 Redrawn with Large Numerals Similar to Redrawn Regular Issue of 1962

1962 *Perf. 13*

C341 AP81 5p carmine rose 1.10 .20
C342 AP82 40p deep claret 6.25 .40

Hand Reaching for Malaria Eradication Emblem — AP89

Bas-relief of Isis, Kalabsha Temple, Nubia — AP90

Design: 70p, Malaria eradication emblem.

1962, July 2 Litho. *Perf. 13½x13*

C349 AP89 30p tan & brown 1.00 .20
C350 AP89 70p bluish lil & vio 1.25 .50

WHO drive to eradicate malaria.

1962, Aug. 1 Unwmk. *Perf. 13*

C351 AP90 30p yellow green 2.00 .25
C352 AP90 50p slate 4.00 .60

Campaign to save historic monuments in Nubia.

Spade, Heart, Diamond, Club — AP91

College Student — AP92

1962, Sept.

C353 AP91 25p car rose, blk & red 3.25 1.25
C354 AP91 40p multicolored 4.50 1.25

European Bridge Championship Tournament.

1962, Oct. 1 *Perf. 12*

C355 AP92 45p multicolored .90 .20

Issued for Students' Day, Oct. 1.

Sword Severing Chain — AP93

Harvest — AP94

1962, Nov. 22 Litho. *Perf. 13*

C356 AP93 25p vio, lt bl & red 1.00 .25
C357 AP93 25p bl, lt bl & red 1.00 .25
C358 AP93 25p grn, lt bl & red 1.00 .25
Nos. C356-C358 (3) 3.00 .75

19th anniversary of independence.

Fruit Type of Regular Issue, 1962

5p, Apricots. 10p, 30p, Plums. 20p, 40p, Apples. 50p, Pears. 70p, Medlar. 100p, Lemons.

1962

Vignette Multicolored

C359 A72 5p orange brown .50 .20
C360 A72 10p black .55 .20
C361 A72 20p brown .60 .20
C362 A72 30p gray .75 .20
C363 A72 40p dark gray 1.00 .20
C364 A72 50p light brown 1.25 .20
C365 A72 70p gray olive 1.50 .30
C366 A72 100p blue 3.00 .50
Nos. C359-C366 (8) 9.15 2.00

1963, Mar. 21 Litho. *Perf. 13*

Design: 15p, 20p, UN Emblem and hand holding Wheat Emblem, horiz.

C367 AP94 2.50p ultra & yel .50 .20
C368 AP94 5p gray grn & yel .50 .20
C369 AP94 7.50p rose lil & yel .50 .20
C370 AP94 15p rose brn & pale grn .80 .20
C371 AP94 20p rose & pale grn 1.00 .20
Nos. C367-C371 (5) 3.30 1.00

FAO "Freedom from Hunger" campaign.

Redrawn Type of 1962, Dated "1963"

Design: Arab League Building, Cairo.

1963, Mar. Unwmk. *Perf. 12*

C372 AP86 5p violet & lt blue .50 .20
C373 AP86 10p green & lt blue .50 .20
C374 AP86 15p claret & lt blue .55 .20
C375 AP86 20p gray & lt blue .70 .25
Nos. C372-C375 (4) 2.25 .85

Issued for Arab League Week.

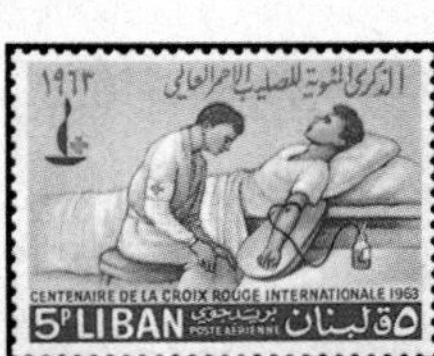

Blood Transfusion AP95

Design: 35p, 40p, Nurse and infant, vert.

1963, Oct. 5 Unwmk. *Perf. 13*

C376 AP95 5p green & red .50 .20
C377 AP95 20p grnsh bl & red .55 .20
C378 AP95 35p org, red & blk .70 .20
C379 AP95 40p purple & red 1.00 .20
Nos. C376-C379 (4) 2.75 .80

Centenary of International Red Cross.

Lyre Player and Columns — AP96

Lebanon Flag, Rising Sun — AP97

1963, Nov. 7 Unwmk. *Perf. 13*

C380 AP96 35p lt bl, org & blk 1.50 .30

International Festival at Baalbek.

1964, Jan. 8 Litho.

C381 AP97 5p bluish grn, ver & yel .50 .20
C382 AP97 10p yel grn, ver & yel .55 .20
C383 AP97 25p ultra, ver & yel .75 .25
C384 AP97 40p gray, ver & yel 1.10 .35
Nos. C381-C384 (4) 2.90 1.00

20th anniversary of Independence.

Sports Type of Regular Issue, 1964

1964, Feb. 11 Unwmk. *Perf. 13*

C385 A76 15p Tennis .55 .20
C386 A76 17.50p Swimming, horiz. .65 .20
C387 A76 30p Skiing, horiz. 1.00 .20
a. Souvenir sheet of 3 13.50 10.50
Nos. C385-C387 (3) 2.20 .60

No. C387a contains three imperf. stamps similar to Nos. C385-C387 with simulated orange brown perforations and green marginal inscription. Sold for 100p.

Anemone AP98

Flame and UN Emblem — AP100

Girls Jumping Rope AP99

1964, June 9 Unwmk. *Perf. 13*

C391 AP98 5p Lily .50 .20
C392 AP98 10p Ranunculus .60 .20
C393 AP98 20p shown .75 .20
C394 AP98 40p Tuberose 1.00 .20
C395 AP98 45p Rhododendron 1.10 .20
C396 AP98 50p Jasmine 1.25 .20
C397 AP98 70p Yellow broom 2.00 .30
Nos. C391-C397 (7) 7.20 1.50

1964, Apr. 8

Children's Day: 20p, 40p, Boy on hobby-horse, vert.

C398 AP99 5p emer, org & red .50 .20
C399 AP99 10p yel brn, org & red .55 .20
C400 AP99 20p dp ultra, lt bl & org .60 .20
C401 AP99 40p lil, lt bl & yel 1.00 .30
Nos. C398-C401 (4) 2.65 .90

1964, May 15 Litho. Unwmk.

40p, Flame, UN emblem and broken chain.

C402 AP100 20p salmon, org & brn .50 .20
C403 AP100 40p lt bl, gray bl & org .75 .20

15th anniv. (in 1963) of the Universal Declaration of Human Rights.

Arab League Conference — AP101

1964, Apr. 20 ***Perf. 13x13½***

C404 AP101 5p blk & pale sal 1.00 .20
C405 AP101 10p black 1.25 .35
C406 AP101 15p green 1.75 .50
C407 AP101 20p dk brn & pink 2.25 .65
Nos. C404-C407 (4) 6.25 1.70

Arab League meeting.

Child in Crib — AP102

Beit-ed-Din Palace and Children — AP103

1964, July 20 ***Perf. 13½x13, 13½***

C408 AP102 2.50p multicolored .50 .20
C409 AP102 5p multicolored .50 .20
C410 AP102 15p multicolored .60 .20
C411 AP103 17.50p multicolored .80 .20
C412 AP103 20p multicolored .90 .20
C413 AP103 40p multicolored 1.00 .20
Nos. C408-C413 (6) 4.30 1.20

Ball of the Little White Beds, Beirut, for the benefit of children's hospital beds.

Clasped Hands and Map of Lebanon AP104

1964, Oct. 16 Litho. ***Perf. 13½x13***

C414 AP104 20p yel grn, yel & gray .65 .20
C415 AP104 40p slate, yel & gray 1.10 .40

Congress of the Intl. Lebanese Union.

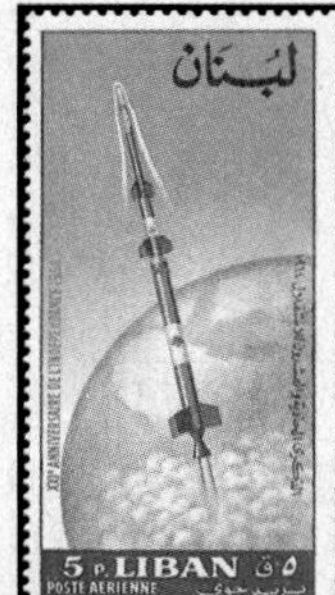

Rocket Leaving Earth — AP105

Woman in Costume AP107

Battle Scene — AP106

1964, Nov. 24 Unwmk. ***Perf. 13½***

C416 AP105 5p multicolored .50 .20
C417 AP105 10p multicolored .50 .20
C418 AP106 40p sl blue & blk 1.00 .30
C419 AP106 70p dp claret & blk 2.00 .50
Nos. C416-C419 (4) 4.00 1.20

21st anniversary of independence.

1965, Jan. 11 Litho. ***Perf. 13½***

Design: 10p, 15p, Man in costume.

C420 AP107 10p multicolored .70 .20
C421 AP107 15p multicolored .90 .20
C422 AP107 25p green & multi 1.25 .35
C423 AP107 40p brown & multi 1.50 .50
Nos. C420-C423 (4) 4.35 1.25

International Festival at Baalbek.

Equestrian AP108

1965, Jan. 23 Engr. ***Perf. 13***

C424 AP108 15p shown .50 .20
C425 AP108 25p Target shooting, vert. .60 .20
C426 AP108 40p Gymnast on rings .75 .20
a. Souvenir sheet of 3, #C424-C426, imperf. 18.00 9.25
Nos. C424-C426 (3) 1.85 .60

18th Olympic Games, Tokyo, Oct. 10-25, 1964. No. 426a sold for 100p.

Heliconius Cybria AP109

30p, Pericallia matronula. 40p, Red admiral. 45p, Satyrus semele. 70p, Machaon. 85p, Aurore. 100p, Morpho cypris. 200p, Erasmia sanguiflua. 300p, Papilio crassus. 500p, Charaxes ameliae.

1965 Unwmk. ***Perf. 13***
Size: 36x22mm

C427 AP109 30p multi 2.75 .20
C428 AP109 35p multi 4.00 .35
C429 AP109 40p multi 5.00 .35
C430 AP109 45p multi 5.50 .50
C431 AP109 70p multi 6.75 .75
C432 AP109 85p multi 7.50 .90
C433 AP109 100p multi 11.00 1.00
C434 AP109 200p multi 18.00 1.25
C435 AP109 300p multi 24.50 3.50

Engr. and Litho.
Perf. 12
Size: 35x25mm

C436 AP109 500p lt ultra & blk 50.00 7.00
Nos. C427-C436 (10) 135.00 15.80

For surcharges see Nos. C654-C656.

Pope Paul VI and Pres. Charles Helou — AP110

1965, June 28 Photo. ***Perf. 12***

C437 AP110 45p gold & brt vio 5.25 1.00
a. Souv. sheet of 1, imperf. 52.50 32.50

Visit of Pope Paul VI to Lebanon. No. C437a sold for 50p.

Cedars of Friendship AP111

1965, Oct. 16 Photo. ***Perf. 13x12½***

C438 AP111 40p multicolored 1.50 .20

Cocoon, Spindle and Silk — AP112

15p, 30p, 40p, 50p, Silk weaver at loom.

1965, Oct. 16 ***Perf. 12½x13***
Design in Buff and Bright Green

C439 AP112 2.50p brown 1.25 .20
C440 AP112 5p dk olive grn 1.25 .20
C441 AP112 7.50p Prus blue 1.25 .20
C442 AP112 15p deep ultra 1.25 .20
C443 AP112 30p deep claret 1.50 .20
C444 AP112 40p brown 2.40 .20
C445 AP112 50p rose brown 3.50 .60
Nos. C439-C445 (7) 12.40 1.80

Parliament Building AP113

1965, Oct. 26 ***Perf. 13x12½***

C446 AP113 35p red, buff & brn .80 .20
C447 AP113 40p emer, buff & brn 1.00 .20

Centenary of the Lebanese parliament.

UN Headquarters, NYC, UN Emblem and Lebanese Flags — AP114

1965, Nov. 10 Engr. ***Perf. 12***

C448 AP114 2.50p dull blue .50 .20
C449 AP114 10p magenta .50 .20
C450 AP114 17.50p dull violet .50 .20
C451 AP114 30p green .60 .20
C452 AP114 40p brown .85 .20
Nos. C448-C452 (5) 2.95 1.00

UN, 20th anniv. A souvenir sheet contains one 40p imperf. stamp in bright rose lilac. Sold for 50p. Value $15.

Playing Card King, Laurel and Cedar AP115

Dagger in Map of Palestine AP116

1965, Nov. 15 Photo. ***Perf. 12½x13***

C453 AP115 2.50p multicolored .70 .20
C454 AP115 15p multicolored 1.10 .20
C455 AP115 17.50p multicolored 1.25 .20
C456 AP115 40p multicolored 1.40 .20
Nos. C453-C456 (4) 4.45 .80

Intl. Bridge Championships. A souvenir sheet contains two imperf. stamps similar to Nos. C454 and C456. Sold for 75p. Value $22.50.

1965, Dec. 12 ***Perf. 12½x11***

C457 AP116 50p multicolored 4.50 .55

Deir Yassin massacre, Apr. 9, 1948.

ITU Emblem, Old and New Communication Equipment and Syncom Satellite — AP117

1966, Apr. 13 ***Perf. 13x12½***

C458 AP117 2.50p multi .50 .20
C459 AP117 15p multi .55 .20
C460 AP117 17.50p multi .60 .20
C461 AP117 25p multi 1.00 .20
C462 AP117 40p multi 1.25 .20
Nos. C458-C462 (5) 3.90 1.00

ITU, centenary (in 1965).

Folk Dancers Before Temple of Bacchus — AP118

Designs: 7.50p, 15p, Dancers before Temple of Jupiter, vert. 30p, 40p, Orchestra before Temple of Bacchus.

1966, July 20 Unwmk. ***Perf. 12***
Gold Frame

C463 AP118 2.50p brn vio, bl & orange .50 .20
C464 AP118 5p mag, bl & org .50 .20
C465 AP118 7.50p vio bl, bl & pink .50 .20

LESOTHO

lə-'sō-ˌtō

LOCATION — An enclave within the Republic of South Africa
GOVT. — Independent state in British Commonwealth
AREA — 11,720 sq. mi.
POP. — 2,128,950 (1999 est.)
CAPITAL — Maseru

Basutoland, the British Crown Colony, became independent, October 4, 1966, taking the name Lesotho.

100 Cents = 1 Rand
100 Lisente (s) = 1 Maloti (1979)

Catalogue values for all unused stamps in this country are for Never Hinged items.

Watermark

Wmk. 362 — Basotho Hat Multiple

Moshoeshoe I and II — A1

Perf. 12½x13

1966, Oct. 4 Photo. Unwmk.

1 A1 2½c red brn, blk & red .20 .20
2 A1 5c red brn, blk & brt bl .20 .20
3 A1 10c red brn, blk & brt green .30 .25
4 A1 20c red brn, blk & red lilac .50 .45
Nos. 1-4 (4) 1.20 1.10

Lesotho's independence, Oct. 4, 1966.

Basutoland Nos. 72-74, 76-82 Overprinted

Perf. 13½

1966, Nov. 1 Wmk. 4 Engr.

5 A7 ½c dk brown & gray .20 .20
6 A7 1c dp grn & gray blk .20 .20
7 A7 2c orange & dp blue .70 .20
8 A7 3½c dp blue & indigo .35 .20
9 A7 5c dk grn & org brn .20 .20
10 A7 10c rose vio & dk ol .30 .20
11 A7 12½c aqua & brown 5.75 .35
12 A7 25c lil rose & dp ultra .50 .20
13 A7 50c dp car & black 1.00 .65

Perf. 11½

14 A8 1r dp claret & blk 1.00 *2.50*
a. "Lseotho" 100.00
Nos. 5-14 (10) 10.20 4.90

Same Overprint on Nos. 87-91 and Type of 1954

Wmk. 314 *Perf. 13½*

15 A7 1c green & gray blk .20 .20
16 A7 2½c car & ol green 1.00 .20
17 A7 5c dk grn & org brn .40 .20
18 A7 12½c aqua & brown .60 .40
19 A7 50c dp car & black 1.25 .75

Perf. 11½

20 A8 1r dp claret & blk 1.50 1.50
a. "Lseotho" 55.00
Nos. 15-20 (6) 4.95 3.25

UNESCO Emblem, Microscope, Book, Violin and Retort — A2

Unwmk.

1966, Dec. 1 Litho. *Perf. 14*

21 A2 2½c green & ocher .20 .20
22 A2 5c olive & brt green .20 .20
23 A2 12½c ver & lt blue .40 .20
24 A2 25c dull blue & orange .75 .50
Nos. 21-24 (4) 1.55 1.10

20th anniv. of UNESCO.

King Moshoeshoe II and Corn — A3

King Moshoeshoe II — A4

Designs: 1c, Bull. 2c, Aloes. 2½c, Basotho hat. 3½c, Merino sheep. 5c, Basotho pony. 10c, Wheat. 12½c, Angora goat. 25c, Maletsunyane Falls. 50c, Diamonds. 1r, Coat of Arms.

Perf. 13½x14½

1967, Apr. 1 Photo. Unwmk.

25 A3 ½c violet & green .20 .20
26 A3 1c dk red & brown .20 .20
27 A3 2c green & yellow .20 .20
28 A3 2½c yel bister & blk .20 .20
29 A3 3½c yellow & black .20 .20
30 A3 5c brt blue & yel bis .30 .20
31 A3 10c gray & ocher .40 .20
32 A3 12½c orange & blk .50 .45
33 A3 25c ultra & blk .95 .85
34 A3 50c Prus green & blk 6.75 2.00
35 A3 1r gray & multi 1.25 1.50

Perf. 14½x13½

36 A4 2r mag, blk & gold 1.75 3.00
Nos. 25-36 (12) 12.90 9.20

See Nos. 47-59.

University Buildings and Graduates — A4a

1967, Apr. 7 *Perf. 14x14½*

37 A4a 1c yel, sep & dp blue .20 .20
38 A4a 2½c blue, sep & dp bl .20 .20
39 A4a 12½c dl rose, sep & dp bl .20 .20
40 A4a 25c lt vio, sep & dp bl .30 .20
Nos. 37-40 (4) .90 .80

1st conferment of degrees by the Univ. of Botswana, Lesotho and Swaziland at Roma, Lesotho.

Statue of Moshoeshoe I — A5

1st Anniv. of Independence: 12½c, Flag of Lesotho. 25c, Crocodile.

1967, Oct. 4 Photo. *Perf. 14*

41 A5 2½c apple green & black .20 .20
42 A5 12½c multicolored .55 .55
43 A5 25c tan, blk & dp green 1.00 1.00
Nos. 41-43 (3) 1.75 1.75

Boy Scout and Lord Baden-Powell — A6

1967, Nov. 1 Unwmk. *Perf. 14x14½*

44 A6 15c lt ol grn, dk grn & brn .40 .25

60th anniversary of the Boy Scouts.

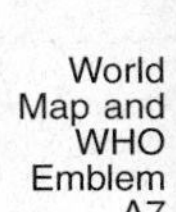

World Map and WHO Emblem A7

20th anniv. of WHO: 25c, Nurse and child, arms of Lesotho and WHO emblem.

1968, Apr. 8 Photo. *Perf. 14x14½*

45 A7 2½c dp bl, car rose & gold .20 .20
46 A7 25c gold, gray grn & redsh brown .50 .40

Types of 1967

Design: 3c, Sorghum. Others as before.

Perf. 13½x14½

1968-69 Photo. Wmk. 362

47 A3 ½c violet & green .20 .20
48 A3 1c dk red & brown .20 .20
49 A3 2c green & yellow .20 .20
50 A3 2½c yel bister & blk .20 .20
51 A3 3c lt brn, dk brn & green .20 .20
52 A3 3½c yellow & black .20 .20
53 A3 5c brt bl & yel bis .35 .20
54 A3 10c gray & ocher .70 .60
55 A3 12½c org & blk ('69) 1.10 1.00
56 A3 25c ultra & blk ('69) 2.10 1.60
57 A3 50c Prussian grn & black ('69) 14.00 3.50
58 A3 1r gray & multi 4.00 4.00

Perf. 14½x13½

59 A4 2r magenta, blk & gold ('69) 11.50 15.00
Nos. 47-59 (13) 34.95 27.10

Hunters, Rock Painting A8

Rock Paintings: 3½c, Baboons. 5c, Javelin thrower, vert. 10c, Archers. 15c, Cranes, vert. 20c, Eland. 25c, Hunting scene.

Perf. 14½x14, 14x14½

1968, Nov. 1 Photo. Wmk. 362

60 A8 3c dk & lt green & brn .35 .20
61 A8 3½c dk brown & yel .45 .20
62 A8 5c sepia, yel & red brn .50 .20
63 A8 10c black, brt rose & org .65 .30
64 A8 15c olive brn & buff 1.00 .50
65 A8 20c black, yel & lt grn 1.25 .70
66 A8 25c dk brown, yel & org 1.40 1.10
Nos. 60-66 (7) 5.60 3.20

Protection for Lesotho's rock paintings.

Queen Elizabeth II Hospital A9

Designs: 10c, Radio Lesotho. 12½c, Leabua Jonathan Airport. 25c, Royal Palace.

1969, Mar. 11 Litho. *Perf. 14x13½*

67 A9 2½c multicolored .20 .20
68 A9 10c multicolored .20 .20
69 A9 12½c multicolored .40 .20
70 A9 25c multicolored .25 .20
Nos. 67-70 (4) 1.05 .80

Centenary of Maseru, capital of Lesotho.

Mosotho Horseman and Car — A10

Designs: 12½c, Car on mountain pass. 15c, View from Sani Pass and signal flags. 20c, Map of Lesotho and Independence Trophy.

1969, Sept. 26 Photo. *Perf. 14½x14*

71 A10 2½c brown & multi .20 .20
72 A10 12½c multicolored .25 .25
73 A10 15c multicolored .30 .30
74 A10 20c yellow & multi .35 .35
Nos. 71-74 (4) 1.10 1.10

Roof of Africa Auto Rally, Sept. 19-20.

Gryponyx A11

Prehistoric Reptile Footprints, Moyeni: 3c, Dinosaur. 10c, Plateosauravus and Footprints. 15c, Tritylodon. 25c, Massospondylus.

Perf. 14½x14

1970, Jan. 5 Wmk. 362

Size: 60x23mm

75 A11 3c brown, yel & black 1.00 .75

Perf. 15x14

Size: 40x23mm

76 A11 5c maroon, blk & pink 1.40 .40
77 A11 10c sepia, blk & yel 1.75 .45
78 A11 15c slate grn, blk & yel 2.75 3.00
79 A11 25c gray blue, blk & bl 3.75 3.00
Nos. 75-79 (5) 10.65 7.60

Moshoeshoe I A12

Design: 25c, Moshoeshoe I with top hat.

Perf. 14x13½

1970, Mar. 11 Litho. Wmk. 362

80 A12 2½c brt grn & car rose .20 .20
81 A12 25c lt blue & org brn .25 .25

Cent. of the death of Moshoeshoe I, chief of the Bakoena clan of the Basothos.

UN Headquarters, New York — A13

2½c, UN emblem. 12½c, UN emblem, people. 25c, UN emblem, peace dove.

1970, June 26 Litho. *Perf. 14½x14*

82 A13 2½c pink, red brn & bl .20 .20
83 A13 10c blue & multi .20 .20
84 A13 12½c olive, ver & lt blue .20 .20
85 A13 25c tan & multi .20 .20
Nos. 82-85 (4) .80 .80

25th anniversary of the United Nations.

Basotho Hat Gift Shop, Maseru A14

Tourism: 5c, Trout fishing. 10c, Horseback riding. 12½c, Skiing, Maluti Mountains. 20c, Holiday Inn, Maseru.

1970, Oct. 27 ***Perf. 14x14½***

No.	Type	Description	Unused	Used
86	A14	2½c multicolored	.20	.20
87	A14	5c multicolored	.20	.20
88	A14	10c multicolored	.40	.30
89	A14	12½c multicolored	.40	.30
90	A14	20c multicolored	.50	.40
		Nos. 86-90 (5)	1.70	1.40

Corn — A15

Designs: 1c, Bull. 2c, Aloes. 2½c, Basotho hat. 3c, Sorghum. 3½c, Merino sheep. 4c, National flag. 5c, Basotho pony. 10c, Wheat. 12½c, Angora goat. 25c, Maletsunyane Falls. 50c, Diamonds. 1r, Coat of Arms. 2r, Statue of King Moshoeshoe I in Maseru, vert.

1971 Litho. Wmk. 362 ***Perf. 14***

No.	Type	Description	Unused	Used
91	A15	½c lilac & green	.20	.20
92	A15	1c brn red & brn	.20	.20
93	A15	2c yel brn & yel	.20	.20
94	A15	2½c dull yel & blk	.20	.20
95	A15	3c bis, brn & grn	.20	.20
96	A15	3½c yellow & black	.20	.20
97	A15	4c ver & multi	.20	.20
98	A15	5c blue & brown	.20	.20
99	A15	10c gray & ocher	.35	.30
100	A15	12½c orange & brn	.40	.35
101	A15	25c ultra & black	.70	.60
102	A15	50c lt bl grn & blk	6.50	3.25
103	A15	1r gray & multi	2.40	2.10
104	A15	2r ultra & brown	2.40	*4.50*
a.		Unwmkd. ('80)	1.75	*2.00*
		Nos. 91-104 (14)	14.35	12.70

Issue dates: 4c, Apr. 1; others, Jan. 4.

For overprints and surcharges see #132-135, 245, 312.

Lammergeier A16

Birds: 5c, Bald ibis. 10c, Rufous rock jumper. 12½c, Blue korhaan (bustard). 15c, Painted snipe. 20c, Golden-breasted bunting. 25c, Ground woodpecker.

1971, Mar. 1 ***Perf. 14***

No.	Type	Description	Unused	Used
105	A16	2½c multicolored	3.00	.25
106	A16	5c multicolored	4.00	1.90
107	A16	10c multicolored	4.00	1.40
108	A16	12½c multicolored	4.50	3.00
109	A16	15c multicolored	5.25	4.00
110	A16	20c multicolored	5.25	4.00
111	A16	25c multicolored	6.25	4.00
		Nos. 105-111 (7)	32.25	18.55

Lionel Collett Dam A17

Designs: 10c, Contour farming. 15c, Earth dams. 25c, Beaver dams.

1971, July 15 Litho. Wmk. 362

No.	Type	Description	Unused	Used
112	A17	4c multicolored	.20	.20
113	A17	10c multicolored	.20	.20
114	A17	15c multicolored	.30	.30
115	A17	25c multicolored	.40	.40
		Nos. 112-115 (4)	1.10	1.10

Soil conservation and erosion control.

Diamond Mining A18

10c, Potter. 15c, Woman weaver at loom. 20c, Construction worker and new buildings.

1971, Oct. 4

No.	Type	Description	Unused	Used
116	A18	4c olive & multi	.95	.40
117	A18	10c ocher & multi	.40	.20
118	A18	15c red & multi	.60	.60
119	A18	20c dk brown & multi	.80	1.25
		Nos. 116-119 (4)	2.75	2.45

Mail Cart, 19th Century A19

Designs: 10c, Postal bus. 15c, Cape of Good Hope No. 17, vert. 20c, Maseru Post Office.

1972, Jan. 3

No.	Type	Description	Unused	Used
120	A19	5c pink & black	.20	.20
121	A19	10c lt blue & multi	.25	.20
122	A19	15c gray, black & blue	.40	.20
123	A19	20c yellow & multi	.50	.50
		Nos. 120-123 (4)	1.35	1.10

Centenary of mail service between Maseru and Aliwal North in Cape Colony.

Runner and Olympic Rings — A20

1972, Sept. 1

No.	Type	Description	Unused	Used
124	A20	4c shown	.20	.20
125	A20	10c Shot put	.25	.25
126	A20	15c Hurdles	.40	.35
127	A20	25c Broad jump	.60	.60
		Nos. 124-127 (4)	1.45	1.40

20th Olympic Games, Munich, 8/26-9/11.

Adoration of the Shepherds, by Matthias Stomer — A21

1972, Dec. 1 Litho. ***Perf. 14***

No.	Type	Description	Unused	Used
128	A21	4c blue & multi	.20	.20
129	A21	10c red & multi	.25	.25
130	A21	25c emerald & multi	.35	.35
		Nos. 128-130 (3)	.80	.80

Christmas.

WHO Emblem — A22

1973, Apr. 7 Litho. ***Perf. 13½***

No.	Type	Description	Unused	Used
131	A22	20c blue & yellow	.50	.50

WHO, 25th anniversary.

Nos. 94, 97-99 overprinted: "O.A.U. / 10th Anniversary / Freedom in Unity"

1973, May 25 Wmk. 362 ***Perf. 14***

No.	Type	Description	Unused	Used
132	A15	2½c dull yellow & black	.20	.20
133	A15	4c vermilion & multi	.20	.20
134	A15	5c blue & brown	.20	.20
135	A15	10c gray & ocher	.30	.30
		Nos. 132-135 (4)	.90	.90

Basotho Hat, WFP/FAO Emblem — A23

Designs: 15c, School lunch. 20c, Child drinking milk and cow. 25c, Map of mountain roads and farm workers.

1973, June 1 ***Perf. 13½***

No.	Type	Description	Unused	Used
136	A23	4c ultra & multi	.20	.20
137	A23	15c buff & multi	.20	.20
138	A23	20c yellow & multi	.20	.20
139	A23	25c violet & multi	.40	.40
		Nos. 136-139 (4)	1.00	1.00

World Food Program, 10th anniversary.

Christmas Butterfly A24

Designs: Butterflies of Lesotho.

1973, Sept. 3 ***Perf. 14x14½***

No.	Type	Description	Unused	Used
140	A24	4c Mountain Beauty	1.40	.20
141	A24	5c shown	1.60	.60
142	A24	10c Painted lady	2.40	.60
143	A24	15c Yellow pansy	4.00	2.25
144	A24	20c Blue pansy	4.00	2.40
145	A24	25c African monarch	4.75	3.25
146	A24	30c Orange tip	4.75	4.50
		Nos. 140-146 (7)	22.90	13.80

Map of Northern Lesotho and Location of Diamond Mines — A25

Designs: 15c, Kimberlite (diamond-bearing) rocks. 20c, Diagram of Kimberlite volcano, vert. 30c, Diamond prospector, vert.

Perf. 13½x14, 14x13½

1973, Oct. 1 Litho. Wmk. 362

No.	Type	Description	Unused	Used
147	A25	10c gray & multi	2.50	.40
148	A25	15c multicolored	2.75	2.10
149	A25	20c multicolored	2.75	2.25
150	A25	30c multicolored	4.50	6.25
		Nos. 147-150 (4)	12.50	11.00

International Kimberlite Conference.

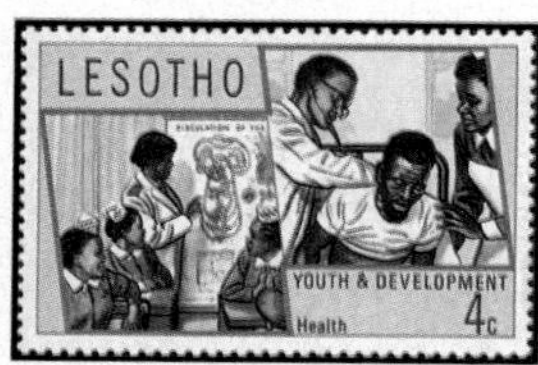

Nurses' Training and Medical Care — A26

Designs: 10c, Classroom, student with microscope. 20c, Farmers with tractor and bullock team and crop instruction. 25c, Potter and engineers with lathe. 30c, Boy scouts and young bricklayers.

1974, Feb. 18 Litho. ***Perf. 13½x14***

No.	Type	Description	Unused	Used
151	A26	4c lt blue & multi	.20	.20
152	A26	10c ocher & multi	.20	.20
153	A26	20c multicolored	.30	.20
154	A26	25c bister & multi	.35	.25
155	A26	30c yellow & multi	.35	.30
		Nos. 151-155 (5)	1.40	1.15

Youth and development.

Open Book and Wreath — A27

Designs: 15c, Flags of Botswana, Lesotho and Swaziland; cap and diploma. 20c, Map of Africa and location of Botswana, Lesotho and Swaziland. 25c, King Moshoeshoe II, Chancellor of UBLS, capping graduate.

1974, Apr. 7 Litho. ***Perf. 14***

No.	Type	Description	Unused	Used
156	A27	10c multicolored	.20	.20
157	A27	15c multicolored	.25	.20
158	A27	20c multicolored	.30	.25
159	A27	25c multicolored	.35	.35
		Nos. 156-159 (4)	1.10	1.00

10th anniversary of the University of Botswana, Lesotho and Swaziland.

Senqunyane River Bridge, Marakabei — A28

5c, Tsoelike River Bridge. 10c, Makhaleng River Bridge. 15c, Seaka Bridge, Orange/Senqu River. 20c, Masianokeng Bridge, Phuthiatsana River. 25c, Mahobong Bridge, Hlotse River.

1974, June 26 Wmk. 362 ***Perf. 14***

No.	Type	Description	Unused	Used
160	A28	4c multicolored	.20	.20
161	A28	5c multicolored	.20	.20
162	A28	10c multicolored	.30	.30
163	A28	15c multicolored	.60	.45
164	A28	20c multicolored	.75	.60
165	A28	25c multicolored	.95	.70
		Nos. 160-165 (6)	3.00	2.45

Bridges and rivers of Lesotho.

UPU Emblem A29

1974, Sept. 6 Litho. ***Perf. 14x13***

No.	Type	Description	Unused	Used
166	A29	4c shown	.20	.20
167	A29	10c Map of Lesotho	.20	.20
168	A29	15c GPO, Maseru	.20	.40
169	A29	20c Rural mail delivery	.80	1.00
		Nos. 166-169 (4)	1.40	1.80

Centenary of Universal Postal Union.

Siege of Thaba-Bosiu — A30

King Moshoeshoe I A31

5c, King Moshoeshoe II laying wreath at grave of Moshoeshoe I. 20c, Makoanyane, warrior hero.

Perf. 12½x12, 12x12½

1974, Nov. 25

170	A30	4c multicolored	.20	.20
171	A30	5c multicolored	.20	.20
172	A31	10c multicolored	.25	.20
173	A31	20c multicolored	.60	.40
		Nos. 170-173 (4)	1.25	1.00

Sesquicentennial of Thaba-Bosiu becoming the capital of Basutoland and Lesotho.

Mamokhorong — A32

Musical Instruments of the Basotho: 10c, Lesiba. 15c, Setolotolo. 20c, Meropa (drums).

Perf. 14x14½

1975, Jan. 25 **Wmk. 362**

174	A32	4c multicolored	.20	.20
175	A32	10c multicolored	.20	.20
176	A32	15c multicolored	.30	.30
177	A32	20c multicolored	.50	.50
a.		Souvenir sheet of 4, #174-177	2.00	2.00
		Nos. 174-177 (4)	1.20	1.20

View, Sehlabathebe National Park — A33

5c, Natural arch. 15c, Mountain stream. 20c, Lake and mountains. 25c, Waterfall.

1975, Apr. 8 **Litho.** ***Perf. 14***

178	A33	4c multicolored	.35	.20
179	A33	5c multicolored	.35	.20
180	A33	15c multicolored	.70	.70
181	A33	20c multicolored	.70	.70
182	A33	25c multicolored	.90	.90
		Nos. 178-182 (5)	3.00	2.70

Sehlabathebe National Park.

Moshoeshoe I (1824-1870) A34

Mofumahali Mantsebo Seeiso (1940-1960) A35

Leaders of Lesotho: 4c, Moshoeshoe II. 5c, Letsie I (1870-1891). 6c, Lerotholi (1891-1905). 10c, Letsie II (1905-1913). 15c, Griffith (1913-1939). 20c, Seeiso Griffith Lerotholi (1939-1940).

1975, Sept. 10 **Litho.** **Wmk. 362**

183	A34	3c dull blue & black	.20	.20
184	A34	4c lilac rose & black	.20	.20
185	A34	5c pink & black	.20	.20
186	A34	6c brown & black	.20	.20
187	A34	10c rose car & black	.20	.20
188	A34	15c orange & black	.25	.25
189	A34	20c olive & black	.30	.30
190	A35	25c lt blue & black	.35	.35
		Nos. 183-190 (8)	1.90	1.90

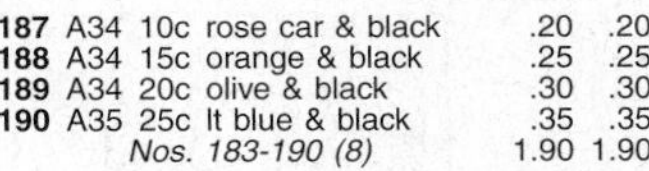

No. 190 issued for Intl. Women's Year.

Mokhibo, Women's Dance A36

Traditional Dances: 10c, Ndlamo, men's dance. 15c, Raleseli, men and women. 20c, Mohobelo, men's dance.

1975, Dec. 17 ***Perf. 14x14½***

191	A36	4c blue & multi	.20	.20
192	A36	10c black & multi	.25	.25
193	A36	15c black & multi	.30	.30
194	A36	20c blue & multi	.40	.40
a.		Souvenir sheet of 4, #191-194	5.50	5.50
		Nos. 191-194 (4)	1.15	1.15

Enrollment in Junior Red Cross — A37

Designs: 10c, First aid team and truck. 15c, Red Cross nurse on horseback in rural area. 25c, Supplies arriving by plane.

1976, Feb. 20 **Litho.** ***Perf. 14***

195	A37	4c red & multi	.60	.40
196	A37	10c red & multi	.85	.60
197	A37	15c red & multi	1.10	.75
198	A37	25c red & multi	1.75	1.25
		Nos. 195-198 (4)	4.30	3.00

Lesotho Red Cross, 25th anniversary.

Mosotho Horseman — A38

King Moshoeshoe II A39

2c, Tapestry (weavers and citation). 4c, Map of Lesotho. 5c, Hand holding Lesotho brown diamond. 10c, Lesotho Bank. 15c, Flags of Lesotho and Organization of African Unity. 25c, Sehlabathebe National Park. 40c, Pottery. 50c, Pre-historic rock painting.

1976, June 2 ***Perf. 14***

199	A38	2c multicolored	.20	.20
200	A38	3c multicolored	.20	.20
201	A38	4c multicolored	1.10	.20
202	A38	5c multicolored	.40	.20
203	A38	10c multicolored	.30	.30
204	A38	15c multicolored	1.10	.60
205	A38	25c multicolored	.80	.95
206	A38	40c multicolored	1.25	1.90
207	A38	50c multicolored	2.25	1.90
208	A39	1r multicolored	1.40	*2.50*
		Nos. 199-208 (10)	9.00	8.95

For surcharges see Nos. 302-311.

Soccer A40

Rising Sun of Independence A41

Olympic Rings and: 10c, Weight lifting. 15c, Boxing. 25c, Discus.

1976, Aug. 9 **Litho.** **Wmk. 362**

209	A40	4c citron & multi	.20	.20
210	A40	10c lilac & multi	.25	.20
211	A40	15c salmon & multi	.30	.25
212	A40	25c blue & multi	.65	.50
		Nos. 209-212 (4)	1.40	1.15

21st Olympic Games, Montreal, Canada, July 17-Aug. 1.

1976, Oct. 4 ***Perf. 14***

Designs: 10c, Opening gates. 15c, Broken chain. 25c, Plane over Molimo Restaurant.

213	A41	4c yellow & multi	.20	.20
214	A41	10c pink & multi	.20	.20
215	A41	15c blue & multi	.60	.20
216	A41	25c dull blue & multi	.70	.50
		Nos. 213-216 (4)	1.70	1.10

Lesotho's independence, 10th anniversary.

Telephones, 1876 and 1976 — A42

Designs: 10c, Woman using telephone, and 1895 telephone. 15c, Telephone operators and wall telephone. 25c, A.G. Bell and 1905 telephone.

Perf. 13x13½

1976, Dec. 6 **Wmk. 362**

217	A42	4c multicolored	.20	.20
218	A42	10c multicolored	.30	.30
219	A42	15c multicolored	.40	.40
220	A42	25c multicolored	.60	.60
		Nos. 217-220 (4)	1.50	1.50

Centenary of first telephone call by Alexander Graham Bell, Mar. 10, 1876.

Aloe Striatula — A43

Aloes and Succulents: 4c, Aloe aristata. 5c, Kniphofia caulescens. 10c, Euphorbia pulvinata. 15c, Aloe saponaria. 20c, Caralluma lutea. 25c, Aloe polyphylla.

1977, Feb. 14 **Litho.** ***Perf. 14***

221	A43	3c multicolored	.35	.20
222	A43	4c multicolored	.40	.20
223	A43	5c multicolored	.50	.20
224	A43	10c multicolored	.65	.20
225	A43	15c multicolored	2.10	.40
226	A43	20c multicolored	2.10	.60
227	A43	25c multicolored	2.25	.80
		Nos. 221-227 (7)	8.35	2.60

Rock Rabbits A44

Perf. 14x14½

1977, Apr. 25 **Wmk. 362**

228	A44	4c shown	*8.25*	.55
229	A44	5c Porcupine	*8.25*	.75
230	A44	10c Polecat	*8.25*	.90
231	A44	15c Klipspringers	*24.50*	3.75
232	A44	25c Baboons	*30.00*	5.00
		Nos. 228-232 (5)	*79.25*	10.95

Man with Cane, Concentric Circles — A45

Man with Cane: 10c, Surrounded by flames of pain. 15c, Surrounded by chain. 25c, Man and globe.

1977, July 4 **Litho.** ***Perf. 14***

233	A45	4c red & yellow	.20	.20
234	A45	10c dk blue & lt blue	.20	.20
235	A45	15c blue green & yellow	.60	.20
236	A45	25c black & orange	.70	.70
		Nos. 233-236 (4)	1.70	1.30

World Rheumatism Year.

Small-mouthed Yellow-fish — A46

Fresh-water Fish: 10c, Orange River mud fish. 15c, Rainbow trout. 25c, Oreodaimon quathlambae.

1977, Sept. 28 **Wmk. 362** ***Perf. 14***

237	A46	4c multicolored	.45	.20
238	A46	10c multicolored	.85	.25
239	A46	15c multicolored	1.60	.60
240	A46	25c multicolored	1.75	1.25
		Nos. 237-240 (4)	4.65	2.30

White and Black Equal — A47

Designs: 10c, Black and white jigsaw puzzle. 15c, White and black cogwheels. 25c, Black and white handshake.

1977, Dec. 12 **Litho.** ***Perf. 14***

241	A47	4c lilac rose & black	.20	.20
242	A47	10c brt blue & black	.20	.20
243	A47	15c orange & black	.20	.20
244	A47	25c lt green & black	.40	.30
		Nos. 241-244 (4)	1.00	.90

Action to Combat Racism Decade.

No. 99 Surcharged

1977, Dec. 7

245	A15	3c on 10c gray & ocher	1.50	1.25

Poppies — A48

Edward Jenner Vaccinating Child — A49

Flowers of Lesotho: 3c, Diascia integerrima. 4c, Helichrysum trilineatum. 5c, Zaluzianskya maritima. 10c, Gladioli. 15c, Chironia krebsii. 25c, Wahlenbergia undulata. 40c, Brunsvigia radulosa.

1978, Feb. 13 Litho. Wmk. 362

246 A48 2c multicolored .20 .30
247 A48 3c multicolored .20 .30
248 A48 4c multicolored .20 .20
249 A48 5c multicolored .20 .20
250 A48 10c multicolored .40 .30
251 A48 15c multicolored .65 .45
252 A48 25c multicolored 1.00 .95
253 A48 40c multicolored 1.75 1.90
Nos. 246-253 (8) 4.60 4.60

1978, May 8 Litho. *Perf. 13½x13*

Global Eradication of Smallpox: 25c, Child's head and WHO emblem.

254 A49 5c multicolored .40 .20
255 A49 25c multicolored 1.40 1.50

Tsoloane Falls — A50

Lesotho Waterfalls: 10c, Qiloane Falls. 15c, Tsoelikana Falls. 25c, Maletsunyane Falls.

1978, July 28 Litho. *Perf. 14*

256 A50 4c multicolored .20 .20
257 A50 10c multicolored .40 .40
258 A50 15c multicolored .65 .65
259 A50 25c multicolored 1.00 1.00
Nos. 256-259 (4) 2.25 2.25

Flyer 1 A51

25c, Orville and Wilbur Wright, Flyer 1.

1978, Oct. 9 Wmk. 362 *Perf. 14½*

260 A51 5c multicolored .20 .20
261 A51 25c multicolored 1.00 1.00

75th anniversary of 1st powered flight.

Dragonflies A52

Trees A53

Insects: 10c, Winged grasshopper. 15c, Wasps. 25c, Praying mantis.

1978, Dec. 18 Litho. *Perf. 14*

262 A52 4c multicolored .20 .20
263 A52 10c multicolored .30 .30
264 A52 15c multicolored .45 .45
265 A52 25c multicolored .75 .75
Nos. 262-265 (4) 1.70 1.70

1979, Mar. 26 Litho. *Perf. 14*

266 A53 4c Leucosidea Sericea .20 .20
267 A53 10c Wild olive .25 .25
268 A53 15c Blinkblaar .40 .40
269 A53 25c Cape holly .65 .65
Nos. 266-269 (4) 1.50 1.50

Reptiles A54

1979, June 4 Wmk. 362 *Perf. 14*

270 A54 4s Agama Lizard .20 .20
271 A54 10s Berg adder .35 .30
272 A54 15s Rock lizard .50 .45
273 A54 25s Spitting snake .85 .75
Nos. 270-273 (4) 1.90 1.70

A55 A56

1979, Oct. 22 Litho. *Perf. 14½*

274 A55 4s Basutoland No. 2 .20 .20
275 A55 15s Basutoland No. 72 .40 .40
276 A55 25s Penny Black .60 .60
Nos. 274-276 (3) 1.20 1.20

Souvenir Sheet

277 A55 50s Lesotho No. 122 1.25 1.25

Sir Rowland Hill (1795-1879), originator of penny postage.

1979, Dec. 10 Wmk. 362 *Perf. 14½*

Children's Games, by Brueghel the Elder, and IYC emblem: 4s, Children Climbing Tree. 10s, Follow the leader. 15s, Three cup montie. 25s, Entire painting.

278 A56 4s multicolored .20 .20
279 A56 10s multicolored .20 .20
280 A56 15s multicolored .35 .35
Nos. 278-280 (3) .75 .75

Souvenir Sheet

281 A56 25s multicolored .80 .80

International Year of the Child.

Beer Strainer, Brooms and Mat A57

1980, Feb. 18 Litho. *Perf. 14½*

282 A57 4s shown .20 .20
283 A57 10s Winnowing basket .20 .20
284 A57 15s Basotho hat .30 .30
285 A57 25s Grain storage pots .50 .50
Nos. 282-285 (4) 1.20 1.20

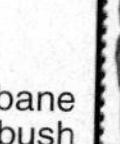

Qalabane Ambush A58

Gun War Centenary: 4s, Praise poet, text. 5s, Basotho army commander Lerotholi. 15s, Snider and Martini-Henry rifles. 25s, Map of Basutoland showing battle sites.

1980, May 6 Litho. *Perf. 14*

286 A58 4s multicolored .20 .20
287 A58 5s multicolored .20 .20
288 A58 10s multicolored .30 .30
289 A58 15s multicolored .70 .40
290 A58 25s multicolored .90 .65
Nos. 286-290 (5) 2.30 1.75

St. Basil's, Moscow, Olympic Torch A59

1980, Sept. 20 Litho. *Perf. 14½*

291 A59 25s shown .35 .35
292 A59 25s Torch and flags .35 .35
293 A59 25s Soccer .35 .35
294 A59 25s Running .35 .35
295 A59 25s Misha and stadium .35 .35
a. Strip of 5, #291-295 2.25 2.25

Souvenir Sheet

296 A59 1.40m Classic and modern torch bearers 2.25 2.25

22nd Summer Olympic Games, Moscow, July 19-Aug. 3.

Beer Mug and Man Drinking A60

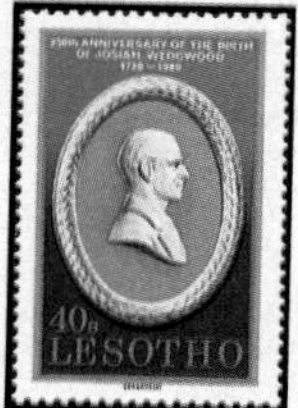

Prince Philip — A61

Wmk. 362

1980, Oct. 1 Litho. *Perf. 14*

297 A60 4s shown .20 .20
298 A60 10s Beer brewing pot .20 .20
299 A60 15s Water pot .20 .20
300 A60 25s Pots and jugs .30 .20
Nos. 297-300 (4) .90 .80

Souvenir Sheet

Perf. 14x14½

301 Sheet of 4 1.80 1.80
a. A61 40s shown .40 .40
b. A61 40s Queen Elizabeth .40 .40
c. A61 40s Prince Charles .40 .40
d. A61 40s Princess Anne .40 .40

Traditional pottery; 250th birth anniversary of Josiah Wedgewood, potter.

Nos. 104, 199-208 Surcharged

Wmk. 362

1980, Oct. 20 Litho. *Perf. 14*

302 A38 2s on 2c multi .20 .20
303 A38 3s on 3c multi .20 .20
304 A38 5s on 5c multi .20 .20
a. 5s on 6s on 5c multi .20 .20
305 A38 6s on 4c multi .20 .20
306 A38 10s on 10c multi .20 .20
307 A38 25s on 25c multi .35 .35
308 A38 40s on 40c multi .55 .55
309 A38 50s on 50c multi .80 .80
310 A38 75s on 15c multi 2.00 2.00
311 A39 1m on 1r multi 2.40 2.40
312 A15 2m on 2r multi 4.50 4.50
Nos. 302-312 (11) 11.60 11.60

Numerous surcharge errors exist (double triple, inverted, etc.).

Souvenir Sheet

Queen Mother Elizabeth and Prince Charles — A62

Basutoland No. 36, Flags of Lesotho and Britain — A63

1980, Dec. 1 Unwmk. *Perf. 14½*

313 Sheet of 9 3.25 3.25
a. A62 5s shown .20 .20
b. A62 10s Portrait .20 .20
c. A63 1m shown .90 .90

Queen Mother Elizabeth, 80th birthday. No. 313 contains 3 each Nos. 313a-313c.

St. Agnes' Anglican Church, Teyateyaneng — A63a

Nativity — A64

1980, Dec. 8 *Perf. 14x14½*

314 A63a 4s Lesotho Evangelical Church, Morija .20 .20
315 A63a 15s shown .20 .20
316 A63a 25s Our Lady's Victory Cathedral, Maseru .20 .20
317 A63a 75s University Chapel, Roma .40 .40
Nos. 314-317 (4) 1.00 1.00

Souvenir Sheet

318 A64 1.50m shown 1.00 1.00

Christmas.

Voyager Satellite and Saturn — A65

1981, Mar. 15 Litho. *Perf. 14*

319 Strip of 5 2.75 2.75
a. A65 25s Voyager, planet .45 .40
b. A65 25s shown .45 .40
c. A65 25s Voyager, Saturn's rings .45 .40
d. A65 25s Columbia space shuttle .45 .40

e. A65 25s Columbia, diff. .45 .40

Souvenir Sheet

320 A65 1.40m Saturn 2.75 2.75

Voyager expedition to Saturn and flight of Columbia space shuttle.

Rock Pigeons — A66

1981, Apr. 20 Unwmk. *Perf. 14½*

321 A66 1s Greater kestrel, vert. .20 .20
322 A66 2s shown .20 .20
323 A66 3s Crowned cranes, vert. .25 .20
324 A66 5s Bokmakierie, vert. .25 .20
325 A66 6s Cape robins, vert. .40 .20
326 A66 7s Yellow canary, vert. .40 .20
327 A66 10s Red-billed teal .40 .25
328 A66 25s Malachite kingfisher, vert. 1.00 .60
329 A66 40s Malachite sunbirds 1.25 1.00
330 A66 60s Orange-throated longclaw 1.60 1.50
331 A66 75s African hoopoe 2.00 1.75
332 A66 1m Red bishops 2.50 2.50
333 A66 2m Egyptian goose 4.75 4.75
334 A66 5m Lilac-breasted rollers 10.00 10.00
Nos. 321-334 (14) 25.20 23.55

For surcharges see Nos. 558A, 561-563, 598A, 599, 600B, 600C.

1981 *Perf. 13*

321a A66 1s 1.40 .70
322a A66 2s 1.60 .70
324a A66 5s 2.00 .70
327a A66 10s 2.00 .70
Nos. 321a-327a (4) 7.00 2.80

1982, June 14 Wmk. 373 *Perf. 14½*

321b A66 1s .20 .40
322b A66 2s .20 .40
323a A66 3s .35 .40
324b A66 5s .35 .45
325a A66 6s .35 .20
326a A66 7s .35 .20
327b A66 10s .35 .20
328a A66 25s 1.00 .45
329a A66 40s 1.10 .50
330a A66 60s 1.50 .90
331a A66 75s 2.00 .90
332a A66 1m 2.40 *2.75*
333a A66 2m 3.00 *4.00*
334a A66 5m 6.00 *10.00*
Nos. 321b-334a (14) 19.15 21.75

Common Design Types pictured following the introduction.

Royal Wedding Issue

Common Design Type and

Royal Wedding — A66a

Unwmk.

1981, July 22 Litho. *Perf. 14*

335 CD331 25s Bouquet .20 .20
a. Booklet pane of 3 + label .80
336 CD331 50s Charles .40 .40
a. Booklet pane of 3 + label 1.60
337 CD331 75s Couple .60 .60
b. Booklet pane of 3 + label 2.00
c. Bklt. pane of 3, #335-337 + label 1.50
Nos. 335-337 (3) 1.20 1.20

1981 Litho. *Perf. 14½*

337A A66a 1.50m Couple 1.75 1.75

Nos. 335-337A exist imperf.

Tree Planting A67

1981, Oct. 30 Litho. *Perf. 14½*

338 A67 6s Duke of Edinburgh .20 .20
339 A67 7s shown .20 .20
340 A67 25s Digging .35 .35
341 A67 40s Mountain climbing .55 .55
342 A67 75s Emblem 1.00 1.00
Nos. 338-342 (5) 2.30 2.30

Souvenir Sheet

343 A67 1.40m Duke of Edinburgh, diff. 2.10 2.10

Duke of Edinburgh's Awards, 25th anniv. #343 contains 1 45x29mm stamp, perf. 13½.

Santa Claus at Globe, by Norman Rockwell A68

The Mystic Nativity, by Botticelli — A69

Christmas: Saturday Evening Post covers by Norman Rockwell.

1981, Oct. 5 *Perf. 13½x14*

344 A68 6s multicolored .20 .20
345 A68 10s multicolored .20 .20
346 A68 15s multicolored .25 .25
347 A68 20s multicolored .35 .35
348 A68 25s multicolored .40 .40
349 A68 60s multicolored 1.00 1.00
Nos. 344-349 (6) 2.40 2.40

Souvenir Sheet

350 A69 1.25m multicolored 2.25 2.25

Chacma Baboons A70

Perf. 14x13½, 14½ (20s, 40s, 50s)

1982, Jan. 15 Litho.

351 A70 6s African wild cat *3.00* .45
352 A70 20s shown *4.00* 1.10
353 A70 25s Cape eland *5.00* 1.60
354 A70 40s Porcupine *6.00* 2.10
355 A70 50s Oribi *6.25* 2.75
Nos. 351-355 (5) *24.25* 8.00

Souvenir Sheet

Perf. 14

356 A70 1.50m Black-backed jackal 13.50 11.00

6s, 25s; 50x37mm. No. 356 contains one stamp 48x31mm.

Scouting Year — A71

1982, Mar. 5 Litho. *Perf. 14x13½*

357 A71 6s Bugle call .20 .20
358 A71 30s Hiking .60 .60
359 A71 40s Drawing .80 .80
360 A71 50s Holding flag 1.00 1.00
361 A71 75s Salute 1.50 1.50
a. Booklet pane of 10 + sheet 12.50
Nos. 357-361 (5) 4.10 4.10

Souvenir Sheet

362 A71 1.50m Baden-Powell 2.75 2.75

No. 361a contains 2 each Nos. 357-361 with gutter and No. 362.

#357-361 issued in sheets of 8 with gutter.

1982 World Cup Soccer A72

Championships, 1930-1978: a, Uruguay, 1930. b, Italy, 1934. c, France, 1938. d, Brazil, 1950. e, Switzerland, 1954. f, Sweden, 1958. g, Chile, 1962. h, England, 1966. i, Mexico, 1970. j, Germany, 1974. k, Argentina, 1978. l, World Cup.

1982, Apr. 14 *Perf. 14½*

363 Sheet of 12 4.25 4.25
a.-l. A72 15s any single .25 .25

Souvenir Sheet

364 A72 1.25m Stadium 2.50 2.50

Nos. 363b, 363c, 363f, 363g, 363j, 363k exist se-tenant in sheets of 72.

George Washington's Birth Bicentenary — A73

Designs: Paintings.

1982, June 7

365 A73 6s Portrait .20 .20
366 A73 7s With children .20 .20
367 A73 10s Indian Chief's Prophecy .20 .20
368 A73 25s With troops .40 .40
369 A73 40s Arriving at New York .60 .60
370 A73 1m Entry into New York 1.25 1.25
Nos. 365-370 (6) 2.85 2.85

Souvenir Sheet

371 A73 1.25m Crossing Delaware 2.00 2.00

Princess Diana Issue

Common Design Type

Wmk. 373

1982, July 1 Litho. *Perf. 14*

372 CD333 30s Arms .90 .90
373 CD333 50s Diana .90 .90
374 CD333 75s Wedding 1.25 1.25
375 CD333 1m Portrait 1.90 1.90
Nos. 372-375 (4) 4.95 4.95

Sesotho Bible Centenary A74

Birth of Prince William of Wales, June 21 — A75

1982, Aug. 20 Litho. *Perf. 14½*

376 A74 6s Man reading bible .20 .20
377 A74 15s Angels, bible .20 .20

Size: 59½x40½mm

378 A74 1m Bible, Maseru Cathedral .50 .50
Nos. 376-378 (3) .90 .90

Issued in sheets of 9 (3 each Nos. 376-378).

1982, Sept. 30

379 A75 6s Congratulation 4.00 4.00
380 A75 60s Diana, William 2.00 2.00

Issued in sheets of 6 (No. 379, 5 No. 380).

Christmas — A76

Designs: Scenes from Walt Disney's The Twelve Days of Christmas. Stamps of same denomination se-tenant.

1982, Dec. 1 Litho. *Perf. 11*

381 A76 2s multicolored .20 .20
382 A76 2s multicolored .20 .20
383 A76 3s multicolored .20 .20
384 A76 3s multicolored .20 .20
385 A76 4s multicolored .20 .20
386 A76 4s multicolored .20 .20
387 A76 75s multicolored 2.25 2.25
388 A76 75s multicolored 2.25 2.25
Nos. 381-388 (8) 5.70 5.70

Souvenir Sheet

Perf. 14x13½

389 A76 1.50m multicolored 5.00 5.00

Local Mushrooms — A77

1983, Jan. 11 *Perf. 14½*

390 A77 10s Lepista caffrorum .20 .20
391 A77 30s Broomexia congregate .50 .40
a. Booklet pane of 2, #390, 391 .75
392 A77 50s Afroboletus luteolus .90 .80
393 A77 75s Lentinus tuberregium 1.25 1.10
a. Booklet pane of 4, #390-393 2.75
Nos. 390-393 (4) 2.85 2.50

Commonwealth Day — A78

1983, Mar. 14 **Litho.** ***Perf. 14½***

No.	Type	Value	Design	Unused	Used
394	A78	5s	Ba-Leseli dance	.20	.20
395	A78	30s	Tapestry weaving	.20	.20
396	A78	60s	Elizabeth II	.35	.35
397	A78	75s	Moshoeshoe II	.40	.40
			Nos. 394-397 (4)	1.15	1.15

Trance Dancers A79

Hunters — A79a

Rock Paintings: 25s, Baboons, Sehonghong Thaba Tseka. 60s, Hunter attacking mountain reedbuck, Makhetha Berera. 75s, Eland, Leribe.

1983, May 20 **Litho.** ***Perf. 14½***

No.	Type	Value	Design	Unused	Used
398	A79	6s	multicolored	.45	.40
399	A79	25s	multicolored	.85	.85
400	A79	60s	multicolored	.95	.90
401	A79	75s	multicolored	1.00	1.00
			Nos. 398-401 (4)	3.25	3.15

Souvenir Sheet

No.	Type	Value	Design	Unused	Used
402			Sheet of 5, #398-401, 402a	3.75	3.75
a.	A79a	10s	multicolored	.35	.20

Manned Flight Bicentenary — A80

1983, July 11 **Litho.** ***Perf. 14½***

No.	Type	Value	Design	Unused	Used
403	A80	7s	Montgolfier, 1783	.20	.20
404	A80	30s	Wright brothers	.45	.35
405	A80	60s	1st airmail plane	.85	.75
406	A80	1m	Concorde	3.00	3.00
			Nos. 403-406 (4)	4.50	4.30

Souvenir Sheet

No.	Type	Value	Design	Unused	Used
407			Sheet of 5	4.00	4.00
a.	A80	6s	Dornier 228	.40	.40

#407 contains #403-406, 407a (60x60mm).

Sesquicentennial of French Missionaries' Arrival — A81

1983, Sept. 5 **Litho.** ***Perf. 13½x14***

No.	Type	Value	Design	Unused	Used
408	A81	6s	Rev. Eugene Casalis, flags	.40	.40
409	A81	25s	Morija, 1833	.40	.40
410	A81	40s	Baptism of Libe	.40	.40
411	A81	75s	Map of Basutoland, 1834	.80	.80
			Nos. 408-411 (4)	2.00	2.00

Christmas — A82

Scenes from Disney's Old Christmas, from Washington Irving's Sketch Book.

1983, Dec. **Litho.** ***Perf. 14***

No.	Type	Value	Design	Unused	Used
412	A82	1s	shown	.20	.20
413	A82	2s	Christmas Eve, diff.	.20	.20
414	A82	3s	Christmas Day	.20	.20
415	A82	4s	Christmas Day, diff.	.20	.20
416	A82	5s	Christmas dinner	.20	.20
417	A82	6s	Christmas dinner, diff.	.20	.20
418	A82	75s	Christmas games	2.75	2.75
419	A82	1m	Christmas dancers	3.25	3.25
			Nos. 412-419 (8)	7.20	7.20

Souvenir Sheet

No.	Type	Value	Design	Unused	Used
420	A82	1.75m	Christmas Eve	6.00	6.00

African Monarch A83

Butterflies.

1984, Jan. 20 **Litho.**

No.	Type	Value	Design	Unused	Used
421	A83	1s	shown	.45	.35
422	A83	2s	Mountain Beauty	.45	.35
423	A83	3s	Orange Tip	.50	.40
424	A83	4s	Blue Pansy	.50	.40
425	A83	5s	Yellow Pansy	.50	.40
426	A83	6s	African Migrant	.50	.40
427	A83	7s	African Leopard	.50	.40
428	A83	10s	Suffused Acraea	.60	.50
429	A83	15s	Painted Lady	1.00	1.10
430	A83	20s	Lemon Traveller	1.25	1.25
431	A83	30s	Foxy Charaxes	1.50	1.75
432	A83	50s	Broad-Bordered Grass Yellow	1.50	1.75
433	A83	60s	Meadow White	1.50	1.75
434	A83	75s	Queen Purple Tip	1.60	2.00
435	A83	1m	Diadem	1.60	2.00
436	A83	5m	Christmas Butterfly	2.50	3.25
			Nos. 421-436 (16)	16.45	18.05

For surcharges see Nos. 559-560, 561A, 564-566, 600, 600A, 600D, 617A-617B.

Easter A84

Designs: Nos. 437a-437j, The Ten Commandments. 1.50m, Moses holding tablets.

1984, Mar. 30 **Litho.** ***Perf. 14***

No.	Type	Value	Design	Unused	Used
437			Sheet of 10 + 2 labels	7.00	7.00
a.-j.	A84	20s	any single	.35	.35

Souvenir Sheet

No.	Type	Value	Design	Unused	Used
438	A84	1.50m	multicolored	2.50	2.50

No. 438 contains one stamp 45x29mm.

1984 Summer Olympics — A85

1984, May 5 **Litho.** ***Perf. 13½***

No.	Type	Value	Design	Unused	Used
439	A85	10s	Torch bearer	.20	.20
440	A85	30s	Equestrian	.20	.20
441	A85	50s	Swimming	.35	.35
442	A85	75s	Basketball	.45	.45
443	A85	1m	Running	.55	.55
			Nos. 439-443 (5)	1.75	1.75

Souvenir Sheet

No.	Type	Value	Design	Unused	Used
444	A85	1.50m	Flags, flame, stadium	2.00	2.00

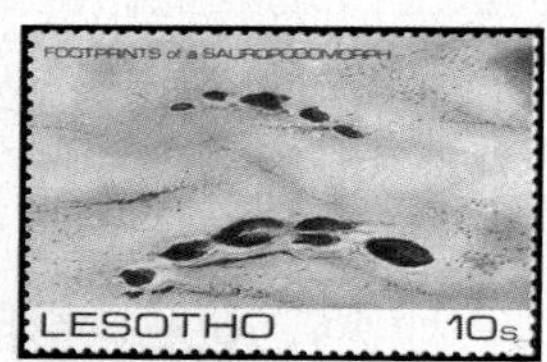

Prehistoric Footprints — A86

1984, July 2 **Litho.** ***Perf. 13½***

No.	Type	Value	Design	Unused	Used
445	A86	10s	Sauropodomorph	.35	.35
446	A86	30s	Lesothosaurus	1.00	1.00
447	A86	50s	Carnivorous dinosaur	1.75	1.75
			Nos. 445-447 (3)	3.10	3.10

Mail Coach Bicentenary and Ausipex '84 — A87

6s, Wells Fargo, 1852. 7s, Basotho mail cart, 1900. 10s, Bath mail coach, 1784. 30s, Cobb coach, 1853. 50s, Exhibition buildings. 1.75m, Penny Black, Basutoland #O4, Western Australia #3.

1984, Sept. 5 **Litho.** ***Perf. 14***

No.	Type	Value	Design	Unused	Used
448	A87	6s	multicolored	.20	.20
449	A87	7s	multicolored	.20	.20
450	A87	10s	multicolored	.20	.20
451	A87	30s	multicolored	.20	.20

Size: 82x26mm

No.	Type	Value	Design	Unused	Used
451A	A87	50s	multicolored	.45	.45
			Nos. 448-451A (5)	1.25	1.25

Souvenir Sheet

No.	Type	Value	Design	Unused	Used
452	A87	1.75m	multicolored	3.75	3.75

No. 452 contains one stamp 82x26mm.

Trains — A88

1984, Nov. 5 **Litho.** ***Perf. 13½***

No.	Type	Value	Design	Unused	Used
453	A88	6s	Orient Express, 1900	.20	.20
454	A88	15s	05.001, Class 5, 1935	.30	.30
455	A88	30s	Cardean, Caledonian, 1906	.55	.55
456	A88	60s	Santa Fe, Super Chief, 1940	1.10	1.10
457	A88	1m	Flying Scotsman, 1934	2.00	2.00
			Nos. 453-457 (5)	4.15	4.15

Souvenir Sheet

Perf. 14x13½

No.	Type	Value	Design	Unused	Used
458	A88	2m	The Blue Train, 1972	2.50	2.50

Indigenous Young Animals — A89

1984, Dec. 20 ***Perf. 14½***

No.	Type	Value	Design	Unused	Used
459	A89	15s	Cape Eland calf	.25	.25
460	A89	20s	Chacma baboons	.30	.30
461	A89	30s	Oribo calf	.45	.45
462	A89	75s	Red rock hares	1.10	1.10

Size: 47x28mm

Perf. 13½

No.	Type	Value	Design	Unused	Used
463	A89	1m	Black-backed jackals	1.60	1.60
			Nos. 459-463 (5)	3.70	3.70

King Moshoeshoe II — A90

1985, Jan. 30 **Litho.** ***Perf. 15***

No.	Type	Value	Design	Unused	Used
464	A90	6s	Royal crown, 1974	.20	.20
465	A90	30s	Moshoeshoe II, 1966	.20	.20
466	A90	75s	In Basotho dress	.50	.50
467	A90	1m	In military uniform	.70	.70
			Nos. 464-467 (4)	1.60	1.60

25th anniversary of reign.

Miniature Sheet

Easter A91

Stations of the Cross: a, Condemned to death. b, Bearing cross. c, Falls the first time. d, Meets his mother. e, Cyrenean helps carry cross. f, Veronica wipes His face. g, Second fall. h, Consoles women of Jerusalem. i, Third fall. j, Stripped. k, Nailed to cross. l, Dies on cross. m, Taken down from cross. n, Laid in sepulchre. No. 469, The Crucifixion, detail, by Mathias Grunewald (c. 1460-1528).

1985, Mar. 8 ***Perf. 11***

No.	Type	Value	Design	Unused	Used
468			Sheet of 14 + label	7.00	
a.-n.	A91	20s	any single	.20	.20

Souvenir Sheet

Perf. 14

No.	Type	Value	Design	Unused	Used
469	A91	2m	multicolored	3.00	3.00

Queen Mother, 85th Birthday — A92

Photographs: 10s, Queen Mother, Princess Elizabeth, 1931. 30s, 75th birthday portrait. 60s With Queen Elizabeth II and Princess Margaret, 80th birthday. No. 473, With Queen Elizabeth II, Princess Diana, Princess Henry and Charles, christening of Prince Henry. No. 474, like No. 473, with Prince William.

1985, May 30 *Perf. 13½x14*

470 A92 10s multicolored .20 .20
471 A92 30s multicolored 1.10 1.10
472 A92 60s multicolored 1.25 1.25
473 A92 2m multicolored 2.25 2.25
Nos. 470-473 (4) 4.80 4.80

Souvenir Sheet

474 A92 2m multicolored 2.25 2.25

No. 474 contains one stamp 38x51mm.

Automobile Centenary — A93

Luxury cars.

1985, June 10 *Perf. 14*

475 A93 6s BMW 732i .40 .20
476 A93 10s Ford LTD Crown Victoria .60 .20
477 A93 30s Mercedes-Benz 500SE .90 .60
478 A93 90s Cadillac Eldorado Biarritz 1.75 1.50
479 A93 2m Rolls Royce Silver Spirit 3.50 3.50
Nos. 475-479 (5) 7.15 6.00

Souvenir Sheet

480 A93 2m 1907 Rolls Royce Silver Ghost Tourer, vert. 6.00 6.00

No. 480 contains one stamp 38x51mm.

Audubon Birth Bicentenary — A94

Illustrations of North American bird species by artist and naturalist John J. Audubon.

1985, Aug. 5 *Perf. 14½*

481 A94 5s Cliff swallow, vert. .55 .45
482 A94 6s Great crested grebe .70 .45
483 A94 10s Vesper sparrow 1.25 .60
484 A94 30s Greenshank 1.75 1.75
485 A94 60s Stilt sandpiper 2.25 2.25
486 A94 2m Glossy ibis 3.50 3.50
Nos. 481-486 (6) 10.00 9.00

Nos. 481-486 printed in sheets of 5 with labels picturing various birds.

Intl. Youth Year, Girl Guides 75th Anniv. — A95

1985, Sept. 26 *Perf. 15*

487 A95 10s Mountain climbing .20 .20
488 A95 30s Medical research .65 .60
489 A95 75s Guides on parade 1.40 1.25
490 A95 2m Guide saluting 2.75 2.25
Nos. 487-490 (4) 5.00 4.30

Souvenir Sheet

491 A95 2m Lady Baden-Powell, World Chief Guide 4.00 4.00

UN, 40th Anniv. — A96

Wildflowers — A97

Designs: 10s, UN No. 1, flag, horiz. 30s, Dish satellite, Ha Sofonia Earth Satellite Station, ITU emblem. 50s, Aircraft, Maseru Airport, ICAO emblem, horiz. 2m, Maimonides (1135-1204), medieval Jewish scholar, WHO emblem.

1985, Oct. 15 **Litho.** *Perf. 15*

492 A96 10s multicolored .35 .35
493 A96 30s multicolored .65 .65
494 A96 50s multicolored 1.25 1.25
495 A96 2m multicolored 6.00 5.00
Nos. 492-495 (4) 8.25 7.25

1985, Nov. 11 *Perf. 11*

496 A97 6s Cosmos .55 .20
497 A97 10s Small agapanthus .70 .20
498 A97 30s Pink witchweed 1.25 .75
499 A97 60s Small iris 2.00 2.00
500 A97 90s Wild geranium 2.50 2.50
501 A97 1m Large spotted orchid 3.50 3.50
Nos. 496-501 (6) 10.50 9.15

Mark Twain, Author, Jacob and Wilhelm Grimm, Fabulists A98

Disney characters acting out Mark Twain quotes or portraying characters from The Wishing Table, by the Grimm Brothers.

1985, Dec. 2 *Perf. 11*

502 A98 6s multicolored .20 .20
503 A98 10s multicolored .20 .20
504 A98 50s multicolored 1.50 1.50
505 A98 60s multicolored 2.10 2.10
506 A98 75s multicolored 2.50 2.50
507 A98 90s multicolored 3.00 3.00
508 A98 1m multicolored 3.25 3.25
509 A98 1.50m multicolored 5.50 5.50
Nos. 502-509 (8) 18.25 18.25

Souvenir Sheets

Perf. 14

510 A98 1.25m multicolored 7.00 7.00
511 A98 1.50m multicolored 7.00 7.00

Christmas. #505, 507 printed in sheets of 8.

World Wildlife Fund — A99

Flora and Fauna — A100

Lammergeier vulture.

1986, Jan. 20 *Perf. 15*

512 A99 7s Male *2.00 .75*
513 A99 15s Male, female *3.75 1.00*
514 A99 50s Male in flight *5.50 2.00*
515 A99 1m Adult, young *7.00 3.50*
Nos. 512-515 (4) 18.25 7.25

1986, Jan. 20

516 A100 9s Prickly pear .50 .20
517 A100 12s Stapelia .50 .20
518 A100 35s Pig's ears .75 .50
519 A100 2m Columnar cereus 2.75 2.50
Nos. 516-519 (4) 4.50 3.40

Souvenir Sheet

520 A100 2m Black eagle 11.00 8.25

1986 World Cup Soccer Championships, Mexico — A101

Various soccer plays.

1986, Mar. 17 *Perf. 14*

521 A101 35s multicolored 1.25 1.25
522 A101 50s multicolored 1.75 1.75
523 A101 1m multicolored 3.50 3.50
524 A101 2m multicolored 7.00 7.00
Nos. 521-524 (4) 13.50 13.50

Souvenir Sheet

525 A101 3m multicolored 11.00 11.00

New Currency, 1st Anniv. (in 1980) A101a

No. 525A — Both sides of: b, 1979 Intl. Year of the Child gold coin. c, Five-maloti banknote. d, 1979 50-lisente coin. e, Ten-maloti banknote. f, 1979 1-sente coin.

1986, Apr. 1 **Litho.** *Perf. 13¾x14*

525A Horiz. strip of 5 *37.50 37.50*
b.-f. A101a 30s Any single *7.50 7.50*

A102

Halley's Comet — A103

Designs: 9s, Hale Telescope, Mt. Palomar, Galileo. 15s, Pioneer Venus 2 probe, 1985 sighting. 70s, 684 sighting illustration, Nuremberg Chronicles. 3m, 1066 sighting, Norman conquest of England. 4m, Comet over Lesotho.

1986, Apr. 5

526 A102 9s multicolored .75 .20
527 A102 15s multicolored 1.00 .20
528 A102 70s multicolored 2.25 .75
529 A102 3m multicolored 6.00 6.00
Nos. 526-529 (4) 10.00 7.15

Souvenir Sheet

530 A103 4m multicolored 10.00 10.00

Queen Elizabeth II, 60th Birthday
Common Design Type

Designs: 90s, In pantomime during youth. 1m, At Windsor Horse Show, 1971. 2m, At Royal Festival Hall, 1971. 4m, Age 8.

1986, Apr. 21

531 CD339 90s lt yel bis & black .60 .60
532 CD339 1m pale grn & multi .70 .70
533 CD339 2m dull vio & multi 1.40 1.40
Nos. 531-533 (3) 2.70 2.70

Souvenir Sheet

534 CD339 4m tan & black 3.00 3.00

For overprints see Nos. 636-639.

Statue of Liberty, Cent. A104

Statue and famous emigrants: 15s, Bela Bartok (1881-1945), composer. 35s, Felix Adler (1857-1933), philosopher. 1m, Victor Herbert (1859-1924), composer. No. 538, David Niven (1910-1983), actor. No. 539, Statue, vert.

1986, May 1

535 A104 15s multicolored 1.00 .20
536 A104 35s multicolored 1.00 .35
537 A104 1m multicolored 3.50 1.75
538 A104 3m multicolored 5.50 3.00
Nos. 535-538 (4) 11.00 5.30

Souvenir Sheet

539 A104 3m multicolored 7.00 7.00

AMERIPEX '86 — A105

Walt Disney characters.

1986, May 22 *Perf. 11*

540 A105 15s Goofy, Mickey 1.10 .20
541 A105 35s Mickey, Pluto 1.40 .45
542 A105 1m Goofy 3.00 1.90
543 A105 2m Donald, Pete 3.50 2.50
Nos. 540-543 (4) 9.00 5.05

Souvenir Sheet

Perf. 14

544 A105 4m Goofy, Chip'n'Dale 12.00 12.00

Royal Wedding Issue, 1986
Common Design Type

Designs: 50s, Prince Andrew and Sarah Ferguson. 1m, Andrew. 3m, Andrew at helicopter controls. 4m, Couple, diff.

1986, July 23 *Perf. 14*

545 CD340 50s multicolored .50 .50
546 CD340 1m multicolored .95 .95
547 CD340 3m multicolored 2.50 2.50
Nos. 545-547 (3) 3.95 3.95

Souvenir Sheet

548 CD340 4m multicolored 4.00 4.00

Natl. Independence, 20th Anniv. — A106

1986, Oct. 20 **Litho.** *Perf. 15*

549 A106 9s Basotho pony, rider .20 .20
550 A106 15s Mohair spinning .20 .20
551 A106 35s River crossing .35 .35
552 A106 3m Thaba Tseka P.O. 3.00 3.00
Nos. 549-552 (4) 3.75 3.75

Souvenir Sheet

553 A106 4m Moshoeshoe I 8.00 8.00

Christmas A107

Walt Disney characters.

1986, Nov. 4 Litho. *Perf. 11*
554 A107 15s Chip'n'Dale .95 .20
555 A107 35s Mickey, Minnie 1.40 .40
556 A107 1m Pluto 1.90 1.60
557 A107 2m Aunt Matilda 2.75 2.75
Nos. 554-557 (4) 7.00 4.95

Souvenir Sheet
Perf. 14

558 A107 5m Huey and Dewey 11.00 11.00

Butterfly and Bird Type of 1981-84 Surcharged

1986 Litho. *Perf. 14, 14½*
558A A66 9s on 10s #327b
b. 9s on 10s #327
559 A83 9s on 30s No. 431 .20 .20
a. 9s on 30s #431 (surcharge smaller & sans serif)
560 A83 9s on 60s No. 433 .20 .20
561 A66 15s on 1s No. 321 .20 .20
b. 15s on 1s #321a
c. 15s on 1s #321b
561A A83 15s on 1s No. 421 2.00 2.00
562 A66 15s on 2s No. 322 .20 .20
563 A66 15s on 60s No. 330 .20 .20
a. 15s on 60s #330a
564 A83 15s on 2s No. 422 .20 .20
565 A83 15s on 3s No. 423 .20 .20
566 A83 35s on 75s No. 434 .35 .35
a. 35s on 75s #434, small "s"
Nos. 558A-566 (10) 3.75 3.75

Issued: Nos. 559-560, July 1. Nos. 561-563, Aug. 22. Nos. 561A, 564-566, June 25.
See Nos. 617A-617B.

Roof of Africa Rally — A108

1988 Summer Olympics, Seoul — A109

1987, Apr. 28 Litho. *Perf. 14*
567 A108 9s White car .45 .20
568 A108 15s Motorcycle #26 .55 .20
569 A108 35s Motorcycle #25 .75 .35
570 A108 4m Red car 4.00 4.00
Nos. 567-570 (4) 5.75 4.75

1987, May 29 *Perf. 14*
571 A109 9s Tennis .90 .20
572 A109 15s Judo .90 .20
573 A109 20s Running 1.00 .20
574 A109 35s Boxing 1.10 .45
575 A109 1m Diving 1.40 1.10
576 A109 3m Bowling 3.25 3.25
Nos. 571-576 (6) 8.55 5.40

Souvenir Sheet

577 A109 2m Tennis, diff. 2.75 2.75
577A A109 4m Soccer 5.25 5.25

See Nos. 606-611.
No. 577A shows green at lower left diagonal half of the flag.

Inventors and Innovators A110

Designs: 5s, Sir Isaac Newton, reflecting telescope. 9s, Alexander Graham Bell, telephone. 75s, Robert H. Goddard, liquid fuel rocket. 4m, Chuck Yeager (b. 1923), test pilot. No. 582, Mariner 10 spacecraft.

1987, June 30 *Perf. 15*
578 A110 5s multicolored .45 .20
579 A110 9s multicolored .45 .20
580 A110 75s multicolored 1.00 .75
581 A110 4m multicolored 4.00 4.00
Nos. 578-581 (4) 5.90 5.15

Souvenir Sheet

582 A110 4m multicolored 5.00 5.00

Fauna and Flora A111

1987, Aug. 14
583 A111 5s Gray rhebuck .50 .20
584 A111 9s Cape clawless otter .50 .20
585 A111 15s Cape gray mongoose .70 .20
586 A111 20s Free state daisy .80 .20
587 A111 35s River bells .90 .35
588 A111 1m Turkey flower 2.00 1.00
589 A111 2m Sweet briar 2.50 2.00
590 A111 3m Mountain reedbuck 3.00 3.00
Nos. 583-590 (8) 10.90 7.15

Souvenir Sheet

591 A111 2m Pig-lily 3.25 3.25
592 A111 4m Cape wildebeest 5.75 5.75

Nos. 586-589 and 591 vert.

16th World Scout Jamboree, Australia, 1987-88 — A112

1987, Sept. 10 Litho. *Perf. 14*
593 A112 9s Orienteering .20 .20
594 A112 15s Playing soccer .20 .20
595 A112 35s Kangaroos .65 .65
596 A112 75s Salute, flag 1.25 1.25
597 A112 4m Windsurfing 7.25 7.25
Nos. 593-597 (5) 9.55 9.55

Souvenir Sheet

598 A112 4m Map, flag of Australia 6.00 6.00

Nos. 324, 425, 424, 328 and 427 Surcharged

1987 Litho. *Perf. 14½, 14*
598A A66 9s on 5s No. 324 .20 .20
599 A66 15s on 5s No. 324 .20 .20
600 A83 15s on 5s No. 425 .20 .20
600A A83 20s on 4s No. 424 .20 .20
600B A66 35s on 25s No. 328 .35 .35
e. 35s on 25s #328, small "s"
f. 35s on 25s #328a
g. 35s on 25s #328a, small "s"
600C A66 35s on 75s #331
h. 35s on 75s #331, small "s"
600D A83 40s on 7s No. 427 .40 .40

Issued: #599-600, Nov. 16; #600B, Dec. 15; #598A, 600A, 600D, Dec. 30.

A113

A114

Religious paintings (details) by Raphael: 9s, Madonna and Child. 15s, Marriage of the Virgin. 35s, Coronation of the Virgin. 90s, Madonna of the Chair. 3m, Madonna and Child Enthroned with Five Saints.

1987, Dec. 21 *Perf. 14*
601 A113 9s multicolored .20 .20
602 A113 15s multicolored .20 .20
603 A113 35s multicolored 1.25 1.25
604 A113 90s multicolored 3.25 3.25
Nos. 601-604 (4) 4.90 4.90

Souvenir Sheet

605 A114 3m multicolored 5.00 5.00

Christmas.

Summer Olympics Type of 1987

1987, Nov. 30 Litho. *Perf. 14*
606 A109 5s like 9s .20 .20
607 A109 10s like 15s .20 .20
608 A109 25s like 20s .25 .25
609 A109 40s like 35s .35 .35
610 A109 50s like 1m .50 .50
611 A109 3.50m like 3m 3.50 3.50
Nos. 606-611 (6) 5.00 5.00

Souvenir Sheet

612 A109 4m Soccer 4.00 4.00

No. 612 shows green at lower right diagonal half of the flag.

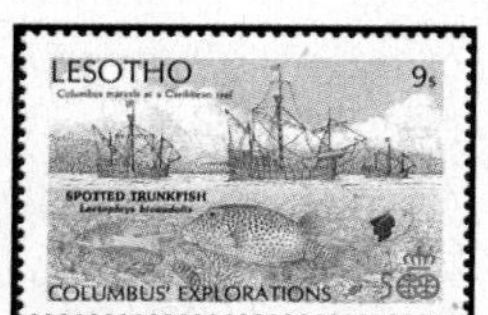

Discovery of America, 500th Anniv. (in 1992) A115

Columbus's fleet and marine life: 9s, Spotted trunkfish. 15s, Green sea turtle. 35s, Common dolphin. 5m, White-tailed tropicbird. 4m, Ship.

1987, Dec. 14 Litho. *Perf. 14*
613 A115 9s multicolored .20 .20
614 A115 15s multicolored .20 .20
615 A115 35s multicolored .60 .60
616 A115 5m multicolored 8.50 8.50
Nos. 613-616 (4) 9.50 9.50

Souvenir Sheet

617 A115 4m multicolored 7.00 7.00

Nos. 328, 559 Surcharged

1988
Methods and Perfs as Before
617A A83 3s on 9s on 30s
617B A83 7s on 9s on 30s
617C A66 16son 25s No. 328 — —

Issued: Nos. 617A, 617B, 2/2/88; No. 617C, 3/88.

Birds A116

1988, Apr. 5 Litho. *Perf. 15*
618 A116 2s Pied kingfisher .20 .20
619 A116 3s Three-banded plover .20 .20
620 A116 5s Spurwing goose .20 .20
621 A116 10s Clapper lark .20 .20
622 A116 12s Red-eyed bulbul .20 .20
623 A116 16s Cape weaver .20 .20
624 A116 20s Red-headed finch .20 .20
625 A116 30s Mountain chat .30 .30
626 A116 40s Stone chat .40 .40
627 A116 55s Pied barbet .55 .55
628 A116 60s Cape glossy starling .60 .60
629 A116 75s Cape sparrow .75 .75
630 A116 1m Cattle egret 1.00 1.00
631 A116 3m Giant kingfisher 3.00 3.00
632 A116 10m Crowned guinea fowl 10.00 10.00
Nos. 618-632 (15) 18.00 18.00

For surcharges see Nos. 755, 805-806.

1989, Sept. 18 *Perf. 14*
620a A116 5s multicolored .20 .20
622a A116 12s multicolored .20 .20
623a A116 16s multicolored .20 .20
624a A116 20s multicolored .20 .20
630a A116 1m multicolored .80 .80
631a A116 3m multicolored 2.40 2.40
632a A116 10m multicolored 8.00 8.00
Nos. 620a-632a (7) 12.00 12.00

Dated 1989.

1990 *Perf. 12½x12*
620b A116 5s multicolored .20 .20
622b A116 12s multicolored .20 .20
623b A116 16s multicolored .20 .20
624b A116 20s multicolored .20 .20
630b A116 1m multicolored .80 .80
631b A116 3m multicolored 2.40 2.40
632b A116 10m multicolored 8.00 8.00
Nos. 620b-632b (7) 12.00 12.00

Dated 1989.

1991 (?) *Perf. 11½x13*
620c A116 5s multicolored .20 .20
622c A116 12s multicolored .20 .20
623c A116 16s multicolored .20 .20
624c A116 20s multicolored .20 .20
630c A116 1m multicolored .80 .80
631c A116 3m multicolored 2.40 2.40
632c A116 10m multicolored 8.00 8.00
Nos. 620c-632c (7) 12.00 12.00

Dated 1989.

Nos. 531-534 Overprinted "40th WEDDING ANNIVERSARY / H.M. QUEEN ELIZABETH II / H.R.H. THE DUKE OF EDINBURGH" in Silver

1988, May 3 *Perf. 14*
636 CD339 90s lt yel bis & blk 1.00 1.00
637 CD339 1m pale grn & multi 1.10 1.10
638 CD339 2m dull vio & multi 2.25 2.25
Nos. 636-638 (3) 4.35 4.35

Souvenir Sheet

639 CD339 4m tan & black 4.50 4.50

FINLANDIA '88, Helsinki, June 1-12 — A117

Disney animated characters and Helsinki sights.

1988, June 2 Litho. *Perf. 14x13½*
640 A117 1s Touring President's Palace .20 .20
641 A117 2s Sauna .20 .20
642 A117 3s Lake Country fishing .20 .20
643 A117 4s Finlandia Hall .20 .20
644 A117 5s Photographing Sibelius Monument .20 .20

645 A117 10s Pony trek, youth hostel .30 .30
646 A117 3m Olympic Stadium 4.75 3.50
647 A117 5m Santa Claus, Arctic Circle 6.00 4.75
Nos. 640-647 (8) 12.05 9.55

Souvenir Sheets

Perf. 14x13½, 13½x14

648 A117 4m Market Square 4.75 4.75
649 A117 4m Lapp encampment, vert. 4.75 4.75

Mickey Mouse, 60th anniv.

A118

A119

1988, Sept. 1 Litho. *Perf. 14*

650 A118 55s Pope giving communion .55 .55
651 A118 2m Leading procession 2.00 2.00
652 A118 3m Walking in garden 3.00 3.00
653 A118 4m Wearing scullcap 4.00 4.00
Nos. 650-653 (4) 9.55 9.55

Souvenir Sheet

654 A118 5m Pope, Archbishop Morapeli of Lesotho, horiz. 8.50 8.50

Visit of Pope John Paul II, Sept. 14-16.

1988, Oct. 13 Litho. *Perf. 14*

Small indigenous mammals.

655 A119 16s Rock hyrax .20 .20
656 A119 40s Honey badger .85 .85
657 A119 75s Genet 1.50 1.50
658 A119 3m Yellow mongoose 6.25 6.25
Nos. 655-658 (4) 8.80 8.80

Souvenir Sheet

659 A119 4m Meerkat 6.00 6.00

Birth of Venus, 1480, by Botticelli A120

Paintings: 25s, View of Toledo, 1608, by El Greco. 40s, Maids of Honor, 1656, by Diego Velazquez. 50s, The Fifer, 1866, by Manet. 55s, The Starry Night, 1889, by Van Gogh. 75s, Prima Ballerina, 1876, by Degas. 2m, Bridge over Water Lilies, 1899, by Monet. 3m, Guernica, 1937, by Picasso. No. 668, The Presentation of the Virgin in the Temple, c. 1534, by Titian. No. 669, The Miracle of the Newborn Infant, 1511, by Titian.

1988, Oct. 17 Litho. *Perf. 13½x14*

660 A120 15s multicolored .40 .20
661 A120 25s multicolored .55 .25
662 A120 40s multicolored .65 .40
663 A120 50s multicolored .75 .50
664 A120 55s multicolored .80 .55
665 A120 75s multicolored .90 .90
666 A120 2m multicolored 2.00 2.00
667 A120 3m multicolored 3.00 3.00
Nos. 660-667 (8) 9.05 7.80

Souvenir Sheets

668 A120 4m multicolored 4.00 4.00
669 A120 4m multicolored 4.00 4.00

1988 Summer Olympics, Seoul — A121

Intl. Tennis Federation, 75th Anniv. — A122

1988, Nov. 11 Litho. *Perf. 14*

670 A121 12s Wrestling, horiz. .20 .20
671 A121 16s Equestrian .20 .20
672 A121 55s Shooting, horiz. .40 .40
673 A121 3.50m like 16s 2.75 2.75
Nos. 670-673 (4) 3.55 3.55

Souvenir Sheet

674 A121 4m Olympic flame 5.25 5.25

1988, Nov. 18

Tennis champions, views of cities or landmarks: 12s, Yannick Noah, Eiffel Tower, horiz. 20s, Rod Laver, Sydney Opera House and Harbor Bridge, horiz. 30s, Ivan Lendl, Prague, horiz. 65s, Jimmy Connors, Tokyo. 1m, Arthur Ashe, Barcelona. 1.55m, Althea Gibson, NYC. 2m, Chris Evert, Vienna. 2.40m, Boris Becker, London. 3m, Martina Navratilova, Golden Gate Bridge, horiz. 4m, Steffi Graf, Berlin, West Germany.

675 A122 12s multi .70 .20
676 A122 20s multi .90 .20
677 A122 30s multi .80 .35
678 A122 65s multi .95 .80
679 A122 1m multi 1.25 1.25
680 A122 1.55m multi 1.75 1.75
681 A122 2m multi 2.40 2.40
682 A122 2.40m multi 2.75 2.75
683 A122 3m multi 3.50 3.50
Nos. 675-683 (9) 15.00 13.20

Souvenir Sheet

684 A122 4m multi 5.00 5.00

No. 676 has "Sidney" instead of "Sydney." No. 679 has "Ash" instead of "Ashe."

Paintings by Titian A123

Designs: 12s, The Averoldi Polyptych. 20s, Christ and the Adulteress (Christ). 35s, Christ and the Adulteress (adultress). 45s, Angel of the Annunciation. 65s, Saint Dominic. 1m, The Vendramin Family. 2m, Mary Magdalen. 3m, The Tribute Money. No. 693, Christ and the Woman Taken in Adultery. No. 694, The Mater Dolorosa.

1988, Dec. 1 *Perf. 14x13½*

685 A123 12s multicolored .40 .20
686 A123 20s multicolored .50 .20
687 A123 35s multicolored .60 .35
688 A123 45s multicolored .70 .45
689 A123 65s multicolored .70 .65
690 A123 1m multicolored 1.00 1.00
691 A123 2m multicolored 2.00 2.00
692 A123 3m multicolored 3.00 3.00
Nos. 685-692 (8) 8.90 7.85

Souvenir Sheets

693 A123 5m multicolored 5.00 5.00
694 A123 5m multicolored 5.00 5.00

Birth of Titian, 500th anniv. Nos. 685-693 inscribed "Christmas 1988."

Intl. Red Cross, 125th Anniv. A124

Anniv. emblem, supply and ambulance planes: 12s, Pilatus PC-6 Turbo Porter. 20s, Cessna Caravan. 55s, De Havilland DHC-6 Otter. 3m, Douglas DC-3 in thunderstorm. 4m, Douglas DC-3, diff.

1989, Jan. 30 Litho. *Perf. 14*

695 A124 12s multicolored .20 .20
696 A124 20s multicolored .20 .20
697 A124 55s multicolored 1.25 1.25
698 A124 3m multicolored 6.00 6.00
Nos. 695-698 (4) 7.65 7.65

Souvenir Sheet

699 A124 4m multi, vert. 10.00 10.00

Landscapes by Hiroshige — A125

Designs: 12s, Dawn Mist at Mishima. 16s, Night Snow at Kambara. 20s, Wayside Inn at Mariko Station. 35s, Shower at Shono. 55s, Snowfall on the Kisokaido Near Oi. 1m, Autumn Moon at Seba. 3.20m, Evening Moon at Ryogaku Bridge. 5m, Cherry Blossoms, Arashiyama. No. 708, Listening to the Singing Insects at Dokanyama. No. 709, Moonlight, Nagakubo.

1989, June 19 Litho. *Perf. 14x13½*

700 A125 12s multi .40 .20
701 A125 16s multi .45 .20
702 A125 20s multi .45 .20
703 A125 35s multi .45 .30
704 A125 55s multi .70 .45
705 A125 1m multi 1.00 .80
706 A125 3.20m multi 2.75 2.75
707 A125 5m multi 4.50 4.50
Nos. 700-707 (8) 10.70 9.40

Souvenir Sheets

708 A125 4m multi 4.50 4.50
709 A125 4m multi 4.50 4.50

Hirohito (1901-1989) and enthronement of Akihito as emperor of Japan.

PHILEXFRANCE '89, French Revolution Bicent. — A126

Disney characters wearing insurgent uniforms.

1989, July 10 *Perf. 13½x14, 14x13½*

710 A126 1s General .20 .20
711 A126 2s Infantry .20 .20
712 A126 3s Grenadier .20 .20
713 A126 4s Cavalry .20 .20
714 A126 5s Hussar .20 .20
715 A126 10s Marine .20 .20
716 A126 3m Natl. guard 3.50 3.50
717 A126 5m Admiral 5.75 5.75
Nos. 710-717 (8) 10.45 10.45

Souvenir Sheets

718 A126 4m Natl. guard, royal family, horiz. 5.50 5.50
719 A126 4m La Marseillaise 5.50 5.50

Maloti Mountains A127

Mushrooms A128

No. 720: a, Sotho thatched dwellings. b, Two trees, cliff edge. c, Waterfall. d, Tribesman.

1989, Sept. Litho. *Perf. 14*

720 Strip of 4 4.25 4.25
a.-d. A127 1m any single .80 .80

Souvenir Sheet

721 A127 4m Flora 4.50 4.50

1989, Sept. 8 Litho. *Perf. 14*

722 A128 12s *Paxillus involutus* .35 .20
723 A128 16s *Ganoderma applanatum* .35 .20
723A A128 55s *Suillus granulatus* .65 .55
724 A128 5m *Stereum hirsutum* 5.00 4.75
Nos. 722-724 (4) 6.35 5.70

Souvenir Sheet

725 A128 4m *Scleroderma flavidum* 6.75 6.75

Birds A129

1989, Oct. 23 Litho. *Perf. 14*

726 A129 12s Marsh sandpipers .20 .20
727 A129 65s Little stints 1.10 1.10
728 A129 1m Ringed plovers 1.75 1.75
729 A129 4m Curlew sandpipers 7.00 7.00
Nos. 726-729 (4) 10.05 10.05

Souvenir Sheet

730 A129 5m Ruff, vert. 12.00 12.00

1st Moon Landing, 20th Anniv. A130

Highlights of the Apollo 11 mission.

1989, Nov. 6 *Perf. 14*

731 A130 12s Liftoff .20 .20
732 A130 16s Eagle landing .20 .20
733 A130 40s Astronaut on ladder .40 .40
734 A130 55s Buzz Aldrin .60 .60
735 A130 1m Solar wind experiment 1.10 1.10
736 A130 2m Eagle lifting off 2.25 2.25
737 A130 3m Columbia in orbit 3.25 3.25
738 A130 4m Splashdown 4.50 4.50
Nos. 731-738 (8) 12.50 12.50

Souvenir Sheet

739 A130 5m Astronaut, Eagle 7.50 7.50

Nos. 731, 733, 738-739 vert.

World Stamp Expo '89 A131

Cathedral Church of Sts. Peter and Paul, Washington, DC — A132

No. 740: a, Postal marking, England, 1680. b, Wax seal and feather, Germany, 1807. c, Crete #1. d, Perot postmaster's provisional, Bermuda, 1848. e, Pony Express handstamp, US, 1860. f, Finland #1. g, Fiji #1. h, Swedish newspaper handstamp, 1823. i, Bhor #1.

1989, Nov. 17 Litho. *Perf. 14*

740 Sheet of 9 9.00 9.00
a.-i. A131 75s any single .40 .40

Souvenir Sheet

741 A132 4m shown 4.50 4.50

Christmas — A133

Religious paintings by Velazquez: 12s, The Immaculate Conception. 20s, St. Anthony Abbot and St. Paul the Hermit. 35s, St. Thomas the Apostle. 55s, Christ in the House of Martha and Mary. 1m, St. John Writing the Apocalypse on Patmos. 3m, The Virgin Presenting the Chasuble to St. Ildephonsus. 4m, The Adoration of the Magi. 5m, The Coronation of the Virgin.

1989, Dec. 18

742 A133 12s multicolored .20 .20
743 A133 20s multicolored .20 .20
744 A133 35s multicolored .35 .35
745 A133 55s multicolored .55 .55
746 A133 1m multicolored .90 .90
747 A133 3m multicolored 2.75 2.75
748 A133 4m multicolored 3.50 3.50
Nos. 742-748 (7) 8.45 8.45

Souvenir Sheet

749 A133 5m multicolored 11.00 11.00

1990 World Cup Soccer Championships, Italy — A134

Various athletes, emblem and name of previous championship host nations.

1989, Dec. 27

750 A134 12s England, 1966 .20 .20
751 A134 16s Mexico, 1970 .20 .20
752 A134 55s West Germany, 1974 1.00 1.00
753 A134 5m Spain, 1982 7.50 7.50
Nos. 750-753 (4) 8.90 8.90

Souvenir Sheet

754 A134 4m Diego Maradona, Argentina 8.00 8.00

No. 622a Surcharged

1990 Litho. *Perf. 14*

755 A116 16s on 12s multi .20 .20

Orchids A135

1990, Mar. 12 Litho. *Perf. 14*

756 A135 12s Satyrium princeps .20 .20
757 A135 16s Huttonaea pulchra .20 .20
758 A135 55s Herschelia graminifolia .90 .90
759 A135 1m Ansellia gigantea 1.60 1.60
760 A135 1.55m Polystachya pubescens 2.50 2.50
761 A135 2.40m Penthea filicornis 3.75 3.75
762 A135 3m Disperis capensis 4.75 4.75
763 A135 4m Disa uniflora 6.50 6.50
Nos. 756-763 (8) 20.40 20.40

Souvenir Sheet

764 A135 5m Stenoglottis longifolia 11.00 11.00

Expo '90.

Butterflies — A136

1990, Feb. 26 Litho. *Perf. 14*

765 A136 12s Pseudo ergolid .95 .20
766 A136 16s Painted lady 1.10 .20
767 A136 55s Ringed pansy 1.60 .55
768 A136 65s False acraea 1.75 .65
769 A136 1m Eyed pansy 2.40 1.10
770 A136 2m Golden pansy 3.75 2.25
771 A136 3m African monarch 5.25 3.25
772 A136 4m African giant swallowtail 6.50 5.50
Nos. 765-772 (8) 23.30 13.70

Souvenir Sheet

773 A136 5m Citrus swallowtail 12.00 12.00

Queen Mother, 90th Birthday — A137

1990, July 5 Litho. *Perf. 14*

774 1.50m In hat 1.25 1.25
775 1.50m Two children 1.25 1.25
776 1.50m Young woman 1.25 1.25
a. A137 Strip of 3, #774-776 4.50 4.50
Nos. 774-776 (3) 3.75 3.75

Souvenir Sheet

777 A137 5m Child 6.00 6.00

A139 A140

Designs: 12s, King Moshoeshoe II, Prince Mohato wearing blankets. 16s, Prince Mohato in Seana-Marena blanket. 1m, Pope John Paul II in Seana-Marena blanket. 3m, Basotho men on horses. 5m, Pope with blanket and hat.

1990, Aug. 17 Litho. *Perf. 14*

778 A139 12s multicolored .20 .20
779 A139 16s multicolored .20 .20
780 A139 1m multicolored 1.40 1.40
781 A139 3m multicolored 4.00 4.00
Nos. 778-781 (4) 5.80 5.80

Souvenir Sheet

782 A139 5m multi, horiz. 8.25 8.25

1990, Aug. 24

Highland Water Project: 16s, Moving gravel. 20s, Fuel truck. 55s, Piers for bridge construction. 2m, Road construction. 5m, Drilling blasting holes.

783 A140 16s multicolored .20 .20
784 A140 20s multicolored .20 .20
785 A140 55s multicolored .90 .90
786 A140 2m multicolored 2.75 2.75
Nos. 783-786 (4) 4.05 4.05

Souvenir Sheet

787 A140 5m multicolored 8.25 8.25

Phila Nippon '91 — A144

A141 A142

1990, Sept. 26 Litho. *Perf. 14*

788 A141 12s Breastfeeding .20 .20
789 A141 55s Oral rehydration 1.75 1.75
790 A141 1m Baby being weighed 2.50 2.50
Nos. 788-790 (3) 4.45 4.45

UNICEF Save the Children campaign.

1990, Oct. 5

791 A142 16s Triple jump .20 .20
792 A142 55s 200-meter race 1.00 1.00
793 A142 1m 5000-meter race 1.50 1.50
794 A142 4m Equestrian show jumping 6.00 6.00
Nos. 791-794 (4) 8.70 8.70

Souvenir Sheet

795 A142 5m Lighting Olympic flame 9.00 9.00

1992 Summer Olympics, Barcelona.

Christmas A143

Different details from paintings by Rubens: 12s, 1m, 3m, Virgin and Child. 16s, 80s, 2m, 4m, Adoration of the Magi. 55s, Head of One of the Three Kings, diff. 5m, Assumption of the Virgin.

1990, Dec. 5 Litho. *Perf. 13½x14*

796 A143 12s multicolored .20 .20
797 A143 16s multicolored .20 .20
798 A143 55s multicolored .55 .55
799 A143 80s multicolored .85 .85
800 A143 1m multicolored 1.00 1.00
801 A143 2m multicolored 2.10 2.10
802 A143 3m multicolored 3.00 3.00
803 A143 4m multicolored 4.25 4.25
Nos. 796-803 (8) 12.15 12.15

Souvenir Sheet

804 A143 5m multicolored 7.50 7.50

Nos. 625-626 Surcharged

1991, Jan. 18 Litho. *Perf. 15*

805 A116 16s on 30s #625 .20 .20
806 A116 16s on 40s #626 .20 .20

Walt Disney characters visit Japan: 20s, Mickey at Nagasaki Peace Park. 30s, Mickey at Kamakura Beach. 40s, Mickey, Donald entertain at Bunraku Puppet Theater. 50s, Mickey, Donald eat soba at noodle shop. 75s, Minnie, Mickey at tea house. 1m, Mickey, Bullet Train. 3m, Mickey, deer at Todaiji Temple. 4m, Mickey, Minnie before Imperial Palace. No. 815, Mickey skiing at Happo-One, Nagano. No. 816, Mickey, Minnie at Suizenji Park.

1991, June 10 Litho. *Perf. 14x13½*

807 A144 20s multicolored .20 .20
808 A144 30s multicolored .25 .25
809 A144 40s multicolored .50 .50
810 A144 50s multicolored .70 .70
811 A144 75s multicolored 1.40 1.40
812 A144 1m multicolored 1.40 1.40
813 A144 3m multicolored 4.00 4.00
814 A144 4m multicolored 5.50 5.50
Nos. 807-814 (8) 13.95 13.95

Souvenir Sheets

815 A144 6m multicolored 6.25 6.25
816 A144 6m multicolored 6.25 6.25

Entertainers in Films About Africa — A145

Designs: 12s, Stewart Granger, King Solomon's Mines. 16s, Johnny Weissmuller, Tarzan, the Ape Man. 30s, Clark Gable, Grace Kelly, Mogambo. 55s, Sigourney Weaver, Gorillas in the Mist. 70s, Humphrey Bogart, Katharine Hepburn, The African Queen. 1m, John Wayne, Hatari. 2m, Meryl Streep, Out of Africa. 4m, Eddie Murphy, Arsenio Hall, Coming to America. 5m, Elsa, Born Free.

1991, June 20 Litho. *Perf. 14*

817 A145 12s multicolored .65 .20
818 A145 16s multicolored .65 .20
819 A145 30s multicolored .80 .25
820 A145 55s multicolored .95 .70
821 A145 70s multicolored 1.25 .90
822 A145 1m multicolored 1.60 1.25
823 A145 2m multicolored 2.50 2.50
824 A145 4m multicolored 5.25 5.25
Nos. 817-824 (8) 13.65 11.25

Souvenir Sheet

825 A145 5m multicolored 7.25 7.25

Butterflies A146

1991, Aug. 1 Litho. *Perf. 13½*

No date inscription below design

827 A146 2s Satyrus aello .20 .20
828 A146 3s Erebia medusa .20 .20
829 A146 5s Melanargia galathea .20 .20
830 A146 10s Erebia aethiops .20 .20
831 A146 20s Coenonympha pamphilus .30 .20
832 A146 25s Pyrameis atalanta .30 .20
833 A146 30s Charaxes jasius .45 .30
834 A146 40s Colias palaeno .45 .35

835 A146 50s Colias cliopatra .50 .45
836 A146 60s Colias philodice .60 .55
837 A146 70s Rhumni gonepterix .60 .60
838 A146 1m Colias caesonia .90 .90
839 A146 2m Pyrameis cardui 1.75 1.75
840 A146 3m Danaus chrysippus 2.50 2.50
840A A146 10m Apatura iris 8.75 8.75
Nos. 827-840A (15) 17.90 17.35

For surcharge see No. 1062.

1992, Apr.

Inscribed "1992"

827a A146 2s multicolored .20 .20
828a A146 3s multicolored .20 .20
829a A146 5s multicolored .20 .20
830a A146 10s multicolored .20 .20
831a A146 20s multicolored .30 .20
832a A146 25s multicolored .30 .20
833a A146 30s multicolored .45 .30
834a A146 40s multicolored .50 .35
835a A146 50s multicolored .65 .45
836a A146 60s multicolored .70 .70
837a A146 70s multicolored 1.00 1.00
838a A146 1m multicolored 1.25 1.25
839a A146 2m multicolored 2.75 2.75
840a A146 3m multicolored 4.00 4.00
840Aa A146 10m multicolored 8.75 8.75
Nos. 827a-840Aa (15) 21.45 20.75

SADCC, 10th Anniv. A147

Tourism: 12s, Wattled cranes. 16s, Butterfly, flowers in national parks. 25s, Tourist bus and Mukurub, the Finger of God. 3m, People in traditional dress.

1991, Oct. 10 Litho. *Perf. 14x13½*

841 A147 12s multicolored 2.00 2.00
842 A147 16s multicolored 2.00 2.00
843 A147 25s multicolored 2.00 2.00
Nos. 841-843 (3) 6.00 6.00

Souvenir Sheet

844 A147 3m multicolored 6.00 6.00

Say No to Drugs A148

1991, Oct. 10

845 A148 16s multicolored 2.40 2.40

Charles de Gaulle, Birth Cent. — A149

DeGaulle: 40s, Wearing brigadier general's kepi. 50s, Facing left. 60s, Facing right. 4m, In later years.

1991, Dec. 6 Litho. *Perf. 14*

846 A149 20s black & brown .20 .20
847 A149 40s black & violet .65 .65
848 A149 50s black & olilve .85 .85
849 A149 60s black & dk blue 1.00 1.00
850 A149 4m black & brn org 6.75 6.75
Nos. 846-850 (5) 9.45 9.45

Christmas A150

Engravings by Albrecht Durer: 20s, St. Anne with Mary and the Child Jesus. 30s, Mary on the Grass Bench. 50s, Mary with the Crown of Stars. 60s, Mary with Child beside a Tree. 70s, Mary with Child beside the Wall. 1m, Mary in a Halo on the Crescent Moon. 2m, Mary Breastfeeding Her Child. 4m, Mary with the Infant in Swaddling Clothes. No. 859, Holy Family with the Dragonfly. No. 860, The Birth of Christ.

1991, Dec. 13 Litho. *Perf. 12*

851 A150 20s rose & black .20 .20
852 A150 30s blue & black .50 .50
853 A150 50s green & black .80 .80
854 A150 60s red & black 1.00 1.00
855 A150 70s yellow & black 1.10 1.10
856 A150 1m yel org & black 1.60 1.60
857 A150 2m violet & black 3.00 3.00
858 A150 4m dk blue & black 6.50 6.50
Nos. 851-858 (8) 14.70 14.70

Souvenir Sheets

Perf. 14½

859 A150 5m blue & black 6.00 6.00
860 A150 5m pink & black 6.00 6.00

Games A151

Walt Disney characters playing games: 20s, Mickey, Pluto playing pin the tail on the donkey. 30s, Mickey enjoying board game, Mancala. 40s, Mickey hoop rolling. 50s, Minnie with hula hoops. 70s, Mickey throwing Frisbee to Pluto. 1m, Donald trying to play Diabolo. 2m, Huey, Dewey and Louie playing marbles. 3m, Donald frustrated by Rubik's cube. No. 869, Donald and Mickey's nephews in tug-of-war. No. 870, Mickey, Donald stick fighting.

1991, Dec. 16 *Perf. 13½x14*

861 A151 20s multicolored .20 .20
862 A151 30s multicolored .55 .55
863 A151 40s multicolored .65 .65
864 A151 50s multicolored .90 .90
865 A151 70s multicolored 1.25 1.25
866 A151 1m multicolored 1.75 1.75
867 A151 2m multicolored 3.50 3.50
868 A151 3m multicolored 5.75 5.75
Nos. 861-868 (8) 14.55 14.55

Souvenir Sheets

869 A151 5m multicolored 6.50 6.50
870 A151 5m multicolored 6.50 6.50

Royal Family Birthday, Anniversary

Common Design Type

1991, Dec. 9 Litho. *Perf. 14*

871 CD347 50s multicolored .70 .70
872 CD347 70s multicolored .95 .95
873 CD347 1m multicolored 1.40 1.40
874 CD347 3m multicolored 4.25 4.25
Nos. 871-874 (4) 7.30 7.30

Souvenir Sheet

875 CD347 4m Charles, Diana, sons 7.00 7.00

Charles and Diana, 10th wedding anniversary. Numbers have been reserved for additional values in this set.

Queen Elizabeth II's Accession to the Throne, 40th Anniv.

Common Design Type

1992, Feb. 6 Litho. *Perf. 14*

881 CD348 20s multicolored .20 .20
882 CD348 30s multicolored .40 .40
883 CD348 1m multicolored 1.25 1.25
884 CD348 4m multicolored 4.75 4.75
Nos. 881-884 (4) 6.60 6.60

Souvenir Sheet

885 CD348 5m multicolored 6.75 6.75

Birds — A152

Designs: a, Lanner falcon. b, Bataleur. c, Red-headed finch. d, Lesser-striped swallow. e, Alpine swift. f, Diederik cuckoo. g, Malachite sunbird. h, Crimson-breasted shrike. i, Pin-tailed whydah. j, Lilac-breasted roller. k, Black korhaan. l, Black-collared barbet. m, Secretary bird. n, Red-billed quelea. o, Red bishop. p, Ring-necked dove. q, Yellow canary. r, Orange-throated longclaw. s, Blue waxbill. t, Golden bishop.

1992, Feb. 10 *Perf. 14½*

886 A152 30s Sheet of 20, #a.-t. 16.00 16.00

World Columbian Stamp Expo '92, Chicago A153

Walt Disney characters depicting native Americans: 30s, Donald Duck making arrowheads. 40s, Goofy playing lacrosse. 1m, Mickey, Donald planting corn. 3m, Minnie Mouse mastering art of beading. No. 891, Mickey as "Blackhawk" hunting for moose.

1992, Apr. Litho. *Perf. 13½x14*

887 A153 30s multicolored .55 .55
888 A153 40s multicolored .65 .65
889 A153 1m multicolored 1.75 1.75
890 A153 3m multicolored 5.25 5.25
Nos. 887-890 (4) 8.20 8.20

Souvenir Sheet

891 A153 5m multicolored 8.50 8.50

Granada '92 — A154

Walt Disney characters in Spanish costumes: 20s, Minnie Mouse as Lady of Rank, 1540-1660. 50s, Mickey as conqueror of Lepanto, 1571. 70s, Donald Duck from Galicia, 1880. 2m, Daisy Duck from Aragon, 1880. No. 901, Goofy as bullfighter.

1992, Apr. 13 Litho. *Perf. 13½x14*

897 A154 20s multicolored .20 .20
898 A154 50s multicolored 1.25 1.25
899 A154 70s multicolored 1.60 1.60
900 A154 2m multicolored 4.75 4.75
Nos. 897-900 (4) 7.80 7.80

Souvenir Sheet

901 A154 5m multicolored 8.50 8.50

Dinosaurs A155

1992, June 9 *Perf. 14*

907 A155 20s Stegosaurus .20 .20
908 A155 30s Ceratosaurus .65 .65
909 A155 40s Procompsognathus .75 .75
910 A155 50s Lesothosaurus 1.00 1.00
911 A155 70s Plateosaurus 1.40 1.40
912 A155 1m Gasosaurus 2.00 2.00
913 A155 2m Massospondylus 4.00 4.00
914 A155 3m Archaeopteryx 6.00 6.00
Nos. 907-914 (8) 16.00 16.00

Souvenir Sheet

915 A155 5m Archaeopteryx, diff. 8.50 8.50
916 A155 5m Lesothosaurus, diff. 8.50 8.50

No. 915 printed in continuous design.

1992 Olympics, Barcelona and Albertville — A156

Designs: 20s, Discus. 30s, Long jump. 40s, Women's 4x100-meter relay. 70s, Women's 100-meter dash. 1m, Parallel bars. 2m, Two-man luge, horiz. 3m, Women's cross-country skiing, horiz. 4m, Biathlon. No. 925, Ice hockey, horiz. No. 926, Women's figure skating.

1992, Aug. 5 Litho. *Perf. 14*

917 A156 20s multicolored .20 .20
918 A156 30s multicolored .25 .25
919 A156 40s multicolored .30 .30
920 A156 70s multicolored .65 .65
921 A156 1m multicolored .95 .95
922 A156 2m multicolored 1.90 1.90
923 A156 3m multicolored 2.75 2.75
924 A156 4m multicolored 4.00 4.00
Nos. 917-924 (8) 11.00 11.00

Souvenir Sheet

925 A156 5m multicolored 6.00 6.00
926 A156 5m multicolored 6.00 6.00

Christmas A158

Details or entire paintings: 20s, Virgin and Child, by Sassetta. 30s, Coronation of the Virgin, by Master of Bonastre. 40s, Virgin and Child, by Master of Saints Cosmas and Damian. 70s, The Virgin of Great Panagia, by Russian School, 12th cent. 1m, Madonna and Child, by Vincenzo Foppa. 2m, Madonna and Child, by School of Lippo Memmi. 3m, Virgin and Child, by Barnaba da Modena. 4m, Virgin and Child, by Simone Dei Crocifissi. No. 935, Virgin & Child Enthroned & Surrounded by Angels, by Cimabue. No. 936, Virgin and Child with Saints (entire triptych), by Dei Crocifissi.

1992, Nov. 2 Litho. *Perf. 13½x14*

927 A158 20s multicolored .20 .20
928 A158 30s multicolored .45 .45
929 A158 40s multicolored .55 .55
930 A158 70s multicolored 1.10 1.10
931 A158 1m multicolored 1.50 1.50
932 A158 2m multicolored 2.75 2.75
933 A158 3m multicolored 4.25 4.25
934 A158 4m multicolored 5.75 5.75
Nos. 927-934 (8) 16.55 16.55

Souvenir Sheets

935 A158 5m multicolored 7.00 7.00
936 A158 5m multicolored 7.00 7.00

Souvenir Sheet

World Trade Center, New York City — A159

1992, Oct. 28 Litho. *Perf. 14*
937 A159 5m multicolored 8.50 8.50

Postage Stamp Mega Event '92, NYC.

Anniversaries and Events — A160

Designs: 20s, Baby harp seal. 30s, Giant panda. 40s, Graf Zeppelin, globe. 70s, Woman grinding corn. 4m, Zeppelin shot down over Cuffley, UK by Lt. Leefe Robinson flying BE 2c, WWI. No. 943, Valentina Tereshkova, first woman in space. No. 944, West African crowned cranes. No. 945, Dr. Ronald McNair.

1993, Jan. Litho. *Perf. 14*
938 A160 20s multicolored .20 .20
939 A160 30s multicolored .40 .40
940 A160 40s multicolored .50 .50
941 A160 70s multicolored .90 .90
942 A160 4m multicolored 5.25 5.25
943 A160 5m multicolored 6.25 6.25
Nos. 938-943 (6) 13.50 13.50

Souvenir Sheets
944 A160 5m multicolored 7.25 7.25
945 A160 5m multicolored 7.25 7.25

Earth Summit, Rio de Janeiro (#938-939, 944). Count Zeppelin, 75th death anniv. (#940, 942). Intl. Conference on Nutrition, Rome (#941). Intl. Space Year (#943, 945).

A number has been reserved for an additional value in this set.

Louvre Museum, Bicent. A161

No. 947 — Details or entire paintings, by Nicolas Poussin: a, Orpheus and Eurydice. b-c, Rape of the Sabine Women (left, right). d-e, The Death of Sapphira (left, right). f-g, Echo and Narcissus (left, right). h, Self-portrait.

No. 948, The Moneychanger and His Wife, by Quentin Metsys.

1993, Mar. 19 Litho. *Perf. 12*
947 A161 70s Sheet of 8, #a.-h. + label 9.50 9.50

Souvenir Sheet
Perf. 14½
948 A161 5m multicolored 8.00 8.00

No. 948 contains one 55x88mm stamp.

Flowers — A162

1993, June Litho. *Perf. 14*
949 A162 20s Healing plant .20 .20
950 A162 30s Calla lily .25 .25
951 A162 40s Bird of Paradise .30 .30
952 A162 70s Belladonna .75 .75
953 A162 1m African lily 1.00 1.00
954 A162 2m Veldt lily 2.00 2.00
955 A162 4m Watsonia 4.25 4.25
956 A162 5m Gazania 5.25 5.25
Nos. 949-956 (8) 14.00 14.00

Souvenir Sheets
957 A162 7m Leadwort 6.25 6.25
958 A162 7m Desert rose 6.25 6.25

Miniature Sheet

Coronation of Queen Elizabeth II, 40th Anniv. — A163

No. 959: a, 20s, Official coronation photograph. b, 40s, St. Edward's Crown, Scepter with the Cross. c, 1m, Queen Mother. d, 5m, Queen, family.

7m, Conversation Piece at Royal Lodge, Windsor, by Sir James Gunn, 1950.

1993, June 2 Litho. *Perf. 13½x14*
959 A163 Sheet, 2 each, #a.-d. 16.00 16.00

Souvenir Sheet
Perf. 14
960 A163 7m multicolored 7.50 7.50

Butterflies A164

1993, June 30 Litho. *Perf. 14*
961 A164 20s Bi-colored pansy .20 .20
962 A164 40s Golden pansy .35 .35
963 A164 70s Yellow pansy .55 .55
964 A164 1m Pseudo ergolid .90 .90
965 A164 2m African giant swallowtail 1.75 1.75
966 A164 5m False acraea 4.50 4.50
Nos. 961-966 (6) 8.25 8.25

Souvenir Sheets
967 A164 7m Seasonal pansy 5.75 5.75
968 A164 7m Ringed pansy 5.75 5.75

African Trains A165

Designs: 20s, East African Railways Vulcan 2-8-2, 1929. 30s, Zimbabwe Railways Class 15A, 1952. 40s, South African Railways Class 25 4-8-4, 1953. 70s, East African Railways A58 Class Garratt. 1m, South Africa Class 9E Electric. 2m, East African Railways Class 87, 1971. 3m, East African Railways Class 92, 1971. 5m, South Africa Class 26 2-D-2, 1982. #977, Algeria 231-132BT Class, 1937. #978, South African Railway Class 6E Bo-Bo, 1969.

1993, Sept. 24 Litho. *Perf. 14*
969 A165 20s multicolored .20 .20
970 A165 30s multicolored .40 .40
971 A165 40s multicolored .45 .45
972 A165 70s multicolored .90 .90
973 A165 1m multicolored 1.25 1.25
974 A165 2m multicolored 2.40 2.40
975 A165 3m multicolored 3.75 3.75
976 A165 5m multicolored 6.00 6.00
Nos. 969-976 (8) 15.35 15.35

Souvenir Sheets
977 A165 7m multicolored 7.50 7.50
978 A165 7m multicolored 7.50 7.50

Taipei '93 — A166

Disney characters in Taiwan: 20s, Chung Cheng Park, Keelung. 30s, Chiao-Tienkung Temple Festival. 40s, Procession. 70s, Temple Festival. 1m, Queen's Head Rock Formation, Yehliu, vert. 1.20m, Natl. Concert Hall, Taiwan, vert. 2m, C.K.S. Memorial Hall, Taiwan, vert. 2.50m, Grand Hotel, Taipei.

No. 987, 5m, Natl. Palace Museum, Taipei. No. 988, 6m, Presidential Palace Museum, Taipei, vert.

1993 Litho. *Perf. 14x13½, 13½x14*
979-986 A166 Set of 8 14.00 14.00

Souvenir Sheets
987-988 A166 Set of 2 12.00 12.00

Domestic Cats — A167

Various cats: 20s, 30s, 70s, 5m.

No. 992A, Brown cat eating mouse, vert.

1993, Oct. 29 Litho. *Perf. 14*
989-992 A167 Set of 4 7.00 7.00

Souvenir Sheet
992A A167 5m multicolored 6.00 6.00

Traditional Houses A168

Designs: 20s, Khoaling, Khotla. 30s, Lelapa le seotloana morao ho, 1833. 70s, Thakaneng, Baroetsana. 4m, Mohlongoafatse pele ho, 1833.

No. 996A, Lelapa litema le mekhabiso.

1993, Sept. 24
993-996 A168 Set of 4 8.00 8.00

Souvenir Sheet
996A A168 4m multicolored 6.00 6.00

A169

A170

Players, country: 20s, Khomari, Lesotho. 30s, Mohale, Lesotho. 40s, Davor, Yugoslavia; Rincon, Colombia. 50s, Lekhotla, Lesotho. 70s, Khali, Lesotho. 1m, Milla, Cameroun. 1.20m, Platt, England. 2m, Rummenigge, Germany; Lerby, Denmark.

No. 1005, Stejskal & Hasek, Czechoslovakia; Baresi, Italy, horiz. No. 1006, Lindenberger, Czechoslovakia; Schillaci, Italy.

1993 Litho. *Perf. 13½x14*
997-1004 A169 Set of 8 10.50 10.50

Souvenir Sheets
Perf. 13
1005-1006 A169 6m Set of 2 12.00 12.00

1994 World Cup Soccer Championships, US.

1994, Apr. 2 Litho. *Perf. 14*

New Democratic Government: 20s, King Letsie III signs oath of office under new constitution. 30s, Parliament building. 50s, Dr. Ntsu Mokhehle sworn in as prime minister. 70s, Transfer of power from Major Gen. P. Ramaema to Dr. Mokhehle.

30s, 50s, 70s are horizontal.

1007 A170 20s multicolored .20 .20
1008 A170 30s multicolored .45 .45
1009 A170 50s multicolored .70 .70
1010 A170 70s multicolored 1.00 1.00
Nos. 1007-1010 (4) 2.35 2.35

A171

PHILAKOREA '94 — A172

Frogs: 35s, Aquatic river. 50s, Bubbling kassina. 1m, Guttural toad. 1.50m, Common river.

No. 1015, 5m, Green frog statue. No. 1016, 5m, Black spotted frog, oriental white-eye bird, vert.

1994, Aug. 16 Litho. *Perf. 14*
1011-1014 A171 Set of 4 3.25 3.25

Souvenir Sheets
1015-1016 A172 Set of 2 12.00 12.00

ICAO, 50th Anniv. A173

Designs: 35s, Airplane, passengers on ground. 50s, Airplane, control tower. 1m, Airplane banking, terminal, control tower. 1.50m, Airplane ascending.

1994 Litho. *Perf. 14*
1017 A173 35s multicolored .20 .20
1018 A173 50s multicolored .65 .65
1019 A173 1m multicolored 1.25 1.25
1020 A173 1.50m multicolored 2.00 2.00
Nos. 1017-1020 (4) 4.10 4.10

Medicinal Plants — A174

Designs: 35s, Tagetes minuta. 50s, Plantago lanceolata. 1m, Amaranthus spinosus. 1.50m, Taraxacum officinale. 5m, Datura stramonium.

1995, May 22 Litho. *Perf. 14*
1021-1024 A174 Set of 4 2.25 2.25

Souvenir Sheet
1025 A174 5m multicolored 3.00 3.00

Pius XII Natl. University, 50th Anniv. A175

Designs: 35s, Pius XII College, 1962. 50s, Univ. of Basutoland, Bechuanaland Protectorate & Swaziland, 1965. 70s, Univ. of Botswana, Lesotho & Swaziland, 1970. 1m, Univ. of Bostswana, Lesotho & Swaziland, 1975. 1.50m, Natl. Univ. of Lesotho, 1988. 2m, Natl. Univ. of Lesotho, procession of vice-chancellors at celebration.

1995, July 26 Litho. *Perf. 14*
1026-1031 A175 Set of 6 4.50 4.50

A176

A177

Designs: 35s, Qiloane Pinnacle, Thaba-Bosiu, horiz. 50s, Rock Formation, Ha Mohalenyane, horiz. 1m, Botsoela Falls, Malealea. 1.50m, Backpacking, Makhaleng River Gorge, horiz.
4m, Red hot pokers.

1995, Aug. 28 Litho. *Perf. 14*
1032-1035 A176 Set of 4 3.00 3.00

Souvenir Sheet

1036 A176 4m multicolored 2.50 2.50

No. 1036 contains one 38x58mm stamp.
World Tourism Organization, 20th anniv.
No. 1036 withdrawn 9/15 because "Pokers" was misspelled "Porkers."

1995, Sept. 26

UN emblem and: 35s, Peace dove. 50s, Scales of justice. 1.50m, Handshake of reconciliation, horiz.

1037-1039 A177 Set of 3 2.50 2.50

UN, 50th anniv.

Christmas A178

Roses: 35s, Sutter's Gold. 50s, Michele Meilland. 1m, J. Otto Thilow. 2m, Papa Meilland.

1995, Nov. 1 Litho. *Perf. 14*
1040-1043 A178 Set of 4 3.00 3.00

A179

A180

UNICEF, 50th Anniv.: 35s, Using iodized salt. 50s, Taking care of livestock, horiz. 70s, Children in classroom. horiz. 1.50m, Children learning traditional dance, singing, horiz.

1996, July 30 Litho. *Perf. 14*
1044-1047 A179 Set of 4 2.50 2.50

1996, Aug. 1

1996 Summer Olympic Games, Atlanta: 1m, US Basketball team, 1936, horiz. 1.50m, Olympic Stadium, Brandenburg Gate, Berlin, horiz. 2m, Jesse Owens, 1936. 3m, Motor boating, horiz.

Past Olympic medalists: No. 1052a, Glen Morris, long jump, decathlon, 1936. b, Said Aouita, 5000-meters, 1984. c, Arnie Robinson, long jump, 1976. d, Hans Woellke, shot put, 1936. e, Renate Stecher, 100-meters, 1972. f, Evelyn Ashford, 100-meters, 1984. g, Willie Davenport, 110-meter hurdles, 1968. h, Bob Beamon, long jump, 1968. i, Heidi Rosendhal, long jump, 1972.

No. 1053, 8m, Michael Gross, swimming, 1984. No. 1054, 8m, Kornelia Ender, swimming, 1976.

1048-1051 A180 Set of 4 4.50 4.50
1052 A180 1.50m Sheet of 9, #a.-i. 11.50 11.50

Souvenir Sheets

1053-1054 A180 Set of 2 12.50 12.50

Maps of Lesotho — A181

No. 1055 — 1911 map: a, Lephaqlioa. b, Maqaleng. c, Molapo. d, Nkeu. e, No area specified. f, Rafanyane. g, No area specified (7800). h, Madibomatso River. i, Konyani. j, Semena River.

No. 1056 — 1978 map: a, No area specified. b, Lepaqoa. c, Mamoha (name). d, Ha Nkisi. e, Ha Rafanyan, Ha Thoora. f, Ha Mikia, Ha Ntseli. g, Ha Kosetabole, Ha Mpeli. h, Ha Selebeli, Ha Theko. i, Ha Rapooane, Ha Ramabotsa. j, Ha Ramani, Khohlontso (Kolberg).

No. 1057 — Locations on 1994 Map: a, Mafika-Lisiu Pass. b, Rampai's Pass, Ha Lesaoana. c, Ha Masaballa. d, Ha Nkisi, Ha Molotanyan. e, Ha Rafanyane, Kobong. f, Laitsoka Pass. g, Katse Reservoir. h, Seshote. i, Ha Rapoeea, Ha Kennan. j, Katse (i, name), Ha Mense.

1996

Sheets of 10, #a-j

1055-1057 A181 35s Set of 3 15.00 15.00

Trains A182

No. 1058, 1.50m: a, ETR 450, Italy. b, TGV, France. c, XPT, Australia. d, Blue Train, South Africa. e, IC 255, Great Britain. f, Bullet Train, Japan.

No. 1059, 1.50m: a, WP Streamlined 4-6-2, India. b, Canadian Pacific 2471, Canada. c, The Caledonian 4-2-2, Scotland. d, William Mason 4-4-0, US. e, Trans-Siberian Express, Russia. f, Swiss Federal 4-6-0, Switzerland.

No. 1060, 8m, 52 Class, Germany. No. 1061, 8m, ICE, Germany.

1996, Sept. 1 Litho. *Perf. 14*

Sheets of 6, #a-f

1058-1059 A182 Set of 2 12.50 12.50

Souvenir Sheets

1060-1061 A182 Set of 2 12.00 12.00

Nos. 1060-1061 each contain one 56x42mm stamp.

No. 833 Surcharged

1996 Litho. *Perf. 13½*
1062 A146 20s on 30s multi .20 .20

Christmas — A183

Women from Mother's Unions: 35s, Methodist Church. 50s, Roman Catholic Church. 1m, Lesotho Evangelical Church. 1.50m, Anglican Church.

1996, Dec. 10 Litho. *Perf. 14*
1063-1066 A183 Set of 4 2.75 2.75

Highlands Water Project A184

Designs: 35s, "Cooperation for Development." 50s, "Nature and Heritage." 1m, "An Engineering Feat." 1.50m, "LHDA 10th Anniv., 1986-1996."

1997, Apr. 21 Litho. *Perf. 14*
1067-1070 A184 Set of 4 3.25 3.25

No. 1070 is 72x25mm.

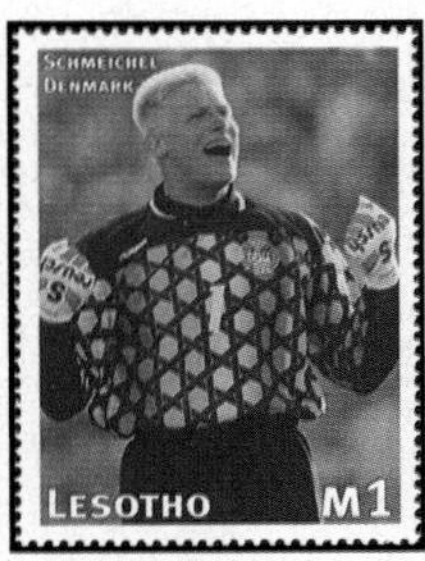

1998 World Cup Soccer Championships, France — A185

Players: 1m, Schmeichel, Denmark. 1.50m, Bergkamp, Holland. 2m, Southgate, England. 2.50m, Asprilla, Colombia. 3m, Gascoigne, England. 4m, Giggs, Wales.

No. 1077: Various action scenes of Argentina vs. Holland, 1978.

No. 1078, 8m, Littbarski, W. Germany, horiz. No. 1079, 8m, Shearer, England.

1997, Oct. 31 Litho. *Perf. 13½*
1071-1076 A185 Set of 6 7.00 7.00
1077 A185 1.50m Sheet of 6, #a.-f. 11.50 11.50

Souvenir Sheets

1078-1079 A185 Set of 2 9.50 9.50

Butterflies A186

No. 1080: a, Spialia spio. b, Cyclyrius pirithous. c, Acraea satis. d, Belenois aurota. e, Spindasis natalensis. f, Torynesis orangica. g, Lepidochrysops variabilis. h, Pinacopteryx eriphea. i, Anthene butleri.

No. 1081, 8m, Bematistes aganice. No. 1082, 8m, Papilio demodocus.

1997, Nov. 28 *Perf. 14*
1080 A186 1.50m Sheet of 9, #a.-i. 7.00 7.00

Souvenir Sheets

1081-1082 A186 Set of 2 12.00 12.00

Morija Museum and Archives, 40th Anniv. A187

Designs: 35s, Rock paintings, child, vert. 45s, Lower jaw of hippopotamus, hippo walking in water. 50s, Traditional attire, vert. 1m, Traditional musical instruments, vert. 1.50m, Award, Man with ceremonial garb, vert. 2m Boy riding bull.

Perf. 14½ Syncopated Type A

1998, Jan. 30 Litho.
1083-1088 A187 Set of 6 3.50 3.50

Diana, Princess of Wales (1961-97) — A188

Designs: No. 1089, Various portaits. No. 1090, Taking flowers from child.

1998, Mar. 16 Litho. *Perf. 13½*
1089 A188 3m Sheet of 6, #a.-f. 9.00 9.00

Souvenir Sheet

1090 A188 9m multicolored 9.50 9.50

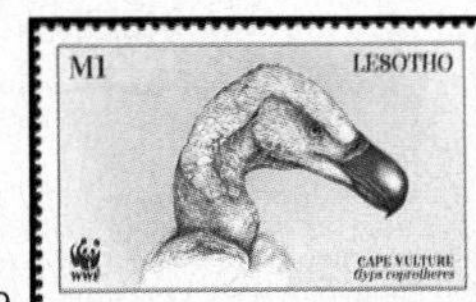

A189

A190

Wildlife — A191

No. 1091 — Cape vulture: a, Head. b, Perched on rock with head down. c, Looking left. d, Looking right.

No. 1092: a, Atitlan grebe. b, Cabot's tragopan. c, Spider monkey. d, Dibatag. e, Right whale. f, Imperial parrot. g, Cheetah. h, Brown-eared pheasant. i, Leatherback turtle. j, Imperial woodpecker. k, Andean condor. l, Barbary deer. m, Grey gentle lemur. n, Cuban parrot. o, Numbat. p, Short-tailed albatross. q, Green turtle. r, White rhinoceros. s, Diademed sifaka. t, Galapagos penguin.

No. 1093: a, Impala. b, Black bear. c, Buffalo. d, Elephant. e, Kangaroo. f, Lion. g, Panda. h, Tiger. i, Zebra.

No. 1094, 8m, Nectarinia talatala. No. 1095, 8m, Psephotus chrysopterygius. No. 1096, 8m, Percina tanasi.

No. 1097, 8m, Monkey.

1998, Apr. 27 Litho. *Perf. 14*
1091 A189 1m Strip of 4, #a.-d. *5.00 5.00*
1092 A190 1m Sheet of 20, #a.-t. 12.00 12.00
1093 A191 1.50m Sheet of 9, #a.-i. 7.50 7.50

Souvenir Sheets

1094-1096 A190 Set of 3 12.00 12.00
1097 A191 8m multicolored 4.00 4.00

No. 1091 was issued in sheets of 12 stamps. World Wildlife Fund (#1091).

Cats A192

Designs: 70s, Siamese. 1m, Chartreux. 2m, Korat. 3m, Egyptian mau. 4m, Bombay. 5m, Burmese.

No. 1104, 2m: a, Japanese bobtail. b, British white. c, Bengal. d, Abyssinian. e, Snowshoe. f, Scottish fold.

No. 1105, 2m: a, Maine coon. b, Balinese. c, Persian. d, Javanese. e, Turkish angora. f, Tiffany.

No. 1106, 8m, Singapura. No. 1107, 8m, Tonkinese.

1998, May 18
1098-1103 A192 Set of 6 7.75 7.75

Sheets of 6, #a-f

1104-1105 A192 Set of 2 16.00 16.00

Souvenir Sheets

1106-1107 A192 Set of 2 10.00 10.00

Mushrooms — A193

Designs: 70s, Laccaria laccata. 1m, Mutinus caninus. 1.50m, Tricholoma lascivum. 2m, Clitocybe geotrapa. 3m, Amanita excelsa. 4m, Red-capped bolete.

No. 1114: a, Parrot wax cap. b, Cortinarius obtusus. c, Volvariella bombycina. d, Cortinarius caerylescens. e, Laccaria amethystea. f, Tricholoma aurantium. g, Amanita excelsa. h, Clavaria helvola. i, Cortinarius caerylescens. j, Russula queletii. k, Amanita phalloides. l, Lactarius delicious.

No. 1115, 8m, Amanita pantherina. No. 1116, 8m, Boletus satanus.

1998, June 15 Litho. *Perf. 14*
1108-1113 A193 Set of 6 7.00 7.00
1114 A193 1m Sheet of 12, #a.-l. 7.00 7.00

Souvenir Sheets

1115-1116 A193 Set of 2 10.00 10.00

Japanese Film Stars A194

No. 1117: a, Takamine Hideko. b, James Shigeta. c, Miyoshi Umeki. d, May Ishimara. e, Sessue Hayakawa. f, Miiko Taka. g, Mori Masayuki. h, Hara Setsuko. i, Kyo Machiko.

10m, Toshiro Mifune.

1998, July 14 Litho. *Perf. 14*
1117 A194 2m Sheet of 9, #a.-i. 8.00 8.00

Souvenir Sheet

1118 A194 10m multicolored 4.00 4.00

Prehistoric Animals — A195

No. 1119, 2m: a, Nyctosaurus (b). b, Volcanoes, wings of nyctosaurus, eudimorphadon. c, Eudimorphodon (b). d, Apatosaurus (g). e, Peteinosaurus (d, f, i). f, Tropeognathus. g, Pteranodon ingens (d). h, Ornithodesmus (g, i). i, Wuerhosaurus.

No. 1120, 2m: a, Ceresiosaurus (b, c, d). b, Rhomaleosaurus (d, e, f). c, Anomalocaris (b, f). d, Mixosaurus (e, g, h). e, Stethacanthus. f, Dunklosteus (c, e, i). g, Tommotia. h, Sanctacaris. i, Ammonites (a, f, h).

No. 1121, 2m: a, Rhamphorhynchus (b, d). b, Brachiosaurus (c, f). c, Mamenchisaurus hochuanensis (a, d, e, f). d, Ceratosaurus nasicornis (e, g, h). e, Archaeopteryx (b). f, Leaellynasaura amicargraphica (e, h, i). g, Chasmosaurus belli (h). h, Deinonychus, Pachyrhinosaurus (g). i, Deinonychus (h).

No. 1122, 10m, Woolly rhinoceros. No. 1123, 10m, Tyrannosaurus. No. 1124, 10m, Coelophysis.

1998, Aug. 10

Sheets of 9, #a-i

1119-1121 A195 Set of 3 27.00 27.00

Souvenir Sheets

1122-1124 A195 Set of 3 18.00 18.00

Intl. Year of the Ocean A196

Fish: No. 1125, 1m, Treefish. No. 1126, 1m, Tiger barb. No. 1127, 1m, Bandtail puffer. No. 1128, 1m, Cod. No. 1129, 1.50m, Filefish. No. 1130, 1.50m, Clown loach. No. 1131, 1.50m, Sicklefin killie. No. 1132, 1.50m, Christy's lyretail. No. 1133, 2m, Brook trout. No. 1134, 2m, Pacific electric ray. No. 1135, 2m, Bighead searobin. No. 1136, 2m, Emerald betta. 3m, Harlequin tuskfish. 4m, Half-moon angelfish. 5m, Spotted trunkfish. 6m, Wolf-eel. 7m, Cherubfish.

No. 1142, 2m: a, Platy variatus. b, Archerfish. c, Clown knifefish. d, Angelicus. e, Black arowana. f, Spotted scat. g, Kribensis. h, Golden pheasant.

No. 1143, 2m: a, Bluegill. b, Grayling. c, Walleye. d, Brown trout. e, Atlantic salmon. f, Northern pike. g, Large mouth bass. h, Rainbow trout.

No. 1144, 2m: a, Purple firefish. b, Halequin sweetlips. c, Clown wrasse. d, Bicolor angelfish. e, False cleanerfish. f, Mandarinfish. g, Regal tang. h, Clownfish.

No. 1145, 2m: a, Weakfish. b, Red drum. c, Blue marlin. d, Yellowfin tuna. e, Barracuda. f, Striped bass. g, White shark. h, Permit.

No. 1146, 12m, Cyprinus carpio. No. 1147, 12m,Oncorhychus. No. 1148, 12m,Pseudopleuronectes americanus. No. 1149, 12m, Heterodontus francisci.

1998, Oct. 15 Litho. *Perf. 14*
1125-1141 A196 Set of 17 17.25 17.25

Sheets of 8, #a-h

1142-1145 A196 Set of 4 26.00 26.00

Souvenir Sheets

1146-1149 A196 Set of 4 19.00 19.00

Africa in Films A197

No. 1150: a, "Simba." b, "Call to Freedom." c, "Cry the Beloved Country." d, "King Solomon's Mines." e, "Flame and the Fire." f, "Cry Freedom." g, "Bopha!" h, "Zulu."

10m "Born Free," horiz.

1998, July 14 Litho. *Perf. 14*
1150 A197 2m Sheet of 8, #a.-h. 8.00 8.00

Souvenir Sheet

1151 A197 10m multicolored 4.00 4.00

Flowers — A198

Designs: 10s, Pelargonium sidoides. 15s, Aponogeton ranunculiflorus. 20s, Sebaea leiostyla. 40s, Sebaea grandis. 50s, Satyrium neglectum. 60s, Massonia jasminiflora. 70s, Ajuga ophrydis. 80s, Nemesia fruticans. 1m, Aloe broomii. 2m, Wahlenbergia androsacea. 2.50m, Phygelius capensis. 3m, Dianthus basuticus. 4.50m, Rhodohypoxis baurii. 5m, Turbina oblongata. 6m, Hibiscus microcarpus. 10m, Lobelia erinus, moraea stricta.

1998 Litho. *Perf. 14*

1152	A198	10s	multicolored	.20	.20
1153	A198	15s	multicolored	.20	.20
1154	A198	20s	multicolored	.20	.20
1155	A198	40s	multicolored	.20	.20
1156	A198	50s	multicolored	.20	.20
1157	A198	60s	multicolored	.20	.20
1158	A198	70s	multicolored	.25	.25
1159	A198	80s	multicolored	.40	.40
1160	A198	1m	multicolored	.50	.50
1161	A198	2m	multicolored	1.00	1.00
1162	A198	2.50m	multicolored	1.25	1.25
1163	A198	3m	multicolored	1.50	1.50
1164	A198	4.50m	multicolored	2.25	2.25
1165	A198	5m	multicolored	2.40	2.40
1166	A198	6m	multicolored	3.00	3.00
1167	A198	10m	multicolored	5.25	5.25
	Nos. 1152-1167 (16)			19.00	19.00

Nos. 1152-1167 are dated 1997.

Coronation of King Letsie III, 1st Anniv. — A199

No. 1168: a, Receiving crown. b, Waving. c, Facing left.

1998, Oct. 31
1168 A199 1m Strip of 3, #a.-c. 2.40 2.40

Dogs A200

Designs: 70s, Akita. 1m, Canaan. 2m, Eskimo. 4.50m, Norwegian elkhound.

No. 1173, 2m: a, Cirneco dell'etna. b, Afghan hound. c, Finnish spitz. d, Dalmatian. e, Basset hound. f, Shar-pei.

No. 1174, 2m: a, Boxer. b, Catalan sheepdog. c, English toy spaniel. d, Greyhound. e, Keeshond. f, Bearded collie.

No. 1175, 8m, Rough collie. No. 1176, 8m, Borzoi.

1999, May 18 Litho. *Perf. 14*
1169-1172 A200 Set of 4 4.00 4.00

Sheets of 6, #a-f

1173-1174 A200 Set of 2 11.00 11.00

Souvenir Sheets

1175-1176 A200 Set of 2 11.00 11.00

Birds A201

Designs: 70s, Belted kingfisher. 1.50m, Palm cockatoo, vert. 2m, Red-tailed hawk. 3m, Tufted puffin. 4m, Reddish egret. 5m, Hoatzin, vert.

No. 1183, 2m: a, Evening grosbeak. b, Lesser blue-winged pitta. c, Altamira oriole. d, Rose-breasted grosbeak. e, Yellow warbler. f, Akiapolaau. g, American goldfinch. h, Northern flicker. i, Western tanager.

No. 1184, 2m, vert: a, Blue jay. b, Northern cardinal. c, Yellow-headed blackbird. d, Red. crossbill. e, Cedar waxwing. f, Vermilion flycatcher. g, Pileated woodpecker. h, Western meadowlark. i, Kingfisher.

No. 1185, 8m, Great egret. No. 1186, 8m, Zosterops erythropleura.

1999, June 28 Litho. *Perf. 14*
1177-1182 A201 Set of 6 8.00 8.00

Sheets of 9, #a-i

1183-1184 A201 Set of 2 19.00 19.00

Souvenir Sheets

1185-1186 A201 Set of 2 11.00 11.00

No. 1183c is incorrectly inscribed "Atlamira."

Orchids — A202

Chinese Art — A203

Designs: 1.50m, Cattleya dowiana. 3m, Diurus behri. 4m, Ancistrochilus rothchildianus. 5m, Aerangis curnowiana. 7m, Arachnis flos-aeris. 8m, Aspasia principissa.

No. 1193, 2m: a, Dendrobium bellaudum. b, Dendrobium trigonopus. c, Dimerandra emarginata. d, Dressleria eburnea. e, Dracula tubeana. f, Disa kirstenbosch. g, Encyclia alata. h, Epidendrum pseudepidendrum. i, Eriopsis biloba.

No. 1194, 2m: a, Apasia epidendroides. b, Barkaria lindleyana. c, Bifrenaria terragona. d, Bulbophyllum graveolens. e, Brassavola flagellaris. f, Bollea lawrenceana. g, Caladenia carnea. h, Catasetum macrocarpum. i, Cattleya aurantiaca.

No. 1195, 2m: a, Cochleanthes discolor. b, Cischweinfia dasyandra. c, Ceratostylis retisquama. d, Comparettia speciosa. e, Cryptostylis subulata. f, Cycnoches ventricsum. g, Dactylorhiza maculata. h, Cypripedium calceolus. i, Cymbidium finlaysonianum.

No. 1196, 10m, Paphiopedilum tonsum. No. 1197, 10m, Laelia rubescens. No. 1198, 10m, Ansellium africana. No. 1199, 10m, Ophrys apifera.

1999, July 30 Litho. *Perf. 14*
1187-1192 A202 Set of 6 13.00 13.00

Sheets of 9, #a-i

1193-1195 A202 Set of 3 22.50 22.50

Souvenir Sheets

1196-1199 A202 Set of 4 16.00 16.00

1999, Aug. 16 *Perf. 13x13¼*

No. 1200 — Paintings by Pan Tianshou (1897-1971): a, Water Lily at Night. b, Hen and Chicks. c, Plum Blossom and Orchid. d, Plum Blossom and Banana Tree. e, Crane and Pine. f, Swallows. g, Eagle on the Pine (black eagle). h, Palm Tree. i, Eagle on the Pine (gray eagle). j, Orchids.

No. 1201: a, Sponge Gourd. b, Dragonfly.

1200 A203 1.50m Sheet of 10, #a.-j. 9.00 9.00

Souvenir Sheet

1201 A203 6m Sheet of 2, #a.-b. 7.00 7.00

China 1999 World Philatelic Exhibition. No. 1201 contains two 51x40mm stamps.

Souvenir Sheet

UN Rights of the Child Convention, 10th Anniv. — A204

No. 1202: a, Black boy. b, Asian girl. c, Caucasian boy.

1999, Aug. 16 ***Perf. 14***
1202 A204 2m Sheet of 3, #a.-c. 4.00 4.00

Paintings by Hokusai (1760-1849) — A205

No. 1203, 3m: a, Nakamaro Watching the Moon from a Hill. b, Peonies and Butterfly. c, The Blind (bald man, both eyes open). d, The Blind (bald man, one eye shut). e, People Crossing an Arched Bridge (two at crest). f, People Crossing an Arched Bridge (river).

No. 1204, 3m: a, A View of Sumida River in Snow. b, Two Carp. c, The Blind (man with hair, both eyes shut). d, The Blind (man with hair, one eye open). e, Fishing by Torchlight. f, Whaling off the Goto Islands.

No. 1205, 10m, The Moon Above Yodo River and Osaka Castle, vert. No. 1206, 10m, Bellflower and Dragonfly, vert.

1999, Aug. 16 ***Perf. 13¾***
Sheet of 6, #a-f
1203-1204 A205 Set of 2 14.00 14.00
Souvenir Sheets
1205-1206 A205 Set of 2 8.00 8.00

Queen Mother (b. 1900) — A206

No. 1207: a, Wearing hat, 1938. b, With King George VI, 1948. c, Wearing tiara, 1963. d, Wearing hat, 1989.
15m, Waving at Clarence House.

1999, Aug. 16 ***Perf. 14***
1207 A206 5m Sheet of 4, #a.-d., + label 9.00 9.00
Souvenir Sheet
Perf. 13¾
1208 A206 15m multicolored 7.00 7.00

No. 1208 contains one 38x51mm stamp.

Johann Wolfgang von Goethe (1749-1832) — A207

No. 1209: a, Mephistopheles appears as a dog in Faust's study. b, Portraits of Goethe and Friedrich von Schiller. c, Mephistopheles disguised as dog scorching the earth.
12m, Mephistopheles.

1999, Aug. 16 ***Perf. 14***
1209 A207 6m Sheet of 3, #a.-c. 7.00 7.00
Souvenir Sheet
1210 A207 12m multicolored 5.00 5.00

IBRA '99, Nuremberg, Germany — A208

Designs: 7m, Austerity 2-10-10 locomotive, building in Frankfurt am Main. 8m, Adler locomotive, Brandenburg Gate.

1999, Aug. 16 ***Perf. 14x14½***
1211 A208 7m multicolored 3.00 3.00
1212 A208 8m multicolored 3.50 3.50

Ships A209

No. 1213, 4m: a, James Watt. b, Savannah. c, Amistad. d, Brick. e, Great Briain. f, Sirius.

No. 1214, 4m: a, France. b, Queen Elizabeth II. c, United States. d, Queen Elizabeth I. e, Michelangelo. f, Mauretania.

No. 1215, 4m: a, New Jersey. b, Aquila. c, De Zeven Provincien. d, Formidable. e, Vittorio Veneto. f, Hampshire.

No. 1216, 4m: a, Shearwater. b, British submarine. c, Hovercraft SRN 130. d, Italian submarine. e, Sr. N/3. f, Soucoupe Plongeante.

No. 1217, 15m, E. W. Morrison. No. 1218, 15m, Titanic. No. 1219, 15m, German U-boat. No. 1220, 15m, Enterprise.

1999, Dec. 31 **Litho.** ***Perf. 14***
Sheets of 6, #a.-f.
1213-1216 A209 32.00 32.00
Souvenir Sheets
1217-1220 A209 Set of 4 22.50 22.50

Names of ships are only found on sheet margins.

Millennium A210

No. 1221 — Highlights of the 12th century: a, Chinese make first rocket. b, Burmese temple guardian. c, Troubador. d, Abbé Suger. e, Pope Adrian IV. f, King Henry II of England. g, Holy Roman Emperor Barbarossa. h, Yoritomo establishes shogunate in Japan. i, Crusader monument. j, Ibn Rushd translates Aristotle. k, Archbishop Thomas Becket. l, Leaning Tower of Pisa. m, Pivot windmill. n, Saladin. o, Richard the Lion-Hearted. p, Easter Island statues (60x40mm) q, Third Crusade begins.

1999, Dec. 31 ***Perf. 12¾x12½***
1221 A210 1.50m Sheet of 17, #a.-q. 11.00 11.00

Wedding of King Letsie III to Karabo Anne Motsoeneng A211

No. 1222: a, King, bride in Western attire. b, Bride. c, King. d, King, bride in native attire.

2000, Feb. 18 **Litho.** ***Perf. 14***
1222 A211 1m Sheet of 4, #a.-d., + label 4.00 4.00

Prince William, 18th Birthday — A212

No. 1223: a, Wearing bow tie. b, Wearing scarf. c, Wearing striped shirt. d, Wearing sweater, holding car door.
15m, Wearing sweater, diff.

2000, June 21 **Litho.** ***Perf. 14***
1223 A212 4m Sheet of 4, #a-d 7.00 7.00
Souvenir Sheet
Perf. 13¾
1224 A212 15m multi 7.00 7.00

No. 1223 contains four 28x42mm stamps.

First Zeppelin Flight, Cent. — A213

No. 1225 — Ferdinand von Zeppelin and: a, LZ- 127. b, LZ-130. c, LZ-10.
15m, LZ-130, diff.

2000, July 6 ***Perf. 14***
1225 A213 8m Sheet of 3, #a-c 9.00 9.00
Souvenir Sheet
1226 A213 15m multi 7.00 7.00

No. 1225 contains three 42x28mm stamps.

Berlin Film Festival, 50th Anniv. — A214

No. 1227: a, Gena Rowlands. b, Vlastimil Brodsky. c, Carlos Saura. d, La Collectioneuse. e, Le Depart. f, Le Diable Probablement.
15m, Stammheim.

2000, July 6
1227 A214 6m Sheet of 6, #a-f 13.00 13.00
Souvenir Sheet
1228 A214 15m multi 7.00 7.00

Souvenir Sheets

2000 Summer Olympics, Sydney — A215

No. 1229: a, Nedo Nadi. b, Swimming. c, Aztec Stadium, Mexico City and Mexican flag. d, Ancient Greek boxers.

2000, July 6
1229 A215 6m Sheet of 4, #a-d 9.00 9.00

Public Railways, 175th Anniv. — A216

No. 1230: a, George Stephenson. b, Stephenson's patent locomotive engine. c, Stephenson's Britannia Tubular Bridge.

2000, July 6
1230 A216 8m Sheet of 3, #a-c 9.00 9.00

Johann Sebastian Bach (1685-1750) — A217

2000, July 6
1231 A217 15m multi 7.00 7.00

Flowers — A218

Designs: 4m, Moore's crinum. 5m, Flame lily. 6m, Cape clivia. 8m, True sugarbush.

No. 1236, 3m: a, Spotted leaved arum. b, Christmas bells. c, Lady Monson. d, Wild pomegranate. e, Blushing bride. f, Bot River protea.

No. 1237, 3m: a, Starry gardenia. b, Pink hibiscus. c, Dwarf poker. d, Coast kaffirboom. e, Rose cockade. f, Pride of Table Mountain.

No. 1238, 3m: a, Drooping agpanthus. b, Yellow marsh afrikander. c, Weak stemmed painted lady. d, Impala lily. e, Beatrice watsonia. f, Pink arum.

No. 1239, 15m, Green arum. No. 1240, 15m, Red hairy erica, horiz.

2000, July 12

1232-1235 A218 Set of 4 9.00 9.00

Sheets of 6, #a-f

1236-1238 A218 Set of 3 21.00 21.00

Souvenir Sheets

1239-1240 A218 Set of 2 16.00 16.00

Apollo-Soyuz Mission, 25th Anniv. — A219

No. 1241: a, Apollo 18 and Soyuz 19 docked. b, Apollo 18. c, Soyuz 19.

2000, July 6 Litho. *Perf. 14*

1241 A219 8m Sheet of 3, #a-c 10.00 10.00

Souvenir Sheet

1242 A219 15m shown 7.00 7.00

Souvenir Sheet

Albert Einstein (1879-1955) — A220

2000, July 6 *Perf. 14¼*

1243 A220 15m multi 7.00 7.00

Endangered Wildlife — A221

No. 1244, 4m, horiz.: a, Alethe. b, Temminck's pangolin. c, Cheetah. d, African elephant. e, Chimpanzee. f, Northern white rhinoceros.

No. 1245, 4m, horiz.: a, African black rhinoceros. b, Leopard. c, Roseate tern. d, Mountain gorilla. e, Mountain zebra. f, Zanzibar red colobus monkey.

No. 1246, horiz: a, Wildebeest. b, Tree hyrax. c, Red lechwe. d, Eland.

No. 1247, 15m, Dugong. No. 1248, 15m, West African manatee.

2000, Aug. 10 Litho. *Perf. 14*

Sheets of 6, #a-f

1244-1245 A221 Set of 2 18.00 18.00

1246 A221 5m Sheet of 4, #a-d 7.75 7.75

Souvenir Sheets

1247-1248 A221 Set of 2 16.00 16.00

The Stamp Show 2000, London.

Automobiles — A222

No. 1249, 3m: a, 1960 Cadillac El Dorado Seville. b, 1955-75 Citroen DS. c, 1961 Ford Zephyr Zodiac Mk II. d, 1945-55 MG TF. e, 1949-65 Porsche 356. f, 1955 Ford Thunderbird.

No. 1250, 3m: a, 1948-52 Cisitalia 202 Coupe. b, 1990s Dodge Viper. c, 1968-69, TVR Vixen SI. d, 1957-70 Lotus 7. e, 1964-68 Ferrari 275 GTB/4. f, 1951 Pegasus Touring Spider.

No. 1251, 4m: a, 1913 Fiat Type O. b, 1914 Stutz Bearcat. c, 1924 French Levat. d, 1888 Benz Motorwagen. e, 1925 Isota Fraschini Type 8A. f, 1887 Markus Motor Carriage.

No. 1252, 4m: a, 1951 Morris Minor. b, 1935 Hispano-Suiza Type 68. c, 1949 MG TC. d, 1955 Morgan 4/4. e, 1950 Jaguar XK120. f, 1946-49 Triumph 1800/2000 Roadster.

No. 1253, 15m, 1896 Bersey Electric Car. No. 1254, 15m, 1948-71 Morris Minor 1000. No. 1255, 15m, 1953-63 AC Ace. No. 1256, 15m, Ferrari F40, vert.

Illustration reduced.

2000, Sept. 1

Sheets of 6, #a-f

1249-1252 A222 Set of 4 32.50 32.50

Souvenir Sheets

1253-1256 A222 Set of 4 26.50 26.50

Fight Against AIDS A223

Designs: 70s, "Fight AIDS, not people living with it." 1m, "Speed kills, so does AIDS. Go Slow!" 1.50m, "People with AIDS need friends, not rejection," vert. 2.10m, "Even when you're off duty, protect the nation."

2001, Jan. 22 Litho. *Perf. 14*

1257-1260 A223 Set of 4 4.25 4.25

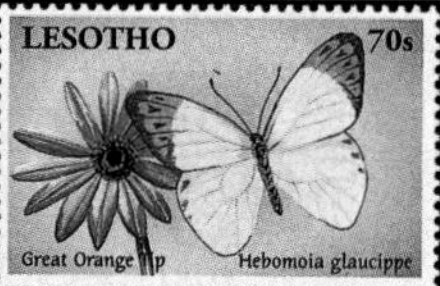

Butterflies A224

Designs: 70s, Great orange tip. 1m, Red-banded pereute. 1.50m, Sword grass brown. No. 1264, 2m, Striped blue crow. No. 1265, 3m, Alfalfa. 4m, Doris.

No. 1267, 2m: a, African migrant. b, Large oak blue. c, Wanderer. d, Tiger swallowtail. e, Union jack. f, Saturn. g, Broad-bordered grass yellow. h, Hewitson's uraneis.

No. 1268, 2m: a, Orange-banded sulfur. b, Large wood nymph. c, Postman. d, Palmfly. e, Gulf fritillary. f, Cairns birdwing. g, Common morpho. h, Common dotted border.

No. 1269, 3m: a, Bertoni's antwren (bird). b, Clorinde. c, Iolas blue. d, Mocker swallowtail. e, Common Indian crow. f, Grecian shoemaker. g, Small flambeau. h, Orchid swallowtail.

No. 1270, 15m, Crimson tip. No. 1271, 15m, Forest queen.

2001, Mar. 1 Litho. *Perf. 13¼x13¾*

1261-1266 A224 Set of 6 5.00 5.00

Sheets of 8, #a-h

1267-1269 A224 Set of 3 21.00 21.00

Souvenir Sheets

1270-1271 A224 Set of 2 13.50 13.50

Phila Nippon '01, Japan A225

Designs: 1.50m, Man in carriage from The Battle of Lepanto and the Map of the World, by unknown artist. 2m, Battle scene from The Battle of Lepanto and the Map of the World. 3m, Crane from Birds and Flowers of the Four Seasons, by Eitoku Kano. 4m, The Four Elegant Pastimes. 7m, Maple Viewing at Mount Takao, by unknown artist. 8m, The Four Accomplishments, by Yusho Kaiho.

No. 1278, 5m: a, Portrait of a Lady, by unknown artist. b, Portrait of Tadakatsu Honda, by unknown artist. c, Portrait of the Wife of Tokujo Goto, by unknown aritst. d, Portrait of Emperor Go-yosei, by Takanobu Kano. e, Portrait of Tenzuiin, Hideyoshi's Mother, by Sochin Hoshuku.

No. 1279, 6m: a, Portrait of Yusai Hosokawa, by Suden Ishin. b, Portrait of Sen No Rikyu, attributed to Tohaku Hasegawa. c, Portrait of Oichi No Kata, by unknown artist. d, Portrait of Ittetsu Inaba, attributed to Hasegawa. e, Portrait of Nobunaga Oda, by Sochin Kokei.

No. 1280, 15m, Portrait of Ieyasu Tokugawa, by unknown artist. No. 1281, 15m, Portrait of Hideyoshi Toyotomi, by unknown artist.

Perf. 13¾, 14 (#1278-1279)

2001, May 31 Litho.

1272-1277 A225 Set of 6 6.00 6.00

Sheets of 5, #a-e

1278-1279 A225 Set of 2 30.00 30.00

Souvenir Sheets

1280-1281 A225 Set of 2 14.00 14.00

Size of stamps on Nos. 1278-1279: 85x28mm.

Nos. 1274-1275 are incorrectly inscribed. No. 1274 actually depicts "Landscape with Flowers and Birds." No. 1275 shows a detail from"The Four Elegant Pastimes," by Eitoku Kano.

Mushrooms A226

Designs: No. 1282, 5m, Bell-shaped panaeolus. No. 1283, 5m, Golden false pholiota. No. 1284, 5m, Shiny cap. No. 1285, 5m, Sooty brown waxy cap.

No. 1286, 3m: a, Violet cortinarius. b, Angel's wings. c, Collybia velutibes. d, Lentinellus. e, Anthurus aseroiformis. f, Caesar's mushroom.

No. 1287, 4m: a, Pungent cortinarius. b, Peziza sarcosphaera. c, Emetic russula. d, Questionable stropharia. e, Apricot jelly mushroom. f, Anise-scented clitocybe.

No. 1288, 15m, Cone-shaped waxy cap, horiz. No. 1289, 15m, Boletus, horiz.

2001, June 29 *Perf. 14*

1282-1285 A226 Set of 4 9.00 9.00

Sheets of 6, #a-f

1286-1287 A226 Set of 2 19.00 19.00

Souvenir Sheets

1288-1289 A226 Set of 2 14.00 14.00

Belgica 2001 Intl. Stamp Exhibition, Brussels (Nos. 1286-1289).

UN High Commissioner for Refugees, 50th Anniv. — A227

Designs: 70s, Silhouette of woman and child. 1m, Child and animal. 1.50m, Woman, vert. 2.10m, Information technology, vert.

2001, Aug. 20 *Perf. 14*

1290-1293 A227 Set of 4 3.00 3.00

Birds of Prey — A228

Designs: 70s, Black kite. 1m, Martial eagle. 1.50m, Bateleur. 2.10m, African goshawk. 2.50m, Bearded vulture. 3m, Jackal buzzard.

2001, Oct. 1 Litho. *Perf. 14*

1294-1299 A228 Set of 6 5.00 5.00

Southern African Wildlife A229

Designs: 1m, Grass owl. 2.10m, Klipspringer. 3m, Saddlebacked jackal. 5m, Black wildebeest.

No. 1304, 4m: a, Damara zebra. b, Bontebok. c, Eland. d, Lion. e, Saddlebacked jackal, diff. f, Yellow-billed kite.

No. 1305, 4m: a, Aardvark. b, Rock kestrel. c, Black-footed cat. d, Springhare. e, Aardwolf. f, Rock hyrax.

No. 1306, 15m, black-shouldered kite. No. 1307, 15m, Caracal, vert.

2001, Oct. 15 Litho. *Perf. 14*

1300-1303 A229 Set of 4 4.25 4.25

Sheets of 6, #a-f

1304-1305 A229 Set of 2 18.00 18.00

Souvenir Sheets

1306-1307 A229 Set of 2 14.00 14.00

Reign of Queen Elizabeth II, 50th Anniv. — A230

No. 1308: a, Queen seated. b, Queen with Prince Philip and British flag. c, Queen with man. c, Prince Philip.
20m, Queen wearing black suit.

2002, Feb. 6 Litho. *Perf. 14¼*

1308 A230 8m Sheet of 4, #a-d 10.00 10.00

Souvenir Sheet

1309 A230 20m multi 8.00 8.00

United We Stand — A231

2002, Aug. 13 *Perf. 14*

1310 A231 7m multi 4.25 4.25

Printed in sheets of 4.

SOS Children's Village, Lithabaneng — A232

2002, Aug. 13

1311 A232 10m multi 5.00 5.00

Rotary International in Lesotho, 25th Anniv. — A233

Designs: 8m, Horner Wood. 10m, Paul Harris.
No. 1314, 25m, Stylized globe and clasped hands. No. 1315, 25m, Golden Gate Bridge, horiz.

2002, Aug. 13

1312-1313 A233 Set of 2 7.00 7.00

Souvenir Sheets

1314-1315 A233 Set of 2 16.00 16.00

20th World Scout Jamboree, Thailand — A234

No. 1316: a, Sheet bend knots. b, Pup and forester tents. c, Canoeing. d, Water rescue.
25m, A night under the stars.

2002, Aug. 13

1316 A234 9m Sheet of 4, #a-d 9.50 9.50

Souvenir Sheet

1317 A234 25m multi 9.00 9.00

Intl. Year of Mountains — A235

No. 1318, horiz.: a, Mt. Machache. b, Mt. Thabana Li-Mèle. c, Mt. Qiloane. d, Mt. Thaba Bosiu.
25m, Mt. Rainier, US.

2002, Aug. 13

1318 A235 8m Sheet of 4, #a-d 6.00 6.00

Souvenir Sheet

1319 A235 25m multi 4.75 4.75

Intl. Year of Ecotourism — A236

No. 1320, horiz.: a, Plant. b, Flowers. c, Man and horses. d, Lion. e, Frog. f, House.
20m, Bird.

2002, Aug. 13

1320 A236 6m Sheet of 6, #a-f 6.75 6.75

Souvenir Sheet

1321 A236 20m multi 3.75 3.75

Flowers, Insects and Spiders — A237

No. 1322, 6m — Flowers: a, Angel's fishing rod. b, Marigold. c, Joan's blood. d, Mule pink. e, Tiger lily. f, Comtesse de Bouchaud.
No. 1323, 6m — Orchids: a, Phragmipedium besseae. b, Cypripedium calceolus. c, Cattleya Louise Georgiana. d, Brassocattleya binosa. e, Laelia gouldiana. f, Paphiopedilum maudiae.
No. 1324, 6m, horiz. — Insects: a, Leaf grasshopper. b, Golden-ringed dragonfly. c, Weevil-hunting wasp. d, European grasshopper. e, Thread-waisted wasp. f, Mantid.
No. 1325, 20m, Bleeding heart. No. 1326, 20m, Brassavola tuberculata. No. 1327, 20m, Orb web spider.

2002, Aug. 30 *Perf. 14*

Sheets of 6, #a-f

1322-1324 A237 Set of 3 21.00 21.00

Souvenir Sheets

1325-1327 A237 Set of 3 11.50 11.50

Coronation of Queen Elizabeth II, 50th Anniv. (in 2003) — A238

No. 1328: a, Wearing blue hat. b, Wearing white hat. c, Wearing black hat.
15m, Wearing red hat.

2004, May 17 Litho. *Perf. 14*

1328 A238 8m Sheet of 3, #a-c 7.50 7.50

Souvenir Sheet

1329 A238 15m multi 4.75 4.75

Prince William, 21st Birthday (in 2003) — A239

No. 1330: a, Wearing sunglasses. b, Wearing suit and tie c, Wearing sports shirt.
15m, As young boy.

2004, May 17

1330 A239 8m Sheet of 3, #a-c 7.50 7.50

Souvenir Sheet

1331 A239 15m multi 4.75 4.75

Intl. Year of Fresh Water (in 2003) — A240

No. 1332: a, Top of Qiloane Falls (gray water at top). b, Middle portion of Qiloane Falls (narrow at top). c, Bottom portion of Qiloane Falls.
15m, Orange River.

2004, May 17 *Perf. 14¼*

1332 A240 8m Sheet of 3, #a-c 7.50 7.50

Souvenir Sheet

1333 A240 15m multi 4.75 4.75

Powered Flight, Cent. (in 2003) — A241

No. 1334: a, Louis Blériot's Canard at Bagatelle, 1906. b, Blériot's Double-winged Libellule, 1907. c, Cross-country flight of Blériot VIII, Toury to Artenay, 1908. d, Blériot XII test flight, 1909.
15m, Blériot XI.

2004, May 17

1334 A241 6m Sheet of 4, #a-d 7.50 7.50

Souvenir Sheet

1335 A241 15m multi 4.75 4.75

Worldwide Fund for Nature (WWF) — A242

No. 1336 — Southern bald ibis: a, On nest, country name in white at LR. b, Flying to right, black denomination. c, Standing on rock, black denomination. d, Facing left.
No. 1337 — Southern bald ibis: a, Standing on rock, red denomination. b, Flying to left, red denomination. c, On nest, country name in black at UR.

2004, May 17 *Perf. 14*

1336 Horiz. strip of 4 3.75 3.75
a.-d. A242 3m Any single .90 .90
1337 Horiz. strip of 4, #1336d, 1337a-1337c 3.75 3.75
a.-c. A242 3m Any single .90 .90

No. 1336 printed in sheets of 4 strips. No. 1337 printed in sheets of 2 strips.

Mammals A243

Designs: 1m, Cape porcupine. 1.50m, Brown rat. 2.10m, Springhare, vert. No. 1341, 5m, South African galago, vert.
No. 1342, 5m: a, Striped grass mouse. b, Greater galago. c, Ground pangolin. d, Banded mongoose.
15m, Egyptian rousette, vert.

2004, May 17

1338-1341 A243 Set of 4 3.00 3.00
1342 A243 5m Sheet of 4, #a-d 6.25 6.25

Souvenir Sheet

1343 A243 15m multi 4.75 4.75

Birds — A244

Designs: 1.50m, Secretary bird. 2.10m, Gray-crowned crane. 3m, Pied avocet. 5m, Common kestrel.
No. 1348: a, European roller. b, Common cuckoo. c, Great spotted cuckoo. d, Pel's fishing owl.
15m, Kori bustard.

2004, May 17

1344-1347	A244	Set of 4	3.50	3.50
1348	A244	6m Sheet of 4, #a-d	7.50	7.50

Souvenir Sheet

1349	A244	15m multi	4.75	4.75

Butterflies A245

Designs: 1.50m, Acraea rabbaiae. 2.10m, Alaena margaritacea. 4m, Bematistes aganice. No. 1353, 6m, Acraea quirina.
No. 1354, 6m: a, Bematistes excisa male. b, Bematistes excisa female. c, Bematistes epiprotea. d, Bematistes poggei.
15m, Acraea satis.

2004, May 17

1350-1353	A245	Set of 4	4.25	4.25
1354	A245	6m Sheet of 4, #a-d	7.50	7.50

Souvenir Sheet

1355	A245	15m multi	4.75	4.75

Flowers — A246

Designs: 1.50m, Sparaxis grandiflora. 2.10m, Agapanthus africanus. 3m, Protea linearis. No. 1359, 5m, Nerine cultivars.
No. 1360, 5m: a, Kniphofia uvaria. b, Amaryllis belladonna. c, Cazania splendens. d, Erica coronata.
15m, Saintpaulia cultivars.

2004, May 17

1356-1359	A246	Set of 4	3.50	3.50
1360	A246	5m Sheet of 4, #a-d	6.25	6.25

Souvenir Sheet

1361	A246	15m multi	4.75	4.75

Houses A247

Designs: 70s, Mokhoro. 1m, Heisi. 1.50m, Lesotho. 2.10m, Mohlongoa-Fat'se.

2005, Feb. 21 Litho. *Perf. 14*

1362-1365	A247	Set of 4	1.90	1.90

Girl Guides A248

Girl Guides: 70s, Dancing. 1m, Marching in parade. 1.50m, Collecting cans, vert. 2.10m, Standing near building.
10m, Leader holding microphone, vert.

2005, May 20 Litho. *Perf. 14*

1366-1369	A248	Set of 4	1.60	1.60

Souvenir Sheet

1370	A248	10m multi	3.00	3.00

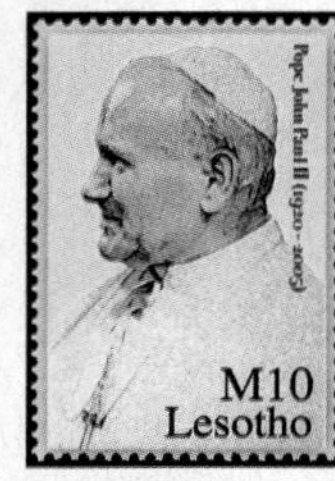

Pope John Paul II (1920-2005) A249

2005, Aug. 22 *Perf. 12¾*

1371	A249	10m multi	3.25	3.25

Printed in sheets of 4.

Souvenir Sheet

Rotary International, Cent. — A250

No. 1372: a, Alleviating poverty. b, Advancement of literacy. c, Helping at-risk children.

2005, Aug. 22

1372	A250	8m Sheet of 3, #a-c	7.75	7.75

World Cup Soccer Championships, 75th Anniv. — A251

No. 1373, horiz. — Players from final match from: a, 1930. b, 1938. c, 1990.
15m, Bodo Illgner, 1990 goalie for Germany.

2005, Aug. 22 *Perf. 12*

1373	A251	8m Sheet of 3, #a-c	7.75	7.75

Souvenir Sheet

1374	A251	15m multi	4.75	4.75

Hans Christian Andersen (1805-75), Author — A252

No. 1375: a, Statue of Andersen, Copenhagen. b, Childhood home of Andersen, Odense, Denmark. c, Scene from "The Steadfast Tin Soldier".
15m, Little Mermaid statue, Copenhagen.

2005, Aug. 22 *Perf. 12¾*

1375	A252	8m Sheet of 3, #a-c	7.75	7.75

Souvenir Sheet

1376	A252	15m multi	4.75	4.75

Jules Verne (1828-1905), Writer — A253

No. 1377, horiz.: a, Journey to the Center of the Earth. b, Verne, without hat. c, 20,000 Leagues Under the Sea.
15m, Verne wearing hat.

2005, Aug. 22

1377	A253	8m Sheet of 3, #a-c	7.75	7.75

Souvenir Sheet

1378	A253	15m multi	4.75	4.75

Albert Einstein (1879-1955), Physicist — A254

No. 1379, horiz. — Einstein and: a, Country name in black. b, Nikola Tesla, Charles Steinmetz. c, Country name in red violet.
15m, Time Magazine "Person of the Century" cover.

2005, Aug. 22

1379	A254	8m Sheet of 3, #a-c	7.75	7.75

Souvenir Sheet

1380	A254	15m multi	4.75	4.75

Battle of Trafalgar, Bicent. — A255

No. 1381: a, HMS Victory. b, Admiral Horatio Nelson facing left. c, Nelson wounded in battle. d, Ships in battle.
25m, Nelson facing right.

2005, Aug. 22 *Perf. 12¾*

1381	A255	8m Sheet of 4, #a-d	10.50	10.50

Souvenir Sheet

Perf. 12

1382	A255	25m multi	8.00	8.00

No. 1381 contains four 42x28mm stamps.

End of World War II, 60th Anniv. — A256

No. 1383, 4m — V-E Day: a, U.S. troops land on Omaha Beach, 1944. b, Gen. George C. Marshall. c, German Field Marshal Wilhelm Keitel signing surrender. d, Generals Dwight D. Eisenhower and George S. Patton. e, Soldiers sifting through war damage.
No. 1384, 4m — V-J Day: a, USS Arizona. b, Bunker, Chula Beach, Tinian Island. c, Bockscar flight crew. d, Newspaper announcing Japanese surrender. e, Historic marker commemorating loading of second atomic bomb on Tinian Island.

2005, Aug. 22 *Perf. 12¾*

Sheets of 5, #a-e

1383-1384	A256	Set of 2	13.00	13.00

A257

People and Livestock — A258

Designs: 70 l, Boy riding calf. 1m, Man feeding cattle. 1.50m, Cattle tenders playing game. 2.10m, Shepherd carrying lamb.
10m, Dancers.

2006, Mar. 13 Litho. *Perf. 14*

1385-1388	A257	Set of 4	1.75	1.75

Souvenir Sheet

1389	A258	10m multi	3.25	3.25

A259

Women Balancing Items on Heads — A260

Women carrying: 70 l, Sticks. 1m, Cooking pot. 1.50m, Water jar. 2.10m, Bowl of fruit.
10m, Bowl of grain.

2006, June 19
1390-1393 A259 Set of 4 1.50 1.50
Souvenir Sheet
1394 A260 10m multi 3.00 3.00

A261

Handicrafts — A262

Designs: 70 l, Baskets. 1m, Artist and drawing, vert. 1.50m, Painted pottery. 2.10m, Figurines of stork and fish, decorated bull's horn. 10m, Boy, native costume.

2006, Oct. 9 Litho. *Perf. 14¼*
1395-1398 A261 Set of 4 1.40 1.40
Souvenir Sheet
1399 A262 10m multi 2.75 2.75

Birds — A263

Designs: 1m, Crested caracara. 1.50m, Wood storks. 2.10m, Tawny-shouldered blackbird. No. 1403, 15m, Jabiru.
No. 1404: a, Great blue heron. b, Anna's hummingbird. c, Gray silky flycatcher. d, Limpkin.
No. 1405, 15m, Western reef heron. No. 1406, 15m, Monk parakeet.

2007, Aug. 20 Litho. *Perf. 14*
1400-1403 A263 Set of 4 5.50 5.50
1404 A263 6m Sheet of 4, #a-d 6.75 6.75
Souvenir Sheets
1405-1406 A263 Set of 2 8.50 8.50

Butterflies — A264

Designs: 1m, Mylothris erlangeri. 1.50m, Papilio nireus. 2.10m, Acraea terpiscore. 10m, Salamis temora.
No. 1411: a, Danaus chrysippus. b, Myrina silenus. c, Chrysiridia madagascariensis. d, Hypolimnas dexithea.
No. 1412, 15m, P. demodocus. No. 1413, 15m, Amphicallia tigris.

2007, Aug. 20
1407-1410 A264 Set of 4 4.25 4.25
1411 A264 6m Sheet of 4, #a-d 6.75 6.75
Souvenir Sheets
1412-1413 A264 Set of 2 8.50 8.50

Orchids — A265

Designs: 1.50m, Spiranthes laciniata. 2.10m, Triphora craigheadii. 3m, Arethusa bulbosa. 10m, Calypso bulbosa.
No. 1418: a, Encyclia tampensis. b, Prosthechea cochleata. c, Vanilla pompona. d, Cypripedium acaule.
No. 1419, 15m, Vanilla barbellata. No. 1420, 15m, Epidendrum radicans.

2007, Aug. 20
1414-1417 A265 Set of 4 4.75 4.75
1418 A265 6m Sheet of 4, #a-d 6.75 6.75
Souvenir Sheets
1419-1420 A265 Set of 2 8.50 8.50

A266

A267

Mushrooms — A268

Designs: 1m, Amanita pantherina. 1.50m, Agaricus xanthodermus. 2.10m, Amanita rubescens. No. 1424, 15m, Amanita phalloides.
No. 1425: a, Amanita phalloides, diff. b, Amanita pantherina, diff. c, Panaeolus papilionaceus. d, Amanita rubescens, diff.
No. 1426, 15m, Amanite panther. No. 1427, 15m, Podaxis pistillaris.

2007, Aug. 20
1421-1424 A266 Set of 4 5.50 5.50
1425 A267 6m Sheet of 4, #a-d 6.75 6.75
Souvenir Sheets
1426 A267 15m multi 4.25 4.25
1427 A268 15m multi 4.25 4.25

Miniature Sheet

2008 Summer Olympics, Beijing — A269

No. 1428: a, Rowing. b, Softball. c, Wrestling. d, Volleyball.

2008, Aug. 18 Litho. *Perf. 12*
1428 A269 3.50m Sheet of 4, #a-d 3.75 3.75

POSTAGE DUE STAMPS

Basutoland Nos. J9-J10 Overprinted: "LESOTHO"

Wmk. 314

1966, Nov. 1 Typo. *Perf. 14*
J1 D2 1c carmine .20 .25
a. "Lseotho" *50.00*
J2 D2 5c dark purple .75 .60
a. "Lseotho" *85.00*

D1

D2

Perf. 13½
1967, Apr. 1 Unwmk. Litho.
J3 D1 1c dark blue .20 .20
J4 D1 2c dull rose .25 .30
J5 D1 5c emerald .55 .70
Nos. J3-J5 (3) 1.00 1.20

1976, Nov. 30 Wmk. 362
J7 D1 2c dull rose 3.00 3.00
J8 D1 5c emerald 3.00 3.00

1986 Litho. *Perf. 13x13½*
J9 D2 2s green .50 .50
J10 D2 5s blue .50 .50
J11 D2 25s purple .50 .50
Nos. J9-J11 (3) 1.50 1.50

This is an expanding set. Numbers will change if necessary.

LIBERIA

lī-ˈbir-ē-ə

LOCATION — West coast of Africa, between Ivory Coast and Sierra Leone
GOVT. — Republic
AREA — 43,000 sq. mi.
POP. — 2,602,100 (1997 est.)
CAPITAL — Monrovia

100 Cents = 1 Dollar

Catalogue values for unused stamps in this country are for Never Hinged items, beginning with Scott 330 in the regular postage section, Scott B19 in the semi-postal section, Scott C67 in the airpost section, and Scott CB4 in the airpost semi-postal section.

Values for unused stamps are for examples with original gum as defined in the catalogue introduction. Any exceptions will be noted. Very fine examples of Nos. 1-3, 13-21 and 157-159 will have perforations just clear of the design due to the narrow spacing of the stamps on the plates and/or imperfect perforating methods.

Watermarks

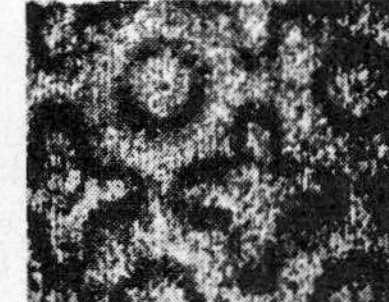
Wmk. 116 — Crosses and Circles

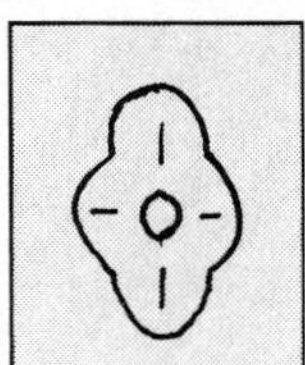
Wmk. 143

For watermarks 373 and 384 see British Watermark page.

"Liberia" — A1

1860 Unwmk. Litho. *Perf. 12*
Thick Paper
1 A1 6c red 400.00 *300.00*
a. Imperf, pair 500.00
2 A1 12c deep blue 22.50 *50.00*
a. Imperf, pair 250.00
3 A1 24c green 50.00 *50.00*
a. Imperf, pair 300.00
Nos. 1-3 (3) 472.50 *400.00*

Stamps set very close together. Examples of the 12c occasionally show traces of a frame line around the design.

Medium to Thin Paper
With a single-line frame around each stamp, about 1mm from the border

1864 *Perf. 11, 12*
7 A1 6c red 62.50 *77.50*
a. Imperf, pair 200.00
8 A1 12c blue 72.50 *87.50*
a. Imperf, pair 200.00
9 A1 24c lt green 82.50 *95.00*
a. Imperf, pair 200.00
Nos. 7-9 (3) 217.50 *260.00*

Stamps set about 5mm apart. Margins large and perforation usually outside the frame line.

Without Frame Line

1866-69
13 A1 6c lt red 25.00 *30.00*
14 A1 12c lt blue 25.00 *30.00*
15 A1 24c lt yellow grn 25.00 *30.00*
Nos. 13-15 (3) 75.00 90.00

Stamps set 2-2½mm apart with small margins. Stamps are usually without frame line but those from one transfer show broken and irregular parts of a frame.

With Frame Line

1880 *Perf. 10½*
16 A1 1c ultra 5.00 7.50
17 A1 2c rose 5.00 *5.25*
a. Imperf, pair 175.00
18 A1 6c violet 5.00 5.25
19 A1 12c yellow 5.00 *5.25*
20 A1 24c rose red 5.00 5.25
Nos. 16-20 (5) 25.00 28.50

Unused values for Nos. 16-20 are for stamps without gum.
For surcharges see Nos. 157-159.

Counterfeits
Counterfeits exist of Nos. 1-28, 32 and 64.

From Arms of Liberia — A2

1881
21 A2 3c black 15.00 10.00

Unused value is for a stamp without gum.

A3

A4

1882				*Perf. 11½, 12, 14*	
22	A3	8c	blue	50.00	10.00
23	A4	16c	red	8.00	5.00

On No. 22 the openings in the figure "8" enclose a pattern of slanting lines. Compare with No. 32.

Canceled to Order

Beginning with the issue of 1885, values in the used column are for "canceled to order" stamps. Postally used examples sell for much more.

A5

A6

From Arms of Liberia — A7

A8

Perf. 10½, 11, 12, 11½x10½, 14, 14½

1885					
24	A5	1c	carmine	2.00	2.00
a.		1c rose		2.00	2.00
25	A5	2c	green	2.00	2.00
26	A5	3c	violet	2.00	2.00
27	A5	4c	brown	2.00	2.00
28	A5	6c	olive gray	2.00	2.00
29	A6	8c	bluish gray	4.00	4.00
a.		8c lilac		7.00	7.00
30	A6	16c	yellow	12.00	12.00
31	A7	32c	deep blue	29.00	29.00
			Nos. 24-31 (8)	55.00	55.00

In the 1885 printing, the stamps are spaced 2mm apart and the paper is medium. In the 1892 printing, the stamps are 4½mm apart.

For surcharges see Nos. J1-J2.

Imperf., Pair

24b	A5	1c	3.00	
25a	A5	2c	4.25	
26a	A5	3c	5.00	
27a	A5	4c	5.00	
28a	A5	6c	4.25	4.25
29b	A6	8c	12.50	
30a	A6	16c	15.00	
31a	A7	32c	30.00	

Imperf. pairs with 2mm spacing sell for higher prices.

1889				*Perf. 12, 14*	
32	A8	8c	blue	4.25	4.25
a.		Imperf., pair		20.00	

The openings in the figure "8" are filled with network. See No. 22.

A9

Elephant — A10

Oil Palm — A11

Pres. Hilary R. W. Johnson — A12

Vai Woman in Full Dress — A13

Coat of Arms — A14

Liberian Star — A15

Coat of Arms — A16

Hippopotamus A17

Liberian Star — A18

President Johnson — A19

1892-96	**Wmk. 143**	**Engr.**		*Perf. 15*	
33	A9	1c	vermilion	.50	.40
a.		1c blue (error)		40.00	
34	A9	2c	blue	.50	.40
a.		2c vermilion (error)		40.00	
35	A10	4c	green & blk	1.75	1.00
a.		Center inverted		175.00	
36	A11	6c	blue green	.70	.50
37	A12	8c	brown & blk	.95	.95
a.		Center inverted		600.00	600.00
b.		Center sideways		750.00	
38	A12	10c	chrome yel & indigo ('96)	.95	.65
39	A13	12c	rose red	.95	.65
40	A13	15c	slate ('96)	.95	.65
41	A14	16c	lilac	3.50	1.75
a.		16c deep greenish blue (error)		110.00	
42	A14	20c	vermilion ('96)	3.50	1.75
43	A15	24c	ol grn, *yel*	2.00	1.10
44	A15	25c	yel grn ('96)	2.00	1.40
45	A16	30c	steel bl ('96)	6.25	4.50
46	A16	32c	grnsh blue	3.50	2.75
a.		32c lilac (error)		*110.00*	
47	A17	$1	ultra & blk	10.00	9.00
a.		$1 blue & black		11.00	11.00
48	A18	$2	brown, *yel*	9.00	8.00
49	A19	$5	carmine & blk	10.00	10.00
a.		Center inverted		500.00	500.00
			Nos. 33-49 (17)	57.00	45.45

Many imperforates, part-perforated and misperforated varieties exist.

The 1c, 2c and 4c were issued in sheets of 60; 6c, sheet of 40; 8c, 10c, sheets of 30; 12c, 15c, 24c, 25c, sheets of 20; 16c, 20c, 30c, sheets of 15; $1, $2, $5, sheets of 10.

For overprints & surcharges see #50, 64B-64F, 66, 71-77, 79-81, 85-93, 95-100, 160, O1-O13, O15-O25, O37-O41, O44-O45.

No. 36 Surcharged:

a

Five Cents
b

1893			
50	A11 (a) 5c on 6c blue grn	1.75	1.10
a.	"5" with short flag	6.00	6.00
b.	Both 5's with short flags	5.00	5.00
c.	"i" dot omitted	19.00	19.00
d.	Surcharge "b"	30.00	30.00

"Commerce," Globe and Krumen — A22

1894	**Unwmk.**	**Engr.**	*Imperf.*	
52	A22 5c carmine & blk		5.00	5.00

Rouletted

53	A22 5c carmine & blk	10.00	7.50

For overprints see Nos. 69, O26-O27.

Oil Palm A23

Hippopotamus A24

Elephant — A25

Liberty — A26

1897-1905	**Wmk. 143**			*Perf. 14 to 16*	
54	A23	1c	lilac rose	1.00	.65
a.		1c violet		1.00	.65
55	A23	1c	deep green ('00)	1.25	.95
56	A23	1c	lt green ('05)	3.00	1.60
57	A24	2c	bister & blk	2.50	1.60
58	A24	2c	org red & blk ('00)	5.00	2.10
59	A24	2c	rose & blk ('05)	2.50	1.60
60	A25	5c	lake & black	2.50	1.60
a.		5c lilac rose & black		2.50	1.60
61	A25	5c	gray bl & blk ('00)	5.00	5.00
62	A25	5c	ultra & blk ('05)	3.50	2.75
a.		Center inverted		1,250.	
63	A26	50c	red brn & blk	3.25	3.50
			Nos. 54-63 (10)	29.50	21.35

For overprints & surcharges see #65, 66A-68. 70, 78, 82-84, M1, O28-O36, O42, O92.

A27

Two types:
I — 13 pearls above "Republic Liberia."
II — 10 pearls.

1897	**Unwmk.**	**Litho.**	*Perf. 14*	
64	A27 3c red & green (I)		.25	*.60*
a.	Type II		*10.00*	.20

No. 64a is considered a reprint, unissued. "Used" examples are CTO.

For surcharge see No. 128.

Official Stamps Handstamped in Black **ORDINARY**

1901-02				**Wmk. 143**	

On Nos. O7-O8, O10-O12

64B	A14	16c	lilac	*525.00*	*500.00*
64C	A15	24c	ol grn, *yel*	*575.00*	*400.00*
64D	A17	$1	blue & blk	*3,000.*	*2,000.*
64E	A18	$2	brown, *yel*	—	—
64F	A19	$5	carmine & blk	—	—

On Stamps with "O S" Printed

65	A23	1c	green	*37.50*	*40.00*
66	A9	2c	blue	*100.00*	*100.00*
66A	A24	2c	bister & blk	—	*150.00*
67	A24	2c	org red & blk	*45.00*	*40.00*
68	A25	5c	gray bl & blk	*37.50*	*35.00*
69	A22	5c	vio & grn (No. O26)	*300.00*	*300.00*
70	A25	5c	lake & blk	*275.00*	*225.00*
71	A12	10c	yel & blue blk	*37.50*	*60.00*
a.		"O S" omitted		—	
72	A13	15c	slate	*40.00*	*60.00*
73	A14	16c	lilac	*475.00*	*300.00*
74	A14	20c	vermilion	*42.50*	*50.00*
75	A15	24c	ol grn,*yel*	*52.50*	*50.00*
76	A15	25c	yellow grn	*42.50*	*50.00*
a.		"O S" omitted		*750.00*	
77	A16	30c	steel blue	*42.50*	*40.00*
78	A26	50c	red brn & blk	*100.00*	*52.50*
79	A17	$1	ultra & blk	*325.00*	*275.00*
a.		"O S" omitted			
80	A18	$2	brn, *yel*	*2,000.*	*1,800.*
81	A19	$5	car & blk	*2,250.*	*2,000.*
a.		"O S" omitted		*3,000.*	*2,750.*

On Stamps with "O S" Handstamped

82	A23	1c	deep green	62.50	—
83	A24	2c	org red & blk	75.00	—
84	A25	5c	lake & blk	200.00	—
85	A12	10c	yel & bl blk	125.00	—
86	A14	20c	vermilion	140.00	—
87	A15	24c	ol grn, *yel*	140.00	—
88	A15	25c	yel grn	160.00	—
89	A16	30c	steel blue	525.00	—
90	A16	32c	grnsh blue	210.00	—

Varieties of Nos. 65-90 include double and inverted overprints.

Nos. 47, O10, O23a Surcharged in Carmine

1902			
91	A17 75c on $1 #47	15.00	13.00
a.	Thin "C" and comma	19.00	19.00
b.	Inverted surcharge	62.50	62.50
c.	As "a," inverted		
92	A17 75c on $1 #O10	*2,500.*	
a.	Thin "C" and comma	*3,500.*	
93	A17 75c on $1 #O23a	*3,500.*	
a.	Thin "C" and comma	*4,250.*	

Liberty — A29

1903	**Unwmk.**	**Engr.**	*Perf. 14*	
94	A29 3c black		.30	.20
a.	Printed on both sides		45.00	
b.	Perf. 12		20.00	6.00

For overprint see No. O43.

Stamps of 1892 Surcharged in Blue

a

b

1903		**Wmk. 143**	
95	A14 (a) 10c on 16c lilac	3.00	4.00
96	A15 (b) 15c on 24c ol grn, *yel*	4.50	5.50

97 A16 (b) 20c on 32c grnsh bl 6.25 7.75
Nos. 95-97 (3) 13.75 17.25

Nos. 50, O3 and 45 Surcharged in Black or Red

1904

98 A11 1c on 5c on 6c bl grn .60 .55
- *a.* "5" with short flag 4.25 4.25
- *b.* Both 5's with short flags 8.75 8.75
- *c.* "i" dot omitted 10.00 10.00
- *d.* Surcharge on #50d 12.50 12.50
- *e.* Inverted surcharge 6.75 6.75

99 A10 2c on 4c grn & blk 1.50 2.75
- *a.* Pair, one without surcharge 35.00
- *b.* Double surcharge
- *c.* Double surcharge, red and blk 62.50
- *d.* Surcharged on back also 19.00
- *e.* "Official" overprint missing 30.00

100 A16 2c on 30c stl bl (R) 8.75 14.00
Nos. 98-100 (3) 10.85 17.30

African Elephant — A33

Mercury — A34

Chimpanzee A35

Great Blue Touraco — A36

Agama — A37

Egret — A38

Head of Liberty From Coin — A39

A40

Liberian Flag — A41

Pygmy Hippopotamus A42

Liberty with Star of Liberia on Cap — A43

Mandingos — A44

Executive Mansion and Pres. Arthur Barclay — A45

1906 **Unwmk.** **Engr.** ***Perf. 14***

101 A33 1c green & blk 1.50 .50
102 A34 2c carmine & blk .30 .20
103 A35 5c ultra & blk 2.75 .65
104 A36 10c red brn & blk 4.00 .65
105 A37 15c pur & dp grn 14.50 3.00
106 A38 20c orange & blk 8.50 2.00
107 A39 25c dull blue & gray .85 .20
108 A40 30c deep violet 1.00 .20
109 A41 50c dp green & blk 1.00 .20
110 A42 75c brown & blk 12.00 2.00
111 A43 $1 rose & gray 3.00 .20
112 A44 $2 dp green & blk 4.50 .35
113 A45 $5 red brown & blk 9.25 .50
Nos. 101-113 (13) 63.15 10.65

For surcharges see Nos. 114, 129, 130, 141, 145-149, 161, M2, M5, O72-O73, O82-O85, O96. For overprints see Nos. O46-O58.

Center Inverted

101a	A33	1c	110.00	55.00
102a	A34	2c	120.00	35.00
103a	A35	5c	175.00	175.00
104a	A36	10c	80.00	80.00
105a	A37	15c	175.00	175.00
106b	A38	20c	175.00	175.00
107a	A39	25c	75.00	75.00
109b	A41	50c	75.00	75.00
110b	A42	75c	125.00	125.00
111a	A43	$1	100.00	100.00
112a	A44	$2	95.00	95.00

Imperf., Pairs

101b	A33	1c	11.00	
102b	A34	2c	4.50	
106a	A38	20c	17.00	
107b	A39	25c	45.00	45.00
109a	A41	50c	17.00	
110a	A42	75c	17.00	
113a	A45	$5	22.50	

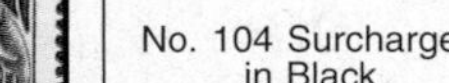

No. 104 Surcharged in Black

1909

114 A36 3c on 10c red brn & blk 6.00 6.00

Coffee Plantation — A46

Pres. Barclay — A47

S. S. Pres. Daniel E. Howard, former Gunboat Lark — A48

Commerce with Caduceus — A49

Vai Woman Spinning Cotton — A50

Blossom and Fruit of Pepper Plants — A51

Circular House — A52

President Barclay — A53

Men in Canoe — A54

Liberian Village — A55

1909-12 ***Perf. 14***

115 A46 1c yel grn & blk .70 .55
116 A47 2c lake & blk .70 .55
117 A48 5c ultra & blk .70 .55
118 A49 10c plum & blk, perf. 12½ ('12) .70 .55
- *a.* Imperf., pair 19.00
- *b.* Perf 14 ('12) 2.25 2.25
- *c.* As "b," pair, imperf between 27.50
- *d.* Perf 12½x14 2.75 2.25

119 A50 15c indigo & blk 3.50 .60
120 A51 20c rose & grn 4.50 .60
- *b.* Imperf.

121 A52 25c dk brn & blk 1.40 .60
- *a.* Imperf.

122 A53 30c dark brown 4.50 .60
123 A54 50c green & blk 4.50 .60
124 A55 75c red brn & blk 4.50 .60
Nos. 115-124 (10) 25.70 5.80

Rouletted

125 A49 10c plum & blk .75 .45

For surcharges see Nos. 126-127E, 131-133, 136-140, 142-144, 151-156, 162, B1-B2, M3-M4, M6-M7, O70-O1, O74-O81, O86-O91, O97.

For overprints see Nos. O59-O69.

Center Inverted

116a	A47	2c	70.00	60.00
117a	A48	5c	62.50	55.00
119a	A50	15c	100.00	60.00
120a	A51	20c	70.00	55.00
121b	A52	25c	47.50	42.50
123a	A54	50c	95.00	80.00

Stamps and Types of 1909-12 Surcharged in Blue or Red

1910-12 ***Rouletted***

126 A49 3c on 10c plum & blk (Bl) .40 .25
- *a.* "3" inverted

126B A49 3c on 10c blk & ultra (R) 30.00 5.00

#126B is roulette 7. It also exists in roulette 13.

Perf. 12½, 14, 12½x14

127 A49 3c on 10c plum & blk (Bl) ('12) .40 .25
- *a.* Imperf., pair 22.50
- *b.* Double surcharge, one invtd. 22.50
- *c.* Double vertical surcharge

127E A49 3c on 10c blk & ultra (R) ('12) 17.00 .55
Nos. 126-127E (4) 47.80 6.05

Nos. 64, 64a Surcharged in Dark Green

1913

128 A27 8c on 3c red & grn (I) .30 .20
- *a.* Surcharge on No. 64a 3.00 .20
- *b.* Double surcharge 6.25
- *c.* Imperf., pair 20.00
- *d.* Inverted surcharge 25.00

Stamps of Preceding Issues Surcharged

a

b

1914

On Issue of 1906

129 A39 (a) 2c on 25c dl bl & gray 11.50 3.25
130 A40 (b) 5c on 30c dp violet 11.50 3.25

On Issue of 1909

131 A52 (a) 2c on 25c brn & blk 11.50 3.25
132 A53 (b) 5c on 30c dk brown 11.50 3.25
133 A54 (a) 10c on 50c grn & blk 11.50 3.25
Nos. 129-133 (5) 57.50 16.25

Liberian House A57

Providence Island, Monrovia Harbor A58

1915 **Engr.** **Wmk. 116** ***Perf. 14***

134 A57 2c red	.20	.20
135 A58 3c dull violet	.20	.20

For overprints see Nos. 196-197, O113-O114, O128-O129.

Nos. 109, 111-113, 119-124 Surcharged with New Values in Dark Blue, Black or Red:

c

d

e

f

g

1915-16 **Unwmk.**

136 A50 (c) 2c on 15c (R)	.90	.90
137 A52 (d) 2c on 25c (R)	8.00	8.00
138 A51 (e) 5c on 20c (Bk)	1.10	5.75
139 A53 (f) 5c on 30c (R)	4.50	4.50
a. Double surcharge	14.00	14.00
140 A53 (g) 5c on 30c (R)	40.00	40.00

h

i

141 A41 (h) 10c on 50c (R)	8.00	8.00
a. Double surch., one invtd.		
142 A54 (i) 10c on 50c (R)	14.00	14.00
a. Double surcharge red & blk	35.00	35.00
b. Blue surcharge	35.00	35.00
143 A54 (i) 10c on 50c (Bk)	20.00	15.00

j

k

144 A55 (j) 20c on 75c (Bk)	3.50	5.75
145 A43 (k) 25c on $1 (Bk)	42.50	42.50

l

m

146 A44 (l) 50c on $2 (R)	11.00	11.00
a. "Ceuts"	22.50	22.50
147 A44 (m) 50c on $2 (R)	800.00	800.00

n

1

=

148 A45 $1 on $5 (Bk)	65.00	65.00
a. Double surcharge	90.00	90.00

o

149 A45 $1 on $5 (R)	52.50	52.50

The color of the red surcharge varies from light dull red to almost brown.

Handstamped Surcharge, Type "i"

150 A54 10c on 50c (Dk Bl)	14.00	14.00

No. 119 Surcharged in Black

2

151 A50 2c on 15c	800.00	800.00

No. 119 Surcharged in Red

152 A50 2c on 15c	45.00	40.00
a. Double surcharge	92.50	

Nos. 116-117 Surcharged in Black or Red

a1

1c

b1

c1 one cemt

d1 1ct

e1 one one

f1 1c

g1 1cent * * * * * *

h1 1 c 1

i1 one c one

j1 1cts

k2 Two cemts

l2 Two cents

m2 2cents

n2 Two cts

o2 2c

p2 2. 2.

q2 two c two

r2 2 2

s2 two

t2 2cent

153 A47 1c on 2c lake & blk	2.50	2.50
a. Strip of 10 types	35.00	
154 A48 2c on 5c ultra & blk (R)	3.50	2.50
a. Black surcharge	14.00	14.00
b. Strip of 10 types (R)	35.00	
c. Strip of 10 types (Bk)	165.00	

The 10 types of surcharge are repeated in illustrated sequence on 1c on 2c in each horiz. row and on 2c on 5c in each vert. row of sheets of 100 (10x10).

No. 116 and Type of 1909 Surcharged:

one ct.

155 A47 1c on 2c lake & blk	190.00	190.00

2ct

156 A48 2c on 5c turq & blk	140.00	140.00

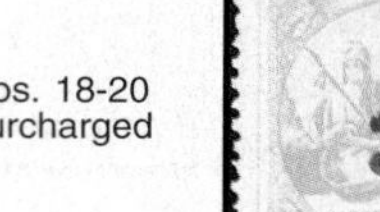

Nos. 18-20 Surcharged

1916

157 A1 3c on 6c violet	42.50	42.50
a. Inverted surcharge	75.00	75.00
158 A1 5c on 12c yellow	3.00	3.00
a. Inverted surcharge	12.50	12.50
b. Surcharge sideways	12.50	
159 A1 10c on 24c rose red	2.75	3.00
a. Inverted surcharge	15.00	15.00
b. Surcharge sideways	12.50	
Nos. 157-159 (3)	48.25	48.50

Unused values for Nos. 157-159 are for examples without gum.

Nos. 44 and 108 Surcharged

p

r

1917 **Wmk. 143**

160 A15 (p) 4c on 25c yel grn	11.00	11.00
a. "OUR"	25.00	25.00
b. "FCUR"	25.00	25.00

Unwmk.

161 A40 (r) 5c on 30c dp vio	90.00	90.00

No. 118 Surcharged in Red

1918

162 A49 3c on 10c plum & blk	2.25	2.25
a. "3" inverted	9.25	9.25

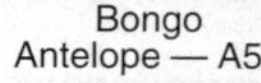

Bongo Antelope — A59

Symbols of Liberia — A61

Two-spot Palm Civet A60

A62

Palm-nut Vulture — A66

Oil Palm — A63

Mercury — A64

Traveler's Tree — A65

"Mudskipper" or Bommi Fish — A67

Mandingos A68

"Liberia" A71

Coast Scene A69

Liberia College A70

1918 **Engr.** ***Perf. 12½, 14***

163 A59 1c dp grn & blk .65 .20
164 A60 2c rose & blk .80 .20
165 A61 5c gray bl & blk .20 .20
166 A62 10c dark green .20 .20
167 A63 15c blk & dk grn 3.00 .20
168 A64 20c claret & blk .35 .20
169 A65 25c dk grn & grn 3.25 .20
170 A66 30c red vio & blk 15.00 .80
171 A67 50c ultra & blk 26.50 3.50
172 A68 75c ol bis & blk .90 .20
173 A69 $1 yel brn & bl 7.25 .20
174 A70 $2 lt vio & blk 6.50 .20
175 A71 $5 dark brown 7.00 .40
Nos. 163-175 (13) 71.60 6.70

For surcharges see Nos. 176-177, 228-229, 248-270, B3-B15, O111-O112, O155-O157.
For overprints see Nos. O98-O110.

Nos. 163-164, F10-F14 Surcharged

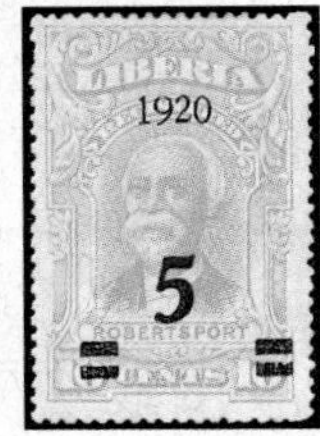

1920

176 A59 3c on 1c grn & blk 1.00 1.00
a. "CEETS" 17.00 17.00
b. Double surcharge 10.00 10.00
c. Triple surcharge 15.00 15.00
177 A60 4c on 2c rose & blk 1.00 1.00
a. Inverted surcharge 20.00 20.00
b. Double surcharge 10.00 10.00
c. Double surcharge, one invtd. 18.00
d. Triple surcharge, one inverted 25.00 25.00
e. Quadruple surcharge 30.00 30.00
f. Typewritten surcharge
g. Same as "f" but inverted
h. Printed and typewritten surcharges, both inverted
178 R6 5c on 10c bl & blk 2.50 2.50
a. Inverted surcharge 10.00 10.00
b. Double surcharge 10.00 10.00
c. Double surcharge, one invtd. 15.00 15.00
d. Typewritten surcharge ("five") 100.00
e. Printed and typewritten surcharges 100.00
179 R6 5c on 10c org red & blk 2.50 2.50
a. 5c on 10c orange & black 4.00 2.75
b. Inverted surcharge 15.00
c. Double surcharge 15.00
d. Double surcharge, one invtd. 18.00 15.00
e. Typewritten surch. in violet 100.00 100.00
f. Typewritten surch. in black
g. Printed and typewritten surcharges 100.00
180 R6 5c on 10c grn & blk 2.50 2.50
a. Double surcharge 10.00 10.00
b. Double surcharge, one invtd. 18.00 18.00
c. Inverted surcharge 18.00
d. Quadruple surcharge 25.00 25.00
e. Typewritten surcharge 100.00
f. Printed and typewritten surcharges
181 R6 5c on 10c vio & blk (Monrovia) 4.00 4.00
a. Double surcharge, one invtd. 25.00 25.00
182 R6 5c on 10c mag & blk (Robertsport) 2.00 2.00
a. Double surcharge 15.00 15.00
b. Double surcharge, one invtd. 15.00 15.00
c. Double surcharge, both invtd. 25.00
Nos. 176-182 (7) 15.50 15.50

Cape Mesurado A75

Pres. Daniel E. Howard — A76

Arms of Liberia — A77

Crocodile A78

Pepper Plant A79

Leopard A80

Village Scene A81

Krumen in Dugout A82

Rapids in St. Paul's River A83

Bongo Antelope A84

Hornbill A85

Elephant A86

1921 **Wmk. 116** ***Perf. 14***

183 A75 1c green .20 .20
184 A76 5c dp bl & blk .20 .20
185 A77 10c red & dl bl .20 .20
186 A78 15c dl vio & grn 6.50 .30
187 A79 20c rose red & grn 2.75 .20
188 A80 25c org & blk 7.50 .30
189 A81 30c grn & dl vio .40 .20
190 A82 50c org & ultra .45 .20
191 A83 75c red & blk brn .80 .20
a. Center inverted 70.00
192 A84 $1 red & blk 32.50 1.75
193 A85 $2 yel & ultra 10.50 .70
194 A86 $5 car rose & vio 32.50 .95
Nos. 183-194 (12) 94.50 5.40

For overprints see Nos. 195, 198-208, O115-O127, O130-O140.

Nos. 134-135, 183-194 Overprinted "1921"

195 A75 1c green 22.50 .40
196 A57 2c red 22.50 .40
197 A58 3c dull violet 32.50 .40
198 A76 5c dp bl & blk 3.50 .30
199 A77 10c red & dull bl 50.00 .40
200 A78 15c dull vio & grn 22.50 1.40
201 A79 20c rose red & grn, ovpt. invtd. 7.25 .75
202 A80 25c orange & blk 22.50 1.40
203 A81 30c grn & dull vio 2.50 .30
204 A82 50c orange & ultra 3.50 .30
205 A83 75c red & blk brn 4.75 .30
206 A84 $1 red & blk 62.50 2.10
207 A85 $2 yellow & ultra 22.50 2.10
208 A86 $5 car rose & vio 60.00 2.75
Nos. 195-208 (14) 339.00 13.30

Overprint exists inverted in Nos. 195-208 and normal on No. 201.

First Settlers Landing at Cape Mesurado from U. S. S. Alligator A87

1923 **Litho.**

209 A87 1c lt blue & blk 18.00 .30
210 A87 2c claret & ol gray 26.00 .30
211 A87 5c ol grn & ind 26.00 .30
212 A87 10c bl grn & vio 1.00 .30
213 A87 $1 rose & brn 3.25 .30
Nos. 209-213 (5) 74.25 1.50

Centenary of founding of Liberia.

Memorial to J. J. Roberts, 1st Pres. — A88

Hall of Representatives, Monrovia — A89

Liberian Star — A90

A91

Pres. Charles Dunbar Burgess King — A92

Hippopotamus — A93

Antelope A94

West African Buffalo A95

Grebos Making Dumboy A96

Pineapple A97

Carrying Ivory Tusk A98

Rubber Planter's House — A99

Stockton Lagoon — A100

Grebo Houses — A101

1923 *Perf. 13½x14½, 14½x13½*

White Paper

No.	Type	Description	Unused	Used
214	A88	1c yel grn & dp grn	7.50	1.25
215	A89	2c claret & brn	7.50	.20
216	A90	3c lilac & blk	.35	.20
217	A91	5c bl vio & blk	115.00	.20
218	A92	10c slate & brn	.35	.20
219	A93	15c bister & bl	35.00	.50
220	A94	20c bl grn & vio	2.50	.35
221	A95	25c org red & brn	160.00	.60
222	A96	30c dk brn & vio	.60	.20
223a	A97	50c dull vio & org	1.00	.20
224	A98	75c gray & bl	1.90	.40
225a	A99	$1 dp red & dk vio	4.50	.60

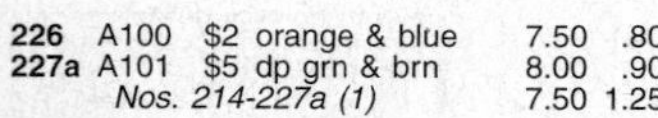

No.	Type	Description	Unused	Used
226	A100	$2 orange & blue	7.50	.80
227a	A101	$5 dp grn & brn	8.00	.90
		Nos. 214-227a (1)	7.50	1.25
224a	A98	75c gray & bl	1.90	45

Nos. 222-227 exist on white, buff or brownish paper. Values are for the most common variety. See the Scott Classic Specialized Catalogue for detailed listings.

For overprints see Nos. O141-O154.

No. 163 Surcharged

1926 **Unwmk.** *Perf. 14*

No.	Type	Description	Unused	Used
228	A59	2c on 1c dp grn & blk	3.50	3.50
a.		Surcharge with ornamental design as on #O155	17.00	

No. 163 Surcharged in Red

1927

No.	Type	Description	Unused	Used
229	A59	2c on 1c dp grn & blk	9.50	9.50
a.		"Ceuts"	14.00	
b.		"Vwo"	14.00	
c.		"Twc"	14.00	
d.		Double surcharge	27.50	
e.		Wavy lines omitted	17.50	

Palms A102

Map of Africa — A103

President King — A104

1928 **Engr.** *Perf. 12*

No.	Type	Description	Unused	Used
230	A102	1c green	.75	.50
231	A102	2c dark violet	.50	.35
232	A102	3c bister brn	.50	.35
a.		Horiz. pair, imperf vert.	—	
233	A103	5c ultra	1.00	.55
234	A104	10c olive gray	1.40	.55
235	A103	15c dull violet	6.25	2.25
236	A103	$1 red brown	77.50	26.50
		Nos. 230-236 (7)	87.90	31.05

For surcharges & overprints see Nos. 288A, 289A, 290A-291, 292A, C1-C3, O158-O165.

Nos. 164-168, 170-175 Surcharged in Various Colors and Styles, "1936" and New Values

1936 *Perf. 12½, 14*

No.	Type	Description	Unused	Used
248	A60	1c on 2c (Bl)	.55	*3.50*
249	A61	3c on 5c (Bl)	.20	*2.00*
250	A62	4c on 10c (Br)	.20	*2.00*
251	A63	6c on 15c (Bl)	.55	*3.50*
252	A64	8c on 20c (V)	.20	*2.00*
253	A66	12c on 30c (V)	1.00	*9.75*
254	A67	14c on 50c (Bl)	1.10	*11.00*
255	A68	16c on 75c (Br)	.55	*5.50*
256	A69	18c on $1 (Bk)	.55	*5.50*
a.		22c on $1 yellow brown & blue	7.25	
257	A70	22c on $2 (V)	.75	*7.75*
258	A71	24c on $5 (Bk)	1.00	*9.75*
		Nos. 248-258 (11)	6.65	62.25

Official Stamps, Nos. O99-O110, Surcharged or Overprinted in various colors and styles with 6 pointed star and "1936"

1936

No.	Type	Description	Unused	Used
259	A60	1c on 2c (Bl)	.40	*4.00*
260	A61	3c on 5c (Bl)	.40	*4.00*
261	A62	4c on 10c (Bl)	.40	*4.00*
262	A63	6c on 15c (Bl)	.40	*4.00*
263	A64	8c on 20c (V)	.40	*4.00*
264	A66	12c on 30c (V)	1.50	*20.00*
a.		"193" instead of "1936"	19.00	
265	A67	14c on 50c (Bl)	2.00	*21.00*
266	A68	16c on 75c (Bk)	1.00	*12.00*
267	A69	18c on $1 (Bk)	1.00	*12.00*
268	A70	22c on $2 (Bl)	1.25	*15.00*
269	A71	24c on $5 (Bk)	1.50	*17.00*
270	A65	25c (Bk)	2.00	*21.00*
		Nos. 259-270 (12)	12.25	138.00

Hornbill — A106

Designs: 2c, Bushbuck. 3c, West African dwarf buffalo. 4c, Pygmy hippopotamus. 5c, Lesser egret. 6c, Pres. E. J. Barclay.

Perf. Compound of 11½, 12, 12½, 14

1937, Apr. 10 **Engr.** **Unwmk.**

No.	Type	Description	Unused	Used
271	A106	1c green & blk	1.50	.80
272	A106	2c carmine & blk	1.50	.20
273	A106	3c violet & blk	1.50	.80
274	A106	4c orange & blk	2.25	1.25
275	A106	5c blue & blk	2.25	.95
276	A106	6c green & blk	.80	.20
		Nos. 271-276 (6)	9.80	4.20

Coast Line of Liberia, 1839 — A107

Seal of Liberia, Map and Farming Scenes — A108

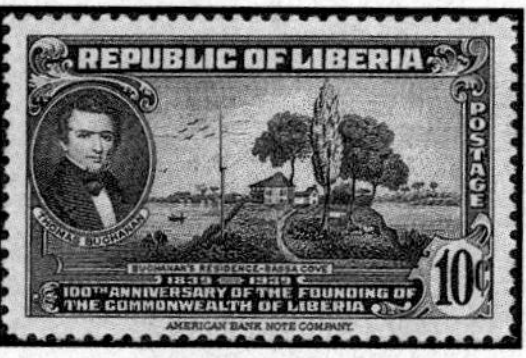

Thomas Buchanan and Residence at Bassa Cove — A109

1940, July 29 **Engr.** *Perf. 12*

No.	Type	Description	Unused	Used
277	A107	3c dark blue	.35	.35
278	A108	5c dull red brn	.35	.35
279	A109	10c dark green	.35	.35
		Nos. 277-279 (3)	1.05	1.05

100th anniv. of the founding of the Commonwealth of Liberia.

For overprints & surcharges see Nos. 280-282, B16-B18, C14-C16, CB1-CB3, CE1, CF1, E1, F35.

Imperforates

Many stamps of Liberia exist imperforate or with various perforation errors, in issued and trial colors, and also in small presentation sheets in issued colors.

Nos. 277-279 Overprinted in Red or Blue

1941, Feb. 21

No.	Type	Description	Unused	Used
280	A107	3c dk blue (R)	2.50	2.50
281	A108	5c dull red brn (Bl)	2.50	2.50
282	A109	10c dark green (R)	2.50	2.50
		Nos. 280-282,C14-C16 (6)	15.75	15.75

Royal Antelope A110

Bay-thighed Diana Monkey — A115

2c, Water chevrotain. 3c, White-shouldered duiker. 4c, Bushbuck. 5c, Zebra antelope.

1942 **Engr.**

No.	Type	Description	Unused	Used
283	A110	1c violet & fawn	1.10	.20
284	A110	2c brt ultra & yel brn	1.40	.20
285	A110	3c brt grn & yel brn	1.90	.90
286	A110	4c blk & red org	2.40	1.90
287	A110	5c olive & fawn	3.00	1.90
288	A115	10c red & black	5.25	2.40
		Nos. 283-288 (6)	15.05	7.50

Nos. 231, 233-234, 271-276 Surcharged with New Values and Bars or X's in Violet, Black, Red Brown or Blue

Perf. 12, 12x12½, 14

1944-46 **Unwmk.**

No.	Type	Description	Unused	Used
288A	A102	1c on 2c (Bk)	9.25	6.50
289	A106	1c on 4c (Bk)	50.00	47.50
289A	A104	1c on 10c (R Br)	12.50	9.50
b.		Double surcharge, one red brown, one violet	25.00	19.00
290	A106	2c on 3c	62.50	50.00
290A	A103	2c on 5c (Bk)	2.75	2.75
290B	A103	2c on 5c (Bl)	21.00	9.25
291	A102	3c on 2c	30.00	30.00
292	A106	4c on 5c	11.00	7.25
292A	A104	4c on 10c (Bk)	3.25	3.25
b.		Double surch., one inverted		
293	A106	5c on 1c (Bk)	100.00	50.00
294	A106	6c on 2c (Bk)	11.00	9.50
295	A106	10c on 6c	11.00	9.50
		Nos. 288A-295 (12)	324.25	235.00

Surcharges on Nos. 289, 290, 293, 294 are found double or inverted. Such varieties command a small premium.

Pres. Franklin D. Roosevelt Reviewing Troops — A116

1945, Nov. 26 **Engr.** *Perf. 12½*

Grayish Paper

No.	Type	Description	Unused	Used
296	A116	3c brt violet & blk	.20	.20
297	A116	5c dk blue & blk	.45	.45
		Nos. 296-297,C51 (3)	1.90	2.05

In memory of Pres. Franklin D. Roosevelt (1882-1945).

Monrovia Harbor — A117

1947, Jan. 2
298 A117 5c deep blue .20 .20

Opening of the Monrovia Harbor Project, Feb. 16, 1946. See No. C52.

Without Inscription at Top

1947, May 16
299 A117 5c violet .20 .20

See No. C53.

1st US Postage Stamps and Arms of Liberia — A118

1947, June 6
300 A118 5c carmine rose .20 .20
Nos. 300,C54-C56 (4) .80 .80

Cent. of US postage stamps and the 87th anniv. of Liberian postal issues.

Matilda Newport Firing Cannon — A119

1947, Dec. 1 Engr. & Photo.
Center in Gray Black
301 A119 1c brt blue green .20 .20
302 A119 3c brt red violet .20 .20
303 A119 5c brt ultra .60 .20
304 A119 10c yellow 3.25 .80
Nos. 301-304,C57 (5) 5.50 1.70

125th anniv. of Matilda Newport's defense of Monrovia, Dec. 1, 1822.

Liberian Star — A120

Cent. of Independence: 2c, Liberty. 3c, Liberian Arms. 5c, Map of Liberia.

1947, Dec. 22 Engr.
305 A120 1c dark green .55 .20
306 A120 2c brt red vio .55 .20
307 A120 3c brt purple .55 .20
308 A120 5c dark blue .55 .20
Nos. 305-308,C58-C60 (7) 3.80 1.65

Centenary of independence.

Natives Approaching Village — A124

Rubber Tapping and Planting A125

Landing of First Colonists — A126

Jehudi Ashmun and Defenders — A127

1949, Apr. 4 Litho. *Perf. 11½*
309 A124 1c multicolored .45 .75
310 A125 2c multicolored .45 .75
311 A126 3c multicolored .45 .75
312 A127 5c multicolored .45 .75
Nos. 309-312,C63-C64 (6) 2.50 4.30

Nos. 309-312 exist perf. 12½ and sell at a much lower price. The status of the perf. 12½ set is indefinite.

Stephen Benson — A128

Liberian Presidents: 1c, Pres. Joseph J. Roberts. 3c, Daniel B. Warner. 4c, James S. Payne. 5c, Executive mansion. 6c, Edward J. Roye. 7c, A. W. Gardner and A. F. Russell. 8c, Hilary R. W. Johnson. 9c, Joseph J. Cheeseman. 10c, William D. Coleman. 15c, Garretson W. Gibson. 20c, Arthur Barclay. 25c, Daniel E. Howard. 50c, Charles D. B. King. $1, Edwin J. Barclay.

1948-50 Unwmk. Engr. *Perf. 12½*
Caption and Portrait in Black
313 A128 1c green ('48) 2.75 *7.00*
314 A128 2c salmon pink .40 *.65*
315 A128 3c rose violet .40 *.65*
a. "1876-1878" added 16.00 *40.00*
316 A128 4c lt olive grn .90 .90
317 A128 5c ultra .50 *.90*
318 A128 6c red orange .90 *1.75*
319 A128 7c lt blue ('50) 1.10 *2.10*
320 A128 8c carmine 1.10 *2.40*
321 A128 9c red violet 1.25 *2.10*
322 A128 10c yellow ('50) .85 .55
323 A128 15c yellow orange 1.00 .70
324 A128 20c blue gray 1.40 1.40
325 A128 25c cerise 2.00 2.10
326 A128 50c aqua 3.75 1.40
327 A128 $1 rose lilac 6.25 1.40
Nos. 313-327,C65 (16) 25.15 *26.65*

Issued: 1c, 11/18; 7c, 10c, 1950; others, 7/21/49.
See Nos. 328, 371-378, C118.

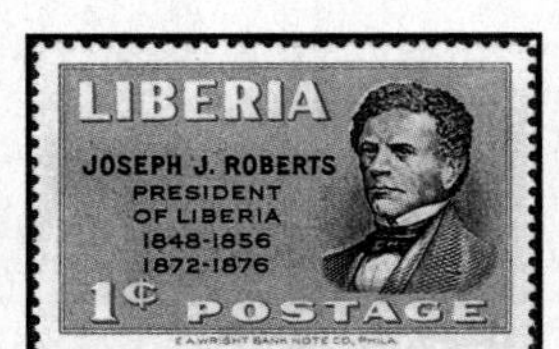

Pres. Joseph J. Roberts — A129

1950
328 A129 1c green & blk .25 .25

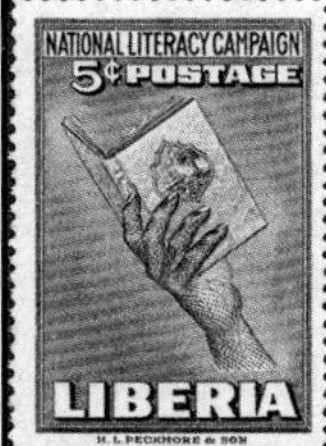

Hand Holding Book — A130

1950, Feb. 14
329 A130 5c deep blue .45 .20

National Literacy Campaign. See No. C66.

Catalogue values for unused stamps in this section, from this point to the end of the section, are for Never Hinged items.

UPU Monument — A131

First UPU Building, Bern — A132

1950, Apr. 21 Engr. Unwmk.
330 A131 5c green & blk .25 .25
331 A132 10c red vio & blk .25 .25
Nos. 330-331,C67 (3) 3.25 3.25

UPU, 75th anniv. (in 1949).
Exist imperf., same value.

Jehudi Ashmun and Seal of Liberia — A133

John Marshall, Ashmun and Map of Town of Marshall — A134

Designs (Map or View and Two Portraits): 2c, Careysburg, Gov. Lott Carey (1780-1828), freed American slave, and Jehudi Ashmun (1794-1828), American missionary credited as founder of Liberia. 3c, Town of Harper, Robert Goodloe Harper (1765-1825), American statesman, and Ashmun. 5c, Upper Buchanan, Gov. Thomas Buchanan and Ashmun. 10c, Robertsport, Pres. Joseph J. Roberts and Ashmun.

1952, Apr. 10 *Perf. 10½*
332 A133 1c deep green .25 .25
333 A133 2c scarlet & ind .25 .25
334 A133 3c purple & grn .25 .25
335 A134 4c brown & grn .25 .25
336 A133 5c ultra & org red .25 .25
337 A134 10c org red & dk bl .25 .25
Nos. 332-337,C68-C69 (8) 2.40 2.40

Nos. 332-337 exist imperf. Value about two and one-half times that of the perf. set.
No. 334 exists with center inverted. Value $50.
See No. C69a.

UN Headquarters Building A135

Scroll and Flags A136

10c, Liberia arms, letters "UN" and emblem.

1952, Dec. 20 Unwmk. *Perf. 12½*
338 A135 1c ultra .30 .30
339 A136 4c car & ultra .30 .30
340 A136 10c red brn & yel .30 .30
a. Souvenir sheet of 3, #338-340 2.00 2.00
Nos. 338-340,C70 (4) 1.80 1.55

Nos. 338-340 and 340a exist imperforate.

Pepper Bird — A137

Roller A138

1953, Nov. 18 *Perf. 10½*
341 A137 1c shown 1.00 .20
342 A138 3c shown 1.00 .20
343 A137 4c Hornbill 1.60 .20
344 A137 5c Kingfisher 1.75 .20
345 A138 10c Jacana 1.90 .20
346 A138 12c Weaver 2.50 .20
Nos. 341-346 (6) 9.75 1.20

Exist imperf. Value, set unused $20.

Tennis A139

Callichilia Stenosepala A140

1955, Jan. 26 Litho. *Perf. 12½*

347 A139 3c shown .25 .25
348 A139 5c Soccer .25 .25
349 A139 25c Boxing .25 .25
Nos. 347-349,C88-C90 (6) 1.65 1.65

1955, Sept. 28 Unwmk.

Various Native Flowers: 7c, Gomphia subcordata. 8c, Listrostachys caudata. 9c, Musaenda isertiana.

350 A140 6c yel grn, org & yel .30 .30
351 A140 7c emer, yel & car .30 .30
352 A140 8c yel grn, buff & bl .30 .30
353 A140 9c orange & green .30 .30
Nos. 350-353,C91-C92 (6) 1.80 1.80

Rubber Tapping A141

1955, Dec. 5 *Perf. 12½*

354 A141 5c emerald & yellow .25 .25
Nos. 354,C97-C98 (3) 1.15 .65

50th anniv. of Rotary Intl. No. 354 exists printed entirely in emerald.

Statue of Liberty A142

Coliseum, New York City — A143

Design: 6c, Globe inscribed FIPEX.

1956, Apr. 28 *Perf. 12*

355 A142 3c brt grn & dk red brn .20 .20
356 A143 4c Prus grn & bis brn .20 .20
357 A143 6c gray & red lilac .20 .20
Nos. 355-357,C100-C102 (6) 1.90 1.20

Fifth International Philatelic Exhibition (FIPEX), NYC, Apr. 28-May 6, 1956.

Kangaroo and Emu — A144

Discus Thrower A145

Designs: 8c, Goddess of Victory and Olympic symbols. 10c, Classic chariot race.

1956, Nov. 15 Litho. Unwmk.

358 A144 4c lt ol grn & gldn brn .20 .20
359 A145 6c emerald & gray .20 .20
360 A144 8c lt ultra & redsh brn .20 .20
361 A144 10c rose red & blk .20 .20
Nos. 358-361,C104-C105 (6) 1.80 1.80

16th Olympic Games at Melbourne, Nov. 22-Dec. 8, 1956.

Idlewild Airport, New York A146

5c, Roberts Field, Liberia, plane & Pres. Tubman.

Lithographed and Engraved

1957, May 4 *Perf. 12*

362 A146 3c orange & dk blue .20 .20
363 A146 5c red lilac & blk .20 .20
Nos. 362-363,C107-C110 (6) 2.95 1.20

1st anniv. of direct air service between Roberts Field, Liberia, and Idlewild (Kennedy), NY.

Orphanage Playground — A147

Orphanage and: 5c, Teacher and pupil. 6c, Singing boys and natl. anthem. 10c, Children and flag.

1957, Nov. 25 Litho. *Perf. 12*

364 A147 4c green & red .20 .20
365 A147 5c bl grn & red brn .20 .20
366 A147 6c brt vio & bis .20 .20
367 A147 10c ultra & rose car .20 .20
Nos. 364-367,C111-C112 (6) 2.00 1.20

Founding of the Antoinette Tubman Child Welfare Foundation.

Windmill and Dutch Flag — A148

Designs: No. 369, German flag and Brandenburg Gate. No. 370, Swedish flag, palace and crowns.

Engraved and Lithographed

1958, Jan. 10 Unwmk. *Perf. 10½*

Flags in Original Colors

368 A148 5c reddish brn .20 .20
369 A148 5c blue .20 .20
370 A148 5c lilac rose .20 .20
Nos. 368-370,C114-C117 (7) 2.40 2.40

European tour of Pres. Tubman in 1956.

Presidential Types of 1948-50

Designs as before.

1958-60 Engr. *Perf. 12*

Caption and Portrait in Black

371 A129 1c salmon pink .45 .20
372 A128 2c brt yellow .45 .20
373 A128 10c blue gray .55 .55
374 A128 15c brt bl & blk ('59) .20 .20
375 A128 20c dark red .65 .65
376 A128 25c blue .65 .65
377 A128 50c red lil & blk ('59) .75 .65
378 A128 $1 bister brn ('60) 5.75 .75
Nos. 371-378,C118 (9) 10.70 4.75

Many shades of 1c.

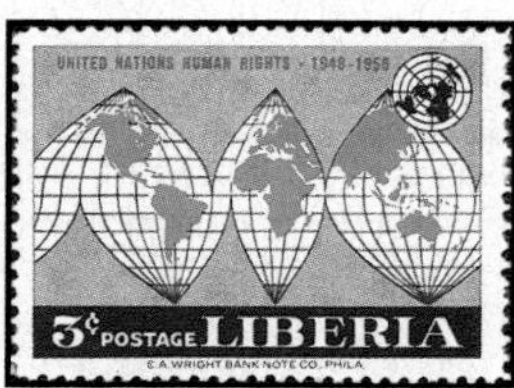

Open Globe Projection — A149

Designs: 5c, UN Emblem and building. 10c, UN Emblem. 12c, UN Emblem and initials of agencies.

1958, Dec. 10 Litho. *Perf. 12*

379 A149 3c gray, bl & blk .20 .20
380 A149 5c blue & choc .20 .20
381 A149 10c black & org .20 .20
382 A149 12c black & car 1.10 1.10
Nos. 379-382 (4) 1.70 1.70

10th anniv. of the Universal Declaration of Human Rights. See No. C119.

People of Africa on the March — A150

Symbols of UNESCO A151

1959, Apr. 15

383 A150 20c orange & brown .45 .45

African Freedom Day, Apr. 15. See No. C120.

1959, May 11 Unwmk.

384 A151 25c dp plum & emer .55 .55

Opening of UNESCO Headquarters in Paris, Nov. 3, 1958.
See Nos. C121, C121a.

Abraham Lincoln — A152

1959, Nov. 20 Engr. *Perf. 12*

385 A152 10c ultra & blk .40 .40
386 A152 15c orange & blk .40 .40
a. Souv. sheet of 3, Nos. 385-386, C122, imperf. 2.50 4.00
Nos. 385-386,C122 (3) 1.70 1.70

150th anniv. of the birth of Abraham Lincoln.

Touré, Tubman and Nkrumah A153

1960, Jan. 27 Litho. Unwmk.

387 A153 25c crimson & blk .55 .55

1959 "Big Three" conference of Pres. Sékou Touré of Guinea, Pres. William V. S. Tubman of Liberia and Prime Minister Kwame Nkrumah of Ghana at Saniquellie, Liberia. See No. C123.

World Refugee Year Emblem — A154

Map of Africa — A155

1960, Apr. 7 *Perf. 11½*

388 A154 25c emerald & blk .70 1.00

World Refuge Year, July 1, 1959-June 30, 1960. See No. C124, C124a.

1960, May 11 Litho. *Perf. 11½*

389 A155 25c green & black .60 .60

10th anniv. of the Commission for Technical Cooperation in Africa South of the Sahara (C.C.T.A.). See No. C125.

Weight Lifter and Porter — A156

Liberian Stamps of 1860 — A157

Designs: 10c, Rower and canoeists, horiz. 15c, Walker and porter.

1960, Sept. 6 Unwmk.

390 A156 5c dk brn & emer .20 .20
391 A156 10c brown & red lil .20 .20
392 A156 15c brown & org .70 .75
Nos. 390-392,C126 (4) 2.00 1.85

17th Olympic Games, Rome, 8/25-9/11.

1960, Dec. 1 Litho. *Perf. 11½*

393 A157 5c multicolored .20 .20
394 A157 20c multicolored .70 .70
Nos. 393-394,C128 (3) 1.90 1.90

Liberian postage stamps, cent.

Laurel Wreath — A158

1961, May 19 Unwmk. *Perf. 11½*

395 A158 25c red & dk blue .60 .60

Liberia's membership in the UN Security Council. Exists imperf. See Nos. C130-C131 and note after No. C131.

Anatomy Class A159

1961, Sept. 8 *Perf. 11½*

396 A159 25c green & brown .60 .60

15th anniv. of UNESCO. See #C132-C133.

Joseph J. Roberts Monument, Monrovia — A160

Design: 10c, Pres. Roberts and old and new presidential mansions, horiz.

1961, Oct. 25 Litho.

397 A160 5c orange & sepia .40 .40

398 A160 10c ultra & sepia .40 .40

Nos. 397-398,C134 (3) 1.50 1.50

150th anniv. of the birth of Joseph J. Roberts, 1st pres. of Liberia.

Boy Scout A161

Design: Insignia and Scouts camping.

1961, Dec. 4 Unwmk. *Perf. 11½*

399 A161 5c lilac & sepia .20 .20

400 A161 10c ultra & bister .50 .50

Nos. 399-400,C135 (3) 2.10 2.10

Boy Scouts of Liberia. Exist imperf.

Dag Hammarskjold and UN Emblem — A162

1962, Feb. 1 *Perf. 12*

401 A162 20c black & ultra .45 .45

Dag Hammarskjold, Secretary General of the UN, 1953-61. See Nos. C137-C138.

Malaria Eradication Emblem — A163

1962, Apr. 7 Litho. *Perf. 12½*

402 A163 25c dk green & red .55 .45

WHO drive to eradicate malaria. See Nos. C139-C140.

United Nations Emblem A164

1962, Oct. 22 *Perf. 12x12½*

403 A164 20c green & yel bister .35 .35

Issued to mark the observance of United Nations Day, Oct. 24, as a national holiday. See Nos. C144-C145.

Executive Mansion, Monrovia A165

1c, 80c, Executive Mansion, Monrovia. 5c, Treasury Department Building, Monrovia. 10c, Information Service. 15c, Capitol.

1962-64

403A A165 1c vio bl & dp org ('64) .20 .20

404 A165 5c lt blue & pur .20 .20

405 A165 10c bister & brn .20 .20

406 A165 15c salmon & dk bl .20 .20

406A A165 80c brn & yel ('64) 1.75 .85

Nos. 403A-406A,C146-C148 (9) 9.10 8.20

"FAO" Emblem and Food Bowl — A166

1963, Mar. 21 *Perf. 12½*

407 A166 5c aqua & dk car .25 .25

FAO "Freedom from Hunger" campaign. See Nos. C149-C150.

Rocket in Space A167

Design: 15c, Space capsule and globe.

1963, May 27 Litho. *Perf. 12½*

408 A167 10c dp vio bl & yel .20 .20

409 A167 15c blue & red brn .60 .60

Nos. 408-409,C151 (3) 1.50 1.50

Achievements in space exploration for peaceful purposes.

Red Cross A168

10c, Centenary emblem and torch, vert.

1963, Aug. 26 Unwmk. *Perf. 11½*

410 A168 5c blue grn & red .20 .20

411 A168 10c gray & red .20 .20

Nos. 410-411,C153-C154 (4) 1.50 1.50

Intl. Red Cross, cent.

Palm Tree and Scroll — A169

Ski Jump — A170

1963, Oct. 28 *Perf. 12½*

412 A169 20c brown & green .45 .45

Conference of African heads of state for African Unity, Addis Ababa, May, 1963. See No. C156.

1963, Dec. 11 Unwmk. *Perf. 12½*

413 A170 5c rose red & dk vio bl .25 .25

Nos. 413,C157-C158 (3) 1.25 1.25

9th Winter Olympic Games, Innsbruck, Austria, Jan. 29-Feb. 9, 1964.

John F. Kennedy A171

1964, Apr. 6 Litho.

414 A171 20c blk & brt blue .35 .35

John F. Kennedy (1917-63). See #C160-C161.

Syncom Satellite A172

Satellites: 15c, Relay I, vert. 25c, Mariner II.

1964, June 22 Unwmk. *Perf. 12½*

415 A172 10c orange & emer .20 .20

416 A172 15c brt car rose & vio .20 .20

417 A172 25c blue, org & blk .70 .70

Nos. 415-417 (3) 1.10 1.10

Progress in space communications and the peaceful uses of outer space. See No. C162.

Mt. Fuji A173

Designs: 15c, Torii and Olympic flame. 25c, Cherry blossoms and stadium.

1964, Sept. 15 Litho.

418 A173 10c orange yel & emer .20 .20

419 A173 15c lt red & purple .20 .20

420 A173 25c ocher & red .95 .95

Nos. 418-420 (3) 1.35 1.35

Issued for the 18th Olympic Games, Tokyo, Oct. 10-25, 1964. See No. C163.

Boy Scout Emblem and Scout Sign — A174

"Emancipation" by Thomas Ball — A175

10c, Bugle and Liberian Scout emblem, horiz.

1965, Mar. 8 Litho. *Perf. 12½*

421 A174 5c lt blue & brown .25 .25

422 A174 10c dk green & ocher .25 .25

Nos. 421-422,C164 (3) 1.30 1.30

Liberian Boy Scouts.

1965, May 3 Unwmk. *Perf. 12½*

Designs: 20c, Abraham Lincoln and John F. Kennedy, horiz. 25c, Lincoln by Augustus St. Gaudens, Lincoln Park, Chicago.

423 A175 5c dk gray & brn org .20 .20

424 A175 20c emer & lt gray .50 .50

425 A175 25c maroon & blue .65 .65

Nos. 423-425 (3) 1.35 1.35

Centenary of the death of Abraham Lincoln. See No. C166.

ICY Emblem A176

1965, June 21 Litho. *Perf. 12½*

426 A176 12c orange & brn .20 .20

427 A176 25c vio blue & brn .40 .40

428 A176 50c emerald & brn .85 .85

Nos. 426-428 (3) 1.45 1.45

Intl. Cooperation Year. See No. C167.

ITU Emblem, Old and New Communication Equipment — A177

1965, Sept. 21 Unwmk. *Perf. 12½*

429	A177	25c brt grn & red brn	.40	.40
430	A177	35c black & car rose	.50	.50
		Nos. 429-430,C168 (3)	1.70	1.60

Cent. of the ITU.

Pres. Tubman and Liberian Flag A178

1965, Nov. 29 Litho.

431	A178	25c red, ultra & brn	.60	.60

Pres. William V. S. Tubman's 70th birthday. See No. C169, C169a.

Churchill in Admiral's Uniform A179

Pres. Joseph J. Roberts — A180

Designs: 15c, Churchill giving "V" sign, vert.

1966, Jan. 18 Litho. *Perf. 12½*

432	A179	15c orange & blk	.20	.20
433	A179	20c black & brt grn	.90	.90
		Nos. 432-433,C170 (3)	1.80	1.65

Issued in memory of Sir Winston Spencer Churchill (1874-1965), statesman and World War II leader.

1966-69 Litho. *Perf. 12½*

Presidents: 2c, Stephen Benson. 3c, Daniel Bashiel Warner. 4c, James S. Payne. 5c, Edward James Roye. 10c, William D. Coleman. 25c, Daniel Edward Howard. 50c, Charles Dunbar Burgess King. 80c, Hilary R. W. Johnson. $1, Edwin J. Barclay. $2, Joseph James Cheeseman ("Cheesman" on stamp).

434	A180	1c black & brick red	.20	.20
435	A180	2c black & yellow	.20	.20
436	A180	3c black & lilac	.20	.20
437	A180	4c ap grn & blk ('67)	.20	.20
438	A180	5c black & dull org	.20	.20
439	A180	10c pale grn & blk ('67)	.20	.20
440	A180	25c black & lt blue	.60	.20
441	A180	50c blk & brt lil rose	1.25	.90
442	A180	80c dp rose & blk ('67)	1.90	1.10
443	A180	$1 black & ocher	2.25	.20

Perf. 11½x11

443A	A180	$2 blk & dp red lil ('69)	4.50	3.00
		Nos. 434-443A,C182 (12)	12.30	6.90

Soccer Players and Globe A181

Designs: 25c, World Championships Cup, ball and shoes, vert. 35c, Soccer player dribbling, vert.

1966, May 3 Litho. *Perf. 12½*

444	A181	10c brt green & dk brn	.20	.20
445	A181	25c brt pink & brn	.60	.20
446	A181	35c brown & orange	.80	.45
		Nos. 444-446 (3)	1.60	.85

World Cup Soccer Championships, Wembley, England, July 11-30. See No. C172.

Pres. Kennedy Taking Oath of Office A182

20c, 1964 Kennedy stamps, #414, C160.

1966, Aug. 16 Litho. *Perf. 12½*

447	A182	15c red & blk	.35	.35
448	A182	20c brt bl & red lil	.35	.35
		Nos. 447-448,C173-C174 (4)	1.80	1.10

3rd anniv. of Pres. Kennedy's death (Nov. 22).

Children on Seesaw and UNICEF Emblem A183

Design: 80c, Boy playing doctor.

1966, Oct. 25 Unwmk. *Perf. 12½*

449	A183	5c brt blue & red	.20	.20
450	A183	80c org brn & yel grn	1.10	1.10

20th anniv. of UNICEF.

Giraffe — A184

Jamboree Badge — A185

Designs: 3c, Lion. 5c, Slender-nosed crocodile, horiz. 10c, Baby chimpanzees. 15c, Leopard, horiz. 20c, Black rhinoceros, horiz. 25c, Elephant.

1966, Dec. 20

451	A184	2c multicolored	1.25	1.25
452	A184	3c multicolored	1.25	1.25
453	A184	5c multicolored	1.25	1.25
a.		Black omitted ("5¢ LIBERIA" and imprint)		*50.00*
454	A184	10c multicolored	1.25	1.25
455	A184	15c multicolored	1.60	1.25
456	A184	20c multicolored	2.25	1.25
457	A184	25c multicolored	3.25	1.25
		Nos. 451-457 (7)	12.10	8.75

1967, Mar. 23 Litho. *Perf. 12½*

Designs: 25c, Boy Scout emblem and various sports, horiz. 40c, Scout at campfire and vision of moon landing, horiz.

458	A185	10c brt lil rose & grn	.20	.20
459	A185	25c brt red & blue	.65	.55
460	A185	40c brt grn & brn org	1.10	.85
		Nos. 458-460 (3)	1.95	1.60

12th Boy Scout World Jamboree, Farragut State Park, Idaho, Aug. 1-9. See No. C176.

A186

A187

Pre-Hispanic Sculpture of Mexico: 25c, Aztec Calendar and Olympic rings. 40c, Mexican pottery, sombrero and guitar, horiz.

1967, June 20 Litho. *Perf. 12½*

461	A186	10c ocher & violet	.20	.20
462	A186	25c lt bl, org & blk	.35	.25
463	A186	40c yel grn & car	.55	.40
		Nos. 461-463 (3)	1.10	.85

Issued to publicize the 19th Olympic Games, Mexico City. See No. C177.

1967, Aug. 28 Litho. *Perf. 12½*

Designs: 5c, WHO Office for Africa, horiz. 80c, WHO Office for Africa.

464	A187	5c blue & yellow	.20	.20
465	A187	80c brt grn & yel	2.10	2.10

Inauguration of the WHO Regional Office for Africa in Brazzaville, Congo.

Boy Playing African Rattle A188

Africans Playing Native Instruments: 3c, Tom-tom and soko violin, horiz. 5c, Mang harp, horiz. 10c, Alimilim. 15c, Xylophone drums. 25c, Large tom-toms. 35c, Large harp.

1967, Oct. 16 Litho. *Perf. 14*

466	A188	2c violet & multi	.20	.20
467	A188	3c blue & multi	.20	.20
468	A188	5c lilac rose & multi	.20	.20
469	A188	10c yel grn & multi	.20	.20
470	A188	15c violet & multi	.40	.20
471	A188	25c ocher & multi	.90	.40
472	A188	35c dp rose & multi	1.40	.65
		Nos. 466-472 (7)	3.50	2.05

Ice Hockey — A189

Pres. William Tubman — A190

Designs: 25c, Ski jump. 40c, Bobsledding.

1967, Nov. 20 Litho. *Perf. 12½*

473	A189	10c emer & vio bl	.20	.20
474	A189	25c grnsh bl & dp plum	.40	.20
475	A189	40c ocher & org brn	.70	.50
		Nos. 473-475 (3)	1.30	.90

10th Winter Olympic Games, Grenoble, France, Feb. 6-18, 1968. See No. C178.

1967, Dec. 22 Litho. *Perf. 12½*

476	A190	25c ultra & brown	1.00	.50

Souvenir Sheet

Imperf

477	A190	50c ultra & brown	2.50	2.50

Inauguration of President Tubman, Jan. 1, 1968. No. 477 contains one stamp with simulated perforations and picture frame.

Human Rights Flame — A191

Martin Luther King, Jr. — A192

1968, Apr. 26 Litho. *Perf. 12½*

478	A191	3c ver & dp bl	.20	.20
479	A191	80c brown & emer	1.40	1.40

Intl. Human Rights Year. See No. C179.

1968, July 11 Unwmk. *Perf. 12½*

Designs: 15c, Mule-drawn hearse and Dr. King. 35c, Dr. King and Lincoln monument by Daniel Chester French, horiz.

480	A192	15c brt bl & brn	.20	.20
481	A192	25c indigo & brn	.40	.20
482	A192	35c olive & blk	.65	.40
		Nos. 480-482 (3)	1.25	.80

Rev. Dr. Martin Luther King, Jr. (1929-1968), American civil rights leader. See No. C180.

Javelin and Diana Statue, Mexico City A193

Designs: 25c, Discus, pyramid and serpent god Quetzalcoatl. 35c, Woman diver and Xochicalco from ruins near Cuernavaca.

1968, Aug. 22 Litho. *Perf. 12½*

483	A193	15c dp vio & org brn	.40	.20
484	A193	25c red & brt blue	.70	.20
485	A193	35c brown & emer	1.00	.45
		Nos. 483-485 (3)	2.10	.85

19th Olympic Games, Mexico City, Oct. 12-27. See No. C181.

Pres. Wm. V. S. Tubman A194

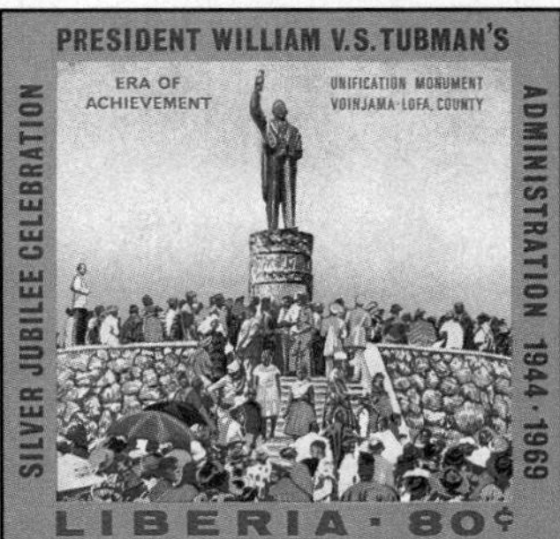

Unification Monument, Voinjama-Lofa County — A195

1968, Dec. 30 Unwmk. *Perf. 12½*
486 A194 25c silver, blk & brn 1.60 1.00

Souvenir Sheet

Imperf

487 A195 80c silver, ultra & red 3.25 3.25

25th anniv. of Pres. Tubman's administration.

"ILO" with Cogwheel and Wreath A196

1969, Apr. 16 Litho. *Perf. 12½*
488 A196 25c lt blue & gold .70 .40

50th anniv. of the ILO. See No. C183.

Red Roofs, by Camille Pissarro — A197

Paintings: 3c, Prince Balthasar Carlos on Horseback, by Velazquez, vert. 10c, David and Goliath, by Caravaggio. 12c, Still Life, by Jean Baptiste Chardin. 15c, The Last Supper, by Leonardo da Vinci. 20c, Regatta at Argenteuil, by Claude Monet. 25c, Judgment of Solomon, by Giorgione. 35c, Sistine Madonna, by Raphael.

1969, June 26 Litho. *Perf. 11*
489 A197 3c gray & multi .20 .20
490 A197 5c gray & multi .20 .20
491 A197 10c lt blue & multi .20 .20
492 A197 12c gray & multi .50 .20
493 A197 15c gray & multi .50 .20
494 A197 20c gray & multi .80 .20
495 A197 25c gray & multi .95 .20
496 A197 35c gray & multi 1.25 .40
Nos. 489-496 (8) 4.60 1.80

See Nos. 502-509.

African Development Bank Emblem — A198

1969, Aug. 12 Litho. *Perf. 12½*
497 A198 25c blue & brown .60 .50
498 A198 80c yel grn & red 1.90 1.00

5th anniversary of the African Development Bank.

Moon Landing and Liberia No. C174 A199

15c, Memorial tablet left on moon, rocket, earth & moon, horiz. 35c, Take-off from moon.

1969, Oct. 15 Litho. *Perf. 12½*
499 A199 15c blue & bister .65 .20
500 A199 25c dk vio bl & org 1.00 .20
501 A199 35c gray & red 1.50 .40
Nos. 499-501 (3) 3.15 .80

Man's 1st landing on the moon, July 20, 1969. US astronauts Neil A. Armstrong and Col. Edwin E. Aldrin, Jr., with Lieut. Col. Michael Collins piloting Apollo 11. See No. C184.

Painting Type of 1969

1969, Nov. 18 Litho. *Perf. 11*

Paintings: 3c, The Gleaners, by Francois Millet. 5c, View of Toledo, by El Greco, vert. 10c, Heads of Negroes, by Rubens. 12c, The Last Supper, by El Greco. 15c, Dancing Peasants, by Brueghel. 20c, Hunters in the Snow, by Brueghel. 25c, Detail from Descent from the Cross, by Rogier van der Weyden, vert. 35c, The Ascension, by Murillo (inscribed "The Conception"), vert.

502 A197 3c lt blue & multi .20 .20
503 A197 5c lt blue & multi .20 .20
504 A197 10c lt blue & multi .20 .20
505 A197 12c gray & multi .40 .20
506 A197 15c gray & multi .55 .20
507 A197 20c lt blue & multi .70 .20
508 A197 25c gray & multi .95 .40
509 A197 35c lt blue & multi 1.25 .40
Nos. 502-509 (8) 4.45 2.00

Peace Dove, UN Emblem and Atom — A200

1970, Apr. 16 Litho. *Perf. 12½*
510 A200 5c green & silver .30 .30

25th anniv. of the UN. See No. C185.

Official Emblem — A201

Designs: 10c, Statue of rain god Tlaloc, vert. 25c, Jules Rimet cup and sculptured wall, vert. 35c, Sombrero and soccer ball. 55c, Two soccer players.

1970, June 10 Litho. *Perf. 12½*
511 A201 5c pale blue & brn .20 .20
512 A201 10c emerald & ocher .20 .20
513 A201 25c dp rose lil & gold .70 .20
514 A201 35c ver & ultra 1.00 .35
Nos. 511-514 (4) 2.10 .95

Souvenir Sheet

Perf. 11½

515 A201 55c brt bl, yel & grn 1.75 1.60

9th World Soccer Championships for the Jules Rimet Cup, Mexico City, May 30-June 21, 1970.

EXPO '70 Emblem, Japanese Singer and Festival Plaza — A202

Designs (EXPO '70 Emblem and): 3c, Male Japanese singer, EXPO Hall and floating stage. 5c, Tower of the Sun and view of exhibition. 7c, Tanabata Festival. 8c, Awa Dance Festival. 25c, Sado-Okesa Dance Festival. 50c, Ricoh Pavilion with "eye," and Mt. Fuji, vert.

1970, July Litho. *Perf. 11*
516 A202 2c multicolored .20 .20
517 A202 3c multicolored .20 .20
518 A202 5c multicolored .45 .20
519 A202 7c multicolored .60 .20
520 A202 8c multicolored .75 .20
521 A202 25c multicolored 1.75 .65
Nos. 516-521 (6) 3.95 1.65

Souvenir Sheet

522 A202 50c multicolored 3.25 1.00

Issued to publicize EXPO '70 International Exhibition, Osaka, Japan, Mar. 15-Sept. 13.

UPU Headquarters and Monument, Bern — A203

Design: 80c, Like 25c, vert.

1970, Aug. 25 *Perf. 12½*
523 A203 25c blue & multi 1.25 1.10
524 A203 80c multicolored 3.00 2.50

Inauguration of the new UPU Headquarters in Bern.

Napoleon as Consul, by Joseph Marie Vien, Sr. A204

Paintings of Napoleon: 5c, Visit to a School, by unknown painter. 10c, Napoleon Bonaparte, by François Pascal Gerard. 12c, The French Campaign, by Ernest Meissonier. 20c, Napoleon Signing Abdication at Fontainebleau, by François Bouchot. 25c, Napoleon Meets Pope Pius VII, by Jean-Louis Demarne. 50c, Napoleon's Coronation, by Jacques Louis David.

1970, Oct. 20 Litho. *Perf. 11*
525 A204 3c blue & multi .20 .20
526 A204 5c blue & multi .20 .20
527 A204 10c blue & multi .55 .20
528 A204 12c blue & multi .75 .20
529 A204 20c blue & multi 1.10 .20
530 A204 25c blue & multi 2.10 .20
Nos. 525-530 (6) 4.90 1.20

Souvenir Sheet

Imperf

531 A204 50c blue & multi 3.25 .80

200th anniv. of the birth of Napoleon Bonaparte (1769-1821). No. 531 contains one stamp with simulated perforations.

Pres. Tubman A205

1970, Nov. 20 Litho. *Perf. 13½*
532 A205 25c multicolored 1.10 .55

Souvenir Sheet

Imperf

533 A205 50c multicolored 2.00 1.10

Pres. Tubman's 75th birthday. No. 533 contains one imperf. stamp with simulated perforations.

Adoration of the Kings, by Rogier van der Weyden — A206

Paintings (Adoration of the Kings, by): 5c, Hans Memling. 10c, Stefan Lochner. 12c, Albrecht Altdorfer, vert. 20c, Hugo van der Goes, Adoration of the Shepherds. 25c, Hieronymus Bosch, vert. 50c, Andrea Mantegna (triptych).

Perf. 13½x14, 14x13½

1970, Dec. 21 Litho.
534 A206 3c multicolored .20 .20
535 A206 5c multicolored .20 .20
536 A206 10c multicolored .20 .20
537 A206 12c multicolored .35 .20
538 A206 20c multicolored .50 .20
539 A206 25c multicolored .75 .20
Nos. 534-539 (6) 2.20 1.20

Souvenir Sheet

Imperf

540 A206 50c multicolored 3.00 .85

Christmas 1970.
No. 540 contains one 60x40mm stamp.

Dogon Tribal Mask A207

African Tribal Ceremonial Masks: 2c, Bapendé. 5c, Baoulé. 6c, Dédougou. 9c, Dan. 15c, Bamiléké. 20c, Bapendé mask and costume. 25c, Bamiléké mask and costume.

1971, Feb. 24 Litho. *Perf. 11*

541	A207	2c lt green & multi	.20	.20
542	A207	3c pink & multi	.20	.20
543	A207	5c lt blue & multi	.20	.20
544	A207	6c lt green & multi	.20	.20
545	A207	9c lt blue & multi	.20	.20
546	A207	15c pink & multi	.45	.20
547	A207	20c lt green & multi	.85	.55
548	A207	25c pink & multi	.45	.20
		Nos. 541-548 (8)	2.75	1.95

Astronauts on Moon — A208

Designs: 5c, Astronaut and lunar transport vehicle. 10c, Astronaut with US flag on moon. 12c, Space capsule in Pacific Ocean. 20c, Astronaut leaving capsule. 25c, Astronauts Alan B. Shepard, Stuart A. Roosa and Edgar D. Mitchell.

1971, May 20 Litho. *Perf. 13½*

549	A208	3c vio blue & multi	.20	.20
550	A208	5c vio blue & multi	.20	.20
551	A208	10c vio blue & multi	.45	.20
552	A208	12c vio blue & multi	.60	.20
553	A208	20c vio blue & multi	.85	.20
554	A208	25c vio blue & multi	1.00	.35
		Nos. 549-554 (6)	3.30	1.35

Apollo 14 moon landing, Jan. 31-Feb. 9. See No. C186.

Map, Liberian Women and Pres. Tubman A209

3c, Pres. Tubman & women at ballot box, vert.

1971, May 27 *Perf. 12½*

555	A209	3c ultra & brn	.20	.20
556	A209	80c green & brn	2.10	2.10

25th anniversary of women's suffrage.

Hall of Honor, Munich, and Olympic Flag — A210

Munich Views and Olympic Flag: 5c, General view. 10c, National Museum. 12c, Max Joseph's Square. 20c, Propylaeum on King's Square. 25c, Liesel-Karlstadt Fountain.

1971, June 28 Litho. *Perf. 11*

557	A210	3c multicolored	.20	.20
558	A210	5c multicolored	.20	.20
559	A210	10c multicolored	.20	.20
560	A210	12c multicolored	.25	.20
561	A210	20c multicolored	1.10	.20
562	A210	25c multicolored	1.90	.90
		Nos. 557-562 (6)	3.85	1.90

Publicity for the 20th Summer Olympic Games, Munich, Germany, 1972. See No. C187.

Boy Scout, Emblem and US Flag A211

Boy Scout, Natl. Flag & Boy Scout Emblem of: 5c, German Federal Republic. 10c, Australia. 12c, Great Britain. 20c, Japan. 25c, Liberia.

1971, Aug. 6 Litho. *Perf. 13½*

563	A211	3c multicolored	.20	.20
564	A211	5c multicolored	.20	.20
565	A211	10c multicolored	.20	.20
566	A211	12c multicolored	.35	.20
567	A211	20c multicolored	.60	.20
568	A211	25c multicolored	.75	.20
		Nos. 563-568 (6)	2.30	1.20

13th Boy Scout World Jamboree, Asagiri Plain, Japan, Aug. 2-10. See No. C188.

Pres. Tubman (1895-1971) A212

1971, Aug. 23 *Perf. 12½*

569	A212	3c black, ultra & brn	.20	.20
570	A212	25c blk, brt rose lil & brn	1.10	1.10

Zebra and UNICEF Emblem — A213

Animals (UNICEF Emblem and Animals with their Young): 7c, Koala. 8c, Llama. 10c, Red fox. 20c, Monkey. 25c, Brown bear.

1971, Oct. 1 *Perf. 11*

571	A213	5c multicolored	.20	.20
572	A213	7c multicolored	.50	.20
573	A213	8c multicolored	.50	.20
574	A213	10c multicolored	.65	.20
575	A213	20c multicolored	1.25	.50
576	A213	25c multicolored	1.60	.65
		Nos. 571-576 (6)	4.70	1.95

25th anniv. of UNICEF. See No. C189.

Sapporo 72 Emblem, Long-distance Skiing, Sika Deer — A214

3c, Sledding & black woodpecker. 5c, Ski Jump & brown bear. 10c, Bobsledding & murres. 15c, Figure skating & pikas. 25c, Downhill skiing & Japanese cranes.

1971, Nov. 4 *Perf. 13x13½*

577	A214	2c multicolored	.20	.20
578	A214	3c multicolored	.20	.20
579	A214	5c multicolored	.20	.20
580	A214	10c multicolored	.30	.20
581	A214	15c multicolored	1.75	.20
582	A214	25c multicolored	3.75	.20
		Nos. 577-582 (6)	6.40	1.20

11th Winter Olympic Games, Sapporo, Japan, Feb. 3-13, 1972. See No. C190.

Dove Carrying Letter, APU Emblem A215

1971, Dec. 9 *Perf. 12½*

583	A215	25c ultra & dp org	.60	.55
584	A215	80c gray & dp brn	2.00	1.60

10th anniversary of African Postal Union.

Pioneer Fathers' Monument, Monrovia A216

Pres. William R. Tolbert, Jr. — A217

Designs: 3c, 25c, Sailing ship "Elizabeth," Providence Island, horiz. 35c, as 20c.

1972, Jan. 1

585	A216	3c blue & brt grn	.20	.20
586	A216	20c orange & blue	.95	.70
587	A216	25c orange & purple	1.00	.85
588	A216	35c lil rose & brt grn	1.75	1.25
		Nos. 585-588 (4)	3.90	3.00

Founding of Liberia, sesqui. See No. C191.

1972, Jan. 1

25c, Pres. Tolbert and map of Liberia, horiz.

589	A217	25c emerald & brown	.65	.40
590	A217	80c blue & brown	2.25	.70

Inauguration of William R. Tolbert, Jr. as 19th president of Liberia.

Soccer and Swedish Flag — A218

Olympic Rings, "Motion" Symbol and: 5c, Swimmers at start, Italian flag. 10c, Equestrian, British flag. 12c, Bicycling, French flag. 20c, Long jump, US flag. 25c, Running and Liberian flag.

1972, May 19 Litho. *Perf. 11*

591	A218	3c lemon & multi	.20	.20
592	A218	5c lt lilac & multi	.20	.20
593	A218	10c multicolored	.75	.20
594	A218	12c gray & multi	1.00	.20
595	A218	20c lt blue & multi	1.40	.60
596	A218	25c pink & multi	1.90	.75
		Nos. 591-596 (6)	5.45	2.15

20th Olympic Games, Munich, Aug. 26-Sept. 10. See No. C192.

Y's Men's Club Emblem, Map A219

Design: 90c, Y's Men's Club emblem and globe; inscribed "fifty and forward."

1972, June 12 *Perf. 13½*

597	A219	15c purple & gold	.50	.20
598	A219	90c vio bl & emer	2.40	2.00

Intl. Y's Men's Club, 50th anniv.

Astronaut and Lunar Rover — A220

5c, Moon scene reflected in astronaut's helmet. 10c, Astronauts with cameras. 12c, Astronauts placing scientific equipment on moon. 20c, Apollo 16 badge. 25c, Astronauts riding lunar rover.

1972, June 26

599	A220	3c lt blue & multi	.20	.20
600	A220	5c red org & multi	.20	.20
601	A220	10c pink & multi	.50	.20
602	A220	12c yellow & multi	.80	.20
603	A220	20c lt vio & multi	1.00	.20
604	A220	25c emerald & multi	1.40	.20
		Nos. 599-604 (6)	4.10	1.20

Apollo 16 US moon mission, Apr. 15-27, 1972. See No. C193.

Emperor Haile Selassie — A221

1972, July 21 *Perf. 14x14½*

605	A221	20c olive grn & yel	.70	.70
606	A221	25c maroon & yel	.85	.85
607	A221	35c brown & yel	1.25	1.25
		Nos. 605-607 (3)	2.80	2.80

80th birthday of Emperor Haile Selassie of Ethiopia.

Ajax, 1809, and Figurehead — A222

1972, Sept. 6 *Perf. 11*

608	A222	3c *shown*	.20	.20
609	A222	5c *Hogue, 1811*	.20	.20
610	A222	7c *Ariadne, 1816*	.55	.20
611	A222	15c *Royal Adelaide, 1828*	1.00	.20
612	A222	20c *Rinaldo, 1860*	1.25	.20
613	A222	25c *Nymphe, 1888*	1.45	.45
		Nos. 608-613 (6)	4.65	1.45

Famous sailing ships and their figureheads. See No. C194.

Pres. Tolbert Taking Oath, Richard A. Henries — A223

1972, Oct. 23 Litho. *Perf. 13½*

614 A223 15c green & multi 1.10 .95
615 A223 25c vio blue & multi 1.50 1.45

Pres. William R. Tolbert, Jr. sworn in as 19th President of Liberia, July 23, 1971. See No. C195.

Klaus Dibiasi, Italy, Diving — A224

8c, Valery Borzov, USSR, running. 10c, Hideaki Yanagida, Japan, wrestling. 12c, Mark Spitz, US, swimming. 15c, Kipchoge Keino, Kenya, 3000-meter steeplechase. 25c, Richard Meade, Great Britain, equestrian. 55c, Hans Winkler, Germany, grand prix jumping.

1973, Jan. 5 Litho. *Perf. 11*

616 A224 5c lt blue & multi .20 .20
617 A224 8c violet & multi .20 .20
618 A224 10c multicolored .20 .20
619 A224 12c green & multi .55 .20
620 A224 15c orange & multi .80 .20
621 A224 25c pale salmon & multi 1.10 .55
Nos. 616-621 (6) 3.05 1.55

Souvenir Sheet

622 A224 55c multicolored 4.50 2.25

Gold medal winners in 20th Olympic Games.

Astronaut on Moon and Apollo 17 Badge — A225

Designs (Apollo 17 Badge and): 3c, Astronauts on earth in lunar rover. 10c, Astronauts collecting yellow lunar dust. 15c, Astronauts in lunar rover exploring moon crater. 20c, Capt. Eugene A. Cernan, Dr. Harrison H. Schmitt and Comdr. Ronald E. Evans on launching pad. 25c, Astronauts on moon with scientific equipment.

1973, Mar. 28 Litho. *Perf. 11*

623 A225 2c blue & multi .20 .20
624 A225 3c blue & multi .20 .20
625 A225 10c blue & multi .20 .20
626 A225 15c blue & multi .70 .20
627 A225 20c blue & multi 1.00 .50
628 A225 25c blue & multi 1.25 .60
Nos. 623-628 (6) 3.55 1.90

Apollo 17 US moon mission, Dec. 7-19, 1972. See No. C196.

Locomotive, England — A226

Designs: Locomotives, 1895-1905.

1973, May 4

629 A226 2c shown .20 .20
630 A226 3c Netherlands .20 .20
631 A226 10c France .90 .20
632 A226 15c United States 1.25 .20
633 A226 20c Japan 2.25 .20
634 A226 25c Germany 3.25 .75
Nos. 629-634 (6) 8.05 1.75

See No. C197.

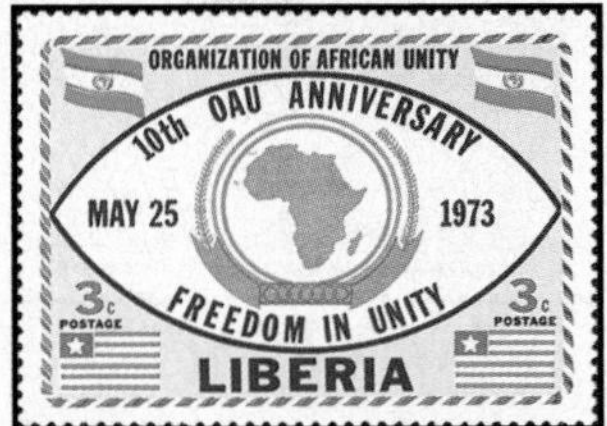

OAU Emblem and Flags — A227

1973, May 24 Litho. *Perf. 13½*

635 A227 3c multicolored .20 .20
636 A227 5c multicolored .20 .20
637 A227 10c multicolored .20 .20
638 A227 15c multicolored .45 .20
639 A227 25c multicolored .55 .45
640 A227 50c multicolored 1.25 .95
Nos. 635-640 (6) 2.85 2.20

10th anniv. of the Organization for African Unity.

WHO Emblem, Edward Jenner and Roses — A228

Designs (WHO Emblem and): 4c, Sigmund Freud and pansies. 10c, Jonas E. Salk and chrysanthemums. 15c, Louis Pasteur and scabiosa caucasia. 20c, Emil von Behring and rhododendron. 25c, Alexander Fleming and tree mallows.

1973, June 26 Litho. *Perf. 11*

641 A228 1c gray & multi .20 .20
642 A228 4c orange & multi .20 .20
643 A228 10c lt blue & multi .20 .20
644 A228 15c rose & multi .40 .20
645 A228 20c blue & multi .50 .20
646 A228 25c yel grn & multi .75 .40
Nos. 641-646 (6) 2.25 1.40

25th anniv. of WHO. See No. C198.

Stanley Steamer, 1910 — A229

Designs: Classic automobiles.

1973, Sept. 11 Litho. *Perf. 11*

647 A229 2c shown .20 .20
648 A229 3c Cadillac, 1903 .20 .20
649 A229 10c Clement-Bayard, 1904 .40 .20
650 A229 15c Rolls Royce, 1907 .55 .20
651 A229 20c Maxwell, 1905 .80 .20
652 A229 25c Chadwick, 1907 1.00 .50
Nos. 647-652 (6) 3.15 1.50

See No. C199.

Copernicus, Armillary Sphere, Satellite Communication — A230

Portraits of Copernicus and: 4c, Eudoxus solar system. 10c, Aristotle, Ptolemy, Copernicus and satellites. 15c, Saturn and Apollo spacecraft. 20c, Orbiting astronomical observatory. 25c, Satellite tracking station.

1973, Dec. 14 Litho. *Perf. 13½*

653 A230 1c yellow & multi .20 .20
654 A230 4c lt violet & multi .20 .20
655 A230 10c lt blue & multi .20 .20
656 A230 15c yel grn & multi .50 .20
657 A230 20c bister & multi .65 .20
658 A230 25c pink & multi .80 .40
Nos. 653-658 (6) 2.55 1.40

Nicolaus Copernicus (1473-1543), Polish astronomer. See No. C200.

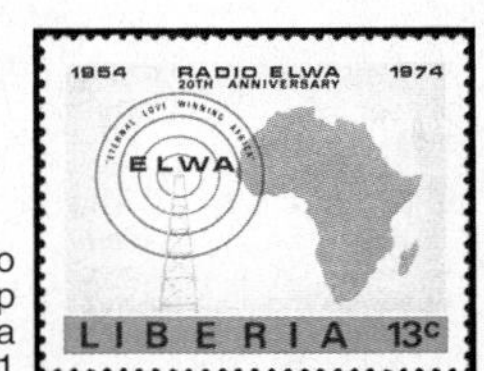

Radio Tower, Map of Africa A231

15c, 25c, Map of Liberia, Radio tower and man listening to broadcast. 17c, like 13c.

1974, Jan. 16 Litho. *Perf. 13½*

659 A231 13c multicolored .60 .60
660 A231 15c yellow & multi .60 .50
661 A231 17c lt gray & multi .75 .60
662 A231 25c brt green & multi 1.00 .65
Nos. 659-662 (4) 2.95 2.35

20th anniv. of Radio ELWA, Monrovia.

Thomas Coutts, 1817; Aureal, 1974; UPU Emblem — A232

Designs (UPU Emblem and): 3c, Jet, satellite, Post Office, Monrovia, ship. 10c, US and USSR telecommunication satellites. 15c, Mail runner and jet. 20c, Futuristic mail train and mail truck. 25c, American Pony Express rider.

1974, Mar. 4 Litho. *Perf. 13½*

663 A232 2c ocher & multi .20 .20
664 A232 3c lt green & multi .20 .20
665 A232 10c lt blue & multi .20 .20
666 A232 15c pink & multi .50 .20
667 A232 20c gray & multi .65 .20
668 A232 25c lt lilac & multi .85 .40
Nos. 663-668 (6) 2.60 1.40

Cent. of UPU. See No. C201.

Fox Terrier — A233

1974, Apr. 16 Litho. *Perf. 13½*

669 A233 5c shown .20 .20
670 A233 10c Boxer .20 .20
671 A233 16c Chihuahua .65 .20
672 A233 19c Beagle .70 .20
673 A233 25c Golden retriever .80 .20
674 A233 50c Collie 1.75 .40
Nos. 669-674 (6) 4.30 1.40

See No. C202.

Soccer Game, West Germany and Chile — A234

Designs: Games between semi-finalists, and flags of competing nations.

1974, June 4 Litho. *Perf. 11*

675 A234 1c shown .20 .20
676 A234 2c Australia and East Germany .20 .20
677 A234 5c Brazil and Yugoslavia .20 .20
678 A234 10c Zaire and Scotland .20 .20
679 A234 12c Netherlands and Uruguay .20 .20
680 A234 15c Sweden and Bulgaria .45 .20
681 A234 20c Italy and Haiti .65 .20
682 A234 25c Poland and Argentina .75 .45
Nos. 675-682 (8) 2.85 1.85

World Cup Soccer Championship, Munich, June 13-July 7. See No. C203.

Chrysiridia Madagascariensis — A235

Tropical Butterflies: 2c, Catagramma sorana. 5c, Erasmia pulchella. 17c, Morpho cypris. 25c, Agrias amydon. 40c, Vanessa cardui.

1974, Sept. 11 Litho. *Perf. 13½*

683 A235 1c gray & multi .20 .20
684 A235 2c gray & multi .20 .20
685 A235 5c gray & multi .20 .20
686 A235 17c gray & multi .95 .20
687 A235 25c gray & multi 1.25 .40
688 A235 40c gray & multi 2.40 .65
Nos. 683-688 (6) 5.20 1.85

See No. C204.

Pres. Tolbert and Medal — A236

$1, Pres. Tolbert, medal & Liberian flag.

1974, Dec. 10 Litho. *Perf. 13½*

689 A236 3c multi .20 .20
690 A236 $1 multi, vert. 2.75 2.75

Pres. William R. Tolbert, Jr., recipient of 1974 Family of Man Award.

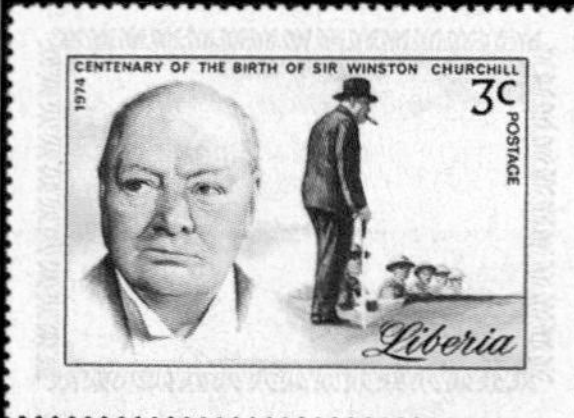

Winston Churchill, 1940 — A237

Churchill and: 10c, RAF planes in dog fight. 15c, In naval launch on way to Normandy. 17c, In staff car reviewing troops in desert. 20c, Aboard landing craft crossing Rhine. 25c, In conference with Pres. Roosevelt.

1975, Jan. 17 Litho. *Perf. 13½*

691 A237 3c multicolored .20 .20
692 A237 10c multicolored .20 .20
693 A237 15c multicolored .20 .20
694 A237 17c multicolored .45 .20
695 A237 20c multicolored .55 .20
696 A237 25c multicolored .90 .45
Nos. 691-696 (6) 2.50 1.45

Sir Winston Churchill (1874-1965), birth centenary. See No. C205.

Women's Year Emblem and Marie Curie — A238

3c, Mahalia Jackson with microphone. 5c, Joan of Arc. 10c, Eleanor Roosevelt and children. 25c, Matilda Newport firing cannon. 50c, Valentina Tereshkova in space suit.

1975, Mar. 14 Litho. *Perf. 14½*

697 A238 2c citron & multi .20 .20
698 A238 3c dull orange & multi .20 .20
699 A238 5c lilac rose & multi .20 .20
700 A238 10c yellow & multi .20 .20
701 A238 25c yellow grn & multi .55 .20
702 A238 50c lilac & multi 1.00 .65
Nos. 697-702 (6) 2.35 1.65

Intl. Women's Year 1975. See No. C206.

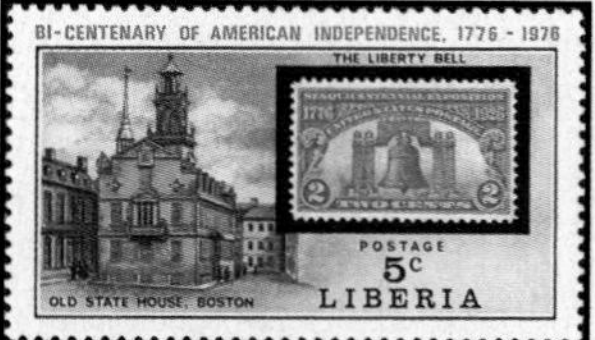

Old State House, Boston, US No. 627 — A239

10c, George Washington, US #645. 15c, Town Hall & Court House, Philadelphia, US #798. 20c, Benjamin Franklin, US #835. 25c, Paul Revere's Ride, US #618. 50c, Santa Maria, US #231.

1975, Apr. 25 Litho. *Perf. 13½*

703 A239 5c multicolored .20 .20
704 A239 10c multicolored .50 .20
705 A239 15c multicolored .60 .20
706 A239 20c multicolored .80 .20
707 A239 25c multicolored 1.25 .20
708 A239 50c multicolored 2.50 .50
Nos. 703-708 (6) 5.85 1.50

American Revolution Bicentennial. See No. C207.

Dr. Schweitzer, Hospital and Baboon Mother — A240

Designs (Dr. Schweitzer and): 3c, Elephant, and tribesmen poling boat. 5c, Water buffalo, egret, man and woman paddling canoe. 6c, Antelope and dancer. 25c, Lioness, woman cooking outdoors. 50c, Zebra and colt, doctor's examination at clinic.

1975, June 26 Litho. *Perf. 13½*

709 A240 1c multicolored .20 .20
710 A240 3c multicolored .20 .20
711 A240 5c multicolored .20 .20
712 A240 6c multicolored .20 .20
713 A240 25c multicolored .55 .20
714 A240 50c multicolored 1.25 .65
Nos. 709-714 (6) 2.60 1.65

Dr. Albert Schweitzer (1875-1965), medical missionary, birth centenary. See No. C208.

American-Russian Handshake in Space — A241

Designs (Apollo-Soyuz Emblem and): 5c, Apollo. 10c, Soyuz. 20c, Flags and maps of US and USSR. 25c, A. A. Leonov, and V. N. Kubasov. 50c, D. K. Slayton, V. D. Brand, T. P. Stafford.

1975, Sept. 18 Litho. *Perf. 13½*

715 A241 5c multicolored .20 .20
716 A241 10c multicolored .20 .20
717 A241 15c multicolored .40 .20
718 A241 20c multicolored .55 .20
719 A241 25c multicolored .75 .20
720 A241 50c multicolored 1.40 .45
Nos. 715-720 (6) 3.50 1.45

Apollo Soyuz space test project (Russo-American cooperation), launching July 15; link-up, July 17. See No. C209.

Presidents Tolbert, Siaka Stevens; Treaty Signing; Liberia and Sierra Leone Maps — A242

1975, Oct. 3 Litho. *Perf. 13½*

721 A242 2c gray & multi .20 .20
722 A242 3c gray & multi .20 .20
723 A242 5c gray & multi .20 .20
724 A242 10c gray & multi .20 .20
725 A242 25c gray & multi .65 .40
726 A242 50c gray & multi 1.25 .80
Nos. 721-726 (6) 2.70 2.00

Mano River Union Agreement between Liberia and Sierra Leone, signed Oct. 3, 1973.

Figure Skating — A243

Designs (Winter Olympic Games Emblem and): 4c, Ski jump. 10c, Slalom. 25c, Ice hockey. 35c, Speed skating. 50c, Two-man bobsled.

1976, Jan. 23 Litho. *Perf. 13½*

727 A243 1c lt blue & multi .20 .20
728 A243 4c lt blue & multi .20 .20
729 A243 10c lt blue & multi .20 .20
730 A243 25c lt blue & multi .90 .20
731 A243 35c lt blue & multi 1.25 .20
732 A243 50c lt blue & multi 1.75 .90
Nos. 727-732 (6) 4.50 1.90

12th Winter Olympic Games, Innsbruck, Austria, Feb. 4-15. See No. C210.

Pres. Tolbert Taking Oath of Office — A244

25c, Pres. Tolbert at his desk, vert. $1, Seal & flag of Liberia, $400 commemorative gold coin.

1976, Apr. 5 Litho. *Perf. 13½*

733 A244 3c multicolored .20 .20
734 A244 25c multicolored .50 .50
735 A244 $1 multicolored 2.50 2.50
Nos. 733-735 (3) 3.20 3.20

Inauguration of President William R. Tolbert, Jr., Jan. 5, 1976.

Weight Lifting and Olympic Rings — A245

Designs (Olympic Rings and): 3c, Pole vault. 10c, Hammer and shot put. 25c, Yachting. 35c, Women's gymnastics. 50c, Hurdles.

1976, May 4 Litho. *Perf. 13½*

736 A245 2c gray & multi .20 .20
737 A245 3c orange & multi .20 .20
738 A245 10c lt violet & multi .20 .20
739 A245 25c lt green & multi .90 .20
740 A245 35c yellow & multi 1.25 .70
741 A245 50c pink & multi 1.75 .70
Nos. 736-741 (6) 4.50 2.20

21st Olympic Games, Montreal, Canada, July 17-Aug. 1. See No. C211.

A. G. Bell, Telephone and Receiver, 1876, UPU Emblem — A246

UPU Emblem and: 4c, Horsedrawn mail coach and ITU emblem. 5c, Intelsat IV satellite, radar and ITU emblem. 25c, A. G. Bell, ship laying underwater cable, 1976 telephone. 40c, A. G. Bell, futuristic train, telegraph and telephone wires. 50c, Wright brothers' plane, Zeppelin and Concorde.

1976, June 4 Litho. *Perf. 13½*

742 A246 1c green & multi .20 .20
743 A246 4c ocher & multi .20 .20
744 A246 5c orange & multi .20 .20
745 A246 25c green & multi .90 .20
746 A246 40c lilac & multi 1.25 .20
747 A246 50c blue & multi 1.50 .70
Nos. 742-747 (6) 4.25 1.70

Cent. of 1st telephone call by Alexander Graham Bell, Mar. 10, 1876. See No. C212.

Gold Nugget on Chain, Gold Panner — A247

1976-81 Litho. *Perf. 14½*

749 A247 1c Mano River Bridge .20 .20
750 A247 3c shown .20 .20
751 A247 5c "V" ring .20 .20
752 A247 7c like 5c ('81) .20 .20
753 A247 10c Rubber tire, tree .45 .20
754 A247 15c Harvesting .75 .60
755 A247 17c like 55c ('81) .80 .60
756 A247 20c Hydroelectric plant 1.00 .80
757 A247 25c Mesurado shrimp 1.25 .20
758 A247 27c Woman tie-dying cloth 1.40 1.00
759 A247 55c Lake Piso, barracuda 2.75 .75
760 A247 $1 Train hauling iron ore 5.00 3.50
Nos. 749-760 (12) 14.20 8.45

See Nos. 945-953.

Rhinoceros — A249

African Animals: 3c, Zebra antelope. 5c, Chimpanzee, vert. 15c, Pigmy hippopotamus. 25c, Leopard. $1, Gorilla, vert.

1976, Sept. 1 Litho. *Perf. 13½*

763 A249 2c orange & multi .60 .60
764 A249 3c gray & multi .60 .60
765 A249 5c blue & multi .60 .60
766 A249 15c brt blue & multi .60 .60
767 A249 25c ultra & multi 1.00 .75
768 A249 $1 multicolored 3.50 2.25
Nos. 763-768 (6) 6.90 5.40

See No. C213.

Maps of US and Liberia; Statue of Liberty, Unification Monument, Voinjama and Liberty Bell — A250

$1, George Washington, Gerald R. Ford, Joseph J. Roberts (1st Pres. of Liberia), William R. Tolbert, Jr., Bicentennial emblem, US & Liberian flags.

1976, Sept. 21 Litho. *Perf. 13½*

769 A250 25c multicolored .55 .40
770 A250 $1 multicolored 1.75 .95

American Bicentennial and visit of Pres. William R. Tolbert, Jr. to the US, Sept. 21-30. See No. C214.

Baluba Masks and Festival Emblem A251

Tribal Masks: 10c, Bateke. 15c, Basshilele. 20c, Igungun. 25c, Masai. 50c, Kifwebe.

1977, Jan. 20 Litho. *Perf. 13½*

771	A251	5c	yellow & multi	.20	.20
772	A251	10c	green & multi	.20	.20
773	A251	15c	salmon & multi	.20	.20
774	A251	20c	lt blue & multi	.65	.20
775	A251	25c	violet & multi	.80	.20
776	A251	50c	lemon & multi	1.50	.65
			Nos. 771-776 (6)	3.55	1.65

FESTAC '77, 2nd World Black and African Festival, Lagos, Nigeria, Jan. 15-Feb. 12. See No. C215.

Latham's Francolin — A252

Birds of Liberia: 10c, Narina trogon. 15c, Rufous-crowned roller. 20c, Brown-cheeked hornbill. 25c, Common bulbul. 50c, Fish eagle. 80c, Gold Coast touraco.

1977, Feb. 18 Litho. *Perf. 14*

777	A252	5c	multicolored	.20	.20
778	A252	10c	multicolored	.55	.20
779	A252	15c	multicolored	.75	.20
780	A252	20c	multicolored	1.10	.20
781	A252	25c	multicolored	1.40	.20
782	A252	50c	multicolored	3.50	.65
			Nos. 777-782 (6)	7.50	1.65

Souvenir Sheet

783	A252	80c	multicolored	4.50	3.00

Edmund Coffin, Combined Training, US — A253

Designs: 15c, Alwin Schockemohle, single jump. Germany, vert. 20c, Christine Stuckelberger, Switzerland, individual dressage. 25c, Prix de Nations (team), France.

1977, Apr. 22 Litho. *Perf. 13½*

784	A253	5c	ocher & multi	.20	.20
785	A253	15c	ocher & multi	.95	.20
786	A253	20c	ocher & multi	1.10	.20
787	A253	25c	ocher & multi	1.40	.80
			Nos. 784-787,C216 (5)	6.90	3.00

Equestrian gold medal winners in Montreal Olympic Games. See No. C217.

Elizabeth II Wearing Crown — A254

Designs: 25c, Elizabeth II Prince Philip, Pres. and Mrs. Tubman. 80c, Elizabeth II, Prince Philip, royal coat of arms.

1977, May 23 Litho. *Perf. 13½*

788	A254	15c	silver & multi	.45	.20
789	A254	25c	silver & multi	.85	.20
790	A254	80c	silver & multi	2.50	.70
			Nos. 788-790 (3)	3.80	1.10

25th anniversary of the reign of Queen Elizabeth II. Nos. 788-790 exist imperf.
See No. C218.

Jesus Blessing Children A255

Christmas: 25c, The Good Shepherd. $1, Jesus and the Samaritan Woman. Designs after stained-glass windows, Providence Baptist Church, Monrovia.

1977, Nov. 3 Litho. *Perf. 13½*

791	A255	20c	lt blue & multi	.45	.20
792	A255	25c	lt blue & multi	.60	.45
793	A255	$1	lt blue & multi	1.90	1.10
			Nos. 791-793 (3)	2.95	1.75

Dornier DOX, 1928 — A256

Progress of Aviation: 3c, Piggyback space shuttle, 1977. 5c, Eddie Rickenbacker and Douglas DC 3. 25c, Charles A. Lindbergh and Spirit of St. Louis. 35c, Louis Bleriot and Bleriot XI. 50c, Orville and Wilbur Wright and flying machine, 1903. 80c, Concorde landing at night at Dulles Airport, Washington, DC.

1978, Jan. 6 Litho. *Perf. 13½*

794	A256	2c	multicolored	.20	.20
795	A256	3c	multicolored	.20	.20
796	A256	5c	multicolored	.20	.20
797	A256	25c	multicolored	.65	.20
798	A256	35c	multicolored	.90	.55
799	A256	50c	multicolored	1.60	.75
			Nos. 794-799 (6)	3.75	2.10

Souvenir Sheet

800	A256	80c	multicolored	3.50	2.50

Baladeuse by Santos-Dumont, 1903 — A257

Airships: 3c, Baldwin's, 1908, and US flag. 5c, Tissandier brothers', 1883. 25c, Parseval PL VII, 1912. 40c, Nulli Secundus II, 1908. 50c, R34 rigid airship, 1919.

1978, Mar. 9 Litho. *Perf. 13½*

801	A257	2c	multicolored	.20	.20
802	A257	3c	multicolored	.20	.20
803	A257	5c	multicolored	.20	.20
804	A257	25c	multicolored	.55	.20
805	A257	40c	multicolored	.85	.20
806	A257	50c	multicolored	1.10	.20
			Nos. 801-806 (6)	3.10	1.20

75th anniv. of the Zeppelin. See No. C219.

Soccer, East Germany and Brazil — A258

Soccer Games: 2c, Poland and Argentina, vert. 10c, West Germany and Netherlands. 25c, Yugoslavia and Brazil. 35c, Poland and Italy, vert. 50c, Netherlands and Uruguay.

1978, May 16 Litho. *Perf. 13½*

807	A258	2c	multicolored	.20	.20
808	A258	3c	multicolored	.20	.20
809	A258	10c	multicolored	.20	.20
810	A258	25c	multicolored	.75	.20
811	A258	35c	multicolored	1.00	.50
812	A258	50c	multicolored	1.50	.75
			Nos. 807-812 (6)	3.85	2.05

11th World Cup Soccer Championships, Argentina, June 1-25. See No. C220.

Coronation Chair — A259

Designs: 25c, Imperial state crown. $1, Buckingham Palace, horiz.

1978, June 12

813	A259	5c	multicolored	.20	.20
814	A259	25c	multicolored	.75	.20
815	A259	$1	multicolored	2.75	1.00
			Nos. 813-815 (3)	3.70	1.40

25th anniversary of coronation of Queen Elizabeth II. See No. C221.

Jinnah, Liberian and Pakistani Flags — A260

1978, June Litho. *Perf. 13*

816	A260	30c	multicolored	*37.50*	8.25

Mohammed Ali Jinnah (1876-1948), first Governor General of Pakistan.

Carter and Tolbert Families — A261

Designs: 25c, Pres. Tolbert, Rosalynn Carter and Pres. Carter at microphone, Robertsfield Airport. $1, Jimmy Carter and William R. Tolbert, Jr. in motorcade from airport.

1978, Oct. 26 Litho. *Perf. 13½*

817	A261	5c	multicolored	.20	.20
818	A261	25c	multicolored	.85	.85
819	A261	$1	multicolored	3.50	3.50
			Nos. 817-819 (3)	4.55	4.55

Pres. Carter's visit to Liberia, Apr. 1978.

Soccer Game: Italy-France — A262

Soccer Games: 1c, Brazil-Spain, horiz. 10c, Poland-West Germany, horiz. 27c, Peru-Scotland. 35c, Austria-West Germany. 50c, Argentina the victor.

1978, Dec. 8 Litho. *Perf. 13½*

820	A262	1c	multicolored	.20	.20
821	A262	2c	multicolored	.20	.20
822	A262	10c	multicolored	.40	.20
823	A262	27c	multicolored	.95	.65
824	A262	35c	multicolored	1.25	.80
825	A262	50c	multicolored	1.75	1.25
			Nos. 820-825 (6)	4.75	3.30

1978 World Cup Soccer winners. See No. C222.

Liberian Lumbermen — A263

Designs: 10c, Hauling timber by truck, vert. 25c, Felling trees with chain saw. 50c, Moving logs.

1978, Dec. 15 Litho. *Perf. 13½x14*

826	A263	5c	multicolored	.20	.20
827	A263	10c	multicolored	.20	.20
828	A263	25c	multicolored	.85	.25
829	A263	50c	multicolored	1.75	1.25
			Nos. 826-829 (4)	3.00	1.90

8th World Forestry Congress, Djakarta, Indonesia.

"25" and Waves — A264

Design: $1, Radio tower and waves.

1979, Apr. 6 Litho. *Perf. 14x13½*

830	A264	35c multicolored	.70	.70
831	A264	$1 multicolored	1.90	1.90

25th anniversary of Radio ELWA.

Emblems of IYC, African Child's Decade and SOS Village — A265

Designs: 25c, $1, like 5c, with UNICEF emblem replacing SOS emblem. 35c, like 5c.

1979, Apr. 6 *Perf. 13½x14*

832	A265	5c multicolored	.20	.20
833	A265	25c multicolored	.20	.20
834	A265	35c multicolored	.60	.60
835	A265	$1 multicolored	1.40	1.40
		Nos. 832-835 (4)	2.40	2.40

IYC and Decade of the African Child.

Presidents Gardner and Tolbert, and Post Office, Monrovia — A266

Design: 35c, Anthony W. Gardner, William R. Tolbert, Jr. and UPU emblem.

1979, Apr. 2 Litho. *Perf. 13½x14*

836	A266	5c multicolored	.20	.20
837	A266	35c multicolored	1.10	1.10

Cent. of Liberia's joining UPU.

Unity Problem, Map of Africa, Torches — A267

Designs: 27c, Masks. 35c, Elephant, giraffe, lion, antelope, cheetah and map of Africa. 50c, Huts, pepper birds and map of Africa.

1979, July 6 Litho. *Perf. 14x13½*

838	A267	5c multicolored	.20	.20
839	A267	27c multicolored	.75	.75
840	A267	35c multicolored	1.00	1.00
841	A267	50c multicolored	1.50	1.50
		Nos. 838-841 (4)	3.45	3.45

Organization for African Unity, 16th anniversary, and OAU Summit Conference.

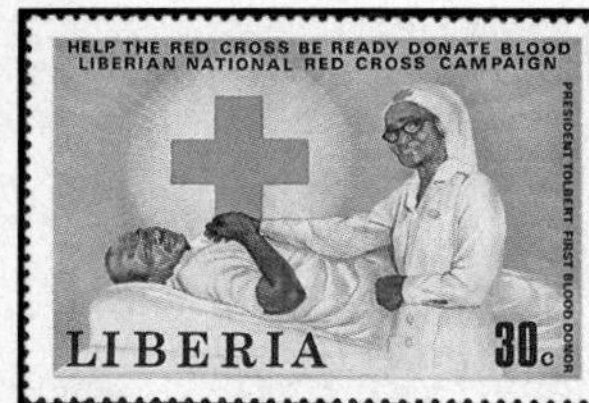

Liberia No. 666, Rowland Hill — A268

10c, Pony Express rider, 1860. 15c, British mail coach, 1800. 25c, Mail steamship John Penn, 1860. 27c, Stanier Pacific train, 1939. 50c, Concorde. $1, Curtiss Jenny, 1916.

1979, July 20

842	A268	3c multicolored	.20	.20
843	A268	10c multicolored	.20	.20
844	A268	15c multicolored	.45	.45
845	A268	25c multicolored	.85	.65
846	A268	27c multicolored	1.00	.75
847	A268	50c multicolored	1.75	1.40
		Nos. 842-847 (6)	4.45	3.65

Souvenir Sheet

848	A268	$1 multicolored	3.50	2.50

Sir Rowland Hill (1795-1879), originator of penny postage.

Red Cross, Pres. Tolbert Donating Blood — A269

Design: 50c, Red Cross, Pres. Tolbert.

1979, Aug. 15 Litho. *Perf. 13½*

849	A269	30c multicolored	.65	.65
850	A269	50c multicolored	1.25	1.25

National Red Cross, 30th anniversary and blood donation campaign.

M.S. World Peace — A270

Design: $1, M.S. World Peace, diff.

1979, Aug. 15

851	A270	5c multicolored	.20	.20
852	A270	$1 multicolored	3.25	3.25

2nd World Maritime Day, March 16; Liberia Maritime Program, 30th anniversary.

A Good Turn, by Norman Rockwell A271

Paintings — Scouting through the eyes of Norman Rockwell (1925-76): #853: a, Stories. b, 3 branches of Scouts. c, camping. d, Church. e, Animal care. f, advancements. g, Scout, Lincoln. h, First aid on puppy. i, Reading with elderly and dog. j, Scout teaching cubs..

#854: a, "1910." b, Feeding dog. c, Man, dog, Scout on top of rock. d, Merit badges. e, Hiking in mountains. f, With explorer and eagle. g, Wearing new uniform. h, Indian lore. i, First camping. j, Group saluting.

#855: a, Eagle ceremony. b, Hiking with compass. c, The Scouting Trail. d, Phyical fitness. e, Prayer. f, Tales of the sea. g, Foreign and US scouts dancing. h, Building a birdhouse. i, In front of flag. j, Rescueing girl and kitten.

#856: a, Painting outdoors. b, Scout saluting in front of flag. c, Scout, Lincoln, Washington, eagle. d, Starting on hike. e, Knot tying. f, Reading instructions. g, Scouts of 6 nations. h, Boy, Girl Scouts and leaders. i, "On my honor..." j, Cooking outdoors.

#857: a, Portaging. b, "Spirit of '76." c, Saluting flag with astronaut. d, 5 branches of scouting. e, Planting trees. f, Washington praying. g, First aid on dog. h, Saying grace in mess tent. i, First time in Scout uniform. j, Rock climbing.

1979, Sept. 1 Litho. *Perf. 11*

853	A271	5c #a.-j, any single	.50	.30
854	A271	10c #a.-j, any single	.50	.30
855	A271	15c #a.-j, any single	.80	.40
856	A271	25c #a.-j, any single	1.40	.45
857	A271	35c #a.-j, any single	2.00	.85
		Nos. 853-857, Set of 50 in 5 strips of 10	85.00	85.00

Mrs. Tolbert, Children, Children's Village Emblem — A272

40c, Mrs. Tolbert, children, emblem, vert.

1979, Nov. 14 Litho. *Perf. 14*

858	A272	25c multicolored	.60	.60
859	A272	40c multicolored	1.40	1.40

SOS Children's Village in Monrovia, Liberia.

Rotary International Headquarters, Evanston, Ill., Emblem — A273

Rotary Emblem and: 5c, Vocational services. 17c, Man in wheelchair, nurse, vert. 27c, Flags of several nations. 35c, People of various races holding hands around globe. 50c, Pres. Tolbert, map of Africa, vert. $1, "Gift of Life."

1979, Dec. 28 *Perf. 11*

860	A273	1c multicolored	.20	.20
861	A273	5c multicolored	.20	.20
862	A273	17c multicolored	.40	.40
863	A273	27c multicolored	.85	.85
864	A273	35c multicolored	1.00	1.00
865	A273	50c multicolored	1.75	1.75
		Nos. 860-865 (6)	4.40	4.40

Souvenir Sheet

866	A273	$1 multicolored	3.25	3.25

Rotary International, 75th anniversary.

Ski Jump, Lake Placid '80 Emblem — A274

Lake Placid '80 Emblem and: 5c, Figure skating. 17c, Bobsledding. 27c, Cross-country skiing. 35c, Women's speed skating. 50c, Ice hockey. $1, Slalom.

1980, Jan. 21

867	A274	1c multicolored	.20	.20
868	A274	5c multicolored	.20	.20
869	A274	17c multicolored	.95	.95
870	A274	27c multicolored	1.90	1.90
871	A274	35c multicolored	1.90	1.90
872	A274	50c multicolored	2.75	2.75
		Nos. 867-872 (6)	7.90	7.90

Souvenir Sheet

873	A274	$1 multicolored	3.50	3.50

13th Winter Olympic Games, Lake Placid, NY, Feb. 12-24.

Pres. Tolbert, Pres. Stevens, Maps of Liberia and Sierra Leone, Mano River — A275

1980, Mar. 6 Litho. *Perf. 14x13½*

874	A275	8c multicolored	.20	.20
875	A275	27c multicolored	.80	.80
876	A275	35c multicolored	1.10	1.10
877	A275	80c multicolored	2.40	2.40
		Nos. 874-877 (4)	4.50	4.50

Mano River Agreement, 5th anniversary; Mano River Postal Union, 1st anniversary.

Sgt. Doe and Soldiers, Clenched Hands Angel — A276

1981 Litho. *Perf. 14*

878	A276	1c Redemption horn, vert.	.20	.20
879	A276	6c like 1c	.20	.20
880	A276	10c shown	.20	.20
881	A276	14c Citizens, map, Flag	.20	.20
882	A276	23c like 10c	.30	.30
883	A276	31c like 14c	.45	.45
884	A276	41c like $2	.60	.60
885	A276	$2 Sgt. Samuel Doe, vert.	3.00	3.00
		Nos. 878-885 (8)	5.15	5.15

Establishment of new government under the People's Redemption Council, Apr. 12, 1980.

Soccer Players, World Cup, Flags of 1930 and 1934 Finalists — A277

Soccer Players, Cup, Flags of Finalists from: 5c, 1938, 1950. 20c, 1954, 1958. 27c, 1962, 1966. 40c, 1970, 1974. 55c. 1978. $1, Spanish team.

1981, Mar. 4 Litho. *Perf. 14*

886	A277	3c multicolored	.20	.20
887	A277	5c multicolored	.20	.20
888	A277	20c multicolored	.55	.55
889	A277	27c multicolored	.80	.80
890	A277	40c multicolored	1.25	1.25
891	A277	55c multicolored	1.75	1.75
		Nos. 886-891 (6)	4.75	4.75

Souvenir Sheet

892	A277	$1 multicolored	3.50	3.50

ESPANA '82 World Cup Soccer Championship.

Sgt. Samuel Doe and Citizens — A278

1981, Apr. 7 Litho. *Perf. 14*

893 A278 22c shown .70 .70
894 A278 27c Doe, Liberian flag .90 .90
895 A278 30c Clasped arms 1.40 1.40
896 A278 $1 Doe, soldiers, Justice 3.50 3.50
Nos. 893-896 (4) 6.50 6.50

People's Redemption Council government, first anniversary.

Royal Wedding A279

1981, Aug. 12 Litho. *Perf. 14x13½*

897 A279 31c Couple .85 .85
898 A279 41c Initials, roses 1.10 1.10
899 A279 62c St. Paul's Cathedral 2.10 2.10
Nos. 897-899 (3) 4.05 4.05

Souvenir Sheet

900 A279 $1 Couple 3.50 3.50

John Adams, US President, 1797-1801 A280

Washington Crossing the Delaware — A281

1981, July 4 *Perf. 11*

901 A280 4c shown .20 .20
902 A280 5c Wm. H. Harrison .20 .20
903 A280 10c Martin Van Buren .20 .20
904 A280 17c James Monroe .50 .40
905 A280 20c John Q. Adams .60 .50
906 A280 22c James Madison .70 .55
907 A280 27c Thomas Jefferson .75 .65
908 A280 30c Andrew Jackson .85 .70
909 A280 40c John Tyler 1.25 .95
910 A280 80c George Washington 2.40 1.50
Nos. 901-910 (10) 7.65 5.85

Souvenir Sheet

911 A281 $1 multi 3.50 3.50

1981, Nov. 26 Litho. *Perf. 11*

912 A280 6c Rutherford B. Hayes .20 .20
913 A280 12c Ulysses S. Grant .20 .20
914 A280 14c Millard Fillmore .20 .20
915 A280 15c Zachary Taylor .20 .20
916 A280 20c Abraham Lincoln .60 .20
917 A280 27c Andrew Johnson .70 .60
918 A280 31c James Buchanan .80 .60
919 A280 41c James A. Garfield 1.00 .80
920 A280 50c James K. Polk 1.25 .95
921 A280 55c Franklin Pierce 1.40 1.00
Nos. 912-921 (10) 6.55 4.95

Souvenir Sheet

922 A281 $1 Washington at Valley Forge 5.50 5.50

1982, Apr. 7 Litho. *Perf. 11*

923 A280 4c William H. Taft .20 .20
924 A280 5c Calvin Coolidge .20 .20
925 A280 6c Benjamin Harrison .20 .20
926 A280 10c Warren G. Harding .20 .20
927 A280 22c Grover Cleveland .65 .50
928 A280 27c Chester Arthur .75 .55
929 A280 31c Woodrow Wilson .80 .65
930 A280 41c William McKinley 1.25 .95
931 A280 80c Theodore Roosevelt 2.25 1.75
Nos. 923-931 (9) 6.50 5.20

Souvenir Sheet

932 A281 $1 Signing Constitution, horiz. 3.50 3.50

1982, July 15 Litho. *Perf. 11*

933 A280 4c Jimmy Carter .20 .20
934 A280 6c Gerald Ford .20 .20
935 A280 14c Harry Truman .20 .20
936 A280 17c F. D. Roosevelt .20 .20
937 A280 23c L. B. Johnson .55 .20
938 A280 27c Richard Nixon .65 .20
939 A280 31c John F. Kennedy .75 .55
940 A280 35c Ronald Reagan .90 .65
941 A280 50c Herbert Hoover 1.25 .90
942 A280 55c Dwight D. Eisenhower 1.40 1.00
Nos. 933-942 (10) 6.30 4.30

Souvenir Sheet

Perf. 14x13½

943 A281 $1 Battle of Yorktown 3.50 3.50

See No. 1113.

Type of 1976

1981-83 Litho. *Perf. 14½x13½*

Size: 34x20mm

945 A247 1c like #749 .20 .20
946 A247 3c like #750 .20 .20
947 A247 6c like #753 .20 .20
948 A247 15c like #754 .60 .60
949 A247 25c like #757 1.00 1.00
950 A247 31c like #756 1.25 1.25
951 A247 41c like #758 1.75 1.75
952 A247 80c like #759 3.50 3.50
953 A247 $1 like #760 5.00 5.00
Nos. 945-953 (9) 13.70 13.70

Issued: #946-947, 949, 950, 11/27/81; #945, 953, 10/12/82; #948, 951, 12/10/82; #952, 11/3/83.

Intl. Year of the Disabled (1981) — A282

Designs: Various disabled people.

1982, Mar. 24 Litho. *Perf. 14*

954 A282 23c multi, vert. .55 .55
955 A282 62c multicolored 1.25 1.25

30th Anniv. of West African Examinations Council — A283

1982, Mar. 24

956 A283 6c multicolored .20 .20
957 A283 31c multicolored 1.25 1.25

21st Birthday of Princess Diana — A284

31c, 41c, 62c, Diana portraits. $1, Wedding.

1982, July 1 *Perf. 14x13½*

958 A284 31c multicolored .85 .85
959 A284 41c multicolored 1.25 1.25
960 A284 62c multicolored 2.25 2.25
Nos. 958-960 (3) 4.35 4.35

Souvenir Sheet

961 A284 $1 multicolored 3.50 3.50

Nos. 958-961 Overprinted in Silver: "ROYAL BABY / 21-6-82 / PRINCE WILLIAM"

1982, Aug. 30 Litho. *Perf. 14x13½*

962 A284 31c multicolored .85 .85
963 A284 41c multicolored 1.25 1.25
964 A284 62c multicolored 2.25 2.25
Nos. 962-964 (3) 4.35 4.35

Souvenir Sheet

965 A284 $1 multicolored 3.50 3.50

Birth of Prince William of Wales, June 21.

3rd Natl. Redemption Day — A285

1983, Apr. 5 Litho. *Perf. 13½*

966 A285 3c Fallah Varney .20 .20
967 A285 6c Samuel Doe .20 .20
968 A285 10c Jlatoh N. Podier, Jr. .20 .20
969 A285 15c Jeffry S. Gbatu .40 .40
970 A285 31c Thomas G. Quiwonkpa .95 .95
971 A285 41c Abraham D. Kollie 1.75 1.75
Nos. 966-971 (6) 3.70 3.70

Souvenir Sheet

972 A285 $1 like 6c 3.50 3.50

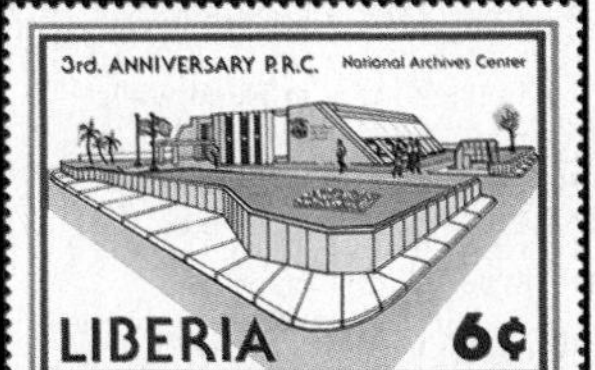

Natl. Archives Opening — A286

Building views.

1983, Apr. 5

973 A286 6c multicolored 1.60 1.60
974 A286 31c multicolored 2.75 2.75

Christmas 1983 A287

Raphael Paintings: 6c, Circumcision of Christ. 15c, Adoration of the Magi. 25c, Announcement to Mary. 31c, Madonna with Baldachin. 41c, Holy Family. 62c, Detail of Madonna with Child Surrounded by Five Saints. $1.25 Madonna of Foligno.

1983, Dec. 14 Litho. *Perf. 13½*

975 A287 6c multicolored .20 .20
976 A287 15c multicolored .20 .20
977 A287 25c multicolored .50 .50
978 A287 31c multicolored .70 .70
979 A287 41c multicolored .85 .85
980 A287 62c multicolored 1.10 1.10
Nos. 975-980 (6) 3.55 3.55

Souvenir Sheet

981 A287 $1.25 multicolored 2.50 2.50

Sheets of 1 showing entire painting exist.

Mano River Union, 10th Anniv. (1983) — A288

1984, Apr. 6 Litho. *Perf. 14x13½*

982 A288 6c Training school graduates .20 .20
983 A288 25c Emblem .85 .85
984 A288 31c Maps, leaders 1.10 1.10
985 A288 41c Guinea's accession 1.75 1.75
Nos. 982-985 (4) 3.90 3.90

Souvenir Sheet

986 A288 75c Guinea's accession, diff. 3.50 3.50

4th Natl. Redemption Day — A289

1984, Apr. 12 *Perf. 14½*

987 A289 3c Hospital, New Kru Town .20 .20
988 A289 10c Ganta-Harper Highway construction .20 .20
989 A289 20c Constitution Assembly opening .60 .60
990 A289 31c Doe at highway construction 1.10 1.10
991 A289 41c Draft Constitution presentation 1.75 1.75
Nos. 987-991 (5) 3.85 3.85

Adoration of the Wise Men, by Rubens (1577-1640) — A290

1984, June 1 Litho. *Perf. 13½*

992 A290 6c shown .20 .20
993 A290 15c Crowning of Katharina .20 .20
994 A290 25c Mother and Child Adored by Wise Men .55 .55
995 A290 31c Madonna and Child with Halo .75 .75
996 A290 41c Adoration of the Shepherds .95 .95
997 A290 62c Madonna and Child with Saints 1.50 1.50
Nos. 992-997 (6) 4.15 4.15

Souvenir Sheet

998 A290 $1.25 Madonna Adored by Saints *5.50 5.50*

Sheets of 1 showing entire painting exist.

1984 Summer Olympics A291

1984, July 2 *Perf. 13½x14*

999 A291 3c Jesse Owens, 1936 .20 .20
1000 A291 4c Rafer Johnson, 1960 .20 .20
1001 A291 25c Miruts Yifter, 1980 1.00 1.00
1002 A291 41c Kipchoge Keino, 1968, 1972 1.60 1.60
1003 A291 62c Muhammad Ali, 1960 2.25 2.25
Nos. 999-1003 (5) 5.25 5.25

Souvenir Sheet

Perf. 14x13½

1004 A291 $1.25 Wilma Rudolph, 1960, horiz. 5.50 5.50

1984 Louisiana Expo — A292

1984, July 24 *Perf. 14½*

1005 A292 6c Water birds .20 .20
1006 A292 31c Ship, Buchanan Harbor 1.25 1.25
1007 A292 41c Fish 1.50 1.50
1008 A292 62c Train carrying iron ore 2.50 2.50
Nos. 1005-1008 (4) 5.45 5.45

Pygmy Hippopotamus, World Wildlife Fund Emblem — A293

Various pygmy hippopotomi.

1984, Nov. 22 Litho. *Perf. 14½*

1009 A293 6c multicolored .75 .75
1010 A293 10c multicolored 1.00 1.00
1011 A293 20c multicolored 2.75 2.75
1012 A293 31c multicolored 4.00 4.00
Nos. 1009-1012 (4) 8.50 8.50

Indigent Children Home, Bensonville — A294

First Lady Mrs. Nancy Doe and various children.

1984, Dec. 14

1013 A294 6c multicolored .20 .20
1014 A294 31c multicolored 1.25 1.25

Natl. Redemption Day, Apr. 12 — A295

1985, Apr. 5 Litho. *Perf. 14½*

1015 A295 6c Army barracks, Monrovia .20 .20
1016 A295 31c Pan-African Plaza, Monrovia 1.25 1.25

Liberian Revolution, fifth anniv.

Audubon Birth Bicentenary — A296

Illustrations by artist/naturalist J. J. Audubon.

1985, Apr. 5

1017 A296 1c Bohemian waxwing .20 .20
1018 A296 3c Bay-breasted warbler .20 .20
1019 A296 6c White-winged crossbill .20 .20
1020 A296 31c Red phalarope 1.10 1.10
1021 A296 41c Eastern bluebird 1.60 1.60
1022 A296 62c Northern cardinal 2.40 2.40
Nos. 1017-1022 (6) 5.70 5.70

Venus and Mirror A297

Paintings (details) by Rubens: 15c, Adam & Eve in Paradise. 25c, Andromeda. 31c, The Three Graces. 41c, Venus & Adonis. 62c, The Daughters of Leucippus. $1.25, The Judgement of Paris.

1985, Nov. 14 Litho. *Perf. 14*

1023 A297 6c multicolored .20 .20
1024 A297 15c multicolored .70 .70
1025 A297 25c multicolored 1.00 1.00
1026 A297 31c multicolored 1.25 1.25
1027 A297 41c multicolored 1.75 1.75
1028 A297 62c multicolored 3.00 3.00
Nos. 1023-1028 (6) 7.90 7.90

Souvenir Sheet

1029 A297 $1.25 multicolored 4.50 4.50

Sheets of 1 showing entire painting exist.

1986 World Cup Soccer Championships, Mexico — A298

1985, Nov. 14

1030 A298 6c Germany-Morocco, 1970 .20 .20
1031 A298 15c Zaire-Brazil, 1974 .50 .50
1032 A298 25c Tunisia-Germany, 1978 .85 .85
1033 A298 31c Cameroun-Peru, 1982, vert. 1.00 1.00
1034 A298 41c Algeria-Germany, 1982 1.25 1.25
1035 A298 62c 1986 Senegal team 2.10 2.10
Nos. 1030-1035 (6) 5.90 5.90

Souvenir Sheet

1036 A298 $1.25 Liberia-Nigeria 4.50 4.50

Queen Mother, 85th Birthday — A299

World Food Day — A300

1985, Dec. 12 Litho. *Perf. 14½*

1037 A299 31c Elizabeth in garter robes .80 .80
1038 A299 41c At the races 1.00 1.00
1039 A299 62c In garden, waving 1.60 1.60
Nos. 1037-1039 (3) 3.40 3.40

Souvenir Sheet

1040 A299 $1.25 Wearing diadem 3.00 3.00

1985, Dec. 12

1041 A300 25c multicolored .50 .50
1042 A300 31c multicolored .75 .75

AMERIPEX '86 — A301

Statue of Liberty, Cent. — A302

1986, June 10 Litho. *Perf. 14½*

1043 A301 25c The Alamo 1.25 1.25
1044 A301 31c Liberty Bell 1.40 1.40
1045 A301 80c #344, 802, C102 3.75 3.75
Nos. 1043-1045 (3) 6.40 6.40

1986, June 10

1046 A302 20c Unveiling, 1886 .40 .40
1047 A302 31c Frederic A. Bartholdi .60 .60
1048 A302 $1 Statue close-up 2.00 2.00
Nos. 1046-1048 (3) 3.00 3.00

1988 Winter Olympics, Calgary — A303

1984 Gold medalists: 3c, Max Julen, Switzerland, men's giant slalom. 6c, Debbie Armstrong, U.S., women's giant slalom. 31c, Peter Angerer, West Germany, biathlon. 60c, Bill Johnson, U.S., men's downhill. 80c, East Germany, 4-man bobsled. $1.25, H. Stangassinger, F. Wembacher, West Germany, 2-man luge.

1987, Aug. 21 Litho. *Perf. 14*

1049 A303 3c multicolored .20 .20
1050 A303 6c multicolored .20 .20
1051 A303 31c multicolored .75 .75
1052 A303 60c multicolored 1.75 1.75
1053 A303 80c multicolored 2.25 2.25
Nos. 1049-1053 (5) 5.15 5.15

Souvenir Sheet

1054 A303 $1.25 multicolored 2.50 2.50

City of Berlin, 750th Anniv. — A304

6c, State (Royal) Theater in the Gendarmenmarkt, c. 1820, architect Schinkel. 31c, Kaiser Friedrich Museum, Museum Is. on River Spree. 60c, Charlottenburg Castle, 17th cent. 80c, Modern church bell tower & Kaiser Wilhelm Gedachtniskirche. $1.50, MIRAK rocket development, Spaceship Society Airfield, Reinickendorf, 1930.

1987, Sept. 4

1055 A304 6c multicolored .20 .20
1056 A304 31c multicolored .85 .85
1057 A304 60c multicolored 1.60 1.60
1058 A304 80c multicolored 2.00 2.00
Nos. 1055-1058 (4) 4.65 4.65

Souvenir sheet

Perf. 11½

1059 A304 $1.50 buff & dk brown 4.50 4.50

No. 1059 contains one 25x61mm stamp.

Shakespearean Plays — A305

1987, Nov. 6 Litho. *Perf. 14*

1060 Sheet of 8 8.50 8.50
a. A305 3c Othello .35 .35
b. A305 6c Romeo & Juliet .35 .35
c. A305 10c The Merry Wives of Windsor .35 .35
d. A305 15c Henry IV .35 .35
e. A305 31c Hamlet .60 .60
f. A305 60c Macbeth .60 .60
g. A305 80c King Lear 1.50 1.50
h. A305 $2 Shakespeare and the Globe Theater, 1598 3.50 3.50

Amateur Radio Association, 25th Anniv. — A306

1987, Nov. 23 Litho. *Perf. 14*

1061 A306 10c Emblem .45 .45
1062 A306 10c Village .45 .45
1063 A306 35c On-the-Air certificate 1.50 1.50
1064 A306 35c Globe, flags 1.50 1.50
Nos. 1061-1064 (4) 3.90 3.90

Miniature Sheets

Statue of Liberty, Cent. (in 1986) — A307

#1065: a, Torch, southern view of NYC. b, Overhead view of crown and scaffold. c, 4 workmen repairing crown. d, 5 workmen, crown. e, Statue's right foot.

#1066: a, Tall ship, statue. b, Bay Queen ferry. c, Statue on poster at a construction site, NYC. d, Tug boat, tall ship. e, Building frieze.

#1067: a, Statue flanked by fireworks. b, Lighting of the statue. c, Crown observatory illuminated. d, Statue surrounded by fireworks. e, Crown and torch observatories illuminated.

#1068: a, Liberty "Happy Birthday" poster at a construction site. b, Ships in NY Harbor. c, Woman renovating statue nose. d, Man & woman renovating nose. e, Man, nose. #1068a-1068e vert.

1987, Dec. 10 *Perf. 13½*

1065 Sheet of 5 + label .95
a.-e. A307 6c any single .20 .20
1066 Sheet of 5 + label 3.00
a.-e. A307 15c any single .50 .50
1067 Sheet of 5 + label 5.75
a.-e. A307 31c any single .95 .95
1068 Sheet of 5 + label 10.00
a.-e. A307 60c any single 1.75 1.75
Nos. 1065-1068 (4) 19.70

Nos. 1065-1068 contain label inscribed "CENTENARY OF THE STATUE OF LIBERTY" in two or five lines.

Second Republic, 2nd Anniv. A308

Design: Natl. flag, coat of arms, hand grip, Pres. Doe and Vice Pres. Moniba.

1988, Jan. 6 *Perf. 14½*

1069 A308 10c multicolored .60 .60
1070 A308 35c multicolored 1.90 1.90

UN Child Survival Campaign — A309

1988, Jan. 15 *Perf. 13x13½, 13½x13*

1071 A309 3c Breast-feeding .20 .20
1072 A309 6c Oral rehydration therapy, vert. .20 .20
1073 A309 31c Immunization 2.00 2.00
1074 A309 $1 Growth monitoring, vert. 5.75 5.75
Nos. 1071-1074 (4) 8.15 8.15

Inauguration of the Second Republic — A310

Design: Pres. Doe greeting Chief Justice Emmanuel N. Gbalazeh.

1988, Jan. 15 *Perf. 13x13½*

1075 A310 6c multicolored 1.50 1.50

Samuel Kanyon Doe Sports Complex, Opened Apr. 12, 1986 A311

1988, Jan. 15

1076 A311 31c multicolored .65 .65

Green (Agricultural) Revolution — A312

1988, Apr. 4 *Perf. 15*

1077 A312 10c multicolored .40 .40
1078 A312 35c multicolored 1.50 1.50

US Peace Corps in Liberia, 25th Anniv. A313

1988, Apr. 4

1079 A313 10c multicolored .40 .40
1080 A313 35c multicolored 1.50 1.50

Souvenir Sheet

1988 Summer Olympics, Seoul — A314

1988, Apr. 14 *Perf. 14*

1081 A314 $3 multicolored 10.00 10.00

Organization of African Unity, 25th Anniv. — A315

1988, May 25

1082 A315 10c multicolored .45 .45
1083 A315 35c multicolored 1.50 1.50
1084 A315 $1 multicolored 4.50 4.50
Nos. 1082-1084 (3) 6.45 6.45

Rail Transport A316

1988, July 30 Litho. *Perf. 14½*

1085 A316 10c GP10 at Nimba .30 .30
1086 A316 35c Triple-headed iron ore train .90 .90

Souvenir Sheets

Perf. 11

1087 A316 $2 King Edward II, 1930 *5.50 5.50*
1088 A316 $2 GWR 57 No. 3697, 1941 *5.50 5.50*
1089 A316 $2 GWR 0-4-2T No. 1408, 1932 *5.50 5.50*
1090 A316 $2 GWR No. 7034 Ince Castle, 1950 *5.50 5.50*

#1087-1090 contain one 64x44mm stamp each.

Nos. 1087-1090 with Added Text

1993, Aug. 3

Souvenir Sheets

1087a With added text in margin 7.50 7.50
1088a With added text in margin 7.50 7.50
1089a With added text in margin 7.50 7.50
1090a With added text in margin 7.50 7.50

Added text on Nos. 1087a-1090a reads: "25th ANNIVERSARY OF THE LAST STEAM TRAIN TO / RUN ON BRITISH RAIL 1968-1993."

1988 Summer Olympics, Seoul — A317

1988, Sept. 13 Litho.

1091 A317 10c Baseball .20 .20
1092 A317 35c Hurdles .85 .85
1093 A317 45c Fencing 1.00 1.00
1094 A317 80c Synchronized swimming 1.90 1.90
1095 A317 $1 Yachting 2.25 2.25
Nos. 1091-1095 (5) 6.20 6.20

Souvenir Sheet

1096 A317 $1.50 Tennis 3.00 3.00

Intl. Tennis Federation, 75th anniv. ($1.50).

St. Joseph's Catholic Hospital, 25th Anniv. A318

1988, Aug. 26 Litho. *Perf. 14½*

1097 A318 10c shown .20 .20
1098 A318 10c Hospital, 4 staff members .20 .20
1099 A318 35c St. John of God .80 .80
1100 A318 $1 Doctor, nurse, map 2.25 2.25
Nos. 1097-1100 (4) 3.45 3.45

Common Design Types pictured following the introduction.

Lloyds of London, 300th Anniv.

Common Design Type

CD341

Designs: 10c, Royal Exchange destroyed by fire, 1838, vert. 35c, Air Liberia BN2A aircraft. 45c, Supertanker Chevron Antwerp. $1, Lakonia on fire off Madeira, 1963, vert.

1988, Oct. 31 Litho. *Perf. 14*

1101 CD341 10c multicolored .20 .20
1102 CD341 35c multicolored 1.00 1.00
1103 CD341 45c multicolored 1.25 1.25
1104 CD341 $1 multicolored 2.75 2.75
Nos. 1101-1104 (4) 5.20 5.20

Sasa Players A319

Perf. 14x14½, 14½x14

1988, Sept. 30 Litho.

1105 A319 10c Monkey bridge, vert. .50 .50
1106 A319 35c shown 1.40 1.40
1107 A319 45c Snake dancers, vert. 1.90 1.90
Nos. 1105-1107 (3) 3.80 3.80

Intl. Fund for Agricultural Development, 10th Anniv. — A320

1988, Oct. 7 Litho. *Perf. 14x14½*

1108 A320 10c Crops .50 .50
1109 A320 35c Spraying crops, livestock 1.90 1.90

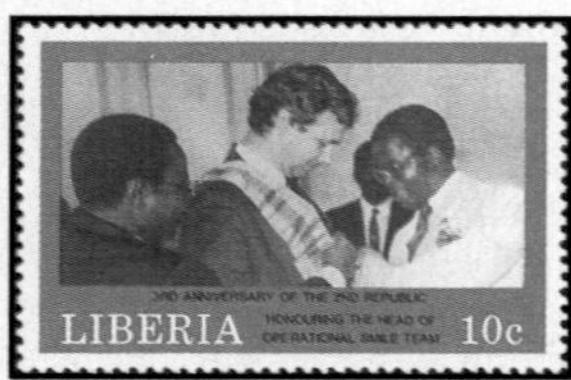

3rd Anniv. of the 2nd Republic — A321

1989, Jan. 6 Litho. *Perf. 14*

1110 A321 10c Pres. Doe, officials .50 .50
1111 A321 35c like 10c 1.90 1.90
1112 A321 50c Pres. Doe, doctor 2.40 2.40
Nos. 1110-1112 (3) 4.80 4.80

US Presidents Type of 1981-82

1989, Jan. 20 *Perf. 13½x14*

1113 A280 $1 George Bush 4.75 4.75

Rissho Kosei-Kai Buddhist Assoc., Tokyo, 50th Anniv. — A322

Natl. flags and: No. 1114, "Harmony" in Japanese. No. 1115, Organization headquarters, Tokyo. No. 1116, Nikkyo Niwano, founder. 50c, Statue of Buddha in the Great Sacred Hall.

1989, Feb. 28 Litho. *Perf. 14x14½*

1114 A322 10c multicolored .60 .60
1115 A322 10c multicolored .60 .60
1116 A322 10c multicolored .60 .60
1117 A322 50c multicolored 2.50 2.50
Nos. 1114-1117 (4) 4.30 4.30

Liberian-Japanese friendship.

Souvenir Sheet

LIBERIA COMMEMORATIVE COINAGE
1989 END OF Shō Wa AND BEGINNING OF Hei Sei
1989 昭和の終わり そして 平成の始まり
LIBERIA 75c
リベリア 記念貨幣

Emperor Hirohito of Japan (1901-1989) — A323

Commemorative coins: a, Silver. b, Gold.

1989, Feb. 28 Unwmk. *Perf. 14½*

1118 A323 Sheet of 2 8.00 8.00
a.-b. 75c any single 3.25 3.25

For overprint see No. 1147.

Mano River Union, 15th Anniv. A324

Natl. flag, crest and: 10c, Union Glass Factory, Gardnersville, Monrovia. 35c, Pres. Doe, Momoh of Sierra Leone and Conte of Guinea. 45c, Monrovia-Freetown Highway. 50c, Sierra Leone-Guinea land postal services. $1, Communique, 1988 summit.

Unwmk.

1989, May 8 Litho. *Perf. 14*

1119 A324 10c multicolored .20 .20
1120 A324 35c multicolored 1.25 1.25
1121 A324 45c multicolored 1.75 1.75
1122 A324 50c multicolored 1.90 1.90
1123 A324 $1 multicolored 3.75 3.75
Nos. 1119-1123 (5) 8.85 8.85

World Telecommunications Day — A325

1989, May 17 Litho. *Perf. 12½*

1124 A325 50c multicolored 1.40 1.40

Moon Landing, 20th Anniv.
Common Design Type

CD342

Apollo 11: 10c, Recovery ship USS Okinawa. 35c, Buzz Aldrin, Neil Armstrong and Michael Collins. 45c, Mission emblem. $1, Aldrin steps on the Moon. $2, Aldrin preparing to conduct experiments on the Moon's surface.

Perf. 14x13½, 14 (35c, 45c)

1989, July 20 Litho. Wmk. 384

Size of Nos. 1126-1127: 29x29mm

1125 CD342 10c multicolored .20 .20
1126 CD342 35c multicolored .90 .90
1127 CD342 45c multicolored 1.25 1.25
1128 CD342 $1 multicolored 2.75 2.75
Nos. 1125-1128 (4) 5.10 5.10

Souvenir Sheet

1129 CD342 $2 multicolored 5.50 5.50

Souvenir Sheet

The Women's March on Versailles — A326

1989, July 7 Wmk. 384 *Perf. 14*

1130 A326 $1.50 multicolored 4.00 4.00

French revolution, bicent., PHILEXFRANCE '89.

Souvenir Sheet

Renovation and Re-dedication of the Statue of Liberty, 1986 — A327

Photographs: a, Workman. b, French dignitary, US flag. c, Dignitaries at ceremony, statue.

Perf. 14x13½

1989, Oct. 2 Litho. Wmk. 373

1131 Sheet of 3 2.25 2.25
a.-c. A327 25c any single .75 .75

World Stamp Expo '89 and PHILEXFRANCE '89.

Souvenir Sheet

A328

1989, Nov. 17 Unwmk. *Perf. 14½*

1132 A328 $2 black 5.50 5.50

World Stamp Expo '89, Washington, DC.

Jawaharlal Nehru, 1st Prime Minister of Independent India — A329

1989, Dec. 22 Unwmk. *Perf. 14*

1133 A329 45c Nehru, signature, flag 1.50 1.50
1134 A329 50c Nehru, signature 3.25 3.25

New Standard-A Earth Satellite Station — A330

1990, Jan. 5

1135 A330 10c shown .20 .20
1136 A330 35c multi, diff. 1.25 1.25

US Educational & Cultural Foundation in Liberia, 25th Anniv. (in 1989) — A331

1990, Jan. 5

1137 A331 10c multicolored .20 .20
1138 A331 45c multicolored 1.40 1.40

Pan-African Postal Union, 10th Anniv. — A332

1990, Jan. 18 *Perf. 13x12½*

1139 A332 35c multicolored 1.00 1.00

Flags of Liberian Counties — A333

Designs: a, Bomi. b, Bong. c, Grand Bassa. d, Grand Cape Mount. e, Grand Gedeh. f, Grand Kru. g, Lofa. h, Margibi. i, Maryland. j, Montserrado. k, Nimba. l, Rivercess. m, Sinoe.

Perf. 14x13½

1990, Mar. 2 Litho. Unwmk.

1140 Strip of 13 5.00 5.00
a.-m. A333 10c any single .30 .30
1141 Strip of 13 17.00 17.00
a.-m. A333 35c any single 1.00 1.00
1142 Strip of 13 22.50 22.50
a.-m. A333 45c any single 1.50 1.50
1143 Strip of 13 25.00 25.00
a.-m. A333 50c any single 1.60 1.60
1144 Strip of 13 50.00 50.00
a.-m. A333 $1 any single 3.00 3.00
Nos. 1140-1144 (5) 119.50 119.50

Queen Mother, 90th Birthday
Common Design Types

Designs: 10c, At age 6. $2, At age 22.

Perf. 14x15

1991, Oct. 28 Wmk. 384

1145 CD343 10c multicolored .20 .20

Perf. 14½

1146 CD344 $2 brn & blk 4.00 4.00

For overprints see Nos. 1162-1163.

Souvenir Sheet

No. 1118 Overprinted

Perf. 14½

1991, Nov. 16 Litho. Unwmk.

1147 A323 Sheet of 2 4.50 4.50
a.-b. 75c any single 2.25 2.25

National Unity — A334

Designs: 35c, Hands clasp over map of Liberia. 45c, Liberian flag, hands, African map. 50c, All Liberia conference, March 1991, conferees, flag, map.

1991, Dec. 30 *Perf. 13½*

1148 A334 35c multicolored 1.10 1.10
1149 A334 45c multicolored 1.60 1.60
1150 A334 50c multicolored 1.75 1.75
Nos. 1148-1150 (3) 4.45 4.45

1992 Summer Olympics, Barcelona — A335

1992, Aug. 7 Litho. *Perf. 14*

1151 A335 45c Boxing 2.00 2.00
1152 A335 50c Soccer 2.25 2.25
1153 A335 $1 Weight lifting 4.50 4.50
1154 A335 $2 Water polo 8.25 8.25
Nos. 1151-1154 (4) 17.00 17.00

Souvenir Sheet

1155 A335 $1.50 Running 6.00 6.00

Disarmament — A336

Designs: 50c, Disarm today. $1, Join your parents & build Liberia. $2, Peace must prevail in Liberia.

1993, Feb. 10 Litho. *Perf. 13½x14*

1156 A336 50c multicolored 1.90 1.90
1157 A336 $1 multicolored 3.75 3.75
1158 A336 $2 multicolored 7.25 7.25
Nos. 1156-1158 (3) 12.90 12.90

See Nos. 1237-1239.

Miniature Sheets

Flora and Fauna — A337

No. 1159 — Flora: a, Papaya. b, Sausage tree. c, Angraecum eichlerianum. d, Arachnis flos-aeris. e, Screw pine. f, African tulip tree. g, Coffee tree. h, Bolusiella talbotii. i, Bulbophyllum lepidum. j, Oeceoclades maculata. k, Plectrelminthus caudatus. l, Diaphananthe rutila.

No. 1160 — Fauna: a, Diana monkey. b, Flying squirrel. c, Egyptian rousette. d, Serval. e, Potto. f, Chimpanzee. g, African horned chameleon. h, Royal python. i, Golden cat. j, Banded duiker. k, Pygmy hippopotamus. l, Water chevrotain.

No. 1161 — Birds: a, Grey heron. b, Bat hawk. c, Martial eagle. d, Little sparrow hawk. e, Hoopoe. f, Red bishop. g, Purple-throated sunbird. h, African fish eagle. i, African grey parrot. j, Black-crowned night heron. k, Swallow. l, Great white egret.

1993-94 Litho. *Perf. 14*

1159 A337 70c Sheet of 12, #a.-l. 35.00 35.00
1160 A337 90c Sheet of 12, #a.-l. 37.50 37.50
1161 A337 $1 Sheet of 12, #a.-l. 37.50 37.50
Nos. 1159-1161 (3) 110.00 110.00

Issued: 70c, 10/14; 90c, 11/18; $1, 1/14/94.

Nos. 1145-1146 Ovptd. with Hong Kong '94 Emblem

Perf. 14x15

1994, Feb. 18 Litho. Wmk. 384

1162 CD343 10c multicolored .20 .20

Perf. 14½

1163 CD344 $2 multicolored 7.75 7.75

Miniature Sheet

Roberts Field, Monrovia, 50th Anniv. A338

No. 1164: a, Vickers Supermarine Spitfire Mk IX. b, Boeing B-17G. c, Douglas A-20 Boston. d, North American B-25J Mitchell. e, Beech C-45 Expeditor. f, Douglas C-54. g, Piper L4 Cub. h, Martin PBM-3C.

1994, July 11 Litho. *Perf. 13½x13*

1164 A338 35c Sheet of 8, #a.-h. + label 11.00 11.00

Souvenir Sheets

Locomotives — A339

Designs: No. 1165, $1, Class A3 #60044 Melton, Class A4 #60017 Silver Fox. No. 1166, $1, GWR 2-6-2 Prairie Tank #4561. No. 1167, $1, GWR 2-6-2 Small Prairie. No. 1168, $1, GWR Castle Class 4-6-0 No. Kinswear Castle. No. 1169, $1, GWR 0-6-0 Pannier Tank. No. 1170, $1, Bong Mining Company diesel hauling iron ore.

1994, Aug. 16 Litho. *Perf. 14*

1165-1170 A339 Set of 6 18.00 18.00

See Nos. 1194-1199, 1205.

Liberian Natl. Red Cross, 75th Anniv. — A340

Designs: 70c, No. 1172, Globe. No. 1173, $2, Jean-Henri Dunant.

1994, Oct. 3 Litho. *Perf. 14½x14*

1171 A340 70c multicolored 2.50 2.50
1172 A340 $1 multicolored 3.50 3.50
1173 A340 $1 multicolored 3.50 3.50
1174 A340 $2 multicolored 7.25 7.25
Nos. 1171-1174 (4) 16.75 16.75

End of World War II, 50th Anniv.

Common Design Types

Designs: 70c, Sunderland on U-boat patrol. 90c, US Army Engineer Task Force. $1, MV Abosso sunk off Liberia, 1942. #1178, MV Adda sunk off Liberia, 1941.

#1179, Obverse of U.S. Victory Medal depicting Liberty.

1995, May 8 Litho. *Perf. 13½*

1175 CD351 70c multicolored 2.10 2.10
1176 CD351 90c multicolored 2.75 2.75
1177 CD351 $1 multicolored 3.00 3.00
1178 CD351 $2 multicolored 5.75 5.75
Nos. 1175-1178 (4) 13.60 13.60

Souvenir Sheet

Perf. 14

1179 CD352 $2 multicolored 6.00 6.00

Wild Animals A341

1995, June 1 *Perf. 14*

1180 A341 70c Cheetah 2.50 2.50
1181 A341 70c Giraffe 2.50 2.50
1182 A341 90c Rhinoceros 3.25 3.25
1183 A341 $1 Elephant 3.75 3.75
1184 A341 $2 Lion 7.50 7.50
Nos. 1180-1184 (5) 19.50 19.50

Souvenir Sheet

1995 IAAF World Track & Field Championships, Gothenburg — A342

No. 1185: a, Merlene Ottey. b, Heike Drechsler.

1995, Aug. 4 Litho. *Perf. 14*

1185 A342 $1 Sheet of 2, #a.-b. 8.50 8.50

Miniature Sheet

Orchids — A343

No. 1186: a, Ancistrochilus rothschildianus. b, Disa uniflora. c, Polystachya ottoniana. d, Aerangis brachycarpa. e, Plectrelminthus caudatus. f, Polystachya bella. g, Ansellia africana. h, Bulbophyllum cochleatum.

1995, Sept. 1 *Perf. 13*

1186 A343 70c Sheet of 8, #a.-h. + label 24.00 24.00

Singapore '95.

UN, 50th Anniv.

Common Design Type

Designs: 25c, UN Land Rovers. 50c, Delivering food supplies. $1, Ilyushin IL-76 freighter airlifting supplies. $2, MIL MI-8 helicopter.

1995, Oct. 24 Litho. *Perf. 14*

1187 CD353 25c multicolored 1.00 1.00
1188 CD353 50c multicolored 2.00 2.00
1189 CD353 $1 multicolored 4.00 4.00
1190 CD353 $2 multicolored 8.00 8.00
Nos. 1187-1190 (4) 15.00 15.00

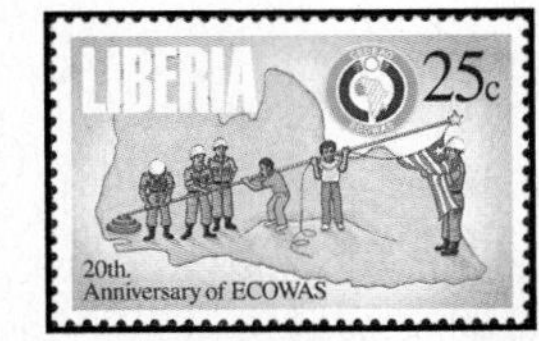

Economic Community of West African States, 20th Anniv. — A344

Designs: 25c, Map, Liberian flag, soldiers, civilians. 50c, Soldier carrying child, vert. $1, Logo, vert.

Perf. 13½x13, 13½x13

1995, Nov. 10 Litho.

1191 A344 25c multicolored 1.00 1.00
1192 A344 50c multicolored 2.00 2.00
1193 A344 $1 multicolored 4.00 4.00
Nos. 1191-1193 (3) 7.00 7.00

Train Type of 1994

Souvenir Sheets

Designs: No. 1194, $1, 4-4-0 locomotive 11 "The Reno," galloping horses. No. 1195, $1, Halwill station, Southern Region T9 class locomotive #30719. No. 1196, $1, GWR 0-4-2T "1400" class locomotive #1408, cricket match. No. 1197, $1, LMS Jubilee class 4-6-0, #45684 "Jutland," Kettering station. No. 1198, $1, GWR 2-6-2 "Prairie" locomotive #4547, Lustleigh station. No. 1199, $1, Wainwright "H" class 0-4-4T locomotive, winter countryside.

1996, Feb. 29 Litho. *Perf. 14x15*

1194-1199 A339 Set of 6 18.00 18.00

Modern Olympic Games, Cent. — A345

1996, Apr. 22 Litho. *Perf. 13*

1200 A345 20c Runners .70 .70
1201 A345 35c Boxing 1.25 1.25
1202 A345 50c Javelin 1.75 1.75
1203 A345 $1 Hurdles 3.50 3.50
Nos. 1200-1203 (4) 7.20 7.20

Butterflies A346

No. 1204: a, Papilio zalmoxis. b, Papilio dardanus. c, Charaxes varanes. d, Acraea natalica. e, Euphaedra neophron. f, Graphium antheus. g, Salamis anacardii. h, Kallima cymodoce. i, Precis hierta.

1996, May 22 Litho. *Perf. 13½*

1204 A346 70c Sheet of 9, #a.-i. 18.00 18.00

Train Type of 1994

Souvenir Sheet

Design: G4a Class Pacific locomotive, Canadian Pacific Railroad.

1996, June 8 Litho. *Perf. 14x15*

1205 A339 $1 multi 3.00 3.00

CAPEX '96.

Fish A347

No. 1206: a, Atlantic Sailfish. b, Guinean flyingfish. c, Blue marlin. d, Little tunny (e). e, Common dolphinfish (f). f, Guachanche barracuda. g, Guinean parrotfish. h, Cadenat's chromis (g). i, Dusky grouper (h). j, Hoefler's butterflyfish (k). k, African hind (l). l, West African Angelfish.

1996, July 15 Litho. *Perf. 14*

1206 A347 90c Sheet of 12, #a.-l. 32.50 32.50

Butterflies — A348

No. 1207: a, Euphaedra judith. b, Euphaedra eleus. c, Acraea encedon. d, Euphaedra neophron. e, Liptena praestans. f, Neptis exalenca. g, Palla decius. h, Salamis cytora. i, Pseudacraea dolomena. j, Anaphaeis eriphia. k, Euphaedra themis. l, Hadrodontes varanes.

No. 1208: a, Papilio mnestheus. b, Papilio nobilis. c, Graphium antheus. d, Asterope benguelae. e, Graphium illyris. f, Emphaedra eupalus. g, Charaxes protoclea. h, Cymothoe beckeri. i, Euphaedra cyparissa. j, Coliades chalybe. k, Mimacraea neokoton. l, Charaxes ethalion.

$2, Charaxes pelias.

1996 Litho. *Perf. 14*

1207 A348 20c Sheet of 12, #a.-l. 7.00
1208 A348 25c Sheet of 12, #a.-l. 9.00

Souvenir Sheet

1209 A348 $2 multicolored 6.00

Birds — A349

Designs, horiz: 35c, African jacana. 50c, Pel's fishing owl. $1, Paradise whydah.

No. 1213: a, Turtle dove. b, Bee-eater. c, Golden oriole. d, Pied flycatcher. e, Sardinian warbler. f, Goliath heron. g, Rock thrush. h, Kestrel. i, Cattle egret. j, Woodchat shrike. k, Hoopoe. l, Great egret.

No. 1214, horiz: a, Red faced crimsonwing. b, Egyptian goose. c, African pitta. d, Paradise flycatcher. e, Garganey. f, Southern carmine bee-eater. g, Fulvous whistling duck. h, Village weaver. i, Martial eagle.

$2, Pintail duck, horiz.

1996

1210-1212 A349 Set of 3 5.50
1213 A349 25c Sheet of 12, #a.-l. 9.50
1214 A349 35c Sheet of 9, #a.-i. 9.50

Souvenir Sheet

1215 A349 $2 multicolored 6.00

Marilyn Monroe (1926-62) A350

1996

1216 A350 20c multicolored .70

No. 1216 was issued in sheets of 16.

UNICEF, 50th Anniv. — A351

Designs: 35c, Education for all. 70c, Health care. $1, Children first.

1996, Sept. 16 *Perf. 13½x13*

1217-1219 A351 35c Set of 3 7.00

1996 Summer Olympic Games, Atlanta A352

Designs: No. 1220, 20c, Cricket (discontinued sport), vert. No. 1221, 20c, Babe Didrikson, vert. No. 1222, 35c, Vitaly Scherbo, winner of 6 gold medals, 1992, vert. No. 1223, 35c, Betty Robinson, vert. No. 1224, 50c, Cuban baseball team, gold medal, 1992. No. 1225, 50c, Ancient Greek wall painting of boxers, vert. No. 1226, $1, Stadium, Barcelona, 1992. No. 1227, $1, Stadium, Amsterdam, 1928, vert.

No. 1228, 35c, vert. — Olympic events: a, Men's athletics. b, Men's gymnastics. c, Weight lifting. d, Women's volleyball. e, Women's diving. f, Women's gymnastics. g, Women's track. h, Women's tennis. i, Discus.

No. 1229, 35c, vert. — Boxing gold medalists, boxing: a, Tyrell Biggs, U.S. b, Isan Gura, Tanzania (no medal). c, Mark Breland, U.S. d, Teofilo Stevenson, Cuba. e, Ray Leonard, U.S. f, Michael Spinks, U.S. g, Joe Frazier, U.S. h, Floyd Patterson, US. i, George Foreman, US.

$2, Evelyn Ashford.

1996 Litho. *Perf. 14*

1220-1227 A352 Set of 8 14.00

Sheets of 9, #a-i

1228-1229 A352 Set of 2 22.50

Souvenir Sheet

1230 A352 $2 multicolored 7.00

Flowers and Flowering Trees — A353

No. 1231: a, Olive tree. b, Olive flower. c, Fig tree. d, Almond tree. e, Almug tree. f, Cedar. g, Pomegranate (b). h, Citron. i, Date palm (d, e, j). j, Date palm (fruit). k, Cedar of Lebanon. l, Rock rose. m, Narcissus. n, Oleander (i). o, Date palm (flower). p, Shittah tree. q, Hyacinth. r, Barley, flax (s). s, Grape vine. t, Lily of the field. u, Mandrake. v, Caper desire. w, Madonna lily. x, Aloe (s). y, Date palm tree.

1996

1231 A353 25c Sheet of 25, #a.-y. 30.00

History of Rock and Roll A354

No. 1232: a, Wilson Pickett. b, Bill Haley. c, Otis Redding. d, Fats Domino. e, Buddy Holly. f, Chubby Checker. g, Marvin Gaye. h, Jimi Hendrix.

1996 *Perf. 13½x14*

1232 A354 35c Sheet of 8, #a.-h. + label 10.00

Kingfisher A355

No. 1233 — Kingfishers: a, Striped. b, Grey-headed. c, Pied. d, Giant. e, Shining-blue.

1996, Oct. 7 Litho. *Perf. 13½*

1233 A355 75c Strip of 5, #a.-e. 11.00

See No. 1236.

Mao Zedong, 20th Anniv. of Death — A356

1996, Nov. 1 Litho. *Perf. 14½x14*

1234 A356 $1 shown 3.25
1235 A356 $1 As older man 3.25

Kingfisher Type of 1996
Souvenir Sheet

1997, Feb. 3 Litho. *Perf. 14*

1236 A355 $1 Like #1233b 3.00

Hong Kong '97. No. 1236 contains one 29x43mm stamp.

Disarmament Type of 1993
Inscribed "PEACE TODAY"

1997 Litho. 13½x14

1237 A336 $1 Like #1157 *4.00*
1238 A336 $2 Like #1158 *8.25*
1239 A336 $3 Like #1156 *12.50*
Nos. 1237-1239 (3) 24.75

Nos. 1237-1239 are dated 1996.

Wildlife — A357

No. 1240: a, Olive baboon. b, Leopard. c, African tree pangolin. d, Vervet. e, Aardvark. f, Spotted hyena. g, Hunting dog. h, Thomson's gazelle. i, Warthog. j, African civet. k, Nile crocodile. l, African polecat.

1997, Apr. 2 Litho. *Perf. 14*

1240 A357 50c Sheet of 12, #a.-l. 18.00

Deng Xiaoping (1904-97), British Transfer of Hong Kong — A358

Different portraits of Deng Xiaoping, "July 1, 1997," Hong Kong: 70c, In daylight, vert. $1, At night.

No. 1243: a, 50c. b, 70c. c, $1.20.

1997 Litho. *Perf. 14*

1241 A358 70c multicolored 2.00
1242 A358 $1 multicolored 3.25
1243 A358 Sheet of 3, #a.-c. 7.75

No. 1241 is 28x44mm, and was issued in sheets of 4. No. 1242 was issued in sheets of 3.

UNESCO, 50th Anniv. — A359

No. 1244, 50c, vert.: a, Canals, Venice, Italy. b, Mosque of Badshahi, Gardens of Shalamar, Lahore, Pakistan. c, Palace of Orando, Spain. d, Grounds of Temple of Hera, Greece. e, Church and Monastery of Daphni, Greece. f, Fraser Island, Australia. g, Canadian Rocky Mountains Park, Canada. h, Church of Santo Domingo Puebla, Mexico.

No. 1245, 50c, vert.: a, City of Ohrid and lake, Macedonia. b, Thracian Tomb of Sveshtari, Bulgaria. c, Monastery of Hossios Luckas, Greece. d, Church of Santa Cristina of Lena, Spain. e, Church of Santa Maria Della Salute, Venice, Italy. f, Center of Puebla, Mexico. g, Bagrati Cathedral, Georgia. h, Quebec City, Canada.

No. 1246: a, Ngorongoro Conservation Area, Tanzania. b, Garamba Natl. Park, Zaire. c, Canaima Natl. Park, Venezuela. d, Simien Natl. Park, Ethiopia. e, Mana Pools Natl. Park, Zimbabwe.

No. 1247, $2, Palace of Diocletian, Split, Croatia. No., 1248, $2, Monument of Nubia at Abu Simbel, Egypt. No. 1249, $2, Quedlinberg, Germany.

Perf. 13½x14, 14x13½

1997, June 17 Litho.

Sheets of 8, #a-h + Label

1244-1245 A359 Set of 2 27.50
1246 A359 70c Sheet of 5, #a.-e, + label 12.50

Souvenir Sheets

1247-1249 A359 Set of 3 21.00

Queen Elizabeth II, Prince Philip, 50th Wedding Anniv. — A360

No. 1250: a, Queen holding umbrella. b, Royal arms. c, Prince in white uniform, Queen. d, Queen waving, Prince. e, Windsor Castle. f, Prince Philip.

No. 1251, $2, Queen seated on sofa. No. 1252, $2, Queen, Prince wearnig robes of Order of the Garter.

1997, June 17 *Perf. 14*

1250 A360 50c Sheet of 6, #a.-f. 11.00

Souvenir Sheet

1251-1252 A360 $2 Set of 2 14.00

Grimm's Fairy Tales A361

Mother Goose — A362

No. 1253 — Scenes from Rapunzel: a, Girl. b, Wicked person, raven. c, Prince.
No. 1254, Prince rescuing girl.
No. 1255, Little Bo Peep, sheep.

1997, June 17 *Perf. 13½x14*
1253 A361 $1 Sheet of 3, #a.-c. 10.00

Souvenir Sheets

1254 A361 $2 multicolored 7.00

Perf. 14

1255 A362 $2 multicolored 7.00

1998 Winter Olympics, Nagano — A363

Designs: 50c, Olympic Stadium, Lillehammer, 1994. 70c, Johann Koss, speed skating. $1, Katarina Witt, figure skating. $1.50, Sonia Henie, figure skating.
No. 1260: a, K. Seizinger, Alpine downhill skiing. b, J. Weissflog, 120-m ski jump. c, T. Kono, Nordic combined. d, G. Hackl, luge.
No. 1261: a, E. Bredesen, 90-m ski jump. b, L. Kjus, downhill skiing. c, B. Daehlie, cross-country skiing. d, P. Wiberg, combined Alpine skiing. e, S.L. Hattestad, freestyle skiing. f, G. Weder, D. Acklin, 2-man bobsled. g, Swedish hockey player. h, T. Alsgaard, cross-country skiing.
No. 1262, $2, German biathlete, 1994. No. 1263, $2, M. Wasmeier, giant slalom. No. 1264, $2, J. Koss, speed skating, diff. No. 1265, $2, V. Schneider, slalom.

1997, June 23 *Perf. 14*
1256-1259 A363 Set of 4 13.00
1260 A363 50c Strip or block of 4, #a.-d. 7.00
1261 A363 50c Sheet of 8, #a.-h. 14.00

Souvenir Sheets

1262-1265 A363 Set of 4 27.50

No. 1260 was issued in sheets of 8 stamps.

Flowers — A364

No. 1266, 50c: a, Sugar cane dahlia. b, Windsor tall phlox. c, Creative art daylily. d, Columbine. e, Infinite Grace bearded iris. f, Fairy lilies mini amaryllis.
No. 1267, 50c: a, White coneflower. b, Peggy Lee hybrid tea rose. c, Daffodil. d, Bowl of Beauty peony. e, Hardy lily. f, Windflower.
No. 1268, $2, Lily-flowered tulip. No. 1269, $2, Chrysanthemum Potomac.

1997, July 1 **Litho.** *Perf. 14*

Sheets of 6, #a-f

1266-1267 A364 Set of 2 20.00 20.00

Souvenir Sheets

1268-1269 A364 Set of 2 16.00 16.00

Flora and Fauna A365

No. 1270: a, Lovebirds. b, Genet. c, Leopard, crowned night heron. d, Gorilla. e, Giant wild boar. f, Elephant. g, Sterculia flower, skink. h, Ladybugs, bush baby. i, Cape primroses, ground hornbill.
No. 1271, $2, Rufus-crowned roller. No. 1272, $2, Gray heron.

1997, July 1
1270 A365 50c Sheet of 9, #a.-i. 13.00 13.00

Souvenir Sheets

1271-1272 A365 Set of 2 12.00 12.00

Chernobyl Disaster, 10th Anniv. A366

1997, June 17 **Litho.** *Perf. 13½x14*
1273 A366 $1 UNESCO 3.25 3.25

Marcello Mastroianni (1923-96), Actor — A367

No. 1274 — Scenes from motion pictures: a, Casanova, 1970. b, Divorce Italian Style. c, 8½. d, La Dolce Vita.

1997, Sept. 3
1274 A367 75c Sheet of 4, #a.-d. 10.00 10.00

Contemporary Artists and Paintings — A368

No. 1275, 50c: a, Andy Warhol (1927-87). b, "Multicolored Retrospective," by Warhol, 1979. c, "The Three Musicians," by Picasso, 1921. d, Pablo Picasso (1881-1973). e, Henri Matisse (1869-1954). f, "The Dance," by Matisse, 1910. g, "Lavender Mist," by Pollock, 1950. h, Jackson Pollock (1912-56).
No. 1276, 50c: a, Piet Mondrian (1872-1944). b, "Broadway Boogie Woogie," by Mondrian, 1942-43. c, "Persistence of Memory," by Dali, 1931. d, Salvador Dali (1904-89). e, Roy Lichtenstein (1923-97). f, "Artist's Studio: The Dance," by Lichtenstein, 1974. g, "Europe After the Rain," by Ernst, 1940-42. h, Max Ernst (1891-1976).

1997, Sept. 3 *Perf. 14*

Sheets of 8, #a-h

1275-1276 A368 Set of 2 27.50 27.50

Nos. 1275b-1275c, 1275f-1275g, 1276b-1276c, 1276f-1276g are 53x38mm.

Owls — A369

No. 1277: a, Akun eagle owl. b, Shelley's eagle owl. c, African wood owl. d, Rufous fishing owl. e, Maned owl. f, Sandy scops owl.

1997
1277 A369 50c Sheet of 6, #a.-f. 9.00 9.00

Birds — A370

Designs: 1c, Black bee-eater. 2c, Yellow-billed barbet. 3c, Carmine bee-eater. 4c, Malachite kingfisher. 5c, Emerald cuckoo. 10c, Blue-throated roller. 15c, Blue-headed bee-eater. 20c, Black-collared lovebird. 25c, Broad-billed roller. 50c, Blue-breasted kingfisher. 70c, Little bee-eater. 75c, Yellow spotted barbet. 90c, White-throated bee-eater. $1, Double-toothed barbet. $2, Blue-cheeked bee-eater. $3, Narina's trogon.

1997

1278	A370	1c	multicolored	.20	.20
1279	A370	2c	multicolored	.20	.20
1280	A370	3c	multicolored	.20	.20
1281	A370	4c	multicolored	.20	.20
1282	A370	5c	multicolored	.20	.20
1283	A370	10c	multicolored	.20	.20
1284	A370	15c	multicolored	.40	.40
1285	A370	20c	multicolored	.50	.50
1286	A370	25c	multicolored	.65	.65
1287	A370	50c	multicolored	1.25	1.25
1288	A370	70c	multicolored	1.90	1.90
1289	A370	75c	multicolored	2.00	2.00
1290	A370	90c	multicolored	2.40	2.40
1291	A370	$1	multicolored	2.75	2.75
1292	A370	$2	multicolored	5.25	5.25
1293	A370	$3	multicolored	7.75	7.75
	Nos. 1278-1293 (16)			26.05	26.05

1998 World Cup Soccer — A371

Players, country, vert: 50c, Salenko, Russia. 70c, Schillaci, Italy. $1, Lineker, England. $1.50, Pele, Brazil. $2, Fontaine, France. $2, Rahn, W. Germany.
No. 1300, 50c, vert: a, Ardiles, Argentina. b, Romario, Brazil. c, Rummenigge, Germany. d, Charlton, England. e, Villa, Argentina. f, Matthäus, Germany. g, Maradona, Argentina. h, Lineker, England.
No. 1301, 50c: a, Paulo Rossi, Italy. b, Ademir, Brazil. c, Grzegorz Lato, Poland. d, Gary Lineker, England. e, Gerd Muller, W. Germany. f, Johan Cruyff, Holland. g, Karl-Heinz Rummenigge, Germany. h, Mario Kempes, Argentina.
No. 1302, $6, Beckenbauer, W. Germany, vert. No. 1303, $6, Maier, W. Germany, vert.

Perf. 13½x14, 14x13½

1997, Oct. 1 **Litho.**
1294-1299 A371 Set of 6 18.00 18.00

Sheets of 8, #a-h, + Label

1300-1301 A371 Set of 2 27.50 27.50

Souvenir Sheets

1302-1303 A371 Set of 2 40.00 40.00

Marine Life A372

No. 1304: a, Flamingoes (beach, palm trees). b, Six flamingoes. c, Sailfish (d). d, Egret. e, Yellow-tail snapper. f, Manatee. g, Clown coris. h, White-collar butterflyfish. i, Royal angelfish. j, Titan triggerfish. k, Three-striped wrasse. l, Pacific blue-eye. m, Wobbegono. n, Jellyfish. o, Sea urchin, red sea triggerfish. p, Harlequin fish.
No. 1305, $2, Seahorses, vert. No. 1306, $2, Anemone fish.

1998, Mar. 9 **Litho.** *Perf. 14*
1304 A372 20c Sheet of 16, #a.-p. 9.50 9.50

Souvenir Sheets

Perf. 13½x14, 14x13½

1305-1306 A372 Set of 2 12.00 12.00

No. 1305 contains one 38x51mm stamp, No. 1306 contains one 51x38mm stamp.

Butterflies — A373

Designs: No. 1307, 50c, Orange tip. No. 1308, 50c, Saturn. No. 1309, 50c, Queen of Spain fritillary. No. 1310, 50c, Plain tiger. No. 1311, 50c, Doris. No. 1312, 50c, Forest queen. No. 1313, 50c, Figure-of-eight. No. 1314, 50c, Orange-barred sulphur.
No. 1315, 50c: a, Alfalfa. b, Orange-barred sulphur, diff. c, Union jack. d, Mocker swallowtail. e, Large green-banded blue. f, Common dotted border.
No. 1316, 50c: a, Cairns birdwing. b, Leafwing. c, Banded kin shoemaker. d, Tiger swallowtail. e, Adonis blue. f, Palmfly.
No. 1317, $2, Great orange tip. No. 1318, $2, Japanese emperor.

1998, Apr. 6 **Litho.** *Perf. 14*
1307-1314 A373 Set of 8 12.00 12.00

Sheets of 6, #a-f

1315-1316 A373 Set of 2 18.00 18.00

Souvenir Sheets

1317-1318 A373 Set of 2 12.00 12.00

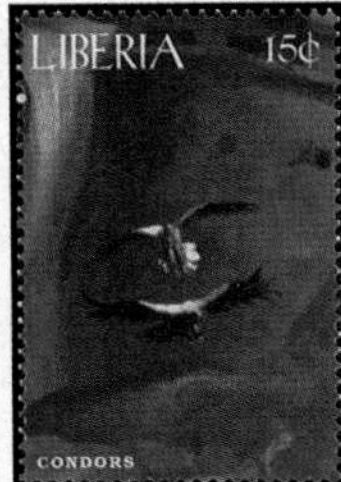

Noah's Ark — A374

No. 1319: a, Condors. b, Giraffes, skunks. c, Mallard ducks. d, Snowy owl. e, Snowy owl (face forward). f, Noah. g, Noah's wife. h, Polar bears. i, Elephants. j, Zebras. k, Rhinoceros. l, Sheep. m. Ruby-throated hummingbird. n, Wives of Noah's sons. o, Bats. p, Ring-necked pheasant. q, Tiger. r, Deer. s, Kangaroos. t, Camels. u, Red-eyed frogs. v, Raccoons. w, Rooster, hen. x, Marmosets. y, Lions.
$2, Black-legged kittiwake gull, ark on top of mountain, horiz.

1998, May 4 Litho. *Perf. 14*
1319 A374 15c Sheet of 25, #a.-y. 11.00 11.00

Souvenir Sheet
1320 A374 $2 multicolored 6.00 6.00

World Wildlife Fund A375

No. 1321 — Liberian Mongoose: a, Looking straight ahead. b, Holding object between front paws. c, With front legs on branch. d, With mouth wide open.

1998, June 16 Litho. *Perf. 14*
1321 A375 32c Block or strip of 4, #a.-d. 5.50 5.50

Issued in sheets of 12 stamps.

Mushrooms A376

Designs: 10c, Lepiota cristata. 15c, Russula emetica. 20c, Coprinus comatus. 30c, Russula cyanoxantha. 50c, Cortinarius violaceus. 75c, Amanita cothurnata. $1, Stropharia cyanea. $1.20, Panaeolus semiovatus.

No. 1330, 40c: a, Collybia butryacea. b, Asterophora parasitica. c, Tricholomopsis rutilans. d, Marasmius alliaceus. e, Mycena crocata. f, Mycena polygramma. g, Oudemansiella mucida. h, Entoloma conferendum. i, Entoloma serrulatum.

No. 1331, 40c: a, Cordyceps militaris. b, Xylaria hypoxlon. c, Sarcoscypha austriaca. d, Auriscalpium. e, Fomitopsis pinicola. f, Pleurotus ostreatus. g, Lepista flaccida. h, Clitocybe metachroa. i, Hygrocybe conica.

No. 1332, $2, Gomphidus roseus. No. 1333, $2, Paxillus atrotomentosus. No. 1334, $2, Russula occidentalis. No. 1335, $2, Cantharellus cibarius.

1998, July 1
1322-1329 A376 Set of 8 14.00 14.00

Sheets of 9, #a-i
1330-1331 A376 Set of 2 24.00 24.00

Souvenir Sheets
1332-1335 A376 Set of 4 27.50 27.50

Monarchs A377

No. 1336, 50c: a, Kaiser Wilhelm II, Germany. b, Qabus Bin Said, Oman. c, King Albert, Belgium. d, Haile Selassie, Ethiopia. e, King Hussein, Jordan. f, Sheik Jaber Al-Ahmad Al-Sabah, Kuwait.

No. 1337, 50c: a, Alexander the Great, Greece. b, Charlemagne, France. c, Cleopatra, Egypt. d, Henry VIII, England. e, Peter the Great, Russia. f, Frederick the Great, Prussia.

No. 1338, 50c: a, Queen Beatrix, Netherlands. b, King Juan Carlos, Spain. c, Queen Elizabeth II, England. d, Franz Joseph I, Austria-Hungary. e, Princess Grace, Monaco. f, King Carl XVI Gustaf, Sweden.

No. 1339, $2, Empress Michiko, Japan. No. 1340, $2, Emperor Akihito, Japan. No. 1341, $2, Kublai Khan, China.

1998, July 27 Litho. *Perf. 14*

Sheets of 6, #a-f
1336-1338 A377 Set of 3 24.00 24.00

Souvenir Sheets
1339-1341 A377 Set of 3 21.00 21.00

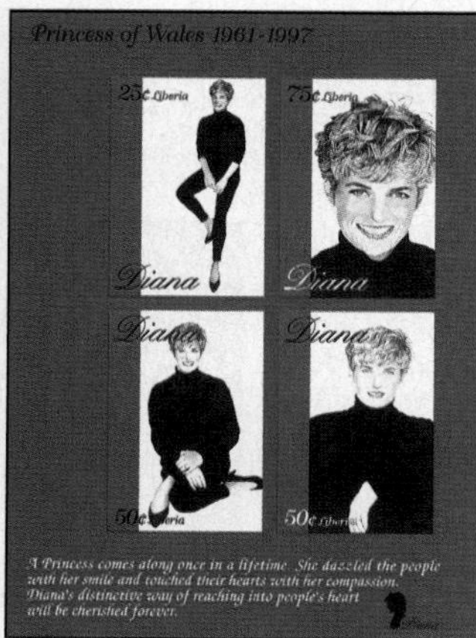
Diana, Princess of Wales (1961-97) — A378

Various portraits of Diana in black outfit.

1998 *Imperf.*
1342 A378 50c Sheet of 4, #a.-d. 4.00 4.00

Birds A379

No. 1343, 32c, Great green macaw. No. 1344, 32c, Crowned pigeon, vert. No. 1345, 32c, Blue-gray tanager. No. 1346, 32c, Roseate spoonbill, vert. No. 1347, 32c, Red-capped manakin. No. 1348, 32c, Groove-billed ani. No. 1349, 32c, South African crowned crane, vert.

No. 1350, vert: a, African sunbird. b, Seven-colored tanager. c, Red-throated bee-eater. d, Blue-crowned motmot. e, Duvaucel's trogon. f, Green bulbul. g, Grass-green tanager. h, Turaco. i, Hammer-head. j, Sarus crane. k, Limpkin. l, Ground hornbill.

No. 1351, $2, Red-crested touraco. No. 1352, $2, Flamingo, vert.

1998, Aug. 31 Litho. *Perf. 14*
1343-1349 A379 Set of 7 7.00 7.00
1350 A379 32c Sheet of 12, #a.-l. 12.00 12.00

Souvenir Sheets
1351-1352 A379 Set of 2 12.00 12.00

Children's Stories A380

No. 1354: a, Tom Sawyer, by Mark Twain. b, Peter Rabbit, by Beatrix Potter. c, The Nutcracker, by E.T.A. Hoffman. d, Hansel & Gretel, by The Brothers Grimm. e, The Princess and the Pea, by Hans Christian Andersen. f, Oliver Twist, by Charles Dickens. g, Little Red Riding Hood, by The Brothers Grimm. h, Rumpelstiltskin, by The Brothers Grimm. i, The Wind & the Willows, by Kenneth Grahame.

$2, Rapunzel, by Brothers Grimm.

1998, Sept. 16 Litho. *Perf. 14½*
1354 A380 40c Sheet of 9, #a.-i. 12.00 12.00

Souvenir Sheet
Perf. 13½
1355 A380 $2 multicolored 7.00 7.00

No. 1355 contains one 38x51mm stamp.

Island, Marine Life A381

No. 1356: a, Litoria peronii. b, Volcano, denomination UL. c, Volcano, denomination UR. d, Egretta alba. e, Graphium antiphates itamputi. f, Rhododendron zoelleri. g, Boat. h, Lava flow. i, Cormorants. j, Vaccinium. k, Caranx latus. l, Dugongs. m, Underwater lava flow. n, Cetocarus bicolor. o, Chilomycterus spilostylus. p, Lienardella fasliatus. q, Aerobatus. r, Gray reef shark. s, Acanthurus leucosternon, denomination UR. t, Hippocampus kuda. u, Coral, denomination UR. v, Chelonia. w, Myripristis hexogona. x, Coral, denomination, UL. y, Acanthurus leucosternon, denonination UL.

No. 1357: a, Sperm whale (b, c). b, Lollipop tang. c, Bottlenose dolphin (b, f). d, Jackass penguin (h). e, Harlequin tuskfish. f, Manta ray (a, b, e, j). g, Sealion. h, Grouper (g, l). i, Hammerhead shark (m). j, Butterfly fish. k, Garibaldi (g). l, Marine iguana (p). m, Loggerhead turtle (n). n, Seahorse. o, Horseshow crab (n, p). p, Moray eel.

No. 1358, 32c: a, Walrus. b, Pockfish-harlequin. c, Striped marlin. d, Whale shark. e, Spiny boxfish. f, Porcupine fish. g, Octopus. h, Dragonfish. i, Sea krait.

No. 1359, 32c: a, Snapping turtle. b, Atlantic spadefish. c, Bottlenose dolphin. d, Humpback whale. e, Whitetip shark. f, Twilight and deep seafish. g, Moorish idol. h, American lobster. i, Stingrays.

No. 1360, $2, Great white shark. No. 1361, $2, Banner fish. No. 1362, $2, Killer whale. No. 1363, $2, Surgeon fish.

1998, Oct. 15 *Perf. 14*
1356 A381 15c Sheet of 25, #a.-y. 12.00 12.00
1357 A381 20c Sheet of 16, #a.-p. 10.00 10.00

Sheets of 9, #a-i
1358-1359 A381 Set of 2 18.00 18.00

Souvenir Sheets
1360-1363 A381 Set of 4 22.50 22.50

International Year of the Ocean.

Diana, Princess of Wales (1961-97) A382

Design: a, 50c, Inscription panel on left. b, 50c, panel on right.

1998, Oct. 26 Litho. *Perf. 14½x14*
1364 A382 50c Pair, a.-b. 3.25 3.25

No. 1364 was issued in sheets of 6.

Pablo Picasso (1881-1973) — A383

Entire paintings or details: 50c, Woman Throwing a Stone, 1931. 70c, Man with Sword and Flower, 1969, vert. $1, Large Bather with a Book, 1937, vert.

$2, French Cancan, 1901.

1998, Oct. 26 *Perf. 14½*
1365-1367 A383 Set of 3 7.50 7.50

Souvenir Sheet
1368 A383 $2 multicolored 7.00 7.00

Mahatma Gandhi (1869-1948) A384

1998, Oct. 26 *Perf. 14*
1369 A384 50c shown 1.75 1.75

Souvenir Sheet
1370 A384 $2 Portrait, diff. 7.00 7.00

No. 1369 was issued in sheets of 4.

1998 World Scout Jamboree, Chile — A385

No. 1371: a, Daniel Carter Beard, Ernest Thompson Seton, award scouts, 1912. b, Robert Baden-Powell in Matabeleland, 1896. c, Scout repairing small girl's wagon.

1998, Oct. 26
1371 A385 $1 Sheet of 3, #a.-c. 10.00 10.00

Enzo Ferrari (1898-1988), Automobile Manufacturer — A386

No. 1372: a, King Leopold Cabriolet. b, 195 S. c, 250 GTO 64.

$2, 250MM Cabriolet.

1998, Oct. 26 Litho. *Perf. 14*
1372 A386 $1 Sheet of 3, #a.-c. 9.00 9.00

Souvenir Sheet
1373 A386 $2 multicolored 8.50 8.50

No. 1373 contains one 91x35mm stamp.

Royal Air Force, 80th Anniv. A387

No. 1374: a, Hawker Hurricane XII. b, Avro Lancaster in flight. c, Avro Lancaster B2. d, Supermarine Spitfire HG Mk 1XB.

No. 1375, $2, Bristol F2B fighter, Eurofighter. No. 1376, $2, Hawk, biplane.

1998, Oct. 26
1374 A387 70c Sheet of 4, #a.-d. 9.50 9.50

Souvenir Sheet
1375-1376 A387 Set of 2 14.00 14.00

Famous People and Events of the Twentieth Cent. — A388

No. 1380, 40c: a, Mao Tse-tung. b, Cultural Revolution begins. c, Promoting Third World unity. d, Zhou Enlai. e, Deng Xiaoping. f, Hong Kong returns to China, 1997. g, Shanghai, an Asian metropolis. h, Jiang Zemin.

No. 1381, 40c: a, Robert E. Peary. b, Expedition to the North Pole. c, Climbing Mt. Everest. d, Sir Edmund Hillary. e, Neil Armstrong. f, Walking on the moon. g, Expedition to the South Pole. h, Roald Amundsen.

$2, Matthew Henson.

1998, Dec. 1 Litho. *Perf. 14*

Sheets of 8, #a-h

1380-1381 A388 Set of 2 22.50 22.50

Souvenir Sheet

1382 A388 $2 multicolored 6.50 6.50

Nos. 1380b-1380c, 1380f-1380g, 1381b-1381c, 1380f-1381g are each 53x38mm.

Classic Cars A389

Designs: No. 1383, 32c, 1966-72 Lamborghini Miura. No. 1384, 32c, 1966-93 Alfa Romeo Spider. No. 1385, 32c, 1948-61 Jaguar XK140. No. 1386, 32c, 1959-63 Lotus Elite.

No. 1387, 50c: a, 1949-53 Bristol 401. b, 1952-55 Bentley Continental R. c, 1973-75 Lancia stratos. d, 1963-67 Chevrolet Corvette Stingray. e, 1948-52 Austin A90 Atlantic. f, 1969-90 Aston Martin V8.

No. 1388, 50c: a, 1961-75 Jaguar E-Type. b, 1955-57 Ford Thunderbird. c, 1964-73, Ford Mustang GT350. d, 1957-77 Fiat 500. e, 1955-59 BMW 507. f, 1963-65 Buick Riviera.

No. 1389, $2, 1945-55 MG TD. No. 1390, $2, 1959-65 Rolls Royce Silver Cloud.

1998, Dec. 24

1383-1386 A389 Set of 4 4.00 4.00

Sheets of 6, #a-f

1387-1388 A389 Set of 2 20.00 20.00

Souvenir Sheets

1389-1390 A389 Set of 2 13.00 13.00

New Year 1999 (Year of the Rabbit) — A390

Paintings, by Liu Jiyou (1918-83): No. 1391, Two rabbits. No. 1392, Three rabbits.

No. 1393, Two rabbits, flowers, vert.

1999, Jan. 5

1391 A390 50c multicolored 1.75 1.75
1392 A390 50c multicolored 1.75 1.75

Souvenir Sheet

1393 A390 $2 multicolored 6.50 6.50

Nos. 1391-1392 were issued in sheets of 2 each. No. 1393 contains one 43x52mm stamp.

US Presidents A391

No. 1394, 75c, Various portraits of Abraham Lincoln. No. 1395, 75c, Various portraits of Bill Clinton.

1998, Dec. 1 Litho. *Perf. 14*

Sheets of 4, #a-d

1394-1395 A391 Set of 2 20.00 20.00

Zhou Enlai (1898-1976), Chinese Premier — A392

Various portraits.

1999 Litho. *Perf. 14*

1396 A392 50c Sheet of 6, #a.-f. 10.00 10.00

Souvenir Sheet

1397 A392 $2 multicolored 7.00 7.00

Raptors — A393

Designs: 50c, Snowy owl. 70c, Barn owl. $1, American kestrel $1.50, Golden eagle.

No. 1402, 50c: a, Eurasian eagle owl. b, Osprey. c, Egyptian vulture. d, Lizard buzzard. e, Pale chanting goshawk. f, Bald eagle.

No. 1403, 50c: a, Goshawk. b, Laughing falcon. c, Oriental bay-owl. d, Swallow-tailed kite. e, Secretary bird. f, Brown falcon.

No. 1404, $2, Northern harrier. No. 1405, $2, Peregrine falcon.

1999, Jan. 4

1398-1401 A393 Set of 4 11.00 11.00

Sheets of 6, #a-f

1402-1403 A393 Set of 2 20.00 20.00

Souvenir Sheets

1404-1405 A393 Set of 2 13.00 13.00

Dinosaurs — A395

No. 1406, 50c, Pachyrinosaur. No. 1407, 50c, Centrosaurus, vert. No. 1408, 70c, Pentaceratops, vert. No. 1409, 70c, Oviraptor, vert. $1, Corythosaur. $1.50, Stegosaurus, vert.

No. 1412, 40c: a, Baryonyx (e). b, Pachycephalosaur (a, c). c, Homalocephale. d, Pterodustro (c, g). e, Pycnosteroides. f, Giant nautiloid. g, Kronosaur (e, f). h, Giant cephalopod (g).

No. 1413, 40c: a, Camarasaur. b, Albertosaur (c, f, g). c, Eudimorhodon (b, d). d, Dimorphodon (c). e, Compsognathus. f, Torosaurus. g, Nodosaurid (h). h, Probactrosaurus.

No. 1414, $2, Tarbosaurus, vert. No. 1415, $2, Shunosaurus, vert.

1999, Jan. 18

1406-1411 A395 Set of 6 12.00 12.00

Sheets of 8, #a-h

1412-1413 A395 Set of 2 22.50 22.50

Souvenir Sheets

1414-1415 A395 Set of 2 13.00 13.00

Dinosaurs — A396

Designs: 50c, Brachiosaurus, vert. 70c, Tyrannosaurus, vert. $1, Mosasaurus. $1.50, Triceratops.

No. 1420: a, Albertosaurus. b, Parasaurolophus. c, Styracosaurus. d, Struthiomimus. e, Ankylosaurus. f, Chasmosaurus.

No. 1421, $2, Deinonychus. No. 1422, $2, Stegosaurus.

1999

1416-1419 A396 Set of 4 9.00 9.00
1420 A396 50c Sheet of 6, #a.-f. 10.00 10.00

Souvenir Sheets

1421-1422 A396 Set of 2 13.00 13.00

Flowers — A397

Designs: No. 1423, 50c, Tecophilaea cyanocrocus. 70c, Nymphoides peltata. $1, Angraecum scottianum. $1.50, Grevillea dielsiana.

No. 1427, 50c: a, Cyrtopodium parvilforum. b, Catharanthus roseus. c, Acacia acuminata. d, Herbertia lahue. e, Protea venusta. f, Clianthus formosus.

No. 1428, 50c: a, Dendrobium rarum. b, Cyrtorchis arcuata. c, Zygopetalum intermedium. d, Cassia fistula. e, Saintpaulia ionantha. f, Heliconia collinsiana.

No. 1429, $2, Hibiscus tilliaceus. No. 1430, $2, Rhododendron thomsonii.

1999, Feb. 8

1423-1426 A397 Set of 4 11.00 11.00

Sheets of 6, #a-f

1427-1428 A397 Set of 2 20.00 20.00

Souvenir Sheets

1429-1430 A397 Set of 2 13.00 13.00

Orchids — A398

Designs: No. 1431, 50c, Tridactyle bicaudata. No. 1432, 50c, Angraecum infundibulare. No. 1433, 70c, Oeceoclades maculata. No. 1434, 70c, Ophyrs fusca. No. 1435, $1, Sobennikoffia robusta. No. 1436, $1, Stenoglottis fimbriata. No. 1437, $1.50, Plectrelminthus caudatus. No. 1438, $1.50, Satyrium erectum.

No. 1439, 50c: a, Angraecrum eichlerianum. b, Ansellia africana. c, Cymbidiella pardalina. d, Angraecum eburnium. e, Ancistrochilus rothchildianus. f, Aerangis luteoalba.

No. 1440, 50c: a, Dis cardinalis. b, Cytorchus arcuata. c, Cynorkis compacta. d, Disa kewensis. e, Eulophia guineensis. f, Eulophia speciosa.

No. 1441, Angraecum compactum. No. 1442, Calanthe vestita.

1999, Mar. 13

1431-1438 A398 Set of 8 22.50 22.50

Sheets of 6, #a-f

1439-1440 A398 Set of 2 19.00 19.00

Souvenir Sheets

1441-1442 A398 Set of 2 13.00 13.00

Orchids — A399

Designs: No. 1443, 50c, Calypso bulbosa. No. #1444, 50c, Maclellanara pagan lovesong. No. 1445, 70c, Masdevallia chimaera. No. 1446, 70c, Yamadara midnight. $1, Cleistes divaricata. $1.50, Oncidium golden sunset.

No. 1449: a, Trichopilia tortilis. b, Stenoglottis longifolia. c, Telipogon pulcher. d, Esmeralda clarkei. e, Papilionanthe teres. f, Mormodes rolfeanum. g, Cypripedium acaule. h, Serapias lingua.

1999, Mar. 13

1443-1448 A399 Set of 6 15.00 15.00
1449 A399 30c Sheet of 8, #a.-h. 9.00 9.00

Wildlife — A400

No. 1450: a, Mink. b, Arctic fox. c, Lynx. d, Snowy owl. e, Polar bear. f, Golden eagle.

$2, Big horn sheep.

1999, Feb. 24 Litho. *Perf. 14*

1450 A400 50c Sheet of 6, #a.-f. 7.00 7.00

Souvenir Sheet

1451 A400 $2 multicolored 5.00 5.00

Flora and Fauna A401

No. 1452: a, Madgascan red fody. b, Indri (e). c, Coral-billed nuthatch. d, Safaka (g, j). e, Golden piper. f, Aye aye (i). g, Croad-bordered grass yellowy. h, Ring-tailed lemur (g, j, k). i, Parson's chameleon. j, Madagascar day gecko. k, Leaf-tailed gecko. l, Orchid.

No. 1453, $2, Wattled false sunbird. No. 1454, $2, Parson's chameleon. No. 1455, $2, Ring-tailed lemur.

1999, Apr. 1

1452 A401 20c Sheet of 12, #a.-l. 7.00 7.00

Souvenir Sheets

1453-1455 A401 Set of 3 15.00 15.00

Seabirds — A402

Designs: No. 1456, 50c, Harlequin duck. No. 1457, 50c, Eleonor's falcon, vert. No. 1458, 70c, Wilson's plover. No. 1459, 70c, Common eider. No. 1460, $1, Little tern. No. 1461, $1, American oystercatcher. No. 1462, $1.50, Herring gull, vert. No. 1463, $1.50, Brown pelican, vert.

No. 1464, 30c, vert: a, Great cormorant. b, Crested cormorant. c, Red faced cormorant. d, Whimbrel. e, Tufted puffin. f, Ivory gull. g, Common murre. h, Shelduck. i, Razorbill.

No. 1465, 30c: a, Common tern. b, Black-legged kittiwake. c, Bernacle goose. d, Black-headed gull. e, Semipalmated plover. f, Northern gannet. g, King eider. h, Iceland gull. i, Ring-billed gull.

No. 1466, $2, Arctic loon. No. 1467, $2, Atlantic puffin. No. 1468, $2, California gull, vert.

1999, Apr. 1 Litho. *Perf. 14*
1456-1463 A402 Set of 8 17.00 17.00

Sheets of 9, #a-i

1464-1465 A402 Set of 2 13.00 13.00

Souvenir Sheets

1466-1468 A402 Set of 3 15.00 15.00

Queen Mother (b. 1900) — A404

No. 1475: a, With King George VI at wedding, 1923. b, In Nairobi, 1959. c, Wearing tiara, 1953. d, Wearing hat, 1990.
$2, Wearing hat, 1990, diff.

1999, Aug. 4 *Perf. 14*
1475 A404 $1 Sheet of 4, #a.-d., + label 9.00 9.00

Souvenir Sheet

Perf. 13¾

1476 A404 $2 multicolored 5.00 5.00

No. 1476 contains one 38x51mm stamp.

Trains A405

Designs: 32c, Nozomi Train, Japan. 40c, 401 Intercity Express, Germany. 50c, C53, Japan Railways. 70c, Beuth 2-2-2, Germany.
No. 1481, 40c: a, "Adler," Germany. b, Suburban EMU, Japan. c, Class 01, 4-6-2, Germany. d, Class 120 Bo-Bo, Germany. e, Class P8, 4-6-0, Germany. f, Fujikawa Express, Japan. g, Class 081, Germany. h, Kodama 8-car train, Japan. i, Class C62, 4-6-4, Japan.
No. 1482, 40c: a, KF Type, 4-8-4, China. b, Minobu Line train, Japan. c, Class S34-40, Germany. d, Class EF81, Bo-Bo, Japan. e, V200, B-B, Germany. f, SVT 877 "Flying Hamburger," Japan. g, C51, 4-6-2 Japan Railways. h, AEO Single rail car, Germany. i, Class D51, Japan.
No. 1483, $2, Yamonote Line train, Japan. No. 1484, $2, Class B8, Germany.

1999, Aug. 25 Litho. *Perf. 14*
1477-1480 A405 Set of 4 4.50 4.50

Sheets of 9, #a-i

1481-1482 A405 Set of 2 17.00 17.00

Souvenir Sheets

1483-1484 A405 Set of 2 10.00 10.00

Dogs A406

No. 1485, Lhasa apso. 70c, Samoyed.
No. 1487, vert.: a, Dalmatian. b, Pyrennean Mountain dog. c, Golden retriever. d, Bearded collie. e, Basset hound. f, Bernese Mountain dog.
No. 1488, Beagle, vert.

1999, Aug. 30 *Perf. 14*
1485 A406 50c multicolored 1.25 1.25
1486 A406 70c multicolored 1.75 1.75
1487 A406 50c Sheet of 6, #a.-f. 7.50 7.50

Souvenir Sheet

1488 A406 $2 multicolored 5.00 5.00

During 1999-2004 Liberia was torn by a brutal and chaotic civil war that reduced the nation to a state of anarchy. Government services, including postal operations, functioned erratically, if at all, for months at a time. During this period, overseas stamp agents continued to produce stamps under pre-war contracts, and a large number of issues appeared that were marketed to overseas collectors. It appears that some of these stamps have been released in Liberia since the end of hostilities. These will be listed when their sale and postal use has been confirmed.

Paintings by Norman Rockwell A580

Paintings: $15, Playing Party Games. $30, Saturday Night Out. $35, The Portrait. No, 2328, $50, Grandpa's Little Ballerina.
No. 2329, $50: a, The Cave of the Winds. b, Redhead Loves Hatty. c, The Rivals. d, Three's Company.
No. 2330, $50: a, Distortion. b, Summer Vacation. c, Runaway Pants. d, Tumble.
No. 2331, $50: a, Daydreams. b, A Patient Friend. c, Lands of Enchantment. d, The Little Spooners.
No. 2332, $50: a, The Skating Lesson. b, The Fortune Teller. c, God Bless You. d, Knowledge is Power.

2005, Jan. 10 Litho. *Perf. 14¼*
2325-2328 A580 Set of 4 7.00 7.00

Sheets of 4, #a-d

2329-2332 A580 Set of 4 40.00 40.00

Jules Verne (1828-1905), Writer — A581

No. 2333, $30: a, The Adventures of Captain Hatteras. b, The Mysterious Island (deflated balloon). c, The Mysterious Island (Men looking at ape). d, 20,000 Leagues Under the Sea (spotlights on ship).
No. 2334, $30: a, Around the World in Eighty Days. b, From the Earth to the Moon (people watching man on space capsule ladder). c, Paris in the Twentieth Century. d, Master of the World (ship captain at wheel).
No. 2335, $30: a, The Chase of the Golden Meteor. b, Master of the World (flying machine, country name in white). c, Five Weeks in a Balloon. d, From the Earth to the Moon (rocket in space).
No. 2336, $30: a, The Mysterious Island (People in balloon basket). b, Robur the Conqueror. c, Round the Moon. d, Master of the World (flying machine, country name in black).
No. 2337, $30 — Scenes from 20,000 Leagues Under the Sea: a, Ships on water. b, Shark and octopus attacking ship. c, Shark attacking diver. d, Squid attacking ship.
No. 2338, $100, Deep sea divers. No. 2339, $100, Admiral Richard E. Byrd. No. 2340, $100, Radio satellite communication. No. 2341, $100, Long range ballistic missile. No. 2342, $100, Extravehicular satellite repair.

2005, Jan. 11 *Perf. 13¼x13½*

Sheets of 4, #a-d

2333-2337 A581 Set of 5 32.50 32.50

Souvenir Sheets

2338-2342 A581 Set of 5 27.50 27.50

Marilyn Monroe (1926-62), Actress — A582

2005, Jan. 26 *Perf. 14*
2343 A582 $12 multi .70 .70

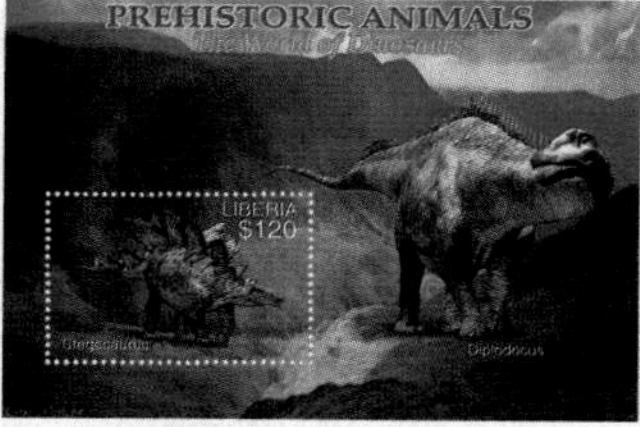

Prehistoric Animals — A583

No. 2344, $50: a, Torosaurus. b, Tyrannosaurus. c, Polacanthus. d, Stegosaurus.
No. 2345, $50: a, Smilodon. b, Brontothere. c, Doedicurus. d, Moeritherium.
No. 2346, $50: a, Cymbospondylus. b, Archelon. c, Xiphactinus. d, Dunkleosteus.
No. 2347, $120, Stegosaurus, diff. No. 2348, $120, Woolly rhinoceros. No. 2349, $120, Odobenocetops.

2005, Jan. 26 *Perf. 13¼x13½*

Sheets of 4, #a-d

2344-2346 A583 Set of 3 32.50 32.50

Souvenir Sheet

2347-2349 A583 Set of 3 18.00 18.00

Battle of Trafalgar, Bicent. — A584

Various ships: $10, $20, $40, $50.
$100, Death of Admiral Horatio Nelson.

2005, May 4 *Perf. 14¼*
2350-2353 A584 Set of 4 6.00 6.00

Souvenir Sheet

2354 A584 $100 multi 5.50 5.50

Hans Christian Andersen (1805-75), Author — A585

No. 2355: a, Medal. b, Open book. c, Andersen.
$100, Sketch of Little Mermaid.

2005, May 4 *Perf. 14¼*
2355 A585 $50 Sheet of 3, #a-c 7.50 7.50

Souvenir Sheet

2356 A585 $100 multi 5.50 5.50

Friedrich von Schiller (1759-1805), Writer — A586

No. 2357: a, Bust of Schiller on round pedestal. b, Bust and foliage. c, Bust on monument.
$100, Statue of Schiller, Chicago.

2005, May 4 *Perf. 14¼*
2357 A586 $50 Sheet of 3, #a-c 7.50 7.50

Size: 48x67mm

Imperf

2358 A586 $100 multi 5.50 7.50

No. 2357 contains three 28x42mm stamps.

Miniature Sheets

Elvis Presley (1935-77) — A587

No. 2359, $35 — Presley in: a, 1956. b, 1969. c, 1969 (country name in yellow). d, 1969 (country name in pink). e, 1970.
No. 2360, $35 — Presley wearing: a, Red suit and white shirt. b, Yellow sweater. c, Red shirt. d, Brown suit. e, Gray suit.

2005, May 19 *Perf. 13½x13¼*

Sheets of 5, #a-e

2359-2360 A587 Set of 2 19.00 19.00

Pope John Paul II (1920-2005) A588

2005, Aug. 22 *Perf. 12¾*
2361 A588 $50 multi 2.50 2.50

Printed in sheets of 4.

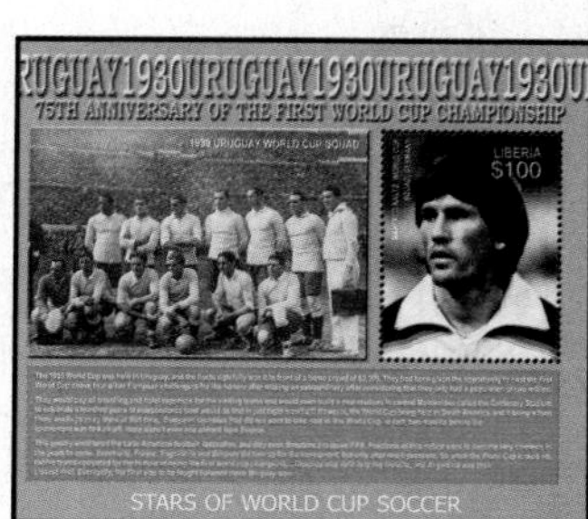

World Cup Soccer Championships, 75th Anniv. — A589

No. 2362: a, Norbert Eder. b, Paul Breitner. c, Thomas Helmer.
$100, Manfred Kaltz.

2005, Aug. 22 ***Perf. 13¼***
2362 A589 $60 Sheet of 3, #a-c 10.00 10.00

Souvenir Sheet
Perf. 12
2363 A589 $100 multi 5.50 5.50

Albert Einstein (1879-1955), Physicist — A590

No. 2364 — Einstein and: a, Charlie Chaplin. b, Max Planck. c, William Allen White.
$100, J. Robert Oppenheimer

2005, Aug. 22 ***Perf. 12¾***
2364 A590 $60 Sheet of 3, #a-c 7.50 7.50

Souvenir Sheet
2365 A590 $100 multi 4.25 4.25

End of World War II, 60th Anniv. — A591

No. 2366, $40 — V-E Day: a, Gen. Dwight D. Eisenhower. b, Prime Minister Winston Churchill. c, Gen. George Patton. d, Field Marshal Bernard Montgomery.
No. 2367, $40 — V-E Day: a, Air Marshal Sir Arthur "Bomber" Harris. b, Gen. Douglas MacArthur. c, Field Marshal Alan Brooke. d, Pres. Franklin D. Roosevelt.
No. 2368, $40 — V-J Day: a, RAF Wellington bomber. b, Mitsubishi A6M Zero. c, RAF Hudson bomber. d, B-17 bomber.
No. 2369, $40 — V-J Day: a, P-51 Mustang. b, RAF Hamilcar glider. c, P-38 Lightning. d, RAF Supermarine Spitfire.

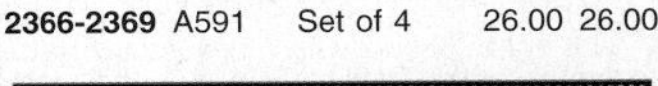

2005, Aug. 22 ***Perf. 13¼x13½***
Sheets of 4, #a-d
2366-2369 A591 Set of 4 26.00 26.00

Worldwide Fund for Nature (WWF) — A592

No. 2370: a, Jentink's duiker. b, Head of Ogilby's duiker. c, Ogilby's duiker. d, Head of Jentink's duiker.

2005, Aug. 31 ***Perf. 14***
2370 A592 $20 Block or vert. strip of 4, #a-d 3.25 3.25
e. Miniature sheet, 2 each #2370a-2370d 6.50 6.50

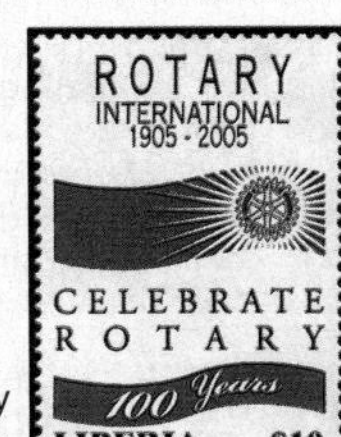

Rotary International, Cent. — A593

Emblem: $10, $25, $35, $50.
$100, Mother Teresa.

2005, Sept. 22 ***Perf. 14***
2371-2374 A593 Set of 4 5.00 5.00

Souvenir Sheet
2375 A593 $100 multi 4.25 4.25

Christmas — A594

Paintings: $20, Glory to God, by Kim Kichang. $25, Flight Into Egypt, by Fra Angelico. $30, Christmas Mom, by Will Hickock Low. $50, The Nativity, by Bernadino Luini.
$100, Adoration of the Magi, by Nicolas Poussin.

2005, Dec. 1
2376-2379 A594 Set of 4 5.25 5.25

Souvenir Sheet
2380 A594 $100 multi 4.25 4.25

Elvis Presley (1935-77) — A595

Variable Serpentine Die Cut
2006, Jan. 17 **Litho. & Embossed**
Without Gum
2381 A595 $350 gold & multi 14.50 14.50

African Antelopes — A596

No. 2382: a, Gemsbok. b, Kudu. c, Sable antelope. d, Impala.
$100, Springbok.

2006, Jan. 17 **Litho.** ***Perf. 13½***
2382 A596 $45 Sheet of 4, #a-d 7.50 7.50

Souvenir Sheet
2383 A596 $100 multi 4.25 4.25

Mammals — A597

No. 2384: a, Jackal. b, Fox. c, Wolf. d, Coyote.
$100, Hyena.

2006, Jan. 17
2384 A597 $45 Sheet of 4, #a-d 7.50 7.50

Souvenir Sheet
2385 A597 $100 multi 4.25 4.25

Wild Cats — A598

No. 2386: a, Jaguar. b, Lion. c, Puma. d, Cheetah.
$100, Siberian tiger.

2006, Jan. 17
2386 A598 $45 Sheet of 4, #a-d 7.50 7.50

Souvenir Sheet
2387 A598 $100 multi 4.25 4.25

Animals of the Bible — A599

No. 2388, $45: a, Lions. b, Camels. c, Doves. d, Donkey.
No. 2389, $45: a, Foxes. b, Vultures. c, Turtles. d, Ducks.
No. 2390, $45: a, Goat. b, Bear. c, Ravens. d, Sheep.
No. 2391, $120, Pig. No. 2392, $120, Whale. No. 2393, $120, Snake.

2006, Jan. 17
Sheets of 4, #a-d
2388-2390 A599 Set of 3 22.50 22.50

Souvenir Sheets
2391-2393 A599 Set of 3 15.00 15.00

Snakes — A600

No. 2394: a, Rough green snake. b, Speckled king snake. c, Garter snake. d, Brown snake.
$100, Red milk snake.

2006, Jan. 27
2394 A600 $45 Sheet of 4, #a-d 7.50 7.50

Souvenir Sheet
2395 A600 $100 multi 4.25 4.25

2006 Winter Olympics, Turin — A601

Designs: $20, Austria #B337. $25, Poster for 1976 Innsbruck Winter Olympics, vert. $35, Austria #B338. $50, Austria #B335. $70, US #3555. $100, Poster for 2002 Salt Lake City Winter Olympics, vert.

2006, Apr. 6 ***Perf. 13½***
2396-2399 A601 Set of 4 5.50 5.50
2399A A601 $70 multi 3.00 3.00
2399B A601 $100 multi 4.25 4.25

Nos. 2399A-2399B were not made available until 2007.

Souvenir Sheet

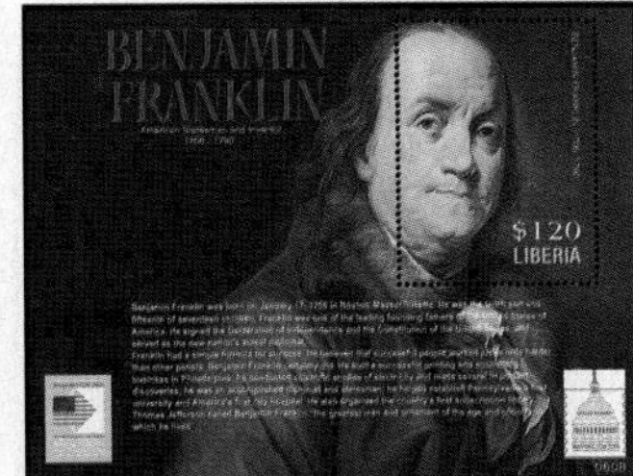

Benjamin Franklin (1706-90), Statesman — A602

2006, May 27 ***Perf. 13½***
2400 A602 $120 multi 5.00 5.00

Washington 2006 World Philatelic Exhibition.

Queen Elizabeth II, 80th Birthday — A603

No. 2401 — Hat color: a, Green. b, Blue. c, Beige. d, Black.
$120, Queen wearing tiara.

2006, June 13 ***Perf. 14¼***
2401 A603 $40 Sheet of 4, #a-d 6.50 6.50

Souvenir Sheet

2402 A603 $120 multi 5.00 5.00

Rembrandt (1606-69), Painter A604

Artwork: $15, Young Man in a Turban. $30, Man Leaning on a Windowsill. $40, Officer with a Gold Chain. $45, The Art Dealer Clement de Jonghe.
No. 2407, $60: a, Self-portrait, 1633. b, Self-portrait, 1634. c, Self-portrait, 1639. d, Self-portrait, 1640.
No. 2408, $60: a, Christ and the Canaanite Woman. b, The Mocking of Christ. c, Head of an Old Man (Three-quarters view). d, Head of an Old Man (profile).
No. 2409, $60: a, David and Jonathan. b, Nude Woman with a Snake. c, The Abduction of Europa. d, Daniel and Cyrus Before the Idol Bel.
No. 2410, $60: a, Shah Jahan and Dara Shikoh. b, Farm Building Surrounded by Trees. c, Two Thatched Cottages with Figures at Window. d, A Sailing Boat on Wide Expanse of Water.
No. 2411, $120, Bearded Old Man with a Gold Chain. No. 2412, $120, A Scholar in His Study. No. 2413, $120, Rembrandt's Mother. No. 2414, $120, Portrait of Jan Six.

2006, June 13 **Litho.**
2403-2406 A604 Set of 4 5.50 5.50

Sheets of 4, #a-d

2407-2410 A604 Set of 4 40.00 40.00

Imperf

Size: 76x103mm

2411-2414 A604 Set of 4 20.00 20.00

Souvenir Sheet

Wolfgang Amadeus Mozart (1756-91), Composer — A605

2006, July 25 ***Perf. 12¾***
2415 A605 $120 multi 5.00 5.00

Miniature Sheet

Chinese Ceramics — A606

No. 2416: a, Bowl with red, black and white exterior, brown interior. b, Bowl with blue and white exterior, blue, red and white interior. c, Bowl with green on white exterior, square opening. d, Bowl with red, white and blue exterior, brown interior. e, Bowl with green on white exterior, circular opening. f, Bowl with red, white and green exterior, square opening.

2006, Aug. 16 ***Perf. 12x12¼***
2416 A606 $35 Sheet of 6, #a-f 8.75 8.75

Inauguration of Pres. Ellen Johnson-Sirleaf — A607

Designs: $10, Pres. Johnson-Sirleaf and flag. $25, Certification by National Election Commission, horiz. $30, Casting of ballots. $40, Pres. Johnson-Sirleaf holding child, horiz.
$100, Pres. Johnson-Sirleaf at microphone.

2006, Aug. 22 ***Perf. 13¼***
2417-2420 A607 Set of 4 4.25 4.25

Souvenir Sheet

2421 A607 $100 multi 4.25 4.25

Millennium Development Goals — A608

Goals: No. 2422, $10, Achieve universal primary education (graduates). No. 2423, $10, Promote gender equality and empower women. No. 2424, $25, Eradicate extreme hunger and poverty. No. 2425, $25, Reduce child mortality. No. 2426, $30, Develop a global partnership for development (map). No. 2427, $30, Develop a global partnership for development (ships and airplane). $40, Improve maternal health. $50, Achieve universal primary education (classroom). No. 2430, $100, Ensure environmental sustainability. No. 2431, $100, Combat HIV/AIDS, malaria and other diseases.
No. 2432, Achieve universal primary education (classroom), vert.

2006, Sept. 22
2422-2431 A608 Set of 10 17.50 17.50

Souvenir Sheet

2432 A608 $100 multi 4.25 4.25

Space Achievements — A609

No. 2433, $40 — Intl. Space Station: a, Country name and denomination in black, at top. b, Country name in black, denomination in white. c, Country name and denomination in white, at top. d, Country name and denomination in black, at bottom. e, Space shuttle (country name and denomination in white, at bottom). f, Astronaut (country name and denomination in white, at bottom.
No. 2434, $40, vert. — Apollo 11: a, Lunar module. b, Rocket on launch pad. c, Nose cone of rocket. d, Astronaut on moon. e, Command module. f, Astronauts and rocket.
No. 2435, $55, vert. — First Flight of Space Shuttle Columbia: a, Astronaut Bob Crippen. b, Front of space shuttle. c, Astronaut John Young. d, Tail of space shuttle.
No. 2436, $55 — Space Shuttle returns to space: a, Wing. b, Fuselage, reflection of sunlight. c, Wing inscribed "Discovery." d, Fuselage and Earth.
No. 2437, $120, Apollo-Soyuz. No. 2438, $120, Mars Reconnaissance Orbiter. No. 2439, $120, Venus Express. No. 2440, $120, Deep Impact Probe.

2006, Oct. 3 **Litho.** ***Perf. 12¾***

Sheets of 6, #a-f

2433-2434 A609 Set of 2 20.00 20.00

Sheets of 4, #a-d

2435-2436 A609 Set of 2 18.00 18.00

Souvenir Sheets

2437-2440 A609 Set of 4 20.00 20.00

Christopher Columbus (1451-1506), Explorer — A610

Designs: $25, Columbus, drawings of ships. $50, Columbus, ships, horiz. $70, Columbus and Santa Maria, horiz. $100, Ship, crew encountering natives, horiz.
$120, Men on shore.

2006, Nov. 15
2441-2444 A610 Set of 4 10.00 10.00

Souvenir Sheet

2445 A610 $120 multi 5.00 5.00

Souvenir Sheet

Christmas — A611

No. 2446 — Details from The Adoration of the Magi, by Peter Paul Rubens: a, Man and boy. b, Mary. c, Man with headcovering. d, Infant Jesus.

2006, Dec. 21 **Litho.** ***Perf. 14***
2446 A611 $40 Sheet of 4, #a-d 6.75 6.75

A612

Concorde — A613

No. 2447, $30 — Concorde: a, G-BOAF. b, G-BOAB.
No. 2448, $35 — Concorde: a, F-BVFA on runway. b, G-BOAA taking off.

2007, Mar. 1 **Litho.** ***Perf. 13½***

Horiz. Pairs, #a-b

2447-2448 A612 Set of 2 5.50 5.50

Litho. & Embossed

Without Gum

Irregular Serpentine Die Cut

2449 A613 $350 gold & multi 14.50 14.50

Souvenir Sheet

Ludwig Durr (1878-1956), Engineer — A614

No. 2450: a, Durr and Zeppelin. b, Interior cabin plan for LZ-127. c, Count Ferdinand von Zeppelin.

2007, Mar. 1 **Litho.** ***Perf. 13¼***
2450 A614 $60 Sheet of 3, #a-c 7.50 7.50

Souvenir Sheet

Marilyn Monroe (1926-62), Actress — A615

Various portraits.

2007, Mar. 1
2451 A615 $50 Sheet of 4, #a-d 8.25 8.25

Pres. John F. Kennedy (1917-62) — A616

No. 2452, $45: a, Signing executive order establishing the Peace Corps. b, With Sargent Shriver. c, Peace Corps volunteers in Tanganyika. d, Jack Hood Vaughn, second director of Peace Corps.
No. 2453, $45 — Kennedy: a, And Eleanor Roosevelt. b, Delivering Alliance for Progress speech. c, With Mrs. Kennedy in Venezuela. d, And Secretary of State Dean Rusk.

2007, Mar. 1 **Litho.**

Sheets of 4, #a-d

2452-2453 A616 Set of 2 15.00 15.00

Mushrooms A617

Designs: $25, Boletus edulis. $35, Begriipt russula. No. 2456, $45, Lactarius helvus. $50, Amanita pantherina.
No. 2458, $45: a, Russula cyanoxantha. b, Cantharellus subalbidus. c, Leccinum oxydalile. d, Boletus badius.
No. 2459, $45: a, Amanita bingensis. b, Chlorophyllum molybdites. c, Calvatia utriformis. d, Amanita loosii.

No. 2460, $100, Amanita muscaria. No. 2461, $100, Chlorophyllum molybdites, diff. No. 2462, $100, Agaricus silvaticus.

2007, Mar. 1
2454-2457 A617 Set of 4 6.50 6.50

Sheets of 4, #a-d

2458-2459 A617 Set of 2 15.00 15.00

Souvenir Sheets

2460-2462 A617 Set of 3 12.50 12.50

Scouting, Cent. A618

Designs: $50, Scouts and 2006 World Jamboree emblem. $150, Scouts, horiz.

2007, Mar. 15
2463 A618 $50 multi 1.75 1.75

Souvenir Sheet

2464 A618 $150 multi 5.00 5.00

No. 2463 was printed in sheets of 4.

Pope Benedict XVI — A619

2007, Nov. 30 Litho. *Perf. 13¼*
2465 A619 $30 multi 1.00 1.00

Miniature Sheet

New Year 2007 (Year of the Boar) — A620

No. 2466 — Wild Boar, by Liu Jiyou with text "Year of the Boar" in: a, Red. b, Green. c, Brown. d, Blue.

2007, Nov. 30
2466 A620 $30 Sheet of 4, #a-d 4.00 4.00

Miniature Sheet

Wedding of Queen Elizabeth II and Prince Philip, 60th Anniv. — A621

No. 2467: a, Couple, denomination in white. b, Queen, denomination in yellow. c, Couple, denomination in lilac. d, Queen, denomination in white. e, Couple, denomination in yellow. f, Queen, denomination in lilac.

2007, Nov. 30
2467 A621 $35 Sheet of 6, #a-f 7.00 7.00

Princess Diana (1961-97) — A622

No. 2468 — Various depictions of Diana with denomination in: a, Red violet. b, Blue. c, Green. d, Red.
$125, Red denomination.

2007, Nov. 30
2468 A622 $45 Sheet of 4, #a-d 6.00 6.00

Souvenir Sheet

2469 A622 $125 multi 4.25 4.25

Souvenir Sheets

Pres. Ellen Johnson-Sirleaf and Foreign Dignitaries — A623

Pres. Johnson-Sirleaf meeting with: No. 2470, $100, Chinese Pres. Hu Jintao. No. 2471, $100, U.S. Pres. George W. Bush.

2007, Nov. 30
2470-2471 A623 Set of 2 6.50 6.50

Miniature Sheet

Elvis Presley (1935-77) — A624

No. 2472 — Presley: a, Wearing red and white sweater, country name in white. b, Holding guitar, country name in blue. c, Wearing cap, country name in white. d, Holding guitar, country name in purple. e, Wearing cap, country name in red violet. f, Wearing red and white sweater, country name in yellow.

2007, Nov. 30
2472 A624 $35 Sheet of 6, #a-f 7.00 7.00

Souvenir Sheet

Japanese Prime Minister Junchiro Koizumi, U.S. Pres. George W. Bush and Wife at Graceland — A625

2007, Nov. 30
2473 A625 $100 multi 3.25 3.25

New Year 2008 (Year of the Rat) A626

2007, Dec. 26 Litho. *Perf. 11½x12*
2474 A626 $25 multi .85 .85

Printed in sheets of 4.

Birds — A627

Designs: $20, Pin-tailed whydahs. $30, Lesser honeyguides. $40, African jacanas. $50, Malachite sunbirds.
No. 2479, $45, horiz.: a, White-brown sparrow weavers. b, Parasitic weavers. c, Black-winged orioles. d, Crested guineafowl.
No. 2480, $45, horiz.: a, Red-billed francolins. b, Rufous-crowned rollers. c, African golden orioles. d, Black-crowned tchagras.
No. 2481, $100, Kori bustard. No. 2482, $100, Ostrich. No. 2483, $100, Great white pelican, horiz.

2007, Dec. 26 *Perf. 14*
2475-2478 A627 Set of 4 4.75 4.75

Sheets of 4, #a-d

2479-2480 A627 Set of 2 12.00 12.00

Souvenir Sheets

2481-2483 A627 Set of 3 10.00 10.00

Butterflies — A628

Designs: $20, Appias epaphia. $30, Papilio bromius. $40, Charaxes jasius. $50, Mimacraea marshalli dohertyi.
No. 2488, $45: a, Belenois thysa. b, Papilio pelodorus. c, Cymothoe sangaris. d, Colotis aurigineus.
No. 2489, $45: a, Junonia hierta. b, Myrina silenus. c, Byblia ilithyia. d, Argyrogrammana attsonii.
No. 2490, $100, Iolaus menas. No. 2491, $100, Leptomyrina hirundo. No. 2492, $100, Pinacopteryx eriphia.

2007, Dec. 26
2484-2487 A628 Set of 4 4.75 4.75

Sheets of 4, #a-d

2488-2489 A628 Set of 2 12.00 12.00

Souvenir Sheets

2490-2492 A628 Set of 3 10.00 10.00

Orchids — A629

Designs: $20, Neobenthamia gracilis. $30, Eulophia guineensis. $40, Aerangis curnowiana. $50, Cymbidiella pardalina.
No. 2497, $45: a, Ophrys lutea. b, Ophrys holoserica. c, Ophrys fusca. d, Ophrys scolopax.
No. 2498, $45: a, Disa veitchii. b, Disa racemosa. c, Disa kewensis. d, Disa diores.
No. 2499, $100, Disa crassicornis. No. 2500, $100, Aerangis citrata. No. 2501, $100, Angraecum sororium.

2007, Dec. 26
2493-2496 A629 Set of 4 4.75 4.75

Sheets of 4, #a-d

2497-2498 A629 Set of 2 12.00 12.00

Souvenir Sheets

2499-2501 A629 Set of 3 10.00 10.00

Christmas A630

Designs: $30, Madonna and Child. $40, Holy Family. $45, Flight into Egypt. $50, The Three Magi, horiz.

2007, Dec. 26 *Perf. 14x14¾, 14¾x14*
2502-2505 A630 Set of 4 5.50 5.50

Miniature Sheet

2008 Summer Olympics, Beijing — A631

No. 2506: a, Babe Didrikson. b, 1932 Summer Olympics poster. c, Helene Madison. d, Chuhei Nambu.

2008, Apr. 8 *Perf. 12¾*
2506 A631 $30 Sheet of 4, #a-d 4.00 4.00

National Basketball Association Players — A632

No. 2507 — NBA and Boston Celtics emblems and Kevin Garnett: a, Wearing white uniform, not holding basketball. b, Wearing green uniform. c, Wearing white uniform, holding basketball.
No. 2508 — NBA and Boston Celtics emblems and Paul Pierce: a, Wearing white uniform, hands at side. b, Wearing green uniform. c, Wearing white uniform, pointing.
No. 2509 — NBA and Washington Wizards emblems and Gilbert Arenas: a, Wearing white uniform, hands on hips. b, Wearing blue uniform. c, Wearing white uniform, with basketball.
No. 2510 — NBA and Milwaukee Bucks emblems and Yi Jianlian: a, Wearing white uniform, basketball at left. b, Wearing blue

green uniform. c, Wearing white uniform, basketball at right.

2008, Apr. 30 *Perf. 13½x13¼*

2507	Vert. strip of 3	4.00	4.00
a.-c.	A632 $40 Any single	1.25	1.25
2508	Vert. strip of 3	4.00	4.00
a.-c.	A632 $40 Any single	1.25	1.25
2509	Vert. strip of 3	4.00	4.00
a.-c.	A632 $40 Any single	1.25	1.25
2510	Vert. strip of 3	4.00	4.00
a.-c.	A632 $40 Any single	1.25	1.25
	Nos. 2507-2510 (4)	16.00	16.00

Nos. 2507-2510 each printed in sheets of 6 containing 2 of each stamp in strip.

Souvenir Sheet

Meeting of Liberian Pres. Ellen Johnson-Sirleaf and US Pres. George W. Bush. — A633

No. 2511: a, Pres. Bush. b, Pres. Johnson-Sirleaf.

2008, June 12 *Perf. 13¼*

2511 A633 $125 Sheet of 2, #a-b 8.00 8.00

Elvis Presley (1935-77) — A634

No. 2512 — Presley: a, Holding microphone, red background. b, Holding microphone, "Elvis" in lights. c, Holding microphone, blue background. d, Wearing glasses.

2008, June 12 *Perf. 13¼*

2512 A634 $60 Sheet of 4, #a-d 7.75 7.75

Space Achievements — A635

No. 2513, $40 — International Space Station with denomination at: a, UR. b, UL. c, LR.

No. 2514, $40 — Chandra X-ray Observatory: a, Observatory below nebula. b, Interior of Observatory. c, Observatory above nebula.

No. 2515: a, Calisto, Europa, Voyager I, Jupiter and Io. b, Lift-off of Voyager I. c, Voyager I record cover. d, Voyager I, Titan and Saturn.

No. 2516, $150, International Space Station, horiz. No. 2517, $150, Chandra X-ray Observatory, horiz. No. 2518, $150, Voyager I and rings of Saturn, horiz.

Illustration reduced.

2008, June 12 *Perf. 13¼*

Horiz. Strips of 3, #a-c

2513-2514 A635 Set of 2 7.75 7.75

Miniature Sheet

2515 A635 $60 Sheet of 4, #a-d 7.75 7.75

Souvenir Sheets

2516-2518 A635 Set of 3 14.50 14.50

Nos. 2513-2514 were each printed in sheets of 6 containing 2 of each stamp in strip.

Pope Benedict XVI — A636

2008, June 30 **Litho.**

2519 A636 $45 multi 1.50 1.50

Printed in sheets of 4.

County Flags A637

Flag of: No. 2520, $10, Maryland County. No. 2521, $10, Montserrado County. No. 2522, $25, Gbarpolu County. No. 2523, $25, Grand Bassa County. No. 2524, $30, Grand Cape Mount County. No. 2525, $30, Nimba County. No. 2526, $40, Lofa County. No. 2527, $40, Sinoe County. No. 2528, $50, Bong County. No. 2529, $50, Margibi County. No. 2530, $100, Bomi County. No. 2531, $100, Grand Gedeh County. No. 2532, $100, Grand Kru County. No. 2533, $100, River Cess County. No. 2534, $100, River Gee County.

2008, June 30

2520-2534 A637 Set of 15 26.00 26.00

Miniature Sheet

Ferrari F2008 — A638

No. 2535: a, "F" under "E" of "Liberia." b, "F" under "B" of Liberia. c, Side view of car. d, Car straddling yellow line on track.

2008, Sept. 5 **Litho.** *Perf. 13½*

2535 A638 $60 Sheet of 4, #a-d 7.75 7.75

A639

Election of Barack Obama as US President — A640

Inscriptions: No. 2537, Joseph Biden. No. 2539a, Joseph Robinette Biden, Jr.

No. 2539B: c, Barack Obama. d, Joseph Biden.

Perf. 14¼x14¾, 12¼x11¾ (#2538)

2008, Nov. 5

2536	A639 $45 shown	1.50	1.50
2537	A639 $45 multi	1.50	1.50
2538	A640 $65 shown	2.10	2.10
	Nos. 2536-2538 (3)	5.10	5.10

Souvenir Sheet

2539	Sheet of 2, #2536, 2539a	3.00	3.00
a.	A639 $45 multi	1.50	1.50
2539B	Sheet of 2	10.50	10.50
c.-d.	A639 $160 Either single	5.25	5.25

No. 2536 was printed in sheets of 9 and in No. 2539. No. 2537 was printed in sheets of 9. No. 2538 was printed in sheets of 4.

A641

Solo Aerial Circumnavigation of the World by Wiley Post, 75th Anniv. — A642

No. 2540: a, Post arriving in Cleveland. b, Harold Gatty, navigator. c, Post wearing pressure suit. d, Post atop plane. e, Post and wife Mae. f, The Winnie Mae.

$100, Post and map of flight.

2008, Nov. 24 *Perf. 13¼*

2540 A641 $40 Sheet of 6, #a-f 7.75 7.75

Souvenir Sheet

2541 A642 $100 multi 3.25 3.25

Christmas A643

Paintings: $10, The Nativity, by Martin Schongauer. $25, Birth of Christ, by Robert Campin. $30, Adoration of the Magi, by Geertgen tot Sint Jans. $40, The Birth of Christ, by Sandro Botticelli.

2008, Dec. 1 **Litho.** *Perf. 14¼x14¾*

2542-2545 A643 Set of 4 3.50 3.50

New Year 2009 (Year of the Ox) A644

2009, Jan. 2 *Perf. 12*

2546 A644 $60 multi 1.90 1.90

Printed in sheets of 4.

Blindness A645

Designs: $10, Blind student reading Braille. $30, Blind man in crosswalk. $45, Blind man, map of Liberia. $100, Sighted man leading blind man.

2009, Jan. 4 *Perf. 14¾x14¼*

2547-2550 A645 Set of 4 5.75 5.75

Miniature Sheets

Star Trek — A646

No. 2551: a, Captain Kirk. b, USS Enterprise. c, Scotty. d, Uhura. e, Spock. f, Spock, Rand and Kirk.

No. 2552: a, Scotty. b, Spock and Kirk. c, Dr. McCoy. d, Sulu.

2009, Jan. 14 *Perf. 11½*

2551 A646 $35 Sheet of 6, #a-f 6.75 6.75

Perf. 13½x13¼

2552 A646 $60 Sheet of 4, #a-d 7.50 7.50

No. 2552 contains four 38x51mm stamps.

Miniature Sheet

Abraham Lincoln (1809-65), US President — A647

No. 2553: a, US #1282. b, US #555. c, US #367. d, US #222.

2009, Feb. 2 *Perf. 13¼x13½*
2553 A647 $60 Sheet of 4, #a-d 7.50 7.50

Miniature Sheet

John F. Kennedy (1917-63), US President — A648

No. 2554 — Kennedy: a, Greeting Cuban-exile Bay of Pigs invasion force, with wife Jackie, shaking hand. b, Standing with Jackie. c, In White House. d, With Jackie at stadium.

2009, Feb. 25 *Perf. 11¼x11½*
2554 A648 $50 Sheet of 4, #a-d 6.25 6.25

A649

Peonies — A650

No. 2556: a, White peony, tan background. b, Pink peony, white background.

2009, Apr. 10 *Perf. 13¼*
2555 A649 $32 multi 1.00 1.00

Souvenir Sheet

2556 A650 $65 Sheet of 2, #a-b 4.00 4.00

No. 2555 was printed in sheets of 6.

Miniature Sheets

A651

A652

China 2009 World Stamp Exhibition, Luoyang — A653

No. 2557: a, Panda, Chengdu. b, West Lake, Hangzhou. c, Bonsai Garden, Suzhou. d, Fuzi Miao and Qinhuai River, Nanjing.

No. 2558: a, Ornamental plaque (770-476 B.C.). b, Vessel (206 B.C.-A.D. 8). c, Covered jar (1279-1368). d, Head of a Bodhisattva (618-907).

No. 2559: a, Wheel of mountain bike. b, Hand holding tennis racquet. c, Hand holding water polo ball. d, Hand holding handball.

2009, Apr. 10 *Perf. 12½*
2557 A651 $35 Sheet of 4, #a-d 4.50 4.50

Perf. 12

2558 A652 $35 Sheet of 4, #a-d 4.50 4.50
2559 A653 $35 Sheet of 4, #a-d 4.50 4.50
Nos. 2557-2559 (3) 13.50 13.50

Pope Benedict XVI — A654

2009, May 4 *Perf. 11¼x11½*
2560 A654 $60 multi 1.75 1.75

Printed in sheets of 4.

Miniature Sheet

Felix Mendelssohn (1809-47), Composer — A655

No. 2561: a, Portrait of young Mendelssohn, by Carl Begas. b, Fanny Mendelssohn, sister of Felix. c, Mendelssohn's sketch of Thomasschule, Leipzig. d, Leipzig Conservatory. e, Portrait of Mendelssohn, by James Warren Childe. f, Mendelssohn drawing made during visit to Scotland.

2009, May 4 *Perf. 11¼x11½*
2561 A655 $50 Sheet of 6, #a-f 8.75 8.75

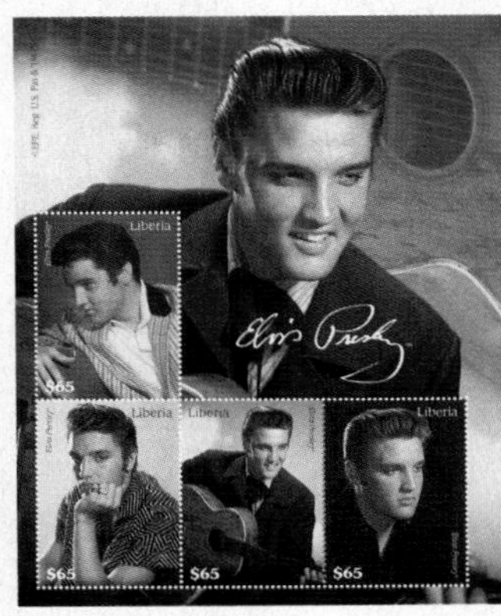

A656

A657

A658

A659

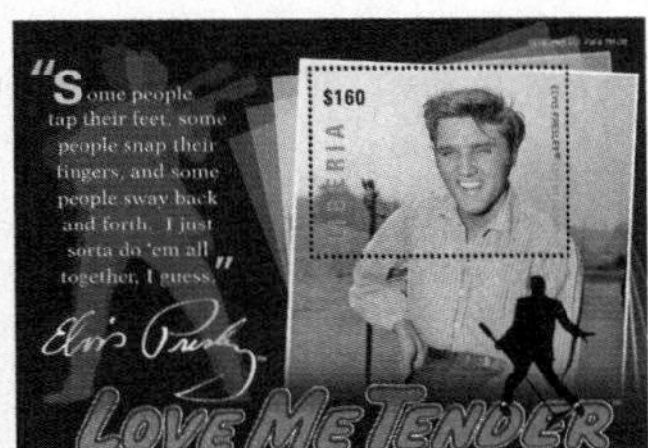

Elvis Presley (1935-77) — A660

No. 2562 — Background color: a, Red brown. b, Tan. c, Gray green. d, Black.

2009, May 4 *Perf. 13¼*
2562 A656 $65 Sheet of 4, #a-d 7.50 7.50

Souvenir Sheets

Perf. 14¼

2563 A657 $160 multi 4.75 4.75
2564 A658 $160 multi 4.75 4.75
2565 A659 $160 multi 4.75 4.75
2566 A660 $160 multi 4.75 4.75
Nos. 2563-2566 (4) 19.00 19.00

US Presidents — A661

No. 2567, $20, vert.: a, George Washington. b, John Adams. c, Thomas Jefferson. d, James Madison. e, James Monroe. f, John Quincy Adams. g, Andrew Jackson. h, Martin Van Buren. i, William Henry Harrison. j, John Tyler. k, James K. Polk. l, Zachary Taylor. m, Millard Fillmore. n, Franklin Pierce. o. James Buchanan.

No. 2568, $20, vert.: a, Abraham Lincoln. b, Andrew Johnson. c, Ulysses S. Grant. d, Rutherford B. Hayes. e, James A. Garfield. f, Chester A. Arthur. g, Grover Cleveland (1885-89). h, Benjamin Harrison. i, Grover Cleveland (1893-97). j, William McKinley. k, Theodore Roosevelt. l, William Howard Taft. m, Woodrow Wilson. n, Warren G. Harding. o, Calvin Coolidge.

No. 2569, $20, vert.: a, Herbert Hoover. b, Franklin D. Roosevelt. c, Harry S Truman. d, Dwight D. Eisenhower. e, John F. Kennedy. f, Lyndon B. Johnson. g, Richard M. Nixon. h, Gerald R. Ford. i, Jimmy Carter. j, Ronald Reagan. k, George H. W. Bush (1989-93). l, William J. Clinton. m, George W. Bush (2001-09). n, Barack H. Obama. o, Presidential seal.

$320, Barack Obama.

2009, May 4 *Perf. 13¼*

Sheets of 15, #a-o

2567-2569 A661 Set of 3 26.00 26.00
2568p Sheet of 9 #2568a 5.25 5.25
2569p Miniature sheet, #2569o, 14 #2569n 8.50 8.50

Souvenir Sheet

Perf. 14¼

2570 A661 $320 multi 9.25 9.25

Nos. 2567-2569 each contain fifteen 28x42mm stamps. Issued: No. 2568p, 3/23/10. 2569p, 9/4.

Famous People — A662

Designs: No. 2571, $50, Madame Suakoko (1816-1927), first female paramount chief. No. 2572, $50, Chief Flomo Doughba Barwulor.

2009, Aug. 2 **Litho.** *Perf. 11¼x11½*
2571-2572 A662 Set of 2 2.75 2.75

Masks — A663

Designs: $10, Korkpor mask. $25, Landa mask. $35, Borwhoo mask. $45, Zoba mask. $100, Kote mask.

2009, Aug. 2 ***Perf. 13¼***

2573-2577 A663 Set of 5 6.00 6.00

Dance — A664

Designs: $30, Traditional dancers. $40, Traditional dancers, diff. $45, Poro dancers.

2009, Aug. 2

2578-2580 A664 Set of 3 3.25 3.25

Souvenir Sheet

Monkey Bridge — A665

2009, Aug. 2

2581 A665 $100 multi 2.75 2.75

Miniature Sheets

Players in 2009 National Basketball Association All-Star Game — A666

No. 2582, $30 — Eastern All-stars: a, Ray Allen. b, Kevin Garnett. c, Danny Granger. d, Devin Harris. e, Dwight Howard. f, Allen Iverson. g, LeBron James. h, Joe Johnson. i, Rashard Lewis. j, Paul Pierce. k, Dwayne Wade. l, Mo Williams.

No. 2583, $30 — Western All-stars: a, Chauncey Billups. b, Kobe Bryant. c, Tim Duncan. d, Pau Gasol. e, Yao Ming. f, Dirk Nowitzki. g, Shaquille O'Neal. h, Tony Parker. i, Chris Paul. j, Brandon Roy. k, Amar'e Stoudemire. l, David West.

2009, Aug. 2 ***Perf. 11¼x11½***

Sheets of 12, #a-l

2582-2583 A666 Set of 2 20.00 20.00

Liberian Presidents — A667

Designs: $10, Ellen Johnson-Sirleaf. $25, Moses Z. Blah. $35, Charles M.G. Taylor. $45, Samuel K. Doe. $50, William Richard Tolbert. $70, William V.S. Tubman.

Nos. 2590, 2611, Joseph Jenkins Roberts. Nos. 2591, 2612, Stepehen Allen Benson. Nos. 2592, 2613, Daniel Bashiel Warner. Nos. 2593, 2614, James Spriggs Payne. Nos. 2594, 2615, Edward James Roye. Nos. 2595, 2616, Anthony Williams Gardiner. Nos. 2596, 2617, Alfred Francis Russell. Nos. 2597, 2618, Hilary R.W. Johnson. Nos. 2598, 2619, Joseph James Cheeseman. Nos. 2599, 2620, William David Coleman. Nos. 2600, 2621, Garretson W. Gibson. Nos. 2601, 2622, Arthur Barclay. Nos. 2602, 2623, Daniel E. Howard. Nos. 2603, 2624, Charles D.B. King. Nos. 2604, 2625, Edwin James Barclay. No. 2605, Tubman. No. 2606, Tolbert. No. 2607, Doe. No. 2608, Taylor. No. 2609, Blah. No. 2610, Johnson-Sirleaf.

2009, Aug. 22 ***Perf. 12¾***

No.	Type	Value	Color	Unused	Used
2584	A667	$10	multi	.30	.30
2585	A667	$25	multi	.70	.70
2586	A667	$35	multi	1.00	1.00
2587	A667	$45	multi	1.25	1.25
2588	A667	$50	multi	1.40	1.40
2589	A667	$70	multi	2.00	2.00
2590	A667	$100	multi	2.75	2.75
2591	A667	$100	multi	2.75	2.75
2592	A667	$100	multi	2.75	2.75
2593	A667	$100	multi	2.75	2.75
2594	A667	$100	multi	2.75	2.75
2595	A667	$100	multi	2.75	2.75
2596	A667	$100	multi	2.75	2.75
2597	A667	$100	multi	2.75	2.75
2598	A667	$100	multi	2.75	2.75
2599	A667	$100	multi	2.75	2.75
2600	A667	$100	multi	2.75	2.75
2601	A667	$100	multi	2.75	2.75
2602	A667	$100	multi	2.75	2.75
2603	A667	$100	multi	2.75	2.75
2604	A667	$100	multi	2.75	2.75
2605	A667	$100	multi	2.75	2.75
2606	A667	$100	multi	2.75	2.75
2607	A667	$100	multi	2.75	2.75
2608	A667	$100	multi	2.75	2.75
2609	A667	$100	multi	2.75	2.75
2610	A667	$100	multi	2.75	2.75
2611	A667	$500	multi	14.00	14.00
2612	A667	$500	multi	14.00	14.00
2613	A667	$500	multi	14.00	14.00
2614	A667	$500	multi	14.00	14.00
2615	A667	$500	multi	14.00	14.00
2616	A667	$500	multi	14.00	14.00
2617	A667	$500	multi	14.00	14.00
2618	A667	$500	multi	14.00	14.00
2619	A667	$500	multi	14.00	14.00
2620	A667	$500	multi	14.00	14.00
2621	A667	$500	multi	14.00	14.00
2622	A667	$500	multi	14.00	14.00
2623	A667	$500	multi	14.00	14.00
2624	A667	$500	multi	14.00	14.00
2625	A667	$500	multi	14.00	14.00
	Nos. 2584-2625 (42)			274.40	274.40

Chinese Aviation, Cent. — A668

No. 2626: a, H-2 missiles. b, H-2B missiles. c, H-12 missiles on trucks. d, H-12 missiles on truck.

$150, H-9 missiles.

2009, Nov. 12 ***Perf. 14***

2626 A668 $50 Sheet of 4, #a-d 6.00 6.00

Souvenir Sheet

Perf. 14¼

2627 A668 $150 multi 4.50 4.50

No. 2626 contains four 42x32mm stamps.

Miniature Sheet

Charles Darwin (1809-82), Naturalist — A669

No. 2628: a, Rhea darwinii. b, Proctotretus fitzingerii. c, Vespertilio chiloensis. d, Geospiza fortis.

2009, Dec. 10 ***Perf. 12x11½***

2628 A669 $60 Sheet of 4, #a-d 7.50 7.50

Miniature Sheet

The Three Stooges — A670

No. 2629: a, Stooges with open book. b, Moe sticking drill into Curly's mouth. c, Stooges at table looking at book. d, Curly pointing stick at man.

2009, Dec. 10 ***Perf. 11½x12***

2629 A670 $60 Sheet of 4, #a-d 7.50 7.50

Miniature Sheet

Pres. John F. Kennedy and Wife, Jacqueline — A671

No. 2630: a, Pres. Kennedy with Jacqueline, wearing cape. b, Pres. Kennedy. c, Pres. Kennedy with Jacqueline in limousine. d, Jacqueline Kennedy and crowd. e, Pres. Kennedy and wife (Jacqueline holding arm of husband). f, Jacqueline Kennedy.

2009, Dec. 10 ***Perf. 11¼x11½***

2630 A671 $60 Sheet of 6, #a-f 11.00 11.00

Intl. Year of Astronomy — A672

No. 2631, horiz.: a, Sergei Korolev and Luna 9. b, Luna 9 horizontal on transporter. c, Lift-off of Luna 9. d, Luna 9 over Moon. e, Luna 9 open, with antennae erect. f, Luna 9 open, antennae not erect.

$160, Lift-off of Apollo 11.

2009, Dec. 10 ***Perf. 13½***

2631 A672 $40 Sheet of 6, #a-f 7.50 7.50

Souvenir Sheet

2632 A672 $160 multi 5.00 5.00

Nos. 2631a, 2631b and 2631d have country name misspelled as "Libeira."

Christmas A673

Paintings: $25, Nativity (Holy Night), by Correggio. $40, Adoration of the Magi, by Bartolomé Esteban Murillo. $50, Adoration of the Magi, by Vicente Gil. $100, Adoration of the Magi, by Peter Paul Rubens.

2009, Dec. 10 ***Perf. 13¼x13***

2633-2636 A673 Set of 4 6.50 6.50

Miniature Sheet

Awarding of Nobel Peace Prize to US Pres. Barack Obama — A674

No. 2637 — Pres. Obama wearing: a, Red tie, facing right. b, Red tie, facing forward. c, Blue tie, facing forward. d, Blue tie, facing left.

2009, Dec. 30 Litho. ***Perf. 12x11½***

2637 A674 $60 Sheet of 4, #a-d 7.00 7.00

Miniature Sheet

Chinese Zodiac Animals — A675

No. 2638: a, Dragon. b, Snake. c, Horse. d, Goat. e, Monkey. f, Rooster. g, Dog. h, Pig. i, Rat. j, Ox. k, Tiger. l, Rabbit.

2010, Jan. 4 ***Perf. 12½***
2638 A675 $15 Sheet of 12, #a-l 5.25 5.25

Souvenir Sheet

New Year 2010 (Year of the Tiger) — A676

No. 2639: a, Tiger. b, Tiger and Chinese characters.

2010, Jan. 4 ***Perf. 14¾x14¼***
2639 A676 $130 Sheet of 2, #a-b 7.50 7.50

Miniature Sheets

Dogs — A677

No. 2640, $65 — German shorthaired pointer: a, At duckpond. b, With trees and building in background. c, On rocks. d, Sniffing flowers.

No. 2641, $65 — Chihuahua: a, On pink dog bed. b, Standing. c, At pond. d, In small pot.

2010, Jan. 19 ***Perf. 11½x12***

Sheets of 4, #a-d

2640-2641 A677 Set of 2 15.00 15.00

Miniature Sheets

A678

Visit of Pope Benedict XVI to Great Synagogue of Rome — A679

No. 2642: a, Great Synagogue. b, Pope Benedict XVI and Rome's Chief Rabbi Riccardo Di Segni. c, Pope Benedict XVI and Cardinal. d, Rabbi Di Segni and man wearing white yarmulke.

No. 2643: a, Pope Benedict XVI and Rabbi Di Segni seated. b, Rome's former Chief Rabbi Elio Toaff. c, Pope Benedixt XVI, standing and reaching for Toaff. d, Pope Benedict XVI with hands clasped.

2010, Mar. 23 ***Perf. 12x11½***
2642 A678 $110 Sheet of 4, #a-d 12.50 12.50

Perf. 11½

2643 A679 $110 Sheet of 4, #a-d 12.50 12.50

Miniature Sheets

Boy Scouts of America, Cent. — A680

No. 2644, $55 — Merit badges: a, Swimming, First Aid. b, Environmental Science, Family Life. c, Citizenship in the Community, Personal Management. d, Camping, Lifesaving. e, Citizenship in the Nation, Communications. f, Personal Fitness, Citizenship in the World.

No. 2645, $55 — Merit badges: a, Aviation, Fishing. b, Engineering, Electronics. c, Medicine, Music. d, Graphic Arts, Soil and Water Conservation. e, Cinematography, Oceanography. f, Animal Science, Art.

2010, Mar. 23 ***Perf. 13¼***

Sheets of 6, #a-f

2644-2645 A680 Set of 2 19.00 19.00

Whales and Dolphins — A681

No. 2646: a, Harbor porpoise. b, Killer whale. c, Sowerby's beaked whale. d, Atlantic spotted dolphin. e, Atlantic hump-backed dolphin. f, Clymene dolphin.

$180, Gervais beaked whale.

2010, Apr. 26 ***Perf. 14¾x14¼***
2646 A681 $60 Sheet of 6, #a-f 10.50 10.50

Souvenir Sheet

2647 A681 $180 multi 5.25 5.25

US Pres. Barack Obama and Wife, Michelle — A682

No. 2648: a, Pres. Obama. b, Pres Obama with arm around wife's waist. c, Pres. Obama and wife dancing. d, Michelle Obama.

No. 2649, Head of Michelle Obama. No. 2650, Michelle Obama (30x81mm).

2010, Apr. 26 ***Perf. 14¼x14¾***
2648 A682 $60 Sheet of 4, #a-d 7.00 7.00

Souvenir Sheets

2649 A682 $100 multi 3.00 3.00
2650 A682 $100 multi 3.00 3.00

Miniature Sheets

A683

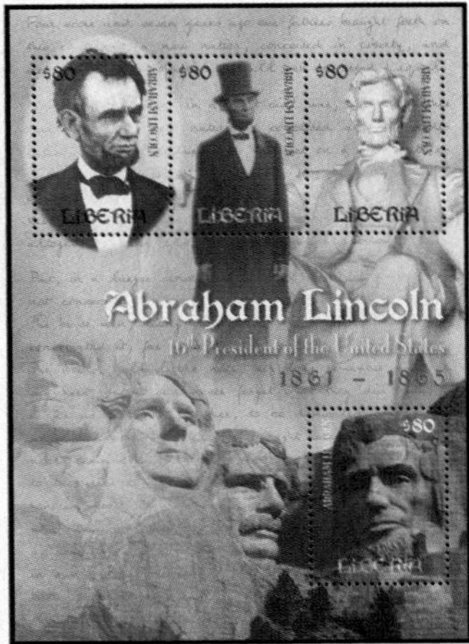

Pres. Abraham Lincoln (1809-65) — A684

No. 2651, $80 — Lincoln: a, Facing right, hand visible at LR. b, Facing left. c, Facing right, no hand visible. d, Facing right, hand visible at center bottom.

No. 2652, $80 — Lincoln: a, Photograph without hat. b, Photograph with hat. c, Lincoln Memorial sculpture. d, Mount Rushmore sculpture.

2010, June 25 ***Perf. 12x11½***
2651 A683 $80 Sheet of 4, #a-d 9.00 9.00
2652 A684 $80 Sheet of 4, #a-d 9.00 9.00

Girl Guides, Cent. — A685

No. 2653, horiz.: a, Three Girl Guides, one wearing cap. b, Three Girl Guides wearing neckerchiefs. c, Three Girl Guides. d, Five Girl Guides in uniform.

$160, Girl Guide wearing cap.

2010, June 25 ***Perf. 13x13¼***
2653 A685 $65 Sheet of 4, #a-d 7.25 7.25

Souvenir Sheet

Perf. 13¼x13

2654 A685 $160 multi 4.50 4.50

Lech Kaczynski (1949-2010), President of Poland — A686

2010, Aug. 27 ***Perf. 11½***
2655 A686 $75 multi 2.10 2.10

Printed in sheets of 4.

Paintings by Michelangelo Merisi da Caravaggio (1573-1610) — A687

No. 2656, horiz.: a, The Beheading of St. John the Baptist. b, Judith Beheading Holofernes. c, Abraham's Sacrifice. d, Medusa.
$180, The Penitent Mary Magdalene.

2010, Aug. 27 ***Perf. 11½x11¼***
2656 A687 $80 Sheet of 4, #a-d 9.00 9.00

Souvenir Sheet
Perf. 11¼x11½
2657 A687 $180 multi 5.25 5.25

Henri Dunant (1828-1910), Founder of the Red Cross — A688

No. 2658 — Red Cross, Florence Nightingale, depictions of war casualties and nurses, and portrait of Dunant in: a, Gray green. b, Brown. c, Purple. d, Gray blue.
$180, Red Cross, Nightingale, war casualties at Red Cross station, Dunant in purple.

2010, Aug. 27 ***Perf. 11½x12***
2658 A688 $80 Sheet of 4, #a-d 9.00 9.00

Souvenir Sheet
Perf. 11½x11¼
2659 A688 $180 multi 5.25 5.25

Miniature Sheets

A689

A690

Princess Diana (1961-97) — A691

No. 2660 — Princess Diana with: a, Bare shoulders and single-stand pearl necklace. b, Pink and white hat. c, White dress, earrings, no hat. d, White hat, dark blue and white dress.
No. 2661 — Princess Diana with: a, Tiara. b, Pink hat and dress. c, Green sweater, white blouse. d, Red and white jacket, white blouse.
No. 2662 — Princess Diana with: a, Red dress and flower bouquet. b, White dress, pendant earrings, no hat. c, Bare shoulders and multi-strand pearl necklace. d, White dress, pearl necklace, no hat.

2010, Aug. 27 ***Perf. 13¼***
2660 A689 $75 Sheet of 4, #a-d 8.50 8.50
2661 A690 $75 Sheet of 4, #a-d 8.50 8.50
2662 A691 $75 Sheet of 4, #a-d 8.50 8.50
Nos. 2660-2662 (3) 25.50 25.50

Miniature Sheets

A692

A693

Elvis Presley (1935-77) — A694

No. 2663 — Presley: a, With hands pointing left. b, Holding microphone. c, With guitar, holding microphone.
No. 2664 — Paintings of Presley with backgrounds of: a, Green and black. b, Orange and bister. c, Black and red.
No. 2665: a, Presley's face in orange and yellow. b, Presley's face in light blue and white. c, Presley's face in blue and gray. d, Silhouette of Presley.

2010, Aug. 27 ***Perf. 11½x11¼***
2663 A692 $90 Sheet of 3, #a-c 7.75 7.75

Perf. 11¼x11½
2664 A693 $90 Sheet of 3, #a-c 7.75 7.75

Perf. 13
2665 A694 $90 Sheet of 4, #a-d 10.00 10.00
Nos. 2663-2665 (3) 25.50 25.50

Cats — A695

No. 2666, vert.: a, Siberian. b, Turkish Angora. c, British shorthair. d, Maine coon. e, Abyssinian. f, Scottish fold.
$180, Bluepoint Himalayan.

2010, Oct. 27 ***Perf. 11¼x11½***
2666 A695 $60 Sheet of 6, #a-f 10.50 10.50

Souvenir Sheet
Perf. 11½x11¼
2667 A695 $180 multi 5.25 5.25

Miniature Sheets

Pres. John F. Kennedy (1917-63) — A696

No. 2668, $80 — Olive bister frames with Kennedy: a, Walking with Vice-president Lyndon B. Johnson. b, On telephone. c, At lectern. d, Looking upwards.
No. 2669, $80 — Blue frames with Kennedy: a, At lectern. b, Walking with McGeorge Bundy. c, Campaigning in New York City. d, With hands clasped.
No. 2670, $80 — Red frames with Kennedy: a, With Dr. Wernher von Braun. b, With wife, Jacqueline, watching space flight on television. c, At lectern. d, Viewing Friendship 7 space capsule.

2010, Oct. 27 ***Perf. 12x11½***
Sheets of 4, #a-d
2668-2670 A696 Set of 3 28.00 28.00

Christmas — A697

Paintings: $25, The Annunciation, by Fra Angelico. $40, The Angelic Announcement to the Shepherds, by Taddeo Gaddi. $50, Adoration of the Shepherds, by Guido Reni. $100, Virgin and Child with Angels and Saints, by Felice Torelli.

2010, Oct. 27 **Litho.** ***Perf. 11½***
2671-2674 A697 Set of 4 6.25 6.25

Liberian Politicians A698

Designs: $25, Pres. Ellen Johnson-Sirleaf receiving gift. $45, Pres. Johnson Sirleaf standing with Chinese Pres. Hu Jintao, vert. No. 2677, $50, Pres. Johnson-Sirleaf reading. No. 2678, $50, Vice-president Joseph N. Boakai. No. 2679, $100, Pres. Johnson-Sirleaf sitting with Pres. Hu. No. 2680, $100, Pres. Johnson-Sirleaf shaking hands with Vice-president Boakai. No. 2681, $100, Pres. Johnson-Sirleaf wearing sash of office, vert. No. 2682, $500, Pres. Johnson-Sirleaf meeting with international investors. No. 2683, $500, Pres. Johnson-Sirleaf with Vice-president Boakai and cabinet.

2010, Dec. 16 ***Perf. 12***
2675-2683 A698 Set of 9 *5.00 5.00*

Nos. 2675-2683 were sold to the philatelic trade at prices well below that indicated by currency exchange rates at the date of issue.

Mother Teresa (1910-97), Humanitarian A699

Various photos with frame color of: No. 2684, $80, Olive bister. No. 2685, $80, Blue.

2010, Dec. 16
2684-2685 A699 Set of 2 4.50 4.50

Nos. 2684-2685 each were printed in sheets of 4.

Pope John Paul II (1920-2005) A700

No. 2686 — Red background: a, Without crucifix. b, With crucifix.
No. 2687 — Purple background: a, With crucifix. b, Without crucifix.

2010, Dec. 16
2686 A700 $80 Pair, #a-b 4.50 4.50
2687 A700 $80 Horiz. pair, #a-b 4.50 4.50

Nos. 2686-2687 each were printed in sheets containing two pairs.

Paintings of Sandro Botticelli (1455-1510) — A701

No. 2688 — Details from The Birth of Venus: a, Head of Venus. b, Reversed image of torso of winged zephyrs. c, Reversed image of heads of winged zephyrs. d, Nymph.
$160, Portrait of St. Augustine, vert.

2010, Dec. 16 ***Perf. 12***

2688 A701 $80 Sheet of 4, #a-d 9.00 9.00

Souvenir Sheet

Perf. 12½x12¾

2689 A701 $160 multi 4.50 4.50

No. 2689 contains one 38x50mm stamp.

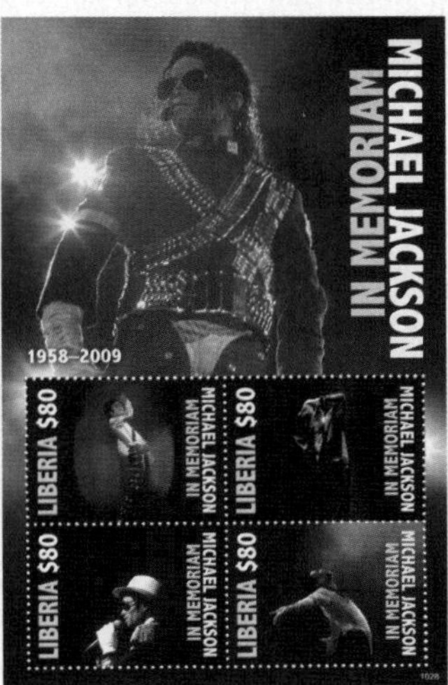

A702

Michael Jackson (1958-2009), Singer — A703

No. 2690 — Jackson: a, With arched back, holding microphone. b, Moving hat to cover face. c, Wearing white glove and hat. d, With arched back, arms stretched outward.

No. 2691 — Jackson: a, Wearing red shirt. b, Holding microphone. c, With arm outstretched. d, With spotlights in background, holding microphone.

$180, Jackson singing.

2010, Dec. 16 ***Perf. 12***

2690 A702 $80 Sheet of 4, #a-d 9.00 9.00
2691 A703 $80 Sheet of 4, #a-d 9.00 9.00

Souvenir Sheet

2692 A703 $180 multi 5.00 5.00

SEMI-POSTAL STAMPS

No. 127 Surcharged in Red

1915 **Unwmk.** ***Perf. 14***

B1 A49 2c + 3c on 10c 1.00 *3.50*
- *a.* Double red surcharge
- *b.* Double blue surcharge
- *c.* Both surcharges double
- *d.* Pair, one without "2c"

Same Surcharge On Official Stamp of 1912

B2 A49 2c + 3c on 10c blk & ultra 1.00 *3.50*
- *a.* Double surcharge

Regular Issue of 1918 Surcharged in Black and Red

1918 ***Perf. 12½, 14***

B3	A59	1c + 2c dp grn & blk	1.40	*10.50*
B4	A60	2c + 2c rose & blk	1.40	*10.50*
a.		Double surch., one inverted		
b.		Invtd. surch., cross double		
c.		Invtd. surch., cross omitted	17.00	
B5	A61	5c + 2c gray bl & blk	.65	*3.00*
a.		Imperf., pair	19.00	
B6	A62	10c + 2c dk green	1.25	*3.00*
a.		Inverted surcharge	5.75	27.50
B7	A63	15c + 2c blk & dk grn	5.25	10.50
B8	A64	20c + 2c claret & blk	2.10	*8.50*
B9	A65	25c + 2c dk grn & grn	4.25	*15.00*
B10	A66	30c + 2c red vio & blk	10.00	*10.50*
B11	A67	50c + 2c ultra & blk	8.50	*16.00*
B12	A68	75c + 2c ol bis & blk	3.75	*30.00*
B13	A69	$1 + 2c yel brn & bl	6.25	*57.50*
B14	A70	$2 + 2c lt vio & blk	8.50	*80.00*
B15	A71	$5 + 2c dk brown	20.00	*200.00*
		Nos. B3-B15 (13)	73.30	*455.00*

Used values are for postally canceled stamps.

Nos. 277-279 Surcharged in Red or Blue

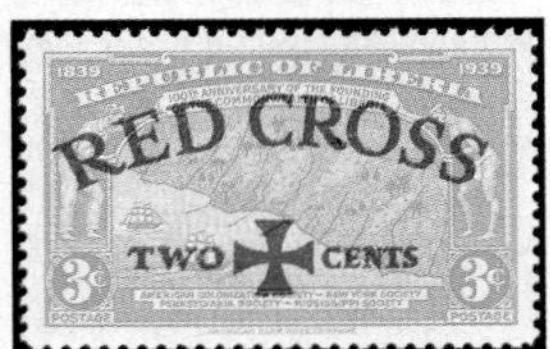

1941 **Unwmk.** ***Perf. 12***

B16	A107	3c + 2c dk blue (R)	2.25	2.25
B17	A108	5c + 2c dull red brn	2.25	2.25
B18	A109	10c + 2c dk grn (R)	2.25	2.25
		Nos. B16-B18 (3)	6.75	6.75

Catalogue values for unused stamps in this section, from this point to the end of the section, are for Never Hinged items.

Research — SP1

Lithographed and Engraved

1954 **Unwmk.** ***Perf. 12½***

B19 SP1 5c + 5c rose lilac & blk .20 .20
Nos. B19,CB4-CB6 (4) .80 .80

The surtax was for the Liberian Government Hospital. No. B19 exists imperforate.

Remember the African Child SP2

Designs: 25c + 10c, Village life. 70c + 20c, Mr. Sean feeding children. 75c + 15c, Fleeing conflict. 80c + 20c, Nuns teaching children. No. B24, Nuns killed in Oct. 1992, vert. No. B25, Sean Devereux (1964-93), vert.

Perf. 13½x14

1994, Jan. 6 **Unwmk.** **Litho.**

B20	SP2	25c +10c multi	1.00	1.00
B21	SP2	70c +20c multi	3.25	3.25
B22	SP2	75c +15c multi	3.25	3.25
B23	SP2	80c +20c multi	3.50	3.50
		Nos. B20-B23 (4)	11.00	11.00

Souvenir Sheets

B24	SP2	$1.50 +50c multi	7.50	7.50
B25	SP2	$1.50 +50c multi	7.50	7.50

Surtax for Sean Devereux Liberian Children's Fund.

Charities — SP3

Designs: 25c+10c, No. B30, Natl. map in flag colors, blind man with cane. No. B27, Logo depicting children. No. B28, Blind man crossing street. No. B29, Dr. Herman Gmeiner, children.

1995 **Litho.** ***Perf. 14***

B26	SP3	25c +10c multi	1.25	1.25
B27	SP3	80c +20c multi	3.50	3.50
B28	SP3	80c +20c multi	3.50	3.50
B29	SP3	$1.50 +50c multi	6.75	6.75
B30	SP3	$1.50 +50c multi	6.75	6.75
		Nos. B26-B30 (5)	21.75	21.75

Christian Assoc. of the Blind, 10th anniv. (#B26, B28, B30). SOS Children's Village (#B27, B29).

Issued: #B27, B29, 4/26; others, 4/28.

George Weah, Soccer Player — SP4

Designs: 50c+20c, In AC Milan strip. 75c+25c, In Liberia Natl. strip. 80c+20c, With 1989 Golden Ball Award. $1.50+50c, Two-time Golden Ball Winner.

1995, Oct. 6 **Litho.** ***Perf. 13x13½***

B31	SP4	50c +20c multi	2.50	2.50
B32	SP4	75c +25c multi	3.50	3.50
B33	SP4	80c +20c multi	3.50	3.50
B34	SP4	$1.50 +50c multi	7.25	7.25
a.		Souvenir sheet of 1, perf. 13	7.25	7.25
		Nos. B31-B34 (4)	16.75	16.75

Issued: No. B34a, 6/24/96. Surcharge for Liberian charities supported by George Weah.

AIR POST STAMPS

Regular Issue of 1928 Surcharged in Black "AIR MAIL" and New Values

1936, Feb. 28 **Unwmk.** ***Perf. 12***

C1	A102	6c on 2c violet	250.00	*275.00*
C2	A102	6c on 3c bis brn	250.00	*275.00*

Same Surcharge on Official Stamp of 1928

C3	A102	6c on 1c green	250.00	*275.00*
m.		On No. 230 (error)		*750.00*
		Nos. C1-C3 (3)	750.00	825.00

Values are for stamps with disturbed gum. Many counterfeits exist.

Waco Plane — AP1

1936, Sept. 30 **Engr.** ***Perf. 14***

C3A	AP1	1c yellow grn & blk	.20	.20
C3B	AP1	2c carmine & blk	.20	.20
C3C	AP1	3c purple & blk	.20	.20
C3D	AP1	4c orange & blk	.20	.20
C3E	AP1	5c blue & blk	.20	.20
C3F	AP1	6c green & blk	.20	.20
		Nos. C3A-C3F (6)	1.20	1.20

Liberia's 1st air mail service of Feb. 28, 1936.

Nos. C3A-C3F exist in pairs imperf. between (value, $50 each) and in pairs imperf. (value $15 each).

Eagle in Flight — AP2

Sikorsky Amphibian — AP5

Trimotor Plane AP3

Egrets — AP4

Designs: 3c, 30c, Albatross.

1938, Sept. 12 **Photo.** ***Perf. 12½***

C4	AP2	1c green	.20	.20
C5	AP3	2c red orange	.40	.20
C6	AP3	3c olive green	.50	.20
C7	AP4	4c orange	.60	.20
C8	AP4	5c brt blue grn	1.00	.20
C9	AP3	10c violet	1.00	.20
C10	AP5	20c magenta	1.25	.20
C11	AP3	30c gray black	2.25	.20
C12	AP2	50c brown	3.00	.20
C13	AP5	$1 blue	5.25	.20
		Nos. C4-C13 (10)	15.45	2.00

For surcharges see Nos. C17-C36, C45-C46, C47-C48, C49-C50.

Nos. 280-282 Overprinted in Red or Dark Blue

1941, Feb. 25 *Perf. 12*

C14	A107	3c dark blue (R)	2.75	2.75
C15	A108	5c dull red brn (DB)	2.75	2.75
C16	A109	10c dark green (R)	2.75	2.75
		Nos. C14-C16 (3)	8.25	8.25

Nos. C4-C13 Surcharged in Black

1941 *Perf. 12½*

C17	AP2	50c on 1c green	*3,000.*	325.00
C18	AP3	50c on 2c red org	175.00	105.00
C19	AP3	50c on 3c ol grn	175.00	105.00
C20	AP4	50c on 4c orange	70.00	60.00
C21	AP4	50c on 5c brt bl grn	70.00	60.00
C22	AP3	50c on 10c violet	70.00	50.00
C23	AP5	50c on 20c magenta	*2,500.*	70.00
C24	AP3	50c on 30c gray blk	55.00	40.00
C25	AP2	50c brown	55.00	40.00
C26	AP5	$1 blue	70.00	40.00

Nos. C17 to C26 with Additional Overprint of Two Bars, Obliterating "1941"

1942

C27	AP2	50c on 1c green	6.75	6.75
C28	AP3	50c on 2c red org	6.75	5.75
C29	AP3	50c on 3c ol grn	6.00	5.75
C30	AP4	50c on 4c orange	4.75	6.00
C31	AP4	50c on 5c brt bl grn	3.00	3.00
C32	AP3	50c on 10c violet	4.25	4.25
C33	AP5	50c on 20c magenta	4.25	4.25
C34	AP3	50c on 30c gray blk	4.75	4.75
C35	AP2	50c brown	4.75	4.75
C36	AP5	$1 blue	4.25	4.25
		Nos. C27-C36 (10)	49.50	49.50

Plane and Air Route from United States to South America and Africa AP6

Plane over House AP7

1942-44 **Engr.** *Perf. 12*

C37	AP6	10c rose	.20	.20
C38	AP7	12c brt ultra ('44)	.20	.20
C39	AP7	24c turq grn ('44)	.20	.20
C40	AP6	30c brt green	.20	.20
C41	AP6	35c red lilac ('44)	.20	.20
C42	AP6	50c violet	.20	.20
C43	AP6	70c olive gray ('44)	.60	.20
C44	AP6	$1.40 scarlet ('44)	1.50	.60
		Nos. C37-C44 (8)	3.30	2.00

No. C3A-C3C, C5-C8, C12 Surcharged with New Values and Large Dot, Bar or Diagonal Line in Violet, Blue, Black or Violet and Black

1944-45 *Perf. 12½*

C45	AP3	10c on 2c (V+Bk)	35.00	25.00
C46	AP4	10c on 5c (V+Bk) ('45)	12.00	12.00
C46A	AP1	30c on 1c (Bk)	140.00	70.00
C47	AP3	30c on 3c (V)	150.00	65.00
C48	AP4	30c on 4c (V+Bk)	12.00	12.00
C48A	AP1	50c on 3c (Bk)	32.50	32.50
C48B	AP1	70c on 2c (Bk)	60.00	60.00
C49	AP3	$1 on 3c (Bl)	22.50	22.50
C50	AP2	$1 on 50c (V)	35.00	26.50
		Nos. C45-C50 (9)	499.00	325.50

These surcharges were handstamped with the possible exception of the large "10 CTS." of No. C46 and the "30 CTS." of No. C48. On No. C47, the new value was created by handstamping a small, violet, broken "O" beside the large "3" of the basic stamp.

Surcharges on Nos. C46A, C48A, C48B are found inverted. Values same as normal.

Roosevelt Type of Regular Issue

1945, Nov. 26 **Engr.**

C51	A116	70c brn & blk, *grysh*	1.25	1.40

Examples on thick white paper appeared later on the stamp market at reduced prices.

Monrovia Harbor Type

1947, Jan. 2

C52	A117	24c brt bluish grn	1.00	1.25

Without Inscription at Top

1947, May 16

C53	A117	25c dark carmine	.40	.45

1st US Postage Stamps Type

1947, June 6

C54	A118	12c green	.20	.20
C55	A118	25c brt red violet	.20	.20
C56	A118	50c brt blue	.20	.20
a.		Souv. sheet of 4, #300, C54-C56	42.50	
		Nos. C54-C56 (3)	.60	.60
		Set, never hinged	2.10	

No. C56a exists imperf. Values: hinged $65; never hinged $160.

Matilda Newport Firing Cannon — AP11

1947, Dec. 1 **Engr. & Photo.**

C57	AP11	25c scar & gray blk	1.25	.30

See note after No. 304.

Monument to Joseph J. Roberts — AP12

Centenary Monument AP14

Design: 25c, Flag of Liberia.

1947, Dec. 22 **Engr.**

C58	AP12	12c brick red	.30	.20
C59	AP12	25c carmine	.50	.20
C60	AP14	50c red brown	.80	.45
		Nos. C58-C60 (3)	1.60	.85
		Set, never hinged	5.50	

Centenary of independence.

L. I. A. Plane in Flight AP15

1948, Aug. 17 *Perf. 11½*

C61	AP15	25c red	1.50	1.50
C62	AP15	50c deep blue	1.00	1.00
		Set, never hinged	5.00	

1st flight of Liberian Intl. Airways, Aug. 17, 1948.

Map and Citizens — AP16

Farm Couple, Arms and Agricultural Products — AP17

1949, Apr. 12 **Litho.** *Perf. 11½*

C63	AP16	25c multicolored	.35	.65
C64	AP17	50c multicolored	.35	.65
		Set, never hinged	2.00	

Nos. C63-C64 exist perf. 12½. Definite information concerning the status of the perf. 12½ set has not reached the editors. The set also exists imperf.

Type of Regular Issue of 1948-50

Design: William V. S. Tubman.

1949, July 21 **Engr.** *Perf. 12½*

C65	A128	25c blue & black	.60	.65
		Set, never hinged	1.60	

See No. C118.

Sun and Open Book — AP18

UPU Monument AP19

1950, Feb. 14 **Engr.** *Perf. 12½*

C66	AP18	25c rose carmine	1.00	.50
		Set, never hinged	2.75	
a.		Souv. sheet of 2, #329, C66, imperf.	1.75	1.75
		Set, never hinged	4.75	

Campaign for National Literacy.

Catalogue values for unused stamps in this section, from this point to the end of the section, are for Never Hinged items.

1950, Apr. 21

C67	AP19	25c orange & vio	2.75	2.75
a.		Souv. sheet of 3, #330-331, C67, imperf.	24.00	24.00

UPU, 75th anniv. (in 1949).

No. C67 exists imperf.

Map of Monrovia, James Monroe and Ashmun — AP20

50c, Jehudi Ashmun, President Tubman & map.

1952, Apr. 1 *Perf. 10½*

C68	AP20	25c lilac rose & blk	.20	.20
C69	AP20	50c dk blue & car	.70	.70
a.		Souvenir sheet of 8	24.00	

Nos. C68-C69 exist imperf. Value about two and one half times that of the perf. set.

Nos. C68-C69 exist with center inverted. Value $50 each.

No. C69a contains one each of Nos. 332 and C68, and types of Nos. 333-337 and C69 with centers in black; imperf.

The 25c exists in colors of the 50c and vice versa. Value, each $8.

Flags of Five Nations — AP21

1952, Dec. 10 *Perf. 12½*

C70	AP21	25c ultra & carmine	.90	.65
a.		Souvenir sheet	2.25	2.25

Nos. C70 and C70a exist imperforate.

Road Building — AP22

Designs: 25c, Ships in Monrovia harbor. 35c, Diesel locomotive. 50c, Free port, Monrovia. 70c, Roberts Field. $1, Wm. V. S. Tubman bridge.

1953, Aug. 3 **Litho.**

C71	AP22	12c orange brown	.20	.20
C72	AP22	25c lilac rose	.20	.20
C73	AP22	35c purple	1.00	.20
C74	AP22	50c orange	1.00	.20
C75	AP22	70c dull green	1.75	.20
C76	AP22	$1 blue	2.25	1.00
		Nos. C71-C76 (6)	6.40	2.00

See Nos. C82-C87.

Flags, Emblem and Children — AP23

1954, Sept. 27

Size: 51x39mm

C77 AP23 $5 bl, red, vio bl & blk 40.00 40.00

A reproduction of No. C77, size 63x49mm, was prepared for presentation purposes. Value $35.

Half the proceeds from the sale of No. C77 was given to the UNICEF.

UN Technical Assistance Agencies — AP24

Designs: 15c, Printing instruction. 20c, Sawmill maintenance. 25c, Geography class.

1954, Oct. 25

C78 AP24 12c black & blue .20 .20
C79 AP24 15c dk brown & yel .20 .20
C80 AP24 20c black & yel grn .20 .20
C81 AP24 25c vio blue & red .80 .20
Nos. C78-C81 (4) 1.40 .80

UN Technical Assistance program.

Type of 1953 Inscribed: "Commemorating Presidential Visit U. S. A.-1954"

Designs as before.

1954, Nov. 19

C82 AP22 12c vermilion .20 .20
C83 AP22 25c blue .20 .20
C84 AP22 35c carmine rose .30 .20
C85 AP22 50c rose violet .40 .20
C86 AP22 70c orange brown .55 .25
C87 AP22 $1 dull green .80 .30
Nos. C82-C87 (6) 2.45 1.35

Visit of Pres. William V.S. Tubman to the US. Exist imperforate.

Baseball AP25

1955, Jan. 26 **Litho.** ***Perf. 12½***

C88 AP25 10c shown .30 .30
C89 AP25 12c Swimming .30 .30
C90 AP25 25c Running .30 .30
a. Souvenir sheet 18.00 18.00
Nos. C88-C90 (3) .90 .90

#C90a contains 1 each of #349, C90 with colors transposed. Exists imperf.; same value.

Costus AP26

Design: 25c, Barteria nigritiana.

1955, Sept. 28 **Unwmk.** ***Perf. 12½***

C91 AP26 20c violet, grn & yel .30 .30
C92 AP26 25c green, red & yel .30 .30

UN Emblem — AP27

UN Charter AP28

15c, General Assembly. 25c, Gabriel L. Dennis signing UN Charter for Liberia.

1955, Oct. 24 **Unwmk.** ***Perf. 12***

C93 AP27 10c ultra & red .20 .20
C94 AP27 15c violet & blk .20 .20
C95 AP27 25c green & red brn .60 .20
C96 AP28 50c brick red & grn 1.50 .20
Nos. C93-C96 (4) 2.50 .80

10th anniv. of the UN, Oct. 24, 1955.

Rotary International Headquarters, Evanston, Ill. — AP29

Design: 15c, View of Monrovia.

1955, Dec. 5 **Litho.** ***Perf. 12½***

C97 AP29 10c deep ultra & red .20 .20
C98 AP29 15c redsh brn, red & bis .70 .20

Souvenir Sheet

C99 AP29 50c deep ultra & red 1.75 1.75
Nos. C97-C99 (3) 2.65 2.15

No. C99 design as No. C97, but redrawn and with leaves omitted.

50th anniversary of Rotary International.

Nos. C97-C99 exist without Rotary emblem; No. C97 printed entirely in deep ultramarine; No. C98 with bister impression omitted.

FIPEX Type of Regular Issue

10c, New York Coliseum. 12c, Globe inscribed FIPEX. 15c, 50c, Statue of Liberty.

1956, Apr. 28 **Unwmk.** ***Perf. 12***

C100 A143 10c rose red & ultra .20 .20
C101 A143 12c orange & purple .20 .20
C102 A142 15c aqua & red lilac .90 .20
Nos. C100-C102 (3) 1.30 .60

Souvenir Sheet

C103 A142 50c lt green & brn 1.75 1.75

Olympic Park, Melbourne — AP32

20c, 40c, Map of Australia & Olympic torch.

1956, Nov. 15 **Unwmk.** ***Perf. 12***

C104 AP32 12c emerald & vio .50 .50
C105 AP32 20c multicolored .50 .50

Souvenir Sheet

C106 AP32 40c multicolored 7.50 7.50
Nos. C104-C106 (3) 8.50 8.50

16th Olympic Games, Melbourne, 11/22-12/8.

Type of Regular Issue, 1957.

12c, 25c, Idlewild airport, NYC. 15c, 50c, Roberts Field, Liberia, plane & Pres. Tubman.

Lithographed and Engraved

1957, May 4 ***Perf. 12***

C107 A146 12c brt grn & dk bl .20 .20
C108 A146 15c red brn & blk .20 .20
C109 A146 25c carmine & dk bl .75 .20
C110 A146 50c lt ultra & blk 1.40 .20
Nos. C107-C110 (4) 2.55 .80

Type of Regular Issue, 1957

Orphanage and: 15c, Nurse inoculating boy. 35c, The Kamara triplets. 70c, Children and flag.

1957, Nov. 25 **Litho.** ***Perf. 12***

C111 A147 15c lt blue & brn .20 .20
C112 A147 35c maroon & lt gray 1.00 .20

Souvenir Sheet

C113 A147 70c ultra & rose car 1.50 1.25
Nos. C111-C113 (3) 2.70 1.65

Type of Regular Issue, 1958

10c, Italian flag & Colosseum. #C115, French flag & Arc de Triomphe. #C116, Swiss flag & chalet. #C117, Vatican flag & St. Peter's.

Engr. and Litho.

1958, Jan. 10 ***Perf. 10½***

Flags in Original Colors

C114 A148 10c dark gray .45 .45
C115 A148 15c dp yellow grn .45 .45
C116 A148 15c ultra .45 .45
C117 A148 15c purple .45 .45
Nos. C114-C117 (4) 1.80 1.80

Type of Regular Issue, 1948-50

Design: William V. S. Tubman.

1958 **Engr.** ***Perf. 12***

C118 A128 25c lt green & blk 1.25 .90

Souvenir Sheet

Preamble to Declaration of Human Rights — AP33

1958, Dec. 17 **Litho.** ***Perf. 12***

C119 AP33 20c blue & red 2.75 2.75

10th anniv. of the signing of the Universal Declaration of Human Rights.

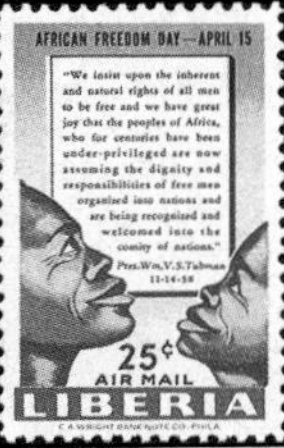

Liberians Reading Proclamation AP34

1959, Apr. 15 **Unwmk.**

C120 AP34 25c blue & brown .60 .60

African Freedom Day, Apr. 15.

UNESCO Building, Paris AP35

1959, May 1

C121 AP35 25c ultra & red .60 .50
a. Souvenir sheet 1.75 1.75

Opening of UNESCO Headquarters in Paris, Nov. 3, 1958.

Lincoln Type of Regular Issue

1959, Nov. 20 **Engr.** ***Perf. 12***

C122 A152 25c emerald & black .90 .90

For souvenir sheet see No. 386a.

Touré, Tubman and Nkrumah AP36

1960, Jan. 27 **Litho.** **Unwmk.**

C123 AP36 25c beige, vio bl & blk .60 .80

See note after No. 387.

WRY Type of Regular Issue, 1960

1960, Apr. 7 ***Perf. 11½***

C124 A154 25c ultra & black .80 .70
a. Souv. sheet of 2, #388, C124, imperf. 2.75 2.75

Map of Africa — AP37

1960, May 11 ***Perf. 11½***

C125 AP37 25c ultra & brown .80 .80

See note after No. 389.

Olympic Games Type of 1960

Designs: 25c, Javelin thrower and hunter, horiz. 50c, Runner and stadium, horiz.

1960, Sept. 6 ***Perf. 11½***

C126 A156 25c brown & brt ultra .90 .70

Souvenir Sheet

Imperf

C127 A156 50c lilac & brown 3.50 3.50

Stamp Centenary Type of 1960

1960, Dec. 1 **Litho.** ***Perf. 11½***

C128 A157 25c multicolored 1.00 1.00

Souvenir Sheet

C129 A157 50c multicolored 1.75 1.75

Globe, Dove and UN Emblem AP38

Design: 50c, Globe and dove.

1961, May 19 **Unwmk.** ***Perf. 11½***

C130 AP38 25c indigo & red .50 .50

Souvenir Sheet

C131 AP38 50c red brn & emerald 2.25 2.25

Liberia's membership in the UN Security Council.

A second souvenir sheet contains one each of Nos. 395, C130 and the 50c from No. C131, imperf. Size: 133x83mm.

No. C130 exists imperf.

Science Class AP39

Design: 50c, Science class, different design.

1961, Sept. 8 **Litho.**
C132 AP39 25c purple & brown .50 .20

Souvenir Sheet

C133 AP39 50c blue & brown 1.75 1.75

15th anniv. of UNESCO.

Joseph J. Roberts and Providence Island — AP40

1961, Oct. 25 **Litho.** ***Perf. 11½***
C134 AP40 25c emerald & sepia .70 .70
a. Souvenir sheet of 3 1.75 1.75

150th anniv. of the birth of Joseph J. Roberts, 1st pres. of Liberia.

No. C134a contains three imperf. stamps similar to Nos. 397-398 and C134, but printed in different colors; 5c, emerald & sepia. 10c, orange & sepia. 25c, ultramarine & sepia.

Scout Type of Regular Issue and

Boy Scout — AP41

1961, Dec. 4 **Unwmk.** ***Perf. 11½***
C135 AP41 25c emerald & sepia 1.40 1.40

Souvenir Sheet

Design: Like No. 399.

C136 A161 35c dull blue & sepia 5.00 5.00

Dag Hammarskjold Type of 1962

1962, Feb. 1 **Unwmk.** ***Perf. 12***
C137 A162 25c black & red lilac .60 .60

Souvenir Sheet

Imperf

C138 A162 50c black & ultra 1.75 1.75

Malaria Eradication Emblem AP42

1962, Apr. 7 ***Perf. 12½***
C139 AP42 25c purple & orange .60 .50

Souvenir Sheet

Imperf

C140 AP42 50c dark red & ultra 1.50 1.50

Pres. Tubman, Statue of Liberty, New York Skyline and Flags of US and Liberia AP43

1962, Sept. 17 **Litho.** ***Perf. 11½x12***
C141 AP43 12c multicolored .20 .20
C142 AP43 25c multicolored .60 .50
C143 AP43 50c multicolored 1.25 .85
Nos. C141-C143 (3) 2.05 1.55

Pres. Tubman's visit to the US in 1961.

United Nations Emblem and Flags AP44

Design: 50c, UN emblem.

1962, Oct. 22 ***Perf. 12x12½***
C144 AP44 25c lt ultra & dk bl .50 .50

Souvenir Sheet

Imperf

C145 AP44 50c brt grnsh bl & blk 1.25 1.25

Observance of UN Day, Oct. 24, as a national holiday.

Building Type of Regular Issue

12c, 70c, Capitol. 50c, Information Service. $1, Treasury Department Building, Monrovia.

1962-63 ***Perf. 12x12½, 12 (70c)***
C146 A165 12c brt yel grn & mar .20 .20
C147 A165 50c orange & ultra 1.50 1.50
C147A A165 70c brt pink & dk bl ('63) 2.10 2.10
C148 A165 $1 salmon & blk ('63) 2.75 2.75
Nos. C146-C148 (4) 6.55 6.55

"FAO" Emblem and Globe — AP45

Design: 50c, "FAO" and UN Emblems.

1963, Mar. 21 **Unwmk.** ***Perf. 12½***
C149 AP45 25c dk green & yel .70 .70

Souvenir Sheet

Perf. 12

C150 AP45 50c emerald & ultra 1.75 1.75

FAO "Freedom from Hunger" campaign.

Type of Regular Issue, 1963

Designs: 25c, Telstar satellite, vert. 50c, Telstar and rocket, vert.

1963, May 27 **Litho.** ***Perf. 12½***
C151 A167 25c Prus blue & org .70 .70

Souvenir Sheet

Perf. 12

C152 A167 50c dp violet & yel 3.00 1.60

Red Cross Type of Regular Issue

Design: 25c, Red Cross and globe. 50c, Centenary emblem and globe.

1963, Aug. 26 **Unwmk.** ***Perf. 12***
C153 A168 25c purple & red .40 .40
C154 A168 50c deep ultra & red .70 .70

Map of Africa — AP46

1963, Oct. 28 ***Perf. 12½***
C156 AP46 25c red orange & grn .40 .40

See note after No. 412.

Olympic Type of Regular Issue

10c, Torch and mountains. 25c, Mountains, horiz. 50c, Torch, background like No. 413.

1963, Dec. 11 **Litho.** ***Perf. 12½***
C157 A170 10c vio blue & red .20 .20
C158 A170 25c green & orange .80 .80

Souvenir Sheet

Perf. 12

C159 A170 50c gray & red 1.75 1.75

Kennedy Type of Regular Issue, 1964

Designs: 25c, John F. Kennedy, vert. 50c, John F. Kennedy (like No. 414).

1964, Apr. 6 **Unwmk.** ***Perf. 12½***
C160 A171 25c blk & red lil .60 .50

Souvenir Sheet

Perf. 12

C161 A171 50c blk & red lil 1.75 1.40

An imperf. miniature sheet containing one of No. C160 exists. No marginal inscription.

Satellite Type of Regular Issue

Souvenir Sheet

Design: Launching rocket separating from booster in space, vert.

1964, June 22 **Litho.**
C162 A172 50c vio bl & red 3.00 3.00

Olympic Type of Regular Issue

Souvenir Sheet

Design: 50c, Runner and Olympic rings.

1964, Sept. 15 **Unwmk.** ***Perf. 12***
C163 A173 50c grnsh bl & red 3.00 1.25

Scout Type of Regular Issue, 1965

Designs: 25c, Liberian flag and fleur-delis. 50c, Globe and Scout emblem.

1965, Mar. 8 **Litho.** ***Perf. 12½***
C164 A174 25c crimson & ultra .80 .80

Souvenir Sheet

Perf. 12

C165 A174 50c yellow & lilac 4.00 4.00

Lincoln Type of Regular Issue

Souvenir Sheet

50c, Lincoln and John F. Kennedy, horiz.

1965, May 3 **Unwmk.** ***Perf. 12***
C166 A175 50c dp plum & lt gray 1.75 1.75

ICY Type of Regular Issue, 1965

Souvenir Sheet

1965, June 21 **Litho.**
C167 A176 50c car rose & brn 1.75 1.75

ITU Type of Regular Issue, 1965

1965, Sept. 21 **Unwmk.** ***Perf. 12½***
C168 A177 50c red org & vio bl .80 .70

Tubman Type of Regular Issue

25c, Pres. Tubman and coat of arms.

1965, Nov. 29 **Litho.** ***Perf. 12½***
C169 A178 25c ultra, red & brn .70 .70
a. Souv. sheet of 2, #431, C169, imperf. 1.75 1.75

Churchill Type of Regular Issue

25c, "Angry Lion" portrait by Karsh & Parliament, London. 50c, "Williamsburg Award Dinner" portrait by Karsh & map of Europe.

1966, Jan. 18 **Litho.** ***Perf. 12½***
C170 A179 25c blk & vio bl .70 .55

Souvenir Sheet

Perf. 12

C171 A179 50c blk & red lil 1.75 1.75

Soccer Type of Regular Issue

Souvenir Sheet

Design: 50c, Soccer match in stadium.

1966, May 3 **Litho.** ***Perf. 11½***
C172 A181 50c ultra & red brn 2.50 2.50

Kennedy Type of Regular Issue

25c, UN General Assembly & Pres. Kennedy. 35c, Pres. Kennedy & rocket on launching pad, Cape Kennedy. 40c, Flame on grave at Arlington.

1966, Aug. 16 **Litho.** ***Perf. 12½***
C173 A182 25c ultra, blk & ocher .50 .20
C174 A182 35c dk vio bl & pink .60 .20

Souvenir Sheet

Perf. 11½

C175 A182 40c dk vio bl & multi 2.50 2.50

Boy Scout Type of Regular Issue

Souvenir Sheet

50c, Scout at campfire & vision of moon landing.

1967, Mar. 23 **Litho.** ***Perf. 12½***
C176 A185 50c brt red lil & scar 5.00 5.00

Olympic Type of Regular Issue

Souvenir Sheet

Design: 50c, Pre-Hispanic sculpture, serape and Olympic rings, horiz.

1967, June 20 **Litho.** ***Perf. 12½***
C177 A186 50c vio & car 3.75 1.60

Winter Olympic Games Type of Regular Issue

Souvenir Sheet

Design: 50c, Woman skater.

1967, Nov. 20 **Litho.** ***Perf. 11½***
C178 A189 50c ver & blk 2.25 .70

Human Rights Type of Regular Issue

Souvenir Sheet

1968, Apr. 26 **Litho.** ***Perf. 11½***
C179 A191 80c bl & red 3.00 1.10

M. L. King Type of Regular Issue

Souvenir Sheet

55c, Pres. Kennedy congratulating Dr. King.

1968, July 11 **Litho.** ***Perf. 11½***
C180 A192 55c brn & blk 3.75 1.00

Olympic Type of Regular Issue

Souvenir Sheet

Design: 50c, Steeplechase and ancient sculpture.

1968, Aug. 22 **Litho.** ***Perf. 11½***
C181 A193 50c brt bl & org brn 2.25 1.10

President Type of Regular Issue 1966-69

Design: 25c, Pres. William V. S. Tubman.

1969, Feb. 18 **Litho.** ***Perf. 11½x11***
C182 A180 25c blk & emer .60 .30

ILO Type of Regular Issue

Design: 80c, "ILO" surrounded by cogwheel and wreath, vert.

1969, Apr. 16 **Litho.** ***Perf. 12½***
C183 A196 80c emer & gold 2.50 1.10

Apollo 11 Type of Regular Issue

Souvenir Sheet

65c, Astronauts Neil A. Armstrong, Col. Edwin E. Aldrin, Jr., & Lieut. Col. Michael Collins, horiz.

1969, Oct. 15 **Litho.** ***Perf. 11½***
C184 A199 65c dk vio bl & brt red 2.50 1.10

UN Type of 1970

Design: $1, UN emblem, olive branch and plane as symbols of peace and progress, vert.

1970, Apr. 16 **Litho.** ***Perf. 12½***
C185 A200 $1 ultra & sil 2.40 1.40

Apollo 14 Type of Regular Issue

Souvenir Sheet

Design: 50c, Moon, earth and star.

1971, May 20 **Litho.** ***Imperf.***
C186 A208 50c multi 3.50 3.50

Souvenir Sheet

Olympic Yachting Village, Kiel, and Yachting — AP47

1971, June 28 Litho. *Perf. 14½x14*

C187 AP47 Sheet of 2 3.50 3.50
a. 25c multi .50 .50
b. 30c multi .60 .60

Publicity for the 20th Summer Olympic Games, and the yachting races in Kiel, Germany, 1972.

Boy Scout Type of Regular Issue

Souvenir Sheet

Boy Scouts of various nations cooking, horiz.

1971, Aug. 6 Litho. *Perf. 15*

C188 A211 50c multi 4.25 4.25

UNICEF Type of Regular Issue

Souvenir Sheet

UNICEF emblem & Bengal tigress with cubs.

1971, Oct. 1 *Imperf.*

C189 A213 50c multi 3.00 3.00

Souvenir Sheet

Japanese Royal Family — AP48

1971, Nov. 4 *Perf. 15*

C190 AP48 50c multi 4.25 4.25

11th Winter Olympic Games, Sapporo, Japan, Feb. 3-13, 1972.

Sesquicentennial Type of Regular Issue

Souvenir Sheet

Design: 50c, Sailing ship "Elizabeth" between maps of America and Africa, horiz.

1972, Jan. 1 Litho. *Imperf.*

C191 A216 50c car & vio bl 3.00 3.00

Olympic Type of Regular Issue

Souvenir Sheet

Design: 55c, View of Olympic Stadium and symbol of "Motion."

1971, May 19 Litho. *Perf. 15*

C192 A218 55c multi 5.50 5.50

Apollo 16 Type of Regular Issue

Souvenir Sheet

Lt. Comdr. Thomas K. Mattingly, 2nd, Capt. John W. Young & Lt. Col. Charles M. Duke, Jr.

1972, June 26 Litho. *Perf. 15*

C193 A220 55c pink & multi 2.50 2.50

Ship Type of 1972

Souvenir Sheet

Design: Lord Nelson's flagship Victory, and her figurehead (1765).

1972, Sept. 6 Litho. *Perf. 15*

C194 A222 50c multi 3.00 3.00

Pres. Tolbert Type of 1972.

Souvenir Sheet

1972, Oct. 23 Litho. *Perf. 15*

C195 A223 55c multi 2.00 2.00

Apollo 17 Type of Regular Issue

Souvenir Sheet

55c, Apollo 17 badge, moon and earth.

1973, Mar. 28 Litho. *Perf. 11*

C196 A225 55c bl & multi 2.50 2.50

Locomotive Type of Regular Issue

Souvenir Sheet

Design: 55c, Swiss locomotive.

1973, May 4 Litho. *Perf. 11*

C197 A226 55c multi 4.00 4.00

WHO Type of Regular Issue 1973

Souvenir Sheet

Design: 55c, WHO emblem, Paul Ehrlich and poppy anemones.

1973, June 26 Litho. *Perf. 11*

C198 A228 55c lt vio & multi 2.50 2.50

Automobile Type of Regular Issue

Souvenir Sheet

Franklin 10 HP cross-engined 1904-05 models.

1973, Sept. 11 Litho. *Perf. 11*

C199 A229 55c multi 2.50 2.50

Copernicus Type of Regular Issue

Souvenir Sheet

Design: 55c, Copernicus and concept of orbiting station around Mars.

1973, Dec. 14 Litho. *Perf. 13½*

C200 A230 55c gray & multi 2.25 2.25

UPU Type of Regular Issue

Souvenir Sheet

55c, UPU emblem and English coach, 1784.

1974, Mar. 4 Litho. *Perf. 13½*

C201 A232 55c multi 3.00 3.00

Dog Type of Regular Issue

Souvenir Sheet

Design: Hungarian sheepdog (kuvasz).

1974, Apr. 16 Litho. *Perf. 13½*

C202 A233 75c multi 4.50 4.50

Soccer Type of Regular Issue

Souvenir Sheet

Design: 60c, World Soccer Championship Cup and Munich Stadium.

1974, June 4 Litho. *Perf. 11*

C203 A234 60c multi 2.50 2.50

Butterfly Type of Regular Issue

Souvenir Sheet

Tropical butterfly: 60c, Pierella nereis.

1974, Sept. 11 Litho. *Perf. 13½*

C204 A235 60c gray & multi *4.50 4.50*

Churchill Type of 1974

Souvenir Sheet

60c, Churchill at easel painting landscape.

1975, Jan. 17 Litho. *Perf. 13½*

C205 A237 60c multi 2.00 2.00

Women's Year Type of 1975

Souvenir Sheet

Design: 75c, Vijaya Lakshmi Pandit, Women's Year emblem and dais of UN General Assembly.

1975, Mar. 14 Litho. *Perf. 13*

C206 A238 75c gray & multi 1.50 1.50

American Bicentennial Type

Souvenir Sheet

Design: 75c, Mayflower and US No. 548.

1975, Apr. 25 Litho. *Perf. 13½*

C207 A239 75c multi 3.50 3.50

Dr. Schweitzer Type, 1975

Souvenir Sheet

Schweitzer as surgeon in Lambarene Hospital.

1975, June 26 Litho. *Perf. 13½*

C208 A240 60c multi 3.00 3.00

Apollo-Soyuz Type, 1975

Souvenir Sheet

75c, Apollo-Soyuz link-up and emblem.

1975, Sept. 18 Litho. *Perf. 13½*

C209 A241 75c multi 2.50 2.50

Winter Olympic Games Type, 1976

Souvenir Sheet

Downhill skiing & Olympic Games emblem.

1976, Jan. 23 Litho. *Perf. 13½*

C210 A243 75c multi 2.00 2.00

Olympic Games Type, 1976

Souvenir Sheet

Design: 75c, Dressage and jumping.

1976, May 4 Litho. *Perf. 13½*

C211 A245 75c multi 2.50 2.50

Bell Type

Souvenir Sheet

Design: 75c, A. G. Bell making telephone call, UPU and ITU emblems.

1976, June 4 Litho. *Perf. 13½*

C212 A246 75c ocher & multi 3.00 3.00

Animal Type of 1976

Souvenir Sheet

Design: 50c, Elephant, vert.

1976, Sept. 1 Litho. *Perf. 13½*

C213 A249 50c org & multi 4.00 4.00

Bicentennial Type of 1976

Souvenir Sheet

Design: 75c, Like No. 770.

1976, Sept. 21 Litho. *Perf. 13½*

C214 A250 75c multi 3.00 3.00

Mask Type of 1977

Souvenir Sheet

75c, Ibo mask and Festival emblem.

1977, Jan. 20 Litho. *Perf. 13½*

C215 A251 75c lil & multi 2.25 2.25

Equestrian Type of 1977

Designs: 55c, Military dressage (team), US. 80c, Winners receiving medals, vert.

1977, Apr. 22 Litho. *Perf. 13½*

C216 A253 55c ocher & multi 3.25 1.60

Souvenir Sheet

C217 A253 80c ocher & multi 3.00 3.00

Elizabeth II Type of 1977

Souvenir Sheet

75c, Elizabeth II, laurel and crowns.

1977, May 23 Litho. *Perf. 13½*

C218 A254 75c sil & multi 1.75 1.25

Zeppelin Type of 1978

Souvenir Sheet

75c, Futuristic Goodyear aerospace airship.

1978, Mar. 9 Litho. *Perf. 13½*

C219 A257 75c multi 2.50 2.50

Soccer Type of 1978

Souvenir Sheet

Soccer game Netherlands & Uruguay, vert.

1978, May 16 Litho. *Perf. 13½*

C220 A258 75c multi 2.50

Coronation Type of 1978

Souvenir Sheet

Design: 75c, Coronation coach, horiz.

1978, June 12

C221 A259 75c multi 3.25

Soccer Winners' Type of 1978

Souvenir Sheet

Design: 75c, Argentine team, horiz.

1978, Dec. 8 Litho. *Perf. 13½*

C222 A262 75c multi 3.25

AIR POST SEMI-POSTAL STAMPS

Nos. C14-C16 Overprinted in Red or Blue Like Nos. B16-B18

1941 Unwmk. *Perf. 12*

CB1 A107 3c +2c dk bl (R) 4.00 4.00
CB2 A108 5c +2c dl red brn (Bl) 4.00 4.00
CB3 A109 10c +2c dk grn (R) 4.00 4.00
Nos. CB1-CB3 (3) 12.00 12.00

Catalogue values for unused stamps in this section, from this point to the end of the section, are for Never Hinged items.

Nurses Taking Oath — SPAP1

Designs: 20c+5c, Liberian Government Hospital. 25c+5c, Medical examination.

1954, June 21 Litho. & Engr.

Size: 39½x28½mm

CB4 SPAP1 10c +5c car & blk .20 .20
CB5 SPAP1 20c +5c emer & blk .20 .20

Size: 45x34mm

CB6 SPAP1 25c +5c ultra, car & blk .20 .20
Nos. CB4-CB6 (3) .60 .60

Surtax for the Liberian Government Hospital. Nos. CB4-CB6 exist imperf. No. CB6 exists with carmine omitted.

AIR POST SPECIAL DELIVERY STAMP

No. C15 Overprinted in Dark Blue Like No. E1

1941 Unwmk. *Perf. 12*

CE1 A108 10c on 5c dl red brn 2.00 2.00

AIR POST REGISTRATION STAMP

No. C15 Overprinted in Dark Blue Like No. F35

1941 Unwmk. *Perf. 12*

CF1 A108 10c on 5c dl red brn 2.00 2.00

SPECIAL DELIVERY STAMP

No. 278 Surcharged in Dark Blue

1941 Unwmk. *Perf. 12*

E1 A108 10c on 5c dl red brn 2.00 2.00

REGISTRATION STAMPS

R1

1893 Unwmk. Litho. *Perf. 14, 15*

Without Value Surcharged

F1 R1 (10c) blk (Buchanan) 250. 250.
F2 R1 (10c) blk (Greenville) *4,500.* —
F3 R1 (10c) blk (Harper) *4,500.* —
F4 R1 (10c) blk (Monrovia) 30. 30.
F5 R1 (10c) blk (Robertsport) 1,000. 1,000.

Types of 1893 Surcharged in Black

1894 ***Perf. 14***

F6	R1	10c bl, *pink* (Buchanan)	5.00	5.25
F7	R1	10c grn, *buff* (Harper)	5.00	5.25
F8	R1	10c red, *yel* (Monrovia)	5.00	5.25
F9	R1	10c rose, *blue* (Roberts - port)	5.00	5.25
		Nos. F6-F9 (4)	20.00	21.00

Exist imperf or missing one 10. Value, each $10.

President Garretson W. Gibson — R6

1903 **Engr.** ***Perf. 14***

F10	R6	10c bl & blk (Buchanan)	1.10	.20
a.		Center inverted	100.00	
F11	R6	10c org red & blk ("Grenville")	1.10	
a.		Center inverted	100.00	
b.		10c orange & black	1.90	.20
F12	R6	10c grn & blk (Harper)	1.10	.20
a.		Center inverted	100.00	
F13	R6	10c vio & blk (Monrovia)	1.10	.20
a.		Center inverted	100.00	
b.		10c lilac & black	1.90	
F14	R6	10c magenta & blk (Robertsport)	1.10	.20
a.		Center inverted	100.00	
		Nos. F10-F14 (5)	5.50	
		Nos. F10, F11b, F12-F14		.75

For surcharges see Nos. 178-182.

S.S. Quail on Patrol — R7

1919 **Litho.** ***Serrate Roulette 12***

F15	R7	10c blk & bl (Buchanan)	1.40	2.75

Serrate Roulette 12, Perf. 14

F16	R7	10c ocher & blk ("Grenville")	1.40	2.75
F17	R7	10c grn & blk (Harper)	1.40	2.75
F18	R7	10c vio & bl (Monrovia)	1.40	2.75
F19	R7	10c rose & blk (Robertsport)	1.40	2.75
		Nos. F15-F19 (5)	7.00	13.75

Gabon Viper — R8

Wmk. Crosses and Circles (116)

1921 **Engr.** ***Perf. 13x14***

F20	R8	10c cl & blk (Buchanan)	90.00	3.50
F21	R8	10c red & blk (Greenville)	22.50	3.50
F22	R8	10c ultra & blk (Harper)	22.50	3.50
F23	R8	10c org & blk (Monrovia)	22.50	3.50
a.		Imperf., pair	225.00	
F24	R8	10c grn & blk (Robertsport)	22.50	3.50
a.		Imperf., pair	225.00	
		Nos. F20-F24 (5)	180.00	17.50

Preceding Issue Overprinted "1921"

F25	R8	10c (Buchanan)	20.00	6.25
F26	R8	10c (Greenville)	20.00	6.25
F27	R8	10c (Harper)	70.00	6.25
F28	R8	10c (Monrovia)	20.00	6.25
F29	R8	10c (Robertsport)	20.00	6.25
		Nos. F25-F29 (5)	150.00	31.25

Nos. F20-F24 are printed tete-beche. Thus, the "1921" overprint appears upright on half the stamps in a sheet and inverted on the other half. Values are the same for either variety.

Passengers Going Ashore from Ship — R9

Designs: No. F31, Transporting merchandise, shore to ship (Greenville). No. F32, Sailing ship (Harper). No. F33, Ocean liner (Monrovia). No. F34, Canoe in surf (Robertsport).

1924 **Litho.** ***Perf. 14***

F30	R9	10c gray & carmine	7.00	.60
F31	R9	10c gray & blue grn	7.00	.60
F32	R9	10c gray & orange	7.00	.60
F33	R9	10c gray & blue	7.00	.60
F34	R9	10c gray & violet	7.00	.60
		Nos. F30-F34 (5)	35.00	3.00

No. 278 Surcharged in Dark Blue

1941 **Unwmk.** ***Perf. 12***

F35	A108	10c on 5c dull red brn	2.00	2.00

POSTAGE DUE STAMPS

Nos. 26, 28 Surcharged

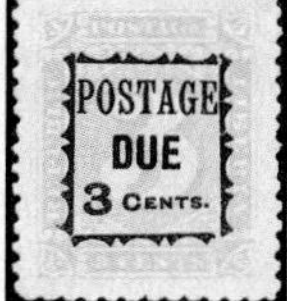

1892 **Unwmk.** ***Perf. 11***

J1	A5	3c on 3c violet	6.50	4.25
a.		Imperf., pair	22.50	
b.		Inverted surcharge	45.00	45.00
c.		As "a," inverted surcharge	110.00	

Perf. 12

J2	A5	6c on 6c olive gray	15.00	13.50
a.		Imperf., pair	32.50	
b.		Inverted surcharge	52.50	35.00

D2

Engr.; Figures of Value Typographed in Black

1893 **Wmk. 143** ***Perf. 14, 15***

J3	D2	2c org, *yel*	2.00	1.00
J4	D2	4c rose, *rose*	2.00	1.00
J5	D2	6c brown, *buff*	2.00	1.25
J6	D2	8c blue, *blue*	2.00	1.25
J7	D2	10c grn, *lil rose*	2.25	1.50
J8	D2	20c vio, *gray*	2.25	1.50
a.		Center inverted	110.00	110.00
J9	D2	40c ol brn, *grnsh*	4.50	3.00
		Nos. J3-J9 (7)	17.00	10.50

All values of the above set exist imperforate.

MILITARY STAMPS

"LFF" are the initials of "Liberian Frontier Force." Nos. M1-M7 were issued for the use of troops sent to guard the frontier.

Issues of 1905, 1906 and 1909 Surcharged

1916 **Wmk. 143**

M1	A23	1c on 1c lt grn	175.00	175.00
a.		2nd "F" inverted	250.00	250.00
b.		"FLF"	250.00	250.00
c.		Inverted surcharge	250.00	250.00

Unwmk.

M2	A33	1c on 1c grn & blk	500.00	500.00
a.		2nd "F" inverted	550.00	550.00
b.		"FLF"	550.00	550.00
M3	A46	1c on 1c yel grn & blk	3.75	4.50
a.		2nd "F" inverted	7.50	7.50
b.		"FLF"	7.50	7.50
M4	A47	1c on 2c lake & blk	3.75	4.50
a.		2nd "F" inverted	7.50	7.50
b.		"FLF"	7.50	7.50

Surcharge exists sideways on Nos. M2, M5; double on Nos. M1-M4; inverted on Nos. M2-M4.

Nos. O46, O59-O60 Surcharged

M5	A33	1c on 1c	400.00	400.00
a.		2nd "F" inverted	550.00	550.00
b.		"FLF"	550.00	550.00
M6	A46	1c on 1c	3.75	4.50
a.		2nd "F" inverted	7.50	7.50
b.		"FLF"	7.50	7.50
c.		"LFF 1c" inverted	10.00	10.00
d.		As "a" and "1c" inverted		14.00
e.		"FLF 1c" inverted		14.00
M7	A47	1c on 2c	2.75	3.25
a.		2nd "F" inverted	5.75	5.75
b.		"FLF"	5.75	5.75
c.		Pair, one without "LFF 1c"		

OFFICIAL STAMPS

Types of Regular Issues Overprinted "OFFICIAL" in Various Colors

Perf. 12½ to 15 and Compound

1892 **Wmk. 143**

O1	A9	1c vermilion	.80	.80
O2	A9	2c blue	.80	.80
O3	A10	4c grn & blk	.80	.80
O4	A11	6c bl grn	.80	.80
O5	A12	8c brn & blk	.80	.80
O6	A13	12c rose red	2.00	2.00
O7	A14	16c red lilac	2.00	2.00
O8	A15	24c ol grn, *yel*	2.00	2.00
O9	A16	32c grnsh bl	2.00	2.00
O10	A17	$1 bl & blk	40.00	16.00
O11	A18	$2 brn, *yel*	16.00	11.50
O12	A19	$5 car & blk	24.00	9.00
		Nos. O1-O12 (12)	92.00	48.50

1893

O13	A11	5c on 6c bl grn (No. 50) (a)	.95	.95
a.		"5" with short flag	5.00	5.00
b.		Both 5's with short flags	5.00	5.00
c.		"i" dot omitted	19.00	19.00
d.		Overprinted on #50d	45.00	45.00

1894

Overprinted "O S" in Various Colors

O15	A9	1c vermilion	.70	.35
O16	A9	2c blue	.85	.40
a.		Imperf.		
O17	A10	4c grn & blk	1.00	.55
O18	A12	8c brn & blk	1.00	.55
O19	A13	12c rose red	1.40	.60
O20	A14	16c red lilac	1.40	.60
O21	A15	24c ol grn, *yel*	1.40	.70
O22	A16	32c grnsh bl	2.75	.80
O23	A17	$1 bl & blk	27.50	21.00
a.		$1 ultra & black	27.50	21.00
O24	A18	$2 brn, *yel*	27.50	21.00
O25	A19	$5 car & blk	125.00	87.50
		Nos. O15-O25 (11)	190.50	134.05

Unwmk.

Imperf

O26	A22	5c vio & grn	3.00	1.90

Rouletted

O27	A22	5c vio & grn	3.00	1.90

Regular Issue of 1896-1905 Overprinted "O S" in Black or Red

1898-1905 **Wmk. 143** ***Perf. 14, 15***

O28	A23	1c lil rose	.90	.90
O29	A23	1c dp grn ('00)	.90	.90
O30	A23	1c lt grn (R) ('05)	.90	.90
O31	A24	2c bis & blk	1.75	.60
a.		Pair, one without overprint	*900.00*	
O32	A24	2c org red & blk ('00)	2.75	1.50
O33	A24	2c rose & blk ('05)	4.50	2.75
O34	A25	5c lake & blk	3.00	1.50
O35	A25	5c gray bl & blk ('00)	3.50	1.50
O36	A25	5c ultra & blk (R) ('05)	6.00	3.75
O37	A12	10c chr yel & ind	1.75	1.75
O38	A13	15c slate	1.75	1.75
O39	A14	20c vermilion	3.00	2.10
O40	A15	25c yel grn	1.75	1.75
O41	A16	30c steel blue	4.50	2.75
O42	A26	50c red brn & blk	4.50	2.75
		Nos. O28-O42 (15)	41.45	27.15

For surcharge see No. O92.

Official stamps overprinted "ORDINARY" or with a bar with an additional surcharge are listed as Nos. 64B-90, 92-93, 99.

Red Overprint

1903 **Unwmk.** ***Perf. 14***

O43	A29	3c green	.20	.20
a.		Overprint omitted	5.00	
b.		Inverted overprint		

Two overprint types: I — Thin, sharp, dark red. II — Thick, heavier, orange red. Same value.

On No. 50

— O3

1904 Black Surcharge Wmk. 143

O44 A11 1c on 5c on 6c bl grn 1.25 1.50
a. "5" with short flag 4.25
b. Both "5s" with straight flag 8.00 8.00

Red Surcharge

O45 O3 2c on 30c steel blue 8.00 8.00
a. Double surcharge, red and black
b. Surcharge also on back

Types of Regular Issue Overprinted in Various Colors — a

1906 Unwmk.

O46 A33 1c grn & blk (R) .65 .40
O47 A34 2c car & blk (Bl) .20 .20
a. Center and overprint inverted 30.00 3.00
b. Inverted overprint 6.00
O48 A35 5c ultra & blk (Bk) .65 .40
a. Inverted overprint 15.00 15.00
b. Center and overprint invtd. 50.00
O49 A36 10c dl vio & blk (R) .75 .55
a. Inverted overprint 10.00 10.00
b. Center and overprint invtd. 50.00
O50 A37 15c brn & blk (Bk) 3.00 .55
a. Inverted overprint 4.50
b. Overprint omitted 12.00 6.00
c. Center and overprint invtd. 60.00
O51 A38 20c dp grn & blk (R) .75 .55
a. Overprint omitted 15.00
O52 A39 25c plum & gray (Bl) .50 .20
a. With 2nd ovpt. in blue, invtd. 15.00
O53 A40 30c dk brn (Bk) .55 .20
O54 A41 50c org brn & dp grn (G) .75 .20
a. Inverted overprint 5.00 4.00
O55 A42 75c ultra & blk (Bk) 1.40 .95
a. Inverted overprint 9.50 5.75
b. Overprint omitted 22.50
O56 A43 $1 dp grn & gray (R) .90 .20
a. Inverted overprint
O57 A44 $2 plum & blk (Bl) 2.75 .20
a. Overprint omitted 22.50 15.00
O58 A45 $5 org & blk (Bk) 5.50 .20
a. Overprint omitted 11.00
b. Inverted overprint 12.00 8.00
Nos. O46-O58 (13) 18.35 4.80

Nos. O52, O54, O55, O56 and O58 are known with center inverted.

For surcharges see Nos. O72, O82-O85, O96.

(b)

1909-12

O59 A46 1c emer & blk (R) .40 .20
O60 A47 2c car rose & brn (Bl) .40 .20
a. Overprint omitted
O61 A48 5c turq & blk (Bk) .45 .20
a. Double overprint, one inverted 7.50
O62 A49 10c blk & ultra (R) ('12) .60 .20
O63 A50 15c cl & blk (Bl) .60 .45
O64 A51 20c bis & grn (Bk) 1.10 .55
O65 A52 25c ultra & grn (Bk) 1.10 .55
a. Double overprint 4.75 4.75
O66 A53 30c dk bl (R) .85 .20
O67 A54 50c brn & grn (Bk) 1.40 .40
a. Center inverted 27.50
b. Inverted overprint 4.00 2.75
O68 A55 75c pur & blk (R) 1.50 .20
Nos. O59-O68 (10) 8.40 3.15

Nos. O63, O64, O67 and O68 are known without overprint and with center inverted.

For surcharges see Nos. O74-O81, O86-O90, O97.

Rouletted

O69 A49 10c blk & ultra (R) .70 .70

Nos. 126B and 127E Overprinted type "a" ("OS") in Red

1910-12 ***Rouletted***

O70 A49 3c on 10c blk & ultra .60 1.00

Perf. 12½, 14, 12½x14

O71 A49 3c on 10c blk & ultra ('12) .60 .30
a. Pair, one without surch., the other with dbl. surch., one invtd.
b. Double surcharge, one inverted 3.75

Stamps of Preceding Issues Surcharged with New Values like Regular Issue and

c

1914

On Nos. O52 and 110

O72 A39 (a) 2c on 25c plum & gray 25.00 10.50
O73 A42 (c) 20c on 75c brn & blk 8.75 5.25

On Nos. O66 and O68

O74 A53 (b) 5c on 30c dk bl 8.75 5.25
O75 A55 (c) 20c on 75c pur & blk (R) 13.00 5.25
Nos. O72-O75 (4) 55.50 26.25

Official Stamps of 1906-09 Surcharged Like Regular Issues of Same Date

1915-16

O76 A50 (c) 2c on 15c (Bk) .75 .50
O77 A52 (d) 2c on 25c (Bk) 4.25 4.25
O78 A51 (e) 5c on 20c (Bk) .75 .50
O79 A53 (g) 5c on 30c (R) 7.00 7.00
O80 A54 (i) 10c on 50c (Bk) 4.50 2.75
O81 A55 (j) 20c on 75c (R) 2.25 2.25
O82 A43 (k) 25c on $1 (R) 16.00 16.00
a. "25" double 22.50
b. "OS" inverted 22.50
O83 A44 (l) 50c on $2 (Bk) 50.00 50.00
a. "Ceuts" 70.00 70.00
O84 A44 (m) 50c on $2 (Br) 18.00 18.00
O85 A45 (n) $1 on $5 (Bk) 17.00 17.00

Handstamped Surcharge

O86 A54 (i) 10c on 50c (Bk) 8.50 8.50

Nos. O60-O61 Surcharged like Nos. 153-154 in Black or Red

a1, b1

c1, d1

e1, f1

g1, h1

i1, j1

O87 A47 1c on 2c 2.25 2.25
Strip of 10 types 25.00
O88 A48 2c on 5c (R) 2.25 2.25
Strip of 10 types (R) 25.00
a. Black surcharge 8.50 8.50
Strip of 10 types (Bk) 125.00

See note following Nos. 153-154.

#O60-O61 Surcharged like #155-156

O90 A47 1c on 2c 125.00 125.00
O91 A48 2c on 5c 100.00 100.00

No. O42 Surcharged

O92 A26 10c on 50c (Bk) 11.00 11.00

No. O53 Surcharged like No. 161

1917

O96 A40 5c on 30c dk brn 17.00 17.00
a. "FIV" 27.50 27.50

The editors consider the 1915-17 issues unnecessary and speculative.

#O62 Surcharged in Red like #162

1918

O97 A49 3c on 10c blk & ultra 1.90 1.90

Types of Regular Issue of 1918 Overprinted Type "a" ("OS") in Black, Blue or Red

1918 Unwmk. *Perf. 12½, 14*

O98 A59 1c dp grn & red brn (Bk) .60 .20
O99 A60 2c red & blk (Bl) .60 .20
O100 A61 5c ultra & blk (R) 1.10 .20
O101 A62 10c ultra (R) .60 .20
O102 A63 15c choc & dk grn (Bl) 2.75 .60
O103 A64 20c gray lil & blk (R) .85 .20
O104 A65 25c choc & grn (Bk) 5.25 .65
O105 A66 30c brt vio & blk (R) 6.50 .65
O106 A67 50c mar & blk (Bl) 7.75 .65
a. Overprint omitted 11.00
O107 A68 75c car brn & blk (Bl) 3.00 .20
O108 A69 $1 ol bis & turq bl (Bk) 6.00 .20
O109 A70 $2 ol bis & blk (R) 9.25 .20
O110 A71 $5 yel grn (Bk) 12.00 .40
Nos. O98-O110 (13) 56.25 4.55

For surcharges see Nos. 259-269, O111-O112, O155-O157. For overprint see No. 270.

Official Stamps of 1918 Surcharged like Regular Issue

1920

O111 A59 3c on 1c grn & red brn .90 .55
a. "CEETS" 15.00 15.00
b. Double surcharge 8.00 8.00
c. Double surch., one invtd. 15.00 15.00
d. Triple surcharge 20.00 20.00
O112 A60 4c on 2c red & blk .55 .55
a. Inverted surcharge 12.00 12.00
b. Double surcharge 12.00 12.00
c. Double surch., one invtd. 10.00 10.00
d. Triple surcharge 15.00 15.00

Types of Regular Issues of 1915-21 Overprinted

1921 Wmk. 116 *Perf. 14*

O113 A57 2c rose red 8.25 .20
O114 A58 3c brown 1.75 .20
O115 A79 20c brn & ultra 2.25 .40

Same, Overprinted "O S"

O116 A75 1c dp grn 1.75 .20
O117 A76 5c dp bl & brn 1.75 .20
O118 A77 10c red vio & blk .85 .20
O119 A78 15c blk & grn 4.75 .60
a. Double overprint
O120 A80 25c org & grn 6.50 .60
O121 A81 30c brn & red 1.75 .20
O122 A82 50c grn & blk 1.75 .20
a. Overprinted "S" only
O123 A83 75c bl & vio 3.25 .20
O124 A84 $1 bl & blk 22.50 .65
O125 A85 $2 grn & org 12.00 .95
O126 A86 $5 grn & bl 13.50 2.10
Nos. O113-O126 (14) 82.60 6.90

Preceding Issues Overprinted "1921"

1921

O127 A75 1c dp grn 7.50 .20
O128 A57 2c rose red 7.50 .20
O129 A58 3c brown 7.50 .20
O130 A76 5c dp bl & brn 4.50 .20
O131 A77 10c red vio & blk 7.50 .20
O132 A78 15c blk & grn 8.50 .20
O133 A79 20c brn & ultra 8.50 .40
O134 A80 25c org & grn 8.25 .80
O135 A81 30c brn & red 7.50 .20
O136 A82 50c grn & blk 8.75 .20
O137 A83 75c bl & vio 5.50 .20
O138 A84 $1 bl & blk 15.00 2.00
O139 A85 $2 org & grn 19.00 2.25
O140 A86 $5 grn & bl 15.00 3.25
Nos. O127-O140 (14) 130.50 10.50

Types of Regular Issue of 1923 Overprinted "O S"

1923 *Perf. 13½x14½, 14½x13½*

White Paper

O141 A88 1c bl grn & blk 8.75 .20
O142 A89 2c dl red & yel brn 8.75 .20
O143 A90 3c gray bl & blk 8.75 .20
O144 A91 5c org & dk grn 8.75 .20
O145 A92 10c ol bis & dk vio 8.75 .20
O146 A93 15c yel grn & bl 1.10 .40
O147 A94 20c vio & ind 1.10 .40
O148 A95 25c brn & red brn 32.50 .40

White, Buff or Brownish Paper

O149a A96 30c dp ultra & brn 1.10 .30
b. Overprint omitted 2.00
O150a A97 50c dl bis & red brn 2.25 .45
O151 A98 75c gray & grn 2.25 .20
O152a A99 $1 red org & grn 2.25 .65
b. Overprint omitted 11.00
O153 A100 $2 red lil & ver 6.00 .20
O154a A101 $5 bl & brn vio 4.50 2.25
Nos. O141-O154a (14) 96.80 6.25

Nos. O149-154 exist on white, buff or brownish paper. Values are for the most common varieties. For detailed listings, see the *Scott Classic Specialized Catalogue.*

No. O98 Surcharged in Red Brown

1926 Unwmk. Perf. 14

O155	A59 2c on 1c	2.25	2.25
a.	"Gents"	7.25	
b.	Surcharged in black	5.75	
c.	As "b," "Gents"	9.50	

No. O98 Surcharged in Black

1926

O156	A59 2c on 1c	.85	.85
a.	Inverted surcharge	20.00	
b.	"Gents"	10.00	

No. O98 Surcharged in Red

1927

O157	A59 2c on 1c	35.00	35.00
a.	"Ceuts"	55.00	
b.	"Vwo"	55.00	
c.	"Twc"	55.00	

Regular Issue of 1928 Overprinted in Red or Black

1928 Perf. 12

O158	A102	1c grn (R)	1.10	.55
O159	A102	2c gray vio (R)	3.50	2.10
O160	A102	3c bis brn (Bk)	3.75	4.25
O161	A103	5c ultra (R)	1.10	.55
O162	A104	10c ol gray (R)	3.50	1.75
O163	A103	15c dl vio (R)	3.50	1.00
O164	A103	$1 red brn (Bk)	77.50	22.50
		Nos. O158-O164 (7)	93.95	32.70

For surcharges see Nos. C3, O165.

No. O162 Surcharged with New Value and Bar in Black

1945 Unwmk. Perf. 12

O165	A104 4c on 10c (Bk)	12.00	12.00

LIBYA

'li-bē-ə

(Libia)

LOCATION — North Africa, bordering on the Mediterranean Sea
GOVT. — Republic
AREA — 679,358 sq. mi.
POP. — 4,992,838 (1999 est.)
CAPITAL — Tripoli

In 1939, the four northern provinces of Libya, a former Italian colony, were incorporated in the Italian national territory. Included in the territory is the former Turkish Vilayet of Tripoli, annexed in 1912. Libya became a kingdom on Dec. 24, 1951. The Libyan Arab Republic was established Sept. 1, 1969. "People's Socialist . . ." was added to its name in 1977. See Cyrenaica and Tripolitania.

100 Centesimi = 1 Lira
Military Authority Lira (1951)
Franc (1951)
1,000 Milliemes = 1 Pound (1952)
1,000 Dirhams = 1 Dinar (1972)

Watermarks

Wmk. 140 — Crown

Wmk. 195 — Multiple Crown and Arabic F

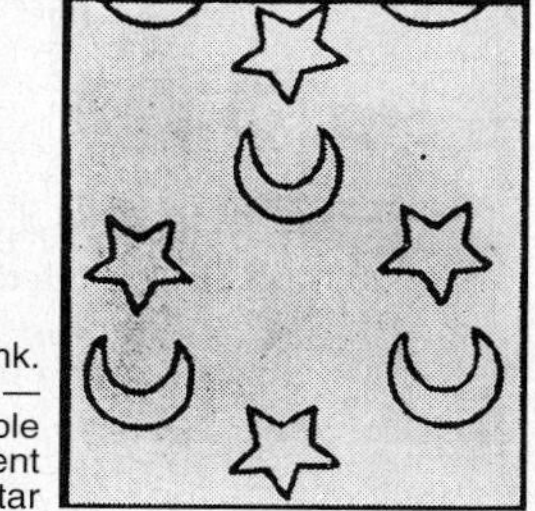

Wmk. 310 — Multiple Crescent and Star

Catalogue values for unused stamps in this country are for Never Hinged items, beginning with Scott 102 in the regular postage section, Scott C51 in the airpost section, Scott E13 in the special delivery section, Scott J25 in the postage due section, Scott O1 in the official section, Scott N1 in the Fezzan-Ghadames section, Scott 2N1 in the Fezzan section, Scott 2NB1 in the Fezzan semi-postal section, Scott 2NC1 in the Fezzan airpost section, Scott 2NJ1 in the Fezzan postage due section, Scott 3N1 in the Ghadames section, and Scott 3NC1 in the Ghadames airpost section.

Used values in italics are for postally used stamps. CTO's sell for about the same as unused, hinged stamps.

Stamps of Italy Overprinted in Black

1912-22 Wmk. 140 Perf. 14

1	A42	1c brown ('15)	1.75	1.00
a.		Double overprint	260.00	260.00
2	A43	2c orange brn	1.75	.65
3	A48	5c green	1.75	.40
a.		Double overprint	160.00	160.00
b.		Imperf., pair	400.00	
c.		Inverted overprint		—
d.		Pair, one without overprint	425.00	425.00
4	A48	10c claret	17.00	.40
a.		Pair, one without overprint	425.00	425.00
b.		Double overprint	190.00	190.00
5	A48	15c slate ('22)	4.75	*8.00*
6	A45	20c orange ('15)	6.50	.40
a.		Double overprint	210.00	*210.00*
b.		Pair, one without overprint	750.00	750.00
7	A50	20c brn org ('18)	4.75	*6.50*
8	A49	25c blue	6.50	.40
b.		Double overprint	175.00	175.00
9	A49	40c brown	16.00	1.25
10	A45	45c ol grn ('17)	36.00	30.00
a.		Inverted overprint	600.00	
11	A49	50c violet	40.00	1.75
12	A49	60c brn car ('18)	19.00	*25.00*
13	A46	1 l brown & green ('15)	85.00	2.10
14	A46	5 l bl & rose ('15)	425.00	450.00
15	A51	10 l gray green & red ('15)	47.50	*200.00*
		Nos. 1-15 (15)	713.25	*727.85*

Two types of overprint were applied to this issue. Type I has bold letters, with dots close within "i"; type II has thinner letters, with dots further away within "i." All values, along with Nos. E1 and E2, received the type I overprint, and values shown are for this type. Nos. 1, 3-4, 6, 8, 11, 13-15 and E1-E2 also received the type II overprint. For detailed listings, see the *Scott Classic Specialized Catalogue of Stamps and Covers.*

For surcharges see Nos. 37-38.

Overprinted in Violet

1912 Unwmk.

16	A58	15c slate	300.00	2.10
a.		Blue black overprint	*21,000.*	40.00

No. 16 Surcharged CENT 20

1916, Mar. Unwmk.

19	A58	20c on 15c slate	47.50	11.00

Roman Legionary — A1

Diana of Ephesus — A2

Ancient Galley Leaving Tripoli — A3

"Victory" — A4

1921 Engr. Wmk. 140 Perf. 14

20	A1	1c blk & gray brn	3.25	*8.00*
21	A1	2c blk & red brn	3.25	*8.00*
22	A1	5c black & green	4.25	.85
a.		5c black & red brown (error)	2,000.	
b.		Center inverted	65.00	92.50
c.		Imperf., pair	600.00	600.00
23	A2	10c blk & rose	4.25	.85
a.		Center inverted	65.00	92.50
24	A2	15c blk brn & brn org	110.00	3.25
a.		Center inverted	140.00	*275.00*
25	A2	25c dk bl & bl	4.25	.20
a.		Center inverted	21.00	30.00
b.		Imperf., pair	875.00	875.00
26	A3	30c blk & blk brn	36.00	.85
a.		Center inverted	2,800.	2,800.
27	A3	50c blk & ol grn	16.00	.20
a.		50c black & brown (error)	600.00	
b.		Center inverted		*4,400.*
28	A3	55c black & vio	16.00	28.00
29	A4	1 l dk brn & brn	47.50	.20
30	A4	5 l blk & dk blue	32.50	25.00
31	A4	10 l dk bl & ol grn	360.00	180.00
		Nos. 20-31 (12)	637.25	255.40

Nos. 20-31 also exist perf. 14x13. Values substantially higher.

See #47-61. For surcharges see #102-121.

Italy Nos. 136-139 Overprinted

1922, Apr.

33	A64	5c olive green	2.10	*7.50*
a.		Double overprint	360.00	360.00
34	A64	10c red	2.10	*7.50*
a.		Double overprint	360.00	360.00
b.		Inverted overprint	725.00	725.00
35	A64	15c slate green	2.10	*12.00*
36	A64	25c ultramarine	2.10	*12.00*
		Nos. 33-36 (4)	8.40	*39.00*

3rd anniv. of the victory of the Piave.

Nos. 11, 8 Surcharged

1922, June 1

37	A49	40c on 50c violet	3.25	2.50
38	A49	80c on 25c blue	3.25	*7.50*

Libyan Sibyl — A6

1924-31 Unwmk. Perf. 14½x14

39	A6	20c deep green	.85	.20
c.		Vert. pair, imperf between and top	1,325.	
d.		Horiz. pair, imperf between and at right	1,325.	
e.		Horiz. pair, imperf between and at left	1,325.	
40	A6	40c brown	2.40	.85
b.		Imperf single	325.00	*450.00*
41	A6	60c deep blue	.85	.20
b.		Imperf single	300.00	
42	A6	1.75 l orange ('31)	.80	.20
43	A6	2 l carmine	4.00	1.20
b.		Imperf single	300.00	*350.00*
44	A6	2.55 l violet ('31)	8.00	14.50
		Nos. 39-44 (6)	16.90	17.15

1926-29 Perf. 11

39a	A6	20c	40.00	.35
40a	A6	40c	35.00	3.00
41a	A6	60c	35.00	.55
43a	A6	2 l ('29)	16.00	6.25
		Nos. 39a-43a (4)	126.00	10.15

Type of 1921

1924-40 Unwmk. Perf. 13½ to 14

47	A1	1c blk & gray brown	3.25	6.50
48	A1	2c blk & red brn	3.25	6.50
49	A1	5c blk & green	4.25	.85
50	A1	7½c blk & brown ('31)	.80	9.50
51	A2	10c blk & dl red	3.50	.35
b.		10c blk & carmine	3.50	.35
c.		As "b," center inverted	210.00	
52	A2	15c blk brn & org	9.50	1.25
b.		Center inverted, perf. 11	*3,500.*	*6,000.*
53	A2	25c dk bl & bl	50.00	.65
a.		Center inverted	300.00	400.00
54	A3	30c blk & blk brn	3.40	.65
55	A3	50c blk & ol grn	3.40	.35
b.		Center inverted	3,500.	
56	A3	55c black & vio	725.00	950.00
57	A4	75c violet & red ('31)	4.00	.20
58	A4	1 l dk brn & brn	12.00	.45
59	A3	1.25 l indigo & ultra ('31)	.80	.20
60	A4	5 l blk & dark blue ('40)	160.00	*160.00*
		Nos. 47-60 (14)	983.15	1,137.

Perf. 11

47a	A1	1c	400.00	
48a	A1	2c	400.00	
49a	A1	5c	80.00	16.00
51a	A2	10c	50.00	6.75
52a	A2	15c	475.00	47.50
54a	A3	30c	160.00	2.50
55a	A3	50c	850.00	.20
58a	A4	1 l	350.00	.45
60a	A4	5 l ('37)	*2,750.*	475.00

61	A4	10 l dk bl & olive grn ('37)	650.00	550.00

Nos. 47a and 48a were not sent to the colony. A few philatelically inspired covers exist.

Italy #197 and 88 Overprinted Like #1-15

1929 Wmk. 140 *Perf. 14*

62	A86	7½c light brown	8.00	*47.50*
a.		Double overprint	—	—
63	A46	1.25 l blue & ultra	55.00	24.00
a.		Inverted overprint	3,000.	

Italy #193 Overprinted Like #33-36

1929 Unwmk. *Perf. 11*

64	A85	1.75 l deep brown	72.50	2.50
h.		Perf 13¾		*11,000.*

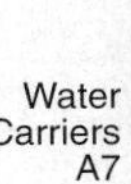

Water Carriers A7

Man of Tripoli — A8

Designs: 25c, Minaret. 30c, 1.25 l, Tomb of Holy Man near Tagiura. 50c, Statue of Emperor Claudius at Leptis. 75c, Ruins of gardens.

1934, Feb. 17 Photo. *Perf. 14*

64A	A7	10c brown	5.00	*17.50*
64B	A8	20c car rose	5.00	*16.00*
64C	A8	25c green	5.00	*16.00*
64D	A7	30c dark brown	5.00	*16.00*
64E	A8	50c purple	5.00	*14.50*
64F	A7	75c rose	5.00	*27.50*
64G	A7	1.25 l blue	55.00	*80.00*
		Nos. 64A-64G (7)	85.00	*187.50*
		Nos. 64A-64G,C14-C18 (12)	489.00	*883.50*

8th Sample Fair, Tripoli.

Bedouin Woman — A15

Highway Memorial Arch — A16

1936, May 11 Wmk. 140 *Perf. 14*

65	A15	50c purple	1.70	*3.25*
66	A15	1.25 l deep blue	1.70	*9.25*

10th Sample Fair, Tripoli.

1937, Mar. 15

67	A16	50c copper red	2.50	*5.00*
68	A16	1.25 l sapphire	2.50	*12.00*
		Nos. 67-68,C28-C29 (4)	10.00	*33.75*

Coastal road to the Egyptian frontier, opening.

Nos. 67-68 Overprinted in Black

1937, Apr. 24

69	A16	50c copper red	15.00	*37.50*
70	A16	1.25 l sapphire	15.00	*37.50*
		Nos. 69-70,C30-C31 (4)	60.00	*150.00*

11th Sample Fair, Tripoli.

Roman Wolf and Lion of St. Mark A17

View of Fair Buildings A18

1938, Mar. 12

71	A17	5c brown	.25	1.25
72	A18	10c olive brown	.25	.85
73	A17	25c green	.60	1.50
74	A18	50c purple	.70	.65
75	A17	75c rose red	1.25	*2.50*
76	A18	1.25 l dark blue	1.40	*6.00*
		Nos. 71-76,C32-C33 (8)	6.95	*21.25*

12th Sample Fair, Tripoli.

Augustus Caesar (Octavianus) A19

Goddess Abundantia A20

1938, Apr. 25

77	A19	5c olive brown	.25	1.70
78	A20	10c brown red	.25	1.70
79	A19	25c dk yel green	.60	.75
80	A20	50c dk violet	.60	.55
81	A19	75c orange red	1.70	*2.10*
82	A20	1.25 l dull blue	1.70	*3.40*
		Nos. 77-82,C34-C35 (8)	6.75	*16.80*

Birth bimillenary of Augustus Caesar (Octavianus), first Roman emperor.

Desert City — A21

View of Ghadames A22

1939, Apr. 12 Photo.

83	A21	5c olive brown	.40	1.25
84	A22	20c red brown	.85	1.25
85	A21	50c rose violet	.85	1.25
86	A22	75c scarlet	.85	*2.50*
87	A21	1.25 l gray blue	.85	*3.75*
		Nos. 83-87,C36-C38 (8)	5.70	*16.70*

13th Sample Fair, Tripoli.

Modern City — A23

Oxen and Plow A24

Mosque — A25

1940, June 3 Wmk. 140 *Perf. 14*

88	A23	5c brown	.35	1.25
89	A24	10c red orange	.35	.85
90	A25	25c dull green	.75	*1.25*
91	A23	50c dark violet	.75	*.85*
92	A24	75c crimson	.85	*3.40*
93	A25	1.25 l ultramarine	1.25	*5.00*
94	A24	2 l + 75c rose lake	1.25	*17.00*
		Nos. 88-94,C39-C42 (11)	9.25	*50.95*

Triennial Overseas Exposition, Naples.

"Two Peoples, One War," Hitler and Mussolini A26

1941, May 16

95	A26	5c orange	2.40	*8.00*
96	A26	10c brown	2.40	*8.00*
97	A26	20c dull violet	4.00	*8.00*
98	A26	25c green	4.00	*8.00*
99	A26	50c purple	4.00	*8.00*
100	A26	75c scarlet	4.00	*19.50*
101	A26	1.25 l sapphire	4.00	*19.50*
		Nos. 95-101,C43 (8)	28.05	*126.50*
		Set, never hinged	42.50	

The Rome-Berlin Axis.

Catalogue values for unused stamps in this section, from this point to the end of the section, are for Never Hinged items.

United Kingdom of Libya

Stamps of Cyrenaica 1950 Surcharged in Black

For Use in Tripolitania

1951, Dec. 24 Unwmk. *Perf. 12½*

102	A2	1mal on 2m rose car	.25	.25
103	A2	2mal on 4m dk grn	.25	.25
104	A2	4mal on 8m red org	.25	.25
105	A2	5mal on 10m pur	.45	.45
106	A2	6mal on 12m red	.45	.45
a.		Inverted surcharge	30.00	30.00
107	A2	10mal on 20m dp bl	.85	.85
a.		Arabic "20" for "10"	25.00	25.00
108	A3	24mal on 50m choc & ultra	3.25	3.25
109	A3	48mal on 100m bl blk & car rose	13.50	13.50
110	A3	96mal on 200m vio & pur	30.00	30.00
111	A3	240mal on 500m dk grn & org	75.00	75.00
		Nos. 102-111 (10)	124.25	*124.25*

The surcharge is larger on Nos. 108 to 111.

Same Surcharge in Francs

For Use in Fezzan

112	A2	2fr on 2m rose car	.25	.50
113	A2	4fr on 4m dk grn	.25	.50
114	A2	8fr on 8m red org	.35	.70
115	A2	10fr on 10m pur	.50	1.00
116	A2	12fr on 12m red	.90	1.75
117	A2	20fr on 20m dp bl	2.00	*4.50*
118	A3	48fr on 50m choc & ultra	42.50	*45.00*
119	A3	96fr on 100m bl blk & car rose	42.50	*240.00*
120	A3	192fr on 200m vio & pur	120.00	*240.00*
121	A3	480fr on 500m dk grn & org	225.00	*260.00*
		Nos. 112-121 (10)	434.25	*793.95*

The surcharge is larger on Nos. 118-121.

A second printing of Nos. 118-121 has an elongated first character in second line of Arabic surcharge.

Cyrenaica Nos. 65-77 Overprinted in Black

For Use in Cyrenaica

122	A2	1m dark brown	.20	.40
123	A2	2m rose carmine	.30	.40
124	A2	3m orange	.30	.50
125	A2	4m dark green	35.00	55.00
126	A2	5m gray	.30	*.50*
127	A2	8m red orange	.75	*1.25*
128	A2	10m purple	1.25	*1.90*
129	A2	12m red	1.40	*2.25*
130	A2	20m deep blue	2.00	*3.75*
131	A3	50m choc & ultra	9.50	*19.00*
132	A3	100m bl blk & car rose	17.50	*24.00*
133	A3	200m violet & pur	55.00	*70.00*
134	A3	500m dk grn & org	180.00	*190.00*
		Nos. 122-134 (13)	303.50	*368.95*

Wider spacing between the two lines on Nos. 131-134.

King Idris

A27 A28

1952, Apr. 15 Engr. *Perf. 11½*

135	A27	2m yellow brown	.20	.20
136	A27	4m gray	.20	.20
137	A27	5m blue green	20.00	.65
138	A27	8m vermilion	.85	.55
139	A27	10m purple	20.00	.40
140	A27	12m lilac rose	1.75	.40
141	A27	20m deep blue	22.50	.90
142	A27	25m chocolate	22.50	.90
143	A28	50m brown & blue	3.00	1.40
144	A28	100m gray blk & car rose	5.25	3.00
145	A28	200m dk blue & pur	11.00	6.00
146	A28	500m dk grn & brn orange	37.50	21.00
		Nos. 135-146 (12)	144.75	35.60

For surcharge and overprints see #168, O1-O8.

Globe — A29

Perf. 13½x13

1955, Jan. 1 Photo. Wmk. 195

147	A29	5m yellow brown	2.00	1.30
148	A29	10m green	3.00	2.00
149	A29	30m violet	5.50	3.50
		Nos. 147-149 (3)	10.50	6.80

Arab Postal Union founding, July 1, 1954.

Nos. 147-149 Overprinted

1955, Aug. 1

No.	Type	Description	Unused	Used
150	A29	5m yellow brn	1.00	.65
151	A29	10m green	2.00	1.10
152	A29	30m violet	3.75	2.00
		Nos. 150-152 (3)	6.75	3.75

Arab Postal Congress, Cairo, Mar. 15.

Emblems of Tripolitania, Cyrenaica and Fezzan with Royal Crown — A30

1955 Engr. Wmk. 310 *Perf. 11½*

No.	Type	Description	Unused	Used
153	A30	2m lemon	2.00	.70
154	A30	3m slate blue	.20	.20
155	A30	4m gray green	2.75	1.25
156	A30	5m light blue grn	.85	.20
157	A30	10m violet	1.50	.20
158	A30	18m crimson	.25	.20
159	A30	20m orange	.50	.20
160	A30	30m blue	.85	.25
161	A30	35m brown	1.25	.25
162	A30	40m rose carmine	2.00	.60
163	A30	50m olive	1.25	.60
		Size: 27½x32½mm		
164	A30	100m dk green & pur	2.75	1.20
165	A30	200m ultra & rose car	13.00	2.50
166	A30	500m grn & orange	20.00	12.00
		Size: 26½x32mm		
167	A30	£1 ocher, brn & grn, *yel*	30.00	18.00
		Nos. 153-167 (15)	79.15	38.35

See Nos. 177-179, 192-206A.

No. 136 Surcharged

1955, Aug. 25 Unwmk.

No.	Type	Description	Unused	Used
168	A27	5m on 4m gray	2.00	.90

Tomb of El Senussi, Jagbub A31

Perf. 13x13½

1956, Sept. 14 Photo. Wmk. 195

No.	Type	Description	Unused	Used
169	A31	5m green	.50	.50
170	A31	10m bright violet	.60	.50
171	A31	15m rose carmine	1.40	1.25
172	A31	30m sapphire	2.25	1.40
		Nos. 169-172 (4)	4.75	3.65

Death centenary of the Imam Seyyid Mohammed Aly El Senussi (in 1859).

Map, Flags and UN Headquarters A32

Globe and Postal Emblems A33

1956, Dec. 14 Litho. *Perf. 13½x13*

No.	Type	Description	Unused	Used
173	A32	15m bl, ocher & ol bis	.75	.35
174	A32	35m bl, ocher & vio brn	1.60	.75

Libya's admission to the UN, 1st anniv.

1957 Wmk. 195 *Perf. 13½x13*

No.	Type	Description	Unused	Used
175	A33	15m blue	1.50	1.50
176	A33	500m yellow brown	22.00	12.00

Arab Postal Congress, Tripoli, Feb. 9.

Emblems Type of 1955

1957 Wmk. 310 Engr. *Perf. 11½*

No.	Type	Description	Unused	Used
177	A30	1m black, *yellow*	.20	.20
178	A30	2m bister brown	.20	.20
179	A30	4m brown carmine	.35	.35
		Nos. 177-179 (3)	.75	.75

UN Emblem and Broken Chain — A34

Unwmk.

1958, Dec. 10 Photo. *Perf. 14*

No.	Type	Description	Unused	Used
180	A34	10m bluish violet	.35	.25
181	A34	15m green	.60	.35
182	A34	30m ultramarine	1.50	.85
		Nos. 180-182 (3)	2.45	1.45

Universal Declaration of Human Rights, 10th anniv.

Date Palms and FAO Emblem A35

1959, Dec. 5 Unwmk. *Perf. 14*

No.	Type	Description	Unused	Used
183	A35	10m pale vio & black	.40	.25
184	A35	15m bluish grn & blk	.60	.45
185	A35	45m light blue & blk	1.50	1.20
		Nos. 183-185 (3)	2.50	1.90

1st Intl. Dates Conf., Tripoli, Dec. 5-11.

Arab League Center, Cairo, and Arms of Libya A36

Perf. 13x13½

1960, Mar. 22 Wmk. 328

No.	Type	Description	Unused	Used
186	A36	10m dull grn & blk	.60	.35

Opening of the Arab League Center and the Arab Postal Museum in Cairo.

Emblems of WRY and UN, Arms of Libya — A37

Palm Tree and Radio Mast — A38

1960, Apr. 7 Unwmk. *Perf. 14*

No.	Type	Description	Unused	Used
187	A37	10m violet & black	.60	.35
188	A37	45m blue & black	1.75	1.25

World Refugee Year, 7/1/59-6/30/60.

1960, Aug. 4 Engr. *Perf. 13x13½*

No.	Type	Description	Unused	Used
189	A38	10m violet	.35	.25
190	A38	15m blue green	.50	.25
191	A38	45m dk carmine rose	1.80	1.25
		Nos. 189-191 (3)	2.65	1.75

3rd Arab Telecommunications Conf., Tripoli, Aug. 4.

Emblems Type of 1955

1960 Wmk. 310 Engr. *Perf. 11½*

Size: 18x21½mm

No.	Type	Description	Unused	Used
192	A30	1m black, *gray*	.20	.20
193	A30	2m bis brn, *buff*	.20	.20
194	A30	3m blue, *bluish*	.20	.20
195	A30	4m brn car, *rose*	.20	.20
196	A30	5m grn, *greenish*	.20	.20
197	A30	10m vio, *pale vio*	.25	.20
198	A30	15m brown, *buff*	.25	.20
199	A30	20m orange, *buff*	.50	.20
200	A30	30m red, *pink*	.50	.20
201	A30	40m rose car, *rose*	.75	.25
202	A30	45m blue, *bluish*	.85	.25
203	A30	50m olive, *buff*	.85	.25
		Size: 27½x32½mm		
204	A30	100m dk grn & pur, *gray*	1.50	.70
205	A30	200m bl & rose car, *bluish*	4.25	1.40
206	A30	500m green & org, *greenish*	30.00	9.00
		Size: 26½x32mm		
206A	A30	£1 ocher, brn & grn, *brn*	35.00	18.00
		Nos. 192-206A (16)	75.70	31.65

Watchtower and Broken Chain — A39

1961, Aug. 9 Photo. Unwmk.

No.	Type	Description	Unused	Used
207	A39	5m lt yel grn & brn	.50	.25
208	A39	15m light blue & brn	.85	.35

Issued for Army Day, Aug. 9, 1961.

Map of Zelten Oil Field and Tanker at Marsa Brega — A40

1961, Oct. 25 *Perf. 11½*

No.	Type	Description	Unused	Used
209	A40	15m ol grn & buff	.50	.25
210	A40	50m red brn & pale vio	1.50	1.00
211	A40	100m ultra & blue	3.50	1.25
		Nos. 209-211 (3)	5.50	2.50

Opening of first oil pipe line in Libya.

Hands Breaking Chain, Tractor and Cows — A41

Designs: 50m, Modern highways and buildings. 100m, Machinery.

1961, Dec. 24 *Perf. 11½*

Granite Paper

No.	Type	Description	Unused	Used
212	A41	15m pale grn, grn & brown	.25	.25
213	A41	50m buff & brown	.90	.60
214	A41	100m sal, vio & brn	3.25	1.25
		Nos. 212-214 (3)	4.40	2.10

10th anniversary of independence.

Camel Riders — A42

15m, Well. 50m, Oil installations in desert.

1962, Feb. 20 Photo. *Perf. 12*

No.	Type	Description	Unused	Used
215	A42	10m choc & org brn	.85	.25
216	A42	15m plum & yel grn	1.00	.60
217	A42	50m emer & ultra	2.75	2.10
a.		Souv. sheet of 3, #215-217, imperf.	65.00	30.00
		Nos. 215-217 (3)	4.60	2.95

Intl. Fair, Tripoli, Feb. 20-Mar. 20.

Nos. 215-217 exist imperf. Value about twice that of perf.

Malaria Eradication Emblem and Palm — A43

Ahmed Rafik El Mehdawi (1898-1961), Poet — A44

1962, Apr. 7 Unwmk. *Perf. 11½*

No.	Type	Description	Unused	Used
218	A43	15m multicolored	.60	.50
219	A43	50m grn, yel & brn	1.50	1.20

WHO drive to eradicate malaria.

Exist imperf. Value $10.

Two imperf. souvenir sheets exist, one containing the 15m, the other the 50m. Sold for 20m and 70m respectively. Value for both, $34.

1962, July 6 Engr. *Perf. 13x14*

No.	Type	Description	Unused	Used
220	A44	15m green	.40	.20
221	A44	20m brown	.85	.50

El Mehdawi, 1st death anniv.

Clasped Hands and Scout Emblem — A45

Drop of Oil with New City, Desert, Oil Wells and Map of Coast Line — A46

Designs: 10m, 30m, Boy Scouts. 15m, 50m, Scout emblem and tents.

1962, July 13 Photo. *Perf. 12*

No.	Type	Description	Unused	Used
222	A45	5m yel, blk & red	.25	.20
223	A45	10m bl, blk & yel	.50	.25
224	A45	15m multicolored	.60	.50
		Nos. 222-224 (3)	1.35	.95

Souvenir Sheet

Imperf

No.	Type	Description	Unused	Used
225		Sheet of 3	20.00	20.00
a.		A45 20m yellow, black & red	5.00	5.00
b.		A45 30m blue, black & yellow	5.00	5.00
c.		A45 50m blue gray, yel, blk & grn	5.00	5.00

Third Libyan Scout meeting (Philia).

Nos. 222-224 exist imperf. Value for set, $3.

1962, Nov. 25 *Perf. 11x11½*

No.	Type	Description	Unused	Used
226	A46	15m grn & vio blk	.50	.25
227	A46	50m brn org & ol	1.40	.75

Opening of the Essider Terminal Sidrah pipeline system.

Centenary Emblem — A47

Litho. & Photo.

1963, Jan. 1 *Perf. 11½*

228 A47 10m rose, blk, red & bl .75 .40
229 A47 15m citron, blk, red & bl .85 .60
230 A47 20m gray, blk, red & bl 1.60 .85
Nos. 228-230 (3) 3.20 1.85

Centenary of the International Red Cross.

Rainbow and Arches over Map of Africa and Libya — A48

1963, Feb. 28 **Litho.** *Perf. 13½*

231 A48 15m multicolored .50 .35
232 A48 30m multicolored .85 .35
233 A48 50m multicolored 1.80 1.00
Nos. 231-233 (3) 3.15 1.70

Tripoli Intl. Fair "Gateway of Africa," Feb. 28-Mar. 28. Every other horizontal row inverted in sheet of 50 (25 tête bêche pairs). Value, set of tête bêche pairs, $6.50.

Date Palm and Well — A49

Designs: 15m, Camel and flock of sheep. 45m, Sower and tractor.

1963, Mar. 21 **Photo.** *Perf. 11½*

234 A49 10m green, lt bl & bis .50 .25
235 A49 15m pur, lt grn & bis .60 .50
236 A49 45m dk bl, sal & sep 1.60 1.00
Nos. 234-236 (3) 2.70 1.75

FAO "Freedom from Hunger" campaign.

Man with Whip and Slave Reaching for UN Emblem A50

1963, Dec. 10 **Unwmk.** *Perf. 11½*

237 A50 5m red brown & bl .25 .20
238 A50 15m deep claret & bl .50 .25
239 A50 50m green & blue 1.25 .75
Nos. 237-239 (3) 2.00 1.20

Universal Declaration of Human Rights, 15th anniv.

Exhibition Hall and Finger Pointing to Libya — A51

1964, Feb. 28 **Photo.** *Perf. 11½*

240 A51 10m red brn, gray grn & brn 1.00 .25
241 A51 15m pur, gray grn & brn 1.40 .60
242 A51 30m dk bl, gray grn & brn 2.00 1.40
Nos. 240-242 (3) 4.40 2.25

3rd Intl. Fair, Tripoli, Feb. 28-Mar. 20.

Child Playing with Blocks — A52

Design: 15m, Child in bird's nest.

1964, Mar. 22 *Perf. 11½*

243 A52 5m multicolored .25 .25
244 A52 15m multicolored .60 .25
245 A52 45m multicolored 1.75 .85
a. Souvenir sheet of 3, #243-245, imperf. 5.00 5.00
Nos. 243-245 (3) 2.60 1.35

Children's Day. Exist imperf. Value about 1½ times that of perf.
No. 245a sold for 100m.

Lungs and Stethoscope — A53

1964, Apr. 7 **Photo.** *Perf. 13½x14*

246 A53 20m deep purple 1.25 .60

Campaign against tuberculosis.

Map of Libya A54

1964, Apr. 27 **Unwmk.** *Perf. 11½*

247 A54 5m emerald & org .25 .20
248 A54 50m blue & yellow 1.50 .60

First anniversary of Libyan union.

Moth Emerging from Cocoon, Veiled and Modern Women — A55

Hand Giving Scout Sign, Scout and Libyan Flags — A56

1964, June 15 **Litho. & Engraved**

249 A55 10m vio bl & lt grn .35 .25
250 A55 20m vio blue & yel .75 .60
251 A55 35m vio bl & pink 1.25 1.10
a. Souv. sheet of 3, #249-251 5.50 5.50
Nos. 249-251 (3) 2.35 1.95

To honor Libyan women in a new epoch. No. 251a sold for 100m.

1964, July 24 **Photo.** *Perf. 12x11½*

Design: 20m, Libyan Scout emblem and hands.

252 A56 10m lt bl & multi .85 .35
253 A56 20m multicolored 1.75 .85
a. Souvenir sheet of 2, #252-253, imperf. 11.50 11.50

Opening of new Boy Scout headquarters; installation of Crown Prince Hassan al-Rida el Senussi as Chief Scout. No. 253a sold for 50m.

Nos. 252-253 exist imperf. Value about 1½ times that of perf.

Bayonet, Wreath and Map A57

Ahmed Bahloul el-Sharef A58

1964, Aug. 9 **Litho.** *Perf. 14x13½*

254 A57 10m yel grn & brn .25 .20
255 A57 20m org & blk .75 .35

Founding of the Senussi Army.

1964, Aug. 11 **Engr.** *Perf. 11½*

256 A58 15m lilac .50 .20
257 A58 20m greenish blue .85 .50

Poet Ahmed Bahloul el-Sharef, died 1953.

Soccer A59

1964, Oct. 1 **Litho.** *Perf. 14*

Black Inscriptions and Gold Olympic Rings

258 A59 5m shown .75 .50
259 A59 10m Bicycling .75 .50
260 A59 20m Boxing .75 .50
261 A59 30m Sprinter .75 .60
262 A59 35m Woman diver .75 .60
263 A59 50m Hurdling .75 .60
a. Block of 6, #258-263 5.00 5.00

18th Olympic Games, Tokyo, Oct. 10-25. No. 263a printed in sheet of 48. The two blocks in each double row are inverted in relation to the two blocks in the next row, providing various tete beche and se-tenant arrangements.

#258-263 exist imperf. Value for set, $27.50.

Perf. and imperf. souvenir sheets exist containing six 15m stamps in the designs and colors of Nos. 258-263. Sheets sold for 100m. Value for both, $32.50.

Arab Postal Union Emblem — A59a

1964, Dec. 1 **Photo.** *Perf. 11x11½*

264 A59a 10m yellow & blue .25 .20
265 A59a 15m pale vio & org brn .50 .25
266 A59a 30m lt yel grn & brn 1.40 .85
Nos. 264-266 (3) 2.15 1.30

Permanent Office of the APU, 10th anniv.

International Cooperation Year Emblem — A60

1965, Jan. 1 **Litho.** *Perf. 14½x14*

267 A60 5m vio bl & gold .50 .25
268 A60 15m rose car & gold 1.50 .70

Imperfs. exist. Value about twice that of perfs.

See Nos. C51-C51a.

European Bee Eater — A61

Birds: 5m, Long-legged buzzard, vert. 15m, Chestnut-bellied sandgrouse. 20m, Houbara bustard. 30m, Spotted sandgrouse. 40m, Libyan Barbary partridge, vert..

1965, Feb. 10 **Photo.** *Perf. 11½*

Granite Paper

Birds in Natural Colors

269 A61 5m gray & black 1.25 .50
270 A61 10m lt bl & org brn 2.00 .55
271 A61 15m lt green & blk 2.25 .60
272 A61 20m pale lil & blk 3.75 .85
273 A61 30m tan & dark brn 4.75 1.50
274 A61 40m dull yel & blk 5.50 1.90
Nos. 269-274 (6) 19.50 5.90

Map of Africa with Libya A62

1965, Feb. 28 **Photo.** *Perf. 11½*

Granite Paper

275 A62 50m multicolored 1.00 .55

4th Intl. Tripoli Fair, Feb. 28-Mar. 20.

Compass Rose, Rockets, Balloons and Stars — A63

1965, Mar. 23 **Litho.**

276 A63 10m multicolored .25 .20
277 A63 15m multicolored .50 .35
278 A63 50m multicolored 1.50 1.00
Nos. 276-278 (3) 2.25 1.55

Fifth World Meteorological Day.

ITU Emblem, Old and New Communication Equipment — A64

1965, May 17 **Unwmk.**

279 A64 10m sepia .25 .20
280 A64 20m red lilac .35 .20
281 A64 50m lilac rose 1.25 .90
Nos. 279-281 (3) 1.85 1.30

ITU, centenary.

Library Aflame and Lamp — A65

1965, June **Litho.** *Perf. 11½*

282 A65 15m multicolored .50 .25
283 A65 50m multicolored 1.25 .55

Burning of the Library of Algiers, June 7, 1962.

Rose — A66

Jet Plane and Globe — A67

1965, Aug. **Litho.** *Perf. 14*

284 A66 1m shown .25 .20
285 A66 2m Iris .25 .20
286 A66 3m Opuntia .35 .20
287 A66 4m Sunflower .75 .20
Nos. 284-287 (4) 1.60 .80

1965, Oct. Photo. *Perf. 11½*
288 A67 5m multicolored .25 .20
289 A67 10m multicolored .50 .20
290 A67 15m multicolored 1.00 .20
Nos. 288-290 (3) 1.75 .60

Issued to publicize Libyan Airlines.

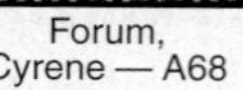

Forum, Cyrene — A68

Mausoleum at Germa — A69

Designs: 100m, Arch of Trajan. 200m, Temple of Apollo, Cyrene. 500m, Antonine Temple of Jupiter, Sabratha, horiz. £1, Theater, Sabratha.

Perf. 12x11½, 11½x12

1965, Dec. 24 Engr. Wmk. 310
291 A68 50m vio blue & olive 2.00 .60
292 A68 100m Prus bl & dp org 2.75 .85
293 A68 200m pur & Prus bl 6.50 1.50
294 A68 500m car rose & grn 15.00 4.00
295 A68 £1 grn & dp org 32.50 10.00
Nos. 291-295 (5) 58.75 16.95

Nos. 293-295 with "Kingdom of Libia" in both Arabic and English blocked out with a blue felt-tipped pen were issued June 21, 1970, by the Republic.

Perf. 11½

1966, Feb. 10 Unwmk. Litho.
296 A69 70m purple & salmon 3.00 1.00

"POLIGRAFICA & CARTEVALORI-NAPLES" and Libyan Coat of Arms printed on back in yellow green. See No. E13.

Booklet pane containing 4 No. 296 and 4 No. E13 exists. Value $30.

Globe in Space, Satellites — A70

1966, Feb. 28 *Perf. 12*
297 A70 15m multicolored .50 .20
298 A70 45m multicolored 1.00 .45
299 A70 55m multicolored 1.25 .65
Nos. 297-299 (3) 2.75 1.30

5th Intl. Fair at Tripoli, Feb. 28-Mar. 20.

Arab League Center, Cairo, and Emblem — A71

Litho. & Photo.

1966, Mar. 22 *Perf. 11*
300 A71 20m car, emer & blk .35 .35
301 A71 55m brt bl, ver & blk 1.50 .65

Issued to publicize the Arab League.

Souvenir Sheet

WHO Headquarters, Geneva, and Emblem — A72

1966, May 3 Litho. *Imperf.*
302 A72 50m multicolored 9.50 *15.00*

Inauguration of the WHO headquarters. See Nos. C55-C57.

Tuareg and Camel — A73

A74

Three Tuareg Riders — A75

Design: 20m, like 10m, facing left.

1966, June 20 Unwmk. *Perf. 10*
303 A73 10m bright red 1.25 .80
304 A73 20m ultramarine 2.75 1.50
305 A74 50m multicolored 6.00 4.00
a. Strip of 3, Nos. 303-305 11.00 8.50

Imperf

306 A75 100m multicolored 16.00 16.00

Gazelle — A76

Emblem — A77

Perf. 13x11, 11x13

1966, Aug. 12 Litho.
307 A76 5m lt grn, blk & red .50 .25
308 A77 25m multicolored .90 .35
309 A77 65m multicolored 2.50 .65
Nos. 307-309 (3) 3.90 1.25

1st Arab Girl Scout Camp (5m); 7th Arab Boy Scout Camp, Good Daim, Libya, Aug. 12 (25m, 60m).

UNESCO Emblem A78

1967, Jan. Litho. *Perf. 10x10½*
310 A78 15m multicolored .50 .25
311 A78 25m multicolored 1.10 .45

UNESCO, 20th anniv. (in 1966).

Castle of Columns, Tolemaide A79

Fair Emblem A80

Design: 55m, Sebha Fort, horiz.

Perf. 13x13½, 13½x13

1966, Dec. 24 Engr.
312 A79 25m lil, red brn & blk .65 .35
313 A79 55m blk, lil & red brn 1.25 .65

1967, Feb. 28 Photo. *Perf. 11½*
314 A80 15m multicolored .65 .20
315 A80 55m multicolored 1.00 .55

6th Intl. Fair, Tripoli, Feb. 28-Mar. 20.

Oil Tanker, Marsa Al Hariga Terminal — A81

1967, Feb. 14 Litho. *Perf. 10*
316 A81 60m multicolored 2.25 .75

Opening of Marsa Al Hariga oil terminal.

Tourist Year Emblem — A82

1967, May 1 Litho. *Perf. 10½x10*
317 A82 5m gray, blk & brt bl .20 .20
318 A82 10m lt bl, blk & brt bl .25 .25
319 A82 45m pink, blk & brt bl .75 .35
Nos. 317-319 (3) 1.20 .80

International Tourist Year.

Map of Mediterranean and Runners — A83

1967, Sept. 8 Litho. *Perf. 10½*
320 A83 5m shown .20 .20
321 A83 10m Javelin .20 .20
322 A83 15m Bicyling .25 .20
323 A83 45m Soccer .75 .55
324 A83 75m Boxing 1.10 .75
Nos. 320-324 (5) 2.50 1.90

5th Mediterranean Games, Tunis, Sept. 8-17.

A84 A85

Arab League emblem and hands reaching for knowledge.

1967, Oct. 1 Litho. *Perf. 12½x13*
325 A84 5m orange & dk pur .25 .20
326 A84 10m brt grn & dk pur .25 .20
327 A84 15m lilac & dk pur .25 .25
328 A84 25m blue & dk pur .50 .25
Nos. 325-328 (4) 1.25 .90

Literacy campaign.

1968, Jan. 15 Litho. *Perf. 13½x14*

Human rights flame.

329 A85 15m grn & vermilion .35 .20
330 A85 60m org & vio bl .90 .55

International Human Rights Year.

Map, Derrick, Plane and Camel Riders — A86

1968, Feb. 28 Photo. *Perf. 11½*
331 A86 55m car rose, brn & yel 1.25 .75

7th Intl. Fair, Tripoli, Feb. 28-Mar. 20.

Arab League Emblem A87

1968, Mar. 22 Engr. *Perf. 13½*
332 A87 10m blue gray & car .25 .20
333 A87 45m fawn & green .90 .65

Issued for Arab League Week.

Children, Statuary Group A88

Children's Day: 55m, Mother and children.

1968, Mar. 21 Litho. *Perf. 11*

334 A88 25m gray, blk & mag .65 .35
335 A88 55m gray & multi 1.25 .65

Hands Reaching for WHO Emblem — A89

1968, Apr. 7 Photo. *Perf. 13½x14½*

336 A89 25m rose cl, dk bl & gray bl .60 .25
337 A89 55m bl, blk & gray .90 .55

WHO, 20th anniversary.

From Oil Field to Tanker A90

1968, Apr. 23 Litho. *Perf. 11*

338 A90 10m multicolored .50 .20
339 A90 60m multicolored 1.50 .80

Opening of the Zueitina oil terminal.

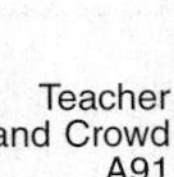

Teacher and Crowd A91

1968, Sept. 8 Litho. *Perf. 13½*

340 A91 5m bright pink .25 .20
341 A91 10m orange .25 .20
342 A91 15m blue .25 .25
343 A91 20m emerald .50 .50
Nos. 340-343 (4) 1.25 1.15

Literacy campaign.

Arab Labor Emblem A92

1968, Nov. 3 Photo. *Perf. 14x13½*

344 A92 10m multicolored .25 .20
345 A92 15m multicolored .50 .20

4th session of the Arab Labor Ministers' Conf., Tripoli, Nov. 3-10.

Wadi el Kuf Bridge and Road Sign — A93

1968, Dec. 25 Litho. *Perf. 11x11½*

346 A93 25m ultra & multi .40 .35
347 A93 60m emer & multi 1.00 .90

Opening of the Wadi el Kuf Bridge.

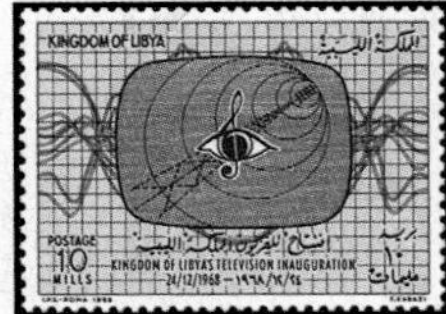

Television Screen and Chart A94

1968, Dec. 25 Photo. *Perf. 14x13½*

348 A94 10m yellow & multi .25 .20
349 A94 30m lilac & multi .90 .45

Inauguration of television service, Dec. 24.

Melons — A95

1969, Jan. Photo. *Perf. 11½*
Granite Paper

350 A95 5m shown .25 .20
351 A95 10m Peanuts .25 .20
352 A95 15m Lemons .25 .20
353 A95 20m Oranges .40 .20
354 A95 25m Peaches .65 .35
355 A95 35m Pears 1.25 .55
Nos. 350-355 (6) 3.05 1.70

Nos. 350-355 with "Kingdom of Libya" in both English and Arabic blocked out with a blue felt-tipped pen were issued in December, 1971, by the Republic.

Tripoli Fair Emblem A96

1969, Apr. 8
Granite Paper

356 A96 25m silver & multi .40 .20
357 A96 35m bronze & multi .65 .35
358 A96 40m gold & multi .75 .45
Nos. 356-358 (3) 1.80 1.00

8th Intl. Fair, Tripoli, Mar. 6-26.

Weather Balloon and Observer A97

1969, Mar. 21 Photo. *Perf. 14x13*

359 A97 60m gray & multi 1.50 .80

World Meteorological Day, Mar. 23.

Cogwheel and Workers A98

1969, Mar. 29 Litho. *Perf. 13½*

360 A98 15m blue & multi .25 .20
361 A98 55m salmon & multi .75 .55

10th anniversary of Social Insurance.

ILO Emblem — A99

1969, June 1 Photo. *Perf. 14*

362 A99 10m bl grn, blk & lt ol .25 .20
363 A99 60m car rose, blk & lt ol .90 .65

ILO, 50th anniversary.

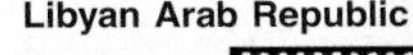

African Tourist Year Emblem — A100

1969, July *Perf. 11½*
Emblem in Emerald, Light Blue & Red

364 A100 15m emer & silver .45 .20
365 A100 30m blk & gold .90 .65

Issued to publicize African Tourist Year.

Libyan Arab Republic

Soldiers, Tanks and Planes — A101

Radar, Flags and Carrier Pigeon — A102

1969, Dec. 7 Photo. *Perf. 12x12½*

366 A101 5m org & multi .45 .20
367 A101 10m ultra & multi .70 .40
368 A101 15m multicolored 1.00 .50
369 A101 25m multicolored 1.50 .70
370 A101 45m brt bl & multi 1.75 1.10
371 A101 60m multicolored 3.00 1.50
Nos. 366-371 (6) 8.40 4.40

Establishment of the Libyan Arab Republic, Sept. 1, 1969. See Nos. 379-384.

1970, Mar. 1 Photo. *Perf. 11½*
Granite Paper

372 A102 15m multicolored .70 .20
373 A102 20m multicolored 1.10 .40
374 A102 25m multicolored 1.50 .50
375 A102 40m multicolored 2.10 1.10
Nos. 372-375 (4) 5.40 2.20

Map of Arab League Countries, Flag and Emblem A102a

1970, Mar. 22

376 A102a 10m lt bl, brn & grn .35 .20
377 A102a 15m org, brn & grn .60 .20
378 A102a 20m ol, brn & grn 1.00 .45
Nos. 376-378 (3) 1.95 .85

25th anniversary of the Arab League.

Type A101 Redrawn — A103

1970, May 2 Photo. *Perf. 12x12½*

379 A103 5m org & multi .40 .20
380 A103 10m ultra & multi .70 .60
381 A103 15m multicolored 1.00 .50
382 A103 25m multicolored 1.50 1.40
383 A103 45m brt bl & multi 1.75 1.10
384 A103 60m multicolored 3.00 1.50
Nos. 379-384 (6) 8.35 5.30

On Nos. 379-384 the numerals are in black, the bottom inscription is in 2 lines and several other changes.

Inauguration of UPU Headquarters, Bern — A104

1970, May 20 Photo. *Perf. 11½x11*

385 A104 10m multicolored .25 .20
386 A104 25m multicolored .60 .20
387 A104 60m multicolored 1.25 .65
Nos. 385-387 (3) 2.10 1.05

Arms of Libyan Arab Republic A105

Flags, Soldiers and Tank A106

1970, June 20 Photo. *Perf. 11*

388 A105 15m black & brt rose .25 .20
389 A105 25m vio bl, yel & brt rose .50 .20
390 A105 45m emer, yel & brt rose 1.75 .45
Nos. 388-390 (3) 2.50 .85

Evacuation of US military base in Libya.

1970, Sept. 1 Photo. *Perf. 11x11½*

391 A106 20m multicolored .75 .20
392 A106 25m multicolored 1.00 .55
393 A106 30m blue & multi 1.60 .75
Nos. 391-393 (3) 3.35 1.50

Libyan Arab Republic, 1st anniv.

UN Emblem, Dove and Scales — A107

1970, Oct. 24 Photo. *Perf. 11x11½*

394 A107 5m org & multi .60 .35
395 A107 10m olive & multi .90 .45
396 A107 60m multicolored 2.50 .90
Nos. 394-396 (3) 4.00 1.70

25th anniversary of the United Nations.

Map and Flags of UAR, Libya, Sudan A107a

1970, Dec. 27 Photo. *Perf. 11½*
397 A107a 15m lt grn, car & blk 7.00 2.25

Signing of the Charter of Tripoli affirming the unity of UAR, Libya and the Sudan, Dec. 27, 1970.

UN Emblem, Dove and Globe — A108

1971, Jan. 10 Litho. *Perf. 12x11½*
398 A108 15m multicolored .60 .20
399 A108 20m multicolored .90 .45
400 A108 60m lt vio & multi 2.50 .90
Nos. 398-400 (3) 4.00 1.55

UN declaration on granting of independence to colonial countries and peoples, 10th anniv.

Education Year Emblem — A109

Al Fatah Fighter — A110

1971, Jan. 16
401 A109 5m red, blk & ocher .25 .20
402 A109 10m red, blk & emer .60 .55
403 A109 20m red, blk & vio bl 1.60 .80
Nos. 401-403 (3) 2.45 1.55

International Education Year.

1971, Mar. 14 Photo. *Perf. 11*
404 A110 5m ol & multi .50 .20
405 A110 10m yel & multi .80 .20
406 A110 100m multicolored 1.90 .20
Nos. 404-406 (3) 3.20 .60

Fight for the liberation of Palestine.

Tripoli Fair Emblem — A111

10th Anniv. of OPEC — A112

1971, Mar. 18 Litho. *Perf. 14*
407 A111 15m multicolored .35 .20
408 A111 30m org & multi .90 .45

9th International Fair at Tripoli.

1971, May 29 Litho. *Perf. 12*
409 A112 10m yellow & brown .25 .20
410 A112 70m pink & vio bl 1.60 .65

Globe and Waves A113

1971, June 10 *Perf. 14½x13½*
411 A113 25m brt grn, blk & vio bl .50 .20
412 A113 35m gray & multi 1.25 1.00

3rd World Telecommunications Day, May 17, 1971.

Map of Africa and Telecommunications Network — A114

1971, June 10
413 A114 5m yel, blk & grn .20 .20
414 A114 15m dl bl, blk & grn .40 .20

Pan-African telecommunications system.

Torchbearer and Banner — A115

Ramadan Suehli — A116

1971, June 15 Photo. *Perf. 11½x12*
415 A115 5m yel & multi .25 .20
416 A115 10m org & multi .35 .35
417 A115 15m multicolored .50 .45
Nos. 415-417 (3) 1.10 1.00

Evacuation of US military base, 1st anniv.

1971, Aug. 24 *Perf. 14x14½*
418 A116 15m multicolored .20 .20
419 A116 55m bl & multi 1.00 .55

Ramadan Suehli (1879-1920), freedom fighter.

See #422-423, 426-427, 439-440, 479-480.

Date Palm — A117

Gamal Abdel Nasser (1918-1970), President of Egypt — A118

1971, Sept. 1
420 A117 5m multicolored .20 .20
421 A117 15m multicolored 1.25 1.25

Sept. 1, 1969 Revolution, 2nd anniv.

Portrait Type of 1971

Portrait: Omar el Mukhtar (1858-1931), leader of the Martyrs.

1971, Sept. 16 *Perf. 14x14½*
422 A116 5m lt grn & multi .20 .20
423 A116 100m multicolored 2.50 1.50

1971, Sept. 28 Photo. *Perf. 11x11½*
424 A118 5m lil, grn & blk .35 .20
425 A118 15m grn, lil & blk 1.25 .20

Portrait Type of 1971

Ibrahim Usta Omar (1908-50), patriotic poet.

1971, Oct. 8 Litho. *Perf. 14x14½*
426 A116 25m vio bl & multi .60 .60
427 A116 30m multicolored 1.10 .45

Racial Equality Emblem A119

Arab Postal Union Emblem — A120

1971, Oct. 24 *Perf. 13½x14½*
428 A119 25m multicolored .60 .20
429 A119 35m multicolored 1.10 .45

Intl. Year Against Racial Discrimination.

1971, Nov. 6 Litho. *Perf. 14½*
Emblem in Black, Yellow and Blue
430 A120 5m red .25 .20
431 A120 10m violet .40 .20
432 A120 15m bright rose lilac .40 .20
Nos. 430-432 (3) 1.05 .60

Conference of Sofar, Lebanon, establishing Arab Postal Union, 25th anniv.

Postal Union Emblem and Letter A121

25m, 55m, APU emblem, letter and dove.

1971, Dec. Photo. *Perf. 11½x11*
433 A121 10m org brn, bl & blk .35 .20
434 A121 15m org, lt bl & blk .50 .35
435 A121 25m lt grn, org & blk .75 .55
436 A121 55m lt brn, yel & blk 1.60 .70
Nos. 433-436 (4) 3.20 1.80

10th anniversary of African Postal Union.
Issued: 25m, 55m, 12/2; 10m, 15m, 12/12.

Despite the change from milliemes to dirhams in 1972, both currencies appear on stamps until August.

Book Year Emblem A122

Coat of Arms A123

1972, Jan. 1 Litho. *Perf. 12½x13*
437 A122 15m ultra, brn, gold & blk .35 .35
438 A122 20m gold, brn, ultra & blk .60 .60

International Book Year.

Portrait Type of 1971

Ahmed Gnaba (1898-1968), poet of unity.

1972, Jan. 12 *Perf. 14x14½*
439 A116 20m red & multi .60 .20
440 A116 35m olive & multi .85 .45

1972, Feb. 10 Photo. *Perf. 14½*
Size: 19x23mm
441 A123 5m gray & multi .20 .20
442 A123 10m lt ol & multi .20 .20
443 A123 15d lilac & multi .20 .20
445 A123 25m lt bl & multi .25 .20
446 A123 30m rose & multi .35 .20
447 A123 35m lt ol & multi .45 .20
448 A123 40m dl yel & multi .60 .20
449 A123 45m lt grn & multi .75 .35
451 A123 55m multicolored 1.00 .50
452 A123 60m bister & multi 1.90 .65
453 A123 65d multicolored .75 .55
454 A123 70d lt vio & multi 1.00 .65
455 A123 80d ocher & multi 1.50 .80
456 A123 90m bl & multi 1.90 .90

Size: 27x32mm
Perf. 14x14½
457 A123 100d multicolored 2.25 1.20
458 A123 200d multicolored 3.75 2.25
459 A123 500d multicolored 9.50 6.50
460 A123 £1 multicolored 17.50 11.00
Nos. 441-460 (18) 44.05 26.75

During the transition from milliemes and pounds to dirhams and dinars, stamps were issued in both currencies.

A124

A124a

A124b

Coil Stamps

1972, July 27 Photo. *Perf. 14½x14*
461 A124 5m sl bl, ocher & black 2.75 2.25
462 A124a 20m bl, lil & blk 12.00 2.25
463 A124b 50m bl, ol & blk 27.50 5.50
Nos. 461-463 (3) 42.25 10.00

See Nos. 496-498, 575-577.

Tombs at Ghirza — A125

Fair Emblem A126

Designs: 10m, Kufic inscription, Agedabia, horiz. 15m, Marcus Aurelius Arch, Tripoli. 25m, Exchange of weapons, mural from Wan Amil Cave. 55m, Garamanthian (Berber) chariot, petroglyph, Wadi Zigza. 70m, Nymph Cyrene strangling a lion, bas-relief, Cyrene.

1972, Feb. 15 Litho. *Perf. 14*
464 A125 5m lilac & multi .50 .50
465 A125 10m multicolored .50 .50
466 A125 15m dp org & multi 1.00 .35
467 A125 25m emer & multi 1.50 .90
468 A125 55m scar & multi 3.50 .90
469 A125 70m ultra & multi 7.00 1.25
Nos. 464-469 (6) 14.00 4.40

1972, Mar. 1
470 A126 25d gray & multi .60 .20
471 A126 35d multicolored .65 .20
472 A126 50d multicolored 1.40 .35
473 A126 70d multicolored 1.60 .60
Nos. 470-473 (4) 4.25 1.35

10th International Fair at Tripoli.

Dissected Arm, and Heart — A127

"Arab Unity" — A128

1972, Apr. 7 *Perf. 14½*

474 A127 15d multicolored 1.50 .45
475 A127 25d multicolored 3.25 1.00

"Your heart is your health," World Health Day.

Litho. & Engr.

1972, Apr. 17 *Perf. 13½x13*

476 A128 15d bl, yel & blk .25 .20
477 A128 20d lt grn, yel & blk .60 .20
478 A128 25d lt ver, yel & blk 1.25 .80
Nos. 476-478 (3) 2.10 1.20

Fed. of Arab Republics Foundation, 1st anniv.

Portrait Type of 1971

Suleiman el Baruni (1870-1940), patriotic writer.

1972, May 1 **Litho.** *Perf. 14x14½*

479 A116 10m yellow & multi 1.25 .80
480 A116 70m dp org & multi 2.00 1.00

Environment Emblem A129

Olympic Emblems A130

1972, Aug. 15 **Litho.** *Perf. 14½*

481 A129 15m red & multi .60 .20
482 A129 55m green & multi 1.40 .40

UN Conference on Human Environment, Stockholm, June 5-16.

1972, Aug. 26

483 A130 25d brt bl & multi 2.00 .60
484 A130 35d red & multi 3.00 1.25

20th Olympic Games, Munich, 8/26-9/11.

Emblem and Broken Chain A131

Dome of the Rock, Jerusalem A132

1972, Oct. 1 **Litho.** *Perf. 14x13½*

485 A131 15d blue & multi .40 .20
486 A131 25d yellow & multi .90 .35

Libyan Arab Republic, 3rd anniv.

1972 *Perf. 12½x13*

487 A132 10d multicolored .40 .20
488 A132 25d multicolored .60 .20

Nicolaus Copernicus (1473-1543), Polish Astronomer A133

Blind Person, Books, Loom and Basket A135

Eagle and Fair Buildings A134

Design: 25d, Copernicus in Observatory, by Jan Matejko, horiz.

Perf. 14½x13½, 13½x14½

1973, Feb. 26

489 A133 15d yellow & multi .40 .20
490 A133 25d blue & multi .60 .35

1973, Mar. 1 *Perf. 13½x14½*

491 A134 5d dull red & multi .40 .20
492 A134 10d blue grn & multi .60 .20
493 A134 15d vio blue & multi 1.25 .20
Nos. 491-493 (3) 2.25 .60

11th International Fair at Tripoli.

1973, Apr. 18 **Photo.** *Perf. 12x11½*

494 A135 20d gray & multi 8.25 1.60
495 A135 25d dull yel & multi 12.00 5.25

Role of the blind in society.

Coil Stamps
Numeral Type of 1972 Denominations in Dirhams

A135a

A135b

A135c

1973, Apr. 26 **Photo.** *Perf. 14½x14*

496 A135a 5d sl bl, ocher & blk 1.00 1.00
497 A135b 20d blue, lilac & blk 1.50 1.50
498 A135c 50d blue, olive & blk 5.50 5.50
Nos. 496-498 (3) 8.00 8.00

Map of Africa — A136

1973, May 25 **Photo.** *Perf. 11x11½*

499 A136 15d yel, green & brown .50 .20
500 A136 25d lt yel grn, grn & blk 1.00 .50

"Freedom in Unity" (Org. for African Unity).

INTERPOL Emblem and General Secretariat, Paris — A138

Perf. 13½x14½

1973, June 30 **Litho.**

501 A138 10d lilac & multi .25 .20
502 A138 15d ocher & multi .50 .20
503 A138 25d lt grn & multi .75 .20
Nos. 501-503 (3) 1.50 .60

50th anniv. of Intl. Criminal Police Org.

Map of Libya, Houses, People, Factories, Tractor A139

1973, July 15 **Photo.** *Perf. 11½*

504 A139 10d rose red, black & ultra 4.25 .85
505 A139 25d ultra, blk & grn 6.00 1.90
506 A139 35d grn, blk & org 11.50 3.75
Nos. 504-506 (3) 21.75 6.50

General census.

UN Emblem — A140

1973, Aug. 1 *Perf. 12½x11*

507 A140 5d ver, blk & bl .25 .20
508 A140 10d yel grn, blk & bl .50 .50

Intl. meteorological cooperation, cent.

Soccer — A141

1973, Aug. 10 **Photo.** *Perf. 11½*

509 A141 5d yel grn & dk brn .50 .20
510 A141 25d orange & dk brn 1.10 .70

2nd Palestinian Cup Soccer Tournament.

Torch and Grain — A142

Writing Hand, Lamp and Globe — A143

1973, Sept. 1 **Litho.** *Perf. 14*

511 A142 15d brown & multi .50 .20
512 A142 25d emer & multi 1.40 .20

4th anniv. of Sept. 1 Revolution.

1973, Sept. 8

513 A143 25d multicolored .60 .60

Literacy campaign.

Gate of First City Hall A144

Militia, Flag and Factories A145

1973, Sept. 18 *Perf. 13*

514 A144 10d shown .50 .50
515 A144 25d Khondok fountain .60 .60
516 A144 35d Clock tower .90 .35
Nos. 514-516 (3) 2.00 1.45

Centenary of Tripoli as a municipality.

1973, Oct. 7 **Photo.** *Perf. 11½x11*

517 A145 15d yel, blk & red .50 .20
518 A145 25d green & multi .75 .35

Libyan Militia.

Revolutionary Proclamation by Khadafy — A146

70d, as 25d, with English inscription.

1973, Oct. 15 **Litho.** *Perf. 12½*

519 A146 25d orange & multi .50 .50
520 A146 70d green & multi 1.50 .75

Proclamation of People's Revolution by Pres. Muammar Khadafy.

FAO Emblem, Camel Pulling Plow A147

1973, Nov. 1 **Photo.** *Perf. 11*

521 A147 10d ocher & multi .20 .20
522 A147 25d dk brn & multi .50 .50
523 A147 35d black & multi .75 .35
Nos. 521-523 (3) 1.45 1.05

World Food Org., 10th anniv.

Human Rights Flame — A148

1973, Dec. 20 **Photo.** *Perf. 11x11½*

524 A148 25d pur, car & dk bl .35 .35
525 A148 70d lt grn, car & dk bl 1.50 .65

Universal Declaration of Human Rights, 25th anniv.

Fish A149

Designs: Various fish from Libyan waters.

1973, Dec. 31 Photo. *Perf. 14x13½*

526	A149	5d light blue & multi	.65	.50
527	A149	10d light blue & multi	1.25	.45
528	A149	15d light blue & multi	1.90	.55
529	A149	20d light blue & multi	2.75	.60
530	A149	25d light blue & multi	5.25	1.50
		Nos. 526-530 (5)	11.80	3.60

1975, Jan. 5

526a	A149	5d greenish blue & multi	2.25	1.50
527a	A149	10d greenish blue & multi	4.50	1.50
528a	A149	15d greenish blue & multi	4.50	1.50
529a	A149	20d greenish blue & multi	6.50	.75
530a	A149	25d greenish blue & multi	8.50	2.75
		Nos. 526a-530a (5)	26.25	8.00

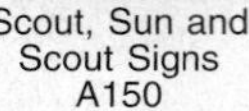

Scout, Sun and Scout Signs A150

Fair Emblem, Flags of Participants A151

1974, Feb. 1 Litho. *Perf. 11½*

531	A150	5d blue & multi	1.25	.40
532	A150	20d light lilac & multi	3.50	.65
533	A150	25d light green & multi	5.75	2.60
		Nos. 531-533 (3)	10.50	3.65

Libyan Boy Scouts.

1974, Mar. 1 Litho. *Perf. 12x11½*

534	A151	10d lt ultra & multi	.65	.40
535	A151	25d tan & multi	1.00	.55
536	A151	35d lt green & multi	1.90	.25
		Nos. 534-536 (3)	3.55	1.20

12th Tripoli International Fair.

Protected Family, WHO Emblem — A152

Minaret and Star — A153

1974, Apr. 7 Litho. *Perf. 12½*

537	A152	5d lt green & multi	.35	.20
538	A152	25d red & multi	.60	.60

World Health Day.

1974, Apr. 16 *Perf. 11½x11*

539	A153	10d pink & multi	.50	.50
540	A153	25d yellow & multi	1.00	.60
541	A153	35d orange & multi	1.40	.50
		Nos. 539-541 (3)	2.90	1.60

City University of Bengazi, inauguration.

UPU Emblem and Star — A154

Traffic Signs — A156

1974, May 22 Litho. *Perf. 13½x14½*

542	A154	25d multicolored	7.50	1.10
543	A154	70d multicolored	14.00	2.25

Centenary of Universal Postal Union.

1974, June 8 Photo. *Perf. 11*

547	A156	5d gold & multi	.20	.20
548	A156	10d gold & multi	.40	.20
549	A156	25d gold & multi	.50	.20
		Nos. 547-549 (3)	1.10	.60

Automobile and Touring Club of Libya.

Tank, Oil Refinery, Book — A157

Symbolic "5" — A158

1974, Sept. 1 Litho. *Perf. 14*

550	A157	5d red & multi	.20	.20
551	A157	20d violet & multi	.40	.40
552	A157	25d vio bl & multi	.40	.40
553	A157	35d green & multi	.50	.50
		Nos. 550-553 (4)	1.50	1.50

Souvenir Sheet

Perf. 13

554	A158	55d yel & maroon	9.50	9.50

Revolution of Sept. 1, 5th anniv. English inscription on No. 553.

WPY Emblem and Crowd — A159

Libyan Woman — A160

1974, Oct. 19 *Perf. 14*

555	A159	25d multicolored	.35	.20
556	A159	35d lt brn & multi	.75	.60

World Population Year.

1975, Mar. 1 Litho. *Perf. 13x12½*

Libyan Costumes: 10d, 15d, Women. 20d, Old man. 25d, Man riding camel. 50d, Man on horseback.

557	A160	5d org yel & multi	.20	.20
558	A160	10d org yel & multi	.20	.20
559	A160	15d org yel & multi	.50	.20
560	A160	20d org yel & multi	.75	.20
561	A160	25d org yel & multi	1.50	.75
562	A160	50d org yel & multi	2.75	.75
		Nos. 557-562 (6)	5.90	2.30

Congress Emblem — A161

1975, Mar. 4 Litho. *Perf. 12x12½*

563	A161	10d brown & multi	.20	.20
564	A161	25d vio & multi	.40	.40
565	A161	35d gray & multi	.75	.20
		Nos. 563-565 (3)	1.35	.80

Arab Labor Congress.

Teacher Pointing to Blackboard A162

1975, Mar. 10 *Perf. 11½*

566	A162	10d gold & multi	.20	.20
567	A162	25d gold & multi	.50	.20

Teacher's Day.

Bodies, Globe, Proclamation A163

Woman and Man in Library — A164

1975, Apr. 7 Litho. *Perf. 12½*

568	A163	20d lilac & multi	.40	.40
569	A163	25d emer & multi	.50	.20

World Health Day.

1975, May 25 Litho. *Perf. 12½*

570	A164	10d bl grn & multi	.20	.20
571	A164	25d olive & multi	.50	.50
572	A164	35d lt vio & multi	.60	.60
		Nos. 570-572 (3)	1.30	1.30

Libyan Arab Book Exhibition.

Festival Emblem — A165

Games Emblem and Arms — A166

1975, July 5 Litho. *Perf. 13x12½*

573	A165	20d lt bl & multi	.40	.40
574	A165	25d orange & multi	.50	.50

2nd Arab Youth Festival.

Coil Stamps

Redrawn Type of 1973 Without "LAR"

1975, Aug. 15 Photo. *Perf. 14½x14*

575	A124	5d blue, org & blk	.50	.50
576	A124	20d blue, yel & blk	1.00	1.00
577	A124	50d blue, grn & blk	2.00	2.00
		Nos. 575-577 (3)	3.50	3.50

1975, Aug. 23 *Perf. 13x12½*

578	A166	10d salmon & multi	.20	.20
579	A166	25d lilac & multi	.50	.50
580	A166	50d yellow & multi	1.40	.40
		Nos. 578-580 (3)	2.10	1.10

7th Mediterranean Games, Algiers, 8/23-9/6.

Peace Dove, Symbols of Agriculture and Industry — A167

Khadafy's Head Over Desert — A168

Design: 70d, Peace dove, diff.

1975, Sept. Litho. *Perf. 13x12½*

581	A167	25d multicolored	.40	.20
582	A167	70d multicolored	1.40	.50

Souvenir Sheet

Imperf

Litho. & Embossed

583	A168	100d multicolored	6.00	6.00

6th anniversary of Sept. 1 revolution. No. 583 contains one stamp with simulated perforations.

Khalil Basha Mosque — A169

Al Kharruba Mosque — A170

Mosques: 10d, Sidi Abdulla El Shaab. 15d, Sidi Ali El Fergani. 25d, Katikhtha. 30d, Murad Agha. 35d, Maulai Mohammed.

1975, Dec. 13 Litho. *Perf. 12½*

584	A169	5d gray & multi	.20	.20
585	A169	10d purple & multi	.20	.20
586	A169	15d green & multi	.20	.20
587	A170	20d ocher & multi	.40	.20
588	A170	25d multicolored	.40	.20
589	A170	30d multicolored	.50	.20
590	A170	35d lilac & multi	.75	.60
		Nos. 584-590 (7)	2.65	1.80

Mohammed's 1405th birthday.

Arms of Libya and People — A171

Islamic- Christian Dialogue Emblem — A172

1976, Jan. 15 Photo. *Perf. 13*

591 A171 35d blue & multi .50 .20
592 A171 40d multicolored .60 .20

General National (People's) Congress.

1976, Feb. 5 Litho. *Perf. 13x12½*

593 A172 40d gold & multi .60 .20
594 A172 115d gold & multi 1.90 .90

Seminar of Islamic-Christian Dialogue, Tripoli, Feb. 1-5.

Woman Blowing Horn — A173

National Costumes: 20d, Lancer. 30d, Drummer. 40d, Bagpiper. 100d, Woman carrying jug on head.

1976, Mar. 1 Litho. *Perf. 13x12½*

595 A173 10d multicolored .20 .20
596 A173 20d multicolored .50 .40
597 A173 30d pink & multi 1.00 .20
598 A173 40d multicolored 1.25 .20
599 A173 100d yel & multi 3.00 .50
Nos. 595-599 (5) 5.95 1.50

14th Tripoli International Fair.

Telephones, 1876 and 1976, ITU and UPU Emblems — A174

70d, Alexander Graham Bell, telephone, satellites, radar, ITU & UPU emblems.

1976, Mar. 10 Photo. *Perf. 13*

600 A174 40d multicolored 2.50 .80
a. Souvenir sheet of 4 10.00 10.00
601 A174 70d multicolored 4.00 .80
a. Souvenir sheet of 4 16.50 16.50

Centenary of first telephone call by Alexander Graham Bell, Mar. 10, 1876.

Nos. 600a and 601a exist imperf. Value, both sheets $100.

Mother and Child — A175

Hands, Eye and Head — A176

1976, Mar. 21 *Perf. 12*

602 A175 85d gray & multi 1.50 1.25
603 A175 110d pink & multi 1.60 1.50

International Children's Day.

1976, Apr. 7 Photo. *Perf. 13½x13*

604 A176 30d multicolored .35 .35
605 A176 35d multicolored .50 .50
606 A176 40d multicolored .60 .60
Nos. 604-606 (3) 1.45 1.45

"Foresight prevents blindness;" World Health Day.

Little Bittern A177

Birds of Libya: 10d, Great gray shrike. 15d, Songbird. 20d, European bee-eater, vert. 25d, Hoopoe.

Perf. 13x13½, 13½x13

1976, May 1 Litho.

607 A177 5d orange & multi .65 .50
608 A177 10d ultra & multi 1.40 1.10
609 A177 15d rose & multi 2.75 1.40
610 A177 20d yellow & multi 4.75 1.50
611 A177 25d blue & multi 9.50 2.75
Nos. 607-611 (5) 19.05 7.25

Al Barambekh A178

Bicycling — A179

Designs: 15d, Whale, horiz. 30d, Lizard (alwaral), horiz. 40d, Mastodon skull, horiz. 70d, Hawk. 115d, Wild mountain sheep.

1976, June 20 Litho. *Perf. 12½*

612 A178 10d multicolored 1.40 1.10
613 A178 15d multicolored 2.50 1.90
614 A178 30d multicolored 3.00 2.40
615 A178 40d multicolored 5.00 4.25
616 A178 70d multicolored 8.75 7.25
617 A178 115d multicolored 14.50 12.25
Nos. 612-617 (6) 35.15 29.15

Museum of Natural History.

1976, July 17 Litho. *Perf. 12x11½*

Granite Paper

618 A179 15d shown .20 .20
619 A179 25d Boxing .50 .50
620 A179 70d Soccer 1.50 1.50
Nos. 618-620 (3) 2.20 2.20

Souvenir Sheet

621 A179 150d Symbolic of various sports 16.00 16.00

21st Olympic Games, Montreal, Canada, July 17-Aug. 1.

Tree Growing from Globe — A180

Symbols of Agriculture and Industry — A181

Drummer and Pipeline — A182

1976, Aug. 9 *Perf. 13*

622 A180 115d multicolored 1.25 .90

5th Conference of Non-Aligned Countries, Colombo, Sri Lanka, Aug. 9-19.

Beginning with No. 622 numerous issues are printed with multiple coats of arms in pale green on back of stamps.

1976, Sept. 1 *Perf. 14½x14*

623 A181 30d yel & multi .40 .20
624 A181 40d multicolored .50 .20
625 A181 100d multicolored 1.25 .90
Nos. 623-625 (3) 2.15 1.30

Souvenir Sheet

Perf. 13

626 A182 200d multicolored 6.00 6.00

Sept. 1 Revolution, 7th anniv.

Sports, Torch and Emblems A183

Chess Board, Rook, Knight, Emblem — A184

145d, Symbolic wrestlers and various emblems.

1976, Oct. 6 Litho. *Perf. 13*

627 A183 15d multicolored .20 .20
628 A183 30d multicolored .35 .35
629 A183 100d multicolored 1.60 .90
Nos. 627-629 (3) 2.15 1.45

Souvenir Sheet

630 A183 145d multi, horiz. 4.50 4.50

5th Arab Games, Damascus, Syria.

1976, Oct. 24 Photo. *Perf. 11½*

631 A184 15d pink & multi 2.10 .45
632 A184 30d buff & multi 3.50 1.00
633 A184 100d multicolored 10.50 2.00
Nos. 631-633 (3) 16.10 3.45

The "Against" (protest) Chess Olympiad, Tripoli, Oct. 24-Nov. 15.

A185

Designs: Various local flowers.

1976, Nov. 1 Photo. *Perf. 11½*

Granite Paper

634 A185 15d lilac & multi .35 .35
635 A185 20d multicolored .35 .35
636 A185 35d yellow & multi .80 .20
637 A185 40d salmon & multi 1.25 .35
638 A185 70d multicolored 3.00 .50
Nos. 634-638 (5) 5.75 1.75

International Archives Council Emblem and Document — A186

1976, Nov. 10 Litho. *Perf. 13x13½*

639 A186 15d brown, org & buff .20 .20
640 A186 35d brn, brt grn & buff .35 .35
641 A186 70d brown, blue & buff .75 .75
Nos. 639-641 (3) 1.30 1.30

Arab Regional Branch of International Council on Archives, Baghdad.

Holy Ka'aba and Pilgrims A187

Numeral A188

1976, Dec. 12 Litho. *Perf. 14*

642 A187 15d multicolored .20 .20
643 A187 30d multicolored .20 .20
644 A187 70d multicolored .80 .80
645 A187 100d multicolored 1.00 1.00
Nos. 642-645 (4) 2.20 2.20

Pilgrimage to Mecca.

Coil Stamps

1977, Jan. 15 Photo. *Perf. 14½x14*

646 A188 5d multicolored .20 .20
647 A188 20d multicolored .35 .35
648 A188 50d multicolored .90 .90
Nos. 646-648 (3) 1.45 1.45

Covered Basket — A189

Designs: 20d, Leather bag. 30d, Vase. 40d, Embroidered slippers. 50d, Ornate saddle. 100d, Horse with saddle and harness.

1977, Mar. 1 Litho. *Perf. 12½x12*

649 A189 10d multicolored .20 .20
650 A189 20d multicolored .20 .20
651 A189 30d multicolored .35 .20
652 A189 40d multicolored .60 .35
653 A189 50d multicolored 1.00 .35
Nos. 649-653 (5) 2.35 1.30

Souvenir Sheet
Imperf

654 A189 100d multicolored 4.50 4.50

15th Tripoli International Fair. No. 654 contains one stamp 49x53mm with simulated perforations.

Girl and Flowers, UNICEF Emblem A190

Children's drawings, UNICEF Emblem and: 30d, Clothing store. 40d, Farm yard.

1977, Mar. 28 Litho. ***Perf. 13x13½***

655 A190 10d multicolored	.35	.20
656 A190 30d multicolored	.60	.35
657 A190 40d multicolored	.75	.50
Nos. 655-657 (3)	1.70	1.05

Children's Day.

Gun, Fighters, UN Headquarters A191

1977, Mar. 13 ***Perf. 13½***

658 A191 15d multicolored	*.25*	.20
659 A191 25d multicolored	*.25*	.20
660 A191 70d multicolored	*1.25*	1.25
Nos. 658-660 (3)	*1.75*	1.65

Battle of Al-Karamah, 9th anniversary.

Child, Raindrop, WHO Emblem — A192

Arab Postal Union, 25th Anniv. — A193

1977, Apr. 7 Litho. ***Perf. 13x12½***

661 A192 15d multicolored	.20	.20
662 A192 30d multicolored	.50	.50

World Health Day.

1977, Apr. 12 ***Perf. 13½***

663 A193 15d multicolored	.20	.20
664 A193 30d multicolored	.35	.35
665 A193 40d multicolored	.50	.50
Nos. 663-665 (3)	1.05	1.05

Map of Libya and Heart — A195

Maps of Africa and Libya A194

1977, May 8 Litho. ***Perf. 14x13½***

666 A194 40d multicolored	1.50	1.25
667 A194 70d multicolored	2.25	1.90

African Labor Day.

1977, May 10 ***Perf. 14½x14***

668 A195 5d multicolored	.35	.20
669 A195 10d multicolored	.50	.35
670 A195 30d multicolored	1.40	.60
Nos. 668-670 (3)	2.25	1.15

Libyan Red Crescent Society.

Electronic Tree, ITU Emblem, Satellite and Radar A196

Electronic Tree, ITU Emblem and: 115d, Communications satellite, Montreal Olympics emblem, boxer on TV screen. 200d, Spacecraft over earth. 300d, Solar system.

1977, May 17 Litho. ***Perf. 13½x13***

671 A196 60d multicolored	.80	.80
672 A196 115d multicolored	2.00	2.00
673 A196 200d multicolored	3.75	3.75
Nos. 671-673 (3)	6.55	6.55

Souvenir Sheet

674 A196 300d multicolored *8.50* 6.50

9th World Telecommunications Day. No. 674 contains one stamp 52x35mm.

Nos. 671-673 exist imperf. Value, set $45. They also exist in miniature sheets of 4, perf and imperf. Values: set perf, $100; set imperf, $135.

Plane over Tripoli, Messenger A197

UPU Emblem and: 25d, Concorde, messenger on horseback. 150d, Loading transport plane and messenger riding camel. 300d, Graf Zeppelin LZ127 over Tripoli.

1977, May 17 Litho. ***Perf. 13½***

675 A197 20d multicolored	.80	.80
676 A197 25d multicolored	1.75	1.75
677 A197 150d multicolored	3.50	3.50
Nos. 675-677 (3)	6.05	6.05

Souvenir Sheet

678 A197 300d multicolored *8.50* 6.50

UPU centenary (in 1974). No. 678 contains one stamp 52x35mm.

Nos. 675-678 exist imperf. Values: set $45; souvenir sheet, $50. Nos. 675-677 also exist in miniature sheets of 4, perf and imperf. Values: set perf, $60; set imperf, $125.

Mosque A198

Various Mosques. 50d, 100d, vertical.

1977, June 1 Photo. ***Perf. 14***

679 A198 40d multicolored	.55	.55
680 A198 50d multicolored	.80	.80
681 A198 70d multicolored	1.10	1.10
682 A198 90d multicolored	1.40	1.40
683 A198 100d multicolored	1.60	1.60
684 A198 115d multicolored	2.10	2.10
Nos. 679-684 (6)	7.55	7.55

Palestinian Archbishop Hilarion Capucci, Jailed by Israel in 1974, Map of Palestine — A199

1977, Aug. 18 Litho. ***Perf. 13½***

687 A199 30d multicolored	.40	.40
688 A199 40d multicolored	.55	.55
689 A199 115d multicolored	2.10	1.00
Nos. 687-689 (3)	3.05	1.95

Raised Hands, Pylons, Wheel, Buildings — A200

Star and Ornament — A201

1977, Sept. 1 Litho. ***Perf. 13½x12½***

690 A200 15d multicolored	.20	.20
691 A200 30d multicolored	.35	.35
692 A200 85d multicolored	1.25	.60
Nos. 690-692 (3)	1.80	1.15

Souvenir Sheet
Perf. 12½

693 A201 100d gold & multi 5.00 3.50

8th anniversary of Sept. 1 Revolution.

Team Handball — A202

1977, Oct. 8 ***Perf. 13½***

694 A202 5d Swimmers, vert.	.20	.20
695 A202 10d shown	.20	.20
696 A202 15d Soccer, vert.	.20	.20
697 A202 25d Table tennis	.75	.75
698 A202 40d Basketball, vert.	1.60	.90
Nos. 694-698 (5)	2.95	2.25

7th Arab School Games.

Steeplechase — A203

Show Emblem and: 10d, Bedouin on horseback. 15d, Show emblem (Horse and "7"), vert. 45d, Steeplechase. 100d, Hurdles. 115d, Bedouins on horseback.

1977, Oct. 10 ***Perf. 14½***

699 A203 5d multicolored	.20	.20
700 A203 10d multicolored	.20	.20
701 A203 15d multicolored	.35	.35
702 A203 45d multicolored	.90	.90
703 A203 115d multicolored	2.00	2.00
Nos. 699-703 (5)	3.65	3.65

Souvenir Sheet

704 A203 100d multicolored 4.50 4.50

7th Intl. Turf Championships, Tripoli, Oct. 1977.

Dome of the Rock, Jerusalem — A204

1977, Oct. 14 ***Perf. 14½x14***

705 A204 5d multicolored	.30	.20
706 A204 10d multicolored	.45	.20

Palestinian fighters and their families.

"The Green Book" — A205

35d, Hands with broken chain holding hook over citadel. 40d, Hands above chaos. 115d, Dove and Green Book rising from Africa, world map.

1977 Litho. ***Perf. 14***

707 A205 Strip of 3	2.75	2.75
a. 35d multicolored	.35	.35
b. 40d multicolored	.50	.50
c. 115d multicolored	1.75	1.75

The Greek Book, by Khadafy outlines Libyan democracy. Green descriptive inscription on back beneath gum, in English on 35d, French on 40d, Arabic on 115d.

Emblems A206

1977 ***Perf. 12½x13***

708 A206 5d multicolored	.60	.20
709 A206 15d multicolored	.80	.20
710 A206 30d multicolored	1.10	.35
Nos. 708-710 (3)	2.50	.75

Standardization Day.

Elephant hunt. A207

Rock Carvings, Wadi Mathendous, c. 8000 B.C.: 10d, Crocodile and Young. 20d, Giraffe, vert. 30d, Antelope. 40d, Trumpeting elephant.

1978, Jan. 1 ***Perf. 12½x13, 13x12½***

711 A207 10d multicolored	.20	.20
712 A207 15d multicolored	.20	.20
713 A207 20d multicolored	.35	.35
714 A207 30d multicolored	.60	.60
715 A207 40d multicolored	1.00	1.00
Nos. 711-715 (5)	2.35	2.35

Silver Pendant — A208

Emblem, Compass and Lightning — A209

Silver Jewelry: 10d, Ornamental plate. 20d, Necklace with pendants. 25d, Crescent-shaped brooch. 115d, Armband.

1978, Mar. 1 Litho. *Perf. 13x12½*

716 A208 5d multicolored .20 .20
717 A208 10d multicolored .20 .20
718 A208 20d multicolored .20 .20
719 A208 25d multicolored .20 .20
720 A208 115d multicolored 1.50 1.50
Nos. 716-720 (5) 2.30 2.30

Tripoli International Fair.

1978, Mar. 10 *Perf. 13½*

721 A209 30d multicolored .50 .50
722 A209 115d multicolored 2.00 2.00

Arab Cultural Education Organization.

Children's Drawings and UNICEF Emblem A210

a, Dancing. b, Children with posters. c, Shopping street. d, Playground. e, Bride and attendants.

1978, Mar. 21

723 A210 40d Strip of 5, #a.-e. 7.25 7.25

Children's Day.

Clenched Fist, Made of Bricks A211

1978, Mar. 22

728 A211 30d multicolored .65 .40
729 A211 115d multicolored 1.50 .70

Determination of Arab people.

Blood Pressure Gauge, WHO Emblem — A212

Games Emblem — A214

Antenna and ITU Emblem A213

1978, Apr. 7 *Perf. 13x12½*

730 A212 30d multicolored .35 .35
731 A212 115d multicolored 1.75 .90

World Health Day, drive against hypertension.

1978, May 17 Photo. *Perf. 13½*

732 A213 30d silver & multi .35 .20
733 A213 115d gold & multi 1.50 .65

10th World Telecommunications Day.

1978, July 13 Litho. *Perf. 12½*

734 A214 15d multicolored .20 .20
735 A214 30d multicolored .35 .35
736 A214 115d multicolored 1.50 1.50
Nos. 734-736 (3) 2.05 2.05

3rd African Games, Algiers, 1978.

Inauguration of Tripoli International Airport — A215

1978, Aug. 10 Litho. *Perf. 13½*

737 A215 40d shown .50 .50
738 A215 115d Terminal 2.00 .90

View of Ankara — A216

Soldiers, Jet, Ship — A217

1978, Aug. 17

739 A216 30d multicolored .50 .20
740 A216 35d multicolored .60 .35
741 A216 115d multicolored 1.60 1.60
Nos. 739-741 (3) 2.70 2.15

Turkish-Libyan friendship.

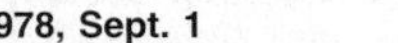
1978, Sept. 1 *Perf. 14½*

35d, Tower, Green Book, oil derrick. 100d, View of Tripoli with mosque and modern buildings. 115d, View of Tripoli within cogwheel.

742 A217 30d multicolored .50 .50
743 A217 35d org & multi .35 .35
744 A217 115d blue & multi 1.50 1.25
Nos. 742-744 (3) 2.35 2.10

Souvenir Sheet

745 A217 100d multicolored 2.75 2.75

9th anniversary of Sept. 1 Revolution. No. 745 contains one 50x41mm stamp.

Quarry and Symposium Emblem — A218

Designs: 40d, Oasis lake. 115d, Crater.

1978, Sept. 16 *Perf. 13½*

746 A218 30d multicolored .50 .50
747 A218 40d multicolored .60 .60
748 A218 115d multicolored 2.00 2.00
Nos. 746-748 (3) 3.10 3.10

2nd Symposium on Libyan Geology.

Green Book and Three Races A219

1978, Oct. 18 *Perf. 12½*

749 A219 30d multicolored .20 .20
750 A219 40d multicolored .50 .50
751 A219 115d multicolored 1.25 1.25
Nos. 749-751 (3) 1.95 1.95

International Anti-Apartheid Year.

Pilgrims, Minarets, Holy Kaaba A220

1978, Nov. 9 Photo. *Perf. 12*

752 A220 5d multicolored .20 .20
753 A220 10d multicolored .20 .20
754 A220 15d multicolored .20 .20
755 A220 20d multicolored .20 .20
Nos. 752-755 (4) .80 .80

Pilgrimage to Mecca.

Handclasp over Globe — A221

Fists, Guns, Map of Israel — A222

1978, Nov. 10 Litho. *Perf. 13½*

756 A221 30d multicolored .40 .30
757 A221 40d multicolored .50 .40
758 A221 115d multicolored 1.50 1.25
Nos. 756-758 (3) 2.40 1.95

Technical Cooperation Among Developing Countries Conf., Buenos Aires, Argentina, Sept. 1978.

1978, Dec. 5 Litho. *Perf. 13½*

40d, 115d, Map of Arab countries and Israel, eagle and crowd. 145d, like 30d.

759 A222 30d multi .35 .35
760 A222 40d multi, horiz. .50 .50
761 A222 115d multi, horiz. 1.25 1.25
762 A222 145d multi 1.50 .90
Nos. 759-762 (4) 3.60 3.00

Anti-Israel Summit Conf., Baghdad, Dec. 2-8.

Scales, Globe and Human Rights Flame — A223

Libyan Fort and Horse Racing — A224

1978, Dec. 10

763 A223 15d multicolored .20 .20
764 A223 30d multicolored .50 .50
765 A223 115d multicolored 1.25 1.25
Nos. 763-765 (3) 1.95 1.95

Universal Declaration of Human Rights, 30th anniv.

1978, Dec. 11

766 A224 20d multicolored .40 .20
767 A224 40d multicolored .50 .50
768 A224 115d multicolored 1.50 1.50
Nos. 766-768 (3) 2.40 2.20

Libyan Study Center.

Lilienthal's Glider, 1896 A225

Mounted Stag's Head — A226

25d, Spirit of St. Louis, 1927. 30d, Adm. Byrd's Polar flight, 1929. 50d, Graf Zeppelin, 1934, hydroplane and storks. 115d, Wilbur and Orville Wright and Flyer A. No. 774, Icarus falling. No. 775, Eagle and Boeing 727.

1978, Dec. 26 Litho. *Perf. 14*

769 A225 20d multicolored .25 .25
770 A225 25d multicolored .45 .45
771 A225 30d multicolored 1.40 1.40
772 A225 50d multicolored 1.60 1.60
773 A225 115d multicolored 1.40 1.40
Nos. 769-773 (5) 5.10 5.10

Souvenir Sheets

774 A225 100d multicolored 3.00 3.00
775 A225 100d multicolored 3.00 3.00

75th anniversary of 1st powered flight.
Nos. 769-773 issued also in sheets of 4. Value, set perf. $45. Also exists imperf.
Nos. 774-775 exist imperf. Value, pair $50.

Coil Stamps

1979, Jan. 15 Photo. *Perf. 14½x14*
776 A226 5d multicolored .35 .35
777 A226 20d multicolored .75 .75
778 A226 50d multicolored 1.50 1.50
Nos. 776-778 (3) 2.60 2.60

Carpobrotus Acinaciformis A227

Flora of Libya: 15d, Caralluma europaea. 20d, Arum cirenaicum. 35d, Lavatera arborea. 40d, Capparis spinosa. 50d, Ranunculus asiaticus.

1979, May 15 Litho. *Perf. 14*
779 A227 10d multicolored .20 .20
780 A227 15d multicolored .20 .20
781 A227 20d multicolored .20 .20
782 A227 35d multicolored .60 .60
783 A227 40d multicolored .60 .60
784 A227 50d multicolored .75 .75
Nos. 779-784 (6) 2.55 2.55

People, Torch, Olive Branches — A228

1979 Litho. *Perf. 13x12½*
Size: 18x23mm
785 A228 5d multi .20 .20
786 A228 10d multi .20 .20
787 A228 15d multi .20 .20
788 A228 30d multi .35 .20
789 A228 50d multi .50 .20
790 A228 60d multi .60 .35
791 A228 70d multi .75 .35
792 A228 100d multi 1.25 .60
793 A228 115d multi 1.25 .60
Perf. 13½
Size: 26½x32mm
794 A228 200d multi 1.90 1.25
795 A228 500d multi 4.75 2.50
796 A228 1000d multi 10.00 6.25
Nos. 785-796 (12) 21.95 12.90

See Nos. 1053-1055.

Tortoise A229

Animals: 10d, Antelope. 15d, Hedgehog. 20d, Porcupine. 30d, Arabian camel. 35d, African wildcat. 45d, Gazelle. 115d, Cheetah. 10d, 30d, 35d, 45d, vert.

1979, Feb. 1 Litho. *Perf. 14½*
797 A229 5d multicolored .25 .20
798 A229 10d multicolored .25 .20
799 A229 15d multicolored .65 .65
800 A229 20d multicolored .65 .65
801 A229 30d multicolored 1.10 .65
802 A229 35d multicolored 1.50 .65
803 A229 45d multicolored 1.75 .80
804 A229 115d multicolored 3.50 1.25
Nos. 797-804 (8) 9.65 5.05

Rug and Tripoli Fair Emblem — A230

Tripoli Fair emblem and various rugs.

1979, Mar. 1 Litho. *Perf. 11*
805 A230 10d multicolored .20 .20
806 A230 15d multicolored .20 .20
807 A230 30d multicolored .35 .35
808 A230 45d multicolored .50 .50
809 A230 115d multicolored 1.25 1.25
Nos. 805-809 (5) 2.50 2.50

17th Tripoli Fair.
Exist imperf. Value, set $30.

Children's Drawings and IYC Emblem A231

a, Families and planes. b, Shepherd, sheep and dog. c, Beach umbrellas. d, Boat in storm. e, Traffic policeman.

1979, Mar. 20 *Perf. 13½*
810 A231 20d Strip of 5, #a.-e. 5.00 3.50

Intl. Year of the Child.
Exists imperf. Value $30.

Book, World Map, Arab Achievements A232

1979, Mar. 22 *Perf. 13*
815 A232 45d multicolored .50 .50
816 A232 70d multicolored .75 .75

WMO Emblem, Weather Map and Tower — A233

1979, Mar. 23
817 A233 15d multicolored .20 .20
818 A233 30d multicolored .35 .35
819 A233 50d multicolored .60 .60
Nos. 817-819 (3) 1.15 1.15

World Meteorological Day.

Medical Services, WHO Emblem — A234

1979, Apr. 7
820 A234 40d multicolored .60 .60

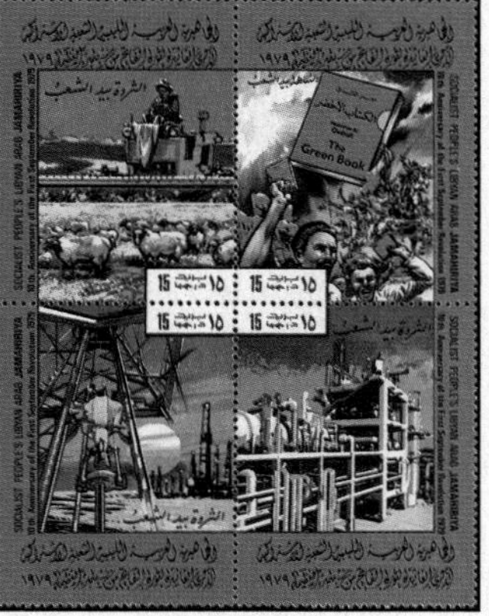

Farmer Plowing and Sheep — A235

1979, Sept. 1 Litho. *Perf. 14½*
821 Block of 4 1.00 1.00
a. A235 15d shown .20 .20
b. A235 15d Men holding Green Book .20 .20
c. A235 15d Oil field .20 .20
d. A235 15d Oil refinery .20 .20
822 Block of 4 2.00 2.00
a. A235 30d Dish antenna .40 .40
b. A235 30d Hospital .40 .40
c. A235 30d Doctor examining patient .40 .40
d. A235 30d Surgery .40 .40
823 Block of 4 3.00 3.00
a. A235 40d Street, Tripoli .50 .50
b. A235 40d Steel mill .50 .50
c. A235 40d Tanks .50 .50
d. A235 40d Tuareg horsemen .50 .50
824 Block of 4 4.00 4.00
a. A235 70d Revolutionaries, Green Book .90 .90
b. A235 70d Crowd, map of Libya .90 .90
c. A235 70d Mullah .90 .90
d. A235 70d Student .90 .90
Nos. 821-824 (4) 10.00 10.00

Souvenir Sheets
Imperf

825 A235 50d Revolution symbols, Green Book 2.50 2.50
826 A235 50d Monument 2.50 2.50

Sept. 1st revolution, 10th anniversary.

Volleyball A236

1979, Sept. 10
827 A236 45d shown .50 .50
828 A236 115d Soccer 1.25 1.25

Universiade '79 World University Games, Mexico City, Sept.
Exists imperf. Value, set $17.50.

Mediterranean Games, Split, Yugoslavia — A237

1979, Sept. 15 Litho. *Perf. 12x11½*
829 A237 15d multicolored .50 .50
830 A237 30d multicolored 1.40 .50
831 A237 70d multicolored 3.50 1.00
Nos. 829-831 (3) 5.40 2.00

Exhibition Emblem — A238

1979, Sept. 25 Photo. *Perf. 11½x11*
832 A238 45d multicolored .50 .50
833 A238 115d multicolored 1.50 1.50

TELECOM '79, 3rd World Telecommunications Exhibition, Geneva, Sept. 20-26.

A239

#834a, 10d, Seminar emblem, Green Book, crowd. #834b, 35d, Meeting hall (Size: 67x43½mm). #834c, 100d, Col. Khadafy. #835, Central portion of #834c.

1979, Oct. 1
834 A239 Strip of 3, #a.-c. 2.50 2.50
Size: 87x114mm
Imperf
835 A239 100d multicolored 3.50 3.50

Intl. Seminar of the Green Book, Benghazi, Oct. 1-3. No. 834 has continuous design.

Evacuation of Foreign Forces — A240

1979, Oct. 7
837 A240 30d shown .60 .40
838 A240 40d Tuareg horsemen .90 .50

Souvenir Sheet
Imperf

839 A240 100d Vignettes 3.00 3.00

Cyclist, Championship Emblem — A241

1979, Nov. 21
840 A241 15d shown .20 .20
841 A241 30d Cyclists, emblem, diff. .50 .50

Junior Cycling Championships, Tripoli, Nov. 21-23. Issued in sheetlets of 4.

Hurdles, Olympic Rings, Moscow '80 Emblem — A242

1979, Nov. 21

842 A242 45d Equestrian .50 .50
843 A242 60d Javelin .75 .75
844 A242 115d Hurdles 1.50 1.50
845 A242 160d Soccer 1.75 1.75
Nos. 842-845 (4) 4.50 4.50

Souvenir Sheets

846 A242 150d shown 3.75 3.75
847 A242 150d like #845 3.75 3.75

Pre-Olympics (Moscow '80 Olympic Games). Nos. 842-845 issued in sheetlets of 4 and sheets of 20 (4x5) with silver Moscow '80 Emblem covering background of every 20 stamps. Value, set of sheetlets of 4, $45.

Nos. 842-847 exist imperf. Values: set $55; souvenir sheets, $90.

Intl. Day of Cooperation with Palestinian People — A242a

1979, Nov. 29 Photo. *Perf. 12*

847A A242a 30d multicolored .25 .25
847B A242a 115d multicolored 1.75 1.75

Tug of War, Jumping — A243

National Games: No. 848, Polo, leap frog. No. 849, Racing, ball game, No. 850, Wrestling, log rolling. No. 852, Horsemen.

1980, Feb. 15

848 A243 Block of 4, #a.-d. 1.00 1.00
849 A243 Block of 4, #a.-d. 1.00 1.00
850 A243 Block of 4, #a.-d. 1.00 1.00
851 A243 Block of 4, #a.-d. 2.00 2.00
852 A243 Block of 4, #a.-d. 3.50 3.50
Nos. 848-852 (5) 8.50 8.50

Battles — A244

#853a, 20d, Gardabia, 1915. #853b, 35d, same. #854a, 20d, Shoghab, 1913. #854b, 35d, same. #855a, 20d, Fundugh Al-Shibani, 1922. #855b, 35d, same. #856a, 20d, Ghira. #856b, 35d, same.

Pairs have continuous design.

1980 Litho. *Perf. 14½*

853 A244 Pair, #a.-b. *1.25 1.25*
854 A244 Pair, #a.-b. *1.25 1.25*
855 A244 Pair, #a.-b. *1.25 1.25*
856 A244 Pair, #a.-b. *1.25 1.25*
Nos. 853-856 (4) *5.00 5.00*

Issued: #853, 4/28; #854, 5/25; #855, 6/1; #856, 8/15.

See Nos. 893-896, 921-932, 980-991, 1059-1070.

Girl Guides Examining Plant — A245

1980, Aug. 22 *Perf. 13½*

861 A245 15d shown .25 .25
862 A245 30d Guides cooking .35 .35
863 A245 50d Scouts at campfire .60 .60
864 A245 115d Scouts reading map 1.50 1.50
Nos. 861-864 (4) 2.70 2.70

Souvenir Sheets

865 A245 100d like #861 2.25 2.25
866 A245 100d like #863 2.25 2.25

8th Pan Arab Girl Guide and 14th Pan Arab Scout Jamborees, Aug.

Men Holding OPEC Emblem A246

1980, Sept. 15 *Perf. 14½*

867 A246 45d Emblem, globe .50 .50
868 A246 115d shown 1.50 1.50

20th anniversary of OPEC.

Martyrdom of Omar Muktar, 1931 — A247

1980, Sept. 16

869 A247 20d multicolored .25 .25
870 A247 35d multicolored .50 .50

Souvenir Sheet

870A A247 100d multicolored 2.50 2.50

UNESCO Emblem and Avicenna A248

1980, Sept. 20

871 A248 45d Scientific symbols .50 .50
872 A248 115d shown 1.50 1.50

School Scientific Exhibition, Sept. 20-24 and birth millenium of Arab physician Avicenna (115d).

18th Tripoli Fair A249

Various musical instruments. 15d vert.

1980 Litho. *Perf. 13½*

873 A249 5d multicolored .25 .25
874 A249 10d multicolored .25 .25
875 A249 15d multicolored .25 .25
876 A249 20d multicolored .25 .25
877 A249 25d multicolored .40 .40
Nos. 873-877 (5) 1.40 1.40

Souvenir Sheet

878 A249 100d Musicians 2.50 2.50

World Olive Oil Year A250

1980, Jan. 15 Litho. *Perf. 13½*

879 A250 15d multicolored .25 .25
880 A250 30d multicolored .35 .35
881 A250 45d multicolored .50 .50
Nos. 879-881 (3) 1.10 1.10

Intl. Year of the Child (1979) A251

Children's drawings: a, Riding horses. b, water sports. c, Fish. d, Gift sale. e, Preparing feast.

1980, Mar. 21

882 Strip of 5 5.00 5.00
a.-e. A251 20d any single .50 .40

The Hegira, 1500th Anniv. A252

1980, Apr. 1

883 A252 50d multicolored .60 .60
884 A252 115d multicolored 1.50 1.50

Operating Room, Hospital — A253

1980, Apr. 7 Litho. *Perf. 13½*

885 A253 20d multicolored .40 .40
886 A253 50d multicolored .75 .75

World Health Day.

Sheik Zarruq Festival, Misurata, June 16-20 — A254

Arabian Towns Organization A255

1980, June 16

887 A254 40d multicolored .50 .50
888 A254 115d multicolored 1.50 1.50

Souvenir Sheet

889 A254 100d multicolored 2.75 2.75

1980, July 1 *Perf. 11½x12*

890 A255 15d Ghadames .25 .25
891 A255 30d Derna .35 .35
892 A255 50d Tripoli .60 .60
Nos. 890-892 (3) 1.20 1.20

Battles Type of 1980

#893a, 20d, Yefren, 1915, #893b, 35d, same. #894a, 20d, El Hani, 1911, #894b, 35d, same. #895a, 20d, Sebha, 1914, #895b, 35d, same. #896a, 20d, Sirt, 1912, #896b, 35d, same.

Pairs have continuous design.

1980 *Perf. 13½*

893 A244 Pair, #a.-b. 1.25 1.25
894 A244 Pair, #a.-b. 1.25 1.25
895 A244 Pair, #a.-b. 1.25 1.25
896 A244 Pair, #a.-b. 1.25 1.25
Nos. 893-896 (4) 5.00 5.00

Issued: #893, 7/16; #894, 10/23; #895, 11/27; #896, 12/31.

Sept. 1 Revolution, 11th Anniv. — A256

Achievements of the Revolution.

1980, Sept. 1

901 A256 5d Oil industry .25 .25
902 A256 10d Youth festival .25 .25
903 A256 15d Agriculture .50 .50
904 A256 25d Transportation 1.25 .50
905 A256 40d Education 1.25 .50
906 A256 115d Housing 3.00 1.25
Nos. 901-906 (6) 6.50 3.25

Souvenir Sheet

907 A256 100d Montage of achievements 2.75 2.75

No. 907 contains one stamp 30x50mm.

World Tourism Conference A257

1980, Sept. 10

908 A257 45d multicolored .50 .50
909 A257 115d multicolored 1.50 1.50

Intl. Year of the Disabled — A258

1981, Jan. 1 *Perf. 15*

910	A258	20d multicolored	.25	.25
911	A258	45d multicolored	.35	.25
912	A258	115d multicolored	1.50	.50
		Nos. 910-912 (3)	2.10	1.00

Redrawn

1981, Nov. 21 **Litho.** *Perf. 15*

913	A258	45d multicolored	.35	.25
914	A258	115d multicolored	1.10	1.10

UPA Disabled Persons Campaign. Design redrawn to include Arab League Emblem.

Mosaics — A259

1981, Jan. 15 *Perf. 13½*

915	A259	10d Horse	1.00	.25
916	A259	20d Sailing ship	1.00	.50
917	A259	30d Peacocks	2.00	.50
918	A259	40d Panther	2.00	.50
919	A259	50d Musician	2.50	.50
920	A259	115d Fish	6.50	1.00
		Nos. 915-920 (6)	15.00	3.25

Battles Type of 1980

#921a, 20d, Dernah, 1912, #921b, 35d, same. #922a, 20d, Bir Tagreft, 1928. #922b, 35d, same. #923a, 20d, Tawargha, 1923. #923b, 35d, same. #924a, 20d, .Funduk El-Jamel Misurata, 1915 #924b, 35d, same. #925a, 20d, Zuara, 1912. #925b, 35d, same. #926a, 20d, Sidi El-Khemri, 1915. #926b, 35d, same. #927a, 20d, El-Khoms, 1913. #927b, 35d, same. #928a, 20d, Roghdalin, 1912. #928b, 35d, same. #929a, 20d, Rughbat El-Naga, 1925. #929b, 35d, same. #930a, 20d, Tobruk. 1911. 1922, #930b, 35d, same. #931a, 20d, Bir Ikshadia, 1924. #931b, 35d, same. #932a, 20d, Ain Zara, 1924. #932b, 35d, same.

Pairs have continuous design.

1981 *Perf. 13½, 14½ (#926, 932)*

921	A244	Pair, #a.-b.	1.25	1.25
922	A244	Pair, #a.-b.	1.25	1.25
923	A244	Pair, #a.-b.	1.25	1.25
924	A244	Pair, #a.-b.	1.25	1.25
925	A244	Pair, #a.-b.	1.25	1.25
926	A244	Pair, #a.-b.	1.25	1.25
927	A244	Pair, #a.-b.	1.25	1.25
928	A244	Pair, #a.-b.	1.25	1.25
929	A244	Pair, #a.-b.	1.25	1.25
930	A244	Pair, #a.-b.	1.25	1.25
931	A244	Pair, #a.-b.	1.25	1.25
932	A244	Pair, #a.-b.	1.25	1.25
		Nos. 921-932 (12)	15.00	15.00

Issued: #921, 1/17; #922, 2/25; #923, 3/20; #924, 4/13; #925, 5/26; #926, 6/4; #927, 7/27; #928, 8/15; #929, 9/16; #930, 10/27; #931, 11/19; #932, 12/4.

Tripoli Intl. Fair — A260

No. 707b, Crowd — A261

Ceramicware.

1981, Mar. 1 *Perf. 13½*

945	A260	5d Bowls, horiz.	.25	.25
946	A260	10d Lamp	.25	.25
947	A260	15d Vase	.25	.25
948	A260	45d Water jar, horiz.	.60	.25
949	A260	115d Spouted water jar, horiz.	1.75	.60
		Nos. 945-949 (5)	3.10	1.60

1981, Mar. 2 *Perf. 15*

950	A261	50d multicolored	.35	.35
951	A261	115d multicolored	1.50	.50

People's Authority Declaration, The Green Book.

Children's Day, IYC — A262

Children's illustrations: a, Desert camp. b, Women doing chores. c, Village scene. d, Airplane over playground. e, Minaret, camel, man.

1981, Mar. 21 **Litho.** *Perf. 13½*

952	Strip of 5	5.00	5.00
a.-e.	A262 20d any single	.50	.40

Bank of Libya, 25th Anniv. — A263

1981, Apr. 1 **Litho.** *Perf. 13½*

953	A263	45d multicolored	.50	.35
954	A263	115d multicolored	1.75	1.10

Souvenir Sheet

955	A263	50d multicolored	1.50	1.50

World Health Day A264

1981, Apr. 7 *Perf. 14*

956	A264	45d multicolored	.50	.50
957	A264	115d multicolored	1.50	.75

Intl. Year for Combating Racial Discrimination A265

1981, July 1 *Perf. 15*

958	A265	45d multicolored	1.10	.65
959	A265	50d multicolored	1.50	.75

September 1 Revolution, 12th Anniv. — A266

#960a-960b, Helicopter and jets. #960c-960d, Paratroopers. #961a-961b, Tanks. #961c-961d, Frogman parade. #962a-962b, Twelve-barrel rocket launchers. #962c-962d, Trucks with rockets. #963a-963b, Sailor parade. #963c-963d, Jeep and trucks with twelve-barrel rocket launchers. #964a-964b, Wheeled tanks and jeeps. #964c-964d, Tank parade. Nos. 960-962 vert. Pairs have continuous designs.

1981, Sept. 1 *Perf. 14½*

960	A266	5d Block of 4, #a.-d.	1.40	1.40
961	A266	10d Block of 4, #a.-d.	1.40	1.40
962	A266	15d Block of 4, #a.-d.	1.40	1.40
963	A266	20d Block of 4, #a.-d.	1.40	1.40
964	A266	25d Block of 4, #a.-d.	2.75	2.75
		Nos. 960-964 (5)	8.35	8.35

Souvenir Sheet

Perf. 11

965	A266	50d Naval troop marching	7.00	7.00

No. 965 contains one 63x38mm stamp.

Miniature Sheet

Butterflies — A267

1981, Oct. 1 *Perf. 14½*

966	Sheet of 16	11.00	
a.-d.	A267 5d, any single	.25	.25
e.-h.	A267 10d, any single	.45	.25
i.-l.	A267 15d, any single	.50	.40
m.-p.	A267 25d, any single	1.00	.60

No. 966 printed in a continuous design, stamps of same denomination in blocks of 4. Sheetlets exist containing blocks of 4 for each denomination. Value, set of 4 sheets, $20.

A268

A269

1981, Oct. 16 *Perf. 15*

967	A268	45d multicolored	.50	.50
968	A268	200d multicolored	2.50	2.50

World Food Day.

1981, Nov. 17 *Perf. 13½*

969	A269	5d Grapes	.25	.25
970	A269	10d Dates	.25	.25
971	A269	15d Lemons	.25	.25
972	A269	20d Oranges	.40	.25
973	A269	35d Cactus fruit	.80	.35
974	A269	55d Pomegranates	1.50	.60
		Nos. 969-974 (6)	3.45	1.95

Miniature Sheet

A270

Mosaics: a, Animals facing right. b, Orpheus playing music. c, Animals facing left. d, Fish. e, Fishermen. f, Fish in basket. g, Farm yard. h, Birds eating fruit. i, Milking a goat.

1982, Jan. 1 *Perf. 13½*

975	A270	Sheet of 9	9.00	9.00
a.-i.		45d any single	.75	.75

Nos. 975a-975c, shown in illustration, printed in continuous design.

3rd Intl. Koran Reading Contest — A271

Designs: 10d, Stone tablets, Holy Ka'aba, Mecca. 35d, Open Koran, creation of the world. 115d, Scholar, students.

1982, Jan. 7

976	A271	10d multicolored	.20	.20
977	A271	35d multicolored	.50	.25
978	A271	115d multicolored	1.50	.75
		Nos. 976-978 (3)	2.20	1.20

Souvenir Sheet

979	A271	100d like 115d	3.50	3.50

Battles Type of 1980

#980a, 20d, Hun Gioffra, 1915. #980b, 35d, same. #981a, 20d, Gedabia, 1914. #981b, 35d, same. #982a, 20d, El-Asaba, 1913. #982b, 35d, same. #983a, 20d, El-Habela, 1917. #983b, 35d, same. #984a, 20d, Suk El-Ahad, 1915. #984b, 35d, same. #985a, 20d, El-Tangi, 1913. #985b, 35d, same. #986a, 20d, Sokna, 1913. #986b, 35d, same. #987a, 20d, Wadi Smalus, 1925. #987b, 35d, same. #988a, 20d, Sidi Abuagela, 1917. #988b, 35d, same. #989a, 20d, Sidi Surur, 1914. #989b, 35d, same. #990a, 20d, Kuefia, 1911. #990b, 35d, same. #991a, 20d, Abunjeim, 1940. #991b, 35d, same.

Pairs have continuous design.

1982 *Perf. 13½, 14½ (#985-988)*

980	A244	Pair, #a.-b.	1.25	1.25
981	A244	Pair, #a.-b.	1.25	1.25
982	A244	Pair, #a.-b.	1.25	1.25
983	A244	Pair, #a.-b.	1.25	1.25
984	A244	Pair, #a.-b.	1.25	1.25
985	A244	Pair, #a.-b.	1.25	1.25
986	A244	Pair, #a.-b.	1.25	1.25
987	A244	Pair, #a.-b.	1.25	1.25
988	A244	Pair, #a.-b.	1.25	1.25
989	A244	Pair, #a.-b.	1.25	1.25
990	A244	Pair, #a.-b.	1.25	1.25
991	A244	Pair, #a.-b.	1.25	1.25
		Nos. 980-991 (12)	15.00	15.00

Issued: #980, 1/26; #981, 3/8; #982, 3/23; #983, 4/24; #984, 5/15; #985, 6/19; #986, 7/23; #987, 8/11; #988, 9/4; #989, 10/14; #990, 11/28; #991, 12/13.

Tripoli Intl. Fair — A272

1982, Mar. 1 *Perf. 13x12½*

1004 A272 5d Grinding stone .20 .20
1005 A272 10d Ox-drawn plow .20 .20
1006 A272 25d Pitching hay .25 .25
1007 A272 35d Tapestry weaving .50 .25
1008 A272 45d Traditional cooking .75 .35
1009 A272 100d Grain harvest 1.50 .75
Nos. 1004-1009 (6) 3.40 2.00

People's Authority Declaration, The Green Book — A273

1982, Mar. 2 *Perf. 13½*

1010 Strip of 3 8.00 8.00
a. A273 100d Harvester combine 1.25 .60
b. A273 200d Khadafy, scholar, rifles 2.50 2.25
c. A273 300d Govt. building, citizens 3.25 2.25

Scouting Movement, 75th Anniv. — A274

13th African Soccer Cup Championships A275

1982, Mar. 2

1011 Strip of 4 22.50 22.50
a. A274 100d Cub scout, blimp 1.75 .80
b. A274 200d Scouts, dog 3.25 1.60
c. A274 300d Scholar, scout 4.75 2.00
d. A274 400d Boy scout, rocket 7.25 3.75

Souvenir Sheets

1012 A274 500d Green Book 8.00 8.00
1013 A274 500d Khadafy, scouts 8.00 8.00

Nos. 1012-1013 each contain one stamp 39x42mm.
Nos. 1011-1013 exist imperf.

1982, Mar. 5

1014 A275 100d multi 1.50 .75
1015 A275 200d multi 3.00 1.50

1982 World Cup Soccer Championships, Spain — A276

World Cup trophy and various soccer plays.

1982, Mar. 15 *Perf. 14½*

1016 A276 45d multi .60 .60
1017 A276 100d multi 1.50 1.50
1018 A276 200d multi 2.75 2.75
1019 A276 300d multi 3.25 3.25
Nos. 1016-1019 (4) 8.10 8.10

Souvenir Sheets

1020 A276 500d like 45d 7.50 7.50
1021 A276 500d like 100d 7.50 7.50

Nos. 1016-1019 issued in sheets of 8 overprinted in silver with soccer ball in motion. Value $75. Sheetlets of 4 in each denomination exist without overprint.

Nos. 1020-1021 have Arabic text in green on reverse. Value $35.

Nos. 1016-1019 exist imperf. Value $15. Nos. 1020-1021 also exist imperf.

Palestinian Children's Day — A277

Designs: a, Two children. b, Girl with bowl. c, Girl with kaffiyeh. d, Girl hiding. e, Boy.

1982, Mar. 7 *Perf. 13½*

1022 Strip of 5 2.75 2.75
a.-e. A277 20d, any single .40 .40

Birds — A278

Arab Postal Union, 30th — A280

Teaching Hospitals Anniv. A279

Miniature Sheet

1982, Apr. 1 *Perf. 14½*

1023 Sheet of 16 20.00 20.00
a.-d. A278 15d, any single .50 .45
e.-h. A278 25d, any single .75 .60
i.-l. A278 45d, any single 1.10 1.00
m.-p. A278 95d, any single 2.40 1.80

No. 1023a-1023p printed se-tenant in a continuous design; stamps of same denomination in blocks of 4.

Each denomination was also printed in a sheet of 16, each sheet containing four se-tenant blocks of the same denomination. Value, set of four sheets, $75.

1982, Apr. 7 *Perf. 13x12½*

1024 A279 95d multi 1.25 1.25
1025 A279 100d multi 1.25 1.25
1026 A279 205d multi 2.75 2.75
Nos. 1024-1026 (3) 5.25 5.25

1982, Apr. 12 *Perf. 13½*

1027 A280 100d multi 1.50 .75
1028 A280 200d multi 2.75 1.50

1982 World Chess Championships — A281

Board positions and chessmen: a, Chinese piece. b, African piece. c, Modern piece. d, European piece.

1982, May 1

1029 Block of 4 10.00 10.00
a.-d. A281 100d, any single 2.25 1.10

Souvenir Sheet

1030 A281 500d Overhead view of chessboard 10.00 10.00

No. 1030 contains one stamp 39x42mm.
Nos. 1029 and 1030 exist imperf.

World Telecommunications Day — A282

1982, May 17

1031 A282 100d multi 1.25 1.25
1032 A282 200d multi 2.50 2.50

Map of Libya, Green Book A283

1982, June 11

1033 A283 200d multi 2.50 1.50

Souvenir Sheet

1034 A283 300d multi 5.00 5.00

Post Day, FIP 51st anniv.

Organization of African Unity, 19th Summit A284

1982, Aug. 5 *Perf. 14*

1035 A284 50d OAU flag, Arab family .75 .75
1036 A284 100d Map of Africa, emblem 1.25 1.25

Size: 69x40mm

1037 A284 200d Khadafy, Green Book 2.50 2.50
Nos. 1035-1037 (3) 4.50 4.50

Souvenir Sheet

Perf. 13x13½

1038 A284 300d Fist, map 5.00 5.00

No. 1038 contains one stamp 29x42mm.

September 1 Revolution, 13th Anniv. — A285

Khadafy in uniforms and various armed forces' exercises.

1982, Sept. 1 *Perf. 11½*

1039 A285 15d multi .25 .25
1040 A285 20d multi .25 .25
1041 A285 30d multi 1.00 1.00
1042 A285 45d multi .60 .60
1043 A285 70d multi 1.00 1.00
1044 A285 100d multi 1.50 1.50
Nos. 1039-1044 (6) 4.60 4.60

Souvenir Sheet

Imperf

1045 A285 200d multi 4.00 4.00

Libyan Red Crescent, 25th Anniv. — A286

Intl. Day of Cooperation with Palestinian People — A287

1982, Oct. 5 *Perf. 13½*

1046 A286 100d Palm tree 1.75 1.25
1047 A286 200d "25," crescents 3.50 2.50

1982, Nov. 29

1048 A287 100d gray grn & blk 1.50 .75
1049 A287 200d brt bl, gray grn & blk 2.75 1.50

Al-Fateh University Symposium on Khadafy's Green Book — A288

1982, Dec. 1 *Perf. 12*

1050 A288 100d Khadafy in uniform 1.25 1.10
1051 A288 200d Khadafy, map, Green Book 2.50 2.50

Flowers — A289

Customs Cooperation Council, 30th Anniv. — A290

Miniature Sheet

Designs: a, Philadelphus. b, Hypericum. c, Antinhinum. d, Lily. e, Capparis. f, Tropaeolum. g, Rose. h, Chrysanthemum. i, Nigella damascena. j, Gaillardia lanceolata. k, Dahlia. l, Dianthus carophyllus. m, Notobasis syriaca. n, Nerium oleander. o, Iris histriodes. p, Scolymus hispanicus.

1983, Jan. 1 ***Perf. 14½***
1052 Sheet of 16 10.00 10.00
a.-p. A289 25d, any single .50 .40

Torch Type of 1979

1983, Jan. 2 ***Perf. 13½***

Size: 26½x32mm

1053 A228 250d multi 3.25 2.00
1054 A228 1500d multi 20.00 12.50
1055 A228 2500d multi 37.50 25.00
Nos. 1053-1055 (3) 60.75 39.50

1983, Jan. 15 ***Perf. 14½x14***
1056 A290 25d Arab riding horse .25 .25
1057 A290 50d Riding camel .60 .60
1058 A290 100d Drawing sword 1.50 1.50
Nos. 1056-1058 (3) 2.35 2.35

Battles Type of 1980

#1059a, 1059b, Ghaser Ahmed, 1922. #1060a, 1060b, Sidi Abuarghub, 1923. #1061a, 1061b, Ghar Yunes, 1913. #1062a, 1062b, Bir Otman, 1926. #1063a, 1063b, Sidi Sajeh, 1922. #1064a, 1064b, Ras El-Hamam, 1915. #1065a, 1065b, Zawiet Ishghefa, 1913. #1066a, 1066b, Wadi Essania, 1930. #1067a, 1067b, El-Meshiashta, 1917. #1068a, 1068b, Gharara, 1925. #1069a, 1069b, Abughelan, 1922. #1070a, 1070b, Mahruka, 1913.

Pairs have continuous design.

1983 ***Perf. 13½***
1059 A244 50d Pair, #a.-b. 2.00 2.00
1060 A244 50d Pair, #a.-b. 2.00 2.00
1061 A244 50d Pair, #a.-b. 2.00 2.00
1062 A244 50d Pair, #a.-b. 2.00 2.00
1063 A244 50d Pair, #a.-b. 2.00 2.00
1064 A244 50d Pair, #a.-b. 2.00 2.00
1065 A244 50d Pair, #a.-b. 2.00 2.00
1066 A244 50d Pair, #a.-b. 2.00 2.00
1067 A244 50d Pair, #a.-b. 2.00 2.00
1068 A244 50d Pair, #a.-b. 2.00 2.00
1069 A244 50d Pair, #a.-b. 2.00 2.00
1070 A244 50d Pair, #a.-b. 2.00 2.00
Nos. 1059-1070 (12) 24.00 24.00

Issued: #1059, 1/26; #1060, 2/2; #1061, 3/26; #1062, 4/9; #1063, 5/2; #1064, 6/24; #1065, 7/13; #1066, 8/8; #1067, 9/9; #1068, 10/22; #1069, 11/17; #1070, 12/24.

Miniature Sheet

Farm Animals — A291

Designs: a, Camel. b, Cow. c, Horse. d, Bull. e, Goat. f, Dog. g, Sheep. h, Ram. i, Goose. j, Turkey hen. k, Rabbit. l, Pigeon. m, Turkey. n, Rooster. o, Hen. p, Duck.

1983, Feb. 15 ***Perf. 14½***
1083 Sheet of 16 10.00 10.00
a.-p. A291 25d any single .50 .40

Tripoli Intl. Fair A292

Libyans playing traditional instruments.

1983, Mar. 5 ***Perf. 14½x14, 14x14½***
1084 A292 40d multi, vert. .60 .40
1085 A292 45d multicolored .75 .50
1086 A292 50d multi, vert. .75 .50
1087 A292 55d multicolored 1.00 .60
1088 A292 75d multi, vert. 1.25 .90
1089 A292 100d multi, vert. 1.60 1.10
Nos. 1084-1089 (6) 5.95 4.00

Intl. Maritime Organization, 25th Anniv. — A293

Early sailing ships.

1983, Mar. 17 ***Perf. 14½***
1090 A293 100d Phoenician 2.00 .75
1091 A293 100d Viking 2.00 .75
1092 A293 100d Greek 2.00 .75
1093 A293 100d Roman 2.00 .75
1094 A293 100d Libyan 2.00 .75
1095 A293 100d Pharoah's ship 2.00 .75
Nos. 1090-1095 (6) 12.00 4.50

Children's Day (1983) A294

Children's illustrations: a, Car. b, Tractor towing trailer. c, Children, dove. d, Boy Scouts. e, Dinosaur.

1983, Mar. 21 ***Perf. 14x14½***
1096 Strip of 5 2.75 2.75
a.-e. A294 20d, any single .40 .30

1st Intl. Symposium on Khadafy's Green Book — A295

1983, Apr. 1 ***Perf. 13½***
1097 A295 50d Khadafy, Green Book, map .60 .40
1098 A295 70d Lecture hall, emblem 1.00 .50
1099 A295 80d Khadafy, Green Book, emblem 1.10 .75
Nos. 1097-1099 (3) 2.70 1.65

Souvenir Sheet

Perf. 12½

1100 A295 100d Khadafy, Green Books 3.00 3.00

No. 1100 contains one stamp 57x48mm.

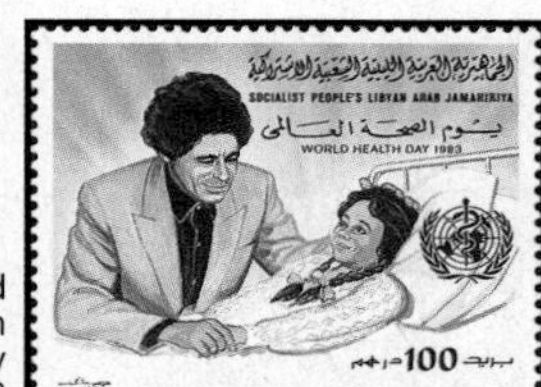

World Health Day A296

1983, Apr. 7 ***Perf. 12½***
1101 A296 25d Healthy children, vert. .25 .25
1102 A296 50d Man in wheelchair, vert. .60 .40
1103 A296 100d Girl in hospital bed 1.25 .75
Nos. 1101-1103 (3) 2.10 1.40

Pan-African Economic Committee, 25th Anniv. — A297

1983, Apr. 20 ***Perf. 13½***
1104 A297 50d multi .60 .40
1105 A297 100d multi 1.25 .75
1106 A297 250d multi 3.00 2.00
Nos. 1104-1106 (3) 4.85 3.15

Miniature Sheet

Fish A298

Designs: a, Labrus bimaculatus. b, Trigloporus lastoviza. c, Thalassoma pavo. d, Apogon imberbis. e, Scomber scombrus. f, Spondyliosoma cantharus. g, Trachinus draco. h, Blennius pavo. i, Scorpaena notata. j, Serranus scriba. k, Lophius piscatorius. l, Uranoscopus scaber. m, Auxis thazard. n, Zeus faber. o, Dactylopterus volitans. p, Umbrina cirrosa.

1983, May 15 ***Perf. 14½***
1107 Sheet of 16 10.00 10.00
a.-p. A298 25d any single .40 .30

Still-life by Gauguin (1848-1903) — A299

Paintings: No. 1108b, Abstract, unattributed. c, The Conquest of Tunis by Charles V, by Rubens. d, Arab Musicians in a Carriage, unattributed.

No. 1109a, Khadafy Glorified on Horseback, unattributed, vert. b, Triumph of David over the Syrians, by Raphael, vert. c, Laborers, unattributed, vert. d, Flower Vase, by van Gogh, vert.

1983, June 1 ***Perf. 11***
1108 Strip of 4 3.00 3.00
a.-d. A299 50d, any single .50 .35
1109 Strip of 4 3.00 3.00
a.-d. A299 50d, any single .50 .35

Souvenir Sheet

Ali Siala — A300

Scientists: No. 1110b, Ali El-Najar.

1983, June 1
1110 A300 Sheet of 2 3.50 3.50
a.-b. 100d, any single 1.50 1.50

1984 Summer Olympic Games, Los Angeles — A301

1983, June 15 ***Perf. 13½***
1111 A301 10d Basketball .25 .20
1112 A301 15d High jump .25 .20
1113 A301 25d Running .25 .25
1114 A301 50d Gymnastics .50 .40
1115 A301 100d Wind surfing 1.25 .75
1116 A301 200d Shot put 2.50 1.60
Nos. 1111-1116 (6) 5.00 3.40

Souvenir Sheets

1117 A301 100d Equestrian *3.00 3.00*
1118 A301 100d Soccer *3.00 3.00*

#1111-1116 exist imperf. Value, set $22.50. Nos. 1117-1118 also exist imperf.

Nos. 1111-1116 exist printed together in a miniature sheet of 6. Values: perf $35; imperf $50. Each value was also printed in a miniature sheet of 4. Value, set of 6 sheets, $45.

World Communications Year — A302

1983, July 1 ***Perf. 13***
1119 A302 10d multicolored .40 .30
1120 A302 50d multicolored .90 .60
1121 A302 100d multicolored 2.00 1.25
Nos. 1119-1121 (3) 3.30 2.15

The Green Book, by Khadafy A303

Ideologies: 10d, The House is to be served by its residents. 15d, Power, wealth and arms are in the hands of the people. 20d, Masters in their own castles, vert. 35d, No democracy without popular congress. 100d, The authority of the people, vert. 140d, The Green Book is the guide of humanity for final release.

1983, Aug. 1 ***Perf. 13½***
1122 A303 10d multi .25 .25
1123 A303 15d multi .25 .25
1124 A303 20d multi .25 .25
1125 A303 35d multi .40 .25
1126 A303 100d multi 1.25 .75
1127 A303 140d multi 1.75 1.25
Nos. 1122-1127 (6) 4.15 3.00

Souvenir Sheet

Litho. & Embossed

1128 A303 200d Khadafy in uniform 4.50 4.50

No. 1128 contains one gold embossed stamp 36x51mm.

2nd African Youth Sports Festival — A304

Designs: a, Team Handball. b, Basketball. c, Javelin. d, Running. e, Soccer.

1983, Aug. 22 **Litho.**
1129 Strip of 5 7.50 4.00
a.-e. A304 100d, any single 1.25 .75

September 1 Revolution, 14th Anniv. — A305

Women in the Armed Forces.

1983, Sept. 1 *Perf. 11½*

1130 A305 65d multi .75 .75
1131 A305 75d multi .90 .90
1132 A305 90d multi 1.00 1.00
1133 A305 100d multi 1.25 1.25
1134 A305 150d multi 1.75 1.75
1135 A305 250d multi 3.25 3.25
Nos. 1130-1135 (6) 8.90 8.90

Souvenir Sheet

Perf. 11

1136 A305 200d multi 4.50 4.50

No. 1136 contains one stamp 63x38mm.

2nd Islamic Scout Jamboree — A306

1983, Sept. 2 *Perf. 12½*

1137 A306 50d Saluting .75 .75
1138 A306 100d Camping 2.00 2.00

Souvenir Sheet

1139 Sheet of 2 4.50 4.50
a. A306 100d like 50d 2.00 2.00

No. 1139 contains Nos. 1138 and 1139a.

Traffic Day — A307

Saadun (1893-1923) A308

1983, Oct. 1 *Perf. 14½x14*

1140 A307 30d Youth traffic monitors 1.25 .75
1141 A307 70d Traffic officer 2.50 1.00
1142 A307 200d Motorcycle police 8.00 3.50
Nos. 1140-1142 (3) 11.75 5.25

1983, Oct. 11 *Perf. 13½*

1143 A308 100d multicolored 1.50 .75

1st Manned Flight, Bicent. — A309

Early aircraft and historic flights: a, Americana, 1910. b, Nulli Secundus, 1907. c, J. B. Meusnier, 1785. d, Blanchard and Jeffries, 1785, vert. e, Pilatre de Rozier, 1784, vert. f, Montgolfiere, Oct. 19, 1783, vert.

1983, Nov. 1

1144 Strip of 6 11.00 11.00
a.-f. A309 100d, any single 1.60 .85

Intl. Day of Cooperation with Palestinian People — A310

1983, Nov. 29 *Perf. 14½x14*

1145 A310 30d pale vio & lt bl grn .50 .30
1146 A310 70d lil & lt yel grn 1.40 .55
1147 A310 200d lt ultra & grn 3.75 2.00
Nos. 1145-1147 (3) 5.65 2.85

Miniature Sheet

Roman Mosaic — A311

Designs: Nos. 1148a-1148c, Gladiators. Nos. 1148d-1148f, Musicians, Nos. 1148g-1148i, Hunters.

1983, Dec. 1 *Perf. 12*

1148 A311 Sheet of 9 7.00 7.00
a.-i. 50d, any single .75 .35

#1148a-1148c, 1148d-1148f and 1148g-1148i se-tenant in a continuous design.

Achievements of the Sept. 1 Revolution — A312

1983, Dec. 15 *Perf. 13½*

1149 A312 10d Mosque .20 .20
1150 A312 15d Agriculture .20 .20
1151 A312 20d Industry .40 .25
1152 A312 35d Office building .50 .25
1153 A312 100d Health care 1.50 .60
1154 A312 140d Airport 2.25 1.10
Nos. 1149-1154 (6) 5.05 2.60

Souvenir Sheet

Litho. & Embossed

1155 A312 200d Khadafy 4.50 4.50

No. 1155 contains one gold embossed stamp 36x51mm.

Khadafy, Irrigation Project Survey Map A313

1983, Dec. 15

1156 A313 150d multicolored 2.25 1.25

A314

A315

Famous men: No. 1157a, Mahmud Burkis. No. 1157b, Ahmed El-Bakbak. No. 1157c, Mohamed El-Misurati. No. 1157d, Mahmud Ben Musa. No. 1157e, Abdulhamid Ben Ashiur. No. 1158a, Hosni Fauzi El-Amir. No. 1158b, Ali Haidar El-Saati. No. 1159, Mahmud Mustafa Dreza. No. 1160, Mehdi El-Sherif. No. 1161a, Ali El-Gariani. No. 1161b, Muktar Shakshuki. No. 1161c, Abdurrahman El-Busayri. No. 1161d, Ibbrahim Bakir. No. 1161e, Mahmud El-Janzuri. No. 1162a, Ahmed El-Feghi Hasan. No. 1162b, Bashir El Jawab.

1984 **Litho.** *Perf. 13½*

1157 Strip of 5 6.00 6.00
a.-e. A314 100d any single 1.10 1.10
1158 Pair 3.50 1.50
a.-b. A314 100d any single 1.50 .60
1159 A314 100d multi 1.75 .60
1160 A315 100d multi 1.75 .60
1161 Strip of 5 15.00 15.00
a.-e. A314 200d any single 2.50 2.50
1162 Pair 6.00 6.00
a.-b. A315 200d any single 2.50 2.50
Nos. 1157-1162 (6) 34.00 29.70

Issued: #1157, 1161-1162, 1/1; #1158-1160, 2/20.

Miniature Sheet

Water Sports — A316

Designs: a, Two windsurfers. b, Two-man craft. c, Two-man craft, birds. d, Wind sailing, skis. e, Water skier facing front. f, Fisherman in boat. g, Power boating. h, Water skier facing right. i, Fisherman in surf. j, Kayaking. k, Surfing. l, Water skier wearing life jacket. m, Scuba diver sketching underwater. n, Diver. o, Snorkel diver removing fish from harpoon. p, Scuba diver surfacing.

1984, Jan. 10 *Perf. 14½*

1164 Sheet of 16 8.50 8.50
a.-p. A316 25d any single .50 .50

African Children's Day — A317

Designs: a, Khadafy, girl scouts. b, Khadafy, children. c, Map, Khadafy, children (size: 63x44mm).

1984, Jan. 15 **Litho.** *Perf. 14½*

1165 Strip of 3 3.50 3.50
a.-b. A317 50d, any single .80 .80
c. A317 100d multi 2.00 2.00

Women's Emancipation — A318

70d, Women, diff., vert. 100d, Soldiers, Khadafy.

1984, Jan. 20 *Perf. 12*

1166 A318 55d multicolored .75 .40
1167 A318 70d multicolored 1.25 .45
1168 A318 100d multicolored 1.50 .75
Nos. 1166-1168 (3) 3.50 1.60

Irrigation A319

#1169: a, Desert, water. b, Produce, sheep grazing. c, Khadafy, irrigation of desert (size: 63x44mm). #1170-1171, Khadafy, map.

1984, Feb. 1 *Perf. 14½*

1169 Strip of 3 2.50 2.50
a.-b. A319 50d any single .50 .25
c. A319 100d multicolored 1.50 .60

Size: 72x36mm

Perf. 13½

1170 A319 100d multicolored 1.50 .60

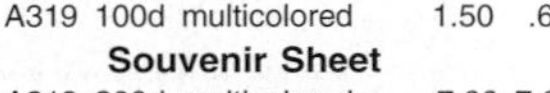

Souvenir Sheet

1171 A319 300d multicolored *7.00 7.00*

World Heritage — A320

Architectural ruins. No. 1174 vert.

1984, Feb. 10 *Perf. 12*

1172 A320 50d Theater, Sabratha .60 .25
1173 A320 60d Temple, Cyrene .75 .30
1174 A320 70d Monument, Sabratha .90 .35
1175 A320 100d Arena, Leptis Magna 1.50 .60
1176 A320 150d Temple, Cyrene, diff. 2.00 .90
1177 A320 200d Basilica, Leptis Magna 2.75 1.40
Nos. 1172-1177 (6) 8.50 3.80

Silver Dirhams Minted A.D. 671-757 — A321

Designs: a, Hegira 115. b, Hegira 93. c, Hegira 121. d, Hegira 49. e, Hegira 135.

Litho. & Embossed

1984, Feb. 15 *Perf. 13½*

1178 Strip of 5 15.00 15.00
a.-e. A321 200d, any single 2.75 1.25

Tripoli Intl. Fair A322

Tea served in various settings.

1984, Mar. 5 Litho. *Perf. 12½*

1179	A322	25d multicolored	.25	.25
1180	A322	35d multicolored	.40	.25
1181	A322	45d multicolored	.75	.25
1182	A322	55d multicolored	.90	.40
1183	A322	75d multicolored	1.10	.40
1184	A322	100d multicolored	1.75	.95
		Nos. 1179-1184 (6)	5.15	2.50

Musicians — A323

Designs: a, Muktar Shiaker Murabet. b, El-Aref El-Jamal. c, Ali Shiaalia. d, Bashir Fehmi.

1984, Mar. 15 *Perf. 14½*

1185	Strip of 4 + label	9.00	9.00
a.-d.	A323 100d, any single	1.90	1.00

Children's Day, IYC A324

Children's drawings: a, Recreation. b, Rainy day. c, Military strength. d, Playground. e, Porch swing, children, motorcycle.

1984, Mar. 21 *Perf. 14*

1186	Strip of 5	2.75	2.75
a.-e.	A324 20d, any single	.45	.25

Arab League Constitution, 39th Anniv. A325

1984, Mar. 22 *Perf. 13½*

1187	A325	30d multicolored	.60	.60
1188	A325	40d multicolored	.70	.70
1189	A325	50d multicolored	1.00	1.00
		Nos. 1187-1189 (3)	2.30	2.30

Miniature Sheet

Automobiles, Locomotives — A326

1984, Apr. 1

1190	Sheet of 16	30.00	30.00
a.-h.	A326 100d, Car, any single	1.75	.90
i.-p.	A326 100d, Locomotive, any single	1.75	.90

No. 1190 pictures outline of two camels in gold. Size: 214x135mm.

World Health Day A327

1984, Apr. 7 *Perf. 14½*

1191	A327	20d Stop Polio	.25	.25
1192	A327	30d No. 910	.40	.25
1193	A327	40d Arabic text	.90	.40
		Nos. 1191-1193 (3)	1.55	.90

Crafts A328

Designs: a, Shoemaker. b, Saddler. c, Women, wool. d, Spinner. e, Weaver. f, Tapestry weavers.

1984, May 1 *Perf. 12½*

1194	Strip of 6	15.00	15.00
a.-f.	A328 150d, any single	2.25	1.25

Postal and Telecommunications Union Congress — A329

Designs: a, Telephones, mail. b, Computer operators. c, Emblem.

1984, May 15 *Perf. 14½*

1195	Strip of 3	3.50	3.50
a.-b.	A329 50d, any single	.75	.40
c.	A329 100d multicolored	1.50	.75

Armed Crowd — A330

Map, Fire, Military — A331

Designs: No. 1197b, Soldiers. No. 1197c, Khadafy. No. 1198, Khadafy giving speech.

1984, May 17 *Perf. 12, 14½ (#1197)*

1196	A330	50d multi	.90	.40
1197		Strip of 3	3.00	3.00
a.-b.		A331 50d, any single	.75	.25
c.		A331 100d multi	1.75	.90
1198	A330	100d multi	1.50	.75
		Nos. 1196-1198 (3)	5.40	4.15

Abrogation of the May 17 Treaty. Size of No. 1197c: 63x45mm.

Youth War Casualties A332

1984, June 4 *Perf. 10*

1199	A332	70d Damaged flag	1.00	.40
1200	A332	100d Children imprisoned	1.50	.75

Miniature Sheet

Green Book Quotations A333

Designs: a, The Party System Aborts Democracy. b, Khadafy. c, Partners Not Wage-Workers. d, No Representation in Lieu of the People . . . e, Green Book. f, Committees Everywhere. g, Forming Parties Splits Societies. h, Party building, text on track. i, No Democracy without Popular Congresses.

1984, June 20 *Perf. 14*

1201	Sheet of 9	14.00	14.00
a.-i.	A333 100d, any single	1.50	.75

See No. 1270.

Folk Costumes — A334

Background colors: a, Green. b, Beige. c, Violet. d, Pale greenish blue. e, Salmon rose. f, Blue.

1984, July 1 *Perf. 14½x14*

1202	Strip of 6	12.50	12.50
a.-f.	A334 100d, any single	1.75	1.00

Miniature Sheet

Natl. Soccer Championships — A335

Stadium, star, world cup and various action scenes.

1984, July 15 *Perf. 13½*

1203	Sheet of 16	20.00	20.00
a.-p.	A335 70d, any single	1.10	.60

1984 Los Angeles Olympics — A336

World Food Day — A337

1984, July 28

1204	A336	100d Soccer	2.00	1.10
1205	A336	100d Basketball	2.00	1.10
1206	A336	100d Swimming	2.00	1.10
1207	A336	100d Sprinting	2.00	1.10
1208	A336	100d Windsurfing	2.00	1.10
1209	A336	100d Discus	2.00	1.10
		Nos. 1204-1209 (6)	12.00	6.60

Souvenir Sheets

1210	A336	250d Equestrian	6.25	6.25
1211	A336	250d Arab equestrian	6.25	6.25

1984, Aug. 1 *Perf. 12*

1212	A337	100d Forest scenes	1.75	.75
1213	A337	200d Men riding camels, oasis	3.50	1.25

Miniature Sheet

Sept. 1 Revolution, 15th Anniv. — A338

Designs: a, Green books, building at right angle. b, Green book, building, minaret. c, Minaret, party building and grounds. d, Revolution leader. e, Eight-story building. f, Construction, dome. g, Highway, bridge. h, Green book, building at left angle. i, Shepherd, sheep. j, Harvester. k, Tractors. l, Industry. m, Khadafy. n, Irrigation pipe, man drinking. o, Silos, factory. p, Shipping.

1984, Sept. 15 *Perf. 14½*

1214	Sheet of 16	9.00	9.00
a.-p.	A338 25d any single	.50	.25

A339

Evacuation Day — A340

#1215b, Warrior facing left. #1215c, Khadafy leading battle (size: 63x45mm). #1216, Female rider. #1217, Battle scene. #1218, Italian whipping Libyan.

1984, Oct. 7

1215	Strip of 3	3.50	3.50
a.-b.	A339 50d, any single	.75	.40

c. A339 100d multi 1.50 .60

Perf. 11½

1216 A340 100d multicolored 1.50 .60
1217 A340 100d multicolored 1.50 .60
1218 A340 100d multicolored 1.50 .60
Nos. 1215-1218 (4) 8.00 5.30

Miniature Sheet

Equestrians — A341

Various jumping, racing and dressage exercises printed in a continuous design.

1984, Oct. 15 ***Perf. 13½***
1219 Sheet of 16 9.00 .90
a.-p. A341 25d any single .50 .50

PHILAKOREA '84.

Agricultural Traditions — A342

Designs: a, Farmer. b, Well, man, ox. c, Basket weaver. d, Shepherd, ram. e, Tanning hide. f, Coconut picker.

1984, Nov. 1 ***Perf. 13½***
1220 Strip of 6 12.50 12.50
a.-f. A342 100d, any single 1.75 1.00

Union of Arab Pharmacists, 9th Congress — A343

1984, Nov. 6 ***Perf. 12***
1221 A343 100d multicolored 1.75 1.75
1222 A343 200d multicolored 3.50 3.50

Arab-African Union — A344

1984, Nov. 15 ***Perf. 12***
1223 A344 100d Map, banner, crowd 1.75 1.75
1224 A344 100d Men, flags 1.75 1.75

Nos. 1046, 1147 A345

1984, Nov. 29 ***Perf. 12½***
1225 A345 100d pink & multi 3.75 3.75
1226 A345 150d brt yel grn & multi 4.75 4.75

Intl. Day of Cooperation with the Palestinian People.

Miniature Sheet

Intl. Civil Aviation Organization, 40th Anniv. — A346

Aircraft: a, Boeing 747 SP, 1975. b, Concorde, 1969. c, Lockheed L1011-500 Tristar, 1978. d, Airbus A310, 1982. e, Tupolev TU-134A, 1962. f, Shorts 360, 1981. g, Boeing 727, 1963. h, Caravelle 10, 1965. i, Fokker F27, 1955. j, Lockheed 749A Constellation, 1946. k, Martin 130, 1955. l, Douglas DC-3, 1936. m, Junkers JU-52, 1932. n, Lindbergh's Spirit of St. Louis, 1927 Ryan. o, De Havilland Moth, 1925. p, Wright Flyer, 1903.

1984, Dec. 7 ***Perf. 13½***
1227 Sheet of 16 27.50 27.50
a.-p. A346 70d any single 1.50 .75

African Development Bank, 20th Anniv. — A347

UN Child Survival Campaign A348

"20" in different configurations and: 70d, Map, symbols of industry, education and agriculture. 100d, Symbols of research and development.

1984, Dec. 15
1228 A347 50d multicolored .90 .90
1229 A347 70d multicolored 1.25 1.25
1230 A347 100d multicolored 1.75 1.75
Nos. 1228-1230 (3) 3.90 3.90

1985, Jan. 1 ***Perf. 12***
1231 A348 70d Mother, child 1.50 .75
1232 A348 70d Children 1.50 .75
1233 A348 70d Boys at military school 1.50 .75
1234 A348 70d Khadafy, children 1.50 .75
Nos. 1231-1234 (4) 6.00 3.00

Irrigation — A349

Drop of Water, Map — A350

1985, Jan. 15 ***Perf. 14½x14***
1235 A349 100d shown 2.00 1.00
1236 A349 100d Flowers 2.00 1.00
1237 A349 100d Map, water 2.00 1.00
Nos. 1235-1237 (3) 6.00 3.00

Souvenir Sheet

Perf. 14x14½

1238 A350 200d shown 4.00 4.00

Musicians — A351

#1239a, Kamel El-Ghadi. #1239b, Lute. #1240a, Ahmed El-Khogia. #1240b, Violin. #1241a, Mustafa El-Fallah. #1241b, Zither. #1242a, Mohamed Hamdi. #1242b, Mask.

1985, Feb. 1 ***Perf. 14½***
1239 A351 Pair 5.00 3.75
a.-b. 100d, any single 2.25 1.75
1240 A351 Pair 5.00 3.75
a.-b. 100d, any single 2.25 1.75
1241 A351 Pair 5.00 3.75
a.-b. 100d, any single 2.25 1.75
1242 A351 Pair 5.00 3.75
a.-b. 100d, any single 2.25 1.75
Nos. 1239-1242 (4) 20.00 15.00

Nos. 1239-1242 printed in sheets of 20, four strips of 5 consisting of two pairs each musician flanking center stamps picturing instruments.

Gold Dinars Minted A.D. 699-727 — A352

#1243a, Hegira 105. #1243b, Hegira 91. #1243c, Hegira 77. #1244, Dinar from Zuela.

Litho. and Embossed

1985, Feb. 15 ***Perf. 13½***
1243 Strip of 3 12.50 12.50
a.-c. A352 200d, any single 4.00 2.50

Souvenir Sheet

1244 A352 300d multi 7.50 7.50

Fossils A353

1985, Mar. 1 **Litho.** ***Perf. 13½***
1245 A353 150d Frog 6.00 3.00
1246 A353 150d Fish 6.00 3.00
1247 A353 150d Mammal 6.00 3.00
Nos. 1245-1247 (3) 18.00 9.00

People's Authority Declaration A354

Khadafy wearing: a, Folk costume. b, Academic robe. c, Khaki uniform. d, Black uniform. e, White uniform.

1985, Mar. 2 **Litho.** ***Perf. 14½***
1248 Strip of 5 10.00 10.00
a.-e. A354 100d, any single 2.00 1.50

Tripoli Intl. Fair — A355

Musicians playing: a, Cymbals. b, Double flute, bongo. c, Wind instrument, drum. d, Drum. e, Tambourine.

1985, Mar. 5 ***Perf. 14***
1249 Strip of 5 10.00 10.00
a.-e. A355 100d, any single 1.90 1.75

Children's Day, IYC A356

Children's drawings, various soccer plays: a, Goalie and player. b, Four players. c, Players as letters of the alphabet. d, Goalie save. e, Player heading the ball.

1985, Mar. 21 ***Perf. 12***
1250 Strip of 5 7.50 7.50
a.-e. A356 20d, any single .40 .25

Intl. Program for Development of Telecommunications A357

World Health Day — A358

1985, Apr. 1
1251 A357 30d multicolored .40 .40
1252 A357 70d multicolored 1.00 1.00
1253 A357 100d multicolored 2.00 2.00
Nos. 1251-1253 (3) 3.40 3.40

1985, Apr. 7
1254 A358 40d Invalid, nurses 1.00 .60
1255 A358 60d Nurse, surgery 1.50 1.00
1256 A358 100d Nurse, child 2.50 1.60
Nos. 1254-1256 (3) 5.00 3.20

Miniature Sheet

Sea Shells — A359

Designs: a, Mytilidae. b, Muricidae (white). c, Cardiidae. d, Corallophilidae. e, Muricidae. f, Muricacea. g, Turridae. h, Argonautidae. i, Tonnidae. j, Aporrhaidae. k, Trochidae. l, Cancellariidae. m, Epitoniidae. n, Turbnidae. o, Mitridae. p, Pectinidae.

1985, Apr. 20

1257 Sheet of 16 13.00 13.00
a.-p. A359 25d, any single .60 .25

Tripoli Intl. Book Fair — A360

Intl. Youth Year — A361

1985, Apr. 28 ***Perf. 13½***

1258 A360 100d multi 2.00 1.50
1259 A360 200d multi 4.00 3.00

1985, May 1

Games: No. 1260a, Jump rope. No. 1260b, Board game. No. 1260c, Hopscotch. No. 1260d, Stickgame. No. 1260e, Tops. No. 1261a, Soccer. No. 1261b, Basketball.

1260 Strip of 5 6.00 6.00
a.-e. A361 20d, any single .40 .25

Souvenir Sheet

1261 Sheet of 2 9.00 9.00
a.-b. A361 100d, any single 3.00 1.00

No. 1261 contains 2 stamps 30x42mm.

Miniature Sheet

Mosque Minarets and Towers — A362

Mosques: a, Abdussalam Lasmar. b, Zaoviat Kadria. c, Zaoviat Amura. d, Gurgi. e, Mizran. f, Salem. g, Ghat. h, Ahmed Karamanli. i, Atya. j, El Kettani. k, Benghazi. l, Derna. m, El Derug. n, Ben Moussa. o, Ghadames. p, Abdulwahab.

1985, May 15 ***Perf. 12***

1262 Sheet of 16 15.00 15.00
a.-p. A362 50d, any single .75 .60

A363

A364

1985, June 1 **Litho.** ***Perf. 13½***

1263 A363 100d Hamida El-Anezi 2.00 1.50
1264 A363 100d Jamila Zemerli 2.00 1.50

Teachers' Day.

1985 June 12

Battle of the Philadelphia: a, Ship sinking. b, Militia. c, Hand-to-hand combat.

1265 Strip of 3 4.00 4.00
a.-b. A364 50d, any single 1.00 1.00
c. A364 100d multicolored 1.75 1.75

Size of No. 1265c: 60x48mm. Continuous design with No. 1265c in middle.

A365

Khadafy's Islamic Pilgrimage — A366

"The Holy Koran is the Law of Society" and Khadafy: a, Writing. b, Kneeling. c, With Holy Kaaba. d, Looking in window. e, Praying at pilgrimage ceremony.

1985, June 16

1266 Strip of 5 22.50 22.50
a.-e. A365 200d, any single 4.00 2.50

Souvenir Sheet

1267 A366 300d multicolored 6.50 6.50

Miniature Sheet

Mushrooms — A367

Designs: a, Leucopaxillus lepistoides. b, Amanita caesarea. c, Coriolus hirsutus. d, Cortinarius subfulgens. e, Dermocybe pratensis. f, Macrolepiota excoriata. g, Amanita curtipes. h, Trametes ljubarskyi. i, Pholiota aurivella. j, Boletus edulis. k, Geastrum sessile. l, Russula sanguinea. m, Cortinarius herculeus. n, Pholiota lenta. o, Amanita rubenscens. p, Scleroderma polyrhizum.

1985, July 15

1268 Sheet of 16 17.50 17.50
a.-p. A367 50d, any single 1.00 .40

No. 1268 exists imperf. Value $50.

Women's Folk Costumes — A368

Designs: a, Woman in violet. b, In white. c, In brown and blue. d, In blue. e, In red.

1985, Aug. 1 ***Perf. 14½x14***

1269 Strip of 5 10.00 10.00
a.-e. A368 100d, any single 1.75 1.50

Green Book Quotations Type of 1984
Miniature Sheet

Designs: a, In Need Freedom Is Latent. b, Khadafy reading. c, To Make A Party You Split Society. d, Public Sport Is for All the Masses. e, Green Books, doves. f, Wage-Workers Are a Type of Slave . . . g, People Are Only Harmonious with Their Own Arts and Heritages. h, Khadafy orating. i, Democracy Means Popular Rule Not Popular Expression.

1985, Aug. 15 ***Perf. 14***

1270 Sheet of 9 17.50 17.50
a.-i. A333 100d, any single 1.75 1.50

A369

September 1 Revolution, 16th Anniv. — A370

Designs: a, Food. b, Oil pipeline, refinery. c, Capital, olive branch. d, Mosque, modern buildings. e, Flag, mountains. f, Telecommunications apparatus.

1985, Sept. 1 ***Perf. 12½***

1271 Strip of 6 12.50 12.50
a.-f. A369 100d, any single 2.00 1.50
1272 A370 200d multi 4.50 4.50

Mosque Entrances A371

Designs: a, Zauiet Amoura, Janzour. b, Shiaieb El-ain, Tripoli. c, Zauiet Abdussalam El-asmar, Zliten. d, Karamanli, Tripoli. e, Gurgi, Tripoli.

1985, Sept. 15 ***Perf. 14***

1273 Strip of 5 10.00 10.00
a.-e. A371 100d, any single 2.00 1.50

Miniature Sheet

Basketball A372

Various players in action.

1985, Oct. 1 **Litho.** ***Perf. 13x12½***

1274 Sheet of 16 9.00 9.00
a.-p. A372 25d any single .50 .40

Evacuation A373

Designs: a, Man on crutches, web, tree. b, Man caught in web held by disembodied hands. c, Three men basking in light.

1985, Oct. 7 ***Perf. 15***

1275 Strip of 3 7.00 7.00
a.-c. A373 100d any single 1.75 1.50

Stamp Day — A374

Italia 85: a, Man sitting at desk, Type A228, Earth. b, Magnifying glass, open stock book, Type A228. c, Stamps escaping envelope.

1985, Oct. 25 ***Perf. 12***

1276 Strip of 3 4.00 4.00
a.-c. A374 50d, any single 1.00 .60

1986 World Cup Soccer Championships — A375

1985, Nov. 1 ***Perf. 13½***

1277 A375 100d Block, heading the ball 2.00 1.50
1278 A375 100d Kick, goalie catching ball 2.00 1.50
1279 A375 100d Goalie, block, dribble 2.00 1.50
1280 A375 100d Goalie, dribble, sliding block 2.00 1.50
1281 A375 100d Goalie catching the ball 2.00 1.50
1282 A375 100d Block 2.00 1.50
Nos. 1277-1282 (6) 12.00 9.00

Souvenir Sheet

1283 A375 200d Four players 8.50 8.50

Intl. Day of Cooperation with the Palestinian People A376

1985, Nov. 29 Litho. *Perf. 12½*

1284	A376	100d multi	1.75	1.50
1285	A376	150d multi	3.25	2.25

A377a — Khadafy
A377

Perf. 12½x13, 13¼x13

1986, Jan. 1 Engr.

1286	A377	50d vermilion	20.00	20.00
1287	A377	60d blue	20.00	20.00
1288	A377	70d carmine	20.00	20.00
1289	A377	80d violet	20.00	20.00
1290	A377	90d brown	20.00	20.00
1291	A377	100d dk green	20.00	20.00
1292	A377	200d dk rose	20.00	20.00
1293	A377	250d brt green	20.00	20.00
1294	A377a	300d grysh blue	20.00	20.00
1295	A377a	500d redsh brown	20.00	20.00
1296	A377a	1500d grysh green	20.00	20.00
1297	A377a	2500d purple	20.00	20.00
	Nos. 1286-1297 (12)		240.00	240.00

Supposedly Nos. 1286-1297 were on sale for two hours. Value on first day cover, $350.

Importation Prohibited

Importation of the stamps of Libya was prohibited as of Jan. 7, 1986.

General Post and Telecommunications Co. — A378

1986, Jan. 15 *Perf. 12*

1298	A378	100d yel & multi	2.25	1.50
1299	A378	150d yel grn & multi	2.75	2.00

Peoples Authority Declaration — A379

Designs: b, Hand holding globe and paper. c, Dove, Khadafy's Green Book (size: 53x37mm).

1986, Mar. 2 *Perf. 12½x13*

1300	Strip of 3	4.50	4.50
a.-b.	A379 50d, any single	1.00	.60
c.	A379 100d multicolored	2.00	1.25

Musical Instruments — A380

Designs: a, Flute. b, Drums. c, Horn. d, Cymbals. e, Hand drum.

1986, Mar. 5

1301	Strip of 5	10.00	10.00
a.-e.	A380 100d any single	2.00	1.50

Tripoli International Fair.

Intl. Children's Day — A381

Designs: a, Boy Scout fishing. b, Riding camel. c, Chasing butterflies. d, Beating drum. e, Soccer game.

1986, Mar. 21 *Perf. 13½*

1302	Strip of 5	8.50	8.50
a.-e.	A381 50d any single	1.25	.75

World Health Day — A382

1986, Apr. 7

1303	A382	250d sil & multi	5.00	3.00
1304	A382	250d gold & multi	5.00	3.00

Government Programs A383

Designs: a, Medical examinations. b, Education. c, Farming (size: 63x42mm).

1986, May 1 *Perf. 14½*

1305	Strip of 3	3.75	3.75
a.-b.	A383 50d any single	.85	.60
c.	A383 100d multicolored	1.75	1.25

Miniature Sheet

World Cup Soccer Championships, Mexico — A384

Designs: No. 1306a, 2 players. No. 1306b, 3 players in red and white shirts, one in green. No. 1306c, 2 players, referee. No. 1306d, Shot at goal. No. 1306e, 2 players with striped shirts. No. 1306f, 2 players with blue shirts, one with red. No. 1307, 7 players. No. 1308, 1st Libyan team, 1931.

1986, May 31 *Perf. 13½*

1306	Sheet of 6	7.50	7.50
a.-f.	A384 50d any single	1.10	.75

Souvenir Sheets

1307	A384	200d multicolored	6.50	6.50
1308	A384	200d multicolored	6.50	6.50

Nos. 1307-1308 each contain one 52x37mm stamp.

Miniature Sheet

Vegetables A385

Designs: a, Peas. b, Zucchini. c, Beans. d, Eggplant. e, Corn. f, Tomato. g, Red pepper. h, Cucumbers. i, Garlic. j, Cabbage. k, Cauliflower. l, Celery. m, Onions. n, Carrots. o, Potato. p, Radishes.

1986, June 1 *Perf. 13x12½*

1309	Sheet of 16	15.00	15.00
a.-p.	A385 50d any single	.85	.75

No. 1309 has a continuous design.

Miniature Sheet

Khadafy and Irrigation Project A386

Khadafy and: a, Engineer reviewing plans, drill rig. b, Map. c, Well. d, Drought conditions. e, Water pipe. f, Pipes, pulleys, equipment. g, Lowering water pipe. h, Construction workers, trailer. i, Hands holding water. j, Opening water valve. k, Laying pipeline. l, Trucks hauling pipes. m, Khadafy holding green book, city. n, Giving vegetables to people. o, Boy drinking, man cultivating field. p, Men in prayer, irrigation. (Khadafy not shown on Nos. 1310h, 1310i, 1310k, 1310 l, 1310o.)

1986, July 1 *Perf. 13½*

1310	Sheet of 16	35.00	35.00
a.-p.	A386 100d any single	2.00	1.40

A387

A388

American Attack on Libya, Apr. 15 — A389

Designs: Nos. 1311a-1311p, Various scenes in Tripoli during and after air raid. No. 1312a. F14 aircraft. No. 1312b, Aircraft carrier, people. No. 1312c, Sinking of USS *Philadelphia,* 1801.

1986, July 13

1311	A387	Sheet of 16, #a.-p.	26.00	26.00
1312		Strip of 3	3.50	3.50
a.-b.		A388 50d multicolored	.85	.65
c.		A388 100d multicolored	1.75	1.25
1313	A389	100d multicolored	2.10	1.50

No. 1312 has a continuous design. Size of No. 1312b: 60x38mm.

Khadafy's Peace Methods A390

Khadafy: b, Reading Green Book. c, With old woman. d, Praying with children. e, Visiting sick. f, Driving tractor.

1986, July 13

1314	Sheet of 6	12.50	12.50
a.-f.	A390 100d any single	2.00	1.40

Miniature Sheet

Green Book Quotations A391

Designs: a, The House Must be Served by its Own Tenant. b, Khadafy. c, The Child is Raised by His Mother. d, Democracy is the Supervision of the People by the People. e, Green Books. f, Representation is a Falsification of Democracy. g, The Recognition of Profit is an Acknowledgement of Exploitation. h, Flowers. i, Knowledge is a Natural Right of Every Human Being...

1986, Aug. 1 *Perf. 14*

1315	Sheet of 9	19.00	19.00
a.-i.	A391 100d any single	2.00	1.40

Sept. 1st Revolution, 17th Anniv. A392

a, Public health. b, Agriculture. c, Sunflowers by Vincent Van Gogh. d, Defense. e. Oil industry.

1986, Sept. 1

1316	Strip of 5	22.50	22.50
a.-e.	A392 200d any single	4.00	2.75

A393

Arab-African Union, 1st Anniv. — A394

1986, Sept. 15 *Perf. 12*

1317 A393 250d Libyan, Arab horsemen 5.00 4.00
1318 A394 250d Women in native dress 5.00 4.00

Evacuation Day — A395

Designs: a, Mounted warrior. b, Two horsemen, infantry. c, Cavalry charge.

1986, Oct. 7 *Perf. 13½*

1319 Strip of 3 6.00 6.00
a. A395 50d multicolored 1.00 .60
b. A395 100d multicolored 2.00 1.10
c. A395 150d multicolored 2.75 2.40

Intl. Peace Year A396

1986, Oct. 24 *Perf. 14½*

1320 A396 200d bl & multi 4.00 3.00
1321 A396 200d grn & multi 4.00 3.00

Solidarity with the Palestinians — A397

1986, Nov. 29 *Perf. 12½*

1322 A397 250d pink & multi 5.00 4.00
1323 A397 250d blue & multi 5.00 4.00

Music and Dance — A398

Designs: a, Man beating drum. b, Masked dancer. c, Woman dancing with jugs on her head. d, Man playing bagpipe. e, Man beating hand drum.

1986, Dec. 1 *Perf. 12*

1324 Strip of 5 8.00 8.00
a.-e. A398 70d any single 1.50 1.25

Gazella Leptoceros — A399

1987, Mar. 2 *Perf. 13½*

1325 A399 100d Two adults 3.00 2.00
1326 A399 100d Fawn nursing 3.00 2.00
1327 A399 100d Adult sleeping 3.00 2.00
1328 A399 100d Adult drinking 3.00 2.00
Nos. 1325-1328 (4) 12.00 8.00

World Wildlife Fund.

Nos. 1325-1328 exist imperf. Value, set $27.50.

A400

A401

Crowd of People and: a, Oilfields. b, Buildings. c, Khadafy, buildings, globe.

1987, Mar. 2 *Perf. 13½*

1329 Strip of 3 40.00 40.00
a.-b. A400 500d multicolored 10.00 8.00
c. A400 1000d multicolored 20.00 15.00

People's Authority declaration.

No. 1329 has a continuous design. Size of No. 1329c: 42x37mm.

1987, Sept. 1 *Perf. 13½*

Sept. 1st Revolution, 18th Anniv.: a, Shepherd, sheep. b, Khadafy. c, Mosque. d, Irrigation pipeline. e, Combine in field. f, Khadafy at microphones. g, Harvesting grain. h, Irrigation. i, Soldier. j, Militiaman. k, Fountain. l, Skyscrapers. m, House, women. n, Children. o, Assembly hall. p, Two girls.

Miniature Sheet

1330 Sheet of 16 65.00 65.00
a.-p. A401 150d any single 3.00 2.25

No. 1330 has a continuous design.

Libyan Freedom Fighters — A402

No. 1331: a, Omer Abed Anabi Al Mansuri. b, Ahmed Ali Al Emrayd. c, Khalifa Said Ben Asker. d, Mohamed Ben Farhat Azawi. e, Mohamed Souf Al Lafi Al Marmori.

1988, Feb. 15

1331 Strip of 5 29.00 29.00
a. A402 100d multicolored 2.00 1.25
b. A402 200d multicolored 5.75 4.25
c. A402 300d multicolored 8.00 4.50
d. A402 400d multicolored
e. A402 500d multicolored 9.00 6.50

Freedom Festival Day — A403

1988, June 1

1332 A403 100d yel & multi 1.75 1.25
1333 A403 150d grn & multi 3.00 2.00
1334 A403 250d brn org & multi 5.00 3.50
Nos. 1332-1334 (3) 9.75 6.75

Miniature Sheet

American Attack on Libya, 2nd Anniv. A404

Khadafy: a, With woman and children. b, Playing chess. c, Fleeing from bombing with children. d, Praying in desert. e, Praying with children. f, Visiting wounded child. g, With infants and children, horiz. h, Delivering speech, horiz. i, With family, horiz.

#1336, In desert, vert. #1337, Making speech.

1988, July 13

1335 Sheet of 9 25.00 25.00
a.-i. A404 150d any single 2.75 2.00

Souvenir Sheets

Litho. & Embossed

1336 A404 500d gold & multi 10.00 10.00
1337 A404 500d gold & multi 10.00 10.00

No. 1335 exists imperf.

September 1st Revolution, 19th Anniv. — A405

1988, Sept. 19 **Litho.**

1338 A405 100d brt bl & multi 1.75 1.25
1339 A405 250d gray & multi 4.50 3.00
1340 A405 300d cit & multi 5.00 4.25
1341 A405 500d bl grn & multi 10.00 7.00
Nos. 1338-1341 (4) 21.25 15.50

1988 Summer Olympics, Seoul — A406

1988, Sept. 17

1342 A406 150d Tennis 2.75 2.00
1343 A406 150d Equestrian 2.75 2.00
1344 A406 150d Relay race 2.75 2.00
1345 A406 150d Soccer 2.75 2.00
1346 A406 150d Distance race 2.75 2.00
1347 A406 150d Cycling 2.75 2.00
Nos. 1342-1347 (6) 16.50 12.00

Souvenir Sheet

1348 A406 750d Soccer, diff. 13.00 13.00

#1348 contains one 30x42mm stamp. Exists imperf. #1342-1347 exist in miniature sheets of 1. Value, set $37.50.

Miniature Sheet

1988 Summer Olympics, Seoul — A407

1988, Sept 17

1350 Sheet of 3 8.50 8.50
a. A407 100d Bedouin rider 2.00 2.00
b. A407 200d shown 3.00 3.00
c. A407 200d Show jumping, diff. 3.00 3.00

Olymphilex '88, Seoul.

A408

A409

Design: Libyan Palm Tree.

1988, Nov. 1

1351 A408 500d Fruit 10.00 6.50
1352 A408 1000d Palm tree 18.00 12.00

1988

1353 Strip of 3 11.50 11.50
a. A409 100d shown 2.00 1.40
b. A409 200d Boy with rocks 3.50 2.75
c. A409 300d Flag, map 5.75 4.25

Palestinian uprising. #1353b, size: 45x39mm.

People's Authority Declaration — A410

1989

1354 A410 260d dk grn & multi 5.00 3.00
1355 A410 500d gold & multi 10.00 6.00

Miniature Sheet

September 1 Revolution, 20th Anniv. — A411

Designs: a, Crowd, Green Books, emblem. b, Soldiers, Khadafy, irrigation pipeline. c, Military equipment, Khadafy, communication and transportation. d, Mounted warriors. e, Battle scenes.

1989 *Perf. 13½*

1356 A411 Sheet of 5 14.00 14.00
a.-e. 150d any single 2.75 2.00
f. Bklt. pane of 5, perf. 13½ horiz. 14.00 14.00

Souvenir Sheet

1357 A411 250d Khadafy 4.00 4.00

No. 1357 contains one 36x51mm stamp. Stamps from No. 1356f have gold border at right.

Libyans Deported to Italy — A412

#1359, Libyans in boats. #1360, Khadafy, crescent moon. #1361, Khadafy at left, in desert. #1362, Khadafy at right, soldiers. #1363, Khadafy in center, Libyans.

1989

1358 A412 100d shown 1.75 1.25
1359 A412 100d multicolored 1.75 1.25
1360 A412 100d multicolored 1.75 1.25
1361 A412 100d multicolored 1.75 1.25
1362 A412 100d multicolored 1.75 1.25
Nos. 1358-1362 (5) 8.75 6.25

Souvenir Sheet

1363 A412 150d multicolored 3.00 3.00

No. 1363 contains one 72x38mm stamp.

A413

A414

1989 ***Perf. 12***

1364 A413 150d multicolored 2.75 2.75
1365 A413 200d multicolored 4.25 4.25

Demolition of Libyan-Tunisian border fortifications.

1989 ***Perf. 12x11½***

1366 A414 100d shown 2.25 2.25
1367 A414 300d Man, flag, crowd 6.50 6.50
1368 A414 500d Emblem 10.00 10.00
Nos. 1366-1368 (3) 18.75 18.75

Solidarity with the Palestinians.

Ibn Annafis, Physician A415

1989 ***Perf. 12***

1369 A415 100d multicolored 2.75 2.75
1370 A415 150d multicolored 4.00 4.00

A416

A417

1990, Oct. 18 **Litho.** ***Perf. 14***

Granite Paper

1371 A416 100d multicolored 1.75 1.75
1372 A416 300d multicolored 8.00 8.00

Intl. Literacy Year.

1990, Oct. 18

Granite Paper

1373 A417 100d multicolored 1.75 1.75
1374 A417 400d multicolored 5.25 5.25

Organization of Petroleum Exporting Countries (OPEC), 30th anniv.

A418

A419

1990, June 28 ***Perf. 11½x12***

1375 A418 100d brt org & multi 1.75 1.75
1376 A418 400d grn & multi 8.00 8.00

Evacuation of US military base, 20th anniv.

1990, Apr. 24

1377 A419 300d bl & multi 5.00 5.00
1378 A419 500d vio & multi 10.00 10.00

People's authority declaration.

A420

A421

Plowing Season in Libya: 2000d, Man on tractor plowing field.

1990, Dec. 4 ***Perf. 14***

Granite Paper

1379 A420 500d multicolored 11.00 11.00
1380 A420 2000d multicolored 37.50 37.50

1990, Nov. 5 ***Perf. 14***

Granite Paper

1381 A421 100d grn & multi 1.75 1.75
1382 A421 400d vio & multi 8.00 8.00
1383 A421 500d bl & multi 9.25 9.25
Nos. 1381-1383 (3) 19.00 19.00

Souvenir Sheet

Perf. 11½

1384 A421 500d Trophy, map, horiz. 11.00 11.00

World Cup Soccer Championships, Italy. No. 1384 contains one 38x33mm stamp.

Sept. 1st Revolution, 21st Anniv. A422

1990, Sept. 3 ***Perf. 14***

Granite Paper

1385 A422 100d multicolored 2.00 2.00
1386 A422 400d multicolored 8.50 8.50
1387 A422 1000d multicolored 21.00 21.00
Nos. 1385-1387 (3) 31.50 31.50

Imperf

Size: 120x90mm

1388 A422 200d multi, diff. 8.50 8.50

Maghreb Arab Union, 2nd Anniv. — A423

1991, Mar. 10 **Litho.** ***Perf. 13½***

1389 A423 100d multicolored 2.00 2.00
1390 A423 300d gold & multi 5.75 5.75

People's Authority Declaration — A424

1991, Mar. 10

1391 A424 300d multicolored 5.00 5.00
1392 A424 400d silver & multi 10.00 10.00

Children's Day — A425

World Health Day — A426

1991, Mar. 22

1393 A425 100d Butterflies, girl 2.75 2.75
1394 A425 400d Bird, boy 10.00 10.00

1991, Apr. 7

1395 A426 100d blue & multi 1.75 1.75
1396 A426 200d green & multi 3.50 3.50

Scenes from Libya A427

1991, June 20

1397 A427 100d Wadi el Hayat, vert. 1.75 1.75
1398 A427 250d Mourzuk 5.00 5.00
1399 A427 500d Ghadames 10.00 10.00
Nos. 1397-1399 (3) 16.75 16.75

Irrigation Project A428

a, Laborers, heavy equipment. b, Khadafy, heavy equipment. c, Livestock, fruit & vegetables.

1991, Aug. 28 ***Perf. 12***

1400 A428 50d Strip of 3, #a.-c. 3.50 3.50

No. 1400 has a continuous design. Size of No. 1400b: 60x36mm.

Sept. 1st Revolution, 22nd Anniv. — A429

1991, Sept. 1 ***Perf. 13½***

1401 A429 300d Chains, roses & "22" 5.75 5.75
1402 A429 400d Chains, "22" 7.25 7.25
a. Souv. sheet of 2, #1401-1402 16.00 16.00

Telecom '91 A430

1991, Oct. 7 **Litho.** ***Perf. 13½***

1403 A430 100d Emblems, vert. 1.75 1.75
1404 A430 500d Buildings, satellite dish 9.25 9.25

Libyans Deported to Italy A431

1991, Oct. 26 **Litho.** ***Perf. 13½***

1405 A431 100d Monument, soldier 1.75 1.75
1406 A431 400d Ship, refugees, soldiers 7.25 7.25
a. Souv. sheet of 2, #1405-1406 10.00 10.00

Arab Unity A432

1991, Nov. 15 ***Perf. 12***

1407 A432 50d tan & multi 1.00 1.00
1408 A432 100d blue & multi 2.00 2.00

Miniature Sheet

Trucks, Automobiles and Motorcycles A433

Designs: a-d, Various trucks. e-h, Various off-road race cars. i-p, Various motorcycles.

1991, Dec. 28 ***Perf. 14***

1409 A433 50d Sheet of 16, #a.-p. 17.50 17.50

Eagle — A434

Col. Khadafy — A434a

1992 ***Perf. 11½***

Granite Paper (#1412-1419)

Background Colors

No.	Type	Denom.	Color	Unused	Used
1412	A434	100d	yellow	1.40	.85
1413	A434	150d	blue gray	2.25	1.25
1414	A434	200d	bright blue	2.75	1.75
1415	A434	250d	orange	3.75	2.00
1416	A434	300d	purple	4.25	2.50
1418	A434	400d	bright pink	5.75	3.50
1419	A434	450d	bright green	7.25	3.75

Perf. 13½

No.	Type	Denom.	Color	Unused	Used
1420	A434a	500d	yellow green	6.50	3.50
1421	A434a	1000d	rose	13.00	7.00
1422	A434a	2000d	blue	26.00	14.00
1423	A434a	5000d	violet	65.00	37.50
1424	A434a	6000d	yellow brown	80.00	45.00
			Nos. 1412-1424 (12)	217.90	122.60

Issued: #1412-1416, 1418-1419, 1/1/92; #1420-1424, 9/1/92.

This is an expanding set. Numbers may change.

People's Authority Declaration A435

1992, Mar. **Litho.** ***Perf. 12***

No.	Type	Description	Unused	Used
1425	A435	100d yellow & multi	1.50	1.50
1426	A435	150d blue & multi	2.25	2.25

African Tourism Year (in 1991) A436

1992, Apr. 5 ***Perf. 14½***

Granite Paper

No.	Type	Description	Unused	Used
1427	A436	50d purple & multi	.75	.75
1428	A436	100d pink & multi	1.40	1.40

1992 Summer Olympics, Barcelona A437

1992, June 15 ***Perf. 12***

No.	Type	Description	Unused	Used
1429	A437	50d Tennis	.75	.75
1430	A437	50d Long jump	.75	.75
1431	A437	50d Discus	.75	.75
		Nos. 1429-1431 (3)	2.25	2.25

Size: 106x82mm

Imperf

No.	Type	Description	Unused	Used
1432	A437	100d Olympic torch, rings	1.50	1.50

Revolutionary Achievements — A438

Designs: 100d, Palm trees. 150d, Steel mill. 250d, Cargo ship. 300d, Libyan Airlines. 400d, Natl. Assembly, Green Books. 500d, Irrigation pipeline, Khadafy.

1992, June 30 ***Perf. 14***

Granite Paper

No.	Type	Description	Unused	Used
1433	A438	100d multicolored	1.40	1.40
1434	A438	150d multicolored	2.25	2.25
1435	A438	250d multicolored	3.75	3.75
1436	A438	300d multicolored	4.25	4.25
1437	A438	400d multicolored	5.75	5.75
1438	A438	500d multicolored	7.25	7.25
		Nos. 1433-1438 (6)	24.65	24.65

Tripoli Intl. Fair — A439

1992, Mar. ***Perf. 12***

No.	Type	Description	Unused	Used
1439	A439	50d Horse & buggy		
1440	A439	100d Horse & sulky		

Mahgreb Arab Union Philatelic Exhibition — A440

1992, Feb. 17 ***Perf. 14½***

No.	Type	Description	Unused	Used
1441	A440	75d blue green & multi	2.50	1.75
1442	A440	80d blue & multi	2.50	1.75

Miniature Sheet

Fish A441

Designs: a, Fish with spots near eye. b, Thin fish. d, Brown fish, currents. e, Fish, plants at LR. f, Fish, plants at LL.

1992, Apr. 15 ***Perf. 14***

No.	Type	Description	Unused	Used
1443	A441	100d Sheet of 6, #a.-f.	14.00	14.00

Miniature Sheet

Horsemanship — A442

Designs: a, Woman rider with gun. b, Man on white horse. c, Mongol rider. d, Roman officer. e, Cossack rider. f, Arab rider. 250d, Two Arab riders.

1992, Apr. 25 ***Perf. 13½x14***

No.	Type	Description	Unused	Used
1444	A442	100d Sheet of 6, #a.-f.	9.50	9.50

Souvenir Sheet

No.	Type	Description	Unused	Used
1445	A442	250d multicolored	5.00	5.00

Khadafy — A443

Designs: No. 1450a, like No. 1446. b, like No. 1447. c, like No. 1448. d, like No. 1449.

1992, Jan. 1 ***Perf. 14x13½***

No.	Type	Description	Unused	Used
1446	A443	100d blue green & multi	2.00	2.00
1447	A443	100d gray & multi	2.00	2.00
1448	A443	100d rose lake & multi	2.00	2.00
1449	A443	100d yellow & multi	2.00	2.00
		Nos. 1446-1449 (4)	8.00	8.00

Souvenir Sheet

No.	Type	Description	Unused	Used
1450	A443	150d Sheet of 4, #a.-d.	11.00	11.00

Evacuation of Foreign Forces — A444

Costumes A445

1992, Oct. 7 **Litho.** ***Perf. 14***

No.	Type	Description	Unused	Used
1451	A444	75d Horse, broken chain	1.00	1.00
1452	A444	80d Flag, broken chain	1.00	1.00

1992, Dec. 15 **Litho.** ***Perf. 12***

Women wearing various traditional costumes.

Denomination color: a, green. b, black. c, violet blue. d, sky blue. e, yellow brown.

No.	Type	Description	Unused	Used
1453	A445	50d Strip of 5, #a.-e.	4.00	4.00

Sept. 1st Revolution, 23rd Anniv. — A446

1992, Sept. 1

No.	Type	Description	Unused	Used
1454	A446	50d Torch, "23"	.75	.75
1455	A446	100d Flag, "23"	1.40	1.40

Souvenir Sheet

No.	Type	Description	Unused	Used
1456	A446	250d Eagle, "23"	3.50	3.50

No. 1456 contains one 50x40mm stamp.

Libyans Deported to Italy — A447

1992, Oct. 26

No.	Type	Description	Unused	Used
1457	A447	100d tan & multi	1.40	1.40
1458	A447	250d blue & multi	3.00	3.00

Oasis A448

Designs: 100d, Gazelle drinking. 200d, Camels, palm trees, vert. 300d, Palm trees, camel and rider.

1992, Oct. 1 ***Perf. 14***

No.	Type	Description	Unused	Used
1459	A448	100d multicolored	1.50	1.50
1460	A448	200d multicolored	3.00	3.00
1461	A448	300d multicolored	5.00	5.00
		Nos. 1459-1461 (3)	9.50	9.50

Palestinian Intifada — A449

Designs: 100d, Palestinian holding rock and flag. 300d, Map of Israel and Palestine, Dome of the Rock, Palestinian flag, olives, hand holding rock, vert.

1992, Nov. 26 **Litho.** ***Perf. 12***

No.	Type	Description	Unused	Used
1462-1463	A449	Set of 2	4.50	4.50

Doctors — A450

Designs: 40d, Dr. Mohamed Ali Imsek (1883-1945). 60d, Dr. Aref Adhani Arif (1884-1935).

1993, Feb. 1

No.	Type	Description	Unused	Used
1464-1465	A450	Set of 2	1.25	1.25

Intl. Conference on Nutrition, Rome — A451

Background colors: 70d, Blue. 80d, Green.

1993, Feb. 15

No.	Type	Description	Unused	Used
1466-1467	A451	Set of 2	1.75	1.75

People's Authority Declaration — A452

Col. Khadafy, map of Libya, crowd, eagle, oil rig, pipeline and tanker: 60d, 65d, 75d.

1993, Mar. 2 *Perf. 14¾*
1468-1470 A452 Set of 3 2.25 2.25

Tripoli Intl. Fair A453

Various Fair participants, Fair emblem and panel color of: No. 1471, 60d, Pink. No. 1472, 60d, Yellow green. No. 1473, 60d, Blue, vert. No. 1474, 60d, Orange, vert.
100d, People on horses.

1993, Mar. 15 *Perf. 14*
1471-1474 A453 Set of 4 2.50 2.50

Souvenir Sheet

Perf. 11¾

1475 A453 100d multi 1.50 1.50

No. 1475 contains one 38x32mm stamp.

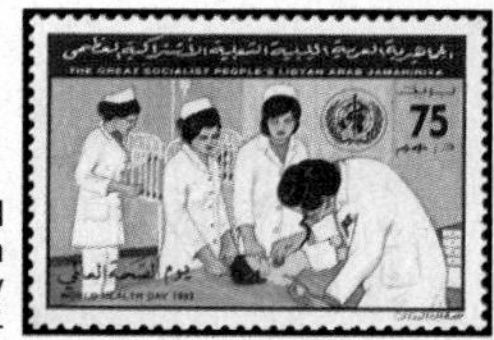

World Health Day A454

Designs: 75d, Doctor and three nurses examining child. 85d, Doctor and two nurses examining woman.

1993, Apr. 7 *Perf. 13¼*
1476-1477 A454 Set of 2 1.60 1.60

Children's Day — A455

No. 1478 — Various girls with background of: a, Gray green (red headdress). b, Red curtains. c, Gray. d, Home furnishings. e, Beige.

1993, May 1 *Perf. 13¾*
1478 Horiz. strip of 5 4.25 4.25
a.-e. A455 75d Any single .80 .80

Miniature Sheet

Watercraft — A456

No. 1479: a, Ship with swan's head figurehead. b, Ship with triangular sail and oars. c, Ship with one large white sail. d, Ship with rectangular sail and oars. e, Ship with three triangular sails. f, Sailboat, map of Western Mediterranean area. g, Sailboat, map of Eastern Mediterranean area. h, Ship with two red triangular sails. i, Ship with four sails, red flag. j, Sailboat, map of Western Libya. k, Sailboat, map of Eastern Libya. l, Ship with three sails on main mast. m, Ocean liner with black hull. n, Ship with six tan sails. o, Ship with furled sails. p, Ocean liner with white hull.

1993, July 15 *Perf. 13¼*
1479 A456 50d Sheet of 16, #a-p 10.00 10.00

Miniature Sheet

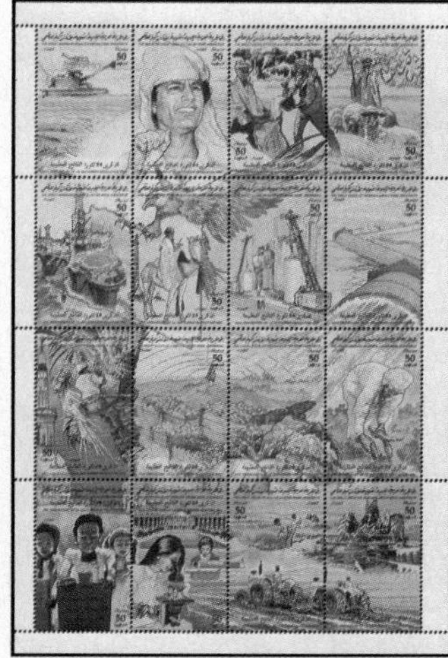

Sept. 1 Revolution, 24th Anniv. — A457

No. 1480: a, Grain combine. b, Col. Khadafy. c, Cows, man with feed bucket. d, Shepherd and sheep. e, Oil platform, map of Western Libya. f, Eagle, man on camel, map of Eastern Libya. g, Cranes lifting large tanks. h, Water pipeline. i, Man picking dates. j, Man in field, crates of vegetables. k, Crates of vegetables. l, Man picking vegetables. m, Three children. n, Building, women at typewriter and microscope. o, Man in field, tractor. p, Tractors in field.

1993, Dec. 10 *Perf. 14*
1480 A457 50d Sheet of 16, #a-p 12.00 12.00

Miniature Sheet

Libyans Deported to Italy — A458

No. 1481: a, Guard tower, soldier with gun, woman tending to sick man. b, Soldier with gun and bayonet guarding Libyans. c, Col. Khadafy with headdress. d, Man holding box and walking stick. e, Soldiers whipping man. f, Man on horse. g, Four men. h, Soldier guarding people looking at hanged man. i, Soldier standing near wooden post, soldier guarding Libyans. j, Woman on camel, soldiers. k, Soldiers on horses among Libyans. l, Boat with deportees. m, Col. Khadafy without headdress. n, Libyan with arm raised, hand of Col. Khadafy. o, Soldier pointing gun at horseman with sword. p, Horseman carrying gun.

1993, Dec. 15 *Perf. 14½*
1481 A458 50d Sheet of 16, #a-p 12.00 12.00

Miniature Sheet

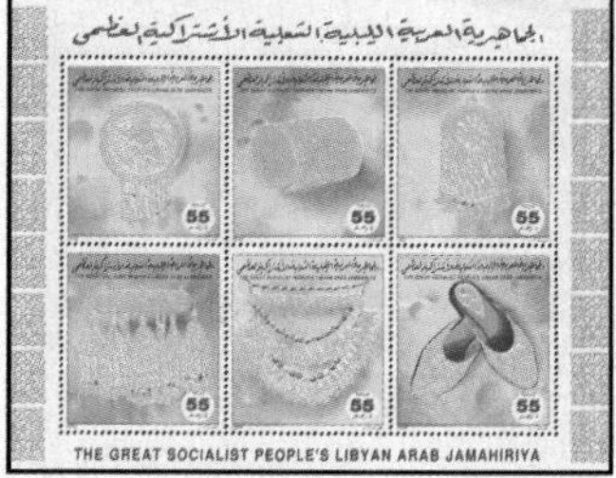

Items Made of Silver — A459

No. 1482: a, Medallion with five-pointed star and tassels. b, Wristband. c, Medallion with star with ten rays and tassels. d, Rod with tassels. e, Necklace. f, Slippers.

Litho. & Embossed With Foil Application

1994, Aug. 10 *Perf. 13¼*
1482 A459 55d Sheet of 6, #a-f 4.25 4.25

A460

Sept. 1 Revolution, 25th Anniv. — A461

No. 1483: a, Jet, Col. Khadafy in robe (40x40mm). b, Warriors on horseback, mother and child, Col. Khadafy in military uniform (60x40mm). c, Ship, shepherd, man and woman, man on camel (40x40mm).

1994, Sept. 1 **Litho.** *Perf. 12*
1483 A460 100d Horiz. strip of 3, #a-c 4.25 4.25

Souvenir Sheet

1484 A461 1000d multi 13.50 13.50

1994 World Cup Soccer Championships, United States — A462

World Cup, and various soccer players with horizontal stripes in: No. 1485, 100d, Red and brown. No. 1486, 100d, Red violet, purple, and green. No. 1487, 100d, Green and purple. No. 1488, 100d, Green, black and yellow. No. 1489, 100d, Orange, brown and red. No. 1490, 100d, Yellow orange, brown and orange.
No. 1491, 500d, Soccer players, World Cup, red violet background. No. 1492, 500d, Soccer player, ball, "1990," horiz.

1994, Oct. 15 *Perf. 13¼*
1485-1490 A462 Set of 6 8.50 8.50

Souvenir Sheets

1491-1492 A462 Set of 2 14.00 14.00

No. 1491 contains one 42x51mm stamp; No. 1492 contains one 51x42mm stamp.

Miniature Sheet

Libyans Deported to Italy — A463

No. 1493: a, Col. Khadafy. b, Airplane, man with rifle. c, Two men, one with rifle, nose of airplane. d, Tail of airplane, man with rifle. e, Soldier with bayoneted rifle, Libyans looking at dead animal. f, Libyans with rifles, camel. g, Nose of camel, horsemen and soldiers. h, Man carrrying child, drawn swords, horsemen. i, Soldier with whip. j, Man with open mouth. k, Tank and soldiers. l, Soldiers on horseback, women. m, Woman tending to injured man, man with bound hands, rifles. n, Soldier bayoneting man. o, Building, women, soldiers on horseback. p, Deportees in boats.

1994, Oct. 26 *Perf. 12*
1493 A463 95d Sheet of 16, #a-p 22.50 22.50

Mosques — A464

No. 1494 — Mosques in: a, Darghut. b, Benghazi. c, Kabao. d, Gouzgu. e, Siala. f, El Kettani.

1994, Nov. 15 **Litho.**
1494 Horiz. strip of 6 11.50 11.50
a.-f. A464 70d Any single 1.50 1.50

Miniature Sheet

People's Authority Declaration — A465

No. 1495: a, Navy ship, jet, women soldiers. b, Wheat, hand holding Green Book, tractor trailer cab. c, Family, water pipeline, tractor trailers. d, Fruit, vegetables, people holding Green Book. e, Col. Khadafy, butterfly, flowers. f, Young men, fruit and vegetables.

1994, Dec. 1 *Perf. 14¾*
1495 A465 80d Sheet of 6, #a-f 12.00 12.00

Evacuation of Foreign Forces — A466

Denomination in: 65d, Blue. 95f, Green.

1994, Dec. 15 *Perf. 14*
1496-1497 A466 Set of 2 2.75 2.75

Miniature Sheet

Khadafy Prize for Human Rights — A467

No. 1498: a, Helmeted soldiers, men with sticks, South African flag. b, Men with sticks, South African flag. c, South African Pres. Nelson Mandela. d, Col. Khadafy. e, Indian at fire, crescent moon. f, Armed Indians on horses. g, Indian chief. h, Indian dancer. i, Men with rifles, jets. j, Women, jet, open book. k, Open book. l, Surgeons. m, Palestinians with flag, denomination at left. n, Palestinians with flag, denomination at right. o, Palestinians throwing rocks. p, Palestinians, soldiers.

1994, Dec. 31 *Perf. 13¼*
1498 A467 95d Sheet of 16, #a-p 24.50 24.50

No. 1498 exists with marginal inscription with correct spelling of "Prize."

People's Authority Declaration A468

Background color: No. 1499, 100d, Green. No. 1500, 100d, Blue. No. 1501, 100d, Yellow.

1995, July 1 *Perf. 12*
1499-1501 A468 Set of 3 2.25 2.25

Arab League, 50th Anniv. A469

Background color: No. 1502, 200d, Green. No. 1503, 200d, Blue.
No. 1504: a, Emblem in silver. b, Emblem in gold.

1995, July 20 **Litho.** *Perf. 13¼*
1502-1503 A469 Set of 2 7.50 7.50

Litho. & Embossed With Foil Application

1504 A469 1000d Sheet of 2, #a-b 13.00 13.00

Miniature Sheet

Libyan Soccer Players — A470

No. 1505: a, Messaud Zentuti. b, Salem Shermit. c, Ottoman Marfua. d, Ghaleb Siala. e, 1935 Libyan Team. f, Senussi Mresila.

1995, Aug. 1 **Litho.**
1505 A470 100d Sheet of 6, #a-f 9.50 9.50

Miniature Sheet

Zoo Animals — A471

No. 1506: a, Camel. b, Secretary bird. c, African wild dog. d, Oryx. e, Baboon. f, Golden jackal. g, Crowned eagle. h, Eagle owl. i, Desert hedgehog. j, Sand gerbil. k, Addax. l, Fennec. m, Lanner falcon. n, Desert wheatear. o, Pintailed sandgrouse. p, Jerboa.

1995, Aug. 15 *Perf. 13¾x14*
1506 A471 100d Sheet of 16, #a-p 25.00 25.00

Miniature Sheet

Fruit — A472

No. 1507: a, Grapefruit. b, Wild cherries. c, Mulberries. d, Strawberry tree fruit (arbutus). e, Plums. f, Pears. g, Apricots. h, Almonds. i, Prickly pears. j, Lemons. k, Peaches. l, Dates. m, Olives. n, Oranges. o, Figs. p, Grapes.

1995, Aug. 20
1507 A472 100d Sheet of 16, #a-p 24.00 24.00

Miniature Sheet

Sept. 1 Revolution, 26th Anniv. — A473

No. 1508: a, Students and chemist. b, Minaret, fist of Col. Khadafy, men. c, Col. Khadafy. d, Scientists and buildings. e, Nurses, doctor and patients. f, Surgeons. g, Woman at keyboard, shoemakers. h, Audio technicians, musician. i, Crane, bulldozer and buildings. j, Grain elevator. k, Offshore oil rig, nose of airplane. l, Tail of airplane, ship. m, Goats and sheep. n, Water pipeline. o, Camels, vegetables, water. p, Fruit, grain combine.

1995, Sept. 1
1508 A473 100d Sheet of 16, #a-p 22.50 22.50

Scouts — A474

No. 1509 — Scouting emblem and: a, Antelope, Scout and butterflies (40x40mm). b, Scouts, butterflies, antelope and cat (60x40mm). c, Scouts, wheat, butterfly, flower.

1995, Sept. 10 *Perf. 12*
1509 A474 250d Horiz. strip of 3, #a-c 17.00 17.00

American Attack on Libya, 9th Anniv. — A475

No. 1510: a, Ships and people (40x50mm). b, Airplanes, helicopters and people, hand holding Green Book (60x50mm). c, Airplane, mother and child (40x50mm).

1995, Sept. 15
1510 A475 100d Horiz. strip of 3, #a-c 4.50 4.50

Tripoli Intl. Fair — A476

Horsemen with background colors of: No. 1511, 100d, Light blue. No. 1512, 100d, Blue. No. 1513, 100d, Violet. No. 1514, 100d, Blue green, vert. No. 1515, 100d, Blue green with black stripes, vert. No. 1516, 100d, Orange, vert.
1000d, Col. Khadafy on horse.

1995, Sept. 20
1511-1516 A476 Set of 6 9.00 9.00

Souvenir Sheet

1517 A476 1000d multi 14.00 14.00

No. 1517 contains one 80x50mm stamp.

Miniature Sheet

City of Ghadames — A477

No. 1518: a, Camel, woman with water jugs. b, Woman with bread on wooden board. c, Seated woman with vase. d, Woman feeding chickens. e, Woman at spinning wheel. f, Woman standing. g, Woman cooking. h, Woman milking goat. i, Shoemaker. j, Man at loom. k, Metalworker with hammer. l, Date picker. m, Men at religious school. n, Potter. o, Tanner. p, Man picking tomatoes.

Perf. 14½x14¼

1995, Sept. 30 **Litho.**
1518 A477 100d Sheet of 16, #a-p 21.00 21.00

Evacuation of Foreign Forces — A478

Panel color: 50d, Pink. 100d, Green. 200d, Lilac.

1995, Oct. 7 **Litho.** *Perf. 14¾x14¼*
1519-1521 A478 Set of 3 5.00 5.00

Bees and Flowers A479

Panel color: No. 1522, 100d, Green. No. 1523, 100d, Pink. No. 1524, 100d, Purple.

1995, Oct. 10 *Perf. 14¼x14¾*
1522-1524 A479 Set of 3 4.50 4.50

Dr. Mohamed Feituri — A480

1995, Oct. 20 *Perf. 14¾x14¼*
1525 A480 200d multi 2.75 2.75

Campaign Against Smoking — A481

Color of central stripe: No. 1526, 100d, Orange. No. 1527, 100d, Yellow.

1995, Oct. 20
1526-1527 A481 Set of 2 3.25 3.25

Miniature Sheet

Libyans Deported to Italy — A482

No. 1528: a, Col. Khadafy. b, Horsemen. c, Battle scene with blue sky, denomination at LR. d, Battle scene with blue sky, airplane, denomination at LL. e, Battle scene, arch. f, Battle scene, red building at UR. g, Battle scene with red sky, soldier holding pistol. h, Battle scene with red sky, building at UR. i, Three Libyans in foreground. j, Battle scene with running soldiers. k, Battle scene of horsemen and riflemen facing right. l, Soldiers, Libyan man in foreground at LR. m, Two horesemen with arms raised. n, Man in foreground shooting at horsemen. o, Children. p, Child, deportees in boats.

1995, Oct. 26 ***Perf. 12***
1528 A482 100d Sheet of 16, #a-p 22.00 22.00

Miniature Sheet

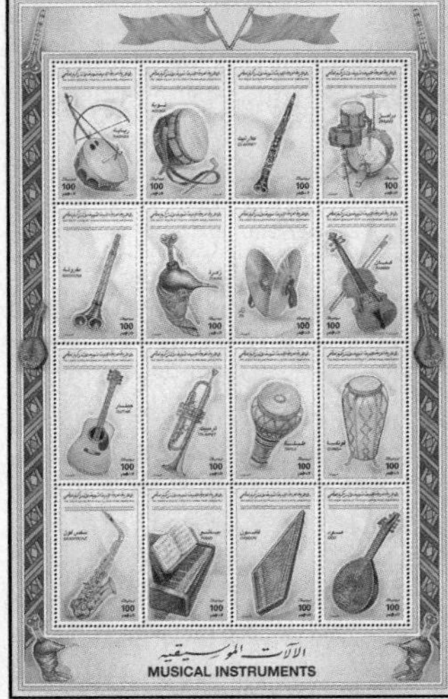

Musical Instruments — A483

No. 1529: a, Rababa. b, Nouba (drum). c, Clarinet. d, Drums. e, Magruna. f, Zukra. g, Zil (cymbals). h, Kaman (violin). i, Guitar. j, Trumpet. k, Tapla (drum). l, Gonga (drum). m, Saxophone. n, Piano. o, Gandon (zither). p, Ood.

1995, Nov. 1 ***Perf. 13¾x14***
1529 A483 100d Sheet of 16, #a-p 21.00 21.00

Doors of Mizda — A484

No. 1530: a, Blue door. b, Door with arched design in rectangular doorway. c, Log door. d, Door with rounded top in archway. e, Door of planks in rectangular doorway.

1995, Nov. 10 ***Perf. 13¼***
1530 Horiz. strip of 5 3.50 3.50
a.-e. A484 100d Any single .65 .65

Intl. Olympic Committee, Cent. — A485

Denomination color: No. 1531, 100d, Red. No. 1532, 100d, Black.

1995, Nov. 15 ***Perf. 13½***
1531-1532 A485 Set of 2 1.40 1.40

Prehistoric Animals — A486

No. 1533: a, Baryonyx. b, Oviraptor. c, Stenonychosaurus. d, Tenontosaurus. e, Yangchuanosaurus. f, Stegotetrabelodon, denomination at LR. g, Stegotetrabelodon, denomination at LL. h, Psittacosaurus. i, Heterodontosaurus. j, Loxodonta atlantica. k, Mammuthus. l, Erlikosaurus. m, Cynognathus. n, Plateosaurus. o, Staurikosaurus. p, Lystrosaurus.
500d, Stegotetrabelodon, horiz.

1995, Nov. 20 ***Perf. 13½***
1533 Miniature sheet of 16 12.50 12.50
a.-p. A486 100d Any single .75 .70

Souvenir Sheet
Perf. 13¼

1534 A486 500d multi 4.25 4.25

No. 1534 contains one 53x49mm stamp.

Children's Day A487

No. 1535: a, Boy, dinosaur with cane. b, Boy on elephant. c, Boy, Scout emblem, turtle and mushroom. d, Dinosaur and soccer ball. e, Boy with gun, pteranodon.

1995, Nov. 25 ***Perf. 13½***
1535 Horiz. strip of 5 15.00 15.00
a.-e. A487 100d Any single 2.75 2.75

Palestinian Intifada — A488

No. 1536: a, Boy throwing object at helicopter. b, Dome of the Rock, Palestinian with flag. c, People, Palestinian flag.

1995, Nov. 29 ***Perf. 14***
1536 A488 100d Horiz. strip of 3, #a-c 4.50 4.50

Intl. Civil Aviation Organization, 50th Anniv. — A489

Denomination color: No. 1537, 100d, Black. No. 1538, 100d, Blue.

1995, Dec. 7 ***Perf. 13½x13¼***
1537-1538 A489 Set of 2 1.40 1.40

United Nations, 50th Anniv. — A490

Background color: No. 1539, 100d, Dark red lilac. No. 1540, 100d, Light red lilac.

1995, Dec. 20 ***Perf. 13½***
1539-1540 A490 Set of 2 1.40 1.40

Miniature Sheet

Flowers — A491

No. 1541: a, Iris germanica. b, Canna edulis. c, Nerium oleander. d, Papaver rhoeas. e, Strelitzia reginae. f, Amygdalus communis.

1995, Dec. 31 ***Perf. 14¾***
1541 A491 200d Sheet of 6, #a-f 11.00 11.00

People's Authority Declaration A492

Panel color: 100d, Pink. 150d, Light blue. 200d, Light green.

1996, Mar. 2 ***Perf. 13¼***
1542-1544 A492 Set of 3 5.00 5.00

1996 Summer Olympics, Atlanta — A493

No. 1545: a, Soccer. b, Long jump. c, Tennis. d, Cycling. e, Boxing. f, Equestrian.
No. 1546, 500d, Runner. No. 1547, 500d, Equestrian, diff.

1996, Aug. 15 ***Perf. 14½***
1545 A493 100d Sheet of 6, #a-f 6.75 6.75

Souvenir Sheets

1546-1547 A493 Set of 2 11.00 11.00

Miniature Sheet

Sept. 1 Revolution, 27th Anniv. — A494

No. 1548: a, Camel, man, fruits, water. b, Water pipeline, fruit. c, Tractor, water, women. d, Oil worker. e, Tailor. f, Seamstress, Col. Khadafy's fist. g, Col. Khadafy. h, Building, women with microscope. i, Nurses at anatomy lesson, man with microscope. j, School child. k, Woman with open book. l, Man playing zither. m, Airplanes. n, Dish antenna, ship, man on camel. o, Ship, television camera. p, Television actress, woman at microphone.

1996, Sept. 1 ***Perf. 13¾x14***
1548 A494 100d Sheet of 16, #a-p 17.50 17.50

Miniature Sheet

American Attack on Libya, 10th Anniv. — A495

No. 1549: a, Left side of missile, explosion. b, Right side of missile, man with raised arms. c, Casualties, airplanes. d, Airplane at left, man on ground. e, Firefighter spraying burning car. f, Damaged vehicles. g, Col. Khadafy. h, Casualties, airplane at top. i, Rescuers assisting casualties. j, Man with extended hand. k, Woman with hands to face. l, Stretcher bearers. m, Three men and casualty. n, Man with bloody hand. o, Woman and child casualties. p, Burning car, rescuers attending to bleeding casualty.

1996, Sept. 15 ***Perf. 13¾***
1549 A495 100d Sheet of 16, #a-p 17.50 17.50

Miniature Sheet

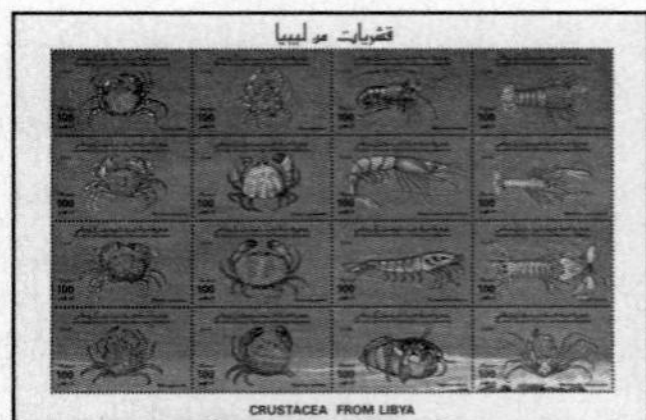

Crustaceans — A496

No. 1550: a, Necora puber. b, Lissa chiragra. c, Palinurus elephas. d, Scyllarus arctus. e, Carcinus maenas. f, Calappa granulata. g, Parapenaeus longirostris. h, Nephrops norvegicus. i, Eriphia verrucosa. j, Cancer pagurus. k, Penaeus kerathurus. l, Squilla mantis. m, Maja squinado. n, Pilumnus hirtellus. o, Pagurus alatus. p, Macropodia tenuirostris.

1996, Oct. 1 ***Perf. 14x13¾***
1550 A496 100d Sheet of 16, #a-p 17.50 17.50

Miniature Sheet

Intl. Day of Maghreb Handicrafts — A497

Various handicrafts.

1996, Oct. 15 ***Perf. 13¾x14***
1551 A497 100d Sheet of 16, #a-p 17.50 17.50

Miniature Sheet

Libyans Deported to Italy — A498

No. 1552: a, Guard tower, soldier with gun, woman tending to sick man. b, Soldier with gun and bayonet, soldier on horseback. c, Col. Khadafy with headdress. d, Man holding box and walking stick. e, Soldiers whipping man. f, Man on horse. g, Four men. h, Soldier guarding people looking at hanged man. i, Soldier standing near wooden post, soldier guarding Libyans. j, Woman on camel, soldiers. k, Soldiers on horses among Libyans. l, Boat with deportees. m, Col. Khadafy without headdress. n, Libyan with arm raised, hand of Col. Khadafy. o, Soldier pointing gun at horseman with sword. p, Horseman carrying gun.

1996, Oct. 26 **Litho.**
1552 A498 100d Sheet of 16, #a-p 17.50 17.50

Miniature Sheet

Horses — A499

No. 1553: a, Brown horse, lake at right. b, Brown horse in front of lake, tree at right. c, Brown horse in front of lake, tree at right. d, Dark brown horse, trees in background. e, Dark brown horse with raised leg. f, Horse at base of tree. g, Gray horse galloping. h, Piebald horse. i, Gray horse, palm tree at left. j, Head of black horse and tail of brown horse. k, Brown horse, palm fronds at upper right. l, Brown horse with gray mane, palm tree at right. m, Head of black horse, body of gray horse, tail of brown horse. n, Head of brown horse, body of black horse, hindquarters of two brown horses. o, Head of brown horse, parts of three other brown horses. p, Head of brown horse, chest of another brown horse, palm tree at right.

1996, Oct. 30 ***Perf. 14x13¾***
1553 A499 100d Sheet of 16, #a-p 17.50 17.50

Miniature Sheet

Camels — A500

No. 1554: a, Camelus dromedarius with head at right. b, Head of Camelus dromedarius. c, Camelus dromedarius with head at left. d, Camelus ferus bactrianus with head at right. e, Camelus ferus ferus. f, Camelus ferus bactrianus with head at left.

1996, Nov. 15 ***Perf. 12***
1554 A500 200d Sheet of 6, #a-f 13.50 13.50

Press and Information A501

Designs: 100d, Photographer, newspapers, computer. 200d, Musicians, video technician, computer, dish antenna.

1996, Nov. 20
1555-1556 A501 Set of 2 3.25 3.25

Miniature Sheet

Fossils and Prehistoric Animals — A502

No. 1557: a, Mene rhombea fossil. b, Mesodon macrocephalus fossil. c, Eyron arctiformis fossil. d, Stegosaurus. e, Pteranodon. f, Allosaurus.

1996, Nov. 25
1557 A502 200d Sheet of 6, #a-f 16.00 16.00

Palestinian Intifada — A503

Frame color: 100d, Yellow. 150d, Green. 200d, Blue.

1996, Nov. 29
1558-1560 A503 Set of 3 5.00 5.00

African Children's Day — A504

Designs: 50d, Child, beige frame. 150d, Child, blue frame. 200d, Mother, child, dove.

1996, Dec. 5 ***Perf. 13¼***
1561-1563 A504 Set of 3 2.50 2.50

Children's Day — A505

No. 1564 — Various cats with background colors of: a, Rose. b, Blue green. c, Blue. d, Yellow green. e, Gray green.

1996, Dec. 5
1564 Horiz. strip of 5 5.50 5.50
a.-e. A505 100d Any single 1.00 1.00

Intl. Family Day — A506

No. 1565 — Family and: a, 150d, Building (21x27mm). b, 150d, Automobile (21x27mm). c, 200d, Stylized globe (46x27mm).

1996, Dec. 10 ***Perf. 13x13¼***
1565 A506 Horiz. strip of 3, #a-c 3.00 3.00

Miniature Sheet

Teachers — A507

No. 1566: a, Mohamed Kamel El-Hammali. b, Mustafa Abdulla Ben-Amer. c, Mohamed Messaud Fesheka. d, Kairi Mustafa Serraj. e, Muftah El-Majri. f, Mohamed Hadi Arafa.

1996, Dec. 15 ***Perf. 13¼***
1566 A507 100d Sheet of 6, #a-f 3.75 3.75

Miniature Sheet

Singers — A508

No. 1567: a, Mohamed Salim and zither. b, Mohamed M. Sayed Bumedyen and flute. c, Otman Najim and ood. d, Mahmud Sherif and tapla. e, Mohamed Ferjani Marghani and piano. f, Mohamed Kabazi and violin.

1996, Dec. 15
1567 A508 100d Sheet of 6, #a-f 3.75 3.75

Miniature Sheet

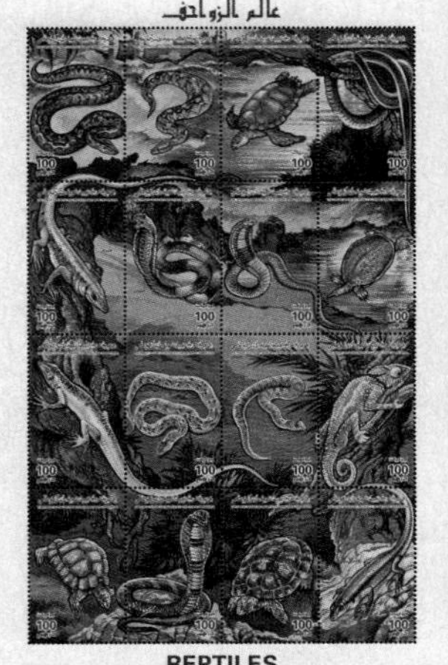

Reptiles — A509

No. 1568: a, Snake, leaves and building at top. b, Snake, building at top. c, Turtle, water and part of snake. d, Snake on tree branch. e, Brown lizard on rock. f, Cobra with head at left. g, Cobra and water. h, Turtle, water, tail of cobra. i, Green lizard on rock. j, Snake, foliage at bottom. k, Snake, foliage at bottom and right. l, Lizard with curled tail. m, Turtle on rock. n, Cobra with head at right. o, Turtle on grass. p, Gray lizard on rock.

1996, Dec. 20 ***Perf. 13¾x14***

1568 A509 100d Sheet of 16, #a-p 18.50 18.50

Miniature Sheet

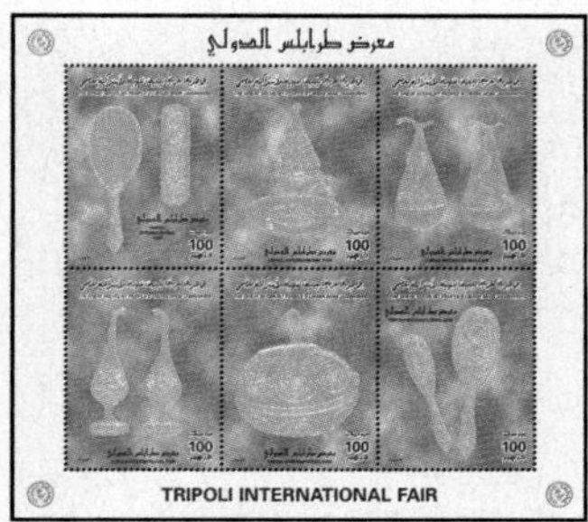

Tripoli Intl. Fair — A510

No. 1569: a, Mirror and brush. b, Container and plate. c, Two containers with rounded bases. d, Two containers on pedestals. e, Oval ornament. f, Brushes.

Litho. & Embossed with Foil Application

1996, Dec. 30 ***Perf. 13¾***

1569 A510 100d Sheet of 6, #a-f 6.75 6.75

A511

People's Authority Declaration, 20th Anniv. — A512

Frame color: 100d, Yellow. 200d, Blue. 300d, Green.

1997, Mar. 2 **Litho.** ***Perf. 12***

1570-1572 A511 Set of 3 7.75 7.75

Souvenir Sheet

Imperf

1573 A512 10,000d multi 90.00 90.00

No. 1573 has a perforated label that bears the denomination but lacks the country name.

Scouts and Philately — A513

No. 1574: a, 50d, Group of scouts, open album, wheat, flag. b, 50d, Two scouts, two albums, wheat. c, 100d, Butterflies, books, scouts and flags.

1997, Mar. 15 ***Perf. 14***

1574 A513 Horiz. strip of 3, #a-c 2.75 2.75

Health Care — A514

No. 1575: a, 50d, Doctor looking at test tube. b, 50d, Doctor, microscope. c, 100d, Doctor and nurse examining baby.

1997, Apr. 7

1575 A514 Horiz. strip of 3, #a-c 2.25 2.25

Buildings A515

Designs: 50d, Shown. 100d, Building with attached tower, vert. 200d, Tower, vert.

Perf. 14¼x14¾, 14¾x14¼

1997, Apr. 15

1576-1578 A515 Set of 3 5.00 5.00

Campaign Against Smoking — A516

Frame color: 100d, Blue. 150d, Green. 200d, Pink.

1997, Apr. 30 ***Perf. 14¾x14¼***

1579-1581 A516 Set of 3 2.75 2.75

Arab National Central Library — A517

Building, map, open book, and olive branches with background in: 100d, Blue. 200d, Green.

1000d, Building, map, books, computer and Col. Khadafy, horiz.

1997, Aug. 10 ***Perf. 13¼***

1582-1583 A517 Set of 2 1.75 1.75

Souvenir Sheet

1584 A517 1000d multi 6.00 6.00

No. 1584 contains one 116x49mm stamp.

Arab Tourism Year — A518

Perf. 13¼x13½

1997, Aug. 20 **Litho.**

1585 Horiz. strip of 3 10.50 10.50

a. A518 100d Black denomination 2.00 2.00

b. A518 200d Red denomination 3.75 3.75

c. A518 250d Blue denomination 4.75 4.75

Miniature Sheet

A519

Sept. 1 Revolution, 28th Anniv. — A520

No. 1586: a, 100d, Mother and child. b, 100d, Col. Khadafy as student. c, 100d, Khadafy at microphone. d, 100d, People on tank. e, 100d, Khadafy and man in suit. f, 100d, Khadafy with fist raised. g, 100d, Woman, child, corner of Green Book. h, 100d, Three people, corner of Green Book. i, 100d, Khadafy with pen. j, 100d, Man and child. k, 100d, Government buildings, helicopters. l, 100d, Khadafy in military uniform. m, 500d, Khadafy on horse. Size of Nos. 1586a-1586l: 28x43mm. Size of No. 1586m: 56x86mm.

Litho., Litho with Foil Application (#1586m)

1997, Sept. 1 ***Perf. 14***

1586 A519 Sheet of 13, #a-m 17.50 17.50

Souvenir Sheet

Perf. 13¾

1587 A520 500d multi 6.00 6.00

Miniature Sheet

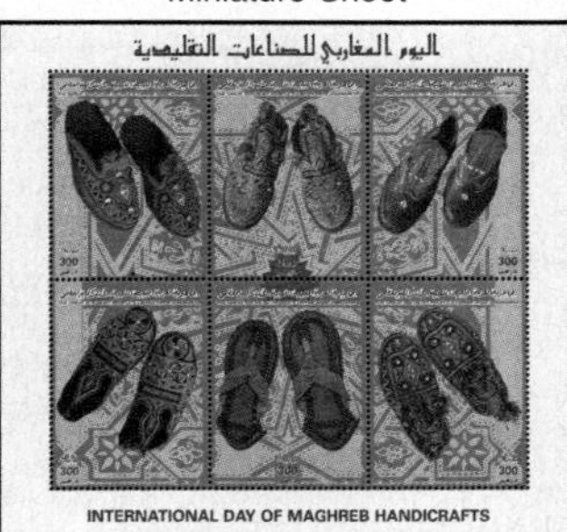

Intl. Day of Maghreb Handicrafts — A521

No. 1588 — Various shoes with toes pointing to: a, LR corner. b, Bottom. c, LL corner. d, UR corner. e, Top. f, UL corner.

Litho. With Foil Application

1997, Sept. 20 ***Perf. 13¾***

1588 A521 300d Sheet of 6, #a-f 18.00 18.00

Miniature Sheet

Tripoli Intl. Fair — A522

No. 1589 — Items made of silver: a, Medallion with tassels. b, Round medallion. c, Diamond-shaped medallion with tassels. d, Curved medallion. e, Necklace. f, Ring.

Litho. & Embossed With Foil Application

1997, Sept. 20

1589 A522 500d Sheet of 6, #a-f 29.00 29.00

Evacuation of Foreign Forces — A523

Denominations: 100d, 150d, 250d.

1997, Oct. 7 **Litho.** ***Perf. 14¾x14¼***

1590-1592 A523 Set of 3 2.75 2.75

Miniature Sheet

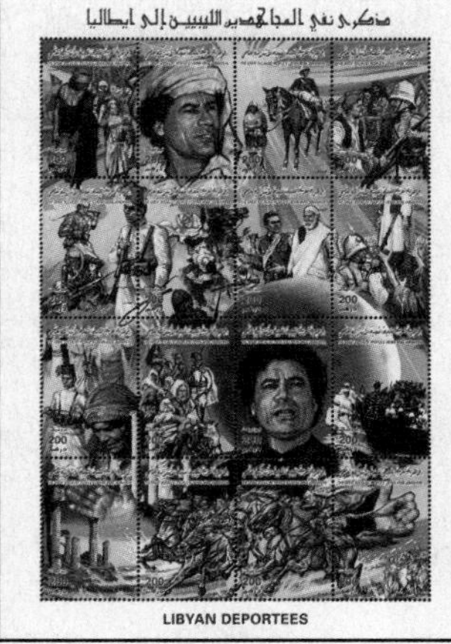

Libyans Deported to Italy — A524

No. 1593: a, Person carrying water jug. b, Col. Khadafy with headdress. c, Man, soldier on horse. d, Soldier and Libyans. e, Soldier whipping man. f, Soldier, man on horse. g, Libyan man and man in uniform. h, People at hanging. i, Man with purple fez, woman with red headdress. j, People, horse and camel. k, Col. Khadafy without headdress. l, Deportees on boats. m, Hand of Khadafy above pillars. n, Horsemen and pillars. o, Horsemen. p, Horsemen and hand of Khadafy.

1997, Oct. 26 ***Perf. 14***

1593 A524 200d Sheet of 16, #a-p 32.50 32.50

Worldwide Fund for Nature (WWF) A525

No. 1594 — Felis lybica: a, With prey at water. b, Adult and kittens. c, Under tree. d, Two adults.

1997, Nov. 1 ***Perf. 13¼***
1594 Horiz. strip of 4 7.50 7.50
a.-d. A525 200d Any single 1.75 1.75

Printed in sheets containing two strips.

Souvenir Sheet

Natl. Society for Wildlife Conservation — A526

No. 1595: a, Antelope facing forward. b, Ram. c, Antelope facing left.

1997, Nov. 1 ***Perf. 13¼***
1595 A526 100d Sheet of 3, #a-c 14.00 14.00

Miniature Sheet

American Attack on Libya, 11th Anniv. — A527

No. 1596: a, Explosion. b, Green Book, Libyan airplanes. c, Minarets, hand of Col. Khadafy. d, Col. Khadafy without headdress. e, Wing of American airplane. f, Nose of American airplane. g, Libyan airplanes. h, People looking at tail of American airplane. i, Rockets hitting American airplane. j, Arm of Col. Khadafy. k, Col. Khadafy with headdress. l, Man, fist of Col. Khadafy. m, Rockets and people. n, Col. Khadafy visiting injured person. o, Col. Khadafy kissing girl's hand. p, People with fists raised.

1997, Nov. 15 ***Perf. 14***
1596 A527 200d Sheet of 16, #a-p 34.00 34.00

Miniature Sheet

Great Man-Made River — A528

No. 1597: a, Fist, outline map of Libya. b, Col. Khadafy pointing to pipeline. c, Technicians reading paper, equipment. d, Col. Khadafy pointing to map. e, Col. Khadafy. f, Pipe, crane lifting cylinders. g, Col. Khadafy, pipe, vertical cylinder. h, Col. Khadafy, vertical cylinder. i, Col. Khadafy, construction trailer. j, Technician and equipment. k, Col. Khadafy, pipes lifted by crane. l, Col. Khadafy, line of trucks carrying pipe. m, Man with hand on spigot. n, Col. Khadafy with clasped hands. o, Hands under faucet, crops. p, Woman, child, flowers and fruit.

1997, Dec. 1 ***Perf. 14***
1597 A528 200d Sheet of 16, #a-p 34.00 34.00

People's Authority Declaration — A529

Panel color: 150d, Blue green. 250d, Purple. 300d, Blue.

1998, Mar. 2 ***Perf. 13¼***
1598-1600 A529 Set of 3 10.50 10.50

Miniature Sheet

Tripoli Intl. Fair — A530

No. 1601 — Items made of silver: a, Container with two spouts. b, Bowl on pedestal. c, Amphora. d, Container on tray. e, Lidded bowl. f, Three-legged container.

Litho. & Embossed With Foil Application

1998, Mar. 5 ***Perf. 13¾***
1601 A530 400d Sheet of 6, #a-f 24.00 24.00

Children's Day — A531

No. 1602 — Various girls in native dress with background colors of: a, Light blue. b, Yellow green. c, Red orange. d, Lilac. e, Yellow brown.

1998, Mar. 21 **Litho.** ***Perf. 13¼***
1602 Horiz. strip of 5 5.50 5.50
a.-e. A531 100d Any single 1.00 1.00

World Health Day — A532

Panel color: 150d, Buff. 250d, Light blue. 300d, Lilac.

1998, Apr. 7
1603-1605 A532 Set of 3 7.75 7.75

American Attack on Libya, 12th Anniv. — A533

No. 1606 — Airplanes, ships and: a, Helicopters, people with raised fists (28x48mm). b, Mother and child, Col. Khadafy (60x48mm). c, Man, boy and birds (28x48mm).

1998, Apr. 15
1606 A533 100d Horiz. strip of 3, #a-c 3.50 3.50

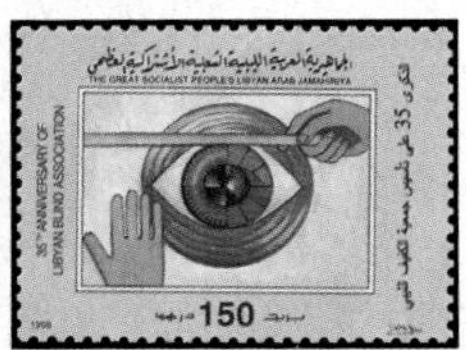

Libyan Blind Association, 35th Anniv. — A534

Designs: 150d, Eye, hand with cane, raised hand. 250d, Blind people, stringed instrument, books.

1998, May 1 ***Perf. 12***
1607-1608 A534 Set of 2 4.75 4.75

Arab Bee Union — A535

Frame color: 250d, Blue. 300d, Yellow. 400d, Light green.

1998, June 1
1609-1611 A535 Set of 3 13.50 13.50

1998 World Cup Soccer Championships, France — A536

No. 1612 — Soccer player with: a, Ball at LR, orange and white lines at bottom. b, Top of World Cup. c, Ball at left, orange and white lines at bottom. d, No visible uniform number, left part of stadium at bottom. e, Bottom of World Cup, stadium. f, Uniform No. 5, right part of stadium at bottom.

No. 1613, 1000d, Player, World Cup, denomination at LL. No. 1614, 1000d, Player, World Cup, denomination at LR.

1998, June 10 ***Perf. 13¼***
1612 A536 200d Sheet of 6, #a-f *15.00 15.00*

Souvenir Sheets

1613-1614 A536 Set of 2 *24.00 24.00*

Nos. 1613-1614 each contain one 42x51mm stamp.

Miniature Sheet

World Book Day — A537

No. 1615: a, Man, boy, mosque. b, Gymnasts. c, Science teacher at blackboard, student, ear. d, Men picking vegetables. e, Men at blackboard, man with machinery. f, Man with headset microphone, world map. g, Teacher with compass, student. h, Scientists with microscope. i, Girl writing, horseman. j, Teacher, student, map of Libya, globe. k, Music teacher at blackboard, student. l, Woman at sewing machine. m, Chemistry teacher and student. n, Teacher and women at typewriters. o, Cooks. p, Woman at computer keyboard, computer technician.

1998, June 23
1615 A537 100d Sheet of 16, #a-p 17.50 17.50

Map of the Great Man-Made River — A538

Denomination color: 300d, Green. 400d, Blue.
2000d, Bister.

Litho. & Embossed With Foil Application

1998, July 1
1616-1617 A538 Set of 2 8.50 8.50

Souvenir Sheet

1618 A538 2000d gold & multi 22.00 22.00

Miniature Sheet

Great Man-Made River and Vegetables — A539

No. 1619: a, Garlic. b, Peas. c, Potatoes. d, Corn. e, Leeks. f, Tomatoes. g, Carrots. h, Radishes. i, Beans. j, Peppers. k, Eggplant. l,

Lettuce. m, Squash. n, Cucumbers. o, Onions, p, Cauliflower.

1998, Sept. 1 Litho. *Perf. 14*
1619 A539 100d Sheet of 16, #a-p 21.00 21.00

Miniature Sheet

Children's Day — A540

No. 1620 — Scouting trefoil and: a, Scouts, dog. b, Scouts saluting, birds. c, Scouts saluting, flags, tents. d, Scouts, sheep. e, Scouts playing musical instruments, tying down tent. f, Scouts at campfire, bird, boat.

1998, Aug. 1 *Perf. 14¼*
1620 A540 400d Sheet of 6, #a-f *55.00 55.00*

A541

Sept. 1 Revolution, 29th Anniv. — A542

No. 1621: a, Col. Khadafy. b, Horseman, pipeline, vegetables. c, Fruit, pipeline, head of eagle. d, Tail of eagle, minaret. e, Surgeons, students. f, Book, map of Northwestern Africa. g, Book, men, map of Northeastern Africa and Arabian Peninsula. h, Mosque. i, People with flags, grain combine. j, Ship. k, Apartment buildings, l, Boy. m, People, irrigation rig, building. n, Building with flagpole at right. o, Building with flagpole at right, irrigation rig. p, Building, irrigation rig.

1998, Sept. 1 Litho. *Perf. 14¼*
1621 A541 200d Sheet of 16, #a-p *37.50 37.50*

Souvenir Sheet
Litho. & Embossed
Perf. 13½x13¾

1622 A542 200d shown 2.50 2.50

Evacuation of Foreign Forces — A543

Panel color: 100d, Pink. 150d, Light green. 200d, Light blue.

1998, Oct. 7 Litho. *Perf. 13¼*
1623-1625 A543 Set of 3 5.00 5.00

Stamp Day — A544

Panel color: 300d, Buff. 400d, Blue.

1998, Oct. 9 *Perf. 12*
1626-1627 A544 Set of 2 10.00 10.00

Miniature Sheet

Libyans Deported to Italy — A545

No. 1628: a, Ship, trucks. b, Bound woman, barbed wire. c, Man, barbed wire. d, Soldiers marching Libyans at gunpoint. e, Airplane, battle scene. f, Barbed wire, line of Libyans. g, Barbed wire, soldier and Libyan. h, Soldiers aiming rifles at Libyans, man with camel. i, Horseman, man ladling water. j, Soldier in boat. k, Boats with deportees. l, Boats with deportees, ships. m, Horsemen, man carrying woman. n, Horsemen raising rifles. o, Horseman and flag. p, Mother and child.

1998, Oct. 26 *Perf. 13¼*
1628 A545 150d Sheet of 16, #a-p 26.00 26.00

Miniature Sheet

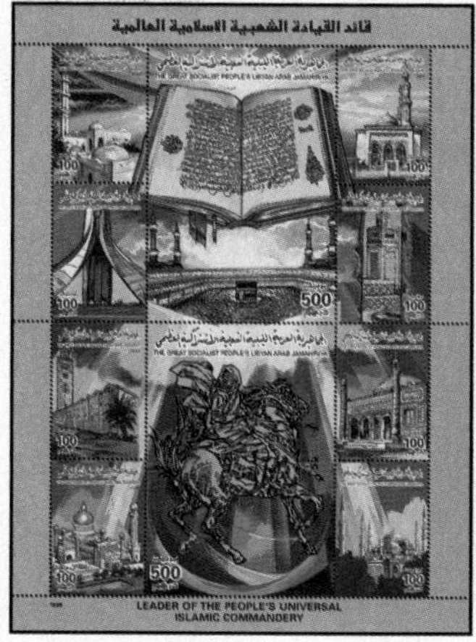

Leadership of Islam — A546

No. 1629: a, 100d, White mosque, minaret at left. b, 100d, White mosque, minaret at right. c, 100d, Modern mosque. d, 100d, Mosque seen through arch. e, 100d, Mosque and palm tree, minaret at left. f, 100d, Mosque with blue dome. g, 100d, Mosque with brown dome, six minarets. h, 100d, Mosque, five minarets. i, 500d, Koran, Holy Kaaba. j, 500d, Col. Khadafy on horse. Sizes: 100d stamps, 28x42mm; 500d stamps, 56x84mm.

Litho., Litho. With Foil Application (#1629j)

1998, Nov. 1 *Perf. 14*
1629 A546 Sheet of 10, #a-j 22.00 22.00

Miniature Sheet

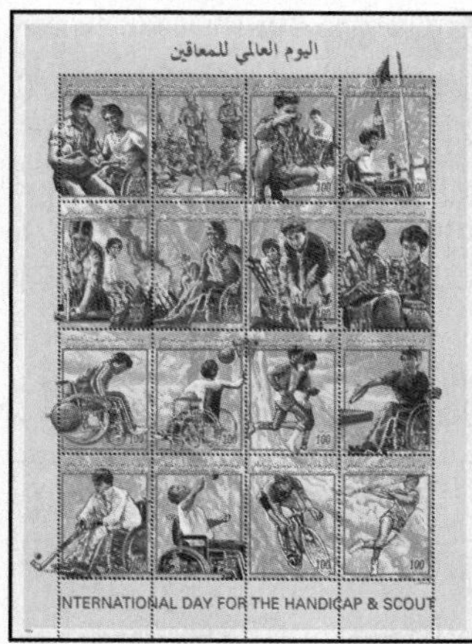

Scouts and the Handicapped — A547

No. 1630: a, Scout reading to boy in wheelchair, butterfly. b, Scout leader instructing group of Scouts. c, Scout photographing bird, boy in wheelchair. d, Scout raising flag, boy in wheelchair. e, Scout sawing log, boy in wheelchair. f, Scout near campfire, boy in wheelchair. g, Scouts with pots in fire, crutches. h, Scouts with pad of paper and pencil. i, Wheelchair basketball player in purple uniform. j, Wheelchair basketball player making shot. k, Handicapped runners. l, Man in wheelchair playing table tennis. m, Man in wheelchair playing hockey. n, Man in wheelchair throwing shot put. o, Handicapped cyclist. p, Handicapped javelin thrower.

1998, Nov. 15 Litho. *Perf. 13¼*
1630 A547 100d Sheet of 16, #a-p 27.50 27.50

Miniature Sheet

A548

Sept. 1 Revolution, 30th Anniv. — A549

No. 1631: a, 100d, Antelopes and "30." b, 100d, Mosque. c, 100d, Woman playing stringed instrument. d, 100d, Horsemen in desert. e, 100d, Grain combine. f, 100d, Ship. g, 100d, Ship, horsemen, flag. h, 100d, Horsemen, flag. i, 100d, Water pipeline, fruit. j, 100d, Butterflies, shepherd and sheep. k, 100d, Building, ship, horse's legs. l, 100d, Dates. m, 200d, Col. Khadafy on horse. Sizes: 100d stamps; 28x42mm, 200d, 56x84mm.

Litho., Litho. With Foil Application (#1631m, 1632)

1999, Sept. 1 *Perf. 14*
1631 A548 Sheet of 13, #a-m 12.00 12.00

Souvenir Sheet
Perf. 13¾

1632 A549 200d shown 2.00 2.00

A550

Organization of African Unity Assembly of Heads of State and Government, Tripoli — A551

No. 1633: a, Pipeline worker, musicians, minarets. b, Surgeons, woman carrying jug. c, Artisan, camel rider, satellite. d, Col. Khadafy, butterflies. e, Pipeline worker, fruit picker. f, Fruit picker, grain combine.

1999, Sept. 8 Litho. ***Perf. 14¼x14½***
1633 A550 300d Sheet of 6, #a-f 13.50 13.50

Souvenir Sheet
Perf. 13¾x14

1634 A551 500d shown 4.00 4.00

Evacuation of Foreign Forces — A552

Frame color: 150d, Pink. 250d, Beige. 300d, Light blue.

1999, Oct. 7 ***Perf. 12***
1635-1637 A552 Set of 3 8.25 8.25

A553

People's Authority Declaration — A554

No. 1638: a, Col. Khadafy with fist raised, man on camel. b, People looking at book. c, Airplane, building, dish antenna. d, Antelope, weaver, tractor. e, Open faucet, pipeline. f, Pipleine, fruit pickers.

No. 1639, 300d, Map of Libya, Col. Khadafy with raised fist, building. No. 1640, 300d, Dove, people, Col. Khadafy.

2000, Mar. 2 Litho. ***Perf. 14½x14¼***
1638 A553 100d Sheet of 6, #a-f 4.75 4.75

Souvenir Sheets
Perf. 13¾
Litho. & Embossed with Foil Application

1639-1640 A554 Set of 2 5.00 5.00

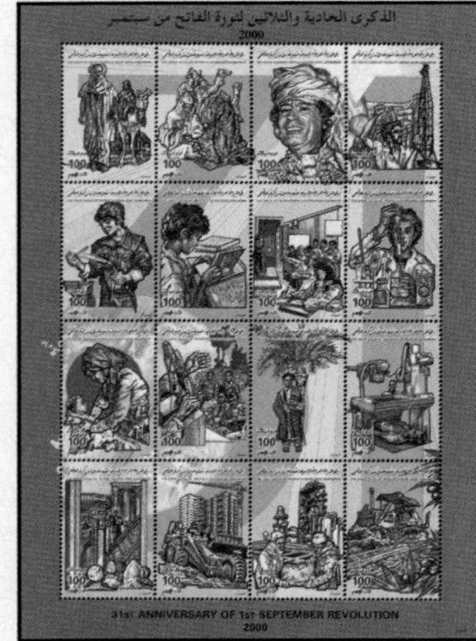

A555

Sept. 1 Revolution, 31st Anniv. — A556

No. 1641: a, Man walking, camel rider. b, Tea drinkers, camels. c, Col. Khadafy. d, Men with raised fists. e, Machinist with torch. f, Boy reading. g, Classroom. h, Scientist. i, Mother and child. j, People attending speech. k, Man and palm tree. l, Patient in X-ray machine. m, Mosque, n, Bulldozer, crane and building. o, Oil workers. p, Bulldozer.

No. 1642, 300d, Col. Khadafy, minaret. No. 1643, 300d, Col. Khadafy, boy and palm tree.

2000, Sept. 1 Litho. ***Perf. 14***
1641 A555 100d Sheet of 16, #a-p 12.50 12.50

Souvenir Sheets
Litho. With Foil Application
Perf. 13¾

1642-1643 A556 Set of 2 5.00 5.00

El-Mujahed Mohamed Abdussalam Ahmeda Abouminiar El-Gaddafi — A557

No. 1644: a, Man holding box. b, Palm tree and horsemen. c, Horsemen and soldiers on horseback. d, Soldiers and armed horsemen. e, Horseman raising rifle above head. f, Men raising rifles, Col. Khadafy.

300d, Man reading book.

2000, Sept. 9 Litho. ***Perf. 13¼***
1644 A557 200d Sheet of 6, #a-f 9.50 9.50

Souvenir Sheet
Litho. & Embossed With Foil Application

1645 A557 300d multi 2.50 2.50

Souvenir Sheet

España 2000 Intl. Philatelic Exhibition — A558

No. 1646: a, A. Castellano (1926-97). b, M. B. Karamanli (1922-95).

2000, Oct. 6 Litho. ***Imperf.***
1646 A558 250d Sheet of 2, #a-b 4.00 4.00

People's Authority Declaration A559

Denomination color: 150d, Pink. 200d, Blue.

2001, Mar. 2 ***Perf. 14***
1647-1648 A559 Set of 2 2.75 2.75

Miniature Sheet

Organization of African Unity Assemby of Heads of State and Government — A560

No. 1649: a, Heads of various states. b, Heads of state, horsemen. c, Men on camels. d, People with hands raised. e, Man holding picture of Col. Khadafy. f, Col. Khadafy at microphone.

2001, Mar. 2 Litho. ***Perf. 13½x13¼***
1649 A560 200d Sheet of 6, #a-f 9.50 9.50

Souvenir Sheets

Organization of African Unity Assembly of Heads of State and Government — A561

Background colors: No. 1650, 500d, Gold. No. 1651, 500d, Silver.

Litho. & Embossed With Foil Application

2001, Mar. 2 ***Perf. 13¼***
1650-1651 A561 Set of 2 8.50 8.50

Miniature Sheet

Tripoli Intl. Fair — A562

No. 1652: a, Rear view of saddle. b, Side view of saddle. c, Front view of saddle. d, Stirrup. e, Four pieces of tack. f, Two pieces of tack.

Litho. & Embossed with Foil Application

2001, Apr. 2 ***Perf. 13¾***
1652 A562 300d Sheet of 6, #a-f 22.00 22.00

Miniature Sheet

Fight Against American Aggression — A563

No. 1653: a, Exploding jet. b, American jet. c, Pilot. d, American plane shooting missile. e, Parachute. f, Airplanes. g, Child crying. h, Palm tree, explosion. i, Missiles. j, Broken egg. k, Teddy bear. l, Clock. m, Explosion in city. n, Man rescuing casualty. o, Man holding child casualty. p, Family fleeing.

2001, Apr. 15 Litho. ***Perf. 13¼***
1653 A563 100d Sheet of 16, #a-p *16.00 16.00*

Desertification Project — A564

No. 1654: a, Man with hoe (30x39mm). b, Men near stream (60x39mm). c, Camels (30x39mm).

2001, June 26 Litho. ***Perf. 13¼***
1654 A564 250d Horiz. strip of 3, #a-c 12.00 12.00

Miniature Sheet

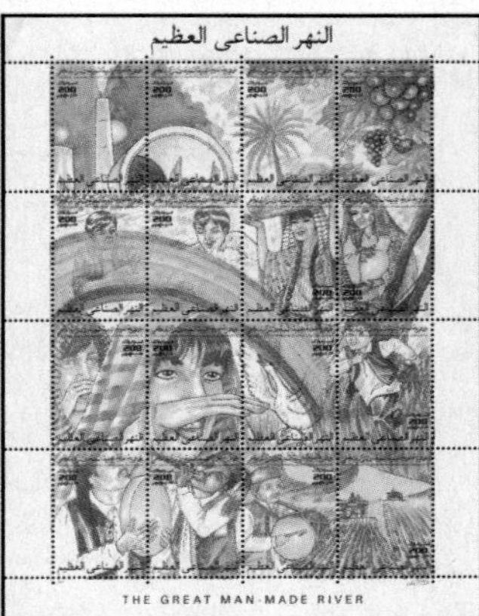

Great Man-Made River — A565

No. 1655: a, Smokestack. b, Pipeline and flags. c, Palm tree, fruit. d, Grapes. e, Clothed boy, rainbow. f, Bathing boy, rainbow. g, Woman carrying fruit. h, Woman holding jug. i, Woman with red and black headdress. j, Woman with green striped headdress. k, Duck, rainbow. l, Boy running. m, Drummer hitting drum with hand. n, Horn player. o, Drummer hitting drum with stick. p, Tractors in field.

2001, Sept. 15 Litho. *Perf. 11¾*
1655 A565 200d Sheet of 16, #a-p *32.50 32.50*

A566

Sept. 1 Revolution, 32nd Anniv. — A567

No. 1656: a, Col. Khadafy in headdress. b, Buildings, water pipeline, helicopters, tank, horsemen. c, Ship, airplane, camel rider. d, Tea drinkers. e, Children. f, Pillars, antelopes, woman. g, Man walking, camel rider. h, Camels, birds. i, Woman with container. j, Sword fight. k, Man and camel rider. l, Camels, pipeline worker, fruit. m, Potter. n, Musicians and weaver. o, Artisan. p, Col. Khadafy with clasped hands.

No. 1657, 300d, Col. Khadafy, pipeline and fruit (gold background). No. 1658, 300d, Col. Khadafy, pipeline and fruit (silver background).

Litho. and Hologram

2001, Sept. 1 *Perf. 13¼*
1656 A566 100d Sheet of 16, #a-p *27.50 27.50*
q. Booklet pane, #a-p, litho. *27.50* —
Complete booklet, #1656q *27.50*

Souvenir Sheets
Litho. & Embossed With Foil Application

1657-1658 A567 Set of 2 *5.50 5.50*

Intl. Day of the Orphan — A568

Panel color: 100d, Blue. 200d, Red violet. 300d, Olive green.

2001, Oct. 1 Litho. *Perf. 14¾x14½*
1659-1661 A568 Set of 3 9.25 9.25

Health Care — A569

Arabic inscription color: 200d, Green. 300d, Yellow orange.

2001, Dec. 1 Litho. *Perf. 14*
1662-1663 A569 Set of 2 6.50 6.50

Miniature Sheet

Tourism — A570

Various tourist attractions.

2002, May 1 *Perf. 11¾*
1664 A570 200d Sheet of 16, #a-p *52.50 52.50*

Intl. Customs Day — A571

Designs: 200d, 400d.

2002, July 1 *Perf. 14*
1665-1666 A571 Set of 2 8.25 8.25

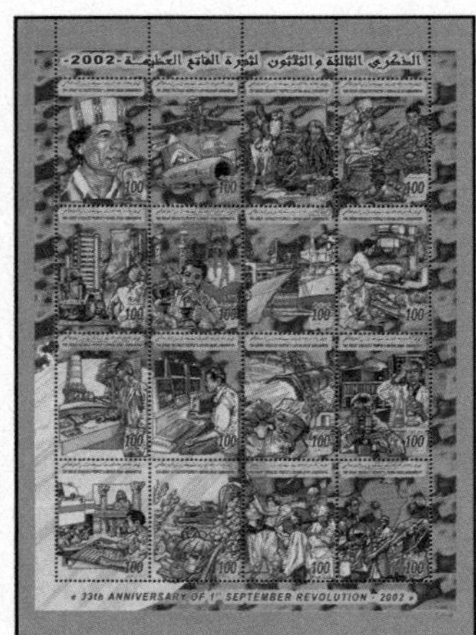

A572

Sept. 1 Revolution, 33rd Anniv. — A573

No. 1667: a, Col. Khadafy. b, Airplanes. c, Camel rider, woman pouring tea. d, Artisans. e, Bulldozer, building. f, Chemist, oil rig. g, Ships. h, Doctors and patients. i, Technician at industrial plant. j, Man at computer, k, Man, spigot, water pipeline, crane. l, Chemist, man at microscope. m, Television camera and technician. n, Fruit, vegetables, grain combine. o, Spear carriers, musician. p, Map of Africa, musicians.

No. 1668, 300d, Col. Khadafy, map of Africa (gold background). No. 1669, 300d, Col. Khadafy, map of Africa (silver background).

Litho. & Hologram

2002, Sept. 1 *Perf. 13¼*
1667 A572 100d Sheet of 16, #a-p *22.50 22.50*
q. Booklet pane, #a-p, litho. *40.00* —
Complete booklet, #1667q *50.00*

Souvenir Sheets
Litho. & Embossed With Foil Application

1668-1669 A573 Set of 2 *8.00 8.00*

Universal Declaration of Human Rights, 50th Anniv. — A576

Panel color: 250d, Red orange. 500d, Blue green.

2002, Nov. 1 Litho. *Perf. 14*
1672-1673 A576 Set of 2 9.50 9.50

Universal Postal Union, 125th Anniv. — A577

Panel color: 200d, Blue. 250d, Red violet.

2002, Dec. 1
1674-1675 A577 Set of 2 5.50 5.50

A580

September 1 Revolution, 34th Anniv. — A581

No. 1679: a, 300d, Doctors and microscope (30x40mm). b, 300d, Nurses studying anatomy (30x40mm). c, 300d, Mother and child (30x40mm). d, 300d, Soldiers, white flag (30x40mm). e, 500d, Teachers, students, building (60x40mm). f, 500d, Helicopter, pilot, women, nurse and patients (60x40mm). g, 500d, Marching band, soldiers in vehicle (60x40mm). h, 1000d, Col. Khadafy, airplane, satellite dish.

2003, May 20 Litho. *Perf. 12*
1679 A580 Sheet of 8, #a-h *22.50 22.50*

Souvenir Sheet
Litho. & Embossed With Foil Application

1680 A581 2000d multi *17.00 17.00*

September 1 Revolution, 35th Anniv. A582

Background color: 750d, Gray green. 1000d, Yellow green.

2004 Litho. *Perf. 13*
1681-1682 A582 Set of 2 4.50 4.50

Khairi Khaled Nuri (1943-2004), Philatelist — A583

2004 Litho. & Hologram *Perf. 13¼*
1683 A583 500d multi 2.00 2.00

People's Authority Declaration, 27th Anniv. A584

Color of rays: 400d, Yellow brown. 1000d, Blue green.

2004 **Litho.** ***Perf. 13***
1684-1685 A584 Set of 2 *12.00 12.00*

1st Communication and Information Technology Exhibition — A585

2005, July 29 ***Perf. 13***
1686 A585 750d multi *5.00 5.00*

Souvenir Sheet
Imperf

1687 A585 1000d multi *6.00 6.00*

People's Authority Declaration, 28th Anniv. — A586

Delegates: 300d, Seated. 1000d, Voting.

2005 ***Perf. 13***
1688-1689 A586 Set of 2 *12.00 12.00*

September 1 Revolution, 36th Anniv. A587

Background color: 750d, Yellow orange. 1000d, Blue.

2005
1690-1691 A587 Set of 2 *15.00 15.00*

Miniature Sheet

Total Solar Eclipse of March 29, 2006 — A588

No. 1692 — Eclipse and: a, Band of totality over map of Libya. b, Buildings, map of Libya. c, Altitude and duration figures. d, Stylized fish, camel, cactus, palm tree and Libyan. e, Saddled camel. f, Camels and riders.

2006, Mar. 29
1692 A588 250d Sheet of 6, #a-f *11.00 11.00*

People's Authority Declaration, 29th Anniv. A589

Wheat ear, flag, fist and torch with background color of: 400d, Yellow. 1000d, Blue.

2006, Nov. 1
1693-1694 A589 Set of 2 *11.00 11.00*

September 1 Revolution, 37th Anniv. — A590

2006
1695 A590 1000d multi *8.00 8.00*

Famous African Leaders — A591

Map of Africa and: No. 1696, 500d, Gamal Abdel Nasser (1918-70), Egyptian President. No. 1697, 500d, Kwame Nkrumah (1909-72), President of Ghana. No. 1698, 500d, Ahmed Ben Bella, President of Algeria. No. 1699, 500d, Patrice Lumumba (1925-61), Congolese Prime Minister. No. 1700, 500d, Kenneth Kaunda, President of Zambia. No. 1701, 500d, Julius Nyerere (1922-99), President of Tanzania. No. 1702, 500d, Modibo Keita (1915-77), President of Mali.

1000d, Map of Africa, Nasser, Nkrumah, Ben Bella, Lumumba, Kaunda, Nyerere and Keita, horiz.

2007, Mar. 6 ***Perf. 12¾***
1696-1702 A591 Set of 7 *32.50 32.50*
1702a Miniature sheet of 7, #1696-1702 *32.50 32.50*

Size: 98x75mm
Imperf

1703 A591 1000d multi *8.00 8.00*

Third Communication and Information Technology Exhibition — A592

2007, May 27 ***Perf. 13***
1704 A592 750d multi *6.50 6.50*

Tripoli, Capital of Islamic Culture A593

2007, June 16 **Litho.**
1705 A593 500d multi *4.50 4.50*

Intl. Day Against Drug Abuse and Illicit Trafficking A594

2007, June 26
1706 A594 750d multi *6.50 6.50*

People's Authority Declaration, 30th Anniv. A595

2007, July 4
1707 A595 750d multi *6.50 6.50*

36th Tripoli Intl. Fair — A596

No. 1708: a, Ring (orange background). b, Pendant (green background). c, Ring (purple background).
Illustration reduced.

2007, July 4 ***Perf. 13x13x13¼***
1708 Strip of 3 *16.00 16.00*
a.-c. A596 500d Any single *3.50 3.00*

Printed in sheets containing 2 strips + 2 labels. Value, $32.50.

Mosque A597

2007, Aug. 24 **Litho.** ***Perf. 13***
1709 A597 500d multi *5.00 5.00*
a. Souvenir sheet of 1 *5.00 5.00*

African Soccer Federation, 50th Anniv. A598

2007, Aug. 25
1710 A598 750d multi *6.50 6.50*

Values are for stamps with surrounding selvage.

September 1 Revolution, 38th Anniv. — A599

2007, Sept. 1 **Litho.** ***Perf. 13***
1711 A599 1000d multi *8.00 8.00*
a. Souvenir sheet of 1 *8.00 8.00*

Khadafy Project for African Women, Children and Youth A600

2007, Sept. 9
1712 A600 500d multi *4.25 4.25*

Libyan Red Crescent Society, 50th Anniv. A601

Red Crescent emblem and: 500d, Red Crescent volunteers. 1000d, 50th anniversary emblem.

2007 *Perf. 13*
1713-1714 A601 Set of 2 *12.50 12.50*

People's Authority Declaration, 31st Anniv. — A602

Type I — Two dots and vertical line in Arabic inscription directly above second "A" in "Jamahiriya."
Type II — No dots or vertical line in Arabic inscription directly above second "A" in "Jamahiriya."

2008, Mar. 2 **Litho.** *Perf. 13*
1715 A602 500d multi, type I *50.00 50.00*
a. Type II *4.50 4.50*

37th Tripoli International Fair — A603

No. 1716: a, Emblems, colored rectangles. b, Emblems. c, Emblems, buildings, displays.
Illustration reduced.

2008, Apr. 2 *Perf. 13x12¾*
1716 A603 500d Horiz. strip of 3, #a-c *13.00 13.00*

Printed in sheets of 6 containing two of each stamp.

Worldwide Fund for Nature (WWF) A604

Rueppell's fox: No. 1717, Head. No. 1718, Walking. No. 1719, Curled up. No. 1720, Sitting.

2008, May 1 *Perf. 12*

1717 A604 750f multi		1.50	1.50
a.	Imperf.	6.00	6.00
1718 A604 750f multi		1.50	1.50
a.	Imperf.	6.00	6.00
1719 A604 750f multi		1.50	1.50
a.	Imperf.	6.00	6.00
1720 A604 750f multi		1.50	1.50
a.	Imperf.	6.00	6.00
b.	Horiz. strip of 4, #1717-1720	8.00	8.00
c.	Horiz. strip of 4, #1717a-1720a	35.00	35.00

Fourth Telecommunications and Information Technology Exhibition — A605

2008, May 25 *Perf. 13*
1721 A605 1000d multi 6.75 6.75

Gamal Abdel Nasser (1918-70), Egyptian President A606

2008, July 23
1722 A606 500d multi 5.00 5.00

Egyptian Revolution, 56th anniv.

Khadafy 6+6 Mediterranean Project — A607

2008, July 27
1723 A607 750d multi *5.00 5.00*

Tenth Meeting of Leaders and Heads of State of Community of Sahel-Sahara Countries — A608

2008, Aug. 3
1724 A608 1000d multi *6.00 6.00*

Libyan Participation in 2008 Summer Olympics, Beijing A609

2008, Aug. 18
1725 A609 1000d multi 8.00 8.00

September 1 Revolution, 39th Anniv. — A610

Col. Khadafy with denomination in: No. 1726, White. No. 1727, Green.

2008, Sept. 1 *Perf. 13x12¾*
1726 A610 1000d multi *8.00 8.00*

Souvenir Sheet

1727 A610 1000d multi *8.00 8.00*

Total Mobile Phone Penetration in Libya A611

2008, Sept. 11 *Perf. 13*
1728 A611 750d multi 6.00 6.00

Fourth Intl. Waatasemu Women's Competition for Koran Memorization — A612

2008, Sept. 23
1729 A612 750d multi 5.00 5.00

Koran Exhibition A613

2008, Sept. 26
1730 A613 500d multi 3.50 3.50

People's Authority Declaration, 32nd Anniv. — A614

2009, Mar. 9
1731 A614 500d multi 3.00 3.00

Support for Gaza Palestinians A615

2009, May 7
1732 A615 1000d multi *5.00 5.00*

American Aggression Against Libya — A616

2009, May 14 **Litho.** *Perf. 13*
1733 A616 500d multi *4.00 4.00*

Fifth Telecommunications and Information Technology Exhibition — A617

2009, May 30
1734 A617 500d multi 3.00 3.00

Omar Bongo (1935-2009), President of Gabon A618

2009, June 20 **Litho.** *Perf. 13*
1735 A618 750d multi 3.00 3.00

16th Mediterranean Games, Pescara, Italy — A619

2009, June 26
1736 A619 500d multi 3.00 3.00

Jerusalem, Capital of Arab Culture — A620

2009, Aug. 3
1737 A620 1000d multi 4.50 4.50

25th African Men's Basketball Championships, Libya — A621

2009

1738 A621 500d multi 3.00 3.00

Souvenir Sheet

September 1 Revolution, 40th Anniv. — A622

No. 1739 — Col. Khadafy and background color of: a, 400d, Yellow. b, 600d, White. c, 750d, Green.

2009

1739 A622 Sheet of 3, #a-c 7.50 7.50

Col. Khadafy, Map of Africa and African Union Emblem — A623

Litho. & Embossed With Foil Application

2009 ***Serpentine Die Cut 11***

Self-Adhesive

1740 A623 1000d multi 4.50 4.50

Souvenir Sheet

1741 A623 2000d multi 9.00 9.00

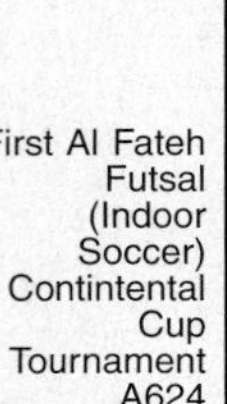

First Al Fateh Futsal (Indoor Soccer) Contintental Cup Tournament A624

2009, Oct. 12 **Litho.** ***Perf. 13***

1742 A624 500d multi 1.50 1.50

Pan-African Postal Union, 30th Anniv. — A625

2010, Jan. 18

1743 A625 500d multi 1.50 1.50

People's Authority Declaration, 33rd Anniv. — A626

Litho. With Foil Application

2010, Mar. 2 ***Serpentine Die Cut 10***

Self-Adhesive

1744 A626 500d multi 1.50 1.50

22nd Session of the Council of the League of Arab States, Sirt — A627

Serpentine Die Cut 10

2010, Mar. 27

Self-Adhesive

1745 A627 500d multi 1.50 1.50

Organization of Petroleum Exporting Countries, 50th Anniv. — A628

2010, June 1 **Litho.** ***Perf. 13***

1746 A628 1000d multi 2.75 2.75

Evacuation of US Forces From Bases in Libya, 40th Anniv. A629

2010, June 9

1747 A629 1000d multi 3.00 3.00

SEMI-POSTAL STAMPS

Many issues of Italy and Italian Colonies include one or more semipostal denominations. To avoid splitting sets, these issues are generally listed as regular postage, semipostals or airmails, etc.

Semi-Postal Stamps of Italy Overprinted

1915-16 **Wmk. 140** ***Perf. 14***

B1 SP1 10c + 5c rose 4.25 *17.00*

a. Double overprint 725.00

B2 SP2 15c + 5c slate 24.00 *30.00*

B3 SP2 20c + 5c org ('16) 5.00 *35.00*

Nos. B1-B3 (3) 33.25 *82.00*

No. B2 with Additional Surcharge

1916, Mar.

B4 SP2 20c on 15c + 5c slate 24.00 *35.00*

a. Double surcharge 725.00

View of Port, Tripoli SP1

Designs: B5, B6, View of port, Tripoli. B7, B8, Arch of Marcus Aurelius. B9, B10, View of Tripoli.

1927, Feb. 15 **Litho.**

B5 SP1 20c + 5c brn vio & black 4.25 *16.00*

B6 SP1 25c + 5c bl grn & black 4.25 *16.00*

B7 SP1 40c + 10c blk brn & black 4.25 *16.00*

B8 SP1 60c + 10c org brn & black 4.25 *16.00*

B9 SP1 75c + 20c red & black 4.25 *16.00*

B10 SP1 1.25 l + 20c bl & blk 24.00 *40.00*

Nos. B5-B10 (6) 45.25 120.00

First Sample Fair, Tripoli. Surtax aided fair. See Nos. EB1-EB2.

View of Tripoli — SP2

Knights of Malta Castle SP3

Designs: 50c+20c, Date palm. 1.25 l+20c, Camel riders. 2.55 l+50c, View of Tripoli. 5 l+1 l, Traction well.

1928, Feb. 20 **Wmk. 140** ***Perf. 14***

B11 SP2 30c + 20c mar & blk 4.00 *17.50*

B12 SP2 50c + 20c bl grn & blk 4.00 *17.50*

B13 SP2 1.25 l + 20c red & blk 4.00 *17.50*

B14 SP3 1.75 l + 20c bl & blk 4.00 *17.50*

B15 SP3 2.55 l + 50c brn & blk 6.50 *22.50*

B16 SP3 5 l + 1 l pur & blk 9.50 *35.00*

Nos. B11-B16 (6) 32.00 *127.50*

2nd Sample Fair, Tripoli, 1928. The surtax was for the aid of the Fair.

Olive Tree — SP4

Herding SP5

Designs: 50c+20c, Dorcas gazelle. 1.25 l+20c, Peach blossoms. 2.55 l+50c, Camel caravan. 5 l+1 l, Oasis with date palms.

1929, Apr. 7

B17 SP4 30c + 20c mar & blk 12.00 *24.00*

B18 SP4 50c + 20c bl grn & blk 12.00 *24.00*

B19 SP4 1.25 l + 20c scar & blk 12.00 *24.00*

B20 SP5 1.75 l + 20c bl & blk 12.00 *24.00*

B21 SP5 2.55 l + 50c yel brn & blk 12.00 *24.00*

B22 SP5 5 l + 1 l pur & blk 130.00 *300.00*

Nos. B17-B22 (6) 190.00 *420.00*

3rd Sample Fair, Tripoli, 1929. The surtax was for the aid of the Fair.

Harvesting Bananas — SP6

Water Carriers SP7

Designs: 50c, Tobacco plant. 1.25 l, Venus of Cyrene. 2.55 l+45c, Black bucks. 5 l+1 l, Motor and camel transportation. 10 l+2 l, Rome pavilion.

1930, Feb. 20 **Photo.**

B23 SP6 30c dark brown 3.25 *16.00*

B24 SP6 50c violet 3.25 *16.00*

B25 SP6 1.25 l deep blue 3.25 *16.00*

B26 SP7 1.75 l + 20c scar 4.75 *24.00*

B27 SP7 2.55 l + 45c dp grn 16.00 *35.00*

B28 SP7 5 l + 1 l dp org 16.00 *47.50*

B29 SP7 10 l + 2 l dk vio 16.00 *50.00*

Nos. B23-B29 (7) 62.50 *204.50*

4th Sample Fair at Tripoli, 1930. The surtax was for the aid of the Fair.

Statue of Ephebus — SP8

Exhibition Pavilion SP9

Designs: 25c, Arab musician. 50c, View of Zeughet. 1.25 l, Snake charmer. 1.75 l+25c, Windmill. 2.75 l+45c, "Zaptie." 5 l+1 l, Mounted Arab.

1931, Mar. 8

B30	SP8	10c black brown	4.75	*11.00*
B31	SP8	25c green	4.75	*11.00*
B32	SP8	50c purple	4.75	*11.00*
B33	SP8	1.25 l blue	4.75	*16.00*
B34	SP8	1.75 l + 25c car rose	4.75	*19.00*
B35	SP8	2.75 l + 45c org	4.75	*24.00*
B36	SP8	5 l + 1 l dl vio	17.50	*35.00*
B37	SP9	10 l + 2 l brn	47.50	*75.00*
		Nos. B30-B37 (8)	93.50	*202.00*
		Nos. B30-B37,C3,EB3 (10)	102.00	246.00

Fifth Sample Fair, Tripoli. Surtax aided fair.

Papaya Tree SP10

Dorcas Gazelle SP12

Ar Tower, Mogadiscio SP11

Designs: 10c, 50c, Papaya tree. 20c, 30c, Euphorbia abyssinica. 25c, Fig cactus. 75c, Mausoleum, Ghirza. 1.75 l+25c, Lioness. 5 l+1 l, Bedouin with camel.

1932, Mar. 8

B38	SP10	10c olive brn	5.00	*14.50*
B39	SP10	20c brown red	5.00	*14.50*
B40	SP10	25c green	5.00	*14.50*
B41	SP10	30c olive blk	5.00	*14.50*
B42	SP10	50c dk violet	5.00	*14.50*
B43	SP10	75c carmine	6.75	*14.50*
B44	SP11	1.25 l dk blue	6.75	*20.00*
B45	SP11	1.75 l + 25c ol brn	29.00	*67.50*
B46	SP11	5 l + 1 l dp bl	29.00	*160.00*
B47	SP12	10 l + 2 l brn violet	120.00	*280.00*
		Nos. B38-B47 (10)	216.50	*614.50*
		Nos. B38-B47,C4-C7 (14)	380.50	*987.00*

Sixth Sample Fair, Tripoli. Surtax aided fair.

Ostrich — SP13

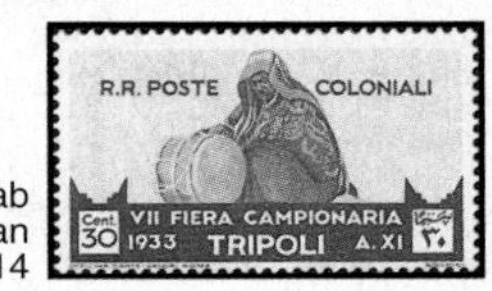

Arab Musician SP14

Designs: 25c, Incense plant. 30c, Arab musician. 50c, Arch of Marcus Aurelius. 1.25 l, African eagle. 5 l+1 l, Leopard. 10 l+2.50 l, Tripoli skyline and fasces.

1933, Mar. 2 Photo. Wmk. 140

B48	SP13	10c dp violet	35.00	35.00
B49	SP13	25c dp green	19.00	*35.00*
B50	SP14	30c orange brn	19.00	*35.00*
B51	SP13	50c purple	17.50	*35.00*
B52	SP13	1.25 l dk blue	45.00	*65.00*
B53	SP14	5 l + 1 l ol brn	87.50	*140.00*
B54	SP13	10 l + 2.50 l car	87.50	*225.00*
		Nos. B48-B54 (7)	310.50	*570.00*
		Nos. B48-B54,C8-C13 (13)	426.00	*905.00*

Seventh Sample Fair, Tripoli. Surtax aided fair.

Pomegranate Tree — SP15

Designs: 50c+10c, 2 l+50c, Musician. 75c+15c, 1.25 l+25c, Tribesman.

1935, Feb. 16

B55	SP15	10c + 10c brown	1.60	*4.75*
B56	SP15	20c + 10c rose red	1.60	*4.75*
B57	SP15	50c + 10c purple	1.60	*4.75*
B58	SP15	75c + 15c car	1.60	*4.75*
B59	SP15	1.25 l + 25c dl blue	1.60	*4.75*
B60	SP15	2 l + 50c ol grn	1.60	*9.50*
		Nos. B55-B60 (6)	9.60	*33.25*
		Nos. B55-B60,C19-C24 (12)	25.10	*97.75*

Ninth Sample Fair, Tripoli. Surtax aided fair.

AIR POST STAMPS

Italy Nos. C3 and C5 Overprinted

1928-29 Wmk. 140 *Perf. 14*

C1	AP2	50c rose red	12.00	*24.00*
C2	AP2	80c brn vio & brn ('29)	35.00	*65.00*

Airplane AP1

1931, Mar. 8 Photo. Wmk. 140

C3	AP1	50c blue	1.75	*16.00*

See note after No. B37.

Seaplane over Bedouin Camp AP2

Designs: 50c, 1 l, Seaplane over Bedouin camp. 2 l+1 l, 5 l+2 l, Seaplane over Tripoli.

1932, Mar. 1 *Perf. 14*

C4	AP2	50c dark blue	10.00	*40.00*
C5	AP2	1 l org brown	10.00	*40.00*
C6	AP2	2 l + 1 l dk gray	24.00	*92.50*
C7	AP2	5 l + 2 l car	120.00	*200.00*
		Nos. C4-C7 (4)	149.00	*332.00*

See note after No. B47.

Seaplane Arriving at Tripoli AP3

Designs: 50c, 2 l+50c, Seaplane arriving at Tripoli. 75c, 10 l+2.50 l, Plane over Tagiura. 1 l, 5 l+1 l, Seaplane leaving Tripoli.

1933, Mar. 1

C8	AP3	50c dp green	11.00	*20.00*
C9	AP3	75c carmine	11.00	*20.00*
C10	AP3	1 l dk blue	11.00	*20.00*
C11	AP3	2 l + 50c pur	17.50	*47.50*
C12	AP3	5 l + 1 l org brn	32.50	*67.50*
C13	AP3	10 l + 2.50 l gray blk	32.50	*160.00*
		Nos. C8-C13 (6)	99.50	*315.00*

See note after No. B54.

Seaplane over Tripoli Harbor AP4

Airplane and Camel — AP5

Designs: 50c, 5 l+1 l, Seaplane over Tripoli harbor. 75c, 10 l+2 l, Plane and minaret.

1934, Feb. 17 Photo. Wmk. 140

C14	AP4	50c slate bl	12.00	*28.00*
C15	AP4	75c red org	12.00	*28.00*
C16	AP4	5 l + 1 l dp grn	120.00	*190.00*
C17	AP4	10 l + 2 l dl vio	120.00	*190.00*
C18	AP5	25 l + 3 l org brn	140.00	*260.00*
		Nos. C14-C18 (5)	352.00	*627.00*

Eighth Sample Fair, Tripoli. Surtax aided fair. See Nos. CE1-CE2.

Plane and Ancient Tower — AP6

Camel Train AP7

Designs: 25c+10c, 3 l+1.50 l, Plane and ancient tower. 50c+10c, 2 l+30c, Camel train. 1 l+25c, 10 l+5 l, Arab watching plane.

1935, Apr. 12

C19	AP6	25c + 10c green	1.20	*5.50*
C20	AP7	50c + 10c slate bl	1.20	*5.50*
C21	AP7	1 l + 25c blue	1.20	*5.50*
C22	AP7	2 l + 30c rose red	1.20	*8.00*
C23	AP6	3 l + 1.50 l brn	1.20	*8.00*
C24	AP7	10 l + 5 l dl vio	9.50	*32.00*
		Nos. C19-C24 (6)	12.75	*57.50*

See note after No. B60.

Cyrenaica No. C6 Overprinted in Black

1936, Oct.

C25	AP2	50c purple	16.00	.40

Same on Tripolitania Nos. C8 and C12

1937

C26	AP1	50c rose carmine	.40	.20
C27	AP2	1 l deep blue	2.10	1.00
		Set, never hinged	6.25	

See Nos. C45-C50.

Ruins of Odeon Theater, Sabrata AP8

1937, Mar. 15 Photo.

C28	AP8	50c dark violet	2.50	*6.75*
C29	AP8	1 l vio black	2.50	*10.00*
		Set, never hinged	12.50	

Opening of a coastal road to the Egyptian frontier.

Nos. C28-C29 Overprinted "XI FIERA DI TRIPOLI"

1937, Mar. 15

C30	AP8	50c dark violet	15.00	*37.50*
C31	AP8	1 l violet blk	15.00	*37.50*
		Set, never hinged	75.00	

11th Sample Fair, Tripoli.

View of Tripoli AP9

Eagle Attacking Serpent AP10

1938, Mar. 12 *Perf. 14*

C32	AP9	50c dk olive grn	1.25	*2.50*
C33	AP9	1 l slate blue	1.25	*6.00*
		Set, never hinged	6.25	

12th Sample Fair, Tripoli.

1938, Apr. 25 Wmk. 140

C34	AP10	50c olive brown	.40	*2.10*
C35	AP10	1 l brn violet	1.25	*4.50*
		Set, never hinged	4.25	

Birth bimillenary Augustus Caesar (Octavianus), first Roman emperor.

Arab and Camel AP11

Design: 50c, Fair entrance.

1939, Apr. 12 Photo.

C36	AP11	25c green	.40	*2.10*
C37	AP11	50c olive brown	.65	*2.10*
C38	AP11	1 l rose violet	.85	*2.50*
		Nos. C36-C38 (3)	1.90	*6.70*
		Set, never hinged	4.25	

13th Sample Fair, Tripoli.

Plane Over Modern City
AP12

Design: 1 l, 5 l+2.50 l, Plane over oasis.

1940, June 3

C39 AP12 50c brn blk .60 *1.00*
C40 AP12 1 l brn vio .60 *2.10*
C41 AP12 2 l + 75c indigo 1.25 *6.25*
C42 AP12 5 l + 2.50 l cop-per brn 1.25 *12.00*
Nos. C39-C42 (4) 3.70 *21.35*
Set, never hinged 8.50

Triennial Overseas Exposition, Naples.

Hitler, Mussolini and Inscription "Two Peoples, One War"
AP13

1941, Apr. 24

C43 AP13 50c slate green 3.25 *47.50*
Never hinged 8.00

Rome-Berlin Axis.

Cyrenaica No. C9 Overprinted in Black Like No. C25

1941

C44 AP3 1 l black 11.00 *55.00*
Never hinged 28.00

Same Overprint on Tripolitania Nos. C9-C11, C13-C15

C45 AP1 60c red orange .85
C46 AP1 75c deep blue .85 47.50
C47 AP1 80c dull violet .85 80.00
C48 AP2 1.20 l dark brown .85 110.00
C49 AP2 1.50 l orange red .85 140.00
C50 AP2 5 l green .85
Nos. C45-C50 (6) 5.10
Set, never hinged 12.50

Catalogue values for unused stamps in this section, from this point to the end of the section, are for Never Hinged items.

United Kingdom of Libya

ICY Type of Regular Issue

Perf. 14½x14

1965, Jan. 1 Litho. Unwmk.

C51 A60 50m dp lil & gold 1.90 .90
a. Souvenir sheet 5.00 5.00

No. C51a exists imperf.; same value.

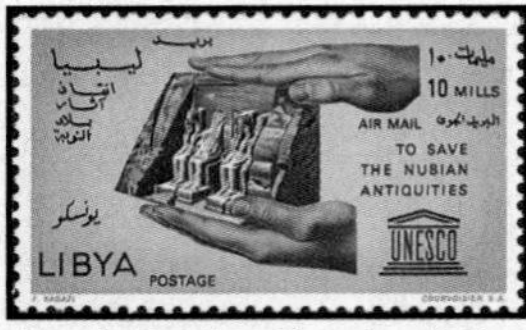

Hands Holding Facade of Abu Simbel — AP14

1966, Jan. 1 Photo. *Perf. 11½*

Granite Paper

C52 AP14 10m bis & dk brn .40 .20
a. Souvenir sheet of 4 2.00 3.75
C53 AP14 15m gray grn & dk grn .50 .20
a. Souvenir sheet of 4 2.50 5.00
C54 AP14 40m dl sal & dk brn 1.60 .65
a. Souvenir sheet of 4 6.50 13.00
Nos. C52-C54 (3) 2.50 1.05

UNESCO world campaign to save historic monuments in Nubia.

Inauguration of WHO Headquarters, Geneva — AP15

Perf. 10x10½

1966, May 3 Litho. Unwmk.

C55 AP15 20m blk, yel & bl .20 .20
C56 AP15 50m blk, yel grn & red .90 .65
C57 AP15 65m blk, sal & brn red 1.40 1.40
Nos. C55-C57 (3) 2.50 2.25

Flag and Globe — AP16

1966, Oct. 1 Photo. *Perf. 11½*

Granite Paper

C58 AP16 25m multicolored .50 .40
C59 AP16 60m multicolored 1.40 1.00
C60 AP16 85m gray & multi 1.90 1.40
Nos. C58-C60 (3) 3.80 2.80

Inauguration of Kingdom of Libya Airlines, 1st anniv.

AIR POST SPECIAL DELIVERY STAMPS

APSD1

Wmk. 140

1934, Feb. 17 Photo. *Perf. 14*

CE1 APSD1 2.25 l olive blk 47.50 *65.00*
CE2 APSD1 4.50 l + 1 l gray blk 47.50 *65.00*
Set, never hinged 240.00

8th Sample Fair at Tripoli. The surtax was for the aid of the Fair.

SPECIAL DELIVERY STAMPS

Special Delivery Stamps of Italy Overprinted

Two types of overprint. See note preceding No. 1 for descriptions.

1915-16. Wmk. 140 *Perf. 14*

E1 SD1 25c rose red, ovpt. type I 87.50 32.00
E2 SD2 30c blue & rose, ovpt. type I 8.00 *35.00*
Set, never hinged 240.00

Issued: Nos. E1, E2, Nov. 1915.
For surcharges see Nos. E7-E8.

"Italia"
SD3

1921-23 Engr. *Perf. 13½*

E3 SD3 30c blue & rose 2.50 *7.50*
E4 SD3 50c rose red & brn 4.00 *12.00*
E5 SD3 60c dk red & brn ('23) 8.50 *19.00*
E6 SD3 2 l dk bl & red ('23) 16.00 *35.00*
Nos. E3-E6 (4) 31.00 *73.50*
Set, never hinged 75.00

30c, 2 l inscribed "EXPRES."
For surcharges see Nos. E9-E12.

Nos. E1-E2 Surcharged

1922, June 1

E7 SD1 60c on 25c rose red 14.50 *16.00*
E8 SD2 1.60 l on 30c bl & rose 16.00 *37.50*
Set, never hinged 75.00

Nos. E5-E6 Surcharged in Blue or Red:

No. E9

Nos. E10, E12

No. E11

1926-36

E9 SD3 70c on 60c 8.25 *19.00*
E10 SD3 2.50 l on 2 l (R) 16.00 *35.00*

Perf. 11

E11 SD3 1.25 l on 60c 6.00 2.00
a. Perf. 14 ('36) 24.00 4.25
Never hinged 60.00
b. Black surcharge *135,000.* *15,000.*
E12 SD3 2.50 l on 2 l (R) 240.00 *800.00*
Nos. E9-E12 (4) 270.25 *856.00*
Set, never hinged 675.00

Issued: #E9-E10, July 1926; #E11-E12, 1927.

Catalogue values for unused stamps in this section, from this point to the end of the section, are for Never Hinged items.

United Kingdom of Libya

Zuela Saracen Castle
SD4

Perf. 11½

1966, Feb. 10 Unwmk. Litho.

E13 SD4 90m car rose & lt grn 2.75 1.60

Coat of Arms of Libya and "POLIGRAFICA & CARTEVALORI — NAPLES" printed on back in yellow green.

SEMI-POSTAL SPECIAL DELIVERY STAMPS

Camel Caravan
SPSD1

Wmk. 140

1927, Feb. 15 Litho. *Perf. 14*

EB1 SPSD1 1.25 l + 30c pur & blk 10.00 40.00
EB2 SPSD1 2.50 l + 1 l yel & blk 10.00 40.00
Set, never hinged 50.00

See note after No. B10.
No. EB2 is inscribed "EXPRES."

War Memorial
SPSD2

1931, Mar. 8 Photo.

EB3 SPSD2 1.25 l + 20c car rose 6.75 *28.00*
Never hinged 17.00

See note after No. B37.

AUTHORIZED DELIVERY STAMPS

Italy No. EY1 Overprinted in Black

1929, May 11 Wmk. 140 *Perf. 14*

EY1 AD1 10c dull blue 35.00 *72.50*
Never hinged 90.00
a. Perf. 11 140.00 280.00
Never hinged 350.00

Italy No. EY2 Overprinted in Black

1941, May *Perf. 14*

EY2 AD2 10c dark brown 12.00 47.50
Never hinged 30.00

A variety of No. EY2, with larger "LIBIA" and yellow gum, was prepared in 1942, but not issued. Value 85 cents, never hinged $2.10.

AD1

1942 Litho. Wmk. 140

EY3 AD1 10c sepia .85
Never hinged 2.10

No. EY3 was not issued.

POSTAGE DUE STAMPS

Italian Postage Due Stamps, 1870-1903 Overprinted in Black

1915, Nov. Wmk. 140 Perf. 14

J1	D3	5c buff & magenta	2.50	*12.00*
J2	D3	10c buff & magenta	2.50	*6.50*
J3	D3	20c buff & magenta	3.25	*9.50*
a.		Double overprint	550.00	
b.		Inverted overprint	550.00	
J4	D3	30c buff & magenta	8.00	*12.00*
J5	D3	40c buff & magenta	12.00	*14.50*
a.		"40" in black	*5,000.*	
J6	D3	50c buff & magenta	8.00	*9.50*
J7	D3	60c buff & magenta	12.00	*22.50*
J8	D3	1 l blue & magenta	8.00	*22.50*
a.		Double overprint	*9,500.*	*14,500.*
J9	D3	2 l blue & magenta	65.00	*110.00*
J10	D3	5 l blue & magenta	80.00	*200.00*
		Nos. J1-J10 (10)	201.25	*419.00*

1926

J11	D3	60c buff & brown	140.00	*240.00*

Postage Due Stamps of Italy, 1934, Overprinted in Black

1934

J12	D6	5c brown	.40	*3.25*
J13	D6	10c blue	.40	*3.25*
J14	D6	20c rose red	1.75	1.75
J15	D6	25c green	1.75	1.75
J16	D6	30c red orange	1.75	*6.75*
J17	D6	40c black brn	1.75	*4.25*
J18	D6	50c violet	2.10	.40
J19	D6	60c black	2.10	*20.00*
J20	D7	1 l red orange	1.75	.40
J21	D7	2 l green	47.50	20.00
J22	D7	5 l violet	110.00	45.00
J23	D7	10 l blue	14.50	*60.00*
J24	D7	20 l carmine	14.50	*80.00*
		Nos. J12-J24 (13)	200.25	*246.80*

In 1942 a set of 11 "Segnatasse" stamps, picturing a camel and rider and inscribed "LIBIA," was prepared but not issued. Values for set: hinged $12; never hinged $30.

Catalogue values for unused stamps in this section, from this point to the end of the section, are for Never Hinged items.

United Kingdom of Libya

Postage Due Stamps of Cyrenaica, 1950 Surcharged in Black

For Use in Tripolitania

1951 Unwmk. Perf. 12½

J25	D1	1mal on 2m dk brown	9.00	18.00
J26	D1	2mal on 4m dp grn	15.00	*30.00*
J27	D1	4mal on 8m scar	25.00	*50.00*
J28	D1	10mal on 20m org yel	50.00	*100.00*
a.		Arabic "20" for "10"	—	
J29	D1	20mal on 40m dp bl	80.00	*160.00*
		Nos. J25-J29 (5)	179.00	*358.00*

Cyrenaica Nos. J1-J7 Overprinted in Black

For Use in Cyrenaica

Overprint 13mm High

1952 Unwmk. Perf. 12½

J30	D1	2m dark brown	10.00	*20.00*
J31	D1	4m deep green	10.00	*20.00*
J32	D1	8m scarlet	15.00	*30.00*
J33	D1	10m vermilion	20.00	*4.00*
J34	D1	20m orange yel	30.00	*60.00*
J35	D1	40m deep blue	42.50	*85.00*
J36	D1	100m dk gray	92.50	*180.00*
		Nos. J30-J36 (7)	220.00	*399.00*

D1

Castle at Tripoli — D2

1952 Litho. Perf. 11½

J37	D1	2m chocolate	1.00	.35
J38	D1	5m blue green	1.60	.90
J39	D1	10m carmine	3.00	1.50
J40	D1	50m violet blue	11.00	4.00
		Nos. J37-J40 (4)	16.60	6.75

1964, Feb. 1 Photo. Perf. 14

J41	D2	2m red brown	.25	.25
J42	D2	6m Prus green	.50	.50
J43	D2	10m rose red	1.00	1.00
J44	D2	50m brt blue	2.00	2.00
		Nos. J41-J44 (4)	3.75	3.75

Men in Boat, Birds, Mosaic — D3

Ancient Mosaics: 10d, Head of Medusa. 20d, Peacock. 50d, Fish.

1976, Nov. 15 Litho. Perf. 14

J45	D3	5d bister & multi	.25	.25
J46	D3	10d orange & multi	.25	.25
J47	D3	20d blue & multi	.35	.35
J48	D3	50d emerald & multi	.80	.80
		Nos. J45-J48 (4)	1.65	1.65

Nos. J45-J48 have multiple coat of arms printed on back in pale green beneath gum.

OFFICIAL STAMPS

Catalogue values for unused stamps in this section are for Never Hinged items.

United Kingdom of Libya

Nos. 135-142 Overprinted in Black

1952 Unwmk. Perf. 11½

O1	A27	2m yel brn	.90	.60
O2	A27	4m gray	1.50	.90
O3	A27	5m bl grn	7.50	3.00
O4	A27	8m vermilion	5.50	2.50
O5	A27	10m purple	7.00	3.00
O6	A27	12m lil rose	11.00	6.25
O7	A27	20m dp bl	19.00	9.50
O8	A27	25m chocolate	25.00	12.50
		Nos. O1-O8 (8)	77.40	38.25

PARCEL POST STAMPS

These stamps were used by affixing them to the way bill so that one half remained on it following the parcel, the other half staying on the receipt given the sender. Most used halves are right halves. Complete stamps were obtainable canceled, probably to order. Both unused and used values are for complete stamps.

Italian Parcel Post Stamps, 1914-22, Overprinted

1915-24 Wmk. 140 Perf. 13½

Q1	PP2	5c brown	3.25	*14.00*
a.		Double overprint	425.00	
Q2	PP2	10c deep blue	3.25	*14.00*
Q3	PP2	20c blk ('18)	4.00	*14.00*
Q4	PP2	25c red	4.00	*14.00*
Q5	PP2	50c orange	6.50	*14.00*
Q6	PP2	1 l violet	6.50	*20.00*
Q7	PP2	2 l green	8.00	*20.00*
Q8	PP2	3 l bister	14.00	*20.00*
Q9	PP2	4 l slate	14.00	*20.00*
Q10	PP2	10 l rose lil ('24)	80.00	*130.00*
Q11	PP2	12 l red brn ('24)	160.00	*350.00*
Q12	PP2	15 l ol grn ('24)	160.00	*450.00*
Q13	PP2	20 l brn vio ('24)	275.00	*475.00*
		Nos. Q1-Q13 (13)	738.50	*1,555.*

Halves Used

Q1	1.00
Q2	1.50
Q3	1.50
Q4	1.50
Q5	1.50
Q6	1.50
Q7	1.50
Q8	1.50
Q9	1.50
Q10	10.00
Q11	11.00
Q12	25.00
Q13	65.00

Same Overprint on Parcel Post Stamps of Italy, 1927-36

1927-38

Q14	PP3	10c dp bl ('36)	4.25	*9.50*
Q15	PP3	25c red ('36)	4.25	*9.50*
Q16	PP3	30c ultra ('29)	1.75	*4.75*
Q17	PP3	50c orange	75.00	325.00
a.		Overprint 8¾x2mm ('31)	125.00	*475.00*
Q18	PP3	60c red ('29)	1.75	*4.75*
Q19	PP3	1 l lilac ('36)	40.00	*130.00*
Q20	PP3	2 l grn ('38)	47.50	*130.00*
Q21	PP3	3 l bister	2.50	*12.00*
Q22	PP3	4 l gray	2.50	*16.00*
Q23	PP3	10 l rose lil ('36)	350.00	650.00
Q24	PP3	20 l brn vio ('36)	400.00	*800.00*
		Nos. Q14-Q24 (11)	929.50	*2,091.*

Halves Used

Q14	.50
Q15	.50
Q16	.50
Q17	12.50
Q17a	22.50
Q18	.50
Q19	7.50
Q20	7.50
Q21	1.50
Q22	2.50
Q23	30.00
Q24	35.00

The overprint measures 10x1½mm on No. Q17.

Same Overprint on Italy No. Q24

1939

Q25	PP3	5c brown	*17,500.*	
		Never hinged	*26,500.*	

The overprint was applied to the 5c in error. Few examples exist.

OCCUPATION STAMPS

Catalogue values for unused stamps in this section are for Never Hinged items.

Issued under French Occupation

Stamps of Italy and Libya were overprinted in 1943: "FEZZAN Occupation Française" and "R. F. FEZZAN" for use in this region when General Leclerc's forces 1st occupied it.

Fezzan-Ghadames

Sebha Fort — OS1

Mosque and Fort Turc Murzuch OS2

Map of Fezzan-Ghadames, Soldier and Camel — OS3

1946 Unwmk. Engr. Perf. 13

1N1	OS1	10c black	.40	.40
1N2	OS1	50c rose	.40	.40
1N3	OS1	1fr brown	.50	.50
1N4	OS1	1.50fr green	.65	.65
1N5	OS1	2fr ultramarine	.85	.85
1N6	OS2	2.50fr violet	1.00	1.00
1N7	OS2	3fr rose carmine	1.40	1.40
1N8	OS2	5fr chocolate	1.40	1.40
1N9	OS2	6fr dark green	1.30	1.30
1N10	OS2	10fr blue	1.40	1.40
1N11	OS3	15fr violet	1.75	1.75
1N12	OS3	20fr red	2.00	1.90
1N13	OS3	25fr sepia	2.00	1.90
1N14	OS3	40fr dark green	2.50	2.50
1N15	OS3	50fr deep blue	2.75	2.75
		Nos. 1N1-1N15 (15)	20.30	20.10

FEZZAN

Catalogue values for unused stamps in this section are for Never Hinged items.

Monument, Djerma Oasis — OS1

Tombs of the Beni-Khettab — OS2

Well at Gorda OS3

Col. Colonna d'Ornano and Fort at Murzuch OS4

Philippe F. M. de Hautecloque (Gen. Jacques Leclerc) — OS5

1949 Unwmk. Engr. Perf. 13

2N1	OS1	1fr black	1.25	1.25
2N2	OS1	2fr lil pink	1.25	1.25
2N3	OS2	4fr red brn	2.50	2.50
2N4	OS2	5fr emerald	2.50	2.50
2N5	OS3	8fr blue	3.25	3.25
2N6	OS3	10fr brown	5.25	5.25
2N7	OS3	12fr dk grn	8.00	8.00
2N8	OS4	15fr sal red	12.00	12.00
2N9	OS4	20fr brn blk	5.50	5.50
2N10	OS5	25fr dk bl	6.75	6.75
2N11	OS5	50fr cop red	12.00	12.00
		Nos. 2N1-2N11 (11)	60.25	60.25

Camel Raising OS6

Agriculture OS7

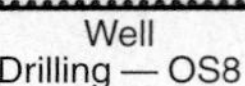

Well Drilling — OS8 Ahmed Bey — OS9

1951

2N12	OS6	30c brown	1.60	1.60
2N13	OS6	1fr dp bl	1.60	1.60
2N14	OS6	2fr rose car	1.60	1.60
2N15	OS7	4fr red	2.40	2.40
2N16	OS7	5fr green	2.40	2.40
2N17	OS7	8fr dp bl	2.40	2.40
2N18	OS8	10fr sepia	6.50	6.50
2N19	OS8	12fr dp grn	7.50	7.25
2N20	OS8	15fr brt red	8.00	8.00
2N21	OS9	20fr blk brn & vio brn	8.00	8.00
2N22	OS9	25fr dk bl & bl	9.25	9.00
2N23	OS9	50fr ind & brn org	9.50	9.50
		Nos. 2N12-2N23 (12)	60.75	60.25

OCCUPATION SEMI-POSTAL STAMPS

Catalogue values for unused stamps in this section are for Never Hinged items.

"The Unhappy Ones"
OSP1 OSP2

1950 Unwmk. Engr. *Perf. 13*

2NB1	OSP1	15fr + 5fr red brn	3.50	3.50
2NB2	OSP2	25fr + 5fr blue	3.50	3.50

The surtax was for charitable works.

OCCUPATION AIR POST STAMPS

Catalogue values for unused stamps in this section are for Never Hinged items.

Airport in Fezzan OAP1

Plane over Fezzan — OAP2

1948 Unwmk. Engr. *Perf. 13*

2NC1	OAP1	100fr red	8.50	8.50
2NC2	OAP2	200fr indigo	12.00	12.00

Oasis OAP3

Murzuch OAP4

1951

2NC3	OAP3	100fr dark blue	11.00	11.00
2NC4	OAP4	200fr vermilion	16.00	16.00

OCCUPATION POSTAGE DUE STAMPS

Catalogue values for unused stamps in this section are for Never Hinged items.

Oasis of Brak — D1

1950 Unwmk. Engr. *Perf. 13*

2NJ1	D1	1fr brown black	1.75	1.75
2NJ2	D1	2fr deep green	1.75	1.75
2NJ3	D1	3fr red brown	2.40	2.40
2NJ4	D1	5fr purple	2.50	2.50
2NJ5	D1	10fr red	4.75	4.75
2NJ6	D1	20fr deep blue	7.25	7.25
		Nos. 2NJ1-2NJ6 (6)	20.40	20.40

GHADAMES

Catalogue values for unused stamps in this section are for Never Hinged items.

Cross of Agadem — OS1

1949 Unwmk. Engr. *Perf. 13*

3N1	OS1	4fr sep & red brn	4.00	4.00
3N2	OS1	5fr pck bl & dk grn	4.00	4.00
3N3	OS1	8fr sep & org brn	5.75	5.75
3N4	OS1	10fr blk & dk ultra	5.75	5.75
3N5	OS1	12fr vio & red vio	14.00	14.00
3N6	OS1	15fr brn & red brn	10.00	10.00
3N7	OS1	20fr sep & emer	12.00	12.00
3N8	OS1	25fr sepia & blue	14.50	14.50
		Nos. 3N1-3N8 (8)	70.00	70.00

OCCUPATION AIR POST STAMPS

Catalogue values for unused stamps in this section are for Never Hinged items.

Cross of Agadem — OAP1

1949 Unwmk. Engr. *Perf. 13*

3NC1	OAP1	50fr pur & rose	18.50	18.50
3NC2	OAP1	100fr sep & pur brn	22.00	22.00

LIECHTENSTEIN

'lik-tən-ˌshtin

LOCATION — Central Europe southeast of Lake Constance, between Austria and Switzerland
GOVT. — Principality
AREA — 61.8 sq. mi.
POP. — 31,320 (1997)
CAPITAL — Vaduz

The Principality of Liechtenstein is a sovereign state consisting of the two counties of Schellenberg and Vaduz. Since 1921 the post office has been administered by Switzerland.

100 Heller = 1 Krone
100 Rappen = 1 Franc (1921)

Catalogue values for unused stamps in this country are for Never Hinged items, beginning with Scott 368 in the regular postage section, Scott B22 in the semi-postal section, Scott C24 in the air post section, and Scott O30 in the offical section.

Watermarks

Greek Cross — Wmk. 183

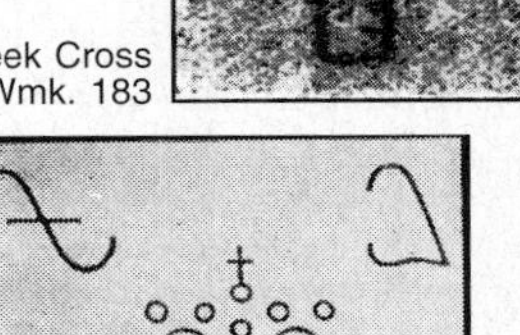

Crown and Initials — Wmk. 296

Austrian Administration of the Post Office

Prince Johann II — A1

Perf. 12½x13

1912, Feb. 1 Unwmk. Typo.

Thick Chalky Paper

1	A1	5h yellow green	35.00	13.00
2	A1	10h rose	70.00	13.00
3	A1	25h dark blue	70.00	40.00
		Nos. 1-3 (3)	175.00	66.00
		Set, never hinged	725.00	

1915

Thin Unsurfaced Paper

1a	A1	5h yellow green	12.00	*15.00*
2a	A1	10h rose	75.00	22.50
3a	A1	25h dark blue	575.00	150.00
b.		25h ultramarine	350.00	350.00
		Never hinged	1,300.	
		#1a-3a, never hinged	2,500.	

Coat of Arms — A2

Prince Johann II — A3

1917-18

4	A2	3h violet	1.40	1.50
5	A2	5h yellow green	1.40	1.50
6	A3	10h claret	1.40	1.50
7	A3	15h dull red	1.40	1.50
8	A3	20h dark green	1.40	1.50
9	A3	25h deep blue	1.40	1.50
		Nos. 4-9 (6)	8.40	9.00
		Set, never hinged	37.50	

Exist imperf. Value set unused original gum, $350.

For surcharges see Nos. 11-16.

Prince Johann II — A4

1918, Nov. 12

Dates in Upper Corners

10	A4	20h dark green	.45	*2.00*
		Never hinged	3.25	

Accession of Prince Johann II, 60th anniv. Exists imperf. Value $150.

National Administration of the Post Office

Stamps of 1917-18 Overprinted or Surcharged

a

b

c

1920

11	A2(a)	5h yellow green	1.90	*7.50*
a.		Inverted overprint	75.00	*175.00*
		Never hinged	200.00	
b.		Double overprint	15.00	*100.00*
		Never hinged	40.00	
12	A3(a)	10h claret	1.90	*7.50*
a.		Inverted overprint	75.00	175.00
		Never hinged	200.00	
b.		Double overprint	15.00	*100.00*
		Never hinged	40.00	
c.		Overprint type "c"	15.00	*100.00*
		Never hinged	35.00	
13	A3(a)	25h deep blue	1.90	*7.50*
a.		Inverted overprint	75.00	*175.00*
		Never hinged	200.00	
b.		Double overprint	15.00	*100.00*
		Never hinged	35.00	
14	A2(b)	40h on 3h violet	1.90	*7.50*
a.		Inverted surcharge	75.00	*175.00*
		Never hinged	200.00	
15	A3(c)	1k on 15h dull red	1.90	*7.50*
a.		Inverted surcharge	75.00	*175.00*
		Never hinged	200.00	
b.		Overprint type "a"	67.50	*150.00*
		Never hinged	250.00	
16	A3(c)	2½k on 20h dk grn	1.90	*7.50*
a.		Inverted surcharge	75.00	*175.00*
		Never hinged	200.00	
		Nos. 11-16 (6)	11.40	*45.00*
		Set, never hinged	50.00	

Coat of Arms A5

Chapel of St. Mamertus A6

Coat of Arms with Supporters A15

Designs: 40h, Gutenberg Castle. 50h, Courtyard, Vaduz Castle. 60h, Red Tower, Vaduz. 80h, Old Roman Tower, Schaan. 1k, Castle at Vaduz. 2k, View of Bendern. 5k, Prince Johann I. 7½k, Prince Johann II.

1920 Engr. *Imperf.*

18	A5	5h olive bister	.25	5.75
19	A5	10h deep orange	.25	5.75
20	A5	15h dark blue	.25	5.75
21	A5	20h deep brown	.25	5.75
22	A5	25h dark green	.25	5.75
23	A5	30h gray black	.25	5.75
24	A5	40h dark red	.25	5.75
25	A6	1k blue	.25	5.75

Perf. 12½

32	A5	5h olive bister	.25	*.50*
33	A5	10h deep orange	.25	*.50*
34	A5	15h deep blue	.25	*.50*
35	A5	20h red brown	.25	*.50*
36	A6	25h olive green	.25	*.50*
37	A5	30h dark gray	.25	*.50*
38	A6	40h claret	.25	*.50*
39	A6	50h yellow green	.25	*.50*
40	A6	60h red brown	.25	*.50*
41	A6	80h rose	.25	*.50*
42	A6	1k dull violet	.45	*.90*
43	A6	2k light blue	.45	*1.00*
44	A6	5k black	.45	*1.10*
45	A6	7½k slate	.45	*1.50*
46	A15	10k ocher	.45	*1.50*
		Nos. 18-46 (23)	6.75	*57.00*
		Set, never hinged	27.50	

Used values for Nos. 18-46 are for canceled to order stamps. Value with postal cancels approximately $45.

Many denominations of Nos. 32-46 are found imperforate, imperforate vertically and imperforate horizontally.

For surcharges see Nos. 51-52.

Madonna and Child — A16

1920, Oct. 5

47	A16	50h olive green	.45	*1.40*
48	A16	80h brown red	.45	*1.40*
49	A16	2k dark blue	.45	*2.10*
		Nos. 47-49 (3)	1.35	*4.90*
		Set, never hinged	7.50	

80th birthday of Prince Johann II.

Imperf., Singles

47a	A16	50h	6.00	—
48a	A16	80h	6.00	—
49a	A16	2k	6.00	—
		Set, never hinged	24.00	

On 1/31/21 the Swiss took over the Post Office administration. Previous issues were demonitized and remainders of Nos. 4-49 were sold.

Swiss Administration of the Post Office

No. 19 Surcharged

No. 51

No. 52

1921 Unwmk. Engr. *Imperf.*

51	A5	2rp on 10h dp org	.90	*27.50*
		Never hinged	3.50	
a.		Double surcharge	97.50	*140.00*
		Never hinged	160.00	
b.		Inverted surcharge	80.00	*140.00*
		Never hinged	140.00	
c.		Double surch., one inverted	100.00	*87.50*
		Never hinged	175.00	
52	A5	2rp on 10h dp org	.60	*20.00*
		Never hinged	1.40	
		First day cover (2/27/21)		*750.00*
a.		Double surcharge	80.00	*175.00*
		Never hinged	140.00	
b.		Inverted surcharge	80.00	*175.00*
		Never hinged	140.00	
c.		Double surch., one inverted	92.50	*190.00*
		Never hinged	160.00	

Arms with Supporters A19

Chapel of St. Mamertus A20

View of Vaduz A21

Designs: 25rp, Castle at Vaduz. 30rp, View of Bendern. 35rp, Prince Johann II. 40rp, Old Roman Tower at Schaan. 50rp, Gutenberg Castle. 80rp, Red Tower at Vaduz.

1921 *Perf. 12½, 9½ (2rp, 10rp, 15rp)*

Surface Tinted Paper (#54-61)

54	A19	2rp lemon	1.00	*10.00*
55	A19	2½rp black	1.10	*11.00*
a.		Perf. 9½	1.25	*57.50*
		Never hinged	2.75	
56	A19	3rp orange	1.10	*10.00*
a.		Perf. 9½	140.00	*3,750.*
		Never hinged	350.00	
57	A19	5rp olive green	11.50	1.75
a.		Perf. 9½	67.50	*13.00*
		Never hinged	200.00	

58 A19 7½rp dark blue 6.75 *35.00*
a. Perf. 9½ 275.00 *875.00*
Never hinged 675.00
59 A19 10rp yellow green 26.00 8.75
a. Perf. 12½ 35.00 6.00
Never hinged 90.00
60 A19 13rp brown 8.25 *77.50*
a. Perf. 9½ 95.00 *2,150.*
Never hinged 300.00
b. Perf. 12½x9½ 125.00 —
Never hinged 400.00
61 A19 15rp dark violet 22.50 20.00
a. Perf. 12½ 21.00 *24.00*
Never hinged 67.50
62 A20 20rp dull vio & blk 67.50 1.90
63 A20 25rp rose red & blk 3.50 3.00
64 A20 30rp dp grn & blk 75.00 17.00
65 A20 35rp brn & blk, *straw* 6.50 *13.50*
66 A20 40rp dk blue & blk 9.75 5.50
67 A20 50rp dk grn & blk 17.00 6.75
68 A20 80rp gray & blk 30.00 *67.50*
69 A21 1fr dp claret & blk 57.50 45.00
Nos. 54-69 (16) 344.95 *334.15*
Set, never hinged 1,150.

Nos. 54-69 exist imperforate; Nos. 54-61, partly perforated. See Nos. 73, 81. For surcharges see Nos. 70-71.

Nos. 58, 60a Surcharged in Red

1924 ***Perf. 12½, 9½***
70 A19 5rp on 7½rp 1.25 *2.00*
Never hinged 3.50
a. Perf. 9½ 15.00 6.75
Never hinged 45.00
71 A19 10rp on 13rp .70 *15.00*
Never hinged 2.00
a. Perf. 12½ 19.00 *40.00*
Never hinged 35.00

Type of 1921

1924 **Wmk. 183** ***Perf. 11½***

Granite Paper

73 A19 10rp green 14.00 2.00
Never hinged 65.00

Peasant A28

Government Palace and Church at Vaduz A30

10rp, 20rp, Courtyard, Vaduz Castle.

1924-28 **Typo.** ***Perf. 11½***
74 A28 2½rp ol grn & red vio ('28) 1.25 *5.00*
75 A28 5rp brown & blue 2.25 .75
76 A28 7½rp bl grn & brn ('28) 1.90 *5.50*
77 A28 15rp red brn & bl grn ('28) 8.75 *27.50*

Engr.

78 A28 10rp yellow grn 11.50 .60
79 A28 20rp deep red 37.50 .90
80 A30 1½fr blue 82.50 *87.50*
Nos. 74-80 (7) 145.65 *127.75*
Set, never hinged 350.00

Bendern Type of 1921

1925
81 A20 30rp blue & blk 11.50 2.00
Never hinged 55.00

Prince Johann II — A31

Prince Johann II as Boy and Man A32

1928, Nov. 12 **Typo.** **Wmk. 183**
82 A31 10rp lt brn & ol grn 4.50 5.00
83 A31 20rp org red & ol grn 6.75 10.00
84 A31 30rp sl bl & ol grn 22.50 17.50
85 A31 60rp red vio & ol grn 45.00 *75.00*

Engr.

Unwmk.

86 A32 1.20fr ultra 37.50 *87.50*
87 A32 1.50fr black brown 67.50 *190.00*
88 A32 2fr deep car 67.50 *190.00*
89 A32 5fr dark green 67.50 *225.00*
Nos. 82-89 (8) 318.75 *800.00*
Set, never hinged 1,000.

70th year of the reign of Prince Johann II.

Prince Francis I, as a Child — A33

Prince Francis I as a Man — A34

Princess Elsa — A35

Prince Francis and Princess Elsa — A36

1929, Dec. 2 **Photo.**
90 A33 10rp olive green .35 *3.00*
91 A34 20rp carmine .55 *5.00*
92 A35 30rp ultra .90 *17.50*
93 A36 70rp brown 16.00 *100.00*
Nos. 90-93 (4) 17.80 *125.50*
Set, never hinged 55.00

Accession of Prince Francis I, Feb. 11, 1929.

Grape Girl — A37

Chamois Hunter — A38

Mountain Cattle — A39

Courtyard, Vaduz Castle — A40

Mt. Naafkopf — A41

Chapel at Steg — A42

Rofenberg Chapel — A43

Chapel of St. Mamertus — A44

Alpine Hotel, Malbun — A45

Gutenberg Castle — A46

Schellenberg Monastery — A47

Castle at Vaduz — A48

Mountain Cottage — A49

Prince Francis and Princess Elsa — A50

1930 ***Perf. 10½, 11½, 11½x10½***
94 A37 3rp brown lake .70 2.00
95 A38 5rp deep green 1.90 5.00
96 A39 10rp dark violet 1.60 5.00
a. Perf. 11½x10½ 6.75 *75.00*
Never hinged 19.00
97 A40 20rp dp rose red 27.50 5.00
98 A41 25rp black 5.50 *32.50*
a. Perf. 11½ 67.50 *250.00*
Never hinged 275.00
99 A42 30rp dp ultra 5.50 7.50
a. Perf. 11½x10½ 675.00 *1,800.*
Never hinged 1,700.
Never hinged 22.50

100 A43 35rp dark green 6.75 *15.00*
a. Perf. 11½ *5,750.* *10,000.*
Never hinged *10,500.*
101 A44 40rp lt brown 6.75 6.00
102 A45 50rp black brown 67.50 15.00
a. Perf. 11½ 110.00 *175.00*
Never hinged 400.00
103 A46 60rp olive blk 67.50 30.00
104 A47 90rp violet brn 67.50 *250.00*
105 A48 1.20fr olive brn 82.50 *275.00*
a. Perf. 11½x10½ *5,750.* *10,000.*
Never hinged *10,500.*
106 A49 1.50fr black violet 45.00 55.00
107 A50 2fr gray grn & red brn 55.00 *100.00*
a. Perf. 11½x10½ *2,500.* *5,500.*
Never hinged *5,250.*
Nos. 94-107 (14) 441.20 *803.00*
Set, never hinged 1,500.

For overprints see Nos. O1-O8.

Mt. Naafkopf A51

Gutenberg Castle A52

Vaduz Castle — A53

1933, Jan. 23 ***Perf. 14½***
108 A51 25rp red orange 175.00 62.50
109 A52 90rp dark green 6.75 *75.00*
110 A53 1.20fr red brown 91.00 *250.00*
Nos. 108-110 (3) 272.75 *387.50*
Set, never hinged 825.00

For overprints see Nos. O9-O10.

Prince Francis I
A54 A55

1933, Aug. 28 ***Perf. 11***
111 A54 10rp purple 18.00 *35.00*
112 A54 20rp brown carmine 18.00 *35.00*
113 A54 30rp dark blue 18.00 *35.00*
Nos. 111-113 (3) 54.00 *105.00*
Set, never hinged 165.00

80th birthday of Prince Francis I.

1933, Dec. 15 **Engr.** ***Perf. 12½***
114 A55 3fr violet blue 82.50 *175.00*
Never hinged 225.00

See No. 152.

Agricultural Exhibition Issue

Souvenir Sheet

Arms of Liechtenstein — A56

Judo and Olympic Rings — A274

Rubens' Sons, Albrecht and Nikolas — A275

Designs (Olympic Rings and): 50rp, volleyball. 80rp, Relay race. 1.10fr, Long jump, women's.

1976, June 10 *Perf. 11½*

591	A274	35rp multicolored	.25	.25
592	A274	50rp multicolored	.45	.45
593	A274	80rp multicolored	.65	.65
594	A274	1.10fr multicolored	.90	.90
		Nos. 591-594 (4)	2.25	2.25

21st Olympic Games, Montreal, Canada, July 17-Aug. 1.

1976, Sept. 9 Engr. *Perf. 13½x14*

Rubens Paintings: 50rp, Singing Angels. 1fr, The Daughters of Cecrops, horiz. (from Collection of Prince of Liechtenstein).

Size: 24x38mm

595	A275	50rp gold & multi	1.40	1.40
596	A275	70rp gold & multi	2.00	2.00

Size: 48x38mm

597	A275	1fr gold & multi	5.50	5.50
		Nos. 595-597 (3)	8.90	8.90

400th anniversary of the birth of Peter Paul Rubens (1577-1640), Flemish painter. Sheets of 8 (2x4).

Zodiac Signs — A276

1976-78 Photo. *Perf. 11½*

598	A276	20rp Pisces	.20	.20
599	A276	40rp Aries	.35	.35
600	A276	40rp Cancer ('77)	.40	.35
601	A276	40rp Scorpio ('78)	.45	.45
602	A276	50rp Sagittarius ('78)	.50	.45
603	A276	70rp Leo ('77)	.65	.65
604	A276	80rp Taurus	.75	.70
605	A276	80rp Virgo ('77)	.75	.75
606	A276	80rp Capricorn ('78)	.75	.70
607	A276	90rp Gemini	1.00	.75
608	A276	1.10fr Libra ('77)	1.10	1.10
609	A276	1.50fr Aquarius ('78)	1.25	1.25
		Nos. 598-609 (12)	8.15	7.70

Flight into Egypt — A277

Ortlieb von Brandis, Sarcophagus A278

Monastic Wax Works: 20rp, Holy Infant of Prague, horiz. 80rp, Holy Family and Trinity. 1.50fr, Holy Family, horiz.

1976, Dec. 9 Photo. *Perf. 11½*

610	A277	20rp multicolored	.20	.20
611	A277	50rp multicolored	.40	.40
612	A277	80rp multicolored	.55	.55
613	A277	1.50fr multicolored	1.25	1.25
		Nos. 610-613 (4)	2.40	2.40

Christmas 1976.

Photogravure and Engraved

1976, Dec. 9 *Perf. 13½x14*

614	A278	1.10fr gold & dk brown	.90	.70

Ortlieb von Brandis, Bishop of Chur (1458-1491).

Map of Liechtenstein, by J. J. Heber, 1721 — A279

Europa: 80rp, View of Vaduz, by Ferdinand Bachmann, 1815.

1977, Mar. 10 Photo. *Perf. 12½*

615	A279	40rp multicolored	*.40*	*.40*
616	A279	80rp multicolored	*.80*	*.80*

Treasure Type of 1975

40rp, Holy Lance and Particle of the Cross. 50rp, Imperial Evangel of St. Matthew. 80rp, St. Stephen's Purse. 90rp, Tabard of Imperial Herald.

Engraved and Photogravure

1977, June 8 *Perf. 14*

617	A266	40rp gold & multi	.40	.30
618	A266	50rp gold & multi	.50	.45
619	A266	80rp gold & multi	.70	.65
620	A266	90rp gold & multi	1.00	.90
		Nos. 617-620 (4)	2.60	2.30

Treasures of the Holy Roman Empire from the Treasury of the Hofburg in Vienna.

Emperor Constantius II Coin — A280

Coins: 70rp, Lindau bracteate, c. 1300. 80rp, Ortlieb von Brandis, 1458-1491.

1977, June 8 Photo. *Perf. 11½*

Granite Paper

621	A280	35rp gold & multi	.35	.30
622	A280	70rp silver & multi	.60	.55
623	A280	80rp silver & multi	.80	.65
		Nos. 621-623 (3)	1.75	1.50

Frauenthal Castle A281

Castles: 50rp, Gross Ullersdorf. 80rp, Liechtenstein Castle near Mödling, Austria. 90rp, Liechtenstein Palace, Vienna.

Engraved and Photogravure

1977, Sept. 8 *Perf. 13½x14*

624	A281	20rp slate grn & gold	.20	.20
625	A281	50rp magenta & gold	.50	.50
626	A281	80rp dk violet & gold	.80	.80
627	A281	90rp dk blue & gold	.90	.90
		Nos. 624-627 (4)	2.40	2.40

Children — A282

Traditional Costumes: 70rp, Two girls. 1fr, Woman in festival dress.

1977, Sept. 8 Photo. *Perf. 11½*

Granite Paper

628	A282	40rp multicolored	.50	.40
629	A282	70rp multicolored	.75	.70
630	A282	1fr multicolored	1.25	1.10
		Nos. 628-630 (3)	2.50	2.20

Princess Tatjana A283

1977, Dec. 7 Photo. *Perf. 11½*

631	A283	1.10fr brown & gold	.90	.85

Angel — A284

Liechtenstein Palace, Vienna A285

Sculptures by Erasmus Kern: 50rp, St. Rochus. 80rp, Virgin and Child. 1.50fr, God the Father.

1977, Dec. 7

632	A284	20rp multicolored	.20	.20
633	A284	50rp multicolored	.45	.45
634	A284	80rp multicolored	.75	.75
635	A284	1.50fr multicolored	1.50	1.50
		Nos. 632-635 (4)	2.90	2.90

Christmas 1977.

Photogravure and Engraved

1978, Mar. 2 *Perf. 14*

Europa: 80rp, Feldsberg Castle.

636	A285	40rp gold & slate blue	*.35*	*.30*
637	A285	80rp gold & claret	*.75*	*.70*

Farmhouse, Triesen — A286

Designs: 20rp, Houses, Upper Village, Triesen. 35rp, Barns, Balzers. 40rp, Monastery, Bendern. 50rp, Residential Tower, Balzers-Mäls. 70rp, Parish house. 80rp, Farmhouse, Schellenberg. 90rp, Parish house, Balzers. 1fr, Rheinberger House, Music School, Vaduz. 1.10fr, Street, Mitteldorf, Vaduz. 1.50fr, Town Hall, Triesenberg. 2fr, National Museum and Administrator's Residence, Vaduz.

1978 Photo. *Perf. 11½*

638	A286	10rp multicolored	.20	.20
639	A286	20rp multicolored	.20	.20
640	A286	35rp multicolored	.30	.30
641	A286	40rp multicolored	.30	.30
642	A286	50rp multicolored	.40	.40
643	A286	70rp multicolored	.55	.55
644	A286	80rp multicolored	.60	.60
645	A286	90rp multicolored	.70	.70
646	A286	1fr multicolored	.75	.75
647	A286	1.10fr multicolored	.90	.90
648	A286	1.50fr multicolored	1.10	1.10
649	A286	2fr multicolored	1.50	1.50
		Nos. 638-649 (12)	7.50	7.50

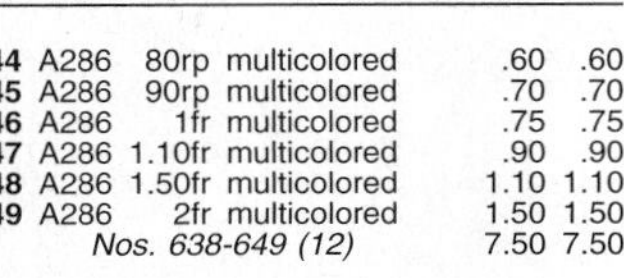

Vaduz Castle A287

Vaduz Castle: 50rp, Courtyard. 70rp, Staircase. 80rp, Triptych from High Altar, Castle Chapel.

Engraved and Photogravure

1978, June 1 *Perf. 13½x14*

650	A287	40rp gold & multi	.45	.45
651	A287	50rp gold & multi	.60	.60
652	A287	70rp gold & multi	.85	.85
653	A287	80rp gold & multi	1.10	1.10
		Nos. 650-653 (4)	3.00	3.00

40th anniversary of reign of Prince Franz Joseph II. Sheet of 8.

Prince Karl I, Coin, 1614 A288

Adoration of the Shepherds A289

Designs: 50rp, Prince Johann Adam, medal, 1694. 80rp, Prince Josef Wenzel, medal, 1773.

1978, Sept. 7 Photo. *Perf. 11½*

654	A288	40rp multicolored	.35	.35
655	A288	50rp multicolored	.50	.50
656	A288	80rp multicolored	.95	.95
		Nos. 654-656 (3)	1.80	1.80

1978, Dec. 7 Photo. *Perf. 11½*

Stained-glass Windows, Triesenberg: 50rp, Holy Family. 80rp, Adoration of the Kings.

657	A289	20rp multicolored	.20	.20
658	A289	50rp multicolored	.50	.50
659	A289	80rp multicolored	.80	.80
		Nos. 657-659 (3)	1.50	1.50

Christmas 1978.

Piebald, by Hamilton and Faistenberger A290

Golden Carriage of Prince Joseph Wenzel, by Martin von Meytens — A291

Design: 80rp, Black stallion, by Johann Georg von Hamilton.

Photo. & Engr.

1978, Dec. 7 *Perf. 13½x14*

660 A290 70rp multicolored .60 .60
661 A290 80rp multicolored .70 .70

Perf. 12

662 A291 1.10fr multicolored .95 .95
Nos. 660-662 (3) 2.25 2.25

Sheets of 8.

Mail Plane over Schaan A292

Europa: 80rp, Zeppelin over Vaduz Castle.

1979, Mar. 8 **Photo.** *Perf. 11½*

663 A292 40rp multicolored *.50* *.45*
664 A292 80rp multicolored *.65* *.60*

First airmail service, St. Gallen to Schaan, Aug. 31, 1930, and first Zeppelin flight to Liechtenstein, June 10, 1931.

Child Drinking — A293

90rp, Child eating. 1.10fr, Child reading.

1979, Mar. 8

665 A293 80rp silver & multi .75 .70
666 A293 90rp silver & multi .85 .85
667 A293 1.10fr silver & multi .95 .95
Nos. 665-667 (3) 2.55 2.50

International Year of the Child.

Ordered Wave Fields A294

Sun over Continents A296

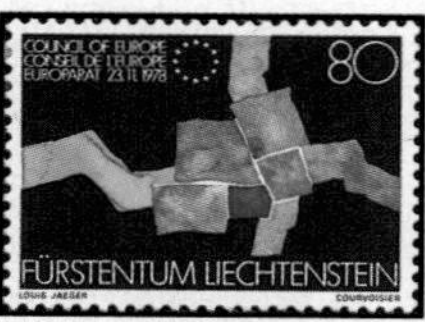

Council of Europe A295

1979, June 7 **Litho.** *Perf. 11½*

668 A294 50rp multicolored .35 .35

Photo.

669 A295 80rp multicolored .75 .75
670 A296 100rp multicolored .75 .75
Nos. 668-670 (3) 1.85 1.85

Intl. Radio Consultative Committee (CCIR) of the Intl. Telecommunications Union, 50th anniv. (50rp); Entry into Council of Europe (80rp); aid to developing countries (100rp).

Heraldic Panel of Carl Ludwig von Sulz — A297

Heraldic Panels of: 70rp, Barbara von Sulz, née zu Staufen. 1.10fr, Ulrich von Ramschwag and Barbara von Hallwil.

Photogravure and Engraved

1979, June 1 *Perf. 13½*

671 A297 40rp multicolored .30 .30
672 A297 70rp multicolored .50 .50
673 A297 1.10fr multicolored .95 .95
Nos. 671-673 (3) 1.75 1.75

Sts. Lucius and Florin, Fresco in Waltensburg-Vuorz Church — A298

Photogravure and Engraved

1979, Sept. 6 *Perf. 13½*

674 A298 20fr multicolored 14.00 13.00

Patron saints of Liechtenstein. Printed in sheets of 4.

Annunciation, Embroidery — A299

Christmas (Ferdnand Nigg Embroideries): 50rp, Christmas. 80rp, Blessed Are the Peacemakers.

1979, Dec. 6 **Engr.** *Perf. 13½*

675 A299 20rp multicolored .20 .20
676 A299 50rp multicolored .40 .35
677 A299 80rp multicolored .60 .50
Nos. 675-677 (3) 1.20 1.05

Cross-Country Skiing A300

Olympic Rings and: 70rp, Oxhead Mountain. 1.50fr, Ski lift.

1979, Dec. 6 **Photo.** *Perf. 12*

678 A300 40rp multicolored .30 .25
679 A300 70rp multicolored .50 .45
680 A300 1.50fr multicolored 1.10 1.00
Nos. 678-680 (3) 1.90 1.70

13th Winter Olympic Games, Lake Placid, NY, Feb. 12-24, 1980.

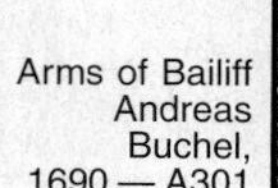

Arms of Bailiff Andreas Buchel, 1690 — A301

Designs: Various arms.

1980, Mar. 10 **Photo.** *Perf. 11½*

Granite Paper

681 A301 40rp shown .30 .25
682 A301 70rp Georg Marxer, 1745 .50 .45
683 A301 80rp Luzius Frick, 1503 .55 .50
684 A301 1.10fr Adam Oehri, 1634 .75 .70
Nos. 681-684 (4) 2.10 1.90

See Nos. 704-707, 729-732.

Princess Maria Leopoldine Esterhazy, by Antonio Canova — A302

Europa: 80rp, Maria Theresa, Duchess of Savoy, by Martin van Meytens.

1980, Mar. 10

685 A302 40rp multicolored *.40* *.35*
686 A302 80rp multicolored *.60* *.50*

Milking Pail — A303

Liechtenstein No. 94 — A304

Old Alpine Farm Tools: 50rp, Wooden heart, ceremonial cattle decoration. 80rp, Butter churn.

1980, Sept. 8

687 A303 20rp multicolored .20 .20
688 A303 50rp multicolored .40 .35
689 A303 80rp multicolored .65 .55
Nos. 687-689 (3) 1.25 1.10

1980, Sept 8

690 A304 80rp multicolored .65 .60

Postal Museum, 50th anniversary.

Crossbow with Spanning Device A305

1980, Sept. 8 **Engr.** *Perf. 13½x14*

691 A305 80rp shown .60 .55
692 A305 90rp Spear, knife .65 .60
693 A305 1.10fr Rifle, powderhorn .75 .65
Nos. 691-693 (3) 2.00 1.80

Triesenberg Family In Traditional Costumes A306

1980, Sept. 8 **Photo.** *Perf. 12*

Granite Paper

694 A306 40rp shown .30 .25
695 A306 70rp Folk dancers, Schellenberg .55 .50
696 A306 80rp Brass band, Mauren .65 .60
Nos. 694-696 (3) 1.50 1.35

Green Beeches, Matrula Forest — A307

Glad Tidings — A308

Photogravure and Engraved

1980, Dec. 9 *Perf. 14*

697 A307 40rp shown .35 .35
698 A307 50rp White firs, Valorsch Valley .45 .45
699 A307 80rp Beech forest, Schaan .65 .65
700 A307 1.50fr Forest, Oberplanken 1.25 1.25
Nos. 697-700 (4) 2.70 2.70

1980, Dec. 9 **Photo.** *Perf. 11½*

Granite Paper

701 A308 20rp shown .20 .20
702 A308 50rp Creche .45 .45
703 A308 80rp Epiphany .70 .70
Nos. 701-703 (3) 1.35 1.35

Christmas 1980.

Bailiff Arms Type of 1980

1981, Mar. 9 **Photo.** *Perf. 11½*

Granite Paper

704 A301 40rp Anton Meier, 1748 .30 .30
705 A301 70rp Kaspar Kindle, 1534 .50 .50
706 A301 80rp Hans Adam Negele, 1600 .60 .60
707 A301 1.10fr Peter Matt, 1693 .90 .90
Nos. 704-707 (4) 2.30 2.30

Fireworks at Vaduz Castle — A309

Europa: 80rp, National Day procession.

1981, Mar. 9 *Perf. 12½*

Granite Paper

708 A309 40rp multicolored *.35* *.30*
709 A309 80rp multicolored *.65* *.60*

Souvenir Sheet

Prince Alois, Princess Elisabeth and Prince Franz Joseph II — A310

1981, June 9 **Photo.** *Perf. 13*

Granite Paper

710 A310 Sheet of 3 2.50 2.50
a. 70rp shown .50 .50
b. 80rp Princes Alois and Franz Joseph II .55 .55
c. 150rp Prince Franz Joseph II 1.00 1.00

75th birthday of Prince Franz Joseph II.

Scout Emblems A311

Man in Wheelchair A312

1981, June 9
711 A311 20rp multicolored .20 .20

50th anniversary of Boy Scouts and Girl Guides.

1981, June 9
712 A312 40rp multicolored .25 .25

International Year of the Disabled.

St. Theodul, 1600th Birth Anniv. — A313

Mosses and Lichens A314

1981, June 9
713 A313 80rp multicolored .55 .55

Photogravure and Engraved

1981, Sept. 7 ***Perf. 13½***
714 A314 40rp Xanthoria parietina .30 .30
715 A314 50rp Parmelia physodes .35 .35
716 A314 70rp Sphagnum palustre .50 .50
717 A314 80rp Amblystegium .60 .60
Nos. 714-717 (4) 1.75 1.75

Gutenberg Castle A315

1981, Sept. 7
718 A315 20rp shown .20 .20
719 A315 40rp Castle yard .30 .30
720 A315 50rp Parlor .35 .35
721 A315 1.10fr Great Hall .85 .85
Nos. 718-721 (4) 1.70 1.70

St. Charles Borromeo (1538-1584) A316

St. Nicholas — A317

Famous Visitors to Liechtenstein (Paintings): 70rp, Goethe (1749-1832), by Angelica Kauffmann. 80rp, Alexander Dumas (1824-1895). 1fr, Hermann Hesse (1877-1962), by Cuno Amiet.

Lithographed and Engraved

1981, Dec. 7 ***Perf. 14***
722 A316 40rp multicolored .35 .35
723 A316 70rp multicolored .60 .60
724 A316 80rp multicolored .70 .70
725 A316 1fr multicolored .80 .80
Nos. 722-725 (4) 2.45 2.45

See Nos. 747-750.

1981, Dec. 7 Photo. ***Perf. 11½***
Granite Paper
726 A317 20rp shown .20 .20
727 A317 50rp Adoration of the Kings .45 .45
728 A317 80rp Holy Family .70 .70
Nos. 726-728 (3) 1.35 1.35

Christmas 1981.

Bailiff Arms Type of 1980

1982, Mar. 8 **Photo.**
Granite Paper
729 A301 40rp Johann Kaiser, 1664 .35 .35
730 A301 70rp Joseph Anton Kaufmann, 1748 .55 .55
731 A301 80rp Christoph Walser, 1690 .70 .70
732 A301 1.10fr Stephan Banzer, 1658 1.00 1.00
Nos. 729-732 (4) 2.60 2.60

Europa 1982 — A318

1982, Mar. 8
Granite Paper
733 A318 40rp Peasants' Uprising, 1525 *.35 .30*
734 A318 80rp Imperial Direct Rule, 1396 *.65 .60*

Hereditary Prince Hans Adam — A319

1982, June 7 **Granite Paper**
735 A319 1fr shown .75 .75
736 A319 1fr Princess Marie Aglae .75 .75

LIBA '82, 10th Liechtenstein Philatelic Exhibition, Vaduz, July 31-Aug. 8.

1982 World Cup — A320

Designs: Sports arenas.

1982, June 7 **Granite Paper**
737 A320 15rp Triesenberg .20 .20
738 A320 25rp Mauren .20 .20
739 A320 1.80fr Balzers 1.25 1.25
Nos. 737-739 (3) 1.65 1.65

Farming A321

1982, Sept. 20 Photo. ***Perf. 11½***
Granite Paper
740 A321 30rp shown .25 .25
741 A321 50rp Horticulture .40 .40
742 A321 70rp Forestry .50 .50
743 A321 150rp Dairy farming 1.10 1.10
Nos. 740-743 (4) 2.25 2.25

View of Neu-Schellenberg, 1861, by Moriz Menzinger (1832-1914) — A322

Photogravure and Engraved

1982, Sept. 20 ***Perf. 13½x14***
744 A322 40rp shown .30 .30
745 A322 50rp Vaduz, 1860 .35 .35
746 A322 100rp Bendern, 1868 .85 .85
Nos. 744-746 (3) 1.50 1.50

Visitor Type of 1981

Paintings: 40rp, Emperor Maximilian I (1459-1519), by Bernhard Strigel. 70rp, Georg Jenatsch (1596-1639). 80rp, Angelika Kaufmann (1741-1807), self portrait. 1fr, Fidelis von Sigmaringen (1577-1622).

1982, Dec. 6 ***Perf. 14***
747 A316 40rp multicolored .30 .30
748 A316 70rp multicolored .50 .50
749 A316 80rp multicolored .60 .60
750 A316 1fr multicolored .75 .75
Nos. 747-750 (4) 2.15 2.15

Christmas 1982 — A323

Europa 1983 — A324

Designs: Chur Cathedral sculptures.

1982, Dec. 6 Photo. ***Perf. 11½***
Granite Paper
751 A323 20rp Angel playing lute .20 .20
752 A323 50rp Virgin and Child .40 .40
753 A323 80rp Angel playing organ .65 .65
Nos. 751-753 (3) 1.25 1.25

1983, Mar. 7 **Photo.**

Designs: 40rp, Notker Balbulus of St. Gall (840-912), Benedictine monk, poet and liturgical composer. 80rp, St. Hildegard of Bingen (1098-1179).

754 A324 40rp multicolored *.40 .30*
755 A324 80rp multicolored *.65 .55*

A325

A326

Shrovetide and Lenten customs: 40rp, Last Thursday before Lent. 70rp, Begging for eggs on Shrove Tuesday. 180fr, Bonfire, first Sunday in Lent.

Photogravure and Engraved

1983, Mar. 7 ***Perf. 14***
756 A325 40rp multicolored .35 .35
757 A325 70rp multicolored .60 .60
758 A325 1.80fr multicolored 1.50 1.50
Nos. 756-758 (3) 2.45 2.45

See Nos. 844-846, 915-917, 952-954.

1983, June 6 Photo. ***Perf. 12***

Landscapes by Anton Ender (b. 1898).

759 A326 40rp Schaan, on the Zollstrasse .35 .35
760 A326 50rp Balzers with Gutenberg Castle .40 .40
761 A326 2fr Stag by the Reservoir 1.75 1.75
Nos. 759-761 (3) 2.50 2.50

Protection of Shores and Coasts — A327

1983, June 6
762 A327 20rp shown .25 .25
763 A327 40rp Manned flight bicentenary .35 .35
764 A327 50rp World communications year .45 .45
765 A327 80rp Humanitarian aid .70 .70
Nos. 762-765 (4) 1.75 1.75

Pope John Paul II A328

1983, Sept. 5 **Photo.**
766 A328 80rp multicolored 1.00 1.00

Princess Gina — A329

1983, Sept. 5 ***Perf. 12x11½***
767 A329 2.50fr shown 2.25 2.25
768 A329 3fr Prince Franz Joseph II 2.75 2.75

Christmas 1983 — A330

1983, Dec. 5 Photo. ***Perf. 12***
Granite Paper
769 A330 20rp Seeking shelter .20 .20
770 A330 50rp Child Jesus .40 .40
771 A330 80rp The Three Magi .70 .70
Nos. 769-771 (3) 1.30 1.30

1984 Winter Olympics, Sarajevo — A331

Snowflakes.

1983, Dec. 5 Photo. ***Perf. 11½x12***
Granite Paper
772 A331 40rp multicolored .40 .40
773 A331 80rp multicolored .80 .80
774 A331 1.80fr multicolored 1.65 1.65
Nos. 772-774 (3) 2.85 2.85

Famous Visitors to Liechtenstein A332

Paintings: 40rp, Count Alexander Wassiljewitsch Suworow-Rimnikski (1730-1800), Austro-Russian Army general. 70rp, Karl Rudolf Count von Buol-Schauenstein (1760-1833). 80rp, Carl Zuckmayer (1896-1977), playwright. 1fr, Curt Goetz (1888-1960), actor and playwright.

Photogravure and Engraved

1984, Mar. 12 *Perf. 14*

775 A332 40rp multicolored .40 .40
776 A332 70rp multicolored .70 .70
777 A332 80rp multicolored .80 .80
778 A332 1fr multicolored 1.00 1.00
Nos. 775-778 (4) 2.90 2.90

A333

A334

1984, Mar. 12 **Photo.** *Perf. 12*

Granite Paper

779 A333 50rp multicolored *.45 .40*
780 A333 80rp multicolored *.65 .60*

Europa (1959-1984).

Photogravure and Engraved

1984, June 12 *Perf. 14*

The Destruction of Trisona Fairy Tale Illustrations: Root Carvings by Beni Gassner.

781 A334 35rp Warning messenger .35 .35
782 A334 50rp Buried town .50 .50
783 A334 80rp Spared family .80 .80
Nos. 781-783 (3) 1.65 1.65

1984 Summer Olympics A335

1984, June 12 **Photo.** *Perf. 11½*

Granite Paper

784 A335 70rp Pole vault .65 .65
785 A335 80rp Discus .75 .75
786 A335 1fr Shot put 1.00 1.00
Nos. 784-786 (3) 2.40 2.40

Industries and Occupations — A336

1984, Sept. 10 **Photo.** *Perf. 11½*

787 A336 5rp Banking & trading .20 .20
788 A336 10rp Construction, plumbing .20 .20
789 A336 20rp Production, factory worker .25 .25
790 A336 35rp Contracting, draftswoman .35 .35
791 A336 45rp Manufacturing, sales rep .45 .45
792 A336 50rp Catering .50 .50
793 A336 60rp Carpentry .60 .60
794 A336 70rp Public health .70 .70
795 A336 80rp Industrial research .80 .80
796 A336 1fr Masonry 1.00 1.00
797 A336 1.20fr Industrial management 1.25 1.25
798 A336 1.50fr Post & communications 1.50 1.50
Nos. 787-798 (12) 7.80 7.80

Princess Marie Aglae — A337

Christmas 1984 — A338

Photogravure and Engraved

1984, Dec. 10 *Perf. 14x13½*

799 A337 1.70fr shown 1.50 1.50
800 A337 2fr Prince Hans Adam 1.90 1.90

1984, Dec. 10 **Photo.** *Perf. 11*

801 A338 35rp Annunciation .35 .35
802 A338 50rp Holy Family .55 .55
803 A338 80rp Three Kings .80 .75
Nos. 801-803 (3) 1.70 1.65

Europa 1985 A339

1985, Mar. 11 **Photo.** *Perf. 11½*

804 A339 50rp Three Muses *.45 .40*
805 A339 80rp Pan and Muses *.70 .65*

Orders and Monestaries A340

Photogravure and Engraved

1985, Mar. 11 *Perf. 13½x14*

806 A340 50rp St. Elisabeth .55 .55
807 A340 1fr Schellenberg Convent 1.10 1.10
808 A340 1.70fr Gutenberg Mission 1.90 1.90
Nos. 806-808 (3) 3.55 3.55

Cardinal Virtues — A341

1985, June 10 **Photo.** *Perf. 11½x12*

809 A341 35rp Justice .35 .35
810 A341 50rp Temperance .50 .50
811 A341 70rp Prudence .70 .70
812 A341 1fr Fortitude 1.00 1.00
Nos. 809-812 (4) 2.55 2.55

Princess Gina, President of Natl. Red Cross, 40th Anniv. A342

Portrait and: 20rp, Helping refugees, 1945. 50rp, Rescue service. 1.20fr, Child refugees, 1979.

1985, June 10 *Perf. 12x11½*

813 A342 20rp multicolored .20 .20
814 A342 50rp multicolored .55 .55
815 A342 1.20fr multicolored 1.40 1.40
Nos. 813-815 (3) 2.15 2.15

Souvenir Sheet

State Visit of Pope John Paul II — A343

Designs: 50rp, Papal coat of arms. 80rp, Chapel of St. Maria zum Trost, Dux, Schaan. 1.70fr, Our Lady of Liechtenstein, St. Mary the Comforter.

1985, Feb. 2 *Perf. 11½*

816 A343 Sheet of 3 4.25 4.25
a. 50rp multi 1.40 1.40
b. 80rp multi 1.40 1.40
c. 1.70fr multi 1.40 1.40

Paintings from the Princely Collections A344

Christmas 1985 — A345

50rp, Portrait of a Canon, by Quintin Massys (1466-1530). 1fr, Portrait of Clara Serena Rubens, by Peter Paul Rubens (1577-1640). 1.20fr, Portrait of the Duke of Urbino, by Raphael (1483-1520).

Photogravure and Engraved

1985, Sept. 2 *Perf. 14*

817 A344 50rp multicolored .50 .50
818 A344 1fr multicolored 1.10 1.10
819 A344 1.20fr multicolored 1.40 1.40
Nos. 817-819 (3) 3.00 3.00

1985, Dec. 9 **Photo.** *Perf. 11½x12*

820 A345 35rp Frankincense .35 .35
821 A345 50rp Gold .50 .50
822 A345 80rp Myrrh .85 .85
Nos. 820-822 (3) 1.70 1.70

Kirchplatz Theater, 15th Anniv. — A346

Photogravure and Engraved

1985, Dec. 9 *Perf. 14*

823 A346 50rp Tragedy .40 .40
824 A346 80rp Commedia dell'arte .55 .55
825 A346 1.50rp Opera buffa 1.75 1.75
Nos. 823-825 (3) 2.70 2.70

Weapons from the Prince's Armory A347

Designs: 35rp, Halberd, bodyguard of Prince Charles I. 50rp, German morion, 16th cent. 80rp, Halberd, bodyguard of Prince Carl Eusebius.

1985, Dec. 9 *Perf. 13½x14½*

826 A347 35rp multicolored .35 .35
827 A347 50rp multicolored .50 .50
828 A347 80rp multicolored .85 .85
Nos. 826-828 (3) 1.70 1.70

A348

A349

1986, Mar. 10 **Photo.** *Perf. 12*

829 A348 50rp Swallows *.45 .40*
830 A348 90rp Robin *.95 .90*

Europa 1986.

1986-89 **Photo.** *Perf. 11½x12*

Views of Vaduz Castle.

Granite Paper

832 A349 20rp Outer courtyard .20 .20
833 A349 25rp View from the south ('89) .35 .35
835 A349 50rp Castle, mountains .40 .40
838 A349 90rp Inner gate ('87) 1.10 1.10
840 A349 1.10fr Back view .90 .90
841 A349 1.40fr Inner courtyard ('87) 1.75 1.75
Nos. 832-841 (6) 4.70 4.70

This is an expanding set. Numbers will change if necessary.

Fasting Sacrifice — A350

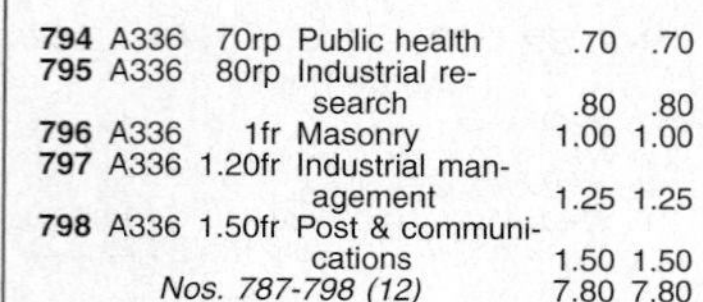

A352

1986, Mar. 10 **Photo.** *Perf. 12*

843 A350 1.40fr multicolored 1.40 1.40

Customs Type of 1983

Photogravure and Engraved

1986, June 9 *Perf. 13½*

844 A325 35rp Palm Sunday procession .40 .40
845 A325 50rp Wedding .60 .60
846 A325 70rp Rogation Day procession .80 .80
Nos. 844-846 (3) 1.80 1.80

1986, June 9 **Photo.** *Perf. 11½*

Karl Freiherr Haus von Hausen (1823-89), founder.

847 A352 50rp multicolored .55 .55

Natl. Savings Bank, Vaduz, 125th anniv.

A353

Hunting — A354

Photogravure and Engraved

1986, June 9 *Perf. 13½*

848 A353 3.50fr multicolored 4.50 4.50

Prince Franz Joseph II, 80th birthday.

1986, Sept. 9 *Perf. 13x13½*

849 A354 35rp Roebuck, Ruggeller Riet .40 .40
850 A354 50rp Chamois in winter, Rappenstein .60 .60
851 A354 1.70fr Rutting stag, Lawena 2.00 2.00
Nos. 849-851 (3) 3.00 3.00

Crops A355

1986, Sept. 9 Photo. *Perf. 12x11½*

852 A355 50rp White cabbage, beets .65 .65
853 A355 80rp Red cabbage 1.10 1.10
854 A355 90rp Potatoes, onions, garlic 1.25 1.25
Nos. 852-854 (3) 3.00 3.00

Christmas A356

Trees A357

Archangels.

1986, Dec. 9 *Perf. 11½*

855 A356 35rp Michael .45 .40
856 A356 50rp Gabriel .65 .65
857 A356 90rp Raphael 1.25 1.25
Nos. 855-857 (3) 2.35 2.30

1986, Dec. 9

858 A357 25rp Silver fir .30 .30
859 A357 90rp Spruce 1.10 1.10
860 A357 1.40fr Oak 1.65 1.65
Nos. 858-860 (3) 3.05 3.05

Europa 1987 — A358

Nicholas Among the Thorns — A359

Modern architecture: 50rp, Primary school, 1980, Gamprin. 90rp, Parish church, c. 1960, Schellenburg.

1987, Mar. 9 Photo. *Perf. 11½x12*
Granite Paper

861 A358 50rp multicolored *.60 .55*
862 A358 90rp multicolored *1.25 1.00*

1987, Mar. 9 *Perf. 11½*
Granite Paper

863 A359 1.10fr multicolored 1.50 1.50

Nicholas von der Flue (1417-1487), canonized in 1947.

Hereditary Prince Alois — A360

Fish — A361

Photo. & Engr.

1987, June 9 *Perf. 14*

864 A360 2fr multicolored 2.50 2.50

No. 864 printed in sheets of 8.

1987, June 9 Photo. *Perf. 11½*

865 A361 50rp Cottus gobio .60 .60
866 A361 90rp Salmo trutta fario 1.10 1.10
867 A361 1.10fr Thymallus thymallus 1.40 1.40
Nos. 865-867 (3) 3.10 3.10

A362

A363

Liechtenstein City Palace, Vienna.

1987, Sept. 7 Photo. *Perf. 11½*
Granite Paper

868 A362 35rp Arch .45 .45
869 A362 50rp Entrance .60 .60
870 A362 90rp Staircase 1.10 1.10
Nos. 868-870 (3) 2.15 2.15

1987, Sept. 7 *Perf. 11½*

871 A363 1.40fr House of Liechtenstein coat of arms 1.90 1.90

Purchase of County of Vaduz, 275th anniv.

Diet, 125th Anniv. A364

1987, Sept. 7 *Perf. 11½*

872 A364 1.70fr Constitution of 1862 2.25 2.25

Christmas — A365

The Evangelists, illuminated codices from the Golden Book, c. 1100, Abbey of Pfafers, purportedly made under the direction of monks from Reichenau Is.

Photo. & Engr.

1987, Dec. 7 *Perf. 14*

873 A365 35rp St. Matthew .30 .30
874 A365 50rp St. Mark .40 .40
875 A365 60rp St. Luke .50 .50
876 A365 90rp St. John .75 .75
Nos. 873-876 (4) 1.95 1.95

1988 Winter Olympics, Calgary A366

Humorous drawings by illustrator Paul Flora of Austria: 25rp, The Toil of the Cross-country Skier. 90rp, Courageous Pioneer of Skiing. 1.10fr, As Grandfather Used to Ride on a Bobsled.

1987, Dec. 7 *Perf. 14x13½*

877 A366 25rp multicolored .30 .30
878 A366 90rp multicolored 1.10 1.10
879 A366 1.10fr multicolored 1.40 1.40
Nos. 877-879 (3) 2.80 2.80

See Nos. 888-891.

Europa 1988 — A367

Modern communication & transportation.

1988, Mar. 7 Photo. *Perf. 11½x12*
Granite Paper

880 A367 50rp Satellite dish *.60 .55*
881 A367 90rp High-speed monorail *1.00 .90*

European Campaign to Protect Undeveloped and Developing Lands — A368

1988, Mar. 7 *Perf. 12*
Granite Paper

882 A368 80rp Forest preservation 1.00 1.00
883 A368 90rp Layout for village development 1.10 1.10
884 A368 1.70rp Traffic planning 2.00 2.00
Nos. 882-884 (3) 4.10 4.10

Balancing nature conservation with natl. development.

Souvenir Sheet

Succession to the Throne — A369

Portraits: a, Crown Prince Hans Adam. b, Prince Alois, successor to the crown prince. c, Prince Franz Josef II, ruler.

Photo. & Engr.

1988, June 6 *Perf. 14½x13½*

885 A369 Sheet of 3 4.00 4.00
a. 50rp black, gold & bright blue .65 .65
b. 50rp black, gold & sage green .65 .65
c. 2fr black, gold & deep rose 2.50 2.50

North and South Campaign A370

1988, June 6 Photo. *Perf. 12x11½*
Granite Paper

886 A370 50rp Public radio .65 .65
887 A370 1.40fr Adult education 1.75 1.75

Cultural cooperation with Costa Rica. See Costa Rica Nos. 401-402.

Olympics Type of 1988

Humorous drawings by illustrator Paul Flora of Austria: 50rp, Cycling. 80rp, Gymnastics. 90rp, Running. 1.40fr, Equestrian.

Photo. & Engr.

1988, Sept. 5 *Perf. 14x13½*

888 A366 50rp multicolored .65 .65
889 A366 80rp multicolored 1.00 1.00
890 A366 90rp multicolored 1.10 1.10
891 A366 1.40fr multicolored 1.75 1.75
Nos. 888-891 (4) 4.50 4.50

Roadside Shrines — A371

Christmas — A372

1988, Sept. 5 Photo. *Perf. 11½x12*
Granite Paper

892 A371 25rp Kaltweh Chapel, Balzers .35 .35
893 A371 35rp Oberdorf, Vaduz, c. 1870 .45 .45
894 A371 50rp Bangstrasse, Ruggell .65 .65
Nos. 892-894 (3) 1.45 1.45

1988, Dec. 5 Photo. *Perf. 11½x12*
Granite Paper

895 A372 35rp Joseph, Mary .40 .40
896 A372 50rp Christ child .55 .55
897 A372 90rp Adoration of the Magi 1.00 1.00
Nos. 895-897 (3) 1.95 1.95

The Letter — A373

Europa 1989 — A374

Details of Portrait of Marie-Therese de Lamballe (The Letter), by Anton Hickel (1745-1798): 90rp, Handkerchief and writing materials in open desk. 2fr, Entire painting.

Photo. & Engr.

1988, Dec. 5 *Perf. 13x13½*

898 A373 50rp shown .65 .65
899 A373 90rp multicolored 1.10 1.10
900 A373 2fr multicolored 2.50 2.50
Nos. 898-900 (3) 4.25 4.25

1989, Mar. 6 Photo. *Perf. 11½x12*

Traditional children's games.

Granite Paper

901 A374 50rp Cat and Mouse *.70 .65*
902 A374 90rp Stockleverband *1.40 1.25*

Josef Gabriel Rheinberger (1839-1901), Composer, and Score — A375

Photo. & Engr.

1989, Mar. 6 *Perf. 14x13½*

903 A375 2.90fr multicolored 3.50 3.50

Fish — A376

1989, June 5 Photo. *Perf. 12x11½*

Granite Paper

904	A376	50rp *Esox lucius*	.65	.65
905	A376	1.10fr *Salmo trutta lacustris*	1.40	1.40
906	A376	1.40fr *Noemacheilus barbatulus*	1.75	1.75
		Nos. 904-906 (3)	3.80	3.80

World Wildlife Fund — A377

1989, June 5 *Perf. 12*

Granite Paper

907	A377	25rp *Charadrius dubius*	.65	.65
908	A377	35rp *Hyla arborea*	1.10	1.10
909	A377	50rp *Libelloides coccajus*	1.50	1.50
910	A377	90rp *Putorius putorius*	2.75	2.75
		Nos. 907-910 (4)	6.00	6.00

Mountains A378

1989, Sept. 4 Photo. *Perf. 11½*

Granite Paper

911	A378	50rp Falknis	.60	.60
912	A378	75rp Plassteikopf	.90	.90
913	A378	80rp Naafkopf	.95	.95
914	A378	1.50fr Garselliturm	1.75	1.75
		Nos. 911-914 (4)	4.20	4.20

See Nos. 930-939.

Customs Type of 1983

Autumn activities: 35rp, Alpine herdsman and flock return from pasture. 50rp, Shucking corn. 80rp, Cattle market.

Photo. & Engr.

1989, Sept. 4 *Perf. 14*

915	A325	35rp multicolored	.40	.40
916	A325	50rp multicolored	.60	.60
917	A325	80rp multicolored	.95	.95
		Nos. 915-917 (3)	1.95	1.95

Christmas A379

Details of the triptych *Adoration of the Magi*, by Hugo van der Goes (50rp) and student (35rp, 90rp), late 15th cent.: 35rp, Melchior and Balthazar. 50rp, Caspar and holy family. 90rp, Donor with St. Stephen.

1989, Dec. 4 *Perf. 13½*

Size of 35rp and 90rp: 23x41mm

918	A379	35rp multicolored	.45	.45
919	A379	50rp shown	.60	.60
920	A379	90rp multicolored	1.10	1.10
		Nos. 918-920 (3)	2.15	2.15

Minerals A380

1989, Dec. 4 *Perf. 13½x13*

921	A380	50rp Scepter quartz	.55	.55
922	A380	1.10fr Pyrite ball	1.25	1.25
923	A380	1.50fr Calcite	1.65	1.65
		Nos. 921-923 (3)	3.45	3.45

Europa 1990 — A381

Postage Stamps, 150th Anniv. — A382

Post offices.

1990, Mar. 5 Photo. *Perf. 11½x12*

Granite Paper

924	A381	50rp shown	*.70*	*.60*
925	A381	90rp Modern p.o.	*1.25*	*1.10*

1990, Mar. 5 *Perf. 11½*

Granite Paper

926 A382 1.50fr Penny Black 1.65 1.65

1990 World Cup Soccer Championships, Italy — A383

1990, Mar. 5 Granite Paper *Perf. 12*

927 A383 2fr multicolored 2.50 2.50

Princess Gina A384

1990, June 5 Litho. *Perf. 11½*

Granite Paper

928	A384	2fr shown	2.75	2.75
929	A384	3fr Prince Franz Joseph II	4.00	4.00

1st anniv of death.

Mountains Type of 1989

1990-93

Granite Paper

930	A378	5rp Augstenberg	.20	.20
931	A378	10rp Hahnenspiel	.20	.20
933	A378	35rp Nospitz	.50	.50
933A	A378	40rp Ochsenkopf	.50	.50
934	A378	45rp Drei Schwestern	.60	.60
935	A378	60rp Kuhgrat	.90	.90
936	A378	70rp Galinakopf	.95	.95
938	A378	1fr Schonberg	1.25	1.25
939	A378	1.20fr Bleikaturm	1.75	1.75
940	A378	1.60fr Schwarzhorn	2.00	2.00
941	A378	2fr Scheienkopf	2.50	2.50
		Nos. 930-941 (11)	11.35	11.35

Issued: 5, 45, 70rp, 1fr, 6/5; 10, 35, 60rp, 1.20fr, 9/3; 40rp, 6/3/91; 1.60fr, 3/2/92; 2fr, 3/1/93.

This is an expanding set. Numbers will change if neccessary.

A385

A386

Paintings by Benjamin Steck (1902-1981).

Photo. & Engr.

1990, June 5 *Perf. 14*

942	A385	50rp shown	.65	.65
943	A385	80rp Fruit, dish	1.00	1.00
944	A385	1.50fr Basket, fruit, stein	2.00	2.00
		Nos. 942-944 (3)	3.65	3.65

Photo. & Engr.

1990, Sept. 3 *Perf. 13x13½*

Game birds.

945	A386	25rp Pheasant	.35	.35
946	A386	50rp Blackcock	.65	.65
947	A386	2fr Mallard duck	2.75	2.75
		Nos. 945-947 (3)	3.75	3.75

European Postal Communications, 500th Anniv. — A387

1990, Dec. 3 *Perf. 13½x14*

948 A387 90rp multicolored 1.25 1.25

A388

A389

Christmas (Lenten Cloth of Bendern): 35rp, The Annunciation. 50rp, Birth of Christ. 90rp, Adoration of the Magi.

1990, Dec. 3 Photo. *Perf. 12*

Granite Paper

949	A388	35rp multicolored	.50	.50
950	A388	50rp multicolored	.70	.70
951	A388	90rp multicolored	1.25	1.25
		Nos. 949-951 (3)	2.45	2.45

Photo. & Engr.

1990, Dec. 3 *Perf. 14*

Holiday Customs: 35rp, St. Nicholas Visiting Children on Feast of St. Nicholas. 50rp, Waking "sleepyheads" on New Year's Day. 1.50fr, Good wishes on New Year's Day.

952	A389	35rp multicolored	.45	.45
953	A389	50rp multicolored	.65	.65
954	A389	1.50fr multicolored	2.00	2.00
		Nos. 952-954 (3)	3.10	3.10

Europa — A390

Designs: 50rp, Telecommunications satellite, Olympus I. 90rp, Weather satellite, Meteosat.

1991, Mar. 4 Photo. *Perf. 11½*

Granite Paper

955	A390	50rp multicolored	*.80*	*.60*
956	A390	90rp multicolored	*1.25*	*1.10*

St. Ignatius of Loyola (1491-1556), Founder of Jesuit Order — A391

90rp, Wolfgang Amadeus Mozart.

1991, Mar. 4 *Perf. 11½*

Granite Paper

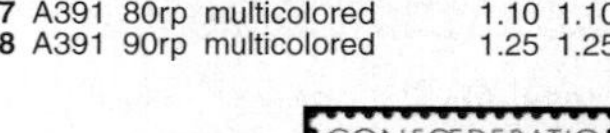

957	A391	80rp multicolored	1.10	1.10
958	A391	90rp multicolored	1.25	1.25

A392 A393

1991, Mar. 4 *Perf. 11½*

Granite Paper

959 A392 2.50fr multicolored 3.50 3.50

UN membership, 1990.

1991, June 3 Photo. *Perf. 11½*

Paintings: 50rp, Maloja, by Giovanni Giacometti. 80rp, Rheintal, by Ferdinand Gehr. 90rp, Bergell, by Augusto Giacometti. 1.10fr, Hoher Kasten, by Hedwig Scherrer.

Granite Paper

960	A393	50rp multicolored	.60	.60
961	A393	80rp multicolored	.95	.95
962	A393	90rp multicolored	1.00	1.00
963	A393	1.10fr multicolored	1.40	1.40
		Nos. 960-963 (4)	3.95	3.95

Swiss Confederation, 700th anniv.

Military Uniforms A394

Designs: 50rp, Non-commissioned officer, private. 70rp, Uniform tunic, trunk. 1fr, Sharpshooters, officer and private.

Photo. & Engr.

1991, June 3 *Perf. 13½x14*

964	A394	50rp multicolored	.60	.60
965	A394	70rp multicolored	.85	.85
966	A394	1fr multicolored	.95	.95
		Nos. 964-966 (3)	2.40	2.40

Last action of Liechtenstein's military, 1866 (70rp).

Princess Marie — A395

Photo. & Engr.

1991, Sept. 2 *Perf. 13x13½*

967 A395 3fr shown 3.75 3.75
968 A395 3.40fr Prince Hans Adam II 4.25 4.25

LIBA 92, Natl. Philatelic Exhibition A396

1991, Sept. 2 Photo. *Perf. 11½*

Granite Paper

969 A396 90rp multicolored 1.10 1.10

A397 A398

Christmas (Altar of St. Mamertus Chapel, Triesen): 50rp, Mary. 80rp, Madonna and Child. 90rp, Angel Gabriel.

Photo. & Engr.

1991, Dec. 2 *Perf. 13½x14*

970 A397 50rp multicolored .70 .70
971 A397 80rp multicolored 1.10 1.10
972 A397 90rp multicolored 1.25 1.25
Nos. 970-972 (3) 3.05 3.05

1991, Dec. 2 Photo. *Perf. 11½x12*

1992 Winter Olympics, Albertville: 70rp, Cross-country skiers, doping check. 80rp, Hockey players, good sportsmanship. 1.60rp, Downhill skier, safety precautions.

Granite Paper

973 A398 70rp multicolored .95 .95
974 A398 80rp multicolored 1.10 1.10
975 A398 1.60fr multicolored 2.25 2.25
Nos. 973-975 (3) 4.30 4.30

1992, Mar. 2 Photo. *Perf. 11½*

1992 Summer Olympics, Barcelona: 50rp, Women's relay, drugs, broken medal. 70rp, Cycling, safety precautions. 2.50fr, Judo, good sportsmanship.

Granite Paper

976 A398 50rp multicolored .65 .65
977 A398 70rp multicolored .90 .90
978 A398 2.50fr multicolored 3.25 3.25
Nos. 976-978 (3) 4.80 4.80

Discovery of America, 500th Anniv. A400

1992, Mar. 2

Granite Paper

979 A400 80rp shown *1.10 1.00*
980 A400 90rp New York skyline *1.40 1.25*

Europa.

Postillion Blowing Horn — A401

Clown in Envelope A402

Designs: No. 982, Postillion delivering valentine. No. 984, Wedding violinist.

Photo. & Engr.

1992, June 1 *Perf. 14x13½*

981 A401 50rp multicolored .65 .65
982 A401 50rp multicolored .65 .65

Photo.

Perf. 12½

Granite Paper

983 A402 50rp multicolored .65 .65
984 A402 50rp multicolored .65 .65
Nos. 981-984 (4) 2.60 2.60

Souvenir Sheet

Prince Hans-Adam and Princess Marie, 25th Wedding Anniv. — A403

Designs: a, 2fr, Coat of Arms of Liechtenstein-Kinsky Alliance. b, 2.50fr, Prince Hans-Adam and Princess Marie.

1992, June 1 *Perf. 11½*

Granite Paper

985 A403 Sheet of 2, #a.-b. 5.75 5.75

Ferns — A404

40rp, Blechnum spicant. 50rp, Asplenium trichomanes. 70rp, Phyllitis scolopendrium. 2.50fr, Asplenium ruta-muraria.

Photo. & Engr.

1992, Sept. 7 *Perf. 14*

986 A404 40rp multicolored .65 .65
987 A404 50rp multicolored .75 .75
988 A404 70rp multicolored 1.10 1.10
989 A404 2.50fr multicolored 4.00 4.00
Nos. 986-989 (4) 6.50 6.50

Creation of Vaduz County, 650th Anniv. A405

1992, Sept. 7 *Perf. 13½x14*

990 A405 1.60fr multicolored 2.50 2.50

Christmas A406 — Hereditary Prince Alois A407

Scenes in Triesen: 50rp, Chapel, St. Mamertus. 90rp, Nativity scene, St. Gallus Church. 1.60rp, St. Mary's Chapel.

1992, Dec. 7 Photo. *Perf. 11½*

Granite Paper

991 A406 50rp multicolored .60 .60
992 A406 90rp multicolored 1.10 1.10
993 A406 1.60fr multicolored 2.00 2.00
Nos. 991-993 (3) 3.70 3.70

Photo. & Engr.

1992, Dec. 7 *Perf. 13x13½*

994 A407 2.50fr multicolored 3.50 3.50

A408

A409

Europa (Contemporary paintings): 80rp, 910805, by Bruno Kaufmann. 1fr, The Little Blue, by Evi Kliemand.

1993, Mar. 1 Photo. *Perf. 11½x12*

Granite Paper

995 A408 80rp multicolored *.90* *.75*
996 A408 1fr multicolored *1.10* *.90*

1993, Mar. 1 *Perf. 11½*

Paintings by Hans Gantner (1853-1914): 50rp, Chalets in Steg and Naafkopf. 60rp, Sass Mountain with Hunting Lodge. 1.80fr, Red House in Vaduz.

Granite Paper

997 A409 50rp multicolored .65 .65
998 A409 60rp multicolored .75 .75
999 A409 1.80fr multicolored 2.25 2.25
Nos. 997-999 (3) 3.65 3.65

Tibetan Art — A410

60rp, Detail from Thangka painting, Tale of the Ferryman. 80rp, Religious dance mask. 1fr, Detail from Thangka painting, The Tale of the Fish.

1993, June 7 Photo. *Perf. 11½*

Granite Paper

1000 A410 60rp multicolored .75 .75
1001 A410 80rp multicolored 1.00 1.00
1002 A410 1fr multicolored 1.25 1.25
Nos. 1000-1002 (3) 3.00 3.00

A411 A412

1993, June 7 *Perf. 11½x12*

Granite Paper

1003 A411 1.80fr Tree of life 2.25 2.25

Church Missionary Work.

Photo. & Engr.

1993, June 7 *Perf. 14x13½*

Contemporary painting: Black Hatter, by Friedensreich Hundertwasser.

1004 A412 2.80fr multicolored 3.50 3.50

Souvenir Sheet

Marriage of Hereditary Prince Alois and Duchess Sophie of Bavaria, July 3 — A413

1993, June 7 Photo. *Perf. 11½*

Granite Paper

1005 A413 4fr multicolored 5.25 5.25

Wild Animals — A414 Meadow Plants — A415

Photo. & Engr.

1993, Sept. 6 *Perf. 13x13½*

1006 A414 60rp Badger .80 .80
1007 A414 80rp Marten 1.00 1.00
1008 A414 1fr Fox 1.25 1.25
Nos. 1006-1008 (3) 3.05 3.05

1993, Sept. 6

1009 A415 50rp Origanum vulgare .65 .65
1010 A415 60rp Salvia pratensis .80 .80
1011 A415 1fr Seseli annuum 1.25 1.25
1012 A415 2.50fr Prunella grandiflora 3.25 3.25
Nos. 1009-1012 (4) 5.95 5.95

See Nos. 1056-1059.

Christmas — A416

A417

Calligraphic Christmas texts by: 60rp, Rainer Maria Rilke. 80rp, Th. Friedrich. 1fr, Rudolph Alexander Schroder.

1993, Dec. 6 Photo. *Perf. 11½x12*
Granite Paper

1013	A416	60rp multicolored	.80	.80
1014	A416	80rp multicolored	1.00	1.00
1015	A416	1fr multicolored	1.25	1.25
		Nos. 1013-1015 (3)	3.05	3.05

1993, Dec. 6
Granite Paper

1016	A417	60rp Ski jump	.80	.80
1017	A417	80rp Slalom skiing	1.00	1.00
1018	A417	2.40fr Bobsled	3.00	3.00
		Nos. 1016-1018 (3)	4.80	4.80

1994 Winter Olympics, Lillehammer.

Anniversaries and Events A418

A419

A420

1994, Mar. 7 Photo. *Perf. 11½*
Granite Paper

1019	A418	60rp multicolored	.75	.75
1020	A419	1.80fr multicolored	2.25	2.25
1021	A420	2.80fr multicolored	3.50	3.50
		Nos. 1019-1021 (3)	6.50	6.50

Principality of Liechtenstein, 275th anniv. (#1019). Intl. Olympic Committee, cent. (#1020). 1994 World Cup Soccer Championships, US (#1021).

Alexander von Humboldt (1769-1859) A421

Europa: 80rp, Vultur gryphus. 1fr, Rhexia cardinalis.

Photo. & Engr.
1994, Mar. 7 *Perf. 13x13½*

1022	A421	80rp multicolored	*1.10*	*.90*
1023	A421	1fr multicolored	*1.40*	*1.00*

Mobile, by Jean Tinguely (1925-91) A422

Photo. & Engr.
1994, June 6 *Perf. 13½x14*

1024	A422	4fr multicolored	5.50	5.50

Letter Writing — A423

1994, June 6 Photo. *Perf. 12½*
Granite Paper

1025	A423	60rp Elephant	.80	.80
1026	A423	60rp Cherub	.80	.80
1027	A423	60rp Pig	.80	.80
1028	A423	60rp Dog	.80	.80
		Nos. 1025-1028 (4)	3.20	3.20

Life Cycle of Grape Vine A424

Designs: No. 1029, Spring, vine beginning to flower. No. 1030, Summer, green grapes on vine. No. 1031, Autumn, ripe grapes ready for harvest. No. 1032, Winter, bare vine in snow.

1994, Sept 5 Photo. *Perf. 11½*
Granite Paper

1029	A424	60rp multicolored	.80	.80
1030	A424	60rp multicolored	.80	.80
1031	A424	60rp multicolored	.80	.80
1032	A424	60rp multicolored	.80	.80
a		Block of 4, #1029-1032	3.25	3.25

No. 1032a is continuous design.

Minerals A425

Photo. & Engr.
1994, Sept. 5 *Perf. 13½x12½*

1033	A425	60rp Strontianite	.80	.80
1034	A425	80rp Faden quartz	1.10	1.10
1035	A425	3.50fr Ferrous dolomite	4.75	4.75
		Nos. 1033-1035 (3)	6.65	6.65

A426

A427

Christmas contemporary art, by Anne Frommelt: 60rp, The True Light. 80rp, Peace on Earth. 1fr, See the House of God.

1994, Dec. 5 Photo. *Perf. 11½*
Granite Paper

1036	A426	60rp multicolored	.90	.90
1037	A426	80rp multicolored	1.25	1.25
1038	A426	1fr multicolored	1.50	1.50
		Nos. 1036-1038 (3)	3.65	3.65

Photo. & Engr.
1994, Dec. 5 *Perf. 14*

The Four Elements, by Ernst Steiner.

1039	A427	60rp Earth	.90	.90
1040	A427	80rp Water	1.25	1.25
1041	A427	1fr Fire	1.50	1.50
1042	A427	2.50fr Air	4.00	4.00
		Nos. 1039-1042 (4)	7.65	7.65

Peace and Freedom A428

Europa: 80rp, 1fr, Excerpts from speeches of Prince Franz Josef II.

1995, Mar. 6 Photo. *Perf. 11½*
Granite Paper

1043	A428	80rp multicolored	*1.10*	*.90*
1044	A428	1fr multicolored	*1.40*	*1.10*

A429

Anniversaries and Events A430 A431

60rp, Princess Marie, Bosnian children.

1995, Mar. 6
Granite Paper

1045	A429	60rp multicolored	.95	.95
1046	A430	1.80fr multicolored	3.00	3.00
1047	A431	3.50fr multicolored	5.50	5.50
		Nos. 1045-1047 (3)	9.45	9.45

Liechtenstein Red Cross, 50th anniv. (#1045). UN, 50th anniv. (#1046). The Alps, European Landscape of the Year 1995-96 (#1047).

Falknis Group, by Anton Frommelt (1895-1975) A432

Paintings: 80rp, Three Oaks. 4.10fr, Rhine below Triesen.

1995, June 6 Photo. *Perf. 12*
Granite Paper

1048	A432	60rp multicolored	1.00	1.00
1049	A432	80rp multicolored	1.40	1.40
1050	A432	4.10fr multicolored	7.25	7.25
		Nos. 1048-1050 (3)	9.65	9.65

Letter Writing — A433

No. 1051, Girl, boy building heart with bricks. No. 1052, Boy, girl bandaging sunflower. No. 1053, Girl, boy & rainbow. No. 1054, Boy in hot air balloon delivering letter to girl.

1995, June 6 *Perf. 12½*
Granite Paper

1051	A433	60rp multicolored	1.00	1.00
1052	A433	60rp multicolored	1.00	1.00
1053	A433	60rp multicolored	1.00	1.00
1054	A433	60rp multicolored	1.00	1.00
a.		Vert. strip of 4, #1051-1054 + label	4.00	4.00

Liechtenstein-Switzerland Postal Relationship — A434

Litho. & Engr.
1995, Sept. 5 *Perf. 13½*

1055	A434	60rp multicolored	1.00	1.00

See Switzerland No. 960.

No. 1055 and Switzerland No. 960 are identical. This issue was valid for postage in both countries.

Plant Type of 1993
Photo. & Engr.
1995, Sept. 5 *Perf. 13x13½*

1056	A415	60rp Arnica montana	1.00	1.00
1057	A415	80rp Urtica dioica	1.40	1.40
1058	A415	1.80fr Valeriana officinalis	3.00	3.00
1059	A415	3.50fr Ranunculus ficaria	6.00	6.00
		Nos. 1056-1059 (4)	11.40	11.40

A435

A436

Paintings by Lorenzo Monaco: 60rp, Angel kneeling, facing right. 80rp, Madonna and Child, two angels at her feet. 1fr, Angel kneeling, facing left.

Photo. & Engr.
1995, Dec. 4 *Perf. 14½x13½*

1060	A435	60rp multicolored	1.00	1.00
1061	A435	80rp multicolored	1.40	1.40
1062	A435	1fr multicolored	1.75	1.75
		Nos. 1060-1062 (3)	4.15	4.15

Christmas.

1995, Dec. 4

Painting: 4fr, Lady with Lap Dog, by Paul Wunderlich.

1063	A436	4fr multicolored	6.75	6.75

Bronze Age in Europe — A437

1996, Mar. 4 Photo. *Perf. 11½*

Granite Paper

1064 A437 90rp Crucible, pin 1.50 1.50

Countess Nora Kinsky (1888-1923), Nurse, Mother of Princess Gina — A438

Profile and: 90rp, Mar. 7, 1917 diary entry. 1.10fr, Feb. 28, 1917 diary entry.

1996, Mar. 4

Granite Paper

1065 A438 90rp multicolored *1.75 1.00*
1066 A438 1.10fr multicolored *2.25 1.25*

Paintings of Village Views, by Marianne Siegl, Based on Sketches by Otto Zeiller A439

10rp, Eschen. 20rp, Farmhouse, St. Joseph's Chapel, Planken. 80rp, Farmhouse, Ruggell. 1fr, Postal auxiliary office, Nendeln. 1.20fr, Buildings, Triesen. 1.30fr, Upper Village, Triesen. 1.70fr, St. Theresa's Church, Schaanwald. 2fr, Rural houses, barns, Gamprin. 4fr, Parish Church, center of village, Triesenberg. 5fr, Vaduz Castle.

1996-99 Photo. *Perf. 12*

Granite Paper

1068 A439 10rp multicolored .20 .20
1069 A439 20rp multicolored .40 .30
1070 A439 80rp multicolored 1.50 1.10
1071 A439 1fr multicolored 2.00 1.40
1072 A439 1.20fr multicolored 2.40 1.75
1073 A439 1.30fr multicolored 2.60 1.75
1074 A439 1.70fr multicolored 3.25 2.25
1075 A439 2fr multicolored 4.00 2.70
1076 A439 4fr multicolored 8.00 5.25
1077 A439 5fr multicolored 10.00 8.25
Nos. 1068-1077 (10) 34.35 24.95

Issued: 10rp, 5fr, 3/4/96; 20rp, 1.30fr, 1.70fr, 3/3/97; 2fr, 4fr, 6/2/98; 80rp, 1fr, 1.20fr, 3/1/99.

See Nos. 1167-1175A

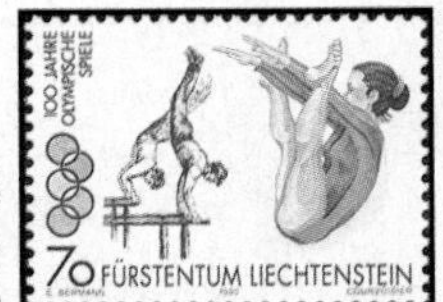

Modern Olympic Games, Cent. A440

1996, June 3 Photo. *Perf. 11½*

Granite Paper

1079 A440 70rp Gymnastics 1.40 1.10
1080 A440 90rp Hurdles 1.75 1.50
1081 A440 1.10fr Cycling 2.25 1.75
Nos. 1079-1081 (3) 5.40 4.35

Ferdinand Gehr, 100th Birthday A441

Various paintings of flowers.

1996, June 3

Granite Paper

1083 A441 70rp multicolored 1.40 1.10
1084 A441 90rp multicolored 1.75 1.50
1085 A441 1.10fr multicolored 2.25 1.75

Size: 33x23mm

1086 A441 1.80fr multicolored 3.50 3.00
Nos. 1083-1086 (4) 8.90 7.35

Austria, Millennium A442

Photo. & Engr.

1996, Sept. 2 *Perf. 13½*

1087 A442 90rp multicolored 1.75 1.75

New Constitution, 75th Anniv. — A443

Litho., Engr. & Embossed

1996, Sept. 2 *Perf. 14*

1088 A443 10fr Natl. arms 20.00 20.00

A444

A445

Paintings by Russian Artist, Eugen Zotow (1881-1953): 70rp, "Country Estate in Poltava." 1.10fr, "Three Bathers in a Park in Berlin." 1.40fr, "View of Vaduz."

Photo. & Engr.

1996, Dec. 2 *Perf. 14*

1089 A444 70rp multicolored 1.40 1.10
1090 A444 1.10fr multicolored 2.25 1.75
1091 A444 1.40fr multicolored 2.75 2.25
Nos. 1089-1091 (3) 6.40 5.10

1996, Dec. 2

Christmas: Illuminated manuscripts, symbols of the Evangelists.

1092 A445 70rp Matthew 1.40 1.10
1093 A445 90rp Mark 1.75 1.40
1094 A445 1.10fr Luke 2.25 1.75
1095 A445 1.80fr John 3.50 3.00
Nos. 1092-1095 (4) 8.90 7.25

A446

A447

Photo. & Engr.

1997, Mar. 3 *Perf. 13½*

1096 A446 70rp multicolored 1.40 .95

Franz Schubert (1797-1828), composer.

1997, Mar. 3 Photo. *Perf. 12*

Europa, Liechtenstein Myths: 90rp, Wild Gnomes. 1.10fr, Foal of Planken.

Granite Paper

1097 A447 90rp multicolored *1.75 1.00*
1098 A447 1.10fr multicolored *2.25 1.10*

St. Lucius, Virgin Mary Holding Infant Jesus, St. Florin, by Gabriel Dreher A448

Photo. & Engr.

1997, June 2 *Perf. 13½x13*

1099 A448 20fr multicolored 40.00 40.00

A449

A450

Painting, "Jeune Fille en Fleur," by Enrico Baj.

1997, Aug. 22 Photo. *Perf. 11½*

Granite Paper

1100 A449 70rp multicolored 1.40 1.40

Photo. & Engr.

1997, Aug. 22 *Perf. 14*

Mushrooms: 70rp, Phaeolepiota aurea. 90rp, Helvella silvicola. 1.10fr, Aleuria aurantia.

1101 A450 70rp multicolored 1.40 .95
1102 A450 90rp multicolored 1.75 1.20
1103 A450 1.10fr multicolored 2.25 1.50
Nos. 1101-1103 (3) 5.40 3.65

Railway in Liechtenstein, 125th Anniv. — A451

Train stations: 70rp, Schaanwald. 90rp, Nendeln. 1.80fr, Schaan-Vaduz.

1997, Aug. 22 Photo. *Perf. 11½*

Granite Paper

1104 A451 70rp multicolored 1.40 .95
1105 A451 90rp multicolored 1.75 1.20
1106 A451 1.80fr multicolored 3.50 2.40
Nos. 1104-1106 (3) 6.65 4.55

Christmas Tree Decorations A452

Photo. & Engr.

1997, Dec. 1 *Perf. 14*

1107 A452 70rp shown 1.40 1.00
1108 A452 90rp Bell 1.75 1.25
1109 A452 1.10fr Oval with pointed ends 2.25 1.50
Nos. 1107-1109 (3) 5.40 3.75

A453

A454

Skiing, 1998 Winter Olympic Games, Nagano.

1997, Dec. 1 *Perf. 12½*

Granite Paper

1110 A453 70rp Cross-country 1.40 1.00
1111 A453 90rp Slalom 1.75 1.25
1112 A453 1.80fr Downhill 3.50 2.50
Nos. 1110-1112 (3) 6.65 4.75

1998, Mar. 2 Photo. *Perf. 12*

Contemporary Art, Paintings by Heinz Mack: No. 1113, Verano (Der Sommer). No. 1114, Hommage An Liechtenstein. No. 1115, Zwischen Tag Und Traum. No. 1116, Salute Chirico!.

Granite Paper

1113 A454 70rp multicolored 1.40 .95
1114 A454 70rp multicolored 1.40 .95
1115 A454 70rp multicolored 1.40 .95
1116 A454 70rp multicolored 1.40 .95
a. Block or strip of 4, #1113-1116 6.00 3.80

Festivals A455

Europa: 90rp, National holiday. 1.10fr, Festival of the Musical Societies.

1998, Mar. 2

Granite Paper

1117 A455 90rp multicolored *1.75 1.00*
1118 A455 1.10fr multicolored *2.25 1.10*

Customs Treaty with Switzerland, 75th Anniv. — A456

1998, Mar. 2

Granite Paper

1119 A456 1.70fr multicolored 3.25 2.25

1998 World Cup Soccer Championships, France — A457

1998, Mar. 2

Granite Paper

1120 A457 1.80fr multicolored 3.50 2.50

Letter Writing — A458

Clown: No. 1121, With woman. No. 1122, Holding four leaf clovers. No. 1123, Tipping hat. No. 1124, Holding paper with heart.

Photo. & Engr.

1998, June 2 *Perf. 14*

1121	A458 70rp multicolored	1.40	.95
1122	A458 70rp multicolored	1.40	.95
1123	A458 70rp multicolored	1.40	.95
1124	A458 70rp multicolored	1.40	.95
a.	Strip of 4, #1121-1124	6.00	3.80

1848 Protest March A459

1998, Sept. 7 Photo. *Perf. 12*

Granite Paper

1125	A459 1.80fr multicolored	3.50	2.50

A460

A461

Traditional Crafts: 90rp, Cooper's tools, tub. 2.20fr, Wooden shoemaker's tools, clog. 3.50fr, Cartwright's tools, wheel.

1998, Sept. 7

Granite Paper

1126	A460 90rp multicolored	1.75	1.25
1127	A460 2.20fr multicolored	4.25	3.00
1128	A460 3.50fr multicolored	7.00	4.75
	Nos. 1126-1128 (3)	13.00	9.00

See Nos. 1215-1217.

Photo. & Engr.

1998, Dec. 7 *Perf. 14*

Christmas (Nativity Scene in high relief): 70rp, Soldier, Virgin Mary. 90rp, Entire nativity scene. 1.10fr, Joseph, donkey.

1129	A461 70rp multicolored	1.40	1.00
1130	A461 90rp multicolored	1.75	1.25
1131	A461 1.10fr multicolored	2.25	1.60
	Nos. 1129-1131 (3)	5.40	3.85

No. 1130 is 34x26mm.

Preservation of Historic Sites — A462

Older buildings, Hinterschellengerg: 90rp, Guest house. 1.70fr, St. George's Chapel, vert. 1.80fr, Farmhouse.

1998, Dec. 7 Photo. *Perf. 11½*

Granite Paper

1132	A462 90rp multicolored	1.75	1.25
1133	A462 1.70fr multicolored	3.25	2.50
1134	A462 1.80fr multicolored	3.50	2.50
	Nos. 1132-1134 (3)	8.50	6.25

A463

A464

1998, Dec. 7

Granite Paper

1135	A463 2.80fr multicolored	5.50	4.00

Telephone in Liechtenstein, cent.

1999, Mar. 1 Photo. *Perf. 11½x12*

Europa (Conservation Areas): 90rp, Snake, Schwabbrünnen-Aescher marshland. 1.10fr, Bird, Ruggell marsh.

Granite Paper

1136	A464 90rp multicolored	*1.75*	*1.00*
1137	A464 1.10fr multicolored	*2.25*	*1.25*

Unterland, 300th Anniv. — A465

Continuous scene of villages: a, Schellenberg, buildings, fortress. b, Mauren, domed steeple on church. c, Eschen,, church, houses. d, Ruggell, road leading into village. e, Gamprin, gray-roofed buildings, church.

1999, Mar. 1 *Perf. 12*

Granite Paper

1138	A465 Sheet of 5 + label	9.00	6.25
a.-e.	90rp any single	1.75	1.25

Anniversaries A466

Stylized designs: No. 1139, Council of Europe 50th anniv. emblem. No. 1140, Bird holding letter. No. 1141, Hand holding heart.

1999, May 25 Photo. *Perf. 11½x12*

Granite Paper

1139	A466 70rp multicolored	1.40	.95
1140	A466 70rp multicolored	1.40	.95
1141	A466 70rp multicolored	1.40	.95
	Nos. 1139-1141 (3)	4.20	2.85

No. 1140, UPU, 125th anniv. No. 1141, Caritas Liechtenstein, 75th anniv.

8th Games of the Small European States A467

1999, May 25

Granite Paper

1142	A467 70rp Judo	1.40	.95
1143	A467 70rp Swimming	1.40	.95
1144	A467 70rp Javelin	1.40	.95
1145	A467 90rp Volleyball	1.75	1.25
1146	A467 90rp Squash	1.75	1.25
1147	A467 90rp Tennis	1.75	1.25
1148	A467 90rp Table tennis	1.75	1.25
1149	A467 90rp Cycling	1.75	1.25
1150	A467 90rp Shooting	1.75	1.25
	Nos. 1142-1150 (9)	14.70	10.35

Johann Wolfgang von Goethe (1749-1832), Poet — A468

Quotations and scenes from Faust: 1.40fr, "Grey, dear friend, is all theory and green the golden tree of life." 1.70fr, "I'll take the wager!...Done! And again, and again!"

Photo. & Engr.

1999, Sept. 9 *Perf. 14*

1151	A468 1.40fr multicolored	2.75	1.90
1152	A468 1.70fr multicolored	3.25	2.25

Paintings by Eugen Verling (1891-1968) A469

Designs: 70rp, Herrengasse. 2fr, Old Vaduz with Castle. 4fr, House in Fürst-Franz-Josef-Strasse, Vaduz.

1999, Sept. 9

1153	A469 70rp multicolored	1.40	.95
1154	A469 2fr multicolored	4.00	2.75
1155	A469 4fr multicolored	8.00	5.50
	Nos. 1153-1155 (3)	13.40	9.20

A470

A471

Walser house identification marks.

1999, Dec. 6 Photo. *Perf. 11¾*

Granite Paper

1156	A470 70rp Door mark	1.40	.90
1157	A470 90rp Picture mark	1.75	1.10
1158	A470 1.80fr Axe mark	3.50	2.40
	Nos. 1156-1158 (3)	6.65	4.40

Photo. & Engr.

1999, Dec. 6 *Perf. 13½*

1159	A471 3.60fr multicolored	4.75	4.75

Johann Gutenberg, inventor of letterpress printing.

Christmas Paintings by Joseph Walser A472

1999, Dec. 6 *Perf. 13½x14¼*

1160	A472 70rp The Annunciation	1.40	.90
1161	A472 90rp Nativity	1.75	1.10
1162	A472 1.10fr Presentation of Jesus	2.25	1.40
	Nos. 1160-1162 (3)	5.40	3.40

Souvenir Sheet

Millennium — A473

Designs: 70rp, The Adoration of the Shepherds, by Matthias Stomer. 1.10fr, The Magi, by Ferdinand Gehr.

2000, Jan. 1 Photo. *Perf. 12*

Granite Paper

1163	Sheet of 2	4.00	2.25
a.	A473 70rp multi	1.40	.85
b.	A473 1.10fr multi	2.25	1.40

Christianity, 2000th anniv.

Creation of Liechtenstein Post, Ltd. — A474

2000, Jan. 1 *Perf. 11¾*

Granite Paper

1164	A474 90rp multi	1.75	1.10

Village Views Type of 1996

Designs: 50rp, Church and vicarage, Ruggell. 60rp, Chapel of St. Peter, Balzers. 70rp, Parish church, Schellenberg. 1.10fr, Holy Cross Chapel, Eschen. 1.40fr, Farmhouse, parish church, Mauren. 1.80fr, Chapel of Peace, Malbun. 1.90fr, Tower of Church of St. Lawrence, Schaan. 2.20fr, Höfle District, Balzers. 4.50fr, Church mound, Bendern.

2000-01 Photo. *Perf. 11¾*

Granite Paper

1167	A439 50rp multi	1.00	.60
1168	A439 60rp multi	1.25	.75
1169	A439 70rp multi	1.40	.85
1171	A439 1.10fr multi	2.25	1.40
1172	A439 1.40fr multi	2.75	1.75
1173	A439 1.80fr multi	3.50	2.25
1174	A439 1.90fr multi	3.75	2.25
1175	A439 2.20fr multi	4.50	2.60
1175A	A439 4.50fr multi	9.00	5.50
	Nos. 1167-1175A (9)	29.40	17.95

Issued: 70rp, 1.80fr, 2.20fr, 4.50fr, 6/5/01.

"Gods Once Walked" Exhibition at Vaduz Museum of Art — A475

Designs: 70rp, Mars and Rhea Silvia, by Peter Paul Rubens. 1.80fr, Cupid With Soap Bubble, by Rembrandt.

Photo. & Engr.

2000, Mar. 6 *Perf. 13½x12¾*

1176	A475 70rp multi	1.40	.85
1177	A475 1.80fr multi	3.50	2.25

Europa, 2000

Common Design Type

2000, May 9 Photo. *Perf. 11½x11¾*

Granite Paper

1178	CD17 1.10fr multi	*2.25*	*1.75*

Expo 2000, Hanover — A476

Art by Friedensreich Hundertwasser: 70rp, Fragrance of Humus. 90rp, Do Not Wait Houses — Move. 1.10fr, The Car: A Drive Towards Nature and Creation.

Photo. & Engr.

2000, May 9 *Perf. 14¼x13½*

1179	A476 70rp multi	1.40	.80
1180	A476 90rp multi	1.75	1.00
1181	A476 1.10fr multi	2.25	1.25
	Nos. 1179-1181 (3)	5.40	3.05

Images of Peace A477

Art by mouth and foot painters: 1.40fr, Dove of Peace, by Antonio Martini. 1.70fr, Universal Peace, by Alberto Alvarez. 2.20fr, Rainbow, by Eiichi Minami.

2000, May 9 Photo. ***Perf. 11¾x11½***

1182 A477 1.40fr multi 2.75 1.60

1183 A477 1.70fr multi 3.25 1.90

1184 A477 2.20fr multi 4.50 2.50

Nos. 1182-1184 (3) 10.50 6.00

2000 Summer Olympics, Sydney A478

Designs: 80rp, Koalas on rings. 1fr, High jump by kangaroo joey. 1.30fr, Emus racing. 1.80fr, Platypuses swimming.

2000, Sept. 4 Photo. ***Perf. 11¾***

Granite Paper

1185 A478 80rp multi 1.60 .95

1186 A478 1fr multi 2.00 1.10

1187 A478 1.30fr multi 2.50 1.50

1188 A478 1.80fr multi 3.50 2.10

Nos. 1185-1188 (4) 9.60 5.65

Organization for Security and Co-operation In Europe, 25th Anniv. A479

2000, Sept. 4 Granite Paper

1189 A479 1.30fr multi 2.50 1.50

Issued in sheets of 20 stamps and 5 labels.

Opening Of Liechtenstein Art Museum — A480

Designs: 80rp, The Dreaming Bee, by Joan Miró. 1.20fr, Cube by Sol LeWitt. 2fr, A Bouquet of Flowers, by Roelant Savery.

2000, Sept. 4 Photo. ***Perf. 11¾***

Granite Paper (#1190-1191)

1190 A480 80rp multi 1.60 .95

1191 A480 1.20fr multi 2.40 1.40

Size: 31x46mm

Photo. & Engr.

Perf. 13¾

1192 A480 2fr multi 4.00 2.40

Nos. 1190-1192 (3) 8.00 4.75

Mushrooms A481

90rp, Mycena adonis. 1.10fr, Chalciporus amarellus. 2fr, Hygrocybe caylptriformis.

Photo. & Engr.

2000, Dec. 4 ***Perf. 14¼***

1193-1195 A481 Set of 3 8.00 4.50

Christmas A482

Various creches: 80rp, 1.30fr, 1.80fr.

2000, Dec. 4 ***Perf. 13¾x14***

1196-1198 A482 Set of 3 7.75 4.50

Europa — A483

2001, Mar. 5 Photo. ***Perf. 11½x11¾***

Granite Paper

1199 A483 1.30fr multi *2.50 2.25*

Liechtenstein's Presidency of Council of Europe — A484

2001, Mar. 5 ***Perf. 11¾***

Granite Paper

1200 A484 1.80fr multi 3.50 2.10

Scratch-off Greetings A485

Postman in: No. 1201, 70rp, Red uniform (hidden flower bouquet). No. 1202, 70rp, Blue uniform (hidden envelope).

2001, Mar. 5 Granite Paper

1201-1202 A485 Set of 2 unscratched 3.00 1.75

Set, scratched 1.75

Easter Eggs of the Russian Czars — A486

Designs: 1.20fr, Silver egg. 1.80fr, Cloisonné egg. 2fr, Porcelain egg.

Photo. & Engr.

2001, Mar. 5 ***Perf. 13¾***

1203-1205 A486 Set of 3 10.00 6.00

Liechtenstein Historical Association, Cent. — A487

Designs: No. 1206, 70rp, Mars of Gutenberg. No. 1207, Carolignian cruciform fibula.

2001, June 5 Photo. ***Perf. 11¾***

Granite Paper

1206-1207 A487 Set of 2 2.75 1.75

Josef Gabriel Rheinberger (1839-1901), Musician A488

Photo. & Engr.

2001, Sept. 3 ***Perf. 14***

1208 A488 3.50fr multi 7.00 4.25

Votive Pictures — A489

Designs: 70rp, 1733 picture, Chapel of Our Lady, Dux. 1.20fr, 1802 picture, St. George's Chapel, Schellenberg. 1.30fr, 1718 picture, Chapel of Our Lady, Dux.

2001, Sept. 3 ***Perf. 13½***

1209-1211 A489 Set of 3 6.50 4.00

Building Preservation A490

Designs: 70rp, St. Theresa's Chapel, Schaanwald. 90rp, St. Johann's winery, Mauren. 1.10fr, Pirsch transformer station, Schaanwald.

2001, Sept. 3 Photo. ***Perf. 11¾***

Granite Paper

1212-1214 A490 Set of 3 5.25 3.25

See Nos. 1232-1233, 1251-1252, 1295-1296, 1323-1324, 1361-1362, 1394-1395, 1424.

Traditional Crafts Type of 1998

Designs: 70rp, Blacksmith's tools, horseshoe, yoke bars. 90rp, Rakemaker's tools, rake. 1.20fr, Saddler's tools, horse collar.

2001, Dec. 3 Photo. ***Perf. 11¾***

Granite Paper

1215-1217 A460 Set of 3 5.50 3.50

Abstract Art by Gottfried Honegger A491

Untitled works: 1.80fr, 2.20fr.

2001, Dec. 3 ***Perf. 11½***

Granite Paper

1218-1219 A491 Set of 2 8.00 5.00

Christmas — A492

Medallions: 70rp, Annunciation. 90rp, Nativity. 1.30fr, The Presentation of the Lord.

2001, Dec. 3 ***Perf. 12x11¾***

Granite Paper

1220-1222 A492 Set of 3 4.00 3.50

Liechtenstein Students' Spice Bees Experiment on Space Shuttle A493

2002, Mar. 4 Photo. ***Perf. 13½x14¼***

1223 A493 90rp multi 1.75 1.10

LIBA.02 Stamp Exhibition, Vaduz — A494

2002, Mar. 4 ***Perf. 13¾***

1224 A494 1.20fr multi 2.40 1.40

Europa — A495

Designs: 90rp, Tightrope walker. 1.30fr, Juggler.

Photo. & Engr.

2002, Mar. 4 ***Perf. 14¼x14***

1225-1226 A495 Set of 2 *4.25 3.75*

Intl. Year of Mountains A496

Intl. Commision for Protection of the Alps A497

2002, Mar. 4 Photo. ***Perf. 13¾x13½***

1227 A496 70rp multi 1.40 .85

1228 A497 1.20fr multi 2.40 1.40

Paintings by Friedrich Kaufmann (1892-1972) A498

Views of: 70rp, Schellenberg. 1.30fr, Schaan. 1.80fr, Steg.

2002, Mar. 4 ***Perf. 13½x13¾***

1229-1231 A498 Set of 3 7.50 4.50

Building Preservation Type of 2001

Designs: 70rp, House, Popers, horiz. 1.20fr, House, Weiherring, horiz.

Perf. 13¾x13½

2002, June 3 Photo.

1232-1233 A490 Set of 2 3.75 2.40

2002 World Cup Soccer Championships, Japan and Korea — A499

2002, June 3 *Perf. 13½x14¼*
1234 A499 1.80fr multi 3.50 2.25

Royalty A500

Designs: 3fr, Princess Marie. 3.50fr, Prince Hans Adam II.

2002, June 3 *Perf. 13¾x13½*
1235-1236 A500 Set of 2 13.00 8.25

Liba.02 Stamp Exhibition, Vaduz — A501

Liechtenstein stamps depicting: 90rp, Various topics. 1.30fr, Royalty.

2002, Aug. 8 **Photo.** *Perf. 13½*
1237-1238 A501 Set of 2 4.25 3.00

Royalty Type of 2002

Designs: 2fr, Hereditary Princess Sophie. 2.50fr, Hereditary Prince Alois.

2002, Aug. 8 *Perf. 13¾x13½*
1239-1240 A500 Set of 2 9.00 6.00

Orchids — A502

Designs: 70rp, Epipogium aphyllum. 1.20fr, Ophrys insectifera. 1.30fr, Nigritella nigra.

2002, Aug. 8 *Perf. 13½x13¾*
1241-1243 A502 Set of 3 6.25 4.25

See Nos. 1288-1290.

Inn Sign Art — A503

Designs: 1.20fr, Eagle, Vaduz. 1.80fr, Angel, Balzers. 3fr, Eagle, Bendern.

Photo. & Engr.

2002, Nov. 25 *Perf. 13½x14¼*
1244-1246 A503 Set of 3 12.00 8.25

Christmas — A504

Batik art by Sister Regina Hassler: 70rp, Search for Shelter. 1.20fr, Nativity. 1.80fr, Flight to Egypt.

Perf. 14¼x13½

2002, Nov. 25 **Photo.**
1247-1249 A504 Set of 3 7.50 5.25

Europa A505

2003, Mar. 3 **Photo.** *Perf. 13½x12¾*
1250 A505 1.20fr multi *2.40 2.25*

Building Preservation Type of 2001

Designs: 70rp, St. Fridolin Church, Ruggell. 2.50fr, House, Spidach, horiz..

Perf. 13½x13¾, 13¾x3½

2003, Mar. 3
1251-1252 A490 Set of 2 6.25 4.75

Viticulture Throughout the Year — A506

Designs: 1.30fr, Pruning (February). 1.80fr, Tying vines to arbor (March). 2.20fr, Hoeing soil (April).

2003, Mar. 3 *Perf. 14¼*
1253-1255 A506 Set of 3 10.50 7.75

2003, June 2 **Photo.** *Perf. 14¼*

Designs: 1.20fr, Looping vines (May). 1.80fr, Leaf work (June). 3.50fr, Removing high growth (July).

1256-1258 A506 Set of 3 13.00 10.00

2003, Sept. 1 **Photo.** *Perf. 14¼*

Designs: 70rp, Thinning out of vines (August). 90rp, Harvesting grapes (September). 1.10fr, Pressing grapes (October).

1259-1261 A506 Set of 3 5.25 4.00

2003, Nov. 24

Designs: 70rp, First tasting of wine (November). 90rp, Harvest of frozen grapes (December). 1.20fr, Bottling wine (January).

1262-1264 A506 Set of 3 5.50 4.25

Liechtenstein Association for the Disabled, 50th Anniv. — A507

2003, June 2 **Photo.** *Perf. 14¼*
1265 A507 70rp multi 1.40 1.10

Reopening of National Museum — A508

Museum building and: 1.20fr, Ammonite fossil. 1.30fr, Shield of bailiff of Vaduz.

2003, June 2 *Perf. 14*
1266-1267 A508 Set of 2 5.00 3.75

White Storks and Nest — A509

Photo. & Engr.

2003, Sept. 1 *Perf. 12¾x13½*
1268 A509 2.20fr multi 4.50 3.25

Saints — A510

Designs: No. 1269, 1.20fr, St. Blasius. No. 1270, 1.20fr, St. George. No. 1271, 1.30fr, St. Erasmus. No. 1272, 1.30fr, St. Vitus.

2003, Sept. 1 *Perf. 13½*
1269-1272 A510 Set of 4 10.00 7.25

Stamps of the same denomination were printed in sheets of 20 arranged in blocks of 10 of each stamp separated by a horizontal gutter.

See Nos. 1280-1285, 1308-1311.

Children's Drawings A511

Designs: 70rp, Cow, by Laura Beck. No. 1274, 1.80fr, Apple Tree, by Patrick Marxer, vert. No. 1275, 1.80fr, Bee, by Laura Lingg.

Perf. 13½x14¼, 14¼x13½

2003, Nov. 24 **Photo.**
1273-1275 A511 Set of 3 8.50 6.25

Christmas — A512

Reverse glass paintings: 70rp, Archangel Gabriel. 90rp, Nativity. 1.30fr, Three Magi.

2003, Nov. 24 *Perf. 14¼x13½*
1276-1278 A512 Set of 3 5.75 4.25

AHV Old Age and Survivor's Insurance, 50th Anniv. — A513

2004, Jan. 3 **Photo.** *Perf. 14*
1279 A513 85rp multi 1.40 1.40

Saints Type of 2003

Designs: No. 1280, 1fr, St. Achatius. No. 1281, 1fr, St. Margareta. No. 1282, 1.20fr, St. Christophorus. No. 1283, 1.20fr, St. Pantaleon. No. 1284, 2.50fr, St. Aegidius. No. 1285, 2.50fr, St. Cyriakus.

Photo. & Engr.

2004, Mar. 1 *Perf. 13½*
1280-1285 A510 Set of 6 19.00 15.50

Stamps of the same denomination were printed in sheets of 20 arranged in blocks of 10 of each stamp separated by a horizontal gutter.

Europa — A514

2004, Mar. 1 **Photo.** *Perf. 13¾x13½*
1286 A514 1.30fr multi *2.50 2.25*

2004 Summer Olympics, Athens — A515

2004, June 1 **Photo.** *Perf. 14¼*
1287 A515 85rp multi 1.75 1.40

Orchid Type of 2002

Designs: 85rp, Ophrys apifera. 1fr, Orchis ustulata. 1.20fr, Epipactis purpurata.

2004, June 1 *Perf. 13½x13¾*
1288-1290 A502 Set of 3 6.00 4.75

Aerial Views A516

2004, June 1 *Perf. 13½*

1291	A516	15rp	Bendern	.30	.25
1292	A516	85rp	Gross-Steg	1.75	1.40
1293	A516	1fr	Tuass	2.00	1.60
1294	A516	6fr	Gutenberg	12.00	9.25
	Nos. 1291-1294 (4)			16.05	12.50

See No. 1312, 1331-1333, 1340-1341, 1375-1377.

Building Preservation Type of 2001

Designs: 2.20fr, House on Unterdorfstrasse, horiz. 2.50fr, Row of houses, Dorfstrasse, horiz.

Perf. 13¾x13½

2004, Sept. 6 **Photo.**
1295-1296 A490 Set of 2 9.50 7.50

Sciences — A517

Designs: 85rp, Mathematics. 1fr, Physics. 1.30fr, Chemistry. 1.80fr, Astronomy.

2004, Sept. 6 *Perf. 13¾x14*
1297-1300 A517 Set of 4 10.00 8.00

Digital Palimpsest Research A518

Photo. & Engr.

2004, Nov. 22 *Perf. 14¼*
1301 A518 2.50fr multi 5.00 4.25

Fossils — A519

Designs: 1.20fr, Ammonite. 1.30fr, Sea urchin. 2.20fr, Shark tooth.

2004, Nov. 22
1302-1304 A519 Set of 3 9.50 8.00

Christmas A520

Designs: 85rp, Annunciation. 1fr, Holy Family. 1.80fr, Adoration of the Magi.

2004, Nov. 22 Photo. *Rouletted 6¾*
1305-1307 A520 Set of 3 7.25 6.25

Punched holes are in stamp frames to give stamps a lace-like appearance.

Saints Type of 2003

Designs: No. 1308, 85rp, St. Eustachius. No. 1309, 85rp, St. Dionysius. No. 1310, 1.80fr, St. Catharine. No. 1311, 1.80fr, St. Barbara.

Photo. & Engr.

2005, Mar. 7 *Perf. 13½*
1308-1311 A510 Set of 4 10.50 9.25

Aerial Views Type of 2004

2005, Mar. 7 Photo.
1312 A516 3.60fr Triesenberg 7.25 6.25

Europa A521

2005, Mar. 7
1313 A521 1.30fr multi *2.50 2.25*

Venus at a Mirror, by Peter Paul Rubens A522

2005, Mar. 7 Photo. & Engr.
1314 A522 2.20fr multi 4.50 4.00

See Austria No. 1980.

Paintings of Flower Arrangements A523

Designs: No. 1315, 85rp, Magnolia Flowers, by Chen Hongshou (shown). No. 1316, 85rp, Flower Vase in a Windoe Niche, by Ambrosius Bosschaert the Elder.

2005, May 18 Photo. *Perf. 14*
1315-1316 A523 Set of 2 3.25 3.00

See People's Republic of China Nos. 3433-3434.

Inn Signs — A524

Designs: 1fr, Stallion, Rössle Inn, Schaan. 1.40fr, Edelweiss Inn, Triesenberg. 2.50fr, Lion, Löwen Inn, Bendern.

Photo. & Engr.

2005, June 6 *Perf. 14¼x13½*
1317-1319 A524 Set of 3 10.00 8.25

Postal Museum, 75th Anniv. A525

Designs: 1.10fr, Hermann E. Sieger, museum founder. 1.30fr, Liechtenstein stamps on stock page. 1.80fr, 1930 Zeppelin cover.

Perf. 13½x14¼

2005, June 6 Photo.
1320-1322 A525 Set of 3 8.25 7.00

Building Preservation Type of 2001

Designs: 85rp, Oberbendern. 2.20fr, Church Hill, Bendern.

Perf. 13¾x13½

2005, Sept. 5 Photo.
1323-1324 A490 Set of 2 6.00 5.00

Bats — A526

Designs: 1.80fr, Plecotus auritus. 2fr, Myotis myotis.

2005, Sept. 5 *Perf. 14¼*
1325-1326 A526 Set of 2 7.50 6.25

Pastures A527

Designs: 85rp, Bargälla. 1fr, Pradamee. 1.30fr, Gritsch. 1.80fr, Valüna.

2005, Sept. 5 *Perf. 13½x14¼*
1327-1330 A527 Set of 4 10.00 8.00

See nos. 1356-1358, 1384-1386, 1403-1404.

Aerial Views Type of 2004

2005, Nov. 21 Photo. *Perf. 13½*
1331 A516 1.50fr Oberland 3.00 2.40
1332 A516 1.60fr Ruggeller Riet 3.25 2.50
1333 A516 3fr Naafkopf 6.00 4.75
Nos. 1331-1333 (3) 12.25 9.65

2006 Winter Olympics, Turin, Italy — A528

Designs: 1.20fr, Ski jumping. 1.30fr, Biathlon. 1.40fr, Slalom skiing.

2005, Nov. 21 *Perf. 14¼x14*
1334-1336 A528 Set of 3 8.00 6.25

Christmas A529

Wood sculptures by Toni Gstöhl: 85rp, The Annunciation. 1fr, Holy Family. 1.30fr, Adoration of the Shepherds.

Photo. & Engr.

2005, Nov. 21 *Perf. 14¼x13½*
1337-1339 A529 Set of 3 6.25 5.00

Aerial Views Type of 2004

2006, Mar. 6 Photo. *Perf. 13½*
1340 A516 2.50fr Rhine Canal 5.00 4.00
1341 A516 3.50fr Rhine Valley 7.00 5.50

Lost in Her Dreams, by Friedrich von Amerling A530

2006, Mar. 6 Photo. & Engr.
1342 A530 2.20fr multi 4.50 3.50

See Austria No. 2041.

Paintings by Eugen Wilhelm Schüepp (1915-74) A531

Designs: 1fr, Peat Cutters, Ruggell Marsh. 1.80fr, Neugut, Schaan.

2006, Mar. 6 Photo. *Perf. 13½x14¼*
1343-1344 A531 Set of 2 5.50 4.50

Europa A532

Winning designs from stamp design contest: 1.20fr, Bridge, by Nadja Beck. 1.30fr, Face of Integration, by Elisabeth Müssner.

2006, Mar. 6
1345-1346 A532 Set of 2 *5.00 4.00*

2006 World Cup Soccer Championships, Germany — A533

Perf. 13½x14¼

2006, June 6 Photo.
1347 A533 3.30fr multi 6.50 5.50

A534

A535

Designs: 85rp, Woman holding G clef. 1fr, Backpacker. 1.20fr, Restaurant patron. 1.80fr, Skier.

2006, June 6 *Perf. 13¾*
1348-1351 A534 Set of 4 9.75 8.25

Tourism promotion.

2006, June 6 Litho. & Engr.

Designs: 85rp, Prince Johann I. 1fr, National flag. 1.30fr, Flag of the Princely House of Liechtenstein. 1.80fr, National arms.

1352-1355 A535 Set of 4 10.00 8.25

Full sovereignty, bicent.

Pastures Type of 2005

Designs: 85rp, Lawena. 1.30fr, Gapfahl. 2.40fr, Gafadura.

Perf. 13½x14¼

2006, Sept. 4 Photo.
1356-1358 A527 Set of 3 9.00 7.50

Wolfgang Amadeus Mozart (1756-91), Composer — A536

2006, Sept. 4 *Perf. 13¾x14¼*
1359 A536 1.20fr multi 2.50 2.00

Miniature Sheet

Classical Music — A537

No. 1360: a, The Magic Flute, by Wolfgang Amadeus Mozart. b, Radetzky March, by Johann Strauss. c, Rhapsody in Blue, by George Gershwin. d, Water Music, by George Frideric Handel. e, Pastoral Symphony, by Ludwig van Beethoven. f, Waltz of the Flowers, by Peter Ilich Tchaikovsky. g, The Swan, by Camille Saint-Saens. h, A Midsummer Night's Dream, by Felix Mendelssohn.

2006, Sept. 4 *Perf. 13½x14¼*
1360 A537 Sheet of 8 16.00 13.00
a.-h. 1fr Any single 2.00 1.60

Building Preservation Type of 2001

Designs: 1.80fr, Governor's residence and Liechtenstein Institute, Bendern. 3.50fr, Bühl House, Gamprin, horiz.

Perf. 13½x13¾, 13¾x13½
2006, Nov. 20 **Photo.**
1361-1362 A490 Set of 2 10.50 8.50

Inventions A538

Designs: 1.30fr, Curta calculator. 1.40fr, Carena film camera. 2.40fr, PAV sliding caliper.

2006, Nov. 20 *Perf. 14¼x14*
1363-1365 A538 Set of 3 10.00 8.25

Christmas A539

Frescos from Chapel of St. Mary, Dux: 85rp, The Annunciation. 1fr, Nativity. 1.30fr, Presentation at the Temple.

Photo. & Engr.
2006, Nov. 20 *Perf. 13½*
1366-1368 A539 Set of 3 6.25 5.00

Scouting, Cent. — A540

2007, Mar. 5 **Photo.** *Perf. 14¼*
1369 A540 1.30fr multi 2.50 2.10

Portrait of a Lady, by Bernardino Zaganelli da Cotignola A541

Litho. & Engr.
2007, Mar. 5 *Perf. 13¾*
1370 A541 2.40fr multi 4.75 4.00

See Austria No. 2086.

Musical Terms A542

Designs: 85rp, Allegro. 1.80fr, Capriccio. 2fr, Crescendo. 3.50fr, Con fuoco.

2007, Mar. 5 **Photo.** *Perf. 13½*
1371-1374 A542 Set of 4 16.00 13.50

Aerial Views Type of 2004

2007, June 4 **Photo.** *Perf. 13½*
1375 A516 1.10fr Nendeln 2.00 2.00
1376 A516 1.80fr Malbun 3.25 3.25
1377 A516 2.60fr Ackerland 4.75 4.75
Nos. 1375-1377 (3) 10.00 10.00

Greeting Card Art — A543

Designs: 85rp, Boy delivering flower and letter to girl. 1fr, Two children carrying litter with cake, flowers and letter. 1.30fr, Bird carrying letter.

2007, June 4 *Rouletted 6¾*
1378-1380 A543 Set of 3 5.25 5.25

Punched holes are in stamp frames to give stamps a lacelike appearance.

Paintings of Rhine Landscapes by Johann Ludwig Bleuler (1792-1850) A544

Designs: 1fr, Castle and Village of Vaduz. 1.30fr, Rätikon Mountain. 2.40fr, Confluence of the Ill and Rhine.

Perf. 13½x14¼
2007, June 4 **Photo. & Engr**
1381-1383 A544 Set of 3 8.50 8.50

Pastures Type of 2005

Designs: 1fr, Hintervalorsch. 1.40fr, Sücka. 2.20fr, Guschgfiel.

Perf. 13½x14¼
2007, Sept. 3 **Photo.**
1384-1386 A527 Set of 3 8.50 8.50

Technical Innovations From Liechtenstein A545

Designs: 1.30fr, Hilti hammer and drill. 1.80fr, Kaiser mobile walking excavator. 2.40fr, Hoval AluFer composite heating tube.

2007, Sept. 3 *Perf. 14¼*
1387-1389 A545 Set of 3 9.25 9.25

See Nos. 1425-1427.

Beetles A546

Designs: 85rp, Trichodes apiarius. 100rp, Cetania aurata. 130rp, Dytiscus marginalis.

2007, Sept. 3 **Litho.** *Perf. 13¾x14*
1390-1392 A546 Set of 3 5.75 5.75

Panoramic View of Liechtenstein — A547

2007, Oct. 1 **Litho.** *Perf. 14*
1393 A547 130rp multi 2.50 2.50

Building Preservation Type of 2001

Designs: 2fr, St. Martin's Church, Eschen. 2.70fr, Mill, Eschen, horiz.

Perf. 13½x13¾, 13¾x13½
2007, Nov. 19 **Photo.**
1394-1395 A490 Set of 2 8.25 8.25

New Parliament Building A548

2007, Nov. 19 *Perf. 13¾*
1396 A548 130rp multi 2.25 2.25

Natural Phenomena A549

Designs: 85rp, Rainbow above Three Sisters Massif. 100rp, Lightning over Bendern. 180rp, Ice crystal halo around Moon over Malbun.

2007, Nov. 19 **Litho.** *Perf. 14¼*
1397-1399 A549 Set of 3 6.50 6.50

Christmas A550

Designs: 85rp, Chapel of St. Mary, Gamprin-Oberbühl. 1fr, Büel Chapel, Eschen. 1.30fr, Chapel of St. Wolfgang, Triesen.

Perf. 13½x14¼
2007, Nov. 19 **Photo.**
1400-1402 A550 Set of 3 5.75 5.75

Pastures Type of 2005

Designs: 2.60fr, Guschg. 3fr, Güschgle.

2008, Mar. 3 **Photo.** *Perf. 13½x14¼*
1403-1404 A527 Set of 2 11.00 11.00

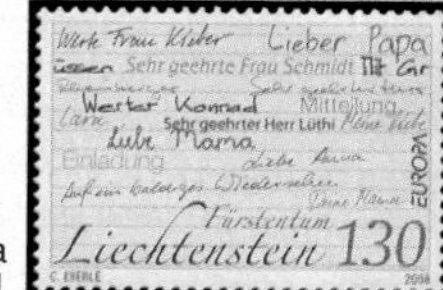

Europa A551

2008, Mar. 3 **Litho.** *Perf. 13½x13¾*
1405 A551 130rp multi 2.60 2.60

Volunteer Fire Fighters A552

2008, Mar. 3 *Perf. 13½*
1406 A552 1fr multi 2.00 2.00

Sleeping Princess Marie Franziska, by Friedrich von Amerling A553

2008, Mar. 3 **Photo. & Engr.**
1407 A553 2.40fr multi 4.75 4.75

See Austria No. 2144.

Spoerry-Areal, Vaduz — A554

Chapel of St. Mamertus, Triesen — A555

Vaduz Castle — A556

2008, Mar. 3 Litho. *Perf. 14*

1408 A554 85rp multi 1.75 1.75
1409 A555 1fr multi 2.00 2.00
1410 A556 1.30fr multi 2.60 2.60
Nos. 1408-1410 (3) 6.35 6.35

Mother and Queen of the Precious Blood with Child, by Unknown Artist — A557

2008, June 2 Litho. *Perf. 12¾x13½*

1411 A557 220rp multi 5.00 5.00

Schellenberg Convent, 150th anniv.

2008 Summer Olympics, Beijing — A558

Mascots involved in: 85rp, Martial arts. 100rp, Soccer.

2008, June 2 *Perf. 14¼x13½*

1412-1413 A558 Set of 2 4.25 4.25

2008 Paralympics, Beijing — A559

Designs: 130rp, Marathon. 180rp, Table tennis.

2008, June 2 *Perf. 13½x14¼*

1414-1415 A559 Set of 2 7.25 7.25

2008 European Soccer Championships, Austria and Switzerland — A560

Designs: No. 1416, 130rp, St. Stephen's Cathedral, Vienna, soccer player waltzing, violinist. No. 1417, 130rp, Soccer fans holding Liechtenstein flag, wearing Swiss hat, and Austrian scarf. No. 1418, 130rp, Alphorn player, Matterhorn, soccer player.

2008, June 2 *Perf. 14*

1416-1418 A560 Set of 3 9.00 9.00

Nos. 1416-1418 printed in sheets containing 4 #1417 and 6 each #1416 and 1418.

Hymenopterans A561

Designs: 85rp, Osmia brevicornis. 1fr, Epeoloides coecutiens. 1.30fr, Odynerus spinipes.

2008, June 2 *Perf. 14¼*

1419-1421 A561 Set of 3 7.25 7.25

Souvenir Sheet

Prince Karl I (1569-1627) — A562

Photo. & Engr.

2008, Sept. 1 *Perf. 13¾x13½*

1422 A562 5fr multi 11.50 11.50

Princely house of Liechtenstein, 400th anniv.

Miniature Sheet

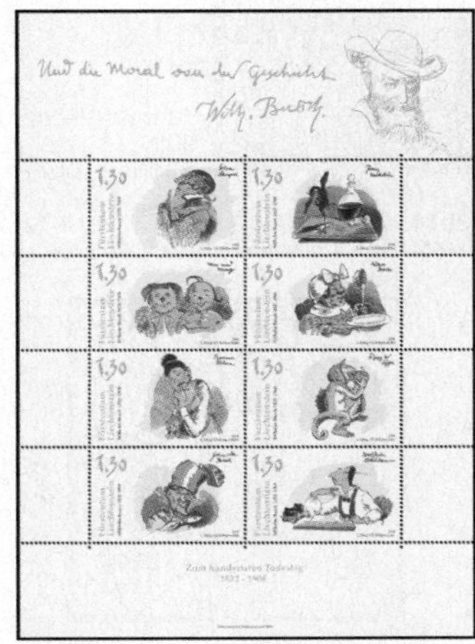

Drawings by Wilhelm Busch (1832-1908) — A563

No. 1423: a, Schoolmaster Lampel. b, Hans Huckebein. c, Max and Moritz. d, Widow Bolte. e, Pious Helene. f, Fipps the Monkey. g, Tailor Böck. h, Balduin Bählamm.

2008, Sept. 1 Photo. *Perf. 14x13¾*

1423 A563 Sheet of 8 24.00 24.00
a.-h. 1.30fr Any single 3.00 3.00

Building Preservation Type of 2001

Design: Schädler Ceramics Building, Nendeln, horiz.

Perf. 13¾x13½

2008, Nov. 17 Photo.

1424 A490 3.80fr multi 8.75 8.75

Technical Innovations Type of 2007

Designs: 1.20fr, Neutrik NC3MX audio cable connectors. 1.40fr, Ivoclar Vivadent bluephase polymerization unit. 2.20fr, Presta DeltaValveControl variable valve-lift system.

2008, Nov. 17 *Perf. 14¼*

1425-1427 A545 Set of 3 8.75 8.75

Christmas A564

Designs: 85rp, Candles, flowers and evergreen branches. 100rp, Children carrying holly, horiz. 130rp, Christmas tree and gifts.

Perf. 14¼x14½, 14½x14¼

2008, Nov. 17 Litho.

1428-1430 A564 Set of 3 7.25 7.25

Civil Protection Volunteers — A565

2009, Mar. 2 Litho. *Perf. 13¾x13½*

1431 A565 1fr multi 2.25 2.25

See Nos. 1471-1472.

Europa — A566

Litho. With Hologram Affixed

2009, Mar. 2 *Perf. 14¼*

1432 A566 1.30fr multi 3.00 3.00

Land Registry, 200th Anniv. A567

2009, Mar. 2 Litho. *Perf. 13¾*

1433 A567 330rp multi 7.50 7.50

Liechtenstein Post AG, 10th Anniv. — A568

Designs: 85rp, Counter clerk handling package. 100rp, Mail deliverer. 130rp, Mail sorter.

2009, Mar. 2 *Perf. 13¾x13½*

1434-1436 A568 Set of 3 7.25 7.25

Linoleum Prints by Stephan Sude — A569

Designs: 1fr, Unfolding. 1.30fr, Awareness. 2.70fr, Fulfillment.

2009, Mar. 2 *Perf. 14x13¼*

1437-1439 A569 Set of 3 11.50 11.50

Alpine Association, Cent. A570

Crosses on summits of: 100rp, Kuegrat. 130rp, Langspitz, vert. 220rp, Rappastein, vert. 240rp, Jahn-Turm and Wolan.

Perf. 13¾x13½, 13½x13¾

2009, June 8 Litho.

1440-1443 A570 Set of 4 16.00 16.00

Forests — A571

Designs: 85rp, Ants in forest. 1fr, Path in forest. 1.40fr, Boulder against tree on hillside. 1.60fr, Cut timber.

2009, June 8 *Perf. 13½*

1444-1447 A571 Set of 4 11.00 11.00

Vaduz Castle A572

Castle in: 130rp, Spring. 180rp, Summer.

2009, June 8 Photo. *Perf. 13¾*

1448-1449 A572 Set of 2 7.00 7.00

See Nos. 1488-1489.

Liechtenstein Philatelic Society, 75th Anniv. — A573

2009, Sept. 7 Litho. *Perf. 13x13¼*

1450 A573 130rp multi 3.00 3.00

Holes are drilled along the map border.

Badminton Cabinet Ornamentation — A574

Panels with bird and flower designs: 1.30fr, Bird with blue head. 2fr, Three birds, vert. (35x50mm). 4fr, Bird with red head.

Perf. 14, 13¾ (2fr)

2009, Sept. 7 Photo. & Engr.

1451-1453 A574 Set of 3 17.00 17.00

Butterflies A575

Designs: 85rp, Pieris rapae. 100rp, Parnassius apollo. 130rp, Melanargia galathea. 200rp, Vanessa atalanta.

2009, Sept. 7 Litho. *Perf. 12x12½*

Self-Adhesive

1454-1457 A575 Set of 4 12.00 12.00

Chapel of St. Mamerta, Triesen — A576

2009, Sept. 16 *Perf. 14*
1458 A576 130rp multi 3.00 3.00

Contemporary Architecture — A577

Designs: 85rp, University of Applied Sciences, Vaduz. 260rp, Art Museum, Vaduz. 350rp, Border crossing, Rugell.

Perf. 13½x13¾
2009, Nov. 16 **Litho.**
1459-1461 A577 Set of 3 17.00 17.00

See Nos. 1473-1474.

Lifestyle Museum, Schellenberg A578

Former Customs House, Vaduz — A579

Parish House, Bendern A580

2009, Nov. 16 *Perf. 12¼*
Self-Adhesive

1462 A578 20rp multi		.40	.40
1463 A579 50rp multi		1.00	1.00
1464 A580 60rp multi		1.25	1.25
Nos. 1462-1464 (3)		2.65	2.65

Christmas — A581

Advent windows by children: 85rp, Annunciation. 100rp, Journey to Bethlehem. 130rp, Nativity. 180rp, Magi and Star of Bethlehem.

2009, Nov. 16 *Perf. 13½x13¾*
1465-1468 A581 Set of 4 10.00 10.00

2010 Winter Olympics, Vancouver A582

Designs: 1fr, Downhill skier. 1.80fr, Cross-country skier, horiz.

2010, Feb. 12 **Litho.** *Perf. 13¾*
1469-1470 A582 Set of 2 5.25 5.25

Civil Protection Volunteers Type of 2009

Designs: 85rp, Mountain rescuers. 1.30rp, Water rescuers.

2010, Mar. 1 *Perf. 13¾x13½*
1471-1472 A565 Set of 2 4.00 4.00

Contemporary Architecture Type of 2009

Designs: 260rp, Natural gas filling station, Vaduz. 360rp, Liechtenstein Electric Power Authority transformer station, Schaan.

2010, Mar. 1 *Perf. 13½x13¾*
1473-1474 A577 Set of 2 11.50 11.50

Agriculture — A583

Designs: 85rp, Fields. 1fr, Flowers, hillside farmers. 1.10fr, Combine in field. 1.30fr, Cattle.

2010, Mar. 1 **Photo.** *Perf. 13½x13¼*
1475-1478 A583 Set of 4 8.00 8.00

Souvenir Sheet

Expo 2010, Shanghai — A584

No. 1479: a, Atmospheric View of Vaduz, by Johann Jakob Schmidt (40x36mm). b, Tidal Bore on the Qiantang River, by Xu Gu (32x60mm).

Photo. & Engr.

2010, May 1 *Perf. 14*

1479 A584	Sheet of 2	6.50	6.50
a.	1.60fr multi	3.00	3.00
b.	1.90fr multi	3.50	3.50
c.	As #1479, imperf.	6.50	6.50
d.	As "a," imperf.	3.00	3.00
e.	As "b," imperf.	3.50	3.50

Butterflies Type of 2009

Designs: 140rp, Coenonympha oedippus. 160rp, Gonepteryx rhamni. 260rp, Papilio machaon.

2010, June 7 **Litho.** *Perf. 12x12½*
Self-Adhesive
1480-1482 A575 Set of 3 9.75 9.75

Liechtenstein Disability Insurance, 50th Anniv. — A585

2010, June 7 *Perf. 14x13¼*
1483 A585 1fr multi 1.75 1.75

European Free Trade Association, 50th Anniv. A586

2010, June 7 *Perf. 12x12½*
1484 A586 140rp multi 2.50 2.50

Interpol Vaduz, 50th Anniv. — A587

2010, June 7 *Perf. 12¼*
1485 A587 1.90fr multi 3.50 3.50

Ceiling Frescoes in Liechtenstein Museum, Vienna — A588

Frescoes by Johann Michael Rottmayr: 1fr, Ariadne Giving Theseus the Thread. 1.40fr, Surrender of the Golden Fleece to Jason.

Photo. & Engr.

2010, June 7 *Perf. 14*
1486-1487 A588 Set of 2 4.25 4.25

Values are for stamps with surrounding selvage.

Vaduz Castle Type of 2009

Castle in: 140rp, Autumn, vert. 190rp, Winter, vert.

2010, Sept. 6 **Photo.** *Perf. 13¾*
1488-1489 A572 Set of 2 6.50 6.50

Europa — A589

2010, Sept. 6 **Litho.** *Perf. 14*
1490 A589 140rp multi 2.75 2.75

Renewable Energy A590

Designs: 100rp, Water. 140rp, Wood. 280rp, Geothermal.

Litho. & Photo.

2010, Sept. 6 *Perf. 14x13¾*
1491-1493 A590 Set of 3 10.50 10.50

Parts of the designs of Nos. 1491-1493 were printed with thermochromic ink that changes color when warmed.

Rhine Valley Landscape — A591

No. 1494: a, Eschnerberg and Dreischwestern Mountains, cart path, denomination at LL. b, Alvier Mountains, denomination at LR.

2010, Sept. 6 **Litho.** *Perf. 14x13¼*

1494	Horiz. pair	4.00	4.00
a.-b.	A591 1fr Either single	2.00	2.00

Schaan-Vaduz Railroad Station — A592

Red House, Vaduz — A593

St. Joseph Church, Triesenberg A594

2010, Nov. 15 **Litho.** *Perf. 12¼*
Self-Adhesive

1495 A592 1.10fr multi		2.25	2.25
1496 A593 1.80fr multi		3.75	3.75
1497 A594 1.90fr multi		4.00	4.00
Nos. 1495-1497 (3)		10.00	10.00

Works From Liechtenstein Museum of Art — A595

Designs: 100rp, Normale e Anormale, embroidery by Alighiero Boetti. 220rp, Testa, sculpture by Marisa Merz. 360rp, Untitled sculpture by Jannis Kounellis.

2010, Nov. 15 *Perf. 13¾x13½*
1498-1500 A595 Set of 3 14.00 14.00

Christmas A596

Ceiling frescoes from Maria-Hilf Chapel, Mäls: 85rp, Annunciation. 1fr, Visitation of

Mary. 1.40fr, Presentation of Jesus in the Temple.

2010, Nov. 15 Photo. *Perf. 14*
1501-1503 A596 Set of 3 6.75 6.75

SEMI-POSTAL STAMPS

Prince Johann II — SP1

Coat of Arms — SP2

Wmk. 183

1925, Oct. 5 Engr. *Perf. 11½*
B1 SP1 10rp yellow green 27.50 14.00
B2 SP1 20rp deep red 20.00 14.00
B3 SP1 30rp deep blue 6.00 4.50
Nos. B1-B3 (3) 53.50 32.50
Set, never hinged 145.00

85th birthday of the Prince Regent. Sold at a premium of 5rp each, the excess being devoted to charities.

1927, Oct. 5 Typo.
B4 SP2 10rp multicolored 6.75 *15.00*
B5 SP2 20rp multicolored 6.75 *15.00*
B6 SP2 30rp multicolored 5.00 *12.50*
Nos. B4-B6 (3) 18.50 *42.50*
Set, never hinged 45.00

87th birthday of Prince Johann II.
These stamps were sold at premiums of 5, 10 and 20rp respectively. The money thus obtained was devoted to charity.

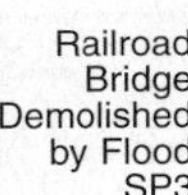

Railroad Bridge Demolished by Flood SP3

Designs: 10rp+10rp, Inundated Village of Ruggel. 20rp+10rp, Austrian soldiers rescuing refugees. 30rp+10rp, Swiss soldiers salvaging personal effects.

1928, Feb. 6 Litho. Unwmk.
B7 SP3 5rp + 5rp brn vio & brn 10.00 20.00
B8 SP3 10rp + 10rp bl grn & brn 14.00 22.50
B9 SP3 20rp + 10rp dl red & brn 14.00 22.50
B10 SP3 30rp + 10rp dp bl & brn 11.00 22.50
Nos. B7-B10 (4) 49.00 87.50
Set, never hinged 175.00

The surtax on these stamps was used to aid the sufferers from the Rhine floods.

Coat of Arms — SP7

Princess Elsa — SP8

Design: 30rp, Prince Francis I.

1932, Dec. 21 Photo.
B11 SP7 10rp (+ 5rp) olive grn 15.00 *25.00*
B12 SP8 20rp (+ 5rp) rose red 15.00 *25.00*
B13 SP8 30rp (+ 10rp) ultra 20.00 *30.00*
Nos. B11-B13 (3) 50.00 *80.00*
Set, never hinged 125.00

The surtax was for the Child Welfare Fund.

Postal Museum Issue
Souvenir Sheet

SP10

1936, Oct. 24 Litho. *Imperf.*
B14 SP10 Sheet of 4 12.50 *37.50*
Never hinged 37.50

Sheet contains 2 each, #120, 122. Sold for 2fr.

"Protect the Child" — SP11

Designs: No. B16, "Take Care of the Sick." No. B17, "Help the Aged."

Perf. 11½
1945, Nov. 27 Photo. Unwmk.
B15 SP11 10rp + 10rp multi .65 *1.75*
B16 SP11 20rp + 20rp multi .65 *2.25*
B17 SP11 1fr + 1.40fr multi 4.75 *20.00*
Nos. B15-B17 (3) 6.05 *24.00*
Set, never hinged 11.00

Souvenir Sheet

Post Coach — SP14

1946, Aug. 10
B18 SP14 Sheet of 2 21.00 *32.50*
Never hinged 35.00
a. 10rp dark violet brown & buff 5.00 *15.00*
Never hinged 12.50

25th anniv. of the Swiss-Liechtenstein Postal Agreement. Sheet, size: 82x60½mm, sold for 3fr.

Canal by Albert Cuyp — SP15

Willem van Huythuysen by Frans Hals — SP16

40rp+10rp, Landscape by Jacob van Ruysdael.

1951, July 24 *Perf. 11½*
B19 SP15 10rp + 10rp olive grn 5.00 7.00
B20 SP16 20rp + 10rp dk vio brn 5.00 *14.00*
B21 SP15 40rp + 10rp blue 5.00 7.00
Nos. B19-B21 (3) 15.00 *28.00*
Set, never hinged 30.00

Issued in sheets of 12. For surcharges see Nos. 281-283.

Catalogue values for unused stamps in this section, from this point to the end of the section, are for Never Hinged items.

Nos. 324-325 Surcharged with New Value and Uprooted Oak Emblem

1960, Apr. 7
B22 A190 30rp + 10rp on 40rp .55 *1.00*
B23 A190 50rp + 10rp on 25rp .90 *2.00*

World Refugee Year, July 1, 1959-June 30, 1960. The surtax was for aid to refugees.

Growth Symbol SP17

1967, Dec. 7 Photo. *Perf. 11½*
B24 SP17 50rp + 20rp multi .50 .60

Surtax was for development assistance.

AIR POST STAMPS

Airplane over Snow-capped Mountain Peaks — AP1

Airplane above Vaduz Castle — AP2

Airplane over Rhine Valley — AP3

Perf. 10½, 10½x11½
1930, Aug. 12 Photo. Unwmk.
Gray Wavy Lines in Background
C1 AP1 15rp dark brown 5.00 *16.00*
C2 AP1 20rp slate 12.00 *20.00*
C3 AP2 25rp olive brown 6.50 *35.00*
C4 AP2 35rp slate blue 10.00 *32.50*
C5 AP3 45rp olive green 24.00 *67.50*
C6 AP3 1fr lake 27.50 *47.50*
Nos. C1-C6 (6) 85.00 *218.50*
Set, never hinged 335.00

For surcharge see No. C14.

Zeppelin over Naafkopf, Falknis Range AP4

Design: 2fr, Zeppelin over Valüna Valley.

1931, June 1 *Perf. 11½*
C7 AP4 1fr olive black 37.50 *75.00*
C8 AP4 2fr blue black 72.50 *200.00*
Set, never hinged 325.00

Golden Eagle — AP6

15rp, Golden Eagle in flight, diff. 20rp, Golden Eagle in flight, diff. 30rp, Osprey. 50rp, Eagle.

1934-35
C9 AP6 10rp brt vio ('35) 6.00 *26.00*
C10 AP6 15rp red org ('35) 15.00 *35.00*
C11 AP6 20rp red ('35) 15.00 *35.00*
C12 AP6 30rp brt bl ('35) 15.00 *35.00*
C13 AP6 50rp emerald 9.00 *26.00*
Nos. C9-C13 (5) 60.00 157.00
Set, never hinged 200.00

No. C6 Surcharged with New Value

1935, June 24 *Perf. 10½x11½*
C14 AP3 60rp on 1fr lake 25.00 37.50
Never hinged 75.00

Airship "Hindenburg" — AP11

Design: 2fr, Airship "Graf Zeppelin."

1936, May 1 *Perf. 11½*
C15 AP11 1fr rose carmine 30.00 62.50
C16 AP11 2fr violet 20.00 62.50
Set, never hinged 120.00

AP13

10rp, Barn swallows. 15rp, Black-headed Gulls. 20rp, Gulls. 30rp, Eagle. 50rp, Northern Goshawk. 1fr, Lammergeier. 2fr, Lammergeier.

1939, Apr. 3 Photo.
C17 AP13 10rp violet .30 .65
C18 AP13 15rp red orange .30 1.40
C19 AP13 20rp dark red 2.50 1.20
C20 AP13 30rp dull blue .65 1.25
C21 AP13 50rp brt green 2.90 2.50
C22 AP13 1fr rose car 1.60 *9.50*
C23 AP13 2fr violet 1.60 *9.50*
Nos. C17-C23 (7) 9.85 *26.00*
Set, never hinged 20.00

Catalogue values for unused stamps in this section, from this point to the end of the section, are for Never Hinged items.

AP20

1948

Designs: 10rp, Leonardo da Vinci. 15rp, Joseph Montgolfier. 20rp, Jacob Degen. 25rp, Wilhelm Kress. 40rp, E. G. Robertson. 50rp, W. S. Henson. 1fr, Otto Lilienthal. 2fr, S. A. Andrée. 5fr, Wilbur Wright. 10fr, Icarus.

C24 AP20 10rp dark green .55 .20
C25 AP20 15rp dark violet .55 .80
C26 AP20 20rp brown .90 .20
a. 20rp reddish brown 65.00 2.75
C27 AP20 25rp dark red 1.10 1.25
C28 AP20 40rp violet blue 1.25 1.25
C29 AP20 50rp Prus blue 1.40 1.25
C30 AP20 1fr chocolate 8.00 2.75
C31 AP20 2fr rose lake 4.50 3.50

C32	AP20	5fr	olive green	5.75	4.75
C33	AP20	10fr	slate black	26.00	14.00
			Nos. C24-C33 (10)	50.00	29.95

Issued in sheets of 9.
Exist imperf. Value, set $6,500.

Helicopter, Bell 47-J AP21

Planes: 40rp, Boeing 707 jet. 50rp, Convair 600 jet. 75rp, Douglas DC-8.

1960, Apr. 7 Unwmk. *Perf. 11½*

C34	AP21	30rp	red orange	2.25	2.25
C35	AP21	40rp	blue black	3.75	2.25
C36	AP21	50rp	deep claret	9.50	4.00
C37	AP21	75rp	olive green	2.00	2.25
			Nos. C34-C37 (4)	17.50	10.75

30th anniv. of Liechtenstein's air post stamps.

POSTAGE DUE STAMPS

National Administration of the Post Office

D1

1920 Unwmk. Engr. *Perf. 12½*

J1	D1	5h	rose red	.20	.20
J2	D1	10h	rose red	.20	.20
J3	D1	15h	rose red	.20	.20
J4	D1	20h	rose red	.20	.20
J5	D1	25h	rose red	.20	.20
J6	D1	30h	rose red	.20	.20
J7	D1	40h	rose red	.20	.20
J8	D1	50h	rose red	.20	.20
J9	D1	80h	rose red	.20	.20
J10	D1	1k	dull blue	.20	.40
J11	D1	2k	dull blue	.20	.40
J12	D1	5k	dull blue	.20	.40
			Nos. J1-J12 (12)	2.40	3.00
			Set, never hinged	4.00	

Nos. J1-J12 exist imperf. and part perf.

Swiss Administration of the Post Office

D2

Post Horn — D3

1928 Litho. Wmk. 183 *Perf. 11½*
Granite Paper

J13	D2	5rp	purple & orange	.70	*1.75*
J14	D2	10rp	purple & orange	.85	*1.75*
J15	D2	15rp	purple & orange	1.40	*8.50*
J16	D2	20rp	purple & orange	1.40	*2.50*
J17	D2	25rp	purple & orange	1.40	*5.00*
J18	D2	30rp	purple & orange	4.00	*7.50*
J19	D2	40rp	purple & orange	4.75	*8.50*
J20	D2	50rp	purple & orange	5.50	*12.50*
			Nos. J13-J20 (8)	20.00	*48.00*
			Set, never hinged	68.00	

Engraved; Value Typographed in Dark Red

1940 Unwmk. *Perf. 11½*

J21	D3	5rp	gray blue	1.10	*2.10*
J22	D3	10rp	gray blue	.50	.40
J23	D3	15rp	gray blue	.60	*2.10*
J24	D3	20rp	gray blue	.75	*1.25*
J25	D3	25rp	gray blue	1.25	*2.50*
J26	D3	30rp	gray blue	2.50	*3.25*
J27	D3	40rp	gray blue	2.50	*3.25*
J28	D3	50rp	gray blue	2.50	*3.75*
			Nos. J21-J28 (8)	11.70	*18.60*
			Set, never hinged	25.00	

OFFICIAL STAMPS

Regular Issue of 1930 Overprinted in Various Colors with Crown and:

1932 Unwmk. *Perf. 11½*

O1	A38	5rp	dk grn (Bk)	5.50	9.00
O2	A39	10rp	dark vio (R)	37.50	7.50
b.			Perf 11½x10½	600.00	*1,000.*
			Never hinged	950.00	
O3	A40	20rp	dp rose red (Bl)	50.00	7.50
a.			Perf. 10½	160.00	40.00
			Never hinged	400.00	
O4	A42	30rp	ultra (R)	10.00	10.00
a.			Perf. 10½	15.00	17.50
			Never hinged	45.00	
O5	A43	35rp	dp grn (Bk)	3,750.	*6,000.*
a.			Perf 10½	8.00	*20.00*
			Never hinged	24.00	
O6	A45	50rp	blk brn (Bl)	90.00	*140.00*
a.			Perf. 11½x10½	37.50	12.00
			Never hinged	130.00	
O7	A46	60rp	olive blk (R)	8.50	*35.00*
O8	A48	1.20fr	olive brn (G)	82.50	275.00
			Nos. O1-O8 (8)	4,034.	6,484.
			Set, Never Hinged	700.00	

Nos. 108, 110 Overprinted in Black

1933 *Perf. 14½*

O9	A51	25rp	red orange	25.00	30.00
O10	A53	1.20fr	red brown	55.00	*150.00*
			Set, never hinged	175.00	

Same Overprint in Various Colors on Regular Issue of 1934-35

1934-36 *Perf. 11½*

O11	A58	5rp	emerald (R)	.50	*2.25*
O12	A59	10rp	dp vio (Bk)	2.25	*3.50*
O13	A60	15rp	red org (V)	.40	*2.25*
O14	A61	20rp	red (Bk)	.35	*2.25*
O15	A62	25rp	brown (R)	27.50	*60.00*
O16	A62	25rp	brown (Bk)	1.50	*11.00*
O17	A63	30rp	dark bl (R)	1.90	*6.50*
O18	A66	50rp	lt brown (V)	.90	*2.75*
O19	A68	90rp	dp grn (Bk)	5.50	*32.50*
O20	A70	1.50fr	brown car (Bl)	27.50	*140.00*
			Nos. O11-O20 (10)	68.30	*263.00*
			Set, never hinged	150.00	

Regular Issue of 1937-38 Overprinted in Black, Red or Blue

1937-41

O21	A76	5rp	emerald (Bk)	.20	.50
O22	A76	10rp	vio & buff (R)	.40	1.25
O23	A76	20rp	brown org (Bl)	.95	1.25
O24	A76	20rp	brn org (Bk) ('41)	.95	1.25
O25	A76	25rp	chestnut (Bk)	.60	1.25
O26	A77	30rp	blue & gray (Bk)	1.25	1.25
O27	A79	50rp	dk brn & buff (R)	.60	1.50
O28	A80	1fr	red brown (Bk)	.85	*5.00*
O29	A80	1.50fr	slate bl (Bk) ('38)	2.75	*7.50*
			Nos. O21-O29 (9)	8.55	*20.75*
			Set, never hinged	27.00	

Catalogue values for unused stamps in this section, from this point to the end of the section, are for Never Hinged items.

Stamps of 1944-45 Overprinted in Black

1947

O30	A136	5rp	slate grn & buff	1.25	.75
O31	A136	10rp	gray & buff	1.25	.75
O32	A136	20rp	org red & buff	1.50	.75
O33	A136	30rp	blue & buff	1.90	1.40
O34	A136	50rp	bluish blk & pale gray	2.00	3.00
O35	A136	1fr	dp cl & buff	9.00	9.00
O36	A136	150rp	royal blue	9.00	9.00
			Nos. O30-O36 (7)	25.90	24.65

Crown — O1

Government Building, Vaduz — O2

Engr.; Value Typo.

1950-68 Unwmk. *Perf. 11½*
Buff Granite Paper
Narrow Gothic Numerals

O37	O1	5rp	red vio & gray	.20	.20
O38	O1	10rp	ol grn & mag	.20	.20
O39	O1	20rp	org brn & bl	.20	.20
O40	O1	30rp	dk red brn & org red	.25	.25
O41	O1	40rp	blue & hn brn	.35	.35
O42	O1	55rp	dk gray grn & red	.70	1.10
a.			White paper ('68)	45.00	*125.00*
O43	O1	60rp	slate & mag	.70	1.10
a.			White paper ('68)	6.00	*22.50*
O44	O1	80rp	red org & gray	.70	.90
O45	O1	90rp	choc & blue	.90	1.25
O46	O1	1.20fr	grnsh bl & org	1.10	1.25
			Nos. O37-O46 (10)	5.30	6.80

1968-69 *Perf. 11½*
White Granite Paper
Broad Numerals, Varying Thickness

O47	O1	5rp	olive brn & org	.20	.20
O48	O1	10rp	violet & car	.20	.20
O49	O1	20rp	ver & emer	.20	.20
O50	O1	30rp	green & red	.20	.20
O51	O1	50rp	ultra & red	.35	.35
O52	O1	60rp	orange & ultra	.40	.40
O53	O1	70rp	maroon & emer	.50	.50
O54	O1	80rp	bl grn & car	.55	.55
O55	O1	95rp	slate & red ('69)	.65	.65
O56	O1	1fr	rose cl & grn	.70	.70
O57	O1	1.20fr	lt red brn & grn	.80	.80
O58	O1	2fr	brn & org ('69)	1.25	1.25
			Nos. O47-O58 (12)	6.00	6.00

Engr., Value Typo.

1976-89 *Perf. 14*

O59	O2	10rp	yel brn & vio	.20	.20
O60	O2	20rp	car lake & bl	.20	.20
O61	O2	35rp	blue & red	.25	.25
O62	O2	40rp	dull pur & grn	.30	.30
O63	O2	50rp	slate & mag	.40	.40
O64	O2	70rp	vio brn & bl grn	.55	.55
O65	O2	80rp	green & mag	.60	.60
O66	O2	90rp	vio & bl grn	.70	.70
O67	O2	1fr	olive & mag	.80	.80
O68	O2	1.10fr	brown & ultra	.85	.85
O69	O2	1.50fr	dull grn & red	1.25	1.25
O70	O2	2fr	orange & blue	1.60	1.60
O75	O2	5fr	rose vio & brn org	5.75	5.75
			Nos. O59-O75 (13)	13.45	13.45

Issued: 5fr, 9/4/89; others, 12/9/76.
This is an expanding set. Numbers will change if necessary.

LITHUANIA

ˌli-thə-ˈwā-nē-ə

(Lietuva)

LOCATION — Northern Europe bordering on the Baltic Sea
GOVT. — Independent republic
AREA — 25,170 sq. mi.
POP. — 3,584,966 (1999 est.)
CAPITAL — Vilnius

Lithuania was under Russian rule when it declared its independence in 1918. The League of Nations recognized it in 1922. In 1940 it became a republic in the Union of Soviet Socialist Republics.

Lithuania declared its independence on March 11, 1990. Lithuanian independence was recognized by the Soviet Union on Sept. 6, 1991.

100 Skatiku = 1 Auksinas
100 Centai = 1 Litas (1922, 1993)
100 Kopecks = 1 Ruble (1991)

Catalogue values for unused stamps in this country are for Never Hinged items, beginning with Scott 70, Scott B43 in the semi-postal section, Scott C1 in the air post section, Scott CB1 in the air post semi-postal section and Scott 2N9 in the Russian occupation section.

Nos. 1-26 were printed in sheets of 20 (5x4) which were imperf. at the outer sides, so that only 6 stamps in each sheet were fully perforated. Values are for the stamps partly imperf. The stamps fully perforated sell for at least double these values. There was also a printing of Nos. 19-26 in a sheet of 160, composed of blocks of 20 of each stamp. Pairs or blocks with different values se-tenant sell for considerably more than the values for the stamps singly.

Nos. 1-26 are without gum.

Watermarks

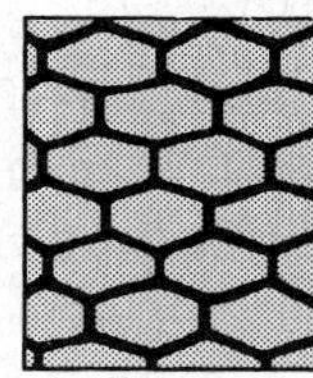
Wmk. 109 — Webbing

Wmk. 144 — Network

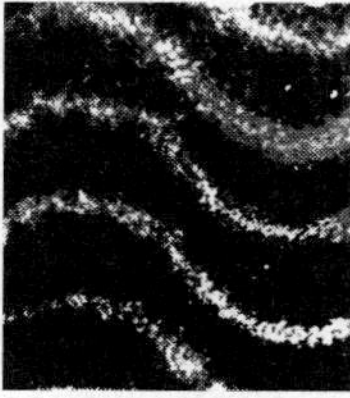
Wmk. 145 — Wavy Lines

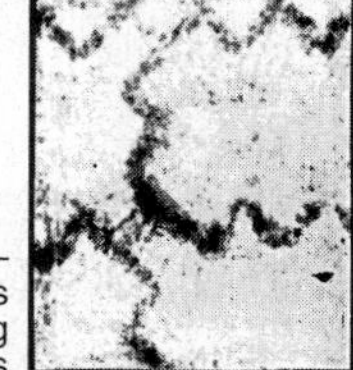
Wmk. 146 — Zigzag Lines Forming Rectangles

Wmk. 147 — Parquetry

Wmk. 198 — Intersecting Diamonds

Wmk. 209 — Multiple Ovals

Wmk. 238 — Multiple Letters

A1

A2

Perf. 11½

1918, Dec. 27 Unwmk. Typeset

First Vilnius Printing

Thin Figures

No.	Type	Description	Unused	Used
1	A1	10sk black	125.00	100.00
2	A1	15sk black	125.00	100.00

1918, Dec. 31

Second Vilnius Printing

Thick Figures

No.	Type	Description	Unused	Used
3	A1	10sk black	70.00	55.00
4	A1	15sk black	70.00	55.00
5	A1	20sk black	30.00	16.00
6	A1	30sk black	35.00	17.50
7	A1	40sk black	50.00	25.00
8	A1	50sk black	40.00	17.50
		Nos. 3-8 (6)	295.00	186.00

First Kaunas Issue

1919, Jan. 29

No.	Type	Description	Unused	Used
9	A2	10sk black	8.00	4.50
10	A2	15sk black	8.00	4.50
a.		"5" for "15"	95.00	72.50
11	A2	20sk black	8.00	4.50
12	A2	30sk black	8.00	4.50
		Nos. 9-12 (4)	32.00	18.00

A3

A4

Second Kaunas Issue

1919, Feb. 18

No.	Type	Description	Unused	Used
13	A3	10sk black	4.25	2.00
14	A3	15sk black	4.25	2.00
15	A3	20sk black	4.25	2.00
a.		"astas" for "pastas"	80.00	75.00
16	A3	30sk black	4.25	2.00
17	A3	40sk black	4.25	2.00
18	A3	50sk black	4.25	2.00
19	A3	60sk black	4.25	2.00
		Nos. 13-19 (7)	29.75	14.00

Third Kaunas Issue

1919, Mar. 1

No.	Type	Description	Unused	Used
20	A4	10sk black	4.25	2.00
21	A4	15sk black	4.25	2.00
22	A4	20sk black	4.25	2.00
23	A4	30sk black	4.25	2.00
24	A4	40sk black	4.25	2.00
25	A4	50sk black	4.25	2.00
26	A4	60sk black	4.25	2.00
		Nos. 20-26 (7)	29.75	14.00

The White Knight "Vytis"

A5 A6

A7

A8

Perf. 10½ to 14 & Compound

1919 Litho. Wmk. 144

Gray Granite Paper

No.	Type	Description	Unused	Used
30	A5	10sk deep rose	1.00	.40
a.		Wmk. vert.	17.50	15.00
31	A5	15sk violet	1.00	.40
a.		Wmk. vert.	17.50	15.00
32	A5	20sk dark blue	1.25	.40
33	A5	30sk deep orange	1.25	.40
a.		Wmk. vert.	17.50	15.00
34	A5	40sk dark brown	1.25	.40
35	A6	50sk blue green	1.25	.50
36	A6	75sk org & dp rose	1.25	.50
37	A7	1auk gray & rose	2.50	.50
38	A7	3auk bis brn & rose	2.50	.50
39	A7	5auk blue grn & rose	2.50	.80
		Nos. 30-39 (10)	15.75	4.80

Nos. 30a, 31a and 33a are from the first printing with watermark vertical showing points to left; various perforations.

Nos. 30-39 exist imperf. Value in pairs, $50.

Issued: #30a, 31a, 33a, 2/17/19; #30-36, 3/20/19.

1919 Wmk. 145

Thick White Paper

No.	Type	Description	Unused	Used
40	A5	10sk dull rose	.35	.25
41	A5	15sk violet	.35	.25
42	A5	20sk dark blue	.35	.25
43	A5	30sk orange	.35	.25
44	A5	40sk red brown	.35	.25
45	A6	50sk green	.35	.25
46	A6	75sk yel & dp rose	.35	.25
47	A7	1auk gray & rose	.95	.35
48	A7	3auk yellow brn & rose, perf. 12½	.60	.40
49	A7	5auk bl grn & rose	1.00	.40
		Nos. 40-49 (10)	5.00	2.90

Nos. 40-49 exist imperf. Value in pairs, $42.50.

Perf. 10½ to 14 & Compound

1919, May 8

Thin White Paper

No.	Type	Description	Unused	Used
50	A5	10sk red	.40	.20
51	A5	15sk lilac	.40	.20
52	A5	20sk dull blue	.40	.20
53	A5	30sk buff	.40	.20
54	A5	40sk gray brn	.40	.20
55	A6	50sk lt green	.40	.20
56	A6	60sk violet & red	.40	.20
57	A6	75sk bister & red	.40	.20
58	A8	1auk gray & red	.40	.20
59	A8	3auk lt brown & red	.40	.30
60	A8	5auk blue grn & red	.40	.45
		Nos. 50-60 (11)	4.40	2.55

Nos. 50-60 exist imperf. Value, pairs $70.

See Nos. 93-96. For surcharges see Nos. 114-115, 120-139, 149-150.

Catalogue values for unused stamps in this section, from this point to the end of the section, are for Never Hinged items.

"Lithuania" Receiving Benediction — A9

The Spirit of Lithuania Rises — A10

"Lithuania" with Chains Broken — A11

White Knight — A12

1920, Feb. 16 Wmk. 146 ***Perf. 11½***

No.	Type	Description	Unused	Used
70	A9	10sk dp rose	3.75	2.25
71	A9	15sk lt violet	3.75	2.25
72	A9	20sk gray blue	3.75	2.25
73	A10	30sk yellow brn	3.75	2.25
74	A11	40sk brown & grn	3.75	2.25
75	A10	50sk deep rose	3.75	2.25
76	A10	60sk lt violet	3.75	2.25
77	A11	80sk purple & red	3.75	2.25
78	A11	1auk green & red	3.75	2.25
79	A12	3auk brown & red	3.75	2.25
80	A12	5auk green & red	3.75	2.25
a.		Right "5" dbl., grn and red	90.00	90.00
		Nos. 70-80 (11)	41.25	24.75

Anniv. of natl. independence. The stamps were on sale only 3 days in Kaunas. The stamps were available in other cities after that. Only a limited number of stamps was sold at post offices but 40,000 sets were delivered to the bank of Kaunas.

All values exist imperforate.

White Knight — A13

Grand Duke Vytautas — A14

Grand Duke Gediminas A15

Sacred Oak and Altar A16

1920, Aug. 25

No.	Type	Description	Unused	Used
81	A13	10sk rose	.95	.50
a.		Imperf., pair	40.00	
82	A13	15sk dark violet	.95	.50
83	A14	20sk grn & lt grn	.95	.50
84	A13	30sk brown	.95	.50
a.		Pair, #82, 84	40.00	
85	A15	40sk gray grn & vio	.95	.50
86	A14	50sk brn & brn org	2.75	1.25
87	A14	60sk red & org	1.50	1.00
88	A15	80sk blk, db & red	1.50	1.00
89	A16	1auk orange & blk	1.75	1.00
90	A16	3auk green & blk	1.75	1.00
91	A16	5auk gray vio & blk	4.50	2.00
		Nos. 81-91 (11)	18.50	9.75

Opening of Lithuanian National Assembly. On sale for three days.

1920

No.	Type	Description	Unused	Used
92	A14	20sk green & lilac	150.00	
92A	A15	40sk gray grn, buff & vio	150.00	
92B	A14	50sk brown & gray lil	150.00	
92C	A14	60sk red & green	150.00	
92D	A15	80sk black, grn & red	150.00	
		Nos. 92-92D (5)	750.00	

Nos. 92 to 92D were trial printings. By order of the Ministry of Posts, 2,000 examples of each were placed on sale at post offices.

Type of 1919 Issue

1920 Unwmk. ***Perf. 11½***

No.	Type	Description	Unused	Used
93	A5	15sk lilac	6.50	4.00
94	A5	20sk deep blue	6.50	4.00

Wmk. 109

No.	Type	Description	Unused	Used
95	A5	20sk deep blue	5.50	5.50
96	A5	40sk gray brown	12.00	9.00
		Nos. 93-96 (4)	30.50	22.50

Watermark horizontal on Nos. 95-96.

No. 96 exists perf. 10½x11½.

Imperf., Pairs

No.	Type	Description	Unused	Used
93a	A5	15sk	32.00	32.00
94a	A5	20sk	32.00	32.00
95a	A5	20sk	17.00	17.00
96a	A5	40sk	48.00	48.00

Sower A17

Peasant Sharpening Scythe A18

Prince Kestutis A19

Black Horseman A20

Perf. 11, 11½ and Compound

1921-22

No.	Type	Description	Unused	Used
97	A17	10sk brt rose	.85	.55
98	A17	15sk violet	.35	*.70*
99	A17	20sk ultra	.25	.20
100	A18	30sk brown	2.50	*1.10*
101	A19	40sk red	.25	.20
102	A18	50sk olive	.35	.20
103	A18	60sk grn & vio	2.50	*1.65*
104	A19	80sk brn org & car	.35	.20
105	A19	1auk brown & grn	.35	.20
106	A19	2auk gray bl & red	.35	.20
107	A20	3auk yel brn & dk bl	1.00	.40
108	A17	4auk yel & dk bl ('22)	.45	.20
109	A20	5auk gray blk & rose	1.00	*1.50*
110	A17	8auk grn & blk ('22)	.45	.20
111	A20	10auk rose & vio	1.00	.55
112	A20	25auk bis brn & grn	1.25	.85
113	A20	100auk dl red & gray blk	12.50	8.00
		Nos. 97-113 (17)	25.75	16.90

Imperf., Pairs

No.	Type	Description	Unused	Used
97a	A17	10sk	—	
98a	A17	15sk	—	
99a	A17	20sk	—	
100a	A18	30sk	—	
101a	A19	40sk	25.00	
102a	A18	50sk	25.00	
103a	A18	60sk	—	
104a	A19	80sk	—	
105a	A19	1auk	—	
106a	A19	2auk	120.00	
107a	A20	3auk	120.00	
109a	A20	5auk	120.00	
110a	A17	8auk	10.00	10.00
111a	A20	10auk	50.00	
112a	A20	25auk	50.00	
113a	A20	100auk	50.00	

For surcharges see Nos. 140-148, 151-160.

No. 57 Surcharged

Perf. 12½x11½

1922, May Wmk. 145

No.	Type	Description	Unused	Used
114	A6	4auk on 75sk bis & red	.90	.20
a.		Inverted surcharge	35.00	35.00

Same with Bars over Original Value

No.	Type	Description	Unused	Used
115	A6	4auk on 75sk bis & red	4.00	*8.00*
a.		Double surcharge	30.00	30.00

Povilas Luksis — A20a

Justinas Staugaitis, Antanas Smetona, Stasys Silingas — A20b

Portraits: 40s, Lt. Juozapavicius. 50s, Dr. Basanavicius. 60s, Mrs. Petkeviciute. 1auk, Prof. Voldemaras. 2auk, Pranas Dovidaitis. 3auk, Dr. Slezevicius. 4auk, Dr. Galvanauskas. 5auk, Kazys Grinius. 6auk, Dr. Stulginskis. 8auk, Pres. Smetona.

1922 Litho. Unwmk.

No.	Type	Description	Unused	Used
116	A20a	20s blk & car rose	1.25	.90
116A	A20a	40s bl grn & vio	1.25	.90
116B	A20a	50s plum & grnsh bl	1.25	.90
117	A20a	60s pur & org	1.25	.90
117A	A20a	1auk car & lt bl	1.25	.90
117B	A20a	2auk dp bl & yel brn	1.25	.90
c.		Center inverted	100.00	100.00
118	A20a	3auk mar & ultra	1.25	.90
118A	A20a	4auk dk grn & red vio	1.25	.90
118B	A20a	5auk blk brn & dp rose	1.25	.90
119	A20a	6auk dk bl & grnsh bl	1.25	.90
a.		Cliché of 8auk in sheet of 6auk	175.00	*175.00*
119B	A20a	8auk ultra & bis	1.25	.90
119C	A20b	10auk dk vio & bl grn	1.25	.90
		Nos. 116-119C (12)	15.00	10.80

League of Nations' recognition of Lithuania. Sold only on Oct. 1, 1922.

Forty sheets of the 6auk each included eight examples of the 8auk.

Stamps of 1919-22 Surcharged in Black, Carmine or Green

On Nos. 37-39

1922 Wmk. 144 *Perf. 11½x12*

Gray Granite Paper

No.	Type	Description	Unused	Used
120	A7	3c on 1auk	175.00	125.00
121	A7	3c on 3auk	175.00	125.00
122	A7	3c on 5auk	140.00	100.00
		Nos. 120-122 (3)	490.00	350.00

White Paper

Perf. 14, 11½, 12½x11½

Wmk. 145

No.	Type	Description	Unused	Used
123	A5	1c on 10sk red	2.75	1.50
124	A5	1c on 15sk lilac	4.00	1.50
125	A5	1c on 20sk dull bl	2.50	1.50
126	A5	1c 30sk orange	250.00	110.00
127	A5	1c on 30sk buff	.40	.40
128	A5	1c on 40sk gray brn	8.00	1.50
129	A6	2c on 50sk green	3.50	1.50
130	A6	2c on 60sk vio & red	.20	.20
131	A6	2c on 75sk bis & red	2.00	1.50
132	A8	3c on 1auk gray & red	.45	.45
133	A8	3c on 3auk brn & red	.25	.20
134	A8	3c on 5auk bl grn & red	.25	.20
		Nos. 123-125,127-134 (11)	24.30	10.45

On Stamps of 1920

1922 Unwmk. *Perf. 11*

No.	Type	Description	Unused	Used
136	A5	1c on 20sk dp bl (C)	4.00	2.00

Wmk. Webbing (109)

Perf. 11, 11½

No.	Type	Description	Unused	Used
138	A5	1c on 20sk dp bl (C)	3.75	2.00
139	A5	1c on 40sk gray brn (C)	8.00	1.25

On Stamps of 1921-22

No.	Type	Description	Unused	Used
140	A18	1c on 50sk ol (C)	.25	.20
a.		Imperf., pair	45.00	
b.		Inverted surcharge	40.00	
c.		Double surch., one invtd.		
141	A17	3c on 10sk	12.00	8.00
142	A17	3c on 15sk	.25	.20
143	A17	3c on 20sk	.45	1.50
144	A18	3c on 30sk	20.00	12.00
145	A19	3c on 40sk	.45	.45
a.		Imperf., pair		
146	A18	5c on 50sk	.20	.20
147	A18	5c on 60sk	20.00	20.00
148	A19	5c on 80sk	.60	.50
a.		Imperf., pair	35.00	15.00

Wmk. Wavy Lines (145)

Perf. 12½x11½

No.	Type	Description	Unused	Used
149	A6	5c on 4auk on 75sk (No. 114) (G)	1.75	10.00
150	A6	5c on 4auk on 75sk (No. 115) (G)	17.50	17.50

Wmk. Webbing (109)

Perf. 11, 11½

No.	Type	Description	Unused	Used
151	A19	10c on 1auk	.85	.20
a.		Inverted surcharge	55.00	
152	A19	10c on 2auk	.25	.20
a.		Inverted surcharge	50.00	
b.		Imperf., pair	45.00	
153	A17	15c on 4auk	.25	.20
a.		Inverted surcharge	45.00	
154	A20	25c on 3auk	20.00	20.00
155	A20	25c on 5auk	12.00	5.00
156	A20	25c on 10auk	2.50	1.50
a.		Imperf., pair	45.00	
157	A17	30c on 8auk (C)	1.25	.35
a.		Inverted surcharge	45.00	25.00
158	A20	50c on 25auk	4.00	2.50
160	A20	1 l on 100auk	4.25	2.50
		Nos. 136-160 (23)	134.55	108.25

A21

Ruin — A22

Seminary Church, Kaunas — A23

1923 Litho. Wmk. 109 *Perf. 11*

No.	Type	Description	Unused	Used
165	A21	10c violet	6.75	.20
166	A21	15c scarlet	2.50	.20
167	A21	20c olive brown	2.50	.20
168	A21	25c deep blue	2.50	.20
169	A22	50c yellow green	2.50	.20
170	A22	60c red	2.50	.20
171	A23	1 l orange & grn	11.00	.20
172	A23	3 l red & gray	15.00	.45
173	A23	5 l brown & blue	22.50	1.00
		Nos. 165-173 (9)	67.75	2.85

See Nos. 189-209, 281-282. For surcharges see Nos. B1-B42.

Memel Coat of Arms — A24

Lithuanian Coat of Arms — A25

Biruta Chapel — A26

Kaunas, War Memorial A27

Trakai Ruins A28

Memel Lighthouse — A29

Memel Harbor A30

Perf. 11, 11½, 12

1923, Aug. Unwmk.

No.	Type	Description	Unused	Used
176	A24	1c rose, grn & blk	2.25	1.60
177	A25	2c dull vio & blk	2.25	1.60
178	A26	3c yellow & blk	2.25	1.60
179	A24	5c bl, buff & blk	4.50	1.90
180	A27	10c orange & blk	3.50	1.90
181	A27	15c green & blk	3.50	2.50
182	A28	25c brt vio & blk	3.50	2.50
183	A25	30c red vio & blk	7.50	5.00
184	A29	60c ol grn & blk	4.00	2.75
185	A30	1 l bl grn & blk	4.00	2.75
186	A26	2 l red & black	15.00	7.50
187	A28	3 l blue & black	15.00	7.50
188	A29	5 l ultra & black	15.00	7.50
		Nos. 176-188 (13)	82.25	46.60

This series was issued ostensibly to commemorate the incorporation of Memel with Lithuania.

Type of 1923

1923 Unwmk. *Perf. 11*

No.	Type	Description	Unused	Used
189	A21	5c pale green	9.00	.50
190	A21	10c violet	12.00	.50
a.		Imperf., pair	50.00	
191	A21	15c scarlet	14.00	.50
a.		Imperf., pair	50.00	
193	A21	25c blue	25.00	.50
		Nos. 189-193 (4)	60.00	2.00

1923 Wmk. 147

No.	Type	Description	Unused	Used
196	A21	2c pale brown	1.25	.25
197	A21	3c olive bister	1.40	.20
198	A21	5c pale green	1.40	.20
199	A21	10c violet	3.25	.20
202	A21	25c deep blue	7.00	.20
a.		Imperf., pair	40.00	
204	A21	36c orange brown	11.00	.75
		Nos. 196-204 (6)	25.30	1.80

Perf. 11½, 14½, 11½x14½

1923-25 Wmk. 198

No.	Type	Description	Unused	Used
207	A21	25c deep blue	750.00	450.00
208	A22	50c deep green ('25)	4.00	.50
209	A22	60c carmine ('25)	4.50	.50

Double- barred Cross A31

Dr. Jonas Basanavicius A32

1927, Jan. *Perf. 11½, 14½*

No.	Type	Description	Unused	Used
210	A31	2c orange	2.00	.30
211	A31	3c deep brown	2.00	.30
212	A31	5c green	3.00	.30
a.		Imperf., pair	25.00	
213	A31	10c violet	4.50	.30
214	A31	15c red	4.50	.30
a.		Imperf., pair	25.00	
215	A31	25c blue	4.50	.30
		Nos. 210-215 (6)	20.50	1.80

1927-29 Wmk. 147 *Perf. 14½*

No.	Type	Description	Unused	Used
216	A31	5c green	250.00	*150.00*
217	A31	30c blue ('30)	100.00	10.00

See Nos. 233-240, 278-280.

1927 Unwmk. *Perf. 11½, 14½x11½*

No.	Type	Description	Unused	Used
219	A32	15c claret & blk	4.00	1.25
220	A32	25c dull blue & blk	4.00	1.25
221	A32	50c dk green & blk	4.00	1.25
222	A32	60c dk violet & blk	7.50	2.00
		Nos. 219-222 (4)	19.50	5.75

Dr. Jonas Basanavicius (1851-1927), patriot and folklorist.

National Arms — A33

1927, Dec. 23 Wmk. 109 *Perf. 14½*

No.	Type	Description	Unused	Used
223	A33	1 l blue grn & gray	2.50	.75
224	A33	3 l vio & pale grn	7.50	.75
225	A33	5 l brown & gray	9.00	1.25
		Nos. 223-225 (3)	19.00	2.75

Pres. Antanas Smetona — A34

Decade of Independence A35

Dawn of Peace — A36

1928, Feb. Wmk. 109

No.	Type	Description	Unused	Used
226	A34	5c org brn & grn	1.00	.30
227	A34	10c violet & blk	1.25	.30
228	A34	15c orange & brn	1.25	.35
229	A34	25c blue & indigo	1.25	.35
230	A35	50c ultra & dl vio	1.50	.45
231	A35	60c carmine & blk	1.75	.55
232	A36	1 l blk brn & drab	2.00	.70
		Nos. 226-232 (7)	10.00	3.00

10th anniv. of Lithuanian independence.

Type of 1926

1929-31

No.	Type	Description	Unused	Used
233	A31	2c orange ('31)	18.50	1.00
234	A31	5c green	4.75	.20
235	A31	10c violet ('31)	14.00	1.00
237	A31	15c red	5.50	.20
a.		Tête bêche pair	45.00	35.00
239	A31	30c dark blue	8.50	.20

Unwmk.

240 A31 15c red ('30) 14.00 .60
Nos. 233-240 (6) 65.25 3.20

Grand Duke Vytautas A37

Grand Duke, Mounted A38

1930, Feb. 16 *Perf. 14*

242 A37 2c yel brn & dk brn .55 .20
243 A37 3c dk brn & vio .55 .20
244 A37 5c yel grn & dp org .55 .20
245 A37 10c vio & emer .55 .20
246 A37 15c dp rose & vio .55 .20
247 A37 30c dk bl & brn vio 1.00 .20
248 A37 36c brn vio & ol blk 1.50 .30
249 A37 50c dull grn & ultra 1.00 .35
250 A37 60c dk blue & rose 1.00 .40
251 A38 1 l bl grn, db & red brn 4.25 1.00
252 A38 3 l dk brn, sal & dk vio 6.50 1.75
253 A38 5 l ol brn, gray & red 15.00 2.75
254 A38 10 l multicolored 40.00 16.00
255 A38 25 l multicolored 85.00 55.00
Nos. 242-255 (14) 158.00 78.75

5th cent. of the death of the Grand Duke Vytautas.

Kaunas, Railroad Station A39

Cathedral at Vilnius — A39a

Designs: 15c, 25c, Landscape on the Neman River. 50c, Main Post Office, Kaunas.

Perf. 14, Imperf.

1932, July 21 **Wmk. 238**

256 A39 10c dk red brn & ocher .50 .45
257 A39 15c dk brown & ol 1.00 .80
258 A39 25c dk blue & ol 1.50 1.25
259 A39 50c gray blk & ol 3.25 2.50
260 A39a 1 l dk blue & ol 8.50 5.00
261 A39a 3 l red brn & gray grn 8.50 6.50

Wmk. 198

262 A39 5c vio bl & ocher .50 .45
263 A39a 60c grnsh blk & lil 8.50 5.00
Nos. 256-263 (8) 32.25 21.95

Issued for the benefit of Lithuanian orphans.

In September, 1935, a red overprint was applied to No. 259: "ORO PASTAS / LITUANICA II / 1935 / NEW YORK-KAUNAS." Value, $400.

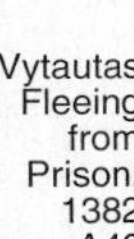

Vytautas Fleeing from Prison, 1382 A40

Designs: 15c, 25c, Conversion of Ladislas II Jagello and Vytautas (1386). 50c, 60c, Battle at Tannenberg (1410). 1 l, 3 l, Meeting of the Nobles (1429).

1932 **Wmk. 209** *Perf. 14, Imperf.*

264 A40 5c red & rose lake .75 .35
265 A40 10c ol bis & org brn .85 .35
266 A40 15c rose lil & ol grn 1.00 .50
267 A40 25c dk vio brn & ocher 2.25 1.25
268 A40 50c dp grn & bis brn 2.25 1.75
269 A40 60c ol grn & brn car 5.50 2.50
270 A40 1 l ultra & ol grn 6.00 3.00
271 A40 3 l dk brn & dk grn 6.50 4.00
Nos. 264-271 (8) 25.10 13.70

15th anniversary of independence.

A. Visteliauskas A41

Mother and Child — A42

Designs: 15c, 25c, Petras Vileišis. 50c, 60c, Dr. John Sliupas. 1 l, 3 l, Jonas Basanavicius.

1933 *Perf. 14, Imperf.*

272 A41 5c yel grn & car .60 .30
273 A41 10c ultra & car .80 .40
274 A41 15c orange & red 1.00 .50
275 A41 25c dk bl & blk brn 1.50 .90
276 A41 50c ol gray & dk bl 2.50 1.50
277 A41 60c org brn & chnt 8.00 4.00
277A A41 1 l red & vio brn 10.00 4.75
277B A41 3 l turq grn & vio brn 11.00 6.00
Nos. 272-277B (8) 35.40 18.35

50th anniv. of the 1st newspaper, "Ausra," in lithuanian language.

1933, Sept. *Perf. 14, Imperf.*

Designs: 15c, 25c, Boy reading. 50c, 60c, Boy playing with blocks. 1 l, 3 l, Woman and boy at the Spinning Wheel.

277C A42 5c dp yel grn & org brn .45 .25
277D A42 10c rose brn & ultra .50 .30
277E A42 15c ol grn & plum .50 .45
277F A42 25c org & gray blk 1.75 1.25
277G A42 50c ol grn & car 2.25 2.00
277H A42 60c blk & yel org 7.50 3.25
277I A42 1 l dk brn & ultra 8.50 3.75
277K A42 3 l rose lil & ol grn 10.00 *10.00*
Nos. 277C-277K (8) 31.45 *21.25*

Issued for the benefit of Lithuanian orphans.

Types of 1923-26

1933-34 **Wmk. 238** *Perf. 14*

278 A31 2c orange 42.50 6.50
279 A31 10c dark violet 60.00 9.50
280 A31 15c red 42.50 4.50
281 A22 50c green 42.50 9.50
282 A22 60c red 42.50 9.50
Nos. 278-282 (5) 230.00 39.50

Pres. Antanas Smetona, 60th Birthday — A43

1934 **Unwmk.** **Engr.** *Perf. 11½*

283 A43 15c red 11.00 .25
284 A43 30c green 14.00 .35
285 A43 60c blue 17.50 .50
Nos. 283-285 (3) 42.50 1.10

A44

A47

Arms — A45

Knight A48

Girl with Wheat — A46

Wmk. 198; Wmk. 209 (35c, 10 l)

1934-35 **Litho.** *Perf. 14*

286 A44 2c rose & dull org 1.25 .20
287 A44 5c bl grn & grn 1.25 .20
288 A45 10c chocolate 2.75 .20
289 A46 25c dk brn & emer 4.50 .20
290 A45 35c carmine 4.50 .20
291 A46 50c dk blue & blue 8.00 .20
292 A47 1 l sl & mar 75.00 .20
293 A47 3 l grn & gray grn .35 .20
294 A48 5 l maroon & gray bl .55 .45
295 A48 10 l choc & yel 3.50 3.75
Nos. 286-295 (10) 101.65 5.80

No. 290 exists imperf. Value, pair $65.
For overprint see No. 2N9.

1936-37 **Wmk. 238** *Perf. 14*

Size: 17½x23mm

296 A44 2c orange ('37) .25 .20
297 A44 5c green .30 .20

Pres. Smetona A49

25 CT LIETUVA

Arms A50

1936-37 **Unwmk.**

298 A49 15c carmine 9.00 .20
299 A49 30c green ('37) 12.00 .20
300 A49 60c ultra ('37) 11.00 .20
Nos. 298-300 (3) 32.00 .60

1937-39 **Wmk. 238** *Perf. 14*

Paper with Gray Network

301 A50 10c green 1.75 .20
302 A50 25c magenta .25 .20
303 A50 35c red 1.00 .20
304 A50 50c brown .60 .20
305 A50 1 l dp vio bl ('39) .75 .45
Nos. 301-305 (5) 4.35 1.25

No. 304 exists in two types:
I — "50" is fat and broad, with "0" leaning to right.
II — "50" is thinner and narrower, with "0" straight.
For overprint see No. 2N10.

Jonas Basanavicius Reading Act of Independence A51

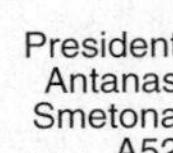

President Antanas Smetona A52

Perf. 13x13½

1939, Jan. 15 **Engr.** **Unwmk.**

306 A51 15c dark red .50 .30
307 A52 30c deep green 1.00 .30
308 A51 35c red lilac 1.25 .45
309 A52 60c dark blue 1.50 .60
a. Souvenir sheet of 2, #308-309 10.00 15.00
b. As "a," imperf. 72.50 72.50
Nos. 306-309 (4) 4.25 1.65

20th anniv. of Independence.
Nos. 309a, 309b sold for 2 l.

Same Overprinted in Blue

1939

310 A51 15c dark red .85 .90
311 A52 30c deep green .90 .90
312 A51 35c red lilac 2.00 1.00
313 A52 60c dark blue 2.25 1.00
Nos. 310-313 (4) 6.00 3.80

Recovery of Vilnius.

View of Vilnius A53

Gediminas — A54

Trakai Ruins A55

Unwmk.

1940, May 6 **Photo.** *Perf. 14*

314 A53 15c brn & pale brn .60 .25
315 A54 30c dk grn & lt grn 1.25 .85
316 A55 60c dk bl & lt bl 2.25 1.00
a. Souv. sheet of 3, #314-316, imperf. 16.00 16.00
Nos. 314-316 (3) 4.10 2.10

Return of Vilnius to Lithuania, Oct. 10, 1939. Exist imperf.

No. 316a has simulated perforations in gold. Sold for 2 l.

White Knight — A56

Angel — A57

Woman Releasing Dove A58

Mother and Children A59

Liberty Bell — A60

Mythical Animal — A61

1940

317 A56	5c brown carmine	.25	.30
318 A57	10c green	.85	.45
319 A58	15c dull orange	.25	.30
320 A59	25c light brown	.25	*.40*
321 A60	30c Prussian green	.30	.30
322 A61	35c red orange	.40	.35
	Nos. 317-322 (6)	2.30	2.10

Nos. 317-322 exist imperf.
For overprints see Nos. 2N11-2N16.

Nos. 371-399 were issued before the Soviet Union recognized the independence of Lithuania on Sept. 6, 1991, but were available and valid for use after that date.

Angel and Map — A66

Colors: 5k, Green. 10k, Brown violet. 20k, Blue. 50k, Red.

1990, Oct. 7 Litho. ***Imperf.***
Without Gum

371-374 A66 Set of 4 2.10 2.10

Simulated Perforations and Denomination in Brownish Gray

Denominations and colors as before.

1990, Dec. 22 Without Gum

375-378 A66 Set of 4 1.60 1.60

White Knight "Vytis" — A67

Hill With Crosses, Siauliai — A68

Design: 200k, Liberty Bell.

1991 Photo. ***Perf. 14***

379 A67	10k multi	.30	.20
380 A67	15k multi	.30	.20
381 A67	20k multi	.30	.20
382 A67	30k multi	.30	.20
383 A68	50k multi	.30	.20
384 A68	200k multi	.40	.20

Litho.
Imperf
Without Gum

385 A67	15k dl grn & blk	.30	.20
386 A67	25k brn & blk	.30	.20
387 A67	30k plum & blk	.30	.20
	Nos. 379-387 (9)	2.80	1.80

Issued: 10k, 20k, #382, 50k, 200k, 1/10; #380, 3/15; #385, 3/13; 25k, #387, 7/23.
No. 385 has a simulated outline of a perforated stamp.

See Nos. 411-418.

Liberty Statue — A69

1991, Feb. 16 Photo. ***Perf. 13¾x14***

388 A69 20k multi .25 .20

Declaration of Independence from Soviet Union, 1st Anniv. — A70

1991, Mar. 11 Litho. ***Perf. 13¼x13***

389 A70 20k multi .25 .20

Religious Symbols — A71

Designs: 40k, Crosses. 70k, Madonna. 100k, Spires, St. Anne's Church, Vilnius.

1991, Mar. 15 Photo. ***Perf. 13¾x14***

390-392 A71 Set of 3 1.25 .75

Resistance to Soviet and German Occupation, 50th Anniv. — A72

Designs: 20k, Candle, barbed wire. 50k, Heart, daggers. 70k, Sword, wreath.

1991, June 14 Litho. ***Perf. 13¼***

393-395 A72 Set of 3 1.25 .75

Fourth World Lithuanian Games A73

Emblem and: 20k, Map. 50k+25k, Head.

1991, July 27 Photo. ***Perf. 13¼x13***

396-397 A73 Set of 2 .85 .50

A74

A75

Denominations: 20k, 70k.

1991. Aug. 20 Litho. ***Perf. 12½x13***

398-399 A74 Set of 2 1.25 .75

Expedition to Mt. Everest.

1991, Sept. 28 Litho. ***Perf. 13x13½***

400 A75	30k Castle	.30	.30
401 A75	50k Grand Duke	.55	.55
402 A75	70k Early view of Vilnius	.85	.85
	Nos. 400-402 (3)	1.70	1.70

Grand Duke Gediminas, 650th dath anniv.

Ciconia Nigra — A76

Design: 50k, Grus grus.

1991, Nov. 21 Litho. ***Perf. 14***

403 A76	30k +15k multi	.65	.55
404 A76	50k multicolored	.75	.65

White Knight Type of 1991

1991, Dec. 20 Photo. ***Perf. 14***
Background Colors

411 A67	40k black	.20	.20
412 A67	50k purple	.20	.20
415 A67	100k dark green	.25	.25
418 A67	500k blue	.90	.55
	Nos. 411-418 (4)	1.55	1.20

For surcharges see Nos. 450-452.

A78

A79

1992, Mar. 15 Litho. ***Perf. 13x13½***

421 A78 100k multicolored .30 .30

Lithuanian admission to UN.

1992, Mar. 22

Emblems.

422 A79	50k +25k Olympic Committee	.30	.30
423 A79	130k Albertville	.45	.45
424 A79	280k Barcelona	1.25	1.25
	Nos. 422-424 (3)	2.00	2.00

Lithuanian Olympic participation. Surtax for Lithuanian Olympic Committee.

A80

A81

1992, July 11 ***Perf. 12½x13***

425 A80	200k Cypripedium	.30	.30
426 A80	300k Eringium maritimum	.50	.50

Litho. & Engr.

1992, Oct. 3 ***Perf. 12½x13***

Birds of the Baltic Shores: No. 427, Pandion haliaetus. No. 428, Limosa limosa. No. 429, Mergus merganser. No. 430, Tadorna tadorna.

Booklet Stamps

427 A81	B grn & grnsh blk	.70	.50
428 A81	B grn & red brn	.70	.50
429 A81	B grn, red brn & brn	.70	.50
430 A81	B grn & red brn	.70	.50
a.	Booklet pane of 4, #427-430	3.50	

Sold for 15r on day of issue.
See Estonia Nos. 231-234a, Latvia Nos. 332-335a and Sweden Nos. 1975-1978a.

Coats of Arms — A82

19th Cent. Costumes — A83

1992, Oct. 11 Litho. ***Perf. 14***

431 A82	2r Kedainiai	.20	.20
432 A82	3r Vilnius	.20	.20
433 A82	10r National	.55	.55
	Nos. 431-433 (3)	.95	.95

See Nos. 454-456, 497-499, 521-522, 554-556, 586-588, 607-609, 642-644, 677-679, 704-706, 716-718, 736-740, 762-764, 788-789, 813-815, 833-835, 879-881, 887-889.

1992, Oct. 18 ***Perf. 13x13½***

Couples in different traditional costumes of the Suwalki region.

434 A83	2r multicolored	.20	.20
435 A83	5r multicolored	.25	.25
436 A83	7r multicolored	.40	.35
	Nos. 434-436 (3)	.85	.80

See #465-467, 493-495, 511-513, 539-541.

Churches — A84

300k, Zapishkis Church, 16th cent. 1000k, Saints Peter & Paul Church, Vilnius, 17th cent. 1500k, Christ Church of the Resurrection, Kaunas, 1934.

1993, Jan. 15 Litho. ***Perf. 12***

437 A84	300k bister & blk	.20	.20
438 A84	1000k blue green & blk	.30	.20
439 A84	1500k gray & blk	.50	.30
	Nos. 437-439 (3)	1.00	.70

See Nos. 502-504

Independence — A85

Designs: A, Jonas Basanavicius (1851-1927), journalist and politician. B, Jonas Vileisis (1872-1942), lawyer and politician.

1993, Feb. 16

440 A85 (A) red & multi .25 .20
441 A85 (B) green & multi .95 .65

No. 440 sold for 3r and No. 441 sold for 15r on day of issue.

See Nos. 479-480, 506-507, 536-537, 563-564, 592-593, 622-623, 660-661, 686-687, 711-712.

A86

Grand Duke Vytautas, 600th Birth Anniv. — A87

Designs: 500k, Royal Seal. 1000k, 5000k, Portrait. 1500k, Vytautas in Battle of Grunwald, by Jan Matejko.

1993, Feb. 27

442 A86 500k bister, red & blk .20 .20
443 A87 1000k citron, blk & red .40 .30
444 A87 1500k lem, blk & red .60 .50
Nos. 442-444 (3) 1.20 1.00

Souvenir Sheet

445 A87 5000k citron, black & red 1.60 1.60

Famous Lithuanians A88

Designs: 1000k, Simonas Daukantas (1793-1864), educator and historian. 2000k, Vydunas (1868-1953), preserver of Lithuanian traditional culture. 4500k, Vincas Mykolaitis Putinas (1893-1967), philosopher and psychologist.

1993, Mar. 13

446 A88 1000k multicolored .25 .25
447 A88 2000k multicolored .50 .50
448 A88 4500k multicolored 1.00 .90
Nos. 446-448 (3) 1.75 1.65

See Nos. 475-477, 514-516, 533-535, 560-562, 599-601, 624-626.

No. 382, 387 and 411 Surcharged

1993 Photo, Litho. (#451) Perf. 14

450 A67 100k on 30k magenta .20 .20
451 A67 100k on 30k magenta, imperf, without gum .20 .20
452 A67 300k on 40k #411 .20 .20
Nos. 450-452 (3) .60 .60

Issued: 300k, 1/19; #450, 1/26; #451, 3/10.

Coat of Arms Type of 1992

Size: 24x31mm

1993, July 3 Litho. Perf. 11

454 A82 5c Skuodas .20 .20
a. Tete-beche pair .40 .40
455 A82 30c Telsiai .35 .30
a. Tete-beche pair 1.20 .60
456 A82 50c Klaipeda .55 .45
a. Tete-beche pair 1.70 .90
Nos. 454-456 (3) 1.10 .95

World Lithuanian Unity Day — A89

5c, The Spring, by M. K. Ciurlionis. 80c, Capts. Steponas Darius and Stasys Girenas.

1993, July 17 Perf. 13

457 A89 5c multicolored .20 .20
a. Tete-beche pair .30
458 A89 80c multicolored .75 .75
a. Tete-beche pair 2.40

Deaths of Darius and Girenas, 60th anniv. (#458).

Natl. Arms — A90

1993, July 21 Litho. Perf. 13x12½

459 A90 (A) bister & multi .30 .20
460 A90 (B) green & multi .80 .20

No. 459 sold for 5c, No. 460 for 80c on day of issue.

Dated 1992.

Visit of Pope John Paul II — A91

1993, Sept. 3 Litho. Perf. 13½x13

461 A91 60c Kryziu Kalnas .50 .30
462 A91 60c Siluva .50 .30
463 A91 80c Vilnius .70 .35
464 A91 80c Kaunas .70 .35
Nos. 461-464 (4) 2.40 1.30

Natl. Costumes Type of 1992

Couples in different traditional costumes of the Dzukai.

1993, Oct. 30 Litho. Perf. 12

Size: 23x36mm

465 A83 60c multicolored .40 .25
466 A83 80c multicolored .60 .35
467 A83 1 l multicolored 1.00 .45
Nos. 465-467 (3) 2.00 1.05

Lithuanian Postal System, 75th Anniv. — A92

Post offices: No. 468, Klaipeda. No. 469, Kaunas. 80c, Vilnius. 1 l, No. 1.

1993, Nov. 16

468 A92 60c multicolored .40 .20
469 A92 60c multicolored .40 .20
470 A92 80c multicolored .60 .30
471 A92 1 l multicolored .90 .40
Nos. 468-471 (4) 2.30 1.10

Europa — A93

Endangered Species — A94

80c, The Old Master, by A. Gudaitis, 1939.

1993, Dec. 24 Litho. Perf. 12

472 A93 80c multicolored 1.40 1.40
a. Tete-beche pair 3.50 3.50

1993, Dec. 30 Litho. Perf. 12

473 A94 80c Emys orbicularis .60 .30
474 A94 1 l Bufo calamita 1.00 .40

See Nos. 500-501, 519-520.

Famous Lithuanians Type of 1993

Designs: 60c, Kristijonas Donelaitis (1714-80), poet. 80c, Vincas Kudirka (1858-99), physician, writer. 1 l, Maironis (1862-1932), poet.

1994, Mar. 26 Litho. Perf. 12

475 A88 60c multicolored .35 .20
476 A88 80c multicolored .55 .30
477 A88 1 l multicolored .85 .40
Nos. 475-477 (3) 1.75 .90

1994 Winter Olympics, Lillehammer A95

1994, Feb. 11

478 A95 1.10 l multicolored .75 .40

Independence Type of 1993

No. 479, Pres. Antanas Smetona (1874-1944). No. 480, Aleksandras Stulginskis.

1994, Feb. 16

479 A85 1 l red brown & multi .80 .35
480 A85 1 l brown & multi .80 .35

A96

Natl. Arms — A96a

Perf. 12, 13½ (40c), 13½x13 (50c)

1994-97 Litho.

481 A96 5c dark brown .20 .20
482 A96 10c deep violet .20 .20
483 A96 20c dark green .20 .20
484 A96 40c deep rose mag .20 .20
485 A96 50c green blue .30 .20
486 A96a 1 l gray & multi .50 .25
a. Souvenir sheet of 4 3.00 3.00
487 A96a 2 l buff & multi 1.50 .50
488 A96a 3 l green & multi 2.00 .75
Nos. 481-488 (8) 5.10 2.50

Independence, 5th anniv. (#486a).

Issued: 5c, 10c, 4/9/94; 20c, 11/19/94; 2 l, 3 l, 7/23/94; 1 l, 3/11/95; 40c, 5/4/96; 50c, 4/5/97.

This is an expanding set. Numbers may change.

Europa — A97

1994, May 7 Litho. Perf. 12

491 A97 80c Artillery rockets, 17th cent. .70 .40

Souvenir Sheet

100th Postage Stamp — A98

1994, May 21 Litho. Perf. 12

492 A98 10 l multicolored 9.00 9.00

No. 492 sold for 12 l.

Natl. Costumes Type of 1992

Couples in different traditional costumes of Samogitia.

1994, June 25 Litho. Perf. 12

493 A83 5c multicolored .30 .20
494 A83 80c multicolored .60 .25
495 A83 1 l multicolored .70 .30
Nos. 493-495 (3) 1.60 .75

Lithuanian World Song Festival — A99

1994, July 6

496 A99 10c multicolored .25 .20

Coat of Arms Type of 1992

1994, Sept. 10 Litho. Perf. 12

Size: 25x32mm

497 A82 10c Punia .25 .20
498 A82 60c Alytus .45 .20
499 A82 80c Perloja .60 .30
Nos. 497-499 (3) 1.30 .70

Endangered Species Type of 1993

1994, Oct. 22 Litho. Perf. 12

500 A94 20c Nyctalus noctula .30 .20
501 A94 20c Glis glis .30 .20

Church Type of 1993

1994, Nov. 12

502 A84 10c Kaunus, 16th cent. .25 .20
503 A84 60c Kedainiu, 17th cent. .45 .25
504 A84 80c Vilnius, 18th cent. .60 .35
Nos. 502-504 (3) 1.30 .80

Christmas A101

1994, Dec. 3 Litho. Perf. 12

505 A101 20c multicolored .25 .20

Independence Type of 1993

No. 506, Pranas Dovydaitis. No. 507, Steponas Kairys.

1995, Feb. 16 Litho. Perf. 12

506 A85 20c multicolored .20 .20
507 A85 20c multicolored .20 .20

Via Baltica Highway Project — A102

No. 509: a, Parnu. b, Bauska. c, Like #508.

1995, Apr. 20 Litho. *Perf. 14*

508 A102 20c multicolored .20 .20

Souvenir Sheet

509 A102 1 l Sheet of 3, #a.-c. 2.25 2.25

See Estonia Nos. 288-289, Latvia Nos. 394-395.

Sculpture, Mother's School — A103

1995, Apr. 29 Litho. *Perf. 12*

510 A103 1 l multicolored 1.40 1.40

Europa.

Natl. Costumes Type of 1992

Couples in traditional costumes of Aukstaiciai.

1995, May 20 Litho. *Perf. 12*

511 A83 20c multicolored .25 .20
512 A83 70c multicolored .60 .25
513 A83 1 l multicolored .75 .30
Nos. 511-513 (3) 1.60 .75

Europa.

Famous People Type of 1993

Writers: 30c, Motiejus Valancius (1801-75). 40c, Zemaite (1845-1921). 70c, Kipras Petrauskas (1885-1968).

1995, May 27 Litho. *Perf. 12*

514 A88 30c multicolored .20 .20
515 A88 40c multicolored .40 .20
516 A88 70c multicolored .60 .25
Nos. 514-516 (3) 1.20 .65

A104

A105

1995, June 14 Litho. *Perf. 12*

517 A104 20c multicolored .25 .20

Day of mourning & hope.

1995, July 30 Litho. *Perf. 12*

518 A105 30c multicolored .25 .20

5th World Sports Games.

Endangered Species Type of 1993

1995, Aug. 26 Litho. *Perf. 12*

519 A94 30c Arctia villica .25 .20
520 A94 30c Baptria tibiale .25 .20

Coat of Arms Type of 1992

Size: 25x32mm

Arms of villages in Suvalkija: 40c, Virbalis. 1 l, Kudirkos Naumiestis, horiz.

1995, Sept. 16 Litho. *Perf. 12*

521 A82 40c multicolored .30 .20
522 A82 1 l multicolored .90 .30

Valerie Mesalina, by Pranciskus Smuglevicius — A106

1995, Oct. 6 Litho. *Perf. 12½*

523 A106 40c multicolored .35 .20

Castles — A107

1995, Nov. 18 *Perf. 11½x12*

524 A107 40c Vilnius .30 .20
525 A107 70c Trakai .60 .30
526 A107 1 l Birzai .90 .45
Nos. 524-526 (3) 1.80 .95

Christmas A108

Designs: 40c, People celebrating Christmas in outdoor snow scene. 1 l, People with lanterns walking toward church.

1995, Dec. 2 Litho. *Perf. 13*

527 A108 40c multicolored .30 .20
528 A108 1 l multicolored .90 .45

Bison Bonasus A109

1996, Jan. 20 *Perf. 13x13½*

529 A109 30c shown .25 .25
530 A109 40c Two adults .40 .25
531 A109 70c Adult, calf .75 .40
532 A109 1 l Two adults, calf 1.00 1.00
a. Miniature sheet, 2 each #529-532 4.50 4.50
Nos. 529-532 (4) 2.40 1.90

World Wildlife Fund.

Famous Lithuanians Type of 1993

Designs: 40c, Kazys Grinius (1866-1950). No. 534, Antanas Zmudzinavicius (1876-1966). No. 535, Balys Sruoga (1896-1947).

1996, Feb. 2 Litho. *Perf. 13x13½*

533 A88 40c multicolored .20 .20
534 A88 1 l multicolored .65 .30
535 A88 1 l multicolored .65 .30
Nos. 533-535 (3) 1.50 .80

Independence Type of 1993

#536, Vladas Mironas. #537, Jurgis Saulys.

1996, Feb. 16 Litho. *Perf. 13½x13*

536 A85 40c gray, blk & buff .30 .20
537 A85 40c olive, blk & buff .30 .20

Barbora Radvilaite (1520-51) — A110

1996, Apr. 27 Litho. *Perf. 13½x13*

538 A110 1 l multicolored 1.50 1.50

Europa.

19th Cent. Costumes Type of 1992

Couples in different traditional costumes of the Klaipeda region: No. 540, Man in blue coat. No. 541, Man wearing wooden shoes.

1996, May 25 Litho. *Perf. 13½*

539 A83 40c multicolored .35 .20
540 A83 1 l multicolored .75 .35
541 A83 1 l multicolored .75 .35
Nos. 539-541 (3) 1.85 .90

A116

A117

1996, June 14 Litho. *Perf. 13½*

547 A116 40c Christ .35 .20
548 A116 40c Angel .35 .20

Day of Mourning and Hope.

1996, July 19 *Perf. 13½x13*

Designs: No. 549, Greek discus thrower. No. 550, Basketball players.

549 A117 1 l multicolored 1.00 .50
550 A117 1 l multicolored 1.00 .50

1996 Summer Olympic Games, Atlanta.

Paintings, by M.K. Ciurlionis — A118

No. 551, Kapines, 1909. No. 552, Auka, 1909.

No. 553: a, Andante, 1908. b, Allegro, 1908.

1996, Sept. 21 Litho. *Perf. 13½x13*

551 A118 40c multicolored .35 .20
552 A118 40c multicolored .35 .20

Souvenir Sheet

Perf. 12½x11½

553 A118 3 l Sheet of 2, #a.-b. 5.00 5.00

No. 553 contains 26x53mm stamps.

Coat of Arms Type of 1992

Size: 25x33mm

1996, Oct. 19 Litho. *Perf. 13½x13*

554 A82 50c Seduva .45 .20
555 A82 90c Panevezys .70 .35
556 A82 1.20 l Zarasai 1.00 .50
Nos. 554-556 (3) 2.15 1.05

Souvenir Sheet

Lithuanian Basketball Team, Bronze Medalists, 1996 Summer Olympic Games, Atlanta — A119

1996, Nov. 16 *Perf. 12½*

557 A119 4.20 l multicolored 3.50 3.50

Christmas A120

1996, Nov. 30 *Perf. 13½x13*

558 A120 50c Angels .35 .20
559 A120 1.20 l Santa on horse 1.00 .50

Famous Lithuanians Type of 1993

Designs: 50c, Ieva Simonaityte (1897-1978). 90c, Jonas Sliupas (1861-1944). 1.20 l, Vladas Jurgutis (1885-1966).

1997, Jan. 23 Litho. *Perf. 13x13½*

560 A88 50c brown & greem .40 .20
561 A88 90c gray & yellow .70 .35
562 A88 1.20 l blue green & orange .90 .45
Nos. 560-562 (3) 2.00 1.00

Independence Type of 1993

No. 563, Mykolas Birziska. No. 564, Kazimieras Saulys.

1997, Feb. 16 Litho. *Perf. 13½x13*

563 A85 50c multicolored .40 .25
564 A85 50c multicolored .40 .25

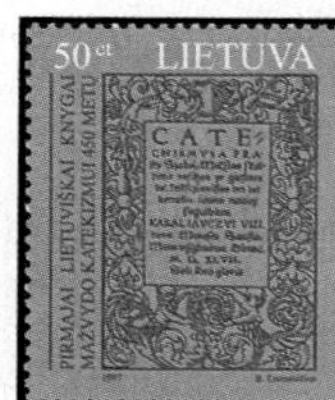

First Lithuanian Book, 450th Anniv. — A121

1997, Feb. 15 Litho. *Perf. 13½x13*

565 A121 50c gray & red .45 .25

Souvenir Sheet

566 A121 4.80 l like #565 3.50 3.50

No. 566 contains one 29x38mm stamp.

Souvenir Sheet

Flag on Mountain Top — A122

1997, Feb. 25 *Perf. 11½x12½*
567 A122 4.80 l multicolored 4.00 4.00

Expeditions to highest peaks on each continent.

Stories and Legends A123

Children's drawings: No. 568, Girl, horse. No. 569, King, moon, stars, bird, vert.

1997, Apr. 12 **Litho.** *Perf. 13*
568 A123 1.20 l multicolored 1.25 1.25
569 A123 1.20 l multicolored 1.25 1.25

Europa.

A124

A125

1997, May 9 **Litho.** *Perf. 13*
570 A124 50c multicolored .45 .25

First Lithuanian School, 600th Anniv.

1997, May 10 *Perf. 14x14½*

Old Ships of the Baltic Sea: 50c, Kurenas, 16th cent.

No. 572: a, Kurenas, 16th cent., diff. b, Maasilinn ship, 16th cent. c, Linijkugis, 17th cent.

571 A125 50c multicolored .45 .25
572 A125 1.20 l Sheet of 3, #a.-c. 3.00 3.00

See Estonia Nos. 322-323, Latvia Nos. 443-444.

Palanga Botanical Park, Cent. — A126

1997, June 1 **Litho.** *Perf. 13½x13*
573 A126 50c multicolored .45 .25
a. Tete-beche pair .90 .90

Numbers 574-577 are unassigned.

2nd Baltic Sea Games — A127

1997, June 25 **Litho.** *Perf. 13½*
578 A127 90c multicolored .75 .35

Museum Art A128

Designs: 90c, Animal face carved on ritual staff. 1.20 l, Coins, 15th cent.

1997, July 12 *Perf. 13½x13*
579 A128 90c multicolored .75 .35
580 A128 1.20 l multicolored 1.00 .50

Double Barred Crosses A129

Mushrooms A130

1997, Aug. 2 **Litho.** *Perf. 13½*
581 A129 20c olive .25 .20
582 A129 50c brown .35 .20
a. Inscribed "1998" .35 .20

Nos. 581 and 582 are inscribed "1997." See Nos. 602, 604, 617-619.

1997, Sept. 20 **Litho.** *Perf. 13½x13*

Designs: No. 583, Morchella elata. No. 584, Boletus aereus.

583 A130 1.20 l multicolored 1.00 .50
a. Tete-beche pair 2.00 2.00
584 A130 1.20 l multicolored 1.00 .50
a. Tete-beche pair 2.00 2.00

Letters of Grand Duke Gediminas A131

1997, Oct. 4 *Perf. 14*
585 A131 50c multicolored .45 .25

Coat of Arms Type of 1992

Size: 25x33mm

1997, Oct. 18 **Litho.** *Perf. 13½x13*
586 A82 50c Neringa .40 .20
587 A82 90c Vilkaviskis .70 .35
588 A82 1.20 l Pasvalys .90 .45
Nos. 586-588 (3) 2.00 1.00

Christmas and New Year — A132

1997, Nov. 22 **Litho.** *Perf. 13*
589 A132 50c shown .40 .20
590 A132 1.20 l Snow on trees 1.00 .50

1998 Winter Olympic Games, Nagano — A133

1998, Jan. 17 **Litho.** *Perf. 14*
591 A133 1.20 l multicolored 1.00 .45
a. Tete-beche pair 2.00 2.00

Independence Type of 1993 and

Declaration of Independence — A134

Designs: 50c, Alfonsas Petrulis. 90c, Jokubas Sernas.

Perf. 13½x12½

1998, Feb. 16 **Litho.**
592 A85 50c olive and black .35 .20
593 A85 90c brown and black .85 .40

Souvenir Sheet

Perf. 12½x11½

594 A134 6.60 l multicolored 5.25 5.25

Independence, 80th anniv.

Souvenir Sheet

National Anthem, Cent. — A135

1998, Feb. 16 *Perf. 12½*
595 A135 5.20 l multicolored 4.25 4.25

Antanas Gustaitis, Aviator, Birth Cent. A136

Designs: 2 l, Portrait of Gustaitis, ANBO 41. 3 l, Design drawings, ANBO-VIII.

1998, Mar. 27 **Litho.** *Perf. 14*
596 A136 2 l multicolored 1.75 .85
597 A136 3 l multicolored 2.25 1.10

Natl. Song Festival — A137

1998, Apr. 18 *Perf. 13½*
598 A137 1.20 l multicolored 1.75 1.75
a. Tete-beche pair 3.75 3.75

Europa.

Famous Lithuanians Type of 1993

50c, Tadas Ivanauskas (1882-1971), scientist. #600, Jurgis Baltrusaitis (1873-1944), writer, Jurgis Baltrusaitis (1903-88), historian. #601, Stasys Lozoraitis (1898-1983), Stasys Lozoraitis (1924-94), politicians.

1998, Apr. 25 *Perf. 13x13½*
599 A88 50c multicolored .40 .20

Size: 45x26mm

600 A88 90c multicolored .70 .35
601 A88 90c multicolored .70 .35
Nos. 599-601 (3) 1.80 .90

Double-Barred Crosses Type of 1997

1998, June 1 **Litho.** *Perf. 13½*
602 A129 70c yellow bister .60 .30
a. Inscribed "1999" .75 .30

No. 602 is inscribed "1998."

2nd Lithuanian Olympic Games, 6th World Lithuanian Games A138

1998, June 23 *Perf. 14*
603 A138 1.35 l multicolored 1.10 .55
a. Tete beche pair 2.25 2.25

Double-Barred Crosses Type of 1997

1998, July 4 **Litho.** *Perf. 13½*
604 A129 35c plum & pink .30 .20

Red Book of Lithuania A139

Fish: No. 605, Coregonus lavaretus holsatus. No. 606, Salmo salar.

1998, July 11 *Perf. 13x13½*
605 A139 1.40 l multicolored 1.10 .55
606 A139 1.40 l multicolored 1.10 .55

Coat of Arms Type of 1992

Size: 25x33mm

1998, Sept. 12 **Litho.** *Perf. 13*
607 A82 70c Kernave .55 .25
608 A82 70c Trakai .55 .25
609 A82 1.35 l Kaunas 1.10 .55
Nos. 607-609 (3) 2.20 1.05

Vilnius-Cracow Post Route Established, 1562 — A141

1998, Oct. 9 **Litho.** *Perf. 14*
611 A141 70c multicolored .60 .30

Souvenir Sheet

Lithuanian Post, 80th Anniv. — A142

1998, Oct. 9 Litho. *Perf. 12*

612 A142 13 l multicolored 11.00 11.00

No. 612 contains a holographic image. Soaking in water may affect the hologram.

Museum Paintings — A143

70c, "Through the Night," by Antanas Zmuidzinavicius (1876-1966). 1.35 l, "The Garden of Bernardines, Vilnius," by Juozapas Marsevskis (1825-83).

1998, Oct. 17 Litho. *Perf. 13½x13*

613 A143 70c multicolored .60 .30

614 A143 1.35 l multicolored 1.00 .50

New Year — A144

Christmas: 1.35 l, Winter scene, people walking through giant tree, village.

1998, Nov. 14 Litho. *Perf. 12½*

615 A144 70c multicolored .50 .25

616 A144 1.35 l multicolored 1.10 .55

Double-Barred Crosses Type of 1997

1998, Nov. 14 Litho. *Perf. 13½*

617 A129 5c lt & dk citron .25 .20

a. Inscribed "1999" .25 .20

618 A129 10c tan & brown .25 .20

a. Inscribed "1999" .25 .20

619 A129 20c lt & dk olive green .25 .20

a. Inscribed "1999" .25 .20

Nos. 617-619 (3) .75 .60

Nos. 617-619 inscribed "1998."

Adam Mickiewicz (1798-1855), Poet — A145

1998, Dec. 24 *Perf. 14*

620 A145 70c multicolored .60 .30

a. Tete beche pair 1.25 1.25

Souvenir Sheet

Publication of "Postile," by M. Dauksa (1527-1613), 400th Anniv. — A146

1999, Jan. 23 Litho. *Perf. 12½*

621 A146 5.90 l brown & gray 5.00 5.00

Independence Type of 1993

Designs: No. 622, Petras Klimas. No. 623, Donatas Malinauskas.

Perf. 13½x12½

1999, Feb. 16 Litho.

622 A85 70c red & black .60 .30

623 A85 70c blue & black .60 .30

Famous Lithuanians Type of 1993

Designs: No. 624, Juozas Matulis (1899-1993). No. 625, Augustinas Gricius (1899-1972). 1.35 l, Pranas Skardzius (1899-1975).

1999, Mar. 19 Litho. *Perf. 13*

624 A88 70c multicolored .60 .30

625 A88 70c multicolored .60 .30

626 A88 1.35 l multicolored 1.10 .55

Nos. 624-626 (3) 2.30 1.15

NATO, 50th Anniv. — A147

1999, Mar. 27 Litho. *Perf. 13¾x14*

627 A147 70c multicolored .60 .30

National Parks — A148

Europa: No. 628, Traditional homes, lake, islands, Aukstaitija Natl. Park. No. 629, Sand dunes, amber, Curonian Spit Natl. Park.

1999, Apr. 10 Litho. *Perf. 13x13¼*

628 A148 1.35 l multicolored 1.40 1.40

629 A148 1.35 l multicolored 1.40 1.40

Council of Europe, 50th Anniv. — A149

1999, May 1 Litho. *Perf. 14*

630 A149 70c multicolored .60 .30

Melniai Windmill — A150

1999, May 8 Litho. *Perf. 14*

631 A150 70c shown .70 .35

632 A150 70c Pumpenai Windmill .70 .35

Bees — A151

Designs: 70c, Dasypoda argentata. 2 l, Bombus pomorum.

1999, June 12 *Perf. 13¼x13*

633 A151 70c multicolored .70 .35

634 A151 2 l multicolored 1.60 .80

UPU, 125th Anniv. A152

1999, July 3 Litho. *Perf. 14*

635 A152 70c multicolored .60 .30

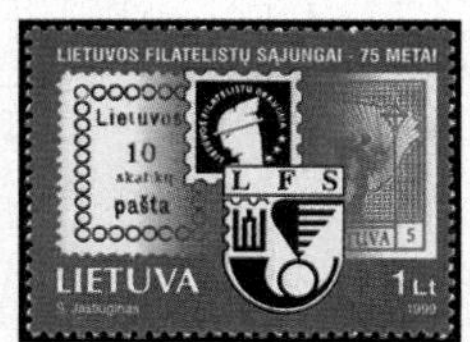

Lithuanian Philatelic Society Emblems, No. 1, Pre-independence Stamp — A153

1999, July 31 Litho. *Perf. 14*

636 A153 1 l multicolored .90 .50

Complete booklet, 10 #636 10.00

Lithuanian Philatelic Society, 75th Anniv.

Souvenir Sheet

Centenary of First Performance of Play, "America in the Baths" — A154

Designs: a, Producers. b, Theater poster.

1999, Aug. 20 Litho. *Perf. 12½*

637 A154 4 l Sheet of 2, #a.-b. 5.00 5.00

A155

A156

Baltic Chain, 10th Anniv. — Family and flags: 1 l, No. 640a, Lithuanian.
No. 640: b, Estonian. c, Latvian.

1999, Aug. 23 Litho. *Perf. 12¾*

639 A155 1 l multicolored .75 .40

Souvenir Sheet

640 A155 2 l Sheet of 3, #a.-c. 4.00 4.00

See Estonia Nos. 366-367, Latvia Nos. 493-494.

1999, Aug. 28 Litho. *Perf. 14*

641 A156 70c multicolored .50 .25

Freedom fight movement, 50th anniv.

Coat of Arms Type of 1992

Size: 25x33mm

1999, Sept. 18 *Perf. 13½x13*

642 A82 70c Marijampole .50 .25

643 A82 1 l Siaulai .75 .35

644 A82 1.40 l Rokiskis 1.00 .45

Nos. 642-644 (3) 2.25 1.05

Museum Pieces — A157

Designs: 70c, Sword of Gen. S. Zukauskas. 3 l, Hussar armor.

1999, Oct. 9 *Perf. 13¼x13½*

645 A157 70c multicolored .50 .25

646 A157 3 l multicolored 2.00 1.00

A158

A159

1999, Oct. 23 Litho. *Perf. 14*

647 A158 70c multicolored .50 .25

Simonas Stanevicius (1799-1848), writer.

Perf. 12½x13½

1999, Nov. 13 Litho.

648 A159 70c shown .50 .25

649 A159 1.35 l Buildings, candles 1.00 .50

Christmas and New Year's Day.

Lighthouses A198

Designs: 1 l, Pervalka. 3 l, Uostodvaris.

2003, Mar. 15
741-742 A198 Set of 2 3.00 1.50

Europa — A199

2003, Apr. 19 Litho. ***Perf. 13½x13***
743 A199 1.70 l multi 1.50 1.50
a. Tete beche pair 3.25 3.25

Rebuilding of Palace of Lithuania's Rulers — A200

2003, Apr. 26 ***Perf. 12***
744 A200 1 l multi .85 .40

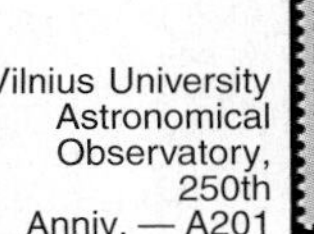
Vilnius University Astronomical Observatory, 250th Anniv. — A201

2003, May 10 ***Perf. 12***
745 A201 1 l multi .85 .40

Insects From Red Book of Lithuania A202

Designs: No. 746, 3 l, Lucanus cervus. No. 747, 3 l, Cerambyx cerdo.

2003, May 24 ***Perf. 13x13½***
746-747 A202 Set of 2 5.00 2.50

Souvenir Sheet

Lithuania, 1000th Anniv. (in 2009) — A203

No. 748: a, Rise of Lithuania, 1183. b, Battle of Siauliai, 1236. c, Coronation of Mindaugas, 1253. d, Selection of Vilnius as capital of Lithuania, 1323.

2003, June 21 ***Perf. 11***
748 A203 2 l Sheet of 4, #a-d, + 2 labels 6.50 3.25

Souvenir Sheet

Coronation of Mindaugas, 750th Anniv. — A204

2003, July 5 ***Perf. 11½x12¼***
749 A204 5 l multi 4.00 2.00

13th European Hot Air Balloon Championships — A205

2003, Aug. 8 ***Perf. 12***
750 A205 1.30 l multi 1.10 .55

Vincentas Cardinal Sladkevicius (1920-2000) A206

2003, Aug. 20
751 A206 1 l multi .85 .40

Panevezys, 500th Anniv. — A207

2003, Sept. 7
752 A207 1 l multi .85 .40

Map of Kaunas-Vilnius-Grodno Postal Route, 1664 — A208

2003, Oct. 4
753 A208 1 l multi .85 .40

Christmas and New Year's Day — A209

Villages at: 1 l, Christmas. 1.70 l, New Year's Eve.

2003, Nov. 8
754-755 A209 Set of 2 2.10 1.00

Souvenir Sheet

Lithuania, 2003 European Men's Basketball Champions — A210

2003, Dec. 6 Litho. ***Perf. 12x11½***
756 A210 5 l multi 4.00 2.00

Gliders in Lithuanian Aviation Museum A211

Designs: No. 757, 1 l, BK-7. No. 758, 1 l, BRO-12.

2003, Dec. 17 ***Perf. 12***
757-758 A211 Set of 2 1.60 .80

Famous Lithuanians Type of 2002

Designs: No. 759, 1 l, Jonas Aistis (1904-73), poet. No. 760, 1 l, Kazimieras Buga (1879-1924), philologist. No. 761, Adolfas Jucys (1904-74), physicist.

2004, Jan. 24 Litho. ***Perf. 12***
759-761 A185 Set of 3 2.50 1.25

Coat of Arms Type of 1992

Designs: 1 l, Mazeikiai. 1.30 l, Radviliskis. 1.40 l, Ukmerge.

2004, Feb. 14
Size: 25x33mm
762-764 A82 Set of 3 3.00 1.50

Vilnius University, 425th Anniv. — A213

2004, Mar. 20
765 A213 1 l multi .85 .40

Europa — A214

Designs: No. 766, 1.70 l, Sailboat. No. 767, 1.70 l, Beach umbrella.

2004, Apr. 10 Litho. ***Perf. 12***
766-767 A214 Set of 2 3.00 3.00

Return to Printing Lithuanian in Latin Letters, Cent. A215

2004, May 1 Litho. ***Perf. 12***
768 A215 1.30 l multi 1.00 .50

Admission to European Union — A216

No. 769: a, Stars, flags of newly-added countries, map of Europe. b, Stars and Lithuanian flag, map and arms.

2004, May 1
769 A216 1.70 l Horiz. pair, #a-b 2.50 1.25

FIFA (Fédération Internationale de Football Association), Cent. A217

2004, May 15
770 A217 3 l multi 2.25 1.10

Chiune Sugihara (1900-86), Japanese Diplomat Who Issued Transit Visas to Jews in World War II — A218

2004, June 19 Litho. ***Perf. 12***
771 A218 1 l multi .85 .40

Souvenir Sheet

Lithuania, 1000th Anniv. — A219

No. 772: a, Defense of Pilenai Castle, 1336. b, Battle at the Blue Waters, 1362. c, Christening of Lithuania, 1387. d, Battle of Zalgiris, 1410.

2004, July 3 ***Perf. 11***
772 A219 2 l Sheet of 4, #a-d, + 2 labels 6.00 3.00

Exhibits in Tadas Ivanauskas Zoology Museum, Kaunas — A220

No. 773: a, Aquila chrysaetos. b, Iguana iguana.

2004, July 10 ***Perf. 12***
773 A220 1 l Horiz. pair, #a-b 1.60 .80

2004 Summer Olympics, Athens
A221

2004 Olympic emblem and: 2 l, Pentathlon equestrian event. 3 l, Canoeing.

2004, July 31
774-775 A221 Set of 2 4.00 2.00

Owls From Red Book of Lithuania — A222

Designs: 1.30 l, Bubo bubo. 3 l, Asio flammeus.

2004, Oct. 2 Litho. ***Perf. 12***
776-777 A222 Set of 2 3.50 1.75

Kaunas Funiculars
A223

Designs: 1 l, Aleksotas Funicular. 1.30 l, Zaliakalnis Funicular.

2004, Oct. 16
778-779 A223 Set of 2 1.90 .95

Christmas
A224

Stars and: 1 l, Christmas tree. 1.70 l, Bird.

2004, Nov. 6
780-781 A224 Set of 2 2.00 2.00

Famous Lithuanians Type of 2002

Designs: No. 782, 1 l, Kazys Boruta (1905-65), writer. No. 783, 1 l, Petras Kalpokas (1880-1945), painter. No. 784, 1 l, Jonas Puzinas (1905-78), archaeologist.

2005, Jan. 8 Litho. ***Perf. 12***
782-784 A185 Set of 3 2.25 2.25

Congratulations
A225

Designs: No. 785, 1 l, Gerbera daisies, freesias and scroll. No. 786, 1 l, Lilies, freesias and box.

Serpentine Die Cut 6¾
2005, Jan. 29 Litho.
Booklet Stamps
Self-Adhesive
785-786 A225 Set of 2 1.50 1.50
786a Booklet pane, 4 each #785-786 6.00

Sartai Horse Race, Cent.
A226

2005, Feb. 5 ***Perf. 12***
787 A226 1 l multi .75 .75

Coat of Arms Type of 1992

Designs: No. 788, 1 l, Druskininkai. No. 789, 1 l, Vabalninkas.

2005, Mar. 5 **Size: 25x33mm**
788-789 A82 Set of 2 1.60 1.60

Europa
A227

Designs: No. 790, 1.70 l, Cow, cheese. No. 791, 1.70 l, Loaf of black bread.

2005, Apr. 9 Litho. ***Perf. 12***
790-791 A227 Set of 2 3.00 3.00

National Museum, 150th Anniv. — A228

No. 792: a, Brass jewelry, 1st-2nd cent. b, Illustration of first exhibition in Aula Hall, Vilnius University.

2005, May 7
792 A228 1 l Pair, #a-b 1.40 1.40

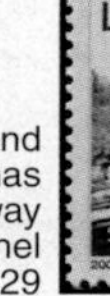

Train and Kaunas Railway Tunnel
A229

2005, June 11
793 A229 3 l multi 2.10 2.10

Souvenir Sheet

Lithuania, 1000th Anniv. — A230

No. 794: a, Battle of Pabaiskas, 1435. b, Valakai Reform, 1557. c, First Lithuanian statute, 1529. d, Union of Lublin, 1569.

2005, July 2 ***Perf. 11***
794 A230 2 l Sheet of 4, #a-d, + 2 labels 6.00 6.00

90th World Esperanto Congress, Vilnius
A231

2005, July 23 Litho. ***Perf. 12***
795 A231 1 l multi .75 .75

Churches
A232

Designs: 1 l, Vilnius Evangelical Lutheran Church. 1.30 l, St. Casimir Church, Vilnius.

2005, Sept. 3 ***Perf. 13½***
796-797 A232 Set of 2 1.75 1.75

Flora and Fauna from Red Book of Lithuania — A233

No. 798: a, Gavia arctica. b, Trapa natans.

2005, Sept. 10
798 A233 1 l Horiz. pair, #a-b 1.50 1.50

Souvenir Sheet

Mikolajus Konstantinas Ciurlionis (1875-1911), Painter and Composer — A234

No. 799 — Details from Sonata of the Sea triptych: a, Allegro. b, Andante. c, Finale.

2005, Sept. 24 ***Perf. 14***
799 A234 2 l Sheet of 3, #a-c, + label 4.50 4.50

Map of St. Petersburg-Warsaw Post Road, 1830-36 — A235

2005, Oct. 8 Litho. ***Perf. 14¼x14***
800 A235 1 l multi .75 .75

Christmas
A236

Designs: 1 l, Candle and snow-covered evergreen branch. 1.70 l, Santa Claus in sleigh.

2005, Nov. 5 ***Perf. 12¾x13***
801-802 A236 Set of 2 1.90 1.90

Dr. Jonas Basanavicius, Vilnius City Hall and Commemorative Medal — A237

2005, Dec. 3 ***Perf. 14¼x14***
803 A237 1 l multi .75 .75

Congress of Lithuanians, cent.

2006 Winter Olympics, Turin — A238

2006, Jan. 28 Litho. ***Perf. 14x14¼***
804 A238 1.70 l multi 1.25 1.25

Famous Lithuanians Type of 2002

Designs: No. 805, 1 l, Adolfas Sapoka (1906-61), historian. No. 806, 1 l, Petras Rimsa (1881-1961), sculptor. No. 807, 1 l, Antanas Vaiciulaitis (1906-92), writer.

2006, Feb. 11 ***Perf. 13½***
805-807 A185 Set of 3 2.10 2.10

Vilnius Album, by Jonas K. Vilcinskis, 160th Anniv. of Publication
A239

2006, Feb. 25 ***Perf. 13x12¾***
808 A239 1 l multi .70 .70

Social Insurance System, 80th Anniv.
A240

2006, Mar. 18 ***Perf. 14¼x14***
809 A240 1 l multi .70 .70

Lithuanian Theater, Music and Cinema Museum, 80th Anniv. — A241

No. 810: a, Parvo camera, 1930s. b, Music box, 1900.

2006, Mar. 18 ***Perf. 13½***
810 A241 1 l Pair, #a-b 1.40 1.40

Printed in sheets containing 10 of each stamp + 5 labels. Each sheet contains se-tenant pairs of the same stamp.

Europa A242

Designs: No. 811, 1.70 l, Woman dancing with man in wheelchair. No. 812, 1.70 l, People in wheelchairs being pushed around track.

2006, Apr. 15
811-812 A242 Set of 2 3.00 3.00

Coat of Arms Type of 1992

Designs: No. 813, 1 l, Kupiskis. No. 814, 1 l, Sakiai. No. 815, 1 l, Silute.

2006, May 13 ***Perf. 14x14¼***
Size: 25x33mm
813-815 A82 Set of 3 2.25 2.25

Souvenir Sheet

Lithuania, 1000th Anniv. — A243

No. 816: a, Establishment of Vilnius University, 1579. b, Truce of Andrusov, 1667. c, Four-year Sejm, 1788. d, Uprising of 1794.

2006, July 1 ***Perf. 11***
816 A243 2 l Sheet of 4, #a-d, + 2 labels 6.00 6.00

Basilicas A244

Designs: 1 l, Vilnius Basilica. 1.70 l, Kaunas Basilica.

2006, Aug. 5 ***Perf. 12¾x13***
817-818 A244 Set of 2 2.00 2.00

Birds and Fish From Red Book of Lithuania A245

No. 819: a, Polysticta stelleri. b, Acipenser sturio.

2006, Sept. 16 ***Perf. 13½***
819 A245 1 l Vert. pair, #a-b 1.50 1.50

Establishment of Lithuania Post and First Postage Stamps, 1918 — A246

2006, Oct. 7 ***Perf. 14¼x14***
820 A246 1 l multi .75 .75

Premiere of Opera "Birute," Cent. — A247

2006, Nov. 4 Litho. ***Perf. 13¼x12¾***
821 A247 2 l multi 1.60 1.60

Christmas A248

Designs: 1 l, Birds, triangular window. 1.70 l, Trees, star, berries, straw.

2006, Nov. 18 ***Perf. 12¾x13¼***
822-823 A248 Set of 2 2.10 2.10

18th Century Wooden Church Belfries — A249

Belfries from churches in: 10c, Pasvalys. 20c, Rozalimas. 50c, Tryskiai. 1 l, Saukenai. 1.30 l, Vaiguva. 1.70 l, Vajasiskis.

Die Cut Perf. 12½
2007, Jan. 1 Litho.
Self-Adhesive

824	A249	10c blue & blk	.20	.20
825	A249	20c org & blk	.20	.20
826	A249	50c bl grn & blk	.40	.40
a.		Dated 2009	.40	.40
827	A249	1 l brn & blk	.80	.80
a.		Dated 2009	.80	.80
828	A249	1.30 l lil & blk	1.00	1.00
829	A249	1.70 l ol brn & blk	1.40	1.40
		Nos. 824-829 (6)	4.00	4.00

Issued: Nos. 826a, 827a, 2/21/09.
See Nos. 842-846.

Famous Lithuanians Type of 2002

Designs: No. 830, 1 l, Bernardas Brazdzionis (1907-2002), writer. No. 831, 1 l, Vytautas Kazimieras Jonynas (1907-97), artist. 3 l, Leonas Sapiega (1557-1633), state chancellor of the Grand Duchy of Lithuania.

2007, Jan. 27 ***Perf. 13½***
830-832 A185 Set of 3 3.75 3.75

Coat of Arms Type of 1992

Designs: 1 l, Svencionys. 1.30 l, Kelme. 2 l, Moletai.

2007, Mar. 3 ***Perf. 14x14¼***
Size: 25x33mm
833-835 A82 Set of 3 3.25 3.25

Europa A250

Designs: No. 836, 1.70 l, Scouting flag, musical score. No. 837, 1.70 l, Symbols of Lithuanian Scouts.

2007, Apr. 14 Litho. ***Perf. 13½***
836-837 A250 Set of 2 2.75 2.75

Scouting, cent.

Churches A251

Designs: 1 l, St. Anne's and Bernardine Churches, Vilnius. 1.30 l, Church buildings, Pazaislis.

2007, May 12 ***Perf. 12¾x13***
838-839 A251 Set of 2 2.10 2.10

Souvenir Sheet

Lithuania, 1000th Anniv. — A252

No. 840: a, Publication of first Lithuanian newspaper, "Ausra," 1883. b, Abolition of the prohibition on printing in Latin characters, 1904. c, Great Seimas of Vilnius, 1905. d, Lithuanian Declaration of Independence, 1918.

2007, June 23 Litho. ***Perf. 11***
840 A252 3 l Sheet of 4, #a-d, + 2 labels 9.50 9.50

Trakai History Museum — A253

No. 841: a, Map of New Trakai in 1600, by J. Kamarauskas. b, Chess pieces, 15th cent.

2007, July 28 Litho. ***Perf. 13½***
841 A253 2 l Pair, #a-b 3.25 3.25

Printed in sheets containing 10 of each stamp + 5 labels.

Wooden Church Belfries Type of 2007

Belfries from churches in: 5c, Vabalininkas, 19th cent. 35c, Varputenai, 18th cent. 1.35 l, Deguciai, 19th cent. 1.55 l, Geidziai, 19th cent. 2.15 l, Pavandenes, 17th cent.

Die Cut Perf. 12½
2007, Sept. 1 Litho.
Self-Adhesive

842	A249	5c yel grn & blk	.20	.20
843	A249	35c gray & blk	.30	.30
844	A249	1.35 l yel & blk	1.10	1.10
845	A249	1.55 l brn org & blk	1.25	1.25
846	A249	2.15 l rose lake & blk	1.75	1.75
		Nos. 842-846 (5)	4.60	4.60

Juozas Miltinis (1907-94), Actor and Theater Founder A254

2007, Sept. 1 Litho. ***Perf. 12¾x13***
847 A254 2.45 l multi 2.00 2.00

Birds — A255

No. 848 — Birds of the Cepkeliai Nature Reserve, Lithuania and Katra Sanctuary, Belarus: a, Gallinago media. b, Crex crex.

2007, Oct. 3 ***Perf. 14***
848 Horiz. pair + central label 5.00 5.00
a.-b. A255 2.90 l Either single 2.25 2.25

See Belarus No. 625.

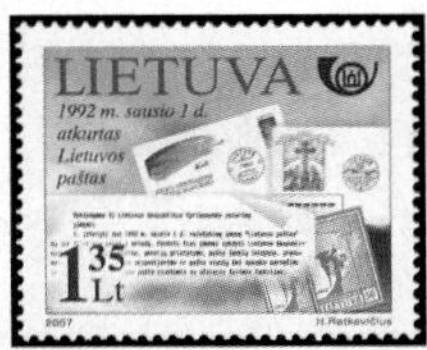

Stamps and Covers From Establishment of Lithuania Post in 1992 — A256

2007, Oct. 6
849 A256 1.35 l multi 1.25 1.25

Christmas A257

Conifer sprigs and: 1.35 l, Snowflake, Christmas ornaments. 2.45 l, Stars, globe.

2007, Nov. 10 ***Perf. 13x12¾***
850-851 A257 Set of 2 3.25 3.25

Wooden Churches — A258

Churches in: 5c, Antazave, 1794. 10c, Deguciai, 1757. 20c, Inturke, 1855. 35c, Prienai, 1750. 1.35 l, Siaudine, 1775. 1.55 l, Uzventis, 1703.

Die Cut Perf. 12½
2008, Jan. 5 Litho.
Self-Adhesive

852	A258	5c multi	.20	.20
853	A258	10c multi	.20	.20
854	A258	20c multi	.20	.20
855	A258	35c multi	.30	.30
856	A258	1.35 l multi	1.10	1.10
857	A258	1.55 l multi	1.25	1.25
		Nos. 852-857 (6)	3.25	3.25

Nos. 853, 854, 856 exist dated "2009."

Famous Lithuanians Type of 2002

Designs: 2 l, Martynas Jankus (1858-1946), publisher. 2.15 l, Zenonas Ivinskis (1908-71), historian. 2.90 l, Antanas Maceina (1908-87), philosopher.

2008, Jan. 19 Litho. ***Perf. 13½***
858-860 A185 Set of 3 6.00 6.00

Restoration of Independence, 90th Anniv. — A259

2008, Feb. 16

861 A259 1.35 l multi 1.25 1.25

State Awards of the Baltic Countries — A260

Designs: Nos. 862, 863a, Order of Vytautas the Great, Lithuania. No. 863b, Order of the National Coat of Arms, Estonia. No. 863c, Order of Three Stars, Latvia.

Perf. 13½x13¾

2008, Mar. 15 **Litho.**

862 A260 7 l multi 6.50 6.50

Souvenir Sheet

863 A260 5 l Sheet of 3, #a-c, + label 14.00 14.00

See Estonia Nos. 592-593, Latvia Nos. 701-702.

Items From Rokiskis Regional Museum — A261

No. 864: a, Wood carving, by Lionginas Sepka. b, 19th cent. women's clothing. Illustration reduced.

2008, Apr. 19 **Litho.** ***Perf. 14***

864 A261 1.55 l Horiz. pair, #a-b 2.75 2.75

Europa A262

Designs: No. 865, 2.45 l, Grand Duke Gediminas and his letters of 1323. No. 866, 2.45 l, Vilnius, 2009 European Cultural Capital.

2008, May 3

865-866 A262 Set of 2 4.00 4.00

Sajudis Party, 20th Anniv. A263

2008, May 31

867 A263 1.35 l multi 1.25 1.25

Expo Zaragoza 2008 — A264

2008, June 7 ***Die Cut Perf. 12½***

Self-Adhesive

868 A264 2.45 l multi 2.25 2.25

Miniature Sheet

Lithuania, 1000th Anniv. — A265

No. 869: a, First Lithuanian Cabinet of Ministers, 1918. b, Consitituent Assembly, 1920. c, Opening of Kaunas University, 1922. d, Occupation of Memel (Klaipeda) by Lithuania, 1923. e, Opening of Zemaiciai Road (man signing document, 1939). f, Return of Vilnius to Lithuania from Poland, 1939.

2008, June 28 ***Perf. 14***

869 A265 3 l Sheet of 6, #a-f 15.00 15.00

Crashed Transatlantic Flight of Captains Steponas Darius and Stasys Girenas, 75th Anniv. — A266

2008, July 12

870 A266 2.90 l multi 2.60 2.60

2008 Summer Olympics, Beijing — A267

Designs: 2.15 l, Women's marathon. 2.45 l, Yachting.

2008, July 26

871-872 A267 Set of 2 4.25 4.25

Apparitions of the Virgin Mary at Siluva, 400th Anniv. — A268

2008, Aug. 30 **Litho.** ***Perf. 14***

873 A268 1.55 l multi 1.40 1.40

Worldwide Fund for Nature (WWF) A269

Coracias garrulus: Nos. 874, 878a, 1.35 l, On branch with beak closed, denomination at LR. Nos. 875, 878b, 1.35 l, In flight. Nos. 876, 878c, 1.35 l, On branch with beak open, denomination at LL. Nos. 877, 878d, 1.35 l, On branch with beak closed, denomination at LL.

2008, Sept. 6 ***Perf. 14***

Stamps With White Frames

874-877 A269 Set of 4 4.50 4.50

Souvenir Sheet

Stamps Without White Frames

878 A269 1.35 l Sheet of 4, #a-d 4.50 4.50

Arms Type of 1992

Designs: No. 879, 1.35 l, Jurbarkas. No. 880, 1.35 l, Joniskis. 3 l, Sirvintos.

2008, Oct. 4 **Litho.**

Size: 26x31mm

879-881 A82 Set of 3 4.50 4.50

Christmas and New Year's Day A270

Designs: 1.35 l, Holiday lights. 2.45 l, Snow-covered evergreen branch.

2008, Nov. 8 ***Perf. 14***

882-883 A270 Set of 2 3.00 3.00

Famous Lithuanians Type of 2002

Designs: 1.35 l, Jonas Zemaitas (1909-54), military officer. 2 l, Vaclovas Birziska (1884-1956), educator and library founder. 2.15 l, Mecislovas Reinys (1884-1953), archbishop.

2009, Jan. 17 **Litho.** ***Perf. 14***

884-886 A185 Set of 3 4.25 4.25

Arms Type of 1992

Designs: No. 887, 1.35 l, Krekenava. No. 888, 1.35 l, Pakruojis. 3 l, Salcininkai.

2009, Feb. 21 **Litho.** ***Perf. 14***

Size: 26x31mm

887-889 A82 Set of 3 4.25 4.25

Souvenir Sheet

Protection of Polar Regions and Glaciers — A271

No. 890 — Glacier with sky in: a, Dark blue. b, Light blue.

2009, Mar. 27

890 A271 2.90 l Sheet of 2, #a-b 4.50 4.50

Vilnius, 2009 European Cultural Capital A272

2009, Apr. 11

891 A272 2.15 l multi 1.75 1.75

Europa — A273

Telescope and: No. 892, Galileo Galilei, Moon. No. 893, Vilnius University Observatory, Sun.

2009, Apr. 25 **Litho.** ***Perf. 14***

892 A273 2.45 l multi 1.90 1.90

893 A273 2.45 l multi 1.90 1.90

Intl. Year of Astronomy.

Great Synagogue of Vilnius — A274

2009, May 23

894 A274 1.35 l multi 1.10 1.10

Palanga Amber Museum — A275

No. 895: a, "Sun Stone" (large piece of amber). b, Museum building. Illustration reduced.

2009, June 13

895 A275 1.55 l Pair, #a-b 2.50 2.50

Spindle A276

2009, June 27 **Litho.** ***Perf. 14***

896 A276 3.35 l multi 2.75 2.75

Millennium Song Festival, Vilnius.

Miniature Sheet

Lithuania, 1000th Anniv. — A277

No. 897: a, Acceptance of declaration of the Council of the Movement for the Freedom of Lithuania, 1949. b, Illegal production of "Chronicle of the Catholic Church in Lithuania," 1972. c, Lithuanian Reform Movement, 1988. d, Signing of declaration of Lithuanian independence, 1990. e, Entry into European Union, 2004. f, Acceptance into Schengen Area, 2007.

2009, July 4 **Litho.** ***Perf. 14***

897 A277 3 l Sheet of 6, #a-f 15.00 15.00

Tall Ships Regatta — A278

Illustration reduced.

Perf. 13½x13¾

2009, Sept. 25 **Litho.**
898 A278 3 l multi + label 2.50 2.50

Railways in Lithuania, 150th Anniv. — A279

2009, Aug. 8 **Litho.** *Perf. 14*
899 A279 2.90 l multi 2.40 2.40

Order of the Cross of Vytis — A280

2009, Sept. 19 *Perf. 13½x13¾*
900 A280 7 l multi 6.00 6.00

Flora and Fauna From Red Book of Lithuania — A281

No. 901: a, Papilio machaon. b, Gentiana pneumonanthe.
Illustration reduced.

2009, Oct. 10 *Perf. 14*
901 A281 1.55 l Horiz. pair, #a-b 2.75 2.75

Struve Geodetic Arc UNESCO World Heritage Site — A282

Designs: No. 902, 2 l, Friedrich Georg Wilhelm von Struve and map of Europe. No. 903, 2 l, Arc post in Meskonys, map of triangulation points.

2009, Oct. 24
902-903 A282 Set of 2 3.50 3.50

Christmas and New Year's Day — A283

Designs: 1.35 l, Village church. 2.45 l, Houses.

2009, Nov. 7
904-905 A283 Set of 2 3.25 3.25

SEMI-POSTAL STAMPS

Regular Issue of 1923-24 Surcharged in Blue, Violet or Black:

On A21

On A22

On A23

1924, Feb. **Wmk. 147** *Perf. 11*
B1 A21 2c + 2c pale brn (Bl) 1.25 *2.25*
B2 A21 3c + 3c ol bis (Bl) 1.25 *2.25*
B3 A21 5c + 5c pale grn (V) 1.25 *2.25*
B4 A21 10c + 10c vio (Bk) 3.00 *3.25*
B5 A21 36c + 34c org brn (V) 6.50 *12.00*

Wmk. Webbing (109)
B6 A21 10c + 10c vio (Bk) 10.00 *20.00*
B7 A21 15c + 15c scar (V) 1.50 *2.50*
B8 A21 20c + 20c ol brn (Bl) 3.00 *4.00*
B9 A21 25c + 25c bl (Bk) 27.50 *55.00*
B10 A22 50c + 50c yel grn (V) 7.00 *12.00*
B11 A22 60c + 60c red (V) 7.00 *12.00*
B12 A23 1 l + 1 l org & grn (V) 8.00 *16.00*
B13 A23 3 l + 2 l red & gray (V) 12.00 *32.50*
B14 A23 5 l + 3 l brn & bl (V) 20.00 *40.00*

Unwmk.
B15 A21 25c + 25c dp bl (Bk) 6.50 *12.00*
Nos. B1-B15 (15) 115.75 228.00

For War Invalids

Semi-Postal Stamps of 1924 Surcharged

Surcharged in Gold or Copper

1926, Dec. 3 **Wmk. 147**
B16 A21 1 + 1c on #B1 1.00 1.25
a. Inverted surcharge 40.00
B17 A21 2 + 2c on #B2 (C) 1.00 1.25
B19 A21 2 + 2c on #B3 1.00 1.25
a. Double surch., one inverted 40.00
B20 A21 5 + 5c on #B4 2.00 2.00
B21 A21 14 + 14c on #B5 6.00 7.00

Wmk. Webbing (109)
B22 A21 5 + 5c on #B6 10.00 10.00
B23 A21 5 + 5c on #B7 2.00 2.00
B24 A21 10 + 10c on #B8 2.00 2.00
B25 A21 10 + 10c on #B9 65.00 65.00

Unwmk.
B26 A21 10 + 10c on #B15 4.00 5.00

Surcharged in Copper or Silver:

On A22

On A23

Wmk. Webbing (109)
B27 A22 20 + 20c on #B10 4.00 5.00
B28 A22 25 + 25c on #B11 6.00 7.00
B29 A23 30 + 30c on #B12 (S) 9.00 11.00
Nos. B16-B29 (13) 113.00 119.75

For War Orphans

Surcharged in Gold

1926, Dec. 3 **Wmk. 147**
B30 A21 1 + 1c on #B1 .90 .90
B31 A21 2 + 2c on #B2 .90 .90
a. Inverted surcharge 260.00
B32 A21 2 + 2c on #B3 .90 .90
a. Inverted surcharge 30.00
B33 A21 5 + 5c on #B4 2.00 2.25
B34 A21 19 + 19c on #B5 4.00 5.00

Wmk. Webbing (109)
B35 A21 5 + 5c on #B6 10.00 10.00
B36 A21 10 + 10c on #B7 1.75 2.00
B37 A21 15 + 15c on #B8 2.00 2.25
B38 A21 15 + 15c on #B9 65.00 65.00

Unwmk.
B39 A21 15 + 15c on #B15 3.00 3.00

Surcharged in Gold:

On A22

On A23

Wmk. 109
B40 A22 25c on #B10 5.00 6.00
B41 A22 30c on #B11 8.00 7.00
B42 A23 50c on #B12 10.00 11.00
Nos. B30-B42 (13) 113.45 116.20

Catalogue values for unused stamps in this section, from this point to the end of the section, are for Never Hinged items.

Javelin throwing — SP1

Natl. Olympiad, July 15-20: 5c+5c, Archery. 30c+10c, Diving. 60c+15c, Running.

Unwmk.
1938, July 13 **Photo.** *Perf. 14*
B43 SP1 5c + 5c grn & dk grn 6.50 6.50
B44 SP1 15c + 5c org & red org 6.50 6.50
B45 SP1 30c + 10c bl & dk bl 12.00 12.00
B46 SP1 60c + 15c tan & brn 16.00 16.00
Nos. B43-B46 (4) 41.00 41.00

Same Overprinted in Red, Blue or Black:

Nos. B47, B50

Nos. B48-B49

1938, July 13
B47 SP1 5c + 5c (R) 12.00 7.50
B48 SP1 15c + 5c (Bl) 12.00 7.50
B49 SP1 30c + 10c (R) 15.00 7.50
B50 SP1 60c + 15c (Bk) 20.00 12.50
Nos. B47-B50 (4) 59.00 35.00

National Scout Jamboree, July 12-14. Forged cancellations exist.

Basketball Players
SP6

SP7

Flags of Competing Nations and Basketball — SP8

1939 **Photo.** *Perf. 14*
B52 SP6 15c + 10c copper brn & brn 6.50 6.50
B53 SP7 30c + 15c myrtle grn & grn 6.50 6.50
B54 SP8 60c + 40c blue vio & gray vio 12.00 12.00
Nos. B52-B54 (3) 25.00 25.00

3rd European Basketball Championships held at Kaunas. The surtax was used for athletic equipment. Nos. B52-B54 exist imperf. Value, set pairs, $500.

AIR POST STAMPS

Catalogue values for unused stamps in this section are for Never Hinged items.

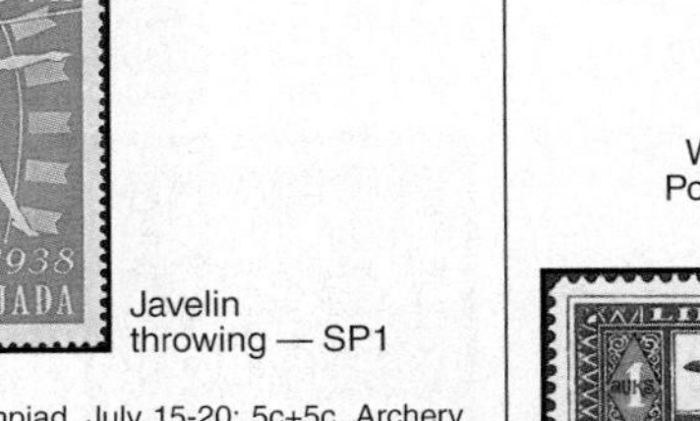

Winged Posthorn AP1

Airplane over Neman River — AP2

Air Squadron AP3

Plane over Gediminas Castle — AP4

1921 **Litho.** **Wmk. 109** *Perf. 11½*
C1 AP1 20sk ultra 1.75 .75
C2 AP1 40sk red orange 1.40 .75
C3 AP1 60sk green *1.50* .75
a. Imperf., pair *45.00*
C4 AP1 80sk lt rose 2.00 .75
a. Horiz. pair, imperf. vert. *50.00* *40.00*
C5 AP2 1auk green & red *2.00* .75
a. Imperf., pair 90.00 *175.00*
C6 AP3 2auk brown & blue 2.25 .75
C7 AP4 5auk slate & yel 2.75 1.75
Nos. C1-C7 (7) 13.65 6.25

For surcharges see Nos. C21-C26, C29.

Allegory of Flight — AP5

1921, Nov. 6

C8	AP5	20sk org & gray bl	2.50	1.50
C9	AP5	40sk dl bl & lake	2.50	1.50
C10	AP5	60sk vio bl & ol grn	2.50	1.50
C11	AP5	80sk ocher & dp grn	2.50	1.50
a.		Vert. pair, imperf. btwn.	35.00	35.00
C12	AP5	1auk bl grn & bl	2.50	1.50
C13	AP5	2auk gray & brn org	2.50	1.50
C14	AP5	5auk dl lil & Prus bl	2.50	1.50
		Nos. C8-C14 (7)	17.50	10.50

Opening of airmail service.

Plane over Kaunas — AP6

Black Overprint

1922, July 16 *Perf. 11, 11½*

C15	AP6	1auk ol brn & red	3.25	2.75
a.		Imperf., pair	60.00	
C16	AP6	3auk violet & grn	3.25	2.75
C17	AP6	5auk dp blue & yel	3.25	4.00
		Nos. C15-C17 (3)	9.75	9.50

Nos. C15-C17, without overprint, were to be for the founding of the Air Post service but they were not put in use at that time. Subsequently the word "ZENKLAS" (stamp) was overprinted over "ISTEIGIMAS" (founding) and the date "1921, VI, 25" was obliterated by short vertical lines.

For surcharge see No. C31.

Plane over Gediminas Castle — AP7

1922, July 22

C18	AP7	2auk blue & rose	1.60	.85
C19	AP7	4auk brown & rose	1.60	.85
C20	AP7	10auk black & gray bl	1.75	1.40
		Nos. C18-C20 (3)	4.95	3.10

For surcharges see Nos. C27-C28, C30.

Nos. C1-C7, C17-C20 Surcharged like Regular Issues in Black or Carmine

1922

C21	AP1	10c on 20sk	5.75	2.50
C22	AP1	10c on 40sk	3.00	1.50
C23	AP1	10c on 60sk	3.00	1.50
a.		Inverted surcharge	45.00	
C24	AP1	10c on 80sk	3.00	1.50
C25	AP2	20c on 1auk	20.00	6.00
C26	AP3	20c on 2auk	20.00	7.50
a.		Without "CENT"	200.00	140.00
C27	AP7	25c on 2auk	1.75	1.00
a.		Inverted surcharge	45.00	40.00
C28	AP7	30c on 4auk (C)	1.75	1.00
a.		Double surcharge	50.00	45.00
C29	AP4	50c on 5auk	3.50	1.50
C30	AP7	50c on 10auk	1.75	1.00
a.		Inverted surcharge	50.00	45.00
C31	AP6	1 l on 5auk	29.00	15.00
a.		Double surcharge	50.00	
		Nos. C21-C31 (11)	92.50	40.00

Airplane and Carrier Pigeons AP8

"Flight" AP9

1924, Jan. 28 **Wmk. 147** *Perf. 11*

C32	AP8	20c yellow	1.75	.75
C33	AP8	40c emerald	1.75	.75
a.		Horiz. or vert. pair, imperf. between	60.00	
C34	AP8	60c rose	1.75	.75
a.		Imperf., pair	75.00	
C35	AP9	1 l dk brown	3.75	.75
		Nos. C32-C35 (4)	9.00	3.00

Most stamps, if not all, of the "unwatermarked" varieties show faint traces of watermark, according to experts.

For surcharges see Nos. CB1-CB4.

Swallow — AP10

1926, June 17 **Wmk. 198** *Perf. 14½*

C37	AP10	20c carmine rose	1.25	.75
a.		Horiz. or vert. pair, imperf. between	55.00	
C38	AP10	40c violet & red org	1.25	.75
a.		Horiz. or vert. pair, imperf. between	55.00	
C39	AP10	60c blue & black	2.50	.75
a.		Horiz. or vert. pair, imperf. between	55.00	
c.		Center inverted	250.00	160.00
		Nos. C37-C39 (3)	5.00	2.25

Juozas Tubelis — AP11

Vytautas and Airplane over Kaunas AP12

Vytautas and Antanas Smetona AP13

1930, Feb. 16 **Wmk. 109** *Perf. 14*

C40	AP11	5c blk, bis & brn	.70	.35
C41	AP11	10c dk bl, db & blk	.70	.35
C42	AP11	15c mar, gray & bl	.70	.35
C43	AP12	20c dk brn, org & dl red	.70	.80
C44	AP12	40c dk bl, lt bl & vio	1.25	.80
C45	AP13	60c bl grn, lil & blk	2.00	.85
C46	AP13	1 l dl red, lil & blk	3.75	1.60
		Nos. C40-C46 (7)	9.80	5.10

5th cent. of the death of the Grand Duke Vytautas.

Map of Lithuania, Klaipeda and Vilnius — AP14

15c, 20c, Airplane over Neman. 40c, 60c, City Hall, Kaunas. 1 l, 2 l, Church of Vytautas, Kaunas.

Wmk. Multiple Letters (238)

1932, July 21 *Perf. 14, Imperf.*

C47	AP14	5c ver & ol grn	.85	.65
C48	AP14	10c dk red brn & ocher	.85	.65
C49	AP14	15c dk bl & org yel	.85	.65
C50	AP14	20c sl blk & org	5.50	.90
C51	AP14	60c ultra & ocher	7.50	3.50
C52	AP14	2 l dk bl & yel	8.00	4.50

Wmk. 198

C53	AP14	40c vio brn & yel	6.25	5.00
C54	AP14	1 l vio brn & grn	8.50	5.75
		Nos. C47-C54 (8)	38.30	21.60

Issued for the benefit of Lithuanian orphans.

Mindaugas in the Battle of Shauyai, 1236 — AP15

15c, 20c, Coronation of Mindaugas (1253). 40c, Grand Duke Gediminas and his followers. 60c, Founding of Vilnius by Gediminas (1332). 1 l, Gediminas capturing the Russian Fortifications. 2 l, Grand Duke Algirdas before Moscow (1368).

Perf. 14, Imperf.

1932, Nov. 28 **Wmk. 209**

C55	AP15	5c grn & red lil	.90	.75
C56	AP15	10c emer & rose	.90	.75
C57	AP15	15c rose vio & bis brn	.90	.75
C58	AP15	20c rose red & blk brn	3.75	1.00
C59	AP15	40c choc & dk gray	5.50	3.50
C60	AP15	60c org & gray blk	7.00	6.50
C61	AP15	1 l rose vio & grn	8.00	5.50
C62	AP15	2 l dp bl & brn	9.00	7.50
		Nos. C55-C62 (8)	35.95	26.25

Anniv. of independence.

Nos. C58-C62 exist with overprint "DARIUS-GIRENAS / NEW YORK-1933- KAUNAS" below small plane. The overprint was applied in New York with the approval of the Lithuanian consul general. Lithuanian postal authorities seem not to have been involved in the creation or release of these overprints.

Trakai Castle, Home of the Grand Duke Kestutis — AP16

Designs: 15c, 20c, Meeting of Kestutís and the Hermit Birute. 40c, 60c, Hermit Birute. 1 l, 2 l, Kestutis and his Brother Algirdas.

1933, May 6 *Perf. 14, Imperf.*

C63	AP16	5c ol gray & dp bl	.50	.45
C64	AP16	10c gray vio & org brn	.50	.45
C65	AP16	15c dp blue & lilac	.80	.60
C66	AP16	20c org brn & lilac	1.75	1.00
C67	AP16	40c lt ultra & lilac	3.50	1.75
C68	AP16	60c brown & lt ultra	5.00	3.50
C69	AP16	1 l ol gray & dp bl	6.00	4.00
C70	AP16	2 l vio gray & yel grn	7.00	*8.00*
		Nos. C63-C70 (8)	25.05	*19.75*

Reopening of air service to Berlin-Kaunas-Moscow, and 550th anniv. of the death of Kestutis.

Joseph Maironis — AP17

Joseph Tumas-Vaizgantas — AP17a

Designs: 40c, 60c, Vincas Kudirka. 1 l, 2 l, Julia A. Zemaite.

1933, Sept. 15 *Perf. 14, Imperf.*

C71	AP17	5c crim & dp bl	.65	.65
C72	AP17	10c bl vio & grn	.65	.65
C73	AP17a	15c dk grn & choc	.65	.65
C74	AP17a	20c brn car & ultra	1.00	.90
C75	AP17	40c red brn & ol grn	2.25	1.50
C76	AP17	60c dk bl & choc	2.75	2.50
C77	AP17	1 l citron & indigo	4.00	3.50
C78	AP17	2 l dp grn & red brn	6.25	5.75
		Nos. C71-C78 (8)	18.20	16.10

Issued for the benefit of Lithuanian orphans.

Capts. Steponas Darius and Stas. Girenas AP18

Ill-Fated Plane "Lituanica" AP19

The Dark Angel of Death — AP20

"Lituanica" over Globe — AP21

"Lituanica" and White Knight — AP22

Perf. 11½

1934, May 18 **Unwmk.** **Engr.**

C79	AP18	20c scarlet & blk	.20	.20
C80	AP19	40c dp rose & bl	.20	.20
C81	AP18	60c dk vio & blk	.20	.20
C82	AP20	1 l black & rose	.35	.20
C83	AP21	3 l gray grn & org	.90	.50
C84	AP22	5 l dk brn & bl	3.50	3.25
		Nos. C79-C84 (6)	5.35	4.55

Death of Capts. Steponas Darius and Stasys Girenas on their New York-Kaunas flight of 1933.

No. C80 exists with diagonal overprint: "F. VAITKUS / nugalejo Atlanta / 21-22-IX-1935." Value $300.

Felix Waitkus and Map of Transatlantic Flight — AP23

Wmk. 238

1936, Mar. 24 **Litho.** *Perf. 14*

C85	AP23	15c brown lake	3.25	.85
C86	AP23	30c dark green	4.50	.85
C87	AP23	60c blue	6.00	2.50
		Nos. C85-C87 (3)	13.75	4.20

Transatlantic Flight of the Lituanica II, Sept. 21-22, 1935.

AIR POST SEMI-POSTAL STAMPS

Catalogue values for unused stamps in this section are for Never Hinged items.

Nos. C32-C35 Surcharged like Nos. B1-B9 (No. CB1), Nos. B10-B11 (Nos. CB2-CB3), and Nos. B12-B14 (No. CB4) in Red, Violet or Black

1924 Wmk. 147 *Perf. 11*

CB1 AP8 20c + 20c yellow (R) 20.00 12.00
CB2 AP8 40c + 40c emerald (V) 20.00 12.00
CB3 AP8 60c + 60c rose (V) 20.00 12.00
CB4 AP9 1 l + 1 l dk brown 20.00 12.00
Nos. CB1-CB4 (4) 80.00 48.00

Surtax for the Red Cross. See note following No. C35.

SOUTH LITHUANIA

GRODNO DISTRICT

Russian Stamps of 1909-12 Surcharged in Black or Red

1919 Unwmk. *Perf. 14, 14½x15*

L1 A14 50sk on 3k red 60.00 57.50
a. Double surcharge 250.00 250.00
L2 A14 50sk on 5k claret 60.00 57.50
a. Imperf., pair 550.00 475.00
L3 A15 50sk on 10k dk bl (R) 60.00 57.50
L4 A11 50sk on 15k red brn & bl 60.00 57.50
a. Imperf., pair 650.00 550.00
L5 A11 50sk on 25k grn & gray vio (R) 60.00 57.50
L6 A11 50sk on 35k red brn & grn 60.00 57.50
L7 A8 50sk on 50k vio & grn 60.00 57.50
L8 A11 50sk on 70k brn & org 60.00 57.50
Nos. L1-L8 (8) 480.00 460.00

Excellent counterfeits are plentiful.
This surcharge exists on Russia No. 119, the imperf. 1k orange of 1917. Value, unused $90, used $60.

OCCUPATION STAMPS

ISSUED UNDER GERMAN OCCUPATION

German Stamps Overprinted in Black

On Stamps of 1905-17

1916-17 Wmk. 125 *Perf. 14, 14½*

1N1 A22 2½pf gray .65 *1.00*
1N2 A16 3pf brown .25 .20
1N3 A16 5pf green .65 *1.00*
1N4 A22 7½pf orange .65 *1.00*
1N5 A16 10pf carmine .65 *1.00*
1N6 A22 15pf yel brn 3.00 2.00
1N7 A22 15pf dk vio ('17) .65 *1.00*
1N8 A16 20pf ultra 1.00 1.00
1N9 A16 25pf org & blk, *yel* .50 *.50*
1N10 A16 40pf lake & blk 1.00 *3.75*
1N11 A16 50pf vio & blk, *buff* 1.00 *1.50*
1N12 A17 1m car rose 12.00 3.50
Nos. 1N1-1N12 (12) 22.00 *17.45*
Set, never hinged 40.00

These stamps were used in the former Russian provinces of Suvalki, Vilnius, Kaunas, Kurland, Estland and Lifland.

ISSUED UNDER RUSSIAN OCCUPATION

Catalogue values for unused stamps in this section are for Never Hinged items.

Lithuanian Stamps of 1937-40 Overprinted in Red or Blue

1940 Wmk. 238 *Perf. 14*

2N9 A44 2c orange (Bl) .30 .40
2N10 A50 50c brown (Bl) .75 .50

Unwmk.

2N11 A56 5c brown car (Bl) .30 .40
2N12 A57 10c green (R) 10.00 10.00
2N13 A58 15c dull orange (Bl) .30 .40
2N14 A59 25c lt brown (R) .30 .40
2N15 A60 30c Prus green (R) .65 .50
2N16 A61 35c red orange (Bl) .90 1.00
Nos. 2N9-2N16 (8) 13.50 13.60

Values for used stamps are for CTOs. Postally used examples are considerably more.
The Lithuanian Soviet Socialist Republic was proclaimed July 21, 1940.

LOURENCO MARQUES

lə-ˈren‚t‚-‚sō-‚mär-ˈkes

LOCATION — In the southern part of Mozambique in Southeast Africa
GOVT. — Part of Portuguese East Africa Colony
AREA — 28,800 sq. mi. (approx.)
POP. — 474,000 (approx.)
CAPITAL — Lourenço Marques

Stamps of Mozambique replaced those of Lourenço Marques in 1920. See Mozambique No. 360.

1000 Reis = 1 Milreis
100 Centavos = 1 Escudo (1913)

King Carlos — A1

Perf. 11½, 12½, 13½

1895 Typo. Unwmk.

1 A1 5r yellow .75 .25
2 A1 10r redsh violet .75 .35
3 A1 15r chocolate 1.00 .50
4 A1 20r lavender 1.00 .50
5 A1 25r blue green 1.00 .30
a. Perf. 11½ 3.50 1.00
6 A1 50r light blue 2.00 1.00
a. Perf. 13½ 15.00 5.00
b. Perf. 11½ — —
7 A1 75r rose 1.50 1.25
8 A1 80r yellow grn 4.75 3.00
9 A1 100r brn, *yel* 3.00 1.00
a. Perf. 12½ 5.00 3.25
10 A1 150r car, *rose* 5.00 3.00
11 A1 200r dk bl, *bl* 6.00 3.00
12 A1 300r dk bl, *sal* 7.50 4.00
Nos. 1-12 (12) 34.25 18.15

For surcharges and overprints see Nos. 29, 58-69, 132-137, 140-143, 156-157, 160.

Saint Anthony of Padua Issue

Regular Issues of Mozambique, 1886 and 1894, Overprinted in Black

1895 Without Gum *Perf. 12½*

On 1886 Issue

13 A2 5r black 20.00 12.00
14 A2 10r green 25.00 12.00
15 A2 20r rose 35.00 14.00
16 A2 25r lilac 40.00 14.00
17 A2 40r chocolate 35.00 15.00
18 A2 50r bl, perf. 13½ 30.00 14.00
a. Perf. 12½ 50.00 27.50
19 A2 100r yellow brn 110.00 90.00
20 A2 200r gray vio 42.50 32.50
21 A2 300r orange 70.00 40.00

On 1894 Issue
Perf. 11½

22 A3 5r yellow 35.00 25.00
23 A3 10r redsh vio 40.00 15.00
24 A3 50r light blue 50.00 32.50
a. Perf. 12½ 275.00 275.00
25 A3 75r rose, perf. 12½ 65.00 50.00
26 A3 80r yellow grn 80.00 65.00
27 A3 100r brown, *buff* 350.00 160.00
28 A3 150r car, *rose*, perf. 12½ 50.00 40.00
Nos. 13-28 (16) 1,077. 631.00

No. 12 Surcharged in Black

1897, Jan. 2

29 A1 50r on 300r 200.00 150.00

Most examples of No. 29 were issued without gum.

King Carlos — A2

1898-1903 *Perf. 11½*
Name, Value in Black except 500r

30 A2 2½r gray .35 .30
31 A2 5r orange .35 .30
32 A2 10r lt green .35 .30
33 A2 15r brown 1.25 .85
34 A2 15r gray green ('03) .75 .50
a. Imperf.
35 A2 20r gray violet .65 .40
a. Imperf.
36 A2 25r sea green .70 .40
a. Perf. 13½ 35.00 8.50
b. 25r light green (error) 32.50 32.50
c. Perf. 12½ 50.00 35.00
37 A2 25r car ('03) .35 .30
a. Imperf.
38 A2 50r blue 2.00 .50
39 A2 50r brown ('03) .90 .75
40 A2 65r dull bl ('03) 20.00 8.50
41 A2 75r rose 2.00 1.50
42 A2 75r lilac ('03) 1.25 .95
a. Imperf.
43 A2 80r violet 2.50 1.25
44 A2 100r dk blue, *blue* 1.75 .65
a. Perf. 13½ 14.50 5.00
45 A2 115r org brn, *pink* ('03) 6.00 5.00
46 A2 130r brn, *straw* ('03) 6.00 5.00
47 A2 150r brn, *straw* 2.25 1.40
48 A2 200r red lil, *pnksh* 2.75 1.25
49 A2 300r dk bl, *rose* 3.25 1.50
50 A2 400r dl bl, *straw* ('03) 7.00 5.00
51 A2 500r blk & red, *bl* ('01) 6.00 3.00
52 A2 700r vio, *yelsh* ('01) 12.00 7.00
Nos. 30-52 (23) 80.40 46.60

For surcharges and overprints see Nos. 57, 71-74, 76-91, 138, 144-155.

Coat of Arms — A3

Surcharged On Upper and Lower Halves of Stamp

1899 *Imperf.*

53 A3 5r on 10r grn & brn 20.00 7.00
54 A3 25r on 10r grn & brn 20.00 7.00
55 A3 50r on 30r grn & brn 30.00 11.00
a. Inverted surcharge
56 A3 50r on 800r grn & brn 40.00 20.00
Nos. 53-56 (4) 110.00 45.00

The lower half of No. 55 can be distinguished from that of No. 56 by the background of the label containing the word "REIS." The former is plain, while the latter is formed of white intersecting curved horizontal lines over vertical shading of violet brown.
Values are for undivided stamps. Halves sell for ¼ as much.

Most examples of Nos. 53-56 were issued without gum. Values are for stamps without gum.

No. 41 Surcharged in Black

1899 *Perf. 11½*

57 A2 50r on 75r rose 5.00 2.50

Most examples of No. 57 were issued without gum. Values are for stamp without gum.

Surcharged in Black

On Issue of 1895

1902 *Perf. 11½, 12½*

58 A1 65r on 5r yellow 4.00 2.50
59 A1 65r on 15r choc 4.00 2.50
60 A1 65r on 20r lav 5.00 2.50
a. Perf. 12½ 25.00 15.00
61 A1 115r on 10r red vio 5.00 3.00
62 A1 115r on 200r bl, *bl* 5.00 3.00
63 A1 115r on 300r bl, *sal* 5.00 3.00
64 A1 130r on 25r grn, perf. 12½ 2.00 2.00
a. Perf. 11½ 30.00 22.50
65 A1 130r on 80r yel grn 3.00 3.00
66 A1 130r on 150r car, *rose* 4.00 3.00
67 A1 400r on 50r lt bl 8.00 6.00
68 A1 400r on 75r rose 8.00 6.00
69 A1 400r on 100r brn, *buff* 7.00 6.00

On Newspaper Stamp of 1893

70 N1 65r on 2½ brn 4.00 2.00
Nos. 58-70 (13) 64.00 44.50

Surcharge exists inverted on Nos. 61, 70.
Nos. 64, 67 and 68 have been reprinted on thin white paper with shiny white gum and clean-cut perforation 13½. Value $6 each.
For overprints see Nos. 132-137, 140-143, 156-157, 160.

Issue of 1898-1903 Overprinted in Black

1903 *Perf. 11½*

71 A2 15r brown 2.00 .85
72 A2 25r sea green 1.50 .85
73 A2 50r blue 2.50 .85
74 A2 75r rose 3.00 1.40
a. Inverted overprint 50.00 50.00
Nos. 71-74 (4) 9.00 3.95

Surcharged in Black

1905

76 A2 50r on 65r dull blue 2.25 2.00

Regular Issues Overprinted in Carmine or Green

1911

77 A2 2½r gray .30 .25
78 A2 5r orange .30 .25
a. Double overprint 10.00 10.00
b. Inverted overprint 10.00 10.00
79 A2 10r lt grn .40 .35
80 A2 15r gray grn .40 .35
a. Inverted overprint 10.00 10.00
81 A2 20r dl vio .40 .40
82 A2 25r car (G) .90 .50

83	A2	50r brown	.80	.50
84	A2	75r lilac	1.00	.50
85	A2	100r dk bl, *bl*	.80	.55
86	A2	115r org brn, *pink*	9.00	3.50
87	A2	130r brn, *straw*	.80	.60
88	A2	200r red lil, *pnksh*	.85	.60
89	A2	400r dl bl, *straw*	1.25	1.10
90	A2	500r blk & red, *bl*	1.50	1.10
91	A2	700r vio, *yelsh*	1.75	1.25
		Nos. 77-91 (15)	20.45	11.80

Vasco da Gama Issue of Various Portuguese Colonies Common Design Types Surcharged

1913 ***Perf. 12½-16***

On Stamps of Macao

92	CD20	¼c on ½a bl grn	2.25	2.25
93	CD21	½c on Ia red	2.25	2.25
94	CD22	1c on 2a red vio	2.25	2.25
95	CD23	2½c on 4a yel grn	2.25	2.25
96	CD24	5c on 8a dk bl	2.25	2.25
97	CD25	7½c on 12a vio brn	4.25	4.25
98	CD26	10c on 16a bis brn	3.50	3.50
a.		Inverted surcharge	40.00	40.00
99	CD27	15c on 24a bister	3.75	3.75
		Nos. 92-99 (8)	22.75	22.75

On Stamps of Portuguese Africa

100	CD20	¼c on 2½r bl grn	1.75	1.75
101	CD21	½c on 5r red	1.75	1.75
102	CD22	1c on 10r red vio	1.75	1.75
103	CD23	2½c on 25r yel grn	1.75	1.75
104	CD24	5c on 50r dk bl	1.75	1.75
105	CD25	7½c on 75r vio brn	4.00	4.00
106	CD26	10c on 100r bis brn	2.75	2.75
107	CD27	15c on 150r bis	2.75	2.75
		Nos. 100-107 (8)	18.25	18.25

On Stamps of Timor

108	CD20	¼c on ½a bl grn	1.75	1.75
109	CD21	½c on 1a red	1.75	1.75
110	CD22	1c on 2a red vio	1.75	1.75
111	CD23	2½c on 4a yel grn	1.75	1.75
112	CD24	5c on 8a dk bl	2.00	1.75
113	CD25	7½c on 12a vio brn	4.00	4.00
114	CD26	10c on 16a bis brn	2.75	2.75
115	CD27	15c on 24a bister	2.75	2.75
		Nos. 108-115 (8)	18.50	18.25
		Nos. 92-115 (24)	59.50	59.25

Ceres — A4

1914 **Typo.** ***Perf. 15x14***

Name and Value in Black

116	A4	¼c olive brn	.25	.20
117	A4	½c black	.25	.20
a.		Value omitted	15.00	
118	A4	1c blue grn	.25	.20
119	A4	1½c lilac brn	.25	.20
a.		Imperf.		
120	A4	2c carmine	.25	.20
121	A4	2½c lt vio	.25	.20
122	A4	5c dp blue	.25	.20
123	A4	7½c yellow brn	.50	.40
124	A4	8c slate	.50	.40
125	A4	10c orange brn	1.50	.85
126	A4	15c plum	1.00	.70
127	A4	20c yellow grn	2.50	.90
128	A4	30c brown, *green*	3.50	1.00
129	A4	40c brown, *pink*	9.00	4.00
130	A4	50c orange, *sal*	8.00	3.00
131	A4	1e green, *blue*	10.00	3.00
		Nos. 116-131 (16)	38.25	15.65

Values of Nos. 116-124 are for stamps on ordinary paper. Those on chalky paper sell for 8 to 12 times as much. Nos. 127-131 issued only on chalky paper.

For surcharges see Nos. 139, 159, 161-162, B1-B12.

In 1921 Nos. 117 and 119 were surcharged 10c and 30c respectively, for use in Mozambique as Nos. 230 and 231. These same values, surcharged 5c and 10c respectively, with the addition of the word "PORTEADO," were used in Mozambique as postage dues, Nos. J44 and J45.

Provisional Issue of 1902 Overprinted Locally in Carmine

1914 ***Perf. 11½, 12½***

132	A1	115r on 10r red vio	1.00	.45
a.		"Republica" inverted	20.00	
133	A1	115r on 200r bl, *bl*	1.00	.45
134	A1	115r on 300r bl, *sal*	1.10	.45
a.		Double overprint	40.00	40.00
135	A1	130r on 25r grn	1.50	.70
a.		Perf. 12½	3.25	1.60
136	A1	130r on 80r yel grn	1.10	.35
137	A1	130r on 150r car, *rose*	1.10	.35
		Nos. 132-137 (6)	6.80	2.75

No. 135a was issued without gum.

Nos. 78 and 117 Perforated Diagonally and Surcharged in Carmine

1915 ***Perf. 11½***

138	A2	¼c on half of 5r org, pair	5.00	5.00
a.		Pair without dividing perfs.	20.00	20.00

Perf. 15x14

139	A4	¼c on half of ½c blk, pair	9.00	9.00

The added perforation on Nos. 138-139 runs from lower left to upper right corners, dividing the stamp in two. Values are for pairs, both halves of the stamp.

Provisional Issue of 1902 Overprinted in Carmine

1915 ***Perf. 11½, 12½***

140	A1	115r on 10r red vio	.55	.40
141	A1	115r on 200r bl, *bl*	.70	.40
142	A1	115r on 300r bl, *sal*	.70	.40
143	A1	130r on 150r car, *rose*	.75	.40
		Nos. 140-143 (4)	2.70	1.60

Nos. 34 and 80 Surcharged

1915

On Issue of 1903

144	A2	2c on 15r gray grn	.90	.80

On Issue of 1911

145	A2	2c on 15r gray grn	.90	.80
a.		New value inverted	22.50	

Regular Issues of 1898-1903 Overprinted Locally in Carmine

1916

146	A2	15r gray grn	1.50	1.00
147	A2	50r brown	3.50	2.00
a.		Inverted overprint		
148	A2	75r lilac	3.50	2.00
149	A2	100r blue, *bl*	3.00	1.00
150	A2	115r org brn, *pink*	2.50	1.00
151	A2	130r brown, *straw*	10.00	5.00
152	A2	200r red lil, *pnksh*	7.00	2.00
153	A2	400r dull bl, *straw*	12.00	4.00
154	A2	500r blk & red, *bl*	7.00	3.00
155	A2	700r vio, *yelsh*	12.00	5.00
		Nos. 146-155 (10)	62.00	26.00

Same Overprint on Nos. 67-68

1917

156	A1	400r on 50r lt blue	1.25	.65
a.		Perf. 13½	11.50	9.00
157	A1	400r on 75r rose	2.50	1.00

No. 69 exists with this overprint. It was not officially issued.

Type of 1914 Surcharged in Red

1920 ***Perf. 15x14***

159	A4	4c on 2½c violet	1.00	.30

Stamps of 1914 Surcharged in Green or Black

a

b

1921

160	A1(a)	¼c on 115r on 10r red vio (G)	.80	.80
161	A4(b)	1c on 2½c vio (Bk)	.60	.40
a.		Inverted surcharge	40.00	
162	A4(b)	1½c on 2½c vio (Bk)	.80	.60
		Nos. 160-162 (3)	2.20	1.80

Nos. 159-162 were postally valid throughout Mozambique.

SEMI-POSTAL STAMPS

Regular Issue of 1914 Overprinted or Surcharged:

a

b

c

1918 ***Perf. 15x14½***

B1	A4(a)	¼c olive brn	2.00	*3.00*
B2	A4(a)	½c black	2.00	*4.00*
B3	A4(a)	1c bl grn	2.00	*4.00*
B4	A4(a)	2½c violet	4.00	4.00
B5	A4(a)	5c blue	4.00	*6.00*
B6	A4(a)	10c org brn	5.00	*7.00*
B7	A4(b)	20c on 1½c lil brn	5.00	*8.00*
B8	A4(a)	30c brn, *grn*	5.00	*9.00*
B9	A4(b)	40c on 2c car	5.00	*10.00*
B10	A4(b)	50c on 7½c bis	8.00	*12.00*
B11	A4(b)	70c on 8c slate	10.00	*15.00*
B12	A4(c)	$1 on 15c mag	10.00	*15.00*
		Nos. B1-B12 (12)	62.00	*97.00*

Nos. B1-B12 were used in place of ordinary postage stamps on Mar. 9, 1918.

NEWSPAPER STAMPS

Numeral of Value — N1

Perf. 11½

1893, July 28 **Typo.** **Unwmk.**

P1	N1	2½r brown	.25	.65
a.		Perf. 12½	20.00	17.50

For surcharge see No. 70.

Saint Anthony of Padua Issue

Mozambique No. P6 Overprinted

1895, July 1 ***Perf. 11½, 13½***

P2	N3	2½r brown	20.00	17.50
a.		Inverted overprint	30.00	30.00

LUXEMBOURG

'lək-səm-,bərg

LOCATION — Western Europe between southern Belgium, Germany and France
GOVT. — Grand Duchy
AREA — 999 sq. mi.
POP. — 476,200 (2007)
CAPITAL — Luxembourg

12½ Centimes = 1 Silbergroschen
100 Centimes = 1 Franc
100 Cents = 1 Euro (2002)

Catalogue values for unused stamps in this country are for Never Hinged items, beginning with Scott 321 in the regular postage section, Scott B216 in the semi-postal section.

Watermarks

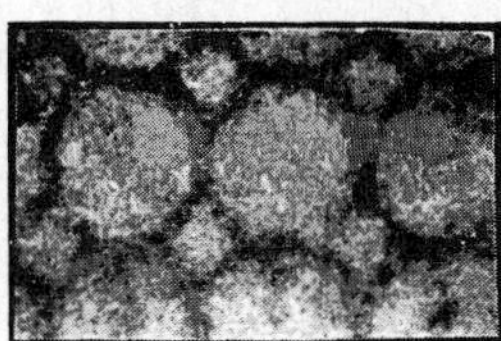

Wmk. 110 — Octagons

Wmk. 149 — W

Wmk. 213 — Double Wavy Lines

Wmk. 216 — Multiple Airplanes

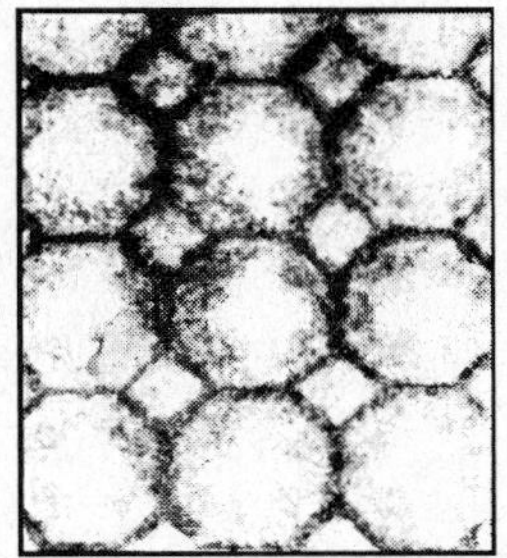

Wmk. 246 — Multiple Cross Enclosed in Octagons

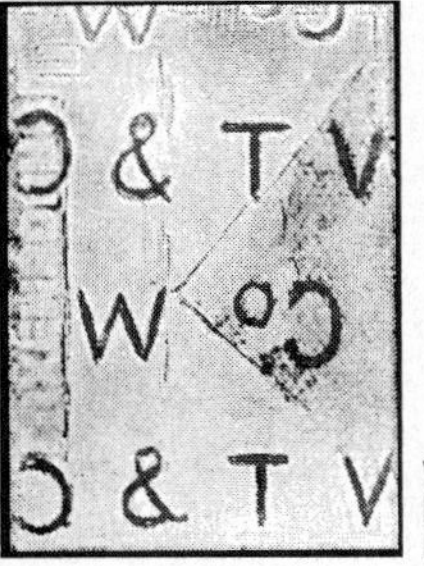

Wmk. 247 — Multiple Letters

Unused values of Nos. 1-47 are for stamps without gum. Though these stamps were issued with gum, most examples offered are without gum. Stamps with original gum sell for more.

Grand Duke William III — A1

Luxembourg Print
Wmk. 149

1852, Sept. 15 Engr. *Imperf.*

No.	Type	Description	Unused	Used
1	A1	10c gray black	*2,850.*	72.50
a.		10c greenish black ('53)	*3,000.*	82.50
b.		10c intense black ('54)	*3,650.*	160.00
2	A1	1sg brown red ('53)	1,950.	125.00
a.		1sg brick red	1,950.	125.00
b.		1sg orange red ('54)	1,950.	125.00
c.		1sg blood red	3,400.	625.00
3	A1	1sg rose ('55)	1,875.	100.00
a.		1sg carmine rose ('56)	1,875.	115.00
b.		1sg dark carmine rose, thin paper ('59)	*1,950.*	*300.00*
		Nos. 1-3 (3)		297.50

Reprints of both values exist on watermarked paper. Some of the reprints show traces of lines cancelling the plates, but others can be distinguished only by an expert.

See Nos. 278-279, 603.

Coat of Arms
A2 A3

No. 26

No. 39

Frankfurt Print

1859-64 Typo. Unwmk.

No.	Type	Description	Unused	Used
4	A2	1c buff ('63)	175.00	*575.00*
5	A2	2c black ('60)	125.00	*700.00*
6	A2	4c yellow ('64)	240.00	225.00
a.		4c orange ('64)	250.00	250.00
7	A3	10c blue	250.00	25.00
8	A3	12½c rose	350.00	200.00
9	A3	25c brown	475.00	350.00
10	A3	30c rose lilac	400.00	300.00
11	A3	37½c green	400.00	250.00
12	A3	40c red orange	1,200.	300.00

Counterfeits of Nos. 1-12 exist.

See Nos. 13-25, 27-38, 40-47. For surcharges and overprints see Nos. 26, 39, O1-O51.

1865-71 *Rouletted*

No.	Type	Description	Unused	Used
13	A2	1c red brown	225.00	325.00
14	A2	2c black ('67)	25.00	21.00
15	A2	4c yellow ('67)	775.00	225.00
16	A2	4c green ('71)	52.50	30.00
		Nos. 13-16 (4)	1,077.	601.00

1865-74 *Rouletted in Color*

No.	Type	Description	Unused	Used
17	A2	1c red brn ('72)	52.50	10.50
18	A2	1c orange ('69)	52.50	10.50
a.		1c brown orange ('67)	150.00	52.50
b.		1c red orange ('69)	1,825.	475.00
19	A3	10c rose lilac	175.00	5.25
a.		10c lilac	150.00	5.25
b.		10c gray lilac	150.00	5.25
20	A3	12½c carmine ('71)	225.00	10.50
a.		12½c rose	250.00	10.50
21	A3	20c gray brown ('72)	150.00	10.50
a.		20c yellow brown ('69)	175.00	8.50
22	A3	25c blue ('72)	1,050.	15.00
22A	A3	25c ultra ('65)	1,050.	15.00
23	A3	30c lilac rose	1,150.	100.00
24	A3	37½c bister ('66)	1,050.	325.00
25	A3	40c pale orange ('74)	52.50	100.00
a.		40c orange red ('66)	1,400.	77.50
26	A4	1fr on 37½c bis ('73)	1,175.	100.00
a.		Surcharge inverted		*3,600.*

Luxembourg Print

1874 Typo. *Imperf.*

No.	Type	Description	Unused	Used
27	A2	4c green	150.00	150.00

1875-79 *Perf. 13*

Narrow Margins

No.	Type	Description	Unused	Used
29	A2	1c red brown ('78)	52.50	10.50
30	A2	2c black	175.00	35.00
31	A2	4c green	3.00	*13.00*
32	A2	5c yellow ('76)	225.00	35.00
a.		5c orange yellow	775.00	150.00
b.		Imperf.	925.00	1,100.
33	A3	10c gray lilac	600.00	3.00
b.		10c lilac	1,700.	40.00
c.		Imperf.	2,700.	*3,250.*
34	A3	12½c lilac rose ('77)	775.00	26.00
35	A3	12½c car rose ('76)	550.00	35.00
36	A3	25c blue ('77)	1,050.	21.00
37	A3	30c dull rose ('78)	1,000.	600.00
38	A3	40c orange ('79)	3.00	*13.00*
39	A5	1fr on 37½c bis ('79)	10.50	*37.50*
a.		"Pranc"	*6,750.*	*7,800.*
b.		Without surcharge	675.00	
c.		As "b," imperf.	825.00	
		As "c," pair	*1,800.*	

In the Luxembourg print the perforation is close to the border of the stamp. Excellent forgeries of No. 39a are plentiful, as well as faked cancellations on Nos. 31, 38 and 39.

Nos. 32b and 33c are said to be essays; Nos. 39b and 39c printer's waste.

Haarlem Print

1880-81 *Perf. 11½x12, 12½x12, 13½*

Wide Margins

No.	Type	Description	Unused	Used
40	A2	1c yel brn ('81)	9.50	6.00
41	A2	2c black	8.50	1.75
42	A2	5c yellow ('81)	250.00	110.00
43	A3	10c gray lilac	190.00	1.00
44	A3	12½c rose ('81)	225.00	225.00
45	A3	20c gray brown ('81)	55.00	19.00
46	A3	25c blue	300.00	5.00
47	A3	30c dull rose ('81)	4.00	*22.50*

Gray Yellowish Paper

Perf. 12½

No.	Type	Description	Unused	Used
42a	A2	5c	7.25	
43a	A3	10c	3.50	
44a	A3	12½c	9.50	
46a	A3	25c	5.00	
		Nos. 42a-46a (4)	25.25	

Nos. 42a-46a were not regularly issued.

"Industry" and "Commerce" A6

Grand Duke Adolphe A7

Perf. 11½x12, 12½x12, 12½, 13½

1882, Dec. 1 Typo.

No.	Type	Description	Unused	Used
48	A6	1c gray lilac	.20	*.40*
49	A6	2c olive gray	.20	*.40*
50	A6	4c olive bister	.25	*2.50*
51	A6	5c lt green	.50	.40
52	A6	10c rose	6.00	.40
53	A6	12½c slate	1.75	*30.00*
54	A6	20c orange	3.00	1.90
55	A6	25c ultra	190.00	1.90
56	A6	30c gray green	19.00	14.50
57	A6	50c bister brown	.75	*11.00*
58	A6	1fr pale violet	.75	*30.00*
59	A6	5fr brown orange	37.50	*190.00*
		Nos. 48-59 (12)	259.90	*283.40*

For overprints see Nos. O52-O64.

Perf. 11, 11½, 11½x11, 12½

1891-93 Engr.

No.	Type	Description	Unused	Used
60	A7	10c carmine	.20	*.40*
a.		Sheet of 25, perf. 11½	100.00	
61	A7	12½c slate grn ('93)	.50	*.70*
62	A7	20c orange ('93)	12.00	.70
a.		20c brown, perf. 11½	*110.00*	300.00
63	A7	25c blue	.70	.60
a.		Sheet of 25, perf. 11½	*1,000.*	
64	A7	30c olive grn ('93)	1.40	1.25
65	A7	37½c green ('93)	2.75	2.50
66	A7	50c brown ('93)	7.25	3.00
67	A7	1fr dp violet ('93)	14.50	6.50
68	A7	2½fr black ('93)	1.50	*25.00*
69	A7	5fr lake ('93)	37.50	80.00
		Nos. 60-69 (10)	78.30	120.65

No. 62a was never on sale at any post office, but exists postally used.

Perf. 11½ stamps are from the sheets of 25.

For overprints see Nos. O65-O74.

Grand Duke Adolphe — A8

1895, May 4 Typo. *Perf. 12½*

No.	Type	Description	Unused	Used
70	A8	1c pearl gray	2.10	.50
71	A8	2c gray brown	.20	*.20*
72	A8	4c olive bister	.20	*.50*
73	A8	5c green	2.10	.20
74	A8	10c carmine	8.25	.20
		Nos. 70-74 (5)	12.85	1.60

For overprints see Nos. O75-O79.

Coat of Arms — A9

Grand Duke William IV — A10

1906-26 Typo. *Perf. 12½*

No.	Type	Description	Unused	Used
75	A9	1c gray ('07)	.20	.20
76	A9	2c olive brn ('07)	.20	.20
77	A9	4c bister ('07)	.20	*.40*
78	A9	5c green ('07)	.20	.20
79	A9	5c lilac ('26)	.20	.20
80	A9	6c violet ('07)	.20	*.50*
81	A9	7½c orange ('19)	.20	*3.50*

Engr.

Perf. 11, 11½x11

No.	Type	Description	Unused	Used
82	A10	10c scarlet	1.50	.20
a.		Souvenir sheet of 10	450.00	*1,200.*
83	A10	12½c slate grn ('07)	1.75	.60
84	A10	15c orange brn ('07)	1.75	.70
85	A10	20c orange ('07)	2.50	.70
86	A10	25c ultra ('07)	60.00	.50
87	A10	30c olive grn ('08)	1.00	.70

88 A10 37½c green ('07) 1.00 .80
a. Perf. 12½ 30.00 14.50
89 A10 50c brown ('07) 5.00 1.25
90 A10 87½c dk blue ('08) 1.75 11.00
91 A10 1fr violet ('08) 6.00 2.10
92 A10 2½fr vermilion ('08) 55.00 *92.50*
93 A10 5fr claret ('08) 9.50 60.00
Nos. 75-93 (19) 148.15 *176.25*

No. 82a for accession of Grand Duke William IV to the throne.

For surcharges and overprints see Nos. 94-96, 112-117, O80-O98.

Nos. 90, 92-93 Surcharged in Red or Black

1912-15

94 A10 62½c on 87½c (R) 1.75 *2.50*
95 A10 62½c on 2½fr (Bk) ('15) 2.50 *5.00*
96 A10 62½c on 5fr (Bk) ('15) .70 *3.50*
Nos. 94-96 (3) 4.95 *11.00*

Grand Duchess Marie Adelaide A11

Grand Duchess Charlotte A12

1914-17 Engr. *Perf. 11½, 11½x11*

97 A11 10c lake .20 .20
98 A11 12½c dull green .20 .20
99 A11 15c sepia .20 *.20*
100 A11 17½c dp brown ('17) .20 *.60*
101 A11 25c ultra .20 .20
102 A11 30c bister .20 *.70*
103 A11 35c dark blue .20 *.60*
104 A11 37½c black brn .20 *.60*
105 A11 40c orange .20 *.50*
106 A11 50c dark gray .20 *.70*
107 A11 62½c blue green .40 *3.50*
108 A11 87½c orange ('17) .30 *3.50*
109 A11 1fr orange brown 2.50 1.00
110 A11 2½fr red .60 *3.50*
111 A11 5fr dark violet 9.50 *55.00*
Nos. 97-111 (15) 15.30 *71.00*

For surcharges and overprints see Nos. 118-124, B7-B10, O99-O113. Nos. 97, 98, 101, 107, 109 and 111 overprinted "Droits de statistique" are revenue stamps.

Stamps of 1906-19 Surcharged with New Value and Bars in Black or Red

1916-24

112 A9 2½c on 5c ('18) .20 .20
a. Double surcharge 75.00
113 A9 3c on 2c ('21) .20 *.20*
114 A9 5c on 1c ('23) .20 *.20*
115 A9 5c on 4c ('23) .20 *.60*
116 A9 5c on 7½c ('24) .20 *.20*
117 A9 6c on 2c (R) ('22) .20 *.25*
118 A11 7½c on 10c ('18) .20 .20
119 A11 17½c on 30c .20 *.60*
120 A11 20c on 17½c ('21) .20 *.20*
121 A11 25c on 37½c ('23) .20 *.20*
a. Double surcharge 90.00
122 A11 75c on 62½c (R) ('22) .20 *.20*
123 A11 80c on 87½c ('22) .20 *.20*
124 A11 87½c on 1fr .60 *7.25*
Nos. 112-124 (13) 3.00 *10.50*

1921, Jan. 6 Engr. *Perf. 11½*

125 A12 15c rose .20 *.40*
a. Sheet of 5, perf 11 150.00 *250.00*
b. Sheet of 25, perf. 11½, 11x11½, 12x11½ 5.50 *17.00*

Birth of Prince Jean, first son of Grand Duchess Charlotte, Jan. 5 (No. 125a). No. 125 was printed in sheets of 100.

See Nos. 131-150. For surcharges and overprints see Nos. 154-158, O114-O131, O136.

Vianden Castle — A13

Foundries at Esch — A14

Adolphe Bridge — A15

1921-34 *Perf. 11, 11½, 11x11½*

126 A13 1fr carmine .20 *.45*
127 A13 1fr dk blue ('26) .20 *.55*

Perf. 11½x11; 11½ (#129, 130)

128 A14 2fr indigo .20 *.65*
129 A14 2fr dk brown ('26) 2.50 2.25
130 A15 5fr dk violet 8.75 8.75
Nos. 126-130 (5) 11.85 12.65

For overprints see Nos. O132-O135, O137-138, O140.

See No. B85.

Charlotte Type of 1921

1921-26 *Perf. 11½*

131 A12 2c brown .20 .20
132 A12 3c olive green .20 .20
a. Sheet of 25 10.00 25.00
133 A12 6c violet .20 .20
a. Sheet of 25 10.00 25.00
134 A12 10c yellow grn .20 .40
135 A12 10c olive brn ('24) .20 .20
136 A12 15c brown olive .20 .20
137 A12 15c pale green ('24) .20 .20
138 A12 15c dp orange ('26) .20 .40
139 A12 20c dp orange .20 .20
a. Sheet of 25 60.00 *110.00*
140 A12 20c yellow grn ('26) .20 .40
141 A12 25c dk green .20 .20
142 A12 30c carmine rose .20 .20
143 A12 40c brown orange .20 .20
144 A12 50c deep blue .20 .60
145 A12 50c red ('24) .20 .40
146 A12 75c red .20 1.50
a. Sheet of 25 325.00
147 A12 75c deep blue ('24) .20 .40
148 A12 80c black .20 1.25
a. Sheet of 25 325.00
Nos. 131-148 (18) 3.60 7.35

For surcharges and overprints see Nos. 154-158, O114-O131, O136.

Philatelic Exhibition Issue

1922, Aug. 27 *Imperf.*

Laid Paper

149 A12 25c dark green 1.50 5.50
150 A12 30c carmine rose 1.50 5.50

Nos. 149 and 150 were sold exclusively at the Luxembourg Phil. Exhib., Aug. 1922.

Souvenir Sheet

View of Luxembourg — A16

1923, Jan. 3 *Perf. 11*

151 A16 10fr dp grn, sheet 1,100. *1,800.*

Birth of Princess Elisabeth.

1923, Mar. *Perf. 11½*

152 A16 10fr black 7.25 *12.50*
a. Perf. 12½ ('34) 7.25 *11.00*

For overprint see No. O141.

The Wolfsschlucht near Echternach — A17

1923-34 *Perf. 11½*

153 A17 3fr dk blue & blue 1.10 1.10
a. Perf. 12½ ('34) .90 .65

For overprint see No. O139.

Stamps of 1921-26 Surcharged with New Values and Bars

1925-28

154 A12 5c on 10c yel grn .20 .20
155 A12 15c on 20c yel grn ('28) .20 .20
a. Bars omitted
156 A12 35c on 40c brn org ('27) .20 .20
157 A12 60c on 75c dp bl ('27) .25 .20
158 A12 60c on 80c blk ('28) .40 .35
Nos. 154-158 (5) 1.25 1.15

Grand Duchess Charlotte — A18

1926-35 Engr. *Perf. 12*

159 A18 5c dk violet .20 .20
160 A18 10c olive grn .20 .20
161 A18 15c black ('30) .25 .25
162 A18 20c orange .40 .20
163 A18 25c yellow grn .50 .20
164 A18 25c vio brn ('27) .45 .20
165 A18 30c yel grn ('27) .45 .50
166 A18 30c gray vio ('30) .50 .40
167 A18 35c gray vio ('28) .25 .20
168 A18 35c yel grn ('30) .20 .20
169 A18 40c olive gray .20 .20
170 A18 50c red brown .20 .20
171 A18 60c blue grn ('28) .25 .20
172 A18 65c black brn .25 .50
173 A18 70c blue vio ('35) .20 .20
174 A18 75c rose .25 .25
175 A18 75c bis brn ('27) .20 .20
176 A18 80c bister brn .25 .60
177 A18 90c rose ('27) 1.50 .90
178 A18 1fr black 1.25 .60
179 A18 1fr rose ('30) .60 .50
180 A18 1¼fr dk blue .20 .45
181 A18 1¼fr yellow ('30) 7.25 .90
182 A18 1¼fr blue grn ('31) .60 .20
183 A18 1¼fr rose car ('34) 12.00 1.40
184 A18 1½fr dp blue ('27) 2.50 .90
185 A18 1¾fr dk blue ('30) .40 .50
Nos. 159-185 (27) 31.50 11.25
Set, never hinged 90.00

For surcharges and overprints see Nos. 186-193, N17-N29, O142-O178.

Stamps of 1926-35, Surcharged with New Values and Bars

1928-39

186 A18 10(c) on 30c yel grn ('29) .50 .20
187 A18 15c on 25c yel grn .40 .30
187A A18 30c on 60c bl grn ('39) .20 1.00
188 A18 60c on 65c blk brn .25 .25
189 A18 60c on 75c rose .25 .25
190 A18 60c on 80c bis brn .45 .50
191 A18 70(c) on 75c bis brn ('35) 6.00 .20
192 A18 75(c) on 90c rose ('29) 1.75 .20
193 A18 1¾(fr) on 1½fr dp bl ('29) 3.50 1.60
Nos. 186-193 (9) 13.30 4.50
Set, never hinged 30.00

The surcharge on No. 187A has no bars.

View of Clervaux A19

1928-34 *Perf. 12½*

194 A19 2fr black ('34) 1.00 .50
Never hinged 3.50
a. Perf. 11½ ('28) 1.25 .60
Never hinged 6.00

See No. B66. For overprint see No. O179.

Coat of Arms — A20

1930, Dec. 20 Typo. *Perf. 12½*

195 A20 5c claret .40 .20
196 A20 10c olive green .60 .20
Set, never hinged 3.00

View of the Lower City of Luxembourg A21

Gate of "Three Towers" A22

1931, June 20 Engr.

197 A21 20fr deep green 3.25 9.50
Never hinged 5.50

For overprint see No. O180.

1934, Aug. 30 *Perf. 14x13½*

198 A22 5fr blue green 1.25 3.50
Never hinged 3.25

For surcharge and overprint see Nos. N31, O181.

Castle From Our Valley A23

1935, Nov. 15 *Perf. 12½x12*

199 A23 10fr green 2.10 5.75
Never hinged 4.50

For surcharge and overprint see Nos. N32, O182.

Municipal Palace — A24

1936, Aug. 26 Photo. *Perf. 11½*

Granite Paper

200 A24 10c brown .20 .20
201 A24 35c green .20 .50
202 A24 70c red orange .20 *.70*
203 A24 1fr carmine rose 1.25 *5.50*
204 A24 1.25fr violet 2.10 *7.00*
205 A24 1.75fr brt ultra 1.25 *6.00*
Nos. 200-205 (6) 5.20 *19.90*
Set, never hinged 13.00

11th Cong. of Intl. Federation of Philately. See No. 859.

Arms of Luxembourg A25

William I A26

Designs: 70c, William II. 75c, William III. 1fr, Prince Henry. 1.25fr, Grand Duke Adolphe. 1.75fr, William IV. 3fr, Regent Marie Anne. 5fr, Grand Duchess Marie Adelaide. 10fr, Grand Duchess Charlotte.

1939, May 27 Engr. *Perf. 12½x12*

No.	Type	Description	Unused	Used
206	A25	35c brt green	.25	.20
207	A26	50c orange	.25	.25
208	A26	70c slate green	.20	.20
209	A26	75c sepia	.65	*1.25*
210	A26	1fr red	1.60	*3.25*
211	A26	1.25fr brown violet	.20	.20
212	A26	1.75fr dark blue	.20	.20
213	A26	3fr lt brown	.25	.50
214	A26	5fr gray black	.50	*1.00*
215	A26	10fr copper red	.75	*2.75*
		Nos. 206-215 (10)	4.85	*9.80*
		Set, never hinged	7.75	

Centenary of Independence.

Allegory of Medicinal Baths — A35

1939, Sept. 18 Photo. *Perf. 11½*

No.	Type	Description	Unused	Used
216	A35	2fr brown rose	.50	1.40
		Never hinged	1.00	

Elevation of Mondorf-les-Bains to town status.

See No. B104. For surcharge see No. N30.

Souvenir Sheet

A36

1939, Dec. 20 Engr. *Perf. 14x13*

No.	Type	Description	Unused	Used
217	A36	Sheet of 3	35.00	*90.00*
		Sheet, never hinged	90.00	
a.		2fr vermilion, *buff*	5.75	*22.50*
b.		3fr dark green, *buff*	5.75	*22.50*
c.		5fr blue, *buff*	5.75	*22.50*

20th anniv. of the reign of Grand Duchess Charlotte (Jan. 15, 1919) and her marriage to Prince Felix (Nov. 6, 1919).

See Nos. B98-B103.

Grand Duchess Charlotte A37

Lion from Duchy Arms A38

1944-46 Unwmk. *Perf. 12*

No.	Type	Description	Unused	Used
218	A37	5c brown red	.20	.20
219	A37	10c black	.20	.20
219A	A37	20c orange ('46)	.20	.20
220	A37	25c sepia	.20	.20
220A	A37	30c carmine ('46)	.20	.20
221	A37	35c green	.20	.20
221A	A37	40c dk blue ('46)	.20	.20
222	A37	50c dk violet	.20	.20
222A	A37	60c orange ('46)	1.10	.20
223	A37	70c rose pink	.20	.20
223A	A37	70c dp green ('46)	.35	*.90*
223B	A37	75c sepia ('46)	.20	.20
224	A37	1fr olive	.20	.20
225	A37	1¼fr red orange	.20	*.55*
226	A37	1½fr red orange ('46)	.20	.20
227	A37	1¾fr blue	.20	.25
228	A37	2fr rose car ('46)	1.60	.25
229	A37	2½fr dp violet ('46)	2.50	*4.50*
230	A37	3fr dp yel grn ('46)	.35	.50
231	A37	3½fr brt blue ('46)	.50	*.75*
232	A37	5fr dk blue grn	.20	.20
233	A37	10fr carmine	.20	.60
234	A37	20fr deep blue	.35	*17.50*
		Nos. 218-234 (23)	9.95	*28.60*
		Set, never hinged	15.00	

1945 Engr. *Perf. 14x13*

No.	Type	Description	Unused	Used
235	A38	20c black	.20	.20
236	A38	30c brt green	.20	.20
237	A38	60c deep violet	.20	.20
238	A38	75c brown red	.20	.20
239	A38	1.20fr red	.20	.20
240	A38	1.50fr rose lilac	.20	.20
241	A38	2.50fr lt blue	.20	.20
		Set, never hinged	1.00	

Issued: 1.20fr, 5/15/45; 30c, 1.50fr, 2.50fr, 7/19; 20c, 75c, 10/1; 60c, 12/13.

Patton's Grave, US Military Cemetery, Hamm A39

Gen. Patton, Broken Chain and Advancing Tanks A40

1947, Oct. 24 Photo. *Perf. 11½*

No.	Type	Description	Unused	Used
242	A39	1.50fr dk carmine	.20	*.20*
243	A40	3.50fr dull blue	.70	*3.25*
244	A39	5fr dk slate grn	.70	*3.25*
245	A40	10fr chocolate	3.25	*37.50*
		Nos. 242-245 (4)	4.85	*44.20*
		Set, never hinged	14.50	

George S. Patton, Jr. (1885-1945), American general.

Esch-sur-Sûre Fortifications A41

Luxembourg A44

Moselle River A42

Steel Mills — A43

Perf. 11½x11, 11x11½

1948, Aug. 5 Engr. Unwmk.

No.	Type	Description	Unused	Used
246	A41	7fr dark brown	5.50	.70
247	A42	10fr dark green	.40	.20
248	A43	15fr carmine	.40	.65
249	A44	20fr dark blue	.55	.65
		Nos. 246-249 (4)	6.85	2.20
		Set, never hinged	22.50	

Grand Duchess Charlotte — A45

1948-49 *Perf. 11½*

No.	Type	Description	Unused	Used
250	A45	15c olive brn ('49)	.20	.20
251	A45	25c slate	.20	.20
252	A45	60c brown ('49)	.25	.20
253	A45	80c green ('49)	.25	.20
254	A45	1fr red lilac	.70	.20
255	A45	1.50fr grnsh bl	.70	.20
256	A45	1.60fr slate gray ('49)	.70	*1.40*
257	A45	2fr dk vio brn	.70	.20
258	A45	4fr violet blue	1.40	.55
259	A45	6fr brt red vio ('49)	2.25	.70
260	A45	8fr dull green ('49)	2.25	1.40
		Nos. 250-260 (11)	9.60	5.45
		Set, never hinged	35.00	

See Nos. 265-271, 292, 337-340, B151.

Self-Inking Canceller A46

1949, Oct. 6 Photo.

No.	Type	Description	Unused	Used
261	A46	80c blk, Prus grn & pale grn	.20	.60
262	A46	2.50fr dk brn, brn red & sal rose	1.10	*1.60*
263	A46	4fr blk, bl & pale bl	3.00	*6.50*
264	A46	8fr dk brn, brn & buff	9.50	*30.00*
		Nos. 261-264 (4)	13.80	38.70
		Set, never hinged	27.50	

UPU, 75th anniv.

Charlotte Type of 1948-49

1951, Mar. 15 Engr. Unwmk.

No.	Type	Description	Unused	Used
265	A45	5c red orange	.20	.20
266	A45	10c ultra	.20	.20
267	A45	40c crimson	.20	.20
268	A45	1.25fr dk brown	.70	.35
269	A45	2.50fr red	.70	.20
270	A45	3fr blue	4.50	.35
271	A45	3.50fr rose lake	1.90	.45
		Nos. 265-271 (7)	8.40	1.95
		Set, never hinged	35.00	

Agriculture and Industry A47

Globe and Scales A48

1fr, 3fr, People of Europe & Charter of Freedom.

1951, Oct. 25 Photo. *Perf. 11½*

No.	Type	Description	Unused	Used
272	A47	80c deep green	*4.00*	*3.50*
273	A47	1fr purple	*2.75*	*.45*
274	A48	2fr black brown	*11.00*	*.45*
275	A47	2.50fr dk carmine	*14.00*	*10.00*
276	A47	3fr orange brn	*20.00*	*15.00*
277	A48	4fr blue	*25.00*	*20.00*
		Nos. 272-277 (6)	*76.75*	*49.40*
		Set, never hinged	*125.00*	

Issued to promote a united Europe.

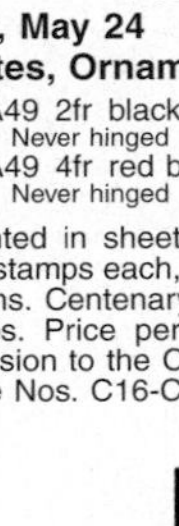
Grand Duke William III — A49

Perf. 13½x13

1952, May 24 Engr. Unwmk.

Dates, Ornaments in Olive Green

No.	Type	Description	Unused	Used
278	A49	2fr black	22.50	*55.00*
		Never hinged	32.50	
279	A49	4fr red brown	22.50	*55.00*
		Never hinged	32.50	

Printed in sheets containing two panes of eight stamps each, alternating the two denominations. Centenary of Luxembourg's postage stamps. Price per set, 26fr, which included admission to the CENTILUX exhibition.

See Nos. C16-C20.

Hurdle Race — A50

Designs: 2fr, Football. 2.50fr, Boxing. 3fr, Water polo. 4fr, Bicycle racing. 8fr, Fencing.

1952, Aug. 20 Photo. *Perf. 11½*

Designs in Black

No.	Type	Description	Unused	Used
280	A50	1fr pale green	.20	.30
281	A50	2fr brown buff	.65	.35
282	A50	2.50fr salmon pink	1.50	1.10
283	A50	3fr buff	1.90	1.75
284	A50	4fr lt blue	9.25	9.00
285	A50	8fr lilac	5.50	6.00
		Nos. 280-285 (6)	19.00	18.50
		Set, never hinged	37.50	

15th Olympic Games, Helsinki; World Bicycling Championships of 1952.

Wedding of Princess Josephine-Charlotte of Belgium and Hereditary Grand Duke Jean — A51

1953, Apr. 1

No.	Type	Description	Unused	Used
286	A51	80c dull violet	.20	.20
287	A51	1.20fr lt brown	.20	.20
288	A51	2fr green	.55	.20
289	A51	3fr red lilac	.90	.65
290	A51	4fr brt blue	3.25	1.25
291	A51	9fr brown red	3.25	1.25
		Nos. 286-291 (6)	8.35	3.75
		Set, never hinged	16.00	

Charlotte Type of 1948-49

1953, May 18 Engr.

No.	Type	Description	Unused	Used
292	A45	1.20fr gray	.45	.30
		Never hinged	1.00	

Radio Luxembourg — A52

Victor Hugo's Home, Vianden A53

1953, May 18 *Perf. 11½x11*

No.	Type	Description	Unused	Used
293	A52	3fr purple	2.75	1.50
294	A53	4fr Prussian blue	1.75	1.50
		Set, never hinged	8.75	

150th birth anniv. of Victor Hugo (No. 294).

St. Willibrord Basilica Restored — A54

Pierre d'Aspelt — A55

Design: 2.50fr, Interior view.

1953, Sept. 18 *Perf. 13x13½*

No.	Type	Description	Unused	Used
295	A54	2fr red	1.60	.45
296	A54	2.50fr dk gray grn	2.75	7.25
		Set, never hinged	8.75	

Consecration of St. Willibrord Basilica at Echternach.

1953, Sept. 25

No.	Type	Description	Unused	Used
297	A55	4fr black	5.25	5.50
		Never hinged	9.00	

Pierre d'Aspelt (1250-1320), chancellor of the Holy Roman Empire and Archbishop of Mainz.

Fencing Swords, Mask and Glove — A56

Winged "L" Over Map — A57

1954, May 6 *Perf. 13½x13*

No.	Type	Description	Unused	Used
298	A56	2fr red brn & blk brn, *gray*	2.25	.90
		Never hinged	4.50	

World Fencing Championship Matches, Luxembourg, June 10-22.

1954, May 6 **Photo.** *Perf. 11½*

No.	Type	Description	Unused	Used
299	A57	4fr dp bl, yel & red	6.50	6.50
		Never hinged	11.00	

6th Intl. Fair, Luxembourg, July 10-25.

Flowers — A58

Artisan, Wheel and Tools — A59

1955, Apr. 1

No.	Type	Description	Unused	Used
300	A58	80c Tulips	.20	.20
301	A58	2fr Daffodils	.20	.20
302	A58	3fr Hyacinths	1.50	3.25
303	A58	4fr Parrot tulips	1.75	5.00
		Nos. 300-303 (4)	*3.65*	*8.65*
		Set, never hinged	8.75	

Flower festival at Mondorf-les-Bains. See Nos. 351-353.

1955, Sept. 1 **Engr.** *Perf. 13*

No.	Type	Description	Unused	Used
304	A59	2fr dk gray & blk brn	.70	.35
		Never hinged	1.40	

Natl. Handicraft Exposition at Luxembourg — Limpertsburg, Sept. 3-12.

Dudelange Television Station A60

1955, Sept. 1 **Unwmk.**

No.	Type	Description	Unused	Used
305	A60	2.50fr dk brn & redsh brn	.65	.35
		Never hinged	1.90	

Installation of the Tele-Luxembourg station at Dudelange.

United Nations Emblem and Children Playing A61

UN, 10th anniv.: 80c, "Charter." 4fr, "Justice" (Sword and Scales). 9fr, "Assistance" (Workers).

1955, Oct. 24 *Perf. 11x11½*

No.	Type	Description	Unused	Used
306	A61	80c black & dk bl	.25	.65
307	A61	2fr red & brown	1.90	.35
308	A61	4fr dk blue & red	1.50	4.25
309	A61	9fr dk brn & sl grn	.60	1.50
		Nos. 306-309 (4)	*4.25*	*6.75*
		Set, never hinged	11.00	

A62

A63

2fr, Anemones. 2.50fr, 4fr, Roses. 3fr, Crocuses.

1956 **Photo.** *Perf. 11½*

Flowers in Natural Colors

No.	Type	Description	Unused	Used
310	A62	2fr gray violet	.25	.20
311	A62	2.50fr brt blue	2.50	5.00
312	A62	3fr red brown	1.00	1.60
313	A62	4fr purple	1.25	1.60
		Nos. 310-313 (4)	*5.00*	*8.40*
		Set, never hinged	10.00	

Flower Festival at Mondorf-les-Bains (Nos. 310, 312). Nos. 311 and 313 are inscribed: "Luxembourg-Ville des Roses."

Issued: #310, 312, Apr. 27; #311, 313, May 30.

1956, May 30

Steel beam and city emblem.

No.	Type	Description	Unused	Used
314	A63	2fr brt grnsh bl, red & blk	.70	.50
		Never hinged	2.50	

50th anniversary of Esch-sur-Alzette.

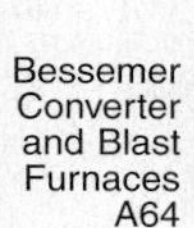

Bessemer Converter and Blast Furnaces A64

Steel Beam and Model of City of Luxembourg A65

"Rebuilding Europe" A66

Design: 4fr, 6-link chain, miner's lamp.

Perf. 11x11½, 11½x11

1956, Aug. 10 **Engr.**

No.	Type	Description	Unused	Used
315	A64	2fr dull red	12.00	.55
316	A65	3fr dark blue	12.00	*22.50*
317	A64	4fr green	3.25	*4.75*
		Nos. 315-317 (3)	*27.25*	*27.80*
		Set, never hinged	55.00	

4th anniv. of the establishment in Luxembourg of the headquarters of the European Coal and Steel Community.

1956, Sept. 15 *Perf. 13*

No.	Type	Description	Unused	Used
318	A66	2fr brown & black	*55.00*	*.25*
319	A66	3fr brick red & car	*17.50*	*17.50*
320	A66	4fr brt bl & dp bl	*1.75*	*3.75*
		Nos. 318-320 (3)	*74.25*	*21.50*
		Set, never hinged	*200.00*	

Cooperation among the six countries comprising the Coal and Steel Community.

Catalogue values for unused stamps in this section, from this point to the end of the section, are for Never Hinged items.

Central Station from Train Window A67

1956, Sept. 29 *Perf. 13x12½*

No.	Type	Description	Unused	Used
321	A67	2fr black & sepia	2.25	.45

Electrification of Luxembourg railways.

Ignace de la Fontaine A68

Design: 7fr, Grand Duchess Charlotte.

1956, Nov. 7 *Perf. 11½*

No.	Type	Description	Unused	Used
322	A68	2fr gray brown	1.25	.30
323	A68	7fr dull purple	2.50	.70

Centenary of the Council of State.

Lord Baden-Powell and Luxembourg Scout Emblems — A69

Designs: 2.50fr, Lord Baden-Powell and Luxembourg Girl Scout emblems.

1957, June 17 *Perf. 11½x11*

No.	Type	Description	Unused	Used
324	A69	2fr ol grn & red brn	1.00	.50
325	A69	2.50fr dk vio & claret	2.50	*2.00*

Birth centenary of Robert Baden-Powell and 50th anniv. of the founding of the Scout movement.

Prince Henry — A70

Children's Clinic — A71

Design: 4fr, Princess Marie-Astrid.

1957, June 17 **Photo.** *Perf. 11½*

No.	Type	Description	Unused	Used
326	A70	2fr brown	1.00	.25
327	A71	3fr bluish grn	3.25	*3.25*
328	A70	4fr ultra	2.25	*2.75*
		Nos. 326-328 (3)	*6.50*	*6.25*

Children's Clinic of the Prince Jean-Princess Josephine-Charlotte Foundation.

"United Europe" — A72

Fair Building and Flags — A73

1957, Sept. 16 **Engr.** *Perf. 12½x12*

No.	Type	Description	Unused	Used
329	A72	2fr reddish brn	*5.50*	*1.75*
330	A72	3fr red	*37.50*	*10.00*
331	A72	4fr rose lilac	*35.00*	*8.00*
		Nos. 329-331 (3)	*78.00*	*19.75*
		Set, hinged	20.00	

A united Europe for peace and prosperity.

1958, Apr. 16 *Perf. 12x11½*

No.	Type	Description	Unused	Used
332	A73	2fr ultra & multi	.25	.20

10th International Luxembourg Fair.

Luxembourg Pavilion, Brussels A74

1958, Apr. 16 **Unwmk.**

No.	Type	Description	Unused	Used
333	A74	2.50fr car & ultra	.25	.20

International Exposition at Brussels.

St. Willibrord — A75

1fr, Sts. Willibrord & Irmina from "Liber Aureus." 5fr, St. Willibrord, young man & wine cask.

1958, May 23 **Engr.** *Perf. 13x13½*

No.	Type	Description	Unused	Used
334	A75	1fr red	.25	.30
335	A75	2.50fr olive brn	.35	.20
336	A75	5fr blue	.90	*1.00*
		Nos. 334-336 (3)	*1.50*	*1.50*

1300th birth anniv. of St. Willibrord, apostle of the Low Countries and founder of Echternach Abbey.

Charlotte Type of 1948-49

1958 Unwmk. *Perf. 11½*

337 A45 20c dull claret .20 .20
338 A45 30c olive .20 .20
339 A45 50c dp org .35 .20
340 A45 5fr violet 8.25 .40
Nos. 337-340 (4) 9.00 1.00

Issued: No. 337, 8/1; Nos. 338-340, 7/1.

Common Design Types pictured following the introduction.

Europa Issue, 1958

Common Design Type

1958, Sept. 13 Litho. *Perf. 12½x13*
Size: 21x34mm

341 CD1 2.50fr car & bl *.30* .20
342 CD1 3.50fr green & org *1.00* *.35*
343 CD1 5fr blue & red *1.10* *.55*
Nos. 341-343 (3) 2.40 1.10

Wiltz Open-Air Theater A76

Vintage, Moselle A77

1958, Sept. 13 Engr. *Perf. 11x11½*

344 A76 2.50fr slate & sepia .50 .20
345 A77 2.50fr lt grn & sepia .50 .20

No. 345 issued to publicize 2,000 years of grape growing in Luxembourg region.

Grand Duchess Charlotte — A78

NATO Emblem — A79

1959, Jan. 15 Photo. *Perf. 11½*

346 A78 1.50fr pale grn & dk grn 1.00 .50
347 A78 2.50fr pink & dk brn 1.00 .50
348 A78 5fr lt bl & dk bl 1.65 *1.25*
Nos. 346-348 (3) 3.65 *2.25*

40th anniv. of the accession to the throne of the Grand Duchess Charlotte.

1959, Apr. 3 *Perf. 12½x12*

349 A79 2.50fr brt ol & bl .20 .20
350 A79 8.50fr red brn & bl .50 .35

NATO, 10th anniversary.

Flower Type of 1955, Inscribed "1959"

1fr, Iris. 2.50fr, Peonies. 3fr, Hydrangea.

1959, Apr. 3 *Perf. 11½*
Flowers in Natural Colors

351 A58 1fr dk bl grn .35 .35
352 A58 2.50fr deep blue .50 .35
353 A58 3fr deep red lilac .65 .65
Nos. 351-353 (3) 1.50 1.35

Flower festival, Mondorf-les-Bains.

Europa Issue, 1959

Common Design Type

Perf. 12½x13½
1959, Sept. 19 Litho.
Size: 22x33mm

354 CD2 2.50fr olive *1.75* *.45*
355 CD2 5fr dk blue *3.25* *1.75*

Locomotive of 1859 and Hymn — A80

1959, Sept. 19 Engr. *Perf. 13½*

356 A80 2.50fr red & ultra 1.60 .35

Centenary of Luxembourg's railroads.

Man and Child Knocking at Door — A81

Holy Family, Flight into Egypt A82

Perf. 11½x11, 11x11½
1960, Apr. 7 Unwmk.

357 A81 2.50fr org & slate .20 .20
358 A82 5fr pur & slate .30 .30

World Refugee Year, July 1, 1959-June 30, 1960.

Steel Worker Drawing CECA Initials and Map of Member Countries A83

1960, May 9 *Perf. 11x11½*

359 A83 2.50fr dk car rose .60 .20

10th anniv. of the Schumann Plan for a European Steel and Coal Community.

European School and Children A84

1960, May 9

360 A84 5fr bl & gray blk .90 .90

Establishment of the first European school in Luxembourg.

Heraldic Lion and Tools A85

1960, June 14 Photo. *Perf. 11½*

361 A85 2.50fr gray, red, bl & blk 1.40 .30

Natl. Exhibition of Craftsmanship, Luxembourg-Limpertsberg, July 9-18.

Grand Duchess Charlotte — A86

1960-64 Engr. Unwmk.

362 A86 10c claret ('61) .20 .20
363 A86 20c rose red ('61) .20 .20
363A A86 25c org ('64) .20 .20
364 A86 30c gray olive .20 .20
365 A86 50c dull grn .60 .20
366 A86 1fr vio blue .75 .20
367 A86 1.50fr rose lilac .75 .20
368 A86 2fr blue ('61) .80 .20
369 A86 2.50fr rose vio 1.40 .20
370 A86 3fr vio brn ('61) 1.60 .20
371 A86 3.50fr aqua ('64) 2.25 1.90
372 A86 5fr lt red brn 2.25 .25
373 A86 6fr slate ('64) 2.75 .20
Nos. 362-373 (13) 13.95 4.35

The 50c, 1fr and 3fr were issued in sheets and in coils. Every fifth coil stamp has control number on back.

Europa Issue, 1960

Common Design Type

1960, Sept. 19 *Perf. 11x11½*
Size: 37x27mm

374 CD3 2.50fr indigo & emer *.40* *.40*
375 CD3 5fr maroon & blk *1.10* *.40*

Great Spotted Woodpecker A87

Clervaux and Abbey of St. Maurice and St. Maur A88

Designs: 1.50fr, Cat, horiz. 3fr, Filly, horiz. 8.50fr, Dachshund.

1961, May 15 Photo. *Perf. 11½*

376 A87 1fr multicolored .20 .20
377 A87 1.50fr multicolored .20 .20
378 A87 3fr gray, buff & red brn .40 .40
379 A87 8.50fr lt grn, blk & ocher .80 .60
Nos. 376-379 (4) 1.60 1.40

Issued to publicize animal protection.

1961, June 8 Engr. *Perf. 11½x11*

380 A88 2.50fr green .50 .25

General Patton Monument, Ettelbruck A89

1961, June 8 *Perf. 11x11½*

381 A89 2.50fr dark blue & gray .50 .25

The monument commemorates the American victory of the 3rd Army under Gen. George S. Patton, Jr., Battle of the Ardennes Bulge, 1944-45.

Europa Issue, 1961

Common Design Type

1961, Sept. 18 *Perf. 13x12½*
Size: 29½x27mm

382 CD4 2.50fr red *.35* *.30*
383 CD4 5fr blue *.25* *.25*

Cyclist Carrying Bicycle — A90

St. Laurent's Church, Diekirch — A91

Design: 5fr, Emblem of 1962 championship.

1962, Jan. 22 Photo. *Perf. 11½*

384 A90 2.50fr lt ultra, crim & blk .25 .20
385 A90 5fr multicolored .45 .40

Intl. Cross-country Bicycle Race, Esch-sur-Alzette, Feb. 18.

Europa Issue, 1962

Common Design Type

1962, Sept. 17 Unwmk. *Perf. 11½*
Size: 32½x23mm

386 CD5 2.50fr ol bis, yel grn & brn blk *.35* *.30*
387 CD5 5fr rose lil, lt grn & brn blk *.50* *.40*

1962, Sept. 17 Engr. *Perf. 11½x11*

388 A91 2.50fr brown & blk .40 .25

Bock Rock Castle, 10th Century A92

Gate of Three Towers, 11th Century — A93

Designs (each stamp represents a different century): No. 391, Benedictine Abbey, Munster. No. 392, Great Seal of Luxembourg, 1237. No. 393, Rham Towers. No. 394, Black Virgin, Grund. No. 395, Grand Ducal Palace. No. 396, The Citadel of the Holy Ghost. No. 397, Castle Bridge. No. 398, Town Hall. No. 399, Municipal theater, bridge and European Community Center.

Perf. 14x13 (A92), 11½ (A93)
Engr. (A92), Photo. (A93)
1963, Apr. 13

389 A92 1fr slate blue .45 .45
390 A93 1fr multicolored .20 .20
391 A92 1.50fr dl red brn .45 .45
392 A93 1.50fr multicolored .20 .20
393 A92 2.50fr gray grn .45 .45
394 A93 2.50fr multicolored .20 .20
395 A92 3fr brown .45 .45
396 A93 3fr multicolored .20 .20
397 A92 5fr brt violet .60 .60
398 A93 5fr multicolored .60 .60
399 A92 11fr multicolored .90 .90
Nos. 389-399 (11) 4.70 4.70

Millennium of the city of Luxembourg; MELUSINA Intl. Phil. Exhib., Luxembourg, Apr. 13-21. Set sold only at exhibition. Value of 62fr included entrance ticket. Nos. 390, 392, 394 and 396 however were sold without restriction.

Blackboard Showing European School Buildings — A94

1963, Apr. 13 Photo. *Perf. 11½*

400 A94 2.50fr gray, grn & mag .20 .20

10th anniv. of the European Schools in Luxembourg, Brussels, Varese, Mol and Karlsruhe.

Colpach Castle and Centenary Emblem A95

1963, May 8 Engr. *Perf. 13*

401 A95 2.50fr hn brn, gray & red .20 .20

Centenary of the Intl. Red Cross. Colpach Castle, home of Emile Mayrisch, was donated to the Luxembourg League of the Red Cross for a rest home.

Twelve Stars of Council of Europe — A96

Brown Trout Taking Bait — A97

1963, June 25 *Perf. 13x14*

402 A96 2.50fr dp ultra, *gold* .20 .20

10th anniv. of the European Convention of Human Rights.

Europa Issue, 1963

Common Design Type

1963, Sept. 16 Photo. *Perf. 11½*

Size: 32½x23mm

403 CD6 3fr bl grn, lt grn & org *.40* *.35*
404 CD6 6fr red brn, org red & org *.60* *.40*

1963, Sept. 16 Engr. *Perf. 13*

405 A97 3fr indigo .25 .20

World Fly-Fishing Championship, Wormeldange, Sept. 22.

Map of Luxembourg, Telephone Dial and Stars — A98

Power House — A99

1963, Sept. 16 Photo. *Perf. 11½*

406 A98 3fr ultra, brt grn & blk .25 .20

Completion of telephone automation.

1964, Apr. 17 Engr. *Perf. 13*

3fr, Upper reservoir, horiz. 6fr, Lohmuhle dam.

407 A99 2fr red brn & sl .20 .20
408 A99 3fr red, sl grn & lt bl .20 .20
409 A99 6fr choc, grn & bl .25 .20
Nos. 407-409 (3) .65 .60

Inauguration of the Vianden hydroelectric station.

Barge Entering Lock at Grevenmacher Dam — A100

1964, May 26 **Unwmk.**

410 A100 3fr indigo & brt bl .35 .20

Opening of Moselle River canal system.

Europa Issue, 1964

Common Design Type

1964, Sept. 14 Photo. *Perf. 11½*

Size: 22x38mm

411 CD7 3fr org brn, yel & dk bl *.35* *.25*
412 CD7 6fr yel grn, yel & dk brn *.55* *.30*

New Atheneum Educational Center and Students A101

1964, Sept. 14 **Unwmk.**

413 A101 3fr dk bl grn & blk .20 .20

Benelux Issue

King Baudouin, Queen Juliana and Grand Duchess Charlotte — A101a

1964, Oct. 12

Size: 45x26mm

414 A101a 3fr dull bl, yel & brn .25 .20

20th anniv. of the customs union of Belgium, Netherlands and Luxembourg.

Grand Duke Jean and Grand Duchess Josephine Charlotte A102

1964, Nov. 11 Photo. *Perf. 11½*

415 A102 3fr indigo .35 .20
416 A102 6fr dk brown .35 .30

Grand Duke Jean's accession to throne.

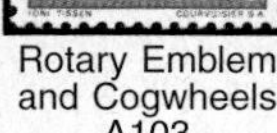

Rotary Emblem and Cogwheels A103

Grand Duke Jean A104

1965, Apr. 5 Photo. *Perf. 11½*

417 A103 3fr gold, car, gray & ultra .40 .20

Rotary International, 60th anniversary.

1965-71 Engr. **Unwmk.**

418 A104 25c olive bister ('66) .20 .20
419 A104 50c rose red .25 .20
420 A104 1fr ultra .25 .20
421 A104 1.50fr dk vio brn ('66) .20 .20
422 A104 2fr magenta ('66) .20 .20
423 A104 2.50fr orange ('71) .35 .25
424 A104 3fr gray .50 .20
425 A104 3.50fr brn org ('66) .35 .40
426 A104 4fr vio brn ('71) .30 .20
427 A104 5fr green ('71) .35 .20
428 A104 6fr purple .95 .20
429 A104 8fr bl grn ('71) .80 .20
Nos. 418-429 (12) 4.70 2.65

The 50c, 1fr, 2fr, 3fr, 4fr, 5fr and 6fr were issued in sheets and in coils. Every fifth coil stamp has control number on back.

See Nos. 570-576.

ITU Emblem, Old and New Communication Equipment — A105

1965, May 17 Litho. *Perf. 13½*

431 A105 3fr dk pur, claret & blk .20 .20

ITU, centenary.

Europa Issue, 1965

Common Design Type

Perf. 13x12½

1965, Sept. 27 Photo. **Unwmk.**

Size: 30x23½mm

432 CD8 3fr grn, maroon & blk .35 *.30*
433 CD8 6fr tan, dk bl & grn .55 *.45*

Inauguration of WHO Headquarters, Geneva — A106

1966, Mar. 7 Engr. *Perf. 11x11½*

434 A106 3fr green .20 .20

Torch and Banner — A107

Key and Arms of City of Luxembourg, and Arms of Prince of Chimay — A108

1966, Mar. 7 Photo. *Perf. 11½*

435 A107 3fr gray & brt red .20 .20

50th anniversary of the Workers' Federation in Luxembourg.

1966, Apr. 28 Engr. *Perf. 13x14*

Designs: 2fr, Interior of Cathedral of Luxembourg, painting by Juan Martin. 3fr, Our Lady of Luxembourg, engraving by Richard Collin. 6fr, Column and spandrel with sculptured angels from Cathedral.

436 A108 1.50fr green .20 .20
437 A108 2fr dull red .20 .20
438 A108 3fr dk blue .20 .20
439 A108 6fr red brown .25 .25
Nos. 436-439 (4) .85 .85

300th anniv. of the Votum Solemne (Solemn Promise) which made the Virgin Mary Patron Saint of the City of Luxembourg.

Europa Issue, 1966

Common Design Type

Perf. 13½x12½

1966, Sept. 26 **Litho.**

Size: 25x37mm

440 CD9 3fr gray & vio bl .40 *.30*
441 CD9 6fr olive & dk grn .70 *.50*

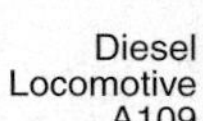

Diesel Locomotive A109

Design: 3fr, Electric locomotive.

1966, Sept. 26 Photo. *Perf. 11½*

442 A109 1.50fr multicolored *.30* .20
443 A109 3fr multicolored *.60* .30

5th Intl. Philatelic Exhibition of Luxembourg Railroad Men, Sept. 30-Oct. 3.

Grand Duchess Charlotte Bridge A110

1966, Sept. 26 Engr. *Perf. 13*

444 A110 3fr dk car rose .20 .20

Tower Building, Kirchberg, Seat of European Community — A111

Design: 13fr, Design for Robert Schuman monument, Luxembourg.

1966, Sept. 26

445 A111 1.50fr dk green .20 .20
446 A111 13fr deep blue .55 .25

"Luxembourg, Center of Europe."

View of Luxembourg, 1850, by Nicolas Liez — A112

Map of Luxembourg Fortress, 1850, by Theodore de Cederstolpe — A113

1967, Mar. 6 Engr. *Perf. 13*

447 A112 3fr bl, vio brn & grn .20 .20
448 A113 6fr blue, brn & red .25 .20

Centenary of the Treaty of London, which guaranteed the country's neutrality after the dismantling of the Fortress of Luxembourg.

Europa Issue, 1967

Common Design Type

1967, May 2 Photo. *Perf. 11½*

Size: 33x22mm

449 CD10 3fr cl brn, gray & buff *.50* *.35*
450 CD10 6fr dk brn, vio gray & lt bl *.75* *.50*

Lion, Globe and Lions Emblem — A115

NATO Emblem and European Community Administration Building — A116

1967, May 2 Photo. *Perf. 11½*
451 A115 3fr multicolored .20 .20

Lions International, 50th anniversary.

> Canceled to Order
> Luxembourg's Office des Timbres, Direction des Postes, was offering, at least as early as 1967, to sell commemorative issues canceled to order.

1967, June 13 Litho. *Perf. 13x12½*
452 A116 3fr lt grn & dk grn .25 .20
453 A116 6fr dp rose & dk car .40 .40

NATO Council meeting, Luxembourg, June 13-14.

Youth Hostel, Ettelbruck A117

Home Gardener A118

1967, Sept. 14 Photo. *Perf. 11½*
454 A117 1.50fr multicolored .20 .20

Luxembourg youth hostels.

1967, Sept. 14
455 A118 1.50fr brt grn & org .20 .20

16th Congress of the Intl. Assoc. of Home Gardeners.

Shaving Basin with Wedding Scene, 1819 — A119

Design: 3fr, Ornamental vase, 1820, vert.

1967, Sept. 14
456 A119 1.50fr ol grn & multi .20 .20
457 A119 3fr ultra & lt gray .25 .20

Faience industry in Luxembourg, 200th anniv.

Wormeldange - Moselle River — A120

Mertert, Moselle River Port A121

1967, Sept. 14 Engr. *Perf. 13*
458 A120 3fr dp bl, claret & ol .25 .20
459 A121 3fr violet bl & slate .25 .20

Swimming — A122

Sport: 1.50fr, Soccer. 2fr, Bicycling. 3fr, Running. 6fr, Walking. 13fr, Fencing.

1968, Feb. 22 Photo. *Perf. 11½*
460 A122 50c bl & grnsh bl .20 .20
461 A122 1.50fr brt grn & emer .20 .20
462 A122 2fr yel grn & lt yel grn .20 .20
463 A122 3fr dp org & dl org .20 .20
464 A122 6fr grnsh bl & pale grn .30 .20
465 A122 13fr rose cl & rose .50 .50
Nos. 460-465 (6) 1.60 1.50

Issued to publicize the 19th Olympic Games, Mexico City, Oct. 12-27.

Europa Issue, 1968
Common Design Type

1968, Apr. 29 Photo. *Perf. 11½*
Size: 32½x23mm
466 CD11 3fr ap grn, blk & org brn *.40 .35*
467 CD11 6fr brn org, blk & ap grn *.70 .50*

Kind Spring Pavilion A123

1968, Apr. 29 Photo. *Perf. 11½*
468 A123 3fr multicolored .20 .20

Issued to publicize Mondorf-les-Bains.

Fair Emblem A124

1968, Apr. 29
469 A124 3fr dp vio, dl bl gold & red .20 .20

20th Intl. Fair, Luxembourg City, May 23-June 2.

Children's Village of Mersch A125

Orphan and Foster Mother — A126

1968, Sept. 18 Engr. *Perf. 13*
470 A125 3fr slate grn & dk red brn .20 .20
471 A126 6fr slate bl, blk & brn .30 .20

Mersch children's village. (Modeled after Austrian SOS villages for homeless children.)

Red Cross and Symbolic Blood Transfusion — A127

1968, Sept. 18 Photo. *Perf. 11½*
472 A127 3fr lt blue & car .20 .20

Voluntary Red Cross blood donors.

Luxair Plane over Luxembourg — A128

1968, Sept. 18 Engr. *Perf. 13*
473 A128 50fr olive, bl & dk bl 1.65 .70

Issued for tourist publicity.

Souvenir Sheet

"Youth and Leisure" — A129

Designs, a, 3fr, Doll. b, 6fr, Ballplayers. c, 13fr, Book, compass rose and ball.

1969, Apr. 3 Photo. *Perf. 11½*
Granite Paper
474 A129 Sheet of 3 4.00 3.25
a.-c. any single 1.25 1.00

1st Intl. Youth Phil. Exhib., JUVENTUS 1969, Luxembourg, Apr. 3-8.
No. 474 was on sale only at the exhibition. Sold only with entrance ticket for 40fr.

Europa Issue, 1969
Common Design Type

1969, May 19 Photo. *Perf. 11½*
Size: 32½x23mm
475 CD12 3fr gray, brn & org *.50 .35*
476 CD12 6fr vio gray, blk & yel *.60 .35*

Boy on Hobbyhorse, by Joseph Kutter (1894-1941) — A130

Design: 6fr, View of Luxembourg, by Kutter.

1969, May 19 Engr. *Perf. 12x13*
477 A130 3fr multicolored .25 .20
a. Green omitted *150.00 150.00*
478 A130 6fr multicolored .35 .35

ILO, 50th Anniv. A131

Photo.; Gold Impressed (Emblem)
1969, May 19 *Perf. 14x14½*
479 A131 3fr brt grn, vio & gold .20 .20

Mobius Strip in Benelux Colors — A131a

1969, Sept. 8 Litho. *Perf. 12½x13½*
480 A131a 3fr multicolored .30 .20

25th anniv. of the signing of the customs union of Belgium, Netherlands and Luxembourg.

NATO, 20th Anniv. A132

Grain and Mersch Agricultural Center — A133

1969, Sept. 8 *Perf. 13½x12½*
481 A132 3fr org brn & dk brn .30 .20

1969, Sept. 8 Photo. *Perf. 11½*
482 A133 3fr bl grn, gray & blk .20 .20

Issued to publicize agricultural progress.

St. Willibrord's Basilica and Abbey, Echternach A134

#484, Castle and open-air theater, Wiltz.

1969, Sept. 8 Engr. *Perf. 13*
483 A134 3fr dark blue & indigo .25 .20
484 A134 3fr slate green & indigo .25 .20

Pasqueflower A135

Design: 6fr, Hedgehog and 3 young.

1970, Mar. 9 Photo. *Perf. 11½*
485 A135 3fr multicolored .25 .20
486 A135 6fr green & multi .45 .40

European Conservation Year.

Goldcrest A136

1970, Mar. 9 Engr. *Perf. 13*
487 A136 1.50fr org, grn & blk brn .20 .20

Luxembourg Society for the protection and study of birds, 50th anniv.

Traffic Sign and Street Scene A137

1970, May 4 Photo. *Perf. 11½*
488 A137 3fr rose mag, red & blk .25 .20

The importance of traffic safety.

Europa Issue, 1970
Common Design Type

1970, May 4
Size: 32½x23mm

489 CD13 3fr brown & multi *.50 .30*
490 CD13 6fr green & multi *.75 .45*

Empress Kunigunde and Emperor Henry II, Window, Luxembourg Cathedral — A138

1970, Sept. 14 Photo. *Perf. 12*
491 A138 3fr multicolored .20 .20

Centenary of the Diocese of Luxembourg.

Census Symbol A139

1970, Sept. 14 *Perf. 11½*
492 A139 3fr dk grn, grnsh bl & red .20 .20

Census of Dec. 31, 1970.

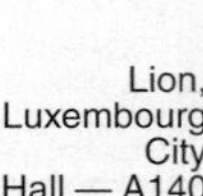

Lion, Luxembourg City Hall — A140

1970, Sept. 14
493 A140 3fr bister, lt bl & dk brn .20 .20

50th anniversary of the City of Luxembourg through the union of 5 municipalities.

UN Emblem A141

Perf. 12½x13½
1970, Sept. 14 Litho.
494 A141 1.50fr bl & vio bl .20 .20

25th anniversary of the United Nations.

Monks in Abbey Workshop A142

Olympic Rings, Arms of Luxembourg A143

Miniatures Painted at Echternach, about 1040: 3fr, Laborers going to the vineyard (Matthew 20:1-6). 6fr, Laborers toiling in vineyard. 13fr, Workers searching for graves of the saints.

1971, Mar. 15 Photo. *Perf. 12*
495 A142 1.50fr gold & multi .20 .20
496 A142 3fr gold & multi .20 .20
497 A142 6fr gold & multi .25 .20
498 A142 13fr gold & multi .50 .45
Nos. 495-498 (4) 1.15 1.05

1971, May 3 Photo. *Perf. 12½*
499 A143 3fr ultra & multi .25 .20

Intl. Olympic Committee, 71st session.

Europa Issue, 1971
Common Design Type

1971, May 3 *Perf. 12½x13*
Size: 34x25mm

500 CD14 3fr ver, brn & blk *.55 .30*
501 CD14 6fr brt grn, brn & blk *.80 .65*

A145

1971, May 3 Litho. *Perf. 13x13½*
502 A145 3fr org, dk brn & yel .20 .20

Christian Workers Union, 50th anniv.

Artificial Lake, Upper Sure A146

Designs: No. 504, Water treatment plant, Esch-sur-Sure. 15fr, ARBED Steel Corporation Headquarters, Luxembourg.

1971, Sept. 13 Engr. *Perf. 13*
503 A146 3fr ol, grnsh bl & indigo .20 .20
504 A146 3fr brn, sl grn & grnsh bl .25 .20
505 A146 15fr indigo & blk brn .70 .40
Nos. 503-505 (3) 1.15 .80

School Girl with Coin — A147

1971, Sept. 13 Photo. *Perf. 11½*
506 A147 3fr violet & multi .20 .20

School children's savings campaign.

Coins of Luxembourg and Belgium — A148

Bronze Mask — A149

1972, Mar. 6
507 A148 1.50fr lt grn, sil & blk .20 .20

Economic Union of Luxembourg and Belgium, 50th anniversary.

1972, Mar. 6

Archaeological Objects, 4th to 1st centuries, B.C.: 1fr, Earthenware bowl, horiz. 8fr, Limestone head. 15fr, Glass jug in shape of head.

508 A149 1fr lemon & multi .20 .20
509 A149 3fr multicolored .20 .20
510 A149 8fr multicolored .60 .60
511 A149 15fr multicolored .80 .80
Nos. 508-511 (4) 1.80 1.80

Europa Issue 1972
Common Design Type

1972, May 2 Photo. *Perf. 11½*
Size: 22x33mm

512 CD15 3fr rose vio & multi .70 *.25*
513 CD15 8fr gray blue & multi 1.10 *.60*

Archer A150

1972, May 2
514 A150 3fr crimson, blk & olive .40 .20

3rd European Archery Championships.

Robert Schuman Medal — A151

The Fox Wearing Tails — A152

1972, May 2 Engr. *Perf. 13*
515 A151 3fr gray & slate green .50 .20

Establishment in Luxembourg of the European Coal and Steel Community, 20th anniv.

1972, Sept. 11 Photo. *Perf. 11½*
516 A152 3fr scarlet & multi .35 .20

Centenary of the publication of "Renert," satirical poem by Michel Rodange.

National Monument A153

Court of Justice of European Communities, Kirchberg — A154

1972, Sept. 11 Engr. *Perf. 13*
517 A153 3fr sl grn, olive & vio .20 .20
518 A154 3fr brn, bl & slate grn .30 .20

Epona on Horseback — A155

Archaeological Objects: 4fr, Panther killing swan, horiz. 8fr, Celtic gold stater inscribed Pottina. 15fr, Bronze boar, horiz.

1973, Mar. 14 Photo. *Perf. 11½*
519 A155 1fr salmon & multi .20 .20
520 A155 4fr beige & multi .20 .20
521 A155 8fr multicolored .65 .65
522 A155 15fr multicolored .65 .65
Nos. 519-522 (4) 1.70 1.70

Europa Issue 1973
Common Design Type

1973, Apr. 30 Photo. *Perf. 11½*
Size: 32x22mm

523 CD16 4fr org, dk vio & lt bl *.85 .35*
524 CD16 8fr ol, vio blk & yel *1.50 .70*

Bee on Honeycomb A156

Nurse Holding Child A157

1973, Apr. 30 Photo. *Perf. 11½*
525 A156 4fr ocher & multi .35 .20

Publicizing importance of beekeeping.

1973, Apr. 30
526 A157 4fr multicolored .30 .20

Publicizing importance of day nurseries.

Laurel Branch A158

1973, Sept. 10 Photo. *Perf. 11½*
527 A158 3fr violet bl & multi .25 .20

50th anniv. of Luxembourg Board of Labor.

Jerome de Busleyden A159

National Strike Memorial, Wiltz A160

1973, Sept. 10 Engr. *Perf. 13*
528 A159 4fr black, brn & pur .30 .20

Council of Mechelen, 500th anniv.

1973, Sept. 10
529 A160 4fr ol bis, sl & sl grn .25 .20

In memory of the Luxembourg resistance heroes who died during the great strike of 1942.

Capital, Byzantine Hall, Vianden — A161

St. Gregory the Great — A161a

Designs: No. 534, Sts. Cecilia and Valerian crowned by angel, Hollenfels Church. No. 535, Interior, Septfontaines Church. 8fr, Madonna and Child, St. Irmina's Chapel, Rosport. 12fr, St. Augustine Sculptures by Jean-Georges Scholtus from pulpit in Feulen parish church, c. 1734.

1973-77 ***Perf. 13x12½, 14 (6fr, 12fr)***

533	A161	4fr green & rose vio	.25	.20
534	A161	4fr red brn, grn & lil	.40	.20
535	A161	4fr gray, brn & dk vio	.40	.20
536	A161a	6fr maroon	.30	.25
537	A161	8fr sepia & vio bl	.70	.60
538	A161a	12fr slate blue	.75	.65
		Nos. 533-538 (6)	2.80	2.10

Architecture of Luxembourg: Romanesque, Gothic, Baroque.

Issued: #533, 8fr, 9/10/73; #534-535, 9/9/74; 6fr, 12fr, 9/16/77.

Princess Marie Astrid — A162

1974, Mar. 14 **Photo.** ***Perf. 11½***

540 A162 4fr blue & multi .65 .20

Princess Marie-Astrid, president of the Luxembourg Red Cross Youth Section.

Torch — A163

1974, Mar. 14

541 A163 4fr ultra & multi .20 .20

50th anniversary of Luxembourg Mutual Insurance Federation.

Royal Seal of Henri VII — A164

Seals from 13th-14th Centuries: 3fr, Equestrian, seal of Jean, King of Bohemia. 4fr, Seal of Town of Diekirch. 19fr, Virgin and Child, seal of Convent of Marienthal.

1974, Mar. 14

542	A164	1fr purple & multi	.20	.20
543	A164	3fr green & multi	.30	.25
544	A164	4fr multicolored	.45	.20
545	A164	19fr multicolored	1.50	1.25
		Nos. 542-545 (4)	2.45	1.90

Hind, by Auguste Trémont — A165

Winston Churchill, by Oscar Nemon — A166

Europa: 8fr, "Growth," abstract sculpture, by Lucien Wercollier.

1974, Apr. 29 **Photo.** ***Perf. 11½***

546	A165	4fr ocher & multi	*3.00*	.75
547	A165	8fr brt blue & multi	*6.00*	*2.25*

1974, Apr. 29

548 A166 4fr lilac & multi .30 .20

Sir Winston Churchill (1874-1965), statesman.

Fairground, Aerial View — A167

Theis, the Blind — A168

1974, Apr. 29

549 A167 4fr silver & multi .30 .20

Publicity for New International Fairground, Luxembourg-Kirchberg.

1974, Apr. 29

550 A168 3fr multicolored .30 .20

Mathias Schou, Theis the Blind (1747-1824), wandering minstrel.

UPU Emblem and "100" — A169

1974, Sept. 9 **Photo.** ***Perf. 11½***

551	A169	4fr multicolored	.30	.30
552	A169	8fr multicolored	.80	.80

Centenary of Universal Postal Union.

"BENELUX" A170

1974, Sept. 9

553 A170 4fr bl grn, dk grn & lt bl .80 .20

30th anniversary of the signing of the customs union of Belgium, Netherlands and Luxembourg.

View of Differdange A171

1974, Sept. 9 **Engr.** ***Perf. 13***

554 A171 4fr rose claret .20 .20

Bourglinster A172

Designs: 1fr, Fish Market, Old Luxembourg, vert. 4fr, Market Square, Echternach. 19fr, St. Michael's Square, Mersch, vert.

Perf. 14x13½, 13½x14

1975, Mar. 10 **Engr.**

555	A172	1fr olive green	.75	.20
556	A172	3fr deep brown	1.40	.40
557	A172	4fr dark purple	1.50	.60
558	A172	19fr copper red	1.25	1.00
		Nos. 555-558 (4)	4.90	2.20

European Architectural Heritage Year.

Joseph Kutter, Self-portrait A173

Moselle Bridge, Remich, by Nico Klopp — A174

Paintings: 8fr, Still Life, by Joseph Kutter. 20fr, The Dam, by Dominique Lang.

1975, Apr. 28 **Photo.** ***Perf. 11½***

559	A173	1fr multicolored	.25	.20
560	A174	4fr multicolored	*1.75*	*.40*
561	A174	8fr multicolored	*2.75*	*1.25*
562	A173	20fr multicolored	1.25	.50
		Nos. 559-562 (4)	6.00	2.35

Cultural series. #560-561 are Europa Issue.

Robert Schuman, Gaetano Martino, Paul-Henri Spaak Medals A175

1975, Apr. 28

563 A175 4fr yel grn, gold & brn 1.10 .25

Robert Schuman's declaration establishing European Coal and Steel Community, 25th anniv.

Albert Schweitzer (1875-1965), Medical Missionary — A176

1975, Apr. 28 **Engr.** ***Perf. 13***

564 A176 4fr bright blue .90 .20

Civil Defense Emblem — A177

Figure Skating — A178

1975, Sept. 8 **Photo.** ***Perf. 11½***

565 A177 4fr multicolored .65 .25

Civil Defense Org. for protection and rescue.

1975, Sept. 8 **Engr.** ***Perf. 13***

4fr, Water skiing, horiz. 15fr, Mountain climbing.

566	A178	3fr green, bl & lilac	.25	.20
567	A178	4fr dk brn, grn & lt brn	.40	.30
568	A178	15fr brown, indigo & grn	1.25	.70
		Nos. 566-568 (3)	1.90	1.20

Grand Duke Type of 1965-71

1975-91 **Engr.** ***Perf. 11½***

Granite Paper (14fr, 22fr)

570	A104	7fr orange	.45	.20
571	A104	9fr yellow green	.65	.20
572	A104	10fr black	.50	.20
573	A104	12fr brick red	1.00	.20
573A	A104	14fr dark blue	.65	.30
574	A104	16fr green	1.00	.25
574A	A104	18fr brown olive	.80	.40
575	A104	20fr blue	.80	.20
576	A104	22fr orange brown	1.10	.80
		Nos. 570-576 (9)	6.95	2.75

Issued: 10fr, 1/9; 9fr, 12fr, 20fr, 12/23; 16fr, 2/25/82; 7fr, 7/1/83; 18fr, 3/3/86; 14fr, 1/2/90; 22fr, 9/23/91.

Grand Duchess Charlotte A179

Design: No. 580, Prince Henri.

1976, Mar. 8 **Litho.** ***Perf. 14x13½***

579	A179	6fr green & multi	.40	.20
580	A179	6fr dull blue & multi	.90	.25

80th birthday of Grand Duchess Charlotte and 21st birthday of Prince Henri, heir to the throne.

Gold Brooch — A180

5fr, Footless beaker, horiz. 6fr, Decorated vessel, horiz. 12fr, Gold coin. All designs show excavated items of Franco-Merovingian period.

Perf. 13½x12½, 12½x13½

1976, Mar. 8

581	A180	2fr blue & multi	.20	.20
582	A180	5fr black & multi	.30	.30
583	A180	6fr lilac & multi	.45	.30
584	A180	12fr multicolored	1.00	1.10
		Nos. 581-584 (4)	1.95	1.90

Soup Tureen A181

Europa: 12fr, Deep bowl. Tureen and bowl after pottery from Nospelt, 19th century.

1976, May 3 Photo. *Perf. 11½*

585 A181 6fr lt violet & multi *1.00* .30
586 A181 12fr yel grn & multi *1.75* 1.00

Independence Hall, Philadelphia A182

Boomerang A183

1976, May 3

587 A182 6fr lt blue & multi .35 .25

American Bicentennial.

1976, May 3

588 A183 6fr brt rose lil & gold .35 .20

21st Olympic Games, Montreal, Canada, July 17-Aug. 1.

"Vibrations of Sound" A184

1976, May 3

589 A184 6fr red & multi .35 .20

Jeunesses Musicales (Young Music Friends), association to foster interest in music and art.

Alexander Graham Bell — A185

Virgin and Child with St. Anne — A186

1976, Sept. 9 Engr. *Perf. 13*

590 A185 6fr slate green .35 .25

Centenary of first telephone call by Alexander Graham Bell, Mar. 10, 1876.

1976, Sept. 9 Photo. *Perf. 11½*

Renaissance sculptures: 12fr, Grave of Bernard de Velbruck, Lord of Beaufort.

591 A186 6fr gold & multi .35 .20
592 A186 12fr gold, gray & blk .70 .70

Johann Wolfgang von Goethe A187

Old Luxembourg A188

Portraits: 5fr, J. M. William Turner. 6fr, Victor Hugo. 12fr, Franz Liszt.

1977, Mar. 14 Engr. *Perf. 13*

593 A187 2fr lake .20 .20
594 A187 5fr purple .30 .25
595 A187 6fr slate green .35 .30
596 A187 12fr violet blue .70 .65
Nos. 593-596 (4) 1.55 1.40

Famous visitors to Luxembourg.

1977, May 3 Photo. *Perf. 11½*

Europa: 12fr, Adolphe Bridge and European Investment Bank headquarters.

597 A188 6fr multicolored *1.00* .25
598 A188 12fr multicolored *2.00* .60

Esch-sur-Sure A189

Marguerite de Busbach A190

Design: 6fr, View of Ehnen.

1977, May 3 Engr. *Perf. 13*

599 A189 5fr Prus blue .40 .25
600 A189 6fr deep brown .35 .25

1977, May 3 Photo. *Perf. 11½*

#602, Louis Braille, by Lucienne Filippi.

601 A190 6fr multicolored .35 .20
602 A190 6fr multicolored .35 .20

Notre Dame Congregation, founded by Marguerite de Busbach, 350th anniversary; Louis Braille (1809-1852), inventor of the Braille system of writing for the blind.

Souvenir Sheet

Luxembourg Nos. 1-2 — A191

Engr. & Photo.

1977, Sept. 15 *Perf. 13½*

603 A191 40fr gray & red brown 5.25 5.25

125th anniv. of Luxembourg's stamps.

Head of Medusa, Roman Mosaic, Diekirch, 3rd Century A.D. — A192

1977, Sept. 15 Photo. *Perf. 11½*

604 A192 6fr multicolored .50 .30

Orpheus and Eurydice, by C. W. Gluck A193

1977, Sept. 15 *Perf. 11½x12*

605 A193 6fr multicolored .60 .25

Intl. Wiltz Festival, 25th anniv.

Europa Tamed, by R. Zilli, and Map of Europe A194

1977, Dec. 5 Photo. *Perf. 11½*

606 A194 6fr multicolored .60 .30

20th anniversary of the Treaties of Rome, setting up the European Economic Community and the European Atomic Energy Commission.

Souvenir Sheet

Grand Duke and Grand Duchess of Luxembourg — A195

Photogravure and Engraved

1978, Apr. 3 *Perf. 13½x14*

607 A195 Sheet of 2 2.00 2.00
a. 6fr dark blue & multi .90 .90
b. 12fr dark red & multi .90 .90

Silver wedding anniversary of Grand Duke Jean and Grand Duchess Josephine Charlotte.

Souvenir Sheet

Youth Fountain, Streamer and Dancers — A196

1978, Apr. 3 Photo. *Perf. 11½*

608 A196 Sheet of 3 4.25 4.25
a. 5fr ultra & multi 1.40 1.40
b. 6fr orange & multi 1.40 1.40
c. 20fr yellow green & multi 1.40 1.40

Juphilux 78, 5th International Young Philatelists' Exhibition, Luxembourg, Apr. 6-10.

Charles IV, Statue, Charles Bridge, Prague A197

Emile Mayrisch, by Theo Van Rysselberghe A198

Europa: 12fr, Pierre d'Aspelt, tomb, Mainz Cathedral.

1978, May 18 Engr. *Perf. 13½*

609 A197 6fr dark violet blue *1.40* .30
610 A197 12fr dull rose lilac *3.25* .70

Charles IV (1316-78), Count of Luxembourg, Holy Roman Emperor. Pierre d'Aspelt (c. 1250-1320), Archbishop of Mainz and Prince-Elector.

1978, May 18 *Perf. 11½*

611 A198 6fr multicolored .85 .30

Emile Mayrisch (1862-1928), president of International Steel Cartel and promoter of United Europe.

Our Lady of Luxembourg A199

Trumpeters and Old Luxembourg A200

1978, May 18 Photo. *Perf. 11½*

612 A199 6fr multicolored .25 .25
613 A200 6fr multicolored .25 .25

Our Lady of Luxembourg, patroness, 300th anniv.; 135th anniv. of Grand Ducal Military Band.

Starving Child, Helping Hand, Millet — A201

League Emblem, Lungs, Open Window — A202

Open Prison Door — A203

1978, Sept. 11 Photo. *Perf. 11½*

614 A201 2fr multicolored .20 .20
615 A202 5fr multicolored .25 .25
616 A203 6fr multicolored .40 .30
Nos. 614-616 (3) .85 .75

"Terre des Hommes," an association to help underprivileged children; Luxembourg Anti-Tuberculosis League, 70th anniv.; Amnesty Intl. and 30th anniv. of Universal Declaration of Human Rights.

Squared Stone Emerging from Rock, City of Luxembourg — A204

1978, Sept. 11 Engr. *Perf. 13½x13*

617 A204 6fr violet blue .45 .25

Masonic Grand Lodge of Luxembourg, 175th anniversary.

Julius Caesar on Denarius, c. 44 B.C. A205

St. Michael's Church, Mondorf-les-Bains A206

Roman Coins, Found in Luxembourg: 6fr, Empress Faustina I on Sestertius, 141 A.D. 9fr, Empress Helena on Follis, c. 324-330. 26fr, Emperor Valens on Solidus, c. 367-375.

1979, Mar. 5 Photo. *Perf. 11½*

618 A205 5fr multicolored .20 .20
619 A205 6fr multicolored .20 .20
620 A205 9fr multicolored .65 .55
621 A205 26fr multicolored 1.25 1.00
Nos. 618-621 (4) 2.30 1.95

1979, Mar. 5 Engr. *Perf. 13*

Design: 6fr, Luxembourg Central Station.

622 A206 5fr multicolored .30 .20
623 A206 6fr rose claret .60 .30

Troisvierges Stagecoach A207

Europa: 12fr, Early wall telephone, vert.

1979, Apr. 30 Photo. *Perf. 11½*

624 A207 6fr multicolored *5.75* .35
625 A207 12fr multicolored *5.75 1.50*

Michel Pintz Facing Jury A208

1979, Apr. 30 Engr. *Perf. 13*

626 A208 2fr rose lilac .30 .20

180th anniversary of peasant uprising against French occupation.

Antoine Meyer — A209

Abundance Crowning Work and Thrift, by Auguste Vinet — A210

Design: 6fr, Sidney Gilchrist Thomas.

1979, Apr. 30

627 A209 5fr carmine .30 .20
628 A209 6fr light blue .30 .25
629 A210 9fr black .50 .35
Nos. 627-629 (3) 1.10 .80

Antoine Meyer (1801-1857), mathematician and first national poet; centenary of acquisition of Thomas process for production of high-quality steel; 50th anniversary of Luxembourg Stock Exchange.

European Parliament A211

1979, June 7 Photo. *Perf. 11½*

630 A211 6fr multi 5.00 .90

European Parliament, first direct elections, June 7-10.

Angel with Chalice, by Barthelemy Namur — A212

Rococo Art: 12fr, Angel with anchor, by Namur, from High Altar, St. Michael's Church, Luxembourg.

Engraved and Photogravure

1979, Sept. 10 *Perf. 13½*

631 A212 6fr multi .35 .25
632 A212 12fr multi .65 .50

Road Safety for Children A213

1979, Sept. 10 Photo. *Perf. 11½*

633 A213 2fr multi .20 .20

International Year of the Child.

Radio Tele-Luxembourg Emblem — A214

1979, Sept. 10

634 A214 6fr ultra, blue & red .45 .25

50 years of broadcasting in Luxembourg.

John the Blind, Silver Coin, 1331 — A215

Ettelbruck Town Hall — A216

14th Century Coins: 2fr, Sts. Gervase and Protais, silver grosso. 6fr, Easter lamb, gold coin. 20fr, Crown and arms, silver grosso.

1980, Mar. 5 Photo. *Perf. 11½*

635 A215 2fr multi .20 .20
636 A215 5fr multi .25 .25
637 A215 6fr multi .35 .35
638 A215 20fr multi 1.20 1.20
Nos. 635-638 (4) 2.00 2.00

See Nos. 651-654.

1980, Mar. 5 Engr. *Perf. 13*

No. 640, State Archives Building, horiz.

639 A216 6fr brn & dk red .35 .25
640 A216 6fr multi .35 .25

Jean Monnet — A217

Sports for All — A218

Europa: 12fr, St. Benedict of Nursia.

1980, Apr. 28 *Perf. 13½*

641 A217 6fr dark blue *1.50* .35
642 A217 12fr olive green *2.50* .65

1980, Apr. 28 Photo. *Perf. 11½*
Granite Paper

643 A218 6fr multi .95 .20

Worker Pouring Molten Iron — A219

Mercury by Jean Mich — A220

Design: 6fr, Man, hand, gears, horiz.

1980, Apr. 28

644 A219 2fr multi .20 .20
645 A219 6fr multi .40 .20

9th World Congress on Prevention of Occupational Accidents & Diseases, Amsterdam, May 6-9.

1980, Sept. 10 Engr. *Perf. 14*

Art Nouveau Sculpture by Jean Mich.

646 A220 8fr shown .50 .40
647 A220 12fr Ceres .70 .55

Introduction of Postal Code — A221

1980, Sept. 10 Photo. *Perf. 11½*

648 A221 4fr multi .40 .20

Police Car and Officers A222

1980, Sept. 10

649 A222 8fr multi .50 .30

State control of police force, 50th anniv.

Grand Duke Jean, Personal Arms — A223

Photo. & Engr.

1981, Jan. 5 *Perf. 13½*

650 A223 Sheet of 3 2.50 2.50
a. 8fr multi .65 .65
b. 12fr multi .75 .75
c. 30fr multi 1.00 1.00

Grand Duke Jean, 60th birthday.

Coin type of 1980

Silver Coins: 4fr, Philip IV patagon, 1635. 6fr, Empress Maria Theresa 12 sol, 1775. 8fr, Emperor Joseph II 12 sol, 1789. 30fr, Emperor Francois II 72 sol, 1795.

1981, Mar. 5 Photo. *Perf. 11½*

651 A215 4fr multi .20 .20
652 A215 6fr multi .25 .20
653 A215 8fr multi .30 .30
654 A215 30fr multi 1.25 1.10
Nos. 651-654 (4) 2.00 1.80

National Library A225

1981, Mar. 5 Engr. *Perf. 13*

655 A225 8fr shown .35 .20
656 A225 8fr European Hemicycle, Kirchberg .35 .20

Hammelsmarsch (Sheep Procession) A226

Europa: 12fr, Bird-shaped whistle, Eimaischen market.

1981, May 4 Photo. *Perf. 13½*

657 A226 8fr multi *1.00 .35*
658 A226 12fr multi *2.25 .45*

Knight on Chessboard A227

Savings Account Book, State Bank A228

First Bank Note, 1856 — A229

1981, May 4 *Perf. 11½*
Granite Paper

659 A227 4fr multi .25 .20
660 A228 8fr multi .35 .35
661 A229 8fr multi .35 .35

Luxembourg Chess Federation, 50th anniv.; State Savings Bank, 125th anniv.; Intl. Bank of Luxembourg, 125th anniv. of issuing rights.

Wedding of Prince Henri and Maria Teresa Mestre, Feb. 14 A230

Photo. & Engr.

1981, June 22 *Perf. 13½*

662 A230 8fr multi .50 .40

Sheets of 12.

Single-seater Gliders A231

Energy Conservation A232

1981, Sept. 28 Photo. *Perf. 11½*

Granite Paper

663 A231 8fr shown .30 .30
664 A231 16fr Propeller planes, horiz. .60 .60
665 A231 35fr Jet, Luxembourg Airport, horiz. 1.50 1.40
Nos. 663-665 (3) 2.40 2.30

1981, Sept. 28

Granite Paper

666 A232 8fr multi .35 .35

Apple Trees in Blossom, by Frantz Seimetz (1858-1914) A233

World War II Resistance — A234

Landscape Paintings: 6fr, Summer Landscape, by Pierre Blanc (1872-1946). 8fr, The Larger Hallerbach, by Guido Oppenheim (1862-1942). 16fr, Winter Evening, by Eugene Mousset (1877-1941).

1982, Feb. 25 Engr. *Perf. 11½*

667 A233 4fr multi .20 .20
668 A233 6fr multi .30 .30
669 A233 8fr multi .40 .40
670 A233 16fr multi .80 .80
Nos. 667-670 (4) 1.70 1.70

1982, Feb. 25

Design: Cross of Hinzert (Natl. Monument of the Resistance and Deportation) and Political Prisoner, by Lucien Wercollier.

671 A234 8fr multi .40 .35

Europa 1982 A235

St. Theresa of Avila (1515-1582) A236

1982, May 4 Photo.

Granite Paper

672 A235 8fr Treaty of London, 1867 *4.00* .45
673 A235 16fr Treaty of Paris, 1951 *6.00* 1.25

1982, May 4

Design: 8fr, Raoul Follereau (1903-1977), "Apostle of the Lepers."

Granite Paper

674 A236 4fr multi .20 .20
675 A236 8fr multi .40 .40

State Museum A237

1982, May 4 Photo. & Engr.

676 A237 8fr shown .45 .35
677 A237 8fr Synagogue of Luxembourg .45 .35

Bourscheid Castle — A238

Intl. Youth Hostel Federation, 50th Anniv. — A239

Designs: Restored castles.

1982, Sept. 9 Engr. *Perf. 11½*

Granite Paper

678 A238 6fr shown .30 .25
679 A238 8fr Vianden, horiz. .45 .35

1982, Sept. 9 Photo.

680 A239 4fr shown .30 .20
681 A239 8fr Scouting year, vert. .60 .35

Civilian and Military Deportation Monument — A240

1982, Sept. 9

682 A240 8fr multi .50 .35

Mercury, Sculpture by Auguste Tremont — A241

NATO Emblem, Flags — A242

1983, Mar. 7 Photo. *Perf. 11½*

Granite Paper

683 A241 4fr multi .20 .20

FOREX '83, 25th Intl. Assoc. of Foreign Exchange Dealers' Congress, June 2-5.

1983, Mar. 7

Granite Paper

684 A242 6fr multi .25 .25

25th anniv. of NAMSA (NATO Maintenance and Supply Agency).

Echternach Cross of Justice, 1236 — A243

Globe, CCC Emblem — A244

1983, Mar. 7

Granite Paper

685 A243 8fr multi .45 .35

30th Cong. of Intl. Union of Barristers, July 3-9.

1983, Mar. 7

Granite Paper

686 A244 8fr multi .45 .35

30th anniv. of Council of Customs Cooperation.

Natl. Federation of Fire Brigades Centenary A245

1983, Mar. 7

Granite Paper

687 A245 8fr Fire engine, 1983 .45 .35
688 A245 16fr Hand pump, 1740 .85 .65

Europa 1983 — A246

The Good Samaritan, Codex Aureus Escorialensis Miniatures, 11th Cent., Echternach.

1983, May 3 Photo.

689 A246 8fr Highway robbers *2.00* *.45*
690 A246 16fr Good Samaritan *3.75* *1.00*

Giant Bible, 11th Cent. — A247

World Communications Year — A248

Illuminated Letters.

Photo. & Engr.

1983, May 3 *Perf. 14*

691 A247 8fr "h," Book of Baruch .45 .35
692 A247 35fr "B," letter of St. Jerome 2.00 1.50

1983, May 3 Photo. *Perf. 11½*

693 A248 8fr Post code .40 .35
694 A248 8fr Satellite relay, horiz. .40 .35

Town Hall, Dudelange A249

7fr, St. Lawrence Church, Diekirch, vert.

1983, Sept. 7 Photo. & Engr.

695 A249 7fr multi .40 .25
696 A249 10fr multi .55 .35

Basketball Fed., 50th Anniv. A250

European Working Dog Championship A251

Tourism — A252

1983, Sept. 7 Photo.

Granite Paper

697 A250 7fr multi .40 .25
698 A251 10fr Alsatian sheepdog .55 .35
699 A252 10fr View of Luxembourg .55 .35
Nos. 697-699 (3) 1.50 .95

Environment Protection A253

1984, Mar. 6 Photo. *Perf. 11½*

Granite Paper

700 A253 7fr Pedestrian zoning .35 .20
701 A253 10fr Water purification .50 .25

2nd European Parliament Election — A254

1984, Mar. 6

Granite Paper

702 A254 10fr Hands holding emblem .60 .40

A255

A256

1984, Mar. 6 Engr. *Perf. 12½x13*

703 A255 10fr No. 1 .50 .35
704 A255 10fr Union meeting .50 .35
705 A255 10fr Mail bag .50 .35
706 A255 10fr Train .50 .35
Nos. 703-706 (4) 2.00 1.40

Philatelic Federation (1934); Civil Service Trade Union (1909); Postal Workers' Union (1909); Railroad (1859).

1984, May 7 Photo. *Perf. 11½x12*

707 A256 10fr The Race, by Jean Jacoby (1891-1936) .55 .35

1984 Summer Olympics.

Europa (1959-84)
A257

1984, May 7 *Perf. 11½*

Granite Paper

708 A257 10fr green *3.00 .40*
709 A257 16fr orange *4.50 1.00*

Young Turk Caressing His Horse, by Delacroix
A258

Paintings: 4fr, The Smoker, by David Teniers the Younger (1610-90). 10fr, Epiphany, by Jan Steen (1626-79). 50fr, The Lacemaker, by Pieter van Slingelandt (1640-91). 4fr, 50fr vert.

Photo. & Engr.

1984, May 7 *Perf. 14*

710 A258 4fr multi .25 .20
711 A258 7fr multi .40 .25
712 A258 10fr multi .60 .35
713 A258 50fr multi 2.75 2.00
Nos. 710-713 (4) 4.00 2.80

Marine Life Fossils — A259

Restored Castles — A260

1984, Sept. 10 Photo. *Perf. 11½*

714 A259 4fr Pecten sp. .20 .20
715 A259 7fr Gryphaea arcuata .40 .25
716 A259 10fr Coeloceras raqyinianum .55 .35
717 A259 16fr Daildius .90 .60
Nos. 714-717 (4) 2.05 1.40

1984, Sept. 10 Engr.

718 A260 7fr Hollenfels .40 .25
719 A260 10fr Larochette .55 .40

A261

A262

1984, Sept. 10 *Perf. 12x12½*

720 A261 10fr Soldier, US flag .75 .35

40th Anniv. of D Day (June 6).

1985, Mar. 4 Photo. *Perf. 11½*

Portrait medals in the state museum: 4fr, Jean Bertels (1544-1607), Historian, Abbott of Echternach. 7fr, Emperor Charles V (1500-1558). 10fr, King Philip II of Spain (1527-1598). 30fr, Prince Maurice of Orange-Nassau, Count of Vianden (1567-1625).

Granite Paper

721 A262 4fr multi .25 .20
722 A262 7fr multi .40 .20
723 A262 10fr multi .60 .30
724 A262 30fr multi 1.75 .90
Nos. 721-724 (4) 3.00 1.60

See Nos. 739-742.

Anniversaries
A263

#725, Benz Velo, First automobile in Luxembourg, 1895. #726, Push-button telephone, sound waves. #727, Fencers.

1985, Mar. 4 *Perf. 12x11½*

Granite Paper

725 A263 10fr multi .65 .40
726 A263 10fr multi .65 .40
727 A263 10fr multi .65 .40
Nos. 725-727 (3) 1.95 1.20

Centenary of the first automobile; Luxembourg Telephone Service, cent.; Luxembourg Fencing Federation, 50th anniv.

Visit of Pope John Paul II — A264

Europa 1985 — A265

1985, Mar. 4 *Perf. 11½x12*

Granite Paper

728 A264 10fr Papal arms .75 .40

1985, May 8 *Perf. 11½*

Designs: 10fr, Grand-Duke Adolphe Music Federation. 16fr, Luxembourg Music School.

729 A265 10fr multi *4.00 .45*
730 A265 16fr multi *5.00 .90*

Souvenir Sheet

End of World War II, 40th Anniv. — A266

Designs: a, Luxembourg resistance fighters, Wounded Fighters medal. b, Luxembourg War Cross. c, Badge of the Union of Luxembourg Resistance Movements. d, Liberation of the concentration camps.

1985, May 8 *Perf. 11½x12*

Granite Paper

731 A266 Sheet of 4 2.75 2.75
a.-d. 10fr, any single .60 .40

Endangered Wildlife — A267

1985, Sept. 23 Photo. *Perf. 12x11½*

732 A267 4fr Athene nocturna, vert. .20 .20
733 A267 7fr Felis silvestris .40 .20
734 A267 10fr Vanessa atalantica .55 .35
735 A267 50fr Hyla arborea, vert. 2.75 1.65
Nos. 732-735 (4) 3.90 2.40

Historic Monuments
A268

1985, Sept. 23 Engr. *Perf. 11½*

736 A268 7fr Echternach Orangery, 1750 .45 .20
737 A268 10fr Mohr de Waldt House, 17th cent. .65 .45

Natl. Art Collection
A269

Photo. & Engr.

1985, Sept. 23 *Perf. 14*

738 A269 10fr 18th cent. book cover, Natl. Library .40 .20

Portrait Medals Type of 1985

1986, Mar. 3 Photo. *Perf. 11½*

Granite Paper

739 A262 10fr Count of Monterey, 1675 .65 .40
740 A262 12fr Louis XIV, 1684 .70 .45
741 A262 18fr Pierre de Weyms, c. 1700 1.10 .70
742 A262 20fr Duke of Marlborough, 1706 1.25 .80
Nos. 739-742 (4) 3.70 2.35

Federation of Luxembourg Beekeepers' Associations, Cent.
A270

Mondorf State Spa, Cent. — A271

Natl. Table Tennis Federation, 50th Anniv. — A272

1986, Mar. 3 *Perf. 11½*

743 A270 12fr Bee collecting pollen .75 .50
744 A271 12fr Mosaic .75 .50
745 A272 12fr Boy playing table tennis .75 .50
Nos. 743-745 (3) 2.25 1.50

Europa 1986
A273

Fortifications
A274

1986, May 5 Photo. *Perf. 12*

Granite Paper

751 A273 12fr Polluted forest, city *2.75 .50*
752 A273 20fr Man, pollution sources *3.75 1.00*

1986, May 5

Granite Paper

753 A274 15fr Ft. Thungen, horiz. 1.60 .60
754 A274 18fr Invalid's Gate 1.60 .70
755 A274 50fr Malakoff Tower 3.00 2.00
Nos. 753-755 (3) 6.20 3.30

Robert Schuman (1886-1963), European Cooperation Promulgator — A275

1986, June 26 *Perf. 12 on 3 Sides*

Granite Paper

756 A275 2fr pink & blk .20 .20
a. Bklt. pane of 4 .30
757 A275 10fr lt bl & blk .50 .40
a. Bklt. pane of 4 2.75
b. Bklt. pane of 2, #756-757 + 2 labels 1.40

Nos. 756-757 issued in booklets only.

European Road Safety Year — A276

Countess Ermesinde (1186-1247), Ruler of Luxembourg
A278

Bas-relief, Town Hall, Esch-Sur-Alzette — A277

1986, Sept. 15 Photo. *Perf. 11½*

758 A276 10fr multi .55 .40

Photogravure & Engraved

1986, Sept. 15 *Perf. 14x13½*

Design: No. 760, Stairs to the Chapel of the Cross, Grevenmacher.

759 A277 12fr shown .75 .50
760 A277 12fr multi .75 .50

1986, Sept. 15 *Perf. 13½x14*

Designs: No. 761, Presentation of the letter of freedom to Echternach inhabitants, 1236, engraving (detail) by P.H. Witkamp, c. 1873. 30fr, Charter seal, Marienthal Convent, 1238.

761 A278 12fr multi .70 .50
762 A278 30fr multi 1.65 1.20

A279

A280

A281

1987, Mar. 9 Photo. *Perf. 11½*

763 A279 6fr Eliomys quercinus, horiz. .65 .35
764 A279 10fr Calopteryx splendens 1.00 .50
765 A279 12fr Cinclus cinclus 1.60 .35
766 A279 25fr Salamandra salamandra terrestris, horiz. 2.25 1.25
Nos. 763-766 (4) 5.50 2.45

Wildlife conservation.

1987, Mar. 9

767 A280 12fr multi .60 .50

Natl. Home Amateur Radio Operators Network, 50th anniv.

1987, Mar. 9

768 A281 12fr multi .60 .50

Luxembourg Intl. Fair, 50th anniv.

Europa 1987 — A282

12fr, Aquatic Sports Center. 20fr, European Communities Court of Justice and abstract sculpture by Henry Moore (1898-1986).

1987, May 4 Photo. *Perf. 11½*

769 A282 12fr multi *3.00* .40
770 A282 20fr multi *5.00* .90

St. Michael's Church Millenary A283

Designs: 12fr, Consecration of the church by Archbishop Egbert of Trier, 987, stained glass window by Gustav Zanter. 20fr, Baroque organ-chest, 17th century.

Photogravure & Engraved

1987, May 4 *Perf. 14*

771 A283 12fr multi .75 .50
772 A283 20fr multi 1.25 .80

15th Century Paintings by Giovanni Ambrogio Bevilacqua A284

Polyptych panels in the State Museum: 10fr, St. Bernard of Sienna and St. John the Baptist. 18fr, St. Jerome and St. Francis of Assisi.

1987, May 4 *Perf. 11½*

773 A284 10fr multi .55 .40
774 A284 18fr multi 1.00 .70

Rural Architecture A285

Photo. & Engr.

1987, Sept. 14 *Perf. 13½*

775 A285 10fr Hennesbau Bark Mill, 1826, Niederfeulen .50 .40
776 A285 12fr Health Center, 18th cent., Mersch .60 .50
777 A285 100fr Post Office, 18th cent., Bertrange 5.00 4.00
Nos. 775-777 (3) 6.10 4.90

Chamber of Deputies (Parliament) 139th Anniv. — A286

Designs: 6fr, Charles Metz (1799-1853), first President. 12fr, Parliament, 1860, designed by Antoine Hartmann (1817-1891).

1987, Sept. 14 Engr. *Perf. 14*

778 A286 6fr violet brn .25 .25
779 A286 12fr blue black .50 .50

Flowers by Botanical Illustrator Pierre-Joseph Redoute (1759-1840) A287

1988, Feb. 8 Photo. *Perf. 11½x12*

780 A287 6fr Orange lily, water lily .40 .40
781 A287 10fr Primula, double narcissus .65 .65
782 A287 12fr Tulip .80 .80
783 A287 50fr Iris, gorteria 3.25 3.25
Nos. 780-783 (4) 5.10 5.10

European Conf. of Ministers of Transport A288

Eurocontrol, 25th Anniv. A289

1988, Feb. 8 *Perf. 12*

784 A288 12fr multi .70 .70
785 A289 20fr multi 1.25 1.25

Souvenir Sheet

Family of Prince Henri — A290

1988, Mar. 29 Photo. *Perf. 12*

786 A290 Sheet of 3 5.50 5.50
a. 12fr Maria Theresa .70 .70
b. 18fr Guillaume, Felix and Louis 1.00 1.00
c. 50fr Prince Henri 2.75 2.75

JUVALUX '88, 9th intl. youth philatelic exhibition, Mar. 29-Apr. 4.

Europa 1988 — A291

Communication.

1988, June 6 Photo. *Perf. 11½*

787 A291 12fr Automatic mail handling *3.75* .50
788 A291 20fr Electronic mail *4.00* 1.25

Tourism — A292

Designs: 10fr, Wiltz town hall and Cross of Justice Monument, c. 1502. 12fr, Castle, Differdange, 16th cent., vert.

Photo. & Engr.

1988, June 6 *Perf. 13½*

789 A292 10fr multi .60 .60
790 A292 12fr multi .70 .70

See Nos. 824-825, 841-842.

League of Luxembourg Student Sports Associations (LASEL), 50th Anniv. A293

1988, June 6 Photo. *Perf. 11½*

791 A293 12fr multi .70 .70

Doorways A294

Architectural drawings by Joseph Wegener (1895-1980) and his students, 1949-1951: 12fr, Septfontaines Castle main entrance, 1785. 25fr, National Library regency north-wing entrance, c. 1720. 50fr, Holy Trinity Church baroque entrance, c. 1740.

Litho. & Engr.

1988, Sept. 12 *Perf. 14*

792 A294 12fr black & buff .65 .65
793 A294 25fr blk & citron 1.25 1.25
794 A294 50fr blk & yel bister 2.60 2.60
Nos. 792-794 (3) 4.50 4.50

Jean Monnet (1888-1979), French Economist — A295

1988, Sept. 12 Engr.

795 A295 12fr multi .65 .65

European Investment Bank, 30th Anniv. A296

1988, Sept. 12 Litho. & Engr.

796 A296 12fr yel grn & blk .65 .65

A297

A298

1988, Sept. 12 Photo. *Perf. 11½*

797 A297 12fr multi .65 .65

1988 Summer Olympics, Seoul.

1989, Mar. 6 Photo. *Perf. 11½x12*

Design: 12fr, Portrait and excerpt from his speech to the Chamber of Deputies, 1896.

798 A298 12fr multi .60 .60

C.M. Spoo (1837-1914), advocate of Luxembourgish as the natl. language.

Book Workers' Fed., 125th Anniv. — A299

Natl. Red Cross, 75th Anniv. — A300

1989, Mar. 6

799 A299 18fr multi .95 .95

1989, Mar. 6

800 A300 20fr Henri Dunant 1.00 1.00

Independence of the Grand Duchy, 150th Anniv. — A301

Design: 12fr, Lion, bronze sculpture by Auguste Tremont (1892-1980) guarding the grand ducal family vault, Cathedral of Luxembourg.

Photo. & Engr.

1989, Mar. 6 *Perf. 14*

801 A301 12fr multi .60 .60

Astra Telecommunications Satellite — A302

1989, Mar. 6 Photo. *Perf. 11½*
802 A302 12fr multi .60 .60

Europa 1989 — A303

Tour de France — A304

Paintings (children at play): 12fr, *Three Children in a Park,* 19th cent., anonymous. 20fr, *Child with Drum,* 17th cent., anonymous.

1989, May 8 Photo. *Perf. 11½x12*
803 A303 12fr multi *2.00 .55*
804 A303 20fr multi *3.00 .90*

1989, May 8 *Perf. 11½*
805 A304 9fr multi .50 .50

Start of the bicycle race in Luxembourg City.

A305

PARLEMENT EUROPEEN EP PE 12F LUXEMBOURG
A306

1989, May 8 *Perf. 11½x12*
806 A305 12fr multi .60 .60

Interparliamentary Union, cent.

1989, May 8
807 A306 12fr multi .60 .60

European Parliament 3rd elections.

Council of Europe, 40th Anniv. A307

1989, May 8 *Perf. 12x11½*
808 A307 12fr multi .60 .60

Reign of Grand Duke Jean, 25th Anniv. A308

Charles IV (1316-1378) A309

1989, Sept. 18 Photo. *Perf. 12x11½*
Booklet Stamps
810 A308 3fr black & orange .20 .20
a. Bklt. pane of 4 .55
811 A308 9fr black & blue green .40 .40
a. Bklt. pane of 4 1.70
b. Bklt. pane, 1 each #810, 811 + 2 labels .55
Booklet, 1 each #810a, 811a, 811b 2.85

Photo. & Engr.
1989, Sept. 18 *Perf. 13½x14*

Stained-glass windows by Joseph Oberberger in the Grand Ducal Loggia, Cathedral of Luxembourg: 20fr, John the Blind (1296-1346). 25fr, Wenceslas II (1361-1419).

821 A309 12fr shown .60 .60
822 A309 20fr multi .95 .95
823 A309 25fr multi 1.25 1.25
Nos. 821-823 (3) 2.80 2.80

Independence of the Grand Duchy, 150th anniv.

Tourism Type of 1988

Designs: 12fr, Clervaux Castle interior courtyard, circa 12th cent. 18fr, Bronzed wild boar of Titelberg, 1st cent., vert.

Litho. & Engr.
1989, Sept. 18 *Perf. 13½*
824 A292 12fr multi .60 .60
825 A292 18fr multi .90 .90

Views of the Former Fortress of Luxembourg, 1814-1815, Engravings by Christoph Wilhelm Selig (1791-1837) — A310

1990, Mar. 5 Photo. *Perf. 12x11½*
826 A310 9fr shown .40 .35
827 A310 12fr multi, diff. .45 .40
828 A310 20fr multi, diff. 1.10 .95
829 A310 25fr multi, diff. 1.50 .95
Nos. 826-829 (4) 3.45 2.65

Congress of Vienna, 1815, during which the Duchy of Luxembourg was elevated to the Grand Duchy of Luxembourg.

Schueberfouer Carnival, 650th Anniv. — A311

1990, Mar. 15 *Perf. 11½x12*
830 A311 9fr Carnival ride .65 .45

Batty Weber (1860-1940), Writer — A312

18F LUXEMBOURG
ITU, 125th Anniv. — A313

1990, Mar. 15
831 A312 12fr multi .50 .40

1990, Mar. 15
832 A313 18fr multicolored .85 .65

A314

A315

Europa (Post Offices): 12fr, Luxembourg City. 20fr, Esch-Sur-Alzette, vert.

Litho. & Engr.
1990, May 28 *Perf. 13½*
833 A314 12fr buff & blk *6.00 .40*
834 A314 20fr lt bl & blk *9.00 1.25*

Photo. & Engr.
1990, May 28 *Perf. 14x13½*

Prime Ministers: 9fr, Paul Eyschen (1841-1915). 12fr, Emmanuel Servais (1811-1890).

835 A315 9fr multicolored .45 .35
836 A315 12fr multicolored .55 .35

A316

A317

1990, May 28 Photo. *Perf. 11½*
837 A316 12fr Psallus Pseudoplatani .55 .35

Luxembourg Naturalists' Society, cent.

Litho. & Engr.
1990, Sept. 24 *Perf. 14*

Fountains: 12fr, Sheep's march by Will Lofy. 25fr, Fountain of Doves. 50fr, "Maus Ketty" by Lofy.

838 A317 12fr multicolored .50 .35
839 A317 25fr multicolored 1.10 .90
840 A317 50fr multicolored 2.10 2.25
Nos. 838-840 (3) 3.70 3.50

Tourism Type of 1988
1990, Sept. 24 *Perf. 13½*
841 A292 12fr Mondercange .50 .25
842 A292 12fr Schifflange .50 .25

Souvenir Sheet

Nassau-Weilburg Dynasty, Cent. — A318

Designs: a, Grand Duke Adolphe. b, Grand Duchess Marie-Adelaide. c, Grand Ducal House arms. d, Grand Duchess Charlotte. e, Grand Duke Guillaume. f, Grand Duke Jean.

Photo. & Engr.
1990, Nov. 26 *Perf. 14x13½*
843 A318 Sheet of 6 8.00 8.00
a.-b. 12fr mulitcolored 1.00 1.00
c.-d. 18fr mulitcolored 1.00 1.00
e.-f. 20fr multicolored 1.00 1.00

View From the Trier Road by Sosthene Weis (1872-1941) — A319

Paintings: 18fr, Vauban Street and the Viaduct. 25fr, St. Ulric Street.

Perf. 12x11½, 11½x12
1991, Mar. 4 Photo.
844 A319 14fr multicolored .65 .40
845 A319 18fr multicolored .65 .65
846 A319 25fr multi, vert. 1.25 1.00
Nos. 844-846 (3) 2.55 2.05

Fungi — A320

1991, Mar. 4 *Perf. 11½*
847 A320 14fr Geastrum varians .65 .45
848 A320 14fr Agaricus (Gymnopus) thiebautii .65 .45
849 A320 18fr Agaricus (lepiota) lepidocephalus .90 .90
850 A320 25fr Morchella favosa 1.40 .90
Nos. 847-850 (4) 3.60 2.70

Europa A321

1991, May 13 Photo. *Perf. 12x11½*
851 A321 14fr Astra 1A, 1B satellites *3.75 .50*
852 A321 18fr Betzdorf ground station *5.00 1.40*

Natl. Miners' Monument, Kayl — A322

Art by Emile Kirscht — A323

Designs: No. 854, Magistrates' Court, Redange-Sur-Attert, horiz.

1991, May 23 ***Perf. 11½x12, 12x11½***

853	A322	14fr multicolored	.70	.40
854	A322	14fr multicolored	.70	.40

1991, May 23 ***Perf. 11½***

#856, Edmund de la Fontaine (1823-91), poet.

855	A323	14fr multicolored	.70	.40
856	A323	14fr multicolored	.70	.40

Labor Unions, 75th anniv. (No. 855).

Post and Telecommunications Museum — A324

Perf. 11½ on 3 sides

1991, Sept. 23 **Photo.**

Booklet Stamps

857	A324	4fr Old telephone	1.90	1.40
a.		Bklt. pane of 1 + 3 labels	2.00	
858	A324	14fr Old postbox	.50	.45
a.		Bklt. pane of 4	2.00	

A325

A326

1991, Sept. 23 ***Perf. 11½***

859	A325	14fr Stamp of Type A24	.70	.40

Stamp Day, 50th anniv.

Photo. & Engr.

1991, Sept. 23 ***Perf. 14***

Designs: Gargoyles.

860	A326	14fr Young girl's head	.65	.40
861	A326	25fr Woman's head	1.10	1.00
862	A326	50fr Man's head	2.00	1.60
		Nos. 860-862 (3)	3.75	3.00

See Nos. 874-876.

Jean-Pierre Pescatore Foundation, Cent. A327

Buildings: No. 864, High Technology Institute. No. 865, New Fair and Congress Centre.

1992, Mar. 16 **Photo.** ***Perf. 11½***

863	A327	14fr lil rose & multi	.70	.55
864	A327	14fr grn & multi	.70	.55
865	A327	14fr brt bl & multi	.70	.55
		Nos. 863-865 (3)	2.10	1.65

Bettembourg Castle A328

1992, Mar. 16

866	A328	18fr shown	.70	.65
867	A328	25fr Walferdange station	1.10	.90

Europa A329

Emigrants to US: 14fr, Nicholas Gonner (1835-1892), newspaper editor. 22fr, N. E. Becker (1842-1920), journalist.

Photo. & Engr.

1992, May 18 ***Perf. 13½x14½***

868	A329	14fr multicolored	*3.50*	*.50*
869	A329	22fr multicolored	*4.50*	*1.25*

Lions Clubs Intl., 75th Anniv. — A330

General Strike, 50th Anniv. — A331

1992, May 18 **Photo.** ***Perf. 11½***

870	A330	14fr multicolored	.65	.40
871	A331	18fr sepia & lake	.75	.70

1992 Summer Olympics, Barcelona A332

1992, May 18 ***Perf. 12x11½***

872	A332	14fr multicolored	1.25	.40

Expo '92, Seville A333

1992, May 18 ***Perf. 11½***

873	A333	14fr Luxembourg pavilion	.60	.35

Gargoyle Type of 1991

Photo. & Engr.

1992, Oct. 5 ***Perf. 14***

874	A326	14fr Ram's head	.60	.45
875	A326	22fr Lion's head	1.10	1.10
876	A326	50fr Satyr's head	1.90	1.75
		Nos. 874-876 (3)	3.60	3.30

Stained Glass Windows, by Auguste Tremont — A334

1992, Oct. 5 **Photo.** ***Perf. 11½x12***

877	A334	14fr Post horn, letters	.50	.40
878	A334	22fr Post rider	1.40	1.25
879	A334	50fr Insulators	1.75	1.60
		Nos. 877-879 (3)	3.65	3.25

Luxembourg Post and Telecommunications, 150th anniv.

Single European Market A335

1992, Oct. 5 ***Perf. 11½x12***

880	A335	14fr multicolored	.60	.35

Fountain of the Children with Grapes, Schwebsingen — A336

Design: No. 882, Old Ironworks Cultural Center, Steinfort.

1993, Mar. 8 **Photo.** ***Perf. 12x11½***

881	A336	14fr multicolored	.70	.50
882	A336	14fr multicolored	.70	.50

Grand Duke Jean — A337

Litho. & Engr.

1993-95 ***Perf. 13½x13***

Background Color

883	A337	1fr yellow brown	.20	.20
883A	A337	2fr olive gray	.20	.20
884	A337	5fr yellow green	.20	.20
885	A337	7fr brick red	.30	.20
886	A337	10fr blue	.30	.25
887	A337	14fr pink	1.40	.30
888	A337	15fr green	.55	.45
889	A337	16fr orange	.60	.50
890	A337	18fr orange	.70	.35
891	A337	20fr red	.70	.55
892	A337	22fr dark green	.90	.75
893	A337	25fr gray blue	.90	.65
894	A337	100fr brown	3.25	2.40
		Nos. 883-894 (13)	10.20	7.00

Issued: 5, 7, 14, 18, 22, 25fr, 3/8/93; 1, 15, 20, 100fr, 3/7/94; 2, 10, 16fr, 1/30/95.

See Nos. 957, 1026.

New Technologies in Surgery A338

1993, May 10 **Photo.** ***Perf. 11½***

895	A338	14fr multicolored	.60	.50

Contemporary Paintings — A339

Europa: 14fr, Rezlop, by Fernand Roda. 22fr, So Close, by Sonja Roef.

1993, May 10

896	A339	14fr multicolored	*1.25*	*.40*
897	A339	22fr multicolored	*1.75*	*.80*

A340

A341

Designs: 14fr, Burgundy Residence. 20fr, Simons House. 50fr, Cassal House.

Photo. & Engr.

1993, May 10 ***Perf. 14***

898	A340	14fr multicolored	.50	.35
899	A340	20fr multicolored	.85	.65
900	A340	50fr multicolored	2.40	1.90
		Nos. 898-900 (3)	3.75	2.90

1993, Sept. 20 **Photo.** ***Perf. 11½***

901	A341	14fr multicolored	.60	.35

Environmental protection.

A342

A343

1993, Sept. 20

902	A342	14fr multicolored	.60	.40
903	A343	14fr multicolored	.60	.40

Jean Schortgen (1880-1918), 1st worker elected to Parliament (#902); Artistic Circle of Luxembourg, cent.

Museum Exhibits A344

14fr, Electric tram, Tram & Bus Museum, City of Luxembourg. 22fr, Iron ore tipper wagon, Natl. Mining Museum, Rumelange. 60fr, Horse-drawn carriage, Wiltz Museum of Ancient Crafts.

Photo. & Engr.

1993, Sept. 20 ***Perf. 14***

904	A344	14fr multicolored	.60	.35
905	A344	22fr multicolored	1.00	1.00
906	A344	60fr multicolored	2.40	1.75
		Nos. 904-906 (3)	4.00	3.10

See Nos. 933-935.

Snow-Covered Landscape, by Joseph Kutter (1894-1941) — A345

Design: No. 908, The Moselle, by Nico Klopp (1894-1930).

1994, Mar. 7 Photo. *Perf. 11½x12*

907 A345 14fr multicolored .60 .40
908 A345 14fr multicolored .60 .40

4th General Elections to European Parliament A346

1994, May 16 Photo. *Perf. 11½*

909 A346 14fr multicolored .60 .40

European Inventions, Discoveries A347

1994, May 16

910 A347 14fr Armillary sphere *1.75 .40*
911 A347 22fr Sail boats, map *2.25 1.00*

Europa.

21st Intl. Congress of Genealogy & Heraldry — A348

14th World Congress of Intl. Police Assoc. — A349

Intl. Year of the Family A350

1994, May 16 *Perf. 11½*

912 A348 14fr multicolored .60 .40
913 A349 18fr multicolored .65 .60
914 A350 25fr multicolored 1.00 .85
Nos. 912-914 (3) 2.25 1.85

Europe A351

1994, Sept. 19 *Perf. 11½*

915 A351 14fr Dove, stars .50 .35
916 A351 14fr Circle of stars .50 .35
917 A351 14fr Bronze Age bowl 2.00 .75
Nos. 915-917 (3) 3.00 1.45

Western European Union, 40th anniv. (#915). Office for Official Publications of European Communities, 25th anniv. (#916). European Bronze Age Research Campaign (#917).

Liberation, 50th Anniv. A352

1994, Sept. 19 Photo. *Perf. 12x11½*

918 A352 14fr multicolored .60 .45

Former Refuges in Luxembourg A353

Designs: 15fr, Munster Abbey. 25fr, Holy Spirit Convent. 60fr, St. Maximine Abbey of Trier.

Photo. & Engr.

1994, Sept. 19 *Perf. 14*

919 A353 15fr multicolored .75 .75
920 A353 25fr multicolored 1.00 1.00
921 A353 60fr multicolored 2.25 1.75
Nos. 919-921 (3) 4.00 3.50

A354

City of Luxembourg, 1995 European City of Culture — A355

A356

Paintings by Hundertwasser A357

Panoramic view of city showing buildings and: No. 923a, Steeples, trees. b, Gateway through fortress wall. c, Angles in fortress wall. d, Roof of church.

Designs: No. 924, The King of the Antipodes. No. 925, The House with the Arcades and the Yellow Tower. No. 926, Small Path.

Perf. 12x11½, 11½x12

1995, Mar. 6 Photo.

922 A354 16fr multicolored .75 .60
923 Strip of 4 3.25 3.00
a.-d. A355 16fr any single .75 .50

Photo. & Engr.

Perf. 14

924 A356 16fr gold, silver & multi 1.00 .60
925 A357 16fr black & multi 1.00 .60
926 A357 16fr yellow & multi 1.00 .60
Nos. 922-926 (5) 7.00 5.40

No. 923 is a continuous design.

Liberation of the Concentration Camps, 50th Anniv. — A358

Europa: 25fr, Barbed wire, cracked plaster.

1995, May 15 Photo. *Perf. 11½x12*

927 A358 16fr multicolored *1.00 .50*
928 A358 25fr multicolored *1.25 .80*

European Nature Conservation Year — A359

1995, May 15 Litho. *Perf. 13½*

929 A359 16fr multicolored .70 .50

A360 A362

European Geodynamics and Seismology Center A361

1995, May 15 Photo. *Perf. 11½x12*

930 A360 16fr multicolored .75 .60

Small States of Europe Games, Luxembourg.

1995, May 15 *Perf. 11½*

931 A361 32fr multicolored 1.40 1.10

1995, May 15 *Perf. 11½x12*

932 A362 80fr multicolored 3.25 2.50

UN, 50th anniv.

Museum Exhibits Type of 1993

Designs, vert: 16fr, Churn, Country Art Museum, Vianden. 32fr, Wine press, Wine Museum, Ehnen. 80fr, Sculpture of a Potter, by Leon Nosbusch, Pottery Museum, Nospelt.

Photo. & Engr.

1995, Sept. 18 *Perf. 14*

933 A344 16fr multicolored .65 .40
934 A344 32fr multicolored 1.10 .90
935 A344 80fr multicolored 3.25 2.25
Nos. 933-935 (3) 5.00 3.55

Luxembourg-Reykjavik, Iceland Air Route, 40th Anniv. — A363

1995, Sept. 18 Litho. *Perf. 13*

936 A363 16fr multicolored .70 .55

See Iceland No. 807.

Tourism A364

1995, Sept. 18 Photo. *Perf. 11½*

937 A364 16fr Erpeldange .65 .50
938 A364 16fr Schengen .65 .50

Portrait of Emile Mayrisch (1862-1928), by Théo Van Rysselberghe (1862-1926) — A365

1996, Mar. 2 Photo. *Perf. 11½*

939 A365 (A) multicolored 1.25 .50

On day of issue No. 939 was valued at 16fr. See Belgium No. 1602.

National Railway, 50th Anniv. — A366

Passenger train: a, Cab facing left. b, Hooked together. c, Cab facing right.

1996, Mar. 4 Photo. *Perf. 11½*

940 Strip of 3 2.25 2.25
a.-c. A366 16fr Any single .70 .60

No. 940 is a continuous design.

Grand Duchess Charlotte (1896-1985) — A367

Design: Statue, Luxembourg City.

1996, Mar. 4

Booklet Stamp

941 A367 16fr multicolored .65 .40
a. Booklet pane of 8 5.00
Complete booklet, #941a 5.00

Mihály Munkácsy (1844-1900), Hungarian Painter — A368

Designs: No. 942, Portrait of Munkácsy, by Edouard Charlemont, 1884. No. 943, Portrait of Marie Munchen, by Munkácsy, 1885, vert.

1996, May 20 Photo. *Perf. 11½*

942 A368 16fr multicolored .70 .50
943 A368 16fr multicolored .70 .50

Famous Women — A369

Europa: 16fr, Marie de Bourgogne (1457-82), duchess of Luxembourg. 25fr, Empress Maria-Theresa of Austria (1717-80), duchess of Luxembourg.

Photo. & Engr.

1996, May 20 *Perf. 14x13½*

944 A369 16fr multicolored *1.40* *.70*
945 A369 25fr multicolored *1.75* *.90*

Luxembourg Confederation of Christian Trade Unions, 75th Anniv. A370

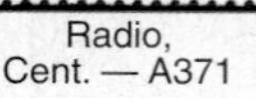

Radio, Cent. — A371

Modern Olympic Games, Cent. — A372

Motion Pictures, Cent. — A373

Perf. 12x11½, 11½x12

1996, May 20 **Photo.**

946 A370 16fr multicolored .75 .60
947 A371 20fr multicolored .80 .70
948 A372 25fr multicolored 1.25 1.25
949 A373 32fr multicolored 1.40 1.25
Nos. 946-949 (4) 4.20 3.80

Registration and Property Administration, Bicent. — A374

1996, Sept. 23 **Photo.** *Perf. 11½*

950 A374 16fr multicolored .75 .60

Let Us Live Together A375

#951, Four children. #952, "L'Abbraccio," bronze statue by M.J. Kerschen, vert.

1996, Sept. 23

951 A375 16fr multicolored .70 .50
952 A375 16fr multicolored .70 .50

Mustelidae A376

Litho. & Engr.

1996, Sept. 23 *Perf. 13½*

953 A376 16fr Meles meles .80 .50
954 A376 20fr Mustela putorius .80 .60
955 A376 80fr Lutra lutra 3.50 2.75
Nos. 953-955 (3) 5.10 3.85

John the Blind (1296-1346), King of Bohemia, Count of Luxembourg A377

Litho. & Engr.

1996, Dec. 9 *Perf. 13½*

956 A377 32fr multicolored 1.40 1.25

Grand Duke Jean Type of 1993

Litho. & Engr.

1997, Jan. 2 *Perf. 13½x13*

957 A337 8fr green & black .35 .30

Treaties of Rome, 40th Anniv. A378

Belgian-Luxembourg Economic Union, 75th Anniv. — A379

1997, Mar. 3 **Photo.** *Perf. 11½*

958 A378 16fr multicolored .65 .50
959 A379 20fr multicolored .85 .55

Tourism A380

Designs: No. 960, Servais House, Mersch. No. 961, Baroque Church, Koerich, vert.

1997, Mar. 3

960 A380 16fr multicolored .65 .50
961 A380 16fr multicolored .65 .50

11th World Congress of Rose Societies — A381

Roses: 16fr, Grand Duchess Charlotte. 20fr, Beautiful Sultana. 80fr, In Memory of Jean Soupert.

1997, Mar. 3 *Perf. 11½*

962 A381 16fr multicolored .75 .60

Size: 33x25mm

963 A381 20fr multicolored .75 .75
964 A381 80fr multicolored 3.50 3.25
Nos. 962-964 (3) 5.00 4.60

Stories and Legends — A382

Europa: 16fr, Melusina of Luxembourg. 25fr, Hunter of Hollenfels.

1997, May 12

965 A382 16fr multicolored *1.25* *.60*
966 A382 25fr multicolored *1.75* *.80*

A383

A384

Mondorf Spa, 150th Anniv. A385

1997, May 12

967 A383 16fr multicolored .75 .55
968 A384 16fr multicolored .75 .55
969 A385 16fr multicolored .75 .55
Nos. 967-969 (3) 2.25 1.65

Grand-Ducal Gendarmerie, bicent. (#967). Union of Small Domestic Animals Farming Societies, 75th anniv. (#968).

JUVALUX 98 — A386

1997, May 12

970 A386 16fr Emblem .85 .60
971 A386 80fr Postal history 3.25 2.75

Saar-Lorraine-Luxembourg Summit — A387

1997, Oct. 16 **Photo.** *Perf. 11½*

972 A387 16fr multicolored .75 .50

See Germany #1982 & France #2613.

Mills — A388

Clocks — A389

Litho. & Engr.

1997, Oct. 16 *Perf. 13½*

973 A388 16fr Kalborn Mill, horiz. .80 .60
974 A388 50fr Ramelli Mill 2.00 1.75

Photo. & Engr.

1997, Oct. 16 *Perf. 13x13½*

Designs: 16fr, Oak wall clock, 1816. 32fr, Astronomic clock with walnut case, mid 19th cent. 80fr, Pear tree wood wall clock, 1815.

975 A389 16fr multicolored .85 .60
976 A389 32fr multicolored 1.40 1.25
977 A389 80fr multicolored 3.50 3.00
Nos. 975-977 (3) 5.75 4.85

Henry V, the Blonde (1247-81), Count of Luxembourg A390

1997, Dec. 8 **Photo.** *Perf. 11½*

978 A390 32fr multicolored 1.50 1.25

Tourism A391

#979, Hesperange. #980, Rodange Church, vert.

1998, Mar. 23 **Photo.** *Perf. 11½*

979 A391 16fr multicolored .70 .50
980 A391 16fr multicolored .70 .50

See Nos. 1023-1024, 1048-1049.

Freshwater Fish A392

Designs: 16fr, Salmo trutta. 25fr, Cottus gobio. 50fr, Alburnoides bipunctatus.

Litho. & Engr.

1998, Mar. 23 *Perf. 13½x13*

981 A392 16fr multicolored 1.00 .50
982 A392 25fr multicolored 1.60 1.40
983 A392 50fr multicolored 2.25 2.00
Nos. 981-983 (3) 4.85 3.90

NGL (Independent Luxembourg Trade Union), 50th Anniv. — A393

Broom Festival, Wiltz, 50th Anniv. — A394

Jean Antoine Zinnen (1827-98), Composer A395

Abolition of Censorship, 150th Anniv. A396

1998, Mar. 23 **Photo.** *Perf. 11½*

984 A393 16fr multicolored .85 .60
985 A394 16fr multicolored .85 .60
986 A395 20fr multicolored .85 .80
987 A396 50fr multicolored 2.00 2.00
Nos. 984-987 (4) 4.55 4.00

King Henri VII (1275?-1313) of Luxembourg, King of Germany, Holy Roman Emperor — A397

1998, June 18 Photo. *Perf. 11½*
988 A397 (A) multicolored 1.25 .60

Granting of the Right to hold a Luxembourg Fair, 700th anniv.
No. 988 was valued at 16fr on the day of issue.

Natl. Holidays and Festivals — A398

Juvalux 98 — A399

A400

Europa: 16fr, Fireworks over bridge, National Day. 25fr, Flame, stained glass window, National Remembrance Day.

1998, June 18
989 A398 16fr multicolored *1.40 .50*
990 A398 25fr multicolored *1.60 .65*

1998, June 18 Photo. & Engr.

16fr, Town postman, 1880. 25fr, Letter, 1590, horiz. 50fr, Country postman, 1880.
#994, Engraving showing 1861 view of Luxembourg.

991 A399 16fr multicolored .80 .60
992 A399 25fr multicolored 1.00 1.00
993 A399 50fr multicolored 2.00 1.75
Nos. 991-993 (3) 3.80 3.35

Souvenir Sheet

994 Sheet of 2 5.25 5.25
a. A400 16fr multicolored .80 .80
b. A400 80fr multicolored 3.50 3.50

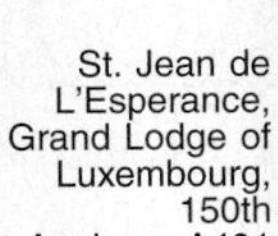

St. Jean de L'Esperance, Grand Lodge of Luxembourg, 150th Anniv. — A401

1998, Sept. 21 Litho. *Perf. 13½*
995 A401 16fr multicolored .75 .50

Abbey of Echternach, 1300th Anniv. A402

Various architectural drawings.

1998, Sept 21 Photo. *Perf. 11½*
996 A402 16fr multicolored .75 .60
997 A402 48fr multicolored 2.25 1.90
998 A402 60fr multicolored 2.25 1.90
Nos. 996-998 (3) 5.25 4.40

Museum Exhibits A403

City of Luxembourg History Museum: 16fr, Spanish army helmet, 16th cent. 80fr, Wayside Cross, Hollerich, 1718.

Litho. & Engr.

1998, Sept. 21 *Perf. 13½*
999 A403 16fr multicolored .85 .60
1000 A403 80fr multicolored 3.25 2.75

NAMSA (NATO Maintenance and Supply Organization), 40th Anniv. — A404

1998, Dec. 7 Photo. *Perf. 11½*
1001 A404 36fr multicolored 1.60 1.25

Introduction of the Euro A405

1999, Mar. 8 Photo. *Perf. 11½*
1002 A405 (A) multicolored 1.25 .60

No. 1002 was valued at 16fr on the day of issue.

Council of Europe, 50th Anniv. — A406

1999, Mar. 8
1003 A406 16fr multicolored .85 .65

Owls A407

1999, Mar. 8 *Perf. 12*
1004 A407 (A) Strix aluco, vert. 1.25 .65
1005 A407 32fr Bubo bubo 1.60 1.75
1006 A407 60fr Tyto alba 3.25 2.50
Nos. 1004-1006 (3) 6.10 4.90

No. 1004 was valued at 16fr on the day of issue.

NATO, 50th Anniv. A408

1999, Mar. 8 *Perf. 11½*
1007 A408 80fr multicolored 4.25 3.50

Europa — A409

National Parks: 16fr, Haute-Sûre. 25fr, Ardennes-Eifel.

1999, May 17 Photo. *Perf. 11½x12*
1008 A409 16fr multicolored *1.00 .50*
1009 A409 25fr multicolored *1.25 .80*

Natl. Federation of Mutuality, 75th Anniv. — A410

Intl. Year of Older Persons — A411

UPU, 125th Anniv. A412

A413 A414

1999, May 17 *Perf. 11½*
1010 A410 16fr multicolored .85 .65
1011 A411 16fr multicolored .85 .65
1012 A412 16fr multicolored .85 .65
1013 A413 32fr multicolored 1.75 1.60
1014 A414 80fr multicolored 4.25 3.25
Nos. 1010-1014 (5) 8.55 6.80

Luxembourg Federation of Amateur Photographers, 50th anniv. (#1013). Luxembourg Gymnastics Federation, cent. (#1014).

18th Birthday of Prince Guillaume A415

Photo. & Engr.

1999, Sept. 21 *Perf. 13½*
1015 A415 16fr multicolored .85 .65

Aline Mayrisch-de Saint-Hubert (1874-1947), President of Luxembourg Red Cross — A416

1999, Sept. 21 Litho. & Engr.
1016 A416 20fr multicolored 1.00 .90

Travelling Into the Future A417

1999, Sept. 21 Photo. *Perf. 11¾*
1017 A417 16fr Communication by road .85 .70
1018 A417 20fr Information age 1.00 1.00
1019 A417 80fr Conquering space 4.25 3.25
Nos. 1017-1019 (3) 6.10 4.95

See Nos. 1063-1065.

Johann Wolfgang von Goethe (1749-1832), German Poet — A418

1999, Nov. 30 Photo. *Perf. 11¾*
1020 A418 20fr henna & dk brn 1.00 .90

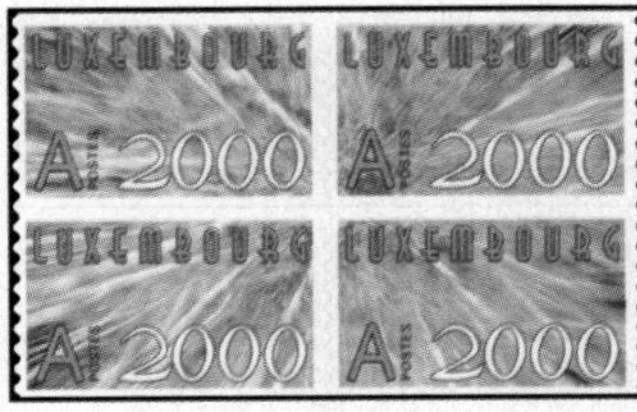

Year 2000 — A419

No. 1021: a, Large white area under A and 2000. b, Large blue area under A. c, Large blue area under A and URG. d, Large blue area under LUX.

Serpentine Die Cut 8 Vert.

2000, Jan. 3 Photo.

Self-Adhesive

Booklet Stamps

1021 A419 Booklet pane of 4 5.00
a.-d. (A) Any single 1.25 .60
Booklet, 2 #1021 10.00

Nos. 1021a-1021d sold for 16fr on day of issue.

Holy Roman Emperor Charles V (1500-58) A420

Litho. & Engr.

2000, Mar. 7 *Perf. 13½*
1022 A420 A multi 1.25 .50

Sold for 16fr on day of issue.

Tourism Type of 1998

Designs: No. 1023, Walferdange Castle. No. 1024, Wasserbillig railway station, vert.

Perf. 11¾x11½, 11½x11¾

2000, Mar. 7 Photo.

Granite Paper

1023 A391 A multi 1.25 .50
1024 A391 A multi 1.25 .50

Sold for 16fr on day of issue.

World Mathematics Year A421

2000, Mar. 7 *Perf. 11½x11¾*
1025 A421 80fr multi 3.00 2.75

Grand Duke Jean Type of 1993
Litho. & Engr.
2000, Mar. 31 *Perf. 13¼x13*
Background Color
1026 A337 9fr pink .40 .30

Musical Instruments — A422

Perf. 11½x11¾
2000, Mar. 31 **Photo.**
Granite Paper
1027 A422 3fr French horn .20 .20
1028 A422 12fr Saxophone .55 .45
1029 A422 21fr Violin .95 .65
1030 A422 30fr Piano 1.40 1.10
Nos. 1027-1030 (4) 3.10 2.40

See Nos. 1045-1046.

Ducks A423

Designs: 18fr, Anas platyrhynchos. 24fr, Aythya ferina, vert. 30fr, Aythya fuligula.

2000, May 9 *Perf. 11¾x11½*
Granite Paper
1031 A423 18fr multi .80 .60
Perf. 11½x11¾
1032 A423 24fr multi 1.10 .90
1033 A423 30fr multi 1.40 1.25
Nos. 1031-1033 (3) 3.30 2.75

Esch-sur-Alzette Gas Works, Cent. (in 1999) — A424

2000, May 9 *Perf. 11¾x11½*
Granite Paper
1034 A424 18fr multi .80 .60

Europa, 2000
Common Design Type
2000, May 9 *Perf. 11½x11¾*
Granite Paper
1035 CD17 21fr multi *2.00 1.00*

Robert Schuman's European Unity Plan, 50th Anniv. A425

2000, May 9 *Perf. 11½x11¾*
1036 A425 21fr multi .95 .75

Art Collection of Luxembourg Posts & Telecommunications — A426

Art by: 21fr, Will Kesseler. 24fr, Joseph Probst, vert. 36fr, Mett Hoffmann.

Perf. 11¾x11½, 11½x11¾
2000, Sept. 27 **Photo.**
Granite Paper
1037 A426 21fr multi .95 .50
1038 A426 24fr multi 1.10 .75
1039 A426 36fr multi 1.60 1.25
Nos. 1037-1039 (3) 3.65 2.50

Towers on Historic Walking Trails A427

Designs: 18fr, Tower of Jacob, Wenzel trail. 42fr, Bons Malades Gate, Vauban trail.

Photo. & Engr.
2000, Sept. 27 *Perf. 13½x14¼*
1040 A427 18fr multi .80 .60
1041 A427 42fr multi 1.90 1.75

Blast Furnace "B," Esch-Belval A428

2000, Sept. 27 *Perf. 11¾x11½*
1042 A428 A multi .80 .60

No. 1042 sold for 18fr on day of issue.

Accession of Grand Duke Henri A429

Designs: 18fr, Prince Henri in uniform, Princess Maria Teresa in pink suit. 100fr, Prince in suit, Princess in red blouse.

2000, Sept. 27 **Photo.** *Perf. 11¾*
Granite Paper (18fr)
1043 A429 18fr multi .80 .70

Souvenir Sheet
Photo. (margin Photo. & Engr.)
Perf. 11½
1044 A429 100fr multi 4.25 4.25

No. 1043 issued in sheets of 12, five of which (positions 6, 8, 9, 10 and 11) have a red and blue "ribbon" running diagonally through stamp margin. No. 1044 contains one 46x35mm stamp.

Musical Instruments Type of 2000
2000, Dec. 5 **Photo.** *Perf. 11½x11¾*
Granite Paper
1045 A422 9fr Electric guitar .40 .30
1046 A422 24fr Accordion 1.00 .80

Treaty Establishing European Coal and Steel Community, 50th Anniv. — A430

Perf. 11¼x11½
2001, Mar. 20 **Photo.**
1047 A430 21fr multi 1.25 .75

Tourism Type of 1998

Designs: No. 1048, 18fr, Bestgen Mill, Schifflange. No. 1049, 18fr, Chapel, Wormeldange, and millstone, Ahn, vert.

Perf. 11¾x11½, 11½x11¾
2001, Mar. 20
Granite Paper
1048-1049 A391 Set of 2 2.10 1.25

Writers — A431

Designs: 18fr, Nik Welter (1871-1951). 24fr, André Gide (1869-1951). 30fr, Michel Rodange (1827-76).

Perf. 13½x13¼
2001, Mar. 20 **Litho. & Engr.**
1050-1052 A431 Set of 3 4.25 2.40

Europa A432

Designs: A (18fr), Stream, Mullerthal region. 21fr, Pond and Kaltreis water tower, Luxembourg-Bonnevoie.

Perf. 11¾x11½, 11½x11¾
2001, May 22 **Photo.**
Granite Paper
1053-1054 A432 Set of 2 2.00 1.60

Rescue Workers — A433

Designs: 18fr, Air rescue. 30fr, Rescue divers. 45fr, Fire fighters.

2001, May 22 *Perf. 11½x11¾*
Granite Paper
1055-1057 A433 Set of 3 5.50 4.00

Humanitarian Services — A434

Designs: 18fr, Humanitarian aid. 24fr, Intl. Organization for Migration, 50th anniv.

2001, May 22 *Perf. 11½*
1058-1059 A434 Set of 2 2.50 1.75

Old Postal Vehicles — A435

Designs: 3fr, Citroen 2CV Mini-van, 1960s. 18fr, Volkswagen Beetle, 1970s.

Serpentine Die Cut 8¼ Vert.
2001, May 22
Booklet Stamps
Granite Paper
1060 A435 3fr multi .20 .20
1061 A435 18fr multi 1.10 .75
a. Booklet, 6 each #1060-1061 8.00

European Year of Languages A436

2001, Oct. 1 **Photo.** *Perf. 11¾x11½*
Granite Paper
1062 A436 A multi 1.10 .80

Luxembourg postal officials state that No. 1062 sold for 45 eurocents on the day of issue, though euro currency was not in circulation on the day of issue. On the day of issue, 45 eurocents was the equivalent of approximately 18fr.

Nos. 1063-1071, 1074, 1076, 1078, 1080, 1084, and B425-B429 are denominated solely in euro currency though euro currency would not circulate until Jan. 1, 2002. From their date of issue until Dec. 31, 2001, these stamps could be purchased for Luxembourg francs. The official pegged rate of 40.3399 francs to the euro made rounding the franc purchase price a necessity for such purchases. The approximate franc equivalent of the euro denominations is shown in parentheses in the listings.

Traveling Into the Future Type of 1999

Designs: 45c (18fr), Renewable energy. 59c (24fr), Waste recycling. 74c (30fr), Biological research.

2001, Oct. 1 *Perf. 11¾*
Granite Paper
1063-1065 A417 Set of 3 4.50 3.25

Euro Coinage A437

Designs : Coin obverses with values of stamp denominations.

2001, Oct. 1 *Perf. 11½*
1066 A437 5c (2fr) multi .20 .20
1067 A437 10c (4fr) multi .25 .20
1068 A437 20c (8fr) multi .50 .40
1069 A437 50c (20fr) multi 1.25 .90
1070 A437 €1 (40fr) multi 2.50 1.75
1071 A437 €2 (80fr) multi 5.25 3.75
Nos. 1066-1071 (6) 9.95 7.20

Grand Duke Henri — A438

Photo. & Engr.
2001-03 *Perf. 11¾x11½*
Vignette Color
1072 A438 1c blue .20 .20
1073 A438 3c green .20 .20
1074 A438 7c (3fr) blue .20 .20

1075 A438 22c (9fr) brown .55 .40
1076 A438 30c (12fr) green .75 .45
1077 A438 45c (18fr) violet 1.10 .65
1078 A438 52c brown 1.40 .90
1079 A438 59c blue 1.50 .90
1080 A438 74c brown 1.90 1.10
1081 A438 89c red violet 2.25 1.25
Nos. 1072-1081 (10) 10.05 6.25

Issued: 7c, 22c, 30c, 45c, 10/1/01. 52c, 59c, 74c, 89c, 3/5/02. 1c, 3c, 10/1/03.
See Nos. 1126, 1129-1133A.

Kiwanis International A439

2001, Dec. 6 **Photo.** ***Perf. 11½***
1084 A439 52c (21fr) multi 1.40 .95

100 Cents = 1 Euro (€)

Art Collection of Luxembourg Posts & Telecommunications — A440

Art by: 22c, Moritz Ney, vert. 45c, Dany Prüm. 59c, Christiane Schmit, vert.

Perf. 14¼x14, 14x14¼
2002, Mar. 5 **Photo.**
1085-1087 A440 Set of 3 3.25 2.25

European Court Anniversaries A441

Designs: 45c, European Court of Auditors, 25th anniv. 52c, Court of Justice of the European communities, 50th anniv.

2002, Mar. 5 **Litho.** ***Perf. 13½***
1088-1089 A441 Set of 2 2.50 1.75

Sports — A442

No. 1090: a, Snowboarding. b, Skateboarding. c, Rollerblading. d, Bicycling. e, Volleyball. f, Basketball.

Die Cut Perf. 10 on 3 Sides
2002, Mar. 5
Booklet Stamps
Self-Adhesive

1090 Booklet pane of 6 4.00
a.-c. A442 7c Any single .20 .20
d.-f. A442 45c Any single 1.10 .80
Booklet, 2 #1090 8.00

Europa — A443

Designs: 45c, Tightrope walker. 52c, Clown.

2002, May 14 **Litho.** ***Perf. 13½***
1091-1092 A443 Set of 2 *3.00 1.75*

Cultural Anniversaries — A444

Designs: A, 50th Wiltz Festival. €1.12, Victor Hugo (1802-85), writer.

2002, May 14 ***Perf. 13¼***
1093-1094 A444 Set of 2 4.00 3.00

No. 1093 sold for 45c on day of issue.

Start of Tour de France in Luxembourg A445

Designs: 45c, Stylized bicycle. 52c, François Faber (1887-1915), 1909 champion. €2.45, The Champion, by Joseph Kutter.

Litho. (45c), Litho. & Engr.
Perf. 13¼x13½, 13½x13¼
2002, May 14
1095-1097 A445 Set of 3 9.00 6.25

Grevenmacher Charter of Freedom, 750th Anniv. — A446

2002, Sept. 14 **Litho.** ***Perf. 13¼x13***
1098 A446 74c multi 1.90 1.50

Nature Museum, Museum of Natural History A447

No. 1099: a, Water drop on spruce needle. b, Butterfly. c, Leaf rosette of *Echeveria* plant. d, Berries.

Serpentine Die Cut 8 Vert.
2002, Sept. 14 **Photo.**
Self-Adhesive

1099 Booklet pane of 4 4.50
a.-d. A447 A Any single 1.10 .80
Booklet, 2 #1099 9.00

Nos. 1099a-1099d had franking value of 45c on day of issue, but booklet sold for discounted price of €3.35.

Souvenir Sheet

Luxembourg Stamps, 150th Anniv. — A448

No. 1100: a, Grand Duke William II, man and woman, 1852 (47x27mm). b, Grand Duke Adolphe, woman, 1902 (47x27mm). c, Grand Duchess Charlotte, street scene, 1952 (47x27mm). d, Grand Duke Henri, hot air balloons in street, 2002 (71x27mm).

Photo. & Engr.
2002, Sept. 14 ***Perf. 11¾***
1100 A448 45c Sheet of 4, #a-d 4.75 4.75

The Post in 50 Years A449

Designs: 22c, Postmen in spacecraft, buildings, vert. A, Spacecraft in flight, cell phone, letter and "@" in orbit around planet.

Perf. 14x14½, 14½x14
2002, Oct. 19 **Litho.**
1101-1102 A449 Set of 2 1.75 1.40

No. 1102 sold for 45c on day of issue.

Grand Duke Jean and Princess Joséphine-Charlotte, 50th Wedding Anniv. — A450

Perf. 14¼x14½
2003, Mar. 18 **Litho.**
1103 A450 45c multi 1.10 .95

Official Journal of the European Communities, 50th Anniv. — A451

2003, Mar. 18 ***Perf. 14½x14***
1104 A451 52c multi 1.40 1.10

Famous Women A452

Designs: No. 1105, 45c, Catherine Schleimer-Kill (1884-1973), feminist leader. No. 1106, 45c, Lou Koster (1889-1973), composer.

2003, Mar. 18 **Photo.** ***Perf. 11½***
1105-1106 A452 Set of 2 2.40 1.90

Tourism A453

Designs: 50c, Fontaine Marie Convent, Differdange. €1, Castle, Mamer. €2.50, St. Joseph Church, Esch-sur-Alzette, vert.

Perf. 14½x14, 14x14½
2003, Mar. 18 **Litho.**
1107-1109 A453 Set of 3 10.50 9.50

Luxembourg Athénée, 400th Anniv. A454

2003, May 20 **Litho.** ***Perf. 14¼x14½***
1110 A454 45c multi 1.10 1.00

Europa A455

Poster art: 45c, 1952 poster for National Lottery, by Roger Gerson. 52c, 1924 poster for Third Commercial Fair, by Auguste Trémont.

2003, May 20 ***Perf. 13¼x13***
1111-1112 A455 Set of 2 *2.75 1.75*

Bridges — A456

Designs: 45c, Adolphe Bridge, 1903. 59c, Stierchen Bridge, 14th cent. (36x26mm). 89c, Victor Bodson Bridge, 1994 (36x26mm).

Photo. & Engr.
2003, May 20 ***Perf. 11½***
1113-1115 A456 Set of 3 5.00 4.25

Electrification of Luxembourg, 75th Anniv. — A457

Litho. & Embossed
2003, Sept. 23 ***Perf. 13¼x13***
1116 A457 A multi 1.25 1.25

Sold for 50c on day of issue.

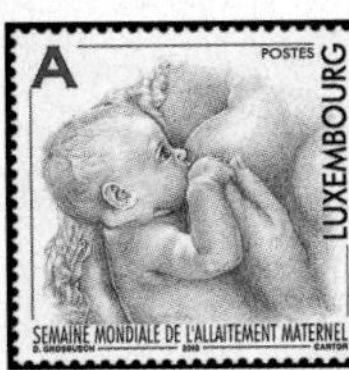

Breastfeeding A458

2003, Sept. 23 **Litho.** ***Perf. 13½***
1117 A458 A multi 1.25 1.25

Sold for 50c on day of issue.

Gaart an Heem Agricultural Cooperatives, 75th Anniv. — A459

Gardeners with: 25c, Spade. A, Basket and rake. €2, Watering can.

2003, Sept. 23 *Perf. 14½x14*
1118-1120 A459 Set of 3 7.00 6.50

No. 1119 sold for 50c on day of issue.

Industrial Products Made in Luxembourg A460

Designs: 60c, Steel. 70c, Industrial valve. 80c, Polyester film.

2003, Oct. 1 **Photo.** *Perf. 11½*
1121-1123 A460 Set of 3 5.00 5.00

Grand Duke Henri Type of 2001-03
Photo. & Engr.
2004-2010 *Perf. 11¾x11½*
Vignette Color

1124	A438	5c violet brn	.20	.20
1125	A438	10c black	.30	.30
1126	A438	25c claret	.65	.65
1129	A438	50c black	1.25	1.25
1130	A438	60c blue	1.50	1.50
1131	A438	70c purple	1.75	1.75
1132	A438	80c olive black	2.10	2.00
1133	A438	90c brown	2.25	2.25
1133A	A438	€1 blue	2.60	2.60
	Nos. 1126-1133A (7)		12.10	12.00

Issued: 25c, 50c, 60c, 80c, 3/16/04; 70c, 90c, €1, 9/26/06; 5c, 10c, 12/7/10.

Emigrants to the United States A461

Designs: 50c, Edward Steichen (1879-1973), photographer. 70c, Hugo Gernsbach (1884-1967), science fiction writer.

Photo. & Engr.
2004, Mar. 16 *Perf. 11½*
1134-1135 A461 Set of 2 3.25 3.00

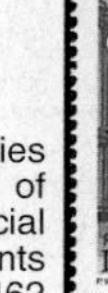

Anniversaries of Commercial Events A462

Designs: No. 1136, 50c, Commercial Union of Esch-sur-Alzette, cent. No. 1137, 50c, Luxembourg City Annual Street Market, 75th anniv.

2004, Mar. 16 **Litho.** *Perf. 14¼*
1136-1137 A462 Set of 2 2.60 2.60

Mushrooms — A463

No. 1138: a, Cantharellus tubaeformis. b, Ramaria flava. c, Stropharia cyanea. d, Helvella lacunosa. e, Anthurus archeri. f, Clitopilus prunulus.

Die Cut Perf. 10
2004, Mar. 16 **Litho.**
Self-Adhesive

1138	Booklet pane of 6	4.50	
a.-c.	A463 10c Any single	.25	.25
d.-f.	A463 50c Any single	1.25	1.25
	Complete booklet, 2 #1138	9.00	

European Parliament Elections A464

2004, May 9 **Litho.** *Perf. 13¼x13*
1139 A464 50c multi 1.25 1.25

2004 Summer Olympics, Athens A465

European Sports Education Year A466

2004, May 9 **Photo.** *Perf. 11½x11¾*
1140 A465 50c multi 1.25 1.25
1141 A466 60c multi 1.40 1.40

European School, 50th Anniv. A467

2004, May 9 **Litho.** *Perf. 14¼x14½*
1142 A467 70c multi 1.75 1.75

Europa A468

Designs: 50c, Stone bridge over Schiessentuempel. 60c, Bourscheid Beach, Bourscheid Castle.

2004, May 9 *Perf. 13¼x13*
1143-1144 A468 Set of 2 *3.00 3.00*

Luxembourg Stock Exchange, 75th Anniv. — A469

Perf. 11¼x11½
2004, Sept. 28 **Litho. & Engr.**
1145 A469 50c multi 1.25 1.25

Food Products Made in Luxembourg — A470

Designs: 35c, Baked goods, beer. 60c, Meats, wine. 70c, Dairy products.

Perf. 13½x13¾
2004, Sept. 28 **Litho.**
1146-1148 A470 Set of 3 4.00 4.00

National Museum of History and Art — A471

Designs: 50c, Museum building. €1.10, Young Woman with a Fan, by Luigi Rubio. €3, Charity, by Lucas Cranach the Elder or Lucas Cranach the Younger.

2004, Sept. 28 **Photo.** *Perf. 11¾*
1149-1151 A471 Set of 3 11.50 11.50

World War II Liberation, 60th Anniv. A472

2004, Dec. 7 **Litho.** *Perf. 14x13½*
1152 A472 70c multi 1.90 1.90

Luxembourg's Presidency of European Union — A473

No. 1153: a, Building with glass facade. b, Arch, Echternach Basilica. c, Vineyard along Moselle River. d, Rusted iron girder.

Serpentine Die Cut 8¼ Vert.
2005, Jan. 25 **Photo.**
Self-Adhesive

1153	Booklet pane of 4	5.00	
a.-d.	A473 A any single	1.25	1.25
	Complete booklet, 2 #1153	10.00	

On the day of issue, Nos. 1153a-1153d each had a franking value of 50c, but complete booklet sold for €3.80.

Rotary International, Cent. — A474

2005, Mar. 15 **Litho.** *Perf. 13½x13*
1154 A474 50c multi 1.40 1.40

Ettelbrück Neuro-psychiatric Medical Center, 150th Anniv. — A475

2005, Mar. 15 *Perf. 13½*
1155 A475 50c multi 1.40 1.40

76th Intl. Congress of Applied Mathematics and Mechanics A476

2005, Mar. 15
1156 A476 60c multi 1.60 1.60

Benelux Parliament, 50th Anniv. — A477

2005, Mar. 15 *Perf. 13¼x12¾*
1157 A477 60c multi 1.60 1.60

Tourism A478

Designs: 50c, Shoe factory, Kayl-Tétange. 60c, Village scene and website address of National Tourist Office (44x31mm). €1, Statue of St. Eloi, Rodange, and foundry worker.

Perf. 14x13¼, 12¾ (60c)
2005, Mar. 15
1158-1160 A478 Set of 3 5.50 5.50

Opening of Grand Duchess Joséphine-Charlotte Concert Hall — A479

2005, May 24 *Perf. 13¼x13¾*
1161 A479 50c multi 1.25 1.25

Europa A480

Designs: 50c, Judd mat Gaardebounen (pork and beans). 60c, Feirstengszalot (beef, egg and pickle salad).

2005, May 24 *Perf. 13½*
1162-1163 A480 Set of 2 *2.75 2.75*

Railways A481

Designs: 50c, Niederpallen Station, CVE 357 car of De Jhangeli narrow-gauge railway. 60c, AL-T3 locomotive. €2.50, PH 408 passenger car.

2005, May 24 **Photo.** *Perf. 11½*
1164-1166 A481 Set of 3 9.00 9.00

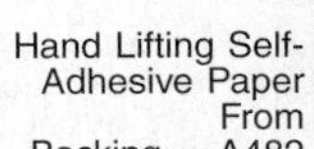

Hand Lifting Self-Adhesive Paper From Backing — A482

Serpentine Die Cut 11x11¼

2005, May 24

Self-Adhesive

Coil Stamps

1167 Vert. strip of 4 2.50
- *a.* A482 25c dark red & multi .60 .60
- *b.* A482 25c red orange & multi .60 .60
- *c.* A482 25c orange & multi .60 .60
- *d.* A482 25c yellow & multi .60 .60

1168 Vert. strip of 4 5.00
- *a.* A482 50c dark green & multi 1.25 1.25
- *b.* A482 50c green & multi 1.25 1.25
- *c.* A482 50c emerald & multi 1.25 1.25
- *d.* A482 50c yellow green & multi 1.25 1.25

Rolls of 100 of the 25c stamps sold for €24, and rolls of 100 of the 50c stamps sold for €48.

Famous People A483

Designs: 50c, Jean-Pierre Pescatore (1793-1855), philanthropist. 90c, Marcel Reuland (1905-56), writer. €1, Marie-Henriette Steil (1898-1930), writer, vert.

Photo. & Engr.

2005, Sept. 27 ***Perf. 11½***

1169-1171 A483 Set of 3 6.00 6.00

Butterflies A484

Designs: 35c, Papilio machaon. 70c, Argynnis paphia, vert. €1.80, Lysandra coridon.

2005, Sept. 27 **Litho.**

1172-1174 A484 Set of 3 7.25 7.25

Rocks A485

No. 1175: a, Schist. b, Rocks with iron (minerai de fer). c, Luxembourg sandstone. d, Conglomerate rocks.

Serpentine Die Cut 12¾ Vert.

2005, Sept. 27

Self-Adhesive

1175 Booklet pane of 4 4.75
- *a.-d.* A485 A Any single 1.10 1.10
- Complete booklet, 2 #1175 9.50

The complete booklet sold for €3.80, but each stamp had a franking value of 50c on the day of issue.

Seeing Eye Dog A486

Litho. & Embossed

2005, Dec. 6 ***Perf. 13x13¼***

1176 A486 70c dk blue & lemon 1.75 1.75

25th Wedding Anniversary of Grand Duke Henri and Grand Duchess Maria Teresa — A487

2006, Feb. 7 **Litho.** ***Perf. 13¼x13¾***

1177 A487 50c multi 1.25 1.25

Souvenir Sheet

Perf. 13¼x13

1178 A487 €2.50 multi 6.25 6.25

No. 1178 contains one 26x37mm stamp.

Blood Donation A488

2006, Mar. 14 **Litho.** ***Perf. 13¼***

1179 A488 50c multi 1.25 1.25

Tourism A489

Designs: No. 1180, 50c, Parc Merveilleux, Bettembourg. No. 1181, 50c, Birelerhaff Pigeon Tower, Sandweiler, vert.

2006, Mar. 14 ***Perf. 11½***

1180-1181 A489 Set of 2 2.40 1.25

Electrification of Railway Network, 50th Anniv. — A490

Designs: 50c, Train passing station. 70c, Train on bridge. €1, Railway workers repairing electrical wires, vert.

2006, Mar. 14 ***Perf. 13¼x13, 13x13¼***

1182-1184 A490 Set of 3 5.25 5.25

Personalized Stamp Website "meng.post.lu" — A491

2006, May 16 **Litho.** ***Perf. 11½***

1185 A491 A multi + label 1.40 1.40

No. 1185 sold for 50c on day of issue. Labels could be personalized for a fee.

Esch-sur-Alzette, Cent. — A492

2006, May 16 ***Perf. 13½***

1186 A492 50c multi 1.40 1.40

Soccer Teams in Luxembourg, Cent. — A493

2006 World Cup Soccer Championships, Germany — A494

2006, May 16 ***Perf. 13x13¼***

1187 A493 50c multi 1.40 1.40

1188 A494 90c multi 2.40 2.40

Europa A495

Contest-winning cell phone photos: 50c, Hands making heart. 70c, People holding globe.

2006, May 16 ***Perf. 12½***

1189-1190 A495 Set of 2 3.25 3.25

State Council, 150th Anniv. — A496

Litho. & Embossed

2006, Sept. 26 ***Perf. 13½***

1191 A496 50c multi 1.25 1.25

Luxembourg Chess Federation, 75th Anniv. — A497

2006, Sept. 26

1192 A497 90c multi 2.25 2.25

Bank Sesquicentenaries — A498

Designs: No. 1193, 50c, State Savings Bank (Spuerkeess). No. 1194, 50c, Dexia-BIL Bank.

2006, Sept. 26 **Litho.** ***Perf. 13¼x13***

1193-1194 A498 Set of 2 2.60 2.60

Fight Against Drug Addiction A499

Designs: 50c, Children's drawing of man and "No Drugs" sign. €1, Ashtray with vegetables and cheese, vert.

2006, Sept. 26 ***Perf. 11½***

1195-1196 A499 Set of 2 3.75 3.75

Luxembourg Horticultural Federation, 75th Anniv. — A500

No. 1197: a, Flowers. b, Fruits and vegetables.

2006, Dec. 5 **Litho.** ***Perf. 13¼x13¾***

1197 A500 Horiz. pair 3.75 3.75
- *a.-b.* 70c Either single 1.75 1.75

Luxembourg, 2007 European Cultural Capital — A501

No. 1198 — Silhouettes of deer and men with deer heads with background color of: a, Blue. b, Orange. c, Bright yellow green. d, Red violet.

Serpentine Die Cut 8½ Vert.

2007, Jan. 30 **Litho.**

1198 Booklet pane of 4 5.25
- *a.-d.* A501 A Any single 1.25 1.25
- Complete booklet, 2 #1198 10.50

Nos. 1198a-1198d each sold for 50c on day of issue.

Luxembourg Caritas, 75th Anniv. A502

2007, Mar. 20 **Litho.** ***Perf. 11½***

1199 A502 50c multi 1.40 1.40

Luxembourg Automobile Club, 75th Anniv. A503

2007, Mar. 20

1200 A503 50c multi 1.40 1.40

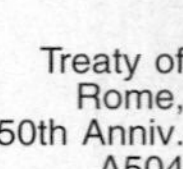

Treaty of Rome, 50th Anniv. A504

Designs: 70c, Delegates. €1, Text and stars.

2007, Mar. 20 ***Perf. 13x13¼***
1201-1202 A504 Set of 2 4.75 4.75

"Postes" A505

Denomination A506

Serpentine Die Cut 11x11¼
2007, Mar. 20 **Photo.**
Self-Adhesive
Coil Stamps

1203 A505 25c pur & multi .70 .70
1204 A506 25c brn & multi .70 .70
1205 A505 25c dk bl & multi .70 .70
1206 A506 25c dk grn & multi .70 .70
a. Vert. strip of 4, #1203-1206 2.80
1207 A505 50c red vio & multi 1.40 1.40
1208 A506 50c red & multi 1.40 1.40
1209 A505 50c bl & multi 1.40 1.40
1210 A506 50c grn & multi 1.40 1.40
a. Vert. strip of 4, #1207-1210 5.60
Nos. 1203-1210 (8) 8.40 8.40

Europa A507

Designs: 50c, Scout campground. 70c, Scouts, globe, knot.

2007, May 22 **Litho.** ***Perf. 13x13¼***
1211-1212 A507 Set of 2 3.25 3.25

Scouting, cent.

Town Centenaries — A508

Designs: No. 1213, 50c, Differdange. No. 1214, 50c, Dudelenge. No. 1215, 50c, Ettelbruck. No. 1216, 50c, Rumelange.

2007, May 22 **Photo.** ***Perf. 11½***
1213-1216 A508 Set of 4 5.50 5.50

Places of Culture A509

Designs: 50c, Rockhal. 70c, Grand Duke Jean Museum of Modern Art. €1, Neumünster Abbey.

2007, May 22 ***Perf. 12½***
1217-1219 A509 Set of 3 6.00 6.00

"Transborderism" A510

2007, Sept. 3 **Photo.** ***Perf. 11½***
1220 A510 50c multi 1.40 1.40

Rotunda of Luxembourg Train Station — A511

2007, Sept. 3 **Photo. & Engr.**
1221 A511 70c multi 1.90 1.90

See Belgium No. 2253.

Casa Luxemburg, Sibiu, Romania — A512

2007, Sept. 3 **Litho.** ***Perf. 13x13¼***
1222 A512 70c multi 1.90 1.90

See Romania Nos. 4993-4994.

Luxembourg Army Peace-keeping Missions — A513

2007, Sept. 3 **Photo.** ***Perf. 11½***
1223 A513 70c multi 1.90 1.90

Souvenir Sheet

Roman Mosaic, Vichten — A514

No. 1224: a, Thalia and Euterpe. b, Terpsichore and Melpomene. c, Clio and Urania. d, Polymnia and Erato. e, Calliope and Homer. Nos. 1224a-1224d are 58x29mm octagonal stamps, No. 1224e is a 55x55mm diamond-shaped stamp.

2007, Sept. 3 **Litho.** ***Perf. 14¼***
1224 A514 Sheet of 5 8.25 8.25
a.-d. 50c Any single 1.40 1.40
e. €1 multi 2.60 2.60

Esch-sur-Sure Dam — A515

Uewersauer Stauséi — A516

Serpentine Die Cut 12½x13½
2007, Dec. 4 **Litho.**
Self-Adhesive

1225 Horiz. pair 4.25
a. A515 70c multi 2.10 2.10
b. A516 70c multi 2.10 2.10

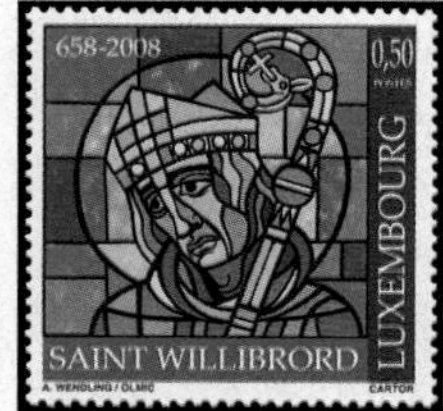

St. Willibrord (658-739) A517

2008, Mar. 18 **Litho.** ***Perf. 13***
1226 A517 50c multi 1.60 1.60

European Investment Bank, 50th Anniv. A518

2008, Mar. 18 ***Perf. 13x13¼***
1227 A518 70c purple & silver 2.25 2.25

Eurosystem, 10th Anniv. — A519

2008, Mar. 18 ***Perf. 13½x13¾***
1228 A519 €1 multi 3.25 3.25

Luxembourg Philharmonic Orchestra, 75th Anniv. — A520

Henri Pensis (1900-58), Conductor — A521

2008, Mar. 18
1229 A520 50c multi 1.60 1.60
1230 A521 70c multi 2.25 2.25

2008 Summer Olympics, Beijing A522

2008, May 20 **Litho.** ***Perf. 14x13½***
1231 A522 70c multi 2.25 2.25

Luxembourg Basketball Federation, 75th Anniv. — A523

Luxembourg Soccer Federation, Cent. — A524

2008, May 20 ***Perf. 12½***
1232 A523 A multi 1.60 1.60
1233 A524 A multi 1.60 1.60

Nos. 1232 and 1233 each sold for 50c on day of issue.

Europa A525

Smiling letter with wings: 50c, Standing on hand. 70c, Flying.

2008, May 20
1234-1235 A525 Set of 2 4.00 4.00

Tourism A526

Designs: No. 1236, A, Bridge, Diekirch, and city arms. No. 1237, A, Building, Leudelange, and city arms. No. 1238, A, Rindschleiden Church, Wahl, vert.

2008, May 20 ***Perf. 11½***
1236-1238 A526 Set of 3 4.75 4.75

Diekirch, 125th anniv., Leudelange, 150th anniv. Nos. 1236-1238 each sold for 50c on day of issue.

Medico-social League, Cent. — A527

2008, Sept. 30 **Litho.** ***Perf. 13¾***
1239 A527 A multi 1.40 1.40

Sold for 50c on day of issue.

Agricultural Technical School, Ettelbruck, 125th Anniv. A528

2008, Sept. 30
1240 A528 A multi 1.40 1.40

Sold for 50c on day of issue.

Federation of Popular Education Associations, Cent. — A529

2008, Sept. 30 ***Perf. 13x13¼***
1241 A529 A multi 1.40 1.40

Sold for 50c on day of issue.

Natl. League for the Protection of Animals, Cent. A530

2008, Sept. 30
1242 A530 A multi 1.40 1.40

Sold for 50c on day of issue.

NATO Maintenance and Supply Agency, 50th Anniv. — A531

2008, Sept. 30
1243 A531 70c multi 2.00 2.00

Greetings A532

Winning art from children's stamp design contest by: 70c, A. Wainer. €1, S. Rauschenberger.

2008, Sept. 30 ***Perf. 11½***
1244-1245 A532 Set of 2 4.75 4.75

A533

A534

Different shapes of colored background lines with "ATR" at: No. 1246, LR. No. 1247, UL. No. 1248, LL. No. 1249, UR.

Different shapes of colored background lines with "A" at: No. 1250, LL. No. 1251, UL. No. 1252, LR. No. 1253, UR.

Serpentine Die Cut 11
2008, Sept. 30
Coil Stamps
Self-Adhesive

1246 A533 ATR blue	.70	.70
1247 A533 ATR purple	.70	.70
1248 A533 ATR green	.70	.70
1249 A533 ATR red	.70	.70
a. Vert. strip of 4, #1246-1249	2.80	
1250 A534 A multi	1.40	1.40
1251 A534 A multi	1.40	1.40
1252 A534 A multi	1.40	1.40
1253 A534 A multi	1.40	1.40
a. Vert. strip of 4, #1250-1253	5.60	
Nos. 1246-1253 (8)	8.40	8.40

On day of issue, Nos. 1246-1249 each sold for 25c, Nos. 1250-1253, for 50c.

Happiness — A535

No. 1254: a, Bowling pins, denomination over red violet. b, Gift, denomination over yellow green. c, Wrapped candies, denomination over green. d, Wrapped candies, denomination over blue. e, Gift, denomination over green. f, Bowling pins, denomination over yellow green. g, Dice, "A" over red violet. h, Drum and sticks, "A" over yellow green. i, Four-leaf clovers, "A" over green. j, Four-leaf clovers, "A" over blue. k, Drum and sticks, "A" over green. l, Dice, "A" over yellow green.

Die Cut Perf. 10 on 3 Sides
2008, Sept. 30
Self-Adhesive

1254 Booklet pane of 12	12.00	
a.-f. A535 20c Any single	.55	.55
g.-l. A535 A Any single	1.40	1.40

Nos. 1254g-1254l each sold for 50c on day of issue.

New Courthouse of Court of Justice of the European Communities — A536

2008, Dec. 2 Litho. ***Perf. 14x13¼***
1255 A536 70c multi 1.90 1.90

Election of Holy Roman Emperor Henry VII (c. 1269-1313), 700th Anniv. — A537

2008, Dec. 2 ***Perf. 13¼x13***
1256 A537 €1 multi 2.60 2.60

Introduction of the Euro, 10th Anniv. — A538

2009, Mar. 17 Litho. ***Perf. 12½***
1257 A538 A multi 1.25 1.25

No. 1257 sold for 50c on day of issue.

Luxembourg Aero Club, Cent. — A539

New Airport Terminal A540

No. 1258: a, Satellite, airplane, hang glider, left half of balloon. b, Right half of balloon, glider, parachutist, jet plane.

2009, Mar. 17 ***Perf. 11½***
1258 A539 50c Horiz. pair, #a-b 2.60 2.60
1259 A540 90c multi 2.25 2.25

Natl. Federation of Fire Fighters, 125th Anniv. A541

Designs: 20c, Modern fire truck. A, Fire fighter rescuing child. €2, Antique fire truck.

2008, Mar. 17 ***Perf. 13x13¼***
1260-1262 A541 Set of 3 7.00 7.00

No. 1261 sold for 50c on day of issue.

Postmen's Federation, Cent. A542

General Confederation of the Civil Service, Cent. — A543

Natl. Federation of Railroad and Transportation Workers, Cent. — A544

2009, Mar. 17 ***Perf. 14x13¼***

1263 A542 50c multi	1.25	1.25
1264 A543 A multi	1.25	1.25
1265 A544 A multi	1.25	1.25
Nos. 1263-1265 (3)	3.75	3.75

On day of issue, Nos. 1264-1265 each sold for 50c.

June 7 European Elections — A545

2009, May 12 Litho. ***Perf. 13***
1266 A545 50c multi 1.40 1.40

National Research Fund, 10th Anniv. — A546

2009, May 12 ***Perf. 13½***
1267 A546 A multi 1.40 1.40

No. 1267 sold for 50c on day of issue.

Children's Houses, 125th Anniv. — A547

2009, May 12 ***Perf. 12½***
1268 A547 A multi 1.40 1.40

No. 1268 sold for 50c on day of issue.

Europa A548

Designs: 50c, Father and child watching comet. 70c, Galileo, telescope, planets.

2009, May 12 ***Perf. 13½***
1269-1270 A548 Set of 2 3.25 3.25

Intl. Year of Astronomy.

Personalized Stamps — A549

Stripe color: A, Red. A Europe, Blue.

2009, May 12 ***Perf. 11¾x11½***
Stamp + Label
1271-1272 A549 Set of 2 3.25 3.25

On day of issue, No. 1271 sold for 50c; No. 1272, 70c. Labels bearing text "PostMusée" and pictures are generic and sold for these prices. Labels could be personalized for an additional fee.

Famous People A550

Designs: 70c, Foni Tissen (1909-75), painter. 90c, Charles Bernhoeft (1859-1933), photographer. €1, Henri Tudor (1859-1928), electrical engineer.

Litho. & Engr.
2009, May 12 ***Perf. 13½***
1273-1275 A550 Set of 3 7.00 7.00

Vianden Castle A551

Perf. 13¼x12¾

2009, Sept. 16 **Litho.**

1276 A551 70c multi 2.00 2.00

Louis Braille (1809-52), Educator of the Blind — A552

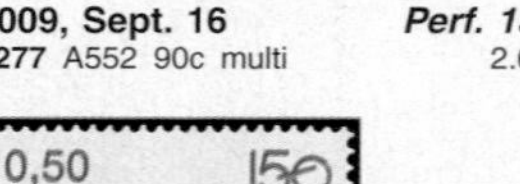

Litho. & Embossed

2009, Sept. 16 ***Perf. 13¼x13***

1277 A552 90c multi 2.60 2.60

Railroads in Luxembourg, 150th Anniv. — A553

Designs: 50c, Modern electric train. €1, Older electric train. €3, Steam locomotive.

2009, Sept. 16 **Litho.** ***Perf. 12½***

1278-1280 A553 Set of 3 13.00 13.00

Souvenir Sheet

Luxembourg Federation of Philatelic Societies, 75th Anniv. — A554

No. 1281: a, Luxembourg #198. b, Gate of Three Towers.

Litho. & Embossed

2009, Sept. 16 ***Perf. 13¾x14***

1281 A554 Sheet of 2 3.50 3.50
- *a.* 50c multi 1.50 1.50
- *b.* 70c multi 2.00 2.00

Johannes Gutenberg (c. 1390-1468), Inventor of Movable Type Presses A555

Website Addresses and Movable Type — A556

2009, Dec. 1 **Litho.** ***Perf. 13¼x13½***

1282 A555 50c multi 1.50 1.50

1283 A556 70c multi 2.10 2.10

See Switzerland No. 1344.

Schengen Convention, 25th Anniv. — A557

2010, Mar. 16 **Litho.** ***Perf. 13½x13***

1284 A557 70c multi 1.90 1.90

Luxembourg Pavilion, Expo 2010, Shanghai — A558

2010, Mar. 16 ***Perf. 14x13½***

1285 A558 90c multi 2.50 2.50

Eisch Valley Castles — A559

No. 1286 — Various castles with country name at: a, UL. b, LR.

Serpentine Die Cut 12¼x13¼

2010, Mar. 16

Self-Adhesive

1286 Horiz. pair 4.00
- *a.-b.* A559 A Either single 1.90 1.90

On day of issue, Nos. 1286a-1287a each sold for 70c.

Countdown 2010 — A560

Designs: 70c, Arnica montana. €1, Mussels.

2010, Mar. 16 ***Perf. 11½***

1287-1288 A560 Set of 2 4.75 4.75

A561

Royalty — A562

Designs: 50c, Grand Duke Henri. €1, Grand Duchess Charlotte (1896-1985).

€3, Grand Duke Henri and Grand Duchess Maria Teresa.

2010, Mar. 16 ***Perf. 11½***

1289-1290 A561 Set of 2 4.25 4.25

Souvenir Sheet

1291 A562 €3 multi 8.25 8.25

Grand Duke Henri's accession to the throne, 10th anniv. (No. 1289).

Marriage of John of Luxembourg and Elizabeth of Bohemia, 700th Anniv. — A563

Photo. & Engr.

2010, June 16 ***Perf. 11¾x11¼***

1292 A563 70c multi 1.75 1.75

Accession to the throne of Bohemia by the House of Luxembourg. See Czech Republic No. 3457.

Europa — A564

Designs: 50c, Child and dragon reading book. 70c, Girl with lasso riding book.

2010, June 16 **Litho.** ***Perf. 13½***

1293-1294 A564 Set of 2 3.00 3.00

Outdoor Activities — A565

Designs: No. 1295, A, Motorcycling. No. 1296, A Europe, Camping.

2010, June 16 ***Perf. 13½x13***

1295-1296 A565 Set of 2 3.00 3.00

On day of issue, No. 1295 sold for 50c, and No. 1296 sold for 70c.

Souvenir Sheet

Philalux 2011 Intl. Philatelic Exhibition, Luxembourg — A566

No. 1297 — Various sites in Luxembourg: a, 50c (38x38mm). b, 70c, (38x38mm). c, €3, (60x38mm).

Perf. 13¾, 13¼x13¾ (#1297c)

2010, June 16

1297 A566 Sheet of 3 10.50 10.50
- *a.* 50c multi 1.25 1.25
- *b.* 70c multi 1.75 1.75
- *c.* €3 multi 7.50 7.50

Souvenir Sheet

Superjhemp, Comic Strip by Lucien Czuga — A567

No. 1298: a, Bernie the Dog. b, Man smoking pipe. c, Woman, vert. d, Superjhemp. e, Man with glasses, vert.

Serpentine Die Cut 12¼

2010, June 16

Self-Adhesive

1298 A567 Sheet of 5 6.25 6.25
- *a.-e.* A Any single 1.25 1.25

On day of issue, Nos. 1298a-1298e each sold for 50c.

A568

Winning Art in Children's "Fight Against Poverty" Stamp Design Contest A569

2010, Sept. 27 **Litho.** ***Perf. 11½***

1299 A568 A multi 1.25 1.25

1300 A569 A Europe multi 1.75 1.75

On day of issue No. 1299 sold for 50c and No. 1300 sold for 70c.

Famous People A570

Designs: 70c, Anne Beffort (1880-1966), educator and writer. 90c, Jean Soupert (1834-1910), rose cultivator. €1, Nicolas Frantz (1899-1985), cyclist.

Litho. & Engr.

2010, Sept. 27 ***Perf. 13½***

1301-1303 A570 Set of 3 6.75 6.75

Bagatelle Rose — A571

Bona Rose — A572

Bordeaux Rose — A573

Reine Marguerite d'Italie Rose — A574

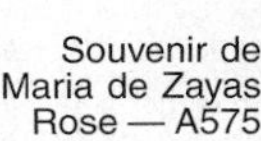

Souvenir de Maria de Zayas Rose — A575

Clotilde Rose — A576

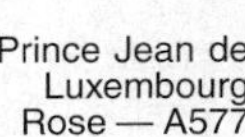

Prince Jean de Luxembourg Rose — A577

Pierre Watine Rose — A578

Ivan Misson Rose — A579

William Notting Rose — A580

Serpentine Die Cut 9¾

2010, Sept. 27 **Litho.**

Self-Adhesive

1304	Booklet pane of 10	12.50	
a.	A571 A multi	1.25	1.25
b.	A572 A multi	1.25	1.25
c.	A573 A multi	1.25	1.25
d.	A574 A multi	1.25	1.25
e.	A575 A multi	1.25	1.25
f.	A576 A multi	1.25	1.25
g.	A577 A multi	1.25	1.25
h.	A578 A multi	1.25	1.25
i.	A579 A multi	1.25	1.25
j.	A580 A multi	1.25	1.25

Nos. 1304a-1304j each sold for 50c on day of issue.

Luxembourg Maritime Cluster — A581

No. 1305 — Ships with lion emblem at: a, Left. b, Right.

2010, Dec. 7 **Litho.** ***Perf. 11½***

1305	A581 A Horiz. pair, #a-b	4.75	4.75

Nos. 1305a and 1305b each sold for 85c on day of issue.

European Year of Volunteering A582

2011, Mar. 15 ***Perf. 13¼x13***

1306	A582 A multi	1.75	1.75

No. 1306 sold for 60c on day of issue.

Royalty A583

Designs: 85c, Prince Guillaume, 30th birthday. €1.10, Grand Duke Jean, 90th birthday.

2011, Mar. 15 ***Perf. 11½***

1307-1308	A583	Set of 2	5.50	5.50

Anniversaries A584

Designs: No. 1309, 60c, Luxembourg Federation of Quilleurs (nine-pin bowling), 50th anniv. No. 1310, 60c, Amnesty International, 50th anniv. No. 1311, 60c, Stamp Day, 75th anniv.

2011, Mar. 15

1309-1311	A584	Set of 3	5.00	5.00

SEMI-POSTAL STAMPS

Clervaux Monastery SP1

Designs: 15c+10c, View of Pfaffenthal. 25c+10c, View of Luxembourg.

Engr.; Surcharge Typo. in Red

1921, Aug. 2 **Unwmk.** ***Perf. 11½***

B1	SP1	10c + 5c green	.20	*4.50*
B2	SP1	15c + 10c org red	.20	*5.75*
B3	SP1	25c + 10c dp grn	.20	*4.50*
		Nos. B1-B3 (3)	.60	*14.75*
		Set, never hinged	2.25	

The amount received from the surtax on these stamps was added to a fund for the erection of a monument to the soldiers from Luxembourg who died in World War I.

Nos. B1-B3 with Additional Surcharge in Red or Black

1923, May 27

B4	SP1	25c on #B1 (R)	1.10	*14.50*
B5	SP1	25c on #B2	1.10	*17.50*
B6	SP1	25c on #B3	1.10	*14.50*
		Nos. B4-B6 (3)	3.30	*46.50*
		Set, never hinged	8.75	

Unveiling of the monument to the soldiers who died in World War I.

Regular Issue of 1914-15 Surcharged in Black or Red

1924, Apr. 17 ***Perf. 11½x11***

B7	A11	12½c + 7½c grn	.20	*2.75*
B8	A11	35c + 10c dk bl (R)	.20	*2.75*
B9	A11	2½fr + 1fr red	1.10	*27.50*
B10	A11	5fr + 2fr dk vio	.55	*17.50*
		Nos. B7-B10 (4)	2.05	*50.50*
		Set, never hinged	3.50	

Nurse and Patient SP4

Prince Jean SP5

1925, Dec. 21 **Litho.** ***Perf. 13***

B11	SP4	5c (+ 5c) dl vio	.20	.70
B12	SP4	30c (+ 5c) org	.20	3.00
B13	SP4	50c (+ 5c) red brn	.20	*5.50*
B14	SP4	1fr (+ 10c) dp bl	.40	*14.00*
		Nos. B11-B14 (4)	1.00	*23.20*
		Set, never hinged	1.75	

1926, Dec. 15 **Photo.** ***Perf. 12½x12***

B15	SP5	5c (+ 5c) vio & blk	.20	.55
B16	SP5	40c (+ 10) grn & blk	.20	.90
B17	SP5	50c (+ 15c) lem & blk	.20	.95
B18	SP5	75c (+ 20c) lt red & blk	.25	*11.00*
B19	SP5	1.50fr (+ 30c) gray bl & blk	.35	*12.00*
		Nos. B15-B19 (5)	1.20	*25.40*
		Set, never hinged	2.50	

Grand Duchess Charlotte and Prince Felix — SP6

1927, Sept. 4 **Engr.** ***Perf. 11½***

B20	SP6	25c dp vio	1.10	*10.00*
B21	SP6	50c green	1.50	*16.00*
B22	SP6	75c rose lake	1.10	*10.00*
B23	SP6	1fr gray blk	1.10	*10.00*
B24	SP6	1½fr dp bl	1.10	*10.00*
		Nos. B20-B24 (5)	5.90	*56.00*
		Set, never hinged	17.00	

Introduction of postage stamps in Luxembourg, 75th anniv. These stamps were sold exclusively at the Luxembourg Philatelic Exhibition, September 4-8, 1927, at a premium of 3 francs per set, which was donated to the exhibition funds.

Princess Elisabeth SP7

Princess Marie Adelaide SP8

1927, Dec. 1 **Photo.** ***Perf. 12½***

B25	SP7	10c (+ 5c) turq bl & blk	.20	*.55*
B26	SP7	50c (+ 10c) dk brn & blk	.20	*.95*
B27	SP7	75c (+ 20c) org & blk	.20	*1.50*
B28	SP7	1fr (+ 30c) brn lake & blk	.25	*11.00*
B29	SP7	1½fr (+ 50c) ultra & blk	.20	*11.00*
		Nos. B25-B29 (5)	1.05	*25.00*
		Set, never hinged	2.25	

The surtax was for Child Welfare societies.

1928, Dec. 12 ***Perf. 12½x12***

B30	SP8	10c (+ 5c) ol grn & brn vio	.20	*1.10*
B31	SP8	60c (+ 10c) brn & ol grn	.40	*2.75*
B32	SP8	75c (+ 15c) vio rose & bl grn	.70	*7.25*
B33	SP8	1fr (+ 25c) dk grn & brn	1.75	*22.50*
B34	SP8	1½fr (+ 50c) cit & bl	1.75	*22.50*
		Nos. B30-B34 (5)	4.80	*56.10*
		Set, never hinged	11.00	

Princess Marie Gabrielle SP9

Prince Charles SP10

1929, Dec. 14 ***Perf. 13***

B35	SP9	10c (+ 10c) mar & dp grn	.20	*1.10*
B36	SP9	35c (+ 15c) dk grn & red brn	1.50	*7.25*
B37	SP9	75c (+ 30c) ver & blk	1.75	*9.00*
B38	SP9	1¼fr (+ 50c) mag & bl grn	2.25	*22.50*
B39	SP9	1¾fr (+ 75c) Prus bl & sl	2.75	*27.50*
		Nos. B35-B39 (5)	8.45	*67.35*
		Set, never hinged	20.00	

The surtax was for Child Welfare societies.

1930, Dec. 10 ***Perf. 12½***

B40	SP10	10c (+ 5c) bl grn & ol brn	.20	1.10
B41	SP10	75c (+ 10c) vio brn & bl grn	1.10	*4.75*
B42	SP10	1fr (+ 25c) car rose & vio	2.50	*17.50*
B43	SP10	1¼fr (+ 75c) ol bis & dk brn	4.00	*22.50*
B44	SP10	1¾fr (+ 1.50fr) ultra & red brn	4.50	*22.50*
		Nos. B40-B44 (5)	12.30	*68.35*
		Set, never hinged	50.00	

The surtax was for Child Welfare societies.

Princess Alix SP11

Countess Ermesinde SP12

1931, Dec. 10

B45	SP11	10c (+ 5c) brn org & gray	.40	1.10
B46	SP11	75c (+ 10c) claret & bl grn	4.00	*14.50*
B47	SP11	1fr (+ 25c) dp grn & gray	7.25	*29.00*
B48	SP11	1¼fr (+ 75c) dk vio & bl grn	7.25	*29.00*
B49	SP11	1¾fr (+ 1.50fr) bl & gray	11.00	*55.00*
		Nos. B45-B49 (5)	29.90	*128.60*
		Set, never hinged	110.00	

The surtax was for Child Welfare societies.

1932, Dec. 8

B50	SP12	10c (+ 5c) ol bis	.40	1.10
B51	SP12	75c (+ 10c) dp vio	2.75	*14.50*
B52	SP12	1fr (+ 25c) scar	11.00	*32.50*
B53	SP12	1¼fr (+ 75c) red brn	11.00	*32.50*
B54	SP12	1¾fr (+ 1.50fr) dp bl	11.00	*32.50*
		Nos. B50-B54 (5)	36.15	*113.10*
		Set, never hinged	92.50	

The surtax was for Child Welfare societies.

Count Henry VII — SP13

John the Blind — SP14

1933, Dec. 12

B55	SP13	10c (+ 5c) yel brn	.40	1.10
B56	SP13	75c (+ 10c) dp vio	4.75	*14.50*
B57	SP13	1fr (+ 25c) car rose	11.00	*35.00*
B58	SP13	1¼fr (+ 75c) org brn	14.50	*47.50*

B59 SP13 1¾fr (+ 1.50fr) brt bl 14.50 *50.00*
Nos. B55-B59 (5) 45.15 *148.10*
Set, never hinged 125.00

1934, Dec. 5

B60 SP14 10c (+ 5c) dk vio .20 1.10
B61 SP14 35c (+ 10c) dp grn 2.50 *9.00*
B62 SP14 75c (+ 15c) rose lake 2.50 *9.00*
B63 SP14 1fr (+ 25c) dp rose 14.50 *47.50*
B64 SP14 1¼fr (+ 75c) org 14.50 *47.50*
B65 SP14 1¾fr (+ 1.50fr) brt bl 14.50 *47.50*
Nos. B60-B65 (6) 48.70 *161.60*
Set, never hinged 125.00

Teacher SP15

Sculptor and Painter — SP16

Journalist SP17

Engineer SP18

Scientist SP19

Lawyer — SP20

Savings Bank and Adolphe Bridge — SP21

Surgeon SP22

1935, May 1 Unwmk. *Perf. 12½*

B65A SP15 5c violet .20 *1.10*
B65B SP16 10c brn red .25 *1.10*
B65C SP17 15c olive .40 *1.75*
B65D SP18 20c orange .55 *3.50*
B65E SP19 35c yel grn .70 *3.25*
B65F SP20 50c gray blk .95 *4.75*
B65G SP21 70c dk green 1.40 *5.50*
B65H SP22 1fr car red 1.75 *7.25*
B65J SP19 1.25fr turq 7.25 *50.00*
B65K SP18 1.75fr blue 9.00 *52.50*
B65L SP16 2fr lt brown 27.50 *110.00*
B65M SP17 3fr dk brown 37.50 *150.00*
B65N SP20 5fr lt blue 65.00 *275.00*
B65P SP15 10fr red vio 160.00 *450.00*
B65Q SP22 20fr dk green 175.00 *550.00*
Nos. B65A-B65Q (15) 487.45 *1,665.*
Set, never hinged 1,000.

Sold at double face, surtax going to intl. fund to aid professional people.

Philatelic Exhibition Issue

Type of Regular Issue of 1928

Wmk. 246

1935, Aug. 15 Engr. *Imperf.*

B66 A19 2fr (+ 50c) blk 4.75 *16.00*
Never hinged 13.00

Philatelic exhibition held at Esch-sur-Alzette.

Charles I — SP23

Perf. 11½

1935, Dec. 2 Photo. Unwmk.

B67 SP23 10c (+ 5c) vio .20 .40
B68 SP23 35c (+ 10c) grn .40 *.55*
B69 SP23 70c (+ 20c) dk brn .95 *1.50*
B70 SP23 1fr (+ 25c) rose lake 14.50 *37.50*
B71 SP23 1.25fr (+ 75c) org brn 14.50 *37.50*
B72 SP23 1.75fr (+ 1.50fr) bl 14.50 *47.50*
Nos. B67-B72 (6) 45.05 *124.95*
Set, never hinged 110.00

Wenceslas I, Duke of Luxembourg — SP24

1936, Dec. 1 *Perf. 11½x13*

B73 SP24 10c + 5(c) blk brn .20 .25
B74 SP24 35c + 10(c) bl grn .20 *.55*
B75 SP24 70c + 20(c) blk .40 *.90*
B76 SP24 1fr + 25(c) rose car 2.50 *14.50*
B77 SP24 1.25fr + 75(c) vio 2.25 *29.00*
B78 SP24 1.75fr + 1.50(fr) saph 1.60 *17.50*
Nos. B73-B78 (6) 7.15 *62.70*
Set, never hinged 32.50

Wenceslas II — SP25

1937, Dec. 1 *Perf. 11½x12½*

B79 SP25 10c + 5c car & blk .20 .40
B80 SP25 35c + 10c red vio & grn .20 .55
B81 SP25 70c + 20c ultra & red brn .25 .55
B82 SP25 1fr + 25c dk grn & scar 1.60 *17.00*
B83 SP25 1.25fr + 75c dk brn & vio 2.25 *17.00*
B84 SP25 1.75fr + 1.50fr blk & ultra 2.75 *17.50*
Nos. B79-B84 (6) 7.25 *53.00*
Set, never hinged 17.50

Souvenir Sheet

SP26

Wmk. 110

1937, July 25 Engr. *Perf. 13*

B85 SP26 Sheet of 2 4.00 *11.50*
Never hinged 11.00
a. 2fr red brown, single stamp 1.50 *5.50*

National Philatelic Exposition at Dudelange on July 25-26.

Sold for 5fr per sheet, of which 1fr was for the aid of the exposition.

Portrait of St. Willibrord — SP28

St. Willibrord, after a Miniature SP29

Abbey at Echternach — SP30

Designs: No, B87, The Rathaus at Echternach. No. B88, Pavilion in Abbey Park, Echternach. No. B91, Dancing Procession in Honor of St. Willibrord.

Perf. 14x13, 13x14

1938, June 5 Engr. Unwmk.

B86 SP28 35c + 10c dk bl grn .40 *.55*
B87 SP28 70c + 10c ol gray .70 *.55*
B88 SP28 1.25fr + 25c brn car 1.50 *2.50*
B89 SP29 1.75fr + 50c sl bl 2.50 *2.75*
B90 SP30 3fr + 2fr vio brn 5.50 *9.00*
B91 SP30 5fr + 5fr dk vio 6.50 *7.25*
Nos. B86-B91 (6) 17.10 22.60
Set, never hinged 60.00

12th centenary of the death of St. Willibrord. The surtax was used for the restoration of the ancient Abbey at Echternach.

Duke Sigismond SP32

Prince Jean SP33

1938, Dec. 1 Photo. *Perf. 11½*

B92 SP32 10c + 5c lil & blk .20 .40
B93 SP32 35c + 10c grn & blk .20 .55
B94 SP32 70c + 20c buff & blk .25 *.55*
B95 SP32 1fr + 25c red org & blk 1.90 *14.50*
B96 SP32 1.25fr + 75c gray bl & blk 1.90 *14.50*
B97 SP32 1.75fr + 1.50fr bl & blk 3.25 *22.50*
Nos. B92-B97 (6) 7.70 *53.00*
Set, never hinged 22.50

1939, Dec. 1 Litho. *Perf. 14x13*

Designs: Nos. B99, B102, Prince Felix. Nos. B100, B103, Grand Duchess Charlotte.

B98 SP33 10c + 5c red brn, *buff* .20 .40
B99 SP33 35c + 10c sl grn, *buff* .20 1.10
B100 SP33 70c + 20c blk, *buff* .95 *1.50*
B101 SP33 1fr + 25c red org, *buff* 4.00 *32.50*
B102 SP33 1.25fr + 75c vio brn, *buff* 4.75 *50.00*
B103 SP33 1.75fr + 1.50fr lt bl, *buff* 5.50 *65.00*
Nos. B98-B103 (6) 15.60 *150.50*
Set, never hinged 45.00

See No. 217 (souvenir sheet).

Allegory of Medicinal Baths — SP36

1940, Mar. 1 Photo. *Perf. 11½*

B104 SP36 2fr + 50c gray, blk & slate grn 1.10 *20.00*
Never hinged 4.00

Stamps of 1944, type A37, surcharged "+50C," "+5F" or "+15F" in black, were sold only in canceled condition, affixed to numbered folders. The surtax was for the benefit of Luxembourg evacuees. Value for folder, $15.

Homage to France SP37

Thanks to: No. B118, USSR. No. B119, Britannia. No. B120, America.

1945, Mar. 1 Engr. *Perf. 13*

B117 SP37 60c + 1.40fr dp grn .20 .20
B118 SP37 1.20fr + 1.80fr red .20 .20
B119 SP37 2.50fr + 3.50fr dp bl .20 .20
B120 SP37 4.20fr + 4.80fr dp vio .20 .20
Nos. B117-B120 (4) .80 .80
Set, never hinged .95

Issued to honor the Allied Nations. Exist imperf. Value, set $60.

Statue Carried in Procession SP41

Statue of Our Lady "Patrona Civitatis" SP42

"Our Lady of Luxembourg" SP43

Cathedral Façade SP44

Altar with Statue of Madonna — SP45

1945, June 4

B121 SP41 60c + 40c grn .20 1.10
B122 SP42 1.20fr + 80c red .20 1.10
B123 SP43 2.50fr + 2.50fr dp bl .20 *5.50*
B124 SP44 5.50fr + 6.50fr dk vio .65 *77.50*
B125 SP45 20fr + 20fr choc .65 *80.00*
Nos. B121-B125 (5) 1.90 *165.20*
Set, never hinged 4.00

Exist imperf. Value, set $250.

Souvenir Sheet

"Our Lady of Luxembourg" — SP46

1945, Sept. 30 **Engr.** ***Imperf.***

B126 SP46 50fr + 50fr blk 1.10 *55.00*
Never hinged 2.10

Young Fighters — SP47

Refugee Mother and Children — SP48

Political Prisoner — SP49

Executed Civilian — SP50

1945, Dec. 20 **Photo.** ***Perf. 11½***

B127 SP47 20c + 30c sl grn & buff .20 *1.10*
B128 SP48 1.50fr + 1fr brn red & buff .20 *1.10*
B129 SP49 3.50fr + 3.50fr bl, dp bl & buff .20 *10.50*
B130 SP50 5fr + 10fr brn, dk brn & buff .20 *10.50*
Nos. B127-B130 (4) .80 *23.20*
Set, never hinged 1.40

Souvenir Sheet

1946, Jan. 30 **Unwmk.** ***Perf. 11½***

B131 Sheet of 4 8.75 *300.00*
Never hinged 25.00
a. SP47 2.50fr + 2.50fr sl grn & buff 2.25 *50.00*
b. SP48 3.50fr + 6.50fr brown red & buff 2.25 *50.00*
c. SP49 5fr + 15fr bl, dp bl & buff 2.25 *50.00*
d. SP50 20fr + 20fr brown, dark brown & buff 2.25 *50.00*

Tribute to Luxembourg's heroes and martyrs.
The surtax was for the National Welfare Fund.

Souvenir Sheet

Old Rolling Mill, Dudelange — SP52

1946, July 28 **Engr. & Typo.**

B132 SP52 50fr brn & dk bl, *buff* 5.50 *35.00*
Never hinged 13.00

National Postage Stamp Exhibition, Dudelange, July 28-29, 1946. The sheets sold for 55fr.

Jean l'Aveugle — SP53

1946, Dec. 5 **Photo.**

B133 SP53 60c + 40c dk grn .20 *1.75*
B134 SP53 1.50fr + 50c brn red .20 *3.00*
B135 SP53 3.50fr + 3.50fr dp bl .60 *27.50*
B136 SP53 5fr + 10fr sepia .40 *22.50*
Nos. B133-B136 (4) 1.40 *54.75*
Set, never hinged 2.50

600th anniv. of the death of Jean l'Aveugle (John the Blind), Count of Luxembourg.

Ruins of St. Willibrord Basilica — SP54

Twelfth Century Miniature of St. Willibrord SP59

Designs: #B138, Statue of Abbot Jean Bertels. #B139, Emblem of Echternach Abbey. #B140, Ruins of the Basilica's Interior. #B141, St. Irmine and Pepin of Hersta Holding Model of the Abbey.

Perf. 13x14, 14x13

1947, May 25 **Engr.**

B137 SP54 20c + 10c blk .20 .25
B138 SP54 60c + 10c dk grn .40 .55
B139 SP54 75c + 25c dk car .55 .75
B140 SP54 1.50fr + 50c dk brn .70 .75
B141 SP54 3.50fr + 2.50fr dk bl 2.25 *4.75*
B142 SP59 25fr + 25fr dk pur 15.00 *25.00*
Nos. B137-B142 (6) 19.10 *32.05*
Set, never hinged 50.00

The surtax was to aid in restoring the Basilica of Saint Willibrord at Echternach.

Michel Lentz — SP60

Edmond de La Fontaine (Dicks) — SP61

1947, Dec. 4 **Photo.** ***Perf. 11½***

B143 SP60 60c + 40c sep & buff .25 1.10
B144 SP60 1.50fr + 50c dp plum & buff .25 1.10
B145 SP60 3.50fr + 3.50fr dp bl & gray 2.75 *17.50*
B146 SP60 10fr + 5fr dk grn & gray 2.40 *17.50*
Nos. B143-B146 (4) 5.65 *37.20*
Set, never hinged 17.00

1948, Nov. 18

B147 SP61 60c + 40c brn & pale bis .25 .95
B148 SP61 1.50fr + 50c brn car & buff .45 .95
B149 SP61 3.50fr + 3.50fr dp bl & gray 5.50 *19.00*
B150 SP61 10fr + 5fr dk grn & gray 4.50 *19.00*
Nos. B147-B150 (4) 10.70 *39.90*
Set, never hinged 19.00

125th anniversary of the birth of Edmond de La Fontaine, poet and composer.

Type of Regular Issue of 1948
Souvenir Sheet

1949, Jan. 8 **Unwmk.** ***Perf. 11½***

B151 Sheet of 3 50.00 55.00
Never hinged 100.00
a. A45 8fr + 3fr blue gray 14.00 17.00
b. A45 12fr + 5fr green 14.00 17.00
c. A45 15fr + 7fr brown 14.00 17.00

30th anniversary of Grand Duchess Charlotte's ascension to the throne. Border and dates "1919-1949" in gray.

Michel Rodange — SP62

1949, Dec. 5

B152 SP62 60c + 40c ol grn & gray .40 .55
B153 SP62 2fr + 1fr dk vio & rose 2.75 *5.00*
B154 SP62 4fr + 2fr sl blk & gray 4.50 *7.50*
B155 SP62 10fr + 5fr brn & buff 4.50 *17.50*
Nos. B152-B155 (4) 12.15 *30.55*
Set, never hinged 22.50

Wards of the Nation
SP63 SP64

1950, June 24 **Engr.** ***Perf. 12½x12***

B156 SP63 60c + 15c dk sl bl 1.25 1.50
B157 SP64 1fr + 20c dk car rose 3.25 1.50
B158 SP63 2fr + 30c red brn 2.25 1.50
B159 SP64 4fr + 75c dk bl 7.50 *17.00*
B160 SP63 8fr + 3fr blk 21.00 *45.00*
B161 SP64 10fr + 5fr lil rose 22.50 *45.00*
Nos. B156-B161 (6) 57.75 *111.50*
Set, never hinged 90.00

The surtax was for child welfare.

Jean A. Zinnen SP65

Laurent Menager SP66

1950, Dec. 5 **Photo.** ***Perf. 11½***

B162 SP65 60c + 10c ind & gray .35 .25
B163 SP65 2fr + 15c cer & buff .35 .40
B164 SP65 4fr + 15c vio bl & bl gray 3.25 *6.50*
B165 SP65 8fr + 5fr dk brn & buff 9.25 *25.00*
Nos. B162-B165 (4) 13.20 *32.15*
Set, never hinged 27.50

1951, Dec. 5

Gray Background

B166 SP66 60c + 10c sepia .25 .40
B167 SP66 2fr + 15c dl ol grn .25 .40
B168 SP66 4fr + 15c blue 2.50 *4.00*
B169 SP66 8fr + 5fr vio brn 10.50 *30.00*
Nos. B166-B169 (4) 13.50 *34.80*
Set, never hinged 29.00

50th anniversary of the death of Laurent Menager, composer.

J. B. Fresez — SP67

Candlemas Singing — SP68

1952, Dec. 3

B170 SP67 60c + 15c dk bl grn & pale bl .25 .40
B171 SP67 2fr + 25c chnt brn & buff .25 .40
B172 SP67 4fr + 25c dk vio bl & gray 1.90 *4.00*
B173 SP67 8fr + 4.75fr dp plum & lil gray 13.00 *35.00*
Nos. B170-B173 (4) 15.40 *39.80*
Set, never hinged 32.50

1953, Dec. 3

Designs: 80c+20c, 4fr+50c, Procession with ratchets. 1.20fr+30c, 7fr+3.35fr, Breaking Easter eggs.

B174 SP68 25c + 15c red org & dp car .25 .40
B175 SP68 80c + 20c vio brn & bl gray .25 .40
B176 SP68 1.20fr + 30c bl grn & ol grn .50 .95
B177 SP68 2fr + 25c brn car & brn .40 .40
B178 SP68 4fr + 50c grnsh bl & vio bl 3.00 *9.00*
B179 SP68 7fr + 3.35fr vio & pur 9.00 *22.50*
Nos. B174-B179 (6) 13.40 *33.65*
Set, never hinged 27.50

The surtax was for the National Welfare Fund of Grand Duchess Charlotte.

Clay Censer and Whistle — SP69

Toys for St. Nicholas Day — SP70

Designs: 80c+20c, 4fr+50c, Sheep and bass drum. 1.20fr+30c, 7fr+3.45fr, Merry-go-round horses. 2fr+25c, As No. B180.

1954, Dec. 3

B180 SP69 25c + 5c car lake & cop brn .25 .55
B181 SP69 80c + 20c dk gray .25 .55
B182 SP69 1.20fr + 30c dk bl grn & cr .60 1.90
B183 SP69 2fr + 25c brn & ocher .35 .55
B184 SP69 4fr + 50c brt bl 3.00 *6.50*
B185 SP69 7fr + 3.45fr pur 8.75 *25.00*
Nos. B180-B185 (6) 13.20 *35.05*
Set, never hinged 32.50

1955, Dec. 5 Unwmk. *Perf. 11½*

Designs: 80c+20c, 4fr+50c, Christ child and lamb (Christmas). 1.20fr+30c, 7fr+3.45fr, Star, crown and cake (Epiphany).

B186 SP70 25c + 5c sal & dk car .20 .40
B187 SP70 80c + 20c gray & gray blk .20 .40
B188 SP70 1.20fr + 30c ol grn & sl grn .35 .95
B189 SP70 2fr + 25c buff & dk brn .40 .40
B190 SP70 4fr + 50c lt bl & brt bl 3.25 *11.00*
B191 SP70 7fr + 3.45fr rose vio & claret 6.50 *15.00*
Nos. B186-B191 (6) 10.90 *28.15*
Set, never hinged 22.50

Coats of Arms — SP71

Arms: 25c+5c, 2fr+25c, Echternach. 80c+20c, 4fr+50c, Esch-sur-Alzette. 1.20fr+30c, 7fr+3.45fr, Grevenmacher.

1956, Dec. 5 Photo.

Arms in Original Colors

B192 SP71 25c + 5c blk & sal pink .20 .40
B193 SP71 80c + 20c ultra & yel .20 .40
B194 SP71 1.20fr + 30c ultra & gray .20 1.10
B195 SP71 2fr + 25c blk & buff .20 .40
B196 SP71 4fr + 50c ultra & lt bl 1.90 *5.50*
B197 SP71 7fr + 3.45fr ultra & pale vio 3.50 *11.50*
Nos. B192-B197 (6) 6.20 *19.30*
Set, never hinged 14.50

1957, Dec. 4 Unwmk. *Perf. 11½*

25c+5c, 2fr+25c, Luxembourg. 80c+20c, 4fr+50c, Mersch. 1.20fr+30c, 7fr+3.45fr, Vianden.

Arms in Original Colors

B198 SP71 25c + 5c ultra & org .20 *.40*
B199 SP71 80c + 20c blk & lem .20 *.40*
B200 SP71 1.20fr + 30c ultra & lt bl grn .20 *.70*
B201 SP71 2fr + 25c ultra & pale brn .20 *.40*
B202 SP71 4fr + 50c blk & pale vio bl .50 *5.50*
B203 SP71 7fr + 3.45fr ultra & rose lil 3.25 *8.00*
Nos. B198-B203 (6) 4.55 15.40
Set, never hinged 11.00

1958, Dec. 3 *Perf. 11½*

30c+10c, 2.50fr+50c, Capellen. 1fr+25c, 5fr+50c, Diekirch. 1.50fr+25c, 8.50fr+4.60fr, Redange.

Arms in Original Colors

B204 SP71 30c + 10c blk & pink .20 *.40*
B205 SP71 1fr + 25c ultra & buff .20 *.40*
B206 SP71 1.50fr + 25c ultra & pale grn .20 *.55*
B207 SP71 2.50fr + 50c blk & gray .20 *.40*
B208 SP71 5fr + 50c ultra 2.25 *5.50*
B209 SP71 8.50fr + 4.60fr ultra & lil 2.50 *8.00*
Nos. B204-B209 (6) 5.55 *15.25*
Set, never hinged 11.00

1959, Dec. 2

30c+10c, 2.50fr+50c, Clervaux. 1fr+25c, 5fr+50c, Remich. 1.50fr+25c, 8.50fr+4.60fr, Wiltz.

Arms in Original Colors

B210 SP71 30c + 10c ultra & pink .20 .40
B211 SP71 1fr + 25c ultra & pale lem .20 .40
B212 SP71 1.50fr + 25c blk & pale grn .20 .55
B213 SP71 2.50fr + 50c ultra & pale fawn .20 .40
B214 SP71 5fr + 50c ultra & lt bl .65 *2.25*
B215 SP71 8.50fr + 4.60fr blk & pale vio 2.75 *11.00*
Nos. B210-B215 (6) 4.20 *15.00*
Set, never hinged 9.25

Catalogue values for unused stamps in this section, from this point to the end of the section, are for Never Hinged items.

Princess Marie-Astrid SP72

Prince Jean SP73

1fr+25c, 5fr+50c, Princess in party dress. 1.50fr+25c, 8.50fr+4.60fr, Princess with book.

1960, Dec. 5 Photo. *Perf. 11½*

B216 SP72 30c + 10c brn & lt bl .35 .20
B217 SP72 1fr + 25c brn & pink .35 .20
B218 SP72 1.50fr + 25c brn & lt bl .65 .50
B219 SP72 2.50fr + 50c brn & yel .50 .35
B220 SP72 5fr + 50c brn & pale lil 1.00 *2.50*
B221 SP72 8.50fr + 4.60fr brn & pale ol 9.25 *11.50*
Nos. B216-B221 (6) 12.10 15.25

Type of 1960

Prince Henri: 30c+10c, 2.50fr+50c, Infant in long dress. 1fr+25c, 5fr+50c, Informal portrait. 1.50fr+25c, 8.50fr+ 4.60fr, In dress suit.

1961, Dec. 4 Unwmk. *Perf. 11½*

B222 SP72 30c + 10c brn & brt pink .35 .25
B223 SP72 1fr + 25c brn & lt vio .35 .25
B224 SP72 1.50fr + 25c brn & sal .50 .50
B225 SP72 2.50fr + 50c brn & pale grn .50 .25
B226 SP72 5fr + 50c brn & cit 3.00 2.50
B227 SP72 8.50fr + 4.60fr brn & gray 5.00 *6.50*
Nos. B222-B227 (6) 9.70 10.25

1962, Dec. 3 Photo. *Perf. 11½*

Designs: Different portraits of the twins Prince Jean and Princess Margaretha. Nos. B228 and B233 are horizontal.

Inscriptions and Portraits in Dark Brown

B228 SP73 30c + 10c org yel .25 .20
B229 SP73 1fr + 25c lt bl .25 .20
B230 SP73 1.50fr + 25c pale ol .35 .35
B231 SP73 2.50fr + 50c rose .35 .25
B232 SP73 5fr + 50c lt yel grn 1.25 *2.25*
B233 SP73 8.50fr + 4.60fr lil gray 3.25 *4.50*
Nos. B228-B233 (6) 5.70 7.75

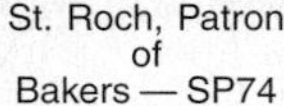
St. Roch, Patron of Bakers — SP74

Three Towers — SP75

Patron Saints: 1fr+25c, St. Anne, tailors. 2fr+25c, St. Eloi, smiths. 3fr+50c, St. Michael, shopkeepers. 6fr+50c, St. Bartholomew, butchers. St. Theobald, seven crafts.

1963, Dec. 2 Unwmk. *Perf. 11½*

Multicolored Design

B234 SP74 50c + 10c pale lil .20 .20
B235 SP74 1fr + 25c tan .20 .20
B236 SP74 2fr + 25c lt grnsh bl .20 .20
B237 SP74 3fr + 50c lt bl .20 .25
B238 SP74 6fr + 50c buff 1.00 *1.60*
B239 SP74 10fr + 5.90fr pale yel grn 1.60 *3.00*
Nos. B234-B239 (6) 3.40 5.45

1964, Dec. 7 Photo. *Perf. 11½*

Children's paintings: 1fr+25c, 6fr+50c, Grand Duke Adolphe Bridge, horiz. 2fr+25c, 10fr+5.90fr, The Lower City.

B240 SP75 50c + 10c multi .20 .20
B241 SP75 1fr + 25c multi .20 .20
B242 SP75 2fr + 25c multi .20 .30
a. Value omitted 300.00
B243 SP75 3fr + 50c multi .20 .30
B244 SP75 6fr + 50c multi 1.00 1.50
B245 SP75 10fr + 5.90fr multi 1.25 *2.50*
Nos. B240-B245 (6) 3.05 5.00

The Roman Lady of Titelberg — SP76

Fairy Tales of Luxembourg: 1fr+25c, Schäppchen, the Huntsman. 2fr+25c, The Witch of Koerich. 3fr+50c, The Gnomes of Schoenfels. 6fr+50c, Tollchen, Watchman of Hesperange. 10fr+5.90fr, The Old Spinster of Heispelt.

1965, Dec. 6 Photo. *Perf. 11½*

B246 SP76 50c + 10c multi .20 .20
B247 SP76 1fr + 25c multi .20 .20
B248 SP76 2fr + 25c multi .20 .20
B249 SP76 3fr + 50c multi .20 .20
B250 SP76 6fr + 50c multi .50 *1.25*
B251 SP76 10fr + 5.90fr multi 1.25 *3.00*
Nos. B246-B251 (6) 2.55 5.05

Fairy Tale Type of 1965

Fairy Tales of Luxembourg: 50c+10c, The Veiled Matron of Wormeldange. 1.50fr+25c, Jekel, Warden of the Wark. 2fr+25c, The Black Man of Vianden. 3fr+50c, The Gracious Fairy of Rosport. 6fr+1fr, The Friendly Shepherd of Donkolz. 13fr+6.90fr, The Little Sisters of Trois-Vièrges.

1966, Dec. 6 Photo. *Perf. 11½*

B252 SP76 50c + 10c multi .20 .20
B253 SP76 1.50fr + 25c multi .20 .20
B254 SP76 2fr + 25c multi .20 .20
B255 SP76 3fr + 50c multi .20 .30
B256 SP76 6fr + 1fr multi .50 *1.00*
B257 SP76 13fr + 6.90fr multi .85 *2.25*
Nos. B252-B257 (6) 2.15 4.15

Prince Guillaume SP77

Castle of Berg SP78

Portraits: 1.50fr+25c, Princess Margaretha. 2fr+25c, Prince Jean. 3fr+50c, Prince Henri as Boy Scout. 6fr+1fr, Princess Marie-Astrid.

1967, Dec. 6 Photo. *Perf. 11½*

B258 SP77 50c + 10c yel & brn .20 .20
B259 SP77 1.50fr + 25c gray bl & brn .20 .20
B260 SP77 2fr + 25c pale rose & brn .20 .20
B261 SP77 3fr + 50c lt ol & brn .65 .20
B262 SP77 6fr + 1fr lt vio & brn .50 *1.00*
B263 SP78 13fr + 6.90fr multi .65 *3.00*
Nos. B258-B263 (6) 2.40 4.80

Medico-professional Institute at Cap — SP79

Deaf-mute Child Imitating Bird — SP80

Handicapped Children: 2fr+25c, Blind child holding candle. 3fr+50c, Nurse supporting physically handicapped child. 6fr+1fr, Cerebral palsy victim. 13fr+6.90fr, Mentally disturbed child.

1968, Dec. 5 Photo. *Perf. 11½*

Designs and Inscriptions in Dark Brown

B264 SP79 50c + 10c lt bl .20 .20
B265 SP80 1.50fr + 25c lt grn .20 .20
B266 SP80 2fr + 25c yel .25 .25
B267 SP80 3fr + 50c bl .25 .25
B268 SP80 6fr + 1fr buff .50 1.10
B269 SP80 13fr + 6.90fr pink 1.60 *3.00*
Nos. B264-B269 (6) 3.00 5.00

Vianden Castle SP81

Children of Bethlehem SP82

Luxembourg Castles: 1.50fr+25c, Lucilinburhuc. 2fr+25c, Bourglinster. 3fr+50c, Hollenfels. 6fr+1fr, Ansembourg. 13fr+6.90fr, Beaufort.

1969, Dec. 8 Photo. *Perf. 11½*

B270 SP81 50c + 10c multi .20 .20
B271 SP81 1.50fr + 25c multi .20 .20
B272 SP81 2fr + 25c multi .20 .20
B273 SP81 3fr + 50c multi .20 .20
B274 SP81 6fr + 1fr multi .60 *1.25*
B275 SP81 13fr + 6.90fr multi 1.00 *3.00*
Nos. B270-B275 (6) 2.40 5.05

1970, Dec. 7 Photo. *Perf. 11½*

Luxembourg Castles: 50c+10c, Clervaux. 1.50fr+25c, Septfontaines. 2fr+25c, Bourscheid. 3fr+50c, Esch-sur-Sure. 6fr+1fr, Larochette. 13fr+6.90fr, Brandenbourg.

B276 SP81 50c + 10c multi .20 .20
B277 SP81 1.50fr + 25c multi .20 .20
B278 SP81 2fr + 25c multi .20 .20
B279 SP81 3fr + 50c multi .20 .20
B280 SP81 6fr + 1fr multi .60 *1.25*
B281 SP81 13fr + 6.90fr multi 1.00 *3.00*
Nos. B276-B281 (6) 2.40 5.05

The surtax on Nos. B180-B281 was for charitable purposes.

1971, Dec. 6 Photo. *Perf. 11½*

Wooden Statues from Crèche of Beaufort Church: 1.50fr+25c, Shepherds. 3fr+50c, Nativity. 8fr+1fr, Herdsmen. 18fr+6.50fr, King offering gift.

Sculptures in Shades of Brown

B282 SP82 1fr + 25c lilac .25 .20
B283 SP82 1.50fr + 25c olive .25 .20
B284 SP82 3fr + 50c gray .35 .20
B285 SP82 8fr + 1fr lt ultra 1.10 *2.25*
B286 SP82 18fr + 6.50fr grn 1.90 *4.50*
Nos. B282-B286 (5) 3.85 7.35

The surtax was for various charitable organizations.

Angel — SP83

Sts. Anne and Joachim — SP84

Stained Glass Windows, Luxembourg Cathedral: 1.50fr+25c, St. Joseph. 3fr+50c, Virgin and Child. 8fr+1fr, People of Bethlehem. 18fr+6.50fr, Angel facing left.

1972, Dec. 4

B287 SP83 1fr + 25c multi .20 .20
B288 SP83 1.50fr + 25c multi .20 .20
B289 SP83 3fr + 50c multi .20 .20
B290 SP83 8fr + 1fr multi 1.00 *2.25*
B291 SP83 18fr + 6.50fr multi 2.75 *6.00*
Nos. B287-B291 (5) 4.35 8.85

Surtax was for charitable purposes.

1973, Dec. 5 Photo. *Perf. 11½*

Sculptures: 3fr+25c, Mary meeting Elizabeth. 4fr+50c, Virgin and Child and a King. 8fr+1fr, Shepherds. 15fr+7fr, St. Joseph holding candle. Designs from 16th century reredos, Hermitage of Hachiville.

B292 SP84 1fr + 25c multi .20 .20
B293 SP84 3fr + 25c multi .20 .20
B294 SP84 4fr + 50c multi .25 .20
B295 SP84 8fr + 1fr multi 1.10 *2.25*
B296 SP84 15fr + 7fr multi 3.00 *6.00*
Nos. B292-B296 (5) 4.75 8.85

Annunciation — SP85

Crucifixion — SP86

Designs: 3fr+25c, Visitation. 4fr+50c, Nativity. 8fr+1fr, Adoration of the King. 15fr+7fr, Presentation at the Temple. Designs of Nos. B297-B301 are from miniatures in the "Codex Aureus Epternacensis" (Gospel from Echternach Abbey). The Crucifixion is from the carved ivory cover of the Codex, by the Master of Echternach, c. 983-991.

1974, Dec. 5 Photo. *Perf. 11½*

B297 SP85 1fr + 25c multi .20 .20
B298 SP85 3fr + 25c multi .20 .20
B299 SP85 4fr + 50c multi .20 .20
B300 SP85 8fr + 1fr multi 1.10 *3.00*
B301 SP85 15fr + 7fr multi 2.00 *5.50*
Nos. B297-B301 (5) 3.70 9.10

Souvenir Sheet

Photogravure & Engraved

Perf. 13½

B302 SP86 20fr + 10fr multi 3.50 8.00

50th anniversary of Caritas issues. No. B302 contains one 34x42mm stamp.

Fly Orchid — SP87

Lilies of the Valley — SP88

Flowers: 3fr+25c, Pyramidal orchid. 4fr+50c, Marsh hellebore. 8fr+1fr, Pasqueflower. 15fr+7fr, Bee orchid.

1975, Dec. 4 Photo. *Perf. 11½*

B303 SP87 1fr + 25c multi .20 .20
B304 SP87 3fr + 25c multi .35 .25
B305 SP87 4fr + 50c multi .50 .20
B306 SP87 8fr + 1fr multi 1.00 *1.60*
B307 SP87 15fr + 7fr multi 2.75 *5.00*
Nos. B303-B307 (5) 4.80 7.25

The surtax on Nos. B303-B317 was for various charitable organizations.

1976, Dec. 6

Flowers: 2fr+25c, Gentian. 5fr+25c, Narcissus. 6fr+50c, Red hellebore. 12fr+1fr, Late spider orchid. 20fr+8fr, Two-leafed squill.

B308 SP87 2fr + 25c multi .20 .30
B309 SP87 5fr + 25c multi .25 .30
B310 SP87 6fr + 50c multi .30 .30
B311 SP87 12fr + 1fr multi 1.00 *2.00*
B312 SP87 20fr + 8fr multi 2.75 *5.50*
Nos. B308-B312 (5) 4.50 8.40

1977, Dec. 5 Photo. *Perf. 11½*

Flowers: 5fr+25c, Columbine. 6fr+50c, Mezereon. 12fr+1fr, Early spider orchid. 20fr+8fr, Spotted orchid.

B313 SP88 2fr + 25c multi .20 .20
B314 SP88 5fr + 25c multi .25 .25
B315 SP88 6fr + 50c multi .50 .25
B316 SP88 12fr + 1fr multi 1.40 *2.75*
B317 SP88 20fr + 8fr multi 2.25 *5.50*
Nos. B313-B317 (5) 4.60 8.95

St. Matthew — SP89

Spring — SP90

Behind-glass Paintings, 19th Century: 5fr+25c, St. Mark. 6fr+50c, Nativity. 12fr+1fr, St. Luke. 20fr+8fr, St. John.

1978, Dec. 5 Photo. *Perf. 11½*

B318 SP89 2fr + 25c multi .20 .20
B319 SP89 5fr + 25c multi .25 .30
B320 SP89 6fr + 50c multi .35 .30
B321 SP89 12fr + 1fr multi 1.25 .90
B322 SP89 20fr + 8fr multi 1.90 *4.00*
Nos. B318-B322 (5) 3.95 5.70

Surtax was for charitable organizations.

1979, Dec. 5 Photo. *Perf. 12*

Behind-glass Paintings, 19th Century: 5fr+25c, Summer. 6fr+50c, Charity. 12fr+1fr, Autumn. 20fr+8fr, Winter.

B323 SP90 2fr + 25c multi .20 .20
B324 SP90 5fr + 25c multi .25 .25
B325 SP90 6fr + 50c multi .35 .25
B326 SP90 12fr + 1fr multi .85 *1.25*
B327 SP90 20fr + 8fr multi 1.75 *4.50*
Nos. B323-B327 (5) 3.40 6.45

St. Martin — SP91

Behind-glass Paintings, 19th Century: 6fr+50c, St. Nicholas. 8fr+1fr, Madonna and Child. 30fr+1fr, St. George the Martyr.

1980, Dec. 5 Photo. *Perf. 11½*

B328 SP91 4fr + 50c multi .20 .20
B329 SP91 6fr + 50c multi .25 .25
B330 SP91 8fr + 1fr multi .45 .45
B331 SP91 30fr + 10fr multi 1.75 1.75
Nos. B328-B331 (4) 2.65 2.65

Surtax was for charitable organizations.

Arms of Petange SP92

Nativity, by Otto van Veen (1556-1629) SP93

1981, Dec. 4 Photo.

Granite Paper

B332 SP92 4fr + 50c shown .25 .30
B333 SP92 6fr + 50c Larochette .30 .35
B334 SP93 8fr + 1fr shown .50 .60
B335 SP92 16fr + 2fr Stadtbredimus .90 1.10
B336 SP92 35fr + 12fr Weiswampach 2.25 2.75
Nos. B332-B336 (5) 4.20 5.10

Surtax was for charitable organizations.

1982, Dec. 6 Photo. *Perf. 11½*

Design: 8fr+1fr, Adoration of the Shepherds, stained-glass window, by Gust Zanter, Hoscheid Parish Church.

Granite Paper

B337 SP92 4fr + 50c Bettembourg .25 .25
B338 SP92 6fr + 50c Frisange .35 .35
B339 SP93 8fr + 1fr multi .45 .45
B340 SP92 16fr + 2fr Mamer .90 .90
B341 SP92 35fr + 12fr Heinerscheid 2.25 2.25
Nos. B337-B341 (5) 4.20 4.20

Surtax was for charitable organizations.

1983, Dec. 5 Photo.

B342 SP92 4fr + 1fr Winseler .20 .20
B343 SP92 7fr + 1fr Beckerich .40 .40
B344 SP93 10fr + 1fr Nativity .50 .50
B345 SP92 16fr + 2fr Feulen .85 .85
B346 SP92 40fr + 13fr Mertert 3.00 3.00
Nos. B342-B346 (5) 4.95 4.95

Surtax was for charitable organizations.

Inquisitive Child — SP94

Children Exhibiting Various Moods.

1984, Dec. 5 Photo.

B347 SP94 4fr + 1fr shown .20 .20
B348 SP94 7fr + 1fr Daydreaming .45 .45
B349 SP94 10fr + 1fr Nativity .55 .55
B350 SP94 16fr + 2fr Sulking .95 .95
B351 SP94 40fr + 13fr Admiring 3.25 3.25
Nos. B347-B351 (5) 5.40 5.40

Surtax was for charitable organizations.

1985, Dec. 5 Photo.

B352 SP94 4fr + 1fr Girl drawing .20 .20
B353 SP94 7fr + 1fr Two boys .30 .30
B354 SP94 10fr + 1fr Adoration of the Magi .40 .40
B355 SP94 16fr + 2fr Fairy tale characters 1.00 1.00
B356 SP94 40fr + 13fr Embarrassed girl 2.75 2.75
Nos. B352-B356 (5) 4.65 4.65

Surtax was for charitable organizations.

SP95

SP96

Book of Hours, France, c. 1550, Natl. Library — SP97

Christmas: illuminated text.

1986, Dec. 8 Photo. *Perf. 11½*

B357 SP95 6fr + 1fr Annunciation .45 .45
B358 SP95 10fr + 1fr Angel appears to the Shepherds .55 .55
B359 SP95 12fr + 2fr Nativity .70 .70
B360 SP95 18fr + 2fr Adoration of the Magi 1.00 1.00
B361 SP95 20fr + 8fr Flight into Egypt 1.40 1.40
Nos. B357-B361 (5) 4.10 4.10

1987, Dec. 1 *Perf. 12*

B362 SP96 6fr + 1fr Annunciation .40 .40
B363 SP96 10fr + 1fr Visitation .65 .65
B364 SP96 12fr + 2fr Adoration of the Magi .85 .85
B365 SP96 18fr + 2fr Presentation in the Temple 1.10 1.10
B366 SP96 20fr + 8fr Flight into Egypt 1.60 1.60
Nos. B362-B366 (5) 4.60 4.60

1988, Dec. 5 *Perf. 11½*

B367 SP97 9fr +1fr Annunciation to the Shepherds .55 .55
B368 SP97 12fr +2fr Adoration of the Magi .75 .75
B369 SP97 18fr +2fr Virgin and Child 1.10 1.10
B370 SP97 20fr +8fr Pentecost 1.50 1.50
Nos. B367-B370 (4) 3.90 3.90

Surtax for charitable organizations.

Christmas SP98

Chapels: No. B371, St. Lambert and St. Blase, Fennange, vert. No. B372, St. Quirinus, Luxembourg. No. B373, St. Anthony the Hermit, Reisdorf, vert. No. B374, The Hermitage, Hachiville.

1989, Dec. 11 Photo. *Perf. 12x11½*

B371 SP98 9fr +1fr multi .50 .50
B372 SP98 12fr +2fr multi .70 .70
B373 SP98 18fr +3fr multi 1.10 1.10
B374 SP98 25fr +8fr multi 1.60 1.60
Nos. B371-B374 (4) 3.90 3.90

Surtax for social work.

1990, Nov. 26 Photo. *Perf. 11½*

Chapels: No. B375, Congregation of the Blessed Virgin Mary, Vianden, vert. No. B376, Our Lady, Echternach. No. B377, Our Lady, Consoler of the Afflicted, Grentzingen. B378, St. Pirmin, Kaundorf, vert.

B375 SP98 9fr +1fr multi .60 .60
B376 SP98 12fr +2fr multi .85 .85
B377 SP98 18fr +3fr multi 1.25 1.25
B378 SP98 25fr +8fr multi 2.00 2.00
Nos. B375-B378 (4) 4.70 4.70

Surtax for charitable organizations.

1991, Dec. 9 Photo. *Perf. 11½*

Chapels: No. B379, St. Donatus, Arsdorf, vert. No. B380, Our Lady of Sorrows,

Brandenbourg. No. B381, Our Lady, Luxembourg. No. B382, The Hermitage, Wolwelange, vert.

B379	SP98 14fr +2fr multi		.95	.95
B380	SP98 14fr +2fr multi		.95	.95
B381	SP98 18fr +3fr multi		1.25	1.25
B382	SP98 22fr +7fr multi		1.75	1.75
	Nos. B379-B382 (4)		4.90	4.90

Surtax used for philanthropic work.

Endangered Birds — SP99

Designs: No. B383, Hazel grouse. No. B384, Golden oriole, vert. 18fr+3fr, Black stork. 22fr+7fr, Red kite, vert.

1992, Dec. 7 Photo. *Perf. 11½*

B383	SP99 14fr +2fr multi	1.00	1.00
B384	SP99 14fr +2fr multi	1.00	1.00
B385	SP99 18fr +3fr multi	1.25	1.25
B386	SP99 22fr +7fr multi	1.75	1.75
	Nos. B383-B386 (4)	5.00	5.00

Surtax for Luxembourg charitable organizations.

1993, Dec. 6 Photo. *Perf. 11½*

Designs: No. B387, Snipe. No. B388, Kingfisher, vert. 18fr+3fr, Little ringed plover. 22fr+7fr, Sand martin, vert.

B387	SP99 14fr +2fr multi	.90	.90
B388	SP99 14fr +2fr multi	.90	.90
B389	SP99 18fr +3fr multi	1.25	1.25
B390	SP99 22fr +7fr multi	1.60	1.60
	Nos. B387-B390 (4)	4.65	4.65

Surtax for Luxembourg charitable organizations.

1994, Sept. 19 Photo. *Perf. 11½*

Designs: No. B391, Partridge. No. B392, Stonechat, vert. 18fr+3fr, Blue-headed wagtail. 22fr+7fr, Great grey shrike, vert.

B391	SP99 14fr +2fr multi	1.00	1.00
B392	SP99 14fr +2fr multi	1.00	1.00
B393	SP99 18fr +3fr multi	1.25	1.25
B394	SP99 22fr +7fr multi	1.90	1.90
	Nos. B391-B394 (4)	5.15	5.15

Christmas SP100

Trees SP101

Design: 16fr + 2fr, Stained glass window, parish church of Alzingen.

1995, Dec. 4 Photo. *Perf. 11½*

B395	SP100 16fr +2fr multi	1.25	1.25

Surtax for Luxembourg charitable organizations.

1995, Dec. 4

Designs: No. B396, Tilia platyphyllos. No. B397, Aesculus hippocastanum, horiz. 20fr+3fr, Quercus pedunculata, horiz. 32fr+7fr, Betula pendula.

B396	SP101 16fr +2fr multi	1.25	1.25
B397	SP101 16fr +2fr multi	1.25	1.25
B398	SP101 20fr +3fr multi	1.50	1.50
B399	SP101 32fr +7fr multi	2.75	2.75
	Nos. B396-B399 (4)	6.75	6.75

Surtax for Luxembourg charitable organizations.

See Nos. B400-B403, B405-B408.

1996, Dec. 9

Designs: No. B400, Fraxinus excelsior. No. B401, Salix SSP, horiz. 20fr+3fr, Sorbus domestica, horiz. 32fr+7fr, Fagus silvatica.

B400	SP101 16fr +2fr multi	1.00	1.00
B401	SP101 16fr +2fr multi	1.00	1.00
B402	SP101 20fr +3fr multi	1.25	1.25
B403	SP101 32fr +7fr multi	2.25	2.25
	Nos. B400-B403 (4)	5.50	5.50

Surtax for Luxembourg charitable organizations.

Christmas SP102

1996, Dec. 9

B404	SP102 16fr +2fr multi	1.00	1.00

Surtax for Luxembourg charitable organizations.

Tree Type of 1995

Designs: No. B405, Ulmus glabra. No. B406, Acer platanoides. 20fr+3fr, Prunus avium. 32fr+7fr, Juglans regia, horiz.

1997, Dec. 8 Photo. *Perf. 11½*

B405	SP101 16fr +2fr multi	1.00	1.00
B406	SP101 16fr +2fr multi	1.00	1.00
B407	SP101 20fr +3fr multi	1.25	1.25
B408	SP101 32fr +7fr multi	2.25	2.25
	Nos. B405-B408 (4)	5.50	5.50

Christmas SP103

1997, Dec. 8

B409	SP103 16fr +2fr multi	1.00	1.00

Christmas SP104

1998, Dec. 7 Photo. *Perf. 11½*

B410	SP104 16fr +2fr multi	1.00	1.00

Charity Stamps SP105

Drawings of villages by Abbot Jean Bertels, 16th cent.: No. B411, Bech. No. B412, Ermesturf (Ermsdorf). 20fr+3fr, Itsich (Itzig). 32fr+7fr, Steinhem (Steinheim).

1998, Dec. 7

B411	SP105 16fr +2fr green & multi	1.00	1.00
B412	SP105 16fr +2fr brown & multi	1.00	1.00
B413	SP105 20fr +3fr red & multi	1.25	1.25
B414	SP105 32fr +7fr blue & multi	2.25	2.25
	Nos. B411-B414 (4)	5.50	5.50

See #B415-B418, B420-B423.

Perf. 11¾x11½

1999, Nov. 30 Photo.

Drawings of villages by Abbot Jean Bertels, 16th cent.: No. B415, Oswiler (Osweiler). No. B416, Bettemburch (Bettembourg). 20fr+3fr, Cruchte auf der Alset (Cruchten). 32fr+7fr, Berchem.

B415	SP105 16fr +2fr red vio & multi	1.00	1.00
B416	SP105 16fr +2fr blue & multi	1.00	1.00
B417	SP105 20fr +3fr bl grn & multi	1.25	1.25
B418	SP105 32fr +7fr brown & multi	2.00	2.00
	Nos. B415-B418 (4)	5.25	5.25

Surtax for Luxembourg charitable organizations.

Christmas SP106

1999, Nov. 30 *Perf. 11¾*

B419	SP106 16fr +2fr multi	1.00	1.00

Surtax for Luxembourg charitable organizations.

Village Drawings Type of 1998

By Abbot Jean Bertels, 16th cent.: 18fr+2fr, Lorentzwiler (Lorentzweiler). 21fr+3fr, Costurf (Consdorf). 24fr+3fr, Elfingen (Elvange). 36fr+7fr, Sprenckigen (Sprinkange).

2000, Dec. 5 Photo. *Perf. 11¾x11½*
Granite Paper

B420	SP105 18fr +2fr grn & multi	.85	.85
B421	SP105 21fr +3fr brn & multi	1.00	1.00
B422	SP105 24fr +3fr red & multi	1.10	1.10
B423	SP105 36fr +7fr bl & multi	1.90	1.90
	Nos. B420-B423 (4)	4.85	4.85

Surtax for Luxembourg charitable organizations.

Christmas SP107

2000, Dec. 5 *Perf. 11¾*
Granite Paper

B424	SP107 18fr +2fr multi	.85	.85

Surtax for Luxembourg charitable organizations.

Christmas SP108

2001, Dec. 6 Photo. *Perf. 14*

B425	SP108 45c +5c (18fr+2fr) multi	1.25	1.25

See note before No. 1063. A star-shaped hole is found at the UL portion of the design.

Fauna SP109

Designs: 45c+5c (18fr+2fr), Squirrel. 52c+8c (21fr+3fr), Wild boar. 59c+11c (24fr+4fr), Hare, vert. 89c+21c (36fr+8fr), Wood pigeon, vert.

Perf. 11¾x11½, 11½x11¾
2001, Dec. 6
Granite Paper

B426-B429	SP109	Set of 4	6.25	6.25

Christmas SP110

2002, Dec. 10 Photo. *Perf. 13¾*

B430	SP110 45c +5c multi	1.25	1.25

Surtax for Grand Duchess Charlotte charities.

Fauna SP111

Designs: 45c+5c, Red fox. 52c+8c, Hedgehog and snail, vert. 59c+11c, Pheasant. 89c+21c, Deer, vert.

2002, Dec. 10 *Perf. 11½*

B431-B434	SP111	Set of 4	6.25	6.25

Christmas — SP112

No. B435: a, Round Church of Ehnen, Christmas tree. b, Wormer Koeppchen Chapel.

2003, Dec. 9 Litho. *Perf. 14¼*

B435	SP112 50c +5c Pair, #a-b	2.75	2.75

Surtax for Luxembourg charitable organizations.

Fauna SP113

Designs: 50c+5c, Roe deer, vert. 60c+10c, Raccoons. 70c+10c, Weasel, vert. €1+25c, Goshawk.

2003, Dec. 9 Photo. *Perf. 11½*

B436-B439	SP113	Set of 4	8.00	8.00

Surtax for Luxembourg charitable organizations.

Christmas SP114

Litho. & Embossed

2004, Dec. 7 *Perf. 13*

B440	SP114 50c +5c multi	1.50	1.50

Sports SP115

Designs: 50c+5c, Skiing. 60c+10c, Running, vert. 70c+10c, Swimming. €1+25c, Soccer, vert.

Perf. 13x13½, 13½x13

2004, Dec. 7 **Litho.**
B441-B444 SP115 Set of 4 8.75 8.75

Christmas SP116

2005, Dec. 6 **Litho.** ***Perf. 13¼***
B445 SP116 50c +5c multi 1.40 1.40

Sports Type of 2004

Designs: 50c+5c, Figure skating, vert. 70c+10c, Basketball, vert. 90c+10c, Judo, vert. €1+25c, Tennis, vert.

2005, Dec. 6 ***Perf. 13½x13***
B446-B449 SP115 Set of 4 8.50 8.50

Christmas SP117

2006, Dec. 5 **Litho.** ***Perf. 12½***
B450 SP117 50c +5c multi 1.40 1.40

Modern Pipe Organs SP118

Organ from: 50c+5c, Grand Auditorium of the Luxembourg Music Conservatory. 70c+10c, Bridel. 90c+10c, Mondercange Parish Church. €1+25c, Luxembourg-Grund.

2006, Dec. 5 ***Perf. 13¼x13***
B451-B454 SP118 Set of 4 9.25 9.25

Christmas SP119

2007, Dec. 4 **Litho.** ***Perf. 12½***
B455 SP119 50c +5c multi 1.60 1.60

Modern Pipe Organs Type of 2006

Organ from: 50c+5c, Church of Niederwiltz. 70c+10c, Sandweiler, horiz. 90c+10c, Echternacht Basilica, horiz. €1+25c, St. Joseph's Church, Esch-sur-Alzette.

2007, Dec. 4 ***Perf. 13½x13, 13x13½***
B456-B459 SP118 Set of 4 10.50 10.50

Christmas SP120

2008, Dec. 2 **Litho.** ***Perf. 12½***
B460 SP120 50c +5c multi 1.40 1.40

Modern Pipe Organs Type of 2006

Organ from: 50c+5c, Junglinster. 70c+10c, Church, Mondorf-les-Bains, horiz. 90c+10c, Church, Vianden. €1+25c, Notre Dame Cathedral, Luxembourg.

2008, Dec. 2 ***Perf. 13½x13, 13x13½***
B461-B464 SP118 Set of 4 9.25 9.25

Christmas SP121

2009, Dec. 1 **Litho.** ***Perf. 12½***
B465 SP121 50c + 5c multi 1.75 1.75

Modern Pipe Organs Type of 2006

Organ from: 50c+5c, Luxembourg Philharmonic. 70c+10c, St. Martin's Church, Dudelange. 90c+10c, Church, Nommern. 1fr+25c, Saint-Pierre aux Liens Church, Heiderscheid.

2009, Dec. 1 ***Perf. 13½x13***
B466-B469 SP118 Set of 4 11.00 11.00

Christmas SP122

2010, Dec. 7 **Litho.** ***Perf. 12½***
B470 SP122 60c + 5c multi 1.90 1.90

Occupations of the Past — SP123

Designs: 60c+5c, Blacksmith. 85c+10c, Basketmaker. €1.10+10c, Grinder, horiz. €1.20+25c, Cooper, horiz.

Litho. & Embossed With Foil Application

2010, Dec. 7 ***Perf. 13¼x13, 13x13¼***
B471-B474 SP123 Set of 4 12.00 12.00

AIR POST STAMPS

Airplane over Luxembourg — AP1

1931-33 **Unwmk.** **Engr.** ***Perf. 12½***

C1	AP1	50c green ('33)	.55	*1.10*
C2	AP1	75c dark brown	.55	*1.50*
C3	AP1	1fr red	.55	*1.50*
C4	AP1	1¼fr dark violet	.55	*1.50*
C5	AP1	1¾fr dark blue	.55	*1.50*
C6	AP1	3fr gray black ('33)	1.10	*6.00*
		Nos. C1-C6 (6)	3.85	*13.10*
		Set, never hinged	8.25	

Aerial View of Moselle River — AP2

Wing and View of Luxembourg AP3

Vianden Castle — AP4

1946, June 7 **Photo.** ***Perf. 11½***

C7	AP2	1fr dk ol grn & gray	.20	.20
C8	AP3	2fr chnt brn & buff	.20	*.25*
c9	AP4	3fr sepia & brown	.20	*.25*
C10	AP2	4fr dp vio & gray vio	.25	*.40*
C11	AP3	5fr dp mag & buff	.20	*.40*
C12	AP4	6fr dk brown & gray	.25	*.55*
C13	AP2	10fr henna brn & buff	.40	*.55*
C14	AP3	20fr dk blue & cream	.90	*1.50*
C15	AP4	50fr dk green & gray	1.75	1.75
		Nos. C7-C15 (9)	4.35	5.85
		Set, never hinged	8.75	

1852 and 1952 AP5

1952, May 24

Stamps in Gray and Dark Violet Brown

C16	AP5	80c olive grn	.40	.55
C17	AP5	2.50fr brt car	.80	1.40
C18	AP5	4fr brt blue	1.60	3.00
C19	AP5	8fr brown red	30.00	*55.00*
C20	AP5	10fr dull brown	22.50	*47.50*
		Nos. C16-C20 (5)	55.30	*107.45*
		Set, never hinged	100.00	

Centenary of Luxembourg's postage stamps. Nos. C16-C18 were available at face, but complete sets sold for 45.30fr, which included admission to the CENTILUX exhibition.

POSTAGE DUE STAMPS

Coat of Arms — D1

1907 **Unwmk.** **Typo.** ***Perf. 12½***

J1	D1	5c green & black	.20	*.25*
J2	D1	10c green & black	1.40	.25
J3	D1	12½c green & black	.45	*.90*
J4	D1	20c green & black	.70	*.80*
J5	D1	25c green & black	17.50	1.50
J6	D1	50c green & black	.65	*4.25*
J7	D1	1fr green & black	.35	*3.50*
		Nos. J1-J7 (7)	21.25	11.45

See Nos. J10-J22.

Nos. J3, J5 Surcharged

1920

J8	D1	15c on 12½c	2.25	*7.25*
J9	D1	30c on 25c	2.25	*9.00*

Arms Type of 1907

1921-35

J10	D1	5c green & red	.20	*.40*
J11	D1	10c green & red	.20	*.35*
J12	D1	20c green & red	.20	*.35*
J13	D1	25c green & red	.20	*.35*
J14	D1	30c green & red	.55	*.60*
J15	D1	35c green & red ('35)	.55	.35
J16	D1	50c green & red	.55	*.60*
J17	D1	60c green & red ('28)	.45	*.50*
J18	D1	70c green & red ('35)	.55	.35
J19	D1	75c green & red ('30)	.55	.25
J20	D1	1fr green & red	.55	*1.10*
J21	D1	2fr green & red ('30)	.55	*6.50*
J22	D1	3fr green & red ('30)	1.60	*18.00*
		Nos. J10-J22 (13)	6.70	29.70
		Set, never hinged	27.50	

D2

D3

1946-48 **Photo.** ***Perf. 11½***

J23	D2	5c bright green	.20	*.65*
J24	D2	10c bright green	.20	*.50*
J25	D2	20c bright green	.20	*.50*
J26	D2	30c bright green	.20	*.50*
J27	D2	70c bright green	.20	*.70*
J28	D2	70c bright green	.20	*.70*
J29	D3	75c brt green ('48)	.70	.25
J30	D3	1fr carmine	.20	*.25*
J31	D3	1.50fr carmine	.20	*.25*
J32	D3	2fr carmine	.20	*.25*
J33	D3	3fr carmine	.20	*.35*
J34	D3	5fr carmine	.55	.45
J35	D3	10fr carmine	.95	*4.00*
J36	D3	20fr carmine	2.75	*22.50*
		Nos. J23-J36 (14)	6.95	31.85
		Set, never hinged	13.00	

OFFICIAL STAMPS

Forged overprints on Nos. O1-O64 abound.

Unused values of Nos. O1-O51 are for stamps without gum. Though these stamps were issued with gum, most examples offered are without gum. Stamps with original gum sell for somewhat more.

Regular Issues Overprinted Reading Diagonally Up or Down

Frankfurt Print

Rouletted in Color except 2c

1875 **Unwmk.**

O1	A2	1c red brown	27.50	37.50
O2	A2	2c black	27.50	37.50
O3	A3	10c lilac	2,100.	2,100.
O4	A3	12½c rose	475.00	575.00
O5	A3	20c gray brn	37.50	57.50
O6	A3	25c blue	250.00	140.00
O7	A3	25c ultra	1,900.	1,400.
O8	A3	30c lilac rose	32.50	*75.00*
O9	A3	40c pale org	160.00	225.00
	a.	40c org red, thick paper	250.00	325.00
	c.	As "a," thin paper	1,650.	1,400.
O10	A3	1fr on 37½c bis	150.00	22.50

Double overprints exist on Nos. O1-O6, O8-O10.

Overprints reading diagonally down sell for more.

Inverted Overprint

O1a	A2	1c	190.00	225.00
O2a	A2	2c	190.00	225.00
O3a	A3	10c	2,500.	2,500.
O4a	A3	12½c	650.00	925.00
O5a	A3	20c	55.00	75.00

O6a A3 25c 1,100. 1,300.
O7a A3 25c 2,100. 1,500.
O8a A3 30c 650.00 925.00
O9b A3 40c pale orange 325.00 450.00
O10a A3 1fr on 37½c 175.00 75.00

Luxembourg Print

1875-76 ***Perf. 13***

O11 A2 1c red brown 11.00 27.50
O12 A2 2c black 14.00 32.50
O13 A2 4c green 100.00 190.00
O14 A2 5c yellow 65.00 85.00
a. 5c orange yellow 75.00 110.00
O15 A3 10c gray lilac 92.50 100.00
O16 A3 12½c rose 85.00 100.00
O17 A3 12½c lilac rose 225.00 275.00
O18 A3 25c blue 11.00 *32.50*
O19 A3 1fr on 37½c bis 42.50 65.00
Nos. O11-O19 (9) 646.00 907.50

Double overprints exist on Nos. O11-O15.

Inverted Overprint

O11a A2 1c 92.50 *110.00*
O12a A2 2c 150.00 190.00
O13a A2 4c 160.00 190.00
O14b A2 5c 500.00 650.00
O15a A3 10c 500.00 190.00
O16a A3 12½c 400.00 550.00
O17a A3 12½c 450.00 525.00
O18a A3 25c 125.00 175.00
O19a A5 1fr on 37½c 190.00 250.00
Nos. O11a-O19a (9) 2,567. 2,830.

Haarlem Print

1880 ***Perf. 11½x12, 12½x12, 13½***

O22 A3 25c blue 2.25 2.75

Overprinted

Frankfurt Print

1878 ***Rouletted in Color***

O23 A2 1c red brown 140.00 160.00
O25 A3 20c gray brn 190.00 225.00
O26 A3 30c lilac rose 750.00 575.00
O27 A3 40c orange 325.00 450.00
O28 A3 1fr on 37½c bis 550.00 110.00
Nos. O23-O28 (5) 1,955. 1,520.

Inverted Overprint

O23a A2 1c 225.00 300.00
O25a A3 20c 325.00 400.00
O26a A3 30c 925.00 700.00
O27a A3 40c 875.00 925.00
O28a A3 1fr on 37½c 650.00 1540.00

Luxembourg Print

1878-80 ***Perf. 13***

O29 A2 1c red brown 750.00 925.00
O30 A2 2c black 190.00 225.00
O31 A2 4c green 190.00 225.00
O32 A2 5c yellow 375.00 450.00
O33 A3 10c gray lilac 375.00 400.00
O34 A3 12½c rose 65.00 110.00
O35 A3 25c blue 525.00 550.00
Nos. O29-O35 (7) 2,470. 2,885.

Inverted Overprint

O29a A2 1c 140.00 160.00
O30a A2 2c 14.50 27.50
O31a A2 4c 150.00 190.00
O32a A2 5c 1,500. 1,500.
O33a A3 10c 92.50 110.00
O34a A3 12½c 525.00 600.00
O35a A3 25c 850.00 1,000.

Overprinted

Frankfurt Print

1881 ***Rouletted in Color***

O39 A3 40c orange 37.50 65.00
a. Inverted overprint 210.00 275.00

"S.P." are initials of "Service Public."

Luxembourg Print
Perf. 13

O40 A2 1c red brown 140.00 160.00
O41 A2 4c green 210.00 210.00
a. Inverted overprint 250.00
O42 A2 5c yellow 600.00 750.00
O43 A3 1fr on 37½c bis 32.500 47.50
Nos. O40-O43 (4) 982.50 1,167.

Haarlem Print
Perf. 11½x12, 12½x12, 13½

O44 A2 1c yellow brn 8.50 9.25
O45 A2 2c black 9.25 9.25
O46 A2 5c yellow 140.00 190.00
a. Inverted overprint 225.00

O47 A3 10c gray lilac 125.00 160.00
O48 A3 12½c rose 225.00 250.00
O49 A3 20c gray brown 65.00 92.50
O50 A3 25c blue 72.50 92.50
O51 A3 30c dull rose 75.00 110.00
Nos. O44-O51 (8) 720.25 913.50

Stamps of the 1881 issue with the overprint of the 1882 issue shown below were never issued.

Overprinted

Perf. 11½x12, 12½x12, 12½, 13½

1882

O52 A6 1c gray lilac .25 .50
O53 A6 2c ol gray .25 .50
a. "S" omitted 110.00
O54 A6 4c ol bister .35 .60
O55 A6 5c lt green .55 .80
O56 A6 10c rose 12.00 20.00
O57 A6 12½c slate 1.90 4.75
O58 A6 20c orange 1.90 4.00
O59 A6 25c ultra 19.00 27.50
O60 A6 30c gray grn 4.25 10.00
O61 A6 50c bis brown 1.10 2.75
O62 A6 1fr pale vio 1.10 2.75
O63 A6 5fr brown org 12.00 27.50
Nos. O52-O63 (12) 54.65 101.65

Nos. O52-O63 exist without one or both periods, also with varying space between "S" and "P." Nine denominations exist with double overprint, six with inverted overprint.

Overprinted

1883 ***Perf. 13½***

O64 A6 5fr brown org *2,200. 2,200.*

Overprinted

1891-93 ***Perf. 11, 11½, 11½x11, 12½***

O65 A7 10c carmine .20 .50
a. Sheet of 25 55.00
O66 A7 12½c slate grn 6.50 8.75
O67 A7 20c orange 12.00 8.50
O68 A7 25c blue .35 .50
a. Sheet of 25 65.00
O69 A7 30c olive grn 8.25 8.50
O70 A7 37½c green 8.25 10.00
O71 A7 50c brown 6.50 10.00
O72 A7 1fr dp vio 6.50 11.50
O73 A7 2½fr black 37.50 72.50
O74 A7 5fr lake 32.50 55.00
Nos. O65-O74 (10) 118.55 185.75

1895 ***Perf. 12½***

O75 A8 1c pearl gray 1.90 1.90
O76 A8 2c gray brn 1.40 1.90
O77 A8 4c olive bis 1.40 1.90
O78 A8 5c green 4.00 5.00
O79 A8 10c carmine 32.50 35.00
Nos. O75-O79 (5) 41.20 45.70

Nos. O66-O79 exist without overprint and perforated "OFFICIEL" through the stamp. Value for set, $25.

Nos. O65a and O68a were issued to commemorate the coronation of Grand Duke Adolphe.

Regular Issue of 1906-26 Overprinted

1908-26 ***Perf. 11x11½, 12½***

O80 A9 1c gray .20 .20
a. Inverted overprint 125.00

O81 A9 2c olive brn .20 .20
O82 A9 4c bister .20 .20
a. Double overprint 140.00
O83 A9 5c green .20 .20
O84 A9 5c lilac ('26) .20 .20
O85 A9 6c violet .20 .20
O86 A9 7½c org ('19) .20 .20
O87 A10 10c scarlet .25 .45
O88 A10 12½c slate grn .25 *.55*
O89 A10 15c orange brn .40 *.70*
O90 A10 20c orange .40 *.70*
O91 A10 25c ultra .40 *.70*
O92 A10 30c olive grn 4.00 *6.50*
O93 A10 37½c green .65 .65
O94 A10 50c brown 1.10 *1.50*
O95 A10 87½c dk blue 2.75 *3.25*
O96 A10 1fr violet 3.25 *4.00*
O97 A10 2½fr vermilion 65.00 65.00
O98 A10 5fr claret 55.00 47.50
Nos. O80-O98 (19) 134.85 132.90

On Regular Issue of 1914-17

1915-17

O99 A11 10c lake .35 *.65*
O100 A11 12½c dull grn .35 *.65*
O101 A11 15c olive blk .35 *.65*
O102 A11 17½c dp brn ('17) .35 .65
O103 A11 25c ultra .35 *.65*
O104 A11 30c bister 1.40 *5.00*
O105 A11 35c dk blue .35 *1.10*
O106 A11 37½c blk brn .35 *1.50*
O107 A11 40c orange .45 *1.10*
O108 A11 50c dk gray .45 *.95*
O109 A11 62½c blue grn .45 *1.50*
O110 A11 87½c org ('17) .45 *1.75*
O111 A11 1fr orange brn .45 *1.50*
O112 A11 2½fr red .45 *2.75*
O113 A11 5fr dk violet .45 *3.25*
Nos. O99-O113 (15) 7.00 23.65

On Regular Issues of 1921-26 in Black

1922-26 ***Perf. 11½, 11½x11, 12½***

O114 A12 2c brown .20 .20
O115 A12 3c olive grn .20 .20
O116 A12 6c violet .20 .20
O117 A12 10c yellow grn .20 .35
O118 A12 10c ol grn ('24) .20 .35
O119 A12 15c brown ol .20 .35
O120 A12 15c pale grn ('24) .20 .35
O121 A12 15c dp org ('26) .20 .25
O122 A12 20c dp orange .20 .35
O123 A12 20c yel grn ('26) .20 .25
O124 A12 25c dk green .20 .35
O125 A12 30c car rose .20 .35
O126 A12 40c brown org .20 .35
O127 A12 50c dp blue .20 .45
O128 A12 50c red ('24) .20 .35
O129 A12 75c red .20 .45
O130 A12 75c dp bl ('24) .20 .45
O131 A12 80c black 4.75 11.00
O132 A13 1fr carmine .40 .90
O133 A14 2fr indigo 3.00 6.50
O134 A14 2fr dk brn ('26) 1.75 5.00
O135 A15 5fr dk vio 17.50 42.50
Nos. O114-O135 (22) 30.80 71.50

On Regular Issues of 1921-26 in Red

1922-34 ***Perf. 11, 11½, 11½x11, 12½***

O136 A12 80c blk, perf. 11½ .20 .35
O137 A13 1fr dk bl, perf. 11½ ('26) .20 .55
O138 A14 2fr ind, perf. 11½x11 .45 1.25
O139 A17 3fr dk bl & bl, perf. 11 2.75 2.75
a. Perf. 11½ .90 1.40
b. Perf. 12½ 1.60 2.25
O140 A15 5fr dk vio, perf. 11½x11 4.00 7.50
a. Perf. 12½ ('34) 27.50 27.50
O141 A16 10fr blk, perf. 11½ 10.00 21.00
a. Perf. 12½ 27.50 27.50
Nos. O136-O141 (6) 17.60 33.40

On Regular Issue of 1926-35

1926-27 ***Perf. 12***

O142 A18 5c dk violet .20 .20
O143 A18 10c olive grn .20 .20
O144 A18 20c orange .20 .20
O145 A18 25c yellow grn .20 .20
O146 A18 25c blk brn ('27) .35 .55
O147 A18 30c yel grn ('27) .65 1.10
O148 A18 40c olive gray .20 .20
O149 A18 50c red brown .20 .20
O150 A18 65c black brn .20 .20
O151 A18 75c rose .20 .20
O152 A18 75c bis brn ('27) .45 .70
O153 A18 80c bister brn .20 .40
O154 A18 90c rose ('27) .35 .55
O155 A18 1fr black .20 .40
O156 A18 1¼fr dk blue .20 .20
O157 A18 1½fr dp blue ('27) .55 .95
Nos. O142-O157 (16) 4.55 6.45

Type of Regular Issue, 1926-35, Overprinted

1928-35 **Wmk. 213**

O158 A18 5c dk violet .20 .20
O159 A18 10c olive grn .20 .20
O160 A18 15c black ('30) .20 .65
O161 A18 20c orange .45 .65
O162 A18 25c violet brn .45 .65
O163 A18 30c yellow grn .50 .70
O164 A18 30c gray vio ('30) .20 .65
O165 A18 35c yel grn ('30) .20 .65
O166 A18 35c gray vio .50 .70
O167 A18 40c olive gray .50 .70
O168 A18 50c red brown .45 .65
O169 A18 60c blue grn .45 .65
O170 A18 70c blue vio ('35) 3.50 7.25
O171 A18 75c bister brn .45 .65
O172 A18 90c rose .50 .70
O173 A18 1fr black .50 .70
O174 A18 1fr rose ('30) .20 .65
O175 A18 1¼fr yel ('30) 1.75 4.50
O176 A18 1¼fr bl grn ('31) 1.75 4.50
O177 A18 1½fr deep blue .50 .70
O178 A18 1¾fr dk blue ('30) .20 .65
Nos. O158-O178 (21) 13.65 27.35

Type of Regular Issues of 1928-31 Overprinted Like Nos. O80-O98

1928-31 **Wmk. 216** ***Perf. 11½***

O179 A19 2fr black .50 1.00

Wmk. 110 ***Perf. 12½***

O180 A21 20fr dp green ('31) 2.25 5.00

No. 198 Overprinted Like Nos. O80-O98

1934 **Unwmk.** ***Perf. 14x13½***

O181 A22 5fr blue green 2.25 3.25

Type of Regular Issue of 1935 Overprinted Like Nos. O158-O178 in Red

1935 **Wmk. 247** ***Perf. 12½x12***

O182 A23 10fr green 1.60 4.00

OCCUPATION STAMPS

Issued under German Occupation
Stamps of Germany, 1933-36, Overprinted in Black

1940, Oct. 1 **Wmk. 237** ***Perf. 14***

N1 A64 3pf olive bis .25 *.50*
N2 A64 4pf dull blue .25 *.55*
N3 A64 5pf bright green .25 *.50*
N4 A64 6pf dark green .25 *.50*
N5 A64 8pf vermilion .25 *.50*
N6 A64 10pf chocolate .25 *.50*
N7 A64 12pf deep carmine .25 *.50*
N8 A64 15pf maroon .25 *.70*
a. Inverted overprint *450.00* *1,300.*
N9 A64 20pf bright blue .25 *1.25*
N10 A64 25pf ultra .35 *1.75*
N11 A64 30pf olive green .35 *1.75*
N12 A64 40pf red violet .50 *1.90*
N13 A64 50pf dk green & blk .50 *2.00*
N14 A64 60pf claret & blk .50 *2.75*
N15 A64 80pf dk blue & blk 1.00 *3.75*
N16 A64 100pf orange & blk 1.25 *5.75*
Nos. N1-N16 (16) 6.70 *25.15*
Set, never hinged 20.00

Nos. 159-162, 164, 168-171, 173, 175, 179, 182, 216, 198-199 Surcharged in Black

b

a

c

d

Perf. 12, 14x13½, 12½x12, 11½

1940, Dec. 5 **Unwmk.**

No.	Type	Description	Unused	Used
N17	A18(a)	3rpf on 15c	.20	*.35*
N18	A18(a)	4rpf on 20c	.20	*.40*
N19	A18(a)	5rpf on 35c	.20	*.40*
N20	A18(a)	6rpf on 10c	.20	*.40*
N21	A18(a)	8rpf on 25c	.20	*.40*
N22	A18(a)	10rpf on 40c	.20	*.40*
N23	A18(a)	12rpf on 60c	.20	*.40*
N24	A18(a)	15rpf on 1fr rose	.20	*.40*
N25	A18(a)	20rpf on 50c	.20	*.75*
N26	A18(a)	25rpf on 5c	.20	*1.25*
N27	A18(a)	30rpf on 70c	.20	*.60*
N28	A18(a)	40rpf on 75c	.20	*1.00*
N29	A18(a)	50rpf on 1¼fr	.20	*.60*
N30	A35(b)	60rpf on 2fr	1.40	*12.50*
N31	A22(c)	80rpf on 5fr	.40	*2.25*
N32	A23(d)	100rpf on 10fr	.50	*3.00*
		Nos. N17-N32 (16)	4.90	*25.10*
		Set, never hinged	7.00	

OCCUPATION SEMI-POSTAL STAMPS

Semi-Postal Stamps of Germany, 1940 Overprinted in Black

1941, Jan. 12 **Unwmk.** ***Perf. 14***

No.	Type	Description	Unused	Used
NB1	SP153	3pf + 2pf dk brn	.20	*.85*
NB2	SP153	4pf + 3pf bluish blk	.20	*.85*
NB3	SP153	5pf + 3pf yel grn	.20	*.85*
NB4	SP153	6pf + 4pf dk grn	.20	*.85*
NB5	SP153	8pf + 4pf dp org	.20	*.85*
NB6	SP153	12pf + 6pf carmine	.20	*.85*
NB7	SP153	15pf + 10pf dk vio brn	.30	*1.90*
NB8	SP153	25pf + 15pf dp ultra	.85	*3.75*
NB9	SP153	40pf + 35pf red lil	1.50	*6.25*
		Nos. NB1-NB9 (9)	3.85	*17.00*
		Set, never hinged	7.50	

MACAO

mə-ˈkau

LOCATION — Off the Chinese coast at the mouth of the Canton River

GOVT. — Special Administrative Area of China (PRC) (as of 12/20/99)

AREA — 8 sq. mi.

POP. — 415,850 (1998)

CAPITAL — Macao

Formerly a Portuguese overseas territory. The territory includes the two small adjacent islands of Coloane and Taipa.

1000 Reis = 1 Milreis
78 Avos = 1 Rupee (1894)
100 Avos = 1 Pataca (1913)

Catalogue values for unused stamps in this country are for Never Hinged items, beginning with Scott 339 in the regular postage section, Scott C16 in the air post section, Scott J50 in the semi-postal section, and Scott RA11 in the postal tax section.

Watermark

Wmk. 232 — Maltese Cross

Portuguese Crown — A1

Perf. 12½, 13½

1884-85 **Typo.** **Unwmk.**

No.	Type	Description	Unused	Used
1	A1	5r black	13.00	9.00
2	A1	10r orange	25.00	12.00
3	A1	10r green ('85)	30.00	9.00
4	A1	20r bister	32.50	22.50
5	A1	20r rose ('85)	45.00	18.00
6	A1	25r rose	22.50	5.25
7	A1	25r violet ('85)	30.00	13.50
8	A1	40r blue	115.00	40.00
9	A1	40r yellow ('85)	42.50	20.00
10	A1	50r green	250.00	75.00
11	A1	50r blue ('85)	57.50	25.00
12	A1	80r gray ('85)	57.50	30.00
13	A1	100r red lilac	75.00	24.00
a.		100r lilac	75.00	24.00
14	A1	200r orange	70.00	20.00
15	A1	300r chocolate	100.00	25.00
		Nos. 1-15 (15)	965.50	348.25

All values exist both perf 12½ and 13½. The cheaper variety is listed above. For detailed listings, see the Scott Classic Specialized Catalogue of stamps and Covers.

The reprints of the 1885 issue are printed on smooth, white chalky paper, ungummed and on thin white paper with shiny white gum and clean-cut perforation 13½.

For surcharges see Nos. 16-28, 108-109.

No. 13a Surcharged in Black

1884 ***Perf. 12½***

Without Gum

No.	Type	Description	Unused	Used
16	A1	80r on 100r lilac	90.00	45.00
a.		Inverted surcharge	*200.00*	*75.00*
b.		Without accent on "e" of "reis"	80.00	47.50
c.		Perf. 13½	125.00	55.00
d.		As "b," perf. 13½	140.00	62.50

Nos. 6 and 10 Surcharged in Black, Blue or Red:

b

c

1885

Without Gum

No.	Type	Description	Unused	Used
17	A1(b)	5r on 25r rose, perf. 12½ (Bk)	21.00	6.50
a.		With accent on "e" of "Reis"	35.00	12.00
b.		Double surcharge	200.00	150.00
c.		Inverted surcharge	175.00	110.00
d.		Perf. 13½	125.00	100.00
e.		As "d," inverted surcharge	*175.00*	*125.00*
18	A1(b)	10r on 25r rose (Bl)	47.50	18.00
a.		Accent on "e" of "Reis"		
b.		Pair, one without surcharge	—	
19	A1(b)	10r on 50r grn, perf. 13½ (Bl)	625.00	225.00
a.		Perf. 12½	625.00	260.00
20	A1(b)	20r on 50r green, perf. 12½ (Bk)	47.50	10.00
a.		Double surcharge		150.00
b.		Accent on "e" of "Reis"	—	—
21	A1(b)	40r on 50r grn, perf. 12½ (R)	175.00	50.00
a.		Perf. 13½	240.00	50.00
		Nos. 17-21 (5)	916.00	309.50

1885

Without Gum

No.	Type	Description	Unused	Used
22	A1(c)	5r on 25r rose (Bk)	32.50	18.00
a.		Original value not obliterated		
23	A1(c)	10r on 50r green (Bk)	32.50	18.00
a.		Inverted surcharge		
b.		Perf. 12½	32.50	18.00

Nos. 12, 13a and 14 Surcharged in Black

1887

Without Gum

No.	Type	Description	Unused	Used
24	A1	5r on 80r gray	32.50	9.00
a.		"R" of "Reis" 4mm high	125.00	50.00
b.		Perf. 12½	150.00	45.00
25	A1	5r on 100r lilac	125.00	90.00
a.		Perf. 12½	95.00	60.00
26	A1	10r on 80r gray	65.00	20.00
a.		"R" 4mm high	140.00	47.50
27	A1	10r on 200r orange	140.00	62.50
a.		"R" 4mm high, "e" without accent	200.00	80.00
b.		Perf. 13½	140.00	62.50
28	A1	20r on 80r gray	100.00	35.00
a.		"R" 4mm high	175.00	47.50
b.		Perf. 12½	100.00	50.00
c.		"R" 4mm high, "e" without accent	160.00	47.50
		Nos. 24-28 (5)	462.50	216.50

The surcharges with larger "R" (4mm) have accent on "e." Smaller "R" is 3mm high.

Occasionally Nos. 24, 26 and 28 may be found with original gum. Values the same.

Coat of Arms — A6

Red Surcharge

1887, Oct. 20 ***Perf. 12½***

Without Gum

No.	Type	Description	Unused	Used
32	A6	5r green & buff	15.00	7.00
a.		With labels, 5r on 10r	77.50	65.00
b.		With labels, 5r on 20r	90.00	65.00
c.		With labels, 5r on 60r	77.50	65.00
33	A6	10r green & buff	22.50	9.00
a.		With labels, 10r on 10r	95.00	75.00
b.		With labels, 10r on 60r	110.00	75.00
34	A6	40r green & buff	37.50	*14.00*
a.		With labels, 40r on 20r	150.00	*110.00*
		Nos. 32-34 (3)	75.00	30.00

Nos. 32-34 were local provisionals, created by perforating contemporary revenue stamps to remove the old value inscriptions and then surcharging the central design portion. The unused portion of the design was normally removed prior to use. For simplicity's sake, we refer to these extraneous portions of the original revenue stamps as "labels."

The 10r also exists with 20r labels, and 40r with 10r labels. Value, $250 each.

King Luiz — A7

King Carlos — A9

Typographed and Embossed

1888, Jan. ***Perf. 12½, 13½***

Chalk-surfaced Paper

No.	Type	Description	Unused	Used
35	A7	5r black	21.00	4.00
36	A7	10r green	21.00	6.00
a.		Perf. 13½	75.00	37.50
37	A7	20r carmine	35.00	13.00
38	A7	25r violet	35.00	13.00
39	A7	40r chocolate	35.00	18.00
a.		Perf. 13½	60.00	26.00
40	A7	50r blue	60.00	13.50
41	A7	80r gray	95.00	22.50
a.		Imperf., pair	—	
42	A7	100r brown	45.00	22.50
43	A7	200r gray lilac	90.00	45.00
44	A7	300r orange	72.50	45.00
		Nos. 35-44 (10)	509.50	202.50

Nos. 37-44 were issued without gum.

For surcharges and overprints see Nos. 45, 58-66B, 110-118, 164-170, 239.

No. 43 Surcharged in Red

1892

Without Gum

45 A7 30r on 200r gray lilac 60.00 24.00
a. Inverted surcharge 275.00 165.00

1894, Nov. 15 Typo. *Perf. 11½*

46 A9 5r yellow 8.25 3.75
47 A9 10r redsh violet 8.25 3.75
48 A9 15r chocolate 12.50 5.25
49 A9 20r lavender 14.00 6.00
50 A9 25r green 35.00 11.25
51 A9 50r lt blue 37.50 22.50
a. Perf. 13½ *500.00 300.00*
52 A9 75r carmine 70.00 30.00
53 A9 80r yellow green 37.50 22.50
54 A9 100r brown, *buff* 40.00 22.50
55 A9 150r carmine, *rose* 45.00 22.50
56 A9 200r dk blue, *blue* 62.50 34.00
57 A9 300r dk blue, *sal* 82.50 45.00
Nos. 46-57 (12) 453.00 229.00

Nos. 49-57 were issued without gum, No. 49 with or without gum.

For surcharges and overprints see Nos. 119-130, 171-181, 183-186, 240, 251, 257-258.

Stamps of 1888 Surcharged in Red, Green or Black

1894 Without Gum *Perf. 12½*

58 A7 1a on 5r black (R) 11.00 4.50
a. Short "1" 11.00 4.50
b. Inverted surcharge 100.00 100.00
c. Double surcharge *400.00*
d. Surch. on back instead of face *200.00 200.00*
59 A7 3a on 20r carmine (G) 19.00 4.50
a. Inverted surcharge — —
60 A7 4a on 25r violet (Bk) 19.00 9.00
a. Inverted surcharge 60.00 50.00
61 A7 6a on 40r choc (Bk) 25.00 6.75
a. Perf. 13½ 19.00 12.00
62 A7 8a on 50r blue (R) 55.00 18.00
a. Double surch., one inverted — —
b. Inverted surcharge 125.00 60.00
c. Perf. 13½ 62.50 40.00
63 A7 13a on 80r gray (Bk) 22.50 7.00
a. Double surcharge — —
64 A7 16a on 100r brown (Bk) 45.00 18.00
a. Inverted surcharge — —
b. Perf. 13½ 115.00 110.00
65 A7 31a on 200r gray lil (Bk) 72.50 25.00
a. Inverted surcharge 150.00 125.00
b. Perf. 13½ 75.00 25.00
66 A7 47a on 300r orange (G) 72.50 11.00
a. Double surcharge — —
Nos. 58-66 (9) 341.50 103.75

The style of type used for the word "PROVISORIO" on Nos. 58 to 66 differs for each value.

A 2a on 10r green was unofficially surcharged and denounced by the authorities.

On No. 45

66B A7 5a on 30r on 200r 150.00 50.00

Common Design Types pictured following the introduction.

Vasco da Gama Issue

Common Design Types

1898, Apr. 1 Engr. *Perf. 12½ to 16*

67 CD20 ½a blue green 10.00 2.25
68 CD21 1a red 10.00 3.75
69 CD22 2a red violet 10.00 5.25
70 CD23 4a yellow green 10.00 7.50
71 CD24 8a dark blue 19.00 12.00
72 CD25 12a violet brown 30.00 22.00
73 CD26 16a bister brown 26.00 22.00
74 CD27 24a bister 30.00 22.00
Nos. 67-74 (8) 145.00 96.75

For overprints and surcharges see Nos. 187-194.

King Carlos — A11

1898-1903 Typo. *Perf. 11½*

Name and Value in Black except #103

75 A11 ½a gray 4.50 1.00
a. Perf. 12½ 15.00 7.50
76 A11 1a orange 4.50 1.00
a. Perf. 12½ 15.00 7.50
77 A11 2a yellow green 5.75 1.50
78 A11 2a gray green ('03) 6.25 1.50
79 A11 2½a red brown 7.50 2.25
80 A11 3a gray violet 7.50 2.25
81 A11 3a slate ('03) 6.25 1.65
82 A11 4a sea green 9.00 5.00
83 A11 4a carmine ('03) 6.25 1.50
84 A11 5a gray brn ('00) 14.00 3.75
85 A11 5a pale yel brn ('03) 9.00 2.25
86 A11 6a red brown ('03) 10.00 2.00
87 A11 8a blue 12.50 3.75
88 A11 8a gray brn ('03) 15.00 4.00
89 A11 10a slate blue ('00) 15.00 3.75
90 A11 12a rose 15.00 6.50
91 A11 12a red lilac ('03) 62.50 15.00
92 A11 13a violet 18.00 6.50
93 A11 13a gray lilac ('03) 22.50 6.00
94 A11 15a pale ol grn ('00) 90.00 23.00
95 A11 16a dk blue, *bl* 17.00 7.50
96 A11 18a org brn, *pink* ('03) 32.50 11.50
97 A11 20a brn, *yelsh* ('00) 45.00 11.50
98 A11 24a brown, *buff* 27.50 7.50
99 A11 31a red lilac 27.50 9.00
100 A11 31a red lil, *pink* ('03) 32.50 11.50
101 A11 47a dk blue, *rose* 50.00 11.50
102 A11 47a dull bl, *straw* ('03) 60.00 13.00
103 A11 78a blk & red, *bl* ('00) 77.50 17.50
Nos. 75-103 (29) 710.50 194.65

Issued without gum: Nos. 76a, 77, 79-80, 82, 84, 89, 94, 97 and 103.

For surcharges and overprints see Nos. 104-107, 132-136, 141, 147-157D, 159-161, 182, 195-209, 253-255, 258A.

Nos. 92, 95, 98-99 Surcharged in Black

1900

Without Gum

104 A11 5a on 13a violet 20.00 3.50
105 A11 10a on 16a dk bl, *bl* 22.50 5.00
106 A11 15a on 24a brn, *buff* 22.50 8.25
107 A11 20a on 31a red lilac 25.00 13.50
Nos. 104-107 (4) 90.00 30.25

Nos. 106-107 were issued without gum.

Regular Issues Surcharged

On Stamps of 1884-85

1902 *Perf. 11½*

Black Surcharge

108 A1 6a on 10r orange 30.00 9.75
a. Double surcharge *300.00 175.00*
109 A1 6a on 10r green 21.00 6.00

On Stamps of 1888

Red Surcharge

Perf. 12½, 13½

110 A7 6a on 5r black 10.00 3.50
a. Inverted surcharge 110.00 60.00

Black Surcharge

111 A7 6a on 10r green 8.25 3.50
112 A7 6a on 40r choc 8.25 3.50
a. Double surcharge 125.00 50.00
b. Perf. 13½ 30.00 10.00
113 A7 18a on 20r rose 17.00 4.50
a. Double surcharge 160.00 70.00
b. Inverted surcharge 175.00 —
114 A7 18a on 25r violet 175.00 60.00
115 A7 18a on 80r gray 190.00 67.50
a. Double surcharge 225.00 175.00
116 A7 18a on 100r brown 42.50 26.00
a. Perf. 13½ 90.00 35.00
117 A7 18a on 200r gray lil 175.00 67.50
a. Perf. 12½ 190.00 60.00
118 A7 18a on 300r orange 30.00 10.00
a. Perf. 13½ 57.50 25.00

Issued without gum: Nos. 110-118.

Nos. 109 to 118 inclusive, except No. 111, have been reprinted. The reprints have white gum and clean-cut perforation 13½ and the colors are usually paler than those of the originals.

On Stamps of 1894

1902-10 *Perf. 11½, 13½*

119 A9 6a on 5r yellow 7.75 2.75
a. Inverted surcharge 82.50 65.00
120 A9 6a on 10r red vio 26.00 5.25
121 A9 6a on 15r choc 26.00 5.25
122 A9 6a on 25r green 7.75 2.75
123 A9 6a on 80r yel grn 7.75 2.75
124 A9 6a on 100r brn, *buff* 15.00 6.00
a. Perf. 11½ 26.00 10.00
125 A9 6a on 200r bl, *bl* 10.00 2.75
a. Vert. half used as 3a on cover ('10) *40.00*
126 A9 18a on 20r lavender 21.00 6.75
127 A9 18a on 50r lt blue 26.00 6.75
a. Perf. 13½ 77.50 17.00
128 A9 18a on 75r carmine 21.00 6.75
129 A9 18a on 150r car, *rose* 21.00 7.50
130 A9 18a on 300r bl, *salmon* 26.00 6.75

On Newspaper Stamp of 1893

Perf. 12½

131 N3 18a on 2½r brown 10.00 3.25
a. Perf. 13½ 27.50 9.00
b. Perf. 11½ 45.00 14.00
Nos. 108-131 (24) 932.25 327.00

Issued without gum: Nos. 122-130, 131b.

Stamps of 1898-1900 Overprinted in Black

1902 *Perf. 11½*

132 A11 2a yellow green 21.00 4.00
133 A11 4a sea green 32.50 10.00
134 A11 8a blue 21.00 7.00
135 A11 10a slate blue 26.00 8.00
136 A11 12a rose 70.00 26.00
Nos. 132-136 (5) 170.50 55.00

Issued without gum: Nos. 133, 135.

Reprints of No. 133 have shiny white gum and clean-cut perforation 13½. Value $1.

No. 91 Surcharged

1905

Without Gum

141 A11 10a on 12a red lilac 30.00 12.50

Nos. J1-J3 Overprinted

1910, Oct. *Perf. 11½x12*

144 D1 ½a gray green 12.50 6.75
a. Inverted overprint 30.00 25.00
b. Double overprint 40.00 40.00
145 D1 1a yellow green 15.00 6.75
a. Inverted overprint 30.00 25.00
146 D1 2a slate 20.00 7.50
a. Inverted overprint *60.00* 25.00
Nos. 144-146 (3) 47.50 21.00

No. 144 issued without gum, Nos. 145-146 with and without gum.

Stamps of 1898-1903 Overprinted in Carmine or Green

Lisbon Overprint

Overprint 24½mm long. "A" has flattened top.

1911, Apr. 2 *Perf. 11½*

147 A11 ½a gray 2.10 .75
a. Inverted overprint 20.00 20.00
147B A11 1a orange 2.00 .75
c. Inverted overprint 20.00 20.00
148 A11 2a gray green 2.00 .75
a. Inverted overprint 5.00 5.00
149 A11 3a slate 6.25 .75
a. Inverted overprint 12.50 5.00
150 A11 4a carmine (G) 6.25 2.00
a. 4a pale yel brn (error) *55.00 50.00*
b. As No. 150, inverted overprint 25.00 25.00
151 A11 5a pale yel brn 6.25 4.00
152 A11 6a red brown 6.25 4.00
153 A11 8a gray brown 6.25 4.00
154 A11 10a slate blue 6.25 4.00
155 A11 13a gray lilac 10.00 5.00
a. Inverted overprint 60.00 60.00
156 A11 16a dk blue, *bl* 10.00 5.00
a. Inverted overprint 60.00 60.00
157 A11 18a org brn, *pink* 16.00 6.00
157A A11 20a brown, *straw* 16.00 6.00
157B A11 31a red lil, *pink* 30.00 8.00
157C A11 47a dull bl, *straw* 50.00 10.00
157D A11 78a blk & red, *bl* 82.50 12.00
Nos. 147-157D (16) 258.10 73.00

Issued without gum: Nos. 151, 153-157D.

Coat of Arms — A14

1911 *Perf. 11½x12*

Red Surcharge

158 A14 1a on 5r brn & buff 32.50 12.50
a. "1" omitted 67.50 50.00
b. Inverted surcharge 45.00 25.00

Stamps of 1900-03 Surcharged

Diagonal Halves

1911 Without Gum *Perf. 11½*

Black Surcharge

159 A11 2a on half of 4a car 32.50 32.50
a. "2" omitted 80.00 80.00
b. Inverted surcharge *150.00* 82.50
d. Entire stamp 67.50 65.00
159C A11 5a on half of 10a sl bl (#89) *4,000.* —
e. Entire stamp *8,500.* —

Red Surcharge

160 A11 5a on half of 10a sl bl (#89) *4,500. 1,500.*
a. Inverted surcharge *5,000. 1,750.*
b. Entire stamp *11,000.* 5,000.
161 A11 5a on half of 10a sl bl (#135) 125.00 80.00
a. Inverted surcharge 350.00 200.00
b. Entire stamp 275.00 165.00

A15

1911 *Perf. 12x11½*

Laid or Wove Paper

162 A15 1a black 525.00 —
a. "Corrieo" 1,900. —
163 A15 2a black 600.00 —
a. "Corrieo" 1,900. —

The vast majority of used stamps were not canceled.

Surcharged Stamps of 1902 Overprinted in Red or Green

Local Overprint

Overprint 23mm long. "A" has pointed top.

1913 Without Gum *Perf. 11½*

164 A1 6a on 10r green (R) 37.50 12.00
a. "REPUBLICA" double 65.00 65.00

Perf. 12½, 13½

165 A7 6a on 5r black (G) 15.00 3.50
166 A7 6a on 10r green (R) 31.00 8.00
167 A7 6a on 40r choc (R) 10.50 3.00
a. Perf. 13½ 50.00 20.00
168 A7 18a on 20r car (G) 21.00 6.00
169 A7 18a on 100r brown (R) 82.50 40.00
a. Perf. 13½ 100.00 50.00
170 A7 18a on 300r org (R) 32.50 9.00
a. Perf. 13½ 50.00 10.00
Nos. 164-170 (7) 230.00 81.50

"Republica" overprint exists inverted on Nos. 164-170.

"Republica" overprint exists double on No. 164.

1913 Without Gum *Perf. 11½, 13½*

171 A9 6a on 10r red vio (G) 14.50 4.50
172 A9 6a on 10r red vio (R) 175.00 26.00
173 A9 6a on 15r choc (R) 14.50 5.00
174 A9 6a on 25r green (R) 16.00 5.00
175 A9 6a on 80r yel grn (R) 14.50 5.00
176 A9 6a on 100r brn, *buff*(R) 30.00 7.00
a. Perf. 11½ 32.50 8.00
177 A9 18a on 20r lav (R) 19.00 5.00
178 A9 18a on 50r lt bl (R) 19.00 5.00
a. Perf. 13½ 21.00 6.00
179 A9 18a on 75r car (G) 19.00 5.50
180 A9 18a on 150r car, *rose* (G) 21.00 6.00
181 A9 18a on 300r dk bl, *buff* (R) 32.50 10.00

On No. 141

182 A11 10a on 12a red lil (R) 13.00 4.50
Nos. 171-182 (12) 388.00 88.50

"Republica" overprint exists inverted on Nos. 171-181.

Stamps of Preceding Issue Surcharged

1913 Without Gum *Perf. 11½*

183 A9 2a on 18a on 20r (R) 10.00 4.00
184 A9 2a on 18a on 50r (R) 10.00 4.00
a. Perf. 13½ 11.00 4.25
185 A9 2a on 18a on 75r (G) 10.00 4.00
186 A9 2a on 18a on 150r (G) 10.00 4.00
Nos. 183-186 (4) 40.00 16.00

"Republica" overprint exists inverted on Nos. 183-186. Value, each $20.

The 2a surcharge exists inverted or double on Nos. 183-186. For values, see Classic Specialized Catalogue.

Vasco da Gama Issue Overprinted or Surcharged:

j

k

187 CD20 (j) ½a blue green 7.75 2.00
188 CD21 (j) 1a red 8.50 2.00
189 CD22 (j) 2a red violet 8.50 2.00
a. Double ovpt., one inverted 100.00
190 CD23 (j) 4a yellow grn 7.75 2.00
191 CD24 (j) 8a dk blue 13.00 2.00
192 CD25 (k) 10a on 12a vio brn 24.00 5.00
193 CD26 (j) 16a bister brn 17.00 4.00
194 CD27 (j) 24a bister 27.50 5.00
Nos. 187-194 (8) 114.00 24.00

Stamps of 1898-1903 Overprinted in Red or Green

1913 Without Gum *Perf. 11½*

195 A11 4a carmine (G) 250.00 100.00
196 A11 5a yellow brn 27.50 20.00
a. Inverted overprint 50.00 40.00
197 A11 6a red brown 77.50 40.00
198 A11 8a gray brown 625.00 300.00
198A A11 10a dull blue —
199 A11 13a violet 77.50 32.50
a. Inverted overprint 95.00
200 A11 13a gray lilac 37.50 20.00
201 A11 16a blue, *bl* 45.00 20.00
202 A11 18a org brn, *pink* 45.00 20.00
203 A11 20a brown, *yelsh* 45.00 20.00
204 A11 31a red lil, *pink* 67.50 30.00
205 A11 47a dull bl, *straw* 100.00 40.00

Only 20 examples of No. 198A were sold by the Post Office.

Stamps of 1911-13 Surcharged

On Stamps of 1911 With Lisbon "Republica"

1913

206 A11 ½a on 5a yel brn (R) 15.00 3.00
a. "½ Avo" inverted 125.00 70.00
207 A11 4a on 8a gray brn (R) 30.00 4.00
a. "4 Avos" inverted 150.00 70.00

On Stamps of 1913 With Local "Republica"

208 A11 1a on 13a violet (R) 125.00 30.00
209 A11 1a on 13a gray lil (R) 15.00 3.00
Nos. 206-209 (4) 185.00 40.00

Issued without gum: Nos. 207-209.

"Ceres" — A16

1913-24 *Perf. 12x11½, 15x14*

Name and Value in Black

210 A16 ½a olive brown 1.75 .20
a. Inscriptions inverted 50.00
211 A16 1a black 1.75 .20
a. Inscriptions inverted 50.00
b. Inscriptions double 50.00
212 A16 1½a yel grn ('24) 1.75 .20
213 A16 2a blue green 1.75 .20
a. Inscriptions inverted 40.00
214 A16 3a orange ('23) 10.00 3.00
215 A16 4a carmine 6.75 1.00
216 A16 4a lemon ('24) 14.00 2.25
217 A16 5a lilac brown 7.75 3.00
218 A16 6a lt violet 7.75 3.00
219 A16 6a gray ('23) 47.50 7.50
220 A16 8a lilac brown 7.75 3.00
221 A16 10a deep blue 7.75 3.00
222 A16 10a pale blue ('23) 27.50 6.00
223 A16 12a yellow brn 11.00 3.00
224 A16 14a lilac ('24) 42.50 12.00
225 A16 16a slate 20.00 5.00
226 A16 20a orange brn 20.00 5.00
227 A16 24a slate grn ('23) 25.00 7.00
228 A16 32a orange brn ('24) 25.00 8.00
229 A16 40a plum 21.00 5.00
230 A16 56a dull rose ('24) 50.00 15.00
231 A16 58a brown, *grn* 35.00 12.00
232 A16 72a brown ('23) 67.50 20.00
233 A16 76a brown, *pink* 50.00 14.00
234 A16 1p orange, *sal* 67.50 20.00
235 A16 1p orange ('24) 200.00 30.00
236 A16 3p green, *bl* 200.00 55.00
237 A16 3p pale turq ('24) 425.00 95.00
238 A16 5p car rose ('24) 350.00 82.50
Nos. 210-238 (29) 1,753. 421.05

For surcharges see Nos. 256, 259-267.

Preceding Issues and No. P4 Overprinted in Carmine

On Stamps of 1902

Perf. 11½, 12, 12½, 13½, 11½x12

1915

239 A7 6a on 10r green 14.50 4.00
240 A9 6a on 5r yellow 14.50 4.00
241 A9 6a on 10r red vio 14.50 4.00
242 A9 6a on 15r choc 12.50 3.25
243 A9 6a on 25r green 12.00 4.00
244 A9 6a on 80r yel grn 12.00 4.00
245 A9 6a on 100r brn, *buff* 21.00 4.00
246 A9 6a on 200r bl, *bl* 11.00 6.00
247 A9 18a on 20r lav 21.00 6.00
248 A9 18a on 50r lt bl 45.00 6.75
249 A9 18a on 75r car 40.00 6.75
250 A9 18a on 150r car, *rose* 45.00 8.00
251 A9 18a on 300r bl, *sal* 40.00 10.00
252 N3 18a on 2½r brn 32.50 6.00

With Additional Overprint

253 A11 8a blue 14.50 8.25
254 A11 10a slate blue 14.50 6.00
a. "Provisorio" double 110.00

On Stamp of 1905

255 A11 10a on 12a red lilac 19.00 9.75
Nos. 239-255 (17) 383.50 100.75

Issued without gum: Nos. 243-251 and 255.

No. 217 Surcharged

1919-20

Without Gum

256 A16 ½a on 5a lilac brn 100.00 32.50

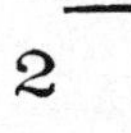

Nos. 243 and 244 Surcharged

257 A9 2a on 6a on 25r green 500.00 125.00
258 A9 2a on 6a on 80r yel grn 100.00 70.00

No. 152 Surcharged

258A A11 2a on 6a red brown 175.00 70.00
Nos. 256-258A (4) 875.00 297.50

Issued without gum: Nos. 256-258A.

Stamps of 1913-24 Surcharged

1931-33

259 A16 1a on 24a slate grn ('33) 14.50 4.00
260 A16 2a on 32a org brn ('33) 14.50 4.00
261 A16 4a on 12a bis brn ('33) 14.50 4.00
262 A16 5a on 6a lt gray ('33) 57.50 20.00
263 A16 5a on 6a lt vio ('33) 30.00 11.00
264 A16 7a on 8a lil brn 24.00 5.00
265 A16 12a on 14a lil 24.00 5.00
266 A16 15a on 16a dk gray ('33) 24.00 5.00
267 A16 20a on 56a dl rose ('33) 50.00 11.00
Nos. 259-267 (9) 253.00 69.00

"Portugal" and Vasco da Gama's Flagship "San Gabriel" — A17

Wmk. 232

1934, Feb. 1 Typo. *Perf. 11½*

268 A17 ½a bister .45 .40
269 A17 1a olive brown .45 .20
270 A17 2a blue green 1.10 .50
271 A17 3a violet 1.40 .50
272 A17 4a black 1.75 .50
273 A17 5a gray 1.75 .80
274 A17 6a brown 1.75 .80
275 A17 7a brt rose 3.25 1.00
276 A17 8a brt blue 3.25 1.00
277 A17 10a red orange 7.25 2.00
278 A17 12a dark blue 7.25 2.00
279 A17 14a olive green 7.25 2.00
280 A17 15a maroon 7.25 2.00
281 A17 20a orange 7.25 2.00
282 A17 30a apple green 14.00 3.50
283 A17 40a violet 14.00 3.50
284 A17 50a olive bister 21.00 5.00
285 A17 1p lt blue 110.00 27.50
286 A17 2p brown org 140.00 35.00
287 A17 3p emerald 225.00 40.00
288 A17 5p dark violet 350.00 87.50
Nos. 268-288 (21) 925.40 217.70

See Nos. 316-323. For overprints and surcharges see Nos. 306-315, C1-C6, J43-J49.

Common Design Types

Perf. 13½x13

1938, Aug. 1 Engr. Unwmk.

Name and Value in Black

289 CD34 1a gray green 1.00 .35
290 CD34 2a orange brown 1.25 .55
291 CD34 3a dk vio brn 1.25 .55
292 CD34 4a brt green 1.25 .55
293 CD35 5a dk carmine 1.25 .55
294 CD35 6a slate 1.25 .55
295 CD35 8a rose violet 2.10 2.25
296 CD36 10a brt red vio 2.50 2.25
297 CD36 12a red 3.25 2.60
298 CD36 15a orange 3.25 2.60
299 CD37 20a blue 16.50 2.90
300 CD37 40a gray black 16.50 3.50
301 CD37 50a brown 16.50 3.75
302 CD38 1p brown car 50.00 7.25
303 CD38 2p olive green 100.00 11.00
304 CD38 3p blue violet 125.00 22.50
305 CD38 5p red brown 250.00 37.50
Nos. 289-305 (17) 592.85 101.20

For surcharge see No. 315A.

Stamps of 1934 Surcharged in Black:

a

b

1941 Wmk. 232 *Perf. 11½x12*

306 A17(a) 1a on 6a brown 7.50 3.00
307 A17(b) 2a on 6a brown 3.00 1.50
308 A17(b) 3a on 6a brown 3.00 1.50
309 A17(a) 5a on 7a brt rose 120.00 50.00
310 A17(b) 5a on 7a brt rose 17.50 8.25
311 A17(a) 5a on 8a brt blue 19.50 9.75
312 A17(b) 5a on 8a brt blue 12.00 8.25
313 A17(b) 8a on 30a apple grn 9.00 4.00
314 A17(b) 8a on 40a violet 9.00 4.00
315 A17(b) 8a on 50a olive bis 9.00 4.50
Nos. 306-315 (10) 209.50 94.75

No. 294 Surcharged in Black:

1941 Unwmk. *Perf. 13½x13*

315A CD35 3a on 6a slate 70.00 32.50

Counterfeits exist.

"Portugal" Type of 1934

1942 Litho. *Rough Perf. 12*

Thin Paper Without Gum

316 A17 1a olive brown 1.90 .75
317 A17 2a blue green 1.90 .75
318 A17 3a vio, perf. 11 22.50 2.50
a. Perf. 12 27.50 3.25
319 A17 6a brown 27.50 3.00
a. Perf. 10 55.00 7.00
b. Perf. 11 47.50 6.00
320 A17 10a red orange 15.00 1.50
321 A17 20a orange 15.00 1.50
a. Perf. 11 47.50 5.00
322 A17 30a apple green 27.50 2.50
323 A17 40a violet 37.50 3.25
Nos. 316-323 (8) 148.80 15.75

Macao Dwelling A18

Pagoda of Barra — A19

Designs: 2a, Mountain fort. 3a, View of Macao. 8a, Praia Grande Bay. 10a, Leal Senado Square. 20a, Sao Jeronimo Hill. 30a, Marginal Ave. 50a, Relief of Goddess Ma. 1p, Gate of Cerco. 3p, Post Office. 5p, Solidao Walk.

1948, Dec. 20 Litho. *Perf. 10½*

324 A18 1a dk brn & org 2.25 .50
325 A19 2a rose brn & rose 1.60 .50
326 A18 3a brn vio & lil 3.75 .75
327 A18 8a rose car & rose 2.25 .90
328 A18 10a lilac rose & rose 3.75 1.25
329 A18 20a dk blue & gray 4.75 1.50
330 A18 30a black & gray 9.25 2.50
331 A18 50a brn & pale bis 14.00 5.00
332 A19 1p emer & pale grn 110.00 15.00
333 A19 2p scarlet & rose 92.50 15.00
334 A19 3p dl grn & gray grn 140.00 16.00
335 A18 5p vio bl & gray 275.00 22.50
Nos. 324-335 (12) 659.10 81.40

See Nos. 341-347A.

Catalogue values for unused stamps in this section, from this point to the end of the section, are for Never Hinged items.

Lady of Fatima Issue
Common Design Type

1949, Feb. 1 Unwmk. *Perf. 14½*

336 CD40 8a scarlet 40.00 12.00

Symbols of the UPU — A20

Dragon — A21

1949, Dec. 24 Litho. Unwmk.

337 A20 32a claret & rose 50.00 15.00

75th anniv. of the formation of the UPU.

Holy Year Issue
Common Design Types

1950, July 26 *Perf. 13x13½*

339 CD41 32a dk slate gray 27.50 6.00
340 CD42 50a carmine 27.50 6.50

Scenic Types of 1948

Designs as before.

1950-51 *Perf. 14*

341 A18 1a violet & rose 2.75 .75
342 A19 2a ol bis & yel 2.75 .75
343 A18 3a org red & buff 8.50 1.25
344 A18 8a slate & gray 11.00 1.25
345 A18 10a red brn & org 15.00 3.25
346 A18 30a vio bl & bl 17.50 3.25
347 A18 50a ol grn & yel grn 42.50 4.00
347A A19 1p dk org brn & org brn 110.00 24.00
Nos. 341-347A (8) 210.00 38.50

A 1p ultra & vio, perf. 11, was not sold in Macao. Value $100.
#341-347 issued in 1951, the 1p in 1950.

1951 *Perf. 11½x12*

348 A21 1a org yel, *lemon* 2.25 .50
349 A21 2a dk grn, *blue* 2.25 .50
350 A21 10a vio brn, *blue* 8.00 2.50
351 A21 10a brt pink, *blue* 7.50 2.50
Nos. 348-351 (4) 20.00 6.00

Nos. 348-351 were issued without gum.
For overprints see Nos. J50-J52.

Holy Year Extension Issue
Common Design Type

1951, Dec. 3 Litho. *Perf. 14*

352 CD43 60a magenta & pink + label *50.00* 9.00

Stamp without label sells for much less.

Fernao Mendes Pinto — A22

Portraits: 2a and 10a, St. Francis Xavier. 3a and 50a, Jorge Alvares. 6a and 30a, Luis de Camoens.

1951, Aug. 27 *Perf. 11½*

353 A22 1a steel bl & gray bl .90 .50
354 A22 2a dk brown & ol grn 1.90 .50
355 A22 3a deep grn & grn 2.25 .75
356 A22 6a purple 3.00 1.00
357 A22 10a red brn & org 7.25 1.50
358 A22 20a brown car 14.00 3.25
359 A22 30a dk brn & ol grn 21.00 4.50
360 A22 50a red & orange 57.50 11.00
Nos. 353-360 (8) 107.80 23.00

Sampan — A23

Junk — A24

Design: 5p, Junk.

1951, Nov. 1 Unwmk.

361 A23 1p vio bl & bl 37.50 2.25
362 A24 3p black & vio 140.00 15.00
363 A23 5p henna brown 175.00 24.00
Nos. 361-363 (3) 352.50 41.25

Medical Congress Issue
Common Design Type

Design: Sao Rafael Hospital.

1952, June 16 Unwmk. *Perf. 13½*

364 CD44 6a black & purple 9.75 3.50

Statue of St. Francis Xavier — A25

Statue of Virgin Mary — A26

St. Francis Xavier Issue

16a, Arm of St. Francis. 40a, Tomb of St. Francis.

1952, Nov. 28 Litho. *Perf. 14*

365 A25 3a blk, *grnsh gray* 4.00 .90
366 A25 16a choc, *buff* 17.00 3.00
367 A25 40a blk, *blue* 21.00 5.25
Nos. 365-367 (3) 42.00 9.15

400th anniv. of the death of St. Francis Xavier.

1953, Apr. 28 Unwmk. *Perf. 13½*

368 A26 8a choc & dull ol 3.75 1.00
369 A26 10a blue blk & buff 15.00 4.00
370 A26 50a slate grn & ol grn 26.00 6.00
Nos. 368-370 (3) 44.75 11.00

Exhibition of Sacred Missionary Art, held at Lisbon in 1951.

Stamp of Portugal and Arms of Colonies — A27

1954, Mar. 9 Photo. *Perf. 13*

371 A27 10a multicolored 10.00 2.00

Cent. of Portugal's first postage stamps.

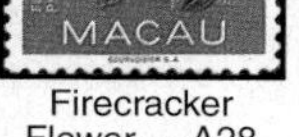
Firecracker Flower — A28

Map of Colony — A29

Flowers: 3a, Forget-me-not. 5a, Dragon claw. 10a, Nunflower. 16a, Narcissus. 30a, Peach flower. 39a, Lotus flower. 1p, Chrysanthemum. 3p, Cherry blossoms. 5p, Tangerine blossoms.

1953, Sept. 22 *Perf. 11½*

Flowers in Natural Colors

372 A28 1a dark red .60 .25
373 A28 3a dark green .60 .25
374 A28 5a dark brown .60 .25
375 A28 10a dp grnsh blue .60 .35
376 A28 16a yellow brown 1.25 .35
377 A28 30a dk olive grn 2.75 .40
378 A28 39a violet blue 3.25 .40
379 A28 1p deep plum 7.25 .90
380 A28 3p dark gray 16.50 2.00
381 A28 5p deep carmine 27.50 3.25
Nos. 372-381 (10) 60.90 8.40

For surcharges see #443-444.

Sao Paulo Issue
Common Design Type

1954, Aug. 4 Litho. *Perf. 13½*

382 CD46 39a org, cream & blk 14.00 2.75

Sao Paulo founding, 400th anniversary.
For surcharge see #445.

Perf. 12½x13½

1956, May 10 Photo.

Inscriptions and design in brown, red, green, ultra & yellow (buff on 10a, 40a, 90a)

383 A29 1a gray .50 .40
384 A29 3a pale gray 1.10 .50
385 A29 5a pale pink 1.50 .75
386 A29 10a buff 3.00 .90
387 A29 30a lt blue 7.50 1.25
388 A29 40a pale green 10.00 1.50
389 A29 90a pale gray 14.00 2.75
390 A29 1.50p pink 25.00 3.75
Nos. 383-390 (8) 62.60 11.80

Exhibition Emblems and View — A30

Armillary Sphere — A31

1958, Nov. 8 Litho. *Perf. 14½*

391 A30 70a multicolored 6.00 1.75

World's Fair, Brussels, Apr. 17-Oct. 19.

Tropical Medicine Congress Issue
Common Design Type

Design: Cinnamomum camphora.

1958, Nov. 15 *Perf. 13½*

392 CD47 20a multicolored 8.00 2.50

1960, June 25 Litho. *Perf. 13½*

393 A31 2p multicolored 11.50 3.50

500th anniversary of the death of Prince Henry the Navigator.

Sports Issue
Common Design Type

Sports: 10a, Field hockey. 16a, Wrestling. 20a, Table tennis. 50a, Motorcycling. 1.20p, Relay race. 2.50p, Badminton.

1962, Feb. 9 *Perf. 13½*

Multicolored Design

394 CD48 10a blue & yel grn 2.00 .40
395 CD48 16a brt pink 2.50 .60
396 CD48 20a orange 3.50 .80
397 CD48 50a rose 6.00 .80
398 CD48 1.20p blue & beige 25.00 2.75
399 CD48 2.50p gray & brown 35.00 6.25
Nos. 394-399 (6) 74.00 11.60

Anti-Malaria Issue
Common Design Type

Design: Anopheles hyrcanus sinensis.

1962, Apr. 7 Litho. *Perf. 13½*

400 CD49 40a multicolored 7.00 2.00

Bank Building — A32

1964, May 16 Unwmk. *Perf. 13½*
401 A32 20a multicolored 10.00 2.25

Centenary of the National Overseas Bank of Portugal.

ITU Issue
Common Design Type

1965, May 17 Litho. *Perf. 14½*
402 CD52 10a pale grn & multi *5.50* 1.50

National Revolution Issue
Common Design Type

Design: 10a, Infante D. Henrique School and Count de S. Januario Hospital.

1966, May 28 Litho. *Perf. 11½*
403 CD53 10a multicolored 5.00 1.50

Drummer, 1548 — A32a

Designs: 15a, Soldier with sword, 1548. 20a, Harquebusier, 1649. 40a, Infantry officer, 1783. 50a, Infantry soldier, 1783. 60a, Colonial infantry soldier (Indian), 1902. 1p, Colonial infantry soldier (Chinese), 1903. 3p, Colonial infantry soldier (Chinese) 1904.

1966, Aug. 8 Litho. *Perf. 13*
404 A32a 10a multicolored 1.25 .40
405 A32a 15a multicolored 2.25 .75
406 A32a 20a multicolored 2.50 .75
407 A32a 40a multicolored 4.50 .85
408 A32a 50a multicolored 5.00 1.50
409 A32a 60a multicolored 12.00 1.75
410 A32a 1p multicolored 15.00 3.00
411 A32a 3p multicolored 27.50 6.25
Nos. 404-411 (8) 70.00 15.25

Navy Club Issue, 1967
Common Design Type

Designs: 10a, Capt. Oliveira E. Carmo and armed launch Vega. 20a, Capt. Silva Junior and frigate Dom Fernando.

1967, Jan. 31 Litho. *Perf. 13*
412 CD54 10a multicolored 3.25 1.00
413 CD54 20a multicolored 6.25 2.75

Arms of Pope Paul VI and Golden Rose — A33

Cabral Monument, Lisbon — A34

1967, May 13 *Perf. 12½x13*
414 A33 50a multicolored 5.75 2.00

50th anniversary of the apparition of the Virgin Mary to three shepherd children at Fatima.

Cabral Issue

Design: 70a, Cabral monument, Belmonte.

1968, Apr. 22 Litho. *Perf. 14*
415 A34 20a multicolored 4.25 1.00
416 A34 70a multicolored 6.00 2.25

500th anniversary of the birth of Pedro Alvares Cabral, navigator who took possession of Brazil for Portugal.

Admiral Coutinho Issue
Common Design Type

Design: 20a, Adm. Coutinho with sextant, vert.

1969, Feb. 17 Litho. *Perf. 14*
417 CD55 20a multicolored 3.75 1.50

Church of Our Lady of the Relics, Vidigueira A35

Bishop D. Belchior Carneiro A36

Vasco da Gama Issue

1969, Aug. 29 Litho. *Perf. 14*
418 A35 1p multicolored 11.00 1.50

Vasco da Gama (1469-1524), navigator.

Administration Reform Issue
Common Design Type

1969, Sept. 25 Litho. *Perf. 14*
419 CD56 90a multicolored 5.00 1.00

1969, Oct. 16 Litho. *Perf. 13*
420 A36 50a multicolored 3.25 .75

4th centenary of the founding of the Santa Casa da Misericordia in Macao.

King Manuel I Issue

Portal of Mother Church, Golega — A37

1969, Dec. 1 Litho. *Perf. 14*
421 A37 30a multicolored 6.25 .90

500th anniversary of the birth of King Manuel I.

Marshal Carmona Issue
Common Design Type

5a, Antonio Oscar Carmona in general's uniform.

1970, Nov. 15 Litho. *Perf. 14*
422 CD57 5a multicolored 1.50 .75

Dragon Mask — A38

1971, Sept. 30 *Perf. 13½*
423 A38 5a lt blue & multi 1.10 .20
424 A38 10a Lion mask 2.25 .50

Lusiads Issue

Portuguese Delegation at Chinese Court — A39

1972, May 25 Litho. *Perf. 13*
425 A39 20a citron & multi 13.00 3.75

4th centenary of publication of The Lusiads by Luiz Camoens.

Olympic Games Issue
Common Design Type

Design: Hockey and Olympic emblem.

1972, June 20 *Perf. 14x13½*
426 CD59 50a multicolored 3.50 1.00

Lisbon-Rio de Janeiro Flight Issue
Common Design Type

Design: "Santa Cruz" landing in Rio de Janeiro.

1972, Sept. 20 Litho. *Perf. 13½*
427 CD60 5p multicolored 22.50 7.50

Pedro V Theater and Lyre — A42

1972, Dec. 25 Litho. *Perf. 13½*
428 A42 2p multicolored 10.00 2.50

Centenary of Pedro V Theater, Macao.

WMO Centenary Issue
Common Design Type

1973, Dec. 15 Litho. *Perf. 13*
429 CD61 20a blue grn & multi 6.25 1.00

Viscount St. Januario A44

Design: 60a, Hospital, 1874 and 1974.

1974, Jan. 25 Litho. *Perf. 13½*
430 A44 15a multicolored .85 .50
431 A44 60a multicolored 3.75 .90

Viscount St. Januario Hospital, Macao, cent.
For surcharge see No. 457.

George Chinnery, Self-portrait A45

1974, Sept. 23 Litho. *Perf. 14*
432 A45 30a multicolored 3.50 1.25

George Chinnery (1774-1852), English painter who lived in Macao.

Macao-Taipa Bridge — A46

Design: 2.20p, Different view of bridge.

1974, Oct. 7 Litho. *Perf. 14x13½*
433 A46 20a multicolored 1.50 .40
434 A46 2.20p multicolored 12.50 1.25

Inauguration of the Macao-Taipa Bridge.
For surcharge see #446.

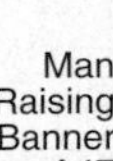

Man Raising Banner A47

1975, Apr. 25 *Perf. 12*
435 A47 10a ocher & multi 2.00 .75
436 A47 1p multicolored 13.50 3.25

Revolution of Apr. 25, 1974, 1st anniv.

Pou Chai Pagoda — A48

Design: 20p, Tin Hau Pagoda.

1976, Jan. 30 Litho. *Perf. 13½x13*
437 A48 10p multicolored *15.00* 1.75
438 A48 20p multicolored *32.50* 3.75

A 1p stamp for the 400th anniv. of the Macao Diocese was prepared but not issued. Some stamps were sold in Lisbon. Value $100.

"The Law" — A50

1978 Litho. *Perf. 13½*
440 A50 5a blk, dk & lt blue *3.00* 1.00
441 A50 2p blk, org brn & buff *125.00* 5.00
442 A50 5p blk, ol & yel grn *25.00* 4.50
Nos. 440-442 (3) 153.00 10.50

Legislative Assembly, Aug. 9, 1976.

Nos. 376, 378, 382, 434 Surcharged

1979, Nov.
443 A28 10a on 16a *7.50* 2.00
444 A28 30a on 39a (#378) *9.50* 2.00
445 CD46 30a on 39a (#382) *65.00* 9.00
446 A46 2p on 2.20p *11.00* 3.00
Nos. 443-446 (4) *93.00* 16.00

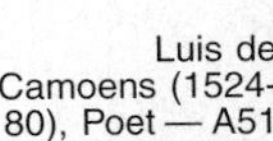

Luis de Camoens (1524-80), Poet — A51

Buddha, Macao Cathedral — A52

1981, June Litho. *Perf. 13½*
447 A51 10a multicolored *.95* .35
448 A51 30a multicolored *1.90* .45
449 A51 1p multicolored *4.25* .75
450 A51 3p multicolored *6.25* 1.60
Nos. 447-450 (4) *13.35* 3.15

1981, Sept.
451 A52 15a multicolored .25 .20
452 A52 40a multicolored .50 .20
453 A52 50a multicolored 1.00 .20
454 A52 60a multicolored 1.90 .20
455 A52 1p multicolored 2.40 .60
456 A52 2.20p multicolored 6.00 1.10
Nos. 451-456 (6) 12.05 2.50

Transcultural Psychiatry Symposium.

No. 431 Surcharged

1981 Litho. *Perf. 13½*
457 A44 30a on 60a multi 6.00 1.00

Health Services Building A53

Designs: Public Buildings and Monuments.

1982, June 10 Litho. *Perf. 12x12½*
458 A53 30a shown .65 .20
459 A53 40a Guia Lighthouse 1.90 .20
460 A53 1p Portas do Cerco 2.50 .25
461 A53 2p Luis de Camoes Museum 3.25 .50
462 A53 10p School Welfare Service Building 7.50 2.50
Nos. 458-462 (5) 15.80 3.65

See Nos. 472-476, 489-493.

Autumn Festivals A54

Designs: Painted paper lanterns.

1982, Oct. 1 *Perf. 12x11½*
463 A54 40a multicolored 3.25 .90
464 A54 1p multicolored 8.75 1.40
465 A54 2p multicolored 10.50 2.25
466 A54 5p multicolored 25.00 4.50
Nos. 463-466 (4) 47.50 9.05

Geographical Position — A55

1982, Dec. 1 Litho. *Perf. 13*
467 A55 50a Aerial view *14.50* 1.75
468 A55 3p Map *52.50* 6.00

World Communications Year — A56

1983, Feb. 16 *Perf. 13½*
469 A56 60a Telephone operators 1.75 .20
470 A56 3p Mailman, mailbox 3.40 1.40
471 A56 6p Globe, satellites 6.75 3.00
Nos. 469-471 (3) 11.90 4.60

Architecture Type of 1982

1983, May 12 Litho. *Perf. 13*
472 A53 10a Social Welfare Institute .85 .20
473 A53 80a St. Joseph's Seminary 1.75 .40
474 A53 1.50p St. Dominic's Church 2.25 .75
475 A53 2.50p St. Paul's Church ruins 3.50 1.40
476 A53 7.50p Senate House 8.50 3.25
Nos. 472-476 (5) 16.85 6.00

Medicinal Plants A57

1983, July 14 Litho. *Perf. 13½x14*
477 A57 20a Asclepias curassavica 1.00 .70
478 A57 40a Acanthus ilicifolius 1.50 .70
479 A57 60a Melastoma sanguineum 2.00 .70
480 A57 70a Nelumbo nucifera 3.25 1.50
481 A57 1.50p Bombax malabaricum 4.25 2.25
482 A57 2.50p Hibiscus mutabilis 8.00 4.25
a. Souvenir sheet of 6, #477-482 *200.00*
Nos. 477-482 (6) 20.00 10.10

No. 482a sold for 6.50p.

16th Century Discoveries — A58

1983, Nov. 15 Litho. *Perf. 13½x14*
483 A58 4p multicolored *6.00* 2.40
484 A59 4p multicolored *6.00* 2.40
a. Pair, #483-484 *16.00* 8.00

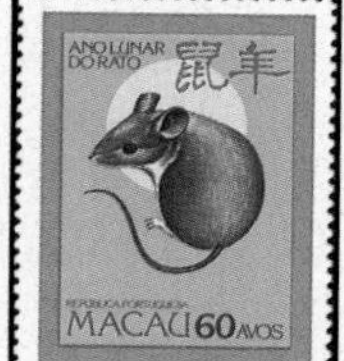

A60

A61

1984, Jan. 25 Litho. *Perf. 13½*
485 A60 60a multicolored *8.00* 1.75
a. Booklet pane of 5 *45.00*

New Year 1984 (Year of the Rat).
No. 485a has straight edges.
See Nos. 504, 522, 540, 560, 583, 611, 639, 662, 684, 718, 757, 804.

1984, Mar. 1 Litho. *Perf. 12½*

Design of First Stamp Issue, 1884.

486 A61 40a orange & blk 1.50 .20
487 A61 3p gray & blk 3.25 .90
488 A61 5p sepia & blk 7.25 1.60
a. Souvenir sheet of 3, #486-488 *40.00*
Nos. 486-488 (3) 12.00 2.70

Centenary of Macao postage stamps.

Architecture Type of 1982

1984, May 18 Litho. *Perf. 13½*
489 A53 20a Holy House of Mercy .35 .20
490 A53 60a St. Lawrence Church .70 .20
491 A53 90a King Peter V Theater 1.10 .20
492 A53 3p Palace of St. Sancha 2.10 .25
493 A53 15p Moorish barracks 4.25 1.25
Nos. 489-493 (5) 8.50 2.10

Birds, Ausipex '84 Emblem A62

1984, Sept. 21 Litho. *Perf. 13*
494 A62 30a Kingfishers .85 .40
495 A62 40a European jay .90 .40
496 A62 50a White eyes 1.75 .40
497 A62 70a Hoopoe 2.50 .40
498 A62 2.50p Peking nightingale 7.00 1.10
499 A62 6p Wild duck 8.75 2.25
Nos. 494-499 (6) 21.75 4.95

Philakorea '84 Emblem, Fishing Boats A63

1984, Oct. 22 Litho.
500 A63 20a Hok lou t'eng .85 .25
501 A63 60a Tai t'ong 1.75 .65
502 A63 2p Tai mei chai 4.25 1.10
503 A63 5p Ch'at pong t'o 8.50 2.00
Nos. 500-503 (4) 15.35 4.00

New Year Type of 1984

1985, Feb. 13 Litho. *Perf. 13½*
504 A60 1p Buffalo 7.25 1.40
a. Booklet pane of 5 *20.00*

Intl. Youth Year — A65

1985, Apr. 19 Litho. *Perf. 13½*
505 A65 2.50p shown *4.75* .65
506 A65 3p Clasped hands *5.75* 1.90

Visit of President Eanes of Portugal A66

1985, May 27 Litho.
507 A66 1.50p multicolored 3.50 .50

Luis de Camoens Museum, 25th Anniv. — A67

Silk paintings by Chen Chi Yun.

1985, June 27 Litho.
508 A67 2.50p Two travelers, hermit 6.00 1.50
509 A67 2.50p Traveling merchant 6.00 1.50
510 A67 2.50p Conversation in a garden 6.00 1.50
511 A67 2.50p Veranda of a house 6.00 1.50
a. Block or strip of 4, #508-511 32.00 11.00
Nos. 508-511 (4) 24.00 6.00

Butterflies, World Tourism Assoc. Emblem — A68

1985, Sept. 27 Litho.
512 A68 30a Euploea midamus 1.40 .20
513 A68 50a Hebomoia glaucippe 1.40 .20
514 A68 70a Lethe confusa 2.25 .35
515 A68 2p Heliophorus epicles 3.25 .85
516 A68 4p Euthalia phemius seitzi 6.50 2.40
517 A68 7.50p Troides helena 9.25 3.50
a. Sheet of 6, #512-517 *160.00*
Nos. 512-517 (6) 24.05 7.50

World Tourism Day.

Cargo Boats A69

Designs: 50a, Tou. 70a, Veng Seng Lei motor junk. 1p, Tong Heng Long No. 2 motor junk. 6p, Fong Vong San cargo ship.

1985, Oct. 25 *Perf. 14*
518 A69 50a multicolored .75 .20
519 A69 70a multicolored 2.25 .50
520 A69 1p multicolored 4.00 1.10
521 A69 6p multicolored 6.50 2.75
Nos. 518-521 (4) 13.50 4.55

New Year Type of 1984

1986, Feb. 3 *Perf. 13½*
522 A60 1.50p Tiger 6.00 1.00
a. Booklet pane of 5 24.00

No. 522a has straight edges.

City of Macau, 400th Anniv. A71

1986, Apr. 10 Litho. *Perf. 13½*
523 A71 2.20p multicolored *4.75* 1.60

Musical Instruments A72

1986, May 22
524 A72 20a Suo-na 4.25 1.25
525 A72 50a Sheng 5.00 1.50
526 A72 60a Er-hu 6.00 1.50
527 A72 70a Ruan 10.25 3.00
528 A72 5p Cheng 24.00 4.50
529 A72 8p Pi-pa 30.00 9.50
a. Souvenir sheet of 6, #524-529 *400.00*
Nos. 524-529 (6) 79.50 21.25

AMERIPEX '86.

Ferries A73

1986, Aug. 28 **Litho.** ***Perf. 13***

530 A73 10a Hydrofoil .50 .20
531 A73 40a Hovermarine 3.50 .65
532 A73 3p Jetfoil 4.00 1.40
533 A73 7.5p High-speed ferry 9.50 2.75
Nos. 530-533 (4) 17.50 5.00

Fortresses — A74

1986, Oct. 3 **Litho.** ***Perf. 12½***

534 A74 2p Taipa 12.00 2.40
535 A74 2p Sao Paulo do Monte 12.00 2.40
536 A74 2p Our Lady of Guia 12.00 2.40
537 A74 2p Sao Francisco 12.00 2.40
a. Block or strip of 4, #534-537 87.50 15.50
Nos. 534-537 (4) 48.00 9.60

Macao Security Forces, 10th anniv. No. 537a has continuous design.

A75

Dr. Sun Yat-sen — A76

1986, Nov. 12 **Litho.** ***Perf. 12½***

538 A75 70a multicolored *4.00 1.40*

Souvenir Sheet

539 A76 1.30p shown *62.50 45.00*

New Year Type of 1984

1987, Jan. 21 ***Perf. 13½***

540 A60 1.50p Hare 6.50 1.25
a. Booklet pane of 5 27.50

No. 540a has straight edges.

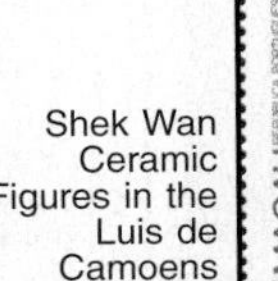

Shek Wan Ceramic Figures in the Luis de Camoens Museum — A78

1987, Apr. 10 **Litho.** ***Perf. 13½***

541 A78 2.20p Medicine man (4/1) 8.00 2.50
542 A78 2.20p Choi San, god of good fortune (4/2) 8.00 2.50
543 A78 2.20p Yi, sun god (4/3) 8.00 2.50
544 A78 2.20p Chung Kuei, conqueror of demons (4/4) 8.00 2.50
a. Block or strip of 4, #541-544 47.50 26.50
Nos. 541-544 (4) 32.00 10.00

Dragon Boat Festival A79

1987, May 29 **Litho.** ***Perf. 13½***

545 A79 50a Dragon boat race 4.50 .90
546 A79 5p Figurehead 11.50 3.00

Decorated Fans — A80

Casino Gambling — A81

1987, July 29 **Litho.** ***Perf. 12½***

547 A80 30a multicolored 4.00 1.90
548 A80 70a multi, diff. 9.00 2.75
549 A80 1p multi, diff. 24.50 3.25
550 A80 6p multi, diff. 24.50 9.00
a. Souvenir sheet of 4, #547-550 *300.00*
Nos. 547-550 (4) 62.00 16.90

1987, Sept. 30 ***Perf. 13½***

551 A81 20a Fan-tan 12.00 3.25
552 A81 40a Cussec 12.00 3.25
553 A81 4p Baccarat 12.00 3.25
554 A81 7p Roulette 12.00 3.25
Nos. 551-554 (4) 48.00 13.00

Traditional Transportation — A82

1987, Nov. 18 **Litho.** ***Perf. 13½***

555 A82 10a Market wagon .50 .20
556 A82 70a Sedan chair 2.25 .20
557 A82 90a Rickshaw 4.75 .80
558 A82 10p Tricycle rickshaw 12.50 3.25
Nos. 555-558 (4) 20.00 4.45

Souvenir Sheet

559 A82 7.50p Sedan chair, diff. *52.50*

New Year Type of 1984

1988, Feb. 10 **Litho.** ***Perf. 13½***

560 A60 2.50p Dragon 6.50 1.90
a. Booklet pane of 5 29.00

No. 560a has straight edges.

Wildlife Protection A84

1988, Apr. 14 **Litho.** ***Perf. 12½x12***

561 A84 3p Erinaceus europaeus 6.00 1.75
562 A84 3p Meles meles 6.00 1.75
563 A84 3p Lutra lutra 6.00 1.75
564 A84 3p Manis pentadactyla 6.00 1.75
a. Block or strip of 4, #561-564 32.50 12.00
Nos. 561-564 (4) 24.00 7.00

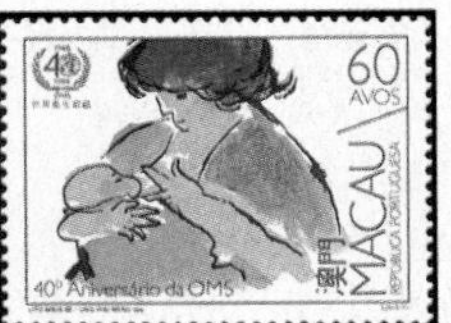

World Health Organization, 40th Anniv. — A85

1988, June 1 **Litho.** ***Perf. 13½***

565 A85 60a Breast-feeding 2.75 .55
566 A85 80a Immunization 4.25 .55
567 A85 2.40p Blood donation 8.50 1.90
Nos. 565-567 (3) 15.50 3.00

Modes of Transportation — A86

1988, July 15 **Litho.**

568 A86 20a Bicycles 1.00 .40
569 A86 50a Vespa, Lambretta 2.00 .80
570 A86 3.30p 1907 Rover 20hp 5.25 1.10
571 A86 5p 1912 Renault delivery truck 7.75 2.40
Nos. 568-571 (4) 16.00 4.70

Souvenir Sheet

572 A86 7.50p 1930s Sedan *62.50*

1988 Summer Olympics, Seoul A87

1988, Sept. 19 **Litho.**

573 A87 40a Hurdles 1.40 .45
574 A87 60a Basketball 2.25 .45
575 A87 1p Soccer 4.00 1.25
576 A87 8p Table tennis 7.75 2.50
Nos. 573-576 (4) 15.40 4.65

Souvenir Sheet

577 Sheet of 5, #573-576, 577a *80.00*
a. A87 5p Tae kwon do *35.00*

World Post Day — A88

35th Macao Grand Prix — A89

1988, Oct. 10 **Litho.** ***Perf. 14***

578 A88 13.40p Electronic mail 5.25 .50
579 A88 40p Express mail 10.50 2.50

1988, Nov. 24 **Litho.** ***Perf. 12½***

580 A89 80a Sedan 1.50 .20
581 A89 2.80p Motorcycle 5.50 .65
582 A89 7p Formula 3 13.00 2.25
a. Souvenir sheet of 3, #580-582 *95.00*
Nos. 580-582 (3) 20.00 3.10

New Year Type of 1984

1989, Jan. 20 **Litho.** ***Perf. 13½***

583 A60 3p Snake 9.50 1.10
a. Booklet pane of 5 40.00

No. 583a has straight edges. Value for No. 583 is for stamp perfed on 4 sides.

Occupations A91

1989, Mar. 1 **Litho.** ***Perf. 12x12½***

584 A91 50a Water carrier .75 .20
585 A91 1p Tan-kya woman 1.75 .45
586 A91 4p Tin-tin (junk) man 3.25 .75
587 A91 5p Tofu peddler 4.75 1.50
Nos. 584-587 (4) 10.50 2.90

See Nos. 612-615, 640-643.

Watercolors by George Smirnoff in the Luis de Camoens Museum — A92

1989, Apr. 10 **Litho.** ***Perf. 12½x12***

588 A92 2p multi (4-1) 2.40 .65
589 A92 2p multi (4-2) 2.40 .65
590 A92 2p multi (4-3) 2.40 .65
591 A92 2p multi (4-4) 2.40 .65
a. Block or strip of 4, #588-591 14.50 2.50
Nos. 588-591 (4) 9.60 2.60

Snakes A93

1989, July 7 **Litho.**

592 A93 2.50p *Naja naja* 4.00 1.10
593 A93 2.50p *Bungarus fasciatus* 4.00 1.10
594 A93 2.50p *Trimeresurus albolabris* 4.00 1.10
595 A93 2.50p *Elaphe radiata* 4.00 1.10
a. Block or strip of 4, #592-595 19.00 4.75
Nos. 592-595 (4) 16.00 4.40

Traditional Games — A94

1989, July 31 **Litho.** ***Perf. 13½***

596 A94 10a Talu .90 .20
597 A94 60a Triol 2.75 .20
598 A94 3.30p Chiquia 5.25 1.10
599 A94 5p Xadrez Chines 7.00 1.90
Nos. 596-599 (4) 15.90 3.40

Airplanes A95

1989, Oct. 9 **Litho.**
600 A95 50a Over church .50 .20
601 A95 70a American over lighthouse 1.00 .20
602 A95 2.80p Over wharf 1.50 .70
603 A95 4p Over junk 3.00 1.00
Nos. 600-603 (4) 6.00 2.10

Souvenir Sheet

604 A95 7.50p Over harbor *35.00* 11.50

No. 604 contains one 40x30mm stamp.

World Stamp Expo '89, Washington, DC — A96

1989, Nov. 17 **Litho.** ***Perf. 12½***
605 A96 40a Malacca .45 .25
606 A96 70a Thailand .90 .25
607 A96 90a India 1.40 .50
608 A96 2.50p Japan 2.25 .65
609 A96 7.50p China 4.50 1.60
Nos. 605-609 (5) 9.50 3.25

Souvenir Sheet

610 Sheet of 6, #605-609, 610a *65.00* 37.50
a. A96 3p Macao *18.00* 18.00

Influence of the Portuguese in the Far East.

New Year Type of 1984

1990, Jan. 19 **Litho.** ***Perf. 13½***
611 A60 4p Horse 4.75 1.40
a. Booklet pane of 5 24.00

No. 611a has straight edges. Value for No. 611 is for stamp perfed on 4 sides.

Occupations Type of 1989

1990, Mar. 1 **Litho.** ***Perf. 12x12½***
612 A91 30a Long chau singer .90 .45
613 A91 70a Cobbler 1.75 .85
614 A91 1.50p Scribe 2.75 .85
615 A91 7.50p Net fisherman 8.00 2.10
Nos. 612-615 (4) 13.40 4.25

Souvenir Sheet

Penny Black, 150th Anniv. — A99

1990, May 3 **Litho.** ***Perf. 12***
616 A99 10p multicolored *40.00 12.50*

Stamp World London 90.

Lutianus Malabaricus — A100

1990, June 8 ***Perf. 12x12½***
617 A100 2.40p shown 2.40 1.10
618 A100 2.40p Epinephelus megachir 2.40 1.10
619 A100 2.40p Macropodus opercularis 2.40 1.10
620 A100 2.40p Ophiocephalus maculatus 2.40 1.10
a. Block or strip of 4, #617-620 16.00 5.25
Nos. 617-620 (4) 9.60 4.40

Decorative Porcelain A101

1990, Aug. 24 **Litho.** ***Perf. 12½***
621 A101 3p shown 2.40 1.10
622 A101 3p Furniture 2.40 1.10
623 A101 3p Toys 2.40 1.10
624 A101 3p Artificial flowers 2.40 1.10
a. Souvenir sheet of 4, #621-624 *40.00 12.50*
b. Block or strip of 4, #621-624 20.00 8.00
Nos. 621-624 (4) 9.60 4.40

Asian Games, Beijing — A102

1990, Sept. 22 **Litho.** ***Perf. 13½***
625 A102 80a Cycling .70 .20
626 A102 1p Swimming 1.25 .30
627 A102 3p Judo 3.50 1.10
628 A102 4.20p Shooting 5.50 1.50
Nos. 625-628 (4) 10.95 3.10

Souvenir Sheet

629 Sheet of 5, #625-628, 629a *47.50 22.50*
a. A102 6p Martial arts *13.00 13.00*

Compass Roses from Portuguese Charts — A103

Charts by 16th century cartographers: Lazaro Luis, Diogo Homem, Fernao Vaz Dourado, and Luiz Teixeira.

1990, Oct. 9 **Litho.** ***Perf. 13½***
630 A103 50a shown .90 .40
631 A103 1p multi, diff. 1.75 .40
632 A103 3.50p multi, diff. 3.50 1.10
633 A103 6.50p multi, diff. 8.00 1.50
Nos. 630-633 (4) 14.15 3.40

Souvenir Sheet

634 A103 5p multi, diff. *62.50 20.00*

Games with Animals A104

1990, Nov. 15 **Litho.** ***Perf. 14***
635 A104 20a Cricket fight .80 .20
636 A104 80a Bird fight 2.40 .60
637 A104 1p Greyhound race 3.00 .85
638 A104 10p Horse race 9.75 1.75
Nos. 635-638 (4) 15.95 3.40

New Year Type of 1984

1991, Feb. 8 **Litho.** ***Perf. 13½***
639 A60 4.50p Sheep 4.75 .95
b. Booklet pane of 5 *32.50*

No. 639b has straight edges.

Occupations Type of 1987

1991, Mar. 1 ***Perf. 14***
640 A91 80a Knife grinder .85 .45
641 A91 1.70p Flour puppet vender 1.75 .45
642 A91 3.50p Street barber 4.25 .90
643 A91 4.20p Fortune teller 6.75 1.75
Nos. 640-643 (4) 13.60 3.55

Shells A106

1991, Apr. 18 **Litho.** ***Perf. 14***
644 A106 3p Murex pecten 3.00 1.40
645 A106 3p Harpa harpa 3.00 1.40
646 A106 3p Chicoreus rosarius 3.00 1.40
647 A106 3p Tonna zonata 3.00 1.40
a. Strip of 4, #644-647 14.50 9.50
Nos. 644-647 (4) 12.00 5.60

Chinese Opera — A107

Various performers in costume.

1991, June 5 **Litho.** ***Perf. 13½***
648 A107 60a multicolored 1.50 .35
649 A107 80a multicolored 2.50 .40
650 A107 1p multicolored 4.00 .95
651 A107 10p multicolored 12.00 2.25
Nos. 648-651 (4) 20.00 3.95

Flowers A108

Designs: 1.70p, Delonix regia. 3p, Ipomoea cairica. 3.50p, Jasminum mesnyi. 4.20p, Bauhinia variegata.

1991, Oct. 9 **Litho.** ***Perf. 13½***
652 A108 1.70p multicolored 1.50 .50
653 A108 3p multicolored 2.25 1.00
654 A108 3.50p multicolored 4.00 1.60
655 A108 4.20p multicolored 5.00 2.25
a. Souvenir sheet of 4, #652-655 *62.50 24.00*
Nos. 652-655 (4) 12.75 5.35

Cultural Exchange A109

Namban screen: No. 656, Unloading boat.

1991, Nov. 16 **Litho.** ***Perf. 12***
656 A109 4.20p multicolored 3.00 .95
657 A109 4.20p shown 3.00 .95
a. Souvenir sheet of 2, #656-657 *35.00 16.00*

Holiday Greetings A110

1991, Nov. 29 **Litho.** ***Perf. 14½***
658 A110 1.70p Lunar New Year 1.25 .35
659 A110 3p Santa Claus, Christmas 1.90 .35
660 A110 3.50p Old man 3.00 .75
661 A110 4.20p Girl at New Year party 6.25 1.50
Nos. 658-661 (4) 12.40 2.95

New Year Type of 1984

1992, Jan. 28 **Litho.** ***Perf. 13½***
662 A60 4.50p Monkey 4.50 1.10
a. Booklet pane of 5 24.00

No. 662a has straight edges.

Paintings of Doors and Windows A111

1992, Mar. 1 ***Perf. 14***
663 A111 1.70p multicolored 1.25 .50
664 A111 3p multi, diff. 2.25 1.25
665 A111 3.50p multi, diff. 3.25 1.25
666 A111 4.20p multi, diff. 4.50 2.00
Nos. 663-666 (4) 11.25 5.00

Mythological Chinese Gods — A112

1992, Apr. 3 **Litho.** ***Perf. 14***
667 A112 3.50p T'it Kuai Lei (4-1) 8.00 3.50
668 A112 3.50p Chong Lei Kun (4-2) 8.00 3.50
669 A112 3.50p Cheong Kuo Lou (4-3) 8.00 3.50
670 A112 3.50p Loi Tong Pan (4-4) 8.00 3.50
a. Block or strip of 4, #667-670 *47.50 24.00*
Nos. 667-670 (4) 32.00 14.00

See Nos. 689-692.

Lion Dance Costume A113

Designs: 2.70p, Lion, diff. 6p, Dragon.

1992, May 18
671 A113 1p multicolored 1.00 .50
672 A113 2.70p multicolored 2.00 .50
673 A113 6p multicolored 3.75 1.00
Nos. 671-673 (3) 6.75 2.00

World Columbian Stamp Expo '92, Chicago.

1992 Summer Olympics, Barcelona — A114

1992, July 1 Litho. *Perf. 13*

674 A114	80a High jump		1.00	.65
675 A114	4.20p Badminton		2.00	.65
676 A114	4.70p Roller hockey		3.00	.80
677 A114	5p Yachting		4.00	2.00
a.	Souvenir sheet of 4, #674-677		*20.00*	*9.50*
	Nos. 674-677 (4)		10.00	4.10

Temples A115

1992, Oct. 9 *Perf. 14*

678 A115	1p Na Cha	.95	.50
679 A115	1.50p Kun Iam	1.40	.50
680 A115	1.70p Hong Kon	1.90	.95
681 A115	6.50p A Ma	3.75	1.90
	Nos. 678-681 (4)	8.00	3.85

See Nos. 685-688.

Portuguese-Chinese Friendship — A116

1992, Nov. 1 Litho. *Perf. 14*

682 A116	10p multicolored	3.25	1.10
a.	Souv. sheet, perf. 13½	*16.00*	*6.50*

Tung Sin Tong Charity Organization, Cent. — A117

1992, Nov. 27 *Perf. 12x11½*

683 A117	1p multicolored	1.75	.40

New Year Type of 1984

1993, Jan. 18 Litho. *Perf. 13½*

684 A60	5p Rooster	3.25	1.40
a.	Booklet pane of 5	17.00	

No. 684a has straight edges.

Temple Type of 1992

1993, Mar. 1 Litho. *Perf. 14*

685 A115	50a T'am Kong	.50	.20
686 A115	2p T'in Hau	1.00	.30
687 A115	3.50p Lin Fong	1.50	.50
688 A115	8p Pau Kong	2.00	1.00
	Nos. 685-688 (4)	5.00	2.00

Mythological Chinese Gods Type of 1992

Designs: No. 689, Lam Ch'oi Wo seated on crane in flight. No. 690, Ho Sin Ku, seated on peach flower.No. 691, Hon Seong Chi throwing peonies from basket. No. 692, Ch'ou Kuok K'ao seated on gold plate.

1993, Apr. 1 Litho. *Perf. 14*

689 A112	3.50p multi (4-1)	*3.50*	*2.00*
690 A112	3.50p multicolored (4-2)	*3.50*	*2.00*
691 A112	3.50p multicolored (4-3)	*3.50*	*2.00*
692 A112	3.50p multicolored (4-4)	*3.50*	*2.00*
a.	Strip of 4, #689-692	*14.00*	*8.00*

Chinese Wedding — A118

#693, Three children celebrating. #694, Bride. #695, Groom. #696, Woman with parasol, person being carried. 8p, Bride & groom.

1993, May 19 *Perf. 14*

693 A118	3p multicolored	*1.60*	*1.25*
694 A118	3p multicolored	*1.60*	*1.25*
695 A118	3p multicolored	*1.60*	*1.25*
696 A118	3p multicolored	*1.60*	*1.25*
a.	Strip of 4, #693-696	*13.00*	*10.50*

Souvenir Sheet

Perf. 14½x14

697 A118	8p multicolored	*14.50*	*11.50*

No. 697 contains one 50x40mm stamp.

World Environment Day — A119

Birds — A120

1993, June 5 Litho. *Perf. 14*

698 A119	1p multicolored	1.75	.55

1993, June 27

699 A120	3p Falco peregrinus	1.60	1.10
700 A120	3p Aquila obrysaetos	1.60	1.10
701 A120	3p Asio otus	1.60	1.10
702 A120	3p Tyto alba	1.60	1.10
a.	Block or strip of 4, #699-702	8.00	5.75
b.	Souvenir sheet of 4, #699-702	*16.00*	*10.00*

Union of Portuguese Speaking Capitals — A121

1993, July 30 Litho. *Perf. 13½*

703 A121	1.50p multicolored	1.25	.65

Portuguese Arrival in Japan, 450th Anniv. A122

50a, Japanese using musket. 3p, Catholic priests. 3.50p, Exchanging items of trade.

1993, Sept. 22 Litho. *Perf. 12x11½*

704 A122	50a multicolored	.60	.20
705 A122	3p multicolored	1.25	.30
706 A122	3.50p multicolored	1.75	.75
	Nos. 704-706 (3)	3.60	1.25

See Portugal Nos. 1964-1966.

Flowers A123

Designs: 1p, Spathodea campanulata. 2p, Tithonia diversifolia. 3p, Rhodomyrtus tomentosa. 8p, Passiflora foetida.

1993, Oct. 9 *Perf. 14½*

707 A123	1p multicolored	.85	.60
708 A123	2p multicolored	1.75	1.00
709 A123	3p multicolored	1.75	1.40
710 A123	8p multicolored	3.50	4.00
a.	Souvenir sheet of 4, #707-710	*20.00*	*12.50*
	Nos. 707-710 (4)	7.85	7.00

Portuguese Ships A124

1993, Nov. 5 Litho. *Perf. 14*

711 A124	1p Caravel	.65	.30
712 A124	2p Round caravel	1.25	.65
713 A124	3.50p Nau	1.25	.75
714 A124	4.50p Galleon	1.90	1.60
a.	Souvenir sheet of 4, #711-714	*10.50*	*6.00*
	Nos. 711-714 (4)	5.05	3.30

Macao Grand Prix, 40th Anniv. A125

1993, Nov. 16 Litho. *Perf. 13½*

715 A125	1.50p Stock car	.65	.65
716 A125	2p Motorcycle	1.25	.65
717 A125	4.50p Formula 1 race car	2.50	1.90
	Nos. 715-717 (3)	4.40	3.20

New Year Type of 1984

1994, Feb. 3 Litho. *Perf. 13½*

718 A60	5p Dog	3.25	1.50
a.	Booklet pane of 5	20.00	

New Year 1994 (Year of the Dog). No. 718a has straight edges.

Prince Henry the Navigator (1394-1460) — A126

1994, Mar. 4 Litho. *Perf. 12*

719 A126	3p multicolored	2.40	1.10

See Portugal No. 1987.

Scenes of Macao, by George Chinnery (1774-1852) — A127

Designs: No. 720, Hut, natives. No. 721, S. Tiago Fortress. No. 722, Overview of Praia Grande. No. 723, S. Francisco Church.

1994, Mar. 21 *Perf. 14*

720 A127	3.50p multi (4-1)	1.75	1.00
721 A127	3.50p multi (4-2)	1.75	1.00
722 A127	3.50p multi (4-3)	1.75	1.00
723 A127	3.50p multi (4-4)	1.75	1.00
a.	Block or strip of 4, #720-723	5.50	3.25
b.	Souvenir sheet of 4, #720-723	*16.00*	*9.00*

Spring Festival of New Lunar Year A128

Designs: 1p, Girl, woman shopping. 2p, Celebration. 3.50p, Couple preparing food at table. 4.50p, Old man making decorations.

1994, Apr. 6

724 A128	1p multicolored	.50	.25
725 A128	2p multicolored	1.00	.50
726 A128	3.50p multicolored	1.00	.60
727 A128	4.50p multicolored	1.75	1.25
	Nos. 724-727 (4)	4.25	2.60

Mythological Chinese Gods — A129

Statuettes: No. 728, Happiness. No. 729. Prosperity. No. 730, Longevity.

1994, May 9 Litho. *Perf. 12*

728 A129	3p multi (3-1)	*3.00*	*1.75*
729 A129	3p multi (3-2)	*3.00*	*1.75*
730 A129	3p multi (3-3)	*3.00*	*1.75*
a.	Strip of 3, #728-730	*9.00*	*4.00*
b.	Souvenir sheet of 3, #728-730	*14.50*	*6.50*

A130

A131

1994 World Cup Soccer Championships, US: Various soccer players.

1994, June 1

731 A130	2p multicolored	.75	.60
732 A130	3p multicolored	1.10	.85
733 A130	3.50p multicolored	1.40	1.00
734 A130	4.50p multicolored	1.75	1.40
a.	Souvenir sheet of 4, #731-734	*14.50*	*8.00*
	Nos. 731-734 (4)	5.00	3.85

1994, June 27 Litho. *Perf. 12*

Traditional Chinese shops.

735 A131	1p Rice shop	.55	.25
736 A131	1.50p Medicinal drink shop	.85	.40
737 A131	2p Salt fish shop	1.25	.55
738 A131	3.50p Pharmacy	2.10	.95
	Nos. 735-738 (4)	4.75	2.15

Navigation Instruments
A132

1994, Sept. 13 Litho. *Perf. 12*

739 A132 3p Astrolabe 1.25 .80
740 A132 3.50p Quadrant 1.40 .95
741 A132 4.50p Sextant 1.75 1.25
Nos. 739-741 (3) 4.40 3.00

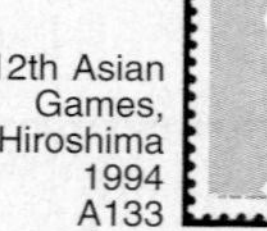

12th Asian Games, Hiroshima 1994
A133

1994, Sept. 30 Litho. *Perf. 12*

742 A133 1p Fencing .40 .30
743 A133 2p Gymnastics .85 .55
744 A133 3p Water polo 1.25 .80
745 A133 3.50p Pole vault 1.50 .95
Nos. 742-745 (4) 4.00 2.60

Bridges
A134

1994, Oct. 8

746 A134 1p Nobre de Carvalho .50 .35
747 A134 8p Friendship 2.75 2.40

Fortune Symbols — A135

Designs: 3p, Child, carp, water lily. 3.50p, Basket of peaches, child, bats. 4.50p, Flower, child playing mouth organ.

1994, Nov. 7 Litho. *Perf. 12*

748 A135 3p multicolored 1.50 1.00
749 A135 3.50p multicolored 1.65 1.25
750 A135 4.50p multicolored 2.25 1.50
Nos. 748-750 (3) 5.40 3.75

Religious Art — A136

Designs: 50a, Stained glass, angel's head. 1p, Stained glass, Holy Ghost. 1.50p, Silver sacrarium. 2p, Silver salver. 3p, Ivory sculpture, Escape to Egypt. 3.50p, Gold & silver chalice.

1994, Nov. 30

751 A136 50a multicolored .20 .20
752 A136 1p multicolored .40 .25
753 A136 1.50p multicolored .65 .40
754 A136 2p multicolored .90 .55
755 A136 3p multicolored 1.25 .80
756 A136 3.50p multicolored 1.50 .95
Nos. 751-756 (6) 4.90 3.15

New Year Type of 1984

1995, Jan. 23 Litho. *Perf. 13½*

757 A60 5.50p Boar 3.00 1.50
a. Booklet pane of 5 20.00

Tourism
A138

Scenes of Macao, by Lio Man Cheong: 50a, Walkway beside pond. 1p, Lighthouse. 1.50p, Temple. 2p, Buildings along coast. 2.50p, Columns, temple. 3p, Ruins on hill overlooking city. 3.50p, Bridge. 4p, Trees in park.

1995, Mar. 1 Litho. *Perf. 12*

758 A138 50a multicolored .25 .20
759 A138 1p multicolored .50 .30
760 A138 1.50p multicolored .65 .40
761 A138 2p multicolored .90 .55
762 A138 2.50p multicolored 1.10 .65
763 A138 3p multicolored 1.25 .80
764 A138 3.50p multicolored 1.50 .95
765 A138 4p multicolored 1.75 1.10
Nos. 758-765 (8) 7.90 4.95

World Day of the Consumer
A139

1995, Mar. 15

766 A139 1p multicolored 1.00 .30

Asian Pangolin — A140

1995, Apr. 10

767 A140 1.50p Facing left (4-1) *2.25* .50
768 A140 1.50p Hanging by tail (4-2) *2.25* .50
769 A140 1.50p On tree limb (4-3) *2.25* .50
770 A140 1.50p On tree stump (4-4) *2.25* .50
a. Block or strip of 4, #767-770 *9.50* 6.50

World wildlife Fund.
Issued in sheets of 16 stamps.

Legend of Buddhist Goddess Kun Iam — A141

#772, Seated atop dragon, holding flower. #773, Meditating. #774, Holding infant.
8p, Goddess with many faces, hands.

1995, May 5 Litho. *Perf. 12*

771 A141 3p multicolored 3.00 .80
772 A141 3p multicolored 3.00 .80
773 A141 3p multicolored 3.00 .80
774 A141 3p multicolored 3.00 .80
a. Block or strip of 4, #771-774 14.50 11.00

Souvenir Sheet

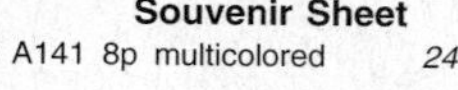

775 A141 8p multicolored *24.00 19.00*

Senado Square — A142

Designs: No. 776, Street, bell tower. No. 777, Street, plaza, shops. No. 778, Fountain, plaza. No. 779, Plaza, buildings.
8p, Bell tower, building, horiz.

1995, June 24 Litho. *Perf. 12*

776 A142 2p multicolored 1.25 .65
777 A142 2p multicolored 1.25 .65
778 A142 2p multicolored 1.25 .65
779 A142 2p multicolored 1.25 .65
a. Strip of 4, #776-779 5.00 2.75

Souvenir Sheet

780 A142 8p multicolored 12.50 7.50

Temple Type of 1992

1995, July 17 Litho. *Perf. 12*

781 A115 50a Kuan Tai .20 .20
782 A115 1p Pak Tai .40 .25
783 A115 1.50p Lin K'ai .65 .40
784 A115 3p Sek Kam Tong 1.25 .80
785 A115 3.50p Fok Tak 1.60 .95
Nos. 781-785 (5) 4.10 2.60

Singapore '95 — A143

Birds: No. 786, Gurrulax canorus. No. 787, Serinus canarius. No. 788, Zosterops japonica. No. 789, Leiothrix lutea. 10p, Copsychus saularis.

1995, Sept. 1 Litho. *Perf. 12*

786 A143 2.50p multicolored 2.25 .65
787 A143 2.50p multicolored 2.25 .65
788 A143 2.50p multicolored 2.25 .65
789 A143 2.50p multicolored 2.25 .65
a. Strip of 4, #786-789 9.00 2.60

Souvenir Sheet

790 A143 10p multicolored *20.00 11.00*

Intl. Music Festival — A144

1995, Oct. 9 Litho. *Perf. 12*

791 A144 1p Pipa (6-1) 1.50 .35
792 A144 1p Erhu (6-2) 1.50 .35
793 A144 1p Gongo (6-3) 1.50 .35
794 A144 1p Sheng (6-4) 1.50 .35
795 A144 1p Xiao (6-5) 1.50 .35
796 A144 1p Tambor (6-6) 1.50 .35
a. Block of 6, #791-796 12.00 3.00

Souvenir Sheet

797 A144 8p Musicians, horiz. *12.00 6.00*

UN, 50th Anniv.
A145

1995, Oct. 24 Litho. *Perf. 12*

798 A145 4.50p multicolored 1.75 1.25

Macao Intl. Airport
A146

Designs: 1p, Airplane above terminal. 1.50p, Boeing 747 on ground, terminal. 2p, Hangars, 747 with boarding ramp at door. 3p, Airplane, control tower. 8p, Boeing 747 over runway.

1995, Dec. 8 Litho. *Perf. 12*

799 A146 1p multicolored .50 .25
800 A146 1.50p multicolored .80 .40
801 A146 2p multicolored 1.00 .50
802 A146 3p multicolored 1.50 .75
Nos. 799-802 (4) 3.80 1.90

Souvenir Sheet

Perf. 12½

803 A146 8p multicolored *14.50 7.25*

No. 803 contains one 51x38mm stamp.

New Year Type of 1984
Miniature Sheet of 12

Designs: a, like #485. b, like #504. c, like #522. d, like #540. e, like #560. f, like #583. g, like #611. h, like #639. i, like #662. j, like #684. k, like #718. l, like #757.

1995, Dec. 15 Litho. *Perf. 13½*

804 A60 1.50p #a.-l. + label *20.00 6.50*

New Year 1996 (Year of the Rat)
A147

1996, Feb. 12 Litho. *Perf. 12*

805 A147 5p multicolored 4.75 1.25

Souvenir Sheet

806 A147 10p like No. 805 *12.00* 7.50

Traditional Chinese Bird Cages — A148

Various styles.

1996, Mar. 1 Litho. *Perf. 12*

807 A148 1p multi (4-1) .35 .25
808 A148 1.50p multi (4-2) .55 .40
809 A148 3p multi (4-3) 1.00 .75
810 A148 4.50p multi (4-4) 1.60 1.10
Nos. 807-810 (4) 3.50 2.50

Souvenir Sheet

811 A148 10p purple & multi *16.00* 6.50

Paintings, by Herculano Estorninho
A149

Scenes of Macao: 50a, Boats. 1.50p, Street, buildings at night, vert. 3p, Fronts of buildings during day, vert. 5p, Townhouse complex.
10p, Entrance to building, vert.

1996, Apr. 1

812 A149 50a multi (4-1) .20 .20
813 A149 1.50p multi (4-2) .65 .45
814 A149 3p multi (4-3) 1.10 .85
815 A149 5p multi (4-4) 2.00 1.40
Nos. 812-815 (4) 3.95 2.90

Souvenir Sheet

816 A149 10p multi *9.50* 4.00

Myths and Legends — A150

Designs: No. 817, Man holding staff. No. 818, Man riding tiger. No. 819, Man on top of fireplace.

1996, Apr. 30 Litho. *Perf. 12*

817 A150 3.50p Tou Tei (3-1) 1.40 .90
818 A150 3.50p Choi San (3-2) 1.40 .90
819 A150 3.50p Chou Kuan (3-3) 1.40 .90
a. Strip of 3, #817-819 4.75 4.75
b. Souvenir sheet of 3, #817-819 *14.50* 4.75

Traditional Chinese Tea Houses A151

Designs: No. 820, Two men seated at table. No. 821, Cook holding steaming tray of food, woman, baby. No. 822, Woman holding up papers. No. 823, Waiter pouring tea, man seated.
8p, Food, serving bowl.

1996, May 17 *Perf. 12*

820 A151 2p multi (4-1) 1.60 .55
821 A151 2p multi (4-2) 1.60 .55
822 A151 2p multi (4-3) 1.60 .55
823 A151 2p multi (4-4) 1.60 .55
a. Block of 4, #820-823 6.50 2.25

Souvenir Sheet

824 A151 8p multi *13.00* 3.25

No. 823a is a continuous design. China '96 (#824).

Greetings Stamps A152

Designs: 50a, Get well. 1.50p, Congratulations on new baby. 3p, Happy birthday. 4p, Marriage congratulations.

1996, June 14 Litho. *Perf. 12*

825 A152 50a multi (4-1) .20 .20
826 A152 1.50p multi (4-2) .65 .40
827 A152 3p multi (4-3) 1.25 .75
828 A152 4p multi (4-4) 1.60 1.00
Nos. 825-828 (4) 3.70 2.35

1996 Summer Olympic Games, Atlanta A153

1996, July 19

829 A153 2p Swimming (4-1) .50 .35
830 A153 3p Soccer (4-2) .80 .55
831 A153 3.50p Gymnastics (4-3) .90 .60
832 A153 4.50p Sailboarding (4-4) 1.10 .80
Nos. 829-832 (4) 3.30 2.30

Souvenir Sheet

833 A153 10p Boxing *8.75* 3.50

Civil and Military Emblems A154

#834, Bird looking left. #835, Dragon. #836, Bird looking right. #837, Leopard.

1996, Sept. 18

834 A154 2.50p bl & multi (4-1) 1.50 .75
835 A154 2.50p grn & multi (4-2) 1.50 .75
836 A154 2.50p grn & multi (4-3) 1.50 .75
837 A154 2.50p pur & multi (4-4) 1.50 .75
a. Block of 4, #834-837 6.50 3.25

See Nos. 947-951.

Fishing with Nets — A155

Boats, fish in sea: No. 838, Six small nets extended from mast of boat. No. 839, Modern trawler. No. 840, Junk trawling. No. 841, Sailboat with nets extended from both sides.

1996, Oct. 9 Litho. *Perf. 12*

838 A155 3p multi (4-1) 1.60 1.10
839 A155 3p multi (4-2) 1.60 1.10
840 A155 3p multi (4-3) 1.60 1.10
841 A155 3p multi (4-4) 1.60 1.10
a. Strip of 4, #838-841 6.50 5.25

Legislative Assembly, 20th Anniv. — A156

1996, Oct. 15 Litho. *Perf. 12x12½*

842 A156 2.80p multicolored .95 .60

Souvenir Sheet

843 A156 8p like No. 842 *12.00* 6.00

Paper Kites A157

1996, Oct. 21 Litho. *Perf. 12*

844 A157 3.50p Dragonfly (4-1) 1.60 1.00
845 A157 3.50p Butterfly (4-2) 1.60 1.00
846 A157 3.50p Owl in flight (4-3) 1.60 1.00
847 A157 3.50p Standing owl (4-4) 1.60 1.00
a. Block of 4, #844-847 9.00 6.50

Souvenir Sheet

Perf. 12½

848 A157 8p Dragon *12.00* 9.00

No. 848 contains one 51x38mm stamp.

Traditional Chinese Toys — A158

1996, Nov. 13 Litho. *Perf. 12*

849 A158 50a shown .20 .20
850 A158 1p Fish 1.25 .65
851 A158 3p Doll 4.00 2.25
852 A158 4.50p Dragon 5.75 3.50
Nos. 849-852 (4) 11.20 6.60

New Year 1997 (Year of the Ox) A159

1997, Jan. 23 Litho. *Perf. 12*

853 A159 5.50p multicolored *3.25* *2.10*

Souvenir Sheet

854 A159 10p multicolored *9.50* *6.25*

No. 854 is a continuous design.

Lucky Numbers A160

1996 Litho. *Perf. 12*

855 A160 2p "2," Simplicity .70 .50
856 A160 2.80p "8," Prosperity .90 .60
857 A160 3p "3," Progress 1.00 .65
858 A160 3.90p "9," Longevity 1.40 1.00
Nos. 855-858 (4) 4.00 2.75

Souvenir Sheet

859 A160 9p Man outside house *6.00* *4.00*

Hong Kong '97 (#859).

Paintings of Macao, by Kwok Se — A161

2p, Junks. 3p, Fortress on side of mountain. 3.50p, Retreat house. 4.50p, Cerco Gate.
8p, Rooftop of building, horiz.

1997, Mar. 1 Litho. *Perf. 12*

860 A161 2p multicolored .65 .65
861 A161 3p multicolored 1.25 1.25
862 A161 3.50p multicolored 1.60 1.60
863 A161 4.50p multicolored 2.00 2.00
Nos. 860-863 (4) 5.50 5.50

Souvenir Sheet

864 A161 8p multicolored 8.00 6.25

A162

A163

Boat People: 1p, Old woman seated. 1.50p, Woman wearing hat. 2.50p, Woman carrying baby. 5.50p, Man, boy.

1997, Mar. 26 Litho. *Perf. 12*

865 A162 1p multicolored .60 .40
866 A162 1.50p multicolored .70 .50
867 A162 2.50p multicolored 1.10 .80
868 A162 5.50p multicolored 2.60 1.75
a. Block of 4, #865-868 5.00 4.00

1997, Apr. 29 Litho. *Perf. 12*

Temple A-Ma: No. 869, Steps leading to entrance. No. 870, People strolling past temple, one with umbrella. No. 871, People outside pagoda, pedicab. No. 872, Towers from temple, one emiting smoke.

869 A163 3.50p multicolored .60 .40
870 A163 3.50p multicolored .60 .40
871 A163 3.50p multicolored .60 .40
872 A163 3.50p multicolored .60 .40
a. Strip of 4, #869-872 3.25 3.25

Souvenir Sheet

873 A163 8p Boat *4.75* *4.75*

Drunken Dragon Festival — A164

Stylized designs: 2p, Two men, one holding dragon. 3p, Man holding up dragon. 5p, Two men, one holding horn.
9p, Dragon, man, horiz.

1997, May 14

874 A164 2p multicolored .75 .75
875 A164 3p multicolored 1.10 1.10
876 A164 5p multicolored 1.75 1.75
a. Strip of 3, #874-876 3.50 3.50

Souvenir Sheet

877 A164 9p multicolored *5.00* *5.00*

Father Luís Fróis, 400th Death Anniv. A165

No. 879, Father Fróis, cathedral, vert.

1997, June 9 Litho. *Perf. 12*

878 A165 2.50p multi (2-1) .65 .65
879 A165 2.50p multi (2-2) .65 .65

See Portugal Nos. 2165-2167.

Legends and Myths — A166

Gods of Protection: #880, Wat Lot. #881, San Su. #882, Chon Keng. #883, Wat Chi Kong.
10p, Chon Keng and Wat Chi Kong.

1997, June 18 Litho. *Perf. 12*

880 A166 2.50p multicolored .60 .60
881 A166 2.50p multicolored .60 .60
882 A166 2.50p multicolored .60 .60
883 A166 2.50p multicolored .60 .60
a. Block of 4, #880-883 3.00 3.00
Nos. 880-883 (4) 2.40 2.40

Souvenir Sheet

884 A166 10p multicolored 4.00 4.00

No. 884 contains one 40x40mm stamp.

Macao Red Cross, 77th Anniv. — A167

1997, July 12 *Perf. 12½*

885 A167 1.50p multicolored .40 .40

No. 885 is printed se-tenant with label.

Verandas A168

Various architectural styles.
8p, Close up of veranda, vert.

1997, July 30 Litho. *Perf. 12*

No.	Type	Description	Unused	Used
886	A168	50a multi (6-1)	.20	.20
887	A168	1p multi (6-2)	.25	.25
888	A168	1.50p multi (6-3)	.40	.40
889	A168	2p multi (6-4)	.50	.50
890	A168	2.50p multi (6-5)	.65	.65
891	A168	3p multi (6-6)	.75	.75
a.		Block of 6, #886-891	2.75	2.75

Souvenir Sheet

No.	Type	Description	Unused	Used
892	A168	8p multicolored	2.10	2.10

Traditional Chinese Fans — A169

Fong Soi (Chinese Geomancy) A170

1997, Sept. 24 Litho. *Perf. 12*

No.	Type	Description	Unused	Used
893	A169	50a Planta (4-1)	.20	.20
894	A169	1p Papel (4-2)	.25	.25
895	A169	3.50p Seda (4-3)	.95	.95
896	A169	4p Pluma (4-4)	1.10	1.10
a.		Block of 4, #893-896	2.40	2.40

Souvenir Sheet

No.	Type	Description	Unused	Used
897	A169	9p Sandalo	5.00	4.00

1997, Oct. 9 Litho. *Perf. 12*

Chinese principles of Yin and Yang related to the five elements of the ancient Zodiac.

No.	Type	Description	Unused	Used
898	A170	50a green & multi	.20	.20
899	A170	1p orange & multi	.30	.30
900	A170	1.50p brown & multi	.45	.45
901	A170	2p yellow & multi	.60	.60
902	A170	2.50p blue & multi	.70	.70
a.		Strip of 5, #898-902	2.25	2.25

Souvenir Sheet

No.	Type	Description	Unused	Used
903	A170	10p green & multi	4.00	4.00

Martial Arts — A171

1997, Nov. 19

No.	Type	Description	Unused	Used
904	A171	1.50p Kung Fu	.40	.40
905	A171	3.50p Judo	.95	.95
906	A171	4p Karate	1.10	1.10
a.		Strip of 3, #904-906	2.40	2.40

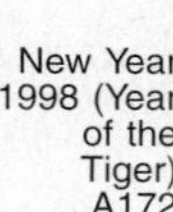

New Year 1998 (Year of the Tiger) A172

1998, Jan. 18 Litho. *Perf. 12*

No.	Type	Description	Unused	Used
907	A172	5.50p multicolored	1.50	1.50

Souvenir Sheets

No.	Type	Description	Unused	Used
908	A172	10p multicolored	3.25	3.25
a.		Ovptd. in sheet margin	3.25	3.25

No. 908 is a continuous design.

No. 908a overprinted in Gold in Sheet Margin with "Amizade Luso-Chinesa / Festival de Macao" & Chinese Text.

Street Vendors A173

Vendors at stands, carts: No. 909, 1p, Frying foods. 1.50p, Food products, eggs. 2p, Clothing items. 2.50p, Balloons. 3p, Flowers. 3.50p, Fruits and vegetables.
6p, Vendor at fruit and vegetable stand, diff.

1998, Feb. 13 Litho. *Perf. 12*

No.	Type	Description	Unused	Used
909	A173	1p multi (6-1)	.25	.25
910	A173	1.50p multi (6-2)	.40	.40
911	A173	2p multi (6-3)	.55	.55
912	A173	2.50p multi (6-4)	.65	.65
913	A173	3p multi (6-5)	.80	.80
914	A173	3.50p multi (6-6)	.95	.95
a.		Block of 6, #909-914	3.60	3.60

Souvenir Sheets

No.	Type	Description	Unused	Used
915	A173	6p multicolored	2.00	2.00
a.		Ovptd. in sheet margin	2.00	2.00

No. 915a overprinted in Gold in Sheet Margin with "Amizade Luso-Chinesa / Festival de Macao" & Chinese Text.

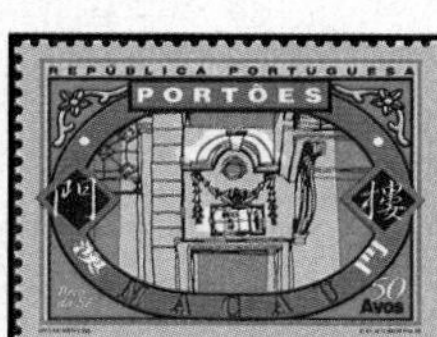

Traditional Gates A174

Inscriptions: 50a, "Beco da Sé." 1p, "Pátio da Ilusao." 3.50p, "Travessa da galinhas." 4p, "Beco das Felicidades."
9p, "Seminário d S. José," vert.

1998, Mar. 1

No.	Type	Description	Unused	Used
916	A174	50a multi (4-1)	.20	.20
917	A174	1p multi (4-2)	.25	.25
918	A174	3.50p multi (4-3)	.95	.95
919	A174	4p multi (4-4)	1.10	1.10
		Nos. 916-919 (4)	2.50	2.50

Souvenir Sheets

No.	Type	Description	Unused	Used
920	A174	9p multicolored	2.40	2.40
a.		Ovptd. in sheet margin	2.40	2.40

No. 920a overprinted in Gold in Sheet Margin with "Amizade Luso-Chinesa / Festival de Macao" & Chinese Text.

Myths and Legends — A175

Gods of Ma Chou: No. 921, Holding baby. No. 922, Watching image appear in smoke. No. 923, With cherubs. No. 924, Hovering over junks.
10p, Face.

1998, Apr. 23 Litho. *Perf. 12*

No.	Type	Description	Unused	Used
921	A175	4p multi (4-1)	1.10	1.10
922	A175	4p multi (4-2)	1.10	1.10
923	A175	4p multi (4-3)	1.10	1.10
924	A175	4p multi (4-4)	1.10	1.10
a.		Strip of 4, #921-924	4.40	4.40

Souvenir Sheets

No.	Type	Description	Unused	Used
925	A175	10p multicolored	2.60	2.60
a.		Ovptd. in sheet margin	2.60	2.60

No. 925a overprinted in Gold in Sheet Margin with "Amizade Luso-Chinesa / Festival de Macao" & Chinese Text.

Voyage to India by Vasco da Gama, 500th Anniv. A176

Designs: 1p, Sailing ship. 1.50p, Vasco da Gama. 2p, Map, sailing ship.
8p, Compass rose.

1998, May 20 Litho. *Perf. 12*

No.	Type	Description	Unused	Used
926	A176	1p multi (3-1)	*.40*	*.40*
927	A176	1.50p multi (3-2)	*.70*	*.70*
928	A176	2p multi (3-3)	*.90*	*.90*
a.		Strip of 3, #926-928	*2.00*	*2.00*

Souvenir Sheet

No.	Type	Description	Unused	Used
929	A176	8p multicolored	*3.75*	*3.75*

Nos. 926-929 are inscribed "1598" instead of "1498," and were withdrawn after two days. For corrected version, see Nos. 943-946.

Oceans A177

Stylized designs: 2.50p, Mermaid, shells, sailing ship, compass rose. 3p, Compass rose, fish, oil derrick.
9p, Sailing ship, seagull, fish, cloud, sun.

1998, May 22

No.	Type	Description	Unused	Used
930	A177	2.50p multi (2-1)	.65	.65
931	A177	3p multi (2-2)	.75	.75
a.		Pair, #930-931	1.40	1.40

Souvenir Sheets

No.	Type	Description	Unused	Used
932	A177	9p multicolored	2.25	2.25
a.		Ovptd. in sheet margin	2.25	2.25

No. 932a overprinted in Gold in Sheet Margin with "Amizade Luso-Chinesa / Festival de Macao" & Chinese Text.

1998 World Cup Soccer Championships, France — A178

Various soccer plays.

1998, June 10 Litho. *Perf. 12*

No.	Type	Description	Unused	Used
933	A178	3p multicolored	.80	.80
934	A178	3.50p multicolored	.95	.95
935	A178	4p multicolored	1.00	1.00
936	A178	4.50p multicolored	1.25	1.25
		Nos. 933-936 (4)	4.00	4.00

Souvenir Sheets

No.	Type	Description	Unused	Used
937	A178	9p multicolored	2.75	2.75
a.		Ovptd. in sheet margin	3.00	3.00

No. 937a overprinted in Gold in Sheet Margin with "Amizade Luso-Chinesa / Festival de Macao" & Chinese Text.

Chinese Opera Masks A179

1998, July 28 Litho. *Perf. 12*

No.	Type	Description	Unused	Used
938	A179	1.50p Lio, Seak Chong (4-1)	.40	.40
939	A179	2p Wat, Chi Kong (4-2)	.55	.55
940	A179	3p Kam, Chin Pao (4-3)	.80	.80
941	A179	5p Lei, Kwai (4-4)	1.25	1.25
a.		Strip of 4, #938-941	3.00	3.00

Souvenir Sheets

No.	Type	Description	Unused	Used
942	A179	8p Masked player	2.25	2.25
a.		Ovptd. in sheet margin	2.25	2.25

No. 942a overprinted in Gold in Sheet Margin with "Amizade Luso-Chinesa / Festival de Macao" & Chinese Text.

Vasco da Gama Type of 1998 Inscribed "1498"

1998, Sept. 4 Litho. *Perf. 12*

No.	Type	Description	Unused	Used
943	A176	1p like #926	.35	.35
944	A176	1.50p like #927	.60	.60
945	A176	2p like #928	.80	.80
a.		Strip of 3, #943-945	1.90	1.90

Souvenir Sheets

No.	Type	Description	Unused	Used
946	A176	8p like #929	2.25	2.25
a.		Ovptd. in sheet margin	2.25	2.25

Issued to correct the error on #926-929.

No. 946a overprinted in Gold in Sheet Margin with "Amizade Luso-Chinesa / Festival de Macao" & Chinese Text.

Civil and Military Emblems Type of 1996

Designs: 50a, Lion. 1p, Dragon. 1.50p, Bird looking right. 2p, Bird looking left.
9p, Bird flying.

1998, Sept. 9

No.	Type	Description	Unused	Used
947	A154	50a multi (4-1)	.20	.20
948	A154	1p multi (4-2)	.30	.30
949	A154	1.50p multi (4-3)	.45	.45
950	A154	2p multi (4-4)	.65	.65
a.		Strip of 4, #947-950	1.50	1.50

Souvenir Sheets

No.	Type	Description	Unused	Used
951	A154	9p multicolored	2.50	2.50
a.		Ovptd. in sheet margin	2.50	2.50

No. 951a overprinted in Gold in Sheet Margin with "Amizade Luso-Chinesa / Festival de Macao" & Chinese Text.

Kun Iam Temple A180

Scenes inside temple compound: No. 952, Buddha figure standing. No. 953, Entrance gate, man running, benches. No. 954, Entrance to building, people. No. 955, People, stream, pagoda, flowers.
10p, Table, chairs, top of incense burner.

1998 Litho. *Perf. 12*

No.	Type	Description	Unused	Used
952	A180	3.50p multicolored	.90	.90
953	A180	3.50p multicolored	.90	.90
954	A180	3.50p multicolored	.90	.90
955	A180	3.50p multicolored	.90	.90
a.		Block of 4, #952-955	3.60	3.60

Souvenir Sheets

No.	Type	Description	Unused	Used
956	A180	10p multicolored	2.50	2.50
a.		Ovptd. in sheet margin	2.50	2.50

No. 956a overprinted in Gold in Sheet Margin with "Amizade Luso-Chinesa / Festival de Macao" & Chinese Text.

Paintings of Macao, by Didier Rafael Bayle A181

Designs: 2p, Street scene, buggy, vert. 3p, People standing outside of buildings. 3.50p, Building atop wall. 4.50p, Buildings, house along street, vert.
8p, Top of building.

1998, Nov. 11 Litho. *Perf. 12*

No.	Type	Description	Unused	Used
957	A181	2p multi (4-1)	.50	.50
958	A181	3p multi (4-2)	.75	.75
959	A181	3.50p multi (4-3)	.90	.90
960	A181	4.50p multi (4-4)	1.10	1.10
		Nos. 957-960 (4)	3.25	3.25

Souvenir Sheets

No.	Type	Description	Unused	Used
961	A181	8p multicolored	2.25	2.25
a.		Ovptd. in sheet margin	2.25	2.25

No. 961a overprinted in Gold in Sheet Margin with "Amizade Luso-Chinesa / Festival de Macao" & Chinese Text.

Tiles A182

Designs: 1p, Dragon. 1.50p, Sailing ship. 2.50p, Chinese junk. 5.50p, Peacock.
10p, Building, lighthouse.

1998, Dec. 8

No.	Type	Description	Unused	Used
962	A182	1p multi (4-1)	.25	.25
963	A182	1.50p multi (4-2)	.40	.40
964	A182	2.50p multi (4-3)	.65	.65

965 A182 5.50p multi (4-4) 1.40 1.40
a. Block of 4, #962-965 2.75 2.75

Souvenir Sheets

966 A182 10p multicolored 6.50 6.50
a. Ovptd. in sheet margin 6.50 6.50

No. 966a overprinted in Gold in Sheet Margin with "Amizade Luso-Chinesa / Festival de Macao" & Chinese Text.

New Year 1999 (Year of the Rabbit) A183

1999, Feb. 8 Litho. *Perf. 12*

967 A183 5.50p multicolored 1.40 1.40

Souvenir Sheet

968 A183 10p multicolored 2.75 2.75
a. Ovptd. in sheet margin 2.75 2.75

No. 968 is a continuous design.
No. 968a overprinted in gold in sheet margin with "Amizade Luso-Chinesa / Transferencia da Soberania de / MACAU 1999 / Sichuan Chengdu," dates and Chinese text.

Characters from Novel, "Dream of the Red Mansion," by Cao Xuequin — A184

1999, Mar. 1 Litho. *Perf. 12*

969 A184 2p Bao Yu (6-1) .55 .55
970 A184 2p Dayiu (6-2) .55 .55
971 A184 2p Bao Chai (6-3) .55 .55
972 A184 2p Xi Feng (6-4) .55 .55
973 A184 2p San Jie (6-5) .55 .55
974 A184 2p Qing Wen (6-6) .55 .55
a. Block of 6, #969-974 3.25 3.25

Souvenir Sheet

975 A184 8p Bao Yu & Dayiu 2.25 2.25
a. Ovptd. in sheet margin 2.25 2.25

No. 975a overprinted in gold in sheet margin with "Amizade Luso-Chinesa / Transferencia da Soberania de / MACAU 1999 / Sichuan Chengdu," dates and Chinese text.

Maritime Heritage A185

1999, Mar. 19 Litho. *Perf. 12*

976 A185 1.50p Sailing ships .50 .50
977 A185 2.50p Marine life .70 .70
a. Pair, #976-977 1.25 1.25

Souvenir Sheet

978 A185 6p Whale, vert. 1.60 1.60
a. Ovptd. in sheet margin 1.60 1.60

Australia '99, World Stamp Expo.
No. 978a overprinted in gold in sheet margin with "Amizade Luso-Chinesa / Transferencia da Soberania de / MACAU 1999 / Sichuan Chengdu," dates and Chinese text.

First Portugal-Macao Flight, 75th Anniv. — A186

Airplanes: No. 979, Breguet 16 Bn2, "Patria." No. 980, DH9.

1999, Apr. 19 Litho. *Perf. 12*

979 A186 3p multicolored .95 .95
980 A186 3p multicolored .95 .95
a. Souvenir sheet, #979-980 2.00 2.00
b. As "a," ovptd. in sheet margin 2.25 2.25

See Portugal Nos. 2289-2290.
No. 980a is a continuous design.
No. 980b overprinted in gold in sheet margin with "Amizade Luso-Chinesa / Transferencia da Soberania de / MACAU 1999 / Sichuan Chengdu," dates and Chinese text.

A187

A188

Traditional Water Carrier: a, 1p, Woman carrying container (4-1). b, 1.50p, Filling container from pump (4-2). c, 2p, Drawing water from well (4-3). d, 2.50p, Filling containers from faucet (4-4).
7p, Woman carrying containers up stairs.

1999, Apr. 28 *Perf. 12*

Horiz. Strip or Block of 4

981 A187 #a.-d. 2.00 2.00

Souvenir Sheet

982 A187 7p multicolored 1.90 1.90
a. Ovptd. in sheet margin 1.90 1.90

No. 981 was issued in sheets of 4 strips or blocks, each in a different order.
No. 982a overprinted in gold in sheet margin with "Amizade Luso-Chinesa / Transferencia de Soberania de / MACAU 1999 / China Shanghai," date and Chinese text.

1999, May 5 Litho. *Perf. 12*

Telecommunications — #983: a, 50a, Sea-Me-We cable. b, 1p, Satellite dishes. c, 3.50p, Cellular phones. d, 4p, Television. e, 4.50p, Internet.
8p, Computer mouse.

983 A188 Strip of 5, #a.-e. 3.50 3.50

Souvenir Sheet

984 A188 8p multi 2.25 2.25
a. Ovptd. in sheet margin 2.25 2.25

No. 984 has a holographic image. Soaking in water may affect hologram.
No. 984a is overprinted in gold in sheet margin with "Amizade Luso-Chinesa / Transferencia de Soberania de / MACAU 1999 / China Shanghai," date and Chinese text.

Modern Buildings, Construction — A189

1p, Cultural Center. 1.50p, Museum of Macao. 2p, Maritime Museum. 2.50p, Maritime Terminal. 3p, University of Macao. 3.50p, Public Administration Building. 4.50p, World Trade Center. 5p, Coloane Go-kart Track. 8p, Bank of China. 12p, Ultramarine National Bank.

1999, June 2 Litho. *Perf. 12*

989 A189 1p multi .25 .25
990 A189 1.50p multi .40 .40
991 A189 2p multi .55 .55
992 A189 2.50p multi .65 .65
993 A189 3p multi .80 .80
994 A189 3.50p multi, vert. .90 .90
995 A189 4.50p multi, vert. 1.25 1.25
996 A189 5p multi, vert. 1.25 1.25
997 A189 8p multi, vert. 2.00 2.00
998 A189 12p multi, vert. 2.50 2.50
Nos. 989-998 (10) 10.55 10.55

TAP SEAC Buildings — A190

#999 — Various buildings with enominations in: a, Greenish blue. b, Orange. c, Dull yellow. d, Blue green (blue door).
10p, Orange.

1999, June 24

999 A190 1.50p Strip of 4, #a.-d. 1.50 1.50

Souvenir Sheet

1000 A190 10p multicolored 2.50 2.50
a. Ovptd. in sheet margin 2.50 2.50

#1000 overprinted in gold in sheet margin with "Amizade Luso-Chinesa / Transferencia de Soberania de / MACAU 1999 / Guangdong Cantao," date and Chinese text.

Dim Sum — A191

#1001 — Table settings with: a, Brown teapot. b, Two food platters. c, Two bamboo steamers. d, Flowered teapot.
9p, Various platters.

1999, Aug. 21

1001 A191 2.50p Strip of 4, #a.-d. 2.50 2.50

Souvenir Sheet

1002 A191 9p multicolored 2.25 2.25
a. Ovptd. in sheet margin 2.25 2.25

China 1999 World Philatelic Exhibition (No. 1002).
#1002 overprinted in gold in sheet margin with "Amizade Luso-Chinesa / Transferencia de Soberania de / MACAU 1999 / Guangdong Cantao," date and Chinese text.

Modern Sculpture A192

Various unidentified sculptures.

1999, Oct. 9 Litho. *Perf. 12*

Background Color

1003 A192 1p red violet .25 .25
1004 A192 1.50p brown, vert. .40 .40
1005 A192 2.50p gray brn, vert. .65 .65
1006 A192 3.50p blue grn .90 .90
Nos. 1003-1006 (4) 2.20 2.20

Souvenir Sheet

1007 A192 10p blue gray 2.50 2.50
a. Ovptd. in sheet margin 2.50 2.50

No. 1007a overprinted in gold in sheet margin with "Amizade Luso-Chinesa / Transferencia da Soberania de / MACAU 1999 / Zhejiang Hangzhou," date and Chinese text.

Meeting of Portuguese and Chinese Cultures — A193

No. 1008: a, 1p, Ships. b, 1.50p, Building. c, 2p, Bridge. d, 3p, Fort.
10p, Fort, diff.

1999, Nov. 19 Litho. *Perf. 12¼*

1008 A193 Strip of 4, #a.-d. 1.90 1.90

Souvenir Sheet

1009 A193 10p multi 2.50 2.50
a. Ovptd. in sheet margin 2.50 2.50

Perforations in corners of stamps on Nos. 1008-1009 are star-shaped.
No. 1009a overprinted in gold in sheet margin with "Amizade Luso-Chinesa / Transferencia da Soberania de / MACAU 1999 / Zhejiang Hangzhou," date and Chinese text.
See Portugal No. 2339.

Retrospective of Macao's Portuguese History — A194

No. 1010: a, 1p, Globe. b, 1.50p, Fort. c, 2p, Chinese, Portuguese people. d, 3.50p, Skyline, Nobre de Carvalho bridge.
9p, Arms.

1999, Dec. 19

1010 A194 Block or strip of 4, #a.-d. 2.50 2.50

Souvenir Sheet

1011 A194 9p multi 2.25 2.25
a. Ovptd. in sheet margin 2.25 2.25

No. 1011a overprinted in gold in sheet margin with "Amizade Luso-Chinesa / Transferencia da Soberania de / MACAU 1999 / Macau," date and Chinese text.
Perforations in corners of stamps on Nos. 1010-1011 are star-shaped.
See Portugal No. 2340.

Special Administrative Region of People's Republic of China

Establishment of Special Administrative Region — A195

No. 1012: a, 1p, Temple, dragon. b, 1.50p, Friendship Bridge, dragon boats. c, 2p, Cathedral, Santa Claus, Christmas tree. d, 2.50p, Lighthouse, race cars. e, 3p, Building, dragons. f, 3.50p, Building, crowd.
8p, Flower.

1999, Dec. 20 Litho. *Perf. 12*

1012 A195 Block of 6, #a.-f. 3.50 3.50

Souvenir Sheet

1013 A195 8p multi 2.25 2.25
a. Ovptd. in sheet margin 2.25 2.25

No. 1013a overprinted in gold in sheet margin with "Amizade Luso-Chinesa / Transferencia da Soberania de / MACAU 1999 / China — Macau," dte, "O futuro de Macau será melhor" and Chinese text.

Souvenir Sheet

Millennium — A196

2000, Jan. 1 Litho. *Perf. 12¼*

1014 A196 8p multi 2.25 2.25

Perforations in corners of stamp are star-shaped.

New Year 2000 (Year of the Dragon) A197

2000, Jan. 28 *Perf. 12¼*

1015 A197 5.50p multi 1.40 1.40

Souvenir Sheet

1016 A197 10p multi 2.50 2.50

Perforations in corners of stamps on Nos. 1015-1016 are star-shaped.

Historic Buildings — A198

2000, Mar. 1 Litho. *Perf. 12¼*

1017 Strip of 4 1.90 1.90
- *a.* A198 1p green circles .25 .25
- *b.* A198 1.50p pink circles .40 .40
- *c.* A198 2p brown circles .50 .50
- *d.* A198 3p blue circles .75 .75

Souvenir Sheet

1018 A198 9p Brown circles 2.25 2.25

Perforations in corners of stamps are star-shaped.

Chinese Calligraphy A199

#1019 — Characters: a, Rectangle with bisecting line. b, Rectangle with lines inside. c, 8 horizontal lines, 3 vertical lines. d, 3 spots to left of 6 touching lines.

8p, Characters shown on #1019a-1019d.

2000, Mar. 23

1019 Block of 4 3.00 3.00
- *a.-d.* A199 3p any single .75 .75

Souvenir Sheet

1020 A199 8p multi 2.25 2.25

Bangkok 2000 Stamp Exhibition (#1020).

Perforations in corners of stamps are star-shaped.

Scenes From "A Journey to the West" — A200

No. 1021: a, 1p, Monkey and tiger. b, 1.50p, Monkey on tree. c, 2p, Monkey and spear carrier. d, 2.50p, Spear carrier and dog. e, 3p, Man in robe. f, 3.50p, Monkey in palm of hand.

9p, Monkey with stick, horiz.

2000, May 5 Litho. *Perf. 12¼*

1021 A200 Block of 6, #a-f 3.50 3.50

Souvenir Sheet

1022 A200 9p multi 2.50 2.50

Perforations in corners of stamps are star-shaped.

Board Games A201

Designs: 1p, Chinese chess. 1.50p, Chess. 2p, Go. 2.50p, Parcheesi.

2000, June 8

1023-1026 A201 Set of 4 1.75 1.75

Souvenir Sheet

1027 A201 9p Chinese checkers 2.25 2.25

Perforations in corners of stamps are star-shaped.

Tea Rituals A202

2000, July 7

1028 Horiz. strip of 4 3.25 3.25
- *a.* A202 2p Square table, 4 people .50 .50
- *b.* A202 3p Round table, 5 people .75 .75
- *c.* A202 3.50p Round table, 3 people .90 .90
- *d.* A202 4.50p Square table, 3 people 1.10 1.10

Souvenir Sheet

1029 A202 8p Woman pouring tea 2.10 2.10

Perforations in corners are star-shaped.

World Stamp Expo 2000, Anaheim (#1029).

Tricycle Drivers — A203

No. 1030: a, Driver pointing. b, Driver wearing yellow cap. c, Driver sitting on saddle. d, Driver with feet on saddle. e, Driver with crossed legs. f, Driver repairing tricycle.

8p, Driver standing next to tricycle, vert.

2000, Sept. 1 Granite Paper

1030 A203 2p Block of 6, #a-f 3.00 3.00

Souvenir Sheet

1031 A203 8p multi 2.10 2.10

Perforations in corners of stamps are star-shaped.

Sculpture Type of 1999 Inscribed "Macau, China"

Various unidentified sculptures with background colors of: 1p, Brown. 2p, Green, vert. 3p, Purple, vert. 4p, Purple.

10p, Gray blue.

2000, Oct. 9 Granite Paper

1032-1035 A192 Set of 4 2.75 2.75

Souvenir Sheet

1036 A192 10p multi 2.75 2.75

Perforations in corners of stamps are star-shaped.

Ceramics and Chinaware — A204

No. 1037; a, Style. b, Color. c, Form. d, Function. e, Design. f, Export.

2000, Oct. 31 Granite Paper

1037 A204 2.50p Sheet of 6, #a-f 4.00 4.00

Souvenir Sheet

1038 A204 8p Plate design 2.10 2.10

No. 1038 contains one 38mm diameter stamp. Perforations in corners of No. 1037 are star-shaped.

Jade Ornaments A205

Various ornaments. Colors of country name: 1.50p, Purple. 2p, Green, vert. 2.50p, Red, vert. 3p, Blue.

9p, Red, vert.

2000, Nov. 22 Granite Paper

1039-1042 A205 Set of 4 2.50 2.50

Souvenir Sheet

1043 A205 9p multi 2.50 2.50

Perforations in corners of stamps are star-shaped.

Special Administrative Region, 1st Anniv. — A206

No. 1044: a, 2p, Dancers, flags. b, 3p, Monument, dragon.

2000, Dec. 20 Litho. *Perf. 12¼*

Granite Paper (#1044)

1044 A206 Horiz. pair, #a-b 1.50 1.50

Souvenir Sheet

Litho. & Embossed

Perf. 13½x13

1045 A206 18p Flags, monument 4.50 4.50

No. 1045 contains one 60x40mm stamp. Perforations in corners of No. 1044 are star-shaped.

New Year 2001 (Year of the Snake) A207

2001, Jan. 18 Litho. *Perf. 13x13¼*

1046 A207 5.50p multi 1.60 1.60

Souvenir Sheet

Granite Paper

1047 A207 10p multi 2.50 2.50

Seng-Yu Proverbs — A208

Designs: No. 1048, Sleeping on a woodpile and tasting gall (4-1). No. 1049, Watching over a stump waiting for a rabbit (4-2). No. 1050, The fox making use of the tiger's fierceness (4-3). No. 1051, Meng Mu moving house three times (4-4).

8p, Man and bell.

2001, Feb. 1 Photo. *Perf. 11¾*

Granite Paper

1048 A208 2p multi .60 .60
- *a.* Booklet pane of 1, plain paper 3.50

1049 A208 2p multi .60 .60
- *a.* Booklet pane of 1, plain paper 3.50

1050 A208 2p multi .60 .60
- *a.* Booklet pane of 1, plain paper 3.50

1051 A208 2p multi .60 .60
- *a.* Booklet pane of 1, plain paper 3.50
- Booklet, #1048a-1051a 15.00
- *Nos. 1048-1051 (4)* 2.40 2.40

Souvenir Sheet

1052 A208 8p multi 2.10 2.10

Hong Kong 2001 Stamp Exhibition (#1052). Booklet containing Nos. 1048a-1051a sold for 35p.

Traditional Implements A209

Designs: 1p, Abacus. 2p, Plane. 3p, Iron. 4p, Balance scale.

8p, Abacus, plane, iron, balance scale.

2001, Mar. 1 Litho. *Perf. 14½x14*

1053-1056 A209 Set of 4 2.75 2.75

Souvenir Sheet

1057 A209 8p multi 2.25 2.25

Religious Beliefs A210

No. 1058: a, Buddha. b, People in prayer. c, Re-enactment of Christ carrying cross. d, People in procession.

8p, Symbols.

2001, Apr. 12 Litho. *Perf. 14½x14*

1058 Horiz. strip of 4 2.25 2.25
- *a.* A210 1p multi .30 .30
- *b.* A210 1.50p multi .45 .45
- *c* A210 2p multi .65 .65
- *d.* A210 2.50p multi .85 .85

Souvenir Sheet

Photo.

Perf.

1059 A210 8p multi 2.40 2.40

No. 1059 contains one 60mm diameter stamp.

Rescue Workers A211

No. 1060: a, Fireman. b, Hazardous materials worker. c, Fireman, diff. d, Ambulance crew.
8p, Firemen, diff

2001, May 2 Litho. *Perf. 14½x14*

1060	Horiz. strip of 4	3.50	3.50
a.	A211 1.50p multi	.45	.45
b.	A211 2.50p multi	.80	.80
c.	A211 3p multi	.90	.90
d.	A211 4p multi	1.25	1.25

Souvenir Sheet

Perf. 14x14½

1061 A211 8p multi 3.25 3.25

No. 1061 contains one 60x40mm stamp.

Internet and E-Commerce — A212

Designs: 1.50p, Keys. 2p, Envelope with "@" symbol. 2.50p, Hand-held computer. 3p, Computer.
6p, Linked computers.

2001, June 30 Litho. *Perf. 14½x14*

1062-1065 A212 Set of 4 2.75 2.75

Souvenir Sheet

1066 A212 6p multi 2.00 2.00

Emblem of 2008 Summer Olympics, Beijing — A213

2001, July 14 Photo. *Perf. 13x13¼*

1067 A213 1p multi + label .80 .80

No. 1067 printed in sheets of 12 stamp + label pairs with one large central label. See People's Republic of China No. 3119, Hong Kong No. 940. No. 1067 with different label is from People's Republic of China No. 3119a.

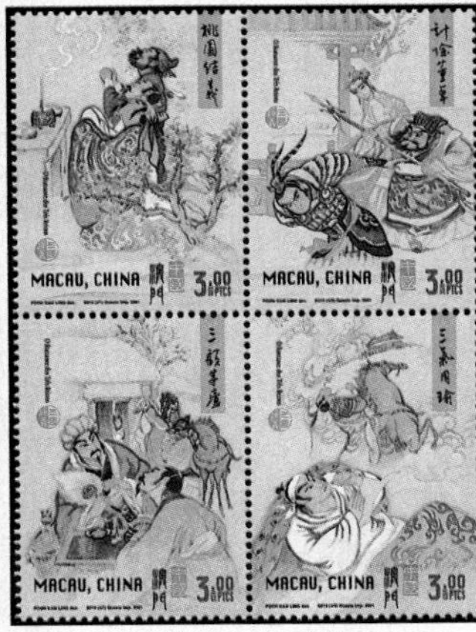

The Romance of Three Kingdoms — A214

Designs: a, Men praying (4-1). b, Man with spear (4-2). c, Men at outdoors table (4-3). d, Man on horseback (4-4).
7p, Man with sword, horiz.

2001, Aug. 1 Litho. *Perf. 14x14½*

1068 A214 3p Block of 4, #a-d 3.25 3.25

Souvenir Sheet

Perf. 14½x14

1069 A214 7p multi 2.50 2.50

2001 Census — A215

Designs: 1p, Buildings, students, child health care. 1.50p, Buildings, street scene. 2.50p, Bridge, people.
6p, Buildings, students, child health care, street scene, bridge, people.

2001, Aug. 23 Litho. *Perf. 14x14½*

1070-1072 A215 Set of 3 1.50 1.50

Souvenir Sheet

1073 A215 6p multi 1.75 1.75

No. 1073 contains one 89x39mm stamp.

Stores — A216

No. 1074: a, 1.50p, Municipal market. b, 2.50p, Store with red window frames. c, 3.50p, Store, parked bicycles. d, 4.50p, Store, parked cars.
7p, Store tower and windows.

2001, Sept. 13 *Perf. 14½x14*

1074 A216 Block of 4, #a-d 3.25 3.25

Souvenir Sheet

Perf. 14x14½

1075 A216 7p multi 2.25 2.25

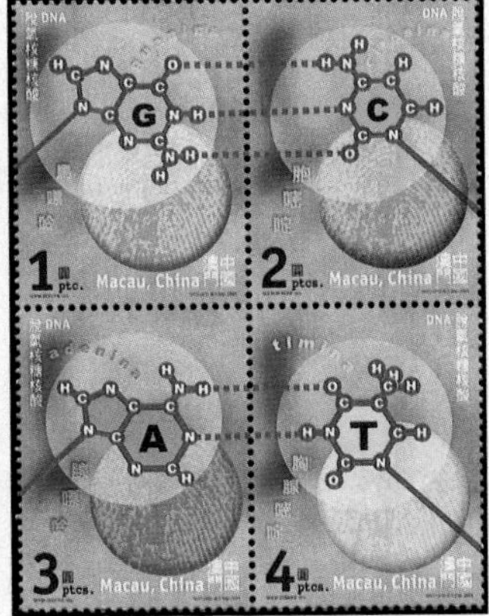

DNA — A217

Fingerprint and: a, 1p, Guanine. b, 2p, Cytosine. c, 3p, Adenine. d, 4p, Thymine.
8p, Adenine, horiz.

2001, Oct. 9 Photo. *Perf. 14x13½*

Granite Paper

1076 A217 Block of 4, #a-d 3.25 3.25

Souvenir Sheet

Perf. 13½x14

1077 A217 8p multi 2.50 2.50

No. 1077 contains one 44x29mm stamp.

Parks and Gardens — A218

No. 1078: a, 1.50p, Comendador Ho Yin Garden. b, 2.50p, Mong Há Hill Municipal Park. c, 3p, City of Flowers Garden. 4.50p, Taipa Grande Nature Park.
8p, Art Garden.

2001, Nov. 30 Litho. *Perf. 13½x14*

Granite Paper

1078 A218 Block of 4, #a-d 3.25 3.25

Souvenir Sheet

1079 A218 8p multi 2.50 2.50

I Ching A219

A219a

No. 1080 — Position of broken bars in trigrams (pa kua): a, No broken bars. b, First and second. c, Second and third. d, Second. e, First and third. f, First. g, Third. h, First, second and third.

2001, Dec. 10 Photo. *Perf. 13*

Granite Paper

1080 A219 2p Sheet of 8, #a-h 4.75 4.75

Souvenir Sheet

Perf. 13½x13¼

1081 A219a 8p shown 2.50 2.50

No. 1080 contains eight 39x34mm hexagonal stamps. See Nos. 1111, 1126, 1135, 1203, 1241, 1306.

New Year 2002 (Year of the Horse) A220

Horse's head: 5.50p, With frame. 10p, With continuous design.

2002, Jan. 28 Litho. *Perf. 14½x14*

1082 A220 5.50p multi 1.75 1.75

Souvenir Sheet

1083 A220 10p multi 2.75 2.75

Characters From Novel "Dream of the Red Mansion II," by Cao Xuequin — A221

No. 1084: a, Lao Lao (6/1). b, Jin Chuan (6/2). c, Zi Juan (6/3). d, Xiang Yun (6/4). e, Liu Lang (6/5). f, Miao Yu (6/6).
8d, Woman reading book.

2002, Mar. 1 *Perf. 14x14½*

1084 A221 2p Block of 6, #a-f 3.50 3.50

Souvenir Sheet

1085 A221 8p multi 2.50 2.50

Tou-tei Festival — A222

No. 1086: a, 1.50p, Opera. b, 2.50p, Dinner in appreciation of the elderly. c, 3.50p, Burning of religious objects. d, 4.50p, Preparing roasted pork.
8p, People watching performance, vert.

2002, Mar. 15 *Perf. 14½x14*

1086 A222 Block of 4, #a-d 3.25 3.25

Souvenir Sheet

Perf. 14x14½

1087 A222 8p multi 2.50 2.50

Church of St. Paul, 400th Anniv. — A223

Various church statues: 1p, 3.50p.
8p, Statue in niche.

2002, Apr. 12 *Perf. 14½x14*

1088-1089 A223 Set of 2 1.50 1.50

Souvenir Sheet

Perf. 14x14½

1090 A223 8p multi 2.50 2.50

No. 1090 contains one 30x40mm stamp.

Participation of Chinese Team in 2002 World Cup Soccer Championships — A224

No. 1091: a, 1p, Goalie. b, 1.50p, Two players.

Perf. 12 Syncopated

2002, May 16 **Photo.**

1091 A224 Horiz. pair, #a-b .95 .95

A souvenir sheet containing Nos. 1091a-1091b, People's Republic of China No. 3198 and Hong Kong Nos. 978a-978b exists.

Environmental Protection — A225

Designs: 1p, Conservation of maritime resources. 1.50p, Reforestation. 2p, Recycling. 2.50p, Protection of swamps. 3p, Reuse of resources. 3.50p, Municipal cleaning. 4p, Air purification. 4.50p, Health and hygiene. 8p, Quiet and comfort.

2002, June 5 **Litho.** ***Perf. 13x13¼***

1092-1100 A225 Set of 9 7.50 7.50

Zheng Guanying (1842-1921), Reformer and Author — A226

Zheng and: a, 1p, Another man. b, 2p, Harbor scene. c, 3p, Men at table. d, 3.50p, Chinese text.

6p, Zheng seated at table.

2002, July 24 ***Perf. 14***

1101 A226 Block of 4, #a-d 2.75 2.75

Souvenir Sheet

1102 A226 6p multi 1.90 1.90

No. 1102 contains one 40x60mm stamp.

Honesty and Equality A227

Various buildings: 1p, 3.50p.

2002, Sept. 13 **Litho.** ***Perf. 14½x14***

1103-1104 A227 Set of 2 1.25 1.25

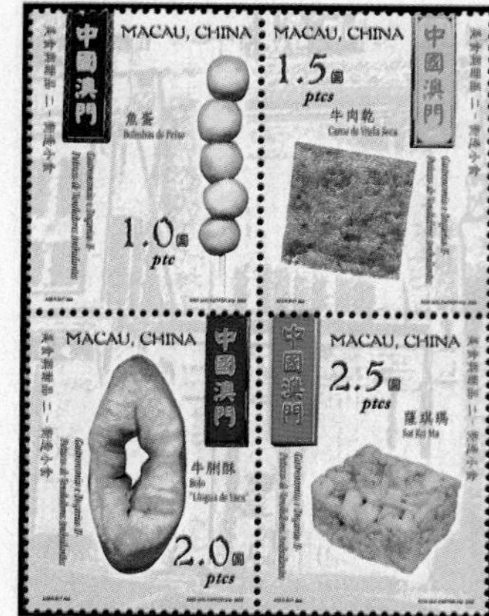

Macao Snack Food — A228

No. 1105: a, 1p, Bolinhas de peixe (fish balls). b, 1.50p, Carne de vitela seca (dried veal). c, 2p, Bolo (cake). d, 2.50p, Sat Kei Ma.

7p, Pastry.

2002, Sept. 26 **Litho.** ***Perf. 13¼x13***

1105 A228 Block of 4, #a-d 1.75 1.75

Souvenir Sheet

1106 A228 7p multi 1.75 1.75

Portions of Nos. 1105-1106 were applied by a thermographic process, producing a raised, shiny effect. No. 1106 contains one 50x50mm diamond-shaped stamp.

Filial Love — A229

No. 1107: a, 1p, Farmer and elephant (O amor filial comove a Deus). b, 1.50p, Man and woman (Abanar a almofada e aquecer a manta). c, 2p, Man and bamboo plants (Chorar sobre o bambu fez crescer rebentos). d, 2.50p, Man and fish (Pescar para a mae deitado no gelo).

No. 1107E: f, Man with arms extended (Mal agasalhado mas tolerante com a madrasta). g, Man and woman (Saltaram carpas da nascente). h, Man with hat (Quem tem amor filial é também fiel). i, Man (Lealdade de pai, amor filial do filho).

7p, Man wearing deer's head (Dar leite de veado aos pais).

2002, Oct. 9 **Litho.** ***Perf. 14***

1107 A229 Block of 4, #a-d 2.25 2.25

1107E Souvenir booklet 5.50

f.-i. A229 4.50p Any booklet pane of 1 1.40 1.40

Souvenir Sheet

Perf. 13½x13

1108 A229 7p multi 2.25 2.25

Particle Physics — A230

No. 1109: a, Unified electroweak interaction theory developed by Steven Weinberg, Sheldon Lee Glashow and Abdus Salam. b, Discovery of W and Z subatomic particles by Carlo Rubbia, 1983. c, Higgs diagram, developed by Richard Feynman and Peter Higgs. d, CERN large electron positron collider, 1989. e, Classification of particles and prediction of quarks by Murray Gell-Mann and George Zweig. f, Unification theory of Albert Einstein.

8p, Detection of positive and negative W particles, CERN LEP, 1996.

2002, Nov. 22 ***Perf. 14x14½***

1109 A230 1.50p Block of 6, #a-f 3.00 3.00

Souvenir Sheet

1110 A230 8p multi 2.50 2.50

I Ching Type of 2001 and

A231

Peace Dance — A231a

No. 1111 — Position of broken bars in trigrams (pa kua): a, Fourth. b, First, second and fourth. c, Second, third and fourth. d, Second and fourth. e, First, third and fourth. f, First and fourth. g, Third and fourth. h, First, second, third and fourth.

2002, Dec. 13 ***Perf. 14***

Granite Paper

1111 A231 2p Sheet of 8, #a-h 4.25 4.25

Souvenir Sheet

Perf. 114x13½

1112 A231a 8p multi 2.25 2.25

No. 1111 contains eight 39x34 hexagonal stamps. Stamps from No. 1111 have Roman numeral II below "I Ching" and "Pa Kua."

New Year 2003 (Year of the Ram) A232

2003, Jan. 2 ***Perf. 14½x14***

1113 A232 5.50p multi 1.60 1.60

Souvenir Sheet

1113A A232 10p multi 2.75 2.75

Legend of Liang Shanbo and Zhu Yingtai A233

No. 1114: a, People seated and reading. b, People on bridge. c, People, tea pot and cups. d, Man holding red paper.

9p, People with butterfly wings.

2003, Feb. 15 **Litho.** ***Perf. 13x13½***

1114 Horiz. strip of 4 3.75 3.75

a.-d. A233 3.50p Any single .90 .90

Souvenir Sheet

1115 A233 9p multi 2.50 2.50

No. 1115 contains one 40x60mm stamp.

The Outlaws of the Marsh — A234

No. 1116: a, Song Jiang. b, Lin Chong. c, Wu Song. d, Lu Zhishen. e, Wu Yong. f, Hua Rong.

8p, Heróis do Monte Liang Shan.

2003, Mar. 1 ***Perf. 13½x14***

Granite Paper (#1116)

1116 A234 2p Block of 6, #a-f 3.50 3.50

Souvenir Sheet

Perf. 14x14½

1117 A234 8p multi 2.25 2.25

Basic Law of Macao, 10th Anniv. A235

Designs: 1p, Building, doves, cover of book of laws. 4.50p, Children, dove, flags of Macao and People's Republic of China, law book

2003, Mar. 31 ***Perf. 14***

1118-1119 A235 Set of 2 1.60 1.60

Traditional Chinese Medicine — A236

No. 1120 — Various medicines: a, 1.50p. b, 2p. c, 3p. d, 3.50p.

8p, Man holding bowl of medicine, horiz.

2003, May 28

1120 A236 Block of 4, #a-d 2.50 2.50

Souvenir Sheet

1121 A236 8p multi 2.00 2.00

Historic Buildings on Taipa and Coloane Islands — A237

Various buildings.

2003, June 18

1122	Horiz. strip of 4	2.00	2.00
a.	A237 1p multi	.25	.25
b.	A237 1.50p multi	.40	.40
c.	A237 2p multi	.50	.50
d.	A237 3.50p multi	.85	.85

Souvenir Sheet

1123 A237 9p multi 2.25 2.25

Everyday Life in the Past — A238

No. 1124: a, Calligrapher at table. b, Puppet maker. c, Man with food cart. d, Washerwoman. e, Woman with decorative lanterns. f, Man carrying food tray above head, man with baskets. g, Photographer. h, Man in chicken costume playing horn.

8p, Barber.

2003, July 30 ***Perf. 13½x13***

1124	Block of 8	3.25	3.25
a.-h.	A238 1.50p Any single	.40	.40

Souvenir Sheet

Perf. 14x14½

1125 A238 8p multi 2.25 2.25

I Ching Type of 2001 and

Woman and Child — A239

No. 1126 — Position of broken bars in trigrams (pa kua): a, Second. b, Second, fifth and sixth. c, Second, fourth and fifth. d, Second and fifth. e, Second, fourth and sixth. f, Second and sixth. g, Second and fourth. h, Second, fourth, fifth and sixth.

2003, Sept. 10 ***Perf. 14***

Granite Paper

1126 A219 2p Sheet of 8, #a-h 4.00 4.00

Souvenir Sheet

Perf. 14x13½

1127 A239 8p multi 2.00 2.00

No. 1126 contains eight 39x34mm hexagonal stamps. Stamps from No. 1126 have Roman numeral III below text "Pa Kua" and "I Ching."

Launch of First Manned Chinese Spacecraft A240

No. 1128: a, 1p, Astronaut. b, 1.50p, Ship, Shenzhou spacecraft.

2003, Oct. 16 ***Perf. 13x13½***

1128 A240 Pair, #a-b 1.10 1.10

A booklet containing No. 1128, People's Republic of China No. 3314 and Hong Kong No. 1062 exists. The booklet sold for a premium over face value. Value $10.

50th Grand Prix of Macao — A241

No. 1129: a, 1p, Race car #5. b, 1.50p, Yellow race car #11. c, 2p, Red race car #11. d, 3p, Motorcycle #5. e, 3.50p, Race car #15. f, 4.50p, Race car #3.

12p, Race car and motorcycle.

Litho. & Embossed

2003, Oct. 29 ***Perf. 14***

1129 A241 Sheet of 6, #a-f 4.00 4.00

Souvenir Sheet

Litho. With Hologram Applied

Perf.

1130 A241 12p multi 3.00 3.00

No. 1129 contains six 36x27mm stamps that have varnish applied to raised portions.

Macao Museum of Art — A242

No. 1131 — Artwork depicting: a, 1p, Man in hooded cloak. b, 1.50p, Hill overlooking harbor. c, 2p, Ruins of St. Paul's Church. d, 2.50p, Two men.

7p, Waterfront buildings, boats in harbor.

2003, Dec. 1 **Litho.** ***Perf. 14½x14***

1131 A242 Block of 4 #a-d 1.75 1.75

Souvenir Sheet

1132 A242 7p multi 1.75 1.75

No. 1132 contains one 57x55mm stamp.

New Year 2004 (Year of the Monkey) A243

2004, Jan. 8 ***Perf. 14½x14***

1133 A243 5.50p shown 1.40 1.40

Souvenir Sheet

1134 A243 10p Monkey, diff. 2.50 2.50

I Ching Type of 2001 and

Man Chiseling Stone — A244

No. 1135 — Position of broken bars in trigrams (pa kua): a, Second and third. b, Second, third, fifth and sixth. c, Second, third, fourth and fifth. d, Second, third and fifth. e, Second, third, fourth and sixth. f, Second, third and sixth. g, Second, third and fourth. h, Second, third, fourth, fifth and sixth.

2004, Mar. 1 ***Perf. 14***

Granite Paper

1135 A219 2p Sheet of 8, #a-h 4.50 4.50

Souvenir Sheet

Perf. 14x13½

1136 A244 8p multi 2.25 2.25

No. 1135 contains eight 39x34mm hexagonal stamps. Stamps from No. 1135 have Roman numeral IV below text "Pa Kua" and "I Ching."

Li Sao — A245

No. 1137: a, Orientaçao. b, Cultivo. c, Aconselhamento pela Irma. d, Transmissao de esperança pela fénix. e, Viagens e reflexoes. f, Local da vida eterna.

8p, Li Sao, horiz.

2004, May 28 ***Perf. 13½x14***

Granite Paper

1137 A245 1.50p Block of 6, #a-f 2.50 2.50

Souvenir Sheet

Perf. 14x13½

1138 A245 8p multi 2.25 2.25

God of Guan Di — A246

2004, June 30 ***Perf. 13½x14***

Granite Paper

1139	Horiz. strip of 4	3.00	3.00
a.	A246 1.50p shown	.35	.35
b.	A246 2.50p God, diff.	.65	.65
c.	A246 3.50p God, diff.	.90	.90
d.	A246 4.50p God, diff.	1.10	1.10

Souvenir Sheet

Perf. 14x13½

1140 A246 9p God, diff. 2.25 2.25

No. 1140 contains one 40x40mm stamp.

2004 Summer Olympics, Athens — A247

Designs: 1p, Woman runner. 1.50p, Long jump. 2p, Discus. 3.50p, Javelin.

2004, July 30 ***Perf. 13¼***

Granite Paper

1141-1144 A247 Set of 4 2.00 2.00

Deng Xiaoping (1904-97), Chinese Leader A248

Designs: 1p, Saluting. 1.50p, Wearing white shirt.

8p, As young man.

2004, Aug. 22 **Litho.** ***Perf. 13x13¼***

1145-1146 A248 Set of 2 .65 .65

Souvenir Sheet

Litho. & Embossed

Perf.

1147 A248 8p multi 2.00 2.00

No. 1147 contains one 40mm diameter stamp.

Intl. Fireworks Display Contest — A249

No. 1148 — Various landmarks and fireworks displays: a, 1p. b, 1.50p. c, 2p. d, 4.50p.

9p, Statue and fireworks, vert.

Litho. & Silk Screened

2004, Sept. 2 ***Perf. 13¼***

Granite Paper

1148 A249 Block of 4, #a-d 2.25 2.25

Souvenir Sheet

Perf. 13x13¼

1149 A249 9p multi 2.25 2.25

No. 1149 contains one 40x60mm stamp.

People's Republic of China, 55th Anniv. — A250

No. 1150 — Buildings and: a, 1p, Flag of People's Republic of China. b, 1.50p, Flag of Macao. c, 2p, Arms of People's Republic of China. d, 3p, Arms of Macao.

7p, Buildings.

2004, Oct. 1 **Litho.** ***Perf. 13x13¼***

Granite Paper

1150 A250 Block of 4, #a-d 1.90 1.90

Souvenir Sheet

Perf. 13¼x13

1151 A250 7p multi 1.75 1.75

No. 1151 contains one 60x40mm stamp.

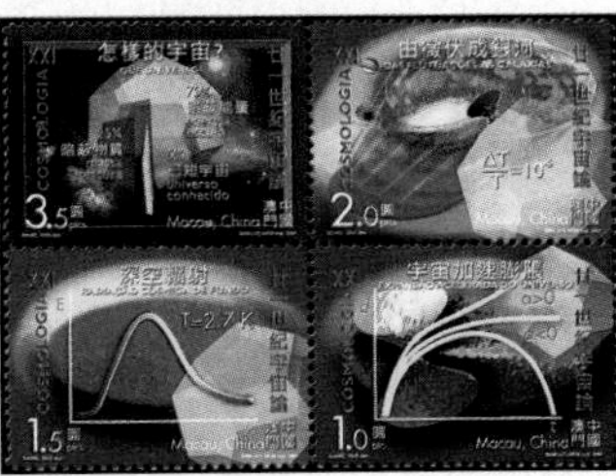

Cosmology — A251

No. 1152: a, 1p, Expansion and acceleration of the Universe. b, 1.50p, Cosmic radiation. c, 2p, Fluctuations of galaxies. d, 3.50p, What is the Universe?

8p, Big Bang Theory.

2004, Oct. 9 ***Perf. 12¼***

1152 A251 Block of 4, #a-d 2.00 2.00

Souvenir Sheet

1153 A251 8p multi 2.00 2.00

Macao Garrison of the People's Liberation Army — A252

No. 1154 — Flag and, in foreground: a, 1p, Soldier holding sword. b, 1p, Soldier in tank. c, 1.50p, Soldiers in car. d, 1.50p, Soldiers giving blood. e, 3.50p, Soldier at attention holding gun. f, 3.50p, Soldier with helmet and rifle with bayonet.

8p, Soldiers in car, vert.

2004, Dec. 1 ***Perf. 13x13¼***

1154 A252 Block of 6, #a-f 3.00 3.00

Souvenir Sheet

1155 A252 8p multi 2.00 2.00

No. 1155 contains one 40x60mm stamp.

Establishment of Special Administrative District, 5th Anniv. — A253

Lotus flowers and various buildings.

2004, Dec. 20 Litho. ***Perf. 14½x14***

1156		Horiz. strip of 4	2.50	2.50
a.	A253	1.50p multi	.45	.45
b.	A253	2p multi	.55	.55
c.	A253	2.50p multi	.65	.65
d.	A253	3p multi	.80	.80

Souvenir Sheet

Litho. & Embossed

1157 A253 10p multi 2.75 2.75

Souvenir Sheet

Air Macau, 10th Anniv. — A254

2004, Dec. 28 Litho. ***Perf. 14***

1158 A254 8p multi 2.00 2.00

New Year 2005 (Year of the Rooster) A255

2005, Jan. 13 Litho. ***Perf. 14½x14***

1159 A255 5.50p shown 1.40 1.40

Souvenir Sheet

1160 A255 10p Rooster, diff. 2.50 2.50

Everyday Life in the Past — A256

No. 1161: a, Cook (8/1). b, Man holding pole with hanging bottles (8/2). c, Man at work at small table (8/3). d, Textile worker (8/4). e, Man cutting coconuts (8/5). f, Cook at cart (8/6). g, Cook under lantern (8/7). h, Seamstress (8/8).

8p, Mailman on bicycle.

2005, Mar. 1 ***Perf. 12¼***

1161		Block of 8	3.00	3.00
a.-h.	A256	1.50p Any single	.35	.35

Souvenir Sheet

1162 A256 8p multi 2.00 2.00

Sai Van Bridge A257

Designs: 1p, Bridge. 3.50p, Bridge and approaches.

8p, Bridge tower, vert.

2005, Mar. 23 ***Perf. 14***

1163-1164 A257 Set of 2 1.10 1.10

Souvenir Sheet

1165 A257 8p multi 2.00 2.00

Libraries A258

2005, Apr. 15

1166		Horiz. strip of 4	2.00	2.00
a.	A258	1p Central Library	.25	.25
b.	A258	1.50p Sir Robert Ho Tung Library	.35	.35
c.	A258	2p Coloane Library	.50	.50
d.	A258	3.50p Mong Há Library	.90	.90

Souvenir Sheet

1167 A258 8p Public Commercial Assoc. Library 2.00 2.00

No. 1167 contains one 60x40mm stamp.

Mothers and Offspring — A259

2005, May 8 ***Perf. 14½x14***

1168		Horiz. strip of 4 + 4 alternating labels	2.00	2.00
a.	A259	1p Humans + label	.25	.25
b.	A259	1.50p Kangaroos + label	.35	.35
c.	A259	2p Birds and nest + label	.50	.50
d.	A259	3.50p Ducks + label	.90	.90

Labels could be personalized, with sheets containing 5 strips and 20 labels selling for 60p.

The Romance of the Western Chamber — A260

No. 1169 — Inscriptions: a, Espreitando a Beldade à Luz da Lua (6/1). b, Ying Ying Ouvindo Música (6/2). c, O Amor e Ansiedade de Zhang Sheng (6/3). d, A Interrogaçao da Dama (6/4). e, Sonhando com Ying Ying na Pensao (6/5). f, A Uniao dos Amados (6/6).

8p, A Espera da Lua.

2005, June 10 ***Perf. 13¼x14***

Granite Paper

1169 A260 2p Block of 6, #a-f 3.00 3.00

Souvenir Sheet

Perf. 14x13¼

1170 A260 8p multi 2.00 2.00

Voyages of Admiral Zheng He, 600th Anniv. A261

No. 1171: a, Admiral Zheng He. b, Giraffe. c, Ship and map.

8p, Ships.

2005, June 28 Litho. ***Perf. 13x13½***

1171		Horiz. strip of 3	2.75	2.75
a.	A261	1p multi	.65	.65
b.-c.	A261	1.50p Either single	.90	.90

Souvenir Sheet

Perf. 13¼

1172 A261 8p multi 2.75 2.75

No. 1172 contains one 50x30mm stamp.

UNESCO World Heritage Sites — A262

Various buildings in Historical Center of Macao World Heritage Site with background colors of: a, 1p, White. b, 1.50p, Red. c, 2p, Orange. d, 3.50p, Dark green.

8p, Green.

2005, July 16 ***Perf. 14***

1173 A262 Block of 4, #a-d 2.00 2.00

Souvenir Sheet

1174 A262 8p multi 2.00 2.00

4th East Asian Games, Macao — A263

No. 1175 — Stylized athletes and: a, 1p, Olympic Swimming Pool of Macao. b, 1.50p, Nautical Center, Praia Grande. c, 2p, Tennis Academy. d, 2.50p, IPM Sports Pavilion. e, 3.50p, Macao Stadium. f, 4.50p, Tap Seac Sports Pavilion.

8p, Sports Arena.

2005, Aug. 30 ***Perf. 14x13¼***

Granite Paper

1175 A263 Block of 6, #a-f 3.75 3.75

Souvenir Sheet

Perf.

1176 A263 8p multi 2.00 2.00

No. 1176 contains one 55x38mm oval stamp.

Macao Bank Notes, Cent. — A264

Designs: 1p, 1 pataca note. 1.50p, 5 pataca note. 3p, 10 pataca note. 4.50p, 50 pataca note.

8p, 100 pataca note.

2005, Sept. 2 ***Perf. 13½x14***

Granite Paper

1177-1180 A264 Set of 4 2.50 2.50

Souvenir Sheet

1181 A264 8p multi 2.00 2.00

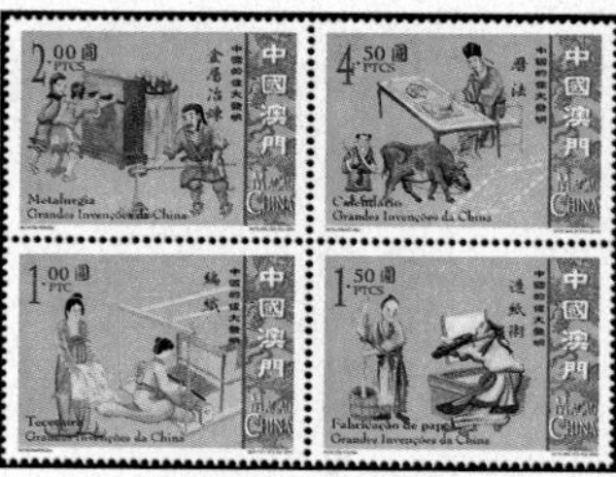

Great Chinese Inventions — A265

No. 1182: a, 1p, Textile loom. b, 1.50p, Paper. c, 2p, Metal smelting. d, 4.50p, Calendar.

8p, Seismograph.

2005, Oct. 9 ***Perf. 14x13½***

Granite Paper

1182 A265 Block of 4, #a-d 2.25 2.25

Souvenir Sheet

1183 A265 8p multi 2.00 2.00

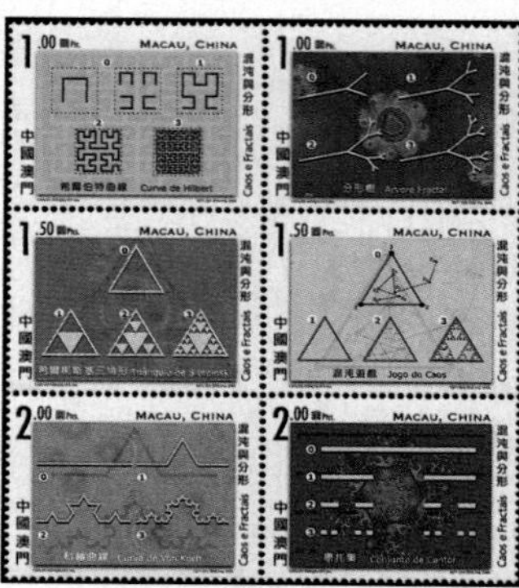

Chaos and Fractal Mathematics — A266

No. 1184: a, 1p, Hilbert's Curve. b, 1p, Tree Fractal. c, 1.50p, Sierpinski Triangle. d, 1.50p, Chaos Game. e, 2p, Von Koch Curve. f, 2p, Cantor Set.

8p, Julia Set.

2005, Nov. 16 ***Perf. 14***

1184 A266 Block of 6, #a-f 2.25 2.25

Souvenir Sheet

1185 A266 8p multi 2.00 2.00

New Year 2006 (Year of the Dog) A267

2006, Jan. 9 Litho. *Perf. 13x13¼*

1186 A267 5.50p multi 1.40 1.40

Souvenir Sheet

1187 A267 10p multi 2.50 2.50

Lanterns — A268

No. 1188 — Various lanterns: a, (4/1). b, (4/2). c, (4/3). d, (4/4).

2006, Feb. 12 *Perf. 13¼x13*

1188 Horiz. strip of 4 1.25 1.25
a.-b. A268 1p Either single .25 .25
c.-d. A268 1.50p Either single .35 .35

Souvenir Sheet

Perf. 13x13¼

1189 A268 8p multi 2.00 2.00

Everyday Life in the Past — A269

No. 1190: a, Cook (8/1). b, Food vendor (8/2). c, Man holding scissors (8/3). d, Man with small round table (8/4). e, Cobbler (8/5). f, Man with pots (8/6). g, Man hammering pails (8/7). h, Man carrying goods suspended from stick (8/8).
8p, Man looking at kettle.

2006, Mar. 1 *Perf. 14*

1190 Block of 8 3.00 3.00
a.-h. A269 1.50p Any single .35 .35

Souvenir Sheet

1191 A269 8p multi 2.00 2.00

Items from Communications Museum — A270

No. 1192: a, Rubber stamp (8/1). b, Scale (8/2). c, Mail box (8/3). d, Mail sorting boxes (8/4). e, Telephone (8/5). f, Telephone switching equipment (8/6). g, Radio (8/7). h, Submarine cable (8/8).
10p, Macao #1, horiz.

2006, May 18 *Perf. 13¼x14*

Granite Paper

1192 Block of 8 3.00 3.00
a.-h. A270 1.50p Any single .35 .35

Souvenir Sheet

1193 A270 10p multi 2.50 2.50

2006 World Cup Soccer Championships, Germany — A271

Various soccer players.

Litho. & Embossed

2006, June 9 *Perf. 13¼*

1194 Block of 4 3.00 3.00
a. A271 1.50p multi .35 .35
b. A271 2.50p multi .65 .65
c. A271 3.50p multi .90 .90
d. A271 4p multi 1.00 1.00

Fans — A272

No. 1195 — Various pictures on fans: a, (5/1). b, (5/2). c, (5/3). d, (5/4). e, (5/5).
10p, Three children.

2006, June 28 Litho. *Perf. 14x13¼*

Granite Paper

1195 Vert. strip of 5 3.00 3.00
a.-b. A272 1.50p Either single .35 .35
c.-d. A272 2.50p Either single .65 .65
e. A272 3.50p multi .90 .90

Souvenir Sheet

1196 A272 10p multi 2.50 2.50

No. 1196 contains one 40x30mm stamp.

21st China Adolescents Invention Contest — A273

No. 1197: a, 1.50p, Models of molecules, laboratory equipment (4/1). b, 2p, Dish antenna, Earth, windmills (4/2). c, 2.50p, Gear, compass, pyramid and diagrams (4/3). d, 3.50p, Invention, computer keyboard and mouse (4/4).
10p, Atomic model, contest venue, vert.

2006, July 28 *Perf. 14*

1197 A273 Block of 4, #a-d 2.40 2.40

Souvenir Sheet

1198 A273 10p multi 2.50 2.50

No. 1198 contains one 40x60mm stamp.

Street Scenes — A274

No. 1199: a, Rua de S. Domingos (4/1). b, Rua de Camilo Pessanha (4/2). c, Calcada de S. Francisco Xavier (4/3). d, Travessa da Paixao (4/4).
10p, Largo de Santo Agostinho.

2006, Sept. 13 *Perf. 13½x14*

Granite Paper

1199 Block of 4 2.25 2.25
a.-b. A274 1.50p Either single .35 .35
c. A274 2.50p multi .65 .65
d. A274 3.50p multi .90 .90

Souvenir Sheet

Perf. 14x13½

1200 A274 10p multi 2.50 2.50

University of Macao, 25th Anniv. A275

No. 1201 — Inscriptions for Faculty of: a, Social Sciences and Humanities (5/1). b, Law (5/2). c, Science and Education (5/3). d, Science and Technology (5/4). e, Business Management (5/5).
10p, University emblem.

2006, Sept. 28 *Perf. 13x13½*

1201 Horiz. strip of 5 1.90 1.90
a.-e. A275 1.50p Any single .35 .35

Souvenir Sheet

1202 A275 10p multi 2.50 2.50

I Ching Type of 2001 and

Two Women — A276

No. 1203 — Position of broken bars in trigrams (pa kua): a, Sixth. b, First, second and sixth. c, Second, third and sixth. d, Second and sixth. e, First, third and sixth. f, First and sixth. g, Third and sixth. h, First, second, third and sixth.

2006, Oct. 9 *Perf. 13*

1203 A219 2p Sheet of 8, #a-h 4.00 4.00

Souvenir Sheet

1204 A276 10p shown 2.50 2.50

No. 1204 contains eight 39x34mm hexagonal stamps. Stamps from No. 1135 have Roman numeral "V" below text "Pa Kua" and "I Ching."

Jesuits — A277

Designs: No. 1205, 1.50p, Matteo Ricci (1552-1610), missionary, and red Chinese chop. No. 1206, 1.50p, St. Francis Xavier (1506-52), missionary, and cross. No. 1207, 3.50p, Allesandro Valignano (1539-1606), missionary, and capital. No. 1208, 3.50p, Melchior Carneiro (c. 1516-83), in red bishop's stole.
10p, St. Ignatius Loyola (1491-1556), founder of Society of Jesus.

2006, Nov. 30 Litho. *Perf. 13½x14*

1205-1208 A277 Set of 4 2.50 2.50

Souvenir Sheet

Perf. 14x13½

1209 A277 10p multi 2.50 2.50

New Year 2007 (Year of the Pig) A278

2007, Jan. 8 Litho. *Perf. 13x13¼*

1210 A278 5.50p multi 1.40 1.40

Souvenir Sheet

1211 A278 10p multi 2.50 2.50

Shek Wan Ceramics — A279

No. 1212: a, 1.50p, Lao Zi (4/1). b, 1.50p, Lu Yu (4/2). c, 1.50p, Philosopher (4/3). d, 2.50p, Luo Han Seated (4/4).
8p, Concubine After Bath.

2007, Feb. 3

1212 A279 Block of 4, #a-d 1.75 1.75

Souvenir Sheet

1213 A279 8p multi 2.00 2.00

Everyday Life in the Past — A280

No. 1214: a, Man carrying tray on head (8/1). b, Man pouring tea into bowls (8/2). c, Rickshaw (8/3). d, People around table looking into bowl (8/4). e, Seamstress (8/5). f, Shoemaker (8/6). g, Ceramics artists (8/7). h, Embroiderer at booth (8/8).
10p, Festival dragon.

2007, Mar. 1 *Perf. 14*

1214 Block of 8 3.00 3.00
a.-h. A280 1.50p Any single .35 .35

Souvenir Sheet

1215 A280 10p multi 2.50 2.50

Traditional Chinese Shops — A281

No. 1216: a, 1.50p, Seamstress's shop (4/1). b, 1.50p, Acupuncturist and herbalist (4/2). c, 2.50p, Print shop (4/3). d, 3.50p, Restaurant (4/4).
10p, Street scene with man carting sign from shop.

2007, May 8 *Perf. 14½x14*

1216 A281 Block of 4, #a-d 2.25 2.25

Souvenir Sheet

1217 A281 10p multi 2.50 2.50

Seng Yu Proverbs — A282

Designs: Nos. 1218, 1223a, 1.50p, The Foolish Old Man Moved a Mountain (pink frame, 4/1). Nos. 1219, 1223b, 1.50p, The Friendship Between Guan and Bao (blue green frame, 4/2). Nos. 1220, 1223c, 3.50p, Calling Black White (lilac frame, 4/3). Nos. 1221, 1223d, 3.50p, The Quarrel Between Snipe and Clam (orange frame, 4/4).
10p, Horses and riders before riderless horse pulling cart, horiz.

2007, June 1 *Perf. 14*

1218-1221 A282 Set of 4 13.00 13.00

Souvenir Sheet

1222 A282 10p multi 13.00 13.00

Self-Adhesive Booklet Stamps

Serpentine Die Cut 14

1223 Booklet pane, #1223a-1223d 13.00 13.00
Complete booklet, 2 #1223 27.50

No. 1222 contains one 60x40mm stamp.

A Journey to the West — A283

No. 1224: a, 1.50p, King and entourage, sprite with stick on cloud (6/1). b, 1.50p, Sprite on cloud, woman dreaming of horned spirit (6/2). c, 2p, Man with foot pierced by spear tip, woman, sprite without stick on cloud (6/3). d, 2p, Sprite on cloud battling other sprites (6/4). e, 2.50p, Sprite with stick, sprite with rake, sprite with swords (6/5). f, 2.50p, Sprite with rake on cloud, spirit with eight hands, spider (6/6).

10p, Sprite and sun.

2007, June 18 *Perf. 14*

1224 A283 Block of 6, #a-f 3.00 3.00

Souvenir Sheet

1225 A283 10p multi 2.50 2.50

Scouting, Cent. A284

Lord Robert Baden-Powell, Macao Scouting emblem, flag ceremony and: 1.50p, Scout with semaphore flags. 2p, Scouts saluting. 2.50p, Scouts setting up campfire. No. 1229, 3.50p, Scouts lashing sticks together. No. 1230, 3.50p, Scout giving directions to other Scout.

10p, Flag, cannon and buildings, vert.

2007, July 9 *Perf. 13x13¼*

1226-1230 A284 Set of 5 3.25 3.25

Souvenir Sheet

Perf. 13¼x13

1231 A284 10p multi 2.50 2.50

Arrival of Robert Morrison (1782-1834), First Protestant Missionary in China, Bicent. — A285

Morrison and: 1.50p, Lilac panel. 3.50p, Yellow panel.

2007, Sept. 28 Litho. *Perf. 13x13¼*

1232-1233 A285 Set of 2 1.25 1.25

Souvenir Sheet

Mount Kangrinboqe, Tibet — A286

2007, Oct. 9 *Perf. 14*

1234 A286 10p multi 2.50 2.50

Applications of the Golden Ratio — A287

No. 1235: a, 1.50p, Fibonacci sequence. b, 2p, Sunflower spirals. c, 2.50p, Penrose tiling. d, 3.50p, Nautilus shell.

10p, Phi and equation.

2007, Oct. 26 *Perf. 13¼x13*

1235 A287 Block of 4, #a-d 2.40 2.40

Souvenir Sheet

1236 A287 10p multi 2.50 2.50

Chinese Philosophers — A288

No. 1237 Chinese character and: a, 1.50p, Lao Tzu (Lao Zi). b, 2.50p, Chuang Tzu (Zhuang Zi). c, 3.50p, Confucius (Confúcio). d, 4p, Meng Tzu (Méncio).

10p, Lao Tzu, Chuang Tzu, Confucius, Meng Tzu.

Litho. & Embossed

2007, Nov. 30 *Perf. 13x13¼*

1237 A288 Block of 4, #a-d 3.00 3.00

Souvenir Sheet

Perf.

1238 A288 10p multi 2.50 2.50

No. 1238 contains one 42mm diameter stamp.

New Year 2008 (Year of the Rat) — A289

No. 1239: a, Metal sculpture of rat. b, Wood carving of rat. c, Watercolor painting of rat. d, Fireworks and laser light image of rat. e, Clay teapot depicting rat.

10p, Clay teapot depicting rat and 2008 Beijing Summer Olympics emblem.

Litho., Litho. & Embossed with Foil and Hologram Application (#1239e, 1240)

2008, Jan. 23 *Perf. 14¼*

1239 Horiz. strip of 5 2.75 2.75
a.-d. A289 1.50p Any single .35 .35
e. A289 5p multi 1.25 1.25

Souvenir Sheet

1240 A289 10p multi 2.50 2.50

No. 1240 contains one 50x50mm diamond-shaped stamp.

I Ching Type of 2001 and

Man Steering Raft — A290

No. 1241 — Position of broken bars in trigrams (pa kua): a, Fourth and sixth. b, First, second, fourth and sixth. c, Second, third, fourth and sixth. d, Second, fourth and sixth. e, First, third, fourth and sixth. f, First, fourth and sixth. g, Third, fourth and sixth. h, First, second, third, fourth and sixth.

2008, Mar. 1 Litho. *Perf. 14*

Granite Paper

1241 A219 2p Sheet of 8, #a-h 4.00 4.00

Souvenir Sheet

1242 A290 10p multi 2.50 2.50

No. 1241 contains eight 39x34mm hexagonal stamps. Stamps from No. 1241 have Roman numeral "VI" below text "Pa Kua" and "I Ching."

Olympic Torch Relay A291

Designs: 1.50p, Man holding Olympic torch, Parthenon. 3.50p, Mascot holding Olympic torch, lotus flower.

10p, Olympic torch, doves, vert.

2008, May 3 *Perf. 13x13¼*

1243-1244 A291 Set of 2 1.25 1.25

Souvenir Sheet

Perf. 13

1245 A291 10p multi 2.50 2.50

No. 1245 contains one 40x70mm stamp.

Western Legends — A292

No. 1246: a, The Golden Apple. b, The Gordian Knot. c, The Trojan Horse. d, The Riddle of the Sphinx.

10p, Cupid and Psyche, horiz.

2008, June 2 *Perf. 13¼x14*

Granite Paper

1246 Horiz. strip of 4 3.00 3.00
a. A292 1.50p multi .35 .35
b. A292 2.50p multi .65 .65
c. A292 3.50p multi .90 .90
d. A292 4.00p multi 1.00 1.00

Souvenir Sheet

Perf. 14x13¼

1247 A292 10p multi 2.50 2.50

Native Cuisine of Macao and Singapore A293

No. 1248: a, Panqueca Indiana. b, Arroz de Frango à Hainan. c, Carne de Porco à Alentejana. d, Lombo de Bacalhau Braseado em Lascas. e, Laksa. f, Saté. g, Arroz Frito à Yangzhou. h, Frango Frito.

No. 1249, vert.: a, Arroz no Tacho de Porcelana. b, Caranguejo con Piri-piri.

2008, July 4 *Perf. 13¼x14*

Granite Paper

1248 Block of 8 5.00 5.00
a.-d. A293 1.50p Any single .35 .35
e.-h. A293 3.50p Any single .90 .90

Souvenir Sheet

1249 Sheet of 2 2.50 2.50
a.-b. A293 5p Either single 1.25 1.25

See Singapore Nos. 1318-1320.

Historic Center of Macau UNESCO World Heritage Site A294

Designs: 1.50p, Fortaleza do Monte. 2p, Largo do Lilau. 2.50p, Lou Kau House. 3p, Largo do Senado. 3.50p, Sam Kai Vui Kun. 4p, Igreja da Sé. 4.50p, Quartel dos Mouros. 5p, St. Anthony's Church.

2008, July 31 Litho. *Perf. 13x13½*

1250 A294 1.50p multi .35 .35
1251 A294 2p multi .50 .50
1252 A294 2.50p multi .65 .65
1253 A294 3p multi .75 .75
1254 A294 3.50p multi .90 .90
1255 A294 4p multi 1.00 1.00
1256 A294 4.50p multi 1.10 1.10
1257 A294 5p multi 1.25 1.25
Nos. 1250-1257 (8) 6.50 6.50

2008 Summer Olympics, Beijing A295

Designs: 5p, National Aquatics Center. 10p, National Stadium.

2008, Aug. 8 *Perf. 13x13½*

1258 A295 5p multi 1.25 1.25

Souvenir Sheet

Perf. 13

1259 A295 10p multi 2.50 2.50

No. 1259 contains one 54x74mm irregular, six-sided stamp.

20th Macao Intl. Fireworks Display Contest — A296

No. 1260 — Fireworks displays over various sections of Macao: a, 1.50p. b, 2.50p. c, 3.50p. d, 5p.

2008, Oct. 1 Litho. *Perf. 14x13½*

Granite Paper

1260 A296 Sheet of 4, #a-d 3.25 3.25

Souvenir Sheet

1261 A296 10p shown 2.50 2.50

Celebration — A297

No. 1262: a, 1.50p, "Celebration" in many languages. b, 3.50p, UPU emblem.

2008, Oct. 9 ***Perf. 14***
1262 A297 Horiz. pair, #a-b 1.25 1.25

Souvenir Sheet

Lijiang, People's Republic of China — A298

2008, Nov. 7
1263 A298 10p multi 2.50 2.50

Traditional Handicrafts A299

Designs: 1.50p, Ivory carving. 2p, Ceramic painting. 2.50p, Basket weaving. 3.50p, Wood carving.
10p, Beaded embroidery.

2008, Dec. 1 ***Perf. 13x13¼***
1264-1267 A299 Set of 4 2.40 2.40

Souvenir Sheet
Perf. 13¼x13
1268 A299 10p multi 2.50 2.50

No. 1268 contains one 60x40mm stamp.

Louis Braille (1809-52), Educator of the Blind — A300

2009, Jan. 4 Litho. ***Perf. 13¼***
1269 A300 5p black 1.25 1.25

New Year 2009 (Year of the Buffalo) A301

No. 1270: a, Metal sculpture of buffalo head. b, Wood carving of buffalo head. c, Watercolor drawing of buffalo head. d, Fireworks display of buffalo head. e, Clay teapot with buffalo design.
10p, Clay teapot with buffalo design, diff.

Litho. (1.50p), Litho. & Embossed With Foil Application (5p, 10p)
2009, Jan. 8 ***Perf. 14¼***
1270 Horiz. strip of 5 2.75 2.75
a.-d. A301 1.50p Any single .35 .35
e. A301 5p multi 1.25 1.25

Souvenir Sheet
1271 A301 10p multi 2.50 2.50

No. 1271 contains one 50x50mm diamond-shaped stamp.

Opening of Kun Iam Treasury — A302

No. 1272 — Crowd of worshipers and holders of incense sticks with red chop at: a, Top. b, Lower left. c, Lower right. d, Left.
10p, Woman praying, horiz.

2009, Feb. 20 Litho. ***Perf. 13¼x13***
1272 Horiz. strip of 4 3.00 3.00
a. A302 1.50p multi .40 .40
b. A302 2.50p multi .65 .65
c. A302 3.50p multi .90 .90
d. A302 4p multi 1.00 1.00

Souvenir Sheet
Perf. 13x13¼
1273 A302 10p multi 2.50 2.50

Traditional Tools A303

Designs: 1.50p, Sand basin for compacting firecrackers. 2.50p, Whetstone. 3.50p, Stone grain mill. 4p, Cake mold.
10p, All four tools.

2009, Mar. 1 ***Perf. 14½x14***
1274-1277 A303 Set of 4 3.00 3.00

Souvenir Sheet
Perf. 14x14½
1278 A303 10p multi 2.50 2.50

No. 1278 contains one 60x40mm stamp.

Souvenir Sheet

Buddha, Longmen Cave — A304

2009, Apr. 8 ***Perf. 14***
1279 A304 10p multi 2.50 2.50

China 2009 World Stamp Exhibition, Luoyang.

Labor Day A305

"5," "1" and: 1.50p, Construction workers, Macao Tower. 5p, Haulers, ruins of St. Paul's Church.
10p, Men lifting diamond-shaped "5.1." box.

2009, May 1 ***Perf. 13x13¼***
1280-1281 A305 Set of 2 1.75 1.75

Souvenir Sheet
1282 A305 10p multi 2.50 2.50

The Mantis Stalking the Cicada — A306

A Fond Dream on Nanke — A307

Songs of Chu on All Sides — A308

Give the Last Measure of Devotion — A309

Design: 10p, Marking the boat to find the sword, horiz.

2009, June 1 Litho. ***Perf. 14***
1283 A306 1.50p multi .40 .40
1284 A307 1.50p multi .40 .40
1285 A308 3.50p multi .90 .90
1286 A309 3.50p multi .90 .90
Nos. 1283-1286 (4) 2.60 2.60

Souvenir Sheet
1287 A309 10p multi 2.50 2.50

Booklet Stamps
Self-Adhesive
Serpentine Die Cut 14
1288 A306 1.50p multi .40 .40
1289 A307 1.50p multi .40 .40
1290 A308 3.50p multi .90 .90
1291 A309 3.50p multi .90 .90
a. Booklet pane of 8, 2 each #1288-1291 5.25
Nos. 1288-1291 (4) 2.60 2.60

Seng Yu proverbs. No. 1287 contains one 60x40mm stamp.

People's Republic of China, 60th Anniv. — A310

No. 1292 — Lanterns and: a, 1.50p, Archway. b, 2.50p, Soldier in tank. c, 3.50p, Children exercising. d, 4p, Soldiers and flag of People's Republic of China.
10p, Archway, soldiers and flag of People's Republic of China, horiz.

2009, Oct. 1 Litho. ***Perf. 13¼x13***
1292 A310 Block of 4, #a-d 3.00 3.00

Souvenir Sheet
Photo.
Perf. 13
1293 A310 10p multi 2.50 2.50

No. 1293 contains one 60x40mm stamp.

Porcelain Plate Paintings by Sou Farong A311

Designs: 1.50p, Bodhisattva Ksitigarbha. 5p, Bodhisattva Avalokitsavara.

2009, Oct. 9 Litho. ***Perf. 13x13¼***
1294-1295 A311 Set of 2 1.75 1.75

Pui Ching Middle School, 120th Anniv. — A312

No. 1296: a, 1.50p, Building and basketball court. b, 2p, Building, diff. c, 2.50d, Buildings. d, 3.50p, Bust and fireplace.
10p, Building and fountain.

2009, Nov. 29 Litho. ***Perf. 13½x14***
Granite Paper
1296 A312 Block or strip of 4, #a-d 2.40 2.40

Souvenir Sheet
1297 A312 10p multi 2.50 2.50

Macao Science Center — A313

No. 1298: a, 1.50p, Aerial view of entire complex. b, 2.50p, Exhibition Center and Planetarium. c, 3.50p, Ground-level view of entire complex. d, 4p, Ground-level view of Exhibition Center and Convention Center.
10p, Top of Exhibition Center.

2009, Dec. 19 ***Perf. 13½x14***
Granite Paper
1298 A313 Block or strip of 4, #a-d 3.00 3.00

Souvenir Sheet
1299 A313 10p multi 2.50 2.50

People's Liberation Army Garrison in Macao, 10th Anniv. A314

No. 1300: a, Soldiers with martial arts stances. b, Two women officers. c, Soldiers with gun. d, Soldiers and children with cannon. e, Soldiers and children planting tree. f, Soldiers repairing tank.
10p, Soldiers on parade, vert.

2009, Dec. 20 *Perf. 13x13¼*

1300 Block of 6 2.25 2.25
a.-f. A314 1.50p Any single .35 .35

Souvenir Sheet

Perf. 13x13½

1301 A314 10p multi 2.50 2.50

No. 1301 contains one 40x60mm stamp.

Return of Macao to China, 10th Anniv. A315

No. 1302: a, Golden Lotus sculpture, flags of People's Republic of China and Macao. b, Senado Square and Macao Tower. c, Macao waterfront.
10p, Golden Lotus, gate, vert.

Perf. 13¼x13 Syncopated

2009, Dec. 20 **Photo.**

1302 Horiz. strip of 3 1.10 1.10
a.-c. A315 1.50p Any single .35 .35

Souvenir Sheet

Perf. 13x13½

1303 A315 10p multi 2.50 2.50

No. 1303 contains one 40x60mm stamp. See People's Republic of China Nos. 3791-3793.

New Year 2010 (Year of the Tiger) — A316

No. 1304: a, Clay sculpture of tiger and cub. b, Fireworks display of tiger's head. c, Watercolor drawing of tiger. d, Wood carving of tiger. e, Metal sculpture of tiger.
10p, Metal sculpture of tiger, diff.

Litho. (1.50p), Litho. & Embossed with Hologram and Foil Application (5p, 10p)

2010, Jan. 2 *Perf. 14¼*

1304 Horiz. strip of 5 2.75 2.75
a.-d. A316 1.50p Any single .35 .35
e. A316 5p multi 1.25 1.25

Souvenir Sheet

1305 A316 10p multi 2.50 2.50

No. 1305 contains one 50x50mm diamond-shaped stamp.

I Ching Type of 2001 and

Child With Toy — A317

No. 1306 — Position of broken bars in trigrams (pa kua): a, First and second. b, First, second, fifth and sixth. c, First, second, fourth and fifth. d, First, second and fifth. e, First, second, fourth and sixth. f, First, second and sixth. g, First, second and fourth. h, First, second, fourth, fifth and sixth.

2010, Mar. 1 **Litho.** *Perf. 13*

Granite Paper

1306 A219 2p Sheet of 8, #a-h 4.00 4.00

Souvenir Sheet

Perf. 13½

1307 A317 10pmulti 2.50 2.50

No. 1306 contains eight 39x34 hexagonal stamps. Stamps from No. 1306 have Roman numeral "VII" below text "Pa Kua" and "I Ching."

Intl. Women's Day, Cent. — A318

No. 1308 — Women in various costumes: a, 1.50p. b, 2.50p. c, 3.50p. d, 4p.
10p, Three women, vert.

2010, Mar. 8 *Perf. 13¼x14*

Granite Paper

1308 A318 Block of 4, #a-d 3.00 3.00

Souvenir Sheet

1309 A318 10p multi 2.50 2.50

No. 1309 contains one 40x60mm stamp.

Expo 2010, Shanghai — A319

Designs: 3.50p, Rabbits. 4p, Chinese lanterns.
10p, Rabbit and Chinese lanterns.

2010, May 1 *Perf. 13¼x14*

Granite Paper

1310-1311 A319 Set of 2 1.90 1.90

Souvenir Sheet

1312 A319 10p multi 2.50 2.50

Macau Branch of Bank of China, 60th Anniv. — A320

No. 1313 — Yellow ribbons forming "60," Bank of China emblem and: a, 1.50p, Street lamp, ruins of St. Paul's Church. b, 2.50p, Buildings. c, 3.50p, "10" from banknote, 1000-pataca banknote. d, 4p, Child, stylized people, people shaking hands.
10p, Buildings, lotus flower, Bank of China emblem.

2010, June 21 *Perf. 13¼x14*

Granite Paper

1313 A320 Block of 4, #a-d 3.00 3.00

Souvenir Sheet

1314 A320 10p multi 2.50 2.50

No. 1314 contains one 60x40mm stamp.

Historic Center of Macao UNESCO World Heritage Site — A321

No. 1315 — Buildings near St. Augustine's Square: a, 1.50p, Dom Pedro V Theater. b, 2.50p, Sir Robert Ho Tung Library. c, 3.50p, St. Augustine's Church. d, 4p, Seminary and Church of St. Joseph.
10p, Building on Square.

2010, July 15 *Perf. 14x13¼*

Granite Paper

1315 A321 Block of 4, #a-d 3.00 3.00

Souvenir Sheet

1316 A321 10p multi 2.50 2.50

Stained-Glass Windows — A322

Stained-glass window from St. Lawrence's Church, Macao: 5.50p, Detail. 10p, Entire window, horiz.

2010, Aug. 30 *Perf. 13¼x13*

Granite Paper

1317 A322 5.50p multi 1.40 1.40

Souvenir Sheet

Perf. 13x13¼

1318 A322 10p multi 2.50 2.50

See Aland Islands Nos. 306-307.

Carvings of Religious Figures — A323

No. 1319: a, 1.50p, Buddha. b, 2.50p, Na Tcha. c, 3.50p, Kun Iam. d, 4p, Tin Hau.
10p, The Eight Immortals, horiz.

2010, Sept. 7 *Perf. 14*

1319 A323 Block or strip of 4, #a-d 3.00 3.00

Souvenir Sheet

1320 A323 10p multi 2.50 2.50

No. 1320 contains one 60x30mm stamp.

Old Telephones — A324

No. 1321 — Various old telephones with background color of: a, 1.50p, Green. b, 2.50p, Pink. c, 3.50p, Yellow. d, 4p, Blue.
10p, Old telephone, horiz.

2010, Sept. 1 **Litho.** *Perf. 14*

1321 A324 Block or strip of 4, #a-d 3.00 3.00

Souvenir Sheet

1322 A324 10d multi 2.50 2.50

No. 1322 contains one 60x40mm stamp.

Macao Food Festival, 10th Anniv. — A325

Designs: 1.50p, Wonton soup. 2.50p, Xiao Long Bao (steamed buns). 3.50p, Sushi. 4p, Pastel de nata (egg tart).
10p, Portuguese chicken.

2010, Nov. 5 *Perf. 13¼x13*

1323-1326 A325 Set of 4 3.00 3.00

Souvenir Sheet

1327 A325 10p multi 2.50 2.50

Traditional Clothing — A326

No. 1328: a, 1.50p, Man in Tang suit. b, 2.50p, Woman in qipao. c, 3.50p, Woman in blouse and long skirt. d, 4p, Man in tunic suit.
10p, Two women, horiz.

2010, Nov. 30

1328 A326 Block of 4, #a-d 3.00 3.00

Souvenir Sheet

1329 A326 10p multi 2.50 2.50

No. 1329 contains one 60x40mm stamp.

Giant Pandas — A327

Panda, domed building and: 1.50p, Chapel of Our Lady of Penha. 5p, Ruins of St. Paul's Church.

10p, Two pandas, domed building, Ruins of St. Paul's Church.

2010, Dec. 18 ***Perf. 13¼x13***

1330-1331 A327 Set of 2 1.75 1.75

Souvenir Sheet

Perf. 13x13¼

1332 A327 10p multi 2.50 2.50

No. 1332 contains one 40x60mm stamp.

New Year 2011 (Year of the Rabbit) A328

No. 1333: a, Clay sculpture of rabbit. b, Fireworks and laser light image of rabbit. c, Watercolor painting of rabbit. d, Wood carving rabbit. e, Metal sculpture of rabbit.

10p, Metal sculpture of rabbit, diff.

Litho., Litho. & Embossed with Foil and Hologram Application (5p, 10p)

2011, Jan. 5 ***Perf. 13¼x13***

1333 Horiz. strip of 5 2.75 2.75
a.-d. A328 1.50p Any single .35 .35
e. A328 5p multi 1.25 1.25

Souvenir Sheet

Perf. 14¼

1334 A328 10p multi 2.50 2.50

No. 1334 contains one 50x50mm diamond-shaped stamp.

AIR POST STAMPS

Stamps of 1934 Overprinted or Surcharged in Black

a

b

1936 **Wmk. 232** ***Perf. 11½***

C1 A17 (a) 2a blue green 2.50 .75
C2 A17 (a) 3a violet 4.25 .75
C3 A17 (b) 5a on 6a brown 4.25 .75
C4 A17 (a) 7a brt rose 4.25 .75
C5 A17 (a) 8a brt blue 11.00 1.00
C6 A17 (a) 15a maroon 27.50 4.00
Nos. C1-C6 (6) 53.75 8.00

Common Design Type
Name and Value in Black

Perf. 13½x13

1938, Aug. 1 **Engr.** **Unwmk.**

C7 CD39 1a scarlet .90 .50
C8 CD39 2a purple 1.10 .50
C9 CD39 3a orange 1.60 .90
C10 CD39 5a ultra 3.25 1.25
C11 CD39 10a lilac brn 5.50 1.25
C12 CD39 20a dk green 11.00 3.00
C13 CD39 50a red brown 18.00 4.00
C14 CD39 70a rose car 22.50 5.00
C15 CD39 1p magenta 45.00 18.00
Nos. C7-C15 (9) 108.85 34.40

No. C13 exists with overprint "Exposicao Internacional de Nova York, 1939-1940" and Trylon and Perisphere. Value $325.

Catalogue values for unused stamps in this section, from this point to the end of the section, are for never hinged items.

Plane over Bay of Grand Beach — AP1

1960, Dec. 11 **Litho.** ***Perf. 14***

C16 AP1 50a shown 3.00 .40
C17 AP1 76a Penha Chapel 5.00 1.25
C18 AP1 3p Macao 16.00 2.00
C19 AP1 5p Bairro de Mong Ha 20.00 2.00
C20 AP1 10p Penha and Bay 32.50 2.25
Nos. C16-C20 (5) 76.50 7.90
Set, hinged 40.00

No. C17 Surcharged

1979, Aug. 3 **Litho.** ***Perf. 14***

C21 AP1 70a on 76a multi *37.50* 3.25

POSTAGE DUE STAMPS

Numeral of Value — D1

Perf. 11½x12

1904, July **Typo.** **Unwmk.**

Name and Value in Black

J1 D1 ½a gray green 1.50 1.25
a. Name & value inverted 125.00 60.00
J2 D1 1a yellow grn 2.00 1.25
J3 D1 2a slate 2.00 1.25
J4 D1 4a pale brown 2.75 1.25
J5 D1 5a red orange 3.50 2.00
J6 D1 8a gray brown 4.00 2.00
J7 D1 12a red brown 6.00 2.00
J8 D1 20a dull blue 10.00 4.50
J9 D1 40a carmine 20.00 6.00
J10 D1 50a orange 26.50 12.00
J11 D1 1p gray violet 52.50 25.00
Nos. J1-J11 (11) 130.75 58.50

Issued without gum: Nos. J7-J11. Issued with or without gum: No. J4. Others issued with gum.

For overprints see Nos. 144-146, J12-J32.

Issue of 1904 Overprinted in Carmine or Green

Lisbon Overprint

Overprint 24½mm long. "A" has flattened top.

1911

J12 D1 ½a gray green .50 .30
J13 D1 1a yellow green 1.00 .50
J14 D1 2a slate 1.25 .65
J15 D1 4a pale brown 1.50 .75
J16 D1 5a orange 2.00 1.00
J17 D1 8a gray brown 4.00 1.75
J18 D1 12a red brown 7.00 2.00
J19 D1 20a dull blue 9.50 3.00
J20 D1 40a carmine (G) 12.50 4.00
J21 D1 50a orange 16.00 5.00
J22 D1 1p gray violet 30.00 7.50
Nos. J12-J22 (11) 85.25 26.45

Issued without gum: Nos. J19-J22.

Issue of 1904 Overprinted in Red or Green

Local Overprint

Overprint 23mm long. "A" has pointed top.

1914

J22A D1 ½a gray green *1,600. 600.00*
J23 D1 1a yellow green 3.00 .50
J24 D1 2a slate 3.00 .50
J25 D1 4a pale brown 3.00 .75
J26 D1 5a orange 3.50 .75
J27 D1 8a gray brown 3.50 .90
J28 D1 12a red brown 3.50 .80
J29 D1 20a dull blue 12.50 3.00
J30 D1 40a car (G) 35.00 5.00
a. Double ovpt., red and green 100.00 27.50
J31 D1 50a orange 35.00 8.00
J32 D1 1p gray violet 70.00 10.00
Nos. J23-J32 (10) 172.00 30.20

Issued without gum: Nos. J28, J30-J32.

D2

Name and Value in Black

1947 **Typo.** ***Perf. 11½x12***

J33 D2 1a red violet 1.00 1.00
J34 D2 2a purple 1.50 1.00
J35 D2 4a dark blue 2.50 1.00
J36 D2 5a chocolate 3.50 1.00
J37 D2 8a red violet 4.50 1.00
J38 D2 12a orange brown 7.50 1.00
J39 D2 20a yellow green 8.50 3.00
J40 D2 40a brt carmine 10.00 3.50
J41 D2 50a orange yellow 19.00 7.75
J42 D2 1p blue 30.00 9.00
Nos. J33-J42 (10) 88.00 29.25

Stamps of 1934 Surcharged "PORTEADO" and New Values in Carmine

1949, May 1 **Wmk. 232**

J43 A17 1a on 4a black 3.75 .85
J44 A17 2a on 6a brown 3.75 .85
J45 A17 4a on 8a brt blue 4.25 .85
J46 A17 5a on 10a red org 4.75 .85
J47 A17 8a on 12a dk blue 4.75 1.40
J48 A17 12a on 30a apple grn 6.50 1.50
J49 A17 20a on 40a violet 6.50 1.50
Nos. J43-J49 (7) 34.25 7.80

Catalogue values for unused stamps in this section, from this point to the end of the section, are for Never Hinged items.

Nos. 348, 349 and 351 Overprinted or Surcharged in Black or Carmine

1951, June 6 **Unwmk.**

J50 A21 1a org yel, *lem* 1.40 .20
J51 A21 2a dk grn, *bl* (C) 1.40 .20
J52 A21 7a on 10a brt pink, *bl* 1.40 .20
Nos. J50-J52 (3) 4.20 .60

Common Design Type

1952 **Photo. & Typo.** ***Perf. 14***

Numeral in Red; Frame Multicolored

J53 CD45 1a violet blue .75 .20
J54 CD45 3a chocolate .75 .20
J55 CD45 5a indigo .75 .20
J56 CD45 10a dark red 3.00 .40
J57 CD45 30a indigo 3.75 .50
J58 CD45 1p chocolate 11.50 1.50
Nos. J53-J58 (6) 20.50 3.00

WAR TAX STAMPS

Victory WT1

1919, Aug. 11 **Unwmk.** ***Perf. 15x14***

Overprinted in Black or Carmine

MR1 WT1 2a green 2.25 1.00
MR2 WT1 11a green (C) 3.50 1.40

Nos. MR1-MR2 were also for use in Timor.

A 9a value was issued for revenue use. Value $10.

NEWSPAPER STAMPS

Nos. P1-P2

No. P3

Typographed and Embossed

1892-93 **Unwmk.** ***Perf. 12½***

Black Surcharge

Without Gum

P1 A7 2½r on 40r choc 6.00 2.50
a. Inverted surcharge 45.00 30.00
b. Perf. 13½ 7.00 4.50
P2 A7 2½r on 80r gray 9.00 4.00
a. Inverted surcharge 60.00 50.00
b. Double surcharge
c. Perf. 13½ 45.00 35.00
P3 A7 2½r on 10r grn ('93) 6.00 4.00
a. Double surcharge
b. Perf. 13½ 7.00 5.75
Nos. P1-P3 (3) 21.00 10.50

N3

N4

1893-94 **Typo.** ***Perf. 12½***

P4 N3 2½r brown 3.25 2.00
a. Perf. 12½ 3.25 2.25
b. Perf. 13½ 3.50 2.00
P5 N4 ⅛a on 2½r brn (Bk) ('94) 4.50 2.75
a. Double surcharge

For surcharges see Nos. 131, 252.

POSTAL TAX STAMPS

Pombal Commemorative Issue

Common Design Types

Perf. 12½

1925, Nov. 3 **Engr.** **Unwmk.**

RA1 CD28 2a red org & blk 3.25 .70
RA2 CD29 2a red org & blk 3.25 .70
RA3 CD30 2a red org & blk 3.25 .70
Nos. RA1-RA3 (3) 9.75 2.10

PT1

PT2

Symbolical of Charity

1930, Dec. 25 **Litho.** ***Perf. 11***
RA4 PT1 5a dk brown, *yel* 7.00 5.00

1945-47 ***Perf. 11½, 12, 10***
RA5 PT2 5a blk brn, *yel* 10.50 7.50
RA6 PT2 5a bl, *bluish* ('47) 30.00 6.75
RA7 PT2 10a grn, *citron* 10.00 3.75
RA8 PT2 15a org, *buff* 1.50 3.75
RA9 PT2 20a rose red, *sal* 60.00 6.75
RA10 PT2 50a red vio, *pnksh* 3.00 3.00
Nos. RA5-RA10 (6) 115.00 31.50

Catalogue values for unused stamps in this section, from this point to the end of the section, are for Never Hinged items.

1953-56 ***Perf. 10½x11½***
RA11 PT2 10a bl, *pale grn* ('56) 2.00 1.50
RA12 PT2 20a chocolate, *yel* 11.00 5.00
RA13 PT2 50a car, *pale rose* 10.00 4.50
Nos. RA11-RA13 (3) 23.00 11.00

1958 ***Perf. 12x11½***
RA14 PT2 1a gray grn, *grnsh* .75 .35
RA15 PT2 2a rose lilac, *grysh* 1.50 .75

Type of 1945-47 Redrawn
Imprint: "Lito. Imp. Nac.-Macau"

1961-66 ***Perf. 11***
RA16 PT2 1a gray grn, *grnsh* 1.50 .80
RA17 PT2 2a rose lil, *grysh* 1.50 .80
RA18 PT2 10a bl, *pale grn* ('62) 1.50 .80
RA19 PT2 20a brn, *yel* ('66) 1.75 1.00
Nos. RA16-RA19 (4) 6.25 3.40

Nos. RA16-RA19 have accent added to "E" in "Assistencia."
Nos. RA4-RA19 were issued without gum.

Type of 1945-47 Redrawn and Surcharged

1979 **Litho.** ***Perf. 11x11½***
RA20 PT2 20a on 1p yel grn, *cream* 5.00 —

No. RA20 has no accent above "E," no imprint and was not issued without surcharge.

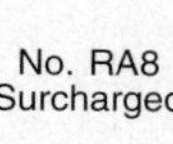
No. RA8 Surcharged

Methods and Perfs As Before
1981
RA20A PT2 10a on 15a #RA8 — —

No. RA17 Surcharged

Methods and Perfs As Before
1981

Without Gum
RA21 PT2 20a on 2a #RA17 6.00 —

POSTAL TAX DUE STAMPS

Pombal Commemorative Issue
Common Design Types

1925 **Unwmk.** ***Perf. 12½***
RAJ1 CD28 4a red orange & blk 3.25 .70
RAJ2 CD29 4a red orange & blk 3.25 .70
RAJ3 CD30 4a red orange & blk 3.25 .70
Nos. RAJ1-RAJ3 (3) 9.75 2.10

MACEDONIA

ˌma-sə-ˈdō-nē-ə

LOCATION — Central Balkans, bordered by on the north by Serbia, to the east by Bulgaria, on the south by Greece and by Albania on the west.
GOVT. — Republic
AREA — 9,928 sq. mi.
POP. — 2,022,604 (1999 est.)
CAPITAL — Skopje

Formerly a constituent republic in the Socialist Federal Republic of Yugoslavia. Declared independence on Nov. 21, 1991.

100 Deni (de) = 1 Denar (d)

Catalogue values for all unused stamps in this country are for Never Hinged items.

Watermark

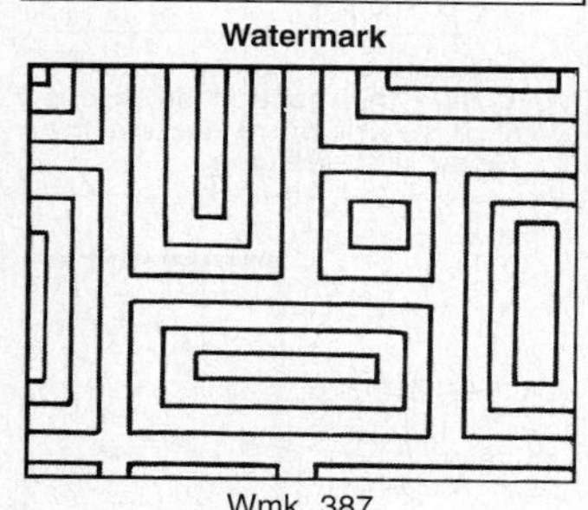
Wmk. 387

Bas Relief — A1

1992-93 **Litho.** ***Perf. 13½x13***
1 A1 30d multicolored .60 .35

Perf. 10
2 A1 40d multicolored .60 .25

Issued: 30d, 9/8/92; 40d, 3/15/93.
For surcharges see Nos. 21, 42.

Christmas — A2

Frescoes: 100d, Nativity Scene, 16th cent. 500d, Virgin and Child, 1422.

1992, Dec. 10 **Litho.** ***Perf. 13x13½***
3 A2 100d multicolored 1.25 1.25
4 A2 500d multicolored 2.75 2.75

Natl. Flag — A3

1993, Mar. 15 ***Perf. 13½x13***
5 A3 10d multicolored 1.00 .35
6 A3 40d multicolored 1.75 .35
7 A3 50d multicolored 1.75 .70
Nos. 5-7 (3) 4.50 1.40

For surcharges see Nos. 23, 40-41.

Fish — A4

Designs: 50d, 1000d, Rutilus macedonicus. 100d, 2000d, Salmothymus achridanus.

1993, Mar. 15 ***Perf. 10***
8 A4 50d multicolored .40 .20
9 A4 100d multicolored .40 .20
10 A4 1000d multicolored 4.50 2.10
11 A4 2000d multicolored 5.50 3.25
Nos. 8-11 (4) 10.80 5.75

Easter — A5

1993, Apr. 16
12 A5 300d multicolored 3.75 3.00

Trans-Balkan Telecommunications Network — A6

1993, May 6
13 A6 500d multicolored 1.40 .80

Admission to the UN, Apr. 8, 1993 — A7

1993, July 28
14 A7 10d multicolored 1.60 .95

A8

A9

1993, Aug. 2
15 A8 10d multicolored 1.60 .95

Souvenir Sheet
Imperf
16 A8 30d multicolored 5.00 5.00

Ilinden Uprising, 90th anniv.

1993, Nov. 4
17 A9 4d multicolored .60 .60

Size: 85x67mm
Imperf
18 A9 40d multicolored 5.50 5.50

Macedonian Revolutionary Organization, cent.

Christmas A10

1993, Dec. 31 ***Perf. 10***
19 A10 2d Nativity Scene 1.00 1.00
20 A10 20d Adoration of the Magi 3.50 2.75

Nos. 1, 5, RA1 Surcharged

1994, Apr. 2 ***Perfs., Etc. as Before***
21 A1 2d on 30d multi .30 .30
22 PT1 8d on 2.50d multi 1.25 1.25
23 A3 15d on 10d multi 2.75 2.75
Nos. 21-23 (3) 4.30 4.30

Size and location of surcharge varies.

Easter — A11

Revolutionaries — A12

1994, Apr. 29 Litho. *Perf. 10*
24 A11 2d multicolored *.60 .30*

1994, May 23

Designs: 8d, Kosta Racin (1908-43), writer. 15d, Grigor Prlicev (1830-93), writer. 20d, Nikola Vapzarov (1909-42), poet. 50d, Goce Delchev (1872-1903), politician.

25 A12 8d multicolored *1.00 .70*
26 A12 15d multicolored *1.50 1.25*
27 A12 20d multicolored *3.00 1.90*
28 A12 50d multicolored *3.50 2.60*
Nos. 25-28 (4) 9.00 6.45

Intl. Year of the Family — A13

1994, June 21
29 A13 2d multicolored *.70 .25*

Liberation Day, 50th Anniv. — A14

Swimming Marathon, Ohrid Lake — A15

Designs: 5d, St. Prohor Pcinski Monastery, up close. 50d, View of entire grounds.

1994, Aug. 2 Litho. *Perf. 10*
30 A14 5d multicolored *.70 .45*

Size: 108x73mm

Imperf

31 A14 50d multicolored *4.25 3.25*

1994, Aug. 22
32 A15 8d multicolored *.95 .45*

Stamp Day — A16

1994, Sept. 12
33 A16 2d multicolored *1.00 .65*

Nova Makedonija, Mlad Boretz, & Makedonka Newspapers, 50th Anniv. — A17

1994, Sept. 13 Litho. *Perf. 10*
34 A17 2d multicolored *1.00 .65*

St. Kliment of Ohrid Library, 50th Anniv. A18

Manuscripts: 2d, 15th cent. 10d, 13th cent.

1994, Sept. 29 Litho. *Perf. 10*
35 A18 2d multi *.30 .20*
36 A18 10d multi, vert. *1.90 1.40*

Macedonian Radio, 50th Anniv. — A19

1994, Dec. 26 Litho. *Perf. 10*
37 A19 2d multicolored *.70 .30*

Wildlife Conservation — A20

1994, Dec. 26 Litho. *Perf. 10*
38 A20 5d Pinus peluse *.65 .45*
39 A20 10d Lynx lynx martinoi *1.60 1.10*

Nos. 2, 6 Surcharged in Black or Gold

a

b

Perfs., Etc. as Before

1995, Mar. 13 Litho.
40 A3(a) 2d on 40d #6 *2.50 2.50*
41 A3(b) 2d on 40d #6 *1.25 1.25*
42 A1(a) 5d on 40d #2 (G) *.85 .85*
Nos. 40-42 (3) 4.60 4.60

Easter — A21

1995, Apr. 23 Litho. *Perf. 10*
43 A21 4d multicolored *.65 .35*

End of World War II, 50th Anniv. A22

1995, May 9 Litho. *Perf. 10*
44 A22 2d multicolored *1.25 .65*

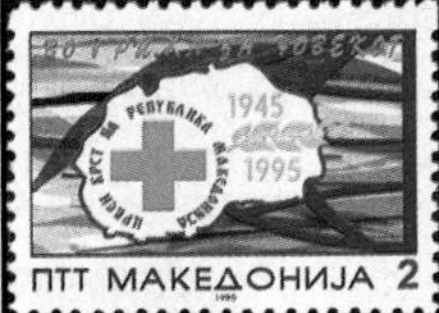

Macedonian Red Cross, 50th Anniv. — A23

1995, May 20 Litho. *Perf. 10*
45 A23 2d multicolored *1.50 .65*

Wilhelm Röntgen (1845-1923), Discovery of the X-Ray, Cent. — A24

1995, May 20
46 A24 2d multicolored *1.50 .65*

Vojdan Cernodrinski (1875-1951), Theater Festival, 50th Anniv. — A25

1995, June 8
47 A25 10d multicolored *1.40 .65*

Death of Prince Marko Kraljevic, 600th Anniv. A26

1995, June 22
48 A26 20d multicolored *2.50 2.00*

Gorgi Puleski (1818-95), Writer A27

1995, July 8
49 A27 2d multicolored *1.25 .65*

Writer's Festival, Struga A28

1995, Aug. 23 Litho. *Perf. 10*
50 A28 2d multicolored *1.90 1.25*

A29

A30

1995, Oct. 4
51 A29 15d Mosque of Tetovo *1.90 1.25*

1995, Oct. 4 Litho. *Perf. 10*

Architecture.

52 A30 2d Malesevija *.35 .25*
53 A30 20d Krakornica *2.40 1.25*

See #81-83 and design A63a.

Motion Pictures, Cent. A31

Film strip of early movie and: No. 54, Auguste and Louis Lumiére. No. 55, Milton and Janaki Manaki, Macedonian cinematographers.

1995, Oct. 6 *Perf. 10 on 3 Sides*
54 A31 10d multicolored *1.75 1.75*
55 A31 10d multicolored *1.75 1.75*
a. Pair, #54-55 *3.50 3.50*

UN, 50th Anniv. A32

1995, Oct. 24
56 A32 20d Blocks, globe in nest *3.00 5.00*
57 A32 50d Blocks, sun *5.75 5.75*

Christmas
A33

1995, Dec. 13
58 A33 15d multicolored *1.90 1.90*

Birds
A34

15d, Pelecanus crispus. 40d, Gypaetus barbatus.

1995, Dec. 14
59 A34 15d multicolored *2.75 2.75*
60 A34 40d multicolored *4.75 4.75*

Reform of Macedonian Language, 50th Anniv. — A35

1995, Dec. 18
61 A35 5d multicolored *.70 .70*

St. Bogorodica Church, Ohrid, 700th Anniv. — A36

Designs: 8d, Detail of fresco, exterior view, St. Kliment of Ohrid (840-916). 50d, Portion of fresco inside church, #62.

1995, Dec. 19
62 A36 8d multicolored *1.00 1.00*

Size: 80x61mm

Imperf

62A A36 50d multicolored *75.00 75.00*

Macedonia's Admission to UPU, 1st Anniv. — A37

1995, Dec. 27
62B A37 10d Post office, Skopje *1.25 1.25*

Admission to Council of Europe (CE) and Organization for Security and Cooperation in Europe (OSCE) — A37a

1995, Dec. 27
62C A37a 20d multicolored *2.75 2.75*

Modern Olympic Games, Cent., 1996 Summer Olympic Games, Atlanta
A38

1996, May 20 Litho. *Perf. 10*
63 A38 2d Kayak race *.70 .70*
64 A38 8d Basketball, vert. *.90 .90*
65 A38 15d Swimming *1.90 1.90*
66 A38 20d Wrestling *3.00 3.00*
67 A38 40d Boxing, vert. *4.75 4.75*
68 A38 50d Running, vert *6.50 6.50*
Nos. 63-68 (6) 17.75 17.75

Intl. Decade to Fight Illegal Drugs — A39

1996, July 11 Litho. *Perf. 10*
69 A39 20d multicolored *2.40 2.40*

Children's Paintings — A40

1996, July 15
70 A40 2d Boy *.30 .30*
71 A40 8d Girl *.95 .95*

Peak of Czar Samuel of Bulgaria's Power, 1000th Anniv.
A41

1996, July 19
72 A41 40d multicolored *5.00 5.00*

Independence, 5th Anniv. — A43

G. Petrov (1865-1921), Revolutionary
A42

1996, Aug. 2
73 A42 20d multicolored *2.00 2.00*

1996, Sept. 8
74 A43 10d multicolored *1.00 1.00*

Vera Ciriviri-Trena (1920-44), Freedom Fighter — A44

Mother Teresa (1910-97) — A45

1996, Nov. 22 Litho. *Perf. 13x13½*
75 A44 20d multicolored *4.75 3.00*
76 A45 40d multicolored *9.50 6.50*

Europa.

Christmas — A46

Terra Cotta Tiles — A47

Designs: No. 77, Tree, children caroling in snow. No. 78, Candle, nuts, apples.

1996, Dec. 14 Litho. *Perf. 10*
77 A46 10d multicolored *.95 .95*
78 A46 10d multicolored *.95 .95*
a. Pair, #77-78 *1.90 1.90*

1996, Dec. 19

#79a, 80a, 4d, Daniel in lions den. #79b, 80b, 8d, Sts. Christopher & George. #79c, 80c, 20d, Joshua, Caleb. #79d, 80d, 50d, Unicorn.

Blocks of 4, #a.-d.
79 A47 bl grn & multi *8.00 8.00*
80 A47 yel grn & multi *8.00 8.00*

Traditional Architecture Type of 1995

1996
81 A30 2d House, Nistrovo *.25 .25*
82 A30 8d House, Brodets *.90 .90*
83 A30 10d House, Niviste *1.05 1.05*
Nos. 81-83 (3) 2.20 2.20

Issued: 8d, 12/20; 2d, 10d, 12/25.
See Nos. 112-116.

Butterflies
A49

4d, Pseudochazara cingovskii. 40d, Colias balcanica.

1996, Dec. 21
84 A49 4d multicolored *.35 .35*
85 A49 40d multicolored *5.00 5.00*

UNICEF, 50th Anniv.
A50

1996, Dec. 31 *Perf. 14½*
86 A50 20d shown *2.40 2.40*
87 A50 40d UNESCO, 50th anniv. *4.25 4.25*

Alpine Skiing Championships, 50th Anniv. — A51

1997, Feb. 7 *Perf. 10*
88 A51 20d multicolored *2.25 2.25*

Alexander Graham Bell (1847-1922) — A52

1997, Mar. 12
89 A52 40d multicolored *3.50 3.50*

Ancient Roman Mosaics, Heraklia and Stobi
A53

1997, Mar. 26 *Perf. 10*
90 A53 2d Wild dog *.40 .40*
91 A53 8d Bull *.70 .70*
92 A53 20d Lion *2.00 2.00*
93 A53 40d Leopard with prey *3.50 3.50*
Nos. 90-93 (4) 6.60 6.60

Size: 79x56mm

Imperf

94 A53 50d Deer, peacocks *6.00 6.00*

No. 94 has simulated perforations within the design.

Cyrilic Alphabet, 1100th Anniv.
A54

Cyrillic inscriptions and: No. 95, Gold embossed plate. No. 96, St. Cyril (827-69), St. Methodius (825-84), promulgators of Cyrillic alphabet.

1997, May 2 *Perf. 10*
95 A54 10d multicolored *.65 .65*
96 A54 10d multicolored *.65 .65*
a. Pair, #95-96 *1.40 1.40*

A55

A56

Europa (Stories and Legends): 20d, Man kneeling down, another seated in background. 40d, Man, tree, bird dressed as man.

1997, June 6 ***Perf. 15x14***

97	A55 20d multicolored	*2.25*	*2.00*
98	A55 40d multicolored	*5.00*	*3.50*

1997, June 5 ***Perf. 10***

99	A56 15d multicolored	*1.00*	*1.00*

5th Natl. Ecology Day.

St. Naum A57

1997, July 3 ***Perf. 10***

100	A57 15d multicolored	*1.90*	*1.90*

Mushrooms — A58

2d, Cantharellus cibarius. 15d, Boletus aereus. 27d, Amanita caesarea. 50d, Morchella conica.

1997, Nov. 7 **Litho.** ***Perf. 10***

101	A58 2d multicolored	*.65*	*.65*
102	A58 15d multicolored	*1.40*	*1.40*
103	A58 27d multicolored	*2.40*	*2.40*
104	A58 50d multicolored	*4.00*	*4.00*
	Nos. 101-104 (4)	*8.45*	*8.45*

Week of the Child — A59

Minerals — A60

1997, Oct. 11

105	A59 27d multicolored	*2.75*	*2.75*

1997, Oct. 10

106	A60 27d Stibnite	*2.50*	*2.50*
107	A60 40d Lorandite	*4.00*	*4.00*

Mahatma Gandhi (1869-1948) A61

1998, Feb. 4 **Litho.** ***Perf. 13½***

108	A61 30d multicolored	*2.40*	*2.40*

Pythagoras (c. 570-c. 500 BC), Greek Philosopher, Mathematician — A62

1998, Feb. 6

109	A62 16d multicolored	*1.40*	*1.40*

1998 Winter Olympic Games, Nagano — A63

1998, Feb. 7

110	A63 4d Slalom skier + label	*.55*	*.55*
111	A63 30d Cross country skiers + label	*4.00*	*4.00*

Nos. 110-111 were each printed with a se-tenant label.

Traditional Architecture A63a

Location of home: 2d, Novo Selo. 4d, Jablanica. 16d, Kiselica. 20d, Konopnica. 30d, Ambar. 50d, Galicnik.

1998

112	A63a 2d multicolored	*.25*	*.25*
113	A63a 4d multicolored	*.25*	*.25*
113A	A63a 16d multicolored	*.90*	*.90*
114	A63a 20d multicolored	*1.10*	*1.10*
115	A63a 30d multicolored	*1.75*	*1.75*
116	A63a 50d multicolored	*2.75*	*2.75*
	Nos. 112-116 (6)	*7.00*	*7.00*

Issued: 2d, 4d, 30d, 2/9; 20d, 50d, 2/12; 16d, 6/10.

See Nos. 146-148.

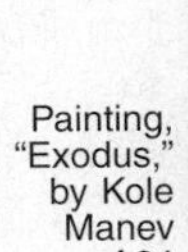

Painting, "Exodus," by Kole Manev A64

1998, Feb. 11

117	A64 30d multicolored	*3.00*	*3.00*

Exodus from Aegean Macedonia, 50th anniv.

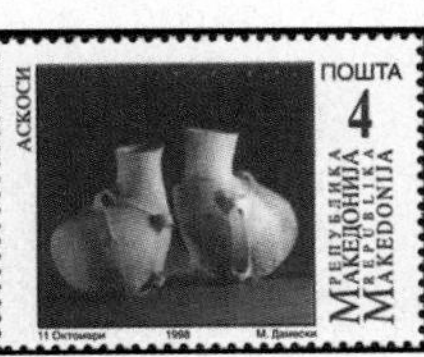

Neolithic Artifacts A65

Designs: 4d, Water flasks. 18d, Animal-shaped bowl. 30d, Woman figure. 60d, Bowl.

1998, Apr. 29 **Litho.** ***Perf. 13½***

118	A65 4d multicolored	*.30*	*.30*
119	A65 18d multicolored	*1.10*	*1.10*
120	A65 30d multicolored	*1.40*	*1.40*
121	A65 60d multicolored	*3.75*	*3.75*
	Nos. 118-121 (4)	*6.55*	*6.55*

1998 World Cup Soccer Championships, France — A66

4d, Looking down at soccer field, ball. 30d, Soccer field with world map in center.

1998, Apr. 30

122	A66 4d multicolored	*.35*	*.35*
123	A66 30d multicolored	*2.50*	*2.50*

Natl. Festivals A67

Europa: 30d, Dancers, Strumica. 40d, People wearing masks, Vevcani.

1998, May 5 **Litho.** ***Perf. 13½***

124	A67 30d multicolored	*3.50*	*1.90*
125	A67 40d multicolored	*4.00*	*2.50*

Carnival Cities Congress, Strumica — A68

1998, May 10 **Litho.** ***Perf. 13½***

126	A68 30d multicolored	*2.75*	*2.75*

World Ecology Day — A69

4d, Stylized flower. 30d, Smokestack uprooting tree.

1998, June 5 **Litho.** ***Perf. 13½***

127	A69 4d multicolored	.40	.40
128	A69 30d multicolored	2.25	2.25

Dimitri Cupovski, 120th Birth Anniv. — A70

1998, June 30

129	A70 16d multicolored	1.25	1.25

Railroads in Macedonia, 125th Anniv. — A72

30d, Document, building, early steam locomotive, vert. 60d, Locomotive, 1873.

1998, Aug. 9 **Litho.** ***Perf. 13½***

130	A72 30d multicolored	2.25	2.25
131	A72 60d multicolored	4.50	4.50

Fossil Skulls Found in Macedonia A73

Designs: 4d, Ursus spelaeus. 8d, Mesopithecus pentelici. 18d, Tragoceros. 30d, Aceratherium incisivum.

1998, Sept. 17

132	A73 4d multicolored	.35	.35
133	A73 8d multicolored	.60	.60
134	A73 18d multicolored	1.25	1.25
135	A73 30d multicolored	2.25	2.25
	Nos. 132-135 (4)	4.45	4.45

The Liturgy of St. John Chrysostom, Cent. — A74

Design: Atanas Badev, composer.

1998, Sept. 21

136	A74 25d multicolored	1.90	1.90

Children's Day — A75

1998, Oct. 5

137	A75 30d multicolored	2.40	2.40

Beetles A76

4d, Cerambyx cerdo. 8d, Rosalia alpina. 20d, Oryctes nasicornis. 40d, Lucanus cervus.

1998, Oct. 20

138	A76 4d multicolored	.25	.25
139	A76 8d multicolored	.50	.50
140	A76 20d multicolored	1.25	1.25
141	A76 40d multicolored	2.50	2.50
	Nos. 138-141 (4)	4.50	4.50

A77

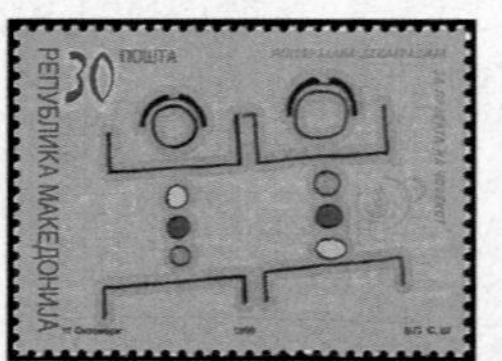
Christmas and New Year A77a

1998, Nov. 20

142	A77	4d multicolored	.30 .30
143	A77a	30d multicolored	2.25 2.25

Universal Declaration of Human Rights, 50th Anniv. — A78

1998, Dec. 10

144	A78	30d multicolored	2.25 2.25

Sharplaninec Dog — A79

1999, Jan. 20 Litho. *Perf. 13¼*

145	A79	15d multi	1.10 1.10

Architecture Type of 1998

"Republica Macedonia" in Cyrillic

Location of home: 1d, Bogomila. 4d, Svekani. 5d, Teovo.

1999 Litho. *Perf. 13¼*

146	A63A	1d multi	.25 .25
147	A63A	4d multi	.25 .25
148	A63A	5d multi	.30 .30
		Nos. 146-148 (3)	.80 .80

Issued: 4d, 2/1; 5d, 2/25; 1d, 11/5.

Icons — A80

Designs: 4d, 1535 Slepche Monastery Annunciation icon, Demir Hisar, by Dimitar Zograf. 8d, 1862 St. Nicholas Church icon, Ohrid. 18d, 1535 Slepche Monastery Madonna and Child icon, Demir Hisar. 30d, 1393-94 Zrze Monastery Jesus icon, Prilep.

50d, 1626 Lesnovo Monastery Jesus icon, Probishtip.

1999, Mar. 3 *Perf. 11¾*

149	A80	4d multi	.30 .30
150	A80	8d multi	.60 .60
151	A80	18d multi	1.25 1.25
152	A80	30d multi	2.25 2.25
		Nos. 149-152 (4)	4.40 4.40

Souvenir Sheet

153	A80	50d multi	3.75 3.75

Dimitar A. Pandilov (1899-1963), Painter — A81

1999, Mar. 14 *Perf. 13¼*

154	A81	4d multi	.50 .50

Telegraphy in Macedonia, Cent. A82

1999, Apr. 22

155	A82	4d multi	.50 .50

Saints Cyril and Methodius University, Skopje, 50th Anniv. A83

1999, Apr. 24

156	A83	8d multi	.70 .70

Issued in sheets of 8 + label.

Council of Europe, 50th Anniv. A84

1999, May 5

157	A84	30d multi	2.25 2.25

Europa A85

Natl. Parks: 30d, Pelister. 40d, Mavrovo.

1999, May 5

158	A85	30d multi	*2.50 1.25*
159	A85	40d multi	*3.00 1.75*

Ecology — A86

1999, June 5

160	A86	30d multi	2.00 2.00

Macedonian Leaders from the Middle Ages — A87

Designs: a, 30d, Strez (1204-14). b, 8d, Gorgi Voytech (1072-1073). c, 18d, Dobromir Hrs (1195-1203). d, 4d, Petar Deljan (1040-41).

1999, June 25

161	A87	Block of 4, #a.-d.	4.00 4.00

Kuzman Sapkarev (1834-1909), Folklorist — A88

1999, Sept. 1 Litho. *Perf. 13¼*

162	A88	4d multi	.55 .55

Flowers — A89

Designs: 4d, Crocus scardicus. 8d, Astragalus mayeri. 18d, Campanula formanekiana. 30d, Viola kosaninii.

1999, Sept. 16

163	A89	4d multi	.30 .30
164	A89	8d multi	.65 .65
165	A89	18d multi	1.25 1.25
166	A89	30d multi	1.90 1.90
		Nos. 163-166 (4)	4.10 4.10

Children's Day — A90

1999, Oct. 4

167	A90	30d multi	1.90 1.90

UPU, 125th Anniv. A91

1999, Oct. 9

168	A91	5d Post horn, emblem	.30 .30
169	A91	30d Emblem, post horn	1.90 1.90

Krste Petkov Misirkov (1875-1926), Writer — A92

1999, Nov. 18

170	A92	5d multi	.55 .55

Christmas — A93

1999, Nov. 24

171	A93	30d multi	1.90 1.90

New Year's Day — A94

1999, Nov. 24 *Perf. 13¼*

172	A94	5d multi	.35 .35

Slavic Presence in Macedonia, 1400th Anniv. — A95

1999, Oct. 27 Litho. *Perf. 13¼*

173	A95	5d multi	.55 .55

Christianity, 2000th Anniv. — A96

Icons and frescoes: 5d, Altar cross, St. Nikita Monastery, vert. 10d, Fresco of Holy Mother of God, St. Mark's Monastery. 15d, St. Clement of Ohrid, vert. 30d, Fresco of Apostle Paul St. Andrew's Monastery, vert.

50d, St. Sophia's Cathedral, Ohrid, vert.

2000, Jan. 19

174-177	A96	Set of 4	4.00 4.00

Souvenir Sheet

178	A96	50d multi	2.75 2.75

No. 178 contains one 30x31mm stamp.

Millennium A97

No. 179: a, 5d, "2000." b, 30d, Religious symbols.

2000, Feb. 16

179	A97	Vert. pair, #a-b	2.25 2.25

Silver Jewelry — A98

Designs: 5d, Pin with icon, Ohrid, 19th cent. 10d, Bracelet, Bitola, 20th cent. 20d, Earrings, Ohrid, 18th cent. 30d, Brooch, Bitola, 19th-20th cent.

2000, Mar. 1 Litho. *Perf. 13¼*
180-183 A98 Set of 4 4.25 4.25

Macedonian Philatelic Society, 50th Anniv. — A99

2000, Mar. 19
184 A99 5d multi .35 .35

World Meteorological Organization, 50th Anniv. — A100

2000, Mar. 23 Litho. *Perf. 13¼*
185 A100 30d multi 2.00 2.00

Easter — A101

2000, Apr. 21 Litho. *Perf. 13¼*
186 A101 5d multi .35 .35

Europa, 2000
Common Design Type

2000, May 9 *Perf. 14*
187 CD17 30d multi *3.50 3.50*

2000 Summer Olympics, Sydney A102

Designs: 5d: Runners. 30d, Wrestlers.

2000, May 17 *Perf. 13¼*
188-189 A102 Set of 2 2.75 2.75

Ecology — A103

2000, June 5 Litho. *Perf. 13¼*
190 A103 5d multi .35 .35

Architecture Type of 1998

2000, July 28
191 A63a 6d House, Zdunje .55 .55

Printing Pioneers — A104

Designs: 6d, Theodosius Sinaitski. 30d, Johannes Gutenberg.

2000, July 28
192-193 A104 Set of 2 2.50 2.50

Mother Teresa (1910-97) A105

2000, Aug. 26
194 A105 6d multi .50 .50

Birds — A106

Designs: 6d, Egretta garzeta. 10d, Ardea cinerea. 20d, Ardea purpurea. 30d, Plegadis falcinellus.

2000, Sept. 14
195-198 A106 Set of 4 5.00 5.00

Children's Week A107

2000, Oct. 2 Litho. *Perf. 13¼*
199 A107 6d multi .55 .55

Duke Dimo Hadi Dimov (1875-1924) A108

2000, Oct. 20
200 A108 6d multi .55 .55

Economics Faculty of Sts. Cyril & Methodius Univ., 50th Anniv. — A109

2000, Nov. 1
201 A109 6d multi .50 .50

Joachim Krchovski, 250th Anniv. of Birth A110

2000, Nov. 8
202 A110 6d multi .55 .55

Christmas A111

2000, Nov. 22
203 A111 30d multi 2.10 2.10

UN High Commissioner For Refugees, 50th Anniv. — A112

Designs: 6d, Handprints. 30d, Globe, hands.

2001, Jan. 10 Litho. *Perf. 13¼*
204-205 A112 Set of 2 2.50 2.50

Worldwide Fund for Nature (WWF) — A113

Imperial eagle: a, 6d, Facing right. b, 8d, With chick. c, 10d, In flight, and close-up of head. d, 30d, Close-up of head.

2001, Feb. 1 Litho. *Perf. 14*
206 A113 Block of 4, #a-d 4.00 4.00

Partenija Zografski (1818-1876) A114

2001, Feb. 6 Litho. *Perf. 13¼*
207 A114 6d multi .35 .35

A115

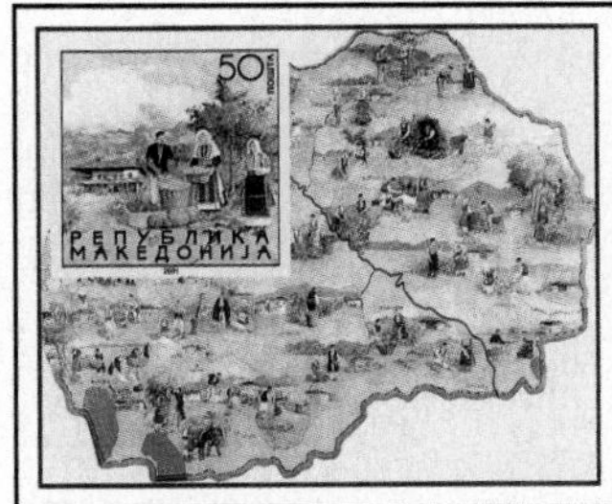

Native Costumes — A116

Designs: 6d, Dolmi Polog. 12d, Albanian. 18d, Reka. 30d, Skopska Crna Gora.
50d, Women, men in costumes, house, vegetables.

2001, Mar. 1 *Perf. 13¼*
208-211 A115 Set of 4 4.50 4.50

Souvenir Sheet
Imperf
Granite Paper

212 A116 50d multi 3.50 3.50

Lazar Licenoski (1901-64), Painter — A117

2001, Mar. 23 *Perf. 13¼*
213 A117 6d multi .55 .55

National Archives, 50th Anniv. — A118

2001, Apr. 1
214 A118 6d multi .35 .35

Easter A119

2001, Apr. 15
215 A119 6d multi .55 .55

Europa — A120

No. 216, Boat on lake: a, 18d. b, 36d.

2001, May 16 Granite Paper
216 A120 Horiz. pair, #a-b *4.00 4.00*

Revolt Against Ottoman Rule, 125th Anniv. A121

2001, May 20 Litho. *Perf. 13¼*
217 A121 6d multi .50 .50

2nd Individual European Chess Championships A122

2001, June 1 Litho. *Perf. 13¼*
218 A122 36d multi 2.50 2.50
a. Booklet pane of 4 10.00 —
Booklet, #218a 10.00

Booklet sold for 145d.

Boats in Lake Dojran A123

2001, June 5 Litho. *Perf. 13¼*
219 A123 6d multi .55 .55

Architecture Type of 1998

Perf. 13¼

2001, June 25 Litho. Unwmk.
220 A63a 6d House, Mitrasinci .50 .50

Independence, 10th Anniv. — A124

2001, Sept. 8 Wmk. 387
221 A124 6d multi .55 .55

Trees A125

Designs: 6d, Juniperus excelsa. 12d, Quercus macedonica. 24d, Arbutus andrachne. 36d, Quercus coccifera.

Perf. 13¼

2001, Sept. 12 Litho. Unwmk.
222-225 A125 Set of 4 5.25 5.25

Children's Day — A126

Perf. 13¼

2001, Oct. 1 Litho. Unwmk.
226 A126 6d multi .50 .50

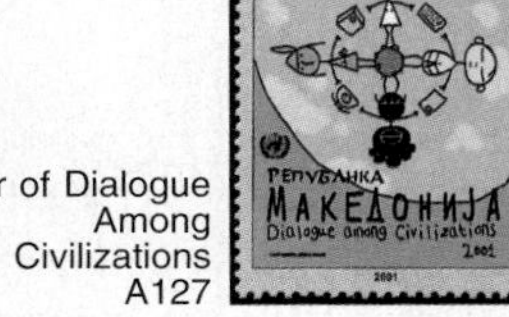

Year of Dialogue Among Civilizations A127

2001, Oct. 9 Granite Paper
227 A127 36d multi 2.75 2.75

Nature Museum, 75th Anniv. A128

2001, Oct. 26
228 A128 6d multi .55 .55

Christmas — A129

2001, Nov. 22
229 A129 6d multi .50 .50

Nobel Prizes, Cent. A130

2001, Dec. 10 Litho. *Perf. 13¼*
230 A130 36d multi 2.50 2.50

2002 Winter Olympics, Salt Lake City — A131

Designs: 6d, Skier. 36d, Skier, diff.

2002, Jan. 16 Litho. *Perf. 14*
231-232 A131 Set of 2 2.75 2.75

Ancient Coins A132

Designs: 6d, King Lykkeios of Paeonia obol, 359-340 B.C. 12d, Alexander III tetradrachm. 24d, Kings of Macedon tetrobol, 185-165 B.C. 36d, Philip II of Macedon gold stater.
50d, Kings of Macedon coin.

2002, Mar. 1
233-236 A132 Set of 4 6.00 6.00

Souvenir Sheet

237 A132 50d multi 3.75 3.75

Petar Mazev (1927-93), Painter A133

2002, Apr. 15
238 A133 6d multi .55 .55

Dimitar Kondovski (1927-93), Painter A134

2002, Apr. 15
239 A134 6d multi .55 .55

Leonardo da Vinci (1452-1519) and Mona Lisa A135

2002, Apr. 15
240 A135 36d multi 2.10 2.10

Easter — A136

2002, Apr. 24
241 A136 6d multi .55 .55

Europa A137

Designs: 6d, Acrobat, bicycle on wire, seal. 36d, Ball on wire, bicycle.

2002, May 9
242-243 A137 Set of 2 *3.25 3.25*

2002 World Cup Soccer Championships, Japan and Korea — A138

2002, May 15
244 A138 6d multi 2.00 2.00

Environmental Protection — A139

2002, June 5
245 A139 6d multi .50 .50

National Arms — A140

Background colors: 10d, Blue. 36d, Greenish blue.

2002, June 18
246-247 A140 Set of 2 3.25 3.25

Architecture A141

Buildings in: 36d, Krushevo. 50d, Bitola.

2002, June 26 *Perf. 13¼*
248-249 A141 Set of 2 5.00 5.00

Metodija Andonov Cento (1902-57), 1st President of Antifascist Council for the Natl. Liberation of Macedonia A142

2002, Aug. 18 Litho. *Perf. 13¼*
250 A142 6d multi .40 .40

Nikola Karev (1877-1905), President of Krushevo Republic, Aug. 1903 — A143

2002, Aug. 18
251 A143 18d multi .90 .90

Fauna — A144

No. 252: a, 6d, Perdix perdix. b, 12d, Sus scrofa. c, 24d, Rupicapra rupicapra. d, 36d, Alectoris graeca.

2002, Sept. 11 *Perf. 14*
252 A144 Block of 4, #a-d 4.50 4.50

Children's Day — A145

2002, Oct. 1
253 A145 6d multi .40 .40

Architecture Type of 1998

2002, Nov. 5 ***Perf. 13¼***
254 A63a 3d House, Jachince .25 .25
255 A63a 9d House, Ratevo .45 .45

Christmas — A146

2002, Nov. 20
256 A146 9d multi .55 .55

Andreja Damjanov (1813-78), Builder of Churches A147

2003, Jan. 21
257 A147 36d multi 2.00 2.00

Musical Instruments A148

Designs: 9d, Gajda. 10d, Tambura. 20d, Kemene. 50d, Tapan.

2003, Feb. 19 **Litho.** ***Perf. 13¼***
258-261 A148 Set of 4 6.50 6.50

Scouting In Macedonia, 50th Anniv. A149

2003, Feb. 22
262 A149 9d multi .65 .65

Krste Petkov Misirkov Macedonian Language Institute, 50th Anniv. A150

2003, Mar. 5
263 A150 9d multi .55 .55

Europa — A151

Poster art: No. 264, 36d, 1966 poster. No. 265, 36d, 1994 Intl. Triennial of Graphic Art poster.

2003, May 9 ***Perf. 13¼x13½***
Granite Paper
264-265 A151 Set of 2 *3.75 3.00*

Ursus Arctos A152

2003, June 5 ***Perf. 13½x13¼***
266 A152 9d multi .60 .60

Building, Skopje A153

Building, Resen A154

2003, June 16
267 A153 10d multi .60 .60
268 A154 20d multi 1.10 1.10

Macedonian Arms — A155

Designs: 9d, Latin lettering. 36d, Cyrillic lettering.

2003, June 23 ***Perf. 13¼x13½***
269-270 A155 Set of 2 3.25 3.25

World Youth Handball Championships A156

2003, July 30
271 A156 36d multi 2.50 2.50

Printed in sheets of 8 + label.

Ilinden Uprising, Cent. A157

Uprising participants and: 9d, Seal. 36d, Memorial.
50d, Seal, diff.

2003, Aug. 2 ***Perf. 13½x13¼***
272-273 A157 Set of 2 2.50 2.50
Souvenir Sheet
274 A157 50d multi + label 2.75 2.75

Paintings — A158

Paintings by: 9d, Nikola Martinovski (1903-73), vert. 36d, Vincent van Gogh (1853-90)

Perf. 13½x13¼, 13¼x13½
2003, Aug. 18
275-276 A158 Set of 2 3.00 3.00

Flowers — A159

Designs: 9d, Colchicum macedonicum. 20d, Viola allchariensis. 36d, Tulipa mariannae. 50d, Thymus oehmianus.

Perf. 13¼x13½
2003, Sept. 25 **Litho.**
277-280 A159 Set of 4 7.50 7.50

Writers A160

Designs: No. 281, 9d, Jeronim de Rada (1814-1903). No. 282, 9d, Said Najdeni (1864-1903).

2003, Sept. 30 ***Perf. 13½x13¼***
281-282 A160 Set of 2 1.00 1.00

Children's Day — A161

2003, Oct. 6 ***Perf. 13¼x13½***
283 A161 9d multi .70 .70

Kresnensko Uprising, 125th Anniv. A162

2003, Oct. 17 ***Perf. 13½x13¼***
284 A162 9d multi .70 .70

Dimitar Vlahov (1878-1953), Politician — A163

2003, Nov. 8 **Litho.** ***Perf. 13½x13¼***
285 A163 9d multi .70 .70

Christmas A164

2003, Nov. 19
286 A164 9d multi .70 .70

Handicrafts A165

DesignsL 5d, Tassels. 9d, Pitcher. 10d, Kettle. 20d, Ornament.

2003-04 **Litho.** ***Perf. 13¼x13½***
287 A165 3d multi .30 .30
288 A165 5d multi .35 .35
289 A165 9d multi .60 .60
290 A165 10d multi .70 .70
291 A165 12d multi .80 .80
292 A165 20d multi 1.50 1.50
Nos. 287-292 (6) 4.25 4.25

Issued: 9d, 12/16; 10d, 1/21/04; 5d, 20d, 6/4/04; 3d, 12d, 6/4/04.

Powered Flight, Cent. A166

Perf. 13½x13¼
2003, Dec. 17 **Litho.**
293 A166 50d multi 4.00 4.00

Paintings Type of 2003

Designs: No. 294, 9d, Street and Buildings, by Tomo Vladimirski (1904-71), vert. No. 295, 9d, Street Scene, by Vangel Kodzoman (1904-94).

Perf. 13½x13¼, 13¼x13½
2004, Feb. 14
294-295 A158 Set of 2 1.25 1.25

Decorated Weapons — A167

Designs: 10d, Sword, 1806. 20d, Saber, 19th cent. 36d, Gun, 18th cent. 50d, Rifle, 18th cent.

2004, Mar. 10 ***Perf. 13¼x13½***
Stamps + Labels
296-299 A167 Set of 4 7.75 7.75

Rugs — A168

Various rugs: 36d, 50d.

2004, Mar. 24
300-301 A168 Set of 2 5.75 5.75

Konstandin Kristoforidhi, Publisher of First Albanian Dictionary in Macedonia
A169

2004, Apr. 19
302 A169 36d multi 2.10 2.10

House, Kratovo
A170

2004, Apr. 23 ***Perf. 13½x13¼***
303 A170 20d multi 1.25 1.25

Macedonian Intention to Enter European Union — A171

2004, May 4
304 A171 36d multi 2.40 2.40

Europa — A172

No. 305 — People at beach: a, Denomination at left. b, Denomination at right.

Perf. 13¼x13½
2004, May 7 **Wmk. 387**
305 A172 50d Horiz. pair, #a-b 6.50 6.50

Prespa Ecopark — A173

Perf. 13¼x13½
2004, June 5 **Litho.** **Unwmk.**
306 A173 36d multi 2.50 2.50

2004 Summer Olympics, Athens — A174

No. 307 — Map of Europe, Olympic rings with flags and 2004 Summer Olympics emblem at: a, Left. b, Right.

Perf. 13½x13¼
2004, June 16 **Wmk. 387**
307 A174 50d Horiz. pair, #a-b 6.00 6.00

Sami Frasheri (1850-1904), Writer — A175

Perf. 13½x13¼
2004, June 18 **Litho.** **Unwmk.**
308 A175 12d multi .80 .80

FIFA (Fédération Internationale de Football Association), Cent. — A176

2004, July 3
309 A176 100d multi 6.00 6.00

Marko Cepenkov (1829-1920), Writer — A177

2004, Sept. 1
310 A177 12d multi .80 .80

Vasil Glavinov (1869-1929), Politician — A178

2004, Sept. 1 ***Perf. 13¼x13½***
311 A178 12d multi .85 .85

Birds — A179

Designs: 12d, Bombycilla garrulus. 24d, Lanius senator. 36d, Monticola saxatilis. 48d, Pyrrhula pyrrhula.
60d, Tichodroma muraria.

Perf. 13¼x13½
2004, Sept. 25 **Litho.**
312-315 A179 Set of 4 8.25 8.25

Souvenir Sheet
Imperf

316 A179 60d multi 4.25 4.25

No. 316 contains one 27x36mm stamp.

Children's Day
A180

2004, Oct. 4 **Litho.** ***Perf. 13½x13¼***
317 A180 12d multi .85 .85

Information Technology Society Summit
A181

2004, Oct. 16
318 A181 36d multi 2.50 2.50

Aseman Gospel, 1000th Anniv.
A182

2004, Oct. 27 **Litho.** ***Perf. 13½x13¼***
319 A182 12d multi .90 .90

Marco Polo (1254-1324), Explorer — A183

2004, Nov. 10
320 A183 36d multi 2.50 2.50

Christmas
A184

2004, Nov. 24 ***Perf. 13¼x13½***
321 A184 12d multi .85 .85

Konstantin Miladinov (1830-62), Poet
A185

2005, Feb. 4 ***Perf. 13½x13¼***
322 A185 36d multi 2.00 2.00

Illuminated Manuscripts
A186

Designs: 12d, Manuscript from 16th-17th cent. 24d, Manuscript from 16th cent.

2005, Mar. 9 ***Perf. 13¼x13½***
323-324 A186 Set of 2 2.00 2.00

A187

Embroidery — A188

2005, Mar. 23 ***Perf. 13½x13¼***
325 A187 36d multi 2.50 2.50
326 A188 50d multi 3.25 3.25

Art
A189

Designs: 36d, Sculpture by Ivan Mestrovic. 50d, Painting by Paja Jovanovic, horiz.

Perf. 13½x13¼, 13¼x13½
2005, Apr. 6
327-328 A189 Set of 2 5.25 5.25

First Book in Albanian Language, 450th Anniv. — A190

2005, Apr. 27 ***Perf. 13¼x13½***
329 A190 12d multi .80 .80

Skanderbeg (1405-68), Albanian National Hero — A191

2005, Apr. 27
330 A191 36d multi 2.50 2.50

Europa — A192

Designs: a, 36d, Wheat, bread. b, 60d, Peppers, plate of food.

2005, May 9 ***Perf. 13½x13¼***
331 A192 Horiz. pair, #a-b 6.75 6.75

Vlachs' Day, Cent. A193

2005, Apr. 27 Litho. ***Perf. 13½x13¼***
332 A193 12d multi .80 .80

Environmental Protection A194

2005, June 4 ***Perf. 13¼x13½***
333 A194 36d multi 2.25 2.25

Friezes — A195

Frieze from: 3d, 16th cent. 4d, 15th cent. 6d, 16th cent., diff. 8d, 1883-84. 12d, 16th cent., diff.

2005, June 8 Litho. ***Perf. 13¼x13½***
334-338 A195 Set of 5 2.50 2.50

First Automobile in Macedonia, Cent. — A196

First Glider in Macedonia, 50th Anniv. — A197

Perf. 13½x13¼
2005, June 15 Litho.
339 A196 12d multi .75 .75
340 A197 36d multi 2.25 2.25

Intl. Year of Physics A198

2005, June 30
341 A198 60d multi 4.25 4.25

Fruit A199

Designs: 12d, Malus Miller (apples). 24d, Prunus persica (peaches). 36d, Prunus avium (cherries). 48d, Prunus sp. (plums).
100d, Pyrus sp. (pears), vert.

Perf. 13½x13¼
2005, Sept. 14 Litho. Wmk. 387
342-345 A199 Set of 4 8.25 8.25

Souvenir Sheet
Perf. 13¼x13½
346 A199 100d multi 7.00 7.00

Smolar Waterfall — A200

Perf. 13¼x13½
2005, Sept. 28 Unwmk.
347 A200 24d multi 1.75 1.75

Hans Christian Andersen (1805-75), Author A201

2005, Oct. 3 Litho. ***Perf. 13½x13¼***
348 A201 12d multi .85 .85

Kozjak Dam A202

2005, Oct. 25
349 A202 12d multi .85 .85

Brsjac Rebellion, 125th Anniv. A203

2005, Oct. 28
350 A203 12d multi .85 .85

Rila Congress, Cent. — A204

2005, Oct. 28 ***Perf. 13¼x13½***
351 A204 12d multi .85 .85

Europa Stamps, 50th Anniv. (in 2006) — A205

Emblems and Europa stamps: Nos. 352a, 353a, 60d, #243. Nos. 352b, 353b, 170d, #158. Nos. 352c, 353c, 250d, #97. Nos. 352d, 353d, 350d, #76.

2005, Nov. 14 ***Perf. 13½x13¼***
352 A205 Block of 4, #a-d 55.00 55.00

Souvenir Sheet
353 A205 Sheet of 4, #a-d 55.00 55.00

Stamp sizes: Nos. 352a-352d, 40x30mm; Nos. 353a-353d, 40x29mm.

Whitewater Kayaker A206

2005, Nov. 23
354 A206 36d multi 2.50 2.50

Christmas A207

2005, Nov. 23 ***Perf. 13¼x13½***
355 A207 12d multi .85 .85

Macedonia Post Emblem — A208

Perf. 13¼x13½
2005, Dec. 14 Litho.
356 A208 12d multi .85 .85

2006 Winter Olympics, Turin — A209

Designs: 36d, Skiing. 60d, Ice hockey.

2006, Jan. 26
357-358 A209 Set of 2 6.50 6.50

Fresco and Matejce Monastery A210

Isaac Celebi Mosque — A211

2006, Mar. 8
359 A210 12d multi .75 .75
360 A211 24d multi 1.75 1.75

Léopold Sédar Senghor (1906-2001), First President of Senegal — A212

2006, Mar. 20 ***Perf. 13½x13¼***
361 A212 36d multi 2.25 2.25

Handicrafts With Inlaid Mother-of-Pearl A213

Designs: 12d, Wooden shoes. 24d, Decorative objects.

2006, Mar. 22 ***Perf. 13¼x13½***
362-363 A213 Set of 2 2.50 2.50

Wood Carving by Makarie Negriev Frckovski A214

Cupola of St. Peter's Basilica, Vatican City, 450th Anniv. A215

2006, Apr. 5 ***Perf. 13½x13¼***
364 A214 12d multi .75 .75
365 A215 36d multi 2.00 2.00

Zivko Firfov (1906-84), Composer A216

2006, Apr. 26 *Perf. 13¼x13½*
366 A216 24d multi 1.60 1.60

Wolfgang Amadeus Mozart (1756-91), Composer A217

2006, Apr. 26
367 A217 60d multi 4.00 4.00

Europa A218

Designs: 36d, Lettered balls. 60d, Lettered blocks.

2006, May 9 *Perf. 13½x13¼*
368-369 A218 Set of 2 6.00 6.00

Souvenir Sheet

Macedonian Europa Stamps, 10th Anniv. — A219

No. 370: a, Pope John Paul II (1920-2005). b, Mother Teresa (1910-97).

2006, May 9 *Perf. 13¼x13½*
370 A219 60d Sheet of 2, #a-b 8.00 8.00

Fight Against Desertification — A220

2006, June 5 Litho. *Perf. 13½x13¼*
371 A220 12d multi .80 .80

Grand Prix Racing, Cent. A221

Perf. 13½x13¼
2006, June 14 **Litho.**
372 A221 36d multi 2.50 2.50

Nikola Tesla (1856-1943), Electrical Engineer — A222

Perf. 13½x13¼
2006, June 28 **Litho.**
373 A222 24d multi 2.00 2.00

Christopher Columbus (1451-1506), Explorer — A223

2006, June 28
374 A223 36d multi 2.10 2.10

Containers — A224

2006, Aug. 30 Litho. *Perf. 12¾x13*
375 A224 3d Carafe .25 .25
376 A224 6d Pitcher, bowl .40 .40

Shells — A225

Designs: 12d, Ancylus scalariformis. 24d, Macedopyrgula pavlovici. 36d, Gyraulus trapezoides. 48d, Valvata hirsutecostata.
72d, Ochridopyrgula macedonica.

2006, Sept. 6 Litho. *Perf. 13¼x13½*
377-380 A225 Set of 4 7.00 7.00

Souvenir Sheet

381 A225 72d multi 4.25 4.25

UNICEF, 60th Anniv. A226

2006, Oct. 2 *Perf. 13½x13¼*
382 A226 12d multi .80 .80

Lynx and Galicica Natl. Park A227

2006, Oct. 2
383 A227 24d multi 1.50 1.50

World Senior Men's and Women's Bowling Championships — A228

2006, Oct. 20
384 A228 36d multi 2.10 2.10

Bishop Frang Bardhi (1606-43) A229

Pres. Boris Trajkovski (1956-2004) A230

Kemal Ataturk (1881-1938), Turkish Statesman A231

Archbishop Dositheus, 100th Anniv. of Birth — A232

2006, Oct. 25 *Perf. 13¼x13½*
385 A229 12d multi .60 .60
386 A230 12d multi .60 .60
387 A231 24d multi 1.40 1.40
388 A232 24d multi 1.40 1.40
Nos. 385-388 (4) 4.00 4.00

Christmas A233

2006, Nov. 22 *Perf. 13½x13¼*
389 A233 12d multi .75 .75

Metal Objects — A234

Designs: 4d, Handled container, Bitola, 19th cent. 5d, Wine flask, Skopje, 20th cent., vert. 10d, Bell, Skopje, 18th cent., vert. 12d, Lidded container, Prilep, 18th-19th cent., vert.

Perf. 13x12¾, 12¾x13
2006, Nov. 30
390 A234 4d multi .25 .25
391 A234 5d multi .25 .25
392 A234 10d multi .55 .55
393 A234 12d multi .70 .70
Nos. 390-393 (4) 1.75 1.75

Kokino Megalithic Observatory A235

Designs: 12d, Mold for amulet. 36d, Sunrise over observatory.

2007, Jan. 31 *Perf. 13¼x13½*
394-395 A235 Set of 2 2.75 2.75

Nos. 394-395 each were printed in sheets of 8 + label.

Monastery Anniversaries — A236

Designs: 12d, Slivnica Monastery, 400th anniv. 36d, St. Nikita Monastery, 700th anniv., vert.

Perf. 13½x13¼, 13¼x13½
2007, Jan. 31
396-397 A236 Set of 2 3.25 3.25

Handicrafts A237

Designs: 12d, Tepelak, Kicevo, 18th-19th cent. 36d, Casket, Ohrid, 19th cent.

2007, Feb. 14 *Perf. 13½x13¼*
398-399 A237 Set of 2 2.75 2.75

Fish A238

Designs: 12d, Cobitis vardarensis. 36d, Zingel balcanicus. 60d, Chondrostoma vardarense. No. 403, 100d, Barbus macedonicus.
No. 404, 100d, Leuciscus cephalus.

2007, Feb. 28
400-403 A238 Set of 4 12.00 12.00

Souvenir Sheet

404 A238 100d multi 5.75 5.75

Epos of Freedom, Mosaic by Borko Lazeski A239

Head of a Woman, by Pablo Picasso — A240

2007, Mar. 14 ***Perf. 13½x13¼***
405 A239 36d multi 2.00 2.00

Perf. 13¼x13½
406 A240 100d multi 6.00 6.00

Cubism, cent.

Intl. Francophone Day — A241

2007, Mar. 20 ***Perf. 13½x13¼***
407 A241 12d multi .70 .70

Cat — A242

2007, Apr. 9 ***Perf. 13¼x13½***
408 A242 12d multi .75 .75

Europa A243

Macedonian Scouting emblem and: 60d, Scout camp. 100d, Scout, tent, vert.

Perf. 13½x13¼, 13¼x13½
2007, May 9 **Litho.**
409-410 A243 Set of 2 9.75 9.75

Souvenir Sheet

Europa — A243a

2007, May 9 **Litho.** ***Perf. 13½x13¼***
411 A243a 160d multi *45.00 45.00*

Scouting, cent.

Discovery of St. Cyril's Grave, 150th Anniv. — A244

2007, May 23 ***Perf. 13¼x13½***
412 A244 50d multi 2.75 2.75

Smokestacks and Clock — A245

2007, June 5 **Litho.** ***Perf. 13¼x13½***
413 A245 12d multi .75 .75

Carl von Linné (1707-78), Botanist — A246

Notes of Dmitri Mendeleev (1834-1907), Chemist — A247

2007, June 20 ***Perf. 13¼x13½***
414 A246 36d multi 2.10 2.10

Perf. 13½x13¼
415 A247 36d multi 2.10 2.10

Euro-Atlantic Partnership Council Security Forum, Ohrid — A248

2007, June 28 ***Perf. 13½x13¼***
416 A248 60d multi 3.25 3.25

Intl. Sailing Federation, Cent. A249

2007, July 31 **Litho.** ***Perf. 13½x13¼***
417 A249 35d multi 2.10 2.10

Maminska River Waterfall — A250

Perf. 13¼x13½
2007, Sept. 19 **Litho.**
418 A250 12d multi .75 .75

Mitrush Kuteli (1907-67), Writer — A251

Fan S. Noli (1882-1965), Albanian Prime Minister — A252

2007, Sept. 25
419 A251 12d multi .75 .75
420 A252 12d multi .75 .75

Children's Day A253

2007, Oct. 1 **Litho.** ***Perf. 13½x13¼***
421 A253 12d multi .75 .75

Launch of Sputnik 1, 50th Anniv. A254

2007, Oct. 4 **Litho.** ***Perf. 13½x13¼***
422 A254 36d multi 2.10 2.10

Petre Prlicko (1905-95), Actor A255

2007, Oct. 31 **Litho.** ***Perf. 13½x13¼***
423 A255 12d multi .75 .75

Jordan Hadzi Konstantinov-Dzinot (1821-82), Educator — A256

2007, Oct. 31
424 A256 12d multi .75 .75

Handbag — A257

2007, Nov. 9 **Litho.** ***Perf. 12¾x13***
425 A257 12d multi .75 .75

Christmas A258

Perf. 13½x13¼
2007, Nov. 21 **Litho.**
426 A258 12d multi .75 .75

Tose Proeski (1981-2007), Singer — A259

2007, Dec. 15 ***Perf. 13¼x13½***
427 A259 12d multi .75 .75

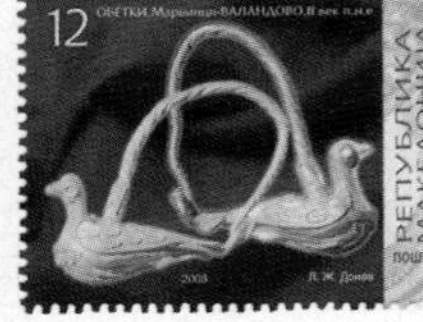

Earrings A260

Designs: 12d, Earrings with pigeon design, 2nd cent. B.C. 24d, Earring with lion design, 4th cent. B.C., vert.

Perf. 13½x13¼, 13¼x13½
2008, Jan. 23 **Litho.**
428-429 A260 Set of 2 2.50 2.50

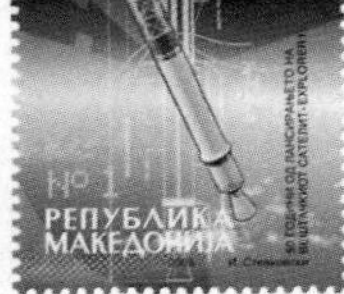

Launch of Explorer 1 Satellite, 50th Anniv. — A261

2008, Jan. 31 **Litho.** ***Perf. 13¼x13½***
430 A261 24d multi 1.75 1.75

High-speed Train — A262

2008, Feb. 27 ***Perf. 13½x13¼***
431 A262 100d multi 6.75 6.75

Worldwide Fund for Nature (WWF) — A263

No. 432 — Upupa epops: a, 12d, In flight. b, 24d, Head. c, 48d, On branch, facing left with insect in beak. d, 60d, On branch, facing right.

Perf. 13½x13¼
2008, Mar. 28 **Litho.**
432 A263 Block of 4, #a-d 7.50 7.50

Bulldog — A264

2008, Apr. 16 **Litho.** ***Perf. 13¼x13½***
433 A264 30d multi 3.25 3.25

Europa — A265

No. 434 — Envelopes over: a, 50d, Western Hemisphere, dark blue panel at top, country name in yellow. b, 100d, Asia, Eastern Europe and Africa, dark blue panel at top, country name in pink.

No. 435, 50d: a, As No. 434a, green panel at top. b, As No. 434b, green panel at top. c, As No. 434a, blue panel at top, country name in orange. d, As No. 434b, blue panel at top, country name in orange.

2008, May 7 **Litho.** ***Perf. 13½x13¼***
434 A265 Horiz. pair, #a-b 8.50 8.50

Miniature Sheet

435 A265 50d Sheet of 4, #a-d *13.50 13.50*

No. 435 was sold with, but not attached to, a booklet cover.

Robert Schuman, Macedonian and European Union Flags — A266

Macedonian and European Union Flags, Eiffel Tower, Paris — A267

Macedonian and European Union Flags, Ljubljana, Slovenia — A268

Perf. 13¼x13½, 13½x13¼
2008, May 22

436	A266 36d multi		2.10	2.10
437	A267 50d multi		3.00	3.00
438	A268 50d multi		3.00	3.00
		Nos. 436-438 (3)	8.10	8.10

Environmental Protection — A269

2008, June 5 **Litho.** ***Perf. 13½x13¼***
439 A269 12d multi .75 .75

Rudolf Diesel (1858-1918), Inventor — A270

2008, June 18 ***Perf. 13¼x13½***
440 A270 30d multi 2.10 2.10

2008 Summer Olympics, Beijing A271

Designs: 12d, Sailing. 18d, Rhythmic gymnastics. 20d, Tennis. 36d, Equestrian.

Perf. 13½x13¼
2008, June 25 **Litho.**
441-444 A271 Set of 4 6.00 6.00

Eqrem Cabej (1908-80), Linguist A272

2008, Aug. 6 **Litho.** ***Perf. 13½x13¼***
445 A272 12d multi .75 .75

14th Intl. Congress of Slavists, Ohrid A273

2008, Sept. 10
446 A273 12d multi .75 .75

Flowers — A274

Designs: 1d, Helichrysum zivojinii. 12d, Pulsatilla halleri, horiz. 50d, Stachys iva, horiz. No. 450, 72d, Fritillaria macedonica.
No. 451, 72d, Centaurea grbavacensis.

Perf. 13¼x13½, 13½x13¼
2008, Sept. 10
447-450 A274 Set of 4 8.00 8.00

Souvenir Sheet

451 A274 72d multi 4.75 4.75

Matka Cave A275

2008, Sept. 24 ***Perf. 13½x13¼***
452 A275 12d multi .85 .85

Children's Day A276

2008, Oct. 6
453 A276 12d multi .75 .75

European Women's Handball Championships — A277

2008, Oct. 15
454 A277 30d multi 1.50 1.50

Religious Song Lyrics by St. John Kukuzel (c. 1280-1360) A278

2008, Oct. 22 **Litho.** ***Perf. 13¼x13½***
455 A278 12d multi .60 .60

Giacomo Puccini (1858-1924), Opera Composer — A279

2008, Oct. 22 ***Perf. 13½x13¼***
456 A279 100d multi 5.25 5.25

Kosta Racin (1908-43), Poet — A280

2008, Nov. 5 ***Perf. 13¼x13½***
457 A280 12d multi .75 .75

Albanian Language, Cent. — A281

Perf. 13¼x13½
2008, Nov. 14 **Litho.**
458 A281 12d multi .75 .75

Christmas A282

Perf. 13½x13¼
2008, Nov. 19 **Litho.**
459 A282 12d multi .75 .75

Cities
A283 A284

Designs: No. 460, Bitola. No. 461, Ohrid. No. 462, Tetovo. No. 463, Skopje. No. 464, Stip.

2008, Dec. 4 **Litho.** ***Perf. 12¾x13***

Denomination Color

460	A283 12d blue		.70	.70
461	A283 12d black		.70	.70
462	A283 12d red		.70	.70
463	A284 12d gray blue		.70	.70
464	A284 12d gray green		.70	.70
		Nos. 460-464 (5)	3.50	3.50

Lech Walesa and Solidarity Emblem — A285

2008, Dec. 8 ***Perf. 13¼x13½***

465 A285 50d multi 2.50 2.50

Friendship between Macedonia and Poland. Printed in sheets of 8 + label.

Blacksmithing A286

Designs: 10d, Blacksmiths and anvil. 20d, Horseshoe.

2009, Jan. 21

466-467 A286 Set of 2 1.90 1.90

Yuri Gagarin (1934-68), First Man in Space A287

2009, Feb. 4 ***Perf. 13½x13¼***

468 A287 50d multi 3.00 3.00

Printed in sheets of 8 + label.

Campaign Against Breast Cancer — A288

2009, Mar. 2 ***Perf. 13¼x13½***

469 A288 15d multi .80 .80

Composers — A289

Designs: 12d, Trajko Prokopiev (1909-79) and Todor Skalovski (1909-2004). 60d, George Friedrich Handel (1685-1759) and Joseph Haydn (1732-1809).

2009, Mar. 18 ***Perf. 13½x13¼***

470-471 A289 Set of 2 4.00 4.00

No. 471 was printed in sheets of 8 + label.

A290

Horses — A291

2009, Apr. 15 Litho. ***Perf. 13¼x13½***

Granite Paper

472 A290 20d multi 1.40 1.40
473 A291 50d multi 3.50 3.50

Prague, Flags of Czech Republic and Macedonia A293

Pippi Longstocking, Flag of Macedonia A294

2009, May 9 Litho. ***Perf. 13½x13¼***

477 A293 10d multi .50 .50

Perf. 13¼x13½

478 A294 60d multi 3.25 3.25

Macedonia in the European Union. No. 478 was printed in sheets of 8 + label.

Vrelo Cave A295

2009, June 5 ***Perf. 13½x13¼***

479 A295 12d multi .70 .70

Louis Braille (1809-52), Educator of the Blind A296

Perf. 13½x13¼

2009, June 17 **Litho.**

480 A296 18d multi 1.00 1.00

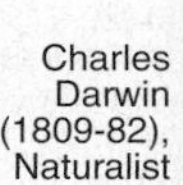

Charles Darwin (1809-82), Naturalist A297

2009, June 17

481 A297 18d multi 1.00 1.00

Boat and Compass Rose A298

Boat's Bow — A299

2009, June 24 ***Perf. 13½x13¼***

482 A298 18d multi 1.00 1.00

Perf. 13¼x13½

483 A299 18d multi 1.00 1.00

Cities Type of 2008

Designs: 16d, Strumica. 18d, Prilep.

2009 ***Perf. 12¾x13***

Denomination Color

484 A283 16d brown .85 .85
485 A283 18d blue 1.00 1.00

Issued: 16d, 8/7; 18d, 7/27.

Organized Soccer in Macedonia, Cent. — A300

2009, Aug. 12 ***Perf. 13¼x13½***

486 A300 18d multi 1.00 1.00

Cyclist — A301

Bicycle Pedal A302

2009, Sept. 2 Litho. ***Perf. 13¼x13½***

487 A301 18d multi 1.00 1.00

Perf. 13½x13¼

488 A302 18d multi 1.00 1.00

Giro d'Italia bicycle race, cent.

Fauna A303

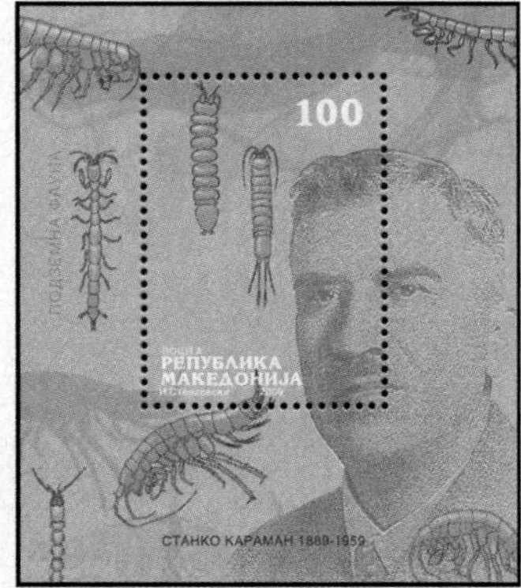

Dr. Stankos Karaman (1889-1959), Zoologist, and Crustaceans — A304

Designs: 2d, Pelobates syriacus balcanicus. 3d, Salmo letnica. 6d, Austropotamobius torrentium macedonicus. 8d, Triturus macedonicus.

2009, Sept. 9 Litho. ***Perf. 13½x13¼***

489-492 A303 Set of 4 1.20 1.20

Souvenir Sheet

Perf. 13¼x13½

493 A304 100d multi 5.00 5.00

Dimitar Andronov Papardishki (1859-1954), Painter — A305

2009, Sept. 30 ***Perf. 13½x13¼***

494 A305 16d multi .90 .90

Elbasan Normal School and Pedagogical High School, 150th Anniv. — A306

2009, Oct. 14 ***Perf. 13¼x13½***

495 A306 16d multi .90 .90

Filip Shiroka (1859-1935), Poet — A307

Krume Kepeski (1909-88), Linguist — A308

Petre M. Amdreevski (1934-2006), Writer — A309

2009, Nov. 4 Litho. ***Perf. 13¼x13½***

496 A307 16d multi .90 .90
497 A308 16d multi .90 .90

Perf. 13½x13¼

498 A309 16d multi .90 .90
Nos. 496-498 (3) 2.70 2.70

Cities Type of 2008 and

Struga — A309a

Delchevo — A309b

Kumanovo — A309c

Resen — A309d

Designs: No. 499, Gostivar. No. 500, Kichevo.

2009, Nov. 11 Litho. ***Perf. 12¾x13***
Denomination Color

499 A283 16d gray blue .80 .80
500 A283 16d Prus blue .80 .80
501 A309a 16d brown .80 .80
502 A309b 16d brown .80 .80
503 A309c 18d brown .90 .90
504 A309d 18d black .90 .90
Nos. 499-504 (6) 5.00 5.00

Christmas A310

Perf. 13¼x13½

2009, Nov. 18 Litho.
505 A310 16d multi .90 .90

Helicopter A311

2010, Feb. 10 ***Perf. 13½x13¼***
506 A311 50d multi 2.50 2.50

2010 Winter Olympics, Vancouver A312

Olympic rings, Vancouver Olympics emblem, inukshuk and: 50d, Ski jumper. 100d, Ice hockey goalie.

2010, Feb. 12 ***Perf. 13¼x13½***
507-508 A312 Set of 2 6.75 6.75

Nos. 507-508 each were printed in sheets of 8 + label.

Souvenir Sheet

International Women's Day — A313

No. 509 — Flower with denomination in: a, UL. b, UR.

2010, Mar. 8
509 A313 18d Sheet of 2, #a-b 1.60 1.60

St. Peter's Church, Golem Grad Island, 650th Anniv. A314

Perf. 13½x13¼

2010, Mar. 25 Litho.
510 A314 18d multi .80 .80

A315

Parrots A316

2010, Apr. 14 ***Perf. 13¼x13½***
511 A315 20d multi .90 .90

Perf. 13½x13¼

512 A316 40d multi 1.75 1.75

Macedonian Chairmanship of the Council of Europe — A318

2010, May 8 Litho. ***Perf. 13½x13¼***
514 A318 18d multi .70 .70

Macedonia in the European Union A319

Buildings: 20d, European Parliament, Brussels. 50d, Main Post Office, Madrid.

2010, May 8
515-516 A319 Set of 2 2.75 2.75

Castanea Sativa A320

2010, June 5 Litho. ***Perf. 13½x13¼***
522 A320 20d multi .80 .80

Robert Schumann (1810-56), Composer A321

Frédéric Chopin (1810-49), Composer A322

2010, June 8 ***Perf. 13½x13¼***
523 A321 50d multi 2.00 2.00

Perf. 13¼x13½

524 A322 60d multi 2.40 2.40

2010 World Cup Soccer Championships, South Africa — A323

Emblem and: 50d, Soccer ball in goal net. 100d, Soccer ball at midfield, vert. 150d, Soccer ball, map of South Africa.

Perf. 13½x13¼, 13¼x13½

2010, June 11
525-526 A323 Set of 2 6.00 6.00

Souvenir Sheet

527 A323 150d multi 6.00 6.00

50th Ohrid Summer Festival — A324

2010, June 30 ***Perf. 13¼x13½***
528 A324 18d multi .75 .75

Bayram Festival — A326

2010, Sept. 9 Litho. ***Perf. 13¼x13½***
530 A326 50d multi 2.10 2.10

Awarding of First Prize in Poetry Contest to "The Serdar," by Gligor Prlicev, 150th Anniv. A327

2010, Sept. 10 ***Perf. 13¼***
531 A327 100d multi 4.25 4.25

POSTAL TAX STAMPS

Men Blowing Horns — PT1

1991, Dec. 30 Litho. ***Perf. 13½***
RA1 PT1 2.50d multicolored *1.50 1.50*

No. RA1 was required on mail Dec. 31, 1991-Sept. 8, 1992. For surcharge see No. 22.

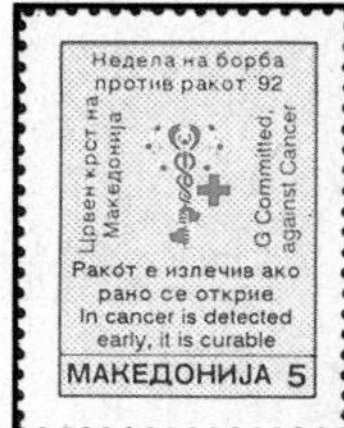

Anti-Cancer Week — PT2

Designs: Nos. RA2, RA6, Emblems, inscriptions. Nos. RA3, RA7, Magnetic resonance imaging scanner. Nos. RA4, RA8, Overhead scanner, examination table. No. RA5, RA9c, Mammography imager. No. RA9, Ultra sound computer.

1992, Mar. 1 Litho. ***Perf. 10***

RA2 PT2 5d multicolored *1.00 1.00*
RA3 PT2 5d multicolored *1.00 1.00*
RA4 PT2 5d multicolored *1.00 1.00*
RA5 PT2 5d multicolored *1.00 1.00*
a. Block of 4, #RA2-RA5 *4.00 4.00*
RA6 PT2 5d multicolored *.30 .30*
RA7 PT2 5d multicolored *.30 .30*
RA8 PT2 5d multicolored *.30 .30*
RA9 PT2 5d multicolored *.30 .30*
a. Block of 4, #RA6-RA9 *1.25 1.25*
b. Souv. sheet of 3, #RA7-RA9, RA9c *22.50 22.50*
c. PT2 5d multicolored *.40 .40*
Nos. RA2-RA9 (8) *5.20 5.20*

Inscription at right reads up on No. RA2 and down on No. RA6. Designs on Nos. RA7-RA8, RA9c are without red cross symbol.

Souvenir folders with perf. and imperf. sheets of RA9b sold for 40d. Value for both sheets in folder, $50.

Obligatory on mail Mar. 1-8.

See Nos. RA28-RA31.

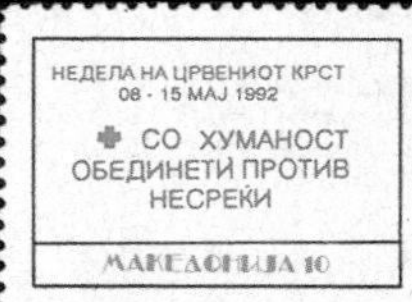

Red Cross Week PT3

Designs: RA10, Slogans. No. RA11, Airplanes dropping supplies. No. RA12, Aiding traffic accident victim. No. RA13, Evacuating casualties from building.

1992, May 8 ***Perf. 10***

RA10 PT3 10d multicolored *.20 .20*
RA11 PT3 10d multicolored *.20 .20*
RA12 PT3 10d multicolored *.20 .20*
RA13 PT3 10d multicolored *.20 .20*
a. Block of 4, #RA10-RA13 *.65 .65*

Nos. RA10-RA13 exist with silver-colored borders in perf. and imperf. miniature sheets that sold for 80d. Value for both sheets $7.50.

Obligatory on mail May 8-15.

PT4

PT5

Solidarity Week: #RA14, Skopje earthquake. #RA15, Woman holding girl. #RA16, Mother carrying infant. #RA17, Mother, children, airplane.

130d, Woman, child, airport control tower.

1992, June 1 ***Perf. 10***

RA14	PT4	20d multicolored	.20	.20
RA15	PT4	20d multicolored	.20	.20
RA16	PT4	20d multicolored	.20	.20
RA17	PT4	20d multicolored	.20	.20
a.		Block of 4	.65	.65

Size: 74x97mm

Imperf

RA18	PT4	130d multicolored	3.25	3.25

No. RA18 also exists with perf. vignette. Same value.

Obligatory on mail June 1-7.

See No. RA55.

1992, Sept. 14 ***Perf. 10***

Anti-Tuberculosis Week: No. RA20, Nurse, infant. No. RA21, Nurse giving oxygen to patient. No. RA22, Infant in bed.

200d, Child being treated by nurse.

RA19	PT5	20d multicolored	.20	.20
RA20	PT5	20d multicolored	.20	.20
RA21	PT5	20d multicolored	.20	.20
RA22	PT5	20d multicolored	.20	.20
a.		Block of 4, #RA19-RA22	.65	.65

Size: 74x97mm

Imperf

RA23	PT5	200d vermilion & multi	2.75	2.75

No. RA23 exists with magenta inscriptions, and also with perf. vignette and either magenta or vermilion inscriptions. Obligatory on mail Sept. 14-21.

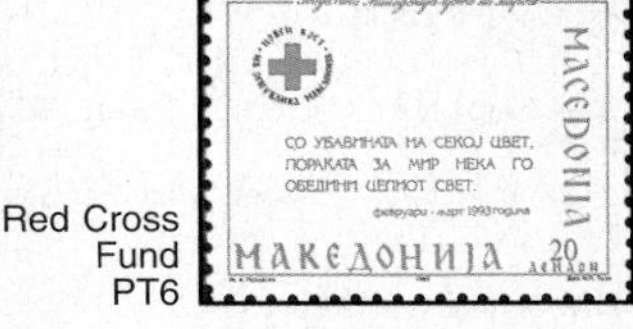

Red Cross Fund PT6

1993, Feb. 1 **Litho.** ***Perf. 10***

RA24	PT6	20d Shown	.35	.35
RA25	PT6	20d Marguerites	.35	.35
RA26	PT6	20d Carnations	.35	.35
RA27	PT6	20d Mixed bouquet	.35	.35
a.		Block of 4, #RA24-RA27	1.40	1.40

Nos. RA24-RA27 exist in perf. or imperf. miniature sheets with either gold or silver backgrounds and inscriptions, that sold for 500d each. Value for both sheets $12.

Obligatory on mail Feb. 1-28.

Cancer Therapy Type of 1992

Designs: No. RA28, Nuclear medicine caduceus, inscriptions. No. RA29, Radiographic equipment. No. RA30, Radiology machine. No. RA31, Scanner.

1993, Mar. 1 **Litho.** ***Perf. 10***

RA28	PT2	20d multicolored	.35	.35
RA29	PT2	20d multicolored	.35	.35
RA30	PT2	20d multicolored	.35	.35
RA31	PT2	20d multicolored	.35	.35
a.		Block of 4, #RA28-RA31	1.40	1.40

Nos. RA28-RA31 exist in perf. & imperf. miniature sheets with gold background or inscription, that sold for 500d each. Value for both sheets $6.50.

Obligatory on mail Mar. 1-8.

Red Cross Week PT7

1993, May 8 **Litho.** ***Perf. 10***

RA32	PT7	50d Inscriptions	.30	.30
RA33	PT7	50d Man holding baby	.30	.30
RA34	PT7	50d Patient in wheelchair	.30	.30
RA35	PT7	50d Carrying stretcher	.30	.30
a.		Block of 4, #RA32-RA35	1.20	1.20

Perf. & imperf. miniature sheets of Nos. RA32-RA35 exist with yellow inscription tablets that sold for 700d each. Value for both sheets $7.

Obligatory on mail May 8-15.

1993, June 1 ***Perf. 10***

RA36	PT7	50de Skopje earthquake	.30	.30
RA37	PT7	50de Unloading boxes	.30	.30
RA38	PT7	50de Labeling boxes	.30	.30
RA39	PT7	50de Boxes, fork lift	.30	.30
a.		Block of 4, #RA36-RA39	1.20	1.20

Perf. & imperf. miniature sheets of Nos. RA36-RA39 exist with gold inscription tablets that sold for 7d each. Value for both sheets $5.

Obligatory on mail June 1-7.

1993, Sept. 14 ***Perf. 10***

Designs: Nos. RA40, Inscriptions. Nos. RA41, Children in meadow. Nos. RA42, Bee on flower. No. RA43, Goat behind rock.

RA40	PT7	50de black, gray & red	.20	.20
RA41	PT7	50de green & multi	.20	.20
RA42	PT7	50de green & multi	.20	.20
RA43	PT7	50de green & multi	.20	.20
a.		Block of 4, #RA40-RA43	.65	.65

Nos. RA41-RA43 exist in perf. & imperf. miniature sheets that sold for 15d each. Values for both sheets $3.25. Nos. RA40-RA43 exist with yellow omitted, resulting in blue stamps. Value of the blue set $4.25.

Obligatory on mail Sept. 14-21.

See Nos. RA52-RA54.

Anti-Cancer Week — PT8

1994, Mar. 1 ***Perf. 10***

RA44	PT8	1d Inscription, emblem	.20	.20
RA45	PT8	1d Lily	.20	.20
RA46	PT8	1d Mushroom	.20	.20
RA47	PT8	1d Swans	.20	.20
a.		Block of 4, #RA44-RA47	.90	.90

Nos. RA44-RA47 without silver color exist in perf. & imperf. miniature sheets and sold for 20d. Value for both sheets $7.

Obligatory on mail Mar. 1-8.

Red Cross Type of 1993 and

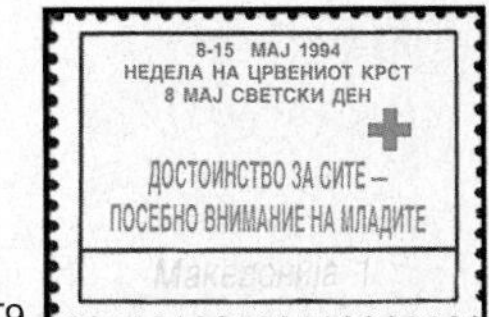

PT9

1994, May 8 **Litho.** ***Perf. 10***

RA51	PT9	1d shown	.20	.20
RA52	PT7	1d like #RA41	.20	.20
RA53	PT7	1d like #RA39	.20	.20
RA54	PT7	1d like #RA33	.20	.20
a.		Block of 4, #RA51-RA54	.65	.65

Nos. RA51-RA54 exist without denomination in perf. & imperf. miniature sheets and sold for 30d each. Value for both sheets $9.

Obligatory on mail May 8-15, 1994.

Skopje Earthquake Type of 1993

1994, June 1

RA55	PT4	1d like #RA14	.65	.65

Obligatory on mail June 1-7, 1994.

Red Cross Fund PT10

1994, Dec. 1 **Litho.** ***Perf. 10***

RA56	PT10	2d shown	.30	.30
RA57	PT10	2d Globe	.30	.30
RA58	PT10	2d AIDS awareness	.30	.30
RA59	PT10	2d Condoms	.30	.30
a.		Block of 4, Nos. RA56-RA59	1.20	1.20

Size: 80x95mm

Imperf

RA60	PT10	40d like RA57	4.50	4.50

Country name and value omitted from vignette on No. RA60, which also exists with perf. vignette. Obligatory on mail Dec. 1-8.

Anti-Cancer Week — PT11

Red Cross Fund — PT12

1995, Mar. 1

RA61	PT11	1d shown	.30	.30
RA62	PT11	1d White lilies	.30	.30
RA63	PT11	1d Red lilies	.30	.30
RA64	PT11	1d Red roses	.30	.30
a.		Block of 4, Nos. RA61-RA64	1.20	1.20

Size: 97x74mm

Imperf

RA65	PT11	30d like #RA61, RA64	3.75	3.75

Blue inscriptions, country name, and value omitted from vignette on No. RA65, which also exists with perf. vignette. Obligatory on mail Mar. 1-8.

1995, May 8

Designs: No. RA66, Red Cross emblem. No. RA67, Red Cross volunteers holding clipboards. No. RA68, Young volunteers wearing white shirts. No. RA69, RA70, Red Cross, Red Crescent symbols, globe.

RA66	PT12	1d multicolored	.30	.30
RA67	PT12	1d multicolored	.30	.30
RA68	PT12	1d multicolored	.30	.30
RA69	PT12	1d blue & multi	.30	.30
a.		Strip of 4, Nos. RA70-RA73	1.20	1.20

Size: 68x85mm

Imperf

RA70	PT12	30d multicolored	3.75	3.75

No. RA70 also exists with perf. vignette. Obligatory on mail May 8-15.

Solidarity Week PT13

1995, June 1

RA71	PT13	1d shown	.45	.45

Size: 85x70

Imperf

RA72	PT13	30d like No. RA75	3.00	3.00

No. RA72 also exists with perf. vignette. Obligatory on mail June 1-7.

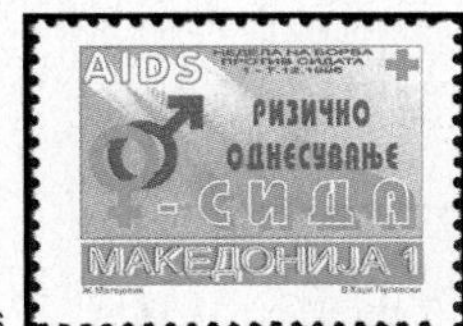

Robert Koch (1843-1910), Bacteriologist — PT14

1995, Sept. 14 **Litho.** ***Perf. 10***

RA73	PT14	1d shown	.45	.45

Size: 90x73mm

Imperf

RA74	PT14	30d like No. RA73	2.50	2.50

No. RA74 exists with perf. vignette. Obligatory on mail Sept. 14-21.

PT15

PT16

1995, Oct. 2 **Litho.** ***Die Cut***

Self-Adhesive

RA75	PT15	2d blue violet & red	.45	.45

Children's Week. Obligatory on mail 10/2-8.

1995, Nov. 1 **Litho.** ***Perf. 10***

RA76	PT16	1d multicolored	.40	.40

Size: 90x72mm

Imperf

RA77	PT16	30d like #RA76	2.50	2.50

Red Cross, AIDS awareness.

No. RA77 also exists with perf. vignette.

Obligatory on mail Nov. 1-7.

Red Cross PT17

1996, Mar. 1 **Litho.** ***Perf. 10***

RA78	PT17	1d multicolored	.45	.45

Size: 98x76mm

Imperf

RA79	PT17	30d like #RA78	3.00	3.00

No. RA79 also exists with perf. vignette. Obligatory on mail Mar. 1-8.

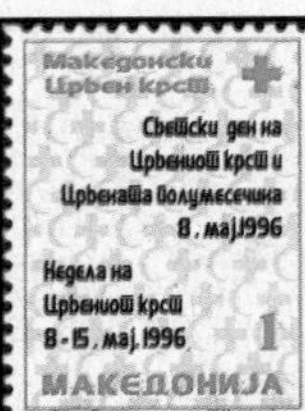

PT18

Red Cross Week — PT19

Fundamental principles of Red Cross, Red Crescent Societies, inscriptions in: No. RA81, Macedonian. No. RA82, English. No. RA83, French. RA84, Spanish.

1996, May 8 Litho. *Perf. 10*

RA80	PT18 1d multicolored	.25	.25
RA81	PT19 1d multicolored	.25	.25
RA82	PT19 1d multicolored	.25	.25
RA83	PT19 1d multicolored	.25	.25
RA84	PT19 1d multicolored	.25	.25
a.	Strip of 5, #RA80-RA84	1.40	1.40

Obligatory on mail May 8-15.

Red Cross, Solidarity Week — PT20

1996, June 1 Litho. *Perf. 10*

RA86 PT20 1d multicolored .40 .40

No. RA86 exists without country name or denomination in perf. & imperf. miniature sheets and sold for 30d each. Value for both sheets $5.50. Obligatory on mail June 1-7, 1996.

Red Cross, Fight Tuberculosis Week — PT21

1996, Sept. 14 Litho. *Perf. 10*

RA87 PT21 1d multicolored .65 .65

Size: 80x90mm

Imperf

RA88 PT21 30d like #RA87 2.75 2.75

No. RA88 also exists with perf. vignette. Obligatory on mail Sept. 14-21.

Red Cross, AIDS Awareness PT22

1996, Dec. 6

RA89 PT22 1d multicolored .55 .55

Size: 90x73mm

Imperf

RA90 PT22 30d like #RA89 2.75 2.75

No. RA90 also exists with perf. vignette. Obligatory on mail Dec. 1-7.

Red Cross, Cancer Week — PT23

Red Cross — PT24

1997, Apr. 1

RA91	PT23 1d Cross in pale org	.50	.50
a.	Cross in red	.70	.70

No. RA91 obligatory on mail Apr. 1-8. No. RA91a issued 5/8.

1997, May 8

RA92 PT24 1d multicolored 2.00 2.00

Obligatory on mail May 8-15.

Children's Day — PT25

Red Cross, Anti-Tuberculosis PT26

1997, June 1

RA93	PT25 1d Cross in deep vermilion	.50	.50
a.	Cross in red	.70	.70

Obligatory on mail June 1-8.

1997, Sept. 14

RA94 PT26 1d multicolored .50 .50

Obligatory on mail, Sept. 14-21.

Red Cross — PT27

1997, Dec. 1 Litho. *Perf. 10*

RA95 PT27 1d multicolored .50 .50

Obligatory on mail Dec. 1-7.

Red Cross Fight Against Cancer PT28

1998, Mar. 1 *Perf. 13½*

RA96 PT28 1d multicolored .50 .50

Obligatory on mail Mar. 1-8.

Red Cross, Humanity PT29

1998, May 8

RA97 PT29 2d multicolored .50 .50

Obligatory on mail May 8-15.

Red Cross — PT30

PT31

1998, June 1 Litho. *Perf. 13½*

RA98 PT30 2d multicolored .30 .30

Obligatory on mail June 1-7, 1998.

1998, Sept. 14 Litho. *Perf. 13½*

RA99 PT31 2d multicolored .30 .30

Fight tuberculosis. Obligatory on mail Sept. 14-21, 1998.

PT32

PT33

1998, Dec. 1

RA100 PT32 2d multicolored .50 .50

AIDS awareness. Obligatory on mail Dec. 1-7, 1998.

1999, Mar. 1 Litho. *Perf. 13¼*

RA101 PT33 2d multi .50 .50

Red Cross fight against cancer. Obligatory on mail Mar. 1-7, 1999.

Red Cross PT34

1999, May 8

RA102 PT34 2d multi .50 .50

Obligatory on mail May 8-15, 1999.

PT35

PT36

1999, June 1

RA103 PT35 2d multi .30 .30

Red Cross, solidarity week. Obligatory on mail June 1-7, 1999.

1999, Sept. 14 Litho. *Perf. 13¼*

RA104 PT36 2d multi .30 .30

Fight tuberculosis. Obligatory on mail Sept. 14-21.

AIDS Awareness PT37

1999, Dec. 1

RA105 PT37 2.50d multi .55 .55

Obligatory on mail Dec. 1-7.

Anti-Cancer Week — PT38

2000, Mar. 1 **Litho.** ***Perf. 13¼***
RA106 PT38 2.50d multi .55 .55

Obligatory on mail Mar. 1-8.

Red Cross PT39

2000, May 8
RA107 PT39 2.50d multi .55 .55

Obligatory on mail May 8-15.

Red Cross — PT40

2000, June 1
RA108 PT40 2.50d multi .30 .30

Obligatory on mail June 1-7.

Red Cross — PT41

2000 Sept. 14 **Litho.** ***Perf. 13¼***
RA109 PT41 3d multi .30 .30

Obligatory on mail Sept. 14-21.

Fight Against AIDS — PT42

2000 Dec. 1
RA110 PT42 3d multi .55 .55

Obligatory on mail Dec. 1-7.

Fight Against Cancer — PT43

2001, Mar. 1 **Litho.** ***Perf. 13¼***
RA111 PT43 3d multi .30 .30

Obligatory on mail Mar. 1-8.

Red Cross PT44

2001, May 8
RA112 PT44 3d multi .55 .55

Obligatory on mail May 8-15.

Red Cross Solidarity Week — PT45

2001, June 1
RA113 PT45 3d multi .30 .30

Obligatory on mail June 1-7.

Fight Against Tuberculosis PT46

2001, Sept. 14
RA114 PT46 3d multi .30 .30

Obligatory on mail Sept. 14-21.

Campaign Against AIDS — PT47

2001, Dec. 1 **Litho.** ***Perf. 13¼***
RA115 PT47 3d multi .55 .55

Obligatory on mail Dec. 1-7.

Campaign Against Cancer PT48

2002, Mar. 1
RA116 PT48 3d multi .30 .30

Obligatory on mail Mar. 1-8.

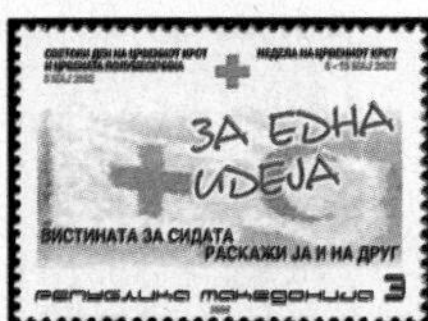

Red Cross Week PT49

2002, May 8 **Litho.** ***Perf. 13¼***
RA117 PT49 3d multi .30 .30

Obligatory on mail May 8-15.

Red Cross Solidarity Week PT50

2002, June 1
RA118 PT50 3d multi .30 .30

Obligatory on mail June 1-7.

Tuberculosis Prevention PT51

2002, Sept. 14
RA119 PT51 3d multi .50 .50

Obligatory on mail Sept. 14-21.

Campaign Against AIDS PT52

2002, Dec. 1
RA120 PT52 3d multi .50 .50

Campaign Against Cancer — PT53

2003, Mar. 1 **Litho.** ***Perf. 13¼***
RA121 PT53 4d multi .50 .50

Obligatory on mail Mar. 1-8.

Campaign Against AIDS — PT54

2003, May 8
RA122 PT54 4d multi .55 .55

Obligatory on mail May 8-15.

Red Cross Solidarity — PT55

2003, June 1 ***Perf. 13¼x13½***
RA123 PT55 4d multi .50 .50

Obligatory on mail June 1-7.

Tuberculosis Prevention PT56

Perf. 13½x13¼

2003, Sept. 14 **Litho.**
RA124 PT56 4d multi .50 .50

Obligatory on mail Sept. 14-21.

Campaign Against AIDS — PT57

2003, Dec. 1 **Litho.** ***Perf. 13¼x13½***
RA125 PT57 4d multi .50 .50

Obligatory on mail Dec. 1-7.

Campaign Against Cancer — PT58

2004, Mar. 1
RA126 PT58 4d multi .50 .50

Obligatory on mail Mar. 1-8.

Red Cross Week — PT59

2004, May 8
RA127 PT59 4d multi .50 .50

Obligatory on mail May 8-15.

Red Cross Solidarity Week — PT60

2004, June 1 Litho. ***Perf. 13¼x13½***
RA128 PT60 6d multi .50 .50

Obligatory on mail June 1-7.

Tuberculosis Week — PT61

2004, Sept. 14 ***Perf. 13½x13¼***
RA129 PT61 6d multi .50 .50

Obligatory on mail Sept. 14-21.

Campaign Against AIDS PT62

2004, Dec. 1 Litho. ***Perf. 13½x13¼***
RA130 PT62 6d multi .50 .50

Obligatory on mail Dec. 1-7.

Campaign Against Cancer — PT63

2005, Mar. 1 ***Perf. 13¼x13½***
RA131 PT63 6d multi .50 .50

Obligatory on mail Mar. 1-8.

Red Cross PT64

2005, May 8 Litho. ***Perf. 13½x13¼***
RA132 PT64 6d multi .50 .50

Obligatory on mail May 8-15.

Campaign Against Tuberculosis — PT65

Perf. 13½x13¼
2005, Sept. 14 Litho.
RA133 PT65 6d multi .50 .50

Obligatory on mail Sept. 14-21.

Campaign Against AIDS — PT66

2005, Dec. 1 ***Perf. 13¼x13½***
RA134 PT66 6d multi .50 .50

Obligatory on mail Dec. 1-7.

Campaign Against Breast Cancer — PT67

2006, Mar. 1 Litho. ***Perf. 13¼x13½***
RA135 PT67 6d multi .60 .60

Obligatory on mail Mar. 1-7.

Red Cross Week — PT68

2006, May 18 Litho. ***Perf. 13¼x13½***
RA136 PT68 6d multi .60 .60

Obligatory on mail May 8-15.

Campaign Against Tuberculosis — PT69

2006, Sept. 14 ***Perf. 13½x13¼***
RA137 PT69 6d multi .60 .60

Obligatory on mail Sept. 14-21.

Campaign Against AIDS PT70

2006, Dec. 1
RA138 PT70 6d multi .60 .60

Obligatory on mail Dec. 1-7.

Campaign Against Cancer — PT71

2007, Mar. 1 Litho. ***Perf. 13¼x13½***
RA139 PT71 6d multi .35 .35

Obligatory on mail Mar. 1-8.

Red Cross Week — PT72

2007, May 8
RA140 PT72 6d multi .35 .35

Obligatory on mail May 8-15.

Campaign Against Tuberculosis PT73

2007, Sept. 14
RA141 PT73 6d multi .35 .35

Obligatory on mail Sept. 14-21.

Campaign Against AIDS PT74

2007, Dec. 1 ***Perf. 13½x13¼***
RA142 PT74 6d multi .35 .35

Obligatory on mail Dec. 1-8.

Campaign Against Cancer PT75

2008, Mar. 1 Litho. ***Perf. 13½x13¼***
RA143 PT75 6d multi .35 .35

Obligatory on mail Mar. 1-8.

Red Cross Week PT76

2008, May 8
RA144 PT76 6d multi .35 .35

Obligatory on mail May 8-15.

Campaign Against Tuberculosis PT77

2008, Sept. 14 ***Perf. 13¼x13½***
RA145 PT77 6d multi .35 .35

Obligatory on mail Sept. 14-21.

Campaign Against AIDS PT78

2008, Dec. 1 ***Perf. 13½x13¼***
RA146 PT78 6d multi .60 .60

Obligatory on mail Dec. 1-8.

Campaign Against Cancer — PT79

2009, Mar. 1 ***Perf. 13¼x13½***
RA147 PT79 6d multi .25 .25

Obligatory on mail Mar. 1-8.

Red Cross Week PT80

2009, May 8 ***Perf. 13½x13¼***
RA148 PT80 6d multi .30 .30

Obligatory on mail May 8-15.

Campaign Against Tuberculosis — PT81

2009, Sept. 14
RA149 PT81 6d multi .30 .30

Obligatory on mail Sept. 14-21.

Campaign Against AIDS PT82

2009, Dec. 1
RA150 PT82 8d multi .40 .40

Obligatory on mail Dec. 1-7.

Campaign Against Cancer — PT83

2010, Mar. 1 *Perf. 13¼x13½*

Granite Paper

RA151	PT83	8d multi	.35	.35

Obligatory on mail Mar. 1-7.

Red Cross Week — PT84

2010, May 8 **Litho.**

Granite Paper

RA152	PT84	8d multi	.35	.35

Obligatory on mail May 8-15.

ISSUED UNDER GERMAN OCCUPATION

During World War II, Yugoslav Macedonia was annexed by Bulgaria. From April 1941 until Sept. 8, 1944, Bulgarian stamps were used in the region. On Sept. 8, 1944, Bulgaria signed an armistace with the Allies, and Macedonia was occupied by German forces. A puppet state was created, which collapsed upon the German withdrawal on Nov. 13.

Catalogue values for all unused stamps in this section are for Never Hinged examples. Hinged stamps are worth approximately 60% of the values shown.

Bulgaria Nos 364//413 Overprinted in Black or Red (R)

Ovpt. I

Ovpt. II

Photo., Typo. (#N1, N2)

1944, Oct. 28 *Perf. 13*

Overprinted I

N1	A177	1 l on 10st red org (#364)	4.00	*16.00*
N2	A178	3 l on 15st blue (#365) (R)	4.00	*16.00*

Overprinted II

N3	A201	6 l on 10st dk blue (#398) (R)	6.50	*26.00*
N4	A201	9 l on 15st Prus blue (#399) (R)	6.50	*26.00*
N5	A201	9 l on 15st dk ol brn (#400) (R)	9.00	*30.00*
N6	A209	15 l on 4 l ol gray (#411) (R)	32.50	*60.00*
N7	A210	20 l on 7 l dp blue (#412) (R)	47.50	*60.00*
N8	A211	30 l on 14 l fawn (#413)	55.00	*110.00*
		Nos. N1-N8 (8)	165.00	*344.00*

There are two types of both overprints, differing in the font of the "9" in the year date. Values for the more common types are given above.

MADAGASCAR

ˌmad-ə-ˈgas-kər

British Consular Mail

Postage stamps issued by the British Consulate in Madagascar were in use for a short period until the British relinquished all claims to this territory in favor of France in return for which France recognized Great Britain's claims in Zanzibar.

See Malagasy Republic for stamps inscribed "Madagascar."

12 Pence = 1 Shilling

British Consular Mail stamps of Madagascar were gummed only in one corner. Unused values are for stamps without gum. Examples having the original corner gum will command higher prices. Most used examples of these stamps have small faults and values are for stamps in this condition. Used stamps without faults are scarce and are worth more. Used stamps are valued with the commonly used crayon or pen cancellations.

"B C M" and Arms — A1

Handstamped "British Vice-Consulate"

1884 **Unwmk.** **Typo.** ***Rouletted***

Black Seal Handstamped

1	A1	1p violet	500.	400.
b.		Seal omitted	6,500.	6,500.
2	A1	2p violet	325.	290.
3	A1	3p violet	350.	300.
4	A1	4p violet 1 oz.	4,250.	4,250.
a.		"1 oz." corrected to "4 oz." in mss.	800.	700.
b.		Seal omitted	*5,750.*	5,750.
5	A1	6p violet	450.	*500.*
6	A1	1sh violet	425.	*475.*
7	A1	1sh6p violet	500.	*500.*
8	A1	2sh violet	700.	*700.*
9	A1	1p on 1sh vio		
10	A1	4½ on 1sh vio		
11	A1	6p red	900.	800.

1886

Violet Seal Handstamped

12	A1	4p violet	1,350.	—
13	A1	6p violet	2,400.	—

Handstamped "British Consular Mail" as on A3

Black Seal Handstamped

14	A1	4p violet	1,850.	—

Violet Seal Handstamped

15	A1	4p violet	5,500.	—

The 1, 2, 3 and 4 pence are inscribed "POSTAL PACKET," the other values of the series are inscribed "LETTER."

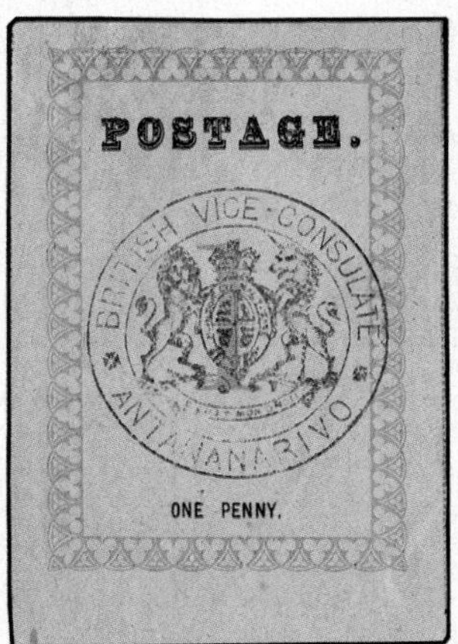

"British Vice-Consulate" — A2

Three types of A2 and A3:

I — "POSTAGE" 29½mm. Periods after "POSTAGE" and value.

II — "POSTAGE" 29½mm. No periods.

III — "POSTAGE" 24½mm. Period after value.

1886

Violet Seal Handstamped

16	A2	1p rose, I	325.	—
a.		Type II	1,050.	—
17	A2	1½p rose, I	1,050.	*875.*
a.		Type II	1,950.	—
18	A2	2p rose, I	350.	—
19	A2	3p rose, I	450.	*375.*
a.		Type II	1,150.	—
20	A2	4p rose, III	500.	—
21	A2	4½p rose, I	550.	*350.*
a.		Type II	1,750.	—
22	A2	6p rose, II	1,350.	—
23	A2	8p rose, I	1,250.	*1,250.*
a.		Type III	600.	—
24	A2	9p rose	1,000.	—
24A	A2	1sh rose, III	—	
24B	A2	1sh6p rose, III	4,250.	—
25	A2	2sh rose, III	2,600.	—

Black Seal Handstamped

Type I

26	A2	1p rose	125.	*150.*
27	A2	1½p rose	2,000.	*1,150.*
28	A2	2p rose	160.	—
29	A2	3p rose	2,000.	*1,100.*
30	A2	4½p rose	1,750.	*575.*
31	A2	8p rose	3,250.	*2,600.*
32	A2	9p rose	3,250.	*2,900.*
32A	A2	2sh rose, III	—	—

"British Consular Mail" — A3

1886

Violet Seal Handstamped

33	A3	1p rose, II	110.	—
34	A3	1½p rose, II	175.	—
35	A3	2p rose, II	185.	—
36	A3	3p rose, II	160.	—
37	A3	4p rose, III	475.	—
38	A3	4½p rose, II	160.	—
39	A3	6p rose, II	375.	—
40	A3	8p rose, III	650.	—
a.		Type I	1,500.	—
41	A3	9p rose, I	300.	—
42	A3	1sh rose, III	1,350.	—
43	A3	1sh6p rose, III	1,500.	—
44	A3	2sh rose, III	1,750.	—

Black Seal Handstamped

45	A3	1p rose, I	90.	—
a.		Type II	90.	*140.*
46	A3	1½p rose, I	90.	—
a.		Type II	80.	110.
47	A3	2p rose, I	115.	—
a.		Type II	82.50	130.
48	A3	3p rose, I	110.	*110.*
a.		Type II	95.	*140.*
49	A3	4p rose, III	225.	—
50	A3	4½p rose, I	110.	*150.*
a.		Type II	95.	*140.*
51	A3	6p rose, II	95.	*140.*
52	A3	8p rose, I	140.	—
a.		Type III	750.	—
53	A3	9p rose, I	150.	*210.*
54	A3	1sh rose, III	525.	—
55	A3	1sh6p rose, III	625.	—
56	A3	2sh rose, III	700.	—

Seal Omitted

45b	A3	1p rose, II	3,000.
46b	A3	1½p rose, II	3,000.
48b	A3	3p rose, II	4,500.
49a	A3	4p rose, III	3,500.
50b	A3	4½p rose, II	5,000.
51a	A3	6p rose, II	5,500.
52b	A3	8p rose, III	3,750.
53a	A3	9p rose, I	4,000.
54a	A3	1sh rose, III	4,500.
55a	A3	1sh6p rose, III	4,000.
56a	A3	2sh rose, III	4,500.

Some students of these issues doubt that the 1886 "seal omitted" varieties were regularly issued.

Red Seal Handstamped

57	A3	3p rose, I		*12,000.*
58	A3	4½p rose, I		*7,000.*

MADEIRA

mə-'dir-ə

LOCATION — A group of islands in the Atlantic Ocean northwest of Africa
GOVT. — Part of the Republic of Portugal
AREA — 314 sq. mi.
POP. — 150,574 (1900)
CAPITAL — Funchal

These islands are considered an integral part of Portugal and since 1898 postage stamps of Portugal have been in use. See Portugal for issues also inscribed Madeira, starting in 1980.

1000 Reis = 1 Milreis
100 Centavos = 1 Escudo (1925)

It is recommended that the rare overprinted 1868-81 stamps be purchased accompanied by certificates of authenticity from competent experts.

King Luiz
A1 A2

Stamps of Portugal Overprinted

1868, Jan. 1 Unwmk. *Imperf.*

Black Overprint

2 A1 20r bister 200.00 120.00
a. Inverted overprint —
b. Rouletted —
3 A1 50r green 200.00 120.00
4 A1 80r orange 225.00 125.00
a. Double overprint —
5 A1 100r lilac 225.00 125.00
Nos. 2-5 (4) 850.00 490.00

The 5r black does not exist as a genuinely imperforate original.

Reprints of 1885 are on stout white paper, ungummed. (Also, 5r, 10r and 25r values were overprinted.) Reprints of 1905 are on ordinary white paper with shiny gum and have a wide "D" and "R." Value, $12 each.

Lozenge Perf.

2c A1 20r —
3a A1 50r —
4b A1 80r —
5a A1 100r —

Overprinted in Red or Black

1868-70 *Perf. 12½*

6 A1 5r black (R) 55.00 37.50
8 A1 10r yellow 90.00 80.00
9 A1 20r bister 140.00 110.00
10 A1 25r rose 57.50 12.00
a. Inverted overprint —
11 A1 50r green 200.00 140.00
a. Inverted overprint —
12 A1 80r orange 180.00 140.00
13 A1 100r lilac 190.00 140.00
a. Inverted overprint —
14 A1 120r blue 110.00 80.00
15 A1 240r violet ('70) 500.00 425.00
Nos. 6-15 (9) 1,522. 1,164.

Two types of 5r differ in the position of the "5" at upper right.

The reprints are on stout white paper, ungummed, with rough perforation 13½, and on thin white paper with shiny white gum and clean-cut perforation 13½. The overprint has the wide "D" and "R" and the first reprints included the 5r with both black and red overprint. Value $10 each.

Overprinted in Red or Black

1871-80 *Perf. 12½, 13½*

16 A2 5r black (R) 11.00 8.00
a. Inverted overprint —
b. Double overprint 55.00 55.00
c. Perf. 14 90.00 55.00
18 A2 10r yellow 35.00 22.50
19 A2 10r bl grn ('79) 140.00 110.00
a. Perf. 13½ 160.00 140.00
20 A2 10r yel grn ('80) 65.00 52.50
21 A2 15r brn ('75) 19.00 11.50
22 A2 20r bister 37.50 22.50
23 A2 25r rose 13.50 4.50
a. Inverted overprint 40.00 40.00
b. Double overprint 40.00 40.00
24 A2 50r green ('72) 67.50 30.00
a. Double overprint —
b. Inverted overprint 200.00 200.00
25 A2 50r blue ('80) 125.00 55.00
26 A2 80r orange ('72) 77.50 67.50
27 A2 100r pale lil ('73) 90.00 60.00
a. Perf. 14 200.00 85.00
b. Perf. 13½ 160.00 75.00
28 A2 120r blue 110.00 80.00
29 A2 150r blue ('76) 160.00 140.00
a. Perf. 13½ 175.00 150.00
30 A2 150r yel ('79) 300.00 240.00
31 A2 240r vio ('74) 700.00 500.00
32 A2 300r vio ('76) 75.00 67.50
Nos. 16-32 (16) 2,026. 1,471.

There are two types of the overprint, the second one having a broad "D."

The reprints have the same characteristics as those of the 1868-70 issues.

A3 A4

King Luiz — A5

1880-81

33 A3 5r black 35.00 21.00
34 A4 25r pearl gray 40.00 21.00
a. Inverted overprint 75.00 75.00
35 A5 25r lilac 42.50 11.00
a. 25r purple brown 32.50 11.00
b. 25r gray 35.00 10.00
Nos. 33-35 (3) 117.50 53.00

Nos. 33, 34 and 35 have been reprinted on stout white paper, ungummed, and the last three on thin white paper with shiny white gum. The perforations are as previously described.

Common Design Types pictured following the introduction.

Vasco da Gama Issue
Common Design Types

1898, Apr. 1 Engr. *Perf. 14-15*

37 CD20 2½r blue grn 2.40 1.25
38 CD21 5r red 2.40 1.25
39 CD22 10r red violet 3.00 1.50
40 CD23 25r yel green 2.75 1.25
41 CD24 50r dk blue 8.50 3.25
42 CD25 75r vio brown 10.00 7.00
43 CD26 100r bister brn 10.00 7.00
44 CD27 150r bister 15.00 11.50
Nos. 37-44 (8) 54.05 34.00

Nos. 37-44 with "REPUBLICA" overprint and surcharges are listed as Portugal Nos. 199-206.

Ceres — A6

1928, May 1 Engr. *Perf. 13½*

Value Typographed in Black

45 A6 3c deep violet .30 *.60*
46 A6 4c orange .30 *.60*
47 A6 5c light blue .30 *.60*
48 A6 6c brown .30 *.60*
49 A6 10c red .30 *.60*
50 A6 15c yel green .30 *.60*
51 A6 16c red brown .35 *.60*
52 A6 25c violet rose .75 .60
53 A6 32c blue grn .75 .60
54 A6 40c yel brown 1.50 *1.75*
55 A6 50c slate 1.50 *1.75*
56 A6 64c Prus blue 1.50 *3.00*
57 A6 80c dk brown 1.50 *5.00*
58 A6 96c carmine rose 7.50 *3.00*
59 A6 1e black 1.25 3.00
a. Value omitted 42.50 *45.00*
60 A6 1.20e light rose 1.25 *3.00*
61 A6 1.60e ultra 1.25 *3.00*
62 A6 2.40e yellow 2.00 *3.50*
63 A6 3.36e dull green 3.00 *5.75*
64 A6 4.50e brown red 4.00 *9.00*
65 A6 7e dark blue 5.00 *17.50*
Nos. 45-65 (21) 34.90 *64.65*

It was obligatory to use these stamps in place of those in regular use on May 1, June 5, July 1 and Dec. 31, 1928, Jan. 1 and 31, May 1 and June 5, 1929. The amount obtained from this sale was donated to a fund for building a museum.

Less than very fine examples sell for much less.

NEWSPAPER STAMP

Numeral of Value — N1

Newspaper Stamp of Portugal Overprinted in Black

Perf. 12½, 13½

1876, July 1 Unwmk.

P1 N1 2½r olive 11.00 4.25
a. Inverted overprint 30.00

The reprints have the same papers, gum, perforations and overprint as the reprints of the regular issues.

POSTAL TAX STAMPS

Pombal Commemorative Issue
Common Design Types

1925 Unwmk. Engr. *Perf. 12½*

RA1 CD28 15c gray & black .60 .65
RA2 CD29 15c gray & black .60 .65
RA3 CD30 15c gray & black .60 .65
Nos. RA1-RA3 (3) 1.80 1.95

POSTAL TAX DUE STAMPS

Pombal Commemorative Issue
Common Design Types

1925 Unwmk. *Perf. 12½*

RAJ1 CD28 30c gray & black .85 3.50
RAJ2 CD29 30c gray & black .85 3.50
RAJ3 CD30 30c gray & black .85 3.50
Nos. RAJ1-RAJ3 (3) 2.55 10.50

MALAGASY REPUBLIC

ˌmal-lə-'gə-sē

Madagascar (French)

Malagasy Democratic Republic

Republic of Madagascar

LOCATION — Large island off the coast of southeastern Africa
GOVT. — Republic
AREA — 226,658 sq. mi.
POP. — 14,062,000 (1995 est.)
CAPITAL — Antananarivo

Madagascar became a French protectorate in 1885 and a French colony in 1896 following several years of dispute among France, Great Britain, and the native government. The colony administered the former protectorates of Anjouan, Grand Comoro, Mayotte, Diego-Suarez, Nossi-Be and Sainte-Marie de Madagascar. Previous issues of postage stamps are found under these individual headings. The Malagasy Republic succeeded the colony in 1958 and became the Democratic Republic of Malagasy in 1975. The official name was again changed in 1993 to Republic of Madagascar.

For British Consular Mail stamps of 1884-1886, see Madagascar.

100 Centimes = 1 Franc
100 Centimes = 1 Ariary (1976)

See France No. 2767 for stamp inscribed "Madagascar."

Catalogue values for unused stamps in this country are for Never Hinged items, beginning with Scott 241 in the regular postage section, Scott B15 in the semi-postal section, Scott C37 in the airpost section, and Scott J31 in the postage due section.

French Offices in Madagascar

The general issues of French Colonies were used in these offices in addition to the stamps listed here.

Stamps of French Colonies Surcharged in Black:

a

b

c

1889 Unwmk. *Perf. 14x13½*

Overprint Type "a"

1 A9 05c on 10c blk, *lav* *650.* *190.*
a. Inverted surcharge *1,500.* *1,100.*
2 A9 05c on 25c blk, *rose* *650.* *190.*
a. Inverted surcharge *1,500.* *1,100.*
b. 25c on 10c lav (error) *9,000.* *7,250.*
3 A9 25c on 40c red, *straw* *575.* *160.*
a. Inverted surcharge *1,200.* *925.*

1891

Overprint Type "b"

4 A9 05c on 40c red, *straw* *200.00* *90.00*
5 A9 15c on 25c blk, *rose* *200.00* *100.00*
a. Surcharge vertical *210.00* *125.00*

Overprint Type "c"

6 A9 5c on 10c blk, *lav* *225.00* *110.00*
a. Double surcharge *750.00* 725.00
7 A9 5c on 25c blk, *rose* *240.00* *125.00*

See Senegal Nos. 4, 8 for similar surcharge on 20c, 30c.

Forgeries of Nos. 1-7 exist.

A4

1891 Type-set *Imperf.*

Without Gum

8 A4 5c blk, *green* 150.00 30.00
9 A4 10c blk, *lt bl* 100.00 30.00
10 A4 15c ultra, *pale bl* 100.00 32.50
11 A4 25c brn, *buff* 21.00 14.00
12 A4 1fr blk, *yellow* 1,000. 275.00
13 A4 5fr vio & blk, *lil* 2,000. 1,000.

Ten varieties of each. Nos. 12-13 have been extensively forged.

Stamps of France 1876-90, Overprinted in Red or Black

1895 *Perf. 14x13½*

14 A15 5c grn, *grnsh* (R) 15.00 7.25
15 A15 10c blk, *lav* (R) 47.50 28.00
16 A15 15c bl (R) 70.00 18.00
17 A15 25c blk, *rose* (R) 100.00 20.00
18 A15 40c red, *straw* (Bk) 80.00 28.00
19 A15 50c rose, *rose* (Bk) 100.00 42.50
20 A15 75c dp vio, *org* (R) 110.00 50.00
21 A15 1fr brnz grn, *straw* (Bk) 130.00 65.00
22 A15 5fr vio, *lav* (Bk) 175.00 80.00
Nos. 14-22 (9) 827.50 338.75

Majunga Issue

Stamps of France, 1876-86, Surcharged with New Value

1895

Manuscript Surcharge in Red

22A A15 0,15c on 25c blk, *rose* *6,500.*
22B A15 0,15c on 1fr brnz grn, *straw* *5,250.*

Handstamped in Black

22C A15 15c on 25c blk, *rose* *6,000.*
22D A15 15c on 1fr brnz grn, *straw* *5,500.*

On most of #22C and all of #22D the manuscript surcharge of #22A-22B was washed off. Three types of "15" were used for No. 22C.

Stamps of France, 1876-84, Surcharged with New Value

1896

23 A15 5c on 1c blk, *bl* *5,500.* *2,100.*
24 A15 15c on 2c brn, *buff* *2,100.* *875.*
25 A15 25c on 3c gray, *grysh* *2,750.* *950.*
26 A15 25c on 4c cl, *lav* *5,500.* *1,600.*
27 A15 25c on 40c red, *straw* *1,350.* *700.*

The oval of the 5c and 15c surcharges is smaller than that of the 25c, and it does not extend beyond the edges of the stamp as the 25c surcharge does.

Excellent counterfeits of the surcharges on Nos. 22A to 27 exist.

Issues of the Colony

Navigation and Commerce — A7

1896-1906 **Typo.** *Perf. 14x13½*

Colony Name in Blue or Carmine

28 A7 1c blk, *lil bl* 1.00 .80
29 A7 2c brn, *buff* 1.75 .95
a. Name in blue black 3.75 3.75
30 A7 4c claret, *lav* 1.90 1.25
31 A7 5c grn, *grnsh* 6.50 1.25
32 A7 5c yel grn ('01) 1.60 .70
33 A7 10c blk, *lav* 6.50 1.75
34 A7 10c red ('00) 2.50 .70
35 A7 15c blue, quadrille paper 12.50 1.25
36 A7 15c gray ('00) 2.25 1.25
37 A7 20c red, *grn* 6.25 1.60
38 A7 25c blk, *rose* 9.00 4.00
39 A7 25c blue ('00) 21.50 20.00
40 A7 30c brn, *bis* 8.00 3.00
41 A7 35c blk, *yel* ('06) 36.00 6.00
42 A7 40c red, *straw* 9.50 4.75
43 A7 50c car, *rose* 11.50 2.40
44 A7 50c brn, *az* ('00) 27.50 25.00
45 A7 75c dp vio, *org* 5.00 3.75
46 A7 1fr brnz grn, *straw* 12.50 2.25
a. Name in blue ('99) 24.00 18.50
47 A7 5fr red lil, *lav* ('99) 32.50 27.50
Nos. 28-47 (20) 215.75 110.15

Perf. 13½x14 stamps are counterfeits.

For surcharges see Nos. 48-55, 58-60, 115-118, 127-128.

Nos. 32, 43, 44 and 46, affixed to pressboard with animals printed on the back, were used as emergency currency in the Comoro Islands in 1920.

Surcharged in Black

1902

48 A7 05c on 50c car, *rose* 6.00 4.00
a. Inverted surcharge 90.00 90.00
49 A7 10c on 5fr red lil, *lav* 19.50 14.50
a. Inverted surcharge 110.00 110.00
50 A7 15c on 1fr ol grn, *straw* 8.00 6.00
a. Inverted surcharge 97.50 97.50
b. Double surcharge 290.00 290.00
Nos. 48-50 (3) 33.50 24.50

Surcharged in Black

51 A7 0,01 on 2c brn, *buff* 8.00 8.00
a. Inverted surcharge 57.50 57.50
b. "00,1" instead of "0,01" 115.00 115.00
c. As "b" inverted — —
d. Comma omitted 160.00 160.00
e. Name in blue black 8.25 8.25
52 A7 0,05 on 30c brn, *bis* 8.50 8.50
a. Inverted surcharge 57.50 57.50
b. "00,5" instead of "0,05" 72.50 72.50
c. As "b" inverted 350.00 350.00
d. Comma omitted 160.00 160.00
53 A7 0,10 on 50c car, *rose* 8.00 8.00
a. Inverted surcharge 57.50 57.50
b. Comma omitted 160.00 160.00
54 A7 0,15 on 75c vio, *org* 6.25 6.25
a. Inverted surcharge 62.50 62.50
b. Comma omitted 160.00 160.00
55 A7 0,15 on 1fr ol grn, *straw* 12.50 12.50
a. Inverted surcharge 80.00 80.00
b. Comma omitted 1,050. 1,050.
Nos. 51-55 (5) 43.25 43.25

Surcharged On Stamps of Diego-Suarez

56 A11 0,05 on 30c brn, *bis* 132.50 110.00
a. "00,5" instead of "0,05" 775.00 775.00
b. Inverted surcharge 1,050. 1,050.
57 A11 0,10 on 50c car, *rose* *4,100.* *4,100.*

Counterfeits of Nos. 56-57 exist with surcharge both normal and inverted.

Surcharged in Black

58 A7 0,01 on 2c brn, *buff* 8.00 8.00
a. Inverted surcharge 57.50 57.50
b. Comma omitted 160.00 160.00
59 A7 0,05 on 30c brn, *bis* 7.25 7.25
a. Inverted surcharge 57.50 57.50
b. Comma omitted 160.00 160.00
60 A7 0,10 on 50c car, *rose* 6.25 6.25
a. Inverted surcharge 57.50 57.50
b. Comma omitted 160.00 160.00
Nos. 58-60 (3) 21.50 21.50

Surcharged On Stamps of Diego-Suarez

61 A11 0,05 on 30c brn, *bis* 110.00 110.00
a. Inverted surcharge 1,050. 1,050.
62 A11 0,10 on 50c car, *rose* *4,100.* *4,100.*

BISECTS

During alleged stamp shortages at several Madagascar towns in 1904, it is claimed that bisects were used. After being affixed to letters, these bisects were handstamped "Affranchissement - exceptionnel - (faute de timbres)" and other inscriptions of similar import. The stamps bisected were 10c, 20c, 30c and 50c denominations of Madagascar type A7 and Diego-Suarez type A11. The editors believe these provisionals were unnecessary and speculative.

Zebu, Traveler's Tree and Lemur — A8

Transportation by Sedan Chair — A9

1903 **Engr.** *Perf. 11½*

63 A8 1c dk violet 1.00 1.00
a. On bluish paper 6.75 5.50
64 A8 2c olive brn 1.00 1.00
65 A8 4c brown 1.10 1.10
66 A8 5c yellow grn 5.75 1.40
67 A8 10c red 10.00 1.00
68 A8 15c carmine 14.00 1.25
a. On bluish paper *140.00* *140.00*
69 A8 20c orange 4.75 2.25
70 A8 25c dull blue 25.00 4.25
71 A8 30c pale red 36.00 13.50
72 A8 40c gray vio 25.00 5.00
73 A8 50c brown org 45.00 24.00
74 A8 75c orange yel 55.00 25.00
75 A8 1fr dp green 55.00 26.00
76 A8 2fr slate 70.00 27.50
77 A8 5fr gray black 72.50 *80.00*
Nos. 63-77 (15) 421.10 214.25

Nos. 63-77 exist imperf. Value of set, $600.

For surcharges see Nos. 119-124, 129.

1908-28 **Typo.** *Perf. 13½x14*

79 A9 1c violet & ol .20 .20
80 A9 2c red & ol .20 .20
81 A9 4c ol brn & brn .20 .20
82 A9 5c bl grn & ol .85 .20
83 A9 5c blk & rose ('22) .20 .20
84 A9 10c rose & brown .85 .20
85 A9 10c bl grn & ol grn ('22) .50 .30
86 A9 10c org brn & vio ('25) .20 .20
87 A9 15c dl vio & rose ('16) .20 .20
88 A9 15c dl grn & lt grn ('27) .40 .35
89 A9 15c dk bl & rose red ('28) 1.40 .80
90 A9 20c org & brn .45 .25
91 A9 25c blue & blk 2.50 .60
92 A9 25c vio & blk ('22) .25 .20
93 A9 30c brown & blk 2.50 1.10
94 A9 30c rose red & brn ('22) .45 .30
95 A9 30c grn & red vio ('25) .40 .20
96 A9 30c dp grn & yel grn ('27) 1.25 .80
97 A9 35c red & black 1.75 .90
98 A9 40c vio brn & blk 1.00 .50
99 A9 45c bl grn & blk .80 .50
100 A9 45c red & ver ('25) .40 .35
101 A9 45c gray lil & mag ('27) 1.25 .80
102 A9 50c violet & blk .85 .50
103 A9 50c blue & blk ('22) .75 .50
104 A9 50c blk & org ('25) .80 .20
105 A9 60c vio, *pnksh* ('25) .60 .50
106 A9 65c black & bl ('25) .80 .70
107 A9 75c rose red & blk .80 .50
108 A9 85c grn & ver ('25) 1.25 .80
109 A9 1fr brown & ol .80 .50
110 A9 1fr dull blue ('25) .95 .95
111 A9 1fr rose & grn ('28) 5.25 4.25
112 A9 1.10fr bis & bl grn ('28) 1.75 1.75
113 A9 2fr blue & olive 3.50 1.40
114 A9 5fr vio & vio brn 12.00 5.25
Nos. 79-114 (36) 48.30 27.35

75c violet on pinkish stamps of type A9 are No. 138 without surcharge.

For surcharges and overprints see Nos. 125-126, 130-146, 178-179, B1, 212-214.

Preceding Issues Surcharged in Black or Carmine

1912, Nov. *Perf. 14x13½*

115 A7 5c on 15c gray (C) 1.00 1.00
116 A7 5c on 20c red, *grn* .90 .90
a. Inverted surcharge 125.00
117 A7 5c on 30c brn, *bis* (C) 1.00 1.00
118 A7 10c on 75c vio, *org* 8.50 8.50
a. Double surcharge 250.00
119 A8 5c on 2c ol brn (C) .50 .50
120 A8 5c on 20c org .80 .80
121 A8 5c on 30c pale red 1.00 1.00
122 A8 10c on 40c gray vio (C) 1.40 1.40
123 A8 10c on 50c brn org 2.75 2.75
124 A8 10c on 75c org yel 5.25 5.25
a. Inverted surcharge 190.00
Nos. 115-124 (10) 23.10 23.10

Two spacings between the surcharged numerals are found on Nos. 115 to 118. For detailed listings, see the *Scott Classic Specialized Catalogue of Stamps and Covers.*

Stamps of Anjouan, Grand Comoro Island, Mayotte and Mohéli with similar surcharges were also available for use in Madagascar and the entire Comoro archipelago.

Preceding Issues Surcharged in Red or Black

g

h

1921

On Nos. 98 & 107

125 A9 (g) 30c on 40c (R) 1.75 1.75
126 A9 (g) 60c on 75c 2.75 2.75

On Nos. 45 & 47

127 A7 (g) 60c on 75c (R) 6.50 6.50
a. Inverted surcharge 175.00 175.00
128 A7 (h) 1fr on 5fr .75 .75

On No. 77

129 A8 (h) 1fr on 5fr (R) 70.00 70.00
Nos. 125-129 (5) 81.75 81.75

Stamps and Type of 1908-16 Surcharged in Black or Red

130 A9 1c on 15c dl vio & rose .70 .70
131 A9 25c on 35c red & blk 5.00 5.00
132 A9 25c on 35c red & blk (R) 15.00 15.00
133 A9 25c on 40c brn & blk 4.25 4.25
134 A9 25c on 45c grn & blk 2.75 2.75
Nos. 130-134 (5) 27.70 27.70
Nos. 125-134 (10) 109.45 109.45

Stamps and Type of 1908-28 Surcharged with New Value and Bars

1922-27

135 A9 25c on 15c dl vio & rose .25 .20
a. Double surcharge 72.50
136 A9 25c on 2fr bl & ol .30 .20
137 A9 25c on 5fr vio & vio brn .55 .20
138 A9 60c on 75c vio, *pnksh* .45 .35
139 A9 65c on 75c rose red & blk .80 .80
140 A9 85c on 45c bl grn & blk 1.25 1.00
141 A9 90c on 75c dl red & rose red .80 .80
142 A9 1.25fr on 1fr lt bl (R) .60 .25
143 A9 1.50fr on 1fr dp bl & dl bl .60 .25
144 A9 3fr on 5fr grn & vio 1.60 1.00
145 A9 10fr on 5fr org & rose lil 7.50 4.75
146 A9 20fr on 5fr rose & sl bl 8.50 6.75
Nos. 135-146 (12) 23.20 16.55

Years of issue: #138, 1922; #136, 137, 1924; #135, 139-140, 1925; #142, 1926; #141, 142-146, 1927.

See Nos. 178-179.

Sakalava Chief — A10

Hova Woman — A12

Hova with Oxen A11

Bétsiléo Woman A13

Perf. 13½x14, 14x13½

1930-44 **Typo.**

147 A11 1c dk bl & bl grn ('33) .20 .20
148 A10 2c brn red & dk brn .20 .20
149 A10 4c dk brn & vio .20 .20
150 A11 5c lt grn & red .25 .20
151 A12 10c ver & dp grn .40 .20
152 A13 15c dp red .25 .20
153 A11 20c yel brn & dk bl .25 .20
154 A12 25c vio & dk brn .25 .20
155 A13 30c Prus blue .65 .45
156 A10 40c grn & red .75 .50
157 A13 45c dull violet .90 .55
158 A11 65c ol grn & vio 1.10 .80
159 A13 75c dk brown .85 .50
160 A11 90c brn red & dk red 1.40 .90
161 A12 1fr yel brn & dk bl 1.75 1.10
162 A12 1fr dk red & car rose ('38) .95 .90
163 A12 1.25fr dp bl & dk brn ('33) 1.60 .90
164 A10 1.50fr dk & dp bl 5.50 1.10
165 A10 1.50fr brn & dk red ('38) .75 .50
165A A10 1.50fr dk red & brn ('44) .50 .50
166 A10 1.75fr dk brn & dk red ('33) 4.25 1.60
167 A10 5fr vio & dk brn 1.25 .70
168 A10 20fr yel brn & dk bl 2.00 1.75
Nos. 147-168 (23) 26.20 14.35

For surcharges and overprints see #211, 215, 217-218, 222-223, 228-229, 233, 235, 239, 257 and note after #B10.

Common Design Types pictured following the introduction.

Colonial Exposition Issue
Common Design Types

1931 **Engr.** ***Perf. 12½***
Name of Country in Black

169 CD70 40c deep green 1.40 1.00
170 CD71 50c violet 2.00 1.25
171 CD72 90c red orange 2.00 1.25
172 CD73 1.50fr dull blue 2.50 1.50
Nos. 169-172 (4) 7.90 5.00

General Joseph Simon Galliéni — A14

1931 **Engr.** ***Perf. 14***
Size: 21½x34½mm

173 A14 1c ultra .50 .45
174 A14 50c orange brn 1.40 .35
175 A14 2fr deep red 5.75 4.25
176 A14 3fr emerald 4.75 2.50
177 A14 10fr dp orange 4.00 2.50
Nos. 173-177 (5) 16.40 10.05

See Nos. 180-190. For overprints and surcharges see Nos. 216, 219, 221, 224, 232, 258.

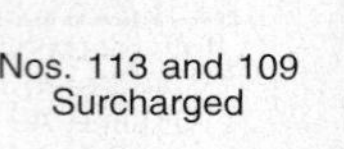
Nos. 113 and 109 Surcharged

1932 ***Perf. 13½x14***

178 A9 25c on 2fr bl & ol .75 .50
179 A9 50c on 1fr brn & ol .75 .50

No. 178 has numerals in thick block letters. No. 136 has thin shaded numerals.

Galliéni Type of 1931

1936-40 **Photo.** ***Perf. 13½, 13x13½***
Size: 21x34mm

180 A14 3c sapphire ('40) .25 .20
181 A14 45c brt green ('40) .50 .40
182 A14 50c yellow brown .25 .20
183 A14 60c brt red lil ('40) .40 .20
184 A14 70c brt rose ('40) .60 .40
185 A14 90c copper brn ('39) .50 .40
186 A14 1.40fr org yel ('40) .90 .50
187 A14 1.60fr purple ('40) .90 .60
188 A14 2fr dk carmine .50 .20
189 A14 3fr green 4.50 2.25
190 A14 3fr olive blk ('39) .90 .70
Nos. 180-190 (11) 10.20 6.05

For overprint see note after #B10.

Paris International Exposition Issue
Common Design Types

1937, Apr. 15 **Engr.** ***Perf. 13***

191 CD74 20c dp violet .95 .95
192 CD75 30c dk green .95 .95
193 CD76 40c car rose 1.00 1.00
194 CD77 50c dk brn & blk 1.40 1.40
195 CD78 90c red 1.40 1.40
196 CD79 1.50fr ultra 1.40 1.40
Nos. 191-196 (6) 7.10 7.10

Colonial Arts Exhibition Issue
Common Design Type
Souvenir Sheet

1937 ***Imperf.***

197 CD74 3fr orange red 5.00 *5.50*

Jean Laborde A15

1938-40 ***Perf. 13***

198 A15 35c green .65 .40
199 A15 55c dp purple .65 .40
200 A15 65c orange red .90 .40
201 A15 80c violet brn .65 .40
202 A15 1fr rose car .90 .40
203 A15 1.25fr rose car ('39) .40 .20
204 A15 1.75fr dk ultra 1.75 .70
205 A15 2.15fr yel brn 2.50 1.75
206 A15 2.25fr dk ultra ('39) .60 .50
207 A15 2.50fr blk brn ('40) .65 .50
208 A15 10fr dk green ('40) 1.25 .80
Nos. 198-208 (11) 10.90 6.45

Nos. 198-202, 204, 205 commemorate the 60th anniv. of the death of Jean Laborde, explorer.

For overprints and surcharges see Nos. 220, 225-227, 230-231, 234, 236-237.

New York World's Fair Issue
Common Design Type

1939, May 10 **Engr.** ***Perf. 12½x12***

209 CD82 1.25fr car lake 1.00 1.00
210 CD82 2.25fr ultra 1.10 1.10

For surcharge see No. 240.

Porters Carrying Man in Chair, and Marshal Petain — A15a

1941 **Engr.** ***Perf. 12x12½***

210A A15a 1fr bister brn .75
210B A15a 2.50fr blue .75

Nos. 210A-210B were issued by the Vichy government in France but were not placed on sale in Madagascar.

For overprints see #B13-B14.

Type of 1930-44 Surcharged in Black with New Value

1942 ***Perf. 14x13½***

211 A11 50c on 65c dk brn & mag 2.25 .50

French Explorers de Hell, Passot & Jehenne — A15b

1942 **Engr.** ***Perf. 13x13½***

211A A15b 1.50fr blue & red brn 1.10

Centenary of French colonies of Mayotte and Nossi Bé.

No. 211A was issued by the Vichy government in France, but was not placed on sale in Madagascar.

Nos. 143, 145-146 with Additional Overprint in Red or Black

1942 **Unwmk.** ***Perf. 14x13½***

212 A9 1.50fr on 1fr (R) 1.75 1.75
213 A9 10fr on 5fr (Bk) 10.00 10.00
214 A9 20fr on 5fr (R) 12.50 12.50

Stamps of 1930-40 Overprinted Like Nos. 212-214 in Black or Red or:

215 A10 2c brn red & dk brn 1.10 1.10
216 A14 3c sapphire (R) 115.00 115.00
217 A13 15c deep red 10.00 10.00
218 A11 65c dk brn & mag .80 .80
219 A14 70c brt rose 1.10 1.10
220 A15 80c violet brn 3.25 3.25
221 A14 1.40fr orange yel 1.40 1.40
222 A10 1.50fr dk bl & dp bl (R) 2.50 2.25
223 A10 1.50fr brn & dk red 2.75 2.75
224 A14 1.60fr purple 1.40 1.40
225 A15 2.25fr dk ultra (R) 1.00 1.00
226 A15 2.50fr black brn (R) 5.00 5.000
227 A15 10fr dk green 6.25 6.25
228 A10 20fr yel brn & dk bl (R) *675.00 750.00*

Stamps of 1930-40 Surcharged in Black or Red

229 A11 5c on 1c dk bl & bl grn .65 .65
230 A15 10c on 55c dp pur 1.60 1.60
231 A15 30c on 65c org red 1.00 1.00
232 A14 50c on 90c cop brn 1.00 1.00
233 A12 1fr on 1.25fr dp bl & dk brn 3.25 3.25
234 A15 1fr on 1.25fr rose car 12.50 12.50
235 A10 1.50fr on 1.75fr dk brn & dk red .95 .95
236 A15 1.50fr on 1.75fr ultra (R) .95 .95
237 A15 2fr on 2.15fr yel brn 1.60 1.60

No. 211 with additional Overprint Like Nos. 217-218 in Black

239 A11 50c on 65c dk brn & mag .50 .50

New York World's Fair Stamp Overprinted Like #217-218 in Red

Perf. 12½x12

240 CD82 2.25fr ultra 1.00 1.00
Nos. 212-227,229-240 (27) 200.80 200.55

Catalogue values for unused stamps in this section, from this point to the end of the section, are for Never Hinged items.

Traveler's Tree — A16

1943 **Unwmk.** **Photo.** ***Perf. 14x14½***

241 A16 5c ol gray .20 .20
242 A16 10c pale rose vio .20 .20
243 A16 25c emerald .20 .20
244 A16 30c dp orange .20 .20
245 A16 40c slate bl .20 .20
246 A16 80c dk red brn .20 .20
247 A16 1fr dull blue .20 .20
248 A16 1.50fr crim rose .35 .30
249 A16 2fr dull yel .35 .30
250 A16 2.50fr brt ultra .35 .30
251 A16 4fr aqua & red .55 .45
252 A16 5fr green & blk .55 .45
253 A16 10fr sal pink & dk bl .95 .75
254 A16 20fr dl vio & brn 1.10 .90
Nos. 241-254 (14) 5.60 4.85

For surcharges see Nos. 255-256, 261-268.

Types of 1930-44 without "RF"

1943-44

254A A11 20c yel brn & dk bl .40
254B A14 60c lilac rose .65
254C A12 1fr dk red & car rose 1.40
254D A10 1.50fr brn & dk red .95
254E A10 5fr vio & dk brn 2.50
Nos. 254A-254E (5) 5.90

On type A10, the two panels at the top of the frame have been reversed, with the value at the left and a blank (RF removed) panel at right.

Nos. 254A-254E were issued by the Vichy government in France, but were not placed on sale in Madagascar.

Nos. 241 and 242 Surcharged with New Values and Bars in Red or Blue

1944

255 A16 1.50fr on 5c (R) .65 .55
256 A16 1.50fr on 10c (Bl) 1.00 .85

Nos. 229 and 224 Surcharged with New Values and Bars in Red or Black

Perf. 14x13½, 14

257 A11 50c on 5c on 1c (R) .85 .70
258 A14 1.50fr on 1.60fr (Bk) 1.10 .95
Nos. 255-258 (4) 3.60 3.05

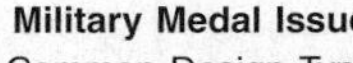

Eboue Issue
Common Design Type

1945	Engr.		*Perf. 13*	
259	CD91	2fr black	.60	.50
260	CD91	25fr Prus green	1.10	.95

Nos. 241, 243 and 250 Surcharged with New Values and Bars in Carmine or Black

1945			*Perf. 14x14½*	
261	A16	50c on 5c ol gray (C)	.40	.35
262	A16	60c on 5c ol gray (C)	.60	.50
263	A16	70c on 5c ol gray (C)	.60	.50
264	A16	1.20fr on 5c ol gray (C)	.60	.50
265	A16	2.40fr on 25c emer	.60	.50
266	A16	3fr on 25c emer	.60	.50
267	A16	4.50fr on 25c emer	.85	.70
268	A16	15fr on 2.50fr brt ultra (C)	.85	.70
		Nos. 261-268 (8)	5.10	4.25

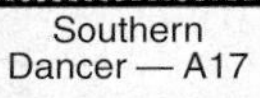
Southern Dancer — A17

Gen. J. S. Galliéni — A20

Herd of Zebus A18

Sakalava Man and Woman A19

Betsimisaraka Mother and Child — A21

General Jacques C. R. A. Duchesne A22

Marshal Joseph J. C. Joffre A23

Perf. 13x13½, 13½x13

1946		Photo.	Unwmk.	
269	A17	10c green	.20	.20
270	A17	30c orange	.20	.20
271	A17	40c brown ol	.20	.20
272	A17	50c violet brn	.20	.20
273	A18	60c dp ultra	.25	.20
274	A18	80c blue grn	.40	.20
275	A19	1fr brown	.25	.20
276	A19	1.20fr green	.25	.20
276A	A20	1.50fr dk red	.25	.20
277	A20	2fr slate blk	.25	.20
278	A20	3fr dp claret	.40	.20
278A	A21	3.60fr dk car rose	.85	.65
279	A21	4fr dp ultra	.40	.20
280	A21	5fr red orange	.65	.20
281	A22	6fr dk grnsh bl	.40	.20
282	A22	10fr red brn	.65	.20
283	A23	15fr violet brn	1.00	.30
284	A23	20fr dk vio bl	1.40	.65
285	A23	25fr brown	2.25	1.00
		Nos. 269-285 (19)	10.45	5.60

Military Medal Issue
Common Design Type

Engraved and Typographed

1952, Dec. 1	Unwmk.		*Perf. 13*	
286	CD101	15fr multicolored	3.75	2.50

Creation of the French Military Medal, cent.

Tropical Flowers — A24

Long-tailed Ground Roller A25

1954			Engr.	
287	A24	7.50fr ind & gray grn	1.25	.20
288	A25	8fr brown carmine	.90	.35
289	A25	15fr dk grn & dp ultra	2.25	.35
		Nos. 287-289 (3)	4.40	.90

Colonel Lyautey and Royal Palace, Tananarive A26

1954-55				
290	A26	10fr vio bl, ind & bl ('55)	.90	.20
291	A26	40fr dk sl bl & red brn	1.60	.20

FIDES Issue
Common Design Type

Designs: 3fr, Tractor and modern settlement. 5fr, Gallieni school. 10fr, Pangalanes Canal. 15fr, Irrigation project.

1956, Oct. 22	Engr.		*Perf. 13x12½*	
292	CD103	3fr gray vio & vio brn	.40	.20
293	CD103	5fr org brn & dk vio brn	.40	.35
294	CD103	10fr indigo & lilac	.60	.35
295	CD103	15fr grn & bl grn	.85	.20
		Nos. 292-295 (4)	2.25	1.10

Coffee A26a

1956, Oct. 22			*Perf. 13*	
296	A26a	20r red brn & dk brn	.55	.20

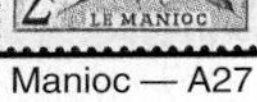
Manioc — A27

Vanilla — A28

Design: 4fr, Cloves.

1957, Mar. 12	Unwmk.		*Perf. 13*	
297	A27	2fr bl, grn & sepia	.20	.20
298	A28	4fr dp grn & red	.55	.20
299	A28	12fr dk vio, dl grn & sepia	.75	.35
		Nos. 297-299 (3)	1.50	.75

Malagasy Republic Human Rights Issue
Common Design Type

1958, Dec. 10	Engr.		*Perf. 13*	
300	CD105	10fr brn & dk bl	.80	.40

Universal Declaration of Human Rights, 10th anniversary.
"CF" stands for "Communauté française."

> **Imperforates**
> Most Malagasy stamps from 1958 onward exist imperforate in issued and trial colors, and also in small presentation sheets in issued colors.

Flower Issue
Common Design Type

Perf. 12½x12, 12x12½

1959, Jan. 31			Photo.	
301	CD104	6fr Datura, horiz.	.60	.20
302	CD104	25fr Poinsettia	.90	.30

Flag and Assembly Building A29

Flag and Map — A30

French and Malagasy Flags and Map — A31

1959, Feb. 28	Engr.		*Perf. 13*	
303	A29	20fr brn vio, car & emer	.30	.20
304	A30	25fr gray, red & emer	.45	.20

Proclamation of the Malagasy Republic.

1959, Feb. 28				
305	A31	60fr multi	1.60	.50

Issued to honor the French Community.

Chionaema Pauliani A32

Ylang-ylang — A33

Designs: 30c, 40c, 50c, 3fr, Various butterflies. 5fr, Sisal. 8fr, Pepper. 10fr, Rice. 15fr, Cotton.

1960	Unwmk.		*Perf. 13*	
306	A32	30c multicolored	.50	.20
307	A32	40c emer, sep & red brn	.50	.20
308	A32	50c vio brn, blk & stl bl	.50	.20
309	A32	1fr ind, red & dl pur	.50	.20
310	A32	3fr ol, vio blk & org	.50	.20
311	A32	5fr red, brn & emer	.50	.20
312	A33	6fr dk grn & brt yel	.55	.20
313	A32	8fr crim rose, emer & blk	.55	.20
314	A33	10fr dk grn, yel grn & lt brn	1.00	.20
315	A32	15fr brown & grn	1.10	.20
		Nos. 306-315 (10)	6.20	2.00

Family Planting Trees — A34

1960, Feb. 1	Engr.		*Perf. 13*	
316	A34	20fr red brn, buff & grn	.90	.30

Issued for the "Week of the Tree," Feb. 1-7.

C.C.T.A. Issue
Common Design Type

1960, Feb. 22				
317	CD106	25fr lt bl grn & plum	.60	.30

Pres. Philibert Tsiranana and Map — A36

1960, Mar. 25	Unwmk.		*Perf. 13*	
318	A36	20fr green & brn	.35	.20

Athletes of Two Races — A37

Pres. Philibert Tsiranana — A38

1960	Engr.		*Perf. 13*	
319	A37	25fr choc, org brn & ultra	.60	.30

First Games of the French Community, Apr. 13-18, at Tananarive.

1960, July 29	Unwmk.		*Perf. 13*	
320	A38	20fr red, blk & brt grn	.35	.20

Issued to honor Pres. Tsiranana, "Father of Independence." For surcharge see No. B18.

Gray Lemur — A39

Designs: 4fr, Ruffed lemur, horiz. 12fr, Mongoose lemur.

1961, Dec. 9			*Perf. 13*	
321	A39	2fr brn & grnsh bl	.25	.20
322	A39	4fr brn, grn & blk	.45	.20
323	A39	12fr grn & red brn	1.10	.20
		Nos. 321-323,C67-C69 (6)	16.80	5.05

Pres. Tsiranana Bridge, Sofia River A40

1962, Jan. 4	Unwmk.		*Perf. 13*	
324	A40	25fr bright blue	1.00	.20

First Train Built at Tananarive A41

1962, Feb. 1

325 A41 20fr dk grn 1.10 .30

UN and Malagasy Flags over Government Building, Tananarive A42

1962, Mar. 14 ***Perf. 13***

326 A42 25fr multicolored .45 .20
327 A42 85fr multicolored 1.90 .55

Malagasy Republic's admission to the UN.
For surcharge see No. 409.

Ranomafana Village — A43

Designs: 30fr, Tritriva crater lake. 50fr, Foulpointe shore. 60fr, Fort Dauphin.

1962, May 7 **Engr.** ***Perf. 13***

328 A43 10fr sl grn, grnsh bl & cl .25 .20
329 A43 30fr sl grn, cl & grnsh bl .65 .20
330 A43 50fr ultra, cl & sl grn .90 .30
331 A43 60fr cl, ultra & sl grn 1.10 .40
Nos. 328-331,C70 (5) 4.65 1.70

African and Malgache Union Issue

Common Design Type

1962, Sept. 8 **Photo.** ***Perf. 12½x12***

332 CD110 30fr grn, bluish grn, red & gold .80 .80

First anniversary of the African and Malgache Union.

Arms of Republic and UNESCO Emblem A44

1962, Sept. 3 **Unwmk.**

333 A44 20fr rose, emer & blk .60 .20

First Conference on Higher Education in Africa, Tananarive, Sept. 3-12.

Power Station — A45

Designs: 8fr, Atomic reactor and atom symbol, horiz. 10fr, Oil derrick. 15fr, Tanker, horiz.

Perf. 12x12½, 12½x12

1962, Oct. 18 **Litho.**

334 A45 5fr blue, yel & red .20 .20
335 A45 8fr blue, red & yel .30 .20
336 A45 10fr multicolored .40 .20
337 A45 15fr bl, red brn & blk .50 .20
Nos. 334-337 (4) 1.40 .80

Industrialization of Madagascar.

Factory and Globe A46

1963, Jan. 7 **Typo.** ***Perf. 14x13½***

338 A46 25fr dp org & blk .55 .20

International Fair at Tamatave.

Hertzian Cable, Tananarive-Fianarantsoa — A47

1963, Mar. 7 **Photo.** ***Perf. 12½x12***

339 A47 20fr multi .55 .20

Madagascar Blue Pigeon — A48 Gastrorchis Humblotii — A49

Birds: 2fr, Blue coua. 3fr, Red fody. 6fr, Madagascar pigmy kingfisher.
Orchids: 10fr, Eulophiella roempleriana. 12fr, Angraecum sesquipedale.

1963 **Unwmk.** ***Perf. 13***

340 A48 1fr multi .45 .30
341 A48 2fr multi .45 .30
342 A48 3fr multi .60 .30
343 A48 6fr multi .75 .30
344 A49 8fr multi 1.00 .30
345 A49 10fr multi 1.90 .45
346 A49 12fr multi 2.10 .50
Nos. 340-346,C72-C74 (10) 21.50 6.60

Arms — A50

Arms of: 1.50fr, Antsirabe. 5fr, Antalaha. 10fr, Tulear. 15fr, Majunga. 20fr, Fianarantsoa. 25fr, Tananarive. 50fr, Diégo-Suarez.

Imprint: "R. Louis del. So. Ge. Im."

1963-65 **Litho.** ***Perf. 13***

Size: 23½x35½mm

347 A50 1.50fr multi ('64) .20 .20
348 A50 5fr multi ('65) .20 .20
349 A50 10fr multi ('64) .20 .20
350 A50 15fr multi ('64) .35 .20
351 A50 20fr multi .50 .20
352 A50 25fr multi .55 .20
353 A50 50fr multi ('65) 1.25 .50
Nos. 347-353 (7) 3.25 1.70

See Nos. 388-390, 434-439.
For surcharge see No. 503.

Map and Centenary Emblem — A51 Globe and Hands Holding Torch — A52

1963, Sept. 2 ***Perf. 12x12½***

354 A51 30fr multi 1.00 .50

Centenary of the International Red Cross.

1963, Dec. 10 **Engr.** ***Perf. 12½***

355 A52 60fr ol, ocher & car .85 .40

Universal Declaration of Human Rights, 15th anniv.

Scouts and Campfire A53

1964, June 6 **Engr.** ***Perf. 13***

356 A53 20fr dk red, org & car .70 .30

40th anniv. of the Boy Scouts of Madagascar.

Europafrica Issue, 1964

Dove and Globe A54

1964, July 20 **Engr.**

357 A54 45fr ol grn, brn red & blk 1.00 .35

First anniversary of economic agreement between the European Economic Community and the African and Malgache Union.

Carved Statue of Woman — A55 University Emblem — A56

Malagasy Art: 30fr, Statue of sitting man.

1964, Oct. 20 **Unwmk.** ***Perf. 13***

358 A55 6fr dk bl, brt bl & sepia .45 .20
359 A55 30fr dp grn, ol bis & dk brn .80 .30
Nos. 358-359,C79 (3) 3.50 1.40

Cooperation Issue

Common Design Type

1964, Nov. 7 **Engr.** ***Perf. 13***

360 CD119 25fr blk, dk brn & org brn .60 .25

1964, Dec. 5 **Litho.** ***Perf. 13x12½***

361 A56 65fr red, blk & grn .70 .35

Founding of the University of Madagascar, Tannanarive. The inscription reads: "Foolish is he who does not do better than his father."

Jejy — A57

Valiha Player A58

Musical instruments: 3fr, Kabosa (lute). 8fr, Hazolahy (sacred drum).

1965 **Engr.** ***Perf. 13***

Size: 22x36mm

362 A57 3fr mag, vio bl & dk brn .50 .20
363 A57 6fr emer, rose lil & dk brn .60 .20
364 A57 8fr brn, grn & blk .90 .20

Photo. ***Perf. 12½x13***

365 A58 25fr multi 1.75 .60
Nos. 362-365,C80 (5) 9.25 3.20

PTT Receiving Station, Foulpointe A59

1965, May 8 **Engr.** ***Perf. 13***

366 A59 20fr red org, dk grn & ocher .50 .25

Issued for Stamp Day, 1965.

ITU Emblem, Old and New Telecommunication Equipment — A60

1965, May 17

367 A60 50fr ultra, red & grn 1.00 .40

ITU, centenary.

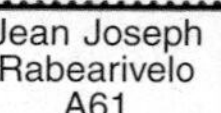

Jean Joseph Rabearivelo A61 Pres. Philibert Tsiranana A62

1965, June 22 **Photo.** ***Perf. 13x12½***

368 A61 40fr dk brn & org .60 .30

Issued to honor the poet Jean Joseph Rabearivelo, pen name of Joseph Casimir, (1901-37).

1965, Oct. 18 ***Perf. 13x12½***

369 A62 20fr multi .25 .20
a. Souv. sheet of 4 1.00 1.00
370 A62 25fr multi .40 .20
a. Souv. sheet of 4 2.00 2.00

55th birthday of President Philibert Tsiranana.

Mail Coach
A63

History of the Post: 3fr, Early automobile. 4fr, Litter. 10fr, Mail runner, vert. 12fr, Mail boat. 25fr, Oxcart. 30fr, Old railroad mail car. 65fr, Hydrofoil.

1965-66 Engr. *Perf. 13*

371 A63 3fr vio, dp bis & sky bl ('66) .40 .25
372 A63 4fr ultra, grn & dk brn ('66) .35 .25
373 A63 10fr multi .35 .25
374 A63 12fr multi .40 .25
375 A63 20fr bis, grn & red brn .90 .30
376 A63 25fr sl grn, dk brn & org .85 .30
377 A63 30fr pck bl, red & sep ('66) 2.50 .50
378 A63 65fr vio, brn & Prus bl ('66) 2.00 .50
Nos. 371-378 (8) 7.75 2.60

Leper's Crippled Hands
A64

1966, Jan. 30

379 A64 20fr dk grn, dk brn & red .70 .30

Issued for the 13th World Leprosy Day.

Couple Planting Trees
A65

1966, Feb. 21

380 A65 20fr dk brn, pur & bl grn .60 .20

Reforestation as a national duty.

Tiger Beetle
A66

Insects: 6fr, Mantis. 12fr, Long-horned beetle. 45fr, Weevil.

1966 Photo. *Perf. 12½x12*
Insects in Natural Colors

381 A66 1fr brick red 1.25 .20
382 A66 6fr rose claret 1.25 .20
383 A66 12fr Prus blue 3.00 .30
384 A66 45fr lt yel grn 4.25 .50
Nos. 381-384 (4) 9.75 1.20

Stamp of 1903 — A67

1966, May 8 Engr. *Perf. 13*

385 A67 25fr red & sepia .75 .30

Issued for Stamp Day 1966.

Betsileo Dancers
A68

1966, June 13 Photo. *Perf. 12½x13*
Size: 36x23mm

386 A68 5fr multi .55 .20

See No. C83.

Symbolic Tree and Emblems — A69

1966, June 26

387 A69 25fr multi .60 .25

Conference of the Organisation Commune Africaine et Malgache (OCAM), Tananarive.

No. 387 dated "JUIN 1966," original date "Janvier 1966" obliterated with bar. Exists without overprint "JUIN 1966" and bar. Value $100.

Arms Type of 1963-65
Imprint: "S. Gauthier So. Ge. Im."

20fr, Mananjary. 30fr, Nossi-Bé. 90fr, Antsohihy.

1966-68 Litho. *Perf. 13*
Size: 23½x35½mm

388 A50 20fr multi ('67) .40 .20
389 A50 30fr multi .45 .20
390 A50 90fr multi ('68) 1.50 .40
Nos. 388-390 (3) 2.35 .80

For surcharge see No. 503.

Singers and Map of Madagascar — A70

1966, Oct. 14 Engr. *Perf. 13*

392 A70 20fr red brn, grn & dk car rose .60 .20

Issued in honor of the National Anthem.

UNESCO Emblem
A71

1966, Nov. 4

393 A71 30fr red, yel & slate .60 .20

UNESCO, 20th anniv.

Lions Emblem — A72

1967, Jan. 14 Photo. *Perf. 13x12½*

394 A72 30fr multi .60 .30

50th anniversary of Lions International.

Rice Harvest
A73

1967, Jan. 27 *Perf. 12½x13*

395 A73 20fr multi .60 .20

FAO International Rice Year.

Adventist Temple, Tanambao-Tamatave — A74

Designs: 5fr, Catholic Cathedral, Tananarive, vert. 10fr, Mosque, Tamatave.

1967, Feb. 20 Engr. *Perf. 13*

396 A74 3fr lt ultra, grn & bis .25 .20
397 A74 5fr brt rose lil, grn & vio .25 .20
398 A74 10fr dp bl, brn & grn .30 .20
Nos. 396-398 (3) .80 .60

Norbert Raharisoa at Piano
A75

1967, Mar. 23 Photo. *Perf. 12½x12*

399 A75 40fr citron & multi .85 .35

Norbert Raharisoa (1914-1963), composer.

Jean Raoult Flying Blériot Plane, 1911
A76

45fr, Georges Bougault and hydroplane, 1926.

1967, Apr. 28 Engr. *Perf. 13*
Size: 35½x22mm

400 A76 5fr gray bl, brn & grn .85 .25
401 A76 45fr brn, stl bl & blk 1.75 .50
Nos. 400-401,C84 (3) 13.60 3.75

History of aviation in Madagascar.

Ministry of Equipment and Communications — A77

1967, May 8 Engr. *Perf. 13*

402 A77 20fr ocher, ultra & grn .60 .20

Issued for Stamp Day, 1967.

Lutheran Church, Tananarive, Madagascar Map — A78

1967, Sept. 24 Photo. *Perf. 12x12½*

403 A78 20fr multi .70 .25

Lutheran Church in Madagascar, cent.

Map of Madagascar and Emblems — A79

1967, Oct. 16 Engr. *Perf. 13*

404 A79 90fr red brn, bl & dk red 1.10 .40

Hydrological Decade (UNESCO), 1965-74.

Dance of the Bilo Sakalavas — A80

Design: 30fr, Atandroy dancers.

1967, Nov. 25 Photo. *Perf. 13x12½*
Size: 22x36mm

405 A80 2fr lt grn & multi .30 .20
406 A80 30fr multi .60 .20
Nos. 405-406,C86-C87 (4) 7.65 2.40

Woman's Face, Scales and UN Emblem
A81

1967, Dec. 16 *Perf. 12½x13*

407 A81 50fr emer, dk bl & brn .70 .30

UN Commission on the Status of Women.

Human Rights Flame — A82

1968, Mar. 16 Litho. *Perf. 13x12½*

408 A82 50fr blk, ver & grn .70 .30

International Human Rights Year.

No. 327 Surcharged with New Value and 3 Bars

1968, June 4 Engr. *Perf. 13*

409 A42 20fr on 85fr multi .70 .40

"Industry"
A83

Designs: 20fr, "Agriculture" (mother and child carrying fruit and grain, and cattle), vert. 40fr, "Communications and Investments," (train, highway, factory and buildings).

1968, July 15

410 A83 10fr rose car, grn & dk pur .25 .20
411 A83 20fr dp car, grn & blk .30 .20
412 A83 40fr brn, vio & sl bl .60 .25
Nos. 410-412 (3) 1.15 .65

Completion of Five-year Plan, 1964-68.

Church, Translated Bible, Cross and Map of Madagascar — A84

1968, Aug. 18 Photo. *Perf. 12½x12*

413 A84 20fr multi .55 .20

Sesquicentennial of Christianity in Madagascar.

Isotry-Fitiavana Protestant Church — A85

12fr, Catholic Cathedral, Fianarantsoa. 50fr, Aga Khan Mosque, Tananarive.

1968, Sept. 10 Engr. *Perf. 13*

414 A85 4fr red brn, brt grn & dk brn .25 .20
415 A85 12fr plum, bl & hn brn .30 .20
416 A85 50fr brt grn, bl & indigo .60 .25
Nos. 414-416 (3) 1.15 .65

President and Mrs. Tsiranana A86

1968, Oct. 14 Photo. *Perf. 12½x12*

417 A86 20fr car, org & blk .30 .20
418 A86 30fr car, grnsh bl & blk .50 .20
a. Souv. sheet of 4, 2 each #417-418 2.00 1.10

10th anniv. of the Republic.

Madagascar Map and Cornucopia with Coins — A87

Striving Mankind — A88

1968, Nov. 3 Photo. *Perf. 12x12½*

419 A87 20fr multi .60 .20

50th anniversary of the Malagasy Savings Bank.

1968, Dec. 3 Photo. *Perf. 12½x12*

15fr, Mother, child and physician, horiz.

420 A88 15fr ultra, yel & crim .30 .20
421 A88 45fr vio bl & multi .55 .20

Completion of Five-Year Plan, 1964-68.

Queen Adelaide Receiving Malagasy Delegation, London, 1836 — A89

1969, Mar. 29 Photo. *Perf. 12x12½*

422 A89 250fr multi 5.75 2.50

Malagasy delegation London visit, 1836-37.

Cogwheels, Wrench and ILO Emblem A90

1969, Apr. 11 *Perf. 12½x12*

423 A90 20fr grn & multi .50 .20

ILO, 50th anniv.

Telecommunications and Postal Building, Tananarive — A91

1969, May 8 Engr. *Perf. 13*

424 A91 30fr bl, brt grn & car lake .60 .20

Issued for Stamp Day 1969.

Steering Wheel, Map, Automobiles — A92

1969, June 1 Photo. *Perf. 12*

425 A92 65fr multi 1.00 .30

Automobile Club of Madagascar, 20th anniv.

Pres. Philibert Tsiranana — A93

Banana Plants — A94

1969, June 26 Photo. *Perf. 12x12½*

426 A93 20fr multi .45 .20

10th anniversary of the inauguration of Pres. Philibert Tsiranana.

1969, July 7 Engr. *Perf. 13*

427 A94 5fr shown .65 .20
428 A94 15fr Lichi tree 1.25 .20

Runners A95

1969, Sept. 9 Engr. *Perf. 13*

429 A95 15fr yel grn, brn & red .55 .20

Issued to commemorate the 19th Olympic Games, Mexico City, Oct. 12-27, 1968.

Malagasy House, Highlands A96

Carnelian A97

Malagasy Houses: #430, Betsileo house, Highlands. #431, Tsimihety house, West Coast, horiz. 60fr, Malagasy house, Highlands.

1969-70 Engr. *Perf. 13*

430 A96 20fr bl, ol & ver .30 .20
431 A96 20fr sl, brt grn & red .30 .20
432 A96 40fr blk, bl & dk red .60 .25
433 A96 60fr vio bl, dp grn & brn .90 .30
Nos. 430-433 (4) 2.10 .95

Issued: 40fr, 60fr, 11/25/69; others, 11/25/70.

Arms Type of 1963-65

1fr, Maintirano. 10fr, Ambalavao. #436, Morondava. #437, Ambatondrazaka. #438, Fenerive-Est. 80fr, Tamatave.

1970-72 Photo. *Perf. 13*

434 A50 1fr multi ('72) .25 .20
435 A50 10fr multi ('72) .35 .20
436 A50 25fr multi ('71) .55 .20
437 A50 25fr multi ('71) .55 .20
438 A50 25fr multi ('72) .70 .20
439 A50 80fr pink & multi 1.10 .30
Nos. 434-439 (6) 3.50 1.30

The 10fr, 80fr are dated "1970." #437 is dated "1971." #434, 438 are dated "1972."

Sizes: #434, 438, 22x37mm; others, 25½x36mm.

Imprints: "S. Gauthier" on Nos. 434, 438; "S. Gauthier Delrieu" on others.

Perf. 12x12½ (5, 20fr), 13 (12, 15fr)
1970-71 Photo.

Semi-precious Stones: 12fr, Yellow calcite. 15fr, Quartz. 20fr, Ammonite.

440 A97 5fr brn, dl rose & yel 4.25 1.00
441 A97 12fr multi ('71) 4.75 1.00
442 A97 15fr multi ('71) 6.25 1.50
443 A97 20fr grn & multi 17.50 2.00
Nos. 440-443 (4) 32.75 5.50

UPU Headquarters Issue
Common Design Type

1970, May 20 Engr. *Perf. 13*

444 CD133 20fr lil rose, brn & ultra .55 .20

UN Emblem and Symbols of Justice A98

1970, June 26 Engr. *Perf. 13*

445 A98 50fr blk, ultra & org .70 .30

25th anniversary of the United Nations.

Fruits of Madagascar — A99

1970, Aug. 18 Photo. *Perf. 13*

446 A99 20fr multi 1.75 .25

Volute Delessertiana — A100

Shells: 10fr, Murex tribulus. 20fr, Spondylus.

1970, Sept. 9 Photo. *Perf. 13*

447 A100 5fr Prus bl & multi .90 .25
448 A100 10fr vio & multi 1.10 .25
449 A100 20fr multi 3.00 .30
Nos. 447-449 (3) 5.00 .80

Aye-aye — A101

1970, Oct. 7 Photo. *Perf. 12½*

450 A101 20fr multi .45 .25

Intl. Conference for Nature Conservation, Tananarive, Oct. 7-10.

Pres. Tsiranana A102

1970, Dec. 30 Photo. *Perf. 12½*

451 A102 30fr grn & lt brn .60 .20

60th birthday of Pres. Philibert Tsiranana.

Tropical Soap Factory, Tananarive A103

Designs: 15fr, Comina chromium smelting plant, Andriamena. 50fr, Textile mill, Majunga.

1971, Apr. 14 Photo. *Perf. 12½x12*

452 A103 5fr multi .30 .20

Engr. *Perf. 13*

453 A103 15fr vio bl, blk & ocher .35 .20

Photo. *Perf. 13*

454 A103 50fr multi .65 .20
Nos. 452-454 (3) 1.30 .60

Economic development.

Globe, Agriculture, Industry, Science
A104

1971, Apr. 22 Photo. *Perf. 12½x12*
455 A104 5fr multi .25 .20

Extraordinary meeting of the Council of the C.E.E.-E.A.M.A. (Communauté Economique Européen-Etats Africains et Malgache Associés).

Mobile Rural Post Office
A105

1971, May 8 *Perf. 13*
456 A105 25fr multi .55 .20

Stamp Day.

Gen. Charles de Gaulle — A106

Madagascar Hilton, Tananarive
A107

1971, June 26 Engr. *Perf. 13*
457 A106 30fr ultra, blk & rose 1.00 .35

In memory of Charles de Gaulle (1890-1970), President of France.
For surcharge see No. B24.

1971, July 23 Photo.

Design: 25fr, Hotel Palm Beach, Nossi-Bé.

458 A107 25fr multi .50 .20

Engr.

459 A107 65fr vio bl, brn & lt grn .85 .30

Trees and Post Horn — A108

1971, Aug. 6 Photo. *Perf. 12½x12*
460 A108 3fr red, yel & grn .30 .20

Forest preservation campaign.

House, South West Madagascar — A109

10fr, House from Southern Madagascar.

1971, Nov. 25 *Perf. 13x12½*
461 A109 5fr lt bl & multi .25 .20
462 A109 10fr lt bl & multi .35 .20

Children Playing, and Cattle
A110

1971, Dec. 11 Litho. *Perf. 13*
463 A110 50fr grn & multi 1.00 .30

UNICEF, 25th anniv.

Cable-laying Railroad Car, PTT Emblem — A111

1972, Apr. 8 Engr. *Perf. 13*
464 A111 45fr slate grn, red & choc 1.50 .40

Coaxial cable connection between Tananarive and Tamatave.

Philibert Tsiranana Radar Station — A112

1972, Apr. 8 Photo. *Perf. 13½*
465 A112 85fr bl & multi 1.00 .40

A113 A114

Voters and Pres. Tsiranana.

1972, May 1 *Perf. 12½x13*
466 A113 25fr yel & multi .55 .35

Presidential election, Jan. 30, 1972.

1972, May 30 Photo. *Perf. 12x12½*
467 A114 10fr Mail delivery .60 .20

Stamp Day 1972.

Emblem and Stamps of Madagascar
A115

Stamps shown are #352, 410, 429, 449.

1972, June 26 *Perf. 13*
468 A115 25fr org & multi .50 .20
469 A115 40fr org & multi .60 .30
470 A115 100fr org & multi 1.50 .50
a. Souv. sheet of 3, #468-470 3.50 3.50
Nos. 468-470 (3) 2.60 1.00

2nd Malgache Philatelic Exhibition, Tananarive, June 26-July 9.

Andapa-Sambava Road and Monument — A116

1972, July 6 *Perf. 12½x12*
471 A116 50fr multi .60 .30

Opening of the Andapa-Sambava road.

Diesel Locomotive
A117

1972, July 6 Engr. *Perf. 13*
472 A117 100fr multicolored 4.50 .50

Razafindrahety College — A118

1972, Aug. 6
473 A118 10fr choc, bl & red brn .25 .20

Razafindrahety College, Tananarive, sesqui.

Volleyball
A119

1972, Aug. 6 Typo. *Perf. 12½x13*
474 A119 12fr orange, blk & brn .45 .20

African volleyball championship.

Oil Refinery, Tamatave
A120

1972, Sept. 18 Engr. *Perf. 13*
475 A120 2fr bl, bister & slate grn .45 .20

Ravoahangy Andrianavalona Hospital — A121

1972, Oct. 14 Photo. *Perf. 13x12½*
476 A121 6fr multi .25 .20

Plowing
A122

1972, Nov. 15 Photo. *Perf. 13½x14*
477 A122 25fr gold & multi .70 .30

Betsimisaraka Costume — A123

Design: 15fr, Merina costume.

1972, Dec. 30 Photo. *Perf. 13x12½*
478 A123 10fr blue & multi .20 .20
479 A123 15fr brown & multi .45 .20

Farmer and Produce — A124

1973, Feb. 6 Photo. *Perf. 13*
480 A124 25fr lt blue & multi .45 .20

10th anniversary of the Malagasy Committee of "Freedom from Hunger Campaign."
For surcharge see No. 499.

Volva Volva
A125

Shells: 10fr, 50fr, Lambis chiragra. 15fr, 40fr, Harpa major. 25fr, Like 3fr.

1973, Apr. 5 Litho. *Perf. 13*
481 A125 3fr olive & multi .35 .20
482 A125 10fr blue grn & multi .55 .25
483 A125 15fr brt blue & multi 1.00 .25
484 A125 25fr lt blue & multi 1.40 .30
485 A125 40fr multicolored 1.75 .30
486 A125 50fr red lilac & multi 3.00 .40
Nos. 481-486 (6) 8.05 1.70

Tsimandoa Mail Carrier — A126

Builders and Map of Africa — A127

1973, May 13 Engr. *Perf. 13*
487 A126 50fr ind, ocher & sl grn .75 .30

Stamp Day 1973.

1973, May 25 Photo. *Perf. 13*
488 A127 25fr multicolored .60 .25

Organization for African Unity, 10th anniversary.

Campani Chameleon A128

Various Chameleons: 5fr, 40fr, Male nasutus. 10fr, 85fr, Female nasutus. 60fr, Like 1fr.

1973, June 15 Photo. *Perf. 13x12½*
489 A128 1fr dp car & multi .35 .20
490 A128 5fr brown & multi .35 .20
491 A128 10fr green & multi .50 .20
492 A128 40fr red lilac & multi 1.40 .25
493 A128 60fr dk blue & multi 1.90 .40
494 A128 85fr brown & multi 3.00 .60
Nos. 489-494 (6) 7.50 1.85

Lady's Slipper A129

Orchids: 25fr, 40fr, Pitcher plant.

1973, Aug. 6 Photo. *Perf. 12½*
495 A129 10fr multicolored .90 .20
496 A129 25fr rose & multi 1.10 .30
497 A129 40fr lt blue & multi 2.50 .35
498 A129 100fr multicolored 5.50 .70
Nos. 495-498 (4) 10.00 1.55

No. 480 Surcharged with New Value, 2 Bars, and Overprinted in Ultramarine: "SECHERESSE / SOLIDARITE AFRICAINE"

1973, Aug. 16 *Perf. 13*
499 A124 100fr on 25fr multi 1.40 .50

African solidarity in drought emergency.

African Postal Union Issue
Common Design Type

1973, Sept. 12 Engr. *Perf. 13*
500 CD137 100fr vio, red & slate grn 1.00 .35

Greater Dwarf Lemur A131

Design: 25fr, Weasel lemur, vert.

1973, Oct. 9 Engr. *Perf. 13*
501 A131 5fr brt green & multi .75 .30
502 A131 25fr ocher & multi 1.75 .60
Nos. 501-502,C117-C118 (4) 10.25 3.20

Lemurs of Madagascar.

No. 389 Surcharged

1974, Feb. 9 Litho. *Perf. 13*
503 A50 25fr on 30fr multi .35 .20

Scouts Helping to Raise Cattle — A132

Mother with Children and Clinic — A133

Design: 15fr, Scouts building house; African Scout emblem.

1974, Feb. 14 Engr. *Perf. 13*
504 A132 4fr blue, slate & emer .20 .20
505 A132 15fr chocolate & multi .30 .25
Nos. 504-505,C122-C123 (4) 5.85 1.80

Malagasy Boy Scouts.

1974, May 24 Photo. *Perf. 13*
506 A133 25fr multicolored .35 .20

World Population Year.

Rainibetsimisaraka — A134

1974, July 26 Photo. *Perf. 13*
507 A134 25fr multicolored .65 .30

In memory of Rainibetsimisaraka, independence leader.

Marble Blocks A135

Design: 25fr, Marble quarry.

1974, Sept. 27 Photo. *Perf. 13*
508 A135 4fr multicolored .80 .25
509 A135 25fr multicolored 2.10 .45

Malagasy marble.

Europafrica Issue, 1974

Links, White and Black Faces, Map of Europe and Africa — A136

1974, Oct. 17 Engr. *Perf. 13*
510 A136 150fr dk brown & org 1.75 .60

Grain and Hand A137

1974, Oct. 29
511 A137 80fr light blue & ocher 1.00 .35

World Committee against Hunger.

Tuléar Dog A138

Design: 100fr, Hunting dog.

1974, Nov. 26 Photo. *Perf. 13x13½*
512 A138 50fr multicolored 2.50 .50
513 A138 100fr multicolored 3.50 .90

Malagasy Citizens — A139

1974, Dec. 9 *Perf. 13½x13*
514 A139 5fr blue grn & multi .25 .20
515 A139 10fr multicolored .25 .20
516 A139 20fr yellow grn & multi .35 .20
517 A139 60fr orange & multi .90 .25
Nos. 514-517 (4) 1.75 .85

Introduction of "Fokonolona" community organization.

Symbols of Development — A140

1974, Dec. 16 Photo. *Perf. 13x13½*
518 A140 25fr ultra & multi .30 .20
519 A140 35fr blue grn & multi .50 .25

National Council for Development.

Woman, Rose, Dove and Emblem — A141

1975, Jan. 21 Engr. *Perf. 13*
520 A141 100fr brown, emer & org 1.10 .40

International Women's Year 1975.

Col. Richard Ratsimandrava — A142

1975, Apr. 25 Photo. *Perf. 13*
521 A142 15fr brown & salmon .20 .20
522 A142 25fr black, bl & brn .35 .25
523 A142 100fr black, lt grn & brn 1.25 .30
Nos. 521-523 (3) 1.80 .75

Ratsimandrava (1933-1975), head of state.

Sofia Bridge A143

1975, May 29 Litho. *Perf. 12½*
524 A143 45fr multicolored .80 .30

Count de Grasse and "Randolph" — A144

Design: 50fr, Marquis de Lafayette, "Lexington" and HMS "Edward."

1975, June 30 Litho. *Perf. 11*
525 A144 40fr multicolored .60 .25
526 A144 50fr multicolored .80 .30
Nos. 525-526,C137-C139 (5) 8.90 2.45

American Bicentennial.

For overprints see Nos. 564-565, C164-C167.

Euphorbia Viguieri A145

Tropical Plants: 25fr, Hibiscus. 30fr, Plumieria rubra acutitolia. 40fr, Pachypodium rosulatum.

1975, Aug. 4 Photo. *Perf. 12½*
527 A145 15fr lemon & multi .30 .25
528 A145 25fr black & multi .50 .25
529 A145 30fr orange & multi .70 .30
530 A145 40fr dk red & multi 1.10 .30
Nos. 527-530,C141 (5) 5.10 2.00

Brown, White, Yellow and Black Hands Holding Globe — A146

1975, Aug. 26 Litho. *Perf. 12*
531 A146 50fr multicolored .70 .25

Namibia Day (independence for South-West Africa.)

Woodpecker — A147

1975, Sept. 16 Litho. *Perf. 14x13½*
532 A147 25fr shown .60 .25
533 A147 40fr Rabbit 1.00 .25
534 A147 50fr Frog 1.40 .30
535 A147 75fr Tortoise 2.50 .45
Nos. 532-535,C145 (5) 7.40 1.70

International Exposition, Okinawa.

Lily Waterfall A148

Design: 40fr, Lily Waterfall, different view.

1975, Sept. 17 Litho. *Perf. 12½*
536 A148 25fr multicolored .45 .25
537 A148 40fr multicolored .65 .25

4-man Bob Sled — A149

100fr, Ski jump. 140fr, Speed skating.

1975, Nov. 19 Litho. *Perf. 14*
538 A149 75fr multicolored .80 .25
539 A149 100fr multicolored 1.10 .30
540 A149 140fr multicolored 1.60 .40
Nos. 538-540,C149-C150 (5) 9.00 2.15

12th Winter Olympic games, Innsbruck, 1976.
For overprints see Nos. 561-563, C161-C163.

Pirogue A150

Designs: 45fr, Boutre (Arabian coastal vessel).

1975, Nov. 20 Photo. *Perf. 12½*
541 A150 8fr multicolored .50 .25
542 A150 45fr ultra & multi 1.75 .40

Canadian Canoe and Kayak — A151

Design: 50fr, Sprint and Hurdles.

1976, Jan. 21 Litho. *Perf. 14x13½*
543 A151 40fr multicolored .45 .25
544 A151 50fr multicolored .55 .25
Nos. 543-544,C153-C155 (5) 7.50 2.30

21st Summer Olympic games, Montreal.
For overprints see Nos. 571-572, C168-C171.

Count Zeppelin and LZ-127 over Fujiyama, Japan — A152

Designs (Count Zeppelin and LZ-127 over): 50fr, Rio. 75fr, NYC. 100fr, Sphinx.

1976, Mar. 3 *Perf. 11*
545 A152 40fr multicolored .50 .25
546 A152 50fr multicolored .70 .25
547 A152 75fr multicolored 1.25 .30
548 A152 100fr multicolored 1.50 .35
Nos. 545-548,C158-C159 (6) 11.20 2.65

75th anniversary of the Zeppelin.

Worker, Globe, Eye Chart and Eye — A153

1976, Apr. 7 Photo. *Perf. 12½*
549 A153 100fr multicolored 1.75 .50

World Health Day: "Foresight prevents blindness."

Aragonite A154

50fr, Petrified wood. 150fr, Celestite.

1976, May 7 Photo. *Perf. 12½*
550 A154 25fr blue & multi 2.75 .50
551 A154 50fr blue grn & multi 3.50 1.00
552 A154 150fr orange & multi 14.00 2.00
Nos. 550-552 (3) 20.25 3.50

Alexander Graham Bell and First Telephone — A155

50fr, Telephone lines, 1911. 100fr, Central office, 1895. 200fr, Cable ship, 1925. 300fr, Radio telephone. 500fr, Telstar satellite and globe.

1976, May 13 Litho. *Perf. 14*
553 A155 25fr multicolored .25 .20
554 A155 50fr multicolored .45 .25
555 A155 100fr multicolored .80 .30
556 A155 200fr multicolored 1.75 .55
557 A155 300fr multicolored 2.75 .75
Nos. 553-557 (5) 6.00 2.05

Souvenir Sheet

558 A155 500fr multicolored 5.25 1.40

Cent. of 1st telephone call by Alexander Graham Bell, Mar. 10, 1876.

Children with Books A156

Design: 25fr, Children with books, vert.

1976, May 25 Litho.
559 A156 10fr multicolored .25 .20
560 A156 25fr multicolored .50 .25

Books for children.

Nos. 538-540 Overprinted

a. VAINQUEUR ALLEMAGNE FEDERALE
b. VAINQUEUR KARL SCHNABL AUTRICHE
c. VAINQUEUR SHEILA YOUNG ETATS-UNIS

1976, June 17
561 A149 (a) 75fr multi .80 .30
562 A149 (b) 100fr multi 1.25 .45
563 A149 (c) 140fr multi 1.75 .60
Nos. 561-563,C161-C162 (5) 8.30 2.75

12th Winter Olympic games winners.

Nos. 525-526 Overprinted "4 Juillet / 1776-1976"

1976, July 4
564 A144 40fr multicolored .60 .30
565 A144 50fr multicolored .80 .40
Nos. 564-565,C164-C166 (5) 7.40 2.50

American Bicentennial.

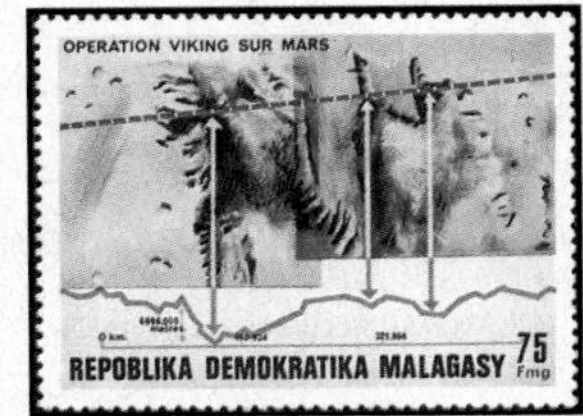

Graph of Projected Landing Spots on Mars — A157

Viking project to Mars: 100fr, Viking probe in flight. 200fr, Viking probe on Mars. 300fr, Viking probe over projected landing spot. 500fr, Viking probe approaching Mars.

1976, July 17 Litho. *Perf. 14*
566 A157 75fr multicolored .60 .25
567 A157 100fr multicolored .85 .30
568 A157 200fr multicolored 1.75 .40
569 A157 300fr multicolored 2.50 .60
Nos. 566-569 (4) 5.70 1.55

Souvenir Sheet

570 A157 500fr multicolored 5.25 1.00

Nos. 543-544 Overprinted

a. A. ROGOV / V. DIBA
b. H. CRAWFORD / J. SCHALLER

1977, Jan.
571 A151 (a) 40fr multi .45 .25
572 A151 (b) 50fr multi .60 .30
Nos. 571-572,C168-C170 (5) 6.80 2.40

21st Summer Olympic games winners.

Rainandriamampandry — A158

Portrait: No. 574, Rabezavana.

1976-77 Litho. *Perf. 12x12½*
573 A158 25fr multicolored .50 .25
574 A158 25fr multicolored .25 .25

Rainandriamampandry was Malagasy Foreign Minister who signed treaties in 1896. Issued: #73, Oct. 15; #74, Mar. 29, 1977.

"Indian Ocean - Zone of Peace." A159

Design: 60fr, Globe with Africa and Indian Ocean, doves, vert. 160fr, Doves, Indian Ocean on Globe.

Perf. 12½x12, 12x12½

1976, Nov. 18
575 A159 60fr multicolored .60 .25
576 A159 160fr shown 1.40 .50

Coat of Arms — A160

1976, Dec. 30 Litho. *Perf. 12*
577 A160 25fr multicolored .30 .20

Democratic Republic of Malagasy, 1st anniv.

Lt. Albert Randriamaromanana — A161

Portrait: #578, Avana Ramanantoanina.

1977, Mar. 29
578 A161 25fr multicolored .25 .20
579 A161 25fr multicolored .25 .20

National Mausoleum — A162

1977, Mar. 29 ***Perf. 12½x12***
580 A162 100fr multicolored 1.25 .40

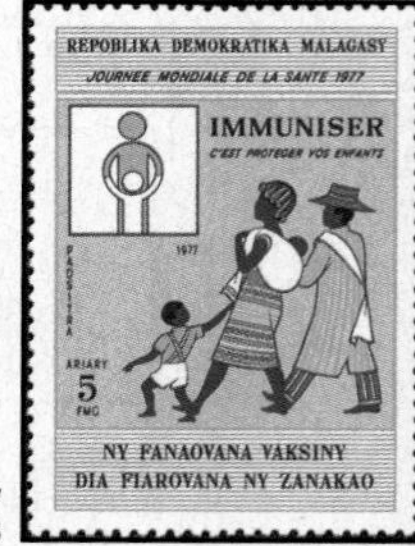

Family A163

1977, Apr. 7 ***Perf. 12x12½***
581 A163 5fr yellow & multi .25 .20

World Health Day: Immunization protects the children.

Tananarive Medical School — A164

1977, June 30 Litho. ***Perf. 12½x12***
582 A164 250fr multicolored 2.50 .80

80th anniversary of Tananarive Medical School.

Mail Bus — A165

1977, Aug. 18 Litho. ***Perf. 12½x12***
583 A165 35fr multicolored .40 .25

Rural mail delivery.

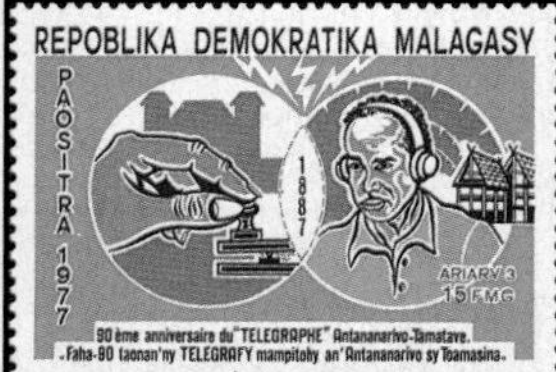

Telegraph Operator — A166

1977, Sept. 13 Litho. ***Perf. 12½x12***
584 A166 15fr multicolored .25 .25

Telegraph service Tananarive-Tamatave, 90th anniv.

Malagasy Art — A167

1977, Sept. 29 ***Perf. 12x12½***
585 A167 10fr multicolored .25 .20

Malagasy Academy, 75th anniversary.

Lenin and Russian Flag — A168

1977, Nov. 7 Litho. ***Perf. 12½x12***
586 A168 25fr multicolored 2.00 .35

60th anniversary of Russian October Revolution.

Raoul Follereau, Map of Malagasy A169

1978, Jan. 28 Litho. ***Perf. 12x12½***
587 A169 5fr multicolored 1.10 .30

25th anniversary of Leprosy Day.

Antenna, ITU Emblem A170

1978, May 17 Litho. ***Perf. 12x12½***
588 A170 20fr multicolored .25 .25

10th World Telecommunications Day.

Black and White Men Breaking Chains of Africa — A171

1978, June 22 Photo. ***Perf. 12½x12***
589 A171 60fr multicolored .60 .25

Anti-Apartheid Year.

Boy and Girl, Arch: Pen, Gun and Hoe A172

Farm Workers, Factory, Tractor A173

1978, July 28 Litho. ***Perf. 12½x12***
590 A172 125fr multicolored 1.00 .40

Youth, the pillar of revolution.

1978, Aug. 24
591 A173 25fr multicolored .25 .20

Socialist cooperation.

Women — A174

Children Bringing Gifts — A175

1979, Mar. 8 Litho. ***Perf. 12½x12***
592 A174 40fr multicolored .35 .20

Women, supporters of the revolution.

1979, June 1 Litho. ***Perf. 12x12½***
593 A175 10fr multicolored .25 .20

International Year of the Child.

Lemur Macaco A176

Fauna: 25fr, Lemur catta, vert. 1000fr, Foussa.

Perf. 12½x12, 12x12½
1979, July 6 Litho.
594 A176 25fr multi .70 .20
595 A176 125fr multi 2.75 .35
596 A176 1000fr multi 9.75 2.50
Nos. 594-596,C172-C173 (5) 15.45 3.50

Jean Verdi Salomon A177

1979, July 25 ***Perf. 12x12½***
597 A177 25fr multicolored .25 .20

Jean Verdi Salomon (1913-1978), poet.

Talapetraka (Medicinal Plant) — A178

1979, Sept. 27 Litho. ***Perf. 12½***
598 A178 25fr multicolored .90 .25

Map of Magagascar, Dish Antenna — A179

1979, Oct. 12
599 A179 25fr multicolored .25 .20

Stamp Day 1979 A180

1979, Nov. 9
600 A180 500fr multicolored 4.50 1.40

Jet, Map of Africa A181

1979, Dec. 12 ***Perf. 12½***
601 A181 50fr multicolored .60 .25

ASECNA (Air Safety Board), 20th anniversary.

Lenin Addressing Workers in the Winter Palace A182

1980, Apr. 22 Litho. ***Perf. 12x12½***
602 A182 25fr multicolored .60 .25

Lenin's 110th birth anniversary.

Bus and Road in Madagascar Colors A183

Flag and Map under Sun — A184

1980, June 15 Litho. ***Perf. 12x12½***
603 A183 30fr multicolored .35 .20

Socialist Revolution, 5th anniversary.

1980, June 26 ***Perf. 12½x12***
604 A184 75fr multicolored .60 .25

Independence, 20th anniversary.

Armed Forces Day — A185

1980, Aug. Litho. ***Perf. 12½x12***
605 A185 50fr multicolored .45 .25

Dr. Joseph Raseta (1886-1979) A186

1980, Oct. 15 Litho. ***Perf. 12x12½***
606 A186 30fr multicolored .30 .20

Anatirova Temple Centenary — A187

1980, Nov. 27 Litho. ***Perf. 12½x12***
607 A187 30fr multicolored .35 .25

Hurdles, Olympic Torch, Moscow '80 Emblem — A188

1980, Dec. 29
608 A188 30fr shown .45 .20
609 A188 75fr Boxing .85 .30
Nos. 608-609,C175-C176 (4) 8.05 2.70

22nd Summer Olympic Games, Moscow, July 19-Aug. 3.

Democratic Republic of Madagascar, 5th Anniversary A189

1980, Dec. 30 ***Perf. 12x12½***
610 A189 30fr multicolored .35 .20

Downhill Skiing — A190

1981, Jan. 26 Litho. ***Perf. 12½x12***
611 A190 175fr multicolored 1.75 .60

13th Winter Olympic Games, Lake Placid, Feb. 12-24, 1980.

Angraecum Leonis A191

1981, Mar. 23 Litho. ***Perf. 11½***
612 A191 5fr shown .50 .20
613 A191 80fr Angraecum ramosum 1.75 .30
614 A191 170fr Angraecum sesquipedale 2.75 .65
Nos. 612-614 (3) 5.00 1.15

For surcharge, see No. 1474B.

A192 A193

1981, June 12 Litho. ***Perf. 12***
615 A192 25fr Student at desk .30 .20
616 A192 80fr Carpenter .75 .30

Intl. Year of the Disabled.

1981, July 10 Litho. ***Perf. 12½x12***
617 A193 15fr multi .25 .20
618 A193 45fr multi .55 .25

13th World Telecommunications Day.

Neil Armstrong on Moon (Apollo 11) — A194

Space Anniversaries.

1981, July 23 ***Perf. 11½***
619 A194 30fr Valentina Tereshkova .30 .20
620 A194 80fr shown .80 .25
621 A194 90fr Yuri Gagarin .90 .25
Nos. 619-621 (3) 2.00 .70

Brother Raphael Louis Rafiringa (1854-1919) A195

1981, Aug. 10 Litho. ***Perf. 12***
622 A195 30fr multi .35 .20

World Literacy Day — A196

1981, Sept. 8
623 A196 30fr multi .35 .20

World Food Day — A197

1981, Oct. 16 Litho. ***Perf. 12x12½***
624 A197 200fr multi 1.90 .60

See No. 635.

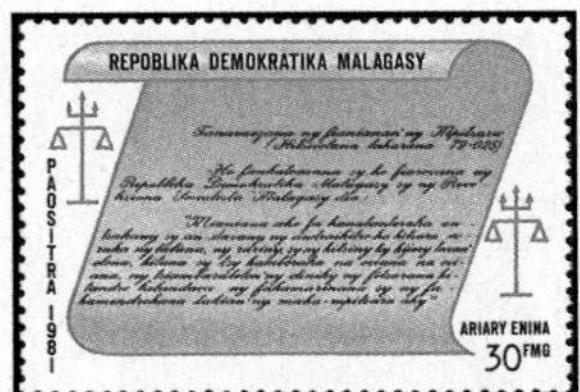
Oaths of Magistracy Renewal — A198

1981, Oct. 30 ***Perf. 12½x12***
625 A198 30fr blk & lil rose .35 .20

Dove, by Pablo Picasso (1881-1973) — A199

1981, Nov. 18 Photo. ***Perf. 11½x12***
626 A199 80fr multi 1.00 .30

20th Anniv. of UPU Membership — A200

Design: Nos. C76, C77, emblem.

1981, Nov. 19 Litho. ***Perf. 12***
627 A200 5fr multi .20 .20
628 A200 30fr multi .35 .20

TB Bacillus Centenary A201

1982, June 21 Litho. ***Perf. 12***
629 A201 30fr multi .45 .20

Jeannette Mpihira (1903-1981), Actress and Singer — A202

Haliaeetus Vociferoides A203

1982, June 24 *Perf. 12½*
630 A202 30fr multi .35 .25

1982, July
631 A203 25fr Vanga curvirostris, horiz. 1.10 .20
632 A203 30fr Leptostomus discolor, horiz. 1.40 .20
633 A203 200fr shown 4.75 .70
Nos. 631-633 (3) 7.25 1.10

Pierre Louis Boiteau (1911-1980), Educator A204

1982, Sept. 13
634 A204 30fr multi .35 .20

World Food Day Type of 1981

1982, Oct. 16 *Perf. 12x12½*
635 A197 80fr multi .75 .25

No. 635 is overprinted "EFA POLO ARIARY" on the text.

25th Anniv. of Launching of Sputnik I — A205

1982, Oct. 4 **Litho.** *Perf. 12*
636 A205 10fr Sputnik I .25 .20
637 A205 80fr Yuri Gagarin, Vostok I .80 .25
638 A205 100fr Soyuz-Salyut 1.00 .30
Nos. 636-638 (3) 2.05 .75

1982 World Cup — A206

Designs: Various soccer players.

1982, Oct. 14 *Perf. 12x12½*
639 A206 30fr multi .30 .20
640 A206 40fr multi .40 .20
641 A206 80fr multi .80 .25
Nos. 639-641 (3) 1.50 .65

Souvenir Sheet

Perf. 11½x12½

642 A206 450fr multi 4.50 1.60

Scene at a Bar, by Edouard Manet (1832-1883) — A207

1982, Nov. 25 *Perf. 12½x12*
643 A207 5fr shown .55 .25
644 A207 30fr Lady in a White Dress .75 .30
645 A207 170fr Portrait of Mallarme 3.50 .70
Nos. 643-645 (3) 4.80 1.25

Souvenir Sheet

Perf. 11½x12½

646 A207 400fr The Fifer, vert. 8.00 2.00

For surcharge, see No. 1475B.

Local Fish — A208

1982, Dec. 14 *Perf. 11½*
647 A208 5fr Lutianus sebae .30 .20
648 A208 20fr Istiophorus platypterus .35 .20
649 A208 30fr Pterois volitans .55 .25
650 A208 50fr Thunnus albacares 1.25 .25
651 A208 200fr Epinephelus fasciatus 3.75 .60
Nos. 647-651 (5) 6.20 1.50

Souvenir Sheet

Perf. 12½x12

652 A208 450fr Latimeria chalumnae 7.00 2.00

No. 652 contains one stamp 38x26mm.

Fort Mahavelona Ruins — A209

1982, Dec. 22 *Perf. 12½x12*
653 A209 10fr shown .20 .20
654 A209 30fr Ramena Beach .25 .20
655 A209 400fr Flowering jacaranda trees 3.00 1.00
Nos. 653-655 (3) 3.45 1.40

60th Anniv. of USSR — A210

1982, Dec. 29
656 A210 10fr Tractors .20 .20
657 A210 15fr Pylon .20 .20
658 A210 30fr Kremlin, Lenin .25 .20
659 A210 150fr Arms 1.25 .50
Nos. 656-659 (4) 1.90 1.10

World Communications Year — A211

80fr, Stylized figures holding wheel.

1983, May 17 **Litho.** *Perf. 12*
660 A211 30fr multi .25 .20
661 A211 80fr multi .80 .30

Organization of African Unity, 20th Anniv. A212

1983, May 25 **Litho.** *Perf. 12*
662 A212 30fr multi .25 .20

Henri Douzon, Lawyer and Patriot — A213

1983, June 27 **Litho.** *Perf. 12*
663 A213 30fr multi .25 .20

Souvenir Sheet

Manned Flight Bicentenary — A214

1983, July 20 **Litho.** *Perf. 12*
664 A214 500fr Montgolfiere balloon 5.75 2.00

Souvenir Sheet

Raphael, 500th Birth Anniv. — A215

1983, Aug. 10 **Litho.** *Perf. 12*
665 A215 500fr The Madonna Connestable 5.75 2.00

Lemur — A216

Various lemurs. Nos. 668-669, 671 vert.

Perf. 12½x12, 12x12½

1983, Dec. 6 **Litho.**
666 A216 30fr Daubentonia madagascariensis .55 .25
667 A216 30fr Microcebus murinus .55 .25
668 A216 30fr Lemur variegatus .55 .25
669 A216 30fr Propithecus verreauxi .55 .25
670 A216 200fr Indri indri 3.50 .80
Nos. 666-670 (5) 5.70 1.80

Souvenir Sheet

671 A216 500fr Perodicticus potto 8.00 2.00

1984 Winter Olympics A217

1984, Jan. 20 **Litho.** *Perf. 11½*
672 A217 20fr Ski jumping .20 .20
673 A217 30fr Speed skating .25 .20
674 A217 30fr Downhill skiing .25 .20
675 A217 30fr Hockey .25 .20
676 A217 200fr Figure skating 2.00 .60
Nos. 672-676 (5) 2.95 1.40

Souvenir Sheet

677 A217 500fr Cross-country skiing 4.75 2.00

No. 677 contains one stamp 48x32mm.

15 FMG ARIARY 3
RENAULT 1907
PAOSITRA 1984
Repoblika Demokratika MALAGASY

Vintage Cars — A218

1984, Jan. 27 *Perf. 12½x12*
678 A218 15fr Renault, 1907 .25 .20
679 A218 30fr Benz, 1896 .30 .20
680 A218 30fr Baker, 1901 .30 .20
681 A218 30fr Blake, 1901 .30 .20
682 A218 200fr FIAL, 1908 2.40 .60
Nos. 678-682 (5) 3.55 1.40

Souvenir Sheet

Perf. 12½x11½

683 A218 450fr Russo-Baltique, 1909 5.50 2.00

Pastor Ravelojaona (1879-1956), Encyclopedist A219

1984, Feb. 14 *Perf. 12x12½*
684 A219 30fr multi .25 .20

See No. 704.

Madonna and Child, by Correggio (1489-1534) A220

Various Correggio paintings.

1984, May 5 Litho. *Perf. 12x12½*

685 A220 5fr multi .20 .20
686 A220 20fr multi .25 .20
687 A220 30fr multi .35 .20
688 A220 80fr multi .75 .30
689 A220 200fr multi 2.10 .60
Nos. 685-689 (5) 3.65 1.50

Souvenir Sheet

690 A220 400fr multi 5.50 2.00

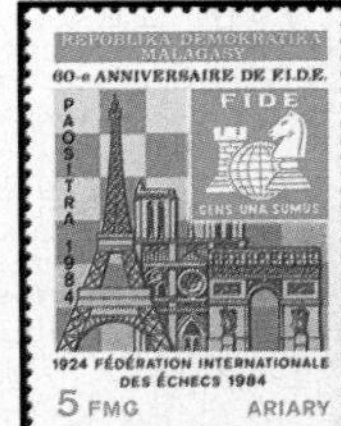

A221

A222

1984, July 27

691 A221 5fr Paris landmarks .20 .20
692 A221 20fr Wilhelm Steinitz .30 .20
693 A221 30fr Champion, cup .50 .25
694 A221 30fr Vera Menchik .50 .25
695 A221 215fr Champion, cup, diff. 3.00 .80
Nos. 691-695 (5) 4.50 1.70

Souvenir Sheet

696 A221 400fr Children playing chess 5.50 2.00

World Chess Federation, 60th anniv.

1984, Aug. 10

697 A222 100fr Soccer 1.00 .35

1984 Summer Olympics.

Butterflies A223

1984, Aug. 30 Litho. *Perf. 11½*

698 A223 15fr Eudaphaenura splendens .45 .20
699 A223 50fr Othreis boseae 1.40 .25
700 A223 50fr Pharmacophagus antenor 1.40 .25
701 A223 50fr Acraea hova 1.40 .25
702 A223 200fr Epicausis smithii 5.50 .65
Nos. 698-702 (5) 10.15 1.60

Miniature Sheet

Perf. 11½x12½

703 A223 400fr Papilio delandii 7.50 2.00

No. 703 contains one stamp 37x52mm.

Famous People Type

Jean Ralaimongo (1884-1944).

1984, Oct. 4 *Perf. 12x12½*

704 A219 50fr Portrait .60 .20

Children's Rights A225

1984, Nov. 20 Litho. *Perf. 12½x12*

705 A225 50fr Youths in school bag .50 .20

Malagasy Orchids — A226

Cotton Seminar, UN Trade and Development Conference A227

1984, Nov. 20 Litho. *Perf. 12*

706 A226 20fr Disa incarnata .30 .20
707 A226 235fr Eulophiella roempleriana 3.25 .70
Nos. 706-707,C180-C182 (5) 6.55 1.50

Miniature Sheet

Perf. 12x12½

708 A226 400fr Gastrorchis tuberculosa 7.50 2.00

No. 708 contains one stamp 30x42mm.

1984, Dec. 15 Litho. *Perf. 13x12½*

709 A227 100fr UN emblem, cotton bolls 1.00 .30

Malagasy Language Bible, 150th Anniv. A228

1985, Feb. 11 Litho. *Perf. 12½x12*

710 A228 50fr multi .50 .20

1985 Agricultural Census — A229

1985, Feb. 21 Litho. *Perf. 12x12½*

711 A229 50fr Census taker, farmer .50 .20

Allied Defeat of Nazi Germany, 40th Anniv. — A230

20fr, Russian flag-raising, Berlin, 1945. 50fr, Normandy-Niemen squadron shooting down German fighter planes. #714, Soviet Victory Parade, Red Square, Moscow. #715, Victorious French troops marching through Arc de Triomphe, vert.

1985 *Perf. 12½x12, 12x12½*

712 A230 20fr multi .30 .20
713 A230 50fr multi .30 .35
714 A230 100fr multi .90 .35
715 A230 100fr multi 3.00 .70
Nos. 712-715 (4) 4.50 1.60

Issue dates: #712-714, May 9; #715, Oct.

Cats and Dogs A231

1985, Apr. 25 *Perf. 12x12½, 12½x12*

716 A231 20fr Siamese .30 .20
717 A231 20fr Bichon .30 .20
718 A231 50fr Abyssinian, vert. .75 .25
719 A231 100fr Cocker spaniel, vert. 1.40 .35
720 A231 235fr Poodle 3.50 .80
Nos. 716-720 (5) 6.25 1.80

Souvenir Sheet

721 A231 400fr Kitten 6.00 2.00

No. 721 contains one stamp 42x30mm, perf. 12½x12.

Gymnastic Event, Natl. Stadium, Atananarivo — A232

1985, July 9 *Perf. 12½x12*

722 A232 50fr multi .45 .20

Natl. Socialist Revolution, 10th anniv.

Commemorative Medal, Memorial Stele — A233

1985, July 9

723 A233 50fr multi 1.25 .25

Independence, 25th anniv.

Intl. Youth Year — A234

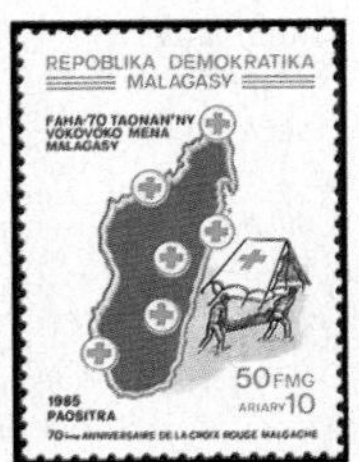

Natl. Red Cross, 70th Anniv. — A235

1985, Sept. 18 *Perf. 12*

724 A234 100fr Emblem, map 1.00 .25

1985, Oct. 3 *Perf. 12x12½*

725 A235 50fr multi .90 .20

Indira Gandhi — A236

22nd World Youth and Student's Festival, Moscow — A237

1985, Oct. 31 *Perf. 13½*

726 A236 100fr multi 1.10 .35

1985, Nov. *Perf. 12*

727 A237 50fr multi .50 .20

Rouen Cathedral at Night, by Monet — A238

UN, 40th Aniv. — A239

Impressionist paintings: No. 729, View of Sea at Sainte-Marie, by van Gogh, horiz. 45fr, Young Women in Black, by Renoir. 50fr, The Red Vineyard at Arles, by van Gogh, horiz. 100fr, Boulevard des Capucines in Paris, by Monet, horiz. 400fr, In the Garden, by Renoir.

1985, Oct. 25 Litho. *Perf. 12*

728 A238 20fr multi .50 .20
729 A238 20fr multi .50 .20
730 A238 45fr multi .90 .20
731 A238 50fr multi 1.10 .20
732 A238 100fr multi 2.40 .50
Nos. 728-732 (5) 5.40 1.30

Souvenir Sheet

Perf. 12x12½

733 A238 400fr multi 6.00 2.75

No. 733 contains one 30x42mm stamp.

1985, Oct. 31 *Perf. 12*

734 A239 100fr multi 1.00 .30

Orchids A240

1985, Nov. 8

735	A240	20fr	Aeranthes grandiflora	1.00	.20
736	A240	45fr	Angraecum magdalanae	1.50	.25
737	A240	50fr	Aerangis stylosa	1.75	.30
738	A240	100fr	Angraecum eburneum longicalcar	3.25	.50
739	A240	100fr	Angraecum sesquipedale	3.25	.50
			Nos. 735-739 (5)	10.75	1.75

Souvenir Sheet

Perf. 12x12½

740	A240	400fr	Angraecum aburneum superbum	8.00	2.50

Nos. 735, 737-740 vert. No. 740 contains one 30x42mm stamp.

INTERCOSMOS — A241

Cosmonauts, natl. flags, rockets, satellites and probes.

1985, Nov. ***Perf. 12x12½***

741	A241	20fr	USSR, Czechoslovakia	.25	.20
742	A241	20fr	Soyuz-Apollo emblem	.25	.20
743	A241	50fr	USSR, India	.55	.25
744	A241	100fr	USSR, Cuba	1.00	.30
745	A241	200fr	USSR, France	1.90	.65
			Nos. 741-745 (5)	3.95	1.60

Souvenir Sheet

746	A241	400fr	Halley's Comet, probe	5.50	1.75

No. 746 contains one stamp 42x30mm.

Democratic Republic, 10th Anniv. — A242

1985, Dec. 30 Litho. ***Perf. 12½x12***

747	A242	50fr	Industrial symbols	.45	.20

Natl. Insurance and Securities Co. (ARO), 10th Anniv. — A243

1986, Jan. 20 ***Perf. 12x12½***

748	A243	50fr	dk brn, yel org & gray brn	.45	.25

Paintings in the Tretyakov Gallery, Moscow — A244

Designs: 20fr, Still-life with Flowers and Fruit, 1839, by I. Chroutzky. No. 750, Portrait of Alexander Pushkin, 1827, by O. Kiprenski, vert. No. 751, Portrait of an Unknown Woman, 1883, by I. Kramskoi. No. 752, The Crows Have Returned, 1872, by A. Sakrassov, vert. 100fr, March, 1895, by I. Levitan. 450fr, Portrait of Pavel Tretyakov, 1883, by I. Repin, vert.

Perf. 12½x12, 12x12½

1986, Apr. 26 **Litho.**

749	A244	20fr	multi	.25	.20
750	A244	50fr	multi	.80	.25
751	A244	50fr	multi	.80	.25
752	A244	50fr	multi	.80	.25
753	A244	100fr	multi	2.25	.40
			Nos. 749-753 (5)	4.90	1.35

Souvenir Sheet

754	A244	450fr	multi	4.50	2.00

1986 World Cup Soccer Championships, Mexico — A245

1986, May 31 ***Perf. 13½***

755	A245	150fr	multi	1.40	.45

Paintings in Russian Museums — A246

#756, David and Urie, by Rembrandt, vert. #757, Danae, by Rembrandt. #758, Portrait of the Nurse of the Infant Isabella, by Rubens, vert. #759, The Alliance of Earth and Water, by Rubens, vert. #760, Portrait of an Old Man in Red, by Rembrandt. #761, The Holy Family, by Raphael.

Perf. 12x12½, 12½x12

1986, Mar. 24 **Litho.**

756	A246	20fr	multi	.25	.20
757	A246	50fr	multi	.70	.25
758	A246	50fr	multi	.70	.25
759	A246	50fr	multi	.70	.25
760	A246	50fr	multi	.75	.25
			Nos. 756-760 (5)	3.10	1.20

Souvenir Sheet

Perf. 11½x12½

761	A246	450fr	multi	3.50	2.50

UN Child Survival Campaign A247

A248

Wildcats — A249

1986, June 1 Litho. ***Perf. 12x12½***

762	A247	60fr	multi	.60	.25

1986, July 17

763	A248	10fr	Sable	.25	.20
764	A248	10fr	Chaus	.25	.20
765	A248	60fr	Serval	.70	.25
766	A248	60fr	Caracal	.70	.25
767	A248	60fr	Bengal	.70	.25
			Nos. 763-767 (5)	2.60	1.15

Souvenir Sheet

Perf. 12½x12

768	A249	450fr	Golden	4.75	2.00

Intl. Peace Year A249a

1986, Sept. 12 ***Perf. 12***

769	A249a	60fr	shown	.55	.25
770	A249a	150fr	Hemispheres, emblem, vert.	1.25	.40

World Post Day — A250

1986, Oct. 9 Litho. ***Perf. 13x12½***

771	A250	60fr	multi	.60	.25
772	A250	150fr	multi	1.40	.40

No. 772 is airmail.

A251

Birds — A252

Perf. 12x12½, 12½x12

1986, Dec. 23 **Litho.**

773	A251	60fr	Xenopirostris daimi, vert.	.80	.25
774	A251	60fr	Falculea palliata	.80	.25
775	A251	60fr	Coua gigas	.80	.25
776	A251	60fr	Coua cristata	.80	.25
777	A251	60fr	Cianolanius madagascariensis, vert.	.80	.25
			Nos. 773-777 (5)	4.00	1.25

Souvenir Sheet

778	A252	450fr	Bubulcus ibis ibis	6.00	2.00

A253

Endangered Species — A254

Perf. 12x12½, 12½x12

1987, Mar. 13 **Litho.**

779	A253	60fr	Lophotibis cristata, vert.	1.10	.25
780	A253	60fr	Coracopsis nigra	1.10	.25
781	A254	60fr	Crocodylus niloticus	1.10	.25
782	A254	60fr	Geochelone yniphora	1.10	.25
			Nos. 779-782 (4)	4.40	1.00

Souvenir Sheet

783	A253	450fr	Centropus toulou, vert.	6.25	2.00

Anti-Colonial Revolt, 40th Anniv. — A255

A256

1987, Mar. 29 ***Perf. 12***

784	A255	60fr	multi	.50	.20
785	A256	60fr	multi	.50	.20

1st Games of Indian Ocean Towns A257

1987, Apr. 15 *Perf. 13½*

786 A257 60fr multi .55 .25
787 A257 150fr multi 1.25 .40

Le Sarimanok — A258

1987, Apr. 15

788 A258 60fr Port side .60 .25
789 A258 150fr Starboard side 1.40 .40

African and Madagascar Coffee Organization, 25th Anniv. — A259

1987, Apr. 24 **Litho.** *Perf. 12*

790 A259 60fr Coffee plant .55 .25
791 A259 150fr Map 1.40 .40

Halley's Comet — A260

Space probes.

1987, May 13 *Perf. 13½*

792 A260 60fr Giotto, ESA .40 .20
793 A260 150fr Vega 1, Russia .90 .25
794 A260 250fr Vega 2, Russia 1.75 .40
795 A260 350fr Planet-A1, Japan 2.50 .60
796 A260 400fr Planet-A2, Japan 2.75 .65
797 A260 450fr ICE, US 3.25 .70
Nos. 792-797 (6) 11.55 2.80

Souvenir Sheet

798 A260 600fr Halley, Giotto 4.50 1.00

Litho. & Embossed 'Gold Foil' Stamps
These stamps generally are of a different design format than the rest of the issue. Since there is a commemorative inscription tying them to the issue a separate illustration is not being shown.

1988 Calgary Winter Olympics — A261

Jean-Joseph Rabearivelo (d. 1937), Poet — A263

Men's Downhill — A262

1987, May 13

799 A261 60fr Biathlon .40 .20
800 A261 150fr shown .90 .25
801 A261 250fr Luge 1.75 .40
802 A261 350fr Speed skating 2.50 .60
803 A261 400fr Hockey 2.75 .65
804 A261 450fr Pairs figure skating 3.25 .70
Nos. 799-804 (6) 11.55 2.80

Litho. & Embossed

804A A261 1500fr Speed skating 11.00

Souvenir Sheets
Litho.

805 A262 600fr shown 4.75 1.25

Litho. & Embossed

805A A262 1500fr Slalom skiing 7.50

No. 804A exists in souvenir sheet of 1.

1987, June 22 *Perf. 13½*

806 A263 60fr multi .40 .25

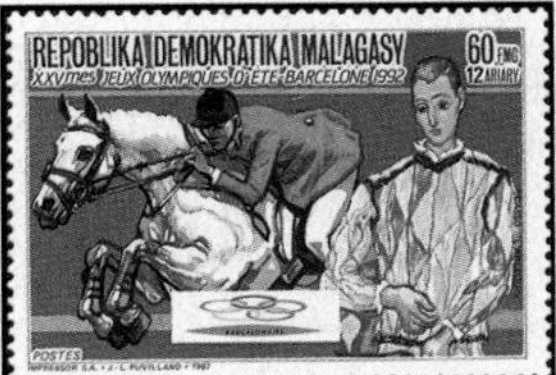

1992 Summer Olympics, Barcelona — A264

Athletes, emblem and art or architecture: 60fr, Equestrian, and the Harlequin, by Picasso. 150fr, Weight lifting, church. 250fr, Hurdles, Canaletas Fountain. 350fr, High jump, amusement park. 400fr, Men's gymnastics, abbey. 450fr, Rhythmic gymnastics, Arc de Triomphe. 600fr, Equestrian, Columbus monument.

1987, Oct. 7 **Litho.** *Perf. 13½*

807 A264 60fr multi .25 .20
808 A264 150fr multi .80 .25
809 A264 250fr multi 1.40 .40
810 A264 350fr multi 2.00 .60
811 A264 400fr multi 2.25 .65
812 A264 450fr multi 2.50 .70
Nos. 807-812 (6) 9.20 2.80

Souvenir Sheet

813 A264 600fr multi 3.75 1.25

Nos. 811-813 are airmail.

A265

Discovery of America, 500th Anniv. (in 1992) — A266

Anniv. emblem and: 60fr, Bartolomeu Dias (c. 1450-1500), Portuguese navigator, departure from De Palos, 1492. 150fr, Henry the Navigator (1394-1460), prince of Portugal, Samana Cay. 250fr, A. De Marchena landing, 1492. 350fr, Paolo Toscanelli dal Pozzo (1397-1482), Italian physician and cosmographer, La Navidad Fort. 400fr, Queen Isabella I, Barcelona, 1493. 450fr, Christopher Columbus, the Nina. 600fr, Landing in New World, 1492.

1987, Sept. 24 **Litho.** *Perf. 13½*

814 A265 60fr multi .30 .20
815 A265 150fr multi .80 .30
816 A265 250fr multi 1.25 .55
817 A265 350fr multi 1.90 .85
818 A265 400fr multi 2.25 1.00
819 A265 450fr multi 2.50 1.10
Nos. 814-819 (6) 9.00 4.00

Souvenir Sheet

820 A266 600fr multi 4.00 1.50

A267

A268

1987, July 27 *Perf. 12½x12*

821 A267 60fr multi .40 .25

Natl. telecommunications research laboratory.

1987, Aug. 14

822 A268 60fr lt blue, blk & brt ultra .40 .25

Rafaravavy Rasalama (d. 1837), Christian martyr.

Antananarivo-Tamatave Telegraph Link, Cent. — A269

1987, Sept. 15 *Perf. 12x12½*

823 A269 60fr multi .40 .25

Pasteur Institute, Paris, Cent. A270

1987, Oct. 26 *Perf. 13½*

824 A270 250fr multi 1.10 .50

City of Berlin, 750th Anniv. — A271

Design: Anniv. emblem, television tower and the Interhotel in East Berlin.

1987, Oct. 18 **Litho.** *Perf. 12½x12*

825 A271 150fr multi .40 .30

Schools Festival A272

1987, Oct. 23 *Perf. 12x12½*

826 A272 60fr multi .25 .20

Paintings in the Pushkin Museum, Moscow — A273

Designs: 10fr, After the Shipwreck (1847), by Eugene Delacroix (1798-1863). No. 828, Still-life with Swan (c. 1620), by Frans Snyders (1579-1647). No. 829, Jupiter and Callisto (1744), by Francois Boucher (1703-1770), vert. No. 830, Chalet in the Mountains (1874), by Jean Desire Gustav Courbet (1819-1877). 150fr, At the Market (1564), by Joachim Bueckelaer. 1000fr, Minerva (1560), by Paolo Veronese (1528-1588), vert.

Perf. 12½x12, 12x12½

1987, Nov. 10

827 A273 10fr multi .30 .20
828 A273 60fr multi .45 .20
829 A273 60fr multi .45 .20
830 A273 60fr multi .45 .20
831 A273 150fr multi 1.00 .25
Nos. 827-831 (5) 2.65 1.05

Souvenir Sheet

832 A273 1000fr multi 7.00 2.75

Pan-African Telecommunications Union, 10th Anniv. — A274

1987, Dec. 28 *Perf. 13x12½*

833 A274 250fr multi .60 .45

Intl. Year of Shelter for the Homeless A275

1988, Feb. 15 **Litho.** *Perf. 12*

834 A275 80fr shown .20 .20
835 A275 250fr Family in shelter, rain, vert. .55 .25

Fauna
A276

1988, Apr. 18 Litho. *Perf. 13½*

836 A276 60fr Hapalemur simus 1.75 .75
837 A276 150fr Propithecus diadema diadema 2.25 .75
838 A276 250fr Indri indri 3.25 1.00
839 A276 350fr Varecia variegata variegata 5.00 1.25
840 A276 550fr Madagascar young heron 1.50 .60
841 A276 1500fr Nossi-Be chameleon 3.50 1.60
Nos. 836-841 (6) 17.25 5.95

Souvenir Sheet

842 A276 1500fr Uratelornis (bird) 6.50 6.50

Conservation and service organization emblems: World Wildlife Fund (60fr, 150fr, 250fr and 350fr); Rotary Intl. (550fr and No. 842); and Scouting trefoil (No. 841).

Nos. 840-841 exist in souvenir sheet of 2.

For overprints see Nos. 1134, 1154.

October Revolution, Russia, 70th Anniv.
A277

1988, Mar. 7 Litho. *Perf. 12x12½*

843 A277 60fr Lenin .60 .20
844 A277 60fr Revolutionaries .60 .20
845 A277 150fr Lenin, revolutionaries 1.25 .20
Nos. 843-845 (3) 2.45 .60

1988 Winter Olympics, Calgary
A278

1988, May 11 *Perf. 11½*

846 A278 20fr Pairs figure skating .20 .20
847 A278 60fr Slalom .20 .20
848 A278 60fr Speed skating .20 .20
849 A278 100fr Cross-country skiing .30 .20
850 A278 250fr Ice hockey .70 .30
Nos. 846-850 (5) 1.60 1.10

Souvenir Sheet

851 A278 800fr Ski jumping 2.50 1.75

Discovery of Radium by Pierre and Marie Curie, 90th Anniv.
A279

1988, July 14 Litho. *Perf. 12*

852 A279 150fr blk & rose lil .50 .20

OAU, 25th Anniv.
A280

1988, May 25 Litho. *Perf. 13*

853 A280 80fr multi .25 .20

Natl. Telecommunications and Posts Institute, 20th Anniv. — A281

1988, June 22 *Perf. 13½*

854 A281 80fr multi .25 .20

Saint-Michel College, Cent. — A282

1988, July 9

855 A282 250fr multi .55 .30

Alma-Ata Declaration, 10th Anniv. — A283

WHO, 40th Anniv. — A284

1988, Aug. 11 Litho. *Perf. 12*

856 A283 60fr multi .30 .20

1988, Aug. 11

857 A284 150fr multi .30 .20

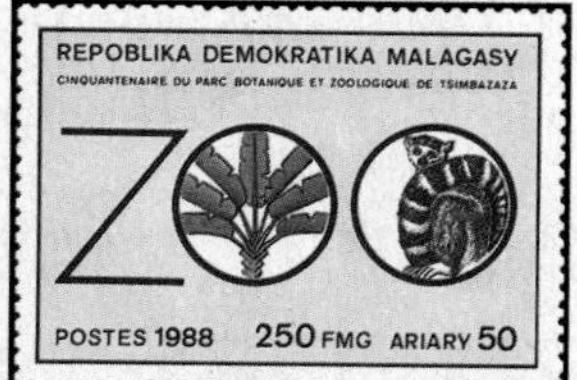

Tsimbazaza Botanical and Zoological Park, 150th Anniv. — A285

Perf. 12x12½, 12½x12

1988, Aug. 22

858 A285 20fr Lemur habitat .55 .25
859 A285 80fr Lemur and young .55 .25
860 A285 250fr shown 1.50 .40
Nos. 858-860 (3) 2.60 .90

Souvenir Sheet

861 A285 1000fr Lemur and mate 3.50 2.25

Size of No. 859: 25x37mm.

Boy Scouts Studying Birds and Butterflies
A286

Designs: 80fr, Upupa epops maginata, Coua caerulea and scout photographing bird. 250fr, Chrysiridia croesus and comparing butterfly to a sketch. 270fr, Nelicurvius nelicourvi, Foudia omissa and constructing bird feeder. 350fr, Papilio dardanus and studying butterflies with magnifying glass. 550fr, Coua critata and tagging bird. No. 867, Argema mittrei and writing observations. No. 868, Merops superciliosus and recording bird calls. No. 868A, Euchloron megaera. No. 868B, Rhynchee.

1988, Sept. 29

862 A286 80fr multi .20 .20
863 A286 250fr multi .55 .30
864 A286 270fr multi .60 .30
865 A286 350fr multi .80 .40
866 A286 550fr multi 1.25 .60
867 A286 1500fr multi 3.75 1.60
Nos. 862-867 (6) 7.15 3.40

Souvenir Sheet

868 A286 1500fr multi 3.50 2.25

Litho. & Embossed

Perf. 13½

868A A286 5000fr gold & multi 8.00

Souvenir Sheet

868B A286 5000fr gold & multi 8.00

No. 868 contains one stamp 36x51mm.

Nos. 868A-868B dated 1989. Nos. 868A-868B exist imperf.

Composers and Entertainers
A287

Designs: 80fr, German-made clavier and Carl Philipp Emanuel Bach (1714-1788), organist and composer. 250fr, Piano and Franz Peter Schubert (1797-1828), Austrian composer. 270fr, Scene from opera Carmen, 1875, and Georges Bizet (1838-1875), French composer. 350fr, Scene from opera Pelleas et Melisande, 1902, and Claude Debussy (1862-1918), French composer. 550fr, George Gershwin (1898-1937), American composer. No. 874, Elvis Presley (1935-1977), American entertainer. No. 875, Rimsky-Korsakov (1844-1908), Russian composer, and Le Coq d'Or from the opera of the same name.

1988, Oct. 28 *Perf. 12x12½, 12½x12*

869 A287 80fr multi .20 .20
870 A287 250fr multi .55 .30
871 A287 270fr multi .60 .30
872 A287 350fr multi .80 .40
873 A287 550fr multi 1.25 .60
874 A287 1500fr multi 3.50 1.60
Nos. 869-874 (6) 6.90 3.40

Souvenir Sheet

875 A287 1500fr multi 3.25 3.25

For overprints see Nos. 1135-1136.

Intl. Fund for Agricultural Development (IFAD), 10th Anniv. — A288

1988, Sept. 4 Litho. *Perf. 12*

876 A288 250fr multi .50 .25

School Feast — A289

1988, Nov. 22

877 A289 80fr multi .25 .20

A290

Ships — A291

Paintings: 20fr, The Squadron of the Sea, Black Feodossia, by Ivan Aivazovski, vert. No. 879, Seascape with Sailing Ships, by Simon de Vlieger, vert. No. 880, The Ship Lesnoie, by N. Semenov, vert. 100fr, The Merchantman, Orel, by N. Golitsine. 250fr, Naval Exercises, by Adam Silo, vert. 550fr, On the River, by Abraham Beerstraten.

1988, Dec. 5 *Perf. 12x12½, 12½x12*

878 A290 20fr multi .20 .20
879 A290 80fr multi .25 .20
880 A290 80fr multi .25 .20
881 A290 100fr shown .35 .20
882 A290 250fr multi .80 .25
Nos. 878-882 (5) 1.85 1.05

Souvenir Sheet

Perf. 11½x12½

883 A291 550fr shown 2.00 1.00

World Wildlife Fund — A292

Insect species in danger of extinction: 20fr, Tragocephala crassicornis. 80fr, Polybothris symptuosa-gema. 250fr, Euchroea auripigmenta. 350fr, Stellognata maculata.

1988, Dec. 13 *Perf. 12*

884 A292 20fr multi *1.00* —
885 A292 80fr multi *6.50* —
886 A292 250fr multi *22.50* —
887 A292 350fr multi *30.00* —
Nos. 884-887 (4) *60.00*

Intl. Red Cross and Red Crescent Organizations, 125th Annivs. — A293

1988, Dec. 27 **Litho.** ***Perf. 12***

888 A293 80fr Globe, stretcher-bearers, vert. .20 .20
889 A293 250fr Emblems, Dunant .55 .30

UN Declaration of Human Rights, 40th Anniv. (in 1988) — A294

1989, Jan. 10

890 A294 80fr shown .25 .20
891 A294 250fr Hands, "4" and "0" .60 .30

Dated 1988.

Transportation — A295

Designs: 80fr, 1909 Mercedes-Benz Blitzen Benz. 250fr, Micheline ZM 517 Tsikirity, Tananarive-Moramanga line. 270fr, Bugatti Coupe Binder 41. 350fr, Electric locomotive 1020-DES OBB, Germany. 1500fr, Souleze Autorail 701 DU CFN, Madagascar. No. 897, 1913 Opel race car. No. 898, Bugatti Presidential Autorail locomotive and Bugatti Type 57 Atalante automobile.

1989, Jan. 24 ***Perf. 13½***

892 A295 80fr multi .20 .20
893 A295 250fr multi .50 .25
894 A295 270fr multi .60 .25
895 A295 350fr multi 1.00 .35
896 A295 1500fr multi 3.50 1.40
897 A295 2500fr multi 5.50 2.40
Nos. 892-897 (6) 11.30 4.85

Souvenir Sheet

898 A295 2500fr multi 5.00 3.50

Nos. 893-897 exist imperf. Value, set $13.

Dinosaurs — A296

1989, Feb. 1 **Litho.** ***Perf. 12½x12***

899 A296 20fr Tyrannosaurus .25 .20
900 A296 80fr Stegosaurus 1.10 .20
901 A296 250fr Arsinoitherium 3.25 .50
902 A296 450fr Triceratops 4.50 1.00
Nos. 899-902 (4) 9.10 1.90

Souvenir Sheet

Perf. 11½x12½

903 A296 600fr Sauralophus, vert. 2.75 1.25

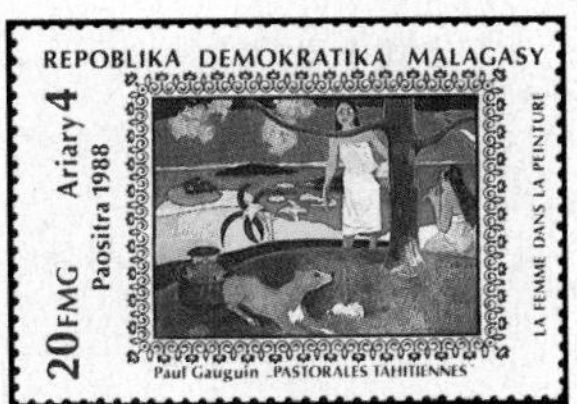

Women as the Subject of Paintings — A297

Designs: 20fr, *Tahitian Pastorales,* by Gauguin. No 905, *Portrait of a Young Woman,* by Titian, vert. No. 906, *Portrait of a Little Girl,* by Jean-Baptiste Greuze (1725-1805), vert. 100fr, *Woman in Black,* by Renoir, vert. 250fr, *Lacemaker,* by Vassili Tropinine, vert. 550fr, *The Annunciation,* by Cima Da Conegliano (c. 1459-1517), vert.

1989, Feb. 10 ***Perf. 12½x12, 12x12½***

904 A297 20fr multi .20 .20
905 A297 80fr multi .25 .20
906 A297 80fr multi .25 .20
907 A297 100fr multi .35 .20
908 A297 250fr multi .75 .30
Nos. 904-908 (5) 1.80 1.10

Souvenir Sheet

Perf. 11½x12½

909 A297 550fr multi 1.60 1.00

Orchids A298

1989, Feb. 28 **Litho.** ***Perf. 12***

910 A298 5fr *Sobennikoffia robusta,* vert. .45 .20
911 A298 10fr *Grammangis fallax* .45 .20
912 A298 80fr *Cymbidiella humblotii,* vert. 1.25 .20
913 A298 80fr *Angraecum sororium,* vert. 1.25 .20
914 A298 250fr *Oenia oncidiiflora,* vert. 3.00 .35
Nos. 910-914 (5) 6.40 1.15

Souvenir Sheet

915 A298 1000fr *Aerangis curnowiana* 5.50 2.75

Jawaharlal Nehru (1889-1964), 1st Prime Minister of Independent India — A299

1989, Mar. 7 **Litho.** ***Perf. 13***

916 A299 250fr multi .50 .25

Ornamental Mineral Industry A300

1989, Apr. 12 **Litho.** ***Perf. 13½***

917 A300 80fr Rose quartz .30 .20
918 A300 250fr Petrified wood .90 .30

Views of Antananarivo A301

Designs: 5fr, Mahamasina Sports Complex, Ampefiloha Quarter. 20fr, Andravoahangy and Anjanahary Quarters. No. 921, Zoma Market and Faravohitra Quarter. No. 922, Andohan'Analakely Quarter and March 29th monument. 250fr, Independence Avenue and Jean Ralaimongo monument. 550fr, Queen's Palace and Andohalo School on Lake Anosy.

1989, Mar. 31 **Litho.** ***Perf. 13½***

919 A301 5fr multi .20 .20
920 A301 20fr multi .20 .20
921 A301 80fr multi .25 .25
922 A301 80fr multi .25 .25
923 A301 250fr multi .50 .25
924 A301 550fr multi .90 .35
Nos. 919-924 (6) 2.30 1.50

Visit of Pope John Paul II — A302

1989, Apr. 28 ***Perf. 12x12½***

925 A302 80fr shown .30 .20
926 A302 250fr Pope, map 1.00 .25

French Revolution, Bicent. A303

1989, July 7 **Litho.** ***Perf. 12½***

927 A303 250fr Storming of the Bastille .60 .25

Phobos Space Program for the Exploration of Mars — A304

1989, Aug. 29 **Litho.** ***Perf. 12½x12***

928 A304 20fr Mars 1 .20 .20
929 A304 80fr Mars 3 .25 .20
930 A304 80fr Sond 2 .25 .20
931 A304 250fr Mariner 9 .55 .25
932 A304 270fr Viking 2 .65 .30
Nos. 928-932 (5) 1.90 1.15

Souvenir Sheet

933 A304 550fr Phobos 1.50 .60

PHILEXFRANCE '89 and French Revolution, Bicent. — A305

Exhibition emblems, key people and scenes from the revolution: 250fr, Honore-Gabriel Riqueti (1749-1791), Count of Mirabeau, at the meeting of Estates-General, June 23, 1789. 350fr, Camille Desmoulins (1760-1794), call to arms, July 12, 1789. 1000fr, Lafayette (1757-1834), women's march on Versailles, Oct. 5, 1789. 1500fr, King tried by the National Convention, Dec. 26, 1792. 2500fr, Charlotte Corday (1768-1793), assassination of Marat, July 13, 1793. 3000fr, Bertrand Barere de Vieuzac, Robespierre, Jean-Marie Collot D'Herbois, Lazare Nicolas Carnot, George Jacques Danton, Georges Auguste Couthon, Pierre-Louis Prieur, Antoine Saint-Just and Marc Guillaume Vadier, Committee of Public Safety, July, 1793. No. 939A, Family saying farewell to Louis XVI. No. 939B, Danton and the Club of the Cordeliers.

1989, July 14 **Litho.** ***Perf. 13½***

934 A305 250fr multicolored .45 .20
935 A305 350fr multicolored .65 .25
936 A305 1000fr multicolored 1.60 .65
937 A305 1500fr multicolored 2.50 1.00
938 A305 2500fr multicolored 4.25 1.60
Nos. 934-938 (5) 9.45 3.70

Souvenir Sheet

939 A305 3000fr multicolored 4.50 4.50

Litho. & Embossed

939A A305 5000fr gold & multi 8.00

Souvenir Sheet

939B A305 5000fr gold & multi 8.00

Nos. 939A-939B exist imperf.

For overprints see #1161-1165, 1166A-1166B.

French Revolution, Bicent. — A306

Paintings and sculpture: 5fr, *Liberty Guiding the People,* by Eugene Delacroix. 80fr, "La Marseillaise" from *Departure of the Volunteers in 1792,* high relief on the Arc de Triomphe, 1833-35, by Francois Rude. 250fr, *The Tennis Court Oath,* by David.

1989, Oct. 25 ***Perf. 12½x12***

940 A306 5fr multicolored .20 .20
941 A306 80fr multicolored .45 .25
942 A306 250fr multicolored .90 .25
Nos. 940-942 (3) 1.55 .70

No. 942 is airmail.

Rene Cassin (1887-1976), Nobel Peace Prize Winner and Institute Founder — A307

1989, Nov. 21 ***Perf. 12***

943 A307 250fr multicolored .40 .20

Intl. Law Institute of the French-Speaking Nations, 25th anniv.

Hapalemur aureus A308

1989, Dec. 5 **Litho.** ***Perf. 12***

944 A308 250fr multicolored 1.10 .35

A309

A309a

Various athletes, cup and: 350fr, Cavour Monument, Turin. 1000fr, Christopher Columbus Monument, Genoa, 1903. 1500fr, Michelangelo's *David.* 2500fr, *Abduction of Prosperina,* by Bernini, Rome. 3000fr, Statue of Leonardo da Vinci, 1903. 5000fr, Castel Nuovo, Naples.

1989, Dec. 12 Litho. *Perf. 13½*

945	A309	350fr multicolored	.65	.25
946	A309	1000fr multicolored	1.60	.65
947	A309	1500fr multicolored	2.25	1.00
948	A309	2500fr multicolored	4.00	1.60
		Nos. 945-948 (4)	8.50	3.50

Souvenir Sheet

949	A309	3000fr multicolored	4.25	2.00

Litho. & Embossed

949A	A309a	5000fr gold & multi	8.00

1990 World Cup Soccer Championships, Italy.

For overprints see Nos. 1137-1140.

A310

1989, Oct. 7 Litho. *Perf. 13½*

950	A310	80fr Long jump	.20	.20
951	A310	250fr Pole vault	.35	.20
952	A310	550fr Hurdles	.80	.40
953	A310	1500fr Cycling	2.25	1.10
954	A310	2000fr Baseball	3.00	1.45
955	A310	2500fr Tennis	3.75	1.75
		Nos. 950-955 (6)	10.35	5.10

Souvenir Sheet

956	A310	3000fr Soccer	4.50	2.10

1992 Summer Olympics, Barcelona.

Scenic Views and Artifacts A311

1990, May 29

Size: 47x33mm (#958, 960)

957	A311	70fr Queen Isalo Rock	.20	.20
958	A311	70fr Sakalava pipe	.20	.20
959	A311	150fr Sakalava combs	.30	.20
960	A311	150fr Lowry Is., Diego Suarez Bay	.30	.20
		Nos. 957-960 (4)	1.00	.80

Fish A312

1990, Apr. 26 Litho. *Perf. 12*

961	A312	5fr Heniochus acuminatus	.35	.20
962	A312	20fr Simenhelys dofleinl	.35	.20
963	A312	80fr Rhinobatos percellens	.35	.20
964	A312	250fr Epinephelus fasciatus	1.50	.25
965	A312	320fr Sphyrna zygaena	1.90	.35
		Nos. 961-965 (5)	4.45	1.20

Souvenir Sheet

966	A312	550fr Latimeria chalumnae	3.50	1.50

Nos. 962-963 vert. Nos. 961-966 inscribed 1989.

Moon Landing, 20th Anniv. — A314

Designs: 80fr, Voyager 2, Neptune. 250fr, Hydro 2000 flying boat. 550fr, NOAA satellite. 1500fr, Magellan probe, Venus. 2000fr, Concorde. 2500fr, Armstrong, Aldrin, Collins, lunar module. 3000fr, Apollo 11 astronauts, first step on moon.

1990, June 19 Litho. *Perf. 13½*

967	A314	80fr multicolored	.20	.20
968	A314	250fr multicolored	.35	.20
969	A314	550fr multicolored	.80	.40
970	A314	1500fr multicolored	2.25	1.10
971	A314	2000fr multicolored	3.00	1.50
972	A314	2500fr multicolored	3.75	1.90
		Nos. 967-972 (6)	10.35	5.30

Souvenir Sheet

973	A314	3000fr multicolored	4.75	2.25

For overprint see No. 1304.

Nos. 967-972 exist in souvenir sheets of 1, and se-tenant in a sheet of 6.

A315

A316

1990, July 17

974	A315	350fr Bobsled	.50	.25
975	A315	1000fr Speed skating	1.50	.75
976	A315	1500fr Nordic skiing	2.25	1.10
977	A315	2500fr Super giant slalom	3.75	1.90
		Nos. 974-977 (4)	8.00	4.00

Souvenir Sheet

978	A315	3000fr Giant slalom	4.50	2.25

Litho. & Embossed

978A	A315	5000fr Pairs figure skating	8.00

Souvenir Sheet

978B	A315	5000fr Ice hockey	8.00

1992 Winter Olympics, Albertville. Nos. 978A-978B exist imperf.

For overprints see Nos. 1141-1145.

1990, June 19 Litho. *Perf. 12*

979	A316	250fr blk, ultra & bl	.45	.20

Intl. Maritime Organization, 30th anniv.

African Development Bank, 25th Anniv. A317

1990, June 19

980	A317	80fr multicolored	.30	.20

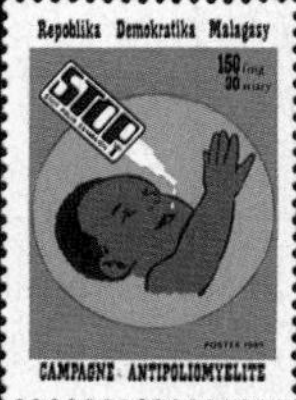

A318

A319

1990, June 28

981	A318	150fr multicolored	.30	.20

Campaign against polio.

1990, Aug. 22

982	A319	100fr multicolored	.30	.20

Independence, 30th anniv.

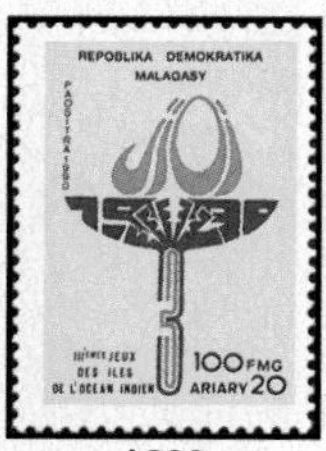

A320

A322

1990, Aug. 24 *Perf. 12½x12*

983	A320	100fr yellow & multi	.35	.20
984	A320	350fr lil rose & multi	.65	.30

3rd Indian Ocean Games.

1990, Oct. 19 Litho. *Perf. 12*

986	A322	350fr multicolored	.65	.30

Ho Chi Minh (1890-1969), Vietnamese leader.

Lemurs A323

1990, Nov. 23 Litho. *Perf. 11½*

987	A323	10fr Avahi laniger	.35	.20
988	A323	20fr Lemur fulvus sanfordi	.35	.20
989	A323	20fr Lemur fulvus albifrons	.35	.20
990	A323	100fr Lemur fulvus collaris	1.25	.20
991	A323	100fr Lepulemur ruficaudatus	1.25	.20
		Nos. 987-991 (5)	3.55	1.00

Souvenir Sheet

992	A323	350fr Lemur fulvus fulvus	3.00	.50

Shells A324

1990, Dec. 21 *Perf. 12½*

993	A324	40fr Tridacna squamosa	.80	.20
994	A324	50fr Terebra demidiata, Terebra subulata	.80	.20

Anniversaries and Events A325

100fr, Charles de Gaulle, liberation of Paris, 1944. 350fr, Galileo probe orbiting Jupiter. 800fr, Apollo 11 crew & Columbia command module, 1st Moon landing, 1969. 900fr, De Gaulle, 1942. 1250fr, Concorde jet, TGV high-speed train. 2500fr, De Gaulle as head of provisional government, 1944. 3000fr, Apollo 11 crew, Eagle lunar module. #1001A, De Gaulle with Roosevelt & Churchill. #1001B, Charles de Gaulle.

1990, Dec. 28 Litho. *Perf. 13½*

995	A325	100fr multi	.20	.20
996	A325	350fr multi	.60	.30
997	A325	800fr multi	1.40	.70
998	A325	900fr multi	1.60	.80
999	A325	1250fr multi	2.25	1.10
1000	A325	2500fr multi	4.50	2.25
		Nos. 995-1000 (6)	10.55	5.35

Souvenir Sheet

1001	A325	3000fr multi	5.25	2.75

Litho. & Embossed

1001A	A325	5000fr gold & multi	7.50

Souvenir Sheet

1001B	A325	5000fr gold & multi	7.50

Nos. 995-1000, 1001A exist in souvenir sheets of 1. A souvenir sheet containing Nos. 996-997 exists.

Mushrooms — A325b

Designs: 25fr, Boletus edulis. 100fr, Suillus luteus. 350fr, Amanita muscaria. 450fr, Boletus calopus. 680fr, Boletus erythropus. 800fr, Leccinum scabrum. 900fr, Leccinum testaceoscabrum.

1500fr, Lycoperdon perlatum.

1990, Dec. 28 Litho. *Perf. 12*

1001C	A325b	25fr multi	.25	.20
1001D	A325b	100fr multi	.40	.20
1001E	A325b	350fr multi	.85	.25
1001F	A325b	450fr multi	1.25	.30
1001G	A325b	680fr multi	1.75	.45
1001H	A325b	800fr multi	1.90	.50
1001I	A325b	900fr multi	2.10	.60

Imperf

Size: 71x91mm

1001J A325b 1500fr multi 4.50 4.50
Nos. 1001C-1001J (8) 13.00 7.00

For surcharge, see No. 1478A.

Intl. Literacy Year A326

1990, Dec. 30 *Perf. 12*
1002 A326 20fr Book, guiding hands, vert. .25 .20
1003 A326 100fr Open Book, hand holding pencil .25 .20

Dogs — A326a

1991, Mar. 20 **Litho.** *Perf. 12*
1003A A326a 30fr Greyhound .25 .20
1003B A326a 50fr Japanese spaniel .25 .20
1003C A326a 140fr Toy terrier .60 .20
1003D A326a 350fr Chow .90 .25
1003E A326a 500fr Miniature pinscher 1.25 .30
1003F A326a 800fr Afghan 2.10 .50
1003G A326a 1140fr Papillon 3.00 .75

Imperf

Size: 70x90mm

1003H A326a 1500fr Shih tzu 4.00 1.40
Nos. 1003A-1003H (8) 12.35 3.80

Nos. 1003D-1003H are airmail.

Democratic Republic of Madagascar, 15th Anniv. (in 1990) — A327

1991, Apr. 8 **Litho.** *Perf. 12*
1004 A327 100fr multicolored .25 .20

Dated 1990.

Trees — A328

1991, June 20 **Litho.** *Perf. 13½*
1005 A328 140fr Adansonia fony .55 .20
1006 A328 500fr Didierea madagascariensis 1.25 .40

Scouts, Insects and Mushrooms A329

Insects: 140fr, Helictopleurus splendidicollis. 640fr, Cocles contemplator. 1140fr, Euchroea oberthurii.

Mushrooms: 500fr, Russula radicans. 1025fr, Russula singeri. 3500fr, Lactariopsis pandani.

4500fr, Euchroea spinnasuta fairmaire and Russula aureotacta.

1991, Aug. 2 **Litho.** *Perf. 13½*
1007 A329 140fr multicolored .35 .20
1008 A329 500fr multicolored .90 .30
1009 A329 640fr multicolored 1.00 .40
1010 A329 1025fr multicolored 1.75 .65
1011 A329 1140fr multicolored 2.10 .70
1012 A329 3500fr multicolored 5.25 2.25
Nos. 1007-1012 (6) 11.35 4.50

Souvenir Sheet

1013 A329 4500fr multicolored 7.00 5.75

#1007-1012 exist in souvenir sheets of 1.
For overprints see Nos. 1149-1156.

Discovery of America, 500th Anniv. A330

Designs: 15fr, Ship, 9th cent.. 65fr, Clipper ship, 1878. 140fr, Golden Hind. 500fr, Galley, 18th cent. 640fr, Galleon Ostrust, 1721, vert. 800fr, Caravel Amsterdam, 1539, vert. 1025fr, Santa Maria, 1492. 1500fr, Map.

1991, Sept. 10 **Litho.** *Perf. 12*
1014 A330 15fr multicolored .20 .20
1015 A330 65fr multicolored .25 .20
1016 A330 140fr multicolored .55 .20
1017 A330 500fr multicolored 1.25 .30
1018 A330 640fr multicolored 1.50 .40
1019 A330 800fr multicolored 1.60 .50
1020 A330 1025fr multicolored 1.75 .65

Size: 90x70mm

1021 A330 1500fr multicolored 3.50 1.50
Nos. 1014-1021 (8) 10.60 3.95

No. 1021 contains one 40x27mm perf. 12 label in center of stamp picturing ships and Columbus.

Domesticated Animals A331

Designs: 140fr, Dog. 500fr, Arabian horse. 640fr, House cats. 1025fr, Himalayan cats. 1140fr, Draft horse. 5000fr, German shepherd. 10,000fr, Horse, cat & dog.

1991, Sept. 27 **Litho.** *Perf. 13½*
1022 A331 140fr multicolored .25 .20
1023 A331 500fr multicolored .90 .30
1024 A331 640fr multicolored 1.00 .40
1025 A331 1025fr multicolored 1.75 .65
1026 A331 1140fr multicolored 2.25 .70
1027 A331 5000fr multicolored 7.25 3.25
Nos. 1022-1027 (6) 13.40 5.50

Souvenir Sheet

1028 A331 10,000fr multicolored 13.00 6.50

Nos. 1022-1028 exist imperf. and in souvenir sheets of 1.

Birds — A332

Designs: 40fr, Hirundo rustica. 55fr, Circus melanoluecos, vert. 60fr, Cuculas canorus, vert. 140fr, Threskiornis aethiopicus. 210fr, Porphyrio poliocephalus. 500fr, Coracias garrulus. 2000fr, Oriolus oriolus. 1500fr, Upupa epops.

Perf. 12½x12, 12x12½

1991, Dec. 10 **Litho.**
1029 A332 40fr multicolored .20 .20
1030 A332 55fr multicolored .20 .20
1031 A332 60fr multicolored .25 .20
1032 A332 140fr multicolored .45 .20
1033 A332 210fr multicolored .70 .25
1034 A332 500fr multicolored 1.00 .35
1035 A332 2000fr multicolored 3.00 1.10

Size: 70x90mm

Imperf

1036 A332 1500fr multicolored 3.00 1.40
Nos. 1029-1036 (8) 8.80 3.90

1992 Winter Olympics, Albertville A333

1991, Dec. 30 **Litho.** *Perf. 12x12½*
1037 A333 5fr Cross-country skiing .20 .20
1038 A333 15fr Biathlon .20 .20
1039 A333 60fr Ice hockey .25 .20
1040 A333 140fr Downhill skiing .45 .25
1041 A333 640fr Figure skating 1.25 .40
1042 A333 1000fr Ski jumping 1.60 .70
1043 A333 1140fr Speed skating 2.00 .75

Imperf

Size: 90x70mm

1044 A333 1500fr Three hockey players 3.00 1.40
Nos. 1037-1044 (8) 8.95 4.10

For surcharge see #1482.

Paul Minault College, 90th Anniv. A333a

1991 **Litho.** *Perf. 13½*
1044A A333a 140fr multicolored .65 .30

Space Program A334

Designs: 140fr, Astronaunts repairing space telescope. 500fr, Soho solar observation probe. 640fr, Topex-Poseidon, observing oceans. 1025fr, Hipparcos probe, Galaxy 3C75. 1140fr, Voyager II surveying Neptune. 5000fr, Adeos, ETS VI, earth observation and communications satellites. 7500fr, Crew of Apollo 11.

1992, Apr. 22 *Perf. 13½*
1045 A334 140fr multi .25 .20
1046 A334 500fr multi .70 .30
1047 A334 640fr multi .90 .40
1048 A334 1025fr multi 1.40 .65
1049 A334 1140fr multi 1.60 .70
1050 A334 5000fr multi 6.75 3.25
a. Souvenir sheet of 6, #1045-1050 19.00 19.00
Nos. 1045-1050 (6) 11.60 5.50

Souvenir Sheet

1051 A334 7500fr multi 12.00 9.75

Nos. 1045-1050 exist in souvenir sheets of one.

Entertainers A335

1992, Apr. 29
1052 A335 100fr Ryuichi Sakamoto .20 .20
1053 A335 350fr John Lennon .60 .25
1054 A335 800fr Bruce Lee 1.50 .50
1055 A335 900fr Sammy Davis, Jr. 1.75 .60
1056 A335 1250fr John Wayne 1.90 .80
1057 A335 2500fr James Dean 3.50 1.60
Nos. 1052-1057 (6) 9.45 3.95

Souvenir Sheet

1058 A335 3000fr Clark Gable & Vivien Leigh 5.25 2.00

Nos. 1052-1057 exist in souvenir sheets of one.

Fight Against AIDS — A336

1990 Sports Festival — A338

Reforestation — A337

1992, July 29 **Litho.** *Perf. 12*
1059 A336 140fr lil rose & black .40 .20

Dated 1991.

1992, July 29 **Litho.** *Perf. 12*
1060 A337 140fr black & green .30 .20

Dated 1991.

1992, Aug. 20
1061 A338 140fr multicolored .35 .20

Dated 1991.

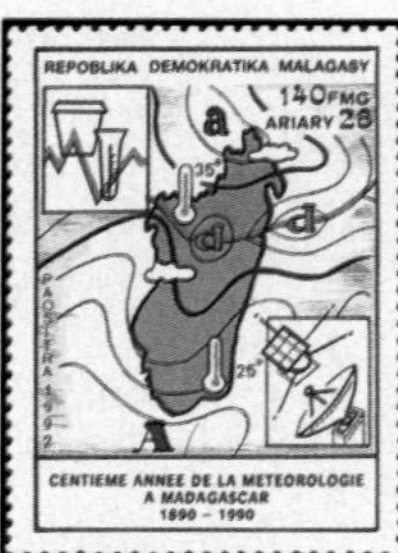

Meteorology in Madgascar, Cent. A339

1992, Nov. 10 Litho. *Perf. 12x12½*

1062 A339 140fr multicolored .40 .20

Fruit — A341

Perf. 12½x12, 12x12½

1992, May 27 Litho.

1064 A341 10fr Litchis .30 .20
1065 A341 50fr Oranges .30 .20
1066 A341 60fr Apples .35 .20
1067 A341 140fr Peaches .50 .25
1068 A341 555fr Bananas, vert. 1.25 .45
1069 A341 800fr Avocados, vert. 1.75 .60
1070 A341 1400fr Mangoes, vert. 3.00 1.25

Size: 89x70mm

Imperf

1071 A341 1600fr Mixed fruit 3.25 1.40
Nos. 1064-1071 (8) 10.70 4.55

For surcharges, see Nos. 1477, 1486.

1992 Summer Olympics, Barcelona A342

1992, June 30 *Perf. 11½*

1072 A342 65fr Women's gymnastics .20 .20
1073 A342 70fr High jump .20 .20
1074 A342 120fr Archery .25 .20
1075 A342 140fr Cycling .30 .20
1076 A342 675fr Weight lifting 1.10 .45
1077 A342 720fr Boxing 1.10 .50
1078 A342 1200fr Canoeing 1.75 .75

Imperf

Size: 90x70mm

1078A A342 1600fr Volleyball 3.00 1.40
Nos. 1072-1078A (8) 7.90 3.90

Litho. & Embossed

Perf. 13½

1079 A342 5000fr Judo 8.00

For surcharge, see No. 1473A.

Butterflies — A344

Designs: 15fr, Eusemia bisma. 35fr, Argema mittrei, vert. 65fr, Alcidis aurora. 140fr, Agarista agricola. 600fr, Trogonoptera croesus. 850fr, Trogonodtera priamus. 1300fr, Pereute leucodrosime. 1500fr, Chrysirridia madagaskariensis.

Perf. 12½x12, 12x12½

1992, June 24 Litho.

1080 A344 15fr multicolored .20 .20
1081 A344 35fr multicolored .20 .20
1082 A344 65fr multicolored .45 .20
1083 A344 140fr multicolored .70 .20
1084 A344 600fr multicolored 1.50 .45
1085 A344 850fr multicolored 2.00 .60
1086 A344 1300fr multicolored 2.50 .85

Imperf

Size: 70x90mm

1087 A344 1500fr multicolored 4.75 1.50
Nos. 1080-1087 (8) 12.30 4.20

For surcharge, see No. 1485.

Anniversaries and Events — A345

Designs: 500fr, Jean-Henri Dunant, delivery of Red Cross supplies. 640fr, Charles de Gaulle, battle of Bir Hacheim. 1025fr, Brandenburg Gate, people on Berlin wall. 1500fr, Village health clinic, Rotary, Lions emblems. 3000fr, Konrad Adenauer. 3500fr, Dirigible LZ4, hanger on Lake Constance, Ferdinand von Zeppelin. 7500fr, Wolfgang Amadeus Mozart at piano, palace, cathedral in Salzburg.

1992, Dec. 8 Litho. *Perf. 13½*

1088 A345 500fr multicolored .70 .30
1089 A345 640fr multicolored .90 .45
1090 A345 1025fr multicolored 1.50 .75
1091 A345 1500fr multicolored 2.00 1.00
1092 A345 3000fr multicolored 4.25 2.00
1093 A345 3500fr multicolored 5.00 2.50
Nos. 1088-1093 (6) 14.35 7.00

Souvenir Sheet

1094 A345 7500fr multicolored 10.00 5.00

Intl. Red Cross (#1088). Battle of Bir Hacheim, 50th anniv. (#1089). Brandenburg Gate, bicent. and destruction of Berlin Wall, 3rd anniv. (#1090). Konrad Adenauer, 25th death anniv. (#1092). Ferdinand von Zeppelin, 75th death anniv. (#1093). Mozart, death bicent. (in 1991), (#1094).

For overprint see No. 1146.

1994 World Cup Soccer Championships, U.S. — A346

Soccer players, Georgia landmarks: 140fr, Ficklin Home, Macon. 640fr, Herndon Home, Atlanta. 1025fr, Cultural Center, Augusta. 5000fr, Old Governor's Mansion, Milledgeville. 7500fr, Player, stars, stripes.

1992, Dec. 15 Litho. *Perf. 13½*

1095 A346 140fr multicolored .20 .20
1096 A346 640fr multicolored .90 .45
1097 A346 1025fr multicolored 1.40 .75
1098 A346 5000fr multicolored 7.00 3.50
Nos. 1095-1098 (4) 9.50 4.90

Souvenir Sheet

1099 A346 7500fr multicolored 10.25 5.25

Miniature Sheet

Inventors and Inventions — A347

No. 1100: a, Gutenberg (1394?-1468), printing press. b, Newton (1642-1727), telescope. c, John Dalton (1766-1844), atomic theory. d, Louis-Jacques-Mande Daguerre (1789-1851), photographic equipment. e, Faraday (1791-1867), electric motor. f, Orville (1871-1948), Wilbur Wright (1867-1912), motor-powered airplane. g, Bell (1847-1922), telephone. h, Edison (1847-1931), phonograph. i, Benz (1844-1929), motor-driven vehicle. j, Charles Parsons (1854-1931), steam turbine. k, Diesel (1858-1913), Diesel engine. l, Marconi, radio. m, Auguste-Marie-Louis Lumiere (1862-1954), Louis-Jean Lumiere (1864-1948), motion pictures. n, Oberth (1894-1989), rocketry. o, John W. Mauchly (1907-1980), John P. Eckert, electronic computer. p, Arthur Schawlow, laser.

1993, Apr. 27

1100 A347 500fr Sheet of 16, #a.-p. 11.00 5.50

Dated 1990.

Transportation — A348

No. 1101 — Race cars: a, 20fr, 1956 Bugatti. b, 20fr, 1968 Ferrari. c, 140fr, 1962 Lotus MK25. d, 140fr, 1970 Matra. e, 1250fr, 1963 Porsche. f, 1250fr, 1980 Ligier JS11. g, 3000fr, 1967 Honda. h, 3000fr, 1992 B192 Benetton.

No. 1102 — Locomotives: a, 20fr, C62, Japan, 1948. b, 20fr, SZD, USSR, 1975. c, 140fr, MU A1A-A1A, Norway, 1954. d, 140fr, Series 26 2-D-2, Africa, 1982. e, 1250fr, Amtrak Metroliner, US, 1967. f, 1250fr, VIA, Canada, 1982. g, 3000fr, Diesel, Union Pacific RR, US, 1969. h, 3000fr, Atlantic, TGV, France, 1990.

1993, Mar. 23

1101 A348 Block of 8, #a.-h. 12.00 6.00
1102 A348 Block of 8, #a.-h. 12.00 6.00

Dated 1990.

Wildlife — A349

No. 1103 — Birds: a, 45fr, Coua verreauxi. b, 45fr, Asio helvola hova. c, 60fr, Coua cristata. d, 60fr, Euryceros prevostii. e, 140fr, Coua gigas. f, 140fr, Foudia madagascariensis. g, 3000fr, Falculea palliata. h, 3000fr, Eutriorchis astur.

No. 1104 — Butterflies: a, 45fr, Chrysiridia madagascariensis. b, 45fr, Hypolimnas misippus. c, 60fr, Charaxes antamboulou. d, 60fr, Papilio antenor. e, 140fr, Hypolimnas dexithea. f, 140fr, Charaxes andranodorus. g, 3000fr, Euxanthe madagascariensis. h, 3000fr, Papilio grosesmithi.

1993, May 27

1103 A349 Block of 8, #a.-h. 8.75 4.25
1104 A349 Block of 8, #a.-h. 8.75 4.25

Dated 1991.

Intl. Conference on Nutrition, Rome — A350

1992, Nov. 3

1105 A350 500fr multicolored 1.00 .40

Automobiles — A351

1993, Jan. 28 Litho. *Perf. 12*

1106 A351 20fr BMW .20 .20
1107 A351 40fr Toyota .20 .20
1108 A351 60fr Cadillac .20 .20
1109 A351 65fr Volvo .20 .20
1110 A351 140fr Mercedes Benz .20 .20
1111 A351 640fr Ford 1.00 .50
1112 A351 3000fr Honda 5.00 2.50

Size: 90x70mm

Imperf

1113 A351 2000fr Renault 3.00 1.50
Nos. 1106-1113 (8) 10.00 5.50

Birds — A352

Designs: 50fr, Anodorhynchus hyacinthinus. 60fr, Nymphicus hollandicus. 140fr, Melopsittacus undulatus. 500fr, Aratinga jandaya. 675fr, Melopsittacus undulatus, diff. 800fr, Cyanoramphus novaezelandiae. 1750fr, Nestor notabilis. 2000fr, Ara militaris.

1993, Feb. 24

1114 A352 50fr multicolored .40 .20
1115 A352 60fr multicolored .40 .20
1116 A352 140fr multicolored .50 .20
1117 A352 500fr multicolored 1.75 .45
1118 A352 675fr multicolored 2.50 .65
1119 A352 800fr multicolored 2.75 .70
1120 A352 1750fr multicolored 6.00 1.50

Size: 71x91mm

Imperf

1121 A352 2000fr multicolored 5.00 2.00
Nos. 1114-1121 (8) 19.30 5.90

For surcharges, see Nos. 1473B, 1488.

Mollusks A353

1993, Feb. 3

1122 A353 40fr Turbo marmoratus .20 .20
1123 A353 60fr Mitra mitra .20 .20
1124 A353 65fr Argonauta argo .20 .20
1125 A353 140fr Conus textile .30 .20
1126 A353 500fr Aplysia depilans 1.10 .45
1127 A353 675fr Harpa amouretta 1.50 .70
1128 A353 2500fr Cypraea tigris 4.50 2.25

Size: 70x90mm

Imperf

1129 A353 2000fr Architectonica maxima 5.00 1.75
Nos. 1122-1129 (8) 13.00 5.95

For surcharge, see No. 1478.

Boat, Barges, Pangalanes Canal A354

1993, Jan. 29 Litho. *Perf. 12*

1130 A354 140fr multicolored .40 .25

Miniature Sheet

Ships A355

No. 1131: a, 5fr, Egyptian ship. b, 5fr, Mediterranean galley. c, 5fr, Great Western, England, 1837. d, 5fr, Mississippi River sidewheeler, US, 1850. e, 15fr, Bireme, Phoenicia. f, 15fr, Viking long ship. g, 15fr, Clermont, US, 1806. h, 15fr, Pourquoi-pas, France, 1936. i, 140fr, Santa Maria, Spain, 1492. j, 140fr, HMS Victory, England, 1765. k, 140fr, Fast motor yacht, Monaco. l, 140fr, Bremen, Germany, 1950. m, 10,000fr, Sovereign of the Seas, England, 1637. n, 10,000fr, Cutty Sark, England, 1869. o, 10,000fr, Savannah, US, 1959. p, 10,000fr, Condor, Australia.

1993, Apr. 6 Litho. *Perf. 13½*
1131 A355 Sheet of 16, #a.-p. 50.00 25.00

Miniature Sheet

Nobel Prize Winners in Physics, Chemistry and Medicine A356

No. 1132: a, Albert Einstein, Niels Bohr. b, Wolfgang Pauli, Max Born. c, Joseph Thomson, Johannes Stark. d, Otto Hahn, Hideki Yukawa. e, Owen Richardson, William Shockley. f, Albert Michelson, Charles Townes. g, Wilhelm Wien, Lev Landau. h, Karl Braun, Sir Edward Appleton. i, Percy Bridgman, Nikolai Semenov. j, Sir William Ramsay, Glenn Seaborg. k, Otto Wallach, Hermann Staudinger. l, Richard Synge, Alex Theorell. m, Thomas Morgan, Hermann Muller. n, Allvar Gullstrand, Willem Einthoven. o, Sir Charles Sherrington, Otto Loewi. p, Jules Bordet, Sir Alexander Fleming.

1993, Mar. 11
1132 A356 500fr Sheet of 16, #a.-p. 11.00 5.50

Alex misspelled on No. 1132l.

Miniature Sheet

Lemurs — A357

No. 1133: a, 60fr, Hapalemur simus. b, 150fr, Propithecus diadema. c, 250fr Indri indri. d, 350fr, Varecia variegata.

1992, Oct. 9 Litho. *Perf. 13½*
1133 A357 Sheet of 4, #a.-d. 5.50 2.00

World Post Day.

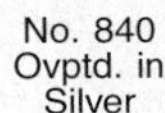

No. 840 Ovptd. in Silver

1993, Sept. 28 Litho. *Perf. 13½*
1134 A276 550fr multicolored *3.75 1.90*

Exists in souvenir sheet of 1.

No. 874 Ovptd. in Silver with Guitar and "THE ELVIS'S GUITAR / 15th ANNIVERSARY OF HIS DEATH / 1977-1992" in English or French

1993, Sept. 28
1135 A287 1500fr English ovpt. 2.50 1.10
1136 A287 1500fr French ovpt. 2.50 1.10
a. Pair, #1135-1136 5.00 2.25

No. 1135 exists in souvenir sheet of 1.

Nos. 945-948 Ovptd. in Gold

1993, Sept. 28
1137 A309 350fr multicolored .50 .30
1138 A309 1000fr multicolored 1.50 .75
1139 A309 1500fr multicolored 2.25 1.25
1140 A309 2500fr multicolored 3.75 1.90
Nos. 1137-1140 (4) 8.00 4.20

Nos. 974-978 Ovptd. in Gold

1993, Sept. 28
1141 A315 350fr multicolored .50 .25
1142 A315 1000fr multicolored 1.50 .75
1143 A315 1500fr multicolored 2.25 1.10
1144 A315 2500fr multicolored 3.75 1.90
Nos. 1141-1144 (4) 8.00 4.00

Souvenir Sheet

1145 A315 3000fr multicolored 4.75 2.50

No. 1088 Overprinted in Red

1993, Sept. 28
1146 A345 500fr multicolored 3.50 1.75

Exists in souvenir sheet of 1, overprinted in red or green.

Miniature Sheet

Commercial Airlines — A358

No. 1147: a, 10fr, Lufthansa, Germany. b, 10fr, Air France. c, 10fr, Air Canada. d. 10fr, ANA, Japan. e, 60fr, British Airways. f, 60fr, DO-X, Germany. g, 60fr, Shinmeiwa, Japan. h, 60fr, Royal Jordanian. i, 640fr, Alitalia, Italy. j, 640fr, Hydro 2000, France-Europe. k, 640fr, Boeing 314 Clipper, US. l, 640fr, Air Madagascar. m, 5000fr, Emirates Airlines, United Arab Emirates n, 5000fr, Scandinavian Airways. o, 5000fr, KLM, Netherlands. p, 5000fr, Air Caledonia.

1993, Nov. 22 Litho. *Perf. 13½*
1147 A358 Sheet of 16, #a.-p. 30.00 15.00

Dated 1990.

Miniature Sheet

Painters — A359

No. 1148: a, 50fr, Da Vinci. b, 50fr, Titian. c, 50fr, Rembrandt. d, 50fr, J.M.W. Turner (1775-1851). e, 640fr, Michelangelo. f, 640fr, Rubens. g, 640fr, Goya. h, 640fr, Delacroix (1798-1863). i, 1000fr, Monet. j, 1000fr, Gauguin. k, 1000fr, Toulouse Lautrec (1864-1901). l, 1000fr, Dali (1904-89). m, 2500fr, Renoir. n, 2500fr, Van Gogh. o, 2500fr, Picasso. p, 2500fr, Andy Warhol.

1993, May 10
1148 A359 Sheet of 16, #a.-p. 22.50 11.50

The local currency on Nos. 1148m-1148p is obliterated by a black overprint.

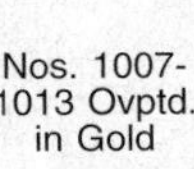

Nos. 1007-1013 Ovptd. in Gold

No. 841 Ovptd. in Metallic Green

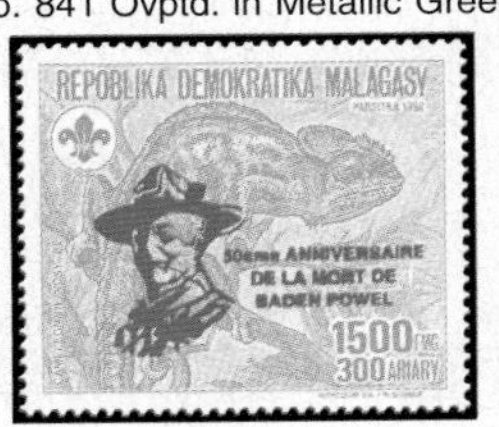

1993, Sept. 28 Litho. *Perf. 13½*
1149 A329 140fr multicolored .20 .20
1150 A329 500fr multicolored .65 .30
1151 A329 640fr multicolored .90 .40
1152 A329 1025fr multicolored 1.25 .60
1153 A329 1140fr multicolored 1.50 .75
1154 A276 1500fr multicolored 2.00 1.00
1155 A329 3500fr multicolored 4.50 2.25
Nos. 1149-1155 (7) 11.00 5.50

Souvenir Sheet

1156 A329 4500fr multicolored 6.00 3.00

Fauna A360

No. 1157 — Dogs: a, 40fr, Golden retriever. b, 140fr, Fox terrier. c, 40fr, Coton de tulear. d, 140fr, Langhaar.

No. 1158 — Cats: a, 40fr, Birman. b, 140fr, Egyptian. c, 40fr, European creme. d, 140fr, Rex du Devon.

No. 1159 — Reptiles: a, 1000fr, Phelsuma madagascariensis. b, 2000fr, Cameleon de parson. c, 1000fr, Laticauda laticaudate. d, 2000fr, Testudo radiata.

No. 1160 — Beetles: a, 1000fr, Euchroea spininasuta. b, 2000fr, Orthophagus minnulus klug. c, 1000fr, Helictopleurus radicollis. d, 2000fr, Euchroea coelestis.

1993, Dec. 7 Litho. *Perf. 13½*
1157 A360 Block of 4, #a.-d. .50 .25
1158 A360 Block of 4, #a.-d. .50 .25
1159 A360 Block of 4, #a.-d. 8.00 4.00
1160 A360 Block of 4, #a.-d. 8.00 4.00
e. Sheet of 16, #1157-1160 18.00 8.50

Dated 1991.

Nos. 934-938 Ovptd. in Metallic Blue
Nos. 939-939B Ovptd. in Metallic Red Lilac

1993, Sept. 28
1161 A305 250fr multicolored .35 .20
1162 A305 350fr multicolored .50 .25
1163 A305 1000fr multicolored 1.50 .75
1164 A305 1500fr multicolored 2.25 1.10
1165 A305 2500fr multicolored 3.75 1.90
Nos. 1161-1165 (5) 8.35 4.20

Souvenir Sheet

1166 A305 3000fr multi 4.50

Litho. & Embossed
Perf. 13½

1166A A305 5000fr gold & multi 8.00

Souvenir Sheet

1166B A305 5000fr gold & multi 8.00

Nos. 1161-1165 exist in souvenir sheets of 1, and in a sheet containing Nos. 1161-1165 plus label.

A number has been reserved for an additional value in this set.

Marine Life — A361

No. 1167 — Shells: a, 15fr, Chicoreus torrefactus. b, 15fr, Fasciolaria filamentosa. c, 30fr, Stellaria solaris. d, 30fr, Harpa ventricosa lamarck.

No. 1168 — Crustaceans: a, 1250fr, Panulirus (#1167c). b, 1250fr, Stenopus hispidus (#1167d). c, 1500fr, Pagure. d, 1500fr, Bernard l'hermite (#1168b).

No. 1169 — Fish: a, 15fr, Pigopytes diacanthus. b, 15fr, Coelacanth latimeria chalumnae. c, 30fr, Ostracion cyanurus. d, 30fr, Coris gaimardi. e, 1250fr, Balistapus undulatus. f, 1250fr, Forcipiger longirostris. g,

1500fr, Adioryx diadema. h, 1500fr, Pterois lunulata.

1993, Nov. 26 ***Perf. 13½***

1167 A361 Block of 4, #a.-d. .20 .20
1168 A361 Block of 4, #a.-d. 7.25 3.50
1169 A361 Block of 8, #a.-h. 7.25 3.50
i. Sheet of 16, #1167-1169 16.50 7.50

Dated "1991."

Flora — A362

No. 1170 — Orchids: a, 45fr, Oceonia oncidiflora. b, 60fr, Cymbidella rhodochica. c, 140fr, Vanilla planifolia. d, 3000fr, Phaius humblotii.

No. 1171 — Fruits: a, 45fr, Artocarpus altilis. b, 60fr, Eugenia malaceensis. c, 140fr, Jambosa domestica. d, 3000fr, Papaya.

No. 1172 — Mushrooms: a, 45fr, Russula annulata. b, 60fr, Lactarius claricolor. c, 140fr, Russula tuberculosa. d, 3000fr, Russula fistulosa.

No. 1173 — Vegetables: a, 45fr, Sweet potatoes. b, 60fr, Yams. c, 140fr, Avocados. d, 3000fr, Mangoes.

1993, Dec. 15 **Litho.** ***Perf. 13***

1170 A362 Strip of 4, #a.-d. 4.25 2.25
1171 A362 Strip of 4, #a.-d. 4.25 2.25
1172 A362 Strip of 4, #a.-d. 4.25 2.25
1173 A362 Strip of 4, #a.-d. 4.25 2.25
e. Sheet of 16, #1170-1173 18.00 9.00

1994 Winter Olympics, Lillehammer A362a

Designs: 140fr, Biathlon. 1250fr, Ice hockey. 2000fr, Figure skating. 2500fr, Slalom skiing. 5000fr, Downhill skiing. #1173K, Ski jumping. #1173L, Speed skating.

1994, Jan. 19 **Litho.** ***Perf. 13***

1173F-1173I A362a Set of 4 *18.50 9.25*

Souvenir Sheet

1173J A362a 5000fr multi *7.25 3.50*

Litho. & Embossed

1173K A362a 10,000fr gold & multi 13.00

Souvenir Sheet

1173L A362a 10,000fr gold & multi 13.00

No. 1173K exists in a souvenir sheet of 1.
For overprints see # 1288A-1288E.

1996 Summer Olympics, Atlanta — A362b

Scene in Atlanta, event: 640fr, 1892 Windsor Hotel Americus, dressage. 1000fr, Covington Courthouse, women's shot put. 1500fr, Carolton Community Activities Center, table tennis. 3000fr, Newman Historic Commercial Court Square, soccer.

7500fr, Relay race runner. No. 1173R, Pole vault, vert. No. 1173S, Hurdles, vert.

1994, Jan. 19

1173M-1173P A362b Set of 4 *19.50 9.50*

Souvenir Sheet

1173Q A362b 7500fr multi *27.00 13.50*

Litho. & Embossed

1173R A362b 5000fr gold & multi 7.50

Souvenir Sheet

1173S A362b 5000fr gold & multi 8.00

Prehistoric Animals — A363

Designs: 35fr, Dinornis maximus, vert. 40fr, Ceratosaurus, vert. 140fr, Mosasavrus, vert. 525fr, Protoceratops. 640fr, Styvacosaurus. 755fr, Smilodon. 1800fr, Uintatherium.

2000fr, Tusks of mammuthus, trees, vert.

1995, Feb. 23 **Litho.** ***Perf. 12***

1174-1180 A363 Set of 7 4.50 4.50

Souvenir Sheet

1181 A363 2000fr multicolored 3.50 1.50

For surcharge see #1474A.

Wild Animals A364

Designs: 10fr, Panthera pardus. 30fr, Martes. 60fr, Vulpes vulpes. 120fr, Canis lupus. 140fr (No. 1186), Fennecus zerda. 140fr (No. 1187), Panthera leo. 3500fr, Uncia uncia.

2000fr, Panthera onca.

1995, Mar. 21

1182-1188 A364 Set of 7 5.00 5.00

Souvenir Sheet

1189 A364 2000fr multicolored 3.50 3.50

D-Day Landings, Normandy, 50th Anniv. — A365

No. 1190: a, 3000fr, American troops, flamethrower. b, 1500fr, Coming ashore. c, 3000fr, Explosion, German commander pointing.

No. 1191 — Liberation of Paris, 50th anniv. : a, 3000fr, Notre Dame, resistance fighters, crowd. b, 1500fr, Arch de Triomphe, woman cheering. c, 3000fr, Eiffel Tower, parade, French troops.

1994 ***Perf. 13½***

1190 A365 Strip of 3, #a.-c. 6.75 3.50
1191 A365 Strip of 3, #a.-c. 6.75 3.50

Nos. 1190b, 1191b are 30x47mm. Nos. 1190-1191 are continuous design.

Aquarium Fish A366

Designs: 10fr, Pomacanthus imperator. 30fr, Betta splendens. 45fr, Trichogaster leeri. 95fr, Labrus bimaculatus. No. 1196, 140fr, Synodontis nigreventris. No. 1197, 140fr, Cichlasoma biocellatum. 3500fr, Fudulus heteroclitus.

2000fr, Carassius auratus, vert.

1994, June 28 **Litho.** ***Perf. 12½x12***

1192-1198 A366 Set of 7 5.75 5.75

Souvenir Sheet

Perf. 12x12½

1199 A366 2000fr multicolored 3.25 3.25

Modern Locomotives — A367

Designs: 5fr, Superviem Odoriko. 15fr, Morrison Knudsen Corporation. 140fr, ER-200. 265fr, General Motors. 300fr, New Jersey Transit. 575fr, Siemens Inter-City Express. 2500fr, Sweden's Fast Train.

2000fr, Alstham T60.

1993, Nov. 10 ***Perf. 12***

1200-1206 A367 Set of 7 5.00 4.50

Souvenir Sheet

1207 A367 2000fr multicolored 3.25 1.50

For surcharge, see No. 1475A, 1477A.

Cathedrals A368

Cathedral, location: 10fr, Antwerp, Belgium. 100fr, Cologne, Germany. 120fr, Antsirabe, Masdagascar. 140fr, Kremlin, Moscow. 525fr, Notre Dame, Paris. 605fr, Toledo, Spain. 2500fr, St. Stephens, Vienna.

2000fr, Westminster Abbey, London.

1995, Feb. 14 ***Perf. 12x12½***

1208-1214 A368 Set of 7 4.50 4.50

Souvenir Sheet

1215 A368 2000fr multicolored 2.75 2.75

Dated 1994.

No. 1215 is inscribed with country name only in the sheet margin.

For surcharge, see No. 1472B.

Insects — A369

Designs: 20fr, Necrophorus tomentosus. 60fr, Dynastes tityus. 140fr, Megaloxantha bicolor. 605fr, Calosoma sycophanta. 720fr, Chrysochroa mirabilis. 1000fr, Crioceris asparaqi. 1500fr, Cetonia aurata.

2000fr, Goliathus goliathus.

1994, Feb. 2 ***Perf. 12***

1216-1222 A369 Set of 7 5.50 5.50

Size: 85x58mm

Imperf

1223 A369 2000fr multicolored 2.25 1.25

For surcharge, see No. 1478B.

Miniature Sheet

PHILAKOREA '94 — A370

No. 1224: a, 100fr, John Lennon, Ella Fitzgerald. b, 140fr, Marilyn Monroe, Elvis Presley. c, 550fr, U.S. Pres. Bill Clinton, Louis Armstrong.

1995, Feb. 23 ***Perf. 12***

1224 A370 Sheet of 2 each, #a.-c. + 3 labels 4.75 2.25

Ancient Art & Architecture — A371

Designs: No. 1225, 350fr, Statue of Augustus, vert. No. 1226, 350fr, Statue, Land Surveyor, vert. No. 1227, 350fr, Painting, "Child of Thera," vert. No. 1228, 350fr, Sarcophagous, Cerveteri and Wife, vert. No. 1229, 350fr, Statue, Athena of Fidia, vert. No. 1230, 405fr, Colosseum, Rome. No. 1231, 405fr, Mask of Agamemnon, vert. No. 1232, 405fr, Forum of Caesar. No. 1233, 405fr, She-Wolf suckling Romulus & Remus. No. 1234, 405fr, Parthenon, Athens. No. 1235, 525fr, Carthaginian mask, vert. No. 1236, 525fr, Bust of Emperor Tiberius, vert. No. 1237, 525fr, Statue of Alexandar the Great, vert. No. 1238, 525fr, Detail, Taormina Theater, vert. No. 1239, 525fr, Denarius of Caesar. No. 1240, 605fr, Forum, Pompeii, vert. No. 1241, 605fr, Bronze statue, Riace, vert. No. 1242, 605fr, Venus de Milo, vert. No. 1243, 605fr, Bronze statue, Archer, vert. No. 1244, 605fr, Pont Du Gard Aqueduct, Nimes.

1994 **Litho.** ***Perf. 13½***

1225-1244 A371 Set of 20 6.50 3.25

Elvis Presley (1935-77) A371a

Design: No. 1244B, "The King," "Presley," Elvis wearing black.

Litho. & Embossed

1994, June 8 ***Perf. 13½***

1244A A371a 10,000fr gold & multi 12.00

Souvenir Sheet

1244B A371a 10,000fr gold & multi 12.00

Exists in sheets of 4.

The Stuff of Heroes, by Philip Kaufman — A372

No. 1245: a, 140fr, Astronaut. b, 140fr, Astronaut up close, walking. c, 5000fr, Spacecraft, astronaut.

1994
1245 A372 Strip of 3, #a.-c. 3.75 1.90

Motion pictures, cent. No. 1245 is a continuous design and exists in souvenir sheet of 1 with scenes from the film "Blade Runner."
No. 1245c is 60x47mm.

Intl. Olympic Committee, Cent. — A373

No. 1246: a, 2500fr, Flag. b, 2500fr, Olympic flame. c, 3500fr, Pierre de Coubertin.

1994
1246 A373 Strip of 3, #a.-c. 5.75 2.75

No. 1246 is a continuous design and exists in souvenir sheet of 1. No. 1246c is 60x47mm.

ILO, 75th Anniv. — A374

1994 Litho. ***Perf. 13½***
1247 A374 140fr multicolored .25 .20

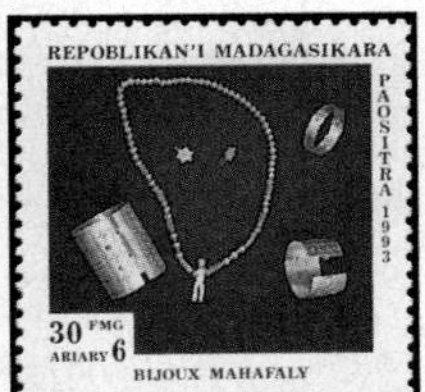

A374a

Designs: 30fr, Mahafaly jewelry. 60fr, Sakalava fork and spoon. 140fr, Antandroy jewelry. 430fr, Sakalava jewelry. 580fr, Antaimoro Ambalavao paper. 1250fr Sakalava jewelry, diff. 1500fr, Inlaid cabinet.
2000fr, Ampanihy tapestry.

1995, Feb. 2 Litho. ***Perf. 11¼***
1247A A374a 30fr multi
1247B A374a 60fr multi
1247C A374a 140fr multi
1247D A374a 430fr multi
1247E A374a 580fr multi
1247F A374a 1250fr multi
1247G A374a 1500fr multi

Souvenir Sheet
Imperf

1247H A374a 2000fr multi

For surcharge, see No. 1472.

Modern Ships — A375

Ships: 45fr, Russian car ferry. 50fr, Australian cargo. 100fr, Japanese cruise. 140fr, US cruise. 300fr, English hovercraft. 350fr, Danish cargo. 3000fr, Korean container ship.
2000fr, Finnish car ferry, vert.

1994 Litho. ***Perf. 12***
1248-1254 A375 Set of 7 4.50 4.50

Souvenir Sheet
1255 A375 2000fr multicolored 3.25 3.25

1994 World Cup Soccer Championships, U.S. — A375a

Player at: No. 1255A, Left. No. 1255B, Right.

Litho. & Embossed
1994, Aug. 24 ***Perf. 13½***
1255A A375a 10,000fr gold & multi 12.00

Souvenir Sheet
1255B A375a 10,000fr gold & multi 12.00

A377

A378

Sports: 5fr, Hurdles. 140fr, Boxing. 525fr, Gymnastics. 550fr, Weight lifting. 640fr, Swimming. 720fr, Equestrian. 1500fr, Soccer.
2000fr, Running, horiz.

1995, Apr. 4 Litho. ***Perf. 12***
1264-1270 A377 Set of 7 5.00 2.50

Souvenir Sheet
1271 A377 2000fr multicolored 3.25 1.25

1993, Nov. 10 Litho. ***Perf. 12***

Orchids: 50fr, Paphiopedilum siamense. 65fr, Cypripedium calceolus. 70fr, Ophrys oestrifera. 140fr, Cephalanthera rubra. 300fr, Cypripedium macranthon. 640fr, Calanthe vestita. 2500fr, Cypripedium guttatum. 2000fr, Oncidium tigrinum.

1272-1278 A378 Set of 7 6.00 2.50

Size: 90x70mm
Imperf
1279 A378 2000fr multicolored 3.25 1.25

Sharks A379

Designs: 10fr, Galeocerdo cuvieri. 45fr, Pristiophorus japonicus. 140fr, Rhincodon typus. 270fr, Sphyrna zygaena. 600fr, Carcharhinus longimanus. 1200fr, Stegostoma tigrinum. 1500fr, Scapanorhynchus owstoni. 2000fr, Galeorhinus zyopterus.

1993, Sept. 22 ***Perf. 12***
1280-1286 A379 Set of 7 5.00 2.50

Size: 70x90mm
Imperf
1287 A379 2000fr multicolored 3.25 1.25

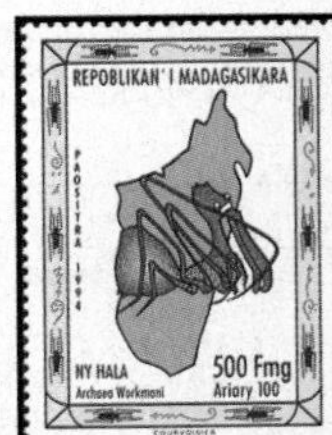

Archaea Workmani A380

1994 ***Perf. 15***
1288 A380 500fr multicolored 1.00 .75

Nos. 1173F-1173J Ovptd. With Names of Winners in Silver or Gold

1994, Aug. 30 Litho. ***Perf. 13***
1288A-1288D A362a Set of 4 *18.50 9.25*

Souvenir Sheet
1288E A362a 5000fr multi *7.25 3.50*

Overprinted in silver: 140fr, "M. BEDARD / CANADA." 1250fr, "MEDAILLE D'OR / SUEDE." 2000fr, "O. BAYUL / UKRAINE." 2500fr, "M. WASMEIER / ALLEMAGNE." 5000fr,
Overprinted in gold: 5000fr, "D. COMPAGNONI / ITALIE."

Marilyn Monroe (1926-62), Elvis Presley (1935-77) — A381

Scenes from films: No. 1289, 100fr, Gentlemen Prefer Blondes. No. 1290, 100fr, Clambake, Roustabout, Viva Las Vegas. 550fr, Some Like it Hot. 1250fr, Girls, Girls, Girls, King Creole. 5000fr, Niagara. 10,000fr, Double Trouble, Kid Gallahad, Speedway.

1995, Aug. 15 Litho. ***Perf. 13½***
1289-1294 A381 Set of 6 12.50 12.50

#1289-1294 exist in souvenir sheets of 1.

Motion Pictures, Cent. A382

Actor, film: No. 1295, 140fr, James Dean, Rebel Without a Cause. No. 1296, 140fr, Burt Lancaster, Vera Cruz. 5000fr, Elvis Presley, Speedway. 10,000fr, Marilyn Monroe, How to Marry a Millionaire.

1995, Aug. 16 Litho. ***Perf. 13½***
1295-1298 A382 Set of 4 11.00 11.00
a. Miniature sheet of 4, #1295-1298 *17.50 17.50*

#1295-1298 exist in souvenir sheets of 1.

Locusts A383

Designs: No. 1299, Assylidae, natural enemy of the locust. No. 1300, Locust eating corn, vert. No. 1301, Gathering locusts for consumption.

1995, Sept. 26 Litho. ***Perf. 13½***
1299 A383 140fr multicolored .90 .20
1300 A383 140fr multicolored .90 .20
1301 A383 140fr multicolored .90 .20
Nos. 1299-1301 (3) 2.70 .60

Malagasyan Bible, 160th Anniv. — A384

World Post Day — A385

1995, June 21 Litho. ***Perf. 15***
1302 A384 140fr multicolored .25 .20

1995, Oct. 9 ***Perf. 13½***
1303 A385 500fr multicolored .80 .35

Nos. 967-972 Ovptd. in Silver

1996, Jan. 21 Litho. ***Perf. 13½***
1304 A314 2000fr on No. 971 *3.50 1.75*
1304A A314 Sheet of 6, #b-g, 1304

No. 1304 exists in souvenir sheet of 1, overprinted in gold or silver. No. 1304A exists with gold overprint.

Death of Charles de Gaulle, 25th Anniv. A386

No. 1305: a, 100fr, World War I battle. b, 100fr, As President of France. c, 100fr, Brazzaville, 1940. d, 500fr, Pierre Brossolette, Churchill, De Gaulle. e, 500fr, Young woman. f, 500fr, Yak 9T, Gen. Leclerc. g, 1500fr, Liberation of Paris. h, 1500fr, De Gaulle as younger man. i, 1500fr, Jean Moulin, Free French barricade in Paris. j, 7500fr, Writing Tourbillon de L'Histoire, Colombey Les Deux Eglises. k, 7500fr, Giving speech as older diplomat. l, 7500fr, Doves, French flag, older De Gaulle standing on hilltop.

1996, Apr. 28 Litho. ***Perf. 13½***
1305 A386 Sheet of 12, #a.-l. 21.50 10.75

See design A390.

Famous People A387

Designs: 1500fr, Wilhelm Steinitz (1836-1900), American chess master. 1750fr, Emmanuel Lasker (1868-1941), German chess master. 2000fr, Enzo Ferrari (1898-1988), automobile designer. 2500fr, Thomas Stafford, American astronaut, A.A. Leonov, Russian cosmonaut. 3000fr, Jerry Garcia (d. 1995), musician. 3500fr, Ayrton Senna (1960-94), race car driver. 5000fr, Paul-Emile Victor (1907-95), polar explorer. 7500fr, Paul Harris (1868-1947), founder of Rotary Intl.

1996, Feb. 20

1306-1313 A387 Set of 8 20.00 10.00

#1306-1313 exist in souvenir sheets of 1.

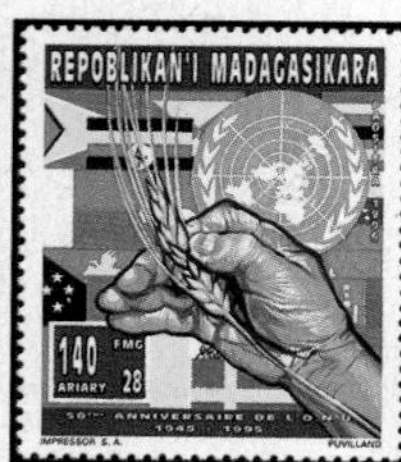

UN and UNICEF, 50th Anniv. A388

Designs: No. 1314, 140fr, Hand holding shaft of grain, UN emblem. No. 1315, 140fr, UN building, flags, map, woman feeding child. No. 1316, 140fr, Child holding plate of food, child holding UNICEF emblem. 7500fr, Two children, UNICEF emblem.

1996, Aug. 30

1314-1317 A388 Set of 4 5.25 2.50

#1314-1317 exist in souvenir sheets of 1.

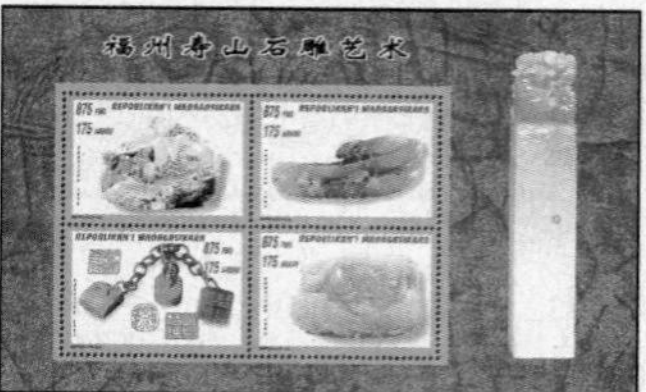

Jade — A389

No. 1318, 175fr: a, People on mountain. b, Carving of insect, leaves. c, Chops on a chain. d, Insect in stone.

1996, Apr. 20 Litho. *Perf. 13½*

1318 A389 Sheet of 4, #a.-d. 2.50 1.25

A390

No. #1319: Bruce Lee (1940-73), various portraits.

No. #1320: John Lennon (1940-80), various portraits.

No. 1321: Locomotives: a, Train going left. b, Train going right. c, ICE Train, Germany. d, Eurostar.

No. 1322: Louis Pasteur (1822-95), various portraits.

No. 1323: Francois Mitterrand (1916-96), various portraits.

No. 1324: Intl. Space Station: a, Shuttle Atlantis, MIR Space Station. b, MIR. c, Intl. Space Station. d, Shuttle, Alpha section of station.

1996 Litho. *Perf. 13½*

1319 A390 500fr Sheet of 4, #a.-d. 2.25 1.10

1320 A390 1500fr Sheet of 4, #a.-d. 3.75 1.90

1321 A390 1500fr Sheet of 4, #a.-d. 3.75 1.90

1322 A390 1750fr Sheet of 4, #a.-d. 4.25 2.10

1323 A390 2000fr Sheet of 4, #a.-d. 5.00 2.50

1324 A390 2500fr Sheet of 4, #a.-d. 6.25 3.00

Post Day — A396

Various local post offices: a, 500fr. b, 1000fr. c, 3500fr. d, 5000fr.

1996, Oct. 16 Litho. *Perf. 13½*

1325 A396 Sheet of 4, #a.-d. 6.25 3.00

Sports Cars — A397

No. 1326: a, Mercedes W196 driven by Juan Manuel Fangio. b, Porsche 911 Carrera. c, Porsche 917-30. d, Mercedes 600 SEC.

1996

1326 A397 3000fr Sheet of 4, #a.-d. 7.50 3.75

1996 Olympic Games, Atlanta

Perf. 11¾x11½

1996, Dec. 27 Litho.

Granite Paper

1326E A397a 140fr Judo

1326F A397a 140fr Tennis

UN, 50th Anniv. — A398

1995, Oct. 24 Litho. *Perf. 11½x11¾*

1327 A398 140fr Private sector promotion

1328 A398 500fr Lemur, tortoise

1330 A398 1500fr Grain stalks

An additional stamp exists in this set. The editors would like to examine it.

1998 Winter Olympics, Nagano A399

Designs: 160fr, Ice hockey. 350fr, Pairs figure skating. 5000fr, Biathlon. 7500fr, Freestyle skiing.

12,500fr, Speed skating.

1997 Litho. *Perf. 13½*

1331-1334 A399 Set of 4 6.75 3.50

Souvenir Sheet

1335 A399 12,500fr multicolored 6.50 3.25

No. 1335 contains one 42x60mm stamp.

1998 World Cup Soccer Championships, France — A400

Various soccer plays: 300fr, 1350fr, 3000fr, 10,000fr.

1997

1336-1339 A400 Set of 4 7.75 4.00

Souvenir Sheet

1340 A400 12,500fr Player, ball 6.50 3.25

No. 1340 contains one 42x60mm stamp.

Greenpeace, 25th Anniv. — A401

Views of Rainbow Warrior I: 1500fr, At anchor. 3000fr, Under sail. 3500fr, Going left, small raft. 5000fr, Going forward at full speed.

12,500fr, Under sail, vert.

1996, Apr. 16 Litho. *Perf. 13½*

1341-1344 A401 Set of 4 5.50 2.75

Souvenir Sheet

1345 A401 12,500fr multicolored 5.50 2.75

Dinosaurs — A402

No. 1346: a, Herrerasaurus, archaeopteryx. b, Segnosaurus, dimorphodon. c, Sauropelta, proavis.

No. 1347: a, Eudimorphodon, eustreptospondylus. b, Triceratops, rhamphorychus. c, Pteranodon, segnosaurus.

12,500fr, Tenontosaurus, deinonychus, vert.

1998, Feb. 25

1346 A402 1350fr Sheet of 3, #a.-c. 2.25 1.10

1347 A402 5000fr Sheet of 3, #a.-c. 8.00 4.00

Souvenir Sheet

1348 A402 12,500fr multicolored 6.50 3.25

Dated 1997.

Meteorites and Minerals — A403

No. 1349 — Meteorites: a, Iron, found in Chile. b, Iron, found in Alvord, Iowa. c, Silicate in lunar meteorite, found in Antarctica.

No. 1350 — Minerals: a, Agate, dioptase. b, Malachite, garnet. c, Chrysolile, wulfenite.

12,500fr, Mars meterorite, found in Antarctica.

1998, Feb. 25

1349 A403 3000fr Sheet of 3, #a.-c. 5.00 2.50

1350 A403 7500fr Sheet of 3, #a.-c. 12.00 6.00

Souvenir Sheet

1351 A403 12,500fr multicolored 6.50 3.25

Dated 1997.

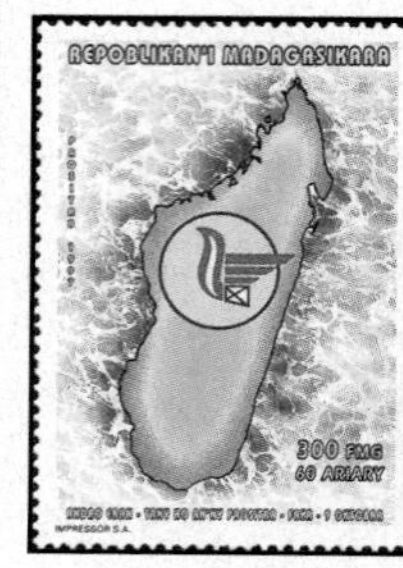

World Post Day — A404

1997, Oct. 21 Litho. *Perf. 13½*

1352 A404 300fr multicolored 5.50 2.75

Radio Nederland in Madagascar, 25th Anniv. — A404a

Perf. 11¾x11½

1997, Sept. 18 Litho.

Granite Paper

1352A A404a 500fr multi — —

Third Francophone Games — A404b

Background colors: 300fr, Light blue. 1850fr, Beige.

1997, Oct. 9 Litho. *Perf. 11½x11¾*

Granite Paper

1352B-1352C A404b Set of 2 1.75 1.75

For surcharge, see No. 1490.

Diana, Princess of Wales (1961-97) A405

No. 1353 — Diana wearing: a, High-collared white dress. b, Halter-style dress. c, Choker necklace, purple dress. d, Wide-brimmed hat. e, Jeweled choker necklace. f, White dress, no necklace. g, Black dress. h, White dress, pearls. i, Red dress.

No. 1354 — Portraits of Diana: a, Wearing jeweled necklace. b, With Pope John Paul II. c, Wearing beaded jacket. d, With Nelson Mandela. e, With man from India. f, With

Chalky Paper

66 A4 20c blk & vio ('23) 5.00 1.75
a. Ordinary paper 50.00 3.50
67 A4 25c red vio & ol vio ('29) 3.50 2.00
68 A4 30c yel & dl vio ('29) 4.00 4.00
69 A4 35c red, *yel*, ordinary paper ('28) 6.00 *24.00*
70 A4 35c dk vio & car ('31) 17.00 15.00
71 A4 50c org & blk ('24) 17.00 15.00
72 A4 50c blk, *bl grn* ('31) 5.50 2.50
73 A3 $1 gray grn & yel grn ('26) 22.50 *50.00*
a. $1 green & blue green 24.00 *95.00*
74 A3 $2 grn & car ('26) 32.00 *87.50*
75 A3 $5 grn & ultra ('25) 150.00 *200.00*
76 A3 $25 grn & org ('28) 1,200. *1,400.*
Nos. 49-75 (27) 307.60 *436.20*

1931-34

77 A4 $1 red & blk, *blue* 15.00 4.75
78 A4 $2 car & green, *yel* ('34) 55.00 50.00
79 A4 $5 car & green, *emer* ('34) 225.00 *240.00*
Nos. 77-79 (3) 295.00 *294.75*

FEDERATION OF MALAYA

GOVT. — Sovereign state in British Commonwealth of Nations
AREA — 50,700 sq. mi.
POP. — 7,139,000 (est. 1961)
CAPITAL — Kuala Lumpur

The Federation comprised the nine states of Johore, Pahang, Negri Sembilan, Selangor, Perak, Kedah, Perlis, Kelantan and Trengganu and the settlements of Penang and Malacca.

Malaya joined the Federation of Malaysia in 1963.

100 Sen (Cents) = 1 Dollar (1957)

Catalogue values for unused stamps in this section are for Never Hinged items.

The Peace Issue of 1946 8c stamp inscribed "MALAYAN UNION" was not issued.

Rubber Tapping — A5

Map of Federation — A6

Designs: 12c, Federation coat of arms. 25c, Tin dredge and flag.

Perf. 13x12½, 12½
Engr., Litho.

1957, May 5 **Wmk. 314**

80 A5 6c blue, red & yel 1.00 .30
a. Yellow omitted 85.00
81 A5 12c car & multi 1.75 1.10
82 A5 25c multicolored 3.75 .40
83 A6 30c dp claret & red org 1.50 .30
Nos. 80-83 (4) 8.00 2.10

Chief Minister Tunku Abdul Rahman and People of Various Races — A7

Perf. 12½

1957, Aug. 31 **Wmk. 4** **Engr.**

84 A7 10c brown .80 .35

Independence Day, Aug. 31.

United Nations Emblem — A8

Design: 30c, UN emblem, vert.

Perf. 13½, 12½

1958, Mar. 5 **Wmk. 314**

85 A8 12c rose red .45 *1.00*
86 A8 30c plum .65 *1.00*

Conf. of the Economic Commission for Asia and the Far East (ECAFE), Kuala Lumpur, Mar. 5-15.

Merdeka Stadium and Flag — A9

Tuanku Abdul Rahman, Paramount Ruler of Malaya — A10

Perf. 13½x14½, 14½x13½

1958, Aug. 31 **Photo.** **Wmk. 314**

87 A9 10c multicolored .30 .30
88 A10 30c multicolored .60 *.90*

1st anniv. of the Independence of the Federation of Malaya.

A11

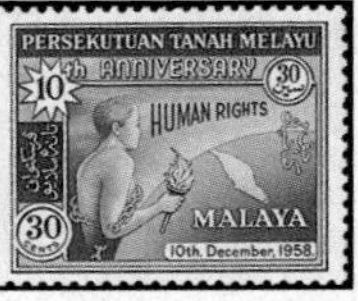

Torch of Freedom and Broken Chain — A12

Perf. 12½x13, 13x12½

1958, Dec. 10 **Litho.** **Wmk. 314**

89 A11 10c multicolored .25 .25

Photo.

90 A12 30c green .70 .70

10th anniv. of the signing of the Universal Declaration of Human Rights.

Mace and People — A13

WRY Emblem A14

Perf. 12½x13½

1959, Sept. 12 **Photo.** **Unwmk.**

91 A13 4c rose red .30 .30
92 A13 10c violet .30 .30
93 A13 25c yellow green .60 .40
Nos. 91-93 (3) 1.20 1.00

1st Federal Parliament of Malaya, inauguration.

Perf. 13½, 13

1960, Apr. 7 **Engr.** **Wmk. 314**

Design: 30c, Similar to 12c, vert.

94 A14 12c lilac .30 *.80*
95 A14 30c dark green .30 .30

World Refugee Year, 7/1/59-6/30/60.

Rubber Tree Seedling on Map of Malaya — A15

Tuanku Syed Putra — A16

Perf. 13x13½

1960, Sept. 19 **Litho.** **Unwmk.**

96 A15 6s red brn, grn & blk .20 *1.25*
97 A15 30s ultra, yel grn & blk .60 *.75*

15th meeting of the Intl. Rubber Study Group and the Natural Rubber Research Conference, Kuala Lumpur, Sept. 26-Oct. 1.

Perf. 13½x14½

1961, Jan. 4 **Photo.** **Wmk. 314**

98 A16 10s blue & black .30 .30

Installation of Tuanku Syed Putra of Perlis as Paramount Ruler (Yang di-Pertuan Agong.)

Colombo Plan Emblem — A17

Malaria Eradication Emblem — A18

1961, Oct. 30 **Unwmk.** ***Perf. 13½***

99 A17 12s rose pink & black .55 *3.25*
100 A17 25s brt yellow & black 1.10 *2.00*
101 A17 30s brt blue & black .90 *1.00*
Nos. 99-101 (3) 2.55 *6.25*

13th meeting of the Consultative Committee for Technical Co-operation in South and South East Asia, Kuala Lumpur, Oct. 30-Nov. 18.

Wmk. PTM Multiple (338)

1962, Apr. 7 ***Perf. 14x14½***

102 A18 25s orange brown .35 *.60*
103 A18 30s dull violet .35 .30
104 A18 50s ultramarine .60 *.80*
Nos. 102-104 (3) 1.30 *1.70*

WHO drive to eradicate malaria.

Palmyra Leaf A19

1962, July 21 **Photo.** ***Perf. 13½***

105 A19 10s violet & gldn brown .35 .35
106 A19 20s bluish grn & gldn brn 1.00 *1.25*
107 A19 50s car rose & gldn brn 2.25 2.25
Nos. 105-107 (3) 3.60 3.85

National Language Month. Watermark inverted on alternating stamps.

Children and their Future Shadows — A20

1962, Oct. 1 **Wmk. 338** ***Perf. 13½***

108 A20 10s bright rose lilac .20 .20
109 A20 25s ocher .70 *1.25*
110 A20 30s bright green 3.00 .20
Nos. 108-110 (3) 3.90 1.65

Free primary education introduced Jan. 1962.

Forms of Food Production and Ears of Wheat — A21

1963, Mar. 21 **Unwmk.** ***Perf. 11½***
Granite Paper

111 A21 25s lt ol grn & lilac rose 3.00 *4.00*
112 A21 30s dk car & lilac rose 3.25 1.75
113 A21 50s ultra & lilac rose 3.25 *4.00*
Nos. 111-113 (3) 9.50 9.75

FAO "Freedom from Hunger" campaign.

Cameron Highlands Dam and Pylon — A22

1963, June 26 **Wmk. 338** ***Perf. 14***

114 A22 20s purple & brt green .80 .25
115 A22 30s ultra & brt green 1.25 *1.50*

Opening of the Cameron Highlands hydroelectric plant.

Check listings for individual states for additional stamps inscribed "Malaya."

POSTAGE DUE STAMPS

D1

D2

Perf. 14½x14

1924-26 **Typo.** **Wmk. 4**

J1 D1 1c violet 4.75 *40.00*
J2 D1 2c black 2.25 7.00
J3 D1 4c green ('26) 3.25 *8.00*
J4 D1 8c red 6.00 *37.50*
J5 D1 10c orange 10.00 *17.50*
J6 D1 12c ultramarine 10.00 *27.50*
Nos. J1-J6 (6) 36.25 *137.50*

1936-38 ***Perf. 14½x14***

J7 D2 1c dk violet ('38) 7.00 1.10
J8 D2 4c yellow green 19.00 1.40
J9 D2 8c scarlet 9.00 5.00
J10 D2 10c yel orange 13.00 .50
J11 D2 12c blue violet 16.00 *17.50*
J12 D2 50c black ('38) 20.00 *8.00*
Nos. J7-J12 (6) 84.00 *33.50*

#J7-J12 were also used in Straits Settlements.

For overprints see #NJ1-NJ20, Malacca #NJ1-NJ6.

1945-49

J13 D2 1c reddish violet 2.50 2.25
J14 D2 3c yel green 5.00 6.00
J15 D2 5c org scarlet 4.50 *3.50*
J16 D2 8c yel org ('49) 9.00 *16.00*
J17 D2 9c yel orange 27.50 *50.00*

J18 D2 15c blue vio 77.50 *35.00*
J19 D2 20c dk blue ('48) 6.00 *10.00*
Nos. J13-J19 (7) 132.00 *122.75*

For surcharge see No. J34.

Catalogue values for unused stamps in this section, from this point to the end of the section, are for Never Hinged items.

1951-54 Wmk. 4 *Perf. 14*
J20 D2 1c dull violet ('52) .70 1.75
J21 D2 2c dk gray ('53) 1.25 2.25
J22 D2 3c green ('52) 28.00 15.00
J23 D2 4c dk brown ('53) .70 7.00
J24 D2 5c vermilion 50.00 13.00
J25 D2 8c yel orange 2.50 6.00
J26 D2 12c magenta ('54) 1.25 6.50
J27 D2 20c deep blue 7.00 6.75
Nos. J20-J27 (8) 91.40 58.25

Nos. J13-J27 were used throughout the Federation and in Singapore, later in Malaysia.

1957-63 *Perf. 12½*
Ordinary Paper
J21a D2 2c ('60) 2.50 *20.00*
b. 2c, chalky paper ('62) 1.75 *13.00*
J23a D2 4c ('60) 2.00 *21.00*
b. 4c, chalky paper ('62) 1.00 *18.00*
J26a D2 12c, chalky paper ('62) 3.25 *27.50*
J27a D2 20c 8.00 *29.00*
b. 20c, chalky paper ('63) 6.50 *40.00*
Nos. J21a-J27a (4) 15.75 *97.50*

1965 Wmk. 314 *Perf. 12*
J28 D2 1c plum 1.50 *16.00*
J29 D2 2c bluish black 1.10 *22.50*
J30 D2 4c brown 1.75 *16.00*
J31 D2 8c yel orange 2.50 *22.50*
J32 D2 12c magenta 6.50 *40.00*
J33 D2 20c dark blue 10.00 *50.00*
Nos. J28-J33 (6) 23.35 *167.00*

Nos. J28-J33 were used in Malaysia.

1964, Apr. 14 *Perf. 12½*
J28a D2 1c .50 *19.00*
J29a D2 2c 1.75 *16.00*
J30a D2 4c 1.00 *16.00*
J32a D2 12c 2.25 *22.50*
J33a D2 20c 3.00 *37.50*
Nos. J28a-J33a (5) 8.50 *111.00*

No. J16 Surcharged

1965, Jan. Wmk. 4
J34 D2 10c on 8c yel orange .60 *3.00*

OCCUPATION STAMPS

Issued Under Japanese Occupation

Malayan Fruit and Fronds OS1

Tin Dredging OS2

Monument to Japanese War Dead OS3

Malayan Plowman OS4

1943 Unwmk. Litho. *Perf. 12½*
N30 OS1 2c emerald 1.00 .20
a. Rouletted 2.25 2.25
b. Imperf., pair 6.50 6.50
N31 OS2 4c rose red 3.00 .20
a. Rouletted 2.25 2.25
b. Imperf., pair 6.50 6.50
N32 OS3 8c dull blue .50 .20
Nos. N30-N32 (3) 4.50 .60

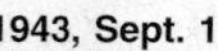

1943, Sept. 1
N33 OS4 8c violet 11.00 3.50
N34 OS4 15c carmine red 8.00 3.50

Publicity for Postal Savings which had reached a $10,000,000 total in Malaya.

Rubber Tapping OS5

Seaside Houses OS6

Japanese Shrine, Singapore OS7

Sago Palms OS8

Johore Bahru and Strait of Johore OS9

Malay Mosque, Kuala Lumpur OS10

1943, Oct. 1
N35 OS5 1c gray green 1.75 .70
N36 OS5 3c olive gray 1.00 .25
N37 OS6 10c red brown 1.25 .25
N38 OS7 15c violet 1.75 *5.00*
N39 OS8 30c olive green 1.50 .50
N40 OS9 50c blue 5.00 5.00
N41 OS10 70c dull blue 22.50 16.00
Nos. N35-N41 (7) 34.75 27.70

Rice Planting and Map of Malaysia — OS11

1944, Feb. 15
N42 OS11 8c carmine 16.00 4.00
N43 OS11 15c violet 5.00 4.00

Issued on the anniversary of the fall of Singapore to commemorate the "Birth of New Malaya".

OCCUPATION POSTAGE DUE STAMPS

Stamps and Type of Postage Due Stamps of 1936-38 Handstamped in Black, Red or Brown

No. NJ7

1942 Wmk. 4 *Perf. 14½x14*
NJ1 D2 1c violet 14.00 *30.00*
a. Brown overprint 160.00 *170.00*
b. Red overprint 190.00 190.00
NJ2 D2 3c yellow green 85.00 *90.00*
a. Red overprint 375.00 *400.00*
NJ3 D2 4c yellow green 80.00 47.50
a. Brown overprint 200.00 200.00
b. Red overprint 65.00 60.00
NJ4 D2 8c red 140.00 110.00
a. Brown overprint 275.00 275.00
b. Red overprint 200.00 150.00
NJ5 D2 10c yellow orange 32.50 *55.00*
a. Brown overprint 100.00 *110.00*
b. Red overprint 375.00 375.00
NJ6 D2 12c blue violet 27.50 *52.50*
a. Red overprint 400.00 400.00
NJ7 D2 50c black 75.00 *100.00*
a. Red overprint 600.00 *650.00*
Nos. NJ1-NJ7 (7) 454.00 485.00

Overprinted in Black

DAI NIPPON
2602
MALAYA

1942
NJ8 D2 1c violet 3.50 *10.50*
NJ9 D2 3c yel green 20.00 *26.00*
NJ10 D2 4c yel green 18.00 *12.50*
NJ11 D2 8c red 30.00 *22.50*
NJ12 D2 10c yel orange 2.00 *17.00*
NJ13 D2 12c blue violet 2.00 *40.00*
Nos. NJ8-NJ13 (6) 75.50 128.50

The 9c and 15c with this overprint were not regularly issued.

Postage Due Stamps of 1936-45 Overprinted

1943
NJ14 D2 1c reddish vio 2.25 *5.00*
NJ15 D2 3c yel green 2.25 *4.50*
NJ15A D2 4c yel green 60.00 52.50
NJ16 D2 5c scarlet 1.50 *5.00*
NJ17 D2 9c yel orange .90 *8.50*
NJ18 D2 10c yel orange 2.25 *9.00*
NJ19 D2 12c blue violet 2.25 *18.00*
NJ20 D2 15c blue violet 2.25 *9.00*
Nos. NJ14-NJ20 (8) 73.65 111.50

#NJ15A is said to have been extensively forged.

ISSUED UNDER THAI OCCUPATION

For use in Kedah, Kelantan, Perlis and Trengganu

War Memorial — OS1

Perf. 12½
1943, Dec. Unwmk. Litho.
2N1 OS1 1c pale yellow 35.00 *37.50*
2N2 OS1 2c buff 14.00 *24.00*
2N3 OS1 3c pale green 22.50 *45.00*
a. Imperf., pair 975.00
2N4 OS1 4c dull lilac 16.00 *32.50*
2N5 OS1 8c rose 16.00 *24.00*
2N6 OS1 15c lt blue 45.00 *72.50*
Nos. 2N1-2N6 (6) 148.50 *235.50*

These stamps, in cent denominations, were for use only in the four Malayan states ceded to Thailand by the Japanese. The states reverted to British rule in September, 1945.

JOHORE

jə-'hōr

LOCATION — At the extreme south of the Malay Peninsula.
AREA — 7,330 sq. mi.
POP. — 1,009,649 (1960)
CAPITAL — Johore Bahru

Stamps of the Straits Settlements Overprinted in Black

Overprinted

1876 Wmk. 1 *Perf. 14*
1 A2 2c brown 20,000. 5,750.
b. Double overprint —

Overprinted

Overprint 13 to 14mm Wide

1884-86 Wmk. 2
1A A2 2c rose 210.00 *225.00*
c. Double overprint 1,200.

Without Period

Overprint 16¾x2mm ("H" & "E" wide)

2 A2 2c rose 2,500. 725.00
a. Double overprint 2,200.

Overprinted

Overprint 11x2½mm
3 A2 2c rose ('86) 115.00 *125.00*

Overprinted

Overprint 17½x2¾mm
4 A2 2c rose ('85) *9,000.* —

Overprinted

Overprint 12½ to 15x2¾mm
5 A2 2c rose 18.00 *22.50*

Overprinted

Overprint 9x2½mm
6 A2 2c brown
7 A2 2c rose ('86) 67.50 60.00
a. Double overprint 850.00

Overprinted

Overprint 9x3mm
8 A2 2c rose ('86) 57.50 57.50

Overprinted

Overprint 14 to 15x3mm
9 A2 2c rose 16.00 13.00

Tall "J" 3½mm high
10 A2 2c rose 225.00 200.00

Overprinted

1888

Overprint 15 to 15½x3mm

11	A2	2c rose	175.00	70.00
b.		Double overprint	950.00	

Overprinted

1890-91

Overprint 12½ to 13x2½mm

12	A2	2c rose	20.00	20.00

Overprint 12x2¾mm

13	A2	2c rose ('91)	*10,500.*	

Surcharged in Black:

a

b

c

d

1891

14	A3(a)	2c on 24c green	47.50	*62.50*
15	A3(b)	2c on 24c green	150.00	160.00
16	A3(c)	2c on 24c green	30.00	45.00
a.		"CENST"	1,000.	525.00
17	A3(d)	2c on 24c green	140.00	150.00
		Nos. 14-17 (4)	367.50	417.50

Sultan Abubakar — A5

1891-94 Typo. Unwmk.

18	A5	1c lilac & vio ('94)	.85	.60
19	A5	2c lilac & yellow	.75	*1.75*
20	A5	3c lilac & car rose ('94)	.75	.60
21	A5	4c lilac & black	3.25	*22.50*
22	A5	5c lilac & green	8.50	*22.50*
23	A5	6c lilac & blue	9.50	*22.50*
24	A5	$1 green & car rose	90.00	*190.00*
		Nos. 18-24 (7)	113.60	*260.45*

For surcharges and overprints see #26-36.

Stamps of 1892-94 Surcharged in Black

1894

26	A5	3c on 4c lilac & blk	3.00	.65
a.		No period after "Cents"	115.00	85.00
27	A5	3c on 5c lilac & grn	2.40	4.25
a.		No period after "Cents"	275.00	175.00
28	A5	3c on 6c lilac & bl	4.00	5.00
a.		No period after "Cents"	210.00	240.00
29	A5	3c on $1 green & car	14.50	85.00
a.		No period after "Cents"	500.00	900.00
		Nos. 26-29 (4)	23.90	94.90

Coronation Issue

Stamps of 1892-94 Overprinted "KEMAHKOTAAN"

1896

30	A5	1c lilac & violet	.60	1.25
31	A5	2c lilac & yellow	.60	1.25
32	A5	3c lilac & car rose	.65	1.25
33	A5	4c lilac & black	1.00	3.00
34	A5	5c lilac & green	6.00	8.00
35	A5	6c lilac & blue	4.00	*7.00*
36	A5	$1 green & car rose	60.00	125.00
		Nos. 30-36 (7)	72.85	146.75

Overprinted "KETAHKOTAAN"

30a	A5	1c	4.50	*6.00*
31a	A5	2c	5.75	*8.50*
32a	A5	3c	11.00	*14.00*
33a	A5	4c	3.50	*15.00*
34a	A5	5c	4.25	*8.50*
35a	A5	6c	9.00	*14.00*
36a	A5	$1	42.50	*190.00*
		Nos. 30a-36a (7)	80.50	*256.00*

Coronation of Sultan Ibrahim.

Sultan Ibrahim — A7

1896-99 Typo. Wmk. 71

37	A7	1c green	1.00	1.75
38	A7	2c green & blue	.60	1.00
39	A7	3c green & vio	4.75	3.00
40	A7	4c green & car rose	1.25	2.40
41	A7	4c yel & red ('99)	1.75	1.75
42	A7	5c green & brn	2.40	3.75
43	A7	6c green & yel	2.40	5.00
44	A7	10c green & black	8.50	*55.00*
45	A7	25c green & vio	10.00	*50.00*
46	A7	50c grn & car rose	19.00	*52.50*
47	A7	$1 lilac & green	37.50	*85.00*
48	A7	$2 lilac & car rose	47.50	*100.00*
49	A7	$3 lilac & blue	42.50	*140.00*
50	A7	$4 lilac & brn	42.50	*100.00*
51	A7	$5 lilac & orange	92.50	*150.00*
		Nos. 37-51 (15)	314.15	*751.15*

On Nos. 44-46 the numerals are on white tablets. Numerals of Nos. 48-51 are on tablets of solid color.

Stamps of 1896-1926 with revenue cancellations sell for a fraction of those used postally.

For surcharges see Nos. 52-58.

Nos. 40-41 Surcharged in Black

1903

52	A7	3c on 4c yel & red	.80	1.25
a.		Without bars	4.00	*24.00*
53	A7	10c on 4c grn & car rose	3.00	10.00
a.		Without bars	27.50	*75.00*

Bars on Nos. 52-53 were handruled with pen and ink.

Surcharged

54	A7	50c on $3 lilac & blue	35.00	*87.50*

Surcharged

55	A7	$1 on $2 lilac & car rose	75.00	*140.00*
a.		Inverted "e" in "one"	1,800.	

Surcharged

1904

56	A7	10c on 4c yel & red	25.00	42.50
a.		Double surcharge	*8,750.*	
57	A7	10c on 4c grn & car rose	10.50	*65.00*
58	A7	50c on $5 lil & org	80.00	170.00
		Nos. 56-58 (3)	115.50	277.50

Sultan Ibrahim — A8

The 10c, 21c, 25c, 50c, and $10 to $500 denominations of type A8 show the numerals on white tablets. The numerals of the 8c, 30c, 40c, and $2 to $5 demoninations are shown on tablets of solid colors.

1904-10 Typo. Wmk. 71

Ordinary Paper

59	A8	1c violet & green	2.00	.40
a.		Chalky paper ('09)	12.00	11.00
60	A8	2c violet & brn org	3.00	4.25
a.		Chalky paper ('10)	14.00	*17.00*
61	A8	3c violet & black	4.75	.60
62	A8	4c violet & red	9.25	3.25
63	A8	5c violet & ol grn	2.50	3.00
64	A8	8c violet & blue	4.25	*13.00*
65	A8	10c violet & black	50.00	11.00
a.		Chalky paper ('10)	120.00	80.00
66	A8	25c violet & green	8.50	*40.00*
67	A8	50c violet & red	45.00	17.50
68	A8	$1 green & vio	19.00	*72.50*
69	A8	$2 green & car	27.50	*62.50*
70	A8	$3 green & blue	32.50	*87.50*
71	A8	$4 green & brn	35.00	*125.00*
72	A8	$5 green & org	50.00	*100.00*
73	A8	$10 green & blk	85.00	*175.00*
74	A8	$50 green & blue	*300.00*	*400.00*
75	A8	$100 green & scar	*450.00*	*700.00*
		Revenue cancel		50.00
		Nos. 59-73 (15)	378.25	*715.50*

Nos. 74 and 75 were theoretically available for postage but were mostly used for revenue purposes.

For surcharge see No. 86.

1912-19 Wmk. 47

Chalky Paper

76	A8	1c violet & green	1.25	.20
77	A8	2c violet & orange	6.00	1.00
78	A8	3c violet & black	10.00	.70
79	A8	4c violet & red	18.00	1.00
80	A8	5c violet & ol grn	8.50	2.75
81	A8	8c violet & blue	4.50	*10.00*
82	A8	10c violet & black	60.00	3.00
83	A8	25c violet & green	18.00	*50.00*
84	A8	50c violet & red ('19)	72.50	*140.00*
85	A8	$1 green & vio ('18)	100.00	*120.00*
		Nos. 76-85 (10)	298.75	*328.65*

#78-79, 82 exist with horizontal watermark.

No. 64 Surcharged

1912 Wmk. 71

86	A8	3c on 8c vio & blue	7.50	*9.00*
a.		"T" of "CENTS" omitted	1,600.	

1918-20 Typo. Wmk. 3

Chalky Paper

87	A8	2c violet & orange	.75	1.75
88	A8	2c violet & grn ('19)	1.00	5.50
89	A8	4c violet & red	1.75	.70
90	A8	5c vio & olive grn ('20)	2.00	10.00
91	A8	10c violet & blue	2.00	1.75
92	A8	21c violet & orange ('19)	3.00	3.25
93	A8	25c vio & grn ('20)	9.00	30.00
94	A8	50c vio & red ('19)	24.00	65.00
95	A8	$1 grn & red vio	14.00	75.00
96	A8	$2 green & scar	27.50	60.00
97	A8	$3 green & blue	65.00	125.00
98	A8	$4 green & brn	80.00	175.00
99	A8	$5 green & org	120.00	200.00
100	A8	$10 green & blk	350.00	500.00
		Nos. 87-100 (14)	700.00	1,252.

1921-40 Wmk. 4

101	A8	1c violet & black	.30	.20
102	A8	2c violet & brn ('24)	1.25	4.25
103	A8	2c green & dk grn ('28)	.50	.40
104	A8	3c green ('25)	2.25	4.75
105	A8	3c dull vio & brn ('28)	1.40	1.50
106	A8	4c vio & red	2.50	.20
107	A8	5c vio & ol grn	.50	.20
108	A8	6c vio & red brown	.50	.50
109	A8	10c vio & blue	20.00	37.50
110	A8	10c vio & yel ('22)	.50	.25
111	A8	12c vio & blue	1.25	1.60
111A	A8	12c ultra ('40)	47.50	4.00
112	A8	21c dull vio & org ('28)	2.75	3.50
113	A8	25c vio & green	4.25	1.25
114	A8	30c dull vio & org ('36)	9.50	10.00
115	A8	40c dull vio & brn ('36)	9.50	11.00
116	A8	50c violet & red	3.75	1.60
117	A8	$1 grn & red violet	3.75	1.25
118	A8	$2 grn & red	10.00	5.00
119	A8	$3 grn & blue	75.00	95.00
120	A8	$4 grn & brn ('26)	110.00	190.00
121	A8	$5 grn & org	62.50	52.50
122	A8	$10 grn & blk	275.00	400.00
123	A8	$50 grn & ultra	1,200.	
		Revenue cancel		100.00
124	A8	$100 grn & red	1,800.	
		Revenue cancel		150.00
125	A8	$500 ultra & org brn ('26)	*23,000.*	
		Revenue cancel		300.00
		Nos. 101-122 (23)	644.45	*826.45*

Nos. 123, 124 and 125 were available for postage but were probably used only fiscally.

A9

A10

1935, May 15 Engr. *Perf. 12½*

126	A9	8c Sultan Ibrahim, Sultana	5.00	3.00
		Never hinged	8.00	

1940, Feb. *Perf. 13½*

127	A10	8c Sultan Ibrahim	17.00	1.00
		Never hinged	26.00	

Catalogue values for unused stamps in this section, from this point to the end of the section, are for Never Hinged items.

Silver Wedding Issue

Common Design Types

Inscribed: "Malaya Johore"

Perf. 14x14½

1948, Dec. 1 Wmk. 4 Photo.

128	CD304	10c purple	.20	.75

Perf. 11½x11

Engr.; Name Typo.

129	CD305	$5 green	29.00	52.50

Common Design Types Pictured following the introduction.

Sultan Ibrahim — A11

1949-55 Wmk. 4 Typo. *Perf. 18*

130	A11	1c black	.50	.25
131	A11	2c orange	.30	.30
132	A11	3c green	1.10	1.10
133	A11	4c chocolate	1.25	.25
134	A11	5c rose vio ('52)	1.25	.30
135	A11	6c gray	1.25	.25
a.		Wmk. 4a (error)	*2,500.*	*1,800.*
136	A11	8c rose red	4.00	1.40
137	A11	8c green ('52)	7.50	2.25
138	A11	10c plum	1.00	.25
a.		Imperf., pair	*3,500.*	
139	A11	12c rose red ('52)	8.00	6.50
140	A11	15c ultra	3.50	.45

141 A11 20c dk grn & blk 2.25 1.25
142 A11 20c ultra ('52) 1.50 .30
143 A11 25c org & rose lil 3.50 .25
144 A11 30c plum & rose red ('55) 2.50 2.75
145 A11 35c dk vio & rose red ('52) 8.50 2.25
146 A11 40c dk vio & rose red 6.50 15.00
147 A11 50c ultra & blk 4.00 .30
148 A11 $1 vio brn & ultra 9.00 2.50
149 A11 $2 rose red & emer 22.50 11.00
150 A11 $5 choc & emer 47.50 16.00
Nos. 130-150 (21) 137.40 64.90

UPU Issue

Common Design Types
Inscribed: "Malaya-Johore"

Engr.; Name Typo. on 15c, 25c

1949, Oct. 10 ***Perf. 13½, 11x11½***

151 CD306 10c rose violet .30 .40
152 CD307 15c indigo 2.00 1.25
153 CD308 25c orange .80 3.50
154 CD309 50c slate 1.60 3.75
Nos. 151-154 (4) 4.70 8.90

Coronation Issue

Common Design Type

1953, June 2 Engr. ***Perf. 13½x13***

155 CD312 10c magenta & black 1.40 .30

Sultan Ibrahim A12

1955, Nov. 1 Wmk. 4 ***Perf. 14***

156 A12 10c carmine lake .35 .35

Sultan Ibrahim's Diamond Jubilee.

Sultan Ismail and Johore State Crest Seal — A13

Perf. 11½

1960, Feb. 10 Unwmk. Photo.

Granite Paper

157 A13 10c multicolored .35 .35

Coronation of Sultan Ismail.

Types of Kedah 1957 with Portrait of Sultan Ismail

1960 Wmk. 314 Engr. ***Perf. 13***

158 A8 1c black .20 *.50*
159 A8 2c red orange .20 *1.25*
160 A8 4c dark brown .20 .20
161 A8 5c dk car rose .20 .20
162 A8 8c dark green 2.25 *3.50*
163 A7 10c violet brown .35 .20
164 A7 20c blue 2.25 1.00
165 A7 50c ultra & black .60 .30
166 A8 $1 plum & ultra 4.50 *6.00*
167 A8 $2 red & green 15.00 *22.50*
168 A8 $5 ol, grn & brn 35.00 *42.50*
Nos. 158-168 (11) 60.75 *78.15*

Starting in 1965, issues of Johore are listed with Malaysia.

POSTAGE DUE STAMPS

D1

Perf. 12½

1938, Jan. 1 Typo. Wmk. 4

J1 D1 1c rose red 18.00 *47.50*
J2 D1 4c green 42.50 *45.00*
J3 D1 8c dull yellow 50.00 *160.00*
J4 D1 10c bister brown 50.00 *57.50*
J5 D1 12c rose violet 60.00 *140.00*
Nos. J1-J5 (5) 220.50 *450.00*

OCCUPATION POSTAGE DUE STAMPS

Issued under Japanese Occupation

Johore Nos. J1-J5 Overprinted in Black, Brown or Red

1942 Wmk. 4 ***Perf. 12½***

NJ1 D1 1c rose red 25.00 75.00
NJ2 D1 4c green 70.00 85.00
NJ3 D1 8c dull yellow 85.00 100.00
NJ4 D1 10c bister brown 18.00 55.00
NJ5 D1 12c rose violet 47.50 60.00
Nos. NJ1-NJ5 (5) 245.50 375.00

Johore Nos. J1-J5 Overprinted in Black

1943

NJ6 D1 1c rose red 10.00 *32.50*
NJ7 D1 4c green 8.00 *37.50*
NJ8 D1 8c dull yellow 10.00 *37.50*
NJ9 D1 10c bister brown 9.50 *47.50*
NJ10 D1 12c rose violet 11.00 *65.00*
Nos. NJ6-NJ10 (5) 48.50 *220.00*

Nos. NJ6-NJ10 exist with second character sideways. See Scott Classic Specialized catalogue for listings.

KEDAH

'ke-də

LOCATION — On the west coast of the Malay Peninsula.
AREA — 3,660 sq. mi.
POP. — 752,706 (1960)
CAPITAL — Alor Star

Sheaf of Rice — A1

Native Plowing — A2

Council Chamber — A3

1912-21 Engr. Wmk. 3 ***Perf. 14***

1 A1 1c green & black .70 .30
2 A1 1c brown ('19) .65 .60
3 A1 2c green ('19) .60 .35
4 A1 3c car & black 5.00 .35
5 A1 3c dk violet ('19) .75 2.25
6 A1 4c slate & car 12.00 .30
7 A1 4c scarlet ('19) 5.50 .40
8 A1 5c org brown & grn 2.75 *3.50*
9 A1 8c ultra & blk 4.25 *4.00*
10 A2 10c black brn & bl 2.75 1.25
11 A2 20c yel grn & blk 6.50 4.50
12 A2 21c red vio & vio ('19) 6.25 *70.00*
13 A2 25c red vio & bl ('21) 2.10 *32.50*
14 A2 30c car & black 3.50 *12.00*
15 A2 40c lilac & blk 4.00 *18.00*
16 A2 50c dull bl & brn 10.00 *14.00*
17 A3 $1 scar & blk, *yel* 17.50 *24.00*
18 A3 $2 dk brn & dk grn 24.00 *95.00*
19 A3 $3 dk bl & blk, *bl* 100.00 *190.00*
20 A3 $5 car & black 110.00 *200.00*
Nos. 1-20 (20) 318.80 *673.30*

There are two types of No. 7, one printed from separate plates for frame and center, the other printed from a single plate.

Overprints are listed after No. 45.

Stamps of 1912 Surcharged

1919

21 A3 50c on $2 dk brn & dk grn 80.00 *90.00*
a. "C" of ovpt. inserted by hand 1,450. 1,650.
22 A3 $1 on $3 dk bl & blk, *blue* 22.50 *110.00*

1921-36 Wmk. 4

Two types of 1c:
I — The 1's have rounded corners, small top serif. Small letters "c."
II — The 1's have square-cut corners, large top serif. Large letters "c."

Two types of 2c:
I — The 2's have oval drops. Letters "c" are fairly thick and rounded.
II — The 2's have round drops. Letters "c" thin and slightly larger.

23 A1 1c brown .90 .20
24 A1 1c blk (I) ('22) 1.00 .20
a. 1c black (II) ('39) 77.50 5.00
25 A1 2c green (I) 1.50 .20
a. 2c green (II) ('40) 160.00 8.00
26 A1 3c dk violet 1.00 .80
27 A1 3c green ('22) 2.75 1.00
28 A1 4c carmine 7.50 .20
29 A1 4c dull vio ('26) 1.50 .20
30 A1 5c yellow ('22) 2.25 .20
31 A1 6c scarlet ('26) 2.50 .80
32 A1 8c gray ('36) 18.00 .20
33 A2 10c blk brn & bl 3.25 1.00
34 A2 12c dk ultra & blk ('26) 6.50 5.00
35 A2 20c green & blk 5.25 3.00
36 A2 21c red vio & vio 3.25 *17.50*
37 A2 25c red vio & bl 3.25 *9.00*
38 A2 30c red & blk ('22) 4.00 *11.00*
39 A2 35c claret ('26) 12.00 *45.00*
40 A2 40c red vio & blk 6.00 *60.00*
41 A2 50c dp blue & brn 4.50 *21.00*
42 A3 $1 scar & blk, *yel* ('24) 75.00 80.00
43 A3 $2 brn & green 17.50 *125.00*
44 A3 $3 dk bl & blk, *bl* 75.00 *110.00*
45 A3 $5 car & black 97.50 *200.00*
Nos. 23-45 (23) 351.90 *691.50*

For overprints see Nos. N1-N6.

Stamps of 1912-21 Overprinted in Black: "MALAYA-BORNEO EXHIBITION." in Three Lines

1922 Wmk. 3

3a A1 2c green 5.00 *27.50*
12a A2 21c red vio & vio 35.00 *95.00*
13a A2 25c red vio & blue 35.00 *110.00*
b. Inverted overprint 1,500.
16a A2 50c dull blue & brn 35.00 *125.00*

Wmk. 4

23a A1 1c brown 5.50 *25.00*
26a A1 3c dark violet 4.75 *47.50*
28a A1 4c carmine 4.75 *30.00*
33a A2 10c blk brn & blue 9.25 *55.00*
Nos. 3a-33a (8) 134.25 *515.00*

Industrial fair at Singapore, Mar. 31-Apr. 15, 1922.

On Nos. 12a, 13a and 16a, "BORNEO" exists both 14mm and 15mm wide.

Sultan of Kedah, Sir Abdul Hamid Halim Shah — A4

1937, July Wmk. 4 ***Perf. 12½***

46 A4 10c sepia & ultra 3.25 2.25
47 A4 12c gray vio & blk 27.50 *5.50*
48 A4 25c brn vio & ultra 6.00 *5.50*
49 A4 30c dp car & yel grn 5.50 *11.50*
50 A4 40c brn vio & blk 3.00 *16.00*
51 A4 50c dp blue & sepia 5.50 *5.00*
52 A4 $1 dk green & blk 3.00 *11.00*
53 A4 $2 dk brn & yel grn 75.00 *85.00*
54 A4 $5 dp car & black 22.50 *170.00*
Nos. 46-54 (9) 151.25 *311.75*
Set, never hinged 265.00

For overprints see Nos. N7-N15.

Catalogue values for unused stamps in this section, from this point to the end of the section, are for Never Hinged items.

Silver Wedding Issue

Common Design Types
Inscribed: "Malaya Kedah"

1948, Dec. 1 Photo. ***Perf. 14x14½***

55 CD304 10c purple .20 .25

Perf. 11½x11

Engraved; Name Typographed

56 CD305 $5 rose car 35.00 50.00

UPU Issue

Common Design Types
Inscribed: "Malaya-Kedah"

Engr.; Name Typo. on 15c, 25c

1949, Oct. 10 ***Perf. 13½, 11x11½***

57 CD306 10c rose violet .25 1.25
58 CD307 15c indigo 2.25 1.75
59 CD308 25c orange .80 2.50
60 CD309 50c slate 1.50 4.75
Nos. 57-60 (4) 4.80 10.25

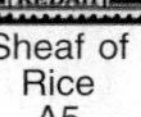

Sheaf of Rice A5

Sultan Tungku Badlishah A6

1950-55 Wmk. 4 Typo. ***Perf. 18***

61 A5 1c black .70 .30
62 A5 2c orange .50 .20
63 A5 3c green 2.00 1.00
64 A5 4c chocolate .75 .20
65 A5 5c rose vio ('52) 3.50 2.50
66 A5 6c gray .70 .20
67 A5 8c rose red 2.25 *4.50*
68 A5 8c green ('52) 3.25 2.00
69 A5 10c plum .70 .20
70 A5 12c rose red ('52) 3.25 3.00
71 A5 15c ultramarine 3.00 .70
72 A5 20c dk green & blk 3.00 3.00
73 A5 20c ultra ('52) 1.50 .35
74 A6 25c org & rose lilac 1.50 .50
75 A6 30c plum & rose red ('55) 4.50 1.50
76 A6 35c dk vio & rose red ('52) 4.00 2.00
77 A6 40c dk vio & rose red 4.75 *8.50*
78 A6 50c ultra & black 4.00 .35
79 A6 $1 vio brown & ultra 5.00 *6.50*
80 A6 $2 rose red & emer 30.00 *35.00*
81 A6 $5 choc & emerald 50.00 *65.00*
Nos. 61-81 (21) 128.85 *137.50*

Coronation Issue

Common Design Type

1953, June 2 Engr. ***Perf. 13½x13***

82 CD312 10c magenta & black 2.25 .60

Fishing Craft — A7

Weaving and Sultan — A8

Portrait of Sultan Tungku Badlishah and: 1c, Copra. 2c, Pineapples. 4c, Rice field. 5c, Mosque. 8c, East Coast Railway. 10c, Tiger. 50c, Aborigines with blowpipes. $1, Government offices. $2, Bersilat.

Perf. 13x12½, 12½x13

1957 Engr. Wmk. 314

83 A8 1c black .35 *.60*
84 A8 2c red orange .50 *1.75*
85 A8 4c dark brown .35 *1.00*
86 A8 5c dk car rose .35 .75
87 A8 8c dark green 3.00 *10.00*
88 A7 10c chocolate 1.00 .50
89 A7 20c blue 3.50 3.25

Perf. 12½, 13½ ($1)

90 A7 50c ultra & black 3.25 *4.25*
91 A8 $1 plum & ultra 9.00 *15.00*
92 A8 $2 red & green 32.50 *45.00*
Revenue cancel .20
93 A8 $5 ol grn & brown 55.00 47.50
Revenue cancel .35
Nos. 83-93 (11) 108.80 129.60

See Nos. 95-105.

Sultan Abdul Halim — A9

Perf. 14x14½

1959, Feb. 20 Photo. Wmk. 314

94 A9 10c ultra, red & yellow .80 .30

Installation of the Sultan of Kedah, Abdul Halim.

Types of 1957

Designs as before with portrait of Sultan Abdul Halim.

Perf. 13x12½, 12½x13, 12½, 13½

1959-62 Engr. Wmk. 314

95 A8 1c black .20 .85
96 A8 2c red orange .20 2.00
97 A8 4c dark brown .20 .85
98 A8 5c dk car rose .20 .30
99 A8 8c dark green 4.00 4.00
100 A7 10c chocolate 1.00 .30
101 A7 20c blue 1.00 1.00
102 A7 50c ultra & blk, perf. 12½x13 ('60) .35 1.75
a. Perf. 12½ .35 .60
103 A8 $1 plum & ultra 2.50 *3.00*
104 A8 $2 red & green 15.00 *22.50*
105 A8 $5 ol grn & brn, perf. 13x12½ ('62) 35.00 19.00
a. Perf. 12½ 20.00 *22.50*
Nos. 95-105 (11) 59.65 55.55

Starting in 1965, issues of Kedah are listed with Malaysia.

OCCUPATION STAMPS

Issued Under Japanese Occupation

Stamps of Kedah 1922-36, Overprinted in Red or Black

1942, May 13 Wmk. 4 *Perf. 14*

N1 A1 1c black (R) 7.00 10.00
N2 A1 2c green (R) 35.00 45.00
N3 A1 4c dull violet (R) 7.00 4.00
N4 A1 5c yellow (R) 5.50 5.50
a. Black overprint 300.00 325.00
N5 A1 6c scarlet (Bk) 4.25 18.00
N6 A1 8c gray (R) 4.75 4.00

Nos. 46 to 54 Overprinted in Red

Perf. 12½

N7 A4 10c sepia & ultra 16.00 18.00
N8 A4 12c gray vio & blk 37.50 55.00
N9 A4 25c brn vio & ultra 12.00 19.00
a. Black overprint 375.00 325.00
N10 A4 30c dp car & yel grn 75.00 85.00
N11 A4 40c brn vio & blk 37.50 50.00
N12 A4 50c dp blue & sep 35.00 50.00
N13 A4 $1 dk grn & blk 160.00 160.00
a. Inverted overprint 750.00 850.00
N14 A4 $2 dk brn & yel green 210.00 190.00
N15 A4 $5 dp car & blk 90.00 125.00
a. Black overprint 1,300. 1,100.
Nos. N1-N15 (15) 736.50 838.50

KELANTAN

kə-'lan-ˌtan

LOCATION — On the eastern coast of the Malay Peninsula.
AREA — 5,750 sq. mi.
POP. — 545,620 (1960)
CAPITAL — Kota Bharu

Symbols of Government — A1

1911-15 Typo. Wmk. 3 *Perf. 14*

Ordinary Paper

1 A1 1c gray green 8.00 1.25
a. 1c green 7.25 .35
2 A1 3c rose red 5.00 .20
3 A1 4c black & red 1.90 .20
4 A1 5c grn & red, *yel* 12.00 1.25
5 A1 8c ultramarine 6.25 1.25
6 A1 10c black & violet 35.00 .90

Chalky Paper

7 A1 30c violet & red 12.50 3.00
8 A1 50c black & org 10.00 3.00
9 A1 $1 green & emer 55.00 45.00
10 A1 $1 grn & brn ('15) 75.00 2.40
11 A1 $2 grn & car rose 1.90 *3.75*
12 A1 $5 green & ultra 4.75 4.00
13 A1 $25 green & org 55.00 *105.00*
Nos. 1-13 (13) 282.30 *171.20*

For overprints see listings after No. 26. For surcharges see Nos. N20-N22.

1921-28 Wmk. 4

Ordinary Paper

14 A1 1c green 5.00 .75
15 A1 1c black ('23) 1.00 .60
16 A1 2c brown 7.50 4.75
17 A1 2c green ('26) 5.50 .60
18 A1 3c brown ('27) 5.00 1.50
19 A1 4c black & red 3.50 .20
20 A1 5c grn & red, *yel* 1.75 .20
21 A1 6c claret 3.50 2.00
22 A1 6c rose red ('28) 5.00 5.00
23 A1 10c black & violet 3.00 .20

Chalky Paper

24 A1 30c dull vio & red ('26) 5.00 *6.00*
25 A1 50c black & orange 7.25 *52.50*
26 A1 $1 green & brown 35.00 *90.00*
Nos. 14-26 (13) 88.00 *164.30*

Stamps of 1911-21 Overprinted in Black: "MALAYA BORNEO EXHIBITION" in Three Lines

1922 Wmk. 3

3a A1 4c black & red 6.50 *50.00*
4a A1 5c green & red, *yel* 7.00 *50.00*
7a A1 30c violet & red 8.00 *80.00*
8a A1 50c black & orange 11.00 *90.00*
10a A1 $1 green & brown 35.00 *125.00*
11a A1 $2 green & car rose 90.00 *225.00*
12a A1 $5 green & ultra 225.00 *525.00*

Wmk. 4

14a A1 1c green 3.50 *55.00*
23a A1 10c black & violet 7.25 *75.00*
Nos. 3a-23a (9) 393.25 1,275.

Industrial fair at Singapore. Mar. 31-Apr. 15, 1922.

Sultan Ismail
A2 A2a

1928-33 Engr. *Perf. 12*

Size: 21½x30mm

27 A2 $1 ultramarine 17.50 *85.00*

Perf. 14

28 A2 $1 blue ('33) 60.00 *47.50*

1937-40 *Perf. 12*

Size: 22½x34½mm

29 A2a 1c yel & ol green 1.40 .65
30 A2a 2c deep green 3.50 .20
31 A2a 4c brick red 3.50 1.00
32 A2a 5c red brown 3.00 .20
33 A2a 6c car lake 8.75 *10.00*
34 A2a 8c gray green 3.00 .20
35 A2a 10c dark violet 14.50 3.50
36 A2a 12c deep blue 3.50 *6.50*
37 A2a 25c vio & red org 4.50 *4.75*
38 A2a 30c scar & dk vio 27.50 24.00
39 A2a 40c blue grn & org 5.75 *35.00*
40 A2a 50c org & ol grn 42.50 9.50
41 A2a $1 dp grn & dk violet 30.00 16.00
42 A2a $2 red & red brn ('40) 175.00 *275.00*
43 A2a $5 rose lake & org ('40) 350.00 *650.00*
Nos. 29-43 (15) 676.40 *1,036.*
Set, never hinged 1,200.

For overprints see Nos. N1-N19.

Catalogue values for unused stamps in this section, from this point to the end of the section, are for Never Hinged items.

Silver Wedding Issue
Common Design Types
Inscribed: "Malaya Kelantan"

Perf. 14x14½

1948, Dec. 1 Wmk. 4 Photo.

44 CD304 10c purple .75 *2.75*

Perf. 11½x11

Engraved; Name Typographed

45 CD305 $5 rose car 35.00 *60.00*

Common Design Types pictured following the introduction.

UPU Issue
Common Design Types
Inscribed: "Malaya-Kelantan"

Engr.; Name Typo. on 15c, 25c

1949, Oct. 10 *Perf. 13½, 11x11½*

46 CD306 10c rose violet .40 .40
47 CD307 15c indigo 2.25 2.25
48 CD308 25c orange .60 5.50
49 CD309 50c slate 1.00 3.00
Nos. 46-49 (4) 4.25 11.15

Sultan Ibrahim — A3

Perf. 18

1951, July 11 Wmk. 4 Typo.

50 A3 1c black .50 .40
51 A3 2c orange 1.25 .40
52 A3 3c green 5.25 1.75
53 A3 4c chocolate 1.75 .30
54 A3 6c gray .75 .30
55 A3 8c rose red 4.25 4.25
56 A3 10c plum .50 .30
57 A3 15c ultramarine 6.00 .80
58 A3 20c dk green & blk 4.50 11.00
59 A3 25c orange & plum 1.50 .80
60 A3 40c vio brn & rose red 14.00 20.00
61 A3 50c dp ultra & blk 6.00 .60
62 A3 $1 vio brown & ultra 10.00 11.00
63 A3 $2 rose red & emer 37.50 50.00
64 A3 $5 choc & emer 72.50 72.50

1952-55

65 A3 5c rose violet 1.50 .50
66 A3 8c green 4.50 2.25
67 A3 12c rose red 4.50 3.00
68 A3 20c ultramarine 1.50 .25
69 A3 30c plum & rose red ('55) 1.60 5.00
70 A3 35c dk vio & rose red 2.00 1.75
Nos. 50-70 (21) 181.85 187.15

Compare with Pahang A8, Perak A16, Selangor A15, Trengganu A5.

Coronation Issue
Common Design Type

1953, June 2 Engr. *Perf. 13½x13*

71 CD312 10c magenta & black 1.60 1.60

Aborigines with Blowpipes
A4

Government Offices and Sultan
A5

Portrait of Sultan Ibrahim and: 1c, Copra. 2c, Pineapples. 4c, Rice field. 5c, Mosque. 8c, East Coast Railway. 10c, Tiger. 20c, Fishing craft. 50c, Aborigines with blowpipes. $1, Government Offices and Sultan. $2, Bersilat. $5, Weaving.

Perf. 13x12½, 12½x13, 13½ ($1)

1957-63 Engr. Wmk. 314

72 A5 1c black .20 .45
73 A5 2c red orange .90 1.50
74 A5 4c dark brown .45 .20
75 A5 5c dk car rose .45 .20
76 A5 8c dark green 2.25 3.25
77 A4 10c chocolate 3.00 .20
78 A4 20c blue 2.50 .45
79 A4 50c ultra & blk ('60) 1.00 .60
a. Perf 12½ 1.00 1.25
80 A5 $1 plum & ultra 8.00 2.00
81 A5 $2 red & grn ('63) 15.00 *32.50*
a. Perf. 12½ 19.00 *9.00*
82 A5 $5 ol grn & brn ('63) 27.50 *37.50*
a. Perf. 12½ 24.00 *14.00*
Nos. 72-82 (11) 61.25 *78.85*

Sultan Yahya Petra — A6

1961, July 17 Photo. *Perf. 14½x14*

83 A6 10s multicolored .55 1.00

Installation of Sultan Yahya Petra.

Types of 1957 with Portrait of Sultan Yahya Petra

Designs as before.

Perf. 13x12½, 12½x13

1961-62 Engr. Wmk. 338

84 A5 1c black .20 *2.75*
85 A5 2c red orange .60 *3.00*
86 A5 4c dark brown 1.75 *2.00*
87 A5 5c dk car rose 1.75 .60
88 A5 8c dark green 14.00 *15.00*
89 A4 10c violet brown ('61) 1.75 .40
90 A4 20c blue 10.00 2.50
Nos. 84-90 (7) 30.05 26.25

Starting in 1965, issues of Kelantan are listed with Malaysia.

OCCUPATION STAMPS

Issued Under Japanese Occupation

Kelantan No. 35 Handstamped in Black

1942 Wmk. 4 *Perf. 12*

N1 A2a 10c dark violet 400.00 500.00

Some authorities believe No. N1 was not regularly issued.

Kelantan Nos. 29-40 Surcharged in Black or Red and Handstamped with Oval Seal "a" in Red

1 Cents

Sunakawa — a

Handa — b

1942

N2 1c on 50c org & ol green 225.00 150.00
a. With "b" seal 160.00 200.00
N3 2c on 40c bl grn & orange 300.00 200.00
a. With "b" seal 160.00 200.00
N4 5c on 12c dp bl (R) 200.00 200.00
N5 8c on 5c red brn (R) 175.00 100.00
a. With "b" seal (R) 110.00 175.00
N6 10c on 6c car lake 475.00 500.00
a. With "b" seal 120.00 200.00
N7 12c on 8c gray green (R) 60.00 140.00
N8 30c on 4c brick red 2,500. 2,250.
N9 40c on 2c dp grn (R) 70.00 100.00
N10 50c on 1c yel & ol green 1,800. 1,500.

Kelantan Nos. 29-40, 19-20, 22 Surcharged in Black or Red and Handstamped with Oval Seal "a" in Red

2 CENTS

N10A 1c on 50c org & ol green 350.00 200.00
N11 2c on 40c bl grn & orange 900.00 350.00
N11A 4c on 30c scar & dark vio 2,500. 1,400.
N12 5c on 12c dp bl (R) 350.00 200.00
N13 6c on 25c vio & red org 375.00 200.00
N14 8c on 5c red brown (R) 500.00 150.00
N15 10c on 6c car lake 100.00 125.00
N16 12c on 8c gray grn (R) 70.00 120.00
a. With "b" seal (R) 225.00 375.00
N17 25c on 10c dk vio 1,600. 1,500.
N17A 30c on 4c brick red 2,500. 2,250.
N18 40c on 2c dp grn (R) 70.00 100.00
N19 50c on 1c yel & ol green 1,800. 1,500.

Perf. 14

N20 $1 on 4c blk & red (R) 60.00 85.00
N21 $2 on 5c grn & red, *yel* 60.00 85.00
N22 $5 on 6c rose red 60.00 85.00

Examples of Nos. N2-N22 without handstamped seal are from the remainder stocks sent to Singapore after Kelantan was ceded to Thailand. Some authorities believe stamps without seals were used before June 1942.

ISSUED UNDER THAI OCCUPATION

OS1

1943, Nov. 15 ***Perf. 11***

2N1 OS1 1c violet & black *240.00 375.00*
2N2 OS1 2c violet & black *300.00 300.00*
2N3 OS1 4c violet & black *300.00 375.00*
2N4 OS1 8c violet & black *300.00 300.00*
2N5 OS1 10c violet & black *450.00 550.00*
Nos. 2N1-2N5 (5) 1,590. 1,900.

Stamps with centers in red are revenues.

MALACCA

mə-ˈla-kə

Melaka

LOCATION — On the west coast of the Malay peninsula.
AREA — 640 sq. mi.
POP. — 318,110 (1960)
CAPITAL — Malacca

Catalogue values for unused stamps in this section are for Never Hinged items.

Silver Wedding Issue

Common Design Types
Inscribed: "Malaya Malacca"

Perf. 14x14½

1948, Dec. 1 Wmk. 4 Photo.

1 CD304 10c purple .40 *2.25*

Engraved; Name Typographed

Perf. 11½x11

2 CD305 $5 lt brown 35.00 *47.50*

Type of Straits Settlements, 1937-41, Inscribed "Malacca"

Perf. 18

1949, Mar. 1 Wmk. 4 Typo.

3 A29 1c black .40 *.85*
4 A29 2c orange 1.00 .60
5 A29 3c green .40 *2.25*
6 A29 4c chocolate .40 .20
7 A29 6c gray .90 *1.10*
8 A29 8c rose red .90 *7.50*
9 A29 10c plum .40 .20
10 A29 15c ultramarine 3.50 .85
11 A29 20c dk green & blk .60 *7.00*
12 A29 25c org & rose lil .60 .85
13 A29 40c dk vio & rose red 1.50 *13.00*
14 A29 50c ultra & black 1.50 1.50
15 A29 $1 vio brn & ultra 15.00 *26.00*
16 A29 $2 rose red & emer 27.50 27.50
17 A29 $5 choc & emer 60.00 50.00
Nos. 3-17 (15) 114.60 *139.40*

See Nos. 22-26.

UPU Issue

Common Design Types
Inscribed: "Malaya-Malacca"

Engr.; Name Typo. on 15c, 25c

Perf. 13½, 11x11½

1949, Oct. 10 Wmk. 4

18 CD306 10c rose violet .35 *.55*
19 CD307 15c indigo 2.40 *2.75*
20 CD308 25c orange .50 *8.50*
21 CD309 50c slate 1.00 *5.50*
Nos. 18-21 (4) 4.25 *17.30*

Type of Straits Settlements, 1937-41, Inscribed "Malacca"

1952, Sept. 1 Wmk. 4 *Perf. 18*

22 A29 5c rose violet 1.25 *1.75*
23 A29 8c green 6.00 *5.25*
24 A29 12c rose red 6.00 *9.50*
25 A29 20c ultramarine 7.50 3.00
26 A29 35c dk vio & rose red 6.00 *3.75*
Nos. 22-26 (5) 26.75 *23.25*

Coronation Issue

Common Design Type

1953, June 2 Engr. *Perf. 13½x13*

27 CD312 10c magenta & black 1.10 *1.50*

Queen Elizabeth II — A1

1954-55 Wmk. 4 Typo. *Perf. 18*

29 A1 1c black .20 .75
30 A1 2c orange .40 1.25
31 A1 4c chocolate 1.50 .20
32 A1 5c rose violet .40 2.75
33 A1 6c gray .20 .40
34 A1 8c green .55 3.00
35 A1 10c plum 2.00 .20
36 A1 12c rose red .40 3.25
37 A1 20c ultramarine .25 1.25
38 A1 25c orange & plum .25 1.75
39 A1 30c plum & rose red ('55) .25 *.40*
40 A1 35c vio brn & rose red .25 *1.50*
41 A1 50c ultra & black 4.00 2.75
42 A1 $1 vio brn & ultra 7.50 *12.00*
43 A1 $2 rose red & grn 29.00 *45.00*
44 A1 $5 choc & emerald 29.00 *47.50*
Nos. 29-44 (16) 76.15 123.95

Types of Kedah with Portrait of Queen Elizabeth II

Perf. 13x12½, 12½x13

1957 Engr. Wmk. 314

45 A8 1c black .20 *.55*
46 A8 2c red orange .20 *.55*
47 A8 4c dark brown .50 .20
48 A8 5c dark car rose .50 .20
49 A8 8c dark green 2.25 *3.00*
50 A7 10c chocolate .45 .20
51 A7 20c blue 2.50 1.00

Perf. 12½, 13½ ($1)

52 A7 50c ultra & black 1.00 1.00
53 A8 $1 plum & ultra 6.00 4.75
54 A8 $2 red & green 20.00 *27.50*
55 A8 $5 olive grn & brn 22.50 *47.50*
Nos. 45-55 (11) 56.10 86.45

Types of Kedah, 1957, With Melaka Tree and Mouse Deer Replacing Portrait of Queen Elizabeth II

Perf. 13x12½, 12½x13, 13½ ($1)

1960, Mar. 15 Engr. Wmk. 314

56 A8 1c black .20 *.50*
57 A8 2c red orange .20 *.70*
58 A8 4c dark brown .20 .20
59 A8 5c dark car rose .20 .20
60 A8 8c dark green 3.50 *3.75*
61 A7 10c violet brown .45 .20
62 A7 20c blue 2.25 1.00
63 A7 50c ultra & black 1.25 1.00
64 A8 $1 plum & ultra 5.00 3.25
65 A8 $2 red & green 7.50 *15.00*
66 A8 $5 ol grn & brn 14.00 *17.50*
Nos. 56-66 (11) 34.75 43.30

Starting in 1965, issues of Malacca (Melaka) are listed with Malaysia.

OCCUPATION STAMPS

Issued Under Japanese Occupation

Stamps of Straits Settlements, 1937-41 Handstamped in Carmine

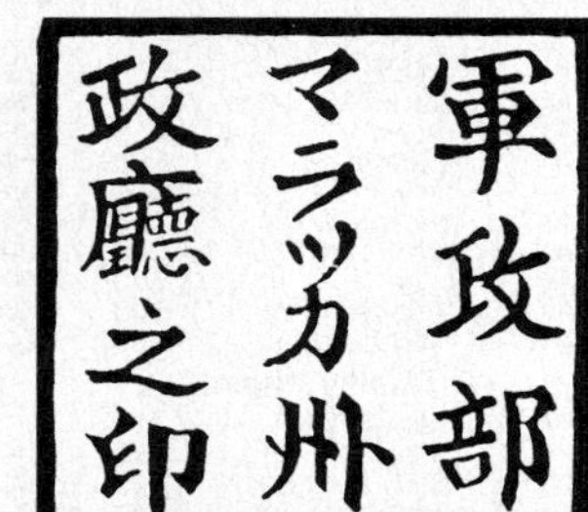

The handstamp covers four stamps. Values are for single stamps. Blocks of four showing complete handstamp sell for six times the price of singles.

1942 Wmk. 4 *Perf. 14*

N1 A29 1c black 125.00 90.00
N2 A29 2c brown orange 75.00 75.00
N3 A29 3c green 80.00 90.00
N4 A29 5c brown 175.00 175.00
N5 A29 8c gray 300.00 150.00
N6 A29 10c dull violet 125.00 125.00
N7 A29 12c ultramarine 140.00 140.00
N8 A29 15c ultramarine 100.00 125.00
N9 A29 30c org & vio *3,500.* —
N10 A29 40c dk vio & rose red 700.00 700.00
N11 A29 50c blk, *emerald* 1,100. 1,100.
N12 A29 $1 red & blk, *bl* 1,350. 1,250.
N13 A29 $2 rose red & gray grn *3,500.* —
N14 A29 $5 grn & red, *grn* *3,500.* —

Some authorities believe Nos. N9, N13, and N14 were not regularly issued.

OCCUPATION POSTAGE DUE STAMPS

Malaya Postage Due Stamps and Type of 1936-38, Handstamped Like Nos. N1-N14 in Carmine

1942 Wmk. 4 *Perf. 14½x14*

NJ1 D2 1c violet *250.00 225.00*
NJ2 D2 4c yel green *275.00 275.00*
NJ3 D2 8c red *3,500. 2,250.*
NJ4 D2 10c yel orange *550.00 525.00*
NJ5 D2 12c blue violet *800.00 725.00*
NJ6 D2 50c black *3,000. 2,000.*
Nos. NJ1-NJ6 (6) 8,375. 6,000.

Pricing note above No. N1 also applies to Nos. NJ1-NJ6.

NEGRI SEMBILAN

ˈne-grē səm-ˈbē-lən

LOCATION — South of Selangor on the west coast of the Malay Peninsula, bordering on Pahang on the east and Johore on the south.
AREA — 2,580 sq. mi.
POP. — 401,742 (1960)
CAPITAL — Seremban

Stamps of the Straits Settlements Overprinted in Black

1891 Wmk. 2 *Perf. 14*

Overprint 14½ to 15mm Wide

1 A2 2c rose 3.50 *8.00*

Tiger — A1

Tiger Head — A2

1891-94 Typo.

2 A1 1c green ('93) 4.00 1.25
3 A1 2c rose 4.00 *11.00*
4 A1 5c blue ('94) 35.00 *47.50*
Nos. 2-4 (3) 43.00 *59.75*

1895-99

5 A2 1c lilac & green 18.00 8.50
6 A2 2c lilac & brown 42.50 *140.00*
7 A2 3c lilac & car rose 18.00 1.50
8 A2 5c lilac & olive 10.00 11.50
9 A2 8c lilac & blue 35.00 20.00
10 A2 10c lilac & orange 32.50 17.00
11 A2 15c green & vio 50.00 *90.00*
12 A2 20c grn & ol ('99) 80.00 *45.00*
13 A2 25c grn & car rose 85.00 *110.00*
14 A2 50c green & black 90.00 80.00
Nos. 5-14 (10) 461.00 *523.50*

For surcharges see Nos. 15-16, 19-20.

Stamps of 1891-99 Surcharged

1899 Green Surcharge

15 A2 4c on 8c lil & blue 8.50 5.00
a. Double surcharge 2,750. 2,500.
b. Pair, one without surcharge 7,250. 4,500.
c. Double surcharge, 1 green, 1 red 925.00 1,000.

Black Surcharge

16 A2 4c on 8c lil & blue 1,400. *1,500.*

Same Surcharge and Bar in Black

17 A1 4c on 1c green 3.00 *20.00*
18 A1 4c on 5c blue 1.50 *17.00*
19 A2 4c on 3c lil & car rose 4.00 *24.00*
a. Double surcharge 2,750. 1,200.
b. Pair, one without surcharge *12,000.* *6,000.*
c. Bar omitted 1,000. 800.00
g. Inverted surcharge 2,100. 1,600.

Bar at bottom on #17-18, at top on #19.

No. 11 Surcharged in Black

1900

20	A2 1c on 15c grn & vio	125.00	*350.00*
a.	Inverted period	500.00	*1,300.*

Arms of Negri Sembilan
A4 A5

1935-41 Typo. Wmk. 4

21	A4	1c black ('36)	1.40	.20
22	A4	2c dp green ('36)	1.40	.20
22A	A4	2c brown org ('41)	2.25	*75.00*
22B	A4	3c green ('41)	4.25	*11.00*
23	A4	4c brown orange	1.25	.20
24	A4	5c chocolate	1.25	.20
25	A4	6c rose red	9.25	2.75
25A	A4	6c gray ('41)	3.00	*140.00*
26	A4	8c gray	1.10	.40
27	A4	10c dull vio ('36)	1.10	.20
28	A4	12c ultra ('36)	1.75	.75
28A	A4	15c ultra ('41)	5.50	*75.00*
29	A4	25c rose red & dull vio ('36)	2.00	1.00
30	A4	30c org & dull vio ('36)	3.00	2.00
31	A4	40c dull vio & car	2.00	*3.00*
32	A4	50c blk, *emer* ('36)	5.00	2.25
33	A4	$1 red & blk, *bl* ('36)	3.00	5.00
34	A4	$2 rose red & grn ('36)	30.00	20.00
35	A4	$5 brn red & grn, *emer* ('36)	20.00	*100.00*
		Nos. 21-35 (19)	98.50	*439.15*
		Set, never hinged	175.00	

For overprints see Nos. N1-N31.

Catalogue values for unused stamps in this section, from this point to the end of the section, are for Never Hinged items.

Silver Wedding Issue

Common Design Types

Inscribed: "Malaya Negri Sembilan"

1948, Dec. 1 Photo. *Perf. 14x14½*

36 CD304 10c purple .60 .70

Perf. 11½x11

Engraved; Name Typographed

37 CD305 $5 green 27.50 37.50

Common Design Types pictured following the introduction.

1949-55 Wmk. 4 Typo. *Perf. 18*

38	A5	1c black	1.25	.20
39	A5	2c orange	1.00	.20
40	A5	3c green	.60	.45
41	A5	4c chocolate	.30	.20
42	A5	5c rose violet	1.00	.45
43	A5	6c gray	2.25	.20
44	A5	8c rose red	.80	.95
45	A5	8c green	5.50	2.25
46	A5	10c plum	.40	.20
47	A5	12c rose red	5.50	3.25
48	A5	15c ultramarine	4.25	.45
49	A5	20c dk green & blk	2.25	2.00
50	A5	20c ultramarine	2.00	.35
51	A5	25c org & rose lilac	1.00	.35
52	A5	30c plum & rose red ('55)	2.00	2.75
53	A5	35c dk vio & rose red	1.50	3.75
54	A5	40c dk vio & rose red	4.75	*6.00*
55	A5	50c ultra & black	5.00	.45
56	A5	$1 vio brn & ultra	6.00	2.25
57	A5	$2 rose red & emer	18.00	27.50
58	A5	$5 choc & emerald	60.00	75.00
		Nos. 38-58 (21)	125.35	129.20

UPU Issue

Common Design Types

Inscribed: "Malaya-Negri Sembilan"

Engr.; Name Typo. on 15c, 25c

1949, Oct. 10 *Perf. 13½, 11x11½*

59	CD306 10c rose violet	.20	.20
60	CD307 15c indigo	1.40	3.50
61	CD308 25c orange	.75	3.00
62	CD309 50c slate	1.10	4.00
	Nos. 59-62 (4)	3.45	10.70

Coronation Issue

Common Design Type

1953, June 2 Engr. *Perf. 13½x13*

63 CD312 10c magenta & black 1.40 .65

Types of Kedah with Arms of Negri Sembilan

Perf. 13x12½, 12½x13, 13½ ($1)

1957-63 Engr. Wmk. 314

64	A8	1c black	.20	.20
65	A8	2c red orange	.20	.20
66	A8	4c dark brown	.20	.20
67	A8	5c dk car rose	.20	.20
68	A8	8c dark green	2.00	*1.60*
69	A7	10c chocolate	2.00	*.20*
70	A7	20c blue	1.00	*.20*
71	A7	50c ultra & blk ('60)	.60	*.20*
a.		Perf. 12½	1.75	*1.50*
72	A8	$1 plum & ultra	4.50	*2.25*
73	A8	$2 red & grn ('63)	20.00	*32.50*
a.		Perf. 12½	15.00	*20.00*
74	A8	$5 ol grn & brn ('62)	27.50	25.00
a.		Perf. 12½	20.00	*26.00*
		Nos. 64-74 (11)	58.40	62.75

Negri Sembilan State Crest and Tuanku Munawir
A6

1961, Apr. 17 Unwmk. *Perf. 14x13*

75 A6 10s blue & multi .45 *.70*

Installation of Tuanku Munawir as ruler (Yang di-Pertuan Besar) of Negri Sembilan.

Starting in 1965, issues of Negri (Negeri) Sembilan are listed with Malaysia.

OCCUPATION STAMPS

Issued under Japanese Occupation

Stamps and Type of Negri Sembilan, 1935-41, Handstamped in Red, Black, Brown or Violet

1942 Wmk. 4 *Perf. 14*

N1	A4	1c black	25.00	16.00
N2	A4	2c brown org	16.00	17.50
N3	A4	3c green	21.00	21.00
N4	A4	5c chocolate	29.00	27.50
N5	A4	6c rose red	600.00	600.00
N6	A4	6c gray	150.00	150.00
N7	A4	8c gray	87.50	87.50
N8	A4	8c rose red	55.00	47.50
N9	A4	10c dark violet	110.00	110.00
N10	A4	12c ultramarine	900.00	900.00
N11	A4	15c ultramarine	20.00	11.00
N12	A4	25c rose red & dk vio	35.00	40.00
N13	A4	30c org & dk vio	175.00	190.00
N14	A4	40c dk vio & car	750.00	750.00
N15	A4	$1 red & blk, *bl*	140.00	140.00
N16	A4	$5 brn red & grn, *emerald*	325.00	350.00

The 8c rose red is not known to have been issued without overprint.

Some authorities believe Nos. N5 and N7 were not regularly issued.

Stamps of Negri Sembilan, 1935-41, Overprinted in Black

N17	A4	1c black	1.40	1.40
a.		Inverted overprint	17.00	27.50
b.		Dbl. ovpt., one invtd.	47.50	67.50
N18	A4	2c brown orange	1.60	1.40
N19	A4	3c green	1.40	1.00
N20	A4	5c chocolate	.90	.90
N21	A4	6c gray	2.00	2.00
a.		Inverted overprint		*1,000.*
N22	A4	8c rose red	2.75	2.75
N23	A4	10c dk violet	5.50	5.50
N24	A4	15c ultramarine	8.00	4.75
N25	A4	25c rose red & dk vio	2.00	*6.75*
N26	A4	30c org & dk vio	4.00	*5.00*
N27	A4	$1 red & blk, *bl*	140.00	175.00
		Nos. N17-N27 (11)	169.55	206.45

The 8c rose red is not known to have been issued without overprint.

Negri Sembilan, Nos. 21, 24 and 29, Overprinted or Surcharged in Black:

a

b

c

1943

N28	A4	1c black	.65	.65
a.		Inverted overprint	17.00	24.00
N29	A4	2c on 5c choc	.55	.65
N30	A4	6c on 5c choc	.65	.90
a.		"6 cts." inverted	350.00	*400.00*
N31	A4	25c rose red & dk violet	2.00	2.75
		Nos. N28-N31 (4)	3.85	4.95

The Japanese characters read: "Japanese Postal Service."

PAHANG

pə-'haŋ

LOCATION — On the east coast of the Malay Peninsula.
AREA — 13,820 sq. mi.
POP. — 338,210 (1960)
CAPITAL — Kuala Lipis

Stamps of the Straits Settlements Overprinted in Black

Overprinted 

Overprint 16x2¾mm

1889 Wmk. 2 *Perf. 14*

1	A2	2c rose	140.00	60.00
2	A3	8c orange	2,000.	2,000.
3	A7	10c slate	250.00	300.00

Overprinted 

Overprint 12½x2mm

4 A2 2c rose 9.00 *10.00*

Overprinted PAHANG

1890 Overprint 15x2½mm

5 A2 2c rose 9,000. 2,500.

Overprinted 

Overprint 16x2¾mm

6 A2 2c rose 125.00 16.00

Surcharged in Black:

PAHANG
Two
CENTS

a

b

c

d

1891

7	A3 (a) 2c on 24c green	1,100.	*1,250.*
8	A3 (b) 2c on 24c green	425.00	*475.00*
9	A3 (c) 2c on 24c green	225.00	*275.00*
10	A3 (d) 2c on 24c green	1,100.	*1,250.*
	Nos. 7-10 (4)	2,850.	3,250.

A5

A6

1892-95 Typo.

11	A5	1c green	5.00	4.00
12	A5	2c rose	5.50	4.00
13	A5	5c blue	12.50	*47.50*
		Nos. 11-13 (3)	23.00	*55.50*

For surcharges see Nos. 21-22.

1895-99

14	A6	3c lilac & car rose	9.75	3.25
14A	A6	4c lil & car rose ('99)	20.00	14.50
15	A6	5c lilac & olive	35.00	*25.00*
		Nos. 14-15 (3)	64.75	*42.75*

For surcharge see No. 28.

Stamps of Perak, 1895-99, Overprinted

1898-99

16	A9	10c lilac & orange	25.00	*30.00*
17	A9	25c green & car rose	95.00	*190.00*
18	A9	50c green & black	500.00	*575.00*
18A	A9	50c lilac & black	350.00	425.00

Overprinted 

Wmk. 1

19	A10	$1 green & lt grn	425.	600.
20	A10	$5 green & ultra	1,700.	2,700.
		Nos. 16-20 (6)	3,095.	4,520.

No. 13 Cut in Half Diagonally and Surcharged in Red With New Value and Initials "J. F. O." in ms.

1897, Aug. 2 Wmk. 2

Red Surcharge

21	A5	2c on half of 5c blue	*1,750.*	*450.*
a.		Black surcharge	*9,500.*	*3,500.*
22	A5	3c on half of 5c blue	*1,750.*	*450.*
a.		Black surcharge	*9,500.*	*3,500.*
d.		Se-tenant pair, #21, 22	*5,500.*	*1,200.*

Perak No. 52 Surcharged

1898
25 A9 4c on 8c lilac & blue 7.50 7.50
b. Inverted surcharge 4,250. 1,700.

Same Surcharge on pieces of White Paper

1898 Without Gum ***Imperf.***
26 4c black 4,500.
27 5c black 3,000.

Pahang No. 15 Surcharged

1899 ***Perf. 14***
28 A6 4c on 5c lilac & olive 21.00 70.00

Sultan Abu Bakar
A7 A8

1935-41 Typo. Wmk. 4 ***Perf. 14***
29 A7 1c black ('36) .20 .20
30 A7 2c dp green ('36) 1.40 .20
30A A7 3c green ('41) 10.00 19.00
31 A7 4c brown orange .70 .20
32 A7 5c chocolate .70 .20
33 A7 6c rose red ('36) 12.00 3.50
34 A7 8c gray 2.00 .20
34A A7 8c rose red ('41) 3.00 60.00
35 A7 10c dk violet ('36) 1.75 .20
36 A7 12c ultra ('36) 2.10 2.00
36A A7 15c ultra ('41) 14.00 65.00
37 A7 25c rose red & pale vio ('36) 3.00 1.50
38 A7 30c org & dk vio ('36) 1.50 1.25
39 A7 40c dk vio & car 1.25 2.40
40 A7 50c black, *emer* ('36) 2.50 2.00
41 A7 $1 red & blk, *blue* ('36) 2.50 8.00
42 A7 $2 rose red & green ('36) 15.00 50.00
43 A7 $5 brn red & grn, *emer* ('36) 6.00 87.50
Nos. 29-43 (18) 79.60 303.35

The 3c was printed on both ordinary and chalky paper; the 15c only on ordinary paper; other values only on chalky paper.

Values for Nos. 34A used and 36A used are for stamps with legible postmarks dated in 1941.

A 2c brown orange and 6c gray, type A7, exist, but are not known to have been regularly issued.

For overprints see Nos. N1-N21.

Catalogue values for unused stamps in this section, from this point to the end of the section, are for Never Hinged items.

Silver Wedding Issue
Common Design Types
Inscribed: "Malaya Pahang"
Perf. 14x14½
1948, Dec. 1 Photo. Wmk. 4
44 CD304 10c purple .50 .55
Perf. 11½x11
Engraved; Name Typopgraphed
45 CD305 $5 green 27.50 37.50

UPU Issue
Common Design Types
Inscribed: "Malaya-Pahang"
Engr.; Name Typo. on 15c, 25c
1949, Oct. 10 ***Perf. 13½, 11x11½***
46 CD306 10c rose violet .30 .25
47 CD307 15c indigo 1.10 1.50
48 CD308 25c orange .60 2.50
49 CD309 50c slate 1.00 3.00
Nos. 46-49 (4) 3.00 7.25

Perf. 18
1950, June 1 Wmk. 4 Typo.
50 A8 1c black .30 .30
51 A8 2c orange .30 .30
52 A8 3c green .30 .80
53 A8 4c chocolate 2.25 .35
54 A8 6c gray .50 .35
55 A8 8c rose red .50 2.00
56 A8 10c plum .30 .30
57 A8 15c ultramarine .75 .35
58 A8 20c dk green & blk 1.00 3.00
59 A8 25c org & rose lilac .50 .30
60 A8 40c dk vio & rose red 2.25 8.50
61 A8 50c dp ultra & black 1.50 .35
62 A8 $1 vio brn & ultra 3.50 3.50
63 A8 $2 rose red & emer 16.00 30.00
64 A8 $5 choc & emer 65.00 90.00

1952-55
65 A8 5c rose violet .50 .70
66 A8 8c green 1.25 1.10
67 A8 12c rose red 1.50 1.25
68 A8 20c ultramarine 2.50 .30
69 A8 30c plum & rose red ('55) 2.75 .50
70 A8 35c dk vio & rose red 1.00 .35
Nos. 50-70 (21) 104.45 144.60

Coronation Issue
Common Design Type
1953, June 2 Engr. ***Perf. 13½x13***
71 CD312 10c magenta & black 2.25 .20

Types of Kedah with Portrait of Sultan Abu Bakar
Perf. 13x12½, 12½x13, 13½ ($1)
1957-62 Engr. Wmk. 314
72 A8 1c black .20 .20
73 A8 2c red orange .20 .20
74 A8 4c dark brown .20 .20
75 A8 5c dark car rose .20 .20
76 A8 8c dark green 2.25 2.25
77 A7 10c chocolate 1.25 .20
78 A7 20c blue 2.75 .25
79 A7 50c ultra & blk ('60) 1.00 .25
a. Perf. 12½ .60 1.00
80 A8 $1 plum & ultra 10.00 2.75
81 A8 $2 red & green ('62) 9.00 22.50
a. Perf. 12½ 7.50 11.00
82 A8 $5 ol grn & brn ('60) 15.00 24.00
a. Perf. 12½ 14.00 17.50
Nos. 72-82 (11) 42.05 53.00

Starting in 1965, issues of Pahang are listed with Malaysia.

OCCUPATION STAMPS

Issued under Japanese Occupation

Stamps of Pahang, 1935-41, Handstamped in Black, Red, Brown or Violet

1942 Wmk. 4 ***Perf. 14***
N1 A7 1c black 35.00 40.00
N1A A7 3c green 125.00 140.00
N2 A7 5c chocolate 15.00 9.50
N3 A7 8c rose red 26.00 11.00
N3A A7 8c gray 240.00 240.00
N4 A7 10c dk violet 60.00 60.00
N5 A7 12c ultramarine 1,200. 1,200.
N6 A7 15c ultramarine 87.50 87.50
N7 A7 25c rose red & pale vio 21.00 37.50
N8 A7 30c org & dk vio 17.00 32.50
N9 A7 40c dk vio & car 17.50 35.00
N10 A7 50c blk, *emerald* 300.00 350.00
N11 A7 $1 red & blk, *bl* 100.00 125.00
N12 A7 $5 brown red & grn, *emer* 575.00 625.00

Some authorities claim the 2c green, 4c brown orange, 6c rose red and $2 rose red and green were not regularly issued with this overprint.

Stamps of Pahang, 1935-41, Overprinted in Black

N13 A7 1c black 2.00 1.10
N14 A7 5c chocolate 2.00 2.00
N15 A7 8c rose red 35.00 3.75
N16 A7 10c violet brown 20.00 9.00
N17 A7 12c ultramarine 2.00 3.00
N18 A7 25c rose red & pale vio 7.50 10.50
N19 A7 30c org & dk vio 2.75 5.50
Nos. N13-N19 (7) 71.25 34.85

Pahang No. 32 Overprinted and Surcharged in Black

e

f

1943
N20 A7(e) 6c on 5c chocolate 1.40 1.40
N21 A7(f) 6c on 5c chocolate 2.00 1.50

The Japanese characters read: "Japanese Postal Service."

PENANG

pə-naŋ

LOCATION — An island off the west coast of the Malay Peninsula, plus a coastal strip called Province Wellesley.
AREA — 400 sq. mi.
POP. — 616,254 (1960)
CAPITAL — Georgetown

Catalogue values for unused stamps in this section are for Never Hinged items.

Common Design Types pictured following the introduction.

Silver Wedding Issue
Common Design Types
Inscribed: "Malaya Penang"
Perf. 14x14½
1948, Dec. 1 Wmk. 4 Photo.
1 CD304 10c purple .50 .30
Perf. 11½x11
Engraved; Name Typographed
2 CD305 $5 lt brown 40.00 37.50

Type of Straits Settlements, 1937-41, Inscribed "Penang"

1949-52 ***Perf. 18***
3 A29 1c black 1.50 .30
4 A29 2c orange 1.50 .30
5 A29 3c green .60 1.25
6 A29 4c chocolate .50 .20
7 A29 5c rose vio ('52) 4.25 4.00
8 A29 6c gray 1.50 .30
9 A29 8c rose red 1.25 5.00
10 A29 8c green ('52) 4.00 3.00
11 A29 10c plum .50 .20
12 A29 12c rose red ('52) 4.50 9.00
13 A29 15c ultramarine 2.00 .40
14 A29 20c dk grn & blk 2.75 1.50
15 A29 20c ultra ('52) 3.25 1.50
16 A29 25c org & rose lilac 3.00 1.25
17 A29 35c dk vio & rose red ('52) 3.25 1.50
18 A29 40c dk vio & rose red 4.25 15.00
19 A29 50c ultra & black 5.50 .30
20 A29 $1 vio brn & ultra 20.00 3.00
21 A29 $2 rose red & emer 26.00 2.50
22 A29 $5 choc & emerald 52.50 3.75
Nos. 3-22 (20) 142.60 54.25

UPU Issue
Common Design Types
Inscribed: "Malaya-Penang"
Engr.; Name Typo. on 15c, 25c
1949, Oct. 10 ***Perf. 13½, 11x11½***
23 CD306 10c rose violet .25 .20
24 CD307 15c indigo 2.50 3.75
25 CD308 25c orange .60 3.75
26 CD309 50c slate 1.75 4.00
Nos. 23-26 (4) 5.10 11.70

Coronation Issue
Common Design Type
1953, June 2 Engr. ***Perf. 13½x13***
27 CD312 10c magenta & black 1.75 .30

Type of Malacca, 1954
1954-55 Wmk. 4 Typo. ***Perf. 18***
29 A1 1c black .20 .85
30 A1 2c orange .60 .40
31 A1 4c chocolate 1.25 .20
32 A1 5c rose violet 2.25 4.25
33 A1 6c gray .20 1.00
34 A1 8c green .30 4.00
35 A1 10c plum .25 .20
36 A1 12c rose red .35 4.00
37 A1 20c ultramarine .60 .20
38 A1 25c orange & plum .40 .20
39 A1 30c plum & rose red ('55) .40 .20
40 A1 35c vio brn & rose red .80 .95
41 A1 50c ultra & black .65 .20
42 A1 $1 vio brn & ultra 2.75 .35
43 A1 $2 rose red & grn 15.00 4.25
44 A1 $5 choc & emerald 47.50 4.25
Nos. 29-44 (16) 73.50 25.50

Types of Kedah with Portrait of Queen Elizabeth II
Perf. 13x12½, 12½x13
1957 Engr. Wmk. 314
45 A8 1c black .30 1.50
46 A8 2c red orange .30 1.25
47 A8 4c dark brown .30 .20
48 A8 5c dk car rose .30 .50
49 A8 8c dark green 2.50 2.75
50 A7 10c chocolate .40 .20
51 A7 20c blue 1.00 .60
Perf. 12½, 13½ ($1)
52 A7 50c ultra & black 1.75 .85
53 A8 $1 plum & ultra 8.50 1.00
54 A8 $2 red & green 22.50 18.00
55 A8 $5 ol green & brown 27.50 15.00
Nos. 45-55 (11) 65.35 41.85

Types of Kedah, 1957 with Penang State Crest and Areca-nut Palm Replacing Portrait of Elizabeth II
Perf. 13x12½, 12½x13, 13½ ($1)
1960, Mar. 15 Engr. Wmk. 314
56 A8 1c black .20 1.75
57 A8 2c red orange .20 1.75
58 A8 4c dark brown .20 .20
59 A8 5c dk car rose .20 .20
60 A8 8c dark green 3.00 5.25
61 A7 10c violet brown .35 .20
62 A7 20c blue .55 .20
63 A7 50c ultra & black .35 .20
64 A8 $1 plum & ultra 7.50 1.90
65 A8 $2 red & green 8.00 7.25
Revenue cancel .20
66 A8 $5 ol green & brown 14.00 9.50
Nos. 56-66 (11) 34.55 28.40

Starting in 1965, issues of Penang (Pulau Pinang) are listed with Malaysia.

OCCUPATION STAMPS

Issued under Japanese Occupation

Stamps of Straits Settlements, 1937-41, Overprinted in Red or Black

1942 Wmk. 4 ***Perf. 14***
N1 A29 1c black (R) 7.00 3.75
a. Inverted overprint 600.00 600.00
b. Double overprint 350.00 350.00
N2 A29 2c brown orange 6.00 4.75
a. Inverted overprint 175.00
b. Double overprint 575.00
N3 A29 3c green (R) 6.00 7.00
a. Double overprint, one inverted 450.00
N4 A29 5c brown (R) 3.50 9.00
a. Double overprint 575.00 475.00
b. "N PPON" for "NIPPON" 200.00
N5 A29 8c gray (R) 2.50 1.60
a. Double overprint, one inverted 525.00
b. "N PPON" for "NIPPON" 60.00 65.00
N6 A29 10c dull vio (R) 1.75 2.50
a. Double overprint 500.00 500.00
b. Double overprint, one inverted 450.00 450.00
N7 A29 12c ultra (R) 4.75 18.00
a. Double overprint 450.00
b. Double overprint, one inverted 675.00 675.00
c. "N PPON" for "NIPPON" 550.00
N8 A29 15c ultra (R) 2.00 4.50
a. Inverted overprint 450.00 475.00
b. Double overprint 600.00 600.00
c. "N PPON" for "NIPPON" 120.00 130.00
N9 A29 40c dk vio & rose red 6.00 18.00
N10 A29 50c black, *emer* (R) 4.25 35.00
N11 A29 $1 red & blk, *bl* 7.00 47.50
a. Inverted overprint 1,200.
N12 A29 $2 rose red & gray grn 65.00 100.00
N13 A29 $5 grn & red, *grn* 675.00 750.00
Nos. N1-N13 (13) 790.75 1,001.

Stamps of Straits Settlements Handstamped in Red

Okugawa Seal

1942 **Wmk. 4** ***Perf. 14***

N14	A29	1c black	12.00	13.50
N15	A29	2c brown orange	27.50	25.00
N16	A29	3c green	22.50	25.00
N17	A29	5c brown	27.50	32.50
N18	A29	8c gray	30.00	42.50
N19	A29	10c dull violet	55.00	55.00
N20	A29	12c ultramarine	47.50	55.00
N21	A29	15c ultramarine	55.00	55.00
N22	A29	40c dk vio & rose red	110.00	125.00
N23	A29	50c blk, *emerald*	250.00	250.00
N24	A29	$1 red & blk, *bl*	275.00	300.00
N25	A29	$2 rose red & gray grn	900.00	800.00
N26	A29	$5 grn & red, *grn*	2,750.	1,700.
		Nos. N14-N26 (13)	4,562.	3,478.

Handstamped in Red

Uchibori Seal

N14a	A29	1c	190.00	150.00
N15a	A29	2c	190.00	130.00
N16a	A29	3c	125.00	125.00
N17a	A29	5c	2,750.	2,750.
N18a	A29	8c	100.00	110.00
N19a	A29	10c	190.00	190.00
N20a	A29	12c	125.00	140.00
N21a	A29	15c	140.00	150.00
		Nos. N14a-N21a (8)	3,810.	3,745.

PERAK

ˈper-ə-ˌak

LOCATION — On the west coast of the Malay Peninsula.
AREA — 7,980 sq. mi.
POP. — 1,327,120 (1960)
CAPITAL — Taiping

Straits Settlements No. 10 Handstamped in Black

1878 **Wmk. 1** ***Perf. 14***

1	A2	2c brown	2,200.	1,800.

Overprinted

Overprint 17x3½mm Wide

1880-81

2	A2	2c brown	40.00	*80.00*

Overprinted

Overprint 10 to 14½mm Wide

3	A2	2c brown, ovpt. 12-13.5mm ('81)	190.00	*200.00*

Same Overprint on Straits Settlements Nos. 40, 41a

1883 **Wmk. 2**

4	A2	2c brown	22.50	*72.50*
a.		Double overprint	750.00	
5	A2	2c rose	35.00	*60.00*
c.		Double overprint	750.00	

Overprinted

Overprint 14 to 15½mm Wide

6	A2	2c rose	5.50	4.00
a.		Inverted overprint	475.00	600.00
b.		Double overprint	700.00	700.00

For surcharge, see No. 19E

Overprinted

Overprint 12¾ to 14mm Wide

1886-90

7	A2	2c rose	2.75	*8.00*
a.		"FERAK" corrected by pen	425.00	*550.00*

Overprinted

Overprint 10x1¾mm

8	A2	2c rose	22.50	*60.00*

Overprinted

Overprint 12-12½x2¾mm

10	A2	2c rose	9.50	*40.00*
a.		Double overprint	1,800.	

Overprinted

Overprint 10½-10¾x2½mm

11	A2	2c rose	160.00	*175.00*

Straits Settlements Nos. 11, 41a, 42 Surcharged in Black or Blue

q

r

s

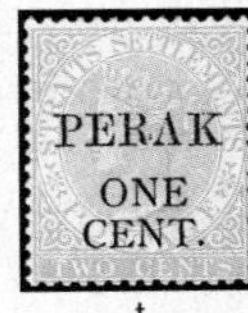

t

12	A2(q)	2c on 4c rose, as #3 ('83)	725.00	300.00
13	A2(t)	1c on 2c rose	350.00	150.00
a.		Without period after "CENT" ('90)	—	300.00
14	A2(r)	1c on 2c rose	75.00	95.00
a.		Without period after "PERAK"	800.00	850.00
b.		Double surcharge	1,250.	
15	A2(s)	1c on 2c rose (Bl)	65.00	85.00
15A	A2(s)	1c on 2c rose (Bk)	2,100.	1,600.

In type "r" PERAK is 11½ to 14mm wide.

Surcharged in Black

16	A2	1c on 2c rose	175.00	175.00
a.		Double surcharge	*2,000.*	2,000.

Surcharged

I
CENT
PERAK

17	A2	1c on 2c rose		

Some authorities question the status of No. 17.

Surcharged

1
CENT
PERAK

18	A2	1c on 2c rose	2,750.	2,750.
b.		Double surcharge, one inverted		
c.		"PREAK"		

Surcharged

18A	A2	1c on 2c rose	1,100.	800.00

Surcharged

19	A2	1c on 2c rose	4.50	*14.00*
a.		Double surcharge, one inverted		
b.		Inverted surcharge		
c.		"One" inverted	*3,500.*	
d.		Double surcharge	*1,400.*	

No. 6 surcharged "1 CENT" in Italic Serifed Capital Letters

1886

19E	A2	1c on 2c rose	3,300.	2,750.

Straits Settlements No. 41a Surcharged

u

v

w

x

y

z

h

1889-90

20	A2(u)	1c on 2c rose	4.00	*7.75*
a.		Italic Roman "K" in "PERAK"	425.00	*550.00*
b.		Double surcharge	*1,400.*	
21	A2(v)	1c on 2c rose	800.00	*975.00*
23	A2(w)	1c on 2c rose	20.00	*50.00*
a.		"PREAK"	775.00	*975.00*
24	A2(x)	1c on 2c rose	150.00	*175.00*
25	A2(y)	1c on 2c rose	11.00	*19.00*
26	A2(z)	1c on 2c rose	13.00	*22.50*
27	A2(h)	1c on 2c rose	24.00	*45.00*

Straits Settlements Nos. 41a, 48, 54 Surcharged in Black:

PERAK One CENT — a

PERAK Two CENTS — b

PERAK One CENT — c

PERAK One CENT — d

PERAK One CENT — e

PERAK One CENT — f

PERAK Two CENTS — g

1891 **Wmk. 2**

28	A2(a)	1c on 2c rose	2.75	10.00
a.		Bar omitted	215.00	
29	A2(a)	1c on 6c violet	60.00	42.50
30	A3(b)	2c on 24c green	22.50	14.50
31	A2(c)	1c on 2c rose	9.75	37.50
a.		Bar omitted	*1,000.*	
32	A2(d)	1c on 2c rose	2.75	14.50
a.		Bar omitted	425.00	
33	A2(d)	1c on 6c violet	100.00	95.00
34	A3(d)	2c on 24c green	85.00	42.50
35	A2(e)	1c on 2c rose	9.75	37.50
a.		Bar omitted	*1,000.*	
36	A2(e)	1c on 6c violet	210.00	210.00
37	A3(e)	2c on 24c green	140.00	80.00
38	A2(f)	1c on 6c violet	210.00	200.00
39	A3(f)	2c on 24c green	140.00	95.00
40	A2(g)	1c on 6c violet	210.00	200.00
41	A3(g)	2c on 24c green	140.00	95.00
		Nos. 28-41 (14)	1,342.	1,174.

A7

1892-95 **Typo.** ***Perf. 14***

42	A7	1c green	2.75	.40
43	A7	2c rose	2.25	.40
44	A7	2c orange ('95)	.70	*5.25*
45	A7	5c blue	4.00	8.50
		Nos. 42-45 (4)	9.70	*14.55*

For overprint see No. O10.

Type of 1892 Surcharged in Black

1895

46	A7	3c on 5c rose	4.25	3.75

A9

A10

1895-99 Wmk. 2 Perf. 14

47 A9 1c lilac & green 3.25 .60
48 A9 2c lilac & brown 3.50 .60
49 A9 3c lilac & car rose 3.75 .25
50 A9 4c lil & car rose ('99) 14.50 6.00
51 A9 5c lilac & olive 6.00 .70
52 A9 8c lilac & blue 50.00 .70
53 A9 10c lilac & orange 17.00 .65
54 A9 25c grn & car rose ('96) 200.00 14.00
55 A9 50c lilac & black 52.50 45.00
56 A9 50c grn & blk ('99) 240.00 190.00

Wmk. 1

57 A10 $1 green & lt grn 250.00 225.00
58 A10 $2 grn & car rose ('96) 400.00 375.00
59 A10 $3 green & ol ('96) 475.00 475.00
60 A10 $5 green & ultra 575.00 575.00
61 A10 $25 grn & org ('96) 10,000. 3,750.
Nos. 47-57 (11) 840.50 483.50

For surcharges and overprint see #62-68, O11, Malaya 9-13A.

Stamps of 1895-99 Surcharged in Black:

i

k

m

1900 Wmk. 2

62 A9(i) 1c on 2c lilac & brown .75 2.75
63 A9(k) 1c on 4c lilac & car rose 1.25 14.50
a. Double surcharge 1,250.
64 A9(i) 1c on 5c lilac & ol 3.00 17.00
65 A9(i) 3c on 8c lilac & blue 7.00 13.00
a. No period after "Cent" 190.00 300.00
b. Double surcharge 575.00 650.00
66 A9(i) 3c on 50c green & black 4.00 8.50
a. No period after "Cent" 150.00 225.00

Wmk. 1

67 A10(m) 3c on $1 grn & lt green 62.50 175.00
a. Double surcharge 1,700.
68 A10(m) 3c on $2 grn & car rose 42.50 95.00
Nos. 62-68 (7) 121.00 325.75

Sultan Iskandar
A14 A15

1935-37 Typo. Wmk. 4
Chalky Paper

69 A14 1c black ('36) 1.00 .20
70 A14 2c dp green ('36) 1.00 .20
71 A14 4c brown orange 1.10 .20
72 A14 5c chocolate .30 .20
73 A14 6c rose red ('37) 6.00 4.25
74 A14 8c gray .50 .30
75 A14 10c dk vio ('36) .40 .20
76 A14 12c ultra ('36) 2.00 1.25
77 A14 25c rose red & pale vio ('36) 1.50 1.25
78 A14 30c org & dark vio ('36) 2.00 2.00
79 A14 40c dk vio & car 2.75 5.00
80 A14 50c blk, *emerald* ('36) 3.75 2.00
81 A14 $1 red & blk, *bl* ('36) 1.50 1.25
82 A14 $2 rose red & green ('36) 17.50 9.00
83 A14 $5 brn red & grn, *emer* ('36) 70.00 37.50
Nos. 69-83 (15) 111.30 64.80
Set, never hinged 200.00

1938-41

84 A15 1c black ('39) 7.00 .20
85 A15 2c dp green ('39) 4.50 .20
85A A15 2c brn org ('41) 1.75 18.00
85B A15 3c green ('41) 1.50 8.00
86 A15 4c brn org ('39) 20.00 .20
87 A15 5c choc ('39) 3.50 .20
88 A15 6c rose red ('39) 14.00 .20
89 A15 8c gray 16.00 .20
89A A15 8c rose red ('41) .55 50.00
90 A15 10c dk violet 18.00 .20
91 A15 12c ultramarine 13.00 2.00
91A A15 15c ultra ('41) 2.25 20.00
92 A15 25c rose red & pale vio ('39) 27.50 4.00
93 A15 30c org & dk vio 5.00 3.00
94 A15 40c dk vio & rose red 27.50 3.00
95 A15 50c blk, *emerald* 17.50 .75
96 A15 $1 red & blk, *bl* ('40) 75.00 25.00
97 A15 $2 rose red & grn ('40) 100.00 75.00
98 A15 $5 red, *emer* ('40) 160.00 425.00
Nos. 84-98 (19) 514.55 635.15
Set, never hinged 950.00

For overprints see Nos. N1-N40.

Catalogue values for unused stamps in this section, from this point to the end of the section, are for Never Hinged items.

Silver Wedding Issue
Common Design Types
Inscribed: "Malaya Perak"

1948, Dec. 1 Photo. Perf. 14x14½

99 CD304 10c purple .30 .20

Perf. 11½x11
Engraved; Name Typographed

100 CD305 $5 green 27.50 37.50

Common Design Types pictured following the introduction.

UPU Issue
Common Design Types
Inscribed: "Malaya-Perak"
Engr.; Name Typo. on 15c, 25c
Perf. 13½, 11x11½

1949, Oct. 10 Wmk. 4

101 CD306 10c rose violet .20 .20
102 CD307 15c indigo 1.50 2.00
103 CD308 25c orange .40 5.00
104 CD309 50c slate 1.50 3.50
Nos. 101-104 (4) 3.60 10.70

Sultan Yussuf Izuddin Shah — A16

1950, Aug. 17 Typo. Perf. 18

105 A16 1c black .25 .40
106 A16 2c orange .25 .40
107 A16 3c green 3.00 1.40
108 A16 4c chocolate .75 .40
109 A16 6c gray .40 .40
110 A16 8c rose red 1.60 2.25
111 A16 10c plum .25 .40
112 A16 15c ultramarine 1.10 .50
113 A16 20c dk grn & blk 1.60 .75
114 A16 25c org & plum .90 .30
115 A16 40c vio brn & rose red 5.00 7.00
116 A16 50c dp ultra & blk 5.00 .30
117 A16 $1 vio brn & ultra 7.00 1.10
118 A16 $2 rose red & emer 17.00 7.50
119 A16 $5 choc & emerald 42.50 22.50

1952-55

120 A16 5c rose violet .50 2.00
121 A16 8c green 1.40 1.25
122 A16 12c rose red 1.40 5.00
123 A16 20c ultramarine 1.10 .30
124 A16 30c plum & rose red ('55) 2.25 .30
125 A16 35c dk vio & rose red 1.40 .40
Nos. 105-125 (21) 94.65 54.85

Coronation Issue
Common Design Type

1953 Engr. Perf. 13½x13

126 CD312 10c magenta & black 1.60 .20

Types of Kedah with Portrait of Sultan Yussuf Izuddin Shah
Perf. 13x12½, 12½x13, 13½ ($1)

1957-61 Engr. Wmk. 314

127 A8 1c black .25 .30
128 A8 2c red orange .45 1.00
129 A8 4c dark brown .25 .25
130 A8 5c dk car rose .25 .25
131 A8 8c dark green 2.50 4.00
132 A7 10c chocolate 2.25 .25
133 A7 20c blue 2.25 .25
134 A7 50c ultra & blk ('60) .45 .25
a. Perf. 12½ .60 1.00
135 A8 $1 plum & ultra 7.50 .50
136 A8 $2 red & grn ('61) 7.00 4.25
a. Perf. 12½ 5.00 5.00
137 A8 $5 ol grn & brn ('60) 14.00 9.00
a. Perf. 12½ 15.00 13.00
Nos. 127-137 (11) 37.15 20.30

Starting with 1963, issues of Perak are listed with Malaysia.

OFFICIAL STAMPS

Stamps and Types of Straits Settlements Overprinted in Black

1890 Wmk. 1 Perf. 14

O1 A3 12c blue 240.00 300.00
O2 A3 24c green 800.00 900.00

Wmk. 2

O3 A2 2c rose 5.50 7.50
a. No period after "S" 85.00 105.00
b. Double overprint 950.00 950.00
O4 A2 4c brown 22.50 27.50
a. No period after "S" 200.00 225.00
O5 A2 6c violet 32.50 60.00
O6 A3 8c orange 42.50 75.00
O7 A7 10c slate 85.00 85.00
O8 A3 12c vio brown 250.00 325.00
O9 A3 24c green 210.00 250.00

P.G.S. stands for Perak Government Service.

Perak No. 45 Overprinted

1894

O10 A7 5c blue 90.00 1.25
a. Inverted overprint 1,200. 550.00

Same Overprint on No. 51

1897

O11 A9 5c lilac & olive 3.50 .60
a. Double overprint 700.00 450.00

OCCUPATION STAMPS

Issued under Japanese Occupation

Stamps of Perak, 1938-41, Handstamped in Black, Red, Brown or Violet

1942 Wmk. 4 Perf. 14

N1 A15 1c black 50.00 35.00
N2 A15 2c brn orange 35.00 21.00
N3 A15 3c green 35.00 37.50
N4 A15 5c chocolate 11.50 11.00
N5 A15 8c gray 55.00 37.50
N6 A15 8c rose red 25.00 35.00
N7 A15 10c dk violet 22.50 27.50
N8 A15 12c ultramarine 150.00 150.00
N9 A15 15c ultramarine 30.00 35.00
N10 A15 25c rose red & pale vio 27.50 30.00
N11 A15 30c org & dk vio 35.00 40.00
N12 A15 40c dk vio & rose red 175.00 190.00
N13 A15 50c blk, *emerald* 57.50 60.00
N14 A15 $1 red & blk, *bl* 275.00 300.00
N15 A15 $2 rose red & grn 1,500. 1,500.
N16 A15 $5 red, *emerald* 750.00 750.00

Some authorities claim No. N6 was not regularly issued. This overprint also exists on No. 85

Stamps of Perak, 1938-41, Overprinted in Black

N16A A15 1c black 40.00 40.00
N17 A15 2c brn org 1.60 1.60
a. Inverted overprint 27.50 29.00
N18 A15 3c green 1.25 1.40
a. Inverted overprint 27.50 30.00
N18B A15 5c chocolate 40.00
N19 A15 8c rose red 1.25 .65
a. Inverted overprint 10.00 10.00
b. Dbl. ovpt., one invtd. 250.00 275.00
c. Pair, one without ovpt. 500.00 475.00
N20 A15 10c dk violet 8.50 9.50
N21 A15 15c ultramarine 6.00 6.75
N21A A15 30c org & dk vio 35.00 35.00
N22 A15 50c blk, *emerald* 4.00 6.00
N23 A15 $1 red & blk, *bl* 350.00 375.00
N24 A15 $5 red, *emerald* 60.00 67.50
a. Inverted overprint 350.00 400.00

Some authorities claim Nos. N16A, N18B and N21A were not regularly issued.

Overprinted on Perak No. 87 and Surcharged in Black "2 Cents"

N25 A15 2c on 5c chocolate 2.00 1.40

Perak Nos. 84 and 89A Overprinted in Black

N26 A15 1c black 3.25 4.00
a. Inverted overprint 35.00 40.00
N27 A15 8c rose red 3.25 2.00
a. Inverted overprint 20.00 24.00

Overprinted on Perak No. 87 and Surcharged in Black "2 Cents"

N28 A15 2c on 5c chocolate 5.00 5.00
a. Inverted overprint 35.00 47.50
b. As "a," "2 Cents" omitted 50.00 57.50

Stamps of Perak, 1938-41, Overprinted or Surcharged in Black:

n

No. N31

No. N32

1943

N29 A15 1c black .65 .65
N30 A15 2c brn orange 35.00 35.00
N31 A15 2c on 5c choc 1.00 1.00
a. "2 Cents" inverted 35.00 40.00
b. Entire surcharge inverted 35.00 40.00
N32 A15 2c on 5c choc 1.40 1.40
a. Vertical characters invtd. 35.00 40.00
b. Entire surcharge inverted 35.00 40.00
N33 A15 3c green 37.50 37.50
N34 A15 5c chocolate 1.00 1.00
a. Inverted overprint 50.00 60.00
N35 A15 8c gray 35.00 35.00
N36 A15 8c rose red 1.00 1.00
a. Inverted overprint 35.00 40.00
N37 A15 10c dk violet 1.25 1.25
N38 A15 30c org & dk vio 2.75 4.00

N39 A15 50c blk, *emerald* 5.50 9.50
N40 A15 $5 red, *emerald* 75.00 85.00
Nos. N29-N40 (12) 197.05 212.30

No. N34 was also used in the Shan States of Burma. The Japanese characters read: "Japanese Postal Service."
Some authorities claim Nos. N30, N33 and N35 were not regularly issued.

PERLIS

ˈper-ləs

LOCATION — On the west coast of the Malay peninsula, adjoining Siam and Kedah.
AREA — 310 sq. mi.
POP. — 97,645 (1960)
CAPITAL — Kangar

Catalogue values for unused stamps in this section are for Never Hinged items.

Silver Wedding Issue
Common Design Types
Inscribed: "Malaya Perlis"

Perf. 14x14½

1948, Dec. 1 Photo. Wmk. 4
1 CD304 10c purple 1.00 *3.00*

Engraved; Name Typographed
Perf. 11½x11
2 CD305 $5 lt brown 32.50 *55.00*

UPU Issue
Common Design Types
Inscribed: "Malaya-Perlis"

Engr.; Name Typo. on 15c, 25c
1949, Oct. 10 ***Perf. 13½, 11x11½***
3 CD306 10c rose violet .40 *2.00*
4 CD307 15c indigo 1.40 *4.50*
5 CD308 25c orange .65 *3.50*
6 CD309 50c slate 1.50 *4.25*
Nos. 3-6 (4) 3.95 14.25

Raja Syed Putra — A1

Perf. 18
1951, Mar. 26 Wmk. 4 Typo.
7 A1 1c black .25 *1.00*
8 A1 2c orange .75 .70
9 A1 3c green 1.75 *5.25*
10 A1 4c chocolate 1.75 1.50
11 A1 6c gray 1.50 2.50
12 A1 8c rose red 3.75 7.50
13 A1 10c plum 1.25 .50
14 A1 15c ultramarine 5.00 8.50
15 A1 20c dk green & blk 4.50 11.50
16 A1 25c org & rose lilac 2.25 3.75
17 A1 40c dk vio & rose red 5.00 *29.00*
18 A1 50c ultra & black 4.75 *7.00*
19 A1 $1 vio brn & ultra 10.00 *27.50*
20 A1 $2 rose red & emer 20.00 *60.00*
21 A1 $5 choc & emerald 70.00 *125.00*

1952-55
22 A1 5c rose violet .75 *3.75*
23 A1 8c green 2.75 *4.50*
24 A1 12c rose red 2.00 *6.25*
25 A1 20c ultramarine 1.25 1.75
26 A1 30c plum & rose red ('55) 2.75 *15.00*
27 A1 35c dk vio & rose red 3.00 *8.50*
Nos. 7-27 (21) 145.00 *330.95*

Coronation Issue
Common Design Type

1953, June 2 Engr. ***Perf. 13½x13***
28 CD312 10c magenta & black 1.75 *4.00*

Types of Kedah with Portrait of Raja Syed Putra

Perf. 13x12½, 12½x13, 12½ ($2, $5), 13½ ($1)

1957-62 Engr. Wmk. 314
29 A8 1c black .25 *.40*
30 A8 2c red orange .25 *.40*
31 A8 4c dark brown .25 .25
32 A8 5c dk car rose .25 .25
33 A8 8c dark green 2.50 2.25
34 A7 10c chocolate 1.50 *3.00*
35 A7 20c blue 3.50 *5.00*
36 A7 50c ultra & blk ('62) 3.50 *4.75*
a. Perf. 12½ 1.50 4.00
37 A8 $1 plum & ultra 10.00 *14.00*
38 A8 $2 red & green 10.00 *10.00*
39 A8 $5 ol green & brown 15.00 *13.00*
Nos. 29-39 (11) 47.00 *53.30*

Starting in 1965, issues of Perlis are listed with Malaysia.

SELANGOR

sə-ˈlaŋ-ər

LOCATION — South of Perak on the west coast of the Malay Peninsula.
AREA — 3,160 sq. mi.
POP. — 1,012,891 (1960)
CAPITAL — Kuala Lumpur

Stamps of the Straits Settlements Overprinted

Handstamped in Black or Red

1878 Wmk. 1 ***Perf. 14***
1 A2 2c brown (Bk) —

Wmk. 2 ***Perf.***
2 A2 2c brown (R) 600.00

The authenticity of Nos. 1-2 is questioned.

S.
Overprinted in Black

1882
3 A2 2c brown — 3,300.
4 A2 2c rose

Overprinted

Overprint 16 to 16¾mm Wide
1881 Wmk. 1
5 A2 2c brown 140.00 140.00
a. Double overprint

Overprint 16 to 17mm Wide
1882-83 Wmk. 2
"S" wide, all other letters narrow
6 A2 2c brown 200.00 160.00
7 A2 2c rose 160.00 125.00

Overprinted

Overprint 14¼x3mm
8 A2 2c rose 11.50 *24.00*
a. Double overprint 975.00 850.00

Overprinted

Overprint 14½ to 15½mm Wide
1886-89
9 A2 2c rose 42.50 *55.00*

Overprinted

Overprint 16½x1¾mm
9A A2 2c rose 67.50 72.50
b. Double overprint 1,000.

Overprinted

Overprint 15½ to 17mm Wide
With Period
10 A2 2c rose 140.00 90.00

Without Period
11 A2 2c rose 14.50 3.25

Same Overprint, but Vertically
12 A2 2c rose 22.50 *37.50*

Overprinted

12A A2 2c rose 150.00 3.75

Overprinted ***Selangor***

Overprint 17mm Wide
13 A2 2c rose 1,700. *1,850.*

Overprinted

14 A2 2c rose 400.00 175.00

Overprinted Vertically

1889
15 A2 2c rose 725.00 40.00

Overprinted Vertically

Overprint 19 to 20¾mm Wide
16 A2 2c rose 325.00 95.00

Similar Overprint, but Diagonally
17 A2 2c rose 3,000.

Overprinted Vertically

18 A2 2c rose 90.00 6.75

Same Overprint Horizontally
18A A2 2c rose *4,500.*

Surcharged in Black:

a

b

c

d

e

1891
19 A3 (a) 2c on 24c green 40.00 *75.00*
20 A3 (b) 2c on 24c green 225.00 *275.00*
21 A3 (c) 2c on 24c green 225.00 *250.00*
22 A3 (d) 2c on 24c green 125.00 *150.00*
23 A3 (e) 2c on 24c green 225.00 *275.00*
Nos. 19-23 (5) 840.00 1,025.

No. 22a occurred ijn the first printing in one position (R. 8/3) in the sheet.

A6

1891-95 Typo. Wmk. 2
24 A6 1c green 1.75 .30
25 A6 2c rose 4.00 1.25
26 A6 2c orange ('95) 3.00 1.00
27 A6 5c blue 27.50 5.25
Nos. 24-27 (4) 36.25 7.80

Type of 1891 Surcharged

1894
28 A6 3c on 5c rose 5.00 .70

A8 A9

1895-99 Wmk. 2 ***Perf. 14***
29 A8 3c lilac & car rose 7.00 .35
30 A8 5c lilac & olive 8.50 .35
31 A8 8c lilac & blue 55.00 8.50
32 A8 10c lilac & orange 13.50 2.50
33 A8 25c grn & car rose 90.00 60.00
34 A8 50c lilac & black 80.00 29.00
35 A8 50c green & black 475.00 140.00

Wmk. 1
36 A9 $1 green & lt grn 65.00 150.00
37 A9 $2 grn & car rose 250.00 300.00
38 A9 $3 green & olive 600.00 500.00
39 A9 $5 green & ultra 300.00 400.00
40 A9 $10 grn & brn vio 800.00 1,000.
41 A9 $25 green & org 4,000. 4,000.

High values with revenue cancellations are plentiful and inexpensive.

Surcharged in Black:

1900 Wmk. 2
42 A8 1c on 5c lilac & olive 75.00 *125.00*
43 A8 1c on 50c grn & blk 3.50 29.00
a. Surcharge reading "cent One cent." 3,500.
44 A8 3c on 50c grn & blk 6.00 *26.00*
Nos. 42-44 (3) 84.50 *180.00*

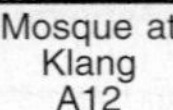
Mosque at Klang
A12

Sultan Sulaiman
A13

1935-41 Typo. Wmk. 4 *Perf. 14*

45 A12 1c black ('36) .30 .20
46 A12 2c dp green ('36) .55 .20
46A A12 2c org brn ('41) 2.25 1.25
46B A12 3c green ('41) 1.25 *8.00*
47 A12 4c orange brown .30 .20
48 A12 5c chocolate .70 .20
49 A12 6c rose red ('37) 4.00 .20
50 A12 8c gray .35 .20
51 A12 10c dk violet ('36) .35 .20
52 A12 12c ultra ('36) .90 .20
52A A12 15c ultra ('41) 7.00 *35.00*
53 A12 25c rose red & pale vio ('36) .60 *.80*
54 A12 30c org & dk vio ('36) .60 *1.10*
55 A12 40c dk vio & car 1.50 1.25
56 A12 50c blk, *emer* ('36) 1.00 .50
57 A13 $1 red & black, *blue* ('36) 6.00 1.10
58 A13 $2 rose red & green ('36) 17.50 9.50
59 A13 $5 brn red & grn, *emer* ('36) 55.00 *30.00*
Nos. 45-59 (18) 100.15 *90.10*
Set, never hinged 170.00

Nos. 46A-46B were printed on both ordinary and chalky paper; 15c only on ordinary paper; other values only on chalky paper.

An 8c rose red was prepared but not issued.

For overprints see Nos. N1-N15, N18A-N24, N26-N39.

Sultan Hisam-ud-Din Alam Shah
A14 A15

1941

72 A14 $1 red & blk, *blue* 11.50 7.00
73 A14 $2 car & green 30.00 *40.00*
Set, never hinged 70.00

A $5 stamp of type A14, issued during the Japanese occupation with different overprints (Nos. N18, N25A, N42), also exists without overprint. The unoverprinted stamp was not issued. Value $125.

For overprints see #N16-N17, N24A, N25, N40-N41.

Catalogue values for unused stamps in this section, from this point to the end of the section, are for Never Hinged items.

Silver Wedding Issue

Common Design Types
Inscribed: "Malaya Selangor"

Perf. 14x14½

1948, Dec. 1 Photo. Wmk. 4

74 CD304 10c purple .20 *.30*

Perf. 11½x11

Engraved; Name Typographed

75 CD305 $5 green 30.00 25.00

Common Design Types pictured following the introduction.

UPU Issue

Common Design Types
Inscribed: "Malaya-Selangor"

Engr.; Name Typo. on Nos. 77 & 78

1949, Oct. 10 *Perf. 13½, 11x11½*

76 CD306 10c rose violet .40 .30
77 CD307 15c indigo 2.50 2.50
78 CD308 25c orange .50 *4.50*
79 CD309 50c slate 1.50 *5.00*
Nos. 76-79 (4) 4.90 12.30

1949, Sept. 12 Typo. *Perf. 18*

80 A15 1c black .25 .60
81 A15 2c orange .30 1.50
82 A15 3c green 4.00 2.00
83 A15 4c chocolate .50 .35
84 A15 6c gray .35 .35
85 A15 8c rose red 2.00 1.25
86 A15 10c plum .25 .25
87 A15 15c ultramarine 8.00 .35
88 A15 20c dk grn & black 5.00 .50
89 A15 25c orange & rose lil 2.00 .35
90 A15 40c dk vio & rose red 11.00 8.00
91 A15 50c ultra & black 3.50 .35
92 A15 $1 vio brn & ultra 4.00 .60
93 A15 $2 rose red & emer 15.00 1.10
94 A15 $5 choc & emerald 55.00 3.00

1952-55

95 A15 5c rose violet 1.00 2.75
96 A15 8c green 1.00 1.75
97 A15 12c rose red 1.25 3.50
98 A15 20c ultramarine 1.25 .35
99 A15 30c plum & rose red ('55) 2.25 2.25
100 A15 35c dk vio & rose red 1.50 1.50
Nos. 80-100 (21) 119.40 32.65

Coronation Issue

Common Design Type

1953, June 2 Engr. *Perf. 13½x13*

101 CD312 10c magenta & black 1.75 .20

A16

Sultan Hisam-ud-Din Alam Shah — A17

Designs as in Kelantan, 1957.

Perf. 13x12½, 12½x13, 13½ ($1)

1957-60 Engr. Wmk. 314

102 A17 1c black .25 *2.50*
103 A17 2c red orange .50 *1.00*
104 A17 4c dark brown .25 .25
105 A17 5c dark car rose .25 .25
106 A17 8c dark green 3.00 *4.00*
107 A16 10c chocolate 2.50 .25
108 A16 20c blue 3.25 .25
109 A16 50c ultra & blk ('60) 1.00 .25
a. Perf. 12½ .40 .20
110 A17 $1 plum & ultra 4.50 .25
111 A17 $2 red & grn ('60) 5.50 3.00
a. Perf. 12½ 4.00 3.00
112 A17 $5 ol grn & brn ('60) 12.00 2.40
a. Perf. 12½ 12.00 3.00
Nos. 102-112 (11) 33.00 14.40

See Nos. 114-120.

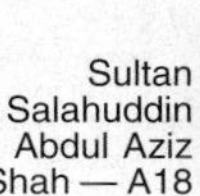

Sultan Salahuddin Abdul Aziz Shah — A18

1961, June 28 Photo. *Perf. 14½x14*

113 A18 10s multicolored .30 .20

Sultan Salahuddin Abdul Aziz Shah, installation.

Types of 1957 with Portrait of Sultan Salahuddin Abdul Aziz Shah

Designs as before.

Perf. 13x12½, 12½x13

1961-62 Engr. Wmk. 338

114 A17 1c black .40 *2.75*
115 A17 2c red orange .40 *3.00*
116 A17 4c dark brown 1.00 .20
117 A17 5c dark car rose 1.00 .20
118 A17 8c dark green 4.75 *6.00*
119 A16 10c vio brown ('61) .90 .20
120 A16 20c blue 8.00 1.50
Nos. 114-120 (7) 16.45 13.85

Starting in 1965, issues of Selangor are listed with Malaysia.

OCCUPATION STAMPS

Issued under Japanese Occupation

Stamps of Selangor 1935-41 Handstamped Vertically or Horizontally in Black, Red, Brown or Violet

1942, Apr. 3 Wmk. 4 *Perf. 14*

N1 A12 1c black 15.00 21.00
N2 A12 2c deep green 600.00 600.00
N3 A12 2c orange brown 55.00 55.00
N4 A12 3c green 35.00 17.00
N5 A12 5c chocolate 10.00 10.00
N6 A12 6c rose red 200.00 200.00
N7 A12 8c gray 27.50 27.50
N8 A12 10c dark violet 22.50 27.50
N9 A12 12c ultramarine 47.50 47.50
N10 A12 15c ultramarine 17.00 20.00
N11 A12 25c rose red & pale vio 80.00 95.00
N12 A12 30c org & dk vio 15.00 30.00
N13 A12 40c dk vio & car 100.00 140.00
N14 A12 50c blk, *emerald* 40.00 47.50
N15 A13 $5 brn red & grn, *emer* 275.00 275.00

Some authorities believe No. N15 was not issued regularly.

Handstamped Vertically on Stamps and Type of Selangor 1941 in Black or Red

N16 A14 $1 red & blk, *bl* 67.50 80.00
N17 A14 $2 car & green 80.00 110.00
N18 A14 $5 brn red & grn, *emer* 110.00 110.00

Stamps and Type of Selangor, 1935-41, Overprinted in Black

1942, May

N18A A12 1c black 110.00 110.00
N19 A12 3c green 1.00 1.00
N19A A12 5c chocolate 110.00 110.00
N20 A12 10c dark violet 35.00 35.00
N21 A12 12c ultramarine 2.75 5.00
N22 A12 15c ultramarine 5.50 4.00
N23 A12 30c org & dk vio 35.00 35.00
N24 A12 40c dk vio & car 4.00 4.00
N24A A14 $1 red & blk, *bl* 35.00 35.00
N25 A14 $2 car & green 24.00 30.00
N25A A14 $5 red & grn, *emer* 55.00 55.00
Nos. N18A-N25A (11) 417.25 424.00

Overprint is horizontal on $1, $2, $5.

On Nos. N18A and N19 the overprint is known reading up, instead of down.

Some authorities claim Nos. N18A, N19A, N20, N23, N24A and N25A were not regularly issued.

Selangor No. 46B Overprinted in Black

DAI NIPPON
YUBIN

1942, Dec.

N26 A12 3c green 400.00 400.00

Stamps and Type of Selangor, 1935-41, Overprinted or Surcharged in Black or Red:

i

k

l

m

1943

N27 A12(i) 1c black 1.40 1.40
N28 A12(k) 1c black (R) .90 .90
N29 A12(l) 2c on 5c choc (R) .90 .90
N30 A12(i) 3c green 1.00 1.00
N31 A12(l) 3c on 5c choc .65 1.00
N32 A12(k) 5c choc (R) .65 1.00
N33 A12(l) 6c on 5c choc .25 *.90*
N34 A12(m) 6c on 5c choc .25 *1.00*
N35 A12(i) 12c ultra 1.40 1.60
N36 A12(i) 15c ultra 6.75 10.00
N37 A12(k) 15c ultra 13.50 13.50
N38 A12(m) $1 on 10c dk vio .50 *1.40*
N39 A12(m) $1.50 on 30c org & dk vio .50 *1.40*
N40 A14(i) $1 red & blk, *blue* 6.75 8.50
N41 A14(i) $2 car & grn 24.00 24.00
N42 A14(i) $5 brn red & grn, *emer* 50.00 55.00
Nos. N27-N42 (16) 109.40 123.50

The "i" overprint is vertical on Nos. N40-N42 and is also found reading in the opposite direction on Nos. N30, N35 and N36.

The overprint reads: "Japanese Postal Service."

Singapore is listed following Sierra Leone.

SUNGEI UJONG

'suŋə ü-juŋ

Formerly a nonfederated native state on the Malay Peninsula, which in 1895 was consolidated with the Federated State of Negri Sembilan.

Stamps of the Straits Settlements Overprinted in Black

Overprinted

1878 Wmk. 1 *Perf. 14*

2 A2 2c brown 3,600. 3,900.

Overprinted

4 A2 2c brown 400.00
5 A2 4c rose *1,950.* 2,000.

No. 5 is no longer recognized by some experts.

Overprinted

1882-83 Wmk. 2

6 A2 2c brown 375.00 —
7 A2 4c rose 4,250. 4,800.

This overprint on the 2c brown, wmk. 1, is probably a trial printing.

Overprinted

11 A2 2c brown 325.00 *400.00*

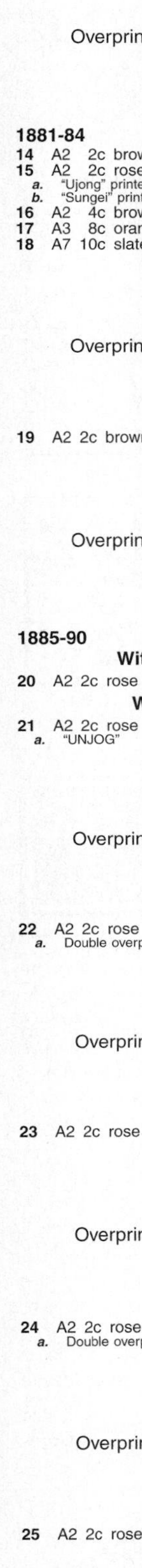
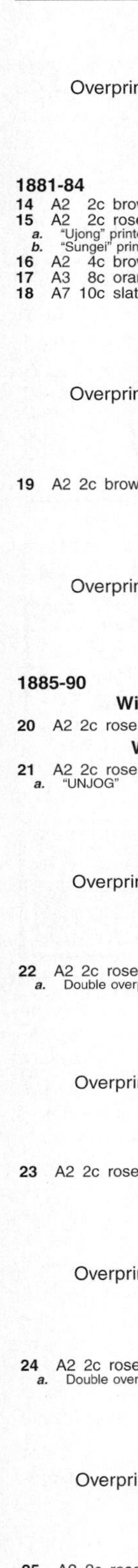

Overprinted

1881-84

14 A2 2c brown 1,200. 550.00
15 A2 2c rose 140.00 140.00
a. "Ujong" printed sideways
b. "Sungei" printed twice
16 A2 4c brown 325.00 425.00
17 A3 8c orange 2,250. 1,700.
18 A7 10c slate 725.00 625.00

Overprinted

19 A2 2c brown 57.50 *160.00*

Overprinted

1885-90

Without Period

20 A2 2c rose 45.00 *77.50*

With Period

21 A2 2c rose 125.00 90.00
a. "UNJOG" 5,750. 4,000.

Overprinted

22 A2 2c rose 95.00 110.00
a. Double overprint 775.00 775.00

Overprinted

23 A2 2c rose 125.00 *150.00*

Overprinted

24 A2 2c rose 30.00 *47.50*
a. Double overprint

Overprinted

25 A2 2c rose 110.00 *125.00*

Overprinted

26 A2 2c rose 175.00 175.00
c. Double overprint

Overprinted

Overprint 14-16x3mm

26A A2 2c rose 12.00 16.00

Overprinted

26B A2 2c rose 50.00 21.00

Stamp of 1883-91 Surcharged:

a b

c d

1891

27 A3 (a) 2c on 24c green 240. *275.*
28 A3 (b) 2c on 24c green 1,100. *1,200.*
29 A3 (c) 2c on 24c green 425. *500.*
30 A3 (d) 2c on 24c green 1,100. *1,200.*
Nos. 27-30 (4) 2,865. 3,175.

On Nos. 27-28, SUNGEI is 14½mm, UJONG 12¾x2½mm.

A3 A4

1891-94 Typo. *Perf. 14*

31 A3 2c rose 40.00 35.00
32 A3 2c orange ('94) 2.25 5.50
33 A3 5c blue ('93) 6.50 7.75
Nos. 31-33 (3) 48.75 48.25

Type of 1891 Surcharged in Black

1894

34 A3 1c on 5c green 1.40 .90
35 A3 3c on 5c rose 3.25 *6.00*

1895

36 A4 3c lilac & car rose 15.00 4.75

Stamps of Sungei Ujong were superseded by those of Negri Sembilan in 1895.

TRENGGANU

treŋ-'gä-ˌnü

LOCATION — On the eastern coast of the Malay Peninsula.
AREA — 5,050 sq. mi.
POP. — 302,171 (1960)
CAPITAL — Kuala Trengganu

Sultan Zenalabidin
A1 A2

1910-19 Typo. Wmk. 3 *Perf. 14*

Ordinary Paper

1a A1 1c blue green 2.10 1.25
2 A1 2c red vio & brn ('15) 1.25 1.10
3 A1 3c rose red 2.75 2.75
4 A1 4c brn orange 4.25 *6.75*
5 A1 4c grn & org brn ('15) 2.50 *5.75*
6 A1 4c scarlet ('19) 1.50 *2.10*
7 A1 5c gray 1.75 *4.50*
8 A1 5c choc & gray ('15) 3.00 2.40
9 A1 8c ultramarine 1.75 11.00
10 A1 10c red & grn, *yel* ('15) 1.75 2.75

Chalky Paper

11a A1 10c violet, *pale yel* 4.00 9.00
12 A1 20c red vio & vio 4.25 *5.75*
13 A1 25c dl vio & grn ('15) 9.75 *42.50*
14 A1 30c blk & dl vio ('15) 8.50 *65.00*
15 A1 50c blk & sep, *grn* 5.75 *11.50*
16 A1 $1 red & blk, *blue* 22.50 *29.00*
17 A1 $3 red & grn, *grn* ('15) 225.00 *500.00*
18 A2 $5 lil & blue grn 225.00 *675.00*
19 A2 $25 green & car 1,200. 2,750.
Revenue Cancel 300.00
Nos. 1a-19 (19) 1,727. 4,128.

On No. 19 the numerals and Arabic inscriptions at top, left and right are in color on a colorless background.

Overprints are listed after No. 41. For surcharges see Nos. B1-B4.

A3

Sultan Badaru'l-alam
A4

1921-38 Wmk. 4 *Perf. 14*

Chalky Paper

20 A3 1c black ('25) 2.75 1.75
21 A3 2c deep green 1.75 2.40
22 A3 3c dp grn ('25) 3.00 1.10
23 A3 3c lt brn ('38) 32.50 *22.50*
24 A3 4c rose red 2.40 2.00
25 A3 5c choc & gray 3.25 8.00
26 A3 5c vio, *yel* ('25) 2.75 2.00
27 A3 6c orange ('24) 6.00 .85
28 A3 8c gray ('38) 42.50 9.50
29 A3 10c ultramarine 3.25 1.50
30 A3 12c ultra ('25) 7.00 *7.25*
31 A3 20c org & dl vio 3.50 *2.40*
32 A3 25c dk vio & grn 3.75 *5.00*
33 A3 30c blk & dl vio 5.50 6.00
34 A3 35c red, *yel* ('25) 7.75 *12.50*
35 A3 50c car & green 11.50 5.25
36 A3 $1 ultra & vio, *bl* ('29) 15.00 6.00
37 A3 $3 red & green, *emer* ('25) 87.50 *240.00*
38 A4 $5 red & grn, *yel* ('38) 500.00 *2,800.*
39 A4 $25 blue & lil 750.00 *1,250.*
40 A4 $50 org & green 1,850. *3,200.*
41 A4 $100 red & green 5,750. 7,500.
Nos. 20-37 (18) 241.65 *336.00*

On Nos. 39 to 41 the numerals and Arabic inscriptions at top, left and right are in color on a colorless background.

A 2c orange, 6c gray, 8c rose red and 15c ultramarine, type A3, exist, but are not known to have been regularly issued.

For surcharges and overprints see Nos. 45-46, N1-N60.

Stamps of 1910-21 Overprinted in Black

1922, Mar. Wmk. 3

8a A1 5c chocolate & gray 4.75 *37.50*
10a A1 10c red & green, *yel* 4.75 *37.50*
12a A1 20c red vio & violet 4.25 *50.00*
13a A1 25c dull vio & green 4.25 *50.00*
14a A1 30c black & dull vio 4.25 *50.00*
15a A1 50c blk & sepia, *grn* 4.25 *50.00*
16a A1 $1 red & blk, *blue* 20.00 *95.00*
17a A1 $3 red & grn, *green* 210.00 *575.00*
18a A2 $5 lil & blue green 300.00 *575.00*

Wmk. 4

21a A3 2c deep green 2.75 *47.50*
24a A3 4c rose red 7.75 *47.50*
Nos. 8a-24a (11) 567.00 *1,615.*

Industrial fair at Singapore, Mar. 31-Apr. 15.

1921 Wmk. 3

Chalky Paper

42 A3 $1 ultra & vio, *bl* 20.00 *40.00*
43 A3 $3 red & grn, *emer* 140.00 *160.00*
44 A4 $5 red & green, *yel* 140.00 *150.00*
Nos. 42-44 (3) 300.00 *350.00*

Types of 1921-25 Surcharged in Black

1941, May 1 Wmk. 4 *Perf. 13½x14*

45 A3 2c on 5c magenta, *yel* 5.50 *6.50*
46 A3 8c on 10c lt ultra 9.50 *6.50*

For overprints see #N30-N33, N46-N47, N59-N60.

Catalogue values for unused stamps in this section, from this point to the end of the section, are for Never Hinged items.

Silver Wedding Issue
Common Design Types
Inscribed: "Malaya Trengganu"

1948, Dec. 1 Photo. *Perf. 14x14½*

47 CD304 10c purple .20 .20

Engraved; Name Typographed
Perf. 11½x11

48 CD305 $5 rose car 35.00 62.50

Common Design Types pictured following the introduction.

UPU Issue
Common Design Types
Inscribed: "Malaya-Trengganu"
Engr.; Name Typo. on 15c, 25c
Perf. 13½, 11x11½

1949, Oct. 10 Wmk. 4

49 CD306 10c rose violet .65 .65
50 CD307 15c indigo .80 2.10
51 CD308 25c orange 1.40 3.50
52 CD309 50c slate 2.10 3.50
Nos. 49-52 (4) 4.95 9.75

Sultan Ismail Nasiruddin Shah — A5

1949, Dec. 27 Typo. *Perf. 18*

53 A5 1c black .40 .45
54 A5 2c orange .40 .50
55 A5 3c green 1.25 1.50
56 A5 4c chocolate .60 .50
57 A5 6c gray 1.25 1.25
58 A5 8c rose red 1.60 1.90
59 A5 10c plum .60 .50
60 A5 15c ultramarine 1.75 1.60
61 A5 20c dk grn & black 2.40 5.00
62 A5 25c org & rose lilac 2.25 3.25
63 A5 40c dk vio & rose red 4.50 27.50

No.	Type	Description	Unused	Used
64	A5	50c dp ultra & black	2.75	2.75
65	A5	$1 vio brn & ultra	5.50	10.00
66	A5	$2 rose red & emer	30.00	24.50
67	A5	$5 choc & emerald	80.00	67.50

1952-55

No.	Type	Description	Unused	Used
68	A5	5c rose violet	.40	.50
69	A5	8c green	1.60	3.25
70	A5	12c rose red	1.60	*6.75*
71	A5	20c ultramarine	1.60	1.50
72	A5	30c plum & rose red ('55)	3.00	6.75
73	A5	35c dk vio & rose red	3.50	6.75
		Nos. 53-73 (21)	146.95	174.20

Coronation Issue

Common Design Type

1953, June 2 Engr. *Perf. 13½x13*

No.	Type	Description	Unused	Used
74	CD312	10c magenta & blk	1.50	1.00

Types of Kedah with Portrait of Sultan Ismail

Perf. 13x12½, 12½x13, 13½ ($1), 12½ ($2)

1957-63 Engr. Wmk. 314

No.	Type	Description	Unused	Used
75	A8	1c black	.30	.50
76	A8	2c red orange	1.00	.50
77	A8	4c dark brown	.30	.50
78	A8	5c dark car rose	.30	.50
79	A8	8c dark green	9.00	.50
80	A7	10c chocolate	.40	.50
81	A7	20c blue	.85	.60
82	A7	50c blue & blk	.40	2.40
a.		Perf. 12½	.50	2.25
83	A8	$1 plum & ultra	9.50	9.50
84	A8	$2 red & green	18.00	12.00
85	A8	$5 ol grn & brn, perf. 12½	27.50	25.00
a.		Perf. 13x12½	32.50	30.00
		Nos. 75-85 (11)	67.55	52.50

Issued: 20c, #85, 6/26/57; 2c, 50c, $1, 7/25/57; 10c, 8/4/57; 1c, 4c, 5c, 8c, $2, 8/21/57; #82a, 5/17/60; #85a, 8/13/63.

Starting in 1965, issues of Trengganu are listed with Malaysia.

SEMI-POSTAL STAMPS

Nos. 3, 4 and 9 Surcharged

1917, Oct. Wmk. 3 *Perf. 14*

No.	Type	Description	Unused	Used
B1	A1	3c + 2c rose red	1.50	*8.00*
a.		"CSOSS"	65.00	*100.00*
b.		Comma after "2c"	4.00	*10.50*
c.		Pair, one without surcharge	2,900.	2,900.
B2	A1	4c + 2c brn org	2.25	*12.50*
a.		"CSOSS"	275.00	*275.00*
b.		Comma after "2c"	16.00	*42.50*
B3	A1	8c + 2c ultra	3.50	*24.00*
a.		"CSOSS"	175.00	*210.00*
b.		Comma after "2c"	13.00	*45.00*
		Nos. B1-B3 (3)	7.25	*44.50*

Same Surcharge on No. 5

1918

No.	Type	Description	Unused	Used
B4	A1	4c + 2c grn & org brn	4.25	*11.50*
a.		Pair, one without surcharge	*2,300.*	

POSTAGE DUE STAMPS

D1

Perf. 14

1937, Aug. 10 Typo. Wmk. 4

No.	Type	Description	Unused	Used
J1	D1	1c rose red	8.25	*65.00*
J2	D1	4c green	9.00	*72.50*
J3	D1	8c lemon	47.50	*400.00*
J4	D1	10c light brown	92.50	*115.00*
		Nos. J1-J4 (4)	157.25	*652.50*
		Set, never hinged	275.00	

For overprints see Nos. NJ1-NJ4.

OCCUPATION STAMPS

Issued under Japanese Occupation

No. N6

No. N17A

Stamps of Trengganu, 1921-38, Handstamped in Black or Brown

1942 Wmk. 4 *Perf. 14*

No.	Type	Description	Unused	Used
N1	A3	1c black	110.00	110.00
N2	A3	2c deep green	190.00	275.00
N3	A3	3c lt brown	140.00	110.00
N4	A3	4c rose red	275.00	190.00
N5	A3	5c violet, *yel*	17.50	19.00
N6	A3	6c orange	13.50	20.00
N7	A3	8c gray	17.50	25.00
N8	A3	10c ultramarine	13.50	27.50
N9	A3	12c ultramarine	15.00	25.00
N10	A3	20c org & dl vio	15.00	22.50
N11	A3	25c dk vio & grn	13.50	27.50
N12	A3	30c blk & dl vio	13.50	25.00
N13	A3	35c red, *yel*	22.50	27.50
N14	A3	50c car & grn	125.00	95.00
N15	A3	$1 ultra & vio, *blue*	1,650.	1,750.
N16	A3	$3 red & grn, *emerald*	125.00	140.00
N17	A4	$5 red & grn, *yellow*	240.00	240.00
N17A	A4	$25 blue & lil	1,500.	
N17B	A4	$50 org & grn	*8,800.*	
N17C	A4	$100 red & grn	950.00	

Handstamped in Red

No.	Type	Description	Unused	Used
N18	A3	1c black	275.00	225.00
N19	A3	2c dp green	140.00	160.00
N20	A3	5c violet, *yel*	35.00	20.00
N21	A3	6c orange	20.00	20.00
N22	A3	8c gray	275.00	240.00
N23	A3	10c ultramarine	275.00	275.00
N24	A3	12c ultramarine	55.00	55.00
N25	A3	20c org & dl vio	35.00	35.00
N26	A3	25c dk vio & grn	40.00	40.00
N27	A3	30c blk & dl vio	35.00	35.00
N28	A3	35c red, *yellow*	35.00	20.00
N29	A3	$3 red & grn, *emerald*	100.00	40.00
N29A	A3	$25 blue & lil	500.00	500.00

Handstamped on Nos. 45 and 46 in Black or Red

No.	Type	Description	Unused	Used
N30	A3	2c on 5c (Bk)	140.00	140.00
N31	A3	2c on 5c (R)	100.00	100.00
N32	A3	8c on 10c (Bk)	25.00	35.00
N33	A3	8c on 10c (R)	35.00	40.00

Stamps of Trengganu, 1921-38, Overprinted in Black

1942

No.	Type	Description	Unused	Used
N34	A3	1c black	15.00	17.00
N35	A3	2c deep green	100.00	*140.00*
N36	A3	3c light brown	16.00	29.00
N37	A3	4c rose red	15.00	20.00
N38	A3	5c violet, *yel*	10.00	20.00
N39	A3	6c orange	10.00	17.00
N40	A3	8c gray	67.50	20.00
N41	A3	12c ultramarine	10.00	13.50
N42	A3	20c org & dl vio	13.50	25.00
N43	A3	25c dk vio & grn	13.50	17.00
N44	A3	30c blk & dl vio	13.50	20.00
N45	A3	$3 red & grn, *emer*	100.00	140.00

Overprinted on Nos. 45 and 46 in Black

No.	Type	Description	Unused	Used
N46	A3	2c on 5c mag, *yel*	13.50	17.00
N47	A3	8c on 10c lt ultra	11.50	20.00
		Nos. N34-N47 (14)	409.00	*515.50*

Stamps of Trengganu, 1921-38, Overprinted in Black

1943

No.	Type	Description	Unused	Used
N48	A3	1c black	13.50	19.00
N49	A3	2c deep green	13.50	27.50
N50	A3	5c violet, *yel*	11.50	27.50
N51	A3	6c orange	15.00	27.50
N52	A3	8c gray	95.00	67.50
N53	A3	10c ultramarine	100.00	175.00
N54	A3	12c ultramarine	19.00	*35.00*
N55	A3	20c org & dl vio	20.00	*35.00*
N56	A3	25c dl vio & grn	19.00	*35.00*
N57	A3	30c blk & dl vio	20.00	*35.00*
N58	A3	35c red, *yellow*	20.00	*40.00*

Overprinted on Nos. 45 and 46 in Black

No.	Type	Description	Unused	Used
N59	A3	2c on 5c mag, *yel*	11.00	*35.00*
N60	A3	8c on 10c lt ultra	27.50	25.00
		Nos. N48-N60 (13)	385.00	*584.00*

The Japanese characters read: "Japanese Postal Service."

OCCUPATION POSTAGE DUE STAMPS

Trengganu Nos. J1-J4 Handstamped in Black or Brown

1942 Wmk. 4 *Perf. 14*

No.	Type	Description	Unused	Used
NJ1	D1	1c rose red	67.50	*95.00*
NJ2	D1	4c green	125.00	*125.00*
NJ3	D1	8c lemon	25.00	*67.50*
NJ4	D1	10c light brown	25.00	*50.00*
		Nos. NJ1-NJ4 (4)	242.50	*337.50*

The handstamp reads: "Seal of Post Office of Malayan Military Department."

MALAYSIA

mə-'lā-zhə̦ē-ə̦

LOCATION — Malay peninsula and northwestern Borneo
GOVT. — Federation within the British Commonwealth
AREA — 127,317 sq. mi.
POP. — 21,376,066 (1999 est.)
CAPITAL — Putrajaya (administrative); Kuala Lumpur (financial)

The Federation of Malaysia was formed Sept. 16, 1963, by a merger of the former Federation of Malaya, Singapore, Sarawak, and North Borneo (renamed Sabah), totaling 14 states. Singapore withdrew in 1965.

Sabah and Sarawak, having different rates than mainland Malaysia, continued to issue their own stamps after joining the federation. The system of individual state issues was extended to Perak in Oct. 1963, and to the 10 other members in Nov. 1965.

100 Cents (Sen) = 1 Dollar (Ringgit)

Catalogue values for all unused stamps in this country are for Never Hinged items.

Watermarks

Wmk. 233 — "Harrison & Sons, London" in Script

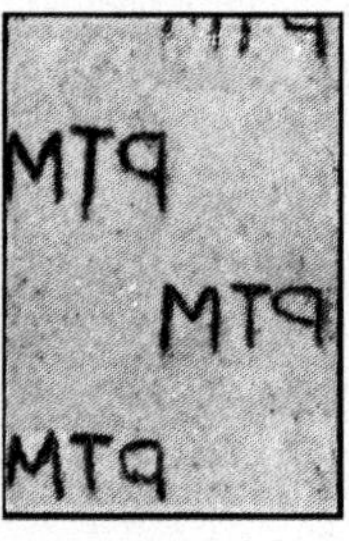

Wmk. 338 — PTM Multiple

Wmk. 378 — Multiple POS in Octagonal Frame

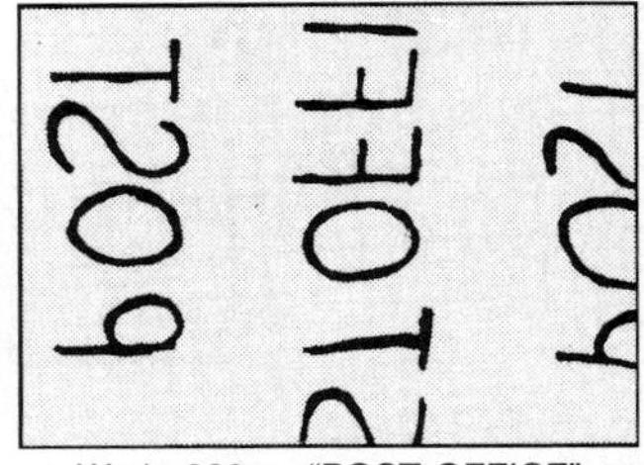

Wmk. 380 — "POST OFFICE"

Wmk. 388 — Multiple "SPM"

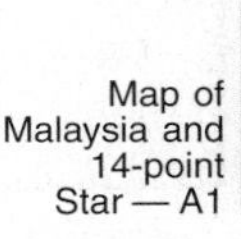

Map of Malaysia and 14-point Star — A1

Wmk. PTM Multiple (338)

1963, Sept. 16 Photo. *Perf. 14*

No.	Type	Description	Unused	Used
1	A1	10s violet & yellow	.30	.25
a.		Yellow omitted	250.00	
2	A1	12s green & yellow	2.10	.70
3	A1	50s dk red brown & yel	1.60	.30
		Nos. 1-3 (3)	4.00	1.25

Formation of the Federation of Malaysia.

Orchids — A2

1963, Oct. 3 Unwmk. *Perf. 13x14*

No.	Type	Description	Unused	Used
4	A2	6s red & multi	1.25	1.25
5	A2	25s black & multi	3.25	2.00

4th World Orchid Conf., Singapore, Oct. 8-11.

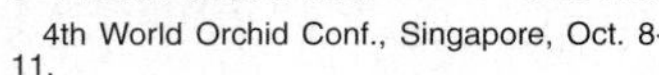

Parliament and Commonwealth Parliamentary Association Emblem — A4

1963, Nov. 4 *Perf. 13½*

No.	Type	Description	Unused	Used
7	A4	20s dk car rose & gold	.50	.40
8	A4	30s dk green & gold	1.50	.75

9th Commonwealth Parliamentary Assoc. Conf.

Globe, Torch, Snake and Hands — A5

1964, Oct. 10 Photo. *Perf. 14x13*

9	A5 25s Prus grn, red & blk	.25	.40
10	A5 30s lt violet, red & blk	.30	.30
11	A5 50s dull yellow, red & blk	.45	.30
	Nos. 9-11 (3)	1.00	1.00

Eleanor Roosevelt, 1884-1962.

ITU Emblem and Radar Tower — A6

1965, May 17 Photo. *Perf. 11½*
Granite Paper

12	A6 2c violet, blk & org	.60	1.50
13	A6 25c brown, blk & org	3.00	1.00
14	A6 50c emerald, blk & brn	2.50	.30
	Nos. 12-14 (3)	6.10	2.80

Cent. of the ITU.

National Mosque, Kuala Lumpur — A7

1965, Aug. 27 Wmk. 338 *Perf. 14½*

15	A7 6c dark car rose	.25	.20
16	A7 15c dark red brown	.30	.20
17	A7 20c Prussian green	.55	.35
	Nos. 15-17 (3)	1.10	.75

Natl. Mosque at Kuala Lumpur, opening.

Control Tower and Airport — A8

Crested Wood Partridge — A9

1965, Aug. 30 *Perf. 14½x14*

18	A8 15c blue, blk & grn	.30	.20
a.	Green omitted	35.00	
19	A8 30c brt pink, blk & grn	.90	.30

Intl. Airport at Kuala Lumpur, opening.

1965, Sept. 9 Photo. *Perf. 14½*

Birds: 30c, Fairy bluebird. 50c, Blacknaped oriole. 75c, Rhinoceros hornbill. $1, Zebra dove. $2, Argus pheasant. $5, Indian paradise flycatcher. $10, Banded pitta.

20	A9 25c orange & multi	.60	.20
21	A9 30c tan & multi	.70	.20
a.	Blue omitted	300.00	
22	A9 50c rose & multi	1.10	.20
a.	Yellow omitted	180.00	
23	A9 75c yel grn & multi	1.25	.20
24	A9 $1 ultra & multi	2.00	.35
25	A9 $2 maroon & multi	4.00	.65
26	A9 $5 dk grn & multi	21.00	2.25
27	A9 $10 brt red & multi	50.00	8.00
	Nos. 20-27 (8)	80.65	12.05

Soccer and Sepak Raga (Ball Game) — A10

National Monument, Kuala Lumpur — A11

1965, Dec. 14 Unwmk. *Perf. 13*

28	A10 25c shown	.40	1.25
29	A10 30c Runner	.40	.30
30	A10 50c Diver	.70	.30
	Nos. 28-30 (3)	1.50	1.85

3rd South East Asia Peninsular Games, Kuala Lumpur, Dec. 14-21.

1966, Feb. 8 Wmk. 338 *Perf. 13½*

31	A11 10c yellow & multi	.25	.20
a.	Blue omitted	150.00	
32	A11 20c ultra & multi	1.25	.45

The National Monument by US sculptor Felix W. de Weldon commemorates the struggle of the people of Malaysia for peace and for freedom from communism.

Tuanku Ismail Nasiruddin — A12

Penang Free School — A13

1966, Apr. 11 Unwmk. *Perf. 13½*

33	A12 15c yellow & black	.25	.20
34	A12 50c blue & black	.90	.35

Installation of Tuanku Ismail Nasiruddin of Trengganu as Paramount Ruler (Yang di-Pertuan Agong).

Perf. 13x12½
1966, Oct. 21 Photo. Wmk. 338

Design: 50c, like 20c with Malayan inscription and school crest added.

35	A13 20c multicolored	.45	.30
36	A13 50c multicolored	1.25	.40

Penang Free School, 150th anniversary.

Mechanized Plowing and Palms — A14

No. 38, Rural health nurse, mother and child, dispensary. No. 39, Communication: train, plane, ship, cars and radio tower. No. 40, School children. No. 41, Dam and rice fields.

1966, Dec. 1 Unwmk. *Perf. 13*

37	A14 15c bister brn & multi	.75	.30
38	A14 15c blue & multi	.75	.30
39	A14 15c crimson & multi	.75	.30
40	A14 15c ol green & multi	.75	.30
41	A14 15c yellow & multi	.75	.30
	Nos. 37-41 (5)	3.75	1.50

Malaysia's First Development Plan.

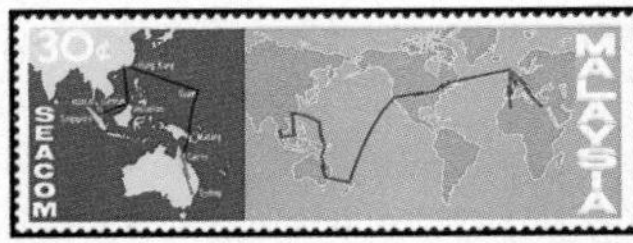

Maps Showing International and South East Asia Telephone Links — A15

1967, Mar. 30 Photo. *Perf. 13*

42	A15 30c multicolored	.50	.50
43	A15 75c multicolored	4.50	4.50

Completion of the Hong Kong-Malaysia link of the South East Asia Commonwealth Cable, SEACOM.

Hibiscus and Rulers of Independent Malaysia — A16

1967, Aug. 31 Wmk. 338 *Perf. 14*

44	A16 15c yellow & multi	.35	.25
45	A16 50c blue & multi	1.25	.80

10th anniversary of independence.

Arms of Sarawak and Council Mace — A17

1967, Sept. 8 Photo.

46	A17 15c yel green & multi	.25	.20
47	A17 50c multicolored	.50	.35

Representative Council of Sarawak, cent.

Straits Settlements No. 13 and Malaysia No. 20 — A18

30c, Straits Settlements #15, Malaysia #21.
50c, Straits Settlements #17, Malaysia #22.

1967, Dec. 2 Unwmk. *Perf. 11½*

48	A18 25c brt blue & multi	1.60	3.00
49	A18 30c dull green & multi	1.90	2.50
50	A18 50c yellow & multi	2.75	3.25
	Nos. 48-50 (3)	6.25	8.75

Cent. of the Malaysian (Straits Settlements) postage stamps.

Tapped Rubber Tree and Molecular Unit — A20

Tapped Rubber Tree and: 30c, Rubber packed for shipment. 50c, Rubber tires for Vickers VC 10 plane.

Wmk. 338
1968, Aug. 29 Litho. *Perf. 12*

53	A20 25c brick red, blk & org	.30	.25
54	A20 30c yellow, black & org	.45	.30
55	A20 50c ultra, black & org	.75	.30
	Nos. 53-55 (3)	1.50	.85

Natural Rubber Conference, Kuala Lumpur.

Olympic Rings, Mexican Hat and Cloth — A21

Tunku Abdul Rahman Putra Al-Haj — A22

75c, Olympic rings & Malaysian batik cloth.

1968, Oct. 12 Wmk. 338 *Perf. 12*

56	A21 30c rose red & multi	.30	.25
57	A21 75c ocher & multi	.60	.35

19th Olympic Games, Mexico City, 10/12-27.

Perf. 13½
1969, Feb. 8 Photo. Unwmk.

Various portraits of Prime Minister Tunku Abdul Rahman Putra Al-Haj with woven pandanus patterns as background. 50c is horiz.

58	A22 15c gold & multi	.40	.20
59	A22 20c gold & multi	1.00	1.25
60	A22 50c gold & multi	1.25	.30
	Nos. 58-60 (3)	2.65	1.75

Issued for Solidarity Week, 1969.

Malaysian Girl Holding Sheaves of Rice — A23

1969, Dec. 8 Wmk. 338 *Perf. 13½*

61	A23 15c silver & multi	.30	.20
62	A23 75c gold & multi	1.60	1.40

International Rice Year.

Kuantan Radar Station — A24

Intelsat III Orbiting Earth A25

Perf. 14x13
1970, Apr. 6 Photo. Unwmk.

63	A24 15c multicolored	.50	.20
64	A25 30c multicolored	1.75	2.50
65	A25 30c gold & multi	1.75	2.50
	Nos. 63-65 (3)	4.00	5.20

Satellite Communications Earth Station at Kuantan, Pahang, Malaysia.

No. 63 was printed tete beche (50 pairs) in sheet of 100 (10x10).

Blue-branded King Crow — A26

ILO Emblem — A27

Butterflies: 30c, Saturn. 50c, Common Nawab. 75c, Great Mormon. $1, Orange albatross. $2, Raja Brooke's birdwing. $5, Centaur oakblue. $10, Royal Assyrian.

1970, Aug. 31 Litho. *Perf. 13x13½*

66 A26 25c multicolored 1.10 .20
67 A26 30c multicolored 1.00 .20
68 A26 50c multicolored 1.50 .20
69 A26 75c multicolored 1.25 .20
70 A26 $1 multicolored 2.25 .25
71 A26 $2 multicolored 3.75 .35
72 A26 $5 multicolored 9.00 2.00
73 A26 $10 multicolored 18.00 5.00
Nos. 66-73 (8) 37.85 8.40

1970, Sept. 7 *Perf. 14½x13½*

74 A27 30c gray & blue .25 .25
75 A27 75c rose & blue .35 .30

50th anniv. of the ILO.

UN Emblem and Doves — A28

Sultan Abdul Halim — A29

Designs: 25c, Doves in elliptical arrangement. 30c, Doves arranged diagonally.

1970, Oct. 24 Litho. *Perf. 13x12½*

76 A28 25c lt brown, blk & yel .35 .25
77 A28 30c lt blue, yel & black .35 .25
78 A28 50c lt ol green & black .40 .40
Nos. 76-78 (3) 1.10 .90

25th anniversary of the United Nations.

Perf. 14½x14

1971, Feb. 20 Photo. Unwmk.

79 A29 10c yellow, blk & gold .50 .35
80 A29 15c purple, blk & gold .50 .35
81 A29 50c blue, blk & gold .75 1.50
Nos. 79-81 (3) 1.75 2.20

Installation of Sultan Abdul Halim of Kedah as Paramount Ruler.

Bank Building and Crescent A30

1971, May 15 Photo. *Perf. 14*

82 A30 25c silver & black 2.75 1.00
83 A30 50c gold & brown 4.25 1.50

Opening of Main office of the Negara Malaysia Bank. Nos. 82-83 have circular perforations around vignette set within a white square of paper, perf. on 4 sides.

Malaysian Parliament — A31

Malaysian Parliament, Kuala Lumpur — A32

1971, Sept. 13 Litho. *Perf. 13½*

84 A31 25c multicolored 1.50 .50

Perf. 12½x13

85 A32 75c multicolored 3.50 1.60

17th Commonwealth Parliamentary Conference, Kuala Lumpur.

Malaysian Festival — A33

1971, Sept. 18 *Perf. 14½*

86 A33 Strip of 3 7.00 5.50
a. 30c Dancing couple 2.00 .75
b. 30c Dragon 2.00 .75
c. 30c Flags and stage horse 2.00 .75

Visit ASEAN (Association of South East Asian Nations) Year.

Elephant and Tiger — A34

Children's Drawings: No. 88, Cat and kittens. No. 89, Sun, flower and chick. No. 90, Monkey, elephant and lion in jungle. No. 91, Butterfly and flowers.

1971, Oct. 2 *Perf. 12½*

Size: 35x28mm

87 A34 15c pale yellow & multi 2.25 .60
88 A34 15c pale yellow & multi 2.25 .60

Size: 21x28mm

89 A34 15c pale yellow & multi 2.25 .60

Size: 35x28mm

90 A34 15c pale yellow & multi 2.25 .60
91 A34 15c pale yellow & multi 2.25 .60
a. Strip of 5, #87-91 12.00 13.00

25th anniv. of UNICEF.

Track and Field — A35

30c, Sepak Raga (a ball game). 50c, Hockey.

1971, Dec. 11 *Perf. 14½*

92 A35 25c orange & multi 1.00 .40
93 A35 30c violet & multi 1.25 .50
94 A35 50c green & multi 1.50 .95
Nos. 92-94 (3) 3.75 1.85

6th South East Asia Peninsular Games. Kuala Lumpur, Dec. 11-18.

South East Asian Tourist Attractions — A36

Designs include stylized map.

1972, Jan. 31 Litho. *Perf. 14½*

95 A36 Strip of 3 10.00 9.00
a. 30c Flag at left 2.75 .60
b. 30c High rise building 2.75 .60
c. 30c Horse & rider 2.75 .60

Pacific Area Tourist Assoc. Conference.

Secretariat Building — A37

50c, Kuala Lumpur Secretariat Building by night.

1972, Feb. 1 *Perf. 14½x14*

96 A37 25c lt blue & multi 1.10 1.25
97 A37 50c black & multi 2.75 1.25

Achievement of city status by Kuala Lumpur.

Social Security Emblem — A38

WHO Emblem — A39

1973, July 2 Litho. *Perf. 14½x13½*

98 A38 10c orange & multi .25 .20
99 A38 15c yellow & multi .25 .20
100 A38 50c gray & multi .50 1.40
Nos. 98-100 (3) 1.00 1.80

Introduction of Social Security System.

1973, Aug. 1 *Perf. 13x12½, 12½x13*

Design: 30c, WHO emblem, horiz.

101 A39 30c yellow & multi .60 .20
102 A39 75c blue & multi 1.40 2.50

25th anniv. of World Health Org.

Flag of Malaysia, Fireworks, Hibiscus — A40

1973, Aug. 31 Litho. *Perf. 14½*

103 A40 10c olive & multi .65 .30
104 A40 15c brown & multi .55 .30
105 A40 50c gray & multi 2.40 1.50
Nos. 103-105 (3) 3.60 2.10

10th anniversary of independence.

INTERPOL and Malaysian Police Emblems A41

Design: 75c, "50" with INTERPOL and Malaysian police emblems.

1973, Sept. 15 *Perf. 12½*

106 A41 25c brown org & multi 1.25 .45
107 A41 75c deep violet & multi 2.75 1.90

50th anniv. of the Intl. Criminal Police Organization (INTERPOL).

MAS Emblem and Plane A42

1973, Oct. 1 Litho. *Perf. 14½*

108 A42 15c green & multi .25 .20
109 A42 30c blue & multi .60 .50
110 A42 50c brown & multi 1.40 1.50
Nos. 108-110 (3) 2.25 2.20

Inauguration of Malaysian Airline System.

View of Kuala Lumpur — A43

1974, Feb. 1 Litho. *Perf. 12½x13*

111 A43 25c multicolored .80 .75
112 A43 50c multicolored 1.60 1.75

Establishment of Kuala Lumpur as a Federal Territory.

Development Bank Emblem and Projects — A44

1974, Apr. 25 Litho. *Perf. 13½*

113 A44 30c gray & multi .60 .45
114 A44 75c bister & multi 1.00 1.60

7th annual meeting of the Board of Governors of the Asian Development Bank.

Map of Malaysia and Scout Emblem — A45

Scout Saluting, Malaysian and Scout Flags — A46

Design: 50c, Malaysian Scout emblem.

Perf. 14x13½, 13x13½ (15c)

1974, Aug. 1 Litho.

115 A45 10c multicolored .55 .80
116 A46 15c multicolored .90 .25
117 A45 50c multicolored 2.50 2.50
Nos. 115-117 (3) 3.95 3.55

Malaysian Boy Scout Jamboree.

Power Installations, NEB Emblem — A47

National Electricity Board Building A48

Perf. 14x14½, 13½x14½

1974, Sept. 1 Litho.

118 A47 30c multicolored .65 .45
119 A48 75c multicolored 1.10 2.00

National Electricity Board, 25th anniversary.

"100," UPU and P.O. Emblems A49

1974, Oct. 9 Litho. *Perf. 14½x13½*

120 A49 25c olive, red & yel	.40	.35
121 A49 30c blue, red & yel	.40	.35
122 A49 75c ocher, red & yel	.80	1.50
Nos. 120-122 (3)	1.60	2.20

Centenary of Universal Postal Union.

Gravel Pump Tin Mine A50

Designs: 20c, Open cast mine. 50c, Silver tin ingot and tin dredge.

1974, Oct. 31 Litho. *Perf. 14*

123 A50 15c silver & multi	.45	.30
124 A50 20c silver & multi	3.25	2.25
125 A50 50c silver & multi	6.50	5.00
Nos. 123-125 (3)	10.20	7.55

4th World Tin Conference, Kuala Lumpur.

Hockey, Cup and Emblem A51

1975, Mar. 1 Litho. *Perf. 14*

126 A51 30c yellow & multi	1.25	.50
127 A51 75c blue & multi	2.75	2.00

Third World Cup Hockey Tournament, Kuala Lumpur, Mar. 1-15.

Trade Union Emblem and Workers — A52

1975, May 1 Litho. *Perf. 14x14½*

128 A52 20c orange & multi	.30	.25
129 A52 25c lt green & multi	.50	.25
130 A52 30c ultra & multi	.50	.50
Nos. 128-130 (3)	1.30	1.00

Malaysian Trade Union Cong., 25th anniv.

National Women's Organization Emblem and Heads — A53

1975, Aug. 25 Litho. *Perf. 14*

131 A53 10c emerald & multi	.65	.30
132 A53 15c lilac rose & multi	.65	.30
133 A53 50c blue & multi	1.75	2.00
Nos. 131-133 (3)	3.05	2.60

International Women's Year.

Ubudiah Mosque, Perak — A54

b, Zahir Mosque, Kedah. c, National Mosque, Kuala Lumpur. d, Sultan Abu Bakar Mosque, Johore. e, Kuching State Mosque, Sarawak.

1975, Sept. 22 Litho. *Perf. 14½x14*

134 Strip of 5	14.50	9.50
a.-e. A54 15c single stamp	2.40	.40

Koran reading competition 1975, Malaysia.

Rubber Plantation and Emblem A55

Designs: 30c, "50" in form of latex cup and tire with emblem. 75c, Six test tubes showing various aspects of natural rubber.

1975, Oct. 22 Litho. *Perf. 14x14½*

135 A55 10c gold & multi	.45	.30
136 A55 30c gold & multi	1.25	.60
137 A55 75c gold & multi	3.00	2.00
Nos. 135-137 (3)	4.70	2.90

Rubber Research Institute of Malaysia, 50th anniversary.

Butterflies A55a

Coil Stamps

1976, Feb. 6 *Perf. 14*

137A A55a 10c Hebomoia glaucippe aturia	*4.00*	*8.00*
137B A55a 15c Precis orithya wallacei	*4.00*	*8.00*

Scrub Typhus — A56

Sultan Jahya Petra — A57

Designs: 25c, Malaria (microscope, blood cells, slides). $1, Beri-beri (grain and men).

1976, Feb. 6 Litho. *Perf. 14*

138 A56 20c red orange & multi	.70	.30
139 A56 25c ultra & multi	.85	.30
140 A56 $1 yellow & multi	1.75	2.25
Nos. 138-140 (3)	3.30	2.85

Institute for Medical Research, Kuala Lumpur, 75th anniversary.

Perf. 14½x13½

1976, Feb. 28 Photo.

141 A57 10c yel, black & bis	.35	.25
142 A57 15c lilac, black & bis	.30	.25
143 A57 50c blue, black & bis	2.75	2.25
Nos. 141-143 (3)	3.40	2.75

Installation of Sultan Jahya Petra of Kelantan as Paramount Ruler (Yang di-Pertuan Agong).

Council and Administrative Buildings — A58

1976, Aug. 17 Litho. *Perf. 12½*

144 A58 15c orange & black	.45	.20
145 A58 20c brt red lilac & black	.55	.35
146 A58 50c blue & black	1.00	1.25
Nos. 144-146 (3)	2.00	1.80

Opening of the State Council Complex and Administrative Building, Sarawak.

Provident Fund Building A59

Provident Fund Emblems — A60

50c, Provident Fund Building at night.

Perf. 13½x14½, 14½ (A60)

1976, Oct. 18 Litho.

147 A59 10c blue & multi	.50	.35
148 A60 25c gray & multi	.45	.60
149 A59 50c violet & multi	.65	1.25
Nos. 147-149 (3)	1.60	2.20

Employees' Provident Fund, 25th anniv.

Rehabilitation of the Blind — A61

75c, Blind man casting large shadow.

1976, Nov. 20 *Perf. 13½x14½*

150 A61 10c multicolored	.50	.30
151 A61 75c multicolored	1.50	2.25

25th anniv. of the Malaysian Assoc. for the Blind.

Abdul Razak and Crowd — A62

Designs: b, Abdul Razak in cap and gown at lectern. c, Abdul Razak pointing to new roads and bridges on map. d, New constitution. e, Abdul Razak addressing Association of Southeast Asian Countries.

1977, Jan. 14 Photo. *Perf. 14x14½*

152 Strip of 5	10.00	8.50
a.-e. A62 15c single stamp	1.25	.40

Prime Minister Tun Haji Abdul Razak bi Dato Hussein (1922-1976).

FELDA Housing Development A63

Design: 30c, View of oil palm settlement area and FELDA emblem.

1977, July 7 Litho. *Perf. 13½x14½*

153 A63 15c multicolored	.60	.30
154 A63 30c multicolored	1.00	1.75

Federal Land Development Authority (FELDA), 21st anniversary.

"10" — A64

ASEAN, 10th anniv.: 75c, Flags of ASEAN members: Malaysia, Philippines, Singapore, Thailand and Indonesia.

1977, Aug. 8 Litho. *Perf. 13½x14½*

155 A64 10c multicolored	.60	.20
156 A64 75c multicolored	1.00	.85

SEA Games Emblems A65

Designs: 20c, Ball, symbolic of 9 participating nations. 75c, Running.

Perf. 13½x14½

1977, Nov. 19 Litho.

157 A65 10c multicolored	.30	.25
158 A65 20c multicolored	.30	.25
159 A65 75c multicolored	.75	1.40
Nos. 157-159 (3)	1.35	1.90

9th South East Asia Games, Kuala Lumpur.

Bank Emblem A66

1978, Mar. 15 Litho. *Perf. 14*

160 A66 30c multicolored	.40	.20
161 A66 75c multicolored	.80	.80

2nd annual meeting of Islamic Development Bank Governors, Kuala Lumpur, Mar. 1978.

Government Building A67

Designs: Views of Shah Alam.

1978, Dec. 7 Litho. *Perf. 13½x14½*

162 A67 10c multicolored	.25	.25
163 A67 30c multicolored	.30	.20
164 A67 75c multicolored	.85	1.60
Nos. 162-164 (3)	1.40	2.05

Inauguration of Shah Alam as state capital of Selangor.

Mobile Post Office in Village — A68

Designs: 25c, General Post Office, Kuala Lumpur. 50c, Motorcyclist, rural mail delivery.

1978, July 10 *Perf. 13*

165 A68 10c multicolored	1.10	.40
166 A68 25c multicolored	1.25	1.75
167 A68 50c multicolored	1.50	2.50
Nos. 165-167 (3)	3.85	4.65

4th Conf. of Commonwealth Postal Administrators.

Jamboree Emblem A69

Bees and Honeycomb A70

1978, July 26 Litho. *Perf. 13½*

168 A69 15c multicolored	1.00	.30
169 A70 $1 multicolored	4.00	3.00

4th Boy Scout Jamboree, Sarawak.

Globe, Crest and WHO Emblem A71

1978, Sept. 30 *Perf. 13½x14½*

170 A71 15c blue, red & black .45 .35
171 A71 30c green, red & black .75 .45
172 A71 50c pink, red & black 1.25 .80
Nos. 170-172 (3) 2.45 1.60

Global eradication of smallpox.

Dome of the Rock A72

1978, Aug. 21 **Litho.** *Perf. 12½*

173 A72 15c red & multi 1.00 .35
174 A72 30c blue & multi 2.50 2.50

For Palestinian fighters and their families.

Tiger — A73

Designs: 40c, Cobego. 50c, Chevrotain. 75c, Pangolin. $1, Leatherback turtle. $2, Tapir. $5, Gaur. $10, Orangutan, vert.

Perf. 15x14½, 14½x15

1979, Jan. 4 **Litho.** **Wmk. 378**

175 A73 30c multicolored .60 .20
176 A73 40c multicolored .70 .20
177 A73 50c multicolored 1.10 .20
178 A73 75c multicolored 1.25 .20
179 A73 $1 multicolored 1.60 .20
180 A73 $2 multicolored 2.50 .75
181 A73 $5 multicolored 7.25 2.00
182 A73 $10 multicolored 13.00 3.00
Nos. 175-182 (8) 28.00 6.75

1983-87

Unwmk.

175a A73 30c ('84) 1.40 .70
176a A73 40c ('84) 1.60 .55
177a A73 50c ('84) 1.90 .55
178a A73 75c ('87) 11.00 8.50
179a A73 $1 5.25 .55
180a A73 $2 7.00 .85
181a A73 $5 ('85) 20.00 7.00
182a A73 $10 ('86) 32.50 10.50
Nos. 175a-182a (8) 80.65 29.20

Central Bank of Malaysia — A74

Year of the Child Emblem — A75

10c, Central Bank of Malaysia & emblem.

Perf. 13½

1979, Jan. 26 **Litho.** **Unwmk.**

183 A74 10c multicolored, horiz. .30 .30
184 A74 75c multicolored 1.10 1.40

Central Bank of Malaysia, 20th anniv.

1979, Feb. 24 *Perf. 14*

Intl. Year of the Child: 15c, Children of the world, globe and ICY emblem. $1, Children at play, ICY emblem.

185 A75 10c multicolored .50 .20
186 A75 15c multicolored .40 .20
187 A75 $1 multicolored 3.25 3.25
Nos. 185-187 (3) 4.15 3.65

Symbolic Rubber Plant — A76

Designs: 10c, Symbolic palm. 75c, Symbolic rubber products.

1978, Nov. 28 **Litho.** *Perf. 13*

188 A76 10c brt green & gold .25 .20
189 A76 20c multicolored .45 .20
190 A76 75c brt green & gold .60 .90
Nos. 188-190 (3) 1.30 1.30

Centenary of rubber production (in 1977).

Rafflesia Hasseltii A77

Flowers: 2c, Pterocarpus indicus. 5c, Lagerstroemia speciosa. 10c, Durio zibethinus. 15c, Hibiscus. 20c, Rhododendron scortechinii. 25c, Phaeomeria speciosa.

Perf. 15x14½

1979, Apr. 30 **Wmk. 378**

191 A77 1c multicolored .20 .20
192 A77 2c multicolored .20 .20
193 A77 5c multicolored .20 .20
a. Unwmkd. ('84)
194 A77 10c multicolored .20 .20
a. White flowers, unwmkd. ('84) .20 .20
195 A77 15c multicolored .25 .20
a. 15c yel & multi, unwmkd. ('83) .20 .20
196 A77 20c multicolored .30 .20
a. 20c greenish & multi, unwmkd. ('83) .25 .20
197 A77 25c multicolored .35 .20
a. Unwmkd. ('85) 5.00
Nos. 191-197 (7) 1.70 1.40

Temengor Hydroelectric Dam — A78

Designs: 25c, 50c, Dam and river, diff.

Perf. 13½x14½

1979, Sept. 19 **Litho.** **Unwmk.**

198 A78 15c multicolored .30 .30
199 A78 25c multicolored .70 .50
200 A78 50c multicolored 1.00 1.25
Nos. 198-200 (3) 2.00 2.05

"TELECOM 79" — A79

Telecom Emblem and: 15c, Telephone receiver and globes. 50c, Modes of communication.

1979, Sept. 20 *Perf. 13½*

Size: 34x25mm

201 A79 10c multicolored .40 .50
202 A79 15c multicolored .30 .20

Perf. 14

Size: 29x28mm

203 A79 50c multicolored .90 2.25
Nos. 201-203 (3) 1.60 2.95

3rd World Telecommunications Exhibition, Geneva, Sept. 20-26.

Haji Ahmad Shah — A80

1980, July 10 **Litho.** *Perf. 14½*

204 A80 10c multicolored .35 .40
205 A80 15c multicolored .25 .20
206 A80 50c multicolored .80 2.25
Nos. 204-206 (3) 1.40 2.85

Installation of Sultan Haji Ahmad Shah of Pahang as Paramount Ruler (Yang di-Pertuan Agong).

Pahang-Sarawak Cable — A81

Designs: 15c, Dial with views of Kuantan and Kuching. 50c, Telephone and maps.

1980, Aug. 31 **Litho.** *Perf. 13½*

207 A81 10c shown .25 .35
208 A81 15c multicolored .25 .20
209 A81 50c multicolored .35 1.75
Nos. 207-209 (3) .85 2.30

National University of Malaysia, 10th Anniversary A82

15c, Jalan Pantai Baru campus. 75c, Great Hall & Tun Haji Abdul Razak (1st chancellor).

1980, Sept. 2 **Litho.** *Perf. 13½*

210 A82 10c shown .25 .20
211 A82 15c multicolored .25 .20
212 A82 75c multicolored .50 2.50
Nos. 210-212 (3) 1.00 2.90

Hegira (Pilgrimage Year) — A83

1980, Nov. 9

213 A83 15c multicolored .30 .20
214 A83 50c multicolored .55 1.25

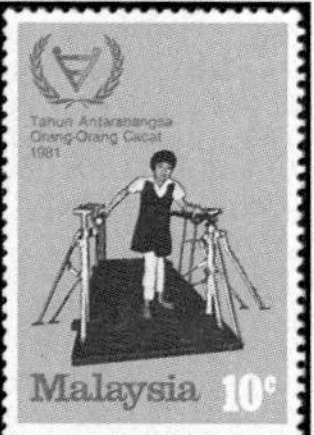

International Year of the Disabled A84

Sultan Mahmud of Trengganu A85

1981, Feb. 14 **Litho.** *Perf. 13½*

215 A84 10c Child learning to walk .60 .25
216 A84 15c Seamstress .55 .20
217 A84 75c Athlete 2.50 3.00
Nos. 215-217 (3) 3.65 3.45

1981, Mar. 21 **Litho.** *Perf. 14½*

218 A85 10c multicolored .20 .20
219 A85 15c multicolored .25 .20
220 A85 50c multicolored .90 .30
Nos. 218-220 (3) 1.35 .70

Industrial Training Seminar A86

Designs: Various workers.

1981, May 2 **Litho.** *Perf. 13½*

221 A86 10c multicolored .35 .20
222 A86 15c multicolored .25 .20
223 A86 30c multicolored .35 .20
224 A86 75c multicolored .60 2.00
Nos. 221-224 (4) 1.55 2.60

World Energy Conference, 25th anniv. — A87

1981, June 17 **Litho.** *Perf. 13½*

225 A87 10c "25" .40 .30
226 A87 15c Sources of Energy .30 .30
227 A87 75c Non-renewable energy 1.40 3.00
Nos. 225-227 (3) 2.10 3.60

Centenary of Sabah — A88

1981, Aug. 31 **Litho.** *Perf. 12*

228 A88 15c Views, 1881 and 1981 .60 .30
229 A88 80c Traditional and modern farming 3.25 4.00

Rain Tree A89

1981, Dec. 16 **Litho.** *Perf. 14*

230 A89 15c shown .50 .20
231 A89 50c Simber tree, vert. 1.50 1.25
232 A89 80c Borneo camphorwood, vert. 3.00 4.00
Nos. 230-232 (3) 5.00 5.45

Scouting Year and Jamboree, Apr. 9- 16 A90

1982, Apr. 10 **Litho.** *Perf. 13½x13*

233 A90 15c Jamboree emblem .40 .30
234 A90 50c Flag, emblem 1.00 .75
235 A90 80c Emblems, knot 1.75 3.00
Nos. 233-235 (3) 3.15 4.05

15th Anniv. of Assoc. of South East Asian Nations (ASEAN) A91

1982, Aug. 8 **Litho.** *Perf. 14*

236 A91 15c Meeting Center .50 .25
237 A91 $1 Flags 1.25 2.00

Dome of the Rock, Jerusalem A92

1982, Aug. 21 *Perf. 13½*

238 A92 15c multicolored 1.25 .35
239 A92 $1 multicolored 6.00 4.75

For the freedom of Palestine.

25th Anniv. of Independence — A93

1982, Aug. 31 **Litho.** ***Perf. 14***

240 A93 10c Kuala Lumpur .20 .20
241 A93 15c Independence celebration .25 .20
242 A93 50c Parade .60 .50
243 A93 80c Independence ceremony .70 2.50
a. Souvenir sheet of 4, #240-243 16.00 16.00
b. Souvenir sheet of 4, #240-243 11.00 11.00
Nos. 240-243 (4) 1.75 3.40

No. 243a has a narrow silver frame around the center vignette of the 10c value. This frame was removed for the second printing, No. 243b.

Traditional Games — A94

1982, Oct. 30 ***Perf. 13½***

244 A94 10c Shadow play 1.00 .35
245 A94 15c Cross top 1.00 .35
246 A94 75c Kite flying 5.25 4.00
Nos. 244-246 (3) 7.25 4.70

Handicrafts — A95

1982, Nov. 26 **Litho.** ***Perf. 13x13½***

247 A95 10c Sabah hats .55 .45
248 A95 15c Gold-threaded cloth .55 .45
249 A95 75c Sarawak pottery 2.50 3.25
Nos. 247-249 (3) 3.60 4.15

Commonwealth Day — A96

1983, Mar. 14 **Litho.** ***Perf. 14***

250 A96 15c Flag .40 .25
251 A96 20c Seri Paduka Baginda .40 .25
252 A96 40c Oil palm refinery .55 .40
253 A96 $1 Globe 1.10 2.00
Nos. 250-253 (4) 2.45 2.90

First Shipment of Natural Gas, Bintulu, Sarawak — A97

1983, Jan. 22 **Litho.** ***Perf. 12***

254 A97 15c Bintulu Port Authority emblem 1.10 .50
a. Perf. 13½ *30.00* 3.25
255 A97 20c LNG Tanker Tenaga Satu 1.40 1.25
a. Perf. 13½ 35.00 3.50
256 A97 $1 Gas plant 4.50 6.00
a. Perf. 13½ *60.00* 12.50
Nos. 254-256 (3) 7.00 7.75
Nos. 254a-256a (3) 125.00 19.25

Freshwater Fish — A98

1983, June 15 ***Perf. 12x12½***

257 Pair 6.00 3.00
a. A98 20c Tilapia nilotica 1.50 .35
b. A98 20c Cyprinus carpio 1.50 .35
c. As #257, perf. 13½x14 11.00 11.00
258 Pair 7.00 3.50
a. A98 40c Puntius gonionotus 1.75 .40
b. A98 40c Ctenopharyngodon idellus 1.75 .40
c. As #258, perf. 13½x14 11.50 11.50

Opening of East-West Highway — A99

1983, July 1 ***Perf. 14x13½***

259 A99 15c Lower Sungei Pergau Bridge 1.25 .40
260 A99 20c Sungei Perak Reservoir Bridge 1.25 .60
261 A99 $1 Map 5.50 5.50
Nos. 259-261 (3) 8.00 6.50

Armed Forces, 50th Anniv. — A100

Designs: 15c, Royal Malaysian Aircraft. 20c, Navy vessel firing missile. 40c, Battle at Pasir Panjang. 80c, Trooping of the Royal colors.

1983, Sept. 16 **Litho.** ***Perf. 13½***

262 A100 15c multicolored .70 .40
263 A100 20c multicolored 1.00 .40
264 A100 40c multicolored 2.00 2.00
265 A100 80c multicolored 4.50 5.00
a. Souvenir sheet of 4, #262-265 15.00 15.00
Nos. 262-265 (4) 8.20 7.80

Helmeted Hornbill — A101

1983, Oct. 26 **Litho.** ***Perf. 13½***

266 A101 15c shown 2.50 .40
267 A101 20c Wrinkled Hornbill 2.50 .45
268 A101 50c White crested Hornbill 3.00 1.75
269 A101 $1 Rhinoceros Hornbill 5.25 5.25
Nos. 266-269 (4) 13.25 7.85

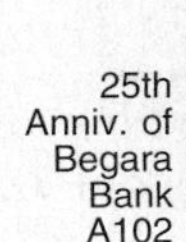

25th Anniv. of Begara Bank A102

Branch offices.

1984, Jan. 26 **Litho.** ***Perf. 13½x14***

270 A102 20c Ipoh 1.25 .35
271 A102 $1 Alor Setar 2.25 3.00

10th Anniv. of Federal Territory A103

Views of Kuala Lumpur. 20c, 40c vert.

Perf. 14x13½, 13½x14

1984, Feb. 1 **Litho.**

272 A103 20c multicolored 1.00 .50
273 A103 40c multicolored 1.40 1.25
274 A103 80c multicolored 4.00 5.50
Nos. 272-274 (3) 6.40 7.25

Labuan Federal Territory A104

Traditional Weapons A105

1984, Apr. 16 **Litho.** ***Perf. 13½x14***

275 A104 20c Development symbols, map, arms 1.50 .40
276 A104 $1 Flag, map 4.75 4.75

1984, May 30 ***Perf. 13x14***

277 A105 40c Keris Semenanjung 1.25 .30
278 A105 40c Keris Pekakak 1.25 .30
279 A105 40c Keris Jawa 1.25 .30
280 A105 40c Tumbuk Lada 1.25 .30
a. Block of 4, #277-280 6.00 6.00

Asia-Pacific Broadcasting Union, 20th Anniv. — A106

1984, June 23 ***Perf. 14x14½***

281 A106 20c Map, waves 1.40 .40
282 A106 $1 "20" 2.50 4.00

Kuala Lumpur Post Office Opening A107

1984, Oct. 29 ***Perf. 12x11½***

283 A107 15c Facsimile transmission .80 .35
284 A107 20c Building .80 .35
285 A107 $1 Mail bag conveyor 2.00 3.00
Nos. 283-285 (3) 3.60 3.70

Installation of Sultan of Johore as 8th Paramount Ruler of Malaysia — A108

Sultan Mahmood, Arms A109

1984, Nov. 15 **Litho.** ***Perf. 12***

286 A108 15c multicolored 1.00 .40
287 A108 20c multicolored 1.00 .35
288 A109 40c multicolored 1.40 .80
289 A109 80c multicolored 2.40 3.50
Nos. 286-289 (4) 5.80 5.05

A110

A111

Malaysian hibiscus.

1984, Dec. 12 **Litho.** ***Perf. 13½***

290 A110 10c White hibiscus 1.00 .40
291 A110 20c Red hibiscus 1.00 .35
292 A110 40c Pink hibiscus 2.00 2.00
293 A110 $1 Orange hibiscus 3.25 4.25
Nos. 290-293 (4) 7.25 7.00

Perf. 13½x14, 14x13½

1985, Mar. 30 **Litho.**

294 A111 20c Badge, vert. 1.25 .30
295 A111 $1 Parliament, Kuala Lumpur 2.75 .45

Parliament, 25th anniv.

Protected Wildlife A112

1985, Apr. 25 ***Perf. 14***

296 A112 10c Prionodon linsang 1.75 .55
297 A112 40c Nycticebus coucang, vert. 2.00 1.25
298 A112 $1 Petaurista elegans, vert. 5.00 6.00
Nos. 296-298 (3) 8.75 7.80

Intl. Youth Year — A113

1985, May 15 ***Perf. 13***

299 A113 20c Youth solidarity 1.25 .40
300 A113 $1 Participation in natl. development 4.00 5.00

Malaya Railways Centenary A114

Locomotives.

1985, June 1 ***Perf. 13***

301 A114 15c Steam engine, 1885 2.00 .50
302 A114 20c Diesel-electric, 1957 2.10 .50
303 A114 $1 Diesel, 1963 5.25 6.00
Nos. 301-303 (3) 9.35 7.00

Souvenir Sheet

Perf. 14x13

304 A114 80c Train leaving Kuala Lumpur Station, 1938 11.00 11.00

No. 304 contains one stamp 48x32mm.

Proton Saga A115

1985, July 9 *Perf. 14*
305 A115 20c multicolored 1.25 .30
306 A115 40c multicolored 1.75 .80
307 A115 $1 multicolored 3.75 5.00
Nos. 305-307 (3) 6.75 6.10

Inauguration of natl. automotive industry.

Sultan Salahuddin Abdul Aziz, Selangor Coat of Arms A116

1985, Sept. 5 *Perf. 13*
308 A116 15c multicolored .75 .60
309 A116 20c multicolored .90 .60
310 A116 $1 multicolored 4.00 6.00
Nos. 308-310 (3) 5.65 7.20

25th anniv. of coronation.

Penang Bridge Opening A117

1985, Sept. 15 Litho. *Perf. 13½x13*
311 A117 20c shown 1.40 .45
312 A117 40c Bridge, map 2.75 .75

Size: 44x28mm
Perf. 12½
313 A117 $1 Map 4.00 5.00
Nos. 311-313 (3) 8.15 6.20

Natl. Oil Industry A118

1985, Nov. 4 *Perf. 12½*
314 A118 15c Offshore rig, vert. 1.40 .45
315 A118 20c 1st refinery 1.40 .45
316 A118 $1 Map of oil and gas fields 5.00 5.00
Nos. 314-316 (3) 7.80 5.90

Coronation of Paduka Seri, Sultan of Perak A119

1985, Dec. 9 *Perf. 14*
317 A119 15c lt blue & multi .55 .40
318 A119 20c lilac & multi .80 .40
319 A119 $1 gold & multi 3.75 5.00
Nos. 317-319 (3) 5.10 5.80

Birds A120

Wmk. 388
1986, Mar. 11 Litho. *Perf. 13¼*
320 A120 20c Lophura ignita, vert. 2.50 .40
a. Perf. 12 4.75 1.25
321 A120 20c Pavo malacense, vert. 2.50 .40
a. Pair, #320-321 5.00 1.50
b. Perf. 12 7.50 2.00
c. Pair, #320a, 321b 12.50 8.25
322 A120 40c Lophura bulweri 4.00 .50
a. Perf. 12 8.25 1.50
323 A120 40c Argusianus argus 5.00 .50
a. Pair, #322-323 9.00 1.90
b. Perf. 12 7.25 1.50
c. Pair, #322a, 323b 15.50 11.50
Nos. 320-323 (4) 14.00 1.80

PATA '86, Pacific Area Travel Assoc. Conference, Persidangan — A121

No. 324: a, Two women dancing. b, Woman in red. c, Man and woman.
No. 325: a, Woman in gold. b, Woman holding fan. c, Woman in violet.

Perf. 15x14½
1986, Apr. 14 Litho. Unwmk.
324 Strip of 3 3.00 3.00
a.-c. A121 20c any single .55 .20
325 Strip of 3 4.00 4.00
a.-c. A121 40c any single .65 .20

Malaysia Games A122

Games Emblem — A123

Flags — A124

Wmk. 388
1986, Apr. 14 Litho. *Perf. 12*
326 A122 20c multicolored 1.60 .50
327 A123 40c multicolored 4.50 2.00
328 A124 $1 multicolored 6.00 4.00
Nos. 326-328 (3) 12.10 6.50

Nephelium Lappaceum A125

Averrhoa Carambola A126

Litho. (#329-332), Photo. (#333-336)
Perf. 12 (#329-332)
1986-2000 Wmk. 388
329 A125 40c shown .40 .20
a. Perf. 13½x14 .65
330 A125 50c Ananas comosus .60 .20
a. Perf. 13½x14 .65
331 A125 80c Durio zibethinus .95 .35
a. Perf. 13½x14 1.00
332 A125 $1 Garcinia mangostana 1.00 .35
a. Perf. 13½x14 1.00

Perf. 13½x14
332C A125 $5 Musa sapientum ('00) 1.75 .80

Perf. 13½
Wmk. 233
333 A126 $2 shown 2.10 .65
334 A126 $5 Musa sapientum 4.00 1.10
335 A126 $10 Mangifera odorata 6.75 3.75
336 A126 $20 Carica papaya 15.00 5.50
Nos. 329-336 (9) 32.55 12.90

No. 332C issued 2000; balance of set issued 6/5/86.

Two additional stamps were issued in this set. The editors would like to examine any examples.
Compare with Nos. 766A-766H.

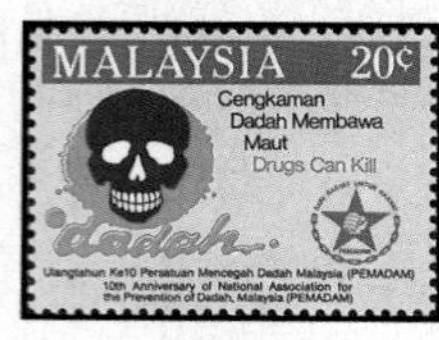

Natl. Assoc. for the Prevention of Drug Abuse, 10th Anniv. A127

1986, June 26 Wmk. 388 *Perf. 13*
337 A127 20c Skull .90 .50
338 A127 40c Dove 1.40 .80
339 A127 $1 Addict, vert. 4.50 4.00
Nos. 337-339 (3) 6.80 5.30

Malaysian Airlines Kuala Lumpur-Los Angeles Inaugural Flight — A128

1986, July 31 *Perf. 14x13½*
340 A128 20c Flight routes map 2.00 .70
341 A128 40c MAS emblem, new route 2.45 .70
342 A128 $1 Emblem, stops 5.50 4.00
Nos. 340-342 (3) 9.95 5.40

Industrial Productivity A129

1986, Nov. 3 Litho. *Perf. 14*
343 A129 20c Construction, vert. 1.00 .40
344 A129 40c Industry 2.00 1.00
345 A129 $1 Automobile factory 5.25 5.25
Nos. 343-345 (3) 8.25 6.65

Historic Buildings A130

15c, Istana Lama Seri Menanti, Negri Sembilan. 20c, Istana Kenangan, Perak. 40c, Bangunan Stadthuys, Malacca. $1, Istana Kuching, Sarawak.

1986, Dec. 20 *Perf. 13*
346 A130 15c multicolored .90 .40
347 A130 20c multicolored .90 .40
348 A130 40c multicolored 2.00 .70
349 A130 $1 multicolored 3.00 4.00
Nos. 346-349 (4) 6.80 5.50

See design A146.

Folk Music Instruments — A131

1987, Mar. 7 Litho. *Perf. 12*
350 A131 15c Sompotan .90 .65
351 A131 20c Sapih .90 .65
352 A131 50c Serunai, vert. 2.40 .65
353 A131 80c Rebab, vert. 4.00 2.00
Nos. 350-353 (4) 8.20 3.95

Intl. Year of Shelter for the Homeless — A132

1987, Apr. 6 Litho. *Perf. 12*
354 A132 20c Model village .80 .40
355 A132 $1 Symbols of family, shelter 4.00 1.50

UN Anti-Drug Campaign and Congress, Vienna A133

1987, June 8 Litho. *Perf. 13½x13*
356 20c Health boy, family, rainbow .75 .75
357 20c Holding drugs .75 .75
a. A133 Pair, #356-357 3.00 3.00
358 40c Child warding off drugs 1.75 .75
359 40c Drugs, damaged body in capsule 1.75 .75
a. A133 Pair, #358-358 7.50 3.00
Nos. 356-359 (4) 5.00 3.00

Nos. 357a, 359a have continuous designs.

Kenyir Hydroelectric Power Station Inauguration — A134

1987, July 13 *Perf. 12*
360 A134 20c Power facility, dam 1.60 .40
361 A134 $1 Side view 3.50 1.75

33rd Commonwealth Parliamentary Conference — A135

1987, Sept. 1 Litho. *Perf. 12*
362 A135 20c Maces, parliament .60 .20
363 A135 $1 Parliament, maces, diff. 1.60 1.10

Transportation and Communications Decade in Asia and the Pacific (1985-94) — A136

Designs: 15c, Satellites, Earth, satellite dish. 20c, Car, diesel train, Kuala Lumpur Station. 40c, MISC container ship. $1, Malaysia Airlines jet, Kuala Lumpur Airport.

1987, Oct. 26 *Perf. 13½x13*
364 A136 15c multicolored 1.25 .60
365 A136 20c multicolored 1.25 .70
366 A136 40c multicolored 2.25 1.25
367 A136 $1 multicolored 4.50 5.50
Nos. 364-367 (4) 9.25 8.05

Protected Wildcats
A137

1987, Nov. 14
368 A137 15c Felis temminckii 3.50 .70
369 A137 20c Felis planiceps 3.50 .70
370 A137 40c Felis marmorata 7.75 1.50
371 A137 $1 Neofelis nebulosa 11.00 6.00
Nos. 368-371 (4) 25.75 8.90

ASEAN, 20th Anniv.
A138

1987, Dec. 14 **Litho.** *Perf. 13*
372 A138 20c "20," flags .35 .25
373 A138 $1 Flags, Earth 1.60 1.50

Opening of Sultan Salahuddin Abdul Aziz Shah Mosque, Selangor
A139

Dome, minarets and: 15c, Arches. 20c, Sultan Abdul Aziz Shah, Selangor crest. $1, Interior, vert.

1988, Mar. 11 **Litho.** *Perf. 12*
374 A139 15c multicolored .50 .35
375 A139 20c multicolored .50 .35
376 A139 $1 multicolored 1.40 2.00
Nos. 374-376 (3) 2.40 2.70

Opening of Sultan Ismail Power Station, Trengganu
A140

1988, Apr. 4 *Perf. 13*
377 A140 20c shown .40 .30
378 A140 $1 Station, diff. 2.00 1.25

Wildlife Protection — A141

Birds.

1988, June 30 **Litho.** *Perf. 13*
379 20c Hypothymis azurea .70 .70
380 20c Dicaeum cruentatum .70 .70
a. A141 Pair, #379-380 3.75 3.75
381 50c Aethopyga siparaja 1.40 1.40
382 50c Cymbirhynchus macrorhynchos 1.40 1.40
a. A141 Pair, #381-382 6.50 6.50
Nos. 379-382 (4) 4.20 4.20

Independence of Sabah and Sarawak, 25th Anniv.
A142 A143

1988, Aug. 31 **Litho.** *Perf. 13x13½*
383 A142 20c Sabah .65 .70
384 A142 20c Sarawak .65 .70
a. Pair, #383-384 1.40 1.50
385 A143 $1 State and natl. symbols 2.25 3.00
Nos. 383-385 (3) 3.55 4.40

A144

Marine Life — A145

Nudibranchs: No. 386: a, Glossodoris atromarginata. b, Phyllidia ocellata. c, Chromodoris annae. d, Flabellina macassarana. e, Fryeria ruppelli.

1988, Dec. 17 **Litho.** *Perf. 12*
386 Strip of 5 7.00 7.00
a.-e. A144 20c any single .75 .25

Souvenir Sheet
Perf. 14
387 A145 $1 Pomacanthus annularis 6.00 6.00

No. 387 contains one stamp 50x40mm.

Historic Buildings, Malacca
A146

#388, Perisytiharan Kemerdekaan Memorial. #389, Istana Kesultanan. $1, Porta da Santiago.

Perf. 13½x13, 13x13½
1989, Apr. 15 **Litho.**
388 A146 20c multicolored .50 .35
389 A146 20c multicolored .50 .35
390 A146 $1 multicolored, vert. 2.50 .70
Nos. 388-390 (3) 3.50 1.40

See design A130.

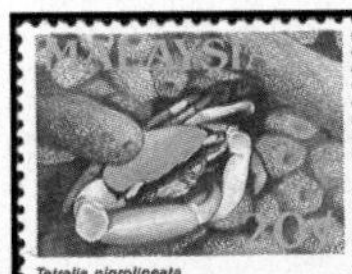

Crustaceans
A147

Wmk. 388
1989, June 29 **Litho.** *Perf. 12*
391 A147 20c *Tetralia nigrolineata* .50 .50
392 A147 20c *Neopetrolisthes maculatus* .50 .50
a. Pair, #391-392 1.60 1.60
393 A147 40c *Periclimenes holthuisi* .90 .90
394 A147 40c *Synalpheus neomeris* .90 .90
a. Pair, #393-394 2.75 2.75
Nos. 391-394 (4) 2.80 2.80

7th Natl. Scout Jamboree
A148

1989, July 26 *Perf. 13½x13, 13x13½*
395 A148 10c Map, badges .50 .45
396 A148 20c Scout salute, natl. flag .50 .45
397 A148 80c Camping out 3.00 3.00
Nos. 395-397 (3) 4.00 3.90

Nos. 395-396 vert.

15th SEA Games, Kuala Lumpur — A149

Installation of Sultan Azlan as Supreme Ruler — A150

Designs: 10c, Cycling, horiz. 20c, Track events, horiz. 50c, Swimming. $1, Torchbearer, stadium and flags.

Perf. 13½x13, 13x13½
1989, Aug. 20 **Litho.** **Wmk. 388**
398 A149 10c multicolored .50 .50
399 A149 20c multicolored .50 .40
400 A149 50c multicolored 1.40 .80
401 A149 $1 multicolored 2.40 3.00
Nos. 398-401 (4) 4.80 4.70

1989, Sept. 18 *Perf. 13x13½*
402 A150 20c multicolored .35 .20
403 A150 40c multicolored .60 .30
404 A150 $1 multicolored 1.40 2.00
Nos. 402-404 (3) 2.35 2.50

Commonwealth Heads of Government Meeting — A151

1989, Oct. 18 *Perf. 13½x13, 13x13½*
405 A151 20c Conference center .40 .30
406 A151 50c Folk dancers, vert. .80 .60
407 A151 $1 Map, flag 1.60 2.25
Nos. 405-407 (3) 2.80 3.15

Malaysia Airlines Inaugural Non-stop Flight to London, Dec. 2
A152

#408, Passenger jet, Malaysian clock tower, Big Ben. #409, Passenger jet, Malaysian skyscraper, Westminster Palace. $1, Map, passenger jet.

1989, Dec. 2 **Wmk. 388** *Perf. 13*
408 A152 20c shown 2.00 2.00
409 A152 20c multicolored 2.00 2.00
a. Pair, #408-409 4.50 4.50
410 A152 $1 multicolored 5.50 5.50
Nos. 408-410 (3) 9.50 9.50

National Park, 50th Anniv. — A153

1989, Dec. 28 *Perf. 13x13½*
411 A153 20c Map, sloth 1.60 .40
412 A153 $1 Crested arguses 4.50 4.50

Visit Malaysia.

Visit Malaysia Year — A154

1990, Jan. 11 *Perf. 12*
413 A154 20c Map .60 .50
414 A154 50c Drummers 1.40 1.10
415 A154 $1 Yachts, scuba divers 2.25 3.00
Nos. 413-415 (3) 4.25 4.60

Wildflowers
A155

1990, Mar. 12
416 A155 15c *Dillenia suffruticosa* .30 .30
417 A155 20c *Mimosa pudica* .30 .30
418 A155 50c *Ipomoea carnea* .80 .80
419 A155 $1 *Nymphaea pubescens* 1.40 2.00
Nos. 416-419 (4) 2.80 3.40

Kuala Lumpur
A156

Wmk. 388
1990, May 14 **Litho.** *Perf. 12*
420 A156 20c Flag, rainbow, vert. .40 .40
421 A156 40c shown .70 .50
422 A156 $1 Cityscape 1.60 2.25
Nos. 420-422 (3) 2.70 3.15

South-South Consultation and Cooperation Conference — A157

1990, June 1 *Perf. 13*
423 A157 20c shown .45 .35
424 A157 80c Emblem 1.75 2.25

Alor Setar, 250th Anniv.
A158

1990, June 2 *Perf. 12*

425 A158 20c shown .40 .30
426 A158 40c Musicians, vert. .70 .35
427 A158 $1 Government bldg., vert. 1.50 2.50
Nos. 425-427 (3) 2.60 3.15

Intl. Literacy Year A159

1990, Sept. 8 *Perf. 12*

428 A159 20c Letters, sign language .35 .35
a. Perf. 13 17.50
429 A159 40c People reading .75 .40
430 A159 $1 Globe, pen nib, vert. 1.50 2.50
Nos. 428-430 (3) 2.60 3.25

Turtles A160

1990, Nov. 17

431 A160 15c Dermochelys coriacea 1.50 .30
432 A160 20c Chelonia mydas 1.50 .30
433 A160 40c Eretmochelys imbricata 1.75 .65
434 A160 $1 Lepidochelys olivacea 3.75 3.75
Nos. 431-434 (4) 8.50 5.00

MARA (Council of Indigenous People), 25th Anniv. A161

1991, Apr. 25

435 A161 20c Construction .35 .35
436 A161 40c Education .65 .35
437 A161 $1 Banking & industry .90 1.75
Nos. 435-437 (3) 1.90 2.45

Wasps — A162

Designs: 15c, Eustenogaster calyptodoma. 20c, Vespa affinis indonensis. 50c, Sceliphorn javanum. $1, Ampulex compressa.

1991, July 29

438 A162 15c multicolored .45 .40
439 A162 20c multicolored .45 .40
440 A162 50c multicolored 1.00 .50
441 A162 $1 multicolored 2.10 2.10
a. Souvenir sheet of 4, #438-441, perf. 14½x14 6.00 6.00
Nos. 438-441 (4) 4.00 3.40

Prime Ministers — A163

#442, Tunku Abdul Rahman Putra Al-Haj (1903-90). #443, Tun Hussein Onn (1922-90). #444, Tun Abdul Razak Hussein (1922-76).

1991, Aug. 30

442 A163 $1 multicolored .90 1.00
443 A163 $1 multicolored .90 1.00
444 A163 $1 multicolored .90 1.00
Nos. 442-444 (3) 2.70 3.00

Historic Buildings A164

Designs: 15c, Istana Maziah, Trengganu. 20c, Istana Besar, Johore. 40c, Istana Bandar, Kuala Langat, Selangor. $1, Istana Jahar, Kelantan.

1991, Nov. 7

445 A164 15c multicolored .35 .30
446 A164 20c multicolored .35 .30
447 A164 40c multicolored .65 .40
448 A164 $1 multicolored 1.50 2.00
Nos. 445-448 (4) 2.85 3.00

Sarawak Museum, Cent. A165

Museum buildings, fabric pattern and: 30c, Brass lamp. $1, Vase.

1991, Dec. 21

449 A165 30c multicolored .45 .30
450 A165 $1 multicolored 1.50 2.00

Malaysian Postal Service — A166

Designs: No. 451a, Postman on bicycle. b, Postman on motorcycle. c, Mail truck. d, Mail truck, diff., oil tank. e, Globe, airplane.

1992, Jan. 1

451 A166 30c Strip of 5, #a.-e. 3.50 3.50

Malaysian Tropical Forests A167

Designs: 20c, Hill Dipterocarp Forest, Dyera costulata. 50c, Mangrove Swamp Forest, Rhizophora apiculata. $1, Lowland Dipterocarp Forest, Neobalanocarpus heimii.

1992, Mar. 23

452 A167 20c multicolored .35 .35
453 A167 50c multicolored .80 .50
454 A167 $1 multicolored 1.10 2.00
Nos. 452-454 (3) 2.25 2.85

Installation of Yang di-Pertuan Besar of Negri Sembilan, Silver Jubilee A168

1992, Apr. 18

455 A168 30c Portrait, arms .35 .20
456 A168 $1 Building 1.25 2.00

1992 Thomas Cup Champions in Badminton — A169

1992, July 25 *Perf. 12*

457 A169 $1 Cup, flag .90 1.10
458 A169 $1 Players .90 1.10

Souvenir Sheet

459 A169 $2 multicolored 2.50 2.50

No. 459 contains one 75x28mm stamp.

ASEAN, 25th Anniv. A170

1992, Aug. 8

460 A170 30c shown .55 .40
461 A170 50c Flora 1.00 .60
462 A170 $1 Architecture 1.60 2.00
Nos. 460-462 (3) 3.15 3.00

Postage Stamps in Malaysia, 125th Annv. A171

#463, Straits Settlements #1, Malaya #84. #464, Straits Settlements #2, Malaysia #2. #465, Straits Settlements #11, Malaysia #421. #466, Straits Settlements #14, Malaysia #467. #467, Flag, simulated stamp.

1992, Sept. 1

463 A171 30c multicolored .60 .25
464 A171 30c multicolored .60 .25
a. Pair #463-464 1.75 1.75
465 A171 50c multicolored 1.00 .25
466 A171 50c multicolored 1.00 .25
a. Pair #465-466 2.25 2.25
Nos. 463-466 (4) 3.20 1.00

Souvenir Sheet

467 A171 $2 multicolored 3.50 3.50

Kuala Lumpur '92.

A173

Coral — A174

No. 471: a, Acropora. b, Dendronephthya. c, Dendrophyllia. d, Sinularia. e, Melithaea. No. 472, Subergorgia.

1992, Dec. 21

471 A173 30c Strip of 5, #a.-e. 7.00 5.00

Souvenir Sheet

472 A174 $2 multicolored 5.50 5.50

16th Asian-Pacific Dental Congress A175

Children from various countries: #473, 4 girls. #474, 4 girls, 1 holding koala.

Dentists, flags of: No. 475, Japan, Malaysia, South Korea. No. 476, New Zealand, Thailand, People's Republic of China, Indonesia.

1993, Apr. 24

473 A175 30c multicolored .60 .60
474 A175 30c multicolored .60 .60
a. Pair, #473-474 1.50 1.50
475 A175 50c multicolored .90 .90
476 A175 $1 multicolored 1.75 1.75
a. Pair, #475-476 3.50 3.50
Nos. 473-476 (4) 3.85 3.85

A176

A177

1993, June 24

477 A176 30c Fairway, vert. .80 .55
478 A176 50c Old, new club houses, vert. 1.60 .70
479 A176 $1 Sand trap 2.50 2.50
Nos. 477-479 (3) 4.90 3.75

Royal Selangor Golf Club, cent.

1993, Aug. 2

Wildflowers.

480 A177 20c Alpinia rafflesiana .65 .50
481 A177 30c Achasma megalocheilos .65 .50
482 A177 50c Zingiber spectabile 1.75 .65
483 A177 $1 Costus speciosus 3.00 3.00
Nos. 480-483 (4) 6.05 4.65

14th Commonwealth Forestry Conference — A178

1993, Sept. 13

484 A178 30c Globe, forest .70 .50
485 A178 50c Hand holding trees 1.25 .60
486 A178 $1 Trees under dome, vert. 2.00 2.00
Nos. 484-486 (3) 3.95 3.10

Nos. 484-486 with Bangkok '93 Emblem Added

Wmk. 388

1993, Oct. 1 **Litho.** *Perf. 12*

486A A178 30c multicolored *4.50 4.00*
486B A178 50c multicolored *5.50 5.00*
486C A178 $1 multicolored *10.00 8.50*
Nos. 486A-486C (3) *20.00 17.50*

Kingfishers — A179

1993, Oct. 23

487 30c Halcyon smyrnensis 1.00 1.00
488 30c Alcedo meninting 1.00 1.00
a. A179 Pair, #487-488 2.50 2.50
489 50c Halcyon concreta 1.60 1.60
490 50c Ceyx erithacus 1.60 1.60
a. A179 Pair, #489-490 4.00 4.00
Nos. 487-490 (4) 5.20 5.20

A180

1993, Dec. 7
491 A180 30c SME MD3-160 airplane .60 .40
492 A180 50c Eagle X-TS airplane 1.25 .70
493 A180 $1 Patrol boat KD Kasturi 1.75 1.75
Nos. 491-493 (3) 3.60 2.85

Souvenir Sheet

494 A180 $2 Map of Malaysia 3.50 3.50

Langkawi Intl. Maritime and Aerospace Exhibition (LIMA '93).

Visit Malaysia Year — A181

1994, Jan. 1
495 A181 20c Jeriau Waterfalls .40 .40
496 A181 30c Flowers .50 .45
497 A181 50c Marine life 1.00 .60
498 A181 $1 Wildlife 1.50 2.00
Nos. 495-498 (4) 3.40 3.45

See Nos. 527A-527D.

Kuala Lumpur Natl. Planetarium A182

Designs: 30c, Exterior. 50c, Interior displays. $1, Theater auditorium.

1994, Feb. 7
499 A182 30c multicolored .60 .40
500 A182 50c multicolored 1.10 .65
501 A182 $1 multicolored 2.10 2.10
Nos. 499-501 (3) 3.80 3.15

Orchids — A183

Designs: 20c, Spathoglottis aurea. 30c, Paphiopedilum barbatum. 50c, Bulbophyllum lobbii. $1, Aerides odorata. $2, Grammatophyllum speciosum.

1994, Feb. 17
502 A183 20c multicolored .55 .35
503 A183 30c multicolored .55 .40
504 A183 50c multicolored .90 .70
505 A183 $1 multicolored 1.60 2.10
Nos. 502-505 (4) 3.60 3.55

Souvenir Sheet

506 A183 $2 multicolored 3.75 3.75

Hong Kong '94 (#506).

A184

A185

1994, June 17
507 A184 20c Decorative bowl .35 .30
508 A184 30c Celestial sphere .40 .30
509 A184 50c Dinar coins .55 .55
510 A184 $1 Decorative tile 1.25 1.25
Nos. 507-510 (4) 2.55 2.40

World Islamic Civilization Festival '94. See Nos. 528-531.

1994, July 26
511 A185 30c shown .70 .40
512 A185 50c Meat processing 1.00 .60
513 A185 $1 Cattle, laboratory 2.00 2.00
Nos. 511-513 (3) 3.70 3.00

Veterinary Services, cent.

Electrification, Cent. — A186

1994, Sept. 3
514 A186 30c Laying cable .55 .40
515 A186 30c Lighted city .55 .40
a. Pair, #514-515 1.40 1.40
516 A186 $1 Futuristic city 1.40 1.40
Nos. 514-516 (3) 2.50 2.20

North-South Expressway A187

1994, Sept. 8
517 A187 30c shown .40 .30
518 A187 50c Interchange .55 .45
519 A187 $1 Bridge 1.25 1.25
Nos. 517-519 (3) 2.20 2.00

A188

A189

1994, Sept. 22
520 A188 30c pink & multi .45 .30
521 A188 50c yellow & multi .60 .40
522 A188 $1 green & multi 1.25 1.25
Nos. 520-522 (3) 2.30 1.95

Installation of 10th Yang Di-Pertuan Agong (Head of State).

Wmk. 388

1994, Oct. 29 **Litho.** ***Perf. 12***
523 A189 $1 shown 1.25 1.25
524 A189 $1 Mascot 1.25 1.25
a. Pair, #523-524 + label 3.00 3.00

1998 Commonwealth Games, Kuala Lumpur.

Official Opening of Natl. Library Building A190

1994, Dec. 16
525 A190 30c Library building .45 .35
526 A190 50c Computer terminal .60 .45
527 A190 $1 Manuscript 1.25 1.25
Nos. 525-527 (3) 2.30 2.05

Nos. 495-498 with Added Inscription

Wmk. 388

1994, Nov. 8 **Litho.** ***Perf. 12***
527A A181 20c multicolored .75 .85
527B A181 30c multicolored 1.25 .95
527C A181 50c multicolored 1.75 1.50
527D A181 $1 multicolored 3.00 2.75
Nos. 527A-527D (4) 6.75 6.05

Nos. 507-510 with Added Inscription

Wmk. 388

1994, Aug. 16 **Litho.** ***Perf. 12***
528 A184 20c multicolored 1.50 1.50
529 A184 30c multicolored 1.25 1.25
530 A184 50c multicolored 3.00 3.00
531 A184 $1 multicolored 6.00 6.00
Nos. 528-531 (4) 11.75 11.75

A191

1994, Nov. 10 **Unwmk.** ***Perf. 14½***
532 A191 30c shown .70 .35
533 A191 $1 Building complex 1.40 1.40

Memorial to Tunku Abdul Rahman Putra Al-Haj (1903-1990), former Prime Minister.

Fungi — A192

1995, Jan. 18 ***Perf. 14½x14***
534 A192 20c Bracket fungus .80 .30
535 A192 30c Cup fungus .90 .30
536 A192 50c Veil fungus 1.40 .40
537 A192 $1 Coral fungus 2.75 2.75
Nos. 534-537 (4) 5.85 3.75

Neofelis Nebulosa A193

1995, Apr. 18 **Wmk. 373** ***Perf. 13½***
538 A193 20c shown .40 .30
539 A193 30c With young .60 .40
540 A193 50c With mouth open 1.00 .75
541 A193 $1 Lying on rock 2.00 2.00
a. Strip of 4, #538-541 5.50 5.50

Nos. 538-541 were issued in sheets of 16 stamps.
World Wildlife Fund.

Marine Life — A194

1995, Apr. 10 **Wmk. 388** ***Perf. 12***

Booklet Stamps

542 A194 20c Feather stars .80 .80
543 A194 20c Sea fans .80 .80
a. Pair, #542-543 1.75 1.75
b. Booklet pane, 5 each #542-543 8.75 8.75
Complete booklet, #543b 9.25
544 A194 30c Soft coral 1.60 1.60
545 A194 30c Cup coral 1.60 1.60
a. Pair, #544-545 3.50 3.50
b. Booklet pane, 5 each #544-545 17.50 17.50
Complete booklet, #543b 18.50
Nos. 542-545 (4) 4.80 4.80

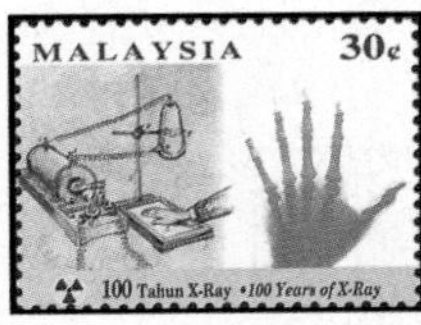

X-Ray, Cent. A195

#546, Early machine x-raying hand. #547, CAT scan machine. $1, Chest x-ray.

1995, May 29
546 A195 30c multicolored .30 .25
547 A195 30c multicolored .30 .25
a. Pair, #546-547 1.10 1.10
548 A195 $1 multicolored 1.50 .50
Nos. 546-548 (3) 2.10 1.00

1998 Commonwealth Games, Kuala Lumpur — A196

Various sporting events: No. 549, Badminton, cricket, shooting, tennis, weight lifting, hurdles, field hockey. No. 550, Cycling, lawn bowling, boxing, basketball, rugby, gymnastics.

Wmk. 388

1995, Sept. 10 **Litho.** ***Perf. 14***
549 A196 $1 multicolored 2.40 .60
550 A196 $1 multicolored 2.40 .60
a. Pair, #549-550 + label 5.50 5.50

Traditional Weapons A197

1995, Sept. 1 **Litho.** ***Perf. 14***
551 A197 20c Jemblah .35 .25
552 A197 30c Keris panjang .35 .25
553 A197 50c Kerambit .50 .35
554 A197 $1 Keris sundang 1.00 1.00
Nos. 551-554 (4) 2.20 1.85

Souvenir Sheet

555 A197 $2 Lading terus 3.75 3.75

Singapore '95.

UN, 50th Anniv. A198

1995, Oct. 24 ***Perf. 13½***
556 A198 30c shown .45 .30
557 A198 $1 UN emblem 1.25 1.25

Intl. Assoc. of Travel Agents (IATA), 50th Anniv. — A199

Jet, globe and: No. 558, Historic buildings. No. 559, Sydney Opera House, Great Wall of China. No. 560, Eiffel Tower, Tower Bridge. No. 561, Hollywood Walk of Fame, Latin American pyramid.

1995, Oct. 30 ***Perf. 14***

558		30c multicolored	.65	.45
559		30c multicolored	.65	.45
a.	A199	Pair, #558-559	1.75	1.75
560		50c multicolored	.90	.45
561		50c multicolored	.90	.45
a.	A199	Pair, #560-561	2.25	2.25
		Nos. 558-561 (4)	3.10	1.80

Turtles A200

Perf. 14x14½

1995, Sept. 26 Litho. Wmk. 388

Booklet Stamps

562	A200	30c Chelonia mydas	2.50	1.25
563	A200	30c Dermochelys coriacea	2.50	1.25
a.		Booklet pane, 5 each #562-563	27.50	16.00
		Complete booklet, #563a	30.00	

Proton Cars, 10th Anniv. — A201

#564, 1985 Saga 1.5. #565, 1992 Iswara 1.5 aeroback. #566, 1992, Iswara 1.5 sedan. #567, 1993 Wira 1.6 sedan. #568, 1993 Wira 1.6 aeroback. #569, 1994 Rally. #570, 1994 Satria 1.6. #571, 1995 Perdana 2.0. #572, 1995 Wira 1.6 aeroback. #573, 1995 Wira 1.8 sedan.

1995, Dec. Litho. ***Perf. 14***

Booklet Stamps

564	A201	30c multicolored	1.00	1.00
565	A201	30c multicolored	1.00	1.00
566	A201	30c multicolored	1.00	1.00
567	A201	30c multicolored	1.00	1.00
568	A201	30c multicolored	1.00	1.00
569	A201	30c multicolored	1.00	1.00
570	A201	30c multicolored	1.00	1.00
571	A201	30c multicolored	1.00	1.00
572	A201	30c multicolored	1.00	1.00
573	A201	30c multicolored	1.00	1.00
a.		Booklet pane, Nos. 564-573	10.00	10.00
		Complete booklet, No. 573a	10.00	

A202 A203

Malaysia East Asia Satellite: 30c, Ariane 4 being launched. 50c, Satellite in Earth orbit over East Asia. $1, Satellite Control Center, Langkawai.
$5, Satellite entering orbit, horiz.

1996, Jan. 13 ***Perf. 13½***

574	A202	30c multicolored	.45	.30
575	A202	50c multicolored	.70	.50
576	A202	$1 multicolored	1.25	1.25
		Nos. 574-576 (3)	2.40	2.05

Souvenir Sheet

Perf. 14

577	A202	$5 multicolored	8.00	8.00

No. 577 contains a holographic image. Soaking in water may affect the hologram.

Wmk. 388

1996, Apr. 16 Litho. ***Perf. 13½***

Pitcher Plants: #578, Nepenthes sanguinea. #579, Nepenthes macfarlanei. #580, Nepenthes rajah. #581, Nepenthes lowii.

578	A203	30c multicolored	.35	.30
579	A203	30c multicolored	.35	.30
a.		Pair, Nos. 578-579	.85	.85
580	A203	50c multicolored	.55	.40
581	A203	50c multicolored	.55	.40
a.		Pair, Nos. 580-581	1.40	1.40
		Nos. 578-581 (4)	1.80	1.40

Birds of Prey A204

Designs: 20c, Haliastur indus. 30c, Spilornis cheela. 50c, Haliaeetus leucogaster. $1, Spizaetus cirrhatus.
$2, Spizaetus alboniger, vert.

Wmk. 388

1996, May 18 Litho. ***Perf. 14***

582	A204	20c multicolored	.45	.45
583	A204	30c multicolored	.55	.55
584	A204	50c multicolored	.75	.75
585	A204	$1 multicolored	1.75	1.75
		Nos. 582-585 (4)	3.50	3.50

Souvenir Sheet

586	A204	$2 multicolored	5.00	5.00

CHINA '96 (#586).

Intl. Day Against Drug Abuse and Illicit Drug Trafficking A205

Designs: No. 587, Family, drugs burning. No. 588, Various sporting activities, marajuana plants. $1, Family, rainbow.

Wmk. 388

1996, June 26 Litho. ***Perf. 14***

587	A205	30c multicolored	.30	.25
588	A205	30c multicolored	.30	.25
a.		Pair, #587-588	.75	.75
589	A205	$1 multicolored	1.25	.45
		Nos. 587-589 (3)	1.85	.95

Butterflies — A206

#590, Graphium sarpedon. #591, Melanocyma faunula. #592, Delias hyparete. #593, Trogonoptera brookiana. #594, Terinos terpander.

1996, Sept. 27 Litho. ***Perf. 14½x14***

Booklet Stamps

590	A206	30c multicolored	1.90	1.25
591	A206	30c multicolored	1.90	1.25
592	A206	30c multicolored	1.90	1.25
593	A206	30c multicolored	1.90	1.25
594	A206	30c multicolored	1.90	1.25
a.		Pane of 10, 2 each #590-594	19.00	19.00

Kuala Lumpur Tower A207

30c, Artist's impression. 50c, Tower head diagram. $1, Tower head, city at night.
$2, Kuala Lumpur Tower, vert.

Perf. 13½

1996, Oct. 1 Litho. Unwmk.

595	A207	30c multicolored	.40	.20
596	A207	50c multicolored	.60	.30
597	A207	$1 multicolored	1.25	1.25
		Nos. 595-597 (3)	2.25	1.75

Souvenir Sheet

598	A207	$2 multicolored	2.75	2.75
a.		With added inscription in sheet margin	2.50	2.50

No. 598a inscribed with TAIPEI '96 emblem, issued 10/16/96.

14th Conference of Confederation of Asian and Pacific Accountants — A208

1996, Oct. 7 ***Perf. 13½x14***

599	A208	30c CAPA logo	.55	.40
600	A208	$1 Globe	1.25	1.25

Natl. Science Center A209

30c, Model of molecular structure. 50c, Model of atom, Science Center. $1, Natl. Science Center.

Unwmk.

1996, Nov. 29 Litho. ***Perf. 14***

601	A209	30c multicolored	.45	.35
602	A209	50c multicolored	.60	.40
603	A209	$1 multicolored	1.25	1.25
		Nos. 601-603 (3)	2.30	2.00

Souvenir Sheet

Stamp Week — A210

Wildlife: a, 20c, Nycticebus coucang. b, 30c, Callosciurus prevostil. c, 50c, Attacus atlas. d, $1, Hylobates lar. e, $1, Buceros rhinoceros. f, $2, Hemigalus derbyanus.

1996, Dec. 2

604	A210	Sheet of 6, #a.-f.	4.50	4.50

No. 604d is 30x60mm. Nos. 605e-605f are 60x30mm.

Birds — A211

Designs: 20c, Muscicapella hodgsoni. 30c, Leiothrix argentauris. 50c, Dicaeum celibicum. $1, Aethopyga mystacalis.

Perf. 13½x14

1997, Jan. 4 Litho. Unwmk.

605	A211	20c multicolored	.40	.40
606	A211	30c multicolored	.50	.40
607	A211	50c multicolored	.75	.40
608	A211	$1 multicolored	1.60	1.60
		Nos. 605-608 (4)	3.25	2.80

16th Commonwealth Games, Kuala Lumpur '98 — A212

1996, Dec. 21 ***Perf. 12***

609	A212	30c Running	.45	.20
610	A212	30c Hurdles	.45	.20
a.		Pair, #609-610	1.10	.90
611	A212	50c High jump	.75	.35
612	A212	50c Javelin	.75	.35
a.		Pair, #611-612	1.75	1.50
		Nos. 609-612 (4)	2.40	1.10

Intl. Cricket Cup Champions A213

1997, Mar. 24 Litho. ***Perf. 14***

613	A213	30c shown	.35	.35
614	A213	50c Batsman	.65	.50
615	A213	$1 Wicket keeper	1.40	1.40
		Nos. 613-615 (3)	2.40	2.25

Aviation in Malaysia, 50th Anniv. A214

Designs: 30c, Jet, world map. 50c, Jet approaching Kuala Lumpur. $1, Airplane tailfins of four Malaysian airlines.

Perf. 14, 13½ (#617)

1997, Apr. 2 Wmk. 388

616	A214	30c multicolored	.65	.40
617	A214	50c multicolored	1.10	.75
618	A214	$1 multicolored	2.25	2.25
a.		Perf. 13½	5.00	2.00
		Nos. 616-618 (3)	4.00	3.40

A215 A216

Light Rail Transit System: No. 620, Two trains, one on bridge, Kuala Lumpur skyline.

Perf. 14x14½

1997, Mar. 1 Litho. Unwmk.

Booklet Stamps

619	A215	30c shown	2.00	.80
620	A215	30c multicolored	2.00	.80
a.		Booklet pane, 5 each #619-620	20.00	20.00
		Complete booklet, #620a	20.00	

1997, May 7 ***Perf. 14½x14***

Highland Flowers: No. 621, Schima wallichi. No. 622, Aeschynanthus longicalyx. No. 623. Aeschynanthus speciosa. No. 624, Phyllagathis tuberculata. No. 625, Didymocarpus quinquevulnerus.

Booklet Stamps

621	A216	30c multicolored	.70	.70
622	A216	30c multicolored	.70	.70
623	A216	30c multicolored	.70	.70
624	A216	30c multicolored	.70	.70
625	A216	30c multicolored	.70	.70
a.		Booklet pane, 2 each #621-625	7.50	7.50
		Complete booklet, #625a	8.00	
		Nos. 621-625 (5)	3.50	3.50

Ruler's Council, Cent. A217

Unwmk.

1997, July 31 Litho. *Perf. 14*

626 A217 30c Photo, 1897 .40 .30
627 A217 50c Emblem, arms .60 .40
628 A217 $1 Emblem 1.00 1.00
Nos. 626-628 (3) 2.00 1.70

ASEAN, 30th Anniv. A218

1997, Aug. 8 Wmk. 388 *Perf. 13½*

629 A218 30c shown .55 .40
630 A218 50c "30," emblem .75 .50
631 A218 $1 Emblem, color bars 1.50 1.50
Nos. 629-631 (3) 2.80 2.40

A219

A220

Coral: 20c, Tubastrea. 30c, Melithaea. 50c, Aulostomus chinensis. $1, Symphillia.

1997, Aug. 23 Unwmk. *Perf. 14½*

632 A219 20c multicolored .30 .30
633 A219 30c multicolored .40 .30
634 A219 50c multicolored .55 .35
635 A219 $1 multicolored 1.10 1.10
Nos. 632-635 (4) 2.35 2.05

1997, Aug. 25 *Perf. 13x13½*

Booklet Stamps

636 A220 30c Career women .75 .40
637 A220 30c Family .75 .40
a. Booklet pane, 5 each #636-637 7.50 7.50
Complete booklet, #637a 7.50

20th Intl. Conf. of Pan-Pacific and Southeast Asia Women's Assoc., Kuala Lumpur.

9th World Youth Soccer Championships A221

30c, Mascot. 50c, Soccer ball, players, flag. $1, Map of Malaysia, silhouettes of players, soccer ball.

Perf. 13½x13

1997, June 16 Unwmk.

638 A221 30c multicolored .40 .40
639 A221 50c multicolored .55 .40

Perf. 13x12½

640 A221 $1 multicolored 1.00 1.00
Nos. 638-640 (3) 1.95 1.80

Souvenir Sheet

Chelonia Mydas — A222

1997, Aug. 23 Litho. *Perf. 14½*

641 A222 $2 multicolored 3.50 3.50

Year of the Coral Reef.

7th Summit Level of the Group of 15 — A223

$1, Emblem, natl. flags of member nations.

Perf. 12, 13½ (#643)

1997, Nov. 3 Litho. Unwmk.

642 A223 30c shown .40 .40
643 A223 $1 multicolored 1.40 1.40

Stamp Week A224

Protected wildlife: a, 20c, Tomistoma schlegelli. b, 30c, Tarsius bancanus, vert. c, 50c, Cervus unicolor, vert. d, $2, Rollulus rouloul. e, $2, Scleropages formosus.

1997, Dec. 1 *Perf. 14½*

644 A224 Sheet of 5, #a.-e. 5.00 5.00

Philately in Malaysia, 50th Anniv. — A225

Malpex '97: a, 20c, Straits Settlements #7. b, 30c, #605-608. c, 50c, #604. d, $1, Early cover from Straits Settlements.

1997, Sept. 9 *Perf. 12½*

645 A225 Sheet of 4, #a.-d. 3.75 3.75
e. Ovptd. in sheet margin in gold 2.50 2.50

No. 645e is inscribed in sheet margin with INDEPEX '97 exhibition emblem.

Rare Fruit — A226

1998, Jan. 10 *Perf. 13½*

646 A226 20c Bouea macrophylla .25 .25
647 A226 30c Sandoricum koetjape .40 .30
648 A226 50c Nephelium ramboutan-ake .60 .30
649 A226 $1 Garcinia atroviridis .75 1.00
Nos. 646-649 (4) 2.00 1.85

Kuala Lumpur '98 Games A227

1998, Feb. 23 *Perf. 12*

650 A227 30c Field hockey .60 .60
651 A227 30c Women's netball .60 .60
a. Pair, #650-651 + label 1.40 1.40
652 A227 50c Cricket .85 .85
653 A227 50c Rugby .85 .85
a. Pair, #652-653 + label 1.90 1.90
Nos. 650-653 (4) 2.90 2.90

Kuala Lumpur '98 Games — A228

Stadiums for the venues: a, 1r, Utama Bukit Jalil. b, 50c, Tertutup. c, 30c, Hoki. d, 20c, Renang Complex.

Wmk. 388

1998, Feb. 23 Litho. *Perf. 13⅓*

654 A228 Sheet of 4, #a.-d. 2.00 2.00

Early Coins A229

Coin's region, date: 20c, Trengganu, 1793-1808. 30c, Kedah, 1661-87. 50c, Johore, 1597-1615. $1, Kelantan, 1400-1780.

Wmk. 388

1998, Apr. 11 Litho. *Perf. 13½*

655 A229 20c multicolored .30 .30
a. Perf. 14¼ 3.00 .25
656 A229 30c multicolored .40 .30
657 A229 50c multicolored .50 .30
a. Perf. 14¼ 4.25 .35
658 A229 $1 multicolored .80 .40
Nos. 655-658 (4) 2.00 1.30

Kuala Lumpur International Airport — A230

Designs: 30c, Tower, tramway, airplanes. 50c, Tower, airplanes at terminal. $1, Tower, airplane in air, airport below. $2, Tower, globe overhead.

1998, June 27 *Perf. 12*

659 A230 30c multicolored .35 .30
a. Perf. 12½ 5.00
660 A230 50c multicolored .65 .30
661 A230 $1 multicolored 1.00
a. Perf. 12½ 6.00 3.75
Nos. 659-661 (3) 2.00 .60

Souvenir Sheet

Perf. 14

662 A230 $2 multicolored 2.75 2.75

No. 662 contains one 26x36mm stamp.

Malaysian Red Crescent Society, 50th Anniv. — A231

1998, May 8 *Perf. 13½*

663 A231 30c Rescue boat .50 .40
a. Perf. 14¼ 2.75 2.75
664 A231 $1 Mobile rescue unit 1.50 .60
a. Perf. 14¼ 10.00 10.00

Medicinal Plants — A234

20c, Solanum torvum. 30c, Tinospora crispa. 50c, Jatropha podagrica. $1, Hibiscus rosa-sinensis.

Wmk. 388

1998, July 18 Litho. *Perf. 13¾*

671 A234 20c multicolored .25 .25
672 A234 30c multicolored .35 .30

Perf. 14¼

673 A234 50c multicolored .50 .30
674 A234 $1 multicolored .70 1.00
Nos. 671-674 (4) 1.80 1.85

1998 Commonwealth Games, Kuala Lumpur — A235

a, 20c, Weight lifting. b, 20c, Badminton. c, 30c, Field hockey goalie. d, 30c, Field hockey. e, 20c, Netball. f, 20c, Shooting. g, 30c, Cycling. h, 30c, Lawn bowling. i, 50c, Gymnastics. j, 50c, Cricket. k, $1, Swimming. l, $1, Squash. m, 50c, Rugby. n, 50c, Running. o, $1, Boxing. p, $1, Bowling.

Perf. 14½x15

1998, Sept. 11 Litho. Wmk. 388

675 A235 Sheet of 16, #a.-p. 7.50 7.50

Modernization of Rail Transport — A236

Designs: 30c, Putra-LRT, 1998. 50c, Star-LRT, 1996. $1, KTM Commuter, 1995.

1998, Oct. 3 *Perf. 13¾, 14¼*

676 A236 30c multicolored .35 .35
a. Perf. 14¼ 3.25
677 A236 50c multicolored .65 .35
a. Perf. 14¼ 1.25 .30
678 A236 $1 multicolored (Perf. 14¼) 1.25 1.25
Nos. 676-678 (3) 2.25 1.95

1998 APEC (Asia-Pacific Economic Cooperation) Conference A237

Design: $1, Petronas Towers, people working with computers, office workers.

1998, Nov. 14

679 A237 30c shown .85 .40
a. Perf. 14¼ 1.40 1.40
680 A237 $1 multicolored .95 .95
a. Perf. 14¼ 4.25 4.25

Insects A238

Designs: a, 20c, Xylotrupes gideon, vert. b, 30c, Pomponia imperatoria, vert. c, 50c, Phyllium pulchrifolium, vert. d, $2, Hymenopus coronatus. e, $2, Macrolyristes corporalis.

Wmk. 388

1998, Nov. 28 Litho. *Perf. 12½*

681 A238 Sheet of 5, #a.-e. 4.00 4.00

Stamp Week.
Nos. 681a-681c are each 30x40mm.

Gold Medal Winners at 16th Commonwealth Games — A238a

No. 681F: h, 30c, Air rifle. i, 30c, 48kg boxing. j, 30c, 50km walk. k, 30c, 69kg clean and jerk weight lifting. l, 50c, Men's doubles, bowling. m, 50c, Men's singles, bowling. n, 50c, Men's doubles, badminton. o, 50c, Men's singles, badminton. p, $1, Rhythmic gymnastics (64x26mm).
$2, Team photograph.

Perf. 13¾x14

1998, Dec. 12 Litho. Wmk. 388

681F A238a Sheet of 9, #h.-p., + 2 labels 10.50 10.50

Souvenir Sheet

681G A238a $2 multi 4.50 4.50

No. 681G contains one 128x80mm stamp.

Intl. Year for Older Persons A239

Wmk. 388

1999, Jan. 28 Litho. *Perf. 14*

682 A239 $1 shown 1.00 1.00
683 A239 $1 World map, people, diff. 1.00 1.00

Fruit — A240

Designs: 20c, Syzgium malaccense. 30c, Garcinia prainiana. 50c, Mangifera caesia. $1, Salacca glabrescens.

1999, Feb. 27 *Perf. 12*

684 A240 20c multicolored .20 .20
685 A240 30c multicolored .35 .20
686 A240 50c multicolored .50 .20
687 A240 $1 multicolored .85 .35
a. Strip of 4, #684-687 2.00 1.75
Nos. 684-687 (4) 1.90 .95

Domestic Cats — A241

Designs: 30c, Kucing Malaysia. 50c, Siamese. $1, Abyssinian.
No. 691: a, British shorthair. b, Scottish fold.
No. 692: a, Birman. b. Persian.

1999, Apr. 1 Litho. *Perf. 12*

688 A241 30c multicolored .40 .30
689 A241 50c multicolored .65 .30
690 A241 $1 multicolored .95 .95
Nos. 688-690 (3) 2.00 1.55

Sheets of 2

691 A241 $1 #a.-b. 1.50 1.50
692 A241 $1 #a.-b. 1.50 1.50

Protected Mammals A242

Wmk. 388

1999, May 28 Litho. *Perf. 12*

693 A242 20c Rhinoceros .20 .20
694 A242 30c Panther .20 .20
695 A242 50c Bear .40 .20
696 A242 1r Elephant .80 .80
697 A242 2r Orangutan 1.60 1.60
a. Strip of 5, #693-697 3.25 3.25
b. Souvenir sheet, #697 2.25 2.25

Nos. 693-697 were issued in sheet containing 4 each. No. 697b is a continuous design.

Intl. Congress on AIDS in Asia and the Pacific, Kuala Lumpur A244

Perf. 14, 13½ (#700, 701)

1999, June 19 Litho. Wmk. 388

699 A244 30c shown .40 .40
700 A244 50c Emblems, hearts .50 .40
701 A244 1r Emblem as heart 1.10 1.10
Nos. 699-701 (3) 2.00 1.90

P. Ramlee (1929-73), Actor, Director — A245

Designs: 20c, Wearing chain around neck. 30c, Wearing bow tie. 50c, Holding gun. No. 705, Behind camera.
No. 706: a, Wearing cap. b, With hands in air. c, Holding microphone. d, Wearing army uniform.
No. 707, Wearing patterned hat. No. 708, Wearing plaid shirt.

Perf. 13½x13¾

1999, July 24 Litho. Wmk. 388

702 A245 20c multicolored .50 .50
703 A245 30c multicolored .60 .50
704 A245 50c multicolored .85 .50
705 A245 $1 multicolored 1.50 1.50
a. Perf. 14¼ 1.10 1.10
Nos. 702-705 (4) 3.45 3.00

Strip of 4

706 A245 30c #a.-d. 3.00 3.00

Souvenir Sheets

Perf. 14¼

707 A245 $1 multicolored 10.00 10.00
708 A245 $1 multicolored 10.00 10.00

No. 706 printed in sheets of 16 stamps.

Water Plants and Fish — A246

#709, Monochoria hastata. #710, Trichopsis vittatus. #711, Limnocharis flava. #712, Betta imbellis. #713, Nymphaea pubescens. #714, Trichogaster trichopterus. #715, Ipomea aquatica. #716, Helostoma temmincki. #717, Eichhornia crassipes. #718, Sphaerichthys osphronemoides.

Perf. 13¾x14

1999, July 31 Litho. Wmk. 388

709 A246 10c multi .40 .40
710 A246 10c multi .40 .40
a. Pair, #709-710 .90 .90
711 A246 15c multi .40 .40
712 A246 15c multi .40 .40
a. Pair, #711-712 .90 .90
713 A246 25c multi .40 .40
714 A246 25c multi .40 .40
a. Pair, #713-714 1.00 1.00
715 A246 50c multi .50 .50
716 A246 50c multi .50 .50
a. Pair, #715-716 1.50 1.50
717 A246 50c multi .50 .50
718 A246 50c multi .50 .50
a. Pair, #717-718 1.50 1.50
b. Block of 10 with bottom row of perforations perf 14½ 4.50 4.50
Nos. 709-718 (10) 4.40 4.40

Trees — A247

Designs: No. 719, Dryobalanops aromatica. No. 720, Alstonia angustiloba. No. 721, Fagraea fragrans. No. 722, Lagerstroemia floribunda. No. 723, Elateriospermum tapos.

Perf. 14x13½

1999, Aug. 14 Litho. Wmk. 388

719 A247 30c multicolored .60 .60
720 A247 30c multicolored .60 .60
721 A247 30c multicolored .60 .60
722 A247 30c multicolored .60 .60
723 A247 30c multicolored .60 .60
a. Strip of 5, #719-723 3.00 3.00
Complete bklt., 4 ea #719-723 12.00

Petronas Towers — A248

Designs: 30c, Daytime view. 50c, Architectural drawing. $1, Nighttime view.
$5, Hologram.

Perf. 14x14¼

1999, Aug. 30 Litho. Unwmk.

724 A248 30c multicolored .40 .40
725 A248 50c multicolored .55 .40
726 A248 $1 multicolored 1.00 1.00
Nos. 724-726 (3) 1.95 1.80

Souvenir Sheet

Perf. 14½x14¼

727 A248 $5 multicolored 5.00 5.00

No. 727 contains one 30x50mm stamp with a holographic image. Soaking in water may affect hologram. No. 727 exists imperf.

Taiping, 125th Anniv. A249

Designs: 20c, Rickshaw, Peace Hotel. 30c, Automobile, building. 50c, Train, train station. $1, Airplanes, airport building.
$2, Building, horse-drawn carriage.

Unwmk.

1999, Sept. 1 Litho. *Perf. 12*

728 A249 20c multi .55 .55
729 A249 30c multi .55 .55
730 A249 50c multi .65 .55
731 A249 $1 multi 1.25 .65
Nos. 728-731 (4) 3.00 2.30

Souvenir Sheet

732 A249 $2 multi 5.25 5.25

Tenaga Nasional, 50th Anniv. A250

Designs: 30c, Power station at night. 50c, High tension wire towers, control room. No. 735, Kuala Lumpur at night.
No. 736, Van, vert. No. 737, High tension wire towers, vert.

Perf. 14¼x14½

1999, Sept. 9 Litho. Unwmk.

733 A250 30c multicolored .60 .60
734 A250 50c multicolored .80 .60
735 A250 $1 multicolored 1.60 1.60
Nos. 733-735 (3) 3.00 2.80

Souvenir Sheets

Perf. 13½x13¾

736 A250 $1 multicolored 1.00 1.00
737 A250 $1 multicolored 1.00 1.00

National Theater — A251

Various performers and views of building.

1999 Litho. Wmk. 388 *Perf. 12¼*

Panel Colors

738 A251 30c red .40 .40
739 A251 50c green .50 .40
740 A251 $1 violet 1.00 1.00
Nos. 738-740 (3) 1.90 1.80

Installation of 11th Yang Di-Pertuan Agong (Head of State) A252

Tuanku Salehuddin Abdul Aziz Shah ibni al-Marhum Hisamuddin Alam Shah and: 30c, Flag. 50c, Old building. $1, Modern building.
No. 744: a, Purple background. b, Yellow background. c, Blue background.

Perf. 13¾x13½

1999, Sept. 23 Litho. Wmk. 388

741 A252 30c multicolored .30 .20

Perf. 14¼

742 A252 50c multicolored .40 .30
743 A252 $1 multicolored .80 .80

Perf. 14x13¾

744 A252 30c Strip of 3, #a.-c. 2.00 2.00
Nos. 741-744 (4) 3.50 3.30

Size of Nos. 744a-744c: 24x30mm.

MALDIVE ISLANDS

ˈmol-ˌdīv ˈī-ləndz

LOCATION — A group of 2,000 islands in the Indian Ocean about 400 miles southwest of Ceylon.
GOVT. — Republic
AREA — 115 sq. mi.
POP. — 300,220 (1999 est.)
CAPITAL — Male

Maldive Islands was a British Protectorate, first as a dependency of Ceylon, then from 1948 as an independent sultanate, except for a year (1953) as a republic. The islands became completely independent on July 26, 1965, and became a republic again on November 11, 1968.

100 Cents = 1 Rupee
100 Larees = 1 Rufiyaa (1951)

Catalogue values for unused stamps in this country are for Never Hinged items, beginning with Scott 20.

Watermarks

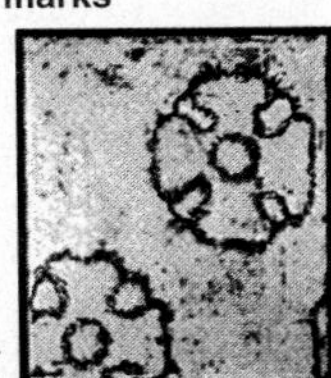

Wmk. 47 — Multiple Rosette

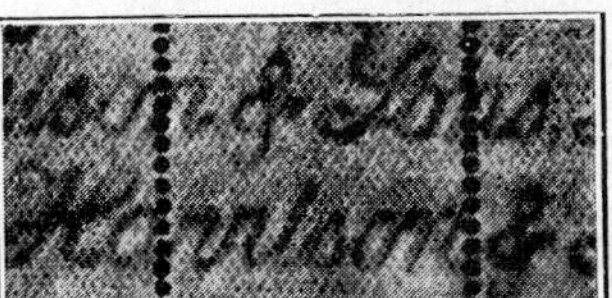

Wmk. 233 — "Harrison & Sons, London" in Script

Stamps of Ceylon, 1904-05, Overprinted

1906, Sept. 9 — Wmk. 3 — *Perf. 14*

No.	Type	Denomination	Unused	Used
1	A36	2c orange brown	22.00	*47.50*
2	A37	3c green	29.00	*47.50*
3	A37	4c yellow & blue	50.00	*90.00*
4	A38	5c dull lilac	5.00	*6.50*
5	A40	15c ultramarine	95.00	*180.00*
6	A40	25c bister	110.00	*190.00*
		Nos. 1-6 (6)	311.00	*561.50*

Minaret of Juma Mosque, near Male — A1

1909 — Engr. — Wmk. 47

No.	Type	Denomination	Unused	Used
7	A1	2c orange brown	2.25	*4.00*
8	A1	3c green	.50	.70
9	A1	5c red violet	.50	.35
10	A1	10c carmine	7.50	.80
		Nos. 7-10 (4)	10.75	5.85

Type of 1909 Issue Redrawn

Perf. 14½x14

1933 — Photo. — Wmk. 233

No.	Type	Denomination	Unused	Used
11	A1	2c gray	2.75	*2.50*
12	A1	3c yellow brown	.75	*1.75*
13	A1	5c brown lake	35.00	10.00
14	A1	6c brown red	1.75	*5.50*
15	A1	10c green	1.00	.50
16	A1	15c gray black	6.50	*20.00*
17	A1	25c red brown	6.50	*20.00*
18	A1	50c red violet	6.50	*22.00*
19	A1	1r blue black	12.50	5.00
		Nos. 11-19 (9)	73.25	87.25

On the 6c, 15c, 25c and 50c, the right hand panel carries only the word "CENTS."

Nos. 11-19 exist with watermark vert. or horiz. The 5c with vert. watermark sells for twice the price of the horiz. watermark.

Catalogue values for unused stamps in this section, from this point to the end of the section, are for Never Hinged items.

Palm Tree and Seascape — A2

Maldive Fish — A3

Unwmk.

1950, Dec. 24 — Engr. — *Perf. 13*

No.	Type	Denomination	Unused	Used
20	A2	2 l olive green	2.25	4.00
21	A2	3 l deep blue	12.50	.85
22	A2	5 l dp blue green	12.50	.85
23	A2	6 l red brown	1.25	1.25
24	A2	10 l red	1.25	1.00
25	A2	15 l orange	1.25	1.00
26	A2	25 l rose violet	1.25	*2.75*
27	A2	50 l violet blue	1.50	*4.00*
28	A2	1r dark brown	14.00	*37.50*
		Nos. 20-28 (9)	47.75	53.20

1952

No.	Type	Denomination	Unused	Used
29	A3	3 l shown	2.00	.75
30	A3	5 l Urns	1.10	2.00

Harbor of Male — A4

Fort and Governor's Palace — A5

Perf. 13½ (A4), 11½x11 (A5)

1956 — Engr. — Unwmk.

No.	Type	Denomination	Unused	Used
31	A4	2 l lilac	.25	.25
32	A4	3 l gray green	.25	.25
33	A4	5 l reddish brown	.25	.25
34	A4	6 l blue violet	.25	.25
35	A4	10 l light green	.25	.25
36	A4	15 l brown	.25	.25
37	A4	25 l rose red	.25	.25
38	A4	50 l orange	.25	.25
39	A5	1r light green	.40	.30
40	A5	5r ultramarine	1.00	.70
41	A5	10r magenta	2.10	1.40
		Nos. 31-41 (11)	5.50	4.40

Bicyclists and Olympic Emblem A6

Design: 25 l, 50 l, 1r, Basketball, vert.

Perf. 11½x11, 11x11½

1960, Aug. 20 — Engr.

No.	Type	Denomination	Unused	Used
42	A6	2 l rose violet & green	.20	.20
43	A6	3 l grnsh gray & plum	.20	.20
44	A6	5 l vio brn & dk blue	.20	.20
45	A6	10 l brt green & brn	.20	.20
46	A6	15 l brown & blue	.20	.20
47	A6	25 l rose red & olive	.20	.20
48	A6	50 l orange & dk vio	.30	.30
49	A6	1r brt green & plum	.50	.50
		Nos. 42-49 (8)	2.00	2.00

17th Olympic Games, Rome, 8/25-9/11.

World Refugee Year Emblem A7

1960, Oct. 15 — *Perf. 11½x11*

No.	Type	Denomination	Unused	Used
50	A7	2 l orange, vio & grn	.20	.20
51	A7	3 l green, brn & red	.20	.20
52	A7	5 l sepia, grn & red	.20	.20
53	A7	10 l dull pur, grn & red	.20	.20
54	A7	15 l gray grn, pur & red	.20	.25
55	A7	25 l redsh brn, ultra & olive	.20	.25
56	A7	50 l rose, olive & blue	.20	.30
57	A7	1r gray, car rose & vio	.35	.75
		Nos. 50-57 (8)	1.75	2.35

WRY, July 1, 1959-June 30, 1960.

Tomb of Sultan — A8

Designs: 3 l, Custom house. 5 l, Cowry shells. 6 l, Old royal palace. 10 l, Road to Minaret, Juma Mosque, Male. 15 l, Council house. 25 l, Government secretariat. 50 l, Prime minister's office. 1r, Tomb and sailboats. 5r, Tomb by the sea. 10r, Port.

1960, Oct. 15 — *Perf. 11½x11*

Various Frames

No.	Type	Denomination	Unused	Used
58	A8	2 l lilac	.45	.45
59	A8	3 l green	.45	.45
60	A8	5 l brown orange	3.75	3.50
61	A8	6 l bright blue	.45	.45
62	A8	10 l carmine rose	.45	.45
63	A8	15 l sepia	.45	.45
64	A8	25 l dull violet	.45	.45
65	A8	50 l slate	.45	.45
66	A8	1r orange	.45	.45
67	A8	5r dark blue	3.50	1.00
68	A8	10r dull green	10.00	2.10
		Nos. 58-68 (11)	20.85	10.20

Stamps in 25r, 50r and 100r denominations were also issued, but primarily for revenue purposes. Value for the three stamps, $350.

Coconuts — A9

Map of Male Showing Population Distribution A10

Perf. 14x14½, 14½x14

1961, Apr. 20 — Photo. — Unwmk.

Coconuts in Ocher

No.	Type	Denomination	Unused	Used
69	A9	2 l green	.20	.20
70	A9	3 l ultramarine	.20	.20
71	A9	5 l lilac rose	.20	.20
72	A9	10 l red orange	.20	.20
73	A9	15 l black	.20	.20
74	A10	25 l multicolored	.20	.20
75	A10	50 l multicolored	.20	.20
76	A10	1r multicolored	.60	.65
		Nos. 69-76 (8)	2.00	2.05

Pigeon and 5c Stamp of 1906 A11

Designs: 10 l, 15 l, 20 l, Post horn and 3c stamp of 1906. 25 l, 50 l, 1r, Laurel branch and 2c stamp of 1906.

1961, Sept. 9 — *Perf. 14½x14*

No.	Type	Denomination	Unused	Used
77	A11	2 l violet blue & mar	.20	.20
78	A11	3 l violet blue & mar	.20	.20
79	A11	5 l violet blue & mar	.20	.20
80	A11	6 l violet blue & mar	.20	.20
81	A11	10 l maroon & green	.20	.20
82	A11	15 l maroon & green	.20	.20
83	A11	20 l maroon & green	.20	.20
84	A11	25 l green, mar & blk	.20	.20
85	A11	50 l green, mar & blk	.20	.20
86	A11	1r green, mar & blk	.35	.35
a.		Souvenir sheet of 4	2.40	3.00
		Nos. 77-86 (10)	2.15	2.15

55th anniv. of the 1st postage stamps of the Maldive Islands.

No. 86a contains 4 No. 86, with simulated perforations.

Malaria Eradication Emblem — A12

1962, Apr. 7 — Engr. — *Perf. 13½x13*

No.	Type	Denomination	Unused	Used
87	A12	2 l orange brown	.20	.20
88	A12	3 l green	.20	.20
89	A12	5 l blue	.20	.20
90	A12	10 l vermilion	.20	.20
91	A12	15 l black	.20	.20
92	A12	25 l dark blue	.20	.20
93	A12	50 l green	.25	.25
94	A12	1r purple	.45	.45
		Nos. 87-94 (8)	1.90	1.90

WHO drive to eradicate malaria.

Children and Map of Far East and Americas A13

UNICEF, 15th Anniv.: 25 l, 50 l, 1r, 5r, Children and Map of Africa, Europe and Asia.

Perf. 14½x14

1962, Sept. 9 — Photo. — Unwmk.

Children in Multicolor

No.	Type	Denomination	Unused	Used
95	A13	2 l sepia	.20	.20
96	A13	6 l violet	.20	.20
97	A13	10 l dark green	.20	.20
98	A13	15 l ultramarine	.20	.20
99	A13	25 l blue	.20	.20
100	A13	50 l bright green	.20	.20
101	A13	1r rose claret	.20	.20
102	A13	5r emerald	.90	.90
		Nos. 95-102 (8)	2.30	2.30

Sultan Mohamed Farid Didi — A14

1962, Nov. 29 — *Perf. 14x14½*

Portrait in Orange Brown and Sepia

No.	Type	Denomination	Unused	Used
103	A14	3 l bluish green	.25	.25
104	A14	5 l slate	.25	.25
105	A14	10 l blue	.40	.40
106	A14	20 l olive	.40	.40
107	A14	50 l dk carmine rose	.40	.40
108	A14	1r dark purple	.75	.75
		Nos. 103-108 (6)	2.45	2.45

9th anniv. of the enthronement of Sultan Mohamed Farid Didi.

Regal Angelfish, Sultan's Crest and Skin Diver — A15

Tropical Fish: 10 l, 25 l, Moorish idol. 50 l, Diadem squirrelfish. 1r, Surgeonfish. 5r, Orange butterflyfish.

1963, Feb. 2 *Perf. 13½*

109	A15	2 l	multicolored	.30	.30
110	A15	3 l	multicolored	.30	.30
111	A15	5 l	multicolored	.35	.35
112	A15	10 l	multicolored	.35	.35
113	A15	25 l	multicolored	.50	.50
114	A15	50 l	multicolored	.95	.95
115	A15	1r	multicolored	1.90	1.90
116	A15	5r	multicolored	12.00	12.00
			Nos. 109-116 (8)	16.65	16.65

Fish in Net — A16

Design: 5 l, 10 l, 50 l, Wheat emblem and hand holding rice, vert.

1963, Mar. 21 **Photo.** *Perf. 12*

117	A16	2 l	green & lt brown	1.00	1.00
118	A16	5 l	dull rose & lt brn	1.00	1.00
119	A16	7 l	grnsh blue & lt brn	1.00	1.00
120	A16	10 l	blue & lt brown	1.00	1.00
121	A16	25 l	brn red & lt brn	2.50	2.50
122	A16	50 l	violet & lt brown	5.00	5.00
123	A16	1r	rose cl & lt brn	10.00	10.00
			Nos. 117-123 (7)	21.50	21.50

FAO "Freedom from Hunger" campaign.

Centenary Emblem A17

1963, Oct. **Unwmk.** *Perf. 14x14½*

124	A17	2 l	dull purple & red	.75	.75
125	A17	15 l	slate green & red	.75	.75
126	A17	50 l	brown & red	.95	.95
127	A17	1r	dk blue & red	1.90	1.90
128	A17	4r	dk ol grn & red	6.50	6.50
			Nos. 124-128 (5)	10.85	10.85

Centenary of the International Red Cross.

Scout Emblem and Knot — A18

1963, Dec. 7 **Unwmk.** *Perf. 13½*

129	A18	2 l	purple & dp green	.30	.30
130	A18	3 l	brown & dp green	.30	.30
131	A18	25 l	dk blue & dp green	.45	.45
132	A18	1r	dp car & dp grn	.95	.95
			Nos. 129-132 (4)	2.00	2.00

11th Boy Scout Jamboree, Marathon, Aug. 1963. Printed in sheets of 12 (3x4) with ornamental borders and inscriptions.

Mosque at Male — A19

Wmk. 314

1964, Aug. 10 **Engr.** *Perf. 11½*

133	A19	2 l	rose violet	.25	.25
134	A19	3 l	green	.25	.25
135	A19	10 l	carmine rose	.50	.50
136	A19	40 l	black brown	.50	.50
137	A19	60 l	blue	.60	.60
138	A19	85 l	orange brown	.85	.85
			Nos. 133-138 (6)	2.95	2.95

Conversion of the Maldive Islanders to Mohammedanism in 1733 (1153 by Islamic calendar).

Shot Put and Maldive Arms A20

15 l, 25 l, 50 l, 1r, Runner, Maldive arms.

Perf. 14x13½

1964, Oct. 6 **Litho.** **Wmk. 314**

139	A20	2 l	grnsh bl & dull vio	.25	.25
140	A20	3 l	red brn & maroon	.25	.25
141	A20	5 l	dk green & gray	.25	.25
142	A20	10 l	plum & indigo	.40	.40
143	A20	15 l	bis brn & dk brn	.40	.40
144	A20	25 l	dk bl & bluish blk	.40	.40
145	A20	50 l	olive & black	.55	.55
146	A20	1r	gray & dk purple	1.10	1.10
a.			Souvenir sheet of 3	4.00	4.00
			Nos. 139-146 (8)	3.60	3.60

18th Olympic Games, Tokyo, Oct. 10-25. #146a contains 3 imperf. stamps similar to #144-146.

General Electric Observation Communication Satellite — A21

Perf. 14½

1965, July 1 **Photo.** **Unwmk.**

147	A21	5 l	dark blue	.20	.20
148	A21	10 l	brown	.20	.20
149	A21	25 l	green	.45	.45
150	A21	1r	magenta	1.75	1.75
			Nos. 147-150 (4)	2.60	2.60

Quiet Sun Year, 1964-65. Printed in sheets of 9 (3x3) with ornamental borders and inscriptions.

Queen Nefertari Holding Sistrum and Papyrus — A22

Designs: 3 l, 10 l, 25 l, 1r, Ramses II.

1965, Sept. 1 **Litho.** **Wmk. 314**

151	A22	2 l	dull bl grn & mar	.30	.30
152	A22	3 l	lake & green	.30	.30
153	A22	5 l	green & lake	.30	.30
154	A22	10 l	dk blue & ocher	.30	.30
155	A22	15 l	redsh brn & ind	.45	.30
156	A22	25 l	dull lil & indigo	.75	.30
157	A22	50 l	green & brown	.95	.45
158	A22	1r	brown & green	1.50	.90
			Nos. 151-158 (8)	4.85	3.15

UNESCO world campaign to save historic monuments in Nubia.

John F. Kennedy and Doves A23

Design: 1r, 2r, President Kennedy and hands holding olive branches.

Unwmk.

1965, Oct. 1 **Photo.** *Perf. 12*

159	A23	2 l	slate & brt pink	.20	.20
160	A23	5 l	brown & brt pink	.20	.20
161	A23	25 l	blue blk & brt pink	.20	.20
162	A23	1r	red lil, yel & grn	.30	.30
163	A23	2r	sl green, yel & grn	.55	.55
a.			Souvenir sheet of 4	2.75	2.75
			Nos. 159-163 (5)	1.45	1.45

#163a contains 4 imperf. stamps similar to #163.

UN Flag — A24

1965, Nov. 24 **Photo.** *Perf. 12*

Flag in Aquamarine

164	A24	3 l	red brown	.30	.30
165	A24	10 l	violet	.30	.30
166	A24	1r	dark olive brown	.60	.45
			Nos. 164-166 (3)	1.20	1.05

20th anniversary of the United Nations.

ICY Emblem A25

1965, Dec. 20 **Photo.** *Perf. 12*

167	A25	5 l	bister & dk brn	.25	.25
168	A25	15 l	dull vio & dk brn	.25	.25
169	A25	50 l	olive & dk brn	.50	.30
170	A25	1r	orange & dk brn	1.40	1.10
171	A25	2r	blue & dk brn	2.00	2.25
a.			Souvenir sheet of 3	8.50	8.50
			Nos. 167-171 (5)	4.40	4.15

Intl. Cooperation Year. No. 171a contains three imperf. stamps with simulated perforation similar to Nos. 169-171.

Sea Shells A26

A27

Coat of Arms and: 2 l, 10 l, 30 l, No. 181, Conus alicus and cymatium maldiviensis (shells). 5 l, 10r, Conus litteratus and distorsia reticulata (shells). 7 l, No. 182, 2r, India-rubber vine flowers. 15 l, 50 l, 5r, Crab plover and gull. 3 l, 20 l, 1.50r, Reinwardtia trigynia.

1966, June 1 **Unwmk.** *Perf. 12*

172	A26	2 l	multicolored	.20	.75
173	A27	3 l	multicolored	.20	.75
174	A26	5 l	multicolored	.40	.50
175	A27	7 l	multicolored	.40	.50
176	A26	10 l	multicolored	.75	.50
177	A26	15 l	multicolored	3.25	.65
178	A27	20 l	multicolored	1.00	.65
179	A26	30 l	multicolored	2.40	.65
180	A26	50 l	multicolored	5.75	1.00
181	A26	1r	multicolored	3.75	1.00
182	A27	1r	multicolored	3.75	1.00
183	A27	1.50r	multicolored	4.50	3.50
184	A27	2r	multicolored	6.25	4.00
185	A26	5r	multicolored	20.00	18.50
186	A26	10r	multicolored	22.50	24.00
			Nos. 172-186 (15)	75.10	57.95

Flag A28

1966, July 26 *Perf. 14x14½*

187	A28	10 l	grnsh blue, red & grn	2.50	.65
188	A28	1r	ocher, brn, red & grn	7.50	1.50

1st anniv. of full independence from Great Britain.

Luna 9 on Moon — A29

Designs: 25 l, 1r, 5r, Gemini 6 and 7, rendezvous in space. 2r, Gemini spaceship as seen from second Gemini spaceship.

1966, Nov. 1 **Litho.** *Perf. 15x14*

189	A29	10 l	gray bl, lt brn & ultramarine	.25	.25
190	A29	25 l	car rose & green	.30	.25
191	A29	50 l	green & dp org	.45	.25
192	A29	1r	org brn & grnsh bl	.75	.40
193	A29	2r	violet & green	1.60	.60
194	A29	5r	Prus blue & pink	2.75	1.60
a.			Souvenir sheet of 3	7.25	6.75
			Nos. 189-194 (6)	6.10	3.35

Rendezvous in space of Gemini 6 and 7 (US), Dec. 4, 1965, and the soft landing on Moon by Luna 9 (USSR), Feb. 3, 1966. No. 194a contains 3 imperf. stamps similar to Nos. 192-194 with simulated perforations.

UNESCO Emblem, Owl and Book — A30

20th anniv. of UNESCO: 3 l, 1r, Microscope, globe and communication waves. 5 l, 5r, Palette, violin and mask.

1966, Nov. 15 **Litho.** *Perf. 15x14*

195	A30	2 l	green & multi	.50	.60
196	A30	3 l	lt violet & multi	.50	.60
197	A30	5 l	orange & multi	.75	.50
198	A30	50 l	rose & multi	4.25	.75
199	A30	1r	citron & multi	8.50	1.25
200	A30	5r	multicolored	26.50	16.50
			Nos. 195-200 (6)	41.00	20.20

Winston Churchill and Coffin on Gun Carriage — A31

10 l, 25 l, 1r, Churchill and catafalque.

1967, Jan. 1 *Perf. 14½x13½*

201	A31	2 l	ol grn, red & dk blue	.50	.45
202	A31	10 l	Prus grn, red & dk blue	2.25	.35
203	A31	15 l	grn, red & dk bl	4.00	.35
204	A31	25 l	vio, red & dk bl	5.00	.40
205	A31	1r	brn, red & dk bl	10.00	1.00
206	A31	2.50r	brn lake, red & dk blue	35.00	12.00
			Nos. 201-206 (6)	56.75	14.55

Sir Winston Spencer Churchill (1874-1965), statesman and World War II leader.

Soccer and Jules Rimet Cup — A32

Designs: 3 l, 5 l, 25 l, 50 l, 1r, Various scenes from soccer and Jules Rimet Cup. 2r, British flag, Games' emblem and Big Ben Tower, London.

Perf. 14x13½

1967, Mar. 22 Photo. Unwmk.

No.	Type	Description	Unused	Used
207	A32	2 l ver & multi	.35	.55
208	A32	3 l olive & multi	.35	.55
209	A32	5 l brt purple & multi	.35	.55
210	A32	25 l brt green & multi	1.25	.35
211	A32	50 l orange & multi	1.90	.35
212	A32	1r brt blue & multi	3.25	.75
213	A32	2r brown & multi	5.75	3.75
a.		Souvenir sheet of 3	12.50	12.50
		Nos. 207-213 (7)	13.20	6.85

England's victory in the World Soccer Cup Championship. No. 213a contains 3 imperf. stamps similar to Nos. 211-213.

Clown Butterflyfish — A33

Tropical Fish: 3 l, 1r, Four-saddled puffer. 5 l, Indo-Pacific blue trunkfish. 6 l, Striped triggerfish. 50 l, 2r, Blue angelfish.

1967, May 1 Photo. *Perf. 14*

No.	Type	Description	Unused	Used
214	A33	2 l brt violet & multi	.25	.35
215	A33	3 l emerald & multi	.25	.35
216	A33	5 l org brn & multi	.25	.25
217	A33	6 l brt blue & multi	.25	.25
218	A33	50 l olive & multi	4.75	.40
219	A33	1r rose red & multi	6.75	.80
220	A33	2r orange & multi	12.00	9.00
		Nos. 214-220 (7)	24.50	11.40

Plane at Hulule Airport — A34

Designs: 5 l, 15 l, 50 l, 10r, Plane over administration building, Hulule Airport.

1967, July 26 *Perf. 14x13½*

No.	Type	Description	Unused	Used
221	A34	2 l citron & lil	.25	.40
222	A34	5 l violet & green	.25	.25
223	A34	10 l lt green & lilac	.35	.25
224	A34	15 l yel bister & grn	.55	.25
225	A34	30 l sky blue & vio bl	1.25	.25
226	A34	50 l brt pink & brn	2.25	.30
227	A34	5r org & vio blue	6.50	5.00
228	A34	10r lt ultra & dp brn	9.50	8.50
		Nos. 221-228 (8)	20.90	15.20

For overprints see Nos. 235-242.

Man and Music Pavilion and EXPO '67 Emblem — A35

Designs: 5 l, 50 l, 2r, Man and his Community Pavilion and EXPO '67 emblem.

Perf. 14x13½

1967, Oct. 1 Photo. Unwmk.

EXPO '67 Emblem in Gold

No.	Type	Description	Unused	Used
229	A35	2 l ol gray, ol & brt rose	.25	.25
230	A35	5 l ultra, grnsh blue & brn	.25	.25
231	A35	10 l brn red, lt grn & red org	.25	.25
232	A35	50 l brn, grnsh blue & org	.45	.25
233	A35	1r vio, grn & rose lil	.85	.45
234	A35	2r dk grn, emer & red brn	1.75	1.10
a.		Souvenir sheet of 2	5.50	5.50
		Nos. 229-234 (6)	3.80	2.55

EXPO '67 Intl. Exhibition, Montreal, Apr. 28-Oct. 27. No. 234a contains 2 imperf. stamps similar to Nos. 233-234 with simulated perforations.

Nos. 221-228 Overprinted in Gold: "International Tourist Year 1967"

1967, Dec. 1 Photo. *Perf. 14x13½*

No.	Type	Description	Unused	Used
235	A34	2 l citron & lilac	.30	.35
236	A34	5 l violet & green	.30	.30
237	A34	10 l lt green & lilac	.30	.30
238	A34	15 l yel bister & grn	.30	.30
239	A34	30 l sky blue & vio bl	.35	.30
240	A34	50 l brt pink & brn	.65	.35
241	A34	5r org & vio blue	4.50	3.75
242	A34	10r lt ultra & dp brn	6.75	6.00
		Nos. 235-242 (8)	13.45	11.65

The overprint is in 3 lines on the 2 l, 10 l, 30 l, 5r; one line on the 5 l, 15 l, 50 l, 10r.

Lord Baden-Powell, Wolf Cubs, Campfire and Flag Signals — A36

Boy Scouts: 3 l, 1r, Lord Baden-Powell, Boy Scout saluting and drummer.

1968, Jan. 1 Litho. *Perf. 14x14½*

No.	Type	Description	Unused	Used
243	A36	2 l yel, brown & green	.20	.20
244	A36	3 l lt bl, ultra & rose car	.20	.20
245	A36	25 l dp org, red brn & vio blue	1.60	.30
246	A36	1r yel grn, grn & red brn	3.70	1.40
		Nos. 243-246 (4)	5.70	2.10

Sheets of 12 (4x3) with decorative border. For overprints see Nos. 278-281.

French Satellites D-1 and A-1 — A37

3 l, 25 l, Luna 10, USSR. 7 l, 1r, Orbiter & Mariner, US. 10 l, 2r, Edward White, Virgil Grissom & Roger Chaffee, US. 5r, Astronaut V. M. Komarov, USSR.

1968, Jan. 27 Photo. *Perf. 14*

No.	Type	Description	Unused	Used
247	A37	2 l dp ultra & brt pink	.20	.20
248	A37	3 l dk ol bis & vio	.20	.20
249	A37	7 l rose car & ol	.30	.20
250	A37	10 l blk, gray & dk bl	.30	.20
251	A37	25 l purple & brt grn	.30	.20
252	A37	50 l brown org & blue	.50	.25
253	A37	1r dk sl grn & vio brn	1.00	.30
254	A37	2r blk, bl & dk brn	1.60	1.00
a.		Souvenir sheet of 2	5.75	5.75
255	A37	5r blk, tan & lil rose	4.00	2.50
		Nos. 247-255 (9)	8.40	5.05

International achievements in space and to honor American and Russian astronauts, who gave their lives during space explorations in 1967. No. 254a contains 2 imperf. stamps similar to Nos. 253-254.

Shot Put — A38

Design: 6 l, 15 l, 2.50r, Discus.

1968, Feb. Litho. *Perf. 14½*

No.	Type	Description	Unused	Used
256	A38	2 l emerald & multi	.25	.25
257	A38	6 l dull yel & multi	.25	.25
258	A38	10 l multicolored	.25	.25
259	A38	15 l orange & multi	.25	.25
260	A38	1r blue & multi	.60	.30
261	A38	2.50r rose & multi	1.60	1.25
		Nos. 256-261 (6)	3.20	2.55

19th Olympic Games, Mexico City, 10/12-27.

On the Adria, by Charles P. Bonington — A39

Seascapes: 1r, Ulysses Deriding Polyphemus (detail), by Joseph M. W. Turner. 2r, Sailboat at Argenteuil, by Claude Monet. 5r, Fishing Boats at Saintes-Maries, by Vincent Van Gogh.

1968, Apr. 1 Photo. *Perf. 14*

No.	Type	Description	Unused	Used
262	A39	50 l ultra & multi	1.00	.30
263	A39	1r dk green & multi	1.50	.40
264	A39	2r multicolored	2.50	1.50
265	A39	5r multicolored	6.75	4.00
		Nos. 262-265 (4)	11.75	6.20

Montgolfier Balloon, 1783, and Zeppelin LZ-130, 1928 — A40

History of Aviation: 3 l, 1r, Douglas DC-3, 1933, and Boeing 707, 1958. 5 l, 50 l, Lilienthal's glider, 1892, and Wright brothers' plane, 1905. 7 l, 2r, British-French Concorde and Supersonic Boeing 733, 1968.

1968, June 1 Photo. *Perf. 14x13*

No.	Type	Description	Unused	Used
266	A40	2 l yel grn, ultra & bis brn	.25	.35
267	A40	3 l org brn, greenish bl & lil	.25	.35
268	A40	5 l grnsh bl, sl grn & lilac	.30	.25
269	A40	7 l org, cl & ultra	1.25	.50
270	A40	10 l rose lil, bl & brn	.75	.30
271	A40	50 l ol, sl grn & mag	2.50	.35
272	A40	1r ver, blue & emer	4.00	.75
273	A40	2r ultra, ol & brn vio	20.00	10.00
		Nos. 266-273 (8)	29.30	12.85

Issued in sheets of 12.

WHO Headquarters, Geneva — A41

1968, July 15 Litho. *Perf. 14½x13*

No.	Type	Description	Unused	Used
274	A41	10 l grnsh bl, bl grn & vio	.85	.25
275	A41	25 l org, ocher & green	1.25	.25
276	A41	1r emer, brt grn & brown	4.25	.70
277	A41	2r rose lil, dp rose lil & dk blue	8.25	4.75
		Nos. 274-277 (4)	14.60	5.95

20th anniv. of WHO.

Nos. 243-246 Overprinted: "International / Boy Scout Jamboree, / Farragut Park, Idaho, / U.S.A. / August 1-9, 1967"

1968, Aug. 1 *Perf. 14x14½*

No.	Type	Description	Unused	Used
278	A36	2 l multicolored	.25	.35
279	A36	3 l multicolored	.25	.35
280	A36	25 l multicolored	1.75	.35
281	A36	1r multicolored	6.00	1.75
		Nos. 278-281 (4)	8.25	2.80

1st anniv. of the Intl. Boy Scout Jamboree in Farragut State Park, ID.

Marine Snail Shells — A42

2 l, 50 l, Common curlew & redshank. 1r, Angel wings (clam shell) & marine snail shell.

1968, Sept. 24 Photo. *Perf. 14x13*

No.	Type	Description	Unused	Used
282	A42	2 l ultra & multi	.70	.70
283	A42	10 l brown & multi	1.50	.30
284	A42	25 l multicolored	1.75	.30
285	A42	50 l multicolored	8.00	1.25
286	A42	1r multicolored	6.50	1.25
287	A42	2r multicolored	7.00	6.00
		Nos. 282-287 (6)	25.45	9.80

Discus A43

50 l, Runner. 1r, Bicycling. 2r, Basketball.

1968, Oct. 12 *Perf. 14*

No.	Type	Description	Unused	Used
288	A43	10 l ultra & multi	.35	.35
289	A43	50 l multicolored	.35	.35
290	A43	1r plum & multi	2.75	.45
291	A43	2r violet & multi	4.25	1.40
		Nos. 288-291 (4)	7.70	2.55

19th Olympic Games, Mexico City, 10/12-27. For overprints see Nos. 302-303.

Republic

Dhow A44

Republic Day: 1r, Coat of arms, map and flag of Maldive Islands.

Perf. 14x14½

1968, Nov. 11 Unwmk.

No.	Type	Description	Unused	Used
292	A44	10 l yel grn, ultra & dk brn	1.25	.30
293	A44	1r ultra, red & emerald	5.00	.85

The Thinker, by Auguste Rodin — A45

Rodin Sculptures and UNESCO Emblem: 10 l, Hands. 1.50r, Sister and Brother. 2.50r, The Prodigal Son.

1969, Apr. 10 Photo. *Perf. 13½*

No.	Type	Description	Unused	Used
294	A45	6 l emerald & multi	.40	.40
295	A45	10 l multicolored	.45	.45
296	A45	1.50r brt blue & multi	2.50	2.50
297	A45	2.50r multicolored	3.50	3.50
a.		Souvenir sheet of 2	9.50	10.00
		Nos. 294-297 (4)	6.85	6.85

Intl. Human Rights Year and honoring UNESCO.

No. 297a contains 2 imperf. stamps similar to Nos. 296-297.

Astronaut Gathering Rock Samples on Moon A46

Designs: 6 l, Lunar landing module. 1.50r, Astronaut on steps of module. 2.50r, Astronaut with television camera.

1969, Sept. 25 Litho. *Perf. 14*

298 A46 6 l multicolored .25 .25
299 A46 10 l multicolored .25 .25
300 A46 1.50r multicolored 3.00 1.40
301 A46 2.50r multicolored 3.25 2.25
a. Souvenir sheet of 4 4.00 4.00
Nos. 298-301 (4) 6.75 4.15

Man's 1st moon landing. See note after US #C76.

Exist imperf.

No. 301a contains stamps similar to Nos. 298-301, with designs transposed on 10 l and 2.50r. Simulated perfs.

For overprints see Nos. 343-345.

Nos. 289-290 Overprinted: "REPUBLIC OF MALDIVES" and Commemorative Inscriptions

Designs: 50 l, overprinted "Gold Medal Winner / Mohamed Gammoudi / 5000m. run / Tunisia." 1r, overprinted "Gold Medal Winner / P. Trentin—Cycling / France."

1969, Dec. 10 Photo. *Perf. 14*

302 A43 50 l multicolored .85 .70
303 A43 1r multicolored 1.40 1.25

Columbia Daumon Victoria, 1899 — A47

Automobiles (pre-1908): 5 l, 50 l, Duryea Phaeton, 1902. 7 l, 1r, Packard S.24, 1906. 10 l, 2r, Autocar Runabout, 1907. 25 l, like 2 l.

1970, Feb. 1 Litho. *Perf. 12*

304 A47 2 l multicolored .20 .20
305 A47 5 l brt pink & multi .30 .20
306 A47 7 l ultra & multi .40 .20
307 A47 10 l ver & multi .45 .20
308 A47 25 l ocher & multi 1.25 .30
309 A47 50 l olive & multi 2.75 .40
310 A47 1r orange & multi 4.00 .70
311 A47 2r multicolored 6.25 4.50
a. Souvenir sheet of 2, #310-311, perf. 11½ 8.00 8.00
Nos. 304-311 (8) 15.60 6.70

Exist imperf.

Orange Butterflyfish — A48

Fish: 5 l, Spotted triggerfish. 25 l, Spotfin turkeyfish. 50 l, Forceps fish. 1r, Imperial angelfish. 2r, Regal angelfish.

1970, Mar. 1 Litho. *Perf. 10½*

312 A48 2 l blue & multi 1.10 .60
313 A48 5 l orange & multi 1.10 .60
314 A48 25 l emerald & multi 1.10 .60
315 A48 50 l brt pink & multi 1.75 .75
316 A48 1r lt vio bl & multi 3.50 1.40
317 A48 2r olive & multi 7.25 3.00
Nos. 312-317 (6) 15.80 6.95

UN Headquarters, New York and UN Emblem — A49

25th anniv. of the UN: 10 l, Surgeons, nurse and WHO emblem. 25 l, Student, performer, musician and UNESCO emblem. 50 l, Children reading and playing, and UNICEF emblem. 1r, Lamb, cock, fish, grain and FAO emblem. 2r, Miner and ILO emblem.

1970, June 26 Litho. *Perf. 13½*

318 A49 2 l multicolored .35 .25
319 A49 10 l multicolored .60 .25
320 A49 25 l multicolored 1.75 .25
321 A49 50 l multicolored 2.40 .30
322 A49 1r multicolored 4.00 .65
323 A49 2r multicolored 6.00 1.25
Nos. 318-323 (6) 15.10 2.95

IMCO Emblem, Buoy and Ship — A50

EXPO Emblem and Australian Pavilion — A51

Design: 1r, Lighthouse and ship.

1970, July 26 Litho. *Perf. 13½*

324 A50 50 l multicolored .75 .30
325 A50 1r multicolored 4.50 .75

10th anniv. of the Intergovernmental Maritime Consultative Organization (IMCO).

1970, Aug. 1 *Perf. 13½x14*

EXPO Emblem and: 3 l, West German pavilion. 10 l, US pavilion. 25 l, British pavilion. 50 l, Russian pavilion. 1r, Japanese pavilion.

326 A51 2 l green & multi .25 .25
327 A51 3 l violet & multi .25 .25
328 A51 10 l brown & multi .40 .25
329 A51 25 l multicolored .95 .25
330 A51 50 l claret & multi 1.60 .35
331 A51 1r ultra & multi 2.10 .70
Nos. 326-331 (6) 5.55 2.05

EXPO '70 International Exhibition, Osaka, Japan, Mar. 15-Sept. 13, 1970.

Guitar Player, by Watteau — A52

Paintings: 7 l, Guitar Player in Spanish Costume, by Edouard Manet. 50 l, Guitar-playing Clown, by Antoine Watteau. 1r, Mandolin Player and Singers, by Lorenzo Costa (inscribed Ercole Roberti). 2.50r, Guitar Player and Lady, by Watteau. 5r, Mandolin Player, by Frans Hals.

1970, Aug. 1 Litho. *Perf. 14*

332 A52 3 l gray & multi .25 .25
333 A52 7 l yellow & multi .25 .25
334 A52 50 l multicolored .60 .60
335 A52 1r multicolored 1.00 1.00
336 A52 2.50r multicolored 2.50 2.50
337 A52 5r multicolored 4.75 4.75
a. Souvenir sheet of 2 8.50 8.00
Nos. 332-337 (6) 9.35 9.35

No. 337a contains 2 stamps similar to Nos. 336-337 but rouletted 13 and printed se-tenant.

Education Year Emblem and Adult Education — A53

Education Year Emblem and: 10 l, Teacher training. 25 l, Geography class. 50 l, Classroom. 1r, Instruction by television.

1970, Sept. 7 Litho. *Perf. 14*

338 A53 5 l multicolored .35 .35
339 A53 10 l multicolored .60 .35
340 A53 25 l multicolored 1.10 .35
341 A53 50 l multicolored 1.40 .60
342 A53 1r multicolored 2.50 1.40
Nos. 338-342 (5) 5.95 3.05

Issued for International Education Year.

Nos. 299-301 Overprinted in Silver: "Philympia / London 1970"

1970, Sept. 18

343 A46 10 l multicolored .30 .30
344 A46 1.50r multicolored 1.00 1.25
345 A46 2.50r multicolored 1.60 2.00
Nos. 343-345 (3) 2.90 3.55

Issued to commemorate Philympia 1970, London Philatelic Exhibition, Sept. 18-26.

This overprint was also applied to No. 301a. Value $10.

Soccer Play, Rimet Cup — A54

Boy Holding UNICEF Flag — A55

Various Soccer Scenes, and Rimet Cup.

1970 Litho. *Perf. 13½*

346 A54 3 l emerald & multi .25 .25
347 A54 6 l rose lilac & multi .40 .25
348 A54 7 l dp orange & multi .40 .25
349 A54 25 l blue & multi .40 .25
350 A54 1r olive & multi 4.50 1.00
Nos. 346-350 (5) 5.95 2.00

Jules Rimet 9th World Soccer Championships, Mexico City, May 30-June 21.

1971, Apr. 1 Litho. *Perf. 12*

UNICEF, 25th. Anniv.: 10 l, 2r, Girl holding balloon with UNICEF emblem.

351 A55 5 l pink & multi .30 .25
352 A55 10 l lt blue & multi .30 .25
353 A55 1r yellow & multi 2.25 .70
354 A55 2r pale lilac & multi 4.00 1.10
Nos. 351-354 (4) 6.85 2.30

Astronauts Swigert, Lovell and Haise — A56

Flowers Symbolizing Races and World — A57

Safe return of Apollo 13: 20 l, Spacecraft and landing module. 1r, Capsule and boat in Pacific Ocean.

1971, Apr. 27 *Perf. 14*

355 A56 5 l dull purple & multi .25 .25
356 A56 20 l multicolored .25 .25
357 A56 1r brt blue & multi 1.40 .70
Nos. 355-357 (3) 1.90 1.20

1971, May 3

358 A57 10 l multicolored .30 .30
359 A57 25 l gray & multi .30 .30

Intl. year against racial discrimination.

Mother and Child, by Auguste Renoir A58

Mother and Child Paintings by: 7 l, Rembrandt. 10 l, Titian. 20 l, Degas. 25 l, Berthe Morisot. 1r, Rubens. 3r, Renoir.

1971, Sept. Litho. *Perf. 12*

360 A58 5 l multicolored .25 .25
361 A58 7 l multicolored .35 .25
362 A58 10 l multicolored .35 .25
363 A58 20 l multicolored 1.25 .25
364 A58 25 l multicolored 1.40 .25
365 A58 1r multicolored 3.75 .70
366 A58 3r multicolored 7.75 5.00
Nos. 360-366 (7) 15.10 6.95

Capt. Alan B. Shepard, Jr. — A59

10 l, Maj. Stuart A. Roosa. 1.50r, Com. Edgar D. Mitchell. 5r, Apollo 14 shoulder patch.

1971, Nov. 11 Photo. *Perf. 12½*

367 A59 6 l dp green & multi .30 .30
368 A59 10 l claret & multi .45 .30

No.	Type	Description	Unused	Used
369	A59	1.50r ultra & multi	5.25	3.00
370	A59	5r multicolored	10.50	9.00
		Nos. 367-370 (4)	16.50	12.60

Apollo 14 US moon landing mission, 1/31-2/9.

Ballerina, by Degas A60

Paintings: 10 l, Dancing Couple, by Auguste Renoir. 2r, Spanish Dancer, by Edouard Manet. 5r, Ballerinas, by Degas. 10r, Moulin Rouge, by Henri Toulouse-Lautrec.

1971, Nov. 19 Litho. *Perf. 14*

No.	Type	Description	Unused	Used
371	A60	5 l plum & multi	.25	.25
372	A60	10 l green & multi	.25	.25
373	A60	2r org brn & multi	2.75	2.10
374	A60	5r dk blue & multi	5.50	4.25
375	A60	10r multicolored	7.75	7.75
		Nos. 371-375 (5)	16.50	14.60

Nos. 371-375 Overprinted Vertically: "ROYAL VISIT 1972"

1972, Mar. 13 Litho. *Perf. 14*

No.	Type	Description	Unused	Used
376	A60	5 l plum & multi	.20	.20
377	A60	10 l green & multi	.20	.20
378	A60	2r org brn & multi	5.00	3.00
379	A60	5r dk blue & multi	9.00	6.00
380	A60	10r multicolored	10.00	8.50
		Nos. 376-380 (5)	24.40	17.90

Visit of Elizabeth II and Prince Philip.

Book Year Emblem A61

1972, May 1 *Perf. 13x13½*

No.	Type	Description	Unused	Used
381	A61	25 l orange & multi	.35	.20
382	A61	5r multicolored	2.50	1.50

International Book Year.

National Costume of Scotland A62

National Costumes: 15 l, Netherlands. 25 l, Norway. 50 l, Hungary. 1r, Austria. 2r, Spain.

1972, May 15 *Perf. 12*

No.	Type	Description	Unused	Used
383	A62	10 l gray & multi	.65	.25
384	A62	15 l lt brown & multi	.70	.25
385	A62	25 l multicolored	1.25	.25
386	A62	50 l lt brown & multi	2.10	.40
387	A62	1r gray & multi	3.00	.70
388	A62	2r lt olive & multi	5.00	2.40
		Nos. 383-388 (6)	12.70	4.25

Stegosaurus — A63

Designs: Prehistoric reptiles.

1972, May 31 *Perf. 14*

No.	Type	Description	Unused	Used
389	A63	2 l shown	.65	.50
390	A63	7 l Edaphosaurus	1.10	.45
391	A63	25 l Diplodocus	2.25	.45
392	A63	50 l Triceratops	2.25	.75
393	A63	2r Pteranodon	6.00	6.00
394	A63	5r Tyrannosaurus	12.00	12.00
		Nos. 389-394 (6)	24.25	20.15

A souvenir sheet has two stamps similar to Nos. 393-394 with simulated perforations. It was not regularly issued. Value, $50.

Sapporo '72 Emblem, Cross Country Skiing A64

1972, June Litho. *Perf. 14*

No.	Type	Description	Unused	Used
395	A64	3 l shown	.25	.25
396	A64	6 l Bobsledding	.25	.25
397	A64	15 l Speed skating	.25	.25
398	A64	50 l Ski jump	1.00	.40
399	A64	1r Figure skating	1.75	.85
400	A64	2.50r Ice hockey	6.25	2.75
		Nos. 395-400 (6)	9.75	4.75

11th Winter Olympic Games, Sapporo, Japan, Feb. 3-13.

Boy Scout Saluting — A65

Olympic Emblems, Bicycling — A66

Scout: 15 l, with signal flags. 50 l, Bugler. 1r, Drummer.

1972, Aug. 1

No.	Type	Description	Unused	Used
401	A65	10 l Prus green & multi	.70	.25
402	A65	15 l dk red & multi	1.00	.25
403	A65	50 l dp green & multi	3.50	1.00
404	A65	1r purple & multi	5.00	1.75
		Nos. 401-404 (4)	10.20	3.25

13th International Boy Scout Jamboree, Asagiri Plain, Japan, Aug. 2-11, 1971.

1972, Oct. Litho. *Perf. 14½x14*

No.	Type	Description	Unused	Used
405	A66	5 l shown	.30	.30
406	A66	10 l Running	.30	.30
407	A66	25 l Wrestling	.30	.30
408	A66	50 l Hurdles, women's	.40	.40
409	A66	2r Boxing	1.60	1.60
410	A66	5r Volleyball	4.00	4.00
		Nos. 405-410 (6)	6.90	6.90

Souvenir Sheet

Perf. 15

No.	Type	Description	Unused	Used
411		Sheet of 2	7.50	7.50
a.		A66 3r like 50 l	2.40	2.40
b.		A66 4r like 10 l	3.00	3.00

20th Olympic Games, Munich, 8/26-9/11.
For overprints see Nos. 417-419.

Globe, Environment Emblem — A67

1972, Nov. 15 Litho. *Perf. 14½*

No.	Type	Description	Unused	Used
412	A67	2 l violet & multi	.25	.25
413	A67	3 l brown & multi	.25	.25
414	A67	15 l blue & multi	.35	.35
415	A67	50 l red & multi	.90	.90
416	A67	2.50r green & multi	4.00	4.00
		Nos. 412-416 (5)	5.75	5.75

UN Conference on Human Environment, Stockholm, June 5-16.

Nos. 409-411 Overprinted in Violet Blue:
a. LEMECHEV / MIDDLE-WEIGHT /GOLD MEDALLIST
b. JAPAN / GOLD MEDAL / WINNER
c. EHRHARDT / 100 METER / HURDLES / GOLD MEDALLIST
d. SHORTER / MARATHON / GOLD MEDALLIST

1973, Feb. Litho. *Perf. 14½x14*

No.	Type	Description	Unused	Used
417	A66(a)	2r multicolored	4.25	3.50
418	A66(b)	5r multicolored	6.00	5.25

Souvenir Sheet

No.	Type	Description	Unused	Used
419		Sheet of 2	10.00	*10.00*
a.		A66(c) 3r multicolored	3.25	*3.25*
b.		A66(d) 4r multicolored	3.50	*3.50*

Gold medal winners in 20th Olympic Games: Viatschesiav Lemechev, USSR, middleweight boxing; Japanese team, volleyball. Annelie Ehrhardt, Germany, 100m. hurdles; Frank Shorter, US, marathon.

Flowers, by Vincent Van Gogh — A68

Paintings of Flowers by: 2 l, 3 l, 1r, 3r, 5r, Auguste Renoir (each different). 50 l, 5 l, Ambrosius Bosschaert.

1973, Feb. *Perf. 13½*

No.	Type	Description	Unused	Used
420	A68	1 l blue & multi	.35	.35
421	A68	2 l tan & multi	.35	.35
422	A68	3 l lilac & multi	.35	.35
423	A68	50 l ultra & multi	.90	.45
424	A68	1r emerald & multi	1.40	.45
425	A68	5r magenta & multi	4.50	4.50
		Nos. 420-425 (6)	7.85	6.45

Souvenir Sheet

Perf. 15

No.	Type	Description	Unused	Used
426		Sheet of 2	9.50	*11.00*
a.		A68 2r black & multi	2.00	*2.25*
b.		A68 3r black & multi	2.50	*2.75*

Scouts Treating Injured Lamb A69

Designs: 2 l, 1r, Lifesaving. 3 l, 5r, Agricultural training. 4 l, 2r, Carpentry. 5 l, Leapfrog.

1973, Aug. Litho. *Perf. 14½*

No.	Type	Description	Unused	Used
427	A69	1 l black & multi	.25	.25
428	A69	2 l black & multi	.25	.25
429	A69	3 l black & multi	.25	.25
430	A69	4 l black & multi	.25	.25
431	A69	5 l black & multi	.25	.25
432	A69	1r black & multi	2.50	.60
433	A69	2r black & multi	5.00	3.75
434	A69	3r black & multi	6.25	6.25
		Nos. 427-434 (8)	15.00	11.85

Souvenir Sheet

No.	Type	Description	Unused	Used
435	A69	5r black & multi	10.00	*11.50*

24th Boy Scout World Conference (1st in Africa), Nairobi, Kenya, July 16-21.
For overprints see Nos. 571-574.

Herschel's Marlin A70

Fish and Ships: 2 l, 4r, Skipjack tuna. 3 l, Bluefin tuna. 5 l, 2.50r, Dolphinfish. 60 l, 75 l, Red snapper. 1.50r, Yellow crescent tail. 3r, Plectropoma maculatum. 5r, Like 1 l. 10r, Spanish mackerel.

1973, Aug. *Perf. 14½*

Size: 38½x24mm

No.	Type	Description	Unused	Used
436	A70	1 l lt green & multi	.25	.25
437	A70	2 l dull org & multi	.25	.25
438	A70	3 l brt red & multi	.25	.25
439	A70	5 l multicolored	.25	.25

Size: 28x22mm

No.	Type	Description	Unused	Used
440	A70	60 l yellow & multi	.80	.40
441	A70	75 l purple & multi	1.00	.40

Size: 38½x24mm

No.	Type	Description	Unused	Used
442	A70	1.50r violet & multi	1.60	1.40
443	A70	2.50r blue & multi	2.00	2.00
444	A70	3r multicolored	2.50	2.50
445	A70	10r orange & multi	6.00	6.50
		Nos. 436-445 (10)	14.90	14.20

Souvenir Sheet

Perf. 15

No.	Type	Description	Unused	Used
446		Sheet of 2	18.50	18.50
a.		A70 4r carmine & multi	5.00	5.00
b.		A70 5r bright green & multi	6.00	6.00

Nos. 436-445 exist imperf.

Goldenfronted Leafbird — A71

2 l, 3r, Fruit bat. 3 l, 50 l, Indian starred tortoise. 4 l, 5r, Kallima inachus (butterfly).

1973, Oct. Litho. *Perf. 14½*

No.	Type	Description	Unused	Used
447	A71	1 l brt pink & multi	.25	.25
448	A71	2 l brt blue & multi	.25	.25
449	A71	3 l ver & multi	.35	.35
450	A71	4 l citron & multi	.50	.35
451	A71	50 l emerald & multi	.90	.50
452	A71	2r lt violet & multi	4.75	4.25
453	A71	3r multicolored	3.50	3.25
		Nos. 447-453 (7)	10.50	9.20

Souvenir Sheet

No.	Type	Description	Unused	Used
454	A71	5r yellow & multi	22.50	22.50

Lantana Camara — A72

Native Flowers: 2 l, Nerium oleander. 3 l, 2r, Rosa polyantha. 4 l, Hibiscus manihot. 5 l, Bougainvillea glabra. 10 l, 3r, Plumera alba. 50 l, Poinsettia pulcherrima. 5r, Ononis natrix.

1973, Dec. 19 Litho. *Perf. 14*

455 A72 1 l ultra & multi .30 .30
456 A72 2 l dp orange & multi .30 .30
457 A72 3 l emerald & multi .30 .30
458 A72 4 l blue grn & multi .30 .30
459 A72 5 l lemon & multi .30 .30
460 A72 10 l lilac & multi .30 .30
461 A72 50 l yel grn & multi .30 .30
462 A72 5r red & multi 3.00 3.00
Nos. 455-462 (8) 5.10 5.10

Souvenir Sheet

463 Sheet of 2 5.75 6.50
a. A72 2r lilac & multi 1.25 1.50
b. A72 3r blue & multi 2.00 2.25

Tiros Weather Satellite A73

Designs: 2 l, 10r, Nimbus satellite. 3 l, 3r, Nomad weather ("weater") station. 4 l, A.P.T. instant weather picture (radar). 5 l, Richard's electrical wind speed recorder. 2r, like 1 l.

1974, Jan. 10 *Perf. 14½*

464 A73 1 l olive & multi .25 .25
465 A73 2 l multicolored .25 .25
466 A73 3 l brt blue & multi .35 .35
467 A73 4 l ocher & multi .35 .35
468 A73 5 l ocher & multi .35 .35
469 A73 2r ultra & multi 2.75 3.50
470 A73 3r orange & multi 4.50 3.00
Nos. 464-470 (7) 8.80 8.05

Souvenir Sheet

471 A73 10r lilac & multi 10.50 *10.50*

World Meteorological Cooperation, cent.

Apollo Spacecraft, John F. Kennedy — A74

Designs: 2 l, 3r, Mercury spacecraft and John Glenn. 3 l, Vostok 1 and Yuri Gagarin. 4 l, Vostok 6 and Valentina Tereshkova. 5 l, Soyuz 11 and Salyut spacecrafts. 2r, Skylab. 10r, Like 1 l.

1974, Feb. 1 Litho. *Perf. 14½*

472 A74 1 l multicolored .25 .25
473 A74 2 l multicolored .25 .25
474 A74 3 l multicolored .35 .35
475 A74 4 l multicolored .35 .35
476 A74 5 l multicolored .35 .35
477 A74 2r multicolored 3.50 3.50
478 A74 3r multicolored 5.50 5.50
Nos. 472-478 (7) 10.55 10.55

Souvenir Sheet

479 A74 10r multicolored 13.50 *13.50*

Space explorations of US and USSR.

Skylab and Copernicus — A75

Copernicus, Various Portraits and: 2 l, 1.50r, Futuristic orbiting station. 3 l, 5r, Futuristic flight station. 4 l, Mariner 2 on flight to Venus. 5 l, Mariner 4 on flight to Mars. 25 l, like 1 l. 10r, Copernicus Orbiting Observatory.

1974, Apr. 10 Litho. *Perf. 14½*

480 A75 1 l multicolored .20 .20
481 A75 2 l multicolored .20 .20
482 A75 3 l multicolored .20 .20
483 A75 4 l multicolored .40 .40
484 A75 5 l multicolored .40 .40
485 A75 25 l multicolored 1.40 1.40
486 A75 1.50r multicolored 4.75 4.75
487 A75 5r multicolored 9.50 9.50
Nos. 480-487 (8) 17.05 17.05

Souvenir Sheet

488 A75 10r multicolored 21.00 *22.50*

"Motherhood," by Picasso — A76

Picasso Paintings: 2 l, Harlequin and his Companion. 3 l, Pierrot Sitting. 20 l, 2r, Three Musicians. 75 l, L'Aficionada. 3r, 5r, Still life.

1974, May *Perf. 14*

489 A76 1 l multicolored .30 .30
490 A76 2 l multicolored .30 .30
491 A76 3 l multicolored .30 .30
492 A76 20 l multicolored .30 .30
493 A76 75 l multicolored .70 .70
494 A76 5r multicolored 4.75 4.75
Nos. 489-494 (6) 6.65 6.65

Souvenir Sheet

495 Sheet of 2 8.50 8.50
a. A76 2r multicolored 1.90 1.90
b. A76 3r multicolored 3.00 3.00

Pablo Picasso (1881-1973), painter.

UPU Emblem, Old and New Trains A77

UPU Emblem and: 2 l, 2.50r, Old and new ships. 3 l, Zeppelin and jet. 1.50r, Mail coach and truck. 4r, 5r, Like 1 l.

1974, May Litho. *Perf. 14½, 13½*

496 A77 1 l lt green & multi .30 .30
497 A77 2 l yellow & multi .30 .30
498 A77 3 l rose & multi .30 .30
499 A77 1.50r yel green & multi 1.00 1.00
500 A77 2.50r blue & multi 1.75 1.75
501 A77 5r ocher & multi 3.00 3.00
Nos. 496-501 (6) 6.65 6.65

Souvenir Sheet

502 A77 4r ver & multi *6.00* 6.00

UPU cent. No. 502 exists imperf.

Nos. 496-501 were printed in sheets of 50, perf. 14½, and also in sheets of 5 plus label, perf. 13½. The label shows UPU emblem, post horn, globe and carrier pigeon.

Capricorn A78

Designs: Zodiac signs and constellations.

1974, July 3

503 A78 1 l shown .25 .25
504 A78 2 l Aquarius .25 .25
505 A78 3 l Pisces .25 .25
506 A78 4 l Aries .25 .25
507 A78 5 l Taurus .25 .25
508 A78 6 l Gemini .25 .25
509 A78 7 l Cancer .25 .25
510 A78 10 l Leo .25 .25
511 A78 15 l Virgo .25 .25
512 A78 20 l Libra .25 .25
513 A78 25 l Scorpio .25 .25
514 A78 5r Sagittarius 7.50 7.50
Nos. 503-514 (12) 10.25 10.25

Souvenir Sheet

515 A78 10r Sun 21.00 *21.00*

Stamp size of 10r: 50x37mm.

Soccer and Games' Emblem — A79

Various soccer scenes & games' emblem.

1974, July 31 Litho. *Perf. 14½*

516 A79 1 l brown & multi .25 .25
517 A79 2 l green & multi .25 .25
518 A79 3 l ultra & multi .25 .25
519 A79 4 l red & multi .25 .25
520 A79 75 l lt blue & multi 1.25 .75
521 A79 4r olive & multi 3.00 2.50
522 A79 5r lilac & multi 3.50 3.00
Nos. 516-522 (7) 8.75 7.25

Souvenir Sheet

523 A79 10r rose & multi 12.50 12.50

World Cup Soccer Championship, Munich, June 13-July 7.

Churchill and WWII Plane A80

Churchill: 2 l, As pilot. 3 l, First Lord of the Admiralty and battleship. 4 l, 10r, Aircraft carrier. 5 l, RAF fighters. 60 l, Anti-aircraft unit. 75 l, Tank. 5r, Seaplane.

1974, Nov. 30 Litho. *Perf. 14½*

524 A80 1 l multicolored .25 .25
525 A80 2 l multicolored .25 .25
526 A80 3 l multicolored .30 .30
527 A80 4 l multicolored .30 .30
528 A80 5 l multicolored .30 .30
529 A80 60 l multicolored 3.00 3.00
530 A80 75 l multicolored 3.50 3.50
531 A80 5r multicolored 12.00 12.00
Nos. 524-531 (8) 19.90 19.90

Souvenir Sheet

532 A80 10r multicolored 20.00 20.00

Sir Winston Churchill (1874-1965).

Cassis Nana — A81 Cypraea Diliculum — A82

1975, Jan. 25 *Perf. 14½, 14 (A82)*

533 A81 1 l shown .25 .25
534 A81 2 l Murex triremus .25 .25
535 A81 3 l Harpa major .30 .30
536 A81 4 l Lambis chiragra .30 .30
537 A81 5 l Conus pennaceus .30 .30
538 A82 60 l shown 2.75 2.75
539 A82 75 l Clanculus pharaonis 3.25 3.25
540 A81 5r Chicoreus ramosus 7.25 *7.25*
Nos. 533-540 (8) 14.65 *14.65*

Souvenir Sheet

Perf. 13½

541 Sheet of 2 14.50 14.50
a. A81 2r like 3 l 3.75 3.75
b. A81 3r like 2 l 4.75 4.75

Sea shells, including cowries.

Throne — A83

Eid-Miskith Mosque — A84

Designs: 10 l, Ornamental candlesticks (dulisa). 25 l, Tree-shaped lamp. 60 l, Royal umbrellas. 3r, Tomb of Al-Hafiz Abu-al Barakath al-Barubari.

1975, Feb. 22 Litho. *Perf. 14*

542 A83 1 l multicolored .20 .20
543 A83 10 l multicolored .20 .20
544 A83 25 l multicolored .20 .20
545 A83 60 l multicolored .30 .30
546 A84 75 l multicolored .40 .40
547 A84 3r multicolored 1.60 1.60
Nos. 542-547 (6) 2.90 2.90

Historic relics and monuments.

Tropical Fruit — A85

1975, Mar. Litho. *Perf. 14½*

548 A85 2 l Guava .25 .25
549 A85 4 l Maldive mulberry .25 .25
550 A85 5 l Mountain apples .25 .25
551 A85 10 l Bananas .25 .25
552 A85 20 l Mangoes .25 .25
553 A85 50 l Papaya .90 .60
554 A85 1r Pomegranates 1.40 .65
555 A85 5r Coconut 8.25 8.75
Nos. 548-555 (8) 11.80 11.25

Souvenir Sheet

Perf. 13½

556 Sheet of 2 10.00 *11.00*
a. A85 2r like 10 l 2.50 *3.00*
b. A85 3r like 2 l 3.00 *3.50*

Phyllangia — A86

Designs: Corals, sea urchins and starfish.

1975, June 6 Litho. *Perf. 14½*

557 A86 1 l shown .25 .25
558 A86 2 l Madrepora oculata .25 .25
559 A86 3 l Acropora gravida .25 .25
560 A86 4 l Stylotella .25 .25
561 A86 5 l Acropora cervicornis .25 .25
562 A86 60 l Strongylocentrotus pupuratus .75 .65
563 A86 75 l Pisaster ochraceus .90 .75
564 A86 5r Marthasterias glacialis 4.50 5.25
Nos. 557-564 (8) 7.40 7.90

Souvenir Sheet

Imperf

565 A86 4r shown 14.00 14.00

"10," Clock Tower and Customs House A87

"10" and: 5 l, Government offices. 7 l, North Eastern waterfront, Male. 15 l, Mosque and Minaret. 10r, Sultan Park and Museum.

1975, July 26 Litho. Perf. 14½

566 A87 4 l salmon & multi .25 .25
567 A87 5 l lt blue & multi .25 .25
568 A87 7 l bister & multi .25 .25
569 A87 15 l lilac & multi .25 .25
570 A87 10r lt green & multi 3.50 *5.75*
Nos. 566-570 (5) 4.50 *6.75*

10th anniversary of independence.

Nos. 432-435 Overprinted: "14th Boy Scout Jamboree / July 29-Aug. 7, 1975"

1975, July 26 Litho. Perf. 14½

571 A69 1r multicolored .65 .65
572 A69 2r multicolored 1.00 1.00
573 A69 3r multicolored 3.00 3.00
Nos. 571-573 (3) 4.65 4.65

Souvenir Sheet

574 A69 5r multicolored 10.50 10.50

Nordjamb 75, 14th World Boy Scout Jamboree, Lillehammer, Norway, July 29-Aug. 7.

Madura-Prau Bedang — A88

Sailing ships, except 5r: 2 l, Ganges patile. 3 l, Indian palla, vert. 4 l, "Odhi," vert. 5 l, Maldivian schooner. 25 l, Cutty Sark. 1r, 10r, Maldivian baggala, vert. 5r, Freighter Maldive Courage.

1975, July 26 Perf. 14½

575 A88 1 l multicolored .25 .25
576 A88 2 l multicolored .25 .25
577 A88 3 l multicolored .25 .25
578 A88 4 l multicolored .25 .25
579 A88 5 l multicolored .25 .25
580 A88 25 l multicolored .65 .30
581 A88 1r multicolored 1.25 .75
582 A88 5r multicolored 3.75 *5.75*
Nos. 575-582 (8) 6.90 8.05

Souvenir Sheet

Perf. 13½

583 A88 10r multicolored 12.50 *12.50*

Brahmaea Wallichii A89

Designs: Butterflies.

1975, Sept. 7 Litho. Perf. 14½

584 A89 1 l shown .25 .25
585 A89 2 l Teoinopalpus imperialis .25 .25
586 A89 3 l Cethosia biblis .30 .30
587 A89 4 l Hestia jasonia .30 .30
588 A89 5 l Apatura .30 .30
589 A89 25 l Kallima horsfieldi 1.50 1.50
590 A89 1.50r Hebomoia leucippe 4.00 4.00
591 A89 5r Papilio memnon 10.00 10.00
Nos. 584-591 (8) 16.90 16.90

Souvenir Sheet

Perf. 13½

592 A89 10r like 25 l 27.50 27.50

Dying Slave by Michelangelo A90

Cup and Vase A91

Works by Michelangelo: 2 l, 4 l, 1r, 5r, paintings from Sistine Chapel. 3 l, Apollo. 5 l, Bacchus. 2r, 10r, David.

1975, Oct. 9 Litho. Perf. 14½

593 A90 1 l blue & multi .25 .25
594 A90 2 l multicolored .25 .25
595 A90 3 l red & multi .25 .25
596 A90 4 l multicolored .25 .25
597 A90 5 l emerald & multi .25 .25
598 A90 1r multicolored .70 .70
599 A90 2r red & multi 1.50 1.50
600 A90 5r multicolored 4.00 4.00
Nos. 593-600 (8) 7.45 7.45

Souvenir Sheet

Perf. 13½

601 A90 10r multicolored 7.50 7.50

Michelangelo Buonarotti (1475-1564), Italian sculptor, painter and architect.

1975, Dec. Litho. Perf. 14

Designs: 4 l, Boxes. 50 l, Vase with lid. 75 l, Bowls with covers. 1r, Worker finishing vases.

602 A91 2 l ultra & multi .20 .20
603 A91 4 l rose & multi .20 .20
604 A91 50 l multicolored .30 .30
605 A91 75 l blue & multi .45 .45
606 A91 1r multicolored .55 .55
Nos. 602-606 (5) 1.70 1.70

Maldivian lacquer ware.

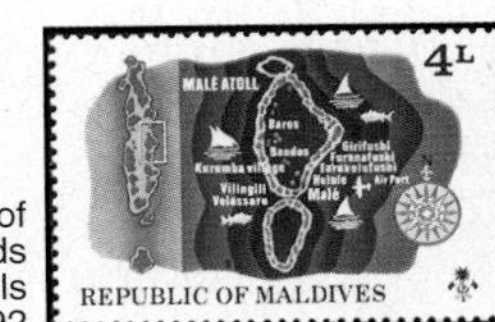

Map of Islands and Atolls A92

Designs: 5 l, Yacht at anchor. 7 l, Sailboats. 15 l, Deep-sea divers and corals. 3r, Hulule Airport. 10r, Cruising yachts.

1975, Dec. 25 Litho. Perf. 14

607 A92 4 l multicolored .30 .30
608 A92 5 l multicolored .30 .30
609 A92 7 l multicolored .30 .30
610 A92 15 l multicolored .30 .30
611 A92 3r multicolored 2.40 2.40
612 A92 10r multicolored 6.50 7.00
Nos. 607-612 (6) 10.10 10.60

Tourist publicity.

Cross-country Skiing — A93

Gen. Burgoyne, by Joshua Reynolds — A94

Winter Olympic Games' Emblem and: 2 l, Speed skating. 3 l, Figure skating, pair. 4 l, Bobsled. 5 l, Ski jump. 25 l, Figure skating, woman. 1.15r, Slalom. 4r, Ice hockey. 10r, Skiing.

1976, Jan. 10 Litho. Perf. 14½

613 A93 1 l multicolored .30 .30
614 A93 2 l multicolored .30 .30
615 A93 3 l multicolored .30 .30
616 A93 4 l multicolored .30 .30
617 A93 5 l multicolored .30 .30
618 A93 25 l multicolored .40 .30
619 A93 1.15r multicolored .75 .75
620 A93 4r multicolored 2.25 2.25
Nos. 613-620 (8) 4.90 4.80

Souvenir Sheet

Perf. 13½

621 A93 10r multicolored 8.00 *9.00*

12th Winter Olympic Games, Innsbruck, Austria, Feb. 4-15. Exist imperf.

1976, Feb. 15 Perf. 14½

Paintings: 2 l, John Hancock, by John S. Copley. 3 l, Death of Gen. Montgomery, by John Trumbull, horiz. 4 l, Paul Revere, by Copley. 5 l, Battle of Bunker Hill, by Trumbull, horiz. 2r, Crossing of the Delaware, by Thomas Sully, horiz. 3r, Samuel Adams, by Copley. 5r, Surrender of Cornwallis, by Trumbull, horiz. 10r, Washington at Dorchester Heights, by Gilbert Stuart.

622 A94 1 l multicolored .25 .25
623 A94 2 l multicolored .25 .25
624 A94 3 l multicolored .25 .25
625 A94 4 l multicolored .25 .25
626 A94 5 l multicolored .25 .25
627 A94 2r multicolored 1.50 1.50
628 A94 3r multicolored 2.10 2.10
629 A94 5r multicolored 3.50 3.50
Nos. 622-629 (8) 8.35 8.35

Souvenir Sheet

Perf. 13½

630 A94 10r multicolored 17.00 *17.00*

American Bicentennial.
For overprints see Nos. 639-642.

Thomas Alva Edison A95

Designs: 2 l, Alexander Graham Bell and his telephone. 3 l, Telephones of 1919, 1937 and 1972. 10 l, Cable tunnel. 20 l, Equalizer circuit assembly. 1r, Ships laying underwater cable. 4r, Telephones of 1876, 1890 and 1879 Edison telephone. 10r, Intelsat IV-A over earth station.

1976, Mar. 10 Litho. Perf. 14½

631 A95 1 l multicolored .25 .25
632 A95 2 l multicolored .25 .25
633 A95 3 l multicolored .25 .25
634 A95 10 l multicolored .25 .25
635 A95 20 l multicolored .25 .25
636 A95 1r multicolored .65 .65
637 A95 10r multicolored 6.50 6.50
Nos. 631-637 (7) 8.40 8.40

Souvenir Sheet

Perf. 13½

638 A95 4r multicolored 11.50 *11.50*

Centenary of first telephone call by Alexander Graham Bell, Mar. 10, 1876.

Nos. 627-630 Overprinted in Silver or Black: MAY 29TH-JUNE 6TH "INTERPHIL" 1976

1976, May 29 Litho. Perf. 14½

639 A94 2r multicolored (S) 1.75 1.75
640 A94 3r multicolored (S) 2.25 2.25
641 A94 5r multicolored (B) 3.50 3.50
Nos. 639-641 (3) 7.50 7.50

Souvenir Sheet

Perf. 13½

642 A94 10r multicolored (S) 13.50 13.50

Interphil 76 Intl. Philatelic Exhibition, Philadelphia, Pa., May 29-June 6. Overprint on 3r and 10r vertical. Same overprint in one horizontal silver line in margin of No. 642.

Wrestling — A96

Bonavist Beans — A97

Olympic Rings and: 2 l, Shot put. 3 l, Hurdles. 4 l, Hockey. 5 l, Women running. 6 l, Javelin. 1.50r, Discus. 5r, Team handball. 10r, Hammer throw.

1976, June 1 Perf. 14½

643 A96 1 l multicolored .20 .20
644 A96 2 l multicolored .20 .20
645 A96 3 l salmon & multi .20 .20
646 A96 4 l multicolored .20 .20
647 A96 5 l pink & multi .20 .20
648 A96 6 l multicolored .20 .20
649 A96 1.50r bister & multi 1.10 1.00
650 A96 5r lilac & multi 3.50 3.75
Nos. 643-650 (8) 5.80 5.95

Souvenir Sheet

Perf. 13½

651 A96 10r lemon & multi 9.25 *10.00*

21st Olympic Games, Montreal, Canada, July 17-Aug. 1.

1976-77 Litho. Perf. 14

Designs: 4 l, 20 l, Beans. 10 l, Eggplant. 50 l, Cucumber. 75 l, 2r, Snake gourd. 1r, Balsam pear.

652 A97 2 l green & multi .25 .25
653 A97 4 l lt blue & multi .60 .60
654 A97 10 l ocher & multi .60 .60
655 A97 20 l blue & multi ('77) .60 .60
656 A97 50 l multicolored .75 .75
657 A97 75 l bister & multi 1.00 1.00
658 A97 1r lilac & multi 1.40 1.40
659 A97 2r bis & multi ('77) 2.50 2.50
Nos. 652-659 (8) 7.70 7.70

1976 stamps issued July 26.

Viking I and Mars A98

Design: 20r, Landing craft on Mars.

1976, Dec. 2 Litho. Perf. 14

660 A98 5r multicolored 3.00 3.00

Souvenir Sheet

661 A98 20r multicolored 13.00 *13.00*

Viking I US Mars Mission.

Coronation Ceremony — A99

Designs: 2 l, Elizabeth II and Prince Philip. 3 l, Queen, Prince Philip, Princes Edward and Andrew. 1.15r, Queen in procession. 3r, State coach. 4r, Queen, Prince Philip, Princess Anne and Prince Charles. 10r, Queen and Prince Charles.

1977, Feb. 6 Perf. 14x13½, 12

662 A99 1 l multicolored .50 .50
663 A99 2 l multicolored .50 .50
664 A99 3 l multicolored .50 .50
665 A99 1.15r multicolored .70 .60
666 A99 3r multicolored 1.40 *1.50*
667 A99 4r multicolored 1.40 *1.60*
Nos. 662-667 (6) 5.00 *5.20*

Souvenir Sheet

668 A99 10r multicolored 5.75 5.75

25th anniv. of the reign of Elizabeth II.

Nos. 662-667 were printed in sheets of 40 (4x10), perf. 14x13½, and sheets of 5 plus label, perf. 12, in changed colors. Nos. 662-668 exist imperf.

Beethoven in Bonn, 1785 — A100

Designs: 2 l, Moonlight Sonata and portrait, 1801. 3 l, Goethe and Beethoven, Teplitz, 1811. 4 l, Beethoven, 1815, and his string instruments. 5 l, Beethoven House, Heiligenstadt, 1817. 25 l, Composer's hands, gold medal. 2r, Missa Solemnis, portrait, 1823. 4r,

Piano, room where Beethoven died, death mask. 5r, Portrait, 1825, hearing aids.

1977, Mar. 26 Litho. *Perf. 14*

No.	Type	Description	Unused	Used
669	A100	1 l multicolored	.25	.25
670	A100	2 l multicolored	.25	.25
671	A100	3 l multicolored	.40	.40
672	A100	4 l multicolored	.40	.40
673	A100	5 l multicolored	.40	.40
674	A100	25 l multicolored	1.40	1.40
675	A100	2r multicolored	4.00	4.00
676	A100	5r multicolored	7.75	7.75
		Nos. 669-676 (8)	14.85	14.85

Souvenir Sheet

No.	Type	Description	Unused	Used
677	A100	4r multicolored	10.50	*10.50*

Ludwig van Beethoven (1770-1827), composer, 150th death anniversary.

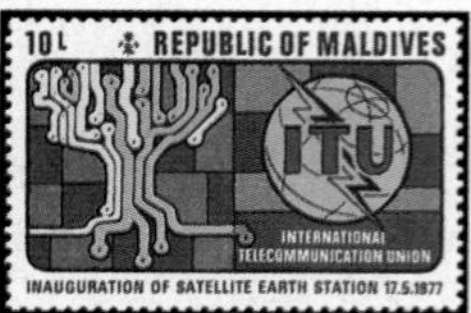

Electronic Tree and ITU Emblem A101

90 l, Central Telegraph Office, Maldives. 5r, Intelsat IV over map. 10r, Parabolic antenna, satellite communications earth station.

1977, May 17 Litho. *Perf. 14*

No.	Type	Description	Unused	Used
678	A101	10 l multicolored	.25	.25
679	A101	90 l multicolored	.50	.50
680	A101	10r multicolored	6.50	6.50
		Nos. 678-680 (3)	7.25	7.25

Souvenir Sheet

No.	Type	Description	Unused	Used
681	A101	5r multicolored	6.25	6.25

Inauguration of Satellite Earth Station and for World Telecommunications Day.

Portrait by Gainsborough A102

Lesser Frigate Birds A103

Paintings: 2 l, 5 l, 10r, Rubens. 3 l, 95 l, 5r, Titian. 4 l, 1r, Gainsborough.

1977, May 20

No.	Type	Description	Unused	Used
682	A102	1 l multicolored	.25	.25
683	A102	2 l multicolored	.25	.25
684	A102	3 l multicolored	.25	.25
685	A102	4 l multicolored	.25	.25
686	A102	5 l multicolored	.25	.25
687	A102	95 l multicolored	.80	.60
688	A102	1r multicolored	.80	.65
689	A102	10r multicolored	4.00	*6.00*
		Nos. 682-689 (8)	6.85	*8.50*

Souvenir Sheet

No.	Type	Description	Unused	Used
690	A102	5r multicolored	5.25	*5.25*

Birth annivs. of Thomas Gainsborough; Peter Paul Rubens; Titian.

1977, July 26 Litho. *Perf. 14½*

Birds: 2 l, Crab plovers. 3 l, Long-tailed tropic bird. 4 l, Wedge-tailed shearwater. 5 l, Gray heron. 20 l, White tern. 95 l, Cattle egret. 1.25r, Blacknaped terns. 5r, Pheasant coucals. 10r, Striated herons.

No.	Type	Description	Unused	Used
691	A103	1 l multicolored	.25	.25
692	A103	2 l multicolored	.25	.25
693	A103	3 l multicolored	.30	.30
694	A103	4 l multicolored	.30	.30
695	A103	5 l multicolored	.30	.30
696	A103	20 l multicolored	1.25	1.25
697	A103	95 l multicolored	2.50	2.50
698	A103	1.25r multicolored	3.50	3.50
699	A103	5r multicolored	6.50	*6.50*
		Nos. 691-699 (9)	15.15	*15.15*

Souvenir Sheet

No.	Type	Description	Unused	Used
700	A103	10r multicolored	35.00	35.00

Charles A. Lindbergh — A104

Designs: 2 l, Lindbergh and Spirit of St. Louis. 3 l, Mohawk plane, horiz. 4 l, Lebaudy I airship, 1902, horiz. 5 l, Count Ferdinand von Zeppelin, and Zeppelin in Pernambuco. 1r, Los Angeles, U. S. Navy airship, 1924, horiz. 3r, Henry Ford and Lindbergh, 1942. 5r, Spirit of St. Louis, Statue of Liberty and Eiffel Tower, horiz. 7.50r, German naval airship over battleship, horiz. 10r, Vickers airship, 1917.

Perf. 13x13½, 13½x13

1977, Oct. 31 Litho.

No.	Type	Description	Unused	Used
701	A104	1 l multicolored	.25	.25
702	A104	2 l multicolored	.25	.25
703	A104	3 l multicolored	.25	.25
704	A104	4 l multicolored	.25	.25
705	A104	5 l multicolored	.25	.25
706	A104	1r multicolored	.60	.30
707	A104	3r multicolored	1.50	1.60
708	A104	10r multicolored	3.50	*4.75*
		Nos. 701-708 (8)	6.85	*7.90*

Souvenir Sheet

No.	Description	Unused	Used
709	Sheet of 2	17.00	17.00
a.	A104 5r multicolored	4.00	4.00
b.	A104 7.50r multicolored	5.00	5.00

Charles A. Lindbergh's solo transatlantic flight from New York to Paris, 50th anniv., and 75th anniv. of first navigable airship.

Boat Building A105

Maldivian Occupations: 15 l, High sea fishing. 20 l, Cadjan weaving. 90 l, Mat weaving. 2r, Lacemaking, vert.

1977, Dec. 12

No.	Type	Description	Unused	Used
710	A105	6 l multicolored	.85	.85
711	A105	15 l multicolored	1.50	1.50
712	A105	20 l multicolored	1.75	1.75
713	A105	90 l multicolored	4.25	4.25
714	A105	2r multicolored	7.25	*7.25*
		Nos. 710-714 (5)	15.60	*15.60*

Rheumatic Heart — A106

X-Ray Pictures: 50 l, Shoulder. 2r, Hand. 3r, Knee.

1978, Feb. 9 *Perf. 14*

No.	Type	Description	Unused	Used
715	A106	1 l multicolored	.20	.20
716	A106	50 l multicolored	.30	.30
717	A106	2r multicolored	1.25	1.25
718	A106	3r multicolored	1.75	1.75
		Nos. 715-718 (4)	3.50	3.50

World Rheumatism Year.

Otto Lilienthal's Glider, 1890 — A107

Designs: 2 l, Chanute's glider, 1896. 3 l, Wright brothers testing glider, 1900. 4 l, A. V. Roe's plane with paper-covered wings, 1908. 5 l, Wilbur Wright showing his plane to King Alfonso of Spain, 1909. 10 l, Roe's second biplane. 20 l, Alexander Graham Bell and Wright brothers in Washington D.C., 1910. 95 l, Clifton Hadley's triplane, 1910. 5r, British B.E.2 planes, Upavon Field, 1914. 10r, Wilbur Wright flying first motorized plane, 1903.

1978, Feb. 27 Litho. *Perf. 13x13½*

No.	Type	Description	Unused	Used
719	A107	1 l multicolored	.30	.35
720	A107	2 l multicolored	.30	.35
721	A107	3 l multicolored	.30	.35
722	A107	4 l multicolored	.35	.35
723	A107	5 l multicolored	.35	.35
724	A107	10 l multicolored	.90	.90
725	A107	20 l multicolored	1.75	1.75
726	A107	95 l multicolored	4.25	4.25
727	A107	5r multicolored	11.50	11.50
		Nos. 719-727 (9)	20.00	20.15

Souvenir Sheet

Perf. 14

No.	Type	Description	Unused	Used
728	A107	10r multicolored	16.00	*16.00*

75th anniversary of first motorized airplane.

Edward Jenner, Vaccination Discoverer A108

TV with Maldives Broadcasting Symbol — A109

Designs: 15 l, Foundling Hospital, London, where children were first inoculated, 1743, horiz. 50 l, Newgate Prison, London, where first experiments were carried out, 1721.

1978, Mar. 15 *Perf. 14*

No.	Type	Description	Unused	Used
729	A108	15 l multicolored	.65	.30
730	A108	50 l multicolored	1.25	.65
731	A108	2r multicolored	3.25	3.25
		Nos. 729-731 (3)	5.15	4.20

World eradication of smallpox.

1978, Mar. 29

Designs: 25 l, Circuit pattern. 1.50r, Station control panel, horiz.

No.	Type	Description	Unused	Used
732	A109	15 l multicolored	.65	.65
733	A109	25 l multicolored	.90	.90
734	A109	1.50r multicolored	4.00	4.00
		Nos. 732-734 (3)	5.55	5.55

Inauguration of Maldive Islands television.

Sailing Ship — A110

The Ampulla — A111

Ships: 1 l, Phoenician. 2 l, Two-master. 5 l, Freighter Maldive Trader. 1r, Trading schooner. 1.25r, 4r, Sailing boat. 3r, Barque Bangala. (1 l, 2 l, 5 l, 1.25r, 4r, horiz.)

1978, Apr. 27 Litho. *Perf. 14½*

No.	Type	Description	Unused	Used
735	A110	1 l multicolored	.25	.25
736	A110	2 l multicolored	.25	.25
737	A110	3 l multicolored	.25	.25
738	A110	5 l multicolored	.25	.25
739	A110	1r multicolored	.50	.50
740	A110	1.25r multicolored	.95	.95
741	A110	3r multicolored	1.60	1.60
742	A110	4r multicolored	1.60	1.60
a.		Souvenir sheet of 2	4.50	4.50
		Nos. 735-742 (8)	5.65	5.65

No. 742a contains No. 742 and a 1r stamp in the design of No. 736.

1978, May 15 *Perf. 14*

Designs: 2 l, Scepter with dove. 3 l, Orb with cross. 1.15r, St. Edward's crown. 2r, Scepter with cross. 5r, Queen Elizabeth II. 10r, Anointing spoon.

No.	Type	Description	Unused	Used
743	A111	1 l multicolored	.30	.30
744	A111	2 l multicolored	.30	.30
745	A111	3 l multicolored	.30	.30
746	A111	1.15r multicolored	.30	.30
747	A111	2r multicolored	.40	.40
748	A111	5r multicolored	.70	.70
		Nos. 743-748 (6)	2.30	2.30

Souvenir Sheet

No.	Type	Description	Unused	Used
749	A111	10r multicolored	2.25	2.25

Coronation of Elizabeth II, 25th anniv.

#743-748 were printed in sheets of 40 and in sheets of 3 + label, in changed colors. Labels show coronation regalia.

Capt. James Cook — A112

Designs: 2 l, Kamehameha I statue, Honolulu. 3 l, "Endeavour" and boat. 25 l, Capt. Cook and route of his 3rd voyage. 75 l, "Discovery" and "Resolution," map of Hawaiian Islands, horiz. 1.50r, Capt. Cook's first meeting with Hawaiians, horiz. 5r, "Endeavour." 10r, Capt. Cook's death, horiz.

1978, July 15 Litho. *Perf. 14½*

No.	Type	Description	Unused	Used
750	A112	1 l multicolored	.25	.25
751	A112	2 l multicolored	.25	.25
752	A112	3 l multicolored	.25	.25
753	A112	25 l multicolored	.50	.35
754	A112	75 l multicolored	1.25	1.25
755	A112	1.50r multicolored	1.75	1.75
756	A112	10r multicolored	6.50	*9.00*
		Nos. 750-756 (7)	10.75	*13.10*

Souvenir Sheet

No.	Type	Description	Unused	Used
757	A112	5r multicolored	20.00	*20.00*

Schizophrys Aspera — A113

Maldivian Crabs and Lobster: 2 l, Atergatis floridus. 3 l, Percnon planissimum. 90 l, Portunus granulatus. 1r, Carpilius maculatus. No. 763, Huenia proteus. No. 765, Panulirus longipes, vert. 25r, Etisus laevimanus.

1978, Aug. 30 Litho. *Perf. 14*

No.	Type	Description	Unused	Used
758	A113	1 l multicolored	.25	.25
759	A113	2 l multicolored	.25	.25
760	A113	3 l multicolored	.25	.25
761	A113	90 l multicolored	.60	.40
762	A113	1r multicolored	.60	.40
763	A113	2r multicolored	.90	*1.25*
764	A113	25r multicolored	7.75	*9.50*
		Nos. 758-764 (7)	10.60	*12.30*

Souvenir Sheet

No.	Type	Description	Unused	Used
765	A113	2r multicolored	3.50	3.50

Four Apostles, by Dürer — A114

Paintings by Albrecht Dürer (1471-1528): 20 l, Self-portrait, age 27. 55 l, Virgin and Child with Pear. 1r, Rhinoceros, horiz. 1.80r, Hare. 3r, The Great Piece of Turf. 10r, Columbine.

1978, Oct. 28 Litho. *Perf. 14*

766 A114 10 l multicolored .25 .25
767 A114 20 l multicolored .25 .25
768 A114 55 l multicolored .25 .25
769 A114 1r multicolored .30 .30
770 A114 1.80r multicolored .60 .60
771 A114 3r multicolored .90 .90
Nos. 766-771 (6) 2.55 2.55

Souvenir Sheet

772 A114 10r multicolored 5.75 5.75

Palms and Fishing Boat A115

Designs: 5 l, Montessori School. 10 l, TV tower and ITU emblem, vert. 25 l, Island with beach. 50 l, Boeing 737 over island. 95 l, Walk along the beach. 1.25r, Fishing boat at dawn. 2r, Presidential residence. 3r, Fishermen preparing nets. 5r, Afeefuddin Mosque.

1978, Nov. 11 Litho. *Perf. 14½*

773 A115 1 l multicolored .20 .20
774 A115 5 l multicolored .20 .20
775 A115 10 l multicolored .20 .20
776 A115 25 l multicolored .20 .20
777 A115 50 l multicolored .25 .20
778 A115 95 l multicolored .35 .25
779 A115 1.25r multicolored .60 .50
780 A115 2r multicolored .75 1.00
781 A115 5r multicolored 1.50 2.00
Nos. 773-781 (9) 4.25 4.75

Souvenir Sheet

782 A115 3r multicolored 3.00 3.00

10th anniversary of Republic.

Human Rights Emblem A116

1978, Dec. 10 *Perf. 14*

783 A116 30 l multicolored .25 .25
784 A116 90 l multicolored .40 .50
785 A116 1.80r multicolored .85 1.00
Nos. 783-785 (3) 1.50 1.75

Universal Declaration of Human Rights, 30th anniversary.

Rare Spotted Cowrie — A117

Bellman Delivering Mail — A118

Sea Shells: 2 l, Imperial cone. 3 l, Green turban. 10 l, Giant spider conch. 1r, Leucodon cowrie. 1.80r, Fig cone. 3r, Glory of the sea. 5r, Top vase.

1979, Jan. Litho. *Perf. 14*

786 A117 1 l multicolored .25 .25
787 A117 2 l multicolored .25 .25
788 A117 3 l multicolored .35 .35
789 A117 10 l multicolored .55 .55
790 A117 1r multicolored 2.25 2.25
791 A117 1.80r multicolored 3.00 3.00
792 A117 3r multicolored 5.00 5.00
Nos. 786-792 (7) 11.65 11.65

Souvenir Sheet

793 A117 5r multicolored 14.00 14.00

1979, Feb. 28 Litho. *Perf. 14*

Designs: 2 l, Royal mail coach, 1840, horiz. 3 l, First London letter box, 1855. 1.55r, Great Britain No. 1 and post horn. 5r, Maldive Islands No. 5 and carrier pigeon. 10r, Rowland Hill.

794 A118 1 l multicolored .30 .30
795 A118 2 l multicolored .30 .30
796 A118 3 l multicolored .30 .30
797 A118 1.55r multicolored .45 .45
798 A118 5r multicolored 1.60 1.60
Nos. 794-798 (5) 2.95 2.95

Souvenir Sheet

799 A118 10r multicolored 3.00 3.75

Sir Rowland Hill (1795-1879), originator of penny postage.

For overprints see Nos. 853-855.

Girl with Teddy Bear — A119

IYC Emblem, Boy and: 1.25r, Model boat. 2r, Rocket launcher. 3r, Blimp. 5r, Train.

1979, May 10 Litho. *Perf. 14*

800 A119 5 l multicolored .20 .20
801 A119 1.25r multicolored .45 .45
802 A119 2r multicolored .55 .55
803 A119 3r multicolored .75 .75
Nos. 800-803 (4) 1.95 1.95

Souvenir Sheet

804 A119 5r multicolored 1.75 1.75

International Year of the Child.

White Feathers, by Matisse A120

Paintings by Henri Matisse (1869-1954): 25 l, Joy of Life. 30 l, Eggplants. 1.50r, Harmony in Red. 4r, Water Pitcher. 5r, Still-life.

1979, Aug. 20 Litho. *Perf. 14*

805 A120 20 l multicolored .55 .55
806 A120 25 l multicolored .55 .55
807 A120 30 l multicolored .55 .55
808 A120 1.50r multicolored 1.10 1.10
809 A120 5r multicolored 3.00 3.00
Nos. 805-809 (5) 5.75 5.75

Souvenir Sheet

810 A120 4r multicolored 4.00 4.00

Sari and Mosque — A121

Gloriosa Superba — A122

National Costumes: 75 l, Sashed apron dress. Male Harbor. 90 l, Serape with necklace, radar station. 95 l, Flowered dress, mosque and minaret.

1979, Aug. 22 Litho. *Perf. 14*

811 A121 50 l multicolored .20 .20
812 A121 75 l multicolored .20 .20
813 A121 90 l multicolored .35 .35
814 A121 95 l multicolored .40 .40
Nos. 811-814 (4) 1.15 1.15

1979, Oct. 29 Litho. *Perf. 14*

815 A122 1 l shown .20 .20
816 A122 3 l Hibiscus .20 .20
817 A122 50 l Barringtonia asiatica .20 .20
818 A122 1r Abutilon indicum .40 .40
819 A122 5r Guettarda speciosa 1.75 1.75
Nos. 815-819 (5) 2.75 2.75

Souvenir Sheet

820 A122 4r Pandanus odoratissimus 2.50 2.50

Maldive wildflowers.

Handicraft Exhibition A123

1979, Nov. 11

821 A123 5 l shown .20 .20
822 A123 10 l Jar and cup .20 .20
823 A123 1.30r Tortoise-shell jewelry .55 .55
824 A123 2r Wooden boxes .75 .75
Nos. 821-824 (4) 1.70 1.70

Souvenir Sheet

825 A123 5r Bracelets, necklace 1.75 1.75

Postal Scenes A123a

1 l, Goofy delivering package. 2 l, Mickey at mailbox. 3 l, Goofy buried in letters. 4 l, Minnie Mouse, Pluto. 5 l, Mickey Mouse on skates. 10 l, Donald Duck at mailbox. 15 l, Chip and Dale carrying letter. 1.50r, Donald Duck on unicycle. 4r, Pluto at mailbox. 5r, Donald Duck wheeling crate.

1979, Dec. Litho. *Perf. 11*

826 A123a 1 l multicolored .25 .25
827 A123a 2 l multicolored .25 .25
828 A123a 3 l multicolored .25 .25
829 A123a 4 l multicolored .25 .25
830 A123a 5 l multicolored .25 .25
831 A123a 10 l multicolored .25 .25
832 A123a 15 l multicolored .25 .25
833 A123a 1.50r multicolored .85 .85
834 A123a 5r multicolored 2.40 *2.75*
Nos. 826-834 (9) 5.00 *5.35*

Souvenir Sheet

835 A123a 4r multicolored 7.50 7.50

National Day A124

Designs: 5 l, Post Ramadan dancing. 15 l, Festival of Eeduu. 95 l, Sultan's ceremonial band. 2r, Music festival. 5r, Sword dance.

1980, Jan. 19 Litho. *Perf. 14*

836 A124 5 l multicolored .20 .20
837 A124 15 l multicolored .20 .20
838 A124 95 l multicolored .45 .45
839 A124 2r multicolored .90 .90
Nos. 836-839 (4) 1.75 1.75

Souvenir Sheet

840 A124 5r multicolored 2.00 2.00

Leatherback Turtle — A125

1980, Feb. 17 Litho. *Perf. 14*

841 A125 1 l shown .20 .20
842 A125 2 l Flatback turtle .20 .20
843 A125 5 l Hawksbill turtle .20 .20
844 A125 10 l Loggerhead turtle .20 .20
845 A125 75 l Olive ridley .40 .40
846 A125 10r Atlantic ridley 5.00 5.00
Nos. 841-846 (6) 6.20 6.20

Souvenir Sheet

847 A125 4r Green turtle 2.75 2.75

Paul Harris in Rotary Emblem — A126

1980, Mar. Litho. *Perf. 14*

848 A126 75 l shown .40 .40
849 A126 90 l Family .45 .45
850 A126 1r Grain .50 .50
851 A126 10r Caduceus 4.00 4.00
Nos. 848-851 (4) 5.35 5.35

Souvenir Sheet

852 A126 5r Anniversary emblem 2.00 2.00

Rotary International, 75th anniversary.

Nos. 797-799 Overprinted "LONDON 1980"

1980, May 6 Litho. *Perf. 14*

853 A118 1.55r multicolored 2.00 1.75
854 A118 5r multicolored 5.50 5.00

Souvenir Sheet

855 A118 10r multicolored 9.00 9.00

London 1980 International Stamp Exhibition, May 6-14. Sheet margin overprinted "Earls Court—London 6-14 May 1980."

Swimming, Moscow '80 Emblem — A127

1980, June 4 Litho. *Perf. 14*

856 A127 10 l shown .20 .20
857 A127 50 l Sprinting .25 .25
858 A127 3r Shot put 1.25 1.25
859 A127 4r High jump 1.50 1.50
Nos. 856-859 (4) 3.20 3.20

Souvenir Sheet

860 A127 5r Weight lifting 2.50 2.50

22nd Summer Olympic Games, Moscow, July 19-Aug. 3.

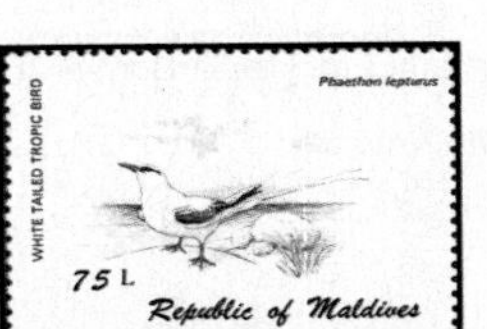

White-tailed Tropic Bird — A128

1980, July 10 Litho. *Perf. 14*

861 A128 75 l shown .30 .25
862 A128 95 l Sooty tern .40 .35
863 A128 1r Brown noddy .40 .35
864 A128 1.55r Eurasian curlew .75 .75
865 A128 2r Wilson's petrel .85 .85
866 A128 4r Caspian tern 1.75 1.75
Nos. 861-866 (6) 4.45 4.30

Souvenir Sheet

867 A128 5r Red-footed & brown boobies 10.00 *10.00*

Seal of Sultan Ibrahim II (1720-1750) — A129

Sultans' Seals: 2 l, Mohamed Imadudeen II (1704-1720). 5 l, Mohamed Bin Haji Ali (1692-1701). 1r, Kuda Mohamed Rasgefaanu (1687-1691). 2r, Ibrahim Iskander I (1648-1687). 3r, Ibrahim Iskander, second seal.

1980, July 26

868 A129 1 l violet brn & blk .20 .20
869 A129 2 l violet brn & blk .20 .20
870 A129 5 l violet brn & blk .20 .20
871 A129 1r violet brn & blk .50 .50
872 A129 2r violet brn & blk .60 .60
Nos. 868-872 (5) 1.70 1.70

Souvenir Sheet

873 A129 3r violet brn & blk 1.25 1.25

Queen Mother Elizabeth, 80th Birthday A130

1980, Sept. 29 ***Perf. 14***

874 A130 4r multicolored 2.00 2.00

Souvenir Sheet

Perf. 12

875 A130 5r multicolored 2.25 2.25

Munnaaru Tower A131

1980, Nov. 9 **Litho.** ***Perf. 15***

876 A131 5 l shown .20 .20
877 A131 10 l Hukuru Miskiiy Mosque .20 .20
878 A131 30 l Medhuziyaaraiy Shrine .20 .20
879 A131 55 l Koran verses on wooden tablets .30 .30
880 A131 90 l Mother teaching son .45 .45
Nos. 876-880 (5) 1.35 1.35

Souvenir Sheet

881 A131 2r Map and arms of Maldives 1.00 1.00

Hegira (Pilgrimage Year).

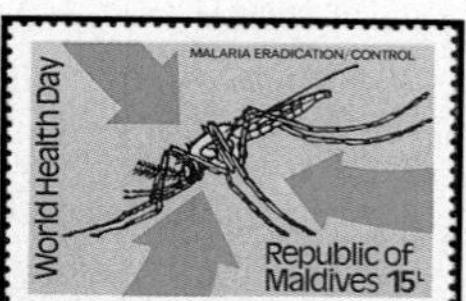

Malaria Eradication Control — A132

1980, Nov. 30 ***Perf. 14***

882 A132 15 l shown .30 .30
883 A132 25 l Balanced diet .30 .30
884 A132 1.50r Oral hygiene 1.00 1.00
885 A132 5r Clinic visit 3.50 3.50
Nos. 882-885 (4) 5.10 5.10

Souvenir Sheet

886 A132 4r like #885 2.50 2.50

World Health Day. No. 886 shows design of No. 885 in changed colors.

The Cheshire Cat — A133

Designs: Scenes from Walt Disney's Alice in Wonderland. 5r, vert.

1980, Dec. 22 ***Perf. 11***

887 A133 1 l multicolored .25 .25
888 A133 2 l multicolored .25 .25
889 A133 3 l multicolored .25 .25
890 A133 4 l multicolored .30 .30
891 A133 5 l multicolored .30 .30
892 A133 10 l multicolored .30 .30
893 A133 15 l multicolored .30 .30
894 A133 2.50r multicolored 1.75 1.75
895 A133 4r multicolored 3.00 3.00
Nos. 887-895 (9) 6.70 6.70

Souvenir Sheet

896 A133 5r multicolored 6.75 *6.75*

Ridley Turtle A134

1980, Dec. 29 **Litho.** ***Perf. 14***

897 A134 90 l shown 2.50 .50
898 A134 1.25r Angel flake fish 3.25 1.10
899 A134 2r Spiny lobster 4.00 1.50
Nos. 897-899 (3) 9.75 3.10

Souvenir Sheet

900 A134 4r Fish 5.00 5.00

Tomb of Ghaazee Muhammad Thakurufaan — A135

National Day (Furniture and Palace of Muhammad Thakurufaan): 20 l, Hanging lamp, 16th century, vert. 30 l, Chair, vert. 95 l, Utheem Palace. 10r, Couch, vert.

1981, Jan. 7 ***Perf. 15***

901 A135 10 l multicolored .20 .20
902 A135 20 l multicolored .20 .20
903 A135 30 l multicolored .20 .20
904 A135 95 l multicolored .40 .40
905 A135 10r multicolored 4.00 4.00
Nos. 901-905 (5) 5.00 5.00

Common Design Types pictured following the introduction.

Royal Wedding Issue

Common Design Type

1981, June 22 **Litho.** ***Perf. 14***

906 CD331a 1r Couple .30 .30
907 CD331a 2r Buckingham Palace .30 .30
908 CD331a 5r Charles .40 .40
Nos. 906-908 (3) 1.00 1.00

Souvenir Sheet

909 CD331 10r Royal state coach 1.00 1.00

Nos. 906-908 also printed in sheets of 5 plus label, perf. 12, in changed colors.

Majlis Chamber, 1932 A136

50th Anniv. of Citizens' Majlis (Grievance Rights); 1r, Sultan Muhammed Shamsuddin III (instituted system, 1932), vert. 4r, Constitution, 1932.

1981, June 27 ***Perf. 15***

910 A136 95 l multicolored .45 .45
911 A136 1r multicolored .50 .50

Souvenir Sheet

912 A136 4r multicolored 3.00 3.00

Self-portrait with Palette, by Picasso (1881-1973) A137

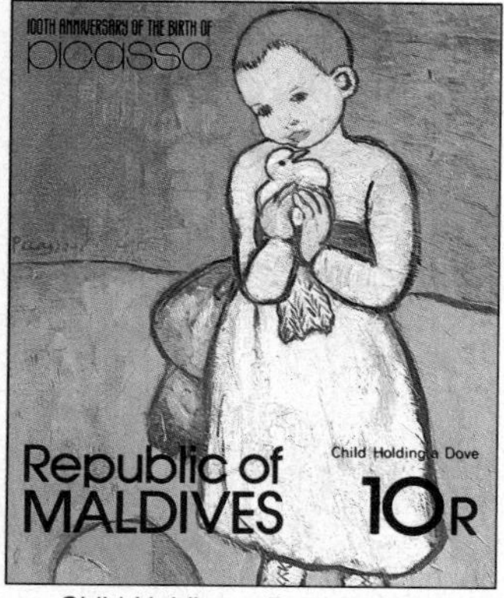

Child Holding a Dove — A138

1981, Aug. 26 **Litho.** ***Perf. 14***

913 A137 5 l shown .40 .40
914 A137 10 l Woman in Blue .40 .40
915 A137 25 l Boy with a Pipe .40 .40
916 A137 30 l Card Player .40 .40
917 A137 90 l Sailor .50 .50
918 A137 3r Self-portrait 1.50 1.50
919 A137 5r Harlequin 2.50 2.50

Imperf

920 A138 10r shown 4.75 4.75
Nos. 913-920 (8) 10.85 10.85

No. 5 on Airmail Cover A139

1981, Sept. 9 **Litho.** ***Perf. 14***

921 A139 25 l multicolored .20 .20
922 A139 75 l multicolored .30 .30
923 A139 5r multicolored 1.25 1.25
Nos. 921-923 (3) 1.75 1.75

Postal service, 75th anniv.

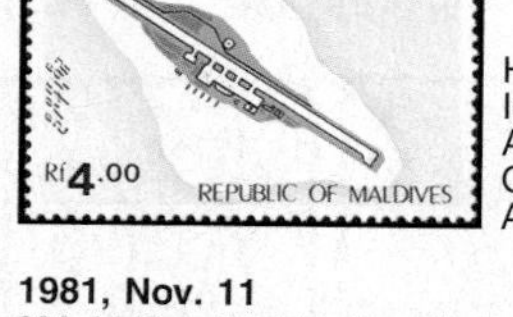

Hulule Intl. Airport Opening A140

1981, Nov. 11

924 A140 5 l Jet taking off .20 .20
925 A140 20 l Passengers leaving jet .20 .20
926 A140 1.80r Refueling 1.00 1.00
927 A140 4r shown 1.50 *2.00*
Nos. 924-927 (4) 2.90 *3.40*

Souvenir Sheet

928 A140 5r Terminal 3.50 3.50

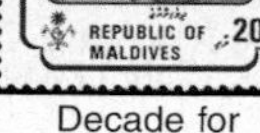

Intl. Year of the Disabled — A141

Decade for Women — A142

1981, Nov. 18 **Litho.** ***Perf. 14½***

929 A141 2 l Homer .25 .25
930 A141 5 l Cervantes .30 .30
931 A141 1r Beethoven 2.25 2.25
932 A141 5r Van Gogh 4.00 *4.00*
Nos. 929-932 (4) 6.80 *6.80*

Souvenir Sheet

933 A141 4r Helen Keller, Anne Sullivan 4.75 *4.75*

1981, Nov. 25 ***Perf. 14***

934 A142 20 l Preparing fish .20 .20
935 A142 90 l 16th cent. woman .45 .45
936 A142 1r Tending yam crop .50 .50
937 A142 2r Making coir rope .75 .75
Nos. 934-937 (4) 1.90 1.90

Fishermen's Day — A143

1981, Dec. 10

938 A143 5 l Collecting bait .60 .25
939 A143 15 l Fishing boats 1.10 .25
940 A143 90 l Fisherman holding catch 1.60 .55
941 A143 1.30r Sorting fish 2.25 .85
Nos. 938-941 (4) 5.55 1.90

Souvenir Sheet

942 A143 3r Loading fish for export 2.25 2.25

World Food Day A144

1981, Dec. 30 **Litho.** ***Perf. 14***

943 A144 10 l Breadfruit .35 .25
944 A144 25 l Hen, chicks .90 .25
945 A144 30 l Corn .90 .25
946 A144 75 l Skipjack tuna 2.10 .45
947 A144 1r Pumpkins 2.50 .60
948 A144 2r Coconuts 3.00 1.75
Nos. 943-948 (6) 9.75 3.55

Souvenir Sheet

949 A144 5r Eggplants 3.50 3.50

50th Anniv. of Walt Disney's Pluto (1980) A145

1982, Mar. 29 **Litho.** ***Perf. 13½x14***

950 A145 4r Scene from Chain Gang, 1930 3.75 3.50

Souvenir Sheet

951 A145 6r The Pointer, 1939 5.25 5.25

Princess Diana Issue
Common Design Type

1982, July 15 Litho. *Perf. 14½x14*
952 CD332 95 l Balmoral .50 .50
953 CD332 3r Honeymoon 1.50 1.50
954 CD332 5r Diana 2.50 2.50
Nos. 952-954 (3) 4.50 4.50

Souvenir Sheet
955 CD332 8r Diana, diff. 3.50 3.50

#952-954 also issued in sheetlets of 5 plus label.
For overprints and surcharges see Nos. 966-969, 1050, 1052, 1054, 1056.

Scouting Year A146

1982, Aug. 9 Litho. *Perf. 14*
956 A146 1.30r Saluting .50 .50
957 A146 1.80r Fire building .75 .75
958 A146 4r Lifesaving 1.50 1.50
959 A146 5r Map reading 2.00 2.00
Nos. 956-959 (4) 4.75 4.75

Souvenir Sheet
960 A146 10r Flag, emblem 3.50 3.50

1982 World Cup — A147

TB Bacillus Cent. — A148

Various soccer players.

1982, Oct. 4 Litho. *Perf. 14*
961 A147 90 l multicolored 1.50 .65
962 A147 1.50r multicolored 2.00 1.10
963 A147 3r multicolored 3.00 2.25
964 A147 5r multicolored 3.75 3.75
Nos. 961-964 (4) 10.25 7.75

Souvenir Sheet
965 A147 10r multicolored 6.00 6.00

Nos. 952-955 Overprinted: "ROYAL BABY/21.6.82"

1982, Oct. 18 *Perf. 14½x14*
966 CD332 95 l multicolored .50 .50
967 CD332 3r multicolored 1.50 1.50
968 CD332 5r multicolored 2.50 2.50
Nos. 966-968 (3) 4.50 4.50

Souvenir Sheet
969 CD332 8r multicolored 5.00 5.00

Birth of Prince William of Wales, June 21.
#966-968 also issued in sheetlets of 5 + label.
For surcharges see #1051, 1053, 1055, 1057.

1982, Nov. 22 *Perf. 14½*
970 A148 5 l Koch isolating bacillus .20 .20
971 A148 15 l Slide, microscope .20 .20
972 A148 95 l Koch, 1905 .20 .20
973 A148 3r Koch, book illus. plates 1.25 1.25
Nos. 970-973 (4) 1.85 1.85

Souvenir Sheet
974 A148 5r Koch in lab 1.75 1.75

Natl. Education — A149

Designs: 90 l, Basic education scheme, 1980-85. 95 l, Formal primary education. 1.30r, Teacher training. 2.50r, Educational materials production. 6r, Thanna typewriter.

1982, Nov. 15
975 A149 90 l multicolored .25 .25
976 A149 95 l multicolored .25 .25
977 A149 1.30r multicolored .35 .35
978 A149 2.50r multicolored .60 .60
Nos. 975-978 (4) 1.45 1.45

Souvenir Sheet
979 A149 6r multicolored 1.75 1.75

Manned Flight Bicentenary — A150

1983, July 28 Litho. *Perf. 14*
980 A150 90 l Blohm & Voss Ha-139 1.00 1.00
981 A150 1.45r Macchi Castoldi MC-72 1.90 1.90
982 A150 4r Boeing F4B-3 5.00 5.00
983 A150 5r Le France 6.25 6.25
Nos. 980-983 (4) 14.15 14.15

Souvenir Sheet
984 A150 10r Nadar's Le Geant 4.75 4.75

For overprints see Nos. 1020-1022.

Roughtooth Dolphin — A151

1983, Sept. 6 Litho. *Perf. 14*
985 A151 30 l shown .60 .60
986 A151 40 l Indopacific humpback dolphin .60 .60
987 A151 4r Finless porpoise 6.00 6.00
988 A151 6r Pygmy sperm whale 9.00 9.00
Nos. 985-988 (4) 16.20 16.20

Souvenir Sheet
989 A151 5r Striped dolphins 7.75 7.75

Classic Cars A152

1983, Aug. 15 Litho. *Perf. 14½x15*
990 A152 5 l Curved Dash Oldsmobile, 1902 .30 .30
991 A152 30 l Aston Martin Tourer, 1932 .30 .30
992 A152 40 l Lamborghini Miura, 1966 .30 .30
993 A152 1r Mercedes-Benz 300sl, 1954 .75 .75
994 A152 1.45r Stutz Bearcat, 1913 1.10 1.10
995 A152 5r Lotus Elite, 1958 3.75 3.75
Nos. 990-995 (6) 6.50 6.50

Souvenir Sheet
996 A152 10r Grand Prix Sunbeam, 1924 9.00 9.00

World Communications Year — A153

50 l, Dish antenna. 1r, Mail transport. 2r, Ship-to-shore communications. 10r, Land-air communications. 20r, Telephone calls.

1983, Oct. 9 *Perf. 14*
997 A153 50 l multicolored .30 .30
998 A153 1r multicolored .60 .60
999 A153 2r multicolored 1.10 1.10
1000 A153 10r multicolored 6.00 6.00
Nos. 997-1000 (4) 8.00 8.00

Souvenir Sheet
1001 A153 20r multicolored 6.00 6.00

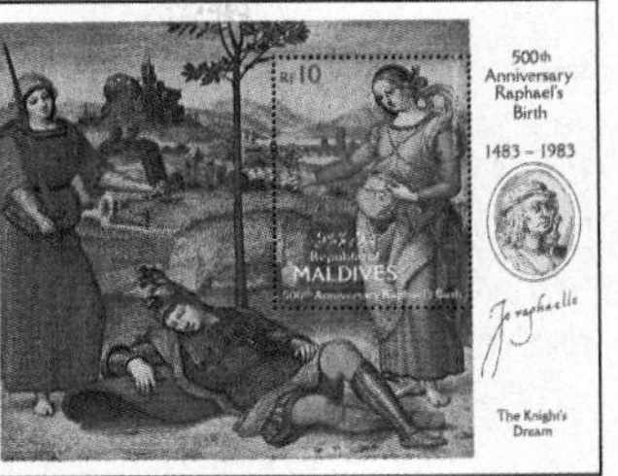

Raphael, 500th Birth Anniv. — A154

1983, Oct. 25 Litho. *Perf. 13½x14*
1002 A154 90 l La Donna Gravida .50 .50
1003 A154 3r Jean of Aragon 1.50 1.50
1004 A154 4r The Woman with the Unicorn 2.00 2.00
1005 A154 6r La Muta 3.00 3.00
Nos. 1002-1005 (4) 7.00 7.00

Souvenir Sheet
1006 A154 10r The Knights Dream 4.75 4.75

Intl. Palestinian Solidarity Day — A155

Various refugees, mosque.

1983, Nov. 29 Litho. *Perf. 14*
1007 A155 4r multicolored 2.00 2.00
1008 A155 5r multicolored 2.50 2.50
1009 A155 6r multicolored 3.00 3.00
Nos. 1007-1009 (3) 7.50 7.50

Natl. Development Programs — A156

1983, Dec. 10 Litho. *Perf. 13½x14*
1010 A156 7 l Education .20 .20
1011 A156 10 l Health care .20 .20
1012 A156 5r Food production 2.50 2.50
1013 A156 6r Fishing industry 3.00 3.00
Nos. 1010-1013 (4) 5.90 5.90

Souvenir Sheet
1014 A156 10r Inter-atoll transportation 3.00 3.00

A157

Tourism — A158

1984, Feb. *Perf. 14*
1015 A157 50 l Baseball .25 .25
1016 A157 1.55r Swimming .80 .80
1017 A157 3r Judo 1.50 1.50
1018 A157 4r Shot put 2.00 2.00
Nos. 1015-1018 (4) 4.55 4.55

Souvenir Sheet
1019 A157 10r Handball 4.75 4.75

23rd Olympic Games, Los Angeles, 7/28-8/12.
For overprints see Nos. 1090-1094.

Nos. 982-984 Overprinted: "19th UPU/CONGRESS HAMBURG"

1984 Litho. *Perf. 14*
1020 A150 4r multicolored 2.00 2.00
1021 A150 5r multicolored 2.50 2.50

Souvenir Sheet
1022 A150 10r multicolored 4.75 4.75

1984, Sept. 21 Litho. *Perf. 14½*
1023 A158 7 l Island resorts .40 .40
1024 A158 15 l Cruising .40 .40
1025 A158 20 l Snorkelling .40 .40
1026 A158 2r Wind surfing 1.00 1.00
1027 A158 4r Scuba diving 2.10 2.10
1028 A158 6r Night fishing 3.25 3.25
1029 A158 8r Big game fishing 4.25 4.25
1030 A158 10r Nature (turtle) 5.25 5.25
Nos. 1023-1030 (8) 17.05 17.05

50th Anniv. of Donald Duck — A160

Scenes from various cartoons and movies.

1984, Nov. Litho. *Perf. 14*
1040 A160 3 l multi .25 .25
1041 A160 4 l multi .25 .25
1042 A160 5 l multi .25 .25
1043 A160 10 l multi .25 .25
1044 A160 15 l multi .25 .25
1045 A160 25 l multi .25 .25
1045A A160 5r multi, perf. 12x12½ 2.00 2.00
1046 A160 8r multi 3.00 3.00
1047 A160 10r multi 4.00 4.00
Nos. 1040-1047 (9) 10.50 10.50

Souvenir Sheets
1048 A160 15r multi 5.00 5.00
1049 A160 15r multi 5.00 5.00

Nos. 952-955, 966-969 Surcharged

1984, July Litho. *Perf. 14½x14*
1050 CD332 1.45r on 95 l #952 *2.50 2.00*
1051 CD332 1.45r on 95 l #966 *2.50 2.00*
1052 CD332 1.45r on 3r #953 *2.50 2.00*
1053 CD332 1.45r on 3r #967 *2.50 2.00*
1054 CD332 1.45r on 5r #954 *2.50 2.00*
1055 CD332 1.45r on 5r #968 *2.50 2.00*
Nos. 1050-1055 (6) *15.00 12.00*

Souvenir Sheet
1056 CD332 1.45r on 8r #955 *10.00 8.00*
1057 CD332 1.45r on 8r #969 *10.00 8.00*

Namibia Day A161

1984, Aug. 26 *Perf. 15*
1058 A161 6r Breaking chain 1.75 1.75
1059 A161 8r Family, rising sun 2.25 2.25

Souvenir Sheet
1060 A161 10r Map, sun 3.50 3.50

Ausipex '84 A162

1984, Sept. 21

1061 A162 5r Frangipani 2.50 2.50
1062 A162 10r Cooktown orchid 5.25 5.25

Souvenir Sheet

1063 A162 15r Sun orchids 12.00 12.00

150th Birth Anniv. of Edgar Degas — A163

1984, Oct. Litho. *Perf. 14*

1064 A163 75 l Portrait of Edmond Iduranty .20 .20
1065 A163 2r Portrait of James Tissot .55 .55
1066 A163 5r Portrait of Achille Degas 1.40 1.40
1067 A163 10r Lady with Chrysanthemums 2.75 2.75
Nos. 1064-1067 (4) 4.90 4.90

Souvenir Sheet

1068 A163 15r Self-Portrait 5.00 5.00

Opening of Islamic Center A164

1984, Nov. 11 Litho. *Perf. 15*

1069 A164 2r Mosque .70 .70
1070 A164 5r Mosque, minaret, vert. 1.75 1.75

40th Anniv., International Civil Aviation Organization — A165

1984, Nov. 19 Litho. *Perf. 14*

1071 A165 7 l Boeing 737 .35 .35
1072 A165 4r Lockheed L-1011 2.40 2.40
1073 A165 6r McDonnell Douglas DC-10 3.25 3.25
1074 A165 8r Lockheed L-1011 4.00 4.00
Nos. 1071-1074 (4) 10.00 10.00

Souvenir Sheet

1075 A165 15r Shorts SC7 Skyvan 5.75 5.75

450th Anniv. of the Death of Correggio — A166

1984, Dec. 10 Litho. *Perf. 14*

1076 A166 5r Detail from The Day 1.40 1.40
1077 A166 10r Detail from The Night 2.75 2.75

Souvenir Sheet

1078 A166 15r Portrait of a Man 5.25 5.25

John J. Audubon A167

Illustrations from Audubon's Birds of America.

1985, Mar. 9 Litho. *Perf. 14*

1079 A167 3r Flesh-footed shearwater, vert. 2.25 1.25
1080 A167 3.50r Little grebe 2.75 1.40
1081 A167 4r Great cormorant, vert. 2.75 1.50
1082 A167 4.50r White-faced storm petrel 2.75 1.60
Nos. 1079-1082 (4) 10.50 5.75

Souvenir Sheet

1083 A167 15r Red-necked phalarope 5.50 5.50

See Nos. 1195-1204.

Natl. Security Services — A168

1985, June 6 Litho. *Perf. 14*

1084 A168 15 l Drill .50 .30
1085 A168 20 l Combat training .50 .30
1086 A168 1r Fire fighting 2.25 .45
1087 A168 2r Coast guard 2.75 .90
1088 A168 10r Parade, vert. 3.50 *4.50*
Nos. 1084-1088 (5) 9.50 6.45

Souvenir Sheet

1089 A168 10r Badge, cannon 4.00 4.00

Nos. 1015-1019 Ovptd. with Country or "Gold Medalist," Winner and Nation in 3 Lines

1985, July 17

1090 A157 50 l Japan .30 .30
1091 A157 1.55r Theresa Andrews .60 .60
1092 A157 3r Frank Wieneke 1.25 1.25
1093 A157 4r Claudia Loch 1.75 1.75
Nos. 1090-1093 (4) 3.90 3.90

Souvenir Sheet

1094 A157 10r US 3.00 3.00

Queen Mother, 85th Birthday A169

Johann Sebastian Bach, Composer A170

1985-86 *Perf. 14, 12 (1r, 4r, 10r)*

1095 A169 1r Wearing tiara .50 .50
1096 A169 3r like 1r .60 .60
1097 A169 4r At Middlesex Hospital, horiz. .70 .70
1098 A169 5r like 4r .95 .95
1099 A169 7r Wearing fur stole 1.25 1.25
1100 A169 10r like 7r 1.90 1.90
Nos. 1095-1100 (6) 5.90 5.90

Souvenir Sheet

1101 A169 15r With Prince of Wales 3.50 3.50

Issued: 1r, 4r, 10r, 1/4/86; 3r, 5r, 7r, 15r, 8/20/85. #1095, 1097, 1100 printed in sheets of 5 + label.

1985, Sept. 3 *Perf. 14*

Portrait, Invention No. 1 in C Major and: 15 l, Lira da Braccio. 2r, Tenor oboe. 4r, Serpent. 10r, Table organ.

1102 A170 15 l multi .25 .25
1103 A170 2r multi .70 .70
1104 A170 4r multi 1.25 1.25
1105 A170 10r multi 2.75 2.75
Nos. 1102-1105 (4) 4.95 4.95

Souvenir Sheet

1106 A170 15r Portrait 4.50 4.50

Ships A171

1985, Sept. 23

1107 A171 3 l Masodi .25 .25
1108 A171 5 l Naalu Baththeli .25 .25
1109 A171 10 l Addu Odi .30 .30
1110 A171 2.60r Masdhoni, 2nd generation 1.40 1.40
1111 A171 2.70r Masdhoni 1.40 1.40
1112 A171 3r Baththeli Dhoni 1.60 1.60
1113 A171 5r Inter 1 2.50 2.50
1114 A171 10r Yacht Dhoni 5.00 5.00
Nos. 1107-1114 (8) 12.70 12.70

For surcharge, see No. 1493B.

World Tourism Org., 10th Anniv. A172

1985, Oct. 2

1115 A172 6r Wind surfing 2.50 2.50
1116 A172 8r Scuba diving 3.50 3.50

Souvenir Sheet

1117 A172 15r Kuda Hithi Resort 6.00 6.00

Maldives Admission to UN, 20th Anniv. — A173

1985, Oct. 24

1118 A173 20 l shown .25 .25
1119 A173 15r Flags, UN building 3.75 3.75

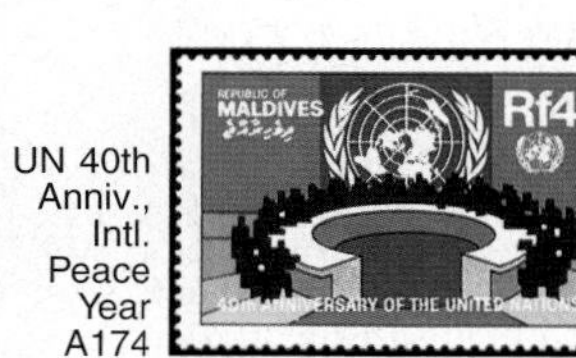

UN 40th Anniv., Intl. Peace Year A174

1985, Oct. 24 Litho. *Perf. 14*

1120 A174 15 l UN Building .25 .25
1121 A174 2r IPY emblem .65 .65
1122 A174 4r Security Council 1.10 1.10
1123 A174 10r Lion, lamb 1.90 1.90
Nos. 1120-1123 (4) 3.90 3.90

Souvenir Sheet

1124 A174 15r UN Building, diff. 3.50 3.50

Nos. 1120-1121, 1123-1124, vert.

Intl. Youth Year A175

1985, Nov. 20 *Perf. 15*

1125 A175 90 l Culture .35 .35
1126 A175 6r Games 1.40 1.40
1127 A175 10r Community service, vert. 2.00 *2.75*
Nos. 1125-1127 (3) 3.75 4.50

Souvenir Sheet

1128 A175 15r Youth camp, vert. 3.50 3.50

Summit Nations Flags, Dedication by Pres. Maumoon — A176

1985, Dec. 8 *Perf. 14*

1129 A176 3r multicolored 2.50 2.50

South Asian Regional Cooperation, SARC, 1st Summit, Dec. 7-8, 1985.

Tuna A177

1985, Dec. 10

1130 A177 25 l Frigate .45 .45
1131 A177 75 l Little tuna .90 .90
1132 A177 3r Dogtooth 2.75 2.75
1133 A177 5r Yellowfin 3.25 3.25
Nos. 1130-1133 (4) 7.35 7.35

Souvenir Sheet

1134 A177 15r Skipjack 7.50 7.50

Fisherman's Day.

Mark Twain, American Novelist A178

Disney characters and Twain quotes.

1985, Dec. 21

1135 A178 2 l multicolored .25 .25
1136 A178 3 l multicolored .25 .25
1137 A178 4 l multicolored .30 .30
1138 A178 20 l multicolored .50 .50
1139 A178 4r multicolored 1.60 1.60
1140 A178 13r multicolored 6.00 6.00
Nos. 1135-1140 (6) 8.90 8.90

Souvenir Sheet

1141 A178 15r multicolored 8.00 8.00

Intl. Youth Year. 4r issued in sheet of 8.

The Brothers Grimm — A179

Disney characters in Doctor Knowall.

1985, Dec. 21

1142 A179 1 l multicolored .25 .25
1143 A179 5 l multicolored .25 .25
1144 A179 10 l multicolored .30 .30
1145 A179 15 l multicolored .30 .30

1146 A179 3r multicolored 1.40 1.40
1147 A179 14r multicolored 6.75 6.75
Nos. 1142-1147 (6) 9.25 9.25

Souvenir Sheet

1148 A179 15r multicolored 7.50 7.50

3r issued in sheets of 8.

World Disarmament Day — A180

1986, Feb. 10 ***Perf. 14½x14***
1149 A180 1.50r shown — —
1150 A180 10r Dove — —

Halley's Comet A181

Designs: 20 l, NASA space telescope. 1.50r, Giotto space probe. 2r, Plant-A probe, Japan. 4r, Edmond Halley, Stonehenge. 5r, Vega probe, USSR. 15r, Comet over Male.

1986, Apr. 29
1151 A181 20 l multicolored .65 .65
1152 A181 1.50r multicolored 1.40 1.40
1153 A181 2r multicolored 1.75 1.75
1154 A181 4r multicolored 2.50 2.50
1155 A181 5r multicolored 2.50 2.50
Nos. 1151-1155 (5) 8.80 8.80

Souvenir Sheet

1156 A181 15r multicolored 9.00 9.00

See Nos. 1210-1215.

Statue of Liberty, Cent. A182

Detail of statue and: 50 l, Walter Gropius (1883-1969), architect. 70 l, John Lennon (1940-1980), musician. 1r, George Balanchine (1904-1983), choreographer. 10r, Franz Werfel (1890-1945), writer. 15r, Close-up of statue, vert.

1986, May 5
1157 A182 50 l multicolored .45 .45
1158 A182 70 l multicolored 1.60 1.60
1159 A182 1r multicolored 1.75 1.75
1160 A182 10r multicolored 4.00 4.00
Nos. 1157-1160 (4) 7.80 7.80

Souvenir Sheet

1161 A182 15r multicolored 8.00 8.00

AMERIPEX '86 — A183

US stamps and Disney portrayals of American legends: 3 l, No. 1317, Johnny Appleseed. 4 l, No. 1122, Paul Bunyan. 5 l, No. 1381, Casey at the Bat. 10 l, No. 1548, Tales of Sleepy Hollow. 15 l, No. 922, John Henry. 20 l, No. 1061, Windwagon Smith. 13r, No. 1409, Mike Fink. 14r, No. 993, Casey Jones. No. 1170, Remember the Alamo, No. 1330. No. 1171, Pocahontas, Nos. 328-330.

1986, May 22 ***Perf. 11***
1162 A183 3 l multicolored .25 .25
1163 A183 4 l multicolored .25 .25
1164 A183 5 l multicolored .30 .30
1165 A183 10 l multicolored .30 .30
1166 A183 15 l multicolored .30 .30
1167 A183 20 l multicolored .30 .30
1168 A183 13r multicolored 8.75 8.75
1169 A183 14r multicolored 10.00 10.00
Nos. 1162-1169 (8) 20.45 20.45

Souvenir Sheets

Perf. 14

1170 A183 15r multicolored 8.50 8.50
1171 A183 15r multicolored 8.50 8.50

Queen Elizabeth II, 60th Birthday
Common Design Type

1986, May 29 ***Perf. 14***
1172 CD339 1r Girl Guides' rally, 1938 .25 .25
1173 CD339 2r Canada visit, 1985 .50 .50
1174 CD339 12r At Sandringham, 1970 2.75 2.75
Nos. 1172-1174 (3) 3.50 3.50

Souvenir Sheet

1175 CD339 15r Royal Lodge, 1940 4.50 4.50

For overprints see Nos. 1288-1291.

1986 World Cup Soccer Championships, Mexico — A184

Various soccer plays.

1986, June 18 **Litho.** ***Perf. 14***
1176 A184 15 l multicolored .85 .85
1177 A184 2r multicolored 2.50 2.50
1178 A184 4r multicolored 4.50 4.50
1179 A184 10r multicolored 8.00 8.00
Nos. 1176-1179 (4) 15.85 15.85

Souvenir Sheet

1180 A184 15r multicolored 7.50 7.50

For overprints see Nos. 1205-1209.

Royal Wedding Issue, 1986
Common Design Type

Designs: 10 l, Prince Andrew and Sarah Ferguson. 2r, Andrew. 12r, Andrew on ship's deck in uniform. 15r, Couple, diff.

1986, July 23
1181 CD340 10 l multi .25 .25
1182 CD340 2r multi .70 .70
1183 CD340 12r multi 4.00 4.00
Nos. 1181-1183 (3) 4.95 4.95

Souvenir Sheet

1184 CD340 15r multi 5.25 5.25

Marine Life A185

1986, Sept. 22 **Litho.** ***Perf. 15***
1185 A185 50 l Sea fan, moorish idol 1.75 1.75
1186 A185 90 l Regal angelfish 2.50 2.50
1187 A185 1r Anemone fish 2.75 2.75
1188 A185 2r Stinging coral, tiger cowrie 3.00 3.00
1189 A185 3r Emperor angelfish, staghorn coral 3.50 3.50
1190 A185 4r Black-naped tern 3.00 3.00
1191 A185 5r Fiddler crab, staghorn coral 3.00 3.00
1192 A185 10r Hawksbill turtle 3.75 3.75
Nos. 1185-1192 (8) 23.25 23.25

Souvenir Sheets

1193 A185 15r Trumpet fish 9.50 9.50
1194 A185 15r Long-nosed butterflyfish 9.50 9.50

Nos. 1185-1187, 1189 and 1193 show the World Wildlife Fund emblem.

Audubon Type of 1985

1986, Oct. 9 **Litho.** ***Perf. 14***
1195 A167 3 l Little blue heron .40 .40
1196 A167 4 l White-tailed kite, vert. .40 .40
1197 A167 5 l Greater shearwater .40 .40
1198 A167 10 l Magnificent frigatebird, vert. .45 .45
1199 A167 15 l Eared grebe, vert. .90 .90
1200 A167 20 l Common merganser, vert. .95 .95
1201 A167 13r Great-footed hawk 5.75 5.75
1202 A167 14r Greater prairie chicken 5.75 5.75
Nos. 1195-1202 (8) 15.00 15.00

Souvenir Sheets

1203 A167 15r White-fronted goose 12.00 12.00
1204 A167 15r Northern fulmar, vert. 12.00 12.00

Nos. 1197, 1199-1201 printed se-tenant with labels picturing a horned puffin, gray kingbird, downy woodpecker and water pipit, respectively.

Nos. 1176-1180 Ovptd. "WINNERS / Argentina 3 / W. Germany 2" in Gold

1986, Oct. 25
1205 A184 15 l multicolored .55 .55
1206 A184 2r multicolored 1.50 1.50
1207 A184 4r multicolored 2.40 2.40
1208 A184 10r multicolored 4.00 4.00
Nos. 1205-1208 (4) 8.45 8.45

Souvenir Sheet

1209 A184 15r multicolored 5.25 5.25

Nos. 1151-1156 Printed with Halley's Comet Symbol in Silver

1986, Oct. 30
1210 A181 20 l multicolored .70 .70
1211 A181 1.50r multicolored 1.40 1.40
1212 A181 2r multicolored 1.60 1.60
1213 A181 4r multicolored 2.25 2.25
1214 A181 5r multicolored 2.25 2.25
Nos. 1210-1214 (5) 8.20 8.20

Souvenir Sheet

1215 A181 15r multicolored 6.75 6.75

UNESCO, 40th Anniv. — A186

1986, Nov. 4 ***Perf. 15***
1216 A186 1r Aviation .30 .30
1217 A186 2r Boat-building .75 .75
1218 A186 3r Education 1.10 1.10
1219 A186 5r Research 2.00 2.00
Nos. 1216-1219 (4) 4.15 4.15

Souvenir Sheet

1220 A186 15r Ocean exploration 4.00 4.00

Mushrooms — A187

1986, Dec. 31 **Litho.** ***Perf. 15***
1221 A187 15 l Hypholoma fasciculare .75 .75
1222 A187 50 l Kuehneromyces mutabilis 1.60 1.60
1223 A187 1r Amanita muscaria 2.00 2.00
1224 A187 2r Agaricus campestris 2.75 2.75
1225 A187 3r Amanita pantherina 2.75 2.75
1226 A187 4r Coprinus comatus 2.75 2.75
1227 A187 5r Pholiota spectabilis 2.75 2.75
1228 A187 10r Pluteus cervinus 4.25 4.25
Nos. 1221-1228 (8) 19.60 19.60

Souvenir Sheets

1229 A187 15r Armillaria mellea 8.50 8.50
1230 A187 15r Stropharia aeruginosa 8.50 8.50

Nos. 1222-1223, 1225-1226 vert.

Flowers — A188

1987, Jan. 29 **Litho.** ***Perf. 15***
1231 A188 10 l Ixora .25 .25
1232 A188 20 l Frangipani .25 .25
1233 A188 50 l Crinum .25 .25
1235 A188 2r Pink rose .85 .85
1236 A188 4r Flamboyant 1.60 1.60
1238 A188 10r Ground orchid 4.00 4.00
Nos. 1231-1238 (6) 7.20 7.20

Souvenir Sheet

1239 A188 15r Gardenia 3.25 3.25
1240 A188 15r Oleander 3.25 3.25

Girl Guides, 75th Anniv. (in 1985) A189

1987, Apr. 4 **Litho.** ***Perf. 15***
1241 A189 15 l Nature study .25 .25
1242 A189 2r Guides, rabbits .65 .65
1243 A189 4r Bird-watching 2.10 2.10
1244 A189 12r Lady Baden-Powell, flag 2.40 2.40
Nos. 1241-1244 (4) 5.40 5.40

Souvenir Sheet

1245 A189 15r Sailing 3.75 3.75

Indigenous Trees and Plants — A190

1987, Apr. 22 **Litho.** ***Perf. 14***
1246 A190 50 l Thespesia populnea, vert. .20 .20
1247 A190 1r Cocos nucifera, vert. .20 .20
1248 A190 2r Calophyllum mophyllum, vert. .40 .40
1249 A190 3r Xyanthosoma indica .60 .60
1250 A190 5r Ipomoea batatas 1.10 1.10
1251 A190 7r Artocarpus altilis, vert. 1.40 1.40
Nos. 1246-1251 (6) 3.90 3.90

Souvenir Sheet

1252 A190 15r Cocos nucifera, diff., vert. 3.75 3.75

A191

America's Cup — A192

1987, May 4 Litho. *Perf. 15*

No.	Type	Denom.	Description	Unused	Used
1253	A191	15 l	Intrepid, 1970	.25	.25
1254	A191	1r	France II, 1974	.35	.35
1255	A191	2r	Gretel, 1962	.60	.60
1256	A191	12r	Volunteer, 1887	3.75	3.75
			Nos. 1253-1256 (4)	4.95	4.95

Souvenir Sheet

No.	Type	Denom.	Description	Unused	Used
1257	A192	15r	Defender Vs. Valkyrie III, 1895	4.00	4.00

Butterflies — A193 Scientists — A194

1987, Dec. 16 Litho. *Perf. 15*

No.	Type	Denom.	Description	Unused	Used
1258	A193	15 l	Precis octavia	.50	.50
1259	A193	20 l	Pachliopta hector	.50	.50
1260	A193	50 l	Teinopalpus imperialis	.90	.90
1261	A193	1r	Kallima horsfieldi	1.10	1.10
1262	A193	2r	Cethosia biblis	2.00	2.00
1263	A193	4r	Hestia jasonia	2.75	2.75
1264	A193	7r	Papilio memnon	4.25	4.25
1265	A193	10r	Meneris tulbaghia	4.75	4.75
			Nos. 1258-1265 (8)	16.75	16.75

Souvenir Sheets

No.	Type	Denom.	Description	Unused	Used
1266	A193	15r	Acraea violae acraeinae	6.00	6.00
1267	A193	15r	Hebomoia leucippe	6.00	6.00

1988, Jan. 10 *Perf. 14*

Designs: 1.50r, Sir Isaac Newton using prism to demonstrate his Theory of Light, horiz. 3r, Euclid (c. 300 B.C.), mathematician. 4r, Gregor Johann Mendel (1822-1884), botanist; father of genetics. 5r, Galileo, 1st man to observe 4 moons of Jupiter, horiz. 15r, Apollo spacecraft orbiting the moon.

No.	Type	Denom.	Description	Unused	Used
1268	A194	1.50r	multicolored	1.50	1.50
1269	A194	3r	multicolored	2.10	2.10
1270	A194	4r	multicolored	2.40	2.40
1271	A194	5r	multicolored	4.00	4.00
			Nos. 1268-1271 (4)	10.00	10.00

Souvenir Sheet

No.	Type	Denom.	Description	Unused	Used
1272	A194	15r	multicolored	7.25	*7.25*

Disney Characters, Space Exploration — A195

1988, Feb. 15

No.	Type	Denom.	Description	Unused	Used
1273	A195	3 l	Weather satellite	.25	.25
1274	A195	4 l	Navigation satellite	.25	.25
1275	A195	5 l	Communication satellite	.25	.25
1276	A195	10 l	Moon rover	.25	.25
1277	A195	20 l	Space shuttle	.25	.25
1278	A195	13r	Space docking	5.75	5.75
1279	A195	14r	Voyager 2	5.75	5.75
			Nos. 1273-1279 (7)	12.75	12.75

Souvenir Sheets

No.	Type	Denom.	Description	Unused	Used
1280	A195	15r	1st Man on Moon	6.50	6.50
1281	A195	15r	Space station colony	6.50	6.50

Nos. 1276-1278 and 1281 vert.

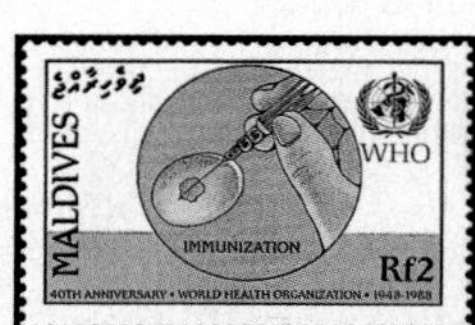

WHO, 40th Anniv. A196

1988, Apr. 7 Litho. *Perf. 14*

No.	Type	Denom.	Description	Unused	Used
1282	A196	2r	Immunization	.60	.60
1283	A196	4r	Clean water	1.10	1.10

For overprints see Nos. 1307-1308.

World Environment Day — A197

1988, May 9 *Perf. 15*

No.	Type	Denom.	Description	Unused	Used
1284	A197	15 l	Save water	.25	.25
1285	A197	75 l	Protect the reef	.30	.30
1286	A197	2r	Conserve nature	.75	.75
			Nos. 1284-1286 (3)	1.30	1.30

Souvenir Sheet

No.	Type	Denom.	Description	Unused	Used
1287	A197	15r	Banyan tree, vert.	4.25	4.25

Nos. 1172-1175 Ovptd. "40th WEDDING ANNIVERSARY/ H.M. QUEEN ELIZABETH II/ H.R.H. THE DUKE OF EDINBURGH" in Gold

1988, July 7 Litho. *Perf. 14*

No.	Type	Denom.	Description	Unused	Used
1288	CD339	1r	multicolored	.35	.35
1289	CD339	2r	multicolored	.65	.65
1290	CD339	12r	multicolored	4.00	4.00
			Nos. 1288-1290 (3)	5.00	5.00

Souvenir Sheet

No.	Type	Denom.	Description	Unused	Used
1291	CD339	15r	multicolored	5.25	5.25

Transportation and Communication Decade for Asia and the Pacific — A198

Globe and: 2r, Postal communications. 3r, Earth satellite telecommunications technology. 5r, Space telecommunications technology. 10r, Automobile, aircraft and ship.

1988, May 31 Litho. *Perf. 14*

No.	Type	Denom.	Description	Unused	Used
1292	A198	2r	multicolored	1.50	1.50
1293	A198	3r	multicolored	2.00	2.00
1294	A198	5r	multicolored	3.00	3.00
1295	A198	10r	multicolored	6.00	6.00
			Nos. 1292-1295 (4)	12.50	12.50

For overprints, see Nos. 1344-1345.

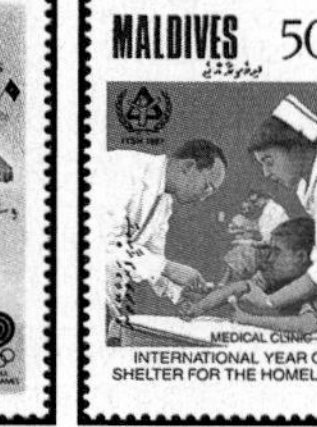

1988 Summer Olympics, Seoul — A199 Intl. Year of Shelter for the Homeless — A200

1988, July 16

No.	Type	Denom.	Description	Unused	Used
1296	A199	15 l	Discus	.20	.20
1297	A199	2r	100-Meter sprint	.60	.60
1298	A199	4r	Gymnastics, horiz.	1.10	1.10
1299	A199	12r	Steeplechase, horiz.	3.50	3.50
			Nos. 1296-1299 (4)	5.40	5.40

Souvenir Sheet

No.	Type	Denom.	Description	Unused	Used
1300	A199	20r	Tennis, horiz.	5.25	5.25

For overprints see Nos. 1311-1315.

1988, July 20

No.	Type	Denom.	Description	Unused	Used
1301	A200	50 l	Medical clinic	.35	.35
1302	A200	3r	Prefab housing	1.60	1.60

Souvenir Sheet

No.	Type	Denom.	Description	Unused	Used
1303	A200	15r	Construction site	4.25	4.25

Intl. Fund for Agricultural Development (IFAD), 10th Anniv. — A201

1988, July 30

No.	Type	Denom.	Description	Unused	Used
1304	A201	7r	Breadfruit	2.00	2.00
1305	A201	10r	Mango, vert.	2.75	2.75

Souvenir Sheet

No.	Type	Denom.	Description	Unused	Used
1306	A201	15r	Coconut palm, yellowtail tuna	4.25	4.25

Nos. 1282-1283 Ovptd.

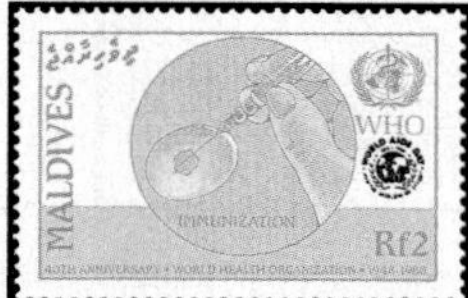

1988, Dec. 1 Litho. *Perf. 14*

No.	Type	Denom.	Description	Unused	Used
1307	A196	2r	multicolored	.60	.60
1308	A196	4r	multicolored	1.10	1.10

Intl. Day for the Fight Against Aids.

John F. Kennedy (1917-1963), 35th US President — A202

Space achievements: a, Apollo launch. b, 1st Man on the Moon. c, Earth and astronaut driving moon rover. d, Space module and Kennedy. 15r, Kennedy addressing the nation.

1989, Feb. 19

No.	Type	Denom.	Description	Unused	Used
1309			Strip of 4	9.50	9.50
a.-d.	A202	5r	any single	2.00	2.00

Souvenir Sheet

No.	Type	Denom.	Description	Unused	Used
1310	A202	15r	multicolored	5.00	5.00

Nos. 1296-1300 Overprinted for Olympic Winners

1989, Apr. 29 Litho. *Perf. 14*

No.	Type	Denom.	Description	Unused	Used
1311	A199	15 l	"J. SCHULT / DDR"	.25	.25
1312	A199	2r	"C. LEWIS / USA"	.75	.75
1313	A199	4r	"MEN'S ALL AROUND / V. ARTEMOV USSR"	1.40	1.40
1314	A199	12r	"TEAM SHOW JUMPING / W. GERMANY"	4.50	4.50
			Nos. 1311-1314 (4)	6.90	6.90

Souvenir Sheet

No.	Type	Denom.	Description	Unused	Used
1315	A199	20r	multi	6.50	6.50

No. 1315 has marginal ovpt. "OLYMPIC WINNERS / MEN'S SINGLES / GOLD M. MECIR / CZECH. / SILVER T. MAYOTTE / USA / BRONZE B. GILBERT / USA."

Paintings by Titian (b. 1489) A203

Designs: 15 l, Portrait of Benedetto Varchi, c. 1540. 1r, Portrait of a Young Man in a Fur, 1515. 2r, King Francis I of France, 1538. 5r, Portrait of Pietro Aretino, 1545. 15r, The Bravo, c. 1520. 20r, The Concert, 1512. No. 1322, An Allegory of Prudence, c. 1565. No. 1323, Portrait of Francesco Maria Della Rovere.

1989, May 15 Litho. *Perf. 13½x14*

No.	Type	Denom.	Description	Unused	Used
1316	A203	15 l	multicolored	.25	.25
1317	A203	1r	multicolored	.30	.30
1318	A203	2r	multicolored	.70	.70
1319	A203	5r	multicolored	1.60	1.60
1320	A203	15r	multicolored	4.75	4.75
1321	A203	20r	multicolored	6.25	6.25
			Nos. 1316-1321 (6)	13.85	13.85

Souvenir Sheets

No.	Type	Denom.	Description	Unused	Used
1322	A203	20r	multicolored	5.00	5.00
1323	A203	20r	multicolored	5.00	5.00

"Thirty-six Views of Mt. Fuji" — A204

Prints by Hokusai (1760-1849): 15 l, Fuji from Hodogaya. 50 l, Fuji from Lake Kawaguchi. 1r, Fuji from Owari. 2r, Fuji from Tsukudajima in Edo. 4r, Fuji from a Teahouse at Yoshida. 6r, Fuji from Tagonoura. 10r, Fuji from Mishima-goe. 12r, Fuji from the Sumida River in Edo. No. 1332, Fuji from Fukagawa in Edo. No. 1333, Fuji from Inume Pass.

1989 *Perf. 14*

No.	Type	Denom.	Description	Unused	Used
1324	A204	15 l	multicolored	.20	.20
1325	A204	50 l	multicolored	.20	.20
1326	A204	1r	multicolored	.30	.30
1327	A204	2r	multicolored	.55	.55
1328	A204	4r	multicolored	1.10	1.10
1329	A204	6r	multicolored	1.60	1.60
1330	A204	10r	multicolored	2.75	2.75
1331	A204	12r	multicolored	3.25	3.25
			Nos. 1324-1331 (8)	9.95	9.95

Souvenir Sheets

No.	Type	Denom.	Description	Unused	Used
1332	A204	18r	multicolored	5.00	5.00
1333	A204	18r	multicolored	5.00	5.00

Hirohito (1901-1989) and enthronement of Akihito as emperor of Japan.

Issue dates: #1332, Oct. 16, others, Sept. 2.

Tropical Fish A205

1989, Oct. 16 Litho. *Perf. 14*

1334 A205 20 l Clown trigger-fish .25 .25
1335 A205 50 l Blue surge-onfish .25 .25
1336 A205 1r Bluestripe snapper .30 .30
1337 A205 2r Oriental sweet-lips .65 .65
1338 A205 3r Wrasse .95 .95
1339 A205 8r Treadfin butter-flyfish 2.50 2.50
1340 A205 10r Bicolor par-rotfish 3.25 3.25
1341 A205 12r Saber squir-relfish 3.75 3.75
Nos. 1334-1341 (8) 11.90 11.90

Souvenir Sheet

1342 A205 15r Butterfly perch 7.50 7.50
1343 A205 15r Semicircle an-gelfish 7.50 7.50

Nos. 1293-1294 Ovptd. "ASIA-PACIFIC / TELECOMMUNITY / 10 YEARS" in Silver

1989, July 5 Litho. *Perf. 14*

1344 A198 3r multicolored 1.90 1.90
1345 A198 5r multicolored 3.00 3.00

World Stamp Expo '89 Emblem, Disney Characters and Japanese Automobiles — A206

Designs: 15 l, 1907 Takuri Type 3. 50 l, 1917 Mitsubishi Model A. 1r, 1935 Datsun Roadstar. 2r, 1940 Mazda. 4r, 1959 Nissan Bluebird 310. 6r, 1958 Subaru 360. 10r, 1966 Honda 5800. 12r, 1966 Daihatsu Fellow. No. 1354, 1981 Isuzu Trooper II. No. 1355, 1985 Toyota Supra.

1989, Nov. 17 Litho. *Perf. 14x13½*

1346 A206 15 l multicolored .25 .25
1347 A206 50 l multicolored .25 .25
1348 A206 1r multicolored .40 .40
1349 A206 2r multicolored .75 .75
1350 A206 4r multicolored 1.50 1.50
1351 A206 6r multicolored 2.40 2.40
1352 A206 10r multicolored 4.00 4.00
1353 A206 12r multicolored 4.50 4.50
Nos. 1346-1353 (8) 14.05 14.05

Souvenir Sheets

1354 A206 20r multicolored 7.00 7.00
1355 A206 20r multicolored 7.00 7.00

Souvenir Sheet

The Marine Corps War Memorial, Arlington, VA — A207

1989, Nov. 17 Litho. *Perf. 14*

1356 A207 8r multicolored 3.00 3.00

World Stamp Expo '89.

1st Moon Landing, 20th Anniv. A208

1989, Nov. 24 *Perf. 14*

1357 A208 1r *Eagle* lunar mod-ule .30 .30
1358 A208 2r Aldrin taking soil samples .60 .60
1359 A208 6r Solar wind experi-ment 1.75 1.75
1360 A208 10r Nixon, astronauts 3.00 3.00
Nos. 1357-1360 (4) 5.65 5.65

Souvenir Sheet

1361 A208 18r Armstrong de-scending ladder 9.50 9.50

Railway Pioneers — A209

Designs: 10 l, Sir William Cornelius Van Horne (1843-1915), chairman of Canadian Pacific Railway, map and locomotive, 1894. 25 l, Matthew Murray, built rack locomotives for Middleton Colliery. 50 l, Louis Favre (1826-1879), built the St. Gotthard (spiral) Tunnel, 1881. 2r, George Stephenson (1781-1848), locomotive, 1825. 6r, Richard Trevithick (1771-1833), builder of 1st rail locomotive, 1804. 8r, George Nagelmackers, Orient Express dining car, 1869. 10r, William Jessop, Surrey horse-drawn cart on rails, 1770. 12r, Isambard Kingdom Brunel (1806-1859), chief engineer of Great Western Railway, introduced broad gauge, 1830's. No. 1370, George Pullman (1831-1897), *Pioneer* passenger car. No. 1371, Rudolf Diesel (1858-1913), inventor of the diesel engine, 1892, and diesel train.

1989, Dec. 26 Litho. *Perf. 14*

1362 A209 10 l multicolored .25 .25
1363 A209 25 l multicolored .25 .25
1364 A209 50 l multicolored .25 .25
1365 A209 2r multicolored .65 .65
1366 A209 6r multicolored 2.00 2.00
1367 A209 8r multicolored 2.50 2.50
1368 A209 10r multicolored 3.25 3.25
1369 A209 12r multicolored 3.75 3.75
Nos. 1362-1369 (8) 12.90 12.90

Souvenir Sheets

1370 A209 18r multicolored 5.00 5.00
1371 A209 18r multicolored 5.00 5.00

Anniversaries and Events (in 1989) — A210

Designs: 20 l, Flag of India, Jawaharlal Nehru, Mahatma Gandhi. 50 l, Syringe, opium poppies, vert. 1r, William Shakespeare, birthplace, Stratford-on-Avon. 2r, Flag of France, storming of the Bastille, Paris, 1789, vert. 3r, Concorde jet, flags of France, Britain. 8r, George Washington, Mount Vernon estate, Virginia. 10r, Capt. William Bligh, the *Bounty.* 12r, Ships in port. No. 1380, 1st Televised baseball game, 1939, vert. No. 1381, Franz von Taxis (1458-1517), vert.

1990, Feb. 15 Litho. *Perf. 14*

1372 A210 20 l multicolored .25 .25
1373 A210 50 l multicolored .25 .25
1374 A210 1r multicolored .60 .60
1375 A210 2r multicolored 1.10 1.10
1376 A210 3r multicolored 1.75 1.75
1377 A210 8r multicolored 5.50 5.50
1378 A210 10r multicolored 7.00 7.00
1379 A210 12r multicolored 8.50 8.50
Nos. 1372-1379 (8) 24.95 24.95

Souvenir Sheets

1380 A210 18r multicolored 8.75 8.75
1381 A210 18r multicolored 8.75 8.75

Birth cent. of Nehru (20 l); SAARC Year for Combatting Drug Abuse (50 l); 425th birth anniv. of Shakespeare (1r); French Revolution, bicent. (2r); first test flight of the Concorde supersonic jet, 20th anniv. (3r); American presidency, bicent. (8r); Mutiny on the *Bounty,* bicent. (10r); Hamburg, 800th anniv. (12r); 1st televised baseball game, 50th anniv. (No. 1380); and European postal communications, 500th anniv. (No. 1381).

Johann von Taxis was the first postmaster of Thurn & Taxis in 1489, not Franz, who is credited on No. 1381.

Natl. Independence, 25th Anniv. — A211

Designs: 20 l, Bodu Thakurufaanu Memorial Center, Utheemu. 25 l, Islamic Center, Male. 50 l, Natl. flag, UN, Islamic Conf., Commonwealth and SAARC emblems. 2r, Muleeaage, Male. 5r, Natl. Security Service, Maldives. 10r, Natl. crest, emblem of the Citizens' Majlis (parliament).

1990, Jan. 1 Litho. *Perf. 14*

1382 A211 20 l multicolored .20 .20
1383 A211 25 l multicolored .20 .20
1384 A211 50 l multicolored .20 .20
1385 A211 2r multicolored .50 .50
1386 A211 5r multicolored 1.25 1.25
Nos. 1382-1386 (5) 2.35 2.35

Souvenir Sheet

1387 A211 10r multicolored 4.50 4.50

French Revolution, Bicent. (in 1989) A212

Paintings: 15 l, *Louis XVI in Coronation Robes,* by Duplessis. 50 l, *Monsieur Lavoisier and His Wife,* by David. 1r, *Madame Pastoret,* by David. 2r, *Oath of Lafayette at the Festival of Federation,* artist unknown. 4r, *Madame Trudaine,* by David. 6r, *Chenard Celebrating the Liberation of Savoy,* by Boilly. 10r, *An Officer Swears Allegiance to the Constitution,* artist unknown. 12r, *Self-portrait,* by David. No. 1396, *The Tennis Court Oath, June 20, 1789,* by David, horiz. No. 1397, *Jean-Jacques Rousseau and the Symbols of the Revolution,* by Jeaurat.

1990, Jan. 11 Litho. *Perf. 14*

1388 A212 15 l multicolored .25 .25
1389 A212 50 l multicolored .25 .25
1390 A212 1r multicolored .40 .40
1391 A212 2r multicolored .85 .85
1392 A212 4r multicolored 1.50 1.50
1393 A212 6r multicolored 2.40 2.40
1394 A212 10r multicolored 4.00 4.00
1395 A212 12r multicolored 4.50 4.50
Nos. 1388-1395 (8) 14.15 14.15

Souvenir Sheets

1396 A212 20r multicolored 6.00 6.00
1397 A212 20r multicolored 6.00 6.00

Stamp World London '90 — A213

Walt Disney characters demonstrating sports popular in Britain.

1990 Litho. *Perf. 14x13½*

1398 A213 15 l Rugby .25 .25
1399 A213 50 l Curling .25 .25
1400 A213 1r Polo .40 .40
1401 A213 2r Soccer .85 .85
1402 A213 4r Cricket 1.50 1.50
1403 A213 6r Horse racing, Ascot 2.50 2.50
1404 A213 10r Tennis 4.00 4.00
1405 A213 12r Lawn bowling 4.50 4.50
Nos. 1398-1405 (8) 14.25 14.25

Souvenir Sheets

1406 A213 20r Fox hunting 8.00 8.00
1407 A213 20r Golf, St. Andrews, Scotland 8.00 8.00

Penny Black, 150th Anniv. A214

1990, May 3 Litho. *Perf. 15x14*

1408 A214 8r Silhouettes 2.50 2.50
1409 A214 12r Silhouettes, diff. 3.75 3.75

Souvenir Sheet

1410 A214 18r Penny Black 5.25 5.25

Queen Mother 90th Birthday
A215 A216

1990, July 8 *Perf. 14*

1411 A215 6r shown 1.25 1.25
1412 A216 6r shown 1.25 1.25
1413 A215 6r As Lady Bowes-Lyon, diff. 1.25 1.25
Nos. 1411-1413 (3) 3.75 3.75

Souvenir Sheet

1414 A216 18r On Wedding Day, diff. 4.00 4.00

Nos. 1411-1413 printed in sheets of 9.

A217

A218

A219

Islamic Heritage Year A220

1990, July 22 Litho. *Perf. 14*

1415 A217 1r blue & black .25 .25
1416 A218 1r blue & black .25 .25
1417 A218 1r Building, diff. .25 .25
1418 A219 2r blue & black .50 .50
1419 A220 2r blue & black .50 .50
1420 A219 2r Building, diff. .50 .50
a. Block of 6, #1415-1420 3.00 3.00

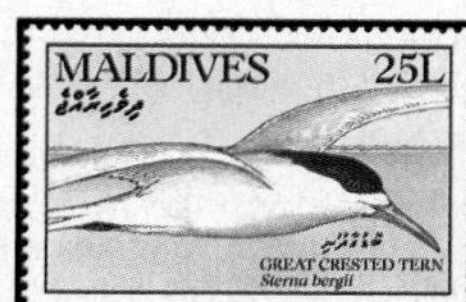

Great Crested Tern
A221

1990, Aug. 9 **Litho.** ***Perf. 14***

1421 A221 25 l shown .20 .20
1422 A221 50 l Koel .20 .20
1423 A221 1r White tern .25 .25
1424 A221 3.50r Cinnamon bittern .90 .90
1425 A221 6r Sooty tern 1.50 1.50
1426 A221 8r Audubon's shearwater 2.00 2.00
1427 A221 12r Brown noddy 3.00 3.00
1428 A221 15r Lesser frigatebird 3.75 3.75
Nos. 1421-1428 (8) 11.80 11.80

Souvenir Sheets

1429 A221 18r White-tailed tropicbird 6.25 6.25
1430 A221 18r Grey heron 6.25 6.25

World War II Milestones — A222

Designs: 15 l, US Marines repulse Japanese invasion of Wake Island, Dec. 11, 1941. 25 l, Gen. Stilwell begins offensive in Burma, Mar. 4, 1944. 50 l, US begins offensive in Normandy, July 3, 1944. 1r, US forces secure Saipan, July 9, 1944. 2.50r, D-Day, June 6, 1944. 3.50r, Allied forces land in Norway, Apr. 14, 1940. 4r, Adm. Mountbatten named Chief of Combined Operations, Mar. 18, 1942. 6r, Gen. MacArthur accepts Japanese surrender, Sept. 2, 1945. 10r, Potsdam Conference, July 16, 1945. 12r, Allied invade Sicily, July 10, 1943. 18r, Atlantic convoys.

1990, Aug. 9 **Litho.** ***Perf. 14***

1431 A222 15 l multicolored .20 .20
1432 A222 25 l multicolored .20 .20
1433 A222 50 l multicolored .20 .20
1434 A222 1r multicolored .25 .25
1435 A222 2.50r multicolored .60 .60
1436 A222 3.50r multicolored 1.10 1.10
1437 A222 4r multicolored 1.25 1.25
1438 A222 6r multicolored 2.00 2.00
1439 A222 10r multicolored 3.25 3.25
1440 A222 12r multicolored 4.00 4.00
Nos. 1431-1440 (10) 13.05 13.05

Souvenir Sheet

1441 A222 18r multicolored 7.75 7.75

A223

5th SAARC Summit — A224

1990, Nov. 21 **Litho.** ***Perf. 14***

1442 A223 75 l Satellite communications .40 .40
1443 A223 3.50r Flags 1.50 1.50

Souvenir Sheet

1444 A224 20r Map 6.75 6.75

Flowers — A225

Bonsai — A226

1990, Dec. 9 **Litho.** ***Perf. 14***

1445 A225 20 l Spathoglottis plicata .25 .25
1446 A225 75 l Hippeastrum puniceum .25 .25
1447 A225 2r Tecoma stans .65 .65
1448 A225 3.50r Catharanthus roseus 1.10 1.10
1449 A225 10r Ixora coccinea 3.25 3.25
1450 A225 12r Clitoria ternatea 4.00 4.00
1451 A225 15r Caesalpinia pulcherrima 4.75 4.75
Nos. 1445-1451 (7) 14.25 14.25

Souvenir Sheets

1452 A225 20r Rosa sp. 5.00 5.00
1453 A225 20r Plumeria obtusa 5.00 5.00
1454 A225 20r Jasminum grandiflorum 5.00 5.00
1455 A225 20r Hibiscus tiliaceous 5.00 5.00

Expo '90, Intl. Garden and Greenery Exposition, Osaka, Japan.
2r, 3.50r, 10r, 12r are horiz.

1990-91

1456 A226 20 l Winged Euonymus .25 .25
1457 A226 50 l Japanese black pine .25 .25
1458 A226 1r Japanese five needle pine .30 .30
1459 A226 3.50r Flowering quince 1.25 1.25
1460 A226 5r Chinese elm 1.60 1.60
1461 A226 8r Japanese persimmon 2.75 2.75
1462 A226 10r Japanese wisteria 3.25 3.25
1463 A226 12r Satsuki azalea 4.00 4.00
Nos. 1456-1463 (8) 13.65 13.65

Souvenir Sheets

1464 A226 20r Sargent juniper 6.25 6.25
1465 A226 20r Trident maple 6.25 6.25

Expo '90, Intl. Garden and Greenery Exposition, Osaka, Japan.
Issued: 50 l, 1r, 8r, 10r, #1464, 12/9/90; 20 l, 3.50r, 5r, 12r, #1465, 1/29/91.

Aesop's Fables — A227

Walt Disney characters: 15 l, Tortoise and the Hare. 50 l, Town Mouse and Country Mouse. 1r, Fox and the Crow. 3.50r, Travellers and the Bear. 4r, Fox and the Lion. 6r, Mice and the Cat. 10r, Fox and the Goat. 12r, Dog in the Manger. No. 1474, Miller, his Son and the Ass, vert. No. 1475. Miser's Gold, vert.

1990, Dec. 11 **Litho.** ***Perf. 14***

1466 A227 15 l multicolored .20 .20
1467 A227 50 l multicolored .20 .20
1468 A227 1r multicolored .35 .35
1469 A227 3.50r multicolored 1.25 1.25
1470 A227 4r multicolored 1.50 1.50
1471 A227 6r multicolored 2.25 2.25
1472 A227 10r multicolored 3.75 3.75
1473 A227 12r multicolored 4.25 4.25
Nos. 1466-1473 (8) 13.75 13.75

Souvenir Sheets

1474 A227 20r multicolored 7.50 7.50
1475 A227 20r multicolored 7.50 7.50

Intl. Literacy Year.

A228

A229

Steam Locomotives: 20 l, "31" Class, East African Railways. 50 l, Mikado, Sudan Railways. 1r, Beyer-Garratt GM Class, South African Railways. 3r, "7th" Class, Rhodesia Railways. 5r, Central Pacific 229. 8r, Reading 415. 10r, Porter Narrow-guage. 12r, Great Northern 515. No. 1484, American Standard 315. No. 1485, East African Railways 5950.

1990, Dec. 15

1476 A228 20 l multicolored .20 .20
1477 A228 50 l multicolored .20 .20
1478 A228 1r multicolored .40 .40
1479 A228 3r multicolored 1.25 1.25
1480 A228 5r multicolored 2.00 2.00
1481 A228 8r multicolored 3.50 3.50
1482 A228 10r multicolored 4.25 4.25
1483 A228 12r multicolored 5.00 5.00
Nos. 1476-1483 (8) 16.80 16.80

Souvenir Sheets

1484 A228 20r multicolored 8.25 8.25
1485 A228 20r multicolored 8.25 8.25

1990, Dec. 27

Various players from participating countries.

1486 A229 1r Holland .40 .40
1487 A229 2.50r England 1.00 1.00
1487A A229 3.50r Argentina 1.60 1.60
1488 A229 5r Brazil 2.10 2.10
1488A A229 7r Italy 2.75 2.75
1489 A229 10r Russia 4.25 4.25
1489A A229 15r West Germany 6.25 6.25
Nos. 1486-1489A (7) 18.35 18.35

Souvenir Sheets

1490 A229 18r Austria 4.50 4.50
1491 A229 18r South Korea 4.50 4.50
1492 A229 20r Italy (dk blue shirt) 5.00 5.00
1493 A229 20r Argentina (blue & white shirt) 5.00 5.00

World Cup Soccer Championships, Italy.

No. 1111 Surcharged

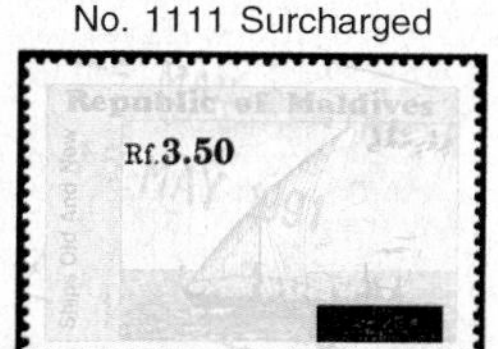

Methods and Perfs As Before

1990

1493B A171 3.50r on 2.70r #1111 —

An additional stamp was issued in this set. The editors would like to examine any examples.

Peter Paul Rubens (1577-1640), Painter — A230

Entire works or details from paintings by Rubens: 20 l, Summer. 50 l, Landscape with Rainbow. 1r, Wreckage of Aeneas. 2.50r, Chateau de Steen. 3.50r, Landscape with Herd of Cows. 7r, Ruins of Palantine. 10r, Landscape with Peasants and Cows. 12r, Wagon Fording a Stream. No. 1502, Landscape with a Sunset. No. 1503, Peasants with Cattle by a Stream in a Woody Landscape. No. 1504, Shepherd with his Flock in a Wooded Landscape. No. 1505, Stuck Wagon.

1991, Feb. 7 **Litho.** ***Perf. 14x13½***

1494 A230 20 l multicolored .20 .20
1495 A230 50 l multicolored .20 .20
1496 A230 1r multicolored .35 .35
1497 A230 2.50r multicolored .80 .80
1498 A230 3.50r multicolored 1.10 1.10
1499 A230 7r multicolored 2.25 2.25
1500 A230 10r multicolored 3.50 3.50
1501 A230 12r multicolored 4.00 4.00
Nos. 1494-1501 (8) 12.40 12.40

Souvenir Sheets

1502-1505 A230 20r each 5.00 5.00

First Marathon Run, 490 B.C. — A231

Events and anniversaries (in 1990): 1r, Anthony Fokker (1890-1939), aircraft builder. 3.50r, Launch of first commercial satellite, 25th anniv. 7r, East, West German foreign ministers sign re-unification documents, Oct. 3, 1990, horiz. 8r, Magna Carta, 775th anniv. 10r, Dwight D. Eisenhower. 12r, Winston Churchill. 15r, Pres. Reagan destroying Berlin Wall, horiz. No. 1514, Brandenburg Gate, horiz. No. 1515, Battle of Britain, 50th anniv., horiz.

1991, Mar. 11 ***Perf. 14***

1506 A231 50 l multicolored .25 .25
1507 A231 1r multicolored .30 .30
1508 A231 3.50r multicolored 1.25 1.25
1509 A231 7r multicolored 2.50 2.50
1510 A231 8r multicolored 2.75 2.75
1511 A231 10r multicolored 3.50 3.50
1512 A231 12r multicolored 4.25 4.25
1513 A231 15r multicolored 5.25 5.25
Nos. 1506-1513 (8) 20.05 20.05

Souvenir Sheets

1514 A231 20r multicolored 7.50 7.50
1515 A231 20r multicolored 7.50 7.50

Global Warming
A232

1991, Apr. 10

1516 A232 3.50r Dhoni 2.00 2.00
1517 A232 7r Freighter 3.75 3.75

Year of the Girl Child — A233

1991, Apr. 14

1518	A233	7r multicolored	2.50	2.50

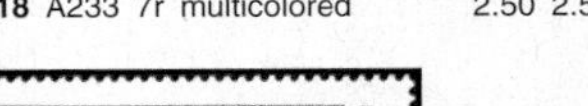

Year of the Child A234

Children's drawings: 3.50r, Beach scene. 5r, City scene. 10r, Visualizing fruit. 25r, Scuba diver.

1991, May 10

1519	A234	3.50r multicolored	1.25	1.25
1520	A234	5r multicolored	1.90	1.90
1521	A234	10r multicolored	3.75	3.75
1522	A234	25r multicolored	9.25	9.25
		Nos. 1519-1522 (4)	16.15	16.15

Paintings by Vincent Van Gogh — A235

Designs: 15 l, Japanese Vase with Roses and Anemones, vert. 20 l, Still Life: Red Poppies and Daisies, vert. 2r, Vincent's Bedroom in Arles. 3.50r, The Mulberry Tree. 7r, Blossoming Chestnut Branches. 10r, Morning: Peasant Couple Going to Work. 12r, Still Life: Pink Roses. 15r, Child with Orange, vert. No. 1531, Courtyard of the Hospital at Arles. No. 1532, Houses in Auvers, vert.

1991, June 6 Litho. *Perf. 13½*

1523	A235	15 l multicolored	.30	.30
1524	A235	20 l multicolored	.30	.30
1525	A235	2r multicolored	.75	.75
1526	A235	3.50r multicolored	1.40	1.40
1527	A235	7r multicolored	2.75	2.75
1528	A235	10r multicolored	4.00	4.00
1529	A235	12r multicolored	4.50	4.50
1530	A235	15r multicolored	5.75	5.75
		Nos. 1523-1530 (8)	19.75	19.75

Sizes: 100x75mm, 75x100mm

Imperf

1531	A235	25r multicolored	8.25	8.25
1532	A235	25r multicolored	8.25	8.25

Royal Family Birthday, Anniversary
Common Design Type

1991, July 4 Litho. *Perf. 14*

1533	CD347	1r multi	.30	.30
1534	CD347	2r multi	.60	.60
1535	CD347	3.50r multi	1.10	1.10
1536	CD347	5r multi	1.50	1.50
1537	CD347	7r multi	2.10	2.10
1538	CD347	8r multi	2.50	2.50
1539	CD347	12r multi	3.75	3.75
1540	CD347	15r multi	4.25	4.25
		Nos. 1533-1540 (8)	16.10	16.10

Souvenir Sheets

1541	CD347	25r Elizabeth, Philip	7.25	7.25
1542	CD347	25r Charles, Diana, sons	7.25	7.25

1r, 3.50r, 7r, 15r, No. 1542, Charles and Diana, 10th wedding anniversary. Others, Queen Elizabeth II, 65th birthday.

Hummel Figurines — A236

Designs: 10 l, No. 1552a, Child painting. 25 l, No. 1552b, Boy reading at table. 50 l, No. 1552c, Boy with back pack. 2r, No. 1551a, School Girl. 3.50r, No. 1551b, The Bookworm (boy sitting and reading). 8r, No. 1551c, Little Brother's Lesson. 10r, No. 1551d, School Girls. 25r, No. 1552d, Three school boys.

1991, July 25 Litho. *Perf. 14*

1543	A236	10 l multicolored	.20	.20
1544	A236	25 l multicolored	.20	.20
1545	A236	50 l multicolored	.20	.20
1546	A236	2r multicolored	.60	.60
1547	A236	3.50r multicolored	1.10	1.10
1548	A236	8r multicolored	2.40	2.40
1549	A236	10r multicolored	3.00	3.00
1550	A236	25r multicolored	7.25	7.25
		Nos. 1543-1550 (8)	14.95	14.95

Souvenir Sheets

1551	A236	5r Sheet of 4, #a.-d.	5.50	5.50
1552	A236	8r Sheet of 4, #a.-d.	9.00	9.00

Japanese Steam Locomotives — A237

1991, Aug. 25 Litho. *Perf. 14*

1553	A237	15 l C 57, vert.	.20	.20
1554	A237	25 l Series 6250	.20	.20
1555	A237	1r D 51, vert.	.35	.35
1556	A237	3.50r Series 8620	1.25	1.25
1557	A237	5r Class 10	1.90	1.90
1558	A237	7r C 61, vert.	2.75	2.75
1559	A237	10r Series 9600	3.75	3.75
1560	A237	12r D 52	4.75	4.75
		Nos. 1553-1560 (8)	15.15	15.15

Souvenir Sheets

1561	A237	20r Class 1080	6.00	6.00
1562	A237	20r C 56	6.00	6.00

Phila Nippon '91.

Butterflies A238

1991, Dec. 2 Litho. *Perf. 14*

1563	A238	10 l Blue salamis	.25	.25
1564	A238	25 l Mountain beauty	.25	.25
1565	A238	50 l Lucerne blue	.35	.35
1566	A238	2r Monarch	.95	.95
1567	A238	3.50r Common rose	1.75	1.75
1568	A238	5r Black witch	2.50	2.50
1569	A238	8r Oriental swallowtail	4.00	4.00
1570	A238	10r Gaudy commodore	5.00	5.00
		Nos. 1563-1570 (8)	15.05	15.05

Souvenir Sheets

1571	A238	20r Pearl crescent	7.25	7.25
1572	A238	20r Friar	7.25	7.25

No. 1570 inscribed "guady."

Japanese Space Program A239

Designs: 15 l, H-11 Launch Vehicle. 20 l, H-II Orbiting plane. 2r, Geosynchronous satellite 5. 3.50r, Marine observation satellite-1. 7r, Communications satellite 3. 10r, Broadcasting satellite-2. 12r, H-1 Launch Vehicle, vert. 15r, Space flier unit, space shuttle. No. 1581, Katsura tracking and data acquisition station. No. 1582, M-3S II Launch vehicle, vert.

1991, Dec. 11

1573	A239	15 l multicolored	.25	.25
1574	A239	20 l multicolored	.25	.25
1575	A239	2r multicolored	.60	.60
1576	A239	3.50r multicolored	1.10	1.10
1577	A239	7r multicolored	2.10	2.10
1578	A239	10r multicolored	3.00	3.00
1579	A239	12r multicolored	3.75	3.75
1580	A239	15r multicolored	4.75	4.75
		Nos. 1573-1580 (8)	15.80	15.80

Souvenir Sheets

1581	A239	20r multicolored	7.25	7.25
1582	A239	20r multicolored	7.25	7.25

Miniature Sheet

Franklin D. Roosevelt A240

World War II Leaders of the Pacific Theater: b, Douglas MacArthur. c, Chester Nimitz. d, Jonathan Wainwright. e, Ernest King. f, Claire Chennault. g, William Halsey. h, Marc Mitscher. i, James Doolittle. j, Raymond Spruance.

1991, Dec. 30 Litho. *Perf. 14½x15*

1583	A240	3.50r Sheet of 10, #a.-j.	16.00	16.00

Grand Prix Race Cars A241

Designs: 20 l, Williams FW-07. 50 l, Brabham BT50 BMW Turbo. 1r, Williams FW-11 Honda. 3.50r, Ferrari 312 T3. 5r, Lotus Honda 99T. 7r, Benetton Ford B188. 10r, Tyrrell P34 Six-wheeler. 21r, Renault RE-30B Turbo. No. 1592, Ferrari F189. No. 1593, Brabham BT50 BMW Turbo, diff.

1991, Dec. 28 Litho. *Perf. 14*

1584	A241	20 l multicolored	.25	.25
1585	A241	50 l multicolored	.25	.25
1586	A241	1r multicolored	.30	.30
1587	A241	3.50r multicolored	1.10	1.10
1588	A241	5r multicolored	1.60	1.60
1589	A241	7r multicolored	2.25	2.25
1590	A241	10r multicolored	3.25	3.25
1591	A241	21r multicolored	6.75	6.75
		Nos. 1584-1591 (8)	15.75	15.75

Souvenir Sheets

1592	A241	25r multicolored	8.25	8.25
1593	A241	25r multicolored	8.25	8.25

Miniature Sheet

Enzo Ferrari (1898-1988) — A242

Ferrari Race cars: a, 1957 Testa Rossa. b, 1966 275GTB. c, 1951 "Aspirarta." d, Testarossa. f, 1958 Dino 246. g, 1952 Type 375. h, Mansell's Formula One. i, 1975 312T.

1991, Dec. 28

1594	A242	5r Sheet of 9, #a.-i.	18.00	18.00

17th World Scout Jamboree A243

Designs: 10r, Scouts diving on reef. 11r, Hand making scout sign, emblem, vert. 18r, Lord Robert Baden-Powell, vert. 20r, Czechoslovakian scout (local) stamp, vert.

1991, Dec. 30

1595	A243	10r multicolored	2.50	2.50
1596	A243	11r multicolored	3.00	3.00

Souvenir Sheets

1597	A243	18r multicolored	4.50	4.50
1598	A243	20r multicolored	5.00	5.00

Wolfgang Amadeus Mozart, Death Bicent. A244

Portrait of Mozart and: 50 l, Schwarzenberg Palace. 1r, Spa at Baden. 2r, Royal Palace, Berlin. 5r, Viennese Masonic seal. 7r, St. Marx. No. 1604, Josepsplatz, Vienna.

1991, Dec. 30

1599	A244	50 l multicolored	.20	.20
1600	A244	1r multicolored	.25	.25
1601	A244	2r multicolored	.55	.55
1602	A244	5r multicolored	1.25	1.25
1603	A244	7r multicolored	1.75	1.75
1604	A244	20r multicolored	5.00	5.00
		Nos. 1599-1604 (6)	9.00	9.00

Souvenir Sheet

1605	A244	20r Bust of Mozart, vert.	5.00	5.00

Brandenburg Gate, Bicent. — A245

Designs: 20 l, Flag. 1.75 l, Man embracing child, Berlin wall. 4r, Soldiers behind barricade, demonstrator. 15r, World War I Iron Cross. No. 1610, Helmet. No. 1611, 1939 helmet. No. 1612, Studded helmet.

1991, Dec. 30

1606	A245	20 l multicolored	.20	.20
1607	A245	1.75r multicolored	.45	.45
1608	A245	4r multicolored	1.00	1.00
1609	A245	15r multicolored	3.75	3.75
		Nos. 1606-1609 (4)	5.40	5.40

Souvenir Sheets

1610	A245	18r multicolored	4.50	4.50
1611	A245	18r multicolored	4.50	4.50
1612	A245	18r multicolored	4.50	4.50

Anniversaries and Events — A246

Designs: No. 1613, Otto Lilienthal, glider No. 16. No. 1614, "D-Day," Normandy 1944, Charles de Gaulle. 7r, Front of locomotive, vert. 8r, Kurt Schwitters, artist and Landesmuseum. 9r, Map, man in Swiss costume. 10r, Charles de Gaulle in Madagascar, 1958. 12r, Steam locomotive. 15r, Portrait of Charles de Gaulle, vert. 20r, Locomotive and coal car.

1991, Dec. 30 Litho. *Perf. 14*

1613	A246	6r multicolored	2.00	2.00
1614	A246	6r multicolored	1.50	1.50
1615	A246	7r multicolored	1.75	1.75
1616	A246	8r multicolored	2.00	2.00
1617	A246	9r multicolored	2.25	2.25
1618	A246	10r multicolored	2.50	2.50
1619	A246	12r multicolored	3.00	3.00
		Nos. 1613-1619 (7)	15.00	15.00

Souvenir Sheets

1620 A246 15r multicolored 4.50 4.50
1621 A246 20r multicolored 5.00 5.00

First glider flight, cent. (#1613). Charles de Gaulle, birth cent. in 1990 (#1614, #1618, & #1620). Trans-Siberian Railway, cent. (#1615, #1619 & #1621). Hanover, 750th anniv. (#1616). Swiss Confederation, 700th anniv. (#1617).

No. 1621 contains one 58x43mm stamp.

Birds — A247

Perf. 14½, 13 (6.50r+50 l, 30r, 40r)

1992-94

1624 A247 10 l Numenius phaeopus .25 .25
1625 A247 25 l Egretta alba .25 .25
1626 A247 50 l Ardea cinerea .25 .25
1627 A247 2r Phalacrocorax aristotelis .60 .60
1628 A247 3.50r Sterna dougallii 1.10 1.10
1629 A247 5r Tringa nebularia 1.50 1.50
1630 A247 6.50r +50 l Neophron percnopterus 1.75 1.75
1631 A247 8r Upupa epops 2.40 2.40
1632 A247 10r Elanus caeruleus 3.00 3.00
1633 A247 25r Eudocimus ruber 4.75 4.75
1634 A247 30r Falco peregrinus 6.00 6.00
1635 A247 40r Milvus migrans 8.50 8.50
1636 A247 50r Pluvialis squatarola 10.50 10.50
Nos. 1624-1636 (13) 40.85 40.85

Issued: 10 l, 25 l, 50 l, 2r, 3.50r, 5r, 8r, 10r, 25r, 2/17/92; 6.50r+50 l, 30r, 11/93; 40r, 1994(?).

See No. 2323.

Queen Elizabeth II's Accession to the Throne, 40th Anniv.

Common Design Type

1992, Feb. 6 ***Perf. 14***

1637 CD348 1r multicolored .30 .30
1638 CD348 3.50r multicolored 1.10 1.10
1639 CD348 7r multicolored 2.25 2.25
1640 CD348 10r multicolored 3.25 3.25
Nos. 1637-1640 (4) 6.90 6.90

Souvenir Sheets

1641 CD348 18r Queen, palm trees 6.75 6.75
1642 CD348 18r Queen, boat 6.75 6.75

This set differs from the common design in that the Queen's portrait and local view are separated by a curved line rather than with a cypher outline.

Disney Characters on World Tour A248

Designs: 25 l, Mickey on Flying Carpet Airways. 50 l, Goofy at Big Ben, London. 1r, Mickey in Holland. 2r, Pluto eating pasta, Italy. 3r, Mickey, Donald do sombero stomp in Mexico. 3.50r, Mickey, Goofy, and Donald form Miki Tiki, Polynesia. 5r, Goofy's Alpine antics, Austria. 7r, Mickey Maus, Germany. 10r, Donald as Samurai Duck. 12r, Mickey in Russia. 15r, Mickey's Oom-pah Band in Germany. No. 1654, Mickey, globe. No. 1655, Donald in Ireland chasing leprechaun with pot of gold at end of rainbow, horiz. No. 1655A, Pluto, kangaroo with joey, Australia.

1992, Feb. 4 ***Perf. 13x13½***

1643 A248 25 l multi .20 .20
1644 A248 50 l multi .20 .20
1645 A248 1r multi .35 .35
1646 A248 2r multi .65 .65
1647 A248 3r multi .90 .90
1648 A248 3.50r multi .90 .90
1649 A248 5r multi 1.25 1.25
1650 A248 7r multi 1.75 1.75
1651 A248 10r multi 2.50 2.50
1652 A248 12r multi 3.25 3.25
1653 A248 15r multi 5.00 5.00
Nos. 1643-1653 (11) 16.95 16.95

Souvenir Sheets

1654 A248 25r multi 6.25 6.25
1655 A248 25r multi 5.00 5.00
1655A A248 25r multi 5.00 5.00

While the rest of the set has the same issue date as Nos. 1644-1645, 1647, 1653-1654, their dollar value was lower when they were released.

Fish A249

1992, Mar. 23 **Litho.** ***Perf. 14***

1656 A249 7 l Blue surgeonfish .30 .30
1657 A249 20 l Bigeye .30 .30
1658 A249 50 l Yellowfin tuna .30 .30
1659 A249 1r Two-spot red snapper .30 .30
1660 A249 3.50r Sabre squirrelfish 1.00 1.00
1661 A249 5r Picasso triggerfish 1.40 1.40
1662 A249 8r Bennet's butterfly fish 2.25 2.25
1663 A249 10r Parrotfish 3.00 3.00
1664 A249 12r Grouper 3.50 3.50
1665 A249 15r Skipjack tuna 4.25 4.25
Nos. 1656-1665 (10) 16.60 16.60

Souvenir Sheets

1666 A249 20r Clownfish 4.00 4.00
1667 A249 20r Sweetlips 4.00 4.00
1667A A249 20r Threadfin butterflyfish 4.00 4.00
1667B A249 20r Clown triggerfish 4.00 4.00

World Columbian Stamp Expo '92, Chicago A250

Walt Disney characters in Chicago: 1r, Mickey as Indian with Jean Baptiste Pointe du Sable, founder of Chicago. 3.50r, Donald at old Chicago post office, 1831. 7r, Donald in old Fort Dearborn. 15r, Goofy, mastodon at Museum of Science and Industry. 25r, Minnie and Mickey at Ferris wheel midway, Columbian Exposition, 1893, horiz.

1992, Apr. 15 ***Perf. 13½x14***

1668 A250 1r multicolored .30 .30
1669 A250 3.50r multicolored 1.10 1.10
1670 A250 7r multicolored 2.25 2.25
1671 A250 15r multicolored 4.75 4.75
Nos. 1668-1671 (4) 8.40 8.40

Souvenir Sheet

Perf. 14x13½

1672 A250 25r multicolored 7.50 7.50

No. 1671 identifies Field Museum as Museum of Science and Industry.

Granada '92 — A251

Disney characters in old Alhambra, Granada: 2r, Minnie in Court of Lions. 5r, Goofy bathing in Lions Fountain. 8r, Mickey walking near Gate of Justice. 12r, Donald Duck serenading Daisy in Vermilion Towers. No. 1682, Goofy and Mickey outside Towers of the Alhambra.

1992, Apr. 15 ***Perf. 13½x14***

1678 A251 2r multicolored .60 .60
1679 A251 5r multicolored 1.50 1.50
1680 A251 8r multicolored 2.50 2.50
1681 A251 12r multicolored 4.00 4.00
Nos. 1678-1681 (4) 8.60 8.60

Souvenir Sheet

1682 A251 25r multicolored 7.50 7.50

A252

Flowers of the World — A253

1992, Apr. 26 **Litho.** ***Perf. 14½***

1688 A252 25 l United States .25 .25
1689 A252 50 l Australia .25 .25
1690 A252 2r England .70 .70
1691 A252 3.50r Brazil 1.25 1.25
1692 A252 5r Holland 1.75 1.75
1693 A252 8r France 2.75 2.75
1694 A252 10r Japan 3.50 3.50
1695 A252 15r Africa 5.25 5.25
Nos. 1688-1695 (8) 15.70 15.70

Souvenir Sheets

Perf. 14

1696 A253 25r org, yel & red vio flowers 6.75 6.75
1696A A253 25r red, pink & yel flowers 6.75 6.75

No. 1696 contains one 57x43mm stamp. No. 1696A contains one 57x34mm stamp.

Natl. Security Service, Cent. A254

1992, Apr. 21 ***Perf. 14***

1697 A254 3.50r Coast Guard 1.25 1.25
1698 A254 5r Infantry 2.25 2.25
1699 A254 10r Aakoatey 4.75 4.75
1700 A254 15r Fire department 7.00 7.00
Nos. 1697-1700 (4) 15.25 15.25

Souvenir Sheet

1701 A254 20r Sultan in procession 7.50 7.50

A255

A256

Mushrooms: 10 l, Laetiporus sulphureus. 25 l, Coprinus atramentarius. 50 l, Gandoderma lucidum. 3.50r, Russula aurata. 5r, Polyporus umbellatus. 8r, Suillus grevillei. 10r, Clavaria zollingeri. No. 1709, Boletus edulis. No. 1710, Trametes cinnabarina. No. 1711, Marasmius oreades.

1992, May 14 **Litho.** ***Perf. 14***

1702 A255 10 l multicolored .20 .20
1703 A255 25 l multicolored .20 .20
1704 A255 50 l multicolored .20 .20
1705 A255 3.50r multicolored 1.00 1.00
1706 A255 5r multicolored 1.40 1.40
1707 A255 8r multicolored 2.40 2.40
1708 A255 10r multicolored 2.75 2.75
1709 A255 25r multicolored 7.50 7.50
Nos. 1702-1709 (8) 15.65 15.65

Souvenir Sheets

1710 A255 25r multicolored 7.00 7.00
1711 A255 25r multicolored 7.00 7.00

1992, June 1

1712 A256 10 l Hurdles .25 .25
1713 A256 1r Boxing .25 .25
1714 A256 3.50r Women's running .90 .90
1715 A256 5r Discus 1.25 1.25
1716 A256 7r Basketball 1.75 1.75
1717 A256 10r Running 2.50 2.50
1718 A256 12r Rhythmic gymnastics 3.25 3.25
1719 A256 20r Fencing 5.25 5.25
Nos. 1712-1719 (8) 15.40 15.40

Souvenir Sheets

1720 A256 25r Torch 5.00 5.00
1721 A256 25r Olympic rings, flags 5.00 5.00

1992 Summer Olympics, Barcelona.

A256a

Dinosaurs — A257

1992 Winter Olympics, Albertville: 5r, Two-man bobsled. 8r, Free-style ski jump. 10r, Women's cross-country skiing. No. 1725, Women's slalom skiing, horiz. No. 1726, Men's figure skating.

1992, June 1 **Litho.** ***Perf. 14***

1722 A256a 5r multicolored 1.00 1.00
1723 A256a 8r multicolored 1.60 1.60
1724 A256a 10r multicolored 2.00 2.00
Nos. 1722-1724 (3) 4.60 4.60

Souvenir Sheets

1725 A256a 25r multicolored 5.00 5.00
1726 A256a 25r multicolored 5.00 5.00

1992, Sept. 15 **Litho.** ***Perf. 14***

1727 A257 5 l Deinonychus .20 .20
1728 A257 10 l Styracosaurus .20 .20
1729 A257 25 l Mamenchisaurus .20 .20
1730 A257 50 l Stenonychosaurus .20 .20
1731 A257 1r Parasaurolophus .20 .20

1732 A257 1.25r Scelidosaurus .30 .30
1733 A257 1.75r Tyrannosaurus .40 .40
1734 A257 2r Stegosaurus .45 .45
1735 A257 3.50r Iguanodon .80 .80
1736 A257 4r Anatosaurus .90 .90
1737 A257 5r Monoclonius 1.10 1.10
1738 A257 7r Tenontosaurus 1.60 1.60
1739 A257 8r Brachiosaurus 1.90 1.90
1740 A257 10r Euoplocephalus 2.25 2.25
1741 A257 25r Triceratops 5.75 5.75
1742 A257 50r Apatosaurus 11.50 11.50
Nos. 1727-1742 (16) 27.95 27.95

Souvenir Sheets

1743 A257 25r Iguanodon, allosaurus 5.00 5.00
1744 A257 25r Hadrosaur 5.00 5.00
1745 A257 25r Tyrannosaurus, triceratops 5.00 5.00
1746 A257 25r Brachiosaurus, iguanodons 5.00 5.00

Genoa '92.

1992 Summer Olympics, Barcelona A258

1992, June 1 Litho. *Perf. 14*
1747 A258 10 l Pole vault, vert. .25 .25
1748 A258 25 l Pommel horse .25 .25
1749 A258 50 l Shot put, vert. .25 .25
1750 A258 1r Horizontal bar .25 .25
1751 A258 2r Triple jump .50 .50
1752 A258 3.50r Table tennis, vert. .90 .90
1753 A258 7r Wrestling 1.90 1.90
1754 A258 9r Baseball, vert. 2.25 2.25
1755 A258 12r Swimming 3.25 3.25
Nos. 1747-1755 (9) 9.80 9.80

Souvenir Sheet

1756 A258 25r Decathlon (high jump) 10.00 10.00

Souvenir Sheets

Mysteries of the Universe — A259

#1757, Loch Ness monster. #1758, Explosion of the Hindenburg. #1759, Crystal skulls. #1760, Black holes. #1761, UFO over Washington State. #1762, UFO near Columbus, Ohio. #1763, Explosion at Chernobyl, 1986. #1764, Crop circles of Great Britain. #1765, Ghosts of English castles and mansions. #1766, Drawings of Plain of Nasca, Peru, vert. #1767, Stonehenge, England, vert. #1768, Bust of Plato, the disappearance of Atlantis. #1769, Footprint of Yeti (abominable snowman), vert. #1770, Pyramids of Giza. #1771, Bermuda Triangle. #1772, The Mary Celeste, vert.

1992, Oct. 28
1757-1772 A259 25r each 5.00 5.00

1994 World Cup Soccer Championships, US — A260

Players of 1990 German team: 10 l, Jurgen Klinsmann. 25 l, Pierre Littbarski. 50 l, Lothar Matthaus. 1r, Rudi Voller. 2r, Thomas Hassler. 3.50r, Thomas Berthold. 4r, Jurgen Kohler. 5r, Berti Vogts, trainer. 6r, Bodo Illgner. 7r, Klaus Augenthaler. 8r, Franz Beckenbauer, coach. 10r, Andreas Brehme. 12r, Guido Buchwald.

No. 1786, Team members, horiz. No. 1787, Unidentified player in action, horiz.

1992, Aug. 10 Litho. *Perf. 14*
1773 A260 10 l multicolored .20 .20
1774 A260 25 l multicolored .20 .20
1775 A260 50 l multicolored .20 .20
1776 A260 1r multicolored .20 .20
1777 A260 2r multicolored .65 .65
1778 A260 3.50r multicolored 1.10 1.10
1779 A260 4r multicolored 1.25 1.25
1780 A260 5r multicolored 1.60 1.60
1781 A260 6r multicolored 2.00 2.00
1782 A260 7r multicolored 2.25 2.25
1783 A260 8r multicolored 2.50 2.50
1784 A260 10r multicolored 3.25 3.25
1785 A260 12r multicolored 3.75 3.75
Nos. 1773-1785 (13) 19.15 19.15

Souvenir Sheets

1786 A260 35r multicolored 7.00 7.00
1787 A260 35r multicolored 7.00 7.00

Souvenir Sheet

New York Public Library — A261

1992, Oct. 28 Litho. *Perf. 14*
1788 A261 20r multicolored 5.25 5.25

Postage Stamp Mega Event '92, New York City.

Walt Disney's Goofy, 60th Anniv. — A262

Scenes from Disney cartoon films: 10 l, Father's Weekend, 1953. 50 l, Symphony Hour, 1942. 75 l, Frank Duck Brings 'Em Back Alive, 1946. 1r, Crazy with the Heat, 1947. 2r, The Big Wash, 1948. 3.50r, How to Ride a Horse, 1950. 5r, Two Gun Goofy, 1952. 8r, Saludos Amigos, 1943, vert. 10r, How to Be a Detective, 1952. 12r, For Whom the Bulls Toil, 1953. 15r, Double Dribble, 1946, vert.

No. 1801, Mickey and the Beanstalk, 1947. No. 1802, Double Dribble, 1946, vert., diff. No. 1803, The Goofy Success Story, 1955.

Perf. 14x13½, 13½x14
1992, Dec. 7 Litho.
1789 A262 10 l multicolored .25 .25
1791 A262 50 l multicolored .25 .25
1792 A262 75 l multicolored .25 .25
1793 A262 1r multicolored .25 .25
1794 A262 2r multicolored .50 .50
1795 A262 3.50r multicolored .90 .90
1796 A262 5r multicolored 1.25 1.25
1797 A262 8r multicolored 2.00 2.00
1798 A262 10r multicolored 2.50 2.50
1799 A262 12r multicolored 3.00 3.00
1800 A262 15r multicolored 3.75 3.75
Nos. 1789-1800 (11) 14.90 14.90

Souvenir Sheets

1801 A262 20r multicolored 4.50 4.50
1802 A262 20r multicolored 4.50 4.50
1803 A262 20r multicolored 4.50 4.50

A number has been reserved for an additional value in this set.

A263

Anniversaries and Events — A264

Designs: 1r, Zeppelin on bombing raid over London during World War I. No. 1805, German, French flags, Konrad Adenauer, Charles de Gaulle. No. 1806, Radio telescope. No. 1807, Columbus studying globe. No. 1808, Indian rhinoceros. 7r, WHO, ICN, and FAO emblems. 8r, Green sea turtle. No. 1822, Scarlet macaw. No. 1811, Lion's Intl. emblem and Melvin Jones, founder. No. 1812, Yacht America, first America's Cup winner, 1851. 12r, Columbus claiming San Salvador for Spain. No. 1814, Voyager 1 approaching Saturn. No. 1815, NATO flag, airplanes, Adenauer. 20r, Graf Zeppelin over New York City. No. 1817, Landsat satellite. No. 1818, Count Zeppelin. No. 1819, Santa Maria. No. 1820, Konrad Adenauer. No. 1821, Zubin Mehta, music director, NY Philharmonic, vert. No. 1823, Friedrich Schmiedl (b. 1902), rocket mail pioneer.

1992-93 Litho. *Perf. 14*
1804 A263 1r multicolored .30 .30
1805 A263 3.50r multicolored .90 .90
1806 A263 3.50r multicolored .70 .70
1807 A263 6r multicolored 1.50 1.50
1808 A263 6r multicolored 1.25 1.25
1809 A263 7r multicolored 1.40 1.40
1810 A263 8r multicolored 1.60 1.60
1811 A263 10r multicolored 2.00 2.00
1812 A263 10r multicolored 2.00 2.00
1813 A263 12r multicolored 3.00 3.00
1814 A263 15r multicolored 3.00 3.00
1815 A263 15r multicolored 4.00 4.00
1816 A263 20r multicolored 6.00 6.00
Nos. 1804-1816 (13) 27.65 27.65

Souvenir Sheets

1817 A263 20r multicolored 6.00 6.00
1818 A263 20r multicolored 6.25 6.25
1819 A263 20r multicolored 6.25 6.25
1820 A263 20r multicolored 6.00 6.00
1821 A264 20r multicolored 6.75 6.75
1822 A263 20r multicolored 6.00 4.60
1823 A263 25r multicolored 6.50 6.50
Nos. 1817-1823 (7) 43.75 42.35

Count Zeppelin, 75th anniv. of death (#1804, 1816, 1818). Konrad Adenauer, 25th anniv. of death (#1805, 1815, 1820). Intl. Space Year (#1806, 1814, 1817). Columbus' discovery of America, 500th anniversary (#1807, 1813, 1819). Earth Summit, Rio de Janeiro (#1808, 1810, 1822). Intl. Conference on Nutrition, Rome (#1809). Lions Intl., 75th anniversary (#1811). America's Cup yacht race (#1812). New York Philharmonic, 150th anniv. (#1821).

No. 1823 contains one 27x35mm stamp.

Issue dates: Nos. 1805, 1808, 1810, 1815, 1820, 1822, Jan. 1993. Others, Nov. 1992.

Miniature Sheet

Western Films — A265

Actors and film: No. 1824a, Jimmy Stewart and Marlene Dietrich, Destry Rides Again, 1939. b, Gary Cooper, The Westerner, 1940. c, Henry Fonda, My Darling Clementine, 1946. d, Alan Ladd, Shane, 1953. e, Kirk Douglas and Burt Lancaster, Gunfight at the O.K. Coral, 1957. f, Steve McQueen, The Magnificent Seven, 1960. g, Robert Redford and Paul Newman, Butch Cassidy & The Sundance Kid, 1969. h, Jack Nicholson and Randy Quaid, The Missouri Breaks, 1976.

No. 1825, Clint Eastwood, Pale Rider. No. 1826, John Wayne, The Searchers, 1956.

1992-93 Litho. *Perf. 13½x14*
1824 A265 5r Sheet of 8, #a.-h. 12.00 12.00

Souvenir Sheets

1825 A265 20r multicolored 5.25 5.25
1826 A265 20r multicolored 5.25 5.25

Issued: #1824-1825, 1992; #1826, Jan. 1993.

Miniature Sheet

Opening of Euro Disney Resort, Paris — A266

Disney characters in paintings by French impressionists — #1827: a, Minnie on theater balcony. b, Goofy playing cards. c, Mickey and Minnie walking by outdoor cafe. d, Mickey fishing. e, Goofy dancing to music of harp player. f, Mickey and Minnie in boat. g, Minnie on dance floor. h, Mickey strolling through country. i, Minnie standing behind Polynesian woman.

1992, Dec. *Perf. 14x13½*
1827 A266 5r Sheet of 9, #a.-i. 15.00 15.00

Souvenir Sheets

1828 A266 20r Goofy 4.00 4.00
1829 A266 20r 4.00 4.00
1830 A266 20r Mickey 4.00 4.00

Perf. 13½x14
1831 A266 20r Donald Duck, vert. 4.00 4.00

SAARC Year of the Environment — A267

Designs: 25 l, Waterfall, drought area. 50 l, Clean, polluted beaches. 5r, Clean, polluted ocean. 10r, Clean island with vegetation, island polluted with trees dying.

1992, Dec. 30 Litho. *Perf. 14*
1832 A267 25 l multicolored .20 .20
1833 A267 50 l multicolored .20 .20
1834 A267 5r multicolored 1.00 1.00
1835 A267 10r multicolored 2.00 2.00
Nos. 1832-1835 (4) 3.40 3.40

Elvis Presley (1935-1977) A268

a, Portrait. b, With guitar. c, With microphone.

1993, Jan. 7
1836 A268 3.50r Strip of 3, #a.-c. 2.50 2.50

A set of 4 stamps commemorating South Asia Tourism year, formerly listed as Nos. 1837-1840, were prepared but not issued.

Miniature Sheets

Madame Seriziat A270

Louvre Museum, Bicent.
Details or entire paintings, by Jacques-Louis David:
#1841: b, Pierre Seriziat. c, Madame de Verninac. d, Madame Recamier. e, Self-portrait. f, General Bonaparte. g-h, The Lictors Returning to Brutus the Bodies of his Sons (left, right).
#1842: a, Self-portrait. b, The Woman in Blue. c, The Jeweled Woman. d, Young Girl in her Dressing Room. e, Haydee. f, Chartres Cathedral. g, The Belfry at Douai. h, The Bridge at Mantes.
Paintings by Jean-Honore Fragonard (1732-1806):
#1843: a, The Study. b, Denis Diderot. c, Marie-Madeleine Guimard. d, The Inspiration. e, Tivoli Cascades. f, The Music Lesson. g, The Bolt. h, Blindman's Buff.
#1844, The Gardens of the Villa D'Este, Tivoli, by Jean-Baptiste-Camille Corot, horiz.
#1845, Young Tiger Playing with its Mother, by Delacroix.

1993, Jan. 7 Litho. *Perf. 12*

Sheets of 8

1841 A270 8r #a.-h. + label 13.00 13.00
1842 A270 8r #a.-h. + label 13.00 13.00
1843 A270 8r #a.-h. + label 13.00 13.00

Souvenir Sheets

Perf. 14½

1844 A270 20r multicolored 6.25 6.25
1845 A270 20r multicolored 6.25 6.25

Nos. 1844-1845 contains one 88x55mm stamp.

Miniature Sheet

Coronation of Queen Elizabeth II, 40th Anniv. A271

Designs: a, 3.50r, Official coronation photograph. b, 5r, St. Edward's crown. c, 10r, Dignataries viewing ceremony. d, 10r, Queen, Prince Philip examining banknote.

1993, June 2 *Perf. 13½x14*

1846 A271 Sheet, 2 ea #a.-d. 13.50 13.50

A number has been reserved for an additional value in this set.

Shells — A272

Endangered Animals — A273

1993, July 15 Litho. *Perf. 14*

1848 A272 7 l Precious wentletrap .25 .25
1849 A272 15 l Purple sea snail .25 .25
1850 A272 50 l Arabian cowrie .25 .25
1850A A272 3.50r Major harp .90 .90
1850B A272 4r Royal paper bubble 1.00 1.00
1851 A272 5r Sieve cowrie 1.25 1.25
1852 A272 6r Episcopal miter 1.60 1.60
1852A A272 7r Camp pitar-venus 1.75 1.75
1853 A272 8r Eyed auger 2.10 2.10
1854 A272 10r Onyx cowrie 2.50 2.50
1854A A272 12r Map cowrie 3.00 3.00
1855 A272 20r Caltrop murex 5.25 5.25
Nos. 1848-1855 (12) 20.10 20.10

Souvenir Sheets

1856 A272 25r Scorpion spider conch 8.00 8.00
1857 A272 25r Black striped triton 8.00 8.00
1857A A272 25r Bull's-mouth helmet 8.00 8.00

1993, July 20 Litho. *Perf. 14*

1857B A273 7 l Sifaka lemur .25 .25
1858 A273 10 l Snow leopard .25 .25
1859 A273 15 l Numbat .25 .25
1859A A273 25 l Gorilla .25 .25
1860 A273 2r Koalas .55 .55
1860A A273 3.50r Cheetah .95 .95
1861 A273 5r Yellow-footed rock wallaby 1.40 1.40
1862 A273 7r Orangutan 2.00 2.00
1863 A273 8r Black lemur 2.25 2.25
1864 A273 10r Black rhinoceros 2.75 2.75
1865 A273 15r Humpback whale 4.25 4.25
1865A A273 20r Mauritius parakeet 5.50 5.50
Nos. 1857B-1865A (12) 20.65 20.65

Souvenir Sheets

1866 A273 25r Asian elephant 8.00 8.00
1867 A273 25r Tiger 8.00 8.00
1867A A273 25r Giant panda 8.00 8.00

Miniature Sheets

Fish A274

#1868: b, Black pyramid butterflyfish. c, Bird wrasse. d, Checkerboard wrasse. e, Blue face angelfish. f, Bannerfish. g, Threadfin butterflyfish. h, Picasso triggerfish. i, Pennantfish. j, Grouper. k, Black back butterflyfish. l, Redfin triggerfish. m, Redfin butterflyfish.
#1868A: n, Yellow goatfish. o, Emperor angelfish. p, Madagascar butterflyfish. q, Empress angelfish. r, Longnose butterfly. s, Racoon butterflyfish. t, Harlequin filefish. u, Wedgetailed triggerfish. v, Clark's anemonefish. w, Clown triggerfish. x, Zebra lionfish. y, Maldive clownfish.
#1869, Goldbelly anemone, vert. #1869A, Klein's butterflyfish, vert.

1993, June 30 *Perf. 14x13½*

Sheets of 12

1868 A274 3.50r #b.-m. 9.50 9.50
1868A A274 3.50r #n.-y. 9.50 9.50

Souvenir Sheets

Perf. 12x13

1869 A274 25r multicolored 6.00 6.00
1869A A274 25r multicolored 6.00 6.00

Miniature Sheets

Birds — A275

No. 1870: a, Pallid harrier. b, Cattle egret. c, Koel (b). d, Tree pipit. e, Short-ear owl. f, European kestrel. g, Yellow wagtail. h, Common heron. i, Black bittern. j, Common snipe. k, Little egret. l, Little stint.
No. 1871: a, Gull-billed tern. b, Long-tailed tropicbird (a). c, Frigate bird. d, Wilson's petrel. e, White tern. f, Brown booby. g, Marsh harrier. h, Common noddy. i, Little heron. j, Turnstone. k, Curlew. l, Crab plover.
No. 1872, Caspian tern, horiz. No. 1873, Audubon's shearwater, horiz.

1993, July 5 *Perf. 13½x14*

1870 A275 3.50r Sheet of 12, #a.-l. 9.50 9.50
1871 A275 3.50r Sheet of 12, #a.-l. 9.50 9.50

Souvenir Sheet

Perf. 13x12

1872 A275 25r multicolored 6.00 6.00
1873 A275 25r multicolored 6.00 6.00

No. 1871 is horiz.

Year of Productivity
A276 A277

1993, July 25 *Perf. 14*

1874 A276 7r multicolored 1.60 1.60
1875 A277 10r multicolored 2.40 2.40

A278 A279

Picasso (1881-1973): 3.50r, Still Life with Pitcher and Apples, 1919. 5r, Bowls and Jug, 1908. 10r, Bowls of Fruit and Loaves, 1908. 20r, Green Still Life, 1914, horiz.

1993, Oct. 11 Litho. *Perf. 14*

1876 A278 3.50r multicolored .90 .90
1877 A278 5r multicolored 1.25 1.25
1878 A278 10r multicolored 2.50 2.50
Nos. 1876-1878 (3) 4.65 4.65

Souvenir Sheet

1879 A278 20r multicolored 5.25 5.25

1993, Oct. 11

Copernicus (1473-1543): 3.50r, Early astronomical instrument. 15r, Astronaut wearing Manned Maneuvering Unit. 20r, Copernicus.

1880 A279 3.50r multicolored 1.00 1.00
1881 A279 15r multicolored 4.25 4.25

Souvenir Sheet

1882 A279 20r multicolored 5.25 5.25

Royal Wedding of Crown Prince Naruhito, Princess Masako — A280

3.50r, Crown Prince Naruhito. 10r, Princess Masako, horiz. 25r, Princess Masako.

1993, Oct. 11

1883 A280 3.50r multicolored .75 .75
1884 A280 10r multicolored 2.25 2.25

Souvenir Sheet

1885 A280 25r multicolored 6.25 6.25

1994 Winter Olympics, Lillehammer, Norway — A281

1993, Oct. 11

8r, Marina Kiehl, gold medalist, women's downhill, 1988. 15r, Vegard Ulvang, gold medalist, cross-country skiing, 1992. 25r, Soviet ice hockey goalie, 1980.

1886 A281 8r multicolored 2.00 2.00
1887 A281 15r multicolored 4.00 4.00

Souvenir Sheet

1888 A281 25r multicolored 6.50 6.50

Polska '93 — A282

Fine arts: 3.50r, Zolte Roze, by Menasze Seidenbeurel, 1932. 5r, Cracow Historical Museum. 18r, Apples and Curtain, by Waclaw Borowski. 25r, Seascape, by Roman Sielski, 1931, horiz.

1993, Oct. 11 Litho. *Perf. 14*

1889 A282 3.50r multicolored .90 .90
1890 A282 5r multicolored 1.25 1.25
1891 A282 8r multicolored 2.00 2.00
Nos. 1889-1891 (3) 4.15 4.15

Souvenir Sheet

1892 A282 25r multicolored 5.00 5.00

Butterflies A283

1993, Oct. 25

1893 A283 7 l Commander .25 .25
1894 A283 20 l Blue tiger .25 .25
1895 A283 25 l Centaur oak-blue .25 .25
1896 A283 50 l Common banded peacock .25 .25
1897 A283 5r Glad-eye bushbrown 1.40 1.40
1898 A283 6.50r + 50 l Common tree nymph 2.00 2.00
1899 A283 7r Lemon emigrant 2.00 2.00
1900 A283 10r Blue pansy 2.75 2.75
1901 A283 12r Painted lady 3.50 3.50
1902 A283 15r Blue mormon 4.25 4.25
1903 A283 18r Tamil yeoman 5.00 5.00
1904 A283 20r Crimson rose 5.50 5.50
Nos. 1893-1904 (12) 27.40 27.40

Souvenir Sheets

1905 A283 25r Common imperial 7.50 7.50
1906 A283 25r Great orange tip 7.50 7.50
1907 A283 25r Black prince 7.50 7.50

Nos. 1905-1907 are vert.

Aviation Anniversaries — A284

Designs: 3.50r, Zeppelin on bombing raid caught in British search lights, vert. 5r, Homing pigeon. 10r, Dr. Hugo Eckener, vert. 15r, Airmal service medal, Jim Edgerton's Jenny, mail truck. 20r, USS Macon approaching mooring mast, vert.

Each 25r: #1913, Blanchard's balloon, 1793, vert. #1914, Santos-Dumont's flight around Eiffel Tower, 1901, vert.

1993, Nov. 22 Litho. *Perf. 14*

1908-1912 A284 Set of 5 14.00 14.00

Souvenir Sheets

1913-1914 A284 Set of 2 10.00 10.00

Dr. Hugo Eckener, 125th birth anniv. (3.50r, 10r, 20r, No. 1913).

Miniature Sheets

First Ford Engine, First Benz Four-Wheeled Car, Cent. — A285

#1915: a, 1915 Model T (b, d-e). b, Henry Ford (e). c, Drawing of 1st Ford engine (b, e-f). d, 1993 Ford Probe GT (e). e, 1947 Ford Sportsman, front (f). f, As "f," rear (e). g, 1915 Ford advertisement (j). h, 1955 Ford Thunderbird (g, i). i, Ford emblem (f, h). j, 1958 Edsel Citation. k, 1941 Ford half-ton pickup. l, Model T.

#1916: a, 1937 Daimler-Benz Straight 8 (b). b, Karl Benz (e). c, Mercedes-Benz advertisement (f). d, 1929 Mercedes 38-250SS (e). e, 1893 Benz Viktoria (f, h). f, Mercedes star emblem (i). g, WWI Mercedes engine. h, 1957 Mercedes-Benz 300SL Gullwing (g). i, 1993 Mercedes Benz SL coupe/roadster (h). j, 1906 Benz 4-cylinder car (k). k, Early Benz advertisement. l, Benz Viktoria, 1893.

1993, Nov. 22

1915 A285 3.50r Sheet of 12, #a.-l. 12.00 12.00
1916 A285 3.50r Sheet of 12, #a.-l. 12.00 12.00

Souvenir Sheets

1917 A285 25r 1933 Ford Model Y 6.50 6.50
1918 A285 25r 1955 Mercedes 300S 6.50 6.50

Peter and the Wolf — A286

Characters and scenes from Disney animated film: 7 l, 15 l, 20 l, 25 l, 50 l, 1r.
Nos. 1925a-1925i: Part 1.
Nos. 1926a-1926i: Part 2.

1993, Dec. 20

1919-1924 A286 Set of 6 1.00 1.00

Miniature Sheets of 9

1925 A286 3.50r #a.-i. 7.50 7.50
1926 A286 3.50r #a.-i. 7.50 7.50

Souvenir Sheets

1927 A286 25r Sonia 5.00 5.00
1928 A286 25r Ivan 5.00 5.00

Fine Art — A287

Paintings by Rembrandt: 50 l, Girl with a Broom. No. 1931, 3.50r, Young Girl at half-open Door. 5r, The Prophetess Hannah (Rembrandt's Mother). 7r, Woman with a Pink Flower. 12r, Lucretia. No. 1939, 15r, Lady with an Ostich Feather Fan.

Paintings by Matisse: 2r, Girl with Tulips (Jeanne Vaderin). No. 1932, 3.50r. Portrait of Greta Moll. 6.50r, The Idol. 9r, Mme. Matisse in Japanese Robe. 10r, Portrait of MMe Matisse (The Green Line). No. 1940, 15r, The Woman with the Hat.

Each 25r: No. 1941, Married Couple with 3 Children (A Family Group), by Rembrandt, horiz. No. 1942, The Painter's Family, by Matisse. No. 1942A: The Music Makers, by Rembrandt.

1994, Jan. 11 Litho. *Perf. 13*

1929-1940 A287 Set of 12 21.00 21.00

Souvenir Sheets

1941-1942A A287 Set of 3 22.50 22.50

No. 1942A issued Feb. 2.

1994 World Cup Soccer US — A288

Players, country: 7 l, Windischmann, US; Giannini, Italy. 20 l, Carnevale, Gascoigne. 25 l, Platt & teammates, England. 3.50r, Koeman, Holland; Klinsmann, Germany. 5r, Quinn, Ireland; Maldini, Italy. 7r, Lineker, England. 15r, Hassam, Egypt; Moran, Ireland. 18r, Canniggia, Argentina.

Each 25r: No. 1951, Conejo, Costa Rica; Mozer, Brazil, horiz. No. 1952, Armstrong & Barboa, US; Orgis, Austria.

1994, Jan. 11 *Perf. 14*

1943-1950 A288 Set of 8 12.50 12.50

Souvenir Sheets

1951-1952 A288 Set of 2 12.00 12.00

A289

Hong Kong '94 — A290

Stamps, Moon-Lantern Festival, Hong Kong: No. 1953, Hong Kong #416, girls, lanterns. No. 1954, Lanterns, #660.

Cloisonne Enamel, Qing Dynasty: No. 1955a, Vase. b, Flower holder. c, Elephant with vase on back. d, Pot (Tibetan-style lama's milk-tea pot. e, Fo-dog. f, Pot with swing handle.

1994, Feb. 18 Litho. *Perf. 14*

1953 A289 4r multicolored .80 .80
1954 A289 4r multicolored .80 .80
a. Pair, #1953-1954 1.60 1.60

Miniature Sheet

1955 A290 2r Sheet of 6, #a.-f. 6.00 6.00

Nos. 1953-1954 issued in sheets of 5 pairs. No. 1954a is a continuous design.

New Year 1994 (Year of the Dog) (#1955e).

Sierra Club, Cent. A290a

Various animals, each 6.50r:

Nos. 1956a-1956b, Prairie dog. c.-e, Woodland caribou. f, Galapagos penguin.

No. 1957, vert: a, Humpback whale. b.-c, Ocelot. d, Snow monkey. e, Prairie dog. f, Golden lion tamarin.

No. 1958: a.-b, Golden lion tamarin. c.-d, Humpback whale. e, Bengal tiger. f, Ocelot. g.-h, Snow monkey.

No. 1959, vert: a.-b, Galapagos penguin. c.-d, Bengal tiger. e.-g, Philippine tarsier. h, Sierra Club centennial emblem.

1994, May 20 Litho. *Perf. 14*

Miniature Sheets of 6, #a-f

1956-1957 A290a Set of 2 18.50 18.50

Miniature Sheets of 8, #a-h

1958-1959 A290a Set of 2 22.50 22.50

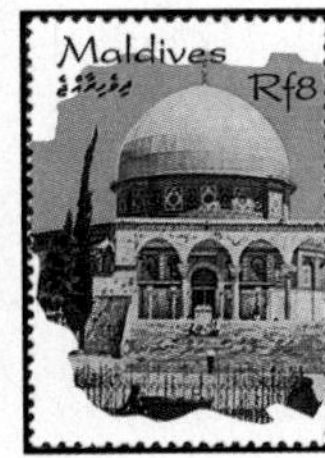

Dome of the Rock, Jerusalem — A291

1994, June 10 *Perf. 13½*

1960 A291 8r multicolored 1.50 1.50

A292

Designs: 25 l, Elasmosaurus. 50 l, Dilophosaurus. 1r, Avimimus. 5r, Chasmosaurus. 8r, Edmontonia. 10r, Anatosaurus. 15r, Velociraptor. 20r, Spinosaurus.

No. 1969, each 3r: a, Dimorphodon. b, Megalosaurus. c, Kuehneosaurus. d, Dryosaurus. e, Kentrosaurus. f, Baraposaurus (c). g, Tenontosaurus. h, Elaphrosaurus (i). i, Maiasaura. j, Huayangosaurus. k, Rutiodon. l, Pianitzkysaurus.

No. 1970, each 3r: a, Quetzalcoatlus. b, Daspletosaurus. c, Pleurocoelus. d, Baryonyx. e, Pentaceratops. f, Kritosaurus. g, Microvenator (h). h, Nodosaurus. i, Montanaceratops. j, Dromiceiomimus. k, Dryptosaurus. l, Parkosaurus.

Each 25r: #1971, Gallimimus. #1972, Plateosaurus, vert.

1994, June 20 *Perf. 14*

1961-1968 A292 Set of 8 16.50 16.50

Miniature Sheets of 12, #a-l

1969-1970 A292 Set of 2 19.50 19.50

Souvenir Sheets

1971-1972 A292 Set of 2 10.00 10.00

Nos. 1969-1970 are continuous design.

Locomotives A293

Domestic Cats — A294

Designs: 25 l, 2-6-6-0 Mallet, Indonesia, horiz. 50 l, C62, Japan, horiz. 1r, D51, Japan. 5r, 4-6-0 Steam, India. 8r, Class 485 electric, Japan, horiz. 10r, Class WP Pacific, India. 15r, "People" class RM 4-6-2, China. 20r, C57, Japan, horiz.

No. 1981: a, W Class 0-6-2, India. b, C53 Class, Indonesia. c, C-10, Japan. d, Hanomag 4-8-0, India. e, Hakari bullet train, Japan. f, C-55, Japan.

Each 25r: No. 1982, 4-4-0, Indonesia. No. 1983, Series 8620, Japan.

1994, July 4

1973-1980 A293 Set of 8 11.00 11.00

Miniature Sheet of 6

1981 A293 6.50r +50 l, #a.-f. 7.50 7.50

Souvenir Sheets

1982-1983 A293 Set of 2 10.00 10.00

1994, July 11

Designs: 7 l, Japanese bobtail, horiz. 20 l, Siamese. 25 l, Persian longhair, horiz. 50 l, Somali. 3.50r, Oriental shorthair, horiz. 5r, Burmese, horiz. 7r, Bombay, horiz. 10r, Turkish van. 12r, Javanese. 15r, Singapura, horiz. 18r, Turkish angora. 20r, Egyptian mau.

Each 25r: #1996, Birman. #1997, Korat. #1998, Abyssinian.

1984-1995 A294 Set of 12 20.00 20.00

Souvenir Sheets

1996-1998 A294 Set of 3 17.50 17.50

Miniature Sheets of 6

1994 World Cup Soccer Championships, US — A295

No. 1999a, 10 l, Franco Baresi, Italy, Stuart McCall, Scotland. b, 25 l, McCarthy, Great Britain, Lineker, Ireland. c, 50 l, J. Helt, Denmark, R. Gordillo, Spain. d, 5r, Martin Vasquez, Spain, Enzo Scifo, Belgium. e, 10r, Emblem. f, 12f, Tomas Brolin, Sweden, Gordon Durie, Scotland.

No. 2000a, Bebeto, Brazil. b, Lothar Matthaus, Great Britain. c, Diego Maradona, Argentina. d, Stephane Chapuasti, Switzerland. e, George Hagi, Romania. f, Carlos Valderama, Colombia.

No. 2001, Hossam Hassan, 2nd Egyptian player.

1994, Aug. 4 Litho. *Perf. 14*

1999 A295 #a.-f. 5.00 5.00
2000 A295 6.50r #a.-f, vert. 7.00 7.00

Souvenir Sheet

2001 A295 10r multicolored 3.75 3.75

D-Day, 50th Anniv. A296

Designs: 2r, Amphibious DUKW approaches Utah Beach. 4r, Landing craft tank, Sword Beach. 18r, Landing craft infantry damaged at Omaha Beach.

No. 2006, Canadian commandos, Juno Beach.

1994, Aug. 8

2003-2005 A296 Set of 3 4.50 4.50

Souvenir Sheet

2006 A296 25r multicolored 5.50 5.50

A297

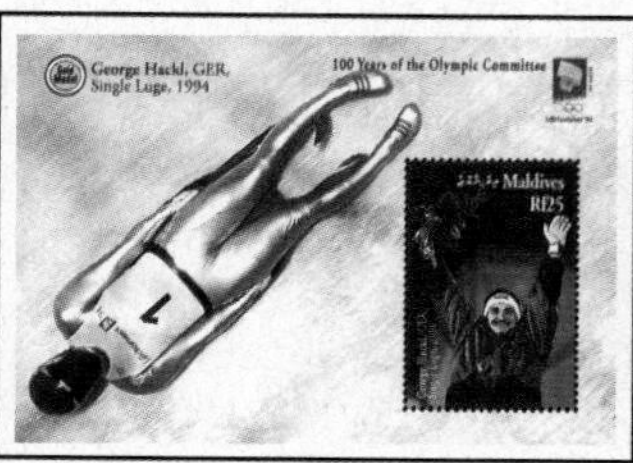

Intl. Olympic Committee, Cent. — A298

Designs: 7r, Linford Christie, Great Britain, track 1988. 12r, Koji Gushiken, Japan, gymnastics, 1984.

25r, George Hackl, Germany, single luge, 1994.

1994, Aug. 8

2007 A297 7r multicolored 1.25 1.25
2008 A297 12r multicolored 2.25 2.25

Souvenir Sheet

2009 A298 25r multicolored 5.25 5.25

A299

PHILAKOREA '94 — A300

Designs: 50 l, Suwan Folk Village duck pond. 3.50r, Youngduson Park. 20r, Ploughing, Hahoe Village, Andong region.

Ceramics, Choson & Koryo Dynasties: No. 2013a, Pear-shaped bottle. b, Vase. c, Vase with repaired lip. d, Labed vase, stoneware. e, Vase, celadon-glazed. f, Vase, unglazed stone. g, Ritual water sprinkler. h, Celadon-glazed vase.

25r, Hunting (detail from eight-panel screen, Choson Dynasty), vert.

1994, Aug. 8 *Perf. 14, 13½ (#2013)*

2010-2012 A299 Set of 3 5.00 5.00

Miniature Sheet of 8

2013 A300 3r #a.-h. 5.00 5.00

Souvenir Sheet

2014 A299 25r multicolored 5.25 5.25

First Manned Moon Landing, 25th Anniv. A301

No. 2015, each 5r: a, Apollo 11 crew. b, Apollo 11 patch, signatures of crew. c, "Buzz" Aldrin, lunar module, Eagle. d, Apollo 12 crew. e, Apollo 12 patch, signatures of crew. f, Alan Bean transporting ALSEP.

No. 2016, each 5r: a, Apollo 16 crew. b, Apollo 16 patch, signatures of crew. c, John Young gives a "Navy salute." d, Apollo 17 crew. e, Apollo 17 patch, signatures of crew. f, Night launch of Apollo 17.

25r, Launch at Baikonur.

1994, Aug. 8 *Perf. 14*

Miniature Sheets of 6, #a-f

2015-2016 A301 Set of 2 13.50 13.50

Souvenir Sheet

2017 A301 25r multicolored 5.25 5.25

UN Development Plan — A302

1r, Woman, baby, undernourished man, city on island. 8r, Island native, case worker, island, ship.

1994 Litho. *Perf. 14*

2018 A302 1r multicolored .20 .20
2019 A302 8r multicolored 1.90 1.90

Miniature Sheet of 12

Space Exploration A304

#2020: a, Voyager 2. b, Sputnik. c, Apollo-Soyuz. d, Apollo 10 descent. e, Apollo 11 mission insignia. f, Hubble space telescope. g, Buzz Aldrin. h, RCA lunar cam. i, Lunar rover. j, Jim Irwin. k, Apollo 12 lunar module. l, Lunar soil extraction.

Each 25r: #2021, David Scott in open hatch of Apollo 9 command module. #2022, Alan Shepard, Jr. waving salute from moon, Apollo 14, horiz.

1994, Aug. 8 Litho. *Perf. 14*

2020 A304 5r #a.-l. 20.00 20.00

Souvenir Sheets

2021-2022 A304 Set of 2 15.00 15.00

Aminiya School, 50th Anniv. A305

15 l, Discipline. 50 l, Arts. 1r, Emblem, hand holding book, vert. 8r, Girls carrying books, vert. 10r, Sports. 11r, Girls cheering, vert. 13r, Science.

1994, Nov. 28

2023-2029 A305 Set of 7 8.50 8.50

ICAO, 50th Anniv. A306

Designs: 50 l, Boeing 747. 1r, De Havilland Comet 4. 2r, Male Intl. Airport, Maldives. 3r, Lockheed 1649 Super Star. 8r, European Airbus. 10r, Dornier Do228. 25r, Concorde.

1994, Dec. 31

2030-2035 A306 Set of 6 8.25 8.25

Souvenir Sheet

2036 A306 25r multicolored 5.50 5.50

Miniature Sheets of 9

Water Birds A307

Designs: No. 2037a, Northern pintail (b, d). b, Comb duck (c). c, Ruddy duck. d, Garganey (a, e, g, h). e, Lesser whistling duck (b, c, f). f, Green winged teal. g, Fulvous whistling duck. h, Northern shoveler (e). i, Cotton pygmy goose (h).

No. 2038, vert.: a, Pochard (b). b, Mallard (c, e, f). c, Wigeon. d, Northern shoveler (e, g). e, Northern pintail (h). f, Garganey (e, i). g, Tufted duck. h, Ferruginous duck (i). i, Red-crested pochard.

Each 25r: No. 2039, Cotton pygmy goose, vert. No. 2040, Garganey, diff.

1995, Feb. 27 Litho. *Perf. 14*

2037 A307 5r #a.-i. 8.25 8.25
2038 A307 6.50r + 50 l #a.-i. 11.50 11.50

Souvenir Sheets

2039-2040 A307 Set of 2 9.00 9.00

Monuments of the World — A308

Designs: 7 l, Taj Mahal. 10 l, Washington Monument. 15 l, Mt. Rushmore Memorial. 25 l, Arc de Triomphe, vert. 50 l, Sphinx, vert. 5r, El Castillo Monument of the Toltec, Chichen Itza, Yucatan, Mexico. 8r, Toltec monument, Tula, Mexico, vert. 12r, Victory Column, Berlin, vert.

Each 25r: No. 2049, Moai statues, Easter Island. No. 2050, Stonehenge.

1995, Feb. 28

2041-2048 A308 Set of 8 6.00 6.00

Souvenir Sheets

2049-2050 A308 Set of 2 9.00 9.00

No. 2049 contains one 43x57mm stamp, No. 2050 one 85x28mm stamp.

Donald Duck, 60th Birthday (in 1994) — A309

Scenes from "Donald and the Wheel:" 3 l, Racing chariot. 4 l, Standing on log. 5 l, Operating steam locomotive. 10 l, Looking at cave drawing, vert. 20 l, Sitting in "junked" car, vert. 25 l, Listening to phonograph. 5r, Climbing on mammoth. 20r, Pushing old car.

Disney Duck family orchestra, vert, each 5r: No. 2059a, Donald Duck, saxophone. b, Moby Duck, violin. c, Feathry Duck, banjo. d, Daisy Duck, harp. e, Gladstone Gander, clarinet. f, Dewey, Louie, Huey, oboe. g, Gus Goose, flute. h, Ludwig von Drake, trombone.

Donald Duck family portraits, vert, each 5r: No. 2060a, Daisy. b, Donald. c, Grandma. d, Gus Goose. e, Gyro Gearloose, f, Huey, Dewey, Louie. g, Ludwig von Drake. h, Scrooge McDuck.

Each 25r: No. 2061, Dixieland band, vert. No. 2062, Donald conducting symphony orchestra. No. 2063, Donald being photographed, vert. No. 2064, Huey, Dewey, Louie in family portrait.

Perf. 13½x13, 13x13½

1995, Mar. 22 Litho.

2051-2058 A309 Set of 8 6.50 6.50

Miniature Sheets of 8, #a-h

2059-2060 A309 Set of 2 17.00 17.00

Souvenir Sheets

2061-2064 A309 Set of 4 18.00 18.00

EID Greetings — A310

1r, Mosque. 1r, Rose. 8r, Hibiscus. 10r, Orchids.

1995, May 1 Litho. *Perf. 14*

2065-2068 A310 Set of 4 3.75 3.75

Whales, Dolphins, & Porpoises A311

Nos. 2069-2072: 1r, Killer whale. 2r, Bottlenose dolphin. 8r, Humpback whale. 10r, Common dolphin.

No. 2073, each 3r: a, Hourglass dolphin. b, Bottlenose dolphin. c, Dusky dolphin. d, Spectacled porpoise. e, Fraser's dolphin. f, Commerson's dolphin. g, Spinner dolphin. h, Dalls dolphin. i, Spotted dolphin. j, Indus river dolphin. k, Hector's dolphin. l, Amazon river dolphin.

No. 2074, each 3r: a, Right whale (d). b, Killer whale (a). c, Humpback whale (f). d, Beluga. e, Narwhale. f, Blue whale (e, g). g, Bowhead whale (h, k). h, Fin whale (d, e, g). i, Pilot whale. j, Grey whale. k, Sperm whale (l). l, Goosebeaked whale.

Each 25r: No. 2075, Hourglass dolphin. No. 2076, Sperm whale.

1995, May 16

2069-2072 A311 Set of 4 4.00 4.00

Miniature Sheets of 12, #a-l

2073-2074 A311 Set of 2 15.50 15.50

Souvenir Sheets

2075-2076 A311 Set of 2 11.00 11.00

Singapore '95.

UN, 50th Anniv. A311a

Designs: 30 l, Emblem, security of small states. 8r, Women in development. 11r, Peace keeping, peace making operations. 13r, Disarmament.

1995, July 6 Litho. *Perf. 14*

2076A-2076D A311a Set of 4 5.75 5.75

UN, 50th Anniv. — A312

No. 2077: a, 6.50r+50 l, Child, dove flying left. b, 8r, Earth from space. c, 10r, Child, Dove flying right.

25r, UN emblem, dove.

1995, July 6 Litho. *Perf. 14*

2077 A312 Strip of 3, #a.-c. 4.50 4.50

Souvenir Sheet

2078 A312 25r multicolored 4.50 4.50

No. 2077 is a continuous design.

FAO, 50th Anniv. — A313
A312a A313

1995 Litho. *Perf. 14*

2078A A312a 7r Food for all 1.25 1.25

2078B A312a 8r Dolphin-friendly fishing 1.40 1.40

1995, July 6

No. 2079: a, 6.50r+50 l, Child eating. b, 8r, FAO emblem. c, 10r, Mother, child.

25r, Food emblem, child, horiz.

2079 A313 Strip of 3, #a.-c. 6.00 6.00

Souvenir Sheet

2080 A313 25r multicolored 6.00 6.00

1995 Boy Scout Jamboree, Holland — A314

No. 2081: a, 10r, Natl. flag, scouts, tents. b, 12r, Scout cooking. c, 15r, Scouts sitting before tents.

25r, Scout playing flute, camp at night, vert.

1995, July 6

2081 A314 Strip of 3, #a.-c. 6.75 6.75

Souvenir Sheet

2082 A314 25r multicolored 4.50 4.50

No. 2081 is a continuous design.

Queen Mother, 95th Birthday — A315

No. 2083: a, Drawing. b, Blue print dress, pearls. c, Formal portrait. d, Blue outfit.

25r, Pale violet hat, violet & blue dress.

1995, July 6 *Perf. 13½x14*

2083 A315 5r Block or strip of 4, #a.-d. 5.25 5.25

Souvenir Sheet

2084 A315 25r multicolored 6.00 6.00

No. 2083 was issued in sheets of 2.

Sheets of Nos. 2083-2084 exist overprinted in margin with black frame and text "In Memoriam 1900-2002."

Natl. Library, 50th Anniv. A316

Designs: 2r, Boys seated at library table. 8r, Two people standing, two at table.

10r, Library entrance.

1995, July 12 *Perf. 14*

2085 A316 2r multicolored .35 .35

2086 A316 8r multicolored 1.40 1.40

Size: 100x70mm

Imperf

2087 A316 10r multicolored 1.75 1.75

Miniature Sheets of 6 or 8

End of World War II, 50th Anniv. A317

No. 2088: a, 203mm Red Army howitzer. b, Ruins of Hitler's residence, Berchtesgaden. c, Operation Manna, Allies drop food to starving Dutch. d, Soviet IL-1 fighter. e, Inmates, British troops burn last hut at Belsen. f, Last V1 Buzz Bomb launched against London. g, US 3rd Armored Division passes through ruins of Cologne. h, Gutted Reichstag, May 7, 1946.

No. 2089: a, Grumman F6F-3 Hellcat. b, F4-U1 attacking with rockets. c, Douglas Dauntless. d, Guadalcanal, Aug. 7, 1942. e, US Marines in Alligator landing craft. f, US Infantry landing craft.

Each 25r: No. 2090, Allied soldiers with smiling faces. No. 2091, Corsair fighters.

1995, July 6 Litho. *Perf. 14*

2088 A317 5r #a.-h. + label 7.25 7.25

2089 A317 6.50r +50 l #a.-f. + label 9.00 9.00

Souvenir Sheets

2090-2091 A317 Set of 2 10.00 10.00

Turtles A318

Hawksbill turtle: No. 2092a, Crawling. b, Two in water. c, One crawling out of water. d, Swimming.

No. 2093: a, Spur-thighed tortoise. b, Aldabra turtle. c, Loggerhead turtle. d, Olive ridley. e, Leatherback turtle. f, Green turtle. g, Atlantic ridley. h, Hawsbill turtle.

25r, Chelonia mydas.

1995, Aug. 22

2092 A318 10r Strip of 4, #a.-d. 9.00 9.00

Miniature Sheet of 8

2093 A318 3r #a.-h. 9.00 9.00

Souvenir Sheet

2094 A318 25r multicolored 13.00 13.00

World Wildlife Fund (#2092). No. 2092 was printed in sheets of 12 stamps.

Fourth World Conference on Women, Beijing — A318a

Designs: 30 l, Woman at computer. 1r, Woman high jumping. 8r, Women dancing. 11r, Woman pilot.

1995, Aug. 24 Litho. *Perf. 12¼*

2094A-2094D A318a Set of 4 — —

Miniature Sheets

Singapore '95 — A319

Mushrooms, butterflies, each 2r: No. 2095a, Russula aurata, papilio demodocus. b, Kallimoides rumia, lepista saeva. c, Lapista nuda, hypolimnas salmacis. d, Precis octavia, boletus subtomentosus.

No. 2096: a, 5r, Gyroporus castaneus, hypolimnas salmacis. b, 8r, Papilio dardanus, Gomphidius glutinosus. c, 10r, Russula olivacea, precis octavia. d, 12r, Prepona praeneste, boletus edulis.

Each 25r: No. 2097, Hypolimnas salmacis, boletus rhodoxanthus, vert. No. 2098, Amanita muscaria, kallimoides rumia, vert.

1995, Oct. 18 Litho. *Perf. 14*

2095 A319 Sheet of 4, #a.-d. 1.50 1.50

2096 A319 Sheet of 4, #a.-d. 7.50 7.50

Souvenir Sheets

2097-2098 A319 Set of 2 10.00 10.00

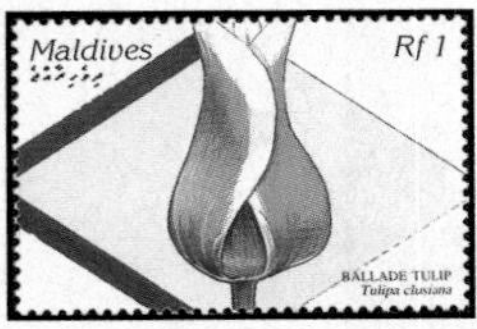

Flowers A320

Designs: 1r, Ballade tulip. 3r, White mallow. 5r, Regale trumpet lily. 7r, Lilactime dahlia. 8r, Blue ideal iris. 10r, Red crown imperial.

No. 2105, a, Dendrobium waipahu beauty. b, Brassocattleya Jean Murray "Allan Christenson." c, Cymbidium Fort George "Lewes." d, Paphiopedilum malipoense. e, Cycnoches chlorochilon. f, Rhyncholaelia digbgana. g, Lycaste deppei. h, Masdevalia constricta. i, Paphiopedilum Clair de Lune "Edgard Van Belle."

Each 25r: No. 2106, Psychopsis krameriana. No. 2107, Cockleshell orchid.

1995, Dec. 4 Litho. *Perf. 14*

2099-2104 A320 Set of 6 7.25 7.25

Miniature Sheet

2105 A320 5r Sheet of 9, #a.-i. 9.25 9.25

Souvenir Sheets

2106-2107 A320 Set of 2 9.00 9.00

Miniature Sheet

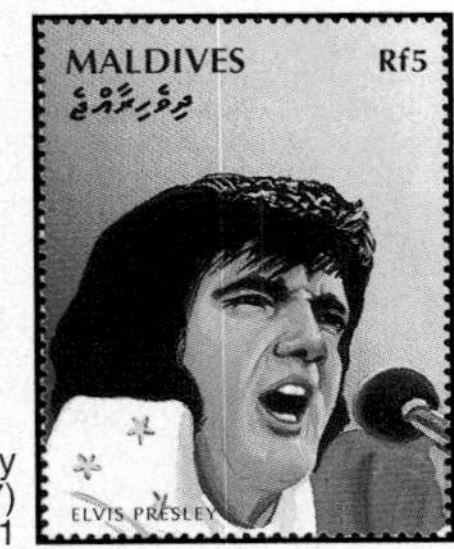

Elvis Presley (1935-77) A321

Various portraits.

1995, Dec. 8 *Perf. 13½x14*

2108 A321 5r Sheet of 9, #a.-i. 8.00 8.00

Souvenir Sheet

Perf. 14x13½

2109 A321 25r multi, horiz. 4.50 4.50

Miniature Sheets

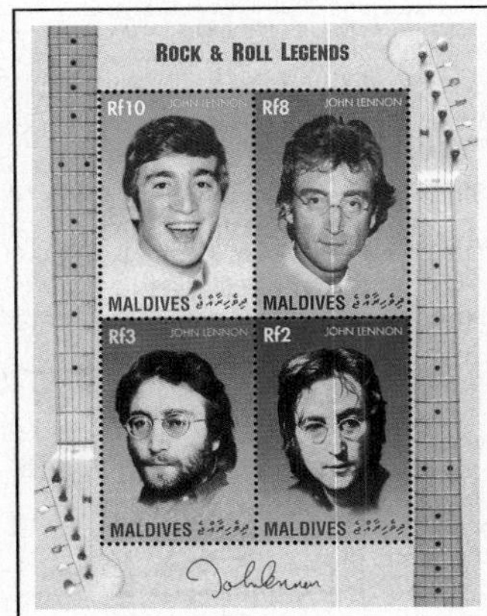

John Lennon (1940-80), Entertainer — A322

No. 2110, Various portraits.

No. 2111: a, 10r, As young man. b, 8r, Younger man with glasses. c, 3r, With beard. d, 2r, Older picture without beard.

No. 2112, Standing at microphone.

1995, Dec. 8

2110 A322 5r Sheet of 6, #a.-f. 8.75 8.75

2111 A322 Sheet of 4, #a.-d. 6.75 6.75

Souvenir Sheet

2112 A322 25r multicolored 7.00 7.00

Nobel Prize Fund Established, Cent. — A323

Recipients: No. 2113, each 5r: a, Bernardo A. Houssay, medicine, 1947. b, Paul H. Müller, medicine, 1948. c, Walter R. Hess, medicine, 1949. d, Sir MacFarlane Burnet, medicine, 1960. e, Baruch S. Blumberg, medicine, 1976. f, Daniel Nathans, medicine, 1978. g, Glenn T. Seaborg, chemistry, 1951. h, Ilya Prigogine, chemistry, 1977. i, Kenichi Fukui, chemistry, 1981.

No. 2114, each 5r: a, Johannes Van Der Waals, physics, 1910. b, Charles Édouard Guillaume, physics, 1920. c, Sir James Chadwick, physics, 1935. d, Willem Einthoven, medicine, 1924. e, Henrik Dam, medicine, 1943. f, Sir Alexander Fleming, medicine, 1945. g, Hermann J. Muller, medicine, 1946. h, Rodney R. Porter, medicine, 1972. i, Werner Arber, medicine, 1978.

No. 2115, each 5r: a, Dag Hammarskjold, peace, 1961. b, Alva R. Myrdal, peace, 1982. c, Archbishop Desmond M. Tutu, peace, 1984. d, Rudolf C. Eucken, literature, 1908. e, Aleksandr Solzhenitsyn, literature, 1970. f, Gabriel Garcia Márquez, literature, 1982. g, Chen N. Yang, physics, 1957. h, Karl A. Müller, physics, 1987. i, Melvin Schwartz, physics, 1988.

No. 2116, each 5r: a, Niels Bohr, physics, 1922. b, Ben R. Mottelson, physics, 1975. c, Patrick White, literature, 1973. d, Elias Canetti, literature, 1981. e, Theodor Kocher, medicine, 1909. f, August Krogh, medicine, 1920. g, William P. Murphy, medicine, 1934. h, John H. Northrop, chemistry, 1946. i, Luis F. Leloir, chemistry, 1970.

No. 2117, each 5r: a, Carl Spitteler, literatue, 1919. b, Henri Bergson, literature, 1927. c, Johannes V. Jensen, literature, 1944. d, Antoine-Henri Becquerel, physics, 1903. e, Sir William H. Bragg, physics, 1915. f, Sir William L. Bragg, physics, 1915. g, Fredrik Bajer, peace, 1908. h, Léon Bourgeois, peace, 1920. i, Karl Branting, peace, 1921.

No. 2118, each 5r: a, Robert A. Millikan, physics, 1923. b, Louis V. de Broglie, physics, 1929. c, Ernest Walton, physics, 1951. d, Richard Willstätter, chemistry, 1915. e, Lars Onsager, chemistry, 1968. f, Gerhard Herzberg, chemistry, 1971. g, William B. Yeats, literature, 1923. h, George B. Shaw, literature, 1925. i, Eugene O'Neill, literature, 1936.

Each 25r: No. 2119, Eisaku Sato, peace, 1974. No. 2120, Robert Koch, medicine, 1905. No. 2121, Otto Wallach, chemistry, 1910. No. 2122, Konrad Bloch, medicine, 1964. No. 2123, Samuel Beckett, literature, 1969. No. 2124, Hideki Yukawa, physics, 1949.

1995, Dec. 28 Litho. *Perf. 14*

Miniature Sheets of 9, #a-i

2113-2118 A323 Set of 6 48.00 48.00

Souvenir Sheets

2119-2124 A323 Set of 6 27.00 27.00

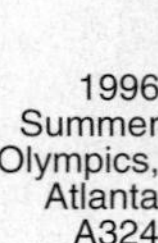

1996 Summer Olympics, Atlanta A324

Designs: 1r, Rhythmic gymnastics, Tokyo, 1964. 3r, Archery, Moscow, 1980. 5r, Diving, Stockholm, 1912. 7r, High jump, London, 1948. 10r, Track and field, Berlin, 1936. 12r, Hurdles, Amsterdam 1928.

No. 2131: a, Montreal 1976. b, Decathlon. c, Olympic pin, Moscow, 1980. d, Fencing. e, Olympic medal. f, Equestrian. g, Sydney, 2000. h, Track and field. i, Seoul, 1988.

Each 25r: No. 2132, Olympic torch, vert. No. 2133, Olympic flame, vert.

1996, Jan. 25 Litho. *Perf. 14*

2125-2130 A324 Set of 6 7.75 7.75

Miniature Sheet

2131 A324 5r Sheet of 9, #a.-i. 9.00 9.00

Souvenir Sheets

2132-2133 A324 Set of 2 10.50 10.50

Paintings from Metropolitan Museum of Art — A325

No. 2134, each 4r: a, Self-portrait, by Degas. b, Andromache & Astyanax, by Prud'hon. c, René Grenier, by Toulouse-Lautrec. d, The Banks of the Biéve Near Bicetre, by Rousseau. e, The Repast of the Lion, by Rousseau. f, Portrait Yves Gobillard-Morisot, by Degas. g, Sunflowers, by Van Gogh. h, The Singer in Green, by Degas.

No. 2135, each 4r: a, Still Life, by Fantin-Latour. b, Portrait of a Lady in Gray, by Degas. c, Apples & Grapes, by Monet. d, The Englishman, by Toulouse-Lautrec. e, Cypresses, by Van Gogh. f, Flowers in Chinese Vase, by Redon. g, The Gardener, by Seurat. h, Large Sunflowers I, by Nolde.

By Manet: No. 2136, each 4r: a, The Spanish Singer. b, Young Man in Costume of Majo. c, Mademoisselle Victorine. d, Boating. e, Peonies. f, Woman with a Parrot. g, George Moore. h, The Monet Family in Their Garden.

No. 2137, each 4r7: a, Goldfish, by Matisse. b, Spanish Woman: Harmony in Blue, by Matisse. c, Nasturtiums & the "Dance" II, by Matisse. d, The House Behind Trees, by Braque. e, Māda Primavesi, by Klimt. f, Head of a Woman, by Picasso. g, Woman in White, by Picasso. h, Harlequin, by Picasso.

Each 25r: No. 2138, Northeaster, by Homer. No. 2139, The Fortune Teller, by Georges de la Tour. No. 2140, Santi (Sanzio), Ritratto di Andrea Navagero E Agostino Beazzano, by Raphael. No. 2141, Portrait of a Woman, by Rubens.

1996, Apr. 22 Litho. *Perf. 13½x14*

Sheets of 8, #a-h + label

2134-2137 A325 Set of 4 32.50 32.50

Souvenir Sheets

Perf. 14

2138-2141 A325 Set of 4 21.00 21.00

Nos. 2138-2141 each contain one 85x57mm stamp.

Nos. 2140-2141 are not in the Metropolitan Museum.

Disney Characters Visit China — A326

No. 2142, each 2r: a, Mickey at the Great Wall. b, Pluto's encounter in the Temple Garden. c, Minnie saves the pandas. d, Mickey sails with the junks. e, Goofy at the grottoes. f, Donald, Daisy at the marble boat.

No. 2143, each 2r: a, Mickey leads terra cotta statues. b, Goofy's masks. c, Traditional fishing with Donald, Goofy. d, Mickey, Minnie in dragon boat. e, Donald at Peking Opera. f, Mickey, Minnie, in Chinese Garden.

No. 2144, vert: a, Mickey, Minnie snowballing at ice pagoda. b, Donald, Mickey fly Chinese kites. c, Goofy plays anyiwu. d, Mickey, Goofy, origami. e, Donald, Mickey in dragon dance.

No. 2145, 5r, Mickey viewing Guilin. No. 2146, 7r, Mickey, Minnie at Moon Festival. No. 2147, 8r, Donald enjoying traditional Chinese food.

1996, May 10 *Perf. 14x13½, 13½x14*

Sheets of 6, #a-f

2142-2143 A326 Set of 2 11.50 11.50

Sheet of 5, #a-e

2144 A326 3r #a.-e. + label 6.00 6.00

Souvenir Sheets

2145 A326 5r multicolored 2.00 2.00
2146 A326 7r multicolored 2.50 2.50
2147 A326 8r multicolored 3.00 3.00

CHINA '96, 9th Asian Intl. Philatelic Exhibition.

1996 Summer Olympic Games, Atlanta A327

Gold medalists: 1r, Stella Walsh, 100-meters, 1932. 3r, Emil Zatopek, 10,000-meters, 1952, vert. 10r, Olga Fikotova, discus throw, 1956. 12r, Joan Benoit, women's marathon, 1984.

No. 2152: a, Ethel Catherwood, high jump, 1928. b, Mildred "Babe" Didrikson, javelin, 1932. c, Francina (Fanny) Blankers-Koen, hurdles, 1948. d, Tamara Press, shot put, 1960. e, Lia Manoliu, discus, 1968. f, Rosa Mota, women's marathon, 1988.

Gold medalists in weight lifting, vert: No. 2153a, Yanko Rusev, lightweight, 1980. b, Peter Baczako, middle heavyweight, 1980. c, Leonid Taranenko, heavyweight, 1980. d, Aleksandr Kurlovich, heavyweight, 1988. e, Assen Zlateu, middleweight, 1980. f, Zeng Guoqiang, flyweight, 1984. g, Yurik Vardanyan, heavyweight, 1980. h, Sultan Rakhmanov, super heavyweight, 1980. i, Vassily Alexeev, super heavyweight, 1972.

Each 25r: No. 2154, Irena Szewinska, gold medal winner, 400-meters, 1976. No. 2155, Naim Suleymanoglu, gold medal winner, weight lifting, 1988, vert.

1996, May 27 Litho. *Perf. 14*

2148-2151 A327 Set of 4 5.75 5.75

Miniature Sheets

2152 A327 5r Sheet of 6, #a.-f. 6.50 6.50
2153 A327 5r Sheet of 9, #a.-i. 9.50 9.50

Souvenir Sheets

2154-2155 A327 Set of 2 11.00 11.00

Olymphilex '96 (#2155).

Queen Elizabeth II, 70th Birthday A329

Designs: a, Portrait. b, As younger woman wearing hat, pearls. c, Younger picture seated at desk.

25r, On balcony with Queen Mother.

1996, June 21 Litho. *Perf. 13½x14*

2164 A329 8r Strip of 3, #a.-c. 7.25 7.25

Souvenir Sheet

2165 A329 25r multicolored 6.25 6.25

No. 2164 was issued in sheets of 9 stamps.

UNICEF, 50th Anniv. — A330

Designs: 5r (#2166), 7r (#2167), 7r (#2167A), girl, blue margin, 10r (#2168), Girls of different races.

25r, Baby girl.

1996, July 10 *Perf. 14*

2166-2168 A330 Set of 4 4.50 4.50

Souvenir Sheet

2169 A330 25r multicolored 4.50 4.50

Butterflies — A331

No. 2170, vert: a, Cymothoe cocccinata. b, Morpho rhetenor. c, Callicore lidwina (b, d). d, Heliconius erato.

No. 2171: a, Epiphora albida. b, Satyrus dryas. c, Satyrus lena. d, Papilio tynderaeus. e, Urota Suraka. f, Satyrus nercis.

No. 2172, vert: a, Spicebush swallowtail. b, Giant swallowtail. c, Lime swallowtail caterpillar (b). d, Painted beauty (c). e, Monarch caterpillar. f, Monarch (e, g). g, Monarch caterpillar & pupa. h, Harris' checkerspot.

Each 25r: No. 2173, Heliconius cydno, vert. No. 2174, Zebra, vert.

1996, July 10

2170 A331 7r Strip of 4, #a.-d. 5.00 5.00
2171 A331 7r Sheet of 6, #a.-f. 7.50 7.50
2172 A331 7r Sheet of 8, #a.-h. 10.00 10.00

Souvenir Sheets

2173-2174 A331 Set of 2 10.00 10.00

No. 2170 was issued in sheets of 8 stamps.

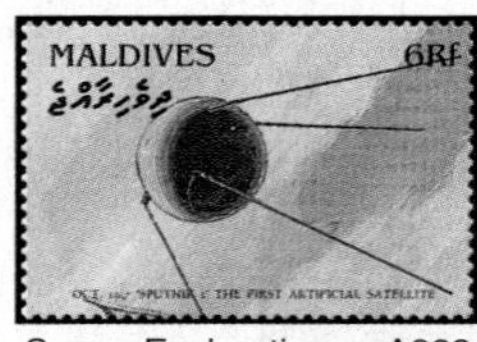
Space Exploration — A332

Designs: No. 2175a, Sputnik I, 1957. b, Apollo 11 Command Module returns to earth, 1969. c, Skylab, 1973. d, Edward White, 1st US astronaut to walk in space, 1965. e, Mariner 9, 1st artificial satellite of Mars, 1971. f, Apollo and Soviet Soyuz dock together, 1975.

25r, Apollo 8 being launched, 1968, vert.

1996, July 10 *Perf. 14*

2175 A332 6r Sheet of 6, #a.-f. 6.50 6.50

Souvenir Sheet

2176 A332 25r multicolored 5.25 5.25

Trains A333

No. 2177, each 3r: a, Electric container train, Germany. b, John Blenkinsop's rack locomotive. c, DB Diesel electric, West Germany. d, Timothy Hackworth's "Royal George," 1827. e, Robert Stephenson (1803-59). f, Trevithick's "New Castle" locomotive. g, Deltic locomotives, British Rail. h, Stockton No. 5, 1826. i, Passenger shuttle, English Channel Tunnel.

No. 2178, each 3r: a, Southern Pacific's "Daylight," San Francisco, US, 1952. b, Timothy Hackworth's "Sans Pareil." c, Chicago & North Western, US. d, Richard Trevithick's "Pen-Y-Darran" locomotive. e, Isambard Kingdom Brunel (1806-59). f, Great Western engine of 1838. g, Passenger train, Canada. h, Mohawk & Hudson Railroad "Experiment," 1832. i, "The ICE," Germany.

No. 2179, each 3r: a, F4 OPH Diesel locomotives, US. b, Stephenson's "Experiment." c, Indian Pacific Intercontinental, Australia. d, George Stephenson's engine, 1815. e, George Stephenson (1781-1848). f, Stephenson's "Rocket," 1829. g, British Rail 125 HST. h, First rail passenger coach, "Experiment," 1825. i, TOFAC, US.

Each 25r: No. 2180, Tom Thumb, 1830. No. 2181, The DeWitt Clinton, 1831. No. 2182, The General, 1855.

1996, Sept. 2 Litho. *Perf. 14*

Sheets of 9, #a-i

2177-2179 A333 Set of 3 21.00 21.00

Souvenir Sheets

2180-2182 A333 Set of 3 15.00 15.00

Fauna A334

Endangered animals:
No. 2183, each 5r: a, Shoebill stork. , Red-billed hornbill. c, Hippopotamus. d, Gorilla. e, Lion. f, Gray-crowned crane.
No. 2184, each 5r: a, Giant panda. b, Indian elephant. c, Arrow poison frog. d, Mandrill. e, Snow leopard. f, California condor.
Wildlife:
No. 2185, vert, each 5r: a, Yellow baboon. b, Zebra duiker. c, Yellow-backed duiker. d, Pygmy hippopotamus. e, Large-spotted genet. f, African spoonbill. g, White-faced whistling duck. h, Helmeted gunieafowl.
No. 2186, vert, each 5r: a, Bongo. b, Bushback. c, Namaqua dove. d, Hoopoe. e, African fish eagle. f, Egyptian goose. g, Saddle-billed stork. h, Blue-breasted kingfisher.
Each 25r: No. 2187, Tiger, vert. No. 2188, Leopard.

1996, Sept. 9

Sheet of 6

2183-2184 A334 Set of 2 11.00 11.00

Sheet of 8

2185-2186 A334 Set of 2 14.50 14.50

Souvenir Sheets

2187-2188 A334 Set of 2 9.00 9.00

Motion Pictures, Cent. — A335

Progressive scenes from "Pluto and the Fly-paper, each 4r:": Nos. 2189a-2189h, Scenes 1-8. No. 2191a-2191i, Scenes 9-17.
Progressive scenes from "Mickey Mouse in The Little Whirlwind, each 4r:" Nos. 2190a-2190h, Scenes 1-8. Nos. 2192a-2192i, Scenes 9-17.
Each 25r: No. 2193, Scene from "Pluto and the Flypaper." No. 2194, Scene from "Mickey Mouse in The Little Whirlwind."

1996, Dec. 2 Litho. *Perf. 13½x14*

Sheets of 8, #a-h, + Label

2189-2190 A335 Set of 2 22.50 22.50

Sheets of 9, #a-i

2191-2192 A335 Set of 2 25.00 25.00

Souvenir Sheets

2193-2194 A335 Set of 2 18.00 18.00

Fauna A336

Designs: a, Saguinus oedipus. b, Bison bonasus. c, Panthera tigris. d, Tetrao urogallus. e, Ailuropoda melanoleuca. f, Trogonoptera brookiana. g, Castor canadensis. h, Leiopelma hamiltoni. i, Trichechus manatus latirostris.
25r, Pan troglodytes.

1996 Litho. *Perf. 14*

2195 A336 7r Sheet of 9, #a.-i. 11.50 11.50

Souvenir Sheet

2196 A336 25r multicolored 4.50 4.50

Turtle Preservation — A336a

1996 ? Litho. *Perf. 12¾*

2196A Horiz. strip of 3 — —
b. A336a 1r Turtle's head — —
c. A336a 7r Turtle's plastron — —
d. A336a 8r Two turtles — —

Hong Kong '97 — A337

Chinese motifs inside letters: No. 2197a, "H." b, "O." c, "N." d, "G" (birds). e, "K." f, "O," diff. g, "N." h, "G" (junk).
25r, "Hong Kong."

1997, Feb. 12 Litho. *Perf. 14*

2197 A337 5r Sheet of 8, #a.-h. 8.25 8.25

Souvenir Sheet

2198 A337 25r multicolored 5.00 5.00

No. 2198 contains one 77x39mm stamp.

Birds — A338

a, Gymnogyps californianus. b, Larus audouinii. c, Fratercula artica. d, Pharomachrus mocinno. e, Amazona vittata. f, Paradisaea minor. g, Nipponia nippon. h, Falco punctatus. i, Strigops habroptilus.
25r, Campephilus principalis.

1997, Feb. 12

2199 A338 5r Sheet of 9, #a.-i. 10.00 10.00

Souvenir Sheet

2200 A338 25r multicolored 6.00 6.00

Eagles
A339 A340

Designs: 1r, Crowned solitary eagle. 2r, African hawk eagle, horiz. 3r, Lesser spotted eagle. 5r, Stellar's sea eagle. 8r, Spanish imperial eagle, horiz. 10r, Harpy eagle. 12r, Crested serpent eagle, horiz.
Bald eagles: No. 2208: a, Wings upward in flight. b, Looking backward on limb. c, Up close, head left. d, Up close, head right. e, On limb. f, In flight.
No. 2209, American bald eagle, horiz. No. 2210, Bald eagle.

1997, Mar. 20 Litho. *Perf. 14*

2201-2207 A339 Set of 7 7.50 7.50
2208 A340 5r Sheet of 6, #a.-f. 5.50 5.50

Souvenir Sheets

2209 A339 25r multicolored 4.50 4.50
2210 A340 25r multicolored 4.50 4.50

Automobiles — A341

No. 2211, each 5r: a, 1911 Blitzer Benz, Germany. b, 1917 Datsun, Japan. c, 1929 Auburn 8-120, US. d, 1996 Mercedes-Benz C280, Germany. e, Suzuki UR-1, Japan. f, Chrysler Atlantic, US.
No. 2212, each 5r: a, 1961 Mercedes-Benz 190SL, Germany. b, 1916 Kwaishinha DAT, Japan. c, 20/25 Rolls-Royce Roadster, England. d, 1997 Mercedes-Benz SLK, Germany. e, 1996 Toyota Camry, Japan. f, 1959 Jaguar MK2, England.
Each 25r: No. 2213, 1939 VW built by Dr. Porsche. No. 2214, Mazda RX-01.

1997, Mar. 27

Sheets of 6, #a-f

2211-2212 A341 Set of 2 11.00 11.00

Souvenir Sheets

2213-2214 A341 Set of 2 9.00 9.00

1998 Winter Olympics, Nagano — A342

Medalists: 2r, Ye Qiabo, 1992 speed skating. 3r, Leonhard Stock, 1980 downhill. 8r, Bjorn Daehlie, 1992 cross-country skiing. 12r, Wolfgang Hoppe, 1984 bobsledding.
No. 2219: a, Herma Von Szabo-Planck, 1924 figure skating. b, Katarina Witt, 1988 figure skating. c, Natalia Bestemianova, Andrei Bukin, 1988 ice dancing. d, Jayne Torvill, Christopher Dean, 1984 ice dancing.
Each 25r: No. 2220, Sonja Henie, 1924 figure skating. No. 2221, Andree Joly, Pierre Brunet, 1932 figure skating.

1997, Mar. 13 Litho. *Perf. 14*

2215-2218 A342 Set of 4 5.25 5.25
2219 A342 5r Block of 4, #a.-d. 4.25 4.25

Souvenir Sheets

2220-2221 A342 Set of 2 11.00 11.00

No. 2219 was issued in sheets of 8 stamps.

Ships A343

Designs: 1r, SS Patris II, 1926, Greece. 2r, MV Infanta Beatriz, 1928, Spain. 8r, SS Stavangerjord, 1918, Norway. 12r, MV Baloeran, 1929, Holland.
No. 2226, each 3r: a, SS Vasilefs Constantinos, 1914, Greece. b, SS Cunene, 1911, Portugal. c, MV Selandia, 1912, Denmark. d, SS President Harding, 1921, US. e, MV Ulster Monarch, 1929, Great Britain. f, SS Matsonia, 1913, US. g, SS France, 1911, France. h, SS Campania, 1893, Great Britain. i, SS Klipfontein, 1922, Holland.
No. 2227, each 3r: a, MV Eridan, 1929, France. b, SS Mount Clinton, 1921, US. c, SS Infanta Isabel, 1912, Spain. d, SS Suwa Maru, 1914, Japan. e, SS Yorkshire, 1920, Great Britain. f, MV Highland Chieftan, 1929, Great Britain. g, MV Sardinia, 1920, Norway. h, SS San Guglielmo, 1911, Italy. i, SS Avila, 1927, Great Britain.
Each 25r: No. 2228, SS Mauritania, 1907, Great Britain. No. 2229, SS United States, 1952, US. No. 2230, SS Queen Mary, 1930, Great Britain. No. 2231, Royal Yacht Brittania sailing into Hong Kong harbor.

1997, Apr. 1

2222-2225 A343 Set of 4 5.50 5.50

Sheets of 9, #a-i

2226-2227 A343 Set of 2 12.00 12.00

Souvenir Sheets

2228-2231 A343 Set of 4 21.00 21.00

No. 2231 contains one 57x42mm stamp.

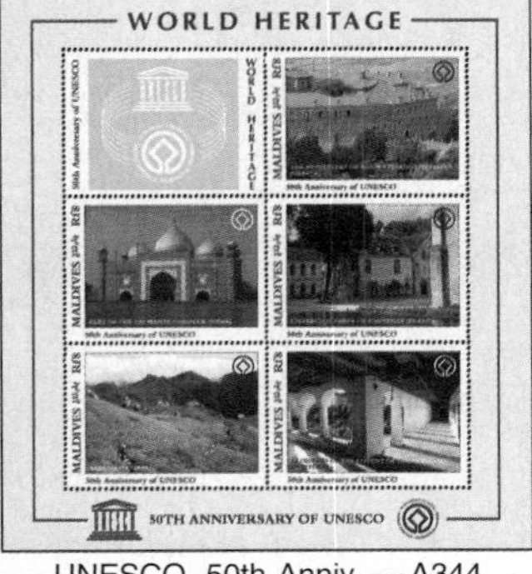

UNESCO, 50th Anniv. — A344

1r, Prayer wheels, Lhasa, vert. 2r, Roman ruins, Temple of Diana, Portugal. 3r, Cathedral of Santa Maria Hildesheim, Germany. 7r, Monument of Nubia at Abu Simbel, Egypt, vert. 8r, Entrance to Port of Mandraki, Rhodes, Greece. 10r, Nature Reserve of Scandola, France. 12r, Temple on the Lake, China.
No. 2232, vert, each 5r: a, Virunga Natl. Park, Zaire. b, Valley of Mai Nature Reserve, Seychelles. c, Kandy, Sri Lanka. d, Taj Mahal, India. e, Istanbul, Turkey. f, Sana'a, Yemen. g, Blenheim Palace, Oxfordshire, England. h, Grand Canyon Natl. Park, US.
No. 2233, vert, each 5r: a, Gondar, Ethiopia. b, Bwindi Natl. Park, Uganda. c, Bemaraha Nature Reserve, Madagascar. d, Buddhist ruins of Takht-i-Bahi, Pakistan. e, Anuradhapura, Sri Lanka. f, Cairo, Egypt. g, Ruins at Petra, Jordan. h, Natl. Park of Ujung Kulon, Indonesia.
Sites in China, vert: No. 2234, each 5r: a-f, Mount Taishan. g-h, Terracotta warriors.
Sites in Japan: No. 2235, each 8r: a-e, Horyu-Ji.
No. 2236, each 8r: a, Monastery of Agios Stefanos Meteora, Greece. b, Taj Mahal, India. c, Cistercian Abbey of Fontenay, France. d, Yakushima, Japan. e, Cloisters of the Convent, San Gonzalo, Portugal.
No. 2237, each 8r: a, Olympic Natl. Park, US. b, Nahanni Waterfalls, Canada. c, Los Glaciares Natl. Park, Argentina. d, Bonfin Salvador Church, Brazil. e, Convent of the Companions of Jesus, Morelia, Mexico.
Each 25r: No. 2238, Temple, Chengde, China. No. 2239, Serengeti Natl. Park, Tanzania. No. 2240, Anuradhapura, Sri Lanka. No. 2241, Monument to Fatehpur Sikri, India.

1997, Apr. 7

2231A-2231G A344 Set of 7 5.75 5.75

Sheets of 8, #a-h, + Label

2232-2234 A344 Set of 3 22.00 22.00

Sheets of 5, #a-e, + Label

2235-2237 A344 Set of 3 22.00 22.00

Souvenir Sheets

2238-2241 A344 Set of 4 18.00 18.00

Queen Elizabeth II, Prince Philip, 50th Wedding Anniv. A345

No. 2242: a, Queen. b, Royal Arms. c, Queen, Prince seated on thrones. d, Queen, Prince holding baby. e, Buckingham Palace. f, Prince.
25r, Queen wearing crown.

1997, June 12 Litho. *Perf. 14*

2242 A345 5r Sheet of 6, #a.-f. 7.50 7.50

Souvenir Sheet

2243 A345 25r multicolored 5.25 5.25

Paintings by Hiroshige (1797-1858) A346

No. 2244: a, Dawn at Kanda Myojin Shrine. b, Kiyomizu Hall & Shinobazu Pond at Ueno. c, Ueno Yamashita. d, Moon Pine, Ueno. e, Flower Pavilion, Dango Slope, Sendagi. f, Shitaya Hirokoji.

Each 25r: No. 2245, Seido and Kanda River from Shohei Bridge. No. 2246, Hilltop View, Yushima Tenjin Shrine.

1997, June 12 ***Perf. 13½x14***

2244 A346 8r Sheet of 6, #a.-f. 8.25 8.25

Souvenir Sheets

2245-2246 A346 Set of 2 9.00 9.00

Heinrich von Stephan (1831-97) A347

a, Early mail messenger, India. b, Von Stephan, UPU emblem. c, Autogiro, Washington DC.

1997, June 12 ***Perf. 14***

2247 A347 2r Sheet of 3, #a.-c. 3.75 3.75

PACIFIC 97.

A number has been reserved for a souvenir sheet with this set.

South Asian Assoc. for Regional Cooperation (SAARC) Summit — A348

1997, May 12 **Litho.** ***Perf. 13***

2249 A348 3r shown .55 .55
2250 A348 5r Flags, "SAARC" .90 .90

A349

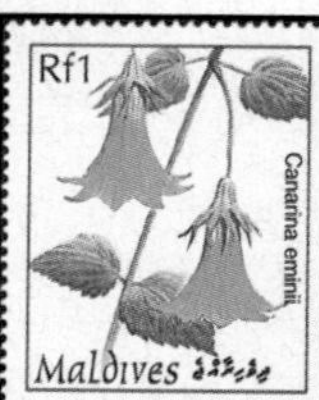

A350

Birds: 30 l, Anous stolidus. 1r, Spectacled owl. 2r, Buffy fish owl. 3r, Peregrine falcon. 5r, Golden eagle. 8r, Bateleur. No. 2257, 10r, Crested caracara. No. 2258, 10r, Childonias hybrida. 15r, Sula sula.

No. 2260: a, Rueppell's parrot. b, Blue-headed parrot. c, St. Vincent parrot. d, Gray parrot. e, Masked lovebird. f, Sun parakeet.

Each 25r: No. 2261, Secretary bird. No. 2262, Bald eagle.

1997 ***Perf. 14***

2251-2259 A349 Set of 9 9.75 9.75
2260 A349 7r Sheet of 6, #a.-f. 7.50 7.50

Souvenir Sheets

2261-2262 A349 Set of 2 11.00 11.00

1997, June 24 **Litho.** ***Perf. 14½x14***

Flowers: 1r, Canarina eminii. 2r, Delphinium macrocentron. 3r, Leucadendron discolor. 5r, Nymphaea caerulea. 7r, Rosa multiflora. 8r, Bulbophyllum barbigerum. 12r, Hibiscus vitifolius.

No. 2270, horiz: a, Acacia seyal. b, Gloriosa superba. c, Gnidia subcordata. d, Platycelphium voense. e, Aspilia mossambicensis. f, Adenium obesum.

Each 25r: No. 2271, Aerangis rhodosticta, horiz. No. 2272, Dichrostachys cinerea, horiz.

2263-2269 A350 Set of 6 7.25 7.25

Perf. 14x14½

2270 A350 8r Sheet of 6, #a.-f. 11.50 11.50

Souvenir Sheets

2271-2272 A350 Set of 2 17.00 17.00

No. 2267 is 16x20mm.

A351

Dinosaurs A352

5r, Archaeopteryx. 8r, Mosasaurus. 12r, Deinonychus. 15r, Triceratops.

No. 2277, each 7r: a, Diplodocus (b, c, d, e, f). b. Tyrannosaurus rex (c, e, f). c, Pteranodon. d, Montanaceratops. e, Dromaeosaurus (d). f, Oviraptor (e).

No. 2278, each 7r: a, Euoplocephalus. b, Compsognathus. c, Herrerasaurus. d, Styracosaurus. e, Baryonyx. f, Lesothosaurus.

No. 2279, each 7r: a, Triceratops. b, Pachycephalosaurus. c, Iguanodon. d, Tyrannosaurus. e, Corythosaurus. f, Stegosaurus.

No. 2280, each 7r: a, Troodon (d). b, Brachosaurus (c). c, Saltasaurus (a, b, d, e, f). d, Oviraptor. e, Parasaurolophus (f). f, Psittacosaurus.

No. 2281, Tyrannosaurus rex. No. 2282, Archaeopteryx.

1997, Nov. 20 **Litho.** ***Perf. 14***

2273-2276 A351 Set of 4 7.25 7.25

Sheets of 6, #a-f

2277 A351 7r #a.-f. 7.50 7.50
2278-2280 A352 Set of 3 22.50 22.50

Souvenir Sheets

2281 A351 25r multicolored 11.00 11.00
2282 A352 25r multicolored 11.00 11.00

1998 World Cup Soccer Championships, France — A353

Past winners: 1r, Brazil, 1994. 2r, West Germany, 1954. 3r, Argentina, 1986. 7r, Argentina, 1978. 8r, England, 1966. 10r, Brazil, 1970.

Various scenes from 1966 finals, England v. West Germany, each 3r: Nos. 2289a-2289h.

Italian tournament winners, each 3r: No. 2290: a, Raulo Rossi, Italy, 1982. b, Zoff & Gentile, Italy, 1982. c, Angelo Schiavio, Italy. d, 1934 team. e, 1934 team entering stadium. f, 1982 team. g, San Paolo Stadium, Italy. h, 1938 team.

Brazilian teams, players, each 3r: No. 2291: a, 1958 team pictue. b, Luis Bellini, 1958. c, 1962 team. d, Carlos Alberto, 1970. e, Mauro, 1962. f, 1970 team. g, Dunga, 1994. h, 1994 team.

Each 25r: No. 2292, Klinsmann, Germany. No. 2293, Ronaldo, Brazil, vert. No. 2294, Schmeichel, Denmark, vert.

Perf. 14x13½, 13½x14

1997, Dec. 10 **Litho.**

2283-2288 A353 Set of 6 5.60 5.60

Sheets of 8 + Label

2289-2291 A353 Set of 3 13.00 13.00

Souvenir Sheets

2292-2294 A353 Set of 3 15.00 15.00

Diana, Princess of Wales (1961-97) — A354

Various portraits, color of sheet margin, each 7r: No. 2295, Pale pink. No. 2296, Pale yellow. No. 2297, Pale blue.

Each 25r: No. 2298, Diana on ski lift. No. 2299, In polka dot dress. No. 2300, Wearing lei.

1998, Feb. 9 **Litho.** ***Perf. 13½***

Sheets of 6, #a-f

2295-2297 A354 Set of 3 22.50 22.50

Souvenir Sheets

2298-2300 A354 Set of 3 13.50 13.50

John F. Kennedy (1917-63) A355

Various portraits.

1998 **Litho.** ***Perf. 13½x14***

2301 A355 5r Sheet of 9, #a.-i. 8.00 8.00

Nelson Mandela, Pres. of South Africa — A356

1998 ***Perf. 14***

2302 A356 4r multicolored 1.50 1.50

Classic Airplanes A357

No. 2303: a, Yakovlev Yak 18. b, Beechcraft Bonanza. c, Piper Cub. d, Tupolev Tu-95. e, Lockheed C-130 Hercules. f, Piper PA-28 Cherokee. g, Mikoyan-Gurevich MiG-21. h, Pilatus PC-6 Turbo Porter. i, Antonov An-2.

25r, KC-135E.

1998

2303 A357 5r Sheet of 9, #a.-i. 8.00 8.00

Souvenir Sheet

2304 A357 25r multicolored 4.50 4.50

No. 2304 contains one 85x28mm stamp.

Cats A358

Designs, vert: 5r, White American shorthair. 8r, Sphinx. 10r, Tabby American shorthair. 12r, Scottish fold.

No. 2309, each 7r: a, American curl, Maine coon (d). b, Maine coon (a, d, e). c, Siberian (f). d, Somali. e, European Burmese (d). f, Nebelung.

No. 2310, each 7r: a, Bicolor British shorthair (b). b, Manx. c, Tabby American shorthair (b, e, f). d, Silver tabby Persian (e). e, Oriental white. f, Norwegian forest cat (e).

Each 30r: No. 2311, Snowshoe, vert. No. 2312, Norwegian forest cat, vert.

1998, June 1 **Litho.** ***Perf. 14***

2305-2308 A358 Set of 4 6.25 6.25

Sheets of 6, #a-f

2309-2310 A358 Set of 2 15.00 15.00

Souvenir Sheets

2311-2312 A358 Set of 2 11.00 11.00

Airplanes A359

Designs: 2r, Boeing 737 HS. 7r, Boeing 727. 8r, Boeing 747, 1970. 10r, Boeing 737.

No. 2317, each 5r: a, FSW Fighter. b, V-Jet II. c, Pilatus PC-12. d, Citation Exel. e, Stutz Bearcat. f, Cessna T-37 (B). g, Peregrine business jet. h, Beech Baron 53.

No. 2318, each 5r: a, CL-215. b, P-3 Orion. c, Yak 54. d, Cessna float plane. e, CL-215 Amphibian. f, CL-215 SAR Amphibian. g, Twin Otter. h, Rockwell Quail.

Each 25r: No. 2319, Falcon Jet. No. 2320, Beechcraft Model 18.

1998, Aug. 10 **Litho.** ***Perf. 14***

2313-2316 A359 Set of 4 4.75 4.75

Sheets of 8, #a-h

2317-2318 A359 Set of 2 14.50 14.50

Souvenir Sheets

2319-2320 A359 Set of 2 10.00 10.00

The Titanic A360

No. 2321: a, Capt. Edward J. Smith's cap. b, Deck chair. c, Fifth Officer Harold Lowe's coat button. d, Lifeboat. e, Steering wheel. f, Lifejacket.

25r, Newpaper picture of the Titanic at sea.

1998, Sept. 27 **Litho.** ***Perf. 14***

2321 A360 7r Sheet of 6, #a.-f. 8.50 8.50

Souvenir Sheet

2322 A360 25r multicolored 5.50 5.50

Bird Type of 1992

1998, Oct. 26 **Litho.** ***Perf. 14½***

2323 A247 100r Anas clypeata 14.00 14.00

IFAD, 20th Anniv. — A361

Designs: 1r, Papaya tree. 5r, Fruits. 7r, Fishermen on boat. 8r, Coconut tree. 10r, Vegetables.

1998, Nov. 30 **Litho.** ***Perf. 14***

2324-2328 A361 Set of 5 5.50 5.50

Ferrari Automobiles — A361a

No. 2328A: c, 250 TR. d, 1957 250 GT TDF. e, 250 GT.
25r, 365 GTC 2+2.

1998, Dec. 15 Litho. *Perf. 14*

2328A A361a 10r Sheet of 3, #c-e 5.25 5.25

Souvenir Sheet

Perf. 13¾x14¼

2328B A361a 25r multi 4.25 4.25

No. 2328A contains three 39x25mm stamps.

1998 World Scout Jamboree, Chile — A362

a, Robert Baden-Powell inspecting Scouts, Amesbury, c. 1909. b, Lord, Lady Baden-Powell, children, South Africa Tour, 1927. c, Robert Baden-Powell pins merit badges on Chicago Scouts, 1926.

1998, Dec. 15

2329 A362 12r Sheet of 3, #a.-c. 6.50 6.50

A363

Diana, Princess of Wales (1961-97) — A364

1998, Dec. 15 *Perf. 14½x14*

2330 A363 10r multicolored 1.75 1.75

Size: 95x56mm

Litho. & Embossed

Die Cut Perf. 7½

2331 A364 50r shown
2332 A364 50r Rose, Diana

No. 2330 was issued in sheets of 6.

Fish A365

Designs: No. 2333, 50 l, Threadfin butterfly fish. No. 2334, 50 l, Queen angelfish. 1r, Oriental sweetlips. No. 2336, 7r, Bandit angelfish. No. 2337, 7r, Achilles tang. 8r, Red-headed butterfly fish. 50r, Blue striped butterfly fish.
No. 2340: a, Mandarinfish. b, Copper-banded butterfly fish. c, Harlequin tuskfish. d, Yellow-tailed demoiselle. e, Wimplefish. f, Red emperor snapper. g, Clown triggerfish. h, Common clown. i, Regal tang.
No. 2341: a, Emperor angelfish. b, Common squirrelfish. c, Lemonpeel angelfish. d, Powderblue surgeon. e, Moorish idol. f, Bicolor cherub. g, Scribbled angelfish. h, Two-banded anemonefish. i, Yellow tang.
Each 25r: No. 2342, Porkfish. No. 2343, Long-nosed butterfly fish.

1998, Dec. 10 Litho. *Perf. 14*

2333-2339 A365 Set of 7 13.50 13.50
2340 A365 3r Sheet of 9, #a.-i. 4.75 4.75
2341 A365 5r Sheet of 9, #a.-i. 8.25 8.25

Souvenir Sheets

2342-2343 A365 Set of 2 9.00 9.00

Intl. Year of the Ocean A366

Marine life: No. 2344, Skipjack tuna.
No. 2345: a, 25 l, Triton. b, 50 l, Napoleon wrasse. c, 1r, Whale shark. d, 3r, Gray reef shark. e, 7r, Blue whale.
No. 2346: a, Harp seal. b, Killer whale. c, Sea otter. d, Beluga. e, Narwhal. f, Walrus. g, Sea lion. h, Humpback salmon. i, Emperor penguin.
No. 2347: a, Ocean sunfish. b, Opalescent squid. c, Electric eel. d, Corded neptune.
Each 25r: No. 2348, Horseshoe crab. No. 2349, Blue whale. No. 2350, Triton, diff.

1999, Apr. 1 Litho. *Perf. 14*

2344 A366 7r multicolored 1.25 1.25

Sheets of 6, 9, 4

2345 A366 #a.-e. + 1 #2344 3.50 3.50
2346 A366 5r #a.-i. 8.00 8.00
2347 A366 8r #a.-d. 5.75 5.75

Souvenir Sheets

2348-2350 A366 Set of 3 13.50 13.50

No. 2344 was issued in sheets of 6.
No. 2350 incorrectly inscribed Coral Reef.

Mickey Mouse, 70th Anniv. (in 1998) — A367

#2351, each 5r: Various pictures of Mickey Mouse.
#2352, each 5r: Various pictures of Minnie Mouse.
#2353, each 7r: Various pictures of Donald Duck.
#2354, each 7r: Various pictures of Daisy Duck.
#2355, each 7r: Various pictures of Goofy.
#2356, each 7r: Various pictures of Pluto.
Each 25r: #2357, Minnie sipping drink. #2358, Minnie looking backward. #2359, Mickey grabbing Donald's hand, horiz. #2360, Minnie wearing pearls. #2361, Mickey with hand on head. #2362, Mickey after throwing ball.

Perf. 13½x14, 14x13½ (#2359)

1999, May 27 Litho.

Sheets of 6, #a-f

2351-2352 A367 Set of 2 11.00 11.00
2353-2356 A367 Set of 4 30.00 30.00

Souvenir Sheets

2357-2362 A367 Set of 6 27.00 27.00

Stamp in No. 2358 is printed se-tenant with label.
Sheets similar to #2351-2352 with "5Rs" denomination and #2353-2356 with "25Rs" exist.

Butterflies A368

50 l, Great orange tip. 1r, Large green aporandria. 2r, Common mormon. 3r, African migrant. 5r, Common pierrot. 10r, Giant redeye.
No. 2369, vert, each 7r: a, Common red flash. b, Burmese lascar. c, Common peirrot. d, Baron. e, Leaf blue. f, Great orange tip.
No. 2370, vert, each 7r: a, Crimson tip. b, Tawny rajah. c, Leafwing butterfly. d, Great egg-fly. e, Blue admiral. f, African migrant.
Each 25r: No. 2371, Crimson tip. No. 2372, Large oak blue.

1999, June 8 Litho. *Perf. 14*

2363-2368 A368 Set of 6 3.75 3.75

Sheets of 6, #a-f

2369-2370 A368 Set of 2 15.00 15.00

Souvenir Sheets

2371-2372 A368 Set of 2 9.00 9.00

Dinosaurs A369

Designs: 1r, Scelidosaurus. 3r, Yansudaurus. 5r, Ornitholestes. 8r, Astrodon.
No. 2377, vert, each 7r: a, Anchisaurus. b, Pterenodon. c, Barosaurus. d, Iguanodon. e, Archaeopteryx. f, Ceratosaurus.
No. 2378, each 7r: a, Stegosaurus. b, Corythosaurus. c, Celiosaurus. d, Avimimus. e, Styracosaurus. f, Massospondylus.
No. 2379, vert, each 7r: a, Dimorphodon. b, Rhamphorhynchus. c, Allosaurus. d, Leaellynasaura. e, Troodon. f, Syntarsus.
Each 25r: No. 2380, Brachiosaurus. No. 2381, Megalosaurus.

1999, June 22

2373-2376 A369 Set of 4 3.25 3.25

Sheets of 6, #a-f

2377-2379 A369 Set of 3 24.50 24.50

Souvenir Sheets

2380-2381 A369 Set of 2 10.00 10.00

Marine Environment Wildlife — A370

30 l, Broderip's cowrie. 1r, Fairy tern. 3r, Darker Maldivian green heron. 7r, Blackflag sandperch. 8r, Coral hind. 10r, Olive ridley turtle.
No. 2388, each 5r: a, Brown booby. b, Red-tailed tropicbird. c, Sooty tern. d, Striped dolphin. e, Long-snouted spinner dolphin. f, Crab plover. g, Hawksbill turtle. h, Indo-Pacific sergeant. i, Yellowfin tuna.
No. 2389, each 5r: a, Manta ray. b, Green turtle. c, Pan-tropical spotted dolphin. d, Moorish idols. e, Threadfin anthias. f, Goldbar wrasse. g, Palette surgeonfish. h, Three spot angelfish. i, Oriental sweetlips.
Each 25r: No. 2390, Cinnamon bittern. No. 2391, Blue-faced angelfish.

1999, Oct. 26 Litho. *Perf. 14*

2382-2387 A370 Set of 6 5.00 5.00

Sheets of 9, #a-i

2388-2389 A370 Set of 2 15.50 15.50

Souvenir Sheets

2390-2391 A370 Set of 2 8.50 8.50

Trains A371

Designs: 50 l, 2-2-2 locomotive, Egypt. 1r, Le Shuttle, France. 2r, 4-4-0 Gowan & Marx, US. 3r, TGV, France. 5r, Ae 6/6 electric locomotive, Switzerland. 8r, Stephenson's Long-boilered 2-4-0 locomotive, Great Britain. 10r, The Philadelphia, Austria. 15r. E class, Great Britain.
No. 2400, each 7r: a, Stephenson's Long-boilered locomotive, diff. b, 4-2-2 Cornwall, Great Britain. c, First locomotive, Germany. d, Great Western, Great Britain. e, Standard Stephenson 2-4-0, France. f, 2-2-2 Meteor, Great Britain.
No. 2401, each 7r: a, Type 4 class 4t, Great Britain. b, 1500 horsepower Diesel-electric locomotive, Malaysia. c, Co-Co 7000 Class, France. d, Diesel-hydraulic passenger locomotive, Thailand. e, Diesel-hydraulic locomotive, Burma. f, Hikari, Japan.
Each 25r: No. 2402, 2-2-2, Passenger locomotive, France. No. 2403, King Arthur class, Great Britain.

1999, Oct. 26

2392-2399 A371 Set of 8 7.50 7.50

Sheets of 6, #a-f

2400-2401 A371 Set of 2 14.50 14.50

Souvenir Sheets

2402-2403 A371 Set of 2 10.00 10.00

A372

Queen Mother (b. 1900) — A373

No. 2404: a, With King George VI, 1936. b, In 1941. c, In 1960. d, In 1981.
25r, At Order of the Garter Service.

Gold Frames

1999, Dec. 1 Litho. *Perf. 14*

2404 A372 7r Sheet of 4, #a.-d., + label 6.00 6.00

Souvenir Sheet

Perf. 13¾

2405 A372 25r multi 6.00 6.00

Litho. & Embossed

Die Cut Perf. 8¾

Without Gum

2406 A373 50r gold & multi

No. 2405 contains one 38x51mm stamp.
See Nos. 2605-2606.

Hokusai Paintings — A374

No. 2407, each 7r: a, A Coastal view. b, Bath House by a Lake. c, Drawings (horse). d, Drawings (two birds). e, Evening Cool at Ryogoku. f, Girls Boating.
No. 2408, each 7r: a, Haunted House. b, Juniso Shrine at Yotsuya. c, Drawings (one bird). d, Drawings (two people). e, Lover in the Snow. f, Mountain Tea House.
Each 25r: No. 2409, Girls Gathering Spring Herbs, vert. No. 2410, Scene in the Yoshiwara, vert.

1999, Dec. 23 *Perf. 13¾*

Sheets of 6, #a.-f.

2407-2408 A374 Set of 2 16.50 16.50

Souvenir Sheets

2409-2410 A374 Set of 2 10.00 10.00

IBRA '99, Nuremberg — A375

Trains (as described): 12r, Drache, 1848. 15r, Der Adler, 1833.

1999, Dec. 23 ***Perf. 14x14½***

2411-2412 A375 Set of 2 6.00 6.00

The illustrations of the two stamps were switched.

Souvenir Sheets

PhilexFrance '99 — A376

Trains: No. 2413, Standard Stephenson 2-4-0, 1837. No. 2414, Long-boilered Stephenson, 1841.

1999, Dec. 23 ***Perf. 13¾***

2413-2414 A376 25r each 4.50 4.50

Rights of the Child — A377

No. 2415: a, Black denomination in UL. b, White denomination in UL. c, Black denomination in UR.

25r, Peter Ustinov, UNICEF goodwill ambassador.

1999, Dec. 23 ***Perf. 14***

2415 A377 10r Sheet of 3, #a.-c. 6.00 6.00

Souvenir Sheet

2416 A377 25r multi 4.25 4.25

Mars Colony of the Future A378

No. 2417, each 5r: a, Phobos and Deimos. b, Improved Hubble Telescope. c, Passenger shuttle. d, Skyscrapers. e, Taxi cab. f, Landing facilities. g, Vegetation. h, Walking on Mars. i, Mars rover.

No. 2418, each 5r: a, Russian Phobos 25. b, Earth and moon. c, Space shuttle. d, Lighthouse. e, Excursion space liner. f, Inner-city shuttle. g, Viking lander. h, Air and water purification plants. i, Life in a Mars city.

Each 25r: No. 2419, Mars, vert. No. 2420, Astronaut, vert.

2000, Jan. 24 **Litho.** ***Perf. 14***

Sheets of 9, #a.-i.

2417-2418 A378 Set of 2 17.50 17.50

Souvenir Sheets

2419-2420 A378 Set of 2 10.00 10.00

Millennium — A379

Highlights of 1750-1800: a, American Declaration of Independence, 1776. b, Hot air balloon flight by Montgolfier brothers, 1783. c, French Revolution begins with storming of the Bastille, 1789. d, James Watt patents steam engine, 1769. e, Wolfgang Amadeus Mozart born, 1756. f, Ts'ao Hsueh-ch'in publishes "Dream of the Red Chamber," 1791. g, Napoleon conquers Egypt, 1798. h, Catherine the Great becomes Empress of Russia, 1762. i, Joseph Priestley discovers oxygen, 1774. j, Benjamin Franklin publishes studies on electricity, 1751. k, Edward Jenner develops vaccination against smallpox, 1796. l, French and Indian War, 1754. m, Jean Honoré Fragonard paints "The Swing," c. 1766. n, Ludwig van Beethoven born, 1770. o, Louis marries Marie Antoinette, 1770. p, Capt. James Cook explores in South Pacific, discovers east coast of Australia, 1770 (60x40mm). q, Luigi Galvani experiments with electricity on nerves and muscles, c. 1780.

2000, Feb. 1 ***Perf. 12¾x12½***

2421 A379 3r Sheet of 17, #a.-q., + label 10.00 10.00

Destination 2000 Tourism Campaign — A380

Designs: a, Yellow flowers. b, School of fish. c, Airplane, boat prow. d, White flowers. e, Lionfish. f, Windsurfers.

2000, Feb. 1 ***Perf. 13¾***

2422 A380 7r Sheet of 6, #a.-f. 9.00 9.00

Solar Eclipse, Aug. 11, 1999 — A381

No. 2423 (Sky background), each 7r: a, First contact. b, Second contact. c, Totality. d, Third contact. e, Fourth contact. f, Observatory.

No. 2424 (Outer space background), each 7r: a, First contact. b, Second contact. c, Totality. d, Third contact. e, Fourth contact. f, Solar and heliospheric observatory.

2000, Mar. 8 **Litho.** ***Perf. 14***

Sheets of 6, #a.-f.

2423-2424 A381 Set of 2 14.50 14.50

Butterflies — A382

No. 2425, each 5r: a, Red lacewing. b, Large oak blue. c, Yellow coster. d, Great orange tip. e, Common pierrot. f, Cruiser. g, Hedge blue. h, Great egg-fly. i, Common tiger.

No. 2426, each 5r: a, Common wall. b, Koh-i-noor. c, Indian red admiral. d, Tawny rajah. e, Blue triangle. f, Orange albatross. g, Common rose swallowtail. h, Jeweled nawab. i, Striped blue crow.

Each 25r: No. 2427, Large tree nymph. No. 2428, Blue pansy.

2000, Apr. 10 **Litho.** ***Perf. 13¼x13½***

Sheets of 9, #a-i

2425-2426 A382 Set of 2 17.50 17.50

Souvenir Sheets

2427-2428 A382 Set of 2 10.00 10.00

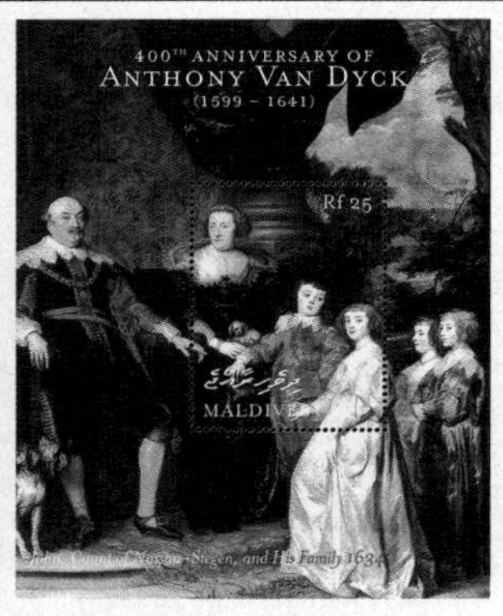

Paintings of Anthony Van Dyck — A383

No. 2429, each 5r: a, Martin Rijckaert. b, Frans Snyders. c, Quentin Simons. d, Lucas van Uffel, 1622. e, Nicolaes Rockox. f, Nicholas Lanier.

No. 2430, each 5r: a, Inigo Jones. b, Lucas van Uffel, (actually detail from John, Count of Nassau-Sieger and his Family) c. 1622-25. c, Margaretha de Vos, Wife of Frans Snyders. d, Peter Breughel the Younger. e, Cornelis van der Geest. f, Francois Langlois as a Savoyard.

No. 2431, each 5r: a, Portrait of a Family. b, Earl and Countess of Denby and Their Daughter. c, Family Portrait. d, A Genoese Nobleman with his Children. e, Thomas Howard, Earl of Arundel, and His Grandson. f, The Woman in Gold (Battonia Balbi with her Children).

Each 25r: No. 2432, John, Count of Nassau-Siegen, and His Family. No. 2433, The Lomellini Family. No. 2434, Lucas and Cornelis de Wael. No. 2435, The Painter Jan de Wael and His Wife Gertrude de Jode. No. 2436, Sir Kenelm and Lady Digby with Their Two Eldest Sons. No. 2437, Sir Philip Herbert, 4th Earl of Pembroke, and His Family.

2000, May 1 ***Perf. 13¾***

Sheets of 6, #a-f

2429-2431 A383 Set of 3 40.00 40.00

Souvenir Sheets

2432-2437 A383 Set of 6 25.00 25.00

Trains A384

Designs: 5r, Shinkansen, Japan. 8r, Super Azusa, Japan. No. 2440, 10r, Spacia, Japan. 15r, Nozomi, Japan.

No. 2442, each 10r: a, 1909 Shanghai-Nanking Railway 4-6-2. b, 1910 Shanghai-Nanking Railway 4-2-2. c, 1914 Manchurian Railway 4-6-2. d, 1934 Chinese National Railway Hankow Line 4-8-4. e, 1949 Chinese National Railway 2-8-2. f, 1949 Chinese National Railway 2-10-0.

No. 2443, each 10r: a, 1856 East Indian Railway "Fawn" 2-2-2. b, 1893 East Indian Railway 4-4-0. c, 1909 Bengal-Nagpur Railway 4-4-2. d, 11924 Great Peninsular Railway 4-6-0. e, 1932 North Western Railway 4-6-2. f, 1949 Indian National Railway 4-6-2.

Each 25r: No. 2444, Chinese National Railways Class JS 2-8-2. No. 2445, Indian National Railway Class WP 4-6-2.

2000, June 8 **Litho.** ***Perf. 14***

2438-2441 A384 Set of 4 6.50 6.50

Sheets of 6, #a-f

2442-2443 A384 Set of 2 20.00 20.00

Souvenir Sheets

2444-2445 A384 Set of 2 10.00 10.00

The Stamp Show 2000, London (Nos. 2442-2445). Nos. 2444-2445 each contain one 57x42mm stamp.

Millennium A385

Designs: 10 l, Republic Monument. 30 l, Bodu Thakurufaanu Memorial Center. 1r, Health services. No. 2449, 7r, Hukuru Miskiiy. No. 2450, 7r, Male Intl. Airport. 10r, Educational development.

No. 2452, 25r, People's Majlis. No. 2453, 25r, Economic development. No. 2454, 25r, Islamic Center.

2000, Aug. 31 **Litho.** ***Perf. 14***

2446-2451 A385 Set of 6 6.00 6.00

Souvenir Sheets

Perf. 13¼

2452-2454 A385 Set of 3 13.00 13.00

Souvenir Sheets

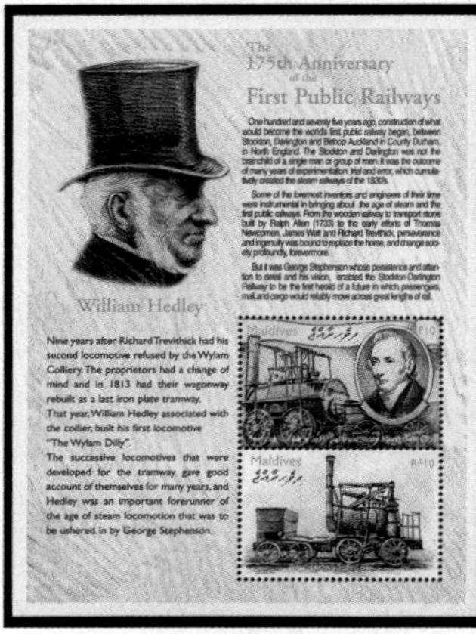

First Public Railways, 175th Anniv. — A386

No. 2455: a, Locomotion No. 1, George Stephenson. b, William Hedley's Puffing Billy.

2000, Sept. 13 ***Perf. 14***

2455 A386 10r Sheet of 2, #a-b 4.50 4.50

2000 Summer Olympics, Sydney — A387

No. 2456: a, Suzanne Lenglen. b, Fencing. c, Olympic Stadium, Tokyo, and Japanese flag. d, Ancient Greek long jumper.

2000, Sept. 13

2456 A387 10r Sheet of 4, #a-d 7.50 7.50

First Zeppelin Flight, Cent. — A388

No. 2457, horiz.: a, Graf Zeppelin. b, Graf Zeppelin II. c, LZ-9.

2000, Sept. 13 ***Perf. 14***

2457 A388 13r Sheet of 3, #a-c 6.75 6.75

Souvenir Sheet

Perf. 13¾

2458 A388 25r LZ-88 6.00 6.00

No. 2457 contains three 39x25mm stamps.

Apollo-Soyuz Mission, 25th Anniv. — A389

No. 2459, vert.: a, Apollo 18 and Soyuz 19. b, Soyuz 19. c, Apollo 18.

2000, Sept. 13 ***Perf. 14***

2459 A389 13r Sheet of 3, #a-c 6.75 6.75

Souvenir Sheet

2460 A389 25r Soyuz 19 5.25 5.25

Orchids — A390

Designs: 50 l, Dendrobium crepidatum. 1r, Eulophia guineensis. 2.50r, Cymbidium finlaysonianum. 3.50r, Paphiopedilum druryi.

No. 2465, 10r: a, Aerides odorata. b, Dendrobium chrysotoxum. c, Dendrobium anosmum. d, Calypso bulbosa. e, Paphiopedilum fairrieanum. f, Cynorkis fastigiata.

No. 2466, 10r: a, Angraecum germinyanum. b, Phalaenopsis amabilis. c, Thrixspermum cantipeda. d, Phaius tankervilleae. e, Rhynchostylis gigantea. f, Papilionanthe teres.

No. 2467, 25r, Cymbidium dayanum. No. 2468, 25r, Spathoglottis plicata.

2000, Sept. 13

2461-2464 A390 Set of 4 1.25 1.25

Sheets of 6, #a-f

2465-2466 A390 Set of 2 21.00 21.00

Souvenir Sheets

2467-2468 A390 Set of 2 10.00 10.00

Birds A391

Designs: 15 l, White tern. 25 l, Brown booby. 30 l, White-collared kingfisher, vert. 1r, Black-winged stilt, vert.

No. 2473, 10r: a, Great frigatebird. b, Common noddy. c, Common tern. d, Sula sula. e, Sooty tern. f, Phaeton leturus.

No. 2474, 10r, vert.: a, White-collared kingfisher. b, Island thrush. c, Red-tailed tropicbird. d, Peregrine falcon. e, Night heron. f, Great egret.

No. 2475, 13r: a, Ringed plover. b, Turnstone. c, Thicknee. d, Black-bellied plover. e, Crab plover. f, Curlew.

No. 2476, 25r, Great cormorant, vert. No. 2477, 25r, Cattle egret, vert.

2000, Sept. 13 ***Perf. 13¾***

2469-2472 A391 Set of 4 3.00 3.00

Sheets of 6, #a-f

2473-2475 A391 Set of 3 35.00 35.00

Souvenir Sheets

2476-2477 A391 Set of 2 10.00 10.00

Motorcycles — A392

No. 2478, 7r: a, 1907 Matchless. b, 1966 Manch 4 1200 TTS. c, 1957 Lambretta LD-150. d, 1990 Yamaha XJP 1200. e, 1885 Daimler. f, 1950-60 John Player Norton.

No. 2479, 7r: a, 1969 Honda CB 750. b, 1913 Harley-Davidson. c, 1925 Bohmerland. d, 1910 American Indian. e, 1993 Triumph Trophy 1200. f, 1928, Moto Guzzi 500S.

No. 2480, 25r, 1960 Electra Glide. No. 2481, 25r, 1950 Harley-Davidson.

2000, Oct. 30 ***Perf. 13¼x13½***

Sheets of 6, #a-f

2478-2479 A392 Set of 2 16.50 16.50

Souvenir Sheets

2480-2481 A392 Set of 2 10.00 10.00

A393

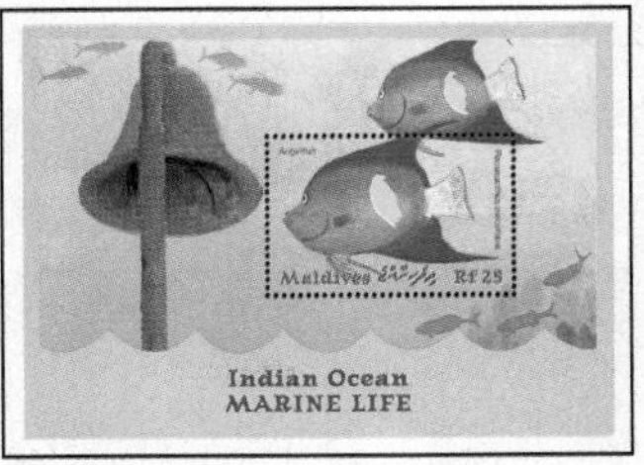

Marine Life — A394

No. 2482: a, Longnosed filefish. b, Hawaiian squirrelfish. c, Freckled hawkfish. d, McCosker's flasher wrasse. e, Pygoplites diacanthus. f, Paraeentzopyge venusta.

No. 2483, 5r: a, Chaetodon lunula. b, Stethojulis albovittata. c, Green turtle. d, Jobfish. e, Damsel fish. f, Chaetodon meyeri. g, Cirrhilabrus exquistus. h, Anemonefish.

No. 2484, 5r: a, Coris aygula. b, Snapper. c, Sea bass. d, Chaetodon bennetti. e, Pelagic snapper. f, Cardinalfish. g, Thalassoma hardwicke. h, Surgeonfish.

No. 2485, 5r: a, Grouper. b, Pygoplites diacanthus. c, Forcipiger flavissimus. d, Goatfish. e, Trumpet fish. f, Anthias. g, Centropyge bispinosus. h, Sweetlips.

No. 2486, 25r, H. aberrans. No. 2487, 25r, Angelfish. No. 2488, 25r, Moray eel. No. 2489, 25r, Spiny butterflyfish.

2000, Nov. 15 Litho. ***Perf. 14***

2482 A393 5r Sheet of 6, #a-f 5.00 5.00

Sheets of 8, #a-h

2483-2485 A394 Set of 3 21.00 21.00

Souvenir Sheets

2486 A393 25r multi 4.25 4.25

2487-2489 A394 Set of 3 13.00 13.00

Flowers — A395

No. 2490, 5r: a, Corn lily. b, Clivia. c, Red hot poker. d, Crown of thorns. e, Cape daisy. f, Geranium.

No. 2491, 5r, horiz.: a, Fringed hibiscus. b, Erica vestita. c, Bird-of-paradise. d, Peacock orchid. e, Mesembryanthemums. f, African violets.

No. 2492, 25r, Gladiolus. No. 2493, 25r, Calla lily, horiz.

2000, Nov. 15

Sheets of 6, #a-f

2490-2491 A395 Set of 2 13.50 13.50

Souvenir Sheets

2492-2493 A395 Set of 2 10.00 10.00

Airplanes, Automobiles and Trains — A396

Designs: 2.50r, Papyrus, vert. 3r, Hiawatha. 12r, Supermarine SGB. 13r, MLX01.

No. 2498, 5r: a, Thrust SSC. b, Curtiss R3C-2. c, Rocket. d, BB-9004. e, Mallard. f, TGV.

No. 2499, 5r: a, Lockheed XP-80. b, Mikoyan MiG-23. c, Tempest. d, Bluebird. e, Blue Flame. f, Thrust 2.

No. 2500, 25r, Bell X-1. No. 2501, 25r, Lockheed SR-71 Blackbird, vert.

2000, Nov. 29

2494-2497 A396 Set of 4 5.25 5.25

Sheets of 6, #a-f

2498-2499 A396 Set of 2 10.00 10.00

Souvenir Sheets

2500-2501 A396 Set of 2 8.50 8.50

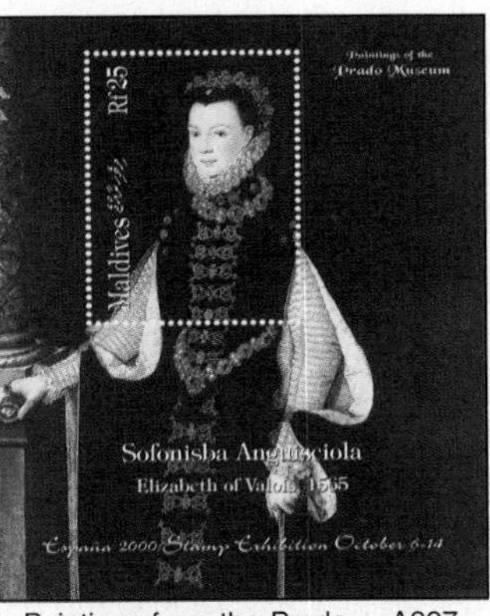

Paintings from the Prado — A397

No. 2502, 7r: a, The Nobleman with the Golden Chain, by Tintoretto. b, Triumphal Arch, by Domenichino. c, Don Garcia de Medici, by Bronzino. d, Micer Marsilio from Micer Marsilio and His Wife, by Lorenzo Lotto. e, La Infanta Maria Antoinetta Fernanda, by Jacopo Amigoni. f, Wife from Micer Marsilio and his Wife.

No. 2503, 7r: a, Two women with headdresses. b, Woman in red. c, Men. d, The Duke of Lerma on Horseback, by Rubens. e, The Death of Seneca, by the Workshop of Rubens. f, Marie de Medici by Rubens. a-c from Achilles Amongst the Daughters of Lycomedes, by Peter Paul Rubens and Anthony Van Dyck.

No. 2504, 7r: a, Self-portrait, by Albrecht Dürer. b, A Woman and Her Daughter, by Adriaen van Cronenburch. c, Portrait of a man, by Dürer. d, Woman and children. e, Artemisia, by Rembrandt. f, The Artist. d, f from The Artist and His Family, by Jacob Jordaens.

No. 2505, 7r: a, The Painter Andrea Sacchi, by Carlo Maratta. b, Two men. c, Charles Cecil Roberts, by Pompeo Girolamo Batoni. d, Francesco Albani, by Sacchi. e, Three men. f, William Hamilton, by Batoni. b, e from The Turkish Ambassador to the Court of Naples, by Giuseppe Bonito

No. 2506, 7r: a, The Marquesa of Villafranca, by Francisco de Goya. b, Maria Ruthven, by Van Dyck. c, Cardinal-Infante Ferdinand, by Van Dyck. d, Frederik Hendrik, Prince of Orange, by Van Dyck. e, Van Dyck from Self-portrait with Endymion Porter. f, Porter from Self-portrait with Endymion Porter.

No. 2507, 7r: a, Philip V, by Hyacinthe Rigaud. b, Louis XIV, by Rigaud. c, Don Luis, Prince of Asturias, by Michel-Ange Houasse. d, Duke Carlo Emanuele II of Savoy with His Wife and Son, by Charles Dauphin. e, Kitchen Maid by Charles-François Hutin. f, Hurdy-gurdy Player, by Georges de La Tour.

No. 2508, 25r, Elizabeth of Valois, by Sofonisba Anguisciola. No. 2509, 25r, Camilla Gonzaga, Countess of San Segundo with Her Three Children, by Parmigianino. No. 2510, 25r, The Turkish Ambassador to the Court of Naples. No. 2511, 25r, Duke Carlo Emanuele of Savoy with His Wife and Son. No. 2512, 25r, The Artist and His Family, horiz. No. 2513, 25r, The Devotion of Rudolf I, by Rubens and Jan Wildens, horiz.

Perf. 12x12¼, 12¼x12

2000, Nov. 29

Sheets of 6, #a-f

2502-2507 A397 Set of 6 42.50 42.50

Souvenir Sheets

2508-2513 A397 Set of 6 26.00 26.00

España 2000 Intl. Philatelic Exhibition.

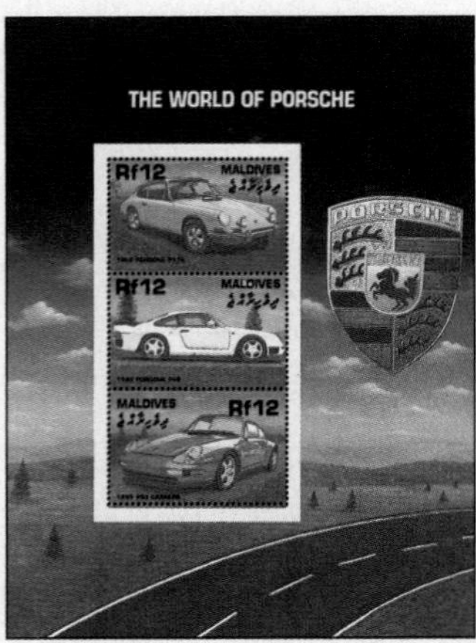

Porsche Automobiles — A398

No. 2514, 12r: a, 1966 911S. b, 1988 959. c, 1995 993 Carrera.
No. 2515, 12r: a, 1963 356 SC. b, 1975 911 Turbo. c, Unidentified.

2000, Nov. 30 Litho. *Perf. 14*
Sheets of 3, #a-c

2514-2515 A398 Set of 2 12.50 12.50

Souvenir Sheet

2516 A398 25r 2000 Boxter 4.25 4.25

No. 2516 contains one 56x42mm stamp.

Mushrooms A399

Designs: 30 l, Cortinarius collinitus. 50 l, Russula ochroleuca. 2r, Lepiota acutesquamosa. 3r, Hebeloma radicosum. 13r, Amanita echinocephala. 15r, Collybia iocephala.
No. 2523, 7r: a, Tricholoma aurantium. b, Pholiota spectabilis. c, Russula caerulea. d, Amanita phalloides. e, Mycena strobilinoides. f, Boletus satanas.
No. 2524, 7r: a, Amanita muscaria. b, Mycena lilacifolia. c, Coprinus comatus. d, Morchella crassipes. e, Russula nigricans. f, Lepiota procera.
No. 2525, 25r, Tricholoma aurantium, diff. No. 2526, 25r, Lepiota procera, diff.

2001, Jan. 2

2517-2522 A399 Set of 6 5.75 5.75

Sheets of 6, #a-f

2523-2524 A399 Set of 2 14.50 14.50

Souvenir Sheets

2525-2526 A399 Set of 2 8.50 8.50

Battle of Britain, 60th Anniv. — A400

No. 2527, 5r: a, German commanders look across the English Channel. b, The armorers make ready. c, The German attack begins. d, Germany bombs the British coast. e, Germany bombs British cities. f, Luftwaffe sets St. Paul's Cathedral ablaze. g, Aerial dogfight. h, A British Spitfire is shot down.
No. 2528, 5r: a, Leaders of Great Britain. b, British pilots prepare to confront the Luftwaffe. c, RAF planes take off. d, British aircraft meet the enemy. e, Luftwaffe meets tough resistance. f, Dogfight above English Channel. g, German planes fall short of their objective. h Many German planes are shot down.
No. 2529, 25r, Hawker Hurricane. No. 2530, 25r, Messerschmitt ME 109.

2001, Jan. 2 *Perf. 14*
Sheets of 8, #a-h

2527-2528 A400 Set of 2 13.50 13.50

Souvenir Sheets

2529-2530 A400 Set of 2 8.50 8.50

Rijksmuseum, Amsterdam, Bicent. (in 2000) — A401

No. 2531, 7r: a, Donkey's head and rider from Donkey Riding on the Beach, by Isaac Lazarus Israels. b, The Paternal Admonition, by Gerard Terborch, the Younger. c, The Sick Woman, by Jan Havicksz Steen. d, Girls with red hats from Donkey Riding on the Beach. e, Pompeius Occo, by Dirck Jacobsz. f, Woman With a Child in a Pantry, by Pieter de Hooch.
No. 2532, 7r: a, The Holy Kinship, by Geertgen tot Sint Jans. b, Sir Thomas Gresham, by Anthonis Mor. c, Self-portrait as St. Paul, by Rembrandt. d, Cleopatra's Banquet, by Gerard Lairesse. e, Still Life With Flowers in a Glass, by Jan Breughel, the Elder. f, Portrait of a Man, Possibly Nicolaes Hasselaer, by Frans Hals.
No. 2533, 7r: a, Rembrandt's Mother, by Gerard Dou. b, Portrait of a Girl Dressed in Blue, by Jan Cornelisz Verspronck. c, Old Woman at Prayer, by Nicolaes Maes. d, Feeding the Hungry from The Seven Works of Charity, by the Master of Alkmaar. e, The Threatened Swan, by Jan Asselyn. f, The Daydreamer, by Maes.
No. 2534, 7r: a, Woman seated in doorway, from The Little Street, by Jan Vermeer. b, Two women from The Love Letter, by Vermeer. c, Woman in Blue Reading a Letter, by Vermeer. d, Woman and pillar from The Love Letter. e, The Milkmaid, by Vermeer. f, Arched doorway, from The Little Street.
No. 2535, 25r, Johannes Wtenbogaert, by Rembrandt. No. 2536, 25r, The Staalmeesters (The Syndics), by Rembrandt. No. 2537, 25r, The Night Watch, by Rembrandt. No. 2538, 25r, Shipwreck on a Rocky Coast, by Wijnandus Johannes Joseph Nuyen, horiz.

2001, Jan. 15 *Perf. 13¾*
Sheets of 6, #a-f

2531-2534 A401 Set of 4 30.00 30.00

Souvenir Sheets

2535-2538 A401 Set of 4 17.00 17.00

Ill-fated Ships — A402

No. 2539, 5r: a, Milton Iatrides, 1970. b, Cyclops, 1918. c, Marine Sulphur Queen, 1963. d, Rosalie, 1840. e, Mary Celeste, 1872. f, Atlanta, 1880.
No. 2540, 5r: a, Windfall, 1962. b, Kobenhavn, 1928. c, Pearl, 1874. d, HMS Bulwark, 1914. e, Patriot, 1812. f, Lusitania, 1915.
No. 2541, 25r, La Baussole and L'Astrolabe, 1789. No. 2542, 25r, Titanic, 1912.

2001, Feb. 12 *Perf. 14*
Sheets of 6, #a-f

2539-2540 A402 Set of 2 10.00 10.00

Souvenir Sheets

2541-2542 A402 Set of 2 8.50 8.50

Flower Type of 1997

2001, Mar. 1 *Perf. 14¾x14*
Size: 16x20mm

2543 A350 10r Like #2267 1.75 1.75

Islam in Maldive Islands, 848th Anniv. — A403

No. 2544: a, Dharumavantha Rasgefaanu Mosque. b, Plaque of Hukurumiskiiy. c, Learning the Holy Koran. d, Institute of Islamic Studies. e, Center for the Holy Koran. f, Islamic Center.

2001, July 9 Litho. *Perf. 13¾*

2544 A403 10r Sheet of 6, #a-f 10.00 10.00

Souvenir Sheet

2545 A403 25r Medhu Ziyaarath 4.25 4.25

Fish — A404

Designs: No. 2546, 10r, Pterois miles. No. 2547, 10r, Pomacanthus imperator.

2001, July 16 *Perf. 14x14¾*

2546-2547 A404 Set of 2 3.50 3.50

Pontiac Trans-Am Automobiles — A405

No. 2548, 12r: a, 1970. b, 1989. c, 1994.
No. 2549, 12r: a, 1976. b, 1988. c, 1988 Coupe.

2001 *Perf. 14*
Sheets of 3, #a-c

2548-2549 A405 Set of 2 12.50 12.50

Souvenir Sheet
Perf. 14¼

2550 A405 25r 1999 4.25 4.25

Nos. 2548-2549 each contain three 42x28mm stamps.

Automobiles — A406

Designs: 1r, 1930 Pierce-Arrow. 2r, 1938 Mercedes-Benz 540K. 8r, 1934 Duesenberg J. 10r, 1931 Bugatti Royale.
No. 2555, 7r: a, 1931 Auburn convertible sedan. b, 1931 Mercedes SSKL. c, 1929 Packard roadster. d, 1940 Chevrolet. e, 1915 Mercer. f, 1941 Packard sedan.
No. 2556, 7r: a, 1932 Chevrolet roadster. b, 1929 Cadillac Fleetwood roadster. c, 1928 Bentley Speed Six. d, 1930 Cadillac Fleetwood. e, 1936 Ford convertible. f, 1929 Hudson Phaeton.
No. 2557, 25r, 1930 Cord Brougham. No. 2558, 25r, 1931 Rolls-Royce P-1.

2001 *Perf. 14*

2551-2554 A406 Set of 4 3.50 3.50

Sheets of 6, #a-f

2555-2556 A406 Set of 2 14.50 14.50

Souvenir Sheets

2557-2558 A406 Set of 2 8.50 8.50

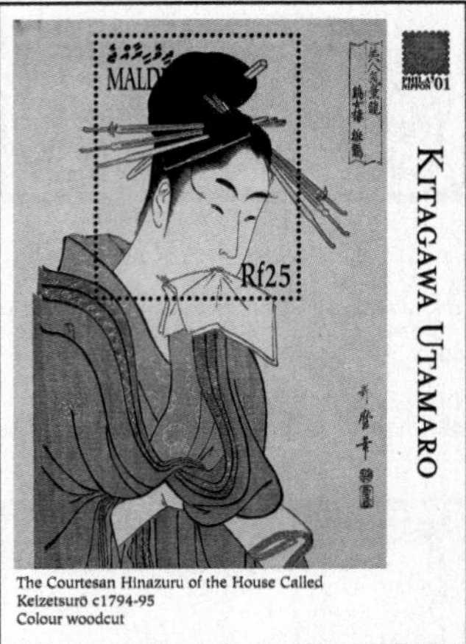

Phila Nippon '01, Japan — A407

No. 2559, 7r (28x42mm) — Prints of women by Utamaro: a, Reed Blind, Model Young Women Woven in Mist. b, Woman with Parasol. c, High-ranked Courtesan, Five Shades of Ink in the Northern Quarter. d, Comparison of Beauties of the Southern Quarter. e, The Barber.
No. 2560, 7r — Actors by Shunsho Katsukawa: a, Danjuro Ichikawa V (black kimono, 28x85mm). b, Danjuro Ichikawa V (arm raised, 28x85mm). c, Danjuro Ichikawa V (arms crossed on chest, 28x85mm). d, Danjuro Ichikawa V (wrapped in kimono, 28x85mm). e, Tomoeman Otani I and Mitsugaro Bando I (56x85mm).
No. 2561, 25r, The Courtesan Hinazuru of the House Called Keizetsuro, by Utamaro. No. 2562, 25r, Jomyo Tsutsui and the Priest Ichirai on the Uji Bridge, by Kiyomasu Torii.

2001, July 18 Litho. *Perf. 14*
Sheets of 5, #a-e

2559-2560 A407 Set of 2 12.00 12.00

Souvenir Sheets
Perf. 13¾

2561-2562 A407 Set of 2 8.50 8.50

Giuseppe Verdi (1813-1901), Opera Composer — A408

No. 2563: a, Alfred Piccaver. b, Rigoletto costume, Heinrich. c, Rigoletto costume, Cologne. d, Cornell MacNeil.
25r, Matteo Manugerra.

2001, Aug. 26 ***Perf. 14***
2563 A408 10r Sheet of 4, #a-d 6.75 6.75

Souvenir Sheet

2564 A408 25r multi 4.25 4.25

Mao Zedong (1893-1976) — A409

No. 2565: a, Red background. b, Blue background. c, Gray background.
25r, Wearing cap.

2001, Aug. 26 ***Perf. 13¾***
2565 A409 15r Sheet of 3, #a-c 7.75 7.75

Souvenir Sheet

2566 A409 25r multi 4.25 4.25

Queen Victoria (1819-1901) — A410

No. 2567: a, Earring at right. b, Earring at left. c, As old woman. d, In black dress.
25r, With hand on chin.

2001, Aug. 26 ***Perf. 14***
2567 A410 10r Sheet of 4, #a-d 6.75 6.75

Souvenir Sheet

2568 A410 25r multi 4.25 4.25

Queen Elizabeth II, 75th Birthday — A411

No. 2569: a, Without hat. b, Wearing large crown. c, Wearing tiara. d, Wearing red uniform. e, Wearing black cape and hat. f, Wearing tan hat.
25r, Wearing crown, diff.

2001, Aug. 26
2569 A411 7r Sheet of 6, #a-f 7.25 7.25

Souvenir Sheet

2570 A411 25r multi 4.25 4.25

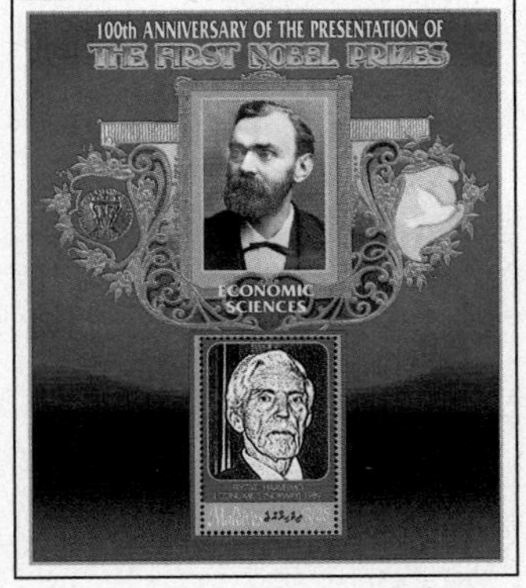

Nobel Prizes, Cent. — A412

No. 2571 — Economics laureates: a, Simon Kuznets, 1971. b, Wassily Leontief, 1973. c, Lawrence R. Klein, 1980. d, Friedrich A. von Hayek, 1974. e, Leonid V. Kantorovich, 1975.

No. 2572, 7r — Peace laureates: a, Ernesto T. Moneta, 1907. b, Albert J. Luthuli, 1960. c, Henri Dunant, 1901. d, Charles Albert Gobat, 1902. e, Sean MacBride, 1974. f, Elie Ducommun, 1902.

No. 2573, 7r — Peace laureates: a, Adolfo Pérez Esquivel, 1980. b, Mikhail S. Gorbachev, 1990. c, Betty Williams, 1976. d, Alfonso Garcia Robles, 1982. e, Paul D'Estournelles de Constant, 1909. f, Louis Renault, 1907.

No. 2574, 25r, Trygve Haavelmo, Economics, 1989. No. 2575, 25r, Vicente Aleixandre, Literature, 1977. No. 2576, 25r, Octavio Paz, Literature, 1990.

2001, Sept. 29 **Litho.** ***Perf. 14***
2571 A412 7r Sheet of 5, #a-e 6.00 6.00

Sheets of 6, #a-f

2572-2573 A412 Set of 2 14.50 14.50

Souvenir Sheets

2574-2576 A412 Set of 3 13.00 13.00

Mercedes-Benz Automobiles, Cent. — A413

Designs: 2.50r, 1939 W165 Grand Prix. 5r, 1928 460 Nürburg Sport Roadster. 8r, 1928 Boattail Speedster. 15r, 1909 Blitzen Benz.

No. 2581, 7r: a, 1927 680S. b, 1934 150. c, 1936 540K Roadster. d, 1933 770 Grosser Mercedes. e, 1958 220SE. f, 1990 500SL.

No. 2582, 7r: a, 1933 290. b, 1927 Model S. c, 1953 300SL Coupe. d, 1911 Benz Victoria. e, 1968 280SL. f, 1937 W125 Grand Prix.

No. 2583, 25r, 1931 370S. No. 2584, 25r, 1955 300SLR.

2001, Oct. 30 **Litho.** ***Perf. 14***
2577-2580 A413 Set of 4 5.25 5.25

Sheets of 6, #a-f

2581-2582 A413 Set of 2 14.50 14.50

Souvenir Sheets

2583-2584 A413 Set of 2 8.50 8.50

2002 World Cup Soccer Championships, Japan and Korea — A414

World Cup Trophy and: 1r, Eusebio, Portugal, Portuguese flag. 3r, Johan Cruyff, Netherlands, Netherlands flag. 7r, French player and flag. 10r, Japanese player and flag. 12r, Seoul World Cup Stadium, horiz. 15r, 1930 World Cup poster.

25r, Gerd Müller's winning goal for West Germany, 1974, vert.

2001, Nov. 28
2585-2590 A414 Set of 6 8.25 8.25

Souvenir Sheet

2591 A414 25r multi 4.25 4.25

No. 2591 contains one 42x56mm stamp.

Princess Diana (1961-97) — A415

No. 2592: a, Pink rose. b, White rose. c, Yellow rose. d, Beige rose.
25r, Wearing pearl necklace.

2001, Dec. 26
2592 A415 10r Sheet of 4, #a-d 6.75 6.75

Souvenir Sheet

2593 A415 25r multi 4.25 4.25

New Year 2002 (Year of the Horse) — A416

No. 2594 — Paintings by Xu Beihong: a, Running Horse (painting 45mm tall). b, Standing Horse. c, Running Horse (painting 49mm tall). d, Horse (painting 44mm tall). e, Horse (painting 48mm tall).
15r, Horse, horiz.

2001, Dec. 26 ***Perf. 14***
2594 A416 5r Sheet of 5, #a-e 4.25 4.25

Souvenir Sheet

Perf. 14x14½

2595 A416 15r multi 2.60 2.60

No. 2594 contains five 31x63mm stamps.

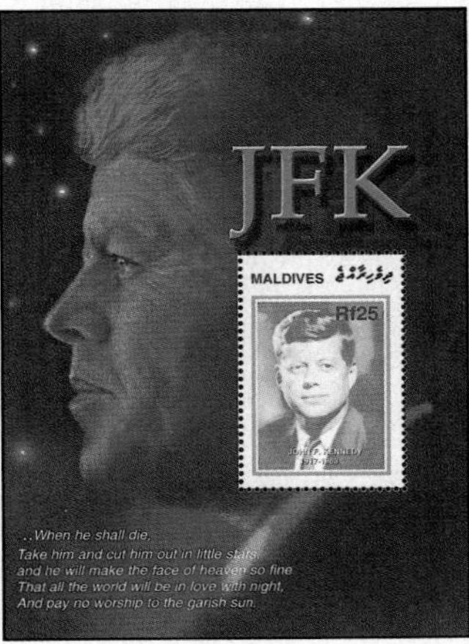

Pres. John F. Kennedy — A417

No. 2596, 5r: a, At Dexter, 1927. b, At Harvard, 1935. c, In Navy, 1943. d, At wedding, 1953. e, With brother Robert, 1956. f, At Presidential inauguration, 1961.

No. 2597, 5r: a, With Nikita Khrushchev, 1961. b, With Harold Macmillan. c, With Charles de Gaulle, 1961. d, With Jawaharlal Nehru, 1962. e, With Konrad Adenauer, 1963. f, With Dr. Martin Luther King, Jr., 1963.

No. 2598, 25r, Portrait. No. 2599, 25r, With wife, 1961.

2001, Dec. 26 ***Perf. 14***

Sheets of 6, #a-f

2596-2597 A417 Set of 2 10.50 10.50

Souvenir Sheets

2598-2599 A417 Set of 2 8.50 8.50

Moths — A418

No. 2600, 7r: a, Cymothoe lucasi. b, Milionia grandis. c, Ornithoptera eroesus. d, Hyantis hodeva. e, Ammobiota festiva. f, Blue salamis.

No. 2601, 7r: a, Zygaena occitanica. b, Campyloes desgodinsi. c, Bhutanitis thaidina. d, Six-tailed helicopsis. e, Parnassius charltonius. f, Acraea ecucogiap.

No. 2602: a, Papilio dardanus. b, Baomisa hieroglyphica. c, Troides prattorum. d, Funonia rhadama.

No. 2603, 25r, Hypolera cassotis. No. 2604, 25r, Euphydryas maturna, vert.

2001, Dec. 26 **Litho.**

Sheets of 6, #a-f

2600-2601 A418 Set of 2 14.50 14.50
2602 A418 10r Sheet of 4, #a-d 6.75 6.75

Souvenir Sheets

2603-2604 A418 Set of 2 8.50 8.50

Queen Mother Type of 1999 Redrawn

No. 2605: a, With King George VI, 1936. b, In 1941. c, In 1960. d, In 1981.
25r, At Order of the Garter Service.

2001, Dec. ***Perf. 14***

Yellow Orange Frames

2605 A372 7r Sheet of 4, #a-d, + label 4.75 4.75

Souvenir Sheet

Perf. 13¾

2606 A372 25r multi 4.25 4.25

Queen Mother's 101st birthday. No. 2606 contains one 38x51mm stamp slightly darker than that found on No. 2405. Sheet margins of Nos. 2605-2606 lack embossing and gold arms and frames found on Nos. 2404-2405.

Reign of Queen Elizabeth II, 50th Anniv. — A419

No. 2607: a, With Princess Margaret. b, Wearing white hat. c, Wearing tiara. d, Holding flowers.
25r, At coronation.

2002, Feb. 6 Litho. *Perf. 14¼*

2607 A419 10r Sheet of 4, #a-d 7.00 7.00

Souvenir Sheet

2608 A419 25r multi 4.25 4.25

Cats — A420

Designs: 3r, Havana brown. 5r, American wirehair. 8r, Norwegian forest cat. 10r, Seal point Siamese.
No. 2613, 7r: a, British blue. b, Red mackerel Manx. c, Scottish fold. d, Somali. e, Balinese. f, Exotic shorthair.
No. 2614, 7r, horiz.: a, Persian. b, Exotic shorthair, diff. c, Ragdoll. d, Manx. e, Tonkinese. f, Scottish fold, diff.
25r, Blue mackerel tabby Cornish rex.

2002, Apr. 8 *Perf. 14*

2609-2612 A420 Set of 4 4.50 4.50

Sheets of 6, #a-f

2613-2614 A420 Set of 2 14.50 14.50

Souvenir Sheet

2615 A420 25r multi 4.25 4.25

Birds A421

Designs: 1r, Swinhoe's snipe. 2r, Oriental honey buzzard. 3r, Asian koel. No. 2619, 5r, Red-throated pipet. No. 2620, 7r, Short-eared owl. 10r, Eurasian spoonbill. 12r, Pied wheatear. 15r, Oriental pratincole.
No. 2624, 5r: a, Lesser noddy. b, Roseate tern. c, Frigate minor. d, Saunder's tern. e, White-bellied storm petrel. f, Red-footed booby.
No. 2625, 5r: a, Cattle egret. b, Barn swallow. c, Osprey. d, Little heron. e, Ruddy turnstone. f, Sooty tern.
No. 2626, 7r: a, Rose-ringed parakeet. b, Common swift. c, Lesser kestrel. d, Golden oriole. e, Asian paradise flycatcher. f, Indian roller.
No. 2627, 7r: a, Pallid harrier. b, Gray heron. c, Blue-tailed bee-eater. d, White-breasted water hen. e, Cotton pygmy goose. f, Maldivian pond heron.
No. 2628, 25r, White-tailed tropicbird. No. 2629, 25r, Greater flamingo. No. 2630, 25r, Cinnamon bittern. No. 2631, 25r, White tern.

2002, Apr. 8

2616-2623 A421 Set of 8 9.50 9.50

Sheets of 6, #a-f

2624-2627 A421 Set of 4 25.00 25.00

Souvenir Sheets

2628-2631 A421 Set of 4 17.00 17.00

Prehistoric Animals — A422

No. 2632, 7r: a, Sivatherium. b, Flat-headed peccary. c, Shasta ground sloth. d, Harlan's ground sloth. e, European woolly rhinoceros. f, Dwarf pronghorn.
No. 2633, 7r: a, Macrauchenia. b, Gyptodon. c, Nesodon. d, Imperial tapir. e, Short-faced bear. f, Mammoth.
No. 2634, 25r, Saber-toothed cat. No. 2635, 25r, Woolly mammoth, vert.

2002, May 21

Sheets of 6, #a-f

2632-2633 A422 Set of 2 14.50 14.50

Souvenir Sheets

2634-2635 A422 Set of 2 8.50 8.50

2002 Winter Olympics, Salt Lake City — A423

Designs: No. 2636, 12r, Freestyle skiing. No. 2637, 12r, Downhill skiing.

2002, July 11 Litho. *Perf. 13½x13¼*

2636-2637 A423 Set of 2 4.00 4.00
a. Souvenir sheet, #2636-2637 4.00 4.00

Intl. Year of Mountains — A424

No. 2638: a, Mt. Ama Dablam, Nepal. b, Mt. Clements, US. c, Mt. Artesonraju, Peru. d, Mt. Cholatse, Nepal.
25r, Balloon and Mt. Jefferson, US.

2002, July 11 *Perf. 14*

2638 A424 15r Sheet of 4, #a-d 10.50 10.50

Souvenir Sheet

2639 A424 25r multi 4.25 4.25

20th World Scout Jamboree, Thailand — A425

No. 2640, vert.: a, Temple. b, Thailand Scout. c, Merit badges.
25r, Mountain climbing merit badge.

2002, July 11

2640 A425 15r Sheet of 3, #a-c 7.75 7.75

Souvenir Sheet

2641 A425 25r multi 4.25 4.25

Souvenir Sheet

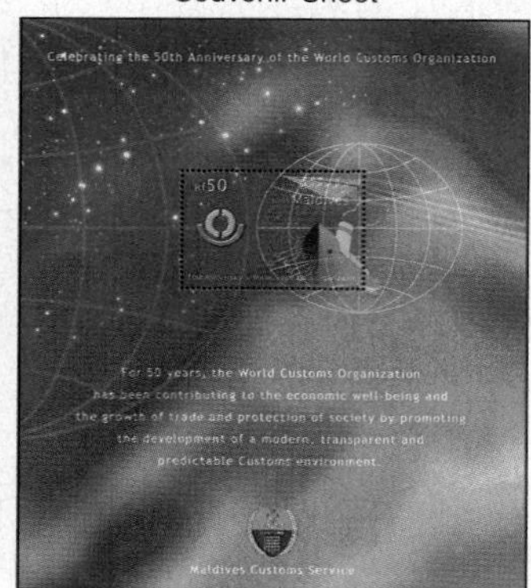

World Customs Organization, 50th Anniv. — A426

2002, Aug. 12 *Perf. 13¾*

2642 A426 50r multi 8.50 8.50

Elvis Presley (1935-77) A427

2002, Oct. 7

2643 A427 5r multi .80 .80

Printed in sheets of 9.

Flowers and Butterflies — A428

No. 2644, 7r — Flowers: a, Morning glory. b, Wedding bell anemone. c, Barrett Browning narcissus. d, Persian jewel nigella. e, Whirligig pink osteospermum. f, Brown lasso iris.
No. 2645, 7r — Orchids: a, Laelia gouldiana. b, Cattleya Louise Georgiana. c, Laeliocattleya Christopher Gubler. d, Miltoniopsis Bert Field Crimson Glow. e, Lemboglossum bictoniense. f, Derosara Divine Victor.
No. 2646, 7r — Butterflies: a, Morpho menelus. b, Small postman. c, Hewitson's blue hairstreak. d, Green swallowtail. e, Cairns birdwing. f, Queen.
No. 2647, 25r, Little pink beauty aster. No. 2648, 25r, Angraecum veitchii, vert. No. 2649, 25r, Cymothoe lurida butterfly.

2002, Nov. 4 Litho. *Perf. 14*

Sheets of 6, #a-f

2644-2646 A428 Set of 3 20.00 20.00

Souvenir Sheets

2647-2649 A428 Set of 3 12.00 12.00

2002 World Cup Soccer Championships, Japan and Korea — A429

No. 2650, 7r: a, Torsten Frings sliding. b, Roberto Carlos. c, Frings kicking. d, Ronaldo pointing. e, Oliver Neuville. f, Ronaldo with ball.
No. 2651, 7r: a, Eul Yong Lee, Alpay Ozalan. b, Myung Bo Hong, Hakan Sukur. c, Emre Belozoglu, Chong Gug Song. d, Ergun Penbe, Chong Gug Song. e, Ergun Penbe, Ki Hyeon Seol. f, Chong Gug Song, Hakan Unsal.
No. 2652, 15r: a, Cafu and Neuville. b, Hands holding World Cup.
No. 2653, 15r: a, Dietmar Hamann. b, Cafu holding World Cup.
No. 2654, 15r: a, Ilhan Mansiz. b, Young Pyo Lee.
No. 2655, 15r: a, Hakan Sukur. b, Sang Chul Yoo.

2002, Nov. 12 *Perf. 13½*

Sheets of 6, #a-f

2650-2651 A429 Set of 2 13.00 13.00

Souvenir Sheets of 2, #a-b

2652-2655 A429 Set of 4 19.00 19.00

Teddy Bears, Cent. — A430

No. 2656: a, Hairdresser. b, Construction worker. c, Gardener. d, Chef.
No. 2657, 12r: a, Mother. b, Sister and brother. c, Father.
No. 2658, 12r: a, Nurse. b, Doctor. c, Dentist.
No. 2659, 30r, Soccer player. No. 2660, 30r, Golfer. No. 2661, 30r, Snow boarder.

2002, Nov. 18 *Perf. 14*

2656 A430 8r Sheet of 4, #a-d 5.00 5.00

Sheets of 3, #a-c

2657-2658 A430 Set of 2 11.50 11.50

Souvenir Sheets

2659-2661 A430 Set of 3 14.00 14.00

First Non-Stop Solo Transatlantic Flight, 75th Anniv. — A430a

No. 2661A, 12r — Various photos of Charles Lindbergh and Spirit of St. Louis: c, Blue. d, Brown. e, Gray. f, Red violet.

No. 2661B, 12r: g, Donald Hall, designer of Spirit of St. Louis. h, Charles Lindbergh. i, Lindbergh, Spirit of St. Louis (Lindbergh distorted). j, Lindbergh, Hall and President Mahoney of Ryan Aircraft.

2002, Dec. 2 **Litho.** ***Perf. 14***

2661A A430a 12r Sheet of 4, #c-f 7.50 7.50
2661B A430a 12r Sheet of 4, #g-j 7.50 7.50

Princess Diana (1961-97)
A431 A432

2002, Dec. 2

2662 A431 12r multi 1.90 1.90
2663 A432 12r multi 1.90 1.90

Nos. 2662-2663 were each printed in sheets of 4.

Pres. John F. Kennedy (1917-63) — A432a

No. 2663A: b, With father Joseph P., and brother Joseph, Jr. c, At age 11. d, Inspecting Boston waterfront, 1951. e, As Navy Ensign, 1941. f, With sister Kathleen in London, 1939. g, With Eleanor Roosevelt, 1951.

2002, Dec. 2 **Litho.** ***Perf. 14***

2663A A432a 7r Sheet of 6, #b-g 6.75 6.75

Pres. Ronald Reagan — A433

Designs: No. 2664, Green background. No. 2665, Blue background.

No. 2666: a, Wearing brown suit. b, Wearing black suit with red tie.

2002, Dec. 2

2664 A433 12r multi 1.90 1.90
2665 A433 12r multi 1.90 1.90
a. Horiz. pair, #2664-2665 4.00 4.00
2666 A433 12r Horiz. pair, #a-b 4.00 4.00
Nos. 2664-2666 (3) 7.80 7.80

Nos. 2664-2665 were printed in sheets containing two of each stamp. No. 2666 was printed in sheets containing two pairs.

Amphilex 2002 Intl. Stamp Exhibition, Amsterdam — A434

No. 2667, 7r — Life of Queen Mother Juliana and Prince Bernhard: a, Wedding, 1937. b, Birth of Princess Beatrix, 1938. c, Exile in Canada, 1940-45. d, Installation of Juliana as queen, 1948. e, Zeeland flood, 1953. f, Royal couple.

No. 2668, 7r — Portraits depicting Queen Beatrix by: a, Pauline Hille. b, John Klinkenberg. c, Beatrice Filius. d, Will Kellermann. e, Graswinckel. f, Marjolijn Spreeuwenberg.

2002, Dec. 8 ***Perf. 14***

Sheets of 6, #a-f

2667-2668 A434 Set of 2 13.00 13.00

Fish A435

Birds and Sharks — A436

Designs: 10 l, Flame basslet. 15 l, Teardrop butterflyfish. 20 l, Hamburg damselfish. 25 l, Bridled tern. 50 l, Blue-lined surgeonfish. 1r, Common tern. 2r, Common noddy. No. 2676, Yellow-breasted wrasse. No. 2677, Blue shark. 4r, Harlequin filefish. 5r, Orangespine unicornfish. 10r, Emperor angelfish. 12r, Bullseye. 20r, Scalloped hammerhead shark.

Perf. 14 (A435), 10¾x13 (25 l, 1r, 2r), 13¼x14 (#2677, 20r)

2002, Dec. 24

2669 A435 10 l multi .20 .20
2670 A435 15 l multi .20 .20
2671 A435 20 l multi .20 .20
2672 A436 25 l multi .20 .20
2673 A435 50 l multi .20 .20
2674 A436 1r multi .20 .20
2675 A436 2r multi .30 .30
2676 A435 2.50r multi .40 .40
2677 A436 2.50r multi .40 .40
2678 A435 4r multi .60 .60
2679 A435 5r multi .75 .75
2680 A435 10r multi 1.50 1.50
2681 A435 12r multi 1.90 1.90
2682 A436 20r multi 3.00 3.00
Nos. 2669-2682 (14) 10.05 10.05

Tourism, 30th Anniv. — A437

No. 2683: a, Atolls. b, Sand spit. c, Surfer. d, Underwater scene.

2002, Dec. 25 ***Perf. 13½***

2683 A437 12r Sheet of 4, #a-d 7.50 7.50

Popeye — A438

No. 2684, vert: a, Diving. b, Surfing. c, Sailboarding. d, Baseball. e, Hurdles. f, Tennis.

25r, Volleyball.

2003, Jan. 27 ***Perf. 14***

2684 A438 7r Sheet of 6, #a-f 6.50 6.50

Souvenir Sheet

2685 A438 25r multi 4.00 4.00

National Museum, 50th Anniv. A439

Various museum items: 3r, 3.50r, 6.50r, 22r.

2003, Jan. 31 **Litho.**

2686-2689 A439 Set of 4 5.50 5.50

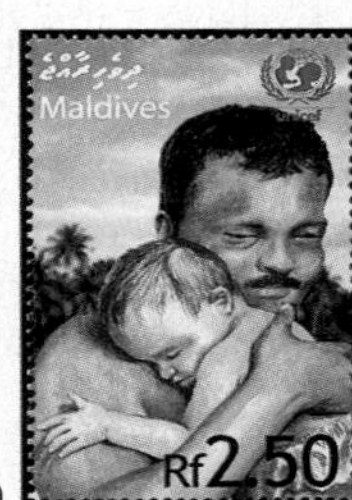

UNICEF — A440

Designs: 2.50r, Father and child. 5r, Mother kissing child. 20r, Child learning to walk.

2003, Jan. 31 ***Perf. 15x14***

2690-2692 A440 Set of 3 4.25 4.25

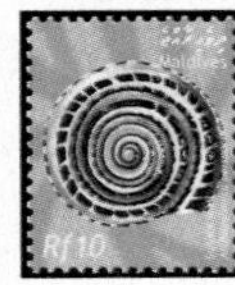

Shells — A441

Designs: No. 2693, 10r, Sundial shell. No. 2694, 10r, Cardita clam. No. 2695, 10r, Corn shell. No. 2696, 10r, Cowrie shell.

2003, Mar. 25 **Litho.** ***Perf. 13¼***

2693-2696 A441 Set of 4 6.25 6.25

Astronauts Killed in Space Shuttle Columbia Accident — A442

No. 2697: a, Mission Specialist 1 David M. Brown. b, Commander Rick D. Husband. c, Mission Specialist 4 Laurel Blair Salton Clark. d, Mission Specialist 4 Kalpana Chawla. e, Payload Commander Michael P. Anderson. f, Pilot William C. McCool. g, Payload Specialist 4 Ilan Ramon.

2003, Apr. 7 ***Perf. 13½x13¼***

2697 A442 7r Sheet of 7, #a-g 7.75 7.75

Coronation of Queen Elizabeth II, 50th Anniv. — A443

No. 2698: a, Wearing hat. b, Wearing crown. c, Wearing tiara.

25r, Wearing tiara, diff.

2003, May 26 ***Perf. 14***

2698 A443 15r Sheet of 3, #a-c 7.00 7.00

Souvenir Sheet

2699 A443 25r multi 4.00 4.00

Prince William, 21st Birthday — A444

No. 2700: a, As toddler. b, Wearing red and blue tie. c, Wearing tie with blue squares.

25r, As toddler, wearing cap.

2003, May 26

2700 A444 15r Sheet of 3, #a-c 7.00 7.00

Souvenir Sheet

2701 A444 25r multi 4.00 4.00

Paintings by Albrecht Dürer (1471-1528) A445

Designs: 3r, Drummer and Piper from wing of the Jabach Altarpiece. 5r, Portrait of a Young Man. 7r, Wire-drawing Mill, horiz. 10r, Innsbruck from the North, horiz.

No. 2706: a, Portrait of Jacob Muffel. b, Portrait of Hieronymus Holzschuher. c, Portrait of Johannes Kleberger. d, Self-portrait.
25r, The Weiden Mill, horiz.

2003, June 17 ***Perf. 14¼***

2702-2705 A445	Set of 4	4.00	4.00
2706 A445 12r Sheet of 4, #a-d		7.50	7.50

Souvenir Sheet

2707 A445 25r multi		4.00	4.00

Japanese Art — A446

Designs: 2r, Detail from The Actor Sojuro Nakamura as Mitsukuni, by Yoshitaki Utagawa. 5r, Detail from The Actor Sojuro Nakamura as Mitsukuni, by Yoshitaki Utagawa, diff. 7r, The Ghost of Koheiji Kohada, by Hokuei Shunkosai. 15r, Ariwara no Narihira as Seigen, by Kunisada Utagawa.
No. 2712: a, The Ghost of Mitsumune Shikibunojo, by Kunisada Utagawa. b, Fuwa Bansakui, by Yoshitoshi Tsukioka. c, The Lantern Ghost of Oiwa, by Shunkosai. d, The Greedy Hag, by Tsukioka.
25r, The Spirit of Sogoro Sakura Haunting Koszuke Hotta.

2003, June 17

2708-2711 A446	Set of 4	4.50	4.50
2712 A446 10r Sheet of 4, #a-d		6.25	6.25

Souvenir Sheet

2713 A446 25r multi		4.00	4.00

Paintings by Joan Miró (1893-1983) — A447

Designs: 3r, Untitled painting, 1934. 5r, Hirondelle Amour. 10r, Two Women. 15r, Women Listening to Music.
No. 2718: a, Woman and Birds. b, Nocturne. c, Morning Star. d, The Escape Ladder.
No. 2719, 25r, Rhythmic Personages, vert. No. 2720, 25r, Women Encircled by the Flight of a Bird, vert.

2003, June 17 ***Perf. 14¼***

2714-2717 A447	Set of 4	5.25	5.25
2718 A447 12r Sheet of 4, #a-d		7.50	7.50

Size: 83x104mm

Imperf

2719-2720 A447	Set of 2	8.00	8.00

Tour de France Bicycle Race, Cent. — A448

No. 2721, 10r: a, Maurice Garin, 1903. b, Henri Cornet, 1904. c, Louis Trousselier, 1905. d, René Pottier, 1906.
No. 2722, 10r: a, Lucien Petit-Breton on Bicycle, 1907. b, Head of Petit-Breton, 1907. c, François Faber, 1909. d, Octave Lapize, 1910.
No. 2723, 10r: a, Eddy Merckx, 1974. b, Bernard Thévenet, 1975. c, Lucien Van Impe, 1976. d, Thévenet, 1977.
No. 2724, 25r, Bernard Hinault, 1979. No. 2725, 25r, Henri Desgranges. No. 2726, 25r, Le Réveil Matin Cafe, Montgeron, France.

2003, July 3 ***Perf. 13¼***

Sheets of 4, #a-d

2721-2723 A448	Set of 3	19.00	19.00

Souvenir Sheets

2724-2726 A448	Set of 3	12.00	12.00

Powered Flight, Cent. — A449

No. 2727, 10r — Alberto Santos-Dumont's: a, Airship No. 1. b, Airship No. 4, c, Airship with 14bis airplane. d, Airship No. 16.
No. 2728, 10r: a, Santos Dumont with Demoiselle airplane. b, Demoiselle airplane. c, Voisin-Farman No. 1 biplane. d, Gold Bug, built by Glenn Curtiss.
No. 2729, 25r, Santos-Dumont's Airship No. 6. No. 2730, 25r, Santos-Dumont's 14bis Airplane.

2003, July 14 ***Perf. 14***

Sheets of 4, #a-d

2727-2728 A449	Set of 2	12.50	12.50

Souvenir Sheets

2729-2730 A449	Set of 2	8.00	8.00

Paintings of Paul Klee (1879-1940) — A450

No. 2731, horiz.: a, Near Taormina, Scirocco. b, Small Town Among the Rocks. c, Still Life with Props. d, North Room.
25r, Dame Demon.

2003, Dec. 4 ***Perf. 13½***

2731 A450 10r Sheet of 4, #a-d		6.25	6.25

Souvenir Sheet

2732 A450 25r multi		4.00	4.00

Maumoon Abdul Gayoom, 25th Anniv. as President — A451

Litho. & Embossed

2003 ***Die Cut Perf. 8***

Without Gum

2733 A451 200r gold & multi		32.50	32.50

Norman Rockwell (1894-1978) — A452

No. 2734 — Four Seasons Calendar: Man and Boy, 1948: a, Winter (ice skating). b, Spring (resting amidst flowers). c, Summer (fishing). d, Autumn (raking leaves).
25r, Illustration for Hallmark Cards, 1937.

2003, Dec. 4 **Litho.** ***Perf. 13¼***

2734 A452 10r Sheet of 4, #a-d		6.25	6.25

Imperf

2735 A452 25r shown		4.00	4.00

No. 2734 contains four 38x50mm stamps.

Intl. Year of Fresh Water — A453

No. 2736: a, Ari Atoll. b, Fresh water for all. c, Desalination plant, Malé.
25r, Community rain water tank.

2003, Dec. 22 ***Perf. 14***

2736 A453 15r Sheet of 3, #a-c		7.00	7.00

Souvenir Sheet

2737 A453 25r multi		4.00	4.00

Fish A454

Designs: 1r, Clown triggerfish. 7r, Sixspot grouper. 10r, Long-nosed butterflyfish. 15r, Longfin bannerfish.
No. 2742: a, Goldtail demoiselle. b, Queen coris. c, Eight-banded butterflyfish. d, Meyer's butterflyfish. e, Exquisite butterflyfish. f, Yellowstripe snapper. g, Yellowback anthias. h, Black-spotted moray. i, Clown anemonefish.
No. 2743: a, Bluestreak cleaner wrasse. b, Threeband demoiselle. c, Palette surgeonfish. d, Emperor snapper. e, Bicolor angelfish. f, Picasso triggerfish.
25r, Chevron butterflyfish.

2003, Dec. 22

2738-2741 A454	Set of 4	5.25	5.25
2742 A454 4r Sheet of 9, #a-i		5.75	5.75
2743 A454 7r Sheet of 6, #a-f		6.75	6.75

Souvenir Sheet

2744 A454 25r multi		4.00	4.00

Nos. 2738-2741 were each printed in sheets of four.

Butterflies — A455

Designs: 3r, Yamfly. 5r, Striped blue crow. 8r, Indian red admiral. 15r, Great eggfly.
No. 2749, horiz.: a, Blue triangle. b, Monarch. c, Broad-bordered grass yellow. d, Red lacewing. e, African migrant. f, Plain tiger.
25r, Beak butterfly.

2003, Dec. 22

2745-2748 A455	Set of 4	5.00	5.00
2749 A455 7r Sheet of 6, #a-f		6.75	6.75

Souvenir Sheet

2750 A455 25r multi		4.00	4.00

Birds A456

Designs: 15 l, Great frigatebird. 20 l, Ruddy turnstone. 25 l, Hoopoe. 1r, Cattle egret.
No. 2755: a, Red-billed tropicbird. b, Red-footed booby. c, Common tern. d, Caspian tern. e, Common curlew. f, Black-bellied plover.
25r, Gray heron.

2003, Dec. 22

2751-2754 A456	Set of 4	.25	.25
2755 A456 7r Sheet of 6, #a-f		6.75	6.75

Souvenir Sheet

2756 A456 25r multi		4.00	4.00

Paintings by Pablo Picasso (1881-1973) — A457

No. 2757: a, Portrait of Jaime Sabartés, 1901. b, Portrait of the Artist's Wife (Olga), 1923. c, Portrait of Olga, 1923. d, Portrait of Jaime Sabartés, 1904.
30r, The Tragedy, 1903.

2003, Dec. 4 **Litho.** ***Perf. 13¼***

2757 A457 10r Sheet of 4, #a-d		6.25	6.25

Imperf

2758 A457 30r multi		4.75	4.75

No. 2757 contains four 37x50mm stamps.

Flowers — A458

Designs: 30 l, Coelogyne asperata. 75 l, Calanthe rosea. 2r, Eria javanica. 10r, Spathoglottis affinis.

No. 2763, horiz.: a, Bird of paradise. b, Flamingo flower. c, Red ginger. d, Cooktown orchid. e, Vanda tricolor. f, Chinese hibiscus.

25r, Morning glory.

2003, Dec. 22 ***Perf. 14***

2759-2762 A458 Set of 4 2.00 2.00
2763 A458 7r Sheet of 6, #a-f 6.75 6.75

Souvenir Sheet

2764 A458 25r multi 4.00 4.00

FIFA (Fédération Internationale de Football Association) Cent. — A459

World Cup winning teams: No. 2765, 5r, Germany, 1974. No. 2766, 5r, Argentina, 1978. No. 2767, 5r, Italy, 1982. No. 2768, 5r, Argentina, 1986. No. 2769, 5r, Germany, 1990. No. 2770, 5r, Brazil, 1994. No. 2771, 5r, France, 1998. No. 2772, 5r, Brazil, 2002.

2004, Mar. 8 ***Perf. 13½***

2765-2772 A459 Set of 8 6.25 6.25

Paintings by Gao Jian-fu (1879-1951) — A460

No. 2773: a, Landscape. b, Moon Night. c, Fox. d, Spider web. e, Woman with mirror. f, Man sitting on ground.

No. 2774: a, Eagle. b, Sunset.

2004, Mar. 8 ***Perf. 13¼***

2773 A460 7r Sheet of 6, #a-f 6.75 6.75
2774 A460 12r Sheet of 2, #a-b 3.75 3.75

2004 Hong Kong Stamp Expo.

Cessation of Concorde Flights — A461

No. 2775: a, F-BVFD, Rio de Janeiro. b, F-BVFC, New York. c, F-BTSD, Honolulu. d, F-BTSD, Lisbon. e, F-BVFA, Washington. f, F-BVFD, Dakar, Senegal. g, G-BOAC, Singapore. h, G-BOAA, Sydney. i, G-BOAD, Hong Kong. j, G-BOAD, Amsterdam. k, G-BOAE, Tokyo. l, G-BOAF, Madrid.

No. 2776, 25r, 214 G-BOAG, Museum of Flight, Seattle. No. 2777, 25r, 214 G-BOAG, horizon. No. 2778, 25r, 204 G-BOAC, British flag.

2004, Mar. 8 ***Perf. 13¼x13½***

2775 A461 1r Sheet of 12, #a-l 1.90 1.90

Souvenir Sheets

2776-2778 A461 Set of 3 12.00 12.00

Paintings in the Hermitage, St. Petersburg, Russia A462

Designs: 1r, Self-portrait, by Anthony van Dyck. 3r, Self-portrait, by Michael Sweerts. 7r, Anna Dalkeith, Countess of Morton, by van Dyck. 12r, Lady Anna Kirk, by van Dyck.

No. 2783: a, Portrait of Prince Alexander Kurakin, by Marie-Louise-Elisabeth Vigée-Lebrun. b, Portrait of a Lady in Waiting to the Infanta Isabella, by Peter Paul Rubens. c, Portrait of a Lady in Blue, by Thomas Gainsborough. d, The Actor Pierre Jéliolte in the Role of Apollo, by Louis Tocqué.

No. 2784, 25r, The Stolen Kiss, by Jean-Honoré Fragonard, horiz. No. 2785, 25r, A Scene from Corneille's Tragedy "La Comte d'Essex," by Nicolas Lancret, horiz.

2004, Mar. 29 ***Perf. 14¼***

2779-2782 A462 Set of 4 3.75 3.75
2783 A462 10r Sheet of 4, #a-d 6.25 6.25

Souvenir Sheets

2784-2785 A462 Set of 2 7.75 7.75

D-Day, 60th Anniv. — A463

No. 2786, 6r: a, Gen. Dwight Eisenhower. b, Field Marshal Guenther von Kluge. c, Air Marshal Sir Trafford Leigh-Mallory. d, Field Marshal Walter Model. e, Field Marshal Gerd von Rundstedt. f, Sir Arthur Tedder.

No. 2787, 6r: a, Maj. Gen. Clarence Huebner. b, Brig. Gen. Anthony McAuliffe. c, Maj. Gen. Leonard Gerow. d, Gen. Adolf Galland. e, Brig. Gen. W. M. Hoge. f, Maj. Gen. Sir Percy Hobart.

No. 2788, 6r: a, Rear Admiral Kirk. b, Field Marshal Erwin Rommel. c, Gen. George Marshall. d, Gen. Jan Smuts. e, Gen. Lt. Gunther Blumentritt. f. Maj. Gen. J. Lawton Collins.

No. 2789, 6r: a, Winston Churchill. b, Adm. Sir Bertram Ramsay. c, Gen. Lt. Dietrich Kraiss. d, Maj. Gen. Richard Gale. e, Gen. George Patton. f, Maj. Gen. Maxwell Taylor.

No. 2790, 6r, horiz.: a, Lt. Gen. Omar Bradley. b, Rear Admiral Hall. c, Maj. Gen. Huebner, diff. d, Adm. Karl Dönitz. e, Rear Admiral Wilkes. f, Capt. Chauncey Camp.

No. 2791, 30r, Gen. Henry Arnold. No. 2792, 30r, Rear Adm. Donald Moon. No. 2793, 30r, Lt. Gen. Sir Frederick Morgan. No. 2794, 30r, Gen. Sir Bernard Montgomery. No. 2795, 30r, Rear Adm. Carlton Bryant, horiz.

Perf. 13½x13¼, 13¼x13½

2004, May 19

Sheets of 6, #a-f

2786-2790 A463 Set of 5 28.00 28.00

Souvenir Sheets

2791-2795 A463 Set of 5 24.00 24.00

Paintings by Paul Cézanne (1839-1906) — A464

No. 2796, horiz.: a, Still Life with Peppermint Bottle and Blue Rug. b, House in Provence. c. Le Château Noir. d, Basket of Apples.

25r, Boy in a Red Waistcoat Leaning on his Elbow.

2004, July 6 ***Perf. 13¼***

2796 A464 10r Sheet of 4, #a-d 6.25 6.25

Imperf

2797 A464 25r multi 4.00 4.00

No. 2796 contains four 50x37mm stamps.

Paintings by Henri Rousseau (1844-1910) — A465

No. 2798, horiz.: a, Nègre Attaqué par un Jaguar. b, Paysage Exotique. c. La Cascade. d, Le Repas du Lion.

25r, Le Rêve.

2004, July 6 ***Perf. 13¼***

2798 A465 10r Sheet of 4, #a-d 6.25 6.25

Imperf

2799 A465 25r multi 4.00 4.00

No. 2798 contains four 50x37mm stamps.

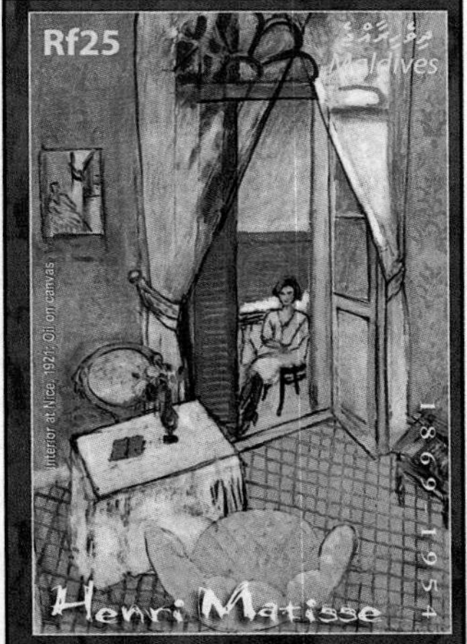

Paintings by Henri Matisse (1869-1954) — A466

No. 2800, horiz.: a, Conversation. b, Still Life with a Blue Tablecloth. c. Seville Still Life II. d, Woman Before an Aquarium.

25r, Interior at Nice.

2004, July 6 ***Perf. 13¼***

2800 A466 10r Sheet of 4, #a-d 6.25 6.25

Imperf

2801 A466 25r multi 4.00 4.00

No. 2800 contains four 50x37mm stamps.

Steam Locomotives, 200th Anniv. — A467

No. 2802, 12r: a, Planet Class 2-2-0. b, American 4-4-0. c, Newmar. d, Class 500 4-6-0.

No. 2803, 12r: a, Firefly Class 2-2-2. b, French "Single." c, Medoc Class 2-4-0. d, German 4-4-0.

No. 2804, 12r: a, Adler 2-2-2. b, Beuth 2-2-2. c, Northumbrian 0-2-2. d, Class 4-6-2.

No. 2805, 12r: a, Woodburning Beyer Garratt 4-8-2+2-8-4. b, Double headed train over Kaaiman River, Africa. c, Garratt 4-8-2+2-8-4. d, Class 15 Garratt.

No. 2806, 12r: a, East African Railways Garratt. b, Rhodesian Railways 12th Class. c, Class 2-6-2. d, Class 19D 4-8-2.

No. 2807, 12r: a, Evening Star. b, Britannia. c, The George Stephenson. d, Sudan Railways 310 2-8-2.

No. 2808, 30r, Claud Hamilton Class 4-4-0. No. 2809, 30r, Class P8 4-6-0. No. 2810, 30r, Vauxhall 2-2-0. No. 2811, 30r, American, diff. No. 2812, 30r, The Lord Nelson. No. 2813, 30r, Flying Scotsman.

2004, July 6 ***Perf. 13¼x13½***

Sheets of 4, #a-d

2802-2807 A467 Set of 6 45.00 45.00

Souvenir Sheets

2808-2813 A467 Set of 6 28.00 28.00

Jules Verne (1828-1905), Writer — A468

No. 2814, 12r: a, Archipelago on Fire. b, Clovis Dardentor. c, The Golden Volcano. d, Le Superbe Orénoque.

No. 2815, 12r — Michael Strogoff, Courier of the Czar: a, People (pink background). b, People in grass (green background). c, People (blue background). d, Animal and head in grass (green background).

No. 2816, 12r — Family Without a Name: a, Woman. b, Soldier. c, Crowd. d, Soldiers and Indian with guns.

No. 2817, 12r — César Cascabel: a, Men pushing train car (blue green background). b, Man (brown background). c, Crevasse (blue green background). d, Crowd and sign (pink background).

No. 2818, 12r — The Lighthouse at the End of the World: a, Men on ship. b, Man with arm extended. c, Rocks. d, Fisherman with hat.

No. 2819, 25r, The Survivors of the Chancellor. No. 2820, 25r, Keraban the Inflexible. No. 2821, 25r, Family Without a Name, diff. No. 2822, 25r, César Cascabel, diff. No. 2823, 25r, The Lighthouse at the End of the World, diff.

2004, July 29 ***Perf. 13¼x13½***

Sheets of 4, #a-d

2814-2818 A468 Set of 5 37.00 37.00

Souvenir Sheets

2819-2823 A468 Set of 5 19.00 19.00

Marilyn Monroe — A469

2004, Aug. 16 ***Perf. 13½x13¼***

2824 A469 7r multi 1.10 1.10

Printed in sheets of 6.

George Herman "Babe" Ruth (1895-1948), Baseball Player — A470

No. 2826: a, Swinging bat. b, Wearing cap, striped uniform. c, Holding two bats. d, Profile of Ruth.

2004

2825 A470 3r shown .45 .45

2826 A470 10r Sheet of 4, #a-d 6.25 6.25

No. 2825 printed in sheets of 16. World Series, 100th anniv.

Paintings by Salvador Dali (1904-89) — A471

No. 2827: a, The Endless Enigma. b, The Persistence of Memory. c, Soft Construction with Boiled Beans — Premonition of Civil War. d, Still Life — Fast Moving.

25r, Figure on the Rocks.

2004, July 6 **Litho.** ***Perf. 13½***

2827 A471 10r Sheet of 4, #a-d 6.25 6.25

Imperf

2828 A471 25r multi 4.00 4.00

No. 2827 contains four 50x37mm stamps.

2004 Summer Olympics, Athens A472

Designs: 2r, Gold medal, 1904 St. Louis Olympics. 5r, Krater depicting Olympic athletes. 7r, Count Jean de Beaumont, Intl. Olympic Committee member. 12r, Pommel horse, horiz.

2004, Sept. 30 ***Perf. 14¼***

2829-2832 A472 Set of 4 4.00 4.00

Sharks — A473

No. 2833: a, Silvertip shark. b, Silky shark. c, Great white shark. d, Gray reef shark.

$25, Starry smoothhound shark.

2004, Nov. 4

2833 A473 10r Sheet of 4, #a-d 6.25 6.25

Souvenir Sheet

2834 A473 25r multi 4.00 4.00

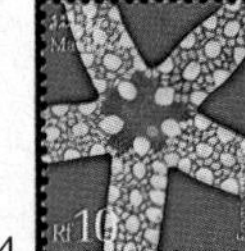
Starfish — A474

Designs: No. 2835, 10r, Fromia monilis (green background). No. 2836, 10r, Linckia laevigata. No. 2837, 10r, Nardoa novaecalidoniae. No. 2838, 10r, Fromia monilis (red background).

2004, Nov. 4 ***Perf. 15x14***

2835-2838 A474 Set of 4 6.25 6.25

Worldwide Fund for Nature (WWF) — A475

No. 2839 — Eurypegasus draconis and: a, Country name at LL, denomination at LR. b, Country name at UL, denomination at LR, dark background. c, Country name at LR, denomination at UL. d, Country name at UL, denomination at LR, light background.

2004, Dec. 15 **Litho.** ***Perf. 14***

2839 A475 7r Block of 4, #a-d 4.50 4.50

e. Miniature sheet, 2 each #2839a-2839d 9.00 9.00

Butterflies — A476

No. 2840, horiz.: a, Red lacewing. b, Amesia sanguiflua. c, Pericallia galactina. d, Limenitis dudu dudu.

25r, Lime butterfly.

2004, Dec. 15

2840 A476 10r Sheet of 4, #a-d 6.25 6.25

Souvenir Sheet

2841 A476 25r multi 4.00 4.00

Dolphins — A477

No. 2842: a, Striped dolphin. b, Amazon River dolphin. c, Bottlenose dolphin. d, Spinner dolphin.

25r, Long-snouted spinner dolphin.

2004, Dec. 15 **Litho.** ***Perf. 14***

2842 A477 10r Sheet of 4, #a-d 6.25 6.25

Souvenir Sheet

2843 A477 25r multi 4.00 4.00

Reptiles and Amphibians — A478

No. 2844, horiz.: a, Eyelash pit viper. b, Basilisk lizard. c, Calico snake. d, Maki frog.

25r, Naja melanoleuca.

2004, Dec. 15

2844 A478 10r Sheet of 4, #a-d 6.25 6.25

Souvenir Sheet

2845 A478 25r multi 4.00 4.00

Mushrooms — A479

No. 2846, horiz.: a, Parrot mushroom. b, Hygrocybe miniata. c, Aleuria aurantia. d, Thaxterogaster porphyreum.

25r, Galerina autumnalis.

2004, Dec. 15

2846 A479 10r Sheet of 4, #a-d 6.25 6.25

Souvenir Sheet

2847 A479 25r multi 4.00 4.00

Prehistoric Animals — A480

No. 2848, 10r: a, Macroplata. b, Ichthyosaurus. c, Shonisaurus. d, Archelon.

No. 2849, 10r, vert.: a, Albertosaurus. b, Iguanodon. c, Deinonychus, name at right. d, Baryonyx.
No. 2850, 10r, vert.: a, Deinonychus, name at left. b, Styracosaurus. c, Ornitholestes. d, Euoplocephalus.
No. 2851, 10r, vert.: a, Pterodactylus. b, Cearadactylus. c, Pterosaur. d, Sordes.
No. 2852, 25r, Muraeonosaurus. No. 2853, 25r, Styracosaurus, diff. No. 2854, 25r, Leptoceratops. No. 2855, 25r, Archaeopteryx.

2004, Dec. 15 *Perf. 14*

Sheets of 4, #a-d

2848-2851 A480 Set of 4 25.00 25.00

Souvenir Sheets

2852-2855 A480 Set of 4 16.00 16.00

Souvenir Sheet

Deng Xiaoping (1904-97), Chinese Leader — A481

2005, Jan. 26

2856 A481 25r multi 4.00 4.00

2004 European Soccer Championships, Portugal — A482

No. 2857, vert.: a, Jupp Derwall. b, René Vandereycke. c, Horst Hrubesch. d, Stadio Olimpico.
25r, 1980 Germany team.

2005, Jan. 26 *Perf. 14*

2857 A482 12r Sheet of 4, #a-d 7.50 7.50

Souvenir Sheet

2858 A482 25r multi 4.00 4.00

No. 2857 contains four 28x42mm stamps.

Rotary International, Cent. — A483

No. 2859 — Chicago skyline: a, Part of Sears Tower at R. b, Sears Tower at L. c, CNA Tower (red brick building) at L.
25r, Telecommunications tower.

2005, July 12 **Litho.** *Perf. 12¾*

2859 A483 15r Sheet of 3, #a-c 7.00 7.00

Souvenir Sheet

2860 A483 25r multi 4.00 4.00

Hans Christian Andersen (1805-75), Author — A484

No. 2861: a, Statue of Andersen wearing hat. b, Photograph of Andersen. c, Statue of Andersen without hat.
25r, Little Mermaid Statue, Copenhagen.

2005, Sept. 20

2861 A484 15r Sheet of 3, #a-c 7.00 7.00

Souvenir Sheet

2862 A484 25r multi 4.00 4.00

World Cup Soccer Championships, 75th Anniv. — A485

No. 2863: a, Oscar. b, Karl-Heinz Rummenigge. c, Oliver Kahn.
25r, Karlheinz Forster..

2005, Sept. 20 *Perf. 13¼*

2863 A485 15r Sheet of 3, #a-c 7.00 7.00

Souvenir Sheet

Perf. 12¼x12

2864 A485 25r multi 4.00 4.00

Battle of Trafalgar, Bicent. — A486

No. 2865, vert.: a, Admiral Cuthbert Collingwood. b, Napoleon Bonaparte. c, Admiral Horatio Nelson. d, Capt. Thomas Masterman Hardy.
25r, Ships at battle.

2005, Sept. 20 *Perf. 12¾*

2865 A486 10r Sheet of 4, #a-d 6.25 6.25

Souvenir Sheet

2866 A486 25r multi 4.00 4.00

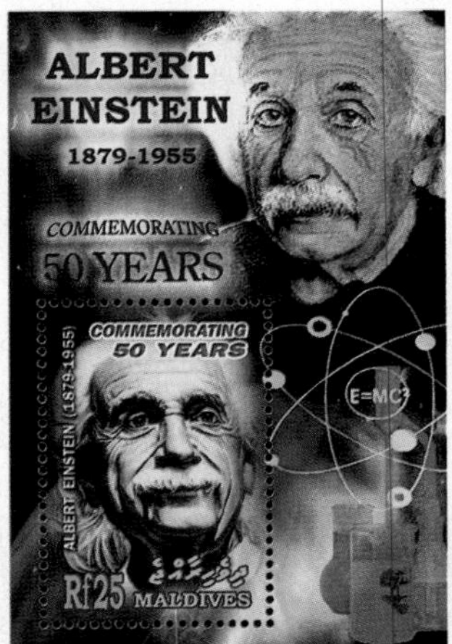

Albert Einstein (1879-1955), Physicist — A487

No. 2867, horiz. — Portraits of Einstein in: a, Red brown (denomination at R). b, Pink & blue (denomination at L). c, Green & pink (denomination at R). d, Brown (denomination at L).
25r, Einstein, diff.

2005, Sept. 20

2867 A487 15r Sheet of 4, #a-d 6.25 6.25

Souvenir Sheet

2868 A487 25r multi 4.00 4.00

Elvis Presley (1935-77) — A488

No. 2869, 7r — Photographs of Presley from: a, 1956 (sepia). b, 1957. c, 1958. d, 1964. e, 1967. f, 1968.
No. 2870, 7r — Photographs of Presley from: a, 1956 (black and white). b, 1960. c, 1962. d, 1969. e, 1973. f, 1975.

2005, Nov. 15 *Perf. 13¾x13¼*

Sheets of 6, #a-f

2869-2870 A488 Set of 2 13.00 13.00

Elvis Presley (1935-77) — A489

Lihto. & Embossed

2006, Jan. 17 *Die Cut Perf 7½*

Without Gum

2871 A489 85r gold & multi 13.50 13.50

Miniature Sheets

Children's Drawings — A490

No. 2872, 10r — Sea Life: a, Bubbles, by Raquel Bobolia. b, Bubble Fish, by Sarah Bowen. c, Lipfish, by Elsa Fleisher. d, Flounder, by Erica Malchowski.
No. 2873, 10r — Birds: a, Purple Bird, by Anna Badger. b, Parrots, by Nick Abrams. c, Pretty Bird, by Jessie Abrams. d, Royal Parrot, by Ashley Mondfrans.
No. 2874, 10r — Flowers: a, Orange Sunflower, by Brett Walker. b, Red Flower, by Jessica Shutt. c, Flower Pot, by Nick Abrams. d, Blue Flower Vase, by Trevor Nielsen.

2006, Jan. 24 **Litho.** *Perf. 13¼*

Sheets of 4, #a-d

2872-2874 A490 Set of 3 19.00 19.00

Skates and Rays — A491

Designs: 20 l, Himantura uamak. 1r, Manta birostris. 2r, Taeniura lymma. 20r, Aetobatus narinari.

2006, Feb. 27 *Perf. 13¾x14¼*

2875-2878 A491 Set of 4 3.75 3.75

Souvenir Sheet

South Asian Association for Regional Cooperation, 20th Anniv. — A492

2006, Mar. 9 *Perf. 13¼*

2879 A492 25r multi 4.00 4.00

2006 Winter Olympics, Turin — A493

Designs: 7r, Norway #B52. 8r, Poster for 1952 Oslo Winter Olympics, vert. 10r, Poster for 1936 Garmisch-Partenkirchen Winter Olympics, vert. 12r, Germany #B79, vert.

2006, May 9 *Perf. 14¼*

2880-2883 A493 Set of 4 5.75 5.75

Miniature Sheet

Wolfgang Amadeus Mozart (1756-91), Composer — A494

No. 2884: a, Portrait in oval frame. b, Mozart looking left. c, Mozart as child. d, Bust.

2006, June 29 *Perf. 12¾*
2884 A494 12r Sheet of 4, #a-d 7.50 7.50

Queen Elizabeth II, 80th Birthday — A495

No. 2885 — Queen and: a, Pres. John F. Kennedy. b, Pres. Ronald Reagan. c, Pres. Gerald R. Ford. d, Pres. George W. Bush.
25r, Portrait of Queen on horse by Chinwe Chukwuogo-Roy.

2006 *Perf. 14¼*
2885 A495 15r Sheet of 4, #a-d 9.50 9.50

Souvenir Sheet

2886 A495 25r multi 4.00 4.00

Souvenir Sheet

Maldive Islands Postal Service, Cent. — A496

2006, Nov. 1 **Litho.** *Perf. 12½*
2887 A496 12r multi 1.90 1.90

Souvenir Sheet

Ludwig Durr (1878-1956), Zeppelin Engineer — A497

No. 2888 — Durr and: a, Zeppelin over Frankfurt. b, Balloons and Festhalle, Frankfurt. c, Hindenburg.

2006, Nov. 15 *Perf. 13¼*
2888 A497 15r Sheet of 3, #a-c 7.00 7.00

Fish — A498

Designs: No. 2889, 10r, Dascyllus aruanus. No. 2890, 10r, Balistoides conspicillum. No. 2891, 10r, Pomacanthus imperator. No. 2892, 10r, Chaetodon meyeri.

2006, Nov. 1 **Litho.** *Perf. 12¾*
2889-2892 A498 Set of 4 6.25 6.25

Miniature Sheet

Elvis Presley (1935-77) — A499

No. 2893 — Presley with: a, Microphone at left, denomination in pink. b, Microphone at center, denomination in white. c, Microphone at center, denomination in light blue. d, Microphone at left, denomination in light green.

2006, Nov. 15 *Perf. 13¼*
2893 A499 12r Sheet of 4, #a-d 7.50 7.50

Space Achievements — A500

No. 2894: a, R-7 missile (Sputnik 1 launcher). b, Sputnik 1. c, Inside Sputnik 1. d, Sputnik 2. e, Map of Earth showing Sputnik 1 orbits. f, Sputnik 3.
No. 2895, 12r: a, Calipso satellite. b, Cloud-Sat satellite. c, Aqua satellite. d, Aura satellite.
No. 2896, 12r: a, Nucleus of Halley's Comet. b, Halley's Comet. c, Giotto Space Probe. d, Close-up image of Halley's Comet taken by Giotto.
No. 2897, 25r, Apollo spacecraft. No. 2898, 25r, Giotto. No. 2899, 25r, Stardust satellite.

2006, Nov. 15 *Perf. 13¼*
2894 A500 8r Sheet of 6, #a-f 7.50 7.50

Sheets of 4, #a-d

2895-2896 A500 Set of 2 15.00 15.00

Souvenir Sheets

2897-2899 A500 Set of 3 12.00 12.00

Birds A501

Designs: 1r, Bar-tailed godwit. 2r, Black-headed gull. No. 2902, 10r, Masked booby, vert. 20r, Kentish plover.
No. 2904, 10r: a, Common swifts. b, Sooty tern. c, Yellow wagtail. d, House sparrow.
No. 2905, 10r: a, Tufted duck. b, Caspian tern. c, Southern giant petrel. d, Glossy ibis.
No. 2906, 30r, Purple herons. No. 2907, 30r, Osprey, vert. No. 2908, 30r, Golden-throated barbet, vert.

2007, Feb. 8 *Perf. 14*
2900-2903 A501 Set of 4 5.25 5.25

Sheets of 4, #a-d

2904-2905 A501 Set of 2 12.50 12.50

Souvenir Sheets

2906-2908 A501 Set of 3 14.00 14.00

Fish A502

Designs: 1r, Ragged-finned lionfish. 2r, Vlaming's unicornfish. No. 2911, 10r, White-spotted grouper. 20r, Maldive anemonefish.
No. 2913, 10r: a, Bicolor parrotfish. b, Blue-barred parrotfish. c, Bullethead parrotfish. d, Dusky parrotfish.
No. 2914, 10r: a, Imperial angelfish. b, Clown triggerfish. c, Black-saddled coral trout. d, Slender grouper.
No. 2915, 30r, Shadow soldierfish. No. 2916, 30r, Picasso triggerfish. No. 2917, 30r, Blue-faced angelfish.

2007, Feb. 8
2909-2912 A502 Set of 4 5.25 5.25

Sheets of 4, #a-d

2913-2914 A502 Set of 2 12.50 12.50

Souvenir Sheets

2915-2917 A502 Set of 3 14.00 14.00

Flowers A503

Designs: 1r, Ranunculus eschscholtzii. 2r, Ratibida columnaris. No. 2920, 10r, Mentzelia laevicaulis. 20r, Clintonia uniflora.
No. 2922, 10r: a, Machaeranthera tanacetifolia. b, Aquilegia coerulea. c, Gentiana detonsa. d, Linum perenne.
No. 2923, 10r: a, Ipomopsis aggregata. b, Rosa woodsii. c, Lewisia rediviva. d, Penstemon rydbergii.
No. 2924, 30r, Ipomoea purpurea. No. 2925, 30r, Encelia farinosa. No. 2926, 30r, Epilobium angustifolium.

2007, Feb. 8
2918-2921 A503 Set of 4 5.25 5.25

Sheets of 4, #a-d

2922-2923 A503 Set of 2 12.50 12.50

Souvenir Sheets

2924-2926 A503 Set of 3 14.00 14.00

Orchids — A504

Designs: 1r, Dendrobium formosum. 2r, Bulbophyllum Elizabeth Ann. No. 2929, 10r, Dendrobium bigibbum. 20r, Spathoglottis gracilis.
No. 2931, 10r: a, Bulbophyllum lasiochilum. b, Phaius Microburst. c, Coelogyne mooreana. d, Bulbophyllum nasseri.
No. 2932, 10r: a, Cymbidium erythrostylum. b, Phaius humboldtii x Phaius tuberculosis. c, Dendrobium farmeri. d, Dendrobium junceum.
No. 2933, 30r, Coelogyne cristata, horiz. No. 2934, 30r, Bulbophyllum graveolens, horiz. No. 2935, 30r, Dendrobium crocatum.

2007, Feb. 8
2927-2930 A504 Set of 4 5.25 5.25

Sheets of 4, #a-d

2931-2932 A504 Set of 2 12.50 12.50

Souvenir Sheets

2933-2935 A504 Set of 3 14.00 14.00

Scouting, Cent. A505

2007, Feb. 21 *Perf. 13¼*

Color of Denomination

2936 A505 15r purple 2.40 2.40

Souvenir Sheet

2937 A505 25r blue 4.00 4.00

No. 2936 was printed in sheets of 3.

Intl. Polar Year — A506

No. 2938 — King penguins with background color of: a, Light blue. b, Lilac. c, Yellow green. d, Blue green. e, Red violet. f, Green.
25r, African penguin with party hat.

2007, May 1 **Litho.** *Perf. 13¼*
2938 A506 12r Sheet of 6, #a-f 11.50 11.50

Souvenir Sheet

2939 A506 25r multi 4.00 4.00

Miniature Sheet

Ferrari Automobiles, 60th Anniv. — A507

No. 2940: a, 1979 312 T4. b, 1992 456 GT. c, 1959 250 GT Berlinetta. d, 1989 F1 89. e, 1998 456M GTA. f, 1955 735 LM. g, 1973 Dino 308 GT4. h, 2001 F 2001.

2007, Aug. 12
2940 A507 8r Sheet of 8, #a-h 10.00 10.00

Princess Diana (1961-97) — A508

No. 2941 — Diana with white hat and: a, Gray jacket, close-up. b, Green dress, close-up. c, White striped jacket, close-up. d, Green dress. e, White striped jacket. f, Gray jacket. 25r, Black and white jacket.

2007, Aug. 12

2941 A508 8r Sheet of 6, #a-f 7.50 7.50

Souvenir Sheet

2942 A508 25r multi 4.00 4.00

Fish — A509

Designs: 10 l, Chaetodon triangulum. 50 l, Chaetodon kleinii. 12r, Chaetodon trifasciatus. 15r, Chaetodon madagascariensis. 20r, Chaetodon lunula.

2007, Oct. 9 Litho. *Perf. 13¼*

2943-2947 A509 Set of 5 7.50 7.50

2008 Summer Olympics, Beijing — A510

No. 2948: a, Rie Mastenbroek, swimming gold medalist, 1936. b, Poster for 1936 Summer Olympics. c, Jesse Owens, long jump gold medalist, 1936. d, Jack Beresford, rowing gold medalist, 1936.

2008, Jan. 8 Litho. *Perf. 13¼*

2948	Horiz. strip of 4	4.50	4.50
a.-d.	A510 7r Any single	1.10	1.10
e.	Souvenir sheet, #2948a-2948d	4.50	4.50

Miniature Sheet

Elvis Presley (1935-77) — A511

No. 2949 — Presley wearing: a, Brown jacket. b, Blue shirt, holding guitar. c, Red jacket and white shirt. d, Gray jacket and black shirt. e, Blue shirt, holding guitar behind microphone. f, Red shirt, holding microphone.

2008, Jan. 8 Litho. *Perf. 13¼*

2949 A511 8r Sheet of 6, #a-f 7.50 7.50

America's Cup Yachting Championships — A512

No. 2950 — Various yachts with panel colors of: a, Yellow orange. b, Red. c, Dark blue. d, Blue green.

2008, Jan. 8

2950	Strip of 4	9.25	9.25
a.	A512 10r multi	1.60	1.60
b.	A512 12r multi	1.90	1.90
c.	A512 15r multi	2.40	2.40
d.	A512 20r multi	3.25	3.25

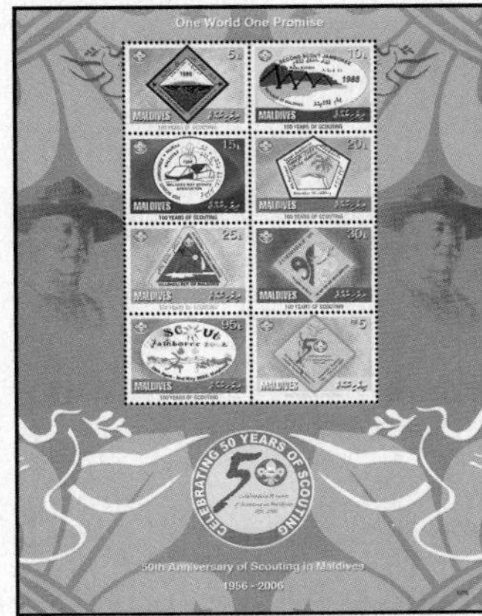

Scouting In Maldive Islands, 50th Anniv. — A513

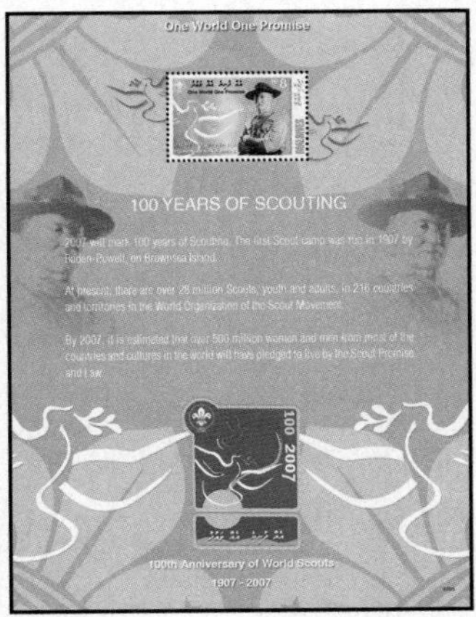

Scouting, Cent. (in 2007) — A514

No. 2951 — Emblems of national jamborees from: a, 5 l, 1986. b, 10 l, 1988. c, 15 l, 1990. d, 20 l, 1992. e, 25 l, 1995. f, 30 l, 1998. g, 95 l, 2002. h, 5r, 2007.

2008, Feb. 19

2951 A513 Sheet of 8, #a-h 1.10 1.10

Souvenir Sheet

2952 A514 8r multi 1.25 1.25

Miniature Sheet

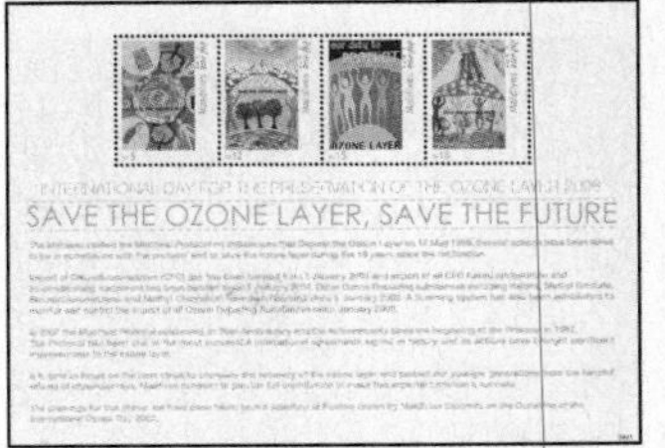

Intl. Day for the Preservation of the Ozone Layer — A515

No. 2953 — Various "Save the Ozone Layer" posters by Maldivian students: a, 5r. b, 12r. c, 15r. d, 18r.

2008, Sept. 10 Litho. *Perf. 12½*

2953 A515 Sheet of 4, #a-d 8.00 8.00

Miniature Sheet

Elvis Presley (1935-77) — A516

No. 2954 — Presley: a, Playing guitar. b, With hand in foreground at right. c, Singing, with legs shown. d, Facing right, holding microphone. e, Singing, with microphone at left. f, Beside car, wearing hat.

2008, Sept. 11 *Perf. 13¼*

2954 A516 8r Sheet of 6, #a-f 7.50 7.50

Miniature Sheet

Royal Air Force, 90th Anniv. — A517

No. 2955: a, Sopwith F-1 Camel. b, Aerospatiale Puma HC1 helicopter. c, Wessex helicopter. d, Armstrong Whitworth Atlas.

2008, Sept. 11 *Perf. 11½*

2955 A517 12r Sheet of 4, #a-d 7.50 7.50

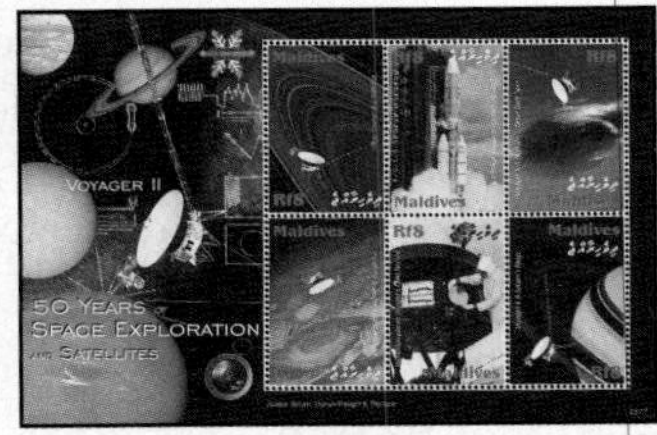

A518

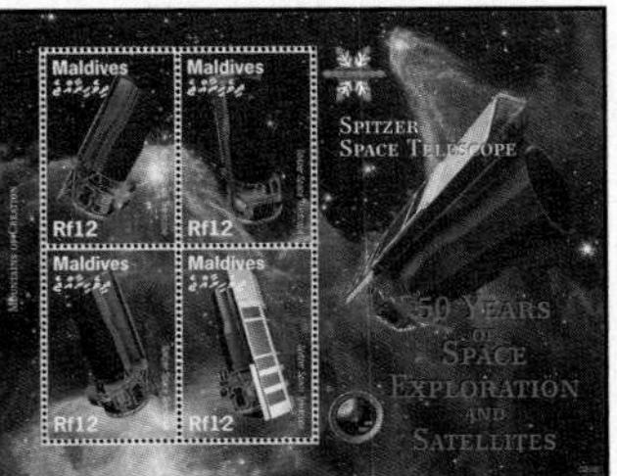

Space Exploration, 50th Anniv. (in 2007) — A519

No. 2956: a, Voyager 2 and rings of Uranus. b, Titan 3E Centaur rocket launching Voyager 2. c, Voyager 2 and Neptune's Great Dark Spot. d, Voyager 2 and Jupiter's Great Red Spot. e, Technician placing gold record into Voyager 2. f, Voyager 2 and rings of Saturn.

No. 2957, 12r — Spitzer Space Telescope: a, Top of telescope pointing to UR corner. b, Top of telescope pointing to top margin. c, Top of telescope pointing to UL corner. d, Solar panels of telescope shown.

No. 2958, 12r — Sputnik 1: a, With black background, denomination at LL. b, With orange background. c, And technician. d, With Moon in background.

No. 2959, 12r — Explorer 1: a, Atop Juno 1 rocket. b, With Earth in background. c, With clouds in background. d, And Dr. James Van Allen.

No. 2960, 12r — Vanguard 1: a, With Earth at top. b, And technicians. c, And rocket. d, With Earth at bottom.

2008, Sept. 11 *Perf. 13¼*

2956 A518 8r Sheet of 6, #a-f 7.50 7.50

Sheets of 4, #a-d

2957-2960 A519 Set of 4 30.00 30.00

Miniature Sheets

End of World War I, 90th Anniv. — A520

No. 2961, 12r: a, Soldiers in trench. b, Two soldiers resting in trench. c, Two soldiers aiming guns in trench. d, Soldier carrying wounded soldier.

No. 2962, 12r, horiz.: a, Soldiers on motorcycles. b, Soldiers moving up hill. c, Tank. d, Two soldiers in machine gun nest.

Perf. 11¼x11½, 11½x11¼

2008, Nov. 11 Litho.

Sheets of 4, #a-d

2961-2962 A520 Set of 2 15.00 15.00

Inauguration of U.S. Pres. Barack Obama — A521

No. 2963, 10r, vert.: a, Pres. Obama waving. b, Obama with dark blue striped tie, facing right. c, First Lady Michelle Obama. d, Obama with red striped tie. e, Michelle Obama clapping. f, Obama with light blue tie.
30r, Couple.

2009, Jan. 20 ***Perf. 11¼x11½***
2963 A521 10r Sheet of 6, #a-f 9.50 9.50

Souvenir Sheet
Perf. 13¼
2964 A521 30r multi 4.75 4.75

No. 2963 contains six 30x40mm stamps.

Miniature Sheet

U.S. Pres. Abraham Lincoln (1809-65) — A522

No. 2965 — Reverse of U.S. $5 banknote and Lincoln: a, Standing, no suit buttons visible. b, Seated, with hand on arm of chair. c, Seated, holding paper. d, Standing, with suit buttons visible.

2009, Feb. 12 ***Perf. 13¼***
2965 A522 12r Sheet of 4, #a-d 7.50 7.50

Fish
A523

Designs: No. 2966, 12r, Black-saddled coral grouper. No. 2967, 12r, Peacock hind. No. 2968, 12r, Four-saddle grouper. No. 2969, 12r, Six-blotch hind.

2009, Sept. 24 **Litho.** ***Perf. 13¼***
2966-2969 A523 Set of 4 7.50 7.50

Miniature Sheet

Visit of Prince Harry to New York — A524

No. 2970: a, At official naming of the British Garden. b, At World Trade Center site. c, Head of Prince Harry. d, Playing polo.

2009, Sept. 29 ***Perf. 11½***
2970 A524 12r Sheet of 4, #a-d 7.50 7.50

Miniature Sheets

A525

Star Trek Characters — A526

No. 2971: a, Fleet crew. b, Lt. Uhura. c, Mr. Spock. d, Dr. McCoy.
No. 2972: a, Scotty. b, Dr. McCoy, diff. c, Captain Kirk. d, Mr. Spock, diff.

2009, Sept. 29 ***Perf. 13¼***
2971 A525 12r Sheet of 4, #a-d 7.50 7.50
2972 A526 12r Sheet of 4, #a-d 7.50 7.50

Miniature Sheet

Marilyn Monroe (1926-62), Actress — A527

No. 2973: a, Face. b, In car. c, Wearing patterned blouse, in room. d, With hand near chin.

2009, Oct. 21 ***Perf. 12½x12¾***
2973 A527 16r Sheet of 4, #a-d 10.00 10.00

Whales — A528

Designs: 10 l, Beluga whale. No. 2975, 12r, Hector's beaked whale. 16r, Beaked whale. 18r, Baird's beaked whale.
No. 2978, 12r, horiz.: a, Dwarf sperm whale. b, Pygmy sperm whale. c, Baird's beaked whale, diff. d, Sperm whale. e, Shepherd's beaked whale. f, Cuvier's beaked whale.

2009, Oct. 21 ***Perf. 12½***
2974-2977 A528 Set of 4 7.25 7.25
2978 A528 12r Sheet of 6, #a-f 11.50 11.50

Butterflies
A529

Designs: 10 l, Crimson rose. 16r, Common Mormon. 18r, Common jay. 20r, Common tiger.
No. 2983, horiz.: a, Small salmon Arab. b, Lemon pansy. c, Tamil yeoman. d, Dark blue tiger.
No. 2984: a, Common jezebel. b, Common gull.

2009, Oct. 21 ***Perf. 12½***
2979-2982 A529 Set of 4 8.50 8.50

Perf. 12
2983 A529 12r Sheet of 4, #a-d 7.50 7.50

Souvenir Sheet
2984 A529 15r Sheet of 2, #a-b 4.75 4.75

Chinese Aviation, Cent. — A530

No. 2985 — Airplanes: a, Y-5. b, Y-7. c, Y-8. d, Y-12
25r, MA60.

2009, Nov. 12 **Litho.** ***Perf. 14¼***
2985 A530 9r Sheet of 4, #a-d 5.75 5.75

Souvenir Sheet
2986 A530 25r multi 4.00 4.00

Aeropex 2009, Beijing. No. 2985 contains four 42x28mm stamps.

Worldwide Fund for Nature (WWF) — A531

No. 2987 — Melon-headed whale: a, Pod of whales underwater. b, Pod of whales at surface, swimming right. c, Whale. d, Pod of whales at surface, swimming left.

2009, Nov. 18 ***Perf. 13¼***
2987 Block or strip of 4 5.00 5.00
a.-d. A531 8r Any single 1.25 1.25
e. Sheet of 8, 2 each #2987a-2987d 10.00 10.00

First Man on the Moon, 40th Anniv. — A532

No. 2988, vert.: a, Apollo 11 Command and Service Modules. b, Apollo 11 Command, Service and Lunar Modules. c, Neil Armstrong. d, Apollo 11 Lunar Module.
30r, Crew of Apollo 11.

2009, July 20 **Litho.** ***Perf. 13¼***
2988 A532 12r Sheet of 4, #a-d 7.50 7.50

Souvenir Sheet
2989 A532 30r multi 4.75 4.75

Intl. Year of Astronomy.

Miniature Sheets

A533

Mushrooms — A534

No. 2990: a, Copelandia bispora. b, Copelandia cyanescens. c, Psilocybe semilanceata. d, Volvariella volvacea.
No. 2991: Various unnamed mushrooms.

2009, Nov. 18 ***Perf. 11½***
2990 A533 8r Sheet of 4, #a-d 5.00 5.00
2991 A534 8r Sheet of 6, #a-f 7.50 7.50

Flowers — A535

No. 2992: a, Nelumbo nucifera. b, Rosa bracteata. c, Freycinetia cumingiata. d, Thespesia lampas. e, Plumeria champa. f, Plumeria cubensis.
No. 2993: a, Lagerstroemia speciosa. b, Plumeria alba.
No. 2994: a, Plumeria rubra. b, Hibiscus tiliaceus.

2009, Dec. 9
2992 A535 10r Sheet of 6, #a-f 9.50 9.50

Souvenir Sheets
2993 A535 15r Sheet of 2, #a-b 4.75 4.75
2994 A535 15r Sheet of 2, #a-b 4.75 4.75

Souvenir Sheet

New Year 2010 (Year of the Tiger) — A536

No. 2995: a, Chinese characters. b, Tiger.

2010, Jan. 4 Litho. *Perf. 12*

2995 A536 25r Sheet of 2, #a-b 8.00 8.00

Shells — A537

Designs: 10 l, Conus abbas. 12r, Conus amadis. 16r, Conus bengalensis. 18r, Pinctada margaritifera.

No. 3000: a, Harpa costata. b, Phalium fimbria. c, Zoila friendii friendii. d, Cyprae leucodon tenuidon.

2010, June 22 *Perf. 11¼x11½*

2996-2999 A537 Set of 4 7.25 7.25

Perf. 12x11½

3000 A537 15r Sheet of 4, #a-d 9.50 9.50

Miniature Sheets

Election of Pres. John F. Kennedy, 50th Anniv. — A538

No. 3001, 15r: a, Pres. Kennedy at lectern. b, Pulitzer Prize medal. c, Civil Rights Act of 1964. d, Peace Corps emblem.

No. 3002, 15r: a, Vice-president Lyndon B. Johnson. b, Pres. Kennedy. c, Brochures for 1960 presidential election. d, Campaign placard.

2010, June 22 *Perf. 13¼*

Sheets of 4, #a-d

3001-3002 A538 Set of 2 19.00 19.00

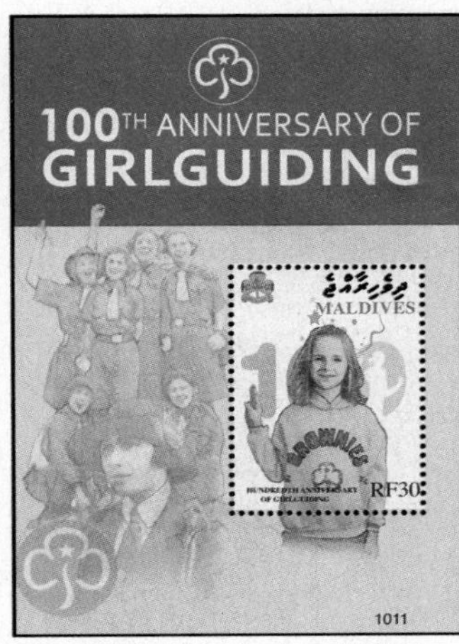

Girl Guides, Cent. — A539

No. 3003, horiz.: a, Three Girl Guides. b, Two Girl Guides, "100." c, Girl Guide climbing rock. d, Two Girl Guides jumping.

30r, Brownie.

2010, June 22 *Perf. 13x13¼*

3003 A539 16r Sheet of 4, #a-d 10.00 10.00

Souvenir Sheet

Perf. 13¼x13

3004 A539 30r multi 4.75 4.75

Reptiles — A540

No. 3005: a, Olive ridley turtle. b, Blood sucker lizard. c, Indian wolf snake. d, Green turtle.

No. 3006: a, Common house gecko. b, Loggerhead turtle.

2010, June 22 *Perf. 11½*

3005 A540 15r Sheet of 4, #a-d 9.50 9.50

Souvenir Sheet

Perf. 11½x12

3006 A540 15r Sheet of 2, #a-b 4.75 4.75

Birds — A541

No. 3007, horiz.: a, White-tailed tropicbird. b, Common tern. c, Bar-tailed godwit. d, Crab plover. e, Whimbrel. f, Black-winged stilt.

30r, Asian koel.

2010, June 22 *Perf. 11½x12*

3007 A541 8r Sheet of 6, #a-f 7.50 7.50

Souvenir Sheet

Perf. 11¼x11½

3008 A541 30r multi 4.75 4.75

Souvenir Sheets

A542

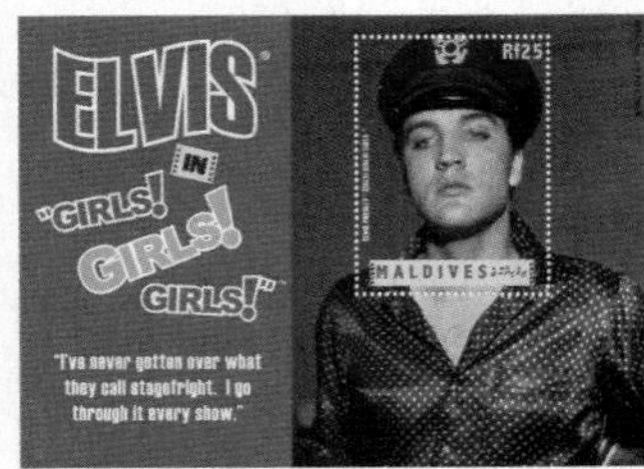

A543

A544

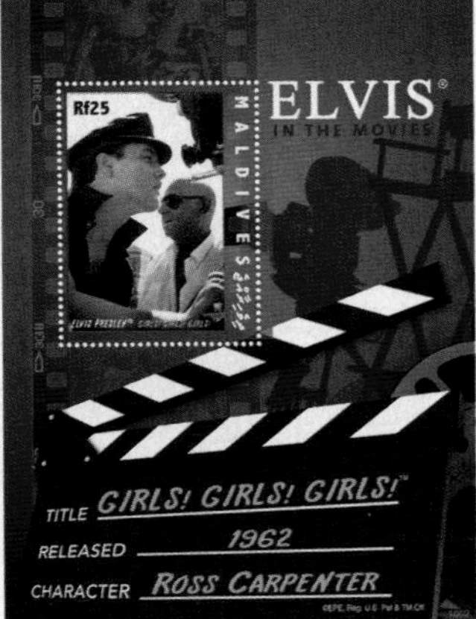

Elvis Presley (1935-77) — A545

2010, June 22 *Perf. 13½*

3009 A542 25r multi 4.00 4.00
3010 A543 25r multi 4.00 4.00
3011 A544 25r multi 4.00 4.00
3012 A545 25r multi 4.00 4.00
Nos. 3009-3012 (4) 16.00 16.00

MALI

'mä-lē

(Federation of Mali)

LOCATION — West Africa
GOVT. — Republic within French Community
AREA — 482,077 sq. mi.
POP. — 5,862,000 (est.)
CAPITAL — Dakar and Bamako

The Federation of Mali, founded Jan. 17, 1959, consisted of the Republic of Senegal and the French Sudan. It broke up in June, 1960. See Senegal.

100 Centimes = 1 Franc

Catalogue values for all unused stamps in this country are for Never Hinged items.

Flag and Map of Mali A1

Unwmk.

1959, Nov. 7 Engr. *Perf. 13*

1 A1 25fr grn, car & dp claret 1.00 .50

Founding of the Federation of Mali.

Imperforates

Most Mali stamps exist imperforate in issued and trial colors, and also in small presentation sheets in issued colors.

Parrotfish A2

Fish: 10fr, Triggerfish. 15fr, Psetta. 20fr, Blepharis crinitus. 25fr, Butterflyfish. 30fr, Surgeonfish. 85fr, Dentex.

1960, Mar. 5

Fish in Natural Colors

2 A2 5fr olive .40 .20
3 A2 10fr brt grnsh blue .40 .20
4 A2 15fr dark blue .55 .20
5 A2 20fr gray green .90 .40
6 A2 25fr slate green 1.10 .55
7 A2 30fr dark blue 2.00 .90
8 A2 85fr dark green 3.75 2.00
Nos. 2-8 (7) 9.10 4.45

For overprints see Nos. 10-12.

Common Design Types pictured following the introduction.

C.C.T.A. Issue

Common Design Type

1960, May 21 *Perf. 13*

9 CD106 25fr lt violet & magenta 1.40 .50

REPUBLIC OF MALI

GOVT. — Republic
AREA — 463,500 sq. mi.
POP. — 10,429,124 (1999 est.)
CAPITAL — Bamako

The Republic of Mali, formerly the French Sudan, proclaimed its independence on June 20, 1960, when the Federation of Mali ceased to exist.

Nos. 5, 6 and 8 Overprinted "REPUBLIQUE DU MALI" and Bar

Unwmk.

1961, Jan. 15 Engr. *Perf. 13*

Fish in Natural Colors

10 A2 20fr gray green 1.60 .65
11 A2 25fr slate green 2.00 .65
12 A2 85fr dark green 3.50 1.60
Nos. 10-12 (3) 7.10 2.90

Pres. Mamadou Konate — A3

Design: 25fr, Pres. Modibo Keita.

1961, Mar. 18

13 A3 20fr green & baclk .40 .20
14 A3 25fr maroon & black .50 .20

For miniature sheet see No. C11a.

Reading Class, Bullock Team and Factory — A4

1961, Sept. 22 Unwmk. *Perf. 13*

15 A4 25fr multi .90 .40

First anniversary of Independence.

Shepherd and Sheep A5

Designs: 1fr, 10fr, 40fr, Cattle. 2fr, 15fr, 50fr, Mali Arts Museum. 3fr, 20fr, 60fr, Plowing. 4fr, 25fr, 85fr, Harvester.

Unwmk.

1961, Dec. 24 Engr. *Perf. 13*

16 A5 50c car rose, blk & dk grn .20 .20
17 A5 1fr grn, bl & bister .20 .20
18 A5 2fr ultra, grn & org red .20 .20
19 A5 3fr bl, grn & brn .20 .20
20 A5 4fr bl grn, indigo & bis .20 .20
21 A5 5fr bl, olive & maroon .20 .20
22 A5 10fr ol blk, bl & sepia .20 .20
23 A5 15fr ultra, grn & bis brn .45 .20
24 A5 20fr bl, grn & org red .45 .20
25 A5 25fr dk bl & yel grn .50 .20
26 A5 30fr vio, grn & dk brn .60 .30
27 A5 40fr sl grn, bl & org red .80 .30
28 A5 50fr ultra, grn & rose car 1.00 .30
29 A5 60fr blue, green & brown 1.25 .30
30 A5 85fr bl, bis & dk red brn 1.90 .45
Nos. 16-30 (15) 8.35 3.65

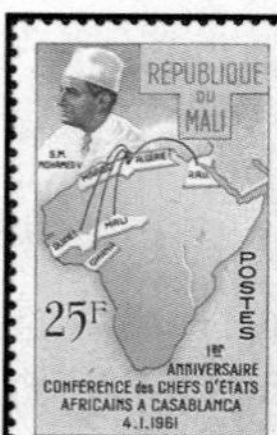

King Mohammed V of Morocco and Map of Africa — A6

1962, Jan. 4 Photo. *Perf. 12*

31 A6 25fr multicolored .45 .20
32 A6 50fr multicolored .55 .20

1st anniv. of the conference of African heads of state at Casablanca.

Patrice Lumumba A7

1962, Feb. 12 Unwmk. *Perf. 12*

33 A7 25fr choc & brn org .70 .20
34 A7 100fr choc & emerald 1.00 .45

Issued in memory of Patrice Lumumba, Premier of the Congo (Democratic) Republic.

Pegasus and UPU Monument, Bern — A8

1962, Apr. 21 *Perf. 12½x12*

35 A8 85fr red brn, yel & brt grn 1.75 .75

1st anniv. of Mali's admission to the UPU.

Map of Africa and Post Horn — A8a

1962, Apr. 23 *Perf. 13½x13*

36 A8a 25fr dk red brn & dp grn .60 .20
37 A8a 85fr dp green & org 1.10 .40

Establishment of African Postal Union.

Sansanding Dam — A9

Cotton Plant A10

1962, Oct. 27 Photo. *Perf. 12*

38 A9 25fr dk gray, ultra & grn .45 .20
39 A10 45fr multicolored 1.60 .40

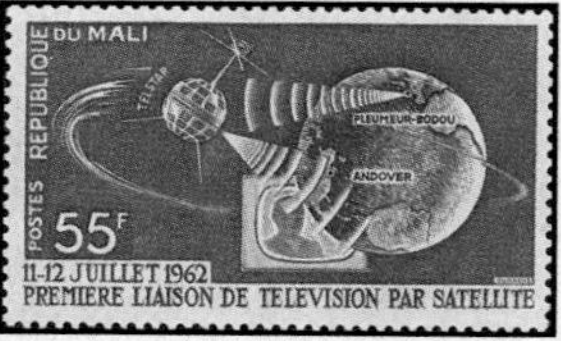

Telstar, Earth and Television Set — A10a

1962, Nov. 24 Engr. *Perf. 13*

40 A10a 45fr dk car, vio & brn 1.00 .45
41 A10a 55fr green, vio & ol 1.40 .55

1st television connection of the US and Europe through the Telstar satellite, 7/11-12.

Bull, Chemical Equipment, Chicks — A11

1963, Feb. 23 Unwmk. *Perf. 13*

42 A11 25fr red brn & grnsh bl .50 .20

Sotuba Zootechnical Institute. See No. C15.

Tractor A12

1963, Mar. 21 Engr.

43 A12 25fr vio bl, dk brn & blk .65 .20
44 A12 45fr bl grn, red brn & grn 1.10 .30

FAO "Freedom from Hunger" campaign.

High Altitude Balloon and WMO Emblem A13

Winners, 800-meter Race — A14

1963, June 12 Photo. *Perf. 12½*

Green Emblem; Yellow and Black Balloon

45 A13 25fr ultra .45 .20
46 A13 45fr carmine rose .80 .30
47 A13 60fr red brown 1.00 .40
Nos. 45-47 (3) 2.25 .90

Studies of the atmosphere.

1963, Aug. 10 Unwmk. *Perf. 12*

20fr, Acrobatic dancers. 85fr, Soccer.

48 A14 5fr multi .20 .20
49 A14 10fr multi .20 .20
50 A14 20fr multi, horiz. .70 .25
51 A14 85fr multi, horiz. 2.10 .60
Nos. 48-51 (4) 3.20 1.25

Issued to publicize Youth Week.

Centenary Emblem — A15

Kaempferia Aethiopica — A16

1963, Sept. 1 *Perf. 13½x13*

Emblem in Gray, Yellow and Red

52 A15 5fr lt ol grn & blk .55 .20
53 A15 10fr yellow & blk .65 .20
54 A15 85fr red & blk 1.50 .75
Nos. 52-54 (3) 2.70 1.15

Centenary of the International Red Cross.

1963, Dec. 23 Unwmk. *Perf. 13*

Tropical plants: 70fr, Bombax costatum. 100fr, Adenium Honghel.

55 A16 30fr multicolored .55 .20
56 A16 70fr multicolored 1.75 .45
57 A16 100fr multicolored 3.75 .60
Nos. 55-57 (3) 6.05 1.25

Plane Spraying, Locust and Village A17

Designs (each inscribed "O.I.C.M.A."): 5fr, Head of locust and map of Africa, vert. 10fr, Locust in flight over map of Mali, vert.

1964, June 15 Engr. *Perf. 13*

58 A17 5fr org brn, dl cl & grn .50 .20
59 A17 10fr org brn, ol & bl grn .75 .25
60 A17 20fr bis, org brn & yel grn 1.10 .30
Nos. 58-60 (3) 2.35 .75

Anti-locust campaign.

Soccer Player and Tokyo Stadium — A18

Designs (stadium in background): 10fr, Boxer, vert. 15fr, Runner, vert. 85fr, Hurdler.

1964, June 27 Unwmk.

61 A18 5fr red, brt grn & dk pur .20 .20
62 A18 10fr blk, dl bl & org brn .35 .20
63 A18 15fr violet & dk red .55 .25
64 A18 85fr vio, dk brn & sl grn 2.50 1.00
a. Min. sheet of 4, #61-64 4.50 4.50
Nos. 61-64 (4) 3.60 1.65

18th Olympic Games, Tokyo, Oct. 10-25.

IQSY Emblem and Eclipse of Sun — A19

1964, July 27 Engr. *Perf. 13*

65 A19 45fr multicolored 1.00 .40

International Quiet Sun Year, 1964-65.

Map of Viet Nam A20

Defassa Waterbuck A21

1964, Nov. 2 Photo. *Perf. 12x12½*

66 A20 30fr multicolored .60 .20

Issued to publicize the solidarity of the workers of Mali and those of South Viet Nam.

1965, Apr. 5 Engr.

Designs: 5fr, Cape buffalo, horiz. 10fr, Scimitar-horned oryx. 30fr, Leopard, horiz. 90fr, Giraffe.

67 A21 1fr choc, brt bl & grn .20 .20
68 A21 5fr grn, ocher & choc .20 .20
69 A21 10fr grn, brt pink & bis brn .55 .20
70 A21 30fr dk red, grn & choc 1.00 .35
71 A21 90fr bis brn, sl & yel grn 3.00 .75
Nos. 67-71 (5) 4.95 1.70

Abraham Lincoln A22

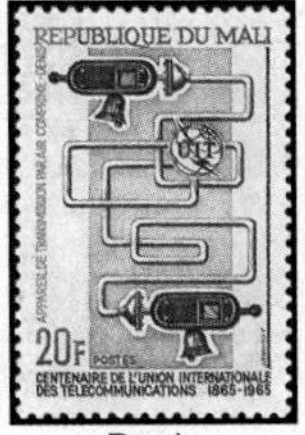

Denis Compressed Air Transmitter A23

1965, Apr. 15 Photo. *Perf. 13x12½*

72 A22 45fr black & multi .75 .50
73 A22 55fr dp green & multi 1.50 .60

Centenary of the death of Lincoln.

1965, May 17 Engr. *Perf. 13*

Designs: 30fr, Hughes telegraph system, horiz. 50fr, Lescurre heliograph.

74 A23 20fr orange, blk & bl .55 .20
75 A23 30fr org, ocher & sl grn .85 .30
76 A23 50fr org, dk brn & sl grn 1.25 .50
Nos. 74-76 (3) 2.65 1.00

Centenary of the ITU.

Mother and infants — A24

Designs: 5fr, Mobile X-ray Unit and Lungs. 25fr, Examination of patient at Marchoux Institute and slide. 45fr, Biology laboratory.

1965, July 5 Unwmk. *Perf. 13*

77 A24 5fr lake, red & vio .20 .20
78 A24 10fr brn ol, red & sl grn .35 .20
79 A24 25fr dk brn, red & grn .65 .25
80 A24 45fr dk brn, red & sl grn 1.25 .50
Nos. 77-80 (4) 2.45 1.15

Issued to publicize the Health Service.

Swimmer A25

1965, July 19 Engr.

81 A25 5fr shown .20 .20
82 A25 15fr Judo .80 .30

1st African Games, Brazzaville, July 18-25.

Globe, Vase, Quill, Trumpet A26

55fr, Mask, palette and microphones. 90fr, Dancers, mask and printed cloth.

1966, Apr. 4 Engr. *Perf. 13*

83 A26 30fr black, red & ocher .45 .20
84 A26 55fr car rose, emer & blk 1.00 .30
85 A26 90fr ultra, org & dk brn 1.60 .45
Nos. 83-85 (3) 3.05 .95

International Negro Arts Festival, Dakar, Senegal, Apr. 1-24.

WHO Headquarters, Geneva — A27

1966, May 3 Photo. *Perf. 12½x13*

86 A27 30fr org yel, bl & ol grn .70 .20
87 A27 45fr org yel, bl & dl red .90 .30

Inauguration of the WHO Headquarters.

Fishermen with Nets — A28

River Fishing: 4fr, 60fr, Group fishing with large net. 20fr, 85fr, Commercial fishing boats.

1966, May 30 Engr. *Perf. 13*

88 A28 3fr ultra & brn .20 .20
89 A28 4fr Prus bl & org brn .20 .20
90 A28 20fr dk brn, ultra & grn .55 .20
91 A28 25fr dk brn, bl & brt grn .70 .20
92 A28 60fr mag, brn & brt grn 1.10 .30
93 A28 85fr dk pur, dl bl & grn 1.60 .60
Nos. 88-93 (6) 4.35 1.70

Initiation of Pioneers A29

Design: 25fr, Dance and Pioneer emblem.

1966, July 25 Engr. *Perf. 13*

94 A29 5fr multicolored .20 .20
95 A29 25fr multicolored .80 .25

Issued to honor the pioneers of Mali.

Inoculation of Zebu A30

1967, Jan. 16 Photo. *Perf. 12½x13*

96 A30 10fr dp grn, yel grn & brn .35 .20
97 A30 30fr Prus bl, bl & brn 1.00 .30

Campaign against cattle plague.

View of Timbuktu and Tourist Year Emblem A31

1967, May 15 Engr. *Perf. 13*

98 A31 25fr Prus bl, red lil & org .70 .20

International Tourist Year, 1967.

Ugada Grandicollis A32

Insects: 5fr, Chelorrhina polyphemus, vert. 50fr, Phymateus cinctus.

1967, Aug. 14 Engr. *Perf. 13*

99 A32 5fr brt bl, sl grn & brn .65 .20
100 A32 15fr sl grn, dk brn & red 1.10 .25
101 A32 50fr sl grn, dk brn & dp org 2.75 .45
Nos. 99-101 (3) 4.50 .90

Teacher and Adult Class A33

1967, Sept. 8 Photo. *Perf. 12½x13*

102 A33 50fr black, grn & car 1.00 .25

International Literacy Day, Sept. 8.

Europafrica Issue

Birds, New Buildings and Map A34

1967, Sept. 18 *Perf. 12½x12*

103 A34 45fr multicolored 1.25 .35

Lions Emblem and Crocodile — A35

1967, Oct. 16 Photo. *Perf. 13x12½*

104 A35 90fr yellow & multi 1.75 .75

50th anniversary of Lions International.

Water Cycle and UNESCO Emblem A36

1967, Nov. 15 Photo. *Perf. 13*

105 A36 25fr multicolored .70 .20

Hydrological Decade (UNESCO), 1965-74.

WHO Emblem A37

1968, Apr. 8 Engr. *Perf. 13*

106 A37 90fr sl grn, dk car rose & bl 1.40 .40

20th anniv. of the World Health Organization.

Linked Hearts and People A38

1968, Apr. 28 Engr. *Perf. 13*

107 A38 50fr sl grn, red & vio bl .90 .25

International Day of Sister Communities.

Books, Student, Chart, and Map of Africa A39

1968, Aug. 12 Engr. *Perf. 13*

108 A39 100fr carmine, ol & blk 1.25 .40

10th anniv. of the Intl. Assoc. for the Development of Libraries and Archives in Africa.

Michaux bicycle, 1861 A40

Designs: 2fr, Draisienne, 1809. 5fr, De Dion-Bouton automobile, 1894, horiz. 45fr, Panhard & Levassor automobile, 1914, horiz.

1968, Aug. 12

109 A40 2fr grn, olive & magenta .40 .20
110 A40 5fr lemon, indigo & red .75 .20
111 A40 10fr brt grn, indigo & brn 1.25 .20
112 A40 45fr ocher, gray grn & blk 2.25 .30
Nos. 109-112,C60-C61 (6) 8.65 1.90

Tourist Emblem with Map of Africa and Dove A41

1969, May 12 Photo. *Perf. 12½x13*

113 A41 50fr lt ultra, grn & red .70 .20

Year of African Tourism.

ILO Emblem and "OIT" A42

1969, May 12 Engr. *Perf. 13*

114 A42 50fr vio, slate grn & brt bl .50 .20
115 A42 60fr slate, red & ol brn .90 .25

Intl. Labor Organization, 50th anniv.

Panhard, 1897, and Citroen 24, 1969 — A43

30fr, Citroen, 1923, Citroen DS 21, 1969.

1969, May 30 Engr. *Perf. 13*

116 A43 25fr blk, maroon & lemon .95 .20
117 A43 30fr blk, brt grn & dk grn 1.60 .20
Nos. 116-117,C71-C72 (4) 6.40 1.35

Play Blocks A44

Toys: 10fr, Mule on wheels. 15fr, Ducks. 20fr, Racing car and track.

1969 Photo. *Perf. 12½x13*

118 A44 5fr red, gray & yel .20 .20
119 A44 10fr red, yel & olive .25 .20
120 A44 15fr red, salmon & yel grn .35 .20
121 A44 20fr red, indigo & org .45 .20
Nos. 118-121 (4) 1.25 .80

Intl. Toy Fair in Nuremberg, Germany.

Ram A45

1969, Aug. 18 Engr. *Perf. 13*

122 A45 1fr shown .20 .20
123 A45 2fr Goat .20 .20
124 A45 10fr Donkey .35 .20
125 A45 35fr Horse 1.00 .30
126 A45 90fr Dromedaries 1.75 .50
Nos. 122-126 (5) 3.50 1.40

Development Bank Issue
Common Design Type

1969, Sept. 10

127 CD130 50fr brt lil, grn & ocher .40 .20
128 CD130 90fr ol brn, grn & ocher .85 .20

Boy Being Vaccinated A46

1969, Nov. 10 Engr. *Perf. 13*

129 A46 50fr brn, indigo & brt grn .90 .25

Campaign against smallbox and measles.

ASECNA Issue
Common Design Type

1969, Dec. 12 Engr. *Perf. 13*

130 CD132 100fr dark slate green 1.00 .30

African and Japanese Women A47

150fr, Flags and maps of Mali and Japan.

1970, Apr. 13 Engr. *Perf. 13*

131 A47 100fr brown, bl & ocher 1.00 .30
132 A47 150fr dk red, yel grn & org 1.50 .40

Issued to publicize EXPO '70 International Exhibition, Osaka, Japan, Mar. 15-Sept. 13.

Satellite Telecommunications, Map of Africa and ITU Emblem — A48

1970, May 17 Engr. *Perf. 13*

133 A48 90fr car rose & brn 1.00 .30

World Telecommunications Day.

UPU Headquarters Issue
Common Design Type

1970, May 20 Engr. *Perf. 13*

134 CD133 50fr dk red, bl grn & ol .55 .20
135 CD133 60fr red lil, ultra & red brn .70 .20

Post Office, Bamako A49

Public Buildings: 40fr, Chamber of Commerce, Bamako. 60fr, Public Works Ministry, Bamako. 80fr, City Hall, Segou.

1970, Nov. 23 Engr. *Perf. 13*

136 A49 30fr brn, brt grn & olive .45 .20
137 A49 40fr brn, sl grn & dp claret .55 .20
138 A49 60fr brn red, sl grn & gray .70 .20
139 A49 80fr brn, brt grn & emer 1.00 .25
Nos. 136-139 (4) 2.70 .85

Gallet 030T, 1882 A50

Old Steam Locomotives: 40fr, Felou 030T, 1882. 50fr, Bechevel 230T, 1882. 80fr, Type 231, 1930. 100fr, Type 141, 1930.

1970, Dec. 14 Engr. *Perf. 13*

140 A50 20fr brt grn, dk car & blk 1.75 .50
141 A50 40fr blk, dk grn & ocher 2.25 .60
142 A50 50fr bis brn, bl grn & blk 3.00 .80
143 A50 80fr car rose, blk & bl grn 4.00 1.00
144 A50 100fr ocher, bl grn & blk 6.75 1.60
Nos. 140-144 (5) 17.75 4.50

Scout Sounding Retreat — A51

Bambara Mask, San — A52

Boy Scouts: 5fr, Crossing river, horiz. 100fr, Canoeing, horiz.

Perf. 13x12½, 12½x13

1970, Dec. 28 Litho.

145 A51 5fr multicolored .20 .20
146 A51 30fr multicolored .55 .20
147 A51 100fr multicolored 1.40 .40
Nos. 145-147 (3) 2.15 .80

1971, Jan. 25 Photo. *Perf. 12x12½*

Designs: 25fr, Dogon mask, Bandiagara. 50fr, Kanaga ideogram. 80fr, Bambara ideogram.

148 A52 20fr orange & multi .25 .20
149 A52 25fr brt green & multi .45 .20
150 A52 50fr dk purple & multi .70 .20
151 A52 80fr blue & multi 1.00 .25
Nos. 148-151 (4) 2.40 .85

Boy, Medical and Scientific Symbols A53

1971, Mar. 22 Engr. *Perf. 13*

152 A53 100fr dp car, ocher & grn 1.40 .40

B.C.G. inoculation (Bacillus-Calmette-Guerin) against tuberculosis, 50th anniv.

Boy Scouts, Mt. Fuji, Japanese Print — A54

1971, Apr. 19

153 A54 80fr lt ultra, dp plum & brt grn .90 .25

13th Boy Scout World Jamboree, Asagiri Plain, Japan, Aug. 2-10.

UNICEF Emblem, Hands and Rose A55

60fr, UNICEF emblem, women & children, vert.

1971, May 24 Engr. *Perf. 13*

154 A55 50fr brn org, car & dk brn .55 .20
155 A55 60fr vio bl, grn & red brn .70 .20

25th anniv. of UNICEF.

Mali Farmer — A56

Map of Africa with Communications Network — A57

Costumes of Mali: 10fr, Mali farm woman. 15fr, Tuareg. 60fr, Embroidered robe, Grand Boubou. 80fr, Ceremonial robe, woman.

1971, June 14 Photo. *Perf. 13*

156 A56 5fr gray & multi .20 .20
157 A56 10fr vio bl & multi .35 .20
158 A56 15fr yellow & multi .45 .20
159 A56 60fr gray & multi .70 .20
160 A56 80fr tan & multi 1.00 .30
Nos. 156-160 (5) 2.70 1.10

1971, Aug. 16 Photo. *Perf. 13*

161 A57 50fr bl, vio bl & org .50 .20

Pan-African telecommunications system.

Hibiscus A58

Flowers: 50fr, Poinsettia. 60fr, Adenium obesum. 80fr, Dogbane. 100fr, Satanocrater berhautii.

1971, Oct. 4 Litho. *Perf. 14x13½*

162 A58 20fr multicolored .55 .20
163 A58 50fr multicolored 1.00 .25
164 A58 60fr multicolored 1.40 .30
165 A58 80fr multicolored 1.75 .40
166 A58 100fr multicolored 2.25 .50
Nos. 162-166 (5) 6.95 1.65

For surcharge see No. 204.

Mother, Child and Bird (Sculpture) A59

1971, Dec. 27 Engr. *Perf. 13x12½*

167 A59 70fr mag, sepia & bl grn .90 .25

Natl. Institute of Social Security, 15th anniv.

ITU Emblem A60

1972, May 17 Photo. *Perf. 13x13½*

168 A60 70fr blue, maroon & blk .90 .25

4th World Telecommunications Day.

Clay Funerary Statuette — A61

Mali Art: 40fr, Female torso, wood. 50fr, Masked figure, painted stone. 100fr, Animals and men, wrought iron.

1972, May 29 *Perf. 12½x13*

169 A61 30fr org red & multi .35 .20
170 A61 40fr yellow & multi .55 .20
171 A61 50fr red & multi .70 .20
172 A61 100fr lt green & multi 1.40 .40
Nos. 169-172 (4) 3.00 1.00

Morse and Telegraph A62

1972, June 5 Engr. *Perf. 13*

173 A62 80fr red, emer & choc 1.10 .35

Centenary of the death of Samuel F. B. Morse (1791-1872), inventor of the telegraph.

Weather Balloon over Africa — A63

1972, July 10 Photo. *Perf. 12½x13*

174 A63 130fr multicolored 1.75 .50

12th World Meteorology Day.

Sarakolé Dance, Kayes — A64

People, Book, Pencil — A65

Designs: Folk dances.

1972, Aug. 21 Photo. *Perf. 13*

175 A64 10fr shown .35 .20
176 A64 20fr LaGomba, Bamako .55 .20
177 A64 50fr Hunters' dance, Bougouni .70 .20
178 A64 70fr Koré Duga, Ségou .90 .25
179 A64 80fr Kanaga, Sanga 1.00 .30
180 A64 120fr Targui, Timbuktu 1.60 .40
Nos. 175-180 (6) 5.10 1.55

1972, Sept. 8 Typo. *Perf. 12½x13*

181 A65 80fr black & yel grn .90 .20

World Literacy Day, Sept. 8.

"Edison Classique," Mali Instruments A66

1972, Sept. 18 Engr. *Perf. 13*

182 A66 100fr multicolored 1.25 .35

First Anthology of Music of Mali.

Aries — A67

Signs of the Zodiac: No. 184, Taurus. No. 185, Gemini. No. 186, Cancer. No. 187, Leo. No. 188, Virgo. No. 189, Libra. No. 190, Scorpio. No. 191, Sagittarius. No. 192, Capricorn. No. 193, Aquarius. No. 194, Pisces.

1972, Oct. 23 Engr. *Perf. 11*

183 A67 15fr lilac & bis brn .40 .20
184 A67 15fr bister brn & blk .40 .20
a. Pair #183-184 .80 .40
185 A67 35fr maroon & indigo .65 .20
186 A67 35fr emerald & mar .65 .20
a. Pair ,#185-186 1.40 .40
187 A67 40fr blue & red brn .70 .20
188 A67 40fr dk pur & red brn .70 .20
a. Pair, #187-188 1.40 .40
189 A67 45fr dk blue & mar .80 .30
190 A67 45fr maroon & brt grn .80 .30
a. Pair, #189-180 1.60 .60
191 A67 65fr dk violet & ind 1.00 .35
192 A67 65fr dk vio & gray ol 1.00 .35
a. Pair, #191-192 2.00 .70
193 A67 90fr brt pink & ind 1.60 .60
194 A67 90fr brt pink & grn 1.60 .60
a. Pair, #193-194 3.25 1.25
Nos. 183-194 (12) 10.30 3.70

Arrival of First Locomotive in Bamako, 1906 A68

Designs (Locomotives): 30fr, Thies-Bamako, 1920. 60fr, Thies-Bamako, 1927. 120fr, Two Alsthom BB, 1947.

1972, Dec. 11 Engr. *Perf. 13*

195 A68 10fr ind, brn & sl grn 1.75 .50
196 A68 30fr sl grn, ind & brn 3.50 1.00
197 A68 60fr sl grn, ind & brn 5.25 1.50
198 A68 120fr sl grn & choc 7.25 2.00
Nos. 195-198 (4) 17.75 5.00

2nd African Games, Lagos, Nigeria, Jan. 7-18 — A69

1973, Jan. 15 Photo. *Perf. 12½*

199 A69 70fr High jump .55 .20
200 A69 270fr Discus 1.40 .50
201 A69 280fr Soccer 1.60 .75
Nos. 199-201 (3) 3.55 1.45

INTERPOL Emblem and Headquarters — A70

1973, Feb. 28 Photo. *Perf. 13*

202 A70 80fr multi .90 .20

50th anniversary of International Criminal Police Organization (INTERPOL).

Blind Man and Disabled Boy — A71

Cora — A72

1973, Apr. 24 Engr. *Perf. 12½x13*

203 A71 70fr dk car, brick red & blk .70 .20

Help for the handicapped.

No. 166 Surcharged with New Value, 2 Bars, and Overprinted: "SECHERESSE / SOLIDARITE AFRICAINE"

1973, Aug. 16 Litho. *Perf. 13½*

204 A58 200fr on 100fr multi 2.25 .65

African solidarity in drought emergency.

Perf. 12½x13, 13x12½

1973, Dec. 10 Engr.

Musical Instruments: 10fr, Balafon, horiz. 15fr, Djembe. 20fr, Guitar. 25fr, N'Djarka. 30fr, M'Bolon. 35fr, Dozo N'Goni. 40fr, N'Tamani.

205 A72 5fr mar, dk grn & brn .35 .20
206 A72 10fr bl & choc .45 .20
207 A72 15fr brn, dk red & yel .55 .20
208 A72 20fr mar & brn ol .65 .20
209 A72 25fr org, yel & blk .70 .20
210 A72 30fr vio bl & blk .80 .20
211 A72 35fr dk red & brn .90 .35
212 A72 40fr dk red & choc 1.10 .35
Nos. 205-212 (8) 5.50 1.90

Farmer with Newspaper, Corn — A73

Soccer, Goalkeeper, Symbolic Globe and Net — A74

1974, Mar. 11 Engr. *Perf. 12½x13*

213 A73 70fr multi .70 .20

"Kibaru," rural newspaper, 2nd anniv.

1974, May 6 Engr. *Perf. 13*

280fr, Games' emblem, soccer and ball.

214 A74 270fr multi 2.00 .90
215 A74 280fr multi 2.25 .90

World Cup Soccer Championships, Munich, June 13-July 7.

For surcharges see Nos. 219-220.

Old and New Ships, UPU Emblem — A75

Artisans of Mali — A76

90fr, Old and new planes, UPU emblem. 270fr, Old and new trains, UPU emblem.

1974, June 2 Engr. *Perf. 12½x13*

216 A75 80fr brn & multir .55 .25
217 A75 90fr ultra & multi .80 .30
218 A75 270fr lt grn & multi 2.25 .75
Nos. 216-218 (3) 3.60 1.30

Centenary of Universal Postal Union.

For surcharges see Nos. 229-230.

Nos. 214-215 Surcharged and Overprinted in Black or Red: "R.F.A. 2 / HOLLANDE 1"

1974, Aug. 28 Engr. *Perf. 13*

219 A74 300fr on 270fr multi 2.50 .90
220 A74 330fr on 280fr multi (R) 2.75 .90

World Cup Soccer Championship, 1974, victory of German Federal Republic.

1974, Sept. 16 Photo. *Perf. 12½x13*

221 A76 50fr Weaver .55 .20
222 A76 60fr Potter .65 .20
223 A76 70fr Smiths .70 .20
224 A76 80fr Sculptor .80 .25
Nos. 221-224 (4) 2.70 .85

Niger River near Gao — A77

Landscapes: 20fr, The Hand of Fatma (rock formation), vert. 40fr, Gouina Waterfall. 70fr, Dogon houses, vert.

Perf. 13x12½, 12½x13

1974, Sept. 23

225 A77 10fr multi .20 .20
226 A77 20fr multi .25 .20
227 A77 40fr multi .55 .20
228 A77 70fr multi .80 .30
Nos. 225-228 (4) 1.80 .90

Nos. 216 and 218 Surcharged and Overprinted in Black or Red: "9 OCTOBRE 1974"

1974, Oct. 9 Engr. *Perf. 13*

229 A75 250fr on 80fr multi 2.00 .90
230 A75 300fr on 270fr multi (R) 2.50 .90

UPU Day.

Mao Tse-tung, Flags, Great Wall — A78

1974, Oct. 21 Engr. *Perf. 13*

231 A78 100fr multi 2.25 .55

People's Republic of China, 25th anniv.

Artisans and Lions Emblem — A79

100fr, View of Samanko and Lions emblem.

1975, Feb. 3 Photo. *Perf. 13*

232 A79 90fr red & multi .70 .20
233 A79 100fr blue & multi .90 .25

5th anniv. of lepers' rehabilitation village, Samanko, sponsored by Lions Intl.

For surcharges see Nos. 303-304.

Tetrodon Fahaka A80

Designs: Fish.

1975, May 12 Engr. *Perf. 13*

234 A80 60fr *shown* 1.10 .30
235 A80 70fr *Malopterurus electricus* 1.25 .35
236 A80 80fr *Citharinus latus* 1.50 .40
237 A80 90fr *Hydrocyon forskali* 1.75 .45
238 A80 110fr *Lates niloticus* 2.25 .50
Nos. 234-238 (5) 7.85 2.00

See Nos. 256-260.

Woman and IWY Emblem — A81

1975, June 9 Engr. *Perf. 13*

239 A81 150fr red & grn 1.25 .35

International Women's Year 1975.

Morris "Oxford," 1913 A82

Automobiles: 130fr, Franklin "E," 1907. 190fr, Daimler, 1900. 230fr, Panhard & Levassor, 1895.

1975, June 16

240 A82 90fr blk, ol & lil .75 .30
241 A82 130fr vio bl, gray & red 1.25 .35
242 A82 190fr bl, grn & indigo 1.75 .50
243 A82 230fr red, ultra & brn ol 2.00 .50
Nos. 240-243 (4) 5.75 1.65

Carthaginian Tristater, 500 B.C. — A83

Ancient Coins: 170fr, Decadrachma, Syracuse, 413 B.C. 190fr, Acanthe tetradrachma, 400 B.C. 260fr, Didrachma, Eritrea, 480-445 B.C.

1975, Oct. 13 Engr. *Perf. 13*

244 A83 130fr bl, cl & blk .70 .25
245 A83 170fr emer, brn & blk 1.00 .45
246 A83 190fr grn, red & blk 1.40 .65
247 A83 260fr dp bl, org & blk 2.00 .90
Nos. 244-247 (4) 5.10 2.25

UN Emblem and "ONU" — A84

1975, Nov. 10 Engr. *Perf. 13*

248 A84 200fr emer & brt bl 1.25 .45

30th anniversary of UN.

A. G. Bell, Waves, Satellite, Telephone — A85

1976, Mar. 8 Litho. *Perf. 12x12½*

249 A85 180fr brn, ultra & ocher 1.25 .35

Centenary of first telephone call by Alexander Graham Bell, Mar. 10, 1876.

Chameleon A86

1976, Mar. 31 Litho. *Perf. 12½*

250 A86 20fr shown .35 .20
251 A86 30fr Lizard .55 .20
252 A86 40fr Tortoise .70 .20
253 A86 90fr Python 1.60 .45
254 A86 120fr Crocodile 2.10 .60
Nos. 250-254 (5) 5.30 1.65

Konrad Adenauer and Cologne Cathedral — A87

1976, Apr. 26 Engr. *Perf. 13*

255 A87 180fr mag & dk brn 1.40 .40

Konrad Adenauer (1876-1967), German Chancellor.

Fish Type of 1975

1976, June 28 Engr. *Perf. 13*

256 A80 100fr *Heterotis niloticus* .75 .20
257 A80 120fr *Synodontis budgetti* 1.00 .20
258 A80 130fr *Heterobranchus bidorsalis* 1.00 .25
259 A80 150fr *Tilapia monodi* 1.25 .35
260 A80 220fr *Alestes macrolepidotus* 1.75 .45
Nos. 256-260 (5) 5.75 1.45

Page from Children's Book — A88

"Le Roi de l'Air" — A89

1976, July 19

261 A88 130fr red & multi .90 .30

Books for children.

1976, July 26 Litho. *Perf. 12½x13*

262 A89 120fr multi 1.40 .40

First lottery, sponsored by L'Essor newspaper.

"Do not overload scaffold" — A90

1976, Aug. 16 Litho. *Perf. 13*

263 A90 120fr multi .70 .20

National Insurance Institute, 20th anniv.

Letters, UPU and UN Emblems — A91

1976, Oct. 4 Engr. *Perf. 13*

264 A91 120fr lil, org & grn .90 .30

UN Postal Administration, 25th anniv.

Moto-Guzzi 254, Italy — A92

Motorcycles: 120fr, BMW 900, Germany. 130fr, Honda-Egli, Japan. 140fr, Motobecane LT-3, France.

1976, Oct. 18 Engr. *Perf. 13*

265 A92 90fr multi 1.00 .20
266 A92 120fr multi 1.25 .25
267 A92 130fr multi 1.25 .35
268 A92 140fr multi 1.50 .35
Nos. 265-268 (4) 5.00 1.15

Fishing Boat, Masgat — A93

180fr, Coaster, Cochin China. 190fr, Fireboat, Dunkirk, 1878. 200fr, Nile river boat.

1976, Dec. 6 Engr. *Perf. 13*

269 A93 160fr multi .80 .30
270 A93 180fr multi .90 .30
271 A93 190fr multi 1.00 .35
272 A93 200fr multi 1.00 .45
Nos. 269-272 (4) 3.70 1.40

Indigo Finch A94

Birds: 25fr, Yellow-breasted barbet. 30fr, Vitelline masked weaver. 40fr, Bee-eater. 50fr, Senegal parrot.

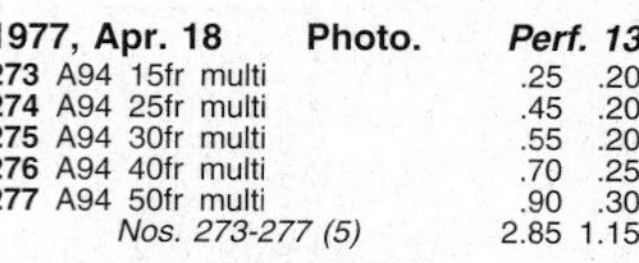

1977, Apr. 18 Photo. *Perf. 13*

273 A94 15fr multi .25 .20
274 A94 25fr multi .45 .20
275 A94 30fr multi .55 .20
276 A94 40fr multi .70 .25
277 A94 50fr multi .90 .30
Nos. 273-277 (5) 2.85 1.15

See Nos. 298-302.

Braille Statue, Script and Reading Hands — A95

1977, Apr. 25 Engr. *Perf. 13*

278 A95 200fr multi 1.40 .45

Louis Braille (1809-1852), inventor of the reading and writing system for the blind.

Electronic Tree, ITU Emblem — A96

1977, May 17 Photo.

279 A96 120fr dk brn & org .50 .20

World Telecommunications Day.

Dragonfly A97

Insects: 10fr, Praying mantis. 20fr, Tropical wasp. 35fr, Cockchafer. 60fr, Flying stag beetle.

1977, June 15 Photo. *Perf. 13x12½*

280 A97 5fr multi .35 .20
281 A97 10fr multi .45 .20
282 A97 20fr multi .55 .20
283 A97 35fr multi .80 .20
284 A97 60fr multi 1.00 .25
Nos. 280-284 (5) 3.15 1.05

Knight and Rook A98

Chess Pieces: 130fr, Bishop and pawn, vert. 300fr, Queen and King.

1977, June 27 Engr. *Perf. 13*

285 A98 120fr multi 1.60 .40
286 A98 130fr multi 1.75 .50
287 A98 300fr multi 3.75 1.10
Nos. 285-287 (3) 7.10 2.00

Europafrica Issue

Symbolic Ship, White and Brown Persons — A99

1977, July 18 Litho. *Perf. 13*

288 A99 400fr multi 2.50 .70

Horse, by Leonardo da Vinci A100

Drawings by Leonardo da Vinci: 300fr, Head of Young Woman. 500fr, Self-portrait.

1977, Sept. 5 Engr. *Perf. 13*

289 A100 200fr dk brn & blk 1.25 .55
290 A100 300fr dk brn & ol 1.75 .55
291 A100 500fr dk brn & red 2.75 .90
Nos. 289-291 (3) 5.75 2.00

Hotel de l'Amitié, Bamako — A101

1977, Oct. 15 Litho. *Perf. 13x12½*

292 A101 120fr multi .70 .20

Opening of the Hotel de l'Amitié, Oct. 15.

Dome of the Rock Jerusalem A102

1977, Oct. 17 *Perf. 12½*

293 A102 120fr multi .90 .20
294 A102 180fr multi 1.10 .30

Palestinian fighters and their families.

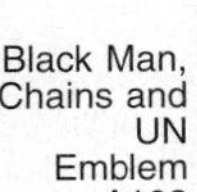

Black Man, Chains and UN Emblem A103

130fr, Statue of Liberty, people & UN emblem. 180fr, Black children & horse behind fence.

1978, Mar. 13 Engr. *Perf. 13*

295 A103 120fr multi .65 .20
296 A103 130fr multi .70 .20
297 A103 180fr multi 1.10 .35
Nos. 295-297 (3) 2.45 .75

International Year against Apartheid.

Bird Type of 1977

Birds: 20fr, Granatine bengala. 30fr, Lagonosticta vinacea. 50fr, Lagonosticta. 70fr, Turtle dove. 80fr, Buffalo weaver.

1978, Apr. 10 Litho. *Perf. 13*

298 A94 20fr multi .65 .20
299 A94 30fr multi .80 .20
300 A94 50fr multi 1.00 .25
301 A94 70fr multi 1.50 .35
302 A94 80fr multi 2.00 .45
Nos. 298-302 (5) 5.95 1.45

Nos. 232-233 Surcharged with New Value, Bar and: "XXe ANNIVERSAIRE DU LIONS CLUB DE BAMAKO 1958-1978"

1978, May 8 Photo.

303 A79 120fr on 90fr multi .80 .20
304 A79 130fr on 100fr multi 1.00 .20

20th anniversary of Bamako Lions Club.

Wall and Desert — A105

1978, May 18 Litho. *Perf. 13*

306 A105 200fr multi 1.25 .35

Hammamet Conference for reclamation of the desert.

Mahatma Gandhi and Roses — A106

1978, May 29 Engr.

307 A106 140fr blk, brn & red 1.50 .25

Mohandas K. Gandhi (1869-1948), Hindu spiritual leader.

Dermestes — A107

Insects: 25fr, Ground beetle. 90fr, Cricket. 120fr, Ladybird. 140fr, Goliath beetle.

1978, June 12 Photo. *Perf. 13*

308 A107 15fr multi .55 .20
309 A107 25fr multi .70 .20
310 A107 90fr multi 1.25 .20
311 A107 120fr multi 1.25 .25
312 A107 140fr multi 1.75 .30
Nos. 308-312 (5) 5.50 1.15

Bridge — A108

Design: 100fr, Dominoes, vert.

1978, June 26 Engr.

313 A108 100fr multi .90 .20
314 A108 130fr multi 1.25 .30

Aristotle — A109

1978, Oct. 16 Engr. *Perf. 13*

315 A109 200fr multi 1.40 .30

Aristotle (384-322 B.C.), Greek philosopher.

Human Rights and UN Emblems — A110

1978, Dec. 11 Engr. *Perf. 13*

316 A110 180fr red, bl & brn 1.25 .25

Universal Declaration of Human Rights, 30th anniversary.

Manatee — A111

Endangered Wildlife: 120fr, Chimpanzee. 130fr, Damaliscus antelope. 180fr, Oryx. 200fr, Derby's eland.

1979, Apr. 23 Litho. *Perf. 12½*

317 A111 100fr multi .90 .20
318 A111 120fr multi 1.00 .20
319 A111 130fr multi 1.10 .20
320 A111 180fr multi 1.60 .30
321 A111 200fr multi 1.75 .30
Nos. 317-321 (5) 6.35 1.20

Boy Praying and IYC Emblem — A112

IYC emblem and: 200fr, Girl and Boy Scout holding bird. 300fr, IYC emblem, boys with calf.

1979, May 7 Engr. *Perf. 13*

322 A112 120fr multi .70 .20
323 A112 200fr multi 1.00 .30
324 A112 300fr multi 1.75 .45
Nos. 322-324 (3) 3.45 .95

International Year of the Child.

Judo and Notre Dame, Paris — A113

1979, May 14 Engr. *Perf. 13*

325 A113 200fr multi 1.40 .40

World Judo Championship, Paris.

Telecommunications A114

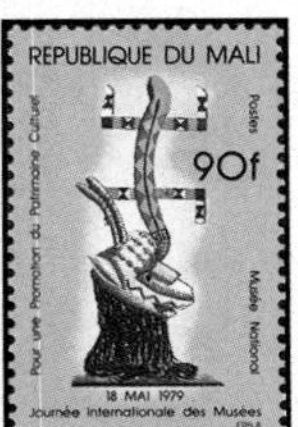
Wood Carving A115

1979, May 17 Litho.

326 A114 120fr multi .70 .20

11th Telecommunications Day.

1979, May 18 *Perf. 13x12½*

Sculptures from National Museum: 120fr, Ancestral figures. 130fr, Animal heads, and kneeling woman.

327 A115 90fr multi .55 .20
328 A115 120fr multi .70 .20
329 A115 130fr multi .90 .25
Nos. 327-329 (3) 2.15 .65

International Museums Day.

Rowland Hill and Mali No. 15 — A116

130fr, Zeppelin & Saxony #1. 180fr, Concorde & France #3. 200fr, Stagecoach & US #2. 300fr, UPU emblem & Penny Black.

1979, May 21 Engr. *Perf. 13*

330 A116 120fr multi .65 .20
331 A116 130fr multi .70 .20
332 A116 180fr multi .90 .30
333 A116 200fr multi 1.00 .30
334 A116 300fr multi 1.75 .55
Nos. 330-334 (5) 5.00 1.55

Sir Rowland Hill (1795-1879), originator of penny postage.

Cora Players — A117

1979, June 4 Litho. *Perf. 13*

335 A117 200fr multi 1.75 .45

Adenium Obesum and Sankore Mosque — A118

Design: 300fr, Satellite, mounted messenger, globe and letter, vert.

1979, June 8 Photo.

336 A118 120fr multi 1.75 .65

Engr.

337 A118 300fr multi 3.00 1.40

Philexafrique II, Libreville, Gabon, June 8-17. Nos. 336, 337 printed in sheets of 10 and 5 labels showing exhibition emblem.

Map of Mali — A119

Design: 300fr, Men planting trees.

1979, June 18 Litho. *Perf. 13x12½*

338 A119 200fr multi 1.25 .35
339 A119 300fr multi 2.00 .60

Operation Green Sahel.

Lemons — A120

Sigmund Freud — A121

1979, June 25 *Perf. 12½x13*

340 A120 10fr shown .25 .20
341 A120 60fr Pineapple .55 .20
342 A120 100fr Papayas .90 .20
343 A120 120fr Soursops 1.00 .20
344 A120 130fr Mangoes 1.10 .25
Nos. 340-344 (5) 3.80 1.05

1979, Sept. 17 Engr. *Perf. 13*

345 A121 300fr vio bl & sepia 1.75 .55

Sigmund Freud (1856-1939), founder of psychoanalysis.

Timbuktu, Man and Camel A122

Design: 130fr, Caillié, Map of Sahara.

1979, Sept. 27 *Perf. 13x12½*

346 A122 120fr multi .90 .25
347 A122 130fr multi 1.00 .30

René Caillié (1799-1838), French explorer, 180th birth anniversary.

Eurema Brigitta A123

1979, Oct. 15 Litho. *Perf. 13*

348 A123 100fr *shown* 1.60 .20
349 A123 120fr *Papilio pylades* 1.75 .25
350 A123 130fr *Melanitis leda satyridae* 2.25 .30
351 A123 180fr *Gonimbrasia belina occidentalis* 2.75 .40
352 A123 200fr *Bunaea alcinoe* 3.00 .45
Nos. 348-352 (5) 11.35 1.60

Greyhound A124

Designs: Dogs.

1979, Nov. 12 Litho. *Perf. 12½*

353 A124 20fr multi .35 .20
354 A124 50fr multi .45 .20
355 A124 70fr multi .55 .20
356 A124 80fr multi .65 .20
357 A124 90fr multi .70 .25
Nos. 353-357 (5) 2.70 1.05

Wild Donkey — A125

1980, Feb. 4 Litho. *Perf. 13x13½*

358 A125 90fr shown .70 .20
359 A125 120fr Addax .90 .20
360 A125 130fr Cheetahs 1.00 .25
361 A125 140fr Mouflon 1.00 .30
362 A125 180fr Buffalo 1.60 .30
Nos. 358-362 (5) 5.20 1.25

Photovoltaic Cell Pumping Station, Koni — A126

Solar Energy Utilization: 100fr, Sun shields, Dire. 120fr, Solar stove, Bamako. 130fr, Heliodynamic solar energy generating station, Dire.

1980, Mar. 10 Litho. *Perf. 13*

363 A126 90fr multi .45 .20
364 A126 100fr multi .55 .20
365 A126 120fr multi .65 .20
366 A126 130fr multi .80 .20
Nos. 363-366 (4) 2.45 .80

For surcharge see No. 511.

Horse Breeding, Mopti A127

1980, Mar. 17

367 A127 100fr shown .80 .20
368 A127 120fr Nioro .90 .20
369 A127 130fr Koro 1.00 .20
370 A127 180fr Coastal zone 1.25 .30
371 A127 200fr Banamba 1.25 .55
Nos. 367-371 (5) 5.20 1.45

Alexander Fleming (Discoverer of Penicillin) A128

1980, May 5 Engr. *Perf. 13*

372 A128 200fr multi 1.50 .45

Avicenna and Medical Instruments A129

Design: 180fr, Avicenna as teacher (12th century manuscript illustration)

1980, May 12 *Perf. 13x12½*

373 A129 120fr multi .60 .20
374 A129 180fr multi .75 .30

Avicenna (980-1037), Arab physician and philosopher, 1000th birth anniversary.

Pilgrim at Mecca — A130

Guavas — A131

1980, May 26 Litho. *Perf. 13*

375 A130 120fr shown .55 .20
376 A130 130fr Praying hands, stars, Mecca .55 .20
377 A130 180fr Pilgrims, camels, horiz. .80 .30
Nos. 375-377 (3) 1.90 .70

Hegira, 1500th Anniversary.

1980, June 9

378 A131 90fr shown .65 .20
379 A131 120fr Cashews .70 .20
380 A131 130fr Oranges .80 .20
381 A131 140fr Bananas 1.00 .25
382 A131 180fr Grapefruit 1.10 .30
Nos. 378-382 (5) 4.25 1.15

League of Nations, 60th Anniversary A132

1980, June 23 Engr. *Perf. 13*

383 A132 200fr multi .90 .30

Festival Emblem, Mask, Xylophone A133

1980, July 5 Litho. *Perf. 12½*

384 A133 120fr multi .60 .20

6th Biennial Arts and Cultural Festival, Bamako, July 5-15.

Sun Rising over Map of Africa — A134

1980, July 7 Engr. *Perf. 13*

385 A134 300fr multi 1.25 .45

Afro-Asian Bandung Conference, 25th anniversary.

Market Place, Conference Emblem A135

1980, Sept. 15 Litho. *Perf. 13*

386 A135 120fr View of Mali, vert. .65 .20
387 A135 180fr shown 1.00 .30

World Tourism Conf., Manila, Sept. 27.

Hydro-electric Dam and Power Station — A136

20th Anniversary of Independence: 120fr, Pres. Traore, flag of Mali, National Assembly building. 130fr, Independence monument, Bamako, Political Party badge, vert.

1980, Sept. 15 *Perf. 13x12½*

388 A136 100fr multi .55 .20
389 A136 120fr multi .70 .20
390 A136 130fr multi .90 .25
Nos. 388-390 (3) 2.15 .65

Utetheisa Pulchella A137

1980, Oct. 6 *Perf. 13½*

391 A137 50fr *shown* 1.10 .20
392 A137 60fr *Mylothis chloris pieridae* 1.25 .20
393 A137 70fr *Hypolimnas misippus* 1.40 .25
394 A137 80fr *Papilio demodocus* 1.75 .30
Nos. 391-394,C402 (5) 11.50 1.95

Fight Against Cigarette Smoking — A138

1980, Oct. 13 Litho. *Perf. 12½x12*

395 A138 200fr multi 1.25 .40

European-African Economic Convention — A139

1980, Oct. 20 *Perf. 12½*
396 A139 300fr multi 2.25 .55

Agricultural Map of West Africa A140

West African Economic Council, 5th anniversary (Economic Maps): 120fr, Transportation. 130fr, Industry. 140fr, Communications.

1980, Nov. 5 *Perf. 13½x13*
397 A140 100fr multi .55 .20
398 A140 120fr multi .65 .20
399 A140 130fr multi .70 .20
400 A140 140fr multi .80 .25
Nos. 397-400 (4) 2.70 .85

African Postal Union, 5th Anniv. — A141

Senuofo Fertility Statue — A142

1980, Dec. 24 Photo. *Perf. 13½*
401 A141 130fr multi .90 .25

1981, Jan. 12 Litho. *Perf. 13*
Designs: Fertility statues.
402 A142 60fr Nomo dogon .35 .20
403 A142 70fr shown .45 .20
404 A142 90fr Bamanan .65 .20
405 A142 100fr Spirit .70 .20
406 A142 120fr Dogon .90 .25
Nos. 402-406 (5) 3.05 1.05

Mambi Sidibe — A143

Hegira (Pilgrimage Year) — A144

Designs: Philosophers.

1981, Feb. 16 *Perf. 12½x13*
407 A143 120fr shown .70 .20
408 A143 130fr Amadou Hampate .70 .20

1981, Feb. 23 *Perf. 13*
409 A144 120fr multi .65 .20
410 A144 180fr multi 1.10 .30

Maure Zebu A145

Designs: Cattle breeds.

1981, Mar. 9 *Perf. 12½*
411 A145 20fr Kaarta zebu .70 .20
412 A145 30fr Peul du Macina zebu .85 .20
413 A145 40fr Maure zebu 1.10 .20
414 A145 80fr Touareg zebu 1.60 .25
415 A145 100fr N'Dama cow 1.75 .30
Nos. 411-415 (5) 6.00 1.15

See Nos. 433-437.

Hibiscus Double Rose — A146

Designs: Flowers.

1981, Mar. 16
416 A146 50fr Crinum de Moore .45 .20
417 A146 100fr Double Rose Hibiscus .90 .20
418 A146 120fr Pervenche 1.10 .20
419 A146 130fr Frangipani 1.25 .25
420 A146 180fr Orgueil de Chine 1.75 .45
Nos. 416-420 (5) 5.45 1.30

See Nos. 442-446.

Wrench Operated by Artificial Hand A147

Perf. 13x12½, 12x13

1981, May 4 Engr.
421 A147 100fr Heads, vert. .65 .20
422 A147 120fr shown .70 .20

Intl. Year of the Disabled.

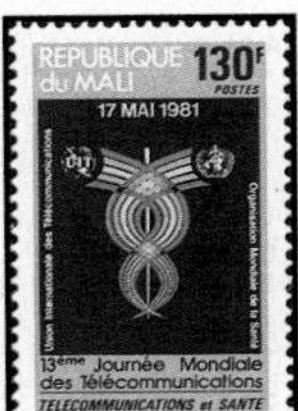

13th World Telecommunications Day — A148

1981, May 17 Litho. *Perf. 13x12½*
423 A148 130fr multi 1.00 .20

Pierre Curie, Lab Equipment A149

1981, May 25 Engr.
424 A149 180fr multi 2.25 .50

Curie (1859-1906), discoverer of radium.

Scouts at Water Hole — A150

1981, June 8 Litho. *Perf. 13*
425 A150 110fr shown 1.50 .25
426 A150 160fr Sending signals 2.25 .40
427 A150 300fr Salute, vert. 4.00 .60
Nos. 425-427 (3) 7.75 1.25

Souvenir Sheet

428 A150 500fr Lord Baden-Powell 8.50 5.00

4th African Scouting Conf., Abidjan, June.

Nos. 425-428 Overprinted in Red in 2 or 3 Lines: "DAKAR 8 AOUT 1981/28e CONFERENCE MONDIALE DU SCOUTISME"

1981, June 29
429 A150 110fr multi 1.50 .25
430 A150 160fr multi 2.25 .40
431 A150 300fr multi 4.00 .60
Nos. 429-431 (3) 7.75 1.25

Souvenir Sheet

432 A150 500fr multi 8.50 5.00

28th World Scouting Conf., Dakar, Aug. 8.

Cattle Type of 1981

Various goats.

1981, Sept. 14 Litho. *Perf. 13x13½*
433 A145 10fr Maure .25 .20
434 A145 25fr Peul .35 .20
435 A145 140fr Sahel 1.25 .20
436 A145 180fr Tuareg 1.60 .25
437 A145 200fr Djallonke 1.90 .30
Nos. 433-437 (5) 5.35 1.15

World UPU Day — A151

1981, Oct. 9 Engr. *Perf. 13*
438 A151 400fr multi 3.00 .60

World Food Day — A152

1981, Oct. 16
439 A152 200fr multi 1.50 .35

Europafrica Economic Convention — A153

1981, Nov. 23 Engr. *Perf. 13*
440 A153 700fr multi 4.00 .95

60th Anniv. of Tuberculosis Inoculation — A154

1981, Dec. 7 *Perf. 13x12½*
441 A154 200fr multi 1.50 .45

Flower Type of 1981

1982, Jan. 18 Litho. *Perf. 13*
442 A146 170fr White water lilies 1.10 .20
443 A146 180fr Red kapok bush 1.10 .20
444 A146 200fr Purple mimosa 1.40 .25
445 A146 220fr Pobego lilies 1.40 .35
446 A146 270fr Satan's chalices 1.75 .45
Nos. 442-446 (5) 6.75 1.45

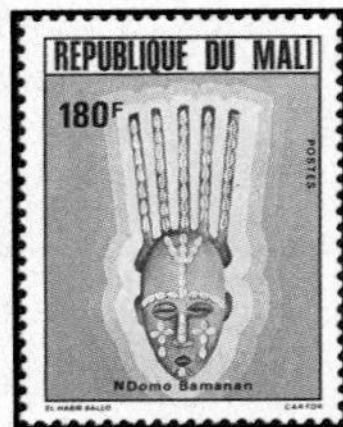

Ceremonial Mask — A155

25th Anniv. of Sputnik I Flight — A156

Designs: Various masks.

1982, Feb. 22 Litho. *Perf. 12½*
447 A155 5fr multi .20 .20
448 A155 35fr multi .30 .20
449 A155 180fr multi 1.25 .30
450 A155 200fr multi 1.40 .35
451 A155 250fr multi 1.75 .35
Nos. 447-451 (5) 4.90 1.40

1982, Mar. 29 Litho. *Perf. 13*
452 A156 270fr multi 1.60 .40

Fight Against Polio — A157

1982, May 3
453 A157 180fr multi 1.10 .30

Lions Intl. and Day of the Blind A158

1982, May 10 Engr.
454 A158 260fr multi 1.60 .25

"Good Friends" Hairstyle — A159

Designs: Various hairstyles.

1982, May 24 **Litho.**

455 A159 140fr multi .60 .20
456 A159 150fr multi .80 .20
457 A159 160fr multi 1.10 .30
458 A159 180fr multi 1.50 .30
459 A159 270fr multi 2.25 .55
Nos. 455-459 (5) 6.25 1.55

Zebu A160

Designs: Various breeds of zebu.

1982, July 5 ***Perf. 12½***

460 A160 10fr multi .45 .20
461 A160 60fr multi .90 .20
462 A160 110fr multi 1.25 .20
463 A160 180fr multi 2.00 .30
464 A160 200fr multi 2.25 .35
Nos. 460-464 (5) 6.85 1.25

Wind Surfing (New Olympic Class) — A161

Pres. John F. Kennedy — A162

Designs: Various wind surfers.

1982, Nov. 22 **Litho.** ***Perf. 12½x13***

465 A161 200fr multi 1.25 .30
466 A161 270fr multi 1.75 .45
467 A161 300fr multi 2.00 .55
Nos. 465-467 (3) 5.00 1.30

1983, Apr. 4 **Engr.** ***Perf. 13***

468 A162 800fr shown 4.25 1.10
469 A162 800fr Martin Luther King 4.25 1.10

Oua Traditional Hairstyle — A163

1983, Apr. 25 **Litho.**

470 A163 180fr shown 1.25 .20
471 A163 200fr Nation 1.40 .20
472 A163 270fr Rond point 1.75 .30
473 A163 300fr Naamu-Naamu 2.00 .35
474 A163 500fr Bamba-Bamba 3.50 .60
Nos. 470-474 (5) 9.90 1.65

World Communications Year — A164

1983, May 17 **Litho.** ***Perf. 13***

475 A164 180fr multi 1.25 .35

Bicent. of Lavoisier's Water Analysis — A165

Musicians — A166

1983, May 27 **Engr.** ***Perf. 13***

476 A165 300fr multi 1.75 .45

1983, June 13 **Litho.** ***Perf. 13x13½***

477 A166 200fr Banzoumana Sissoko 1.00 .20
478 A166 300fr Batourou Sekou Kouyate 1.60 .30

Nicephore Niepce, Photography Pioneer, (1765-1833) A167

1983, July 4 **Engr.** ***Perf. 13***

479 A167 400fr Portrait, early camera 2.25 .40

2nd Pan African Youth Festival — A168

Palestinian Solidarity A169

14th World UPU Day — A170

1983, Aug. 22 **Litho.** ***Perf. 12½***

480 A168 240fr multi 1.50 .25
481 A169 270fr multi 1.75 .35

1983, Oct. 10 **Engr.** ***Perf. 12½***

482 A170 240fr multi 1.50 .30

For surcharge see No. 500.

Sahel Goat A171

1984, Jan. 30 **Litho.** ***Perf. 13***

483 A171 20fr shown .25 .20
484 A171 30fr Billy goat .45 .20
485 A171 50fr Billy goat, diff. .70 .20
486 A171 240fr Kaarta goat 2.25 .30
487 A171 350fr Southern goats 3.25 .45
Nos. 483-487 (5) 6.90 1.35

For surcharges see Nos. 497-499, 501-502.

Rural Development A172

Fragrant Trees A173

1984, June 1 **Litho.** ***Perf. 13***

488 A172 5fr Crop disease prevention .25 .20
489 A172 90fr Carpenters, horiz. 1.00 .20
490 A172 100fr Tapestry weaving, horiz. 1.10 .25
491 A172 135fr Metal workers, horiz. 1.40 .40
Nos. 488-491 (4) 3.75 1.05

1984, June 1

492 A173 515fr Borassus flabelifer 5.00 1.75
493 A173 1225fr Vitelaria paradoxa 12.00 3.50

For surcharge see No. 583.

UN Infant Survival Campaign — A174

1984, June 12 **Engr.**

494 A174 120fr Child, hearts 1.50 .35
495 A174 135fr Children 1.75 .40

1984 UPU Congress — A175

1984, June 18

496 A175 135fr Anchor, UPU emblem, view of Hamburg 1.60 .35

Nos. 482-487 Surcharged

1984

497 A171 10fr on 20fr #483 .30 .20
498 A171 15fr on 30fr #484 .30 .20
499 A171 25fr on 50fr #485 .40 .20
500 A170 120fr on 240fr #482 1.60 .30
501 A171 120fr on 240fr #486 2.00 .30
502 A171 175fr on 350fr #487 2.75 .50
Nos. 497-502 (6) 7.35 1.70

West African Economic Community, CEAO, 10th Anniv. A176

1984, Oct. 22 **Litho.** ***Perf. 13½***

503 A176 350fr multi 3.50 1.75

For surcharge see No. 588.

Prehistoric Animals A177

1984, Nov. 5 **Litho.** ***Perf. 12½***

504 A177 10fr Dimetrodon .25 .20
505 A177 25fr Iguanodon, vert. .55 .20
506 A177 30fr Archaeopteryx, vert. .80 .20
507 A177 120fr Like 10fr 2.50 .40
508 A177 175fr Like 25fr 4.00 .60
509 A177 350fr Like 30fr 7.50 1.50
510 A177 470fr Triceratops 11.00 4.00
Nos. 504-510 (7) 26.60 7.10

For surcharges see Nos. 579, 593.

No. 366 Overprinted "Aide au Sahel 84" and Surcharged

1984 **Litho.** ***Perf. 13***

511 A126 470fr on 130fr 6.00 2.00

Issued to publicize drought relief efforts.

Mali Horses A178

1985, Jan. 21 **Litho.** ***Perf. 13½***

512 A178 90fr Modern horse 1.25 .30
513 A178 135fr Horse from Beledougou 1.75 .40
514 A178 190fr Horse from Nara 2.75 .60
515 A178 530fr Horse from Trait 7.75 1.75
Nos. 512-515 (4) 13.50 3.05

For surcharges see Nos. 586, 591.

Fungi — A179

1985, Jan. 28 Litho. *Perf. 12½*

516 A179 120fr Clitocybe nebularis 1.60 .90
517 A179 200fr Lepiota cortinarius 2.50 .90
518 A179 485fr Agavicus semotus 6.75 1.60
519 A179 525fr Lepiota procera 7.00 1.60
Nos. 516-519 (4) 17.85 5.00

For surcharges see Nos. 589-590.

Health — A180

Designs: 120fr, 32nd World Leprosy Day, Emile Marchoux (1862-1943), Marchoux Institute, 150th anniv. 135fr, Lions Intl., Samanko Convalescence Village, 15th anniv. 470fr, Anti-polio campaign, research facility, victim.

1985, Feb. 18 Litho. *Perf. 13*

520 A180 120fr multi 1.50 .35
521 A180 135fr multi 1.75 .40
522 A180 470fr multi 5.00 1.50
Nos. 520-522 (3) 8.25 2.25

For surcharges see Nos. 580, 584. No. 522 is airmail.

Cultural and Technical Cooperation Agency, 15th Anniv. — A181

1985, Mar. 20

523 A181 540fr brn & brt bl grn 5.25 1.50

Intl. Youth Year A182

Youth activities.

1985, May 13 *Perf. 12½x13*

524 A182 120fr Natl. Pioneers Movement emblem 1.00 .40
525 A182 190fr Agricultural production 2.00 .60
526 A182 500fr Sports 5.00 1.50
Nos. 524-526 (3) 8.00 2.50

For surcharge see No. 587.

PHILEXAFRICA '85, Lome, Togo — A183

1985, June 24 *Perf. 13*

527 A183 250fr Education, telecommunications 2.75 2.00
528 A183 250fr Road, dam, computers 2.75 2.00
a. Pair, #527-528 7.50 2.75
Nos. 527-528,C517-C518 (4) 10.00 6.20

Nos. 527-528 show the UPU emblem.

Cats A184

1986, Feb. 15 Litho. *Perf. 13½*

529 A184 150fr Gray 2.75 .50
530 A184 200fr White 3.75 .75
531 A184 300fr Tabby 4.50 1.00
Nos. 529-531 (3) 11.00 2.25

For surcharge see No. 582.

Fight Against Apartheid — A185

1986, Feb. 24 *Perf. 13*

532 A185 100fr shown 1.50 .30
533 A185 120fr Map, broken chain 1.60 .40

Telecommunications and Agriculture — A186

1986, May 17 Litho. *Perf. 13*

534 A186 200fr multi 2.50 .60

1986 World Cup Soccer Championships, Mexico — A187

Various soccer plays.

1986, May 24 Litho. *Perf. 12½*

535 A187 160fr multi 1.50 .45
536 A187 225fr multi 2.50 .65

Souvenir Sheet

537 A187 500fr multi 5.25 2.25

For overprints surcharges see #539-541, 585.

James Watt (1736-1819), Inventor, and Steam Engine — A188

1986, May 26 *Perf. 12½x12*

538 A188 110fr multi 2.00 .35

For surcharge see No. 581.

Nos. 535-537 Ovptd. "ARGENTINE 3 / R.F.A. 2" in Red

1986, July 30 Litho. *Perf. 12½*

539 A187 160fr multi 2.25 .60
540 A187 225fr multi 3.50 .80

Souvenir Sheet

541 A187 500fr multi 6.50 2.50

World Wildlife Fund — A189

Derby's Eland, Taurotragus derbianus.

1986, Aug. 11 Litho. *Perf. 13*

542 A189 5fr Adult head 2.00 .25
543 A189 20fr Adult in brush 3.75 .25
544 A189 25fr Adult walking 3.75 .25
545 A189 200fr Calf suckling 30.00 4.00
Nos. 542-545 (4) 39.50 4.75

Henry Ford (1863-1947), Auto Manufacturer, Inventor of Mass Production — A190

1987, Feb. 16 Litho. *Perf. 13*

546 A190 150fr Model A, 1903 2.10 .45
547 A190 200fr Model T, 1923 2.75 .90
548 A190 225fr Thunderbird, 1968 3.00 1.00
549 A190 300fr Lincoln Continental, 1963 3.25 1.10
Nos. 546-549 (4) 11.10 3.45

Bees A191

1987, May 11 Litho. *Perf. 13½*

550 A191 100fr Apis florea, Asia 2.00 .50
551 A191 150fr Apis dorsata, Asia 2.40 .60
552 A191 175fr Apis adansonii, Africa 2.50 .75
553 A191 200fr Apis mellifica, worldwide 2.75 .90
Nos. 550-553 (4) 9.65 2.75

Lions Club Activities — A192

1988, Jan. 13 Litho. *Perf. 12½*

554 A192 200fr multi 2.50 .85

World Health Organization, 40th Anniv. — A193

1988, Feb. 22 Litho. *Perf. 12½x12*

555 A193 150fr multi 1.60 .55

For surcharge see No. 557.

John F. Kennedy (1917-1963), 35th US President A194

1988, June 6 Litho. *Perf. 13*

556 A194 640fr multi 6.25 2.50

For surcharge see No. 592.

No. 555 Surcharged in Dark Red

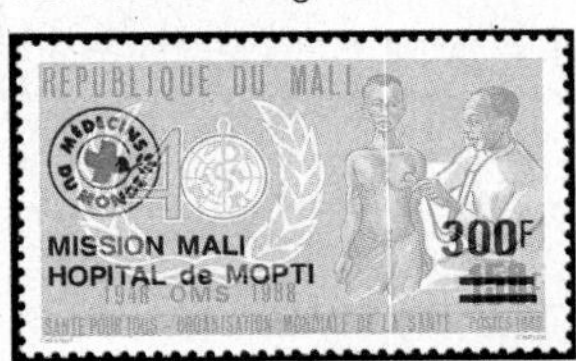

1988, June 13 *Perf. 12½x12*

557 A193 300fr on 150fr multi 3.00 1.40

Mali Mission Hospital in Mopti and World Medicine organization.

Organization of African Unity, 25th Anniv. — A194a

1988, June 27 Litho. *Perf. 12½*

558 A194a 400fr multi 3.75 1.60

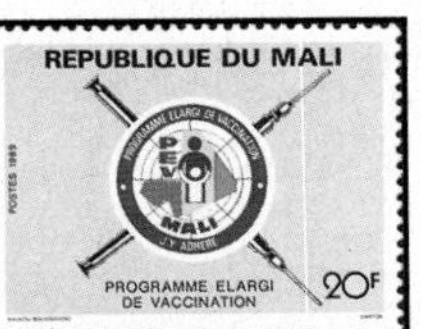

Universal Immunization Campaign — A195

1989, May 2 Litho. *Perf. 13½*

559 A195 20fr shown .25 .20
560 A195 30fr Inoculating woman .35 .20
561 A195 50fr Emblem, needles, diff. .55 .20
562 A195 175fr Inoculating boy 1.90 .80
Nos. 559-562 (4) 3.05 1.40

Intl. Law Institute of the French-Speaking Nations — A196

1989, May 15 *Perf. 12½*

563 A196 150fr multi 1.60 .60
564 A196 200fr multi 2.00 .80

World Post Day — A197

1989, Oct. 9 Litho. *Perf. 13*

565 A197 625fr multicolored 7.25 3.00

For surcharge see No. 594.

Visit of Pope John Paul II — A198

1990, Jan. 28 Litho. *Perf. 13x12½*

566 A198 200fr multicolored 3.00 .90

Multinational Postal School, 20th Anniv. — A199

1990, May 31 Litho. *Perf. 12½*

567 A199 150fr multicolored 1.60 .65

Independence, 30th Anniv. — A200

1990, Sept. 20 Litho. *Perf. 13x12½*

568 A200 400fr multicolored 4.25 1.75

Intl. Literacy Year A201

1990, Sept. 24 Litho. *Perf. 13½*

569 A201 150fr grn & multi 1.40 .65
570 A201 200fr org & multi 2.10 .90

A202

A203

Lions Intl. Water Project, 6th anniv.: No. 572, Rotary Club fight against polio, 30th anniv.

1991, Feb. 25 Litho. *Perf. 13x12½*

571 A202 200fr multicolored 2.25 1.00
572 A202 200fr multicolored 2.25 1.00

1991, Apr. 29 Litho. *Perf. 12½*

Designs: Tribal dances of Mali.

573 A203 50fr Takamba .55 .30
574 A203 100fr Mandiani 1.00 .60
575 A203 150fr Kono 1.60 .90
576 A203 200fr Songho 2.10 1.10
Nos. 573-576 (4) 5.25 2.90

A204

A205

1991, Dec. 2 Litho. *Perf. 12½*

577 A204 200fr multicolored 2.00 1.00

Central Fund for Economic Cooperation, 50th anniv.

1992, Mar. 26 Litho. *Perf. 12½*

578 A205 150fr multicolored 1.60 .75

National Women's Movement.

Various Stamps of 1984-89 Surcharged in Black or Black and Silver

1992, June Litho. *Perfs. as Before*

579 A177 25fr on 470fr #510 .40 .20
580 A180 25fr on 470fr #522 .40 .20
581 A188 30fr on 110fr #538 .50 .20
582 A184 50fr on 300fr #531 .80 .20
583 A173 50fr on 1225fr #493 .80 .20
584 A180 150fr on 135fr #521 (Bk & S) 2.50 .60
585 A187 150fr on 160fr #535 2.50 .60
586 A178 150fr on 190fr #514 2.50 .60
587 A182 150fr on 190fr #525 2.50 .60
588 A176 150fr on 350fr #503 2.50 .60
589 A179 150fr on 485fr #518 2.50 .60
590 A179 150fr on 525fr #519 2.50 .60
591 A178 150fr on 530fr #515 2.50 .60
592 A194 200fr on 640fr #556 3.25 .80
593 A177 240fr on 350fr #509 3.75 1.00
594 A197 240fr on 625fr #565 3.75 1.00
Nos. 579-594 (16) 33.65 8.60

No. 580 is airmail. Size and location of surcharge varies. No. 585 also overprinted "Euro '92."

New Constitution, 1st Anniv. — A205a

1993, Jan. 12 Litho. *Perf. 11½x12*

594A A205a 150fr multi *45.00*
594B A205a 225fr multi *65.00*

Martyr's Day, 2nd Anniv. — A206

1993, Mar. 26 Litho. *Perf. 11½*

595 A206 150fr blue & multi 55.00 55.00
596 A206 160fr yellow & multi 55.00 55.00

Rotary Intl. and World Health Organization (WHO) — A206a

Designs: 150fr, Polio victims, Rotary emblem. 200fr, WHO emblem, pregnant woman receiving vaccination.

1993, Apr. 16 Litho. *Perf. 14*

596A A206a 150fr multi *45.00*
596B A206a 200fr multi *65.00*

Lions Club in Mali, 35th Anniv. A207

1993, Dec. 20 Litho. *Perf. 14½*

597 A207 200fr blue & multi 55.00 55.00
598 A207 225fr red & multi 55.00 55.00

Monument, Liberty Place — A207a

1993, Dec. 20 Photo. *Perf. 11¾*
Granite Paper

598A A207a 20fr multicolored
598B A207a 25fr multicolored
598C A207a 50fr multi
598D A207a 100fr multicolored
598E A207a 110fr multicolored
598F A207a 150fr multicolored
598G A207a 200fr multicolored
598H A207a 225fr multicolored
598I A207a 240fr multicolored
598J A207a 260fr multicolored

1994 Winter Olympics, Lillehammer A208

1994, Feb. 12 Litho. *Perf. 13*

599 A208 150fr Pairs figure skating .90 .50
600 A208 200fr Giant slalom 1.25 .75
601 A208 225fr Ski jumping 1.75 1.00
602 A208 750fr Speed skating 3.00 1.75
Nos. 599-602 (4) 6.90 4.00

Souvenir Sheet

603 A208 2000fr Downhill skiing 9.00 9.00

No. 603 contains one 36x36mm stamp.
For overprints see Nos. 671-676.

1994 World Cup Soccer Championships, US — A209

Designs: 200fr, Juan Schiaffino, Uruguay. 240fr, Diego Maradona, Argentina. 260fr, Paolo Rossi, Italy. 1000fr, Franz Beckenbauer, Germany. 2000fr, Just Fontaine, France.

1994, Mar. 15 Litho. *Perf. 13*

604 A209 200fr multicolored .90 .90
605 A209 240fr multicolored 1.40 .80
606 A209 260fr multicolored 1.60 .90
607 A209 1000fr multicolored 5.00 2.75
Nos. 604-607 (4) 8.90 5.35

Souvenir Sheet

608 A209 2000fr multicolored 9.00 9.00

For overprints see Nos. 677-681.

Miniature Sheet

Dinosaurs A210

a, 5fr, Scaphonyx. b, 10fr, Cynognathus. c, 15fr, Lesothosaurus. d, 20fr, Scutellosaurus. e, 25fr, Ceratosaurus. f, 30fr, Dilophosaurus.

g, 40fr, Dryosaurus. h, 50fr, Heterodontosaurus. i, 60fr, Anatosaurus. j, 70fr, Saurornithoides. k, 80fr, Avimimus. l, 90fr, Saltasaurus. m, 300fr, Dromaeosaurus. n, 400fr, Tsintaosaurus. o, 600fr, Velociraptor. p, 700fr, Ouranosaurus.
2000fr, Daspletosaurus, iguanodon.

1994, Mar. 28

609	A210	Sheet of 16, #a.-p.	15.00	8.00

Souvenir Sheet

610	A210	2000fr multicolored	12.00	12.00

Insects
A211

Designs: 40fr, Sternuera castanea, vert. 50fr, Eudicella gralli. 100fr, Homoderus mellyi, vert. 200fr, Kraussaria angulifera.

1994, Mar. 30 Litho. *Perf. 13*

611	A211	40fr multicolored	.40	.20
612	A211	50fr multicolored	.70	.35
613	A211	100fr multicolored	1.10	.60
614	A211	200fr multicolored	2.00	1.00
		Nos. 611-614 (4)	4.20	2.15

Vaccination Campaign Against Measles — A212

1994, Apr. 7 Litho. *Perf. 13½*

615	A212	150fr black & green	.90	.50
616	A212	200fr black & blue	1.60	.90

Birds
A213

1994, Apr. 25

617	A213	25fr Pigeons	.30	.20
618	A213	30fr Turkeys	.30	.20
619	A213	150fr Crowned cranes, vert.	1.40	.70
620	A213	200fr Chickens, vert.	1.50	.80
		Nos. 617-620 (4)	3.50	1.90

Intl. Year of the Family — A213a

1994, May 2

620A	A213a	220fr multicolored	1.25	.60

Jazz
Musicians
A214

1994, May 23 Litho. *Perf. 13*

621	A214	200fr Ella Fitzgerald	.80	.60
622	A214	225fr Lionel Hampton	1.00	.70
623	A214	240fr Sarah Vaughan	1.25	.85
624	A214	300fr Count Basie	1.75	1.25
625	A214	400fr Duke Ellington	2.25	1.50
626	A214	600fr Miles Davis	3.00	2.00
		Nos. 621-626 (6)	10.05	6.90

Souvenir Sheet

627	A214	1500fr Louis Armstrong	8.00	8.00

No. 627 contains one 45x45mm stamp.

Ancient Art — A215

#628-637: 15fr, Venus of Brassempoury, vert. 25fr, Petroglyphs, Tanum, vert. 45fr, Prehistoric cave drawings, vert. 50fr, Cave paintaings, Lascaux. 55fr, Tomb of Amonherkhopeshef, vert. 65fr, Goddess Anubis and the pharaoh. 75fr, Sphinx. 85fr, Bust of Nefertiti, vert. 95fr, Statue of Shibum, vert. 100fr, Standard of Ur. 130fr, Mesopotamian bull's head harp, vert.
#638-647: 135fr, Mesopotamian scroll. 140fr, Assyrian dignitary, vert. 180fr, Enameled horse, Babylon. 190fr, Assyrian carving of hunters, vert. 200fr, Mona Lisa of Nimrud, vert. 225fr, Carthaginian coin. 250fr, Phoenician sphinx, vert. 275fr, Persian archer, vert. 280fr, Ceramic and glass mask, vert.

1994, Aug. 24 Litho. *Perf. 13½*

628-647	A215	Set of 20	15.00	15.00

D-Day Landings, Normandy, 50th Anniv. — A216

Villiers-Bocage, June 12: No. 648a, Explosion, men being killed. b, Tank firing. c, Tank, men with weapons.
Beaumont-Sur-Sarthe, June 6: No. 649a, Explosion, airplanes. b, British airplanes, tanks. c, German tanks, soldier firing machine gun.
Utah Beach, June 6: No. 650a, Explosion, bow of landing craft. b, Stern of landing craft, soldiers. c, Landing craft filled with troops.
Aerial battle: No. 651a, British planes dropping bombs. b, British, German planes. c, British, German planes, explosion.
Sainte-Mere-Eglise, June 5: No. 652a, German troops firing on paratroopers. b, Church tower. c, Paratroopers, German troops.

1994, June 6

Strips of 3

648	A216	200fr #a.-c.	3.25	1.75
649	A216	300fr #a.-c.	4.00	2.25
650	A216	300fr #a.-c.	4.00	2.25
651	A216	400fr #a.-c.	5.25	3.00
652	A216	400fr #a.-c.	5.25	3.00
		Nos. 648-652 (5)	21.75	12.25

Nos. 648-652 are each continuous designs. Nos. 648b, 649b, 650b, 651b, 652b are each 30x47mm.

Orchids,
Vegetables, &
Mushrooms
A217

Orchids: 25fr, Disa kewensis. 50fr, Angraecum eburneum. 100fr, Ansellia africana.
Vegetables: 140fr, Sorghum. 150fr, Onions. 190fr, Corn.
Mushrooms: 200fr, Lepiota (clitocybe) nebularis. 225fr, Macrolepiota (lepiota) procera. 500fr, Lepiota aspera.

1994, Sept. 12

653	A217	25fr multicolored	.20	.20
654	A217	50fr multicolored	.35	.20
655	A217	100fr multicolored	.65	.35
a.		Souvenir sheet of 3, #653-655	*11.00*	*7.50*
656	A217	140fr multicolored	.70	.40
657	A217	150fr multicolored	.80	.45
658	A217	190fr multicolored	1.00	.60
a.		Souvenir sheet of 3, #656-658	*11.00*	*7.50*
659	A217	200fr multicolored	1.10	.65
660	A217	225fr multicolored	1.25	.75
661	A217	500fr multicolored	2.75	1.50
a.		Souvenir sheet of 3, #659-661	*11.00*	*7.50*
		Nos. 653-661 (9)	8.80	5.10

Moths,
Butterflies &
Insects
A218

Designs: 20fr, Polyptychus roseus. 30fr, Elymniopsis bammakoo. 40fr, Deilephila nerii. 150fr, Utetheisa pulchella. 180fr, Charaxes jasius. 200fr, Mylothris chloris.
Insects: 225fr, Goliath beetle. 240fr, Locust. 350fr, Praying mantis.

1994, Sept. 12

662	A218	20fr multicolored	.20	.20
663	A218	30fr multicolored	.20	.20
664	A218	40fr multicolored	.20	.20
665	A218	150fr multicolored	.90	.50
666	A218	180fr multicolored	1.00	.55
667	A218	200fr multicolored	1.00	.60
a.		Souv. sheet of 6, #662-667	*22.50*	*12.50*
668	A218	225fr multicolored	1.10	.65
669	A218	240fr multicolored	1.25	.70
670	A218	350fr multicolored	1.60	.90
a.		Souv. sheet of 3, #668-670	*11.00*	*6.50*
		Nos. 662-670 (9)	7.45	4.50

Nos. 599-603 Ovptd. in Silver or Gold with Name of Olympic Medalist, Country

Overprints in silver: No. 671a, "Y. GORDEYEVA / S. GRINKOV / RUSSIE." No. 671b, "O. GRISHCHUK / Y. PLATOV / RUSSIE." No. 672a, "D. COMPAGNONI / ITALIE." No. 672b, "M. WASMEIER / ALLEMAGNE." No. 673a, "E. BREDESEN /NORVEGE." No. 673b, "J. WEISSFLOG / ALLEMAGNE." No. 674a, "B. BLAIR, U.S.A." No. 674b, "J.O. KOSS / NORVEGE."
Overprint in gold: No. 675, "L. KJUS / NORVEGE." No. 676, "P. WIBERG / SUEDE."

1994, Sept. 12 Litho. *Perf. 13*

671	A208	150fr Pair, #a.-b.	1.75	1.00
672	A208	200fr Pair, #a.-b.	2.75	1.50
673	A208	225fr Pair, #a.-b.	3.50	2.00
674	A208	750fr Pair, #a.-b.	10.00	5.50
		Nos. 671-674 (4)	18.00	10.00

Souvenir Sheet

675	A208	2000fr multicolored	9.00	5.00
676	A208	2000fr multicolored	9.00	5.00

Nos. 604-608 Ovptd. in Metallic Red

1994, Sept. 15 Litho. *Perf. 13*

677	A209	200fr multicolored	.90	.50
678	A209	240fr multicolored	1.25	.70
679	A209	260fr multicolored	1.40	.80
680	A209	1000fr multicolored	5.25	3.00
		Nos. 677-680 (4)	8.80	5.00

Souvenir Sheet

681	A209	2000fr multicolored	9.00	5.00

Intl. Olympic Committee, Cent. — A218a

1994, June 23 Litho. *Perf. 13½*

681A	A218a	150fr multicolored	1.10	.60
681B	A218a	200fr multicolored	1.60	.90

Exist in imperf souvenir sheets of 1.

Intl. Olympic Committee, Cent. — A219

Pierre de Coubertin and: 225fr, Woman carrying flame, vert. 240fr, Olympic rings, vert. 300fr, Torch bearer. 500fr, Gold medal of Olympic rings.
600fr, Flame, statue of flag bearer.

1994, June 23 *Perf. 13½*

682	A219	225fr multicolored	.90	.50
683	A219	240fr multicolored	1.00	.60
684	A219	300fr multicolored	1.60	.90
685	A219	500fr multicolored	2.75	1.50
		Nos. 682-685 (4)	6.25	3.50

Souvenir Sheet

686	A219	600fr multicolored	3.50	2.00

Anniversaries
& Events
A220

Designs: 150fr, Erst Julius Opik, Galileo probe, impact of comet on Jupiter. 200fr, Clyde Tombaugh, probe moving toward Pluto. 500fr, Intl. Red Cross, Henri Dunant. 650fr, Crew of Apollo 11, 1st manned moon landing. 700fr, Lions Intl., Rotary Intl. 800fr, Gary Kasparov chess champion.

1994, Apr. 10 Litho. *Perf. 13½*

687	A220	150fr multicolored	.60	.30
688	A220	200fr multicolored	.90	.45
689	A220	500fr multicolored	2.25	1.10
690	A220	650fr multicolored	2.75	1.40
691	A220	700fr multicolored	3.00	1.50
692	A220	800fr multicolored	3.50	1.75
		Nos. 687-692 (6)	13.00	6.50

Nos. 687-692 exist in souvenir sheets of 1.

Motion Picture, Cent. — A221

Movie star, movie: 100fr, Kirk Douglas, Spartacus. 150fr, Elizabeth Taylor, Cleopatra. 200fr, Clint Eastwood, Sierra Torrid. 225fr, Marilyn Monroe, The River of No Return. 500fr, Arnold Schwarzenegger, Conan the Barbarian. 1000fr, Elvis Presley, Loving You. 1500fr, Charlton Heston, The Ten Commandments.

1994, May 23 Litho. *Perf. 13½*
693-698 A221 Set of 6 16.00 8.75

Souvenir Sheet

699 A221 1500fr multicolored 8.25 4.50

No. 695 is airmail.

Fight Against AIDS A222

Designs: 150fr, Woman, man holding condoms. 225fr, Nurse with AIDS patient, researcher looking into microscope.

1994, June 30
700 A222 150fr multicolored 1.10 .60
701 A222 225fr multicolored 1.60 .90

Tourism A223

Designs: 150fr, Traditional buildings, statue, vert. 200fr, Sphinx, pyramids, ruins.

1994, Dec. 5
702 A223 150fr multicolored 1.10 .60
703 A223 200fr multicolored 1.60 .90

1996 Summer Olympics, Atlanta — A224

Designs: 25fr, Reiner Klimke, dressage. 50fr, Kristin Otto, swimming. 100fr, Hans-Gunther Winkler, equestrian. 150fr, Birgit Fischer-Schmidt, kayak. 200fr, Nicole Uphoff, dressage, vert. 225fr, Renate Stecher, track, vert. 230fr, Michael Gross, swimming. 240fr, Karin Janz, gymnastics. 550fr, Anja Fichtel, fencing, vert. 700fr, Heide Rosendahl-Ecker, track, vert.

1995, Mar. 27
704-713 A224 Set of 10 12.50 7.00

Dated 1994.

Rotary Intl., 90th Anniv. — A225

1995, Oct. 18 Litho. *Perf. 14*
714 A225 1000fr Paul Harris, logo 6.50 3.50

Souvenir Sheet

715 A225 1500fr 1905, 1995 Logos 8.00 4.50

Miniature Sheets

Birds, Butterflies — A226

No. 716: a, Campephilos imperialis. b, Momotus momota. c, Ramphastos sulfuratus. d, Halcyon malimbica. e, Trochilus polytmus. f, Cardinalis cardinalis. g, Pharomachrus mocinno. h, Aratinga solstitialis. i, Amazona arausiaca. j, Eudocimus ruber. k, Carduelis cucullatus. l, Anodorhynchus hyacinthinus. m, Passerina leclancherii. n, Pipra mentalis. o, Rupicola rupicola. p, Sicalis flaveola.

No. 717: a, Carito niger. b, Chloroceryle amazona. c, Tersina virdis. d, Momotus momota. e, Campephilus menaloleucos. f, Leistes militaris. g, Sarcoramphus papa. h, Pilherodius pileatus. i, Tityra cayana. j, Tangara chilinsis. k, Amazona ochrocephala. l, Saltator maximus. m, Paroaria dominicana. n, Egretta tricolor. o, Piaya melano gaster. p, Thamnophilus doliatus.

No. 718: a, Paradise whydah (g). b, Red-necked francolin. c, Whale-headed stork (i). d, Ruff (j). e, Marabou stork (k). f, White pelican. g, Western curlew. h, Scarlet ibis. i, Great crested crebe. j, White spoonbill. k, African jacana. l, African pygmy goose.

No. 719: a, Ruby-throated hummingbird. b, Grape shoemaker, blue morpho butterflies. c, Northern hobby. d, Cuvier toucan (g). e, Black-necked red cotinga (h). f, Green-winged macaws (i). g, Flamingo (j). h, Malachite kingfisher. i, Bushy-crested hornbill (l). j, Purple swamphen (k). k, Striped body (j, l). l, Painted lady butterfly.

Each 1000fr: No. 720, Topaza pella. No. 721, Sporophila lineola.

1995, Oct. 20 Litho. *Perf. 14*

Sheets of 16 & 12

716 A226 50fr #a.-p. 6.50 3.50
717 A226 100fr #a.-p. 11.00 6.00
718 A226 150fr #a.-l. 12.00 6.50
719 A226 200fr #a.-l. 16.00 8.50
Nos. 716-719 (4) 45.50 24.50

Souvenir Sheets

720-721 A226 Set of 2 12.00 6.75

John Lennon (1940-80) A227

1995 Litho. *Perf. 14*
722 A227 150fr multicolored 1.25 .70

No. 722 was issued in sheets of 16.

Miniature Sheets

Motion Pictures, Cent. A228

Western actors: No. 723:a, Justus D. Barnes (misidentified as George Barnes). b, William S. Hart. c, Tom Mix. d, Wallace Beery. e, Gary Cooper. f, John Wayne.

Actresses and their directors: No. 724: a, Marlene Dietrich, Josef Von Sternberg. b, Jean Harlow, George Cukor. c, Mary Astor, John Huston (Houston on stamp). d, Ingrid Bergman, Alfred Hitchcock. e, Claudette Colbert, Cecil B. De Mille. f, Marilyn Monroe, Billy Wilder.

Musicals and their stars: No. 725: a, Singin' in the Rain, Gene Kelly. b, The Bandwagon, Anne Miller, Ray Bolger. c, Cabaret, Liza Minnelli, Joel Gray. d, The Sound of Music, Julie Andrews. e, Top Hat, Ginger Rogers, Fred Astaire. f, Saturday Night Fever, John Travolta.

Each 1000fr: No. 726, Robert Redford as the Sundance Kid. No. 727, Liv Ullman, actress, Ingmar Bergman, director. No. 728, Judy Garland in the Wizard of Oz.

1995, Dec. 8 Litho. *Perf. 13½x14*

Sheets of 6

723 A228 150fr #a.-f. 5.25 3.00
724 A228 200fr #a.-f. 7.25 4.00
725 A228 240fr #a.-f. 9.00 5.00
Nos. 723-725 (3) 21.50 12.00

Souvenir Sheets

726-728 A228 Set of 3 16.00 9.00

Nos. 723-728 have various styles of lettering.

Miniature Sheet

Stars of Rock and Roll — A229

No. 729: a, Connie Francis. b, The Ronettes. c, Janis Joplin. d, Debbie Harry of Blondie. e, Cyndi Lauper. f, Carly Simon.

No. 730, Bette Midler.

1995, Dec. 8
729 A229 225fr Sheet of 6, #a.-f. 8.00 4.50

Souvenir Sheet

730 A229 1000fr multicolored 5.25 3.00

Traditional Cooking Utensils A230

5fr, Canaris, vert. 50fr, Mortier, calebasse, vert. 150fr, Fourneau. 200fr, Vans, vert. 500fr, Vans.

1995, Nov. 20 Litho. *Perf. 14*
731-734 A230 Set of 4 2.75 1.50

Souvenir Sheet

735 A230 500fr multicolored 3.00 1.75

18th World Scout Jamboree, Holland — A231

Scout examining butterfly or mushroom: 150fr, Saturnia pyri. 225fr, Gonepteryx rhamni. 240fr, Myrina silenus. 500fr, Clitocybe nebularis. 650fr, Agaricus semotus. 725fr, Lepiota procera.
1500fr, Morpho cypris.

1995, Aug. 1 Litho. *Perf. 13½*
736-741 A231 Set of 6 11.50 5.75

Souvenir Sheet

742 A231 1500fr multicolored 9.25 4.50

Nos. 736-741 exist in souvenir sheets of 1.

UN, 50th Anniv. A232

Designs: 20fr, 170fr, UN emblem, scales of justice, doves, vert. 225fr, 240fr, Doves, UN emblem, four men of different races.

1995, Oct. 24 Litho. *Perf. 13*
743 A232 20fr light blue & multi .20 .20
744 A232 170fr light grn & multi 1.00 .55
745 A232 225fr light pur & multi 1.25 .55
746 A232 240fr light org & multi 1.50 .85
Nos. 743-746 (4) 3.95 2.15

Ayrton Senna (1960-94), F-1 Race Car Driver — A233

1000fr, Jerry Garcia (1942-95), entertainer.

1995 *Perf. 13½*
747 A233 500fr multicolored 2.25 1.10
748 A233 1000fr multicolored 4.50 2.25

Nos. 747-748 exist in souvenir sheets of one.

1945-49 Greenland Expeditions of Paul Emile Victor — A234

1995
749 A234 150fr Charles de Gaulle .70 .35
750 A234 200fr De Gaulle, liberation of Paris .90 .45
751 A234 240fr Enzo Ferrari 1.10 .55
752 A234 650fr multicolored 3.00 1.50
753 A234 725fr Paul Harris 3.25 1.60
754 A234 740fr Michael Schumacher 3.50 1.75
Nos. 749-754 (6) 12.45 6.20

Nos. 749-754 exist in souvenir sheets of 1.

A235

A236

Designs: 150fr, Second election party emblems, horiz. 200fr, Pres. Alpha Oumar Konare. 225fr, First election party emblems, horiz. 240fr, Natl. flag, map, party representations.

1995 Litho. *Perf. 13½*

755 A235 150fr multicolored	.70	.35
756 A235 200fr multicolored	.90	.45
757 A235 225fr multicolored	1.00	.50
758 A235 240fr multicolored	1.10	.55
Nos. 755-758 (4)	3.70	1.85

Second Presidential elections.

1995

Economic Community of West African States (ECOWAS): 150fr, Regional integration, horiz. 200fr, Cooperation. 220fr, Prospect of creating one currency, horiz. 225fr, Peace and security, horiz.

759 A236 150fr multicolored	.70	.35
760 A236 200fr multicolored	.90	.45
761 A236 220fr multicolored	1.00	.50
762 A236 225fr multicolored	1.00	.50
Nos. 759-762 (4)	3.60	1.80

Mushrooms — A237

Genus Russula: No. 763: a, Emetica. b, Laurocerasi. c, Rosacea. d, Occidentalis. e, Fragilis. f, Mariae. g, Eeruginea. h, Compacta.
Genus Boletus: No. 764: a, Felleus. b, Elagans. c, Castaneus. d, Edulis. e, Aereus. f, Granulatus. g, Cavipes. h, Badius.
Genus Lactarius: No. 765: a, Deliciosus. b, Luculentus. c, Pseudomucidus. d, Scrobiculatus. e, Deceptivus. f, Indigo. g, Peckii. h, Lignyotus.
Genus Amanita: No. 766a, Caesarea. b, Muscaria. c, Solitaria. d, Verna. e, Malleata. f. Phalloides. g, Citrina. h, Pantherina.
Each 1000fr: No. 767, Coprinus atramentarius. No. 768, Panaeolus subbalteatus.

1996, Mar. 15 Litho. *Perf. 14*

763 A237 25fr Sheet of 8, #a.-h.	1.60	.85
764 A237 150fr Sheet of 8, #a.-h.	9.00	5.00
765 A237 200fr Sheet of 8, #a.-h.	12.00	6.50
766 A237 225fr Sheet of 8, #a.-h.	14.00	7.50

Souvenir Sheets

767-768 A237 Set of 2	14.00	8.00

Sites in Beijing — A238

No. 769: a, Bridge, Gateway to Hall of Supreme Harmony. b, Temple of Heaven. c, Great Wall. d, Hall of Supreme Harmony. e, Courtyard, Gate of Heavenly Purity, f, Younghe Gong Temple. g, Lang Ru Ting, Bridge of Seventeen Arches. h, Meridian Gate (Wu Men). i, Corner Tower.
Each 500fr: No. 770, Pagoda, vert. No. 771, Li Peng.

1996, May 13

769 A238 100fr Sheet of 9, #a.-i.	7.50	4.25

Souvenir Sheets

770-771 A238 Set of 2	7.00	4.25

No. 771 contains one 47x72mm stamp. CHINA '96 (Nos. 769, 771).

Trains A239

Historic: No. 772: a, "Novelty," 1829. b, Premiere class Liverpool & Manchester Line, 1830. c, William Norris, 1843. d, Trevithick, 1808. e, Robert Stephenson "Rocket," 1829. f, "Puffing Billy," William Hedley, 1813.
No. 773: a, Subway Train, London. b, San Francisco cable car. c, Japanese monorail. d, Pantograph car, Stockholm. e, Double-decker tram, Hong Kong. f, Sacre-Coeur Cog Train, Montmartre, France.
No. 774: a, Docklands Light Railway, London. b, British Railway's high-speed diesel train. c, Japanese Bullet Train. d, Germany Inter-City Electric high speed train. e, French TGV high-speed electric train. f, German "Wuppertal" monorail.
Trains of China: No. 775: a, RM Class Pacific. b, Manchurian steam engine. c, SY Class 2-8-2, Tangshan. d, SL Class 4-6-2 Pacific. e, Chengtu-Kunming steam. f, Lanchow passenger train.
Each 500fr: No. 776, Rheingold Express, 1925. No. 777, Matterhorn cable car, vert. No. 778, Superchief, best long-distance diesel, US. No. 779, Shanghai-Nanking Railway.

1996, July 29

772 A239 180fr Sheet of 6, #a.-f.	8.00	4.50
773 A239 250fr Sheet of 6, #a.-f.	12.00	6.50
774 A239 310fr Sheet of 6, #a.-f.	14.00	7.75
775 A239 320fr Sheet of 6, #a.-f.	15.00	8.25

Souvenir Sheets

776-779 A239 Set of 4	16.00	9.00

Nos. 776-779 each contain one 57x43mm stamp.

Express Mail Service, 10th Anniv. A240

Designs: 30fr, Man with package, vert. 40fr, Bird holding package, letter, vert. 90fr, World map, woman with letter holding telephone receiver. 320fr, 320fr, Mail van, hands holding letters, map.

1996, Sept. 1 Litho. *Perf. 14*

780 A240 30fr multicolored	.20	.20
781 A240 40fr multicolored	.30	.20
782 A240 90fr multicolored	.55	.30
783 A240 320fr multicolored	1.75	1.00
Nos. 780-783 (4)	2.80	1.70

Queen Elizabeth II, 70th Birthday A241

Designs: a, Portrait. b, Wearing blue & red hat. c, Portrait as young woman.
1000fr, Portrait as young girl.

1996, Sept. 9 *Perf. 13½x14*

784 A241 370fr Strip of 3, #a.-c.	5.50	2.25

Souvenir Sheet

785 A241 1000fr multicolored	5.25	2.00

No. 784 was issued in sheets of 9 stamps.

Nanking Bridge — A242

1996 Litho. *Perf. 13½*

786 A242 270fr multicolored	2.50	1.25

Mosques A243

1996

787 A243 250fr Djenne	3.50	2.00
788 A243 310fr Sankore	4.50	2.50

Pandas, Dogs, and Cats — A244

Panda, vert: No. 789: a, Climbing on branch. b, On bare limb. c. Closer view. d, Lying in branch with leaves.
Dogs, cats: No. 790: a, Azawakh. b, Basenji. c, Javanais. d, Abyssin.

1996

789 A244 150fr Sheet of 4, #a.-d.	3.25	1.60
790 A244 310fr Sheet of 4, #a.-d.	6.00	3.00

Nos. 789a-789d are 39x42mm.

Marilyn Monroe (1926-62) A245

Various portraits.

1996

791 A245 320fr Sheet of 9, #a.-i.	14.00	7.00

Souvenir Sheet

792 A245 2000fr multicolored	9.50	4.75

No. 792 contains one 42x60mm stamp.

Entertainers A246

#793: a, Frank Sinatra. b, Johnny Mathis. c, Dean Martin. d, Bing Crosby. e, Sammy Davis, Jr. f, Elvis Presley. g, Paul Anka. h, Tony Bennett. i, Nat "King" Cole.
No. 794, Various portraits of John Lennon.

1996

Sheets of 9

793 A246 250fr #a.-i.	10.00	5.00
794 A246 310fr #a.-i.	12.50	6.25

U.S. Space Shuttle, Challenger A247

Designs: a, Halley's Comet, Andromeda Galaxy. b, Mars. c, Challenger, Saturn. d, Moon, Jupiter.
1000fr, Shuttle Challenger.

1996, Oct. 14 *Perf. 14*

795 A247 320fr Sheet of 4, #a.-d.	5.75	3.00

Souvenir Sheet

796 A247 1000fr multicolored	5.25	3.00

No. 796 contains one 85x29mm stamp.

Mickey's ABC's A248

Disney characters in various scenes with: No. 797: a, "MICKEY." b, "A." c, "B." d, "C." e, "D." f, "E." g, "F." h, "G." i, "H."
No. 798: a, "I." b, "J." c, "K." d, "L." e, "M." f, "N." g, "O." h, "P." i, "Q."
No. 799: a, "R." b, "S." c, "T." d, "U." e, "V." f, "W." g, "X." h, "Y." i, "Z."
Each 1000fr: No. 800, Mouse child holding "DE MICKEY" sign, horiz. No. 801, Mouse children with various letters.

1996, Oct. 15 Litho. *Perf. 13½x14*

797 A248 50fr Sheet of 9, #a.-i.	2.25	1.25
798 A248 100fr Sheet of 9, #a.-i.	4.50	2.50
799 A248 200fr Sheet of 9, #a.-i.	9.00	5.00

Souvenir Sheets

800-801 A248 Set of 2	10.50	6.00

Sites in Beijing A249

#802, Hall of Supreme Harmony. #803, Great Wall. #804, Hall of Prayers for Good Harvests, Temple of Heaven.

1996 *Perf. 13½*

802 A249 180fr multicolored 1.75 1.00
803 A249 180fr multicolored 1.75 1.00
804 A249 180fr multicolored 1.75 1.00
Nos. 802-804 (3) 5.25 3.00

Cotton Production A250

Designs: 20fr, Cotton plant, vert. 25fr, People working in cotton fields. 50fr, Holding plant, vert. 310fr, Dumping cotton into cart.

1996 *Perf. 13½*

805 A250 20fr multicolored .20 .20
806 A250 25fr multicolored .20 .20
807 A250 50fr multicolored .25 .20
808 A250 310fr multicolored 1.40 .70
Nos. 805-808 (4) 2.05 1.30

Birds and Snakes A251

a, Crowned eagle in flight. b, Tufted eagle. c, Python. d, Gabon viper.
Songbirds: No. 810: a, Choucador splendide. b, Astrid ondulé. c, Martin chasseur. d, Coucou didric.
Butterfies: No. 811a, Salamis parhassus. b, Charaxes bohemani. c, Coeliades forestan. d, Mimacrea marshalli.

1996

809 A251 180fr Sheet of 4, #a.-d. 3.25 1.60
810 A251 250fr Sheet of 4, #a.-d. 4.50 2.25
811 A251 320fr Sheet of 4, #a.-d. 5.75 3.00

Third World — A252

Design: 250fr, Hot air balloon in flight.

1996

812 A252 180fr shown 2.50 1.25
813 A252 250fr multicolored 3.00 1.50

A253

A254

1996

814 A253 180fr green & multi 1.00 .50
815 A253 250fr bister & multi 1.50 .75

Death of Abdoul Karim Camara (Cabral), 16th anniv.

1997, Jan. 10 **Litho.** *Perf. 14*

Dogs: #816, Airdale terrier. #817, Briard. #818, Schnauzer. #819, Chow chow.
Cats: #820, Turkish van. #821, Sphynx. #822, Korat. #823, American curl.
Dogs, horiz.: #824: a, Basset hound. b, Dachshund. c, Brittany spaniel. d, Saint Bernard. e, Bernese mountain. f, Irish setter. g, Gordon setter. h, Poodle. i, Pointer.
Cats, horiz: #825: a, Scottish fold. b, Javanese. c, Norwegian forest. d, American shorthair. e, Turkish angora. f, British shorthair. g, Egyptian mau. h, Maine coon. i, Burmese.
Each 1000fr: #826, Newfoundland. #827, Flame point Himalayan Persian.

816-819 A254 100fr Set of 4 2.50 1.25
820-823 A254 150fr Set of 4 3.25 1.10
824 A254 150fr Sheet of 9, #a.-i. 7.50 3.75
825 A254 180fr Sheet of 9, #a.-i. 8.50 4.25

Souvenir Sheets

826-827 A254 Set of 2 11.00 6.00

Environmental Protection A255

Fauna: No. 828: a, Dolphin. b, Ok, Rhea. d, Black rhinocrhinoceros. e, Malayan tapir. f, Galapagos tortoise. g, Walrus. h, Gray wolf. i, Giraffe.
1000fr, Koala.

1997, Feb. 3

828 A255 250fr Sheet of 9, #a.-i. 14.00 7.75

Souvenir Sheet

829 A255 1000fr multicolored 6.00 3.25

Ships A256

Warships: No. 830: a, Bellerophon, England, 1867. b, Chen Yuan, China 1882. c, Hiei, Japan, 1877. d, Kaiser, Austria, 1862. e, King Wilhelm, Germany, 1869. f, Re D'Italia, Italy, 1864.
Paddle steamers: No. 831: a, Arctic, US, 1849. b, Washington, France, 1847. c, Esploratore, Italy, 1863. d, Fuad, Turkey, 1864. e, Hope, Confederate States of America, 1864. f, Britannia, England, 1840.
Each 1000fr: No. 832, Arabia, England, 1851. No. 833, Northumberland, England, 1867.

1996, Dec. 20 **Litho.** *Perf. 14*

830 A256 250fr Sheet of 6, #a.-f. 6.00 3.00
831 A256 320fr Sheet of 6, #a.-f. 10.00 3.75

Souvenir Sheets

832-833 A256 Set of 2 12.00 6.75

Wildlife — A257

Designs: a, Hippotragus niger. b, Damaliscus hunter. c, G. demidovii. d, Chimpanzee.

1996 **Litho.** *Perf. 13½*

834 A257 250fr Sheet of 4, #a.-d. 5.00 2.50

UNESCO, 50th anniv.

Red Cross — A258

Dogs: a, Rottweiler. b, Newfoundland. c, German shepherd. d, Bobtail (English sheepdog).

1996

835 A258 250fr Sheet of 4, #a.-d. 4.25 2.10

African Education Year — A259

100fr, Student with book, map, vert. 150fr, Classroom. 180fr, Families watching video program on farming techniques. 250fr, African people being educated, map, vert.

1996, Apr. 4 *Perf. 14*

836 A259 100fr multicolored .45 .45
837 A259 150fr multicolored .65 .65
838 A259 180fr multicolored .80 .80
839 A259 250fr multicolored 1.10 1.10
Nos. 836-839 (4) 3.00 3.00

Nos. 836-839 were not available until March 1997.

Folk Dances — A260

1996 *Perf. 13½*

840 A260 150fr Dounouba .65 .65
841 A260 170fr Gomba .75 .75
842 A260 225fr Sandia 1.40 1.40
843 A260 230fr Sabar 1.50 1.50
Nos. 840-843 (4) 4.30 4.30

Service Organizations — A261

No. 844: a, Man carrying bags. b, Man drinking water. c, Child holding bowl of food. d, Mother feeding infant.
No. 845: a, Girl with food. b, Man holding rice bowl. c, Woman holding bowl of food. d, Child opening box of food.

1996

844 A261 500fr Sheet of 4, #a.-d. 8.50 4.25
845 A261 650fr Sheet of 4, #a.-d. 11.50 5.75

79th Lions Intl. Convention (#844). 91st Rotary Intl. Convention (#845).

City of Canton, 2210th Anniv. A262

Designs: a, Statue of goats. b, Seal. c, Boat. d, Fruits, tea pot. e, Buildings. f, Dragon.

1996

846 A262 50fr Sheet of 6, #a.-f. 1.40 .70

FAO, 50th Anniv. A264

Space satellite, fauna: a, MOP.2, grasshopper. b, Meteosat P.2, lion. c, Envisat, dolphins. d, Radar satellite, whale.

1996 **Litho.** *Perf. 13½*

847 A264 310fr Sheet of 4, #a.-d. 5.00 2.50

Artifacts from Natl. Museum — A265

1996

848 A265 5fr Kara .20 .20
849 A265 10fr Hambe .20 .20
850 A265 180fr Pinge .80 .40
851 A265 250fr Merenkun 1.10 .55
Nos. 848-851 (4) 2.30 1.35

Nos. 848-851 exist in souvenir sheets of 1.

1998 Winter Olympics, Nagano A266

250fr, Speed skating. 310fr, Slalom skiing. 750fr, Figure skating. 900fr, Hockey. 2000fr, Downhill skiing.

1996

852	A266	250fr multicolored	1.25	.60
853	A266	310fr multicolored	1.50	.75
854	A266	750fr multicolored	3.50	1.75
855	A266	900fr multicolored	4.00	2.00
		Nos. 852-855 (4)	10.25	5.10

Souvenir Sheet

856 A266 2000fr multicolored 10.00 5.00

Fauna, Mushrooms A267

a, Ploceus ocularis. b, Hemiolaus coecolus. c, Hebeloma radicosum. d, Sparassus dufouri simon.

1996

857 A267 750fr Sheet of 4, #a.-d. 13.00 6.50

New Year 1997 (Year of the Ox) — A268

1997

858 A268 500fr shown 2.00 1.00

Size: 53x35mm

859 A268 500fr Black porcelain ox 2.00 1.00

Nos. 858-859 exist in souvenir sheets of 1.

Butterflies A269

#860, Black-lined eggar. #861, Common opae. #862, Veined tiger. #863, The basker.

No. 864: a, Natal barred blue. b, Common grass blue. c, Fire grid. d, Mocker swallowtail. e, Azure hairstreak. f, Mother-of-pearl butterfly. g, Boisduval's false asraea. h, Pirate butterfly. i, African moon moth.

No. 865, vert.: a, Striped policeman. b, Mountain sandman. c, Brown-veined white. d, Bowker's widow. e, Foxy charaxes. f, Pirate. g, African clouded yellow. h, Garden inspector.

Each 1000fr: No. 866, Plain tiger. No. 867, Beautiful tiger. No. 868, African clouded yellow, vert. No. 869, Zebra white, vert.

1997, Jan. 27 *Perf. 14*

860-863	A269	180fr Set of 4	3.50	1.75
864	A269	150fr Sheet of 9, #a.-i.	6.25	3.00
865	A259	210fr Sheet of 8, #a.-h.	9.50	4.75

Souvenir Sheets

866-869 A269 Set of 4 24.00 12.00

Disney Characters A270

Greetings stamps: 25fr, Goofy, Bon Voyage. 50fr, Mickey, Happy New Year. 100fr, Goofy, Happy Birthday. 150fr, Donald writing. 180fr, Minnie writing. 250fr, Mickey, Minnie, anniversary. 310fr, Mickey, Minnie going on vacation. 320fr, Mickey, Minnie kissing.

Each 1500fr: No. 878, Daisy Duck, horiz. No. 879, Huey, Dewey, Louie throwing school books in air, horiz.

1997, Mar. 1 *Perf. 13½x14*

870-877 A270 Set of 8 7.00 3.50

Souvenir Sheets

878-879 A270 Set of 2 15.00 7.50

Bridges — A271

1997 **Litho.** *Perf. 14*

880	A271	100fr Mahina	.50	.25
881	A271	150fr Selingue Dam	.80	.40
882	A271	180fr King Fahd	1.00	.50
883	A271	250fr Martyrs	1.50	.75
		Nos. 880-883 (4)	3.80	1.90

Dated 1996.

1998 World Cup Soccer Championships, France — A272

Various action scenes.

1997 *Perf. 13½*

884	A272	180fr multicolored	1.00	.50
885	A272	250fr multicolored	1.25	.60
886	A272	320fr multicolored	1.50	.75
887	A272	1060fr multicolored	4.50	2.25
		Nos. 884-887 (4)	8.25	4.10

Souvenir Sheet

888 A272 2000fr multicolored 9.00 4.25

Dated 1996. No. 888 contains one 36x42mm stamp.

Formula I Race Car Drivers A273

Designs: a, Michael Schumacher. b, Damon Hill. c, Jacques Villeneuve. d, Gerhard Berger.

1996 **Litho.** *Perf. 13½*

889 A273 650fr Sheet of 4, #a.-d. 11.00 5.50

John F. Kennedy (1917-63) A274

Various portraits.

1997

890 A274 390fr Sheet of 9, #a.-i. 15.00 7.50

John Lennon (1940-80) A275

Various portraits.

1997

891 A275 250fr Sheet of 9, #a.-i. 9.50 4.75

Deng Xiaoping (1904-97), Chinese Leader A276

Designs: a, As young man. b, Without hat. c, With hat. d, As middle-aged man. 250fr, Being kissed by child.

1997 *Perf. 13½*

892 A276 250fr Sheet of 4, #a.-d. 4.00 2.00

Souvenir Sheet

Perf. 13x13½

893 A276 250fr multicolored 4.00 2.00

No. 893 contains 69x50mm stamp.

Elvis Presley, 20th Death Anniv. A277

No. 894, Various portraits. No. 895, Portrait, Elvis on motorcycle.

1997 **Litho.** *Perf. 13½*

894 A277 310fr Sheet of 9, #a.-i. 12.00 6.00

Souvenir Sheet

895 A277 2000fr multicolored 9.00 4.50

No. 895 contains one 42x51mm stamp.

Marine Life A278

No. 896: a, Chaetodon auriga. b, Balistoides conspicillum. c, Forcipiger longirostris. d, Chelmon rostratus. e, Plectorhinchus diagrammus. f, Stegastes leucostictus. g, Chaetodon kleinii. h, Synchiropus splendidus. i, Platax orbicularis.

No. 897: a, Amphiprion percula. b, Holacanthus ciliaris. c, Chaetodon reticulatus. d, Pomacanthus imperator. e, Heniochus acuminatus. f, Lienardella fasciata. g, Zanclus cornutus. h, Scarus guacamaia. i, Lutjanus sebae.

No. 898: a, Tursiops truncatus. b, Phaethon lepturus. c, Istiophorus platypterus. d, Sphyma zygaena. e, Reinhardtius hippoglossoides. f, Manta birostris. g, Thunnus albacares. h, Himantolophus groenlandicus. i, Tridacana gigas.

No. 899: a, Cypselurus heterurus. b, Sailboat. c, Delphinus delphis. d, Cacharodon carcharias. e, Orcinus orca (b, f). f, Salmo salar. g, Conger conger. h, Pomatomus saltatrix. i, Sphyraena barracuda.

Each 1000r: No. 900, Balaenoptera musculus. No. 901, Megaptera novaenglaie, vert.

1997, Mar. 2 **Litho.** *Perf. 14*

896	A278	150fr Sheet of 9, #a.-i.	6.00	6.00
897	A278	180fr Sheet of 9, #a.-i	7.00	7.00
898	A278	250fr Sheet of 9, #a.-i.	9.75	9.75
899	A278	310fr Sheet of 9, #a.-i.	11.50	11.50

Souvenir Sheets

900-901 A278 Set of 2 9.00 9.00

Transportation — A279

Cyclists: No. 902: a, Rudolph Lewis, 1912. b, Jacques Anquetil, 4-time Tour de France winner. c, Miguel Indurain, hour record holder.

Sailing ships: No. 903: a, Lightning, by Donald McKay, 1856. b, Olivier de Kersauson, winner of Jules Verne trophy. c. Lockheed Sea Shadow, US.

Motorcycles, cyclists: No. 904: a, Coventry Eagle-Jap 998cm3. b, Michael Doohan, Honda 500 NSRV4. c, Harley-Davidson, Heritage Softail classic FLSTC.

Airships: No. 905: a, "Gifford," steam-powered dirigible, 1852. b, Count Ferdinand von Zeppelin, Zeppelin NT LZ N07. c, Nobile N1, "Norge," 1926.

Trains: No. 906: a, Locomotive G 4/5 2-8-0, Switzerland. b, W.V. Siemens, ICE train, Germany. c, Maglev HSST-5, Japan.

Race cars: No. 907: a, 1949 Ferrari Type 166/MM. b, Michael Schumacher, F1 310B Ferrari. c, Ferrari F50.

Sled dogs: No. 908: a, Eskimo. b, Alaskan malamute. c, Siberian husky.

Aircraft: No. 909: a, Wright Brothers' first flight at Kitty Hawk. b, Andre Turcat, Concorde. c, X34 space vehicle.

1997 **Litho.** *Perf. 13½*

902	A279	180fr Strip of 3, #a.-c.	2.10	1.00
903	A279	250fr Strip of 3, #a.-c.	3.00	1.50
904	A279	320fr Strip of 3, #a.-c.	3.75	2.00
905	A279	370fr Strip of 3, #a.-c.	4.25	2.25
906	A279	460fr Strip of 3, #a.-c.	5.50	2.75
907	A279	490fr Strip of 3, #a.-c.	5.75	3.00
908	A279	530fr Strip of 3, #a.-c.	6.50	3.25
909	A279	750fr Strip of 3, #a.-c.	8.75	4.50

Movie Stars — A281

Designs: a, John Wayne. b, Frank Sinatra. c, Rita Hayworth. d, Sammy Davis, Jr. e, Marilyn Monroe. f, Eddie Murphy. g, Elizabeth Taylor. h, James Dean. i, Robert Mitchum.

1997

910 A281 320fr Sheet of 9, #a.-i. 11.00 5.50

A282

A283

Diana, Princess of Wales (1961-97) — A284

Designs: No. 911, Various close-up portraits. No. 912, Pictures of various times in Diana's life.

Each 1500fr: No. 913, In pink dress with Pres. Clinton (in margin). No. 914, Wearing strapless evening dress. No. 915, Wearing hat and veil. No. 916, In blue dress with Nelson Mandela (in margin).

1997 Litho. ***Perf. 13½***

911 A282 250fr Sheet of 9, #a.-i. 8.75 4.50
912 A283 370fr Sheet of 9, #a.-i. 13.00 6.50

Souvenir Sheets

913-916 A284 Set of 4 26.00 13.00

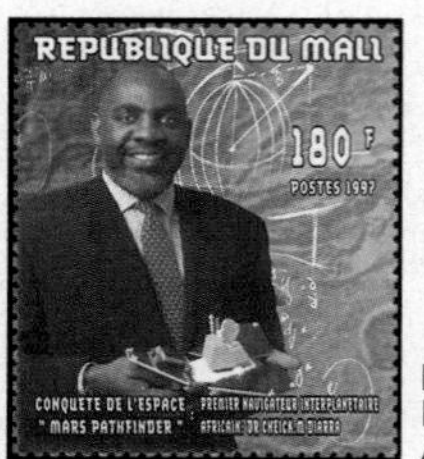

Mars Pathfinder A285

No. 917 - Dr. Cheick M. Diarra with: a, blue & multi background. b, green & multi background. c, Part of Mars in background. d, violet black & multi background.

No. 917E: f, Like #917a. g, Like #917b. h, Like #917c, i, Like #917d.

1997

917 A285 180fr Sheet of 4, #a.-d. 5.50 2.50
917E A285 320fr Sheet of 4, #f-i — —

Crested Porcupine A286

World Wildlife Fund: a, Two adults. b, One adult crawling right. c, Mother with young. d, Adult with quills raised.

1998

918 A286 250fr Block of 4, #a.-d. 6.75 3.00

Churches A287

Pieces from Natl. Museum — A288

1997 Litho. ***Perf. 13½***

919 A287 5fr Kita Basilica .20 .20
920 A287 10fr San Cathedral .20 .20
921 A287 150fr Bamako Cathedral .70 .35
922 A287 370fr Mandiakuy Church 1.75 .85
Nos. 919-922 (4) 2.85 1.60

1997

20fr, Bamanan. 25fr, Dogon couple. 250fr, Tasmasheq. 310fr, Oil lamp, Boo.

923 A288 20fr multicolored .20 .20
924 A288 25fr multicolored .20 .20
925 A288 250fr multicolored 1.25 .60
926 A288 310fr multicolored 1.50 .75
Nos. 923-926 (4) 3.15 1.75

Cotton Industry — A289

1997

927 A289 30fr Spools of threads .20 .20
928 A289 50fr Clothing .20 .20
929 A289 180fr Towels 1.00 .50
930 A289 320fr Textile production 1.50 .75
Nos. 927-930 (4) 2.90 1.65

"Star Wars" Motion Pictures A290

Various scenes from: No. 931, "The Return of the Jedi." No. 932, "Star Wars." No. 933: "The Empire Strikes Back."

1997 Litho. ***Perf. 13½***

Sheets of 9

931 A290 180fr #a.-i. 7.00 7.00
932 A290 310fr #a.-i. 12.00 12.00
933 A290 320fr #a.-i. 13.00 13.00

Wild Animals A291

Lions Intl. — #934: a, Lion. b, Cheetah standing. c, Cheetah lying down. d, Leopard.

Rotary Intl. — #935: a, Giraffe. b, Addax. c, Kob. d, Okapi.

1997

934 A291 310fr Sheet of 4, #a.-d. 5.00 2.50
935 A291 320fr Sheet of 4, #a.-d. 5.75 2.75

Mars Pathfinder — A292

Insignia and various scenes of Pathfinder mission.

1997

936 A292 370fr Sheet of 9, #a.-i. 15.00 7.50

Cats — A293

No. 937: a, Sphynx. b, Siberian brown tabby. c, Somali creme. d, Java cream point.

1500fr, Chartreux.

1997 Litho. ***Perf. 13½***

937 A293 530fr Sheet of 4, #a.-d. 9.00 4.50

Souvenir Sheet

938 A293 1500fr multicolored 6.50 3.25

No. 938 contains one 36x42mm stamp.

Scouts and Birds A294

1997

Color of Bird

939 A294 180fr yellow & black .90 .45
940 A294 490fr black & white 2.75 1.40
941 A294 530fr gray & yel org 3.00 1.50
Nos. 939-941 (3) 6.65 3.35

Souvenir Sheets

942 A294 Sheet of 3, #a.-c. + 3 labels 10.00 5.00
943 A294 1500fr multicolored 7.00 7.00

No. 942 sold for 2200fr. Nos. 942a-942c have the same designs and denominations as Nos. 939-941 but have continuous background showing portion of scouting emblem.

No. 943 contains 42x50mm stamp.

1997

Various mushrooms, scout: 250fr, Frying mushrooms. 320fr, Grilling mushrooms. 1060fr, Gathering mushrooms, placing in bag.

944 A294 250fr multicolored 1.25 .60
945 A294 320fr multicolored 1.50 .75
946 A294 1060fr multicolored 5.00 2.50
Nos. 944-946 (3) 7.75 3.85

Souvenir Sheet

947 A294 Sheet of 3, #a.-c. + 3 labels 11.00 5.50

#947 sold for 2600fr. #947a-947c have the same designs and denominations as #944-946 but have continuous background showing portion of scouting emblem. A number has been reserved for an additional souvenir sheet with this set.

1998

Various minerals, scout: 150fr, Looking at minerals with magnifying glass. 750fr, Reading book. 900fr, Using chisel.

949 A294 150fr multicolored .70 .35
950 A294 750fr multicolored 3.50 1.75
951 A294 900fr multicolored 4.50 2.25
Nos. 949-951 (3) 8.70 4.35

Souvenir Sheet

952 A294 Sheet of 3, #a.-c. + 3 labels 12.00 6.00

No. 952 sold for 2800fr. Nos. 952a-952c have the same designs and denominations as Nos. 949-951 but have continuous background showing portion of scouting emblem.

1998 Litho. ***Perf. 13½***

Various butterflies, scout: 310fr, Photographing butterfly. 430fr, Using book to identify butterfly. 460fr, Holding and looking at butterfly.

954 A294 310fr multicolored 1.40 .70
955 A294 430fr multicolored 2.25 1.10
956 A294 460fr multicolored 2.40 1.25
Nos. 954-956 (3) 6.05 3.05

Souvenir Sheet

957 A294 Sheet of 3, #a.-c. + 3 labels 10.00 5.00

No. 957 sold for 2200fr. Nos. 957a-957c have same designs and denominations as Nos. 954-956 but have continuous background showing portion of scouting emblem. A number has been reserved for an additional souvenir sheet with this set.

Flame of Peace, Timbuktu — A295

Pan-African Postal Union, 18th anniv. — A296

1997

959 A295 180fr yellow & multi 2.00 1.00
960 A295 250fr dull red & multi 3.00 1.50

Dated 1996.

1998

961 A296 250fr Addax 1.50 .75

Local Views — A297

5fr, Mosque, Mopti. 10fr, Fertility doll, Mopti. 15fr, Fishermen. 20fr, Woman carrying bowls on head, Macina. 25fr, Friendship Hotel. 30fr, Sikasso Hill. 40fr, Camel caravan, Azalai. 50fr, Women's hair style, Kayes. 60fr, Old Dogon man. 70fr, Shepherd. 80fr, Playing musical instrument, Wassoulou. 90fr, Crest, Ciwara Bamanan.

1998

962 A297 5fr multi .20 .20
963 A297 10fr multi, vert. .20 .20
964 A297 15fr multi .20 .20
966 A297 20fr multi, vert. .20 .20
966 A297 25fr multi, vert. .30 .30
967 A297 30fr multi, vert. .30 .30
968 A297 40fr multi, vert. .30 .30
969 A297 50fr multi, vert. .30 .30
970 A297 60fr multi, vert. .40 .40
971 A297 70fr multi, vert. .40 .40
972 A297 80fr multi, vert. .40 .40
973 A297 90fr multi, vert. .40 .40
Nos. 962-973 (12) 3.60 3.60

Travels of Pope John Paul II — A298

#974: a, Looking at book with Fidel Castro, Cuba. b, Walking with Castro, Cuba. c, With girl, Castro, Cuba. d, With boy, Nigeria. e, With three nuns, Cuba. f, Reading inscription on monument, Cuba. g, Holding crucifix, blessing child, Nigeria. h, Standing before monument, Nigeria. i, Giving blessing, people in traditional costumes, Nigeria.

Nos. 975a, 975c, 975d, 975e, 975f, 975g, 975i: Various portraits of Mother Teresa with Pope John Paul II. No. 975b, Pope John Paul II. No. 975h, Mother Teresa.

1998 **Litho.** ***Perf. 13½***
Sheets of 9

974 A298 310fr #a.-i. 12.00 6.00
975 A298 320fr #a.-i. 12.00 6.00

Animal Type of 1997

Dogs — #976: a, Dachshund. b, Persian hound. c, Chihuahua. d, Pug.
1500fr, Dalmatian.

1998 **Litho.** ***Perf. 13½***

976 A293 390fr Sheet of 4, #a.-d. 6.50 3.25

Souvenir Sheet

977 A293 1500fr multicolored 6.25 3.00

No. 977 contains one 36x42mm stamp.

Entertainers A299

No. 978, Various portraits of James Dean.
No. 979, opera singers: a, Placido Domingo. b, Luciano Pavarotti. c, Jose Carreras. d, Andrea Bocelli. e, Maria Callas. f, Jose Van Dam. g, Renata Tebaldi. h, Montserrat Caballe. i, Kiri Te Kanawa.
No. 980, actresses: a, Audrey Hepburn. b, Greta Garbo. c, Elizabeth Taylor. d, Grace Kelly. e, Jean Harlow. f, Ava Gardner. g, Lana Turner. h, Marilyn Monroe. i, Vivien Leigh.

1998 **Litho.** ***Perf. 13½***
Sheets of 9

978 A299 250fr #a.-i. 9.50 4.75
979 A299 310fr #a.-i. 13.00 6.50
980 A299 320fr #a.-i. 13.00 6.50

Chess Masters A300

Portraits: a, Adolf Anderssen, 1818-79. b, Wilhelm Steinitz, 1836-1900. c, Emmanuel Lasker, 1868-1941. d, Alexandre Alekhine, 1892-1946. e, Tigran Petrossian, 1929-84. f, Boris Spassky, 1937. g, Bobby Fischer, 1943. h, Garry Kasparov, 1963. i, Anatoli Karpov, 1951.

1998

981 A300 370fr Sheet of 9, #a.-i. 15.00 7.50

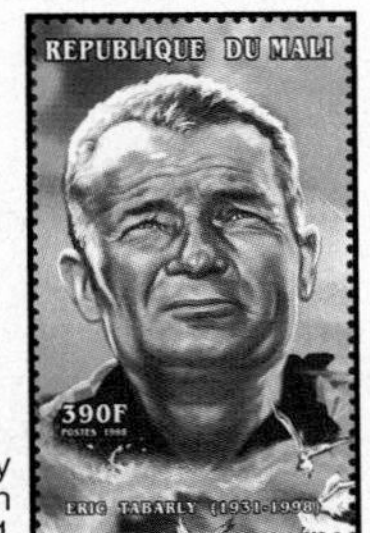

Eric Tabarly (1931-98), French Sailor — A301

Designs: a, Portrait. b, Tabarly at helm, yachts Pen Duick, Pen Duick VI. c, Tabarly, Charles de Gaulle.

1998

982 A301 390fr Sheet of 3, #a.-c. 5.00 2.50

No. 982b is 60x50mm.

France, 1998 World Cup Soccer Champions — A302

No. 983: a, Laurent Blanc. b, Lilian Thurman. c, David Trezeguet.
No. 984: a, Marcel Desailly. b, Fabien Barthez. c, Christian Karembeu.
No. 985: a, Didier Deschamps. b, Emmanuel Petit. c, Bixente Lizarazu.
No. 986: a, Youri Djorkaeff. b, Zinedine Zidane. c, Aime Jacquet.
2000fr, Team picture.

1998 **Litho.** ***Perf. 13½***
Sheets of 3

983 A302 250fr #a.-c. 4.00 2.00
984 A302 370fr #a.-c. 5.00 2.75
985 A302 390fr #a.-c. 6.00 3.00
986 A302 750fr #a.-c. 10.50 5.25

Souvenir Sheet

987 A302 2000fr multicolored 10.00 10.00

No. 987 contains one 57x51mm stamp.

Jacques-Yves Cousteau (1910-97), Underwater Explorer, Environmentalist A303

No. 988: a, Cousteau, ship Calypso. b, Divers, underwater submersibles. c, Diver looking into submarine habitat, man playing chess.
No. 989: a, Portrait, Cousteau with Pres. John F. Kennedy. b, Divers retrieving amphora. c, Hard hat diver, Cousteau wearing early aqualung.

1998
Sheets of 3

988 A303 460fr #a.-c. 6.50 3.25
989 A303 490fr #a.-c. 7.00 3.50

Nos. 988b, 989b are each 60x51mm.

History of Chess A304

Chess pieces, boards — #990: a, India, 18th cent. b, Italy, 1700. c, Siam, 18th cent. d, France, 1880. e, Austria, 1872. f, Germany, 1925. g, Yugoslavia, 20th cent. h, China, 20th cent. i, Russia, 20th cent.
No. 991, Albert V of Bavaria playing chess with his wife, Anne of Austria. No. 992, Arabian chess. No. 993, Japanese chess. No. 994, Nefertari, Ramses II playing chess.

1998 **Litho.** ***Perf. 13½***

990 A304 370fr Sheet of 9, #a.-i. 12.50 6.25

Souvenir Sheets

991-994 A304 1500fr each 5.75 3.00

Nos. 991-994 each contain one 57x51mm stamp.

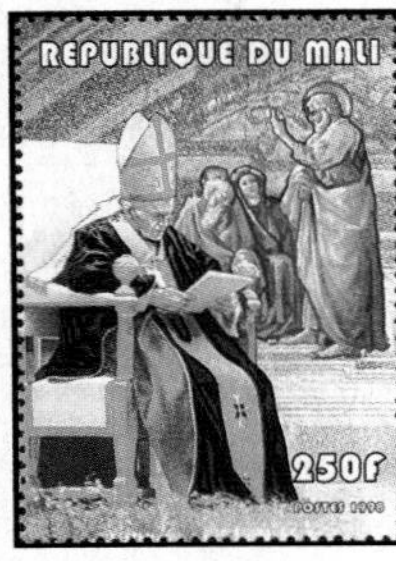

Pope John Paul II — A305

No. 995: Various portraits of John Paul II portrayed with events, popes depicting papal history.
Pope John Paul II, famous cathedrals — #996: a, Chartres. b, Santiago de Compostela. c, St. Sophie, Novgorod, Russia. d, St. Peter's Basilica, Vatican City. e, Our Lady of Peace Basilica, Yamoussoukro, Ivory Coast. f, Milan.
Pope John Paul II, famous cathedrals — #997: a, Sacred Family, Barcelona. b, Saint Sophie, Kiev. c, Notre Dame, Lausanne. d, Cathedral of Mexico. e, Cathedral of Cologne. f, Burgos Cathedral.

1998 **Litho.** ***Perf. 13½***
Sheets of 6 or 9

995 A305 250fr #a.-i. 8.00 4.00
996 A305 370fr #a.-f. 7.50 3.75
997 A305 750fr #a.-f. 15.00 7.50

Granaries A306

1998 **Litho.** ***Perf. 13½***

998 A306 25fr Sénoufo, vert. .20 .20
999 A306 180fr Sarakolé .70 .35
1000 A306 310fr Minianka, vert. 1.40 .70
1001 A306 320fr Boo, vert. 1.40 .70
Nos. 998-1001 (4) 3.70 1.95

Trees A307

1998

1002 A307 100fr Tamarindus indica .50 .25
1003 A307 150fr Adansonia digitata .70 .35
1004 A307 180fr Acacia senegal .80 .40
1005 A307 310fr Parkia biglobosa 1.50 .75
Nos. 1002-1005 (4) 3.50 1.75

National Museum Pieces — A308

1998

1006 A308 50fr Bamanan .20 .20
1007 A308 150fr Dogon .60 .30
1008 A308 250fr Bamanan, diff. 1.00 .50
1009 A308 320fr Minianka 1.40 .70
Nos. 1006-1009 (4) 3.20 1.70

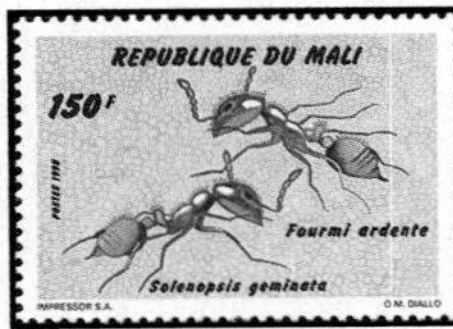

Ants A309

150fr, Solenopsis geminata. 180fr, Camponotus pennsylvanicus. 250fr, Monorium minimum. 310fr, Lasius niger.

1998

1010 A309 150fr multi .60 .30
1011 A309 180fr multi, vert. .80 .40
1012 A309 250fr multi 1.25 .60
1013 A309 310fr multi 1.50 .75
Nos. 1010-1013 (4) 4.15 2.05

Baladji Cisse (1924-77), Boxer — A309a

1999, May 12 **Litho.** ***Perf. 13½***

1013B A309a 250fr shown —

An additional stamp was issued in this set. The editors would like to examine any example.

World Teachers' Day A310

Various views of teachers working.

1999 **Litho.** ***Perf. 13½***

1014	A310 150fr multi, vert.	.60	.30
1015	A310 250fr multi, vert.	1.00	.50
1016	A310 370fr multi, vert.	1.50	.75
1017	A310 390fr multi	1.75	.85
	Nos. 1014-1017 (4)	4.85	2.40

Fight Against Poverty A311

1999 **Litho.** ***Perf. 13¼***

1018	A311 150fr Agriculture	.70	.35
1019	A311 180fr Labor projects	.90	.45
1020	A311 750fr Food, vert.	3.25	1.60
1021	A311 1000fr Potable water	4.25	2.10
	Nos. 1018-1021 (4)	9.10	4.50

UPU, 125th Anniv. A312

UPU emblem and: 150fr, Airplane, train, boat. 250fr, Stick figures with letters. 310fr, Eagles, antelopes with letters. 320fr, Eagle with letter on mud structure, vert.

1999

1022	A312 150fr multi	.60	.30
1023	A312 250fr multi	1.00	.50
1024	A312 310fr multi	1.25	.60
1025	A312 320fr multi	1.40	.70
	Nos. 1022-1025 (4)	4.25	2.10

Flora and Fauna A313

No. 1026 — Reptiles: a, Pseudonaja textilis. b, Litoria chloris. c, Imantodes inornata. d, Pyton arboricole. e, Pachydactylus bibroni. f, Trimeresurus wagleri.

No. 1027 — Orchids: a, Epidendrum ellipticum. b, Oncidium macranthum. c, Miltoniopsis roezlii. d, Oncidium barbatum. e, Miltonia warscewiczii. f, Lockhartia oerstedii.

No. 1028 — Birds: a, Amandava subflava. b, Ploceus bojeri. c, Lagonostica senegala. d, Uraeginthus bengalus. e, Monticola saxatilis. f, Saxicola torquata.

No. 1028G — Birds: a, Tyto alba. b, Pernis apivorus. c, Bubo africanus. d, Gypaetus barbatus meridionalis. e, Strix aluco. f, Milvus migrans.

No. 1029 — Butterflies: a, Cymothoe hypatha. b, Cymothoe sangaris. c, Top view, Charaxes fournierae. d, Male Catopsilia thauruma. e, Bottom view, Charaxes fournierae. f, Female Catopsilia thauruma.

No. 1030 — Mushrooms: a, Amanita muscaria. b, Amanita spissa. c, Helvella acetabulum. d, Pleurotus ostreatus. e, Phallus duplicatus. f, Cortinarius salor.

1999

Sheets of 6

1026	A313 350fr #a.-f.	9.00	4.50
1027	A313 390fr #a.-f.	10.00	5.00
1028	A313 430fr #a.-f.	11.00	5.50
1028G	A313 460fr #h-m	12.00	6.00
1029	A313 490fr #a.-f.	13.00	6.50
1030	A313 530fr #a.-f.	14.00	7.00
	Nos. 1026-1030 (6)	69.00	34.50

Rocks, Dinosaurs and Volcanoes A314

No. 1031 — Dinosaurs and rocks: a, Edmontonia, Ensisheim meteorite. b, Iguanodon, Saint-Mesmin meteorite. c, Allosaurus, Pallasite meteorite. d, Troodon, Lunar meteorite. e, Lesothosaurus, rock from Bouvant. f, Carnotaurus, Axtell meteorite. g, Deinonychus, Orgueil meteorite. h, Dilophosaurus, rock from Douar Mghila. i. Psittacosaurus, L'Aigle meteorite.

No. 1032 — Volcanic eruptions and rocks: a, Popocatepetl, 1519, Peekskill meteorite. b, Santorin, 1645, Tamentit meteorite. c, Mt. Pelee, 1902, Ouallen meteorite. d, Herculaneum during Vesuvius eruption, 79, Chinguetti meteorite. e, Krakatoa, 1883, Pultush meteorite. f, Soufriere, 1979, rock from Sienne. g, Mt. St. Helens, 1980, Allende meteorite. h, Kilauea, 1984, Parnallee meteorite. i, Mt. Etna, 1986, Tamentit meteorite.

1500fr, Pompeii during Vesuvius eruption, 79.

1999 ***Perf. 13¼***

Sheets of 9

1031	A314 250fr #a.-i.	9.00	4.50
1032	A314 310fr #a.-i.	12.00	6.00

Souvenir Sheet

Perf. 13½

1033	A314 1500fr multi	6.75	3.25

No. 1033 contains one 39x56mm stamp.

Space A315

No. 1034: a, Hubble Space Telescope. b, Venera 12. c, Space shuttle. d, Ariane 5.

No. 1035: a, Apollo-Soyuz mission. b, Carl Sagan, Viking 1. c, Voyager 1. d, Giotto probe, Edmond Halley.

1999 ***Perf. 13¼***

Sheets of 4

1034	A315 250fr #a.-d.	4.50	2.25
1035	A315 310fr #a.-d.	5.50	2.75

The Malian government declared that sheets of 9 stamps containing 100, 150, 200, 250, 300, 350, 400, 450 and 500fr stamps with the following topics are "illegal": Trains, Chess, Prehistoric Animals, Ferdinand Magellan, Christopher Columbus, Mushrooms, Computers, Wolves, Minerals, International Red Cross, Composers, Horses, and Wild Animals (tiger, lion, eagle, etc.)

Space Type of 1999

No. 1036: a, Frank Borman, Apollo 8. b, Neil Armstrong, Apollo 11. c, Luna 16 and Lunokhod 2. d, Surveyor 3.

No. 1037: a, Konstantin Tsiolkovsky. b, Robert H. Goddard. c, Hermann Oberth. d, Theodor von Kármán.

No. 1038: a, Laika, Sputnik 2. b, Yuri Gagarin, Vostok 1. c, Edward White, Gemini 4. d, John Glenn, Friendship 7.

No. 1039: a, Apollo 15 Lunar Rover. b, Pioneer 10. c, Skylab. d, Mariner 10.

1999 **Litho.** ***Perf. 13¼***

Sheets of 4

1036	A315 320fr #a-d	5.50	2.75
1037	A315 500fr #a-d	8.75	4.25
1038	A315 750fr #a-d	13.00	6.50
1039	A315 900fr #a-d	15.00	7.50
	Nos. 1036-1039 (4)	42.25	21.00

I Love Lucy — A318

No. 1045: a, Lucy showing Fred open handcuffs. b, Lucy touching reclining Ricky while handcuffed. c, Fred watching Ricky glare at Lucy. d, Handcuffed Lucy and Ricky trying to go in opposite directions. e, Handcuffed Lucy and Ricky seated. f, Lucy and Ricky handcuffed on bed. g, Lucy trying to get off bed while handcuffed to Ricky. h, Handcuffed Ricky with hand between legs. i, Ricky with arm draped over Lucy.

No. 1046, 1000fr, Fred examining handcuffs on Lucy and Ricky. No. 1047, 1000fr, Lucy and Ricky looking down.

1999, May 20 **Litho.** ***Perf. 13¼***

1045	A318 320fr Sheet of 9, #a-i	16.00	16.00

Souvenir Sheets

1046-1047	A318 Set of 2	12.00	12.00

Garfield the Cat — A319

No. 1048: a, With eyes half shut, pink background. b, With eyes open, pink background. c, Touching chin. d, With eyes open and open mouth. e, Showing tongue. f, With eyes open, showing teeth. g, With eyes open, blue background. h, With eyes half shut, blue background. i, Odie.

1000fr, As mailman.

1999, May 20 **Litho.** ***Perf. 13¼***

1048	A319 250fr Sheet of 9, #a-i	10.00	5.00

Souvenir Sheet

1049	A319 1000fr multi	4.50	2.25

No. 1049 contains one 36x42mm stamp.

Miniature Sheet

Millennium — A320

No. 1051: a, Jules Verne, Scene from "20,000 Leagues Under the Sea," 1905. b, Commander William R. Anderson, USS Nautilus, map of Arctic region showing underwater voyage across North Pole, 1958. c, Discovery of tomb of King Tutankhamun, 1922. d, Transatlantic flight of Charles A. Lindbergh, 1927.

No. 1056: a, Mother Teresa holding Nobel diploma, dove. b, Princess Diana, rose, dove. c, Pope John Paul II. d, Fall of the Berlin Wall, doves.

1999, July 2 **Litho.** ***Perf. 13¼***

1051	A320 310fr Sheet of 4, #a-d	—	—
1056	A320 490fr Sheet of 4, #a-d	—	—

Six additional sheets exist in this set. The editors would like to examine any these sheets.

Flags of the World — A321

No. 1058: a, Myanmar. b, Namibia. c, Nepal. d, Niger. e, Nigeria. f, Norway. g, Uganda. h, Pakistan. i, Netherlands. j, Peru. k, Philippines. l, Poland. m, New Zealand. n, Portugal. o, North Korea. p, Romania.

No. 1059: a, Russia. b, Rwanda. c, Singapore. d, Slovakia. e, Sudan. f, Sri Lanka. g, Sweden. h, Switzerland. i, Syria. j, Tanzania. k, Czech Republic. l, Thailand. m, Somalia. n, Tunisia. o, Turkey. p, Ukraine.

No. 1060: a, Finland. b, France. c, Great Britain. d, Greece. e, Guinea. f, Hungary. g, India. h, Indonesia. i, Iran. j, Iraq. k, Ireland. l, Iceland. m, Israel. n, Italy. o, Libya. p, Japan.

No. 1061: a, Cambodia. b, Cameroun. c, Canada. d, Chile. e, People's Republic of China. f, Colombia. g, Democratic Republic of the Congo. h, South Korea. i, Ivory Coast. j, Croatia. k, Cuba. l, Denmark. m, Egypt. n, United Arab Emirates. o, Spain. p, Ethiopia.

No. 1062: a, Afghanistan. b, South Africa. c, Albania. d, Algeria. e, Germany. f, United States. g, Angola. h, Saudi Arabia. i, Argentina. j, Australia. k, Austria. l, Bangladesh. m, Belgium. n, Bolivia. o, Brazil. p, Bulgaria.

No. 1063: a, Jordan. b, Kenya. c, Kuwait. d, Laos. e, Lebanon. f, Lithuania. g, Luxembourg. h, Madagascar. i, Malaysia. j, Mali. k, Viet Nam. l, Morocco. m, Mauritius. n, Mexico. o, Monaco. p, Mongolia.

1999, Aug. 2 **Litho.** ***Perf. 13¼***

1058	A321 20fr Sheet of 16, #a-p	—	—
1059	A321 25fr Sheet of 16, #a-p	—	—
1060	A321 50fr Sheet of 16, #a-p	—	—
1061	A321 100fr Sheet of 16, #a-p	5.00	2.50
q.	Cameroun, flag with green star	—	—
r.	Sheet of 16, #1061a, 1061c-1061q	—	—
1063	A321 100fr Sheet of 16, #a-p	—	—

No. 1061b has a Cameroun flag with a yellow star.

Sikasso Cathedral — A322

No. 1065: a, Photograph. b, Drawing.

1999, Dec. 25 **Litho.** ***Perf. 13¼***

1065	A322 150fr Horiz. pair, #a-b	1.40	.70

Christianity, 2000th Anniv. — A323

No. 1066, 100fr: a, St. Louis. b, Construction of Amiens Cathedral, 13th cent. c, Joan of Arc. d, Pope John Paul II.
No. 1067, 180fr: a, Jesus Christ. b, Persecution of Christians by Nero. c, St. Peter. d, Charlemagne.

1999, Dec. 25
Sheets of 4, #a-d

1066-1067	A323	Set of 2	5.00	2.50

Religious Paintings — A324

No. 1068, 250fr: a, Heller Madonna, by Albrecht Dürer. b, Virgin and Child, by Dürer. c, Madonna with Sts. Francis and Liberale, by Giorgione. d, Virgin and Child, by Giorgione.
No. 1069, 310fr: a, Virgin and Child, by Fra Filippo Lippi. b, Virgin and Child with Two Angels, by Lippi. c, Virgin and Sleeping Child, by Andrea Mantegna. d, Madonna of Victory, by Mantegna.
No. 1070, 320fr: a, Virgin and Child, by Hugo van der Goes. b, Virgin and Child and landscape, by van der Goes. c, Madonna and Child with St. Peter and a Martyred Saint, by Paolo Veronese. d, Adoration of the Magi, by Veronese.
No. 1071, 370fr: a, Madonna and Child Between St. Peter and St. Sebastian, by Giovanni Bellini. b, Madonna and Child with Cherubim, by Bellini. c, Madonna and Child with Two Angels, by Sandro Botticelli. d, Bardi Madonna, by Botticelli.
No. 1072, 390fr: a, Rest During the Flight to Egypt, with St. Francis, by Corregio. b, The Night, by Corregio. c, Senigallia Madonna, by Piero della Francesca. d, Virgin and Child and Four Angels, by della Francesca.
No. 1073, 750fr: a, Virgin and Child (rectangular), by Quentin Massys. b, Virgin and Child (curved top) by Massys. c, Madonna and Saint Sixtus, by Raphael. d, Madonna of the Duke of Alba, by Raphael.

1999, Dec. 25
Sheets of 4, #a-d

1068-1073	A324	Set of 6	40.00	20.00

2000 Summer Olympics, Sydney — A325

No. 1074, 150fr — Equestrian events: a, Show jumping. b, Military jumping. c, Dressage, horse facing left. d, Dressage, horse facing right.
No. 1075, 460fr — Tennis: a, Woman with green trim on dress. b, Man with red trim on shirt. c, Woman, diff. d, Man, diff.
No. 1076, 530fr — Table tennis: a, Green and red shirt and shorts. b, White shirt, red shorts. c, White and red shirt, black shorts. d, Yellow and green shirt, black shorts.
No. 1077, 750fr — Basketball: a, Red and yellow uniform. b, Green uniform. c, White and red uniform. d, Yellow and green uniform.
1000fr, Hurdler, horse and rider, horiz.

2000, June 30
Sheets of 4, #a-d

1074-1077	A325	Set of 4	45.00	22.50

Souvenir Sheet

1078	A325	1000fr multi	6.00	3.00

No. 1078 contains one 57x51mm stamp.

2002 World Cup Soccer Championships, Japan and Korea — A326

No. 1079, 150fr: a, Pedro Cea. b, Schiavo. c, Luigi Colaussi. d, Juan Schiaffino.
No. 1080, 250fr: a, Fritz Walter. b, Pelé. c, Amarildo. d, Bobby Moore.
No. 1081, 320fr: a, Jairzinho. b, Franz Beckenbauer. c, Mario Kempes. d, Paolo Rossi.
No. 1082, 750fr: a, Diego Maradona. b, Jurgen Klinsmann. c, Romario. d, Zinedine Zidane.

2000, June 30
Sheets of 4, #a-d

1079-1082	A326	Set of 4	35.00	17.50

Fauna, Mushrooms and Prehistoric Animals — A327

No. 1083, 150fr — Birds: a, Ganga de Liechtenstein. b, Guepier à gorge blanche. c, Moineau domestique. d, Euplecte de feu. e, Irrisor namaquois. f, Pique-boeuf à bec jaune.
No. 1084, 180fr — Dogs: a, Dalmatian. b, Hungarian Kuvasz. c, Swedish shepherd. d, Ibiza dog. e, Golden retriever. f, Dachshund.
No. 1085, 250fr — Cats: a, White cat with orange eyes. b, Somali. c, Himalayan blue tortie point. d, Korat. e, Bombay. f, La Perm.
No. 1086, 310fr — Butterflies: a, Paralethe dendrophilis. b, Papilio ophidicephalus. c, Kallima jacksoni. d, Hypolimnas antevorta. e, Papilio nobilis. f, Euxanthe wakefieldi.
No. 1087, 320fr — Butterflies: a, Euxanthe eurinome. b, Euryphura chalcis. c, Dira mintha. d, Euphaedra zaddachi. e, Euphaedra neophron. f, Euxanthe tiberius.
No. 1088, 370fr — Mushrooms: a, Volvariella acystidiata. b, Leucopricus birnbaumii. c, Cystoderma elegans. d, Leucoprinus elaidis. e, Leucoprinus discoideus. f, Leucoagaricus carminescens.
No. 1089, 370fr — Birds: a, Pririt du cap. b, Petit duc scops. c, Ouette d'Egypte. d, Rollier d'Europe. e, Promerops du cap. f, Sauteur du cap.
No. 1090, 390fr — Mushrooms: a, Volvariella parvispora. b, Volvariella surrecta. c, Lentinus similis. d, Leucoagaricus holosericeus. e, Leucoagaricus pepinus. f, Agrocybe elegantior.
No. 1091, 460fr — Prehistoric animals: a, Psittacosaurus. b, Phororhacos. c, Coelophysis. d, Saurornithoides. e, Acanthopholis. f, Varannosaurus.
No. 1092, 490fr — Prehistoric animals: a, Dromiceiomimus. b, Placodus. c, Ceratosaurus. d, Heterodontosaurus. e, Diatryma. f, Ouranosaurus.

2000, Sept. 25
Sheets of 6, #a-f

1083-1092	A327	Set of 10	110.00	55.00

Campaign Against Malaria A328

Designs: No. 1093, 150fr, Doctor, mother and child. No. 1094, 150fr, Man with briefcase, man with crutch, syringe. No. 1095, 150fr, Doctor, syringe. 430fr, Mother, child, syringe, quinine tablets.

2000

1093-1096	A328	Set of 4	3.25	1.60

Intl. Volunteers Year (in 2001) — A329

2000

1097	A329	250fr multi	.80	.40

Independence, 40th Anniv. — A330

Designs: 20fr, Provincial map. 375fr, Flag-raising ceremony, front and back of 50-franc banknote, vert.

2001 **Litho.** ***Perf. 13***

1099	A330	20fr multi	—	—
1100	A330	375fr multi	—	—

An additional stamp was issued in this set. The editors would like to examine it.

Senegal River Regional Organization — A331

2001 **Litho.** ***Perf. 12¾***

1101	A331	30fr multi	—	—
1102	A331	100fr multi	—	—
1103	A331	5000fr multi	—	—

No. 1102 exists dated "2003."

A332

A333

Perf. 13¼ (A332), 13x12¾ (A333)

2002 **Litho.**

1104	A332	195fr multi	—	—
1105	A333	255fr multi	—	—
1106	A332	385fr multi	—	—
1107	A333	395fr multi		—
1108	A333	565fr multi		—
1109	A332	975fr multi		—

23rd African Cup Soccer Tournament. Dated "2001."

Bobo Mask — A334

Dogon Mask — A335

Sénoufo Sanctuary Door — A336

Bamanan Fertility Statue — A337

2001-04 **Litho.** ***Perf. 12¾***

1110	A334	5fr multi	—	—
1111	A335	10fr multi	—	—
a.		Dated "2004"	—	—
1112	A336	25fr multi	—	—
a.		Dated "2004"		—
1113	A334	40fr multi		—
1114	A335	75fr multi	—	—
a.		Dated "2004"	—	—
1115	A334	195fr multi	—	—
1116	A335	195fr multi	1.00	.50
a.		Dated "2005"	—	—
1117	A334	235fr multi	—	—
1118	A335	255fr multi	—	—
1119	A337	255fr multi	1.40	.70
1120	A335	325fr multi	—	—
1121	A336	385fr multi	—	—
1122	A336	400fr multi		—
1123	A337	500fr multi	—	—
1124	A337	1000fr multi		—

Issued: Nos. 1115, 1117, 1118, 1120, 1121-1123, 2001; Nos. 1110, 1111-1114, 2002. Nos. 1116, 1119, 2003. No. 1124, 2004.

AIDS Prevention A338

2002, Jan. 10 **Litho.** ***Perf. 12¾***

1125	A338	195fr multi		—

Five additional stamps were issued in this set. The editors would like to examine any examples.

Songhoi Woman's Hairstyle — A340

Peulh Woman — A341

Badiangara Cliffs
A342

Perf. 12¾, 13x12¾ (#1131)

2003, Mar. 7 **Litho.**

1131 A340 50fr multi .25 .25
1132 A341 385fr multi 2.25 2.25
a. Dated "2004" —
1133 A342 485fr multi 2.75 2.75

Balaphone Festival
A343

2003, Mar. 7 **Litho.** ***Perf. 12¾***

1134 A343 565fr multi 3.00 .300

Men Drinking Tea in Desert — A344

2005, Aug. 18 **Litho.** ***Perf. 12¾***

1135 A344 10fr multi —

Djenné Fair — A345

2005, Aug. 18 **Litho.** ***Perf. 12¾***

1136 A345 20fr multi .50 .50

Map of Africa, Water Drop, Lions International Emblem — A346

2005, Aug. 18 **Litho.** ***Perf. 12¾***

1137 A346 465fr multi 3.25 3.25

World Summit on the Information Society, Tunis
A347

2005, Aug. 18 **Litho.** ***Perf. 12¾x13***

1138 A347 195fr multi —
1140 A347 385fr multi —

An additional stamp was issued in this set. The editors would like to examine any example.

23rd Summit of Heads of State of Africa and France
A348 A349

2005, Aug. 18 **Litho.** ***Perf. 13x12¾***

1141 A348 195fr multi —
1142 A349 195fr multi —

Two additional stamps were issued in this set. The editors would like to examine any examples.

Mother Nursing Baby — A350

2009 **Litho.** ***Perf. 13x12¾***

1149 A350 195fr multi —

An additional stamp was issued in this set. The editors would like to examine any example.

SEMI-POSTAL STAMPS

Anti-Malaria Issue

Common Design Type

Perf. 12½x12

1962, Apr. 7 **Engr.** **Unwmk.**

B1 CD108 25fr + 5fr pale vio bl 1.25 .60

Algerian Family — SP1

1962, Dec. 24 **Photo.** ***Perf. 12x12½***

B2 SP1 25fr + 5fr multi .70 .30

Issued for the national campaign to show the solidarity of the peoples of Mali and Algeria.

AIR POST STAMPS

Federation

Composite View of St. Louis, Senegal — AP1

Unwmk.

1959, Dec. 11 **Engr.** ***Perf. 13***

C1 AP1 85fr multi 2.75 1.00

Founding of St. Louis, Senegal, tercentenary, and opening of the 6th meeting of the executive council of the French Community.

Birds — AP2

100fr, Amethyst starling. 200fr, Bateleur eagle, horiz. 500fr, Barbary shrike.

Perf. 12½x13, 13x12½

1960, Feb. 13 **Photo.**

C2 AP2 100fr multi 3.50 2.00
C3 AP2 200fr multi 9.00 2.50
C4 AP2 500fr multi 24.00 11.50
Nos. C2-C4 (3) 36.50 16.00

Republic

Nos. C2-C4 Overprinted or Surcharged "REPUBLIQUE DU MALI" and Bars

1960, Dec. 18

C5 AP2 100fr multi 5.25 1.60
C6 AP2 200fr multi 8.00 2.75
C7 AP2 300fr on 500fr multi 11.50 5.25
C8 AP2 500fr multi 20.00 8.25
Nos. C5-C8 (4) 44.75 17.85

Pres. Modibo Keita — AP3

1961, Mar. 18 **Engr.** ***Perf. 13***

Designs: 200fr, Mamadou Konate.

C9 AP3 200fr claret & gray brn 3.75 .85
C10 AP3 300fr grn & blk 5.50 1.10

Flag, Map, UN Emblem — AP4

1961, Mar. 18

C11 AP4 100fr multicolored 2.25 .75
a. Min. sheet of 3, #13, 14, C11 3.00 3.00

Proclamation of independence and admission to UN.

Sankore Mosque, Timbuktu — AP5

200fr, View of Timbuktu. 500fr, Bamako & arms.

1961, Apr. 15 **Unwmk.** ***Perf. 13***

C12 AP5 100fr Prus bl, red brn & gray 2.75 .50
C13 AP5 200fr grn, brn & red 5.25 1.50
C14 AP5 500fr red brn, Prus bl & dk grn 13.50 3.00
Nos. C12-C14 (3) 21.50 5.00

Inauguration of Timbuktu airport and Air Mali.

Bull, Chemical Equipment and Chicks — AP6

1963, Feb. 23 **Engr.**

C15 AP6 200fr bis, mar & grnsh bl 5.00 1.25

Sotuba Zootechnical Institute.

Air Ambulance — AP7

Designs: 55fr, National Line plane loading. 100fr, Intl. Line Vickers Viscount in flight.

1963, Nov. 2 **Unwmk.** ***Perf. 13***

C16 AP7 25fr dk bl, emer & red brn .45 .20
C17 AP7 55fr bis, bl & red brn 1.10 .30
C18 AP7 100fr dk bl, red brn & yel grn 2.10 .60
Nos. C16-C18 (3) 3.65 1.10

Issued to publicize Air Mali.

Crowned Crane and Giant Tortoise — AP8

1963, Nov. 23 **Unwmk.** ***Perf. 13***

C19 AP8 25fr sepia, org & ver 1.60 .60
C20 AP8 200fr multi 7.00 2.25

Animal protection.

UN Emblem, Flag, Doves — AP9

1963, Dec. 10 **Engr.**

C21 AP9 50fr lt grn, yel & red 1.40 .40

15th anniversary of the Universal Declaration of Human Rights.

Cleopatra and Ptolemy at Kôm Ombo — AP10

1964, Mar. 9 Unwmk. *Perf. 12*

C22 AP10 25fr dp claret & bister 1.00 .35
C23 AP10 55fr dp claret & lt ol grn 2.00 .75

UNESCO world campaign to save historic monuments in Nubia.

Pres. John F. Kennedy — AP11

1964, Oct. 26 Photo. *Perf. 12½*

C24 AP11 100fr sl, red brn & blk 2.50 1.00
a. Souv. sheet of 4 10.00 10.00

Touracos — AP12

200fr, Abyssinian ground hornbills, vert. 300fr, Egyptian vultures, vert. 500fr, Goliath herons.

1965, Feb. 15 Engr. *Perf. 13*

C25 AP12 100fr grn, dk bl & red 2.75 .90
C26 AP12 200fr blk, red & brt bl 8.00 1.25
C27 AP12 300fr blk, sl grn & yel 12.50 2.25
C28 AP12 500fr sl grn, dk brn & claret 20.00 3.50
Nos. C25-C28 (4) 43.25 7.90

UN Headquarters, New York, and ICY Emblem — AP13

1965, Mar. 15 Unwmk. *Perf. 13*

C29 AP13 55fr bis, dk bl & vio brn 1.25 .40

International Cooperation Year.

Pope John XXIII AP14

Perf. 12½x13

1965, Sept. 14 Photo. Unwmk.

C30 AP14 100fr multi 2.50 1.00

Winston Churchill — AP15

1965, Oct. 11 Engr. *Perf. 13*

C31 AP15 100fr brn & indigo 2.50 1.00

Dr. Albert Schweitzer and Sick Child — AP16

1965, Dec. 20 Photo. *Perf. 12½*

C32 AP16 100fr multi 2.75 1.00
a. Souv. sheet of 4 11.00 11.00

Major Edward H. White and Gemini 4 — AP17

#C34, Lt. Col. Alexei A. Leonov. 300fr, Gordon Cooper, Charles Conrad, Alexei Leonov & Pavel Belyayev, Parthenon, Athens, & vase, vert.

1966, Jan. 10

C33 AP17 100fr vio, yel, lt bl & blk 1.75 1.10
C34 AP17 100fr bl, red, yel & blk 1.75 1.10
C35 AP17 300fr multi 5.25 3.00
Nos. C33-C35 (3) 8.75 5.20

Achievements in space research and 16th Intl. Astronautical Congress, Athens, Sept. 12-18, 1965.

Papal Arms and UN Emblem — AP18

1966, July 11 Engr. *Perf. 13*

C36 AP18 200fr brt bl, grnsh bl & grn 3.50 1.75

Visit of Pope Paul VI to the UN, NYC, Oct. 4, 1965.

People and UNESCO Emblem — AP19

1966, Sept. 5 Engr. *Perf. 13*

C37 AP19 100fr dk car rose, sl grn & ultra 2.50 1.25

20th anniv. of UNESCO.

Soccer Players, Ball, Globe, and Jules Rimet Cup — AP20

1966, Oct. 31 Photo. *Perf. 13*

C38 AP20 100fr multi 2.75 1.40

8th International Soccer Championship Games, Wembley, England, July 11-30.

Crab and Mt. Fuji — AP21

UNICEF Emblem and Children — AP22

1966, Nov. 30 Photo. *Perf. 13*

C39 AP21 100fr multi 2.25 .90

9th Intl. Anticancer Cong., Tokyo, Oct. 23-29.

1966, Dec. 10 Engr.

C40 AP22 45fr dp bl, bis brn & red lil 1.00 .40

20th anniv. of UNICEF.

Land Cruisers in Hoggar Mountain Pass — AP23

1967, Mar. 20 Engr. *Perf. 13*

C41 AP23 200fr multi 6.25 2.00

"Black Cruise 1924," which crossed Africa from Beni-Abbes, Algeria to the Indian Ocean and on to Tananarive, Madagascar, Oct. 28, 1924-June 26, 1925.

Diamant Rocket and Francesco de Lana's 1650 Flying Boat — AP24

Designs: 100fr, A-1 satellite and rocket launching adapted from Jules Verne. 200fr, D-1 satellite and Leonardo da Vinci's bird-borne flying machine.

1967, Apr. 17 Engr. *Perf. 13*

C42 AP24 50fr brt bl, pur & grn .90 .25
C43 AP24 100fr dk Prus bl, dk car & lil 1.75 .50
C44 AP24 200fr sl bl, ol & pur 3.50 1.00
Nos. C42-C44 (3) 6.15 1.75

Honoring French achievements in space.

Amelia Earhart and Map of Mali — AP25

1967, May 29 Photo. *Perf. 13*

C45 AP25 500fr bl & multi 11.00 3.00

Amelia Earhart's stop at Gao, West Africa, 30th anniv.

Paul as Harlequin, by Picasso AP26

Picasso Paintings: 50fr, Bird Cage. 250fr, The Flutes of Pan.

1967, June 16 *Perf. 12½*

C46 AP26 50fr multi 1.25 .40
C47 AP26 100fr multi 2.75 .75
C48 AP26 250fr multi 5.75 1.60
Nos. C46-C48 (3) 9.75 2.75

See No. C82.

Jamboree Emblem, Scout Knots and Badges — AP27

Design: 100fr, Scout with portable radio transmitter, tents and Jamboree badge.

1967, July 10 Engr. *Perf. 13*

C49 AP27 70fr dk car, emer & bl grn .90 .25
C50 AP27 100fr dk car lake, sl grn & blk 1.25 .30
a. Strip of 2, #C49-C50 + label 3.00 1.75

12th Boy Scout World Jamboree, Farragut State Park, Idaho, Aug. 1-9.

Head of Horse, by Toulouse-Lautrec — AP28

300fr, Cob-drawn gig, by Toulouse-Lautrec.

Perf. 12x12½, 12½x12

1967, Dec. 11 **Photo.**

C51 AP28 100fr multi	3.25	1.25
C52 AP28 300fr multi, vert.	8.00	2.50

See Nos. C66-C67.

Grenoble AP29

Design: 150fr, Bobsled course on Huez Alp.

1968, Jan. 8 **Engr.** ***Perf. 13***

C53 AP29 50fr bl, yel brn & grn	.90	.25
C54 AP29 150fr brn, vio bl & stl bl	2.25	.75

10th Winter Olympic Games, Grenoble, France, Feb. 6-18.

Roses and Anemones, by Van Gogh — AP30

Paintings: 150fr, Peonies in Vase, by Edouard Manet (36x49mm). 300fr, Bouquet, by Delarcroix (41x42mm). 500fr, Daisies in Vase, by Jean François Millet (49x37mm).

Perf. 13, 12½x12, 12x12½

1968, June 24 **Photo.**

C55 AP30 50fr multi	1.00	.50
C56 AP30 150fr grn & multi	2.40	.65
C57 AP30 300fr grn & multi	4.75	1.40
C58 AP30 500fr car & multi	7.00	2.00
Nos. C55-C58 (4)	15.15	4.55

Martin Luther King, Jr. — AP31

Long Jumper and Satellite — AP32

1968, July 22 ***Perf. 12½***

C59 AP31 100fr rose lil, sal pink & blk	1.40	.40

Bicycle Type of Regular Issue

Designs: 50fr, Bicyclette, 1918. 100fr, Mercedes Benz, 1927, horiz.

1968, Aug. 12 **Engr.** ***Perf. 13***

C60 A40 50fr gray, dk grn & brick red	1.25	.30
C61 A40 100fr lemon, indigo & car	2.75	.70

1968, Nov. 25 **Photo.** ***Perf. 12½***

100fr, Soccer goalkeeper and satellite.

C62 AP32 100fr multi, horiz.	1.40	.60
C63 AP32 150fr multi	2.50	.80

19th Olympic Games, Mexico City, 10/12-27.

PHILEXAFRIQUE Issue

Editorial Department, by François Marius Granet — AP33

1968, Dec. 23 **Photo.** ***Perf. 12½x12***

C64 AP33 200fr multi	3.50	1.75

Issued to publicize PHILEXAFRIQUE Philatelic Exhibition in Abidjan, Feb. 14-23. Printed with alternating light green label.

See Nos. C85-C87, C110-C112, C205-C207, C216-C217.

2nd PHILEXAFRIQUE Issue

Common Design Type

100fr, French Sudan #64, sculpture.

1969, Feb. 14 **Engr.** ***Perf. 13***

C65 CD128 100fr pur & multi	2.00	1.00

Painting Type of 1967

Paintings: 150fr, Napoleon as First Consul, by Antoine Jean Gros, vert. 250fr, Bivouac at Austerlitz, by Louis François Lejeune.

Perf. 12½x12, 12x12½

1969, Feb. 25 **Photo.**

C66 AP28 150fr multi	4.00	1.25
C67 AP28 250fr multi	5.75	1.75

Napoleon Bonaparte (1769-1821).

Montgolfier's Balloon — AP34

Designs: 150fr, Ferber 5, experimental biplane. 300fr, Concorde.

1969, Mar. 10 **Photo.** ***Perf. 13***

C68 AP34 50fr multi	.70	.30
C69 AP34 150fr multi	2.25	.60
C70 AP34 300fr multi	4.50	1.40
a. Strip of 3, #C68-C70	9.00	4.50

1st flight of the prototype Concorde plane at Toulouse, France, Mar. 1, 1969.

For overprints see Nos. C78-C80.

Auto Type of Regular Issue

55fr, Renault, 1898, Renault 16, 1969. 90fr, Peugeot, 1893, Peugeot 404, 1969.

1969, May 30 **Engr.** ***Perf. 13***

C71 A43 55fr rose car, blk & brt pink	1.60	.35
C72 A43 90fr blk, dp car & indigo	2.25	.60

Ronald Clarke, Australia, 10,000-meter Run, 1965 — AP35

World Records: 90fr, Yanis Lusis, USSR, Javelin, 1968. 120fr, Yoshinobu Miyake, Japan, weight lifting, 1967. 140fr, Randy Matson, US, shot put, 1968. 150fr, Kipchoge Keino, Kenya, 3,000-meter run, 1965.

1969, June 23 **Engr.** ***Perf. 13***

C73 AP35 60fr bl & ol brn	.45	.20
C74 AP35 90fr car rose & red brn	.70	.30
C75 AP35 120fr emer & gray ol	1.00	.55
C76 AP35 140fr gray & brn	1.00	.60
C77 AP35 150fr red org & blk	1.25	.65
Nos. C73-C77 (5)	4.40	2.30

Issued to honor sports world records.

Nos. C68-C70 Overprinted in Red with Lunar Landing Module and: "L'HOMME SUR LA LUNE / JUILLET 1969 / APOLLO 11"

1969, July 25 **Photo.** ***Perf. 13***

C78 AP34 50fr multi	.90	.60
C79 AP34 150fr multi	2.25	1.25
C80 AP34 300fr multi	3.50	2.00
a. Strip of 3, #C78-C80	9.00	4.50

Man's 1st landing on moon, July 20, 1969. US astronauts Neil A. Armstrong and Col. Edwin E. Aldrin, Jr., with Lieut. Col. Michael Collins piloting Apollo 11.

Apollo 8, Moon and Earth — AP35a

Embossed on Gold Foil

1969, July 24 ***Die-cut perf 10½***

C81 AP35a 2000fr gold	27.00	27.00

US Apollo 8 mission, the 1st men in orbit around the moon, Dec. 21-27, 1968.

Painting Type of 1967

500fr, Mona Lisa, by Leonardo da Vinci.

1969, Oct. 20 **Photo.** ***Perf. 12½***

C82 AP26 500fr multi	7.25	2.25

Mahatma Gandhi — AP36

1969, Nov. 24 **Engr.** ***Perf. 13***

C83 AP36 150fr brt bl, ol brn & red brn	3.00	.70

Map of West Africa, Post Horns and Lightning Bolts — AP37

1970, Feb. 23 **Photo.** ***Perf. 12½***

C84 AP37 100fr multi	1.00	.40

11th anniversary of the West African Postal Union (CAPTEAO).

Painting Type of 1968

Paintings: 100fr, Madonna and Child, from Rogier van der Weyden school. 150fr, Nativity, by the master of Flemalle. 250fr, Madonna and Child with St. John, from the Dutch School.

1970, Mar. 2

C85 AP33 100fr multi	1.00	.40
C86 AP33 150fr multi	1.60	.80
C87 AP33 250fr multi	3.50	1.40
Nos. C85-C87 (3)	6.10	2.60

Roosevelt AP38

Lenin — AP39

1970, Mar. 30 **Photo.** ***Perf. 12½***

C88 AP38 500fr red, lt ultra & blk	5.00	2.50

Pres. Franklin D. Roosevelt (1882-1945).

1970, Apr. 22

C89 AP39 300fr pink, grn & blk	4.50	1.25

Jules Verne and Firing of Moon Rockets — AP40

150fr, Jules Verne, rockets, landing modules & moon. 300fr, Jules Verne & splashdown.

1970, May 4

C90	AP40	50fr multi	.90	.30
C91	AP40	150fr multi	2.25	.80
C92	AP40	300fr multi	4.00	1.60
		Nos. C90-C92 (3)	7.15	2.70

Nos. C90-C92 Overprinted in Red or Blue: "APOLLO XIII / EPOPEE SPATIALE / 11-17 AVRIL 1970"

1970, June Photo. *Perf. 12½*

C93	AP40	50fr multi (Bl)	.55	.25
C94	AP40	150fr multi (R)	1.60	.80
C95	AP40	300fr multi (Bl)	3.25	1.60
		Nos. C93-C95 (3)	5.40	2.65

Flight and safe return of Apollo 13, Apr. 11-13, 1970.

Intelsat III — AP41

Telecommunications Through Space: 200fr, Molniya I satellite. 300fr, Radar. 500fr, "Project Symphony" (various satellites).

1970, July 13 Engr. *Perf. 13*

C96	AP41	100fr gray, brt bl & org	.90	.40
C97	AP41	200fr bl, gray & red lil	1.75	.50
C98	AP41	300fr org, dk brn & gray	2.75	1.40
C99	AP41	500fr dk brn, sl & grnsh bl	4.50	2.25
		Nos. C96-C99 (4)	9.90	4.55

For surcharges see Nos. C108-C109.

Auguste and Louis Lumière, Jean Harlow and Marilyn Monroe AP42

1970, July 27 Photo. *Perf. 12½x12*

C100	AP42	250fr multi	5.25	2.00

Issued to honor Auguste Lumière (1862-1954), and his brother Louis Jean Lumière (1864-1948), inventors of the Lumière process of color photography and of a motion picture camera.

Soccer — AP43

1970, Sept. 7 Engr. *Perf. 13*

C101	AP43	80fr bl, dp car & brn ol	.90	.30
C102	AP43	200fr dp car, bl grn & ol brn	2.25	.80

9th World Soccer Championships for the Jules Rimet Cup, Mexico City, May 30-June 21, 1970.

Rotary Emblem, Map of Mali and Ceremonial Antelope Heads — AP44

Men Holding UN Emblem, and Doves — AP45

1970, Sept. 21 Photo. *Perf. 12½*

C103	AP44	200fr multi	2.75	1.25

Issued to honor Rotary International.

1970, Oct. 5 Engr. *Perf. 13*

C104	AP45	100fr dk pur, red brn & dk bl	1.25	.50

25th anniversary of the United Nations.

Koran Page, Baghdad, 11th Century AP46

Moslem Art: 200fr, Tree, and lion killing deer, mosaic, Jordan, c. 730, horiz. 250fr, Scribe, miniature, Baghdad, 1287.

1970, Oct. 26 Photo. *Perf. 12½x12*

C105	AP46	50fr multi	.90	.30
C106	AP46	200fr multi	1.75	.65
C107	AP46	250fr multi	2.75	.95
		Nos. C105-C107 (3)	5.40	1.90

Nos. C97-C98 Surcharged and Overprinted: "LUNA 16 / PREMIERS PRELEVEMENTS AUTOMATIQUES / SUR LA LUNE / SEPTEMBRE 1970"

1970, Nov. 9 Engr. *Perf. 13*

C108	AP41	150fr on 200fr multi	1.25	.65
C109	AP41	250fr on 300fr multi	2.25	.95

Unmanned moon probe of the Russian space ship Luna 16, Sept. 12-24.

Painting Type of 1968

100fr, Nativity, Antwerp School, c. 1530. 250fr, St. John the Baptist, by Hans Memling. 300fr, Adoration of the Kings, Flemish School, 17th cent.

1970, Dec. 1 Photo. *Perf. 12½x12*

C110	AP33	100fr brown & multi	1.00	.40
C111	AP33	250fr brown & multi	2.75	.95
C112	AP33	300fr brown & multi	3.50	1.25
		Nos. C110-C112 (3)	7.25	2.60

Christmas 1970.

Gamal Abdel Nasser — AP47

Embossed on Gold Foil

1970, Nov. 25 *Perf. 12½*

C113	AP47	1000fr gold	15.00	15.00

In memory of Gamal Abdel Nasser (1918-1970), President of Egypt.

Charles de Gaulle AP48

Embossed on Gold Foil

1971, Feb. 8 *Die-cut Perf. 10*

C114	AP48	2000fr gold, red & dp ultra	70.00	70.00

In memory of Gen. Charles de Gaulle (1890-1970), President of France.

Alfred Nobel — AP49

Tennis, Davis Cup — AP50

1971, Feb. 22 Engr. *Perf. 13*

C115	AP49	300fr multi	3.50	1.00

Alfred Nobel (1833-1896), inventor of dynamite, sponsor of Nobel Prize.

1971, Mar. 8

Designs: 150fr, Derby at Epsom, horiz. 200fr, Racing yacht, America's Cup.

C116	AP50	100fr bl, lil & slate	1.75	.60
C117	AP50	150fr brn, brt grn & ol	2.75	.90
C118	AP50	200fr brt bl, ol & brn	3.50	1.25
		Nos. C116-C118 (3)	8.00	2.75

The Arabian Nights — AP51

Designs: 180fr, Ali Baba and the 40 Thieves. 200fr, Aladdin's Lamp.

1971, Apr. 5 Photo. *Perf. 13*

C119	AP51	120fr gold & multi	1.75	.60
C120	AP51	180fr gold & multi	2.50	.90
C121	AP51	200fr gold & multi	3.00	1.00
		Nos. C119-C121 (3)	7.25	2.50

Olympic Rings and Sports — AP52

1971, June 28 Photo. *Perf. 12½*

C122	AP52	80fr ultra, yel grn & brt mag	.90	.30

Pre-Olympic Year.

Mariner 4 — AP53

Design: 300fr, Venera 5 in space.

1971, Sept. 13 Engr. *Perf. 13*

C123	AP53	200fr multi	1.75	.70
C124	AP53	300fr multi	2.75	.95

Space explorations of US Mariner 4 (200fr); and USSR Venera 5 (300fr).

Santa Maria, 1492 — AP54

Famous Ships: 150fr, Mayflower, 1620. 200fr, Potemkin, 1905. 250fr, Normandie, 1935.

1971, Sept. 27

C125	AP54	100fr brn, bluish grn & pur	1.25	.40
C126	AP54	150fr sl grn, brn & pur	2.00	.70
C127	AP54	200fr car, bl & dk ol	2.50	.80
C128	AP54	250fr blk, bl & red	3.25	1.00
		Nos. C125-C128 (4)	9.00	2.90

Symbols of Justice and Maps — AP55

1971, Oct. 18

C129	AP55	160fr mar, ocher & dk brn	1.40	.50

25th anniversary of the International Court of Justice in The Hague, Netherlands.

Statue of Zeus, by Phidias — AP56

Nat "King" Cole — AP57

The Seven Wonders of the Ancient World: 80fr, Cheops Pyramid and Sphinx. 100fr, Temple of Artemis, Ephesus, horiz. 130fr, Lighthouse at Alexandria. 150fr, Hanging Gardens of Babylon, horiz. 270fr, Mausoleum of Halicarnassus. 280fr, Colossus of Rhodes.

1971, Dec. 13

C130 AP56 70fr ind, dk red & pink .70 .25
C131 AP56 80fr brn, bl & blk .90 .25
C132 AP56 100fr org, ind & pur 1.00 .30
C133 AP56 130fr rose lil, blk & grnsh bl 1.25 .40
C134 AP56 150fr brn, brt grn & bl 1.50 .50
C135 AP56 270fr sl, brn & plum 2.50 .70
C136 AP56 280fr sl lil & ol 2.75 .80
Nos. C130-C136 (7) 10.60 3.20

1971, Dec. 6 Photo. *Perf. 13x12½*

Famous American Black Musicians: 150fr, Erroll Garner. 270fr, Louis Armstrong.

C137 AP57 130fr blk, brn & yel 2.75 .40
C138 AP57 150fr blk, bl & yel 3.00 .50
C139 AP57 270fr blk, rose car & yel 5.00 .70
Nos. C137-C139 (3) 10.75 1.60

Slalom and Japanese Child AP58

200fr, Ice hockey & character from Noh play.

1972, Jan. 10 Engr. *Perf. 13*

C140 AP58 150fr multicolored 1.25 .50
C141 AP58 200fr multicolored 1.75 .70
a. Souv. sheet of 2, #C140-C141 3.50 3.50

11th Winter Olympic Games, Sapporo, Japan, Feb. 3-13.

Santa Maria della Salute, by Ippolito Caffi — AP59

Paintings of Venice, by Ippolito Caffi: 270fr, Rialto Bridge. 280fr, St. Mark's Square, vert.

1972, Feb. 21 Photo. *Perf. 13*

C142 AP59 130fr gold & multi 1.25 .45
C143 AP59 270fr gold & multi 2.00 .70
C144 AP59 280fr gold & multi 2.10 .75
Nos. C142-C144 (3) 5.35 1.90

UNESCO campaign to save Venice.

Hands of 4 Races Holding Scout Flag — AP60

1972, Mar. 27 Engr. *Perf. 13*

C145 AP60 200fr dk red, ocher & ol gray 2.25 .60

World Boy Scout Seminar, Cotonou, Dahomey, March, 1972.

"Your Heart is your Health" — AP61

1972, Apr. 7 Engr. *Perf. 13*

C146 AP61 150fr brt bl & red 1.75 .50

World Health Day.

Soccer Player and Frauenkirche, Munich — AP62

Designs (Sport and Munich Landmarks): 150fr, Judo and TV Tower, vert. 200fr, Steeplechase and Propylaeum, vert. 300fr, Runner and Church of the Theatines.

1972, Apr. 17

C147 AP62 50fr ocher, dk bl & grn .45 .20
C148 AP62 150fr dk bl, ocher & grn 1.25 .45
C149 AP62 200fr grn, dk bl & ocher 1.60 .60
C150 AP62 300fr dk bl, grn & ocher 2.25 .75
a. Min. sheet of 4, #C147-C150 5.75 5.75
Nos. C147-C150 (4) 5.55 2.00

20th Olympic Games, Munich, 8/26-9/10.
For overprints see Nos. C165-C166, C168.

Apollo 15, Lunar Rover, Landing Module — AP63

Design: 250fr, Cugnot's steam wagon and Montgolfier's Balloon.

1972, Apr. 27

C151 AP63 150fr multicolored 1.75 .60
C152 AP63 250fr multicolored 3.50 1.25

Development of transportation.

Cinderella AP64

Fairy Tales: 80fr, Puss in Boots. 150fr, Sleeping Beauty.

1972, June 19 Engr. *Perf. 13x12½*

C153 AP64 70fr multicolored 1.10 .30
C154 AP64 80fr multicolored 1.25 .35
C155 AP64 150fr multicolored 2.00 .60
Nos. C153-C155 (3) 4.35 1.25

Charles Perrault (1628-1703), French writer.

Astronauts and Lunar Rover on Moon — AP65

1972, July 24 Engr. *Perf. 13*

C156 AP65 500fr multicolored 4.00 1.40

US Apollo 16 moon mission, Apr. 15-27.

Book Year Emblem — AP66

1972, Aug. 7 Litho. *Perf. 12½*

C157 AP66 80fr bl, gold & grn 1.75 .60

International Book Year 1972.

Bamako Rotary Emblem with Crocodiles AP67

1972, Oct. 9 Engr. *Perf. 13*

C158 AP67 170fr dk brn, red & ultra 1.75 .60

10th anniv. of the Bamako Rotary Club.

Hurdler, Olympic Rings, Melbourne Cathedral, Kangaroo — AP68

Designs (Olympic Rings and): 70fr, Boxing, Helsinki Railroad Station, arms of Finland, vert. 140fr, Running, Colosseum, Roman wolf. 150fr, Weight lifting, Tokyo stadium, phoenix, vert. 170fr, Swimming, University Library, Mexico City; Aztec sculpture. 210fr, Javelin, Munich Stadium, Arms of Munich. Stamps inscribed with name of gold medal winner of event shown.

1972, Nov. 13 Engr. *Perf. 13*

C159 AP68 70fr red, ocher & ind .45 .20
C160 AP68 90fr red brn, bl & sl .55 .25
C161 AP68 140fr brn, brt grn & ol gray .90 .30
C162 AP68 150fr dk car, emer & gray ol 1.00 .35
C163 AP68 170fr red lil, brn & Prus bl 1.10 .40
C164 AP68 210fr ultra, emer & brick red 1.25 .50
Nos. C159-C164 (6) 5.25 2.00

Retrospective of Olympic Games 1952-1972.
For overprint see No. C167.

Nos. C148-C150 and C164 Overprinted:

a. JUDO / RUSKA / 2 MEDAILLES D'OR
b. STEEPLE / KEINO / MEDAILLE D'OR
c. MEDAILLE D'OR / 90m. 48
d. 100m.-200m. / BORZOV / 2 MEDAILLES D'OR

1972, Nov. 27 Engr. *Perf. 13*

C165 AP62 150fr multi (a) 1.00 .40
C166 AP62 200fr multi (b) 1.40 .50
C167 AP68 210fr multi (c) 1.60 .55
C168 AP62 300fr multi (d) 2.25 .70
Nos. C165-C168 (4) 6.25 2.15

Gold medal winners in 20th Olympic Games: Wim Ruska, Netherlands, heavyweight judo (#C165); Kipchoge Keino, Kenya, 3000m. steeplechase (#C166); Klaus Wolfermann, Germany, javelin (#C167); Valery Borzov, USSR, 100m., 200m. race (#C168).

Emperor Haile Selassie AP69

1972, Dec. 26 Photo. *Perf. 12½*

C169 AP69 70fr grn & multi .70 .25

80th birthday of Emperor Haile Selassie of Ethiopia.

Plane, Balloon, Route Timbuktu to Bamako — AP70

300fr, Balloon, jet & route Timbuktu to Bamako.

1972, Dec. 29 *Perf. 13½*

C170 AP70 200fr multi 1.25 .50
C171 AP70 300fr bl & multi 2.25 .80

First postal balloon flight in Mali.

Bishop of 14th Century European Chess Set — AP71

Design: 200fr, Knight (elephant), from 18th century Indian set.

1973, Feb. 19 Engr. *Perf. 13*

C172 AP71 100fr dk car, bl & ind 1.75 .60
C173 AP71 200fr blk, red & brn 3.50 1.25

World Chess Championship, Reykjavik, Iceland, July-Sept., 1972.

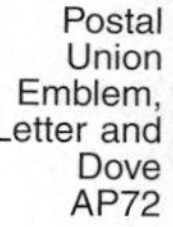

Postal Union Emblem, Letter and Dove AP72

1973, Mar. 9 Photo. *Perf. 11½x11*

C174 AP72 70fr bl, blk & org .70 .25

10th anniv. (in 1971) of African Postal Union. This stamp was to be issued Dec. 8, 1971. It was offered by the agency on Mar. 9, 1973. Copies were sold in Mali as early as July or August, 1972.

No. C20, Collector's Hand and Philatelic Background
AP73

1973, Mar. 12 **Engr.** ***Perf. 13***
C175 AP73 70fr multi 1.75 .50

Stamp Day, 1973.

Astronauts and Lunar Rover on Moon
AP74

1973, Mar. 26
C176 AP74 250fr bl, indigo & bis 2.75 1.00

Souvenir Sheet

C177 AP74 350fr choc, vio bl & ultra 2.75 1.60

Apollo 17 US moon mission, 12/7-19/72.

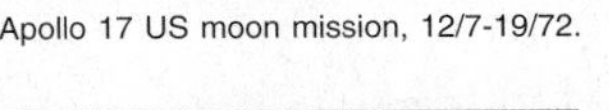

Nicolaus Copernicus — AP75

1973, Apr. 9 **Engr.** ***Perf. 13***
C178 AP75 300fr brt bl & mag 3.50 1.25

500th anniversary of the birth of Nicolaus Copernicus (1473-1543), Polish astronomer.

Dr. Armauer G. Hansen and Leprosy Bacillus — AP76

1973, May 7 **Engr.** ***Perf. 13***
C179 AP76 200fr blk, yel grn & red 2.25 .85

Centenary of the discovery of the Hansen bacillus, the cause of leprosy.

Bentley and Alfa Romeo, 1930 — AP77

Designs: 100fr, Jaguar and Talbot, 1953. 200fr, Matra and Porsche, 1972.

1973, May 21 **Engr.** ***Perf. 13***
C180 AP77 50fr bl, org & grn .50 .25
C181 AP77 100fr grn, ultra & car .90 .30
C182 AP77 200fr ind, grn & car 2.50 .60
Nos. C180-C182 (3) 3.90 1.15

50th anniversary of the 24-hour automobile race at Le Mans, France.

Camp Fire, Fleur-de-Lis
AP78

Designs (Fleur-de-Lis and): 70fr, Scouts saluting flag, vert. 80fr, Scouts with flags. 130fr, Lord Baden-Powell, vert. 270fr, Round dance and map of Africa.

1973, June 4
C183 AP78 50fr dk red, ultra & choc .35 .25
C184 AP78 70fr sl grn, dk brn & red .55 .25
C185 AP78 80fr mag, sl grn & ol .65 .25
C186 AP78 130fr brn, ultra & sl grn 1.00 .40
C187 AP78 270fr mag, gray & vio bl 2.00 .60
Nos. C183-C187 (5) 4.55 1.75

Mali Boy and Girl Scouts and International Scouts Congress.
For surcharges see Nos. C222-C223.

Swimming, US and "Africa" Flags — AP79

80fr, Discus, javelin, vert. 330fr, Runners.

1973, July 30 **Engr.** ***Perf. 13***
C188 AP79 70fr red, sl grn & bl .50 .25
C189 AP79 80fr vio bl, dk ol & red .60 .25
C190 AP79 330fr red & vio bl 2.50 .80
Nos. C188-C190 (3) 3.60 1.30

First African-United States sports meet.

Head and City Hall, Brussels
AP80

Perseus, by Benvenuto Cellini — AP81

1973, Sept. 17 **Engr.** ***Perf. 13***
C191 AP80 70fr brt ultra, ol & vio .70 .25

Africa Weeks, Brussels, Sept. 15-30, 1973.

1973, Sept. 24

Famous Sculptures: 150fr, Pietá, by Michelangelo. 250fr, Victory of Samothrace, Greek 1st century B.C.

C192 AP81 100fr dk car & sl grn 1.00 .30
C193 AP81 150fr dk car & dp cl 1.60 .50
C194 AP81 250fr dk car & dk ol 2.75 .80
Nos. C192-C194 (3) 5.35 1.60

Stephenson's Rocket and Buddicom Engine — AP82

Locomotives: 150fr, Union Pacific, 1890, and Santa Fe, 1940. 200fr, Mistral and Tokaido, 1970.

1973, Oct. 8 **Engr.** ***Perf. 13***
C195 AP82 100fr brn, bl & blk 1.10 .40
C196 AP82 150fr red, brt ultra & dk car 1.75 .70
C197 AP82 200fr ocher, bl & ind 2.50 .90
Nos. C195-C197 (3) 5.35 2.00

Apollo XI on Moon
AP83

75fr, Landing capsule, Apollo XIII. 100fr, Astronauts & equipment on moon, Apollo XIV. 280fr, Rover, landing module % astronauts on moon, Apollo XV. 300fr, Lift-off from moon, Apollo XVII.

1973, Oct. 25
C198 AP83 50fr vio, org & sl grn .35 .25
C199 AP83 75fr slate, red & bl .55 .25
C200 AP83 100fr slate, bl & ol brn .70 .30
C201 AP83 280fr vio bl, red & sl grn 1.75 .55
C202 AP83 300fr slate, red & sl grn 2.00 .80
Nos. C198-C202 (5) 5.35 2.15

Apollo US moon missions.
For surcharges see Nos. C224-C225.

Pablo Picasso — AP84

John F. Kennedy — AP85

1973, Nov. 7 **Litho.** ***Perf. 12½***
C203 AP84 500fr multi 5.50 2.00

Pablo Picasso (1881-1973), painter.

1973, Nov. 12
C204 AP85 500fr gold, brt rose lil & blk 4.75 1.75

Painting Type of 1968

100fr, Annunciation, by Vittore Carpaccio, horiz. 200fr, Virgin of St. Simon, by Federigo Baroccio. 250fr, Flight into Egypt, by Andrea Solario.

Perf. 13x12½, 12½x12, 12½x13

1973, Nov. 30 **Litho.**
C205 AP33 100fr blk & multi .90 .25
C206 AP33 200fr blk & multi 1.75 .60
C207 AP33 250fr blk & multi 2.25 .80
Nos. C205-C207 (3) 4.90 1.65

Christmas 1973.

Soccer Player and Ball — AP86

250fr, Goalkeeper & ball. 500fr, Frauenkirche, Munich, Arms of Munich & soccer ball, horiz.

1973, Dec. 3 **Engr.** ***Perf. 13***
C208 AP86 150fr emer, ol brn & red 1.25 .50
C209 AP86 250fr emer, vio bl & ol brn 2.25 .70

Souvenir Sheet

C210 AP86 500fr bl & multi 4.50 4.50

World Soccer Cup, Munich.

Musicians, Mosaic from Pompeii — AP87

Designs (Mosaics from Pompeii): 250fr, Alexander the Great in battle, vert. 350fr, Bacchants, vert.

1974, Jan. 21 **Engr.** ***Perf. 13***
C211 AP87 150fr sl bl, ol & rose 1.50 .30
C212 AP87 250fr mag, ol & ocher 2.00 .50
C213 AP87 350fr ol, dp brn & ocher 2.50 .70
Nos. C211-C213 (3) 6.00 1.50

Winston Churchill — AP88

1974, Mar. 18 **Engr.** ***Perf. 13***
C214 AP88 500fr black 3.75 1.25

Chess Game — AP89

1974, Mar. 25 **Engr.** ***Perf. 13***
C215 AP89 250fr multi 5.25 1.75

21st Chess Olympic Games, Nice 1974.

Painting Type of 1968

Paintings: 400fr, Crucifixion, Alsatian School, c. 1380, vert. 500fr, Burial of Christ, by Titian.

Perf. 12½x13, 13x12½

1974, Apr. 12			**Photo.**	
C216	AP33	400fr multi	2.75	.90
C217	AP33	500fr multi	3.50	1.25

Easter 1974.

Lenin — AP90

1974, Apr. 22		**Engr.**	***Perf. 13***	
C218	AP90	150fr vio bl & lake	2.75	.60

50th anniversary of the death of Lenin.

Women's Steeplechase — AP91

1974, May 20		**Engr.**	***Perf. 13***	
C219	AP91	130fr bl, lil & brn	2.25	.60

World Horsewomen's Championship, La Baule, France, June 30-July 7.

Skylab Docking in Space — AP92

250fr, Skylab over globe with Africa.

1974, July 1		**Engr.**	***Perf. 13***	
C220	AP92	200fr bl, sl & org	1.40	.50
C221	AP92	250fr lil, sl & org	2.40	.70

Skylab's flight over Africa, 1974.

Nos. C184-C185 Surcharged in Violet Blue with New Value, Two Bars and:

a. 11e JAMBOREE ARABE / AOUT 1974 LIBAN
b. CONGRES PANARABE LIBAN / AOUT 1974

1974, July 8		**Engr.**	***Perf. 13***	
C222	AP78	130fr on 70fr (a)	1.50	.50
C223	AP78	170fr on 80fr (b)	1.90	.60

11th Pan-Arab Jamboree and Pan-Arab Congress, Batrun, Lebanon, Aug. 1974.

Nos. C200-C201 Surcharged in Red with New Value, Two Bars and:

c. Ier DEBARQUEMENT / SUR LA LUNE / 20-VII-69
d. Ier PAS SUR LA / LUNE 21-VII-69

1974, July 15				
C224	AP83	130fr on 100fr (c)	1.00	.40
C225	AP83	300fr on 280fr (d)	3.00	1.25

First manned moon landing, July 20, 1969, and first step on moon, July 21, 1969.

1906 and 1939 Locomotives — AP93

Locomotives: 120fr, Baldwin, 1870, and Pacific, 1920. 210fr, Al., 1925, and Buddicom, 1847. 330fr, Hudson, 1938, and La Gironde, 1839.

1974, Oct. 7		**Engr.**	***Perf. 13***	
C226	AP93	90fr dk car & multi	1.10	.40
C227	AP93	120fr ocher & multi	1.50	.50
C228	AP93	210fr org & multi	2.40	.70
C229	AP93	330fr grn & multi	3.50	1.10
		Nos. C226-C229 (4)	8.50	2.70

Skier, Winter Sports and Olympic Rings AP94

1974, Oct. 7				
C230	AP94	300fr multi	2.75	.80

Holy Family, by Hans Memling AP95

310fr, Virgin & Child, Bourgogne School. 400fr, Adoration of the Kings, by Martin Schongauer.

1974, Nov. 4		**Photo.**	***Perf. 12½***	
C231	AP95	290fr multi	2.10	.60
C232	AP95	310fr multi	2.50	.70
C233	AP95	400fr multi	3.25	1.10
		Nos. C231-C233 (3)	7.85	2.40

Christmas 1974.
See Nos. C238-C240, C267-C269.

Raoul Follereau — AP96

1974, Nov. 18		**Engr.**	***Perf. 13***	
C234	AP96	200fr brt bl	2.75	.85

Raoul Follereau (1903-1977), apostle to the lepers and educator of the blind. See No. C468.

Europafrica Issue

Train, Jet, Cogwheel, Grain, Maps of Africa and Europe — AP97

1974, Dec. 27		**Engr.**	***Perf. 13***	
C235	AP97	100fr brn, grn & indigo	1.00	.30
C236	AP97	110fr ocher, vio bl & pur	1.10	.40

Painting Type of 1974

Designs: 200fr, Christ at Emmaus, by Philipe de Champaigne, horiz. 300fr, Christ at Emmaus, by Paolo Veronese, horiz. 500fr, Christ in Majesty, Limoges, 13th century.

Perf. 13x12½, 12½x13

1975, Mar. 24			**Litho.**	
C238	AP95	200fr multi	1.50	.50
C239	AP95	300fr multi	2.50	.70
C240	AP95	500fr multi	4.50	1.25
		Nos. C238-C240 (3)	8.50	2.45

Easter 1975.

"Voyage to the Center of the Earth" — AP99

Jules Verne's Stories: 170fr, "From Earth to Moon" and Verne's portrait. 190fr, "20,000 Leagues under the Sea." 220fr, "A Floating City."

1975, Apr. 7		**Engr.**	***Perf. 13***	
C241	AP99	100fr multi	.75	.25
C242	AP99	170fr multi	1.40	.45
C243	AP99	190fr multi	1.40	.50
C244	AP99	220fr multi	1.75	.55
		Nos. C241-C244 (4)	5.30	1.75

Dawn, by Michelangelo — AP100

Design: 500fr, Moses, by Michelangelo.

1975, Apr. 28		**Photo.**	***Perf. 13***	
C245	AP100	400fr multi	3.00	.90
C246	AP100	500fr multi	3.75	1.25

Michelangelo Buonarroti (1475-1564), Italian sculptor, painter and architect.

Astronaut on Moon — AP101

Designs: 300fr, Constellations Virgo and Capricorn. 370fr, Statue of Liberty, Kremlin, Soyuz and Apollo spacecraft.

1975, May 19		**Engr.**	***Perf. 13***	
C247	AP101	290fr multi	1.40	.60
C248	AP101	300fr multi	1.40	.60
C249	AP101	370fr multi	2.40	.90
		Nos. C247-C249 (3)	5.20	2.10

Soviet-American space cooperation.
For overprints see Nos. C264-C266.

Boy Scout, Globe, Nordjamb 75 Emblem AP103

150fr, Boy Scout giving Scout sign. 290fr, Scouts around campfire.

1975, June 23		**Engr.**	***Perf. 13***	
C251	AP103	100fr claret, brn & bl	.75	.25
C252	AP103	150fr red, brn & grn	1.10	.30
C253	AP103	290fr bl, grn & claret	2.10	.65
		Nos. C251-C253 (3)	3.95	1.20

Nordjamb 75, 14th Boy Scout Jamboree, Lillehammer, Norway, July 29-Aug. 7.

Battle Scene and Marquis de Lafayette — AP104

300fr, Battle scene & George Washington. 370fr, Battle of Chesapeake Bay & Count de Grasse.

1975, July 7		**Engr.**	***Perf. 13***	
C254	AP104	290fr lt bl & indigo	1.75	.60
C255	AP104	300fr lt bl & indigo	1.75	.60
C256	AP104	370fr lt bl & indigo	2.25	.90
a.		Strip of 3, #C254-C256	8.50	3.50

Bicentenary of the American Revolution. No. C256a has continuous design.

Schweitzer, Bach and Score AP105

Designs: No. C257, Albert Einstein (1879-1955), theoretical physicist. No. No. C258, André-Marie Ampère (1775-1836), French physicist. 100fr, Clément Ader (1841-1925), French aviation pioneer. No. C260, Dr. Albert Schweitzer (1875-1965), Medical missionary and musician. No. C261, Sir Alexander Fleming (1881-1955), British bacteriologist, discoverer of penicillin.

1975		**Engr.**	***Perf. 13***	
C257	AP105	90fr multi	1.10	.40
C258	AP105	90fr pur, org & bister	1.10	.40
C259	AP105	100fr bl, red & lilac	1.10	.40
C260	AP105	150fr grn, bl & dk grn	1.60	.60
C261	AP105	150fr lil, bl & brick red	1.25	.45
		Nos. C257-C261 (5)	6.15	2.25

Issued: #C257, May 26; #C258, Sept. 23; 100fr, Dec. 8; #C260, Jan. 14; #C261, July 21.
For surcharge see No. C358.

Olympic Rings and Globe — AP106

400fr, Montreal Olympic Games' emblem.

1975, Oct.				
C262	AP106	350fr pur & bl	2.50	.75
C263	AP106	400fr blue	3.00	.85

Pre-Olympic Year 1975.

Nos. C247-C249 Overprinted: "ARRIMAGE / 17 Juil. 1975"

1975, Oct. 20		**Engr.**	***Perf. 13***	
C264	AP101	290fr multi	2.10	.60
C265	AP101	300fr multi	2.25	.65
C266	AP101	370fr multi	3.25	1.00
		Nos. C264-C266 (3)	7.60	2.25

Apollo-Soyuz link-up in space, July 17, 1975.

Painting Type of 1974

Designs: 290fr, Visitation, by Ghirlandaio. 300fr, Nativity, Fra Filippo Lippi school. 370fr, Adoration of the Kings, by Velazquez.

1975, Nov. 24 Litho. *Perf. 12½x13*

C267 AP95 290fr multi 2.10 .60
C268 AP95 300fr multi 2.25 .70
C269 AP95 370fr multi 3.25 1.10
Nos. C267-C269 (3) 7.60 2.40

Christmas 1975.

Concorde — AP107

1976, Jan. 12 Litho. *Perf. 13*

C270 AP107 500fr multi 5.25 1.50

Concorde supersonic jet, first commercial flight, Jan. 21, 1976.

For overprint see No. C315.

AP108

AP109

1976, Feb. 16 Litho. *Perf. 13*

C271 AP108 120fr Figure skating .70 .25
C272 AP108 420fr Ski jump 2.25 .70
C273 AP108 430fr Slalom 2.25 .70
Nos. C271-C273 (3) 5.20 1.65

12th Winter Olympic Games, Innsbruck, Austria, Feb. 4-15.

1976, Apr. 5 Litho. *Perf. 12½*

Eye examination, WHO emblem.

C274 AP109 130fr multi 1.00 .25

World Health Day: "Foresight prevents blindness."

Space Ship with Solar Batteries — AP110

Design: 300fr, Astronaut working on orbital space station, vert.

1976, May 10 Engr. *Perf. 13*

C275 AP110 300fr org, dk & lt bl 2.00 .60
C276 AP110 400fr mag, dk bl & org 3.00 .90

Futuristic space achievements.

American Eagle, Flag and Liberty Bell — AP111

Designs: 400fr, Revolutionary War naval battle and American eagle. 440fr, Indians on horseback and American eagle, vert.

1976, May 24 Litho. *Perf. 12½*

C277 AP111 100fr multi .70 .25
C278 AP111 400fr multi 3.00 .75
C279 AP111 440fr multi 3.00 .80
Nos. C277-C279 (3) 6.70 1.80

American Bicentennial. Nos. C278-C279 also for Interphil 76, International Philatelic Exhibition, Philadelphia, Pa, May 29-June 6.

Running AP112

Designs (Olympic Rings and): 250fr, Swimming. 300fr, Field ball. 440fr, Soccer.

1976, June 7 Engr. *Perf. 13*

C280 AP112 200fr red brn & blk 1.10 .30
C281 AP112 250fr multi 1.40 .40
C282 AP112 300fr multi 2.00 .50
C283 AP112 440fr multi 2.75 .75
Nos. C280-C283 (4) 7.25 1.95

21st Olympic Games, Montreal, Canada, July 17-Aug. 1.

Cub Scout and Leader — AP113

Designs: 180fr, Scouts tending sick animal, horiz. 200fr, Night hike.

1976, June 14 Engr. *Perf. 13*

C284 AP113 140fr ultra & red brn 1.00 .35
C285 AP113 180fr dk brn & multi 1.40 .45
C286 AP113 200fr brn org & vio bl 1.50 .50
Nos. C284-C286 (3) 3.90 1.30

First African Boy Scout Jamboree, Nigeria.

Mohenjo-Daro, Bull from Wall Relief — AP114

Design: 500fr, Man's head, animals, wall and UNESCO emblem.

1976, Sept. 6 Engr. *Perf. 13*

C287 AP114 400fr blk, bl & pur 2.40 .60
C288 AP114 500fr dk red, bl & grn 3.25 1.10

UNESCO campaign to save Mohenjo-Daro excavations.

Europafrica Issue

Freighter, Plane, Map of Europe and Africa — AP115

1976, Sept. 20

C289 AP115 200fr vio brn & bl 2.00 .70

Nativity, by Taddeo Gaddi — AP116

Paintings: 300fr, Adoration of the Kings, by Hans Memling. 320fr, Nativity, by Carlo Crivelli.

1976, Nov. 8 Litho. *Perf. 13x12½*

C290 AP116 280fr multi 2.00 .50
C291 AP116 300fr multi 2.25 .60
C292 AP116 320fr multi 2.40 .75
Nos. C290-C292 (3) 6.65 1.85

Christmas 1976.

Viking Flying to Mars — AP117

1000fr, Viking landing craft on Mars.

1976, Dec. 8 Engr. *Perf. 13*

C293 AP117 500fr red, brn & bl 3.00 1.25
C294 AP117 1000fr multi 5.00 1.75
a. Miniature sheet of 2 10.00 3.50

Operation Viking, US Mars mission, No. C294a contains 2 stamps similar to Nos. C293-C294 in changed colors.

Pres. Giscard d'Estaing, Village and Bambara Antelope — AP118

1977, Feb. 13 Photo. *Perf. 13*

C295 AP118 430fr multi 4.25 .90

Visit of Pres. Valéry Giscard d'Estaing of France, Feb. 13-15.

Elizabeth II and Prince Philip — AP119

Designs: 200fr, Charles de Gaulle. vert. 250fr, Queen Wilhelmina, vert. 300fr, King Baudouin and Queen Fabiola. 480fr, Coronation of Queen Elizabeth II, vert.

1977, Mar. 21 Litho. *Perf. 12*

C296 AP119 180fr multi 1.10 .45
C297 AP119 200fr multi 1.25 .45
C298 AP119 250fr multi 1.60 .55
C299 AP119 300fr multi 2.00 .65
C300 AP119 480fr multi 3.00 1.00
Nos. C296-C300 (5) 8.95 3.10

Personalities involved in de-colonization.

Newton, Rocket and Apple — AP120

1977, May 7 Engr. *Perf. 13*

C301 AP120 400fr grn, brn & red 3.25 .90

Isaac Newton (1643-1727), natural philosopher and mathematician, 250th death anniversary.

Charles Lindbergh and Spirit of St. Louis — AP121

430fr, Spirit of St. Louis flying over clouds.

1977, Apr. 4 Litho. *Perf. 12*

C302 AP121 420fr org & pur 2.75 .80
C303 AP121 430fr multi 2.75 .80

Charles A. Lindbergh's solo transatlantic flight from New York to Paris, 50th anniversary.

Sassenage Castle, Grenoble — AP122

1977, May 21 Litho. *Perf. 12½*

C304 AP122 300fr multi 2.00 .60

Intl. French Language Council, 10th anniv.

Zeppelin No. 1, 1900 — AP123

Designs: 130fr, Graf Zeppelin, 1924. 350fr, Hindenburg aflame at Lakehurst, NJ, 1937. 500fr, Ferdinand von Zeppelin and Graf Zeppelin.

1977, May 30 Engr. *Perf. 13*

C305 AP123 120fr multi .70 .25
C306 AP123 130fr multi .90 .25
C307 AP123 350fr multi 2.25 .65
C308 AP123 500fr multi 3.25 .75
Nos. C305-C308 (4) 7.10 1.90

History of the Zeppelin.

Martin Luther King, American and Swedish Flags — AP124

Design: 600fr, Henri Dunant, Red Cross, Swiss and Swedish flags.

1977, July 4 **Engr.** ***Perf. 13***

C309 AP124 600fr multi 2.25 .70
C310 AP124 700fr multi 2.75 .75

Nobel Peace Prize recipients.

Soccer — AP125

Designs: 200fr, 3 soccer players, vert. 420fr, 3 soccer players.

1977, Oct. 3 **Engr.** ***Perf. 13***

C311 AP125 180fr multi .70 .30
C312 AP125 200fr multi .90 .35
C313 AP125 420fr multi 2.00 .75
Nos. C311-C313 (3) 3.60 1.40

World Soccer Cup Elimination Games.

Mao Tse-tung and COMATEX Hall, Bamako — AP126

1977, Nov. 7 **Engr.** ***Perf. 13***

C314 AP126 300fr dull red 5.00 .90

Chairman Mao Tse-tung (1893-1976).

No. C270 Overprinted in Violet Blue: "PARIS NEW-YORK 22.11.77"

1977, Nov. 22 **Litho.** ***Perf. 13***

C315 AP107 500fr multi 11.50 5.50

Concorde, first commerical transatlantic flight, Paris to New York.

Virgin and Child, by Rubens AP127

Rubens Paintings: 400fr, Adoration of the Kings. 600fr, Detail from Adoration of the Kings, horiz.

1977, Dec. 5 ***Perf. 12½x12, 12x12½***

C316 AP127 400fr gold & multi 1.75 .60
C317 AP127 500fr gold & multi 2.25 .80
C318 AP127 600fr gold & multi 3.00 1.00
Nos. C316-C318 (3) 7.00 2.40

Christmas 1977, and 400th birth anniversary of Peter Paul Rubens (1577-1640).

Battle of the Amazons, by Rubens — AP128

Rubens Paintings: 300fr, Return from the fields. 500fr, Hercules fighting the Nemean Lion, vert.

Perf. 12x12½, 12½x12

1978, Jan. 16 **Litho.**

C319 AP128 200fr multi 1.00 .30
C320 AP128 300fr multi 1.60 .50
C321 AP128 500fr multi 2.75 .80
Nos. C319-C321 (3) 5.35 1.60

Peter Paul Rubens, 400th birth anniversary.

Schubert Composing "Winterreise" — AP129

Design: 300fr, Schubert and score, vert.

1978, Feb. 13

C322 AP129 300fr multi 1.60 .50
C323 AP129 420fr multi 2.25 .70

Franz Schubert (1797-1828), Austrian composer.

Capt. Cook Receiving Hawaiian Delegation — AP130

Design: 300fr, Cook landing on Hawaii. Designs after sketches by John Weber.

1978, Feb. 27 **Engr.** ***Perf. 13***

C324 AP130 200fr multi 1.50 .40
C325 AP130 300fr multi 2.50 .55

Capt. James Cook (1728-1779), bicentenary of his arrival in Hawaii.

Soccer — AP131

250fr, One player. 300fr, Two players, horiz.

1978, Mar. 20

C326 AP131 150fr multi 1.00 .30
C327 AP131 250fr multi 1.60 .50
a. "REPUPLIQUE" 3.25 .90
C328 AP131 300fr multi 2.10 .60
a. Min. sheet of 3, #C326-C328 + label 6.00 4.00
b. As "a," #C326, C327a, C328 9.00 6.00
Nos. C326-C328 (3) 4.70 1.40

World Soccer Cup Championships, Argentina, 1978, June 1-25.

Nos. C327 and C328a were issued in July to correct the spelling error.

For overprints see Nos. C338-C340.

Jesus with Crown of Thorns, by Dürer AP132

430fr, Resurrection, by Albrecht Dürer.

1978, Mar. 28

C329 AP132 420fr multi 3.00 .60
C330 AP132 430fr multi 3.25 .60

Easter 1978. See Nos. C359-C361.

Citroen, C3-Trefle, 1922 — AP133

Citroen Cars: 130fr, Croisiere Noire, 1924, tractor. 180fr, B14G, 1927. 200fr, "11" Tractor Avant, 1934.

1978, Apr. 24 **Engr.** ***Perf. 13***

C331 AP133 120fr multi 1.10 .25
C332 AP133 130fr multi 1.25 .25
C333 AP133 180fr multi 1.60 .40
C334 AP133 200fr multi 1.75 .45
Nos. C331-C334 (4) 5.70 1.35

Andre Citroen (1878-1935), automobile designer and manufacturer.

UPU Emblem, World Map, Country Names — AP133a

Design: 130fr, UPU emblem, globe and names of member countries.

1978, May 15

C334A AP133a 120fr multi .80 .25
C335 AP133a 130fr red, grn & emer 1.10 .25

Centenary of Congress of Paris where General Postal Union became the Universal Postal Union.

Europafrica Issue

Zebra, Miniature by Mansur, Jehangir School, 1620 — AP134

Design: 100fr, Ostrich Incubating Eggs, Syrian Manuscript, 14th Century.

1978, July 24 **Litho.** ***Perf. 13x12½***

C336 AP134 100fr multi 3.00 .60
C337 AP134 110fr multi 3.00 .60

Nos. C326-C328a Overprinted in Black:

a. CHAMPION / 1978 / ARGENTINE
b. 2e HOLLANDE
c. 3e BRESIL / 4e ITALIE

1978, Aug. 7 **Engr.** ***Perf. 13***

C338 AP131 150fr multi (a) 1.25 .35
C339 AP131 250fr multi (b) 1.60 .50
C340 AP131 300fr multi (c) 2.25 .60
a. Souvenir sheet of 3 6.50 2.50
Nos. C338-C340 (3) 5.10 1.45

Winners, World Soccer Cup Championship, Argentina. Overprints on No. C340a are green including label overprint: FINALE / ARGENTINA 3 HOLLANDE 1.

Elizabeth II in Coronation Robes AP135

Design: 500fr, Coronation coach.

1978, Sept. 18 **Litho.** ***Perf. 12½x12***

C341 AP135 500fr multi 2.40 .65
C342 AP135 1000fr multi 5.25 1.50

Coronation of Queen Elizabeth II, 25th anniv.

US No. C3a and Douglas DC-3 AP136

History of Aviation: 100fr, Belgium No. 252 and Stampe SV-4. 120fr, France No. C48 and Ader's plane No. 3. 130fr, Germany No. C2 and Junker Ju-52. 320fr, Japan No. C25 and Mitsubishi A-6M "Zero."

1978, Oct. 16 **Engr.** ***Perf. 13***

C343 AP136 80fr multi .45 .20
C344 AP136 100fr multi .55 .20
C345 AP136 120fr multi .65 .20
C346 AP136 130fr multi .70 .20
C347 AP136 320fr multi 1.75 .55
Nos. C343-C347 (5) 4.10 1.35

Annunciation, by Dürer — AP137

Etchings by Dürer: 430fr, Virgin and Child. 500fr, Adoration of the Kings.

1978, Nov. 6

C348 AP137 420fr blk & rose car 1.60 .50
C349 AP137 430fr ol grn & brn 1.75 .60
C350 AP137 500fr blk & red 2.40 .70
Nos. C348-C350 (3) 5.75 1.80

Christmas 1978 and 450th death anniversary of Albrecht Dürer (1471-1528), German painter.

Rocket and Trajectory Around Moon — AP138

Design: 300fr, Spaceship circling moon.

1978, Nov. 20 Engr. *Perf. 13*

C351	AP138 200fr multi		1.50	.60
C352	AP138 300fr multi		2.25	.70
a.	Pair, #C351-C352 + label		4.75	2.00

10th anniversary of 1st flight around moon.

Ader's Plane and Concorde — AP139

Designs: 130fr, Wright Flyer A and Concorde. 200fr, Spirit of St. Louis and Concorde.

1979, Jan. 25 Litho. *Perf. 13*

C353	AP139 120fr multi	.80	.25
C354	AP139 130fr multi	1.00	.30
C355	AP139 200fr multi	1.75	.55
	Nos. C353-C355 (3)	3.55	1.10

1st supersonic commercial flight, 3rd anniv.
For surcharges see Nos. C529-C531.

Philexafrique II-Essen Issue
Common Design Types

Designs: No. C356, Dromedary and Mali No. C26. No. C357, Bird and Lubeck No. 1.

1979, Jan. 29 Litho. *Perf. 13x12½*

C356	CD138 200fr multi	3.00	1.00
C357	CD139 200fr multi	3.00	1.00
a.	Pair, #C356-C357 + label	7.50	3.00

No. C257 Surcharged

1979, Mar. 26 Engr. *Perf. 13*

C358	AP105 130fr on 90fr multi	1.50	.50

Albert Einstein (1879-1955).

Easter Type of 1978

Dürer Etchings: 400fr, Jesus Carrying Cross. 430fr, Crucified Christ. 480fr, Pietà.

1979, Apr. 9

C359	AP132 400fr bl & blk	2.50	.75
C360	AP132 430fr red & blk	2.75	.85
C361	AP132 480fr ultra & blk	3.00	.95
	Nos. C359-C361 (3)	8.25	2.55

Easter 1979.

Basketball and Cathedral, Moscow AP140

430fr, Soccer and St. Basil's Cathedral.

1979, Apr. 17 Litho. *Perf. 13*

C362	AP140 420fr multi	2.25	.80
C363	AP140 430fr multi	2.25	.80

Pre-Olympic Year.

Mali #C92, Apollo Spacecraft AP141

Design: 500fr, Mali No. C176, lift-off.

1979, Oct. 22 Litho. *Perf. 12½x13*

C364	AP141 430fr multi	2.25	.70
C365	AP141 500fr multi	2.40	.80

Apollo 11 moon landing, 10th anniversary.

Capt. Cook, Ship, Kerguelen Island — AP142

Design: 480fr, Capt. Cook, Ship, Hawaii.

1979, Oct. 29 *Perf. 13x12½*

C366	AP142 300fr multi	1.75	.60
C367	AP142 480fr multi	2.40	.85

Capt. James Cook (1728-1779).

David Janowski (1868-1927), Chess Pieces — AP143

Chess Pieces and Grand Masters: 140fr, Alexander Alekhine (1892-1946). 200fr, W. Schlage. 300fr, Effim D. Bogoljubow (1889-1952).

1979, Nov. 30 Engr. *Perf. 13*

C368	AP143 100fr red & brn	1.00	.25
C369	AP143 140fr multi	1.40	.25
C370	AP143 200fr multi	2.00	.40
C371	AP143 300fr multi	2.75	.55
	Nos. C368-C371 (4)	7.15	1.45

For overprints see Nos. C441-C442.

Adoration of the Kings, by Dürer AP144

Christmas 1979: 400fr, 500fr, Adoration of the Kings by Dürer, diff.

1979, Dec. 10 *Perf. 13x13½*

C372	AP144 300fr brn org & brn	1.60	.50
C373	AP144 400fr bl & brn	2.25	.70
C374	AP144 500fr dk grn & brn	2.75	.90
	Nos. C372-C374 (3)	6.60	2.10

Jet, Map of Africa AP145

1979, Dec. 27 Litho. *Perf. 12½*

C375	AP145 120fr multi	.90	.30

ASECNA (Air Safety Board), 20th anniv.

Train, Globe, Rotary Emblem AP146

Rotary Intl., 75th Anniv.: 250fr, Jet. 430fr, Bamako Club emblem, meeting hall.

1980, Jan. 28 Litho. *Perf. 12½*

C376	AP146 220fr multi	1.10	.40
C377	AP146 250fr multi	1.10	.40
C378	AP146 430fr multi	2.00	.70
	Nos. C376-C378 (3)	4.20	1.50

Speed Skating, Lake Placid '80 Emblem, Snowflake AP147

1980, Feb. 11 *Perf. 13*

C379	AP147 200fr shown	.90	.25
C380	AP147 300fr Ski jump	1.25	.50
a.	Souvenir sheet of 2	3.25	2.00

13th Winter Olympic Games, Lake Placid, NY, Feb. 12-24. No. C380a contains Nos. C379-C380 in changed colors.

Stephenson's Rocket, Mali No. 196 — AP148

Liverpool-Manchester Railroad, 150th Anniversary: 300fr, Stephenson's Rocket, Mali No. 142.

1980, Feb. 25 Engr.

C381	AP148 200fr multi	1.10	.25
C382	AP148 300fr multi	1.75	.50

Equestrian, Moscow '80 Emblem — AP149

1980, Mar. 10 Engr. *Perf. 13*

C383	AP149 200fr shown	1.00	.30
C384	AP149 300fr Yachting	1.40	.50
C385	AP149 400fr Soccer	2.25	.70
a.	Souvenir sheet of 3, #C383-C385	5.00	5.00
	Nos. C383-C385 (3)	4.65	1.50

22nd Summer Olympic Games, Moscow, July 19-Aug. 3.
For overprints see Nos. C399-C401.

Jesus Carrying Cross, by Maurice Denis AP150

Easter: 500fr, Jesus before Pilate, by Dürer.

1980, Mar. 31

C386	AP150 480fr brn & org red	2.50	.80
C387	AP150 500fr org red & brn	2.50	.80

Kepler, Copernicus and Solar System Diagram — AP151

200fr, Kepler & diagram of earth's orbit.

1980, Apr. 7 Engr. *Perf. 13*

C388	AP151 200fr multi, vert.	1.25	.30
C389	AP151 300fr multi	1.75	.50

Discovery of Pluto, 50th Anniversary — AP152

1980, Apr. 21

C390	AP152 420fr multi	2.10	.75

Lunokhod I, Russian Flag — AP153

Design: 500fr, Apollo and Soyuz spacecraft, flags of US and Russia.

1980, Apr. 28

C391	AP153 480fr multi	2.25	.70
C392	AP153 500fr multi	2.25	.70

Lunokhod I, 10th anniversary; Apollo-Soyuz space test program, 5th anniversary.

Rochambeau, French Fleet Landing at Newport, R.I. — AP154

French Cooperation in American Revolution: 430fr, Rochambeau and George Washington, eagle.

1980, June 16 Engr. *Perf. 13*

C393 AP154 420fr multi 2.25 .75
C394 AP154 430fr multi 2.25 .75

Jet Flying Around Earth — AP155

Designs: No. C396, Ship, people, attack. No. C397, Astronaut on moon. No. C398, Space craft, scientists, moon. Nos. C395-C396 from "Around the World in 80 Days;" Nos. C397-C398 from "From Earth to Moon."

1980, June 30 Engr. *Perf. 11*

C395 AP155 100fr multi + label .80 .25
C396 AP155 100fr multi + label .80 .25
C397 AP155 150fr multi + label 1.10 .30
C398 AP155 150fr multi + label 1.10 .30
Nos. C395-C398 (4) 3.80 1.10

Jules Verne (1828-1905), French science fiction writer. Nos. C395-C398 each printed se-tenant with label showing various space scenes.

Nos. C383-C385a Overprinted:

200fr — CONCOURS COMPLET/ INDIVIDUEL/ROMAN (It.)/ BLINOV (Urss) /SALNIKOV (Urss)
300fr — FINN/RECHARDT (Fin.)/ MAYRHOFER (Autr.)/ BALACHOV (Urss)
400fr — TCHECOSLOVAQUIE/ ALLEMAGNE DE L'EST/URSS

1980, Sept. 8 Engr. *Perf. 13*

C399 AP149 200fr multi 1.00 .30
C400 AP149 300fr multi 1.40 .50
C401 AP149 400fr multi 2.25 .75
a. Souvenir sheet of 3 5.00 5.00
Nos. C399-C401 (3) 4.65 1.55

Butterfly Type of 1980

1980, Oct. 6 Litho. *Perf. 13x12½*

Size: 48x36mm

C402 A137 420fr *Denaus chrysippus* 6.00 1.00

Charles De Gaulle, Map and Colors of France — AP156

1980, Nov. 9 Litho. *Perf. 13½x13*

C403 AP156 420fr shown 3.50 .90
C404 AP156 430fr De Gaulle, cross 3.50 .90

Charles De Gaulle, 10th anniv. of death.

Mali No. 140, Amtrak Train — AP157

Mali Stamps and Trains: 120fr, No. 195, Tokaido, Japan, vert. 200fr, No. 144, Rembrandt, Germany. 480fr, No. 143, TGV-001 France, vert.

1980, Nov. 17 Engr. *Perf. 13*

C405 AP157 120fr multi .70 .25
C406 AP157 130fr multi .80 .25
C407 AP157 200fr multi 1.10 .40
C408 AP157 480fr multi 2.75 .90
Nos. C405-C408 (4) 5.35 1.80

For overprint see No. C425.

Holy Family, by Lorenzo Lotto — AP158

Christmas 1980 (Paintings): 400fr, Flight to Egypt, by Rembrandt, vert. 500fr, Christmas Night, by Gauguin.

1980, Dec. 1 Litho. *Perf. 13x12½*

C409 AP158 300fr multi 1.60 .55
C410 AP158 400fr multi 2.10 .70
C411 AP158 500fr multi 2.50 .80
Nos. C409-C411 (3) 6.20 2.05

Self-portrait, by Picasso — AP159

1981, Jan. 26 Litho. *Perf. 12½x13*

C412 AP159 1000fr multi 7.50 2.00

Pablo Picasso (1881-1973).

Soccer Players — AP160

Designs: Soccer players.

1981, Feb. 28 *Perf. 13*

C413 AP160 100fr multi .65 .25
C414 AP160 200fr multi 1.10 .35
C415 AP160 300fr multi 1.75 .50
Nos. C413-C415 (3) 3.50 1.10

Souvenir Sheet

C416 AP160 600fr multi 3.75 1.75

World Cup Soccer preliminary games.

Mozart and Instruments — AP161

225th Birth Anniversary of Wolfgang Amadeus Mozart: 430fr, Mozart and instruments, diff.

1981, Mar. 30 Litho. *Perf. 13*

C417 AP161 420fr multi 3.00 .70
C418 AP161 430fr multi 3.00 .70

Jesus Falls on the Way to Calvary, by Raphael AP162

Easter 1981: 600fr, Ecce Homo, by Rembrandt.

1981, Apr. 6 *Perf. 12½x13*

C419 AP162 500fr multi 2.50 .80
C420 AP162 600fr multi 2.75 .90

Alan B. Shepard AP163

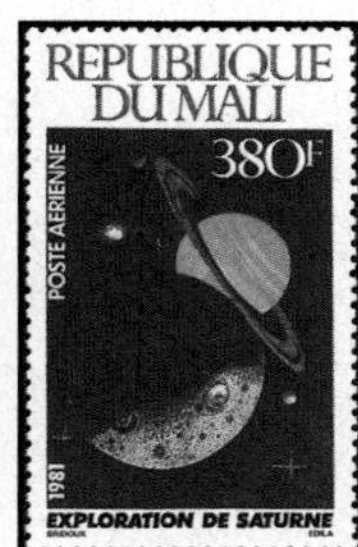

Exploration of Saturn — AP164

Space Anniversaries: No. C422, Yuri Gagarin's flight, 1961. 430fr, Uranus discovery bicentennial, horiz.

1981, Apr. 21 Litho. *Perf. 13*

C421 AP163 200fr multi 1.00 .30
C422 AP163 200fr multi 1.00 .30
C423 AP164 380fr multi 2.00 .55
C424 AP163 430fr multi 2.10 .65
Nos. C421-C424 (4) 6.10 1.80

No. C408 Overprinted:
"26 fevrier 1981
Record du monde de/vitesse-380 km/h."

1981, June 15 Engr.

C425 AP157 480fr multi 3.50 .90

New railroad speed record.

US No. 233, Columbus and His Fleet — AP165

475th Death Anniversary of Christopher Columbus (Santa Maria and): 200fr, Spain No. 418, vert. 260fr, Spain No. 421, vert. 300fr, US No. 232.

1981, June 22

C426 AP165 180fr multi 1.00 .30
C427 AP165 200fr multi 1.25 .35
C428 AP165 260fr multi 1.75 .55
C429 AP165 300fr multi 2.10 .65
Nos. C426-C429 (4) 6.10 1.85

Columbia Space Shuttle — AP166

Designs: Space shuttle.

1981, July 6 Litho. *Perf. 13*

C430 AP166 200fr multi 1.25 .30
C431 AP166 500fr multi 3.00 .90
C432 AP166 600fr multi 3.50 1.00
Nos. C430-C432 (3) 7.75 2.20

Souvenir Sheet

Perf. 12

C433 AP166 700fr multi 5.75 2.00

For overprint see No. C440.

Harlequin on Horseback AP167

Picasso Birth Cent.: 750fr, Child Holding a Dove.

1981, July 15 *Perf. 12½x13*

C434 AP167 600fr multi 4.00 1.00
C435 AP167 750fr multi 5.00 1.10

Prince Charles and Lady Diana, St. Paul's Cathedral AP168

1981, July 20 *Perf. 12½*

C436 AP168 500fr shown 2.25 .70
C437 AP168 700fr Couple, coach 3.50 1.00

Royal wedding.

Christmas 1981 AP169

Designs: Virgin and Child paintings.

1981, Nov. 9 Litho. *Perf. 12½x13*

C438 AP169 500fr Grunewald 2.75 .70
C439 AP169 700fr Correggio 3.50 1.00

See Nos. C451-C452, C464-C466, C475-C477, C488-C489, C511.

No. C433 Overprinted In Blue: "JOE ENGLE / RICHARD TRULY / 2 eme VOL SPATIAL"

1981, Nov. 12 Litho. *Perf. 12*

C440 AP166 700fr multi 5.00 1.50

Nos. C369, C371 Overprinted with Winners' Names and Dates

1981, Dec. Engr. *Perf. 13*

C441 AP143 140fr multi 1.25 .35
C442 AP143 300fr multi 2.75 .60

Lewis Carroll (1832-1908) — AP170

Designs: Scenes from Alice in Wonderland.

1982, Jan. 30 Litho. *Perf. 12½*

C443 AP170 110fr multi 2.50 .60
C444 AP170 130fr multi 2.50 .80
C445 AP170 140fr multi 2.50 1.00
Nos. C443-C445 (3) 7.50 2.40

AP171

AP172

1982, Feb. 8 *Perf. 13*

C446 AP171 700fr Portrait, by Gilbert Stuart 4.50 1.10

George Washington's Birth, 250th anniv. Incorrectly inscribed "Stuart Gilbert."

1982, Mar. 15 Litho. *Perf. 13*

1982 World Cup: Various soccer players.

C447 AP172 220fr multi 1.00 .30
C448 AP172 420fr multi 2.00 .50
C449 AP172 500fr multi 2.25 .75
Nos. C447-C449 (3) 5.25 1.55

Souvenir Sheet

Perf. 12½

C450 AP172 680fr multi 4.50 2.00

For overprints see Nos. C458-C461.

Art Type of 1981

Paintings: 680fr, Transfiguration, by Fra Angelico. 1000fr, Pieta, by Bellini, horiz.

Perf. 12½x13, 13x12½

1982, Apr. 19 Litho.

C451 AP169 680fr multi 3.25 1.75
C452 AP169 1000fr multi 4.25 1.25

Mali No. O30, France No. 1985 — AP174

1982, June 1 *Perf. 13*

C453 AP174 180fr shown 1.00 .25
C454 AP174 200fr No. C356 1.25 .35
a. Pair, #C453-C454 + label 2.75 1.40

PHILEXFRANCE '82 Intl. Stamp Exhibition, Paris, June 11-21.

Fire Engine, France, 1850 — AP175

Designs: French fire engines.

1982, June 14

C455 AP175 180fr shown 1.10 .25
C456 AP175 200fr 1921 1.25 .30
C457 AP175 270fr 1982 1.75 .45
Nos. C455-C457 (3) 4.10 1.00

Nos. C447-C450 Overprinted with Finalists' and Scores in Brown, Black, Blue or Red

1982, Aug. 16 Litho. *Perf. 13*

C458 AP172 220fr multi (Brn) 1.25 .25
C459 AP172 420fr multi 1.75 .55
C460 AP172 500fr multi (Bl) 2.25 .75
Nos. C458-C460 (3) 5.25 1.55

Souvenir Sheet

Perf. 12½

C461 AP172 680fr multi (R) 3.50 1.75

Italy's victory in 1982 World Cup.

Scouting Year — AP176

1982 *Perf. 12½*

C462 AP176 300fr Tent, Baden-Powell 1.25 .45
C463 AP176 500fr Salute, emblem 2.25 .80

Art Type of 1981

Boy with Cherries, by Edouard Manet (1832-83).

1982, Oct. 28 Litho. *Perf. 12½x13*

C464 AP169 680fr multi 4.50 1.25

Art Type of 1981

Madonna and Child Paintings.

1982, Nov. 10

C465 AP169 500fr Titian 2.25 .75
C466 AP169 1000fr Bellini 4.50 1.25

Johann von Goethe (1749-1832), Poet — AP179

1982, Dec. 13 Engr. *Perf. 13*

C467 AP179 500fr multi 3.25 .85

Follereau Type of 1974

1983, Jan. 24

C468 AP96 200fr dk brn 1.40 .35

Vostok VI, 20th Anniv. — AP180

Manned Flight, 200th Anniv. — AP181

1983, Feb. 14 Litho. *Perf. 12½*

C469 AP180 400fr Valentina Tereshkova 2.00 .60

1983, Feb. 28 *Perf. 13*

C470 AP181 500fr Eagle transatlantic balloon 3.25 .75
C471 AP181 700fr Montgolfiere 4.25 1.10

Pre-Olympic Year — AP182

1983, Mar. 14 Litho. *Perf. 13*

C472 AP182 180fr Soccer .90 .25
C473 AP182 270fr Hurdles 1.25 .45
C474 AP182 300fr Wind surfing 1.75 .55
Nos. C472-C474 (3) 3.90 1.25

Art Type of 1981

Raphael paintings.

1983, Mar. 28 *Perf. 12½x13*

C475 AP169 400fr Deposition 2.00 .60
C476 AP169 600fr Transfiguration 3.00 .85

Art Type of 1981

Design: Family of Acrobats with Monkey, by Picasso (1881-1973).

1983, Apr. 30 Litho. *Perf. 12½x13*

C477 AP169 680fr multi 3.75 1.25

Lions Intl. — AP185

1983, May 9 *Perf. 12½*

C478 Pair 15.00 6.50
a. AP185 700fr shown 4.00 1.10
b. AP185 700fr Rotary Intl. 4.00 1.10

Challenger Spacecraft AP186

1983, July 29 Litho. *Perf. 13*

C479 AP186 1000fr multi 4.75 1.25

Printed se-tenant with orange red label showing astronaut Sally Ride.

Paris-Dakar Auto Race — AP187

1983, Sept. 5 Litho. *Perf. 12½*

C480 AP187 240fr Mercedes, 1914 1.60 .35
C481 AP187 270fr SSK, 1929 1.75 .45
C482 AP187 500fr W196, 1954 3.50 .75
Nos. C480-C482 (3) 6.85 1.55

Souvenir Sheet

C483 AP187 1000fr Mercedes van 8.50 2.00

For surcharge see No. C506.

Chess Game — AP188

1983, Oct. 24 Engr. *Perf. 13*

C484 AP188 300fr Pawn, bishop 2.25 .40
C485 AP188 420fr Knight, castle 2.75 .70
C486 AP188 500fr King, Queen 3.75 .80
Nos. C484-C486 (3) 8.75 1.90

Souvenir Sheet

C487 AP188 700fr Various chess pieces 5.75 1.75

Art Type of 1981

Raphael Paintings.

1983, Nov. 7 Litho. *Perf. 12½x13*

C488 AP169 700fr Canigiani Madonna 3.50 .90
C489 AP169 800fr Madonna with Lamb 3.75 1.00

Portrait of Leopold Zborowski, by Amedeo Modigliani (1884-1920) — AP190

1984, Feb. 13 Litho. *Perf. 12½x13*

C490 AP190 700fr multi 4.75 1.25

Abraham Lincoln — AP191

Duke Ellington AP192

1984, Feb. 27 *Perf. 12½*
C491 AP191 400fr Henri Dunant 2.00 .50
C492 AP191 540fr shown 2.50 .60

1984, Mar. 12 *Perf. 13½x13*
C493 AP192 470fr Sidney Bechet 5.00 .90
C494 AP192 500fr shown 6.00 .90

Glider — AP193

1984, Mar. 26
C495 AP193 270fr shown 1.60 .35
C496 AP193 350fr Hang glider 2.00 .55

1984 Summer Olympics — AP194

1984, Apr. 9 *Perf. 13*
C497 AP194 265fr Weight lifting 1.60 .35
C498 AP194 440fr Equestrian 2.50 .55
C499 AP194 500fr Hurdles 3.00 .60

Souvenir Sheet
Perf. 12½
C500 AP194 700fr Wind surfing 5.50 1.75

For surcharges see Nos. C507-C510.

Easter 1984 — AP195

Paintings; 940fr, Crucifixion, by Rubens, vert. 970fr, Resurrection, by Mantegna.

1984, Apr. 24 **Engr.**
C501 AP195 940fr multi 6.25 1.25
C502 AP195 970fr multi 6.25 1.25

Gottlieb Daimler Birth Sesquicentenary — AP196

1984, June 1 **Engr.** *Perf. 13*
C503 AP196 350fr Mercedes Simplex 3.50 1.00
C504 AP196 470fr Mercedes-Benz 370-S 4.75 1.25
C505 AP196 485fr 500-SEC 5.00 1.25
Nos. C503-C505 (3) 13.25 3.50

No. C480 Overprinted and Surcharged

1984 **Litho.** *Perf. 12½*
C506 AP187 120fr on 240fr #C480 1.75 .40

Nos. C497-C500 Overprinted and Surcharged

1984, Oct. **Litho.** *Perf. 13*
C507 AP194 135fr on 265fr 1.00 .50
C508 AP194 220fr on 440fr 1.75 1.00
C509 AP194 250fr on 500fr 2.50 1.25
Nos. C507-C509 (3) 5.25 2.75

Souvenir Sheet
C510 AP194 350fr on 700fr 5.25 3.00

Overprints refer to the winners of the events depicted.

Art Type of 1981

Painting: Virgin and Child, by Lorenzo Lotto.

1984, Nov. 20 **Litho.** *Perf. 12½x13*
C511 AP169 500fr multi 5.00 2.00

Audubon Birth Bicentenary — AP198

1985, Apr. 15 **Litho.** *Perf. 13*
C512 AP198 180fr Kingfisher 2.00 .70
C513 AP198 300fr Bustard, vert. 3.25 1.25
C514 AP198 470fr Ostrich, vert. 5.50 2.00
C515 AP198 540fr Buzzard 6.00 2.10
Nos. C512-C515 (4) 16.75 6.05

For surcharge see No. C560, C562, C567.

ASECNA Airlines, 25th Anniv. — AP199

1985, June 10 *Perf. 12½*
C516 AP199 700fr multi 6.25 2.50

For surcharge see No. C559.

PHILEXAFRICA Type of 1985

1985, June 24 *Perf. 13*
C517 A183 200fr Boy Scouts, lion 2.25 1.10
C518 A183 200fr Satellite communications 2.25 1.10
a. Pair, #C517-C518 5.75 2.00

Halley's Comet — AP200

1986, Mar. 24 **Litho.** *Perf. 12½*
C519 AP200 300fr multi 2.75 1.10

For surcharge see No. C558.

Statue of Liberty, Cent. — AP201

1986, Apr. 7 *Perf. 13*
C520 AP201 600fr multi 6.50 2.25

Gottlieb Daimler Motorcycle — AP202

1986, Apr. 14
C521 AP202 400fr multi 4.75 1.40

1st Internal combustion automotive engine, cent.

Paul Robeson (1898-1976), American Actor, Singer — AP203

1986, May 10
C522 AP203 500fr Portrait, Show Boat 5.75 1.75

Karl Eberth (1835-1926), Bacteriologist, and Typhoid Bacilli — AP204

World Chess Championships AP205

1986, June 7 **Litho.** *Perf. 12x12½*
C523 AP204 550fr multi 5.25 2.50

1986, June 16 *Perf. 12½*
C524 AP205 400fr Chessmen 4.50 1.40
C525 AP205 500fr Knight 5.25 1.75

Disappearance of Jean Mermoz, 50th Anniv. — AP206

Mermoz and: 150fr, Latecoere-300 seaplane. 600fr, Cams 53 Oiseau Tango, seaplane. 625fr, Flight map, Le Comte de La Vaulx aircraft.

1986, Aug. 18 **Litho.** *Perf. 13*
C526 AP206 150fr multi 1.75 .50
C527 AP206 600fr multi 5.25 1.75
C528 AP206 625fr multi 5.25 2.00
Nos. C526-C528 (3) 12.25 4.25

Nos. C353-C355 Surcharged "1986-10e Anniversaire du ler Vol/Commercial Supersonique" and New Value

1986, Sept. 29
C529 AP139 175fr on 120fr 2.00 .60
C530 AP139 225fr on 130fr 2.50 .80
C531 AP139 300fr on 200fr 3.75 1.00
Nos. C529-C531 (3) 8.25 2.40

Hansen, Leprosy Bacillus, Follereau and Lepers — AP207

1987, Jan. 26 **Litho.** *Perf. 13*
C532 AP207 500fr multi 5.50 1.60

Gerhard Hansen (1841-1912), Norwegian physician who discovered the leprosy bacillus (1869); Raoul Follereau (1903-1977), philanthropist.

Konrad Adenauer (1876-1967), West German Chancellor AP208

1987, Mar. 9 **Litho.** *Perf. 13*
C533 AP208 625fr org, buff & blk 6.25 2.25

Pre-Olympics Year — AP209

Buddha and: 400fr, Runners. 500fr, Soccer players.

1987, Apr. 6 **Engr.**
C534 AP209 400fr blk & red brn 4.00 1.40
C535 AP209 500fr lil rose, ol grn & ol 5.00 1.75

25th Summer Olympics, Seoul, 1988.

Al Jolson in The Jazz Singer — AP210

1987, Apr. 20

C536	AP210	550fr dk red brn & car rose	7.75	2.25

Sound films, 60th anniv.

Albert John Luthuli (1899-1967), 1960 Nobel Peace Prize Winner — AP211

1987, May 26 Engr. *Perf. 13*

C537	AP211	400fr multi	3.75	1.10

Service Organizations AP212

1987, June 8 Litho. *Perf. 13*

C538	AP212	500fr Rotary Int'l.	5.00	1.60
C539	AP212	500fr Lions Int'l.	5.00	1.60

Coubertin, Ancient Greek Runners, Contemporary Athletes — AP213

1988, Feb. 14 Litho. *Perf. 13*

C540	AP213	240fr shown	2.25	.80
C541	AP213	400fr 5-ring emblem, stadium	4.00	1.40

125th birth anniv. of Baron Pierre de Coubertin (1863-1937), French educator and sportsman who promulgated revival of the Olympic Games; 1988 Summer Olympics, Seoul.

For surcharge see No. C565

Harlequin, by Pablo Picasso (1881-1973) — AP214

1988, Apr. 4 Litho. *Perf. 13*

C542	AP214	600fr multi	6.25	2.00

For surcharge see No. C563.

1st Scheduled Transatlantic Flight of the Concorde (London-New York), 15th Anniv. — AP215

1988, May 2 *Perf. 13*

C543	AP215	500fr multi	6.00	2.00

Home Improvement for a Verdant Mali — AP216

1989, Feb. 6 Litho. *Perf. 12½*

C544	AP216	5fr shown	.20	.20
C545	AP216	10fr Furnace, tree, field	.25	.20
C546	AP216	25fr like 5fr	.35	.25
C547	AP216	100fr like 10fr	1.25	.45
		Nos. C544-C547 (4)	2.05	1.10

1st Man on the Moon, 20th Anniv. — AP217

1989, Mar. 13 Engr. *Perf. 13*

C548	AP217	300fr multi.	3.00	1.00
C549	AP217	500fr multi, vert.	5.00	1.60

For surcharges see Nos. C561, C564.

French Revolution, Bicent. AP218

1989, July 3 Engr. *Perf. 13*

C550	AP218	400fr Women's march on Versailles	4.50	1.40
C551	AP218	600fr Storming of the Bastille	6.25	1.90

For surcharges see Nos. C566, C568.

World Cup Soccer Championships, Italy — AP219

1990, June 4 Litho. *Perf. 13*

C552	AP219	200fr multi	2.10	.70
C553	AP219	225fr multi, diff.	2.25	.80

Souvenir Sheet

C554	AP219	500fr like #C552	5.25	2.50

No. C552 overprinted in red "ITALIE : 2 / ANGLETERRE : 1"

No. C553 overprinted in red "R.F.A. : 1 / ARGENTINE : 0"

No. C554 overprinted in red in margin "1er : R.F.A. 2eme : ARGENTINE 3eme : ITALIE"

1990

C555	AP219	200fr on #C552	2.10	.85
C556	AP219	225fr on #C553	2.25	.85

Souvenir Sheet

C557	AP219	500fr on #C554	5.25	2.75

#C512-C513, C515-C516, C519, C541-C542, C548-C551 Surcharged Like #579-594

1992, June *Perfs. as Before*

Printing Methods as Before

C558	AP200	20fr on 300fr	.35	.25
C559	AP199	20fr on 700fr	.35	.25
C560	AP198	30fr on 180fr	.90	.25
C561	AP217	30fr on 500fr	.90	.25
C562	AP198	100fr on 540fr	3.00	.50
C563	AP214	100fr on 600fr	3.00	.50
C564	AP217	150fr on 300fr	4.50	.75
C565	AP213	150fr on 400fr	4.50	.75
C566	AP218	150fr on 400fr	4.50	.75
C567	AP198	200fr on 300fr	5.75	1.00
C568	AP218	240fr on 600fr	7.00	1.25
		Nos. C558-C568 (11)	34.75	6.50

Size and location of surcharge varies. No. C565 also overprinted "BARCELONE 92."

POSTAGE DUE STAMPS

Bambara Headpiece — D1

Perf. 14x13½

1961, Mar. 18 Engr. Unwmk.

J1	D1	1fr black	.25	.20
J2	D1	2fr bright ultra	.25	.20
J3	D1	5fr red lilac	.30	.20
J4	D1	10fr orange	.50	.25
J5	D1	20fr bright green	.75	.25
J6	D1	25fr red brown	.95	.30
		Nos. J1-J6 (6)	3.00	1.40

Polyptychus Roseus — D2

No. J8, Deilephila Nerii. No. J9, Gynanisa maja. No. J10, Bunaea alcinoe. No. J11, Teracolus eris. No. J12, Colotis antevippe. No. J13, Charaxes epijasius. No. J14, Manatha microcera. No. J15, Hypokopelates otraeda. No. J16, Lipaphnaeus leonina. No. J17, Gonimbrasia hecate. No. J18, Lobounaea christyi. No. J19, Hypolimnas misippus. No. J20, Catopsilia florella.

1964, June 1 Photo. *Perf. 11*

Butterflies and Moths in Natural Colors

J7	1fr olive green	.30	.20
J8	1fr org & brn	.30	.20
a.	D2 Pair, #J7-J8	.60	.20
J9	2fr emer & brn	.40	.20
J10	2fr emer & brn	.40	.20
a.	D2 Pair, #J9-J10	.80	.20
J11	3fr rose lil & brn	.40	.20
J12	3fr rose lil & brn	.40	.20
a.	D2 Pair, #J11-J12	.80	.20
J13	5fr blk & rose	.40	.20
J14	5fr green	.40	.20
a.	D2 Pair, #J13-J14	.80	.20
J15	10fr yel, org & blk	.85	.35
J16	10fr blue	.85	.35
a.	D2 Pair, #J15-J16	1.75	.70
J17	20fr lt bl & brn	1.60	.70
J18	20fr lt bl & brn	1.60	.70
a.	D2 Pair, #J17-J18	3.25	1.40
J19	25fr grn & yel	2.25	1.00
J20	25fr dp grn & blk	2.25	1.00
a.	D2 Pair, #J19-J20	4.50	2.00
	Nos. J7-J20 (14)	12.40	5.70

Nos. J7-J20 Surcharged

1984 Photo. *Perf. 11*

J21	5fr on 1fr #J7	.30	.20
J22	5fr on 1fr #J8	.30	.20
a.	D2 Pair, #J21-J22	.60	.20
J23	10fr on 2fr #J9	.30	.20
J24	10fr on 2fr #J10	.30	.20
a.	D2 Pair, #J23-J24	.60	.20
J25	15fr on 3fr #J11	.30	.20
J26	15fr on 3fr #J12	.30	.20
a.	D2 Pair, #J25-J26	.60	.20
J27	25fr on 5fr #J13	.40	.20
J28	25fr on 5fr #J14	.40	.20
a.	Pair, #J27-J28	.80	.20
J29	50fr on 10fr #J15	.70	.30
J30	50fr on 10fr #J16	.70	.30
a.	D2 Pair, #J29-J30	1.40	.60
J31	100fr on 20fr #J17	1.60	.70
J32	100fr on 20fr #J18	1.60	.70
a.	D2 Pair, #J31-J32	3.25	1.40
J33	125fr on 25fr #J19	2.00	.85
J34	125fr on 25fr #J20	2.00	.85
a.	Pair, #J33-J34	4.00	1.75
	Nos. J21-J34 (14)	11.20	5.30

OFFICIAL STAMPS

Dogon Mask — O1

Mali Coat of Arms — O2

Perf. 14x13½

1961, Mar. 18 Engr. Unwmk.

O1	O1	1fr gray	.30	.20
O2	O1	2fr red orange	.30	.20
O3	O1	3fr black	.30	.20
O4	O1	5fr light blue	.30	.20
O5	O1	10fr bister brown	.35	.20
O6	O1	25fr brt ultra	.75	.20
O7	O1	30fr car rose	.90	.20
O8	O1	50fr Prus green	1.40	.20
O9	O1	85fr red brown	2.25	.65
O10	O1	100fr emerald	2.75	.65
O11	O1	200fr red lilac	5.50	1.25
		Nos. O1-O11 (11)	15.10	4.15

1964, June 1 Photo. *Perf. 12½*

National Colors and Arms in Multicolor, Background in Light Green

O12	O2	1fr green	.30	.20
O13	O2	2fr light vio	.30	.20
O14	O2	3fr gray	.30	.20
O15	O2	5fr lilac rose	.30	.20
O16	O2	10fr bright blue	.30	.20
O17	O2	25fr ocher	.35	.20
O18	O2	30fr dark green	.50	.20
O19	O2	50fr orange	.75	.20
O20	O2	85fr dark brown	1.10	.60
O21	O2	100fr red	1.40	.60
O22	O2	200fr dk vio bl	2.75	1.10
		Nos. O12-O22 (11)	8.35	3.90

City Coats of Arms — O3

1981, Sept. Photo. *Perf. 12½x13*

O23 O3 5fr Gao .30 .20
O24 O3 15fr Timbuktu .35 .20
O25 O3 50fr Mopti .45 .20
O26 O3 180fr Segou 1.25 .25
O27 O3 200fr Sikasso 1.50 .35
O28 O3 680fr Koulikoro 4.00 .90
O29 O3 700fr Kayes 4.75 1.10
O30 O3 1000fr Bamako 6.25 1.40
Nos. O23-O30 (8) 18.85 4.60

Nos. O23-O30 Surcharged

1984 Photo. *Perf. 12½x13*

O31 O3 15fr on 5fr .30 .20
O32 O3 50fr on 15fr .55 .25
O33 O3 120fr on 50fr 1.25 .25
O34 O3 295fr on 180fr 3.25 .60
O35 O3 470fr on 200fr 4.50 .85
O36 O3 515fr on 680fr 5.00 1.00
O37 O3 845fr on 700fr 8.25 1.75
O38 O3 1225fr on 1000fr 13.00 2.25
Nos. O31-O38 (8) 36.10 7.15

MALTA

'mol-tə

LOCATION — A group of islands in the Mediterranean Sea off the coast of Sicily
GOVT. — Republic within the British Commonwealth
AREA — 122 sq. mi.
POP. — 376,513 (1998)
CAPITAL — Valletta

The former colony includes the islands of Malta, Gozo, and Comino. It became a republic Dec. 13, 1974.

4 Farthings = 1 Penny
12 Pence = 1 Shilling
20 Shillings = 1 Pound
10 Mils = 1 Cent (1972)
100 Cents = 1 Pound (1972)
100 Cents = 1 Euro (2008)

Catalogue values for unused stamps in this country are for Never Hinged items, beginning with Scott 206 in the regular postage section, Scott B1 in the semi-postal section, Scott C2 in the air post section, and Scott J21 in the postage due section.

Watermark

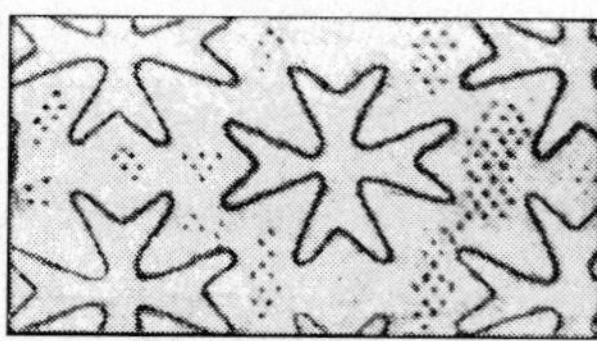
Wmk. 354 — Maltese Cross, Multiple

Values for unused stamps are for examples with original gum as defined in the catalogue introduction. Very fine examples of Nos. 1-7 will have perforations touching the frameline on one or more sides due to the narrow spacing of the stamps on the plate. Stamps with perfs clear of the frameline are scarce and will command higher prices.

Queen Victoria
A1 A2

A3

A4

1860-61 Unwmk. Typo. *Perf. 14*

1 A1 ½p buff ('63) 800.00 400.00
2 A1 ½p buff, *bluish* 1,200. 600.00
a. Imperf. (single) *11,750.*

1863-80 Wmk. 1

3 A1 ½p yellow buff ('75) 80.00 65.00
a. ½p buff 110.00 70.00
b. ½p brown orange ('67) 400.00 110.00
c. ½p orange yellow ('80) 225.00 110.00
4 A1 ½p golden yel (aniline) ('74) 325.00 375.00

1865 *Perf. 12½*

5 A1 ½p buff 160.00 110.00
a. ½p yellow buff 350.00 190.00

1878 *Perf. 14x12½*

6 A1 ½p buff 190.00 100.00
a. Perf. 12½x14 —

No. 6a unused is believed to be unique. It has a small fault.

1882 Wmk. 2 *Perf. 14*

7 A1 ½p reddish orange ('84) 21.00 *57.50*

1885, Jan. 1

8 A1 ½p green 3.75 .60
9 A2 1p car rose 8.00 .40
a. 1p rose 100.00 30.00
10 A3 2p gray 7.50 2.25
11 A4 2½p ultramarine 50.00 1.25
a. 2½p bright ultramarine 50.00 1.25
b. 2½p dull blue 65.00 3.00
12 A3 4p brown 13.00 3.50
a. Imperf., pair *6,000. 6,000.*
13 A3 1sh violet 60.00 22.50
Nos. 8-13 (6) 142.25 30.50

For surcharge see No. 20.

Queen Victoria within Maltese Cross — A5

1886 Wmk. 1

14 A5 5sh rose 125.00 95.00

Gozo Fishing Boat — A6
Ancient Galley — A7

1899, Feb. 4 Engr. Wmk. 2

15 A6 4½p black brown 21.00 16.00
16 A7 5p brown red 42.50 18.00

See Nos. 42-45.

"Malta" — A8

St. Paul after Shipwreck — A9

1899 Wmk. 1

17 A8 2sh6p olive gray 47.50 14.00
18 A9 10sh blue black 105.00 75.00

See No. 64. For overprint see No. 85.

Valletta Harbor — A10

1901, Jan. 1 Wmk. 2

19 A10 1f red brown 1.75 .55

See Nos. 28-29.

No. 11 Surcharged in Black

1902, July 4

20 A4 1p on 2½p dull blue 1.50 2.00
a. "Pnney" *32.50 65.00*
b. Double surcharge *17,500. 4,500.*

King Edward VII — A12

1903-04 Typo.

21 A12 ½p dark green 10.00 1.00
22 A12 1p car & black 17.50 .50
23 A12 2p gray & red vio 32.50 7.00
24 A12 2½p ultra & brn vio 27.50 5.25
25 A12 3p red vio & gray 2.00 .60
26 A12 4p brown & blk ('04) 30.00 19.00
27 A12 1sh violet & gray 25.00 8.25
Nos. 21-27 (7) 144.50 41.60

1904-11 Wmk. 3

28 A10 1f red brown ('05) 8.50 2.00
29 A10 1f dk brown ('10) 5.50 .20
30 A12 ½p green 6.00 .35
31 A12 1p car & blk ('05) 22.50 .25
32 A12 1p carmine ('07) 3.50 .20
33 A12 2p gray & red vio ('05) 12.00 3.00
34 A12 2p gray ('11) 4.00 6.50
35 A12 2½p ultra & brn vio 27.50 .70
36 A12 2½p ultra ('11) 6.50 4.25
37 A12 4p brn & blk ('06) 13.00 7.50
38 A12 4p scar & blk, *yel* ('11) 4.75 4.50
39 A12 1sh violet & gray 57.50 2.40
40 A12 1sh blk, *grn* ('11) 8.75 4.25
41 A12 5sh scar & grn, *yel* ('11) 75.00 87.50

Engr.

42 A6 4½p black brn ('05) 35.00 7.00
43 A6 4½p orange ('11) 5.25 4.00
44 A7 5p red ('04) 35.00 6.50
45 A7 5p ol green ('10) 5.00 4.00
Nos. 28-45 (18) 335.25 145.10

A13

A15

King George V — A16

1914-21 Typo.

Ordinary Paper

49 A13 ¼p brown 1.25 .20
50 A13 ½p green 2.50 .35
51 A13 1p scarlet ('15) 1.75 .45
a. 1p carmine ('14) 1.75 .20
52 A13 2p gray ('15) 11.00 5.50
53 A13 2½p ultramarine 2.50 .60

Chalky Paper

54 A15 3p vio, *yel* 3.00 *14.00*
58 A13 6p dull vio & red vio 13.00 *21.00*
59 A15 1sh black, *green* 14.00 *20.00*
a. 1sh black, *bl grn,* ol back 22.50 27.50
b. 1sh black, *emerald* ('21) 37.50 *82.50*
c. As "b," olive back 10.00 *27.50*
60 A16 2sh ultra & dl vio, *bl* 57.50 35.00
61 A16 5sh scar & grn, *yel* 105.00 *115.00*

Surface-colored Paper

62 A15 1sh blk, *grn* ('15) 16.00 *32.50*
Nos. 49-54,58-62 (11) 227.50 244.60

See Nos. 66-68, 70-72. For overprints see Nos. 77-82, 84.

Valletta Harbor — A17

1915 Engr.

Ordinary Paper

63 A17 4p black 17.50 7.00

St. Paul
A18

George V
A19

1919

64 A8 2sh6p olive green 70.00 *95.00*
65 A18 10sh black 3,500. *4,400.*
Revenue cancel 85.00

For overprint see No. 83.

1921-22 Typo. Wmk. 4

Ordinary Paper

66 A13 ¼p brown 2.75 *35.00*
67 A13 ½p green 5.00 *27.50*
68 A13 1p rose red 5.00 2.00
69 A19 2p gray 7.00 2.00
70 A13 2½p ultramarine 6.00 *32.50*

Chalky Paper

71 A13 6p dull vio & red vio 32.50 80.00
72 A16 2sh ultra & dull vio, *bl* 70.00 *225.00*

Engr.

Ordinary Paper

73 A18 10sh black 400.00 *750.00*
Nos. 66-73 (8) 528.25 1,154.

For overprints and surcharge see Nos. 86-93, 97.

Stamps of 1914-19 Overprinted in Red or Black

1922 Wmk. 3

Ordinary Paper

Overprint 21mm

77 A13 ½p green 1.10 *2.25*
78 A13 2½p ultra 13.00 *40.00*

Chalky Paper

79 A15 3p violet, *yel* 4.50 *24.00*
80 A13 6p dull lil & red vio 3.75 *22.00*
81 A15 1sh black, *emer* 4.50 *22.00*

Overprint 28mm

82 A16 2sh ultra & dull vio, *bl* (R) 250.00 525.00

Ordinary Paper

83 A8 2sh6p olive grn 27.50 52.50

Chalky Paper

84 A16 5sh scar & grn, *yel* 57.50 92.50
Nos. 77-84 (8) 361.85 780.25

Wmk. 1
Ordinary Paper

85 A9 10sh blue black (R) 225.00 *400.00*

Same Overprint on Stamps of 1921

1922 Ordinary Paper Wmk. 4
Overprint 21mm

86 A13 ¼p brown .35 *.75*
87 A13 ½p green 3.75 *8.50*
88 A13 1p rose red 1.10 .20
89 A19 2p gray 4.00 .50
90 A13 2½p ultramarine 1.25 *1.75*

Chalky Paper

91 A13 6p dull vio & red vio 19.00 *47.50*

Overprint 28mm

92 A16 2sh ultra & dull vio, *bl* (R) 50.00 *100.00*

Ordinary Paper

93 A18 10sh black (R) 160.00 *250.00*
Nos. 86-93 (8) 239.45 *409.20*

No. 69 Surcharged

1922, Apr. 15

97 A19 1f on 2p gray .85 .50

"Malta" — A20

Britannia and Malta — A21

1922-26 Typo.
Chalky Paper

98 A20 ¼p brown 3.00 .70
99 A20 ½p green 3.00 .20
100 A20 1p buff & plum 4.50 .20
101 A20 1p violet ('24) 4.25 .90
102 A20 1½p org brn ('23) 5.50 .20
103 A20 2p ol brn & turq 3.25 1.40
104 A20 2½p ultra ('26) 4.50 *12.00*
105 A20 3p ultramarine 5.00 2.00
a. 3p blue 4.25 1.75
106 A20 3p blk, *yel* ('26) 4.25 *18.00*
107 A20 4p yel & ultra 3.00 *4.00*
108 A20 6p ol grn & vio 4.50 3.50
109 A21 1sh ol brn & blue 9.00 3.25
110 A21 2sh ultra & ol brn 14.00 *15.00*
111 A21 2sh6p blk & red vio 12.50 *16.00*
112 A21 5sh ultra & org 24.00 *47.50*
113 A21 10sh ol brn & gray 62.50 *175.00*

Engr.
Ordinary Paper

114 A20 £1 car red & blk ('25) 125.00 *500.00*
a. £1 rose car & blk ('22) 140.00 *350.00*
Nos. 98-114 (17) 291.75 *799.85*

No. 114a has watermark sideways.

For overprints and surcharges see Nos. 115-129.

No. 105 Surcharged

1925, Dec.

115 A20 2½p on 3p ultramarine 2.00 *4.50*

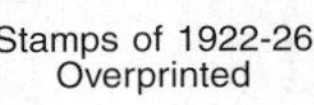
Stamps of 1922-26 Overprinted

1926

116 A20 ¼p brown .80 *5.00*
117 A20 ½p green .80 .20
118 A20 1p violet 1.10 .25
119 A20 1½p orange brown 1.25 .70
120 A20 2p ol brn & turq .85 *2.00*
121 A20 2½p ultramarine 1.40 1.00
122 A20 3p black, *yel* .85 .90
a. Inverted overprint 200.00 *550.00*
123 A20 4p yel & ultra 15.00 *26.00*
124 A20 6p ol grn & vio 3.25 *5.00*
125 A21 1sh ol brn & bl 6.25 *17.50*
126 A21 2sh ultra & ol brown 60.00 *160.00*
127 A21 2sh6p blk & red vio 18.50 *47.50*
128 A21 5sh ultra & org 11.00 *47.50*
129 A21 10sh ol brn & gray 8.50 *21.00*
Nos. 116-129 (14) 129.55 334.55

George V — A22

Valletta Harbor — A23

St. Publius — A24

Notabile (Mdina) — A25

Gozo Fishing Boat — A26

Statue of Neptune — A27

Ruins at Mnaidra — A28

St. Paul — A29

1926-27 Typo. Perf. 14½x14

131 A22 ¼p brown .90 .20
132 A22 ½p green .70 .20
133 A22 1p red 3.50 1.10
134 A22 1½p orange brn 2.25 .20
135 A22 2p gray 5.25 *11.00*
136 A22 2½p blue 4.50 1.10
137 A22 3p dark violet 5.00 4.00
138 A22 4p org red & blk 3.75 *15.00*
139 A22 4½p yel buff & vio 4.00 *4.25*
140 A22 6p red & violet 5.00 *5.50*

Engr. Perf. 12½
Inscribed: "Postage"

141 A23 1sh black 7.50 *8.00*
142 A24 1sh6p green & blk 7.50 *17.50*
143 A25 2sh dp vio & blk 7.50 *22.50*
144 A26 2sh6p ver & black 18.00 *55.00*
145 A27 3sh blue & blk 20.00 *35.00*
146 A28 5sh green & blk 25.00 *70.00*
147 A29 10sh car & blk 65.00 *110.00*
Nos. 131-147 (17) 185.35 *360.55*

See #167-183. For overprints see #148-166.

Stamps and Type of 1926-27 Overprinted in Black

1928 Perf. 14½x14

148 A22 ¼p brown 1.75 .20
149 A22 ½p green 1.75 .20
150 A22 1p red 2.00 *3.75*
151 A22 1p orange brown 5.25 .20
152 A22 1½p yel brown 2.25 1.00
153 A22 1½p red 5.00 .20
154 A22 2p gray 5.00 *10.50*
155 A22 2½p blue 2.25 .20
156 A22 3p dark violet 2.25 1.00
157 A22 4p org red & blk 2.25 2.00
158 A22 4½p yel & violet 2.50 1.10
159 A22 6p red & violet 2.50 1.75

Overprinted in Red

Perf. 12½

160 A23 1sh black 6.25 3.00
161 A24 1sh6p green & blk 11.00 *11.00*
162 A25 2sh dp vio & blk 27.50 *65.00*
163 A26 2sh6p ver & black 20.00 *26.00*
164 A27 3sh ultra & blk 22.50 *35.00*
165 A28 5sh yel grn & blk 32.50 *75.00*
166 A29 10sh car rose & black 70.00 *100.00*
Nos. 148-166 (19) 224.50 337.10

Issued: Nos. 151, 153, Dec. 5; others, Oct. 1.

Types of 1926-27 Issue

1930, Oct. 20 Typo. *Perf. 14½x14*
Inscribed: "Postage & Revenue"

167 A22 ¼p brown .70 .20
168 A22 ½p green .70 .20
169 A22 1p yel brown .70 .20
170 A22 1½p red .80 .20
171 A22 2p gray 1.40 .60
172 A22 2½p blue 2.25 .20
173 A22 3p dark violet 1.75 .20
174 A22 4p org red & blk 1.40 *4.50*
175 A22 4½p yel & violet 3.75 1.40
176 A22 6p red & violet 3.25 1.40

Engr. *Perf. 12½*

177 A23 1sh black 11.00 18.00
178 A24 1sh6p green & blk 9.75 24.00
179 A25 2sh dp vio & blk 11.00 *26.00*
180 A26 2sh6p ver & black 20.00 *60.00*
181 A27 3sh ultra & blk 30.00 62.50
182 A28 5sh yel grn & blk 37.50 75.00
183 A29 10sh car rose & blk 65.00 140.00
Nos. 167-183 (17) 200.95 414.60

Common Design Types pictured following the introduction.

Silver Jubilee Issue
Common Design Type

1935, May 6 *Perf. 11x12*

184 CD301 ½p green & blk .50 .70
185 CD301 2½p ultra & brn 2.50 *4.50*
186 CD301 6p ol grn & lt bl 7.00 7.00
187 CD301 1sh brn vio & ind 15.00 22.50
Nos. 184-187 (4) 25.00 34.70
Set, never hinged 45.00

Coronation Issue
Common Design Type

1937, May 12 Wmk. 4 *Perf. 13½x14*

188 CD302 ½p deep green .20 .20
189 CD302 1½p carmine .55 .55
190 CD302 2½p bright ultra .55 .75
Nos. 188-190 (3) 1.30 1.50
Set, never hinged 2.50

Valletta Harbor — A30

Fort St. Angelo — A31

Verdala Palace — A32

Neolithic Ruins — A33

Victoria and Citadel, Gozo — A34

De l'Isle Adam Entering Mdina — A35

St. John's Co-Cathedral A36

Mnaidra Temple — A37

Statue of Antonio Manoel de Vilhena — A38

Woman in Faldetta — A39

St. Publius — A40

Mdina Cathedral A41

Palace Square — A43

Statue of Neptune — A42

St. Paul — A44

1938-43 Wmk. 4 *Perf. 12½*

No.	Type	Description	Unused	Used
191	A30	1f brown	.20	.20
192	A31	½p green	1.75	.30
192A	A31	½p chnt ('43)	.55	.30
193	A32	1p chestnut	3.50	.40
193A	A32	1p grn ('43)	.30	.20
194	A33	1½p rose red	1.00	*2.00*
194A	A33	1½p dk gray ('43)	.20	.20
195	A34	2p dark gray	1.10	.30
195A	A34	2p rose red ('43)	.40	.25
196	A35	2½p blue	2.00	.60
196A	A35	2½p violet ('43)	.35	.35
197	A36	3p violet	1.25	.80
197A	A36	3p blue ('43)	.40	.20
198	A37	4½p ocher & ol green	.30	.30
199	A38	6p rose red & ol green	1.10	.30
200	A39	1sh black	.90	.55
201	A40	1sh6p sage grn & black	5.00	4.00
202	A41	2sh dk bl & lt grn	2.50	*6.00*
203	A42	2sh6p rose red & black	5.00	*5.50*
204	A43	5sh bl grn & blk	4.75	*8.00*
205	A44	10sh dp rose & blk	15.00	*16.00*
		Nos. 191-205 (21)	47.55	46.75
		Never hinged	75.00	

See #236a. For overprints see #208-222.

Catalogue values for unused stamps in this section, from this point to the end of the section, are for Never Hinged items.

Peace Issue

Common Design Type

Inscribed: "Malta" and Crosses

Perf. 13½x14

1946, Dec. 3 Engr. Wmk. 4

No.	Type	Description	Unused	Used
206	CD303	1p bright green	.20	.20
207	CD303	3p dark ultra	.40	1.50

Stamps of 1938-43 Overprinted in Black or Carmine

a

1948, Nov. 25 *Perf. 12½*

No.	Type	Description	Unused	Used
208	A30	1f brown	.35	.20
209	A31	½p chestnut	.35	.20
210	A32	1p green	.35	.20
211	A33	1½p dk gray (C)	1.40	.20
212	A34	2p rose red	1.40	.30
213	A35	2½p violet (C)	.90	.30
214	A36	3p blue (C)	3.00	.20
215	A37	4½p ocher & ol grn	2.75	1.75
216	A38	6p rose red & ol green	3.50	.45
217	A39	1sh black	3.75	.70
218	A40	1sh6p sage grn & blk	2.75	1.25
219	A41	2sh dk bl & lt grn (C)	5.75	2.75
220	A42	2sh6p rose red & blk	14.00	2.75
221	A43	5sh bl grn & blk (C)	26.00	5.00
222	A44	10sh dp rose & blk	26.00	25.00
		Nos. 208-222 (15)	92.25	41.25

The overprint is smaller on No. 208. It reads from lower left to upper right on Nos. 209 and 221.

See Nos. 235-240.

Silver Wedding Issue

Common Design Types

Inscribed: "Malta" and Crosses

1949, Jan. 4 Photo. *Perf. 14x14½*

No.	Type	Description	Unused	Used
223	CD304	1p dark green	.55	.20

Perf. 11½x11

Engr.

No.	Type	Description	Unused	Used
224	CD305	£1 dark blue	40.00	45.00

UPU Issue

Common Design Types

Inscribed: "Malta" and Crosses

Perf. 13½, 11x11½

1949, Oct. 10 Engr. Wmk. 4

No.	Type	Description	Unused	Used
225	CD306	2½p violet	.35	.20
226	CD307	3p indigo	3.75	1.25
227	CD308	6p dp carmine	.75	1.10
228	CD309	1sh slate	.75	*2.75*
		Nos. 225-228 (4)	5.60	5.30

Princess Elizabeth — A45

Madonna and Child — A46

1950, Dec. 1 Engr. *Perf. 12x11½*

No.	Type	Description	Unused	Used
229	A45	1p emerald	.20	.20
230	A45	3p bright blue	.25	.25
231	A45	1sh gray black	1.50	1.40
		Nos. 229-231 (3)	1.95	1.85

Visit of Princess Elizabeth.

1951, July 12

No.	Type	Description	Unused	Used
232	A46	1p green	.20	.20
233	A46	3p purple	.55	.20
234	A46	1sh slate black	1.25	1.00
		Nos. 232-234 (3)	2.00	1.40

700th anniv. of the presentation of the scapular to St. Simon Stock.

Types of 1938-43 Overprinted Type "a" in Red or Black

1953, Jan. 8 Wmk. 4 *Perf. 12½*

No.	Type	Description	Unused	Used
235	A32	1p gray (R)	.75	.20
236	A33	1½p green	.45	.20
a.		Overprint omitted		*14,000.*
237	A34	2p ocher	.45	.20
238	A35	2½p rose red	.80	*2.25*
239	A36	3p violet (R)	.80	.20
240	A37	4½p ultra & ol grn (R)	.85	*1.25*
		Nos. 235-240 (6)	4.10	4.30

Coronation Issue

Common Design Type

Inscribed: "Malta" and Crosses

1953, June 3 Engr. *Perf. 13½x13*

No.	Type	Description	Unused	Used
241	CD312	1½p dk green black	.55	.20

Type of 1938-43 with Portrait of Queen Elizabeth II Inscribed: "Royal Visit 1954."

1954, May 3 *Perf. 12½*

No.	Type	Description	Unused	Used
242	A36	3p violet	.35	.20

Visit of Elizabeth II and the Duke of Edinburgh, 1954.

Central Altarpiece, Collegiate Parish Church, Cospicua — A47

Perf. 14½x13½

1954, Sept. 8 Photo. Wmk. 4

No.	Type	Description	Unused	Used
243	A47	1½p bright green	.20	.20
244	A47	3p ultramarine	.20	.20
245	A47	1sh gray black	.40	.40
		Nos. 243-245 (3)	.80	.80

Cent. of the promulgation of the Dogma of the Immaculate Conception.

Monument of the Great Siege, 1565 — A48

Auberge de Castille — A49

Designs: ¼p, Wignacourt Aqueduct Horse-trough. 1p, Victory Church. 1½p, War Memorial. 2p, Mosta Dome. 3p, King's Scroll. 4½p, Roosevelt's Scroll. 6p, Neolithic Temples at Tarxien. 8p, Vedette. 1sh, Mdina Gate. 1sh6p, Les Gavroches. 2sh, Monument of Christ the King. 2sh6p, Monument of Nicolas Cottoner. 5sh, Raymond Perellos Monument. 10sh, St. Paul. £1, Baptism of Christ.

1956-57 Engr. *Perf. 11½*

No.	Type	Description	Unused	Used
246	A48	¼p violet	.20	.20
247	A48	½p yel orange	.55	.20
248	A48	1p black	.55	.20
249	A48	1½p brt green	.35	.20
250	A48	2p brown	1.75	.20
251	A49	2½p orange brown	1.75	.35
252	A48	3p rose red	1.75	.20
253	A48	4½p blue	2.75	.25
254	A49	6p slate blue	.85	.20
255	A48	8p olive bister	4.00	*1.10*
256	A48	1sh purple	1.10	.30
257	A48	1sh6p Prus green	14.00	.40
258	A48	2sh olive green	14.00	2.75
		Perf. 13½x13		
259	A48	2sh6p cop brown	10.50	2.50
260	A48	5sh emerald	17.00	3.25
261	A48	10sh dk carmine	42.50	14.00
262	A48	£1 yel brn ('57)	42.50	29.00
		Nos. 246-262 (17)	156.10	55.30

See Nos. 296-297.

First George Cross Issue

Symbol of Malta's War Effort — A50

Searchlights over Malta — A51

Design: 1sh, Bombed houses.

Perf. 14x14½, 14½x14

1957, Apr. 15 Photo.

Cross in Silver

No.	Type	Description	Unused	Used
263	A50	1½p green	.20	.20
264	A51	3p bright red	.20	.20
265	A50	1sh dark red brown	.20	.20
		Nos. 263-265 (3)	.60	.60

Award of the George Cross to Malta for its war effort.

See Nos. 269-274.

Symbols of Architecture — A52

Designs: 3p, Symbols of Industry, vert. 1sh, Symbols of electronics and chemistry and Technical School, Paola.

Perf. 14½x14, 14x14½

1958, Feb. 15 Wmk. 314

No.	Type	Description	Unused	Used
266	A52	1½p dp green & blk	.20	.20
267	A52	3p rose red, blk & gray	.20	.20
268	A52	1sh gray, blk & lilac	.25	.25
		Nos. 266-268 (3)	.65	.65

Technical education on Malta.

Second George Cross Issue

Types of 1957

1½p, Bombed-out family & searchlights. 3p, Convoy entering harbor. 1sh, Searchlight battery.

1958, Apr. 15 *Perf. 14½x14, 14x14½*

Cross in Silver

No.	Type	Description	Unused	Used
269	A51	1½p black & brt green	.20	.20
270	A50	3p black & vermilion	.20	.20
271	A51	1sh black & brt lilac	.25	.25
		Nos. 269-271 (3)	.65	.65

Third George Cross Issue

Types of 1957

Designs: 1½p, Air Raid Precautions Organization helping wounded. 3p, Allegory of Malta. 1sh, Mother and child during air raid.

1959, Apr. 15 *Perf. 14x14½, 14½x14*

No.	Type	Description	Unused	Used
272	A50	1½p gold, green & black	.20	.20
273	A51	3p gold, lilac & black	.20	.20
274	A50	1sh gold, gray & black	.80	1.10
		Nos. 272-274 (3)	1.20	1.50

St. Paul's Shipwreck, Painting in St. Paul's Church, Valletta — A53

Statue of St. Paul, St. Paul's Grotto, Rabat — A54

Designs: 3p, Consecration of St. Publius. 6p, St. Paul leaving Malta; painting, St. Paul's Church, Valletta. 1sh, Angel holding tablet with quotations from Acts of the Apostles. 2sh6p, St. Paul and St. Paul's Bay islets.

Wmk. 314

1960, Feb. 9 Photo. *Perf. 13*

No.	Type	Description	Unused	Used
275	A53	1½p bister, brt bl & gold	.25	.20
a.		Gold dates & crosses omitted	*65.00*	*57.50*
276	A53	3p lt blue, red lil & gold	.30	.20
277	A53	6p car, gray & gold	.40	.20
		Perf. 14x14½		
278	A54	8p black & gold	.60	*.75*
279	A54	1sh brt cl & gold	.60	.50
280	A54	2sh6p brt grnsh bl & gold	2.25	2.25
a.		Gold omitted	*375.00*	
		Nos. 275-280 (6)	4.40	4.10

19th centenary of St. Paul's shipwreck on Malta.

Stamp of 1860 — A55

Perf. 13x13½

1960, Dec. 1 Engr. Wmk. 314

281 A55 1½p multi .20 .20
282 A55 3p multi .35 .20
283 A55 6p multi .50 1.10
Nos. 281-283 (3) 1.05 1.50

Centenary of Malta's first postage stamp.

Fourth George Cross Issue

George Cross A56

Background designs: 3p, Sun and water. 1sh, Maltese crosses.

1961, Apr. 15 Photo. *Perf. 14½x14*

284 A56 1½p gray, bister & buff .20 .20
285 A56 3p ol gray, lt & dk grnsh blue .35 .20
286 A56 1sh ol green, vio & lil .85 2.00
Nos. 284-286 (3) 1.40 2.40

19th anniv. of the award of the George Cross to Malta.

Madonna Damascena A57

David Bruce and Themistocles Zammit A58

Designs: 3p, Great Siege Monument by Antonio Sciortino. 6p, Grand Master La Valette (1557-1568). 1sh, Assault on Fort Elmo (old map).

Perf. 12½x12

1962, Sept. 7 Wmk. 314

287 A57 2p ultramarine .20 .20
288 A57 3p dark red .20 .20
289 A57 6p olive green .25 .25
290 A57 1sh rose lake .25 .45
Nos. 287-290 (4) .90 1.10

Great Siege of 1565 in which the knights of the Order of St. John and the Maltese Christians defeated the Turks.

Freedom from Hunger Issue
Common Design Type

1963, June 4 *Perf. 14x14½*

291 CD314 1sh6p sepia 2.25 2.75

Red Cross Centenary Issue
Common Design Type

1963, Sept. 2 Litho. *Perf. 13*

292 CD315 2p black & red .25 .25
293 CD315 1sh6p ultra & red 3.00 4.75

Type of 1956
Designs as before.

1963-64 Engr. *Perf. 11½*

296 A48 1p black 1.00 .70
297 A48 2p brown ('64) 2.10 *2.40*

Perf. 14x13½

1964, Apr. 14 Photo. Wmk. 314

1sh6p, Goat and laboratory equipment.

298 A58 2p dl grn, blk & brn .20 .20
a. Black omitted *250.00*
299 A58 1sh6p rose lake & blk 1.00 1.00

Anti-Brucellosis (Malta fever) Congress of the UN FAO, Valletta, June 8-13.

Nicola Cottoner Attending Sick Man and Congress Emblem — A59

6p, Statue of St. Luke & St. Luke's Hospital. 1sh6p, Sacra Infermeria, Valletta.

Perf. 13½x14

1964, Sept. 5 Wmk. 354

300 A59 2p multicolored .20 .20
301 A59 6p multicolored .55 .55
302 A59 1sh6p multicolored 1.25 2.10
Nos. 300-302 (3) 2.00 2.85

1st European Cong. of Catholic Physicians, Malta, Sept. 6-10.

Independent State

Dove, Maltese Cross and British Crown — A60

Nativity — A61

Dove, Maltese Cross and: 3p, 1sh6p, Pope's tiara. 6p, 2sh6p, UN Emblem.

Perf. 14½x13½

1964, Sept. 21 Photo.

Gold and

303 A60 2p gray ol & red .40 .20
304 A60 3p dk red brn & red .45 .20
305 A60 6p sl blue & red 1.00 .30
306 A60 1sh ultra & red 1.00 .40
307 A60 1sh6p bl blk & red 2.75 1.50
308 A60 2sh6p vio bl & red 3.00 3.00
Nos. 303-308 (6) 8.60 5.60

Malta's independence.

Perf. 13x13½

1964, Nov. 3 Wmk. 354

309 A61 2p magenta & gold .20 .20
310 A61 4p ultra & gold .25 .25
311 A61 8p dp green & gold 1.25 1.10
Nos. 309-311 (3) 1.70 1.55

Cippus, Phoenician and Greek Inscriptions — A62

British Arms, Armory, Valletta A63

Designs (History of Malta): ½p, Neolithic (sculpture of sleeping woman). 1½p, Roman (sculpture). 2p, Proto-Christian (lamp, Roman temple, Chrismon). 2½p, Saracen (tomb, 12th cent.). 3p, Siculo Norman (arch, Palazzo Gatto-Murina, Notabile). 4p, Knights of Malta (lamp base, cross, and armor of knights). 4½p, Maltese navy (16th cent. galleons). 5p, Fortifications. 6p, French occupation (Cathedral of Notabile, cap, fasces). 10p, Naval Arsenal.

1sh, Maltese Corps of the British Army (insignia). 1sh3p, International Eucharistic Congress, 1913 (angels adoring Eucharist and map of Malta). 1sh6p, Self Government, 1921 (Knights of Malta Hall, present assembly seat). 2sh, Civic Council, Gozo (Statue of Livia, Gozo City Hall). 2sh6p, State of Malta (seated woman and George Cross). 3sh, Independence (doves, UN emblem, British crown, and Pope's tiara).

5sh, "HAFMED," (headquarters and insigne of Allied Forces, Mediterranean). 10sh, Map of Mediterranean. £1, Catholicism (Sts. Paul, Publius and Agatha).

Perf. 14x14½, 14½ (A63)

1965-70 Photo. Wmk. 354

312 A62 ½p violet & yel .20 .20
313 A62 1p multi .20 .20
a. Booklet pane of 6 ('70) .35
314 A62 1½p multi .20 .20
315 A62 2p multi .20 .20
a. Gold omitted 25.00
b. Booklet pane of 6 ('70) .40
316 A62 2½p multi .20 .20
a. Gold ("SARACENIC") omitted 55.00
317 A62 3p multi .20 .20
a. Imperf., pair 250.00
b. Gold (windows) omitted 37.50
318 A62 4p multi .20 .20
a. Black (arms shading) omitted 47.50
b. Silver omitted 45.00
319 A62 4½p multi .20 .20
319A A62 5p multi ('70) .25 .20
b. Booklet pane of 6 ('71) 1.75
320 A62 6p multi .20 .20
a. Black omitted 60.00
b. Silver ("MALTA") omitted 60.00
321 A63 8p multi .20 .20
321A A63 10p multi ('70) .30 .20
322 A63 1sh multi .30 .20
323 A63 1sh3p multi .65 .45
324 A63 1sh6p multi .50 .25
a. Queen's head omitted *225.00*
325 A63 2sh multi .65 .45
326 A63 2sh6p multi .75 .50
327 A63 3sh multi .95 .60
328 A63 5sh multi 1.60 1.00
329 A63 10sh multi 3.25 2.50
330 A63 £1 multi 6.00 4.50
a. Pink (shading on figures) omitted 30.00
Nos. 312-330 (21) 17.20 12.85

Issued: 5p, 10p, 8/1/70; others 1/7/65.
For surcharges see Nos. 447-449, 521.

Dante, by Raphael — A64

1965, July 7 Unwmk. *Perf. 14*

331 A64 2p dark blue .20 .20
332 A64 6p olive green .20 .20
333 A64 2sh chocolate .80 .70
Nos. 331-333 (3) 1.20 1.10

700th birth anniv. of Dante Alighieri.

Turkish Encampment and Fort St. Michael A65

Blockading Turkish Armada — A66

Designs: 3p, Knights and Turks in battle. 8p, Arrival of relief force. 1sh, Trophy, arms of Grandmaster Jean de La Valette. 1sh6p, Allegory of Victory, mural by Calabrese from St. John's Co-Cathedral. 2sh6p, Great Siege victory medal; Jean de La Valette on obverse, David slaying Goliath on reverse.

Perf. 14½x14, 13

1965, Sept. 1 Photo. Wmk. 354

334 A65 2p multicolored .20 .20
335 A65 3p multicolored .20 .20
336 A66 6p multicolored .30 .25
a. Black omitted *140.00*
b. Gold omitted *165.00*
337 A65 8p multicolored .45 .35
338 A66 1sh multicolored 1.10 .90
339 A65 1sh6p multicolored 1.40 1.10
340 A65 2sh6p multicolored 3.50 3.00
Nos. 334-340 (7) 7.15 6.00

Great Siege (Turks against Malta), 4th cent.

The Three Wise Men A67

Perf. 11x11½

1965, Oct. 7 Photo. Wmk. 354

341 A67 1p dk purple & red .20 .20
342 A67 4p dk pur & blue .90 .80
343 A67 1sh3p dk pur & dp mag 1.00 .90
Nos. 341-343 (3) 2.10 1.90

Winston Churchill, Map and Cross of Malta — A68

Winston Churchill: 3p, 1sh6p, Warships in Valletta Harbor and George Cross.

1966, Jan. 24 *Perf. 14½x14*

344 A68 2p blk, gold & red .20 .20
345 A68 3p dk grn, gold & blk .20 .20
346 A68 1sh dp cl, gold & red .30 .30
a. Gold omitted 225.00
347 A68 1sh6p dk bl, gold & vio .50 .45
Nos. 344-347 (4) 1.20 1.15

Grand Master Jean Parisot de la Valette — A69

3p, Pope St. Pius V. 6p, Map of Valletta. 1sh, Francesco Laparelli, Italian architect. 2sh6p, Girolamo Cassar, Maltese architect.

1966, Mar. 28 Unwmk. *Perf. 12*

348 A69 2p gold & multi .20 .20
349 A69 3p gold & multi .20 .20
350 A69 6p gold & multi .20 .20
351 A69 1sh gold & multi .20 .20
352 A69 2sh6p gold & multi .55 .55
Nos. 348-352 (5) 1.35 1.35

400th anniversary of Valletta.

Kennedy — A70

Trade Fair — A71

Perf. 15x14

1966, May 28 Photo. Wmk. 354

353 A70 3p ol gray, blk & gold .20 .20
354 A70 1sh6p dull bl, blk & gold .35 .35

President John F. Kennedy (1917-1963).

1966, June 16 *Perf. 13x13½*

355 A71 2p multicolored .20 .20
356 A71 8p gray & multi .25 .25
357 A71 2sh6p tan & multi .70 .70
Nos. 355-357 (3) 1.15 1.15

The 10th Malta Trade Fair.

Nativity — A72

George Cross — A73

1966, Oct. 7 Photo. Wmk. 354

358	A72	1p multicolored	.20	.20
359	A72	4p multicolored	.20	.20
360	A72	1sh3p multicolored	.20	.20
		Nos. 358-360 (3)	.60	.60

1967, Mar. 1 ***Perf. 14½x14***

361	A73	2p multicolored	.20	.20
362	A73	4p multicolored	.20	.20
363	A73	3sh slate & multi	.30	.30
		Nos. 361-363 (3)	.70	.70

25th anniv. of the award of the George Cross to Malta and Gozo for the war effort.

Crucifixion of St. Peter — A74

Keys, Tiara, Bible, Cross and Sword — A75

Design: 3sh, Beheading of St. Paul.

Perf. 14½, 13½x14
1967, June 28 Photo. Wmk. 354

364	A74	2p black & brn orange	.20	.20
365	A75	8p blk, gold & lt ol grn	.20	.20
366	A74	3sh black & brt blue	.40	.35
		Nos. 364-366 (3)	.80	.75

1900th anniv. of the martyrdom of the Apostles Peter and Paul.

St. Catherine of Siena by Melchior Gafá — A76

Sculptures by Gafá: 4p, St. Thomas from Villanova. 1sh6p, Christ's baptism. 2sh6p, St. John the Baptist.

1967, Aug. 1 ***Perf. 13½***

367	A76	2p black, gold, buff & ultra	.20	.20
368	A76	4p gold, buff, blk & grn	.20	.20
369	A76	1sh6p gold, buff, blk & org brown	.20	.20
370	A76	2sh6p black, gold, buff & dp car	.30	.30
		Nos. 367-370 (4)	.90	.90

Melchior Gafá (1635-67), Maltese sculptor.

Ruins of Megalithic Temples, Tarxien — A77

Designs: 6p, Facade of Palazzo Falzon, Notabile. 1sh, Facade of Old Parish Church, Birkirkara. 3sh, Entrance to Auberge de Castille.

1967, Sept. 12 Photo. ***Perf. 14½***

371	A77	2p gold, Prus bl & blk	.20	.20
372	A77	6p org brn, blk, gray & gold	.20	.20
373	A77	1sh gold, ol, ind & blk	.20	.20
374	A77	3sh dk car, rose, blk, gray & gold	.30	.30
		Nos. 371-374 (4)	.90	.90

Issued to publicize the 15th Congress of the History of Architecture, Malta, Sept. 12-16.

Nativity — A78

Design: 1sh4p, Angels facing left.

1967, Oct. 20 ***Perf. 13½x14***

375	A78	1p slate, gold & red	.20	.20
a.		Red omitted (stars)	50.00	
376	A79	8p slate, gold & red	.20	.20
377	A78	1sh4p slate, gold & red	.30	.30
a.		Triptych, #375-377	.55	.50
		Nos. 375-377 (3)	.70	.70

Sheets of Nos. 375-377 were arranged in 2 ways: sheets containing 60 stamps of the same denomination arranged tête bêche, and sheets containing 20 triptychs.

Arms of Malta — A80

Designs: 4p, Queen Elizabeth II in the robes of the Order of St. Michael and St. George, vert. 3sh, Queen and map of Malta.

Perf. 14½x14, 14x14½
1967, Nov. 13 Photo. Wmk. 354

378	A80	2p slate & multi	.20	.20
379	A80	4p dp claret, blk & gold	.20	.20
380	A80	3sh black & gold	.30	.30
		Nos. 378-380 (3)	.70	.70

Visit of Queen Elizabeth II, Nov. 14-17.

Human Rights Flame and People A81

1968, May 2 Photo. ***Perf. 14½***
Size: 40x19mm

381	A81	2p sepia, dp car, blk & gold	.20	.20

Perf. 12x12½
Size: 24x24mm

382	A81	6p gray, dk blue, blk & gold	.20	.20

Perf. 14½
Size: 40x19mm

383	A81	2sh gray, grnsh blue, blk & gold	.25	.20
		Nos. 381-383 (3)	.65	.60

International Human Rights Year.

Fair Emblem — A82

Perf. 14x14½
1968, June 1 Photo. Wmk. 354

384	A82	4p black & multi	.20	.20
385	A82	8p Prus blue & multi	.20	.20
386	A82	3sh dp claret & multi	.40	.40
		Nos. 384-386 (3)	.80	.80

12th Malta Intl. Trade Fair, July 1-15.

La Valette in Battle Dress — A83

La Valette's Tomb, Church of St. John, Valletta — A84

Designs: 1p, Arms of Order of St. John of Jerusalem and La Valette's arms, horiz. 2sh6p, Putti bearing shield with date of La Valette's death, and map of Malta.

Perf. 13x14, 14x13
1968, Aug. 1 Photo. Wmk. 354

387	A83	1p black & multi	.20	.20
388	A83	8p dull blue & multi	.20	.20
389	A84	1sh6p blue grn & multi	.20	.20
390	A83	2sh6p dp claret & multi	.30	.30
		Nos. 387-390 (4)	.90	.90

400th anniv. of the death of Grand Master Jean de La Valette (1494-1568).

Star of Bethlehem, Shepherds and Angel A85

8p, Nativity. 1sh4p, The Three Wise Men.

Perf. 14½x14
1968, Oct. 3 Wmk. 354

391	A85	1p multicolored	.20	.20
392	A85	8p gray & multi	.20	.20
393	A85	1sh4p tan & multi	.25	.25
		Nos. 391-393 (3)	.65	.65

Christmas. Printed in sheets of 60 with alternate rows inverted.

"Agriculture" A86

Mahatma Gandhi A87

1sh, Greek medal and FAO emblem. 2sh6p, Woman symbolizing soil care.

1968, Oct. 21 Photo. ***Perf. 12½x12***

394	A86	4p ultra & multi	.20	.20
395	A86	1sh gray & multi	.20	.20
396	A86	2sh6p multicolored	.45	.45
		Nos. 394-396 (3)	.85	.85

6th Regional Congress for Europe of the FAO, Malta, Oct. 28-31.

Perf. 12x12½
1969, Mar. 24 Photo. Wmk. 354

397	A87	1sh6p gold, blk & sepia	.35	.35

Birth cent. of Mohandas K. Gandhi (1869-1948), leader in India's struggle for independence.

ILO Emblem A88

1969, May 26 ***Perf. 13½x14½***

398	A88	2p indigo, blue grn & gold	.20	.20
399	A88	6p brn blk, red brn & gold	.20	.20

50th anniv. of the ILO.

Sea Bed, UN Emblem and Dove — A89

Designs: 2p, Robert Samut, bar of music and coat of arms. 10p, Map of Malta and homing birds. 2sh, Grand Master Pinto and arms of Malta University.

1969, July 26 Photo. ***Perf. 13½***

400	A89	2p vio blk, blk, gold & red	.20	.20
401	A89	5p gray, Prus blue, gold & blk	.20	.20
402	A89	10p olive, blk & gold	.20	.20
403	A89	2sh dk olive, blk, red & gold	.30	.30
		Nos. 400-403 (4)	.90	.90

Cent. of the birth of Robert Samut, composer of Natl. Anthem (2p); UN resolution on peaceful uses of the sea bed (5p); convention of Maltese emigrants (10p), Aug. 3-16; bicent. of the founding of Malta University (2sh).

June 17, 1919, Uprising Monument A90

"Tourism" A91

Designs: 5p, Maltese flag and 5 doves, horiz. 1sh6p, Dove and emblems of Malta, UN and Council of Europe. 2sh6p, Dove and symbols of trade and industry.

Perf. 13x12½
1969, Sept. 20 Photo. Wmk. 354

404	A90	2p black, gray, buff & gold	.20	.20
405	A91	5p gray, blk, red & gold	.20	.20
406	A91	10p gold, Prus blue, gray & blk	.20	.20
407	A91	1sh6p gold, olive & multi	.20	.20
408	A91	2sh6p gold, brn ol, gray & blk	.40	.40
		Nos. 404-408 (5)	1.20	1.20

Fifth anniversary of independence.

St. John the Baptist in Robe of Knight of Malta A92

Mortar and Jars from Infirmary — A93

Designs: 1p, The Beheading of St. John By Caravaggio. 5p, Interior of St. John's Co-

Dental Assoc. of Malta, 50th Anniv. — A205

Design: 44c, Dental instrument, teeth.

1994, Feb. 12

827 A205 5c multicolored .50 .50
828 A205 44c multicolored 3.50 3.50

Europa — A206

Designs: 14c, Sir Themistocles Zammit (1864-1935), discoverer of micro-organism causing undulant fever. 30c, Marble candelabrum, 2nd cent. B.C., Natl. Museum of Archaeology, Valletta.

1994, Mar. 29 ***Perf. 14***

829 A206 14c multicolored *.85 .85*
830 A206 30c multicolored *1.90 1.90*

Anniversaries and Events — A207

1994, May 10

831 A207 5c shown .45 .45
832 A207 9c Crosses .70 .70
833 A207 14c Farm animals 1.10 1.10
834 A207 20c Factory worker 1.60 1.60
835 A207 25c Cathedral, vert. 2.00 2.00
Nos. 831-835 (5) 5.85 5.85

Intl. Year of the Family (#831). Malta Red Cross Society, 3rd anniv. (#832). Agrarian Society, 150th anniv. (#833). ILO, 75th anniv. (#834). St. Paul's Anglican Cathedral, 150th anniv. (#835).

1994 World Cup Soccer Championships, U.S. — A208

1994, June 9

836 A208 5c shown .35 .35
837 A208 14c Ball, net, map 1.00 1.00
838 A208 30c Ball, field, map 2.25 2.25
a. Souvenir sheet of 3, #836-838 4.00 4.00
Nos. 836-838 (3) 3.60 3.60

Aviation Anniversaries & Events — A209

Aircraft, related objects: 5c, Trophy, map, Twin Comanche. 14c, Airshow emblem, Phantom jet, demonstration team in silhouette, Alouette helicopter, flag. 20c, Emblem, Avro York, old terminal building, DeHavilland Dove. 25c, Emblem, DeHavilland Comet, new terminal, Airbus 320.

1994, July 2

839 A209 5c multicolored .45 .45
840 A209 14c multicolored 1.25 1.25
841 A209 20c multicolored 1.90 1.90
842 A209 25c multicolored 2.25 2.25
Nos. 839-842 (4) 5.85 5.85

Intl. Air Rally of Malta, 25th anniv. (#839). Malta Intl. Airshow (#840). ICAO, 50th anniv. (#841-842).

First Manned Moon Landing, 25th Anniv. — A210

1994, July 20

843 A210 14c multicolored 1.25 1.25

Christmas — A211

1994, Oct. 26

844 A211 5c shown .30 .30

Size: 28x40mm

845 A211 9c +2c Angel in pink .65 .65
846 A211 14c +3c Madonna & child 1.00 1.00
847 A211 20c +3c Angel in green 1.40 1.40
Nos. 844-847 (4) 3.35 3.35

Antique Maltese Silver — A212

Designs: 5c, Ewer, Vilhena period. 14c, Balsamina, Pinto period. 20c, Coffee pot, Pinto period. 25c, Sugar box, Pinto period.

Wmk. 354

1994, Dec. 12 **Litho.** ***Perf. 14***

848 A212 5c multicolored .40 .40
849 A212 14c multicolored 1.25 1.25
850 A212 20c multicolored 1.75 1.75
851 A212 25c multicolored 2.10 2.10
Nos. 848-851 (4) 5.50 5.50

Anniversaries & Events — A213

1995, Feb. 27

852 A213 2c multicolored .25 .25
853 A213 5c multicolored .35 .35
854 A213 14c multicolored .85 .85
855 A213 20c multicolored 1.25 1.25
856 A213 25c multicolored 1.50 1.50
Nos. 852-856 (5) 4.20 4.20

Natl. Assoc. of Pensioners, 25th anniv. (#852). Natl. Youth Council of Malta, 10th anniv. (#853). 4th World Conf. on Women, Beijing (#854). Malta Memorial District Nursing Assoc., 50th anniv. (#855). Louis Pasteur (1822-95) (#856).

Peace & Freedom A214

Europa: 14c, Hand with olive twig, rainbow, vert. 30c, Doves.

1995, Mar. 29

857 A214 14c multicolored *.75 .75*
858 A214 30c multicolored *1.60 1.60*

50th Anniversaries — A215

Designs: 5c, End of World War II, ships, planes. 14c, Formation of UN, people joining hands. 35c, FAO, hands holding bowl of wheat, FAO emblem.

1995, Apr. 21

859 A215 5c multicolored .35 .35
860 A215 14c multicolored .85 .85
861 A215 35c multi, vert. 2.10 2.10
Nos. 859-861 (3) 3.30 3.30

Telecommunications & Electricity — A216

1995, June 15

862 A216 2c Light bulb .25 .25
863 A216 5c Cable, binary numbers .35 .35
864 A216 9c Satellite dish .55 .55
865 A216 14c Sun's rays, trees .85 .85
866 A216 20c Telephone, satellite 1.25 1.25
Nos. 862-866 (5) 3.25 3.25

European Nature Conservation Year — A217

1995, July 24

867 A217 5c Ruins, Girna .50 .50
868 A217 14c Podarcis filfolensis 1.25 1.25
869 A217 44c Pina halepensis 4.25 4.25
Nos. 867-869 (3) 6.00 6.00

Antique Clocks — A218

Designs: 1c, Pinto's turret clock. 5c, Michelangelo Sapiano, long case & smaller clock. 14c, Arlogg tal-lira (case) clock. 25c, Maltese sundials.

1995, Oct. 5

870 A218 1c multicolored .40 .40
871 A218 5c multicolored .60 .60
872 A218 14c multicolored 1.40 1.40
873 A218 25c multicolored 2.40 2.40
Nos. 870-873 (4) 4.80 4.80

Christmas — A219

Designs: 5c, Christmas Eve children's procession. 5c+2c, Children carrying manger. 14c+3c, Boy carrying manger, boy with lamp. 25c+3c, Boy with lamp, balcony.

Wmk. 354

1995, Nov. 15 **Litho.** ***Perf. 14***

874 A219 5c multi .35 .35

Size: 26x32mm

875 A219 5c +2c multi .45 .45
876 A219 14c +3c multi 1.10 1.10
877 A219 25c +3c multi 1.75 1.75
Nos. 874-877 (4) 3.65 3.65

Surtax for child welfare organizations.

Child and Youth Welfare Organizations — A220

Silhouettes of youth, children, and: 5c, Maltese cross, Palace of the President. 14c, Fr. Nazzareno Camilleri, St. Patricks' School. 20c, St. Maria of St. Euphrasia Pelletier, convent building. 25c, Globe, children looking at pool.

1996, Feb. 29

878 A220 5c multicolored .35 .35
879 A220 14c multicolored .85 .85
880 A220 20c multicolored 1.25 1.25
881 A220 25c multicolored 1.50 1.50
Nos. 878-881 (4) 3.95 3.95

President's Award, 35th anniv. (#878). Fr. Camilleri, 90th death anniv. (#879). St. Maria, death bicent. (#880). UNICEF, 50th anniv. (#881).

Prehistoric Art — A221

Sculptures, pottery from 5000-2500BC: 5c, People, animals. 14c, Two people seated, one with missing head. 20c, Venus figure, vert. 35c, Pitcher, vert.

1996, Mar. 29

882 A221 5c multicolored .35 .35
883 A221 14c multicolored .85 .85
884 A221 20c multicolored 1.25 1.25
885 A221 35c multicolored 2.10 2.10
Nos. 882-885 (4) 4.55 4.55

Famous Women — A222

Europa: 14c, Mabel Strickland (1899-1988). 30c, Inez Soler (1910-1974).

1996, Apr. 24

886 A222 14c multicolored *.80 .80*
887 A222 30c multicolored *1.75 1.75*

Anniversaries and Events — A223

Designs: No. 888, UN, decade against drug abuse. No. 889, Malta Federation of Industry, 50th anniv. 14c, Self-government, 75th anniv. 44c, Guglielmo Marconi, radio, cent.

1996, June 5

888 A223 5c multicolored .35 .35
889 A223 5c multicolored .35 .35
890 A223 14c multicolored .85 .85
891 A223 44c multicolored 2.75 2.75
Nos. 888-891 (4) 4.30 4.30

1996 Summer Olympic Games, Atlanta A224

1996, July 10

892 A224 2c Judo .25 .25
893 A224 5c Running .35 .35
894 A224 14c Swimming .85 .85
895 A224 25c Shooting 1.50 1.50
Nos. 892-895 (4) 2.95 2.95

Paintings, by or of Giuseppe Cali — A225

Designs: 5c, Boy cutting wheat. 14c, Dog. 20c, Woman with hoe standing on hillside, vert. 25c, Portrait of Calì, by Dingli, vert.

1996, Aug. 22

896 A225 5c multicolored .35 .35
897 A225 14c multicolored .85 .85
898 A225 20c multicolored 1.25 1.25
899 A225 25c multicolored 1.50 1.50
Nos. 896-899 (4) 3.95 3.95

Buses A226

2c, Tal-Gallarija "Diamond Star" No. 1990. 5c, Stewart "Tom Mix" No. 434. 14c, Diamond T "Verdala" No. 1764. 30c, Front control No. 3495.

Wmk. 354

1996, Sept. 26 Litho. *Perf. 14*

900 A226 2c multicolored .35 .35
901 A226 5c multicolored .50 .50
902 A226 14c multicolored 1.40 1.40
903 A226 30c multicolored 2.75 2.75
Nos. 900-903 (4) 5.00 5.00

Christmas — A227

Stained glass windows: 5c+2c, Madonna and Child. 14c+3c, Angel flying right. 25c+3c, Angel flying left.

1996, Nov. 7

904 A227 5c shown .30 .30

Size: 26x31mm

905 A227 5c +2c multi .45 .45
906 A227 14c +3c multi 1.00 1.00
907 A227 25c +3c multi 1.75 1.75
Nos. 904-907 (4) 3.50 3.50

City Bicentennials A228

1997, Feb. 20

908 A228 6c Hompesch .50 .50
909 A228 16c Ferdinand 1.40 1.40
910 A228 26c Beland 2.00 2.00
a. Souvenir Sheet of 3, #908-910 5.50 5.50
Nos. 908-910 (3) 3.90 3.90

Treasures of Malta — A229

1997, Apr. 11

911 A229 2c Suggetta .20 .20
912 A229 6c Suggetta, diff. .45 .45
913 A229 16c Sedan chair, vert. 1.00 1.00
914 A229 27c Sedan chair, diff., vert. 1.60 1.60
Nos. 911-914 (4) 3.25 3.25

A230

A231

Europa (Stories and Legends): 16c, Man carrying door, figure in front of house (Gahan). 35c, Woman kneeling in prayer, knight on white horse (St. Dimitri).

1997, May 5

915 A230 16c multicolored *.90 .90*
916 A230 35c multicolored *2.00 2.00*

1997, July 10

917 A231 1c multicolored .20 .20
918 A231 16c multicolored .90 .90

Antonio Sciortino (1879-1947), sculptor.

Gozo Cathedral, 300th Anniv. — A232

1997, July 10

919 A232 6c multi .35 .35
920 A232 11c multi, diff. .60 .60

Joseph Caleia (1897-1975), Actor — A233

1997, July 10

921 A233 6c multicolored .35 .35
922 A233 22c multi, diff. 1.25 1.25

Pioneers of Freedom — A234

Designs: 6c, Dr. Albert V. Laferla (1887-1943). 16c, Sister Emilie de Vialar (1797-1856). 19c, Msgr. Paolo Pullicino (1815-90). 26c, Msgr. Tommaso Gargallo (c. 1544-1614).

Wmk. 354

1997, Sept. 24 Litho. *Perf. 14*

923 A234 6c multicolored .35 .35
924 A234 16c multicolored 1.00 1.00
925 A234 19c multicolored 1.40 1.40
926 A234 26c multicolored 1.75 1.75
Nos. 923-926 (4) 4.50 4.50

Christmas — A235

Designs: 6c, Nativity. 6c+2c, Madonna and Child, vert. 16c+3c, Joseph with donkey, vert. 26c+3c, Shepherd, sheep, vert.

1997, Nov. 12

927 A235 6c multi .35 .35
928 A235 6c +2c multi .45 .45
929 A235 16c +3c multi 1.10 1.10
930 A235 26c +3c multi 1.60 1.60
Nos. 927-930 (4) 3.50 3.50

Victoria Lines, Cent. A236

Designs: 2c, Fort, soldiers in front of wall. 16c, Soldiers with cannon, fort.

1997, Dec. 5

931 A236 2c multicolored .20 .20
932 A236 16c multicolored .90 .90

Self-government, 50th Anniv. — A237

Designs: 6c, Man looking at paper, group of people. 37c, People in line waiting to vote.

1997, Dec. 5

933 A237 6c multicolored .35 .35
934 A237 37c multicolored 2.10 2.10

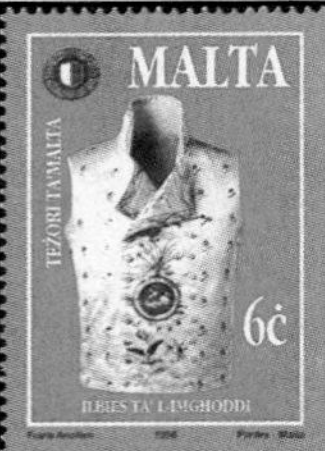

Treasures of Malta — A238

Designs: No. 935, Vest. No. 936, Portrait of a Woman, by Antoine de Favray (1706-98). No. 937, Portrait of Woman Holding Girl, by de Favray. No. 938, Early woman's costume. 26c, Valletta, city of culture.

1998, Feb. 26

935 A238 6c multicolored .40 .40
936 A238 6c multicolored .40 .40
937 A238 16c multicolored .95 .95
938 A238 16c multicolored .95 .95
Nos. 935-938 (4) 2.70 2.70

Souvenir Sheet

Perf. 13x13½

939 A238 26c multicolored 1.75 1.75

No. 939 contains one 39x48mm stamp.

French Occupation of Malta, Bicent. — A239

Designs: No. 940, Ferdinand von Hompesch, commander of Knights of St. John. No. 941, French fleet, map. No. 942, French coming ashore. No. 943, Napoleon Bonaparte.

Wmk. 239

1998, Mar. 28 Litho. *Perf. 14*

940 A239 6c multicolored .40 .40
941 A239 6c multicolored .40 .40
a. Pair, #940-941 .95 .95
942 A239 16c multicolored .95 .95
943 A239 16c multicolored .95 .95
a. Pair, #942-943 2.40 2.40
Nos. 940-943 (4) 2.70 2.70

National Festivals A240

Europa: 16c, 35c, Various boats at annual regatta.

Wmk. 354

1998, Apr. 22 Litho. *Perf. 14*

944 A240 16c multicolored *.90 .90*
945 A240 35c multicolored *2.00 2.00*

Intl. Year of the Ocean A241

Designs: 2c, Diver, dolphin, vert. 6c, Diver, hand holding sea urchin, vert. 16c, Diver, Jacques Cousteau (1910-97), deep sea explorer. 27c, Two divers.

Wmk. 354

1998, May 27 Litho. *Perf. 14*

946 A241 2c multicolored .25 .25
947 A241 6c multicolored .60 .60
948 A241 16c multicolored 1.40 1.40
949 A241 27c multicolored 2.40 2.40
Nos. 946-949 (4) 4.65 4.65

1998 World Cup Soccer Championship, France — A242

Various soccer plays, flags from participating teams.

1998, June 10

950 A242 6c multicolored .65 .65
951 A242 16c multicolored 1.25 1.25
952 A242 22c multicolored 2.10 2.10
a. Souvenir sheet, #950-952 4.50 4.50
Nos. 950-952 (3) 4.00 4.00

Anniversaries and Events — A243

1c, Intl. Maritime Organization, 50th anniv. 6c, Symbolic people, emblem, Universal Declaration of Human Rights. 11c, Cogs in wheels, Assoc. of General Retailers & Traders, 50th anniv. 19c, Roman god Mercury, Malta Chamber of Commerce, 150th anniv. 26c, Stylized planes, Air Malta, 25th anniv.

Wmk. 354

1998, Sept. 17 Litho. *Perf. 14*

953 A243 1c multicolored .30 .30
954 A243 6c multicolored .45 .45
955 A243 11c multicolored .70 .70
956 A243 19c multicolored 1.40 1.40
957 A243 26c multicolored 1.75 1.75
Nos. 953-957 (5) 4.60 4.60

Christmas A244

Paintings by Mattia Preti (1613-99): 6c, Rest on the Flight to Egypt. 6c+2c, Virgin and Child with Saints Anthony the Abbot and John the Baptist. 16c+3c, Virgin and Child with Saints Raphael, Nicholas and Gregory. 26c+3c, Virgin and Child with Saints John the Baptist and Nicholas.

Wmk. 354

1998, Nov. 19 Litho. *Perf. 14*

958 A244 6c multicolored .40 .40
959 A244 6c +2c multi .50 .50
960 A244 16c +3c multi 1.50 1.50
961 A244 26c +3c multi 2.10 2.10
Nos. 958-961 (4) 4.50 4.50

Knights Hospitaller, Order of St. John of Jerusalem, 900th Anniv. — A245

2c, Fort St. Angelo. 6c, Grandmaster L'Isle Adam, vert. 16c, Grandmaster La Valette, vert. 27c, Auberge de Castille.

Wmk. 354

1999, Feb. 26 Litho. *Perf. 14*

962 A245 2c multicolored .35 .35
963 A245 6c multicolored .60 .60
964 A245 16c multicolored 1.40 1.40
965 A245 27c multicolored 2.40 2.40
Nos. 962-965 (4) 4.75 4.75

Council of Europe, 50th Anniv. — A246

Designs: 6c, European Parliament in session. 16c, Human Rights Building.

1999, Apr. 6

966 A246 6c multicolored .60 .60
967 A246 16c multicolored 1.40 1.40

Nature Reserves — A247

Europa: 16c, Charadrius dubius, Ghadira Nature Reserve. 35c, Alcedo atthis, Simar Nature Reserve.

Unwmk.

1999, Apr. 6 Litho. *Perf. 14*

968 A247 16c multicolored *.90 .90*
969 A247 35c multicolored *2.00 2.00*

UPU, 125th Anniv. — A248

UPU emblem and: a, 6c, Sailing ship, Valletta Bastions, Marsamxett Harbor. b, 16c, IBRA '99 emblem, Nuremberg, Germany. c, 22c, Philexfrance emblem, Eiffel Tower, Paris. d, 27c, Beijing '99 emblem, Beijing. e, 37c, Australia '99 emblem, Melbourne.

1999, June 2 *Perf. 13¾x14*

970 A248 Strip of 5, #a.-e. 7.50 7.50

Tourism — A249

Sun shining and: 6c, Man, woman in boat, vert. 16c, Man taking picture of family posed with Knight of Malta, vert. 22c, Man basking in sun while frying egg on stomach. 27c, Girl with flowers, man pushing woman in horse-drawn carriage. 37c, Cave man among ruins pulling luggage, reading travel guide.

Perf. 14x13¾, 13¾x14

1999, June 16

971 A249 6c multicolored .40 .40
972 A249 16c multicolored .95 .95
973 A249 22c multicolored 1.40 1.40
974 A249 27c multicolored 1.60 1.60
975 A249 37c multicolored 2.25 2.25
Nos. 971-975 (5) 6.60 6.60

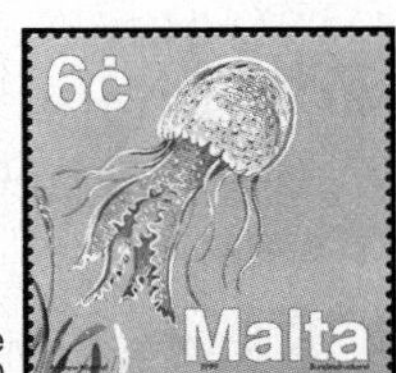

Marine Life — A250

No. 976: a, Pelagia noctiluca (jellyfish). b, Thalassoma pavo (fish with green stripes). c, Sepia officinalis (squid.) d, Sphaerechinus granularis (sea urchin). e, Epinephelus guaza (large fish). f, Diplodus vulgaris (fish with black stripes). g, Astroides calycularis (corals). h, Maia squinado (crab). i, Coris julis (fish with orange stripes). j, Octopus vulgaris (octopus). k, Charonia variegata (shell). l, Sparisoma cretense (red, green and blue fish). m, Hippocampus ramulosus (seahorse). n, Dardanus arrosor (hermit crab). o, Muraena helena (moray eel). p, Echinaster sepositus (starfish).

Perf. 13¾

1999, Aug. 25 Litho. Unwmk.

976 Sheet of 16 10.00 10.00
a.-p. A250 6c Any single .55 .55

Animal names are on sheet margin only.

Uprising Against France, 200th Anniv. A251

#977, Father Mikiel Scerri. #978, Sculpture. #979, French Gen. Belgrand de Vaubois. #980, British Capt. Alexander Ball.

1999, Oct. 6 Litho. *Perf. 14*

977 A251 6c multicolored .40 .40
978 A251 6c multicolored .40 .40
a. Pair, #977-978 1.25 1.25
979 A251 16c multicolored .95 .95
980 A251 16c multicolored .95 .95
a. Pair, #979-980 3.25 3.25
Nos. 977-980 (4) 2.70 2.70

Crowning of Painting of Our Lady of Mellieha, Cent. — A252

1999, Oct. 6

981 A252 35c shown 2.10 2.10

Souvenir Sheet

982 A252 6c Crowned Madonna, vert. .90 .90

Flowers A253

Designs: 2c, Pancratium maritimum. 4c, Iris pseudopumila. 6c, Narcissus tazetta. 16c, Crocus longiflorus. 25c, Ornithogalum arabicum. 46c, Tulipa sylvestris.

1999, Oct. 20 Litho. *Perf. 13¾*

983 A253 2c multi .20 .20
984 A253 4c multi .20 .20
985 A253 6c multi .35 .35
986 A253 16c multi .90 .90
987 A253 25c multi 1.40 1.40
988 A253 46c multi 2.50 2.50
Nos. 983-988 (6) 5.55 5.55

See Nos. 1022-1027, 1061-1066, 1102-1107, 1139-1140, 1213-1214.

Christmas A254

6c, Madonna & Child. 6c+3c, Carolers. 16c+3c, Santa Claus. 26c+3c, Tree, ornament.

1999, Nov. 27

989 A254 6c multi .55 .55
990 A254 6c + 3c multi .70 .70
991 A254 16c + 3c multi 1.50 1.50
992 A254 26c + 3c multi 2.10 2.10
Nos. 989-992 (4) 4.85 4.85

Republic of Malta, 25th Anniv. — A255

6c, Legislative meeting room. 11c, Chambers of House of Representatives. 16c, Central Bank of Malta. 19c, Flags, aerial view of Valletta. 26c, Computer, airplane, port facilities.

1999, Dec. 10 Litho. *Perf. 14*

993 A255 6c multi .40 .40
994 A255 11c multi .65 .65
995 A255 16c multi .95 .95
996 A255 19c multi 1.25 1.25
997 A255 26c multi 1.60 1.60
Nos. 993-997 (5) 4.85 4.85

Greetings — A256

Designs: 3c, Gift, roses. 6c, Roses, letter, picture frame. 16c, Heart, tulips. 20c, Clock, champagne bottle, glass. 22c, Roses, wedding rings.

Unwmk.

2000, Feb. 9 Litho. *Perf. 14*

998 A256 3c multi .25 .25
999 A256 6c multi .40 .40
1000 A256 16c multi .95 .95
1001 A256 20c multi 1.25 1.25
1002 A256 22c multi 1.40 1.40
Nos. 998-1002 (5) 4.25 4.25

Malta in the 20th Century — A257

Designs: 6c, Cruise ship, small boat. 16c, Festival, musicians. 22c, Family walking, view of harbor. 27c, Farm family, Victoria Citadel, Gozo.

2000, Mar. 7 *Perf. 13¾x14*

1003 A257 6c multi .40 .40
1004 A257 16c multi .95 .95
1005 A257 22c multi 1.40 1.40
1006 A257 27c multi 1.60 1.60
Nos. 1003-1006 (4) 4.35 4.35

Sports A258

Designs: 6c, Soccer players, trophy. 16c, Swimmer, sailboats. 26c, Judo, shooting, runners. 37c, Soccer players.

2000, Mar. 28 *Perf. 14*

1007 A258 6c multi .35 .35
1008 A258 16c multi .90 .90
1009 A258 26c multi 1.50 1.50
1010 A258 37c multi 2.10 2.10
Nos. 1007-1010 (4) 4.85 4.85

Malta Soccer Assoc., cent. (6c); 2000 Summer Olympics, Sydney (16c, 26c); European Soccer Championships (37c).

Europa, 2000
Common Design Type

2000, May 9 *Perf. 14*

Color of Large "E"

1011 CD17 16c green *.95 .95*
1012 CD17 46c blue *2.75 2.75*

Air Transportation, Cent. — A259

#1013, D. H. 66 Hercules, 1928. #1014, Zeppelin LZ-127, 1933. #1015, Douglas DC-3 Dakota, 1949. #1016, Airbus A320.

2000, July 28

1013 A259 6c multi .45 .45
1014 A259 6c multi .45 .45
a. Pair, #1013-1014 1.40 1.40
1015 A259 16c multi 1.00 1.00
1016 A259 16c multi 1.00 1.00
a. Pair, #1015-1016 3.50 3.50
b. Souvenir sheet, #1013-1016 4.50 4.50
Nos. 1013-1016 (4) 2.90 2.90

Fireworks — A260

Denominations: 2c, 6c, 16c, 20c, 50c.

2000, July 19 **Litho.** *Perf. 13¾x14*
1017-1021 A260 Set of 5 6.25 6.25

Flower Type of 1999

Designs: 1c, Helichrysum melitense. 3c, Cistus creticus. 10c, Rosa sempervirens. 12c, Cynara cardunculus. 20c, Anacamptis pyramidalis. £2, Adonis microcarpa.

2000, Sept. 13 **Litho.** *Perf. 13¾*

1022 A253 1c multi .20 .20
1023 A253 3c multi .20 .20
1024 A253 10c multi .55 .55
1025 A253 12c multi .70 .70
1026 A253 20c multi 1.10 1.10
1027 A253 £2 multi 11.00 11.00
Nos. 1022-1027 (6) 13.75 13.75

Stampin' the Future Children's Stamp Design Contest Winners A261

Artwork by: #1028, Bettina Paris. #1029, Roxana Caruana. #1030, Jean Paul Zammit. #1031, Chiara Borg.

2000, Oct. 18 *Perf. 14x13¾*
1028-1031 A261 6c Set of 4 1.90 1.90

See also Nos. 1250, B85.

Christmas — A262

Designs: 6c, Children, Holy Family. 6c+3c, Magi. 16c+3c, Christmas tree, Santa Claus, family. 26c, Christmas tree, church, family.

2000, Nov. 18 **Litho.** *Perf. 14*
1032-1035 A262 Set of 4 4.75 4.75
1035a Souv. sheet, #1032-1035 4.75 4.75

Size of No. 1033: 23x27mm.

Carnival — A263

Various scenes and cartoon mascots at LL with: 6c, Horn. 11c, Guitar, vert. 16c, Drum, vert. 19c, Tambourine, vert. 27c, Flute.

No. 1041: a, 12c, Clowns (black and white photo), mascot with tambourine. b, 37c, Clowns (color photo), mascot with drum.

Perf. 13¾x14, 14x13¾

2001, Feb. 23 **Litho.**
1036-1040 A263 Set of 5 5.25 5.25

Souvenir Sheet

Perf. 13¾

1041 A263 Sheet of 2, #a-b 3.00 3.00

No. 1041 contains two 34x34mm stamps.

Lighthouses A264

Designs: 6c, Sant'Iermu. 16c, Gurdan. 22c, Delimara.

2001, Mar. 21 *Perf. 14x13¾*
1042-1044 A264 Set of 3 3.75 3.75

Paintings by Edward Caruana Dingli — A265

Denominations: 2c, 4c, 6c, 10c, 26c.

2001, Apr. 18
1045-1049 A265 Set of 5 4.00 4.00

Visit of Pope John Paul II A266

Designs: 6c, Nazju Falzon, Gorg Preca, and Adeodata Pisani, Maltese beatified by Pope. 16c, Pope, statue.

75c, Falzon, Preca, Pisani and Pope.

2001, May 4 *Perf. 14*
1050-1051 A266 Set of 2 3.00 3.00

Souvenir Sheet

1052 A266 75c multi 5.00 5.00

Europa A267

Designs: 16c, Discoglossus pictus. 46c, Sympetrum fonscolombii.

2001, May 23 **Litho.** *Perf. 14x14¼*
1053-1054 A267 Set of 2 *3.50 3.50*

Birds — A268

No. 1055: a, Larus cachinnans. b, Falco tinnunculus. c, Oriolus oriolus, d, Fringilla coelebs. e, Monticola solitarius. f, Merops apiaster. g, Hirundo rustica. h, Passer hispaniolensis. i, Sylvia conspicillata. j, Streptopelia turtur. k, Anas acuta. l, Ixobrychus minutus. m, Scolopax rusticola. n, Asio flammeus. o, Vanellus vanellus. p, Gallinula chloropus.

2001, June 22 **Litho.** *Perf. 13¾*
1055 A268 6c Sheet of 16, #a-p 11.00 11.00

Musical Instruments A269

Designs: 1c, Whistle flute. 3c, Reed pipe. 14c, Maltese bagpipe. 20c, Friction drum. 25c, Frame drum.

2001, Aug. 22 **Litho.** *Perf. 13¾*
1056-1060 A269 Set of 5 3.75 3.75

Flower Type of 1999

Designs: 5c, Papaver rhoeas. 11c, Silene colorata. 19c, Anthemis arvensis. 27c, Borago officinalis. 50c, Chrysanthemum coronarium. £1, Malva sylvestris.

2001, Sept. 19
1061-1066 A253 Set of 6 12.00 12.00

See No. 1269A.

Dogs A270

Designs: 6c, Kelb tal-Fenek. 16c, Kelb tal-Kacca. 19c, Maltese. 35c, Kelb tal-But.

2001, Oct. 20 **Litho.** *Perf. 14*
1067-1070 A270 Set of 4 5.25 5.25

Worldwide Fund for Nature (WWF) — A271

Seahorses: No. 1071, 6c, Hippocampus guttulatus. No. 1072, 6c, Hippocampus hippocampus. No. 1073, 16c, Hippocampus guttulatus, diff. No. 1074, 16c, Hippocampus hippocampus, diff.

2002 **Litho.** *Perf. 14¼x14*
1071-1074 A271 Set of 4 3.50 3.50

Antique Furniture — A272

Designs: 2c, Credenza. 4c, Bureau, vert. 11c, Table, vert. 26c, Armoire, vert. 60c, Credenza, diff.

2002, Mar. 27 **Litho.** *Perf. 14*
1075-1079 A272 Set of 5 5.75 5.75

Europa — A273

2002, May 9 **Litho.** *Perf. 14*
1080 A273 16c multi *.95 .95*

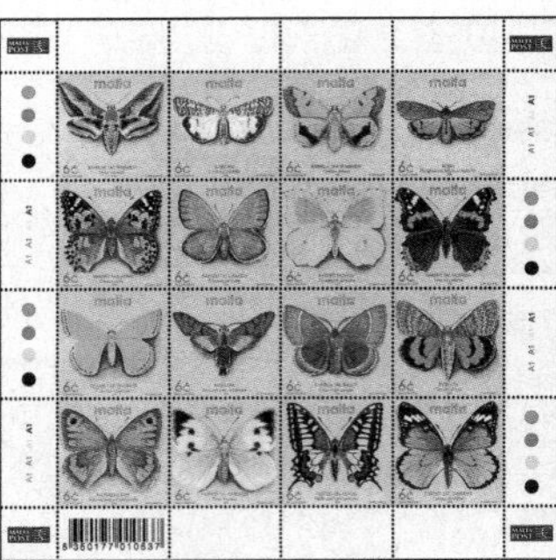

Butterflies and Moths — A274

No. 1081: a, Hyles sammuii. b, Utetheisa pulchella. c, Ophiusa tirhaca. d, Phragmatobia fulginosa melitensis. e, Vanessa cardui. f, Polyommatus icarus. g, Gonepteryx cleopatra. h, Vanessa atalanta. i, Eucrostes indigenata. j, Macroglossum stellatarum. k, Lasiocampa quercus. l, Catoeala elocata. m, Maniola jurtina hyperhispulla. n, Pieris brassicae. o, Papilio machaon melitensis. p, Danaus chrysippus.

2002, June *Perf. 13¾*
1081 A274 6c Sheet of 16, #a-p 7.00 7.00

Maltese Cuisine A275

Designs: 7c, Kusksu bil-ful. 12c, Qaqocc mimli. 16c, Lampuki. 27c, Qaghqa tal-kavatelli. 75c, Stuffat tal-fenek.

2002, Aug. 13 **Litho.** *Perf. 14*
1082-1085 A275 Set of 4 5.25 5.25

Souvenir Sheet

1086 A275 75c multi 6.25 6.25

Succulent Plants — A276

Designs: 1c, Yavia cryptocarpa. 7c, Aztekium hintonii, vert. 28c, Pseudolithos migiurtinus. 37c, Pierrebraunia brauniorum, vert. 76c, Euphorbia turbiniformis.

2002, Sept. 25
1087-1091 A276 Set of 5 8.75 8.75

Famous Men — A277

Designs: 3c, Adrian Dingli (1817-1900), legislator. 7c, Oreste Kirkop (1923-98), opera singer. 15c, Father Athanasius Kircher (1602-80), vulcanologist. 35c, Father Saverio Cassar (1746-1805), Gozo Uprising leader. 50c, Emmanuele Vitale (1759-1802), commander in uprising against the French.

2002, Oct. 18 Litho. *Perf. 14*
1092-1096 A277 Set of 5 6.25 6.25

Christmas A278

Designs: 7c, Mary and Joseph in donkey cart. 16c, Angels, Magi, Holy Family in bus. 22c, Holy Family and Angels on boat. 37c, Shepherds in field, Holy family in horse-drawn carriage. 75c, Angel, Magi, Holy Family and animals on galley.

2002, Nov. 20
1097-1101 A278 Set of 5 8.75 8.75

Flower Type of 1999

Designs: 7c, Vitex agnus-castus. 22c, Spartium junceum. 28c, Crataegus azalorus. 37c, Cercis siliquastrum. 45c, Myrtus communis. 76c, Pistacia lentiscus.

2003, Jan. 30 *Perf. 13¾*
1102 A253 7c multi .40 .40
1103 A253 22c multi 1.25 1.25
1104 A253 28c multi 1.60 1.60
1105 A253 37c multi 2.25 2.25
1106 A253 45c multi 2.75 2.75
1107 A253 76c multi 4.50 4.50
Nos. 1102-1107 (6) 12.75 12.75

Automobiles — A279

Designs: 2c, 1965 Vanden Plas Princess. 7c, 1948 Allard "M" Type. 10c, 1904 Cadillac Model B. 26c, 1936 Fiat Cinquecento Model A Topolino. 35c, 1965 Ford Anglia Super.

2003, Feb. 26 Litho. *Perf. 14*
1108-1112 A279 Set of 5 5.50 5.50

Military Architecture — A280

Designs: 1c, Fort St. Elmo. 4c, Rinella Battery. 11c, Fort St. Angelo. 16c, Reserve Post R15. 44c, Fort Tigné.

2003, Mar. 21 Litho. *Perf. 14*
1113-1117 A280 Set of 5 4.50 4.50

Martyrdom of St. George, 1700th Anniv. — A281

Various paintings depicting St. George: 3c, 7c, 14c, 19c, 27c.

2003, Apr. 23
1118-1122 A281 Set of 5 4.50 4.50

Europa — A282

Poster art: 16c, Cisk Beer. 46c, 1939 Carnival.

2003, May 9
1123-1124 A282 Set of 2 *3.50 3.50*

Games of Small European States A283

Designs: 25c, Track and field. 50c, Shooting. 75c, Volleyball. £3, Swimming.

2003, May 21 Litho. *Perf. 14x14¼*
1125-1128 A283 Set of 4 25.00 25.00

Coronation of Queen Elizabeth II, 50th Anniv. — A284

Queen Elizabeth II: 12c, With woman. 15c, Seated in limousine. 22c, With Prince Philip, reading book. 60c, With Prince Philip, receiving book from man.
£1, Queen and crowd of people.

2003, June 3
1129-1132 A284 Set of 4 6.00 6.00

Souvenir Sheet

1133 A284 £1 multi 6.75 6.75

Souvenir Sheet

Valletta Bastions — A285

2003, July 1 Litho. *Perf. 14x13¾*
1134 A285 £1.50 multi + 4 labels 10.50 10.50

Elton John concert, July 6, 2003.

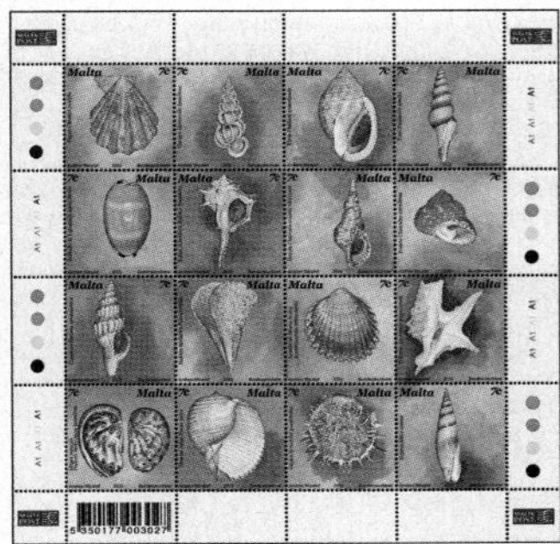

Shells — A286

No. 1135: a, Chlamys pesfelis. b, Gyroscala lamellosa. c, Phalium granulatum. d, Fusiturris similis. e, Luria lurida. f, Bolinus brandaris. g, Charonia tritonis variegata. h, Clanculus corallinus. i, Fusinus syracusanus. j, Pinna nobilis. k, Acanthocardia tuberculata. l, Aporrhais pespelcani. m, Haliotis tuberculata lamellosa. n, Tonna galea. o, Spondylus gaederopus. p, Mitra zonata.

2003, Aug. 20 Litho. *Perf. 13¾*
1135 A286 7c Sheet of 16, #a-p 7.50 7.50

Sailboats A287

Designs: 8c, Malta-Syracuse Race. 22c, Middle Sea Race, vert. 35c, Royal Malta Yacht Club, vert.

2003, Sept. 30 Litho. *Perf. 14*
1136-1138 A287 Set of 3 3.75 3.75

Flower Type of 1999

Designs: 7c, Vitex agnus-castus.16c, Crocus longiflorus.

Serpentine Die Cut 12½ on 2 or 3 Sides

2003, Oct. 22

Booklet Stamps
Self-Adhesive
Size: 23x23mm

1139 A253 7c multi .40 .40
a. Booklet pane of 12 5.00
1140 A253 16c multi .90 .90
a. Booklet pane of 6 5.50

Windmills — A288

Designs: 11c, Is-Sur ta'San Mikiel, Valletta. 27c, Ta'Kola, Xaghra, vert. 45c, Tax-Xarolla, Zurrieq, vert.

2003, Oct. 29 *Perf. 14*
1141-1143 A288 Set of 3 5.25 5.25

Christmas — A289

Designs: 7c, The Annunciation, vert. 16c, Holy Family, vert. 22c, Adoration of the Magi. 50c, Adoration of the Magi.

2003, Nov. 12
1144-1147 A289 Set of 4 6.75 6.75

Letter Boxes — A290

Boxes from era of: 1c, Queen Victoria. 16c, King Edward VII. 22c, King George V, King George VI. 37c, Queen Elizabeth II. 76c, Independent Malta (Malta Post).

2004, Mar. 12
1148-1152 A290 Set of 5 10.50 10.50

Cats — A291

Various cats with denominations and country name in: 7c, Golden brown. 27c, Dark brown. 28c, Lilac. 50c, Red brown. 60c, Green.

2004, Mar. 26 *Perf. 13¾*
1153-1157 A291 Set of 5 10.50 10.50

Souvenir Sheet

Salesians in Malta, Cent. — A292

2004, Apr. 7 *Perf. 14*
1158 A292 75c multi 4.50 4.50

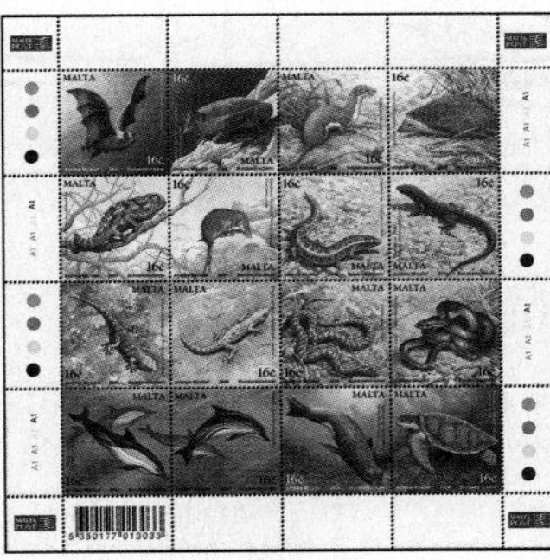

Fauna — A293

No. 1159: a, Pipistrellus pygmaeus. b, Myotis blythi punicus. c, Mustela nivalis. d, Atelerix algirus fallax. e, Chamaeleo chamaeleon. f, Crocidura sicula. g, Chalcides ocellatus. h, Podarcis filfolensis filfolensis. i, Tarentola mauritanica. j, Hemidactylus turcicus. k, Elaphe situla. l, Coluber viridiflavus. m, Delphinus delphis. n, Stenella coeruleoalba. o, Monachus monachus. p, Chelonia mydas.

2004, Apr. 21 *Perf. 13¾*
1159 A293 16c Sheet of 16, #a-p 14.50 14.50

Admission to European Union — A294

Stars, map of Europe and: 16c, Flags of newly-admitted countries. 28c, Officials signing treaty.

2004, May 1 ***Perf. 14***
1160-1161 A294 Set of 2 2.50 2.50

Europa — A295

Designs: 16c, Youths jumping into water. 51c, People at archaeological site.

2004, May 19 ***Perf. 13¾x14***
1162-1163 A295 Set of 2 *3.75 3.75*

Wayside Chapels A296

Designs: 3c, Lunzjata-Hal Milliere, Zurrieq. 7c, San Basilju, Mqabba. 39c, San Cir, Rabat. 48c, Santa Lucija, Mtarfa. 66c, Ta' Santa Marija, Kemmuna.

2004, June 16 Litho. ***Perf. 14***
1164-1168 A296 Set of 5 10.50 10.50

Trams A297

Designs: 19c, Side view of tram. 37c, Tram and conductor (22x40mm). 50c, Ticket (22x40mm). 75c, Tram and archway.

Perf. 13¾, 14 (37c, 50c)
2004, July 14
1169-1172 A297 Set of 4 10.50 10.50

2004 Summer Olympics, Athens A298

Designs: 11c, Discus thrower. 16c, Doric column, olive wreath. 76c, Javelin thrower.

Perf. 14¼
2004, Aug. 13 Litho. Unwmk.
1173-1175 A298 Set of 3 6.00 6.00

Religious Festivals — A299

Designs: 5c, Ascension Day. 15c, St. Gregory's Day. 27c, Pilgrimage on First Sunday in Lent. 51c, St. Martin's Day, vert. £1, Feast of Sts. Peter and Paul, vert.

Perf. 14x14¼, 14¼x14
2004, Sept. 15 Wmk. 354
1176-1180 A299 Set of 5 11.50 11.50

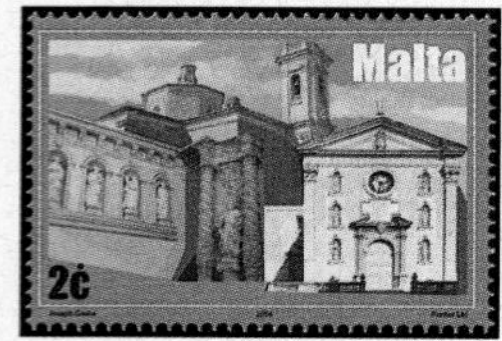
Works of Art A300

Designs: 2c, Church of St. Mary, Attard. 20c, Mdina Cathedral organ, music by Benignon Zerafa, vert. 57c, Statue of St. Agatha, vert. 62c, Books, illustration for poem "The Turkish Galleon," by Gian Antonio Vassallo, vert.
72c, Icon of St. Paul, vert.

Perf. 14x14¼, 14¼x14
2004, Oct. 13 Litho. Wmk. 354
1181-1184 A300 Set of 4 10.50 10.50

Souvenir Sheet

1185 A300 72c multi 5.00 5.00

Christmas — A301

Various effigies of Infant Jesus: 7c, 16c, 22c, 50c. Nos. 1187-1189 vert.

Perf. 14x14¼, 14¼x14
2004, Nov. 10 Litho. Wmk. 354
1186-1189 A301 Set of 4 5.75 5.75

Historic Maps A302

Designs: 1c, Map of Malta by Abbé Jean Quintin, 1536. 12c, Map of Malta by Antonio Lafreri, 1551. 37c, Fresco map of Malta, by Matteo Perez d'Aleccio, 1565. £1.02, Map of Gozo, Comino, Cominotto and Marfa Peninsula, by Fr. Luigi Bartolo, 1745.

Wmk. 354
2005, Jan. 19 Litho. ***Perf. 14***
1190-1193 A302 Set of 4 9.25 9.25

Rotary International, Cent. — A303

Rotary emblem and: 27c, Dar il-Kaptan Home, Mtarfa, woman, man. 76c, Map of Malta.

Perf. 14x14¼
2005, Feb. 23 Litho. Wmk. 354
1194-1195 A303 Set of 2 6.50 6.50

Hans Christian Andersen (1805-75), Author A304

Paper Cutting by Andersen, Scissors — A305

Designs: 60c, Pen, inkwell, illustration of duckling, manuscript handwritten by Andersen. 75c, Andersen's drawing of Casino dell'Orlogio, Rome, and boots.

Perf. 14x13¾
2005, Mar. 3 Litho. Wmk. 354
1196 A304 7c gray & black .45 .45
1197 A305 22c blue & black 1.40 1.40
1198 A305 60c multi 3.75 3.75
1199 A305 75c multi 4.75 4.75
Nos. 1196-1199 (4) 10.35 10.35

See Denmark Nos. 1323-1326.

Pope John Paul II (1920-2005) A306

2005, Apr. 15 ***Perf. 14***
1200 A306 51c multi 4.00 4.00

Miniature Sheet

Insects — A307

No. 1201: a, Coccinella septempunctata. b, Chrysoperla carnea. c, Apis mellifera. d, Crocothermis erythraea. e, Anax imperator. f, Lampyris pallida. g, Henosepilachna elaterii. h, Forficula decipiens. i, Mantis religiosa. j, Eumenes lunulatus. k, Cerambyx cerdo. l, Gryllus bimaculatus. m, Xylocopa violacea. n, Cicada orni. o, Acrida ungarica. p, Oryctes nasicornis.

2005, Apr. 20 ***Perf. 14¼***
1201 A307 16c Sheet of 16, #a-p 15.50 15.50

Europa — A308

Designs: 16c, Stuffed peppers, zucchini and eggplant. 51c, Fried rabbit in wine and garlic.

2005, May 9 ***Perf. 14¼x14***
1202-1203 A308 Set of 2 *4.00 4.00*

Paintings Depicting St. Catherine — A309

Designs: No. 1204, 28c, The Beheading of St. Catherine, by unknown artist. No. 1205, 28c, The Martyrdom of St. Catherine, by Mattia Preti, vert. No. 1206, 45c, St. Catherine Disputing the Philosophers, by Francesco Zahra. No. 1207, 45c, Mystic Marriage, by Sahra, vert.

Perf. 14x14¼, 14¼x14
2005, June 15 Litho. Wmk. 354
1204-1207 A309 Set of 4 8.25 8.25

Famous People A310

Designs: 3c, Monsignor Michael Azzopardi (1910-87), religious educator. 19c, Egidio Lapira (1897-1970), dental surgeon. 20c, Petition of Guzeppi Callus (1505-61), doctor executed for taxation opposition. 46c, Hand and quill pen of Geronimo Matteo Abos (1715-60), composer. 76c, Gio Francesco Abela (1592-1655), historian, ambassador.

Wmk. 354
2005, July 13 Litho. ***Perf. 14¼***
1208-1212 A310 Set of 5 9.50 9.50

Flower Type of 1999 Redrawn

Design: 7c, Vitex agnus-castus. 16c, Crocus longiflorus.

2005 Litho. ***Perf. 14¼***
1213 A253 7c multi + label .40 .40
1214 A253 16c multi + label .95 .95

Nos. 1213-1214 have "2005" year date and "Printex Ltd" inscription at lower right. Additionally, No. 1213 has wider distance between denomination and country name than No. 1102, and No. 1214 has denomination and country name in a different font than No. 986. Nos. 1213-1214 were issued in sheets of 10 stamps and 10 labels. Labels could be personalized for an additional fee.

Horses and Mules at Work A311

Designs: 11c, Horse-drawn hearse. 15c, Mule pulling plow. 62c, Mule at grindstone. 66c, Horse pulling cart.

Perf. 14x14¼
2005, Aug. 19 Litho. Wmk. 354
1215-1218 A311 Set of 4 9.00 9.00

End of World War II, 60th Anniv. A312

Scenes from Battle of Malta: 2c, Civilians on food line. 5c, Royal Navy ships under attack. 25c, Anti-aircraft gunners. 51c, Aviators and planes. £1, Tanker "Ohio."

2005, Sept. 23
1219-1223 A312 Set of 5 10.50 10.50

Christmas — A313

Mosaics of paintings by Envin Cremona from National Sanctuary of Our Lady of Ta' Pinu, Gozo: 7c, Nativity. 16c, Annunciation, vert. 22c, Adoration of the Magi. 50c, Flight into Egypt (68x27mm).

Perf. 14¼, 13¾x14 (50c)
2005, Oct. 12 Litho. Wmk. 354
1224-1227 A313 Set of 4 5.50 5.50

Souvenir Sheets

Commonwealth Heads of Governments Meeting — A314

Flags of Malta, British Commonwealth and: 14c, Commonwealth Heads of Government flag. 28c, Doves. 37c, Maltese cross. 75c, People.

Perf. 14x14¼
2005, Nov. 23 Litho. Wmk. 354
1228-1231 A314 Set of 4 8.50 8.50

Souvenir Sheet

Europa Stamps, 50th Anniv. — A315

No. 1232: a, 5c, #677. b, 13c, #628. c, 23c, #540. d, 24c, #738.

2006, Jan. 3 ***Perf. 13¾x14***
1232 A315 Sheet of 4, #a-d 3.75 3.75

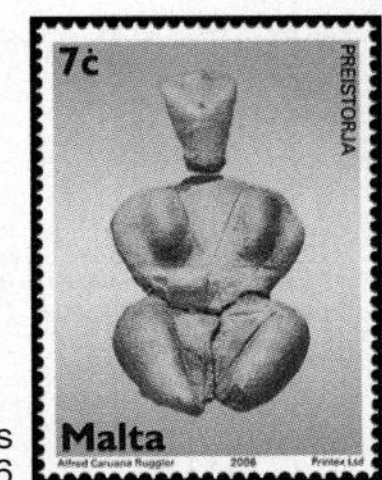

Ceramics A316

Designs: 7c, Neolithic terra-cotta female figurine. 16c, Roman terra-cotta head. 28c, Terra-cotta oil lamp holder. 37c, Sicilian maiolica plate. 60c, Stylized figure in traditional Maltese costume, by Ianni Bonnici.

Wmk. 354
2006, Feb. 25 Litho. ***Perf. 14¼***
1233-1237 A316 Set of 5 8.25 8.25

Miniature Sheet

Pets — A317

No. 1238: a, Shetland pony. b, Chihuahua. c, Goldfish. d, Siamese cat. e, Siamese fighting fish. f, Ferret. g, Canary. h, Turtle. i, Chinchilla. j, Parakeet. k, Rabbit. l, Zebra finch. m, Pointer. n, Pigeon. o, Guinea pig. p, House cat.

Wmk. 354
2006, Mar. 14 Litho. ***Perf. 14¼***
1238 A317 Sheet of 16 13.50 13.50
a.-h. 7c Any single .40 .40
i.-p. 22c Any single 1.25 1.25

Traditional Holy Week Celebrations A318

Designs: 7c, Men carrying crosses. 15c, Men carrying crucifixion scene. 22c, Float. 27c, Men pulling statue of Jesus. 82c, Decorated altar.

2006, Apr. 12 ***Perf. 14¼x14***
1239-1243 A318 Set of 5 9.25 9.25

Europa A319

Designs: 16c, Shown. 51c, Stick figures, diff. (28x41mm).

Perf. 14¼, 14¼x14 (51c)
2006, May 9
1244-1245 A319 Set of 2 4.00 4.00

2006 World Cup Soccer Championships, Germany A320

Designs: 7c, Bobby Charlton. 16c, Pelé. 27c, Franz Beckenbauer. 76c, Dino Zoff.

2006, June 2 ***Perf. 14¼x14***
1246-1249 A320 Set of 4 7.75 7.75
1249a Souvenir sheet, #1246-1249 7.75 7.75

Stampin' The Future Type of 2000 Souvenir Sheet

2006, June 5 ***Perf. 14***
1250 A261 £1.50 Like #1028 9.00 9.00

Ten percent of the sale went to the Rainforest Foundation.

Naval Vessels A321

Designs: 8c, Gran Carraca di Rodi. 29c, Guillaume Tell (HMS Malta). 51c, USS Constitution. 76c, HMS Dreadnought. £1, Slava and USS Belknap.

Wmk. 354
2006, Aug. 18 Litho. ***Perf. 14¼***
1251-1255 A321 Set of 5 16.00 16.00

Greetings A322

Inscriptions: 8c, Happy Birthday. 16c, Happy Anniversary. 27c, Congratulations. 37c, Best Wishes.

2006, Sept. 18
1256-1259 A322 Set of 4 5.25 5.25

Castles and Towers A323

Designs: 7c, Wignacourt Tower. 16c, Verdala Castle. 27c, San Lucjan Tower. 37c, Kemmuna Tower. £1, Selmun Castle.

Perf. 14x14¼
2006, Sept. 29 Litho. Wmk. 354
1260-1264 A323 Set of 5 11.00 11.00

Christmas — A324

Designs: 8c, Paolino Vassallo (1856-1923), composer of "Inno per Natale," Nativity. 16c, Carmelo Pace (1906-93), composer of "They Heard the Angels," Magi on camels. 22c, Paul Nani (1906-86), composer of "Maltese Christmas," angels. 27c, Carlo Diacono (1876-1942), composer of "Notte di Natale," shepherds and angel.

50c, Wolfgang Amadeus Mozart (1756-91), composer of "Alma Dei Creatoris."

2006, Nov. 6 ***Perf. 14¼***
1265-1268 A324 Set of 4 4.50 4.50

Souvenir Sheet
Perf. 13¾
1269 A324 50c multi 3.25 3.25

No. 1269 contains one 40x30mm stamp.

Flower Type of 1999 Redrawn

2006 Litho. Wmk. 354 ***Perf. 14¼***
1269A A253 1c Like #1022 .20 .20

No. 1269A has a "2006" year date and "Printex Ltd." inscription at lower right. Additionally, the country name has a different font than No. 1022, with the lines in the lettering being of equal thickness throughout the letter on No. 1269A. Other differences in the vignette exist.

Due to the scheduled conversion to the euro on Jan. 1, 2008, Nos. 1270-1274 and all stamps issued in 2007 will show denominations in pounds and the not-yet-circulating euros.

Crafts A325

Designs: 8c, Wrought iron window guard, blacksmith and anvil. 16c, Glass ornamental objects, glassblower. 22c, Filigree pendant, silversmith. 37c, Pottery, potter. 60c, Reed baskets, basket maker.

2006, Dec. 29 ***Perf. 14¼***
1270-1274 A325 Set of 5 8.75 8.75

Sculptures from 3000-2500 B.C. — A326

Designs: 15c, Human head. 29c, Animals, horiz. 60c, Spirals, horiz. £1.50, Headless nude female.

Wmk. 354
2007, Feb. 28 Litho. ***Perf. 14¼***
1275-1278 A326 Set of 4 16.00 16.00

Miniature Sheet

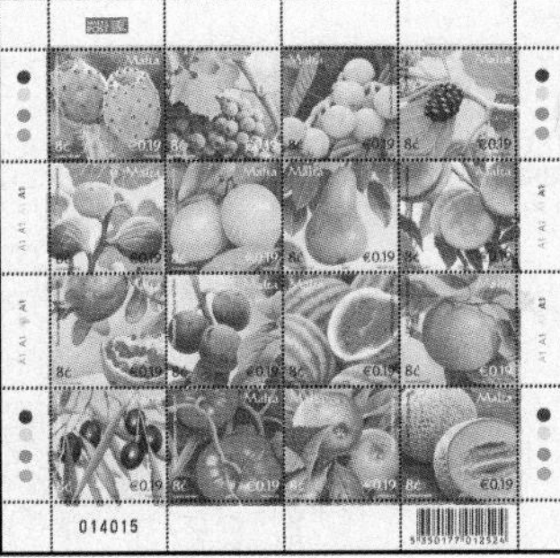

Fruit — A327

No. 1279: a, Opuntia ficus-indica (prickly pears). b, Viris vinifera (grapes). c, Eriobotrya japonica (loquats). d, Morus nigra (black mulberries). e, Ficus carica (figs). f, Citrus limonum (lemons). g, Pyrus communis (pear). h, Prunus persica (peaches). i, Punica granatum (pomegranates). j, Prunus salicina (plums). k, Citrullus vulgaris (watermelons). l, Citrus sinensis (orange). m, Olea europaea (olives). n, Lycopersicon esculentum (tomatoes). o, Malus domestica (apples). p, Cucumis melo (cantaloupe).

2007, Apr. 16
1279 A327 8c Sheet of 16, #a-p 8.00 8.00

Balconies
A328

Designs: 8c, Wrought iron balcony. 22c, Stone balcony. 27c, Balustraded balcony, National Library. 29c, Closed wooden balcony. 46c, Art Deco balcony by Silvio Mercieca.

51c, Ornamented balcony, Hostel de Verdelin, Valletta, horiz.

Wmk. 354

2007, Apr. 28 Litho. *Perf. 14¼*
1280-1284 A328 Set of 5 8.50 8.50

Souvenir Sheet

Perf. 13¾

1285 A328 51c multi 3.25 3.25

No. 1285 contains one 37x28mm stamp.

Europa
A329

Emblems of Scout Association of Malta, Scouting Centenary and: 16c, Lord Robert Baden-Powell. 51c, Maltese scouts at 1957 Jamboree.

2007, May 9 *Perf. 14¼*
1286-1287 A329 Set of 2 4.25 4.25

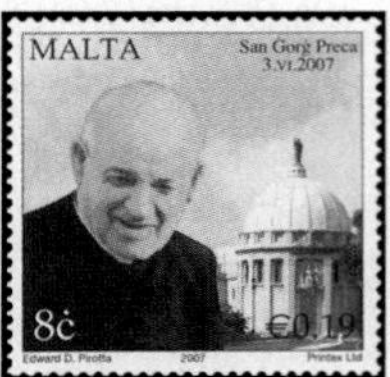
Canonization of St. George Preca (1880-1962)
A330

Background color: 8c, Blue. £1, Orange.

Wmk. 354

2007, May 28 Litho. *Perf. 14¼*
1288-1289 A330 Set of 2 6.75 6.75

Toys — A331

Photographs of children and: 2c, Rocking horse, tricycle, car. 3c, Baby carriage, drums and tops. 16c, Boats, beach pails and shovel. 22c, Dolls. 50c, Truck, motorcycle and race car.

2007, July 11 *Perf. 14¼x14*
1290-1294 A331 Set of 5 6.00 6.00

Paintings by Caravaggio — A332

Designs: 5c, St. Jerome. 29c, The Beheading of St. John the Baptist (48x40mm). £2, The Beheading of St. John the Baptist, vert.

2007, July 20 *Perf. 14¼*
1295-1296 A332 Set of 2 2.25 2.25

Souvenir Sheet

1297 A332 £2 multi 13.00 13.00

Arrival of Caravaggio on Malta, 400th anniv.

Motorcycles — A333

Designs: 1c, 1954 Royal Enfield. 16c, 1941 Matchless G3/L. 27c, 1903 Minerva. 50c, 1965 Triumph Speed Twin.

Perf. 14x14¼

2007, Sept. 12 Litho. Wmk. 354
1298-1301 A333 Set of 4 6.25 6.25

Greetings Stamps
A334

2007, Sept. 28 *Perf. 14¼*

1302	A334 8c Hearts	.55	.55
a.	Sheet of 5 + 5 labels	13.50	13.50
1303	A334 8c Stars	.55	.55
a.	Sheet of 5 + 5 labels	13.50	13.50
1304	A334 8c Roses	.55	.55
a.	Sheet of 5 + 5 labels	13.50	13.50
1305	A334 8c Balloons	.55	.55
a.	Sheet of 5 + 5 labels	13.50	13.50
1306	A334 8c Champagne flutes	.55	.55
a.	Sheet of 5 + 5 labels	13.50	13.50
1307	A334 8c Teddy bears	.55	.55
a.	Sheet of 5 + 5 labels	13.50	13.50
	Nos. 1302-1307 (6)	3.30	3.30

Labels on Nos. 1302a-1307a were personalizable, with full sheets each selling for £2, with a minimum purchase of two sheets of any stamp.

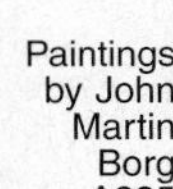

Paintings by John Martin Borg
A335

Designs: 11c, Mdina Skyline. 16c, Qrendi. 37c, Vittoriosa Waterfront. 46c, Mgarr Harbor, Gozo. 76c, Xlendi Bay, Gozo.

2007, Oct. 1 *Perf. 14¼*
1308-1312 A335 Set of 5 12.50 12.50

Fruit Type of 2007

Souvenir Sheet

2007, Oct. 18
1313 A327 75c Like #1279m 5.00 5.00

National Tree Planting Weekend. An unspecified portion of the proceeds of the sale went to the 34U Campaign.

Bands
A336

Various bands: 4c, 15c, 21c, 22c, £1.

2007, Nov. 13
1314-1318 A336 Set of 5 11.00 11.00

Christmas
A337

Maltese arms and nave paintings in St. Andrew's Church, Luqa, by Giuseppe Cali: 8c, Madonna and Child. 16c, Holy Family with Women and Young Girl. 21c, Infant Jesus and Young Girl.

2007, Nov. 20
1319-1321 A337 Set of 3 3.50 3.50

See Vatican City Nos. 1370-1372.

Youth Soccer Association, 25th Anniv. — A338

Society of Christian Doctrine Museum, Cent. — A339

Religious Figures — A340

Treaty of Rome, 50th Anniv. — A341

Designs: 16c, Monsignor Frangisk Bonnici (1852-1905), founder of St. Joseph Institute, Hamrun. 43c, Father Manwel Magri (1851-1907), ethnographer and archaeologist. 86c, Carolina Cauchi (1824-1907), founder of Dominican Sisters of Malta.

Wmk. 354

2007, Dec. 1 Litho. *Perf. 14¼*

1322	A338 4m multi	.20	.20
1323	A339 9c multi	.60	.60
1324	A340 16c multi	1.10	1.10
1325	A340 43c multi	3.00	3.00
1326	A340 86c multi	6.00	6.00
	Nos. 1322-1326 (5)	10.90	10.90

Souvenir Sheet

Perf. 13¾

1327 A341 76c multi 5.25 5.25

No. 1327 contains one 40x30mm stamp.

Souvenir Sheet

Obverse and Reverse of Maltese Pound Coin — A342

Wmk. 354

2007, Dec. 31 Litho. *Perf. 14¼*
1328 A342 £1 multi 7.00 7.00

Last day of use of pound currency.

100 Cents = 1 Euro

Souvenir Sheet

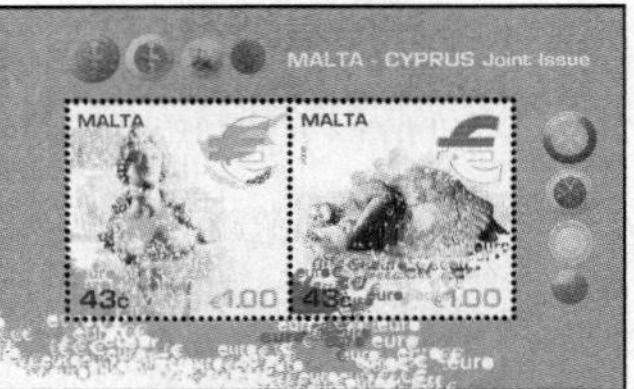
Introduction of Euro Currency — A343

No. 1329: a, Statue of Aphrodite, map of Cyprus. b, Sleeping Lady statue.

Wmk. 354

2008, Jan. 1 Litho. *Perf. 14¼*
1329 A343 €1 Sheet of 2, #a-b 6.00 6.00

See Cyprus No. 1088.

Souvenir Sheet

Obverse and Reverse of Maltese Euro Coin — A344

2008, Jan. 1
1330 A344 €1 multi 3.00 3.00

Door Knockers
A345

Various door knockers with background color of: 26c, Blue. 51c, Red. 63c, Brown. €1.77, Green.

2008, Mar. 5 *Perf. 14¼x14*
1331-1334 A345 Set of 4 9.75 9.75

2008 Summer Olympics, Beijing — A346

Designs: 5c, Shooting. 12c, Swimming. €1.57, Running.

2008, Mar. 7 ***Perf. 14x14¼***
1335-1337 A346 Set of 3 5.50 5.50

Europa — A347

Mail room, postman with bicycle in: 37c, Sepia. €1.19, Black.

Wmk. 354
2008, May 9 **Litho.** ***Perf. 14¼***
1338-1339 A347 Set of 2 5.00 5.00

Birth of St. Paul, 2000th Anniv. — A348

Statues depicting St. Paul from: 19c, Conversion of St. Paul Church, Safi. 68c, St. Paul's Shipwreck Church, Munxar. €1.08, St. Paul's Shipwreck Church, Rabat.
€3, St. Paul's Shipwreck Church, Valletta.

2008, June 28
1340-1342 A348 Set of 3 6.25 6.25

Souvenir Sheet
1343 A348 €3 multi 9.50 9.50

Intl. Year of Planet Earth A349

Emblem and: 7c, Sand dune. 86c, Tree in field. €1, Earth. €1.77, Sea coast.

Wmk. 354
2008, Aug. 11 **Litho.** ***Perf. 14¼***
1344-1347 A349 Set of 4 11.00 11.00

Cruise Liners A350

Designs: 63c, MSC Musica. €1.16, M.S. Voyager of the Seas. €1.40, M. S. Westerdam. €3, RMS Queen Elizabeth 2.

Perf. 14x14¼
2008, Nov. 18 **Litho.** **Wmk. 354**
1348-1351 A350 Set of 4 16.00 16.00

Christmas — A351

Paintings: 19c, Madonna and Child with the Infant St. John the Baptist, by Francesco Trevisani. 26c, Nativity, by Master Alberto. 37c, Virgin and Child with the Infant St. John the Baptist, by Carlo Maratta.

2008, Nov. 27 ***Perf. 14¼***
1352-1354 A351 Set of 3 2.10 2.10

Mushrooms A352

Designs: 5c, Laetiorus sulphureus. 12c, Montagnea arenaria. 19c, Pleurotus eryngii. 26c, Inonotus indicus. €1.57, Suillus collinitus.

Wmk. 354
2009, Mar. 27 **Litho.** ***Perf. 14¼***
1355-1359 A352 Set of 5 6.00 6.00

Postal Transportation A353

Designs: 9c, Airplane. 35c, Motorcycles. €2.50, Bicycles. €3, Mail boat to Gozo.

2009, Apr. 28
1360-1363 A353 Set of 4 16.00 16.00

Introduction of Euro Currency, 10th Anniv. — A354

Wmk. 354
2009, Apr. 30 **Litho.** ***Perf. 14¼***
1364 A354 €2 multi 5.50 5.50

Europa — A355

Designs: 37c, Galileo Galilei, Sketch of Moon by Galileo, Lunar Module. €1.19, Telescope of William Lassell, M42 nebula.

2009, May 9 ***Perf. 14¼x14***
1365 A355 37c multi 1.10 1.10
a. Booklet pane of 5 5.50 —
Complete booklet, #1365a 5.50
1366 A355 €1.19 multi 3.50 3.50

Intl. Year of Astronomy.

13th Games of the Small States of Europe, Cyprus A356

Designs: 10c, Sailing. 19c, Judo. 37c, Shooting. 67c, Swimming. €1.77, Running.

2009, June 1 ***Perf. 14x14¼***
1367-1371 A356 Set of 5 8.75 8.75

Cruise Liners Type of 2008

Designs: 37c, MS Seabourn Pride. 68c, MS Brilliance of the Seas. 91c, Costa Magica and Costa Atlantica. €2, MS MSC Splendida.

2009, July 15
1372-1375 A350 Set of 4 11.50 11.50

Scenic Views A357

Designs: 2c, Mediterranean coast. 7c, Watchtower. 37c, Salt pans, Qbajjar, Gozo. €1.02, Ggantija Temple ruins.

Perf. 14x14¼
2009, Sept. 16 **Litho.** **Wmk. 354**
1376-1379 A357 Set of 4 4.50 4.50

Christmas A358

Designs: 19c, Mater Admirabilis, in the manner of Botticelli by unknown artist. 37c, Madonna and Child, by Corrado Giaquinto. 63c, Madonna and Child, by Follower of Simone Cantarini.

Perf. 14¼x14
2009, Nov. 30 **Litho.** **Wmk. 354**
1380-1382 A358 Set of 3 3.50 3.50

History of Malta A359

Inscriptions: 1c, Pleistocene Period. 2c, Early Temple Period. 5c, Late Temple Period. 7c, Bronze Period. 9c, Phoenician & Punic Period, vert. 10c, Roman Period. 19c, Byzantine Period, vert. 25c, Arab Period. 37c, Norman & Hohenstaufen Period, vert. 50c, Angevin & Aragaonese, vert. 51c, Knights of St. John. 63c, French Period. 68c, British Period, vert. 86c, Independence, vert. €1, Republic, vert. €1.08, E.U. Accession, vert. €5, Coat of arms, vert.

2009, Dec. 29 ***Perf. 14x14¼, 14¼x14***

No.	Type	Value	Unused	Used
1383	A359	1c multi	.20	.20
1384	A359	2c multi	.20	.20
1385	A359	5c multi	.20	.20
1386	A359	7c multi	.20	.20
1387	A359	9c multi	.20	.20
1388	A359	10c multi	.30	.30
1389	A359	19c multi	.55	.55
1390	A359	25c multi	.75	.75
1391	A359	37c multi	1.10	1.10
1392	A359	50c multi	1.50	1.50
1393	A359	51c multi	1.50	1.50
1394	A359	63c multi	1.90	1.90
1395	A359	68c multi	2.00	2.00
1396	A359	86c multi	2.50	2.50
1397	A359	€1 multi	3.00	3.00
1398	A359	€1.08 multi	3.25	3.25
1399	A359	€5 multi	14.50	14.50
a.	Souvenir sheet, #1383-1399		34.00	34.00
Nos. 1383-1399 (17)			33.85	33.85

Miniature Sheet

100-Ton Guns of Malta and Gibraltar — A360

No. 1400 — 100-ton gun from: a, Fort Rinella, Malta, 2010. b, Fort Rinella, 1882. c, Napier of Magdala Battery, Gibraltar, 1880. d, Napier of Magdala Battery, 2010.

Wmk. 354
2010, Feb. 19 **Litho.** ***Perf. 13¾***
1400 A360 75c Sheet of 4, #a-d 8.25 8.25

See Gibraltar No.

Balloons A361

Islands A362

Mortarboard and Diploma — A363

Wedding A364

Champagne Bottle, Bucket and Flutes — A365

Clock Tower and Fireworks A366

Hand Holding Trophy — A367

Map of Malta A368

Wmk. 354

2010, Mar. 17 Litho. ***Perf. 14¼***

1401 A361 19c multi .55 .55
1402 A362 19c multi .55 .55
1403 A363 19c multi .55 .55
1404 A364 19c multi .55 .55
1405 A365 19c multi .55 .55
1406 A366 19c multi .55 .55
1407 A367 19c multi .55 .55
1408 A368 37c multi 1.00 1.00
Nos. 1401-1408 (8) 4.85 4.85

Souvenir Sheet

Visit of Pope Benedict XVI to Malta — A369

2010, Mar. 17
1409 A369 €3 multi 8.25 8.25

Europa — A370

Characters from children's books: 37c, Puttinu u Toninu, by Dr. Philip Farrugia Randon. €1.19, Meta l-Milied Ma Glex (When Christmas Didn't Come), by Clare Azzopardi.

2010, May 4
1410-1411 A370 Set of 2 4.00 4.00
1411a Booklet pane of 5 #1411 4.75 —
Complete booklet, #1411a 4.75

2010 World Cup Soccer Championships, South Africa — A371

Designs: 63c, Flags, map of Africa. €2.50, Mascot, flag and map of South Africa.

Wmk. 354

2010, June 11 Litho. ***Perf. 14¼***
1412-1413 A371 Set of 2 7.75 7.75
1413a Souvenir sheet, #1412-1413 7.75 7.75

Intl. Year of Biodiversity — A372

Designs: 19c, Maltese wall lizard. 68c, Storm petrel, vert. 86c, Maltese pyramidal orchid, vert. €1.40, Freshwater crab.

Perf. 14x14¼, 14¼x14

2010, Sept. 23 Litho. Wmk. 354
1414-1417 A372 Set of 4 8.00 8.00

Coastline Features — A373

Designs: 37c, Azure Window, Gozo. 51c, Blue Grotto, Zurrieq, vert. 67c, Ta' Cenc Cliffs, Gozo, vert. €1.16, Filfla.

Perf. 14x14¼, 14¼x14

2010, Oct. 19 Litho. Wmk. 354
1418-1421 A373 Set of 4 7.75 7.75

Christmas — A374

Designs: 19c, The Adoration of the Magi, by the Studio of Valerio Castello. 37c, The Flight Into Egypt, attributed to Filippo Paladini. 63c, Madonna di Maggio, by Pierre Guillemin, vert.

Perf. 14x14¼, 14¼x14

2010, Nov. 9 Litho. Wmk. 354
1422-1424 A374 Set of 3 3.25 3.25

Compare with type A358.

Souvenir Sheet

First Malta Stamp, 150th Anniv. — A375

2010, Dec. 1 ***Perf. 14¼x14***
1425 A375 €2.80 multi 7.50 7.50

SEMI-POSTAL STAMPS

All semi-postal issues are for Christmas.

Catalogue values for unused stamps in this section are for Never Hinged items.

Two Peasants with Tambourine and Bagpipe SP1

Star of Bethlehem and: 5p+1p, Angels with Trumpet and Harp, Star of Bethlehem and Mdina Cathedral. 1sh6p+3p, Choir boys singing Christmas carols.

The background of the 3 stamps together shows the Cathedral of Mdina, Malta, and surrounding countryside.

Wmk. 354

1969, Nov. 8 Litho. ***Perf. 12½***
B1 SP1 1p +1p multi .20 .20
B2 SP1 5p +1p multi .20 .20
B3 SP1 1sh6p +3p multi .20 *.30*
a. Triptych, #B1-B3 .50 .50
Nos. B1-B3 (3) .60 .70

Nos. B1-B3 were printed each in sheets of 60, and in sheets containing 20 triptychs.

Christmas Eve Procession — SP2

10p+2p, Nativity & Cathedral. 1sh6p+3p, Adoration of the Shepherds & Mdina Cathedral.

1970, Nov. 7 Photo. ***Perf. 14x13½***
B4 SP2 1p +½p multi .20 .20
B5 SP2 10p +2p multi .20 .20
B6 SP2 1sh6p +3p multi .30 *.45*
Nos. B4-B6 (3) .70 *.85*

Surtax for child welfare organizations.

Angel — SP3

#B8, Madonna & Child. #B9, Shepherd.

1971, Nov. 8 ***Perf. 14***
B7 SP3 1p +½p multi .20 .20
B8 SP3 10p +2p multi .25 .25
B9 SP3 1sh6p +3p multi .40 .40
a. Souv. sheet, #B7-B9, perf. 15 1.00 *1.25*
Nos. B7-B9 (3) .85 .85

1972, Dec. Litho. ***Perf. 13½***

Designs: 3c+1c, Angel playing tambourine. 7c5m+1c5m, Angel singing.

B10 SP3 8m +2m dk gray & gold .20 .20
B11 SP3 3c +1c dk purple & gold .20 .20
B12 SP3 7c5m +1c5m slate & gold .50 *.50*
a. Souvenir sheet of 3, #B10-B12 2.00 *2.50*
Nos. B10-B12 (3) .90 .90

1973, Nov. 10 Litho. ***Perf. 13½***

8m+2m, Singers, organ pipes. 3c+1c, Virgin & Child with star. 7c5m+1c5m, Star, candles, buildings, tambourine.

B13 SP3 8m +2m multi .20 .20
B14 SP3 3c +1c multi .30 .30
B15 SP3 7c5m +1c5m multi .80 .80
a. Souvenir sheet of 3, #B13-B15 5.00 *6.00*
Nos. B13-B15 (3) 1.30 1.30
Nos. B7-B15 (9) 3.05 3.05

Star and Holy Family — SP4

Designs: 3c+1c, Star and two shepherds. 5c+1c, Star and three shepherds. 7c5m+1c5m, Star and Three Kings.

1974, Nov. 22 Litho. ***Perf. 14***
B16 SP4 8m +2m multi .20 .20
B17 SP4 3c +1c multi .20 .20
B18 SP4 5c +1c multi .35 .35
B19 SP4 7c5m +1c5m multi .50 .50
Nos. B16-B19 (4) 1.25 1.25

Nativity, by Maestro Alberto — SP5

8m+2m, Shepherds. 7c5m+1c5m, Three Kings.

1975, Nov. 4 ***Perf. 13½***
Size: 24x23mm (#B20, B22); 49x23mm (#B21)
B20 SP5 8m +2m multi .20 .20
B21 SP5 3c +1c multi .50 .40
B22 SP5 7c5m +1c5m multi 2.00 *2.50*
a. Triptych, #B20-B22 3.50 *4.00*
Nos. B20-B22 (3) 2.70 *3.10*

Printed singly and as triptychs. Surtax for child welfare.

SP6

Madonna and Saints, by Domenico di Michelino — SP7

Details of Painting: 5c+1c, Virgin & Child. 7c+1c5m, St. Christopher & Bishop.

1976, Nov. 23 Litho. ***Perf. 13½***
B23 SP6 1c +5m multi .20 .20
B24 SP6 5c +1c multi .40 .30
B25 SP6 7c +1c5m multi .70 .65

Perf. 13½x14
B26 SP7 10c +2c multi 1.50 1.50
Nos. B23-B26 (4) 2.80 2.65

Nativity SP8

Crèche Figurines: 1c+5m, Annunciation to the Shepherds. 11c+1c5m, Shepherds.

Perf. 13½x14

1977, Nov. 16 Wmk. 354
B27 SP8 1c +5m multi .20 .20
B28 SP8 7c +1c multi .45 .45
B29 SP8 11c +1c5m multi .80 .80
a. Triptych, #B27-B29 1.50 1.50
Nos. B27-B29 (3) 1.45 1.45

Nos. B27-B29 printed singly and as triptychs. Surtax was for child welfare.

Christmas Decorations, People and Church — SP9

Designs: 5c+1c, Decorations and angels. 7c+1c5m, Decorations and carolers. 11c+3c, Combined designs of #B30-B32.

1978, Nov. 9 Litho. ***Perf. 14***
Size: 24x30mm
B30 SP9 1c +5m multi .20 .20
B31 SP9 5c +1c multi .35 .35
B32 SP9 7c +1c5m multi .50 .50

Perf. 13½
Size: 58x22½mm

B33 SP9 11c +3c multi .80 .80
Nos. B30-B33 (4) 1.85 1.85

Nativity, by Giuseppe Cali — SP10

Designs (Cali Paintings): 5c+1c, 11c+3c, Flight into Egypt. 7c+1c5m, Nativity.

1979, Nov. 14 Litho. ***Perf. 14x13½***
B34 SP10 1c +5m multi .20 .20
B35 SP10 5c +1c multi .35 .35
B36 SP10 7c +1c5m multi .50 .50
B37 SP10 11c +3c multi .80 .80
Nos. B34-B37 (4) 1.85 1.85

Nativity, by Anton Inglott (1915-1945) — SP11

Details of Painting: 2c+5m, Annunciation. 6c+1c, Angel. 8c+1c5m, Holy Family.

1980, Oct. 7 Litho. ***Perf. 14x13½***
Size: 20x47mm
B38 SP11 2c +5m multi .20 .20
B39 SP11 6c +1c multi .40 .40
B40 SP11 8c +1c5m multi .55 .55

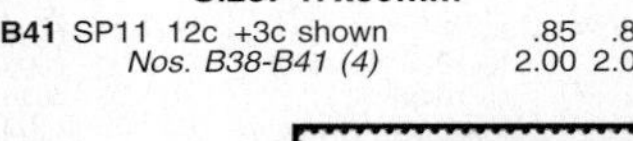

Perf. 14½x14
Size: 47x39mm
B41 SP11 12c +3c shown .85 .85
Nos. B38-B41 (4) 2.00 2.00

SP12

1981, Nov. 18 Wmk. 354 ***Perf. 14***
B42 SP12 2c +1c Children, vert. .20 .20
B43 SP12 8c +2c Procession .55 .55
B44 SP12 20c +3c Service, vert. 1.25 1.25
Nos. B42-B44 (3) 2.00 2.00

SP13

Three Kings Following Star: 2c+1c, Star. 8c+2c, Three Kings. 20c+3c, Entire design.

1982, Oct. 8 Litho. ***Perf. 13½***
B45 SP13 2c +1c multi .20 .20
B46 SP13 8c +2c multi .55 .55

Perf. 14
Size: 45x36mm
B47 SP13 20c +3c multi 1.25 1.25
Nos. B45-B47 (3) 2.00 2.00

SP14

Illuminated Manuscripts, Book of Hours, 15th Cent.: 2c+1c, Annunciation. 8c+2c, Nativity. 20c+3c, Three Kings bearing gifts. Surtax was for child welfare.

1983, Sept. 6 Litho. ***Perf. 14***
B48 SP14 2c +1c multi .25 .25
B49 SP14 8c +2c multi .60 .60
B50 SP14 20c +3c multi 1.40 1.40
Nos. B48-B50 (3) 2.25 2.25

SP15

Paintings by Peter-Paul Caruana, Church of Our Lady of Porto Salvo, Valletta, 1850: 2c+1c, Visitation, vert. 8c+2c, Epiphany. 20c+3c, Jesus Among the Doctors.

1984, Oct. 5 Litho. ***Perf. 14***
B51 SP15 2c +1c multi .30 .30
B52 SP15 8c +2c multi .85 .85
B53 SP15 20c +3c multi 2.00 2.00
Nos. B51-B53 (3) 3.15 3.15

SP16

1985, Oct. 10 Litho. ***Perf. 14***
B54 SP16 2c +1c Adoration of the Magi .35 .35
B55 SP16 8c +2c Nativity .90 .90
B56 SP16 20c +3c Trumpeter Angels 1.90 1.90
Nos. B54-B56 (3) 3.15 3.15

Surtax for child welfare organizations.

SP17

Paintings by Giuseppe D'Arena (1633-1719).

1986, Oct. 10 Wmk. 354 ***Perf. 14½***
B57 SP17 2c +1c The Nativity .55 .55
B58 SP17 8c +2c The Nativity, detail, vert. 1.75 1.75
B59 SP17 20c +3c The Epiphany 4.00 4.00
Nos. B57-B59 (3) 6.30 6.30

Surtax for child welfare organizations.

SP18

Illuminated text from choral books of the Veneranda Assemblea of St. John's Conventual Church, Valletta.

1987, Nov. 6 Litho. ***Perf. 14***
B60 SP18 2c +1c Mary's Visit to Elizabeth .50 .50
B61 SP18 8c +2c Nativity 1.50 1.50
B62 SP18 20c +3c Adoration of the Magi 3.50 3.50
Nos. B60-B62 (3) 5.50 5.50

Surtax for child welfare organizations and the handicapped.

SP19

1988, Nov. 5 Litho. ***Perf. 14½x14***
B63 SP19 3c +1c Shepherd .30 .30
B64 SP19 10c +2c Nativity .75 .75
B65 SP19 25c +3c Magi 1.75 1.75
Nos. B63-B65 (3) 2.80 2.80

Surtax for child welfare organizations and the handicapped.

SP20

Various angels from frescoes by Mattia Preti in the vault of St. John's Co-Cathedral, Valletta, 1666.

1989, Nov. 11 ***Perf. 14***
B66 SP20 3c +1c multi .30 .30
B67 SP20 10c +2c multi 1.10 1.10
B68 SP20 20c +3c multi 2.10 2.10
Nos. B66-B68 (3) 3.50 3.50

Surtax for child welfare organizations and the handicapped.

SP21 SP22

Creche figures.

1990, Nov. 10
Size: #B70, 41x27mm
B69 SP21 3c +1c Carrying water .30 .30
B70 SP21 10c +2c Nativity .85 .85
B71 SP21 25c +3c Shepherd 1.90 1.90
Nos. B69-B71 (3) 3.05 3.05

Surtax for child welfare organizations.

1991, Nov. 6
B72 SP22 3c +1c Wise men .40 .40
B73 SP22 10c +2c Mary, Joseph, Jesus 1.00 1.00
B74 SP22 25c +3c Shepherds 2.50 2.50
Nos. B72-B74 (3) 3.90 3.90

Surtax for child welfare organizations.

SP23

Paintings from dome spandrels of Mosta Parish Church by Giuseppe Cali (1846-1930): 3c+1c, Nativity scene. 10c+2c, Adoration of the Magi. 25c+3c, Christ among the Elders in the Temple.

1992, Oct. 22
B75 SP23 3c +1c multi .40 .40
B76 SP23 10c +2c multi 1.60 1.60
B77 SP23 25c +3c multi 4.00 4.00
Nos. B75-B77 (3) 6.00 6.00

Surtax for child welfare organizations.

SP24

Designs: 3c+1c, Christ Child in manger. 10c+2c, Christmas tree. 25c+3c, Star.

1993, Nov. 20
B78 SP24 3c +1c multi .40 .40
B79 SP24 10c +2c multi .85 .85
B80 SP24 25c +3c multi 1.90 1.90
Nos. B78-B80 (3) 3.15 3.15

Beginning with No. 845, semi-postal stamps are included with the postage portion of the set.

Christmas — SP25

Children's art: 6c+2c, Man with net chasing star. 15c+2c, People, Christmas tree. 16c+2c, People hugging. 19c+3c, Woman with shopping bags.

2001, Nov. 29 Litho. ***Perf. 14***
B81-B84 SP25 Set of 4 4.75 4.75

Stampin' the Future Type of 2000
Souvenir Sheet
Wmk. 354

2006, Dec. 22 Litho. ***Perf. 14***
B85 A261 £1.50 + (16c) Like #1029 10.00 10.00

Surtax was for the Valletta YMCA.

AIR POST STAMPS

No. 140 Overprinted

Perf. 14½x14

1928, Apr. 1 Typo. Wmk. 4
C1 A22 6p red & violet 2.00 1.00

Catalogue values for unused stamps in this section, from this point to the end of the section, are for Never Hinged items.

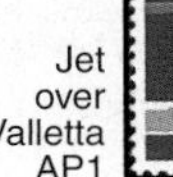

Jet over Valletta AP1

Designs: 3c, 5c, 20c, 35c, Winged emblem. 7c5m, 25c, like 4c.

Wmk. 354

1974, Mar. Litho. *Perf. 13½*

Cross Emblem in Red and Blue

C2	AP1	3c ol brown & gold	.20	.20
C3	AP1	4c dk blue & gold	.20	.20
C4	AP1	5c dk vio bl & gold	.30	.30
C5	AP1	7c5m sl green & gold	.40	.40
C6	AP1	20c vio brn & gold	1.10	1.10
C7	AP1	25c slate & gold	1.40	1.40
C8	AP1	35c brown & gold	2.00	2.00
		Nos. C2-C8 (7)	5.60	5.60

Jet and Megalithic Temple — AP2

Designs: 7c, 20c, Air Malta Boeing 720B approaching Malta. 11c, 75c, Jumbo jet landing at Luqa Airport. 17c, like 5c.

1978, Oct. 3 Litho. *Perf. 13½*

C9	AP2	5c multicolored	.30	.30
C10	AP2	7c multicolored	.40	.40
C11	AP2	11c multicolored	.60	.60
C12	AP2	17c multicolored	.95	.95
C13	AP2	20c multicolored	1.10	1.10
C14	AP2	75c multicolored	4.25	4.25
		Nos. C9-C14 (6)	7.60	7.60

Boeing 737, 1984 AP3

1984, Jan. 26 Wmk. 354 *Perf. 14*

C15	AP3	7c shown	.45	.45
C16	AP3	8c Boeing 720B, 1974	.50	.50
C17	AP3	16c Vickers Vanguard, 1964	.95	.95
C18	AP3	23c Vickers Viscount, 1958	1.40	1.40
C19	AP3	27c Douglas DC3 Dakota, 1948	1.60	1.60
C20	AP3	38c AW Atlanta, 1936	2.40	2.40
C21	AP3	75c Dornier Wal, 1929	4.50	4.50
		Nos. C15-C21 (7)	11.80	11.80

POSTAGE DUE STAMPS

D1

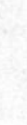

Maltese Cross — D2

1925 Typeset Unwmk. *Imperf.*

J1	D1	½p black, *white*	1.40	8.00
J2	D1	1p black, *white*	3.75	3.50
J3	D1	1½p black, *white*	3.50	4.25
J4	D1	2p black, *white*	8.50	*15.00*
J5	D1	2½p black, *white*	3.25	3.25
a.		"2" of "½" omitted	1,200.	1,400.
J6	D1	3p black, *gray*	10.50	*17.00*
J7	D1	4p black, *orange*	5.75	*11.00*
J8	D1	6p black, *orange*	5.75	*20.00*
J9	D1	1sh black, *orange*	8.50	*25.00*
J10	D1	1sh6p black, *orange*	16.00	*62.50*
		Nos. J1-J10 (10)	66.90	*169.50*
		Set, never hinged	130.00	

These stamps were typeset in groups of 42. In each sheet there were four impressions of a group, two of them being inverted and making tete beche pairs.

Forged examples of No. J5a are known.

Wmk. 4 Sideways

1925 Typo. *Perf. 12*

J11	D2	½p blue green	1.40	.70
J12	D2	1p violet	1.40	.50
J13	D2	1½p yellow brown	1.75	1.00
J14	D2	2p gray	12.50	1.25
J15	D2	2½p orange	2.25	1.40
J16	D2	3p dark blue	4.00	1.40
J17	D2	4p olive green	14.00	*18.00*
J18	D2	6p claret	3.50	4.75
J19	D2	1sh gray black	7.50	*14.00*
J20	D2	1sh6p deep rose	9.75	*32.50*
		Nos. J11-J20 (10)	58.05	*75.50*
		Set, never hinged	85.00	

In 1953-57 six values (½p-2p, 3p, 4p) were reissued on chalky paper in slightly different colors.

Catalogue values for unused stamps in this section, from this point to the end of the section, are for Never Hinged items.

1966 Wmk. 314 *Perf. 12*

J21	D2	2p sepia	22.50	*26.00*

Wmk. 354 Sideways

1968 *Perf. 12½*

J22	D2	½p green	.20	.20
J23	D2	1p rose violet	.20	.20
J24	D2	1½p bister brn	.30	.30
J25	D2	2p brown black	.45	.45
J26	D2	2½p orange	.50	.50
J27	D2	3p Prus blue	.60	.60
J28	D2	4p olive	.90	.90
J29	D2	6p purple	1.50	1.50
J30	D2	1sh black	1.60	1.60
J31	D2	1sh6p rose car	3.75	3.75
		Nos. J22-J31 (10)	10.00	10.00

1967, Nov. 9 *Perf. 12*

J22a	D2	½p	3.25	3.25
J23a	D2	1p	4.50	4.50
J25a	D2	2p	6.75	6.75
J28a	D2	4p	82.50	*110.00*
		Nos. J22a-J28a (4)	97.00	*124.50*

Numeral — D3

Scroll — D4

Perf. 13x13½

1973, Apr. 28 Litho. Wmk. 354

J32	D3	2m brown	.20	.20
J33	D3	3m brown orange	.20	.20
J34	D3	5m carmine	.20	.20
J35	D3	1c deep green	.20	.20
J36	D3	2c black	.20	.20
J37	D3	3c olive	.20	.20
J38	D3	5c violet blue	.30	.30
J39	D3	10c deep magenta	.60	.60
		Nos. J32-J39 (8)	2.10	2.10

Wmk. 354

1993, Jan. 4 Litho. *Perf. 14*

J40	D4	1c brt pink & lt pink	.20	.20
J41	D4	2c brt blue & lt blue	.20	.20
J42	D4	5c brt grn & lt grn	.30	.30
J43	D4	10c org yel & brt yel	.55	.55
		Nos. J40-J43 (4)	1.25	1.25

WAR TAX STAMPS

Nos. 50, 25 Overprinted

1918 Wmk. 3 *Perf. 14*

MR1	A13	½p green	1.75	.30

Wmk. 2

MR2	A12	3p red violet & gray	3.00	*11.00*

MANCHUKUO

'man-'chü-'kwō

LOCATION — Covering Manchuria, or China's three northeastern provinces —Fengtien, Kirin and Heilungkiang—plus Jehol province.

GOVT. — Independent state under Japanese influence

AREA — 503,013 sq. mi. (estimated)

POP. — 43,233,954 (est. 1940)

CAPITAL — Hsinking (Changchun)

Manchukuo was formed in 1932 with the assistance of Japan. In 1934 Henry Pu-yi, Chief Executive, was enthroned as Emperor Kang Teh. In 1945, when Japan surrendered to the Allies, the terms included the return of Manchukuo to China. The puppet state was dissolved.

100 Fen = 1 Yuan

Watermarks

Wmk. 141 — Horizontal Zigzag Lines

Wmk. 239 — Curved Wavy Lines

Wmk. 242 — Characters

Pagoda at Liaoyang A1

Chief Executive Henry Pu-yi A2

Five characters in top label.

Inscription reads "Manchu State Postal Administration."

Lithographed

Perf. 13x13½

1932, July 26 Unwmk.

White Paper

1	A1	½f gray brown	1.75	.70
2	A1	1f dull red	2.00	.35
3	A1	1½f lilac	6.00	5.00
4	A1	2f slate	6.00	1.00
5	A1	3f dull brown	7.50	7.50
6	A1	4f olive green	2.75	.50
7	A1	5f green	3.50	.55
8	A1	6f rose	9.50	3.50
9	A1	7f gray	4.75	1.00
10	A1	8f ocher	17.50	12.50
11	A1	10f orange	5.50	.50
12	A2	13f dull brown	13.50	7.00
13	A2	15f rose	20.00	3.00
14	A2	16f turquoise grn	27.50	9.00
15	A2	20f gray brown	8.75	1.75
16	A2	30f orange	10.00	2.25
17	A2	50f olive green	27.50	3.25
18	A2	1y violet	37.50	9.00
		Nos. 1-18 (18)	211.50	68.35
		Set, never hinged	300.00	

A local provisional overprint of a horizontal line of four characters in red or black, reading "Chinese Postal Administration," was applied to Nos. 1-18 by followers of Gen. Su Ping-wen, who rebelled against the Manchukuo government in September, 1932. Many counterfeits exist.

See #23-31. For surcharges see #36, 59-61.

See note on local handstamps at end of the Manchukuo listings.

Flags, Map and Wreath — A3

Old State Council Building — A4

1933, Mar. 1 *Perf. 12½*

19	A3	1f orange	4.00	4.00
20	A4	2f dull green	12.00	12.00
21	A3	4f light red	4.50	4.50
22	A4	10f deep blue	30.00	30.00
		Nos. 19-22 (4)	50.50	50.50
		Set, never hinged	90.00	

1st anniv. of the establishing of the State. Nos. 19-22 were printed in sheets of 100 with a special printing in sheets of 20.

Type of 1932

Perf. 13x13½

1934, Feb. Engr. Wmk. 239

Granite Paper

23	A1	½f dark brown	4.00	1.65
24	A1	1f red brown	4.00	.90
25	A1	1½f dark violet	5.50	3.00
26	A1	2f slate	7.50	1.50
27	A1	3f brown	4.00	.60
28	A1	4f olive brown	29.00	5.00
29	A1	10f deep orange	14.50	1.00
30	A2	15f rose	475.00	200.00
31	A2	1y violet	50.00	11.00
		Nos. 23-31 (9)	593.50	224.65

For surcharge see No. 60.

Emperor's Palace — A5

Phoenix — A6

1934, Mar. 1 *Perf. 12½*

32	A5	1½f orange brown	5.50	4.00
33	A6	3f carmine	4.50	3.50
34	A5	6f green	13.00	10.00
35	A6	10f dark blue	20.00	17.50
		Nos. 32-35 (4)	43.00	35.00
		Set, never hinged	75.00	

Enthronement of Emperor Kang Teh. Nos. 32-35 were printed in sheets of 100, with a special printing in sheets of 20.

No. 6 Surcharged in Black

Perf. 13x13½

1934 Unwmk. White Paper

36	A1	1f on 4f olive grn	5.50	2.50
		Never hinged	7.00	
a.		Brown surcharge	37.50	37.50
b.		Upper left character of surcharge omitted		
c.		Inverted surcharge	175.00	175.00

Pagoda at Liaoyang A7

Emperor Kang Teh A8

Six characters in top label instead of five as in 1932-34 issues.

Inscription reads "Manchu Empire Postal Administration."

Perf. 13x13½

1934-36 Wmk. 239 Engr.

Granite Paper

37 A7 ½f brown .50 .35
38 A7 1f red brown 1.00 .30
39 A7 1½f dk violet 1.00 .50
a. Booklet pane of 6 90.00
41 A7 3f brown ('35) .75 .35
a. Booklet pane of 6 80.00
42 A7 5f dk blue ('35) 10.00 2.00
43 A7 5f gray ('36) 5.00 2.00
44 A7 6f rose ('35) 3.00 .60
45 A7 7f dk gray ('36) 2.50 2.00
47 A7 9f red orange ('35) 2.50 .75
50 A8 15f ver ('35) 2.50 .85
51 A8 18f Prus grn ('35) 25.00 5.00
52 A8 20f dk brown ('35) 4.00 .90
53 A8 30f orange brn ('35) 4.50 .90
54 A8 50f ol grn ('35) 6.00 2.00
55 A8 1y dk violet ('35) 20.00 6.00
a. 1y violet 20.00 8.00
Nos. 37-55 (15) 88.25 24.50
Set, never hinged 120.00

4f and 8f, type A7, were prepared but not issued. Values $45 and $15, respectively.

1935 Wmk. 242 *Perf. 13x13½*

57 A7 10f deep blue 8.50 1.25
58 A8 13f light brown 11.50 5.75
Set, never hinged 27.50

Nos. 6 and 28 Surcharged in Black

1935 White Paper Unwmk.

59 A1 3f on 4f ol grn 65.00 60.00
Never hinged 90.00

1935 Granite Paper Wmk. 239

60 A1 3f on 4f olive brn 8.00 4.00
Never hinged 15.00

Similar Surcharge on No. 14

1935 White Paper Unwmk.

61 A2 3f on 16f turq grn 14.00 9.00
Never hinged 18.00
Nos. 59-61 (3) 87.00 73.00

Orchid Crest of Manchukuo A9

Sacred White Mountains and Black Waters A10

1935, Jan. 1 Litho. Wmk. 141

Granite Paper

62 A9 2f green 4.00 1.75
63 A10 4f dull ol grn 2.00 1.50
64 A9 8f ocher 3.50 4.00
65 A10 12f brown red 10.00 *17.50*
Nos. 62-65 (4) 19.50 24.75
Set, never hinged 27.50

Nos. 62-65 exist imperforate.

1935 Wmk. 242

66 A9 2f yellow green 3.50 .75
68 A9 8f ocher 5.00 3.00
70 A10 12f brown red 11.00 8.00
Nos. 66-70 (3) 19.50 11.75
Set, never hinged 29.00

Nos. 62-70 issued primarily to pay postage to China, but valid for any postal use.

See Nos. 75-78, 113, 115, 158. For surcharges see Nos. 101, 103-104, 106-109, People's Republic of China No. 2L19.

Mt. Fuji — A11

Phoenix — A12

Perf. 11, 12½ and Compound

1935, Apr. 1 Engr. Wmk. 242

71 A11 1½f dull green 2.50 2.00
72 A12 3f orange 3.50 3.25
a. 3f red orange 6.00 5.00
73 A11 6f dk carmine 5.50 4.75
a. Horiz. pair, imperf. btwn. 250.00
b. Perf. 11x12½ 45.00 37.50
74 A12 10f dark blue 7.50 6.00
a. Perf. 12½x11 50.00 37.50
b. Perf. 12½ 22.50 25.00
Nos. 71-74 (4) 19.00 16.00
Set, never hinged 27.50

Visit of the Emperor of Manchukuo to Tokyo.

Orchid Crest — A13

Types of A9 & A10

Redrawn and Engraved

1936 Wmk. 242 *Perf. 13x13½*

75 A13 2f lt green 1.00 .30
76 A10 4f olive green 3.25 .75
77 A13 8f ocher 3.00 1.25
78 A10 12f orange brn 42.50 27.50
Nos. 75-78 (4) 49.75 29.80
Set, never hinged 67.50

Unbroken lines of shading in the background of Nos. 76 and 78. Shading has been removed from right and left of the mountains. Nearly all lines have been removed from the lake. There are numerous other alterations in the design.

Issued primarily to pay postage to China, but valid for any postal use.

See #112. For surcharges see #102-106.

Wild Goose over Sea of Japan — A14

Communications Building at Hsinking — A15

Perf. 12x12½, 12½x12

1936, Jan. 26 Wmk. 242

79 A14 1½f black brown 3.00 2.50
80 A15 3f rose lilac 3.00 2.00
81 A14 6f carmine rose 7.00 7.00
82 A15 10f blue 10.00 7.00
Nos. 79-82 (4) 23.00 18.50
Set, never hinged 42.50

Postal convention with Japan.

New State Council Building A16

Carting Soybeans A17

North Mausoleum at Mukden A18

Summer Palace at Chengteh A19

1936-37 Wmk. 242 *Perf. 13x13½*

83 A16 ½f brown .40 .20
84 A16 1f red brown .40 .20
85 A16 1½f violet 4.25 2.75
a. Booklet pane of 6 85.00
86 A17 2f lt green ('37) .40 .20
a. Booklet pane of 6 20.00
87 A16 3f chocolate .40 .20
a. Booklet pane of 6 200.00
88 A18 4f lt ol grn ('37) .45 .20
a. Booklet pane of 6 25.00
89 A16 5f gray black 19.00 7.50
90 A17 6f carmine .45 .20
91 A18 7f brown blk .75 .30
92 A18 9f red orange .80 .35
93 A19 10f blue .70 .20
94 A18 12f dp orange ('37) .55 .20
95 A18 13f brown 30.00 35.00
96 A18 15f carmine 3.00 .55
97 A17 20f dk brown 1.10 .35
98 A19 30f chestnut brn 1.10 .35
99 A17 50f olive green 1.60 .50
100 A19 1y violet 4.25 .60
Nos. 83-100 (18) 69.60 49.85
Set, never hinged 110.00

Nos. 83, 84, 86, 88 and 93 are known imperforate but were not regularly issued.

See Nos. 159-163. For overprints see Nos. 140-141, 148-151. For surcharges see People's Republic of China Nos. 2L1-2L2, 2L11-2L18, 2L20-2L37, 2L40-2L52.

a

b

c

d

1937

Surcharged on No. 66

101 A9 (a) 2½f on 2f 2.50 2.50

Surcharged on Nos. 75, 76 and 78

102 A13 (a) 2½f on 2f 2.50 2.50
103 A10 (b) 5f on 4f 3.75 3.75
104 A10 (c) 13f on 12f 10.50 10.00

Surcharged in Black on Nos. 75, 76 and 70

Space between bottom characters of surcharge 4½mm

105 A13 (d) 2½f on 2f 2.00 1.90
a. Inverted surcharge 200.00 *225.00*
b. Vert. pair, one without surch. 95.00
106 A10 (b) 5f on 4f 3.50 2.75
107 A10 (c) 13f on 12f 11.00 9.50

Surcharged on No. 70

Space between characters 6½mm

108 A10 (c) 13f on 12f 175.00 175.00

Same Surcharge on No. 63

Space between characters 4½mm

Wmk. 141

109 A10 (b) 5f on 4f 6.50 5.25
Nos. 101-109 (9) 217.25 213.15
Set, never hinged 310.00

Nos. 101-109 were issued primarily to pay postage to China, but were valid for any postal use.

Rising Sun over Manchurian Plain — A20

Composite Picture of Manchurian City — A21

Perf. 12½

1937, Mar. 1 Litho. Unwmk.

110 A20 1½f carmine rose 3.00 3.00
111 A21 3f blue green 2.50 2.25
Set, never hinged 7.50

5th anniv. of the founding of the State of Manchukuo.

Types of 1936

Perf. 13x13½

1937 Wmk. 242 Engr.

112 A13 2½f dk violet .75 .40
113 A10 5f black .25 .25
115 A10 13f dk red brown .80 .60
Nos. 112-115 (3) 1.80 1.25
Set, never hinged 2.50

Issued primarily to pay postage to China, but were valid for any postal use.

Pouter Pigeon — A22

National Flag and Buildings — A23

Perf. 12x12½

1937, Sept. 16 **Unwmk.**

116	A22	2f dark violet	2.50	1.60
117	A23	4f rose carmine	2.50	1.25
118	A22	10f dark green	5.75	3.25
119	A23	20f dark blue	7.50	5.25
		Nos. 116-119 (4)	18.25	11.35
		Set, never hinged	24.00	

Completion of the national capital, Hsinking, under the first Five-Year Construction Plan.

Map — A24

Dept. of Justice Building — A27

Japanese Residents' Association Building — A25

Postal Administration Building — A26

Perf. 12x12½, 13

1937, Dec. 1 **Litho.** **Unwmk.**

121	A24	2f dark carmine	1.25	.90
122	A25	4f green	2.25	1.10
123	A25	8f orange	4.75	3.25
124	A26	10f blue	5.25	3.75
125	A27	12f lt violet	6.25	5.00
126	A26	20f lilac brown	8.25	6.00
		Nos. 121-126 (6)	28.00	20.00
		Set, never hinged	40.00	

Issued in commemoration of the abolition of extraterritorial rights within Manchukuo.

New Year Greetings — A28

Map and Cross — A29

1937, Dec. 15 **Engr.** ***Perf. 12x12½***

127	A28	2f dk blue & red	1.90	.55
		Never hinged	2.40	
a.		Double impression of border	12.50	

Issued to pay postage on New Year's greeting cards.

Wmk. 242

1938, Oct. 15 **Litho.** ***Perf. 13***

128	A29	2f lake & scarlet	1.25	1.10
129	A29	4f slate grn & scar	1.25	1.10
		Set, never hinged	3.75	

Founding of the Red Cross Soc. in Manchukuo.

Network of State Railroads in Manchukuo A30

Express Train "Asia" A31

1939, Oct. 21

130	A30	2f dk org, blk & dp bl	1.75	1.40
131	A31	4f dp blue & indigo	1.75	1.40
		Set, never hinged	4.50	

Attainment of 10,000 kilometers in the railway mileage in Manchuria.

Stork Flying above Mast of Imperial Flagship — A32

1940 **Photo.** **Unwmk.**

132	A32	2f brt red violet	.70	.70
133	A32	4f brt green	.70	.70
		Set, never hinged	1.75	

Second visit of Emperor Kang Teh to Emperor Hirohito of Japan.

Census Taker and Map of Manchukuo A33

Census Form A34

1940, Sept. 10 **Litho.** **Wmk. 242**

134	A33	2f vio brn & org	.55	.55
135	A34	4f black & green	.60	.60
a.		Double impression of green	50.00	
		Set, never hinged	1.50	

National census starting Oct. 1.

Message of Congratulation from Premier Chang Ching-hui — A35

Dragon Dance A36

1940, Sept. 18 **Engr.**

136	A35	2f carmine	.55	.55
137	A36	4f indigo	.60	.60
a.		Imperf., pair	100.00	
		Set, never hinged	1.75	

2600th anniversary of the birth of the Japanese Empire.

Soldier — A37

1941, May 25 **Photo.** **Unwmk.**

138	A37	2f deep carmine	.60	.60
139	A37	4f bright ultra	.60	.60
		Set, never hinged	2.00	

Conscription Law, effective June 1, 1941.

Nos. 86 and 88 Overprinted in Red or Blue

Perf. 13x13½

1942, Feb. 16 **Wmk. 242**

140	A17	2f lt green (R)	.60	.60
141	A18	4f lt olive grn (Bl)	.60	.60
		Set, never hinged	2.00	

"Return of Singapore to East Asia, 9th year of Kang Teh."

Kengoku Shrine A38

Map of Manchukuo A39

Flag of Manchukuo A40

Perf. 12x12½, 12½x12

1942, Mar. 1 **Engr.**

142	A38	2f carmine	.40	.40
143	A38	4f lilac	.40	.40
144	A39	10f red, *yel*	1.10	1.50
145	A40	20f indigo, *yel*	2.25	2.00
		Nos. 142-145 (4)	4.15	4.30
		Set, never hinged	5.00	

"10th anniv. of Manchukuo, Mar. 1, 1942."

Allegory of National Harmony — A41

Women of Five Races, Dancing — A42

1942, Sept. 15

146	A41	3f orange	.50	.40
147	A42	6f light green	.75	*1.00*
		Set, never hinged	1.75	

"10th anniv. of the founding of Manchukuo, Sept. 15, 1942."

Nos. 87 and 90 Overprinted in Green or Blue

1942, Dec. 8 ***Perf. 13x13½***

148	A16	3f chocolate (G)	.40	.40
149	A17	6f carmine (Bl)	.40	.40
		Set, never hinged	1.10	

1st anniv. of the "Greater East Asia War."

The overprint reads "Asiatic Prosperity Began This Day December 8, 1941."

Nos. 87 and 90 Overprinted in Red or Blue

1943, May 1

150	A16	3f chocolate (R)	.40	.40
151	A17	6f carmine (Bl)	.40	.40
		Set, never hinged	1.10	

Proclamation of the labor service law.

Red Cross Nurse Carrying Stretcher A43

Smelting Furnace A44

1943, Oct. 1 **Photo.**

152	A43	6f green	.60	.60
		Never hinged	.90	

5th anniv. of the founding of the Red Cross Society of Manchukuo, Oct. 1, 1938.

1943, Dec. 8 **Unwmk.** ***Perf. 13***

153	A44	6f red brown	.40	.40
		Never hinged	.55	

2nd anniv. of the "Greater East Asia War."

Chinese Characters A45

Japanese Characters A46

Perf. 13x13½

1944 **Wmk. 242** **Litho.**

154	A45	10f rose	.75	*1.25*
a.		Imperf., vert. pair #154, 155	15.00	
b.		Vert. pair #154, 155	1.50	*2.50*
155	A46	10f rose	.75	*1.25*
156	A45	40f gray green	3.25	3.25
a.		Imperf., vert. pair #156, 157	50.00	
b.		40f with 10f vignette, perf.	140.00	140.00
c.		40f with 10f vignette, imperf.	200.00	
d.		Vert. pair #156, 157	6.50	6.50
157	A46	40f gray green	3.25	3.25
		Nos. 154-157 (4)	8.00	*9.00*
		Set, never hinged	10.00	

"Japan's Progress Is Manchukuo's Progress." Issued as propaganda for the close relationship of Japan and Manchukuo.

Frames of the 10f vignettes have rounded corners, those of the 40f vignettes have indented corners.

Types of 1935 and 1936-37

1944-45 **Litho.**

158	A10	5f gray black	1.00	*1.75*
a.		Imperf., pair	10.00	
159	A17	6f crimson rose	2.25	*3.50*
160	A19	10f light blue	5.00	*6.50*
161	A17	20f brown	1.75	*2.50*
162	A19	30f buff ('45)	1.90	*2.50*
163	A19	1y dull lilac	2.50	*2.75*
		Nos. 158-163 (6)	14.40	*19.50*
		Set, never hinged	20.00	

For surcharges see People's Republic of China Nos. 2L1, 2L14, 2L19, 2L24, 2L27, 2L30-2L31, 2L35, 2L37, 2L49, 2L52.

"One Heart, One Soul" — A47

1945, May 2

164	A47	10f red	.60	*1.50*
		Never hinged	.90	
a.		Imperf., pair	4.00	*5.00*

Emperor's edict of May 2, 1935, 10th anniv.

AIR POST STAMPS

Sheep Grazing AP1

Railroad Bridge AP2

Wmk. Characters (242)

1936-37 Engr. *Perf. 13x13½*

Granite Paper

C1	AP1 18f green		15.00	12.50
C2	AP1 19f blue green ('37)		5.00	3.50
C3	AP2 38f blue		16.00	15.00
C4	AP2 39f deep blue ('37)		1.60	1.75
	Nos. C1-C4 (4)		37.60	32.75
	Set, never hinged		45.00	

With the end of World War II and the collapse of Manchukuo, the Northeastern Provinces reverted to China. In many Manchurian towns and cities, the Manchukuo stamps were locally handstamped in ideograms: "Republic of China," "China Postal Service" or "Temporary Use for China." A typical example is shown above. Many of these local issues also were surcharged.

MARIANA ISLANDS

ˌmar-ē-ˈa-nə ˈī-ləndz

LOCATION — A group of 14 islands in the West Pacific Ocean, about 1500 miles east of the Philippines.
GOVT. — Possession of Spain, then of Germany
AREA — 246 sq. mi.
POP. — 44,025 (1935)
CAPITAL — Saipan

Until 1899 this group belonged to Spain but in that year all except Guam were ceded to Germany.

100 Centavos = 1 Peso
100 Pfennig = 1 Mark (1899)

Values for unused stamps are for examples with original gum as defined in the catalogue introduction. Very fine examples of Nos. 1-6 will have perforations touching or just cutting into the design. Stamps with perfs clear on all sides and well centered are rare and sell for substantially more.

Issued under Spanish Dominion

King Alfonso XIII — A1

Stamps of the Philippines Handstamped Vertically in Blackish Violet Reading Up or Down

1899, Sept. Unwmk. *Perf. 14*

1	A1	2c dark blue green	875.	325.
2	A1	3c dark brown	675.	225.
3	A1	5c car rose	1,000.	350.
4	A1	6c dark blue	*6,500.*	5,000.
5	A1	8c gray brown	500.	200.
6	A1	15c slate green	2,500.	1,300.

Overprint forgeries of Nos. 1-6 exist.
No. 4 was issued in a quantity of 50 stamps.

Issued under German Dominion

Stamps of Germany, 1889-90, Overprinted in Black at 56 degree Angle

1900, May Unwmk. *Perf. 13½x14½*

11	A9	3pf dark brown	12.00	*30.00*
12	A9	5pf green	16.00	*32.50*
13	A10	10pf carmine	19.00	*45.00*
14	A10	20pf ultra	25.00	*125.00*
15	A10	25pf orange	62.50	*160.00*
b.		Inverted overprint	*2,400.*	
16	A10	50pf red brn	65.00	*210.00*
		Nos. 11-16 (6)	199.50	*602.50*

Forged cancellations exist on Nos. 11-16, 17-29.

Stamps of Germany, 1889-90, Overprinted in Black at 48 degree Angle

1899, Nov. 18

11a	A9	3pf light brown	*2,000.*	*2,000.*
12a	A9	5pf green	*2,500.*	*1,700.*
13a	A10	10pf carmine	190.00	*200.00*
14a	A10	20pf ultra	190.00	*200.00*
15a	A10	25pf orange	*2,750.*	*2,750.*
16a	A10	50pf red brown	*2,750.*	*2,750.*

Kaiser's Yacht "Hohenzollern"
A4 A5

1901, Jan. Typo. *Perf. 14*

17	A4	3pf brown	1.10	*1.75*
18	A4	5pf green	1.10	*1.90*
19	A4	10pf carmine	1.10	*4.25*
20	A4	20pf ultra	1.25	*7.25*
21	A4	25pf org & blk, *yel*	1.75	*12.50*
22	A4	30pf org & blk, *sal*	1.75	*13.50*
23	A4	40pf lake & blk	1.75	*13.50*
24	A4	50pf pur & blk, *sal*	2.00	*15.00*
25	A4	80pf lake & blk, *rose*	2.50	*25.00*

Engr.

Perf. 14½x14

26	A5	1m carmine	4.00	*72.50*
27	A5	2m blue	5.50	*92.50*
28	A5	3m blk vio	8.00	*140.00*
29	A5	5m slate & car	140.00	*500.00*
		Nos. 17-29 (13)	171.80	*899.65*

Wmk. Lozenges (125)

1916-19 Typo. *Perf. 14*

30	A4	3pf brown ('19)	1.00

Engr.

Perf. 14½x14

31	A5	5m slate & carmine, 25x17 holes	30.00

Nos. 30 and 31 were never placed in use.

MARIENWERDER

mä-ˈrē-ən-ˌveə̧rd-ər

LOCATION — Northeastern Germany, bordering on Poland
GOVT. — A district of West Prussia

By the Versailles Treaty the greater portion of West Prussia was ceded to Poland but the district of Marienwerder was allowed a plebiscite which was held in 1920 and resulted in favor of Germany.

100 Pfennig = 1 Mark

Plebiscite Issues

Symbolical of Allied Supervision of the Plebiscite — A1

1920 Unwmk. Litho. *Perf. 11½*

No.	Type	Value	Unused	Used
1	A1	5pf green	.75	*1.50*
2	A1	10pf rose red	.75	*1.50*
3	A1	15pf gray	.75	*1.75*
4	A1	20pf brn org	.75	*1.50*
5	A1	25pf deep blue	.75	*1.50*
6	A1	30pf orange	.95	*1.50*
7	A1	40pf brown	.75	*1.50*
8	A1	50pf violet	.75	*1.50*
9	A1	60pf red brown	4.25	*2.75*
10	A1	75pf chocolate	.95	*1.50*
11	A1	1m brn & grn	.75	*1.50*
12	A1	2m dk vio	2.10	3.00
13	A1	3m red	5.00	5.00
14	A1	5m blue & rose	24.00	22.00
		Nos. 1-14 (14)	43.25	48.00
		Set, never hinged	120.00	

These stamps occasionally show parts of two papermakers" watermarks, consisting of the letters "O. B. M." with two stars before and after, or "P. & C. M."

Nos. 1-14 exist imperf.; value for set, $700. Nearly all exist part perf.

Stamps of Germany, 1905-19, Overprinted

1920 Wmk. 125 *Perf. 14, 14½*

No.	Type	Value	Unused	Used
24	A16	5pf green	15.00	*30.00*
a.		Inverted overprint	125.00	
		Never hinged	210.00	
26	A16	20pf bl vio	6.00	*25.00*
a.		Inverted overprint	62.50	
		Never hinged	125.00	
b.		Double overprint	85.00	
		Never hinged	150.00	
28	A16	50pf vio & blk, *buff*	375.00	*850.00*
29	A16	75pf grn & blk	4.25	*7.50*
a.		Inverted overprint	62.50	
		Never hinged	125.00	
30	A16	80pf lake & blk, *rose*	75.00	*120.00*
31	A17	1m car rose	85.00	*160.00*
a.		Inverted overprint	425.00	
		Never hinged	850.00	
		Nos. 24-31 (6)	560.25	*1,192.*
		Set, never hinged	1,200.	

Trial impressions were made in red, green and lilac, and with 2½mm instead of 3mm space between the lines of the overprint. These were printed on the 75pf and 80pf. The 1 mark was overprinted with the same words in 3 lines of large sans-serif capitals. All these are essays. Some were passed through the post, apparently with speculative intent.

Stamps of Germany, 1905-18, Surcharged

No.	Type	Value	Unused	Used
32	A22	1m on 2pf gray	22.50	*47.50*
33	A22	2m on 2½pf gray	9.00	*17.00*
a.		Inverted surcharge	55.00	*100.00*
		Never hinged	100.00	
34	A16	3m on 3pf brown	12.00	*17.00*
a.		Double surcharge	55.00	*100.00*
		Never hinged	100.00	
b.		Inverted surcharge	55.00	*100.00*
		Never hinged	100.00	
35	A22	5m on 7½pf org	9.00	*21.00*
a.		Inverted surcharge	55.00	*100.00*
		Never hinged	100.00	
b.		Double surcharge	55.00	*100.00*
		Never hinged	100.00	
		Nos. 32-35 (4)	52.50	*102.50*
		Set, never hinged	165.00	

There are two types of the letters "M," "C," "i" and "e" and of the numerals "2" and "5" in these surcharges.

Counterfeits exist of Nos. 24-35.

Stamps of Germany, 1920, Overprinted

1920, July *Perf. 15x14½*

No.	Type	Value	Unused	Used
36	A17	1m red	2.50	*5.50*
37	A17	1.25m green	3.25	*5.50*
38	A17	1.50m yellow brown	4.25	*8.00*
39	A21	2.50m lilac rose	2.50	*7.25*
		Nos. 36-39 (4)	12.50	*26.25*
		Set, never hinged	30.00	

A2

1920 Unwmk. *Perf. 11½*

No.	Type	Value	Unused	Used
40	A2	5pf green	3.25	2.00
41	A2	10pf rose red	3.25	2.00
42	A2	15pf gray	11.00	12.00
43	A2	20pf brn org	2.00	*4.50*
44	A2	25pf dp bl	12.50	*17.00*
45	A2	30pf orange	1.60	1.20
46	A2	40pf brown	.80	*1.60*
47	A2	50pf violet	1.60	2.00
48	A2	60pf red brn	6.00	4.75
49	A2	75pf chocolate	6.00	5.00
50	A2	1m brn & grn	1.60	1.20
51	A2	2m dk vio	1.60	1.40
52	A2	3m light red	2.00	2.00
53	A2	5m blue & rose	3.25	2.40
		Nos. 40-53 (14)	56.45	59.05
		Set, never hinged	120.00	

MARSHALL ISLANDS

ˈmär-shəl ˈī-ləndz

LOCATION — Two chains of islands in the West Pacific Ocean, about 2,500 miles southeast of Tokyo
GOVT. — Republic
AREA — 70 sq. mi.
POP. — 65,507 (1999 est.)
CAPITAL — Majuro Atoll

The Marshall Islands were German possession from 1885 to 1914. Seized by Japan in 1914, the islands were taken by the US in WW II and became part of the US Trust Territory of the Pacific in 1947. By agreement with the USPS, the islands began issuing their own stamps in 1984, with the USPS continuing to carry the mail to and from the islands.

On Oct. 21, 1986 Marshall Islands became a Federation as a Sovereign State in Compact of Free Association with the US.

100 Pfennig = 1 Mark
100 Cents = 1 Dollar

Catalogue values for unused stamps in this country are for Never Hinged items, beginning with Scott 31 in the regular postage section, and Scott C1 in the airpost section.

Watermark

Wmk. 125 — Lozenges

Issued under German Dominion

A1

A2

Stamps of Germany Overprinted "Marschall-Inseln" in Black

1897 Unwmk. *Perf. 13½x14½*

No.	Type	Value	Unused	Used
1	A1	3pf dark brown	140.00	*725.00*
a.		3pf light yellowish brn	*4,250.*	*2,200.*
2	A1	5pf green	120.00	*550.00*
3	A1	10pf carmine	50.00	*150.00*
4	A2	20pf ultra	50.00	*150.00*
5	A2	25pf orange	140.00	*925.00*
6	A2	50pf red brown	140.00	*925.00*
		Nos. 1-6 (6)	640.00	3,425.

Nos. 5 and 6 were not placed in use, but canceled stamps exist.

A small quantity of the 3pf, 5pf, 10pf and 20pf were issued at Jaluit. These have yellowish, dull gum. Later overprintings of Nos. 1-6 were sold only at Berlin, and have white, smooth, shiny gum. No. 1a belongs to the Jaluit issue. For detailed listings, see the *Scott Specialized Catalogue of Stamps and Covers.*

Forged cancellations are found on almost all Marshall Islands stamps.

Overprinted "Marshall-Inseln"

1899-1900

No.	Type	Value	Unused	Used
7	A1	3pf dk brn ('00)	4.50	*5.50*
a.		3pf light brown	250.00	*775.00*
8	A1	5pf green	9.25	*12.50*
9	A2	10pf car ('00)	12.00	*16.00*
a.		Half used as 5pf on post-card		*8,000.*
10	A2	20pf ultra ('00)	16.00	*25.00*
11	A2	25pf orange	19.00	*42.50*
12	A2	50pf red brown	30.00	*47.50*
a.		Half used as 25pf on cover		*35,000.*
		Nos. 7-12 (6)	90.75	*149.00*

Values for Nos. 9a and 12a are for properly used items, addressed and sent to Germany.

Kaiser's Yacht "Hohenzollern"
A3 A4

1901 Unwmk. Typo. *Perf. 14*

No.	Type	Value	Unused	Used
13	A3	3pf brown	.65	1.75
14	A3	5pf green	.65	1.75
15	A3	10pf carmine	.65	*5.00*
16	A3	20pf ultra	.95	*9.25*
17	A3	25pf org & blk, *yel*	1.00	*16.00*
18	A3	30pf org & blk, *sal*	1.00	*16.00*
19	A3	40pf lake & blk	1.00	*16.00*
20	A3	50pf pur & blk, *sal*	1.40	*25.00*
21	A3	80pf lake & blk, *rose*	2.50	*35.00*

Engr.

Perf. 14½x14

No.	Type	Value	Unused	Used
22	A4	1m carmine	3.75	*85.00*
23	A4	2m blue	5.50	*120.00*
24	A4	3m blk vio	8.50	*200.00*
25	A4	5m slate & car	135.00	*500.00*
		Nos. 13-25 (13)	162.55	1,030.

Wmk. Lozenges (125)

1916 Typo. *Perf. 14*

No.	Type	Value	Unused	Used
26	A3	3pf brown	.85	

Engr.

Perf. 14½x14

No.	Type	Value	Unused	Used
27	A4	5m slate & carmine, 25x17 holes	35.00	

Nos. 26 and 27 were never placed in use.

The stamps of Marshall Islands overprinted "G. R. I." and new values in British currency were all used in New Britain and are listed among the issues for that country.

Two unauthorized issues appeared in 1979. The 1st, a set of five for the "Establishment of Government, May 1, 1979," consists of 8c, 15c, 21c, 31c and 75c labels. The 75c is about the size of a postcard. The 2nd, a set of four se-tenant blocks of four 10c labels for the Intl. Year of the Child. This set also exists imperf. and with specimen overprints.

Catalogue values for unused stamps in this section, from this point to the end of the section, are for Never Hinged items.

Inauguration of Postal Service — A5

1984, May 2 Litho. *Perf. 14x13½*

No.	Type	Value	Unused	Used
31	A5	20c Outrigger canoe	.50	.50
32	A5	20c Fishnet	.50	.50
33	A5	20c Navigational stick chart	.50	.50
34	A5	20c Islet	.50	.50
a.		Block of 4, #31-34	2.00	2.00

Mili Atoll, Astrolabe — A6

Maps and Navigational Instruments.

1984-85 Litho. *Perf. 15x14*

No.	Type	Value	Unused	Used
35	A6	1c shown	.20	.20
36	A6	3c Likiep, Azimuth compass	.20	.20
37	A6	5c Ebon, 16th cent. compass	.20	.20
38	A6	10c Jaluit, anchor buoys	.20	.20
39	A6	13c Ailinginae, Nocturnal	.25	.25
a.		Booklet pane of 10	*8.00*	—
40	A6	14c Wotho Atoll, navigational stick chart	.30	.30
a.		Booklet pane of 10	*7.50*	—
41	A6	20c Kwajalein and Ebeye, stick chart	.40	.40
a.		Booklet pane of 10	*10.00*	—
b.		Bklt. pane, 5 each 13c, 20c	*9.25*	—
42	A6	22c Eniwetok, 18th cent. lodestone storage case	.45	.45
a.		Booklet pane of 10	*9.50*	—
b.		Bklt. pane, 5 each 14c, 22c	*8.50*	—
43	A6	28c Ailinglaplap, printed compass	.55	.55
44	A6	30c Majuro, navigational stick-chart	.60	.60
45	A6	33c Namu, stick chart	.65	.65
46	A6	37c Rongelap, quadrant	.75	.75
47	A6	39c Taka, map compass, 16th cent. sea chart	.80	.80
48	A6	44c Ujelang, chronograph	.90	.90
49	A6	50c Maloelap and Aur, nocturlabe	1.00	1.00
49A	A6	$1 Arno, 16th cent. sector compass	2.00	2.00
		Nos. 35-49A (16)	9.45	9.45

Issued: 1c, 3c, 10c, 30c, $1, 6/12; 13c, 20c, 28c, 37c, 12/19/84; 14c, 22c, 33c, 39c, 44c, 50c, 6/5/85.

See Nos. 107-109.

No. 7 — A7

1984, June 19 *Perf. 14½x15*

50	A7 40c shown	.60	.60
51	A7 40c No. 13	.60	.60
52	A7 40c No. 4	.60	.60
53	A7 40c No. 25	.60	.60
a.	Block of 4, #50-53	2.40	2.40

Philatelic Salon, 19th UPU Congress, Hamburg, June 19-26.

Ausipex '84 — A8

Dolphins.

1984, Sept. 5 **Litho.** *Perf. 14*

54	A8 20c Common	.40	.40
55	A8 20c Risso's	.40	.40
56	A8 20c Spotter	.40	.40
57	A8 20c Bottlenose	.40	.40
a.	Block of 4, #54-57	1.60	1.60

Christmas — A9

1984, Nov. 7 **Litho.** *Perf. 14*

58	Strip of 4	2.25	2.25
a.-d.	A9 20c any single	.50	.50
e.	Sheet of 16	9.00	

Sheet background shows text from Marshallese New Testament, giving each stamp a different background.

Marshall Islands Constitution, 5th Anniv. — A10

1984, Dec. 19 **Litho.** *Perf. 14*

59	A10 20c Traditional chief	.40	.40
60	A10 20c Amata Kabua	.40	.40
61	A10 20c Chester Nimitz	.40	.40
62	A10 20c Trygve Lie	.40	.40
a.	Block of 4, #59-62	1.60	1.60

Audubon Bicentenary — A11

1985, Feb. 15 **Litho.** *Perf. 14*

63	A11 22c Forked-tailed Petrel	.60	.60
64	A11 22c Pectoral Sandpiper	.60	.60
a.	Pair, #63-64	1.20	1.20
	Nos. 63-64,C1-C2 (4)	3.00	3.00

Sea Shells — A12

1985, Apr. 17 **Litho.** *Perf. 14*

65	A12 22c Cymatium lotorium	.45	.45
66	A12 22c Chicoreus cornucervi	.45	.45
67	A12 22c Strombus aurisdanae	.45	.45
68	A12 22c Turbo marmoratus	.45	.45
69	A12 22c Chicoreus palmarosae	.45	.45
a.	Strip of 5, #65-69	2.25	2.25

See Nos. 119-123, 152-156, 216-220.

Decade for Women A13

1985, June 5 **Litho.** *Perf. 14*

70	A13 22c Native drum	.40	.40
71	A13 22c Palm branches	.40	.40
72	A13 22c Pounding stone	.40	.40
73	A13 22c Ak bird	.40	.40
a.	Block of 4, #70-73	1.65	1.65

Reef and Lagoon Fish A14

1985, July 15 **Litho.** *Perf. 14*

74	A14 22c Acanthurus dussumieri	.45	.45
75	A14 22c Adioryx caudimaculatus	.45	.45
76	A14 22c Ostracion meleacaris	.45	.45
77	A14 22c Chaetodon ephippium	.45	.45
a.	Block of 4, #74-77	1.80	1.80

Intl. Youth Year A15

IYY and Alele Nautical Museum emblems and: No. 78, Marshallese youths and Peace Corps volunteers playing basketball. No. 79, Legend teller reciting local history, girl listening to recording. No. 80, Islander explaining navigational stick charts. No. 81, Jabwa stick dance.

1985, Aug. 31 **Litho.** *Perf. 14*

78	A15 22c multicolored	.45	.45
79	A15 22c multicolored	.45	.45
80	A15 22c multicolored	.45	.45
81	A15 22c multicolored	.45	.45
a.	Block of 4, #78-81	1.80	1.80

1856 American Board of Commissions Stock Certificate for Foreign Missions — A16

Missionary ship Morning Star I: 22c, Launch, Jothan Stetson Shipyard, Chelsea, MA, Aug. 7, 1857. 33c, First voyage, Honolulu to the Marshalls, 1857. 44c, Marshall islanders pulling Morning Star I into Ebon Lagoon, 1857.

1985, Oct. 21 **Litho.** *Perf. 14*

82	A16 14c multicolored	.25	.25
83	A16 22c multicolored	.45	.45
84	A16 33c multicolored	.65	.65
85	A16 44c multicolored	.90	.90
	Nos. 82-85 (4)	2.25	2.25

Christmas.

US Space Shuttle, Astro Telescope, Halley's Comet — A17

Comet tail and research spacecraft: No. 87, Planet A Space Probe, Japan. No. 88, Giotto spacecraft, European Space Agency. No. 89, INTERCOSMOS Project Vega spacecraft, Russia, France, etc. No. 90, US naval tracking ship, NASA observational aircraft, cameo portrait of Edmond Halley (1656-1742), astronomer. Se-tenant in continuous design.

1985, Nov. 21

86	A17 22c multicolored	1.00	1.00
87	A17 22c multicolored	1.00	1.00
88	A17 22c multicolored	1.00	1.00
89	A17 22c multicolored	1.00	1.00
90	A17 22c multicolored	1.00	1.00
a.	Strip of 5, #86-90	5.00	5.00

Medicinal Plants A18

1985, Dec. 31 **Litho.** *Perf. 14*

91	A18 22c Sida fallax	.45	.45
92	A18 22c Scaevola frutescens	.45	.45
93	A18 22c Guettarda speciosa	.45	.45
94	A18 22c Cassytha filiformis	.45	.45
a.	Block of 4, #91-94	1.90	1.90

Maps Type of 1984

1986-87 *Perf. 15x14, 14 ($10)*

107	A6 $2 Wotje and Erikub, terrestrial globe, 1571	4.50	4.50
108	A6 $5 Bikini, Stick chart	9.50	9.50

Size: 31x31mm

109	A6 $10 Stick chart of the atolls	16.00	16.00
	Nos. 107-109 (3)	30.00	30.00

Issued: $2, $5, 3/7/86; $10, 3/31/87.

Marine Invertebrates — A19

1986, Mar. 31 **Litho.** *Perf. 14½x14*

110	A19 14c Triton's trumpet	1.50	1.50
111	A19 14c Giant clam	1.50	1.50
112	A19 14c Small giant clam	1.50	1.50
113	A19 14c Coconut crab	1.50	1.50
a.	Block of 4, #110-113	8.00	8.00

Souvenir Sheet

AMERIPEX '86, Chicago, May 22-June 1 — A20

1986, May 22 **Litho.** *Perf. 14*

114	A20 $1 Douglas C-54 Globester	2.75	2.75

1st Around-the-world scheduled flight, 40th anniv. No. 114 has multicolored margin continuing the design and picturing US Air Transport Command Base, Kwajalein Atoll and souvenir card.

See Nos. C3-C6.

Operation Crossroads, Atomic Bomb Tests, 40th Anniv. — A21

Designs: No. 115, King Juda, Bikinians sailing tibinal canoe. No. 116, USS Sumner, amphibious DUKW, advance landing. No. 117, Evacuating Bikinians. No. 118, Land reclamation, 1986.

1986, July 1 **Litho.** *Perf. 14*

115	A21 22c multicolored	.45	.45
116	A21 22c multicolored	.45	.45
117	A21 22c multicolored	.45	.45
118	A21 22c multicolored	.45	.45
a.	Block of 4, #115-118	1.90	1.90

See No. C7.

Seashells Type of 1985

1986, Aug. 1 **Litho.** *Perf. 14*

119	A12 22c Ramose murex	.45	.45
120	A12 22c Orange spider	.45	.45
121	A12 22c Red-mouth frog shell	.45	.45
122	A12 22c Laciniate conch	.45	.45
123	A12 22c Giant frog shell	.45	.45
a.	Strip of 5, #119-123	2.25	2.25

Game Fish A22

1986, Sept. 10 **Litho.**

124	A22 22c Blue marlin	.40	.40
125	A22 22c Wahoo	.40	.40
126	A22 22c Dolphin fish	.40	.40
127	A22 22c Yellowfin tuna	.40	.40
a.	Block of 4, #124-127	1.60	1.60

Christmas, Intl. Peace Year — A23

1986, Oct. 28 **Litho.** *Perf. 14*

128	A23 22c United Nations UR	.60	.60
129	A23 22c United Nations UL	.60	.60
130	A23 22c United Nations LR	.60	.60
131	A23 22c United Nations LL	.60	.60
a.	Block of 4, #128-131	2.50	2.50

See No. C8.

US Whaling Ships A24

1987, Feb. 20 **Litho.** *Perf. 14*

132	A24 22c James Arnold, 1854	.50	.50
133	A24 22c General Scott, 1859	.50	.50
134	A24 22c Charles W. Morgan, 1865	.50	.50
135	A24 22c Lucretia, 1884	.50	.50
a.	Block of 4, #132-135	2.00	2.00

Historic and Military Flights A25

Designs: No. 136, Charles Lindbergh commemorative medal, Spirit of St. Louis crossing the Atlantic, 1927. No. 137, Lindbergh flying in the Battle of the Marshalls, 1944. No. 138, William Bridgeman flying in the Battle of Kwajalein, 1944. No. 139, Bridgeman testing the Douglas Skyrocket, 1951. No. 140, John Glenn flying in the Battle of the Marshalls. No. 141, Glenn, the first American to orbit the Earth, 1962.

1987, Mar. 12 Litho. *Perf. 14½*

136 A25 33c multicolored .70 .70
137 A25 33c multicolored .70 .70
a. Pair, #136-137 1.40 1.40
138 A25 39c multicolored .75 .75
139 A25 39c multicolored .75 .75
a. Pair, #138-139 1.50 1.50
140 A25 44c multicolored .80 .80
141 A25 44c multicolored .80 .80
a. Pair, #140-141 1.60 1.60
Nos. 136-141 (6) 4.50 4.50

Souvenir Sheet

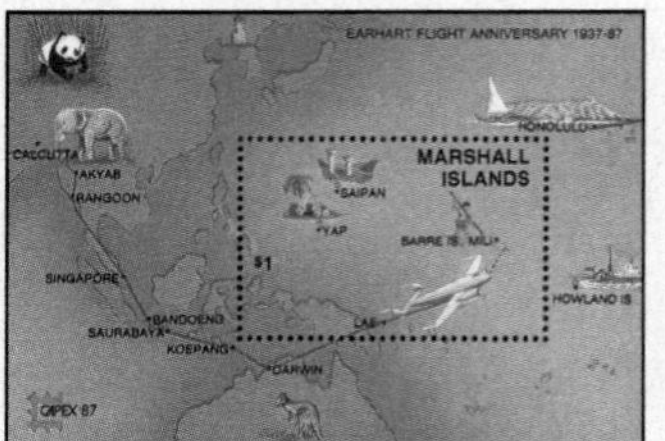

CAPEX '87 — A26

1987, June 15 Litho. *Perf. 14*

142 A26 $1 Map of flight 2.50 2.50

Amelia Earhart (1897-1937), American aviator who died during attempted round-the-world flight, 50th anniv. No. 142 has multicolored margin picturing Earhart's flight pattern from Calcutta, India, to the crash site near Barre Is., Marshall Is.

US Constitution Bicentennial — A27

Excerpts from the Marshall Islands and US Constitutions.

1987, July 16 Litho. *Perf. 14*

143 A27 14c We,... Marshall .30 .30
144 A27 14c National seals .30 .30
145 A27 14c We,... United States .30 .30
a. Triptych, #143-145 1.00 1.00
146 A27 22c All we have... .40 .40
147 A27 22c Flags .40 .40
148 A27 22c to establish... .40 .40
a. Triptych, #146-148 1.25 1.25
149 A27 44c With this Constitution... .80 .80
150 A27 44c Stick chart, Liberty Bell .80 .80
151 A27 44c to promote... .80 .80
a. Triptych, #149-151 2.50 2.50
Nos. 143-151 (9) 4.50 4.50

Triptychs printed in continuous designs.

Seashells Type of 1985

1987, Sept. 1 Litho. *Perf. 14*

152 A12 22c Magnificent cone .40 .40
153 A12 22c Partridge tun .40 .40
154 A12 22c Scorpion spider conch .40 .40
155 A12 22c Hairy triton .40 .40
156 A12 22c Chiragra spider conch .40 .40
a. Strip of 5, #152-156 2.00 2.00

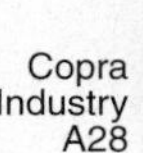

Copra Industry A28

Contest-winning crayon drawings by Amram Enox; design contest sponsored by the Tobular Copra Processing Co.

1987, Dec. 10 Litho. *Perf. 14*

157 A28 44c Planting coconut .65 .65
158 A28 44c Making copra .65 .65
159 A28 44c Bottling coconut oil .65 .65
a. Triptych, #157-159 2.00 2.00

Biblical Verses A29

1987, Dec. 10

160 A29 14c Matthew 2:1 .25 .25
161 A29 22c Luke 2:14 .40 .40
162 A29 33c Psalms 33:3 .60 .60
163 A29 44c Pslams 150:5 .75 .75
Nos. 160-163 (4) 2.00 2.00

Christmas.

Marine Birds A30

1988, Jan. 27

164 A30 44c Pacific reef herons .75 .75
165 A30 44c Bar-tailed godwit .75 .75
166 A30 44c Masked booby .75 .75
167 A30 44c Northern shoveler .75 .75
a. Block of 4, #164-167 3.00 3.00

Fish — A31

Perf. 14½x14, 14 (#187)

1988-89 Litho.

168 A31 1c Damselfish .20 .20
169 A31 3c Blackface butterflyfish .20 .20
170 A31 14c Hawkfish .25 .25
a. Booklet pane of 10 3.75 —
171 A31 15c Balloonfish .25 .25
a. Booklet pane of 10 4.50 —
172 A31 17c Trunk fish .30 .30
173 A31 22c Lyretail wrasse .35 .35
a. Booklet pane of 10 5.00 —
b. Bklt. pane, 5 each 14c, 22c 5.00 —
174 A31 25c Parrotfish .35 .35
a. Booklet pane of 10 7.25 —
b. Bklt. pane, 5 each 15c, 25c 7.25 —
175 A31 33c White-spotted boxfish .60 .60
176 A31 36c Spotted boxfish .65 .65
177 A31 39c Surgeonfish .75 .75
178 A31 44c Long-snouted butterflyfish .80 .80
179 A31 45c Trumpetfish .80 .80
180 A31 56c Sharp-nosed puffer 1.00 1.00
181 A31 $1 Seahorse 1.90 1.90
182 A31 $2 Ghost pipefish 3.50 3.50
183 A31 $5 Big-spotted triggerfish 8.00 8.00
184 A31 $10 Blue jack ('89) 16.00 16.00
Nos. 168-184 (17) 35.90 35.90

Issued: #170a, 173a, 173b, 3/31/88; 15c, 25c, 36c, 45c, 7/19/; #171a, 174a, 174b, 12/15; $10, 3/31/89; others, 3/17/88.

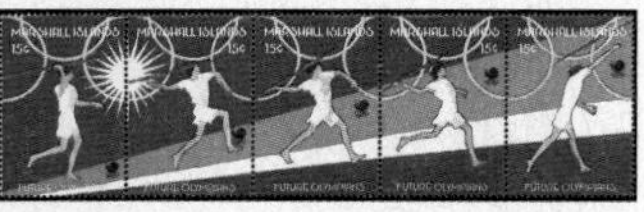

A32

1988 Summer Olympics, Seoul — A33

Athletes in motion: 15c, Javelin thrower. 25c, Runner.

1988, June 30 Litho. *Perf. 14*

188 A32 15c Strip of 5, #a-e 1.65 1.65
189 A33 25c Strip of 5, #a-e 2.25 2.25

Souvenir Sheet

Pacific Voyages of Robert Louis Stevenson — A34

Stick chart of the Marshalls and: a, *Casco* sailing through the Golden Gate. b, At the Needles of Ua-Pu, Marquesas. c, *Equator* departing from Honolulu and Kaiulani, an Hawaiian princess. d, Chief's canoe, Majuro Lagoon. e, Bronze medallion, 1887, by Augustus St. Gaudens in the Tate Gallery, London. f, Outrigger canoe and S.S. *Janet Nicoll* in Majuro Lagoon. g, View of Apemama, Gilbert Is. h, Samoan outrigger canoe, Apia Harbor. i, Stevenson riding horse Jack at his estate, Vallima, Samoa.

1988, July 19 Litho. *Perf. 14*

190 Sheet of 9 6.25 4.50
a.-i. A34 25c any single .50 .50

Robert Louis Stevenson (1850-1894), Scottish novelist, poet and essayist.

Colonial Ships and Flags A35

Designs: No. 191, Galleon *Santa Maria de La Victoria,* 1526, and Spanish "Ragged Cross" ensign in use from 1516 to 1785. No. 192, Transport ships *Charlotte* and *Scarborough,* 1788, and British red ensign, 1707-1800. No. 193, Schooner *Flying Fish,* sloop-of-war *Peacock,* 1841, and U.S. flag, 1837-1845. No. 194, Steamer *Planet,* 1909, and German flag, 1867-1919.

1988, Sept. 2 Litho. *Perf. 14*

191 A35 25c multicolored .50 .50
192 A35 25c multicolored .50 .50
193 A35 25c multicolored .50 .50
194 A35 25c multicolored .50 .50
a. Block of 4, #191-194 2.00 2.00

Christmas — A36

A37

No. 195, Santa Claus riding in sleigh. No. 196, Reindeer, hut and palm trees. No. 197, Reindeer and palm trees. No. 198, Reindeer, palm tree, fish. No. 199, Reindeer and outrigger canoe.

1988, Nov. 7 Litho. *Perf. 14*

195 A36 25c multicolored .50 .50
196 A36 25c multicolored .50 .50
197 A36 25c multicolored .50 .50
198 A36 25c multicolored .50 .50
199 A36 25c multicolored .50 .50
a. Strip of 5, #195-199 2.50 2.50

No. 199a has a continuous design.

1988, Nov. 22 Litho. *Perf. 14*

200 A37 25c Nuclear threat diminished .55 .55
201 A37 25c Signing the Test Ban Treaty .55 .55
202 A37 25c Portrait .55 .55
203 A37 25c US-USSR Hotline .55 .55
204 A37 25c Peace Corps enactment .55 .55
a. Strip of 5, #200-204 2.75 2.75

Tribute to John F. Kennedy. No. 204a has a continuous design.

US Space Shuttle Program and Kwajalein — A38

#205, Launch of *Prime* from Vandenberg Air Force Base downrange to the Kwajalein Missile Range. #206, *Prime* X023A/SV-5D lifting body reentering atmosphere. #207, Parachute landing and craft recovery off Kwajalein Is. #208, Shuttle over island.

1988, Dec. 23 Litho. *Perf. 14*

205 25c multicolored .50 .50
206 25c multicolored .50 .50
207 25c multicolored .50 .50
208 25c multicolored .50 .50
a. A38 Strip of 4, #205-208 2.00 2.00

NASA 30th anniv. and 25th anniv. of the Project PRIME wind tunnel tests.

See No. C21.

Links to Japan A39

Designs: No. 209, Typhoon Monument, Majuro, 1918. No. 210, Seaplane base and railway depot, Djarrej Islet, c. 1940. No. 211, Fishing boats. No. 212, Japanese honeymooners scuba diving, 1988.

1989, Jan. 19 Litho. *Perf. 14*

209 A39 45c multicolored .75 .75
210 A39 45c multicolored .75 .75
211 A39 45c multicolored .75 .75
212 A39 45c multicolored .75 .75
a. Block of 4, #209-212 3.00 3.00

Links to Alaska A40

Paintings by Claire Fejes.

1989, Mar. 31 Litho. *Perf. 14*

213 A40 45c Island Woman .85 .85
214 A40 45c Kotzebue, Alaska .85 .85
215 A40 45c Marshallese Madonna .85 .85
a. Strip of 3, #213-215 2.55 2.55

Printed in sheets of 9.

Seashells Type of 1985

1989, May 15 Litho. *Perf. 14*

216 A12 25c Pontifical miter .50 .50
217 A12 25c Tapestry turban .50 .50
218 A12 25c Flame-mouthed helmet .50 .50
219 A12 25c Prickly Pacific drupe .50 .50
220 A12 25c Blood-mouthed conch .50 .50
a. Strip of 5, #216-220 2.50 2.50

Souvenir Sheet

In Praise of Sovereigns, 1940, by Sanko Inoue — A41

1989, May 15 Litho. *Perf. 14*

221 A41 $1 multicolored 2.00 2.00

Hirohito (1901-89) and enthronement of Akihito as emperor of Japan.

Migrant Birds A42

1989, June 27 Litho. *Perf. 14*

222 A42 45c Wandering tattler .85 .85
223 A42 45c Ruddy turnstone .85 .85
224 A42 45c Pacific golden plover .85 .85
225 A42 45c Sanderling .85 .85
a. Block of 4, #222-225 3.40 3.40

Postal History A43

PHILEXFRANCE '89 — A44

Designs: No. 226, Missionary ship *Morning Star V,* 1905, and Marshall Isls. #15 canceled. No. 227, Marshall Isls. #15-16 on registered letter, 1906. No. 228, *Prinz Eitel Friedrich,* 1914, and German sea post cancel. No. 229, Cruiser squadron led by SMS *Scharnhorst,* 1914, and German sea post cancel.

No. 230: a, SMS *Bussard* and German sea post cancel and Germany #32. b, US Type A924 and Marshall Isls. #34a on FDC. c, LST 119 FPO, 1944, US Navy cancel and pair of US #853. d, Mail boat, 1936, cancel and Japan #222. e, Majuro PO f, Marshall Isls. cancel, 1951, and four US #803.

No. 231, Germany #32 and Marshall Isls. cancel, 1889.

1989, July 7

226 A43 45c multicolored .80 .80
227 A43 45c multicolored .80 .80
228 A43 45c multicolored .80 .80
229 A43 45c multicolored .80 .80
a. Block of 4, #226-229 3.25 3.25

Souvenir Sheets

230 Sheet of 6 10.00 10.00
a.-f. A44 25c any single 1.50 1.50
231 A43 $1 multicolored 10.00 3.00

Nos. 230b and 230e are printed in a continuous design.

1st Moon Landing, 20th Anniv. A45

Apollo 11: No. 232, Liftoff. No. 233, Neil Armstrong. No. 234, Lunar module *Eagle.* No. 235, Michael Collins. No. 236, Raising the American flag on the Moon. No. 237, Buzz Aldrin. $1, 1st step on the Moon and "We came in peace for all mankind."

1989, Aug. 1 Litho. *Perf. 13½*

Booklet Stamps

232 A45 25c multicolored 1.25 1.25
233 A45 25c multicolored 1.25 1.25
234 A45 25c multicolored 1.25 1.25
235 A45 25c multicolored 1.25 1.25
236 A45 25c multicolored 1.25 1.25
237 A45 25c multicolored 1.25 1.25

Size: 75x32mm

238 A45 $1 multicolored 7.00 5.00
a. Booklet pane of 7, #232-238 15.00
Nos. 232-238 (7) 14.50 12.50

Decorative inscribed selvage separates No. 238 from Nos. 232-237 and surrounds it like a souvenir sheet margin. Selvage around Nos. 232-237 is plain.

World War II

A46

A47

Anniversaries and events, 1939: #239, Invasion of Poland. #240, Sinking of HMS *Royal Oak.* #241, Invasion of Finland.

Battle of the River Plate: #242, HMS *Exeter,.* #243, HMS *Ajax,.* #244, *Admiral Graf Spee,.* #245, HMNZS *Achilles,.*

1989 Litho. *Perf. 13½*

239 A46 25c W1 (1-1) .60 .45
240 A46 45c W2 (1-1) 1.00 .75
241 A46 45c W3 (1-1) 1.00 .75
242 A46 45c W4 (4-1) .80 .75
243 A46 45c W4 (4-2) .80 .75
244 A46 45c W4 (4-3) .80 .75
245 A46 45c W4 (4-4) .80 .75
a. Block of 4, #242-245 3.25 3.00

Issued: #239, 9/1; #240, 10/13; #241, 11/30; #245a, 12/13.

1990

1940: #246, Invasion of Denmark. #247, Invasion of Norway. #248, Katyn Forest Massacre. #249, Bombing of Rotterdam. #250, Invasion of Belgium. #251, Winston Churchill becomes prime minister of England. #252, Evacuation of the British Expeditionary Force at Dunkirk. #253, Evacuation at Dunkirk. #254, Occupation of Paris.

246 A46 25c W5 (2-1) .60 .50
247 A46 25c W5 (2-2) .60 .50
a. Pair, #246-247 1.25 1.00
248 A47 25c W6 (1-1) .50 .50
249 A46 25c W8 (2-1) .50 .50
250 A46 25c W8 (2-2) .50 .50
a. Pair, #249-250 1.00 1.00
251 A46 45c W7 (1-1) 1.00 .90
252 A46 45c W9 (2-1) 1.00 .90
253 A46 45c W9 (2-2) 1.00 .90
a. Pair, #252-253 2.00 1.80
254 A47 45c W10 (1-1) 1.00 .90

Issued: #247a, 4/9; #248, 4/16; #249-251, 5/10; #252-253, 6/4; #254, 6/14.

1990

#255, Battle of Mers-el-Kebir, 1940. #256, Battles for the Burma Road, 1940-45.

US Destroyers for British bases: #257, HMS Georgetown (ex-USS Maddox). #258, HMS Banff (ex-USCGC Saranac). #259, HMS Buxton (ex-USS Edwards). #260, HMS Rockingham (ex-USS Swasey).

Battle of Britain: #261, Supermarine Spitfire Mark IA. #262, Hawker Hurricane Mark I. #263, Messerschmitt Bf109E. #264, Junkers JU87B-2. #265, Tripartite Pact Signed 1940.

255 A46 25c W11 (1-1) .60 .50
256 A47 25c W12 (1-1) .60 .50
257 A46 45c W13 (4-1) 1.00 .90
258 A46 45c W13 (4-2) 1.00 .90
259 A46 45c W13 (4-3) 1.00 .90
260 A46 45c W13 (4-4) 1.00 .90
a. Block of 4, #257-260 4.00 3.60
261 A46 45c W14 (4-1) 1.00 .90
262 A46 45c W14 (4-2) 1.00 .90
263 A46 45c W14 (4-3) 1.00 .90
264 A46 45c W14 (4-4) 1.00 .90
a. Block of 4, #261-264 4.00 3.60
265 A46 45c W15 1.10 .90

Issued: #255, 7/3; #256, 7/18; #260a, 9/9; #264a, 9/15; #265, 9/27.

1990-91

Designs: #266, Roosevelt elected to third term, 1940. Battle of Taranto: #267, HMS Illustrious. #268, Fairey Swordfish. #269, RM Andrea Doria. #270, RM Conte di Cavour.

Roosevelt's Four Freedoms Speech: #271, Freedom of Speech. #272, Freedom from Want. #273, Freedom of Worship. #274, Freedom From Fear. #275, Battle of Beda Fomm, Feb. 5-7, 1941.

Germany Invades the Balkans: #276, Invasion of Greece. #277, Invasion of Yugoslavia.

Sinking of the Bismarck: #278, HMS Prince of Wales. #279, HMS Hood. #280, Bismarck. #281, Fairey Swordfish. #282, German Invasion of Russia, 1941.

266 A47 25c W16 .60 .50
267 A46 25c W17 (4-1) .60 .50
268 A46 25c W17 (4-2) .60 .50
269 A46 25c W17 (4-3) .60 .50
270 A46 25c W17 (4-4) .60 .50
a. Block of 4, #266-270 2.50 2.00
271 A46 30c W18 (4-1) .65 .60
272 A46 30c W18 (4-2) .65 .60
273 A46 30c W18 (4-3) .65 .60
274 A46 30c W18 (4-4) .65 .60
a. Block of 4, #271-274 2.60 2.40
275 A46 30c Tanks, W19 .60 .60
276 A47 29c W20 (2-1) .60 .60
277 A47 29c W20 (2-2) .60 .60
a. Pair, #276-277 1.25 1.25
278 A46 50c W21 (4-1) 1.00 1.00
279 A46 50c W21 (4-2) 1.00 1.00
280 A46 50c W21 (4-3) 1.00 1.00
281 A46 50c W21 (4-4) 1.00 1.00
a. Block of 4, #278-281 4.00 4.00
282 A46 30c Tanks, W22 .60 .60

Issued: #266, 11/5/90; #270a, 11/11/90; #274a, 1/6/91; #275, 2/5/91; #277a, 4/6/91; #281a, 5/27/91; #282, 6/22/91.

1991

1941 — Declaration of the Atlantic Charter: #283, Pres. Roosevelt and USS Augusta. #284, Churchill and HMS Prince of Wales. #285, Siege of Moscow.

Sinking of USS Reuben James: #286, Reuben James hit by torpedo. #287, German U-562 submarine.

Japanese attack on Pearl Harbor: #288, American warplanes. # 289, Japanese warplanes. #290, USS Arizona. #291, Japanese aircraft carrier Akagi.

283 A47 29c W23 (2-1) .60 .60
284 A47 29c W23 (2-2) .60 .60
a. Pair, #283-284 1.25 1.25
285 A46 29c W24 .60 .60
286 A46 30c W25 (2-1) .60 .60
287 A46 30c W25 (2-1) .60 .60
a. Pair, #286-287 1.25 1.25
288 A47 50c W26 (4-1) 1.00 1.00
a. Revised inscription 4.75 1.00
289 A47 50c W26 (4-2) 1.00 1.00
290 A47 50c W26 (4-3) 1.00 1.00
291 A47 50c W26 (4-4) 1.00 1.00
a. Block of 4, #288-291 4.00 4.00
b. Block of 4, #288a, 289-291 8.50 4.00

Inscriptions read "Peal" on No. 288 and "Pearl" on No. 288a.

Issued: #284a, 8/14; #285, 10/2; #287a, 10/31; #291a, 12/7.

1991-92

1941-42: #292, Japanese capture Guam. #293, Fall of Singapore.

First combat of the Flying Tigers: #294, Curtiss Tomahawk. #295, Mitsubishi Ki-21 on fire. #296, Fall of Wake Island.

#297, Roosevelt and Churchill at Arcadia Conference. #298, Japanese tank entering Manila. #299, Japanese take Rabaul. #300, Battle of the Java Sea. #301, Rangoon falls to Japanese. #302, Japanese land on New Guinea. #303, MacArthur evacuated from Corregidor. #304, Raid on Saint-Nazaire. #305, Surrender of Bataan / Death March. #306, Doolittle Raid on Tokyo. #307, Fall of Corregidor.

292 A47 29c W27 .60 .60
293 A46 29c W28 .60 .60
294 A46 50c W29 (2-1) 1.00 1.00
295 A46 50c W29 (2-2) 1.00 1.00
a. Pair, #294-295 2.00 2.00
296 A46 29c W30 .60 .60
297 A46 29c W31 .60 .60
298 A46 50c W32 1.00 1.00
299 A46 29c W33 .60 .60
300 A46 29c W34 .60 .60
301 A47 50c W35 1.00 1.00
302 A46 29c W36 .60 .60
303 A46 29c W37 .60 .60
304 A46 29c W38 .60 .60
305 A47 29c W39 .60 .60
306 A47 50c W40 1.00 1.00
307 A46 29c W41 .60 .60

Issued: #292-293, 12/10/91; #295a, 12/20/91; #296, 12/23/91; #297, 1/1/92; #298, 1/2/92; #299, 1/23/92; #300, 2/15/92; #301-302, 3/8/92; #303, 3/11/92; #304, 3/27/92; #305, 4/9/92; #306, 4/18/92; #307, 5/6/92.

1992

1942 — Battle of the Coral Sea: #308, USS Lexington. #309, Japanese Mitsubishi A6M2 Zeros. #310, Douglas SBD Dauntless dive bombers. #311, Japanese carrier Shoho.

Battle of Midway: #312, Japanese aircraft carrier Akagi. #313, U.S. Douglas SBD Dauntless dive bombers. #314, USS Yorktown. #315, Nakajima B5N2 Kate torpedo planes.

#316, Village of Lidice destroyed. #317, Fall of Sevastopol.

Convoy PQ17 destroyed: #318, British merchant ship in convoy. #319, German U-boats.

#320, Marines land on Guadalcanal. #323, Battle of Stalingrad. #324, Battle of Eastern Solomons.

#321, Battle of Savo Island. #322, Dieppe Raid. #325, Battle of Cape Esperance. #326, Battle of El Alamein.

Battle of Barents Sea: #327, HMS Sheffield. #328, Admiral Hipper.

308 A46 50c W42 (4-1) 1.00 1.00
a. Revised inscription 2.00 1.00
309 A46 50c W42 (4-2) 1.00 1.00
a. Revised inscription 2.00 1.00
310 A46 50c W42 (4-3) 1.00 1.00
a. Revised inscription 2.00 1.00
311 A46 50c W42 (4-4) 1.00 1.00
a. Block of 4, #308-311 4.00 4.00
b. Revised inscription 2.00 1.00
c. Block of 4, #308a-310a, 311b 8.50 4.00
312 A46 50c W43 (4-1) 1.00 1.00
313 A46 50c W43 (4-3) 1.00 1.00
314 A46 50c W43 (4-2) 1.00 1.00
315 A46 50c W43 (4-4) 1.00 1.00
a. Block of 4, #312-315 4.00 4.00
316 A46 29c W44 .60 .60
317 A47 29c W45 .60 .60
318 A46 29c W46 (2-1) .60 .60
319 A46 29c W46 (2-2) .60 .60
a. Pair, #318-319 1.25 1.25

320 A46 29c W47 .60 .60
321 A47 29c W48 .60 .60
322 A46 29c W49 .60 .60
323 A47 50c W50 1.25 1.00
324 A46 29c W51 .60 .60
325 A46 50c W52 1.25 1.00
326 A46 29c W53 .60 .60
327 A46 29c W54 (2-1) .60 .60
328 A46 29c W54 (2-2) .60 .60
a. Pair, #327-328 1.25 1.25

Inscription reads "U.S.S. Lexington/Grumman F4F-3 Wildcat" on No. 308a, "Japanese Aichi D3A1 Vals/Nakajima B5N2 Kate" on No. 309a, "U.S. Douglas TBD-1 Devastators" on No. 310a, "Japanese Carrier Shoho/Mitsubishi A6M2 Zeros" on No. 311b.

Issued: #311a, 5/8/92; #315a, 6/4; #316, 6/9/92; #317, 7/4; #319a, 7/5; #320, 8/7; #321, 8/9; #322-323, 8/19; #324, 8/24; #325, 10/11; #326, 10/23; #328a, 12/31.

Vertical pairs, Nos. 312-313 and Nos. 314-315 have continuous designs.

No. 310 incorrectly identifies Douglas TBD torpedo bombers.

1993 Litho. *Perf. 13½*

1943 — #329, Casablanca Conf. #330, Liberation of Kharkov.

Battle of Bismarck Sea: #331, Japanese A6M Zeroes, destroyer Arashio. #332, U.S. P38 Lightnings, Australian Beaufighter. #333, Japanese destroyer Shirayuki. #334, U.S. A-20 Havoc, B-25 Mitchell.

#335, Interception of Admiral Yamamoto.

Battle of Kursk: #336, German Tiger I. #337, Soviet T-34.

329 A46 29c W55 .65 .60
330 A46 29c W56 .65 .60
331 A46 50c W57 (4-1) 1.00 1.00
332 A46 50c W57 (4-2) 1.00 1.00
333 A46 50c W57 (4-3) 1.00 1.00
334 A46 50c W57 (4-4) 1.00 1.00
a. Block of 4, #331-334 4.00 4.00
335 A46 50c W58 1.00 1.00
336 A46 29c W59 (2-1) .85 .60
337 A46 29c W59 (2-2) .85 .60
a. Pair, #336-337 1.70 1.25
Nos. 239-337 (99) 78.50 74.05

Issued: #329, 1/14; #330, 2/16; #334a, 3/3; #335, 4/18; #337a, 7/5.

See #467-524, 562-563.

Christmas A57

Angels playing musical instruments.

1989, Oct. 25 *Perf. 13½*

341 A57 25c Horn .80 .80
342 A57 25c Singing carol .80 .80
343 A57 25c Lute .80 .80
344 A57 25c Lyre .80 .80
a. Block of 4, #341-344 3.25 3.25

Miniature Sheet

Milestones in Space Exploration A58

Designs: a, Robert Goddard and 1st liquid fuel rocket launch, 1926. b, *Sputnik,* 1st man-made satellite, 1957. c, 1st American satellite, 1958. d, Yuri Gagarin, 1st man in space, 1961. e, John Glenn, 1st American to orbit Earth, 1962. f, Valentina Tereshkova, 1st woman in space, 1963. g, Aleksei Leonov, 1st space walk, 1965. h, Edward White, 1st American to walk in space, 1965. i, Gemini-Titan 6A, 1st rendezvous in space, 1965. j, 1st Soft landing on the Moon, 1966. k, Gemini 8, 1st docking in space, 1966. l, 1st probe of Venus, 1967. m, Apollo 8, 1st manned orbit of the Moon, 1968. n, Apollo 11, 1st man on the Moon, 1969. o, Soyuz 11, 1st space station crew, 1971. p, Apollo 15, 1st manned lunar vehicle, 1971. q, *Skylab 2,* 1st American manned space station, 1973. r, 1st Flyby of Jupiter, 1973. s, Apollo-Soyuz, 1st joint space flight, 1975. t, 1st Landing on Mars, 1976. u, 1st flyby of Saturn, 1979. v, *Columbia,* 1st space shuttle flight, 1981. w, 1st probe beyond the solar system, 1983. x, 1st untethered space walk, 1984. y, Launch of space shuttle *Discovery,* 1988.

1989, Nov. 24 Litho. *Perf. 13½*

345 Sheet of 25 25.00 25.00
a.-y. A58 45c any single .90 .90

No. 345 contains World Stamp Expo '89 emblem on selvage.

Birds

A59 A59a

1990-92 Litho. *Perf. 13½*

346 A59 1c Black noddy .20 .20
347 A59 5c Red-tailed tropic bird .20 .20
348 A59 10c Sanderling .20 .20
349 A59 12c Black-naped tern .25 .25
350 A59 15c Wandering tattler .30 .30
351 A59 20c Bristle-thighed curlew .40 .40
352 A59 23c Northern shoveler .45 .45
353 A59 25c Brown noddy .50 .50
354 A59 27c Sooty tern .55 .55
355 A59 29c Wedge-tailed shearwater .60 .60
356 A59a 29c Northern pintail .60 .60
357 A59 30c Pacific golden plover .60 .60
358 A59 35c Brown booby .70 .70
359 A59 36c Red footed booby .75 .75
360 A59 40c White tern .80 .80
361 A59 50c Great frigate bird 1.00 1.00
a. Min. sheet of 4 (#347, 350, 353, 361) 2.25 2.00
362 A59 52c Great crested tern 1.00 1.00
363 A59 65c Lesser sand plover 1.25 1.25
364 A59 75c Little tern 1.50 1.50
365 A59 $1 Pacific reef heron 2.00 2.00
365A A59 $2 Masked booby 4.00 4.00
Nos. 346-365A (21) 17.85 17.85

No. 361a for ESSEN '90, Germany Apr. 19-22.

Issued: 5c, 15c, 25c, 50c, 3/8; 30c, 36c, 40c, $1, 10/11; #361a, 4/19; #355, 20c, 52c, 2/22/91; 27c, 3/8/91; 1c, 12c, 35c, $2, 11/6/91; #356, 2/3/92; 10c, 23c, 65c, 75c, 4/24/92.

See Nos. 430-433.

Children's Games A60

1990, Mar. 15

366 A60 25c Lodidean .80 .75
367 A60 25c Lejonjon .80 .75
368 A60 25c Etobobo .80 .75
369 A60 25c Didmakol .80 .75
a. Block of 4, #366-369 3.25 3.00

Penny Black, 150th Anniv. A61

Designs: No. 370, Penny Black, 1840. No. 371, Essay by James Chalmers. No. 372, Essay by Robert Sievier. No. 373, Essay by Charles Whiting. No. 374, Essay by George Dickinson. No. 375, Medal engraved by William Wyon to celebrate Queen Victoria's first visit to London. $1, Engraver Charles Heath, engraving for master die.

1990, Apr. 6 Booklet Stamps

370 A61 25c multicolored 1.00 1.00
371 A61 25c multicolored 1.00 1.00
372 A61 25c multicolored 1.00 1.00
373 A61 25c multicolored 1.00 1.00
374 A61 25c multicolored 1.00 1.00
375 A61 25c multicolored 1.00 1.00

Size: 73x31mm

376 A61 $1 multicolored 4.00 4.00
a. Booklet pane of 7, #370-376 10.00 —
Nos. 370-376 (7) 10.00 10.00

Decorative inscribed selvage picturing part of a Penny Black proof sheet separates No. 376 from Nos. 370-375 in pane and surrounds it like a souvenir sheet margin. Selvage around Nos. 370-375 is plain.

Endangered Wildlife — A62

Sea Turtles: No. 377, Pacific green turtle hatchlings entering ocean. No. 378, Pacific great turtle under water. No. 379, Hawksbill hatchling, eggs. No. 380, Hawksbill turtle in water.

1990, May 3

377 A62 25c multicolored .80 .75
378 A62 25c multicolored .80 .75
379 A62 25c multicolored .80 .75
380 A62 25c multicolored .80 .75
a. Block of 4, #377-380 3.25 3.00

Stick Chart, Canoe and Flag of the Republic of the Marshall Islands A63

1990, Sept. 28 *Perf. 11x10½*

381 A63 25c multicolored .95 .60

See #615, US #2507, Micronesia #124-126.

German Reunification — A64

1990, Oct. 3 *Perf. 13½*

382 A64 45c multicolored 1.25 1.00

Christmas A65

1990, Oct. 25 Litho. *Perf. 13½*

383 A65 25c Canoe, stick chart .75 .75
384 A65 25c Missionary preaching .75 .75
385 A65 25c Sailors dancing .75 .75
386 A65 25c Youths dancing .75 .75
a. Block of 4, #383-386 3.00 3.00

Breadfruit — A66

1990, Dec. 15 Litho. *Perf. 12x12½*

387 A66 25c Harvesting .75 .75
388 A66 25c Peeling, slicing .75 .75
389 A66 25c Preserving .75 .75
390 A66 25c Kneading dough .75 .75
a. Block of 4, #387-390 3.00 3.00

US Space Shuttle Flights, 10th Anniv. A67

1991, Apr. 12 Litho. *Perf. 13½*

391 A67 50c 747 ferry .90 .90
392 A67 50c Orbital release of LDEF .90 .90
393 A67 50c Lift-off .90 .90
394 A67 50c Landing .90 .90
a. Block of 4, #391-394 3.75 3.75

Flowers — A68

1991, June 10 Litho. *Perf. 13½*

395 A68 52c Ixora carolinensis 1.10 1.00
396 A68 52c Clerodendrum inerme 1.10 1.00
397 A68 52c Messerchmidia argentea 1.10 1.00
398 A68 52c Vigna marina 1.10 1.00
a. Miniature sheet of 4, #395-398 4.75 4.00
b. Block of 4, #395-398, without inscription 4.50 4.00

Phila Nippon '91 (No. 398a). Stamps from miniature sheets inscribed C53A.

Operation Desert Storm — A69

1991, July 4 Litho. *Perf. 13½*

399 A69 29c multicolored .80 .60

Birds — A70

1991, July 16 Booklet Stamps

400 A70 29c Red-footed booby 1.25 .60
401 A70 29c Great frigate bird (7-2) 1.25 .60
402 A70 29c Brown booby 1.25 .60
403 A70 29c White tern 1.25 .60
404 A70 29c Great frigate bird (7-5) 1.25 .60
405 A70 29c Black noddy 1.25 .60

Size: 75x33mm

406 A70 $1 White-tailed tropic bird 6.50 2.00
a. Booklet pane of 7, #400-406 14.00 —
Nos. 400-406 (7) 14.00 5.60

Decorative selvage separates No. 406 from Nos. 400-405 and surrounds it like a souvenir sheet margin.

Aircraft of Air Marshall Islands — A71

1991, Sept. 10 Litho. *Perf. 13½*

407 A71 12c Dornier 228 .25 .20
408 A71 29c Douglas DC-8 .65 .50
409 A71 50c Hawker Siddeley 748 1.10 .85
410 A71 50c Saab 2000 1.10 .85
Nos. 407-410 (4) 3.10 2.40

Admission to United Nations A72

1991, Sept. 24 Litho. *Perf. 11x10½*

411 A72 29c multicolored .70 .65

Christmas — A73

1991, Oct. 25 *Perf. 13½*

412 A73 30c multicolored .75 .75

Peace Corps in Marshall Islands, 25th Anniv. A74

1991, Nov. 26 Litho. *Perf. 11x10½*

413 A74 29c multicolored .75 .60

Ships A75

#414, Bulk cargo carrier, Emlain. #415, Tanker, CSK Valiant. #416, Patrol boat, Ionmeto. #417, Freighter, Micro Pilot.

1992, Feb. 15 Litho. *Perf. 11x10½*

414 A75 29c multicolored .80 .45
415 A75 29c multicolored .80 .45
416 A75 29c multicolored .80 .45
417 A75 29c multicolored .80 .45
a. Strip of 4, #414-417 3.25 2.00

Voyages of Discovery A76

Designs: No. 418, Traditional tipnol. No. 419, Reconstructed Santa Maria. No. 420, Constellation Argo Navis. No. 421, Marshallese sailor, tipnol. No. 422, Columbus, Santa Maria. No. 423, Astronaunt, Argo Navis. $1, Columbus, sailor, and astronaunt.

1992, May 23 Litho. *Perf. 13½*

Booklet Stamps

418 A76 50c multicolored 1.00 1.00
419 A76 50c multicolored 1.00 1.00
420 A76 50c multicolored 1.00 1.00
421 A76 50c multicolored 1.00 1.00
422 A76 50c multicolored 1.00 1.00
423 A76 50c multicolored 1.00 1.00

Size: 75x32mm

424 A76 $1 multicolored 4.00 2.00
a. Booklet pane of 7, #418-424 10.00 —

Decorative selvage separates No. 424 from Nos. 418-423 and surrounds it like a souvenir sheet margin.

Traditional Handicrafts — A77

1992, Sept. 9 Litho. *Perf. 13½*

425 A77 29c Basket weaving .60 .60
426 A77 29c Canoe models .60 .60
427 A77 29c Wood carving .60 .60
428 A77 29c Fan making .60 .60
a. Strip of 4, #425-428 2.40 2.40

Christmas A78

1992, Oct. 29 Litho. *Perf. 11x10½*

429 A78 29c multicolored .70 .60

Bird Type of 1990

1992, Nov. 10 Litho. *Perf. 13½*

430 A59 9c Whimbrel .20 .20
431 A59 22c Greater scaup .45 .45
432 A59 28c Sharp-tailed sandpiper .55 .55
433 A59 45c Common teal .90 .90
Nos. 430-433 (4) 2.10 2.10

Reef Life — A79

1993, May 26 Litho. *Perf. 13½*

434 A79 50c Butterflyfish 1.40 1.00
435 A79 50c Soldierfish 1.40 1.00
436 A79 50c Damselfish 1.40 1.00
437 A79 50c Filefish 1.40 1.00
438 A79 50c Hawkfish 1.40 1.00
439 A79 50c Surgeonfish 1.40 1.00

Size: 75x33mm

440 A79 $1 Parrotfish 5.50 2.00
a. Booklet pane of 7, #434-440 13.00 —
Nos. 434-440 (7) 13.90 8.00

Decorative selvage separates No. 440 from Nos. 434-439 and surrounds it like a souvenir sheet margin.

Ships A80

Marshallese Sailing Vessels — A81

Designs: 10c, Spanish galleon San Jeronimo. 14c, USCG Fisheries Patrol vessel Cape Corwin. 15c, British merchant ship Britannia. 19c, Island transport Micro Palm. 20c, Dutch ship Eendracht. 23c, Frigate HMS Cornwallis. 24c, U.S. naval schooner Dolphin. 29c, Missionary packet Morning Star. 30c, Russian brig Rurick. 32c, Spanish sailing ship Santa Maria de la Vittoria. 35c, German warship SMS Nautilus. 40c, British brig Nautilus. 45c, Japanese warships Nagara, Isuzu. 46c, Trading schooner Equator. 50c, Aircraft carrier USS Lexington CV-16. 52c, HMS Serpent. 55c, Whaling ship Potomac. 60c, Coast Guard cutter Assateague. 75c, British transport Scarborough. 78c, Whaler Charles W. Morgan. 95c, US steam vessel Tanager. $1, Walap, Eniwetok. $1, Barkentine hospital ship Tole Mour. $2, Walap, Jaluit. $2.90, Marshall Islands fishing vessels. $3, Schooner Victoria. $5, Tipnol, Ailuk. $10, Racing canoes.

Perf. 11x10½ (A80), 13½ (A81)

1993-95 Litho.

441 A80 10c multicolored .20 .20
442 A80 14c multicolored .30 .30
443 A80 15c multicolored .30 .30
444 A80 19c multicolored .40 .40
445 A80 20c multicolored .40 .40
446 A80 23c multicolored .45 .45
447 A80 24c multicolored .50 .50
448 A80 29c multicolored .60 .60
449 A80 30c multicolored .60 .60
450 A80 32c multicolored .65 .65
451 A80 35c multicolored .70 .70
452 A80 40c multicolored .80 .80
453 A80 45c multicolored .90 .90
454 A80 46c multicolored .95 .95
455 A80 50c multicolored 1.00 1.00
456 A80 52c multicolored 1.10 1.10
457 A80 55c multicolored 1.10 1.10
458 A80 60c multicolored 1.25 1.25
459 A80 75c multicolored 1.50 1.50
460 A80 78c multicolored 1.65 1.65
461 A80 95c multicolored 1.90 1.90
462 A80 $1 multicolored 2.00 2.00
463 A81 $1 multicolored 2.00 2.00
464 A81 $2 multicolored 4.00 4.00
465 A80 $2.90 multicolored 5.75 5.75
466 A80 $3 multicolored 6.00 6.00
466A A81 $5 multicolored 10.00 10.00
466B A81 $10 multicolored 20.00 20.00
Nos. 441-466B (28) 67.00 67.00

Souvenir Sheet

Stamp Size: 46x26mm

466C A81 Sheet of 4, #d.-g. 3.75 3.50

No. 466C contains 15c, 23c, 52c and 75c stamps. Inscription reads "Hong Kong '94 Stamp Exhibition" in Chinese on Nos. 466Cd, 466Cg, and in English on Nos. 466Ce-466Cf.

Issued: 15c, 24c, 29c, 50c, 6/24/93; 19c, 23c, 52c, 75c, 10/14/93; #463, 5/29/93; $2, 8/26. 10c, 30c, 35c, $2.90, 4/19/94; $5, 3/15/94; $10, 8/18/94; 20c, 40c, 45c, 55c, 9/23/94; #466C, 2/18/94; 14c, 46c, 95c, #462, 9/25/95; 32c, 60c, 78c, $3, 5/5/95.

See #605.

World War II Type of 1989

1943 — Invasion of Sicily: #467, Gen. George S. Patton, Jr. #468, Gen. Bernard L. Montgomery. #469, Americans landing at at Licata. #470, British landing south of Syracuse.

Allied bomber raids on Schweinfurt: #471, B-17F Flying Fortresses and Bf-109 fighter. #472, Liberation of Smolensk. #473, Landings at Bougainville. #474, Invasion of Tarawa, 1943. #475, Teheran Conference, 1943.

Battle of North Cape: #476, HMS Duke of York. #477, Scharnhorst.

1944 — #478, Gen. Dwight D. Eisenhower, SHAEF Commander. #479, Invasion of Anzio. #480, Siege of Leningrad lifted. #481, U.S. liberates Marshall Islands. #482, Japanese defeated at Truk. #483, Big Week, US bombing of Germany.

1993-94 Litho. *Perf. 13½*

467 A46 52c W60 (4-1) 1.10 1.10
468 A46 52c W60 (4-2) 1.10 1.10
469 A46 52c W60 (4-3) 1.10 1.10
470 A46 52c W60 (4-4) 1.10 1.10
a. Block of 4, #467-470 4.50 4.50
471 A46 50c W61 1.00 1.00
472 A47 29c W62 .60 .60
473 A46 29c W63 .60 .60
474 A46 50c W64 1.00 1.00
475 A47 52c W65 1.10 1.10
476 A46 29c W66 (2-1) .60 .60
477 A46 29c W66 (2-2) .60 .60
a. Pair, #476-477 1.25 1.25
478 A46 29c W67 .60 .60
479 A46 50c W68 1.00 1.00
480 A46 52c W69 1.10 1.10
481 A46 29c W70 .60 .60
482 A47 29c W71 .60 .60
483 A46 52c W72 1.10 1.10
Nos. 467-483 (17) 14.90 14.90

Issued: #467-470, 7/10/93; #471, 8/17/93; #472, 9/25/93; #473, 11/1/93; #474, 11/20/93; #475, 12/1/93; #476-477, 12/26/93; #478, 1/16/94; #479, 1/22/94; #480, 1/27/94; #481, 2/4/94; #482, 2/17/94; #483, 2/20/94.

1994 Litho. *Perf. 13½*

1944 — #484, Lt. Gen. Mark Clark, Rome falls to the Allies.

D-Day-Allied landings in Normandy: #485, Horsa gliders. #486, U.S. P-51B Mustangs, British Hurricanes. #487, German gun defenses. #488, Allied amphibious landing.

#489, V-1 flying bombs strike England. #490, U.S. Marines land on Saipan.

First Battle of the Philippine Sea: #491, Grumman F6F-3 Hellcat.

#492, U.S. liberates Guam. #493, Warsaw uprising. #494, Liberation of Paris. #495, U.S. Marines land on Peliliu. #496, MacArthur returns to the Philippines. #497, Battle of Leyte Gulf.

German battleship Tirpitz sunk: #498, Avro Lancaster. #499, Tirpitz.

Battle of the Bulge: #500, Infantry. #501, Armor. #502, Aviation. #503, Lt. Col. Creighton W. Abrams, Brig. Gen. Anthony C. McAuliffe.

484 A47 50c W73 1.00 1.00
485 A46 75c W74 (4-1) 1.60 1.50
a. Revised inscription 3.25 1.50
486 A46 75c W74 (4-2) 1.60 1.50
a. Revised inscription 3.25 1.50
487 A46 75c W74 (4-3) 1.60 1.50
a. Revised inscription 3.25 1.50
488 A46 75c W74 (4-4) 1.60 1.50
a. Block of 4, #485-488 6.50 6.00
b. Block of 4, #485a-487a, 488 12.00 6.00
489 A46 50c W75 1.00 1.00
490 A46 29c W76 .60 .60
491 A46 50c W77 1.00 1.00
492 A46 29c W78 .60 .60
493 A46 50c W79 1.00 1.00
494 A46 50c W80 1.00 1.00
495 A46 29c W81 .60 .60
496 A46 52c W82 1.00 1.00
497 A46 52c multicolored 1.00 1.00
498 A46 50c W84 (2-1) 1.00 1.00
499 A46 50c W84 (2-2) 1.00 1.00
a. Pair, #498-499 2.00 2.00
500 A47 50c W85 (4-1) 1.00 1.00
501 A47 50c W85 (4-2) 1.00 1.00
502 A47 50c W85 (4-3) 1.00 1.00
503 A47 50c W85 (4-4) 1.00 1.00
a. Block of 4, #500-503 5.00 4.00
Nos. 484-503 (20) 21.20 20.80

Inscription reads "Horsa Gliders, Parachute Troops" on #485a, "British Typhoon-1B, U.S. P51B Mustangs" on #486a, "German Gun Defenses, Pointe du Hoc" on #487a.

Issued: #484, 6/4; #485-488, 6/6; #489, 6/13; #490, 6/15; #491, 6/19; #492, 7/21; #493, 8/1; 494, 8/25; #495, 9/15; #496, 10/20; #497, 10/24; #498-499, 11/12; #500-503, 12/16.

1995 Litho. *Perf. 13½*

1945 — #504, Stalin, Churchill, Roosevelt, Yalta Conference. #505, Meissen porcelain, bombing of Dresden, 1945. #506, Iwo Jima invaded by US Marines.

#507, Remagen Bridge taken by US forces.

#508, Okinawa invaded by US forces. #509, Death of Franklin D. Roosevelt.

#510, US/USSR troops meet at Elbe River. #511, Russian troops capture Berlin. #512, Allies liberate concentration camps.

VE Day: #513, German surrender, Rheims. # 514, Times Square, New York. #515, Victory Parade, Moscow. #516, Buckingham Palace, London.

UN Charter signed: #517, 563, U.S. Pres. Harry S Truman, Veteran's Memorial Hall, San Francisco.

#518, Potsdam Conference Convenes. #519, Churchill resigns. #520, B-29 Enola Gay drops atomic bomb on Hiroshima.

V-J Day: #521, Mt. Fuji, ships in Tokyo Bay. #522, USS Missouri. #523, Adm. Nimitz signs surrender document. #524, Japanese delegation.

504 A47 32c W86 .65 .65
505 A47 55c W87 1.10 1.10
506 A47 $1 W88 2.25 2.00
507 A47 32c W89 .65 .65
508 A47 55c W90 1.10 1.10
509 A46 50c W91 1.00 1.00
510 A46 32c W92 .65 .65
511 A46 60c W93 1.25 1.25
512 A46 55c W94 1.10 1.10
513 A46 75c W95 (4-1) 1.60 1.50
514 A46 75c W95 (4-2) 1.60 1.50
515 A46 75c W95 (4-3) 1.60 1.50
516 A46 75c W95 (4-4) 1.60 1.50
a. Block of 4, #513-516 6.50 6.00
517 A46 32c W96 .65 .65
518 A46 55c W97 1.10 1.10
519 A47 60c W98 1.25 1.25
520 A46 $1 W99 2.25 2.00
521 A46 75c W100 (4-1) 1.75 1.50
522 A46 75c W100 (4-2) 1.75 1.50
523 A46 75c W100 (4-3) 1.75 1.50
524 A46 75c W100 (4-4) 1.75 1.50
a. Block of 4, #521-524 7.25 6.00
Nos. 504-524 (21) 28.40 26.50

Issued: #504, 2/4/95; #505, 2/13/95; #506, 2/19/95; #507, 3/7/95; #508, 4/1/95; #509, 4/12/95; #516a, 5/8/95; #517, 6/26/95; #518, 7/7/95; #519, 7/26/95; #520, 8/6/95; #524a, 9/2/95.

Souvenir Sheets

#562a, like #303. #562b, like #496.

1994-95 *Imperf.*

562	Sheet of 2	2.00 2.00
a.-b.	A46 50c any single	1.00 1.00
563	A46 $1 like #517	2.00 2.00

No. 563 contains one 80x50mm stamp with UN 50th anniv. emblem.
Issued: #562, 10/20/94; #563, 6/26/95.
Nos. 525-561, 564-566 are unassigned.

Dedication of Capitol Building Complex A82

Designs: No. 567, Capitol building. No. 568, Nitijela (parliament) building. No. 569, Natl. seal, vert. No. 570, Flag over complex, vert.

1993, Aug. 11 Litho. ***Perf. 11x10½***

567	A82 29c multi (4-1)	.50 .50
568	A82 29c multi (4-2)	.50 .50
	Perf. 10½x11	
569	A82 29c multi (4-3)	.50 .50
570	A82 29c multi (4-4)	.50 .50
	Nos. 567-570 (4)	2.00 2.00

Souvenir Sheet

Christening of Mobil Super Tanker Eagle — A83

1993, Aug. 25 ***Perf. 13½***

571	A83 50c multicolored	.85 .85

Marshallese Life in 1800's — A84

1993, Sept. 15 Litho. ***Perf. 13½***

572	A84 29c Woman, breadfruit (4-1)	.60 .60
573	A84 29c Canoes, warrior (4-2)	.60 .60
574	A84 29c Young chief (4-3)	.60 .60
575	A84 29c Drummer, dancers (4-4)	.60 .60
a.	Block of 4, #572-575	2.40 2.40

Christmas A85

1993, Oct. 25 Litho. ***Perf. 13½***

576	A85 29c multicolored	.60 .60

Souvenir Sheet

Constitution, 15th Anniv. — A86

1994, May 1 Litho. ***Perf. 13½***

577	A86 $2.90 multicolored	4.50 4.50

Souvenir Sheet

Marshall Islands Postal Service, 10th Anniv. — A87

1994, May 2

578	A87 29c multicolored	.60 .60

1994 World Cup Soccer Championships, U.S. — A88

Design: No. 580, Soccer players, diff.

1994, June 17 Litho. ***Perf. 13½***

579	A88 50c red & multi (2-1)	1.60 1.00
580	A88 50c blue & multi (2-2)	1.60 1.00
a.	Pair, #579-580	3.25 2.00

No. 580a has a continuous design.

Miniature Sheet

Solar System — A89

Mythological characters, symbols: a, Solar system. b, Sun. c, Moon. d, Mercury. e, Venus. f, Earth. g, Mars. h, Jupiter. i, Saturn. j, Uranus. k, Neptune. l, Pluto.

1994, July 20 Litho. ***Perf. 13½***

582	A89 50c Sheet of 12, #a.-l.	12.00 12.00

First Manned Moon Landing, 25th Anniv. — A90

Designs: No. 583, First step onto Moon's surface. No. 584, Planting US flag on Moon. No. 585, Astronaut's salute to America, flag. No. 586, Astronaut stepping onto Moon, John F. Kennedy.

1994, July 20

583	A90 75c multi (4-1)	1.10 1.10
584	A90 75c multi (4-2)	1.10 1.10
585	A90 75c multi (4-3)	1.10 1.10
586	A90 75c multi (4-4)	1.10 1.10
a.	Block of 4, #583-586	4.50 4.50
b.	Souvenir sheet of 4, #583-586	4.50 4.50

Souvenir Sheet

Butterflies A91

1994, Aug. 16 Litho. ***Perf. 13½***

587	A91 Sheet of 3	3.75 3.75
a.	29c Meadow argus	.60 .60
b.	52c Brown awl	1.10 1.10
c.	$1 Great eggfly	2.00 2.00

PHILAKOREA '94.

Christmas — A92

1994, Oct. 28 Litho. ***Perf. 13½***

588	A92 29c multicolored	.60 .60

Souvenir Sheet

New Year 1995 (Year of the Boar) — A93

1995, Jan. 2 Litho. ***Perf. 13½***

589	A93 50c multicolored	1.00 1.00

Marine Life — A94

Designs: a, Meyer's butterflyfish, achilles tang, scuba diver. b, Scuba diver, moorish idols (a, d). c, Pacific green turtle, fairy basslets. d, Fairy basslets, emperor angelfish, orange-fin anemonefish.

1995, Mar. 20 Litho. ***Perf. 13½***

590	A94 55c Block of 4, #a.-d.	4.50 4.50

See Nos. 614, 644.

John F. Kennedy (1917-63), 35th Pres. of US — A95

Designs: a, PT-109. b, Taking presidential oath. c, Peace Corps volunteers. d, US aircraft, naval vessels, Cuban Missile Crisis. e, Signing Nuclear Test Ban Treaty. f, Eternal flame, Arlington Natl. Cemetery.

1995, May 29 Litho. ***Perf. 13½***

591	A95 55c Strip of 6, #a.-f.	5.25 5.25

Marilyn Monroe (1926-1962), Actress — A96

Various portraits with background color: a, red. b, green. c, orange. d, violet.

1995, June 1 Litho. ***Perf. 13½***

592	A96 75c Block of 4, #a.-d.	5.75 5.75

No. 592 was issued in sheets of three blocks.

Cats — A97

Designs: a, Siamese, exotic shorthair. b, American shorthair, Persian. c, Maine coon, Burmese. d, Abyssinian, Himalayan.

1995, July 5 Litho. ***Perf. 13½***

593	A97 32c Block of 4, #a.-d.	2.50 2.50

Mir-Space Shuttle Docking & Apollo-Soyuz Link-Up — A98

a, Space station Mir. b, Space shuttle Atlantis. c, Apollo command module. d, Soyuz spacecraft.

1995, June 29 Litho. ***Perf. 13½***

594	A98 75c Block of 4, #a.-d.	4.75 4.75

Nos. 594 is a continuous design.

Pacific Game Fish — A99

a, Pacific sailfish. b, Albacore. c, Wahoo. d, Pacific blue marlin. e, Yellowfin tuna. f, Giant trevally. g, Dolphin fish. h, Mako shark.

1995, Aug. 21 Litho. *Perf. 13½*
595 A99 60c Block of 8, #a.-h. 11.00 11.00

Island Legends — A100

Designs: a, Inedel's Magic Kite. b, Lijebake Rescues Her Granddaughter. c, Jebro's Mother Invents the Sail. d, Limajnon Escapes to the Moon.

1995, Aug. 25 Litho. *Perf. 13½*
596 A100 32c Block of 4, #a.-d. + 4 labels 2.50 2.50

See Nos. 612, 643.

Miniature Sheet

Singapore '95 World Stamp Exhibition A101

Orchids: a, Paphiopedilum armeniacum. b, Masdevallia veitchiana. c, Cattleya francis. d, Cattleya x guatemalensis.

1995, Sept. 1 Litho. *Perf. 13½*
597 A101 32c Sheet of 4, #a.-d. 2.25 2.25

Souvenir Sheet

Intl. Stamp & Coin Expo, Beijing '95 — A102

1995, Sept. 12
598 A102 50c Suzhou Gardens .85 .85

Christmas A103

1995, Oct. 31 Litho. *Perf. 13½*
599 A103 32c multicolored .55 .55

Miniature Sheet

Jet Fighter Planes — A104

a, Me 262-1a Schwalbe. b, Meteor F.MK8. c, F-80 Shooting Star. d, F-86 Sabre. e, F9F-2 Panther. f, MiG-15. g, F-100 Super Sabre. h, F-102A Delta Dagger. i, F-104 Starfighter. j, MiG-21 MT. k, F8U Crusader. l, F-105 Thunderbird. m, Saab J35 Draken. n, Fiat G91Y. o, F-4 Phantom II. p, Saab JA37 Viggen. q, Mirage F1C. r, F-14 Tomcat. s, F-15 Eagle. t, F-16 Fighting Falcon. u, Tornado F.MK3. v, Sukhoi Su-27UB. w, Mirage 2000C. x, Sea Harrier FRS.MK1. y, F-117 Nighthawk.

1995, Nov. 10
600 A104 32c Sheet of 25, #a.-y. 16.00 16.00

No. 600 was sold in uncut sheets of 6 panes.

See Nos. 617, 641, 666, 708, 728.

Yitzhak Rabin (1922-95), Israeli Prime Minister — A105

1995, Nov. 10 Litho. *Perf. 14*
601 A105 32c multicolored .55 .55

No. 601 was issued in sheets of 8.

Souvenir Sheet

New Year 1996 (Year of the Rat) — A106

1996, Jan. 5 Litho. *Perf. 13½*
602 A106 50c multicolored .85 .85

Native Birds A107

Designs: a, Blue-gray noddy. b, Gray-backed tern. c, Masked booby. d, Black-footed albatross.

1996, Feb. 26 Litho. *Perf. 13½*
603 A107 32c Block of 4, #a.-d. 2.50 2.50

Wild Cats — A108

a, Cheetah. b, Tiger. c, Lion. d, Jaguar.

1996, Mar. 8 Litho. *Perf. 13½*
604 A108 55c Block of 4, #a.-d. 3.75 3.75

Sailing Ship Type of 1993
Miniature Sheet

Designs: a, like #443. b, like #447. c, like #448. d, like #455. e, like #444. f, like #446. g, like #456. h, like #459. i, like #441. j, like #449. k, like #451. l, like #465. m, Malmel outrigger sailing canoe. n, like #445. o, like #452. p, like #453. q, like #457. r, like #450. s, like #458. t, like #460. u, like #466. v, like #442. w, like #454. x, like #459A. y, like #462.

1996, Apr. 18 Litho. *Perf. 11x10½*
605 A80 32c Sheet of 25, #a.-y. 16.00 16.00

Olympic Games, Cent. — A109

First Olympic stamps, Greece: a, #119. b, #124. c, #123. d, #125.

1996, Apr. 27 Litho. *Perf. 12*
606 A109 60c Block of 4, #a.-d. 4.00 4.00

Issued in sheets of 4. A small number were were overprinted in gold in the margin for Olymphilex '96.

Miniature Sheet

History of the Marshall Islands A110

a, Undersea eruptions form island bases. b, Coral reefs grow. c, Storms bring birds & seeds. d, Early human inhabitants arrive. e, Seen by Spanish explorers, 1527. f, Capt. John Marshall, RN, charts islands, 1788. g, Islands become German protectorate, 1885. h, Japan seizes islands, 1914. i, US troops liberate islands, 1944. j, Bikiniatoll evacuated for nuclear testing, 1946. k, Islands become UN Trust Territory, 1947. l, Independence, 1986.

1996, May 2 Litho. *Perf. 13x12*
607 A110 55c Sheet of 12, #a.-l. 10.50 10.50

Elvis Presley's First #1 Hit, "Heartbreak Hotel," 40th Anniv. — A111

1996, May 5 *Perf. 10½x11*
608 A111 32c multicolored .65 .65

Issued in sheets of 20.

Souvenir Sheet

China '96, 9th Asian Intl. Philatelic Exhibition — A112

Design: The Palance Museum, Shenyang.

1996, May 17 *Perf. 13½*
609 A112 50c multicolored 1.00 1.00

James Dean (1931-55), Actor — A113

1996, June 1 Litho. *Perf. 10½x11*
610 A113 32c multicolored .65 .65

No. 610 was issued in sheets of 20.

First Ford Automobile, Cent. — A114

Designs: a, 1896 Quadricycle. b, 1903 Model A Roadster. c, 1909 Model T Touring Car. d, 1929 Model A Station Wagon. e, 1955 Thunderbird. f, 1964 ½ Mustang convertible. g, 1995 Explorer. h, 1996 Taurus.

1996, June 4 Litho. *Perf. 13½*
611 A114 60c Sheet of 8, #a.-h. 6.00 6.00

Island Legends Type of 1995

Designs: a, Kijeek An Letao. b, Mennin Jobwodda. c, Wa Kone, Waan Letao. d, Kouj.

1996, July 19
612 A100 32c Block of 4, #a.-d. + 4 labels 2.25 2.25

Steam Locomotives — A115

Designs: a, Pennsylvania K4, U.S. b, "Big Boy," US. c, Mallard, Great Britain. d, RENFE Class 242, Spain. e, DB Class 01, Germany. f, FS Group 691, Italy. g, "Royal Hudson," Canada. h, Evening Star, Great Britain. i, SAR 520 Class, Australia. j, SNCF 232.U1, France. k, QJ "Advance Forward," China. l, C62 "Swallow," Japan.

1996, Aug. 23 Litho. *Perf. 13½*
613 A115 55c Sheet of 12, #a.-l. 11.00 11.00

Marine Life Type of 1995

Designs: a, like #590a. b, like #590b. c, like #590c. d, like #590d.

1996, Oct. 21 Litho. *Perf. 13½*
614 A94 32c Block of 4, #a.-d. 1.75 1.75

Taipei '96, 10th Asian Intl. Philatelic Exhibition. Nos. 614a-614b have Chinese inscription, Nos. 614c-614d English.

Stick Chart, Canoe and Flag of the Republic Type of 1990

1996, Oct. 21 ***Perf. 11x10½***
615 A63 $3 like No. 381 6.00 6.00

No. 615 inscribed "Free Association United States of America."

Angels from "Madonna and Child with Four Saints," by Rosso Fiorentino A116

1996, Oct. 31 **Litho.** ***Perf. 13½***
616 A116 32c multicolored .55 .55

Christmas.

Legendary Planes Type of 1995

Biplanes: a, JN-3 Jenny. b, SPAD XIII. c, Albatros D.III. d, DH-4 LIberty. e, Fokker Dr.1. f, F-1 Camel. g, Martin MB-2. h, MB-3A Tommy. i, Curtiss TS-1. j, P-1 Hawk. k, Boeing PW-9. l, Douglas 0-2H. m, LB-5 Pirate. n, 02U-1 Corsair. o, F8C Heldiver. p, Boeing F4B-4. q, J6B Gerfalcon. r, Martin BM. s, FF-1 Fifi. t, C.R. 32 Cricket. u, Polikarpov I-15 Gull. v, Mk.1 Swordfish. w, Aichi D1A2. x, Grumman F3F. y, SOC-3 Seagull.

1996, Nov. 1
617 A104 32c Sheet of 25, #a.-y. 16.00 16.00

Native Crafts A117

Designs: a, Fan making. b, Canoe models. c, Carving. d, Basketmaking.

1996, Nov. 7 **Litho.** ***Perf. 11x10½***
618 A117 32c Block of 4, #a.-d. 1.60 1.60

See Nos. 629-630.

Souvenir Sheet

New Year 1997 (Year of the Ox) — A118

1997, Jan. 7 **Litho.** ***Perf. 13x13½***
619 A118 60c multicolored 1.25 1.25

Amata Kabua (1928-96), President of Marshall Islands — A119

1997, Jan. 27 **Litho.** ***Perf. 13½***
620 A119 32c multicolored .65 .65
621 A119 60c multicolored 1.25 1.25

No. 621 has vertical inscriptions in English.

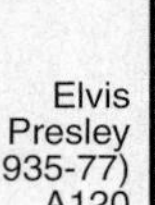

Elvis Presley (1935-77) A120

Designs: a, "Rocking 50's." b, "Soaring 60's." c, "Sensational 70's."

1997, Jan. 8 **Litho.** ***Perf. 13½***
622 A120 32c Strip of 3, #a.-c. 2.00 2.00

Hong Kong '97 — A121

Hong Kong at sunrise, ships: No. 623: a, Walap. b, Junk.

Hong Kong at night, ships: No. 624: a, Canoe. b, Junk, diff.

1997, Feb. 12 ***Perf. 12***

Sheets of 2

623 A121 32c #a.-b. + 3 labels 1.25 1.25
624 A121 32c #a.-b. + 3 labels 1.25 1.25

Christianity in Marshall Islands, 140th Anniv. — A122

Apostles: No. 625: a, Andrew. b, Matthew. c, Philip. d, Simon. e, Thaddeus. f, Thomas. g, Bartholomew. h, John. i, James, the Lesser. j, James, the Greater. k, Paul. l, Peter.

$3, The Last Supper, by Peter Paul Rubens.

1997, Mar. 28 ***Perf. 13½***
625 A122 60c Sheet of 12, #a.-l. 14.50 14.50

Souvenir Sheet

Perf. 13x13½

626 A122 $3 multicolored 6.00 6.00

No. 626 contains one 80x50mm stamp.

First Decade of 20th Century — A123

Designs: a, Family of immigrants. b, Dowager Empress, Boxers, China. c, Photography for every man. d, Dr. Walter Reed, mosquito. e, Sigmund Freud. f, Marconi, wireless transmitter. g, Enrico Caruso, phonograph. h, Wright Brothers, Flyer. i, Einstein. j, HMS Dreadnought. k, San Francisco earthquake, 1906. l, Gandhi, non-violent protestors. m, Picasso. n, Dawn of the automobile age. o, Man, camels, oil derrick amid sand dunes.

1997, Apr. 15 **Litho.** ***Perf. 13½***
627 A123 60c Sheet of 15, #a.-o. 18.00 18.00

See Nos. 646, 654, 657, 679, 702, 711, 723, 726 and 730.

Deng Xiaoping (1904-97), Chinese Leader — A124

1997, Apr. 21
628 A124 60c multicolored 1.25 1.25

Crafts Type of 1996

Designs: Nos. 629a, 630a, Fan making. Nos. 629b, 630b, Canoe models. Nos. 629c, 630c, Wood carving. Nos. 629d, 630d, Basket making.

1997, May 29 **Litho.** ***Perf. 11x10½***

Self-Adhesive

629 A117 32c Block of 4, #a.-d. 2.50 2.50

Serpentine Die Cut Perf. 11

Self-Adhesive

630 A117 32c Strip of 4, #a.-d. 2.50 2.50

No. 629 was issued in sheets of 20 stamps. No. 630 was issued in sheets of 16 stamps. Die cutting does not extend through backing paper on No. 630.

Marshall Islands Stamps, Cent., US Stamps, 150th Anniv. A126

1997, May 29 **Litho.** ***Perf. 13½***

Booklet Stamps

631 A126 50c No. 1 1.00 1.00
632 A126 50c No. 2 1.00 1.00
633 A126 50c No. 3 1.00 1.00
634 A126 50c No. 4 1.00 1.00
635 A126 50c No. 5 1.00 1.00
636 A126 50c No. 6 1.00 1.00
a. Booklet pane, #631-636 6.00

Size: 75x32mm

637 A126 $1 US Nos. 1 & 2 2.00 2.00
a. Booklet pane of 1 2.00
Complete booklet, #636a, #637a 8.00

PACIFIC 97.

Bristle-thighed Curlew — A127

World Wildlife Fund: a, Walking right. b, On tree branch. c, Standing with mouth open. d, In flight.

1997, June 6
638 A127 16c Block or strip of 4, #a.-d. 4.00 4.00

Souvenir Sheet

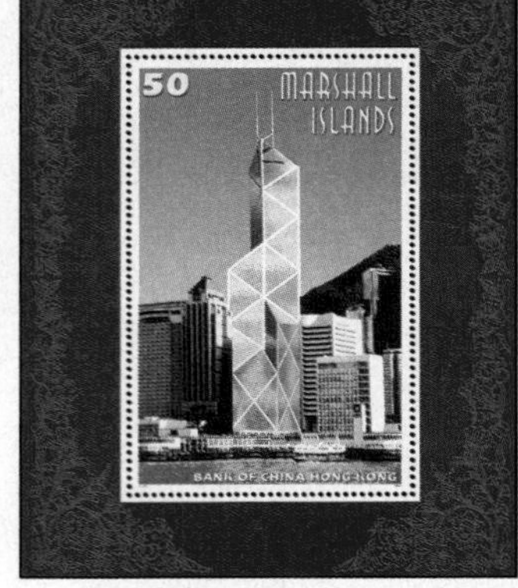

Bank of China, Hong Kong — A128

1997, July 1 **Litho.** ***Perf. 13½***
639 A128 50c multicolored 1.00 1.00

Canoes A129

Designs: a, Pacific Arts Festival canoe, Walap of Enewetak. b, Large Voyaging canoe, Walap of Jaluit. c. Racing canoe. d, Sailing canoe, Tipnol of Ailuk.

1997, July 10 **Litho.** ***Perf. 13½***
640 A129 32c Block or strip of 4, #a.-d. 2.50 2.50

Legendary Aircraft Type of 1995

Designs: a, C-54 Skymaster. b, B-36 Peacemaker. c, F-86 Sabre. d, B-47 Stratojet. e, C-124 Globemaster II. f, C-121 Constellation. g, B-52 Stratofortress. h, F-100 Super Sabre. i, F-104 Starfighter. j, C-130 Hercules. k, F-105 Thunderchief. l, KC-135 Stratotanker. m, B-58 Hustler. n, F-4 Phanton II. o, T-38 Talon. p, C-141 Star Lifter. q, F-111 Aardvark. r, SR-71 "Blackbird." s, C-5 Galaxy. t, A-10 Thunderbolt II. u, F-15 Eagle. v, F-16 Fighting Falcon. w, F-117 Nighthawk. x, B-2 Spirit. y, C-17 Globemaster III.

1997, July 19
641 A104 32c Sheet of 25, #a.-y. 16.00 16.00

USS Constitution, Bicent. — A130

1997, July 21
642 A130 32c multicolored .65 .65

Island Legends Type of 1995

Designs: a, The Large Pool of Mejit. b, The Beautiful Woman of Kwajalein. c, Sharks and Lowakalle Reef. d, The Demon of Adrie.

1997, Aug. 15 **Litho.** ***Perf. 13½***
643 A100 32c Block of 4, #a.-d. +4 labels 2.50 2.50

Marine Life Type of 1995

Designs: a, Watanabe's angelfish, gray reef shark. b, Raccoon butterflyfish. c, Flame angelfish. d, Square-spot fairy basslets.

1997, Aug. 21
644 A94 60c Block of 4, #a.-d. 4.75 4.75

Diana, Princess of Wales (1961-97) A131

Various portraits, background color: a, violet. b, blue. c, yellow orange.

1997, Sept. 30 Litho. *Perf. 13½*
645 A131 60c Strip of 3, #a.-c. 3.75 3.75

No. 645 printed in sheets with two vertical strips flanking three horizontal strips.

Events of the 20th Century Type

1910-19: a, Women mobilize for equal rights. b, Ernest Rutherford, model of atom. c, Sun Yat-sen. d, Sinking of the Titanic. e, Igor Stravinsky, The Rite of Spring. f, Ford begins assembly line production of autos. g, Archduke Franz Ferdinand, wife Sophie. h, German U-boat sinks Lusitania. i, Soldiers in trenches at Battle of Verdun. j, Patrick Pearse proclaims Irish Republic. k, Jews praying at Wailing Wall. l, Cruiser Aurora. m, Baron Manfred von Richtofen. n, German revolutionary troops, 1918. o, Negotiators write Treaty of Versailles.

1997, Oct. 15 Litho. *Perf. 13½*
646 A123 60c Sheet of 15, #a.-o. 18.00 18.00

Christmas A132

Cherubs from Sistine Madonna, by Raphael: No. 647, With hand under chin. No. 648, With arms folded under chin.

1997, Oct. 25

647 A132 32c multicolored	.60	.60
648 A132 32c multicolored	.60	.60
a. Pair, #647-648	1.25	1.25

US State-Named Warships — A133

Designs: a.-z., aa.-ax.: USS Alabama-USS Wyoming in alphabetical order. USS Honolulu shown for Hawaii.

1997, Nov. 1
649 A133 20c Sheet of 50 20.00 20.00

Souvenir Sheet

Shanghai 97, Intl. Stamp and Coin Expo — A134

Treasure ship, Ming Dynasty.

1997, Nov. 19 Litho. *Perf. 13x13½*
650 A134 50c multicolored 1.00 1.00

Souvenir Sheet

New Year 1998 (Year of the Tiger) — A135

1998, Jan. 2 Litho. *Perf. 13x13½*
651 A135 60c multicolored 1.25 1.25

Elvis Presley's 1968 Television Special A136

Scenes from special: a, shown. b, Red background. c, Elvis in white suit.

1998, Jan. 8 *Perf. 13½*
652 A136 32c Strip of 3, #a.-c. 1.75 1.75

Sea Shells A137

a, Chicoreus brunneus. b, Cypraea aurantium. c, Lambis chiragra. d, Tridanca squamosa.

1998, Feb. 13 Litho. *Perf. 13½*
653 A137 32c Strip of 4, #a.-d. 2.50 2.50

Events of the 20th Century Type

1920-29: a, Radio broadcasting reaches the world. b, Quest for peace lurches forward. c, Architects reshape the world. d, Funerary mask of King Tutankhamen. e, USSR emerges as a Communist State. f, Nations emerge from Ottoman Empire, Kemal Ataturk. g, Arrival of the Jazz Age. h, Age of the rocket launched, Robert Goddard. i, Talkies arrive at the movie theater. j, Scourge of Fascism arrives. k, Man's universe expands. l, Penicillin launches antibiotic revolution. m, First glimmers of television. n, Aviation shrinks the world, Graf Zeppelin. o, World suffers economic depression.

1998, Mar. 16 Litho. *Perf. 13½*
654 A123 60c Sheet of 15, #a.-o. 18.00 18.00

Canoes of the Pacific — A138

a, Pahi Sailing canoe, Tuamotu Archipelago. b, Maori war canoe, New Zealand. c, Wa'a Kaukahi fishing canoe, Hawaii. d, Amatasi sailing canoe, Samoa. e, Ndrua sailing canoe, Fiji. f, Tongiaki voyaging canoe, Tonga. g, Tipairua traveling canoe, Tahiti. h, Walap sailing canoe, Marshall Islands.

1998, May 21 Litho. *Perf. 13½*
655 A138 32c Sheet of 8, #a.-h. 5.00 5.00

See Nos. 690-698.

Berlin Airlift, 50th Anniv. — A139

Designs: a, Douglas C-54/R4D-5. b, Avro York. c, Watching the flights of freedom. d, Berliners welcoming supplies.

1998, June 26 Litho. *Perf. 13½*
656 A139 60c Block of 4, #a.-d. 4.75 4.75

Events of the 20th Century Type

1930-39: a, Economic depression engulfs the world. b, Scientists split the atom. c, Stalin's terror reigns in Soviet Union. d, Fascism becomes rampant. e, Engineers harness nature (Dneproges Dam). f, Streamlined design symbolizes bright future. g, Passengers travel airways in comfort. h, Artists protest the scourges of war. i, Media create indelible memories. j, Japanese agression arouses world opinion. k, Era of appeasement. l, Inventions pave way to future. m, Persecution of Jews portends holocaust. n, World War II begins in Europe. o, Movies cheer audiences.

1998, July 15
657 A123 60c Sheet of 15, #a.-o. 17.50 17.50

Czar Nicholas II — A140

#658, Coronation Czar Nicholas II, 1896. #659, Russo-Japanese War and the Cruiser Varyag, 1904-05. #660, Czar's Manifesto, 1905. #661, Peasant sower, Rasputin, 1905. #662, Czar with soldiers at the front, 1915. #663, Ipateva House, Ekaterinburg, 1917. $3, Family portrait.

1998, July 17 *Perf. 13½*

Booklet Stamps

658 A140 60c multicolored	1.25	1.25
659 A140 60c multicolored	1.25	1.25
660 A140 60c multicolored	1.25	1.25
661 A140 60c multicolored	1.25	1.25
662 A140 60c multicolored	1.25	1.25
663 A140 60c multicolored	1.25	1.25

Size: 60x54mm

Perf. 13½ at Top

664 A140 $3 multicolored	6.00	6.00
a. Booklet pane, #658-664	13.50	
Complete booklet, #664a	13.50	

George Herman "Babe" Ruth (1895-1948) A141

1998, Aug. 16 Litho. *Perf. 13½*
665 A141 32c multicolored .65 .65

Legendary Aircraft Type of 1995

US Navy aircraft: a, NC-4. b, PBY-5 Catalina. c, TBD Devastator. d, SB2U Vindicator. e, F4F Wildcat. f, OS2U Kingfisher. g, SBD Dauntless. h, F4U Corsair. i, SB2C Helldiver. j, PV-Ventura. k, TBM Avenger. l, F6F Hellcat. m, PB4Y-2 Privateer. n, A-1J Skyraider. o, F2H Banshee. p, F9F-2B Panther. q, P5M Marlin. r, F-8 Crusader. s, F-4 Phantom II. t, A-6 Intruder. u, P-3 Orion. v, A-7 Corsair II. w, A-4 Skyhawk. x, S-3 Viking. y, F/A-18 Hornet.

1998, Aug. 28
666 A104 32c Sheet of 25, #a.-y. 16.00 16.00

Chevrolet Automobiles — A142

Designs: a, 1912 Classic Six. b, 1931 Sports Roadster. c, 1941 Special Deluxe. d, 1955 Cameo Carrier Fleetside. e, 1957 Corvette. f, 1957 Bel Air. g, 1967 Camaro. h, 1970 Chevelle SS 454.

1998, Sept. 1
667 A142 60c Sheet of 8, #a.-h. 9.50 9.50

Marshallese Language and Alphabet — A143

Letter, example of Marshallese word beginning with letter: a, "A," Amata Kabua, first president. b, "A," Aj, to weave. c, "B," butterfly. d, "D," beautiful lady. e, "E," fish. f, "I," Rainbow. g, "J," mat. h, "K," house of government. i, "L," stars. j, "L," Tropicbird. k, "M," breadfruit. l, "M," Arrowroot plant. m, "N," Coconut tree. n, "N," Ocean wave. o, "N," shark tooth. p, "O," Fish net. q, "O," Tattoo. r, "O," Lionfish. s, "P," Visitor's hut. t, "R," Whale. u, "T," outrigger canoe. v, "U," Fire. w, "U," Dorsal fin of whale. x, "W," Woven sail.

1998, Sept. 14
668 A143 33c Sheet of 24, #a.-x. 16.00 16.00

New Buildings in Marshall Islands — A144

a, Trust Company of the Marshall Islands, 1998. b, Embassy of the People's Republic of China, 1996. c, Outrigger Marshall Islands Resort, 1996.

1998, Oct. 12
669 A144 33c Strip of 3, #a.-c. 2.00 2.00

Christmas A145

1998, Oct. 26
670 A145 32c Midnight angel .65 .65

John Glenn's Return to Space A146

#671, Friendship 7 launch, 1962. #672, Glenn in spacesuit, 1962. #673, Mercury capsule in space, 1962. #674, Shuttle Discovery Launch, 1998. #675, Astronaut and US Senator Glenn, 1998. #676, Shuttle Discovery in space, 1998.
$3, US #1193, astrological drawings.

1998, Oct. 29

Booklet Stamps

671 A146 60c multicolored 1.25 1.25
672 A146 60c multicolored 1.25 1.25
673 A146 60c multicolored 1.25 1.25
674 A146 60c multicolored 1.25 1.25
675 A146 60c multicolored 1.25 1.25
676 A146 60c multicolored 1.25 1.25

Size: 75x32mm

677 A146 $3 multicolored 6.00 6.00
a. Booklet pane, #671-677 13.50
Complete booklet, #677a 13.50

Souvenir Sheet

Antonov An-124 Delivering Drought Relief Supplies — A147

1998, Nov. 3 Litho. *Perf. 13½*
678 A147 $3.20 multicolored 6.50 6.50

Events of the 20th Century Type

1940-49: a, Aviation assumes strategic importance. b, State of war becomes global. c, Missiles announce new age of warfare. d, Music raises spirits. e, Determined peoples fight for survival. f, The Holocaust. g, Mankind faces Atomic Age. h, War's end brings hope. i, Computer age dawns. j, Nations unite for peace. k, World demands justice from war criminals. l, A time for rebuilding. m, Transistor opens door to miniaturization. n, World divided by cold war. o, New China is proclaimed.

1998, Nov. 16 Litho. *Perf. 13½*
679 A123 60c Sheet of 15, #a.-o. 17.50 17.50

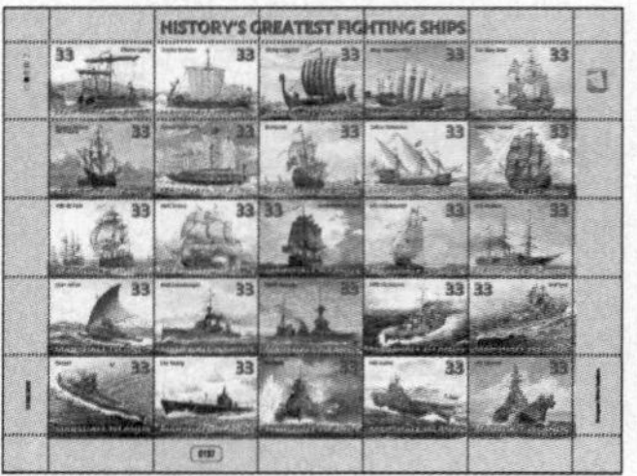

Warships — A148

Designs: a, Trireme Galley. b, Trireme Romano. c, Viking Longship. d, Ming Treasure ship. e, The Mary Rose. f, Nuestra Señora del Rosario. g, Korean Turtle ship. h, Brederode. i, Galera Veneziana. j, Santisima Trinidad. k, Ville de Paris. l, HMS Victory. m, Bonhomme Richard. n, USS Constellation. o, USS Hartford. p, Fijian Ndrua. q, HMS Dreadnought. r, HMAS Australia. s, HMS Dorsetshire. t, Graf Spee. u, Yamato. v, USS Tautog. w, Bismarck. x, USS Hornet. y, USS Missouri.

1998, Dec. 1
680 A148 33c Sheet of 25, #a.-y. 16.00 16.00

Souvenir Sheet

New Year 1999 (Year of the Rabbit) — A149

1999, Jan. 2 Litho. *Perf. 13x13½*
681 A149 60c multicolored 1.25 1.25

Birds — A150

1c, Lesser golden plover. 3c, Siberian tattler. 20c, Brown noddy. 22c, Common fairy tern. 33c, Micronesian pigeon. 55c, Long-tailed cuckoo. $1, Christmas shearwater. $10, Eurasian tree sparrow.

1999, Jan. 9 *Perf. 13½*
682 A150 1c multicolored .20 .20
683 A150 3c multicolored .20 .20
684 A150 20c multicolored .40 .40
685 A150 22c multicolored .45 .45
686 A150 33c multicolored .65 .65
687 A150 55c multicolored 1.10 1.10
688 A150 $1 multicolored 2.00 2.00
689 A150 $10 multicolored 15.00 15.00
Nos. 682-689 (8) 20.00 20.00

See Nos. 714-721.

Canoes of the Pacific Type

Designs: a, like #655a. b, like #655b. c, like #655c. d, like #655f. e, like #655e. f, like #655d. g, like #655g. h, like #655h.

1999, Jan. 25 Litho. *Perf. 13½*
690 A138 33c Sheet of 8, #a.-h. 5.25 5.25

Self-Adhesive

Size: 40x25mm

Perf. 11x10½

691 A138 33c like #690a .65 .65
692 A138 33c like #690b .65 .65
693 A138 33c like #690c .65 .65
694 A138 33c like #690d .65 .65
695 A138 33c like #690e .65 .65
696 A138 33c like #690f .65 .65
697 A138 33c like #690g .65 .65
698 A138 33c like #690h .65 .65
a. Block of 10, #691-697, 3 #698 6.50

Issued in sheets of 20.

Great American Indian Chiefs — A151

Designs: a, Tecumseh. b, Powhatan. c, Hiawatha. d, Dull knife. e, Sequoyah. f, Sitting Bull. g, Cochise. h, Red Cloud. i, Geronimo. j, Chief Joseph. k, Pontiac. l, Crazy Horse.

1999, Feb. 1 *Perf. 13½*
699 A151 60c Sheet of 12, #a.-l. 14.50 14.50

National Flag A152

1999, Feb. 5 *Perf. 14*
700 A152 33c multicolored .65 .65

Flowers of the Pacific A153

Designs: a, Plumeria. b, Vanda. c, Ilima. d, Tiare. e, White ginger. f, Hibiscus.

1999, Feb. 18 *Perf. 13½*
701 A153 33c Block of 6, #a.-f. 4.00 4.00

Events of the 20th Century Type

1950-59: a, World enters age of television. b, Cold war battles erupt. c, Vaccines conquer scourge of polio. d, U.S., USSR engage in arms race. e, Science begins to unravel genetic code. f, Conquests reach unconquered heights. g, Pageantry reassures commonwealth. h, Rock 'n' roll reshapes music beat. i, Suns sets on Colonial Empires. j, World condemns racial discrimination. k, Unrest challenges Communism's march. l, Vision of European Union takes form. m, Space race opens space age. n, Jets shrink time and distance. o, Microchip presages computer revolution.

1999, Mar. 15
702 A123 60c Sheet of 15, #a.-o. 18.00 18.00

Souvenir Sheet

HMAS Australia — A154

1999, Mar. 19
703 A154 $1.20 multicolored 2.50 2.50

Australia '99, World Stamp Expo.

Elvis Presley — A155

1999, Apr. 6 Litho. *Perf. 13½*
704 A155 33c multicolored .65 .65

IBRA '99 World Stamp Exhibition, Nuremberg, Germany A156

Designs: a, #25. b, #24. c, #23. d, #22.

1999, Apr. 27 Litho. *Perf. 13½*
705 A156 60c Sheet of 4, #a.-d. 4.75 4.75

Marshall Islands Constitution, 20th Anniv. — A157

1999, May 1 Litho. *Perf. 13½*
706 A157 33c Constitution Committee .65 .65

Marshall Islands Postal Service, 15th Anniv. — A158

Portions of No. 607 and, clockwise: a, #572, 644, 689, 597d (b). b, #668c, 595c, 655h, 597a. c, #381, 570, 574, 668d. d, #597b, 643b, 621.

1999, May 2
707 A158 33c Block of 4, #a.-d. 2.50 2.50

Legendary Aircraft Type of 1995

a, Martin B-10B. b, Northrop A-17A Nomad. c, Douglas B-18 Bolo. d, Boeing B-17F Flying Fortress. e, Douglas A-20 Havoc. f, North American B-25B Mitchell. g, Consolidated B-24D Liberator. h, North American P-51B Mustang. i, Martin B-26 Marauder. j, Douglas A-26B Invader. k, Bell P-59 Airacomet. l, Boeing KC-97 Stratofreighter. m, Douglas A-1J Skyraider. n, Lockheed P2V-7 Neptune. o, North American B-45 Tornado. p, Boeing B-50 Superfortress. q, North American AJ-2 Savage. r, Grumman F9F Cougar. s, Douglas A-3 Skywarrior. t, Martin B-57E Canberra. u, Douglas EB-66 Destroyer. v, Grumman E-2A Hawkeye. w, Northrop F-5E Tiger II. x, McDonnell Douglas AV-8B Harrier II. y, Rockwell B-1B Lancer.

1999, June 1
708 A104 33c Sheet of 25, #a.-y. 16.00 16.00

Souvenir Sheet

PhilexFrance 99 — A159

1999, July 2 Litho. *Perf. 13½*
709 A159 $1 Astronaut, lunar rover 2.00 2.00

Souvenir Sheet

Tanker Alrehab — A160

1999, July 15 Litho. *Perf. 13x13½*
710 A160 60c multi 1.25 1.25

Events of the 20th Century Type

1960-69: a, Invention of the laser. b, Pill revolutionizes family planning. c, Gagarin becomes the Columbus of the cosmos. d, Communism advertizes failures. e, Planet Earth endangered. f, Superpowers totter on precipice of war. g, Spirit of ecumenism renews Christianity. h, Railways achieve record speeds. i, Cultural Revolution stuns China. j, Arab-Israeli War unsettles Middle East. k, Organ transplants repair human body. l, America engulfed in Vietnam War. m, Political assassinations shock world. n, Supersonic travel becomes a reality. o, Mankind leaps from Earth to Moon.

1999, July 15 *Perf. 13½*

711 A123 60c Sheet of 15, #a.-o. 18.00 18.00

First Manned Moon Landing, 30th Anniv. — A161

Designs: a, Saluting astronaut, Earth. b, Flag. c, Astronaut.

1999, July 20

712 A161 33c Sheet of 3, #a.-c. 2.00 2.00

Ships — A162

Designs: a, Galleon Los Reyes, Spain, 1568. b, Frigate Dolphin, Great Britain, 1767. c, Bark Scarborough, Great Britain, 1788. d, Brig Rurick, Russia, 1817.

1999, Aug. 26

713 A162 33c Block of 4, #a.-d. 2.75 2.75

Bird Type of 1999

Designs: 5c, Black-tailed godwit. 40c, Franklin's gull. 45c, Rufous-necked stint. 75c, Kermadec petrel. $1.20, Purple-capped fruit dove. $2, Mongolian plover. $3.20, Cattle egret. $5, Dunlin.

1999, Sept. 16 **Litho.** *Perf. 13½*

714	A150 5c multi		.20	.20
715	A150 40c multi		.80	.80
716	A150 45c multi		.90	.90
717	A150 75c multi		1.50	1.50
718	A150 $1.20 multi		2.40	2.40
719	A150 $2 multi		4.00	4.00
720	A150 $3.20 multi		6.50	6.50
721	A150 $5 multi		10.00	10.00
	Nos. 714-721 (8)		26.30	26.30

Christmas A163

1999, Oct. 26 **Litho.** *Perf. 13½*

722 A163 33c multi .65 .65

Events of the 20th Century Type

1970-79: a, Jumbo jets enter transatlantic service. b, China advances on world stage. c, Terrorists range the world. d, Space stations orbit earth. e, Oil crisis strangles world. f, China unearths underground army. g, Reign of death devastates Cambodia. h, Superpowers proclaim era of détente. i, America celebrates bicentennial. j, Personal computers reach markets. k, Diagnostic tools revolutionize medicine. l, Automobiles transport millions. m, Prospect of peace in Middle East. n, Compact disc revolutionizes recording. o, Islam's prophets resurgent.

1999, Nov. 15

723 A123 60c Sheet of 15, #a.-o. 18.00 18.00

Millennium — A164

Earth and inscriptions: No. 724, "December 31, 1999." No. 725, "January 1, 2000."

1999, Dec. 31 **Litho.** *Perf. 13½*

724	33c multi	.65	.65
725	33c multi	.65	.65
a.	A164 Pair, #724-725	1.30	1.30

Events of the 20th Century Type

1980-89: a, People unite in freedom's quest. b, Mankind confronts new diseases. c, Royal romance captivates the world. d, Information age begins. e, Armed conflicts upset peace. f, Cell phone revolutionizes communication. g, Every man a movie maker. h, Space exploration makes headlines. i, Disaster alerts public to nuclear risks. j, Perestroika signals change. k, Technology of war advances. l, Terrorism claims innocent victims. m, World's oceans endangered. n, Eys of the world on Tiananmen. o, Events signal "end of history."

2000, Jan. 15

726 A123 60c Sheet of 15, #a.-o. 18.00 18.00

Souvenir Sheet

New Year 2000 (Year of the Dragon) — A165

2000, Jan. 20 *Perf. 13x13½*

727 A165 60c multi 1.25 1.25

Legendary Aircraft Type of 1995

Designs: a, P-26 Peashooter. b, N2S-1 Kaydet. c, P-35A. d, P-36A Hawk. e, P-40B Warhawk. f, P-38 Lightning. g, P-39D Airacobra. h, C-46 Commando. i, P-47D Thunderbolt. j, P-61B Black Widow. k, B-29 Superfortress. l, F7F-3N Tigercat. m, F8F-2 Bearcat. n, F-82, Twin Mustang. o, F-84G Thunderjet. p, FJ-1 Fury. q, C-119C Flying Boxcar. r, F3D-2 Skynight. s, F-89D Scorpion. t, F-94B Starfire. u, F4D Skyray. v, F3H-2 Demon. w, RF-101A/C Voodoo. x, U-2F Dragon Lady. y, OV-10 Bronco.

2000, Feb. 10 *Perf. 13½*

728 A104 33c Sheet of 25, #a.-y. 16.00 16.00

Roses — A166

Rose varieties: a, Masquerade. b, Tuscany Superb. c, Frau Dagmar Hastrup. d, Ivory Fashion. e, Charles De Mills. f, Peace.

2000, Feb. 23

729 A166 33c Block of 6, #a.-f. 4.00 4.00

Events of the 20th Century Type

1990-99: a, Free markets and trade reshape world economy. b, Coalition expels Iraq from Kuwait. c, South Africans freed from apartheid. d, WWW revolutionizes information superhighway. e, Era of Soviet power ends. f, A lasting peace in Middle East is promised. g, Engineering triumphs alter landscape. h, Ethnic conflicts stun world. i, Athletes celebrate peaceful world competition. j, Scientists probe secrets of life. k, Hong Kong and Macao return to China. l, Space exploration captivates millions. m, World mourns global heroines. n, Architecture shows confidence in the future. o, World population soars to new record.

2000, Mar. 15 **Litho.** *Perf. 13½*

730 A123 60c Sheet of 15, #a-o 18.00 18.00

Pandas — A167

a, Adult seated. b, Adult, seated, facing away, & cub. c, Adult holding cub. d, Two adults. e, Adult climbing. f, Adult & cub seated.

2000, Mar. 31 *Perf. 11¾*

731 A167 33c Block of 6, #a-f 4.00 4.00

American Presidents — A168

No. 732: a, 1c, George Washington. b, 2c, John Adams. c, 3c, Thomas Jefferson. d, 4c, James Madison. e, 5c, James Monroe. f, 6c, John Quincy Adams.

No. 733: a, 7c, Andrew Jackson. b, 8c, Martin Van Buren. c, 9c, William Henry Harrison. d, 10c, John Tyler. e, 11c, James K. Polk. f, 12c, Zachary Taylor.

No. 734: a, 13c, Millard Fillmore. b, 14c, Franklin Pierce. c, 15c, James Buchanan. d, 16c, Abraham Lincoln. e, 17c, Andrew Johnson. f, 18c, Ulysses S. Grant.

No. 735: a, 19c, Rutherford B. Hayes. b, 20c, James A. Garfield. c, 21c, Chester A. Arthur. d, 22c, Grover Cleveland. e, 23c, Benjamin Harrison. f, 24c, White House.

No. 736: a, 25c, William McKinley. b, 26c, Theodore Roosevelt. c, 27c, William H. Taft. d, 28c, Woodrow Wilson. e, 29c, Warren G. Harding. f, 30c, Calvin Coolidge.

No. 737: a, 31c, Herbert C. Hoover. b, 32c, Franklin D. Roosevelt. c, 33c, Harry S Truman. d, 34c, Dwight D. Eisenhower. e, 35c, John F. Kennedy. f, 36c, Lyndon B. Johnson.

No. 738: a, 37c, Richard M. Nixon. b, 38c, Gerald R. Ford. c, 39c, James E. Carter. d, 40c, Ronald W. Reagan. e, 41c, George H. W. Bush. f, 42c, William J. Clinton.

Illustration reduced.

2000, Apr. 18 *Perf. 13½*

732	A168 Sheet of 6, #a-f	.45	.45
733	A168 Sheet of 6, #a-f	1.25	1.25
734	A168 Sheet of 6, #a-f	1.90	1.90
735	A168 Sheet of 6, #a-f	2.60	2.60
736	A168 Sheet of 6, #a-f	3.25	3.25
737	A168 Sheet of 6, #a-f	4.00	4.00
738	A168 Sheet of 6, #a-f	4.75	4.75
	Nos. 732-738 (7)	18.20	18.20

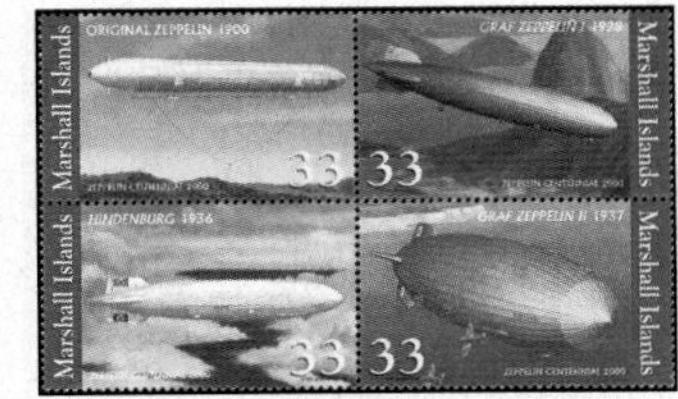

First Zeppelin Flight, Cent. — A169

Designs: a, Original Zeppelin, 1900. b, Graf Zeppelin I, 1928. c, Hindenburg, 1936. d, Graf Zeppelin II, 1937.

2000, May 11 *Perf. 13½*

739 A169 33c Block of 4, #a-d 2.75 2.75

Sir Winston Churchill — A170

#740, War correspondent in South Africa, 1899-1900. #741, Engagement and marriage to Clementine Hozier, 1908. #742, Young statesman, 1900-14. #743, Writer and academic, 1898-1960. #744, First Lord of the Admiralty, 1939-40. #745, Prime Minister, 1940-45. $1, Appointed knight, Nobel Prize for Literature, 1946-65.

2000, June 16 **Litho.** *Perf. 13½*

Booklet Stamps

740	A170 60c multi	1.25	1.25
741	A170 60c multi	1.25	1.25
742	A170 60c multi	1.25	1.25
743	A170 60c multi	1.25	1.25
744	A170 60c multi	1.25	1.25
745	A170 60c multi	1.25	1.25

Size: 87x67mm

Perf. 13½ at Top

746	A170 $1 multi	2.00	2.00
a.	Booklet pane, #740-746	9.50	
	Booklet, #746a	9.50	

US Military, 225th Anniv. A171

No. 747: a, Army. b, Navy, c, Marines.

2000, June 22 *Perf. 13½*

747	Horiz. strip of 3	2.00	2.00
a.-c.	A171 33c Any single	.65	.65

National Government — A172

No. 748: a, National seal. b, Nitijela, horiz. c, National flag. d, Capitol buildijng, horiz.

2000, July 4 Litho. *Perf. 13½*
748 A172 33c Block of 4, #a-d 2.75 2.75

Ships — A173

No. 749: a, Half Moon. b, La Grande Hermine. c, Golden Hind. d, Mathew. e, Victoria. f, Sao Gabriel.

2000, July 20
749 A173 60c Block of 6, #a-f 7.25 7.25

Queen Mother, 100th Birthday — A174

No. 750: a, As child. b, As young wife. c, As Queen. d, As Queen Mother.

2000, Aug. 4
750 A174 60c Block of 4, #a-d 5.00 5.00

Compare with No. 810.

Reef Life A175

No. 751: a, Green sea turtle. b, Blue-girdled angelfish. c, Clown triggerfish. d, Harlequin tuskfish. e, Lined butterflyfish. f, White-bonnet anemonefish. g, Longnose filefish. h, Emperor angelfish.

2000, Aug. 24
751 Sheet of 8 5.50 5.50
a.-h. A175 33c Any single .65 .65

Butterflies — A176

No. 752: a, Holly blue. b, Swallowtail. c, Clouded yellow. d, Small tortoiseshell. e, Nettle tree. f, Long-tailed blue. g, Cranberry blue. h, Small heath. i, Pontic blue. j, Lapland fritillary k, Large blue. l, Monarch.

2000, Sept. 14 *Perf. 11¾*
752 A176 60c Sheet of 12, #a-l 14.50 14.50

See also Nos. 776, 798, 821, 876.

Reunification of Germany, 10th Anniv. — A177

2000, Oct. 3 *Perf. 13½*
753 A177 33c multi .65 .65

Submarines — A178

No. 754: a, USS S-44, 1925. b, USS Gato, 1941. c, USS Wyoming, 1996. d, USS Cheyenne, 1997.

2000, Oct. 12
754 Block of 4 2.75 2.75
a.-d. A178 33c Any single .65 .65

Christmas — A179

2000, Oct. 26 *Perf. 10¼x11¼*
755 A179 33c multi .65 .65

Sun Yat-sen — A180

No. 756: a, As youth in Cuiheng village, 1866. b, As student in Honolulu and Hong Kong, 1879. c, As President of Tong Meng Hui, 1905. d, Revolution, 1911. e, President of the Republic of China, 1912. f, Principles of Democracy. g, Sun Yat-sen Memorial, Nanjing and Great Wall of China (87x62mm).

2000, Nov. 12 Litho. *Perf. 13½*
756 Booklet pane of 7 9.50
a.-f. A180 60c Any single 1.25 1.25
g. A180 $1 multi, perf. 13½ at top 2.00 2.00
Booklet, #756 9.50

Souvenir Sheet

New Year 2001 (Year of the Snake) — A181

2001, Jan. 2 Litho. *Perf. 13x13¾*
757 A181 80c multi 1.60 1.60

Flowers of the Month — A182

2001 *Perf. 11¾*

Stamp + label

758	A182 34c Carnations	.70	.70
759	A182 34c Violets	.70	.70
760	A182 34c Jonquil	.70	.70
761	A182 34c Sweet pea	.70	.70
762	A182 34c Lily of the valley	.70	.70
763	A182 34c Rose	.70	.70
764	A182 34c Larkspur	.70	.70
765	A182 34c Poppy	.70	.70
766	A182 34c Aster	.70	.70
767	A182 34c Marigold	.70	.70
768	A182 34c Chrysanthemum	.70	.70
769	A182 34c Poinsettia	.70	.70
	Nos. 758-769 (12)	8.40	8.40

Issued: No. 758, 1/5; No. 759, 2/1; No. 760, 3/1; No. 761, 4/3; No. 762, 5/1; No. 763, 6/1; No. 764, 7/3; No. 765, 8/1; No. 766, 9/5; No. 767, 10/1; No. 768, 11/1; No. 769, 12/1.

Sailing Canoes A183

Walaps of: $5, Jaluit. $10, Eniwetok.

2001, Jan. 19 Engr. *Perf. 12¼*
770 A183 $5 green 10.00 10.00
771 A183 $10 blue 20.00 20.00

Famous People — A184

Designs: 34c, Pres. Amata Kabua. 55c, Robert Reimers, entrepreneur. 80c, Leonard Hacker, S. J., humanitarian. $1, Dwight Heine, educator.

2001, Jan. 22 Litho. *Perf. 10¼x11¼*

772	A184 34c multi	.70	.70
773	A184 55c multi	1.10	1.10
774	A184 80c multi	1.60	1.60
775	A184 $1 multi	2.00	2.00
	Nos. 772-775 (4)	5.40	5.40

See Nos. 784, 817-819.

Butterflies Type of 2000

No. 776: a, Red admiral. b, Moroccan orange tip. c, Silver-studded blue. d, Marbled white. e, False Apollo. f, Ringlet. g, Map. h, Fenton's wood white. i, Grecian copper. j, Pale Arctic clouded yellow. k, Great banded greyling. l, Cardinal.

2001, Feb. 22 *Perf. 11¾*
776 A176 80c Sheet of 12, #a-l 20.00 20.00

Fairy Tales A185

No. 777: a, Tom Thumb. b, Three Little Pigs. c, Gulliver's Travels. d, Cinderella. e, Gallant John. f, Ugly Duckling. g, Fisher and the Goldfish.

2001, Mar. 22 Litho. *Perf. 13½*
777 Vert. strip of 7 5.00 5.00
a.-g. A185 34c Any single .70 .70

Watercraft Racing — A186

No. 778: a, Canoeing. b, Windsurfing. c, Cruising yachts. d, Sailing dinghy.

2001, Apr. 6
778 A186 34c Block of 4, #a-d 2.75 2.75

Manned Spaceflight, 40th Anniv. A187

No. 779: a, Yuri A. Gagarin. b, Alan B. Shepard, Jr. c, Virgil I. Grissom. d, Gherman S. Titov.

2001, Apr. 12
779 Block of 4 + 4 labels 6.50 6.50
a.-d. A187 80c Any single 1.60 1.60

Stamp Day — A188

2001, May 2
780 A188 34c multi .70 .70
a. Tete-beche pair 1.40 1.40

American Achievements in Space — A189

No. 781: a, First U.S. astronaut in space, 1962. b, First US space walk, 1965. c, First man on the Moon, 1969. d, First space shuttle, 1977.

2001, May 15
781 A189 80c Block of 4, #a-d 6.50 6.50

Marine Life — A190

No. 782: a, Longnose butterflyfish, star puffer, starfish. b, Nautilus. c, Raccoon butterflyfish. d, Porkfish, grouper.

2001, June 7
782 A190 34c Block of 4, #a-d 2.75 2.75

Sports — A191

No. 783: a, Basketball. b, Bowling. c, Table tennis. d, Kayaking.

2001, June 26 ***Perf. 11¾***
783 A191 34c Block of 4, #a-d 2.75 2.75

Famous People Type of 2001

Design: 57c, Atlan Anien, legislator.

2001, July 9 ***Perf. 10¼x11¼***
784 A184 57c multi 1.10 1.10

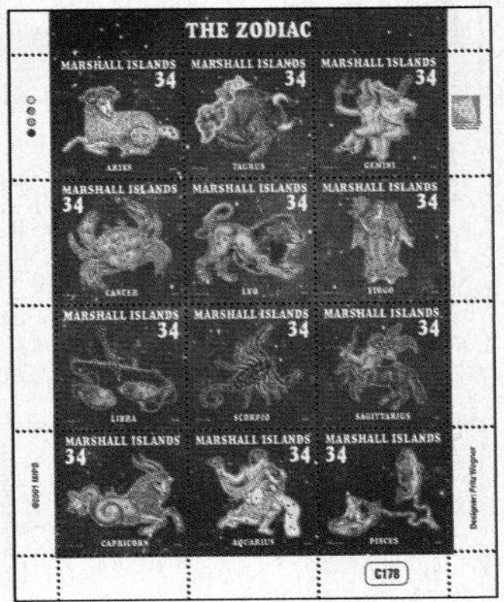

Zodiac Signs — A192

No. 785: a, Aries. b, Taurus. c, Gemini. d, Cancer. e, Leo. f, Virgo. g, Libra. h, Scorpio. i, Sagittarius. j, Capricorn. k, Aquarius. l, Pisces.

2001, July 17 ***Perf. 11¾***
785 A192 34c Sheet of 12, #a-l 8.25 8.25

Phila Nippon '01 — A193

No. 786: a, Black Cat, by Tan Axi. b, Brown Cat, by Tan Axi. c, Cliffs, by Wang Xinhai. d, Boat and Bridge, by Li Yan. e, Rooster, by Wang Xinlan. f, Great Wall, by Liu Zhong. g, Crane, by Wang Lynn. h, Baboon With Basket, by Wang Yani. i, Baboon in Tree, by Wang Yani. j, Umbrella, by Sun Yuan. k, Baboon With Fruit, by Wang Yani. l, Baboon on Ox, by Wang Yani.

2001, Aug. 1 **Litho.** ***Perf. 11¾***
786 A193 80c Sheet of 12, #a-l 20.00 20.00

US Naval Heroes in WWII Pacific Theater — A194

No. 787: a, Adm. Raymond A. Spruance. b, Adm. Arleigh A. Burke. c, Adm. Ernest A. King. d, Adm. Richmond K. Turner. e, Adm. Marc A. Mitscher. f, Adm. Chester W. Nimitz. g, Lt. Edward H. O'Hare. h, Adm. William F. Halsey, Jr. i, The Sullivan Brothers.

2001, Aug. 24 ***Perf. 13½***
787 A194 80c Sheet of 9, #a-i 14.50 14.50

Classic Cars — A195

No. 788: a, 1916 Stutz Bearcat. b, 1909 Stanley Steamer. c, 1934 Citroen 7CV. d, 1910 Rolls-Royce Silver Ghost. e, 1927 Daimler. f, 1935 Hispano-Suiza Type 68V-12. g, 1928 Lancia Lambda V4. h, 1927 Volvo OV4.

2001, Sept. 11
788 A195 34c Block of 8, #a-h 5.50 5.50

See also Nos. 796, 809, 823, 828, 865.

Remembrance of Victims of Sept. 11, 2001 Terrorist Attacks — A196

No. 789: a, U.S. flag, "Blessed are those. . ." b, Statue of Liberty, "United we stand. . ." c, U.S. flag, "An attack on freedom. . ." d, U.S. flag, "In the great struggle. . ." e, Statue of Freedom, "We go forward. . ." f, U.S. flag, "In the face of terrorism. . ." g, American people (75x32mm)

2001, Oct. 11 **Litho.** ***Perf. 13½***

789		Booklet pane of 7	6.25	—
	a.-f.	A196 34c Any single	.70	.70
	g.	A196 $1 multi	2.00	2.00
		Booklet, #789	6.25	

Christmas A197

No. 790: a, Angel on high. b, Adoration of the Magi. c, Nativity scene. d, Adoration of the shepherds.

2001, Oct. 26

790		Vert. strip of 4	2.80	2.80
	a.-d.	A197 34c Any single	.70	.70

Airplanes — A198

No. 791: a, Supermarine Sea Eagle. b, Gloster Sea Gladiator. c, DHC-6 Twin Otter. d, Shorts 330. e, Sandringham Flying Boat. f, De Havilland DHC-7. g, Beech Duke B60. h, Fokker Friendship F27. i, Consolidated B-24J Liberator. j, Vickers 953C Merchantman.

Perf. 11¼x10¼
2001, Nov. 13 **Litho.**
791 A198 80c Block of 10, #a-j 16.00 16.00

Souvenir Sheet

New Year 2002 (Year of the Horse) — A199

2002, Jan. 2 ***Perf. 13x13½***
792 A199 80c multi 1.60 1.60

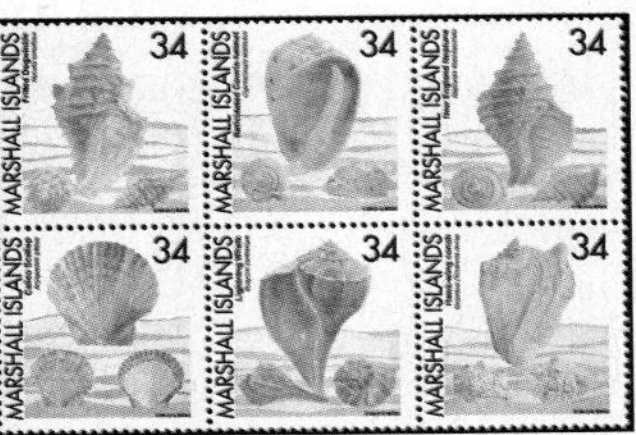

Shells — A200

No. 793: a, Frilled dogwinkle. b, Reticulated cowrie-helmet. c, New England neptune. d, Calico scallop. e, Lightning whelk. f, Hawk-wing conch.

2002, Jan. 22 ***Perf. 11¾***
793 A200 34c Block of 6, #a-f 4.25 4.25

Souvenir Sheet

Reign of Queen Elizabeth II, 50th Anniv. — A201

2002, Feb. 6 **Litho.** ***Perf. 13x13½***
794 A201 80c multi 1.60 1.60

United We Stand — A202

2002, Feb. 11 ***Perf. 13½***
795 A202 34c multi .70 .70

Classic Cars Type of 2001

No. 796: a, 1909 Le Zebre. b, 1886 Hammel. c, 1902 Wolseley. d, 1899 Eysink. e, 1903 Dansk. f, 1907 Spyker. g, 1913 Fiat Model Zero. h, 1902 Weber.

2002, Feb. 26
796 A195 34c Block of 8, #a-h 5.50 5.50

Corals — A203

No. 797: a, Mixed. b, Chalice. c, Elkhorn. d, Finger.

2002, Mar. 13
797 A203 34c Block of 4, #a-d 2.75 2.75

Butterflies Type of 2000

No. 798: a, Grayling. b, Eastern festoon. c, Speckled wood. d, Cranberry fritillary. e, Bath white. f, Meadow brown. g, Two-tailed pasha. h, Scarce swallowtail. i, Dusky grizzled skipper. j, Provençal short-tailed blue. k, Dryal. l, Comma.

2002, Mar. 25 ***Perf. 11¾***
798 A176 80c Sheet of 12, #a-l 20.00 20.00

Horses in Art — A204

No. 799: a, Horses, by Giorgio de Chirico. b, Tartar Envoys Give Horse to Qianlong, by Father Giuseppe Castiglione. c, Gathering Seaweed, by Anton Mauve. d, Mares and Foals, by George Stubbs. e, A Mare and Her Foal in a Spring Meadow, by Wilson Hepple. f, Horse with Child and a Dog, by Natale Attanasio. g, The Horse, by Waterhouse Hawkins. h, Attendants and a Horse, by Edgar Degas. i, Mares and Foals in a Landscape, by Stubbs. j, The Horse, by Guglielmo Ciardi. k, Little Blue Horse, by Franz Marc. l, Sketch for the Set of "Fire Bird," by Pavel Kuznetsov.

80c, Emperor Qianlong Leaving for his Summer Residence, by Castiglione.

2002, Apr. 15 Litho. *Perf. 13½*
799 A204 34c Sheet of 12, #a-l 8.25 8.25

Souvenir Sheet

Perf. 13x13½

800 A204 80c multi 1.60 1.60

No. 800 contains one 80x50mm stamp.

Miniature Sheet

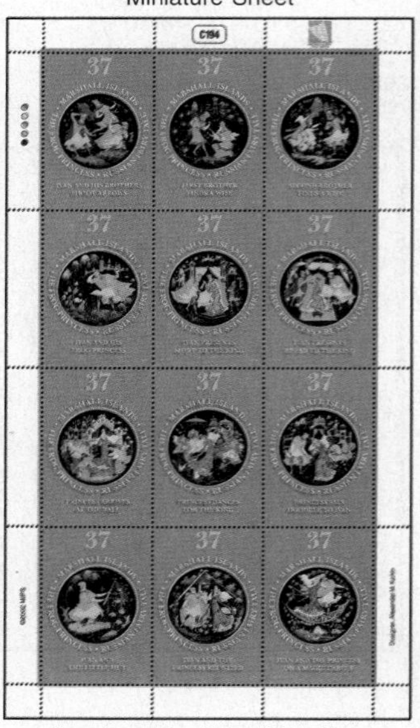

Russian Fairy Tale, "The Frog Princess" — A205

No. 801: a, Ivan and his brothers shoot arrows. b, First brother finds a wife. c, Second brother finds a wife. d, Ivan and his Frog Princess. e, Ivan presents shirt to the king. f, Ivan presents bread to the king. g, Princess arrives at the ball. h, Princess dances for the king. i, Princess says goodbye to ivan. j, Ivan and the little hut. k, Ivan and the Princess reunited. l, Ivan and the Princess on a magic carpet.

2002, Apr. 26 Litho. *Perf. 12½x12¼*
801 A205 37c Sheet of 12, #a-l 9.00 9.00

Carousel Figures — A206

No. 802: a, Armored horse and rabbit. b, Zebra and camel. c, Horse, reindeer and angel. d, Horse, frog and tiger.

2002, May 13 Litho. *Perf. 13½*
802 A206 80c Block of 4, #a-d 6.50 6.50

Birds — A207

No. 803: a, Lesser golden plover. b, Siberian tattler. c, Brown noddy. d, Common fairy tern. e, Micronesian pigeon. f, Long-tailed cuckoo. g, Christmas shearwater. h, Eurasian tree sparrow. i, Black-tailed godwit. j, Franklin's gull. k, Rufous-necked stint. l, Kermadec petrel. m, Purple-capped fruit dove. n, Mongolian plover. o, Cattle egret. p, Dunlin.

2002, May 29
803 A207 37c Sheet of 16, #a-p 12.00 12.00

Benjamin Franklin (1706-90) — A208

No. 804: a, Inventor. b, Scholar.

2002, June 10 Litho. *Perf. 13½*
804 A208 80c Horiz. pair, #a-b 3.25 3.25

Sea Turtles — A209

No. 805: a, Loggerhead. b, Leatherback. c, Hawksbill. d, Green.

2002, June 25
805 A209 37c Block of 4, #a-d 3.00 3.00

Intl. Federation of Stamp Dealers' Associations, 50th Anniv. — A210

No. 806: a, Stamp collector. b, First day of issue. c, Father and daughter collectors. d, Young collector. e, Sharing Dad's stamp collection. f, The new generation.

2002, July 2
806 A210 80c Block of 6, #a-f 9.75 9.75

US Navy Ships — A211

No. 807: a, USS Hartford. b, Bon Homme Richard. c, Prince de Neufchatel. d, USS Ohio. e, USS Onkahye. f, USS Oneida.

2002, July 18
807 A211 37c Block of 6, #a-f 4.50 4.50

See No. 827..

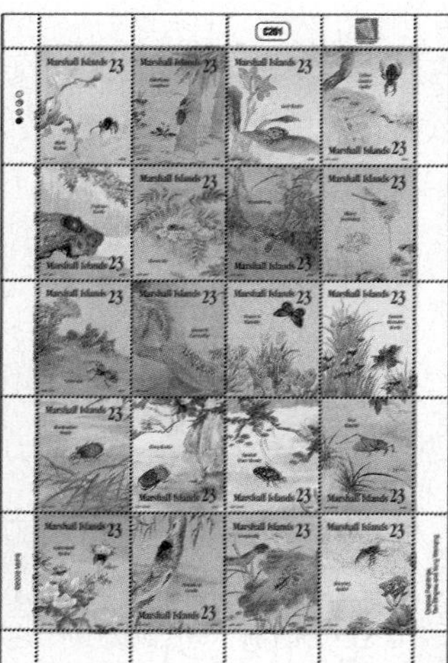

Insects and Spiders — A212

No. 808: a, Black widow spider. b, Elderberry longhorn. c, Ladybug. d, Yellow garden spider. e, Dogbane beetle. f, Flower fly. g, Assassin bug. h, Ebony jewelwing. i, Velvet ant. j, Monarch caterpillar. k, Monarch butterfly. l, Eastern Hercules beetle. m, Bombardier beetle. n, Dung beetle. o, Spotted water beetle. p, True katydid. q, Spiny-back spider. r, Periodical cicada. s, Scorpionfly. t, Jumping spider.

2002, Aug. 2 Litho. *Perf. 13½*
808 A212 23c Sheet of 20, #a-t 9.25 9.25

Classic Cars Type of 2001

No. 809: a, 1934 Hotchkiss. b, 1909 De Dion Bouton. c, 1922 Renault. d, 1927 Amilcar Surbaisse. e, 1943 Austin. f, 1913 Peugeot Bebe. g, 1927 O.M. Type 665 Superba. h, 1922 Elizalde Tipo 20C.

2002, Aug. 15
809 A195 80c Block of 8, #a-h 13.00 13.00

Queen Mother Type of 2000 Redrawn

No. 810: a, As child. b, As young wife. c, As Queen. d, As Queen Mother.

2002, Aug. 30
810 A174 80c Block of 4, #a-d 6.50 6.50

Queen Mother Elizabeth (1900-2002).

Souvenir Sheet

Regal Princess — A213

2002, Sept. 10 *Perf. 13¼x13¾*
811 A213 80c multi 1.60 1.60

World War I Heroes — A214

No. 812: a, Adm. William S. Sims. b, Gen. William E. Mitchell. c, Cpl. Freddie Stowers. d, Maj. Gen. Smedley D. Butler. e, Capt. Edward V. Rickenbacker. f, Sgt. Alvin C. York. g, Maj. Gen. John A. Lejeune. h, Gen. John J. Pershing.

2002, Sept. 23 *Perf. 13½*
812 A214 80c Block of 8, #a-h 13.00 13.00

Christmas — A215

Snowman cookies with denomination in: a, Green. b, Red.

2002, Oct. 26 Litho. *Perf. 13½*
813 A215 37c Horiz. pair, #a-b 1.50 1.50

Souvenir Sheet

New Year 2003 (Year of the Ram) — A216

2003, Jan. 2 Litho. *Perf. 13x13¾*
814 A216 80c multi 1.60 1.60

UN Membership, 12th Anniv. — A217

2003, Jan. 29 *Perf. 11¼x10¼*
815 A217 60c multi 1.25 1.25

Folktales — A218

No. 816: a, Inedel's Magic Kite. b, Lijebake Rescues Her Granddaughter. c, Jebro's Mother Invents the Sail. d, Limajnon Escapes to the Moon.

2003, Jan. 29 *Perf. 13½*
816 A218 50c Block of 4, #a-d, + 4 labels 4.00 4.00

Famous People Type of 2001

Designs: 37c, Oscar deBrum (1929-2002), first Chief Secretary. $3.85, Senator Tipne Philippo (1933-2000). $13.65, Senator Henchi Balos (1946-2000).

Perf. 10¼x11¼
2003, Mar. 25 **Litho.**
817 A184 37c multi .75 .75
818 A184 $3.85 multi 7.75 7.75
819 A184 $13.65 multi 25.00 25.00
Nos. 817-819 (3) 33.50 33.50

The denomination of No. 819 was printed in a thermographic ink that changes color when warmed.

Marshallese Culture — A219

No. 820: a, Lagajimi, c. 1870s, by Franz Hernsheim (21x38mm). b, Old-style house with attic-like roof space (46x38mm). c, Tidal lake on Jabwor (46x38mm). d, Kabua, c. 1870s, by Hernsheim (21x38mm). e, Children in mat dresses (21x38mm). f, Jaluit pass, c. 1870s, by Hernsheim (46x38mm). g, Traditional Canoe c. 1870s, by Hernsheim (46x38mm). h, Man in fishing attire (21x38mm).

2003, Mar. 25 *Perf. 13½*
820 A219 37c Block of 8, #a-h 6.00 6.00

See No. 824.

Butterflies Type of 2000

No. 821: a, False grayling. b, Green hairstreak. c, Purple-shot copper. d, Black-veined white. e, Arctic grayling. f, Greek clouded yellow. g, American painted lady. h, Wall brown. i, Polar fritillary. j, Mountain clouded yellow. k, Camberwell beauty. l, Large white.

2003, May 2 **Litho.** *Perf. 11¾*
821 A176 80c Sheet of 12, #a-l 20.00 20.00

Powered Flight, Cent. — A220

No. 822: a, 1903 Wright Flyer. b, Curtiss JN-3 "Jenny." c, Douglas World Cruiser. d, "Spirit of St. Louis." e, Lockheed Vega. f, Boeing 314 Clipper. g, Douglas C-47 Skytrain. h, Boeing B-50 Superfortress. i, Antonov An-225 Mriya. j, B-2 Spirit.

2003, June 10 *Perf. 13½*
822 A220 37c Block of 10, #a-j 7.50 7.50

Classic Cars Type of 2001

No. 823: a, 1927 Alfa Romeo RLSS. b, 1912 Austro-Daimler Prince Henry. c, 1923 Mors 14/20 HP Tourer. d, 1926 AC Tourer. e, 1903 Scania, 1897 Vabis. f, 1914 Graf und Stift. g, 1919 Pic-Pic. h, 1911 Hispano-Suiza-Alfonso XIII.

2003, July 10 **Litho.** *Perf. 13½*
823 A195 37c Block of 8, #a-h 6.00 6.00

Marshallese Culture Type of 2003

No. 824: a, Kabua's Daughter on Pandanus, c. 1906, by Augustin Krämer (21x38mm). b, Traditional walap (46x38mm). c, Jabwor, Jaluit Atoll (46x38mm). d, Traditional and Modern Dress, by Augustin Erdland (21x38mm). e, Nemedj, c. 1905, by Krämer (21x38mm). f, Typhoon of 1905, by Josef Schmidlin (46x38mm). g, Marshallese Kor Kor, c. 1905, by Richard Deeken (46x38mm). h, Marshallese Grandfather, by Erdland (21x38mm).

2003, Aug. 7 *Perf. 13½x13¼*
824 A219 37c Block of 8, #a-h 6.00 6.00

Christmas Ornaments — A221

No. 825: a, Snowman. b, Jack-in-the-box. c, Toy soldier. d, Reindeer.

2003, Oct. 24 *Perf. 13½*
825 A221 37c Block of 4, #a-d 3.00 3.00

Souvenir Sheet

New Year 2004 (Year of the Monkey) — A222

2004, Jan. 4 **Litho.** *Perf. 13x13¾*
826 A222 $1 multi 2.00 2.00

Ship Type of 2002

No. 827: a, Bonhomme Richard. b, HMS Resolution, denomination at UR. c, HMS Resolution, denomination at UL.

2004, Feb. 14 *Perf. 13½*
827 A211 37c Horiz. strip of 3, #a-c 2.25 2.25

Classic Cars Type of 2001

No. 828: a, 1906 Wolseley-Siddeley. b, 1901 Mors. c, 1908 Hutton. d, 1907 Metallurgique. e, 1902 Benz. f, 1900 Cudell. g, 1906 Peugeot. h, Mercedes 60.

2004, Mar. 15 *Perf. 13½*
828 A195 37c Block of 8, #a-h 6.00 6.00

Greetings — A223

No. 829: a, Thank you! b, Congratulations. c, Happy birthday. d, Best wishes. e, Get well soon. f, Loye you, Dad. g, Love you, Mom. h, Best wishes, Get well soon, Love you, Mom, Congratulations, Love you, Dad, Happy birthday, Thank you.

2004, Apr. 15 **Litho.** *Perf. 13½*
829 A223 37c Sheet of 8, #a-h 6.00 6.00

Marshall Islands Postal Service, 20th Anniv. — A224

Messenger and canoe with background colors of: 37c, Prussian blue. 60c, Brown. $2.30, Purple.

2004, May 2
830-832 A224 Set of 3 6.75 6.75

No. 832 printed in sheets of 8 stamps + 8 adjacent certified mail etiquettes. Value is for set with No. 832 with attached etiquette.

Lewis and Clark Expedition, Bicent. — A225

No. 833 — Inscriptions: a, The saga begins. b, Westward bound. c, Endless bison.

2004, May 14
833 Horiz. strip of 3 2.25 2.25
a.-c. A225 37c Any single .75 .75

See Nos. 840, 845, 855, 867, 871, 885.

D-Day, 60th Anniv. — A226

No. 834: a, Horsa gliders and parachute troops. b, British Typhoon 1B and US P-51B Mustangs. c, German defenses and Pointe du Hoc. d, Allied amphibious landing.

2004, June 6 **Litho.** *Perf. 13½*
834 A226 37c Block of 4, #a-d 3.00 3.00

Marine Life — A227

No. 835: a, Chambered nautilus, map cowrie, fish, coral, trumpet triton (2-1). b, Marlin spike, fish, coral, turban shell, Toulerei's cowrie (2-2).

2004, July 1
835 A227 37c Horiz. pair, #a-b 1.50 1.50

Pres. Ronald Reagan (1911-2004) A228

2004, July 4
836 A228 60c multi 1.25 1.25

First Manned Moon Landing, 35th Anniv. — A229

No. 837: a, Astronaut floating in space (4-1). b, Astronaut in space (4-2). c, Astronaut floating in orbit (4-3). d, Astronaut and Jupiter (4-4).

2004, July 20
837 A229 37c Block of 4, #a-d 3.00 3.00

Festival of Arts — A230

No. 838: a, Woman showing fan making. b, Woman making baskets. c, Men carving. d,

Children making canoe models. e, White ginger. f, Vanda. g, Tiare. h, Hibiscus. i, Breadfruit. j, Tattooed warrior. k, Young chiefs. l, Drummers and dancers.

2004, July 22
838 A230 37c Sheet of 12, #a-l 9.00 9.00

Aircraft — A231

No. 839: a, 1903 Wright Flyer. b, Blériot XI. c, Curtiss Golden Flyer. d, Curtiss Flying Boat. e, Deperdussin Racer. f, Sikorsky Il'ya Muromets. g, Fokker E1. h, Junkers J1. i, S.E. 5A. j, Handley Page O/400. k, Fokker D VII. l, Junkers F13. m, Lockheed Vega. n, M-130 Pan Am Clipper. o, Messerschmitt BF 109. p, Spitfire. q, Junkers Ju-88. r, A6M Zero. s, Ilyushin Il-2. t, Heinkel He-178. u, C-47 Skytrain. v, Piper Cub. w, Avro Lancaster. x, B-17F Flying Fortress. y, Messerschmitt Me-262. z, B-29 Superfortress. aa, P-51 Mustang. ab, Yak-9. ac, Bell Model 47 helicopter. ad, Bell X-1. ae, Beechcraft Bonanza. af, AN-225 Mriya. ag, B-47 Stratojet. ah, MiG-15. ai, Saab J35 Draken. aj, B-52 Stratofortress. ak, Boeing 367-80. al, U-2. am, C-130 Hercules. an, F-4 Phantom II. ao, North American X-15. ap, Sikorsky S-61 (HH-3E). aq, Learjet 23. ar, SR-71 Blackbird. as, Boeing 747. at, Concorde. au, Airbus A300. av, MiG-29. aw, F-117A Nighthawk. ax, F/A-22 Raptor.

Perf. 10¼x11¼

2004, Aug. 12 **Litho.**
839 Sheet of 50 23.00 23.00
a.-ax. A231 23c Any single .45 .45

Lewis and Clark Type of 2004

No. 840 — Inscriptions: a, First Fourth of July. b, Death of Sgt. Charles Floyd. c, Setting the prairie on fire.

2004, Aug. 24 *Perf. 13½*
840 Horiz. strip of 3 2.25 2.25
a.-c. A225 37c Any single .75 .75

John Wayne (1907-79), Actor — A232

2004, Sept. 9 *Perf. 10¼x11¼*
841 A232 37c multi .75 .75

Miniature Sheet

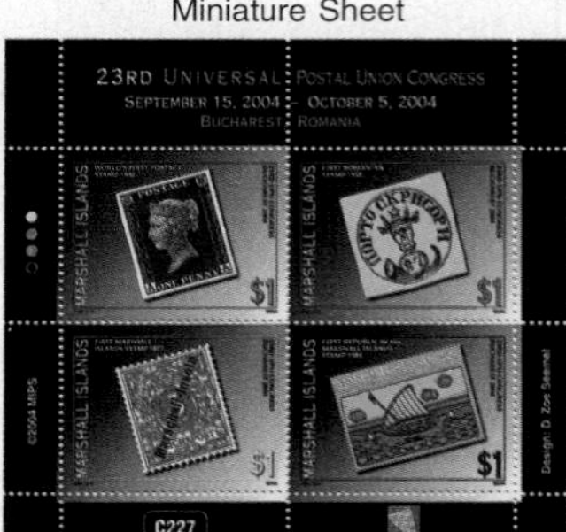
23rd UPU Congress, Bucharest, Romania — A233

No. 842: a, Great Britain #1. b, Romania #1. c, Marshall Islands #1. d, Marshall Islands #31.

2004, Sept. 15 **Litho.** *Perf. 13½*
842 A233 $1 Sheet of 4, #a-d 8.00 8.00

Miniature Sheet

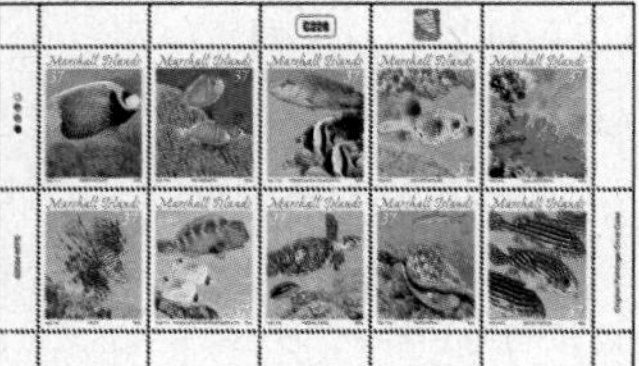
Marine Life — A234

No. 843: a, Emperor angelfish. b, Pink anemonefish. c, Humphead wrasse, Moorish idol. d, Black-spotted puffer. e, Snowflake moray eel. f, Lionfish. g, Bumphead parrotfish, threadfin butterflyfish. h, Hawksbill turtle. i, Triton's trumpet. j, Oriental sweetlips.

2004, Oct. 1
843 A234 37c Sheet of 10, #a-j 7.50 7.50

Miniature Sheet

Christmas — A235

No. 844: a, Angel with bells. b, God Almighty. c, Appears the Star of Bethlehem. d, Three Wise Men. e, Procession of the poor people. f, Pastors with sheep. g, Flight to Egypt. h, Holy Family. i, Animals adoring Jesus.

2004, Oct. 27
844 A235 37c Sheet of 9, #a-i 6.75 6.75

Lewis and Clark Type of 2004

No. 845 — Inscriptions: a, The interpreters. b, Sacred bison calling. c, Teton Sioux rob men.

2004, Nov. 22
845 Horiz. strip of 3 2.25 2.25
a.-c. A225 37c Any single .75 .75

Battle of the Bulge, 60th Anniv. — A236

No. 846: a, Infantry. b, Armor. c, Aviation. d, Lt. Col. Creighton Abrams and Brig. Gen. Anthony McAuliffe.

2004, Dec. 1
846 A236 37c Block of 4, #a-d 3.00 3.00

United States Presidents — A237

No. 847: a, 1c, George Washington. b, 2c, John Adams. c, 3c, Thomas Jefferson. d, 4c, James Madison. e, 5c, James Monroe. f, 6c, John Quincy Adams. g, 7c, Andrew Jackson. h, 8c, Martin Van Buren. i, 9c, William Henry Harrison. j, 10c, John Tyler. k, 11c, James K. Polk. l, 12c, Zachary Taylor. m, 13c, Millard Fillmore. n, 14c, Franklin Pierce. o, 15c, James Buchanan. p, 16c, Abraham Lincoln. q, 17c, Andrew Johnson. r, 18c, Ulysses S. Grant. s, 19c, Rutherford B. Hayes. t, 20c, James A. Garfield. u, 21c, Chester A. Arthur. v, 22c, Grover Cleveland. w, 23c, Benjamin Harrison. x, 24c, Grover Cleveland. y, 25c, William McKinley. z, 26c, Theodore Roosevelt. aa, 27c, William Howard Taft. ab, 28c, Woodrow Wilson. ac, 29c, Warren G. Harding. ad, 30c, Calvin Coolidge. ae, 31c, Herbert Hoover. af, 32c, Franklin D. Roosevelt. ag, 33c, Harry S Truman. ah, 34c, Dwight D. Eisenhower. ai, 35c, John F. Kennedy. aj, 36c, Lyndon B. Johnson. ak, 37c, Richard M. Nixon. al, 38c, Gerald R. Ford. am, 39c, Jimmy Carter. an, 40c, Ronald W. Reagan. ao, 41c, George H. W. Bush. ap, 42c, William J. Clinton. aq, 43c, George W. Bush. ar, 60c, White House. as, $1, White House.

2005, Jan. 20 **Litho.** *Perf. 13½*
847 A237 Sheet of 45, #a-as 31.00 31.00

No. 847 sold for $15.49.

Souvenir Sheet

New Year 2005 (Year of the Rooster) — A238

2005, Feb. 9 **Litho.** *Perf. 13x13½*
848 A238 $1 multi 2.00 2.00

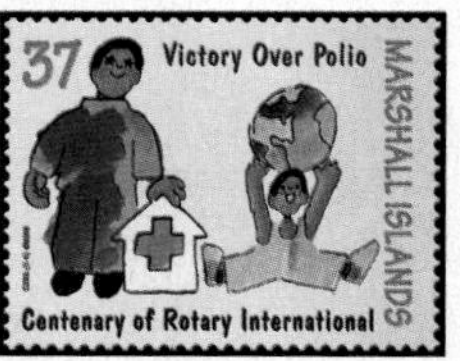

Rotary International, Cent. — A239

2005, Feb. 23 *Perf. 13½*
849 A239 37c multi .75 .75

Hibiscus Varieties — A240

Designs: 37c, Burgundy Blush. 60c, Fiesta. 80c, June's Joy. $1, Norman Lee.

Perf. 10¼x11¼

2005, Mar. 15 **Litho.**
850 A240 37c multi .75 .75
851 A240 60c multi 1.25 1.25
852 A240 80c multi 1.60 1.60
853 A240 $1 multi 2.00 2.00
Nos. 850-853 (4) 5.60 5.60

See Nos. 860-863, 878-881.

Hans Christian Andersen (1805-75), Author — A241

No. 854: a, The Princess and the Pea. b, Thumbelina. c, The Little Mermaid. d, The Emperor's New Suit.

2005, Apr. 2 *Perf. 13½*
854 A241 37c Block of 4, #a-d 3.00 3.00

Lewis and Clark Type of 2004

No. 855 — Inscriptions: a, First grizzly confrontation. b, Lewis reaching the Great Falls. c, Sacajawea and her brother reunite.

2005, Apr. 29
855 Horiz. strip of 3 2.25 2.25
a.-c. A225 37c Any single .75 .75

American First Day Cover Society, 50th Anniv. — A242

No. 856: a, George W. Linn first day cover for US No. 610 (Harding Memorial stamp). b, First day cover for Marshall Islands Nos. 31-34. c, First day cover of US No. C76 with Moon Landing cancel. d, First day cover for Marshall Islands No. 856.

2005, May 2
856 A242 37c Block of 4, #a-d 3.00 3.00

V-E Day, 60th Anniv. — A243

No. 857: a, German surrender, Reims, France. b, Times Square, New York. c, Victory parade, Moscow. d, Royal family and Winston Churchill, Buckingham Palace, London.

2005, May 9
857 A243 37c Block of 4, #a-d 3.00 3.00

Pope John Paul II (1920-2005) — A244

No. 858: a, Wearing red cape, with arm raised. b, Wearing green vestments. c, Close-up. d, Holding crucifix, wearing red vestments. e, Wearing miter.

2005, May 18 Litho. *Perf. 13½*

858 Vert. strip of 5 3.75 3.75
a.-e. A244 37c Any single .75 .75

United Nations, 60th Anniv. — A245

2005, June 26

859 Horiz. pair 2.40 2.40
a. A245 37c Six people .75 .75
b. A245 80c Seven people 1.60 1.60

Hibiscus Varieties Type of 2005

Designs: 1c, Margaret Okano. 24c, Cameo Queen. 39c, Madonna. $4, Estrella Red.

2005, July 13 *Perf. 10¼x11¼*

860 A240 1c multi .20 .20
861 A240 24c multi .50 .50
862 A240 39c multi .80 .80
863 A240 $4 multi 8.00 8.00
Nos. 860-863 (4) 9.50 9.50

Space Shuttles A246

No. 864: a, Columbia. b, Discovery. c, Endeavour. d, Challenger. e, Atlantis.

2005, July 26 *Perf. 13½*

864 Horiz. strip of 5 3.75 3.75
a.-e. A246 37c Any single .75 .75

Classic Cars Type of 2001

No. 865: a, 1925 Excelsior (8-1). b, 1912 Adler K (8-2). c, 1920 Thulin (8-3). d, 1913 Palladium (8-4). e, 1926 Minerva (8-5). f, 1922 Elizalde (8-6). g, 1911 Rolls-Royce Silver Ghost (8-7). h, 1931 Invicta (8-8).

2005, Aug. 4

865 Block of 8 6.00 6.00
a.-h. A195 37c Any single .75 .75

No. 865b is incorrectly inscribed "1926 Minerva."

V-J Day, 60th Anniv. — A247

No. 866: a, Fujiyama and Tokyo Bay. b, USS Missouri. c, US contingent. d, Japanese delegation.

2005, Sept. 2

866 A247 37c Block of 4, #a-d 3.00 3.00

Lewis & Clark Type of 2004

No. 867 — Inscriptions: a, Crossing the Bitterroots. b, Peace agreement. c, Ocean in view.

2005, Sept. 22

867 Horiz. strip of 3 2.25 2.25
a.-c. A225 37c Any single .75 .75

Battle of Trafalgar, Bicent. — A248

No. 868 — Fighting ships: a, Trireme galley. b, Trireme Romano. c, Viking longship. d, Ming treasure ship. e, Mary Rose. f, Nuestra Senora del Rosario. g, Korean turtle ship. h, Brederode. i, Galera Veneziana. j, Santisima Trinidad. k, Ville de Paris. l, HMS Victory. m, Bonhomme Richard. n, USS Constellation. o, USS Hartford. p, Fijian ndrua. q, HMS Dreadnought. r, HMAS Australia. s, HMS Dorsetshire. t, Admiral Graf Spee. u, Yamato. v, USS Tautog. w, Bismarck. x, USS Hornet. y, USS Missouri.

$2, HMS Victory, diff.

Illustration reduced.

2005, Oct. 21 Litho. *Perf. 13½*

868 A248 37c Sheet of 25, #a-y 18.50 18.50

Souvenir Sheet

Imperf

869 A248 $2 multi 4.00 4.00

No. 868 contains twenty-five 40x31mm stamps.

Christmas — A249

No. 870 — Angels with: a, Lute. b, Harp, horn and lute. c, Horn. d, Harp.

2005, Nov. 1 *Perf. 13½*

870 A249 37c Block of 4, #a-d 3.00 3.00

Lewis & Clark Type of 2004

No. 871 — Inscriptions: a, First vote allowed to all. b, Leaving Fort Clatsop. c, At Pompey's Pillar.

2005, Nov. 24

871 Horiz. strip of 3 2.25 2.25
a.-c. A225 37c Any single .75 .75

Marshallese Culture — A250

No. 872 — Photographs: a, First Catholic Church on Jabwor, Jaluit Atoll, by Josef Schmidlin. b, Women on Jaluit Atoll, by Richard Deeken. c, Canoes in Jaluit Harbor, by Deeken. d, Nelu and His Wife Ledagoba, by Augustin Kramer. e, An Old Man from Ebon Atoll, by Augustin Erdland.

2005, Dec. 1

872 Horiz. strip of 5 3.75 3.75
a.-e. A250 37c Any single .75 .75

See also Nos. 886, 901, 929, 950.

Miniature Sheet

Benjamin Franklin (1706-90), Statesman — A251

No. 873 — Franklin: a, Painting by J. S. Duplessis. b, Painting by David K. Stone. c, Painting by Mason Chamberlain. d, Painting by John Trumbull. e, Sculpture, by James Earle Fraser. f, Painting by David Martin. g, Painting by Benjamin West. h, Painting by J. B. Greuze. i, Painting by C. N. Cochin.

2006, Jan. 17 *Perf. 13½*

873 A251 48c Sheet of 9, #a-i 8.75 8.75

Souvenir Sheet

New Year 2006 (Year of the Dog) — A252

2006, Jan. 27 *Perf. 13¼x13½*

874 A252 $1 multi 2.00 2.00

Love — A253

2006, Feb. 14 Litho. *Perf. 13½*

875 A253 39c multi .80 .80

Butterflies Type of 2000

No. 876: a, Peacock. b, Southern comma. c, Pale clouded yellow. d, Common blue. e, Wood white. f, Baltic grayling. g, Purple emperor. h, Silky ringlet. i, Peak white. j, Idas blue. k, Cleopatra. l, Chequered skipper.

2006, Mar. 20 *Perf. 11¾*

876 A176 84c Sheet of 12, #a-l 21.00 21.00

First Spaceflight by Yuri Gagarin, 45th Anniv. — A254

2006, Apr. 12 Litho. *Perf. 11¾*

877 A254 39c multi .80 .80

Hibiscus Varieties Type of 2005

Designs: 10c, Butterscotch Sundae. 63c, Magic Moments. 84c, Joanne Boulin. $4.05, Capsicum Red.

2006, May 2 *Perf. 10¼x11¼*

878 A240 10c multi .20 .20
879 A240 63c multi 1.25 1.25
880 A240 84c multi 1.75 1.75
881 A240 $4.05 multi 8.25 8.25
Nos. 878-881 (4) 11.45 11.45

Miniature Sheet

Washington 2006 World Philatelic Exhibition — A255

No. 882 — Designs of the United States 1922-25 definitive issue inscribed "Marshall Islands Postage": a, ½c, Nathan Hale. b, 1c, Benjamin Franklin. c, 1½c, Warren G. Harding. d, 2c, George Washington. e, 3c, Abraham Lincoln. f, 4c, Martha Washington. g, 5c, Theodore Roosevelt. h, 6c, James A. Garfield. i, 7c, William McKinley. j, 8c, Ulysses S. Grant. k, 9c, Thomas Jefferson. l, 10c, James Monroe. m, 11c, Rutherford B. Hayes. n, 12c, Grover Cleveland. o, 14c, American Indian chief. p, 15c, Statue of Liberty. q, 20c, Golden Gate, horiz. r, 25c, Niagara Falls, horiz. s, 30c, Buffalo, horiz. t, 50c, Arlington Amphitheater, horiz.

2006, May 27 Litho. *Perf. 13½*

882 A255 Sheet of 20, #a-t 4.75 4.75
u. Souvenir sheet, #882o, 882s, imperf. .90 .90

Sharks — A256

No. 883: a, Gray reef shark. b, Silvertip shark. c, Blacktip reef shark. d, Whitetip reef shark.

2006, June 16 *Perf. 13½*

883 A256 39c Block of 4, #a-d 3.25 3.25

Miniature Sheet

Operations Crossroads, 60th Anniv. — A257

No. 884: a, Evacuation of Bikinians. b, Navy preparations. c, "Able" bomb blast. d, "Baker" bomb blast. e, Ghost fleet. f, Effects on the Bikinians.

2006, July 1 **Litho.** ***Perf. 13½***
884 A257 39c Sheet of 6, #a-f, + 6 labels 4.75 4.75

Lewis and Clark Type of 2004

No. 885 — Inscriptions: a, Leaving Sacagawea and Charbonneau. b, Return to St. Louis.

2006, Aug. 24
885 Horiz. pair 1.60 1.60
a.-b. A225 39c Either single .80 .80

Marshallese Culture Type of 2005

No. 886 — Photographs: a, Harbor Front of Jabwor, Jaluit Atoll, by L. Sander. b, Irooj with Family, Jabwor, Jaluit Atoll, by Richard Deeken. c, Traditional Voyaging Canoe at Jaluit Atoll, by Sander. d, Mission Sisters and Girls Doing Laundry, Jaluit, by Hildegard von Bunsen. e, Traditional House on Mile Atoll, by Hans Seidel.

2006, Sept. 22 **Litho.** ***Perf. 13½***
886 Horiz. strip of 5 4.00 4.00
a.-e. A250 39c Any single .80 .80

Ships in the Marshallese Maritime and Corporate Registry — A258

No. 887: a, Cape Norviega. b, Front Century. c, Ashley. d, TI Africa. e, Discoverer Enterprise. f, Genmar Spyridon. g, Rickmers New Orleans. h, LNG Aquarius. i, Centurion. j, Barkald.

2006, Oct. 9
887 A258 39c Sheet of 10, #a-j 8.00 8.00

Christmas — A259

2006, Nov. 1
888 A259 39c multi .80 .80

Greetings — A260

No. 889: a, "Happy Birthday." b, "Congratulations." c, "Thank You." d, "Best Wishes."

2007, Jan. 16 ***Perf. 11¾***
889 A260 39c Block of 4, #a-d 3.25 3.25

Souvenir Sheet

New Year 2007 (Year of the Pig) — A261

2007, Feb. 19 **Litho.** ***Perf. 13x13½***
890 A261 $1 multi 2.00 2.00

Trains — A262

No. 891: a, Art Deco train. b, Pennsylvania. c, Santa Fe Chief. d, Hiawatha. e, 20th Century Limited. f, Daylight.

2007, Mar. 26 ***Perf. 13½***
891 A262 39c Block of 6, #a-f 4.75 4.75

Dolphins — A263

No. 892: a, Spotter dolphins. b, Bottlenose dolphins. c, Risso's dolphin. d, Common dolphin.

2007, Apr. 9
892 A263 39c Block of 4, #a-d 3.25 3.25

Fish A264

Designs: 26c, Achilles tang. 41c, Regal angelfish. 52c, Saddled butterflyfish. 61c, Tinker's butterflyfish.

Perf. 10¼x11¼

2007, June 12 **Litho.**
893 A264 26c multi .55 .55
894 A264 41c multi .85 .85
895 A264 52c multi 1.10 1.10
896 A264 61c multi 1.25 1.25
Nos. 893-896 (4) 3.75 3.75

Miniature Sheet

Space Age, 50th Anniv. — A265

No. 897: a, First man in space. b, First man-made satellite. c, First men on the Moon. d, First docking in space. e, First woman in space. f, First manned lunar vehicle. g, First space walk. h, First landing on Mars. i, First probe of Venus. j, First American in orbit.

2007, June 12 ***Perf. 13½***
897 A265 41c Sheet of 10, #a-j 8.25 8.25

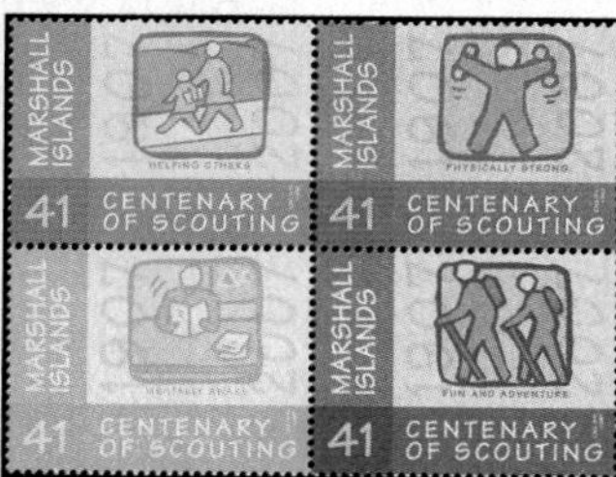

Scouting, Cent. — A266

No. 898 — Inscriptions: a, Helping others. b, Physically strong. c, Mentally awake. d, Fun and adventure.

2007, June 25
898 A266 41c Block of 4, #a-d 3.50 3.50

Purple Heart, 225th Anniv. — A267

2007, July 30 **Litho.** ***Perf. 13½***
899 A267 41c multi .85 .85

Miniature Sheet

United States Air Force, 60th Anniv. — A268

No. 900: a, C-54 Skymaster. b, B-36 Peacemaker. c, F-86 Sabre. d, B-47 Stratojet. e, C-124 Globemaster II. f, C-121 Constellation. g, B-52 Stratofortress. h, F-100 Super Sabre. i, F-104 Starfighter. j, C-130 Hercules. k, F-105 Thunderchief. l, KC-135 Stratotanker. m, B-58 Hustler. n, F-4 Phantom II. o, T-38 Talon. p, C-141 Starlifter. q, F-111 Aardvark. r, SR-71 Blackbird. s, C-5 Galaxy. t, A-10 Thunderbolt II. u, F-15 Eagle. v, F-16 Fighting Falcon. w, F-117 Nighthawk. x, B-2 Spirit. y, C-17 Globemaster III.

2007, Aug. 7
900 A268 41c Sheet of 25, #a-y 21.00 21.00

Marshallese Culture Type of 2005

No. 901 — Photographs by J. Debrum: a, Lonkwon Getting Fish from His Trap. b, Alele Style of Fishing at Bilarek. c, Portrait of Lanju and Family. d, Outrigger with Sail. e, Lien and Litublan Collecting Shells.

2007, Sept. 18 **Litho.** ***Perf. 13½***
901 Horiz. strip of 5 4.25 4.25
a.-e. A250 41c Any single .85 .85

Miniature Sheet

Marshall Islands Yacht Registry — A269

No. 902 — Registered yachts: a, Domani. b, Excellence III. c, Aquasition. d, Perfect Symmetry 5. e, Happy Days. f, Mystique. g, Halcyon Days. h, Man of Steel. i, Marathon. j, Sinbad.

2007, Oct. 8
902 A269 41c Sheet of 10, #a-j 8.25 8.25

Christmas — A270

No. 903 — Santa Claus: a, Reading list. b, Standing by fireplace. c, Holding gift. d, Waving from sleigh.

2007, Dec. 12
903 A270 41c Block of 4, #a-d 3.50 3.50

Miniature Sheet

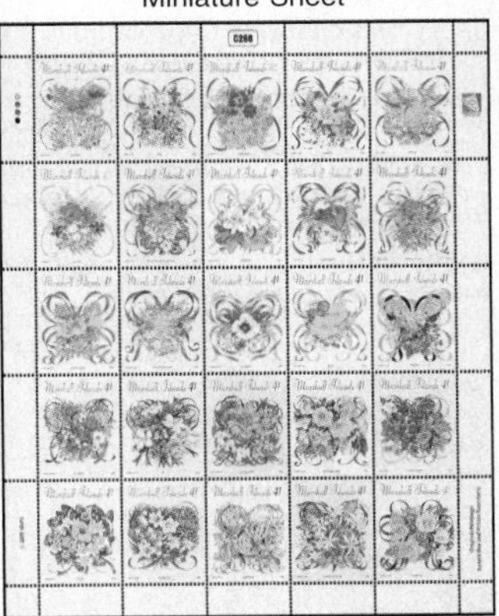

Flower Bouquets — A271

No. 904 — Various bouquets with country name at bottom: a, Scotland. b, Jersey. c, Gibraltar. d, Dominica. e, Canada. f, Cyprus. g, Turks and Caicos Islands. h, Bahamas. i, Montserrat. j, Cayman Islands. k, Bangladesh. l, Falkland Islands. m, Grenada. n, Nevis. o, Jamaica. p, Australia. q, Fiji. r, New Hebrides. s, Pitcairn Islands. t, Cook Islands. u, Tonga. v, Seychelles. w, Zimbabwe. x, Christmas Island. y, Antigua.

2008, Jan. 15 Litho. *Perf. 13½*
904 A271 41c Sheet of 25, #a-y 20.50 20.50

See No. 934.

Miniature Sheet

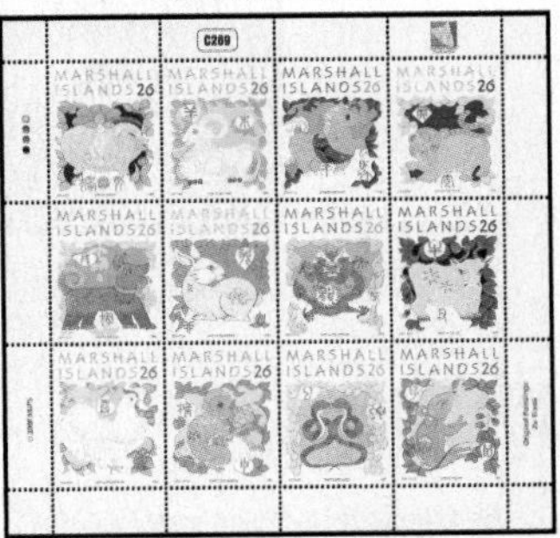

Chinese New Year Animals and Characters — A272

No. 905: a, Pig. b, Ram. c, Horse. d, Tiger. e, Dog. f, Rabbit. g, Dragon. h, Ox. i, Rooster. j, Monkey. k, Snake. l, Rat.

2008, Feb. 7
905 A272 26c Sheet of 12, #a-l 6.25 6.25

United States Lighthouses — A273

No. 906: a, St. Augustine Lighthouse, Florida. b, Old Cape Henry Lighthouse, Virginia. c, Cape Lookout Lighthouse, North Carolina. d, Tybee Island Lighthouse, Georgia. e, Morris Island Lighthouse, South Carolina. f, Hillsboro Inlet Lighthouse, Florida.

2008, Mar. 6 Litho. *Perf. 13½*
906 A273 41c Block of 6, #a-f 5.00 5.00

Miniature Sheet

Wild Cats — A274

No. 907: a, Lion family at rest. b, Ocelot mother with cub sitting in grass. c, White Siberian tiger mother with cubs. d, Mother tiger with cubs lying in grass. e, Serval mother with cubs sitting in tall grass. f, North American cougar mother with cubs. g, Lynx mother with cubs. h, Jaguar with cubs at stream. i, Black panther mother with cubs. j, Clouded leopard mother with cubs. k, Cheetah with cubs lying in grass. l, Snow leopard with cubs.

2008, Mar. 26 Litho. *Perf. 13½*
907 A274 41c Sheet of 12, #a-l 10.00 10.00

Miniature Sheet

Sailing Ships — A275

No. 908: a, H.M.S. Victory. b, La Grande Hermine. c, U.S.S. Constitution. d, Fram. e, Tovarisch I. f, Ark and Dove. g, Rainbow. h, Great Republic. i, H.M.S. Resolution. j, La Dauphine. k, Kreuzenshtern. l, Golden Hind.

2008, Apr. 2
908 A275 41c Sheet of 12, #a-l 10.00 10.00

Miniature Sheet

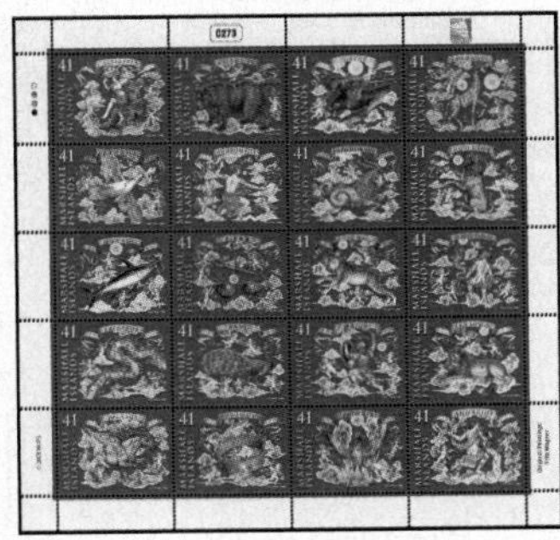

Constellations — A276

No. 909: a, Cassiopeia. b, Ursa Major. c, Corvus. d, Camelopardalis. e, Cygnus. f, Andromeda. g, Capricornus. h, Canis Major. i, Dorado. j, Libra. k, Lynx. l, Serpentarius. m, Eridanus. n, Pavo. o, Orion. p, Leo Minor. q, Pegasus. r, Corona Borealis. s, Phoenix. t, Aquarius.

2008, Apr. 29 Litho. *Perf. 13½*
909 A276 41c Sheet of 20, #a-t 16.50 16.50

See No. 945.

Miniature Sheet

US Marine Corps — A277

No. 910: a, US liberates Marshall Islands. b, John Lejeune. c, Holland Smith. d, Smedley D. Butler. e, Daniel J. Daly. f, Lewis "Chesty" Puller. g, John Basilone. h, Alexander Vandegrift. i, Gregory "Pappy" Boyington. j, Marines raising flag on Iwo Jima.

2008, May 12
910 A277 42c Sheet of 10, #a-j 8.50 8.50

Tropical Fish A278

Designs: 1c, Banded butterflyfish. 3c, Damselfish. 5c, Pink skunk clownfish. 27c, Copperband butterflyfish. 42c, Threadfin butterflyfish. 60c, Beau Gregory damselfish. 61c, Porkfish. 63c, Goatfish. 94c, Common longnose butterflyfish. $1, Royal gramma. $4.80, Longfin bannerfish. $5, Blue-striped blenny. $16.50, Emperor butterflyfish.

2008		**Litho.**		***Perf. 11¼x10¼***	
911	A278	1c	multi	.20	.20
912	A278	3c	multi	.20	.20
913	A278	5c	multi	.20	.20
914	A278	27c	multi	.55	.55
915	A278	42c	multi	.85	.85
916	A278	60c	multi	1.25	1.25
917	A278	61c	multi	1.25	1.25
918	A278	63c	multi	1.25	1.25
919	A278	94c	multi	1.90	1.90
920	A278	$1	multi	2.00	2.00
921	A278	$4.80	multi	9.75	9.75
922	A278	$5	multi	10.00	10.00
923	A278	$16.50	multi	33.00	33.00
	Nos. 911-923 (13)			62.40	62.40

Issued: Nos. 914, 915, 6/24; Nos. 919, 921, 923, 5/12. Nos. 911-913, 916-918, 920, 922, 9/9.

Miniature Sheet

Birds — A279

No. 924: a, Blue-gray tanager. b, St. Vincent parrot. c, Green-throated carib. d, Yellow oriole. e, Blue-hooded euphonia. f, Crested honeycreeper. g, Purple-capped fruit dove. h, Green magpie. i, Bay-headed tanager. j, Bananaquit. k, Cardinal honeyeater. l, Toco toucan. m, Cattle egret. n, Ringed kingfisher. o, Red-necked parrot. p, Purple gallinule. q, Copper-rumped hummingbird. r, Micronesian pigeon. s, Painted bunting. t, Black-naped oriole. u, Channel-billed toucan. v, Saddle-billed stork. w, Blood pheasant. x, Gray-crowned crane. y, Little blue heron.

2008, June 3 Litho. *Perf. 13½*
924 A279 42c Sheet of 25, #a-y 21.00 21.00

Miniature Sheet

Dinosaurs — A280

No. 925: a, Camarasaurus. b, Allosaurus. c, Parasaurolophus. d, Ornithomimus. e, Goniopholis. f, Camptosaurus. g, Edmontia. h, Ceratosaurus. i, Stegosaurus. j, Einiosaurus. k, Brachiosaurus. l, Corythosaurus.

2008, June 19
925 A280 42c Sheet of 12, #a-l 10.50 10.50

Miniature Sheet

Fishing Flies — A281

No. 926: a, Lefty's Deceiver (25x35mm). b, Apte Tarpon (25x35mm). c, Royal Wulff (50x48mm). d, Muddler Minnow (25x35mm). e, Jock Scott (25x35mm).

2008, July 20
926 A281 42c Sheet of 5, #a-e 4.25 4.25

Miniature Sheet

Personalities of the Wild West — A282

No. 927: a, Wild Bill Hickok. b, Jim Bridger. c, Geronimo. d, Charles Goodnight. e, Chief Joseph. f, Kit Carson. g, Jim Beckwourth. h, Wyatt Earp. i, Bat Masterson. j, Bill Pickett. k, Bill Tilghman. l, Annie Oakley. m, Buffalo Bill Cody. n, Nellie Cashman. o, Sacagawea. p, John Fremont.

2008, Aug. 14
927 A282 42c Sheet of 16, #a-p 13.50 13.50

Endangered Species — A283

No. 928: a, Blue whale. b, Amazonian manatee. c, Hawaiian monk seal. d, Green turtle. e, Giant clam. f, Killer whale.

2008, Aug. 19 Litho. *Perf. 13½*
928 A283 42c Block of 6, #a-f 5.25 5.25

Marshallese Culture Type of 2005

No. 929, vert. — Photographs by J. Debrum: a, Lokeinlik Wearing Traditional Mat for Men. b, Limekto Weaving Hat from Kimej. c, Unfinished Outrigger. d, Young Boys in Mejit. e, Lonkoon with Fish Trap.

2008, Sept. 15 Litho. *Perf. 13½*
929 Horiz. strip of 5 4.25 4.25
a.-e. A250 42c Any single .85 .85

Miniature Sheet

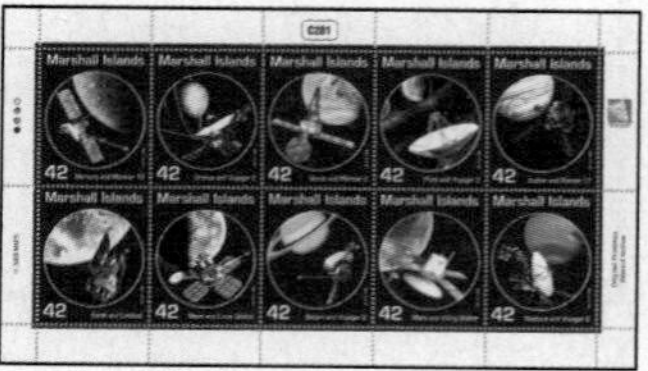

Spacecraft and the Solar System — A284

No. 930: a, Mercury, Mariner 10. b, Uranus, Voyager 2. c, Venus, Mariner 2. d, Pluto, Voyager 2. e, Jupiter, Pioneer 11. f, Earth, Landsat. g, Moon, Lunar Orbiter. h, Saturn, Voyager 2. i, Mars, Viking Orbiter. j, Neptune, Voyager 2.

2008, Oct. 1
930 A284 42c Sheet of 10, #a-j 8.50 8.50

Miniature Sheet

Christmas — A285

No. 931 — Song titles under ornament: a, Silent Night. b, We Three Kings. c, Deck the Halls. d, Hark, the Herald Angels Sing. e, O Little Town of Bethlehem. f, Joy to the World. g, Jingle Bells. h, O Come All Ye Faithful.

2008, Oct. 15 Litho. *Perf. 13½*
931 A285 42c Sheet of 8, #a-h 6.75 6.75

Owls — A286

No. 932: a, Barn owl. b, Barred owl. c, Burrowing owl. d, Snowy owl. e, Great horned owl. f, Spotted owl.

2008, Nov. 5
932 A286 42c Block of 6, #a-f 5.25 5.25

Souvenir Sheet

First United States Airmail Stamp, 90th Anniv. — A287

2008, Dec. 10 *Perf. 13x13½*
933 A287 $1 multi 2.00 2.00

Flower Bouquets Type of 2008
Miniature Sheet

No. 934 — Various bouquets with country name at bottom: a, Isle of Man. b, St. Lucia. c, Grenada. d, Bermuda. e, Anguilla. f, Barbados. g, Belize. h, St. Kitts. i, Hong Kong. j, British Virgin Islands. k, St. Vincent. l, Tristan da Cunha. m, St. Helena. n, British Antarctic Territory. o, St. Vincent and the Grenadines. p, New Zealand. q, Papua New Guinea. r, Western Samoa. s, Solomon Islands. t, Brunei. u, Swaziland. v, Botswana. w, Maldives. x, Ghana. y, Sierra Leone.

2009, Mar. 31 Litho. *Perf. 13½*
934 A271 42c Sheet of 25, #a-y 21.00 21.00

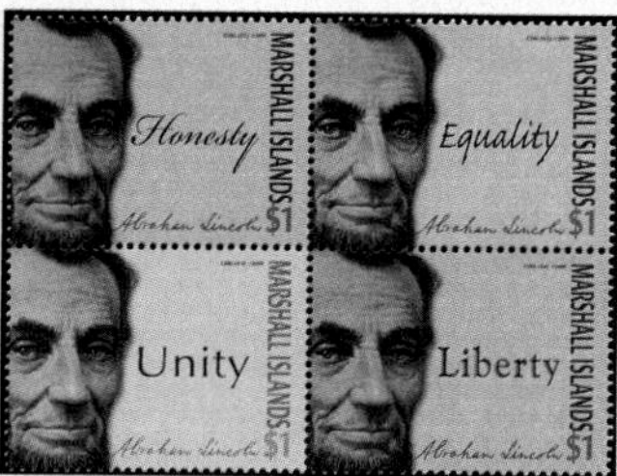

Pres. Abraham Lincoln (1809-65) — A288

No. 935 — Lincoln and: a, "Honesty." b, "Equality." c, "Unity." d, "Liberty."

2009, Apr. 7 Litho. *Perf. 13½*
935 A288 $1 Block of 4, #a-d 8.00 8.00

Arctic Explorers — A289

No. 936: a, Elisha Kent Kane, ships. b, Robert E. Peary, Matthew A. Henson, dog sled. c, Vilhjalmur Stefansson, ship, dog sled. d, Adolphus Washington Greely, ship.

2009, Apr. 14
936 A289 42c Block of 4, #a-d 3.50 3.50

Peary Expedition to North Pole, cent.

Miniature Sheet

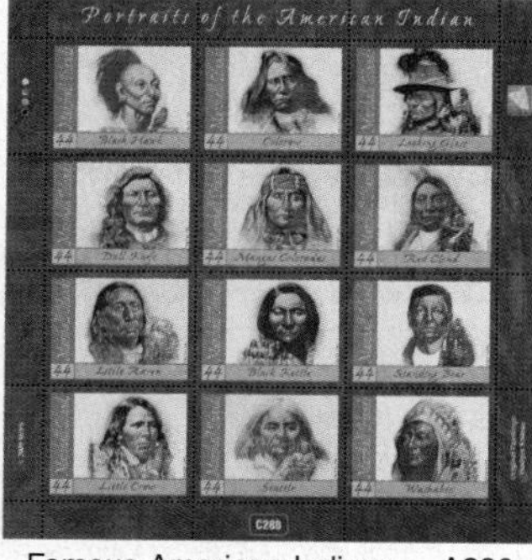

Famous American Indians — A290

No. 937: a, Black Hawk. b, Colorow. c, Looking Glass. d, Dull Knife. e, Mangas Coloradas. f, Red Cloud. g, Little Raven. h, Black Kettle. i, Standing Bear. j, Little Crow. k, Seattle. l, Washakie.

2009, Apr. 21 Litho. *Perf. 13½*
937 A290 44c Sheet of 12, #a-l 11.00 11.00

Miniature Sheet

US Military Heroes of the Air — A291

No. 938: a, Richard I. Bong. b, Charles "Chuck" Yeager. c, Lauris Norstad. d, William "Billy" Mitchell. e, Curtis E. LeMay. f, Edward Henry O'Hare. g, Claire L. Chennault. h, George C. Kenney. i, James "Jimmy" Doolittle. j, Paul W. Tibbets, Jr. k, Benjamin O. Davis, Jr. l, Carl "Tooey" Spaatz. m, Ira C. Eaker. n, Edward "Eddie" Rickenbacker. o, Henry "Hap" Arnold. p, Map of Marshall Islands, birds, outrigger canoe, dolphin.

2009, Apr. 28
938 A291 44c Sheet of 16, #a-p 14.50 14.50

Souvenir Sheet

Marshall Islands Postal Service, 25th Anniv. — A292

2009, May 2 Litho. *Perf. 13x13½*
939 A292 44c multi .90 .90

Marine Life A293

Designs: 28c, Masked butterflyfish. 44c, Queen angelfish. 88c, Clownfish. 98c, Starfish. $1.22, Orca whale.

2009, May 11 Litho. *Perf. 11¼x10¼*

940 A293	28c multi		.60	.60
941 A293	44c multi		.90	.90
942 A293	88c multi		1.75	1.75
943 A293	98c multi		2.00	2.00
944 A293	$1.22 multi		2.50	2.50
	Nos. 940-944 (5)		7.75	7.75

Constellations Type of 2008
Miniature Sheet

No. 945: a, Antinous. b, Aquila. c, Cancer. d, Canis Major. e, Leo. f, Ara. g, Sextans Uraniae. h, Cepheus. i, Apus. j, Indus. k, Ursa Minor. l, Grus. m, Centaurus. n, Cetus. o, Piscis Volans. p, Lupus. q, Equuleus. r, Draco. s, Boötes. t, Scorpius.

2009, June 1 *Perf. 13½*
945 A276 44c Sheet of 20, #a-t 18.00 18.00

2005-09 Rose Varieties of the Year — A294

No. 946: a, Summertime, 2005. b, Champagne Moment, 2006. c, Tickled Pink, 2007. d, Sweet Haze, 2008. e, Lucky!, 2009.

2009, June 18
946 Horiz. strip of 5 4.50 4.50
a.-e. A294 44c Any single .90 .90

Hot Air Balloons A295

No. 947: a, Montgolfier's balloon. b, Intrepid. c, Explorer II. d, Double Eagle. e, Contemporary balloons.

2009, July 13
947 Horiz. strip of 5 4.50 4.50
a.-e. A295 44c Any single .90 .90

July 22, 2009 Solar Eclipse — A296

No. 948 — Eclipse phases: a, Beginning (shown). b, Totality and near-totality. c, Ending.

2009, July 22
948 Horiz. strip of 3 2.75 2.75
a.-c. A296 44c Any single .90 .90

Steam Locomotives — A297

No. 949: a, Samson. b, Best Friend of Charleston. c, John Bull. d, Gowan & Marx. e, Stourbridge Lion. f, Brother Jonathan.

2009, Aug. 6 Litho. *Perf. 13½*
949 A297 44c Block of 6, #a-f 5.50 5.50

Marshallese Culture Type of 2005

No. 950 — Photographs by J. Debrum: a, Making Arrowroot Lagoonside. b, Boats in Lagoon, One Capsized for Repair. c, Family Portrait in Front of Wooden Home with Pandanus Roof. d, Man Carrying Fish Trap. e, Portrait of New Year and LemeLali Weaving Baskets.

2009, Sept. 1 Litho. *Perf. 13½*
950 Horiz. strip of 5 4.50 4.50
a.-e. A250 44c Any single .90 .90

Eagles — A298

No. 951: a, Philippine eagle. b, Tawny eagle. c, Martial eagle. d, Bald eagle. e, African fish eagle. f, Bataleur eagle. g, Golden eagle. h, Harpy eagle.

2009, Sept. 14 Litho. *Perf. 13½*
951 A298 44c Block of 8, #a-h 7.25 7.25

Dogs — A299

No. 952: a, Beagle and Boston terrier. b, Chesapeake Bay retriever and Cocker spaniel. c, Alaskan malamute and Collie. d, Water spaniel and Basset hound. e, Coonhound and Foxhound.

No. 953, horiz.: a, Old English sheepdog. b, Irish setter. c, Welsh springer spaniel. d, West Highland terrier.

2009, Oct. 5 Litho. *Perf. 13½*
952 Horiz. strip of 5 4.50 4.50
a.-e. A299 44c Any single .90 .90
953 Sheet of 4 8.00 8.00
a.-d. A299 98c Any single 2.00 2.00

Christmas A300

No. 954: a, Chili wreath. b, Christmas wreath. c, Traditional wreath. d, Tropical wreath. e, Colonial wreath.

2009, Oct. 15 Litho. *Perf. 13½*
954 Horiz. strip of 5 4.50 4.50
a.-e. A300 44c Any single .90 .90

Miniature Sheet

Endangered Species — A301

No. 955: a, Giant anteater. b, Caracal. c, Wild yak. d, Giant panda. e, Black-footed ferret. f, Black rhinoceros. g, Golden lion tamarin. h, African elephant. i, Persian fallow deer. j, Polar bear. k, Ocelot. l, Gorilla.

2009, Nov. 2 Litho. *Perf. 13½*
955 A301 44c Sheet of 12, #a-l 11.00 11.00

Prehistoric Animals — A302

No. 956: a, Mastodons on prairie. b, Eohippus. c, Woolly mammoth. d, Saber-toothed cat. e, Mastodons in marsh.

2009, Nov. 24
956 Horiz. strip of 5 4.50 4.50
a.-e. A302 44c Any single .90 .90

Shells — A303

No. 957: a, Paper nautilus. b, Giant tun. c, Pilgrim's scallop. d, Gibbula magus.

2009, Dec. 8
957 A303 44c Block of 4, #a-d 3.75 3.75

Miniature Sheet

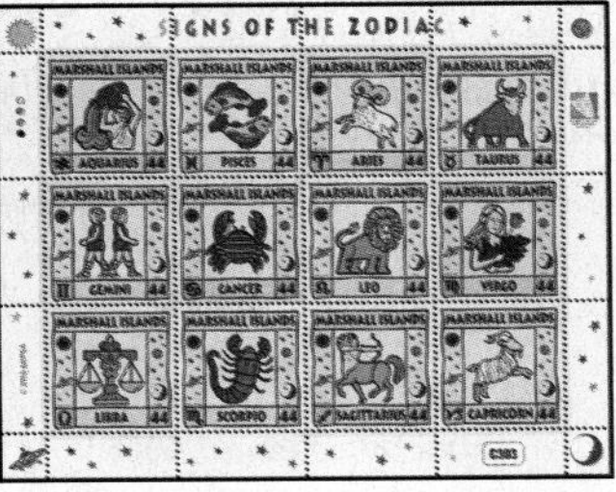

Signs of the Zodiac — A304

No. 958: a, Aquarius. b, Pisces. c, Aries. d, Taurus. e, Gemini. f, Cancer. g, Leo. h, Virgo. i, Libra. j, Scorpio. k, Sagittarius. l, Capricorn.

2010, Jan. 5 *Perf. 11¾*
958 A304 44c Sheet of 12, #a-l 11.00 11.00

Miniature Sheet

Waterfowl — A305

No. 959: a, European wigeon. b, Tufted ducks. c, Mallards. d, Gadwall. e, Snow geese. f, Pintail ducks. g, Northern shoveler. h, Canvasback ducks.

2010, Feb. 10 Litho. *Perf. 11¾*
959 A305 44c Sheet of 8, #a-h 7.25 7.25

Famous American Indians Type of 2009

Miniature Sheet

No. 960: a, Osceola. b, Lone Wolf. c, Menawa. d, Wabasha. e, Captain Jack. f, Quanah Parker. g, Ouray. h, Mannelito. i, Cochise. j, Satanta. k, Massasoit. l, Red Eagle.

2010, Mar. 4 Litho. *Perf. 13½*
960 A290 44c Sheet of 12, #a-l 11.00 11.00

Boy Scouts of America, Cent. — A306

No. 961 — Background color: a, Olive green. b, Red. c, Yellow bister. d, Blue.

2010, Mar. 18 Litho. *Perf. 13½*
961 A306 44c Block of 4, #a-d 3.75 3.75

Shells — A307

No. 962: a, Paper nautilus. b, Giant tun. c, Pilgrim's scallop. d, Gibbula magus.

2010, Mar. 29 Litho. *Perf. 13½*
962 A307 98c Block of 4, #a-d 8.00 8.00

See Nos. 971-972.

Astronomers A308

No. 963: a, Nicolaus Copernicus. b, Johannes Kepler. c, Galileo Galilei. d, Sir Isaac Newton. e, Sir William Herschel.

2010, Apr. 7
963 Horiz. strip of 5 4.50 4.50
a.-e. A308 44c Any single .90 .90

No. 963e is incorrectly inscribed "Hirschel."

Constellations Type of 2008

No. 964: a, Columba. b, Virgo. c, Argo Navis. d, Tucana (Toucan). e, Aries. f, Coma Berenices. g, Delphinus. h, Perseus. i, Taurus. j, Monoceros. k, Gemini. l, Vulpecula. m, Lepus. n, Auriga. o, Pisces. p, Sagittarius. q, Crater. r, Lyra. s, Hercules. t, Canes Venatici.

2010, June 1
964 A276 44c Sheet of 20, #a-t 18.00 18.00

Fish Type of 2009

2010, June 1 *Perf. 11¼x10¼*
965 A293 28c Mandarin goby .60 .60

Marshallese Alphabet — A309

No. 966 — Letters and Marshallese words: a, "A," Amata (first name of first Marshallese president). b, "A with macron," Aj (to weave). c, "B," Babbub (butterfly). d, "D," Deo (beautiful young lady). e, "E," Ek (fish). f, "I," Iokwe (rainbow). g, "J," Jaki (mat). h, "K," Imon Kien (house of government). i, "L," Loktanur (star Capella). j, "L with cedilla," Lokwajek (red-tailed tropic bird). k, "M," Ma (breadfruit). l, "M with cedilla," Makmok (arrowroot plant). m, "N," Ni (coconut tree). n, "N with cedilla," No (ocean wave). o, "N with macron," Niin-pako (shark tooth). p, "O," Ok (fish net). q, "O with cedilla," Eo (tattoo). r, "O with macron," Oo (lionfish). s, "P," Pejak (visitor's hut). t, "R," Raj (whale). u, "T," Tipnol (outrigger sailing canoe). v, "U," Urur (fire). w, "U with macron," Ulin-raj (dorsal fin of whale). x, "W," Wojla (woven pandanus leaf sail).

2010, June 16 Litho. *Perf. 13½*
966 Sheet of 24 22.00 22.00
a.-x. A309 44c Any single .90 .90

Miniature Sheet

Statue of Liberty — A310

No. 967 — Statue of Liberty: a, Red clouds and water (9-1). b, Blue background (9-2). c, Brown and gray clouds (9-3). d, American flag (9-4). e, Frederic Bartholdi (9-5). f, Blue background, diff. (9-6). g, White background around head (9-7). h, Torch (9-8). i, Brown background around head (9-9).

2010, June 17 *Perf. 11¾*
967 A310 44c Sheet of 9, #a-i, + 7 labels 8.25 8.25

Miniature Sheet

Classic Cars — A311

No. 968: a, 1935 Duesenberg. b, 1932 Packard. c, 1928 Locomobile. d, 1931 Cord. e, 1929 Pierce Arrow.

2010, July 7
968 A311 44c Sheet of 5, #a-e, + 4 labels 4.50 4.50

Carousel Horses — A312

No. 969 — Various carousel horses numberd: a, (6-1). b, (6-2). c, (6-3). d, (6-4). e, (6-5). f, (6-6).

2010, Aug. 12 *Perf. 13½*
969 A312 44c Block of 6, #a-f 5.50 5.50

US Warships of World War II — A313

No. 970: a, USS Nevada. b, USS Missouri. c, USS Wisconsin. d, USS Oregon. e, USS Massachusetts. f, USS North Carolina. g, USS Texas. h, USS Idaho. i, USS New Jersey. j, USS Colorado. k, USS South Dakota. l, USS New Mexico. m, USS Washington. n, USS Iowa. o, USS Alabama.

2010, Sept. 2 *Perf. 13½*
970 Sheet of 15 13.50 13.50
a.-o. A313 44c Any single .90 .90

Shells Type of 2010

Designs: 28c, Pilgrim's scallop. 98c, Gibbula magus.

2010, Sept. 20
971 A307 28c multi .60 .60
972 A307 98c multi 2.00 2.00

SEMI-POSTAL STAMPS

Operation Crossroads, Nuclear Testing at Bikini Atoll, 50th Anniv. — SP1

Designs: a, Evacuation of Bikinians. b, Navy preparations. c, Able. d, Baker. e, Ghost fleet. f, Effects on Bikinians.

1996, July 1 **Litho.** *Perf. 13½*
B1 SP1 32c +8c #a.-f. + 6 labels 4.75 4.75

Surtax for the benefit of the people of Bikini.

AIR POST STAMPS

Audubon Type of 1985

1985, Feb. 15 **Litho.** *Perf. 14*
C1 A11 44c Booby Gannet, vert. .90 .90
C2 A11 44c Esquimaux Curlew, vert. .90 .90
a. Pair, #C1-C2 1.80 1.80

AMERIPEX Type of 1986

Designs: No. C3, Consolidated PBY-5A Catalina Amphibian. No. C4, Grumman SA-16 Albatross. No. C5, McDonnell Douglas DC-6B Super Cloudmaster. No. C6, Boeing 727-100.

1986, May 22 **Litho.** *Perf. 14*
C3 A20 44c multicolored .85 .85
C4 A20 44c multicolored .85 .85
C5 A20 44c multicolored .85 .85
C6 A20 44c multicolored .85 .85
a. Block of 4, #C3-C6 3.50 3.50

Operation Crossroads Type of 1986
Souvenir Sheet

1986, July 1 **Litho.** *Perf. 14*
C7 A21 44c USS Saratoga *4.00 4.00*

Statue of Liberty Cent., Intl. Peace Year — AP1

1986, Oct. 28 **Litho.**
C8 AP1 44c multicolored 1.00 .95

Natl. Girl Scout Movement, 20th Anniv. — AP2

1986, Dec. 8 **Litho.**
C9 AP2 44c Community service .75 .75
C10 AP2 44c Salute .75 .75
C11 AP2 44c Health care .75 .75
C12 AP2 44c Learning skills .75 .75
a. Block of 4, #C9-C12 3.00 3.00

Girl Scout Movement in the US, 75th anniv. (1912-1987).

Marine Birds AP3

1987, Jan. 12 **Litho.** *Perf. 14*
C13 AP3 44c Wedge-tailed shearwater .75 .75
C14 AP3 44c Red-footed booby .75 .75
C15 AP3 44c Red-tailed tropic-bird .75 .75
C16 AP3 44c Great frigatebird .75 .75
a. Block of 4, #C13-C16 3.00 3.00

CAPEX '87 AP4

Last flight of Amelia Earhart: No. C17, Take-off at Lae, New Guinea, July 2, 1937. No. C18, USCG Itasca cutter at Howland Is. No. C19, Purported crash landing of the Electra at Mili Atoll. No. C20, Recovery of the Electra by the Koshu, a Japanese survey ship.

1987, June 15 **Litho.** *Perf. 14*
C17 AP4 44c multicolored .75 .75
C18 AP4 44c multicolored .75 .75
C19 AP4 44c multicolored .75 .75
C20 AP4 44c multicolored .75 .75
a. Block of 4, #C17-C20 3.00 3.00

Space Shuttle Type of 1988

1988, Dec. 23 **Litho.** *Perf. 14*
C21 A38 45c Astronaut, shuttle over Rongelap .85 .85

Aircraft — AP5

1989, Apr. 24 **Litho.** *Perf. 14x14½*
C22 AP5 12c Dornier Do228 .25 .25
a. Booklet pane of 10 3.00 —
C23 AP5 36c Boeing 737 .75 .75
a. Booklet pane of 10 8.00 —
C24 AP5 39c Hawker Siddeley 748 .90 .90
a. Booklet pane of 10 9.00 —
C25 AP5 45c Boeing 727 1.00 1.00
a. Booklet pane of 10 10.00 —
b. Bklt. pane, 5 each 36c, 45c 8.75 —
Nos. C22-C25 (4) 2.90 2.90

MARTINIQUE

ˌmär-tən-ˈēk

LOCATION — Island in the West Indies, southeast of Puerto Rico
GOVT. — French Colony
AREA — 385 sq. mi.
POP. — 261,595 (1946)
CAPITAL — Fort-de-France

Formerly a French colony, Martinique became an integral part of the Republic, acquiring the same status as the departments in metropolitan France, under a law effective Jan. 1, 1947.

100 Centimes = 1 Franc

Catalogue values for unused stamps in this country are for Never Hinged items, beginning with Scott 196 in the regular postage section, Scott C1 in the airpost section, and Scott J37 in the postage due section.

See France Nos. 1278, 1508, French West Africa 70, for stamps inscribed "Martinique."

Stamps of French Colonies 1881-86 Surcharged in Black

Nos. 1, 7

MARTINIQUE
5c
No. 2

No. 3

MQE
15 c.
No. 4

Nos. 5-6, 8

Nos. 9-20

1886-91 **Unwmk.** *Perf. 14x13½*
1 A9 5 on 20c 65.00 55.00
a. Double surcharge *750.00 750.00*
2 A9 5c on 20c *15,000. 15,000.*
3 A9 15c on 20c ('87) 275.00 240.00
a. Inverted surcharge *2,500. 2,500.*
4 A9 15c on 20c ('87) 110.00 100.00
a. Inverted surcharge *1,500. 1,500.*
b. Se-tenant pair, #3-4 475.00 475.00
c. Se-tenant pair, #3a-4a *4,750. 4,750.*
5 A9 01 on 20c ('88) 20.00 19.00
a. Inverted surcharge *350.00 350.00*
6 A9 05 on 20c 16.00 13.00
7 A9 15 on 20c ('88) 200.00 180.00
c. Inverted surcharge *750.00 750.00*
8 A9 015 on 20c ('87) 65.00 *65.00*
a. Inverted surcharge *875.00 875.00*
9 A9 01c on 2c ('88) 4.75 3.25
a. Double surcharge *475.00 475.00*
10 A9 01c on 4c ('88) 15.00 4.75
11 A9 05c on 4c ('88) 1,500. 1,500.
12 A9 05c on 10c ('90) 120.00 72.50
a. Slanting "5" *300.00 240.00*
13 A9 05c on 20c ('88) 28.00 20.00
a. Slanting "5" *150.00 120.00*
b. Inverted surcharge *425.00 375.00*
14 A9 05c on 30c ('91) 35.00 28.00
a. Slanting "5" *160.00 150.00*
15 A9 05c on 35c ('91) 20.00 16.00
a. Slanting "5" *160.00 150.00*
b. Inverted surcharge *325.00 300.00*
16 A9 05c on 40c ('91) 65.00 47.50
a. Slanting "5" *260.00 180.00*
17 A9 15c on 4c ('88) *12,000. 11,000.*
18 A9 15c on 20c ('87) 150.00 120.00
a. Slanting "5" *500.00 425.00*
b. Double surcharge *700.00 700.00*
19 A9 15c on 25c ('90) 32.50 20.00
a. Slanting "5" *150.00 130.00*
b. Inverted surcharge *325.00 275.00*
c. Double surcharge 450.00 450.00
20 A9 15c on 75c ('91) 210.00 175.00
a. Slanting "5" *550.00 175.00*

French Colonies No. 47 Surcharged

1891
21 A9 01c on 2c brn, *buff* 11.00 11.00

French Colonies Nos. J5-J9 Surcharged

1891-92 **Black Surcharge** *Imperf.*
22 D1 05c on 5c blk ('92) 17.50 17.00
a. Slanting "5" *72.50 65.00*
23 D1 05c on 15c blk 16.00 16.00
b. Slanting "5" *72.50 65.00*
24 D1 15c on 20c blk 20.00 16.00
a. Inverted surcharge *300.00 300.00*
b. Double surcharge *300.00 300.00*
25 D1 15c on 30c blk 20.00 16.00
a. Inverted surcharge *300.00 300.00*
b. Slanting "5" *80.00 72.50*
Nos. 22-25 (4) 73.50 65.00

Red Surcharge

26 D1 05c on 10c blk 14.50 11.00
a. Inverted surcharge *300.00 300.00*
27 D1 05c on 15c blk 16.00 16.00
28 D1 15c on 20c blk 52.50 45.00
a. Inverted surcharge *450.00 450.00*
Nos. 26-28 (3) 83.00 72.00

French Colonies No. 54 Surcharged in Black

j

k

1892 *Perf. 14x13½*

29 A9 (j) 05c on 25c 65.00 65.00
a. Slanting "5" *300.00 300.00*
30 A9 (j) 15c on 25c 36.00 36.00
a. Slanting "5" *275.00 275.00*
31 A9 (k) 05c on 25c 65.00 65.00
a. "1882" instead of "1892" *675.00 600.00*
b. "95" instead of "05" *850.00 800.00*
c. Slanting "5" *300.00 300.00*
32 A9 (k) 15c on 25c 32.50 32.50
a. "1882" instead of "1892" *600.00 600.00*
b. Slanting "5" *160.00 160.00*
Nos. 29-32 (4) 198.50 198.50

Navigation and Commerce — A15

1892-1906 Typo. *Perf. 14x13½*
"MARTINIQUE" Colony in Carmine or Blue

33 A15 1c blk, *lil bl* 1.50 1.40
a. "MARTINIQUE" in blue 1,000. 1,000.
b. "MARTINIQUE" omitted 5,500.
34 A15 2c brn, *buff* 1.75 1.40
35 A15 4c claret, *lav* 2.00 1.50
36 A15 5c grn, *grnsh* 2.40 1.50
37 A15 5c yel grn ('99) 3.50 1.10
38 A15 10c blk, *lav* 11.00 2.00
39 A15 10c red ('99) 5.25 1.50
40 A15 15c blue, quadrille paper 42.50 8.00
41 A15 15c gray ('99) 13.50 2.10
42 A15 20c red, *grn* 20.00 10.00
43 A15 25c blk, *rose* 24.00 3.25
44 A15 25c blue ('99) 16.00 14.50
45 A15 30c brn, *bis* 36.00 19.00
46 A15 35c blk, *yel* ('06) 16.00 9.50
47 A15 40c red, *straw* 36.00 19.00
48 A15 50c car, *rose* 40.00 24.00
49 A15 50c brn, *az* ('99) 42.50 32.50
50 A15 75c dp vio, *org* 32.50 20.00
51 A15 1fr brnz grn, *straw* 32.50 21.00
52 A15 2fr vio, *rose* ('04) 92.50 75.00
53 A15 5fr lil, *lav* ('03) 110.00 95.00
Nos. 33-53 (21) 581.40 363.25

Perf. 13½x14 stamps are counterfeits.
For surcharges see Nos. 54-61, 101-104.

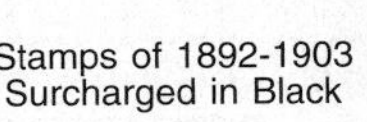

Stamps of 1892-1903 Surcharged in Black

1904

54 A15 10c on 30c brn, *bis* 14.50 14.50
a. Double surcharge 525.00 525.00
b. Inverted surcharge 1,600. 1,600.
55 A15 10c on 5fr lil, *lav* 16.00 16.00

Surcharged

56 A15 10c on 30c brn, *bis* 24.00 24.00
57 A15 10c on 40c red, *straw* 24.00 24.00
a. Double surcharge 600.00 600.00
58 A15 10c on 50c car, *rose* 28.00 28.00
59 A15 10c on 75c dp vio, *org* 20.00 20.00
60 A15 10c on 1fr brnz grn, *straw* 24.00 24.00
a. Double surcharge 350.00 350.00
61 A15 10c on 5fr lil, *lav* 200.00 200.00
Nos. 54-61 (8) 350.50 350.50

Martinique Woman — A16

Girl Bearing Pineapple in Cane Field — A18

View of Fort-de-France — A17

1908-30 Typo.

62 A16 1c red brn & brn .25 .25
63 A16 2c ol grn & brn .30 .25
64 A16 4c vio brn & brn .30 .30
65 A16 5c grn & brn 1.10 .40
66 A16 5c org & brn ('22) .50 .40
67 A16 10c car & brn 1.10 .50
68 A16 10c bl grn & grn ('22) .55 .40
69 A16 10c brn vio & rose ('25) .55 .40
70 A16 15c brn vio & rose ('17) .65 .40
71 A16 15c bl grn & gray grn ('25) .50 .40
72 A16 15c dp bl & red org ('28) 1.60 1.60
73 A16 20c vio & brn 1.40 1.05
74 A17 25c bl & brn 2.25 1.10
75 A17 25c org & brn ('22) .90 .55
76 A17 30c brn org & brn 2.25 1.10
77 A17 30c dl red & brn ('22) .75 .65
78 A17 30c rose & ver ('24) .55 .55
79 A17 30c ol brn & brn ('25) .55 .55
80 A17 30c sl bl & bl grn ('27) 1.60 1.60
81 A17 35c vio & brn .90 .65
a. White chalky paper 4.50 2.75
82 A17 40c gray grn & brn .90 .65
83 A17 45c dk brn & brn .90 .65
a. White chalky paper 2.00 1.60
84 A17 50c rose & brn 2.25 1.10
85 A17 50c bl & brn ('22) 1.40 1.30
86 A17 50c org & grn ('25) .90 .40
87 A17 60c dk bl & lil rose ('25) .75 .75
88 A17 65c vio & ol brn ('27) 2.00 2.00
89 A17 75c slate & brn 1.40 1.05
90 A17 75c ind & dk bl ('25) .90 .90
91 A17 75c org brn & lt bl ('27) 2.75 2.75
92 A17 90c brn red & brt red ('30) 5.50 5.50
93 A18 1fr dl bl & brn 1.20 1.00
94 A18 1fr dk bl ('25) 1.00 .90
95 A18 1fr ver & ol grn ('27) 2.75 2.75
96 A18 1.10fr vio & dk brn ('28) 3.75 *4.50*
97 A18 1.50fr ind & ultra ('30) 5.50 5.50
98 A18 2fr gray & brn 4.50 2.00
99 A18 3fr red vio ('30) 9.50 9.50
100 A18 5fr org red & brn 10.50 8.00
Nos. 62-100 (39) 76.90 64.30

For surcharges see Nos. 105-128, B1.

Nos. 41, 43, 47 and 53 Surcharged in Carmine or Black

1912, Aug.
Spacing between figures of surcharge 1.5mm (5c), 2mm (10c)

101 A15 5c on 15c gray (C) 1.00 1.00
102 A15 5c on 25c blk, *rose* (C) 1.50 1.50
103 A15 10c on 40c red, *straw* 2.40 2.40
104 A15 10c on 5fr lil, *lav* 3.00 3.00
Nos. 101-104 (4) 7.90 7.90

Two spacings between the surcharged numerals are found on Nos. 101 to 104. For detailed listings, see the *Scott Classic Specialized Catalogue of Stamps and Covers.*

Nos. 62, 63, 70 Surcharged

1920, June 15

105 A16 5c on 1c 2.10 2.10
a. Double surcharge 45.00 45.00
b. Inverted surcharge 32.50 32.50
106 A16 10c on 2c 2.10 2.10
a. Double surcharge 130.00
b. Inverted surcharge 45.00 45.00
c. Double surcharge, one inverted 95.00
107 A16 25c on 15c 2.25 2.25
a. Double surcharge 55.00 55.00
b. Inverted surcharge 55.00 55.00
c. Double surcharge, one inverted 100.00
d. Pair, one stamp without surcharge 160.00 160.00
Nos. 105-107 (3) 6.45 6.45

No. 70 Surcharged in Various Colors

1922, Dec.

108 A16 1c on 15c (Bk) .50 .50
a. Double surcharge 190.00 190.00
109 A16 2c on 15c (Bl) .50 .50
110 A16 5c on 15c (R) .65 .65
a. Imperf., pair 260.00
Nos. 108-110 (3) 1.65 1.65

Types of 1908-30 Surcharged

1923-25

111 A17 60c on 75c bl & rose .65 .65
112 A17 65c on 45c ol brn & brn ('25) 1.45 1.45
113 A17 85c on 75c blk & brn (R) ('25) 1.75 1.75
Nos. 111-113 (3) 3.85 3.85

Nos. 63, 73, 76-77, 84-85 Surcharged in Brown

Surcharge is horiz. on #114-115, vert. reading up on #116, 119 and down on #117-118.

1924, Feb. 14

114 A16 1c on 2c 3.25 3.25
a. Double surcharge 550.00 550.00
b. Inverted surcharge 100.00 100.00
115 A16 5c on 20c 4.00 4.00
a. Inverted surcharge 100.00 100.00
116 A17 15c on 30c (#76) 16.00 16.00
a. Surcharge reading down 57.50 57.50
117 A17 15c on 30c (#77) 22.50 22.50
a. Surcharge reading up 67.50 67.50
118 A17 25c on 50c (#84) 325.00 350.00
119 A17 25c on 50c (#85) 10.50 10.50
a. Double surcharge 400.00 400.00
b. Surcharge reading down 47.50
Nos. 114-119 (6) 381.25 406.25

Stamps and Types of 1908-30 Surcharged

1924-27

120 A16 25c on 15c brn vio & rose ('25) .55 .55
121 A18 25c on 2fr gray & brn .50 .50
122 A18 25c on 5fr org red & brn (Bl) 2.10 1.75
123 A17 90c on 75c brn red & red ('27) 3.75 2.75
124 A18 1.25fr on 1fr dk bl ('26) 1.10 1.00
125 A18 1.50fr on 1fr dk bl & ultra ('27) 2.00 1.10
126 A18 3fr on 5fr dl red & grn ('27) 3.00 3.00
127 A18 10fr on 5fr dl grn & dp red ('27) 12.00 12.00
128 A18 20fr on 5fr org brn & red vio ('27) 18.50 17.50
Nos. 120-128 (9) 43.50 40.15

Common Design Types pictured following the introduction.

Colonial Exposition Issue
Common Design Types

1931, Apr. 13 Engr. *Perf. 12½*
Name of Country in Black

129 CD70 40c deep green 5.25 5.25
130 CD71 50c violet 5.25 5.25
131 CD72 90c red orange 5.25 5.25
132 CD73 1.50fr dull blue 5.25 5.25
Nos. 129-132 (4) 21.00 21.00

Village of Basse-Pointe — A19

Government Palace, Fort-de-France — A20

Martinique Women A21

1933-40 Photo. *Perf. 13½*

133 A19 1c red, *pink* .25 .25
134 A20 2c dull blue .25 .25
135 A20 3c sepia ('40) .35 .35
136 A19 4c olive grn .25 .25
137 A20 5c dp rose .35 .35
138 A19 10c blk, *pink* .35 .35
139 A20 15c blk, *org* .35 .35
140 A21 20c org brn .35 .35
141 A19 25c brn vio .35 .35
142 A20 30c green .50 .50
143 A20 30c lt ultra ('40) .40 .40
144 A21 35c dl grn ('38) 1.00 .90
145 A21 40c olive brn .65 .50
146 A20 45c dk brn 2.00 1.90
147 A20 45c grn ('40) .65 .65
148 A20 50c red .50 .30
149 A19 55c brn red ('38) 1.30 1.00
150 A19 60c lt bl ('40) .95 .95
151 A21 65c red, *grn* .50 .50
152 A21 70c brt red vio ('40) .75 .75
153 A19 75c dk brn 1.05 .90
154 A20 80c vio ('38) .75 .65
155 A19 90c carmine 1.90 1.75
156 A19 90c brt red vio ('39) .95 .95
157 A20 1fr blk, *grn* 1.90 1.40
158 A20 1fr rose red ('38) .75 .65
159 A21 1.25fr dk vio .80 .80
160 A21 1.25fr dp rose ('39) .75 .75
161 A19 1.40fr lt ultra ('40) .80 .80
162 A20 1.50fr dp bl .65 .55
163 A20 1.60fr chnt ('40) .80 .80
164 A21 1.75fr ol grn 9.50 5.25
165 A21 1.75fr dp bl ('38) .75 .75
166 A19 2fr dk bl,*grn* .50 .40
167 A21 2.25fr blue ('39) .75 .75
168 A19 2.50fr sepia ('40) .95 .95
169 A21 3fr brn vio .65 .60
170 A21 5fr red, *pink* 1.30 1.10
171 A19 10fr dk bl, *bl* 1.10 .80
172 A20 20fr red, *yel* 1.35 .95
Nos. 133-172 (40) 40.00 32.75

For surcharges see Nos. 190-195.
For type A20 without "RF," see Nos. 189A-189E.

Landing of Bélain d'Esnambuc — A22

Freed Slaves Paying Homage to Victor Schoelcher A23

1935, Oct. 22 Engr. *Perf. 13*

No.	Type	Description	Unused	Used
173	A22	40c blk brn	3.25	3.25
174	A22	50c dl red	3.25	3.25
175	A22	1.50fr ultra	12.00	12.00
176	A23	1.75fr lil rose	12.00	12.00
177	A23	5fr brown	12.00	12.00
a.		5fr ultramarine (error)	950.00	
178	A23	10fr blue grn	9.50	9.50
		Nos. 173-178 (6)	52.00	52.00

Tercentenary of French possessions in the West Indies.

Colonial Arts Exhibition Issue
Common Design Type
Souvenir Sheet

1937 *Imperf.*

No.	Type	Description	Unused	Used
179	CD74	3fr brt grn	8.75	*10.50*
a.		"MARTINIQUE" omitted	3,100.	
b.		Inscriptions inverted	2,200.	

Paris International Exposition Issue
Common Design Types

1937, Apr. 15 *Perf. 13*

No.	Type	Description	Unused	Used
180	CD74	20c dp vio	2.10	2.10
181	CD75	30c dk grn	1.75	1.75
182	CD76	40c car rose	1.75	1.75
183	CD77	50c dk brn & blk	1.60	1.60
184	CD78	90c red	2.00	2.00
185	CD79	1.50fr ultra	2.00	2.00
		Nos. 180-185 (6)	11.20	11.20

New York World's Fair Issue
Common Design Type

1939, May 10 *Perf. 12½x12*

No.	Type	Description	Unused	Used
186	CD82	1.25fr car lake	1.10	1.10
187	CD82	2.25fr ultra	1.25	1.25

View of Fort-de-France and Marshal Pétain — A23a

1941 Engr. *Perf. 12½x12*

No.	Type	Description	Unused	Used
188	A23a	1fr dull lilac	.80	
189	A23a	2.50fr blue	.80	

Nos. 188-189 were issued by the Vichy government in France, but were not placed on sale in Martinique.

For surcharges, see Nos. B10A-B10B.

Types of 1933-40 without "RF"

1942-44 Photo. *Perf. 13½*

No.	Type	Description	Unused	Used
189A	A20	3c sepia	.50	
189B	A20	15c blk, *org*	.55	
189C	A20	30c yel green	.55	
189D	A20	50c red	1.40	
189E	A20	1.50fr dp bl	.65	
		Nos. 189A-189E (5)	3.65	

Nos. 189A-189E were issued by the Vichy government in France, but were not placed on sale in Martinique.

Nos. 134, 135, 136 and 151 Surcharged in Red, Black or Blue

1945 *Perf. 13½, 13x13½*

No.	Type	Description	Unused	Used
190	A20	1fr on 2c dl bl (R)	.65	.65
191	A19	2fr on 4c ol grn	.65	.65
192	A20	3fr on 2c dl bl (R)	.80	.80
193	A21	5fr on 65c red, *grn*	1.40	1.40
194	A21	10fr on 65c red, *grn*	1.50	1.50
195	A20	20fr on 3c sepia (Bl)	1.50	1.50
		Nos. 190-195 (6)	6.50	6.50

Catalogue values for unused stamps in this section, from this point to the end of the section, are for Never Hinged items.

Eboue Issue
Common Design Type

1945 Engr. *Perf. 13*

No.	Type	Description	Unused	Used
196	CD91	2fr black	.75	.55
197	CD91	25fr Prussian green	1.30	1.00

Victor Schoelcher and View of Town of Schoelcher A24

1945 Unwmk. Litho. *Perf. 11½*

No.	Type	Description	Unused	Used
198	A24	10c dp bl vio & ultra	.35	.25
199	A24	30c dk org brn & lt org brn	.35	.25
200	A24	40c grnsh bl & pale bl	.40	.35
201	A24	50c car brn & rose lil	.40	.35
202	A24	60c org yel & yel	.40	.35
203	A24	70c brn & pale brn	.40	.35
204	A24	80c lt bl grn & pale grn	.40	.35
205	A24	1fr bl & lt bl	.40	.35
206	A24	1.20fr rose vio & rose lil	.40	.35
207	A24	1.50fr red org & org	.40	.35
208	A24	2fr blk & gray	.40	.35
209	A24	2.40fr red & pink	1.75	1.00
210	A24	3fr pink & pale pink	.75	.50
211	A24	4fr ultra & lt ultra	.95	.50
212	A24	4.50fr yel grn & lt grn	1.10	.50
213	A24	5fr org brn & lt org brn	.95	.50
214	A24	10fr dk vio & lil	1.10	.65
215	A24	15fr rose car & lil rose	1.50	.75
216	A24	20fr ol grn & lt ol grn	2.25	1.25
		Nos. 198-216 (19)	14.65	9.30

Martinique Girl A25

Mountains A30

Cliffs A26

Gathering Sugar Cane A27

Mount Pelée A28

Tropical Fruit — A29

1947, June 2 Engr. *Perf. 13*

No.	Type	Description	Unused	Used
217	A25	10c red brown	.50	.25
218	A25	30c deep blue	.50	.40
219	A25	50c olive brown	.50	.40
220	A26	60c dark green	.55	.50
221	A26	1fr red brown	.55	.35
222	A26	1.50fr purple	.60	.50
223	A27	2fr blue green	1.10	.75
224	A27	2.50fr blk brn	1.10	.65
225	A27	3fr deep blue	1.10	.65
226	A28	4fr dk brown	1.00	.65
227	A28	5fr dark green	1.10	.65
228	A28	6fr lilac rose	1.00	.65
229	A29	10fr indigo	1.75	1.25
230	A29	15fr red brown	1.90	1.25
231	A29	20fr blk brown	2.50	1.50
232	A30	25fr violet	2.50	1.60
233	A30	40fr blue green	3.00	2.00
		Nos. 217-233 (17)	21.25	14.00

SEMI-POSTAL STAMPS

Regular Issue of 1908 Surcharged in Red

Perf. 13½x14

1915, May 15 Unwmk.

No.	Type	Description	Unused	Used
B1	A16	10c + 5c car & brn	2.75	2.00
		Never hinged	4.00	

Curie Issue
Common Design Type

1938, Oct. 24 *Perf. 13*

No.	Type	Description	Unused	Used
B2	CD80	1.75fr + 50c brt ultra	13.00	13.00
		Never hinged	17.50	

French Revolution Issue
Common Design Type
Photo.; Name & Value Typo. in Black

1939, July 5

No.	Type	Description	Unused	Used
B3	CD83	45c + 25c grn	10.50	10.50
		Never hinged	15.00	
B4	CD83	70c + 30c brn	10.50	10.50
		Never hinged	15.00	
B5	CD83	90c + 35c red org	10.50	10.50
		Never hinged	15.00	
B6	CD83	1.25fr + 1fr rose pink	10.50	10.50
		Never hinged	15.00	
B7	CD83	2.25fr + 2fr blue	10.50	10.50
		Never hinged	15.00	
		Nos. B3-B7 (5)	52.50	52.50

Common Design Type and

Colonial Infantry with Machine Gun SP1

Naval Rifleman SP2

1941 Photo. *Perf. 13½*

No.	Type	Description	Unused	Used
B8	SP1	1fr + 1fr red	1.25	
B9	CD86	1.50fr + 3fr maroon	1.40	
B10	SP2	2.50fr + 1fr blue	1.40	
		Nos. B8-B10 (3)	4.05	

Nos. B8-B10 were issued by the Vichy government in France, but were not placed on sale in Martinique.

Nos. 188-189 Surcharged in Black or Red

1944 Engr. *Perf. 12½x12*

No.	Description	Unused	Used
B10A	50c + 1.50fr on 2.50fr blue (R)	.95	
B10B	+ 2.50fr on 1fr dull lilac	1.00	

Colonial Development Fund.

Nos. B10A-B10B were issued by the Vichy government in France, but were not placed on sale in Martinique.

Red Cross Issue
Common Design Type

1944 *Perf. 14½x14*

No.	Type	Description	Unused	Used
B11	CD90	5fr + 20fr dark purple	1.20	1.20

The surtax was for the French Red Cross and national relief.

AIR POST STAMPS

Catalogue values for unused stamps in this section are for Never Hinged items.

Common Design Type

1945 Unwmk. Photo. *Perf. 14½x14*

No.	Type	Description	Unused	Used
C1	CD87	50fr dark green	1.25	.80
C2	CD87	100fr plum	1.75	.80

Two other values, 8.50fr orange and 18fr red brown, were prepared but not issued. Value, $210 each.

Victory Issue
Common Design Type

1946, May 8 Engr. *Perf. 12½*

No.	Type	Description	Unused	Used
C3	CD92	8fr indigo	1.30	1.00

European victory of the Allied Nations in WWII.

Chad to Rhine Issue
Common Design Types

1946, June 6

No.	Type	Description	Unused	Used
C4	CD93	5fr orange	1.00	.90
C5	CD94	10fr slate grn	1.40	1.10
C6	CD95	15fr carmine	1.40	1.20
C7	CD96	20fr chocolate	1.40	1.20
C8	CD97	25fr deep blue	1.75	1.40
C9	CD98	50fr gray blk	1.90	1.50
		Nos. C4-C9 (6)	8.85	7.30

Seaplane and Beach Scene — AP1

Plane over Tropic Shore — AP2

Albatross — AP3

1947, June 2 *Perf. 13*

No.	Type	Description	Unused	Used
C10	AP1	50fr dk brn vio	6.50	2.75
C11	AP2	100fr dk bl grn	8.00	3.75
C12	AP3	200fr violet	45.00	25.00
		Nos. C10-C12 (3)	59.50	31.50

AIR POST SEMI-POSTAL STAMPS

Nurse with Mother & Child — SPAP1

Unwmk.

1942, June 22 Engr. *Perf. 13*

CB1 SPAP1 1.50fr + 3.50fr green .90
CB2 SPAP1 2fr + 6fr brn & red .90

Native children's welfare fund.

Nos. CB1-CB2 were issued by the Vichy government in France, but were not placed on sale in Martinique.

Colonial Education Fund

Common Design Type

1942, June 22

CB3 CD86a 1.20fr + 1.80fr blue & red 1.00

No. CB3 was issued by the Vichy government in France, but was not placed on sale in Martinique.

POSTAGE DUE STAMPS

The set of 14 French Colonies postage due stamps (Nos. J1-J14) overprinted "MARTINIQUE" diagonally in red in 1887 was not an official issue.

Postage Due Stamps of France, 1893-1926 Overprinted

1927, Oct. 10 *Perf. 14x13½*

J15 D2 5c light blue 1.75 1.75
J16 D2 10c brown 2.10 2.10
J17 D2 20c olive green 2.10 2.10
J18 D2 25c rose 2.75 2.75
J19 D2 30c red 3.75 3.75
J20 D2 45c green 5.25 5.25
J21 D2 50c brn violet 6.50 6.50
J22 D2 60c blue green 6.50 6.50
J23 D2 1fr red brown 8.75 8.75
J24 D2 2fr bright vio 12.00 12.00
J25 D2 3fr magenta 13.00 13.00
Nos. J15-J25 (11) 64.45 64.45

Tropical Fruit — D3

1933, Feb. 15 Photo. *Perf. 13½*

J26 D3 5c dk bl, *green* .50 .50
J27 D3 10c orange brown .50 .50
J28 D3 20c dk blue .95 .95
J29 D3 25c red, *pink* 1.40 1.40
J30 D3 30c dk vio 1.40 1.40
J31 D3 45c red, *yel* 1.10 1.10
J32 D3 50c dk brn 1.75 1.75
J33 D3 60c dl grn 1.75 1.75
J34 D3 1fr blk, *org* 1.75 1.75
J35 D3 2fr dp rose 1.75 1.75
J36 D3 3fr dk blue, *bl* 1.75 1.75
Nos. J26-J36 (11) 14.60 14.60

Type of 1933 Without "RF"

1943

J36A D3 10c orange brown .35
J36B D3 20c dk blue .35
J36C D3 25c red, *pink* .50
J36D D3 30c dk vio .50
Nos. J36A-J36D (4) 1.70

Nos. J36A-J36D were issued by the Vichy government in France, but were not placed on sale in Martinique.

Catalogue values for unused stamps in this section, from this point to the end of the section, are for Never Hinged items.

Map — D4

1947, June 2 Engr. *Perf. 14x13*

J37 D4 10c ultra .40 .30
J38 D4 30c brt bl grn .40 .30
J39 D4 50c slate gray .40 .30
J40 D4 1fr org red .40 .30
J41 D4 2fr dk vio brn .90 .75
J42 D4 3fr lilac rose .95 .80
J43 D4 4fr dk brn .95 .95
J44 D4 5fr red 1.20 .95
J45 D4 10fr black 2.10 1.60
J46 D4 20fr olive grn 2.40 1.75
Nos. J37-J46 (10) 10.10 8.00

PARCEL POST STAMP

Postage Due Stamp of French Colonies Surcharged in Black

1903, Oct. Unwmk. *Imperf.*

Q1 D1 5fr on 60c brn, *buff* 550.00 *675.00*
a. Inverted surcharge 875.00 950.00

MAURITANIA

mor-ə-ta-nē-ə

LOCATION — Northwestern Africa, bordering on the Atlantic Ocean
GOVT. — Republic
AREA — 398,000 sq. mi.
POP. — 2,581,738 (1999 est.)
CAPITAL — Nouakchott

The Islamic Republic of Mauritania was proclaimed Nov. 28, 1958.

Stamps of French West Africa were used in the period between the issues of the colony and the republic.

100 Centimes = 1 Franc
Ouguiya ("um") (1973)

Catalogue values for unused stamps in this country are for Never Hinged items, beginning with Scott 116 in the regular postage section, Scott B16 in the semi-postal section, Scott C14 in the airpost section, Scott J19 in the postage due section, and Scott O1 in the official section.

See French West Africa No. 65 for additional stamp inscribed "Mauritanie" and "Afrique Occidentale Francaise."

General Louis Faidherbe A1

Oil Palms — A2

Dr. Noel Eugène Ballay A3

Perf. 14x13½

1906-07 Typo. Unwmk.

"Mauritanie" in Red or Blue

1 A1 1c slate .75 .75
2 A1 2c chocolate 1.40 1.20
3 A1 4c choc, *gray bl* 2.00 1.60
4 A1 5c green 1.10 .90
5 A1 10c carmine (B) 12.00 4.50
7 A2 20c black, *azure* 22.50 15.00
8 A2 25c blue, *pnksh* 7.50 6.00
9 A2 30c choc, *pnksh* 110.00 65.00
10 A2 35c black, *yellow* 8.25 5.25
11 A2 40c car, *az* (B) 8.25 8.25
12 A2 45c choc, *grnsh* ('07) 9.00 8.25
13 A2 50c deep violet 9.00 7.50
14 A2 75c blue, *org* 8.25 8.25
15 A3 1fr black, *azure* 22.50 22.50
16 A3 2fr blue, *pink* 52.50 52.50
17 A3 5fr car, *straw*(B) 140.00 140.00
Nos. 1-17 (16) 415.00 347.45

Crossing Desert A4

1913-38

18 A4 1c brn vio & brn .30 *.35*
19 A4 2c black & blue .35 *.45*
20 A4 4c violet & blk .35 *.45*
21 A4 5c yel grn & bl grn 1.00 .65
a. Chalky paper 3.00 2.25
22 A4 5c brn vio & rose ('22) .25 .25
23 A4 10c rose & red org 2.25 1.75
a. Chalky paper 3.00 2.25
24 A4 10c yel grn & bl grn ('22) .55 .55
25 A4 10c lil rose, *bluish* ('25) .45 .45
26 A4 15c dk brn & blk ('17) .60 .60
a. Chalky paper .75 .75
27 A4 20c bis brn & org .60 .60
28 A4 25c blue & vio 1.40 1.10
29 A4 25c grn & rose ('22) .30 .30
30 A4 30c bl grn & rose 1.25 1.25
31 A4 30c rose & red org ('22) 1.40 1.40
32 A4 30c black & yel ('26) .30 .30
33 A4 30c bl grn & yel grn ('28) 1.10 1.10
34 A4 35c brown & vio .75 .65
35 A4 35c dp grn & lt grn ('38) 1.25 1.25
36 A4 40c gray & bl grn 2.50 2.25
37 A4 45c org & bis brn 1.60 1.25
38 A4 50c brn vio & rose 1.20 1.20
39 A4 50c dk bl & ultra ('22) .55 .55
40 A4 50c gray grn & dp bl ('26) .85 .85
41 A4 60c vio, *pnksh* ('25) .70 *.75*
42 A4 65c yel brn & lt bl ('26) .85 *1.00*
43 A4 75c ultra & brown .90 .90
44 A4 85c myr grn & lt brn ('26) 1.00 *1.20*
45 A4 90c brn red & rose ('30) 2.00 1.90
46 A4 1fr rose & black 1.00 1.00
47 A4 1.10fr vio & ver ('28) 10.50 *12.00*
48 A4 1.25fr dk bl & blk brn ('33) 2.00 2.00
49 A4 1.50fr lt bl & dp bl ('30) 1.40 *1.50*
50 A4 1.75fr bl grn & brn red ('33) 1.75 1.75
51 A4 1.75fr dk bl & ultra ('38) 2.10 1.75
52 A4 2fr red org & vio 2.00 1.75
53 A4 3fr red violet ('30) 1.75 1.75
54 A4 5fr violet & blue 3.00 3.00
Nos. 18-54 (37) 52.10 51.80

Stamp and Type of 1913-38 Surcharged

1922-25

55 A4 60c on 75c violet, *pnksh* 1.00 1.00
56 A4 65c on 15c dk brn & blk ('25) 1.75 *1.90*
57 A4 85c on 75c ultra & brn ('25) 1.75 *1.90*
Nos. 55-57 (3) 4.50 *4.80*

Stamp and Type of 1913-38 Surcharged with New Value and Bars

1924-27

58 A4 25c on 2fr red org & vio 1.00 1.00
59 A4 90c on 75c brn red & cer ('27) 2.40 *2.60*
60 A4 1.25fr on 1fr dk bl & ultra ('26) .55 *.60*
61 A4 1.50fr on 1fr bl & dp bl ('27) 1.50 *1.60*
62 A4 3fr on 5fr ol brn & red vio ('27) 6.00 6.75
63 A4 10fr on 5fr mag & bl grn ('27) 6.00 6.75
64 A4 20fr on 5fr bl vio & dp org ('27) 6.75 *7.50*
Nos. 58-64 (7) 24.20 *26.80*

Common Design Types pictured following the introduction.

Colonial Exposition Issue

Common Design Types

Engr.; Name of Country Typo. in Black

1931, Apr. 13 *Perf. 12½*

65 CD70 40c deep green 6.75 6.75
66 CD71 50c violet 5.00 5.00
67 CD72 90c red orange 5.00 5.00
68 CD73 1.50fr dull blue 5.00 5.00
Nos. 65-68 (4) 21.75 21.75

Paris International Exposition Issue

Common Design Types

1937, Apr. 15 *Perf. 13*

69 CD74 20c deep violet 1.60 1.60
70 CD75 30c dark green 1.60 1.60
71 CD76 40c carmine rose 1.60 1.60
72 CD77 50c dk brn & blk 1.40 1.40
73 CD78 90c red 1.40 1.40
74 CD79 1.50fr ultra 1.75 1.75
Nos. 69-74 (6) 9.35 9.35

Colonial Arts Exhibition Issue

Common Design Type

Souvenir Sheet

1937 *Imperf.*

75 CD76 3fr dark blue 7.50 *9.00*

Camel Rider — A5

Mauri Couple — A8

Mauris on Camels A6

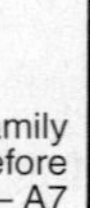

Family Before Tent — A7

1938-40 *Perf. 13*

76 A5 2c violet blk .30 .30
77 A5 3c dp ultra .30 .30
78 A5 4c rose violet .30 .30
79 A5 5c orange red .30 .30
80 A5 10c brown car .40 .40
81 A5 15c dk violet .40 .40
82 A6 20c red .40 .40
83 A6 25c deep ultra .40 .40
84 A6 30c deep brown .30 .30
85 A6 35c Prus green .75 .75
86 A6 40c rose car ('40) .30 .30
87 A6 45c Prus grn ('40) .30 .30
88 A6 50c purple .55 .55
89 A7 55c rose violet .90 .90
90 A7 60c violet ('40) .45 .45
91 A7 65c deep green .90 .90
92 A7 70c red ('40) .75 .75
93 A7 80c deep blue 1.25 1.25
94 A7 90c rose violet ('39) .85 .85
95 A7 1fr red 2.10 2.10
96 A7 1fr dp green ('40) .85 .85
97 A7 1.25fr rose car ('39) 1.40 1.40
98 A7 1.40fr dp blue ('40) .85 .85
99 A7 1.50fr violet .85 .85
99A A7 1.50fr red brn ('40) 100.00 100.00
100 A7 1.60fr black brn ('40) 1.60 1.60
101 A8 1.75fr deep ultra 1.25 *1.40*
102 A8 2fr rose violet .75 *.85*
103 A8 2.25fr dull ultra ('39) .75 .75
104 A8 2.50fr black brn ('40) .90 .90
105 A8 3fr deep green .75 *.85*
106 A8 5fr scarlet .90 *1.00*
107 A8 10fr deep brown 1.60 *1.90*
108 A8 20fr brown car 1.60 *1.90*
Nos. 76-108 (34) 126.25 127.30

Nos. 91 and 109 surcharged with new values are listed under French West Africa.
For surcharges see Nos. B9-B12.

Caillie Issue
Common Design Type

1939, Apr. 5 Engr. *Perf. 12½x12*

109 CD81 90c org brn & org 1.00 1.00
110 CD81 2fr brt violet 1.10 1.10
111 CD81 2.25fr ultra & dk bl 1.10 1.10
Nos. 109-111 (3) 3.20 3.20

New York World's Fair Issue
Common Design Type

1939, May 10

112 CD82 1.25fr carmine lake .75 .75
113 CD82 2.25fr ultra .75 .75

Caravan and Marshal Pétain A9

1941

114 A9 1fr green .50 *1.10*
115 A9 2.50fr deep blue .50 *1.10*

For surcharges, see Nos. B15A-B15B.

Types of 1938-40 Without "RF"

1943-44

115A A5 10c brown car .50
115B A5 15c dk violet .55
115C A6 40c rose car 1.10
115D A6 50c purple 1.10
115E A7 60c violet 1.10
115F A7 1fr dp green 1.10
Nos. 115A-115F (6) 5.45

Nos. 115A-115F were issued by the Vichy government in France, but were not placed on sale in Mauritania.

Catalogue values for unused stamps in this section, from this point to the end of the section, are for Never Hinged items.

Islamic Republic

Camel and Hands Raising Flag — A10

Unwmk.

1960, Jan. 20 Engr. *Perf. 13*

116 A10 25fr multi, *pink* .60 .35

Issued to commemorate the proclamation of the Islamic Republic of Mauritania.

Imperforates
Most Mauritania stamps from 1960 onward exist imperforate in issued and trial colors, and also in small presentation sheets in issued colors.

C.C.T.A. Issue
Common Design Type

1960, May 16

117 CD106 25fr bluish grn & ultra .75 .40

Flag and Map — A11

1960, Dec. 15 Engr. *Perf. 13*

118 A11 25fr org brn, emer & sepia .60 .30

Proclamation of independence, Nov. 28, 1960.

Pastoral Well — A12

Scimitar-horned Oryx — A15

Spotted Hyena A13

Ore Train and Camel Riders A14

Designs: 50c, 1fr, Well. 2fr, Date harvesting. 3fr, Aoudad. 4fr, Fennecs. 5fr, Millet harvesting. 10fr, Shoemaker. 15fr, Fishing boats. 20fr, Nomad school. 25fr, 30fr, Seated dance. No. 130, Religious student. 60fr, Metalworker.

1960-62 Unwmk. *Perf. 13*

119 A12 50c mag, yel & brn ('61) .20 .20
120 A12 1fr brn, yel brn & grn .20 .20
121 A12 2fr dk brn, bl & grn .20 .20
122 A13 3fr bl grn, red brn & gray ('61) .40 .25
123 A13 4fr yel grn & ocher ('61) .40 .25
124 A12 5fr red, dk brn & yel brn .35 .25
125 A14 10fr dk bl & org .40 .25
126 A14 15fr ver, dk brn, grn & bl .70 .25
127 A14 20fr grn, sl grn & red brn .70 .25
128 A12 25fr ultra & gray grn ('61) 1.00 .25
129 A12 30fr lil, bis & indigo 1.00 .25
130 A12 50fr org brn & grn 1.75 .40
131 A14 50fr red brn, bl & ol ('62) 4.75 .80
132 A12 60fr grn, cl & pur 3.00 .40
133 A15 85fr bl, brn & blk ('61) 7.25 1.90
Nos. 119-133 (15) 22.30 6.10

An overprint, "Jeux Olympiques / Rome 1960 / Tokyo 1964," the 5-ring Olympic emblem and a 75fr surcharge were applied to Nos. 126-127 in 1962. Two overprint types, varying in size. Values, set: small overprint, $20; large overprint, $22.50.

An overprint, "Aide aux Rèfugiès" with uprooted oak emblem, was applied in 1962 to No. 132 and to pink-paper printings of Nos. 129-130. Two types: type 1, 26 leaves on tree; type 2, 37 leaves on tree. Values, set: type 1, $24; type 2, $8.

Other overprints, applied to airmail stamps, are noted after No. C16.

1963, July 6

Designs: 50c, Striped hyena. 1.50fr, Cheetah. 2fr, Guinea baboons. 5fr, Dromedaries. 10fr, Leopard. 15fr, Bongo antelopes. 20fr, Aardvark. 25fr, Patas monkeys. 30fr, Crested porcupine. 50fr, Dorcas gazelle. 60fr, Common chameleon.

134 A15 50c sl grn, blk & org brn .20 .20
135 A13 1fr ultra, blk & yel .20 .20
136 A15 1.50fr ol grn, brn & bis .35 .20
137 A13 2fr dk brn, grn & dp org .30 .25
138 A15 5fr brn, ultra & bis .35 .25
139 A13 10fr blk & bis .75 .25
140 A13 15fr vio bl & red brn .75 .25
141 A13 20fr dk red brn, dk bl & bis .85 .30
142 A15 25fr brt grn, red brn & ol bis 1.25 .30
143 A13 30fr dk brn, dk bl & ol bis 2.40 .30
144 A15 50fr grn, ocher & brn 3.00 .90
145 A13 60fr dk bl, emer & ocher 3.75 1.25
Nos. 134-145 (12) 14.15 4.65

UN Headquarters, New York, and View of Nouakchott — A15a

1962, June 1 Engr. *Perf. 13*

167 A15a 15fr blk, ultra & cop red .30 .30
168 A15a 25fr cop red, sl grn & ultra .45 .35
169 A15a 85fr dk bl, dl pur & cop red 1.25 1.10
Nos. 167-169 (3) 2.00 1.75

Mauritania's admission to the UN.

African-Malagasy Union Issue
Common Design Type

1962, Sept. 8 Photo. *Perf. 12½x12*

170 CD110 30fr multi .75 .50

Organization Emblem and View of Nouakchott — A16

1962, Oct. 15 *Perf. 12½*

171 A16 30fr dk red brn, ultra & brt grn .70 .40

8th Conf. of the Organization to Fight Endemic Diseases, Nouakchott, Oct. 15-18.

Map, Mechanized and Manual Farm Work — A17

1962, Nov. 28 Engr. *Perf. 13*

172 A17 30fr blk, grn & vio brn .75 .35

2nd anniversary of independence.

People in European and Mauritanian Clothes — A18

1962, Dec. 24 Unwmk.

173 A18 25fr multicolored .40 .25

First anniversary of Congress for Unity.

Weather and WMO Symbols — A20

1964, Mar. 23 Unwmk. *Perf. 13*

175 A20 85fr dk brn, dk bl & org 1.50 .75

UN 4th World Meteorological Day, Mar. 23.

IQSY Emblem A21

1964, July 3 Engr.

176 A21 25fr dk bl, red & grn .60 .35

International Quiet Sun Year, 1964-65.

Striped Mullet A22

Designs: 5fr, Mauritanian lobster, vert. 10fr, Royal lobster, vert. 60fr, Maigre fish.

1964, Oct. 5 Engr. *Perf. 13*

177 A22 1fr org brn, dk bl & grn .40 .25
178 A22 5fr org brn, sl grn & choc .50 .25
179 A22 10fr dk bl, bis & sl grn .80 .25
180 A22 60fr dk brn, dp grn & dl bl 5.00 .80
Nos. 177-180 (4) 6.70 1.55

Cooperation Issue
Common Design Type

1964, Nov. 7 Unwmk. *Perf. 13*

181 CD119 25fr mag, sl grn & dk brn .60 .35

Water Lilies A23

Tropical Plants: 10fr, Acacia. 20fr, Adenium obesum. 45fr, Caralluma retrospiciens.

1965, Jan. 11 Engr. *Perf. 13*

182	A23	5fr multi	.20	.25
183	A23	10fr multi, vert.	.20	.25
184	A23	20fr multi	.55	.25
185	A23	45fr multi, vert.	1.10	.50
		Nos. 182-185 (4)	2.05	1.25

Hardine A24

Musical Instruments: 8fr, Tobol (drums). 25fr, Tidinit (stringed instruments). 40fr, Musicians.

1965, Mar. 8 *Perf. 13*

186	A24	2fr red brn, brt bl & sep	.20	.25
187	A24	8fr red brn, red & brn	.40	.25
188	A24	25fr red brn, emer & blk	.65	.25
189	A24	40fr vio bl, plum & blk	1.00	.35
		Nos. 186-189 (4)	2.25	1.10

Abraham Lincoln (1809-1865) — A25

1965, Apr. 23 Photo. *Perf. 13x12½*

190	A25	50fr lt ultra & multi	1.00	.35

Palms at Adrar A26

Designs: 4fr, Chinguetti mosque, vert. 15fr, Clay pit and donkeys. 60fr, Decorated door, Oualata.

1965, June 14 Engr. *Perf. 13*

191	A26	1fr brn, bl & grn	.25	.20
192	A26	4fr dk red, bl & brn	.25	.20
193	A26	15fr multi	.40	.25
194	A26	60fr grn, dk brn & red brn	1.25	.50
		Nos. 191-194 (4)	2.15	1.15

Issued for tourist publicity.

Tea Service in Inlaid Box — A27

7fr, Tobacco pouch and pipe, vert. 25fr, Dagger, vert. 50fr, Mederdra ornamental chest.

1965, Sept. 13 Unwmk. *Perf. 13*

195	A27	3fr gray, choc & ocher	.25	.20
196	A27	7fr red lil, Prus bl & org	.25	.20
197	A27	25fr blk, org red & brn	.55	.25
198	A27	50fr brt grn, brn org & mar	1.10	.35
		Nos. 195-198 (4)	2.15	1.00

Choum Railroad Tunnel — A28

10fr, Nouakchott wharf, ships & anchor, horiz. 30fr, as 5fr. 85fr, Nouakchott hospital & caduceus, horiz.

1965, Oct. 18 Engr. *Perf. 13*

199	A28	5fr dk brn & brt grn	.20	.20
200	A28	10fr dk vio bl, brn red & Prus bl	.25	.20
201	A28	30fr brn red, red & red brn	.70	.25
202	A28	85fr dp bl, rose cl & lil	1.10	.55
		Nos. 199-202 (4)	2.25	1.20

Sculptured Heads A29

Designs: 30fr, "Music and Dance." 60fr, Movie camera and huts.

1966, Apr. Engr. *Perf. 13*

203	A29	10fr brt grn, blk & brn	.20	.20
204	A29	30fr brt bl, red lil & blk	.50	.25
205	A29	60fr red, org & dk brn	1.00	.45
		Nos. 203-205 (3)	1.70	.90

Intl. Negro Arts Festival, Dakar, Senegal, Apr. 1-24.

Mimosa — A30

Myrina Silenus — A31

Flowers: 15fr, Schouwia purpurea. 20fr, Ipomea asarifolia. 25fr, Grewia bicolor. 30fr, Pancratium trianthum. 60fr, Blepharis linariifolia.

1966, Aug. 8 Photo. *Perf. 13x12½*

Flowers in Natural Colors

206	A30	10fr dl bl & dk bl	.40	.25
207	A30	15fr dk brn & buff	.60	.35
208	A30	20fr grnsh bl & lt bl	.70	.40
209	A30	25fr brn & buff	1.00	.50
210	A30	30fr lil & vio	1.50	.75
211	A30	60fr grn & pale grn	2.00	1.25
		Nos. 206-211 (6)	6.20	3.50

1966, Oct. 3 Photo. *Perf. 12x12½*

Various Butterflies

212	A31	5fr buff & multi	1.10	.30
213	A31	30fr bl grn & multi	3.50	.45
214	A31	45fr yel grn & multi	4.75	.65
215	A31	60fr dl bl & multi	6.75	1.10
		Nos. 212-215 (4)	16.10	2.50

Hunter, Petroglyph from Adrar A32

Designs: 3fr, Two men fighting, petroglyph from Tenses (Adrar). 30fr, Copper jug, Le Mreyer (Adrar). 50fr, Camel caravan.

1966, Oct. 24 Engr. *Perf. 13*

216	A32	2fr dk brn & brn org	.30	.20
217	A32	3fr bl & brn org	.80	.20
218	A32	30fr sl grn & dk red	1.40	.30
219	A32	50fr mag, sl grn & brn	2.40	.70
		Nos. 216-219 (4)	4.90	1.40

Issued for tourist publicity.

UNESCO, 20th Anniv. A33

1966, Dec. 5 Litho. *Perf. 12½x13*

220	A33	30fr multi	1.00	.40

Plaza of Three Cultures, Mexico City — A34

Olympic Village, Grenoble A35

Designs: 40fr, Olympic torch and skating rink. 100fr, Olympic Stadium, Mexico City.

1967, Mar. 11 Engr. *Perf. 13*

221	A34	20fr dl bl, brn & sl grn	.50	.25
222	A35	30fr dl bl, brn & grn	.60	.35
223	A34	40fr brt bl, dk brn & sep	1.00	.45
224	A35	100fr brn, emer & blk	1.75	.80
		Nos. 221-224 (4)	3.85	1.85

#221, 223 for the 19th Olympic Games, Mexico City; #222, 224 the 10th Winter Olympic Games, Grenoble.

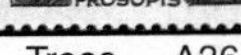

Trees — A36

1967 Jamboree Emblem and Campsite — A37

1967, May 15 Engr. *Perf. 13*

225	A36	10fr Prosopis	.45	.20
226	A36	15fr Jujube	.60	.20
227	A36	20fr Date palm	.70	.25
228	A36	25fr Peltophorum	.90	.30
229	A36	30fr Baobob	1.25	.35
		Nos. 225-229 (5)	3.90	1.30

1967, June 5

Design: 90fr, 1967 Jamboree emblem and Mauritanian Boy Scouts, horiz.

230	A37	60fr brn, ultra & slate grn	.95	.30
231	A37	90fr dl red, bl & slate grn	1.40	.45

12th Boy Scout World Jamboree, Farragut State Park, Idaho, Aug. 1-9.

Weavers A38

10fr, Embroiderer, vert. 20fr, Nurse, mother & infant. 30fr, Laundress, vert. 50fr, Seamstresses.

1967, July 3 Engr. *Perf. 13*

232	A38	5fr plum, blk & cl	.25	.20
233	A38	10fr plum, brt grn & blk	.25	.20
234	A38	20fr brt bl, plum & blk	.50	.25
235	A38	30fr dk bl, brn & blk	.60	.30
236	A38	50fr plum, sl & blk	1.00	.30
		Nos. 232-236 (5)	2.60	1.25

Progress made by working women.

Cattle and Hypodermic Syringe — A39

1967, Aug. 21 Engr. *Perf. 13*

237	A39	30fr sl grn, brt bl & rose cl	.80	.35

Campaign against cattle plague.

Monetary Union Issue

Common Design Type

1967, Nov. 4 Engr. *Perf. 13*

238	CD125	30fr gray & orange	.45	.25

Fruit — A40

Human Rights Flame — A41

1967, Dec. 4 Engr. *Perf. 13*

239	A40	1fr Doom palm	.35	.20
240	A40	2fr Bito, horiz.	.40	.20
241	A40	3fr Baobob	.50	.20
242	A40	4fr Jujube, horiz.	.60	.20
243	A40	5fr Daye	.75	.40
		Nos. 239-243 (5)	2.60	1.20

For surcharges see Nos. 323-327.

1968, Jan. 8 Photo. *Perf. 13x12½*

244	A41	30fr brt grn, blk & yel	.60	.25
245	A41	50fr brn org, blk & yel	.75	.35

International Human Rights Year.

Nouakchott Mosque A42

45fr, Amogjar Pass. 90fr, Cavaliers' Towers.

1968, Apr. 1 Photo. *Perf. 12½x13*

246	A42	30fr multi	.35	.20
247	A42	45fr multi	.50	.20
248	A42	90fr multi	.85	.40
		Nos. 246-248 (3)	1.70	.80

For surcharges see Nos. 332-333.

UPU Building, Bern, Globe and Map of Africa A43

1968, June 3 Engr. *Perf. 13*

249	A43	30fr ver, ultra & olive	.60	.25

Mauritania's admission to the UPU.

Symbolic Water Cycle A44

1968, June 24

250	A44	90fr car, lake, grn & sl grn	.75	.35

Hydrological Decade (UNESCO), 1965-74.

Land Yacht Racing — A45

Donkey and Foal — A46

40fr, Three land yachts racing, horiz. 60fr, Crew changing wheel of land yacht.

1968, Oct. 7 Engr. *Perf. 13*

251 A45 30fr ultra, org & ocher .70 .25
252 A45 40fr ultra, dp org & plum .85 .30
253 A45 60fr brt grn, dp org & ocher 1.40 .55
Nos. 251-253 (3) 2.95 1.10

1968, Dec. 16 Photo. *Perf. 13*

Domestic Animals: 10fr, Ewe and lamb. 15fr, Camel and calf. 30fr, Mare and foal. 50fr, Cow and calf. 90fr, Goat and kid.

254 A46 5fr ocher & multi .30 .20
255 A46 10fr multi .40 .25
256 A46 15fr multi .45 .25
257 A46 30fr multi .85 .30
258 A46 50fr pur & multi 1.25 .40
259 A46 90fr multi 2.40 .60
Nos. 254-259 (6) 5.65 2.00

For surcharge see No. 303.

ILO Emblem and Map — A47

Desert Monitor — A48

1969, Apr. 14 Photo. *Perf. 13x12½*

260 A47 50fr dk & lt bl, pur & org .60 .30

ILO, 50th anniversary.

1969, May 5 Photo. *Perf. 13x12½*

Reptiles: 10fr, Horned viper. 30fr, Common spitting cobra. 60fr, Rock python. 85fr, African crocodile.

261 A48 5fr brn, pink & yel .40 .25
262 A48 10fr brn, lt grn & yel .70 .30
263 A48 30fr dk brn, pink & yel 1.75 .40
264 A48 60fr dk brn, lt bl & yel 3.00 1.10
265 A48 85fr dk brn, yel & red 5.50 1.40
Nos. 261-265 (5) 11.35 3.45

Lady Beetle Eating Noxious Insects A49

1969, May 26 Engr. *Perf. 13*

266 A49 30fr indigo, grn & mar 3.00 .70

Natural protection of date palms.

Development Bank Issue
Common Design Type

1969, Sept. 10 Engr. *Perf. 13*

267 CD130 30fr Prus bl, grn & ocher .60 .25

Pendant — A50

Design: 20fr, Rahla headdress, horiz.

1969, Oct. 13 Engr. *Perf. 13*

268 A50 10fr dk brn, lil & brn .25 .20
269 A50 20fr blk, Prus bl & mag .50 .25

For surcharges see Nos. 309-310.

Desalination Plant A51

Designs: 15fr, Fishing harbor, Nouadhibou. 30fr, Meat refrigeration plant, Kaedi.

1969, Dec. 1 Engr. *Perf. 13*

270 A51 10fr brt rose lil, dk bl & red brn .25 .25
271 A51 15fr dk car, blk & dp bl .25 .25
272 A51 30fr blk, dk bl & rose brn .40 .25
Nos. 270-272 (3) .90 .75

Issued to publicize economic progress.

Lenin (1870-1924) A52

Sternocera Interrupta A53

1970, Feb. 16 Photo. *Perf. 12x12½*

273 A52 30fr car, lt bl & blk 1.75 .50

1970, Mar. 16 Engr. *Perf. 13*

Insects: 10fr, Anoplocnemis curvipes. 20fr, Julodis aequinoctialis. 30fr, Thermophilum sexmaculatum marginatum. 40fr, Plocaederus denticornis.

274 A53 5fr red brn, buff & blk .50 .25
275 A53 10fr red brn, yel & brn .85 .25
276 A53 20fr red brn, lil & dk ol 1.25 .25
277 A53 30fr red brn, grn & vio 2.10 .35
278 A53 40fr red brn, lt bl & brn 3.75 .70
Nos. 274-278 (5) 8.45 1.80

For surcharges see Nos. 311-315.

Soccer Players and Hemispheres — A54

Hemispheres & various views of soccer play.

1970, May 11 Engr. *Perf. 13*

279 A54 25fr bl, vio bl & dk brn .45 .20
280 A54 30fr vio bl, brn & ol brn .45 .20
281 A54 70fr brt pink, mar & dk brn .90 .40
282 A54 150fr brn red, grn & dk brn 2.10 .65
Nos. 279-282 (4) 3.90 1.45

9th World Soccer Championships for the Jules Rimet Cup, Mexico City, 5/29-6/21.

UPU Headquarters Issue
Common Design Type

1970, May 20 Engr. *Perf. 13*

283 CD133 30fr grn, dk brn & red brn .50 .25

Woman Wearing "Boubou" — A55

Various Traditional Costumes: 30fr, 70fr, Men. 40fr, 50fr, Women.

1970, Sept. 21 Engr. *Perf. 12½x13*

284 A55 10fr red brn & org .35 .25
285 A55 30fr ol, red brn & ind .55 .25
286 A55 40fr red brn, plum & dk brn .75 .30
287 A55 50fr dk brn & brt bl 1.00 .35
288 A55 70fr bl, brn & dk brn 1.25 .50
Nos. 284-288 (5) 3.90 1.65

People of Various Races — A55a

Design: 40fr, Outstretched hands, vert.

1971, Mar. 22 Engr. *Perf. 13*

288A A55a 30fr brn vio, ol & brt bl .60 .20
288B A55a 40fr brn red, bl & blk .80 .25

Intl. year against racial discrimination.

Gen. Charles de Gaulle (1890-1970), President of France — A56

Design: 100fr, De Gaulle as President.

1971, June 18 Photo. *Perf. 13*

289 A56 40fr gold, blk & grnsh bl 2.00 .65
290 A56 100fr lt bl, gold & blk 4.50 1.25
a. Souvenir sheet of 2, #289-290 6.50 6.50

Iron Ore Freight Train of Miferma Mines — A57

1971, Nov. 8 Photo. *Perf. 12½x12*

291 35fr ore cars 2.00 .65
292 100fr engines 4.50 1.60
a. A57 Pair, #291-292 8.75 8.75

UNICEF Emblem and Child A59

1971, Dec. 11 Litho. *Perf. 13½*

293 A59 35fr lt ultra, blk & brn .60 .25

UNICEF, 25th anniv.

Samuel F. B. Morse and Telegraph — A60

Designs: 40fr, Relay satellite over globes. 75fr, Alexander Graham Bell.

1972, May 17 Engr. *Perf. 13*

294 A60 35fr lilac, indigo & vio .60 .25
295 A60 40fr bl, ocher & choc .65 .25
296 A60 75fr grn, ol grn & Prus bl 1.00 .45
Nos. 294-296 (3) 2.25 .95

4th World Telecommunications Day.
For surcharge see No. 343.

Fossil Spirifer Shell — A61

1972, July 31 Litho. *Perf. 12½*

297 A61 25fr shown 2.50 .70
298 A61 75fr Phacops rana 4.50 1.25

Fossil shells.
For surcharges see Nos. 306, 308.

West African Monetary Union Issue
Common Design Type

1972, Nov. 2 Engr. *Perf. 13*

299 CD136 35fr brn, yel grn & gray .85 .25

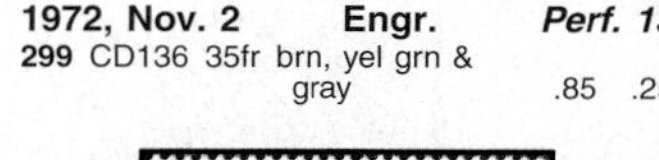

Mediterranean Monk Seal and Pup — A63

1973, Feb. 28 Litho. *Perf. 13*

300 A63 40fr multi 2.75 .70

See #C130. For surcharges see #307, C145.

Food Program Symbols and Emblem A64

1973, Apr. 30 Photo. *Perf. 12x12½*

301 A64 35fr gray bl & multi .45 .25

World Food Program, 10th anniversary.

UPU Monument and Globe A65

1973, May 28 Engr. *Perf. 13*

302 A65 100fr grn, ocher & bl 1.60 .65

Universal Postal Union Day.

Currency Change to Ouguiya ("um")

No. 258 Surcharged with New Value, 2 Bars, and Overprinted: "SECHERESSE / SOLIDARITE / AFRICAINE"

1973, Aug. 16 Photo. *Perf. 13*

303 A46 20um on 50fr multi .90 .40

African solidarity in drought emergency.

African Postal Union Issue

Common Design Type

1973, Sept. 12 Engr. *Perf. 13*

304 CD137 20um org, brn & ocher 1.10 .40

INTERPOL Emblem, Detective, Criminal, Fingerprint A66

1973, Sept. 24

305 A66 15um brn, ver & vio 1.00 .40

50th anniv. of Intl. Criminal Police Org.

Nos. 297-298, 300 and 268-269 Surcharged with New Value and Two Bars in Ultramarine, Red or Black

1973-74 Litho. *Perf. 12½*

306 A61 5um on 25fr (U) ('74) 2.00 .80
307 A63 8um on 40fr (R) .95 .40
308 A61 15um on 75fr (U) ('74) 5.25 1.50

Engr.

Perf. 13

309 A50 27um on 10fr (B) ('74) 2.25 .65
310 A50 28um on 20fr (R) ('74) 1.75 .80
Nos. 306-310 (5) 12.20 4.15

Nos. 274-278 Surcharged with New Value and Two bars in Violet Blue or Red

1974, July 29 Engr. *Perf. 13*

311 A53 5um on 5fr 1.25 .45
312 A53 7um on 10fr 1.10 .30
313 A53 8um on 20fr 1.25 .35
314 A53 10um on 30fr (R) 1.75 .40
315 A53 20um on 40fr 3.50 1.00
Nos. 311-315 (5) 8.85 2.50

UPU Emblem and Globes — A67

1974, Aug. 5 Photo. *Perf. 13*

316 A67 30um multi 1.90 .80
317 A67 50um multi 3.25 1.25

Centenary of Universal Postal Union. For overprints see Nos. 321-322.

5-Ouguiya Coin and Bank Note — A68

Designs: 8um, 10-ouguiya coin. 20um, 20-ouguiya coin. Each design includes picture of different bank note.

1974, Aug. 12 Engr.

318 A68 7um blk, ultra & grn .60 .20
319 A68 8um blk, sl grn & mag .70 .20
320 A68 20um blk, red & bl 1.40 .45
Nos. 318-320 (3) 2.70 .85

First anniversary of currency reform.

Nos. 316-317 Overprinted in Red: "9 OCTOBRE / 100 ANS D'UNION POSTALE / INTERNATIONALE"

1974, Oct. 9 Photo. *Perf. 13*

321 A67 30um multi 2.25 1.00
322 A67 50um multi 4.00 1.40

Centenary of Universal Postal Union.

Nos. 239-243 Surcharged with New Value and Two Bars in Black or Violet Blue

1975, Feb. 14 Engr. *Perf. 13*

323 A40 1um on 5fr multi (B) .30 .20
324 A40 2um on 4fr multi (VB) .30 .20
325 A40 3um on 2fr multi (B) .35 .20
326 A40 10um on 1fr multi (B) .95 .25
327 A40 12um on 3fr multi (VB) 1.10 .30
Nos. 323-327 (5) 3.00 1.15

Hunters, Rock Carvings — A69

White and Black Men, Map of Europe and Africa — A70

Rock Carvings from Zemmour Cave: 5um, Ostrich. 10um, Elephant, horiz.

1975, May 26 Engr. *Perf. 13*

328 A69 4um lt brn & car 1.00 .20
329 A69 5um red lil 1.25 .30
330 A69 10um blue 1.90 .45
Nos. 328-330 (3) 4.15 .95

Europafrica Issue

1975, July 7 Engr. *Perf. 13*

331 A70 40um dk brn & red 2.10 .80

Nos. 247-248 Surcharged in Red or Black

1975, Aug. 25 Photo. *Perf. 12½x13*

332 A42 15um on 45fr (R) 1.25 .50
333 A42 25um on 90fr 2.00 .80

African solidarity in drought emergency.

Map of Africa with Mauritania, Akjoujt Blast Furnace, Camel — A71

Fair Emblem — A72

Design: 12um, Snim emblem, furnace, dump truck, excavator.

1975, Sept. 22 Engr. *Perf. 13*

334 A71 10um brt bl, choc & org .90 .30
335 A71 12um brt bl & multi 1.00 .40

Mining and industry: Somima (Société Minière de Mauritanie) and Snim (Société Nationale Industrielle et Minière).

1975, Oct. 5 Litho. *Perf. 12*

336 A72 10um multi .60 .30

National Nouakchott Fair, Nov. 28-Dec. 7.

Commemorative Medal — A73

Design: 12um, Map of Mauritania, vert.

1975, Nov. 28 Litho. *Perf. 12*

337 A73 10um sil & multi 1.50 .35
338 A73 12um grn, yel & grn 1.50 .35

15th anniversary of independence.

Docked Space Ships and Astronauts — A74

Docked Space Ships and: 10um, Soyuz rocket launch.

1975, Dec. 29 Litho. *Perf. 14*

339 A74 8um multi .70 .25
340 A74 10um multi .85 .25
Nos. 339-340,C156-C158 (5) 7.55 2.65

Apollo Soyuz space test project, Russo-American cooperation, launched July 15, link-up July 17, 1975.

French Legion Infantryman A75

Uniform: 10um, Green Mountain Boy.

1976, Jan. 26 *Perf. 13½x14*

341 A75 8um multi .80 .25
342 A75 10um multi 1.00 .25
Nos. 341-342,C160-C162 (5) 7.30 2.25

American Bicentennial.

No. 296 Surcharged

1976, Mar. 1 Engr. *Perf. 13*

343 A60 12um on 75fr multi .90 .30

Arab Labor Charter, 10th anniversary.

Map of Mauritania with Spanish Sahara Incorporated — A76

1976, Mar. 15 Litho. *Perf. 13x12½*

344 A76 10um grn & multi .80 .30

Reunified Mauritania, Feb. 29, 1976.

LZ-4 over Hangar — A77

75th anniv. of the Zeppelin: 10um, Dr. Hugo Eckener and "Schwaben" (LZ-10). 12um, "Hansa" (LZ-13) over Heligoland. 20um, "Bodensee" (LZ-120) and Dr. Ludwig Dürr.

1976, June 28 Litho. *Perf. 11*

345 A77 5um multi .25 .20
346 A77 10um multi .60 .25
347 A77 12um multi .75 .30
348 A77 20um multi 1.25 .40
Nos. 345-348,C167-C168 (6) 10.10 3.15

Mohenjo-Daro — A78

1976, Sept. 6 Litho. *Perf. 12*

349 A78 15um multi 1.10 .40

UNESCO campaign to save Mohenjo-Daro excavations, Pakistan.

A. G. Bell, Telephone and Satellite — A79

1976, Oct. 11 Engr. *Perf. 13*

350 A79 10um bl, car & red .80 .20

Centenary of first telephone call by Alexander Graham Bell, Mar. 10, 1876.

Mohammed Ali Jinnah (1876-1948), Governor General of Pakistan — A80

1976, Dec. 25 Litho. *Perf. 13*

351 A80 10um multi .60 .30

NASA Control Room, Houston — A81

Design: 12um, Viking components, vert.

1977, Feb. 28 *Perf. 14*

352 A81 10um multi .60 .20
353 A81 12um multi .75 .20
Nos. 352-353,C173-C175 (5) 7.85 1.80

Viking Mars project.

For surcharge and overprints see Nos. 425-426, C192-C195.

Jackals A82

Designs: 5um, Wild rabbits. 12um, Wart-hogs. 14um, Lions. 15um, Elephants.

1977, Mar. 14 Litho. *Perf. 12½*

354 A82 5um multi .40 .20
355 A82 10um multi 1.00 .35
356 A82 12um multi 1.40 .40
357 A82 14um multi 1.50 .50
358 A82 15um multi 3.00 .75
Nos. 354-358 (5) 7.30 2.20

For surcharge see No. 577.

Irene and Frederic Joliot-Curie, Chemistry — A83

Nobel prize winners: 15um, Emil A. von Bering, medicine.

1977, Apr. 29 Litho. *Perf. 14*

359 A83 12um multi 1.10 .20
360 A83 15um multi .90 .20
Nos. 359-360,C177-C179 (5) 10.50 1.80

APU Emblem, Member's Flags — A84

1977, May 30 Photo. *Perf. 13*

361 A84 12um multi .75 .30

Arab Postal Union, 25th anniversary.

Oil Lamp A85

Tegdaoust Pottery: 2um, 4-handled pot. 5um, Large jar. 12um, Jug with filter.

1977, June 13 Engr. *Perf. 13*

362 A85 1um multi .20 .20
363 A85 2um multi .20 .20
364 A85 5um multi .30 .20
365 A85 12um multi .80 .30
Nos. 362-365 (4) 1.50 .90

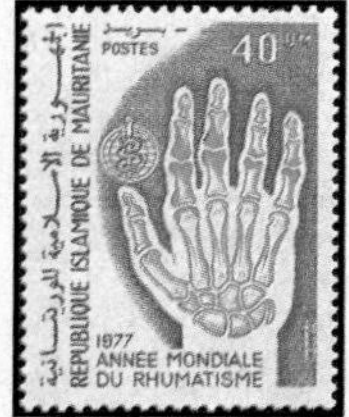

X-ray of Hand — A86

1977, June 27 Engr. *Perf. 12½x13*

366 A86 40um multi 3.00 1.25

World Rheumatism Year.

Charles Lindbergh and "Spirit of St. Louis" — A87

History of aviation: 14um, Clement Ader and "Eole!" 15um, Louis Bleriot over channel. 55um, Italo Balbo and seaplanes. 60um, Concorde. 100um, Charles Lindbergh and "Spirit of St. Louis."

1977, Sept. 19

367 A87 12um multi .65 .20
368 A87 14um multi .70 .20
369 A87 15um multi .85 .30
370 A87 55um multi 3.00 .70
371 A87 60um multi 3.50 .75
Nos. 367-371 (5) 8.70 2.15

Souvenir Sheet

372 A87 100um multi 6.00 1.50

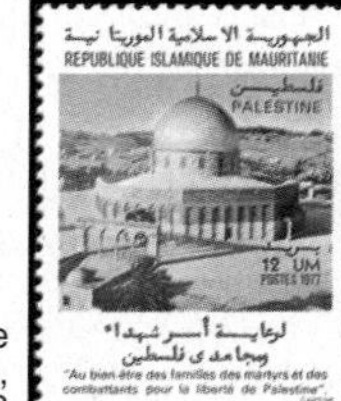

Dome of the Rock, Jerusalem — A88

1977, Oct. 31 Litho. *Perf. 12½*

373 A88 12um multi .60 .25
374 A88 14um multi .75 .40

Palestinian fighters and their families.

Soccer and Emblems — A89

Emblems and: 14um, Alf Ramsey and stadium. 15um, Players and goalkeeper.

1977, Dec. 19 Litho. *Perf. 13½*

375 A89 12um multi .55 .20
376 A89 14um multi .65 .20
377 A89 15um multi .80 .20
Nos. 375-377,C182-C183 (5) 7.50 1.75

Elimination Games for World Cup Soccer Championship, Argentina, 1978.

For overprints see Nos. 399-401, C187-C189.

Helen Fourment and her Children, by Rubens A90

Paintings by Peter Paul Rubens (1577-1640): 14um, Knight in armor. 67um, Three Burghers. 69um, Landscape, horiz. 100um, Rubens with wife and son.

1977, Dec. 26

378 A90 12um multi .75 .20
379 A90 14um multi .90 .35
380 A90 67um multi 4.00 .70
381 A90 69um multi 4.50 .85
Nos. 378-381 (4) 10.15 2.10

Souvenir Sheet

382 A90 100um gold & multi 6.00 1.50

Sable Antelope and Wildlife Fund Emblem — A91

Endangered Animals: 12um, Gazelles, vert. 14um, Manatee. 55um, Aoudad, vert. 60um, Elephant. 100um, Ostrich, vert.

1978, Feb. 28 Litho. *Perf. 13½x14*

383 A91 5um multi *1.10* .30
384 A91 12um multi *2.25* .40
385 A91 14um multi *2.50* .70
386 A91 55um multi *8.50* .70
387 A91 60um multi *10.00* 1.25
388 A91 100um multi *13.00* 2.25
Nos. 383-388 (6) *37.35* 5.60

Nouakchott-Nema Road — A91a

1978, June 19 Litho. *Perf. 13*

388A A91a 12um multicolored *12.00* 8.50
388B A91a 14um multicolored *13.50* 9.00

Soccer and Games' Emblem — A92

14um, Rimet Cup. 20um, Soccer ball & F.I.F.A. flag. 50um, Soccer ball & Rimet Cup, horiz.

1978, June 26 Photo. *Perf. 13*

389 A92 12um multi .60 .20
390 A92 14um multi .70 .30
391 A92 20um multi 1.10 .30
Nos. 389-391 (3) 2.40 .80

Souvenir Sheet

392 A92 50um multi 2.50 1.00

11th World Cup Soccer Championship, Argentina, June 1-25.

Raoul Follereau and St. George Slaying Dragon — A93

1978, Sept. 4 Engr. *Perf. 13*

393 A93 12um brn & dp grn 1.50 .60

25th anniversary of the Raoul Follereau Anti-Leprosy Foundation.

Anti-Apartheid Emblem, Fenced-in People — A94

Design: 30um, Anti-Apartheid emblem and free people, vert.

1978, Oct. 9

394 A94 25um bl, red & brn 1.25 .55
395 A94 30um grn, bl & brn 1.75 .75

Anti-Apartheid Year.

Charles de Gaulle A95

14um, King Baudouin. 55um, Queen Elizabeth II.

1978, Oct. 16 Litho. *Perf. 12½x12*

396 A95 12um multi 1.10 .35
397 A95 14um multi 1.10 .35
398 A95 55um multi 2.50 .90
Nos. 396-398 (3) 4.70 1.60

Rulers who helped in de-colonization. No. 398 also commemorates 25th anniversary of coronation of Queen Elizabeth II.

Nos. 375-377 Overprinted in Arabic and French in Silver: "ARGENTINE- / PAYS BAS 3-1"

1978, Dec. 11 Litho. *Perf. 13½*

399 A89 12um multi .70 .20
400 A89 14um multi .75 .30
401 A89 15um multi 1.00 .50
Nos. 399-401,C187-C188 (5) 7.70 3.50

Argentina's victory in World Cup Soccer Championship 1978.

View of Nouakchott — A96

1978, Dec. 18 Litho. *Perf. 12*

402 A96 12um multi .65 .30

20th anniversary of Nouakchott.

Flame Emblem — A97

Leather Key Holder — A98

1978, Dec. 26 *Perf. 12½*

403 A97 55um ultra & red 2.50 1.10

Universal Declaration of Human Rights, 30th anniv.

1979, Feb. 5 Litho. *Perf. 13½x14*

Leather Craft: 7um, Toothbrush case. 10um, Knife holder.

404 A98 5um multi .30 .20
405 A98 7um multi .40 .20
406 A98 10um multi .55 .30
Nos. 404-406 (3) 1.25 .70

Farmers at Market, by Dürer — A99

Engravings by Albrecht Durer (1471-1528): 14um, Young Peasant and Wife. 55um, Mercenary with flag. 60um, St. George Slaying Dragon. 100um, Mercenaries, horiz.

Litho.; Red Foil Embossed

1979, May 3 *Perf. 13½x14*

407 A99 12um blk, *buff* .60 .20
408 A99 14um blk, *buff* 1.00 .20
409 A99 55um blk, *buff* 2.40 .80
410 A99 60um blk, *buff* 3.00 .95
Nos. 407-410 (4) 7.00 2.15

Souvenir Sheet

Perf. 14x13½

411 A99 100um blk, *buff* 5.00 2.00

Buddha, Borobudur Temple and UNESCO Emblem — A100

UNESCO Emblem and: 14um, Hunter on horseback, Carthage. 55um, Caryatid, Acropolis.

1979, May 14 Photo. *Perf. 12½*

412 A100 12um multi .70 .30
413 A100 14um multi .90 .35
414 A100 55um multi 2.75 1.10
Nos. 412-414 (3) 4.35 1.75

Preservation of art treasures with help from UNESCO.

Paddle Steamer Sirius, Rowland Hill — A101

Sir Rowland Hill (1795-1879), originator of penny postage, and: 14um, Paddle steamer Great Republic. 55um, S.S. Mauritania. 60um, M.S. Stirling Castle. 100um, Mauritania No. 8.

1979, June 4 Litho. *Perf. 13½x14*

415 A101 12um multi .55 .20
416 A101 14um multi .70 .20
417 A101 55um multi 2.40 .55
418 A101 60um multi 2.90 .70
Nos. 415-418 (4) 6.55 1.65

Souvenir Sheet

419 A101 100um multi 5.00 1.25

Embossed Leather Cushion — A102

30um, Satellite, jet, ship, globe & UPU emblem.

1979, June 8 Litho. *Perf. 12½*

420 A102 12um multi 1.10 .50

Engr.

Perf. 13

421 A102 30um multi, vert. 3.00 1.40

Philexafrique II, Libreville, Gabon, June 8-17. Nos. 420, 421 each printed in sheets of 10 and 5 labels showing exhibition emblem.

Mother and Children, IYC Emblem — A103

1979, Oct. 2 Litho. *Perf. 12½*

422 A103 12um multi .55 .20
423 A103 14um multi .70 .35
424 A103 40um multi 2.00 .90
Nos. 422-424 (3) 3.25 1.45

International Year of the Child

Nos. 352-353 Overprinted in Silver: "ALUNISSAGE / APOLLO XI / JUILLET 1969" and Emblem

1979, Oct. 24 Litho. *Perf. 14*

425 A81 10um multi .60 .30
426 A81 12um multi .60 .30
Nos. 425-426,C192-C194 (5) 7.20 3.05

Apollo 11 moon landing, 10th anniversary.

Runner, Moscow '80 Emblem A104

Moscow '80 Emblem and: 14um, 55um, 100um, Running, diff. 60um, Hurdles.

1979, Oct. 26 Litho. *Perf. 13½*

427 A104 12um multi .55 .20
428 A104 14um multi .75 .20
429 A104 55um multi 2.10 .50
430 A104 60um multi 2.50 .60
Nos. 427-430 (4) 5.90 1.50

Souvenir Sheet

431 A104 100um multi 4.75 1.25

Pre-Olympic Year.

Scomberesox Saurus Walbaum — A104a

1979, Nov. 12 Photo. *Perf. 14*

431A A104a 1um shown .75 .30
431B A104a 5um Trigla lucerna .75 .30

A 20m denomination (Xiphias gladius) also exists. Value $250.

Ice Hockey, Lake Placid '80 Emblem — A105

Various ice hockey plays.

1979, Dec. 6 Litho. *Perf. 14½*

432 A105 10um multi .50 .20
433 A105 12um multi .65 .20
434 A105 14um multi .65 .25
435 A105 55um multi 2.40 .50
436 A105 60um multi 2.50 .60
437 A105 100um multi 4.25 1.00
Nos. 432-437 (6) 10.95 2.75

13th Winter Olympic Games. Lake Placid, NY, Feb. 12-24, 1980.

For overprints see Nos. 440-445.

Arab Achievements — A106

1980, Mar. 22 Litho. *Perf. 13*

438 A106 12um multi .70 .35
439 A106 15um multi .80 .35

Nos. 432-437 Overprinted:

a. Médaille / de bronze / SUÈDE
b. MÉDAILLE / DE BRONZE / SUÈDE
c. Médaille / d'argent / U.R.S.S.
d. MÉDAILLE / D'ARGENT/ U.R.S.S.
e. MÉDAILLE / D'OR / ÉTATS-UNIS
f. Médaille / d'or / ÉTATS-UNIS

1980, June 14 Litho. *Perf. 14½*

440 A105(a) 10um multi .55 .20
441 A105(b) 12um multi .60 .20
442 A105(c) 14um multi .60 .30
443 A105(d) 55um multi 2.10 .75
444 A105(e) 60um multi 3.00 .85
445 A105(f) 100um multi 4.50 1.40
Nos. 440-445 (6) 11.35 3.70

Equestrian, Olympic Rings — A107

Designs: Equestrian scenes. 10um, 20um, 70um, 100um, vert.

1980, June Litho. *Perf. 14*

446 A107 10um multi .45 .20
447 A107 20um multi .85 .25
448 A107 50um multi 2.40 .50
449 A107 70um multi 3.25 .70
Nos. 446-449 (4) 6.95 1.65

Souvenir Sheet

450 A107 100um multi 5.50 1.75

22nd Summer Olympic Games, Moscow, July 19-Aug. 3.

For overprints see Nos. 464-468.

Armed Forces Day — A108

1980, July 9 *Perf. 13x12½*

451 A108 12um multi .60 .20
452 A108 14um multi .65 .30

World Red Cross Day — A109

1980, June 14 *Perf. 13*

453 A109 20um multi *12.00* 1.25

Pilgrimage to Mecca — A110

Design: 50um, Mosque, outside view.

1980

454 A110 10um multi 1.00 .35
455 A110 50um multi 3.00 1.25

Man with Turban, by Rembrandt A111

Rembrandt Paintings: 10um, Self-portrait. 20um, His mother. 70um, His son Titus reading. 100um, Polish knight, horiz.

1980, July Litho. *Perf. 12½*

456 A111 10um multi .60 .25
457 A111 20um multi 1.00 .30
458 A111 50um multi 2.60 .50
459 A111 70um multi 3.00 .80
Nos. 456-459 (4) 7.20 1.85

Souvenir Sheet

460 A111 100um multi 5.50 1.50

Tea Time A112

1980, Mar. 11 Litho. *Perf. 12½*

460A A112 1um multi .40 .20
461 A112 5um multi .60 .20
462 A112 12um multi 1.00 .30
Nos. 460A-462 (3) 2.00 .70

Arbor Day — A113

1980, Aug. 29

463 A113 12um multi 1.10 .40

Nos. 446-450 Overprinted with Winner and Country

1980, Oct. Litho. *Perf. 14*

464 A107 10um multi .45 .25
465 A107 20um multi .85 .30
466 A107 50um multi 2.40 .60
467 A107 70um multi 3.00 .80
Nos. 464-467 (4) 6.70 1.95

Souvenir Sheet

468 A107 100um multi 4.50 1.75

Mastodont Locomotive, 1850 — A114

Designs: Various locomotives.

1980, Nov. *Perf. 12½*

469 A114 10um shown .70 .20
470 A114 12um Iron ore train .85 .30
471 A114 14um Chicago-Milwaukee line, 1900 1.10 .40
472 A114 20um Bury, 1837 1.50 .50
473 A114 67um Reseau North line, 1870 5.00 .70
474 A114 100um Potsdam, 1840 7.50 1.10
Nos. 469-474 (6) 16.65 3.20

20th Anniversary of Independence — A115

1980, Nov. 27 *Perf. 13*

475 A115 12um multi .55 .20
476 A115 15um multi .60 .30

El Haram Mosque — A116

1981, Apr. 13 Litho. *Perf. 12½*

477 A116 2um shown .20 .20
478 A116 12um Medina Mosque .60 .30
479 A116 14um Chinguetti Mosque .80 .30
Nos. 477-479 (3) 1.60 .80

Hegira, 1500th anniversary.

Prince Charles and Lady Diana, Coach — A117

Designs: Coaches.

1981, July 8 Litho. *Perf. 14½*

480 A117 14um multi .60 .20
481 A117 18um multi .75 .20
482 A117 77um multi 2.75 .90
Nos. 480-482 (3) 4.10 1.30

Souvenir Sheet

483 A117 100um multi 4.50 1.10

Royal wedding.
For overprints see Nos. 518-521.

Intl. Year of the Disabled A119

1981, June 29 Litho. *Perf. 13x13½*

486 A119 12um multi .80 .40

Battle of Yorktown Bicentenary (American Revolution) — A120

1981, Oct. 5 *Perf. 12½*

487 A120 14um George Washington, vert. .60 .25
488 A120 18um Admiral de Grasse, vert. 1.00 .30
489 A120 63um Surrender of Cornwallis 3.00 1.00
490 A120 81um Battle of Chesapeake Bay 4.00 1.50
Nos. 487-490 (4) 8.60 3.05

475th Death Anniv. of Christopher Columbus (1451-1506) — A121

1981, Oct. 5

491 A121 19um Pinta 1.50 .40
492 A121 55um Santa Maria 4.25 1.10

World Food Day — A122

Kemal Ataturk Birth Cent. — A123

1981, Oct. 16 *Perf. 13*

493 A122 19um multi 1.00 .40

1981, Oct. 29 *Perf. 12½*

494 A123 63um multi 3.00 1.25

Scouting Year — A124

Designs: Boating scenes. 92um vert.

1982, Jan. 20 Litho. *Perf. 12½*

495 A124 14um multi .70 .20
496 A124 19um multi 1.00 .20
497 A124 22um multi 1.10 .25
498 A124 92um multi 4.25 .85
Nos. 495-498 (4) 7.05 1.50

Souvenir Sheet

Perf. 13

499 A124 100um Baden-Powell, scout 5.50 1.25

75th Anniv. of Grand Prix — A125

Designs: Winners and their Cars.

1982, Jan. 23 *Perf. 13½*

500 A125 7um Deusenberg, 1921 .60 .20
501 A125 12um Alfa Romeo, 1932 .85 .20
502 A125 14um Juan Fangio, 1949 .95 .20
503 A125 18um Renault, 1979 1.10 .25
504 A125 19um Niki Lauda, 1974 1.25 .30
Nos. 500-504 (5) 4.75 1.15

Souvenir Sheet

505 A125 100um Race 6.00 1.75

Birds of the Arguin Bank A126

1981, Dec. 17 Photo. *Perf. 13*

506 A126 2um White pelicans 1.00 .20
507 A126 18um Pink flamingoes 3.75 .75

Battle of Karameh A127

1982, Dec. 19 Litho.

508 A127 14um Hand holding tattered flag .80 .35

Deluth Turtle — A128

APU, 30th Anniv. — A129

Designs: Sea turtles.

1981, Dec. 21 Photo. *Perf. 14x13½*

509 A128 1um shown 1.50 .25
510 A128 3um Green turtle 2.00 .25
511 A128 4um Shell turtle 2.50 .35
Nos. 509-511 (3) 6.00 .85

1982, May 14 Litho. *Perf. 13*

512 A129 14um org & brn .65 .30

A130

A131

1982, May 17 Photo. *Perf. 13½x13*

513 A130 21um multi .85 .40

14th World Telecommunications Day.

1982, June 7 Litho. *Perf. 12½*

514 A131 14um grnsh bl .65 .30

UN Conf. on Human Environment, 10th anniv.

21st Birthday of Princess Diana of Wales — A132

Portraits.

1982, July *Perf. 14x13½*

515 A132 21um multi .75 .40
516 A132 77um multi 2.50 .85

Souvenir Sheet

517 A132 100um multi 3.75 1.50

Nos. 480-483 Overprinted in Blue: "NAISSANCE ROYALE 1982"

1982, Aug. 2 *Perf. 14½*

518 A117 14um multi .50 .30
519 A117 18um multi .70 .35
520 A117 77um multi 2.50 1.25
Nos. 518-520 (3) 3.70 1.90

Souvenir Sheet

521 A117 100um multi 3.75 1.50

Birth of Prince William of Wales, June 21.

Manned Flight Bicentenary A133

1982, Dec. 29 Litho. *Perf. 14*

522 A133 14um Montgolfiere balloon, 1783, vert. .95 .25
523 A133 18um Hydrogen balloon, 1783 .95 .25
524 A133 19um Zeppelin, vert. .95 .35
525 A133 55um Nieuport plane 2.50 .50
526 A133 63um Concorde 2.75 .60
527 A133 77um Apollo II, vert. 3.00 .70
Nos. 522-527 (6) 11.10 2.65

Preservation of Ancient Cities — A134

1983, Feb. 16 Litho. *Perf. 14x14½*

528 A134 14um City Wall, Ouadane .75 .25
529 A134 18um Chinguetti .85 .30
530 A134 24um Staircase, panels, Qualata 1.10 .40
531 A134 30um Ruins, Tichitt 1.75 .60
Nos. 528-531 (4) 4.45 1.55

World Communications Year — A135

1983, June 21 Litho. *Perf. 13*

532 A135 14um multi .70 .30

30th Anniv. of Customs Cooperation Council — A136

1983, June 25

533 A136 14um multi .70 .30

Traditional Houses A137

Ancient Manuscript Page — A138

1983, June 14 Photo. *Perf. 13½*

534 A137 14um Peule *2.50* .30
535 A137 18um Toucouleur *3.25* .45
536 A137 19um Tent *3.50* .50
Nos. 534-536 (3) *9.25* 1.25

1983, June 15 Photo. *Perf. 12½x13*

537 A138 2um shown .40 .20
538 A138 5um Ornamental scroll-work .60 .20
539 A138 7um Sheath .75 .20
Nos. 537-539 (3) 1.75 .60

Manned Flight Bicentenary — A139

Early Fliers and their Balloons or Dirigibles. 10um, 14um vert.

1983, Oct. 17 Litho. *Perf. 13½*

540 A139 10um F. Pilatre de Rozier .75 .20
541 A139 14um John Wise .95 .20
542 A139 25um Charles Renard 1.90 .30
543 A139 100um Henri Julliot 5.75 1.10
Nos. 540-543 (4) 9.35 1.80

Souvenir Sheet

544 A139 100um Joseph Montgolfier 6.50 1.25

No. 544 contains one stamp 47x37mm. Nos. 543-544 airmail.

Mortar — A140

Various prehistoric grinding implements.

1983, Dec. 28 Litho. *Perf. 13*

545 A140 10um multi .85 .35
546 A140 14um multi 1.25 .45
547 A140 18um multi 1.75 .75
Nos. 545-547 (3) 3.85 1.55

Pre-Olympics — A141

1983, Dec. 31 Litho. *Perf. 13½*

548 A141 1um Basketball .20 .20
549 A141 20um Wrestling .85 .40
550 A141 50um Equestrian 2.00 .70
551 A141 77um Running 3.50 .95
Nos. 548-551 (4) 6.55 2.25

Souvenir Sheet

552 A141 100um Soccer 4.75 1.25

No. 552 contains one stamp 41x36mm. Nos. 551-552 airmail.

Scouting Year — A142

Artemis, by Rembrandt — A142a

Events & Annivs.: 14um, Johann Wolfgang von Goethe. 25um, Virgin and Child, by Peter Paul Rubens.

1984, Jan. 24

553 A142 5um Flag, Baden-Powell 1.00 .50
553A A142 14um multicolored 1.00 .50
553B A142 25um multicolored 1.50 .50
Nos. 553-553B (3) 3.50 1.50

Souvenir Sheet

553C A142a 100um multicolored 4.25 1.50

No. 553C is airmail and contains one 42x51mm stamp.

Sand Rose A143

1984, Mar. Litho. *Perf. 14*

554 A143 21um multi *10.00* 1.50

Inscribed 1982.

Anniversaries and Events — A145

1984, Apr. 26

555 A145 10um Albrecht Durer (1471-1528) .80 .20
556 A145 12um Apollo XI, 15th anniv. .95 .25
557 A145 50um Chess 3.00 1.00
Nos. 555-557 (3) 4.75 1.45

1984, Apr. 16 Litho. *Perf. 13½*

Designs: 77um, Prince Charles, Princess Diana. 100um, Prince Charles, Princess Diana, vert.

557A A145 77um multi 3.75 1.60

Miniature Sheet

557B A145 100um multi 5.50 3.00

Nos. 557A-557B airmail.

Fishing Industry A146

1984

558 A146 1um Tuna .40 .20
559 A146 2um Mackerel .40 .20
560 A146 5um Haddock .55 .25
561 A146 14um Black chinchard 1.40 .50
562 A146 18um Boat building 1.75 .60
Nos. 558-562 (5) 4.50 1.75

Nouakchott Olympic Complex A148

1984, Sept. 26 Litho. *Perf. 13½*

569 A148 14um multi 1.00 .40

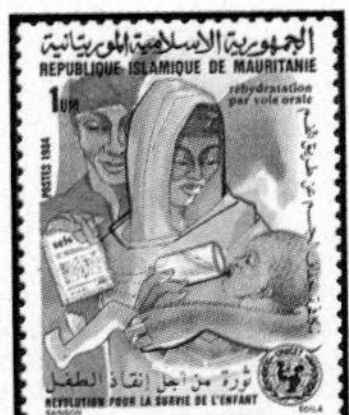

Infant Survival Campaign A149

1984, Sept. 26 Litho. *Perf. 12½*

570	A149	1um Feeding by glass	.40	.20
571	A149	4um Breastfeeding	.40	.20
572	A149	10um Vaccinating	1.00	.20
573	A149	14um Weighing	1.25	.30
		Nos. 570-573 (4)	3.05	.90

Pilgrimage to Mecca — A150

1984, Oct. 3 Litho. *Perf. 13*

574	A150	14um Tents, mosque	.80	.40
575	A150	18um Tents, courtyard	1.25	.60

10th Anniv., West African Union — A151

1984, Nov. Litho. *Perf. 13*

576	A151	14um Map of member nations	.85	.40

No. 355 Overprinted "Aide au Sahel 84" and Surcharged

1984 Litho. *Perf. 12½*

577	A82	18um on 10um	1.25	.50

Issued to publicize drought relief efforts.

Technical & Cultural Cooperation Agency, 15th Anniv. — A152

1985, Mar. 20 Litho. *Perf. 12½*

578	A152	18um Profiles, emblem	1.00	.45

League of Arab States, 40th Anniv. — A153

1985, May 7 *Perf. 13*

579	A153	14um brt yel grn & blk	.75	.40

German Railways 150th Anniv. — A154

Anniversaries and events: 12um, Adler, 1st German locomotive, 1835. 18um, Series 10, 1956, last Fed. German Railways locomotive. 44um, European Music Year, Johann Sebastian Bach, composer, and Angels Making Music, unattributed painting. 77um, George Frideric Handel. 90um, Statue of Liberty, cent., vert. 100um, Queen Mother, 85th birthday, vert.

1985, Sept.

580	A154	12um multi	.65	.25
581	A154	18um multi	1.00	.40
582	A154	44um multi	2.00	1.00
583	A154	77um multi	3.50	1.75
584	A154	90um multi	4.00	2.00
		Nos. 580-584 (5)	11.15	5.40

Souvenir Sheet

585	A154	100um multi	4.75	2.25

World Food Day — A155

1985, Oct. 16 *Perf. 13x12½*

586	A155	18um multi	.70	.40

UN Food and Agriculture Org., 40th anniv.

Fight Against Drought A156

1985 Litho. *Perf. 13*

587	A156	14um Antelope	1.00	.30
588	A156	18um Oasis	1.25	.40

Fight Against Desert Encroachment — A157

1985

589	A157	10um Grain harvest, vert.	.55	.30
590	A157	14um Brush fire	2.50	.75
591	A157	18um Planting brush	2.50	.75
		Nos. 589-591 (3)	5.55	1.80

Natl. Independence, 25th Anniv. — A158

1985 *Perf. 15x14½*

592	A158	18um multi	1.00	.40

Intl. Youth Year A159

1986, Feb. 13 Litho. *Perf. 13*

593	A159	18um Development	.80	.30
594	A159	22um Participation	1.00	.40
595	A159	25um Peace, vert.	1.40	.50
		Nos. 593-595 (3)	3.20	1.20

Toujounine Satellite Station — A160

1986, May 22 Litho. *Perf. 12½*

596	A160	25um multi	1.25	.50

World Wildlife Fund — A161

Monk seal (Monachus monachus).

1986, June 12 *Perf. 13*

597	A161	2um multi	*1.75*	*.35*
598	A161	5um multi	*2.75*	*.60*
599	A161	10um multi	*4.50*	*1.00*
600	A161	18um multi	*8.00*	*2.00*
		Nos. 597-600 (4)	*17.00*	*3.95*

Souvenir Sheet

601	A161	50um multi	*15.00*	*5.00*

Weaving — A162

1986, July 20 Litho. *Perf. 12½*

602	A162	18um multi	.80	.40

Sabra and Chatila Massacre, 4th Anniv. — A163

1986, Oct. 18

603	A163	22um multi	.90	.40

A164

Christopher Columbus — A165

Indians, maps on globe and: 2um, Santa Maria. 22um, Nina. 35um, Pinta. 150um, Columbus.

1986, Oct. 14 Litho. *Perf. 13½*

604	A164	2um multi	.20	.20
605	A164	22um multi	.80	.35
606	A164	35um multi	1.25	.55
607	A164	150um multi	5.50	2.25
		Nos. 604-607 (4)	7.75	3.35

Souvenir Sheet

608	A165	100um Columbus, Earth	4.50	4.00

Nos. 607-608 are airmail.

US Space Shuttle Challenger Explosion, Jan. 28, 1986 — A166

Crew members and: 7um, Space shuttle. 22um, Canadarm. 32um, Sky, moon. 43um, Memorial emblem.

1986, Oct. 14

609	A166	7um multi	.25	.20
610	A166	22um multi	.80	.30
611	A166	32um multi	1.25	.50
612	A166	43um multi	1.75	.65
		Nos. 609-612 (4)	4.05	1.65

Souvenir Sheet

613	A166	100um Crew, lift-off	4.00	1.50

Nos. 612-613 are airmail.

Fish A167

1986, Oct. 16 *Perf. 13*

614	A167	4um Dorade	.50	.20
615	A167	98um Truite de mer	7.50	2.25

See Nos. 631-633.

Birds A168

1986, Oct. 16

616	A168	22um Spatule blanche	2.50	.60
617	A168	32um Sterne bridee	3.00	.80

See Nos. 634-635.

World Food Day
A169

1986, Nov. 6 ***Perf. 12½***
618 A169 22um multi 1.00 .40

A170

Halley's Comet — A171

Space probes and portraits: 5um, J.H. Dort, Giotto probe. 18um, Sir William Huggins (1824-1910), English astronomer, and launch of Giotto on Ariane rocket. 26um, E.J. Opik, Giotto and Vega. 80um, F.L. Whipple, Planet-A. 100um, Edmond Halley, Giotto.

1986, Oct. 14 **Litho.** ***Perf. 13½***
619 A170 5um multi .20 .20
620 A170 18um multi .60 .25
621 A170 26um multi 1.00 .40
622 A170 80um multi 3.25 1.25
Nos. 619-622 (4) 5.05 2.10

Souvenir Sheet

623 A171 100um multi 4.00 2.00

Nos. 622-623 are airmail.

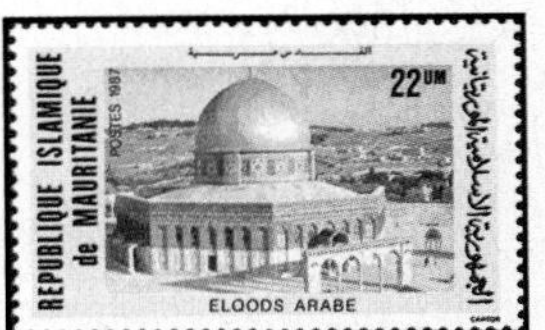

Jerusalem Day — A172

1987, May 21 **Litho.** ***Perf. 13½***
624 A172 22um Dome of the Rock 1.00 .40

Cordoue Mosque, 1200th Anniv.
A173

1987, Sept. 5 **Litho.** ***Perf. 13½***
625 A173 30um multi 1.50 .55

Literacy Campaign
A174

1987, Sept. 12
626 A174 18um Classroom .70 .40
627 A174 22um Family reading, vert. .90 .60

World Health Day — A175

1987, Oct. 1 ***Perf. 13***
628 A175 18um multi 1.00 .40

Natl. Population Census
A176

1988, Aug. 21 **Litho.** ***Perf. 13½***
629 A176 20um multi 1.00 .40

WHO, 40th Anniv. — A177

Arab Scouting Movement, 75th Anniv. — A178

1988, Sept. 19 ***Perf. 13***
630 A177 30um multi 1.25 .45

Fish Type of 1986

1988, Sept. 10 **Litho.** ***Perf. 13***
631 A167 1um Rascasse blanche .60 .25
632 A167 7um Baliste 1.90 .35
633 A167 15um Bonite a ventre raye 2.75 .75
Nos. 631-633 (3) 5.25 1.35

Bird Type of 1986

1988, Sept. 15
634 A168 18um Grand cormorant 2.00 .60
635 A168 80um Royal tern 7.00 2.75

1988, Sept. 29 **Litho.** ***Perf. 13***
636 A178 35um multi 1.40 .60

1st Municipal Elections — A179

1988, Nov. 22 ***Perf. 13½***
637 A179 20um Men casting ballots .65 .30
638 A179 24um Woman casting ballot 1.00 .40

Organization of African Unity, 25th Anniv. (in 1988) — A180

Intl. Fund for Agricultural Development, 10th Anniv. (in 1988) — A181

1988, Dec. 7 **Litho.** ***Perf. 13***
639 A180 40um multi 1.25 .65

1988, Dec. 15
640 A181 35um multi 1.75 .70

Autonomy of Nouakchott (Amitie) Port, 1st Anniv. — A182

1988, Dec. 20 **Litho.** ***Perf. 13***
641 A182 24um multi 1.40 .60

A183

A184

1989, July 7 **Litho.** ***Perf. 13***
642 A183 35um multi 1.60 .60

French Revolution bicent., PHILEXFRANCE '89.

1989, July 17
643 A184 20um multi 1.00 .40

1990 World Cup Soccer Championships, Italy.

Pilgrimage to Mecca
A185

1989, Aug. 26 **Litho.** ***Perf. 13½***
644 A185 20um Mosque 1.00 .40

African Development Bank, 25th Anniv. — A186

1989, Sept. 2
645 A186 37um lt vio & blk 1.25 .60

Tapestry — A187

1989, Oct. 1 ***Perf. 13***
646 A187 50um multicolored 2.00 .85

Locusts, Moths and Ladybugs
A188

1989, Dec. 29
647 A188 2um *Heliothis armigera* .20 .20
648 A188 5um Locust .50 .20
649 A188 6um *Aphis gossypii* .25 .20
650 A188 10um *Agrotis ypsilon* .50 .20
651 A188 20um *Chilo* .95 .35
652 A188 20um Two locusts, egg case 1.00 .35
653 A188 24um Locusts emerging 1.25 .40
654 A188 24um *Plitella xylostella* 1.25 .40
655 A188 30um *Henosepilachna elaterii* 1.60 .50
656 A188 40um Locust flying 2.25 .70

657 A188 42um *Trichoplusia ni* 2.25 .70
658 A188 88um Locust, diff. 5.50 1.40
Nos. 647-658 (12) 17.50 5.60

For surcharge see No. 737.

Revolt — A189

1989, Dec. 8 Litho. *Perf. 13*
659 A189 35um multicolored 1.60 .60

2nd Anniv. of the Palestinian Uprising and 1st anniv. of the declaration of a Palestinian State.

Maghreb Arab Union, 1st Anniv. — A190

1990, Feb. 17 Litho. *Perf. 13½*
660 A190 50um multicolored 1.75 .70

Mineral Resources A191

1990, July 27 *Perf. 11½*
661 A191 60um multicolored 2.75 1.60

Intl. Literacy Year — A192

1990, July 27
662 A192 60um multicolored 2.00 1.00

1992 Summer Olympics, Barcelona A193

Litho. & Typo.

1990, Sept. 2 *Perf. 13½*
663 A193 5um Equestrian .20 .20
664 A193 50um Archery 1.90 .65
665 A193 60um Hammer throw 2.00 1.00
666 A193 75um Field hockey 2.75 1.00
667 A193 90um Handball 3.50 1.25
668 A193 220um Table tennis 8.50 3.00
Nos. 663-668 (6) 18.85 7.10

Souvenir Sheet

669 A193 150um Runner 6.25 2.00

Nos. 668-669 airmail.

A194

A195

1990, July 27 *Perf. 11½*
670 A194 50um multicolored 2.00 .75

Multinational Postal School, 20th anniv.

1990, Nov. 21 Litho. *Perf. 11½*
671 A195 85um multicolored 3.75 1.60

Declaration of the Palestinian State, 2nd anniv.

1992 Winter Olympics, Albertville A196

1990, Dec. 10 Litho. *Perf. 13½*
672 A196 60um Downhill skiing 1.75 .75
673 A196 75um Cross-country skiing 2.00 .90
674 A196 90um Ice hockey 2.75 1.10
675 A196 220um Pairs figure skating 6.25 2.75
Nos. 672-675 (4) 12.75 5.50

Souvenir Sheet

676 A196 150um Slalom skiing 5.00 2.50

Nos. 675-676 are airmail.

Release of Nelson Mandela A197

1990, Dec. 10
677 A197 85um multicolored 5.00 1.75

Return of Senegalese Refugees — A198

1990, Dec. 10
678 A198 50um Cooking at encampment 2.25 1.00
679 A198 75um Women sewing 3.25 1.60
680 A198 85um Drawing water 3.75 1.75
Nos. 678-680 (3) 9.25 4.35

Boy Scouts Observing Nature — A199

Scout: 5um, Picking mushrooms. 50um, Holding mushroom. 60um, Drawing butterfly. 75um, Feeding butterfly. 90um, Photographing butterfly. 220um, Drying mushrooms. No. 687, Using microscope.

1991, Jan. 16 Litho. *Perf. 13½*
681 A199 5um multicolored .40 .20
682 A199 50um multicolored 2.40 .95
683 A199 60um multicolored 2.25 1.10
684 A199 75um multicolored 2.50 1.00
685 A199 90um multicolored 2.50 1.10
686 A199 220um multicolored 5.75 2.75
Nos. 681-686 (6) 15.80 7.10

Souvenir Sheet

687 A199 150um multicolored 6.50 3.00

Nos. 684 and 687 are airmail. Nos. 683-685 exist in souvenir sheets of 1.

Independence, 30th Anniv. — A200

1991, Mar. 5
688 A200 50um Satellite dish antennae 1.90 1.00
689 A200 60um Container ship 2.25 1.40
690 A200 100um Harvesting rice 3.75 1.90
Nos. 688-690 (3) 7.90 4.30

World Meteorology Day — A201

1991, Mar. 23 *Perf. 14x15*
691 A201 100um multicolored 3.75 2.10

World Population Day — A202

1991, July 27 Litho. *Perf. 13½*
692 A202 90um multicolored 3.50 1.75

Domesticated Animals — A203

1991 Litho. *Perf. 13½*
693 A203 50um Cats 3.00 1.00
693A A203 60um Dog 3.50 1.60

Campaign Against Blindness A204

1991, Nov. 10 Litho. *Perf. 13½*
694 A204 50um multicolored 2.00 1.00

Doctors Without Borders, 20th Anniv. A205

1991 Litho. *Perf. 13½*
695 A205 60um multicolored 2.50 1.25

Installation of Central Electric Service (in 1989) A206

1991, Dec. 29 Litho. *Perf. 13½*
696 A206 50um multicolored 2.50 1.00

Mineral Exploration, M'Haoudat A207

1993 Litho. *Perf. 13½*
697 A207 50um shown 2.10 1.00
698 A207 60um Desert landscape 2.50 1.40

1994 Winter Olympics, Lillehammer A208

Intifada, 6th Anniv. — A209

1993
699 A208 10um Bobsled .40 .20
700 A208 50um Luge 1.90 .95
701 A208 60um Figure skating 2.25 1.10
702 A208 80um Downhill skiing 3.00 1.50
703 A208 220um Cross-country skiing 8.25 4.00
Nos. 699-703 (5) 15.80 7.75

Souvenir Sheet

704 A208 150um Downhill skiing, diff. 5.75 2.75

No. 704 is airmail.
No. 700 exists dated "1998."

1993

Design: 60um, Palestinian children, horiz.

705 A209 50um multicolored 2.10 1.00
706 A209 60um multicolored 2.50 1.40

First Multiparty Presidential Elections, 1st Anniv. A209a

Design: 60um, Line at polling place.

1993 Litho. *Perf. 13½*

706B A209a 60um multi — —

An additional stamp was issued in this set. The editors would like to examine any example.

Caravans — A210

1993

707 A210 50um blue & multi 1.90 1.00
708 A210 60um violet & multi 2.25 1.40

Hut A210a

1994 Litho. *Perf. 13¼x13½*

708A A210a 50um Hut, diff. — —
708B A210a 60um multi — —
708C A210a 80um Hut, diff. —

1994 World Cup Soccer Championships, U.S. — A211

Designs: 10um, Soldier Field. 50um, Foxboro Stadium. 60um, Robert F. Kennedy Stadium. 90um, Stanford Stadium. 220um, Giants Stadium. 150um, Rose Bowl.

1994, Feb. 10 Litho. *Perf. 13*

709 A211 10um multicolored .35 .20
710 A211 50um multicolored 1.90 .95
711 A211 60um multicolored 2.25 1.10
712 A211 90um multicolored 3.25 1.60
713 A211 220um multicolored 8.25 4.00
Nos. 709-713 (5) 16.00 7.85

Souvenir Sheet

714 A211 150um multicolored 5.75 2.75

Birds of Banc d'Arguin National Park — A211a

Designs: 10 um, Gulls, horiz. 30um, Various birds. 40um, Terns. 50um, Sandpipers.

1994 Litho. *Perf. 13½*

714A A211a 10um lt blue & multi —
714B A211a 30um lt blue & multi — —
714C A211a 40um lt blue & multi — —
714D A211a 50um lt blue & multi — —

UN, 50th Anniv. A212

1995 Litho. *Perf. 11½*

715 A212 60um Emblem, #167 1.50 .75

FAO, 50th Anniv. A213

1995

716 A213 50um Working in field 1.25 .60
717 A213 60um With fishing boat 1.50 .75
718 A213 90um Planting garden 2.25 1.10
Nos. 716-718 (3) 5.00 2.45

Traditional Handicrafts — A214

1995, Aug. 14 Litho. *Perf. 12*

719 A214 50um Weaving rug .50 .25

Perf. 11½x12

720 A214 60um Kettle .60 .30

1996 Summer Olympics, Atlanta — A216

Design: 20um, Sprinters crouching at starting line. 40um, Five Runners. 50um, Runners.

1996, July 19 Litho. *Perf. 11¾*

725 A216 20um pink & multi —
727 A216 40um blue & multi —
728 A216 50um yel & multi —

An additional stamp was issued in this set. The editors would like to examine any example.

Traditional Games A218

Design: 90um, Women and sticks.

1996, Oct. 25 Litho. *Perf. 11¾*

733 A218 90um multi —

Two additional stamps were issued in this set. The editors would like to examine any examples.

French Pres. Jacques Chirac, Mauritanian Pres. Maaouya Ould Sid Ahmed Taya — A219

1997 Litho. *Perf. 13¼x13*

735A A219 60um multi —

State visit of Chirac to Mauritania.

Universal Declaration of Human Rights, 50th Anniv. A220

1998 Litho. *Perf. 13x13¼*

736 A220 60um multi

The editors suspect that other stamps were issued in this set and would like to examine any examples.

No. 649 Surcharged

2000 Method and Perf. As Before

737 A188 50um on 6um #649 —

Independence, 40th Anniv. — A221

2000 Litho. *Perf. 13¼*

738 A221 50um multi 2.00 1.00

Education A222

Designs: 50um, Man with tablet, woman at computer. 60um, Open-air class. 90um, Reading class. 100um, Mathematics class.

2000

739-742 A222 Set of 4 4.00 4.00

Mauritanian postal officials have declared as "illegal" the following items:

Sheets of 9 stamps with 60um denominations depicting Famous actresses (2 different). Classic actresses, Marilyn Monroe, Elvis Presley, The Beatles, Queen, Walt Disney, The Simpsons, Teddy bears.

Sheets of 6 stamps with 80um denominations depicting Birds and Scout emblem (15 different).

Sheets of 6 stamps with 60um denominations depicting Trains (5 different), Penguins and Rotary emblem (2 different), Cats and Rotary emblem (2 different), Elephants and Rotary emblem (2 different), Polar bears and Rotary emblem (2 different), Lighthouses and Rotary emblem (2 different), Firearms and Rotary emblem, Firearms and Scout emblem, Pope John Paul II, Harry Potter, Scooby-Doo.

Sheets of 4 stamps depicting various sports of the Sydney Olympics (2 different).

Souvenir sheet depicting Various sports of the Sydney Olympics.

Se-tenant sets of 4 stamps depicting sports of the Sydney Olympics (2 different).

Flora, Fauna and Mushrooms — A223

No. 743: a, Chelonia mydas. b, Octopus vulgaris. c, Coelacanth.
No. 744: a, Lepiota aspera. b, Lactarius camphoratus. c, Clitocybe gibba.
No. 745: a, Harpa costata. b, Voluta lapponica. c, Tellina variegata.
No. 746: a, Akhal-Teke horse. b, Arabian horse. c, Lipizzaner horse.
No. 747: a, Tibetan dog, Balinese cat. b, Shetland sheepdog, Ragdoll cat. c, Cao de Serra de Aires sheepdog, Abyssinian cat.
No. 748: a, Acraea igati. b, Mylotris humbolti. c, Mylotris ngaziya.
No. 749: a, Zosterops maderaspatana. b, Otus rutilus. c, Nelicurvitus nelicourvi.
No. 750: a, Maxillaria tenuifolia. b, Crotalaria. c, Maxillaria marginata.
No. 751, Russula virescens. No. 752, Black Russian cat.

2000, Nov. 5 Litho. *Perf. 13½*

743 Horiz. strip of 3 1.60 1.60
a.-c. A223 50um Any single .50 .50
744 Horiz. strip of 3 1.60 1.60
a.-c. A223 50um Any single .50 .50
745 Horiz. strip of 3 1.75 1.75
a.-c. A223 60um Any single .55 .55
746 Horiz. strip of 3 2.75 2.75
a.-c. A223 90um Any single .90 .90
747 Horiz. strip of 3 3.00 3.00
a.-c. A223 100um Any single 1.00 1.00
748 Horiz. strip of 3 6.00 6.00
a.-c. A223 200um Any single 2.00 2.00
749 Horiz. strip of 3 7.00 7.00
a.-c. A223 220um Any single 2.25 2.25
750 Horiz. strip of 3 2.75 2.75
a. A223 60um multi .60 .60
b. A223 90um multi .90 .90
c. A223 100um multi 1.00 1.00
Nos. 743-750 (8) 26.45 26.45

Souvenir Sheets

751 A223 300um multi 4.75 4.75
752 A223 300um multi 4.75 4.75

Nos. 746-749 exist in souvenir sheets containing one strip of 3 with light blue frames. No. 750 exists imperf.

2002 World Cup Soccer Championships, Japan and Korea — A224

No. 753: a, Zinedine Zidane. b, Christian Vieri. c, Alessandro del Piero. d, Lilian Thuram.

No. 754: a, Oliver Bierhoff. b, Jürgen Klinsmann. c, Edgar Davids. d, Dennis Bergkamp.

300um, Jules Rimet Cup, soccer players, horiz.

2000

753	Horiz. strip of 4	4.50	4.50
a.-d.	A224 90um Any single	1.10	1.10
754	Horiz. strip of 4	5.00	5.00
a.-d.	A224 100um Any single	1.25	1.25

Souvenir Sheet

755 A224 300um multi 3.75 3.75

No. 755 contains one 57x51mm stamp. Souvenir sheets of 4 stamps exist with Nos. 753a-753d and 754a-754d with colored stamp frames.

Theodore Monod (1902-2000), Naturalist A225

2003, Jan. 1 ***Perf. 13¼x13***

756 A225 370um multi 3.25 3.25

Trains A226

Designs: 100um, Freight train for minerals. 370um, Passenger train. 440um, Desert train.

2003, Jan. 1 ***Perf. 13x13¼***

757-759 A226 Set of 3 7.25 7.25

Tourist Attractions A227

Designs: 100um, Sailboats, Banc d'Arguin. 220um, Ben Amera. 370um, Desert warthogs, Diawling Park. 440fr, Palms, Tergit, vert.

2003, Jan. 1 ***Perf. 13x13¼, 13¼x13***

760-763 A227 Set of 4 9.00 9.00

Handicrafts A228

Designs: 100um, Wooden chest. 220um, Pipes. 310um, Teapot. 370um, Beads.

2003, Jan. 1 ***Perf. 13x13¼***

764-767 A228 Set of 4 8.00 8.00

Historic Towns A229

Designs: 100um, Mosque, Chinguetti. 220um, Mosque, Ouadane. 660um, Wall design, Oualata. 880um, Mosque, Tichitt.

2003, Jan. 1

768-771 A229 Set of 4 15.00 15.00

Promotion of Books and Reading A230

Open book and: 100um, Stack of books, chair. 220um, Camel. 280um, Tower. 370um, Man, construction equipment.

2003, Jan. 1 **Litho.** ***Perf. 13***

772-775 A230 Set of 4 12.50 12.50

Diplomatic Relations Between Mauritania and People's Republic of China, 40th Anniv. A231

Flags and: 100um, Ships and crane. 370um, Ship and crane, vert.

Perf. 13x13¼, 13¼x13

2005, July 19 **Litho.**

776-777 A231 Set of 2 6.25 6.25

Independence, 45th Anniv. — A232

Denominations: 100um, 370um.

2005, Nov. 16 ***Perf. 13***

778-779 A232 Set of 2 6.25 6.25

World Summit on the Information Society, Tunis A233

Denominations: 100um, 370um.

2005, Nov. 16

780-781 A233 Set of 2 6.25 6.25

Musical Instruments — A234

Designs: 100um, Tidinit and gambré. 220um, Ardines, vert. 370um, Tom-toms. 440um, Kora and djembé, vert.

2005, Nov. 28

782-785 A234 Set of 4 13.00 13.00

Flora A235

Designs: 100um, Acacia tree. 220um, Euphorbia, vert. 370um, Jujube tree. 440um, Baobab tree, vert.

2005, Nov. 28

786-789 A235 Set of 4 13.00 13.00

Fauna A236

Designs: 100um, Starred lizard. 220um, Horned viper, vert. 370um, Lizard. 440um, Scorpion, vert.

2005, Nov. 28

790-793 A236 Set of 4 13.00 13.00

Tourism A237

Designs: 100um, People, fish and dolphins in water. 220um, Hodh El Gharbi. 370um, Adrar. 440um, Tiris Zemour.

2005, Nov. 28

794-797 A237 Set of 4 13.00 13.00

Jewelry A238

Designs: 100um, Necklaces. 220um, Khalkhal bracelets. 370um, Strings of beads. 440fr, Bracelets.

2008 **Litho.** ***Perf. 13***

798-801 A238 Set of 4 17.00 17.00

Exploitation of Natural Resources — A239

Designs: 100um, Zouerate iron mine. 280um, Chinguitti oil platform, vert. 310um, Akjoujt copper mine. 370um, Taziast gold mine, vert.

2008

802-805 A239 Set of 4 17.00 17.00

Animals A240

Designs: 100um, Birds. 220um, Dolphins. 370um, Seal. 440um, Sea turtle.

2009 **Litho.** ***Perf. 13***

806-809 A240 Set of 4 13.50 13.50

Saddles A241

Saddle for: 100um, Horse. 220um, Cow. 370um, Ass. 440um, Camel.

2009

810-813 A241 Set of 4 13.50 13.50

Gear for Nomads A242

Designs: 100um, Rifle holster. 150um, Tassoufra. 220um, Powder horns. 370um, Palanquin, vert. 440um, Prayer rug.

2009

814-818 A242 Set of 5 16.50 16.50

SEMI-POSTAL STAMPS

Nos. 23 and 26 Surcharged in Red

1915-18 **Unwmk.** ***Perf. 14x13½***

B1	A4 10c + 5c rose & red org	1.90	1.90
a.	Double surcharge	200.00	
B2	A4 15c + 5c dk brn & blk ('18)	1.90	1.90
a.	Double surcharge	200.00	
b.	Inverted surcharge	160.00	

Curie Issue

Common Design Type

1938, Oct. 24 ***Perf. 13***

B3 CD80 1.75fr + 50c brt ultra 8.25 8.25

French Revolution Issue

Common Design Type

Photo.; Name and Value Typographed in Black

1939, July 5 **Unwmk.**

B4	CD83	45c + 25c grn	9.00	9.00
B5	CD83	70c + 30c brn	9.00	9.00
B6	CD83	90c + 35c red org	9.00	9.00
B7	CD83	1.25fr + 1fr rose pink	9.00	9.00
B8	CD83	2.25fr + 2fr bl	9.00	9.00
		Nos. B4-B8 (5)	45.00	45.00

Stamps of 1938 Surcharge in Red or Black

1941

B9	A6	50c + 1fr pur (R)	1.75	1.75
B10	A7	80c + 2fr dp bl (R)	5.75	5.75
B11	A7	1.50fr + 2fr vio (R)	5.75	5.75
B12	A8	2fr + 3fr rose vio (Bk)	5.75	5.75
		Nos. B9-B12 (4)	19.00	19.00

Common Design Type and

Moorish Goumier SP1

White Goumier — SP2

1941 **Photo.** ***Perf. 13½***

B13	SP1	1fr + 1fr red	.70
B14	CD86	1.50fr + 3fr claret	.70
B15	SP2	2.50fr + 1fr blue	.70
		Nos. B13-B15 (3)	2.10

Nos. B13-B15 were issued by the Vichy government in France, but were not placed on sale in Mauritania.

Nos. 114-115
Surcharged in Black or Red

1944 Engr. *Perf. 12½x12*

B15A 50c + 1.50fr on 2.50fr deep blue (R) .50
B15B + 2.50fr on 1fr green .50

Colonial Development Fund.

Nos. B15A-B15B were issued by the Vichy government in France, but were not placed on sale in Mauritania.

Catalogue values for unused stamps in this section, from this point to the end of the section, are for Never Hinged items.

Islamic Republic
Anti-Malaria Issue
Common Design Type

1962, Apr. 7 Engr. *Perf. 12½x12*

B16 CD108 25fr + 5f light olive grn .80 .80

Freedom from Hunger Issue
Common Design Type

1963, Mar. 21 Unwmk. *Perf. 13*

B17 CD112 25fr + 5fr multi .80 .80

Nurse Tending Infant SP3

1972, May 8 Photo. *Perf. 12½x13*

B18 SP3 35fr + 5fr grn, red & brn 1.50 1.50

Surtax was for Mauritania Red Crescent Society.

AIR POST STAMPS

Common Design Type
Perf. 12½x12

1940, Feb. 8 Engr. Unwmk.

C1	CD85 1.90fr ultra	.55	.55
C2	CD85 2.90fr dk red	.55	.55
C3	CD85 4.50fr dk gray grn	.70	.70
C4	CD85 4.90fr yel bister	1.00	1.00
C5	CD85 6.90fr deep org	1.00	1.00
	Nos. C1-C5 (5)	3.80	3.80

Common Design Types

1942

C6	CD88 50c car & bl	.20	
C7	CD88 1fr brn & blk	.20	
C8	CD88 2fr dk grn & red brn	.35	
C9	CD88 3fr dk bl & scar	.35	
C10	CD88 5fr vio & brn red	.70	

Frame Engraved, Center Typo.

C11	CD89 10fr ultra, ind & hn	.75	
a.	Center inverted	*750.00*	
C12	CD89 20fr rose car, mag & buff	.75	
a.	Center inverted	*750.00*	
C13	CD89 50fr yel grn, dl grn & org	.85	*3.25*
	Nos. C6-C13 (8)	4.15	

There is doubt whether Nos. C6-C12 were officially placed in use.

Catalogue values for unused stamps in this section, from this point to the end of the section, are for Never Hinged items.

Islamic Republic

Flamingoes AP1

Designs: 200fr, African spoonbills. 500fr, Slender-billed gull, horiz.

Unwmk.

1961, June 30 Engr. *Perf. 13*

C14	AP1 100fr red org, brn & ultra	3.75	2.00
C15	AP1 200fr red org, sep & sl grn	6.00	3.25
C16	AP1 500fr red org, gray & bl	20.00	7.25
	Nos. C14-C16 (3)	29.75	12.50

An overprint, "Europa / CECA / MIFERMA," was applied in carmine to No. C16 in 1962. Two types exist: type 1, no box around "MIFERMA"; box surrounding "MIFERMA". Values: type 1, $35; type 2, $16.

The anti-malaria emblem, including slogan "Le Monde contre le Paludisme," was overprinted on Nos. C14-C15 in 1962. Two types of overprint: type 1, double lines of latitude and longitude on globe; type single lines of latitude and longitude on globe. Values: type 1, $27.50; type 2: $8.

Air Afrique Issue
Common Design Type

1962, Feb. 17

C17 CD107 100fr sl grn, choc & bis 2.50 1.10

UN Headquarters, New York; View of Nouakchott — AP2

1962, Oct. 27 Engr. *Perf. 13*

C18 AP2 100fr bluish grn, dk bl & org brn 2.50 .85

Mauritania's admission to the UN.

Plane, Nouakchott Airport — AP3

1963, May 3 Unwmk. *Perf. 13*

C19 AP3 500fr dp bl, gldn brn & slate grn 12.50 4.00

Miferma Open-pit Mine at Zouerate — AP4

Design: 200fr, Ore transport at Port Etienne.

1963, June Photo. *Perf. 13x12*

C20 AP4 100fr multi 1.90 .50
C21 AP4 200fr multi 4.75 1.00

African Postal Union Issue
Common Design Type

1963, Sept. 8 Unwmk. *Perf. 12½*

C22 CD114 85fr blk brn, ocher & red 1.75 .60

Globe and Telstar — AP5

Design: 150fr, Relay satellite and stars.

1963, Oct. 7 Engr. *Perf. 13*

C23 AP5 50fr yel grn, pur & red brn .75 .40
C24 AP5 150fr red brn & sl grn 2.75 1.25

Communication through space.

Tiros Satellite and Emblem of WMO — AP6

UN Emblem, Doves and Sun — AP7

1963, Nov. 4

C25 AP6 200fr ultra, brn & grn 4.25 1.50

Space research for meteorology and navigation.

1963 Air Afrique Issue
Common Design Type

1963, Nov. 19 Photo. *Perf. 13x12*

C26 CD115 25fr multi .70 .25

1963, Dec. 10 Engr. *Perf. 13*

C27 AP7 100fr vio, brn, & dk bl 2.00 .75

Universal Declaration of Human Rights, 15th anniv.

Symbols of Agriculture and Industry — AP8

Lichtenstein's Sand Grouse — AP9

Europafrica Issue

1964, Jan. 6 Photo.

C28 AP8 50fr multi 1.40 .75

Signing of economic agreement between the European Economic Community and the African and Malgache Union at Yaoundé, Cameroun, July 20, 1963.

1964, Feb. 3 Engr. *Perf. 13*

Birds: 200fr, Long-tailed cormorant. 500fr, Chanting goshawk.

C29	AP9 100fr ocher, ol & dk brn	3.25	1.00
C30	AP9 200fr blk, dk bl & brn	5.00	1.75
C31	AP9 500fr rose red, grn & sl	15.00	5.25
	Nos. C29-C31 (3)	23.25	8.00

Isis, Temple at Philae and Trajan's Kiosk — AP10

1964, Mar. 8 Unwmk. *Perf. 13*

C32	AP10 10fr red brn, Prus bl & blk	.60	.20
C33	AP10 25fr red brn, ind & Prus bl	.90	.40
C34	AP10 60fr blk brn, Prus bl & red brn	1.90	.60
	Nos. C32-C34 (3)	3.40	1.20

UNESCO world campaign to save historic monuments in Nubia.

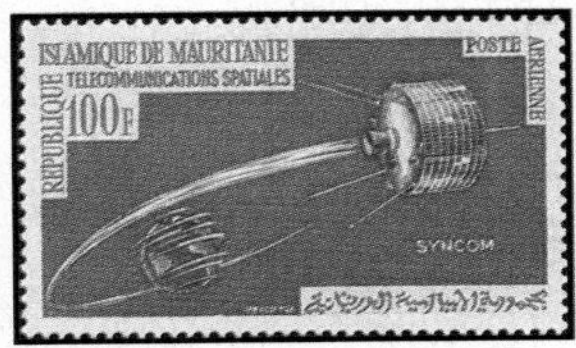

Syncom Satellite, Globe — AP11

1964, May 4 Engr.

C35 AP11 100fr red, red brn & ultra 1.60 .65

Issued to publicize space communications.

Horse Race on Bowl — AP12

Sport Designs from Ancient Pottery: 50fr, Runner, vert. 85fr, Wrestlers, vert. 100fr, Charioteer.

1964, Sept. 27 Unwmk. *Perf. 13*

C36	AP12 15fr ol bis & choc	.60	.30
C37	AP12 50fr bl & org brn	1.25	.50
C38	AP12 85fr crim & brn	2.10	1.00
C39	AP12 100fr emer & dk red brn	2.75	1.25
a.	Min. sheet of 4, #C36-C39	8.50	8.50
	Nos. C36-C39 (4)	6.70	3.05

18th Olympic Games, Tokyo, Oct. 10-25.

Pres. John F. Kennedy (1917-1963) AP13

1964, Dec. 7 Photo. *Perf. 12½*
C40 AP13 100fr red brn, bl grn & dk brn 2.10 1.00
a. Souv. sheet of 4 8.50 8.50

ITU Emblem, Induction Telegraph and Relay Satellite — AP14

1965, May 17 Engr. *Perf. 13*
C41 AP14 250fr multi 5.50 2.75

ITU, centenary.

Fight Against Cancer — AP15

Winston Churchill — AP16

1965, July 19 Unwmk. *Perf. 13*
C42 AP15 100fr bis, Prus bl & red 1.90 .60

Issued to publicize the fight against cancer.

1965, Dec. 6 Photo. *Perf. 13*
C43 AP16 200fr multi 3.25 1.10

Sir Winston Spencer Churchill (1874-1965), statesman and WWII leader.

Diamant Rocket Ascending AP17

French achievements in space: 60fr, Satellite A-1 and earth, horiz. 90fr, Scout rocket and satellite FR-1, horiz.

1966, Feb. 7 Engr. *Perf. 13*
C44 AP17 30fr dp bl, red & grn .60 .30
C45 AP17 60fr mar, Prus grn & bl 1.25 .50
C46 AP17 90fr dp bl, rose cl & vio 1.90 .75
Nos. C44-C46 (3) 3.75 1.55

Dr. Albert Schweitzer and Clinic — AP18

1966, Feb. 21 Photo. *Perf. 12½*
C47 AP18 50fr multi 1.50 .55

Schweitzer (1875-1965), medical missionary to Gabon, theologian and musician.

Thomas P. Stafford, Walter M. Schirra and Gemini 6 — AP19

Designs: 100fr, Frank A. Borman, James A. Lovell, Jr., and Gemini 7. 200fr, Pavel Belyayev, Alexei Leonov, Voskhod 2.

1966, Mar. 7 Photo. *Perf. 12½*
C48 AP19 50fr multi .80 .30
C49 AP19 100fr multi 1.75 .45
C50 AP19 200fr multi 3.50 1.00
Nos. C48-C50 (3) 6.05 1.75

Issued to honor achievements in space.

Map of Africa and Dove — AP20

D-1 Satellite over Earth — AP21

1966, May 9 Photo. *Perf. 13*
C51 AP20 100fr red brn, sl & yel grn 1.10 .40

Organization for African Unity.

1966, June 6 Engr.
C52 AP21 100fr bl, dk pur & ocher 1.50 .70

Launching of the D-1 satellite at Hammaguir, Algeria, Feb. 17, 1966.

Bréguet 14 — AP22

Planes: 100fr, Goliath Farman, and camel caravan. 150fr, Couzinet "Arc-en-Ciel." 200fr, Latécoère 28 hydroplane.

1966, July 4 Engr. *Perf. 13*
C53 AP22 50fr sl bl, dl grn & ol bis 1.00 .25
C54 AP22 100fr brt bl, dk grn & dk red brn 2.10 .45
C55 AP22 150fr dl brn, Prus bl & saph 3.25 .70
C56 AP22 200fr dk red brn, bl & ind 4.75 1.10
Nos. C53-C56 (4) 11.10 2.50

Air Afrique Issue, 1966
Common Design Type

1966, Aug. 31 Photo. *Perf. 13*
C57 CD123 30fr red, blk & gray .80 .30

"The Raft of the Medusa," by Théodore Géricault — AP23

1966, Sept. 5 Photo. *Perf. 12½*
C58 AP23 500fr multi 13.00 6.00

Sinking of the frigate "Medusa" off Mauritania, July 2, 1816.

Symbols of Agriculture and Industry — AP24

1966, Nov. 7 Photo. *Perf. 13x12*
C59 AP24 50fr multi 1.00 .35

Third anniversary, economic agreement between the European Economic Community and the African and Malgache Union.

Crowned Crane — AP25

Eye, Globe and Rockets — AP26

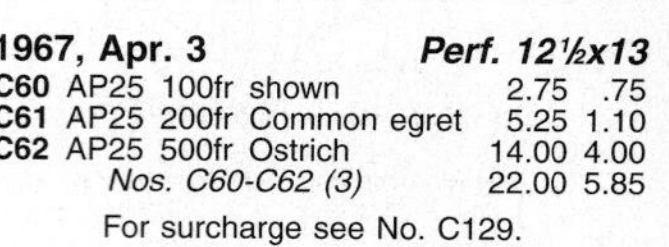

1967, Apr. 3 *Perf. 12½x13*
C60 AP25 100fr shown 2.75 .75
C61 AP25 200fr Common egret 5.25 1.10
C62 AP25 500fr Ostrich 14.00 4.00
Nos. C60-C62 (3) 22.00 5.85

For surcharge see No. C129.

1967, May 2 Engr. *Perf. 13*
C63 AP26 250fr brn, Prus bl & blk 4.25 1.25

EXPO '67 Intl. Exhibition, Montreal, Apr. 28-Oct. 27.

Emblem of Atomic Energy Commission AP27

1967, Aug. 7 Engr. *Perf. 13*
C64 AP27 200fr dk red, brt grn & ultra 3.00 1.10

International Atomic Energy Commission.

African Postal Union Issue, 1967
Common Design Type

1967, Sept. 9 Engr. *Perf. 13*
C65 CD124 100fr brn org, vio brn & brt grn 1.25 .55

Francesca da Rimini, by Ingres AP28

Paintings by and of Ingres: 100fr, Young man's torso. 150fr, "The Iliad" (seated woman). 200fr, Ingres in his Studio, by Alaux. 250fr, "The Odyssey" (seated woman).

1967-68 Photo. *Perf. 12½*
C66 AP28 90fr multi 2.00 .55
C67 AP28 100fr multi ('68) 2.00 .60
C68 AP28 150fr multi ('68) 3.00 .95
C69 AP28 200fr multi 3.50 1.00
C70 AP28 250fr multi ('68) 5.00 1.50
Nos. C66-C70 (5) 15.50 4.60

Jean Dominique Ingres (1780-1867), French painter.

Issued: 90fr, 200fr, 10/2/67; others, 9/2/68.

See No. C79.

Konrad Adenauer AP29

Gymnast AP30

1968, Feb. 5 Photo. *Perf. 12½*

C71 AP29 100fr org brn, lt bl & blk 2.00 .60
a. Souv. sheet of 4 7.50 5.50

Adenauer (1876-1967), chancellor of West Germany (1949-63).

1968, Mar. 4 Engr. *Perf. 13*

Sports: 20fr, Slalom, horiz. 50fr, Ski jump. 100fr, Hurdling, horiz.

C72 AP30 20fr plum, blk & bl .35 .20
C73 AP30 30fr dl pur, brt grn & brn .45 .20
C74 AP30 50fr Prus bl, bis & bl grn .65 .30
C75 AP30 100fr brn, grn & ver 1.40 .45
Nos. C72-C75 (4) 2.85 1.15

1968 Olympic Games.

WHO Emblem, Man and Insects — AP31

1968, May 2 Engr. *Perf. 13*

C76 AP31 150fr red lil, dp bl & org red 2.25 .80

WHO, 20th anniversary.

Martin Luther King — AP32

Design: No. C78, Mahatma Gandhi.

1968, Nov. 4 Photo. *Perf. 12½*

C77 AP32 50fr sl bl, cit & blk 1.00 .30
C78 AP32 50fr sl bl, lt bl & blk 1.00 .30
a. Souv. sheet of 4, 2 each #C77-C78 4.25 4.25

Issued to honor two apostles of peace.

PHILEXAFRIQUE Issue

Painting Type of 1967

Design: 100fr, The Surprise Letter, by Charles Antoine Coypel.

1968, Dec. 9 Photo. *Perf. 12½*

C79 AP28 100fr multi 3.25 1.25

PHILEXAFRIQUE, Phil. Exhib., Abidjan, Feb. 14-23. Printed with alternating brown red label.

2nd PHILEXAFRIQUE Issue

Common Design Type

50fr, Mauritania #89 & family on jungle trail.

1969, Feb. 14 Engr. *Perf. 13*

C80 CD128 50fr sl grn, vio brn & red brn 2.10 .65

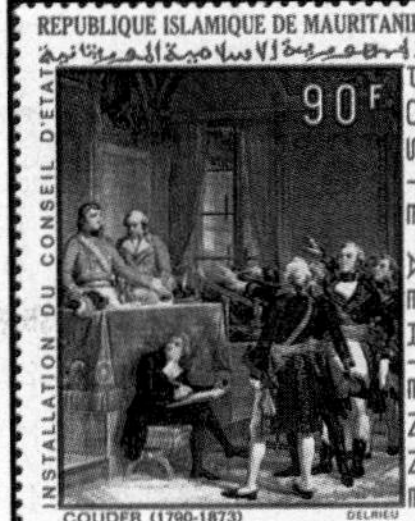

Napoleon Installed in Council of State, by Louis Charles Couder AP33

Paintings: 50fr, Napoleon at Council of the 500, by F. Bouchot. 250fr, Farewell at Fontainebleau, by Horace Vernet.

1969, Feb. 24 Photo. *Perf. 12½*

C81 AP33 50fr pur & multi 2.10 .80
C82 AP33 90fr multi 2.75 1.25
C83 AP33 250fr multi 7.25 3.00
Nos. C81-C83 (3) 12.10 5.05

Napoleon Bonaparte (1769-1821).

Camel, Gazelles, and Tourist Year Emblem — AP34

1969, June 9 Engr. *Perf. 13*

C84 AP34 50fr org, dk brn & lt bl 1.40 .40

Year of African Tourism.

Dancers and Temple Ruins, Baalbek — AP35

1969, June 16

C85 AP35 100fr Prus bl, ol brn & rose car 1.40 .45

International Baalbek Festival, Lebanon.

Apollo 8 and Moon Surface — AP36

Embossed on Gold Foil

1969 *Die-cut Perf. 10*

C86 AP36 1000fr gold 22.50 22.50

Man's first flight around the moon, Dec. 21-28, 1968 (US astronauts Col. Frank Borman, Capt. James Lovell and Maj. William Anders).

Mamo Wolde, Ethiopia, Marathon AP37

Designs: 70fr, Bob Beamon, US, broad jump. 150fr, Vera Caslavska, Czechoslovakia, gymnastics.

1969, July 7 Engr. *Perf. 13*

C87 AP37 30fr multi .45 .25
C88 AP37 70fr multi .80 .35
C89 AP37 150fr multi 2.10 .80
Nos. C87-C89 (3) 3.35 1.40

Issued to honor gold medal winners in the 19th Olympic Games, Mexico City.

Map of London-Istanbul Route — AP38

London to Sydney automobile rally: 20fr, Map showing Ankara to Teheran route, and compass rose. 50fr, Map showing Kandahar to Bombay route, arms of Afghanistan and elephant. 70fr, Map of Australia with Perth to Sydney route, and kangaroo.

1969, Aug. 14 Engr. *Perf. 13*

C90 AP38 10fr multicolored .25 .20
C91 AP38 20fr multicolored .45 .20
C92 AP38 50fr multicolored .75 .30
C93 AP38 70fr multicolored 1.10 .40
a. Min. sheet of 4, #C90-C93 3.50 3.50
Nos. C90-C93 (4) 2.55 1.10

Palette with World Map, Geisha and EXPO '70 Emblem — AP39

EXPO '70 Emblem and: 75fr, Fan & fireworks. 150fr, Stylized bird, map of Japan & boat.

1970, June 15 Photo. *Perf. 12½*

C94 AP39 50fr multi .80 .20
C95 AP39 75fr multi 1.40 .30
C96 AP39 150fr multi 2.50 .70
Nos. C94-C96 (3) 4.70 1.20

Issued to publicize EXPO '70 International Exhibition, Osaka, Japan, Mar. 15-Sept. 13.

UN Emblem, Balloon, Rocket, Farm Woman, Tractor, Old and New Record Players — AP40

1970, June 22 Engr. *Perf. 13*

C97 AP40 100fr ultra, dk brn & grn 1.40 .55

25th anniversary of the United Nations.

Elliott See (1927-1966), American Astronaut AP41

Apollo 13 Capsule with Parachutes AP42

#C99, Vladimir Komarov (1927-67). #C100, Yuri Gagarin (1934-68). #C101, Virgil Grissom (1926-67). #C102, Edward White (1930-67). #C103, Roger Chaffee (1935-67).

1970 Engr. *Perf. 13*

Portrait in Brown

C98 AP41 150fr gray & brt bl 1.50 .70
C99 AP41 150fr gray & org 1.50 .70
C100 AP41 150fr gray & org 1.50 .70
a. Souv. sheet of 3, #C98-C100 5.00 5.00
C101 AP41 150fr ultra & grnsh bl 1.75 .70
C102 AP41 150fr ultra & org 1.75 .70
C103 AP41 150fr ultra & grnsh bl 1.75 .70
a. Souv. sheet of 3, #C101-C103 6.00 6.00
Nos. C98-C103 (6) 9.75 4.20

American and Russian astronauts who died in space explorations.

Gold Embossed

1970, Aug. 17 *Perf. 12½*

C104 AP42 500fr gold, crim & bl 8.00 8.00

Safe return of Apollo 13 crew.

Parliament, Nouakchott, and Coat of Arms — AP43

1970, Nov. 28 Photo. *Perf. 12½*

C105 AP43 100fr multi 1.25 .40

10th anniversary of Independence.

Hercules Wrestling Antaeus — AP44

1971, Mar. 8 Engr. *Perf. 13*

C106 AP44 100fr red lil, brn & ultra 1.90 .75

Pre-Olympic Year. Design from a vase decoration by Euphronius.

Gamal Abdel Nasser (1918-1970), President of U.A.R. — AP46

1971, May 10 Photo. *Perf. 12½*

C109 AP46 100fr gold & multi 1.00 .40

Boy Scout, Emblem and Map of Mauritania
AP47

1971, Aug. 16 Photo. *Perf. 12½*

C110 AP47	35fr yel & multi		.55	.20
C111 AP47	40fr pink & multi		.60	.20
C112 AP47	100fr multi		1.50	.40
	Nos. C110-C112 (3)		2.65	.80

13th Boy Scout World Jamboree, Asagiri Plain, Japan, Aug. 2-10.

African Postal Union Issue, 1971

Common Design Type

Design: 100fr, Women musicians and UAMPT building, Brazzaville, Congo.

1971, Nov. 13 Photo. *Perf. 13x13½*

C113 CD135 100fr bl & multi 1.10 .60

Letter and Postal Emblem
AP48

1971, Dec. 2 *Perf. 13*

C114 AP48 35fr bis & multi .65 .30

10th anniversary of African Postal Union.

Mosul Monarch, from Book of Songs, c. 1218
AP49

Designs from Mohammedan Miniatures: 40fr, Prince holding audience, Egypt, 1334. 100fr, Pilgrim caravan, from "Maquamat," Baghdad, 1237.

1972, Jan. 10 Photo. *Perf. 13*

C115 AP49	35fr gold & multi	.50	.20
C116 AP49	40fr gray & multi	.65	.30
C117 AP49	100fr buff & multi	1.75	.60
	Nos. C115-C117 (3)	2.90	1.10

For surcharges see Nos. C140, C143-C144.

Grand Canal, by Canaletto — AP50

Designs: 45fr, Venice Harbor, by Carlevaris, vert. 250fr, Santa Maria della Salute, by Canaletto.

1972, Feb. 14

C118 AP50	45fr gold & multi	.75	.30
C119 AP50	100fr gold & multi	1.90	.60
C120 AP50	250fr gold & multi	4.25	1.00
	Nos. C118-C120 (3)	6.90	1.90

UNESCO campaign to save Venice.

Hurdles and Olympic Rings — AP51

1972, Apr. 27 Engr. *Perf. 13*

C121 AP51	75fr org, vio brn & blk	.75	.25
C122 AP51	100fr Prus bl, vio brn & brn	1.10	.40
C123 AP51	200fr lake, vio brn & blk	2.40	.60
a.	Min. sheet of 3, #C121-C123	7.00	7.00
	Nos. C121-C123 (3)	4.25	1.25

20th Olympic Games, Munich, Aug. 26-Sept. 11.

For overprints see Nos. C126-C128.

Luna 17 on Moon — AP52

75fr, Luna 16 take-off from moon, vert.

1972, Oct. 9

C124 AP52	75fr vio bl, bis & grn	.80	.25
C125 AP52	100fr dl pur, sl & ol bis	1.10	.40

Russian moon missions, Luna 16, Sept. 12-14, 1970; and Luna 17, Nov. 10-17, 1970.

Nos. C121-C123 Overprinted in Violet Blue or Red:

a. 110m HAIES / MILBURN MEDAILLE D'OR
b. 400m HAIES / AKII-BUA MEDAILLE D'OR
c. 3.000m STEEPLE / KEINO MEDAILLE D'OR

1972, Oct. 16

C126 AP51(a)	75fr multi (VB)	1.00	.30
C127 AP51(b)	100fr multi (R)	1.25	.45
C128 AP51(c)	200fr multi (VB)	2.75	.90
	Nos. C126-C128 (3)	5.00	1.65

Gold medal winners in 20th Olympic Games: Rod Milburn, US, John Akii-Bua, Uganda, and Kipchoge Keino, Kenya.

No. C62 Surcharged with New Value, Two Bars and: "Apollo XVII / December 1972"

1973, Jan. 29 Photo. *Perf. 12½x13*

C129 AP25 250fr on 500fr multi 4.00 1.25

Apollo 17 moon mission, Dec. 7-19, 1972.

Seal Type of Regular Issue

1973, Feb. 28 Litho. *Perf. 13*

C130 A63 135fr Seal's head 4.25 1.75

For surcharge see No. C145.

Lion Eating Caiman, by Delacroix — AP53

Painting: 250fr, Lion Eating Boar, by Delacroix.

1973, Mar. 26 Photo. *Perf. 13x12½*

C131 AP53	100fr blk & multi	2.00	.80
C132 AP53	250fr blk & multi	4.50	2.00

For surcharges see Nos. C148-C149.

Villagers Observing Solar Eclipse — AP54

40fr, Rocket take-off & Concord, vert. 140fr, Scientists with telescopes observing eclipse.

1973, June 20 Engr. *Perf. 13*

C133 AP54	35fr grn & pur	.85	.25
C134 AP54	40fr ultra, pur & scar	.90	.25
C135 AP54	140fr scar & pur	3.50	.70
a.	Souvenir sheet of 3	6.00	6.00
	Nos. C133-C135 (3)	5.25	1.20

Solar eclipse, June 30, 1973. No. C135a contains 3 stamps similar to Nos. C133-C135 in changed colors (35fr, 140fr in magenta and violet blue; 40fr in magenta, violet blue and orange).

For surcharges see Nos. C141-C142, C146.

Soccer
AP55

1973, Dec. 24 Photo. *Perf. 13*

C136 AP55	7um multi	.40	.25
C137 AP55	8um multi	.40	.25
C138 AP55	20um multi	1.25	.60
	Nos. C136-C138 (3)	2.05	1.10

Souvenir Sheet

C139 AP55 30um multi 1.75 1.75

World Soccer Cup, Munich, 1974.

Nos. C115-C117, C130 and C133-C135 Surcharged with New Value and Two Bars in Red, Black or Ultramarine

1973-74 Photo., Litho. or Engr.

C140 AP49	7um on 35fr (R) ('74)	.60	.25
C141 AP54	7um on 35fr (B)	.70	.25
C142 AP54	8um on 40fr (B)	.70	.25
C143 AP49	8um on 40fr (U) ('74)	.60	.25
C144 AP49	20um on 100fr (R) ('74)	2.00	.60
C145 A63	27um on 135fr (R)	3.00	.70
C146 AP54	28um on 140fr (B)	2.25	.70
	Nos. C140-C146 (7)	9.85	3.00

Winston Churchill (1874-1965)
AP56

Lenin (1870-1924)
AP57

1974, June 3 Engr. *Perf. 13*

C147 AP56 40um blk, brn & hn brn 2.00 .90

Nos. C131-C132 Surcharged with New Value and Two Bars in Red

1974, July 15 Photo. *Perf. 13x12½*

C148 AP53	20um on 100fr multi	1.50	.60
C149 AP53	50um on 250fr multi	4.00	1.60

1974, Sept. 16 Engr. *Perf. 13*

C150 AP57 40um slate grn & red 3.75 1.10

Women, IWY Emblem
AP58

40um, Woman's head and IWY emblems.

1975, June 16 Engr. *Perf. 13*

C151 AP58	12um multi	.60	.25
C152 AP58	40um dk brn, lt brn & bl	2.25	.80

International Women's Year.

Albert Schweitzer and Patients Arriving — AP59

1975, Aug. 4 Engr. *Perf. 13*

C153 AP59 60um multi 3.50 1.50

Schweitzer (1875-1965), medical missionary.

Javelin and Olympic Emblem — AP60

52um, Running and Olympic emblem.

1975, Nov. 17 Engr. *Perf. 13*

C154 AP60	50um sl grn, red & ol	2.50	1.25
C155 AP60	52um car, ocher & ultra	2.50	1.25

Pre-Olympic Year 1975.

Apollo Soyuz Type, 1975

Docked Space Ships and: 20um, Apollo rocket launch. 50um, Handshake in linked-up cabin. 60um, Apollo splash-down. 100um, Astronauts and Cosmonauts.

1975, Dec. 29 Litho. *Perf. 14*

C156 A74	20um multi	1.00	.40
C157 A74	50um multi	2.25	.75
C158 A74	60um multi	2.75	1.00
	Nos. C156-C158 (3)	6.00	2.15

Souvenir Sheet

C159 A74 100um multi 4.25 1.25

American Bicentennial Type, 1976

Uniforms: 20um, French Hussar officer. 50um, 3rd Continental Artillery officer. 60um, French infantry regiment grenadier. 100um, American infantryman.

1976, Jan. 26

C160 A75	20um multi	.75	.25
C161 A75	50um multi	2.00	.70
C162 A75	60um multi	2.75	.80
	Nos. C160-C162 (3)	5.50	1.75

Souvenir Sheet

C163 A75 100um multi 4.50 1.25

Running and Olympic Rings AP61

12um, High jump. 52um, Fencing.

1976, June 14 Engr. *Perf. 13*

C164 AP61 10um pur, grn & brn .80 .25
C165 AP61 12um pur, grn & brn .90 .40
C166 AP61 52um pur, grn & brn 3.00 1.40
Nos. C164-C166 (3) 4.70 2.05

21st Olympic Games, Montreal, Canada, July 17-Aug. 1.

Zeppelin Type, 1976

Designs: 50um, "Graf Zeppelin" (LZ-127) over US Capitol. 60um, "Hindenburg" (LZ-130) over Swiss Alps. 100um, "Führersland" (LZ-129) over 1936 Olympic stadium.

1976, June 28 Litho. *Perf. 11*

C167 A77 50um multi 3.25 .90
C168 A77 60um multi 4.00 1.10

Souvenir Sheet

C169 A77 100um multi 6.75 1.50

Marabou Storks — AP62

African Birds: 50um, Sacred ibis, vert. 200um, Long-crested eagles, vert.

1976, Sept. 20 Litho. *Perf. 13½*

C170 AP62 50um multi 3.50 1.00
C171 AP62 100um multi 6.50 1.75
C172 AP62 200um multi 13.00 3.50
Nos. C170-C172 (3) 23.00 6.25

Viking Type, 1977

Designs: 20um, Viking orbiter in flight to Mars. 50um, Viking "B" in descent to Mars. 60um, Various phases of descent. 100um, Viking lander using probe.

1977, Feb. 28 *Perf. 14*

C173 A81 20um multi 1.00 .25
C174 A81 50um multi 2.50 .50
C175 A81 60um multi 3.00 .65
Nos. C173-C175 (3) 6.50 1.40

Souvenir Sheet

C176 A81 100um multi 5.00 1.50

For surcharge & overprints see #C192-C195.

Nobel Prize Type, 1977

14um, George Bernard Shaw, literature. 55um, Thomas Mann, literature. 60um, Intl. Red Cross Society, peace. 100um, George C. Marshall, peace.

1977, Apr. 29 Litho. *Perf. 14*

C177 A83 14um multi 1.00 .25
C178 A83 55um multi 3.25 .50
C179 A83 60um multi 4.25 .65
Nos. C177-C179 (3) 8.50 1.40

Souvenir Sheet

C180 A83 100um multi 8.00 1.50

Holy Kaaba — AP63

1977, July 25 Litho. *Perf. 12½*

C181 AP63 12um multi 1.75 .40

Pilgrimage to Mecca.

Soccer Type of 1977

50um, Soccer ball. 60um, Eusebio Ferreira. 100um, Players holding pennants.

1977, Dec. 19 Litho. *Perf. 13½*

C182 A89 50um multi 2.50 .50
C183 A89 60um multi 3.00 .65

Souvenir Sheet

C184 A89 100um multi 5.00 1.25

For overprints see Nos. C187-C189.

Franco-African Co-operation — AP63a

1978, June 7 Embossed *Perf. 10½*

C184A AP63a 250um silver 12.00 12.00
C184B AP63a 500um gold 25.00 25.00

Philexafrique II — Essen Issue
Common Design Types

No. C185, Hyena and Mauritania #C60. No. C186, Wading bird and Hamburg #1.

1978, Nov. 1 Litho. *Perf. 12½*

C185 CD138 20um multi 1.75 1.00
C186 CD139 20um multi 1.75 1.00
a. Pair #C185-C186 + label 5.25 4.00

Nos. C182-C184 Overprinted in Arabic and French in Silver: "ARGENTINE- / PAYS BAS 3-1"

1978, Dec. 11 Litho. *Perf. 13½*

C187 A89 50um multi 2.25 1.10
C188 A89 60um multi 3.00 1.40

Souvenir Sheet

C189 A89 100um multi 5.00 5.00

Argentina's victory in World Cup Soccer Championship 1978.

Flyer A and Prototype Plane — AP64

Design: 40um, Flyer A and supersonic jet.

1979, Jan. 29 Engr. *Perf. 13*

C190 AP64 15um multi 1.10 .35
C191 AP64 40um multi 2.50 1.00

75th anniversary of first powered flight.

Nos. C173-C176 Overprinted and Surcharged in Silver: "ALUNISSAGE / APOLLO XI / JUILLET 1969" and Emblem

1979, Oct. 24 Litho. *Perf. 14*

C192 A81 14um on 20um multi .75 .30
C193 A81 50um multi 2.50 .90
C194 A81 60um multi 2.75 1.25
Nos. C192-C194 (3) 6.00 2.45

Souvenir Sheet

C195 A81 100um multi 5.00 5.00

Apollo 11 moon landing, 10th anniversary.

Soccer Players — AP65

Designs: Various soccer scenes.

1980, Sept. 29 Litho. *Perf. 12½*

C196 AP65 10um multi .45 .25
C197 AP65 12um multi .55 .25
C198 AP65 14um multi .55 .25
C199 AP65 20um multi 1.00 .25
C200 AP65 67um multi 2.75 .60
Nos. C196-C200 (5) 5.30 1.60

Souvenir Sheet

C201 AP65 100um multi 4.75 1.00

World Soccer Cup 1982.
For overprints see Nos. C212-C217.

Flight of Columbia Space Shuttle — AP66

Designs: Views of Columbia space shuttle.

1981, Apr. 27 Litho. *Perf. 12½*

C202 AP66 12um multi .60 .25
C203 AP66 20um multi 1.00 .25
C204 AP66 50um multi 2.25 .50
C205 AP66 70um multi 3.25 .70
Nos. C202-C205 (4) 7.10 1.70

Souvenir Sheet

C206 AP66 100um multi 5.00 1.25

Dinard Landscape, by Pablo Picasso — AP67

Picasso Birth Centenary: 12um, Harlequin, vert. 20um, Vase of Flowers, vert. 50um, Three Women at the Well. 100um, Picnic.

1981, June 29 Litho. *Perf. 12½*

C207 AP67 12um multi .70 .25
C208 AP67 20um multi 1.10 .30
C209 AP67 50um multi 2.50 .60
C210 AP67 70um multi 3.50 .85
C211 AP67 100um multi 5.00 1.25
Nos. C207-C211 (5) 12.80 3.25

Nos. C196-C201 Overprinted in Red with Finalists and Score on 1 or 2 Lines

1982, Sept. 18 Litho. *Perf. 12½*

C212 AP65 10um multi .45 .25
C213 AP65 12um multi .55 .25
C214 AP65 14um multi .55 .30
C215 AP65 20um multi 1.00 .30
C216 AP65 67um multi 2.75 .75
Nos. C212-C216 (5) 5.30 1.85

Souvenir Sheet

C217 AP65 100um multi 4.75 1.25

Italy's victory in 1982 World Cup.

25th Anniv. of Intl. Maritime Org. — AP68

1983, June 18 Litho. *Perf. 12½x13*

C218 AP68 18um multi .85 .40

Paul Harris, Rotary Founder AP69

1984, Jan. 20 Litho. *Perf. 13½*

C219 AP69 100um multi 4.75 1.00

1984 Summer Olympics — AP70

1984, July 15 Litho. *Perf. 14*

C223 AP70 14um Running, horiz. .70 .30
C224 AP70 18um Shot put .85 .40
C225 AP70 19um Hurdles .95 .40
C226 AP70 44um Javelin 1.90 1.00
C227 AP70 77um High jump 4.00 1.75
Nos. C223-C227 (5) 8.40 3.85

Souvenir Sheet

C228 AP70 100um Steeplechase 6.00 2.00

Olympics Winners — AP71

1984, Dec. 20 Litho. *Perf. 13*

C229 AP71 14um Van den Berg, sailboard, Netherlands .85 .30
C230 AP71 18um Coutts, Finn sailing, N.Z. 1.00 .40
C231 AP71 19um 470 class, Spain 1.10 .45
C232 AP71 44um Soling, US 2.50 1.00
Nos. C229-C232 (4) 5.45 2.15

Souvenir Sheet

C233 AP71 100um Sailing, US 6.00 3.00

PHILEXAFRICA '85, Lome, Togo — AP72

1985, May 23 Litho. *Perf. 13*

C234 AP72 40um Youths, map, IYY emblem 1.90 .75
C235 AP72 40um Oil refinery, Nouadhibou 1.90 .75
a. Pair, #C234-C235 + label 5.00 3.75

Exists with two labels showing map of Africa or Lome '85 emblem.

1985, Nov. 12 *Perf. 13x12½*

C236 AP72 50um Iron mine, train 2.00 .75
C237 AP72 50um Boy reading, herding sheep 2.00 .75
a. Pair, #C236-C237 + label 5.75 5.75

Audubon Birth Bicentenary AP73

1985, Aug. 14

C238 AP73 14um Passeriformes thraupidae .80 .25
C239 AP73 18um Larus philadelphia 1.00 .25
C240 AP73 19um Cyanocitta cristata 1.25 .35
C241 AP73 44um Rhyncops nigra 2.75 .70
Nos. C238-C241 (4) 5.80 1.55

Souvenir Sheet

C242 AP73 100um Anhinga anhinga 8.00 4.00

1st South Atlantic Crossing, 55th Anniv. — AP74

1986, May 19 Litho. *Perf. 13*

C243 AP74 18um Comte de Vaux, 1930 .65 .30
C244 AP74 50um Flight reenactment, 1985 1.75 .90
a. Pair, #C243-C244 + label 2.75 2.75

1986 World Cup Soccer Championships, Mexico — AP75

Various soccer plays.

1986, June 19 Litho. *Perf. 13*

C245 AP75 8um No. 279 .30 .20
C246 AP75 18um No. 280 .75 .30
C247 AP75 22um No. 281 .95 .35
C248 AP75 25um No. 282 1.10 .45
C249 AP75 40um Soccer cup 1.75 .70
Nos. C245-C249 (5) 4.85 2.00

Souvenir Sheet

C250 AP75 100um multi 4.75 2.50

Air Africa, 25th Anniv. — AP76

1986, Oct. 6 Litho. *Perf. 13*

C251 AP76 26um multi .90 .40

1988 Summer Olympics, Seoul — AP77

1987, Aug. 13 Litho. *Perf. 13*

C252 AP77 30um Boxing 1.10 .45
C253 AP77 40um Judo 1.50 .60
C254 AP77 50um Fencing 1.75 .75
C255 AP77 75um Wrestling 3.00 1.10
Nos. C252-C255 (4) 7.35 2.90

Souvenir Sheet

C256 AP77 150um Judo, diff. 5.75 2.25

1988 Winter Olympics, Calgary — AP78

1987, Sept.

C257 AP78 30um Women's slalom 1.10 .45
C258 AP78 40um Speed skating 1.50 .60
C259 AP78 50um Ice hockey 1.75 .75
C260 AP78 75um Women's downhill skiing 3.00 1.10
Nos. C257-C260 (4) 7.35 2.90

Souvenir Sheet

C261 AP78 150um Men's cross-country skiing 5.75 2.25

For overprints see Nos. C267-C271.

1988 Summer Olympics, Seoul AP79

1988, Sept. 17 Litho. *Perf. 13*

C262 AP79 20um Hammer throw .85 .30
C263 AP79 24um Discus .90 .35
C264 AP79 30um Shot put 1.25 .45
C265 AP79 150um Javelin 5.75 2.00
Nos. C262-C265 (4) 8.75 3.10

Souvenir Sheet

C266 AP79 170um Javelin, diff. 6.50 2.50

Nos. C257-C261 Overprinted "Medaille d'or" in Red or Bright Blue and:
a. "Vreni Schneider (Suisse)"
b. "1500 m / Andre Hoffman (R.D.A.)"
c. "U.R.S.S."
d. "Marina Kiehl (R.F.A.)"
e. "15 km / Mikhail Deviatiarov (U.R.S.S.)"

1988, Sept. 18

C267 AP78(a) 30um multi 1.25 .45
C268 AP78(b) 40um multi (BB) 1.75 .60
C269 AP78(c) 50um multi 2.00 .80
C270 AP78(d) 75um multi 3.50 1.25
Nos. C267-C270 (4) 8.50 3.10

Souvenir Sheet

C271 AP78(e) 150um multi 6.50 3.00

World Cup Soccer Championships, Italy — AP80

Map of Italy and various soccer plays.

1990 Litho. *Perf. 13*

C272 AP80 50um multicolored 2.00 .65
C273 AP80 60um multicolored 2.00 .85
C274 AP80 70um multicolored 2.50 .95
C275 AP80 90um multicolored 3.50 1.25
C276 AP80 150um multicolored 7.50 2.75
Nos. C272-C276 (5) 17.50 6.45

AIR POST SEMI-POSTAL STAMPS

Maternity Hospital, Dakar — SPAP1

Dispensary, Mopti — SPAP2

Nurse Weighing Baby — SPAP3

Unwmk.

1942, June 22 Engr. *Perf. 13*

CB1 SPAP1 1.50fr + 3.50fr green .55
CB2 SPAP2 2fr + 6fr brown .55
CB3 SPAP3 3fr + 9fr carmine .55
Nos. CB1-CB3 (3) 1.65

Native children's welfare fund.

Nos. CB1-CB3 were issued by the Vichy government in France, but were not placed on sale in Mauritania.

Colonial Education Fund

Common Design Type

1942, June 22

CB4 CD86a 1.20fr + 1.80fr bl & red .55

No. CB4 was issued by the Vichy government in France, but was not placed on sale in Mauritania.

POSTAGE DUE STAMPS

D1

D2

Perf. 14x13½

1906-07 Unwmk. Typo.

J1 D1 5c grn, *grnsh* 2.60 2.60
J2 D1 10c red brn 4.00 4.00
J3 D1 15c dk bl 8.25 7.50
J4 D1 20c blk, *yellow* 10.50 9.00
J5 D1 30c red, *straw* 12.00 11.00
J6 D1 50c violet 19.00 18.00
J7 D1 60c blk, *buff* 13.50 12.50
J8 D1 1fr blk, *pinkish* 20.00 17.50
Nos. J1-J8 (8) 89.85 82.10

Issue dates: 20c, 1906; others 1907.

Regular postage stamps canceled "T" in a triangle were used for postage due.

1914

J9 D2 5c green .25 *.30*
J10 D2 10c rose .30 *.40*
J11 D2 15c gray .45 *.55*
J12 D2 20c brown .45 *.55*
J13 D2 30c blue .75 *.85*
J14 D2 50c black 1.40 *1.60*
J15 D2 60c orange 1.20 *1.25*
J16 D2 1fr violet 1.20 *1.40*
Nos. J9-J16 (8) 6.00 *6.90*

Type of 1914 Issue Surcharged

1927, Oct. 10

J17 D2 2fr on 1fr lil rose 2.75 2.75
a. Period after "F" omitted 12.50 12.50
J18 D2 3fr on 1fr org brn 3.25 3.25

Catalogue values for unused stamps in this section, from this point to the end of the section, are for Never Hinged items.

Islamic Republic

Oualata Motif — D3

Perf. 14x13½

1961, July 1 Typo. Unwmk.

Denominations in Black

J19 D3 1fr plum & org yel .20 .20
J20 D3 2fr red & gray .20 .20
J21 D3 5fr mar & pink .25 .25
J22 D3 10fr dk grn & grn .30 .25
J23 D3 15fr ol & brn org .30 .25
J24 D3 20fr red brn & lt blue .50 .25
J25 D3 25fr grn & vermilion .75 .50
Nos. J19-J25 (7) 2.50 1.90

Vulture (Ruppell's Griffon) — D4

Birds: #J27, Eurasian crane. #J28, Pink-backed pelican. #J29, Garganey teal. #J30, European golden oriole. #J31, Variable sunbird. #J32, Shoveler ducks. #J33, Great snipe. #J34, Vulturine guinea fowl. #J35, Black stork. #J36, Gray heron. #J37, White stork. #J38, Red-legged partridge. #J39, Paradise whydah. #J40, Sandpiper (little stint). #J41, Sudan bustard.

1963, Sept. 7 Engr. *Perf. 11*

J26	D4	50c blk, yel org & red	.20	.20
J27	D4	50c blk, yel org & red	.20	.20
a.		Pair, #J26-J27	.50	.50
J28	D4	1fr blk, red & yel	.20	.20
J29	D4	1fr blk, red & yel	.20	.20
a.		Pair, #J28-J29	.60	.60
J30	D4	2fr blk, bl grn & yel	.20	.20
J31	D4	2fr blk, bl grn & yel	.20	.20
a.		Pair, #J30-J31	.80	.80
J32	D4	5fr blk, grn & red brn	.35	.35
J33	D4	5fr blk, grn & red brn	.35	.35
a.		Pair, #J32-J33	1.25	1.25
J34	D4	10fr blk, red & tan	.70	.70
J35	D4	10fr blk, red & tan	.70	.70
a.		Pair, #J34-J35	2.50	2.50
J36	D4	15fr blk, emer & red	.75	.75
J37	D4	15fr blk, emer & red	.75	.75
a.		Pair, #J36-J37	2.75	2.75
J38	D4	20fr blk, yel grn & red	1.00	1.00
J39	D4	20fr blk, yel grn & red	1.00	1.00
a.		Pair, #J38-J39	3.25	3.25
J40	D4	25fr blk, yel grn & brn	1.50	1.50
J41	D4	25fr blk, yel grn & brn	1.50	1.50
a.		Pair, #J40-J41	4.50	4.50
		Nos. J26-J41 (16)	9.80	9.80

Ornament D5

1976, May 10 Litho. *Perf. 12½x13*

J42	D5	1um buff & multi	.20	.20
J43	D5	3um buff & multi	.20	.20
J44	D5	10um buff & multi	.45	.45
J45	D5	12um buff & multi	.55	.55
J46	D5	20um buff & multi	.95	.95
		Nos. J42-J46 (5)	2.35	2.35

OFFICIAL STAMPS

Catalogue values for unused stamps in this section are for Never Hinged items.

Islamic Republic

Cross of Trarza — O1

Perf. 14x13½

1961, July 1 Typo. Unwmk.

O1	O1	1fr vio & lilac	.20	.20
O2	O1	3fr red & slate	.20	.20
O3	O1	5fr grn & brown	.25	.20
O4	O1	10fr grn & vio bl	.25	.20
O5	O1	15fr blue & org	.35	.25
O6	O1	20fr sl grn & emer	.45	.25
O7	O1	25fr red org & mar	.50	.30
O8	O1	30fr maroon & grn	.60	.40
O9	O1	50fr dk red & dk brn	1.25	.50
O10	O1	100fr orange & blue	1.90	.90
O11	O1	200fr grn & red org	3.75	1.75
		Nos. O1-O11 (11)	9.70	5.15

Ornament O2

1976, May 3 Litho. *Perf. 12½x13*

O12	O2	1um black & multi	.20	.20
O13	O2	2um black & multi	.20	.20
O14	O2	5um black & multi	.25	.20
O15	O2	10um black & multi	.50	.25
O16	O2	12um black & multi	.70	.30
O17	O2	40um black & multi	2.50	.90
O18	O2	50um black & multi	3.00	1.25
		Nos. O12-O18 (7)	7.35	3.30

MAURITIUS

mo-'ri-sh,ē-,əs

LOCATION — Island in the Indian Ocean about 550 miles east of Madagascar
GOVT. — Republic
AREA — 720 sq. mi.
POP. — 1,182,212 (1999 est.)
CAPITAL — Port Louis

12 Pence = 1 Shilling
100 Cents = 1 Rupee (1878)

The British Crown Colony of Mauritius was granted self-government in 1967 and became an independent state on March 12, 1968.

Nos. 1-6, 14-17 unused are valued without gum.

Nos. 3a-8, 14-15 are printed on fragile paper with natural irregularities which might be mistaken for faults.

Very fine examples of Nos. 22-58 will have perforations touching the design on one or more sides. Examples with perfs clear on four sides are scarce and will sell for more. Inferior examples will sell for much reduced prices.

Catalogue values for unused stamps in this country are for Never Hinged items, beginning with Scott 223 in the regular postage section, Scott J1 in the postage due section.

Queen Victoria
A1 A2

1847 Unwmk. Engr. *Imperf.*

1	A1	1p orange	*1,250,000.*	*900,000.*
2	A1	2p dark blue		*1,000,000.*

Nos. 1 and 2 were engraved and printed in Port Louis. There is but one type of each value. The initials "J. B." on the bust are those of the engraver, J. Barnard.

All unused examples of the 2p are in museums. There is one unused example of the 1p in private hands. There are two used examples of the 1p in private hands, both of which have small faults and are valued thus.

1848

Earliest Impressions
Thick Yellowish Paper

3	A2	1p orange	*55,000.*	*17,500.*
4	A2	2p dark blue	*50,000.*	*20,000.*
d.		"PENOE"	*100,000.*	*35,000.*

Early Impressions
Yellowish White Paper

3a	A2	1p orange	*26,500.*	*7,250.*
4a	A2	2p blue	*28,000.*	*8,000.*
e.		"PENOE"	*50,000.*	*13,000.*

Bluish Paper

5	A2	1p orange	*26,500.*	*7,250.*
6	A2	2p blue	*28,000.*	*8,000.*
c.		"PENOE"	*50,000.*	*13,000.*

Intermediate Impressions
Yellowish White Paper

3b	A2	1p red orange	*16,000.*	2,750.
4b	A2	2p blue	*16,500.*	3,750.
f.		"PENOE"	*26,000.*	*6,500.*

Bluish Paper

5a	A2	1p red orange	*16,000.*	2,750.
6a	A2	2p blue	*16,500.*	3,750.
d.		"PENOE"	*26,000.*	*6,500.*
f.		Double impression		—

Worn Impressions
Yellowish White Paper

3c	A2	1p orange red	6,000.	750.
d.		1p brownish red	6,000.	750.
4c	A2	2p blue	7,250.	1,400.
g.		"PENOE"	*10,000.*	2,500.

Bluish Paper

5b	A2	1p orange red	5,000.	700.
c.		1p brownish red	5,000.	700.
d.		Pair, double impression		
6b	A2	2p blue	7,250.	1,350.
e.		"PENOE"	*10,000.*	2,000.

Latest Impressions
Yellowish or Grayish Paper

3e	A2	1p orange red	4,250.	600.
f.		1p brownish red	4,250.	600.
4h	A2	2p blue	5,250.	950.
i.		"PENOE"	*9,250.*	1,600.

Bluish Paper

5e	A2	1p orange red	4,250.	600.
f.		1p brownish red	4,250.	600.
6g	A2	2p blue	5,250.	950.
h.		"PENOE"	9,250.	1,600.

These stamps were printed in sheets of twelve, four rows of three, and each position differs in details. The "PENOE" error is the most pronounced variety on the plates and is from position 7.

The stamps were in use until 1859. Earliest impressions, Nos. 3-4, show the full background of diagonal and vertical lines with the diagonal lines predominant. Early impressions, Nos. 3a-4a, 5-6, show the full background with the vertical lines predominating. As the plate became worn the vertical lines disappeared, giving the intermediate impressions, Nos. 3b-4b, 5a-6a.

Worn impressions, Nos. 3c-4c, 5b-6b, have little background remaining, and latest impressions, Nos. 3e-4h, 5e-6g, have also lost details of the frame and head. The paper of the early impressions is usually rather thick, that of the worn impressions rather thin. Expect natural fibrous inclusions in the paper of all impressions.

"Britannia"
A3 A4

1849-58

7	A3	red brown, *blue*	25.00
8	A3	blue ('58)	7.50

Nos. 7-8 were never placed in use.

1858-59

9	A3	(4p) green, *bluish*	550.00	240.00
10	A3	(6p) red	50.00	*110.00*
11	A3	(9p) magenta ('59)	775.00	240.00

No. 11 was re-issued in Nov. 1862, as a 1p stamp (No. 11a). When used as such it is always canceled "B53." Price so used, $200.

1858 Black Surcharge

12	A4	4p green, *bluish*	1,650.	525.00

Queen Victoria — A5

Early Impressions

1859, Mar.

14	A5	2p blue, *grayish*	10,000.	2,450.
a.		2p deep blue, *grayish*	12,000.	3,000.
14B	A5	2p blue, *bluish*	10,000.	2,500.
c.		Intermediate impression	6,500.	1,100.
d.		Worn impression	4,000.	750.00

Type A5 was engraved by Lapirot, in Port Louis, and was printed locally. There were twelve varieties in the sheet.

Early impressions have clear and distinct background lines. In the intermediate impressions, the lines are somewhat blurred, and white patches appear. In the worn impressions, the background lines are discontinuous, with many white patches. Analogous wear is also obvious in the background of the inscriptions on all four sides. Values depend on the state of wear. One should expect natural fibrous inclusions in the paper on all printings.

A6

A7

1859, Oct.

15	A6	2p blue, *bluish*	*180,000.*	11,000.

No. 15 was printed from the plate of the 1848 issue after it had been entirely re-engraved by Sherwin. It is commonly known as the "fillet head." The plate of the 1p, 1848, was also re-engraved but was never put in use.

1859, Dec. Litho.

Laid Paper

16	A7	1p vermilion	6,500.	1,200.
a.		1p deep red	*11,000.*	2,100.
b.		1p red	*8,750.*	1,500.
17	A7	2p pale blue	4,250.	700.
a.		2p slate blue	7,250.	1,100.
b.		2p blue	4,500.	875.

Lithographed locally by Dardenne.

"Britannia" — A8

1859 Wove Paper Engr. *Imperf.*
18 A8 6p blue 750.00 55.00
19 A8 1sh vermilion 3,000. 60.00

1861
20 A8 6p gray violet 32.50 *60.00*
21 A8 1sh green 675.00 150.00

1862 *Perf. 14 to 16*
22 A8 6p slate 30.00 *100.00*
a. Horiz. pair, imperf between *8,000.*
23 A8 1sh deep green 2,750. 400.00

Following the change in currency in 1878, a number of issues denominated in sterling were overprinted "CANCELLED" in serifed type and sold as remainders.

A9

A10

1860-63 Typo. *Perf. 14*
24 A9 1p brown lilac 325.00 32.50
25 A9 2p blue 350.00 60.00
26 A9 4p rose 360.00 37.50
27 A9 6p green ('62) 1,000. 175.00
28 A9 6p lilac ('63) 375.00 125.00
29 A9 9p dull lilac 175.00 50.00
30 A9 1sh buff ('62) 350.00 100.00
31 A9 1sh green ('63) 800.00 200.00

For surcharges see Nos. 43-45.

1863-72 Wmk. 1
32 A9 1p lilac brown 85.00 17.50
a. 1p bister brown 160.00 15.00
b. 1p brown 110.00 10.00
33 A9 2p blue 100.00 12.00
a. Imperf., pair 1,950. 2,350.
34 A9 3p vermilion 80.00 18.50
35 A9 4p rose 100.00 4.00
36 A9 6p lilac ('64) 375.00 42.50
37 A9 6p blue grn ('65) 200.00 7.25
a. 6p yellow green ('65) 250.00 16.75
38 A9 9p green ('72) 200.00 *325.00*
39 A9 1sh org yel ('64) 325.00 29.00
a. 1sh yellow 275.00 14.50
40 A9 1sh blue ('70) 155.00 28.50
41 A9 5sh red violet 215.00 65.00
a. 5sh bright violet 300.00 65.00
Nos. 32-41 (10) 1,835. 549.25

For surcharges see Nos. 48-49, 51-58, 87.

1872
42 A10 10p claret 350.00 55.00

For surcharges see Nos. 46-47.

No. 29 Surcharged in Black or Red:

a

b

1876 Unwmk.
43 A9(a) ½p on 9p 21.00 21.00
a. Inverted surcharge *750.00*
b. Double surcharge *2,250.*
44 A9(b) ½p on 9p *4,750.*
45 A9(b) ½p on 9p (R) *3,000.*

Nos. 44 and 45 were never placed in use. No. 45 is valued with perfs cutting into the design.

Stamps of 1863-72 Surcharged in Black:

c

d

1876-77 Wmk. 1
46 A10(a) ½p on 10p claret 3.75 *26.00*
47 A10(c) ½p on 10p cl ('77) 9.25 *42.50*
48 A9(d) 1p on 4p rose ('77) 21.00 24.00
49 A9(d) 1sh on 5sh red vio ('77) 325.00 120.00
a. 1sh on 5sh violet ('77) 325.00 150.00
Nos. 46-49 (4) 359.00 *212.50*

A16

Black Surcharge

1878
50 A16 2c claret 14.00 8.75

Stamps and Type of 1863-72 Surcharged in Black

e

51 A9 4c on 1p bister brn 24.00 8.00
52 A9 8c on 2p blue 90.00 3.75
53 A9 13c on 3p org red 22.50 40.00
54 A9 17c on 4p rose 190.00 4.25
55 A9 25c on 6p sl blue 250.00 7.75
56 A9 38c on 9p violet 37.50 *95.00*
57 A9 50c on 1sh green 100.00 4.50
58 A9 2r50c on 5sh violet 19.50 *22.50*
Nos. 50-58 (9) 747.50 *194.50*

For surcharge see No. 87.

A18

A19

A20

A21

A22

A23

A24

A25

A26

1879-80 Wmk. 1
59 A18 2c red brn ('80) 55.00 22.50
60 A19 4c orange 72.50 4.25
61 A20 8c blue ('80) 35.00 4.50
62 A21 13c slate ('80) 175.00 300.00
63 A22 17c rose ('80) 85.00 8.75
64 A23 25c bister 475.00 15.00
65 A24 38c violet ('80) 200.00 350.00
66 A25 50c green ('80) 4.50 4.25
67 A26 2r50c brn vio ('80) 55.00 *82.50*
Nos. 59-67 (9) 1,157. 791.75

Nos. 59-67 are known imperforate.
For surcharges & overprints see #76-78, 83-86, 122-123.

1882-93 Wmk. 2
68 A18 1c violet ('93) 2.10 .55
69 A18 2c red brown 38.50 6.00
70 A18 2c green ('85) 4.00 .75
71 A19 4c orange 85.00 5.00
72 A19 4c rose ('85) 3.75 1.25
73 A20 8c blue ('91) 3.75 1.80
74 A23 25c bister ('83) 10.00 3.50
75 A25 50c dp orange ('87) 37.50 16.50
Nos. 68-75 (8) 184.60 35.35

For surcharges and overprint see #88-89, 121.

Nos. 63 and Type of 1882 Surcharged in Black:

f

g

1883 Wmk. 1
Surcharge Measures 14x3½mm
76 A22(f) 16c on 17c rose 170.00 60.00
a. Double surcharge 2,750.

Surcharge Measures 15½x3½mm
77 A22(f) 16c on 17c rose 190.00 60.00

Surcharge Measures 15½x2¾mm
78 A22(f) 16c on 17c rose *375.00* *135.00*

Wmk. 2
79 A22(g) 16c on 17c rose 100.00 2.40
Nos. 76-79 (4) *835.00* *257.40*

Queen Victoria — A29

1885-94
80 A29 15c orange brown ('92) 8.00 1.50
81 A29 15c blue ('94) 9.00 1.50
82 A29 16c orange brown 8.00 2.40
Nos. 80-82 (3) 25.00 5.40

For surcharges see Nos. 90, 116.

Various Stamps Surcharged in Black or Red:

h

j

1885-87 Wmk. 1
83 A24(h) 2c on 38c violet 160.00 42.50
a. Inverted surcharge 1,100. 975.00
b. Double surcharge 1,300.
c. Without bar 275.00
84 A21(j) 2c on 13c sl (R) ('87) 75.00 *130.00*
a. Inverted surcharge 250.00 *275.00*
b. Double surcharge *975.00* 850.00
c. As "b," one on back *975.00*
d. Double surcharge, both inverted *1,750.*

k

l

1891
85 A22(k) 2c on 17c rose 130.00 *140.00*
a. Inverted surcharge 525.00 —
b. Double surcharge 875.00 875.00
86 A24(k) 2c on 38c vio 9.25 11.00
a. Double surcharge 225.00 250.00
b. Dbl. surch., one invtd. 250.00 275.00
c. Inverted surcharge 1,100. —
87 A9(e+l) 2c on 38c on 9p vio 8.75 6.00
a. Double surcharge 850.00 850.00
b. Inverted surcharge 550.00 —

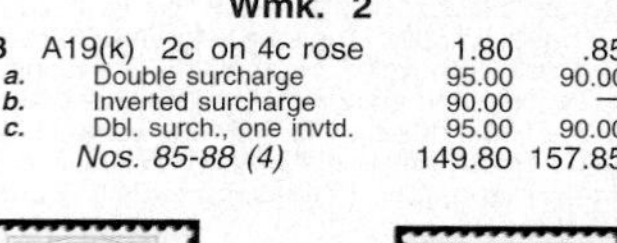

c. Dbl. surch., one invtd. 200.00 225.00

Wmk. 2
88 A19(k) 2c on 4c rose 1.80 .85
a. Double surcharge 95.00 90.00
b. Inverted surcharge 90.00 —
c. Dbl. surch., one invtd. 95.00 90.00
Nos. 85-88 (4) 149.80 157.85

m

n

1893, Jan.
89 A18(m) 1c on 2c violet 2.75 1.35
90 A29(n) 1c on 16c org brown 2.75 *4.00*

Coat of Arms — A38

1895-1904 Wmk. 2
91 A38 1c lilac & ultra .90 1.80
92 A38 1c gray blk & black .60 .25
93 A38 2c lilac & orange 6.00 .60
94 A38 2c dull lil & vio 1.00 .25
95 A38 3c lilac .90 .60
96 A38 3c grn & scar, *yel* 4.50 1.50
97 A38 4c lilac & green 4.50 .60
98 A38 4c dull lil & car, *yel* 1.80 .50
99 A38 4c gray green & pur 1.25 *2.40*
100 A38 4c black & car, *blue* 13.50 .75
101 A38 5c lilac & vio, *buff* 8.75 *75.00*
102 A38 5c lilac & blk, *buff* 3.00 3.00
103 A38 6c grn & rose 5.50 5.00
104 A38 6c violet & scar, *red* 2.40 1.00
105 A38 8c gray grn & blk, *buff* 4.00 *12.00*
106 A38 12c black & car rose 2.50 *2.75*
107 A38 15c grn & org 21.50 *8.75*
108 A38 15c blk & ultra, *blue* 65.00 1.50
109 A38 18c gray grn & ultra 16.00 4.25
110 A38 25c grn & car, *grn,* chalky paper 5.00 *22.50*
111 A38 50c green, *yel* 20.00 *70.00*
Nos. 91-111 (21) 188.60 *215.00*

The 25c is on both ordinary and chalky paper. Ornaments in lower panel omitted on #106-111.
Year of issue: #103, 107, 1899; #92, 94, 98, 1900; #96, 99, 101-102, 104-106, 110-111, 1902; #100, 108, 1904; others, 1895.
See #128-135. For surcharges and overprints see #113, 114, 117-120.

Diamond Jubilee Issue

Arms A39

1898, May 23 Wmk. 46
112 A39 36c brown org & ultra 14.00 *25.00*

60th year of Queen Victoria's reign.
For surcharges see Nos. 114 and 127.

No. 109 Surcharged in Red

1899 Wmk. 2
113 A38 6c on 18c 1.40 1.25
a. Inverted surcharge 725.00 340.00

No. 112 Surcharged in Blue

Wmk. 46

114 A39 15c on 36c 2.25 2.10
a. Without bar 500.00

Admiral Mahe de La Bourdonnais
A40

1899, Dec. Engr. Wmk. 1

115 A40 15c ultra 24.00 5.00

Birth bicent. of Admiral Mahe de La Bourdonnais, governor of Mauritius, 1734-46.

No. 82 Surcharged in Black

1900 Wmk. 2

116 A29 4c on 16c orange brown 10.00 21.00

No. 109 Surcharged in Black

r

1902

117 A38 12c on 18c grn & ultra 2.40 *8.00*

Preceding Issues Overprinted in Black

1902

118 A38 4c lilac & car, *yel* 1.50 .35
119 A38 6c green & rose 1.50 *3.25*
120 A38 15c green & orange 5.00 1.35
121 A23 25c bister 8.00 3.25

Wmk. 1

122 A25 50c green 14.00 5.50
123 A26 2r50c brown violet 135.00 *225.00*
Nos. 118-123 (6) 165.00 238.70

Coat of Arms — A41

1902 Wmk. 1

124 A41 1r blk & car rose 60.00 60.00

Wmk. 2 Sideways

125 A41 2r50c grn & blk, *bl* 30.00 *150.00*
126 A41 5r blk & car, *red* 95.00 *150.00*
Nos. 124-126 (3) 185.00 *360.00*

No. 112 Surcharged type "r" but with longer bar

1902 Wmk. 46

127 A39 12c on 36c 1.50 1.75
a. Inverted surcharge 775.00 525.00

Arms Type of 1895-1904

1904-07 Wmk. 3

Chalky Paper

128 A38 1c gray blk & black ('07) 8.75 5.00
129 A38 2c dl lil & vio ('05) 32.50 2.10
130 A38 3c grn & scar, *yel* 22.50 10.00
131 A38 4c blk & car, *blue* 11.00 .20
132 A38 6c vio & scar, *red* ('06) 10.00 .35
133 A38 15c blk & ultra, *bl* 4.50 .40
135 A38 50c green, *yel* 2.25 *4.25*
136 A41 1r black & car rose ('07) 42.50 *65.00*
Nos. 128-136 (8) 134.00 *87.30*

The 2c, 4c, 6c also exist on ordinary paper.

Ornaments in lower panel omitted on 15c and 50c.

Arms — A42

Edward VII — A43

1910 Wmk. 3

Ordinary Paper

137 A42 1c black 3.25 .35
138 A42 2c brown 3.25 .20
139 A42 3c green 3.50 .20
140 A42 4c ol grn & rose 4.25 .20
141 A43 5c gray & rose 3.25 *3.25*
142 A42 6c carmine 2.75 .20
143 A42 8c brown orange 3.25 *1.50*
144 A43 12c gray 2.75 *3.25*
145 A42 15c ultramarine 21.00 .20

Chalky Paper

146 A43 25c blk & scar, *yel* 2.50 *13.00*
147 A43 50c dull vio & blk 2.50 *20.00*
148 A43 1r blk, *green* 13.00 *13.00*
149 A43 2r50c blk & car, *bl* 24.00 *75.00*
150 A43 5r grn & car, *yel* 37.50 *100.00*
151 A43 10r grn & car, *grn* 150.00 *250.00*
Nos. 137-151 (15) 276.75 *480.35*

Numerals of 12c, 25c and 10r of type A43 are in color on plain tablet.

See Nos. 161-178.

King George V — A44

Die I

For description of dies I and II see "Dies of British Colonial Stamps" in table of contents.

Numeral tablet of 5c, 50c, 1r, 2.50r and 5r of type A44 has lined background with colorless denomination.

1912-22 Wmk. 3

Ordinary Paper

152 A44 5c gray & rose 2.50 *4.25*
153 A44 12c gray 8.00 1.10

Chalky Paper

154 A44 25c blk & red, *yel* .50 1.75
a. 25c gray black & red, *yellow*, Die II 1.10 *24.00*
155 A44 50c dull vio & blk 52.50 *110.00*
156 A44 1r black, *emerald*, die II 2.75 *8.00*
a. 1r black, *emer*, olive back, die I ('21) 11.00 *60.00*
b. 1r blk, *bl grn*, olive back, die I 6.00 *19.00*
157 A44 2r50c blk & red, *bl* 35.00 *75.00*
158 A44 5r grn & red, *yel* 100.00 *175.00*
a. Die II ('22) 75.00 *200.00*
159 A44 10r grn & red, *emer*, die II ('21) 42.50 *160.00*
a. 10r grn & red, *bl grn*, olive back, die I 1,100.
b. 10r green & red, *emer*, die I 75.00 *185.00*
c. 10r grn & red, *emer*, olive back, die I 130.00 *200.00*
d. 10r grn & red, *grn*, die I 100.00 *200.00*

Surface-colored Paper

160 A44 25c blk & red, *yel* ('16) 1.60 *20.00*
Nos. 152-160 (9) 245.35 *555.10*

1921-26 Wmk. 4

Ordinary Paper

161 A42 1c black 1.25 1.25
162 A42 2c brown 1.25 .20
163 A42 2c violet, *yel* ('25) 2.50 1.35
164 A42 3c green ('25) 3.25 3.00
165 A42 4c ol grn & rose 1.75 *2.10*
166 A42 4c green 1.25 .20
167 A42 4c brown ('25) 3.50 2.00
168 A42 6c rose red 13.50 7.25
169 A42 6c violet 1.50 .20
170 A42 8c brown org ('25) 2.75 *22.50*
171 A42 10c gray ('22) 2.50 *3.75*
172 A42 10c rose red ('25) 12.00 4.25
173 A42 12c rose red 1.90 .50
174 A42 12c gray ('25) 2.10 *4.50*
175 A42 15c ultramarine 6.00 6.00
176 A42 15c dull blue ('25) 1.75 .25
177 A42 20c ultra ('22) 2.40 .95
178 A42 20c dull vio ('25) 9.50 *14.00*
Nos. 161-178 (18) 70.65 *74.25*

Ornaments in lower panel omitted on #171-178.

For surcharges see Nos. 201-203.

Die II

1922-34

Ordinary Paper

179 A44 1c black 2.25 *3.00*
180 A44 2c brown 1.10 .20
181 A44 3c green 1.90 .50
182 A44 4c olive grn & red ('27) 2.75 .35
a. Die I ('32) 15.00 *60.00*
183 A44 4c green, die I ('33) 12.00 *.55*
184 A44 5c gray & car 1.10 .20
a. Die I ('32) 7.50 6.50
185 A44 6c olive brn ('28) 5.50 .70
186 A44 8c orange 1.60 *14.00*
187 A44 10c rose red ('26) 3.25 .20
a. Die I ('32) 13.00 *15.00*
188 A44 12c gray, small "c" ('22) 4.00 *21.50*
189 A44 12c gray, "c" larger & thinner ('34) 13.00 .20
190 A44 12c rose red .35 *3.75*
191 A44 15c dk blue ('28) 3.75 .20
192 A44 20c dull vio 3.75 .50
193 A44 20c dk blue ('34) 25.00 .45
a. Die I ('27) 11.00 2.25
194 A44 25c black & red, *yel* .85 .20
a. Die I ('32) 6.00 *65.00*

Chalky Paper

195 A44 50c dull vio & blk 8.00 3.75
196 A44 1r blk, *emerald* 5.00 .60
a. Die I ('32) 22.00 *60.00*
197 A44 2r50c blk & red, *bl* 22.00 15.00
198 A44 5r green & red, *yel* 42.50 *92.50*
199 A44 10r green & red, *emer* ('28) 130.00 *325.00*
Nos. 179-199 (21) 289.65 *483.35*

A45

1924

200 A45 50r lilac & green 900.00 *2,500.*

Nos. 166, 173, 177 Surcharged

1925

201 A42 3c on 4c green 6.00 *5.00*
202 A42 10c on 12c rose red .50 *1.60*
203 A42 15c on 20c ultra .65 1.75
Nos. 201-203 (3) 7.15 8.35

Common Design Types pictured following the introduction.

Silver Jubilee Issue

Common Design Type

1935, May 6 Engr. *Perf. 13½x14*

204 CD301 5c gray black & ultra .60 .20
205 CD301 12c indigo & green 5.50 .20
206 CD301 20c blue & brown 6.50 .25
207 CD301 1r brt vio & indigo 35.00 *57.50*
Nos. 204-207 (4) 47.60 58.15
Set, never hinged 60.00

Coronation Issue

Common Design Type

1937, May 12 Wmk. 4 *Perf. 13½x14*

208 CD302 5c dark purple .30 .20
209 CD302 12c carmine .50 2.40
210 CD302 20c bright ultra 1.25 1.10
Nos. 208-210 (3) 2.05 3.70
Set, never hinged 1.60

King George VI — A46

1938-43 Typo. *Perf. 14*

211 A46 2c gray .20 .20
a. Perf. 15x14 ('43) .85 .20
212 A46 3c rose vio & car 1.50 2.15
213 A46 4c green 3.25 *2.15*
214 A46 5c violet 2.25 .20
a. Perf. 15x14 ('43) 40.00 .20
215 A46 10c carmine 1.90 .20
a. Perf. 15x14 ('43) 25.00 2.50
216 A46 12c salmon pink .70 .20
a. Perf. 15x14 ('43) 40.00 1.35
217 A46 20c blue .70 .20
218 A46 25c maroon 6.00 .20
219 A46 1r brown black 14.00 2.00
220 A46 2.50r pale violet 22.00 22.50
221 A46 5r olive green 21.00 37.50
222 A46 10r rose violet 9.75 *37.50*
Nos. 211-222 (12) 83.25 105.00
Set, never hinged 110.00

Catalogue values for unused stamps in this section, from this point to the end of the section, are for Never Hinged items.

Peace Issue

Common Design Type

Perf. 13½x14

1946, Nov. 20 Engr. Wmk. 4

223 CD303 5c lilac .20 .80
224 CD303 20c deep blue .20 .25

"Post Office" Stamp of 1847 — A47

1948, Mar. 22 *Perf. 11½*

225 A47 5c red vio & orange .20 .55
226 A47 12c green & orange .20 .25
227 A47 20c blue & dp blue .20 .20
228 A47 1r lt red brn & dp blue .35 .35
Nos. 225-228 (4) .95 1.35

Cent. of the 1st Mauritius postage stamps.

Silver Wedding Issue

Common Design Types

1948, Oct. 25 Photo. *Perf. 14x14½*

229 CD304 5c violet .25 .25

Perf. 11½x11

Engraved; Name Typographed

230 CD305 10r lilac rose 17.50 40.00

UPU Issue

Common Design Types

Engr.; Name Typo. on 20c, 35c

Perf. 13½, 11x11½

1949, Oct. 10 Wmk. 4

231 CD306 12c rose carmine .75 1.90
232 CD307 20c indigo 2.40 2.75
233 CD308 35c rose violet .75 1.60
234 CD309 1r sepia .75 .25
Nos. 231-234 (4) 4.65 6.50

Sugar Factory — A48

Aloe Plant — A49

Designs: 2c, Grand Port. 4c, Tamarind Falls. 5c, Rempart Mountain. 10c, Transporting cane. 12c, Map and dodo. 20c, "Paul et Virginie." 25c, Statue of Mahe La Bourdonnais. 35c, Government House. 50c, Pieter Both Mountain. 1r, Sambar. 2.50r, Port Louis. 5r, Beach scene. 10r, Arms.

Perf. 13½x14½, 14½x13½

1950, July 1 Photo.

235	A48	1c	red violet	.25	.55
236	A48	2c	cerise	.25	.25
237	A49	3c	yel green	.70	*2.75*
238	A49	4c	green	.25	*1.40*
239	A48	5c	greenish blue	.25	.25
240	A48	10c	red	.30	*.75*
241	A48	12c	olive green	1.60	*3.25*
242	A49	20c	brt ultra	1.10	.25
243	A49	25c	vio brown	2.15	.45
244	A48	35c	rose violet	.45	.25
245	A49	50c	emerald	3.00	.55
246	A48	1r	sepia	8.50	.25
247	A48	2.50r	orange	18.50	17.50
248	A48	5r	red brown	19.50	17.50
249	A48	10r	gray blue	16.00	*37.50*
			Nos. 235-249 (15)	72.80	83.45

Coronation Issue
Common Design Type

1953, June 2 Engr. *Perf. 13½x13*

250	CD312	10c	dk green & black	1.00	.25

Sugar Factory — A50

Tamarind Falls — A51

Designs: 2c, Grand Port. 3c, Aloe plant. 5c, Rempart Mountain. 15c, Museum, Mahebourg. 20c, Statue of Mahe La Bourdonnais. 25c, "Paul et Virginie." 35c, Government House. 50c, Pieter Both Mountain. 60c, Map and dodo. 1r, Sambar. 2.50r, Port Louis. 5r, Beach scene. 10r, Arms.

Perf. 13½x14½, 14½x13½

1953-54 Photo. Wmk. 4

251	A50	2c	rose car ('54)	.30	.25
252	A51	3c	yel green ('54)	.35	.25
253	A50	4c	red violet	.30	*.60*
254	A50	5c	grnsh blue ('54)	.30	.25
255	A51	10c	dk green	.30	.25
256	A50	15c	scarlet	.30	.25
257	A51	20c	violet brown	.30	.25
a.			Imperf., pair		
258	A51	25c	brt ultra	1.60	.25
259	A50	35c	rose vio ('54)	.30	.25
260	A51	50c	emerald	.75	.75
261	A50	60c	gray grn ('54)	12.00	.25
262	A50	1r	sepia	.35	.25
a.			Imperf., pair		
263	A50	2.50r	orange ('54)	16.00	9.25
264	A50	5r	red brn ('54)	16.00	9.25
265	A50	10r	gray blue ('54)	16.00	1.25
			Nos. 251-265 (15)	65.15	23.60

See Nos. 273-275.

King George III and Queen Elizabeth II — A52

Wmk. 314

1961, Jan. 11 Litho. *Perf. 13½*

266	A52	10c	dk red & dk brown	.20	.20
267	A52	20c	lt blue & dk blue	.20	.20
268	A52	35c	org yel & brown	.30	.30
269	A52	1r	yel green & dk brn	.60	.60
			Nos. 266-269 (4)	1.30	1.30

Sesquicentenary of postal service under British administration.

Freedom from Hunger Issue
Common Design Type

1963, June 4 Photo. *Perf. 14x14½*

270	CD314	60c	lilac	.50	.50

Red Cross Centenary Issue
Common Design Type

1963, Sept. 2 Litho. *Perf. 13*

271	CD315	10c	black & red	.20	.20
272	CD315	60c	ultra & red	.65	.65

Types of 1953-54

Perf. 14½x13½, 13½x14½

1963-64 Photo. Wmk. 314

273	A51	10c	dark green ('64)	.50	.30
274	A50	60c	gray green ('64)	2.75	.30
275	A50	2.50r	orange	9.75	*11.00*
			Nos. 273-275 (3)	13.00	11.60

Gray White-Eye — A53

Birds of Mauritius: 3c, Rodriguez fody. 4c, Olive white-eye. 5c, Mauritius paradise flycatcher. 10c, Mauritius fody. 15c, Rose-ringed parakeet. 20c, Cuckoo shrike. 25c, Mauritian kestrel. 35c, Pink pigeon. 50c, Mauritius olivaceous bulbul. 60c, Mauritius blue pigeon. 1r, Dodo. 2.50r, Rodriguez solitaire. 5r, Van den Broeck's red rail. 10r, Broad-billed Mauritian parrot.

Wmk. 314

1965, Mar. 16 Photo. *Perf. 14½*

Birds in Natural Colors

276	A53	2c	brt yel & brn	.50	.30
a.			Gray (leg, etc.) omitted	210.00	
277	A53	3c	brn & dk brn	1.00	.30
a.			Black (eye, beak) omitted	210.00	
278	A53	4c	dl rose lil & blk	.35	.30
a.			Rose lilac omitted	55.00	
279	A53	5c	gray & ultra	3.25	.30
a.			Wmkd. sideways ('66)	.25	.25
280	A53	10c	dl grn & dk brn	.35	.30
281	A53	15c	lt gray & dk brn	2.10	.30
a.			Carmine (beak) omitted	160.00	
282	A53	20c	pale yel & dk brown	2.10	.30
283	A53	25c	gray & brown	2.10	.30
284	A53	35c	vio bl & blk	2.75	.30
a.			Wmkd. sideways ('67)	.40	.35
285	A53	50c	pale yel & blk	.50	.50
286	A53	60c	pale cit & brn	.60	.30
287	A53	1r	lt yel grn & blk	5.50	.30
a.			Pale gray (ground) omitted	250.00	
b.			Pale orange omitted	175.00	
288	A53	2.50r	pale grn & brn	4.75	6.00
289	A53	5r	pale blue & blk	14.00	9.00
290	A53	10r	pale grn & ultra	26.00	22.50
			Nos. 276-290 (15)	65.85	41.30

On No. 278 the background was printed in two colors. The rose lilac tint is omitted on No. 278a.

See #327-332. For overprints see #306-320.

ITU Issue
Common Design Type

Perf. 11x11½

1965, May 17 Litho. Wmk. 314

291	CD317	10c	dp org & apple grn	.30	.25
292	CD317	60c	yellow & violet	.90	.40

Intl. Cooperation Year Issue
Common Design Type

1965, Oct. 25 *Perf. 14½*

293	CD318	10c	lt green & claret	.20	.20
294	CD318	60c	lt violet & green	.45	.45

Churchill Memorial Issue
Common Design Type

1966, Jan. 24 Photo. *Perf. 14*

Design in Black, Gold and Carmine Rose

295	CD319	2c	brt blue	.40	.40
296	CD319	10c	green	.40	.40
297	CD319	60c	brown	1.00	1.00
298	CD319	1r	violet	2.25	2.25
			Nos. 295-298 (4)	4.05	4.05

UNESCO Anniversary Issue
Common Design Type

1966, Dec. 1 Litho. *Perf. 14*

299	CD323	5c	"Education"	.35	.35
300	CD323	10c	"Science"	.35	.35
301	CD323	60c	"Culture"	1.40	.80
			Nos. 299-301 (3)	2.10	1.50

Red-Tailed Tropic Bird — A54

Birds of Mauritius: 10c, Rodriguez bush warbler. 60c, Newton's parakeet. 1r, Mauritius swiftlet.

1967, Sept. 1 Photo. *Perf. 14½*

302	A54	2c	lt ultra & multi	.40	.40
303	A54	10c	emerald & multi	.40	.40
304	A54	60c	salmon & multi	1.25	1.25
305	A54	1r	yellow & multi	2.40	2.40
			Nos. 302-305 (4)	4.45	4.45

Attainment of self-government, Sept. 1, 1967.

Bird Issue of 1965-67 and Type Overprinted: "SELF GOVERNMENT 1967"

1967, Dec. 1 Photo. Wmk. 314

306	A53	2c	multicolored	.25	.25
307	A53	3c	multicolored	.25	.25
308	A53	4c	multicolored	.25	.25
309	A53	5c	multicolored	.25	.25
310	A53	10c	multicolored	.25	.25
311	A53	15c	multicolored	.25	.25
312	A53	20c	multicolored	.25	.25
313	A53	25c	multicolored	.25	.25
314	A53	35c	multicolored	.25	.25
315	A53	50c	multicolored	.40	.25
316	A53	60c	multicolored	.45	.30
317	A53	1r	multicolored	.75	.45
318	A53	2.50r	multicolored	2.10	2.25
319	A53	5r	multicolored	4.25	4.25
320	A53	10r	multicolored	8.00	8.50
			Nos. 306-320 (15)	18.20	18.25

5c, 10c, 35c watermarked sideways.

Independent State

Flag of Mauritius — A55

Designs: 3c, 20c, 1r, Dodo emerging from egg and coat of arms.

Perf. 13½x13

1968, Mar. 12 Litho. Unwmk.

321	A55	2c	brt violet & multi	.20	.20
322	A55	3c	red brown & multi	.20	.20
323	A55	15c	brown & multi	.20	.20
324	A55	20c	multicolored	.50	.20
325	A55	60c	dk green & multi	.65	.40
326	A55	1r	brt violet & multi	1.00	.65
			Nos. 321-326 (6)	2.75	1.85

Independence of Mauritius.

Bird Type of 1965 in Changed Background Colors

Wmk. 314

1968, July 12 Photo. *Perf. 14½*

Birds in Natural Colors

327	A53	2c	lemon & brown	.30	.25
328	A53	3c	ultra & dk brown	.30	.25
329	A53	15c	tan & dk brown	.90	.25
330	A53	20c	dull yel & dk brn	1.40	.25
331	A53	60c	pink & black	3.50	2.50
332	A53	1r	rose lilac & black	5.50	4.50
			Nos. 327-332 (6)	11.90	8.00

Domingue Rescuing Paul and Virginie — A56

Designs: 15c, Paul and Virginie crossing river, vert. 50c, La Bourdonnais visiting Madame de 1a Tour. 60c, Paul and Virginie, vert. 1r, Departure of Virginie for Europe. 2.50r, Bernardin de St. Pierre, vert. The designs are from old prints illustrating "Paul et Virginie."

Perf. 13½

1968, Dec. 2 Unwmk. Litho.

333	A56	2c	multicolored	.25	.25
334	A56	15c	multicolored	.25	.25
335	A56	50c	multicolored	.30	.30
336	A56	60c	multicolored	.40	.40
337	A56	1r	multicolored	.65	.65
338	A56	2.50r	multicolored	1.75	1.75
			Nos. 333-338 (6)	3.60	3.60

Bicent. of the visit of Bernardin de St. Pierre (1737-1814), author of "Paul et Virginie."

Batardé Fish A57

Marine Life: 3c, Red reef crab. 4c, Episcopal miter shell. 5c, Bourse fish. 10c, Starfish. 15c, Sea urchin. 20c, Fiddler crab. 25c, Spiny shrimp. 30c, Single and double harp shells. 35c, Argonaut shell. 40c, Nudibranch (sea-slug). 50c, Violet and orange spider shells. 60c, Blue marlin. 75c, Conus clytospira. 1r, Dorad. 2.50r, Spiny lobster. 5r, Sacré chien rouge fish. 10r, Moonfish.

Wmk. 314 Sideways (#339-344, 351-352), others Upright

1969, Mar. 12 Photo. *Perf. 14*

339	A57	2c	pink & multi	.30	.30
340	A57	3c	yellow & multi	.30	.30
341	A57	4c	multicolored	.30	.30
342	A57	5c	lt blue & multi	.30	.30
343	A57	10c	salmon & multi	.30	.30
344	A57	15c	pale blue & multi	.30	.30
345	A57	20c	pale gray & multi	.30	.30
346	A57	25c	multicolored	.30	.30
347	A57	30c	multicolored	.30	.40
348	A57	35c	multicolored	.30	.40
349	A57	40c	tan & multi	.40	.50
350	A57	50c	lt vio & multi	.50	.60
351	A57	60c	ultra & multi	.70	.75
352	A57	75c	lemon & multi	.85	.85
353	A57	1r	cream & multi	.90	1.10
354	A57	2.50r	lt vio & multi	3.75	4.75
355	A57	5r	multicolored	7.75	10.00
356	A57	10r	multicolored	13.50	17.50
			Nos. 339-356 (18)	31.35	39.25

For overprints see Nos. 368-369.

Wmk. 314 Upright (#339a-344a, 351a-352a), others Sideways

1972-74

339a	A57	2c	multi ('74)	1.00	1.00
340a	A57	3c	multi ('74)	1.00	1.00
341a	A57	4c	multi ('74)	1.00	1.00
342a	A57	5c	multi ('74)	1.00	1.00
343a	A57	10c	multicolored	1.00	1.00
344a	A57	15c	multi ('74)	1.00	1.00
345a	A57	20c	multicolored	1.00	1.00
346a	A57	25c	multi ('73)	1.00	1.00
347a	A57	30c	multicolored	1.25	1.00
348a	A57	35c	multicolored	1.50	1.25
349a	A57	40c	multicolored	1.50	1.50
350a	A57	50c	multi ('73)	1.50	1.50
351a	A57	60c	multi ('74)	2.00	1.50
352a	A57	75c	multicolored	2.50	2.00
353a	A57	1r	multicolored	3.00	2.50

354a	A57	2.50r	multi ('73)	7.50	7.00
355a	A57	5r	multi ('73)	15.00	12.50
356a	A57	10r	multicolored	29.00	25.00
	Nos. 339a-356a (18)			72.75	63.75

1975-77 **Wmk. 373**

339b	A57	2c	multi ('77)	.75	.75
340b	A57	3c	multi ('77)	.75	.75
341b	A57	4c	multi ('77)	.75	.75
342b	A57	5c	multicolored	.75	.75
344b	A57	15c	multicolored	.75	.75
345b	A57	20c	multi ('76)	.75	.75
346b	A57	25c	multicolored	.95	.75
347b	A57	30c	multicolored	1.10	.95
348b	A57	35c	multi ('76)	1.10	.95
349b	A57	40c	multi ('76)	1.10	1.10
350b	A57	50c	multi ('76)	1.50	1.10
351b	A57	60c	multi ('77)	1.90	1.50
352b	A57	75c	multi ('77)	1.90	1.90
353b	A57	1r	multi ('76)	3.00	2.75
354b	A57	2.50r	multi ('77)	12.50	7.50
355b	A57	5r	multicolored	21.00	16.00
356b	A57	10r	multicolored	50.00	32.50
	Nos. 339b-356b (17)			100.55	71.50

Gandhi as Law Student in London A58

Portraits of Gandhi: 15c, as stretcher bearer during Zulu rebellion. 50c, as member of non-violent movement in South Africa (Satyagrahi). 60c, wearing Indian garment at No. 10 Downing Street, London. 1r, wearing turban in Mauritius, 1901. 2.50r, as old man.

1969, July 1 **Litho.** ***Perf. 13½***

357	A58	2c	dull org & multi	.30	.30
358	A58	15c	brt blue & multi	.30	.30
359	A58	50c	multicolored	.30	.30
360	A58	60c	brick red & multi	.40	.40
361	A58	1r	multicolored	.75	.75
362	A58	2.50r	olive & multi	1.90	1.90
a.	Souvenir sheet of 6, #357-362			7.50	7.50
	Nos. 357-362 (6)			3.95	3.95

Mohandas K. Gandhi (1869-1948), leader in India's struggle for independence.

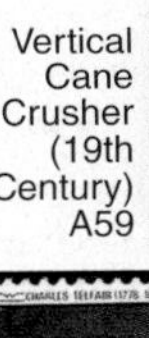

Vertical Cane Crusher (19th Century) A59

Dr. Charles Telfair (1778-1833) A60

Designs: 15c, The Frangourinier, 18th century cane crusher. 60c, Beau Rivage sugar factory, 1867, painting by Numa Desjardin. 1r, Mon Desert-Alma sugar factory, 1969.

Perf. 11x11½, 11½x11

1969, Dec. 22 **Photo.** **Wmk. 314**

363	A59	2c	multicolored	.20	.20
364	A59	15c	multicolored	.20	.20
365	A59	60c	multicolored	.20	.20
366	A59	1r	multicolored	.30	.30
367	A60	2.50r	multicolored	.60	.60
a.	Souvenir sheet of 5			2.75	2.75
	Nos. 363-367 (5)			1.50	1.50

150th anniv. of Telfair's improvements of the sugar industry.

No. 367a contains one each of Nos. 363-367. The 2.50r in the sheet is imperf., the others are perf. 11x11½.

Nos. 351 and 353 Overprinted: "EXPO '70 / OSAKA"

1970, Apr. 7 ***Perf. 14***

368	A57	60c	ultra & multi	.25	.25
369	A57	1r	cream & multi	.40	.40

EXPO '70 Intl. Exhib., Osaka, Japan, Mar. 15-Sept. 13.

Lufthansa Plane over Mauritius — A61

25c, Brabant Hotel, Morne Beach, horiz.

1970, May 2 **Litho.** ***Perf. 14***

370	A61	25c	multicolored	.20	.20
371	A61	50c	multicolored	.40	.40

Lufthansa's inaugural flight from Mauritius to Frankfurt, Germany, May 2, 1970.

Lenin as Student, by V. Tsigal — A62

Design: 75c, Bust of Lenin.

1970, May 15 **Photo.** ***Perf. 12x11½***

372	A62	15c	dk slate blue & sil	.20	.20
373	A62	75c	dk brown & gold	.65	.65

Birth cent. of Lenin (1870-1924), Russian communist leader.

UN Emblem and Symbols of UN Activities — A63

1970, Oct. 24 **Litho.** ***Perf. 14***

374	A63	10c	blue black & multi	.20	.20
375	A63	60c	blue black & multi	.40	.40

25th anniversary of the United Nations.

Mauritius No. 2, and Post Office before 1870 A64

Designs: 15c, General Post Office Building, 1870-1970. 50c, Mauritius mail coach, 1870. 75c, Port Louis harbor, 1970. 2.50r, Arrival of Pierre André de Suffren de St. Tropez in Port Louis harbor, 1783.

1970, Oct. 15 **Litho.** ***Perf. 14***

376	A64	5c	multicolored	.20	.20
377	A64	15c	multicolored	.20	.20
378	A64	50c	multicolored	.20	.20
379	A64	75c	multicolored	.30	.30
380	A64	2.50r	multicolored	1.00	1.00
a.	Souvenir sheet of 5			5.00	5.00
	Nos. 376-380 (5)			1.90	1.90

Centenary of the General Post Office and to show the improvements of Port Louis harbor. No. 380a contains one each of Nos. 376-380 and a label showing map of Mauritius.

Waterfall A65

15c, Trois Mamelles Mountains. 60c, Beach scene with sailboats. 2.50r, Marine life.

1971, Apr. 12 **Litho.** ***Perf. 14***

381	A65	10c	multicolored	.20	.20
382	A65	15c	multicolored	.20	.20
383	A65	60c	multicolored	.40	.40
384	A65	2.50r	multicolored	1.90	1.90
	Nos. 381-384 (4)			2.70	2.70

Tourist publicity. Each stamp has a different 6-line message printed in black on back.

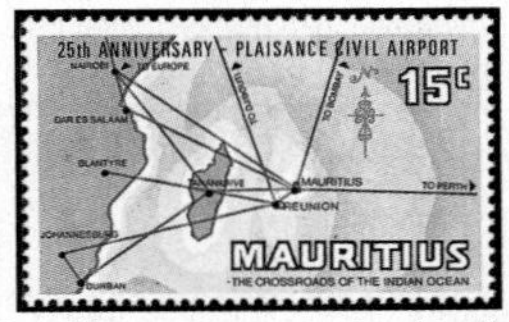

Mauritius at Crossroads of Indian Ocean — A66

60c, Plane at Plaisance Airport. 1r, Stewardesses on plane ramp. 2.50r, Roland Garros' airplane, Choisy Airfield, 1937.

1971, Oct. 23 **Wmk. 314** ***Perf. 14½***

385	A66	15c	multicolored	.25	.25
386	A66	60c	multicolored	.55	.55
387	A66	1r	multicolored	.65	.65
388	A66	2.50r	multicolored	2.75	2.75
	Nos. 385-388 (4)			4.20	4.20

25th anniversary of Plaisance Civil Airport.

Princess Margaret Orthopedic Center — A67

75c, Operating room, National Hospital.

1971, Nov. 2 ***Perf. 14x14½***

389	A67	10c	multicolored	.20	.20
390	A67	75c	multicolored	.30	.30

3rd Commonwealth Medical Conf., Nov. 1971.

Elizabeth II and Prince Philip — A68

Design: 2.50r, Queen Elizabeth II, vert.

1972, Mar. **Litho.** ***Perf. 14½***

391	A68	15c	brown & multi	.30	.30
392	A68	2.50r	ultra & multi	2.75	2.75

Visit of Elizabeth II and Prince Philip.

Port Louis Theater and Masks A69

Design: 1r, Interior view and masks of Comedy and Tragedy.

1972, June 26

393	A69	10c	brown & multi	.25	.25
394	A69	1r	multicolored	.45	.45

Sesquicentennial of Port Louis Theater.

Pirate Dhow Entering Tamarind River A70

Perf. 14x14½, 14½x14

1972, Nov. 17 **Litho.**

395	A70	15c	shown	.30	.30
396	A70	60c	Treasure chest, vert.	.85	.85
397	A70	1r	Lememe and brig Hirondelle, vert.	2.00	2.00
398	A70	2.50r	Robert Surcouf	7.00	7.00
	Nos. 395-398 (4)			10.15	10.15

Pirates and privateers.

Mauritius University — A71

60c, Tea development plant. 1r, Bank of Mauritius.

1973, Apr. 10 ***Perf. 14½***

399	A71	15c	green & multi	.20	.20
400	A71	60c	yellow & multi	.20	.20
401	A71	1r	red & multi	.30	.30
	Nos. 399-401 (3)			.70	.70

5th anniversary of independence.

OCAM Emblem A72

Design: 2.50r, Handshake, map of Africa; inscriptions in French, vert.

1973, Apr. 25

402	A72	10c	multicolored	.20	.20
403	A72	2.50r	lt blue & multi	.60	.60

Conference of the Organisation Commune Africaine, Malgache et Mauricienne (OCAM), Mauritius, Apr. 25-May 6.

WHO Emblem A73

Perf. 14½x14

1973, Nov. 20 **Wmk. 314**

404	A73	1r	green & multi	.40	.40

25th anniv. of WHO.

Meteorological Station, Vacoas — A74

1973, Nov. 27

405	A74	75c	multicolored	.40	.40

Cent. of intl. meteorological cooperation.

Surcouf and Capture of the "Kent" A75

1974, Mar. 21 **Litho.** ***Perf. 14½x14***

406	A75	60c	sepia & multi	1.25	1.25

Bicentenary of the birth of Robert Surcouf (1773-1827), French privateer.

Philibert Commerson and Bougainvillaea A76

1974, Apr. 18 ***Perf. 14***

407 A76 2.50r slate grn & multi .70 .70

Philibert Commerson (1727-1773), French physician and naturalist.

FAO Emblem, Woman Milking Cow A77

1974, Oct. 23 ***Perf. 14½***

408 A77 60c multicolored .35 .35

8th FAO Regional Conference, Aug. 1-17.

Mail Train and UPU Emblem A78

Design: 1r, New General Post Office Building, Port Louis, and UPU emblem.

1974, Dec. 4 **Litho.** ***Perf. 14½***

409 A78 15c multicolored .30 .30
410 A78 1r multicolored .80 .80

Centenary of Universal Postal Union.

Cottage Life, by F. Leroy A79

Paintings: 60c, Milk Seller, by A. Richard, vert. 1r, Entrance to Port Louis Market, by Thuillier. 2.50r, Washerwomen, by Max Boullé, vert.

1975, Mar. 6 **Wmk. 373**

411 A79 15c multicolored .25 .25
412 A79 60c multicolored .40 .40
413 A79 1r multicolored .65 .65
414 A79 2.50r multicolored 1.50 1.50
Nos. 411-414 (4) 2.80 2.80

Artistic views of life on Mauritius.

Mace, Map and Arms of Mauritius, Association Emblem — A80

1975, Nov. 21 **Litho.** **Wmk. 373**

415 A80 75c multicolored .60 .60

French-speaking Parliamentary Association, conf.

Woman and Aladdin's Lamp A81

1975, Dec. 5 ***Perf. 14½***

416 A81 2.50r multicolored .75 .75

International Women's Year.

Parched Land A82

Drought in Africa: 60c, Map of Africa, carcass and desert, vert.

1976, Feb. 26 **Litho.** **Wmk. 373**

417 A82 50c vermilion & multi .20 .20
418 A82 60c blue & multi .30 .30

Pierre Loti, 1953-1970 — A83

Mail Carriers: 15c, Secunder, 1907. 50c, Hindoostan, 1842. 60c, St. Geran, 1740. 2.50r, Maen, 1638.

1976, July 2 **Litho.** **Wmk. 373**

419 A83 10c multicolored .65 .65
420 A83 15c multicolored .65 .65
421 A83 50c multicolored .95 .95
422 A83 60c multicolored 1.25 1.25
423 A83 2.50r multicolored 5.50 5.50
a. Souvenir sheet of 5, #419-423 13.50 13.50
Nos. 419-423 (5) 9.00 9.00

Flame, and "Hindi Carried Across the Sea" A84

Designs: 75c, like 10c. 1.20r, Flame and tablet with Hindi inscription.

1976, Aug. 28 ***Perf. 14½x14***

424 A84 10c multicolored .20 .20
425 A84 75c lt blue & multi .20 .20
426 A84 1.20r multicolored .35 .35
Nos. 424-426 (3) .75 .75

2nd World Hindi Convention.

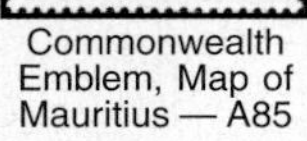

Commonwealth Emblem, Map of Mauritius — A85

King Priest and Steatite Pectoral — A86

2.50r, Commonwealth emblem twice.

1976, Sept. 22 **Litho.** ***Perf. 14x14½***

427 A85 1r multicolored .40 .40
428 A85 2.50r multicolored .90 .90

22nd Commonwealth Parliamentary Association Conference, Mauritius, Sept. 17-30.

1976, Dec. 15 **Wmk. 373** ***Perf. 14***

Designs: 1r, House with well, and goblet. 2.50r, Terracotta goddess and necklace.

429 A86 60c multicolored .35 .35
430 A86 1r multicolored .75 .75
431 A86 2.50r multicolored 1.75 1.75
Nos. 429-431 (3) 2.85 2.85

UNESCO campaign to save Mohenjo-Daro excavations.

Sega Dance A87

1977, Jan. 20 **Litho.** ***Perf. 13***

432 A87 1r multicolored .50 .50

2nd World Black and African Festival, Lagos, Nigeria, Jan. 15-Feb. 12.

Elizabeth II at Mauritius Legislative Assembly — A88

Designs: 75c, Queen holding scepter and orb. 5r, Presentation of scepter and orb.

1977, Feb. 7 ***Perf. 14½x14***

433 A88 50c multicolored .20 .20
434 A88 75c multicolored .20 .20
435 A88 5r multicolored 1.10 1.10
Nos. 433-435 (3) 1.50 1.50

25th anniv. of the reign of Elizabeth II.

Hugonia Tomentosa — A89

Flowers: 1r, Oehna mauritiana, vert. 1.50r, Dombeya acuntangula. 5r, Trochetia blackburniana, vert.

1977, Sept. 22 **Wmk. 373** ***Perf. 14***

436 A89 20c multicolored .20 .20
437 A89 1r multicolored .40 .40
438 A89 1.50r multicolored .60 .60
439 A89 5r multicolored 1.75 1.75
a. Souvenir sheet of 4, #436-439 5.00 5.00
Nos. 436-439 (4) 2.95 2.95

Twin Otter of Air Mauritius — A90

Designs: 50c, Air Mauritius emblem (red-tailed tropic bird) and Twin Otter. 75c, Piper Navajo and Boeing 747. 5r, Air Mauritius Boeing 707 in flight.

1977, Oct. 31 **Litho.** ***Perf. 14½***

440 A90 25c multicolored .60 .60
441 A90 50c multicolored .90 .90
442 A90 75c multicolored 1.00 1.00
443 A90 5r multicolored 5.50 5.50
a. Souvenir sheet of 4, #440-443 12.00 12.00
Nos. 440-443 (4) 8.00 8.00

Air Mauritius International Inaugural Flight.

Mauritius, Portuguese Map, 1519 — A91

Dutch Occupation, 1638-1710 — A92

Designs: 20c, Mauritius, map by Van Keulen, c. 1700. 25c, 1st settlement of Rodrigues, 1708. 35c, Proclamation, arrival of French settlers, 1715. 50c, Construction of Port Louis, c. 1736. 60c, Pierre Poivre and nutmeg tree. 70c, Map by Belin, 1763. 75c, First coin minted in Mauritius, 1810. 90c, Naval battle of Grand Port, 1810. 1r, Landing of the British, Nov. 1810. 1.20r, Government House, c. 1840. 1.25r, Invitation with No. 1 and ball of Lady Gomm, 1847. 1.50r, Indian immigration in Mauritius, 1835. 2r, Champ de Mars race course, c. 1870. 3r, Place D'Armes, c. 1880. 5r, Postal card commemorating visit of Prince and Princess of Wales, 1901. 10r, Curepipe College, 1914. 15r, Raising flag of Mauritius, 1968. 25r, Raman Osman, first Governor General and Seewoosagur Ramgoolan, first Prime Minister.

1978, Mar. 12 **Wmk. 373** ***Perf. 13½***

444 A91 10c multicolored .25 .25
445 A92 15c multicolored .25 .25
446 A92 20c multicolored .25 .25
447 A91 25c multicolored .25 .25
448 A91 35c multicolored .25 .25
b. Perf. 14½, "1986" .25 .25
449 A92 50c multicolored .25 .25
450 A91 60c multicolored .35 .35
451 A92 70c multicolored .40 .35
452 A91 75c multicolored .45 .40
453 A92 90c multicolored .45 .40
454 A92 1r multicolored .45 .45
455 A92 1.20r multicolored .45 .45
456 A91 1.25r multicolored .45 .45
457 A92 1.50r multicolored .55 .60
458 A92 2r multicolored .75 .80
459 A92 3r multicolored 1.10 1.25
460 A92 5r multicolored 1.90 2.00
461 A92 10r multicolored 3.75 4.00
462 A91 15r multicolored 5.25 6.00
463 A92 25r multicolored 8.75 9.75
Nos. 444-463 (20) 26.55 28.75

Nos. 448, 452, 456, 458 reprinted inscribed 1983; Nos. 444, 447-449, 452, 454, 456, 460 reprinted inscribed 1985.

1985-89 **Wmk. 384** ***Perf. 14½***

446a A92 20c "1987" .20 .20
447a A91 25c "1987" .20 .20
448a A91 35c ('85) .20 .20
449a A92 50c ('85) .20 .20
452a A91 75c ('85) .20 .20
458a A92 2r "1987" .20 .20
459a A92 3r "1989" .40 .40
460a A92 5r "1989" .70 .70
463a A92 25r "1989" 3.45 3.45
Nos. 446a-463a (9) 5.75 5.75

Issued: 20c, 25c, 2r, 1/11/87; 3r-25r, 1/19/89.

Nos. 449a and 458a reprinted inscribed 1989.

Elizabeth II Coronation Anniv. Issue

Common Design Types

Souvenir Sheet

1978, Apr. 21 **Unwmk.** ***Perf. 15***

464 Sheet of 6 2.75 2.75
a. CD326 3r Antelope of Bohun .50 .50
b. CD327 3r Elizabeth II .50 .50
c. CD328 3r Dodo .50 .50

No. 464 contains 2 se-tenant strips of Nos. 464a-464c, separated by horizontal gutter with commemorative and descriptive inscriptions and showing central part of coronation procession with coach.

Dr. Fleming, WWI Casualty, Bacteria — A93

1r, Microscope & 1st mold growth, 1928. 1.50r, Penicillium notatum, close-up. 5r, Alexander Fleming & nurse administering penicillin.

Wmk. 373

1978, Aug. 3 Litho. *Perf. 13½*

465 A93 20c multicolored .80 .80
466 A93 1r multicolored 1.60 1.60
467 A93 1.50r multicolored 2.75 2.75
468 A93 5r multicolored 3.75 3.75
a. Souvenir sheet of 4, #465-468 11.00 11.00
Nos. 465-468 (4) 8.90 8.90

Discovery of penicillin by Dr. Alexander Fleming, 50th anniversary.

Citrus Butterfly — A94

Wildlife Protection (Wildlife Fund Emblem and): 1r, Geckos. 1.50r, Flying foxes. 5r, Mauritius kestrels.

1978, Sept. 21 *Perf. 13½x14*

469 A94 20c multicolored *4.00 2.50*
470 A94 1r multicolored *3.50 2.50*
471 A94 1.50r multicolored *3.50 2.50*
472 A94 5r multicolored *18.50 5.00*
a. Souvenir sheet of 4, #469-472 *110.00 80.00*
Nos. 469-472 (4) *29.50 12.50*

Le Reduit — A95

15c, Ornate table. 3r, Reduit gardens.

1978, Dec. 21 *Perf. 14½x14*

473 A95 15c multicolored .20 .20
474 A95 75c multicolored .30 .30
475 A95 3r multicolored 1.00 1.00
Nos. 473-475 (3) 1.50 1.50

Reconstruction of Chateau Le Reduit, 200th anniversary.

Whitcomb, 1949 — A96

Locomotives: 1r, Sir William, 1922. 1.50r, Kitson, 1930. 2r, Garratt, 1927.

1979, Feb. 1 *Perf. 14½*

476 A96 20c multicolored .25 .25
477 A96 1r multicolored .50 .50
478 A96 1.50r multicolored .95 .95
479 A96 2r multicolored 1.25 1.25
a. Souvenir sheet of 4, #476-479 5.25 5.25
Nos. 476-479 (4) 2.95 2.95

Father Laval and Crucifix — A97

Designs: 1.50r, Jacques Desire Laval. 5r, Father Laval's sarcophagus, horiz.

1979, Apr. 30 Wmk. 373 *Perf. 14*

480 A97 20c multicolored .20 .20
481 A97 1.50r multicolored .30 .30
482 A97 5r multicolored 1.00 1.00
a. Souvenir sheet of 3, #480-482 3.75 3.75
Nos. 480-482 (3) 1.50 1.50

Beatification of Father Laval (1803-1864), physician and missionary.

Souvenir Booklet

10th Anniv. of Apollo 11 Moon Landing — A98

Imperf. x Roulette 5

1979, July 20 Litho.

Self-adhesive

483 A98 Booklet of 9 8.00
a. 20c Astronaut and Lunar Module .20
b. 3r Neil Armstrong on moon .90
c. 5r Astronaut walking on moon 3.75
d. Bklt. pane of 3 (20c, 5r, 3r) 5.00
e. Bklt. pane of 6 (3 each 20c, 3r) 3.50

No. 483 contains 2 panes printed on peelable paper backing showing map of moon (d) and details of uniform and spacecraft (e).

Rowland Hill and Great Britain No. 23 — A99

1979, Aug. 29 *Perf. 14½*

Rowland Hill and: 2r, Mauritius No. 261. 3r, Mauritius No. 2. 5r, Mauritius No. 1.

484 A99 25c multicolored .20 .20
485 A99 2r multicolored .50 .50
486 A99 5r multicolored 1.25 1.25
Nos. 484-486 (3) 1.95 1.95

Souvenir Sheet

Perf. 14½

487 A99 3r multicolored 1.75 1.75

Sir Rowland Hill (1795-1879), originator of penny postage. No. 487 contains one stamp.

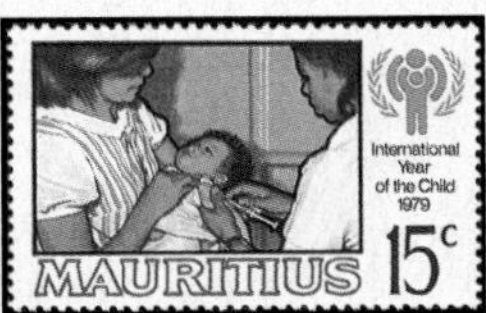

Infant Vaccination — A100

IYC Emblem and: 25c, Children playing. 1r, Coat of arms, vert. 1.50r, Children in laboratory. 3r, Teacher and student working lathe.

Wmk. 373

1979, Oct. 11 Litho. *Perf. 14*

488 A100 15c multicolored .20 .20
489 A100 25c multicolored .20 .20
490 A100 1r multicolored .25 .25
491 A100 1.50r multicolored .35 .35
492 A100 3r multicolored .70 .70
Nos. 488-492 (5) 1.70 1.70

International Year of the Child.

Lienard Obelisk A101

Designs: 25c, Poivre Avenue, 1r, Pandanus. 2r, Giant water lilies, 5r, Mon Plaisir.

1980, Jan. 24 *Perf. 14x14½*

493 A101 20c multicolored .20 .20
494 A101 25c multicolored .20 .20
495 A101 1r multicolored .20 .20
496 A101 2r multicolored .40 .40
497 A101 5r multicolored 1.00 1.00
a. Souvenir sheet of 5, #493-497 4.25 4.25
Nos. 493-497 (5) 2.00 2.00

Pamplemousses Botanical Gardens.

"Emirne," 19th Century, London 1980 Emblem — A102

1980, May 6 Litho. *Perf. 14½*

498 A102 25c shown .25 .25
499 A102 1r Boissevain, 1930's .50 .50
500 A102 2r La Boudeuse, 18th cent. 1.00 1.00
501 A102 5r Sea Breeze, 19th cent. 2.25 2.25
Nos. 498-501 (4) 4.00 4.00

London 80 Intl. Stamp Exhib., May 6-14.

Helen Keller Reading Braille — A103

1980, June 27 Litho. *Perf. 14½*

502 A103 25c Blind men weaving baskets .25 .25
503 A103 1r Teacher and deaf girl .50 .50
504 A103 2.50r shown 1.25 1.25
505 A103 5r Keller graduating college 2.00 2.00
Nos. 502-505 (4) 4.00 4.00

Helen Keller (1880-1968), blind and deaf writer and lecturer.

Prime Minister Seewoosagur Ramgoolan, 80th Birthday — A104

Litho.; Gold Embossed

1980, Sept. 18 *Perf. 13½*

506 A104 15r multicolored 2.00 2.00

Mauritius Institute, Centenary — A105

1980, Oct. 1 Litho. *Perf. 13*

507 A105 25c shown .25 .25
508 A105 2r Rare Veda copy .50 .50
509 A105 2.50r Rare cone .60 .60
510 A105 5r Landscape, by Henri Harpignies 1.25 1.25
Nos. 507-510 (4) 2.60 2.60

Hibiscus Liliiflorus — A106

Arms of Curepipe — A107

1981, Jan. 15 Litho. *Perf. 14*

511 A106 25c shown .20 .20
512 A106 2r Erythrospermum monticolum .70 .70
513 A106 2.50r Chasalia boryana .90 .90
514 A106 5r Hibiscus columnaris 1.75 1.75
Nos. 511-514 (4) 3.55 3.55

Perf. 13½x13

1981, Apr. 10 Litho. Wmk. 373

Designs: City coats of arms.

515 A107 25c Beau-Bassin / Rose Hill .20 .20
516 A107 1.50r shown .30 .30
517 A107 2r Quatre-Bornes .40 .40
518 A107 2.50r Vacoas/Phoenix .50 .50
519 A107 5r Port Louis 1.00 1.00
a. Souv. sheet of 5, #515-519, perf. 14 3.25 3.25
Nos. 515-519 (5) 2.40 2.40

Royal Wedding Issue

Common Design Type

1981, July 22 Litho. *Perf. 14*

520 CD331 25c Bouquet .20 .20
521 CD331 2.50r Charles .50 .50
522 CD331 10r Couple 2.00 2.00
Nos. 520-522 (3) 2.70 2.70

Emmanuel Anquetil and Guy Rozemont — A108

Famous Men: 25c, Remy Ollier, Sookdeo Bissoondoyal. 1.25r, Maurice Cure, Barthelemy Ohsan. 1.50r, Guy Forget, Renganaden Seeneevassen. 2r, Abdul Razak Mohamed, Jules Koenig. 2.50r, Abdoollatiff Mahomed Osman, Dazzi Rama. 5r, Thomas Lewis.

1981, Aug. 13 *Perf. 14½*

523 A108 20c black & red .25 .25
524 A108 25c black & yellow .25 .25
525 A108 1.25r black & green .35 .35
526 A108 1.50r black & vermilion .40 .40
527 A108 2r black & ultra .55 .55
528 A108 2.50r black & red brn .65 .65
529 A108 5r black & blue grn 1.40 1.40
Nos. 523-529 (7) 3.85 3.85

Chinese Pagoda A109

1981, Sept. 16 *Perf. 13½*
530 A109 20c Tamil Women .25 .25
531 A109 2r Swami Sivananda, vert. .75 .75
532 A109 5r shown 1.90 1.90
Nos. 530-532 (3) 2.90 2.90

World Tamil Culture Conference, 1980 (20c).

A110 A111

1981, Oct. 26 **Litho.** *Perf. 14*
533 A110 25c Pottery making .20 .20
534 A110 1.25r Dog grooming .20 .20
535 A110 5r Hiking .75 .75
536 A110 10r Duke of Edinburgh 1.50 1.50
Nos. 533-536 (4) 2.65 2.65

Duke of Edinburgh's Awards, 25th anniv.

1981, Nov. 26 **Wmk. 373** *Perf. 14½*
537 A111 25c Holy Ka'aba, Mecca .30 .30
538 A111 2r Prophet's Mosque .80 .80
539 A111 5r Holy Ka'aba, Prophet's Mosque 1.90 1.90
Nos. 537-539 (3) 3.00 3.00

Hegira, 1,500th anniv.

Scouting Year — A112

1982, Feb. 25 **Litho.** *Perf. 14x14½*
540 A112 25c Emblem .25 .25
541 A112 2r Baden-Powell .60 .60
542 A112 5r Grand howl, sign 1.40 1.40
543 A112 10r Scouts, mountain 2.75 2.75
Nos. 540-543 (4) 5.00 5.00

Darwin Death Centenary — A113

1982, Apr. 19 **Litho.** *Perf. 14*
544 A113 25c Portrait .20 .20
545 A113 2r Telescope .45 .45
546 A113 2.50r Riding elephant .55 .55
547 A113 10r The Beagle 2.25 2.25
Nos. 544-547 (4) 3.45 3.45

Princess Diana Issue
Common Design Type

1982, July 1 **Litho.** *Perf. 13*
548 CD333 25c Arms .20 .20
549 CD333 2.50r Diana .75 .75
550 CD333 5r Wedding 1.50 1.50
551 CD333 10r Portrait 3.00 3.00
Nos. 548-551 (4) 5.45 5.45

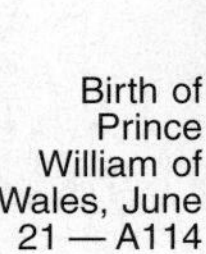

Birth of Prince William of Wales, June 21 — A114

1982, Sept. 22 **Litho.** *Perf. 14½*
552 A114 2.50r multicolored 1.10 1.10

Issued in sheets of 9.

TB Bacillus Centenary — A115

1982, Dec. 15 *Perf. 14*
553 A115 25c Aphloia theiformis .25 .25
554 A115 1.25r Central Market, Port Louis .55 .55
555 A115 2r Gaertnera psychotrioides .85 .85
556 A115 5r Selaginella deliquescens 1.25 1.25
557 A115 10r Koch 3.75 3.75
Nos. 553-557 (5) 6.65 6.65

A116

1983, Mar. 14 *Perf. 13x13½*
558 A116 25c Flag, arms .20 .20
559 A116 2.50r Satellite view .40 .40
560 A116 5r Sugar cane harvest .85 .85
561 A116 10r Port Louis Harbor 1.75 1.75
Nos. 558-561 (4) 3.20 3.20

Commonwealth Day.

World Communications Year — A117

1983, June 24 **Wmk. 373** *Perf. 14*
562 A117 25c Antique telephone, vert. .20 .20
563 A117 1.25r Early telegraph apparatus .35 .35
564 A117 2r Earth satellite station, vert. .50 .50
565 A117 10r 1st hot air balloon in Mauritius, 1784 2.40 2.40
Nos. 562-565 (4) 3.45 3.45

Namibia Day — A118

1983, Aug. 26
566 A118 25c Map .70 .70
567 A118 2.50r Breaking chains 1.60 1.60
568 A118 5r Family, village 3.25 3.25
569 A118 10r Diamond mining 6.00 6.00
Nos. 566-569 (4) 11.55 11.55

Fishery Resources — A119

1983, Oct. 7
570 A119 25c Fish trap, vert. .25 .25
571 A119 1r Fishermen in boat .40 .40
572 A119 5r Game fishing, vert. 1.75 1.75
573 A119 10r Octopus drying 3.75 3.75
Nos. 570-573 (4) 6.15 6.15

Swami Dayananda, Death Centenary — A120

1983, Nov. 3 **Litho.** **Wmk. 373**
574 A120 25c shown .20 .20
575 A120 35c Last meeting with father .20 .20
576 A120 2r Receiving instruction .30 .30
577 A120 5r Demonstrating strength .80 .80
578 A120 10r Religious gathering 1.75 1.75
Nos. 574-578 (5) 3.25 3.25

Adolf von Plevitz (1837-1893), Social Reformer A121

1983, Dec. 8
579 A121 25c shown .30 .30
580 A121 1.25r Government school .65 .65
581 A121 5r Addressing Commission of Enquiry 1.10 1.10
582 A121 10r Indian field workers 2.50 2.50
Nos. 579-582 (4) 4.55 4.55

Mauritius Kestrels A122

1984, Mar. 26 **Wmk. 373** *Perf. 14*
583 A122 25c Courtship chase .40 .40
584 A122 2r Side view, vert. 2.40 2.40
585 A122 2.50r Fledgling 2.75 2.75
586 A122 10r Bird, diff., vert. 12.00 12.00
Nos. 583-586 (4) 17.55 17.55

Lloyd's List Issue
Common Design Type

1984, May 23 **Litho.** *Perf. 14½x14*
587 CD335 25c Tayeb, Port Lewis .35 .35
588 CD335 1r Taher .70 .70
589 CD335 5r East Indiaman Triton 2.40 2.40
590 CD335 10r Astor 5.50 5.50
Nos. 587-590 (4) 8.95 8.95

Palm Trees — A123

Slave Sale — A124

1984, July 23 **Litho.** *Perf. 14*
591 A123 25c Blue latan .30 .30
592 A123 50c Hyophorbe vaughanii .30 .30
593 A123 2.50r Tectiphiala ferox 1.40 1.40

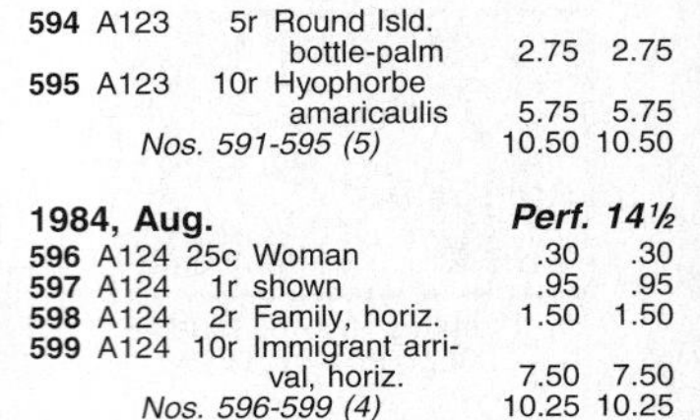

594 A123 5r Round Isld. bottle-palm 2.75 2.75
595 A123 10r Hyophorbe amaricaulis 5.75 5.75
Nos. 591-595 (5) 10.50 10.50

1984, Aug. *Perf. 14½*
596 A124 25c Woman .30 .30
597 A124 1r shown .95 .95
598 A124 2r Family, horiz. 1.50 1.50
599 A124 10r Immigrant arrival, horiz. 7.50 7.50
Nos. 596-599 (4) 10.25 10.25

Alliance Francaise Centenary — A125

1984, Sept. 10 *Perf. 14½*
600 A125 25c Production of Faust, 1959 .25 .25
601 A125 1.25r Award ceremony .65 .65
602 A125 5r Headquarters 2.10 2.10
603 A125 10r Lion Mountain 4.50 4.50
Nos. 600-603 (4) 7.50 7.50

Queen Mother 85th Birthday
Common Design Type

Perf. 14½x14

1985, June 7 **Wmk. 384**
604 CD336 25c Portrait, 1926 .25 .25
605 CD336 2r With Princess Margaret .55 .55
606 CD336 5r On Clarence House balcony 1.50 1.50
607 CD336 10r Holding Prince Henry 2.75 2.75
Nos. 604-607 (4) 5.05 5.05

Souvenir Sheet

608 CD336 15r On Royal Barge, reopening Stratford Canal, 1964 6.75 6.75

2nd Annual Indian Ocean Islands Games — A126

Pink Pigeon — A127

1985, Aug. 24 **Wmk. 373** *Perf. 14½*
609 A126 25c High jump .35 .35
610 A126 50c Javelin .75 .75
611 A126 1.25r Cycling 4.75 4.75
612 A126 10r Wind surfing 8.25 8.25
Nos. 609-612 (4) 14.10 14.10

1985, Sept. 2 **Wmk. 384** *Perf. 14*
613 A127 25c Adult and young *6.25* *1.25*
614 A127 2r Nest site display *11.00* *2.75*
615 A127 2.50r Nesting *12.50* *4.25*
616 A127 5r Preening *20.00* *6.00*
Nos. 613-616 (4) *49.75* *14.25*

World Wildlife Fund.

World Tourism Org., 10th Anniv. A128

1985, Sept. 20 *Perf. 14½*
617 A128 25c Patates Caverns .60 .60
618 A128 35c Colored Earth, Chamarel .60 .60
619 A128 5r Serpent Island 2.75 2.75
620 A128 10r Coin de Mire Is. 11.00 11.00
Nos. 617-620 (4) 14.95 14.95

Port Louis, 250th Anniv. A129

1985, Nov. 22 *Perf. 13½*

621 A129 25c Old Town Hall .30 .30
622 A129 1r Al-Aqsa Mosque .90 .90
623 A129 2.50r Tamil-speaking Indians, settlement 1.75 1.75
624 A129 10r Port Louis Harbor 6.50 6.50
Nos. 621-624 (4) 9.45 9.45

Halley's Comet A130

1986, Feb. 21 **Wmk. 384** *Perf. 14*

625 A130 25c Halley, map .55 .55
626 A130 1.25r Newton's telescope, 1682 sighting .75 .75
627 A130 3r Mauritius from space 1.50 1.50
628 A130 10r Giotto space probe 5.00 5.00
Nos. 625-628 (4) 7.80 7.80

Queen Elizabeth II 60th Birthday
Common Design Type

Designs: 25c, In uniform, Grenadier Guards, 1942. 75c, Investiture of the Prince of Wales, 1969. 2r, State visit with Prince Philip. 3r, State visit to Germany, 1978. 15r, Visiting Crown Agents' offices, 1983.

1986, Apr. 21 **Litho.** *Perf. 14½x14*

629 CD337 25c scar, black & sil .20 .20
630 CD337 75c ultra & multi .20 .20
631 CD337 2r green & multi .40 .40
632 CD337 3r violet & multi .55 .55
633 CD337 15r rose vio & multi 2.25 2.25
Nos. 629-633 (5) 3.60 3.60

Intl. Events — A131

Orchids — A132

Designs: 25c, World Food Day. 1r, African Regional Industrial Property Organization, 10th anniv. 1.25r, Intl. Peace Year. 10r, 1986 World Cup Soccer Championships.

1986, July 25 **Litho.** *Perf. 14*

634 A131 25c FAO emblem, corn .30 .30
635 A131 1r ARIPO emblem .65 .65
636 A131 1.25r IPY emblem .95 .95
637 A131 10r Athlete, MFA 7.25 7.25
Nos. 634-637 (4) 9.15 9.15

1986, Oct. 3 **Litho.** *Perf. 14½*

638 A132 25c Cryptopus elatus .65 .65
639 A132 2r Jumellea recta 1.10 1.10
640 A132 2.50r Angraecum mauritianum 1.75 1.75
641 A132 10r Bulbophyllum longiflorum 6.50 6.50
Nos. 638-641 (4) 10.00 10.00

Bridges A133

1987, May 22 **Wmk. 373**

642 A133 25c Hesketh Bell .25 .25
643 A133 50c Sir Colville Deverell .60 .60
644 A133 2.50r Cavendish 1.50 1.50
645 A133 5r Tamarin 3.00 3.00
646 A133 10r Grand River North West 6.00 6.00
Nos. 642-646 (5) 11.35 11.35

The Bar, Bicent. A134

Perf. 14x14½

1987, June 2 **Wmk. 384**

647 A134 25c Port Louis Supreme Court .25 .25
648 A134 1r Flacq District Court .50 .50
649 A134 1.25r Statue of Justice .55 .55
650 A134 10r Barristers, 1787-1987 3.25 3.25
Nos. 647-650 (4) 4.55 4.55

Intl. Festival of the Sea — A135

1987, Sept. 5 **Wmk. 373**

651 A135 25c Dodo mascot, vert. .75 .75
652 A135 1.50r Sailboats 1.75 1.75
653 A135 3r Water-skier 2.75 2.75
654 A135 5r Tall ship Svanen, vert. 4.75 4.75
Nos. 651-654 (4) 10.00 10.00

Industrialization — A136

1987, Oct. 30 *Perf. 14*

655 A136 20c Toy .30 .30
656 A136 35c Spinning .30 .30
657 A136 50c Rattan .30 .30
658 A136 2.50r Optical .95 .95
659 A136 10r Stone carving 3.25 3.25
Nos. 655-659 (5) 5.10 5.10

Art & Architecture A137

Designs: 25c, Maison Ouvriere, Intl. Year of Shelter for the Homeless emblem. 1r, Paul et Virginie, a lithograph. 1.25r, Chateau Rosney. 2r, Old Farmhouse, Boulle. 5r, Three Peaks, watercolor.

1988, June 29 **Wmk. 384** *Perf. 14½*

660 A137 25c multicolored .20 .20
661 A137 1r gray & black .40 .40
662 A137 1.25r multicolored .50 .50
663 A137 2r multicolored .60 .60
664 A137 5r multicolored 1.60 1.60
Nos. 660-664 (5) 3.30 3.30

Natl. Independence, 20th Anniv. — A138

Designs: 25c, University of Mauritius. 75c, Calisthenics at sunset in stadium. 2.50r, Runners, Sir Maurice Rault Stadium. 5r, Air Mauritius jet at gate, Sir Seewoosagur Ramgoolam Intl. Airport. 10r, Gov.-Gen. Veerasamy Ringadoo and Prime Minister Anerood Jugnauth.

1988, Mar. 11 **Wmk. 373** *Perf. 14*

665 A138 25c multicolored .25 .25
666 A138 75c multicolored .25 .25
667 A138 2.50r multicolored .90 .90
668 A138 5r multicolored 1.60 1.60
669 A138 10r multicolored 3.25 3.25
Nos. 665-669 (5) 6.25 6.25

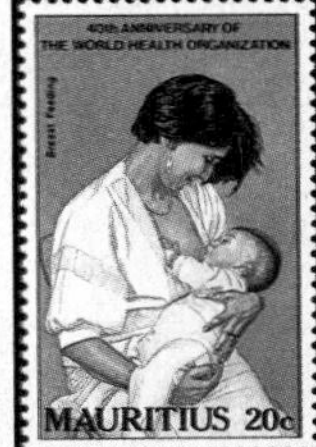

WHO, 40th Anniv. — A139

1988, July 1 **Wmk. 373** *Perf. 13½*

670 A139 20c Breast-feeding .30 .30
671 A139 2r Immunization .90 .90
672 A139 3r Nutrition 1.75 1.75
673 A139 10r Emblem 5.00 5.00
Nos. 670-673 (4) 7.95 7.95

Mauritius Commercial Bank, Ltd., 150th Anniv. A140

1988, Sept. 1 **Wmk. 373** *Perf. 14*

674 A140 25c Bank, 1981, vert. .30 .30
675 A140 1r Bank, 1897 .40 .40
676 A140 1.25r Coat of arms, vert. .50 .50
677 A140 25r 15-Dollar bank note, 1838 8.00 8.00
Nos. 674-677 (4) 9.20 9.20

1988 Summer Olympics, Seoul A141

1988, Oct. 1

678 A141 25c shown .25 .25
679 A141 35c Wrestling .35 .35
680 A141 1.50r Running .65 .65
681 A141 10r Swimming 4.00 4.00
Nos. 678-681 (4) 5.25 5.25

Environmental Protection — A142

Wmk. 384 (20c, 40c, 50c, 1r, 10r), 373 (Others)

1989-97 **Litho.** *Perf. 14*

682 A142 15c Tropical reef .35 .35
683 A142 20c like #682 .35 .35
684 A142 30c Greenshank .40 .40
a. Wmk. 384 .35 .35
685 A142 40c shown .35 .35
a. Wmk. 373 .35 .35
686 A142 50c Round Island, vert. .35 .35
687 A142 60c like #685 .35 .35
688 A142 75c Bassin Blanc .35 .35
689 A142 1r Mangrove, vert. .35 .35
690 A142 1.50r Whimbrel .40 .40
691 A142 2r Le Morne .40 .40
692 A142 3r Fish .75 .75
693 A142 4r Fern tree, vert. 1.00 1.00
694 A142 5r Riviere du Poste Estuary 1.00 1.00
695 A142 6r Ecological scenery, vert. 1.50 1.50
696 A142 10r Phelsuma ornata,vert. 2.40 2.40
a. Wmk. 373 ('97) 2.40 2.40
697 A142 15r Benares surf 3.25 3.25
a. Wmk. 384 3.00 3.00
698 A142 25r Migratory birds, vert. 5.50 5.50
a. Wmk. 384 ('96) 5.25 5.25
Nos. 682-698 (17) 19.05 19.05

Issued: 40c, 3r-10r, 3/11/89; #685a, 2/19/91; 50c, 75c, 2r, 5r, 15r, 10/4/91; 20c, 60c, 3/96; others, 11/22/90.

#682, 685a, 693 exist inscribed "1994," #682-684, 696, "1995," #698, "1996," #685, 687, 696, 698, 698a, "1997." #689, 693-695, 696, 696a, 698, "1998."

For surcharge see No. 781.

A143

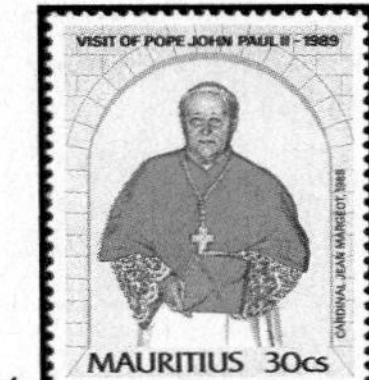

A144

French Revolution, Bicent.: 30c, La Tour Sumeire, Place Du Theatre Municipal. 1r, Salle De Spectacle Du Jardin. 8r, Le Comte De Malartic. 15r, Anniv. emblem.

1989, July 14 **Wmk. 373**

702 A143 30c multicolored .25 .25
703 A143 1r multicolored .25 .25
704 A143 8r multicolored 2.00 2.00
705 A143 15r multicolored 3.75 3.75
Nos. 702-705 (4) 6.25 6.25

1989, Oct. 13 *Perf. 14x13½*

Visit of Pope John Paul II: 30c, Cardinal Jean Margeot. 40c, Pope welcoming Prime Minister Aneerood Jugnauth to the Vatican, 1988. 3r, Mother Mary Magdalene of the Cross (1810-1889) and Filles des Marie Chapel, Port Louis, 1864. 6r, St. Francis of Assisi Church, 1756, Pamplemousses. 10r, Pope John Paul II.

706 A144 30c multicolored .30 .30
707 A144 40c multicolored 1.00 1.00
708 A144 3r multicolored 2.00 2.00
709 A144 6r multicolored 4.25 4.25
710 A144 10r multicolored 6.75 6.75
Nos. 706-710 (5) 14.30 14.30

Jawaharlal Nehru, 1st Prime Minister of India — A145

Designs: 1.50r, Nehru and Indira, Rajiv and Sanjay Gandhi. 3r, With Mahatma Gandhi. 4r, With Nasser and Tito. 10r, With children.

1989, Oct. 13 **Wmk. 384** *Perf. 14*

711 A145 40c shown 1.25 1.25
712 A145 1.50r multicolored 1.50 1.50
713 A145 3r multicolored 3.00 3.00
714 A145 4r multicolored 3.75 3.75
715 A145 10r multicolored 9.00 9.00
Nos. 711-715 (5) 18.50 18.50

Sugar Cane Industry, 350th Anniv. A146

Perf. 13½x14

1990, Jan. 10 Litho. Wmk. 384

716	A146	30c	Cutting cane	.30	.30
717	A146	40c	Refinery, 1867	.30	.30
718	A146	1r	Mechanically loading cane	.75	.75
719	A146	25r	Modern refinery	12.00	12.00
			Nos. 716-719 (4)	13.35	13.35

Prime Minister Jugnauth's 60th Birthday A147

Jugnauth: 35c, And symbols of the industrial estate. 40c, At his desk. 1.50r, And stock exchange emblem. 4r, And Gov.-Gen. Ramgoolam. 10r, And Pope John Paul II, map.

Wmk. 373

1990, Mar. 29 Litho. *Perf. 14*

720	A147	35c	multicolored	.35	.35
721	A147	40c	multicolored	.35	.35
722	A147	1.50r	multicolored	1.60	1.60
723	A147	4r	multicolored	3.50	3.50
724	A147	10r	multicolored	8.75	8.75
			Nos. 720-724 (5)	14.55	14.55

Mauritian Television, 25th Anniv. A148

Anniversaries and Events: 30c, Death of Desjardins, naturalist, 150th anniversary, vert. 6r, Line barracks, 250th anniversary, vert. 8r, Municipality of Curepipe, centenary.

1990, July 5

725	A148	30c	lt orange & multi	.50	.50
726	A148	35c	pink & multi	.50	.50
727	A148	6r	lt blue & multi	5.25	5.25
728	A148	8r	lt green & multi	6.50	6.50
			Nos. 725-728 (4)	12.75	12.75

Intl. Literacy Year A149

Wmk. 373

1990, Sept. 28 Litho. *Perf. 14*

729	A149	30c	shown	.35	.35
730	A149	1r	Blind girl printing braille	1.40	1.40
731	A149	3r	Globe, open book	2.50	2.50
732	A149	10r	Open book, world map	8.75	8.75
			Nos. 729-732 (4)	13.00	13.00

Elizabeth & Philip, Birthdays

Common Design Types

Wmk. 384

1991, June 17 Litho. *Perf. 14½*

733	CD345	8r	multicolored	1.75	1.75
734	CD346	8r	multicolored	1.75	1.75
a.			Pair, #733-734 + label	3.75	3.75

Port Louis, City Incorporation, 25th Anniv. — A150

Anniversaries and Events: 4r, Col. Draper, 150th death anniv., vert. 6r, Joseph Barnard, engraver of first Mauritius stamps, 175th birth anniv., vert. 10r, Spitfire, Mauritius' contribution to Allied war effort, 1939-1945.

Wmk. 373

1991, Aug. 18 Litho. *Perf. 14*

735	A150	40c	multicolored	.30	.30
736	A150	4r	multicolored	2.10	2.10
737	A150	6r	multicolored	3.25	3.25
738	A150	10r	multicolored	5.25	5.25
			Nos. 735-738 (4)	10.90	10.90

Phila Nippon '91 — A151

Butterflies: 40c, Euploea euphon. 3r, Hypolimnas misippus, female. 8r, Papilio manlius. 10r, Hypolimnas misippus, male.

Perf. 14x14½

1991, Nov. 15 Litho. Wmk. 373

739	A151	40c	multicolored	.90	.90
740	A151	3r	multicolored	2.00	2.00
741	A151	8r	multicolored	4.75	4.75
742	A151	10r	multicolored	5.50	5.50
			Nos. 739-742 (4)	13.15	13.15

Flora and Fauna From Mauritius A152

Designs: 40c, Chelonia mydas, Tromelin. 1r, Ibis, Agalega. 2r, Takamaka flowers, Chagos Archipelago. 15r, Lambis violacea, St. Brandon.

1991, Dec. 13 *Perf. 14*

743	A152	40c	multicolored	.75	.75
744	A152	1r	multicolored	1.25	1.25
745	A152	2r	multicolored	1.60	1.60
746	A152	15r	multicolored	9.50	9.50
			Nos. 743-746 (4)	13.10	13.10

Republic

Proclamation of the Republic of Mauritius — A153

1992, Mar. 12

747	A153	40c	President	.30	.30
748	A153	4r	Prime Minister	1.40	1.40
749	A153	8r	Mauritian children	3.00	3.00
750	A153	10r	President's flag	3.50	3.50
			Nos. 747-750 (4)	8.20	8.20

8th African Track and Field Championships A154

Designs: 40c, Games mascot, Tricolo. 4r, Sir Anerood Jugnauth Stadium, horiz. 5r, High jumper, horiz. 6r, Torch, emblem of games.

1992, June 25 *Perf. 13½*

751	A154	40c	multicolored	.25	.25
752	A154	4r	multicolored	.85	.85
753	A154	5r	multicolored	1.25	1.25
754	A154	6r	multicolored	1.50	1.50
			Nos. 751-754 (4)	3.85	3.85

Anniversaries and Events — A155

Designs: 40c, Flower, vert. 1r, Swami Krishnanandji Maharaj, vert. 2r, Boy and dog. 3r, Building, flags. 15r, Radio telescope antennae.

1992, Aug. 13

755	A155	40c	multicolored	.25	.25
756	A155	1r	multicolored	.60	.60
757	A155	2r	multicolored	.95	.95
758	A155	3r	multicolored	1.50	1.50
759	A155	15r	multicolored	6.50	6.50
			Nos. 755-759 (5)	9.80	9.80

Fleurir Maurice, 25th anniv. (#755). 25th anniv. of Swami Maharaj's arrival (#756). Humane education (#757). Indian Ocean Commission, 10th anniv. (#758). Inauguration of radio telescope project (#759).

Bank of Mauritius, Silver Jubilee A156

Designs: 40c, Bank of Mauritius building, vert. 4r, Dodo gold bullion coin. 8r, First bank note issues. 15r, Foreign exchange reserves 1967-1992.

Perf. 14½x14, 14x14½

1992, Oct. 29 Litho. Wmk. 373

760	A156	40c	multicolored	.30	.30
761	A156	4r	multicolored	1.60	1.60
762	A156	8r	multicolored	3.50	3.50
763	A156	15r	multicolored	5.75	5.75
			Nos. 760-763 (4)	11.15	11.15

National Day, 25th Anniv. — A157

30c, Housing development. 40c, Computer showing gross domestic product. 3r, Flag in shape of map of Mauritius. 4r, Ballot box. 15r, Medal for Grand Commander of the Order of the Star & Key of the Indian Ocean.

1993, Mar. 12 *Perf. 15x14*

764	A157	30c	multicolored	.25	.25
765	A157	40c	multicolored	.25	.25
766	A157	3r	multicolored	.55	.55
767	A157	4r	multicolored	.80	.80
768	A157	15r	multicolored	2.75	2.75
			Nos. 764-768 (5)	4.60	4.60

Air Mauritius Ltd., 25th Anniv. A158

40c, Bell 206B Jet Ranger. 3r, Boeing 747SP. 4r, ATR 42. 10r, Boeing 767-200ER.

1993, June 14 *Perf. 14*

769	A158	40c	multicolored	.85	.85
770	A158	3r	multicolored	1.50	1.50
771	A158	4r	multicolored	2.00	2.00
772	A158	10r	multicolored	4.75	4.75
a.			Souvenir sheet of 4, #769-772	11.50	11.50
			Nos. 769-772 (4)	9.10	9.10

5th Francophone Summit — A159

Designs: 1r, 1715 Act of French Seizure of Mauritius, 1810 Act of Surrender. 5r, Signs. 6r, Page from Napoleonic Code. 7r, French publications.

1993, Oct. 16

773	A159	1r	multicolored	.25	.25
774	A159	5r	multicolored	2.50	2.50
775	A159	6r	multicolored	3.00	3.00
776	A159	7r	multicolored	3.50	3.50
			Nos. 773-776 (4)	9.25	9.25

Telecommunications — A160

Designs: 40c, SS Scotia, cable laying. 3r, Morse code, Morse key. 4r, Signal mountain station. 8r, Communications satellite.

1993, Nov. 25 *Perf. 13*

777	A160	40c	multicolored	.65	.65
778	A160	3r	multicolored	1.10	1.10
779	A160	4r	multicolored	1.75	1.75
780	A160	8r	multicolored	3.50	3.50
			Nos. 777-780 (4)	7.00	7.00

No. 686 Surcharged

1993, Sept. 15 Litho. *Perf. 14*

781	A142	40c	on 75c multi	2.00	2.00

Mammals — A161

Wmk. 384

1994, Mar. 9 Litho. *Perf. 14½*

782	A161	40c	Mongoose	.30	.30
783	A161	2r	Hare	1.25	1.25
784	A161	8r	Monkey	4.00	4.00
785	A161	10r	Tenrec	4.50	4.50
			Nos. 782-785 (4)	10.05	10.05

Anniversaries and Events — A162

40c, Dr. E. Brown-Sequard (1817-94). 4r, Silhouettes of family. 8r, World Cup trophy, US map. 10r, Control Tower, SSR Intl. Airport.

Wmk. 373

1994, June 16 Litho. *Perf. 14*
786 A162 40c multicolored .25 .25
787 A162 4r multicolored .75 .75
788 A162 8r multicolored 1.60 1.60
789 A162 10r multicolored 2.00 2.00
Nos. 786-789 (4) 4.60 4.60

Intl. Year of the Family (#787). 1994 World Cup Soccer Championships, US (#788). ICAO, 50th anniv. (#789).

Wreck of the St. Geran, 250th Anniv. A163

Wmk. 384

1994, Aug. 18 Litho. *Perf. 14*
790 A163 40c Leaving L'Orient .35 .35
791 A163 5r In rough seas 1.50 1.50
792 A163 6r Ship's bell 1.75 1.75
793 A163 10r Relics from ship 3.00 3.00
Nos. 790-793 (4) 6.60 6.60

Souvenir Sheet

794 A163 15r St. Geran, vert. 9.00 9.00

Children's Paintings of Leisure Activities — A164

Designs: 30c, "Ring Around the Rosey." 40c, Playing with balls, jump rope. 8r, Water sports. 10r, "Blindman's Buff."

Wmk. 373

1994, Oct. 25 Litho. *Perf. 13½*
795 A164 30c multicolored .25 .25
796 A164 40c multicolored .25 .25
797 A164 8r multicolored 1.50 1.50
798 A164 10r multicolored 1.90 1.90
Nos. 795-798 (4) 3.90 3.90

Spices — A165

Perf. 13x14

1995, Mar. 10 Litho. Wmk. 373
799 A165 40c Nutmeg .30 .30
800 A165 4r Coriander .85 .85
801 A165 5r Cloves 1.25 1.25
802 A165 10r Cardamon 2.40 2.40
Nos. 799-802 (4) 4.80 4.80

End of World War II
Common Design Type

Designs: No. 803, HMS Mauritius. No. 804, Mauritian servicemen, map of North Africa. No. 805, Catalina, Tombeau Bay.

Wmk. 373

1995, May 8 Litho. *Perf. 14*
Size: 35x28mm
803 CD351 5r multicolored 2.50 2.50
804 CD351 5r multicolored 2.50 2.50
805 CD351 5r multicolored 2.50 2.50
Nos. 803-805 (3) 7.50 7.50

Anniversaries & Events — A166

1995, May 8
806 A166 40c multicolored .25 .25
807 A166 4r multicolored 1.25 1.25
808 A166 10r multicolored 2.75 2.75
Nos. 806-808 (3) 4.25 4.25

Construction of Mare Longue Reservoir, 50th anniv. (#806). Construction of Mahebourg-Curepipe Road, bicent. (#807). Great fire of Port Louis, cent. (#808).

A167

A168

Designs: Lighthouses.

Perf. 13x14

1995, Aug. 28 Litho. Wmk. 373
809 A167 30c Ile Plate 1.00 1.00
810 A167 40c Pointe aux Caves 1.00 1.00
811 A167 8r Ile aux Fouquets 4.75 4.75
812 A167 10r Pointe aux Canonniers 6.00 6.00
a. Souvenir sheet of 4, #809-812 15.00 15.00
Nos. 809-812 (4) 12.75 12.75

UN, 50th Anniv.
Common Design Type

Designs: 40c, Silhouettes of children under UNICEF umbrella. 4r, ILO contruction site. 8r, WMO satellite view of hurricane. 10r, Bread, grain representing FAO.

Wmk. 373

1995, Oct. 24 Litho. *Perf. 14*
813 CD353 40c multicolored .25 .25
814 CD353 4r multicolored .65 .65
815 CD353 8r multicolored 1.40 1.40
816 CD353 10r multicolored 1.60 1.60
Nos. 813-816 (4) 3.90 3.90

1995, Dec. 8 Litho. *Perf. 13*
817 A168 60c pink & multi .25 .25
818 A168 4r blue & multi .55 .55
819 A168 8r yellow & multi 1.25 1.25
820 A168 10r green & multi 1.40 1.40
Nos. 817-820 (4) 3.45 3.45

Common Market for Eastern and Southern Africa (COMESA).

Snails A169

Designs: 60c, Pachystyla bicolor. 4r, Gonidomus pagodus. 5r, Harmogenanina implicata. 10r, Tropidophora eugeniae.

Wmk. 373

1996, Mar. 11 Litho. *Perf. 13*
821 A169 60c multicolored .35 .35
822 A169 4r multicolored 1.00 1.00
823 A169 5r multicolored 1.25 1.25
824 A169 10r multicolored 2.50 2.50
Nos. 821-824 (4) 5.10 5.10

Modern Olympic Games, Cent. A170

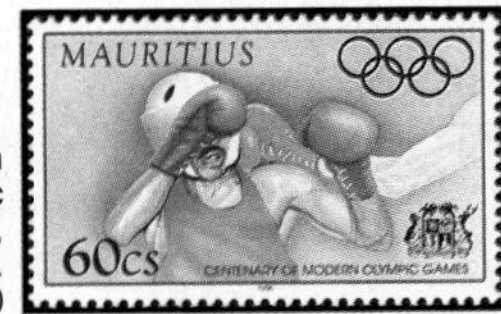

Wmk. 384

1996, June 26 Litho. *Perf. 13½*
825 A170 60c Boxing .30 .30
826 A170 4r Badminton .75 .75
827 A170 5r Basketball .95 .95
828 A170 10r Table tennis 2.00 2.00
Nos. 825-828 (4) 4.00 4.00

Ships A171

Wmk. 373

1996, Sept. 30 Litho. *Perf. 14*
829 A171 60c SS Zambezia .30 .30
830 A171 4r MV Sir Jules .80 .80
831 A171 5r MV Mauritius 1.00 1.00
832 A171 10r MS Mauritius Pride 2.10 2.10
a. Souvenir sheet of 4, #829-832 5.00 5.00
Nos. 829-832 (4) 4.20 4.20

Post Office Ordinance, 150th Anniv. — A172

Wmk. 384

1996, Dec. 2 Litho. *Perf. 13½*
833 A172 60c Pillar box .30 .30
834 A172 4r Early handstamp cancel 1.10 1.10
835 A172 5r Mobile post office 1.50 1.50
836 A172 10r Carriole 3.00 3.00
Nos. 833-836 (4) 5.90 5.90

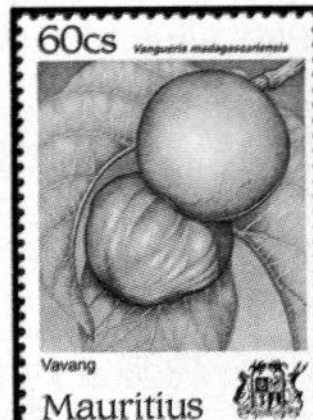

Fruit — A173

Designs: 60c, Vangueria madgascariensis. 4r, Mimusops coriacea. 5r, Syzgium jambos. 10r, Diospyros digyna.

Perf. 14x13½

1997, Mar. 10 Litho. Wmk. 373
837 A173 60c multicolored .25 .25
838 A173 4r multicolored .50 .50
839 A173 5r multicolored .65 .65
840 A173 10r multicolored 1.40 1.40
Nos. 837-840 (4) 2.80 2.80

Anniversaries and Events — A174

Designs: 60c, Ile de France, Mahé de La Bourdonnais. 1r, Exploration, La Perouse. 4r, Lady Gomm's Ball, Sir William Maynard Gomm. 6r, Skeleton of the Dodo, George Clark. 10r, Professor Brian Abel-Smith.

Wmk. 373

1997, June 9 Litho. *Perf. 13½*
841 A174 60c multicolored .45 .45
842 A174 1r multicolored .45 .45
843 A174 4r multicolored .85 .85
844 A174 6r multicolored 1.25 1.25
845 A174 10r multicolored 2.00 2.00
Nos. 841-845 (5) 5.00 5.00

First Postage Stamps of Mauritius, 150th Anniv. A175

Stamps: 60c, #1. 4r, #2. 5r, #2, #1, gold background. 10r, #1, #2, silver background. 20r, #2, #1 on "The Bordeaux Cover."

Wmk. 373

1997, Sept. 22 Litho. *Perf. 13½*
846 A175 60c multicolored .40 .40
847 A175 4r multicolored 1.25 1.25
a. Sheet of 12, 7 #846, 5 #847 6.75 6.75
848 A175 5r multicolored 1.50 1.50
849 A175 10r multicolored 3.25 3.25
Nos. 846-849 (4) 6.40 6.40

Souvenir Sheet

850 A175 20r multicolored 5.75 5.75

Booklet Panes and Booklets

846a Booklet pane of 10 3.50
Complete booklet, #846a 3.50
847b Booklet pane of 10 11.00
Complete booklet, #847b 11.00
848a Booklet pane of 10 14.50
Complete booklet, #848a 14.50
849a Booklet pane of 10 30.00
Complete booklet, #849a 30.00

Local Occupations — A176

Wmk. 373

1997, Dec. 1 Litho. *Perf. 14½*
851 A176 60c Wheelwright .40 .40
852 A176 4r Washerman .70 .70
853 A176 5r Shipwright .90 .90
854 A176 15r Quarryman 2.75 2.75
Nos. 851-854 (4) 4.75 4.75

Geckos A177

Designs: 1r, Phelsuma guentheri. 6r, Nactus serpensinsula. 7r, Nactus coindemirensis. 8r, Phelsuma edwardnewtonii.

Wmk. 373

1998, Mar. 11 Litho. *Perf. 13½*
855 A177 1r multicolored .40 .40
856 A177 6r multicolored 1.25 1.25
857 A177 7r multicolored 1.50 1.50
858 A177 8r multicolored 1.75 1.75
Nos. 855-858 (4) 4.90 4.90

Inland Transportation — A178

Wmk. 373

1998, June 15 Litho. *Perf. 13½*
859 A178 40c Railroad .60 .60
860 A178 5r Truck 1.25 1.25
861 A178 6r Bus, bicycles, cars 1.60 1.60
862 A178 10r Boat 2.50 2.50
Nos. 859-862 (4) 5.95 5.95

Dutch Landing, 400th Anniv. A179

50c, Maurits van Nassau, landing scene. 1r, Otaheite sugar cane, Frederik Hendrik Fort. 7r, Dutch map, 1670. 8r, Landing fleet. 25r, Ships of landing fleet.

Wmk. 373

1998, Sept. 18 Litho. *Perf. 13½*
863 A179 50c multicolored .35 .35
864 A179 1r multicolored .35 .35
865 A179 7r multicolored 1.75 1.75
866 A179 8r multicolored 2.25 2.25
Nos. 863-866 (4) 4.70 4.70

Souvenir Sheet

867 A179 25r multicolored 5.50 5.50

State Visit of South African Pres. Nelson Mandela — A180

1998, Sept. 10 Litho. *Perf. 14*
868 A180 25r multicolored 3.25 3.25

Waterfalls — A181

1r, Balfour Falls. 5r, Rochester Falls. 6r, GRSE Falls, vert. 10r, 500-Foot Falls, vert.

1998 Litho. Wmk. 384 *Perf. 13½*
869 A181 1r multicolored .50 .50
870 A181 5r multicolored 1.00 1.00
871 A181 6r multicolored 1.40 1.40
872 A181 10r multicolored 2.10 2.10
Nos. 869-872 (4) 5.00 5.00

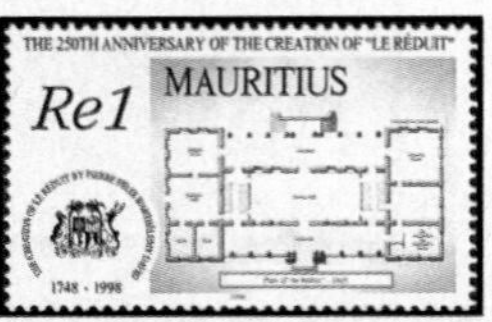

Creation of Presidential Residence "Le Réduit," 250th Anniv. — A182

Designs: 1r, Drawing of floor plan, 1823. 4r, Exterior view, by P.A.F. Thuillier, 1814. 5r, "Le Réduit," by Hassen Edun, 1998. 15r, Commemorative monument, 1998.

1998 Litho. Wmk. 373 *Perf. 14½*
873 A182 1r multicolored .40 .40
874 A182 4r multicolored .70 .70
875 A182 5r multicolored .90 .90
876 A182 15r multicolored 2.50 2.50
Nos. 873-876 (4) 4.50 4.50

Admiral Mahé de la Bourdonnais, 300th Birth Anniv. — A183

Wmk. 373
1999, Feb. 11 Litho. *Perf. 13*
877 A183 7r No. 115 1.75 1.75

Native Flowers A184

Designs: 1r, Clerodendron laciniatum. 2r, Senecio lemarckianus. 5r, Cylindrocline commersonii. 9r, Psiadia pollicina.

1999, Mar. 10 *Perf. 13½*
878 A184 1r multicolored .40 .40
879 A184 2r multicolored .40 .40
880 A184 5r multicolored .70 .70
881 A184 9r multicolored 1.25 1.25
Nos. 878-881 (4) 2.75 2.75

Paintings — A185

Designs: 1r, "The Washerwomen," by Hervé Masson. 3r, "The Casino," by Gaetan de Rosnay. 4r, "The Four Elements," by Andrée Poilly. 6r, "Coming out of Mass," by Xavier Le Juge de Segrais.

1999, June 18 *Perf. 14x15*
882 A185 1r multicolored .50 .50
883 A185 3r multicolored .60 .60
884 A185 4r multicolored .70 .70
885 A185 6r multicolored 1.10 1.10
Nos. 882-885 (4) 2.90 2.90

Old Sugar Mill Chimneys — A186

Wmk. 384
1999, Sept. 17 Litho. *Perf. 14¼*
886 A186 1r Alma .40 .40
887 A186 2r Antoinette .60 .60
888 A186 5r Belle Mare .90 .90
889 A186 7r Grande Rosalie 1.00 1.00
a. Souvenir sheet of 4, #886-889, Wmk. 373 3.25 3.25
Nos. 886-889 (4) 2.90 2.90

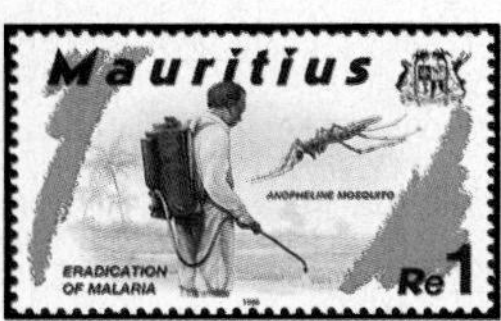

Achievements in the 20th Century — A187

Designs: 1r, Eradication of malaria. 2r, Emancipation of women. 5r, International Conference Center. 9r, Special sugars.

Perf. 13¼x13
1999, Dec. 7 Litho. Wmk. 373
890 A187 1r multi .40 .40
891 A187 2r multi .60 .60
892 A187 5r multi 1.10 1.10
893 A187 9r multi 2.00 2.00
Nos. 890-893 (4) 4.10 4.10

Chamber of Commerce & Industry, 150th Anniv. — A188

1r, Emblem. 2r, Computer chip. 7r, Francis Channell, 1st sec. 15r, Louis Léchelle, 1st pres.

2000, Jan. 25 Litho. *Perf. 13¼*
894 A188 1r multi .40 .40
895 A188 2r multi .60 .60
896 A188 7r multi 1.10 1.10
897 A188 15r multi 2.10 2.10
Nos. 894-897 (4) 4.20 4.20

Insects A189

Designs: 1r, Cratopus striga. 2r, Cratopus armatus. 3r, Cratopus chrysochlorus. 15r, Cratopus nigrogranatus.

Wmk. 373
2000, Mar. 29 Litho. *Perf. 14¼*
898 A189 1r multi .40 .40
899 A189 2r multi .40 .40
900 A189 3r multi .50 .50
901 A189 15r multi 2.40 2.40
a. Souvenir sheet of 4, #898-901 4.00 4.00
Nos. 898-901 (4) 3.70 3.70

2000 Summer Olympics, Sydney — A190

Wmk. 373
2000, June 28 Litho. *Perf. 14½*
902 A190 1r Handball .40 .40
903 A190 2r Archery .60 .60
904 A190 5r Sailing .80 .80
905 A190 15r Judo 2.40 2.40
Nos. 902-905 (4) 4.20 4.20

Sir Seewoosagur Ramgoolam, Birth Cent. — A191

Designs: 1r, Ramgoolam with Mother Teresa. 2r, As elected member of legislative council, vert. 5r, As student, 1926, vert. 15r, As Prime Minister, 1968, vert.

Perf. 13¼x13, 13x13¼
2000, Sept. 18 Litho. Wmk. 373
906-909 A191 Set of 4 4.25 4.25

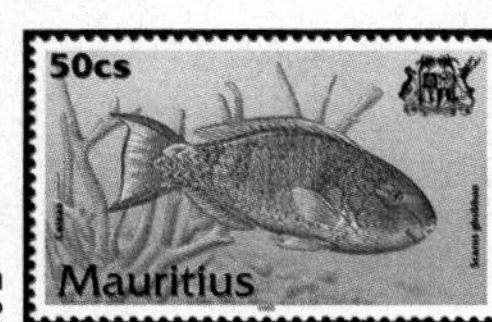

Fish A192

Designs: 50c, Scarus ghobban. 1r, Cephalopholis sonnerati. 2r, Naso brevirostris. 3r, Lethrinus nebulosus. 4r, Centropyge debelius. 5r, Amphiprion chrysogaster. 6r, Forcipiger flavissimus. 7r, Acanthurus leucosternon. 8r, Pterois volitans. 10r, Siderea grisea. 15r, Carcharhinus wheeleri. 25r, Istiophorus platypterus.

Perf. 14½x14¼
2000, Oct. 9 Litho. Wmk. 373
910 A192 50c multi .40 .40
911 A192 1r multi .40 .40
912 A192 2r multi .40 .40
913 A192 3r multi .40 .40
914 A192 4r multi .50 .50
915 A192 5r multi .60 .60
916 A192 6r multi .75 .75
917 A192 7r multi .80 .80
918 A192 8r multi 1.00 1.00
919 A192 10r multi 1.10 1.10
a. Souvenir sheet, #914, 917-919 3.50 3.50
b. As #919, perf. 13½ ('08) .75 .75
920 A192 15r multi 1.90 1.90
a. Souvenir sheet, #913, 915-916, 920 3.50 3.50
921 A192 25r multi 2.75 2.75
a. Souvenir sheet, #910-912, 921 3.50 3.50
Nos. 910-921 (12) 11.00 11.00

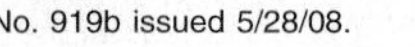
No. 919b issued 5/28/08.

Famous People — A193

Designs: 1r, Affan Tank Wen (1842-1900). 5r, Alphonse Ravaton (1900-92), musician. 7r, Dr. Idrice Goumany (1859-89). 9r, Anjalay Coopen (d. 1943), martyr.

Perf. 14¼x14½
2000, Dec. 13 Wmk. 373
922-925 A193 Set of 4 3.75 3.75

Textile Industry A194

Designs: 1r, Finished sweater. 3r, Computer-aided machinery. 6r, T-shirt folder. 10r, Embroidery machine.

2001, Jan. 10 *Perf. 14½x14¼*
926-929 A194 Set of 4 3.25 3.25

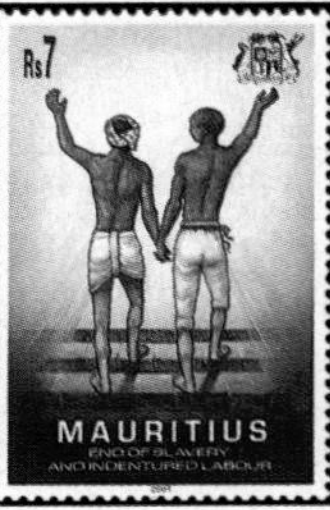

End of Slavery and Indentured Labor, 166th Anniv. — A195

2001, Feb. 1 *Perf. 14x13½*
930 A195 7r multi 2.00 2.00

Trees A196

Designs: 1r, Foetida mauritana. 3r, Diospyros tessellaria. 5r, Sideroxylon puberulum. 15r, Gastonia mauritana.

2001, Mar. 21 Wmk. 373 *Perf. 13½*
931-934 A196 Set of 4 5.00 5.00

Expedition of Nicholas Baudin, Bicent. — A197

Designs: 1r, Ships Géographe and Naturaliste. 4r, Baudin and map of itinerary. 6r, Phedina borbonica. 10r, Napoleon Bonaparte and account of expedition, vert.

Wmk. 373
2001, June 13 Litho. *Perf. 14¼*
935-938 A197 Set of 4 4.00 4.00

20th Century Achievements — A198

Designs: 2r, Hotel School of Mauritius. 3r, Steel bar milling. 6r, Solar energy, Agalega. 10r, Indian Ocean Rim Association for Regional Cooperation.

Wmk. 373

2001, Sept. 12 Litho. ***Perf. 13½***
939-942 A198 Set of 4 3.50 3.50

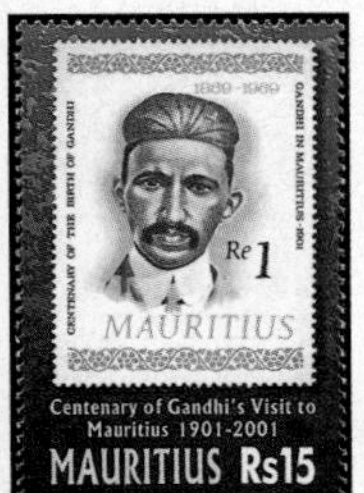

Mahatma Gandhi's Visit to Mauritius, Cent. — A199

2001, Oct. 2 ***Perf. 14¾x14***
943 A199 15r No. 361 3.00 3.00

Copra Industry A200

Designs: 1r, Dehusking of coconuts, vert. 5r, Deshelling of coconuts. 6r, Drying copra. 10r, Oil extraction, vert.

2001, Dec. 5 ***Perf. 13½***
944-947 A200 Set of 4 4.75 4.75

Republic, 10th Anniv. A201

Designs: 1r, Port development. 4r, Financial services. 5r, Water storage. 9r, Road development.

Perf. 13½x13¾

2002, Mar. 12 Litho. Wmk. 373
948-951 A201 Set of 4 4.00 4.00

Cicadas — A202

Designs: 1r, Abricta brunnea. 6r, Fractuosella darwini. 7r, Distantada thomaseti. 8r, Dinarobia claudeae.

Wmk. 373

2002, June 12 Litho. ***Perf. 13½***
952-955 A202 Set of 4 3.50 3.50
a. Souvenir sheet, #952-955 4.00 4.00

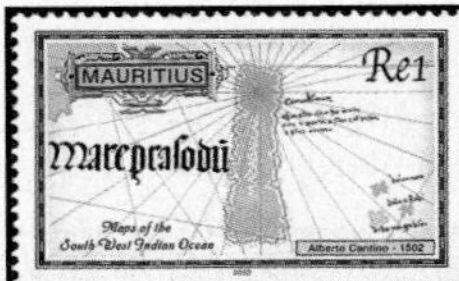

Maps of the Southwest Indian Ocean — A203

Maps by: 1r, Alberto Cantino, 1502. 3r, Jorge Reinel, 1520. 4r, Diogo Ribeiro, 1529. 10r, Gerard Mercator, 1569.

2002, Sept. 18
956-959 A203 Set of 4 5.00 5.00

Constellations A204

Designs: 1r, Orion. 7r, Sagittarius. 8r, Scorpius. 9r, Crux.

Perf. 14¼x14½

2002, Dec. 18 Litho. Wmk. 373
960-963 A204 Set of 4 4.00 4.00

2nd U.S. — Sub-Saharan Africa Trade and Economic Forum — A205

Panel color: 1r, Violet blue. 25r, Red.

2003, Jan. ***Perf. 14¼***
964-965 A205 Set of 2 3.25 3.25

Worldwide Fund for Nature (WWF) — A206

Echo parakeet: 1r, Chick. 2r, Fledgling. 5r, Female. 15r, Male.

Wmk. 373

2003, Mar. 19 Litho. ***Perf. 13½***
966-969 A206 Set of 4 4.00 4.00

Flowers — A207

Designs: 1r, Trochetia boutoniana. 4r, Trochetia uniflora. 7r, Trochetia triflora. 9r, Trochetia parviflora.

Wmk. 373

2003, June 18 Litho. ***Perf. 13½***
970-973 A207 Set of 4 3.75 3.75

Anniversaries and Events — A208

Designs: 2r, Sixth Indian Ocean Games, Mauritius. 6r, Mauritius Chamber of Agriculture, 150th anniv. 9r, Visit of Abbé de la Caille, 250th anniv. 10r, Mauritius Sugar Industry Research Institute, 50th anniv.

2003, Aug. 20
974-977 A208 Set of 4 5.75 5.75

Fortresses — A209

Designs: 2r, Batterie de la Pointe du Diable. 5r, Donjon St. Louis. 6r, Martello tower. 12r, Fort Adelaide,

2003, Dec. 10
978-981 A209 Set of 4 4.00 4.00

Indian Ocean Commission, 20th Anniv. — A210

Wmk. 373

2004, Feb. 16 Litho. ***Perf. 13½***
982 A210 10r multi 2.25 2.25

Mountains — A211

Designs: 2r, Le Pouce. 7r, Corps de Garde. 8r, Le Chat et La Souris. 25r, Piton du Milieu.

2004, Mar. 11 ***Perf. 14½x14¼***
983-986 A211 Set of 4 6.50 6.50

Traditional Trades — A212

Designs: 2r, Tinsmith. 7r, Cobbler. 9r, Blacksmith. 15r, Basket weaver.

Wmk. 373

2004, June 30 Litho. ***Perf. 13½***
987-990 A212 Set of 4 5.00 5.00

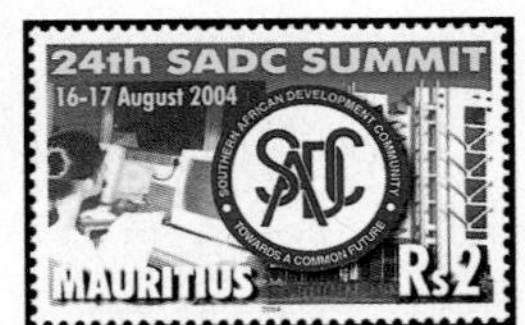

24th Southern Africa Development Community Summit — A213

Emblem, woman at computer, building and panel in: 2r, Gray. 50r, Red.

Wmk. 373

2004, Aug. 16 Litho. ***Perf. 13½***
991-992 A213 Set of 2 7.50 7.50

Rodrigues Regional Assembly — A214

Designs: 2r, Plaine Corail Airport. 7r, Ecotourism. 8r, Agricultural products. 10r, Coat of arms.

Wmk. 373

2004, Oct. 12 Litho. ***Perf. 13½***
993-996 A214 Set of 4 5.50 5.50

Anthurium Andreanum Varieties A215

Designs: 2r, Acropolis. 8r, Tropical. 10r, Paradisio. 25r, Fantasia.

2004, Dec. 1 ***Perf. 13¼***
997-1000 A215 Set of 4 7.00 7.00

Round Island Flora and Fauna A216

Designs: 2r, Juvenile keel scale boa. 8r, Hurricane palm. 9r, Round Island petrel. 25r, Mazambron.

Wmk. 373

2005, Mar. 18 Litho. ***Perf. 13¼***
1001-1004 A216 Set of 4 7.00 7.00

Postal Services A217

Designs: 2r, Counter services. 7r, Mail sorting. 8r, Mail distribution. 10r, Mail transfer.

Wmk. 373

2005, July 14 Litho. ***Perf. 13¼***
1005-1008 A217 Set of 4 4.00 4.00

Stone Buildings — A218

Designs: 2r, Vagrant Depot, Grand River North West. 7r, Postal Museum, Port Louis. 16r, Carnegie Library, Curepipe.

Wmk. 373

2005, Oct. 9 Litho. ***Perf. 13½***
1009-1011 A218 Set of 3 3.75 3.75

Ship Models — A219

Designs: 7r, 100-gun ship. 8r, Sampan. 9r, Roman galley. 16r, Drakkar.
25r, Drakkar, horiz.

Perf. 13¾x13½

2005, Dec. 20 **Litho.**
1012-1015 A219 Set of 4 6.00 6.00

Souvenir Sheet
Perf. 13½x13¾

1016 A219 25r multi 4.25 4.25

Mahebourg, Bicent. — A220

Designs: 2r, Market. 7r, Regattas. 8r, Le Lavoir. No. 1020, 16r, Pointe des Régates.
No. 1021, vert.: a, 16r, Mahé de la Bourdonnais. b, 16r, Gen. Charles Decaen.

Wmk. 373

2006, Feb. 4 **Litho.** ***Perf. 13½***
1017-1020 A220 Set of 4 5.00 5.00

Souvenir Sheet

1021 A220 16r Sheet of 2, #a-b 5.25 5.25

Professor Basdeo Bissoondoyal (1906-91), Educator — A221

Wmk. 373

2006, Apr. 15 **Litho.** ***Perf. 13¾***
1022 A221 10r multi 1.10 1.10

Ecological History — A222

Designs: 2r, Biological control of locusts with introduction of mynah birds, 1763. 8r, Fish repopulation with artificial reefs, 1980. 10r, Erosion control with terraces in Rodrigues, 1958. 25r, First captive breeding of giant tortoises, 1881.

2006, June 5 ***Perf. 13½***
1023-1026 A222 Set of 4 5.50 5.50

Crabs — A223

Designs: 2r, Tourloulou crab. 7r, Land crab. 8s, Freshwater crab. 25r, Coconut crab.

Wmk. 373

2006, Oct. 9 **Litho.** ***Perf. 13¼***
1027-1030 A223 Set of 4 4.50 4.50

Traditional Children's Activities — A224

Designs: 5r, Sapsiwaye. 10r, Marbles, horiz. 15r, Hop Scotch, horiz. 25r, Kite flying.

Perf. 13¾x13½, 13½x13¾

2006, Dec. 7
1031-1034 A224 Set of 4 3.50 3.50

Corals A225

Designs: 3r, Rodrigues endemic coral. 5r, Soft coral. 10r, Chagos coral. 15r, Head coral. 22r, Table coral. 25r, Tube coral.

Wmk. 373

2007, Apr. 30 **Litho.** ***Perf. 13½***
1035-1040 A225 Set of 6 5.25 5.25

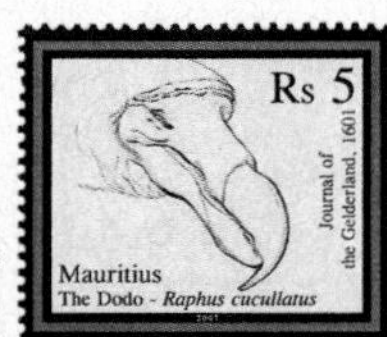

Drawings of Dodo Birds — A226

Drawing: 5r, From Journal of the Gelderland, 1601. 10r, By Adrian van de Venne, 1626. 15r, Published by Harrison, 1798. No. 1044, 25r, By J. W. Frohawk, 1905.
No. 1045, By Julian Pender Hume, 2001, vert.

Wmk. 373

2007, June 25 **Litho.** ***Perf. 13½***
1041-1044 A226 Set of 4 3.50 3.50

Souvenir Sheet
Perf. 13x13¼

1045 A226 25r multi 1.60 1.60

No. 1045 contains one 28x45mm stamp.

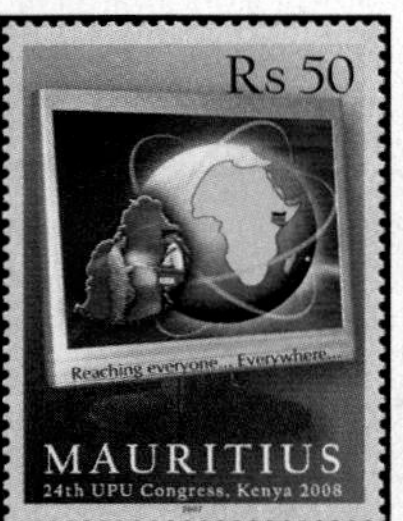

24th UPU Congress, Nairobi A227

Wmk. 373

2007, Oct. 9 **Litho.** ***Perf. 13¼***
1046 A227 50r multi 3.50 3.50

Due to political unrest in Kenya, the UPU Congress was moved to Geneva, Switzerland.

Anniversaries — A228

Designs: 5r, Ministerial System, 50th anniv. 10r, Arrival in Mauritius of Manilall Doctor, cent., vert. 15r, Scouting, cent., vert. 25r, First meteorological observatory in Mauritius, 175th anniv.

2007, Dec. 4 ***Perf. 13½***
1047-1050 A228 Set of 4 3.75 3.75

Ministerial System, 50th Anniv. (With Corrected Photograph) — A229

2007, Dec. 4 **Litho.** ***Perf. 13½***
1051 A229 5r multi .35 .35

The photo in the LR corner on No. 1051 differs from the photo in the LR corner on No. 1047.

Authors Who Mentioned Mauritius — A230

Author and work: 5r, Bernardin de St. Pierre (1737-1814), Paul et Virginie. 10r, Alexandre Dumas (père) (1802-70), Georges. 15r, Charles Baudelaire (1821-67), A une Dame Creole. 22r, Mark Twain (1835-1910), Following the Equator. 25r, Joesph Conrad (1857-1924), A Smile of Fortune.

Wmk. 406

2008, Dec. 8 **Litho.** ***Perf. 13½***
1052-1056 A230 Set of 5 4.75 4.75

Flowers — A231

Designs: 3r, Myonima obovata. 4r, Cylindrocline lorencei. 5r, Crinum mauritianum. 6r, Elaeocarpus bojeri. 7r, Bremeria landia. 8r, Distephanus populifolius. 9r, Gaertnera longifolia. 10r, Dombeya acutangula. 15r, Aphloia theiformis. 22r, Barleria observatrix. 25r, Roussea simplex. 50r, Hibiscus fragilis.

Wmk. 406

2009, Apr. 9 **Litho.** ***Perf. 13½***

1057	A231	3r multi	.20	.20
1058	A231	4r multi	.25	.25
1059	A231	5r multi	.30	.30
1060	A231	6r multi	.35	.35
1061	A231	7r multi	.45	.45
1062	A231	8r multi	.50	.50
a.		Dated "2010"	.55	.55
1063	A231	9r multi	.55	.55
1064	A231	10r multi	.60	.60
1065	A231	15r multi	.90	.90
a.		Dated "2010"	1.00	1.00
1066	A231	22r multi	1.40	1.40
1067	A231	25r multi	1.50	1.50
a.		Dated "2010"	1.75	1.75
1068	A231	50r multi	3.00	3.00
		Nos. 1057-1068 (12)	10.00	10.00

Extinct Mauritian Giant Tortoises — A232

Designs: 5r, Cylindraspis peltastes. 10r, Cylindraspis vosmaeri, vert. 15r, Cylindraspis inepta. 25r, Cylindraspis triserrata, vert.
50r, Cylindraspis peltastes, diff.

Wmk. 406

2009, July 16 **Litho.** ***Perf. 13½***
1069-1072 A232 Set of 4 3.50 3.50

Souvenir Sheet

1073 A232 50r multi 3.25 3.25

New Mauritius Travel Slogan — A233

No. 1074 — New slogan on: a, Yellow background. b, Mountain background.

Perf. 13½x13

2009, Oct. 9 **Litho.** **Wmk. 406**
1074 A233 7r Vert. pair, #a-b .95 .95

Chinese Chamber of Commerce, Cent. (in 2008) — A234

Dr. Kissoonsingh Hazareesingh, Historian, Birth Cent. — A235

Capture of Rodrigues Island by British, Bicent. — A236

Teeluckpersad Callychurn, Postmaster General, Birth Cent. — A237

Wmk. 406

2009, Nov. 30 **Litho.** ***Perf. 13½***

1075	A234	7r multi	.50	.50
1076	A235	14r multi	1.00	1.00
1077	A236	20r multi	1.40	1.40
1078	A237	21r multi	1.50	1.50
		Nos. 1075-1078 (4)	4.40	4.40

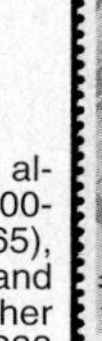

Muhammad al-Idrisi (c.1100-c.1165), Geographer and Cartographer A238

Wmk. 406

2010, Aug. 2 Litho. ***Perf. 13½***

1079	A238	27r multi	1.90	1.90

Mauritius No. 2 — A239

2010, Aug. 20

1080	A239	30r multi	2.00	2.00

Expo 2010, Shanghai.

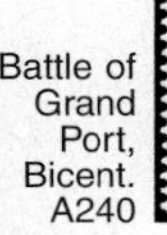

Battle of Grand Port, Bicent. A240

Designs: 14r, Battle scene. 21r, Ile de la Passe.

2010, Aug. 20

1081-1082	A240	Set of 2	2.25	2.25

Sir Seewoosagur Ramgoolam (1900-85), Prime Minister — A241

Litho. & Embossed With Foil Application

2010, Sept. 18 Wmk. 406

1083	A241	100r multi	6.75	6.75

British Conquest of Isle de France, Bicent. — A242

Designs: 2r, Capitulation document. 7r, British landing on Isle de France, horiz.

Wmk. 406

2010, Dec. 3 Litho. ***Perf. 13½***

1084-1085	A242	Set of 2	.60	.60

SPECIAL DELIVERY STAMPS

SD1

1903 Wmk. 1 ***Perf. 14***

Red Surcharge

E1	SD1	15c on 15c ultra	13.00	32.50

SD2

SD3

EXPRESS DELIVERY (INLAND) 15 c

New Setting with Smaller "15c" without period — SD3a

1904

E2	SD2	15c on 15c ultra	60.00	85.00
a.		"INLAND" inverted		3,250.
b.		Inverted "A" in "INLAND"	1,600.	1,100.
E3	SD3	15c on 15c ultra	9.00	3.75
a.		Double surcharge, both inverted	1,825.	1,825.
b.		Inverted surcharge	1,100.	700.00
c.		Vert. pair, imperf between	*5,500.*	
E3F	SD3a	15c on 15c ultra	800.00	750.00
g.		Inverted surcharge		1,725.
h.		Double surcharge		3,500.
i.		Double surcharge, both inverted	—	5,500.
j.		"c" omitted		2,750.

To make No. E2 the word "INLAND" was printed on No. E1. For Nos. E3 and E3F, new settings of the surcharge were made with different spacing between the words.

SD4

SD5

E4	SD4	15c green & red	13.00	6.00
a.		Double surcharge	700.00	725.00
b.		Inverted surcharge	925.00	800.00
c.		"LNIAND."		—
d.		As "c," double surcharge	*800.00*	750.00
E5	SD5	18c green & black	3.00	32.50
a.		Exclamation point (!) instead of "I" in "FOREIGN"	700.00	

POSTAGE DUE STAMPS

Catalogue values for unused stamps in this section are for Never Hinged items.

Numeral — D1

Perf. 14½x14

1933-54 Typo. Wmk. 4

J1	D1	2c black	1.50	.60
J2	D1	4c violet	.60	.80
J3	D1	6c red	.70	*.95*
J4	D1	10c green	.85	*1.90*
J5	D1	20c ultramarine	.60	*2.15*
J6	D1	50c dp red lilac ('54)	.65	*19.00*
J7	D1	1r orange ('54)	.85	*19.00*
		Nos. J1-J7 (7)	5.75	*44.40*

1966-68 Wmk. 314 ***Perf. 14***

J8	D1	2c black ('67)	2.75	3.00

Perf. 14½14

J9	D1	4c rose violet ('68)	1.90	8.50
J10	D1	6c dp orange ('68)	7.00	26.00
J11	D1	10c yel green ('67)	.35	2.25
J12	D1	20c ultramarine	2.50	5.00
J13	D1	50c dp red lilac ('68)	.85	13.00
		Nos. J8-J13 (6)	15.35	57.75

Nos. 445-446, 450, 455, 457, 462 Surcharged "POSTAGE/ DUE" and New Value

Wmk. 373

1982, Oct. 25 Litho. ***Perf. 13½***

J14	A92	10c on 15c multi	.20	.20
J15	A92	20c on 20c multi	.20	.60
J16	A91	50c on 60c multi	.35	.35
J17	A92	1r on 1.20r multi	.45	.35
J18	A92	1.50r on 1.50r multi	.60	.85
J19	A91	5r on 15r multi	1.10	2.50
		Nos. J14-J19 (6)	2.90	4.85

MAYOTTE

mä-ˈyät

LOCATION — One of the Comoro Islands situated in the Mozambique Channel midway between Madagascar and Mozambique (Africa)
GOVT. — French Colony
AREA — 144 sq. mi.
POP. — 149,336 (1999 est.)
CAPITAL — Mamoutzou
See Comoro Islands.

100 Centimes = 1 Franc
100 Cents = 1 Euro (2002)

Stamps of Mayotte were replaced successively by those of Madagascar, Comoro Islands and France. Individual issues were resumed in 1975.

See France No. 2271 for French stamp inscribed "Mayotte."

Catalogue values for unused stamps in this country are for Never Hinged items, beginning with Scott 75 in the regular postage section, and Scott C1 in the airpost section.

Navigation and Commerce — A1

Perf. 14x13½

1892-1907 Typo. Unwmk.

Name of Colony in Blue or Carmine

1	A1	1c blk, *lil bl*	1.40	.90
2	A1	2c brn, *buff*	1.90	1.40
a.		Name double	575.00	500.00
3	A1	4c claret, *lav*	2.40	1.75
4	A1	5c grn, *grnsh*	4.75	3.25
5	A1	10c blk, *lavender*	9.00	4.75
6	A1	10c red ('00)	67.50	52.50
7	A1	15c blue, quadrille paper	17.50	10.50
8	A1	15c gray ('00)	125.00	110.00
9	A1	20c red, *grn*	12.00	10.50
10	A1	25c blk, *rose*	14.50	9.75
11	A1	25c blue ('00)	14.50	13.50
12	A1	30c brn, *bis*	22.00	16.00
13	A1	35c blk, *yel*	11.00	8.00
14	A1	40c red, *straw*	22.00	16.00
15	A1	45c blk, *gray grn* ('07)	21.00	20.00
16	A1	50c carmine, *rose*	32.00	22.50
17	A1	50c brn, *az* ('00)	30.00	30.00
18	A1	75c dp vio, *org*	30.00	21.00
19	A1	1fr brnz grn, *straw*	32.00	22.50
20	A1	5fr red lil, *lav* ('99)	150.00	130.00
		Nos. 1-20 (20)	620.45	504.80

Perf. 13½x14 stamps are counterfeits.

Issues of 1892-1907 Surcharged in Black or Carmine

1912

22	A1	5c on 2c brn, *buff*	3.25	*4.00*
23	A1	5c on 4c cl, *lav* (C)	2.00	2.00
24	A1	5c on 15c bl (C)	2.00	2.00
25	A1	5c on 20c red, *grn*	2.00	*2.40*
26	A1	5c on 25c blk, *rose* (C)	1.60	1.60
a.		Double surcharge	300.00	
b.		Pair, one stamp without surcharge	1,000.	
27	A1	5c on 30c brn, *bis* (C)	2.00	2.00
28	A1	10c on 40c red, *straw*	2.00	*2.40*
a.		Double surcharge	300.00	
29	A1	10c on 45c blk, *gray grn* (C)	2.00	2.00
a.		Double surcharge	300.00	*325.00*
30	A1	10c on 50c car, *rose*	4.50	*5.00*
31	A1	10c on 75c dp vio, *org*	3.50	*4.25*
32	A1	10c on 1fr brnz grn, *straw*	3.50	*4.25*
		Nos. 22-32 (11)	28.35	*31.90*

Two spacings between the surcharged numerals are found on Nos. 22-32. For detailed listings, see the *Scott Classic Specialized Catalogue of Stamps and Covers.*

Nos. 22-32 were available for use in Madagascar and the entire Comoro archipelago.

Catalogue values for unused stamps in this section, from this point to the end of the section, are for Never Hinged items.

Marianne Type of France Ovtpd. "MAYOTTE"

1997, Jan. 2 Engr. ***Perf. 13***

Design A1161

75	10c on #2179	.25	*.30*
76	20c on #2180	.25	*.30*
77	50c on #2181	.25	*.30*
78	1fr on #2182	.55	.55
79	2fr on #2331	1.10	1.10
80	(2.50fr) on #2342	1.25	1.25
81	2.70fr on #2334	1.40	1.40
82	3.80fr on #2337	1.75	1.75
83	5fr on #2194	2.50	2.50
84	10fr on #2195	5.00	5.00
	Nos. 75-84 (10)	14.30	14.45

Ylang Ylang — A5

1997, Jan. 2 Litho. ***Perf. 13½x13***

85	A5	2.70fr multicolored	1.50	1.50

Coat of Arms — A6

1997, Jan. 2 ***Perf. 13x13½***

86	A6	3fr multicolored	1.60	1.60
a.		Sheet of 4	7.25	7.25

#86a issued 6/19/99 for Philex France 99.

Le Banga — A7

1997, May 31 Litho. *Perf. 13*
87 A7 3.80fr multicolored 1.90 1.90

Dzen Dzé Musical Instrument A8

Photo. & Engr.
1997, May 31 *Perf. 12½*
88 A8 5.20fr multicolored 2.50 2.50

Lemur A9

1997, Aug. 30 Engr. *Perf. 12*
89 A9 3fr red & dk brown 1.60 1.60

Face of a Woman A10

1997, Aug. 30 Litho. *Perf. 13*
90 A10 3.50fr multicolored 1.75 1.75

Marine Life — A11

1997, Nov. 29 Litho. *Perf. 13*
91 A11 3fr multicolored 1.60 1.60

Longoni Port — A12

1998, Jan. 31 Litho. *Perf. 13*
92 A12 2.70fr multicolored 1.40 1.40

Chelonia Mydas — A13

1998, Jan. 31
93 A13 3fr multicolored 1.75 1.75

Family Planning — A14

1998, Apr. 1 Litho. *Perf. 13¼x13*
94 A14 1fr multicolored .75 .75

France No. 2604 Ovptd. "MAYOTTE"
Die Cut x Serpentine Die Cut 7
1998, Apr. 15 Engr.
Self-Adhesive
104 A1409 (3fr) red 1.40 1.40
a. Booklet pane of 10 14.00

No. 104a is a complete booklet, the peelable backing serves as a booklet cover.

Children's Carnival A15

1998, May 30 Litho. *Perf. 13*
105 A15 3fr multicolored 1.50 1.50

Ferry, "Salama Djema II" — A16

1998, May 30
106 A16 3.80fr multicolored 1.75 1.75

Mosque of Tsingoni A17

1998, Sept. 5 Litho. *Perf. 13*
107 A17 3fr multicolored 1.50 1.50

Mariama Salim — A18

Photo. & Engr.
1998, Oct. 3 *Perf. 13*
108 A18 2.70fr multicolored 1.25 1.25

Traditional Fishing, Djarifa — A19

1998, Nov. 7 Litho. *Perf. 13*
109 A19 2fr multicolored 1.25 1.25

Pomacanthus — A20

1998, Nov. 7
110 A20 3fr multicolored 1.50 1.50

See Nos. 121-124.

Agricultural Tools — A21

1998, Dec. 19 Litho. *Perf. 13*
111 A21 3fr multicolored 1.50 1.50

France Nos. 2589-2593, 2601, 2603 Ovptd. "MAYOTTE"
1999, Jan. 1 Engr. *Perf. 13*
112 A1409 10c brn (#2589) .25 .25
113 A1409 20c brt bl grn (#2590) .30 .30
114 A1409 50c purple (#2591) .50 .50
115 A1409 1fr brt orange (#2592) .65 .65
116 A1409 2fr brt blue (#2593) .90 .90
117 A1409 5fr brt grn bl (#2601) 2.00 2.00
118 A1409 10fr violet (#2603) 4.50 4.50
Nos. 112-118 (7) 9.10 9.10

Map of Mayotte A22

1999, Feb. 6 *Perf. 12x13*
119 A22 3fr multicolored 1.50 1.50

Combani Dam A23

1999, Feb. 6 Litho. *Perf. 13*
120 A23 8fr multicolored 3.50 3.50

Fish Type of 1998

Designs: 2.70fr, Cephalopholis miniatus, vert. 3fr, Pterois volitans. 5.20fr, Pygoplites diacanthus. 10fr, Acanthurus leucosternon.

Perf. 13¼x13, 13x13¼
1999, Apr. 3 Litho.
121 A20 2.70fr multicolored 1.25 1.25
122 A20 3fr multicolored 1.40 1.40
123 A20 5.20fr multicolored 2.50 2.50
124 A20 10fr multicolored 3.75 3.75
Nos. 121-124 (4) 8.90 8.90

France No. 2691 Ovptd. "MAYOTTE"
1999, May 25 Engr. *Perf. 13*
125 A1470 3fr red & blue 1.25 1.25

Founga — A24

Photo. & Engr.
1999, June 5 *Perf. 13*
126 A24 5.40fr multicolored 2.50 2.50

Baobab Tree — A25

1999, June 5 Litho. *Perf. 13x13½*
127 A25 8fr multicolored 3.50 3.50

Dzaoudzi Prefecture A26

1999, Sept. 25 Litho. *Perf. 13x13¼*
128 A26 3fr multicolored 1.40 1.40

Souvenir Sheet

Pirogues — A27

Designs: a, Pirogues on beach, shown. b, Pirogues, vert. c, Pirogues, close-up.

1999, Sept. 25 *Perf. 13*
129 A27 5fr Sheet of 3, #a.-c. 10.50 10.50

Vanilla A28

1999, Nov. 6 Litho. *Perf. 13*
130 A28 4.50fr multi 1.75 1.75

Soulou Waterfalls — A29

1999, Dec. 11 *Perf. 13½x13*
131 A29 10fr multi 4.00 4.00

Year 2000 A30

1999, Dec. 11 *Perf. 13*
132 A30 3fr multi 1.25 1.25

Indian Ocean Boat — A31

2000, Feb. 5 Litho. *Perf. 13x13¼*
133 A31 3fr multi 1.25 1.25

Whales A32

2000, Feb. 5 Litho. *Perf. 13x13¼*
134 A32 5.20fr multi 2.50 2.50

Inner Wheel Rotary District — A33

2000, Mar. 24 *Perf. 13¼x13*
135 A33 5.20fr multi 2.50 2.50

Lagoon A34

2000, Apr. 29 Litho. *Perf. 13x13¼*
136 A34 3fr multi 1.40 1.40

Souvenir Sheet

Mahoraise Women — A35

Woman in: a, 3fr, red. b, 5.20fr, white.

2000, Apr. 29 *Perf. 13¼x13*
137 A35 Sheet of 2, #a-b 5.00 5.00

Tire Race A36

2000, June 24 *Perf. 13x13¼*
138 A36 3fr multi 1.40 1.40

Tomb of Sultan Andriantsouli — A37

2000, June 24
139 A37 5.40fr multi 2.10 2.10

Souvenir Sheet

Sea Shells — A38

No. 140: a, Cassis cornuta. b, Charonia tritonis. c, Cyraecassis rufa. d, Cyprae mauritania, Cyprae tigris.

2000, Sept. 23 Litho. *Perf. 13x13½*
140 A38 3fr Sheet of 4, #a-d 8.00 8.00

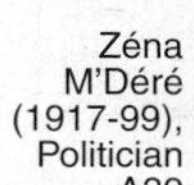

Zéna M'Déré (1917-99), Politician A39

2000, Oct. 27 *Perf. 13*
141 A39 3fr multi 1.40 1.40

Ylang Distillery A40

2000, Nov. 25 Litho. *Perf. 13x13½*
142 A40 2.70fr multi 1.40 1.40

New Hospital — A41

2000, Nov. 25 *Perf. 13½x13*
143 A41 10fr multi 4.50 4.50

Map of Mayotte — A42

2001, Jan. 1 Litho. *Perf. 13*
144 A42 2.70fr grn & blk 1.25 1.25
145 A42 (3fr) red & blk 1.25 1.25

Breastfeeding A43

2001, Jan. 27 *Perf. 13¼x13*
146 A43 3fr multi 1.60 1.60

Return of Pilgrims to Mecca A44

2001, Mar. 10 *Perf. 13x13¼*
147 A44 2.70fr multi 1.40 1.40

Bush Taxi — A45

2001, Mar. 10 *Perf. 13*
148 A45 3fr multi 1.40 1.40

Soccer — A46

2001, May 26 Litho. *Perf. 13¼x13*
149 A46 3fr multi 1.40 1.40

Fish Type of 1998

Design: Pajama fish (gaterin, plectorhinchus orientalis).

2001, May 26 *Perf. 13x13¼*
150 A20 10fr multi 4.50 4.50

Foreign Legion Detachment in Mayotte, 25th Anniv. — A47

2001, Apr. 30 Litho. *Perf. 13*
151 A47 5.20fr multi 2.25 2.25

Souvenir Sheet

Flying Foxes — A48

No. 152: a, 3fr, Hanging from branch. b, 5.20fr, In flight.

2001, July 7 Litho. *Perf. 13x13½*
152 A48 Sheet of 2, #a-b 6.50 6.50

Adapted Military Service Group, 1st Anniv. A49

2001, Sept. 1 Litho. *Perf. 13x13½*
153 A49 3fr multi 1.40 1.40

Flowers A50

Designs: 3fr, Shown. 5.40fr, Fruits.

2001, Sept. 22 ***Perf. 13***
154-155 A50 Set of 2 4.00 4.00

Lake Dziani Dzaha — A51

2001, Nov. 17
156 A51 5.20fr multi 2.40 2.40

Mayotte Post Office A52

2001, Nov. 17
157 A52 10fr multi 5.00 5.00

100 Cents = 1 Euro (€)

Arms — A53

2002, Jan. 1 **Litho.** ***Perf. 13x13½***
158 A53 46c multi 1.75 1.75

France Nos. 2835, 2849-2863 Overprinted

2002, Jan. 1 **Engr.** ***Perf. 13***

159	A1583	1c	yellow	.20	.20
160	A1583	2c	brown	.20	.20
161	A1583	5c	brt bl grn	.30	.30
162	A1583	10c	purple	.40	.40
163	A1583	20c	brt org	.70	.70
164	A1583	41c	brt green	1.25	1.25
165	A1409	(46c)	red	1.40	1.40
166	A1583	50c	dk blue	1.50	1.50
167	A1583	53c	apple grn	1.60	1.60
168	A1583	58c	blue	1.75	1.75
169	A1583	64c	dark org	2.00	2.00
170	A1583	67c	brt blue	2.10	2.10
171	A1583	69c	brt pink	2.25	2.25
172	A1583	€1	Prus blue	3.00	3.00
173	A1583	€1.02	dk green	3.00	3.00
174	A1583	€2	violet	6.00	6.00
	Nos. 159-174 (16)			27.65	27.65

Athletics — A54

2002, Mar. 23 **Litho.** ***Perf. 13***
175 A54 41c multi 1.50 1.50

Kawéni Mangrove Swamp — A55

2002, Mar. 25
176 A55 €1.52 multi 5.00 5.00

Mayotte Communes, 25th Anniv. — A56

2002, June 3 **Litho.** ***Perf. 13¼x13***
177 A56 46c multi 1.60 1.60

Salt Drying — A57

2002, June 3 ***Perf. 13x13¼***
178 A57 79c multi 3.00 3.00

2002 Census — A58

2002, July 29 **Litho.** ***Perf. 13¼x13***
179 A58 46c multi 1.75 1.75

Abandoned Sugar Processing Equipment — A59

2002, Sept. 21 **Litho.** ***Perf. 13***
180 A59 82c multi 2.75 2.75

Miniature Sheet

Birds — A60

No. 181: a, Souimanga. b, Drongo. c, Oiseau-lunette. d, Foudy.

2002, Sept. 21 ***Perf. 13x13¼***
181 A60 46c Sheet of 4, #a-d 8.50 8.50

Mt. Choungui — A61

2002, Nov. 16 **Litho.** ***Perf. 13¼x13***
182 A61 46c multi 1.75 1.75

Breadfruit — A62

2002, Nov. 16
183 A62 €1.22 multi 4.00 4.00

Vanilla and Ylang Museum A63

2003, Jan. 1 **Litho.** ***Perf. 13x13½***
184 A63 46c multi 2.00 2.00

Banana Tree — A64

2003, Feb. 1 ***Perf. 13½x13***
185 A64 79c multi 2.75 2.75

Holiday Face Decorations A65

2003, Apr. 5 **Litho.** ***Perf. 13***
186 A65 46c multi 1.75 1.75

Swordfish — A66

2003, Apr. 5
187 A66 79c multi 3.00 3.00

Gecko — A67

2003, June 14 **Litho.** ***Perf. 13***
188 A67 50c multi 2.00 2.00

Mraha Game — A68

2003, June 14 **Engr.** ***Perf. 13x12½***
189 A68 €1.52 claret & brown 5.50 5.50

Mtzamboro College A69

2003, Sept. 6 **Litho.** ***Perf. 13x13¼***
190 A69 45c multi 1.75 1.75

Ziyara de Pole — A70

2003, Sept. 6 ***Perf. 13¼x13***
191 A70 82c multi 3.00 3.00

Basketball — A71

2003, Nov. 15 Litho. ***Perf. 13¼x13***
192 A71 50c multi 1.75 1.75

Wadaha A72

2004, Jan. 3 ***Perf. 13***
193 A72 50c multi 1.75 1.75

Map Type of 2001 Inscribed "RF" and With Euro Denominations Only

2004

194	A42	1c yel & blk	.25	.25
195	A42	2c gray & blk	.25	.25
196	A42	5c greenish bl & blk	.30	.30
197	A42	10c red vio & blk	.30	.30
198	A42	20c org & blk	.50	.50
199	A42	45c green & black	1.25	1.25
200	A42	50c dk bl & blk	1.25	1.25
201	A42	€1 Prus bl & blk	2.40	2.40
202	A42	€2 violet & blk	5.00	5.00
		Nos. 194-202 (9)	11.50	11.50

Issued: 1c, 2c, 50c, €2, 3/10; 5c, 10c, 20c, €1, 4/17; 45c, 7/17.

Sada Bay — A73

2004, Apr. 3 Litho. ***Perf. 13***
203 A73 90c multi 2.75 2.75

Souvenir Sheet

Butterflies — A74

No. 204: a, Junonia rhadama. b, Papilio demodocus. c, Acraea ranavalona. d, Danaus chrysippus.

2004, Apr. 3 ***Perf. 13x13¼***
204 A74 50c Sheet of 4, #a-d 7.00 7.00

Papaya and Papaya Tree A75

2004, June 12 Litho. ***Perf. 13x13¼***
205 A75 50c multi 1.75 1.75

Gold Jewelry A76

2004, June 12 Litho. ***Perf. 13***
206 A76 €2.40 multi 7.50 7.50

Kwalé River Bridge A77

2004, Sept. 25 Litho. ***Perf. 13x13¼***
207 A77 50c multi 1.75 1.75

Maki and Young A78

2004, Sept. 25 ***Perf. 13***
208 A78 75c multi 2.50 2.50

Woman Cooking Food A79

2004, Nov. 13 ***Perf. 13x13¼***
209 A79 45c multi 1.50 1.50

Domino Players — A80

2004, Nov. 13 ***Perf. 13***
210 A80 75c multi 2.50 2.50

Ylang-ylang Trees — A81

2005, Jan. 3 Litho. ***Perf. 13***
211 A81 50c multi 2.00 2.00

Traditional Women's Clothing A82

2005, Mar. 14 Litho. ***Perf. 13***
212 A82 53c multi 2.00 2.00

Breadfruit and Tree — A83

2005, Mar. 14 ***Perf. 13¼x13***
213 A83 64c multi 2.00 2.00

Rotary International, Cent. — A84

2005, May 13 ***Perf. 13***
214 A84 90c multi 2.75 2.75

Souvenir Sheet

Marine Mammals — A85

No. 215: a, Humpback whale (Baleine à bosse). b, Dolphins. c, Sperm whale (grand cachalot). d, Dugongs.

2005, May 13 ***Perf. 13x13¼***
215 A85 53c Sheet of 4, #a-d 8.00 8.00

Stick Figure Drawings A86

2005, July 4 ***Perf. 13***
216 A86 48c multi 1.75 1.75

Mamoudzou — A87

2005, Sept. 10 Litho. ***Perf. 13***
217 A87 48c multi 1.50 1.50

Fisherman in Pirogue A88

2005, Sept. 10
218 A88 75c multi 2.25 2.25

Blacksmith A89

2005, Nov. 12 Litho. ***Perf. 13x13¼***
219 A89 53c multi 1.75 1.75

Tam-tam Boeuf Celebration — A90

2005, Nov. 12 ***Perf. 13***
220 A90 53c multi 1.75 1.75

Woman Grating Coconuts A91

2006, Jan. 14 Litho. ***Perf. 13x13¼***
221 A91 53c multi 1.75 1.75

Moya Beach — A92

2006, Mar. 18 Litho. *Perf. 13*
222 A92 48c multi 1.75 1.75

Souvenir Sheet

Turtle Protection — A93

No. 223: a, Turtle swimming. b, Turtle laying eggs. c, Hatchlings.

2006, Mar. 18 *Perf. 13x13¼*
223 A93 53c Sheet of 3, #a-c 7.50 7.50

Farmer's Market — A94

Ferries — A95

2006, May 15 Litho. *Perf. 13x12¾*
224 A94 53c multi 1.50 1.50
225 A95 €1.07 multi 3.50 3.50

Aloe Mayottensis A96

2006, July 3 Litho. *Perf. 13¼x13*
226 A96 53c multi 1.75 1.75

Frangipani Shrub and Flowers A97

2006, Sept. 9 *Perf. 13x13¼*
227 A97 53c multi 1.75 1.75

Moulidi Dance — A98

2006, Sept. 9 *Perf. 13*
228 A98 75c multi 2.75 2.75

Tropic Birds A99

2006, Nov. 18 Litho. *Perf. 13*
229 A99 54c multi 2.00 2.00

Resumption of Stamp Issues, 10th Anniv. — A100

2007, Jan. 20 Litho. *Perf. 13½x13*
230 A100 54c multi 1.75 1.75

Phanelopsis Orchid — A101

2007, Jan. 20 *Perf. 13x13½*
231 A101 54c multi 2.00 2.00

Audit Office, Bicent. A102

2007, Mar. 19 Engr. *Perf. 13¼*
232 A102 54c multi 1.75 1.75

Phyllostachys Edulis — A103

2007, Mar. 19 Litho. *Perf. 13¼x13*
233 A103 €1.01 multi 4.00 4.00

Traditional House A104

2007, May 14 *Perf. 13x13¼*
234 A104 54c multi 1.75 1.75

General Council, 30th Anniv. — A105

2007, May 12 Litho. *Perf. 13¼x13*
235 A105 54c multi 2.00 2.00

Souvenir Sheet

Corals — A106

No. 236: a, Corail corne d'elan. b, Gorgone eventail. c, Corail corne de cerf. d, Cerveau de Neptune.

2007, June 16 *Perf. 13x13¼*
236 A106 54c Sheet of 4, #a-d 9.00 9.00

Mangos and Mango Tree A107

2007, Sept. 17 Litho. *Perf. 13x13¼*
237 A107 54c multi 1.75 1.75

Chameleon — A108

2007, Sept. 17
238 A108 54c multi 1.75 1.75

Beach Grill and Shelter — A109

2007, Nov. 10 *Perf. 13*
239 A109 54c multi 1.75 1.75

N'Gouja Beach — A110

2007, Nov. 10 *Perf. 13x13¼*
240 A110 54c multi 2.00 2.00

Zebu A111

2008, Jan. 28 Litho. *Perf. 13x13½*
241 A111 54c multi 1.75 1.75

Coconuts and Coconut Palm — A112

2008, Jan. 28 *Perf. 13x13¼*
242 A112 54c multi 1.75 1.75

Miniature Sheet

Spices — A113

No. 243: a, Cinnamon (cannelle). b, Nutmeg (muscade). c, Turmeric (curcuma). d, Ginger (gingembre).

2008, Mar. 22 Litho. *Perf. 13x13¼*
243 A113 55c Sheet of 4, #a-d 7.75 7.75

Hibiscus — A114

2008, May 26 *Perf. 13¼x13*
244 A114 55c multi 2.00 2.00

Wedding Ceremony A115

2008, May 26 ***Perf. 13***
245 A115 55c multi 2.00 2.00

Younoussa Bamana (1935-2007), Politician — A116

2008, June 23 Litho. ***Perf. 13¼x13***
246 A116 55c multi 1.90 1.90

M'Biwi Dance A117

2008, Sept. 22 Litho. ***Perf. 13x13¼***
247 A117 55c multi 1.75 1.75

Embroidery — A118

2008, Nov. 10 Litho. ***Perf. 13x13¼***
248 A118 55c multi 1.75 1.75

Mamoudzou Town Hall — A119

2008, Dec. 8 ***Perf. 13***
249 A119 55c multi 1.75 1.75

Longoni Power Station — A120

2009, Jan. 12
250 A120 55c multi 1.75 1.75

Cardinals A121

2009, Jan. 12 Litho. ***Perf. 13***
251 A121 55c multi 2.00 2.00

Tamarind Tree and Fruit A122

2009, Mar. 9 ***Perf. 13x13¼***
252 A122 56c multi 1.75 1.75

Fishing by Kerosene Lantern — A123

2009, Mar. 9 ***Perf. 13***
253 A123 56c multi 1.75 1.75

Miniature Sheet

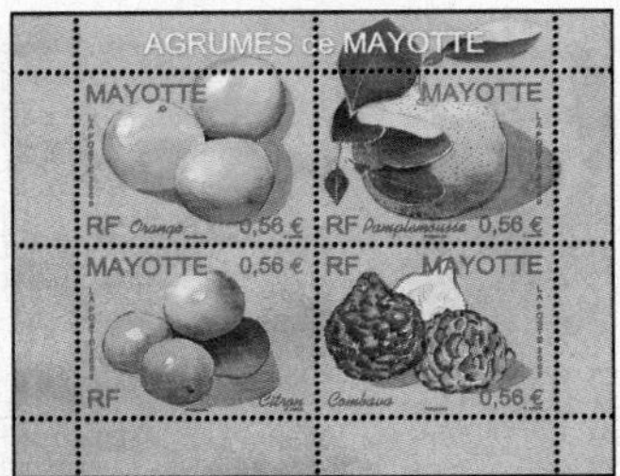

Citrus Fruits — A124

No. 254: a, Oranges. b, Grapefruit (pamplemousse). c, Lemons (citron). d, Kaffir limes (combava).

2009, May 18 ***Perf. 13x13¼***
254 A124 56c Sheet of 4, #a-d 7.75 7.75

Souvenir Sheet

Les Quatres Freres — A125

No. 255: a, Close-up view (blue sky). b, Distant view (yellow sky).

2009, June 29 Litho. ***Perf. 13x13¼***
255 A125 56c Sheet of 2, #a-b 4.00 4.00

Jasmine Flowers A126

2009, Sept. 21 Litho. ***Perf. 13***
256 A126 56c multi 2.00 2.00

Gaboussi Player A127

2009, Nov. 16 ***Perf. 13x13¼***
257 A127 56c multi 1.75 1.75

Welcome to Travelers A128

2010, Jan. 11 Litho. ***Perf. 13***
258 A128 56c multi 1.75 1.75

Basket Weaver — A129

2010, Mar. 8 Litho. ***Perf. 13***
259 A129 56c multi 1.75 1.75

Governor's House — A130

2010, Mar. 8
260 A130 56c multi 1.75 1.75

Sparrow Hawk A131

2010, May 17 Engr. ***Perf. 13¼***
261 A131 56c multi 1.40 1.40

Platycerium Alcicorne A132

2010, May 17 Litho. ***Perf. 13¼***
262 A132 56c multi 1.40 1.40

Decorated Book Rest A133

2010, July 5 Engr. ***Perf. 12¼***
263 A133 58c multi 1.50 1.50

Customs Department Building — A134

2010, July 30 Litho. ***Perf. 13x13½***
264 A134 58c multi 1.50 1.50

Chigoma Dance — A135

2010, Sept. 13
265 A135 95c multi 2.60 2.60

Mail Carrier on All-Terrain Vehicle — A136

2010, Nov. 8 ***Perf. 13¼x13***
266 A136 58c multi 1.60 1.60

AIR POST STAMPS

Catalogue values for unused stamps in this section are for Never Hinged items.

Opening of New Air Terminal — AP1

1997, Mar. 1 Engr. ***Perf. 13x12½***
C1 AP1 20fr multicolored 11.00 11.00

First Mayotte-Réunion Flight, 20th Anniv. — AP2

Photo. & Engr.

1997, Nov. 29 *Perf. 13x12½*
C2 AP2 5fr multicolored 3.00 3.00

Pique-boeuf Bird, Zebu — AP3

1998, Apr. 1 **Litho.** *Perf. 13*
C3 AP3 30fr multicolored 13.00 13.00

Deba Religious Festival — AP4

1999, Nov. 6 **Litho.** *Perf. 13*
C4 AP4 10fr multicolored 5.00 5.00

Dzaoudzi Aero Club — AP5

2001, July 7 **Litho.** *Perf. 13*
C5 AP5 20fr multi 9.50 9.50

Dzaoudzi Rock — AP6

2003, Nov. 15 **Litho.** *Perf. 13*
C6 AP6 €1.50 multi 5.00 5.00

MEMEL

'mā-məl

LOCATION — In northern Europe, bordering on the Baltic Sea
GOVT. — Special commission (see below)
AREA — 1099 sq. mi.
POP. — 151,960

Following World War I this territory was detached from Germany and by Treaty of Versailles assigned to the government of a commission of the Allied and Associated Powers (not the League of Nations), which administered it until January, 1923, when it was forcibly occupied by Lithuania. In 1924 Memel became incorporated as a semi-autonomous district of Lithuania with the approval of the Allied Powers and the League of Nations.

100 Pfennig = 1 Mark
100 Centu = 1 Litas (1923)

Excellent counterfeits of all Memel stamps exist.

Stamps of Germany, 1905-20, Overprinted

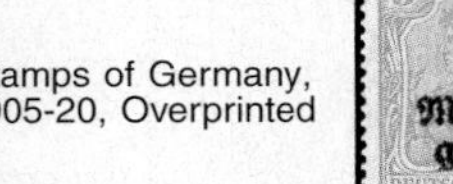

Wmk. Lozenges (125)

1920, Aug. 1 *Perf. 14, 14½*
1 A16 5pf green 1.10 *7.50*
2 A16 10pf car rose 2.25 *9.00*
3 A16 10pf orange .30 *2.60*
4 A22 15pf violet brown 2.60 *8.00*
5 A16 20pf blue violet 1.20 *5.25*
6 A16 30pf org & blk, *buff* 1.30 *7.50*
7 A16 30pf dull blue .40 *2.60*
8 A16 40pf lake & blk .25 *2.60*
9 A16 50pf pur & blk, *buff* .30 *2.60*
10 A16 60pf olive green 1.30 *4.50*
11 A16 75pf grn & blk 2.60 *20.00*
12 A16 80pf blue violet 1.50 *9.00*

Overprinted

13 A17 1m car rose .40 *2.60*
14 A17 1.25m green 13.50 *47.50*
15 A17 1.50m yel brn 4.50 *26.50*
16 A21 2m blue 2.00 *12.00*
17 A21 2.50m red lilac 12.00 *65.00*
Nos. 1-17 (17) 47.50 *234.75*

Stamps of France, Surcharged in Black

On A22

On A18

1920 **Unwmk.** *Perf. 14x13½*
18 A22 5pf on 5c green .50 *2.25*
19 A22 10pf on 10c red .30 *1.90*
20 A22 20pf on 25c blue .90 *3.75*
21 A22 30pf on 30c org .40 *2.25*
22 A22 40pf on 20c red brn .50 *3.00*
23 A22 50pf on 35c vio .30 *1.50*
24 A18 60pf on 40c red & pale bl .35 *1.90*
25 A18 80pf on 45c grn & bl .75 *3.75*
26 A18 1m on 50c brn & lav .50 *3.75*
27 A18 1m 25pf on 60c vio & ultra 1.25 *8.00*
28 A18 2m on 1fr cl & ol grn .35 *1.50*
29 A18 3m on 5fr bl & buff 18.50 *72.50*
Nos. 18-29 (12) 24.60 *106.05*

For stamps with additional surcharges and overprints see Nos. 43-49, C1-C4.

French Stamps of 1900-20 Surcharged like Nos. 24 to 29 in Red or Black

4
Type I

4
Type II

Four Marks

1920-21 **Unwmk.** *Perf. 14x13½*
30 A18 3m on 2fr org & pale bl 16.00 *67.50*
31 A18 4m on 2fr org & pale bl (I) (Bk) .45 *1.50*
a. Type II 26.00 *75.00*
32 A18 10m on 5fr bl & buff 2.75 *16.00*
33 A18 20m on 5fr bl & buff 35.00 *160.00*
Nos. 30-33 (4) 54.20 *245.00*

For stamps with additional overprints see Nos. C5, C19.

New Value with Initial Capital

1921
39 A18 60Pf on 40c red & pale bl 4.25 *18.50*
40 A18 3M on 60c vio & ultra 2.25 *7.50*
41 A18 10M on 5fr bl & buff 2.25 *7.50*
42 A18 20M on 45c grn & bl 4.50 *25.00*
Nos. 39-42 (4) 13.25 *58.50*

The surcharged value on No. 40 is in italics. For stamps with additional overprints see Nos. C6-C7, C18.

Stamps of 1920 Surcharged with Large Numerals in Dark Blue or Red

1921-22
43 A22 15pf on 10pf on 10c .40 *1.90*
a. Inverted surcharge 60.00 *125.00*
44 A22 15pf on 20pf on 25c .40 *2.25*
a. Inverted surcharge 60.00 *82.50*
45 A22 15pf on 50pf on 35c (R) .40 *2.25*
a. Inverted surcharge 60.00 *82.50*
46 A22 60pf on 40pf on 20c .40 *1.90*
a. Inverted surcharge 60.00 *225.00*
47 A18 75pf on 60pf on 40c .60 *2.25*
48 A18 1.25m on 1m on 50c .40 *1.90*
49 A18 5.00m on 2m on 1fr .75 *3.75*
a. Inverted surcharge 160.00 *550.00*
Nos. 43-49 (7) 3.35 *16.20*

Stamps of France Surcharged in Black or Red

On A20, A22

1922
50 A22 5pf on 5c org .25 *1.40*
51 A22 10pf on 10c red .80 *5.25*
52 A22 10pf on 10c grn .50 *1.40*
53 A22 15pf on 10c grn .25 *1.40*
54 A22 20pf on 20c red brn 8.00 *40.00*
55 A22 20pf on 25c bl 8.00 *40.00*
56 A22 25pf on 5c org .25 *1.40*
57 A22 30pf on 30c red 1.10 *5.00*
58 A22 35pf on 35c vio .20 *.75*
59 A20 50pf on 50c dl bl .30 *1.40*
60 A20 75pf on 15c grn .20 *.75*
61 A22 75pf on 35c vio .30 *1.40*
62 A22 1m on 25c blue .20 *.75*
63 A22 1¼m on 30c red .30 *1.40*
64 A22 3m on 5c org .30 *4.00*
65 A20 6m on 15c grn (R) .55 *4.50*
66 A22 8m on 30c red .70 *12.50*

On A18

67 A18 40pf on 40c red & pale bl .25 *1.40*
68 A18 80pf on 45c grn & bl .30 *1.40*
69 A18 1m on 40c red & pale bl .30 *1.40*
70 A18 1.25m on 60c vio & ultra (R) .30 *1.40*
71 A18 1.50m on 45c grn & bl (R) .30 *1.40*
72 A18 2m on 45c grn & bl .50 *2.25*
73 A18 2m on 1fr cl & ol grn .30 *1.40*
74 A18 2¼m on 40c red & pale bl .20 *.75*
75 A18 2½m on 60c vio & ultra .45 *2.25*
76 A18 3m on 60c vio & ultra (R) 1.10 *5.25*
77 A18 4m on 45c grn & bl .20 *.75*
78 A18 5m on 1fr cl & ol grn .30 *1.50*
79 A18 6m on 60c vio & ultra .20 *.75*
80 A18 6m on 2fr org & pale bl .35 *1.50*
81 A18 9m on 1fr cl & ol grn .40 *.75*
82 A18 9m on 5fr bl & buff (R) .40 *2.60*
83 A18 10m on 45c grn & bl (R) .70 *5.00*
84 A18 12m on 40c red & pale bl .25 *1.90*
85 A18 20m on 40c red & pale bl .70 *5.00*
86 A18 20m on 2fr org & pale bl .25 1.90
87 A18 30m on 60c vio & ultra .70 *5.00*
88 A18 30m on 5fr dk bl & buff 2.75 *20.00*
89 A18 40m on 1fr cl & ol grn .70 *6.50*
90 A18 50m on 2fr org & pale bl 11.00 *47.50*
91 A18 80m on 2fr org & pale bl (R) .70 *6.50*
92 A18 100m on 5fr bl & buff .90 *13.50*
Nos. 50-92 (43) 46.70 *262.85*

A 500m on 5fr dark blue and buff was prepared, but not officially issued. Value: unused $950; never hinged $2,400.

For stamps with additional surcharges and overprints see Nos. 93-99, C8-C17, C20-C29.

Nos. 52, 54, 67, 59 Surcharged "Mark"

1922-23
93 A22 10m on 10pf on 10c .90 *7.50*
a. Double surcharge 100.00 *475.00*
94 A22 20m on 20pf on 20c .40 *4.50*
95 A18 40m on 40pf on 40c ('23) .75 *4.50*
96 A20 50m on 50pf on 50c 2.25 *12.50*
Nos. 93-96 (4) 4.30 *29.00*

Nos. 72, 61, 70 Surcharged with New Values in Red or Black

1922-23
97 A18 10m on 2m on 45c 1.90 *12.50*
98 A22 25m on 1m on 25c 1.90 *12.50*
99 A18 80m on 1.25m on 60c (Bk) ('23) 1.10 *7.00*
Nos. 97-99 (3) 4.90 *32.00*

For No. 99 with additional surcharges see Nos. N28-N30.

AIR POST STAMPS

Nos. 24-26, 28, 31, 39-40 Overprinted in Dark Blue

1921, July 6 **Unwmk.** *Perf. 14x13½*
C1 A18 60pf on 40c 40.00 *160.00*
C2 A18 80pf on 45c 3.75 *20.00*
C3 A18 1m on 50c 4.50 *11.50*
C4 A18 2m on 1fr 4.50 *11.50*
a. "Flugpost" inverted 175.00
C5 A18 4m on 2fr (I) 4.25 *20.00*
a. Type II 120.00 *400.00*

New Value with Initial Capital

C6 A18 60Pf on 40c 4.00 *20.00*
a. "Flugpost" inverted 175.00
C7 A18 3M on 60c 3.50 *15.00*
a. "Flugpost" inverted 175.00
Nos. C1-C7 (7) 64.50 *258.00*

The surcharged value on No. C7 is in italics.

Nos. 67-71, 73, 76, 78, 80, 82 Overprinted in Dark Blue

1922, May 12
C8 A18 40pf on 40c .40 *2.75*
C9 A18 80pf on 45c .40 *2.75*
C10 A18 1m on 40c .40 *2.75*
C11 A18 1.25m on 60c .75 *4.75*
C12 A18 1.50m on 45c .75 *4.75*
C13 A18 2m on 1fr .75 *4.75*
C14 A18 3m on 60c .75 *4.75*

C15 A18 5m on 1fr 1.20 *4.75*
C16 A18 6m on 2fr 1.20 *4.75*
C17 A18 9m on 5fr 1.20 *4.75*

Same Overprint On Nos. 40, 31

C18 A18 3m on 60c 120.00 *1,100.*
C19 A18 4m on 2fr .75 *4.00*
Nos. C8-C17,C19 (11) 8.55 *45.50*

Nos. 67, 69-71, 73, 76, 78, 80, 82 Overprinted in Black or Red

1922, Oct. 17

C20 A18 40pf on 40c 1.20 *16.00*
C21 A18 1m on 40c 1.20 *16.00*
C22 A18 1.25m on 60c (R) 1.20 *16.00*
C23 A18 1.50m on 45c (R) 1.20 *16.00*
C24 A18 2m on 1fr 1.20 *16.00*
C25 A18 3m on 60c (R) 1.20 *16.00*
C26 A18 4m on 2fr 1.20 *16.00*
C27 A18 5m on 1fr 1.20 *16.00*
C28 A18 6m on 2fr 1.20 *16.00*
C29 A18 9m on 5fr (R) 1.20 *16.00*
Nos. C20-C29 (10) 12.00 *160.00*

No. C26 is not known without the "FLUGPOST" overprint.

OCCUPATION STAMPS

Issued under Lithuanian Occupation

Surcharged in Various Colors on Unissued Official Stamps of Lithuania Similar to Type O4

On Nos. N1-N6

On Nos. N7-N11

Memel Printing

1923 **Unwmk.** **Litho.** ***Perf. 11***

N1 O4 10m on 5c bl (Bk) 1.20 *12.00*
a. Double overprint 40.00 *275.00*
b. "Memel" and bars omitted 5.75 *60.00*
N2 O4 25m on 5c bl (R) 1.20 *12.00*
a. Double overprint 40.00 *160.00*
N3 O4 50m on 25c red (Bk) 1.20 *12.00*
a. Double overprint 40.00 *275.00*
N4 O4 100m on 25c red (G) 1.20 *12.00*
a. Double overprint 40.00 *275.00*
N5 O4 400m on 1 l brn (R) 1.60 *16.00*
a. Double overprint 40.00 *275.00*
N6 O4 500m on 1 l brn (Bl) 1.60 *16.00*
a. Double overprint 40.00 *275.00*
Nos. N1-N6 (6) 8.00 *80.00*

Kaunas Printing

Black Surcharge

N7 O4 10m on 5c blue .75 *6.75*
N8 O4 25m on 5c blue .75 *6.75*
N9 O4 50m on 25c red .75 *6.75*
N10 O4 100m on 25c red .90 *6.75*
N11 O4 400m on 1 l brn 1.50 *10.50*
Nos. N7-N11 (5) 4.65 *37.50*

No. N8 has the value in "Markes," others of the group have it in "Markiu."

For additional surcharge see No. N87.

Surcharged in Various Colors on Unissued Official Stamps of Lithuania Similar to Type O4

1923

N12 O4 10m on 5c bl (R) 1.60 *9.00*
a. "Markes" instead of "Markiu" 20.00 *100.00*
N13 O4 20m on 5c bl (R) 1.60 *9.00*
N14 O4 25m on 25c red (Bl) 1.60 *12.00*
N15 O4 50m on 25c red (Bl) 3.25 *12.00*
a. Inverted surcharge 40.00 *160.00*
N16 O4 100m on 1 l brn (Bk) 3.25 *16.50*
a. Inverted surcharge 40.00 160.00
N17 O4 200m on 1 l brn (Bk) 4.00 *16.50*
Nos. N12-N17 (6) 15.30 *75.00*

No. N14 has the value in "Markes," others of the group have it in "Markiu."

"Vytis"
O4 O5

1923, Mar.

N18 O4 10m lt brown .40 *6.50*
N19 O4 20m yellow .40 *6.50*
N20 O4 25m orange .40 *7.50*
N21 O4 40m violet .40 *6.50*
N22 O4 50m yellow grn 1.20 *14.50*
N23 O5 100m carmine .55 *6.75*
N24 O5 300m olive grn 6.00 *140.00*
N25 O5 400m olive brn .55 *6.75*
N26 O5 500m lilac 6.00 *140.00*
N27 O5 1000m blue 1.10 *12.00*
Nos. N18-N27 (10) 17.00 *347.00*

No. N20 has the value in "Markes."

For surcharges see Nos. N44-N69, N88-N114.

No. 99 Surcharged in Green

1923, Apr. 13

N28 A18 100m on No. 99 5.00 *72.50*
a. Inverted overprint 110.00
N29 A18 400m on No. 99 5.00 *72.50*
a. Inverted overprint 110.00
N30 A18 500m on No. 99 5.00 *72.50*
a. Inverted overprint 110.00
Nos. N28-N30 (3) 15.00 217.50

The normal position of the green surcharge is sideways, up-reading, with the top at the left. Inverted varieties are reversed, with the overprint down-reading.

Ship — O7

Seal — O8

Lighthouse — O9

1923, Apr. 12 **Litho.**

N31 O7 40m olive grn 3.50 *40.00*
N32 O7 50m brown 3.50 *40.00*
N33 O7 80m green 3.50 *40.00*
N34 O7 100m red 3.50 *40.00*
N35 O8 200m deep blue 3.50 *40.00*
N36 O8 300m brown 3.50 *40.00*
N37 O8 400m lilac 3.50 *40.00*
N38 O8 500m orange 3.50 *40.00*
N39 O8 600m olive grn 3.50 *40.00*
N40 O8 800m deep blue 3.50 *40.00*
N41 O9 1000m lilac 3.50 *40.00*
N42 O9 2000m red 3.50 *40.00*
N43 O9 3000m green 3.50 *40.00*
Nos. N31-N43 (13) 45.50 *520.00*

Union of Memel with Lithuania. Forgeries exist.

For surcharges see Nos. N70-N86.

Nos. N20, N24, N26 Surcharged in Various Colors

1923

Thin Figures

N44 O5 2c on 300m (R) 6.50 *15.00*
a. Double surcharge 80.00 *375.00*
N45 O5 3c on 300m (R) 7.00 *20.00*
a. Double surcharge 175.00 *475.00*
N46 O4 10c on 25m (Bk) 7.00 *15.00*
a. Double surcharge 80.00 *400.00*
b. Inverted surcharge 110.00 *325.00*
N47 O4 15c on 25m (Bk) 7.00 *15.00*
N48 O5 20c on 500m (Bl) 10.50 *32.50*
N49 O5 30c on 500m (Bk) 8.25 *15.00*
a. Double surcharge
N50 O5 50c on 500m (G) 20.00 *32.50*
a. Inverted surcharge 65.00 *240.00*
b. Double surcharge 160.00 *725.00*
Nos. N44-N50 (7) 66.25 *145.00*

Nos. N19, N21-N27 Surcharged:

N51 O4 2c on 20m yellow 3.25 *15.00*
N52 O4 2c on 50c yel grn 3.25 *15.00*
a. Double surcharge 65.00 *325.00*
b. Vert. pair, imperf between 80.00 *350.00*
N53 O4 3c on 40m violet 4.50 *13.50*
a. Double surcharge 65.00 *325.00*
N54 O5 3c on 300m ol grn 3.00 *11.50*
a. Double surcharge 160.00 *550.00*
N55 O5 5c on 100m carmine 7.50 *11.50*
N56 O5 5c on 300m ol grn (R) 3.75 *18.50*
a. Double surcharge 110.00 *400.00*
N57 O5 10c on 400m ol brn 11.50 *22.50*
N58 O5 30c on 500m lilac 6.00 *26.50*
a. Double surcharge 110.00 *400.00*
b. Inverted surcharge 120.00 *450.00*
N59 O5 1 l on 1000m blue 19.00 *67.50*
a. Double surcharge 160.00 *550.00*
Nos. N51-N59 (9) 61.75 *201.50*

There are several types of the numerals in these surcharges. Nos. N56 and N58 have "CENT" in short, thick letters, as on Nos. N44 to N50.

Nos. N18-N23, N25, N27 Surcharged

Thick Figures

N60 O4 2c on 10m lt brn 6.50 *80.00*
N61 O4 2c on 20m yellow 20.00 *140.00*
N62 O4 2c on 50m yel grn 8.00 *95.00*
N63 O4 3c on 10m lt brn 20.00 *130.00*
a. Double surcharge 150.00 *650.00*
N64 O4 3c on 40m violet 24.00 *225.00*
N65 O5 5c on 100m car 12.00 *40.00*
a. Double surcharge 110.00 *350.00*
N66 O5 10c on 400m ol brn 140.00 *675.00*
N67 O4 15c on 25m orange 140.00 *675.00*
N68 O5 50c on 1000m blue 6.00 *12.00*
a. Double surcharge 110.00 *350.00*
N69 O5 1 l on 1000m blue 8.00 *24.00*
a. Double surcharge 110.00 *350.00*
Nos. N60-N69 (10) 384.50 *2,096.*

No. N69 is surcharged like type "b" in the following group.

Nos. N31-N43 Surcharged:

a

b

N70 O7(a) 15c on 40m ol grn 5.50 *32.50*
N71 O7(a) 30c on 50m brown 5.25 *22.50*
a. Double surcharge 65.00 *275.00*
N72 O7(a) 30c on 80m green 5.25 *40.00*
N73 O7(a) 30c on 100m red 5.50 *15.00*
N74 O8(a) 50c on 200m dp blue 6.00 *28.00*
N75 O8(a) 50c on 300m brn 5.25 *20.00*
a. Double surcharge 65.00 *275.00*
b. Inverted surcharge 68.00 *275.00*
N76 O8(a) 50c on 400m lilac 5.50 *28.00*
a. Inverted surcharge 72.50 *325.00*
N77 O8(a) 50c on 500m org 5.50 *15.00*
a. Double surcharge 65.00 *275.00*
N78 O8(b) 1 l on 600m ol grn 5.50 *36.00*
N79 O9(b) 1 l on 800m dp blue 6.50 *36.00*
N80 O9(b) 1 l on 1000m lil 6.00 *36.00*
N81 O9(b) 1 l on 2000m red 6.00 *36.00*
N82 O9(b) 1 l on 3000m grn 6.50 *36.00*
Nos. N70-N82 (13) 74.25 *381.00*

These stamps are said to have been issued to commemorate the institution of autonomous government.

Nos. N32, N34, N36, N38 Surcharged in Green

1923

N83 O7 15c on 50m brn 275. *2,000.*
a. Thick numerals in surcharge *950.* *4,750.*
N84 O7 25c on 100m red 150. *1,200.*
a. Thick numerals in surcharge *550.* *3,250.*
N85 O8 30c on 300m brn 250. *1,300.*
a. Thick numerals in surcharge *725.* *3,500.*
N86 O8 60c on 500m org 150. *1,200.*
a. Thick numerals in surcharge *550.* *2,400.*

Surcharges on Nos. N83-N86 are of two types, differing in width of numerals. Values are for stamps with narrow numerals, as illustrated. Stamps with wide numerals sell for two to four times as much. For detailed listing see the *Scott Classic Specialized Catalogue of Stamps & Covers.*

Nos. N8, N10-N11, N3 Surcharged in Red or Green

N87 O4 10c on 25m on 5c bl (R) 35.00 *120.00*
N88 O4 15c on 100m on 25c red (G) 40.00 *350.00*
a. Inverted surcharge 400.00 *2,250.*
N89 O4 30c on 400m on 1 l brn (R) 17.50 *47.50*
N90 O4 60c on 50m on 25c red (G) 40.00 *325.00*
Nos. N87-N90 (4) 132.50 *842.50*

Nos. N18-N22 Surcharged in Green or Red

N91 O4 15c on 10m 32.50 *210.00*
N92 O4 15c on 20m 3.50 *32.50*
N93 O4 15c on 25m 5.25 *65.00*
N94 O4 15c on 40m 3.50 *32.50*
N95 O4 15c on 50m (R) 2.75 *20.00*
a. Inverted surcharge 65.00 *250.00*
N96 O4 25c on 10m 11.00 *120.00*
N97 O4 25c on 20m 3.50 *32.50*
a. Double surcharge 160.00
N98 O4 25c on 25m 5.25 *47.50*
N99 O4 25c on 40m 4.50 *47.50*
a. Inverted surcharge 60.00
N100 O4 25c on 50m (R) 2.60 *22.50*
a. Inverted surcharge 65.00
N101 O4 30c on 10m 32.50 *200.00*
N102 O4 30c on 20m 3.75 *40.00*
N103 O4 30c on 25m 5.25 *65.00*
N104 O4 30c on 40m 3.75 *24.00*
N105 O4 30c on 50m (R) 2.60 *24.00*
a. Inverted surcharge 65.00
Nos. N91-N105 (15) 122.20 *983.00*

Nos. N23, N25, N27 Surcharged in Green or Red

N106 O5 15c on 100m 2.75 *22.50*
a. Inverted surcharge 60.00
N107 O5 15c on 400m 2.50 *18.50*
N108 O5 15c on 1000m (R) 65.00 *400.00*
a. Inverted surcharge 200.00 *800.00*
N109 O5 25c on 100m 2.50 *22.50*
N110 O5 25c on 400m 2.50 *22.50*
a. Double surcharge 160.00

N111	O5 25c on 1000m (R)	65.00	*400.00*
a.	Inverted surcharge	200.00	*800.00*
N112	O5 30c on 100m	2.60	*22.50*
a.	Inverted surcharge	60.00	
N113	O5 30c on 400m	2.60	*22.50*
N114	O5 30c on 1000m (R)	65.00	*475.00*
a.	Inverted surcharge	200.00	*800.00*
	Nos. N106-N114 (9)	210.45	*1,406.*

Nos. N96 to N100 and N109 to N111 are surcharged "Centai," the others "Centu."

MESOPOTAMIA

ˌme-s(ə-)pə-ˈtā-mē-ə

LOCATION — In Western Asia, bounded on the north by Syria and Turkey, on the east by Persia, on the south by Saudi Arabia and on the west by Trans-Jordan.
GOVT. — A former Turkish Province
AREA — 143,250 (1918) sq. mi.
POP. — 2,849,282 (1920)
CAPITAL — Baghdad

During World War I this territory was occupied by Great Britain. It was recognized as an independent state and placed under British Mandate but in 1932 the Mandate was terminated and the country admitted to membership in the League of Nations as the Kingdom of Iraq. Postage stamps of Iraq are now in use.

16 Annas = 1 Rupee

Watermark

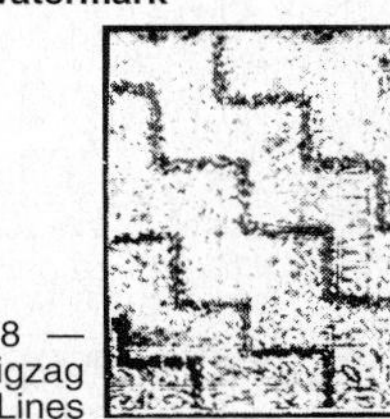

Wmk. 48 — Diagonal Zigzag Lines

Issued under British Occupation

Baghdad Issue

Stamps of Turkey 1901-16 Surcharged

N1

N2

N3

N4

N5

The surcharges were printed from slugs which were arranged to fit the various shapes of the stamps.

1917 Unwmk. *Perf. 12, 13½*

On Turkey Nos. 254, 256, 258-260

N1 ¼a on 2pa red lil 250.00 300.00
a. "IN BRITISH" omitted *12,000.*
N2 ¼a on 5pa vio brown 175.00 185.00
a. "¼ An" omitted *11,000.*
N3 ½a on 10pa green 975.00 *1,250.*
N4 1a on 20pa red 650.00 *750.00*
N5 2a on 1pi blue 300.00 *325.00*
Nos. N1-N5 (5) 2,350. 2,810.

On Turkey No. 249

N6 A22 2a on 1pi ultra 700.00 *875.00*

On Turkey No. 251

N7 A23 ½a on 10pa green 1,850. 2,100.

On Turkey Nos. 272-273

N8 A29 1a on 20pa red 425. *500.*
a. "OCCUPATION" omitted *10,000.*
N9 A30 2a on 1pi blue 5,250. *6,000.*

On Turkey Nos. 346-348

N10 A41 ½a on 10pa car, perf 12½ 700.00 *800.00*
N11 A41 1a on 20pa ultra, perf 12½ 1,500. 2,000.
a. "1 An" omitted *13,000.*
N12 A41 2a on 1pi vio & black, perf 13½ 190.00 *200.00*
a. "BAGHDAD" omitted *9,750.*

On Turkey Nos. 297, 300

N13 A17 ¼a on 5pa purple *10,000.*
N14 A17 2a on 1pi blue 300. 350.

On Turkey No. 306

N15 A18 1a on 20pa car 700.00 *825.00*

On Turkey Nos. 329-331

N16 A22 ½a on 10pa bl grn 175.00 190.00
N17 A22 1a on 20pa car rose 650.00 *700.00*
a. "1 An" omitted *7,000.* *5,750.*
N18 A22 2a on 1pi ultra 190.00 200.00

On Turkey No. 337

N19 A22 1a on 20pa car rose *6,000.* *7,500.*

On Turkey No. P125

N20 A17 1a on 20pa car —

On Turkey Nos. B1, B8

Inscription in crescent is obliterated by another crescent handstamped in violet black on Nos. N21-N27.

N21 A18 ½a on 10pa dull grn 200.00 *250.00*
a. "OCCUPATION" omitted *12,500.*
N22 A21 1a on 20pa car rose 700.00 *750.00*

On Semi-Postal Stamps of 1916

On Turkey No. B29

N23 A21 2a on 1pi ultra 2,500. *2,750.*

No. N25

On Turkey Nos. B33-B34

N24 A22 1a on 20pa car rose 200.00 *250.00*
N25 A22 2a on 1pi ultra 300.00 *350.00*
a. "OCCUPATION" omitted *12,000.*
b. "BAGHDAD" omitted *11,000.*

On Turkey No. B42

N26 A41 ½a on 10pa car, perf 12½ 300.00 *325.00*
a. "BAGHDAD" double *2,500.*

On Turkey No. B38

N27 A11 1a on 10pa on 20pa vio brn 325.00 350.00

Iraq Issue

N28

N29

N30

N32

N33

N34

N35

N36

N37

N38

N39

N40

N41

IRAQ IN BRITISH OCCUPATION 1½An.

N31

Turkey Nos. 256, 258-269 Surcharged

1918-20 *Perf. 12*

N28 ¼a on 5pa vio brn .55 *1.10*
N29 ½a on 10pa grn .75 .20
N30 1a on 20pa red .55 .20
N31 1½a on 5pa vio brn 8.75 5.50
N32 2½a on 1pi blue 1.35 1.50
a. Inverted surcharge *8,500.*
N33 3a on 1½pi car & black 1.60 .25
a. Double surcharge, red & blk *3,500.* *4,500.*
N34 4a on 1¾pi slate & red brn 1.60 .30
a. Center inverted *30,000.*

N35	6a on 2pi grn & black	1.75	2.00
N36	8a on 2½pi org & ol grn	2.25	2.25
N37	12a on 5pi dl vio	2.00	5.00
N38	1r on 10pi red brown	2.50	1.50
N39	2r on 25pi ol grn	8.00	2.75
N40	5r on 50pi car	26.00	30.00
N41	10r on 100pi dp blue	92.50	18.50
	Nos. N28-N41 (14)	150.15	71.05

See #N50-N53. For overprints see #NO1-NO21.

Mosul Issue

A13

A14

A15

A16

A17

A18

A19

1919	**Unwmk.**		***Perf. 11½, 12***
N42 A13	½a on 1pi grn & brn red	2.40	2.10
N43 A14	1a on 20pa *rose*	1.50	1.90
a.	"POSTAGE" omitted		
N44 A15	1a on 20pa *rose*	4.50	4.50
a.	Double surcharge	725.00	

Turkish word at right of tughra ("reshad") is large on No. N43, small on No. N44.

Wmk. Turkish Characters
Perf. 12½

N45 A16	2½a on 1pi vio & yel	1.60	1.60
N46 A17	3a on 20pa grn & yel	75.00	*100.00*

Wmk. 48

N47 A17	3a on 20pa green	1.75	*4.25*
N48 A18	4a on 1pi dull vio	3.50	3.75
a.	Double surcharge	1,100.	
b.	"4" omitted	2,000.	
c.	As "b," double surcharge		
N49 A19	8a on 10pa claret	4.25	*5.50*
a.	Double surcharge	*700.00*	*875.00*
b.	Inverted surcharge	*800.00*	*1,000.*
c.	8a on 1pi dull violet	*3,250.*	
	Nos. N42-N49 (8)	94.50	123.60

Value for No. 49c is for a stamp with the perfs cutting into the design.

Iraq Issue

Types of 1918-20 Issue

1921	**Wmk. 4**		***Perf. 12***
N50 A28	½a on 10pa green	3.25	2.25
N51 A26	1½a on 5pa dp brn	2.50	1.10
N52 A37	2r on 25pi ol grn	24.00	13.00
	Nos. N50-N52 (3)	29.75	16.35

Type of 1918-20 without "Reshad"

1922			**Unwmk.**
N53 A36	1r on 10pi red brn	220.00	26.00

"Reshad" is the small Turkish word at right of the tughra in circle at top center.
For overprint see No. NO22.

OFFICIAL STAMPS

Nos. N29-N41 Overprinted:

1920	**Unwmk.**		***Perf. 12***
NO1 A28	½a on 10pa grn	13.00	2.00
NO2 A29	1a on 20pa red	5.50	.65
NO3 A26	1½a on 5pa vio brown	37.50	2.75
NO4 A30	2½a on 1pi blue	5.50	6.00
NO5 A31	3a on 1½pi car & black	26.00	.85
NO6 A32	4a on 1¾pi sl & red brn	37.50	4.00
NO7 A33	6a on 2pi grn & black	32.50	8.00
NO8 A34	8a on 2½pi org & ol grn	35.00	5.00
NO9 A35	12a on 5pi dull vio	25.00	16.00
NO10 A36	1r on 10pi red brown	32.50	12.00
NO11 A37	2r on 25pi ol green	32.50	17.50
NO12 A38	5r on 50pi car	65.00	48.00
NO13 A39	10r on 100pi dp blue	92.50	*120.00*
	Nos. NO1-NO13 (13)	440.00	242.75

Same Overprint on Types of Regular Issue of 1918-20

1921-22			**Wmk. 4**
NO14 A28	½a on 10pa grn	1.10	1.10
NO15 A29	1a on 20pa red	7.50	1.10
NO16 A26	1½a on 5pa dp brn	3.00	.75
NO17 A32	4a on 1¾pi gray & red brn	2.25	*2.75*
NO18 A33	6a on 2pi grn & black	30.00	*140.00*
NO19 A34	8a on 2½pi org & yel grn	3.50	2.25
NO20 A35	12a on 5pi dl vio	30.00	*85.00*
NO21 A37	2r on 25pi ol grn	85.00	*130.00*
	Nos. NO14-NO21 (8)	162.35	*362.95*

Same Overprint on No. N53

1922			**Unwmk.**
NO22 A36	1r on 10pi red brn	37.50	7.50

MEXICO

'mek-si-ˌkō

LOCATION — Extreme southern part of the North American continent, south of the United States
GOVT. — Republic
AREA — 759,529 sq. mi.
POP. — 100,294,036 (1999 est.)

CAPITAL — Mexico, D.F

8 Reales = 1 Peso
100 Centavos = 1 Peso

Catalogue values for unused stamps in this country are for Never Hinged items, beginning with Scott 792 in the regular postage section, Scott C143 in the airpost section, Scott E8 in the special delivery section, and Scott G4 in the insured letter section.

District Overprints

Nos. 1-149 are overprinted with names of various districts, and sometimes also with district numbers and year dates. Some of the district overprints are rare and command high prices. Values given for Nos. 1-149 are for the more common district overprints.

Watermarks

Wmk. 150 — PAPEL SELLADO in Sheet

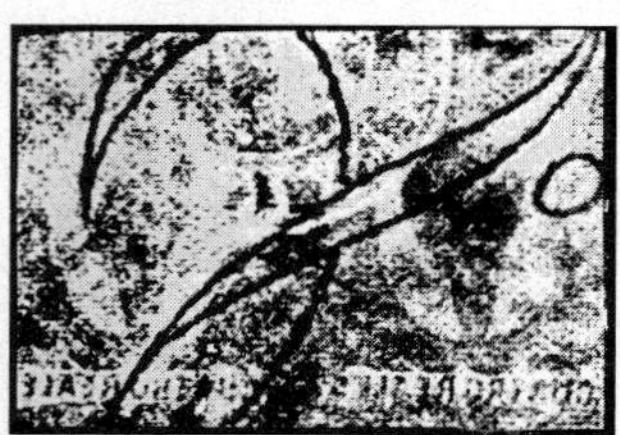
Wmk. 151 — R. P. S. in the Sheet (R.P.S. stands for "Renta Papel Sellado")

Wmk. 152 — "CORREOS E U M" on Every Horizontal Line of Ten Stamps

Wmk. 153 — "R M" Interlaced

Wmk. 154 — Eagle and R M

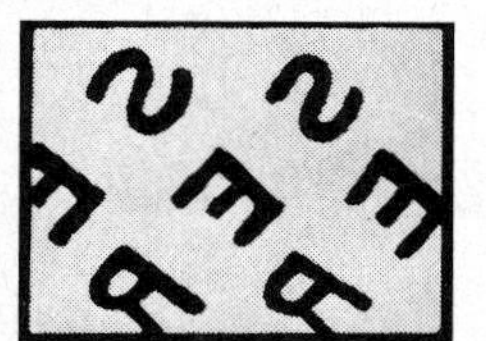
Wmk. 155 — SERVICIO POSTAL DE LOS ESTADOS UNIDOS MEXICANOS

Wmk. 156 — CORREOS MEXICO

Wmk. 248 — SECRETARIA DE HACIENDA MEXICO

Wmk. 260 — Lines and SECRETARIA DE HACIENDA MEXICO

Wmk. 272 — "S. H. C. P. MEXICO" and Eagle in Circle

Wmk. 279 — GOBIERNO MEXICANO and Eagle in Circle

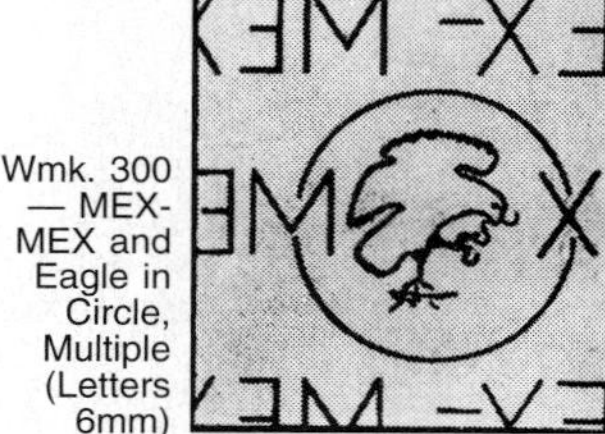
Wmk. 300 — MEX-MEX and Eagle in Circle, Multiple (Letters 6mm)

Wmk. 350 — MEX and Eagle in Circle, Multiple. Letters 8-9mm

Miguel Hidalgo y Costilla — A1

Handstamped with District Name

1856 Unwmk. Engr. *Imperf.*

No.	Stamp	Unused	Used
1	A1 ½r blue	50.00	40.00
b.	Without overprint	45.00	45.00
2	A1 1r yellow	30.00	5.00
b.	Half used as ½r on cover		10,000.
c.	Without overprint	25.00	30.00
d.	1r green (error)		
3	A1 2r yellow grn	27.50	3.50
a.	2r blue green	275.00	40.00
b.	2r emerald	250.00	50.00
c.	Half used as 1r on cover		600.00
d.	Without overprint	40.00	22.50
e.	As "a," without overprint	250.00	45.00
f.	As "b," without overprint		75.00
g.	Printed on both sides (yel green)	300.00	
4	A1 4r red	175.00	110.00
a.	Half used as 2r on cover		250.00
b.	Quarter used as 1r on cover		700.00
c.	Without overprint	140.00	160.00
d.	Three quarters used as 3r on cover		12,000.
5	A1 8r red lilac	350.00	200.00
a.	8r violet	300.00	200.00
b.	Without overprint	225.00	225.00
c.	Eighth used as 1r on cover		17,500.
d.	Quarter used as 2r on cover		225.00
e.	Half used as 4r on cover		900.00
	Nos. 1-5 (5)	632.50	358.50

The 1r and 2r were printed in sheets of 60 with wide spacing between stamps, and in sheets of 190 or 200 with narrow spacing.

No. 3a can be distinguished from the other 2r stamps by the horizontal grain of the paper. The plate for No. 3b has framelines.

All values, except the 1r, have been reprinted, some of them several times. The reprints usually show signs of wear and the impressions are often smudgy. The paper is usually thicker than that of the originals. Reprints are usually on very white paper. Reprints are found with and without overprints and with cancellations made both from the original handstamps and from forged ones.

Counterfeits exist.

See Nos. 6-12. For overprints see Nos. 35-45.

1861

No.	Stamp	Unused	Used
6	A1 ½r black, *buff*	50.00	45.00
a.	Without overprint	34.00	62.50
7	A1 1r black, *green*	20.00	5.50
a.	Impression of 2r on back		450.00
b.	Without overprint	5.00	22.50
d.	As "b," blk, *pink* (error)	8,000	9,000.
f.	Double impression		150.00
8	A1 2r black, *pink*	15.00	4.50
a.	Impression of 1r on back	2,000.	
b.	Half used as 1r on cover		750.00
c.	Without overprint	3.50	22.50
d.	Printed on both sides		2,250.
e.	Double impression		100.00
f.	As "e," without overprint		—
9	A1 4r black, *yellow*	200.00	100.00
a.	Half used as 2r on cover		190.00
b.	Without overprint	50.00	100.00
c.	Quarter used as 1r on cover		700.00
d.	Three-quarters used as 3r on cover		35,000.
10	A1 4r dull rose, *yel*	200.00	70.00
a.	Half used as 2r on cover		950.00
b.	Without overprint	110.00	140.00
c.	Printed on both sides		9,000.
d.	Quarter used as 1r on cover		10,000.
11	A1 8r black, *red brn*	375.00	250.00
a.	⅛ used as 1R on cover front		11,000.
b.	Quarter used as 2r on cover		250.00
c.	Half used as 4r on cover		750.00
d.	Without overprint	110.00	225.00
e.	Three quarters used as 6r on cover		45,000.
12	A1 8r grn, *red brn*	500.00	240.00
a.	Half used as 4r on cover		30,000.
b.	Without overprint	150.00	200.00
c.	Quarter used as 2r on cover		40,000.
d.	Printed on both sides	12,500.	12,500.
	Nos. 6-12 (7)	1,360.	715.00

Nos. 6, 9, 10, 11 and 12 have been reprinted. Most reprints of the ½r, 4r and 8r are on vertically grained paper. Originals are on horizontally grained paper. The original ½r stamps are much worn but the reprints are unworn. The paper of the 4r is too deep and rich in color and No. 10 is printed in too bright red.

Reprints of the 8r can only be told by experts. All these reprints are found in fancy colors and with overprints and cancellations as in the 1856 issue.

Counterfeits exist.

Hidalgo — A3

Coat of Arms — A4

With District Name

1864 *Perf. 12*

No.	Stamp	Unused	Used
14	A3 1r red	750.	3,000.
a.	Without District Name	.75	
15	A3 2r blue	550.	1,000.
a.	Without District Name	.75	
16	A3 4r brown	1,250.	2,400.
a.	Without District Name	1.25	
b.	Vert. pair, imperf. between		
17	A3 1p black	3,250.	22,500.
a.	Without District Name	2.00	

Nos. 14 to 17 were issued with district overprints of Saltillo or Monterrey on the toned paper of 1864. Overprints on the 1867 white paper are fraudulent. Counterfeits and counterfeit cancellations are plentiful. The 1r red with "½" surcharge is bogus.

Overprint of District Name, etc.

1864-66 *Imperf.*

Five types of overprints:

I — District name only.

II — District name, consignment number and "1864" in large figures.

III — District name, number and "1864" in small figures.

IV — District name, number and "1865."

V — District name, number and "1866."

No.	Stamp	Unused	Used
18	A4 3c brn (IV, V)	1,300.	2,500.
a.	Without overprint	700.00	
b.	Laid paper	4,500.	6,000.
19	A4 ½r brown (I)	400.00	250.00
a.	Type II	2,200.	2,250.
b.	Without overprint	200.00	650.00
20	A4 ½r lilac (IV)	60.00	55.00
a.	Type III	140.00	75.00
b.	Type II	200.00	200.00
c.	Type V		3,000.
d.	½r gray (V)	70.00	80.00
e.	Without overprint	5.75	
f.	½r gray lilac	250.00	100.00
21	A4 1r blue (IV, V)	15.00	9.00
a.	Type III	80.00	40.00
b.	Without overprint	2.50	
c.	Half used as ½r on cover		3,000.
22	A4 1r ultra (I, II)	120.00	30.00
a.	Type III	90.00	40.00
b.	Without overprint	160.00	150.00
c.	Half used as ½r on cover		7,250.
23	A4 2r org (III, IV, V)	10.00	4.00
a.	Type II	20.00	6.00
b.	Type I	50.00	7.00
c.	2r dp org, without ovpt., early plate	175.00	65.00
d.	Without ovpt., late plate	2.00	
e.	Half used as 1r on cover		6,000.
24	A4 4r grn (III, IV, V)	100.00	50.00
a.	Types I, II	160.00	77.50
b.	4r dk grn, without ovpt.	4.75	1,700.
d.	Half used as 2r on cover		700.00
25	A4 8r red (IV, V)	150.00	90.00
a.	Types II, III	175.00	125.00
b.	Type I	400.00	175.00
c.	8r dk red, without ovpt.	7.00	575.00
f.	Quarter used as 2r on cover		15,000.
g.	Three-quarters used as 6r on cover		

The 2r printings from the early plates are 25½mm high; those from the late plate, 24½mm.

Varieties listed as "Without overprint" in unused condition are remainders.

Besides the overprints of district name, number and date, Nos. 18-34 often received, in the district offices, additional overprints of numbers and sometimes year dates. Stamps with these "sub-consignment numbers" sell for more than stamps without them.

Genuine examples of No. 20c should bear Mexico district name overprint, together with consignment numbers 1-1866 or 17-1866. Gray lilac stamps of other consignments are examples of No. 20f.

Value unused for No. 18 is for an example without gum. Examples with original gum sell for more. Examples of No. 18a on laid paper are forgeries.

No. 25g does not exist on full cover.

Faked quarterlings and bisects of 1856-64 are plentiful.

The 3c has been reprinted from a die on which the words "TRES CENTAVOS," the outlines of the serpent and some of the background lines have been retouched.

Emperor Maximilian — A5

Overprinted with District Name, Number and Date 1866 or 866; also with Number and Date only, or with Name only

1866 Litho.

No.	Stamp	Unused	Used
26	A5 7c lilac gray	65.00	125.00
a.	7c deep gray	85.00	140.00
27	A5 13c blue	35.00	35.00
a.	Half used as 7c on cover		—
b.	13c cobalt blue	25.00	25.00
c.	Without overprint	2,500.	
28	A5 25c buff	12.50	9.00
a.	Half used as 13c on cover		—
b.	Without overprint	2,500.	
29	A5 25c orange	12.00	12.00
a.	25c red orange	20.00	27.50
b.	25c red brown	85.00	47.50
c.	25c brown	110.00	85.00
30	A5 50c green	25.00	30.00
	Nos. 26-30 (5)	149.50	211.00

Litho. printings have round period after value numerals.

Overprinted with District Name, Number and Date 866 or 867; also with Number and Date only

Engr.

No.	Stamp	Unused	Used
31	A5 7c lilac	450.00	5,500.
a.	Without overprint	3.50	
32	A5 13c blue	12.00	12.00
a.	Without overprint	1.25	
33	A5 25c orange brown	12.00	11.00
a.	Without overprint	1.25	
34	A5 50c green	700.00	70.00
a.	Without overprint	2.50	

See "sub-consignment" note after No. 25.

Engraved printings have square period after value numerals.

Varieties listed as "Without overprint" in unused condition are remainders.

1867

No.	Stamp	Unused	Used
35	A1 ½r blk, *buff*	2,500.	4,000.
36	A1 1r blk, *green*	60.00	10.00
37	A1 2r blk, *pink*	22.50	5.00
a.	Printed on both sides		140.00
38	A1 4r red, *yel*	625.00	50.00
a.	Printed on both sides		175.00
39	A1 4r red	6,000.	3,250.
40	A1 8r blk, *red brn*	3,500.	275.00
41	A1 8r grn, *red brn*		4,000.

Dangerous counterfeits exist of the "Mexico" overprint.

Examples of No. 38 with yellow removed are offered as No. 39.

Same Overprint Thin Gray Blue Paper Wmk. 151

No.	Stamp	Unused	Used
42	A1 ½r gray	275.00	190.00
a.	Without overprint	175.00	175.00
43	A1 1r blue	400.00	65.00
b.	Without overprint	300.00	125.00
44	A1 2r green	200.00	30.00
a.	Printed on both sides	6,000.	3,500.
b.	Without overprint	300.00	50.00
45	A1 4r rose	3,000.	75.00
a.	Without overprint	5,000.	225.00

Most examples of Nos. 42-45 do not show the watermark. Values are for such stamps. Examples showing the watermark sell for more.

Reprints of the ½r and 4r exist on watermarked paper. Reprints of ½r and 8r also exist in gray on thick grayish wove paper, unwatermarked.

Hidalgo — A6

Thin Figures of Value, without Period after Numerals

6 CENT. 12 CENT.

25 CENT. 50 CENT.

100 CENT.

Overprinted with District Name, Number and Abbreviated Date

1868 Unwmk. Litho. *Imperf.*

No.	Stamp	Unused	Used
46	A6 6c blk, *buff*	40.00	20.00
47	A6 12c blk, *green*	45.00	20.00
a.	Period after "12"	65.00	55.00
48	A6 25c bl, *pink*	75.00	20.00
a.	Without overprint	125.00	
49	A6 50c blk, *yellow*	600.00	60.00
50	A6 100c blk, *brown*	775.00	140.00
51	A6 100c brn, *brn*	1,750.	500.00

Perf.

No.	Stamp	Unused	Used
52	A6 6c blk, *buff*	35.00	35.00
a.	Without overprint	150.00	
b.	Period after "6"	100.00	75.00
53	A6 12c blk, *green*	35.00	12.00
a.	Period after "12"	85.00	30.00
b.	Very thick paper	50.00	25.00
c.	Without overprint	110.00	
54	A6 25c blue, *pink*	55.00	10.00
b.	Without overprint	150.00	
55	A6 50c blk, *yellow*	325.00	45.00
56	A6 100c blk, *brown*	375.00	110.00
c.	Without overprint	350.00	
57	A6 100c brn, *brn*	1,000.	375.00
a.	Printed on both sides	1,250.	1,000.

Four kinds of perforation are found in the 1868 issue: serrate, square, pin and regular. The narrow spacing between stamps was inadequate for some of these perforation types.

Thick Figures of Value, with Period after Numerals

6.CENT. 12.CENT
25.CENT. 50.CENT.
100.CENT

Overprinted with District Name, Number and Abbreviated Date

Imperf

58 A6 6c blk, *buff* 9.50 4.50
59 A6 12c blk, *green* 4.25 1.25
a. Very thick paper 10.00
c. 12c black, *buff* (error) 575.00 575.00
d. Printed on both sides *3,000.*
e. No period after "12" —
61 A6 25c blue, *pink* 8.00 1.25
a. No period after "25" 90.00
c. Very thick paper 25.00 6.00
d. "85" for "25" 75.00 50.00
e. "35" for "25" 75.00
f. Printed on both sides —
62 A6 50c blk, *yellow* 125.00 15.00
a. No period after "50" 225.00 35.00
b. 50c blue, *lt pink* (error) *3,000.* *2,000.*
c. Half used as 25c on cover 1,000.
d. Very thick paper 50.00
e. "30" for "50" 750.00 750.00
64 A6 100c blk, *brown* 150.00 90.00
a. No period after "100" 175.00 100.00
b. Very thick paper 75.00
c. Quarter used as 25c on cover *2,000.*
Nos. 58-64 (5) 296.75 112.00

Perf.

65 A6 6c blk, *buff* 40.00 20.00
a. Very thick paper 60.00 35.00
66 A6 12c blk, *green* 5.50 5.50
a. Very thick paper 20.00 15.00
b. 12c black, *buff* (error) 575.00 575.00
c. No period after "12" —
68 A6 25c blue, *pink* 20.00 2.50
a. No period after "25" 80.00 80.00
c. Thick paper 30.00 15.00
d. "85" for "25" 80.00 40.00
69 A6 50c blk, *yellow* 200.00 25.00
a. No period after "50" 200.00 30.00
b. 50c blue, *lt pink* (error) *2,500.* *1,500.*
c. Thick paper 60.00
70 A6 100c blk, *brown* 200.00 60.00
a. No period after "100" 200.00 65.00
b. Very thick paper 80.00
Nos. 65-70 (5) 465.50 113.00

Postal forgeries of Nos. 58-70 were printed from original plates with district name overprints forged. These include the pelure paper varieties and some thick paper varieties. The "Anotado" handstamp was applied to some of the confiscated forgeries and they were issued, including Nos. 73a and 78a.

Stamps of 1868 Handstamped

Overprinted with District Name, Number and Abbreviated Date Thick Figures with Period

1872 *Imperf.*

71 A6 6c blk, *buff* 650.00 675.00
72 A6 12c blk, *green* 85.00 75.00
73 A6 25c bl, *pink* 40.00 45.00
a. Pelure paper 55.00 65.00
b. "85" for "25" 125.00
74 A6 50c blk, *yellow* 850.00 475.00
a. No period after "50" 900.00 475.00
75 A6 100c blk, *brown* 1,250. 1,000.
a. No period after "100" 1,100.

Perf.

76 A6 6c blk, *buff* 750.00
77 A6 12c blk, *green* 90.00 80.00
78 A6 25c blue, *pink* 35.00 42.50
a. Pelure paper 65.00 90.00
79 A6 50c blk, *yellow* 850.00 600.00
a. No period after "50" 550.00
80 A6 100c blk, *brown* 1,200.

Counterfeit "Anotado" overprints abound. Genuine cancellations other than Mexico City or of the Diligencias de Puebla are unknown. It is recommended that these be purchased accompanied by certificates of authenticity from competent experts.

The stamps of the 1872 issue are found perforated with square holes, pin-perf. 13, 14 or 15, and with serrate perforation.

Counterfeits of the 1868 6c, 12c buff, 50c and 100c (both colors) from new plates have clear, sharp impressions and more facial shading lines than the originals. These counterfeits are found perf. and imperf., with thick and thin numerals, and with the "Anotado" overprint.

Hidalgo — A8

Moiré on White Back Overprinted with District Name, Number and Abbreviated Date White Wove Paper

1872 Litho. Wmk. 150 *Imperf.*

81 A8 6c green 150.00 120.00
82 A8 12c blue 100.00 70.00
a. Laid paper 2,000. 350.00
83 A8 25c red 250.00 50.00
a. Laid paper 2,000. 350.00
84 A8 50c yellow 950.00 500.00
a. 50c blue (error) 3,000.
b. Laid paper 4,000.
c. As "a," without ovpt. 130.00
86 A8 100c gray lilac 700.00 400.00
Nos. 81-86 (5) 2,150. 1,140.

Wmk. "LA + F"

81a A8 6c green 500.00 250.00
82b A8 12c blue 325.00 125.00
83b A8 25c red 425.00 95.00
c. Without overprint 500.00
84d A8 50c yellow 3,000. 1,200.
86a A8 100c gray lilac 1,800. 750.00

1872 Wmk. 150 *Pin-perf.*

87 A8 6c green 850.00 850.00
88 A8 12c blue 125.00 100.00
89 A8 25c red 275.00 90.00
b. Laid paper 1,000.
90 A8 50c yellow 1,300. 650.00
a. 50c blue (error) *1,000.* *1,250.*
b. As "a," without overprint 200.00
92 A8 100c gray lilac 750.00 600.00
Nos. 87-92 (5) 3,300. 2,290.

Wmk. "LA + F"

87a A8 6c green 950.00 950.00
88a A8 12c blue 325.00 *350.00*
89a A8 25c red 900.00 225.00
90c A8 50c yellow 2,600. 2,200.
92a A8 100c gray lilac 2,000. 1,350.

The watermark "LA+F" stands for La Croix Frères, the paper manufacturers, and is in double-lined block capitals 13mm high. A single stamp will show only part of this watermark.

Values for Nos. 87-92a are for examples with visible perfs on all sides.

1872 Unwmk. *Imperf.*

93 A8 6c green 12.50 12.50
a. Without moiré on back, without overprint 60.00 65.00
b. Vertically laid paper 3,000. 1,300.
c. Bottom label retouched 100.00 90.00
d. Very thick paper 37.50 37.50
94 A8 12c blue 2.00 1.75
a. Without moiré on back, without overprint 30.00 35.00
b. Vertically laid paper 350.00 210.00
c. Thin gray bl paper of 1867 (Wmk 151) 2,000.
95 A8 25c red 8.50 2.00
a. Without moiré on back, without overprint 30.00 35.00
b. Vertically laid paper 450.00 500.00
c. Thin gray bl paper of 1867 (Wmk 151) 1,500.
96 A8 50c yellow 140.00 35.00
a. 50c orange 140.00 35.00
b. Without moiré on back, without overprint 50.00 70.00
c. Vertically laid paper 2,000.
d. 50c blue (error) 650.00
e. As "d," without overprint 45.00
f. As "e," without moiré on back 65.00
g. Half used as 25c on cover *5,000.*
98 A8 100c gray lilac 90.00 50.00
a. 100c lilac 100.00 42.50
b. Without moiré on back, without overprint 50.00 110.00
c. Vertically laid paper 1,250.
Nos. 93-98 (5) 253.00 101.25

Counterfeits of these stamps are 24½mm high instead of 24mm. The printing is sharper and more uniform than the genuine. Forged district names and consignment numbers exist.

Pin-perf. and Serrate Perf.

99 A8 6c green 90.00 75.00
100 A8 12c blue 3.50 3.00
a. Vertically laid paper 350.00
b. Horiz. pair, imperf. vert. 100.00 100.00
c. Vert. pair, imperf. between 150.00
101 A8 25c red 3.25 1.50
a. Vertically laid paper 500.00
b. Horiz. pair, imperf. vert. 100.00 100.00
102 A8 50c yellow 175.00 50.00
a. 50c orange 160.00 50.00
b. 50c blue (error) 475.00 500.00
c. As "b," without overprint 45.00
104 A8 100c lilac 150.00 80.00
a. 100c gray lilac 125.00 80.00
Nos. 99-104 (5) 421.75 209.50

Values for Nos. 99-104a are for examples with visible perfs on all sides.

Hidalgo
A9 A10

A11

A12

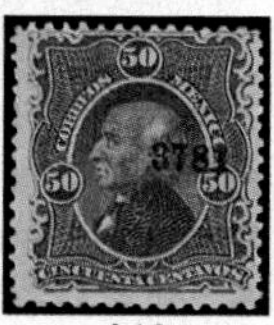

A13

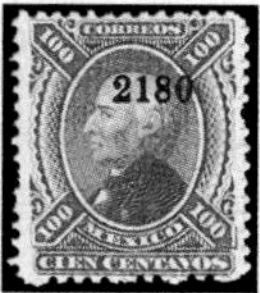

A14

Overprinted with District Name and Number and Date; also with Number and Date only Thick Wove Paper, Some Showing Vertical Ribbing

1874-80 Unwmk. Engr. *Perf. 12*

105 A9 4c org ('80) 12.50 12.00
a. Vert. pair, imperf. btwn. 60.00
b. Without overprint 6.50 12.50
c. Half used as 2c on cover 1,000.
106 A10 5c brown 4.50 3.00
a. Horizontally laid paper 100.00 55.00
b. Imperf., pair 60.00
c. Horiz. pair, imperf. btwn. 50.00 300.00
d. Vert. pair, imperf. btwn. 110.00 110.00
e. Without overprint 37.50 37.50
f. As "a," wmkd. "LACROIX" 350.00 200.00
107 A11 10c black 2.00 1.25
a. Horizontally laid paper 2.50 2.50
b. Horiz. pair, imperf. btwn. 75.00 75.00
c. Without overprint 35.00 27.50
d. Half used as 5c on cover 2,000.
e. Imperf., pair
f. As "a," wmkd. "LACROIX" 70.00 50.00
108 A11 10c org ('78) 2.00 1.25
a. 10c yellow bister 7.50 4.25
b. Imperf., pair
c. Without overprint 55.00 55.00
d. Half used as 5c on cover 100.00
109 A12 25c blue .85 .70
b. Horizontally laid paper 2.25 1.75
c. Imperf., pair 50.00 25.00
d. Without overprint 35.00 20.00
e. Horiz. pair, imperf. btwn. 125.00
f. As "b," horiz. pair, imperf. vert. 200.00
g. As "b," wmkd. "LACROIX" 60.00 50.00
h. Printed on both sides 1,500.
i. Half used as 10c on cover 2,000.
110 A13 50c green 13.00 13.00
a. Without overprint 50.00
b. Half used as 25c on cover 2,500.
111 A14 100c carmine 18.00 15.00
a. Imperf., pair 200.00 200.00
b. Without overprint 50.00
c. Quarter used as 25c on cover 3,000.
Nos. 105-111 (7) 52.85 46.20

The "LACROIX" watermark is spelled out "LACROIX FRERES" in 2 lines of block capitals without serifs once to a sheet of horiz. laid paper.6-12 stamps may have a portion of the wmk.

1875-77 Wmk. 150

112 A10 5c brown 55.00 35.00
113 A11 10c black 55.00 35.00
114 A12 25c blue 55.00 32.50
115 A13 50c green 325.00 225.00
116 A14 100c carmine 300.00 200.00
Nos. 112-116 (5) 790.00 527.50

1881 Unwmk. Thin Wove Paper

117 A9 4c orange 70.00 70.00
a. Without overprint 20.00 20.00
118 A10 5c brown 10.00 6.50
a. Without overprint .50 20.00
b. As "a," vert. pair, imperf. horiz. 1,000.
119 A11 10c orange 6.00 3.50
a. Imperf., pair
b. Vert. pair, imperf. horiz.
c. Without overprint .75 4.50
d. Vert. pair, imperf. btwn.
e. Half used as 5c on cover 1,500.
120 A12 25c blue 4.00 2.25
a. Imperf., pair 100.00
b. Without overprint .50 8.00
c. Double impression 65.00
d. Printed on both sides *1,500.*
121 A13 50c green 45.00 40.00
a. Without overprint 4.00 30.00
122 A14 100c carmine 50.00 50.00
a. Without overprint 6.00 300.00

The stamps of 1874-81 are found with number and date wide apart, close together or omitted, and in various colors.

The thin paper is fragile and easily damaged. Values for Nos. 117-122 are for undamaged, fine examples.

Benito Juárez — A15

Overprinted with District Name and Number and Date; also with Number and Date only Thick Wove Paper, Some Showing Vertical Ribbing

1879 *Perf. 12*

123 A15 1c brown 4.00 4.00
a. Without overprint 75.00 140.00
b. 1c gray 20.00 15.00
124 A15 2c dk violet 4.00 4.50
a. Without overprint 75.00 150.00
b. Printed on both sides
c. 2c dark gray 20.00 14.00
125 A15 5c orange 2.25 1.50
a. Without overprint 75.00 90.00
b. Double impression *500.00*
126 A15 10c blue 3.00 2.50
a. Without overprint 75.00 150.00
b. 10c ultra 160.00 160.00
127 A15 25c rose 8.00 30.00
a. Without overprint 1.75 150.00
128 A15 50c green 15.00 50.00
a. Without overprint 1.25 150.00
b. Printed on both sides 165.00
129 A15 85c violet 20.00 250.00
a. Without overprint 2.50
130 A15 100c black 25.00 75.00
a. Without overprint 3.00 150.00
Nos. 123-130 (8) 81.25 417.50

Used values for Nos. 127-130 are for stamps with postal cancellations. Pen cancelled examples are worth the same as unused stamps.

Forged cancellations on Nos. 127-130 are plentiful.

1882

Thin Wove Paper

131 A15 1c brown 40.00 37.50
a. Without overprint 125.00
132 A15 2c dk violet 27.50 24.00
a. 2c slate 47.50 50.00
b. Without overprint 110.00
c. Half used as 1c on cover
133 A15 5c orange 9.00 6.00
a. Without overprint 1.25
b. Half used as 2c on cover
c. As "a," vert. pair, imperf. btwn.
134 A15 10c blue 9.00 6.00
a. Without overprint 1.25
b. Half used as 5c on cover
135 A15 10c brown 9.00
a. Imperf., pair 3.00
136 A15 12c brown 7.50 8.00
a. Without overprint 2.50 22.50
b. Imperf., pair 75.00
c. Half used as 6c on cover
137 A15 18c orange brn 9.00 15.00
a. Horiz. pair, imperf. btwn. 100.00
b. Without overprint 2.25 18.00
138 A15 24c violet 9.00 11.00
a. Without overprint 2.25 17.50
139 A15 25c rose 45.00 250.00
a. Without overprint 4.50
140 A15 25c orange brn 5.50
141 A15 50c green 45.00 75.00
a. Without overprint 6.25
142 A15 50c yellow 80.00 350.00
a. Without overprint 150.00
143 A15 85c red violet 55.00
144 A15 100c black 75.00 *250.00*
a. Without overprint 5.00
b. Vert. pair, imperf. btwn. 165.00 165.00
145 A15 100c orange 95.00 400.00
a. Without overprint 175.00
Nos. 131-145 (15) 520.50 1,432.

No. 135, 140 and 143 exist only without overprint. They were never placed in use.

Used values for Nos. 139, 141, 142, 144 and 145 are for postally used stamps. Forged cancellations are plentiful. Pen cancelled examples are worth the same as unused stamps.

See note on thin paper after No. 122.

A16

Overprinted with District Name, Number and Abbreviated Date

1882-83

146 A16 2c green 11.00 8.00
a. Without overprint 27.50 20.00
147 A16 3c car lake 11.00 8.00
a. Without overprint 5.25 8.50
148 A16 6c blue ('83) 30.00 40.00
a. Without overprint 30.00 50.00
149 A16 6c ultra 6.00 8.50
a. Without overprint 3.50 6.00
b. As "a," imperf pair 50.00
Nos. 146-149 (4) 58.00 64.50

See note on thin paper after No. 122.

Hidalgo — A17

1884 Wove or Laid Paper *Perf. 12*

150 A17 1c green 4.00 .75
a. Imperf., pair 32.50
b. 1c blue (error) 600.00 475.00
151 A17 2c green 6.75 2.00
a. Imperf., pair 60.00 55.00
b. Half used as 1c on cover
152 A17 3c green 12.50 2.00
a. Imperf., pair 110.00 90.00
b. Horiz. pair, imperf. vert. 125.00 125.00
153 A17 4c green 16.00 2.00
a. Imperf., pair 75.00 65.00
b. Half used as 2c on cover 200.00
154 A17 5c green 17.50 1.50
a. Imperf., pair 110.00 90.00
155 A17 6c green 15.00 1.50
a. Imperf., pair 75.00 65.00
156 A17 10c green 16.00 .75
a. Imperf., pair 75.00 70.00
157 A17 12c green 30.00 3.50
a. Vert. pair, imperf. between 75.00 60.00
b. Half used as 6c on cover 125.00
158 A17 20c green 90.00 2.50
a. Diagonal half used as 10c on cover 200.00
b. Imperf., pair 160.00 125.00
159 A17 25c green 150.00 5.00
a. Imperf., pair 250.00 200.00
160 A17 50c green .60 *5.00*
a. Imperf., pair 25.00 20.00
161 A17 1p blue .60 *11.00*
a. Imperf., pair 60.00 45.00
b. Vert. pair, imperf. between 100.00
162 A17 2p blue .60 *22.50*
a. Imperf., pair 75.00 60.00
163 A17 5p blue 350.00 300.00
164 A17 10p blue 500.00 225.00
Nos. 150-162 (13) 359.55 *60.00*

Imperforate varieties should be purchased in pairs or larger. Single imperforates are usually trimmed perforated stamps.

Beware of examples of No. 150 that have been chemically changed to resemble No. 150b.

Forged cancels on Nos. 161-162 are plentiful.

Some values exist perf. 11.

See Nos. 165-173, 230-231.

1885

165 A17 1c pale green 35.00 7.00
166 A17 2c carmine 25.00 3.50
a. Diagonal half used as 1c on cover 100.00
167 A17 3c orange brn 25.00 6.00
a. Imperf., pair 100.00 100.00
168 A17 4c red orange 42.50 19.00
169 A17 5c ultra 27.50 3.50
170 A17 6c dk brown 32.50 6.00
a. Half used as 3c on cover 210.00
171 A17 10c orange 27.50 1.50
a. 10c yellow 30.00 1.50
b. Horiz. pair, imperf. btwn. 100.00 100.00
172 A17 12c olive brn 57.50 9.00
173 A17 25c grnsh blue 225.00 22.50
Nos. 165-173 (9) 497.50 78.00

Numeral of Value — A18

1886 *Perf. 12*

174 A18 1c yellow green 2.25 .75
a. 1c blue grn 5.50 4.50
b. Horiz. pair, imperf. btwn. 75.00 60.00
c. Perf. 11 45.00 45.00
175 A18 2c carmine 2.60 .90
a. Horiz. pair, imperf. btwn. 80.00 75.00
b. Vert. pair, imperf. between 75.00 75.00
c. Perf. 11 45.00 45.00
d. Half used as 1c on cover 100.00
176 A18 3c lilac 12.00 7.50
177 A18 4c lilac 18.00 5.25
a. Perf. 11 50.00 *55.00*
178 A18 5c ultra 2.25 1.00
a. 5c blue 2.25 .75
179 A18 6c lilac 30.00 7.50
180 A18 10c lilac 22.50 1.10
a. Perf. 11 125.00
181 A18 12c lilac 25.00 14.00
182 A18 20c lilac 190.00 110.00
183 A18 25c lilac 75.00 19.00
Nos. 174-183 (10) 379.60 167.00

Nos. 175, 191, 194B, 196, 202 exist with blue or black surcharge "Vale 1 Cvo." These were made by the Colima postmaster.

1887

184 A18 3c scarlet 1.90 .60
a. Imperf., pair 75.00
185 A18 4c scarlet 7.50 2.25
186 A18 6c scarlet 12.50 2.25
a. Horiz. pair, imperf. btwn. 75.00
187 A18 10c scarlet 2.75 .60
a. Imperf., pair 75.00
b. Horiz. pair, imperf. btwn. 45.00
188 A18 20c scarlet 18.00 1.50
a. Horiz. pair, imperf. btwn. 75.00
189 A18 25c scarlet 15.00 4.00
Nos. 184-189 (6) 57.65 11.20

Perf. 6

190 A18 1c blue grn 45.00 45.00
191 A18 2c brown car 22.50 42.00
192 A18 5c ultra 15.00 4.50
a. 5c blue 15.00 4.50
193 A18 10c lilac 15.00 4.25
193A A18 10c brown lilac 15.00 3.00
194 A18 10c scarlet 35.00 15.00

Perf. 6x12

194A A18 1c blue grn 62.50 42.50
194B A18 2c brown car 85.00 75.00
194C A18 3c scarlet 300.00 350.00
194D A18 5c ultra 60.00 45.00
194E A18 10c lilac 90.00 75.00
194F A18 10c scarlet 80.00 60.00
194G A18 10c brown lilac 90.00 75.00

Many shades exist.

Paper with colored ruled lines on face or reverse of stamp

1887 *Perf. 12*

195 A18 1c green 75.00 45.00
196 A18 2c brown car 190.00 47.50
198 A18 5c ultra 110.00 30.00
199 A18 10c scarlet 110.00 25.00

Perf. 6

201 A18 1c green 60.00 20.00
202 A18 2c brown car 60.00 24.00
204 A18 5c ultra 50.00 12.00
205 A18 10c brown lil 42.50 10.00
206 A18 10c scarlet 250.00 40.00
Nos. 201-206 (5) 462.50 106.00

Perf. 6x12

207 A18 1c green 225.00 140.00
208 A18 2c brown car 325.00 140.00
209 A18 5c ultra 225.00 140.00
210 A18 10c brown lil 290.00 135.00
211 A18 10c scarlet 350.00 225.00
Nos. 207-211 (5) 1,415. 780.00

1890-95 Wmk. 152 *Perf. 11 & 12*

Wove or Laid Paper

212 A18 1c yellow grn .75 .35
a. 1c blue green .75 .35
b. Horiz. pair, imperf. btwn. 35.00 35.00
c. Laid paper 2.50 2.50
d. Horiz. pair, imperf. vert. 35.00 35.00
213 A18 2c carmine 1.50 .75
a. 2c brown car 1.25 1.00
b. Vert. pair, imperf. btwn. 150.00
c. Imperf., pair 200.00
214 A18 3c vermilion 1.00 .60
b. Horiz. pair, imperf. btwn. 80.00
215 A18 4c vermilion 3.25 2.10
a. Horiz. pair, imperf. btwn. 80.00
216 A18 5c ultra .60 .50
a. 5c dull blue 1.00 .50
217 A18 6c vermilion 3.75 2.75
a. Horiz. pair, imperf. btwn. 45.00
218 A18 10c vermilion .50 .35
b. Horiz. or vert. pair, imperf. btwn. 45.00 45.00
c. Vert. pair, imperf. horiz. 45.00
d. Imperf., pair 50.00
219 A18 12c ver ('95) 14.00 18.00
220 A18 20c vermilion 3.50 1.50
220A A18 20c dk violet 160.00 *190.00*
221 A18 25c vermilion 5.00 2.50
Nos. 212-220,221 (10) 33.85 29.40

No. 219 has been reprinted in slightly darker shade than the original.

1892

222 A18 3c orange 4.00 2.00
223 A18 4c orange 4.25 3.00
224 A18 6c orange 5.75 2.00
225 A18 10c orange 27.50 2.00
226 A18 20c orange 50.00 6.00
227 A18 25c orange 16.00 4.50
Nos. 222-227 (6) 107.50 19.50

1892

228 A18 5p carmine 1,250. 900.
229 A18 10p carmine 1,900. 1,250.
230 A17 5p blue green 3,500. 1,200.
231 A17 10p blue green *7,000. 2,700.*

1894 *Perf. 5½, 6*

232 A18 1c yellow grn 3.00 3.00
233 A18 3c vermilion 9.00 9.00
234 A18 4c vermilion 40.00 37.50
235 A18 5c ultra 12.50 5.00
236 A18 10c vermilion 7.50 3.00
236A A18 20c vermilion 110.00 110.00
237 A18 25c vermilion 62.50 62.50
Nos. 232-237 (7) 244.50 230.00

Perf. 5½x11, 11x5½, Compound and Irregular

238 A18 1c yellow grn 7.00 7.00
238A A18 2c brown car 16.00 16.00
238B A18 3c vermilion 47.50 32.50
238C A18 4c vermilion 55.00 55.00
239 A18 5c ultra 17.50 12.50
a. 5c blue 12.50 12.50
239C A18 6c vermilion 75.00 75.00
240 A18 10c vermilion 20.00 7.00
240A A18 20c vermilion 200.00 200.00
241 A18 25c vermilion 62.50 62.50
Nos. 238-241 (9) 500.50 467.50

The stamps of the 1890 to 1895 issues are also to be found unwatermarked, as part of the sheet frequently escaped the watermark.

Letter Carrier — A20

Mounted Courier with Pack Mule — A21

Statue of Cuauhtémoc A22

Mail Coach A23

Mail Train — A24

Regular or Pin Perf. 12

1895 Wmk. 152

Wove or Laid Paper

242 A20 1c green 3.00 .75
a. Vert. pair, imperf. horiz. 100.00
d. Watermarked sideway ('97) 125.00 15.00
243 A20 2c carmine 3.75 1.00
a. Half used as 1c on cover 50.00
c. Watermarked sideways ('97) 80.00 10.00
244 A20 3c orange brown 3.75 1.00
a. Vert. pair, imperf. horiz. 80.00
d. Watermarked sideways ('97) 125.00 10.00
246 A21 4c orange 12.50 1.50
a. 4c orange red 7.50 1.25
247 A22 5c ultra 7.00 .35
a. Imperf., pair 50.00 50.00
b. Horiz. or vert. pair, imperf. between 65.00 50.00
e. Half used as 2c on cover 60.00
f. Watermarked sideways ('97) 15.00 5.00
248 A23 10c lilac rose 4.50 1.00
a. Horiz. or vert. pair, imperf. between 75.00
b. Half used as 5c on cover 60.00

No.	Type	Description	Unused	Used
249	A21	12c olive brown	50.00	12.50
251	A23	15c brt blue	27.50	3.00
b.		Watermarked sideways ('97)		100.00
252	A23	20c brown rose	32.50	3.00
b.		Half used as 10c on cover		60.00
c.		Watermarked sideways ('97)	1,000.	750.00
253	A23	50c purple	70.00	16.00
a.		Half used as 25c on cover		100.00
254	A24	1p brown	90.00	35.00
a.		Watermarked sideways ('97)	750.00	*900.00*
255	A24	5p scarlet	300.00	190.00
256	A24	10p deep blue	650.00	350.00
		Nos. 242-256 (13)	1,254.	615.10

No. 248 exists in perf. 11.

Nos. 242d, 243c, 244d, 247f, 251b, 252c and 254a was a special printing, made in Jan. 1897. The watermark is sideways, the grain of the paper is horizontal (rather than vertical, as appears on Nos. 242-256), and the design is somewhat shorter than the other stamps in this series. The sideways orientation of the watermark is the most easily identifable feature of this printing.

Important: For unwatermarked examples of Nos. 242-256, see the footnote after No. 291.

Perf. 6

No.	Type	Description	Unused	Used
242b	A20	1c green	60.00	35.00
243b	A20	2c carmine	125.00	60.00
244b	A20	3c orange brown	90.00	50.00
247c	A22	5c ultra	90.00	50.00
248c	A23	10c lilac rose	125.00	55.00
249a	A21	12c olive brown	100.00	50.00

Perf. 6x12, 12x6 & Compound or Irregular

No.	Type	Description	Unused	Used
242c	A20	1c green	30.00	20.00
244c	A20	3c orange brown	35.00	20.00
246b	A21	4c orange	75.00	50.00
247d	A22	5c ultra	75.00	50.00
248d	A23	10c lilac rose	35.00	20.00
249b	A21	12c olive brown	50.00	25.00
251a	A23	15c brt blue	60.00	40.00
252a	A23	20c brown rose	100.00	70.00
253b	A23	50c purple	150.00	100.00

See Nos. 257-291. For overprints see Nos. O10-O48A.

"Irregular" Perfs.

Some stamps perf. 6x12, 12x6, 5½x11 and 11x5½ have both perf. 6 and 12 or perf. 5½ and 11 on one or more sides of the stamp. These are known as irregular perfs.

1896-97 Wmk. 153 *Perf. 12*

No.	Type	Description	Unused	Used
257	A20	1c green	14.00	1.25
c.		Imperf., pair		250.00
258	A20	2c carmine	17.50	1.50
a.		Horiz. pair, imperf. vert.		
259	A20	3c orange brn	20.00	1.50
260	A21	4c orange	32.50	1.75
c.		4c deep orange	30.00	6.00
261	A22	5c ultra	9.00	1.25
a.		Imperf., pair	60.00	
b.		Vert. pair, imperf. btwn.	120.00	
262	A21	12c olive brn	160.00	80.00
263	A23	15c brt blue	200.00	13.00
264	A23	20c brown rose	750.00	275.00
265	A23	50c purple	175.00	110.00
266	A24	1p brown	300.00	250.00
267	A24	5p scarlet	800.00	600.00
268	A24	10p dp blue	900.00	525.00
		Nos. 257-268 (12)	3,378.	1,860.

Perf. 6

No.	Type	Description	Unused	Used
257a	A20	1c green	35.00	25.00
259a	A20	3c orange brown	35.00	20.00
260a	A21	4c orange	40.00	25.00
261c	A22	5c ultra	110.00	70.00
263a	A23	15c bright blue	75.00	35.00

Perf. 6x12, 12x6 and Compound or Irregular

No.	Type	Description	Unused	Used
257b	A20	1c green	25.00	20.00
258b	A20	2c carmine	50.00	25.00
259b	A20	3c orange brown	40.00	20.00
260b	A21	4c orange	45.00	20.00
261d	A22	5c ultra	40.00	20.00
262a	A21	12c olive brown	125.00	80.00
263b	A23	15c bright blue	250.00	125.00
264a	A23	20c brown rose		
265a	A23	50c purple		

1897-98 Wmk. 154 *Perf. 12*

No.	Type	Description	Unused	Used
269	A20	1c green	20.00	3.00
270	A20	2c scarlet	35.00	4.50
271	A21	4c orange	52.50	3.75
a.		Horizontal pair, imperf. vertical		—
272	A22	5c ultra	50.00	3.75
a.		Imperf., pair	85.00	
273	A21	12c olive brown	200.00	45.00
275	A23	15c brt blue	275.00	85.00
276	A23	20c brown rose	175.00	15.00
277	A23	50c purple	375.00	75.00
278	A24	1p brown	425.00	200.00
278A	A24	5p scarlet	—	—
		Nos. 269-278 (9)	1,607.	435.00

Perf. 6

No.	Type	Description	Unused	Used
269a	A20	1c green	45.00	25.00
270a	A20	2c scarlet	45.00	25.00
272b	A22	5c ultra	60.00	25.00
273a	A21	12c olive brown	110.00	60.00
276a	A23	20c brown rose		*650.00*

Perf. 6x12, 12x6 and Compound or Irregular

No.	Type	Description	Unused	Used
269b	A20	1c green	25.00	15.00
270b	A20	2c scarlet	30.00	22.50
271b	A21	4c orange	65.00	12.50
272c	A22	5c ultra	50.00	15.00
273b	A21	12c olive brown	125.00	65.00
275a	A23	15c bright blue	125.00	65.00
276b	A23	20c brown rose	240.00	30.00
277a	A23	50c purple	125.00	50.00

1898 Unwmk. *Perf. 12*

No.	Type	Description	Unused	Used
279	A20	1c green	3.00	.50
a.		Horiz. pair, imperf vert	300.00	
b.		Imperf., pair	100.00	
280	A20	2c scarlet	6.25	.75
a.		2c green (error)	*475.00*	
281	A20	3c orange brn	6.00	.75
a.		Imperf., pair	150.00	150.00
b.		Pair, imperf. between	80.00	80.00
282	A21	4c orange	30.00	3.00
b.		4c deep orange	37.50	7.00
283	A22	5c ultra	2.00	.50
a.		Imperf., pair	50.00	50.00
b.		Pair, imperf. between	125.00	
284	A23	10c lilac rose	550.00	175.00
285	A21	12c olive brn	80.00	27.50
a.		Imperf., pair	200.00	
286	A23	15c brt blue	175.00	8.00
287	A23	20c brown rose	35.00	3.00
a.		Imperf., pair	200.00	
288	A23	50c purple	150.00	42.50
289	A24	1p brown	175.00	80.00
290	A24	5p carmine rose	550.00	425.00
291	A24	10p deep blue	800.00	575.00
		Nos. 279-291 (13)	2,562.	1,341.

Warning: Sheets of Nos. 242-256 (watermarked "CORREOS E U M") have a column of stamps without watermarks, because the watermark did not fit the sheet size. As a result, be careful not to confuse unwatermarked examples of Nos. 242-256 with Nos. 279-291. This is especialy important for No. 284. Nos. 242-256 and the watermarked 1895-97 overprinted Officials, Nos. O10-O39, have a vertical grain or mesh to the paper. Nos. 279-291 and the unwatermarked 1898 overprinted Officials, Nos. O40-O48B, have a horizontal grain or mesh to the paper. Be careful not to confuse unwatermarked examples of Nos. O10-O39 with Nos. O40-O48B.

Perf. 6

No.	Type	Description	Unused	Used
279c	A20	1c green	85.00	35.00
280b	A20	2c scarlet	75.00	30.00
281c	A20	3c orange brown	50.00	35.00
283c	A22	5c ultra	65.00	30.00
287b	A23	20c brown rose	125.00	75.00
291a	A24	10p deep blue		

Perf. 6x12, 12x6 and Compound or Irregular

No.	Type	Description	Unused	Used
279d	A20	1c green	25.00	20.00
280c	A20	2c scarlet	25.00	20.00
281d	A20	3c orange brown	30.00	20.00
282a	A21	4c orange	40.00	25.00
283d	A22	5c ultra	20.00	10.00
284a	A23	10c lilac rose	125.00	85.00
285b	A21	12c olive brown	90.00	60.00
286a	A23	15c bright blue	75.00	50.00
287c	A23	20c brown rose	100.00	50.00
288a	A23	50c purple	575.00	575.00

Forgeries of the 6 and 6x12 perforations of 1895-98 are plentiful.

Coat of Arms

A25 A26

A27 A28

A29

A30

A31

Juanacatlán Falls — A32

View of Mt. Popocatépetl A33

Cathedral, Mexico, D. F. — A34

1899, Nov. 1 Wmk. 155 *Perf. 14, 15*

No.	Type	Description	Unused	Used
294	A25	1c green	1.90	.35
295	A26	2c vermilion	4.50	.35
296	A27	3c orange brn	3.00	.35
297	A28	5c dark blue	4.75	.35
298	A29	10c violet & org	6.00	.35
299	A30	15c lav & claret	8.00	.35
300	A31	20c rose & dk bl	9.00	.40
301	A32	50c red lil & blk	35.00	2.25
a.		50c lilac & black	42.50	2.25
302	A33	1p blue & blk	80.00	3.50
303	A34	5p carmine & blk	275.00	12.00
		Nos. 294-303 (10)	427.15	20.25
		Set, never hinged	1,500.	

See Nos. 304-305, 307-309. For overprints see Nos. 420-422, 439-450, 452-454, 482-483, 515-516, 539, 550, O49-O60, O62-O66, O68-O74, O101.

A35

1903

No.	Type	Description	Unused	Used
304	A25	1c violet	1.50	.35
305	A26	2c green	2.00	.35
306	A35	4c carmine	5.00	.45
307	A28	5c orange	1.25	.35
308	A29	10c blue & org	5.00	.35
309	A32	50c carmine & blk	75.00	6.50
		Nos. 304-309 (6)	89.75	8.35
		Set, never hinged	350.00	

For overprints see Nos. 451, O61, O67.

Independence Issue

Josefa Ortiz — A36

Leona Vicario — A37

López Rayón — A38

Juan Aldama — A39

Miguel Hidalgo — A40

Ignacio Allende — A41

Epigmenio González A42

Mariano Abasolo A43

Declaration of Independence A44

Mass on the Mount of Crosses A45

Capture of Granaditas A46

1910 *Perf. 14*

No.	Type	Description	Unused	Used
310	A36	1c dull violet	.35	.35
311	A37	2c green	.35	.35
312	A38	3c orange brn	.60	.35
313	A39	4c carmine	2.50	.45
314	A40	5c orange	.35	.35
315	A41	10c blue & org	1.50	.35
316	A42	15c gray bl & cl	8.00	.50
317	A43	20c red & bl	5.00	.40
318	A44	50c red brn & blk	12.00	1.60
319	A45	1p blue & blk	15.00	2.00
320	A46	5p car & blk	57.50	16.50
		Nos. 310-320 (11)	103.15	23.20
		Set, never hinged	325.00	

Independence of Mexico from Spain, cent.

For overprints and surcharges see Nos. 370-380, 423-433, 455-465, 484-494, 517-538, 540-549, 551-558, 577-590, O75-O85, O102-O112, O191-O192, O195, RA13, Merida 1.

CIVIL WAR ISSUES

During the 1913-16 Civil War, provisional issues with various handstamped overprints were circulated in limited areas.

Sonora

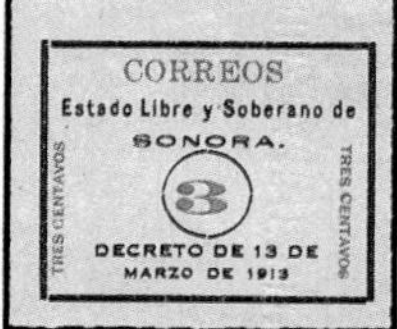

A47

Seal

Typeset in a row of five varieties. Two impressions placed tête bêche (foot to foot) constitute a sheet. The settings show various wrong font and defective letters, "!" for "1" in "1913," etc. The paper occasionally has a manufacturer's watermark.

a *b* *c* *d*

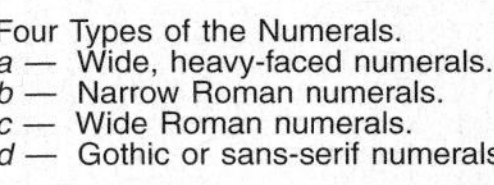

Four Types of the Numerals.
a — Wide, heavy-faced numerals.
b — Narrow Roman numerals.
c — Wide Roman numerals.
d — Gothic or sans-serif numerals.

Nos. 321-346 Issued Without Gum

Embossed "CONSTITUCIONAL"

1913 Typeset Unwmk. *Perf. 12*

321	A47 (a)	5c black & red	*4,250.*	800.00
a.		"CENTAVOB"	*4,750.*	*850.00*

Colorless Roulette

322	A47(b)	1c black & red	22.00	25.00
a.		With green seal	*1,500.*	*1,250.*
323	A47(a)	2c black & red	18.00	15.00
a.		With green seal	*2,000.*	*2,000.*
324	A47(c)	2c black & red	87.50	72.50
a.		With green seal	*5,000.*	*5,000.*
325	A47(a)	3c black & red	97.50	77.50
a.		With green seal	*750.00*	*750.00*
326	A47(a)	5c black & red	190.00	77.50
a.		"CENTAVOB"	200.00	50.00
327	A47(d)	5c black & red	1,200.	350.00
a.		With green seal		*1,000.*
328	A47(b)	10c black & red	35.00	*37.50*

Black Roulette

329	A47(d)	5c black & red	300.00	140.00
a.		"MARO"	87.50	52.50

Stamps are known with the embossing double or omitted.

The varieties with green seal are from a few sheets embossed "Constitucional" which were in stock at the time the green seal control was adopted.

Nos. 322-329 are known with "Peerless Mills" papermaker's watermark.

Without Embossing
With Green Seal
Colorless Roulette

336	A47(b)	1c black & red	15.00	10.00
337	A47(a)	3c black & red	14.50	9.00
a.		Imperf.	*350.00*	
338	A47(a)	5c black & red	750.00	250.00
a.		"CENTAVOB"	*800.00*	275.00
339	A47(b)	10c black & red	8.00	7.50

Colored Roulette

340	A47(d)	5c brnsh blk & red	25.00	6.00
a.		5c lilac brown & red	75.00	22.50
b.		Double seal		*1,250.*
c.		Red printing omitted		*1,000.*

1913-14 *Black Roulette*
With Green Seal

341	A47(a)	1c black & red	4.00	4.00
b.		"erano" ('14)	100.00	60.00
342	A47(d)	2c black & red	4.50	4.00
a.		"erano" ('14)	30.00	35.00
343	A47(a)	3c black & red	4.75	4.00
a.		"CENTAVO"	25.00	25.00
b.		"erano" ('14)	35.00	35.00
344	A47(d)	5c black & red	4.75	4.00
b.		Heavy black penetrating roulette	2.75	1.75
c.		As "b," "MARO"	10.50	5.00
d.		Without green seal	*2,250.*	
		Nos. 341-344 (4)	18.00	16.00

Stamps without seal are unfinished remainders.

On Nos. 341-344 the rouletting cuts the paper slightly or not at all. On Nos. 344b-344c the rouletting is heavy, cutting deeply into the paper.

1914

345	A47(a)	5c black & red	5.00	5.00
346	A47(b)	10c black & red	4.25	5.00

Coat of Arms — A49

Revenue Stamps Used for Postage

1913 Litho. *Rouletted 14, 14x7*

347	A49	1c yellow grn	2.00	*2.50*
a.		With coupon	7.00	6.00
348	A49	2c violet	3.50	*4.00*
a.		With coupon	17.50	14.50
349	A49	5c brown	.60	*.75*
a.		With coupon	2.00	1.50
350	A49	10c claret	2.50	*3.50*
a.		With coupon	15.00	12.00
351	A49	20c gray grn	3.00	*3.50*
a.		With coupon	20.00	18.00
352	A49	50c ultra	11.00	*16.00*
a.		With coupon	60.00	47.50
353	A49	1p orange	45.00	*55.00*
a.		With coupon	175.00	120.00
		Nos. 347-353 (7)	67.60	85.25
		Set, never hinged	275.00	

For a short time these stamps (called "Ejercitos") were used for postage with coupon attached. Later this was required to be removed unless they were to be used for revenue. Stamps overprinted with district names are revenues. Values above 1p were used for revenue. Imperfs exist of all values, but were not issued.

Many examples do not have gum because of a flood.

Use of typeset Sonora revenue stamps for postage was not authorized or allowed.

Coat of Arms
A50 A51

5c (A50): "CINCO CENTAVOS" 14x2mm

1914 *Rouletted 9½x14*

354	A50	1c deep blue	.45	.45
355	A50	2c yellow grn	.60	.35
a.		2c green	3.00	1.75
356	A50	4c blue vio	11.00	2.50
a.		Horiz. pair, imperf. btwn.	250.00	
357	A50	5c gray grn	11.00	3.00
a.		Horiz. pair imperf. btwn.	250.00	
358	A50	10c red	.45	.45
359	A50	20c yellow brn	.60	.60
a.		20c deep brown	2.25	2.25
b.		Horiz. pair, imperf. btwn.	250.00	
360	A50	50c claret	2.50	3.50
a.		Horiz. pair, imperf. btwn.	250.00	
361	A50	1p brt violet	14.00	16.00
a.		Horiz. pair, imperf. btwn.	250.00	
		Nos. 354-361 (8)	40.60	26.85
		Set, never hinged	175.00	

Nos. 354-361 (called "Transitorios") exist imperf. but were not regularly issued.

Many examples do not have gum because of a flood.

See Note after No. 465.

See No. 369. For overprints see Nos. 362-368, 559-565.

Overprinted in Black

1914

362	A50	1c deep blue	200.00	175.00
363	A50	2c yellow green	225.00	200.00
364	A50	4c blue violet	250.00	300.00
365	A50	5c gray green	35.00	50.00
a.		Horiz. pair, imperf. btwn.	550.00	
366	A50	10c red	150.00	150.00
367	A50	20c yellow brn	*2,500.*	*2,500.*
368	A50	50c claret	*3,500.*	*3,500.*

Values are for stamps with design close to, or just touching, the perfs.

Excellent counterfeits of this overprint exist.

Redrawn
"CINCO CENTAVOS" 16x2½mm

1914 *Perf. 12*

369	A51	5c gray green	1.00	.35

Imperfs are printers' waste.

Regular Issue of 1910 Overprinted in Violet, Magenta, Black or Green

1914 Wmk. 155 *Perf. 14*

370	A36	1c dull violet	1.50	.60
371	A37	2c green	3.00	1.25
372	A38	3c orange brn	3.00	1.25
373	A39	4c carmine	5.00	2.00
374	A40	5c orange	1.00	.35
375	A41	10c blue & org	6.00	2.00
376	A42	15c gray bl & cl	10.00	3.00
377	A43	20c red & blue	20.00	6.00
378	A44	50c red brn & blk	25.00	8.00
379	A45	1p blue & blk	55.00	11.00
380	A46	5p carmine & blk	190.00	160.00
		Nos. 370-380 (11)	319.50	195.45
		Set, never hinged	1,000.	

Overprinted On Postage Due Stamps of 1908

381	D1	1c blue	27.50	*30.00*
382	D1	2c blue	27.50	*30.00*
383	D1	4c blue	27.50	*30.00*
384	D1	5c blue	27.50	*30.00*
385	D1	10c blue	27.50	*30.00*
		Nos. 381-385 (5)	137.50	150.00
		Set, never hinged	375.00	

This overprint is found double, inverted, sideways and in pairs with and without the overprint.

There are two or more types of this overprint.

The Postage Due Stamps and similar groups of them which follow were issued and used as regular postage stamps.

Values are for stamps where the overprint is clear enough to be expertised.

Counterfeits abound.

A52

A53

1914 Unwmk. Litho. *Perf. 12*

386	A52	1c pale blue	.35	.50
387	A52	2c light green	.35	.45
388	A52	3c orange	.50	.50
389	A52	5c deep rose	.50	.35
390	A52	10c rose	.70	.85
391	A52	15c rose lilac	1.20	1.75
392	A52	50c yellow	2.00	2.50
a.		50c ocher	1.75	
393	A52	1p violet	8.50	12.00
		Nos. 386-393 (8)	14.10	18.90
		Set, never hinged	50.00	

Nos. 386-393, are known imperforate.

This set is usually called the Denver Issue because it was printed there.

See Note after No. 465.

For overprints and surcharges see Nos. 566-573, 591-592.

Revenue Stamps Used for Postage

1914, July *Perf. 12*

No.	Type	Description	Unused	Used
393A	A53	1c rose	40.00	
393B	A53	2c lt green	35.00	
393C	A53	3c lt orange	75.00	
393D	A53	5c red	15.00	
393E	A53	10c gray green	70.00	
393F	A53	25c blue	150.00	
		Nos. 393A-393F (6)	385.00	

Nos. 393A-393F were used in the northeast. Values are for examples with postal cancellations.

Unused examples are to be considered as revenues.

Pres. Madero

Stamps in this design, featuring Pres. Madero, within a frame very similar to that of the Denver Issue (Nos. 386-393), were ordered in 1915 by Francisco Villa, to be used by the Constitutionalist government. Five values (1c green, 2c brown, 3c carmine, 5c blue, and 10c yellow) were printed by Ellis Brothers & Co., El Paso, Texas. By the time of the stamps' arrival in Mexico City, the Constitutionalist regime had fallen, and the new Conventionist government returned them to the printer, who later sold the unissued stamps within the philatelic market. Value, set $10.

Background as A55 — A54

A55

Nos. 394-410 Issued Without Gum

1914 *Imperf.*

Values and Inscriptions in Black

Inscribed "SONORA"

No.	Type	Description	Unused	Used
394	A54	1c blue & red	.35	.35
a.		Double seal		
b.		Without seal	20.00	
395	A54	2c green & org	.35	.35
a.		Without seal	100.00	
396	A54	5c yellow & grn	.35	.35
a.		5c orange & green	1.50	1.25
b.		Without seal		*300.00*
397	A54	10c lt bl & red	3.50	1.75
a.		10c blue & red	40.00	15.00
398	A54	20c yellow & grn	1.75	2.00
399	A54	20c orange & bl	15.00	17.50
400	A54	50c green & org	1.25	1.25
		Nos. 394-400 (7)	22.55	23.55

Shades. Stamps of type A54 are usually termed the "Coach Seal Issue."

Inscribed "DISTRITO SUR DE LA BAJA CAL"

No.	Type	Description	Unused	Used
401	A54	1c yellow & blue	2.00	*30.00*
a.		Without seal	50.00	
402	A54	2c gray & ol grn	2.50	*25.00*
403	A54	5c olive & rose	2.00	*20.00*
a.		Without seal	50.00	
404	A54	10c pale red & dl vio	2.00	*20.00*
a.		Without seal	50.00	
		Nos. 401-404 (4)	8.50	95.00

Counterfeit cancellations exist.

Inscribed "SONORA"

No.	Type	Description	Unused	Used
405	A55	1c blue & red	6.00	
a.		Without seal	50.00	
406	A55	2c green & org	.50	
407	A55	5c yellow & grn	.50	*2.50*
a.		Without seal	75.00	
408	A55	10c blue & red	.50	*2.50*
409	A55	20c yellow & grn	75.00	*15.00*
a.		Without seal	95.00	
b.		Double seal	*80.00*	
		Nos. 405-409 (5)	*82.50*	*20.00*

With "PLATA" added to the inscription

No.	Type	Description	Unused	Used
410	A55	1c blue & red	1.00	
a.		"PLATA" inverted	60.00	
b.		Pair, one without "PLATA"	15.00	
411	A55	10c blue & red	1.00	
412	A55	20c yellow & grn	2.50	
a.		"PLATA" double	50.00	
413	A55	50c gray grn & org	1.75	
a.		Without seal	1.00	
b.		As "a," "P" of "PLATA" missing	150.00	
		Nos. 410-413 (4)	6.25	

Stamps of type A55 are termed the "Anvil Seal Issue".

Nos. 394-413 were issued without gum.

Nos. 410-413 were not placed in use.

Oaxaca

Coat of Arms — A56

5c:

Type I — Thick numerals, 2mm wide.

Type II — Thin numerals, 1 ½mm wide.

Perf. 8½ to 14

1915 **Typo.** **Unwmk.**

No.	Type	Description	Unused	Used
414	A56	1c dull violet	2.00	1.25
415	A56	2c emerald	3.00	2.25
a.		Inverted numeral	30.00	
e.		Numeral omitted	35.00	
416	A56	3c red brown	4.00	3.50
b.		Inverted numeral	30.00	
417	A56	5c org (type I)	77.50	77.50
a.		Tête bêche pair	175.00	175.00
418	A56	5c org (type II)	.50	.75
a.		Types I and II in pair	70.00	
419	A56	10c blue & car	4.00	4.00
		Nos. 414-419 (6)	91.00	89.25
		Set, never hinged	275.00	

Many printing errors, imperfs and part perfs exist. Mostly these are printers' waste, private reprints or counterfeits.

Nos. 414-419 printed on backs of post office receipt forms.

Regular Issues of 1899-1910 Overprinted in Black

1914 **Wmk. 155** *Perf. 14*

On Issues of 1899-1903

No.	Type	Description	Unused	Used
420	A28	5c orange		
421	A30	15c lav & claret	250.00	250.00
		Never hinged	700.00	
422	A31	20c rose & dk bl	*1,000.*	500.00

Counterfeits exist.

The listing of No. 420 is being re-evaluated. The Catalogue Editors would appreciate any information on the stamp.

On Issue of 1910

No.	Type	Description	Unused	Used
423	A36	1c dull violet	.35	.35
424	A37	2c green	.35	.35
425	A38	3c orange brown	.40	.40
426	A39	4c carmine	.50	.50
427	A40	5c orange	.35	.35
428	A41	10c blue & orange	.35	.35
429	A42	15c gray bl & claret	.70	.60
430	A43	20c red & blue	.75	.70

Overprinted

No.	Type	Description	Unused	Used
431	A44	50c red brn & blk	1.75	1.50
432	A45	1p blue & blk	8.00	5.50
433	A46	5p carmine & blk	42.50	32.50
		Nos. 423-433 (11)	56.00	43.10
		Set, never hinged	170.00	

In the first setting of the overprint on 1c to 20c, the variety "GONSTITUCIONALISTA" occurs 4 times in each sheet of 100. In the second setting it occurs on the last stamp in each row of 10.

The overprint exists reading downward on Nos. 423-430; inverted on Nos. 431-433; double on Nos. 423-425, 427.

See Note after No. 465.

Postage Due Stamps of 1908 Overprinted

No.	Type	Description	Unused	Used
434	D1	1c blue	4.75	5.00
435	D1	2c blue	6.00	5.00
436	D1	4c blue	25.00	25.00
437	D1	5c blue	25.00	25.00
438	D1	10c blue	5.50	5.00
a.		Double overprint		
		Nos. 434-438 (5)	66.25	65.00
		Set, never hinged	200.00	

Preceding Issues Overprinted

This is usually called the "Villa" monogram. Counterfeits abound.

1915

On Issue of 1899

No.	Type	Description	Unused	Used
439	A25	1c green	*210.00*	
440	A26	2c vermilion	*210.00*	
441	A27	3c orange brn	*175.00*	
442	A28	5c dark blue	*210.00*	
443	A29	10c violet & org	*210.00*	
444	A30	15c lav & claret	*750.00*	750.00
445	A31	20c rose & bl	*1,000.*	—
446	A32	50c red lil & blk	*500.00*	—
447	A33	1p blue & blk	*500.00*	
448	A34	5p car & blk	*750.00*	—
		Nos. 439-448 (10)	*4,515.*	

On Issue of 1903

No.	Type	Description	Unused	Used
449	A25	1c violet	*200.00*	
450	A26	2c green	*200.00*	
451	A35	4c carmine	*200.00*	
452	A28	5c orange	45.00	
a.		Inverted overprint	*75.00*	
453	A29	10c blue & org	*750.00*	—
454	A32	50c car & blk	—	—
		Nos. 449-453 (5)	*1,395.*	

In Sept. 1915 Postmaster Hinojosa ordered a special printing of Nos. 439-454 (as valued) for sale to collectors. Earlier a small quantity of Nos. 444-445, 448 and 452-454 was regularly issued. They are hard to distinguish and sell for much more. Counterfeits abound.

On Issue of 1910

No.	Type	Description	Unused	Used
455	A36	1c dull violet	.85	1.00
456	A37	2c green	.40	.60
457	A38	3c orange brown	.60	.75
458	A39	4c carmine	4.00	4.50
459	A40	5c orange	.35	.35
460	A41	10c blue & orange	7.00	7.50
461	A42	15c gray bl & cl	3.00	4.00
462	A43	20c red & blue	5.50	7.00
463	A44	50c red brn & blk	13.00	14.00
464	A45	1p blue & blk	17.00	20.00
465	A46	5p carmine & blk	*150.00*	
		Nos. 455-464 (10)	51.70	59.70
		Nos. 455-464, never hinged	175.00	

Nos. 455-465 are known with overprint inverted, double and other variations. Most were ordered by Postmaster General Hinojosa for philtelic purposes. They were sold at a premium. This applies to Nos. 354-361, 386-393, 431-433 with this monogram as well.

Overprinted On Postage Due Stamps of 1908

No.	Type	Description	Unused	Used
466	D1	1c blue	15.00	20.00
467	D1	2c blue	15.00	20.00
468	D1	4c blue	15.00	20.00
469	D1	5c blue	15.00	20.00
470	D1	10c blue	15.00	20.00
		Nos. 466-470 (5)	75.00	100.00
		Set, never hinged	225.00	

Nos. 466 to 470 are known with inverted overprint. All other values of the 1899 and 1903 issues exist with this overprint. See note after No. 465.

Issues of 1899-1910 Overprinted

This is called the "Carranza" or small monogram. Counterfeits abound.

On Issues of 1899-1903

No.	Type	Description	Unused	Used
482	A28	5c orange	40.00	20.00
		Never hinged	125.00	
483	A30	15c lav & claret	200.00	80.00
		Never hinged	650.00	

On Issue of 1910

No.	Type	Description	Unused	Used
484	A36	1c dull violet	.70	.70
485	A37	2c green	.70	.60
486	A38	3c orange brn	.75	.75
487	A39	4c carmine	2.00	2.00
488	A40	5c orange	.35	.35
489	A41	10c blue & org	1.50	1.50
a.		Double ovpt., one invtd.	25.00	
490	A42	15c gray bl & cl	1.50	1.50
491	A43	20c red & blue	1.50	1.50
492	A44	50c red brn & blk	10.00	10.00
493	A45	1p blue & blk	15.00	15.00
494	A46	5p car & blk	150.00	*150.00*
		Nos. 484-494 (11)	184.00	*183.90*
		Set, never hinged	550.00	

All values exist with inverted overprint; all but 5p with double overprint.

Overprinted On Postage Due Stamps of 1908

No.	Type	Description	Unused	Used
495	D1	1c blue	22.00	*25.00*
496	D1	2c blue	22.00	*25.00*
497	D1	4c blue	22.00	*25.00*
498	D1	5c blue	22.00	*25.00*
499	D1	10c blue	22.00	*25.00*
		Nos. 495-499 (5)	110.00	125.00
		Set, never hinged	325.00	

Nos. 495-499 exist with inverted overprint.

It is stated that, in parts of Mexico occupied by the revolutionary forces, instructions were given to apply a distinguishing overprint to all stamps found in the post offices. This overprint was usually some arrangement or abbreviation of "Gobierno Constitucionalista". Such overprints as were specially authorized or were in general use in large sections of the country are listed. Numerous other handstamped overprints were used in one town or locality. They were essentially military faction control marks necessitated in most instances by the chaotic situation following the split between Villa and Carranza. The fact that some were often struck in a variety of colors and positions suggests the influence of philatelists.

Coat of Arms A57

Statue of Cuauhtémoc A58

Ignacio Zaragoza A59

José María Morelos A60

Francisco Madero — A61

Benito Juárez — A62

1915 **Unwmk.** **Litho.** *Rouletted 14*

No.	Type	Description	Unused	Used
500	A57	1c violet	.20	.20
501	A58	2c green	.25	.20
502	A59	3c brown	.50	.25
503	A60	4c carmine	.50	.25
504	A61	5c orange	.75	.25
505	A62	10c ultra	.35	.30
		Nos. 500-505 (6)	2.55	1.45
		Set, never hinged	4.00	

Nos. 500-505 exists imperf.; some exist imperf. vertically or horizontally; some with rouletting and perforation combined. These probably were not regularly issued in these forms.

See Nos. 506-511. For overprints see Nos. O86-O97.

Map of Mexico — A63

Veracruz Lighthouse A64

Post Office, Mexico, D.F. — A65

TEN CENTAVOS:
Type I — Size 19½x24mm. Crossed lines on coat.
Type II — Size 19x23½mm. Diagonal lines only on coat.

1915-16 ***Perf. 12***
506 A57 1c violet .40 .25
507 A58 2c green .40 .30
508 A59 3c brown .50 .30
509 A60 4c carmine .50 .35
a. "CEATRO" 7.50 7.50
510 A61 5c orange .75 .35
511 A62 10c ultra, type I 1.00 .35
a. 10c ultra, type II .50 .25

Engr.
512 A63 40c slate .75 .35
513 A64 1p brown & blk 1.00 .75
a. Inverted center 200.00 275.00
514 A65 5p cl & ultra ('16) 12.00 4.00
a. Inverted center 450.00
Nos. 506-514 (9) 17.30 7.00
Set, never hinged 60.00

Nos. 507-508, 510-514, exist imperf; Nos. 513-514 imperf with inverted center. These varieties were not regularly issued.

See Nos. 626-628, 647. For overprints see Nos. O92-O100, O121-O123, O132-O133, O142-O144, O153-O154, O162-O164, O174, O188, O193, O207, O222.

Issues of 1899-1910 Overprinted in Blue, Red or Black

1916 **Wmk. 155** ***Perf. 14***

On Issues of 1899-1903
515 A28 5c orange (Bl) 125.00 175.00
Never hinged 400.00
516 A30 15c lav & cl (Bl) 775.00 775.00
Never hinged 2,250.

On Issue of 1910
517 A36 1c dull vio (R) 10.00 *10.00*
518 A37 2c green (R) .50 .35
519 A38 3c orange brn (Bl) .55 .40
a. Double overprint 500.00
520 A39 4c carmine (Bl) 6.00 *8.00*
521 A40 5c orange (Bl) .25 .25
a. Double overprint 75.00
522 A41 10c blue & org (R) 1.25 1.50
523 A42 15c gray bl & cl (Bk) 1.75 3.00
524 A43 20c red & bl (Bk) 1.75 3.00
525 A44 50c red brn & blk (R) 8.50 5.00
526 A45 1p blue & blk (R) 15.00 6.50
527 A46 5p car & blk (R) 175.00 175.00
Nos. 517-527 (11) 220.55 213.00
Nos. 517-527, never hinged 650.00

Nos. 519-524 exist with this overprint (called the "Corbata") reading downward and Nos. 525-527 with it inverted. Of these varieties only Nos. 519-521 were regularly issued.

On Nos. 423-430
528 A36 1c dull vio (R) 2.50 4.00
529 A37 2c green (R) .75 .60
530 A38 3c orange brn (Bl) .60 .60
531 A39 4c carmine (Bl) .60 .60
532 A40 5c orange (Bl) 1.00 .30
533 A41 10c blue & org (R) .75 .60
534 A42 15c gray bl & cl (Bk) .80 .80
535 A43 20c red & bl (Bk) .80 .80

On Nos. 431-433 in Red
536 A44 50c red brn & blk 7.50 6.00
537 A45 1p blue & blk 16.00 16.00
538 A46 5p carmine & blk 150.00 140.00
a. Tablet inverted 300.00
Nos. 528-538 (11) 181.30 170.30
Set, never hinged 550.00

Nos. 529 to 535 are known with the overprint reading downward and Nos. 536 to 538 with it inverted.

On No. 482
539 A28 5c orange (Bl) 400.00 *400.00*

On Nos. 484-494
540 A36 1c dull vio (R) 6.00 *6.00*
541 A37 2c green (R) .75 .75
a. Monogram inverted 100.00
542 A38 3c orange brn (Bl) .75 .75
543 A39 4c carmine (Bl) 8.50 *10.00*
544 A40 5c orange (Bl) 1.25 .35
545 A41 10c blue & org (R) 2.00 *2.50*
546 A42 15c gray bl & cl (Bk) 1.75 .75
a. Tablet double *750.00* *750.00*
b. Monogram double *750.00*
547 A43 20c red & bl (Bk) 1.75 1.50
548 A44 50c red brn & blk (R) 9.00 *10.00*
a. Monogram inverted 75.00
b. Tablet inverted 85.00
549 A45 1p blue & blk (R) 13.00 14.00
a. Tablet double 200.00
b. Monogram inverted 70.00
Nos. 539-549 (11) 444.75 *446.60*
Set, never hinged 1,300.

Nos. 541-547 exist with overprint reading downward. A few 5p were overprinted for the Post Office collection.

On No. 453
550 A28 5c orange (Bl) 125.00 *125.00*

On Nos. 455-462
551 A36 1c dull vio (R) 11.00 *15.00*
552 A37 2c green (R) 1.50 .90
553 A38 3c org brn (Bl) 3.25 *4.50*
554 A39 4c carmine (Bl) 13.00 *15.00*
555 A40 5c orange (Bl) 4.50 *6.00*
556 A41 10c bl & org (R) 12.00 *14.00*
a. Monogram inverted *250.00*
557 A42 15c gray bl & cl (Bk) 12.00 *14.00*
a. Monogram inverted *250.00*
558 A43 20c red & bl (Bk) 12.00 *14.00*
a. Monogram inverted *250.00*
Nos. 550-558 (9) 194.25 *208.40*
Set, never hinged 650.00

Stamps of 50c, 1p and 5p were overprinted for the Post Office collection but were not regularly issued.

Issues of 1914 Overprinted

On "Transitorio" Issue
Rouletted 9½x14
Unwmk.
559 A50 1c dp blue (R) 24.00 24.00
Never hinged 75.00
560 A50 2c yellow grn (R) 12.00 18.00
Never hinged 27.50
561 A50 4c blue vio (R) 425.00 375.00
Never hinged 1,200.
562 A50 10c red (Bl) 2.00 6.00
Never hinged 4.00
a. Vertical overprint 125.00
563 A50 20c yellow brn (Bl) 3.00 6.00
Never hinged 7.50
564 A50 50c claret (Bl) 15.00 20.00
Never hinged 45.00
565 A50 1p violet (Bl) 24.00 24.00
Never hinged 100.00
a. Horiz. pair, imperf. btwn.
Nos. 559-565 (7) 505.00 473.00

Overprinted in Blue On "Denver" Issue
Perf. 12
566 A52 1c pale blue 3.75
567 A52 2c lt green 3.75
568 A52 3c orange .45 *5.00*
569 A52 5c deep rose .45 *5.00*
570 A52 10c rose .45 *5.00*
571 A52 15c rose lilac .45 *5.00*
572 A52 50c yellow 1.10 *15.00*
573 A52 1p violet 9.50 *25.00*
Nos. 566-573 (8) 19.90
Set, never hinged 65.00

Many of the foregoing stamps exist with the "G. P. DE M." overprint printed in other colors than those listed. These "trial color" stamps were not regularly on sale at post offices but were available for postage and used copies are known.

There appears to have been speculation in Nos. 516, 517, 520, 528, 539, 540, 543, 566, and 567. A small quantity of each of these stamps was sold at post offices but subsequently they could be obtained only from officials or their agents at advanced prices.

Venustiano Carranza A66

Coat of Arms A67

1916, June 1 **Engr.** ***Perf. 12***
574 A66 10c blue 1.75 1.00
a. Imperf., pair 25.00
575 A66 10c lilac brown 15.00 15.00
a. Imperf., pair 50.00
Nos. 574-575, never hinged 32.50

Entry of Carranza into Mexico, D.F.
Stamps of type A66 with only horizontal lines in the background of the oval are essays.

1916
576 A67 1c lilac .35 .25
Never hinged .80

Issue of 1910 Surcharged in Various Colors

This overprint is called the "Barril."

1916 **Wmk. 155** ***Perf. 14***
577 A36 5c on 1c dl vio (Br) .50 .50
a. Vertical surcharge 1.25 1.25
b. Double surcharge 150.00
578 A36 10c on 1c dl vio (Bl) .50 .50
a. Double surcharge 100.00
579 A40 20c on 5c org (Br) .50 .50
a. Double surcharge 90.00
580 A40 25c on 5c org (G) .40 .50
581 A37 60c on 2c grn (R) 27.50 20.00
Nos. 577-581 (5) 29.40 22.00
Set, never hinged 100.00

On Nos. 423-424, 427
582 A36 5c on 1c (Br) .50 .50
a. Double tablet, one vertical 100.00
b. Inverted tablet 250.00 250.00
583 A36 10c on 1c (Bl) 1.00 1.00
584 A40 25c on 5c (G) .50 .50
a. Inverted tablet 225.00 225.00
585 A37 60c on 2c (R) 650.00 *425.00*
Nos. 582-584, never hinged 4.50

No. 585 was not regularly issued.
The variety "GONSTITUCIONALISTA" is found on Nos. 582 to 585.

On No. 459
586 A40 25c on 5c org (G) .25 .25
Never hinged .70

On Nos. 484-485, 488
587 A36 5c on 1c (Br) 15.00 20.00
a. Vertical tablet 100.00 125.00
588 A36 10c on 1c (Bl) 5.00 7.50
589 A40 25c on 5c (G) 1.00 1.50
a. Inverted tablet 225.00
590 A37 60c on 2c (R) 650.00
Nos. 587-589, never hinged 60.00

No. 590 was not regularly issued.

Surcharged on "Denver" Issue of 1914

1916 **Unwmk.** ***Perf. 12***
591 A52 60c on 1c pale bl (Br) 3.00 6.00
592 A52 60c on 2c lt grn (Br) 3.00 6.00
a. Inverted surcharge *1,250.*
Set, never hinged 18.00

Postage Due Stamps Surcharged Like Nos. 577-581

1916 **Wmk. 155** ***Perf. 14***
593 D1 5c on 1c blue (Br) 2.50
594 D1 10c on 2c blue (V) 2.50
595 D1 20c on 4c blue (Br) 2.50
596 D1 25c on 5c blue (G) 2.50
597 D1 60c on 10c blue (R) 1.50
598 D1 1p on 1c blue (C) 1.50
599 D1 1p on 2c blue (C) 1.50
600 D1 1p on 4c blue (C) .80 .80
601 D1 1p on 5c blue (C) 2.50
602 D1 1p on 10c blue (C) 2.50
Nos. 593-602 (10) 20.30
Set, never hinged 60.00

There are numerous "trial colors" and "essays" of the overprints and surcharges on Nos. 577 to 602. They were available for postage though not regularly issued.

Postage Due Stamps Surcharged

1916
603 D1 2.50p on 1c blue 1.25 1.25
604 D1 2.50p on 2c blue 10.00
605 D1 2.50p on 4c blue 10.00 250.00
606 D1 2.50p on 5c blue 10.00
607 D1 2.50p on 10c blue 10.00
a. Inverted surcharge *1,500.*
Nos. 603-607 (5) 41.25
Set, never hinged 125.00

Regular Issue

Ignacio Zaragoza A68

Ildefonso Vázquez A69

J. M. Pino Suárez A70

Jesús Carranza A71

Maclovio Herrera — A72

F. I. Madero — A73

Belisario Domínguez A74

Aquiles Serdán A75

Rouletted 14½
1917-20 **Engr.** **Unwmk.**
Thick Paper
608 A68 1c dull violet 2.00 1.00
Never hinged 4.00
609 A68 1c lilac gray ('20) 5.00 .75
Never hinged 9.50
a. 1c gray ('20) 5.00 5.00
610 A69 2c gray green 1.50 .50
Never hinged 3.00
611 A70 3c bister brn 1.50 1.00
Never hinged 3.00
612 A71 4c carmine 2.50 1.00
Never hinged 7.50
613 A72 5c ultra 2.50 .50
Never hinged 5.00
a. Horiz. pair, imperf. btwn. 75.00
b. Imperf., pair 35.00 75.00
614 A73 10c blue 4.00 .50
Never hinged 10.00
a. Without imprint 7.50 1.00
Never hinged 16.00
615 A74 20c brown rose 40.00 2.00
Never hinged 90.00
a. 20c rose 40.00 2.00
Never hinged 80.00
616 A75 30c gray brown 90.00 3.00
Never hinged 250.00

617 A75 30c gray blk ('20) 100.00 4.00
Never hinged 250.00
Nos. 608-617 (10) 249.00 14.25

Perf. 12

Thick or Medium Paper

618 A68 1c dull violet 35.00 25.00
Never hinged 100.00
619 A69 2c gray green 10.00 6.00
Never hinged 20.00
620 A70 3c bis brn ('17) 200.00 200.00
Never hinged 400.00
622 A72 5c ultra 5.00 .25
Never hinged 10.00
623 A73 10c blue ('17) 5.00 .25
Never hinged 10.00
a. Without imprint ('17) 20.00 15.00
Never hinged 40.00
624 A74 20c rose ('20) 140.00 3.00
Never hinged 350.00
625 A75 30c gray blk ('20) 140.00 2.00
Never hinged 350.00

Thin or Medium Paper

626 A63 40c violet 65.00 1.00
Never hinged 200.00
627 A64 1p blue & blk 50.00 1.50
Never hinged 150.00
a. With center of 5p 800.00
b. 1p bl & dark blue (error) 500.00 20.00
c. Vert. pair, imperf. btwn. 250.00
628 A65 5p green & blk 1.50 *10.00*
Never hinged 3.00
a. With violet or red control number 25.00 10.00
b. With center of 1p 800.00

The 1, 2, 3, 5 and 10c are known on thin paper perforated. It is stated they were printed for Postal Union and "specimen" purposes.

All values exist imperf; these are not known to have been regularly issued. Nos. 627a and 628b were not regularly issued.

All values except 3c have an imprint.

For overprints and surcharges see Nos. B1-B2, O113-O165.

Meeting of Iturbide and Guerrero
A77

Entering City of Mexico
A78

1921

632 A77 10c blue & brn 25.00 3.00
Never hinged 82.50
a. Center inverted *40,000.*
633 A78 10p black brn & blk 22.50 *37.50*
Never hinged 75.00

Commemorating the meeting of Augustin de Iturbide and Vicente Guerrero and the entry into City of Mexico in 1821.

For overprint see No. O194.

"El Salto de Agua," Public Fountain
A79

Pyramid of the Sun at Teotihuacán
A80

Chapultepec Castle
A81

Columbus Monument
A82

Juárez Colonnade, Mexico, D. F.
A83

Monument to Josefa Ortiz de Dominguez
A84

Cuauhtémoc Monument — A85

1923 **Unwmk.** ***Rouletted 14½***

634 A79 2c scarlet 2.00 .20
635 A80 3c bister brn 2.00 .25
636 A81 4c green 2.50 .75
637 A82 5c orange 5.00 .20
638 A83 10c brown 3.75 .20
639 A85 10c claret 3.50 .20
640 A84 20c dk blue 52.50 1.75
641 A85 30c dk green 52.50 2.00
Nos. 634-641 (8) 123.75 5.55
Set, never hinged 300.00

See Nos. 642-646, 650-657, 688-692, 727A, 735A-736. For overprints see Nos. O166-O173, O178-O181, O183-O187, O196-O197, O199-O206, O210, O212-O214, O217-O222.

Communications Building — A87

Palace of Fine Arts (National Theater)
A88

Two types of 1p:
I — Eagle on palace dome.
II — Without eagle.

1923 **Wmk. 156** ***Perf. 12***

642 A79 2c scarlet 10.00 10.00
643 A81 4c green 1.40 .30
644 A82 5c orange 10.00 7.00
645 A85 10c brown lake 12.50 6.00
646 A83 30c dark green .95 .20
647 A63 40c violet 1.25 .25
648 A87 50c olive brn 1.00 .25
649 A88 1p red brn & bl (I) 1.00 1.00
a. Type II 3.00 *10.00*
Nos. 642-649 (8) 38.10 25.00
Set, never hinged 90.00

Most of Nos. 642-649 are known imperforate or part perforate but probably were not regularly issued.

For overprints see Nos. O175-O176, O189-O190, O208-O209, O223.

1923-34 ***Rouletted 14½***

650 A79 2c scarlet .25 .20
651 A80 3c bis brn ('27) .25 .20
652 A81 4c green 47.50 35.00
653 A82 4c green ('27) .25 .20
654 A82 5c orange .25 .20
655 A85 10c lake .25 .20
656 A84 20c deep blue .75 .30
657 A83 30c dk green ('34) .75 .30
Nos. 650-657 (8) 50.25 36.60
Set, never hinged 125.00

Nos. 650 to 657 inclusive exist imperforate.

Medallion
A90

Map of Americas
A91

Francisco García y Santos — A92

Post Office, Mexico, D. F. — A93

1926 ***Perf. 12***

658 A90 2c red 2.50 1.00
659 A91 4c green 2.50 1.00
660 A90 5c orange 2.50 .75
661 A91 10c brown red 4.00 1.00
662 A92 20c dk blue 4.00 1.25
663 A92 30c dk green 7.50 4.00
664 A92 40c violet 13.50 3.00
665 A93 1p brown & blue 27.50 10.00
a. 1p red & blue 37.50 15.00
Nos. 658-665 (8) 64.00 22.00
Set, never hinged 150.00

Pan-American Postal Congress.

Nos. 658-665 were also printed in black, on unwatermarked paper, for presentation to delegates to the Universal Postal Congress at London in 1929. Remainders were overprinted in 1929 for use as airmail official stamps, and are listed as Nos. CO3-CO10.

For overprints see Nos. 667-674, 675A-682, CO3-CO10.

Benito Juárez — A94

1926 ***Rouletted 14½***

666 A94 8c orange .30 .20
Never hinged .70

For overprint see No. O182.

Nos. 658-665 Overprinted

1930 ***Perf. 12***

667 A90 2c red 4.00 2.25
a. Reading down 15.00 15.00
668 A91 4c green 4.00 2.50
a. Reading down 15.00 15.00
669 A90 5c orange 4.00 2.00
a. Reading down 15.00 35.00
b. Double overprint 75.00 *75.00*
670 A91 10c brown red 7.50 2.50
671 A92 20c dk blue 9.50 3.50
672 A92 30c dk green 8.50 4.00
a. Reading down 10.00 12.00
673 A92 40c violet 12.50 8.50
a. Reading down 47.50 50.00
674 A93 1p red brn & bl 11.00 7.00
a. Double overprint 250.00
b. Triple overprint 200.00
Nos. 667-674 (8) 61.00 32.25
Set, never hinged 150.00

Overprint horizontal on 1p.

Arms of Puebla — A95

1931, May 1 **Engr.**

675 A95 10c dk bl & dk brn 3.00 .50
Never hinged 7.50

400th anniversary of Puebla.

Nos. 658-665a Overprinted

1931

676 A91 4c green 70.00 *75.00*
a. Inverted overprint *2,500.*
677 A90 5c orange 13.00 *17.00*
678 A91 10c brown red 13.00 *14.00*
679 A92 20c dk blue 13.00 *18.00*
680 A92 30c dk green 22.50 *25.00*
681 A92 40c violet 32.50 *35.00*
682 A93 1p brown & bl 30.00 *35.00*
a. 1p red & blue 42.50 *45.00*
Nos. 676-682 (7) 194.00 219.00
Set, never hinged 475.00

Overprint horizontal on 1p.

Nos. 676 and 682 are not known to have been sold to the public through post offices.

Forgeries of overprint exist.

Bartolomé de las Casas
A96

Emblem of Mexican Society of Geography and Statistics
A97

1933, Mar. 3 **Engr.** ***Rouletted 14½***

683 A96 15c dark blue .30 .20
Never hinged .70

For overprint see No. O215.

1933, Oct. ***Rouletted 14½***

684 A97 2c deep green 1.50 .60
685 A97 5c dark brown 1.75 .50
686 A97 10c dark blue .75 .20
687 A97 1p dark violet 100.00 65.00
Nos. 684-687 (4) 104.00 66.30
Set, never hinged 250.00

XXI Intl. Congress of Statistics and the 1st centenary of the Mexican Society of Geography and Statistics.

Types of 1923 and PT1

1934 ***Perf. 10½, 11 (4c)***

687A PT1 1c brown 1.00 .30
688 A79 2c scarlet .35 .20
689 A82 4c green .35 .20
690 A85 10c brown lake .35 .20
691 A84 20c dark blue .75 .75
692 A83 30c dk blue grn 1.00 1.25
Nos. 687A-692 (6) 3.80 2.90
Set, never hinged 9.00

See 2nd note after Postal Tax stamp No. RA3.

Indian Archer — A99

Indian — A100

Woman Decorating Pottery
A101

Peon
A102

Potter
A103

Sculptor
A104

Craftsman
A105

Offering to the Gods
A106

Worshiper — A107

1934, Sept. 1 Wmk. 156 *Perf. 10½*

698	A99	5c dk green	4.00	1.00
699	A100	10c brown lake	5.50	1.50
700	A101	20c ultra	13.50	8.00
701	A102	30c black	26.00	20.00
702	A103	40c black brn	37.50	25.00
703	A104	50c dull blue	75.00	75.00
704	A105	1p brn lake & blk	150.00	75.00
705	A106	5p brn blk & red brn	325.00	325.00
706	A107	10p brown & vio	1,100.	1,200.
a.		Unwatermarked	*3,250.*	
		Never hinged	5,000.	
		Nos. 698-706 (9)	1,736.	1,730.
		Set, never hinged	4,250.	

National University.

The design of the 1p is wider than the rest of the set. Values are for copies with perfs just touching the design.

See Nos. C54-C61, RA13B.

Yalalteca Indian — A108

Tehuana Indian — A109

Arch of the Revolution
A110

Tower of Los Remedios
A111

Cross of Palenque
A112

Independence Monument
A113

Independence Monument, Puebla
A114

Monument to the Heroic Cadets
A115

Stone of Tizoc — A116

Ruins of Mitla — A117

Coat of Arms
A118

Charro
A119

Imprint: "Oficina Impresora de Hacienda-Mexico"

1934-40 Wmk. 156 *Perf. 10½*

Size: 20x26mm

707	A108	1c orange	.65	.20
a.		Unwmkd.		—
708	A109	2c green	.65	.20
a.		Unwmkd.	3.75	3.75
709	A110	4c carmine	.90	.20
710	A111	5c olive brn	.65	.20
a.		Unwmkd.	400.00	350.00
711	A112	10c dk blue	.80	.20
712	A112	10c violet ('35)	1.25	.20
a.		Unwmkd.	200.00	40.00
713	A113	15c lt blue	4.00	.30
714	A114	20c gray green	1.90	.20
a.		20c olive green	2.00	.20
715	A114	20c ultra ('35)	1.40	.20
a.		Unwmkd.		150.00
716	A115	30c lake	.90	.20
a.		Unwmkd.	350.00	
716B	A115	30c lt ultra ('40)	1.00	.20
717	A116	40c red brown	1.00	.20
718	A117	50c grnsh black	.90	.20
a.		Imperf., pair	110.00	
b.		Unwmkd.		375.00
719	A118	1p dk brn & org	2.50	.20
a.		Imperf., pair	350.00	
720	A119	5p org & vio	7.75	.75
		Nos. 707-720 (15)	26.25	3.65
		Set, never hinged	70.00	

No. 718a was not regularly issued.

The existence of No. 707a has been questioned.

See Nos. 729-733, 733B, 735, 784-788, 795A-800A, 837-838, 840-841, 844, 846-851. For overprints see Nos. 728, O224-O232.

Tractor — A120

1935, Apr. 1 Wmk. 156 *Perf. 10½*

721	A120	10c violet	4.00	.50
		Never hinged	9.00	

Industrial census of Apr. 10, 1935.

Arms of Chiapas
A121

Emiliano Zapata
A122

1935, Sept. 14

722	A121	10c dark blue	.50	.20
		Never hinged	1.40	
a.		Unwmkd.	125.00	100.00

The 111th anniversary of the joining of the state of Chiapas with the federal republic of Mexico. See No. 734.

1935, Nov. 20 Wmk. 156

723	A122	10c violet	.75	.20
		Never hinged	2.00	

25th anniversary of the Plan of Ayala.

US and Mexico Joined by Highways
A123

Matalote Bridge
A124

View of Nuevo Laredo Highway — A125

1936 Wmk. 248 *Perf. 14*

725	A123	5c blue grn & rose	.35	.25
726	A124	10c slate bl & blk	.50	.25
727	A125	20c brn & dk grn	1.50	1.00
		Nos. 725-727,C77-C79 (6)	3.60	2.40
		Set, never hinged	8.50	

Opening of the Mexico City - Nuevo Laredo Highway.

Monument Type of 1923

1936 Wmk. 248 Engr. *Perf. 10½*

727A	A85	10c brown lake	*2,500.*	650.00

No. 712 Overprinted in Green

1936, Dec. 15 Wmk. 156

728	A112	10c violet	.60	.50
		Never hinged	1.50	

1st National Congress of Industrial Hygiene and Medicine.

Type of 1934

Redrawn size: 17½x21mm

Imprint: "Talleres de Imp. de Est. y Valores-Mexico"

1937 Photo. Wmk. 156 *Perf. 14*

729	A108	1c orange	.60	.20
a.		Imperf., pair	12.50	12.50
		Never hinged	25.00	
730	A109	2c dull green	.60	.20
a.		Imperf., pair	12.50	12.50
		Never hinged	30.00	
731	A110	4c carmine	.90	.20
a.		Imperf., pair	12.50	12.50
		Never hinged	30.00	
732	A111	5c olive brn	.80	.20
a.		Unwmkd.		*300.00*
733	A112	10c violet	.70	.20
a.		Imperf., pair	10.00	12.50
		Never hinged	12.00	
		Nos. 729-733 (5)	3.60	1.00
		Set, never hinged	9.00	

The imperfs were not regularly issued.

Types of 1934-35

1937 Wmk. 260

Size: 17½x21mm

733B	A111	5c olive brown	*4,000.*	250.00
		Never hinged	*9,000.*	

1937 Engr. *Perf. 10½*

734	A121	10c dark blue	35.00	35.00
		Never hinged	75.00	

1937

Size: 20x26mm

735	A112	10c violet	350.00	55.00

Types of 1923

1934-37 Wmk. 260 *Perf. 10½*

735A	A79	2c scarlet	*6,000.*
735B	A85	10c brown lake	—

Forged perforations exist.

The listing of No. 735B is being re-evaluated. The Catalogue Editors would appreciate any information on the stamp.

Rouletted 14½

736	A85	10c claret	*5,500.*	*175.00*

Blacksmith
A126

Revolutionary Soldier
A127

Revolutionary Envoy — A128

Wmk. 156

1938, Mar. 26 Photo. *Perf. 14*

737	A126	5c black & brn	.80	.20
738	A127	10c red brown	.35	.25
739	A128	20c maroon & org	6.00	1.00
		Nos. 737-739,C82-C84 (6)	13.15	4.90
		Set, never hinged	32.00	

Plan of Guadalupe, 25th anniv.

Arch of the Revolution
A129

Independence Monument
A131

Design: 10c, National Theater.

1938, July 1

740	A129	5c bister brn	4.25	.60
741	A129	5c red brown	25.00	2.25
742	A129	10c orange	15.00	11.00
743	A129	10c chocolate	1.00	.20
744	A131	20c brown lake	6.00	4.00
745	A131	20c black	18.00	15.00
		Nos. 740-745 (6)	69.25	33.05
		Nos. 740-745,C85-C90 (12)	129.60	63.30
		Set, never hinged	275.00	

16th Intl. Congress of Planning & Housing.

Arch of the Revolution
A132

1939, May 1

746	A132	10c Prus blue	.65	.20
		Nos. 746,C91-C93 (4)	4.75	2.95
		Set, never hinged	11.00	

New York World's Fair.

Indian — A133

1939, May 17

747 A133 10c red orange			.45	.20
Nos. 747,C94-C96 (4)			5.55	2.75
Set, never hinged			13.00	

Tulsa World Philatelic Convention.

Juan Zumárraga
A134

First Printing Shop in Mexico, 1539
A135

Design: 10c, Antonio de Mendoza.

1939, Sept. 1 Engr. *Perf. 10½*

748 A134 2c brown blk	.75	.25
749 A135 5c green	.75	.20
750 A134 10c red brown	.25	.20
Nos. 748-750,C97-C99 (6)	3.75	1.75
Set, never hinged	11.50	

400th anniversary of printing in Mexico.

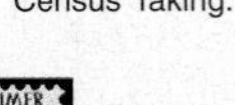

View of Taxco
A137

Allegory of Agriculture
A138

10c, Two hands holding symbols of commerce.

1939, Oct. 1 Photo. *Perf. 12x13*

751 A137 2c dark carmine	1.25	.20
752 A138 5c sl grn & gray grn	.25	.20
753 A138 10c org brn & buff	.25	.20
Nos. 751-753,C100-C102 (6)	6.25	1.80
Set, never hinged	14.00	

Census Taking.

"Penny Black" of 1840
A140

Roadside Monument
A141

1940, May *Perf. 14*

754 A140 5c black & lemon	.90	.50
755 A140 10c dark violet	.25	.20
756 A140 20c lt blue & car	.25	.20
757 A140 1p gray & red org	7.00	4.00
758 A140 5p black & Prus bl	50.00	50.00
Nos. 754-758,C103-C107 (10)	141.00	115.90
Set, never hinged	340.00	

Postage stamp centenary.

1940 Wmk. 156

759 A141 6c deep green	.50	.25
Never hinged	1.25	

Opening of the highway between Mexico, D. F., and Guadalajara. See Nos. 789, 842.

Vasco de Quiroga — A142

Melchor Ocampo — A143

College Seal — A144

1940, July 15 Engr. *Perf. 10½*

760 A142 2c violet	1.30	.50
761 A143 5c copper red	.80	.20
762 A144 10c olive bister	.80	.30
a. Imperf., pair	150.00	
Nos. 760-762,C108-C110 (6)	5.10	2.50
Set, never hinged	11.00	

Founding of the National College of San Nicolas de Hidalgo, 400th anniv.

Coat of Arms of Campeche
A145

1940, Aug. 7 Photo. *Perf. 12x13*

763 A145 10c bis brn & dk car	5.00	1.25
Nos. 763,C111-C113 (4)	12.60	6.70
Set, never hinged	30.00	

400th anniversary of the founding of Campeche.

Man at Helm
A146

1940, Dec. 1

764 A146 2c red org & blk	1.60	.60
765 A146 5c peacock bl & red brn	8.00	3.50
766 A146 10c slate grn & dk brn	4.00	.85
Nos. 764-766,C114-C116 (6)	21.00	9.45
Set, never hinged	45.00	

Inauguration of Pres. Manuel Avila Camacho.

Alternated Perforations

Nos. 763-766, 774-779, 792-795, 801-804, 806-811, 813-818, C100-C102, C111-C116, C123-C128, C143-C162, C430-C431 have alternating small and large perforations.

Javelin Thrower — A147

1941, Nov. 4 *Perf. 14*

767 A147 10c dull yellow grn	5.00	.50

National Athletic Games of the Revolution, Nov. 4-20, 1941.

Serpent Columns, Chichén Itzá
A148

Mayan Sculpture
A149

Coat of Arms of Merída — A150

1942, June 30

768 A148 2c dk olive bis	1.40	.75
769 A149 5c deep orange	2.25	.60
770 A150 10c dark violet	1.60	.25
Nos. 768-770,C117-C119 (6)	11.50	6.35

400th anniversary of the founding of Merida.

Independence Monument to Hidalgo — A151

Government Palace — A152

View of Guadalajara — A153

1942, Feb. 11 Engr. *Perf. 10x10½*

771 A151 2c bl vio & vio brn	.35	.30
772 A152 5c black & cop red	1.25	.50
773 A153 10c red org & ultra	1.25	.40
Nos. 771-773,C120-C122 (6)	7.85	4.20

Founding of Guadalajara, 400th anniv.

No. 773 exists imperf on unwatermarked paper as a color proof.

Black Cloud in Orion
A154

Designs: 5c, Total solar eclipse. 10c, Spiral galaxy in the "Hunting Dogs."

1942, Feb. 17 Photo. *Perf. 12x13*

774 A154 2c lt vio & indigo	10.00	3.00
775 A154 5c blue & indigo	15.00	2.00
776 A154 10c red org & indigo	15.00	.75
Nos. 774-776,C123-C125 (6)	100.00	17.25

Astrophysics Congress and the inauguration of an observatory at Tonanzintla, Feb. 17, 1942.

"Mother Earth"
A157

Sowing Wheat
A158

Western Hemisphere Carrying a Torch — A159

1942, July 1

777 A157 2c chestnut	2.00	.40
778 A158 5c turq blue	3.50	1.10
779 A159 10c red orange	1.50	.55
Nos. 777-779,C126-C128 (6)	12.90	5.50

2nd Inter-American Agricultural Conference.

Fuente Academy
A160

1942, Nov. 16 *Perf. 14*

780 A160 10c grnsh black	2.50	.75

75th anniversary of Fuente Academy.

Las Monjas Church — A161

Generalissimo Ignacio José de Allende — A163

Design: 5c, San Miguel Church.

1943, May 11

781 A161 2c intense blue 1.00 .35
782 A161 5c deep brown 1.10 .30
783 A163 10c dull black 3.50 1.00
Nos. 781-783,C129-C131 (6) 10.60 5.35

400th anniv. of the founding of San Miguel de Allende.

Types of 1937

1944 Photo. Wmk. 272

784 A108 1c orange 2.00 .20
785 A109 2c dull green 2.00 .20
786 A110 4c carmine 4.00 .20
787 A111 5c olive brown 4.00 .20
788 A112 10c violet 2.00 .20

Type of 1940

789 A141 6c green 2.00 .20
Nos. 784-789 (6) 16.00 1.20

"Liberty"
A164

Juan M. de Castorena
A165

1944 Photo.

790 A164 12c violet brown .35 .20

See No. 845.

1944, Oct. 12 Engr. *Perf. 10*

791 A165 12c dark brown .60 .20

Third Book Fair. See No. C142.

Catalogue values for unused stamps in this section, from this point to the end of the section, are for Never Hinged items.

Hands Holding Globe Showing Western Hemisphere
A166

1945, Feb. 27 Photo. *Perf. 12x13*

792 A166 12c dark carmine .60 .20
793 A166 1p slate green 1.00 .25
794 A166 5p olive brown 5.75 4.50
795 A166 10p black 17.50 8.00
Nos. 792-795,C143-C147 (9) 55.25 33.70

Inter-American Conf. held at Chapultepec, Feb. 1945.

Types of 1934-40

Wmk. 272

1945-46 Engr. *Perf. 10½*

795A A113 15c lt grnsh bl ('46) 325.00 60.00
796 A114 20c gray grn 2.50 .20
797 A115 30c lt ultra 3.25 .20
798 A116 40c brown 2.50 .20
799 A117 50c grnsh blk 1.60 .20
800 A118 1p dk brn & org 7.00 .20
b. Imperf., pair
800A A119 5p org & vio ('46) 17.00 6.00
Nos. 795A-800A (7) 358.85 67.00

Theater of Peace, San Luis Potosi
A167

1945, July 27 Photo. *Perf. 12x13*

801 A167 12c blk & vio brn .45 .20
802 A167 1p blk & bl gray .60 .40
803 A167 5p blk & brn lake 5.50 5.00
804 A167 10p blk & grnsh bl 17.00 12.00
Nos. 801-804,C148-C152 (9) 51.65 35.40

Reconstruction of the Peace Theater (Teatro de la Paz), San Luis Potosi.

Fountain of Diana, the Huntress — A168

1945 *Perf. 14*

805 A168 3c violet blue .55 .20

See No. 839.

Removing Blindfold
A169

1945, Nov. 2 *Perf. 12x13*

806 A169 2c bluish grn .40 .20
807 A169 6c orange .40 .20
808 A169 12c ultra .40 .20
809 A169 1p olive .60 .25
810 A169 5p gray & pale rose 3.50 3.00
811 A169 10p bl & yel grn 27.50 20.00
Nos. 806-811 (6) 32.80 23.85
Nos. 806-811,C153-C157 (11) 68.25 55.85

Issued to publicize the national literacy campaign.

M. E. de Almanza — A170

1946 *Perf. 14*

812 A170 8c black 1.25 .25

Martines Enriquez de Almanza, founder of the Mexican posts. See No. 843.

Allegory of World Peace
A171

1946, Apr. 10 *Perf. 12x13*

813 A171 2c dk olive bis .35 .20
814 A171 6c red brown .30 .20
815 A171 12c Prus green .25 .20
816 A171 1p lt green .60 .40
817 A171 5p dull red vio 5.50 5.00
818 A171 10p lt ultra 30.00 20.00
Nos. 813-818 (6) 37.00 26.00
Nos. 813-818,C158-C162 (11) 64.20 40.75

United Nations.

Arms of Zacatecas
A173

Monument to Gen. Gonzalez Ortega
A174

Ramón Lopez Velarde — A175

Francisco Garcia Salinas — A176

Wmk. 279

1946, Sept. 1 Photo. *Perf. 14*

820 A173 2c orange brn .55 .20
821 A173 12c Prus blue .25 .20

Engr.

Perf. 10x10½

822 A174 1p lilac rose .70 .20
823 A175 5p red 5.50 3.00
824 A176 10p dk blue & blk 40.00 10.00
Nos. 820-824 (5) 47.00 13.60
Nos. 820-824,C163-C166 (9) 68.60 32.15

400th anniversary of the founding of the city of Zacatecas.

A177

A178

1947 Photo. *Perf. 14*

825 A177 15c Postman .25 .20
a. Imperf., pair 110.00

1947, May 16

10c, F. D. Roosevelt and Stamp of 1st Mexican Issue. 15c, Arms of Mexico and Stamp of 1st US Issue.

826 A178 10c yellow brown 1.60 1.00
827 A178 15c green .25 .20
Nos. 826-827,C167-C169 (5) 4.60 2.35

Cent. Intl. Phil. Exhib., NYC, 5/17-25/47.

Justo Sierra — A180

Communications Building — A181

Perf. 10x10½, 10½x10

1947, Engr. Wmk. 279

828 A180 10p brown & dl grn 150.00 40.00
829 A181 20p dk green & lil 1.60 2.00

Cadet Juan Escutia — A182

Gen. Manuel Rincón — A186

Flag of San Blas Battalion — A188

Designs: 2c, Cadet Francisco Márquez. 5c, Cadet Fernando Montes de Oca. 10c, Cadet Juan Escutia. 15c, Cadet Agustin Melgar. 1p, Gen. Lucas Balderas.

1947, Sept. 8 Photo. *Perf. 14*

830 A182 2c brown black .45 .20
831 A182 5c red orange .30 .20
832 A182 10c dk brown .25 .20
833 A182 15c dk Prus green .25 .20
834 A186 30c dull olive grn .35 .20

Engr.

Perf. 10x10½

835 A186 1p aqua .45 .45
836 A188 5p dk blue & claret 1.90 1.90
Nos. 830-836 (7) 3.95 3.35
Nos. 830-836,C180-C184 (12) 7.30 6.15

Centenary of the battles of Chapultepec, Churubusco and Molino del Rey.

Types of 1934-46

1947-50 Wmk. 279 Photo. *Perf. 14*

837 A108 1c orange 1.00 .30
a. Imperf., pair 150.00
838 A109 2c dk green .60 .20
839 A168 3c violet blue .60 .20
840 A110 4c dull red 1.90 .20
841 A111 5c olive brown 2.50 .20
842 A141 6c deep green .45 .20
a. Imperf., pair 150.00
843 A170 8c black .35 .20
844 A112 10c violet 1.90 .25
845 A164 12c violet brn 12.00 .75

Types A108 to A112 are in the redrawn size of 1937.

Size: 19x25mm

Engr. *Perf. 10½*

846 A114 20c olive green 1.25 .20
a. 20c green 3.00 .30
847 A115 30c lt ultra 12.00 .40
848 A116 40c red brown 1.40 .25
849 A117 50c green 1.90 .20
a. Imperf., pair 110.00
850 A118 1p dk brn & org 45.00 9.00
851 A119 5p org & vio ('50) 35.00 11.00
Nos. 837-851 (15) 117.85 23.55

A189

Designs: 3c, Modernistic church, Nuevo Leon. 5c, Modern building, Mexico City. 10c, Convent, Morelos. 15c, Benito Juarez. 20, Puebla Cathedral. 30c, Indian dancer, Michoacan. 40c, Stone head, Tabasco. 50c, Carved head, Veracruz. 1p, Convent and carved head, Hidalgo. 5p, Galleon, arms of Campeche. 10p, Francisco I. Madero. 20p, Modern building, Mexico City.

1950-52 Wmk. 279 Photo. *Perf. 14*

856 A189 3c blue vio ('51) .50 .20
857 A189 5c dk red brn .75 .20
858 A189 10c dk green 3.50 .20
859 A189 15c dk green ('51) 1.75 .20
860 A189 20c blue violet 14.00 .20
861 A189 30c red .50 .20
862 A189 40c red orange ('51) 1.00 .20
863 A189 50c blue 1.25 .20

Engr.

864 A189 1p dull brown 4.50 .20
865 A189 5p ultra & bl grn 7.00 4.00
866 A189 10p blk & dp ultra ('52) 7.00 7.00
867 A189 20p pur & grn ('52) 10.00 10.00
Nos. 856-867 (12) 51.75 22.80

See Nos. 875-885, 909, 928-931, 943-952, 1003-1004, 1054-1055, 1072, 1076, 1081, 1090-1091, 1094-1102.

Highway Bridge A190

Symbolical of Construction in 1950 — A191

Railroad Laborer — A192

Perf. 10½x10, 10x10½

1950, May 5 **Engr.**

868 A190 15c purple .60 .20
869 A191 20c deep blue .40 .20
Nos. 868-869,C199-C200 (4) 4.30 .85

Completion of the International Highway between Ciudad Juarez and the Guatemala border.

Inscribed: "Ferrocarril del Sureste 1950"

Design: 20c, Map and locomotive.

1950, May 24 ***Perf. 10x10½***

870 A192 15c chocolate 1.25 .20
871 A192 20c dp carmine .45 .20
Nos. 870-871,C201-C202 (4) 2.55 .90

Opening of the Southeastern Railroad between Veracruz, Coatzocoalcos and Yucatan, 1950.

Postal Service A193

Miguel Hidalgo y Costilla A194

1950, June 25 ***Perf. 10x10½***

872 A193 50c purple .40 .20
Nos. 872,C203-C204 (3) 1.25 .70

75th anniv. (in 1949) of the UPU.

Wmk. 300

1953, May 8 **Photo.** ***Perf. 14***

873 A194 20c grnsh bl & dk brn 1.75 .25
Nos. 873,C206-C207 (3) 3.55 .70

Bicentenary of birth of Miguel Hidalgo y Costilla. See Nos. C206-C207.

Type of 1950-52

Designs as before.
Two types of 5p:
Type I — Imprint ½mm high and blurred.
Type II — Imprint ¾mm high and clear.

1954-67 **Photo.** ***Perf. 14***

875 A189 5c red brown .50 .20
876 A189 10c green, redrawn 2.50 .20
a. 10c dark green 2.50 .20
877 A189 15c dk green .40 .20
878 A189 20c bluish blk, white paper, colorless gum ('67) .60 .20
a. 20c dark blue 3.50 .20
879 A189 30c brown red .75 .20
a. 30c redsh brn .75 .20
880 A189 40c red orange 1.50 .20
881 A189 50c lt blue 1.00 .20

Engr.

882 A189 1p olive grn, perf. 11, vert. wmk. ('58) 12.00 .25
a. 1p olive grn, perf. 14 7.00 .20
b. olive brown 12.00 .20
883 A189 5p ultra & bl grn, I 7.00 1.00
a. Type II 500.00 7.00
884 A189 10p sl & dp ultra ('56) 9.00 5.00
a. 10p slate green & ultra 35.00 5.00
885 A189 20p purple & grn 11.00 9.00
a. 20p brn vio & yel grn 75.00 20.00
Nos. 875-885 (11) 46.25 16.65

Nos. 875-881 come only with watermark vertical, and in various shades. Watermark inverted on Nos. 884, 885.

On No. 876, imprint extends full width of stamp.

Vert. pairs, imperf. horiz. of Nos. 878, 880 are noted after No. 1004.

Aztec Messenger of the Sun A195

Symbolizing Adoption of National Anthem A196

1954, Mar. 6

886 A195 20c rose & bl gray 1.10 .20
Nos. 886,C222-C223 (3) 2.85 .80

7th Central American and Caribbean Games.

1954, Sept. 16 **Photo.**

887 A196 5c rose lil & dk bl .75 .20
888 A196 20c yel brn & brn vio .90 .20
889 A196 1p gray grn & cerise .65 .40
Nos. 887-889,C224-C226 (6) 3.40 1.50

Centenary of the adoption of Mexico's National Anthem.

Torch-Bearer and Stadium — A197

Aztec Designs A198

1955, Mar. 12 **Wmk. 300** ***Perf. 14***

890 A197 20c dk grn & red brn .85 .20
Nos. 890,C227-C228 (3) 2.35 .80

Second Pan American Games, 1955.

1956, Aug. 1

891 A198 5c "Motion" .50 .20
892 A198 10c Bird .50 .20
893 A198 30c Flowers .40 .20
894 A198 50c Corn .50 .20
895 A198 1p Deer .60 .20
896 A198 5p Man 2.25 2.25
a. Souv. sheet, #891-896, imperf. 75.00 75.00
Nos. 891-896,C229-C234 (12) 7.90 5.55

Centenary of Mexico's 1st postage stamps. No. 896a sold for 15p.

Stamp of 1856 A199

Francisco Zarco — A200

1956, Aug. 1

897 A199 30c brn & intense bl .75 .25

Cent. of 1st Mexican Stamp Intl. Philatelic Exhibition, Mexico City, Aug. 16, 1956.

1956-63

Portraits: 25c, 45c, Guillermo Prieto. 60c, Ponciano Arriaga.

897A A200 25c dk brown ('63) .75 .50
898 A200 45c dk blue green .35 .25
899 A200 60c red lilac .35 .35
900 A200 70c violet blue .40 .20
Nos. 897A-900,C236-C237A (7) 4.45 2.60

Centenary of the constitution (in 1957). See Nos. C289, 1075, 1092-1093.

"Mexico" A201

Mexican Eagle and Oil Derrick A202

Design: 1p, National Assembly.

1957, Aug. 31 **Photo.** ***Perf. 14***

901 A201 30c maroon & gold .50 .20
902 A201 1p pale brn & metallic grn .35 .25
Nos. 901-902,C239-C240 (4) 1.70 .90

Constitution, centenary.

1958, Aug. 30 **Wmk. 300** ***Perf. 14***

Design: 5p, Map of Mexico and refinery.

903 A202 30c lt blue & blk .50 .20
904 A202 5p hn brn & Prus grn 6.00 4.00
Nos. 903-904,C243-C244 (4) 7.15 4.60

20th anniv. of the nationalization of Mexico's oil industry.

UNESCO Building and Eiffel Tower — A203

UN Headquarters, New York — A204

1959, Jan. 20

905 A203 30c dull lilac & blk .50 .20

UNESCO Headquarters opening, Paris, Nov. 9.

1959, Sept. 7 **Litho.** ***Perf. 14***

906 A204 30c org yel & bl .50 .20

Meeting of UNESCO.

Carranza A205

Humboldt Statue A206

1960, Jan. 15 **Photo.** **Wmk. 300**

907 A205 30c pale grn & plum .35 .20

Birth centenary of Pres. Venustiano Carranza. See No. C246.

1960, Mar. 16 **Wmk. 300** ***Perf. 14***

908 A206 40c bis brn & grn .35 .20

Cent. of the death (in 1859) of Alexander von Humboldt, German naturalist and geographer.

Type of 1950-52 Inscribed: "HOMENAJE AL COLECCIONISTA DEL TIMBRE DE MEXICO-JUNIO 1960"

1960, June 8 **Engr.** **Wmk. 300**

909 A189 10p lil, brn & grn 100.00 75.00

Visit of the Elmhurst (Ill.) Philatelic Society of Mexico Specialists to Mexico, 25th anniv. See No. C249.

Independence Bell & Monument A207 A208

5p, Bell of Dolores and Miguel Hidalgo.

Wmk. 300

1960, Sept. 15 **Photo.** ***Perf. 14***

910 A207 30c grn & rose red 3.00 .20
911 A208 1p dl grn & dk brn .50 .20
912 A208 5p maroon & dk bl 5.00 5.00
Nos. 910-912,C250-C252 (6) 15.50 8.10

150th anniv. of Mexican independence. See US No. 1157.

Agricultural Reform A209

Symbols of Health Education — A210

Designs: 20c, Sailor and Soldier, 1960, and Fighter of 1910. 30c, Electrification. 1p, Political development (schools). 5p, Currency stability (Bank and money).

1960-61 **Photo.** ***Perf. 14***

913 A209 10c sl grn, blk & red org .75 .20
914 A210 15c grn & org brn 2.75 .50

915 A210 20c brt bl & lt brn ('61) 1.00 .20
916 A210 30c vio brn & sep .40 .20
917 A210 1p redsh brn & slate .50 .20
918 A210 5p maroon & gray 6.00 3.50
Nos. 913-918,C253-C256 (10) 18.80 8.55

50th anniversary (in 1960) of the Mexican Revolution.

Issued: #913, 11/20/60; #914, 916-918, 12/23/60; #915, 3/14/61.

Tunnel — A211

Microscope, Mosquito and Globe — A212

1961, Dec. 7 Wmk. 300 *Perf. 14*
919 A211 40c blk & brt grn .40 .20
Nos. 919,C258-C259 (3) 1.20 .60

Opening of the railroad from Chihuahua to the Pacific Ocean.

1962, Apr. 7
920 A212 40c dl bl & maroon .40 .20

WHO drive to eradicate malaria.

President Joao Goulart of Brazil — A213

Insurgent at Marker for Battle of Puebla — A214

Wmk. 300
1962, Apr. 11 Photo. *Perf. 14*
921 A213 40c brown olive 1.00 .25

Visit of Joao Goulart, president of Brazil, to Mexico.

1962, May 5
922 A214 40c sepia & dk grn .35 .20

Centenary of the Battle of May 5 at Puebla and the defeat of French forces by Gen. Ignacio Zaragoza. See No. C260.

Draftsman and Surveyor A215

Plumbline A216

1962, June 11
923 A215 40c slate grn & dk bl .90 .20

25th anniversary of the National Polytechnic Institute. See No. C261.

1962, June 21
924 A216 20c dp blue & blk 1.40 .20

Issued to publicize the importance of mental health.

"Space Needle" and Gear Wheels A217

Globe A218

1962, July 6
925 A217 40c dk grn & gray .35 .20

"Century 21" International Exposition, Seattle, Wash., Apr. 21-Oct. 12.

1962, Oct. 1 *Perf. 14*
926 A218 40c gray & brn .35 .20

1962 meeting of the Inter-American Economic and Social Council. See No. C263.

Pres. Alessandri of Chile A219

Pres. Betancourt of Venezuela A220

1962, Dec. 20 Wmk. 300 *Perf. 14*
927 A219 20c olive black .75 .20

Visit of President Jorge Alessandri Rodriguez of Chile to Mexico, Dec. 17-20.

Type of 1950-52

Designs as before.

Wmk. 300, Vertical
1962-74 Photo. *Perf. 14*
928 A189 1p ol gray ('67) 1.25 .20
a. 1p green 4.00 .20
929 A189 5p dl bl & dk grn 3.50 .75
a. 5p bluish gray & dark green, white paper ('67) 3.50 .50
930 A189 10p gray & bl ('63) 8.50 5.00
a. 10p green & deep blue ('74) 8.50 5.50
931 A189 20p lil & blk ('63) 9.00 7.50
a. Redrawn, white paper 10.00 10.00
Nos. 928-931 (4) 22.25 13.45

No. 928 is on thick, luminescent paper. No. 929 is 20½mm high; No. 929a, 20¾mm. Nos. 931a and 1102 (unwmkd.) have more shading in sky and spots on first floor windows.

1963, Feb. 23 Wmk. 300
932 A220 20c slate .70 .20

Visit of President Romulo Betancourt of Venezuela to Mexico.

Congress Emblem A221

Wheat Emblem A222

1963, Apr. 22 Wmk. 300 *Perf. 14*
933 A221 40c fawn & blk .60 .20

19th International Chamber of Commerce Congress. See No. C271.

1963, June 23 Wmk. 300 *Perf. 14*
934 A222 40c crim & dk bl .60 .20

FAO "Freedom from Hunger" campaign.

Mercado Mountains and Arms of Durango A223

Belisario Dominguez A224

1963, July 13 Photo.
935 A223 20c dk bl & choc .60 .20

400th anniv. of the founding of Durango.

1963, July 13 Photo.
936 A224 20c dk grn & ol gray .60 .20

Centenary of the birth of Belisario Dominguez, revolutionary leader.

Mexico. No. 897, depicting Mexico No. 1 — A225

1963, Oct. 9 Wmk. 350 *Perf. 14*
937 A225 1p int blue & brn 1.25 .75

77th Annual Convention of the American Philatelic Society, Mexico City, Oct. 7-13. See No. C274.

Tree of Life A226

José Morelos A227

1963, Oct. 26 Wmk. 350 *Perf. 14*
938 A226 20c dl bl grn & car .40 .20

Intl. Red Cross, cent. See No. C277.

1963, Nov. 9
939 A227 40c grn & dk sl grn .55 .20

150th anniv. of the 1st congress of Anahuac.

Pres. Victor Paz Estenssoro A228

Arms of Sinaloa University A229

1963, Nov. 9 Wmk. 350 *Perf. 14*
940 A228 40c dk brn & dk red brn .60 .20

Visit of President Victor Paz Estenssoro of Bolivia.

1963 Photo.
941 A229 40c slate grn & ol bister .60 .20

90th anniversary of the founding of the University of Sinaloa.

Diesel Train, Rail Cross Section and Globe A230

1963, Nov. 29 Photo.
942 A230 20c black & dk brn .90 .50

11th Pan-American Railroad Congress. See No. C279.

Type of 1950-52

Designs as before.

1963-66 Wmk. 350 Photo. *Perf. 14*
943 A189 5c red brn ('65) .60 .20
944 A189 10c dk green ('64) .65 .20
945 A189 15c dk green ('66) .60 .20
946 A189 20c dark blue .60 .20
948 A189 40c red orange .70 .20
949 A189 50c blue ('64) 2.00 .20
950 A189 1p olive grn ('64) 4.00 .20
951 A189 5p dl bl & dk grn ('66) 100.00 30.00
952 A189 10p gray & Prus bl ('65) 35.00 25.00
Nos. 943-952 (9) 144.15 56.40

The 20c is redrawn; clouds almost eliminated and other slight variations.

"F.S.T.S.E." Emblem A231

Academy of Medicine Emblem A232

1964, Feb. 15
954 A231 20c red org & dk brn .40 .20

25th anniv. (in 1963) of the Civil Service Statute affecting federal employees.

1964, May 18 Wmk. 350 *Perf. 14*
955 A232 20c gold & blk .40 .20

National Academy of Medicine, cent.

José Rizal A233

View of Zacatecas A234

40c, Miguel Lopez de Legaspi, Spanish navigator.

1964, Nov. 10 Photo. *Perf. 14*
956 A233 20c dk bl & dp grn .50 .20
957 A233 40c dk bl & brt vio .60 .20
Nos. 956-957,C300-C301 (4) 6.10 1.75

Issued to honor 400 years of Mexican-Philippine friendship.

1964, Nov. 10 Wmk. 350
958 A234 40c slate grn & red .55 .20

50th anniv. of the capture of Zacatecas.

Col. Gregorio Mendez
A235

Morelos Theater, Aguascalientes
A236

1964, Nov. 10

959 A235 40c grysh blk & dk brn .50 .20

Cent. of the Battle of Jahuactal, Tabasco.

1965, Jan. 9 Photo. *Perf. 14*

960 A236 20c dl cl & dk gray .35 .20

50th anniversary of the Aguascalientes Convention, Oct. 1-Nov. 9, 1914.

Andrés Manuel del Río
A237

1965, Feb. 18 Wmk. 350 *Perf. 14*

961 A237 30c gray .40 .20

Bicentenary of the birth of Andrés Manuel del Rio, founder of the National School of Mining and discoverer of vanadium.

José Morelos and Constitution
A238

Trees
A239

1965, Apr. 24 Photo. *Perf. 14*

962 A238 40c brt grn & dk red brn .45 .20

Sesquicentennial (in 1964) of the 1st Mexican constitution.

1965, July 14 Wmk. 350 *Perf. 14*

963 A239 20c blue & green .30 .20

Issued to commemorate Tree Day, July 8.

ICY Emblem
A240

1965, Sept. 13 Photo.

964 A240 40c olive gray & slate grn .30 .20

International Cooperation Year, 1965.

Athlete with Sling, Clay Figure
A241

Design: 40c, Batter. Clay figures on 20c and 40c found in Colima, period 300-650 A.D.

1965, Dec. 17 Wmk. 350 *Perf. 14*

965 A241 20c olive & vio bl 3.25 .20

966 A241 40c pink & black 1.00 .20

Nos. 965-966,C309-C311 (5) 6.70 1.20

19th Olympic Games, Mexico, 1968.

José Morelos by Diego Rivera — A242

Emiliano Zapata — A243

1965, Dec. 22

967 A242 20c lt vio bl & blk .40 .20

José Maria Morelos y Pavon (1765-1815), priest and patriot in 1810 revolution against Spain.

1966, Jan. 10 Photo.

20c, Corn, cotton, bamboo, wheat and cow.

968 A243 20c carmine rose .35 .20

969 A243 40c black .45 .20

50th anniv. of the Agrarian Reform Law.

Mexican Postal Service Emblem
A244

Bartolomé de Las Casas
A245

1966, June 24 Wmk. 300 *Perf. 14*

970 A244 40c brt green & blk .40 .20

Nos. 970,C314-C315 (3) 1.00 .60

Congress of the Postal Union of the Americas and Spain, UPAE, Mexico City, June 24-July 23.

1966, Aug. 1 Photo. Wmk. 300

971 A245 20c black & buff .40 .20

400th anniv. of the death of Bartolomé de Las Casas (1474-1566), "Apostle of the Indies."

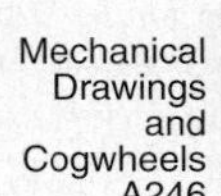

Mechanical Drawings and Cogwheels
A246

1966, Aug. 15 Photo. *Perf. 14*

972 A246 20c gray & grn .30 .20

50th anniversary of the founding of the School of Mechanical and Electrical Engineering (ESIME).

FAO Emblem — A247

1966, Sept. 30 Wmk. 300 *Perf. 14*

973 A247 40c green .30 .20

FAO International Rice Year.

Wrestling, by Diego Rivera
A248

1966, Oct. 15

Size: 35x21mm

974 A248 20c Running and Jumping 1.25 .20

975 A248 40c shown 1.00 .20

a. Souvenir sheet 4.00 4.00

Nos. 974-975,C318-C320 (5) 5.70 1.40

Issued to publicize the 19th Olympic Games, Mexico City, D.F., 1968. No. 975a contains 2 imperf. stamps similar to Nos. 974-975 with simulated perforations. Sold for 90c.

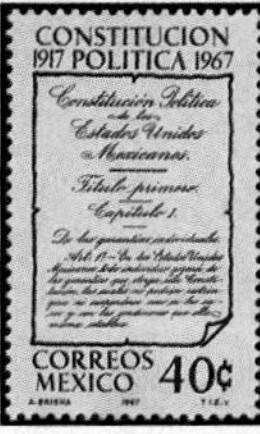

First Page of Constitution
A249

Oil Refinery and Pyramid of the Sun
A250

Wmk. 300

1967, Feb. 5 Photo. *Perf. 14*

976 A249 40c black .50 .20

Constitution, 50th anniv. See #C322.

1967, Apr. 2 Wmk. 300 *Perf. 14*

977 A250 40c lt bl & blk .35 .20

7th Intl. Oil Congress, Mexico City, Sept. 1967.

Nayarit Indian — A251

Wmk. 300

1967, May 1 Photo. *Perf. 14*

978 A251 20c pale grn & blk .30 .20

50th anniversary of Nayarit Statehood.

Degollado Theater, Guadalajara — A252

Wmk. 300

1967, June 12 Photo. *Perf. 14*

979 A252 40c pink & black .35 .20

Centenary of the founding of the Degollado Theater, Guadalajara.

Mexican Eagle over Imperial Crown — A253

Perf. 10x10½

1967, June 19 Litho. Wmk. 350

980 A253 20c black & ocher .30 .20

Centenary of the victory of the Mexican republican forces and of the execution of Emperor Maximilian I.

Canoeing
A254

Designs: 40c, Basketball. 50c, Hockey. 80c, Bicycling. 2p, Fencing.

Wmk. 300

1967, Oct. 12 Photo. *Perf. 14*

981 A254 20c blue & blk .50 .20

982 A254 40c brick red & blk .50 .20

983 A254 50c brt yel grn & blk .50 .20

a. Souvenir sheet of 3, #981-983, imperf. 5.00 3.50

984 A254 80c brt pur & blk 1.25 .25

985 A254 2p orange & blk 2.25 .30

a. Souvenir sheet of 2, #984-985, imperf. 7.00 4.00

Nos. 981-985,C328-C331 (9) 8.75 2.70

Nos. 981-985 (5) 5.00 1.15

Issued to publicize the 19th Olympic Games, Mexico City, Oct. 12-27, 1968.

No. 983a sold for 1.50p; No. 985a sold for 3.50p. Both sheets are watermark 350.

See Nos. 990-995, C335-C338.

Artemio de Valle-Arizpe
A255

Pedro Moreno
A256

1967, Nov. 1 Photo.

986 A255 20c brown & slate .35 .30

Centenary of the Ateneo Fuente, a college at Saltillo, Coahuila.

1967, Nov. 18 Wmk. 300 *Perf. 14*

987 A256 40c blk & lt bl .35 .20

Moreno (1775-1817), revolutionary leader.

Gabino Barreda
A257

Staircase, Palace of Mining
A258

1968, Jan. 27 Photo. *Perf. 14*

988 A257 40c dk bl & rose claret .40 .20
989 A258 40c blk & bl gray .40 .20

Centenary of the founding of the National Preparatory and Engineering Schools.

Type of Olympic Issue, 1967

20c, Wrestling. 40c, Pentathlon. 50c, Water polo. 80c, Gymnastics. 1p, Boxing. 2p, Pistol shoot.

1968, Mar. 21 Wmk. 300 *Perf. 14*

990 A254 20c olive & blk .75 .20
991 A254 40c red lil & blk .75 .20
992 A254 50c brt green & blk .75 .20
a. Souvenir sheet of 3, #990-992, imperf. 7.00 4.00
993 A254 80c brt pink & blk 1.00 .25
994 A254 1p org brn & blk 4.00 3.50
995 A254 2p gray & blk 5.50 3.50
a. Souvenir sheet of 3, #993-995, imperf. 7.50 4.00
Nos. 990-995,C335-C338 (10) 15.45 9.65

19th Olympic Games, Mexico City, Oct. 12-27. No. 992a sold for 1.50p; No. 995a sold for 5p. Both sheets are watermark 350.

Map of Mexico, Peace Dove A259

Arms of Veracruz A261

Symbols of Cultural Events A260

40c, University City Olympic stadium. 50c, Telecommunications tower. 2p, Sports Palace. 10p, Pyramid of the Sun, Teotihuacan, & Olympic torch.

Wmk. 350

1968, Oct. Photo. *Perf. 14*

996 A259 20c blue, yel & grn .75 .20
997 A259 40c multicolored .75 .20
998 A259 50c multicolored .75 .20
a. Souv. sheet of 3, #996-998, imperf. 20.00 10.00
999 A260 2p multicolored 4.00 .50
1000 A260 5p silver & blk 10.00 1.25
a. Souv. sheet of 2, #999-1000, imperf. 25.00 20.00
1001 A259 10p multicolored 7.50 2.00
Nos. 996-1001,C340-C344 (11) 32.35 8.15

19th Olympic Games, Mexico City, Oct. 12-27 (Nos. 996-1000). Arrival of the Olympic torch in Veracruz (No. 1001).

#998a sold for 1.50p. #1000a sold for 9p.

Issued: #996-1000, 10/12/68; #1001, 10/6/68.

1969, May 20 Wmk. 350 *Perf. 14*

1002 A261 40c multicolored .35 .20

450th anniv. of the founding of Veracruz.

Type of 1950-52 Coil Stamps

Perf. 11 Vert.

1969 Wmk. 300 Photo.

1003 A189 20c dk blue 4.00 2.00
1004 A189 40c red orange 5.00 3.00

Vert. pairs, imperf. horiz. may be from uncut rolls of coils.

Subway Train — A262

1969, Sept. 4 Wmk. 350 *Perf. 14*

1005 A262 40c multicolored .35 .20

Inauguration of Mexico City subway.

Honeycomb, Bee and ILO Emblem A263

Gen. Allende, by Diego Rivera A264

1969, Oct. 18 Photo. *Perf. 14*

1006 A263 40c multicolored .30 .20

50th anniversary of the ILO.

1969, Nov. 15 Wmk. 350 *Perf. 14*

1007 A264 40c multicolored .30 .20

Gen. Ignacio Allende Unzaga (1769-1811), hero of Mexican independence.

Tourist Issue

Pyramid of Niches at El Tajin, Veracruz, and Dancers Swinging from Pole A265

Anthropology Museum, Mexico City — A266

Deer Dance, Sonora — A267

Designs: No. 1010, View of Puerto Vallarta. No. 1011, Puebla Cathedral. No. 1012, Calle Belaunzaran. No. 1014, Ocotlan Cathedral, horiz.

1969-73 Photo. Wmk. 350

1008 A265 40c shown .45 .20
1009 A266 40c shown ('70) .45 .20
1010 A266 40c Jalisco ('70) .45 .20
1011 A266 40c Puebla ('70) .45 .20
1012 A266 40c Guanajuato ('70) .45 .20

Wmk. 300

1013 A267 40c shown ('73) .35 .20
1014 A267 40c Tlaxcala ('73) .35 .20
Nos. 1008-1014,C354-C358 (12) 6.35 2.75
Nos. 1008-1014 (7) 2.95 1.40

No. 1010 is inscribed "1970" below the design. Copies inscribed "1969" are from an earlier, unissued printing. Value $500.

Issued: #1008, 12/13/69; #1009-1012, 1/17/70; #1013-1014, 3/6/73.

Luminescence

Fluorescent stamps include Nos. 1013-1014, 1035, 1038, 1041, 1043-1045, 1047-1050, 1054-1059. (See Luminescence note over No. C527.)

"How Many, Who and What are We?" — A268

40c, "What, How & How Much do we produce?" (horse's head & symbols of agriculture).

1970, Jan. 26 Wmk. 350 *Perf. 14*

1024 A268 20c multicolored .30 .20
1025 A268 40c blue & multi .30 .20

Issued to publicize the 1970 census.

Human Eye and Spectrum A269

1970, Mar. 8 Photo. Wmk. 350

1026 A269 40c multicolored .30 .20

21st International Congress of Ophthalmology, Mexico City, Mar. 8-14.

Helmets of 1920 and 1970 A270

1970, Apr. 11 Wmk. 350 *Perf. 14*

1027 A270 40c dk car rose, blk & lt brn .30 .20

50th anniversary of the Military College.

José Maria Pino Suarez — A271

Coat of Arms of Celaya — A272

1970, Apr. 25 Photo.

1028 A271 40c black & multi .30 .20

Centenary of the birth of José Maria Pino Suarez (1869-1913), lawyer, poet and Vice President of Mexico.

1970, Oct. 12 Photo. *Perf. 14*

1029 A272 40c black & multi .30 .20

City of Celaya, 400th anniversary.

Eclipse of Sun — A273

1970, Nov. 27 Wmk. 350 *Perf. 14*

1030 A273 40c black & gray .30 .20

Total eclipse of the sun, Mar. 7, 1970.

Spheres with Dates 1970-1770 A274

1971, June 26 Photo. *Perf. 14*

1031 A274 40c emerald & blk .30 .20

Bicentenary of National Lottery.

Vasco de Quiroga, Mural by O'Gorman A275

1971, July 10 Photo.

1032 A275 40c multicolored .30 .20

500th anniversary of the birth of Vasco de Quiroga (1470-1565), Archbishop of Michoacan, founder of hospitals and schools.

Amado Nervo (1870-1919), Poet — A276

1971, Aug. 7 Wmk. 350 *Perf. 14*

1033 A276 40c multicolored .30 .20

Waves and Transformer A277

1971, Oct. 8

1034 A277 40c blk, lt bl & lt grn .30 .20

50th anniversary of Mexican radio.

Pres. Lazaro Cardenas (1895-1970) — A278

1971, Oct. 19 Wmk. 300

1035 A278 40c blk & pale lil .30 .20

Keyboard and Lara's Signature A279

1971, Nov. 6 Wmk. 350

1036 A279 40c blk, buff & pale bl .30 .20

Agustin Lara (1900-70), composer.

Arms of Monterrey A280

Cardiology Institute and WHO Emblems A281

1971, Dec. 18
1037 A280 40c black & multi .30 .20

375th anniv. of the founding of Monterrey.

1972, Apr. 8 **Wmk. 300**
1038 A281 40c multicolored .30 .20

"Your heart is your health," World Health Day 1972. See No. C395.

Gaceta de Mexico, Jan. 1, 1722 A282

1972, June 24 **Wmk. 350**
1039 A282 40c multicolored .30 .20

250th anniv. of 1st Mexican newspaper.

Lions Intl. Emblem A283

Sailing Ship Zaragoza A284

1972, June 28
1040 A283 40c black & multi .30 .20

55th Lions International Convention.

1972, July 1
1041 A284 40c blue & multi .30 .20

75th anniv. of the Naval School of Veracruz.

Olive Tree and Branch — A285

1972, July 18 **Wmk. 350** ***Perf. 14***
1042 A285 40c lt grn, ocher & blk .30 .20
a. 40c light green, yellow & black 3.00 3.00

Centenary of Chilpancingo as capital of Guerrero State.

Margarita Maza de Juárez A286

Design: 40c, Benito Juárez, by Diego Rivera.

1972, Sept. 15 **Photo.** **Wmk. 300**
1043 A286 20c pink & multi .40 .20
1044 A286 40c dp yellow & multi .40 .20
Nos. 1043-1044,C403-C405 (5) 1.60 1.00

Benito Juárez (1806-1872), revolutionary leader and president of Mexico.

Emperor Justinian I, Mosaic A287

1972, Sept. 30 **Wmk. 300**
1045 A287 40c multicolored .65 .20

Mexican Bar Association, 50th anniv.

Caravel A288

Library, Book Year Emblem A290

Olympic Emblems A289

1972, Oct. 12 **Wmk. 350**
1046 A288 80c buff, pur & ocher .40 .20

Stamp Day of The Americas.

1972, Dec. 9 **Wmk. 300**
1047 A289 40c multicolored 1.00 .20

20th Olympic Games, Munich, Aug. 26-Sept. 11. See Nos. C410-C411.

1972, Dec. 16
1048 A290 40c black & multi .30 .20

International Book Year 1972.

Fish in Clean Water A291

1972, Dec. 16
1049 A291 40c blk & lt bl .40 .20

Anti-pollution campaign. See No. C412.

Metlac Railroad Bridge — A292

1973, Feb. 2 ***Perf. 14***
1050 A292 40c multicolored .85 .20

Centenary of Mexican railroads.

Cadet — A293

1973, Oct. 11 **Photo.** **Wmk. 300**
1051 A293 40c black & multi .45 .20

Sesquicentennial of Military College.

Madero, by Diego Rivera — A294

Antonio Narro — A295

1973, Nov. 9 **Wmk. 350** ***Perf. 14***
1052 A294 40c multicolored .30 .20

Pres. Francisco I. Madero (1873-1913).

1973, Nov. 9 **Photo.**
1053 A295 40c steel gray .35 .20

50th anniversary of the Antonio Narro Agriculture School in Saltillo.

Type of 1950-52

Designs as before.

1973 **Unwmk.** ***Perf. 14***
1054 A189 20c blue violet 5.00 2.00
1055 A189 40c red orange 5.00 2.00

Fluorescent printing on back (or on front of 40c) consisting of network pattern and diagonal inscription.

Unsaturated Hydrocarbon Molecule — A296

Wmk. 300
1973, Dec. 7 **Photo.** ***Perf. 14***
1056 A296 40c blk, dk car & yel .30 .20

Pointing Hand Emblem of Foreign Trade Institute — A297

1974, Jan. 11 **Photo.** **Wmk. 300**
1057 A297 40c dk green & blk .30 .20

Export promotion.

A298

1974, Jan. 18 **Litho.** **Wmk. 300**
1058 A298 40c black .30 .20

EXMEX 73 Philatelic Exhibition, Cuernavaca, Apr. 7-15. See No. C424.

Manuel M. Ponce at Keyboard A299

1974, Jan. 18 **Photo.** **Wmk. 300**
1059 A299 40c gold & multi .30 .20

Manuel M. Ponce (1882-1948), composer.

Silver Statuette of Mexican Woman — A300

1974, Mar. 23 **Photo.** ***Perf. 14***
1060 A300 40c red & multi .30 .20

First World Silver Fair.

Mariano Azuela A301

1974, Apr. 26 **Wmk. 300** ***Perf. 14***
1061 A301 40c multicolored .30 .20

Mariano Azuela (1873-1952), writer.

Dancing Dogs, Pre-Columbian A302

1974, Apr. 10
1062 A302 40c multicolored .30 .20

6th Traveling Dog Exhibition, Mexico City, Nov. 23-Dec. 1.

Aqueduct, Tepotzotlan — A303

1974, July 1 **Photo.** **Wmk. 300**
1063 A303 40c brt blue & blk .45 .20

National Engineers' Day, July 1.

Dr. Rodolfo Robles A304

1974, July 19 *Perf. 14*
1064 A304 40c bister & grn .30 .20

25th anniv. of WHO (in 1973).

EXFILMEX 74 Emblem — A305

1974, July 26 *Perf. 13x12*
1065 A305 40c buff, grn & blk .30 .20

EXFILMEX 74, 5th Inter-American Philatelic Exhibition honoring UPU cent, Mexico City, 10/26-11/3. See #C429.

Demosthenes A306

1974, Aug. 2 **Photo.** *Perf. 14*
1066 A306 20c green & brn .35 .20

2nd Spanish-American Cong. for Reading and Writing Studies, Mexico City, May 7-14.

Map of Chiapas and Head A307

1974, Sept. 14 **Wmk. 300** *Perf. 14*
1067 A307 20c black & grn .30 .20

Sesquicentenary of Chiapas statehood.

Law of 1824 — A308

Sebastian Lerdo de Tejada — A309

1974, Oct. 11 **Wmk. 300**
1068 A308 40c gray & grn .30 .20

Sesquicentennial of the establishment of the Federal Republic of Mexico.

1974, Oct. 11 **Photo.**
1069 A309 40c black & lt bl .30 .20

Centenary of restoration of the Senate.

UPU Monument, Bern A310

1974, Dec. 13 **Wmk. 300** *Perf. 14*
1070 A310 40c ultra & org brn .30 .20
Nos. 1070,C437-C438 (3) .80 .60

Cent. of UPU.

Types of 1950-56

Designs (as 1951-56 issues): 80p, Michoacan dance of the Moors. 2.30p, Guillermo Prieto. 3p, Modernistic church, Nuevo Leon. 50p, Benito Juarez.

1975 **Photo.** **Wmk. 300** *Perf. 14*
1072 A189 80c green .55 .25
1075 A200 2.30p dp violet bl .85 .35
1076 A189 3p brick red .85 .35
1081 A189 50p orange & grn 10.00 7.50
Nos. 1072-1081 (4) 12.25 8.45

See No. 1097 for unwmkd. 3p with no shading under "Leon."

Gov. José Maria Mora — A312

1975, Feb. 21 **Photo.** **Wmk. 300**
1084 A312 20c yellow & multi .30 .20

Sesquicentennial (in 1974) of establishment of the State of Mexico.

Merchants with Pre-Columbian Goods — A313

1975, Apr. 18 **Photo.** **Unwmk.**
1085 A313 80c multicolored .30 .20

Centenary (in 1974) of the National Chamber of Commerce in Mexico City. Design from Florentine Codex.

Juan Aldama, by Diego Rivera A314

1975, June 6 *Perf. 14*
1086 A314 80c multicolored .30 .20

Juan Aldama (1774-1811), officer and patriot, birth bicentenary.

Indians and Eagle on Cactus Destroying Serpent, from Duran Codex A315

1975, Aug. 1 **Photo.** **Unwmk.**
1087 A315 80c multicolored .30 .20

650th anniv. of Tenochtitlan (Mexico City).

Julián Carrillo A316

Academy Emblem A317

1975, Sept. 12 **Photo.** **Unwmk.**
1088 A316 80c brt grn & red brn .30 .20

Julián Carrillo (1875-1965), violinist and composer, birth centenary.

1975, Sept. 13 *Perf. 14*
1089 A317 80c brown & ocher .30 .20

Cent. of Mexican Academy of Languages.

Types of 1950-56

Designs (as 1950-56 issues): 80c, Indian dancer, Michoacan. 2p, Convent, Morelos.

1975-76 **Photo.** **Unwmk.**
1090 A189 40c orange .35 .20
1091 A189 50c blue .40 .20
1092 A200 60c red lilac .50 .20
1093 A200 70c violet blue .50 .20
1094 A189 80c green .50 .20
1095 A189 1p olive green .50 .20
1096 A189 2p scarlet 1.00 .50
1097 A189 3p brick red 1.00 .50
1099 A189 5p gray bl & grn 2.10 1.00
1101 A189 10p grn & dp ultra ('76) 5.00 2.00
1102 A189 20p lilac & blk ('76) 10.00 4.00
Nos. 1090-1102 (11) 21.85 9.20

University of Guadalajara — A318

1975, Oct. 1 **Photo.** *Perf. 14*
1107 A318 80c multicolored .30 .20

University of Guadalajara, 50th anniversary.

Road Workers — A319

1975, Oct. 17 **Photo.** **Unwmk.**
1108 A319 80c gray grn, grn & blk .30 .20

50 years of road building for progress.

Pistons A320

Designs: Export Emblem and 5c, 6p, Steel pipes. 20c, Chemistry flasks. 40c, Cup of coffee. 80c, Meat cuts marked on steer. 1p, Electrical conductor. 2p, Abalone. 3p, Men's shoes. 4p, Tiles. 5p, Minerals. 7p, 8p, 9p, Overalls. 10p, Tequila. 15p, Honey. 20p, Wrought iron. 25p, Copper vase. 35p, 40p, No. 1133, 80p, Books. No. 1132, Jewelry. 100p, Strawberry. 200p, Citrus fruit. 300p, Motor vehicles. 400p, Circuit board. 500p, Cotton.

Some stamps have a gray burelage;
Type I — Burelage lines run lower left to upper right with arch towards lower right.
Type II — Burelage lines run lower left to upper right with arch towards upper left.

1975-87 **Photo.** **Unwmk.** *Perf. 14*
1109 A320 5c slate bl ('77) 1.00 .20
1110 A320 20c black ('76) .20 .20
1111 A320 40c dk brn ('76) .90 .20
a. 40c claret brown ('81) 1.00 .25
1112 A320 50c slate, thin paper ('81) .75 .20
a. 50c slate blue ('76) .90 .20
b. 50c black ('83) .60 .20
c. 50c dull blue ('75) .90 .20
1113 A320 80c brt car ('76) 5.50 .20
a. Perf. 11 .40 .20
b. Perf. 11½x11 .75 .20
c. As "a," thin paper ('81) 1.40 .75
d. As "b," thin paper ('81) .75 .75
1114 A320 1p vio bl & org ('78) .90 .20
1115 A320 1p lt vio & org ('83) 1.50 .20
1116 A320 1p black & org ('84) .20 .20
1117 A320 2p grn & brt bl ('81) 1.25 .20
a. 2p bl grn & dk bl ('76) 1.50 .20
1118 A320 3p red brown 2.75 .20
a. 3p brn, perf 11½x11 ('82) 3.00 .20
b. Golden brn, thin paper ('81) .60 .20
1119 A320 4p tan & dk brn ('80) .20 .20
1120 A320 5p gray olive ('78) 2.25 .20
a. Perf 11½x11 ('84) .20 .20
1121 A320 6p brt org ('83) .30 .20
a. Perf 11½x11 ('83) .30 .20
b. Perf 11 ('84) 3.25 .20
1121C A320 6p gray, perf. 11½x11 ('84) .20 .20
1122 A320 7p Prus blue ('84) .20 .20
a. 7p blue gray ('84) 5.00 .20
1123 A320 8p bis brn, perf 11½x11 ('84) .20 .20
a. Perf 11 ('84) 8.00 .20
1124 A320 9p dk bl ('84) .20 .20
1125 A320 10p dk & lt grn ('78) .35 .20
a. Thin paper ('81) .65 .30
b. Dk ol grn & yel grn ('86) 2.00 .20
c. Dk ol grn & brt ol grn ('87) .30 .20
1126 A320 15p yel org & red brn ('84) .30 .20
1127 A320 20p black ('78) 1.25 .20
1128 A320 20p dk gray ('84) .20 .20
1129 A320 25p org brn ('84) .40 .20
1130 A320 35p brt cer & yel ('84) .20 .20

1131 A320 40p org brn & lt yel ('84) .30 .20
1132 A320 50p gray, sil, brt vio & pur ('80) 6.00 .75
1133 A320 50p brt bl & lt yel ('83) 1.50 .20
1133A A320 80p pink & gold ('85) 1.60 .35
1134 A320 100p scar & brt grn, I ('83) 1.50 .80
1135 A320 200p emer & yel grn, I ('83) 4.50 .50
a. Emer & lemon, I ('87) 6.00 1.25
b. Emer & yel grn, II ('83) 5.00 2.00
1136 A320 300p brt bl & red, I ('83) 4.00 2.00
a. Type II ('87) 125.00 20.00
1137 A320 400p lem & red brn, I ('84) 3.00 .75
1138 A320 500p lt ol grn & yel org, I ('84) 4.00 .75
Nos. 1109-1138 (32) 47.60 10.90

No. 1125b is 2mm wider than No. 1125. Size of No. 1125b: 37x21mm.

Nos. 1117, 1119, 1126, 1135 exist with one or more colors missing. These were not regularly issued.

See Nos. 1166-1176, 1465-1470A, 1491-1505, 1583-1603, 1763-1776, C486-C508, C594-C603.

Aguascalientes Cathedral A323

Jaime Torres Bodet A324

1975, Nov. 28
1140 A323 50c bl grn & blk .75 .20

400th anniversary of Aguascalientes.

1975, Nov. 28
1141 A324 80c blue & brn .30 .20

Jaime Torres Bodet (1920-1974), writer, director general of UNESCO (1958-1962).

Allegory, by José Clemente Orozco — A325

1975, Dec. 9 *Perf. 14*
1142 A325 80c multicolored .30 .20

Sesquicentennial of Supreme Court.

The Death of Cuauhtemoc, by Chavez Morado — A326

1975, Dec. 12 **Photo.**
1143 A326 80c multicolored .30 .20

450th anniv. of the death of Cuauhtemoc (1495?-1525), last Aztec emperor.

Netzahualcoyotl (Water God) — A327

1976, Jan. 9 **Unwmk.** *Perf. 14*
1144 A327 80c blue & vio bl .30 .20

50th anniv. of Mexican irrigation projects.

Arch, Leon A328

1976, Jan. 20
1145 A328 80c dk brn & ocher .30 .20

400th anniversary of León, Guanajuato.

Forest Fire A329

1976, July 8 **Photo.** *Perf. 14*
1146 A329 80c blk, grn & red .30 .20

Prevent fires!

Hat and Scout Emblem A330

Exhibition Emblem A331

1976, Aug. 24 **Photo.** **Unwmk.**
1147 A330 80c olive & red brn .30 .20

Mexican Boy Scout Assoc., 50th anniv.

1976, Sept. 2
1148 A331 80c black, red & grn .30 .20

Mexico Today and Tomorrow Exhibition.

New Building, Military College A332

1976, Sept. 13 *Perf. 14*
1149 A332 50c red brn & ocher .30 .20

Military College, new installations.

Dr. Ricardo Vertiz — A333

1976, Sept. 24 **Photo.** *Perf. 14*
1150 A333 80c blk & redsh brn .30 .20

Our Lady of Light Ophthalmological Hospital, centenary.

National Basilica of Guadeloupe — A334

1976, Oct. 12
1151 A334 50c black & ocher .30 .20

Inauguration of the new National Basilica of Our Lady of Guadeloupe.

"40" and Emblem A335

1976, Oct. 28 **Photo.** *Perf. 14*
1152 A335 80c blk, lt grn & car .30 .20

Natl. Polytechnic Institute, 40th anniv.

Blast Furnace A336

1976, Nov. 4
1153 A336 50c multicolored .30 .20

Inauguration of the Lazaro Cardenas Steel Mill, Las Truchas.

Saltillo Cathedral A337

Electrification A338

1977, July 25 **Photo.** *Perf. 14*
1154 A337 80c yel & dk brn .30 .20

400th anniversary of the founding of Saltillo.

1977, Aug. 14 **Photo.** *Perf. 14*
1155 A338 80c multicolored .30 .20

40 years of Mexican development program.

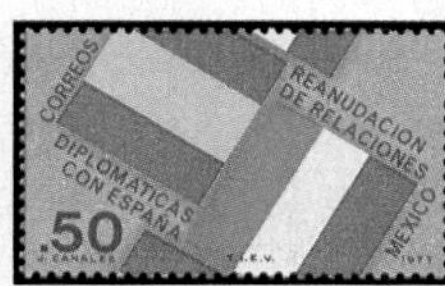

Flags of Spain and Mexico A339

1977, Oct. 8 **Photo.** **Wmk. 300**
1156 A339 50c multicolored .30 .20
1157 A339 80c multicolored .30 .20
Nos. 1156-1157,C537-C539 (5) 1.45 1.00

Resumption of diplomatic relations with Spain.

Aquiles Serdan (1877-1910), Martyr of the Revolution — A340

1977, Nov. 18 **Photo.** *Perf. 14*
1158 A340 80c lt & dk grn & blk .30 .20

Poinsettia A341

1977, Dec. 2 **Wmk. 300** *Perf. 14*
1159 A341 50c multicolored .30 .20

Christmas 1977.

Old and New Telephones — A342

1978, Mar. 15 **Photo.** *Perf. 14*
1160 A342 80c salmon & maroon .30 .20

Centenary of first telephone in Mexico.

Oil Derrick A343

1978, Mar. 18
1161 A343 80c dp org & mar .30 .20
Nos. 1161,C556-C557 (3) .85 .60

Nationalization of oil industry, 40th anniv.

Institute Emblem A344

1978, July 21 **Photo.** *Perf. 14*
1162 A344 80c blue & black .30 .20
Nos. 1162,C574-C575 (3) .90 .60

Pan-American Institute for Geography and History, 50th anniv.

Dahlias A345

Decorations and Candles A346

1978, Sept. 29 Photo. Wmk. 300
1163 A345 50c shown .30 .20
1164 A345 80c Frangipani .75 .20

See No. 1196.

1978, Nov. 22 Photo. *Perf. 14*
1165 A346 50c multicolored .30 .20

Christmas 1978.

Export Type of 1975

Designs as before. 50p, Jewelry.

1979-81 Photo. Wmk. 300 *Perf. 14*
1166 A320 20c black ('81) .40 .20
1167 A320 50c slate blue .20 .20
a. 50c bluish black .30 .20
1168 A320 80c brt car, perf 11 1.00 .20
a. Perf. 14 1.00 .20
1169 A320 1p ultra & org .30 .20
1170 A320 2p brt grn & bl .50 .20
1171 A320 3p dk brown .60 .20
1172 A320 4p tan & dk brn ('80) .75 .20
1173 A320 5p gray olive 1.00 .35
1174 A320 10p dk & lt green 2.75 .75
1175 A320 20p black 2.75 .75
1176 A320 50p gray, sil, brt vio & pur 6.75 2.50
Nos. 1166-1176 (11) 17.00 5.75

A347

Soccer Ball — A348

1979, Apr. 26 Wmk. 300 *Perf. 14*
1177 A347 80c multicolored .30 .20

Centenary of Hermosillo, Sonora.

1979, June 15 Photo. Wmk. 300

Designs: 80c, Aztec ball player. 1p, Wall painting showing athletes. 5p, Runners, horiz.

1178 A348 50c blue & blk .30 .20
1179 A348 80c multicolored .30 .20
1180 A348 1p multicolored .30 .20
Nos. 1178-1180,C606-C607 (5) 1.50 1.00

Souvenir Sheet

Imperf

1181 A348 5p multicolored 3.50 3.50

Universiada '79, World Games, Mexico City, 9/79. #1181 has simulated perforations.

Josefa Ortiz de Dominguez, Wife of the Mayor of Queretaro (Miguel Dominguez), 150th Death Anniv. — A349

1979, July 6 *Perf. 14*
1182 A349 80c multicolored .30 .20

Allegory of National Culture, by Alfaro Siqueiros — A350

3p, Conquest of Energy, by Chavez Morado.

1979, July 10
1183 A350 80c multicolored .30 .20
1184 A350 3p multicolored .30 .20
Nos. 1183-1184,C609-C610 (4) 1.20 .80

National University, 50th anniv. of autonomy.

Emiliano Zapata, by Diego Rivera — A351

1979, Aug. 8 Photo. *Perf. 14*
1185 A351 80c multicolored .30 .20

Emiliano Zapata (1879-1919), revolutionist.

Soccer A352

Designs: 80c, Women's volleyball. 1p, Basketball. 5p, Fencing.

1979, Sept. 2
1186 A352 50c multicolored .30 .20
1187 A352 80c multicolored .30 .20
1188 A352 1p multicolored .30 .20
Nos. 1186-1188,C612-C613 (5) 1.50 1.00

Souvenir Sheet

Imperf

1189 A352 5p multicolored 2.25 2.25

Universiada '79 World University Games, Mexico City. No. 1189 has simulated perforations.

Tepoztlan, Morelos — A353

Tourism: No. 1191, Mexcaltitan, Nayarit.

1979, Sept. 28 Photo. *Perf. 14*
1190 A353 80c multicolored .30 .20
1191 A353 80c multicolored .30 .20
Nos. 1190-1191,C615-C616 (4) 1.10 .80

See #1274-1277, 1318-1321, 1513-1516.

Postmaster Martin de Olivares A354

Shepherd and Sheep A355

1979, Oct. 26 Wmk. 300 *Perf. 14*
1192 A354 80c multicolored .30 .20

Royal proclamation of mail service in the New World (New Spain), 400th anniversary. See Nos. C618-C620.

1979, Nov. 15
1193 A355 50c multicolored .30 .20

Christmas 1979. See No. C623.

Serpent, Mayan Temple A356

1980, Feb. 16 Photo. *Perf. 14x14½*
1194 A356 80c multicolored .30 .20
Nos. 1194,C625-C626 (3) .90 .60

Pre-Hispanic monuments.

North American Turkey — A357

Tajetes Erecta — A358

Wmk. 300

1980, Mar. 8 Photo. *Perf. 14*
1195 A357 80c multicolored .30 .20
1196 A358 80c multicolored .30 .20
Nos. 1195-1196,C632-C633 (4) 1.05 .80

See Nos. 1163-1164, 1234-1237.

A359

A360

Designs: 50c, China Poblana (woman's costume), Puebla. 80c, Jarocha, Veracruz.

Wmk. 300

1980, Apr. 26 Photo. *Perf. 14*
1197 A359 50c multicolored .30 .20
1198 A359 80c multicolored .30 .20
Nos. 1197-1198,C636 (3) .85 .60

See Nos. 1231-1233.

1980, June 4
1200 A360 3p silver & blk .30 .20

10th national census.

Cuauhtemoc (Last Aztec Emperor), 1520, Matritense Codex — A361

Pre-Hispanic Art (Leaders): 1.60p, Nezahualcoyotl (1402-1472), governor of Tetzcoco, poet, Azcatitlan Codex. 5.50p, Eight Deer Tiger's Claw (1011-1063), 11th king of Mixtec, Nuttall Codex.

1980, June 21
1201 A361 80c multicolored .30 .20
1202 A361 1.60p multicolored .30 .20
1203 A361 5.50p multicolored .45 .20
Nos. 1201-1203 (3) 1.05 .60

See Nos. 1285-1287, 1510-1512.

Xipe (Aztec God of Medicine), Bourbon Codex A362

1980, June 29
1204 A362 1.60p multicolored .30 .20

22nd Intl. Biennial Cong. of the Intl. College of Surgeons, Mexico City, 6/29-7/4.

Moscow '80 Bronze Medal, Emblem, Misha, Olympic Rings — A363

1980, July 19 Photo. *Perf. 14*
1205 A363 1.60p shown .30 .20
1206 A363 3p Silver medal .30 .20
1207 A363 5.50p Gold medal .40 .25
Nos. 1205-1207 (3) 1.00 .65

22nd Summer Olympic Games, Moscow, July 19-Aug. 3.

Ceremonial Vessel, Tenochtitlan Temple A364

Wmk. 300

1980, Aug. 23 Photo. *Perf. 14*
1208 A364 80c shown .30 .20
1209 A364 1.60p Caracol .30 .20
1210 A364 5.50p Chacmool .30 .20
Nos. 1208-1210 (3) .90 .60

Pre-Columbian Art.

Sacromonte Sanctuary, Amecameca — A365

Colonial Monuments: No. 1212, St. Catherine's Convent, Patzcuaro. No. 1213, Basilica, Cuilapan, vert. No. 1214, Calvary Hermitage, Cuernavaca.

1980, Sept. 26 Photo. *Perf. 14*
1211 A365 2.50p black .30 .20
1212 A365 2.50p black .30 .20
1213 A365 3p black .30 .20
1214 A365 3p black .30 .20
Nos. 1211-1214 (4) 1.20 .80

See Nos. 1260-1263, 1303-1306, 1338-1341.

Quetzalcoatl (God) — A366

Sinaloa Coat of Arms — A367

1980, Sept. 27
1215 A366 2.50p multicolored .30 .20

World Tourism Conf., Manila, Sept. 27.

1980, Oct. 13
1216 A367 1.60p multicolored .30 .20

Sinaloa state sesquicentennial.

Straw Angel — A368

Christmas 1980: 1.60p, Poinsettias.

1980 Photo. *Perf. 14*
1217 A368 50c multicolored .30 .20
1218 A368 1.60p multicolored .30 .20

Issued: #1217, 11/15/80; #1218, 10/15/80.

Congress Emblem A369

1980, Dec. 1
1219 A369 1.60p multicolored .30 .20

4th International Civil Justice Congress.

Glass Vase and Animals A370

1980, Dec. 13 Wmk. 300
1220 A370 50c shown .30 .20
1221 A370 1p Poncho .30 .20
1222 A370 3p Wooden mask, 17th century .30 .20
Nos. 1220-1222 (3) .90 .60

See Nos. 1267-1269.

Simon Bolivar, by Paulin Guerin A371

Vicente Guerrero A372

1980, Dec. 17
1223 A371 4p multicolored .40 .25

Simon Bolivar death sesquicentennial.

1981, Feb. 14
1224 A372 80c multicolored .30 .20

Vicente Guerrero (1783-1831), statesman.

Valentin Gomez Farias — A373

1981, Feb. 14
1225 A373 80c brt grn & gray .30 .20

First Latin-American Table Tennis Cup — A374

Wmk. 300
1981, Feb. 27 Photo. *Perf. 14*
1226 A374 4p multicolored .40 .25

Jesus Gonzalez Ortega, Politician, Birth Cent. A375

Gabino Barreda (1818-1881), Physician A376

Wmk. 300
1981, Feb. 28 Photo. *Perf. 14*
1227 A375 80c brn & yel org .30 .20

1981, Mar. 10
1228 A376 80c multicolored .30 .20

Benito Juarez, 175th Birth Anniv. A377

1981, Mar. 21
1229 A377 1.60p multicolored .30 .20

450th Anniv. of Puebla City — A378

1981, Apr. 16 Unwmk.
1230 A378 80c multicolored .30 .20
a. Wmk. 300 3.00 .20

Costume Type of 1980

1981, Apr. 25 Unwmk.
1231 A359 50c Purepecha, Michoacan .30 .20
1232 A359 80c Charra, Jalisco .30 .20
1233 A359 1.60p Mestiza, Yucatan .30 .20
Nos. 1231-1233 (3) .90 .60

Flora and Fauna Types of 1980
Wmk. 300 (#1235), Unwmkd.

1981, May 30
1234 A357 80c Mimus polyglottos .30 .20
1235 A358 80c Persea americana .30 .20
1236 A357 1.60p Trogon mexicanus .30 .20
1237 A358 1.60p Theobromo cacao .30 .20
Nos. 1234-1237 (4) 1.20 .80

Workers' Strike, by David Alfaro Siqueiros — A379

Wmk. 300
1981, June 10 Photo. *Perf. 14*
1238 A379 1.60p multicolored .30 .20

Labor strike martyrs of Cananea, 75th anniv.

Intl. Year of the Disabled A380

1981, July 4 Unwmk. *Perf. 14*
1239 A380 4p multicolored .40 .25

450th Anniv. of Queretaro City — A381

1981, July 25 Unwmk.
1240 A381 80c multicolored .30 .20
a. Wmk. 300 3.00 .20

Alexander Fleming (1881-1955), Discoverer of Penicillin — A382

1981, Aug. 6 Unwmk.
1241 A382 5p blue & orange .40 .20

No. 1 A383

1981, Aug. 12
1242 A383 4p multicolored .30 .20
a. Wmk. 300 3.00 .20

125th anniv. of Mexican stamps.

St. Francis Xavier Clavijero, 250th Birth Anniv. — A384

1981, Sept. 9 Unwmk. *Perf. 14*
1243 A384 80c multicolored .30 .20

Union Congress Building Opening — A385

1981, Sept. 1
1244 A385 1.60p red & brt grn .30 .20

1300th Anniv. of Bulgarian State A386

1981, Sept. 19 Photo. *Perf. 14*
1245 A386 1.60p Desislava, mural, 1259 .30 .20
1246 A386 4p Thracian gold cup .30 .20
1247 A386 7p Horseman .50 .20
Nos. 1245-1247 (3) 1.10 .60

Pre-Hispanic Art — A387

1981, Sept. 26

1248 A387 80c Squatting diety .30 .20
1249 A387 1.60p Animal head .30 .20
1250 A387 4p Fish .40 .25
Nos. 1248-1250 (3) 1.00 .65

Pablo Picasso (1881-1973) — A388

1981, Oct. 5

1251 A388 5p lt ol grn & grn .40 .25

Christmas 1981 — A389

1981, Oct. 15

1252 A389 50c Shepherd .30 .20
1253 A389 1.60p Girl .30 .20

World Food Day A390

1981, Oct. 16

1254 A390 4p multicolored .30 .20

50th Death Anniv. of Thomas Edison A391

1981, Oct. 18

1255 A391 4p multicolored .30 .20

Intl. Meeting on Cooperation and Development — A392

1981, Oct. 22

1256 A392 4p multicolored .30 .20

Pan-American Railway Congress — A393

1981, Oct. 25 **Unwmk.**

1257 A393 1.60p multicolored .30 .20

50th Anniv. of Mexican Sound Movies A394

1981, Nov. 3 **Photo.** ***Perf. 14***

1258 A394 4p multicolored .30 .20

Inauguration of Zip Codes — A395

1981, Nov. 12

1259 A395 80c multicolored .30 .20

Colonial Monument Type of 1980

#1260, Mascarones House. #1261, La Merced Order Convent. #1262, Third Order Chapel, Texcoco. #1263, Friar Tembleque Aqueduct, Otumba.

1981, Nov. 28

1260 A365 4p black .30 .20
1261 A365 4p black .30 .20
1262 A365 5p black .30 .20
1263 A365 5p black .30 .20
Nos. 1260-1263 (4) 1.20 .80

Martyrs of Rio Blanco, 75th Anniv. A396

1982, Jan. 7 **Photo.** ***Perf. 14***

1264 A396 80c multicolored .30 .20

Death Sesquicentennial of Ignacio Lopez Rayon — A397

1982, Feb. 2

1265 A397 1.60p multicolored .30 .20

75th Anniv. of Postal Headquarters — A398

1982, Feb. 17

1266 A398 4p green & ocher .30 .20

Crafts Type of 1980

1982, Mar. 6 **Photo.** ***Perf. 14***

1267 A370 50c Huichole art .30 .20
1268 A370 1p Ceramic snail .30 .20
1269 A370 3p Tiger mask, Madera .30 .20
Nos. 1267-1269 (3) .90 .60

"Use Zip Codes" A399

1982, Mar. 20

1270 A399 80c multicolored .30 .20

TB Bacillus Centenary and World Health Day A400

1982, Apr. 7 **Photo.** ***Perf. 14***

1271 A400 4p multicolored .30 .20

50th Anniv. of Military Academy A401

1982, Apr. 15

1272 A401 80c multicolored .30 .20

Oaxaca City, 450th Anniv. — A402

1982, Apr. 25

1273 A402 1.60p multicolored .30 .20

Tourism Type of 1979

#1274, Basaseachic Cascade, Chihuahua. #1275, Silence Zone, Durango. #1276, Ruins, Maya city of Edzna, Campeche. #1277, Olmec sculpture, Tabasco.

1982, May 29 **Photo.** ***Perf. 14***

1274 A353 80c multicolored .30 .20
1275 A353 80c multicolored .30 .20
1276 A353 1.60p multicolored .30 .20
1277 A353 1.60p multicolored .30 .20
Nos. 1274-1277 (4) 1.20 .80

1982 World Cup A403

Designs: Various soccer players.

1982, June 13

1278 A403 1.60p multicolored 1.00 .20
1279 A403 4p multicolored 1.00 .20
1280 A403 7p multicolored 1.00 .20
Nos. 1278-1280 (3) 3.00 .60

Turtles and Map A404

1982, July 3

1281 A404 1.60p shown 1.00 .20
1282 A404 4p Gray whales 2.00 .20

Gen. Vicente Guerrero (1783-1831) — A405

1982, Aug. 9 **Photo.** ***Perf. 14***

1283 A405 80c multicolored .30 .20

2nd UN Conference on Peaceful Uses of Outer Space, Vienna, Aug. 9-21 A406

1982, Aug. 14

1284 A406 4p multicolored .30 .20

Pre-Hispanic Art Type of 1980

Designs: 80c, Tariacuri, founder of Tarasco Kingdom, Chronicle of Michoacan, 16th cent. 1.60p, Acamapichtli, Aztec emperor, 1376-1396, Azcatitlan Codex. 4p, 10-Deer Tiger's Breastplate, wife of Lord 13-Eagle Tlaloc Copal Ball, 12th cent., Nuttal Mixtec Codex.

1982, Sept. 4

1285	A361	80c multicolored		.30	.20
1286	A361	1.60p multicolored		.30	.20
1287	A361	4p multicolored		.30	.20
		Nos. 1285-1287 (3)		.90	.60

Papaya
A407

1982, Sept. 18 Unwmk. *Perf. 14*

1288	A407	80c shown	.30	.20
1289	A407	1.60p Corn	.30	.20

Florentine Codex Illustrations
A408

1982, Oct. 2

1290	A408	80c Astrologer	.30	.20
1291	A408	1.60p School	.30	.20
1292	A408	4p Musicians	.30	.20
		Nos. 1290-1292 (3)	.90	.60

See Nos. 1520-1522.

Manuel Gamio (1883-1960) Anthropologist — A409

Scientists: No. 1294, Isaac Ochoterena (1855-1950), biologist. No. 1295, Angel Maria Garibay K. (1892-1976), philologist. No. 1296, Manuel Sandoval Vallarta (1899-), nuclear physicist. No. 1297, Guillermo Gonzalez Camarena (b. 1917), electronic engineer.

1982, Oct. 16 Photo. *Perf. 14*

1293	A409	1.60p multicolored	.30	.20
1294	A409	1.60p multicolored	.30	.20
1295	A409	1.60p multicolored	.30	.20
1296	A409	1.60p multicolored	.30	.20
1297	A409	1.60p multicolored	.30	.20
a.		Strip of 5, #1293-1297	4.00	4.00

Natl. Archives Opening, Aug. 27 — A410

1982, Oct. 23 *Perf. 14*

1298	A410	1.60p brt grn & blk	.30	.20

Christmas 1982
A411

1982, Oct. 30 *Perf. 14*

1299	A411	50c Dove	.30	.20
1300	A411	1.60p Dove, diff.	.30	.20

Mexican Food System
A412

1982, Nov. 13 Photo. *Perf. 14*

1301	A412	1.60p multicolored	.30	.20

Opening of Revolutionary Museum, Chihuahua — A413

1982, Nov. 17 *Perf. 14*

1302	A413	1.60p No. C232	.30	.20

Colonial Monument Type of 1980

Designs: 1.60p, College of Sts. Peter and Paul, Mexico City, 1576. 8p, Convent of Jesus Maria, Mexico City, 1603. 10p, Open Chapel, Tlalmanalco, 1585. 14p, Convent at Actopan, Hidalgo State, 1548.

1982, Nov. 27

1303	A365	1.60p black & gray	.30	.20
1304	A365	8p black & gray	.30	.20
1305	A365	10p black & gray	.30	.20
1306	A365	14p black & gray	.40	.20
a.		Vert. strip of 4, #1303-1306 + label	*15.00*	*15.00*
		Nos. 1303-1306 (4)	1.30	.80

Alfonso Garcia Robles, 1982 Nobel Peace Prize Winner
A414

1982, Dec. 10 Unwmk. *Perf. 14*

1307	A414	1.60p multicolored	.30	.20
1308	A414	14p multicolored	.30	.20

Jose Vasconcelos, Philosopher — A415

1982, Dec. 11 *Perf. 14*

1309	A415	1.60p bl & blk	.30	.20

World Communications Year — A416

1983, Feb. 12 Photo. *Perf. 14*

1310	A416	16p multicolored	.30	.20

First Philatelic Exposition of the Mexican Revolution
A417

1983, Mar. 13 Photo. *Perf. 14*

1311	A417	6p No. 326	.30	.20

25th Anniv. of Intl. Maritime Org. — A418

1983, Mar. 17

1312	A418	16p multicolored	.35	.20

Year of Constitutional Right to Health Protection — A419

1983, Apr. 7

1313	A419	6p red & olive	.30	.20

Society of Geography and Statistics Sesquicentennial — A420

1983, Apr. 18

1314	A420	6p Founder Gomez Farias	.30	.20

2nd World Youth Soccer Championships
A421

1983, June 2 Photo. *Perf. 14*

1315	A421	6p green & blk	.30	.20
1316	A421	13p red & blk	.35	.20
1317	A421	14p blue & blk	.35	.20
		Nos. 1315-1317 (3)	1.00	.60

Tourism Type of 1979

Designs: No. 1318, Federal Palace Building, Queretaro. No. 1319, Fountain, San Luis Potosi. 13p, Cable car, Zacatecas. 14p, Mayan stone head, Quintana Roo.

1983, June 24 Photo. *Perf. 14*

1318	A353	6p multicolored	.25	.20
1319	A353	6p multicolored	.25	.20
1320	A353	13p multicolored	.35	.20
1321	A353	14p multicolored	.35	.20
a.		Vert. strip of 4, #1318-1321 + label	2.75	2.75
		Nos. 1318-1321 (4)	1.20	.80

Simon Bolivar (1783-1830) — A422

1983, July 24

1322	A422	21p multicolored	.40	.20

Angela Peralta, Opera Singer (1845-1883) — A423

1983, Aug. 30 Photo. *Perf. 14*

1323	A423	9p multicolored	.30	.20

Mexican Flora
A424

1983, Sept. 23 Photo. *Perf. 14*

1324	A424	9p Achras zapota	.30	.20
1325	A424	9p Agave atrovirens	.30	.20

Mexican Fauna
A425

1983, Sept. 23 Photo. *Perf. 14*

1326	A425	9p Boa constrictor imperator	2.00	.20
1327	A425	9p Papilio machaon	2.00	.20

Christmas 1983 — A426

1983, Oct. 15 Photo. *Perf. 14*

1328 A426 9p multicolored .30 .20
1329 A426 20p multicolored .30 .20

Integral Communications and Transportation Systems — A427

1983, Oct. 17 Photo. *Perf. 14*

1330 A427 13p brt blue & blk .30 .20

Carlos Chavez (1899-1978), Musician, Composer — A428

Contemporary Artists: No. 1332, Francisco Goitia (1882-1960), Painter. No. 1333, Salvador Diaz Miron (1853-1927), Lyrical Poet. No. 1334, Carlos Bracho (1899-1966), Sculptor. No. 1335, Fanny Anitua (1887-1968), Singer.

1983, Nov. 7 Photo. *Perf. 14*

1331 A428 9p brown & multi .30 .20
1332 A428 9p brown & multi .30 .20
1333 A428 9p brown & multi .30 .20
1334 A428 9p brown & multi .30 .20
1335 A428 9p brown & multi .30 .20
a. Horiz. strip of 5, #1331-1335 4.00 4.00

Jose Clemente Orozco (1883-1949), Painter — A429

1983, Nov. 23 Photo. *Perf. 14*

1336 A429 9p multicolored .30 .20

35th Anniv. of Human Rights Declaration A430

1983, Dec. 10 *Perf. 14*

1337 A430 20p multicolored .30 .20

Colonial Monument Type of 1980

9p, Convent Garden, Malinalco, 16th cent. 20p, Open Chapel, Cuernavaca Cathedral, Morelos. 21p, Tepeji del Rio Convent, Hidalgo. 24p, Atlatlahuacan Convent, Morelos.

1983, Dec. 16 Photo. *Perf. 14*

1338 A365 9p black & gray .30 .20
1339 A365 20p black & gray .40 .20
1340 A365 21p black & gray .40 .20
1341 A365 24p black & gray .40 .25
a. Vert. strip of 4, #1338-1341 + label 4.00 4.00

Antonio Caso (1883-1946), Philosopher — A431

1983, Dec. 19
Granite Paper

1342 A431 9p multicolored .30 .20

Royal Mining Decree Bicentenary — A432

1983, Dec. 21

1343 A432 9p Joaquin Velazquez Leon, reform author .30 .20

Postal Code Centenary A433

1984, Jan. 2 Photo. *Perf. 14*

1344 A433 12p Envelopes .35 .20

Fight Against Polio A434

1984, Apr. 7 Photo. *Perf. 14*

1345 A434 12p Children dancing .35 .20

Aquatic Birds — A435

1984, May 4 Photo. *Perf. 14*

1346 A435 12p Muscovy duck .40 .20
1347 A435 20p Black-bellied whistling tree duck .45 .20
a. Pair, #1346-1347 + label 3.50 3.50

World Dog Exposition, Mexico City A436

1984, May 27

1348 A436 12p multicolored 1.25 .20

Natl. Bank of Mexico Centenary — A437

1984, June 2

1349 A437 12p multicolored .35 .20

Forest Protection and Conservation — A438

1984, July 12 Photo. *Perf. 14*

1350 A438 20p Hands holding trees .40 .20

1984 Summer Olympics A439

1984, July 28

1351 A439 14p Shot put 1.00 .20
1352 A439 20p Equestrian 1.00 .20
1353 A439 23p Gymnastics 1.00 .20
1354 A439 24p Diving 1.00 .20
1355 A439 25p Boxing 1.00 .20
1356 A439 26p Fencing 1.00 .20

Size: 56x62mm
Imperf

1357 A439 40p Rings 3.50 1.50
Nos. 1351-1357 (7) 9.50 2.70

Mexico-USSR Diplomatic Relations, 60th Anniv. — A440

1984, Aug. 4

1358 A440 23p Flags .40 .20

Intl. Population Conference, Aug. 5-14 — A441

1984, Aug. 6

1359 A441 20p UN emblem, hand .40 .20

Economic Culture Fund, 50th Anniv. — A442

1984, Sept. 3

1360 A442 14p multicolored .35 .20

Gen Francisco J. Mugica A443

1984, Sept. 3

1361 A443 14p black & brown .35 .20

Red Cactus, by Sebastian A444

Airline Emblem A445

1984, Sept. 14 Photo. *Perf. 14*

1362 A444 14p multicolored .30 .20
1363 A445 20p blk & org .30 .20

Aeromexico (airline), 50th anniv.

Palace of Fine Arts, 50th Anniv. A446

1984, Sept. 29

1364 A446 14p multicolored .35 .20

275th Anniv. of Chihuahua City A447

1984, Oct. 12

1365 A447 14p Cathedral exterior detail .35 .20

Coatzacoalcos Bridge Inauguration — A448

1984, Oct. 17 ***Perf. 14***

1366 A448 14p Aerial view .35 .20

UN Disarmament Week — A449

1984, Oct. 24 **Photo.** ***Perf. 14***

1367 A449 20p multicolored .30 .20

Christmas 1984 A450

1984, Oct. 31 **Photo.** ***Perf. 14***

1368 A450 14p Toy train & tree .30 .20

1369 A450 20p Pinata breaking, vert. .30 .20

Politician-Journalist Ignacio M. Altamirano (1834-1893) — A451

1984, Nov. 13 **Photo.** ***Perf. 14***

1370 A451 14p blk & lt red brn .30 .20

State Audit Office, 160th Anniv. A452

1984, Nov. 16

1371 A452 14p multicolored .35 .20

1986 World Cup Soccer Championships, Mexico — A453

1984, Nov. 19

1372 A453 20p multicolored *1.75* *.20*

1373 A453 24p multicolored *2.25* *.20*

a. Pair, #1372-1373 + label *5.50* *5.50*

Romulo Gallegos (1884-1969), Author and Former Pres. of Venezuela — A454

1984, Dec. 6

1374 A454 20p blue & gray .30 .20

State Registry Office, 125th Anniv. A455

1984, Dec. 13

1375 A455 24p slate blue .30 .20

Natl. Flag, 50th Anniv. A456

1985, Feb. 24

1376 A456 22p multicolored .50 .20

Johann Sebastian Bach — A457

Intl. Youth Year — A458

1985, Mar. 21 **Photo.** ***Perf. 14***

1377 A457 35p dl red brn, gold & blk .45 .20

1985, Mar. 28 **Photo.** ***Perf. 14***

1378 A458 35p rose vio, gold & blk .35 .20

Child Survival Campaign A459

1985, Apr. 7 **Photo.** ***Perf. 14***

1379 A459 36p multicolored .45 .20

Mexican Mint, 450th Anniv. A460

1985, May 11 **Photo.** ***Perf. 14***

1380 A460 35p 1st gold & copper coins .45 .20

Victor Hugo A461

1985, May 22 **Photo.** ***Perf. 14***

1381 A461 35p slate .45 .20

MEXFIL '85 — A462

1985, June 9 **Photo.** ***Perf. 14***

1382 A462 22p No. 5 .40 .40

1383 A462 35p No. 574 .40 .40

1384 A462 36p No. 1081 .40 .40

Nos. 1382-1384 (3) 1.20 1.20

Souvenir Sheet

1985, June 27 ***Imperf.***

1385 A462 90p No. 111 on cover 3.50 2.50

Morelos Telecommunications Satellite Launch — A463

1985, June 17 ***Perf. 14***

1386 A463 22p Shuttle launch .25 .20

1387 A463 36p Ground receiver .25 .20

1388 A463 90p Modes of communication .50 .40

a. Strip of 3, #1386-1388 + 2 labels 4.00 4.00

Nos. 1386-1388 (3) 1.00 .80

Souvenir Sheet

Imperf

1389 A463 100p multicolored 3.50 3.00

Nos. 1386-1388 has continuous design. No. 1389 pictures uninscribed continuous design of Nos. 1386-1388.

9th World Forestry Congress, Mexico City, July 1-9 A464

1985, July 1 ***Perf. 14***

1390 A464 22p Conifer .25 .20

1391 A464 35p Silk-cotton tree .25 .20

1392 A464 36p Mahogany .25 .20

a. Strip of 3, #1390-1392 + 2 labels 4.50 4.50

Nos. 1390-1392 (3) .75 .60

Martin Luis Guzman (1887-1977), Journalist, Politician — A465

Contemporary writers: No. 1394, Agustin Yanez (1904-1980), politician. No. 1395, Alfonso Reyes (1889-1959), diplomat. No. 1396, Jose Ruben Romero (1890-1952), diplomat. No. 1397, Artemio de Valle Arizpe (1888-1961), historian.

1985, July 19 ***Perf. 14***

1393 A465 22p multicolored .25 .20

1394 A465 22p multicolored .25 .20

1395 A465 22p multicolored .25 .20

1396 A465 22p multicolored .25 .20

1397 A465 22p multicolored .25 .20

a. Strip of 5, #1393-1397 4.50 4.50

Nos. 1393-1397 (5) 1.25 1.00

Heroes of the Mexican Independence, 1810 — A466

1985, Sept. 15

1398 A466 22p Miguel Hidalgo .25 .20

1399 A466 35p Jose Morelos .25 .20

1400 A466 35p Ignacio Allende .25 .20

1401 A466 36p Leona Vicario .25 .20

1402 A466 110p Vicente Guerre-ro .75 .75
Nos. 1398-1402 (5) 1.75 1.55

Souvenir Sheet

Imperf

1403 A466 90p Bell, church 3.00 2.50

175th anniv. of independence from Spanish rule. #1403 contains one 56x49mm stamp.

University of Mexico, 75th Anniv. A467

1985, Sept. 22 **Photo.** ***Perf. 14***

1404 A467 26p San Ildefonso, 1910 .25 .20
1405 A467 26p University emblem .25 .20
1406 A467 40p Rectory, 1985 .25 .20
1407 A467 45p 1st Rector Justo Sierra, crest, 1910 .25 .20
1408 A467 90p Crest, 1985 .50 .40
a. Strip of 5, #1404-1408 8.50 8.50
Nos. 1404-1408 (5) 1.50 1.20

Interamerican Development Bank, 25th Anniv. — A468

1985, Oct. 23 **Photo.** ***Perf. 14***

1409 A468 26p multicolored .30 .20

UN Disarmament Week — A469

1985, Oct. 24 ***Perf. 14***

1410 A469 36p Guns, doves .30 .20

UN, 40th Anniv. — A470

1985, Oct. 25 ***Perf. 14***

1411 A470 26p Hand, dove .25 .20

Christmas 1985 A471

Children's drawings.

1985, Nov. 15 **Photo.** ***Perf. 14***

1412 A471 26p multicolored .25 .20
1413 A471 35p multicolored .25 .20

1910 Revolution, 75th Anniv. A472

1985, Nov. 18 ***Perf. 14***

1414 A472 26p Soldadera .25 .20
1415 A472 35p Francisco Villa .25 .20
1416 A472 40p Emiliano Zapata .25 .20
1417 A472 45p Venustiano Carranza .25 .20
1418 A472 110p Francisco Madero .75 .25
Nos. 1414-1418 (5) 1.75 1.05

Souvenir Sheet

Imperf

1419 A472 90p Liberty bell 3.00 2.50

No. 1419 contains one 48x40mm stamp.

Astronaut, by Sebastian A473

The Watchman, by Federico Silva A474

Mexican Astronaut, Rodolfo Neri, by Cauduro — A475

Morelos and Telecommunications Satellite Launch — A476

1985, Nov. 26 ***Perf. 14***

1420 A473 26p multicolored .25 .20
1421 A474 35p multicolored .25 .20
1422 A475 45p multicolored .25 .20
Nos. 1420-1422 (3) .75 .60

Miniature Sheet

Imperf

1423 A476 100p multicolored 3.00 2.50

1986 World Cup Soccer Championships, Mexico — A477

1985, Dec. 15 **Photo.** ***Perf. 14***

1424 A477 26p Olympic Stadium 1.50 .20
1425 A477 45p Aztec Stadium 2.00 .20

1st Free Textbook for Primary Education, 25th Anniv. — A478

1985, Dec. 16

1426 A478 26p Book cover .25 .20

Colonial Monuments A479

Landmarks in Mexico City: 26p, College of the Vizcainas, c. 1735. 35p, Palace of the Counts of Heras and Soto. 40p, Palace of the Counts of Calimaya, 16th cent. 45p, San Carlos Academy, 16th cent.

1985, Dec. 27 ***Perf. 14***

1427 A479 26p grnsh blk & fawn .25 .20
1428 A479 35p grnsh blk & fawn .25 .20
1429 A479 40p grnsh blk & fawn .25 .20
1430 A479 45p grnsh blk & fawn .25 .20
a. Strip of 4, #1427-1430 + label 4.00 4.00
Nos. 1427-1430 (4) 1.00 .80

Natl. Polytechnic Institute, 50th Anniv. A480

1986, Feb. 7 ***Perf. 14***

1431 A480 40p Luis Enrique Erro Planetarium .25 .20
1432 A480 65p School of Arts & Communications .25 .20
1433 A480 75p Emblem, founders .30 .25
a. Strip of 3, #1431-1433 + 2 labels 7.00 7.00
Nos. 1431-1433 (3) .80 .65

Fruit — A481

1986, Feb. 21 ***Perf. 14***

1434 A481 40p Cucurbita pepo .25 .20
1435 A481 65p Nopalea coccinellifera .30 .25

World Health Day A482

1986, Apr. 7 **Photo.** ***Perf. 14***

1436 A482 65p Doll .25 .20

Halley's Comet A483

1986, Apr. 25

1437 A483 90p multicolored .50 .20

Natl. Geology Institute, Cent. A484

1986, May 26

1438 A484 40p multicolored .35 .20

1986 World Cup Soccer Championships — A485

Paintings by Angel Zarraga (1886-1946) and Sergio Guerrero Morales: 30p, Three Soccer Players with Cap. 40p, Portrait of Ramon Novaro. 65p, Dimanche. 70p, Portrait of Ernest Charles Gimpel. 90p, Three Soccer Players. 110p, Poster for 1986 championships, by Morales.

1986, May 31

1439 A485 30p multicolored .50 .20
1440 A485 40p multicolored .50 .20
1441 A485 65p multicolored .50 .20

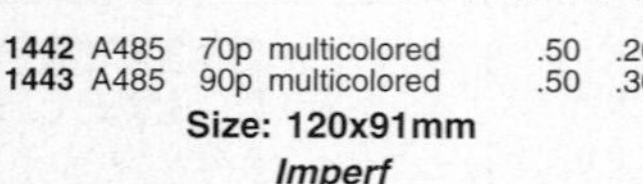

1442 A485 70p multicolored .50 .20
1443 A485 90p multicolored .50 .30

Size: 120x91mm

Imperf

1444 A485 110p multicolored 6.00 3.00
Nos. 1439-1444 (6) 8.50 4.10

Independence War Heroes — A486

175th Death anniv. of: 40p, Ignacio Allende (1769-1811). 65p, Juan Aldama (1774-1811). 75p, Mariano Jimenez (1781-1811).

1986, June 26 Photo. *Perf. 14*
1445 A486 40p multicolored .35 .20
1446 A486 65p multicolored .35 .20
1447 A486 75p multicolored .35 .20
Nos. 1445-1447 (3) 1.05 .60

Miguel Hidalgo y Costilla (1753-1811), Mural by Jose Clemente Orozco — A487

1986, July 30 Photo. *Perf. 14*
1448 A487 40p multicolored .30 .20

Federal Tax Court, 50th Anniv. — A488

1986, Aug. 27 *Perf. 14*
1449 A488 40p gray, bl & blk .30 .20

Gen. Nicolas Bravo (1786-1854) — A489

1986, Sept. 10 *Perf. 14*
1450 A489 40p multicolored .40 .20

Paintings by Diego Rivera — A490

Designs: 50p, Paisaje Zapatista, 1915, vert. 80p, Desnudo con Alcatraces, 1944, vert. 110p, Sueno de una Tarde Dominical en la Alameda Central, 1947-48.

1986, Sept. 26 *Perf. 14*
1451 A490 50p multicolored .25 .20
1452 A490 80p multicolored .45 .20
1453 A490 110p multicolored .55 .35
Nos. 1451-1453 (3) 1.25 .75

See Nos. 1571-1573.

Guadalupe Victoria (1786-1843), 1st President — A491

1986, Sept. 29 *Perf. 14*
1454 A491 50p multicolored .30 .20

Natl. Storage Warehouse, 50th Anniv. — A492

1986, Oct. 3
1455 A492 40p multicolored .30 .20

Intl. Post Day A493

1986, Oct. 9 *Perf. 14*
1456 A493 120p multicolored .50 .20

Natl. Committee Commemorating the 500th Anniv. (1992) of the Meeting of Two Worlds — A494

1986, Oct. 12 *Perf. 14*
1457 A494 50p black & lake .30 .20

15th Pan American Highways Congress, Mexico City A495

1986, Oct. 17 Photo. *Perf. 14*
1458 A495 80p Palacio de Mineria .40 .20

Franz Liszt, Composer, 175th Birth Anniv. — A496

1986, Oct. 22 *Perf. 14*
1459 A496 100p black & brown .45 .20

Intl. Peace Year A497

1986, Oct. 24
1460 A497 80p blk, bl & dk red .40 .20

Interment of Pino Suarez in the Rotunda of Illustrious Men — A498

1986, Nov. 6
1461 A498 50p multicolored .30 .20

Jose Maria Pino Suarez, vice-president of 1st revolutionary government, 1911.

See Nos. 1472, 1475, 1487, 1563.

Christmas — A499

Clay figurines from Tonala, Jalisco.

1986, Nov. 28
1462 A499 50p King .30 .20
1463 A499 80p Angel .30 .20

Diego Rivera (1886-1957), Painter — A500

1986, Dec. 8 Photo. *Perf. 14*
1464 A500 80p Self-portrait .30 .20

Export Type of 1975

Designs as before and: 60p, Men's shoes. 70p, Copperware. 80p, Denim overalls. 90p, Abalone. 100p, Cup of coffee.

1986-87 Unwmk. *Perf. 11½x11*
1465 A320 20p gray .25 .20

Perf. 14

1466 A320 40p pale grn & gold .35 .20

Perf. 11½x11

1467 A320 60p brown .50 .20
1468 A320 70p orange brn 1.50 .20
a. Perf. 14 1.60 .20

Perf. 14

1469 A320 80p blue .50 .20
1470 A320 90p green & blue .75 .25
1470A A320 100p brown ('88) .50 .20
b. 100p dark brown, perf. 11½x11 ('87) .75 .30
Nos. 1465-1470A (7) 4.35 1.45

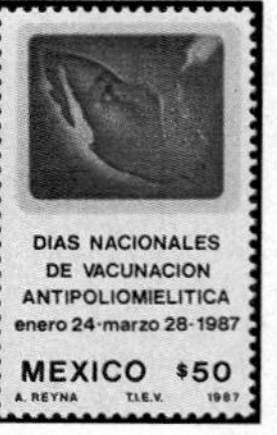

Natl. Polio Vaccination Program, Jan. 24-Mar. 28 — A501

1987, Jan. 20 Photo. *Perf. 14*
1471 A501 50p Oral vaccine .30 .20

Rotunda of Illustrious Men Type of 1986

1987, Feb. 4
1472 A498 100p multicolored .40 .25

Jose Maria Iglesias (1823-1891), president in 1876.

Natl. Teachers' College, 100th Anniv. A503

1987, Feb. 24 *Perf. 14*
1473 A503 100p multicolored .50 .25

Exploration of Pima Indian Territory by Eusebio Francisco Kino, 300th Anniv. — A504

1987, Feb. 27 ***Perf. 14***
1474 A504 100p multicolored .50 .25

Rotunda of Illustrious Men Type of 1986

1987, Mar. 20 **Photo.** ***Perf. 14***
1475 A498 100p Pedro Sainz de Baranda .40 .25

World Health Day, UN Child Survival Program A505

1987, Apr. 7
1476 A505 100p blue & slate blue .50 .25

Autonomous University of Puebla, 50th Anniv. — A506

1987, Apr. 23
1477 A506 200p multicolored .75 .50

Battle of Puebla, 125th Anniv. — A507

1987, May 5 **Photo.** ***Perf. 14***
1478 A507 100p multicolored .40 .20

METROPOLIS '87 — A508

1987, May 19
1479 A508 310p gray blk, grn & red 1.25 .75

Cong. of metropolitan areas, Mexico City.

Handicrafts A509

100p, Lacquerware tray, Uruapan, Michoacan. 200p, Blanket, Santa Ana Chiautempan, Tlaxcala. 230p, Lidded jar, Puebla, Pue.

1987, May 29 **Photo.** ***Perf. 14***
1480 A509 100p multicolored .30 .20
1481 A509 200p multicolored .60 .35
1482 A509 230p multicolored 1.00 .50
Nos. 1480-1482 (3) 1.90 1.05

Genaro Estrada, (1887-1937) Political Reformer — A510

1987, June 2
1483 A510 100p pale pink, blk & pale rose .30 .20

See Nos. 1509, 1568-1569.

Native Traders, 1961, Mural by P. O'Higgins — A511

1987, June 8
1484 A511 100p multicolored .30 .20

Nat'l. Bank of Int'l. Commerce, 50th anniv.

Publication of the 1st Shipbuilding Manual in the Americas, by Diego Garcia Palacio, 400th Anniv. — A512

1987, June 15
1485 A512 100p multicolored .30 .20

Nat'l. Food Program, 50th Anniv. A513

1987, June 22
1486 A513 100p multicolored .30 .20

Rotunda of Illustrious Men Type of 1986

1987, June 22
1487 A498 100p multicolored .30 .20

Leandro Valle (1833-1861), jurist.

Paintings by Saturnino Herran (1887-1918) — A514

1917 paintings: No. 1488, Self-portrait with Skull. No. 1489, The Offering. No. 1490, Creole Woman with Mantilla.

1987, July 9
1488 A514 100p black & red brn .35 .20
1489 A514 100p multicolored .35 .20
1490 A514 400p multicolored 1.10 .75
Nos. 1488-1490 (3) 1.80 1.15

Export Type of 1975

Designs: 10p, Meat cuts marked on steer. 20p, Bicycle. 50p, Tomatoes. 300p, Motor vehicle. 500p, Petroleum valves. 600p, Jewelry. 700p, Film. 800p, Construction materials. 900p, Pistons. 1,000p, Agricultural machinery. 2,000p, Wrought iron. 3,000p, Electric wiring. 4,000p, Honey. 5,000p, Cotton.

1987-88 **Photo.** **Unwmk.** ***Perf. 14***
1491 A320 10p brt carmine .20 .20
1492 A320 20p black & org .20 .20
1493 A320 50p ver & yel grn .45 .20
1494 A320 300p chalky blue & scar, type I .45 .20
1495 A320 300p Prus blue & brt rose .55 .20
a. Thin paper 1.10 .20
b. Brt blue & brt rose .60 .20
1496 A320 500p dark gray & Prus blue .90 .25
1497 A320 600p multicolored 1.75 .30
a. Thin paper 1.50 .20
1498 A320 700p brt yel grn, dark red & blk 1.50 .75
a. Brt yel grn, lilac rose & blk 1.75 .85
1499 A320 800p dark red brn & golden brn 2.50 1.25
1500 A320 900p black 5.00 2.10

Wmk. 300
Granite Paper
Type I Burelage in Gray

1501 A320 1000p dk red & blk 6.00 1.10
1502 A320 2000p black 5.50 1.75
1503 A320 3000p gray blk & org 5.50 1.75
1504 A320 4000p yel org & red brn 5.00 2.50
1505 A320 5000p apple grn & org 6.50 3.25
Nos. 1491-1505 (15) 42.00 16.00

Issue years: 10p-50p, 1987; others, 1988.

A515

10th Pan American Games, Indianapolis — A516

Unwmk.

1987, Aug. 7 **Photo.** ***Perf. 14***
1506 A515 100p multicolored .30 .20
1507 A516 200p blk, brt grn & dk red .30 .20

Federal Power Commission, 50th Anniv. — A517

1987, Aug. 14 **Photo.** ***Perf. 14***
1508 A517 200p multicolored .40 .25

Art and Science Type of 1987

Design: J.E. Hernandez y Davalos (1827-1893), historian.

1987, Aug. 25 ***Perf. 14***
1509 A510 100p buff, blk & dull red brn .30 .20

Pre-Hispanic Art Type of 1980

Designs: 100p, Xolotl (d. 1232), king of Amaquemecan. 200p, Nezahualpilli (1460-1516), king of Texcoco, conqueror. 400p, Motecuhzoma Ilhuicamina (Montezuma I d. 1469), emperor of Tenochtitlan (1440-1469).

1987, Aug. 31 ***Perf. 14***
1510 A361 100p multicolored .30 .20
1511 A361 200p multicolored .50 .30
1512 A361 400p multicolored .90 .35
Nos. 1510-1512 (3) 1.70 .85

Tourism Type of 1979

Designs: 100p, Central Public Library, Mexico State. No. 1514, Patzcuaro Harbor, Michoacan. No. 1515, Garcia Caverns, Nuevo Leon. No. 1516, Beach resort, Mazatlan, Sinaloa.

1987 ***Perf. 14***
1513 A353 100p multicolored .30 .20
1514 A353 150p multicolored .30 .20
1515 A353 150p multicolored .30 .20
1516 A353 150p multicolored .30 .20
Nos. 1513-1516 (4) 1.20 .80

Issue dates: 100p, Sept. 11; others, Oct. 19.

Formula 1 Grand Prix Race, Oct. 18 — A518

1987, Sept. 11
1517 A518 100p multicolored .30 .20

13th Intl. Cartography Conference — A519

1987, Oct. 12
1518 A519 150p Map, 16th cent. .30 .20

Discovery of America, 500th Anniv. (in 1992) A520

Design: Santa Maria, emblem of the Discovery of America Festival to be held in 1992.

1987, Oct. 12 *Perf. 14*
1519 A520 150p multicolored 3.50 .20

For overprint see No. 1698.

Illuminated Codices Type of 1982

Mendocino Codex (c. 1541): No. 1520, Founding of Tenochtitlan by the Aztecs, 1324. No. 1521, Pre-Hispanic wedding. No. 1522, Montezuma's Council.

1987, Nov. 3
1520 A408 150p multicolored .35 .20
1521 A408 150p multicolored .35 .20
1522 A408 150p multicolored .35 .20
Nos. 1520-1522 (3) 1.05 .60

Christmas 1987 A521

1987, Nov. 6
1523 A521 150p brt pink .30 .20
1524 A521 150p dull blue .30 .20

World Post Day A522

Documents: 150p, Ordinance for expediting mail by sea, 1777. 600p, Roster of correspondence transported by coach, 1857.

1987, Nov. 12
1525 A522 150p pale gray & slate gray .30 .20

Size: 129x102mm

Imperf

1526 A522 600p rose lake & yel bis 3.00 1.00

Meeting of Eight Latin American Presidents, 1st Anniv. — A523

1987, Nov. 26 *Perf. 14*
1527 A523 250p shown .40 .20
1528 A523 500p Flags, peace doves .60 .40

Dualidad 1964, by Rufino Tamayo (b. 1899) — A524

1987, Dec. 9
1529 A524 150p multicolored .35 .20

Nationalization of Mexican Railroads, 50th Anniv. — A525

1987, Dec. 15
1530 A525 150p Metlac Bridge 1.00 .20

Antonio Stradivarius (c. 1644-1737), Italian Violin Maker — A526

1987, Dec. 18 *Perf. 14*
1531 A526 150p bluish lilac .40 .20

Constitutional Tribunal of the Supreme Court, Plenum Hall, Jan. 15 — A527

Design: Statue of Manuel Rejon, author of the Mexican constitution.

1988, Jan. 15 **Photo.** *Perf. 14*
1532 A527 300p multicolored .50 .30

Fauna A528

1988, Feb. 29 **Photo.** *Perf. 14*
1533 A528 300p *Ambystoma mexicanum* 1.00 .40
1534 A528 300p *Trichechus manatus* 1.00 .40

A529

Nationalization of the Petroleum Industry, 50th Anniv. — A530

1988, Mar. 18
1535 A529 300p blue & blk .30 .25
1536 A530 300p PEMEX emblem, vert. .30 .25
1537 A530 500p shown .40 .35
Nos. 1535-1537 (3) 1.00 .85

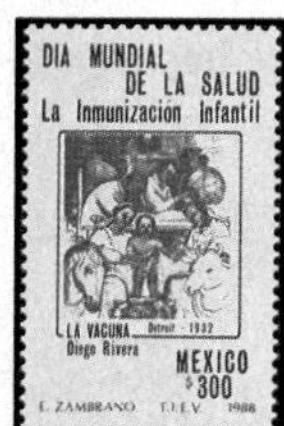

Vaccination, Detroit, 1932, Mural (detail) by Diego Rivera — A531

1988, Apr. 7
1538 A531 300p olive grn & henna brn .35 .25

World Health Day: child immunization.

The People in Pursuit of Health, 1953, by Diego Rivera — A532

1988, Apr. 7
1539 A532 300p multicolored .35 .25

World Health Organization, 40th anniv.

Vallejo in Repose (Large) — A533

Vallejo in Repose (Small) — A534

1988, Apr. 15
1540 A533 300p shown .35 .25
1541 A533 300p Portrait, diff. (large) .35 .25
a. Pair, #1540-1541 + label 3.25 3.25
b. Bklt. pane of 4 (2 each #1540-1541) + label 250.00
1542 A534 300p shown .35 .25
1543 A534 300p As #1541 (small) .35 .25
a. Pair, #1542-1543 + label 3.25 3.25
Nos. 1540-1543 (4) 1.40 1.00

Cesar Vallejo (1892-1938), Peruvian poet. Stamps of the same type printed se-tenant in sheets of 20 stamps containing 10 pairs plus 5 labels between inscribed with various Vallejo quotes or commemorative text.

Issued: #1541b, 11/9/90. Label in No. 1541b is overprinted in red with Mexican Chicagopex '90 souvenir cancel, and had limited distribution.

Sketch of Carlos Pellicer Camara (1897-1977), Poet, by Fontanelly — A535

1988, Apr. 23
1544 A535 300p pale vio, blk & sal .35 .25

MEPSIRREY '88 Philatelic Exhibition, Monterrey, May 27-29 — A536

1988, May 27
1545 A536 300p Youth collectors .35 .25
1546 A536 300p Handstamped cover .35 .25
1547 A536 500p Alfa Planetarium .55 .50
Nos. 1545-1547 (3) 1.25 1.00

Mexico-Elmhurst Philatelic Society Intl. (MEPSI).

1988 Formula I Grand Prix of Mexico — A537

Design: Layout of Hermanos Rodriguez race track, Mexico City, and car.

1988, May 28 **Photo.** *Perf. 14*
1548 A537 500p multicolored .50 .35

A538

Ramon Lopez Velarde (1888-1921), Poet — A539

1988, June 15
1549 A538 300p multicolored .30 .25
1550 A539 300p multicolored .30 .25
a. Bklt. pane of 4 + label 250.00

Issue date: No. 1550a, Nov. 9, 1990. Label in No. 1550a is overprinted in red with Mexican Chicagopex '90 souvenir cancel, and had limited distribution.

University Military Pentathlon, 50th Anniv. — A540

1988, July 9 **Photo.** ***Perf. 14***
1551 A540 300p multicolored .30 .25

1st Mexico-Japan Friendship, Commerce and Navigation Treaty, Cent. — A541

1988, Aug. 16
1552 A541 500p multicolored .50 .35

Joint Oceanographic Assembly, Acapulco, Aug. 23-31 — A542

1988, Aug. 23
1553 A542 500p multicolored .50 .35

1988 Summer Olympics, Seoul — A543

1988, Aug. 31 **Photo.** ***Perf. 14***
1554 A543 500p multicolored 1.00 .35

Size: 71x55mm

Imperf

1555 A543 700p Emblems, torch 3.50 .60

World Boxing Council, 25th Anniv. A544

1988, Sept. 9
1556 A544 500p multi .50 .35

Intl. Red Cross and Red Crescent Organizations, 125th Annivs. — A545

1988, Sept. 23 **Photo.** ***Perf. 14***
1557 A545 300p blk, gray & scar .30 .25

Jose Guadalupe Posada (1852-1913), Painter, Illustrator — A546

1988, Sept. 29
1558 A546 300p sil & blk .30 .25

World Wildlife Fund — A547

Various monarch butterflies, *Danaus plexippus.*

1988, Sept. 30 ***Perf. 14***
1559 A547 300p shown 3.00 .65
1560 A547 300p Three adults 3.00 .65
1561 A547 300p Larva, adult, pupa 3.00 .65
1562 A547 300p Five adults 3.00 .65
Nos. 1559-1562 (4) 12.00 2.60

Rotunda of Illustrious Men Type of 1986

Portrait and eternal flame: Manuel Sandoval Vallarta (1899-1977), physicist.

1988, Oct. 5
1563 A498 300p multi .30 .25

World Post Day A548

1988, Oct. 9 ***Perf. 14***
1564 A548 500p World map .50 .35

Size: 75x44mm

Imperf

1565 A548 700p Envelope, doves, Earth 3.50 1.00

Discovery of America, 500th Anniv. (in 1992) — A549

Illuminations: Aztec painter Tlacuilo from the Mendocine Codex, 1541, and Dominican scribe from the Yanhuitlan Codex, 1541-50.

1988, Oct. 12 ***Perf. 14***
1566 A549 500p multi .50 .35

World Food Day A550

1988, Oct. 16 ***Perf. 14***
1567 A550 500p multi .50 .35

Art and Science Type of 1987

#1568, Alfonso Caso (1896-1970), educator, founder of the Natl. Museum of Anthropology. #1569, Vito Alessio Robles (1879-1957), historian.

1988, Oct. 24 ***Perf. 14***
1568 A510 300p gray & blk .30 .25
1569 A510 300p pale yel, blk & red brn .30 .25

Act of Independence, 175th Anniv. — A551

1988, Nov. 9
1570 A551 300p claret brn & fawn .30 .25

Art Type of 1986

Paintings by Antonio M. Ruiz (1895-1964): No. 1571, *Parade,* 1936. No. 1572, *La Malinche,* 1939. No. 1573, *Self-portrait,* 1925, vert.

1988, Nov. 21 ***Perf. 14***
1571 A490 300p multi .30 .25
1572 A490 300p multi .30 .25
1573 A490 300p multi .30 .25
Nos. 1571-1573 (3) .90 .75

Tempera and Oil Paintings by Jose Reyes (b. 1924) A552

1988, Nov. 25 ***Perf. 14***
1574 A552 300p Feast .30 .25
1575 A552 300p Pinata, vert. .30 .25

Christmas.

Municipal Workers' Trade Union, 50th Anniv. A553

1988, Dec. 5 ***Perf. 14***
1576 A553 300p pale bister & blk .30 .25

Flora — A554

1988, Dec. 20 ***Perf. 14***
1577 A554 300p *Ustilago maydis* .30 .25
1578 A554 300p *Mimosa tenuiflora* .30 .25

Exporta Type of 1975

Designs: 40p, 1400p, Chemistry flasks. 200p, Citrus fruit. 450p, Circuit board. 750p, Film. 950p, Pistons. 1000p, Agricultural machinery. 1100p, Minerals. 1300p, Strawberries. 1500p, Copper vase. 1600p, Steel pipes. 1700p, Tequila. 1900p, Abalone. 2000p, Wrought iron. 2100p, Bicycles. 2500p, Overalls. 5000p, Cotton.

#1588A, 1589, 1592, 1598A, 1599, 1601, 1603 have gray burelage Type I.

1988-92 **Photo.** **Unwmk.** ***Perf. 14***

Design A320

1583 40p black .20 .20
1584 200p emer & brt yel .50 .20
a. Thin paper 1.10 .40
1585 450p yel bister & lil rose .75 .25
a. Thin paper 1.25 .40
1586 750p brt yel grn, dark red & dark gray 2.00 .40
1587 950p indigo 1.75 .60
a. Thin paper 2.25 .75
1588 1000p dark red & blk 1.10 .25
1588A 1000p dark red & blk, type 1 2.50 .25
1589 1100p dark gray, type I 1.75 .40
1590 1100p dark gray 2.25 .50
1591 1300p red & grn 2.25 .55
1592 1300p red & grn, type I 2.00 .55
a. Thin paper 3.00 .75
1593 1400p black 1.75 .50
1594 1500p tan 1.75 .60
a. 1500p orange brown 1.75 .60
1595 1600p red orange 1.60 .55
1596 1700p dk grn & yel grn 1.60 .60
1597 1900p bl grn & bl 1.75 .65
1598 2000p black 2.75 .75
1598A 2000p black, type 1 2.25 .20
1599 2100p black & orange, type I 4.00 .85
1600 2100p black & ver 7.50 1.00
1601 2500p dark blue, type I 4.00 1.00
1602 2500p slate blue 4.00 .90
1603 5000p apple grn & org, type I 4.50 1.90
Nos. 1583-1603 (23) 54.50 13.65

Issued: 40p, 1/5/88; 200p, 2/27/89; 450p, 2/10/89; #1585a, 950p, #1587a, 1589, 3/30/89; 1,000p, 1989; #1590, 1599, 1601, 1991; #1600, 1602, 5000p, 1992; others, 1990.

Graphic Arts Workshop, 50th Anniv. A555

1989, Feb. 9 **Photo.** ***Perf. 14***
1604 A555 450p yel bis, red & blk .45 .35

Coat of Arms and *E Santo Domingo,* the Natl. Hymn — A556

1989, Feb. 27
1605 A556 450p multicolored .45 .35

Dominican Republic independence, 145th anniv.

Intl. Border and Territorial Waters Commission of Mexico and the US, Cent. — A557

1989, Mar. 1
1606 A557 1100p multi 1.25 .80

10th Intl. Book Fair A558

1989, Mar. 4
1607 A558 450p UNAM School of Engineering .45 .35

Lyricists and Composers Soc., 25th Anniv. A559

1989, Mar. 17
1608 A559 450p multi .45 .35

World Day for the Fight Against AIDS — A560

1989, Apr. 7
1609 A560 450p multi .45 .35

Leona Vicario (1779-1842), Heroine of the Independence Movement A561

Alfonso Reyes (1889-1959), Author, Educator A562

1989, Apr. 20 Photo. *Perf. 14*
1610 A561 450p blk, sepia & golden brn .45 .35

1989, May 17
1611 A562 450p multi .45 .35

Formula 1 Grand Prix of Mexico — A563

1989, May 28 *Perf. 14*
1612 A563 450p multi .45 .35

14th Tourism Congress, Acapulco A564

14th Intl. Gerontology Congress, Mexico A565

1989, June 11 *Perf. 14*
1613 A564 1100p multi 1.10 .80

1989, June 18

Statue: The god Huehueteotl as an old man bearing the weight of the world on his shoulders.

1614 A565 450p multi .45 .35

Battle of Zacatecas, 75th Anniv. — A566

1989, June 23
1615 A566 450p black .45 .35

Baseball Hall of Fame of Mexico — A567

1989, June 25
1616 A567 550p Umpire, catcher 3.00 .45
1617 A567 550p Batter 3.00 .45
a. Pair, #1616-1617 + label 15.00 15.00

No. 1617a has continuous design.

35th World Archery Championships, Lausanne, Switzerland, July 4-8 — A568

1989, July 2
1618 A568 650p Bows and arrows 1.50 .50
1619 A568 650p Arrows, target 1.50 .50
a. Pair, #1618-1619 + label 15.00 15.00

No. 1619a has continuous design.

Tijuana, Cent. A569

1989, July 11 Photo. *Perf. 14*
1620 A569 1100p Municipal arms .90 .70

French Revolution, Bicent. A570

1989, July 14
1621 A570 1300p blue, blk & dark red 1.40 .80

Gen. Francisco Xavier Mina (1789-1817), Independence Hero — A571

1989, Sept. 7
1622 A571 450p green, blk & dark red .50 .30

Natl. Museum of Anthropology, Chapultepec, 25th Anniv. — A572

1989, Sept. 17 *Perf. 14*
1623 A572 450p multicolored .50 .30

7th Mexico City Marathon — A573

1989, Sept. 24
1624 A573 450p multicolored .50 .30

Printing in America, 450th Anniv. — A574

1989, Sept. 28
1625 A574 450p multicolored .50 .30

World Post Day A575

1989, Oct. 9 Photo. *Perf. 14*
1626 A575 1100p multicolored 1.10 .65

Sovereign Revolutionary Convention of Aguascalientes, 75th Anniv. — A576

1989, Oct. 10
1627 A576 450p multicolored .90 .25

Exploration and Colonization of the Americas by Europeans — A577

1989, Oct. 12
1628 A577 1300p multicolored 2.00 .75

America Issue — A578

UPAE emblem and symbols like those produced on art by pre-Columbian peoples.

1989, Oct. 12

1629 A578 450p shown .50 .25
1630 A578 450p multi, diff., vert. .50 .25

Natl. Tuberculosis Foundation, 50th Anniv. — A579

1989, Nov. 10

1631 A579 450p multicolored .35 .25

Mask of the Bat God, Zapoteca Culture, c. 200-300 A580

1989, Nov. 28

1632 A580 450p multicolored .50 .25

Serfin Commercial Bank of Mexico, 125th Anniv. A581

1989, Nov. 29

1633 A581 450p deep blue, gold & blk .50 .25

Pres. Adolfo Ruiz Cortines (1889-1973) — A582

1989, Dec. 3

1634 A582 450p multicolored .50 .25

Christmas A583

1989, Dec. 11

1635 A583 450p Candlelight vigil .50 .25
1636 A583 450p Man sees star, vert. .50 .25

Natl. Institute of Anthropology and Natural History, 50th Anniv. — A584

1989, Dec. 13

1637 A584 450p dark red, gold & black .60 .25

Nationalization of the Railway System in Mexico, 80th Anniv. — A585

1989

1638 A585 450p multicolored .70 .25

Issue dates for some 1990-1991 issues are based on First Day cancels. Original printings were small. Later printings, made in 1991, were distributed to the stamp trade and seem to be the ones used for "First Day Covers."

Tampico Bridge — A586

1990, Jan. 11 **Photo.** ***Perf. 14***

1639 A586 600p gold, blk & red .80 .30

Eradication of Polio — A587

1990, Feb. 1

1640 A587 700p multicolored .70 .35

Natl. Census A588

1990, Mar. 12

1641 A588 700p lt grn & yel .75 .35

Mexican Philatelic Assoc., 10th Anniv. — A589

1990, Apr. 19

1642 A589 700p multicolored .75 .35

Natl. Archives, Bicentennial — A590

1990, Apr. 24

1643 A590 700p pale violet .75 .35

Intl. Conf. of Advertising Agencies — A591

1990, Apr. 27

1644 A591 700p multicolored .75 .35

Stamp World London '90 — A592

1990, May 3

1645 A592 700p multicolored .80 .35

First Postage Stamps, 150th Anniv. — A593

1990, May 6

1646 A593 700p lake, gold & blk .80 .35

15th Tourism Exposition — A594

1990, May 6

1647 A594 700p multicolored .75 .35

Visit of Pope John Paul II A595

1990, May 6

1648 A595 700p multicolored .80 .35

Health of Young Mothers A596

1990, May 10

1649 A596 700p multicolored .75 .35

Fight Against Smoking — A597

1990, May 31

1650 A597 700p multicolored .75 .35

World Environment Day — A598

1990, June 5

1651 A598 700p multicolored .75 .35

Formula 1 Grand Prix of Mexico — A599

1990, June 24
1652 A599 700p grn, red & blk .75 .35

Airport & Auxiliary Services, 25th Anniv. — A600

1990, June 25 **Photo.** ***Perf. 14***
1653 A600 700p multicolored .70 .35

Fight Against Drugs — A601

1990, June 26
1654 A601 700p multicolored .75 .35

Protection of Rain Forests — A602

1990, July 6
1655 A602 700p multicolored .90 .35

Solidarity with Poor People — A603

1990, Aug. 8
1656 A603 700p multicolored .70 .35

Solidarity is a governmental social program of Pres. Salinas de Gortari. See No. 1704.

Oaxaca Cultural Heritage — A604

1990, Aug. 10
1657 A604 700p multicolored .75 .35

Nature Conservation — A605

1990, Aug. 21
1658 A605 700p blk, gray & org .85 .35

Mexican Institute of Petroleum, 25th Anniv. A606

1990, Aug. 23
1659 A606 700p black & blue .75 .35

8th Mexico City Marathon — A607

1990, Aug. 24
1660 A607 700p blk, red & grn .75 .35

University of Colima, 50th Anniv. A608

1990, Sept. 16
1661 A608 700p gray, bister, red & grn .70 .35

Mexico City Advisory Council, Founded in 1929 — A609

1990, Sept. 17
1662 A609 700p sil, yel, blk & org .70 .35

Nationalization of Electric Industry, 30th Anniv. — A610

1990, Sept. 27
1663 A610 700p gray, grn, red & blk .75 .35

City of Campeche, 450th Anniv. A611

1990, Oct. 4
1664 A611 700p multicolored .70 .35

Silvestre Revueltas (1899-1940), Musician — A612

1990, Oct. 4
1665 A612 700p multicolored .60 .35

Plan of San Luis, 80th Anniv. A613

1990, Oct. 5
1666 A613 700p multicolored .60 .35

14th World Conference of Supreme Counselors — A614

1990, Oct. 8
1667 A614 1500p vio, sil, gold & grn 1.10 .80

Discovery of America, 498th Anniv. — A615

1990, Oct. 12
1668 A615 700p multicolored .50 .35

Mexican Archaeology, Bicentennial — A616

1990, Nov. 18
1669 A616 1500p multicolored 1.50 .80

16th Central American and Caribbean Games — A617

1990, Nov. 20
1670 A617 750p shown .75 .40
1671 A617 750p Mayan ball player .75 .40
1672 A617 750p Mayan ball player, vert. .75 .40
1673 A617 750p Ball court, stone ring, vert. .75 .40
a. Strip of 4, #1670-1673 4.50 4.50
Nos. 1670-1673 (4) 3.00 1.60

Christmas
A618 A619

1990, Dec. 3
1674 A618 700p Poinsettias .70 .35
1675 A619 700p Candles .70 .35

Mexican Canine Federation, 50th Anniv. A620

1990, Dec. 9
1676 A620 700p multicolored .80 .35

World Post Day A621

1990, Oct. 9 **Photo.** ***Perf. 14***
1677 A621 1500p multicolored 1.50 .80

America Issue A622

#1678, Flowers, galleon. #1679, Galleon, parrot.

1990, Oct. 12
1678 A622 700p multicolored .85 .35
1679 A622 700p multicolored .85 .35
a. Pair, #1678-1679 + blank label 2.75 2.75

No. 1679a has continuous design.

Mexican Brewing Industry, Cent. — A623

1990, Nov. 8 ***Perf. 14***
1680 A623 700p multicolored .75 .35

National Chamber of Industrial Development, 50th Anniv. — A624

1990, Dec. 5 ***Perf. 14***
1681 A624 1500p multicolored 1.40 .80

Naval Secretariat, 50th Anniv. A625

1991, Jan. 4 **Photo.** ***Perf. 14***
1682 A625 1000p bl, blk & gold .90 .50

Prevent Transportation Accidents — A626

1991, Jan. 11 **Photo.** ***Perf. 14***
1683 A626 700p multicolored .75 .40

Natl. Consumers Institute, 15th Anniv. — A627

1991, Feb. 11
1684 A627 1000p multicolored .80 .55

Voter Registration A628

1991, Feb. 13 ***Perf. 14***
1685 A628 1000p org, blk & grn .80 .55

Olympic Basketball — A629

1991, Feb. 25 ***Perf. 14***
1686 A629 1000p black & yellow 1.00 .55

Campaign Against Polio — A630

1991, Mar. 8
1687 A630 1000p multicolored 1.25 .55

Nos. 1688-1691, 1697 with "NP" and Post Office eagle head logo or just the logo, are specimens.

Childrens' Day for Peace and Development — A631

Health and Family Life A632

1991, Apr. 16 ***Perf. 14***
1688 A631 1000p multicolored .95 .55
1689 A632 1000p multicolored .95 .55

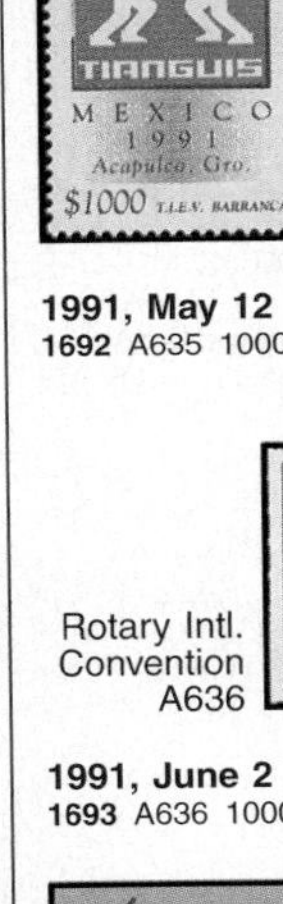

Mining in Mexico, 500th Anniv. — A633

1991, Apr. 25 ***Perf. 14***
1690 A633 1000p multicolored .80 .55

Promotion of Breastfeeding — A634

1991, May 10 ***Perf. 14***
1691 A634 1000p multicolored .80 .55

16th Tourism Exposition — A635

1991, May 12 ***Perf. 14***
1692 A635 1000p brt grn & dk grn .85 .60

Rotary Intl. Convention A636

1991, June 2 ***Rouletted 6½***
1693 A636 1000p blue & gold .85 .60

Integrated Communications and Transportation Systems (SCT), Cent. — A637

Designs: No. 1695a, 1000p, Jet landing. b, 1500p, Airport control tower. c, 1000p, FAX machine. d, 1500p, Upper floors, SCT headquarters. e, 1000p, Communications van. f, 1500p, Satellite. g, 1000p, Satellite in orbit, earth. h, 1000p, Boxcars. i, 1500p, Locomotives. j, 1000p, People using telephones. k, 1500p, Lower floors, SCT headquarters. l, 1000p, Hillside road, left section, highway bridge. m, 1500p, Center section, highway bridge. n, 1000p, Right section of bridge. o, 1000p, Cranes loading cargo ship. p, 1500p, Bow of cargo ship. q, 1000p, Television camera. r, 1500p, Bus. s, 1000p, Truck. t, 1500p, Trailers passing through toll plaza. u, 1000p, Bridge construction. Continuous design.

1991, June 11 ***Rouletted 6½***
1694 A637 1000p gray & multi 1.00 .60
1695 A637 Block of 21, #a.-u. 50.00 *55.00*

Jaguar — A638

1991, June 12 ***Perf. 14***
1696 A638 1000p black & orange 2.00 .60

Conservation of the rain forests.

Formula 1 Grand Prix of Mexico A639

1991, June 16 **Litho.** ***Rouletted 6½***
1697 A639 1000p multicolored .85 .50

No. 1519 Ovptd. in Red 

1991, June 14 **Photo.** ***Perf. 14***
1698 A520 150p multicolored 50.00 *30.00*

No. 1698 was available in strips of 5 only in booklets with limited distribution. Value of booklet, $300.

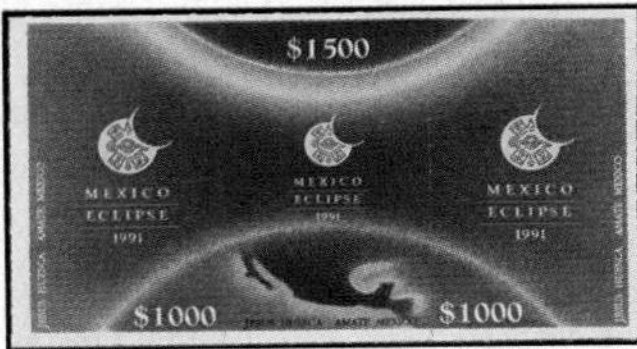

Total Solar Eclipse — A640

Designs: No. 1699a, 1000p, Denomination at lower right. b, Globe showing Mexico. c, 1000p, Denomination at lower left. Continuous design.

1991, July 5 ***Rouletted 6½***
1699 A640 Strip of 3, #a.-c. 6.50 5.00

First Latin American Presidential Summit, Guadalajara A641

1991, July 18
1700 A641 1500p blk, org & yel 1.10 .80

Solidarity Bridge — A642

1991, July 31
1701 A642 2000p multicolored 1.75 1.25

A643

A644

1991, Aug. 22
1702 A643 1000p multicolored .85 .60

Ninth Mexico City marathon.

1991, Aug. 27
1703 A644 1000p blue & silver .85 .60

Federal tax court, 55th anniv.

Solidarity Type of 1990 and

A645

1991 ***Perf. 14***
1704 A603 1000p multicolored .85 .60

Rouletted 6½
1705 A645 1000p multicolored .85 .60

Issued: #1704, Dec. 17; #1705, Sept. 9.

World Post Day — A646

1991, Oct. 9 ***Rouletted 6½***
1706 A646 1000p multicolored .85 .60

Voyages of Discovery A647

Discovery of America, 500th Anniv. (in 1992) A648

Design: No. 1708, Sailing ship, storm.

1991, Oct. 12

1707	A647	1000p multicolored	1.75	.60
1708	A647	1000p multicolored	1.75	.60
a.		Pair, #1707-1708	4.00	1.25
1709	A648	1000p multicolored	2.50	.60
		Nos. 1707-1709 (3)	6.00	1.80

No. 1708a has continuous design. Printed in sheets of 20+5 labels.

A649

Christmas A650

1991, Nov. 26
1710 A649 1000p multicolored .85 .60
1711 A650 1000p multicolored .85 .60

Carlos Merida, Birth Cent. A651

1991, Dec. 2 Photo. ***Rouletted 6½***
1712 A651 1000p multicolored .85 .60

Wolfgang Amadeus Mozart, Death Bicent. A652

1991, Dec. 5
1713 A652 1000p multicolored .85 .60

Self-sufficiency in Corn and Bean Production — A653

1991, Dec. 11 Photo. ***Rouletted 6½***
1714 A653 1000p multicolored .80 .55

City of Morelia, 450th Anniv. A654

1991, Dec. 13
1715 A654 1000p multicolored .80 .55

Merida, 450th Anniv. A655

1992, Jan. 6 Photo. ***Rouletted 6½***
1716 A655 1300p multicolored 1.10 .70

Engineering Education in Mexico, Bicent. A656

1992, Jan. 15
1717 A656 1300p blue & red 1.10 .70

1992 Summer Olympics, Barcelona A657

Design: No. 1719, Stylized Olympic Rings.

1992 Photo. ***Rouletted 6½***
1718 A657 2000p multicolored 1.50 1.00
1719 A657 2000p multicolored 1.50 .95

Issued: No. 1718, Feb. 10; No. 1719, Mar. 1.

Guadalajara, 450th Anniv. — A658

#1720: a, 1300p, Coat of arms. b, 1300p, Municipal buildings. c, 1300p, Guadalajara Cathedral. d, 1900p, Allegory of the city's founding. e, 1900p, Anniversary emblem.

1992, Feb. 14
1720 A658 Strip of 5, #a.-e. 15.00 15.00

Healthy Child Development — A659

1992, Feb. 26
1721 A659 2000p multicolored 1.50 .95

Formula 1 Grand Prix of Mexico A660

1992, Mar. 22
1722 A660 1300p multicolored 1.00 .65

Introduction of the wheel and domesticated horses to America, 500th anniv.

Telecom '92 — A661

1992, Apr. 6
1723 A661 1300p multicolored 1.00 .65

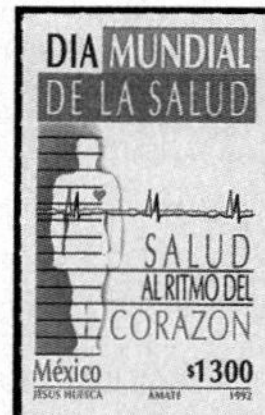
World Health Day — A662

1992, Apr. 7
1724 A662 1300p blk, red & bl 1.00 .65

War College, 60th Anniv. A663

1992, Apr. 15
1725 A663 1300p multicolored 1.00 .65

Discovery of America, 500th Anniv. A664

Paintings: No. 1726, Inspiration of Christopher Columbus, by Jose Maria Obregon. No. 1727, Meeting of the Races, by Jorge Gonzalez Camarena. No. 1728, Spanish, Indian and Mestizo, from the Natl. Historical Museum. No. 1729, Origin of the Sky, from Selden Codex. No. 1730, Quetzalcoatl and Tezcatlipoca, from Borbonico Codex. No. 1731, Human Culture by Camarena.

1992, Apr. 24 Litho. ***Perf. 14***

1726	A664	1300p multicolored	2.25	.65
1727	A664	1300p multicolored	2.25	.65
1728	A664	2000p multicolored	3.50	.95
1729	A664	2000p multicolored	3.50	.95
1730	A664	2000p multicolored	3.50	.95
		Nos. 1726-1730 (5)	15.00	4.15

Size: 107x84mm

Imperf

1731 A664 7000p multicolored 20.00 4.50

Granada '92. For overprints see Nos. 1752-1757.

Natl. Medical Center in the 21st Cent. — A665

1992, Apr. 27 Photo. ***Rouletted 6½***
1732 A665 1300p multicolored 1.00 .65

Rights of the Child A666

1992, Apr. 30
1733 A666 1300p multicolored 1.00 .65

Midwives in Mexico — A667

1992, May 10
1734 A667 1300p multicolored 1.00 .65

Discovery of America, 500th Anniv. — A668

1992, May 22 Litho. *Imperf.*

1735	A668	7000p multicolored	9.00	3.75

World Columbian Stamp Expo, Chicago.

Notary College of Mexico, Mexico City, Bicent. A669

1992, June 18 Litho. *Rouletted 6½*

1736	A669	1300p multicolored	1.00	.70

Arbor Day — A670

1992, July 9 *Rouletted 5*

1737	A670	1300p multicolored	1.00	.70

1992 Summer Olympics, Barcelona A671

1992, July 30 *Perf. 14*

1738	A671	1300p	Boxing	1.25	.70
1739	A671	1300p	Fencing	1.25	.70
1740	A671	1300p	High jump	1.25	.70
1741	A671	1300p	Gymnastics	1.25	.70
1742	A671	1300p	Shooting	1.25	.70
1743	A671	1900p	Swimming	2.50	1.00
1744	A671	1900p	Running	2.50	1.00
1745	A671	1900p	Rowing	2.50	1.00
1746	A671	1900p	Soccer	2.50	1.00
1747	A671	2000p	Equestrian	2.50	1.10
	Nos. 1738-1747 (10)			18.75	8.60

Souvenir Sheet

Perf. 10

1748	A671	7000p Torch bearer	15.00	8.00

10th Intl. Marathon of Mexico City — A672

1992, Aug. 26 Litho. *Rouletted 5*

1749	A672	1300p multicolored	1.00	.65

Solidarity, United for Progress — A673

1992, Sept. 8 *Perf. 10*

1750	A673	1300p multicolored	1.00	.65

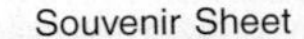

Souvenir Sheet

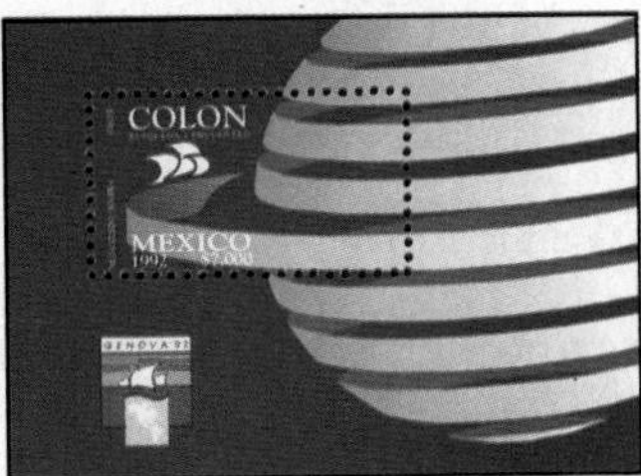

Discovery of America, 500th Anniv. — A674

1992, Sept. 18 *Perf. 10*

1751	A674	7000p multicolored	10.00	3.25

Genoa '92.

Nos. 1726-1731 Ovptd. with emblem of World Columbian Stamp Expo '92, Chicago

1992, Apr. 24 Litho. *Perf. 14*

1752	A664	1300p on #1726	16.00	16.00
1753	A664	1300p on #1727	16.00	16.00
1754	A664	2000p on #1728	16.00	16.00
1755	A664	2000p on #1729	16.00	16.00
1756	A664	2000p on #1730	16.00	16.00
	Nos. 1752-1756 (5)		80.00	80.00

Size: 107x84mm

Imperf

1757	A664	7000p on #1731	85.00	85.00

Nos. 1752-1757 were produced in limited quantities and had limited distribution with no advance release information available.

Natl. Council of Radio and Television, 50th Anniv. A675

1992, Oct. 5 Litho. *Perf. 10*

1758	A675	1300p multicolored	1.00	.65

World Post Day A676

1992, Oct. 9 Litho. *Perf. 10*

1759	A676	1300p multicolored	1.00	.65

Communications System of the Americas — A677

1992, Oct. 12

1760	A677	2000p multicolored	2.00	1.00

Discovery of America, 500th Anniv. A678

Designs: No. 1761, Aztec calendar stone. No. 1762, Snake, fish, compass.

1992, Oct. 12

1761	A678	2000p shown	2.00	1.00
1762	A678	2000p multicolored	2.00	1.00
a.		Pair, #1761-1762	4.50	2.00

Exporta Type of 1975

Designs: 2200p, Cuts of meat marked on steer. 2800p, Chemistry flasks. 3600p, Pistons. 3900p, Petroleum valves. 4000p, Honey. 4800p, Tomatoes. 6000p, Citrus fruit. 7200p, Film.

1992 Photo. *Perf. 14*

1763	A320	2200p red	1.60	.80
1764	A320	2800p black	2.50	1.00

With Gray Burelage

1765	A320	3600p blk, I	2.75	1.40
1766	A320	3900p gray & bl, II	3.50	1.50
1767	A320	4000p yel org & red brn, I	3.50	1.40
1768	A320	4800p red & grn, I	4.00	1.75
1768A	A320	4800p red & green, II	25.00	1.75
1769	A320	6000p yel & grn, I	5.00	2.25
1770	A320	7200p grn, red & blk, I	6.00	2.75
	Nos. 1763-1770 (9)		53.85	14.60

San Luis Potosi, 400th Anniv. A679

1992, Nov. 3 Litho. *Perf. 10*

1777	A679	1300p multicolored	1.00	.65

Values are for copies with perfs touching the design.

United for Conservation — A680

1992, Nov. 17

1778	A680	1300p multicolored	2.00	.65

Navy Day A681

1992, Nov. 23

1779	A681	1300p multicolored	1.00	.65

Values are for copies with perfs touching the design.

Christmas A682

1300p, Christmas tree, children, pinata, vert.

1992, Nov. 26

1780	A682	1300p multicolored	1.00	.65
1781	A682	2000p multicolored	2.00	1.00

Tourism in States of Mexico A683

1993-96 Photo. Unwmk. *Perf. 14*

1782	A683	90c	Campeche	1.25	.50
1783	A683	1p	Guanajuato	1.50	.60
1784	A683	1.10p	Guanajuato	1.75	.25
1785	A683	1.30p	Colima	1.90	.70
1786	A683	1.80p	Coahuila	1.40	.45
1787	A683	1.80p	Campeche	1.00	.40
1788	A683	1.80p	Colima	1.00	.40
1789	A683	1.80p	Chiapas	1.00	.30
1790	A683	1.90p	Michoacan, vert.	3.00	1.10
1791	A683	2p	Coahuila	2.75	1.10
1792	A683	2p	Colima	2.75	.20
1793	A683	2.20p	Queretaro	3.25	1.25
1794	A683	2.30p	Sinaloa	1.50	.35
1795	A683	2.40p	Yucatan	1.75	.40
1796	A683	2.50p	Sonora	4.50	1.40
1797	A683	2.70p	Mexico	3.00	.60
1798	A683	2.80p	Zacatecas, vert.	4.75	1.50
1798A	A683	3p	Campeche	3.75	.30
1799	A683	3.40p	Sinaloa	3.75	.80
1800	A683	3.70p	Sinaloa	10.00	1.90
1801	A683	3.80p	Yucatan	2.90	.85
1802	A683	4.40p	Yucatan	6.75	2.40
1803	A683	4.80p	Chiapas	7.75	2.50
1804	A683	6p	Mexico	10.00	3.25
1805	A683	6.50p	Sonora	5.00	1.50
	Nos. 1782-1805 (25)			87.95	25.00

A 2nd printing of #1797 exists. This printing appears crude, with missing and misregistered color dots.

Issued: 90c, 1p, 1.30p, 1.90p, #1791, 2.20p, 2.30p, 2.40p, 2.50p, 2.80p, 3.70p, 4.40p, 4.80p, 6p, 1993; 1.10p, 1.80p, 2.70p, 3.40p, 3.80p, 6.50p, 1995; #1792, 3p, 1996.

See #1960-1980, 2119, 2122-2140.

A685

A686

Designs: No. 1808, Child's drawing, ball, blocks. No. 1809, Hands.

1993, Jan. 19 Litho. *Perf. 10*

1807	A685	1.30p Doctor, child	.90	.65
1808	A685	1.30p multicolored	1.00	.75
1809	A685	1.30p multicolored	1.00	.75
1810	A686	1.50p multicolored	1.10	.85
	Nos. 1807-1810 (4)		4.00	3.00

Mexican Social Security Institute, 50th anniv. Medical Services (#1807), Day Nursery Social Security Service (#1808), security and solidarity (#1809).

Issued: 1.50p, 1/19; #1807, 5/11; others, 12/7.

Mexican Society of Ophthomolgists, Cent. — A687

1993, Feb. 16 Litho. *Perf. 10*

1811	A687	1.30p multicolored	.95	.70

Children's Month — A688

1993, Feb. 23

1812 A688 1.30p multicolored .95 .70

Mexican Geography and Statistics Society, 160th Anniv. A689

1993, Apr. 19 Litho. *Perf. 10*

1813 A689 1.30p blue, blk & red .95 .70

Miguel Ramos Arizpe (1776-1843), Proponent of Mexican Federalism — A690

1993, Apr. 28

1814 A690 1.30p multicolored .95 .70

Federico Gomez Children's Hospital, 50th Anniv. A691

1993, Apr. 29

1815 A691 1.30p multicolored .95 .70

Health Begins at Home A692

1993, May 31

1816 A692 1.30p multicolored .95 .70

Upper Gulf of California, Nature Preserve A693

1993, June 10 Litho. *Perf. 10*

1817 A693 1.30p multicolored .95 .70

Mario Moreno (Cantinflas), Film Actor — A694

1993, June 24 Photo. *Perf. 14*

1818 A694 1.30p black & blue .95 .70

See Nos. 1847-1851.

Secretariat of Health, 50th Anniv. A695

Designs: No. 1819, Dr. Maximiliano Ruiz Castaneda. No. 1820, Dr. Bernardo Sepulveda Gutierrez. No. 1821, Dr. Ignacio Chavez Sanchez. No. 1822, Dr. Mario Salazar Mallen. No. 1823, Dr. Gustavo Baz Prada.

1993 Litho. *Perf. 10*

1819	A695	1.30p	multicolored	.95	.70
1820	A695	1.30p	multicolored	.95	.70
1821	A695	1.30p	multicolored	.95	.70
1822	A695	1.30p	multicolored	.95	.70
1823	A695	1.30p	multicolored	.95	.70
			Nos. 1819-1823 (5)	4.75	3.50

Issued: #1819, 6/29; #1820, 7/26; #1821, 8/31; #1822, 9/23; #1823, 10/26.

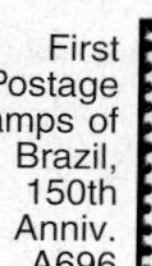

First Postage Stamps of Brazil, 150th Anniv. A696

1993, July 30

1824 A696 2p multicolored 1.50 1.10

A697

1993, Aug. 25

1825 A697 1.30p Runners .95 .70

11th Intl. Marathon of Mexico City.

A698

1993, Sept. 6

1.30p, Open book, lightning bolt. 2p, Buildings.

1826	1.30p multicolored	.95	.70
1827	2p multicolored	1.40	1.00
a.	A698 Pair, #1826-1827	2.50	2.00

Monterrey Institute of Technology and Higher Studies, 50th anniv.

Solidarity Week A699

1993, Sept. 6

1828 A699 1.30p multicolored .95 .70

Confederation of Mexican Chambers of Industry, 75th Anniv. — A700

1993, Sept. 13 Litho. *Perf. 10*

1829 A700 1.30p multicolored .95 .70

City of Torreon, Cent. — A701

1993, Sept. 15

1830 A701 1.30p multicolored .95 .70

Europalia '93 — A702

1993, Sept. 22

1831 A702 2p multicolored 1.50 1.10

A703 A704

1993, Oct. 9

1832 A703 2p multicolored 1.50 1.10

World Post Day.

1993, Oct. 10

1833 A704 1.30p multicolored .95 .70

Guadalupe Victoria (1786-1843), first president of Mexico.

Natl. Civil Protection System — A705

1993, Oct. 13

1834 A705 1.30p multicolored .95 .70

Intl. Day for Reduction of Natural Disasters.

UN Decade for Intl. Law A706

1993, Oct. 19

1835 A706 2p multicolored 1.50 1.10

20th Natl. Wheelchair Games A707

1993, Oct. 21

1836 A707 1.30p multicolored .95 .70

Jose Peon y Contreras, Poet, 150th Anniv. of Birth A708

1993, Oct. 22 Litho. *Perf. 10*

1837 A708 1.30p purple & black .95 .70

Endangered Species — A709

1993, Oct. 25 Litho. *Perf. 10*

1838 A709 2p Quetzal 2.50 1.10

1839 A709 2p Pavon, vert. 2.50 1.10

Christmas A710

Designs: No. 1840, Adoration of the Magi. No. 1841, Christmas trees, presents, vert.

1993, Nov. 26 Litho. *Perf. 10*

1840 A710 1.30p multicolored .95 .70

1841 A710 1.30p multicolored .95 .70

Solidarity A711

1993, Nov. 20

1842 A711 1.30p multicolored 1.00 .75

Natl. Preparatory School, 125th Anniv. — A712

1993, Dec. 2 Litho. *Perf. 10*

1843 A712 1.30p multicolored 1.00 .75

FSTSE, 55th Anniv. A713

1993, Dec. 6 Photo.

1844 A713 1.30p multicolored 1.00 .75

Mescala Bridge A714

1993, Dec. 7

1845 A714 1.30p multicolored 1.00 .75

Highway of the Sun A715

1993, Dec. 7

1846 A715 1.30p multicolored 1.00 .75

Film Actor Type of 1993

#1847, Pedro Armendariz. #1848, Pedro Infante. #1849, Jorge Negrete. #1850, Maria Felix. #1851, Dolores del Rio.

1993, Dec. 9 *Perf. 14*

1847 A694 1.30p black & light blue 1.00 .75
1848 A694 1.30p black & green 1.00 .75
1849 A694 1.30p black & purple 1.00 .75
1850 A694 1.30p black & orange 1.00 .75
1851 A694 1.30p black & rose 1.00 .75
Nos. 1847-1851 (5) 5.00 3.75

Secretariat of Education, 72nd Anniv. A716

Famous educators: #1852, Jose Vasconcelos. #1853, Rafael Ramirez Castaneda. #1854, Estefania Castaneda Nunez. #1855, Moises Saenz Garza. #1856, Rosaura Zapata Cano. #1857, Gregorio Torres Quintero. #1858, Lauro Aguirre Espinosa.

1994, Jan. 26 **Litho.** *Perf. 10*

1852 A716 1.30p multicolored 1.00 .75
1853 A716 1.30p multicolored 1.00 .75
1854 A716 1.30p multicolored 1.00 .75
1855 A716 1.30p multicolored 1.00 .75
1856 A716 1.30p multicolored 1.00 .75
1857 A716 1.30p multicolored 1.00 .75
1858 A716 1.30p multicolored 1.00 .75
Nos. 1852-1858 (7) 7.00 5.25

Emiliano Zapata, (1879-1919), Revolutionary — A717

1994, Apr. 10 **Litho.** *Perf. 10*

1859 A717 1.30p multicolored .95 .70

ILO, 75th Anniv. — A718

1994, Apr. 18 *Perf. 14*

1860 A718 2p multicolored 1.40 1.00

School Construction by CAPFCE, 50th Anniv. — A719

1994, Apr. 19

1861 A719 1.30p multicolored .90 .70

Children for Peace A720

1994, Apr. 28

1862 A720 1.30p multicolored .90 .70

Youth Services A721

1994, May 12 *Rouletted 12*

1863 A721 1.30p green & black .90 .70

United for Conservation — A722

1994, May 6 *Perf. 10*

1864 A722 1.30p multicolored 2.50 .70

Rouletting on many of the 1994 issues leaves individual stamps with rough, unattractive edges. Some copies are separated by scissors because of the difficulty in separating stamps.

The gum on many issues is poorly applied, often having a rough feel and appearance, due to air bubbles. Gum may not cover the entire back side.

Serial numbers are found on the back of some copies of No. 1896. These may appear on other stamps.

A723 A724

1994, Apr. 26 *Rouletted 12*

1865 A723 1.30p Francisco Zuniga .90 .70

1994, May 16 **Litho.** *Rouletted 13*

1866 A724 2p multicolored 1.40 1.00

34th World Congress of Publicists, Cancun.

World Telecommunications Day — A725

1994, May 17 **Litho.** *Rouletted 13*

1867 A725 2p multicolored 1.40 .75

ANIERM (Natl. Assoc. of Importers & Exporters of the Republic of Mexico), 50th Anniv. A726

1994, May 17 *Rouletted 12½*

1868 A726 1.30p multicolored .90 .70

Yumka Natural Wildlife Center A727

1994, May 21 **Litho.** *Rouletted 13*

1869 A727 1.30p multicolored .90 .70

City of Zacatecas A728

1994, May 26 *Rouletted 12½*

1870 A728 1.30p multicolored .90 .70

Prevention of Mental Retardation — A729

1994, June 1 **Litho.** *Perf. 14*

1871 A729 1.30p multicolored .90 .70

Month of the Child.

A730

1994, June 1 **Litho.** *Perf. 14*

1872 A730 1.30p Mother and child .90 .70

Friendship Hospital.

A731

1994, June 7 *Rouletted 13*

Stylized soccer players: a, Kicking ball. b, Behind net.

1873 A731 2p Pair, #a.-b. 3.25 2.25

1994 World Cup Soccer Championships, US.

A732 A733

1994, June 8

1874 A732 1.30p multicolored .90 .70

Intl. Fish Fair, Vera Cruz.

1994, June 5 *Perf. 14*

Wildlife conservation: a, Silhouettes of ornamental songbirds (green). b, Silhouettes of cynegetic birds (blue). c, Silhouettes of fierce-looking wildlife (brown). d, Silhouettes of endangered wildlife (red). e, Perico frente-anaranjada. f, Calandria cola amarilla. g, Cardenal torito. h, Sastrecillo americano. i, Cenzontle norteno. j, Guajolote norteno. k, Paloma de ala blanca. l, Pato pijiji de ala blanca. m, Ganso blanco. n, Codorniz de gambel. o, Peregrin falcon. p, Jaguar. q, Jaguarundi. r, Mono saraguato. s, Lobo fino de guadalupe. t, Berrendo peninsular. u, Guacamaya roja. v, Mexican prairie dog. w, Mexican wolf. x, Manati.

1875 A733 1.30p Block of 24 + label 50.00 50.00

Juvenile Integration Centers, 25th Anniv. — A734

Rouletted 12½

1994, June 29 **Litho.**

1876 A734 1.30p multicolored .90 .70

Mexican-Canadian Diplomatic Relations, 50th Anniv. — A735

1994, July 1

1877 A735 2p multicolored 1.40 1.10

Natl. Population Council, 20th Anniv. A736

1994, July 15

1878 A736 1.30p multicolored .90 .70

A737

A738

1994, July 20
1879 A737 2p multicolored 1.40 1.00
Intl. Year of the Family.

Rouletted 12½

1994, Aug. 22 **Photo.**
1880 A738 1.30p Arbor day .90 .70

A739

A740

1994, July 27
1881 A739 1.30p multicolored .90 .70
12th Mexico City Marathon.

1994, Aug. 1
1882 A740 1.30p Giant panda 1.25 .70
Chapultepec Zoo.

A741

A742

1994, Sept. 5 ***Perf. 13x13½***
1883 A741 1.30p multicolored .90 .70
Metro System, 25th anniv.

1994, Sept. 5
1884 A742 1.30p multicolored .90 .70
Economic Cultural Foundation, 60th Anniv..

A743

A744

1994, Sept. 22
1885 A743 1.30p multicolored .90 .70
Don Adolfo Lopez Mateos, 25th Death Anniv.

1994, Sept. 22
1886 A744 1.30p multicolored .90 .70
Solidarity Week.

City University, 40th Anniv. A745

1994, Sept. 21 **Litho.** ***Perf. 13½***
1887 A745 1.30p blue & yellow .90 .70

Opening of the Natl. Medical Center A746

1994, Oct. 3
1888 A746 1.30p multicolored .90 .70

Natl. Week of Patriot Symbols A747

1994, Sept. 16
1889 A747 1.30p multicolored .90 .70

Intl. Olympic Committee, Cent. — A748

1994, Sept. 29
1890 A748 2p multicolored 2.50 1.00

America Issue — A749

1994, Oct. 12
Mail delivery vehicles: a, bicycle. b, Railroad cycle.
1891 A749 2p Pair, #a.-b. 3.75 2.50

City of Salvatierra Guanajuato, 350th Anniv. — A750

1994, Sept. 12
1892 A750 1.30p multicolored .90 .70

Horses — A751

Designs: a, Saddled Aztec racer. b, Light brown quarter horse. c, Black quarter horse. d, Charro on horseback. e, Aztec racer. f, Chinaco riding galloping horse.

1994, Sept. 30 ***Perf. 14***
1893 A751 1.30p Block of 6, #a.-f. 10.00 10.00
Issued in sheets of 3 #1893 + 7 labels.

Grandparents' Day — A752

1994, Oct. 15 ***Perf. 13½***
1894 A752 1.30p multicolored .90 .70

Palace of Fine Arts, Mexico City, 60th Anniv. A753

1994, Sept. 29 **Litho.** ***Perf. 13½***
1895 A753 1.30p multicolored .90 .70

Antoine de Saint-Exupery (1900-44), Writer — A754

1994, Oct. 6 ***Rouletted 13***
1896 A754 2p multicolored 1.40 1.00

World Post Day A755

1994, Oct. 9 ***Perf. 13½***
1897 A755 2p multicolored 1.40 1.00

Natl. Clean Water Program A756

1994, Oct. 17
1898 A756 1.30p multicolored .90 .70

Dr. Jose Luis Mora (1794-1850), Politician — A757

1994, Oct. 27
1899 A757 1.30p multicolored .90 .70

City Theater, Saltillo, 50th Anniv. A758

1994, Nov. 3
1900 A758 1.30p multicolored .90 .70

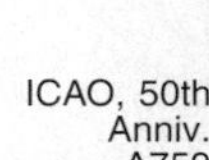

ICAO, 50th Anniv. A759

1994, Nov. 3
1901 A759 2p multicolored 1.40 1.00

Natl. Museum of Anthropology, 30th Anniv. — A760

Natl. Assoc. of Actors, 60th Anniv. — A761

1994, Nov. 8
1902 A760 1.30p multicolored .90 .70

1994, Nov. 9
1903 A761 1.30p multicolored .90 .70

Ignacio Allende (1769-1811), Independence Hero — A762

1994, Nov. 10
1904 A762 1.30p multicolored .90 .70

Natl. Museum of History, 50th Anniv. — A763

1994, Nov. 22 ***Perf. 14***
1905 A763 1.30p multicolored .90 .70

Coahuila Teachers' College, Cent. — A764

Pumas UNAM Soccer Team, 40th Anniv. — A765

1994, Nov. 23 ***Perf. 13½***
1906 A764 1.30p multicolored .90 .70

1994, Nov. 23
1907 A765 1.30p blue & gold .90 .70

Christmas A766

1994, Nov. 29

1908 A766 2p shown 1.40 1.00
1909 A766 2p Tree, vert. 1.40 1.00

Chalco Valley Solidarity A767

1994, Nov. 30

1910 A767 1.30p multicolored .90 .70

Sr. Juana Ines de la Cruz (1648-95), Writer — A768

1995, Apr. 17 **Litho.** ***Perf. 13½***

1911 A768 1.80p multicolored .75 .60

Wilhelm Roentgen (1845-1923), Discovery of the X-Ray, Cent. — A769

1995, May 8

1912 A769 2p multicolored .85 .65

Teachers' Day A770

1995, May 15

1913 A770 1.80p Ignacio M. Altamirano .75 .60

World Telecommunications Day — A771

1995, May 17 ***Perf. 14x14½***

1914 A771 2.70p multicolored 1.10 .85

A772

A773

1995, May 18 ***Perf. 13½***

1915 A772 1.80p multicolored .75 .60

Natl. Institute of Public Administration, 40th anniv.

1995, May 19 ***Perf. 14x14½***

Jose Marti (1853-95), Cuban patriot.

1916 A773 2.70p multicolored 1.10 .85

A774

A775

1.80p, Venustiano Carranza (1859-1920), politician, President of Mexico, 1917-20.

1995, May 23 ***Perf. 13½***

1917 A774 1.80p multicolored .75 .60

1995, June 11

1918 A775 2.70p multicolored 1.10 .85

Tianquis Turistico, travel trade show, 20th anniv.

A776

A777

a, Face becoming skull with pills, needle. b, Person as puppet. c, Faces behind bars.

1995, June 26

1919 A776 1.80p Strip of 3, #a.-c. 2.25 1.75

Intl. Day Against Illegal Drugs.

1995, June 28

1920 A777 1.80p black .75 .60

Lazaro Cardenas (1895-1970), soldier, politician, President of Mexico, 1934-40.

Natl. School for the Blind, 125th Anniv. A778

1995, July 18 **Litho.** ***Perf. 13½***

1921 A778 1.30p sepia & black .45 .35

Migratory Wildlife A781

Designs: a, Danaus plexippus. b, Lasiurus cinereus. c, Anas acuta. d, Ceryle alcyon.

1995, Aug. 15 **Litho.** ***Perf. 13½***

1924 A781 2.70p Block or strip of 4, #a.-d. 8.00 8.00

See Canada Nos. 1563-1567.

13th Mexico City Marathon A782

1995, Aug. 22 **Litho.** ***Perf. 13½***

1925 A782 2.70p multicolored .95 .70

16th Congress of UPAEP — A783

World Post Day — A785

Louis Pasteur (1822-95) A784

World Food Day A786

1995, Sept. 15

1926 A783 2.70p multicolored .95 .70

1995, Sept. 26 ***Perf. 14***

1927 A784 2.70p multicolored .95 .70

1995, Oct. 9

1928 A785 2.70p multicolored .95 .70

1995, Oct. 16 ***Perf. 14x14½***

1929 A786 1.80p multicolored .85 .50

FAO, 50th Anniv. A787

1995, Oct. 16 ***Perf. 14***

1930 A787 2.70p multicolored .95 .70

Plutarco Elias Calles (1877-1945), President of Mexico 1924-28 — A788

1995, Oct. 19 ***Perf. 13½***

1931 A788 1.80p multicolored .85 .50

Birth of Cuauhtemoc, 500th Anniv. — A789

1995, Oct. 21

1932 A789 1.80p multicolored .85 .50

A790

A791

National Symbols: 1.80p, Natl. flag, Constitution of Apatzingan, words of Natl. Anthem.

1995, Oct. 22

1933 A790 1.80p multicolored .85 .50

1995, Oct. 24 **Litho.** ***Perf. 14½x14***

1934 A791 2.70p multicolored .95 .70

UN, 50th anniv.

Intl. Year of Travel A792

1995, Nov. 14 **Litho.** ***Perf. 13½***

1935 A792 2.70p multicolored .85 .65

Viceregal Gallery of Art Painting, The Holy Family, by Andres de Conchas A793

1995, Nov. 16 ***Perf. 14***

1936 A793 1.80p multicolored .75 .40

Famous Generals A794

Designs: No. 1937, Ignacio Zaragoza (1829-62). No. 1938, Sóstenes Rocha (1831-97). No. 1939, Felipe B. Berriozábal (1829-1900). No. 1940, Pedro María Anaya (1795-1854). No. 1941, Leandro Valle (1833-61). No. 1942, Santos Degollado (1811-61).

1995, Nov. 23 ***Perf. 13½***

1937 A794 1.80p yel, blk & bister .75 .40
1938 A794 1.80p yel, blk & bister .75 .40
1939 A794 1.80p yel, blk & bister .75 .40
1940 A794 1.80p yel, blk & bister .75 .40
1941 A794 1.80p yel, blk & bister .75 .40
1942 A794 1.80p yel, blk & bister .75 .40
Nos. 1937-1942 (6) 4.50 2.40

Christmas A795

Children's paintings: 1.80p, Family celebrating Christmas inside house. 2.70p, Adoration of the Magi.

1995, Nov. 27

1943 A795 1.80p multicolored .55 .40
1944 A795 2.70p multicolored .85 .65
a. Pair, Nos. 1943-1944 1.40 1.10

Mexican Health Foundation, 10th Anniv. — A796

1995, Nov. 30 **Litho.** ***Perf. 14***

1945 A796 1.80p multicolored .80 .45

Wildlife Conservation — A797

1995, Dec. 4 ***Perf. 14***
1946 A797 1.80p Ocelot 2.00 .40

Motion Pictures, Cent. — A798

1995, Dec. 12
1947 A798 1.80p violet & black .75 .40

Natl. Library of Education A799

1995, Dec. 13 ***Perf. 13½***
1948 A799 1.80p bl grn & yel .75 .40

A800

A801

1995, Dec. 15
1949 A800 1.80p multicolored .75 .40

Natl. Arts and Sciences Awards, 50th anniv.

1995, Dec. 19 ***Perf. 14***

Radio personalities: a, Pedro Vargas. b, Agustin Lara. c, Hermanas Aguila. d, Toña "La Negra." e, "Cri-Cri," (F. Gabilondo Soler). f, Emilio Tuero. g, Gonzalo Curiel. h, Lola Beltrán.

1950 A801 1.80p Strip or block of 8, #a.-h. 10.00 10.00

Natl. Council of Science and Technology, 25th Anniv. A802

1995, Dec. 20 ***Perf. 13½***
1951 A802 1.80p multicolored .75 .40

Plaza de Toros, Mexico City, 50th Anniv. A803

Matadors: 1.80p, Silverio Perez, Carlos Arruza, Manolo Martinez. 2.70p, Rodolfo Gaona, Fermin Espinosa "Armillita," Lorenzo Garza.

1996, Feb. 5 **Litho.** ***Perf. 13½***
1952 A803 1.80p multicolored .55 .40
1953 A803 2.70p multicolored .85 .65
a. Pair, Nos. 1952-1953 1.40 1.10

No. 1953a is a contiunuous design.

Mexican Aviation Day A804

Designs: a, 2.70p, Patrol jet. b, 2.70p, Jet landing, airport terminal. c, 1.80p, Fighter plane, Squadron 201 (1945), map. d, 1.80p, Commercial biplane (1921), commerical jet.

1996, Jan. 20 **Litho.** ***Perf. 13½***
1954 A804 Strip or block of 4, #a.-d. 7.50 7.50

Dr. Alfonso Caso (1896-1970), Archaeologist — A805

1996, Feb. 1
1955 A805 1.80p multicolored .75 .40

Natl. Consumer Agency, 20th Anniv. A806

1996, Feb. 9 ***Perf. 14***
1956 A806 1.80p multicolored .75 .40

Tourism Type of 1993

Denomination Shown As $

1996-99 **Photo.** **Unwmk.** ***Perf. 14***

Design A683

No.	Value	Design	Unused	Used
1960	1p	Colima ('97)	1.00	.20
1961	1.80p	Chiapas	1.00	.20
1962	2p	Colima	1.00	.25
1963	2p	Guanajuato ('97)	1.00	.25
1964	2.30p	Chiapas ('97)	1.50	.30
1965	2.50p	Queretaro ('97)	1.50	.40
1966	2.70p	Mexico	2.00	.35
1967	3p	Campeche	2.00	.40
1968	3.10p	Coahuila ('97)	2.00	.35
1969	3.40p	Sinaloa	2.50	.45
a.		Pair, #1799, 1969	*125.00*	*125.00*
1970	3.50p	Mexico ('97)	2.50	.60
1971	3.60p	Sonora ('99)	2.50	.35
1972	3.70p	Campeche ('98)	2.50	.35
1973	4p	Michoacan, vert. ('97)	3.00	.50
1974	4.40p	Yucatan ('97)	3.00	.50
1975	5p	Queretaro	3.00	.65
1976	5p	Colima ('98)	4.00	.50
1977	6p	Zacatecas, vert. ('97)	4.00	.70
1978	6.50p	Sinaloa ('98)	5.00	.65
1979	7p	Sonora ('97)	6.00	.80
1980	8.50p	Mexico ('97)	7.50	1.00
		Nos. 1960-1980 (21)	58.50	9.75

Denomination on #1782-1805 was shown as N$.

Two additional printings of the 3.50p appear crude with missing and mis-registered dots. One of these printings is perf 12.

Two additional printings of No. 1975 exist. These appear crude, with missing and mis-registered color dots. One of the reprints is perf 12.

Orthopedics Society, 50th Anniv. — A807

1996, Apr. 29 **Litho.** ***Perf. 13½***
1981 A807 1.80p multicolored .75 .40

Juan Rulfo (1917-86), Writer A808

1996, May 3
1982 A808 1.80p multicolored .75 .40

Natl. Polytechnical Institute, 60th Anniv. — A809

1996, May 21
1983 A809 1.80p multicolored .75 .40

A810

A811

Stylized designs: a, 1.80p, Hands reaching toward one another. b, 1.80p, Person helping another out of hole. c, 2.70p, Two people.

1996, June 26 **Litho.** ***Perf. 13½***
1984 A810 Strip of 3, #a.-c. 3.00 3.00

Decade of United Nations Against Illegal Drug Abuse and Trafficking.

1996, July 19 ***Perf. 14x14½***

1996 Summer Olympic Games, Atlanta: a, Women's gymnastics. b, Soccer. c, Marathon race. d, Hurdles. e, Equestrian show jumping.

1985 A811 Strip of 5, #a.-e. 6.00 6.00

Motion Pictures, Cent. A812

1996, Aug. 6 **Litho.** ***Perf. 13½***

Color of Film Cells

1986 A812 1.80p grn, ocher & vio .45 .35
1987 A812 1.80p pur, grn & red .45 .35
a. Pair, #1986-1987 2.25 2.25

Justice Dept., 60th Anniv. A813

1996, Aug. 18
1988 A813 1.80p multicolored .75 .35

14th Mexico City Marathon A814

1996, Aug. 20
1989 A814 2.70p multicolored .90 .50

City of Zacatecas, 450th Anniv. A815

1996, Sept. 8
1990 A815 1.80p multicolored .90 .35

Natl. Council to Promote Education, 25th Anniv. A816

1996, Sept. 17
1991 A816 1.80p multicolored .90 .35

Souvenir Sheet

City of Monterrey, 400th Anniv. — A817

1996, Sept. 20
1992 A817 7.40p multicolored 4.50 4.50

Family Planning — A818

1996, Sept. 26
1993 A818 1.80p multicolored .90 .35

Independence, 175th Anniv. — A819

1996, Sept. 27
1994 A819 1.80p multicolored .90 .35

Endangered Species — A820

Designs show a wide variety of species, one from each stamp is: a, Aguila arpia. b, Tortola serrana. c, Monarch butterflies. d, Vernado bura. e, Guacamaya roja. f, Quetzal. g, Venado cola blanca. h, Puma. i, Coyote. j, Jaguar. k, Martucha. l, Woodpecker. m, Cuco canelo. n, Lince. o, Oso hormiguero. p, Ocelote. q, Encino. r, Chachalaca. s, Liebre. t, Tapir. u, Crocodile. v, Armadillo. w, Pecari. x, Cacomixtle.

1996, Oct. 2
Sheet of 24
1995 A820 1.80p #a.-x. + label 24.00 24.00
See US No. 3105.

World Post Day — A821

1996, Oct. 9
1996 A821 2.70p multicolored .90 .50

Salvador Zubirán Natl. Nutrition Institute, 50th Anniv. A822

1996, Oct. 12
1997 A822 1.80p multicolored .90 .35

Radio in Mexico, 75th Anniv. — A823

1996, Oct. 13
1998 A823 1.80p multicolored .90 .35

Paintings in Viceregal Gallery A824

Designs: a, 1.80p, Portrait of a Woman, by Baltasar de Echave Ibia. b, 2.70p, Archangel Michael, by Luis Juarez. c, 1.80p, Portrait of young Joaquín Manuel Fernández of Santa Cruz, by Nicolas Rodriguez Xuarez. d, 2.70p. The Virgin of the Apocalypse, by Miguel Cabrera. e, 1.80p, Portrait of Dona Maria Luisa Gonzaga Foncerrada y Labarrieta, by Jose Maria Vazquez.

1996, Oct. 14 ***Perf. 14***
1999 A824 Strip of 5, #a.-e. 4.75 4.75

World Food Day — A825

1996, Oct. 31 ***Perf. 13½***
2000 A825 2.70p multicolored .90 .50

Mexican Science A826

1996, Sept. 2
2001 A826 1.80p multicolored .90 .35

Intl. Subway Conference A828

1996, Nov. 12 **Litho.** ***Perf. 13½***
2003 A828 2.70p multicolored .90 .50

Christmas A829

1996, Nov. 14 **Litho.** ***Perf. 13½***
2004 A829 1p Star pinata .35 .20
2005 A829 1.80p Man carrying pinatas .55 .30

Andres Henestrosa, Writer — A830

1996, Nov. 23 **Litho.** ***Perf. 14***
2006 A830 1.80p multicolored .90 .30

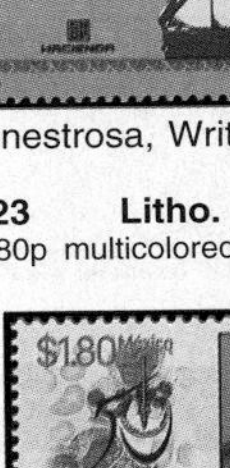

Natl. Cancer Institute, 50th Anniv. A831

1996, Nov. 25 **Litho.** ***Perf. 13½***
2007 A831 1.80p multicolored .90 .30

Paisano Program — A832

1996, Nov. 28 **Litho.** ***Perf. 13½***
2008 A832 2.70p multicolored .90 .50

David Alfaro Siqueiros (1896-1974), Painter — A833

1996, Dec. 5 **Litho.** ***Perf. 13½***
2009 A833 1.80p multicolored .90 .30

32nd Natl. Assembly of Surgeons A834

Dr. José Ma. Barceló de Villagrán

1996, Dec. 6 **Litho.** ***Perf. 13½***
2010 A834 1.80p multicolored .90 .30

Wildlife Conservation — A835

1996, Dec. 11 **Litho.** ***Perf. 14***
2011 A835 1.80p Black bear, cubs 2.25 .75

UNICEF, 50th Anniv. A836

1996, Dec. 11 **Litho.** ***Perf. 13½***
2012 A836 1.80p multicolored .90 .30

Palafoxiana Library, Puebla, 350th Anniv. — A837

1996, Dec. 17 **Litho.** ***Perf. 13½***
2013 A837 1.80p multicolored .90 .30

Natl. Institute of Nuclear Research A838

1996, Dec. 19 **Litho.** ***Perf. 13½***
2014 A838 1.80p multicolored .90 .30

A839

A840

1996, Dec. 19 **Litho.** ***Perf. 13½***
2015 A839 1.80p multicolored .90 .30

Intl. Day for Preservation of the Ozone Layer.

1996, Dec. 20 **Litho.** ***Perf. 13½***
2016 A840 1.80p multicolored .90 .30

30 year career of plastic arts sculptor Sebastian.

Mexican Diplomats A841

Design: Isidro Fabela (b. 1882), lawyer, and Genaro Estrada (1887-1977), journalist, politician.

1996, Oct. 24 **Litho.** ***Perf. 13½***
2017 A841 1.80p multicolored .90 .30

Carlos Pellicer (1897-1977), Poet, Museum Founder — A842

1997, Jan. 16
2018 A842 2.30p multicolored 1.00 .40

Andres Eloy Blanco (1896-1955), Poet — A843

1997, Feb. 6 **Litho.** ***Perf. 13½***
2019 A843 3.40p multicolored 1.40 .60

A844

A845

1997, Feb. 10
2020 A844 3.40p multicolored 1.40 .60

UNESCO Intl. Summit on Education, Confederation of American Educators.

1997, Feb. 14
2021 A845 3.40p multicolored 1.40 .60

Treaty of Tlatelolco prohibiting nuclear weapons in Latin America & Caribbean.

Souvenir Sheet

Mexican Central Post Office, 90th Anniv. — A846

1997, Feb. 20
2022 A846 7.40p multicolored 6.00 6.00

A847

A848

Generals: No. 2023, Francisco L. Urquizo. No. 2024, Mariano Escobedo. No. 2025, Jacinto B. Trevino Gonzalez. No. 2026, Felipe Angeles. No. 2027, Candido Aguilar Vargas. No. 2028, Joaquin Amaro Dominguez.

1997, Mar. 5
2023 A847 2.30p multicolored .90 .40
2024 A847 2.30p multicolored .90 .40
2025 A847 2.30p multicolored .90 .40
2026 A847 2.30p multicolored .90 .40
2027 A847 2.30p multicolored .90 .40
2028 A847 2.30p multicolored .90 .40
Nos. 2023-2028 (6) 5.40 2.40

1997, Mar. 8
2029 A848 2.30p multicolored .80 .40

Intl. Women's Day.

1st Intl. Congress for Spanish Language A849

Painting: Allegory, "La Gramatica," by Juan Correa.

1997, Apr. 7 Litho. *Perf. 13½*
2030 A849 3.40p multicolored .90 .40

Dr. Ignacio Chávez, Pres. of Natl. Academy of Medicine, Birth Cent. A850

1997, Apr. 23
2031 A850 2.30p multicolored .80 .40

Mexican Constitution, 80th Anniv. — A851

1997, Apr. 29
2032 A851 2.30p Venustiano Carranza .80 .40

First Edition of "Al Filo Del Agua," by Agustín Yáñez, 50th Anniv. A852

1997, May 9
2033 A852 2.30p multicolored .80 .40

Prof. Rafael Ramírez (1855-1959), Educator — A853

1997, May 15
2034 A853 2.30p green & gray .80 .40

Japanese Emigration to Mexico, Cent. A854

1997, May 12
2035 A854 3.40p multicolored 1.75 .60

See Japan No. 2569.

A855

A856

1997, May 31
2036 A855 2.30p multicolored .80 .40

Autonomous University of Baja California, 40th Anniv.

1997, June 26

Intl. Day to Stop Use of Illegal Drugs: a, 2.30p, Dove, clouds, sunlight. b, 3.40p, Man with one hand on bars, one hand raised toward sky. c, 3.40p, Dove in window behind bars.

2037 A856 Strip of 3, #a.-c. + label 5.50 5.50

Sigmund Freud — A857

Naval Military School, Cent. — A858

1997, June 28
2038 A857 2.30p multicolored .80 .40

1997, July 1
2039 A858 2.30p multicolored .80 .40

Natl. Bank of Foreign Commerce, 60th Anniv. A859

1997, July 4 Litho. *Perf. 13½*
2040 A859 3.40p multicolored 1.25 .60

United for Conservation — A860

1997, July 16
2041 A860 2.30p Vaquita, calf 2.00 .90

Mexican College of Aviation Pilots, 50th Anniv. A861

1997, July 17
2042 A861 2.30p multicolored .90 .40

15th Mexico City Marathon — A862

1997, Aug. 6
2043 A862 3.40p multicolored 1.25 .60

Juarez Hospital of Mexico, 150th Anniv. A863

1997, Aug. 18
2044 A863 2.30p multicolored .90 .40

Battles of 1847 A864

#2045, Battle of Padierna. #2046, Battle of Churubusco. #2047, Battle of Molino del Rey. #2047A, Defense of the Castle of Chapultepec.

1997
2045 A864 2.30p multicolored .90 .40
2046 A864 2.30p multicolored .90 .40
2047 A864 2.30p multicolored .90 .40
2047A A864 2.30p multicolored .90 .40
Nos. 2045-2047A (4) 3.60 1.60

Issued: #2045, 8/19; #2046, 8/20; #2047, 9/8; #2047A, 9/13.

A865

A866

1997, Sept. 3
2048 A865 2.30p multicolored .90 .40

Guillermo Prieto, poet, death cent.

1997, Sept. 12 Litho. *Perf. 13½*
2049 A866 3.40p multicolored 1.25 .60

Battalion of St. Patrick, 150th anniv. See Ireland No. 1085.

A867

A868

1997, Oct. 6
2050 A867 2.30p multicolored .90 .40

Reproductive health for adolescents month.

1997, Oct. 9
2051 A868 3.40p Stamp Day 1.25 .60

Heinrich von Stephan (1831-97) A869

1997, Oct. 9
2052 A869 3.40p multicolored 1.25 .60

Manuel Gómez Morin (1897-1949), Politician — A870

1997, Oct. 14
2053 A870 2.30p multicolored .90 .40

Dr. Manuel Gea González General Hospital, 50th Anniv. A871

1997, Oct. 14
2054 A871 2.30p multicolored .90 .40

Mexican Bar Assoc. College of Law, 75th Anniv. — A872

1997, Oct. 30
2055 A872 2.30p multicolored .90 .40

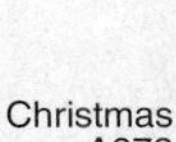

Christmas A873

Children with piñatas: No. 2056, By Ana R. Botello. No. 2057, By Adrián Laris.

1997, Nov. 19
2056 A873 2.30p multicolored .90 .40
2057 A873 2.30p multicolored .90 .40

New Law on Social Security — A874

1997, Dec. 10
2058 A874 2.30p multicolored .90 .40

Central University Hospital, Chihuahua, Cent. — A875

1997, Dec. 5 **Litho.** ***Perf. 13½***
2059 A875 2.30p multicolored .90 .40

Dr. Mario Jose Molina Henriquez, 1995 Nobel Prize Recipient in Chemistry A876

1997, Dec. 8
2060 A876 3.40p multicolored 1.25 .55

Baking Industry Granary, 50th Anniv. A877

Baked goods and: a, Storage shelves. b, Man working at oven. c, Basic ingredients, man working with dough.

1997, Dec. 10
2061 A877 2.30p Vert. strip of 3, #a.-c. + label 4.00 4.00

A878

A879

Modern Mexican art, by Jose Chavez Morado.

1997, Dec. 19
2062 A878 2.30p multicolored .90 .40

Cervantes Festival, Guanajuato, 45th anniv.

1997, Dec. 20
2063 A879 2.30p multicolored .90 .40

City of Loreto, 300th anniv.

Military School of Arms, 50th Anniv. A880

1998, Mar. 1 **Litho.** ***Perf. 13½***
2064 A880 2.30p multicolored .90 .40

Intl. Mother's Day A881

1998, Mar. 8
2065 A881 2.30p multicolored .90 .40

Cinco de Mayo — A882

1998, Apr. 16
2066 A882 3.50p multicolored 1.25 .60

See US No. 3203.

1998 World Cup Soccer Championships, France — A883

Eiffel Tower, national colors of France and Mexico and: No. 2067, Soccer player. No. 2068, Mexican Eagle mascot.
#2069: a, 8.60p, like #2067. b, 6.20p, like #2068.

1998
2067 A883 2.30p multicolored 1.50 1.50
2068 A883 2.30p multicolored 1.50 1.50

Souvenir Sheet

2069 A883 Sheet of 2, #a.-b. 8.00 8.00

Issued: #2067, 4/20; #2068, 5/11; #2069, 5/25. #2069 contains two 24x40mm stamps with a continuous design.

Justo Sierra, Educator, 150th Birth Anniv. — A884

1998, Apr. 23
2070 A884 2.30p multicolored .90 .40

Dr. Salvador Zubiran, Birth Cent. A885

1998, Apr. 24
2071 A885 2.30p multicolored .90 .40

Organization of American States, 50th Anniv. — A886

1998, Apr. 27
2072 A886 3.40p multicolored 1.00 .55

University of Puebla, 25th Anniv. A887

1998, May 6
2073 A887 2.30p multicolored .90 .40

Teacher's Day — A888

1998, May 15
2074 A888 2.30p Soledad Anaya Solorzano .90 .40

State of Tamaulipas (New Santander), 250th Anniv. — A889

1998, May 31
2075 A889 2.30p multicolored .90 .40

Sports Lottery, 20th Anniv. A890

1998, June 2
2076 A890 2.30p multicolored .90 .40

Universal Declaration of Human Rights, 50th Anniv. A891

1998, June 5 **Litho.** ***Perf. 13½***
2077 A891 3.40p multicolored 1.00 .35

Federico García Lorca (1898-1936), Poet — A892

1998, June 5
2078 A892 3.40p multicolored 1.00 .35

Philippine Independence, Cent. — A893

3.40p, Mexican flag, sailing ship. 7.40p, Mexican, Philippine flags, sailing ship.

1998, June 3 **Litho.** ***Perf. 13½***
2079 A893 3.40p multicolored 1.00 .55

Souvenir Sheet

2080 A893 7.40p multicolored 4.75 4.75

See Philippines Nos. 2537-2539, Spain No. 2949.

Intl. Day Against Drugs — A894

1998, June 26
2081 A894 2.30p multicolored .90 .35

Chapultepec Zoological Park, 7th Anniv. — A895

Design: Alfonso L. Herrera, jaguar.

1998, July 6
2082 A895 2.30p multicolored .90 .35

Arbor Day — A896

1998, July 9
2083 A896 2.30p multicolored .90 .35

Opening of the Philatelic Museum, Oaxaca — A897

Designs: No. 2084, Convent of St. Peter and St. Paul, Teposcolula. No. 2085, Burnished vase with carving. No. 2086, San Bartolo Coyotepec, "El Camino," by Francisco Toledo. No. 2087, Golden breast plate from Tomb 7, Monte Alban.

1998, July 9
2084 A897 2.30p multicolored .90 .35
2085 A897 2.30p multicolored .90 .35
2086 A897 3.40p multicolored 1.75 .75
2087 A897 3.40p multicolored 1.75 .75
Nos. 2084-2087 (4) 5.30 2.20

Precinct in Natl. Palace Honoring Benito Juárez (1806-72)
A898

1998, July 18 ***Perf. 14***
2088 A898 2.30p multicolored .90 .35

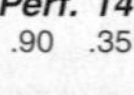

Santo Domingo Cultural Center, Oaxaca — A899

a, Entire complex. b, Portals of museum. c, Francisco da Burgoa Library. d, Ethnobotanical Garden.

1998, July 24 ***Perf. 13½***
2089 A899 2.30p Block of 4, #a.-d. 4.25 4.25

Marine Life
A900

a, Frigatebird, gray whale. b, Albatross. c, Whale's tail flukes. d, Dolphins, flamingos. e, Turtles. f, Sea lions. g, Elegant swallows, dolphin. h, Killer whale. i, Flamingos. j, Alligator. k, Sardines. l, Squid, loggerhead turtle. m, Bluefin tuna, jellyfish. n, Barracudas. o, Manatee. p, Garibaldi. q, Hammerhead shark. r, Huachinango, shrimp, ray. s, Octopus, mero. t, Blowfish, turtle. u, Crab, sandollars. v, Seahorse, angelfish. w, Crab, turtle, moray eel. x, Mariposa de cuatro ojos. y, Shark, coral.

1998, Aug. 14
Sheet of 25
2090 A900 2.30p #a.-y. 25.00 25.00

No. 2090 is a continuous design showing many different species of marine life, aquatic birds, and surrounding vegetation. Just a few species from each stamp are described in the above design note.

16th Mexico City Marathon
A901

1998, Aug. 19 **Litho.** ***Perf. 13½***
2091 A901 3.40p multicolored 1.00 .55

World Tourism Day
A902

1998, Sept. 25
2092 A902 3.40p multicolored 1.00 .55

Natl. Archives, 175th Anniv.
A903

1998, Sept. 29 ***Perf. 14***
2093 A903 2.30p multicolored .90 .35

A904

A905

1998, Oct. 1 ***Perf. 13½***
2094 A904 3.40p multicolored 1.00 .55

Interpol, 75th Anniv.

1998, Oct. 5
2095 A905 2.30p multicolored .60 .35

Reproductive Health Month.

Luis Nishizawa (b. 1918), Painter — A906

1998, Oct. 9
2096 A906 2.30p multicolored .60 .35

World Post Day
A907

1998, Oct. 9
2097 A907 3.40p multicolored 1.00 .55

Heroic Military College, 175th Anniv.
A908

1998, Oct. 11
2098 A908 2.30p multicolored .60 .35

District of Tamaulipas, 250th Anniv.
A909

1998, Oct. 12
2099 A909 2.30p multicolored .60 .35

United for Conservation — A910

1998, Oct. 13
2100 A910 2.30p Aguila real .60 .35

World Food Day
A911

1998, Oct. 16
2101 A911 3.40p multicolored 1.00 .55

Natl. Mexican Migration Week
A912

1998, Oct. 19
2102 A912 2.30p multicolored .60 .35

José Alfredo Jiménez (1926-72), Composer
A913

1998, Nov. 11
2103 A913 2.30p multicolored .60 .35

College of Petroleum Engineers, 25th Anniv. — A914

1998, Nov. 11
2104 A914 3.40p multicolored 1.00 .55

Cultural and Economic Cooperation Between Mexico and France — A915

1998, Nov. 12
2105 A915 3.40p multicolored 1.00 .55

City of Colima, 475th Anniv.
A916

1998, Nov. 16
2106 A916 2.30p multicolored .60 .35

Christmas
A917

Children's drawings: 2.30p, Nativity scene. 3.40p, Pinata, candy, vert.

1998, Nov. 17
Self-Adhesive
2107 A917 2.30p multicolored .60 .35
2108 A917 3.40p multicolored 1.00 .55

Latin American Civil Aviation Commission, 25th Anniv. — A918

1998, Dec. 14 **Litho.** ***Perf. 13½***
2109 A918 3.40p multicolored 1.00 .55

Natl. Institute of Native People, 50th Anniv.
A919

1998, Dec. 4
2110 A919 2.30p multicolored .60 .35

Federation of Govt. Workers, 60th Anniv.
A920

1998, Dec. 7
2111 A920 2.30p multicolored .60 .35

State University of Sinaloa, 125th Anniv. — A921

1998, Dec. 18
2112 A921 2.30p multicolored .60 .35

Mexico's Natl. Program for Women
A922

1999, Mar. 8 **Litho.** ***Perf. 13½***
2113 A922 4.20p multicolored 1.25 .45

A923

1999, Feb. 9
2114 A923 3p multicolored .90 .35

Carnaval '99, Veracruz.

A924

1999, Feb. 27

2115 A924 3p Hammock .65 .35
2116 A924 4.20p Divers .90 .45
a. Pair, #2115-2116 4.00 4.00

Acapulco, 200th Anniv.

Launching of SATMEX 5 — A925

1999, Feb. 9

2117 A925 3p multicolored .90 .35

Souvenir Sheet

Visit of Pope John Paul II — A926

1999, Jan. 22

2118 A926 10p multicolored 5.00 5.00

Tourism Type of 1993
Denomination Shown As $

Unwmk.

1999-2001		Photo.		*Perf. 14*	
2119	A683	50c	Coahuila	.75	.20
2120	A683	70c	Yucatan	.75	.20
2121	A683	1.50p	Chiapas	1.00	.20
2122	A683	2p	Coahuila	1.00	.20
2123	A683	2.50p	Yucatan	1.25	.25
2124	A683	2.60p	Colima	2.00	.30
2125	A683	3p	Michoacan, vert.	1.75	.30
2126	A683	3.60p	Coahuila	1.75	.40
2127	A683	4.20p	Guanajuato	1.75	.45
2128	A683	4.20p	Zacatecas, vert.	3.00	.45
2129	A683	4.50p	Mexico	3.00	.50
2130	A683	4.90p	Sonora	3.00	.50
2131	A683	5.30p	Michoacan, vert.	3.75	.55
2132	A683	5.90p	Queretaro	3.50	.55
2133	A683	6p	Sinaloa	3.50	.70
2134	A683	6p	Michoacan, vert.	4.00	.70
2135	A683	6.50p	Queretaro	4.50	.70
2136	A683	7p	Coahuila	4.50	.75
2137	A683	8p	Zacatecas, vert.	9.00	.85
2138	A683	8p	Sinaloa	4.75	.85
2139	A683	8.50p	Chiapas	4.75	.90
2139A	A683	8.50p	Chiapas, denomination upright	5.50	1.10
2140	A683	8.50p	Zacatecas, vert.	4.75	.95
2141	A683	10p	Campeche	18.00	1.10
2141A	A683	10p	Chiapas	7.50	1.10
2141B	A683	10.50p	Michoacan, vert.	7.00	1.10
2141C	A683	11.50p	Queretaro	8.50	1.25
2141D	A683	30p	Queretaro	19.00	3.25
			Nos. 2119-2141D (28)	133.50	20.35

Issued: #2122, 2124, 2126, 2127, 2130-2133, 2137, 1999; #2120, 2000; #2119, 2121, 2123, 2125, 2128, 2129, 2134-2136, 2138-2141D, 2001.

The denomination of No. 2139 is in italics.

Natl. Commission to Distribute Free Textbooks, 40th Anniv. — A927

1999, Mar. 11 Litho. *Perf. 13½*

2142 A927 3p multicolored 1.00 .35

See Nos. 2155-2156, 2172.

Natl. Population Commission, 25th Anniv. — A928

1999, Mar. 26

2143 A928 3p multicolored 1.00 .35

Souvenir Sheet

Ponciano Díaz Salinas (1856-99), Bullfighter — A929

Sheet Size: 95x240mm.

1999, Apr. 17

2144 A929 10p sheet of 1 5.00 5.00

Ceniceros de Pérez (1908-68), Teacher A930

1999, May 15

2145 A930 3p multicolored .90 .35

Teacher's Day.

AAA Mexican Baseball League, 75th Anniv. A931

Designs: a, Skeleton pitcher, skeleton batter. b, Stylized pitcher. c, Pitcher lifting up large foot, sun. d, Catcher.

1999, May 31

2146 A931 3p Block of 4, #a.-d. 5.00 5.00

Also available in strip of 4 + label.

National Bank of Mexico, 115th Anniv. — A932

Designs: No. 2147, Old, new bank buildings. No. 2148, 10p bill.

1999, June 2

2147 A932 3p multicolored .90 .35
2148 A932 3p multicolored .90 .35

World Dog Show — A933

a, 4.20p, Chihuahua. b, 4.20p, Xoloitzcuintle. c, 3p, German shepherd. d, 3p, Rottweiler.

1999, June 2

2149 A933 Sheet of 4, #a.-d. 7.50 7.50

A934 A935

Perf. 13¼x13½

1999, June 25 Litho.

2150 A934 4.20p multicolored 1.25 .45

Intl. Day Against Illegal Drugs.

1999, July 2 Litho. *Perf. 13¼x13½*

2151 A935 3p multicolored .90 .35

National Bank, 65th anniv.

Arbor Day A936

1999, July 26 *Perf. 13½x13¼*

2152 A936 3p multicolored .90 .35

Civil Register, 140th Anniv. A937

1999, July 27

2153 A937 3p multicolored .90 .35

17th Mexico City Marathon A938

1999, Aug. 11

2154 A938 4.20p multicolored 1.75 .45

Free Textbook Type of 1999

Designs: No. 2155, Children, book, flag, cacti. No. 2156, "Tsuni tsame."

1999 Litho. *Perf. 13¼x13½*

2155 A927 3p green & multi .90 .35
2156 A927 3p orange & multi .90 .35

Issued: #2155, 8/23; #2156, 10/28.

Self-portrait, by Rufino Tamayo (1899-1991) — A939

1999, Aug. 28 *Perf. 13¼x13½*

2157 A939 3p multicolored .90 .35

City of Toluca, Bicent. A940

1999, Sept. 12 *Perf. 13½x13¼*

2158 A940 3p copper & brown .90 .35

State of Mexico, 175th Anniv. A941

1999, Sept. 14

2159 A941 3p multicolored 1.00 .35

Union of Latin American Universities, 50th Anniv. — A942

1999, Sept. 22 *Perf. 13¼x13½*

2160 A942 4.20p multicolored 1.25 .45

Institute of Security & Social Services of State Workers, 40th Anniv. A943

1999, Oct. 1 *Perf. 13½x13¼*

2161 A943 3p multicolored 1.00 .35

State of Baja California Sur, 25th Anniv. A944

1999, Oct. 4

2162 A944 3p multicolored 1.00 .35

Family Planning, 25th Anniv. A945

1999, Oct. 4
2163 A945 3p multicolored 1.00 .35

Nature Conservation — A946

1999, Oct. 5
2164 A946 3p Harpy eagle 1.00 .35

State of Quintana Roo, 25th Anniv. — A947

1999, Oct. 8 Litho. ***Perf. 13¼x13½***
2165 A947 3p multicolored 1.00 .35

UPU, 125th Anniv. — A948

World Post Day — A949

1999, Oct. 9
2166 A948 4.20p multicolored 1.50 .45

1999, Oct. 9
2167 A949 4.20p multicolored 1.50 .45

12th General Assembly of the Int'l Council on Monuments and Sites A950

1999, Oct. 17 ***Perf. 13½x13¼***
2168 A950 4.20p multicolored 1.50 .45

Carlos Chavez (1899-1978) & Silvestre Revueltas (1899-1940), Composers — A951

1999, Oct. 21
2169 A951 3p multicolored 1.00 .35

Autonomous Metropolitan University, 25th Anniv. — A952

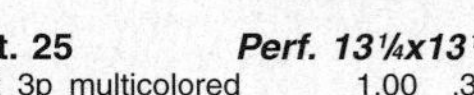

1999, Oct. 25 ***Perf. 13¼x13½***
2170 A952 3p multicolored 1.00 .35

State of Guerrero, 150th Anniv. A953

1999, Oct. 27 Litho. ***Perf. 13½x13¼***
2171 A953 3p multicolored 1.00 .35

Free Textbook Type of 1999

Design: "Ciencias Naturales."

Perf. 13¼x13½
1999, Nov. 12 **Litho.**
2172 A927 3p multi 1.00 .35

Christmas
A954 A955

1999, Nov. 29
2173 A954 3p multi 1.00 .35
2174 A955 4.20p multi 1.75 .45

Natl. Commission of Professional Education, 20th Anniv. — A956

1999, Dec. 1 ***Perf. 13½x 13¼***
2175 A956 3p multi 1.00 .35

Scientific Voyage of Alexander von Humboldt to Americas, Bicent. A957

1999, Dec. 1
2176 A957 3p multi 1.00 .35

The 20th Century A958

Education: a, 3p, Natl. Autonomous University of Mexico. b, 3p, Justo Sierra, José Vasconcelos. c, 3p, Natl. Poytechnic Institute. d, 3p, Free text books. e, 4.20p, Reading programs.

Litho. & Embossed
1999, Dec. 15 ***Perf. 14x14½***
2177 A958 Sheet of 5, #a.-e. 10.00 10.00

Nos. 2177c-2177d are 79x25mm, No. 2177e is oval-shaped and 39x49mm.
See #2180-2181, 2191-2196.

A959 A960

2000, Jan. 24 Litho. ***Perf. 13¼x13½***
2178 A959 3p multi 1.00 .35
2000 census.

2000, Mar. 8 Litho. ***Perf. 13¼x13½***
2179 A960 4.20p multi 1.50 .45
International Women's Day.

The 20th Century Type of 1999

Building Democracy — No. 2180: a, 3p, Mexican presidents from Porfirio Díaz to Lázaro Cárdenas, Mexican Constitution. b, 3p, Pancho Villa, Emiliano Zapata. c, 3p, Mexican presidents from Manuel Avila Camacho to Gustavo Díaz Ordaz. d, 3p, Political figures, protestors, newspaper boy. e, 4.20p, Voter registration card, child at ballot box.
10p, People writing and at computers.

Litho. & Embossed
2000, Mar. 16 ***Perf. 14x14½***
2180 A958 Sheet of 5, #a-e 10.00 10.00

Souvenir Sheet
Litho.
Perf. 13½
2181 A958 10p multi 7.50 7.50

Nos. 2180a and 2180b are 79x25mm, and No. 2180e is oval-shaped and 39x49mm.

Natl. Assoc. of Universities and Institutions of Higher Learning, 50th Anniv. A961

Perf. 13½x13¼
2000, Mar. 24 **Litho.**
2182 A961 3p multi 1.00 .35

25th Mexican Travel Trade Show, Acapulco A962

2000, Apr. 9
2183 A962 4.20p multi 1.50 .45

Discovery of Brazil, 500th Anniv. A963

2000, Apr. 22
2184 A963 4.20p multi 1.50 .45

Teacher's Day — A964

2000, May 15 ***Perf. 13¼x13½***
2185 A964 3p Luis Alvarez Barret 1.00 .35

Stampin' the Future Children's Stamp Design Contest Winners A965

Art by: 3p, Alejandro Guerra Millán. 4.20p, Carlos Hernández García.

2000, May 17 ***Perf. 13½x13¼***
2186 A965 3p multi 1.00 .35
2187 A965 4.20p multi 1.50 .45

Fourth Meeting of Telecommunications Ministers and Information Industry Leaders — A966

2000, May 24
2188 A966 4.20p multi 1.50 .45

Intl. Day Against Illegal Drugs — A967

Perf. 13¼x13½
2000, June 26 **Litho.**
2189 A967 4.20p multi 1.50 .45

National Worker's Housing Fund Institute — A968

#2190, Sculptures: a, 3p, Pre-Hispanic building. b, 3p, Pre-Hispanic building with stairway. c, 10p, Pre-Hispanic natives in circle.

2000, June 27 ***Perf. 14¼x13½***
2190 A968 Sheet of 3, #a-c 7.00 7.00

The 20th Century Type of 1999

Cultural Idenity and Diversity — No. 2191: a, Xóchitl Incuícatl. b, Corre y se va. c, Tercera llamada. . . Cácado! d, Al Hablar como al guisar, su granito de sal. e, Children.

Health — No. 2192: a, Six men, certificate, man in tuberculosis prevention truck. b, Children on line. c, Nine men, posters. d, Poster showing tractor, health care. e, Modern medical equipment.

Art — No. 2193: a, El sello de la casa. b, Espíritu del siglo. c, La luz de México. d, Los nostros en que nos reconocemos. e, Building dome, artists and artwork.

Photography — No. 2194: a, Colchón enrollado, by Manuel Alvarez Bravo. b, Roses, by

Tina Modotti. c, Four vertical photos, four horizontal photos. d, Two vertical photos, six horizontal photos. e, Three photos.

Commercial Development and Industrialization — No. 2195: a, Tractor. b, Truck cab. c, Store. d, Automobile. e, Globe.

Communications — No. 2196: a, Telephones and telegraph. b, Roads and bridges. c, Postal services. d, Railroads. e, Satellite, satellite dish, train.

Litho. & Embossed

2000 *Perf. 14x14¼*

2191	Sheet of 5	10.00	10.00
a.-d.	A958 3p Any single	1.00	.30
e.	A958 4.20p multicolored	1.50	.45
2192	Sheet of 5	10.00	10.00
a.-d.	A958 3p Any single	1.00	.30
e.	A958 4.20p multicolored	1.50	.45
2193	Sheet of 5	10.00	10.00
a.-d.	A958 3p Any single	1.00	.30
e.	A958 4.20p multicolored	1.50	.45
2194	Sheet of 5	10.00	10.00
a.-d.	A958 3p Any single	1.00	.30
e.	A958 4.20p multicolored	1.50	.45
2195	Sheet of 5	10.00	10.00
a.-d.	A958 3p Any single	1.00	.30
e.	A958 4.20p multicolored	1.50	.45
2196	Sheet of 5	10.00	10.00
a.-d.	A958 3p Any single	1.00	.30
e.	A958 4.20p multicolored	1.50	.45
	Nos. 2191-2196 (6)	60.00	60.00

Issued: #2191, 7/18; #2192, 10/24; #2193, 11/10; #2194, 12/9; #2195, 12/20; #2196, 12/21.

Nos. 2191c-2196c, 2191d-2196d are 79x25mm and Nos. 2191e-2196e are oval shaped and 39x49mm.

Natl. Program for Development of Handicapped People, 5th Anniv. — A969

2000, Aug. 2 **Litho.** *Perf. 13¼x13½*
2197 A969 3p multi 1.00 .35

Latin American Integration Association, 20th Anniv. — A970

2000, Aug. 11 *Perf. 13½x13¼*
2198 A970 4.20p multi 1.50 .45

Restoration of the Senate, 125th Anniv. — A971

2000, Aug. 17 *Perf. 13¼x13½*
2199 A971 3p multi 1.00 .35

Souvenir Sheets

Expo 2000, Hanover — A972

a, 1p, Mexican soul. b, 1p, Natl. mosaic. c, 1.80p, Future construction. d, 1.80p, Plaza pyramid. e, 2p, Creation of towns. f, 2p, Millennial construction. g, 3p, Naturea. h, 3p, Humanity. i, 3p, Technology. j, 3.60p, Expo 2000, Hanover. k, 4.20p, Emblem.

Litho. & Embossed

2000, Aug. 20 *Perf. 14½x14*
2200 A972 Sheet of 11, #a-k 12.50 12.50

No. 2200k is oval shaped and 39x49mm.

Bank of Mexico, 75th Anniv. — A973

2000, Aug. 23 **Litho.** *Perf.*
2201 A973 10p multi 5.00 5.00

Stamp is oval-shaped and 49x39mm.

18th Mexico City Marathon A974

2000, Aug. 24 *Perf. 13½x13¼*
2202 A974 4.20p multi 1.50 .45

2000 Summer Olympics, Sydney A975

2000, Sept. 15
2203 A975 4.20p multi 1.50 .45

Paisano Program A976

2000, Sept. 21
2204 A976 4.20p multi 1.50 .45

2nd Intl. Memory of the World Conference A977

2000, Sept. 12
2205 A977 4.20p multi 1.50 .45

Women's Reproductive Health Month — A978

2000, Oct. 5 *Perf. 13¼x13½*
2206 A978 3p multi 1.00 .35

Ciudad Victoria, 250th Anniv. A979

2000, Oct. 6 *Perf. 13½x13¼*
2207 A979 3p multi 1.00 .35

World Post Day — A980

2000, Oct. 9 *Perf. 13¼x13½*
2208 A980 4.20p multi 1.50 .45

Natl. Human Rights Commission, 10th Anniv. — A981

2000, Oct. 23 *Perf. 13½x13¼*
2209 A981 3p multi 1.00 .35

World Meteorological Organization, 50th Anniv. — A982

2000, Oct. 27
2210 A982 3p multi 1.00 .35

Intl. Diabetes Federation, 50th Anniv. A983

2000, Nov. 6
2211 A983 4.20p multi 1.50 .45

Telegraphy in Mexico, 150th Anniv. A984

2000, Nov. 11
2212 A984 3p multi 1.00 .35

Luis Buñuel (1900-83), Film Director A985

2000, Nov. 21
2213 A985 3p multi 1.00 .35

Electrical Investigation Institute, 25th Anniv. — A986

2000, Nov. 25
2214 A986 3p multi 1.00 .35

Customs Administration, Cent. — A987

2000, Nov. 28
2215 A987 3p multi 1.00 .35

Christmas A988

2000, Nov. 29
2216 A988 3p shown 1.00 .35
2217 A988 4.20p Poinsettias 1.50 .45

Television in Mexico, 50th Anniv. A989

2000, Nov. 30
2218 A989 3p multi 1.00 .35

Souvenir Sheet

Postal Headquarters — A990

No. 2219: a, 3p, Adamo Boari (1863-1928), architect. b, 3p, Roofline. c, 3p, Gonzalo Garita y Frontera (1867-1922), engineer. d, 10p, Headquarters building.

Litho. & Embossed

2000, Nov. 30 *Perf. 14¼x13½*
2219 A990 Sheet of 4, #a-d 9.00 9.00

Pre-Hispanic City of El Tajín — A991

Perf. 13½x13¼

2000, Dec. 14 **Litho.**
2220 A991 3p multi 1.00 .35

Nature Conservation — A992

2000, Dec. 15
2221 A992 3p Manatee 1.00 .35

Stamps inscribed 'Aquila Real / Unidos Para Conservacion' with white, yellow or gray backgrounds and 20c denominations have no postal validity.

Francisco Sarabia (1900-39), Aviator — A993

2000, Dec. 20 *Perf. 13¼x13½*
2222 A993 3p multi 1.00 .35

Law Faculty of National Autonomous University of Mexico, 50th Anniv. A994

2001, Mar. 7 **Litho.** *Perf. 13½x13¼*
2223 A994 3p multi 1.00 .30

Intl. Women's Day A995

2001, Mar. 8
2224 A995 4.20p multi 1.50 .45

National Cement Council, 53rd Anniv. A996

2001, Mar. 27
2225 A996 3p multi 1.00 .30

Teacher's Day A997

2001, May 15 *Perf. 14*
2226 A997 3p José Vasconcelos 1.00 .30

World Refugee Day — A998

Frida Kahlo (1907-54), Painter — A999

2001, June 20
2227 A998 4.20p multi 1.50 .45

2001, June 21
2228 A999 4.20p multi 1.50 .45

Intl. Day Against Illegal Drugs — A1000

2001, June 26
2229 A1000 4.20p multi 1.50 .45

Mario de la Cueva, Educator, Cent. of Birth — A1001

2001, July 11 **Litho.** *Perf. 14*
2230 A1001 3p multi 1.00 .30

Intl. Volunteers Year A1002

2001, July 25
2231 A1002 4.20p multi 1.50 .45

Souvenir Sheet

Rodolfo Morales (1925-2001), Painter — A1003

2001, Aug. 4 *Perf. 14¼x13½*
2232 A1003 10p multi 4.50 4.50

Federal Fiscal and Administrative Justice Tribunal, 65th Anniv. — A1004

2001, Aug. 23 *Perf. 14*
2233 A1004 3p multi 1.00 .30

University of Mexico, 450th Anniv. A1005

2001, Sept. 3
2234 A1005 3p multi 1.00 .30

Adela Formoso de Obregón Santcilia (1907-81), Woman's Rights Activist — A1006

2001, Sept. 6
2235 A1006 3p multi 1.00 .30

Daniel Cosío Villegas (1898-1976), Historian — A1007

2001, Sept. 6
2236 A1007 3p multi 1.00 .30

Mexican Pharmacies A1008

2001, Sept. 27 **Litho.** *Perf. 14*
2237 A1008 3p multi 1.00 .30

Year of Dialogue Among Civilizations A1010

Women's Health Day A1012

Intl. Day of the Elderly A1009

2001, Oct. 1
2238 A1009 3p multi 1.00 .30

World Post Day — A1011

2001, Oct. 9
2239 A1010 3p multi 1.00 .30

2001, Oct. 9
2240 A1011 3p multi 1.00 .30

2001, Oct. 31
2241 A1012 3p multi 1.00 .30

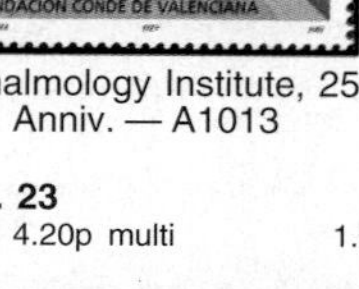

Ophthalmology Institute, 25th Anniv. — A1013

2001, Nov. 23
2242 A1013 4.20p multi 1.50 .45

United for Conservation — A1014

2001, Nov. 26
2243 A1014 5.30p Chara pinta 2.50 .90

Christmas A1015

2001, Dec. 3
2244 A1015 3p shown 1.00 .30
2245 A1015 4.20p Candles 1.50 .45

Souvenir Sheet

Fund for Indigenous People's Health and Education — A1016

2001, Dec. 4 *Perf. 13½x14¼*
2246 A1016 3p multi 1.50 1.50

Souvenir Sheet

National Scholarship Fund — A1017

2001, Dec. 4
2247 A1017 3p multi 1.50 1.50

Children's Protection A1018

World Food Day A1019

2001, Dec. 11 *Perf. 14*
2248 A1018 3p multi 1.00 .30

2001, Dec. 17
2249 A1019 3p multi 1.00 .30

United For Conservation — A1020

2002, Jan. 24 **Litho.** *Perf. 14*
2250 A1020 6p Borrego cimarrón 2.50 .90

Manuel Alvarez Bravo, Photographer, Cent. of Birth — A1021

2002, Feb. 3
2251 A1021 6p gray & blk 2.25 .70

Mexico — People's Republic of China A1022

Designs: No. 2252, green panel at UL and brown panel at LL. No. 2252A, Like #2252, but with brown panel at UL, green panel at LL.

2002, Feb. 14 **Litho.** *Perf. 14*
2252 A1022 6p multi 2.00 .65
2252A A1022 6p multi 2.00 .65
b. Vert. pair, #2252-2252A 5.00 5.00

Conservation — A1023

Designs: 50c, Mangrove swamps. No. 2254, Rivers. No. 2255, Forests. 1.50p, No. 2267, Land mammals. No. 2257, Rain forests. No. 2258, Cacti. 4.50p, Birds. No. 2260, Sea turtles. No. 2261, Reptiles. No. 2262, Butterflies. No. 2263, Eagles. 7p, Reefs. 8.50p, 12p, Tropical forests. No. 2266, Marine mammals. No. 2268, Orchids. No. 2269, Cats. No. 2270, Oceans. No. 2271, Coastal birds. No. 2273, Deserts. No. 2274, Lakes and lagoons.

2002, Feb. 18 **Litho.** *Perf. 14*

2253	A1023	50c	multi	.20	.20
2254	A1023	1p	multi	.20	.20
2255	A1023	1p	multi	.35	.20
2256	A1023	1.50p	multi	.50	.20
2257	A1023	2p	multi	.70	.20
2258	A1023	2p	multi	.70	.20
2259	A1023	4.50p	multi	1.50	.50
2260	A1023	5p	multi	1.75	.55
2261	A1023	5p	multi	1.75	.55
2262	A1023	6p	multi	2.00	.65
2263	A1023	6p	multi	2.00	.65
2264	A1023	7p	multi	2.40	.75
2265	A1023	8.50p	multi	2.75	.95
2266	A1023	10p	multi	3.50	1.10
2267	A1023	10p	multi	3.50	1.10
2268	A1023	10.50p	multi	3.50	1.25
2269	A1023	10.50p	multi	3.50	1.25
2270	A1023	11.50p	multi	3.75	1.25
2271	A1023	11.50p	multi	3.75	1.25
2272	A1023	12p	multi	4.00	1.25
2273	A1023	30p	multi	10.00	3.25
2274	A1023	30p	multi	10.00	3.25
	Nos. 2253-2274 (22)			62.30	20.75

2003 *Perf. 13x13¼*

2253a	A1023	50c	multi	.40	.20
2254a	A1023	1p	multi	1.10	.20
2255a	A1023	1p	multi	1.10	.20
2259a	A1023	4.50p	multi	3.50	.40
2260a	A1023	5p	multi	1.75	.45
2261a	A1023	5p	multi	1.75	.45
2262a	A1023	6p	multi	2.50	.55
2263a	A1023	6p	multi	2.00	.55
2264a	A1023	7p	multi	2.50	.65
2265a	A1023	8.50p	multi	3.75	.75
2266a	A1023	10p	multi	4.00	.90
2267a	A1023	10p	multi	4.25	.90
2268a	A1023	10.50p	multi	5.00	.95
2269a	A1023	10.50p	multi	4.25	.95
2270a	A1023	11.50p	multi	6.00	1.00
2271a	A1023	11.50p	multi	6.00	1.00
	Nos. 2253a-2271a (16)			49.85	10.10

See Nos. 2321-2330, 2362-2377, 2394-2436, 2452-2473.

2002 Winter Olympics, Salt Lake City A1024

2002, Feb. 20 **Litho.** *Perf. 14*
2275 A1024 8.50p multi 2.75 .95

Veracruz Port Modernization, Cent. — A1025

2002, Mar. 4
2276 A1025 6p multi 2.25 .70

Mexico — South Korea Diplomatic Relations, 40th Anniv. A1026

2002, Mar. 5
2277 A1026 8.50p multi 2.75 .95

Council for the Restoration of Historic Central Mexico City — A1027

2002, Mar. 7
2278 A1027 6p multi 2.25 .70

Natl. Women's Institute A1028

José Guadalupe Posada (1851-1913), Printmaker A1029

2002, Mar. 8
2279 A1028 8.50p multi 2.75 .95

2002, Mar. 18
2280 A1029 6p gold & black 2.25 .65

Justo Sierra Mendez (1848-1912), Writer — A1030

2002, May 15 **Litho.** *Perf. 14*
2281 A1030 6p multi 2.25 .65

UN General Assembly Special Session on Children A1031

2002, May 27
2282 A1031 6p multi 2.25 .65

Discovery of the Tomb of Pakal, 50th Anniv. A1032

2002, June 14
2283 A1032 6p multi 2.25 .65

2002 World Cup Soccer Championships, Japan and Korea — A1033

2002, June 15
2284 A1033 8.50p multi 2.75 .85

Intl. Day Against Illegal Drugs — A1034

2002, June 26
2285 A1034 6p multi 2.25 .65

5th Mexico-Central American Summit — A1035

2002, June 27
2286 A1035 6p multi 2.25 .65

Intl. Year of Mountains A1036

2002, July 24 **Litho.** *Perf. 14*
2287 A1036 6p multi 2.25 .65

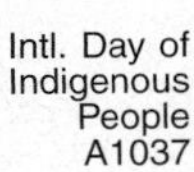

Intl. Day of Indigenous People A1037

2002, Aug. 9 *Perf. 13x13¼*
2288 A1037 6p multi 2.25 .65

Federal Electricity Commission A1038

2002, Aug. 14 *Perf. 14*
2289 A1038 6p multi 2.25 .65

Natl. Blood Donor Day — A1039

2002, Aug. 23 *Perf. 13¼x13*
2290 A1039 6p multi 2.25 .65

Campaign Against Corruption A1040

2002, Sept. 12 **Litho.** *Perf. 13x13¼*
2291 A1040 6p multi 2.25 .60

Code of Ethics for Public Servants — A1041

2002, Sept. 12 *Perf. 13¼x13*
2292 A1041 6p multi 2.25 .60

World Tourism Day A1042

2002, Sept. 27 ***Perf. 13x13¼***
2293 A1042 8.50p multi 2.75 .85

Natl. Organ Transplant and Donation Week — A1043

2002, Oct. 7 ***Perf. 13¼x13***
2294 A1043 6p multi 2.25 .60

World Post Day A1044

2002, Oct. 9 ***Perf. 13x13¼***
2295 A1044 8.50p multi 2.75 .85

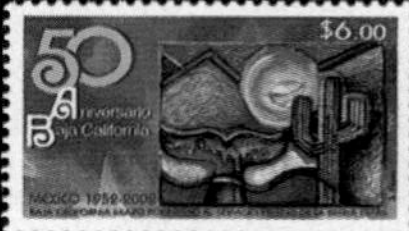

State of Baja California, 50th Anniv. A1045

2002, Nov. 1
2296 A1045 6p multi 2.25 .60

Luis Barragan (1902-88), Architect — A1046

2002, Nov. 7 ***Perf. 13¼x13***
2297 A1046 6p multi 2.25 .60

Renewal of Diplomatic Relations Between Mexico and Spain, 25th Anniv. A1047

2002, Nov. 19 ***Perf. 13x13¼***
2298 A1047 8.50p multi 2.75 .85

Mexico City Intl. Airport, 50th Anniv. — A1048

Details from mural "The Conquest of the Air by Man": a, Indian chief at left, Montgolfier balloon flight at right. b, Charles Lindbergh at left, parachutist at center. c, Wright Brothers at left, Mexico City at center.

2002, Nov. 19 ***Perf. 13¼x13***
2299 Horiz. strip of 3 7.50 7.50
a.-b. A1048 6p Either single 2.25 .60
c. A1048 8.50p multi 2.75 .85

Information Technology Development in Mexico, 75th Anniv. — A1049

2002, Nov. 21
2300 A1049 6p multi 1.75 .60

Anti-Violence Campaign — A1050

2002, Nov. 25 ***Perf. 13x13¼***
2301 A1050 8.50p multi 2.50 .85

Pan-American Health Organization, Cent. — A1051

2002, Dec. 2 ***Perf. 13¼x13***
2302 A1051 8.50p multi 1.75 .85

Acolmiztli Nezahualcóyotl (1402-72), Poet — A1052

2002, Dec. 10
2303 A1052 6p multi 1.75 .60

Christmas A1053

Children's art: 6p, Nativity, by Sara Elisa Miranda Alcaraz. 8.50p, Children with Nativity Scene, by Alejandro Ruíz Sampedro.

2002, Dec. 19 ***Perf. 13x13¼***
2304 A1053 6p multi 1.75 .60
2305 A1053 8.50p multi 2.50 .80

Powered Flight, Cent. A1054

2003, Mar. 6 **Litho.** ***Perf. 13x13¼***
2306 A1054 8.50p multi 2.50 .80

Iberoamerican University, 60th Anniv. — A1055

2003, Mar. 7 ***Perf. 13¼x13***
2307 A1055 6p multi 1.75 .55

Intl. Women's Day — A1056

2003, Mar. 8
2308 A1056 8.50p multi 2.50 .80

Mexicali, Cent. A1057

2003, Mar. 14 ***Perf. 13x13¼***
2309 A1057 6p multi 1.75 .55

Mexican Chamber of Industry and Construction, 50th Anniv. — A1058

2003, Mar. 26
2310 A1058 6p multi 1.75 .55

Federico Gomez Children's Hospital, 60th Anniv. A1059

2003, Apr. 30 **Litho.** ***Perf. 13x13¼***
2311 A1059 6p multi 1.75 .60

Miguel Hidalgo y Costilla (1753-1811), Independence Leader — A1060

2003, May 8 ***Perf. 13¼x13***
2312 A1060 6p multi 1.75 .60
a. Perf 14 *350.00 350.00*

Gregorio Torres Quintero (1866-1934), Educator — A1061

2003, May 15
2313 A1061 6p multi 1.75 .55

Natl. Astronomical Observatory, 125th Anniv. — A1062

2003, May 20 ***Perf. 13x13¼***
2314 A1062 6p multi 1.75 .55

World Day Against Tobacco — A1063

2003, May 30 ***Perf. 13¼x13***
2315 A1063 8.50p multi 2.50 .80

Inauguration of Satellite Internet Network — A1064

2003, June 5
2316 A1064 6p multi 1.75 .55

Intl. Day Against Illegal Drugs A1065

2003, June 26 **Litho.** ***Perf. 13x13¼***
2317 A1065 8.50p multi 2.50 .80

Mexican Baseball Hall of Fame, 30th Anniv. A1066

2003, July 21
2318 A1066 6p multi 1.75 .55

Xavier Villaurrutia (1903-51), Poet A1067

2003, July 24
2319 A1067 6p multi 1.75 .55

Veterinary Medicine Education in Mexico, 150th Anniv. A1068

2003, Aug. 16
2320 A1068 6p multi 1.75 .55

Conservation Type of 2002

Designs: 50c, Oceans. 1p, Reptiles. No. 2323, Land mammals. No. 2324, Rain forests. No. 2325, Coastal birds. 4.50p, Orchids. 6p, Rivers. 8.50p, Cacti. No. 2329, Lakes and lagoons. No. 2330, Sea turtles.

Perf. 13x13¼, 13½ (#2328)

2003-04 **Litho.**
2321 A1023 50c multi ('04) .50 .20
2322 A1023 1p multi ('04) .50 .20
2323 A1023 2.50p multi 1.25 .25

2324	A1023	2.50p multi	1.25	.25
2325	A1023	2.50p multi ('04)	1.25	.25
2326	A1023	4.50p multi ('04)	2.00	.40
2327	A1023	6p multi ('04)	2.75	.55
2328	A1023	8.50p multi ('04)	3.50	.75
2329	A1023	10.50pmulti ('04)	4.00	.95
2330	A1023	10.50pmulti ('04)	4.50	.95
		Nos. 2321-2330 (10)	21.50	4.75

National Pedagogical University, 25th Anniv. — A1069

2003, Aug. 29 Litho. ***Perf. 13¼x13***
2331 A1069 6p multi 1.75 .55

Federico Silva Museum, San Luis Potosí A1070

2003, Sept. 18 ***Perf. 13x13¼***
2332 A1070 6p multi 1.75 .55

National Organ and Tissue Donation Week A1071

2003, Sept. 26
2333 A1071 6p multi 1.75 .55

World Post Day A1072

Woman Suffrage, 50th Anniv. A1073

2003, Oct. 9 ***Perf. 13¼x13***
2334 A1072 8.50p multi 2.25 .75

2003, Oct. 16
2335 A1073 6p multi 1.50 .55

Health Ministry, 60th Anniv. A1074

2003, Oct. 23 ***Perf. 13x13¼***
2336 A1074 6p multi 1.50 .55

Juarez Theater, Cent. A1075

2003, Oct. 27
2337 A1075 6p multi 1.50 .55

Teaching of Law in the Americas, 450th Anniv. — A1076

2003, Nov. 4 ***Perf. 13¼x13***
2338 A1076 8.50p multi 2.25 .80

Central Power and Light, Cent. A1077

2003, Nov. 18 Litho. ***Perf. 13x13¼***
2339 A1077 6p multi 1.50 .55

Christmas A1078

Children's drawings of Nativity by: 6p, Valeria Báez. 8.50p, Octavio Alemán.

2003, Dec. 3
2340 A1078 6p multi 1.50 .55
2341 A1078 8.50p multi 2.25 .75

A1079

A1080

2003, Dec. 5 ***Perf. 13¼x13***
2342 A1079 6p multi 1.50 .55

Children's rights.

2003, Dec. 11
2343 A1080 8.50p multi 2.25 .75

Intl. Year of Fresh Water.

National Technical Education College, 25th Anniv. A1081

2003, Dec. 15 ***Perf. 13x13¼***
2344 A1081 6p multi 1.50 .55

First Visit of Pope John Paul II to Mexico, 25th Anniv. A1082

2004, Jan. 28 Litho. ***Perf. 13x13¼***
2345 A1082 6p multi 1.10 .55

Agustín Yáñez (1904-80), Novelist A1083

2004, May 4
2346 A1083 8.50p multi 1.50 .75

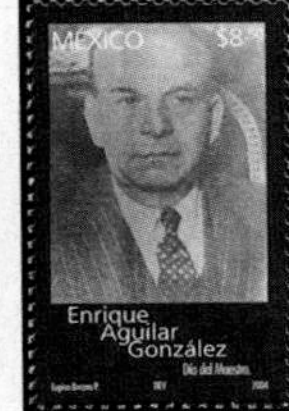

Enrique Aguilar González — A1084

2004, May 15 ***Perf. 13¼x13***
2347 A1084 8.50p multi 1.50 .75

Teacher's Day.

Cable Television in Mexico, 50th Anniv. — A1085

2004, May 19
2348 A1085 6p multi 1.10 .55

Mexican Geological Society, Cent. A1086

2004, June 2 ***Perf. 13x13¼***
2349 A1086 8.50p multi 1.50 .75

Intl. Day Against Illegal Drugs — A1087

2004, June 25 ***Perf. 13¼x13***
2350 A1087 8.50p multi 1.50 .75

Salvador Novo (1904-74), Poet A1088

2004, July 30 ***Perf. 13x13¼***
2351 A1088 7p multi 1.25 .60

Gilberto Owen (1905-52), Poet A1089

2004, Aug. 8 Litho. ***Perf. 13x13¼***
2352 A1089 7p multi 1.25 .60

FIFA (Fédération Internationale de Football Association), Cent. — A1090

2004, Aug. 11
2353 A1090 11.50p multi 2.00 1.00

Mexican Cartooning — A1091

2004, Aug. 13 ***Perf. 13¼x13***
2354 A1091 6p multi 1.00 .50

2004 Summer Olympics, Athens — A1092

2004, Aug. 13
2355 A1092 10.50p multi 1.90 .95

Celestino Gorostiza (1904-67), Writer A1093

2004, Aug. 16 Litho. ***Perf. 13x13¼***
2356 A1093 7p multi 1.25 .60

Fresnillo, 450th Anniv. — A1094

2004, Sept. 2 ***Perf. 13¼x13***
2357 A1094 7p multi 1.25 .60

Economic Culture Fund, 70th Anniv. A1095

2004, Sept. 6 ***Perf. 13x13¼***
2358 A1095 8.50p multi 1.50 .75

Autonomy of National Autonomous University of Mexico, 75th Anniv. — A1096

2004, Sept. 6 *Perf. 13¼x13*

2359 A1096 11.50p multi 2.00 1.00

Autonomous University of Chihuahua, 50th Anniv. — A1097

2004, Sept. 8 *Perf. 13x13¼*

2360 A1097 7p multi 1.25 .60

Palace of Fine Arts, 70th Anniv. A1098

2004, Sept. 29

2361 A1098 7p multi 1.25 .60

Conservation Type of 2002

Designs: 50c, Cats. No. 2363, Oceans. No. 2364, Rain forests. 2.50p, No. 2374, Reefs. 4.50p, Forests. 5p, No. 2370, Land mammals.

Nos. 2368, 2376, Reptiles. No. 2369, Birds. Nos. 2371, 2375, Deserts. No. 2372, Cacti. No. 2373, Tropical forests. No. 2377, Coastal birds.

2004	**Litho.**		*Perf. 13x13¼*	
2362	A1023	50c multi	.45	.20
2363	A1023	1p multi	2.50	.20
2364	A1023	1p multi	.45	.20
2365	A1023	2.50p multi	1.25	.20
2366	A1023	4.50p multi	1.25	.40
2367	A1023	5p multi	1.90	.45
2368	A1023	6p multi	1.90	.55
2369	A1023	6p multi	1.75	.55
2370	A1023	6p multi	2.00	.55
2371	A1023	7p multi	2.00	.60
2372	A1023	7p multi	2.00	.60
2373	A1023	10p multi	3.50	.90
2374	A1023	10p multi	3.50	.90
2375	A1023	10.50p multi	3.50	.95
a.		Microprinting at top in black	4.25	1.00
2376	A1023	30p multi	8.00	2.25
2377	A1023	30p multi	8.00	2.25
	Nos. 2362-2377 (16)		43.95	11.75

Microprinting at top on No. 2375 is in gray.

State Workers' Institute of Social Services and Security — A1099

2004, Oct. 1 **Litho.** *Perf. 13¼x13*

2378 A1099 6p multi 1.10 .55

Termination of Walled District of Campeche, 300th Anniv. — A1100

2004, Oct. 6 *Perf. 13x13¼*

2379 A1100 6p multi 1.10 .55

National Anthem, 150th Anniv. A1101

2004, Oct. 8

2380 A1101 6.50p multi 1.25 .60

World Post Day A1102

2004, Oct. 11

2381 A1102 6p bright rose lilac 1.10 .55

Admission to UPU, 125th Anniv. A1103

2004, Oct. 29

2382 A1103 8.50p multi 1.50 .75

Channel 11 Television — A1104

2004, Nov. 10 *Perf. 13¼x13*

2383 A1104 8.50p multi 1.50 .75

Superior Federation Audit, 180th Anniv. — A1105

2004, Nov. 16

2384 A1105 6.50p multi 1.25 .60

Health Secretary's Building, 75th Anniv. A1106

2004, Nov. 22 *Perf. 13x13¼*

2385 A1106 8.50p multi 1.60 .80

Culture on the Radio — A1107

2004, Nov. 30 *Perf. 13¼x13*

2386 A1107 6.50p multi 1.25 .60

Natl. Communications and Transportation Department Center, 50th Anniv. — A1108

2004, Nov. 30 *Perf. 13¼x13*

2387 A1108 6.50p multi 1.25 .60

Souvenir Sheet

Perf. 14¼x14

2388 A1108 7.50p multi 1.40 .70

Town of General Escobedo, 400th Anniv. A1109

2004, Dec. 3 *Perf. 13x13¼*

2389 A1109 8.50p multi 1.60 .80

Natl. Free Textbook Commission, 45th Anniv. — A1110

2004, Dec. 6

2390 A1110 10.50p multi 1.90 .95

A1111

Christmas — A1112

2004, Dec. 13 *Perf. 13x13¼*

2391 A1111 7.50p multi 1.40 .70

Perf. 13¼x13

2392 A1112 10.50p multi 1.90 .95

Traffic Accident Prevention — A1113

2004, Dec. 17 **Litho.** *Perf. 13¼x13*

2393 A1113 8.50p multi 1.60 .80

Conservation Type of 2002

Designs: Nos. 2394, 2404, Deserts. Nos. 2395, 2406, 2408, 2411, Orchids. Nos. 2396, 2410, 2419, 2435, Sea turtles. Nos. 2397, 2416, Birds. Nos. 2398, 2401, 2421, 2433, Marine mammals. Nos. 2399, 2425, Oceans. Nos. 2400, 2402, 2424, Cats. Nos. 2403, 2430, Rain forests. Nos. 2405, 2412, Eagles. Nos. 2407, 2415, Lakes and lagoons. Nos. 2409, 2436, Butterflies. Nos. 2413, 2423, Tropical forests. Nos. 2414, 2431, Rivers. Nos. 2417, 2429, Reefs. Nos. 2418, 2427, Forests. Nos. 2420, 2434, Coastal birds. No. 2422, Reptiles. Nos. 2426, 2428, Land mammals. No. 2432, Mangrove swamps.

2004-05 **Litho.** *Perf. 13½x13¼*

Inscribed "ROMO" at Lower Right

2394	A1023	50c multi	.20	.20
2395	A1023	1p multi	.20	.20
2396	A1023	2.50p multi	.50	.25
2397	A1023	6.50p multi	1.25	.60
2398	A1023	6.50p multi	150.00	.60
2399	A1023	7p multi	1.40	.70
2400	A1023	7.50p multi	1.40	.70
2401	A1023	8.50p multi	1.50	.75
		Complete booklet, 6 #2401	9.00	
2402	A1023	10.50p multi	1.90	.95
		Complete booklet, 6 #2402	11.50	
2403	A1023	13p multi	2.50	1.25

Inscribed "TIEV" at Lower Right

Perf. 13x13¼

2404	A1023	50c multi	.20	.20
2405	A1023	50c multi	.20	.20
2406	A1023	50p multi	.20	.20
2407	A1023	1p multi	.20	.20
2408	A1023	1p multi	.20	.20
a.		Perf. 14	.20	.20
2409	A1023	2p multi	.20	.20
2410	A1023	2.50p multi	.50	.25
2411	A1023	2.50p multi	.50	.25
2412	A1023	2.50p multi	.50	.25
2413	A1023	5p multi	.95	.45
2414	A1023	5p multi	.95	.45
2415	A1023	5p multi	.95	.45
2416	A1023	6.50p multi	1.25	.60
2417	A1023	6.50p multi	1.25	.60
2418	A1023	6.50p multi	1.25	.60
2419	A1023	6.50p multi	1.25	.60
2420	A1023	6.50p multi	1.25	.60
2421	A1023	6.50p multi	1.25	.60
2422	A1023	6.50p multi	1.25	.60
2423	A1023	7p multi	1.40	.70
2424	A1023	7.50p multi	1.40	.70
2425	A1023	7.50p multi	1.40	.70
2426	A1023	7.50p multi, denomination in black	1.40	.70
a.		Denomination in gray	1.40	.70
2427	A1023	8.50p multi	1.60	.80
2428	A1023	10.50p multi	2.00	1.00
2429	A1023	10.50p multi	2.00	1.00
2430	A1023	13p multi	2.50	1.25
2431	A1023	13p multi	2.50	1.25
2432	A1023	13p multi	2.50	1.25
2433	A1023	14.50p multi	2.75	1.40
2434	A1023	14.50p multi	2.75	1.40
2435	A1023	30.50p multi	5.75	2.75
2436	A1023	30.50p multi	5.75	2.75
	Nos. 2394-2436 (43)		210.85	31.35

Issued: Nos. 2401, 2402, 2004. Others, 2005. Colors are duller on stamps inscribed

"TIEV" than those on similar stamps inscribed "ROMO."

Mexico General Hospital, Cent. — A1114

2005, Feb. 4 Litho. *Perf. 13¼x13*
2437 A1114 6.50p multi 1.25 .60

Intl. Women's Day A1115

2005, Mar. 8 *Perf. 13x13¼*
2438 A1115 6.50p multi 1.25 .60

Publication of Pedro Paramo by Juan Rulfo, 50th Anniv. A1116

2005, Mar. 13
2439 A1116 6.50p multi 1.25 .60

Natl. University Games A1117

World Without Polio A1118

2005, Apr. 18 *Perf. 13¼x13*
2440 A1117 7.50p multi 1.40 .70

2005, Apr. 29
2441 A1118 10.50p multi 1.90 .95

Eulalia Guzmán A1119

2005, May 15 *Perf. 13x13¼*
2442 A1119 6.50p multi 1.25 .60

Teacher's Day.

Souvenir Sheet

Publication of Don Quixote, 400th Anniv. — A1120

No. 2443: a, 6.50p, Silhouette of Don Quixote. b, 10.50p, Crowd, horse and rider. c, 10.50p, Don Quixote.

2005, May 23 *Perf. 13¼x13*
2443 A1120 Sheet of 3, #a-c 5.25 5.25

Intl. Year of Physics — A1121

2005, May 26
2444 A1121 7.50p multi 1.40 .70

Natl. Human Rights Commission — A1122

2005, June 5 *Perf. 13x13¼*
2445 A1122 6.50p multi 1.25 .60

Society of Mexican Architects, Cent. — A1123

2005, June 8 *Perf. 13¼x13*
2446 A1123 6.50p multi 1.25 .60

Intl. Day Against Illegal Drugs — A1124

2005, June 24
2447 A1124 10.50p multi 2.00 1.00

Baseball — A1125

2005, June 27
2448 A1125 7.50p multi 1.40 .70

Information Access and Transparency — A1126

2005, June 27
2449 A1126 6.50p multi 1.25 .60

Memin Pinguin, by Yolanda Vargas Dulche — A1127

Memin Pinguin: a, And comic book page. b, Holding flower. c, Holding open comic book. d, Wearing tuxedo. e, Holding closed book.

2005, June 28 *Perf. 13*
2450 Horiz. strip of 5 *9.50 9.50*
a.-e. A1127 6.50p Any single *1.90 .95*

Multiple Self-portrait, by Juan O'Gorman (1905-82) — A1128

2005, June 29 *Perf. 13¼x13*
2451 A1128 7.50p multi 1.40 .70

Conservation Type of 2002

Designs: No. 2452, Butterflies. Nos. 2453, 2473, Sea turtles. No. 2454, Coastal birds. Nos. 2456, 2463, Marine mammals. Nos. 2457, 2459, Rivers. Nos. 2458, 2462, 2466, Oceans. No. 2460, Lakes and lagoons. Nos. 2461, 2469, Cats. No. 2464, Reptiles. No. 2465, Mangrove swamps. No. 2467, Birds. No. 2468, Cacti. No. 2470, Reefs. No. 2471, Eagles. No. 2472, Tropical forests.

2005 Litho. *Perf. 13x13¼*
Inscribed "TIEV" at Lower Right

2452	A1023	50c multi	.20	.20
2453	A1023	50c multi	.20	.20
2454	A1023	1p multi	.20	.20
2456	A1023	1p multi	.20	.20
2457	A1023	2.50p multi	.50	.25
2458	A1023	5p multi	.95	.50
2459	A1023	6.50p multi	1.25	.60
2460	A1023	6.50p multi	1.25	.60
2461	A1023	6.50p multi	1.25	.60
2462	A1023	7p multi	1.40	.70
2463	A1023	7p multi	1.40	.70
2464	A1023	7.50p multi	1.40	.70
2465	A1023	7.50p multi	1.40	.70
2466	A1023	10.50p multi	2.00	1.00
2467	A1023	10.50p multi	2.00	1.00
2468	A1023	13p multi	2.50	1.25
2469	A1023	13p multi	2.50	1.25
2470	A1023	13p multi	2.50	1.25
2471	A1023	14.50p multi	2.75	1.40
2472	A1023	30.50p multi	5.75	2.75

Inscribed "ROMO" at Lower Right
Booklet Stamp

2473 A1023 (15.75p) multi 3.00 1.50
a. Booklet pane of 4 12.00 —
Complete booklet, 4 #2473 12.00
Nos. 2452-2473 (21) 34.60 17.55

See No. 2399 for 7p Oceans stamp with "ROMO" inscription. No. 2473 is inscribed "Porte mundial" at lower left.

Minerals — A1129

No. 2474: a, Silver. b, Argentite. c, Marcasite, quartz and galena. d, Allende meteorite. e, Gold. f, Galena. g, Pyrargyrite. h, Gypsum. i, Manganocalcite. j, Barite. k, Stephanite. l, Red calcite. m, Calcite. n, Asbestos. o, Valencianite. p, Livingstoneite. q, Beryl. r, Smithsonite. s, Fluorite. t, Amethyst quartz. u, Azurite. v, Hemimorphite. w, Apatite. x, Pyromorphite. y, Actinolite with talc.

2005, Aug. 3 *Perf. 13¼x13*
2474 Sheet of 25 32.50 32.50
a.-y. A1129 6.50p Any single 1.25 .60

Ignacio L. Vallarta (1830-94), Chief Justice A1130

2005, Aug. 23 *Perf. 13x13¼*
2475 A1130 7.50p multi 1.40 .70

Judicial Anniversaries — A1131

Designs: No. 2476, Federal Justice Council, 10th anniv. No. 2477, Supreme Court, 180th anniv. 10.50p, Supreme Justice Tribunal, 190th anniv.

2005, Aug. 23
2476 A1131 6.50p multi 1.25 .60
2477 A1131 6.50p multi 1.25 .60
2478 A1131 10.50p multi 2.00 1.00
a. Souvenir sheet, #2476-2478 4.50 4.50

Expo 2005, Aichi, Japan — A1132

2005, Sept. 15 *Perf. 13¼x13*
2479 A1132 13p multi 2.40 1.25

Federal District Superior Court, 150th Anniv. — A1133

No. 2480 — Buildings from: a, 1855. b, 2005. c, 1964.

2005, Oct. 6

2480 Horiz. strip of 3 4.00 4.00
a.-b. A1133 6.50p Either single 1.25 .60
c. A1133 7.50p multi 1.40 .70

World Post Day — A1134

2005, Oct. 10

2481 A1134 10.50p multi 2.00 1.00

United Nations Day A1135

2005, Oct. 24 ***Perf. 13x13¼***

2482 A1135 10.50p multi 2.00 1.00

Jalisco Philatelic Organization, Cent. — A1136

2005, Oct. 27

2483 A1136 6.50p multi 1.25 .60

Lebanese in Mexico, 125th Anniv. — A1137

2005, Nov. 11 ***Perf. 13¼x13***

2484 A1137 10.50p multi 2.00 1.00

Rodolfo Usigli (1905-79), Playwright — A1138

2005, Nov. 15

2485 A1138 7.50p multi 1.50 .75

San Juan de Ulua, Last Spanish Redoubt — A1139

2005, Nov. 23

2486 A1139 7.50p multi 1.50 .75

Gómez Palacio, Cent. — A1140

2005, Nov. 24

2487 A1140 6.50p multi 1.25 .60

Folk Art — A1141

Designs: 50c, Legged earthen pot. 1p, Lacquered wooden chest. 1.50p, Horn comb. 2p, Black clay jug. 2.50p, Paper bull. 5p, Silk shawl. No. 2494, Model. No. 2495, Glazed basin. No. 2496, Vase. No. 2497, Wooden mask. No. 2498, Tin rooster. 7p, Doll. 7.50p, Copper jar. 9p, Embroidered tablecloth. 10.50p, 11.50p, Woven basket. 13p, 13.50p, Silver pear. 14.50p, 15p, Amber marimba. 30.50p, Obsidian and opal turtle.

2005, Nov. 30 Litho. ***Perf. 13¼x13***

2488 A1141 50c multi .20 .20
a. Dated "2006" .20 .20
b. Dated "2007" .20 .20
c. Dated "2008" .20 .20
d. Magenta panel, dated "2010" .20 .20
2489 A1141 1p multi .20 .20
a. Dated "2006" .20 .20
b. Dated "2007" .20 .20
c. Dated "2008" .20 .20
d. Dated "2010" .20 .20
2490 A1141 1.50p multi .30 .20
a. Dated "2006" .30 .20
b. Dated "2007" .30 .20
c. Dated "2008" .25 .20
d. Dated "2009" .25 .20
2490e Dated "2010" .25 .20
2491 A1141 2p multi .40 .20
a. Dated "2006" .40 .20
b. Dated "2007" .40 .20
c. Dated "2008" .30 .20
d. Dated "2009" .30 .20
e. Dated "2010" .35 .20
2492 A1141 2.50p multi .50 .25
a. Dated "2006" .45 .25
b. Dated "2007" .45 .25
c. Dated "2008" .40 .20
d. Dated "2010" .40 .20
2493 A1141 5p multi .95 .50
a. Dated "2006" .95 .50
b. Dated "2007" .95 .50
c. Dated "2008" .75 .35
d. Dated "2009" .80 .40
e. Dated "2010" .85 .40
2494 A1141 6.50p multi 1.25 .60
a. Dated "2006" 1.25 .60
b. Dated "2007" 1.25 .60
2495 A1141 6.50p multi 1.25 .60
a. Dated "2006" 1.25 .60
b. Dated "2007" 1.25 .60
2496 A1141 6.50p multi 1.25 .60
a. Dated "2006" 1.25 .60
b. Dated "2007" 1.25 .60
2497 A1141 6.50p multi 1.25 .60
a. Dated "2006" 1.25 .60
b. Dated "2007" 1.25 .60
2498 A1141 6.50p multi 1.25 .60
a. Horiz. or vert. strip of 5, #2494-2498 6.25 3.00
b. Dated "2006" 1.25 .60
c. Horiz. or vert. strip of 5, #2494a, 2495a, 2496a, 2497a, 2498b 6.25 3.00
d. Dated "2007" 1.25 .60
e. Horiz. or vert. strip of 5, #2494b, 2495b, 2496b, 2497b, 2498d 6.25 3.00
2499 A1141 7p multi 1.40 .70
a. Dated "2006" 1.40 .70
b. Dated "2007" 1.40 .70
c. Dated "2008" 1.10 .55
d. Dated "2010" 1.25 .60
2500 A1141 7.50p multi 1.50 .75
a. Dated "2006" 1.40 .70
b. Dated "2007" 1.40 .70
c. Dated "2008" 1.10 .55
d. Dated "2009" 1.25 .60
e. Dated "2010" 1.25 .60
2501 A1141 9p multi 1.75 .85
a. Dated "2010" 1.50 .75
2502 A1141 10.50p multi 2.00 1.00
a. Dated "2006" 2.00 1.00
b. Dated "2007" 2.00 1.00
c. Dated "2008" 1.60 .80
d. Dated "2009" 1.60 .80
2502E A1141 11.50p multi 1.90 .95
2503 A1141 13p multi 2.50 1.25
a. Dated "2006" 2.40 1.25
b. Dated "2007" 2.40 1.25
c. Dated "2008" 1.90 .95
2503D A1141 13.50p multi 2.25 1.10
2504 A1141 14.50p multi 2.75 1.40
a. Dated "2006" 2.75 1.40
b. Dated "2007" 2.75 1.40
c. Dated "2008" 2.10 1.10
2504D A1141 15p multi 2.50 1.25
2505 A1141 30.50p multi 6.00 3.00
a. Dated "2006" 5.75 2.75
b. Dated "2007" 5.75 2.75
Nos. 2488-2505 (22) 33.60 17.00

Nos. 2494-2498, 2505 exist dated "2008."

Christian Brothers in Mexico, Cent. — A1142

2005, Dec. 2 ***Perf. 13¼x13***

2506 A1142 6.50p multi 1.25 .60

Jews in Mexico, Cent. — A1143

2005, Dec. 6

2507 A1143 7.50p multi 1.40 .70

Indigenous Popular Culture A1144

2005, Dec. 16 ***Perf. 13x13¼***

2508 A1144 6.50p multi 1.25 .60

A1145

Christmas A1146

2005, Dec. 20

2509 A1145 6.50p multi 1.25 .60
2510 A1146 7.50p multi 1.40 .70

Souvenir Sheet

National Polytechnic Institute, 70th Anniv. — A1147

2006, Feb. 27 Litho. ***Perf. 13¼x13***

2511 A1147 10.50p multi 2.00 1.00

Wolfgang Amadeus Mozart (1756-91), Composer — A1148

2006, Mar. 31

2512 A1148 7.50p multi 1.40 .70

Central Library of National Autonomous University of Mexico, 50th Anniv. — A1149

2006, Apr. 5

2513 A1149 6.50p multi 1.25 .60

Latin American Tower, 50th Anniv. A1150

2006, Apr. 26 ***Perf. 13x13¼***

2514 6.50p multi 1.25 .60
2515 10.50p multi 2.00 1.00
a. A1150 Vert. pair, #2514-2515 3.25 1.60

Isidro Castillo Pérez, Educator — A1151

2006, May 15 *Perf. 13¼x13*

2516 A1151 6.50p multi 1.25 .60

Vasconcelos Library — A1152

2006, May 16

2517 A1152 6.50p multi 1.25 .60

Intl. Women's Day A1153

2006, May 31 *Perf. 13x13¼*

2518 A1153 6.50p multi 1.25 .60

2006 World Cup Soccer Championships, Germany — A1154

2006, June 9 *Perf. 13¼x13*

2519 A1154 13p multi 2.40 1.25

Souvenir Sheet

President Benito Juarez (1806-72) — A1155

2006, June 22 *Perf. 13x13¼*

2520 A1155 13p multi 2.40 1.25

Navy Qualification Center, 50th Anniv. — A1156

2006, Aug. 11 **Litho.**

2521 A1156 6.50p multi 1.25 .60

Popular Television Characters — A1157

No. 2522: a, El Chayo del Ocho and barrel. b, El Chapulín Colorado with arms crossed. c, El Chayo del Ocho, door and window d, El Chapulín Colorado with arms spread. e, El Chayo del Ocho holding suspenders.

2006, Aug. 21 *Perf. 13¼x13*

2522	Horiz. strip of 5	9.75	4.75
a.	A1157 6.50p multi	1.25	.60
b.	A1157 7.50p multi	1.40	.70
c.	A1157 10.50p multi	1.90	.95
d.	A1157 13p multi	2.40	1.25
e.	A1157 14.50p multi	2.60	1.25

Intl. Year of Deserts and Desertification — A1158

2006, Sept. 20

2523 A1158 6.50p multi 1.25 .60

Souvenir Sheet

Dinosaurs — A1159

No. 2524: a, 6.50p, Muzzy (40x24mm). b, 7.50p, Sabinosaurus (40x48mm). c, 10.50p, Aramberri Monster (40x48mm).

2006, Sept. 29 *Perf. 13x13¼*

2524 A1159 Sheet of 3, #a-c 4.50 2.25

Engineering Institute of National Autonomous University of Mexico, 50th Anniv. — A1160

2006, Oct. 5 *Perf. 13¼x13*

2525 A1160 6.50p multi 1.25 .60

Miniature Sheet

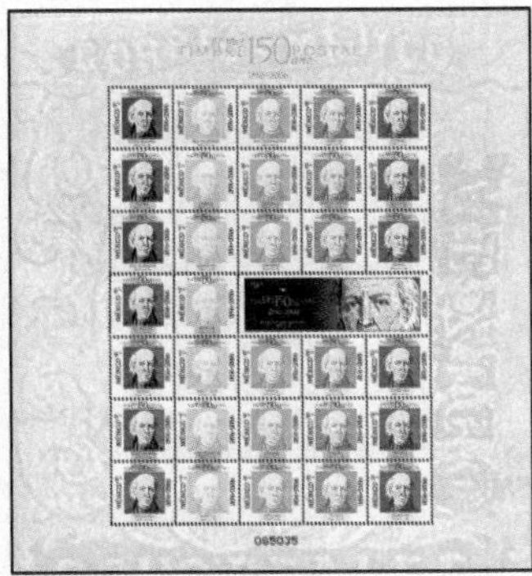
First Mexican Stamps, 150th Anniv. — A1161

No. 2526 — Miguel Hidalgo y Costilla and inscription: a, Aguascalientes. b, Colima. c, Edo. de México. d, Michoacán. e, Nayarit. f, Quintana Roo. g, Tamaulipas. h, Baja California. i, Chiapas. j, Guanajuato. k, Morelos. l, Nuevo León. m, San Luis Potosí. n, Tlaxcala.

o, Baja California Sur. p, Chihuahua. q, Guerrero. r, Oaxaca. s, Sinaloa. t, Veracruz. u, Campeche. v, Distrito Federal. w, Hidalgo. x, Puebla. y, Sonora. z, Yucatán. aa, Coahuila. ab, Durango. ac, Jalisco. ad, Querétaro. ae, Tabasco. af, Zacatecas. ag, Estados Unidos Mexicanos (70x22mm).

Litho., Litho. & Embossed (50p)

2006, Oct. 9

2526	A1161 Sheet of 33	65.00	65.00
a.-g.	6.50p Any single	1.25	.60
h.-n.	7.50p Any single	1.40	.70
o.-t.	9p Any single	1.75	.85
u.-z.	10.50p Any single	1.90	.95
aa.-af.	13p Any single	2.40	1.25
ag.	50p multi	9.25	4.75

World Post Day — A1162

2006, Oct. 9 **Litho.**

2527 A1162 13p multi 2.40 1.25

Popular Television Characters — A1163

Xavier López "Chabelo": 6.50p, Boy with ice cream cone. 10.50p, Man seated.

2006, Oct. 30

2528	6.50p multi	1.25	.60
2529	10.50p multi	2.00	1.00
a.	A1163 Horiz. pair, #2528-2529	3.25	1.60

Letter Carrier's Day — A1164

2006, Nov. 10

2530 A1164 6.50p multi 1.25 .60

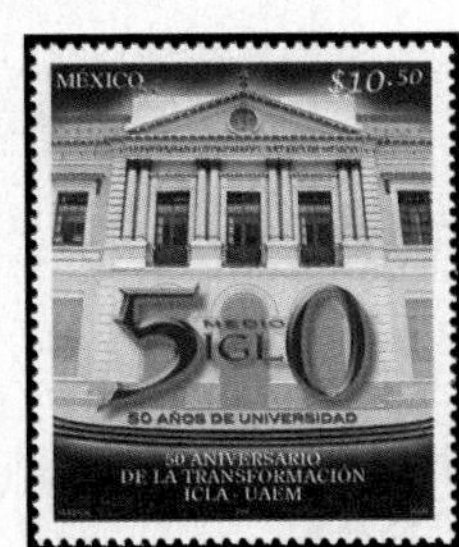
Transformation of the Autonomous Scientific and Literary Institute, Autonomous University of the State of Mexico, 50th Anniv. — A1165

2006, Nov. 17 *Perf. 13x13¼*

2531 A1165 10.50p multi 1.90 .95

"Children, The Future of Mexico" A1166

2006, Nov. 22
2532 A1166 10.50p multi + label 1.90 .95

Andrés Henestrosa, Writer, Cent. of Birth — A1167

2006, Nov. 23 ***Perf. 13¼x13***
2533 A1167 9p multi 1.75 .85

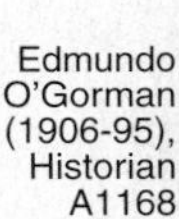

Edmundo O'Gorman (1906-95), Historian A1168

2006, Nov. 28 ***Perf. 13x13¼***
2534 A1168 10.50p multi 1.90 .95

Mexico in Intl. Telecommunications Union, Cent. — A1169

2006, Nov. 30 ***Perf. 13¼x13***
2535 A1169 7p multi 1.40 .70

Christmas A1170

Children's art by: 7.50p, Ricardo Salas Pineda. 10.50p, Maria José Goytia.

2006, Dec. 6 Litho. ***Perf. 13x13¼***
2536 7.50p multi 1.40 .70
2537 10.50p multi 2.00 1.00
a. A1170 Pair, #2536-2537 3.40 1.70

El Universal Newspaper, 90th Anniv. — A1171

2006, Dec. 22 ***Perf. 13¼x13***
2538 A1171 10.50p multi + label 2.00 1.00

Teacher's Day — A1172

2007, May 15
2539 A1172 7.50p multi 1.40 .70

Frida Kahlo (1907-54), Painter A1173

2007, June 13 ***Perf. 13x13¼***
2540 A1173 13p multi 2.40 1.25

Scouting, Cent. — A1174

Designs: 6.50p, Dove and compass. 10.50p, Centenary emblem, compass.

2007, June 30 ***Perf. 13¼x13***
2541 6.50p multi 1.25 .60
2542 10.50p multi 2.00 1.00
a. A1174 Pair, #2541-2542 3.25 1.60

Miniature Sheet

Chichén Itzá — A1175

No. 2543: a, Pelota ring, Jaguar Temple, serpent head. b, Colonnade. c, Observatory. d, Castillo, jaguar head. e, Chac Mool.

2007, July 13
2543 A1175 Sheet of 5 + label 9.25 4.75
a.-b. 6.50p Either single 1.25 .60
c. 10.50p multi 1.90 .95
d.-e. 13p Either single 2.40 1.25

State of Colima, 150th Anniv. — A1176

2007, July 19
2544 A1176 10.50p multi 1.90 .95

Miniature Sheet

Postal Headquarters Building, Cent. — A1177

No. 2545: a, Nude boy writing (40x23mm). b, Nude boy touching item on pedestal (40x23mm). c, Two nude boys, chalice (40x23mm). d, Two nude boys, press (40x23mm). e, Boy, gear (40x23mm). f, Clock and machinery (40x23mm). g, Sculpture of UPU emblem, photographs (80x23mm). h, Mercury and caduceus (40x23mm). i, Two nude boys (40x23mm). j, Two nude boys, diff. (40x23mm). k, Seated nude boy with arms extended, holding bird (40x23mm). l, Seated nude boy holding bird (40x23mm). m, Stairway (40x48mm). n, Glass ceiling (40x48). o, Stairways (80x48mm). p, Building exterior (80x48mm).

2007, Aug. 1 ***Perf. 13x13¼***
2545 A1177 Sheet of 16 35.00 35.00
a.-b. 5.50p Either single 1.00 .50
c.-g. 6.50p Any single 1.25 .60
h.-i. 9p Either single 1.75 .85
j. 10.50p multi 1.90 .95
k.-l. 13p Either single 2.40 1.25
m.-n. 14.50p Either single 2.75 1.40
o. 15.50p multi 3.00 1.50
p. 39.50p multi 7.25 3.50

Torreón, Cent. A1178

No. 2546: a, Locomotive, Torreón Station Museum. b, Bridge, church spires. c, Isauro Martínez Theater. d, Statue of Jesus Christ. e, Bilbao Dunes, Tower.

2007, Sept. 5
2546 Horiz. strip of 5 8.75 4.50
a. A1178 5p multi .90 .45
b.-c. A1178 6.50p Either single 1.25 .60
d.-e. A1178 14.50p Either single 2.60 1.25

Cultural Forum, Monterrey A1179

No. 2547: a, Dove and hand. b, Child and books. c, Children, windmill, hand picking orange. d, Woman and artist. e, Sculpture and figurines.

2007, Aug. 20 Litho. ***Perf. 13x13¼***
2547 Horiz. strip of 5 9.00 4.50
a. A1179 7p multi 1.25 .60
b.-c. A1179 7.50p Either single 1.40 .70
d.-e. A1179 13p Either single 2.40 1.25

Central University City Campus of National Autonomous University of Mexico World Heritage Site — A1180

No. 2548: a, Olympic Stadium and artwork. b, University building, University Library. c, Rectory Building.

2007, Sept. 21
2548 Horiz. strip of 3 5.25 2.75
a. A1180 6.50p multi 1.25 .60
b. A1180 9p multi 1.60 .80
c. A1180 13p multi 2.40 1.25

University of Baja California, 50th Anniv. A1181

2007, Oct. 1
2549 A1181 7.50p multi 1.40 .70

Ozone Layer Protection A1182

No. 2550: a, Doves, tree, leaves. b, Doves, Earth in hands.

2007, Oct. 1
2550 A1182 Vert. pair 4.00 2.00
a. 7p multi 1.25 .60
b. 14.50p multi 2.75 1.40

St. Christopher, by Nicolás Rodríguez Juárez — A1183

2007, Oct. 3
2551 A1183 6.50p multi 1.25 .60

Autonomous University of Coahuila, 50th Anniv. — A1184

2007, Oct. 4 *Perf. 13¼x13*
2552 A1184 7.50p multi 1.40 .70

World Post Day A1185

No. 2553 — Envelope with denomination in: a, Yellow. b, Black.

2007, Oct. 9 *Perf. 13x13¼*
2553 A1185 Vert. pair 3.25 1.60
a. 7p multi 1.25 .60
b. 10.50p multi 2.00 1.00

Rights of People With Disabilities A1186

2007, Oct. 11
2554 A1186 6.50p multi 1.25 .60

Miniature Sheet

Francisco Gabilondo Soler (1907-90), Composer of Children's Songs — A1187

No. 2555: a, Turtle, giraffe, peacock (Caminito de la Escuela). b, Dog, camel, mouse (Caminito de la Escuela). c, Duck and ducklings (La Patita). d, Girl and mouse (La Muñeca Fea). e, Cat with guitar (Gato de Barrio). f, King and cakes (Bombón I). g, Three pigs and cakes (Cochinitos Dormilones). h, Three pigs in bed (Cochinitos Dormilones). i, Old woman and cat (Di Por Qué). j, Mouse in cowboy's clothes (El Ratón Vaquero). k, Boy eating watermelon (Negrito Sandía). l, Cricket holding stick (Cri-Cri). m, Soler. n, Cricket at music stand (Cri-Cri). o, Ant and fountain (El Chorrito).

2007, Oct. 11 *Perf. 13¼x13*
2555 A1187 Sheet of 15 18.50 18.50
a.-b. 5p Either single .90 .45
c.-k. 6.50p Any single 1.25 .60
l.-n. 7p Any single 1.25 .60
o. 7.50p multi 1.40 .70

Degrees in Administration, 50th Anniv. — A1188

2007, Oct. 19 *Perf. 13x13¼*
2556 A1188 7.50p multi 1.40 .70

Cuauhtemoc Sailing School — A1189

2007, Nov. 4 *Perf. 13¼x13*
2557 A1189 7.50p multi 1.40 .70

A1190

A1191

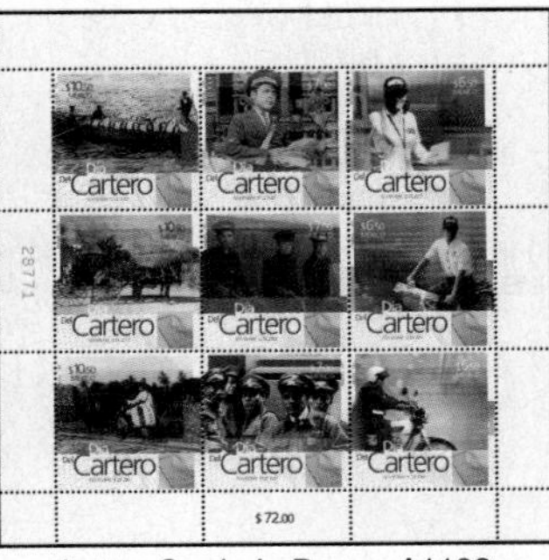
Letter Carrier's Day — A1192

No. 2559: a, Girl writing letter, letter carrier on bicycle. b, Girl mailing letter in mailbox. c, Letter carrier on bicycle. d, Letter carrier delivering letter.

No. 2560: a, Female letter carrier. b, Letter carrier on bicycle. c, Letter carrier on motorcycle. d, Letter carrier with mail bag. e, Three letter carriers. f, Five letter carriers. g, Letter carriers on rowboat. h, Horse-drawn carriage. i, Letter carrier and mail bag on railway hand car.

2007, Nov. 12 *Perf. 13*
2558 A1190 10.50p multi 2.00 1.00
2559 A1191 Block of 4 5.00 2.50
a.-d. 6.50p Any single 1.25 .60
2560 A1192 Sheet of 9 13.50 13.50
a.-c. 6.50p Any single 1.25 .60
d.-f. 7p Any single 1.25 .60
g.-i. 10.50p Any single 2.00 1.00

Mountains — A1193

Designs: No. 2561, Mt. Minya Konka, People's Republic of China. No. 2562, Popocatépetl, Mexico.

2007, Nov. 22 Litho. *Perf. 13¼x13*
2561 A1193 6.50p multi 1.25 .60
2562 A1193 6.50p multi 1.25 .60

See People's Republic of China Nos. 3635-3636.

Intl. Day Against Violence Towards Women — A1194

2007, Nov. 26
2563 A1194 7p multi 1.40 .70

Mariano Otero (1817-50), Judicial and Constitutional Reformer — A1195

2007, Nov. 27 *Perf. 13x13¼*
2564 A1195 10.50p multi 2.00 1.00

Trials of Amparo, legal protection of individual constitutional guarantees in federal courts.

Miniature Sheet

Monte Albán Archaeological Site — A1196

No. 2565: a, Scribe of Cuilapan. b, Head with jaguar helmet. c, Building II, Cocijo urn. d, Building I, Central Plaza, Cocijo urn. e, Observatory, Southern Platform, Central Plaza.

2007, Dec. 11 *Perf. 13¼x13*
2565 A1196 Sheet of 5 + label 9.50 4.75
a.-b. 6.50p Either single 1.25 .60
c. 10.50p multi 2.00 1.00
d.-e. 13p Either single 2.40 1.25

Christmas A1197

2007, Dec. 12 *Perf. 13*
2566 Horiz. strip of 5 10.00 5.00
a. A1197 6.50p Candle 1.25 .60
b. A1197 7p Bell 1.40 .70
c. A1197 10.50p Angel 2.00 1.00
d. A1197 13.50p Magi 2.50 1.25
e. A1197 14.50p Holy Family 2.75 1.40

Miniature Sheet

Dogs — A1198

No. 2567: a, Two English bulldogs. b, Two rottweilers. c, Two boxers. d, Two beagles. e, Head of English Bulldog. f, Head of Rottweiler. g, Head of boxer. h, Head of beagle. i, English bulldog. j, Rottweiler. k, Boxer. l, Beagle.

2007, Dec. 14
2567 A1198 Sheet of 12 19.00 9.50
a.-d. 6.50p Any single 1.25 .60
e.-h. 7p Any single 1.40 .70
i.-l. 10.50p Any single 2.00 1.00

Jesús García Corona (1883-1907), Heroic Railroad Engineer — A1199

2007, Dec. 17 *Perf. 13¼x13*
2568 A1199 10.50p multi 2.00 1.00

Satélite Towers, Naucalpan, 50th Anniv. A1200

2007, Dec. 19 *Perf. 13x13¼*
2569 A1200 6.50p multi 1.25 .60

El Cajón Dam — A1201

Aerial view of: 7p, Open spillway. 13p, Dam.

2007, Dec. 28 *Perf. 13¼x13*
2570 A1201 7p multi 1.40 .70
2571 A1201 13p multi 2.40 1.25

Letter and Heart A1202

2008, Jan. 29 Litho. *Perf. 13½x13¼*
2572 A1202 6.50p multi 1.25 .60

Mother's Day A1203

2008, May 2 *Perf. 13x13¼*
2573 A1203 6.50p multi 1.25 .60

Pres. Miguel Alemán Valdés (1900-83) A1204

2008, May 14 *Perf. 13x13¼*
2574 A1204 6.50p multi 1.25 .60

The Fruits, by Diego Rivera A1205

2008, May 15
2575 A1205 6.50p multi 1.25 .60

Teacher's Day.

Miniature Sheet

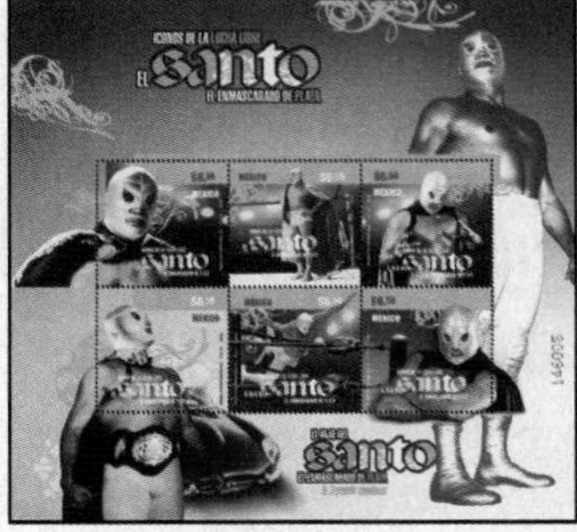

El Santo and El Hijo del Santo — A1206

No. 2576: a, El Santo wearing silver mask and robe. b, El Santo in ring. c, El Hijo del Santo with hands outstretched. d, El Santo with automobile. e, El Hijo del Santo in ring. f, El Hijo del Santo with arms crossed.

2008, June 17 *Perf. 13*
2576 A1206 Sheet of 6 7.50 3.75
a.-f. 6.50p Any single 1.25 .60

El Santo (Rodolfo Guzmán Huerta, 1917-84), El Hijo del Santo (Jorge Guzmán), wrestling legends and film stars.

2008 Summer Olympics, Beijing A1207

Designs: No. 2577, Rowing. No. 2578, Weight lifting. No. 2579, Rhythmic gymnastics.

2008, Aug. 8 *Perf. 13*
2577 A1207 6.50p multi 1.25 .60
2578 A1207 6.50p multi 1.25 .60
2579 A1207 6.50p multi 1.25 .60
Nos. 2577-2579 (3) 3.75 1.80

Electoral Justice — A1208

2008, Aug. 19 Litho. *Perf. 13¼x13*
2580 A1208 6.50p multi 1.25 .60

Mexico Post Emblem — A1209

2008, Sept. 8
2581 A1209 6.50p multi 1.25 .60

Fight for Mexican Independence, Bicent. — A1210

Designs: No. 2582, Ignacio Allende (1769-1811), revolutionary leader. No. 2583, Josefa Ortíz de Dominguez (1768-1829), revolutionary leader. No. 2584, José María Morelos y Pavón (1765-1815), revolutionary leader. No. 2585, Battle of Monte de las Cruces, 1810, horiz. No. 2586, Battle of Alhóndiga de Grandaitas, 1810, horiz. No. 2587, Meeting of Miguel Hidalgo and Morelos, horiz. No. 2588, Querétaro Conspiracy, horiz. No. 2589, Francisco Primo de Verdad y Ramos (1760-1808), promoter of Mexican independence, horiz. No. 2590, Miguel Hidalgo and Cry of Independence. No. 2591, Crowd on Mexico City Alameda.

2008, Sept. 15 *Perf. 13x13¼*
2582 A1210 6.50p multi 1.25 .60
2583 A1210 6.50p multi 1.25 .60
2584 A1210 6.50p multi 1.25 .60

Perf. 13¼x13

2585 A1210 6.50p multi 1.25 .60

Size: 71x30mm

2586 A1210 6.50p multi 1.25 .60
2587 A1210 6.50p multi 1.25 .60
2588 A1210 6.50p multi 1.25 .60
2589 A1210 6.50p multi 1.25 .60
Nos. 2582-2589 (8) 10.00 4.80

Imperf

Size:80x80mm

2590 A1210 10.50p multi 1.90 .95
2591 A1210 10.50p multi 1.90 .95

See Nos. 2627-2636.

Miniature Sheet

Autonomous University of Nuevo León, 75th Anniv. — A1211

No. 2592 — Stained-glass windows by Roberto Montenegro: a, Top of "La Historia." b, Top of "La Agricultura." c, Top of "La Ciencia y la Sabiduría." d, Bottom of "La Historia." e, Bottom of "La Agricultura." f, Bottom of "La Ciencia y la Sabiduría."

2008, Sept. 25 *Perf. 13*
2592 A1211 Sheet of 6 7.50 7.50
a.-f. 6.50p Any single 1.25 .60

World Post Day A1212

2008, Oct. 9 *Perf. 13x13¼*
2593 A1212 10.50p multi 1.60 .80

Flowers — A1213

No. 2594: a, Hylocereus undulatus. b, Curcubita pepo.

2008, Oct. 10 *Perf. 13*
2594 A1213 Horiz. pair 2.00 1.00
a.-b. 6.50p Either single 1.00 .50

Juarez Autonomous University of Tabasco, 50th Anniv. — A1214

2008, Nov. 3 Litho. *Perf. 13x13¼*
2595 A1214 6.50p multi 1.00 .50

Miniature Sheet

Letter Carrier's Day — A1215

No. 2596: a, Letter carrier with large shoulder pouch. b, Letter carrier on bicycle. c, Letter carrier on motorcycle with sidecar. d, Letter carrier on motor scooter. e, Postal service automobile. f, Postal truck. g, Letter carriers, bicycles and truck. h, Postal van, letter carrier on bicycle.

2008, Nov. 12 *Perf. 13*
2596 A1215 Sheet of 8 7.75 7.75
a.-h. 6.50p Any single .95 .50

National Employment Service — A1216

2008, Nov. 19 *Perf. 13¼x13½*
2597 A1216 6.50p multi .95 .50

Mexican Revolution, Cent. (in 2011) A1217

Designs: No. 2598, José María Pino Suárez (1869-1913), politician. No. 2599, Aquiles Serdán (1876-1910), politician. No. 2600, Ricardo Flores Magón (1874-1922), anarchist, and Regeneración Newspaper. No. 2601, Mexican Liberal Party. No. 2602, Cananea Strike. No. 2603, Railway system. No. 2604, Rio Blanco Strike. No. 2605, Revolutionary Junta of Puebla.

No. 2606, Triumphal Entry of Francisco I. Madero. No. 2607, Tienda de raya (company store).

2008, Nov. 20 *Perf. 13x13¼*
2598 A1217 6.50p multi .95 .50
2599 A1217 6.50p multi .95 .50
2600 A1217 6.50p multi .95 .50

Size: 71x30mm

Perf. 13¼x13

2601 A1217 6.50p multi .95 .50
2602 A1217 6.50p multi .95 .50
2603 A1217 6.50p multi .95 .50
2604 A1217 6.50p multi .95 .50
2605 A1217 6.50p multi .95 .50
Nos. 2598-2605 (8) 7.60 4.00

Imperf

Size: 80x80mm

2606 A1217 10.50p multi 1.60 .80
2607 A1217 10.50p multi 1.60 .80

See Nos. 2647-2656.

Parque La Venta Archaeological Museum, La Venta — A1218

2008, Dec. 4 ***Perf. 13***
2608 A1218 6.50p multi .95 .50

Christmas A1219

Designs: 6.50p, Adoration of the Shepherds, by Cristóbal de Villalpando. 10.50p, Adoration of the Magi, by unknown artist.

2008, Dec. 10 ***Perf. 13x13¼***
2609 A1219 6.50p multi 1.00 .50
2610 A1219 10.50p multi 1.60 .80
a. Horiz. pair, #2609-2610 2.60 1.30

Dr. Gonzalo Aguirre Beltrán (1908-96), Anthropologist — A1220

2008, Dec. 16 ***Perf. 13¼x13***
2611 A1220 6.50p multi .95 .50

Miniature Sheet

Palenque Archaeological Site — A1221

No. 2612: a, Mayan hieroglyphic cartouches, tomb, seated figure. b, Jade mask, skull mask, tablet. c, Palace and tower. d, Temple of the Sun, Temples 14 and 15. e, Temple of Inscriptions, incense holder.

2008, Dec. 19 **Litho.**
2612 A1221 Sheet of 5 + label 7.25 7.25
a.-b. 6.50p Either single .95 .50
c. 10.50p multi 1.50 .75
d.-e. 13p Either single 1.90 .95

Mexican Academy of Film Ariel Awards, 50th Anniv. — A1222

2008, Dec. 24 ***Perf. 13¼x13***
2613 A1222 6.50p multi .95 .50

St. Valentine's Day — A1223

2009, Feb. 9 **Litho.** ***Perf. 13x13¼***
2614 A1223 6.50p multi .90 .45

Veracruz Carnival A1224

2009, Feb. 18
2615 A1224 6.50p multi .90 .45

Miniature Sheet

Tajín Archaeological Site — A1225

No. 2616: a, Yoke, eagle-shaped hatchet. b, Decorated panel. c, Terracotta pelota player and pelota pyramid. d, Pyramid, bird's head hatchet, lightning bolt. e, Temple, temple diagram, decorated handle.

2009, Mar. 21 ***Perf. 13¼x13***
2616 A1225 Sheet of 5 + label 7.50 3.75
a.-b. 6.50p Either single .95 .50
c. 10.50p multi 1.60 .80
d.-e. 13p Either single 1.90 .95

Channel 11 Television, 50th Anniv. — A1226

2009, Mar. 27
2617 A1226 6.50p multi .95 .50

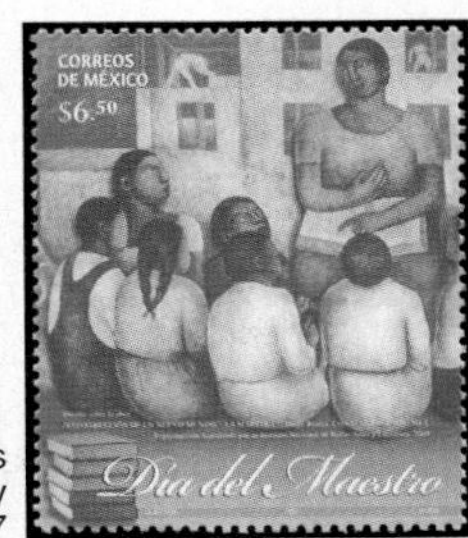

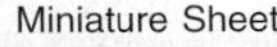

Teacher's Day A1227

2009, May 15 ***Perf. 13x13¼***
2618 A1227 6.50p multi 1.00 .50

Miniature Sheet

National Bank of Mexico, 125th Anniv. — A1228

No. 2619: a, Palacio de los Condes de San Mateo de Valparaiso, Mexico City. b, Main patio, Palacio de los Condes de San Mateo de Valparaiso. c, Column and main door, Palacio de Iturbide, Mexico City. d, Casa Montejo, Mérida. e, Doors, Casa del Mayorazgo de la Canal, San Miguel de Allende. f, Main patio, Palacio de los Condes del Valle de Súchil, Durango.

2009, June 2 ***Perf. 13***
2619 A1228 Sheet of 6 6.00 3.00
a.-f. 6.50p Any single 1.00 .50

World Environment Day — A1229

2009, June 5 ***Perf. 13¼x13***
2620 A1229 10.50p multi 1.60 .80

Aguascalientes Autonomous University — A1230

2009, June 19
2621 A1230 10.50p multi 1.60 .80

Gymnogyps Californianus — A1231

2009, July 27 ***Perf. 13x13¼***
2622 A1231 10.50p multi 1.60 .80

Intl. Day of Indigenous People A1232

2009, Aug. 11
2623 A1232 6.50p multi 1.00 .50

The Country, by Jorge González Camarena — A1233

2009, Aug. 20 **Litho.** ***Perf. 13¼x13***
2624 A1233 6.50p multi 1.00 .50

National Free Textbook Commission, 50th anniv.

Preservation of Polar Regions and Glaciers — A1234

Designs: 10.50p, Mts. Popocatépetl and Iztaccíhuatl. 13p, Mt. Ctilaltépetl.

2009, Sept. 14 ***Perf. 13***
2625 10.50p multi 1.60 .80
2626 13p multi 1.90 .95
a. A1234 Vert. pair, #2625-2626 3.50 1.75

Fight For Mexican Independence Type of 2008

Designs: No. 2627, Congress of Chilpancingo. No. 2628, Establishment of the Supreme Junta. No. 2629, Leona Vicario (1789-1842), supporter of independence movement, and husband, Andrés Quintana Roo (1787-1851), independence movement leader and politician. No. 2630, Execution of José María Morelos y Pavón, horiz. No. 2631, Capture of Miguel Hidalgo and insurgents, horiz. No. 2632, Execution of Hidalgo, horiz. No. 2633, Siege of Cuautla, horiz. No. 2634, Constitution of Apatzingán, horiz.

No. 2635, Map of campaign of Morelos, portraits of compatriots Hermenegildo Galeana, Mariano Matamoros, Pablo Galeana, and Nicolás Bravo. No. 2636, Abolition of slavery.

2009, Sept. 16 ***Perf. 13x13¼***
2627 A1210 6.50p multi 1.00 .50
2628 A1210 6.50p multi 1.00 .50
2629 A1210 6.50p multi 1.00 .50

Perf. 13¼x13

2630 A1210 6.50p multi 1.00 .50
2631 A1210 6.50p multi 1.00 .50
2632 A1210 6.50p multi 1.00 .50

Size: 71x30mm

2633 A1210 6.50p multi 1.00 .50
2634 A1210 6.50p multi 1.00 .50
Nos. 2627-2634 (8) 8.00 4.00

Imperf

Size: 80x80mm

2635 A1210 10.50p multi 1.60 .80
2636 A1210 10.50p multi 1.60 .80

UNI Global Union Post and Logistics Conference, Mexico City — A1235

2009, Sept. 30 ***Perf. 13x13¼***
2637 A1235 6.50p multi 1.00 .50

Autonomous University of San Luis Potosí Scientific and Literary Institute, 150th Anniv. — A1236

2009, Oct. 5 ***Perf. 13¼x13***
2638 A1236 6.50p multi 1.00 .50

World Post Day A1237

2009, Oct. 9 ***Perf. 13x13¼***
2639 A1237 10.50p multi 1.60 .80

City of Chihuahua, 300th Anniv. — A1238

2009, Oct. 12 ***Perf. 13¼x13***
2640 A1238 6.50p multi 1.00 .50

Day of the Dead (All Souls' Day) — A1239

Figurines: No. 2641, Woman honoring dead. No. 2642, Ferris wheel with skeleton riders.

2009, Nov. 2 ***Perf. 13***
2641 6.50p multi 1.00 .50
2642 6.50p multi 1.00 .50
a. A1239 Horiz. pair, #2641-2642 2.00 1.00

Juan Bosch (1909-2001), President of Dominican Republic — A1240

2009, Nov. 4 ***Perf. 13x13¼***
2643 A1240 10.50p multi 1.60 .80

Wilderness Areas A1241

No. 2644: a, El Carmen Mountains, Mexico. b, Nahanni National Park, Canada. c, Zion National Park, US. d, Kronotsky Reserve, Russia. e, Baviaanskloof Reserve, South Africa.

2009, Nov. 6 **Litho.** ***Perf. 13***
2644 Horiz. strip of 5 8.50 4.25
a. A1241 6.50p multi 1.00 .50
b.-c. A1241 10.50p Either single 1.60 .80
d. A1241 13p multi 2.00 1.00
e. A1241 14.50p multi 2.25 1.10

Letter Carrier's Day — A1242

Letter carrier on: No. 2645, Bicycle. No. 2646, Motorcycle.

2009, Nov. 12 ***Perf. 13***
2645 6.50p multi 1.00 .50
2646 6.50p multi 1.00 .50
a. A1242 Horiz. pair, #2645-2646 2.00 1.00

Mexican Revolution Type of 2008

Designs: No. 2647, Emiliano Zapata (1879-1919), General of Liberation Army of the South. No. 2648, Pres. Francisco I. Madero (1873-1913). No. 2649, Proclamation of the Plan of Ayala. No. 2650, Taking of Zacatecas, horiz. No. 2651, Women revolution fighters, horiz. No. 2652, Francisco "Pancho" Villa (1878-1923), General of the Division of the North, horiz. No. 2653, Railroads in the revolution, horiz. No. 2654, The "Ten Tragic Days," horiz.

No. 2655, Venustiano Carranza (1859-1920), revolution leader, and proclamation of Plan of Guadalupe. No. 2656, Revolutionaries, painting by David Alfaro Siqueiros.

2009, Nov. 20 ***Perf. 13x13¼***
2647 A1217 6.50p multi 1.10 .55
2648 A1217 6.50p multi 1.10 .55
2649 A1217 6.50p multi 1.10 .55

Perf. 13¼x13
2650 A1217 6.50p multi 1.10 .55
2651 A1217 6.50p multi 1.10 .55

Size: 71x30mm
2652 A1217 6.50p multi 1.10 .55
2653 A1217 6.50p multi 1.10 .55
2654 A1217 6.50p multi 1.10 .55
Nos. 2647-2654 (8) 8.80 4.40

Imperf
Size: 80x80mm
2655 A1217 10.50p multi 1.75 .85
2656 A1217 10.50p multi 1.75 .85

Traffic Safety A1243

2009, Nov. 23 ***Perf. 13¼x13***
2657 A1243 6.50p multi 1.10 .55

Jaíme Sabínes (1926-99), Poet — A1244

2009, Nov. 27 **Litho.**
2658 A1244 6.50p multi 1.10 .55

Federal Fiscal Auditor, 50th Anniv. — A1245

2009, Nov. 30
2659 A1245 6.50p multi 1.10 .55

Christmas
A1246 A1247

2009, Dec. 1 ***Perf. 13¼x13***
2660 A1246 6.50p Melchior 1.10 .55
2661 A1246 6.50p Gaspar 1.10 .55
2662 A1246 6.50p Balthazar 1.10 .55
2663 A1247 6.50p Santa Claus 1.10 .55
Nos. 2660-2663 (4) 4.40 2.20

Oportunidades Human Development Program — A1248

2009, Dec. 15 ***Perf. 13x13¼***
2664 A1248 6.50p multi 1.00 .50

Energy Conservation — A1249

No. 2665 — Children's drawings: a, Child connecting power cord from house to sun. b, Light bulbs in daytime and nighttime. c, Light bulb people in room.

2009, Dec. 16 ***Perf. 13¼x13***
2665 Horiz. strip of 3 3.00 1.50
a.-c. A1249 6.50p Any single 1.00 .50

Paisano Program A1250

2009, Dec. 18 ***Perf. 13x13¼***
2666 A1250 6.50p multi 1.00 .50

Pres. Venustiano Carranza (1859-1920) — A1251

2009, Dec. 21
2667 A1251 6.50p multi 1.00 .50

Aviation in Mexico, Cent. — A1252

2010, Jan. 8 **Litho.** ***Perf. 13¼x13***
2668 A1252 7p multi 1.10 .55

State Workers' Security and Social Services Institute, 50th Anniv. — A1253

2010, Jan. 19
2669 A1253 7p multi 1.10 .55

St. Valentine's Day — A1254

2010, Feb. 3
2670 A1254 7p multi 1.10 .55

New Year 2010 (Year of the Tiger) A1255

2010, Feb. 11 ***Perf. 13x13¼***
2671 A1255 7p multi 1.10 .55

Mexican Red Cross, Cent. A1256

2010, Feb. 21 *Perf. 13*
2672 A1256 10.50p multi 1.75 .85

Inter-America Development Bank Assembly of Governors, Cancun — A1257

2010, Mar. 19 *Perf. 13x13¼*
2673 A1257 11.50p multi 1.90 .95

Souvenir Sheet

Mexico City Red Devils Baseball Players — A1258

No. 2674: a, José Luis Sandoval. b, Miguel Ojeda. c, Roberto Saucedo.

2010, Apr. 11 *Perf. 13*
2674 A1258 Sheet of 3 3.50 1.75
a.-c. 7p Any single 1.10 .55

Mother's Day A1259

2010, Apr. 23 *Perf. 13x13¼*
2675 A1259 7p multi 1.10 .55

Teacher's Day A1260

2010, May 15
2676 A1260 7p multi 1.10 .55

2010 World Cup Soccer Championships, South Africa — A1261

No. 2677 — 2010 World Cup emblem and: a, Mexican team. b, Gerardo Torrado, Giovani Dos Santos. c, Andrés Guardado, Guillermo Ochoa.

2010, May 15 *Perf. 13¼x13*
2677 Horiz. strip of 3 4.00 2.00
a.-b. A1261 7p Either single 1.10 .55
c. A1261 11.50p multi 1.75 .90

Intl. Mother Language Day — A1262

2010, May 21
2678 A1262 11.50p multi 1.75 .90

Pres. Adolfo López Mateos (1909-69) — A1263

2010, May 26
2679 A1263 7p multi 1.10 .55

Natl. Human Rights Commission — A1264

2010, June 7 **Litho.**
2680 A1264 7p multi 1.10 .55

Scouting in Mexico, 90th Anniv. A1265

2010, July 17 *Perf. 13*
2681 A1265 7p multi 1.10 .55

Grandparent's Day — A1266

2010, Aug. 16
2682 A1266 7p multi 1.10 .55

Mexican Petroleum Institute — A1267

2010, Aug. 23 *Perf. 13¼x13*
2683 A1267 7p multi 1.10 .55

Mexican Independence, Bicent. — A1268

Designs: No. 2684, Pres. Guadalupe Victoria (1789-1843). No. 2685, Pedro Moreno (1775-1817), revolutionary leader. No. 2686, Father Servando Teresa de Mier (1765-1827), politician. No. 2687, Xavier Mina (1789-1817), revolutionary leader. No. 2688, Vicente Guerrero (1783-1831), soldier and politician. No. 2689, Flag of the Army of the Three Guarantees. No. 2690, Gen. Manuel de Mier y Terán (1789-1832), Nicolás Bravo (1786-1854), soldier and politician, horiz. No. 2691, Ignacio López Rayón (1773-1832), leader of revolutionary government, Gen. Ramón Rayón (1775-1839), horiz. No. 2692, O'Donojú Conference, horiz.

No. 2693, Miguel Hidalgo y Costilla (1753-1811), revolutionary leader; Lieutenant Colonel Mariano Jiménez (1781-1811); Juan Aldama (1774-1811), soldier; Leona Vicario (1789-1842), revolution supporter; José María Morelos y Pavón (1765-1815), revolutionary leader; Ignacío Allende (1769-1811), revolutionary leader; Josefa Ortiz de Domínguez (1768-1829), revolution supporter; and Miguel Domínguez (1756-1830), revolutionary leader. No. 2694, Entrance into Mexico City of the Army of the Three Guarantees.

2010, Sept. 16 *Perf. 13x13¼*

2684	A1268	7p multi	1.10	.55
2685	A1268	7p multi	1.10	.55
2686	A1268	7p multi	1.10	.55
2687	A1268	7p multi	1.10	.55
2688	A1268	7p multi	1.10	.55
2689	A1268	7p multi	1.10	.55

Perf. 13¼x13

2690	A1268	7p multi	1.10	.55
2691	A1268	7p multi	1.10	.55
2692	A1268	7p multi	1.10	.55
	Nos. 2684-2692 (9)		9.90	4.95

Imperf

Size: 80x80mm

2693	A1268	11.50p multi	1.90	.95
2694	A1268	11.50p multi	1.90	.95

Miniature Sheet

National University of Mexico, Cent. — A1269

No. 2695: a, University founder Justo Serra, opening of National University. b, National Preparatory School, College of San Ildefonso. c, National School of Law, Academy of San Carlos, National School of Higher Studies. d, Murals by José Clemente Orozco and David Alfaro Siqueiros. e, National University of Mexico Symphonic Orchestra in Nezahualcoyotl Hall, Olympic Stadium, Dancers of National University of Mexico Choreographic Studio. f, University Museum of Contemporaneous Art.

2010, Sept. 21 **Litho.** *Perf. 13*
2695 A1269 Sheet of 6 6.75 3.50
a.-f. 7p Any single 1.10 .55

Girl Guides of Mexico A1270

2010, Sept. 25
2696 A1270 7p multi 1.10 .55

Plenipotentiary Conference of the Intl. Telecommunications Union, Guadalajara — A1271

2010, Oct. 4 *Perf. 13¼x13*
2697 A1271 11.50p multi 1.90 .95

World Post Day A1272

2010, Oct. 9 *Perf. 13x13¼*
2698 A1272 11.50p multi 1.90 .95

Souvenir Sheet

Temples — A1273

No. 2699: a, Pyramid of the Sun, Teotihuacan, Mexico. b, Ateshgah, Baku, Azerbaijan.

2010, Oct. 12
2699 A1273 Sheet of 2 2.25 1.10
a.-b. 7p Either single 1.10 .55

See Azerbaijan No.

National Center for Disaster Prevention, 20th Anniv. A1274

2010, Oct. 13
2700 A1274 7p multi 1.25 .60

All Souls' Day (Day of the Dead) — A1275

2010, Oct. 25

2701 A1275 7p multi 1.25 .60

SEMI-POSTAL STAMPS

Nos. 622, 614 Surcharged in Red

1918, Dec. 25 **Unwmk.** ***Perf. 12***

B1 A72 5c + 3c ultra 20.00 25.00

Rouletted 14½

B2 A73 10c + 5c blue 25.00 25.00
Set, never hinged 57.50

AIR POST STAMPS

Eagle AP1

Unwmk.

1922, Apr. 2 **Engr.** ***Perf. 12***

C1 AP1 50c blue & red brn 67.50 50.00
Never hinged 160.00
a. 50c dark blue & claret ('29) 90.00 90.00
Never hinged 200.00

See #C2-C3. For overprints and surcharges see #C47-C48, CO1-CO2B, CO18-CO19, CO29.

1927, Oct. 13 **Wmk. 156**

C2 AP1 50c dk bl & red brn .75 .25
Never hinged 2.50
a. 50c dark blue & claret ('29) .75 .25
Never hinged 3.00
b. Vert. strip of 3, imperf. btwn. *7,500.*

The vignettes of Nos. C1a and C2a fluoresce a bright rose red under UV light.

1928

C3 AP1 25c brn car & gray brn .45 .20
C4 AP1 25c dk grn & gray brn .45 .20
Set, never hinged 2.50

On May 3, 1929, certain proofs or essays were sold at the post office in Mexico, D. F. They were printed in different colors from those of the regularly issued stamps. There were 7 varieties perf. and 2 imperf. and a total of 225 copies. They were sold with the understanding that they were for collections but the majority of them were used on air mail sent out that day.

Capt. Emilio Carranza and his Airplane "México Excelsior" AP2

1929, June 19

C5 AP2 5c ol grn & sepia 1.10 .65
C6 AP2 10c sep & brn red 1.25 .70
C7 AP2 15c vio & dk grn 3.00 1.25
C8 AP2 20c brown & blk 1.25 .75
C9 AP2 50c brn red & blk 7.50 5.00
C10 AP2 1p black & brn 15.00 10.00
Nos. C5-C10 (6) 29.10 18.35
Set, never hinged 75.00

1st anniv. of death of Carranza (1905-28).
For overprints see Nos. C29-C36, C40-C44.

Coat of Arms and Airplane AP3

1929-34 ***Perf. 11½, 12***

C11 AP3 10c violet .35 .20
C12 AP3 15c carmine 1.35 .20
C13 AP3 20c brown olive 37.50 1.25
C14 AP3 30c gray black .20 .20
C15 AP3 35c blue green .35 .25
a. Imperf., pair 1,200.
C16 AP3 50c red brn ('34) 1.25 .65
C17 AP3 1p blk & dk bl 1.25 .65
C18 AP3 5p claret & dp bl 4.00 3.50
C19 AP3 10p vio & ol brn 6.00 7.00
Nos. C11-C19 (9) 52.25 13.90
Set, never hinged 130.00

1930-32 ***Rouletted 13, 13½***

C20 AP3 5c lt blue ('32) .35 .20
C21 AP3 10c violet .35 .20
C22 AP3 15c carmine .35 .20
a. 15c rose carmine .40 .20
C23 AP3 20c brown olive 1.50 .20
a. 20c brown .50 .20
b. 20c yellow brown .50 .20
c. Horiz. pair, imperf. btwn.
C24 AP3 25c violet .95 .80
C25 AP3 50c red brown .90 .75
Nos. C20-C25 (6) 4.40 2.35
Set, never hinged 13.00

Trial impressions of No. C20 were printed in orange but were never sold at post offices.

See Nos. C62-C64, C75. For overprints and surcharges see Nos. C28, C38-C39, C46, C49-C50, CO17, CO20-CO28, CO30.

Plane over Plaza, Mexico City — AP4

1929, Dec. 10 **Wmk. 156** ***Perf. 12***

C26 AP4 20c black violet 1.25 1.00
C27 AP4 40c slate green 85.00 75.00
Set, never hinged 210.00

Aviation Week, Dec. 10-16.
For overprint see No. CO11.

No. C21 Overprinted in Red

1930, Apr. 20 ***Rouletted 13, 13½***

C28 AP3 10c violet 2.00 1.25
Never hinged 5.50

National Tourism Congress at Mexico, D. F., Apr. 20-27, 1930.

Nos. C5 and C7 Overprinted

1930, Sept. 1 ***Perf. 12***

C29 AP2 5c ol grn & sepia 5.50 4.50
a. Double overprint 225.00 *250.00*
C30 AP2 15c violet & dk grn 9.00 7.75
Set, never hinged 45.00

Nos. C5-C10 Overprinted

1930, Dec. 18

C31 AP2 5c ol grn & sepia 7.00 6.50
C32 AP2 10c sep & brn red 3.50 4.00
a. Double overprint 60.00 60.00
C33 AP2 15c vio & dk grn 7.50 7.00
C34 AP2 20c brown & blk 7.00 5.50
C35 AP2 50c brn red & blk 14.00 10.00
C36 AP2 1p black & brn 4.00 2.75
Nos. C31-C36 (6) 43.00 35.75
Set, never hinged 130.00

Plane over Flying Field AP5

1931, May 15 **Engr.** ***Perf. 12***

C37 AP5 25c lake 4.00 4.50
Never hinged 11.00
a. Imperf., pair 80.00 72.50
Never hinged 175.00

Aeronautic Exhibition of the Aero Club of Mexico. Of the 25c, 15c paid air mail postage and 10c went to a fund to improve the Mexico City airport.
For surcharge see No. C45.

Nos. C13 and C23 Surcharged in Red

1931

C38 AP3 15c on 20c brn ol 32.50 35.00
Never hinged 80.00

Rouletted 13, 13½

C39 AP3 15c on 20c brn ol .30 .20
Never hinged 1.00
a. Inverted surcharge 150.00 *200.00*
b. Double surcharge 150.00 *200.00*
c. Pair, one without surcharge 350.00

Nos. C5 to C9 Overprinted

1932, July 13 ***Perf. 12***

C40 AP2 5c ol grn & sep 6.00 5.00
a. Imperf., pair 60.00 60.00
C41 AP2 10c sep & brn red 5.00 3.00
a. Imperf., pair 60.00 60.00
C42 AP2 15c vio & bk grn 6.00 4.00
a. Imperf., pair 60.00 60.00
C43 AP2 20c brn & blk 5.00 2.75
a. Imperf., pair 60.00 60.00
C44 AP2 50c brn red & blk 35.00 35.00
a. Imperf., pair 60.00 60.00
Nos. C40-C44 (5) 57.00 49.75
Set, never hinged 170.00
Set, C40a-C44a never hinged 650.00

Death of Capt. Emilio Carranza, 4th anniv.

No. C37 Surcharged

1932

C45 AP5 20c on 25c lake .70 .30
Never hinged 2.50
a. Imperf., pair 72.50 72.50
Never hinged 150.00

No. C13 Surcharged

C46 AP3 30c on 20c brn ol 30.00 30.00
Never hinged 75.00

Similar Surcharge on Nos. C3 and C4

C47 AP1 40c on 25c (#C3) .90 .90
Never hinged 3.00
a. Inverted surcharge *11,000.*
C48 AP1 40c on 25c (#C4) 50.00 50.00
Never hinged 125.00

Surcharged on Nos. C23 and C24
Rouletted 13, 13½

C49 AP3 30c on 20c brn ol .35 .20
Never hinged 1.00
a. Inverted surcharge *2,750.*
C50 AP3 80c on 25c dl vio 1.75 1.25
Never hinged 5.00
Nos. C45-C50 (6) 83.70 82.65

Palace of Fine Arts AP6

1933, Oct. 1 Engr. *Perf. 12*

C51	AP6	20c dk red & dl vio	3.50	1.40
C52	AP6	30c dk brn & dl vio	7.00	6.00
C53	AP6	1p grnsh blk & dl vio	72.50	70.00
		Nos. C51-C53 (3)	83.00	77.40
		Set, never hinged	190.00	

21st Intl. Cong. of Statistics and the cent. of the Mexican Soc. of Geography and Statistics.

National University Issue

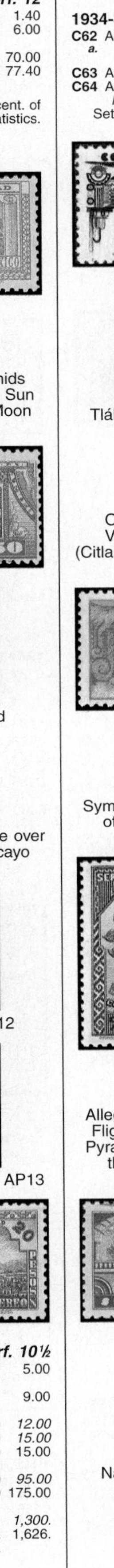

Nevado de Toluca AP7

Pyramids of the Sun and Moon AP8

View of Ajusco AP9

Volcanoes Popocatepetl and Iztaccíhuatl — AP10

Bridge over Tepecayo AP11

Chapultepec Fortress — AP12

Orizaba Volcano (Citlaltépetl) — AP13

Mexican Girl and Aztec Calendar Stone AP14

1934, Sept. 1 Wmk. 156 *Perf. 10½*

C54	AP7	20c orange	5.00	5.00
C55	AP8	30c red lilac & vio	9.00	9.00
C56	AP9	50c ol grn & bis brn	11.00	*12.00*
C57	AP10	75c blk & yel grn	12.00	*15.00*
C58	AP11	1p blk & pck bl	15.00	15.00
C59	AP12	5p bis brn & dk bl	75.00	*95.00*
C60	AP13	10p indigo & mar	240.00	175.00
C61	AP14	20p brn & brn lake	1,250.	*1,300.*
		Nos. C54-C61 (8)	1,617.	1,626.
		Set, never hinged	3,200.	

Type of 1929-34

1934-35 *Perf. 10½, 10½x10*

C62	AP3	20c olive green	.35	.20
a.		20c slate	500.00	500.00
		Never hinged	600.00	
C63	AP3	30c slate	.40	.40
C64	AP3	50c red brn ('35)	2.00	2.00
		Nos. C62-C64 (3)	2.75	2.60
		Set, never hinged	7.00	

Symbols of Air Service AP15

Tláloc, God of Water (Quetzalcóatl Temple) — AP16

Orizaba Volcano (Citlaltépetl) AP17

"Eagle Man" AP18

Symbolical of Flight AP19

Aztec Bird-Man — AP20

Allegory of Flight and Pyramid of the Sun AP21

"Eagle Man" and Airplanes AP22

Natives Looking at Airplane and Orizaba Volcano — AP23

Imprint: "Oficina Impresora de Hacienda-Mexico"

Perf. 10½x10, 10x10½

1934-35 Wmk. 156

C65	AP15	5c black	.45	.20
a.		Imperf., pair		
C66	AP16	10c red brown	.90	.20
C67	AP17	15c gray green	1.25	.20
a.		Imperf., pair	*400.00*	
C68	AP18	20c brown car	3.00	.20
a.		20c lake	4.00	.20
b.		Imperf., pair		
C69	AP19	30c brown olive	.70	.20
C70	AP20	40c blue ('35)	1.25	.20
C71	AP21	50c green	2.50	.20
a.		Imperf., pair	275.00	
C72	AP22	1p gray grn & red brn	3.50	.20
C73	AP23	5p dk car & blk	7.25	.70
		Nos. C65-C73 (9)	20.80	2.30
		Set, never hinged	45.00	

See Nos. C76A, C80, C81, C132-C140, C170-C177A. For overprint see No. C74.

No. C68 Overprinted in Violet

1935, Apr. 16

C74	AP18	20c lake	*3,250.*	*4,000.*
		Never hinged	*6,000.*	

Amelia Earhart's goodwill flight to Mexico.

No. C74 with "Muestra" to left of "Mexico" was not issued for postage.

Arms-Plane Type of 1929-34

1935 Wmk. 248 *Perf. 10½x10*

C75	AP3	30c slate	3.00	*5.00*
		Never hinged	5.00	

Francisco I. Madero AP24

1935, Nov. 20 Wmk. 156

C76	AP24	20c scarlet	.30	.25
		Never hinged	.75	

Plan of San Luis, 25th anniv. See No. C76B.

Eagle Man Type of 1934-35

1936 Wmk. 260

C76A	AP18	20c lake	*4,500.*	60.00
		Never hinged	7,500.	

Madero Type of 1935

C76B	AP24	20c scarlet		*12,500.*

Tasquillo Bridge AP25

Corona River Bridge AP26

Bridge on Nuevo Laredo Highway AP27

Wmk. 248

1936, July 1 Photo. *Perf. 14*

C77	AP25	10c slate bl & lt bl	.35	.20
C78	AP26	20c dl vio & org	.35	.20
C79	AP27	40c dk bl & dk grn	.55	.50
		Nos. C77-C79 (3)	1.25	.90
		Set, never hinged	2.75	

Opening of Nuevo Laredo Highway.

Eagle Man Type of 1934-35

Perf. 10½x10

1936, June 18 Engr. Unwmk.

C80	AP18	20c brown carmine	10.00	7.00
		Never hinged	25.00	

Imprint: "Talleres de Imp. de Est. y Valores-Mexico"

1937 Wmk. 156 Photo. *Perf. 14*

C81	AP18	20c rose red	1.25	.20
		Never hinged	2.50	
a.		20c brown carmine	1.50	.20
		Never hinged	3.00	
b.		20c dark carmine	2.00	.20
		Never hinged	4.50	
c.		Imperf., pair	37.50	50.00
		Never hinged	75.00	

There are two sizes of watermark 156. No. C81c was not regularly issued.

Cavalryman AP28

Early Biplane over Mountains AP29

Venustiano Carranza on Horseback AP30

1938, Mar. 26

C82	AP28	20c org red & bl	.50	.20
C83	AP29	40c bl & org red	.75	*1.00*
C84	AP30	1p bl & bis brn	4.75	2.25
		Nos. C82-C84 (3)	6.00	3.45
		Set, never hinged	18.00	

Plan of Guadalupe, 25th anniversary.

Reconstructed edifices of Chichén Itzá — AP31

Designs: Nos. C85, C86, The Zócalo and Cathedral, Mexico City. Nos. C89, C90, View of Acapulco.

1938, July 1

C85	AP31	20c carmine rose	.35	.25
C86	AP31	20c purple	20.00	10.00
C87	AP31	40c brt green	10.00	5.00
C88	AP31	40c dark green	10.00	5.00
C89	AP31	1p light blue	10.00	5.00
C90	AP31	1p slate blue	10.00	5.00
		Nos. C85-C90 (6)	60.35	30.25
		Set, never hinged	130.00	

16th Intl. Cong. of Planning & Housing.

Statue of José María Morelos — AP34

1939 Engr. *Perf. 10½*

C91	AP34	20c green	.70	.50
		Never hinged	1.00	
C92	AP34	40c red violet	2.00	1.25
		Never hinged	5.00	

C93 AP34 1p vio brn & car 1.40 1.00
Never hinged 1.75
Nos. C91-C93 (3) 4.10 2.75
Set, never hinged 9.50

New York World's Fair. Released in New York May 2, in Mexico May 24.

Type of 1939 Overprinted in Cerise

1939, May 23
C93A AP34 20c blue & red 425.00 425.00
Never hinged 800.00

Issued for the flight of Francisco Sarabia from Mexico City to New York on May 25.

Statue of Pioneer Woman, Ponca City, OK — AP35

1939, May 17
C94 AP35 20c gray brown 1.00 .40
Never hinged 2.00
C95 AP35 40c slate green 2.50 1.25
Never hinged 7.00
C96 AP35 1p violet 1.60 .90
Never hinged 3.00
Nos. C94-C96 (3) 5.10 2.55
Set, never hinged 12.00

Tulsa World Philatelic Convention.

First Engraving Made in Mexico, 1544 — AP36

First Work of Legislation Printed in America, 1563 — AP37

Designs: 1p, Reproduction of oldest preserved Mexican printing.

1939, Sept. 7 **Wmk. 156**
C97 AP36 20c slate blue .25 .20
a. Unwmkd. 50.00
C98 AP37 40c slate green .65 .20
a. Imperf., pair 700.00
C99 AP37 1p dk brn & car 1.10 .70
Nos. C97-C99 (3) 2.00 1.10
Set, never hinged 8.00

400th anniversary of printing in Mexico.

Alternated Perforations

Nos. 763-766, 774-779, 792-795, 801-804, 806-811, 813-818, C100-C102, C111-C116, C123-C128, C143-C162, C430-C431 have alternating small and large perforations.

Transportation — AP39

Designs: 40c, Finger counting and factory. 1p, "Seven Censuses."

Perf. 12x13, 13x12

1939, Oct. 2 **Photo.**
C100 AP39 20c dk bl & bl 1.00 .20
C101 AP39 40c red org & org .75 .25
C102 AP39 1p ind & vio bl 2.75 .75
Nos. C100-C102 (3) 4.50 1.20
Set, never hinged 10.00

National Census of 1939-40.

Penny Black Type of Regular Issue, 1940

1940, May ***Perf. 14***
C103 A140 5c blk & dk grn .65 .55
C104 A140 10c bis brn & dp bl .55 .25
C105 A140 20c car & bl vio .40 .20
C106 A140 1p car & choc 6.00 5.00
C107 A140 5p gray grn & red brn 75.00 55.00
Nos. C103-C107 (5) 82.60 61.00
Set, never hinged 200.00

Issue dates: 5c-1p, May 2; 5p, May 15.

Part of Original College at Pátzcuaro AP43

College at Morelia (18th Century) — AP44

College at Morelia (1940) AP45

1940, July 15 **Engr.** ***Perf. 10½***
C108 AP43 20c brt green .45 .20
C109 AP44 40c orange .50 .30
C110 AP45 1p dp pur, red brn & org 1.25 1.00
Nos. C108-C110 (3) 2.20 1.50
Set, never hinged 5.00

400th anniv. of the founding of the National College of San Nicolas de Hidalgo.

Pirate Ship AP46

Designs: 40c, Castle of San Miguel. 1p, Temple of San Francisco.

Perf. 12x13, 13x12

1940, Aug. 7 **Photo.**
C111 AP46 20c red brn & bis brn 1.10 .70
C112 AP46 40c blk & sl grn 1.50 .75
C113 AP46 1p vio bl & blk 5.00 4.00
Nos. C111-C113 (3) 7.60 5.45
Set, never hinged 20.00

400th anniversary of Campeche.

Inauguration Type of Regular Issue, 1940

1940, Dec. 1 ***Perf. 12x13***
C114 A146 20c gray blk & red org 1.90 1.00
C115 A146 40c chnt brn & dk sl 2.00 1.50
C116 A146 1p brt vio bl & rose 3.50 2.00
Nos. C114-C116 (3) 7.40 4.50
Set, never hinged 20.00

Tower of the Convent of the Nuns AP50

Casa de Montejo — AP51

1p, Campanile of Cathedral at Merída.

1942, Jan. 2 ***Perf. 14***
C117 AP50 20c Prus blue 1.50 .75
C118 AP51 40c grnsh blk (C) 2.25 2.00
a. Without overprint 7.50 7.50
C119 AP50 1p carmine 2.50 2.00
Nos. C117-C119 (3) 6.25 4.75

400th anniversary of Merída.
No. C118 bears the overprint "Servicio Aereo" in carmine.

Church of Zapopan AP53

Our Lady of Guadalupe Church AP54

Guadalajara Arms — AP55

1942, Feb. 11 **Engr.** ***Perf. 10½x10***
C120 AP53 20c green & blk 1.60 .75
C121 AP54 40c ol & yel grn 1.75 1.00
C122 AP55 1p purple & sepia 1.65 1.25
Nos. C120-C122 (3) 5.00 3.00

400th anniversary of Guadalajara.

Astrophysics Type of Regular Issue

Designs: 20c, Spiral Galaxy NGC 4594. 40c, Planetary Nebula in Lyra. 1p, Russell Diagrams.

1942, Feb. 17 **Photo.** ***Perf. 12x13***
C123 A154 20c dk grn & ind 20.00 3.00
C124 A154 40c car lake & ind 15.00 4.00
C125 A154 1p orange & blk 25.00 4.50
Nos. C123-C125 (3) 60.00 11.50

Corn AP59

1942, July 1
C126 AP59 20c shown 1.90 .70
C127 AP59 40c Coffee 1.50 .75
C128 AP59 1p Bananas 2.50 2.00
Nos. C126-C128 (3) 5.90 3.45

2nd Inter-American Agricultural Conf.

View of San Miguel de Allende AP62

Designs: 40c, Birthplace of Allende. 1p, Church of Our Lady of Health.

1943, May 18 ***Perf. 14***
C129 AP62 20c dk slate grn 1.00 .60
C130 AP62 40c purple 1.25 .60
C131 AP62 1p dp carmine 2.75 2.50
Nos. C129-C131 (3) 5.00 3.70

400th anniversary of the founding of San Miguel de Allende.

Types of 1934-35

1944 **Photo.** **Wmk. 272**
C132 AP18 20c brown carmine .75 .20

Perf. 10½x10

1944-46 **Engr.** **Wmk. 272**
C133 AP15 5c black .50 .20
C134 AP16 10c red brn ('45) 1.25 .20
C135 AP17 15c gray grn ('45) .85 .20
C136 AP19 30c brown ol ('45) 12.50 .75
C137 AP20 40c gray bl ('45) 1.10 .20
C138 AP21 50c green .85 .20
C139 AP22 1p gray grn & red brn ('45) 6.00 1.50
C140 AP23 5p dk car & blk ('46) 4.75 2.00
Nos. C133-C140 (8) 27.80 5.25

Symbol of Flight AP65

Microphone, Book and Camera AP66

1944 **Photo.** ***Perf. 14***
C141 AP65 25c chestnut brown .35 .20

See No. C185.

1944, Nov. 8 **Wmk. 272**
C142 AP66 25c dull slate grn .65 .20

Issued to commemorate the third Book Fair.

Catalogue values for unused stamps in this section, from this point to the end of the section, are for Never Hinged items.

Globe-in-Hands Type

1945, Feb. 27 ***Perf. 12x13***
C143 A166 25c red orange .40 .20
C144 A166 1p brt green .50 .30
C145 A166 5p indigo 2.50 2.00
C146 A166 10p brt rose 7.00 5.25
C147 A166 20p brt vio bl 20.00 13.00
Nos. C143-C147 (5) 29.75 20.75

Theater Type

1945, July 27

C148 A167 30c slate & ol .35 .20
C149 A167 1p slate & lil .50 .35
C150 A167 5p slate & blk 3.25 2.50
C151 A167 10p sl & lt ultra 6.00 4.25
C152 A167 20p blk & gray grn 18.00 10.50
Nos. C148-C152 (5) 26.35 17.80

Blindfold Type

1945, Nov. 21

C153 A169 30c slate green .20 .20
C154 A169 1p brown red .50 .30
C155 A169 5p red brn & pale bl 3.75 2.50
C156 A169 10p sl blk & pale lil 6.00 5.00
C157 A169 20p grn & lt brn 25.00 24.00
Nos. C153-C157 (5) 33.55 32.00

Torch, Laurel and Flag-decorated ONU — AP70

1946, Apr. 10

C158 AP70 30c chocolate .20 .20
C159 AP70 1p slate grn .50 .30
C160 AP70 5p chnt & dk grn 2.00 1.25
C161 AP70 10p dk brn & chnt 6.50 4.00
C162 AP70 20p sl grn & org red 18.00 9.00
Nos. C158-C162 (5) 25.15 14.75

Issued to honor the United Nations.

Father Margil de Jesus and Plane over Zacatecas AP71

Zacatecas scene and: 1p, Genaro Codina. 5p, Gen. Enrique Estrada. 10p, Fernando Villalpando.

Perf. 10½x10

1946, Sept. 13 Engr. Wmk. 279

C163 AP71 30c gray .20 .20
C164 AP71 1p brn & Prus grn .40 .35
C165 AP71 5p red & olive 3.00 3.00
C166 AP71 10p Prus grn & dk brn 18.00 15.00
Nos. C163-C166 (4) 21.60 18.55

400th anniversary of Zacatecas.

Franklin D. Roosevelt and Stamp of 1st Mexican Issue AP72

30c, Arms of Mexico & Stamp of 1st US Issue.

1947, May 16 Photo. *Perf. 14*

C167 AP72 25c lt violet bl .90 .50
C168 AP72 30c gray black .60 .25
a. Imperf., pair 325.00
C169 AP72 1p blue & carmine 1.25 .40
Nos. C167-C169 (3) 2.75 1.15

Centenary International Philatelic Exhibition, New York, May 17-25, 1947.

Type of 1934-35

Perf. 10½x10, 10x10½

1947 Engr. Wmk. 279

C170 AP15 5c black 1.50 .20
C171 AP16 10c red brown 3.00 .30
C172 AP17 15c olive grn 3.00 .30
C173 AP19 30c brown ol 2.00 .20
C174 AP20 40c blue gray 2.00 .20
C175 AP21 50c green 12.50 .30
a. Imperf., pair 450.00
C176 AP22 1p gray grn & red brn 3.50 .25
a. Imperf., pair 500.00
C177 AP23 5p red & blk 9.00 1.25
c. 5p dark car & black 200.00 3.00

Perf. 14

C177A AP18 20c brown car 2.75 .50
b. Imperf., pair 250.00
Nos. C170-C177A (9) 39.25 3.50

Emilio Carranza AP74

Douglas DC-4 AP75

1947, June 25 Engr. *Perf. 10½x10*

C178 AP74 10p red & dk brn 1.75 1.50
a. 10p dark carmine & brown 8.00
C179 AP75 20p bl & red brn 2.75 2.75

Cadet Vincente Suárez AP76

Chapultepec Castle — AP78

30c, Lieut. Juan de la Barrera. 1p, Gen. Pedro M. Anaya. 5p, Gen. Antonio de Leon.

1947, Sept. 8 Photo. *Perf. 14*

C180 AP76 25c dull violet .25 .20
C181 AP76 30c blue .25 .20

Engr.

Perf. 10x10½

C182 AP78 50c deep green .35 .20
C183 AP78 1p violet .50 .20
C184 AP78 5p aqua & brn 2.00 2.00
a. Imperf. pair 600.00
Nos. C180-C184 (5) 3.35 2.80

Centenary of the battles of Chapultepec, Churubusco and Molino del Rey.

Flight Symbol Type of 1944

1947 Wmk. 279 Photo. *Perf. 14*

C185 AP65 25c chestnut brown .50 .20
a. Imperf., pair 250.00

Puebla, Dance of the Half Moon AP81

Designs: 5c, Guerrero, Acapulco waterfront. 10c, Oaxaca, dance. 20c, Chiapas, musicians (Mayan). 25c, Michoacan, masks. 30c, Cuauhtemoc. 35c, Guerrero, view of Taxco. 40c, San Luis Potosi, head. 50c, Chiapas, bas-relief profile, Mayan culture. 80c, Mexico City University Stadium. 5p, Queretaro, architecture. 10p, Miguel Hidalgo. 20p, Modern building.

Two types of 20p:
Type I — Blue gray part 21¼mm wide. Child's figure touching left edge.
Type II — Blue gray part 21¾mm wide; "LQ" at lower left corner. Child's figure 1mm from left edge.

Imprint: "Talleres de Impresion de Estampillas y Valores-Mexico"

Perf. 10½x10

1950-52 Wmk. 279 Engr.

C186 AP81 5c aqua ('51) .50 .20
C187 AP81 10c brn org ('51) 2.75 .50
C188 AP81 20c carmine 1.25 .20
C189 AP81 25c redsh brown 1.25 .20
C190 AP81 30c olive bister .50 .20
C191 AP81 35c violet 2.75 .20
a. Retouched die 19.00 .30
b. As "a," imperf., pair 300.00
C192 AP81 40c dk gray bl ('51) 2.25 .20
a. Imperf., pair 300.00
C193 AP81 50c green 3.75 .20
C194 AP81 80c claret ('52) 2.25 .50
a. Imperf., pair 300.00
C195 AP81 1p blue gray 1.40 .20
C196 AP81 5p dk brn & org ('51) 5.00 1.00
a. Imperf., pair 1,800.
C197 AP81 10p blk & aqua ('52) 95.00 20.00
C198 AP81 20p car & bl gray, I ('52) 8.50 9.00
a. Type II 400.00 100.00
Nos. C186-C198 (13) 127.15 32.60

No. C191a: A patch of heavy shading has been added at right of "MEXICO;" lines in sky increased and strengthened. On Nos. C191, C191a, the top of the highest tower is even with the top of the "o" in "Guerrero," and has no frame line at right. No. C220C has frame line at right and tower top is even with "Arquitectura."

Many shades exist of Nos. C186-C198.

See Nos. C208-C221, C249, C265-C268, C285-C288, C290-C298, C347-C349, C422, C444, C446-C450, C471-C480.

Pres. Aleman and Highway Bridging Map of Mexico AP82

Design: 35c, Pres. Juarez and map.

1950, May 21 Engr.

C199 AP82 25c lilac rose 3.00 .25
C200 AP82 35c deep green .30 .20

Completion of the Intl. Highway between Ciudad Juarez and the Guatemala border.

Trains Crossing Isthmus of Tehuantepec — AP83

Design: 35c, Pres. Aleman and bridge.

1950, May 24

C201 AP83 25c green .50 .25
C202 AP83 35c ultra .35 .25

Opening of the Southeastern Railroad between Veracruz, Coatzocoalcos and Yucatan, 1950.

Aztec Courier, Plane, Train AP84

80c, Symbols of universal postal service.

1950, June 15

C203 AP84 25c red orange .35 .20
C204 AP84 80c blue .50 .30

75th anniv. (in 1949) of the UPU.

Miguel Hidalgo AP86

Design: 35c, Hidalgo and Mexican Flag.

Wmk. 300

1953, May 8 Photo. *Perf. 14*

C206 AP86 25c gray bl & dk red brn .90 .20
C207 AP86 35c slate green .90 .25
a. Wmk. 279 —

Bicentenary of birth of Miguel Hidalgo y Costilla (1753-1811), priest and revolutionist.

Type of 1950-52

Designs as before.

Imprint: "Talleres de Impresion de Estampillas y Valores-Mexico"

Wmk. 300, Horizontal

1953-56 Engr. *Perf. 10½x10*

C208 AP81 5c aqua .50 .20
C209 AP81 10c orange brn 5.50 3.50
a. 10c orange 11.50 2.50
C210 AP81 30c gray olive 18.00 10.00
C211 AP81 40c gray bl ('56) 18.00 1.50
C212 AP81 50c green 350.00 250.00
C213 AP81 80c claret 100.00 10.00
C214 AP81 1p blue gray 3.00 .30
C215 AP81 5p dk brn & org 2.75 .60
C216 AP81 10p black & aqua 6.25 1.25
C217 AP81 20p car & bl gray (II) ('56) 75.00 8.00
Nos. C208-C211,C213-C217 (9) 229.00 35.35

Printed in sheets of 30.

Type of 1950-52

Designs as in 1950-52. 2p, Guerrero, view of Taxco. 2.25p, Michoacan, masks.

Two types of 2p:
I — No dots after "Colonial". Frame line at right broken near top.
II — Three dots in a line after "Colonial". Right frame line unbroken.

Wmk. 300, Vertical

1955-65 *Perf. 11½x11*

Design AP81

C218 5c bluish grn ('56) .20 .20

Perf. 11

C219 10c orange brn ('60) .35 .20
a. Perf. 11½x11 1.10 .40
C220 20c carmine ('60) .35 .20
k. Perf. 11½x11 ('57) 1.60 .20
C220A 25c vio brn, perf. 11½x11 1.75 .20
C220B 30c olive gray ('60) .35 .20
l. Perf. 11½x11 .90 .20
C220C 35c dk vio, perf. 11½x11 .90 .20
C220D 40c slate bl ('60) .35 .20
m. Perf. 11½x11 10.00 .20
C220E 50c green, perf. 11½x11 .90 .20
n. Perf. 11 ('60) 1.10 .20
q. 50c yellow green 1.10 .20
C220F 80c claret ('60) 5.00 .70
o. Perf. 11½x11 5.00 .60
C220G 1p grn gray ('60) 1.10 .30
p. Perf. 11½x11 12.50 .30
C220H 2p dk org brn, II ('63) 1.10 .60
i. 2p lt org brn, perf. 11½x11 ('65) 150.00 40.00
j. 2p org brn, I, perf. 11 8.50 1.25
C221 2.25p maroon ('63) .65 .70
Nos. C218-C221 (12) 13.00 3.90

Printed in sheets of 45 and 50. Nos. C218-C221 have been re-engraved.

No. C218 has been redrawn and there are many differences. "CTS" measures 7mm; it is 5½mm on No. C208.

Nos. C208-C221 exist in various shades.

For No. C220C, see note after No. C198.

No. C220En was privately overprinted in red: "25vo Aniversario / Primer Cohete Internacional / Reynosa, Mexico-McAllen, U.S.A. / 1936-1961."

Mayan Ball Court and Player AP87

Design: 35c, Modern Stadium, Mexico.

1954, Mar. 6 Photo. *Perf. 14*

C222 AP87 25c brn & dk bl grn 1.00 .35
C223 AP87 35c dl sl grn & lil rose .75 .25

7th Central American & Caribbean Games.

Allegory AP88

1954, Sept. 15
C224 AP88 25c red brn & dp bl .50 .25
C225 AP88 35c dk bl & vio brn .30 .20
C226 AP88 80c blk & bl grn .30 .25
Nos. C224-C226 (3) 1.10 .70

Centenary of national anthem.

Aztec God Tezcatlipoca and Map — AP89

Design: 35c, Stadium and map.

1955, Mar. 12
C227 AP89 25c dk Prus grn & red brn .75 .30
C228 AP89 35c carmine & brn .75 .30

2nd Pan American Games, 1955.

Ornaments and Mask, Archeological Era — AP90

Designs: 10c, Virrey Enriquez de Almanza, bell tower and coach, colonial era. 50c, Jose Maria Morelos and cannon, heroic Mexico. 1p, Woman and child and horse back rider, revolutionary Mexico. 1.20p, Sombrero and Spurs, popular Mexico. 5p, Pointing hand and school, modern Mexico.

Perf. 11½x11
1956, Aug. 1 Engr. Wmk. 300
C229 AP90 5c black .40 .20
C230 AP90 10c lt blue .40 .20
C231 AP90 50c violet brn .30 .20
C232 AP90 1p blue gray .40 .20
C233 AP90 1.20p magenta .40 .25
C234 AP90 5p blue grn 1.25 1.25
a. Souv. sheet of 6, #C229-C234, perf. 10½x10 60.00 60.00
Nos. C229-C234 (6) 3.15 2.30

Centenary of Mexico's 1st postage stamps. No. C234a sold for 15 pesos.

Paricutín Volcano AP91

1956, Sept. 5 Photo. *Perf. 14*
C235 AP91 50c dk violet bl .50 .20

20th Intl. Geological Cong., Mexico City.

Valentin Gomez Farias and Melchor Ocampo AP92

1.20p, Leon Guzman and Ignacio Ramirez.

1956-63 Wmk. 300 *Perf. 14*
C236 AP92 15c intense blue .50 .20
C237 AP92 1.20p dk grn & pur .85 .35
b. Dark green omitted 110.00
c. Purple omitted 125.00
C237A AP92 2.75p purple ('63) 1.25 .75
Nos. C236-C237A (3) 2.60 1.30

Centenary of the constitution (in 1957). See Nos. C289, C445, C451, C471A.

Map AP93

1956, Dec. 1
C238 AP93 25c gray & dk bl .35 .20

4th Inter-American Regional Tourism Congress of the Gulf of Mexico and the Caribbean (in 1955).

Eagle Holding Scales AP94

1p, Allegorical figure writing the law.

1957, Aug. 31 Photo. *Perf. 14*
C239 AP94 50c metallic red brn & green .35 .20
C240 AP94 1p metallic lilac & ultra .50 .25

Centenary of 1857 Constitution.

Globe, Weights and Measure AP95

1957, Sept. 21
C241 AP95 50c metallic bl & blk .40 .20

Centenary of the adoption of the metric system in Mexico.

Death of Jesus Garcia AP96

1957, Nov. 7 Wmk. 300 *Perf. 14*
C242 AP96 50c car rose & dk vio .35 .20

50th anniversary of the death of Jesus Garcia, hero of Nacozari.

Oil Industry Symbols AP97

Design: 1p, Derricks at night.

1958, Aug. 30
C243 AP97 50c emerald & blk .25 .20
C244 AP97 1p car & bluish blk .40 .20

Nationalization of Mexico's oil industry, 20th anniv.

Independence Monument Figure — AP98

1958, Dec. 15 Engr. *Perf. 11*
C245 AP98 50c gray blue .35 .20

10th anniversary of the signing of the Universal Declaration of Human Rights.

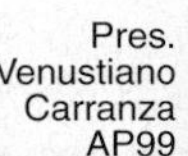

Pres. Venustiano Carranza AP99

1960, Jan. 15 Photo. *Perf. 14*
C246 AP99 50c salmon & dk bl .35 .20

Centenary of the birth of President Venustiano Carranza.

Alberto Braniff's 1910 Plane, Douglas DC-7 and Mexican Airlines Map AP100

1960, May 15 Wmk. 300 *Perf. 14*
C247 AP100 50c lt brn & vio .50 .20
C248 AP100 1p lt brn & bl grn .40 .20

50th anniversary of Mexican aviation.

Type of 1950-52 inscribed: "HOMENAJE AL COLECCIONISTA DEL TIMBRE DE MEXICO-JUNIO 1960"

1960, June 8 Engr. *Perf. 10½x10*
C249 AP81 20p lil, brn & lt grn 100.00 100.00

See note below No. 909.

Flag AP101

Designs: 1.20p, Bell of Dolores and eagle. 5p, Dolores Church.

Wmk. 300
1960, Sept. 16 Photo. *Perf. 14*
C250 AP101 50c dp grn & brt red .40 .20
C251 AP101 1.20p grnsh bl & dk brn .60 .25
C252 AP101 5p sepia & green 6.00 2.25
Nos. C250-C252 (3) 7.00 2.70

150th anniversary of independence.

Aviation (Douglas DC-8 Airliner) AP102

Designs: 1p, Oil industry. 1.20p, Road development. 5p, Water power (dam).

1960, Nov. 20 Photo. *Perf. 14*
C253 AP102 50c gray bl & blk .40 .20
C254 AP102 1p dk grn & rose car .50 .25
C255 AP102 1.20p dk grn & sep .50 .30
C256 AP102 5p blue & lilac 6.00 3.00
Nos. C253-C256 (4) 7.40 3.75

50th anniversary of Mexican Revolution.

Count de Revillaggigedo AP103

1960, Dec. 23
C257 AP103 60c dk car & blk .60 .20

80th census and to honor Juan Vicente Güémez Pacheco de Padilla Horcasitas, Count de Revillagigedo, who conducted the 1st census in America, 1793.

Railroad Tracks and Map AP104

Design: 70c, Railroad bridge.

1961, Nov. Wmk. 300 *Perf. 14*
C258 AP104 60c chlky bl & dk grn .40 .20
C259 AP104 70c dk blue & gray .40 .20

Opening of the railroad from Chihuahua to the Pacific Ocean.

Gen. Ignacio Zaragoza and View of Puebla AP105

1962, May 5
C260 AP105 1p gray grn & slate grn .60 .20

Centenary of the Battle of May 5 at Puebla and the defeat of French forces by Gen. Ignacio Zaragoza.

Laboratory AP106

1962, June 11
C261 AP106 1p olive & vio bl .60 .20

National Polytechnic Institute, 25th anniv.

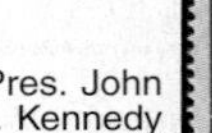

Pres. John F. Kennedy AP107

1962, June 29
C262 AP107 80c brt blue & car 1.75 .40

Commemorates visit of President John F. Kennedy to Mexico, June 29-30.

Globe AP108

1962, Oct. 20
C263 AP108 1.20p violet & dk brn .60 .25

Inter-American Economic and Social Council meeting.

Balloon over Mexico City, 1862 — AP109

1962, Dec. 21 Wmk. 300 *Perf. 14*
C264 AP109 80c lt blue & blk 1.60 .60

Cent. of the 1st Mexican balloon ascension by Joaquin de la Cantolla y Rico.

Type of 1950-52
Imprint: "Talleres de Imp. de Est. y Valores-Mexico"

Designs as before.

Two sizes of 80c:
I — 35½x20mm.

II — 37x20½mm.

Wmk. 300, Vertical

1962-72 Photo. *Perf. 14*

C265 AP81 80c cl, I ('63) 1.40 .30
- *a.* Perf. 11½x11, size II ('63) 4.00 .35
- *b.* Perf. 11, size II ('63) 3.50 .30
- *c.* Perf. 11, size I ('72) 2.50 .20

C266 AP81 5p dk brn & yel org 4.00 1.00

C267 AP81 10p blk & lt grn ('63) 7.00 3.75

C268 AP81 20p car & bl gray 15.00 3.50
- *a.* 20p carmine & aqua 17.00 4.75

Nos. C265-C268 (4) 27.40 8.55

Vert. pairs, imperf. horiz. of No. C265, perf. 11, may be from uncut rolls of No. C348.

ALALC Emblem AP110

1963, Feb. 15 Wmk. 300

C269 AP110 80c orange & dl pur 1.10 .30

2nd general session of the Latin American Free Trade Assoc. (ALALC), held in 1962.

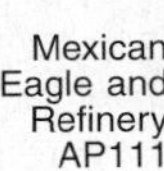

Mexican Eagle and Refinery AP111

1963, Mar. 23

C270 AP111 80c red org & slate .60 .20

Nationalization of the oil industry, 25th anniv.

Polyconic Map AP112

1963, Apr. 22 Photo. *Perf. 14*

C271 AP112 80c blue & blk .85 .30

19th Intl. Chamber of Commerce Congress.

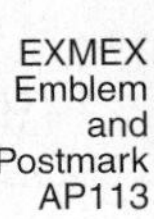

EXMEX Emblem and Postmark AP113

1963, Oct. 9 Wmk. 350 *Perf. 14*

C274 AP113 5p rose red 2.75 1.75

77th Annual Convention of the American Philatelic Society, Mexico City, Oct. 7-13.

Marshal Tito AP114

1963, Oct. 15 Wmk. 350 *Perf. 14*

C275 AP114 2p dk grn & vio 2.00 .70

Visit of Marshal Tito of Yugoslavia.

Modern Architecture — AP115

1963, Oct. 19

C276 AP115 80c dk blue & gray .70 .25

Intl. Architects' Convention, Mexico City.

Dove AP116

1963, Oct. 26

C277 AP116 80c dl bl grn & car 1.25 .35

Centenary of the International Red Cross.

Don Quixote by José Guadalupe Posada AP117

1963, Nov. 9 Engr. *Perf. 10½x10*

C278 AP117 1.20p black 1.75 .50

50th anniversary of the death of José Guadalupe Posada, satirical artist.

Horse-drawn Rail Coach, Old and New Trains — AP118

Wmk. 350

1963, Nov. 29 Photo. *Perf. 14*

C279 AP118 1.20p violet bl & bl .90 .35

11th Pan-American Railroad Congress.

Eleanor Roosevelt, Flame and UN Emblem AP119

1964, Feb. 22 Wmk. 350 *Perf. 14*

C280 AP119 80c lt ultra & red .85 .25

15th anniversary (in 1963) of the Universal Declaration of Human Rights and to honor Eleanor Roosevelt.

Gen. Charles de Gaulle AP120

1964, Mar. 16 Photo.

C281 AP120 2p dl vio bl & brn 2.50 .80

Visit of President Charles de Gaulle of France to Mexico, Mar. 16-18.

Pres. John F. Kennedy and Pres. Adolfo López Mateos and Map AP121

1964, Apr. 11 Photo.

C282 AP121 80c vio bl & gray .85 .25

Ratification of the Chamizal Treaty, returning the Chamizal area of El Paso, Texas, to Mexico, July 18, 1963.

Queen Juliana AP122

1964, May 8 Wmk. 350 *Perf. 14*

C283 AP122 80c bister & vio bl 1.25 .25

Visit of Queen Juliana of the Netherlands.

Lt. José Azueta and Cadet Virgilio Uribe AP123

1964, June 18 Wmk. 350 *Perf. 14*

C284 AP123 40c dk brn & blk .55 .20

50th anniversary of the defense of Veracruz (against US Navy).

Types of 1950-62

Designs as before.

Perf. 11 (20c, 40c, 50c, 80c, 2p); 14

Photo.; Engr. (C296-C298)

1964-73 Wmk. 350

C285 AP81 20c carmine ('71) .75 1.25

C286 AP81 40c gray bl ('71) 125.00 *100.00*

C287 AP81 50c green ('71) .50 .50

C288 AP81 80c claret, I ('73) .50 .50

C289 AP92 1.20p dk grn & pur 6.50 2.50

C290 AP81 2p red brn, II ('71) 1.75 1.40

C296 AP81 5p brn & org ('66) 11.00 9.00

C297 AP81 10p black & aqua 35.00 17.50

C298 AP81 20p car & bl gray 55.00 40.00

Nos. C285-C290,C296-C298 (9) 236.00 *172.65*

National Emblem, Cahill's Butterfly World Map, Sword and Scales of Justice AP124

1964, July 29 Photo.

C299 AP124 40c sepia & dp bl .60 .20

10th conference of the International Bar Association, Mexico City, July 27-31.

Galleon AP125

Map Showing 16th Century Voyages Between Mexico and Philippines — AP126

1964, Nov. 10 Wmk. 350 *Perf. 14*

C300 AP125 80c ultra & indigo 2.25 .35

C301 AP126 2.75p brt yel & blk 2.75 1.00

400 years of Mexican-Philippine friendship.

Netzahualcoyotl Dam, Grijalva River — AP127

1965, Feb. 19 Photo. *Perf. 14*

C302 AP127 80c vio gray & dk brn .50 .20

Radio-electric Unit of San Benito, Chiapas — AP128

80c, Microwave tower, Villahermosa, Tabasco.

1965, June 19 Wmk. 350 *Perf. 14*

C303 AP128 80c lt bl & dk bl .65 .30

C304 AP128 1.20p dk grn & blk .70 .30

Centenary of the ITU.

Campfire, Tent and Scout Emblem AP129

1965, Sept. 27 Photo. *Perf. 14*

C305 AP129 80c lt ultra & vio bl .65 .30

20th World Scout Conference, Mexico City, Sept. 27-Oct. 3.

King Baudouin, Queen Fabiola and Arms of Belgium AP130

1965, Oct. 18 Wmk. 350 *Perf. 14*

C306 AP130 2p slate grn & dl bl 1.00 .40

Visit of the King and Queen of Belgium.

Mayan Antiquities and Unisphere AP131

1965, Nov. 9 Photo.

C307 AP131 80c lemon & emerald .50 .20

Issued for the NY World's Fair, 1964-65.

Dante by Raphael — AP132

Perf. 10x10½

1965, Nov. 23 Wmk. 350 Engr.

C308 AP132 2p henna brown 1.25 .65

700th anniv. of the birth of Dante Alighieri.

Runner in Starting Position, Terra Cotta Found in Colima, 300-650 A.D.
AP133

Designs: 1.20p, Chin cultic disk, ball game scoring stone with ball player in center, Mayan culture, c. 500 A.D., found in Chiapas. 2p, Clay sculpture of ball court, players, spectators and temple. Pieces on 80c and 2p from 300-650 A.D.

1965, Dec. 17 Photo. *Perf. 14*
Size: 35x21mm

C309 AP133 80c orange & sl .80 .25
C310 AP133 1.20p bl & vio bl .90 .30
a. Souv. sheet of 4, #965-966, C309-C310, imperf. 3.50 3.50

Size: 43x36mm

C311 AP133 2p brt bl & dk brn .75 .25
a. Souv. sheet, imperf. 3.50 3.50
Nos. C309-C311 (3) 2.45 .80

19th Olympic Games, Mexico, 1968. No. C310a sold for 3.90p. No. C311a sold for 3p.
Nos. C310a and C311a have large watermark of national arms (diameter 54mm) and "SECRETARIA DE HACIENDA Y CREDITO PUBLICO." Issued without gum.

Ruben Dario — AP134

1966, Mar. 17 Wmk. 350 *Perf. 14*
C312 AP134 1.20p sepia .60 .35

Ruben Dario (pen name of Felix Ruben Garcia Sarmiento, 1867-1916), Nicaraguan poet, newspaper correspondent and diplomat.

Father Andres de Urdaneta and Compass Rose
AP135

Perf. 10½x10
1966, June 4 Engr. Wmk. 350
C313 AP135 2.75p bluish blk 1.25 .60

4th centenary of Father Urdaneta's return trip from the Philippines.

UPAE Type of Regular Issue

Designs: 80c, Pennant and post horn. 1.20p, Pennant and UPAE emblem, horiz.

Wmk. 300
1966, June 24 Photo. *Perf. 14*
C314 A244 80c magenta & blk .25 .20
C315 A244 1.20p lt ultra & blk .35 .20

U Thant and UN Emblem
AP136

1966, Aug. 24 Photo. Wmk. 300
C316 AP136 80c black & ultra .75 .20

Visit of U Thant, Secretary General of the UN.

AP137

1966, Aug. 26 *Perf. 14*
C317 AP137 80c green & red .25 .20

Issued to publicize the year of friendship between Mexico and Central America.

Olympic Type of Regular Issue

Designs by Diego Rivera: 80c, Obstacle race. 2.25p, Football. 2.75p, Lighting Olympic torch.

1966, Oct. 15 Wmk. 300 *Perf. 14*
Size: 57x21mm

C318 A248 80c org brn & blk .55 .20
C319 A248 2.25p green & blk .90 .35
C320 A248 2.75p dp pur & blk 2.00 .45
a. Souvenir sheet of 3 3.00 3.00
Nos. C318-C320 (3) 3.45 1.00

Issued to publicize the 19th Olympic Games, Mexico City, D.F., 1968. No. C320a contains 3 imperf. stamps similar to Nos. C318-C320 with simulated perforations. Sold for 8.70p.

UNESCO Emblem
AP138

Litho. & Engr.
1966, Nov. 4 *Perf. 11*
C321 AP138 80c blk, car, brt grn & org .50 .20
a. Perf. 10½ 5.00 2.00
b. Perf. 10½x11 25.00
c. Perf. 11x10½ 12.50 5.00

UNESCO 20th anniv. The 4th color varies from yellow to orange. A number of perforation varieties exist on the perf 11 stamps.

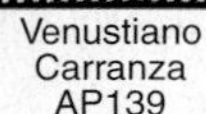

Venustiano Carranza
AP139

Tiros Satellite over Earth
AP140

1967, Feb. 5 Photo. *Perf. 14*
C322 AP139 80c dk red brn & ocher .35 .20

Constitution, 50th anniv. Venustiano Carranza (1859-1920), was president of Mexico 1917-20.

1967, Mar. 23 Photo. Wmk. 300
C323 AP140 80c blk & dk bl .50 .20

World Meteorological Day, Mar. 23.

Medical School Emblem
AP141

Captain Horacio Ruiz Gaviño
AP142

1967, July 10 Wmk. 300 *Perf. 14*
C324 AP141 80c black & ocher .35 .20

Mexican Military Medical School, 50th anniv.

1967, July 17 Photo.

Design: 2p, Biplane, horiz.

C325 AP142 80c black & brown .25 .20
C326 AP142 2p black & brown .45 .25

50th anniv. of the 1st Mexican airmail flight, from Pachuca to Mexico City, July 6, 1917.

Marco Polo and ITY Emblem — AP143

1967, Sept. 9 Wmk. 300 *Perf. 14*
C327 AP143 80c rose cl & blk .25 .20

Issued for International Tourist Year, 1967.

Olympic Games Type of Regular Issue, 1967

Designs: 80c, Diving. 1.20p, Runners. 2p, Weight lifters. 5p, Soccer.

1967, Oct. 12 Photo. *Perf. 14*
C328 A254 80c dp lil rose & blk .45 .20
C329 A254 1.20p brt grn & blk .45 .20
a. Souv. sheet of 2, #C328-C329, imperf. 5.50 3.75
C330 A254 2p yellow & blk 1.25 .40
C331 A254 5p olive & blk 1.60 .75
a. Souv. sheet of 2, #C330-C331, imperf. 7.50 4.00
Nos. C328-C331 (4) 3.75 1.55

No. C329a sold for 2.50p; No. C331a sold for 9p. Both sheets are watermark 350.

Heinrich Hertz and James Clerk Maxwell
AP144

1967, Nov. 15 Photo. Wmk. 300
C332 AP144 80c brt grn & blk .30 .20

2nd Intl. Telecommunications Plan Conf., Mexico City, Oct. 30-Nov. 15.

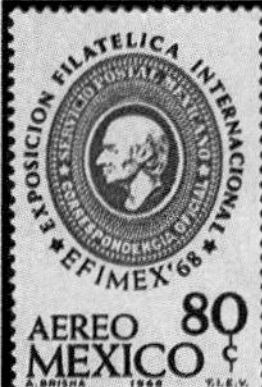

EFIMEX Emblem, Showing Official Stamp of 1884 — AP145

1968, Feb. 24 Wmk. 300 *Perf. 14*
C333 AP145 80c black & grn .45 .25
C334 AP145 2p black & ver .45 .25

EFIMEX '68, International Philatelic Exhibition, Mexico City, Nov. 1-9, 1968.

Olympic Games Type of Regular Issue, 1967

Designs: 80c, Sailing. 1p, Rowing. 2p, Volleyball. 5p, Equestrian.

1968, Mar. 21 Photo. *Perf. 14*
C335 A254 80c ultra & blk .25 .20
C336 A254 1p brt bl grn & blk .35 .20
a. Souv. sheet of 2, #C335-C336, imperf. 3.50 2.75
C337 A254 2p yellow & blk .70 .30
C338 A254 5p red brn & blk 1.40 1.10
a. Souv. sheet of 2, #C337-C338, imperf. 7.50 4.50
Nos. C335-C338 (4) 2.70 1.80

No. C336a sold for 2.40p; No. C338a sold for 9p. Both sheets are watermark 350.

Martin Luther King, Jr. — AP146

1968, June 8 Photo. Wmk. 300
C339 AP146 80c black & gray .35 .20

Rev. Dr. Martin Luther King, Jr. (1929-1968), American civil rights leader.

Olympic Types of Regular Issue, 1968

Designs: 80c, Peace dove and Olympic rings. 1p, Discobolus. 2p, Olympic medals. 5p, Symbols of Olympic sports events. 10p, Symbolic design for Mexican Olympic Games.

1968, Oct. 12 Wmk. 350 *Perf. 14*
C340 A259 80c green, lil & org .35 .20
C341 A259 1p green, bl & blk .45 .20
C342 A259 2p multicolored .90 .50
a. Souvenir sheet of 3, #C340-C342, imperf. 20.00 17.50
C343 A260 5p multicolored 4.00 1.40
C344 A260 10p black & multi 2.90 1.50
a. Souvenir sheet of 2, #C343-C344, imperf. 20.00 17.50
Nos. C340-C344 (5) 8.60 3.80

19th Olympic Games, Mexico City, Oct. 12-27. No. C342a sold for 5p. No. C344a sold for 20p.

Souvenir Sheet

EFIMEX Emblem — AP147

1968, Nov. 1 Photo. *Imperf.*
C345 AP147 5p black & ultra 3.50 2.50

EFIMEX '68 International philatelic exhibition, Mexico City, Nov. 1-9. No. C345 contains one stamp with simulated perforations.

Father Francisco Palóu (See footnote)
AP148

1969, July 16 Wmk. 350 *Perf. 14*
C346 AP148 80c multicolored .40 .20

Issued to honor Father Junipero Serra (1713-1784), Franciscan missionary, founder of San Diego, Calif. The portrait was intended to be that of Father Serra. By error the head of Father Palóu, his coworker, was taken from a painting (c. 1785) by Mariano Guerrero which also contains a Serra portrait.

Type of 1950-52 Redrawn Coil Stamps
Wmk. 300 Vert.
1969 Photo. *Perf. 11 Vert.*
Imprint: "T.I.E.V."

C347 AP81 20c carmine 2.75 2.00

Imprint: "Talleres de Imp de Est y Valores-Mexico"

C348 AP81 80c claret 4.00 2.00

Imprint: "T.I.E.V."

C349 AP81 1p gray grn 4.00 2.25
Nos. C347-C349 (3) 10.75 6.25

Soccer Ball
AP149

Design: 2p, Foot and soccer ball.

1969, Aug. 16 Wmk. 350 ***Perf. 14***
C350 AP149 80c red & multi 1.25 .20
C351 AP149 2p green & multi 1.25 .20

9th World Soccer Championships for the Jules Rimet Cup, Mexico City, May 30-June 21, 1970.

Mahatma Gandhi
AP150

Astronaut's Footprint
AP151

1969, Sept. 27 Photo. ***Perf. 14***
C352 AP150 80c multicolored .30 .20

Mohandas K. Gandhi (1869-1948), leader in India's fight for independence.

1969, Sept. 29 Photo.
C353 AP151 2p black .50 .25

Man's 1st landing on the moon, July 20, 1969. See note after US No. C76.

Tourist Issue

Type of Regular Issue, 1969-73 and

"Sound and Light" at Pyramid, Teotihuacan — AP152

Designs: No. C355, Acapulco Bay. No. C356, El Caracol Observatory, Yucatan. No. C357, Dancer with fruit basket, Oaxaca. No. C358, Sports fishing, Lower California, horiz.

1969-73 Wmk. 350 ***Perf. 14***
C354 AP152 80c shown .90 .30
C355 AP152 80c multicolored .90 .30
C356 AP152 80c multicolored .90 .30

Wmk. 300

C357 A267 80c multicolored .35 .25
C358 A267 80c multicolored .35 .20
Nos. C354-C358 (5) 3.40 1.35

Issue dates: Nos. C354-C356, Nov. 1, 1969. Nos. C357-C358, Mar. 16, 1973.

Red Crosses
AP154

1969, Nov. 8 Photo. Wmk. 350
C370 AP154 80c black & multi .35 .20
a. Red omitted 150.00

50th anniv. of the League of Red Cross Societies.

AP155

AP156

1969, Dec. 6 Wmk. 350 ***Perf. 14***
C371 AP155 80c multicolored .35 .20

Installation of the ground station for communications by satellite at Tulancingo, Hidalgo.

1970, May 31 Wmk. 350 ***Perf. 14***

Design: 80c, Soccer Ball, and Mexican Masks. 2p, Pre-Columbian sculptured heads and soccer ball.

C372 AP156 80c blue & multi 1.25 .20
C373 AP156 2p multicolored 1.25 .20

World Soccer Championships for the Jules Rimet Cup, Mexico City, May 30-June 21, 1970. The design of Nos. C372-C373 is continuous.

SPORTMEX '70 Emblem — AP157

1970, June 19 ***Rouletted 13***
C374 AP157 2p gray & car 5.00 3.00

SPORTMEX '70 philatelic exposition devoted to sports, especially soccer, on stamps. Mexico City, June 19-28. The 2p stamp of No. C374 is imperf.

Ode to Joy and Beethoven's Signature
AP158

1970, Sept. 26 Wmk. 350 ***Perf. 14***
C375 AP158 2p multicolored .50 .25

200th anniversary of the birth of Ludwig van Beethoven (1770-1827), composer.

UN General Assembly Floor Plan
AP159

1970, Oct. 24 Photo. ***Perf. 14***
C376 AP159 80c multicolored .30 .20

25th anniversary of United Nations.

Isaac Newton
AP160

1971, Feb. 27 Wmk. 350 ***Perf. 14***
C377 AP160 2p shown .45 .20
C378 AP160 2p Galileo .45 .20
C379 AP160 2p Johannes Kepler .45 .20
Nos. C377-C379 (3) 1.35 .60

Mayan Warriors, Dresden Codex
AP161

Designs: No. C381, Sister Juana, by Miguel Cabrera (1695-1768). No. C382, José Maria Velasco (1840-1912), self-portrait. No. C383, El Paricutin (volcano), by Gerardo Murillo ("Dr. Atl," 1875-1964). No. C384, Detail of mural, Man in Flames, by José Clemente Orozco (1883-1949).

Imprint includes "1971"

1971, Apr. 24 Photo. Wmk. 350
C380 AP161 80c multicolored .30 .20
C381 AP161 80c multicolored .30 .20
C382 AP161 80c multicolored .30 .20
C383 AP161 80c multicolored .30 .20
C384 AP161 80c multicolored .30 .20
Nos. C380-C384 (5) 1.50 1.00

Mexican art and science through the centuries. See Nos. C396-C400, C417-C421, C439-C443, C513-C517, C527-C531.

Stamps of Venezuela, Mexico and Colombia
AP162

1971, May 22 Photo. Wmk. 350
C385 AP162 80c multicolored .35 .20

EXFILCA 70, 2nd Interamerican Philatelic Exhibition, Caracas, Venezuela, Nov. 27-Dec. 6, 1970.

Francisco Javier Clavijero
AP163

1971, July 10 Wmk. 350 ***Perf. 14***
C386 AP163 2p lt ol bis & dk brn .50 .25

Francisco Javier Clavijero (1731-1786), Jesuit and historian, whose remains were returned from Italy to Mexico in 1970.

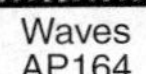

Waves
AP164

Mariano Matamoros, by Diego Rivera
AP165

1971, Aug. 7 Wmk. 350 ***Perf. 14***
C387 AP164 80c multicolored .25 .20

3rd World Telecommunications Day, May 17.

1971, Aug. 28 Photo.
C388 AP165 2p multicolored .45 .20

Bicentenary of the birth of Mariano Matamoros (1770-1814), priest and patriot.

Vicente Guerrero
AP166

Circles
AP167

1971, Sept. 27
C389 AP166 2p multicolored .40 .20

Vicente Guerrero (1783-1831), independence leader, president of Mexico. Painting by Juan O'Gorman.

1971, Nov. 4 Wmk. 300
C390 AP167 80c grnsh bl, dk bl & blk .30 .20

25th anniv. of UNESCO.

Stamps of Venezuela, Mexico, Colombia and Peru
AP168

1971, Nov. 4
C391 AP168 80c multicolored .45 .20

EXFILIMA '71, 3rd Interamerican Philatelic Exhibition, Lima, Peru, Nov. 6-14.

Faces and Hand
AP169

1971, Nov. 29
C392 AP169 2p blk, dk bl & pink .45 .20

5th Congress of Psychiatry, Mexico City, Nov. 28-Dec. 4.

Ex Libris by Albrecht Dürer
AP170

1971, Dec. 18
C393 AP170 2p blk & buff .65 .20

Albrecht Dürer (1471-1528), German painter and engraver.

Retort, Pulley and Burner
AP171

Scientists and WHO Emblem
AP172

1972, Feb. 26 Wmk. 300 *Perf. 14*
C394 AP171 2p lilac, blk & yel .35 .20

Anniversary of the National Council on Science and Technology.

1972, Apr. 8
C395 AP172 80c multicolored .25 .20

World Health Day 1972. Stamp shows Willem Einthoven and Frank Wilson.

Art and Science Type of 1971

Designs: No. C396, King Netzahuacoyotl (1402-1472) of Texcoco, art patron. No. C397, Juan Ruiz de Alarcon (c. 1580-1639), lawyer. No. C398, José Joaquin Fernandez de Lizardi (1776-1827), author. No. C399, Ramon Lopez Velarde (1888-1921), writer. No. C400, Enrique Gonzalez Martinez (1871-1952), poet.

Imprint includes "1972"

1972, Apr. 15 Wmk. 350

Black Inscriptions

C396 AP161 80c ocher 1.25 .25
C397 AP161 80c green 1.25 .25
C398 AP161 80c brown 1.25 .25
C399 AP161 80c carmine 1.25 .25
C400 AP161 80c gray blue 1.25 .25
Nos. C396-C400 (5) 6.25 1.25

Mexican art and science through the centuries.

Rotary Emblem
AP173

1972, Apr. 15
C401 AP173 80c multicolored .30 .20

Rotary Intl. in Mexico, 50th anniv.

Tire Treads
AP174

1972, May 11 Wmk. 300
C402 AP174 80c gray & blk .30 .20

74th Assembly of the International Tourism Alliance, Mexico City, May 8-11.

Benito Juárez
AP175

Designs: 80c, Page of Civil Register. 1.20p, Juárez, by Pelegrin Clavé.

1972 Photo. *Perf. 14*
C403 AP175 80c gray bl & blk .20 .20
C404 AP175 1.20p multi .25 .20
C405 AP175 2p yellow & multi .35 .20
Nos. C403-C405 (3) .80 .60

Benito Juárez (1806-1872), revolutionary leader and president of Mexico.

Issue dates: 80c, 2p, July 18; 1.20p, Sept. 15.

Atom Symbol, Olive Branch — AP176

1972, Oct. 3 Photo. Wmk. 300
C406 AP176 2p gray, bl & blk .40 .20

16th Conference of the Atomic Energy Commission, Mexico City, Sept. 26.

"Over the Waves," by Juventino Rosas
AP177

1972, Oct. 16 *Perf. 14*
C407 AP177 80c olive bister .25 .20

28th Intl. Cong. of the Societies of Authors and Composers, Mexico City, Oct. 16-21.

Child with Doll, by Guerrero Galvan, UNICEF Emblem — AP178

1972, Nov. 4
C408 AP178 80c multicolored .75 .20

25th anniv. (in 1971) of UNICEF.

Pedro de Gante, by Rodriguez y Arangorti
AP179

Map of Americas with Tourists' Footprints
AP180

1972, Nov. 22 *Perf. 14*
C409 AP179 2p multicolored .35 .20

Brother Pedro de Gante (Pedro Moor or van der Moere; 1480?-1572), Franciscan brother who founded first school in Mexico, and writer.

Olympic Games Type of Regular Issue, 1972

Designs: 80c, Olympic emblems and stylized soccer game. 2p, Olympic emblems, vert.

1972, Dec. 9 Photo. Wmk. 300
C410 A289 80c green & multi .35 .20
C411 A289 2p yel grn, blk & bl .65 .20

20th Olympic Games, Munich, Aug. 26-Sept. 11.

Anti-pollution Type of Regular Issue

80c, Bird sitting on ornamental capital, vert.

1972, Dec. 16
C412 A291 80c lt blue & blk .25 .20

Anti-pollution campaign.

1972, Dec. 23
C413 AP180 80c black, yel & grn .25 .20

Tourism Year of the Americas.

Mexico #O1, Brazil #992, Colombia #130, Venezuela #22, Peru #C320
AP181

1973, Jan. 19 *Perf. 14*
C414 AP181 80c multicolored .25 .20

4th Interamerican Philatelic Exhibition, EXFILBRA 72, Rio de Janeiro, Brazil, Aug. 26-Sept. 2, 1972.

Aeolus, God of Winds — AP182

1973, Sept. 14 Photo. Wmk. 300
C415 AP182 80c brt pink, blk & bl .60 .20

Cent. of intl. meteorological cooperation.

Nicolaus Copernicus
AP183

San Martin Monument
AP184

Wmk. 300
1973, Oct. 10 Photo. *Perf. 14*
C416 AP183 80c slate green .30 .20

500th anniversary of the birth of Nicolaus Copernicus (1473-1543), Polish astronomer.

Art and Science Type of 1971

Designs: No. C417, Aztec calendar stone. No. C418, Carlos de Sigüenza y Gongora (1645-1700), mathematician, astronomer. No. C419, Francisco Diaz Covarrubias (1833-1889), topographer. No. C420, Joaquin Gallo (1882-1965), geographer, astronomer. No. C421, Luis Enrique Erro (1897-1955), founder of Tonanzintla Observatory.

Imprint includes "1973"

1973, Nov. 21 Wmk. 350
C417 AP161 80c car & sl grn .20 .20
C418 AP161 80c multicolored .20 .20
C419 AP161 80c multicolored .20 .20
C420 AP161 80c multicolored .20 .20
C421 AP161 80c multicolored .20 .20
Nos. C417-C421 (5) 1.00 1.00

Type of 1950-52

Design: Mexico City University Stadium.

Imprint: "Talleres de Imp. de Est. y Valores-Mexico"

1973 Unwmk. *Perf. 11*
C422 AP81 80c claret, I 3.00 .95

Fluorescent printing on front or back of stamps consisting of beehive pattern and diagonal inscription.

Wmk. 350
1973, Dec. 14 Photo. *Perf. 14*
C423 AP184 80c orange, indigo & yel .25 .20

Erection of a monument to San Martin in Mexico City, a gift of Argentina.

Palace of Cortes, Cuernavaca — AP185

Wmk. 300
1974, Feb. 22 Litho. *Perf. 14*
C424 AP185 80c black & multi .25 .20

EXMEX 73 Philatelic Exhibition, Cuernavaca, Apr. 7-15.

Gold Brooch, Mochica Culture
AP186

1974, Mar. 6 Photo. Wmk. 300
C425 AP186 80c gold & multi .25 .20

Exhibition of Peruvian gold treasures, Mexico City, 1973-74.

Luggage — AP187

1974, Mar. 22 *Perf. 14*
C426 AP187 80c multicolored .25 .20

16th Convention of the Federation of Latin American Tourist Organizations (COTAL), Acapulco, May 1974.

CEPAL Emblem
AP188

1974, Mar. 22
C427 AP188 80c black & multi .25 .20
a. Red omitted 100.00

25th anniversary (in 1973) of the Economic Commission for Latin America (CEPAL).

"The Enameled Casserole," by Picasso — AP189

1974, Mar. 29 Wmk. 300
C428 AP189 80c multicolored .35 .20

Pablo Ruiz Picasso (1881-1973), painter and sculptor.

EXFILMEX Type of 1974

1974, July 26 ***Perf. 13x12***
C429 A305 80c buff, red brn & blk .25 .20

See note after No. 1065.

Biplane — AP190

Perf. 13x12

1974, Aug. 20 Photo. Wmk. 300
C430 AP190 80c shown .25 .20
C431 AP190 2p Jet plane .25 .20

50th anniversary of Mexican Airlines (MEXICANA).

Transmitter and Waves Circling Globe — AP191

1974, Oct. 4 Wmk. 300 ***Perf. 14***
C432 AP191 2p multicolored .25 .20

First International Congress of Electric and Electronic Communications, Sept. 17-21.

Volleyball AP192

1974, Oct. 12 ***Perf. 13x12***
C433 AP192 2p orange, bis & blk .25 .20

8th World Volleyball Championship. Perforation holes are of two sizes.

Souvenir Sheet

Mexico #O1, Colombia #130, Venezuela #22, Peru #C320, Brazil #992, Mexico #123 — AP193

Wmk. 300

1974, Oct. 26 Photo. ***Imperf.***
C434 AP193 10p multicolored 3.50 1.50

EXFILMEX 74, 5th Inter-American Philatelic Exhibition, Mexico City, Oct. 26-Nov. 3.
Exists with red omitted.

Felipe Carrillo Puerto AP194

1974, Nov. 8 ***Perf. 14***
C435 AP194 80c grn & gldn brn .25 .20

Birth centenary of Felipe Carrillo Puerto (1874-1924), politician and journalist.

Mask, Bat and Catcher's Mitt — AP195

1974, Nov. 29 Wmk. 350 ***Perf. 14***
C436 AP195 80c multi .25 .20

Mexican Baseball League, 50th anniversary.

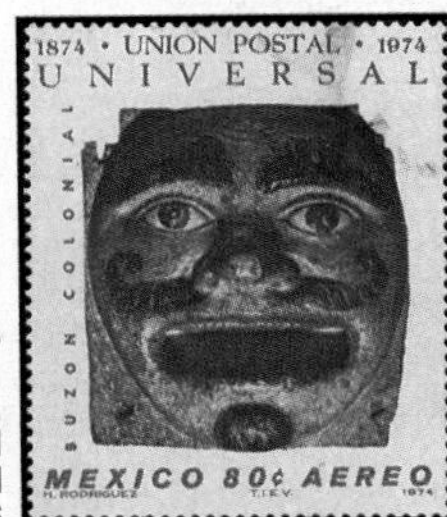

Man's Face, Mailbox, Colonial Period AP196

Design: 2p, Heinrich von Stephan, contemporary engraving.

1974, Dec. 13 Photo. Wmk. 300
C437 AP196 80c multicolored .25 .20
C438 AP196 2p green & ocher .25 .20

Centenary of Universal Postal Union.

Art and Science Type of 1971

Designs: No. C439, Mayan mural (8th century), Bonampak, Chiapas. No. C440, First musical score printed in Mexico, 1556. No. C441, Miguel Lerdo de Tejada (1869-1941), composer. No. C442, Silvestre Revueltas (1899-1940), composer (bronze bust). No. C443, Angela Peralta (1845-1883), singer.

Imprint includes "1974"

1974, Dec. 20 Wmk. 300
C439 AP161 80c multi .25 .20
C440 AP161 80c multi .25 .20
C441 AP161 80c multi .25 .20
C442 AP161 80c multi .25 .20
C443 AP161 80c multi .25 .20
Nos. C439-C443 (5) 1.25 1.00

Types of 1950-56

Designs (as 1950-56 issues): 40c, San Luis Potosi, head. 60c, Leon Guzman and Ignacio Ramirez. 1.60p, Chiapas, Mayan bas-relief. 1.90p, Guerrero, Acapulco waterfront. 4.30p, Oaxaca, dance. 5.20p, Guerrero, view of Taxco. 5.60p, Michoacan, masks. 50p, Valentin Gomez Farias and Melchor Ocampo.

Engraved (40c), Photogravure
Perf. 11 (40c, 1.60p), 14

1975 Wmk. 300

C444	AP81	40c	bluish gray	.35	.20
C445	AP92	60c	yellow grn	.90	.30
C446	AP81	1.60p	red	3.00	.35
C447	AP81	1.90p	rose red	3.00	.35
C448	AP81	4.30p	ultra	1.00	.25
C449	AP81	5.20p	purple	1.75	.40
C450	AP81	5.60p	blue grn	2.25	.50
C451	AP92	50p	dk bl & brick red	15.00	3.50
	Nos. C444-C451 (8)			27.25	5.85

Women's Year Emblem — AP199

1975, Jan. 3 Wmk. 300 ***Perf. 14***
C456 AP199 1.60p brt pink & blk .25 .20

International Women's Year 1975.

Declaration, UN Emblem, Mexican Flag AP200

1975, Feb. 7 Photo. Wmk. 300
C457 AP200 1.60p multi .25 .20

Declaration of Economic Rights and Duties of Nations.

Balsa Raft "Acali" — AP201

1975, Mar. 7 Wmk. 300 ***Perf. 14***
C458 AP201 80c multicolored .25 .20

Trans-Atlantic voyage of the "Acali" from Canary Islands to Yucatan, May-Aug. 1973.

Dr. Miguel Jimenez, by I. Ramirez AP202

Miguel de Cervantes AP203

1975, Mar. 24 Unwmk. ***Perf. 14***
C459 AP202 2p multicolored .25 .20

Fifth World Gastroenterology Congress.

1975, Apr. 26 Photo. Unwmk.
C460 AP203 1.60p bl blk & dk car .25 .20

Third International Cervantes Festival, Guanajuato, Apr. 26-May 11.

Four-reales Coin, 1535 — AP204

1975, May 2
C461 AP204 1.60p bl, gold & blk .25 .20

Intl. Numismatic Convention, Mexico City, Mar. 28-30, 1974.

Salvador Novo, by Roberto Montenegro — AP205

1975, May 9
C462 AP205 1.60p multi .25 .20

Salvador Novo (1904-1974), author.

Mural, Siqueiros — AP206

1975, May 16
C463 AP206 1.60p multi .25 .20

David Alfaro Siqueiros (1896-1974), painter.

UN and IWY Emblems AP207

1975, June 19
C464 AP207 1.60p ultra & pink .25 .20

International Women's Year World Conference, Mexico City, June 19-July 2.

Mexico City Coat of Arms AP208

Unwmk.

1975, Aug. 1 Photo. *Perf. 14*

C465 AP208 1.60p multi .25 .20

650th anniv. of Tenochtitlan (Mexico City).

Domingo F. Sarmiento AP209

Teachers' Monument AP210

Unwmk.

1975, Aug. 9 Photo. *Perf. 14*

C466 AP209 1.60p brown & sl grn .25 .20

1st International Congress of Third World Educators, Acapulco, Aug. 5-9. Domingo Faustino Sarmiento (1811-1888), Argentinian statesman, writer and educator.

1975, Aug. 9

C467 AP210 4.30p green & ocher .35 .20

Mexican-Lebanese friendship. The monument in Mexico City, by I Naffa al Rozzi, shows Cadmus, a mythical Phoenician, teaching the alphabet.

7th Pan American Games' Emblem AP211

1975, Aug. 29

C468 AP211 1.60p multi .25 .20

Pan American Games, Mexico City, Oct. 13-26.

Dr. Atl, Self-portrait AP212

Unwmk.

1975, Oct. 3 Photo. *Perf. 14*

C469 AP212 4.30p multi .35 .20

Geraldo Murillo ("Dr. Atl," 1875-1924), painter and writer, birth centenary.

Globe and Traffic Circle — AP213

1975, Oct. 17

C470 AP213 1.60p bl, blk & gray .25 .20

15th World Road Congress, Mexico City, Oct. 12-26.

Type of 1950-52

Designs: 40c, San Luis Potosi, head. 60c, Leon Guzman & Ignacio Ramirez. 80c, Mexico City University stadium. 1p, Puebla, Half Moon dance. 1.60p, Chiapas, Mayan bas-relief. 5p, Queretaro, architecture. 5.60p, Michoacan, masks. 10p, Miguel Hidalgo. 20p, Modern building.

Engraved (40c, 1p), Photogravure
Perf. 11 (40c, 80c, 1p, 1.60p), 14

1975-76 Unwmk.

C471 AP81 40c bluish gray .35 .35
C471A AP92 60c yel grn 1,200.
C472 AP81 80c claret, II .60 .50
C473 AP81 1p grysh grn 1.00 .80
C474 AP81 1.60p red 1.75 1.00
C476 AP81 5p dk brn & org ('76) 1.50 1.00
a. 5p dark brown & red orange 2.00 2.00
C477 AP81 5.60p bluish grn ('76) 4.75 3.25
C479 AP81 10p blk & grn 4.00 2.50
C480 AP81 20p red & dl grn ('76) 7.50 4.00
Nos. C471,C472-C480 (8) 21.45 13.40

Bicycle and Export Emblem AP214

Designs: Export Emblem and 30c, Copper vase. 80c, Overalls. 1.90p, Oil valves. 2p, Books. 4p, Honey. 4.30p, Strawberry. 5p, Motor vehicles. 5.20p, Farm machinery. 5.60p, Cotton. 20p, Film. 50p, Cotton thread.

1975-82 Unwmk. Photo. *Perf. 14*

C486 AP214 30c copper ('76) .20 .20
C489 AP214 80c dull blue ('76) .25 .20
C491 AP214 1.60p black & org .35 .20
a. Thin paper ('81) 1.00 .20
C492 AP214 1.90p ver & dk grn .35 .20
C493 AP214 2p ultra & gold ('76) .65 .20
C495 AP214 4p yel bis & brn ('82) 1.25 .20
C496 AP214 4.30p brt pink & ol .50 .20
C497 AP214 5p dk bl & ocher ('76) 1.50 .20
C498 AP214 5.20p red & blk ('76) .75 .40
C499 AP214 5.60p yel grn & org ('76) .35 .20
C503 AP214 20p multi, thin paper ('81) 1.00 .20
C508 AP214 50p multi ('82) 4.00 2.00
Nos. C486-C508 (12) 11.15 4.40

See Nos. C594-C603.

Art and Science Type of 1971

Designs: No. C513, Title page of "Medical History of New Spain," by Francisco Hernandez, 1628. No. C514, Alfonso L. Herrera (1868-1942), biologist. No. C515, Title page, Aztec Herbal, 1552. No. C516, Arturo S. Rosenblueth (1900-1970). No. C517, Alfredo Augusto Duges (1826-1910) French-born naturalist.

Imprint includes "1975"

1975, Nov. 21 Unwmk. *Perf. 14*

C513 AP161 1.60p buff, red & blk .25 .20
C514 AP161 1.60p vio bl & multi .25 .20
C515 AP161 1.60p black & multi .25 .20
C516 AP161 1.60p gray & multi .25 .20
C517 AP161 1.60p green & multi .25 .20
a. Thin paper 400.00
Nos. C513-C517 (5) 1.25 1.00

Telephone AP216

60-peso Gold Coin, Oaxaca, 1917 AP217

1976, Mar. 10 Photo.

C518 AP216 1.60p gray & blk .25 .20

Centenary of first telephone call by Alexander Graham Bell, Mar. 10, 1876.

1976, Mar. 25 Photo. Unwmk.

C519 AP217 1.60p black, ocher & yel .25 .20

4th International Numismatic Convention, Mexico City, March 1976.

Rain God Tlaloc and Calles Dam AP218

1976, Mar. 29 *Perf. 14*

C520 AP218 1.60p vio brn & dk grn .25 .20

12th International Great Dams Congress, Mar. 29-Apr. 2.

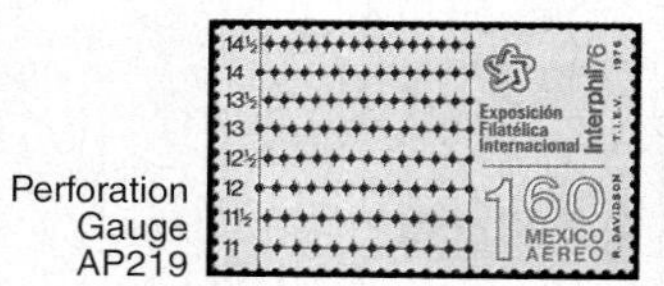

Perforation Gauge AP219

1976, May 7 Photo. Unwmk.

C521 AP219 1.60p blk, red & bl .25 .20

Interphil 76 International Philatelic Exhibition, Philadelphia, Pa., May 29-June 6.

Rainbow over City — AP220

1976, May 31 Unwmk. *Perf. 14*

C522 AP220 1.60p black & multi .25 .20

Habitat, UN Conf. on Human Settlements, Vancouver, Canada, May 31-June 11.

Liberty Bell AP221

"Peace" AP222

1976, July 4 Photo. *Perf. 14*

C523 AP221 1.60p ultra & red .25 .20

American Bicentennial.

1976, Aug. 3 Photo. *Perf. 14*

Design: "Peace" written in Chinese, Japanese, Hebrew, Hindi and Arabic.

C524 AP222 1.60p multi .25 .20

30th Intl. Cong. of Science and Humanities of Asia and North Africa, Mexico, Aug. 3-8.

Television Screen AP223

1976, Aug. 24 Photo. Unwmk.

C525 AP223 1.60p multi .25 .20

1st Latin-American Forum on Children's Television.

Luminescence

Fluorescent airmail stamps include Nos. C265, C265c, C288, C357-C358, C390-C415, C422-C423.

Airmail stamps issued on both ordinary and fluorescent paper include Nos. C220, C220D-C220E, C220G-C220H, C265b, C266-C268, C286.

Sky, Sun, Water and Earth AP224

1976, Nov. 8 Photo. *Perf. 14*

C526 AP224 1.60p multi .25 .20

World Conservation Day.

Art and Science Type of 1971

Designs: No. C527, Coatlicue, Mother of Earth, Aztec sculpture. No. C528, El Caballito, statue of Charles IV of Spain, by Manuel Tolsá. No. C529, Chief Tlahuicole, bronze statue by Manuel Vilar. No. C530, Today's God, Money, seated ceramic figure, by L. Ortiz Monasterio. No. C531, Signal, abstract sculpture by Angela Gurria.

Imprint includes "1976"

1976, Dec. 10 Photo. *Perf. 14*

C527 AP161 1.60p black & yel .25 .20
C528 AP161 1.60p blk & red brn .25 .20
C529 AP161 1.60p black & multi .25 .20
C530 AP161 1.60p car & multi .25 .20
C531 AP161 1.60p carmine & blk .25 .20
Nos. C527-C531 (5) 1.25 1.00

Score for El Pesebre by Casals AP225

1976, Dec. 29

C532 AP225 4.30p lt bl, blk & brn .35 .20

Pablo Casals (1876-1973), cellist and composer, birth centenary.

Mankind Destroyed by Nuclear Power AP226

1977, Feb. 14 Photo. *Perf. 14*
C533 AP226 1.60p multi .25 .20
a. Wmk. 300 50.00 40.00

10th anniv. of the Agreement of Tlatelolco, banning nuclear arms in Latin America.

Soccer AP227

Anniversary Emblem — AP228

1977, Aug. 23 Wmk. 300 *Perf. 14*
C534 AP227 1.60p multicolored .25 .20
C535 AP228 4.30p black, bl & yel .35 .20

Mexican Soccer Fed., 50th anniv.

Hands and Scales AP229

1977, Sept. 23 Photo. *Perf. 14*
C536 AP229 1.60p org, brn & blk .25 .20

Federal Council of Reconciliation and Arbitration, 50th anniversary.

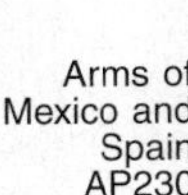

Arms of Mexico and Spain AP230

1.90p, Maps of Mexico & Spain. 4.30p, Pres. José Lopez Portillo & King Juan Carlos.

1977, Oct. 8 *Perf. 14*
C537 AP230 1.60p dull bl & blk .25 .20
C538 AP230 1.90p lt grn & maroon .25 .20
C539 AP230 4.30p tan, grn & brn .35 .20
Nos. C537-C539 (3) .85 .60

Resumption of diplomatic relations with Spain.

Tlaloc, the Rain God AP231

Ludwig van Beethoven AP232

Wmk. 300
1977, Nov. 4 Photo. *Perf. 14*
C540 AP231 1.60p multi .25 .20

National Central Observatory, centenary.

1977, Nov. 10 Photo.
C541 AP232 1.60p brt grn & brn .25 .20
C542 AP232 4.30p lilac rose & bl .30 .20

Tractor and Dam AP233

1977, Nov. 25 Photo. *Perf. 14*
C543 AP233 1.60p multi .25 .20

United Nations Desertification Conference.

Mexico City-Cuernavaca Highway — AP234

1977, Nov. 30
C544 AP234 1.60p multi .25 .20

25th anniversary of first national highway.

Arms of Campeche — AP235

1977, Dec. 3
C545 AP235 1.60p multi .25 .20

200th anniv. of the naming of Campeche.

Congress Emblem AP236

1977, Dec. 9
C546 AP236 1.60p multi .25 .20

20th World Congress for Education, Hygiene and Recreation, July 18-24, 1977.

Freighter Navimex AP237

1977, Dec. 16
C547 AP237 1.60p multi .25 .20

60th anniv. of National Merchant Marine.

Mayan Dancer, Jaina — AP238

Pre-Columbian Sculptures: No. C549, Aztec dance god. No. C550, Snake dancer, bas-relief. No. C551, Monte Alban, bas-relief. No. C552, Totonaca figurine.

1977, Dec. 26 *Perf. 14*
C548 AP238 1.60p sal, blk & car .25 .20
C549 AP238 1.60p lt & dk bl & blk .25 .20
C550 AP238 1.60p yel, blk & gray .25 .20
C551 AP238 1.60p bl grn, blk & grn .25 .20
C552 AP238 1.60p gray, blk & red brn .25 .20
Nos. C548-C552 (5) 1.25 1.00

Mexican art.

Tumor Clinic, by David A. Siqueiros — AP239

4.30p, La Raza Medical Center, by Diego Rivera.

1978, Jan. 19 Photo. Wmk. 300
C553 AP239 1.60p multi .25 .20
C554 AP239 4.30p multi .30 .20

Mexican Social Security Institute, 35th anniv.

Moorish Fountain — AP240

1978, Mar. 1 Photo. *Perf. 14*
C555 AP240 1.60p multi .25 .20

Founding of Chiapa de Corzo, Chiapas, 450th anniv.

Oil Industry Type of 1978

Designs: 1.60p, Gen. Lazaro Cardenas. 4.30p, Offshore oil rig.

Wmk. 300
1978, Mar. 18 Photo. *Perf. 14*
C556 A343 1.60p brt bl & lil rose .25 .20
C557 A343 4.30p bl, brt bl & blk .30 .20

Oil industry nationalization, 40th anniv.

Arms of Diego de Mazariegos AP241

Wmk. 300
1978, Apr. 3 Photo. *Perf. 14*
C558 AP241 1.60p pink, blk & pur .25 .20

400th anniversary of the founding of San Cristobal de las Casas, Chiapas, by Diego de Mazariegos.

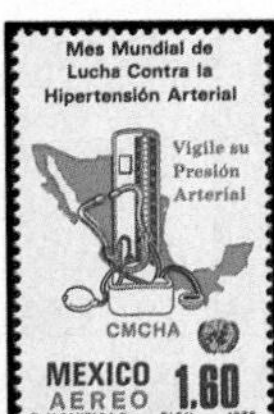

Blood Pressure Gauge, Map of Mexico AP242

Globe, Snake, Hand Holding Stethoscope AP243

1978, Apr. 7
C559 AP242 1.60p dk bl & car .25 .20
C560 AP243 4.30p org & dk bl .30 .20

Drive against hypertension and World Health Day.

X-ABC1 Plane AP244

1978, Apr. 15
C561 AP244 1.60p ultra & multi .25 .20
C562 AP244 4.30p ultra & multi .30 .20

1st Mexican airmail route, 50th anniv.

Globe, Cogwheel, UN Emblem — AP245

4.30p, Globe, flags, cogwheel, UN emblem.

1978, Apr. 21
C563 AP245 1.60p multi .25 .20
C564 AP245 4.30p multi .30 .20

World Conference on Technical Cooperation of Underdeveloped Countries.

Soccer — AP246

Designs: 1.90p, Goalkeeper catching ball. 4.30p, Soccer player.

Wmk. 300
1978, June 1 Photo. *Perf. 14*
C565 AP246 1.60p multi .25 .20
C566 AP246 1.90p multi .25 .20
C567 AP246 4.30p multi .35 .20
Nos. C565-C567 (3) .85 .60

11th World Cup Soccer Championship, Argentina, June 1-25.

Francisco (Pancho) Villa
AP247

1978, June 5

C568 AP247 1.60p multi .25 .20

Pancho Villa (1878-1923), revolutionary leader.

Mexico No. C6, Independence Monument, Washington Monument — AP248

1978, June 11

C569 AP248 1.60p ol gray & red .25 .20

50th anniversary of flight Mexico to Washington by Emilio Carranza (1905-1928).

Woman and Calendar Stone — AP249

Wmk. 300

1978, July 15 Photo. *Perf. 14*

C570 AP249 1.60p rose, blk & brn .25 .20
C571 AP249 1.90p brt grn, blk & brn .25 .20
C572 AP249 4.30p org, blk & brn .35 .20
Nos. C570-C572 (3) .85 .60

Miss Universe contest, Acapulco, July 1978.

Alvaro Obregón
AP250

1978, July 17

C573 AP250 1.60p multi .25 .20

Obregón (1880-1928), president of Mexico.

Geographical Institute Type of 1978

Institute emblem in different arrangements.

1978, July 21 Photo. Wmk. 300

C574 A344 1.60p emerald & blk .25 .20
C575 A344 4.30p ocher & blk .35 .20

Pan-American Institute for Geography and History, 50th anniversary.

Sun Rising over Ciudad Obregón
AP251

1978, Aug. 4 *Perf. 14*

C576 AP251 1.60p multi .25 .20

Founding of the city of Obregón, 50th anniv.

Mayan Figure, Castle and Pawn
AP252

Aristotle (384-322 B.C.), Philosopher
AP253

1978, Aug. 19 Photo. *Perf. 14*

C577 AP252 1.60p multi .25 .20
C578 AP252 4.30p multi .35 .20

World Youth Team Chess Championship, Ajedrez, Aug. 19-Sept. 7.

1978, Aug. 25

Design: 4.30p, Statue of Aristotle.

C579 AP253 1.60p multi .25 .20
C580 AP253 4.30p multi .35 .20

Mule Deer
AP254

Man's Head, Dove, UN Emblem
AP255

1978, Sept. 8 Photo. Wmk. 300

C581 AP254 1.60p shown .25 .20
C582 AP254 1.60p Ocelot .35 .20

Protected animals.

1978, Sept. 22 *Perf. 14*

4.30p, Woman's head, dove, UN emblem.

C583 AP255 1.60p ver, gray & blk .25 .20
C584 AP255 4.30p lil, gray & blk .35 .20

Anti-Apartheid Year.

Emblem — AP256

Wmk. 300

1978, Oct. 23 Photo. *Perf. 14*

C585 AP256 1.60p multi .25 .20

13th Congress of International Union of Architects, Mexico City, Oct. 23-27.

Dr. Rafael Lucio (1819-1886)
AP257

Franz Schubert, "Death and the Maiden"
AP258

1978, Nov. 13 Wmk. 350

C586 AP257 1.60p yellow grn .25 .20

11th International Anti-Leprosy Congress.

1978, Nov. 19 Photo. *Perf. 14*

C587 AP258 4.30p brn, grn & blk .35 .20

Schubert (1797-1828), Austrian composer.

Children, Christmas Decorations
AP259

Antonio Vivaldi
AP260

Wmk. 350

1978, Nov. 22 Photo. *Perf. 14*

C588 AP259 1.60p multi .25 .20

Christmas 1978.

1978, Dec. 1

C589 AP260 4.30p multi .35 .20

Antonio Vivaldi (1675-1741), Italian violinist and composer.

Wright Brothers' Flyer
AP261

Design: 4.30p, Flyer, different view.

1978, Dec. 17

C590 AP261 1.60p multi .25 .20
C591 AP261 4.30p multi .35 .20

75th anniversary of 1st powered flight.

Einstein and his Equation
AP262

Wmk. 300

1979, Apr. 20 Photo. *Perf. 14*

C592 AP262 1.60p multi .25 .20

Albert Einstein (1879-1955), theoretical physicist.

Rowland Hill — AP263

1979, Apr. 27

C593 AP263 1.60p multi .25 .20

Sir Rowland Hill (1795-1879), originator of penny postage.

Export Type of 1975

Designs: Export Emblem and 50c, Circuit board. 1.60p, Bicycle. 1.90p, Oil valves. 2.50p, Tomato. 4p, Honey. 5p, Motor vehicles. 10p, Citrus fruit. 50p, Cotton thread.

1979-81 Photo. Wmk. 300

C594 AP214 50c ocher & red brn .35 .20
C596 AP214 1.60p black & org .35 .20
C597 AP214 1.90p ver & dk grn ('81) .50 .40
C599 AP214 2.50p ver & grn .35 .20
C600 AP214 4p yel bis & brn ('81) .35 .25
C601 AP214 5p dk bl & dl org 4.50 .50
C602 AP214 10p grn & yel grn ('81) .90 .75
C603 AP214 50p multicolored 6.00 1.50
Nos. C594-C603 (8) 13.30 4.00

No. C600 exists with brown omitted.

Children, Child's Drawing — AP264

1979, May 16

C604 AP264 1.60p multi .25 .20

International Year of the Child.

Registered Letter from Mexico to Rome, 1880 — AP265

Wmk. 300

1979, June 7 Photo. *Perf. 14*

C605 AP265 1.60p multi .25 .20

MEPSIPEX '79, 3rd Intl. Exhibition of Elmhurst Philatelic Society, Mexico City, 6/7-10.

Sports Type of 1979

Designs: 1.60p, Games emblem. 4.30p, Symbolic flame and birds. 10p, Women gymnasts, horiz.

1979, June 15

C606 A348 1.60p multi .25 .20
C607 A348 4.30p multi .35 .20

Souvenir Sheet

Imperf

C608 A348 10p multi 2.00 2.00

No. C608 has simulated perforations.

University Type of 1979

Paintings: 1.60p, The Return of Quetzalcoatl, by Chavez Morado. 4.30p, Students Reaching for Culture, by Alfaro Siqueiros.

1979, July 10 *Perf. 14*
C609 A350 1.60p multi .25 .20
C610 A350 4.30p multi .35 .20

Messenger and UPU Emblem AP266

1979, July 27 **Photo.** **Wmk. 300**
C611 AP266 1.60p multi .25 .20

Cent. of Mexico's membership in UPU.

Sports Type of 1979

1979, Sept. 2 **Wmk. 300** *Perf. 14*
C612 A352 1.60p Tennis .25 .20
C613 A352 5.50p Swimming .35 .20

Souvenir Sheet

Imperf

C614 A352 10p Various sports 1.75 1.75

Tourism Type of 1979

#C615, Agua Azul Waterfall, Chiapas. #C616, King Coliman statue, Colima.

Wmk. 300

1979, Sept. 28 **Photo.** *Perf. 14*
C615 A353 1.60p multi .25 .20
C616 A353 1.60p multi .25 .20

Graphic Design AP267

1979, Oct. 14 **Photo.** **Wmk. 300**
C617 AP267 1.60p multi .25 .20

ICSID, 11th Congress and Assembly of the Intl. Industrial Design Council, Oct. 1979.

Mail Service Type of 1979

Designs: 1.60p, Martin Enriquez de Almanza, Viceroy of New Spain. 5.50p, King Philip II of Spain. 10p, Sailing ship, horiz.

1979, Oct. 26
C618 A354 1.60p multi .25 .20
C619 A354 5.50p multi .35 .20

Souvenir Sheet

Imperf

C620 A354 10p multi 4.50 1.50

#C620 contains stamp with simulated perfs.

Early Lamp — AP268

1979, Oct. 21 **Wmk. 300**
C621 AP268 1.60p multi .25 .20

Centenary of invention of electric light.

Union Emblem AP269

Wmk. 300

1979, Nov. 12 **Photo.** *Perf. 14*
C622 AP269 1.60p multi .25 .20

Latin American Universities Union, 8th general assembly.

Christmas Type of 1979

Design: 1.60p, Girl and Christmas tree.

1979, Nov. 15
C623 A355 1.60p multi .25 .20

Moon Symbol from Mexican Codex AP270

1979, Nov. 30
C624 AP270 2.50p multi .25 .20

Apollo 11 moon landing, 10th anniversary.

Monument Type of 1980

Stone Sculptures: 1.60p, Tlaloc, water god. 5.50p, Coyolxauqui, goddess.

1980, Feb. 16 **Photo.** *Perf. 14*
C625 A356 1.60p multi .25 .20
C626 A356 5.50p multi .35 .20

16th Century Church, Acolman AP271

16th Century Churches in: No. C628, Actopan Convent. No. C629, Tlayacapan. No. C630, Yanhuitlan. No. C631, Yuriria. No. C628 actually shows Tlayacapan; No. C629, Actopan convent (inscriptions reversed).

1980, Feb. 1
C627 AP271 1.60p multi .25 .20
C628 AP271 1.60p multi .25 .20
C629 AP271 1.60p multi .25 .20
C630 AP271 1.60p multi .25 .20
C631 AP271 1.60p multi .25 .20
Nos. C627-C631 (5) 1.25 1.00

Flora and Fauna Types of 1980

1980, Mar. 8 *Perf. 14*
C632 A357 1.60p Flamingo .25 .20
C633 A358 1.60p Vanilla plant .20 .20

Jules Verne AP272

Wmk. 300

1980, Mar. 24 **Photo.** *Perf. 14*
C634 AP272 5.50p blk & red brn .35 .20

Jules Verne (1828-1905) French science fiction writer.

Skeleton Smoking Cigar, UN Emblem AP273

1980, Apr. 7 *Perf. 14*
C635 AP273 1.60p multi .25 .20

World Health Day/Fight against cigarette smoking.

Costume Type

1980, Apr. 26 *Perf. 14*
C636 A359 1.60p Chiapaneca, Chiapas .25 .20

Items inscribed "MEXICO" and "correo aereo" picturing Emiliano Zapata are not postage stamps.

AIR POST OFFICIAL STAMPS

Nos. C4 and C3 Overprinted in Black or Red

1929 **Wmk. 156** *Perf. 12*
CO1 AP1 25c dk grn & gray brn 4.50 3.25
a. Without period 20.00 20.00
CO2 AP1 25c dk grn & gray brn (R) 4.00 *5.00*
a. Without period 21.00 21.00
CO2B AP1 25c brn car & gray brn 10.00 *12.50*
c. Without period 25.00 25.00
Nos. CO1-CO2B (3) 18.50 20.75
Set, never hinged 35.00

Types of Regular Issue of 1926 Overprinted in Red

1929, Oct. 15 **Unwmk.**
CO3 A90 2c black 75.00 *90.00*
CO4 A91 4c black 75.00 *90.00*
CO5 A90 5c black 75.00 *90.00*
CO6 A91 10c black 75.00 *90.00*
CO7 A92 20c black 75.00 *90.00*
CO8 A92 30c black 75.00 *90.00*
CO9 A92 40c black 75.00 *90.00*
Nos. CO3-CO9 (7) 525.00 630.00
Set, never hinged 1,100.

Horizontal Overprint

CO10 A93 1p black *2,250.* *2,250.*
Never hinged *4,000.*

#CO3-CO9 also exist with overprint reading up.

No. C26 Overprinted in Black

1930 **Wmk. 156**
CO11 AP4 20c black violet 1.10 *1.75*
Never hinged 2.25
a. Without period 20.00 *20.00*
b. Inverted overprint 18.00 *18.00*
c. As "a," inverted overprint 210.00 210.00

No. CO11 with red overprint is believed not to have been issued for postal purposes.

Plane over Mexico City OA1

1930 **Engr.**
CO12 OA1 20c gray black 6.00 6.00
CO13 OA1 35c lt violet 1.10 *1.90*
CO14 OA1 40c ol brn & dp bl 1.25 *1.75*
CO15 OA1 70c vio & ol gray 1.25 *1.75*
Nos. CO12-CO15 (4) 9.60 *11.40*
Set, never hinged 22.50

No. CO12 Surcharged in Red

1931
CO16 OA1 15c on 20c .85 *1.40*
Never hinged 1.60
a. Inverted surcharge 140.00
b. Double surcharge 140.00

No. C20 Overprinted

1932 *Roulетted 13, 13½*
CO17 AP3 5c light blue .80 *.90*
Never hinged 1.75

Air Post Stamps of 1927-32 Overprinted

On No. C1a

1932 **Unwmk.** *Perf. 12*
CO18 AP1 50c dk bl & cl 1,000. 1,000.
Never hinged 2,000.

On Nos. C2, C2a
Wmk. 156

CO19 AP1 50c dk bl & red brn 1.25 *1.50*
Never hinged 2.25
a. 50c dark blue & claret 1.40 *1.60*

See note after No. C2.

On Nos. C11 and C12

1932 *Perf. 12*
CO20 AP3 10c violet 22.50 *25.00*
Never hinged 45.00
CO21 AP3 15c carmine 350.00 *375.00*
Never hinged 700.00

On Nos. C21 to C23
Rouletted 13, 13½

CO22 AP3 10c violet .35 *.55*
CO23 AP3 15c carmine 1.40 *2.00*
CO24 AP3 20c brn olive 1.40 *2.00*

Nos. C20, C21 C23 and C25 Overprinted

1933-34 *Rouletted 13½*
CO25 AP3 5c light blue .30 *.55*
CO26 AP3 10c violet ('34) .30 *.90*
CO27 AP3 20c brown olive .75 *1.25*
CO28 AP3 50c red brn ('34) 1.25 *1.90*

On No. C2
Perf. 12

CO29 AP1 50c dk bl & red brn 1.10 *2.00*
a. 50c dark blue & claret 1.60 *2.50*

On No. C11
Perf. 12

CO30 AP3 10c violet ('34) 140.00 *175.00*
a. Double overprint *325.00*

Forgeries exist.

SPECIAL DELIVERY STAMPS

Motorcycle Postman SD1

1919 Unwmk. Engr. *Perf. 12*
E1 SD1 20c red & black 70.00 2.75

1923 Wmk. 156
E2 SD1 20c blk car & blk .30 .25

For overprint see No. E7

Messenger with Quipu — SD2

1934
E3 SD2 10c brn red & blue .30 .50

Indian Archer — SD3

Imprint: "Oficina Impresora de Hacienda Mexico."

1934 *Perf. 10x10½*
E4 SD3 10c black violet 1.50 .50

See Nos. E5-E6, E8-E9.

Redrawn

Imprint: "Talleres de Imp. de Est. y Valores-Mexico."

1938-41 Photo. *Perf. 14*
E5 SD3 10c slate violet .75 .25
a. Unwatermarked 50.00
E6 SD3 20c orange red ('41) .50 .15

Imperforate examples of No. E6 were not regularly issued.

No. E2 Overprinted "1940" in Violet

1940 Engr. *Perf. 12*
E7 SD1 20c red & black .40 .20

Catalogue values for unused stamps in this section, from this point to the end of the section, are for Never Hinged items.

Redrawn Archer Type of 1941

1944-47 Wmk. 272 Photo. *Perf. 14*
E8 SD3 20c orange red 1.40 .25

Wmk. 279
E9 SD3 20c orange red ('47) 1.75 .25

Special Delivery Messenger SD4

Messengers' Hands Transferring Letter — SD5

1950-51 Photo. Wmk. 279
E10 SD4 25c bright red .35 .20
E11 SD5 60c dk bl grn ('51) 2.00 .95

Redrawn

1951
E12 SD4 25c bright red 40.00 5.00

Sharper Impression, heavier shading; motorcycle sidecar ½mm from "s" of "centavos;" imprint wider, beginning under "n" of "inmediata."

Second Redrawing

1952
E13 SD4 25c bright red 15.00 2.00

Design 35½mm wide (33mm on Nos. E10 and E12); finer lettering at left, and height of letters in imprint reduced 50 per cent; three distinct lines in tires.

Redrawn Type of 1951

1954 Wmk. 300
E14 SD4 25c red orange .45 .20

Type of 1951

1954
E15 SD5 60c dk blue grn .55 *1.10*

Hands and Pigeon SD6

Plane Circling Globe SD7

1956 Wmk. 300 Photo. *Perf. 14*
E16 SD6 35c red lilac .25 .20
E17 SD7 80c henna brown .35 *1.40*

1962
E18 SD6 50c green .80 .20
E19 SD7 1.20p dark purple 1.25 *1.40*

1964 Wmk. 350
E20 SD6 50c green .65 .20
E21 SD7 1.20p dk purple 1.40 1.00

1973 Unwmk.
E22 SD6 50c green 3.50 3.25

Fluorescent printing on front or back consists of beehive pattern and diagonal inscription.

1975 Wmk. 300
E23 SD6 2p orange .20 *1.00*
E24 SD7 5p vio bl 1.25 .90

1976 Unwmk.
E25 SD6 2p red org .25 .40
E26 SD7 5p dk vio bl .35 1.00

Watch SD8

1976 Unwmk. Photo. *Perf. 14*
E27 SD8 2p org & blk .25 *1.00*

INSURED LETTER STAMPS

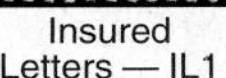

Insured Letters — IL1

Registered Mailbag — IL2

Safe — IL3

1935 Engr. Wmk. 156 *Perf. 10½*
G1 IL1 10c vermilion 1.75 .75
a. Perf. 10x10½
G2 IL2 50c dk bl 10.00 .60
G3 IL3 1p turq grn 1.25 .85
Nos. G1-G3 (3) 13.00 2.20

Nos. G1 and G4 were issued both with and without imprint.

Catalogue values for unused stamps in this section, from this point to the end of the section, are for Never Hinged items.

1944-45 Wmk. 272 *Perf. 10x10½*
G4 IL1 10c ver ('45) 12.50 1.50
G5 IL2 50c dk bl 2.00 .50
G6 IL3 1p turq grn 3.50 .65
Nos. G4-G6 (3) 18.00 2.65

1947 Wmk. 279 *Perf. 10x10½*
G7 IL1 10c vermilion 9.50 .85
G8 IL2 50c dark blue 12.00 1.50
G9 IL3 1p turq grn 4.00 1.00
Nos. G7-G9 (3) 25.50 3.35

Vault — IL4

1950-51 Photo. *Perf. 14*
G10 IL4 20c blue 3.75 .45
G11 IL4 40c purple .40 .20
G12 IL4 1p yel grn ('51) 1.75 .50
G13 IL4 5p dk bl & gray grn ('51) 1.40 1.00
G14 IL4 10p car & ultra ('51) 4.00 4.00
Nos. G10-G14 (5) 11.30 6.15

1954-71 Wmk. 300
G15 IL4 20c blue ('56) .25 .20
G16 IL4 40c lt pur ('56) .25 .20
G17 IL4 1p yel grn .40 .20
a. Size: 37x20¼mm ('71) 2.00 1.10
G18 IL4 5p bl & grn ('59) 1.25 1.00
G19 IL4 10p car & ultra ('63) 4.75 2.50
Nos. G15-G19 (5) 6.90 4.10

No. G17 measures 35x19½mm. Vertical measurement excludes imprint.

1967 Wmk. 350 *Perf. 14*
G21 IL4 40c light purple 2.00 1.50
G22 IL4 1p yellow green 2.00 1.50

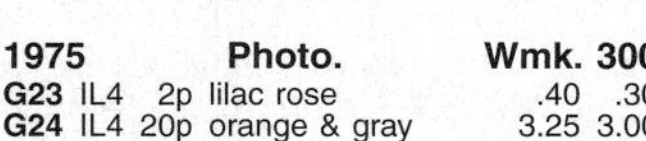

1975 Photo. Wmk. 300
G23 IL4 2p lilac rose .40 .30
G24 IL4 20p orange & gray 3.25 3.00

Padlock — IL5

1976-81 Unwmk. Photo. *Perf. 14*
G25 IL5 40c black & blue .30 .30
G26 IL5 1p black & blue .30 .30
G26A IL5 2p blk & bl ('81) .35 .30
G27 IL5 5p black & blue 1.50 .50
G28 IL5 10p black & blue 1.50 .50
G28A IL5 20p black & blue 2.25 .55
Nos. G25-G28A (6) 6.20 2.45

1979 Photo. Wmk. 300
G29 IL5 40c black & blue .90 .40
G30 IL5 1p black & blue .90 .30
G31 IL5 5p black & blue 1.50 .45
G32 IL5 10p black & blue 4.00 .40
G33 IL5 20p black & blue 4.00 .75
Nos. G29-G33 (5) 11.30 2.30

Perf. 14½x14
1983-86 Photo. Unwmk.
Size of Lock: 20x31mm
G36 IL5 5p black & blue 1.25 .40
G37 IL5 10p black & blue 1.00 .40
G38 IL5 20p black & blue 1.00 .40
G39 IL5 50p black & blue 2.50 .45
G40 IL5 100p blk & bl ('86) 5.00 3.00
Nos. G36-G40 (5) 10.75 4.65

This is an expanding set. Numbers will change if necessary.

POSTAGE DUE STAMPS

D1

1908 Engr. Wmk. 155 *Perf. 14*
J1 D1 1c blue 1.00 *3.00*
J2 D1 2c blue 1.00 *3.00*
J3 D1 4c blue 1.00 *3.00*
J4 D1 5c blue 1.00 *3.00*
J5 D1 10c blue 1.00 *3.00*
Nos. J1-J5 (5) 5.00 *15.00*

For overprints and surcharges see Nos. 381-385, 434-438, 466-470, 495-499, 593-607.

PORTE DE MAR STAMPS

These stamps were used to indicate the amount of cash to be paid to the captains of the mail steamers taking outgoing foreign mail.

PM2

PM3

1875 Unwmk. Litho. *Imperf.*
JX9 PM2 2c black .60 *50.00*
a. "5" added to make 25c 12.00 *100.00*
JX10 PM2 10c black .80 *30.00*
JX11 PM2 12c black .80 *50.00*
JX12 PM2 20c black 1.00 *50.00*
JX13 PM2 25c black 3.25 *50.00*
JX14 PM2 35c black 3.25 *60.00*
JX15 PM2 50c black 3.00 *60.00*
JX16 PM2 60c black 3.00 *75.00*
JX17 PM2 75c black 3.50 *75.00*
JX18 PM2 85c black 3.25 *100.00*
JX19 PM2 100c black 4.00 *100.00*
Nos. JX9-JX19 (11) 26.45 700.00

Same, Numerals Larger

No.	Type	Denom.	Unused	Used
JX20	PM2	5c black	1.00	*50.00*
JX21	PM2	25c black	1.65	*50.00*
JX22	PM2	35c black	250.00	
JX23	PM2	50c black	1.00	*50.00*
JX24	PM2	60c black	125.00	
JX25	PM2	100c black	.60	*100.00*
		Nos. JX20-JX25 (6)	379.25	

In Nos. JX9-JX19 the figures of value are 7mm high and "CENTAVOS" is 7½mm long. On Nos. JX20-JX25 the figures of value are 8mm high and "CENTAVOS" is 9½mm long.

Nos. JX9-JX25 exist with overprints of district names.

Counterfeits exist of Nos. JX9-JX31.

1879

No.	Type	Denom.	Unused
JX26	PM3	2c brown	.50
JX27	PM3	5c yellow	.50
JX28	PM3	10c red	.50
JX29	PM3	25c blue	.50
JX30	PM3	50c green	.50
JX31	PM3	100c violet	.50
		Nos. JX26-JX31 (6)	3.00

Nos. JX26-JX31 were never put in use.

Nos. JX26-JX31 were printed on paper watermarked "ADMINISTRACION GENERAL DE CORREOS MEXICO." Approximately ¾ of the stamps do not show any of the watermark.

Stamps of this design were never issued. Examples appeared on the market in 1884. Value, set, $22.

All were printed in same sheet of 49 (7x7). Sheet consists of 14 of 10c; 7 each of 25c, 35c, 50c; 4 each of 60c, 85c; 3 each of 75c, 100c. There are four varieties of 10c, two of 25c, 35c and 50c.

OFFICIAL STAMPS

Hidalgo — O1

Wove or Laid Paper

1884-93 Unwmk. Engr. *Perf. 12*

No.	Type	Description	Unused	Used
O1	O1	red	1.40	1.00
a.		Vert. pair, imperf. betwn.	120.00	
O1B	O1	scarlet ('85)	1.40	1.00
O2	O1	olive brn ('87)	.90	.70
a.		Horiz. pair, imperf. betwn.	—	
b.		Blue ruled lines on paper		
O3	O1	orange ('88)	2.50	.90
a.		Vert. pair, imperf. betwn.	110.00	
b.		Perf. 11	15.00	12.00
O4	O1	blue grn ('93)	1.40	.80
a.		Imperf., pair	15.00	12.00
b.		Perf. 11	15.00	12.00
		Nos. O1-O4 (5)	7.60	4.40

Pin-perf. 6

No.	Type	Description	Unused	Used
O5	O1	olive brown ('87)	100.00	50.00

Wmk. "Correos E U M" on every Vertical Line of Ten Stamps (152)

1894 *Perf. 5½*

No.	Type	Description	Unused	Used
O6	O1	ultra	3.00	2.75
a.		Vert. pair, imperf. horiz.	35.00	
b.		Imperf., pair	45.00	

Perf. 11, 12

No.	Type	Description	Unused	Used
O7	O1	ultra	1.75	1.60

Perf. 5½x11, 11x5½

No.	Type	Description	Unused	Used
O9	O1	ultra	12.00	8.00
		Nos. O6-O9 (3)	16.75	12.35

Regular Issues with Handstamped Overprint in Black

1895 Wmk. 152 *Perf. 12*

No.	Type	Description	Unused	Used
O10	A20	1c green	17.50	6.00
O11	A20	2c carmine	20.00	6.00
O12	A20	3c orange brn	17.50	6.00
O13	A21	4c red orange	26.00	12.00
a.		4c orange	42.50	14.00
O14	A22	5c ultra	35.00	12.00
O15	A23	10c lilac rose	32.50	3.00
O16	A21	12c olive brn	70.00	30.00
O17	A23	15c brt blue	42.50	18.00
O18	A23	20c brown rose	42.50	18.00
O19	A23	50c purple	90.00	42.50
O20	A24	1p brown	200.00	90.00
O21	A24	5p scarlet	475.00	250.00
O22	A24	10p deep blue	750.00	500.00
		Nos. O10-O22 (13)	1,818.	993.50

Similar stamps with red overprint were not officially placed in use. Nos. O10-O22 have a vertical grain or mesh to the paper.

Black Overprint

1896-97 Wmk. 153

No.	Type	Description	Unused	Used
O23	A20	1c green	60.00	10.00
O24	A20	2c carmine	60.00	12.00
O25	A20	3c orange brn	60.00	12.00
O26	A21	4c red orange	60.00	12.00
a.		4c orange	75.00	22.50
O27	A22	5c ultra	60.00	12.00
O28	A21	12c olive brn	80.00	30.00
O29	A23	15c brt blue	100.00	30.00
O29A	A23	50c purple	650.00	650.00
		Nos. O23-O29A (8)	1,130.	768.00

Nos. O23-O29A have a vertical grain or mesh to the paper.

Black Overprint

1897 Wmk. 154

No.	Type	Description	Unused	Used
O30	A20	1c green	100.00	30.00
O31	A20	2c scarlet	90.00	35.00
O33	A21	4c orange	125.00	60.00
O34	A22	5c ultra	100.00	35.00
O35	A21	12c olive brn	125.00	42.50
O36	A23	15c brt blue	160.00	42.50
O37	A23	20c brown rose	110.00	18.00
O38	A23	50c purple	150.00	30.00
O39	A24	1p brown	375.00	125.00
		Nos. O30-O39 (9)	1,335.	418.00

Nos. O30-O39 have a vertical grain or mesh to the paper.

Black Overprint

1898 Unwmk.

No.	Type	Description	Unused	Used
O40	A20	1c green	35.00	9.50
O41	A20	2c scarlet	35.00	9.50
O42	A20	3c orange brn	35.00	9.50
O43	A21	4c orange	60.00	12.00
O44	A22	5c ultra	60.00	20.00
O45	A23	10c lilac rose	650.00	500.00
O46	A21	12c olive brn	125.00	30.00
O47	A23	15c brt blue	125.00	30.00
O48	A23	20c brown rose	225.00	75.00
O48A	A23	50c purple	375.00	150.00
O48B	A24	10p deep blue		—
		Nos. O40-O48A (10)	1,725.	845.50

The existence of No. O45 has been questioned by specialists. The editors would like to see authenticated evidence of this stamp.

See note following No. 291.

Black Overprint

1900 Wmk. 155 *Perf. 14, 15*

No.	Type	Description	Unused	Used
O49	A25	1c green	37.50	2.50
O50	A26	2c vermilion	50.00	4.00
O51	A27	3c yellow brn	50.00	2.50
O52	A28	5c dark blue	50.00	4.50
O53	A29	10c violet & org	65.00	5.50
O54	A30	15c lavender & cl	65.00	5.50
O55	A31	20c rose & dk bl	75.00	2.50
O56	A32	50c red lil & blk	150.00	25.00
O57	A33	1p blue & blk	300.00	25.00
O58	A34	5p carmine & blk	575.00	75.00
		Nos. O49-O58 (10)	1,417.	152.00

Black Overprint

1903

No.	Type	Description	Unused	Used
O59	A25	1c violet	35.00	4.00
O60	A26	2c green	35.00	4.00
O61	A35	4c carmine	65.00	2.50
O62	A28	5c orange	65.00	13.00
O63	A29	10c blue & org	70.00	4.00
O64	A32	50c carmine & blk	200.00	25.00
		Nos. O59-O64 (6)	470.00	52.50

Regular Issues Overprinted

On Issues of 1899-1903

1910

No.	Type	Description	Unused	Used
O65	A26	2c green	175.00	6.50
O66	A27	3c orange brn	175.00	4.00
O67	A35	4c carmine	200.00	10.00
O68	A28	5c orange	225.00	50.00
O69	A29	10c blue & org	200.00	4.00
O70	A30	15c lav & claret	225.00	6.50
O71	A31	20c rose & dk bl	275.00	3.00
O72	A32	50c carmine & blk	375.00	35.00
O73	A33	1p blue & blk	575.00	125.00
O74	A34	5p carmine & blk	200.00	125.00
		Nos. O65-O74 (10)	2,625.	369.00

On Issue of 1910

1911

No.	Type	Description	Unused	Used
O75	A36	1c violet	5.00	5.00
O76	A37	2c green	3.75	2.25
O77	A38	3c orange brn	5.00	2.50
O78	A39	4c carmine	5.50	2.25
O79	A40	5c orange	12.50	7.00
O80	A41	10c blue & org	5.50	2.50
O81	A42	15c gray bl & cl	13.00	8.50
O82	A43	20c red & blue	10.00	2.50
O83	A44	50c red brn & blk	35.00	15.00
O84	A45	1p blue & blk	60.00	25.00
O85	A46	5p carmine & blk	300.00	125.00
		Nos. O75-O85 (11)	455.25	197.50

Nos. 500 to 505 Overprinted

1915 Unwmk. *Rouletted 14½*

No.	Type	Description	Unused	Used
O86	A57	1c violet	1.00	*2.00*
O87	A58	2c green	1.00	*2.00*
O88	A59	3c brown	1.25	*2.00*
O89	A60	4c carmine	1.00	*2.00*
O90	A61	5c orange	1.00	*2.00*
O91	A62	10c ultra	1.25	*2.00*
		Nos. O86-O91 (6)	6.50	12.00

All values are known with inverted overprint. All values exist imperforate and part perforate but were not regularly issued in these forms.

On Nos. 506 to 514

1915-16 *Perf. 12*

No.	Type	Description	Unused	Used
O92	A57	1c violet	1.50	*2.00*
O93	A58	2c green	1.50	*2.00*
O94	A59	3c brown	1.50	*2.00*
O95	A60	4c carmine	1.50	*2.00*
a.		"CEATRO"	21.00	*30.00*
O96	A61	5c orange	1.50	*2.00*
O97	A62	10c ultra, type II	1.50	*2.00*
a.		Double overprint	*475.00*	
O98	A63	40c slate	8.00	*14.50*
a.		Inverted overprint	24.00	*25.00*
b.		Double overprint	40.00	
O99	A64	1p brown & blk	10.00	*14.50*
a.		Inverted overprint	27.50	27.50
O100	A65	5p claret & ultra	60.00	*60.00*
a.		Inverted overprint	80.00	
		Nos. O92-O100 (9)	87.00	101.00

Nos. O98 and O99 exist imperforate but probably were not issued in that form.

Preceding Issues Overprinted in Red, Blue or Black

On No. O74

1916 Wmk. 155

No.	Type	Description	Unused	Used
O101	A34	5p carmine & blk	900.00	

On Nos. O75 to O85

No.	Type	Description	Unused	Used
O102	A36	1c violet	6.50	
O103	A37	2c green	1.25	
O104	A38	3c orange brn (Bl)	1.75	
O105	A39	4c carmine (Bl)	7.00	
O106	A40	5c orange (Bl)	1.75	
O107	A41	10c blue & org	1.75	
O108	A42	15c gray bl & cl (Bk)	1.75	
O109	A43	20c red & bl (Bk)	1.90	
O110	A44	50c red brn & blk	200.00	
O111	A45	1p blue & blk	11.00	
O112	A46	5p carmine & blk	*3,250.*	
		Nos. O102-O111 (10)	234.65	

No. O102 with blue overprint is a trial color. Counterfeits exist of Nos. O110, O112.

Nos. 608, 610 to 612, 615 and 616 Overprinted Vertically in Red or Black

Thick Paper

1918 Unwmk. *Rouletted 14½*

No.	Type	Description	Unused	Used
O113	A68	1c violet (R)	60.00	35.00
O114	A69	2c gray grn (R)	65.00	35.00
O115	A70	3c bis brn (R)	60.00	35.00
O116	A71	4c carmine (Bk)	60.00	35.00
O117	A74	20c rose (Bk)	125.00	90.00
O118	A75	30c gray brn (R)	190.00	175.00

On Nos. 622-623
Medium Paper
Perf. 12

No.	Type	Description	Unused	Used
O119	A72	5c ultra (R)	40.00	40.00
O120	A73	10c blue (R)	35.00	25.00
a.		Double overprint	400.00	*400.00*
		Nos. O113-O120 (8)	635.00	470.00

Overprinted Horizontally in Red

On Nos. 626-628
Thin Paper

No.	Type	Description	Unused	Used
O121	A63	40c violet (R)	35.00	27.50
O122	A64	1p bl & blk (R)	85.00	70.00
O123	A65	5p grn & blk (R)	*575.00*	*600.00*
		Nos. O121-O123 (3)	*695.00*	*697.50*

Nos. 608 and 610 to 615 Overprinted Vertically Up in Red or Black

Thick Paper

1919 *Rouletted 14½*

No.	Type	Description	Unused	Used
O124	A68	1c dull vio (R)	6.00	6.00
a.		"OFICIAN"	70.00	*80.00*
O125	A69	2c gray grn (R)	9.50	3.50
a.		"OFICIAN"	70.00	*80.00*
O126	A70	3c bis brn (R)	14.00	6.00
a.		"OFICIAN"	95.00	*100.00*
O127	A71	4c car (Bk)	29.00	13.00
c.		"OFICIAN"		—
O127A	A72	5c ultra	200.00	125.00
b.		"OFICIAN"	*500.00*	
O128	A73	10c blue (R)	9.50	2.50
a.		"OFICIAN"	85.00	60.00
O129	A74	20c rose (Bk)	60.00	47.50
a.		"OFICIAN"		140.00

On Nos. 618, 622
Perf. 12

No.	Type	Description	Unused	Used
O130	A68	1c dull violet (R)	47.50	47.50
a.		"OFICIAN"	140.00	100.00
O131	A72	5c ultra (R)	47.50	22.50
a.		"OFICIAN"	140.00	100.00

Overprinted Horizontally On Nos. 626-627
Thin Paper

No.	Type	Description	Unused	Used
O132	A63	40c violet (R)	47.50	35.00
O133	A64	1p bl & blk (R)	60.00	50.00
		Nos. O124-O133 (11)	530.50	358.50

Nos. 608 to 615 and 617 Overprinted Vertically down in Black, Red or Blue

Size: 17½x3mm

1921 ***Rouletted 14½***

O134 A68 1c gray (Bk) 30.00 12.00
a. 1c dull violet (Bk) 17.00 7.00
O135 A69 2c gray grn (R) 5.00 3.00
O136 A70 3c bis brn (R) 8.50 4.50
O137 A71 4c carmine (Bk) 27.50 21.00
O138 A72 5c ultra (R) 25.00 12.00
O139 A73 10c bl, reading down (R) 32.50 12.00
a. Overprint reading up 60.00 60.00
O140 A74 20c rose (Bl) 47.50 27.50
O141 A75 30c gray blk (R) 25.00 25.00

Overprinted Horizontally On Nos. 626-628
Perf. 12

O142 A63 40c violet (R) 32.50 32.50
O143 A64 1p bl & blk (R) 25.00 25.00
O144 A65 5p grn & blk (Bk) 600.00 *600.00*
Nos. O134-O144 (11) *858.50 774.50*

Nos. 609 to 615 Overprinted Vertically Down in Black

1921-30 ***Rouletted 14½***

O145 A68 1c gray 5.00 2.50
a. 1c lilac gray 1.00 .70
O146 A69 2c gray green 1.75 .70
O147 A70 3c bister brn .80 .70
a. "OFICAL" 47.50 25.00
b. "OIFCIAL" 47.50 25.00
c. Double overprint 140.00
O148 A71 4c carmine 22.50 2.50
O149 A72 5c ultra 1.00 .70
O150 A73 10c blue 1.00 .70
a. "OFICAIL" 50.00
O151 A74 20c brown rose 9.00 *9.50*
a. 20c rose 5.00 2.50

On No. 625
Perf. 12

O152 A75 30c gray black 7.25 2.50

Overprinted Horizontally On Nos. 626, 628

O153 A63 40c violet 7.00 5.00
a. "OFICAL" 60.00 60.00
b. "OICIFAL" 60.00 60.00
c. Inverted overprint 90.00 *125.00*
O154 A65 5p grn & blk ('30) 375.00 *375.00*
Nos. O145-O154 (10) 430.30 *399.80*

Overprinted Vertically Down in Red On Nos. 609, 610, 611, 613 and 614

1921-24 ***Rouletted 14½***

O155 A68 1c lilac 1.60 1.00
O156 A69 2c gray green 1.50 .90
O157 A70 3c bister brown 4.00 1.00
O158 A72 5c ultra 1.60 .80
O159 A73 10c blue 35.00 3.50
a. Double overprint

On Nos. 624-625
Perf. 12

O160 A74 20c rose 7.25 1.60
O161 A75 30c gray black 19.00 5.00

Overprinted Horizontally On Nos. 626-628

O162 A63 40c violet 14.00 7.50
a. Vert. pair, imperf. btwn.
O163 A64 1p blue & blk 35.00 25.00
O164 A65 5p green & blk 300.00 *300.00*

Overprinted Vertically Down in Blue on No. 612
Rouletted 14½

O165 A71 4c carmine 7.00 3.50
Nos. O155-O165 (11) 425.95 *349.80*

Same Overprint Vertically Down in Red on Nos. 635 and 637

1926-27 ***Rouletted 14½***

O166 A80 3c bis brn, ovpt. horiz. 12.00 12.00
a. Period omitted 30.00 30.00
O167 A82 5c orange 27.50 *30.00*

Same Overprint Vertically Down in Blue or Red 0n Nos. 650, 651, 655 and 656
Wmk. 156

O168 A79 2c scarlet (Bl) 20.00 20.00
a. Overprint reading up 30.00 30.00
O169 A80 3c bis brn, ovpt. horiz. (R) 5.00 5.00
a. Inverted overprint 60.00
O170 A85 10c claret (Bl) 35.00 16.00
O171 A84 20c deep blue (R) 14.00 12.00
a. Overprint reading up 14.00 12.00

Overprinted Horizontally in Red On Nos. 643, 646-649
Perf. 12

O172 A81 4c green 6.00 6.00
O173 A83 30c dk grn 6.00 6.00
O174 A63 40c violet 16.00 16.00
a. Inverted overprint 80.00
O175 A87 50c olive brn 1.50 1.50
a. 50c yellow brown 18.00 18.00
O176 A88 1p red brn & bl 15.00 15.00
Nos. O168-O176 (9) 118.50 97.50

Same Overprint Horizontally on No. 651, Vertically Up on Nos. 650, 653-656, 666, RA1

1927-31 ***Rouletted 14½***

O177 PT1 1c brown ('31) .70 *1.00*
O178 A79 2c scarlet .70 *1.00*
a. "OFICAIL" 30.00 30.00
b. Overprint reading down 1.50 *2.00*
O179 A80 3c bis brn 2.00 1.50
a. "OFICAIL" 40.00 30.00
O180 A82 4c green 1.50 1.00
a. "OFICAIL" 40.00 40.00
b. Overprint reading down 10.00 2.00
O181 A82 5c orange 4.00 3.00
a. Overprint reading down 4.00 2.50
O182 A94 8c orange 12.00 8.00
a. Overprint reading down 7.00 6.00
O183 A85 10c lake 2.00 2.00
a. Overprint reading down 2.00 2.00
O184 A84 20c dark blue 10.00 4.00
a. "OFICAIL" 40.00 40.00
b. Overprint reading down 20.00 20.00
Nos. O177-O184 (8) 32.90 21.50

Overprinted Vertically Up on #O186, Horizontally On Nos. 643 and 645 to 649

1927-33 ***Perf. 12***

O185 A81 4c green 6.00 5.00
a. Inverted overprint 30.00 30.00
O186 A85 10c brown lake 55.00 45.00
O187 A83 30c dark green 1.40 1.00
a. Inverted overprint 30.00 30.00
b. Pair, tête bêche overprints 35.00 35.00
c. "OFICAIL" 35.00 35.00
O188 A63 40c violet 12.00 8.00
O189 A87 50c olive brn ('33) 3.25 *4.00*
O190 A88 1p red brn & bl 24.00 20.00
Nos. O185-O190 (6) 101.65 83.00

The overprint on No. O186 is vertical.

Nos. 320, 628, 633 Overprinted Horizontally

On Stamp No. 320

1927-28 **Wmk. 155** ***Perf. 14, 15***

O191 A46 5p car & blk (R) 175.00 *250.00*
O192 A46 5p car & blk (Bl) 175.00 *250.00*

Unwmk. ***Perf. 12***

O193 A65 5p grn & blk (Bk) 375.00 *500.00*
a. Inverted overprint — —
O194 A78 10p blk brn & blk (Bl) 200.00 *300.00*

No. 320 Overprinted Horizontally

Wmk. 155 ***Perf. 14***

O195 A46 5p carmine & blk 300.00

Nos. 650 and 655 Overprinted Horizontally

1928-29 **Wmk. 156** ***Rouletted 14½***
Size: 16x2½mm

O196 A79 2c dull red 18.00 12.00
O197 A85 10c rose lake 27.50 12.00

Nos. RA1, 650-651, 653-656 Overprinted

1932-33

O198 PT1 1c brown .70 *1.00*
O199 A79 2c dull red .80 *1.00*
O200 A80 3c bister brn 3.00 3.00
O201 A82 4c green 10.00 8.00
O202 A82 5c orange 12.00 8.00
O203 A85 10c rose lake 3.25 3.00
O204 A84 20c dark blue 15.00 10.00
a. Double overprint *200.00 90.00*
Nos. O198-O204 (7) 44.75 34.00

Nos. 651, 646-649 Overprinted Horizontally

1933 ***Rouletted 14½***

O205 A80 3c bister brn 3.00 3.00

Perf. 12

O206 A83 30c dk green 8.00 3.00
O207 A63 40c violet 15.00 6.00
O208 A87 50c olive brn 2.50 3.00
a. "OFICIAL OFICIAL" 50.00 50.00
O209 A88 1p red brn & bl, type I 3.00 3.00
a. Type II 2.75 *3.50*

Overprinted Vertically On No. 656
Rouletted 14½

O210 A84 20c dark blue 18.00 10.00
Nos. O205-O210 (6) 49.50 28.00

Nos. RA1, 651, 653, 654, 683 Overprinted Horizontally

1934-37 ***Rouletted 14½***
Size: 13x2mm

O211 PT1 1c brown 5.00 *6.00*
O212 A80 3c bister brn .70 .70
O213 A82 4c green 12.00 10.00
O214 A82 5c orange .70 .70
O215 A96 15c dk blue ('37) 1.00 1.00
Nos. O211-O215 (5) 19.40 18.40

See No. O217a.

Same Overprint on Nos. 687A-692

1934-37 ***Perf. 10½***

O216 PT1 1c brown ('37) 1.00 *1.25*
O217 A79 2c scarlet 1.00 *1.50*
a. On No. 650 (error) 350.00
b. Double overprint 275.00
O218 A82 4c green ('35) 1.40 1.60
O219 A85 10c brown lake 1.00 1.00
O220 A84 20c dk blue ('37) 1.25 1.25
O221 A83 30c dk bl grn ('37) 2.00 2.00

On Nos. 647 and 649
Perf. 12, 11½x12

O222 A63 40c violet 3.00 3.50
O223 A88 1p red brn & bl (I) 5.00 *6.00*
a. Type II 4.00 4.00
Nos. O216-O223 (8) 15.65 18.10

On Nos. 707 to 709, 712, 715, 716, 717, 718 and 719

O224 A108 1c orange 2.00 *4.00*
O225 A109 2c green 1.25 *2.00*
O226 A110 4c carmine 1.25 *1.40*
O227 A112 10c violet 1.25 *2.50*
O228 A114 20c ultra 1.60 *2.50*
O229 A115 30c lake 2.00 *4.00*
O230 A116 40c red brown 2.50 *4.00*
O231 A117 50c black 2.75 *2.75*
O232 A118 1p dk brn & org 8.00 *12.00*
Nos. O224-O232 (9) 22.60 *35.15*

PARCEL POST STAMPS

Railroad Train PP1

1941 **Photo.** **Wmk. 156** ***Perf. 14***

Q1 PP1 10c brt rose 2.75 .35
Q2 PP1 20c dk vio bl 1.75 .35

1944-46 **Wmk. 272**

Q3 PP1 10c brt rose 1.75 1.00
Q4 PP1 20c dk vio bl ('46) 5.00 2.50

1947-49 **Wmk. 279**

Q5 PP1 10c brt rose 1.25 .60
Q6 PP1 20c dk vio bl ('49) 1.60 .60

Streamlined Locomotive PP2

1951

Q7 PP2 10c rose pink 5.00 .40
Q8 PP2 20c blue violet 4.00 .70

1954 **Wmk. 300**

Q9 PP2 10c rose pink 4.25 .60
Q10 PP2 20c blue violet 4.25 1.50

POSTAL TAX STAMPS

Morelos Monument — PT1

Rouletted 14½

1925 **Engr.** **Wmk. 156**

RA1 PT1 1c brown .35 .20
a. Imperf. 30.00

1926 ***Perf. 12***

RA2 PT1 1c brown .75 *5.00*
a. Booklet pane of 2 12.00

1925 **Unwmk.** ***Rouletted 14½***

RA3 PT1 1c brown 75.00 19.00

It was obligatory to add a stamp of type PT1 to the regular postage on every article of domestic mail matter. The money obtained from this source formed a fund to combat a plague of locusts.

In 1931, 1c stamps of type PT1 were discontinued as Postal Tax stamps. It was subsequently used for the payment of postage on drop letters (announcement cards and unsealed circulars) to be delivered in the city of cancellation. See No. 687A.

For overprints see Nos. O177, O198, O211, O216, RA4.

Red Overprint

1929 **Wmk. 156**

RA4 PT1 1c brown .35 .20
a. Overprint reading down 75.00 75.00

There were two settings of this overprint. They may be distinguished by the two lines being spaced 4mm or 6mm apart.

The money from sales of this stamp was devoted to child welfare work.

Mother and Child — PT3

1929 **Litho.** ***Rouletted 13, 13½***

RA5 PT3 1c violet .35 .20

PT4

PT5

1929 **Unwmk.**

Size: 18x24½mm

RA6 PT4 2c deep green .40 .20
RA7 PT4 5c brown .40 .20
a. Imperf., pair 60.00 60.00

For surcharges see Nos. RA10-RA11.

1929 **Size: 19x25¼mm**

Two types of 1c:
Type I — Background lines continue through lettering of top inscription. Denomination circle hangs below second background line. Paper and gum white.
Type II — Background lines cut away behind some letters. Circle rests on second background line. Paper and gum yellowish.

RA8 PT5 1c violet, type I .35 .20
a. Booklet pane of 4 10.00
b. Booklet pane of 2 18.00
c. Type II .40 .20
d. Imperf., pair 50.00 50.00
RA9 PT5 2c deep green .65 .20
a. Imperf., pair 12.00

The use of these stamps, in addition to the regular postage, was compulsory. The money obtained from their sale was used for child welfare work.
For surcharge see No. RA12.

Nos. RA6, RA7, RA9 Surcharged

1930
RA10 PT4 1c on 2c dp grn .75 .40
RA11 PT4 1c on 5c brown 1.00 .60
RA12 PT5 1c on 2c dp grn 2.00 1.00
Nos. RA10-RA12 (3) 3.75 2.00

Used stamps exist with surcharge double or reading down.

No. 423 Overprinted

1931, Jan. 30 **Wmk. 155** ***Perf. 14***
RA13 A36 1c dull violet .40 .40
a. "PRO INFANCIA" double 50.00

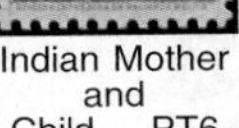
Indian Mother and Child — PT6

Mosquito Attacking Man — PT7

Wmk. 156
1934, Sept. 1 **Engr.** ***Perf. 10½***
RA13B PT6 1c dull orange .30 .20

1939 **Photo.** **Wmk. 156** ***Perf. 14***
RA14 PT7 1c Prus blue 1.50 .20
a. Imperf. 3.00 3.00

This stamp was obligatory on all mail, the money being used to aid in a drive against malaria.
See Nos. RA16, RA19.

Miguel Hidalgo y Costilla PT8

Learning Vowels PT9

1941
RA15 PT8 1c brt carmine .45 .20

Type of 1939
1944 **Wmk. 272** ***Perf. 14***
RA16 PT7 1c Prus blue 1.00 .20

1946 **Photo.** **Wmk. 279**
RA17 PT9 1c black brown .45 .20
a. 1c green black 1.00 1.00

1947 **Wmk. 272**
RA18 PT9 1c black brown 65.00 5.00

Type of 1939
Wmk. 279
RA19 PT7 1c Prus blue 3.50 .30

PROVISIONAL ISSUES

During the struggle led by Juarez to expel the Emperor Maximilian, installed June, 1864 by Napoleon III and French troops, a number of towns when free of Imperial forces issued provisional postage stamps. Maximilian was captured and executed June 19, 1867, but provisional issues continued current for a time pending re-establishment of Republican Government.

Campeche

A southern state in Mexico, comprising the western part of the Yucatan peninsula.

A1

White Paper
Numerals in Black

1876 **Handstamped** ***Imperf.***
1 A1 5c gray blue & blue *2,000.*
2 A1 25c gray blue & blue *1,100.*
3 A1 50c gray blue & blue *4,500.*

The stamps printed in blue-black and blue on yellowish paper, formerly listed as issued in 1867, are now known to be an unofficial production of later years. They are reprints, but produced without official sanction.

Chiapas

A southern state in Mexico, bordering on Guatemala and the Pacific Ocean.

A1

1866 **Typeset**
1 A1 ½r blk, *gray bl* *2,000.* *1,300.*
2 A1 1r blk, *lt grn* *850.*
3 A1 2r blk, *rose* *900.*
4 A1 4r blk, *lt buff* *2,000.*
a. Vertical half used as 2r on cover *3,000.*
5 A1 8r blk, *rose* *15,000.*
a. Quarter used as 2r on cover *4,000.*
b. Half used as 4r on cover *5,000.*

Chihuahua

A city of northern Mexico and capital of the State of Chihuahua.

A1

A2

1872 **Handstamped**
1 A1 12(c) black *3,000.*
2 A2 25(c) black *3,000.*

Cuautla

A town in the state of Morelos.

A1

1867 **Handstamped**
1 A1 (2r) black *7,000.*

All known examples on cover are uncanceled. Examples are known without the "73" inside the oval.

Cuernavaca

A city of Mexico, just south of the capital, and the capital of the State of Morelos.

A1

1867 **Handstamped**
1 A1 (1r) black *1,750.*
2 A1 (2r) black *40,000.*

No. 1 was canceled at Cuernavaca with the district name overprint. Supplies of overprinted stamps were sent to the Tetecala and Yquala sub-offices, where they were canceled with the usual local postmarks.
No. 2 was created by doubling the impression of the basic stamp and applying the district name overprint twice.
Unused examples of Nos. 1 and 2 do not exist.
Counterfeits exist.

Guadalajara

A city of Mexico and capital of the State of Jalisco.

A1

Dated "1867"
1st Printing
Medium Wove Paper

1867 **Handstamped** ***Imperf.***
1 A1 Medio r blk, *white* 350.00 250.00
2 A1 un r blk, *gray bl* 750.00 350.00
a. Overprinted "Cd. Guzman" *1,000.*
3 A1 un r blk, *dk bl* 450.00
4 A1 un r blk, *white* 250.00
a. Overprinted "Cd. Guzman" *750.00*
5 A1 2r blk, *dk grn* 250.00 21.00
a. Overprinted "Cd. Guzman" *500.00*
6 A1 2r blk, *white* 125.00
a. Overprinted "Cd. Guzman" *400.00*
b. Double print 250.00
7 A1 4r blk, *rose* 250.00 *300.00*
a. Half used as 2r on cover 500.00
b. Overprinted "Cd. Guzman" *900.00*
8 A1 4r blk, *white* 500.00
a. Half used as 2r on cover 2,500.
9 A1 un p blk, *lilac* 250.00 *300.00*

Serrate Perf.
10 A1 un r blk, *gray bl* 400.00
11 A1 2r blk, *dk grn* 700.00
12 A1 4r blk, *rose* 350.00
12A A1 un p blk, *lilac* *1,750.*

2nd Printing
No Period after "2" or "4"
Thin Quadrille Paper
Imperf
13 A1 2r blk, *green* 30.00 20.00
a. Half used as 1r on cover 400.00

Serrate Perf.
14 A1 2r blk, *green* 225.00

Thin Laid Batonné Paper
Imperf
15 A1 2r blk, *green* 45.00 24.00

Serrate Perf.
16 A1 2r blk, *green* 225.00

3rd Printing
Capital "U" in "Un" on 1r, 1p
Period after "2" and "4"
Thin Wove Paper
Imperf
16A A1 Un r blk, *white* 125.00
17 A1 Un r blk, *blue* 90.00
17A A1 Un r blk, *lilac* 100.00
18 A1 2r blk, *rose* 50.00
18A A1 4r blk, *blue* 500.00 *1,000.*
18B A1 Un p blue 1,750.

Serrate Perf.
19 A1 Un r blk, *blue* 300.00
19A A1 2r blk, *rose* *750.00*
19B A1 4r blue *500.00*

Thin Quadrille Paper
Imperf
20 A1 2r blk, *rose* 42.50 42.50
21 A1 4r blk, *blue* 15.00 30.00
22 A1 4r blk, *white* 200.00
23 A1 Un p blk, *lilac* 15.00 60.00
24 A1 Un p blk, *rose* 65.00
24A A1 Un p blk, *white* 1,500.

Serrate Perf
24B A1 2r blk, *rose* *500.00*
25 A1 Un p blk, *lilac* 750.00 750.00
25A A1 Un p blk, *rose* 700.00 300.00

Thin Laid Batonné Paper
Imperf
26 A1 Un r blk, *green* 22.50 17.50
27 A1 2r blk, *rose* 27.50 22.50
27A A1 2r blk, *green* 47.50
28 A1 4r blk, *blue* 17.50 42.50
29 A1 4r blk, *white* 100.00
30 A1 Un p blk, *lilac* 30.00 52.50
31 A1 Un p blk, *rose* 65.00

Serrate Perf.
32 A1 Un r blk, *green* 65.00
33 A1 2r blk, *rose* 400.00 *200.00*
34 A1 4r blk, *blue* 425.00
34A A1 4r blk, *white* *1,750.*
34B A1 Un p blk, *lilac* 700.00

Thin Oblong Quadrille Paper
Imperf
35 A1 Un r blk, *blue* 250.00 22.50
35A A1 Un r blk, *white* 1,500.
36 A1 4r blk, *blue* 600.00

Serrate Perf.
37 A1 Un r blk, *blue* 300.00

4th Printing
Dated "1868"
Wove Paper

1868 ***Imperf.***
38 A1 2r blk, *lilac* 30.00 14.00
a. Half used as 1r on cover 500.00
39 A1 2r blk, *rose* 52.50 65.00

Serrate Perf.
40 A1 2r blk, *lilac* 52.50
41 A1 2r blk, *rose* 750.00 95.00

Laid Batonné Paper

Imperf

42	A1	un r blk, *green*	12.50	12.50
43	A1	2r blk, *lilac*	12.50	12.50
a.		Half used as 1r on cover		1,500.
43A	A1	2r blk, *rose*	750.00	

Serrate Perf.

44	A1	un r blk, *green*	250.00	200.00
44A	A1	2r blk, *rose*	500.00	

Quadrille Paper.

Imperf

45	A1	2r blk, *lilac*	25.00	14.00

Serrate Perf.

46	A1	2r blk, *lilac*	300.00	300.00

Laid Paper

Imperf

47	A1	un r blk, *green*	13.00	17.00
a.		Watermarked "LA + F"	*750.00*	*1,000.*
b.		"nu" instead of "un"		750.00
c.		Dated "1863"		300.00
48	A1	2r blk, *lilac*	32.50	32.50
49	A1	2r blk, *rose*	37.50	37.50

Serrate Perf.

50	A1	un r blk, *green*	750.00	55.00
51	A1	2r blk, *rose*	475.00	

Counterfeits of Nos. 1-51 abound.

Merida

A city of southeastern Mexico, capital of the State of Yucatan.

Mexico No. 521 Surcharged **25**

1916 Wmk. 155 *Perf. 14*

1	A40	25(c) on 5c org, on cover	*500.00*

The G.P.DE.M. overprint reads down.

Authorities consider the Monterrey, Morelia and Patzcuaro stamps to be bogus.

Tlacotalpan

A village in the state of Veracruz.

A1

Handstamped Monogram, Value in Manuscript

1856, Oct.

1	A1	½(r) black	*30,000.*

REVOLUTIONARY ISSUES

SINALOA

A northern state in Mexico, bordering on the Pacific Ocean. Stamps were issued by a provisional government.

Coat of Arms — A1

1929 Unwmk. Litho. *Perf. 12*

1	A1	10c blk, red & bl	5.00
a.		Tête bêche pair	35.00
2	A1	20c blk, red & gray	5.00

Just as Nos. 1 and 2 were ready to be placed on sale the state was occupied by the Federal forces and the stamps could not be used. At a later date a few copies were canceled by favor.

A recent find included a number of errors or printer's waste.

YUCATAN

A southeastern state of Mexico.

Chalchiuitlicue, Nahuatl Water Goddess — A1

"Casa de Monjas" — A2

Temple of the Tigers — A3

Without Gum

1924 Unwmk. Litho. *Imperf.*

1	A1	5c violet	10.00	15.00
2	A2	10c carmine	40.00	50.00
3	A3	50c olive green	175.00	

Perf. 12

4	A1	5c violet	50.00	60.00
5	A2	10c carmine	50.00	75.00
6	A3	50c olive green	200.00	

Nos. 3 and 6 were not regularly issued.

MICRONESIA

ˌmī-krə-ˈnē-zhə

LOCATION — A group of over 600 islands in the West Pacific Ocean, north of the Equator.
GOVT. — Republic
AREA — 271 sq. miles
POP. — 131,500 (1999 est.)
CAPITAL — Palikir

These islands, also known as the Caroline Islands, were bought by Germany from Spain in 1899. Caroline Islands stamps issued as a German territory are listed in Vol. 2 of this Catalogue. Seized by Japan in 1914, they were taken by the US in WWII and became part of the US Trust Territory of the Pacific in 1947. By agreement with the USPS, the islands began issuing their own stamps in 1984, with the USPS continuing to carry the mail to and from the islands.

On Nov. 3, 1986 Micronesia became a Federation as a Sovereign State in Compact of Free Association with the US.

100 Cents = 1 Dollar

Catalogue values for all unused stamps in this country are for Never Hinged items.

Postal Service Inauguration — A1

1984, July 12 Litho. *Perf. 14*

1	A1	20c Yap	.45	.45
2	A1	20c Truk	.45	.45
3	A1	20c Pohnpei	.45	.45
4	A1	20c Kosrae	.45	.45
a.		Block of 4, #1-4	1.90	1.90

For surcharges see Nos. 48-51.

Fernandez de Quiros — A2

Men's House, Yap — A3

Designs: 1c, 19c, Pedro Fernandez de Quiros, Spanish explorer, first discovered Pohnpei, 1595. 2c, 20c, Louis Duperrey, French explorer. 3c, 30c, Fyedor Lutke, Russian explorer. 4c, 37c, Dumont d'Urville. 10c, Sleeping Lady, Kosrae. 13c, Liduduhriap Waterfall, Pohnpei. 17c, Tonachau Peak, Truk. 50c, Devil mask, Truk. $1, Sokeh's Rock, Pohnpei. $2, Canoes, Kosrae. $5, Stone money, Yap.

1984, July 12 *Perf. 13½x13*

5	A2	1c Prussian blue	.20	.20
6	A2	2c deep claret	.20	.20
7	A2	3c dark blue	.20	.20
8	A2	4c green	.20	.20
9	A3	5c yellow brown	.20	.20
10	A3	10c dark violet	.20	.20
11	A3	13c dark blue	.20	.20
12	A3	17c brown lake	.25	.25
13	A2	19c dark violet	.30	.30
14	A2	20c olive green	.30	.30
15	A2	30c rose lake	.45	.45
16	A2	37c deep violet	.55	.55
17	A3	50c brown	.75	.75
18	A3	$1 olive	1.75	1.75
19	A3	$2 Prussian blue	3.50	3.50
20	A3	$5 brown lake	8.50	8.50
		Nos. 5-20 (16)	17.75	17.75

See Nos. 33, 36, 38.

Ausipex '84 A4

1984, Sept. 21 Litho. *Perf. 13½*

21	A4	20c Truk Post Office	.40	.40
		Nos. 21,C4-C6 (4)	3.00	3.00

Christmas A5

Child's drawing.

1984, Dec. 20

22	A5	20c Child in manger	.90	.90
		Nos. 22,C7-C9 (4)	3.55	3.55

Ships — A6

1985, Aug. 19

23	A6	22c U.S.S. Jamestown	.55	.55
		Nos. 23,C10-C12 (4)	3.00	3.00

Christmas A7

1985, Oct. 15 Litho. *Perf. 13½*

24	A7	22c Lelu Protestant Church, Kosrae	.75	.60
		Nos. 24,C13-C14 (3)	2.90	2.75

Audubon Birth Bicentenary — A8

1985, Oct. 30 *Perf. 14½*

25	A8	22c Noddy tern	.60	.60
26	A8	22c Turnstone	.60	.60
27	A8	22c Golden plover	.60	.60
28	A8	22c Black-bellied plover	.60	.60
a.		Block of 4, #25-28	2.60	2.60
		Nos. 25-28,C15 (5)	3.40	3.40

Types of 1984 and

Birds — A9

Tall Ship Senyavin A10

Natl. Seal A11

Perf. 13½ (A8a), 13½x13

1985-88 Litho.

31	A9	3c Long-billed white-eye	.20	.20
32	A9	14c Truk monarch	.30	.30
33	A3	15c Liduduhriap Waterfall, Pohnpei	.30	.30
a.		Booklet pane of 10	6.00	—
34	A10	22c bright blue green	.35	.35
35	A9	22c Pohnpei mountain starling	.45	.45
36	A3	25c Tonachau Peak, Truk	.50	.50
a.		Booklet pane of 10	6.50	—
b.		Booklet pane, 5 15c + 5 25c	7.50	—
37	A10	36c ultramarine	.70	.70
38	A3	45c Sleeping Lady, Kosrae	.90	.90
39	A11	$10 bright ultra	15.00	15.00
		Nos. 31-39,C34-C36 (12)	21.70	21.70

Issued: $10, 10/15; #34, 4/14/86; 3c, 14c, #35, 8/1/88; 15c, 25c, 36c, 45c, 9/1/88.

Nan Madol Ruins, Pohnpei A16

1985, Dec. Litho. *Perf. 13½*

45	A16	22c Land of the Sacred Masonry	.60	.60
		Nos. 45,C16-C18 (4)	3.00	3.00

Intl. Peace Year — A17

1986, May 16

46	A17	22c multicolored	.65	.60

Nos. 1-4 Surcharged

1986, May 19 Litho. *Perf. 14*

48	Al	22c on 20c No. 1	.40	.40
49	A1	22c on 20c No. 2	.40	.40
50	A1	22c on 20c No. 3	.40	.40
51	A1	22c on 20c No. 4	.40	.40
a.		Block of 4, #48-51	1.75	1.75

AMERIPEX '86 A18

Bully Hayes (1829-1877), Buccaneer.

1986, May 22 *Perf. 13½*

52	A18	22c At ship's helm	.50	.50
		Nos. 52,C21-C24 (5)	4.00	4.00

First Passport A19

1986, Nov. 4 Litho. *Perf. 13½*

53	A19	22c multicolored	.60	.60

Christmas A20

Virgin and child paintings: 5c, Italy, 18th cent. 22c, Germany, 19th cent.

1986, Oct. 15 Litho. *Perf. 14½*

54	A20	5c multicolored	.20	.20
55	A20	22c multicolored	.75	.75
		Nos. 54-55,C26-C27 (4)	3.35	3.35

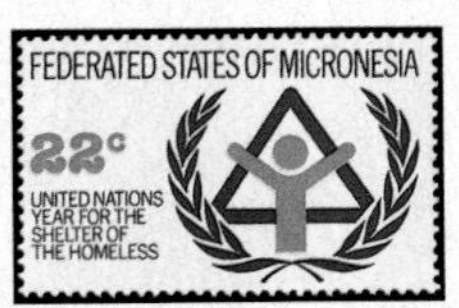

Anniversaries and Events — A21

1987, June 13 Litho. *Perf. 14½*

56	A21	22c Intl. Year of Shelter for the Homeless	.50	.50
		Nos. 56,C28-C30 (4)	3.20	3.20

Souvenir Sheet

57	A21	$1 CAPEX '87	3.25	3.25

Christmas A22

22c, Archangel Gabriel appearing before Mary.

1987, Nov. 16 Litho. *Perf. 14½*

58	A22	22c multicolored	.60	.60
		Nos. 58,C31-C33 (4)	3.30	3.30

Colonial Eras — A23

1988, July 20 Litho. *Perf. 13x13½*

59	A23	22c German	.60	.60
60	A23	22c Spanish	.60	.60
61	A23	22c Japanese	.60	.60
62	A23	22c US Trust Territory	.60	.60
a.		Block of 4, #59-62	2.40	2.40
		Nos. 59-62,C37-C38 (6)	4.30	4.30

Printed se-tenant in sheets of 28 plus 4 center labels picturing flags of Spain (UL), Germany (UR), Japan (LL) and the US (LR).

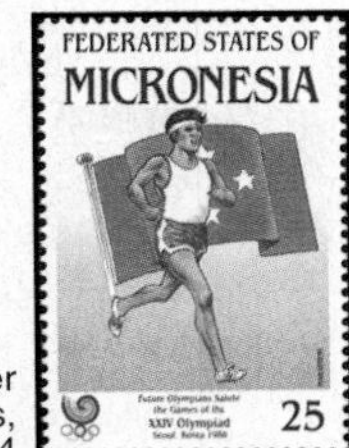

1988 Summer Olympics, Seoul — A24

1988, Sept. 1 Litho. *Perf. 14*

63	A24	25c Running	.50	.50
64	A24	25c Women's hurdles	.50	.50
a.		Pair, #63-64	1.00	1.00
65	A24	45c Basketball	.80	.80
66	A24	45c Women's volleyball	.80	.80
a.		Pair, #65-66	1.65	1.65
		Nos. 63-66 (4)	2.60	2.60

Christmas — A25

Children decorating tree: No. 67, Two girls, UL of tree. No. 68, Boy, girl, dove, UR of tree. No. 69, Boy, girl, LL of tree. No. 70, Boy, girl, LR of tree. Se-tenant in a continuous design.

1988, Oct. 28 Litho. *Perf. 14*

67	A25	25c multicolored	.45	.45
68	A25	25c multicolored	.45	.45
69	A25	25c multicolored	.45	.45
70	A25	25c multicolored	.45	.45
a.		Block of 4, #67-70	1.90	1.90

Miniature Sheet

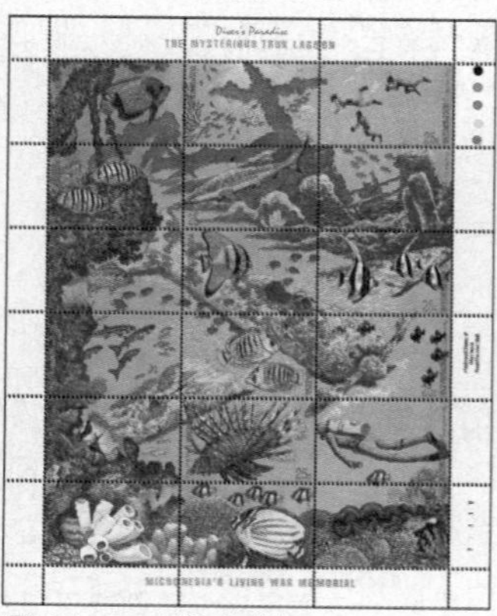

Truk Lagoon State Monument — A26

a, Sun and stars angelfish. b, School of fish. c, 3 divers. d, Goldenjack. e, Blacktip reef shark. f, 2 schools of fish. g, Squirrelfish. h, Batfish. i, Moorish idols. j, Barracudas. k, Spot banded butterflyfish. l, Three-spotted dam-selfish. m, Foxface. n, Lionfish. o, Diver. p, Coral. q, Butterflyfish. r, Bivalve, fish, coral.

1988, Dec. 19 Litho. *Perf. 14*

71 A26 Sheet of 18 9.50 9.50
a.-r. 25c any single .50 .50

Mwarmwarms — A27

1989, Mar. 31 Litho. *Perf. 14*

72 A27 45c Plumeria .65 .65
73 A27 45c Hibiscus .65 .65
74 A27 45c Jasmine .65 .65
75 A27 45c Bougainvillea .65 .65
a. Block of 4, #72-75 2.75 2.75

Souvenir Sheet

Pheasant and Chrysanthemum, 1830s, by Hiroshige (1797-1858) — A28

1989, May 15 Litho. *Perf. 14½*

76 A28 $1 multicolored 1.60 1.60

Hirohito (1901-1989), emperor of Japan.

Sharks A29

1989, July 7

77 A29 25c Whale .40 .40
78 A29 25c Hammerhead .40 .40
a. Pair, #77-78 .80 .80
79 A29 45c Tiger, vert. .75 .75
80 A29 45c Great white, vert. .75 .75
a. Pair, #79-80 1.50 1.50
Nos. 77-80 (4) 2.30 2.30

Miniature Sheet

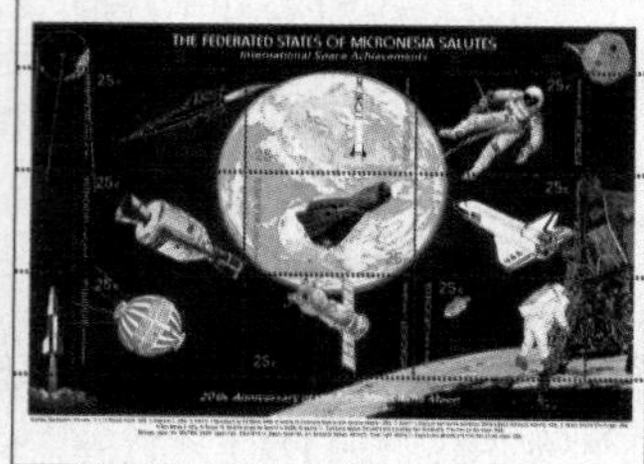

First Moon Landing, 20th Anniv. — A30

Space achievements: a, X-15 rocket plane, 1959. b, *Explorer 1* launched into orbit, 1958. c, Ed White, 1st American to walk in space, Gemini 4 mission, 1965. d, Apollo 18 command module, 1975. e. Gemini 4 capsule. f, Space shuttle *Challenger,* 1983-86. g, *San Marco 2,* satellite engineered by Italy. h, Soyuz 19 spacecraft, 1975. i, *Columbia* command module and Neil Armstrong taking man's first step onto the Moon during the Apollo 11 mission, 1969.

1989, July 20 Litho. *Perf. 14*

81 A30 Sheet of 9 5.25 4.50
a.-i. 25c any single .50 .45

Earth and Lunar Module, by William Hanson, 1st Art Transported to the Moon — A31

1989, July 20 *Perf. 13½x14*

82 A31 $2.40 multicolored 4.50 4.00

First Moon landing, 20th anniv.

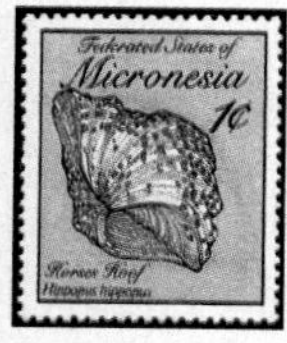

Seashells — A32

1989, Sept. 26 *Perf. 14*

83 A32 1c Horse's hoof .20 .20
84 A32 3c Rare spotted cowrie .20 .20
85 A32 15c Commercial trochus .20 .20
a. Booklet pane of 10 5.00 —
87 A32 20c General cone .30 .30
88 A32 25c Triton's trumpet .40 .40
a. Booklet pane of 10 7.50 —
b. Booklet pane, 5 each 15c, 25c 7.50 —
90 A32 30c Laciniated conch .45 .45
91 A32 36c Red-mouthed olive .55 .55
93 A32 45c Map cowrie .70 .70
95 A32 50c Textile cone .75 .75
100 A32 $1 Orange spider conch 1.75 1.75
101 A32 $2 Golden cowrie 3.50 3.50
102 A32 $5 Episcopal miter 8.50 8.50
Nos. 83-102 (12) 17.50 17.50

Booklet panes issued Sept. 14, 1990.
This is an expanding set. Numbers will change if necessary.

Miniature Sheet

Fruits and Flowers Endemic to Kosrae A33

Designs: a, Orange. b, Lime. c, Tangerine. d, Mango. e, Coconut. f, Breadfruit. g, Sugar cane. h, Thatched dwelling. i, Banana. j, Girl, boy. k, Pineapple picker. l, Taro. m, Hibiscus. n, Ylang ylang. o, White ginger. p, Plumeria. q, Royal poinciana. r, Yellow allamanda.

1989, Nov. 18 Litho. *Perf. 14*

103 Sheet of 18 9.00 9.00
a.-r. A33 25c any single .45 .45

Margin inscribed for World Stamp Expo '89.

Christmas — A34

1989, Dec. 14 Litho. *Perf. 14½*

104 A34 25c Heralding angel .50 .50
105 A34 45c Three wise men .90 .90

World Wildlife Fund A35

Micronesian kingfishers and pigeons.

1990, Feb. 19 Litho. *Perf. 14*

106 A35 10c Kingfisher (juvenile) *.55 .55*
107 A35 15c Kingfisher (adult) *1.25 1.25*
108 A35 20c Pigeon *1.75 1.75*
109 A35 25c Pigeon, diff. *2.50 2.50*
Nos. 106-109 (4) *6.05 6.05*

Stamp World London '90 — A36

Exhibition emblem, artifacts and whaling vessels: No. 110, Wooden whale stamp, *Lyra,* 1826. No. 111, Harpoons, *Prudent,* 1827. No. 112, Scrimshaw (whale), *Rhone,* 1851. No. 113, Scrimshaw on whale tooth, *Sussex,* 1843. $1, Whalers at kill.

1990, May 3 Litho. *Perf. 14*

110 A36 45c multicolored .80 .80
111 A36 45c multicolored .80 .80
112 A36 45c multicolored .80 .80
113 A36 45c multicolored .80 .80
a. Block of 4, #110-113 3.25 3.25

Souvenir Sheet

114 A36 $1 multicolored 2.00 2.00

Souvenir Sheet

Penny Black, 150th Anniv. — A37

1990, May 6 *Perf. 14*

115 A37 $1 Great Britain No. 1 2.00 2.00

Main Building — A38

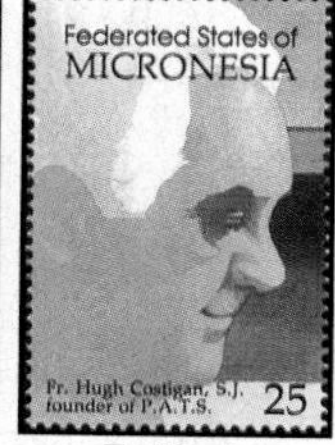

Fr. Hugh Costigan, School Founder — A39

Designs: No. 117, Fr. Costigan, students. No. 119, Fr. Costigan, Isaphu Samuel Hadley. No. 120, New York City Police Badge.

1990, July 31 Litho. *Perf. 14*

116 A38 25c multicolored .50 .50
117 A38 25c multicolored .50 .50
118 A39 25c multicolored .50 .50
119 A38 25c multicolored .50 .50
120 A38 25c multicolored .50 .50
a. Strip of 5, #116-120 2.50 2.50

Pohnpei Agriculture and Trade School, 25th anniversary. Printed in sheets of 15.

Souvenir Sheet

Expo '90, Intl. Garden and Greenery Exposition, Osaka, Japan — A40

1990, July 31 Litho. *Perf. 14*

121 A40 $1 multicolored 1.75 1.75

Loading Mail, Pohnpei Airport, 1990 A41

Pacifica Emblem and: 45c, Japanese mail boat, Truk Lagoon, 1940.

1990, Aug. 24

122 A41 25c multicolored .50 .50
123 A41 45c multicolored 1.25 1.25

Canoe, Flag of Federated States of Micronesia A42

Designs: No. 124, Stick chart, canoe, flag of Marshall Islands. No. 125, Frigate bird, eagle, USS Constitution, flag of US.

1990, Sept. 28 *Perf. 13½*

124 A42 25c multicolored .55 .55
125 A42 25c multicolored .55 .55
126 A42 25c multicolored .55 .55
a. Strip of 3, #124-126 1.75 1.75

Compact of Free Association with the US. Printed in sheets of 15. See #253, US #2506, Marshall Islands #381.

Moths A43

1990, Nov. 10 Litho. *Perf. 14*

127 A43 45c Gracillariidae .80 .80
128 A43 45c Yponomeatidae .80 .80
129 A43 45c shown .80 .80
130 A43 45c Cosmopterigidae, diff. .80 .80
a. Block of 4, #127-130 3.25 3.25

Miniature Sheet

Christmas A44

Designs: a, Cherub. b, Star of Bethlehem. c, Cherub blowing horn. d, Goats. e, Nativity scene. f, Children, outrigger canoe. g, Messenger blowing a conch shell. h, Family walking. i, People carrying bundles.

1990, Nov. 19 Litho. *Perf. 14*

131 Sheet of 9 4.50 4.50
a.-i. A44 25c any single .50 .50

Souvenir Sheets

New Capital of Micronesia — A45

1991, Jan. 15 Litho. *Perf. 14x13½*

132 A45 Sheet of 2 1.40 1.40
a. 25c Executive Branch .50 .50
b. 45c Legislative, Judicial Branches .90 .90
133 A45 $1 New Capitol 2.00 2.00

Turtles — A46

1991, Mar. 14 Litho. *Perf. 14*

134 A46 29c Hawksbill on beach 1.10 1.10
135 A46 29c Green 1.10 1.10
a. Pair, #134-135 2.25 2.25
136 A46 50c Hawksbill 1.40 1.40
137 A46 50c Leatherback 1.40 1.40
a. Pair, #136-137 2.75 2.75
Nos. 134-137 (4) 5.00 5.00

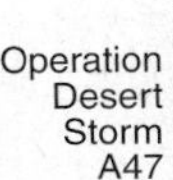

Operation Desert Storm A47

1991, July 30 Litho. *Perf. 14*

138 A47 29c Battleship Missouri .60 .60
139 A47 29c Multiple launch rocket system .60 .60
140 A47 29c F-14 Tomcat .60 .60
141 A47 29c E-3 Sentry (AWACS) .60 .60
a. Block or strip of 4, #138-141 2.40 2.40

Size: 51x38mm

142 A47 $2.90 Frigatebird, flag 5.00 5.00
a. Souvenir sheet of 1 5.50 5.50
Nos. 138-142 (5) 7.40 7.40

Miniature Sheets

Phila Nippon '91 — A48

Ukiyo-e prints by Paul Jacoulet (1902-1960) — #143: a, Evening Flowers, Toloas, Truk, 1941. b, The Chief's Daughter, Mogomog, 1953. c, Yagourouh and Mio, Yap, 1938. No. 144a, Yap Beauty and Orchids, 1934. b, The Yellow-eyed Boys, Ohlol, 1940. c, Violet Flowers, Tomil, 1937. $1, First Love, Yap, 1937, horiz.

1991, Sept. Litho. *Perf. 14*

143 Sheet of 3 2.25 2.25
a.-c. A48 29c any single .75 .75

144 Sheet of 3 3.50 3.50
a.-c. A48 50c any single 1.25 1.25

Souvenir Sheet

145 A48 $1 multicolored 2.40 2.40

Christmas — A49

Handicraft scenes: 29c, Nativity. 40c, Adoration of the Magi. 50c, Adoration of the Shepherds.

1991, Oct. 30 *Perf. 14x13½*

146 A49 29c multicolored .50 .50
147 A49 40c multicolored .75 .75
148 A49 50c multicolored 1.00 1.00
Nos. 146-148 (3) 2.25 2.25

Pohnpei Rain Forest A50

Designs: a, Pohnpei fruit bat. b, Purple capped fruit-dove. c, Micronesian kingfisher. d. Birdnest fern. e, Island swiftlet. f, Long-billed white-eye. g, Brown noddy. h, Pohnpei lory. i, Pohnpei flycatcher. j, Caroline ground-dove. k, White-tailed tropicbird. l, Micronesian honeyeater. m, Ixora. n, Pohnpei fantail. o, Gray white-eye. p, Blue-faced parrotfinch. q, Cicadabird. r, Green skink.

1991, Nov. 18

149 Sheet of 18 13.00 13.00
a.-r. A50 29c any single .65 .65

Peace Corps — A51

Designs: a, Learning crop planting techniques. b, Education. c, John F. Kennedy. d, Public health nurses. e, Recreation.

1992, Apr. 10 Litho. *Perf. 14*

150 A51 29c Strip of 5, #a.-e. 2.50 2.50

Printed in sheets of 15.

Discovery of America, 500th Anniv. — A52

Designs: a, Queen Isabella I. b, Santa Maria. c, Columbus.

1992, May 23 Litho. *Perf. 13½*

151 A52 29c Strip of 3, #a.-c. 5.00 5.00

Admission to the UN, First Anniv. A53

1992, Sept. 24 *Perf. 11x10½*

152 A53 29c multicolored 1.50 1.50
153 A53 50c multicolored 2.25 2.25
a. Souvenir sheet of 2, #152-153 3.50 3.50

Christmas A54

1992, Dec. 4 *Perf. 13½*

154 A54 29c multicolored 1.90 1.90

Pioneers of Flight A55

a, Andrei N. Tupolev. b, John A. Macready. c, Edward V. Rickenbacker. d, Manfred von Richtofen. e, Hugh M. Trenchard. f, Glenn H. Curtiss. g, Charles E. Kingsford-Smith. h, Igor I. Sikorsky.

1993, Apr. 12

155 A55 29c Block of 8, #a.-h. 4.75 4.75

See Nos. 178, 191, 200, 210, 233, 238, 249.

Fish — A56

Designs: 10c, Bigscale soldierfish. 19c, Bennett's butterflyfish. 20c, Peacock grouper. 22c, Great barracuda. 25c, Coral grouper. 29c, Regal angelfish. 30c, Bleeker's parrotfish. 35c, Picassofish. 40c, Mandarinfish. 45c, Bluebanded surgeonfish. 50c, Orange-striped triggerfish. 52c, Palette surgeonfish. 75c, Oriental sweetlips. $1, Zebra moray. $2, Foxface rabbitfish. $2.90, Orangespine unicornfish.

1993-94 Litho. *Perf. 13½*

156 A56 10c multicolored .20 .20
157 A56 19c multicolored .35 .35
158 A56 20c multicolored .35 .35
159 A56 22c multicolored .40 .40
160 A56 25c multicolored .45 .45
161 A56 29c multicolored .55 .55
162 A56 30c multicolored .55 .55
162A A56 35c multicolored .65 .65
163 A56 40c multicolored .70 .70
163A A56 45c multicolored .75 .75
164 A56 50c multicolored .90 .90
164A A56 52c multicolored 1.00 1.00
164B A56 75c multicolored 1.40 1.40
165 A56 $1 multicolored 1.75 1.75
166 A56 $2 multicolored 3.50 3.50
167 A56 $2.90 multicolored 5.50 5.50
Nos. 156-167 (16) 19.00 19.00

Issued: 19c, 29c, 50c, $1, 5/14/93; 22c, 30c, 40c, 45c, 8/26/93; 10c, 20c, 35c, $2.90, 5/20/94; 25c, 52c, 75c, $2, 8/5/94.

See Nos. 213-227, 250.

A57

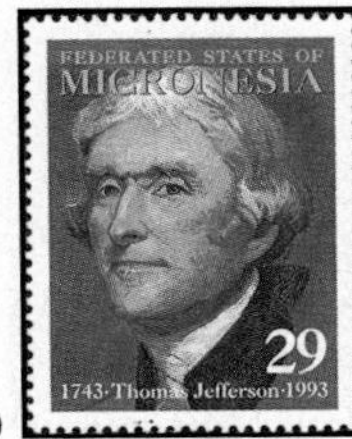

A59

Sailing Ships: a, Great Republic. b, Benjamin F. Packard. c, Stag Hound. d, Herald of the Morning. e, Rainbow. f, Flying Cloud. g, Lightning. h, Sea Witch. i, Columbia. j, New World. k, Young America. l, Courier.

1993, May 21 Litho. *Perf. 13½*

168 A57 29c Sheet of 12, #a.-l. 15.00 15.00

1993, July 4 Litho. *Perf. 13½*

172 A59 29c multicolored .80 .80

Thomas Jefferson, 250th anniv. of birth.

Pacific Canoes — A60

1993, July 21 Litho. *Perf. 13½*

173 A60 29c Yap .80 .80
174 A60 29c Kosrae .80 .80
175 A60 29c Pohnpei .80 .80
176 A60 29c Chuuk .80 .80
a. Block of 4, #173-176 3.25 3.25

Local Leaders — A61

Designs: a, Ambilos Iehsi, (1935-81), educator. b, Andrew Roboman (1905-92), Yap chief. c, Joab N. Sigrah (1932-88), first vice-speaker of Congress. d, Petrus Mailo (1902-71), Chuuk leader.

1993, Sept. 16 Litho. *Perf. 13½*

177 A61 29c Strip of 4, #a.-d. 2.50 2.50

See Nos. 204-207.

Pioneers of Flight Type of 1993

Designs: a, Hugh L. Dryden. b, Theodore von Karman. c, Otto Lilienthal. d, Thomas O.M. Sopwith. e, Lawrence B. Sperry. f, Alberto Santos-Dumont. g, Orville Wright. h, Wilbur Wright.

1993, Sept. 25 Litho. *Perf. 13½*

178 A55 50c Block of 8, #a.-h. 6.75 6.75

Tourist Attractions, Pohnpei — A62

1993, Oct. 5

179 A62 29c Kepirohi Falls .75 .75
180 A62 50c Spanish Wall 1.50 1.50

Souvenir Sheet

181 A62 $1 Sokehs Rock 2.00 2.00

No. 181 contains one 80x50mm stamp.

See Nos. 187-189.

Butterflies — A63

Christmas — A64

#182a, Great eggfly female (typical). #182b, Great eggfly female (local variant). #183a, Monarch. #183b, Great eggfly male.

1993, Oct. 20 Litho. *Perf. 13½*

182 A63 29c Pair, #a.-b.	1.40	1.40
183 A63 50c Pair, #a.-b.	2.00	2.00

See No. 190.

1993, Nov. 11

184 A64 29c We Three Kings	.75	.75
185 A64 50c Silent Night, Holy Night	1.25	1.25

Miniature Sheet

Yap Culture A65

Designs: a, Baby basket. b, Bamboo raft. c, Baskets, handbag. d, Fruit bat. e, Forest. f, Outrigger canoe. g, Dioscorea yams. h, Mangroves. i, Manta ray. j, Cyrtosperma taro. k, Fish weir. l, Seagrass, fish. m, Taro bowl. n, Thatched house. o, Coral reef. p, Lavalava. q, Dance. r, Stone money.

1993, Dec. 15 Litho. *Perf. 13½x14*

186 A65 29c Sheet of 18, #a.-r.	12.50	12.50

Tourist Attractions Type of 1993

Sites on Kosrae: 29c, Sleeping Lady Mountain. 40c, Walung. 50c, Lelu Ruins.

1994, Feb. 11 Litho. *Perf. 13½*

187 A62 29c multicolored	.55	.55
188 A62 40c multicolored	.75	.75
189 A62 50c multicolored	.95	.95
Nos. 187-189 (3)	2.25	2.25

Butterfly Type of 1993 with Added Inscription

Souvenir Sheet

a, 29c, like No. 182a. b, 29c, like No. 182b. c, 50c, like No. 183a. d, 50c, like No. 183b.

1994, Feb. 18

190 A63 Sheet of 4, #a.-d.	4.25	4.25

Inscription reads "Hong Kong '94 Stamp Exhibition" in Chinese on Nos. 190a, 190d, and in English on Nos. 190b-190c.

Inscriptions on Nos. 190a-190d are in black.

Pioneers of Flight Type of 1993

Designs: a, Edwin E. Aldrin, Jr. b, Neil A. Armstrong. c, Michael Collins. d, Wernher von Braun. e, Octave Chanute. f, T. Claude Ryan. g, Frank Whittle. h, Waldo D. Waterman.

1994, Mar. 4 Litho. *Perf. 13½*

191 A55 29c Block of 8, #a.-h.	5.75	5.75

1994 Micronesian Games — A66

Designs: a, Spearfishing. b, Basketball. c, Coconut husking. d, Tree climbing.

1994, Mar. 26 *Perf. 13½x14*

192 A66 29c Block of 4, #a.-d.	2.75	2.75

Native Costumes — A67

a, Pohnpei. b, Kosrae. c, Chuuk. d, Yap.

1994, Mar. 31 *Perf. 13½*

193 A67 29c Block of 4, #a.-d.	2.75	2.75

Constitution, 15th Anniv. — A68

1994, May 10 Litho. *Perf. 11x10½*

194 A68 29c multicolored	1.50	1.50

Flowers — A69

Designs: a, Fagraea berteriana. b, Pangium edule. c, Pittosporum ferrugineum. d, Sonneratia caseolaris.

1994, June 6 Litho. *Perf. 13½*

195 A69 29c Strip of 4, #a.-d.	2.75	2.75

1994 World Cup Soccer Championships, US — A70

Design: No. 197, Soccer players, diff.

1994, June 17 Litho. *Perf. 13½*

196 A70 50c red & multi	2.25	2.25
197 A70 50c blue & multi	2.25	2.25
a. Pair, #196-197	4.50	4.50

No. 197a has a continuous design.

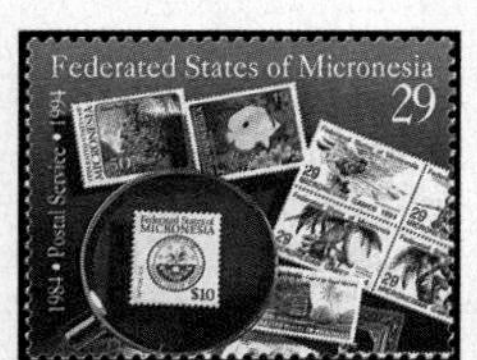

Micronesian Postal Service, 10th Anniv. — A71

Stamps: a, #39, 45, 54 (c), 159, 189, 192 (b). b, #58 (d), 151, 161 (d), 176a, 183a (d). c, #4a, 137a, 184 (a), C12 (d), C39, C41. d, #161 (b), 183a (b), 183b, 193, C12, C40, C42.

1994, July 12 Litho. *Perf. 13½*

198 A71 29c Block of 4, #a.-d.	5.00	5.00

No. 198 is a continuous design.

Souvenir Sheet

PHILAKOREA '94 — A72

Dinosaurs: a, 29c, Iguanodons (b). b, 52c, Coelurosaurs (c). c, $1, Camarasaurus.

1994, Aug. 16 Litho. *Perf. 13½*

199 A72 Sheet of 3, #a.-c.	5.25	5.25

Pioneers of Flight Type of 1993

a, William A. Bishop. b, Karel J. Bossart. c, Marcel Dassault. d, Geoffrey de Havilland. e, Yuri A. Gagarin. f, Alan B. Shepard, Jr. g, John H. Towers. h, Hermann J. Oberth.

1994, Sept. 20 Litho. *Perf. 13½*

200 A55 50c Block of 8, #a.-h.	6.75	6.75

Migratory Birds — A73

Designs: a, Oriental cuckoo. b, Long-tailed cuckoo. c, Short-eared owl. d, Dollarbird.

1994, Oct. 20 Litho. *Perf. 13½*

201 A73 29c Block of 4, #a.-d.	2.50	2.50

Christmas A74

1994, Nov. 2

202 A74 29c Doves	.60	.60
203 A74 50c Angels	1.00	1.00

Local Leaders Type of 1993

Pioneers of island unification: No. 204, Johnny Moses (1900-91), Pohnpei. No. 205, Belarmino Hatheylul (1907-93), Yap. No. 206, Anton Ring Buas (1907-79), Chuuk. No. 207, Paliknoa Sigrah (King John) (1875-1957), Kosrae.

1994, Dec. 15 Litho. *Perf. 13½*

204 A61 32c multicolored	.65	.65
205 A61 32c multicolored	.65	.65
206 A61 32c multicolored	.65	.65
207 A61 32c multicolored	.65	.65
Nos. 204-207 (4)	2.60	2.60

Souvenir Sheet

New Year 1995 (Year of the Boar) — A75

1995, Jan. 2

208 A75 50c multicolored	1.00	1.00

Chuuk Lagoon A76

Underwater scenes: a, Photographer with light. b, Various species of fish, coral. c, Diver. d, Two gold fish.

1995, Feb. 6

209 A76 32c Block of 4, #a.-d.	2.50	2.50

Pioneers of Flight Type of 1993

Designs: a, Robert H. Goddard. b, Leroy R. Grumman. c, Hugo Junkers. d, James A. Lovell, Jr. e, Louis-Charles Breguet. f, Juan de la Cierva. g, Donald W. Douglas. h, Reginald J. Mitchell.

1995, Mar. 4 Litho. *Perf. 13½*

210 A55 32c Block of 8, #a.-h.	5.25	5.25

Dogs A77

a, West Highland white terrier. b, Welsh springer spaniel. c, Irish setter. d, Old English sheepdog.

1995, Apr. 5 Litho. *Perf. 13½*

211 A77 32c Block of 4, #a.-d.	2.50	2.50

Fish Type of 1993

Designs: 23c, Yellow-fin tuna. 32c, Saddled butterflyfish. 46c, Achilles tang. 55c, Moorish idol. 60c, Skipjack tuna. 78c, Square-spot fairy basslet. 95c, Bluelined snapper. $3, Flame angelfish. $5, Cave grouper.

#227: a, like #157. b, like #161. c, like #164. d, like #165. e, like #159. f, like #162. g, like #163. h, like #163A. i, like #156. j, like #158. k, like #162A. l, like #167. m, like #217. n, like #160. o, like #164A. p, like #164B. q, like #166. r, like #214. s, like #218. t, like #222. u, like #225. v, like #213. w, like #219. x, like #223. y, like #226.

1996 Litho. *Perf. 13½*

213 A56 23c multicolored	.45	.45
214 A56 32c multicolored	.65	.65
217 A56 46c multicolored	.95	.95
218 A56 55c multicolored	1.10	1.10
219 A56 60c multicolored	1.25	1.25
222 A56 78c multicolored	1.50	1.50
223 A56 95c multicolored	1.90	1.90
225 A56 $3 multicolored	6.00	6.00
226 A56 $5 multicolored	10.00	10.00
Nos. 213-226 (9)	23.80	23.80

Miniature Sheet

227 A56 32c Sheet of 25, #a.-y.	16.00	16.00

Issued: 32c, 55c, 78c, $3, 5/15/95. 23c, 60c, 95c, $5, 8/4/95; 46c, 4/10/96.

Hibiscus — A78

a, Tiliaceus. b, Huegelii. c, Trionum. d, Splendens.

1995, June 1 Litho. *Perf. 13½*

228 A78 32c Strip of 4, #a.-d.	2.50	2.50

No. 228 is a continuous design.

Souvenir Sheet

UN, 50th Anniv. — A79

1995, June 26 Litho. *Perf. 13½*
229 A79 $1 multicolored 2.00 2.00

Miniature Sheet

Singapore '95 — A80

Orchids: a, Paphiopedilum henrietta fujiwara. b, Thunia alba. c, Lycaste virginalis. d, Laeliocattleya prism palette.

1995, Sept. 1 Litho. *Perf. 13½*
230 A80 32c Sheet of 4, #a.-d. 2.60 2.60

End of World War II, 50th Anniv. — A81

US warships: a, USS Portland. b, USS Tillman. c, USS Soley. d, USS Hyman.

1995, Sept. 2
231 A81 60c Block of 4, #a.-d. 5.00 5.00

Souvenir Sheet

Intl. Stamp & Coin Expo, Beijing '95 — A82

1995, Sept. 14
232 A82 50c Temple of Heaven 1.00 1.00

Pioneers of Flight Type of 1993

Designs: a, Hugh C.T. Dowding. b, William Mitchell. c, John K. Northrop. d, Frederick Handley Page. e, Frederick H. Rohr. f, Juan T. Trippe. g, Konstantin E. Tsiolkovsky. h, Ferdinand Graf von Zeppelin.

1995, Sept. 21 Litho. *Perf. 13½*
233 A55 60c Block of 8, #a.-h. 9.50 9.50

Christmas Poinsettias A83

1995, Oct. 30 Litho. *Perf. 13½*
234 A83 32c gray & multi .65 .65
235 A83 60c bister & multi 1.25 1.25

Yitzhak Rabin (1922-95), Israeli Prime Minister — A84

1995, Nov. 30 Litho. *Perf. 13½*
236 A84 32c multicolored .65 .65

No. 236 was issued in sheets of 8.

Souvenir Sheet

New Year 1996 (Year of the Rat) — A85

1996, Jan. 5 Litho. *Perf. 13½*
237 A85 50c multicolored 1.00 1.00

Pioneers of Flight Type of 1993

Designs: a, James H. Doolittle. b, Claude Dornier. c, Ira C. Eaker. d, Jacob C.H. Ellehammer. e, Henry H. Arnold. f, Louis Blériot. g, William E. Boeing. h, Sydney Camm.

1996, Feb. 21 Litho. *Perf. 13½*
238 A55 32c Block of 8, #a.-h. 5.25 5.25

Tourism in Yap — A86

a, Meeting house. b, Stone money. c, Churu dancing. d, Traditional canoe.

1996, Mar. 13 Litho. *Perf. 13½*
239 A86 32c Block of 4, #a.-d. 2.50 2.50

Sea Stars A87

Designs: a, Rhinoceros. b, Necklace c, Thick-skinned. d, Blue.

1996, Apr. 26 Litho. *Perf. 12*
240 A87 55c Block of 4, #a.-d. 4.50 4.50

Olympic Games, Cent. — A88

First Olympic stamps, Greece: a, #120. b, #122. c, #121. d, #128.

1996, Apr. 27
241 A88 60c Block of 4, #a.-d. 4.75 4.75

Souvenir Sheet

China '96, 9th Asian Intl. Philatelic Exhibition — A89

Design: The Tarrying Garden, Suzhou.

1996, May 15 *Perf. 13x13½*
242 A89 50c multicolored 1.00 1.00

Patrol Boats — A90

1996, May 3 Litho. *Perf. 13½*
243 A90 32c FSS Palikir .65 .65
244 A90 32c FSS Micronesia .65 .65
a. Pair, #243-244 1.30 1.30

No. 244a is a continuous design.

First Ford Automobile, Cent. — A91

a, 1896 Quadricycle. b, 1917 Model T truck. c, 1928 Model A Tudor Sedan. d, 1932 V-8 Sport Roadster. e, 1941 Lincoln Continental. f, 1953 F-100 Truck. g, 1958 Thunderbird convertible. h, 1996 Mercury Sable.

1996, June 4 *Perf. 13½*
245 A91 55c Sheet of 8, #a.-h. 8.75 8.75

Officer Reza, Member of Natl. Police Drug Enforcement Unit — A93

1996, July 31 Litho. *Perf. 13½*
247 A93 32c multicolored .65 .65

Citrus Fruit — A94

a, Orange. b, Lime. c, Lemon. d, Tangerine.

1996, Aug. 24 Litho. *Perf. 13½*
248 A94 50c Strip of 4, #a.-d. 4.00 4.00

Pioneers of Flight Type of 1993

Designs: a, Gianni Caproni. b, Henri Farman. c, Curtis E. LeMay. d, Grover Loening. e, Sergey P. Korolyov. f, Isaac M. Laddon. g, Glenn L. Martin. h, Alliott Verdon Roe.

1996, Sept. 18
249 A55 60c Block of 8, #a.-h. 12.50 12.50

Fish Type of 1993

Designs: a, like #157. b, like #165. c, like #162A. d, like #218.

1996, Oct. 21 Litho. *Perf. 13½*
250 A56 32c Block of 4, #a.-d. 2.50 2.50

Taipei '96, 10th Asian Intl. Philatelic Exhibition. Nos. 250a, 250d have English inscriptions. Nos. 250b-250c have Chinese inscriptions.

Magi Following Star to Bethlehem A95

1996, Oct. 30 Litho. *Perf. 13½*
251 A95 32c dark blue & multi .65 .65
252 A95 60c blue & multi 1.25 1.25

Christmas.

Canoe, Flag of Federated States of Micronesia Type of 1990

1996, Nov. 3 *Perf. 11x10½*
253 A42 $3 like #124 6.00 6.00

No. 253 inscribed "Free Association United States of America."

Deng Xiaoping (1904-97) — A96

Portraits: a, Wearing white-collared shirt. b, Looking left. c, Looking right. d, Wearing hat. $3, Looking left, diff.

1997 Litho. *Perf. 14*
254 A96 60c Sheet of 4, #a.-d. 4.75 4.75

Souvenir Sheet

255 A96 $3 multicolored 6.00 6.00

Souvenir Sheet

Hong Kong — A97

1997
256 A97 $2 multicolored 4.00 4.00

New Year 1997 (Year of the Ox) — A98

1997 **Litho.** ***Perf. 14***
257 A98 32c multicolored .65 .65

Souvenir Sheet

258 A98 $2 like #257 4.00 4.00

Return of Hong Kong to China A99

Flowers, Victoria Harbor: a, Melia azedarach. b, Sail from ship, Victoria Peak. c, Sail from ship, dendrobium chrysotoxum. d, Bauhinia blakeana. e, Cassia surattensis, Chinese junk. f, Junk, nelumbo nucifera.

$3, Strongylodon macrobatrys, pagoda.

1997, July 1
259 A99 60c Sheet of 6, #a.-f. 7.25 7.25

Souvenir Sheet

260 A99 $3 multicolored 6.00 6.00

Sea Goddesses of the Pacific — A100

a, Giant serpent, woman holding child, Walutahanga of Melanesia. b, Sailing ship in storm, woman holding lantern, Tien-Hou of China. c, Woman swimming to bottom of sea gathering fish into basket, Lorop of Micronesia. d, Woman swimming to man in canoe, Oto-Hime of Japan. e, Woman holding seashell, Nomoi of Micronesia. f, Three women in canoe, Junkgowa sisters of Australia.

1997, May 29 **Litho.** ***Perf. 14***
261 A100 32c Sheet of 6, #a.-f. 3.75 3.75

PACIFIC 97.

Paintings by Hiroshige (1797-1858) A101

Whirlpools at Naruto in Awa Province, 1857: No. 262: a, Sailboats in distance. b, Island of trees at left. c, Island of trees at right.

Tale of Genji: Viewing the Plum Blossoms, 1852: No. 263: a, Small evergreen trees in front of woman. b, Woman. c, Trees, house in distance with woman.

Snow on the Sumida River, 1847: No. 264: a, House, river. b, Two women under umbrella. c, Woman with folded umbrella.

Each $2: No. 265, Rapids in Bitchu Province, 1854. No. 266, Fuji from Satta Point, 1858.

1997, July 25 ***Perf. 13½x14***
262 A101 20c Sheet of 3, #a.-c. 1.25 1.25
263 A101 50c Sheet of 3, #a.-c. 3.00 3.00
264 A101 60c Sheet of 3, #a.-c. 3.50 3.50

Souvenir Sheets

265-266 A101 Set of 2 8.00 8.00

Second Federated States of Micronesia Games — A102

a, Tennis. b, Discus. c, Swimming. d, Canoeing.

1997, Aug. 15 **Litho.** ***Perf. 14***
267 A102 32c Block of 4, #a.-d. 2.50 2.50

No. 267 was issued in sheets of 16 stamps.

Elvis Presley (1935-77) A103

Various portraits.

1997, Aug. 16
268 A103 50c Sheet of 6, #a.-f. 6.00 6.00

Ocean Exploration A104

#269: a, Simon Lake, Argonaut, 1897. b, William Beebe, Bathysphere, 1934. c, Auguste Piccard, Bathyscaphe, 1954. d, Harold Edgerton, deep-sea camera, 1954. e, Jacques Piccard, Trieste, 1960. f, Edwin Link, Man-in-Sea Project, 1962. g, Melvin Fisher, search for treasure, 1971. h, Robert Ballard, Alvin, 1978. i, Sylvia Earle, Deep Rover, 1979.

Each $2: No. 270, C. Wyville Thomson, deep-sea dredge, vert. No. 271, Shinkai 6500 exploring bottom of sea, vert. No. 272, Jacques-Yves Cousteau, vert.

1997, Oct. 6 **Litho.** ***Perf. 14***
269 A104 32c Sheet of 9, #a.-i. 4.25 4.25

Souvenir Sheets

270-272 A104 Set of 3 30.00 30.00

Diana, Princess of Wales (1961-97) A105

1997, Nov. 26 **Litho.** ***Perf. 14***
273 A105 60c multicolored 1.25 1.25

No. 273 was issued in sheets of 6.

World Wildlife Fund A106

Butterfly fish: a, Blackback. b, Saddled. c, Threadfin. d, Bennett's.

1997, Nov. 24 **Litho.** ***Perf. 14***
274 A106 50c Block of 4, #a.-d. 8.00 8.00

No. 274 was issued in sheets of 16 stamps.

Christmas Paintings A107

Christ Glorified in the Court of Heaven, by Fra Angelico: No. 275, Angels playing musical instruments. No. 276, Choir of Angels.

A Choir of Angels, by Simon Marmion: No. 277, Two angels blowing long horns. No. 278, One angel blowing horn.

1997, Nov. 25

275	A107 32c multicolored		.65	.65
276	A107 32c multicolored		.65	.65
	a.	Horiz. pair, Nos. 275-276	1.30	1.30
277	A107 60c multicolored		1.25	1.25
278	A107 60c multicolored		1.25	1.25
	a.	Vert. pair, Nos. 277-278	2.50	2.50

Nos. 276a, 278a were each issued in sheets of 8 pairs.

Souvenir Sheets

New Year 1998 (Year of the Tiger) — A108

1998, Jan. 2 **Litho.** ***Perf. 14***
279 A108 50c shown 1.00 1.00
280 A108 50c Chinese toy (face) 1.00 1.00

Souvenir Sheet

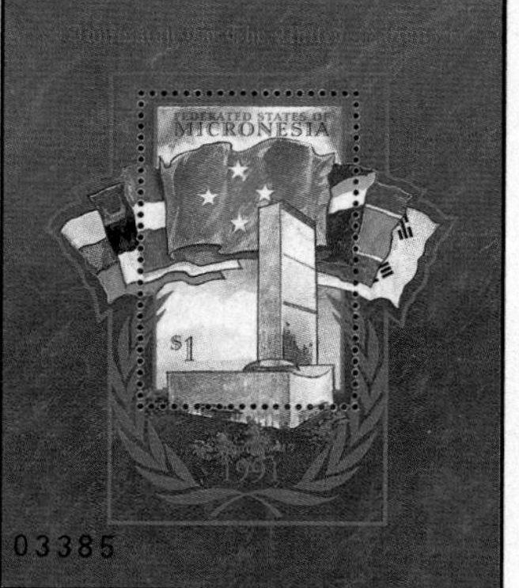

Micronesia's Admission to United Nations, 7th Anniv. — A109

1998, Feb. 13 ***Perf. 13½***
281 A109 $1 multicolored 2.00 2.00

Winnie the Pooh — A110

No. 282: a, Rabbit. b, Owl. c, Eeyore. d, Kanga and Roo. e, Piglet. f, Tigger. g, Pooh. h, Christopher Robin.

Each $2: No. 283, Piglet, Pooh, and Tigger. No. 284, Rabbit and Pooh.

1998, Feb. 16 ***Perf. 14x14½***
282 A110 32c Sheet of 8, #a.-h. 5.25 5.25

Souvenir Sheets

283-284 A110 Set of 2 8.00 8.00

1998 World Cup Soccer Championships, France — A111

Various soccer plays, color of foreground player's shirt & shorts — #285: a, White & black. b, Green & white. c, Yellow & blue, socks with colored stripes. d, Green & black. e, Yellow & black. f, Red & blue. g, Yellow & blue, plain socks. h, Red & white.

Each $2: No. 286, Red & blue. No. 287, Green, black & white.

1998, Mar. 20 **Litho.** ***Perf. 13½***
285 A111 32c Sheet of 8, #a.-h. 5.00 5.00

Souvenir Sheets

286-287 A111 Set of 2 8.00 8.00

Souvenir Sheet

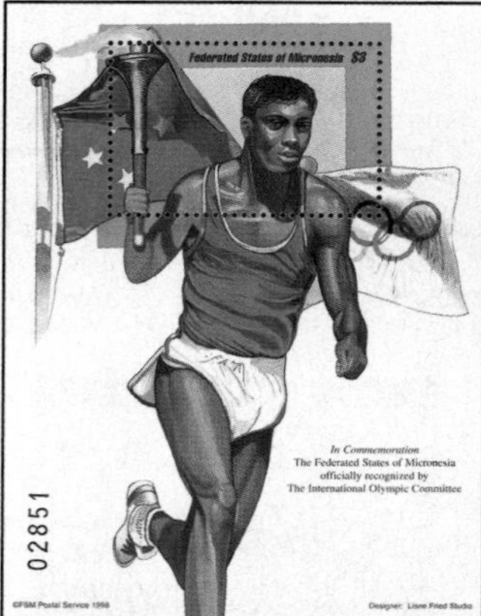

Micronesia's Recognition by Intl. Olympic Committee — A112

1998, Mar. 20
288 A112 $3 multicolored 6.00 6.00

Old Testament Bible Stories — A113

Adam and Eve — #289: a, Land of plenty. b, Adam, Eve before the fall. c, Serpent of temptation.

Joseph and his brethren — #290: a, Brothers plan to sell Joseph. b, Joseph in his many-colored coat. c, Ishmaelites take Joseph.

Rebekah — #291: a, Rebekah at the well. b, Abraham's servant Eliezer. c, Angel sent to prosper Eliezer's way.

Each $2: No. 292, Adam and Eve sent forth from Eden. No. 293, Joseph forgives his brothers. No. 294, Isaac takes Rebekah to wife.

1998, May 13 **Litho.** ***Perf. 13½x14***
289 A113 32c Sheet of 3, #a.-c. 1.90 1.90
290 A113 40c Sheet of 3, #a.-c. 2.50 2.50
291 A113 60c Sheet of 3, #a.-c. 3.50 3.50

Souvenir Sheets

292-294 A113 Set of 3 12.00 12.00

Israel '98.

Intl. Year of the Ocean A114

Deep sea research — #295: a, Marine observation satellite. b, Support vessel, Natsushima. c, Research vessel, Kaiyo. d, Deep sea anemone. e, Shinkai 2000. f, Deep tow. g, Tripod fish. h, Towed deep survey system. i, Black smokers.

Each $2: No. 296, Communications satellite. No. 297, Ocean observation buoy, vert. No. 298, Weather satellite.

1998, June 2 Litho. *Perf. 13*

295 A114 32c Sheet of 9, #a.-i. 5.75 5.75

Souvenir Sheets

296-298 A114 Set of 3 12.00 12.00

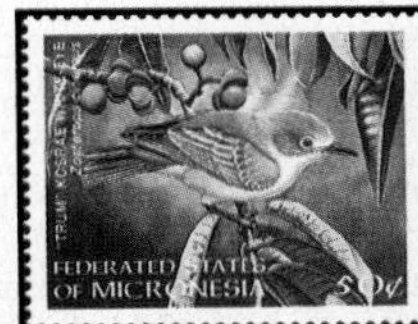

Native Birds A115

No. 299: a, Kosrae white-eye. b, Chuuk monarch. c, Yap monarch. d, Pohnpei lory.

$3, Pohnpei mountain starling.

1998, June 30 *Perf. 14x14½*

299 A115 50c Block or strip of 4, #a.-d. 4.00 4.00

Souvenir Sheet

300 A115 $3 multicolored 6.00 6.00

No. 299 was issued in sheets of 16 stamps.

Fish — A116

Designs: 1c, White-tipped soldierfish. 2c, Red-breasted wrasse. 3c, Bicolor angelfish. 4c, Falco hawkfish. 5c, Convict tang. 10c, Square-spot fairy basslet. 13c, Orangeband surgeonfish. 15c, Multibarred goatfish. 17c, Masked rabbitfish. 20c, White-spotted surgeonfish. 22c, Blue-girdled angelfish. 32c, Wedge picassofish. 39c, Red parrotfish. 40c, Lemonpeel angelfish. 60c, Humphead wrasse. 78c, Sapphire damselfish. $1, Bluefin travally. $3, Whitespot hawkfish. $5, Spotted trunkfish. $10.75, Pinktail triggerfish.

1998		**Litho.**	***Perf. 14½***	
301	A116	1c multi	.20	.20
302	A116	2c multi	.20	.20
303	A116	3c multi	.20	.20
304	A116	4c multi	.20	.20
305	A116	5c multi	.20	.20
306	A116	10c multi	.20	.20
307	A116	13c multi	.25	.25
308	A116	15c multi	.30	.30
309	A116	17c multi	.35	.35
310	A116	20c multi	.40	.40
311	A116	22c multi	.45	.45
312	A116	32c multi	.65	.65
313	A116	39c multi	.75	.75
314	A116	40c multi	.80	.80
315	A116	60c multi	1.25	1.25
316	A116	78c multi	1.50	1.50
317	A116	$1 multi	1.90	1.90
318	A116	$3 multi	5.75	5.75
319	A116	$5 multi	10.00	10.00
319A	A116	$10.75 multi	21.00	21.00
	Nos. 301-319A (20)		46.55	46.55

Issued: $10.75, 9/8; others, 7/20.

See Nos. 328-333.

Fala, Franklin D. Roosevelt's Scottish Terrier — A117

Designs: a, Roosevelt's hand petting dog. b, Radio at right. c, Radio at left. d, In car with FDR. e, Presidential seal. f, Closeup of Fala looking left.

1998, Aug. 27 Litho. *Perf. 13½*

320 A117 32c Sheet of 6, #a.-f. 3.75 3.75

Christmas A118

Twentieth cent. art — #321: a, Eskimo Madonna, by Claire Fejes. b, Madonna, by Man Ray. c, Peasant Mother, by David Siquerios.

No. 322: a, Mother and Child, by Pablo Picasso. b, Gypsy Woman with Baby, by Amedeo Modigliani. c, Mother and Child, by José Orozco.

$2, Detail from The Family, by Marisol, horiz.

1998, Sept. 15 Litho. *Perf. 13½x14*

321 A118 32c Sheet of 3, #a.-c. 1.90 1.90
322 A118 60c Sheet of 3, #a.-c. 3.75 3.75

Souvenir Sheet
Perf. 14x13½

323 A118 $2 multicolored 4.00 4.00

John Glenn's Return to Space — A119

Each 60c: No. 324: Various photos of Friendship 7 mission, 1962.

Each 60c: No. 325: Various photos of Discovery space shuttle mission, 1998.

Each $2: No. 326, Launch of Friendship 7. No. 327, Portrait of Glenn, 1998.

1998, Oct. 29 Litho. *Perf. 14*

Sheets of 8, #a-h

324-325 A119 Set of 2 19.00 19.00

Souvenir Sheets

326-327 A119 Set of 2 8.00 8.00

Fish Type of 1993

Designs: 33c, Black jack. 50c, Whitecheek surgeonfish. 55c, Long-jawed squirrelfish. 77c, Onespot snapper. $3.20, Tan-faced parrotfish. $11.75, Yellow-faced angelfish.

1999		**Litho.**	***Perf. 14½***	
328	A116	33c multicolored	.65	.65
329	A116	50c multicolored	1.00	1.00
330	A116	55c multicolored	1.10	1.10
331	A116	77c multicolored	1.50	1.50
332	A116	$3.20 multicolored	6.50	6.50

Perf. 14
Size: 45x21mm

333 A116 $11.75 multicolored 22.50 22.50
Nos. 328-333 (6) 33.25 33.25

Issued: $11.75, 3/31; others, 2/22.

Russian Space Exploration A120

No. 334: a, Sputnik 1, 1957. b, Leika in Sputnik 2, 1957. c, Luna 1, 1959. d, Luna 3, 1959. e, Yuri Gagarin in Vostok 1, 1961. f, Venera 1, 1961. g, Mars 1, 1962. h, Valentina Tereshkova in Vostok 6, 1963. i, Voskhod 1, 1964. j, Aleksei Leonov in Voskhod 2, 1965. k, Venera 3, 1966. l, Luna 10. m, Luna 9. n, Luna 16, 1970. o, Luna 17, 1970. p, Mars 3, 1971. q, Leonid Popov, Valeri Ryumin, Soyuz 35, 1980. r, Vega 1, 1985. s, Vega 1, Halley's Comet, 1986. t, Mir, 1986-98.

Each $2: No. 335, Russian Space Station, Mir, 1998. No. 336, Docking of USSR Soyuz 19 and Apollo 18, horiz.

1999, Mar. 15 *Perf. 14*

334 A120 33c Sheet of 20, #a.-t. 13.50 13.50

Souvenir Sheets

335-336 A120 Set of 2 8.00 8.00

See Nos. 344-346.

"Romance of the Three Kingdoms," by Lo Kuan-Chung A121

No. 337: a, Men, women conferring. b, Four men, one grabbing on clothes of another. c, Two men jousting. d, Four men looking down at one man. e, Man kneeling before another man in wheelchair.

No. 338: a, Mounted warriors approaching drawbridge. b, Warriors fighting in front of fire, banners. c, Warrior fighting off others, smoke. d, Man, woman kneeling before old man. e, Two men looking up at smoke coming from boiling pot.

No. 339, Three men in boat, raging fire.

1999, Mar. 19 Litho. *Perf. 13½*

Sheets of 5

337 A121 33c #a.-e. 3.25 3.25
338 A121 50c #a.-e. 5.00 5.00

Souvenir Sheet

339 A121 $2 multicolored 4.00 4.00

No. 339 contains one 52x79mm stamp.

IBRA '99, World Stamp Exhibition, Nuremberg, Germany — A122

Designs: No. 340, The Leipzig-Dresden Railway, Caroline Islands #4. No. 341, Gölsdorf 4-4-0, Caroline Islands #16.

$2, Exhibition emblem, Caroline Islands #6, vert.

1999, Apr. 27 *Perf. 14x14½*

340 A122 55c multicolored 1.10 1.10
341 A122 55c multicolored 1.10 1.10

Souvenir Sheet

342 A122 $2 multicolored 4.00 4.00

Voyages of the Pacific A123

Designs: a, Map of Pacific Ocean. b, Parrot. c, Bird in flight, leaves. d, Map, ship's stern. e, Part of ship, various blocks. f, Flower. g, Sailing ship, side view. h, Three flowers, compass rose. i, Fish over ship's drawing. j, Map, flag LL. k, Map, flag UR. l, Map, flag LR. m, Three sections of coconut. n, Three flowers, plant. o, Fish. p, Flag, UL, "Equator." q, Sextant. r, Bottom of plant. s, Fish, compass rose. t, Sailing ship, bow on.

1999, Mar. 19 Litho. *Perf. 13½*

343 A123 33c Sheet of 20, #a.-t. 13.50 13.50

Space Achievements Type of 1999

US space achievements — #344: a, Explorer 1, 1958. b, OSO 1, 1962. c, Mariner 2 to Venus, 1962. d, Mariner 2, 1962. e, Apollo 8, 1968. f, First step onto moon, Apollo 11, 1969. g, First samples from moon, Apollo 11, 1969. h, Apollo 15, 1971. i, Mariner 9, 1971. j, Pioneer 10, 1973. k, Mariner 10, 1974. l, Viking 1, 1976. m, Pioneer 11, 1979. n, STS 1, 1981. o, Pioneer 10, 1983. p, Solar Maximum Mission, 1984. q, Cometary Explorer, 1985. r, Voyager 2, 1989. s, Gallileo to Gaspra, 1992. t, Sojourner, 1997.

Each $2: No. 345, International space station. No. 346, Shuttle mission to repair Hubble Telescope, 1993.

1999, Mar. 15 Litho. *Perf. 14*

344 A120 33c Sheet of 20, #a.-t. 13.50 13.50

Souvenir Sheets

345-346 A120 Set of 2 8.00 8.00

Illustrations on Nos. 344p and 344q are incorrect.

Earth Day — A124

Endangered, extinct, and prehistoric species — #347: a, Black rhinoceros. b, Cheetah. c, Jackass penguin. d, Blue whale. e, Red-headed woodpecker. f, African elephant. g, Aurochs. h, Dodo bird. i, Tasmanian wolf. j, Giant lemur. k, Quagga. l, Steller's sea cow. m, Pteranodon. n, Shonisaurus. o, Stegosaurus. p, Galliminus. q, Tyrannosaurus. r, Archelon. s, Brachiosaurus. t, Triceratops.

Each $2: No. 348, Moa. No. 349, Suchominus tenerensis, horiz.

1999

347 A124 33c Sheet of 20, #a.-t. 13.50 13.50

Souvenir Sheets

348-349 A124 Set of 2 8.00 8.00

Nos. 348-349 contain one 50x38mm and one 38x50mm stamp, respectively.

Paintings by Hokusai (1760-1849) A125

Details or entire paintings — #305, each 33c: a, Ghost of O-Iwa. b, Horse Drawings (head down). c, Abe Nakamaro. d, Ghost of Kasane. e, Horse Drawings (head up). f, The Ghost of Kiku and the Priest Mitazuki.

No. 306, each 33c: a, Belly Band Float. b, Drawing of Women (facing left). c, Swimmers. d, Eel Climb. e, Drawings of Women (facing right). f, Kimo Ga Imo Ni Naru.

Each $2: No. 352, Whaling off Goto. No. 353, Fishing by Torchlight.

1999, July 20 Litho. *Perf. 13¾x14*

Sheets of 6, #a-f

350-351 A125 Set of 2 8.00 8.00

Souvenir Sheets

352-353 A125 Set of 2 8.00 8.00

Flowers A126

Various flowers making up a photomosaic of Princess Diana.

1999 **Litho.** ***Perf. 13¼***

354 A126 50c Sheet of 8, #a.-h.	8.00	8.00

See No. 393, 403.

Millennium A127

No. 355 — Highlights of the 12th Century: a, Death of Emperor Henry IV. b, Taira and Minamoto clans. c, Order of the Knights of the Hospital of St. John founded. d, Nautical compass invented. e, "White Ship" disaster. f, Pope Calixtus and Henry V end dispute. g, Death of Omar Khyyam. h, Death of Duke William IX. i, Roger II crowned King of Sicily. j, Stephen of Blois, Matilda. k, Birth of Maimonides. l, Church condemns Peter Abelard. m, Crusaders defeated at Damascus. n, Fall of city of Tula. o, Completion of Angkor Wat. p, Chimu culture flourishes (60x40mm). q, Honen becomes hermit.

No. 356 — Science and Technology of Ancient China: a, Well drilling. b, Chain pump. c, Magic lantern. d, Seismograph. e, Dial and pointer devices. f, Refined value of pi. g, Porcelain. h, Water mill. i, Stirrup. j, Tea. k, Umbrella. l, Brandy and whiskey. m, Printing. n, Paper money. o, Gunpowder. p, Arch bridge (60x40mm). q, Mercator map projection.

1999, Oct. 4 ***Perf. 12¾x12½***

Sheets of 17

355 A127 20c #a.-q. + label	7.00	7.00
356 A127 33c #a.-q. + label	11.50	11.50

Inscriptions on Nos. 355g, 355o, and perhaps others, are incorrect or misspelled.

See No. 377.

Costumes A128

Designs: a, French princess gown (head at R). b, As "a," (head at B). c, As "a," (bust). d, As "a," (umbrella). e, Scissors. f, Tools for fabric making. g, Micronesian wedding costume (head at R). h, As "g," (midriff). i, As "g," (feet). j, Japanese fabrics. k, Masai warrior costume (head at L). l, As "k," (head at R). m, African fabric details. n, Kabuki theater costume (head). o, As "n," (midriff). p, French Renaissance costume (head at B). q, Textile patterns. r, As "p," (head at R). s, Rulers. t, Iron.

1999, Nov. 22 ***Perf. 14¾***

357 A128 33c Sheet of 20, #a.-t.	13.50	13.50

Vertical strips of 2, 3 or 5 have continuous designs.

Christmas A129

Paintings by Anthony Van Dyck: 33c, Holy Family with St. John. 60c, Madonna with Child. No. 360, The Virgin and Child with Two Donors (detail).

No. 361, The Adoration of the Shepherds.

1999, Dec. 1 **Litho.** ***Perf. 13¾***

358 A129 33c multi	.65	.65
359 A129 60c multi	1.25	1.25
360 A129 $2 multi	4.00	4.00
Nos. 358-360 (3)	5.90	5.90

Souvenir Sheet

361 A129 $2 multi	4.00	4.00

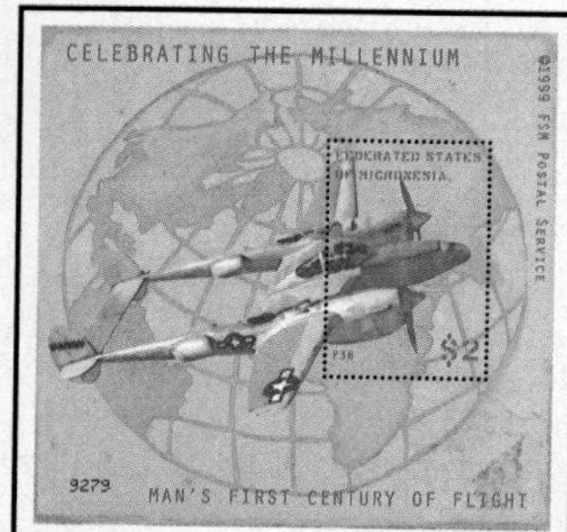

Millennium — A130

Airplanes — No. 362: a, Wright Flyer I. b, Blériot XI. c, Fokker D VII. d, Dornier Komet I. e, Ryan NYP. f, Mitsubishi A6M. g, Boeing B-29. h, Messerschmitt 262A. i, Bell X-1. j, MiG-19. k, Lockheed U-2. l, Boeing 707. m, Concorde. n, McDonnell Douglas DC-10. o, B-2.

No. 363, P38. No. 364, Dornier Do X.

1999, Dec. 9 ***Perf. 14***

362 A130 33c Sheet of 15, #a.-o.	10.00	10.00

Souvenir Sheets

Perf. 13¾

363 A130 $2 multi	4.00	4.00
364 A130 $2 multi	4.00	4.00

No. 363 contains one 32x48mm stamp. No. 364 contains one 48x32mm stamp.

Orchids — A131

No. 365: a, Baptistonia echinata. b, Bulbophyllum lobbii. c, Cattleya bicolor. d, Cischweinfia dasyandra. e, Cochleanthes discolor. f, Dendrobium bellatulum.

No. 366: a, Esmeralda clarkei. b, Gomesa crispa. c, Masdevallia elephanticeps. d, Maxillaria variabilis. e, Mitoniopsis roezlii. f, Oncidium cavendishianum.

No. 367: a, Oncidium obryzatum. b, Oncidium phalaenopsis. c, Oncidium pulvinatum. d, Paphiopedilum armeniacum. e, Paphiopedilum dayanum. f, Paphiopedilum druryi.

No. 368, Paphiopedilum hirutissimum. No. 369, Licoglossum oerstedii.

2000, Jan. 5 ***Perf. 14¼x14***

Sheets of 6

365 A131 33c #a.-f.	4.00	4.00
366 A131 33c #a.-f.	4.00	4.00
367 A131 33c #a.-f.	4.00	4.00

Souvenir Sheets

Perf. 14x14¼

368 A131 $1 multi	2.00	2.00
369 A131 $1 multi	2.00	2.00

Nos. 368-369 each contain one 31x53mm stamp.

Leaders of the 20th Century A132

Designs: a, Martin Luther King, Jr. b, Albert Schweitzer. c, Pope John Paul II. d, Sarvepalli Radhakrishnan. e, Toyohiko Kagawa. f, Mahatma Gandhi. g, Mother Teresa. h, Khyentse Rinpoche. i, Desmond Tutu. j, Chiara Lubich. k, 14th Dalai Lama. l, Abraham Heschel.

2000, Jan. 18 **Litho.** ***Perf. 14¼***

370 A132 33c Sheet of 12, #a.-l.	8.00	8.00

Souvenir Sheet

New Year 2000 (Year of the Dragon) — A133

2000, Feb. 5 ***Perf. 13¾***

371 A133 $2 multi	4.00	4.00

Butterflies A134

No. 372: a, Salamis parhassus. b, Morpho rhetenor. c, Danaus plexippus. d, Phyciodes actinote. e, Idea leucone. f, Actinote negra.

No. 373: a, Graphium sarpedon. b, Papilio machaon. c, Ornithoptera priamus. d, Ornithoptera chimaerea. e, Graphium antiphates. f, Pachliopta aristochiae.

Each $2: No. 374, Hamadryas amphinome, vert. No. 375, Colias croceus, vert. No. 376, Butterfly collector, vert.

2000, Feb. 28 **Litho.** ***Perf. 14***

Sheets of 6

372 A134 20c #a.-f.	2.40	2.40
373 A134 55c #a.-f.	6.75	6.75

Souvenir Sheets

374-376 A134 Set of 3	12.00	12.00

Millennium Type of 1999

Highlights of the 1920s: a, Mahatma Gandhi leads non-violent reform in India. b, International Dada Fair in Berlin. c, American women win right to vote. d, Sacco and Vanzetti case. e, Hermann Rorshach develops inkblot test. f, Thomas J. Watson incorporates IBM. g, First successful commercial 35mm camera. h, Scopes "Monkey Trial." i, Charles Lindbergh makes first solo transatlantic flight. j, George Lemaitre develops "Big Bang" theory of cosmology. k, Chiang Kai-shek becomes generalissimo of China. l, Werner Heisenberg states "uncertainty principle" of physics. m, Alexander Fleming isolates Penicillium mold. n, Hirohito enthroned as Japanese emperor. o, Stock market crash starts Great Depression. p, First round-the-world flight (60x40mm). q, "All Quiet on the Western Front" published.

2000, Mar. 13 ***Perf. 12¾x12½***

Sheet of 17

377 A127 20c #a.-q. + label	7.00	7.00

Inscriptions are incorrect or misspelled on Nos. 377a, 377f and 377m.

Millennium Type of 1999 with "Millennium 2000" Inscription

Perf. 13¼x13½

2000, Mar. 13 **Litho.**

378 A127 33c Like #356o	.65	.65

Peacemakers — A135

a, Mikhail Gorbachev. b, Ending the Cold War. c, Ronald Reagan. d, Le Duc Tho. e, Resolving the conflict in Viet Nam. f, Henry Kissinger. g, Linus Pauling. h, Protest against nuclear weapons. i, Peter Benenson. j, Amnesty Intl. k, Mahatma Gandhi. l, Fasting for peace. m, Initiating the Peace Corps. n, John F. Kennedy. o, Praying for peace. p, The 14th Dalai Lama. q, The UN. r, Cordell Hull. s, F. W. De Klerk. t, Ending apartheid. u, Nelson Mandela. v, Franklin Roosevelt. w, Yalta Conference. x, Winston Churchill.

Illustration reduced.

2000, Mar. 28 ***Perf. 14***

379 A135 33c Sheet of 24, #a-x	16.00	16.00

Philanthropists — A136

a, Andrew Carnegie. b, John D. Rockefeller. c, Henry Ford. d, Madam C. J. Walker. e, James B. Duke. f, Andrew Mellon. g, Charles F. Kettering. h, Robert W. Woodruff. i, Brooke Astor. j, Howard Hughes. k, Jesse H. Jones. l, Paul Mellon. m, J. Paul Getty. n, George Soros. o, Phyllis Wattis. p, Ted Turner.

2000, May 1 ***Perf. 14¼x14½***

380 A136 33c Sheet of 16, #a-p	11.00	11.00

Mushrooms — A137

No. 381, each 33c: a, Fairies' bonnets. b, Black bulgar. c, Amethyst deceiver. d, Common morel. e, Bird's nest fungus. f, Trumpet clitocybe.

No. 382, each 33c: a, Bonnet mycena. b, Horse mushroom. c, Velvet boletus. d, Oyster. d, Aztec mandala. e, Fly agaric.

Each $2: No. 383, Magpie ink cap. No, 384, Brown birch bolete.

2000, May 15 ***Perf. 13¾x14¼***
Sheets of 6, #a-f

381-382 A137 Set of 2 8.00 8.00

Souvenir Sheets

383-384 A137 Set of 2 8.00 8.00

Flowers of the Pacific — A138

Wildflowers — A139

No. 385: a, Freycinetia arborea. b, Mount Cook lily. c, Sun orchid. d, Bossiaea ensata. e, Swamp hibiscus. f, Gardenia brighamii.

No. 386: a, Eleagant brodiaea. b, Skyrocket. c, Hedge bindweed. d, Woods' rose. e, Swamp rose. f, Wake robin.

No. 387, Black-eyed Susan. No. 388, Yellow meadow lily.

2000, May 29 ***Perf. 14x13¾***

385 A138 33c Sheet of 6, #a-f 4.00 4.00
386 A139 33c Sheet of 6, #a-f 4.00 4.00

Souvenir Sheets

387 A138 $2 multi 4.00 4.00
388 A139 $2 multi 4.00 4.00

Souvenir Sheet

2000 Summer Olympics, Sydney — A140

No. 389: a, Henry Taylor. b, Cycling. c, Olympic Stadium, Munich and German flag. d, Ancient Greek wrestling.

2000, July 10 **Litho.** ***Perf. 14***

389 A140 33c Sheet of 4, #a-d 2.75 2.75

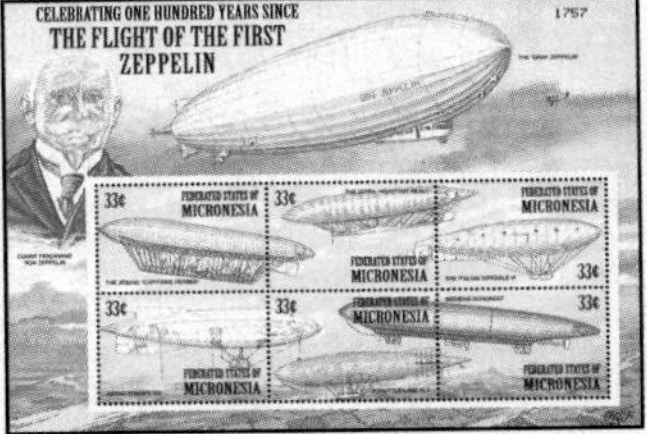

Zeppelins and Airships — A141

No. 390: a, Zodiac Capitaine Ferber. b, Astra Adjutant Reau. c, Italian dirigible IA. d, Astra-Torres XIV. e, Schuttle-Lanz SL3. f, Siemens-Schukert.

Each $2: No. 391, Graf Zeppelin. No. 392, Dupuy de Lome airship.

2000, Aug. 7 **Litho.** ***Perf. 14***

390 A141 33c Sheet of 6, #a-f 4.00 4.00

Souvenir Sheets

391-392 A141 Set of 2 8.00 8.00

First Zeppelin flight, cent. (#390, 391).

Flower Photomosaic Type of 1999

Various flowers making up a photomosaic of the Queen Mother.

2000, Sept. 5 **Litho.** ***Perf. 13¾***

393 A126 33c Sheet of 8, #a-h 5.25 5.25

Souvenir Sheet

2000 Summer Olympics, Sydney — A142

No. 394: a, 33c, Weight lifting. b, 33c, Basketball. c, $1, Weight lifting.

2000, Sept. 11 ***Perf. 14***

394 A142 Sheet of 3, #a-c 3.50 3.50

Olymphilex 2000, Sydney.

Fish A143

Designs: No. 395, Rock beauty. No. 396, Bluestreak cleaner wrasse. No. 397, Chevroned butterflyfish (with frame). No. 398, Longfin bannerfish (with frame).

No. 399: a, Mandarinfish. b, Emperor snapper. c, Copper-banded butterflyfish. d, Chevroned butterflyfish (no frame). e, Lemonpeel angelfish. f, Harlequin tuskfish. g, Clown triggerfish. h, Coral hind. i, Longfin bannerfish (no frame).

No. 400: a, Six-spot grouper. b, Common jellyfish. c, Palette surgeonfish. d, Bicolor angelfish. e, Threadfin butterflyfish. f, Clown anemonefish. g, Three-banded demoiselle. h, Reef shark. i, Starfish.

No. 401, Long-nosed butterflyfish. No. 402, Emperor angelfish.

2000, Nov. 1

395-398 A143 33c Set of 4 2.60 2.60

Sheets of 9, #a-i

399-400 A143 33c Set of 2 12.00 12.00

Souvenir Sheets

401-402 A143 $2 Set of 2 8.00 8.00

Flower Photomosaic Type of 1999

Various photos with religious themes making up a photomosaic of Pope John Paul II.

2000, Nov. 1 **Litho.** ***Perf. 13¾x14***

403 A126 50c Sheet of 8, #a-h 8.00 8.00

Christmas A144

Designs: 20c, The Holy Trinity, by Titian. 33c, The Adoration of the Magi, by Diego Velazquez. 60c, The Holy Nereus, by Peter Paul Rubens. $3.20, St. Gregory With Saints Around Him, by Rubens.

2000, Dec. 1 ***Perf. 14¼***

404-407 A144 Set of 4 8.75 8.75

Dogs and Cats — A145

No. 408, 33c: a, Afghan hound. b, Yellow Labrador retriever. c, Greyhound. d, German shepherd. e, King Charles spaniel. f, Jack Russell terrier.

No. 409, 33c: a, Siamese. b, Mackerel tabby. c, British shorthair. d, Persian. e, Turkish angora. f, Calico.

No. 410, $2, Dog in field. No. 411, $2, Cat stalking bird.

2000, June 26 **Litho.** ***Perf. 14***
Sheets of 6, #a-f

408-409 A145 Set of 2 8.00 8.00

Souvenir Sheets

410-411 A145 Set of 2 8.00 8.00

Souvenir Sheets

New Year 2001 (Year of the Snake) — A146

Designs: No. 412, 60c, Snake on ground. No. 413, 60c, Snake in bamboo, vert.

2001, Jan. 2

412-413 A146 Set of 2 2.40 2.40

Pokémon — A147

No. 414: a, Weepinbell. b, Snorlax. c, Seel. d, Hitmonchan. e, Jynx. f, Ponyta.

2001, Feb. 13 ***Perf. 13¾***

414 A147 50c Sheet of 6, #a-f 6.00 6.00

Souvenir Sheet

415 A147 $2 Farfetch'd 4.00 4.00

Whales — A148

No. 416, 50c: a, Fin. b, Right. c, Pygmy right. d, Humpback. e, Blue. f, Bowhead.

No. 417, 60c: a, True's beaked. b, Cuvier's beaked. c, Shepherd's beaked. d, Baird's beaked. e, Northern bottlenose. f, Pygmy sperm.

No. 418, $2, Killer. No. 419, $2, Sperm.

2001, Feb. 27 ***Perf. 13¼x13¾***
Sheets of 6, #a-f

416-417 A148 Set of 2 13.50 13.50

Souvenir Sheets

418-419 A148 Set of 2 8.00 8.00

Ecology — A149

No. 420: a, Coral reef in peril. b, Galapagos Islands tortoise. c, Tasmanian tiger. d, Yanomani. e, Bird from Florida Keys. f, Eagle, Endangered species act.

No. 421: a, Pollution. b, Deforestation. c, Acid rain. d, Greenhouse effect.

No. 422, $2, Bird in flight. No. 423, Chimpanzee, vert.

Perf. 13¼x13¾, 13¾x13¼

2001, Feb. 27 **Litho.**

420 A149 34c Sheet of 6, #a-f 4.25 4.25
421 A149 60c Sheet of 4, #a-d 5.00 5.00

Souvenir Sheets

422-423 A149 $2 Set of 2 8.00 8.00

Fish Type of 1998

Designs: 11c, Yellow damselfish. 34c, Rainbow runner. 70c, Whitelined grouper. 80c, Purple queen anthias. $3.50, Eibl's angelfish. $12.25, Blue-spotted boxfish.

2001, Mar. 28 *Perf. 14½x14¾*

424 A116	11c multi	.25	.25
425 A116	34c multi	.70	.70
426 A116	70c multi	1.40	1.40
427 A116	80c multi	1.60	1.60
428 A116	$3.50 multi	7.00	7.00
429 A116	$12.25 multi	25.00	25.00
	Nos. 424-429 (6)	35.95	35.95

Japanese Art — A150

Designs: No. 430, 34c, Parody of the Allegory of the Sage Chin Kao Riding a Carp, by Suzuki Harunobu. No. 431, 34c, The Courtesan Hinazuru of the Choji-Ya, by Chokosai Eisho. No. 432, 34c, Girl Tying Her Hair Ribbon, by Tori Kiyomine. No. 433, 34c, The Iris Garden, by Kiyonaga Torii. No. 434, 34c, The Courtesan Mayuzumi of the Daimonji-Ya, by Shunsho Katsukawa. No. 435, 34c, Bath House Scene, by Toyokuni Utagawa.

No. 436 — Paintings by Utamaro: a, Dance of a Kamisha. b, The Courtesan Hinazura at the Keizetsuro. c, Toilet Scene. d, Applying Lip Rouge. e, Beauty Reading a Letter. f, The Geisha Kamekichi.

No. 437, $2, Allegory of Ariwara No Narihira, by Kikugawa Eizan, horiz. No. 438, $2, Girl Seated by a Brook, by Harunobu, horiz.

2001, Apr. 20 *Perf. 14*

430-435 A150 Set of 6 4.25 4.25
436 A150 34c Sheet of 6, #a-f 4.25 4.25

Imperf

Size: 118x88mm

437-438 A150 Set of 2 8.00 8.00

Phila Nippon '01, Japan (Nos. 436-438).

Toulouse-Lautrec Paintings — A151

No. 439: a, Oscar Wilde. b, Doctor Tapie in a Theater Corridor. c, Monsieur Delaporte. $2, The Clowness Cha-U-Kao.

2001, May 15 *Perf. 13¾*

439 A151 60c Sheet of 3, #a-c 3.75 3.75

Souvenir Sheet

440 A151 $2 multi 4.00 4.00

Queen Victoria (1819-1901) — A152

Various portraits.

2001, May 15 *Perf. 14*

441 A152 60c Sheet of 6, #a-f 7.25 7.25

Souvenir Sheet

Perf. 13¾

442 A152 $2 shown 4.00 4.00

No. 441 contains six 28x42mm stamps.

Queen Elizabeth II, 75th Birthday — A153

No. 443: a, With necklace and brooch. b, Color photograph. c, As girl. d, As child. e, With dog. f, Facing left.
$2, Portrait in color.

2001, May 15 *Perf. 14*

443 A153 60c Sheet of 6, #a-f 7.25 7.25

Souvenir Sheet

444 A153 $2 multi 4.00 4.00

Marine Life — A154

No. 445, 60c, horiz.: a, Striped dolphin. b, Olive Ridley turtle. c, Goldrim tang. d, Blue shark. e, Picasso triggerfish. f, Polkadot grouper.

No. 446, 60c, horiz.: a, Loggerhead turtle. b, Striped marlin. c, Bicolor cherub. d, Clown wrasse. e, Clown triggerfish. f, Japanese tang.

No. 447, $2, Adult and juvenile emperor angelfish. No. 448, $2, Harlequin tuskfish, horiz.

2001, July 16 *Perf. 14*

Sheets of 6, #a-f

445-446 A154 Set of 2 14.50 14.50

Souvenir Sheets

Perf. 13¾

447-448 A154 Set of 2 8.00 8.00

Nos. 445-446 each contain six 42x28mm stamps.

Prehistoric Animals — A155

Designs: No. 449, 60c, Allosaurus (with frame). No. 450, 60c, Psittacosaurus. No. 451, 60c, Triceratops. No. 452, 60c, Archaeopteryx (with frame).

No. 453, 60c: a, Tyrannosaurus. b, Pteranodon. c, Brachiosaurus. d, Spinosaurus. e, Deinonychus. f, Teratosaurus.

No. 454, 60c: a, Parasaurolophus. b, Plateosaurus. c, Archaeopteryx (no frame). d, Allosaurus (no frame). e, Torosaurus. f, Euoplocephalus.

No. 455, $2, Tyrannosaurus. No. 456, $2, Parasaurolophus, horiz.

2001, Aug. 12 **Litho.** *Perf. 14*

449-452 A155 Set of 4 4.75 4.75

Sheets of 6, #a-f

453-454 A155 Set of 2 14.50 14.50

Souvenir Sheets

455-456 A155 Set of 2 8.00 8.00

Shells — A156

No. 457, 50c: a, Bat volute. b, Horned helmet. c, Troschel's murex. d, Lotorium triton. e, Orange-mouthed olive. f, Phos whelk.

No. 458, 50c, vert.: a, Oblique nutmeg. b, Imperial volute. c, Pontifical miter. d, Eburneus cone. e, Variegated sundial. f, Heart cockle.

No. 459, $2, Eyed auger. No. 460, $2, Geography cone.

2001, Oct. 15 **Litho.** *Perf. 14*

Sheets of 6, #a-f

457-458 A156 Set of 2 12.00 12.00

Souvenir Sheets

459-460 A156 Set of 2 8.00 8.00

On Nos. 485a-458f, the descriptions of the shells are transposed. Our descriptions are those of the stamps as they are printed.

Birds A157

Designs: 5c, Malleefowl. 22c, Corncrake. 23c, Hooded merganser. $2.10, Purple gallinule.

No. 465, 60c: a, Fairy wren. b, Golden-crowned kinglet warbler. c, Flame-tempered babbler. d, Golden-headed cisticola. e, White-browed babbler. f, White-breasted dipper.

No. 466, 60c: a, Logrunner. b, Eurasian treecreeper. c, Goldfinch. d, Rufous fantail. e, Orange-billed flowerpecker. f, American goldfinch.

No. 467, $2, Emperor bird of paradise. No. 468, $2, Yellow-eyed cuckooshrike, vert.

2001, Oct. 29 **Litho.** *Perf. 14*

461-464 A157 Set of 4 5.25 5.25

Sheets of 6, #a-f

465-466 A157 Set of 2 14.50 14.50

Souvenir Sheets

467-468 A157 Set of 2 8.00 8.00

Nobel Prizes, Cent. — A158

No. 469, 60c — Physiology or Medicine laureates: a, Alexis Carrel, 1912. b, Max Theiler, 1951. c, Niels Finsen, 1903. d, Philip S. Hench, 1950. e, Sune Bergström, 1982. f, John R. Vane, 1982.

No. 470, 60c — Laureates: a, Bengt Samuelsson, Physiology or Medicine, 1982. b, Johannes Fibiger, Physiology or Medicine, 1926. c, Theodore Richards, Chemistry, 1914. d, Tadeus Reichstein, Physiology or Medicine, 1950. e, Frederick Soddy, Chemistry, 1921. f, Albert Szent-Györgyi, 1937.

No. 471, $2, Irving Langmuir, Chemistry, 1932. No. 472, $2, Artturi Illmari Virtanen, Chemistry, 1945.

2001, Nov. 12

Sheets of 6, #a-f

469-470 A158 Set of 2 14.50 14.50

Souvenir Sheets

471-472 A158 Set of 2 8.00 8.00

Christmas A159

Santa Claus: 22c, On cat. 34c, Between Christmas trees. 60c, In sleigh. $1, On dog. $2, Entering chimney, vert.

2001, Dec. 5

473-476 A159 Set of 4 4.50 4.50

Souvenir Sheet

477 A159 $2 multi 4.00 4.00

Attack on Pearl Harbor, 60th Anniv. — A160

No. 478, 60c: a, Rollover of USS Oklahoma. b, Japanese attack Wheeler Air Field. c, Japanese sailors loading bombs onto planes. d, Destroyer USS Ward sinks a Japanese submarine. e, USS Arizona sunk by Japanese bombs. f, Ewa Marine Base attacked by Japanese.

No. 479, 60c: a, Memorial poster showing attack. b, Japanese Prime Minister Hideki Tojo. c, Rescue at Bellows Field. d, Rescue of USS Arizona crew. e, Admiral Isoroku Yamamoto. f, Memorial poster showing soldier and flag.

No. 480, $2, USS Arizona Memorial. No. 481, $2, Pres. Franklin D. Roosevelt.

2001, Dec. 7

Sheets of 6, #a-f

478-479 A160 Set of 2 14.50 14.50

Souvenir Sheets

480-481 A160 Set of 2 8.00 8.00

Souvenir Sheet

New Year 2002 (Year of the Horse) — A161

Various horses.

2002, Jan. 24 ***Perf. 13¾x13¼***

482 A161 60c Sheet of 5, #a-e 6.00 6.00

Reign of Queen Elizabeth II, 50th Anniv. — A162

No. 483: a, Queen wearing flowered dress. b, Prince Philip. c, Queen waving, holding flowers. d, Queen with children.

$2, Queen wearing scarf.

2002, Feb. 6 ***Perf. 14¼***

483 A162 80c Sheet of 4, #a-d 6.50 6.50

Souvenir Sheet

484 A162 $2 multi 4.00 4.00

United We Stand — A163

2002, Feb. 20 ***Perf. 13¾x13¼***

485 A163 $1 multi 2.00 2.00

Issued in sheets of 4.

2002 Winter Olympics, Salt Lake City — A164

Designs: No. 486, $1, Luge. No. 487, $1, Ice hockey.

2002, Mar. 18 ***Perf. 14***

486-487 A164 Set of 2 4.00 4.00

487a Souvenir sheet, #486-487 4.00 4.00

Compare with Nos. 502-503.

Japanese Art — A165

Birds and Flowers of the Twelve Months, by Hoitsu Sakai — No. 488, 60c: a, January. b, February. c, March. d, April. e, May. f, June.

No. 489, 60c: a, July. b, August. c, September. d, October. e, November. f, December.

No. 490, $2, Seashells and Plums by Kiitsu Suzuki. No. 491, Peacock and Peonies, by Rosetsu Nagasawa.

2002, Mar. 25 **Litho.** ***Perf. 14x14¾***

Sheets of 6, #a-f

488-489 A165 Set of 2 14.50 14.50

Imperf

490-491 A165 Set of 2 8.00 8.00

Nos. 488-489 each contain six 77x26mm stamps.

Intl. Year of Mountains — A166

No. 492: a, Matterhorn, Switzerland. b, Maroonbells, U.S. c, Wetterhorn, Switzerland. d, Mt. Tsaranora, Africa.

$2, Cerro Fitzroy, South America.

2002, Mar. 30 ***Perf. 14***

492 A166 80c Sheet of 4, #a-d 6.50 6.50

Souvenir Sheet

493 A166 $2 multi 4.00 4.00

Pres. John F. Kennedy (1917-63) — A167

No. 494: a, Dark blue background. b, Lilac background, name at left. c, Tan background, name at right. d, Light blue background.

$2, Purple background.

2002, Mar. 30

494 A167 60c Sheet of 4, #a-d 5.00 5.00

Souvenir Sheet

495 A167 $2 multi 4.00 4.00

Princess Diana (1961-97) — A168

No. 496: a, Wearing wedding veil. b, Wearing tiara and necklace. c, Wearing brimless hat. d, Wearing scarf. e, Hatless. f, Wearing tiara and large collar.

$2, Wearing hat with brim.

2002, Mar. 30

496 A168 60c Sheet of 6, #a-f 7.25 7.25

Souvenir Sheet

497 A168 $2 multi 4.00 4.00

Intl. Year of Ecotourism — A169

No. 498: a, Lizard. b, Canoes. c, Micronesian house. d, Three children in costume. e, Woman. f, Two dancers, house.

$2, Fishermen.

Perf. 13¼x13½

2002, June 17 **Litho.**

498 A169 80c Sheet of 6, #a-f 9.75 9.75

Souvenir Sheet

499 A169 $2 multi 4.00 4.00

20th World Scout Jamboree, Thailand — A170

No. 500: a, Thai temple. b, American scout insignia. c, Scout cap.

$2, Merit badges.

2002, June 17 ***Perf. 13½x13¼***

500 A170 $1 Sheet of 3, #a-c 6.00 6.00

Souvenir Sheet

501 A170 $2 multi 4.00 4.00

Winter Olympics Type of 2002 Redrawn With White Panel Behind Olympic Rings

Designs: No. 502, $1, Luge. No. 503, $1, Ice hockey.

2002, July 15

502-503 A164 Set of 2 4.00 4.00

503a Souvenir sheet, #502-503 4.00 4.00

Xavier High School, 50th Anniv. A171

2002, July 31 ***Perf. 13½x13¾***

504 A171 37c multi .75 .75

Queen Mother Elizabeth (1900-2002) — A172

No. 505, horiz.: a, At age 7. b, At wedding. c, At birth of Princess Elizabeth. d, At coronation of King George VI, 1937.

$2, As elderly lady.

2002, Aug. 12 ***Perf. 14***

505 A172 80c Sheet of 4, #a-d 6.50 6.50

Souvenir Sheet

506 A172 $2 multi 4.00 4.00

Teddy Bears, Cent. — A173

No. 507: a, Burglar bear. b, White bear with heart. c, Blue bear with flowers. d, Brown bear with heart.

2002, Sept. 23 **Litho.** ***Perf. 14***

507 A173 80c Sheet of 4, #a-d 6.50 6.50

Elvis Presley (1935-77) — A174

Presley with: a, Hand below guitar. b, Head on guitar. c, Hat. d, Checked shirt, no hat. e, Arms raised. f, Microphone.

2002, Oct. 7 ***Perf. 13¾***
508 A174 37c Sheet of 6, #a-f 4.50 4.50

Christmas A175

Paintings: 21c, Madonna and Child, by Filippino Lippi, vert. 37c, Madonna and Child, by Giovanni Bellini, vert. 70c, Madonna and Child Between St. Stephen and St. Ladislaus, by Simone Martini. 80c, Holy Family, by Bronzino, vert. No. 513, $2, Holy Family, by Martini, vert.
No. 514, Sacred Conversation, by Bellini, vert.

2002, Nov. 4 ***Perf. 14***
509-513 A175 Set of 5 8.25 8.25

Souvenir Sheet
Perf. 14x14¼
514 A175 $2 multi 4.00 4.00

Flora, Fauna and Mushrooms — A176

No. 515, 37c — Moths: a, White-lined sphinx. b, Tropical fruit-piercer. c, Coppery dysphania. d, Large agarista. e, Indian moon moth. f, Croker's frother.
No. 516, 55c — Mushrooms: a, Phellinus robustus. b, Purple coincap. c, Shaggy parasol. d, King bolete. e, Boletus crocipodius. f, Sharp-scaled parasol.
No. 517, 60c — Orchids: a, Eria javanica. b, Cymbidium finlaysonianum. c, Coelogyne asperata. d, Spathoglottis affinis. e, Vanda tricolor. f, Calanthe rosea.
No. 518, 60c — Butterflies: a, Meadow argus. b, Cairns birdwing. c, Large green-banded blue. d, Beak butterfly. e, Palmfly. f, Broad-bordered grass yellow.
No. 519, 80c — Insects and spiders: a, Stag beetle. b, Honeybee. c, Black widow spider. d, Mosquito. e, Black ant. f, Cicada.
No. 520, $2, Zodiac moth. No. 521, $2, Lepiota acutesquamosa mushroom. No. 522, $2, Dendrobium phalaenopsis orchid. No. 523, $2, Yamfly butterfly. No. 524, $2, Dragonfly, horiz.

2002, Dec. 16 ***Perf. 14***
Sheets of 6, #a-f
515-519 A176 Set of 5 35.00 35.00

Souvenir Sheets
520-524 A176 Set of 5 20.00 20.00

Birds — A177

Designs: 3c, Greater flame-backed woodpecker. 5c, Red-tailed tropicbird. 21c, Hair-crested drongo. 22c, Pale white-eye. 23c, White-backed munia. 37c, Yap monarch. 60c, Eclectus parrot. 70c, Sulphur-crested cockatoo. 80c, Giant white-eye. $2, Green magpie. $3.85, Dollarbird.

2002, Dec. 30 ***Perf. 14¼x14***

525	A177	3c multi	.20	.20
526	A177	5c multi	.20	.20
527	A177	21c multi	.40	.40
528	A177	22c multi	.45	.45
529	A177	23c multi	.45	.45
530	A177	37c multi	.75	.75
531	A177	60c multi	1.25	1.25
532	A177	70c multi	1.40	1.40
533	A177	80c multi	1.60	1.60
534	A177	$2 multi	4.00	4.00
		Perf. 13¾		
535	A177	$3.85 multi	7.75	7.75
536	A177	$5 multi	10.00	10.00
537	A177	$13.65 multi	27.50	27.50
		Nos. 525-537 (13)	55.95	55.95

First Non-stop Solo Transatlantic Flight, 75th Anniv. (in 2002) — A178

No. 538: a, Charles Lindbergh, Donald Hall, Spirit of St. Louis. b, Spirit of St. Louis, Apr. 28, 1927. c, Towing of Spirit of St. Louis, May 20. d, Lindbergh taking off from Roosevelt Field, May 20. e, Lindbergh's arrival in Paris, May 21. f, Lindbergh in ticker tape parade, New York.

2003, Jan. 13 **Litho.** ***Perf. 14***
538 A178 60c Sheet of 6, #a-f 7.25 7.25

New Year 2003 (Year of the Ram) — A179

No. 539: a, Black ram facing left, country name at left. b, Black ram facing left, country name at right. c, White ram facing right, country name at left. d, White ram facing forward, country name at right.

2003, Feb. 1 **Litho.** ***Perf. 14¼x14***
539 A179 37c Sheet of 6, #a-b, 2 each #c-d 4.50 4.50

Astronauts Killed in Space Shuttle Columbia Accident — A180

No. 540: a, Mission Specialist 1 David M. Brown. b, Commander Rick D. Husband. c, Mission Specialist 4 Laurel Blair Salton Clark. d, Mission Specialist 4 Kalpana Chawla. e, Payload Commander Michael P. Anderson. f, Pilot William C. McCool. g, Payload Specialist Ilan Ramon.

2003, Apr. 7 ***Perf. 13½x13¼***
540 A180 37c Sheet of 7, #a-g 5.25 5.25

Coronation of Queen Elizabeth II, 50th Anniv. — A181

No. 541: a, Wearing pearl necklace. b, Wearing sash and tiara. c, Wearing robe.
$2, Wearing crown.

2003, May 13 ***Perf. 14x14¼***
541 A181 $1 Sheet of 3, #a-c 6.00 6.00

Souvenir Sheet
542 A181 $2 multi 4.00 4.00

Prince William, 21st Birthday — A182

No. 543: a, Wearing checked shirt and striped sweater. b, Facing right, wearing sweater, shirt and tie. c, Wearing suit and tie.
$2, Wearing raincoat.

2003, May 14
543 A182 $1 Sheet of 3, #a-c 6.00 6.00

Souvenir Sheet
544 A182 $2 multi 4.00 4.00

Operation Iraqi Freedom — A183

No. 545, 37c: a, B-52 Bomber. b, F-16 Fighter. c, Cobra Helicopter. d, Apache Helicopter. e, T8000 Tow Missile. f, Bradley Tank.
No. 546, 37c: a, Stealth Fighter. b, AC-130 Cargo plane. c, MH-53j Pave Low II Helicopter. d, Predator. e, Challenger Two Tank. f, Aegis Cruiser.

2003, May 14 ***Perf. 14***
Sheets of 6, #a-f
545-546 A183 Set of 2 9.00 9.00

Tour de France Bicycle Race, Cent. — A184

No. 547: a, Greg LeMond, 1990. b, Miguel Indurain, 1991. c, Indurain, 1992. d, Indurain, 1993.
$2, Marco Pantani, 1998.

2003, July 1 ***Perf. 13½***
547 A184 60c Sheet of 4, #a-d 5.00 5.00

Souvenir Sheet
548 A184 $2 multi 4.00 4.00

Intl. Year of Fresh Water — A185

No. 549: a, Kosrae mangroves. b, Chuuk Lagoon. c, Pohnpei's waterfalls.
$2, Pohnpei Lagoon.

2003, July 21 ***Perf. 13½***
549 A185 $1 Sheet of 3, #a-c 6.00 6.00

Souvenir Sheet
550 A185 $2 multi 4.00 4.00

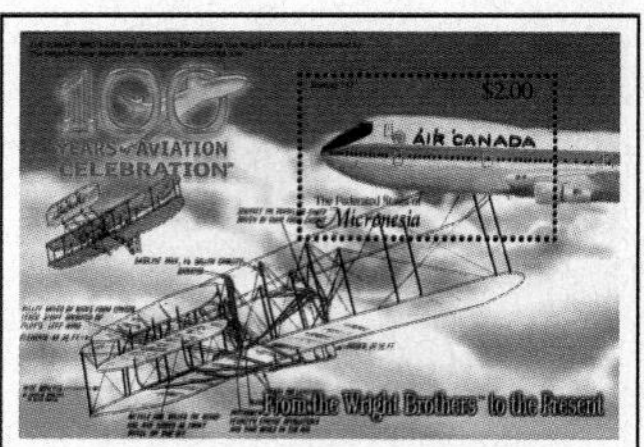

Powered Flight, Cent. — A186

No. 551: a, Concorde. b, Boeing 757. c, Junkers F13a. d, Martin M-130 China Clipper. e, Handley Page H.P.42W. f, Wright Flyer II.
$2, Boeing 747.

2003, Aug. 7 ***Perf. 14***
551 A186 55c Sheet of 6, #a-f 6.75 6.75

Souvenir Sheet
552 A186 $2 multi 4.00 4.00

2003 APS Stampshow, Columbus, Ohio (#551).

Circus Performers — A187

No. 553, 80c: a, Glen Little. b, Joseph Grimaldi. c, Beverly Reno Bergerson. d, Coco Michael Polakov.
No. 554, 80c: a, Jana Mandana. b, Maxim Papazov. c, Harry Keaton. d, Giraffe.

2003, Aug. 25 ***Perf. 14***
Sheets of 4, #a-d
553-554 A187 Set of 2 13.00 13.00

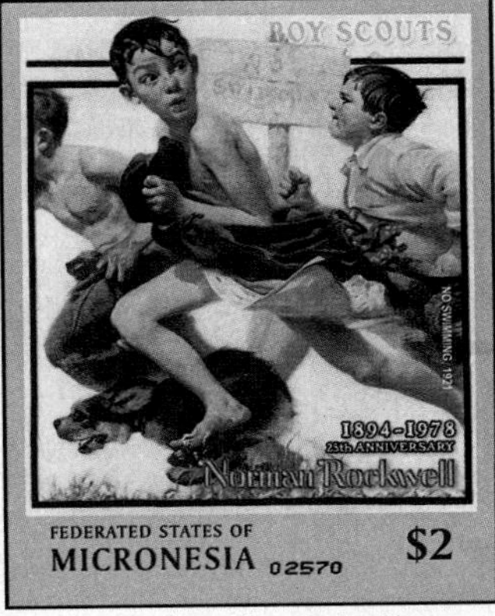

Paintings of Boy Scouts by Norman Rockwell (1894-1978) — A188

No. 555: a, Scout with plaid neckerchief, from 1963 Boy Scout Calendar. b, A Scout is Helpful. c, The Scoutmaster. d, Scout with red neckerchief, from 1963 Boy Scout Calendar.
$2, No Swimming.

2003, Sept. 8 ***Perf. 14***
555 A188 80c Sheet of 4, #a-d 6.50 6.50
Imperf
556 A188 $2 multi 4.00 4.00
No. 555 contains four 28x42mm stamps.

Paintings by Paul Gauguin (1848-1903) — A189

No. 557: a, Vahine No Te Tiare. b, Les Amants. c, Trois Tahitiens Conversation. d, Arearea.
$2, Ta Matete.

2003, Sept. 8 ***Perf. 13¾***
557 A189 80c Sheet of 4, #a-d 6.50 6.50
Imperf
558 A189 $2 multi 4.00 4.00
No. 557 contains four 51x38mm stamps.

Paintings of James McNeill Whistler (1834-1903) — A190

Designs: 37c, Blue and Silver Blue: Wave, Biarritz. 55c, Brown and Silver: Old Battersea Bridge. 60c, Nocturne in Blue and Silver: The Lagoon, Venice. 80c, Crepuscule in Flesh Color and Green: Valparaiso.
No. 563: a, Symphony in White No. 2: The Little White Girl, vert. b, At the Piano (75x50mm). c, Symphony in White No. 1: The White Girl, vert.
$2, Portrait of Thomas Carlyle: Arrangement in Gray and Black No. 2, vert.

2003, Oct. 6 ***Perf. 14¼***
559-562 A190 Set of 4 4.75 4.75
563 A190 $1 Sheet of 3, #a-c 6.00 6.00
Size: 83x104mm
Imperf
564 A190 $2 multi 4.00 4.00

Christmas A191

Designs: 37c, Madonna of the Carnation, by Leonardo da Vinci. 60c, Madonna with Yarn Winder, by da Vinci. 80c, Litta Madonna, by da Vinci. $1, Madonna of the Grand Duke, by Raphael.
$2, The Adoration of the Magi, by Giambattista Tiepolo.

2003, Nov. 5 ***Perf. 14¼***
565-568 A191 Set of 4 5.75 5.75
Souvenir Sheet
569 A191 $2 multi 4.00 4.00

Cats, Dogs, Birds, Reptiles & Amphibians — A192

No. 570, 80c — Cats: a, Ragdoll. b, Calico Shorthaired Japanese Bobtail. c, Blue Mackerel Taffy Exotic Shorthair. d, Dilute Calico.
No. 571, 80c — Dogs: a, Australian shepherd. b, Greyhound. c, English bulldog. d, Schnauzer.
No. 572, 80c, horiz. — Birds: a, Green-winged macaw. b, American flamingo. c, Blue and gold macaw. d, Abyssinian ground hornbill.
No. 573, 80c, horiz. — Reptiles and amphibians: a, Leopard gecko. b, Red-eyed tree frog. c, Panther chameleon. d, Green and black poison frog.
No. 574, $2, Lynx Point Colorpoint Shorthair. No. 575, $2, Toy poodle. No. 576, $2, American flamingo. No. 577, $2, Madagascan chameleon, horiz.

2003, Dec. 22 ***Perf. 14***
Sheets of 4, #a-d
570-573 A192 Set of 4 26.00 26.00
Souvenir Sheets
574-577 A192 Set of 4 16.00 16.00

Pres. Bailey Olter (1932-99) — A193

2004, Feb. 16 **Litho.** ***Perf. 14***
578 A193 37c multi .75 .75

Paintings by Pablo Picasso (1881-1973) — A194

No. 579: a, Marie-Thérèse Leaning on One Elbow. b, Portrait of Jaime Sabartés. c, Portrait of Emilie Marguerite Walter (Mémé). d, Bust of a Woman Leaning on One Elbow.
$2, Seated Bather (Olga).

2004, Mar. 8 ***Perf. 14¼***
579 A194 80c Sheet of 4, #a-d 6.50 6.50
Imperf
580 A194 $2 multi 4.00 4.00
No. 579 contains four 37x50mm stamps.

Paintings in the Hermitage, St. Petersburg, Russia A195

Designs: 22c, A Young Lady in a Theatrical Costume, by Alexis Grimou. 37c, Portrait of Mrs. Harriet Greer, by George Romney. 80c, Portrait of Prince Nikolai Yusupov, by Friedrich Heinrich Füger. $1, Portrait of Richard Brinsley Sheridan, by John Hoppner.
$2, Spanish Concert (Conversation Espagnole), by Carle Vanloo.

2004, Mar. 8 ***Perf. 14¼***
581-584 A195 Set of 4 5.00 5.00
Imperf
Size: 64x81mm
585 A195 $2 multi 4.00 4.00

New Year 2004 (Year of the Monkey) — A196

Designs: 50c, Moon-struck Gibbon, by Gao Qi-feng. $1, Detail from Moon-struck Gibbon.

2004, Mar. 9 ***Perf. 13¼***
586 A196 50c multi 1.00 1.00
Souvenir Sheet
Perf. 13¼x13
587 A196 $1 multi 2.00 2.00
No. 587 contains one 30x40mm stamp. No. 586 printed in sheets of four.

Election of Pope John Paul II, 25th Anniv. (in 2003) — A197

No. 588 — Pope John Paul II: a, Visiting Monaco, 1990. b, With Bill and Hillary Clinton, 1999. c, Visiting Ukraine, 2001. d, Visiting Spain, 2003.

2004, Sept. 1 ***Perf. 14¼x14***
588 A197 80c Sheet of 4, #a-d 6.50 6.50

2004 European Soccer Championships, Portugal — A198

No. 589: a, Lars Olsen. b, Juergen Klinsmann. c, Peter Schmeichel. d, Nya Ullevi Stadium.
$2, 1992 Denmark team, horiz.

2004, Sept. 1 ***Perf. 14***
589 A198 80c Sheet of 4, #a-d 6.50 6.50
Souvenir Sheet
Perf. 14¼
590 A198 $2 multi 4.00 4.00
No. 589 contains four 28x42mm stamps.

D-Day, 60th Anniv. — A199

No. 591: a, Landing craft vehicle personnel. b, Destroyer Thompson. c, LST-391. d, Rhino Ferry 2, Rhino Tug 3. e, HMS Mauritius. f, Battleship Arkansas.
$2, LCI 1539.

2004, Sept. 1 ***Perf. 14***
591 A199 50c Sheet of 6, #a-f 6.00 6.00

Souvenir Sheet

592 A199 $2 multi 4.00 4.00

Souvenir Sheet

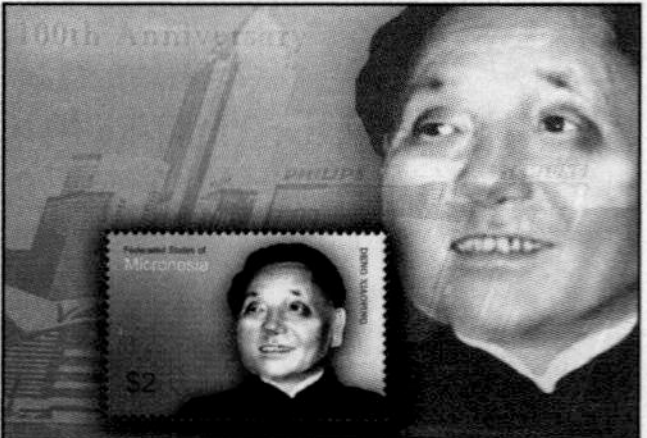

Deng Xiaoping (1904-97), Chinese Leader — A200

2004, Sept. 1 **Litho.** ***Perf. 14***
593 A200 $2 multi 4.00 4.00

Locomotives, Bicent. — A201

No. 594, 80c: a, CFL N5520. b, Inter-region trains. c, SW-600. d, WSOR 3801.
No. 595, 80c: a, Baldwin 2-8-0. b, F-10 #1114 Diesel. c, BNSF locomotive (incorrectly inscribed "Okinawa Hitachi trains". d, Shinkansen.
No. 596, 80c: a, RS-1 #22. b, Diesel class 630. c, Okinawa Hitachi train. d, Eurostar.
No. 597, $2, Eurostar, diff. No. 598, $2, Locomotive 231-065. No. 599, $2, Michigan Central locomotive.

2004, Sept. 1 **Sheets of 4, #a-d**
594-596 A201 Set of 3 19.50 19.50

Souvenir Sheets

597-599 A201 Set of 3 12.00 12.00

Birds Type of 2002

Designs: 2c, Blue-gray gnatcatcher. 10c, Clapper rail.

2004, Nov. 1 ***Perf. 13¼***
600 A177 2c multi .20 .20
601 A177 10c multi .20 .20

Miniature Sheet

Intl. Year of Peace — A202

No. 602: a, Nelson Mandela. b, Dalai Lama. c, Pope John Paul II.

2004, Nov. 1 ***Perf. 14***
602 A202 80c Sheet of 3, #a-c 5.00 5.00

2004 Summer Olympics, Athens — A203

Designs: 37c, Ancient bronze sculpture of horse and rider. 55c, Pin from 1912 Stockholm Olympics, vert. 80c, Baron Pierre de Coubertin, Intl. Olympic Committee President, vert. $1, Poster from 1968 Mexico City Olympics, vert.

2004, Nov. 1 ***Perf. 14¼***
603-606 A203 Set of 4 5.50 5.50

Miniature Sheets

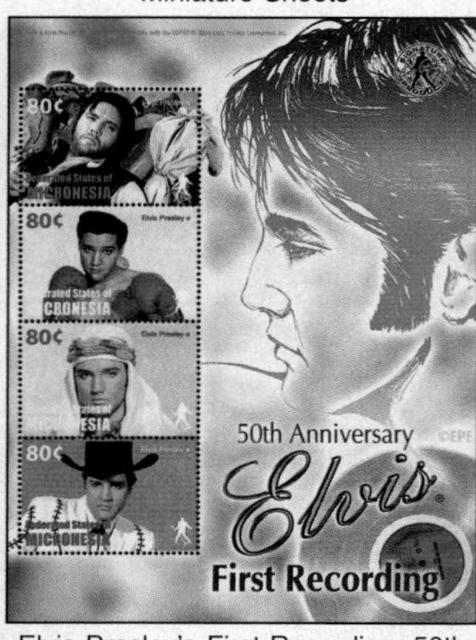

Elvis Presley's First Recording, 50th Anniv. — A204

No. 607, 80c — Presley with: a, Beard. b, Boxing gloves. c, Kaffiyeh. d, Cowboy hat.
No. 608, 80c, vert. — Presley with denomination in: a, Red. b, Purple. c, Blue. d, Orange yellow.

2004, Nov. 1 ***Perf. 14***

Sheets of 4, #a-d

607-608 A204 Set of 2 13.00 13.00

Flowers — A205

No. 609, horiz.: a, Epiphytic aeschynanthus. b, Darwinia collina. c, Rhododendron. d, Rhododendron retusum. e, Eucryphia lucida. f, Microporus xanthopus.
$2, Grevillea.

2004, Nov. 1 ***Perf. 13¼x13½***
609 A205 55c Sheet of 6, #a-f 6.75 6.75

Souvenir Sheet

Perf. 13½x13¼

610 A205 $2 multi 4.00 4.00

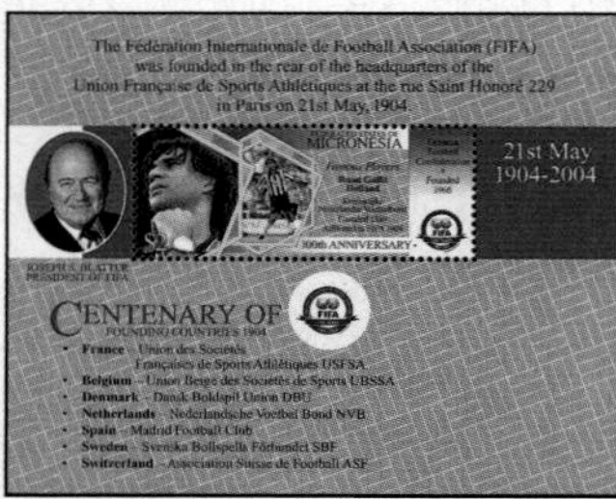

FIFA (Fédération Internationale de Football Association), Cent. — A206

No. 611: a, Herman Crespo. b, Peter Shilton. c, Klaus Augenthaler. d, Bryan Robson.
$2, Ruud Gullit.

2004, Nov. 1 ***Perf. 12¾x12½***
611 A206 80c Sheet of 4, #a-d 6.50 6.50

Souvenir Sheet

612 A206 $2 multi 4.00 4.00

National Basketball Association Players — A207

Designs: No. 613, 20c, Dirk Nowitzki, Dallas Mavericks. No. 614, 20c, Vince Carter, Toronto Raptors.

2004 ***Perf. 14***
613-614 A207 Set of 2 .80 .80

Issued: No. 613, 11/2; No. 614, 11/3. Each stamp issued in sheets of 12.

When Prehistoric Mammals Walked the Earth...

Moeritherium
$2
Federated States of
Micronesia

Prehistoric Animals — A208

No. 615, 80c: a, Indricotheres. b, Hyaenodons. c, Deinotherium. d, Chalicotheres.
No. 616, 80c: a, Apatosaurus. b, Pachyrhinosaurus. c, Kentrosaurus. d, Saltasaurus.
No. 617, 80c, vert.: a, Allosaurus. b, Tyrannosaurus. c, Troodon. d, Carnotaurus.
No. 618, $2, Moeritherium. No. 619, $2, Coelophysis. No. 620, $2, Deinonychus.

Perf. 14½x14, 14x14½

2004, Dec. 13 **Litho.**

Sheets of 4, #a-d

615-617 A208 Set of 3 19.50 19.50

Souvenir Sheets

618-620 A208 Set of 3 12.00 12.00

Fish and Coral — A209

No. 621: a, Clown triggerfish. b, Striped-face unicornfish. c, Firefish. d, Longnose hawkfish. e, Annella mollis. f, Dendronephthya.
$2, Great barracuda.

2004, Nov. 1 **Litho.** ***Perf. 13½***
621 A209 55c Sheet of 6, #a-f 6.75 6.75

Souvenir Sheet

622 A209 $2 multi 4.00 4.00

Reptiles and Amphibians — A210

No. 623: a, Blue coral snake. b, Solomon Islands horned frog. c, Levuka wrinkled ground frog. d, Flying lizard. e, Platymantis vitensis. f, Pacific ground boa.
$2, Loggerhead turtle.

2004, Nov. 1

623 A210 55c Sheet of 6, #a-f 6.75 6.75

Souvenir Sheet

624 A210 $2 multi 4.00 4.00

No. 623c has incorrect inscription as stamp depicts a lizard.

Birds — A211

No. 625, vert.: a, Black-faced woodswallows. b, Brown boobies. c, Rainbow lorikeets. d, Wandering albatross. e, Kagu. f, Great frigatebird.

$2, Golden whistler.

2004, Nov. 1

625 A211 55c Sheet of 6, #a-f 6.75 6.75

Souvenir Sheet

626 A211 $2 multi 4.00 4.00

Christmas A212

Madonna and Child paintings by: 37c, Giovanni Battista Tiepolo. 60c, Raphael. 80c, Jan Gossaert (Mabuse). $1, Fra Filippo Lippi.

$2, Unknown artist.

2004, Dec. 27 ***Perf. 14¼***

627-630 A212 Set of 4 5.75 5.75

Souvenir Sheet

631 A212 $2 multi 4.00 4.00

New Year 2005 (Year of the Rooster) — A213

2005, Jan. 17 ***Perf. 12¾***

632 A213 50c multi 1.00 1.00

Printed in sheets of 4.

Basketball Players Type of 2004

Design: Luke Walton, Los Angeles Lakers.

2005, Feb. 24 ***Perf. 14***

633 A207 20c multi .40 .40

Pres. Ronald Reagan (1911-2004) — A214

No. 634: a, With British Prime Minister Margaret Thatcher. b, With Israeli Prime Minister Yitzhak Shamir.

2005, Mar. 21 ***Perf. 13¼x13½***

634 A214 55c Horiz. pair, #a-b 2.25 2.25

Printed in sheets containing 3 each Nos. 634a and 634b.

Elvis Presley (1935-2005) — A215

No. 635, 60c — Photos from: a, 1955. b, 1956. c, 1960 (with arm outstretched). d, 1968. e, 1970. f, 1973.

No. 636, 60c — Photos from: a, 1957. b, 1960 (in army uniform). c, 1963. d, 1965. e, 1967. f, 1969.

2005, Mar. 21 ***Perf. 13½x13¼***

Sheets of 6, #a-f

635-636 A215 Set of 2 14.50 14.50

End of World War II, 60th Anniv. — A216

No. 637, 60c: a, U.S. soldiers marching in Ireland. b, British troops cross Volturno River, Italy. c, Hawker Typhoon attacks enemy on the Rhine River. d, Damaged Remagen Bridge. e, Meeting of Russian and American armies near Torgau, Germany.

No. 638, 60c: a, Poster remembering Pearl Harbor. b, Chula Beach, Tinian Island. c, Paul Tibbets and the Enola Gay. d, Hiroshima atomic bomb mushroom cloud. e, Newspaper announcing Japanese surrender.

2005, Mar. 31 ***Perf. 14***

Sheets of 5, #a-e

637-638 A216 Set of 2 12.00 12.00

Friedrich von Schiller (1759-1805), Writer — A217

No. 639: a, Wearing red cape. b, Statue. c, With head on hand.

2005, Mar. 31

639 A217 $1 Sheet of 3, #a-c 6.00 6.00

Souvenir Sheet

640 A217 $2 shown 4.00 4.00

Battle of Trafalgar, Bicent. — A218

Various depictions of ships in battle: 37c, 55c, 80c, $1.

$2, Death of Admiral Horatio Nelson.

2005, Mar. 31 ***Perf. 14¼***

641-644 A218 Set of 4 5.50 5.50

Souvenir Sheet

645 A218 $2 multi 4.00 4.00

Pope John Paul II (1920-2005) A219

2005, June 27 ***Perf. 13½x13¼***

646 A219 $1 multi 2.00 2.00

Printed in sheets of 6.

Rotary International, Cent. — A220

No. 647, vert.: a, Child. b, Emblem. c, 2004-05 Rotary International President Glenn E. Estess, Sr.

$2, 2002-03 Rotary International President Bhichai Rattakul.

2005, July 12 ***Perf. 12¾***

647 A220 $1 Sheet of 3, #a-c 6.00 6.00

Souvenir Sheet

648 A220 $2 multi 4.00 4.00

Jules Verne (1828-1905), Writer — A221

No. 649, vert.: a, Around the World in 80 Days. b, Phineas Fogg in India. c, Phineas Fogg, explorer and adventurer.

$2, Nautilus.

2005, June 7 **Litho.** ***Perf. 12¾***

649 A221 $1 Sheet of 3, #a-c 6.00 6.00

Souvenir Sheet

650 A221 $2 multi 4.00 4.00

Souvenir Sheet

Expo 2005, Aichi, Japan — A222

No. 651: a, Gray nurse shark. b, Surfer. c, Krakatoa Volcano. d, Yellow coral.

2005, June 27 ***Perf. 12x12¼***

651 A222 80c Sheet of 4, #a-d 6.50 6.50

Boats — A223

No. 652: a, 37c, Papyrus boat. b, 55c, Outrigger canoe. c, 80c, Papyrus sailboat. d, $1, Arab dhow.

$2, Lateen-rigged Nile riverboat.

2005, June 27 ***Perf. 12¾***

652 A223 Sheet of 4, #a-d 5.50 5.50

Souvenir Sheet

653 A223 $2 multi 4.00 4.00

Kosrae Government Building Complex — A224

Views of various buildings with frame colors of: 4c, Light yellow. 10c, Light blue. 22c, Pink. 37c, Light green.

2005, July 8 ***Perf. 14***

654-657 A224 Set of 4 1.50 1.50

Vatican City No. 67 — A225

2005, Aug. 9 ***Perf. 13x13¼***

658 A225 37c multi .75 .75

Pope John Paul II (1920-2005). Printed in sheets of 12.

Worldwide Fund for Nature (WWF) — A226

No. 659: a, Stephanometra echinus. b, Oxycomanthus bennetti. c, Alloeocomatella polycaldia. d, Dichrometra flagellata.

2005, Aug. 31 ***Perf. 14***

659 A226 50c Block or vert. strip of 4, #a-d 4.00 4.00

e. Souvenir sheet, 2 each #659a-659d 8.00 8.00

Souvenir Sheet

Albert Einstein (1879-1955), Physicist — A227

No. 660 — Various portraits with "Albert Einstein (1879-1955)" in: a, Orange. b, Blue. c, Red. d, Black.

2005, Sept. 20 ***Perf. 12¾***

660 A227 $1 Sheet of 4, #a-d 8.00 8.00

Bananas A228

Designs: 4c, Mother feeding banana to child. 10c, Four bananas. 22c, Bunch of bananas. 37c, Banana plant.

2005, Oct. 14 ***Perf. 14***

661-664 A228 Set of 4 1.50 1.50

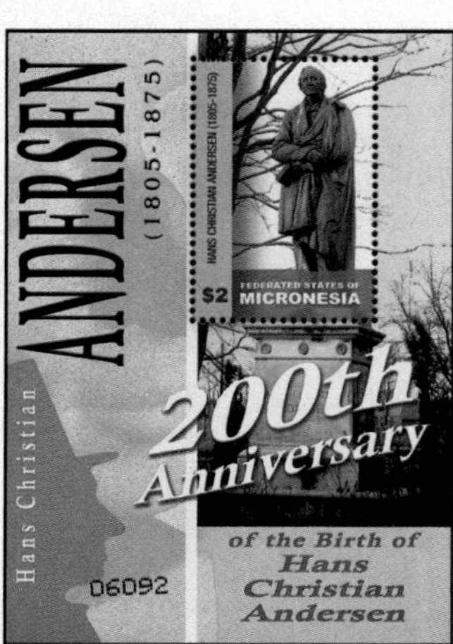

Hans Christian Andersen (1805-75), Author — A229

No. 665: a, Bust of Andersen. b, Statue of seated Andersen. c, Bust of Andersen on pedestal.

$2, Statue of standing Andersen.

2005, Nov. 15 ***Perf. 12¾***

665 A229 80c Sheet of 3, #a-c 5.00 5.00

Souvenir Sheet

666 A229 $2 multi 4.00 4.00

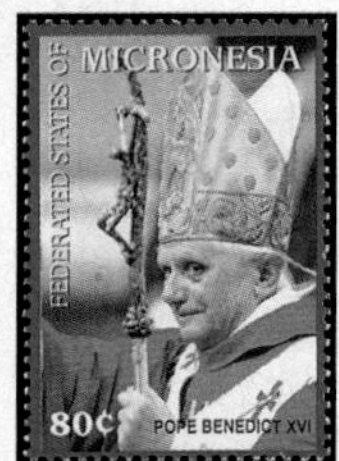

Pope Benedict XVI — A230

2005, Nov. 21 Litho. ***Perf. 13½***

667 A230 80c multi 1.60 1.60

Printed in sheets of 4.

Christmas — A231

Painting details: 37c, Kanigani Madonna, by Raphael. 60c, Madonna with the Fish, by Raphael. 80c, The Holy Family, by Bartolomé Esteban Murillo. $1, Madonna with the Book, by Raphael.

$2, The Holy Family, by Murillo, diff.

2005, Dec. 1 Litho. ***Perf. 14***

668-671 A231 Set of 4 5.75 5.75

Souvenir Sheet

672 A231 $2 multi 4.00 4.00

Flowers — A232

Designs: 4c, Tecoma stans. 10c, Ipomoea fistulosa. 22c, Hibiscus rosa-sinensis. 37c, Gerbera jamesonii. No. 677, 80c, Helianthus annuus. $1, Ixora casei.

No. 679, 80c: a, Tapeinochilos ananassae. b, Bauhnia monandra. c, Galphimia gracilis. d, Hibiscus rosa-sinensis, diff.

No. 680, $2, Helianthus annuus, diff. No. 681, $2, Phinia variegata.

2005, Nov. 15 Litho. ***Perf. 12***

673-678 A232 Set of 6 5.25 5.25

679 A232 80c Sheet of 4, #a-d 6.50 6.50

Souvenir Sheets

680-681 A232 Set of 2 8.00 8.00

New Year 2006 (Year of the Dog) — A233

Paintings by Liu Jiyou: 50c, Wolf Dog. $1, Wolf Dog, horiz.

2006, Jan. 3 ***Perf. 13¼***

682 A233 50c multi 1.00 1.00

Souvenir Sheet

683 A233 $1 multi 2.00 2.00

No. 683 contains one 48x35mm stamp.

No. 682 was issued in sheets of 4.

Birds — A234

Designs: No. 684, Glaucous-winged gull. No. 685, Slaty-headed parakeet. No. 686, Harlequin duck. No. 687, Purple sunbird. 75c, Plum-headed parakeet. 84c, Yellow-wattled lapwing. $4.05, Eurasian collared dove, horiz.

2006 ***Perf. 12***

684	A234	24c multi	.50	.50
685	A234	24c multi	.50	.50
686	A234	39c multi	.80	.80
687	A234	39c multi	.80	.80
688	A234	75c multi	1.50	1.50
689	A234	84c multi	1.75	1.75
690	A234	$4.05 multi	8.25	8.25
		Nos. 684-690 (7)	14.10	14.10

Issued: Nos. 684, 686, 2/21; others, 4/20.

Vice-President Petrus Tun (1936-99) — A235

2006, Mar. 19 ***Perf. 12¾***

691 A235 39c multi .80 .80

Printed in sheets of 4.

Rembrandt (1606-69), Painter — A236

No. 692: a, Saskia as Flora. b, Young Girl at a Window. c, Girl with a Broom. d, Prodigal Son in the Tavern.

$2, Man in Oriental Costume.

2006, June 22 ***Perf. 13¼***

692 A236 $1 Sheet of 4, #a-d 8.00 8.00

Imperf

693 A236 $2 multi 4.00 4.00

No. 692 contains four 38x50mm stamps.

Queen Elizabeth II, 80th Birthday — A237

No. 694 — Dogs and Queen in: a, Red violet dress. b, Beige dress. c, Purple dress. d, Light blue dress.

$2, Green dress.

2006, June 22 ***Perf. 14¼***

694 A237 84c Sheet of 4, #a-d 6.75 6.75

Souvenir Sheet

695 A237 $2 multi 4.00 4.00

Space Achievements — A238

No. 696 — Various views of Venus Express: a, Text in black. b, Country name in black, denomination in white. c, Country name in white, denomination in black. d, Country name and denomination in white. e, Country name and denomination in red, "Venus Express" at left. f, Country name and denomination in red, "Venus Express" at right.

No. 697, $1, horiz. — Return to space of Space Shuttle Discovery: a, Denomination in white. b, Shuttle arm. c, Shuttle with cargo bay open. d, Shuttle tail.

No. 698, $1, horiz. — Spacecraft for future trips to: a, Moon, black denomination. b, Moon, blue denomination. c, Mars, red denomination. d, Mars, white denomination.

No. 699, $2, Space Shuttle Discovery astronaut space-walking. No. 700, $2, Mars Reconnaissance Orbiter. No. 701, $2, Stardust probe, horiz.

2006, July 11 ***Perf. 14¼***

696 A238 75c Sheet of 6, #a-f 9.00 9.00

Sheets of 4, #a-d

697-698 A238 Set of 2 16.00 16.00

Souvenir Sheets

699-701 A238 Set of 3 12.00 12.00

Butterflies A239

Designs: 1c, Papilio euchenor. 2c, Golden birdwing. 4c, Delias henningia. 5c, Bassarona duda. 10c, Common bluebottle. 19c, Arhopala cleander. 20c, Arhopala argentea. 22c, Danaus aspasia. 75c, Arhopala aurea. 84c, Caleta mindaurus. $1, Black and white tit. $4.05, Grand imperial. $5, Jamides abdul. $10, Paralaxita lacoon.

2006, Nov. 15 *Perf. 12*

702	A239	1c multi	.20	.20
703	A239	2c multi	.20	.20
704	A239	4c multi	.20	.20
705	A239	5c multi	.20	.20
706	A239	10c multi	.20	.20
707	A239	19c multi	.40	.40
708	A239	20c multi	.40	.40
709	A239	22c multi	.45	.45
710	A239	75c multi	1.50	1.50
711	A239	84c multi	1.75	1.75
712	A239	$1 multi	2.00	2.00
713	A239	$4.05 multi	8.25	8.25
714	A239	$5 multi	10.00	10.00
715	A239	$10 multi	20.00	20.00
		Nos. 702-715 (14)	45.75	45.75

Christmas — A240

Designs: 22c, Christmas tree. 24c, Stocking. 39c, Snowman. 75c, Candle. 84c, Ornament.

2006, Dec. 4 *Perf. 13½*

716-720 A240 Set of 5 5.00 5.00

Concorde — A241

No. 721, 75c — Concorde's Jubilee Flypast: a, With statue. b, Without statue.
No. 722, 75c — Concorde 001: a, In flight. b, On ground.

Perf. 13¼x13½

2006, Dec. 20 **Litho.**

Pairs, #a-b

721-722 A241 Set of 2 6.00 6.00

New Year 2007 (Year of the Pig) — A242

2007, Jan. 3 *Perf. 13¼*

723 A242 75c multi 1.50 1.50

Printed in sheets of 4.

Souvenir Sheet

Wolfgang Amadeus Mozart (1756-91), Composer — A243

2007, Jan. 11

724 A243 $2 multi 4.00 4.00

Souvenir Sheet

Ludwig Durr (1878-1956), Engineer — A244

No. 725 — Durr and: a, Walrus Hula airship. b, Walrus heavy transport blimp. c, Hindenburg.

2007, Jan. 11

725 A244 $1 Sheet of 3, #a-c 6.00 6.00

Souvenir Sheet

Marilyn Monroe (1926-62), Actress — A245

No. 726: a, Looking right. b, With puckered lips. c, Wearing beret. d, With eyes closed, facing left.

2007, Jan. 11

726 A245 $1 Sheet of 4, #a-d 8.00 8.00

Scouting, Cent. — A246

2007, Jan. 11

727 A246 $1 shown 2.00 2.00

Souvenir Sheet

728 A246 $2 Scouts, flag 4.00 4.00

No. 727 was printed in sheets of 3. No. 728 contains one 37x50mm stamp.

Pope Benedict XVI, 80th Birthday — A247

2007, May 25

729 A247 50c multi 1.00 1.00

Printed in sheets of 8.

Miniature Sheet

Wedding of Queen Elizabeth II and Prince Philip, 60th Anniv. — A248

No. 730 — Queen and Prince: a, Standing, red frame. b, Seated, red frame. c, Seated, white frame. d, Standing, white frame. e, Standing, blue frame. f, Seated, blue frame.

2007, May 25

730 A248 60c Sheet of 6, #a-f 7.25 7.25

Princess Diana (1961-97) — A249

No. 731 — Various portraits with background color of: a, Pink. b, Lilac. c, Bister. d, Light green.
$2, Diana wearing tiara.

2007, May 25

731 A249 90c Sheet of 4, #a-d 7.25 7.25

Souvenir Sheet

732 A249 $2 multi 4.00 4.00

Bananas — A250

Inscriptions: 22c, Utim was. 26c, Utin Iap. 41c, Mangat. 58c, Ipali. 80c, Daiwang. 90c, Akadahn Weitahta, horiz. $1.14, Peleu. $4.60, Utin Kerenis.

Perf. 14x14¾, 14¾x14

2007, June 12

733	A250	22c multi	.45	.45
734	A250	26c multi	.55	.55
735	A250	41c multi	.85	.85
736	A250	58c multi	1.25	1.25
737	A250	80c multi	1.60	1.60
738	A250	90c multi	1.90	1.90
739	A250	$1.14 multi	2.40	2.40
740	A250	$4.60 multi	9.25	9.25
		Nos. 733-740 (8)	18.25	18.25

Miniature Sheet

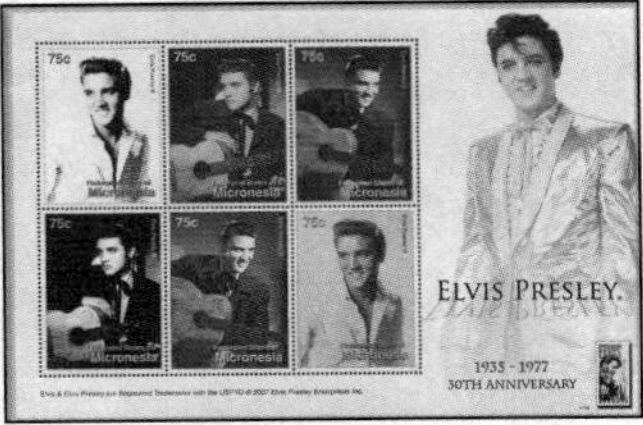

Elvis Presley (1935-77) — A251

No. 741 — Various portraits with denomination color of: a, Blue (country name in gray). b, Pink. c, Blue (country name in blue). d, Green. e, Buff. f, Lilac.

2007, June 20 *Perf. 14¼*

741 A251 75c Sheet of 6, #a-f 9.00 9.00

Fish — A252

No. 742: a, Longnose hawkfish. b, Fingerprint sharpnose puffer. c, Ornate butterflyfish. d, Longnose filefish.
$2, Multi-barred goatfish.

2007, June 21 *Perf. 13¼*

742 A252 90c Sheet of 4, #a-d 7.25 7.25

Souvenir Sheet

743 A252 $2 multi 4.00 4.00

Flowers — A253

No. 744: a, White plumeria. b, Yellow plumeria. c, White lily. d, Yellow ginger lily.
$2, Bougainvillea glabra.

2007, June 21

744 A253 90c Sheet of 4, #a-d 7.25 7.25

Souvenir Sheet

745 A253 $2 multi 4.00 4.00

Souvenir Sheet

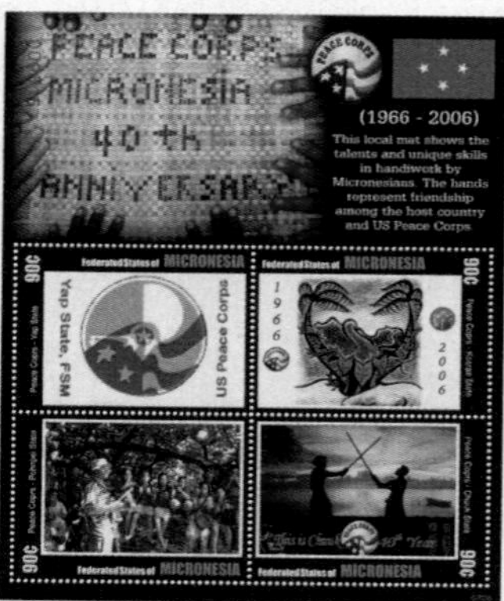

Peace Corps in Micronesia, 40th Anniv. (in 2006) — A254

No. 746 — Inscriptions: a, Yap State. b, Kosrae State. c, Pohnpei State. d, Chuuk State.

2007, June 22
746 A254 90c Sheet of 4, #a-d 7.25 7.25

Miniature Sheet

Pres. Gerald R. Ford (1913-2006) — A255

No. 747 — Ford: a, With hand raised. b, Seated, reading documents. c, With Pres. Richard Nixon, denomination at UL. d, With Nixon, denomination at UR. e, With wife, Betty. f, Signing Nixon's pardon.

2007, Aug. 7
747 A255 $1 Sheet of 6, #a-f 12.00 12.00

Intl. Polar Year — A256

No. 748: a, African penguins. b, Emperor penguins. c, Galapagos penguin. d, Humboldt penguin. e, Magellanic penguin. f, Rockhopper penguin.
$3.50, Gentoo penguins.

2007, Aug. 7
748 A256 75c Sheet of 6, #a-f 9.00 9.00

Souvenir Sheet

749 A256 $3.50 multi 7.00 7.00

Souvenir Sheet

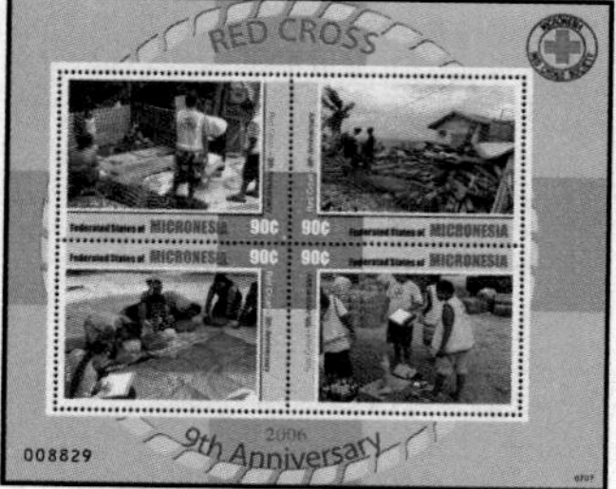

Micronesian Red Cross, 9th Anniv. — A257

No. 750 — Various pictures of relief efforts with denomination at: a, LR. b, LL. c, UR. d, UL.

2007, Aug. 20
750 A257 90c Sheet of 4, #a-d 7.25 7.25

Cats — A258

Designs: 22c, Scottish Fold. 26c, Munchkin. 41c, Abyssinian. 90c, Somali, horiz.
$2, Blue Silver Shaded Tiffanie.

Perf. 13½x13, 13x13½

2007, Sept. 24 **Litho.**
751-754 A258 Set of 4 3.75 3.75

Souvenir Sheet

Perf. 12½x12¾

755 A258 $2 multi 4.00 4.00

No. 755 contains one 29x42mm stamp.

Christmas A259

Churches: 22c, Mother Church, United Church of Christ, Pohnpei. 26c, St. Mary's Church, Yap, horiz. 41c, Sapore Bethesca Church, Fefan, Chuuk, horiz. 90c, Lelu Congregational Church, Kosrae, horiz.

Perf. 14¼x14¾, 14¾x14¼

2007, Nov. 12
756-759 A259 Set of 4 3.75 3.75

America's Cup Yachting Races, Valencia, Spain — A260

Sails of various sailboats.

2007, Dec. 12 ***Perf. 13¼***

760	Strip of 4	8.50 8.50
a.	A260 26c aquamarine & multi	.50 .50
b.	A260 80c red & multi	1.60 1.60
c.	A260 $1.14 yellow & multi	2.40 2.40
d.	A260 $2 orange & multi	4.00 4.00

First Helicopter Flight, Cent. — A261

No. 761: a, AH-1 Huey Cobra. b, 206 Jet Ranger. c, H-43 Huskie. d, AS-350 Ecureuil.
$2.50, Fa 223 Drache.

2007, Dec. 12 ***Perf. 13¼***
761 A261 $1 Sheet of 4, #a-d 8.00 8.00

Souvenir Sheet

762 A261 $2.50 multi 5.00 5.00

Princess Diana (1961-97) — A262

Serpentine Die Cut 7¾

2007, Dec. 12 **Litho. & Embossed**
Without Gum

763 A262 $8 multi 16.00 16.00

Miniature Sheet

Pres. John F. Kennedy (1917-63) — A263

No. 764 — Kennedy: a, With curtain at left. b, Color portrait. c, With Presidential Seal. d, At microphones.

2008, Jan. 2 **Litho.** ***Perf. 14***
764 A263 90c Sheet of 4, #a-d 7.25 7.25

New Year 2008 (Year of the Rat) — A264

2008, Jan. 2 **Litho.** ***Perf. 12***
765 A264 90c multi 1.90 1.90

Printed in sheets of 4.

Miniature Sheet

2008 Olympic Games, Beijing — A265

No. 766: a, Cover of book with music from 1904 World's Fair. b, Poster for 1904 Olympic Games and World's Fair. c, Jim Lightbody. d, Martin Sheridan.

2008, Jan. 8 ***Perf. 14***
766 A265 50c Sheet of 4, #a-d 4.00 4.00

Souvenir Sheet

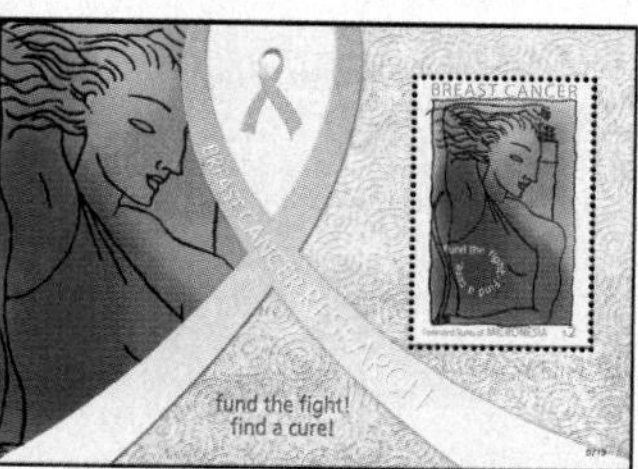

Breast Cancer Awareness — A266

2008, Mar. 12
767 A266 $2 multi 4.00 4.00

Hummer Vehicles — A267

No. 768: a, Front bumper of Hummer H3x, denomination at UR. b, Side view of Hummer H3x, denomination at LR. c, Front view of Hummer H3x, denomination at LR. d, Rear view of Hummer H3x, denomination at UR.
$2, Hummer H3.

2008, May 6 ***Perf. 13¼***
768 A267 90c Sheet of 4, #a-d 7.25 7.25

Souvenir Sheet

769 A267 $2 multi 4.00 4.00

Jerusalem — A268

2008, May 14 ***Imperf.***
770 A268 $3 multi 6.00 6.00

World Stamp Championship, Israel, 2008.

Miniature Sheet

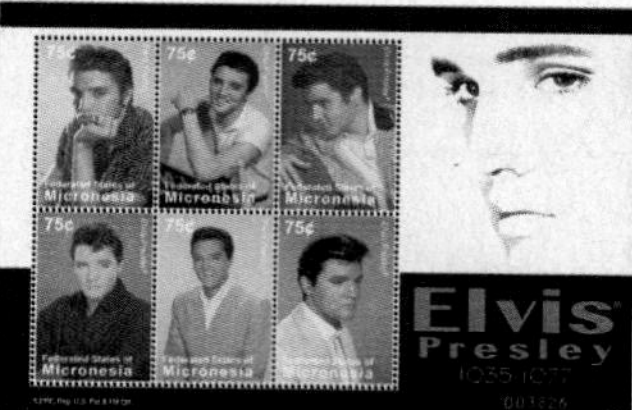

Elvis Presley (1935-77) — A269

No. 771 — Presley: a, With head on hand, buff background. b, Sitting in director's chair, gray background. c, Wearing striped jacket, brown background. d, Wearing brown shirt, red brown background. e, Wearing gray suit, yellow orange background. f, Wearing gray suit, blue gray background.

2008, June 12 ***Perf. 13¼***
771 A269 75c Sheet of 6, #a-f 9.00 9.00

Miniature Sheet

Members of Phoenix Suns Basketball Team — A270

No. 772 — Emblem of National Basketball Association and: a, Amare Stodemire. b, Boris Diaw. c, Brian Skinner. d, D. J. Strawberry. e, Shaquille O'Neal. f, Grant Hill. g, Leandro Barbosa. h, Raja Bell. i, Steve Nash.

2008, June 19
772 A270 42c Sheet of 9, #a-i 7.75 7.75

Miniature Sheet

Royal Air Force, 90th Anniv. — A271

No. 773 — Aircraft: a, Tornado. b, Harrier. c, Typhoon. d, Hawk.

2008, May 6 Litho. ***Perf. 13¼***
773 A271 90c Sheet of 4, #a-d 7.25 7.25

Miniature Sheet

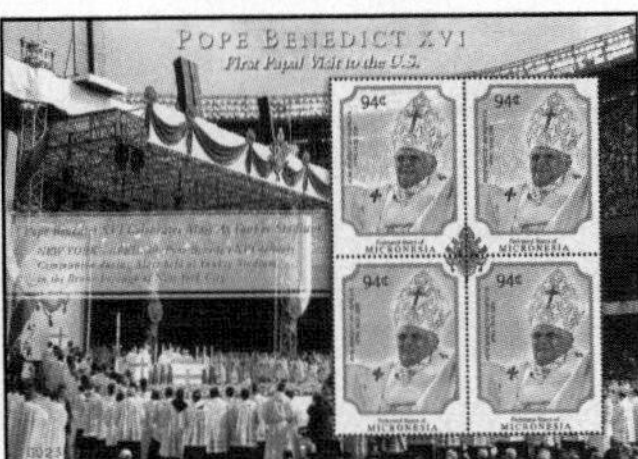

Visit of Pope Benedict XVI to United States — A272

No. 774 — Pope Benedict XVI and one quarter of Papal arms at: a, LR. b, LL. c, UR. d, UL.

2008, Sept. 9 ***Perf. 13¼***
774 A272 94c Sheet of 4, #a-d 7.75 7.75

Miniature Sheets

A273

Muhammad Ali, Boxer — A274

No. 775 — Ali: a, Wearing protective headgear. b, Receiving adjustment of headgear. c, Looking right. d, In boxing ring, looking right. e, In boxing ring, looking left. f, With trainer, looking at hands.

No. 776 — Ali fighting: a, Throwing left jab. b, Ready to deliver punch. c, With hands in front of his chest. d, With opponent's punch missing.

2008, Sept. 9 ***Perf. 11½x11¼***
775 A273 75c Sheet of 6, #a-f 9.00 9.00

Perf. 13¼
776 A274 94c Sheet of 4, #a-d 7.75 7.75

Star Trek — A275

No. 777: a, U.S.S. Enterprise. b, Mr. Spock and woman. c, Captain Kirk. d, Uhura and Chekov. e, Starbase 11. f, Dr. McCoy and Mr. Spock.

No. 778: a, Scotty. b, Captain Kirk. c, Dr. McCoy and Uhura. d, Chekov.

2008, Sept. 9 ***Perf. 12x11½***
777 A275 75c Sheet of 6, #a-f 9.00 9.00

Perf. 13¼
778 A275 94c Sheet of 4, #a-d 7.75 7.75

No. 778 contains four 38x60mm stamps.

Christmas A276

Ornaments: 22c, Angel. 27c, Snowflake. 42c, Cross. 94c, Angel, diff.

2008, Sept. 9 ***Perf. 14x14¾***
779-782 A276 Set of 4 3.75 3.75

Famous Men — A277

No. 783: a, Ioanis Artui, Palikiri chief. b, Dr. Eluel K. Pretrick, Human Resources Secretary.

2008, Oct. 17 ***Perf. 13¼***
783 A277 94c Pair, #a-b 3.75 3.75

Miniature Sheet

Inauguration of US Pres. Barack Obama — A278

No. 784: a, 42c, Obama facing right. b, 42c, Obama facing left, one side of shirt collar showing. c, 42c, Obama facing left, both sides of shirt collar showing. d, 75c, As "c." e, 75c, As "b." f, 75c, As "a."

2009, Jan. 20 Litho. ***Perf. 11½***
784 A278 Sheet of 6, #a-f 7.25 7.25

Miniature Sheet

Marilyn Monroe (1926-62), Actress — A279

No. 785: a, Monroe in dressing gown. b, Head of Monroe. c, Monroe in lilac sweater. d, Monroe in automobile.

2009, Jan. 22
785 A279 94c Sheet of 4, #a-d 7.75 7.75

Surfing — A280

Ocean waves and various surfers. Waves only on 20c, 22c, 59c, 83c.

2009, Jan. 26 ***Perf. 14x14¾***

786	A280	1c multi	.20	.20
787	A280	2c multi	.20	.20
788	A280	17c multi	.35	.35
789	A280	20c multi	.40	.40
790	A280	22c multi	.45	.45
791	A280	27c multi	.55	.55
792	A280	42c multi	.85	.85
793	A280	59c multi	1.25	1.25
794	A280	72c multi	1.50	1.50
795	A280	83c multi	1.75	1.75
796	A280	94c multi	1.90	1.90
797	A280	$1.17 multi	2.40	2.40
798	A280	$4.80 multi	9.75	9.75
799	A280	$16.50 multi	33.00	33.00
	Nos. 786-799 (14)		54.55	54.55

Miniature Sheet

New Year 2009 (Year of the Ox) — A281

No. 800: a, Denomination next to yellow arc, three leaves at top. b, Denomination even with yellow curlicues, two tan arcs going beneath denomination. c, Denomination next to yellow arc, one leaf between yellow and pink curlicues at top. d, Denomination even with yellow curlicues, tip of brown leaf touching "9" in denomination.

2009, Jan. 26 ***Perf. 11½***
800 A281 94c Sheet of 4, #a-d 7.75 7.75

Peonies A282

2009, Apr. 10 ***Perf. 13¼***
801 A282 42c multi .85 .85

Printed in sheets of 6.

Miniature Sheets

A283

China 2009 World Stamp Exhibition — A284

No. 802 — Olympic sports: a, Triathlon. b, Diving. c, Equestrian. d, Table tennis.

No. 803 — Tang Dynasty art: a, Portrait of Emperor Taizong (Li Shih-min). b, Portrait of Emperor Taizong and his subjects. c, Calligraphy of Emperor Taizong. d, Mural of Emperor Taizong, Dunhuang.

2009, Apr. 10 ***Perf. 12***

802 A283 59c Sheet of 4, #a-d 4.75 4.75
803 A284 59c Sheet of 4, #a-d 4.75 4.75

Souvenir Sheets

A285

A286

A287

Elvis Presley (1935-77) — A288

2009, June 10 ***Perf. 13¼***

804 A285 $2.50 multi 5.00 5.00
805 A286 $2.50 multi 5.00 5.00
806 A287 $2.50 multi 5.00 5.00
807 A288 $2.50 multi 5.00 5.00
Nos. 804-807 (4) 20.00 20.00

Miniature Sheets

A289

Michael Jackson (1958-2009) — A290

No. 808 — Shirt color: a, 28c, Yellow. b, 28c, Black. c, 75c, Yellow. d, 75c, Black.

No. 809 — Shirt color: a, 28c, Tan. b, 28c, White. c, 75c, Tan. d, 75c, White.

2009, July 7 **Litho.** ***Perf. 13¼x13***

808 A289 Sheet of 4, #a-d 4.25 4.25
809 A290 Sheet of 4, #a-d 4.25 4.25

Miniature Sheets

A291

First Man on the Moon, 40th Anniv. — A292

No. 810: a, Apollo 11 lift-off. b, Neil Armstrong in space. c, Bust of Armstrong by Paula Slater. d, Apollo 11 Command Module. e, Apollo 11 Lunar Module. f, Buzz Aldrin on moon.

No. 811: a, Apollo 11 Lunar and Command Modules. b, Apollo 11 Command Module. c, Armstrong. d, Silicon disc left on Moon.

2009, July 20 ***Perf. 13¼***

810 A291 75c Sheet of 6, #a-f 9.00 9.00
811 A292 98c Sheet of 4, #a-d 8.00 8.00

Butterflies A293

Designs: 28c, Great orange tip. 44c, Red pierrot. 98c, Plains cupid. $1.05, Blue admiral.

No. 816: a, Tree nymph sinharaja. b, Great Mormon. c, Blue Mormon. d, Tailed jay. e, Gladeye bushbrown. f, Ceylon rose.

2009, Sept. 4 ***Perf. 12***

812-815 A293 Set of 4 5.50 5.50
816 A293 75c Sheet of 6, #a-f 9.00 9.00

Fish A294

Designs: 22c, Powder blue surgeon. 28c, Maroon clownfish. 61c, Flame angelfish. 78c, Moon wrasse. $1.24, Regal angelfish. $2.30, Firefish.

No. 823: a, Clown triggerfish. b, Wreckfish. c, Purple firefish. d, Regal tang.

2009, Sept. 4

817-822 A294 Set of 6 11.00 11.00
823 A294 94c Sheet of 4, #a-d 7.75 7.75

A295

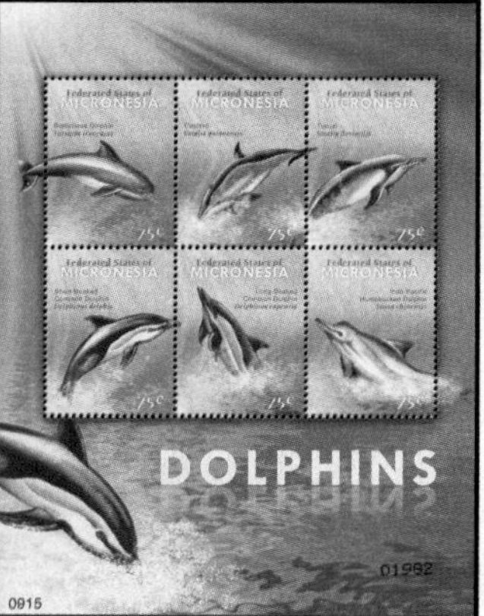

Dolphins — A296

Designs: 22c, Indo-Pacific bottlenose dolphin. 88c, Chinese white dolphin. 95c, Southern right whale dolphin. $2.80, Northern right whale dolphin.

No. 828: a, Bottlenose dolphin. b, Costero. c, Tucuxi. d, Short-beaked common dolphin. e, Long-beaked common dolphin. f, Indo-Pacific humpbacked dolphin.

2009, Sept. 4

824-827 A295 Set of 4 9.75 9.75
828 A296 75c Sheet of 6, #a-f 9.00 9.00

A297

Shells — A298

Designs: 22c, Clea nigericans. 79c, Achatina fulica. $1.39, Pamacea canaliculata. $1.56, Cyclophorus diplochilus.

No. 833: a, Thais bitubercularis. b, Conus caracteristicus. c, Amphidromus glaucolarynx. d, Anadara pilula. e, Cypraea erronea pyriformis. f, Thais aculeata.

2009, Sept. 4

829-832 A297 Set of 4 8.00 8.00
833 A298 75c Sheet of 6, #a-f 9.00 9.00

Corals A299

Designs: 27c, Flat leather coral. 55c, Strawberry coral. 83c, Discosoma sp. 3. $1.44, Porous lettuce coral.

No. 838, vert.: a, Lobophytum sp. 1. b, Nara nematifera. c, Leuconia palaoensis. d, Dendronepithya sp. 1.

No. 839, vert.: a, Sarcophyton sp. 1. b, Echinopora lamellosa.

2009, Sept. 24 ***Perf. 14¾x14***

834-837 A299 Set of 4 5.75 5.75

Perf. 14x14¾

838 A299 98c Sheet of 4, #a-d 8.00 8.00

Souvenir Sheet

839 A299 98c Sheet of 2, #a-b 4.00 4.00

Miniature Sheet

Pres. Abraham Lincoln (1809-65) — A300

No. 840 — Photographs of Lincoln: a, Without beard. b, With beard, top of head not showing. c, With beard, looking right. d, With beard, profile.

2009, Oct. 16 ***Perf. 13¼***

840 A300 98c Sheet of 4, #a-d 8.00 8.00

Chinese Aviation, Cent. — A301

No. 841 — Airplanes: a, CJ-5. b, CJ-6. c, JJ-5. d, JJ-6.
$2, JL-8.

2009, Nov. 12 Litho. *Perf. 14¼*
841 A301 75c Sheet of 4, #a-d 6.00 6.00

Souvenir Sheet

842 A301 $2 multi 4.00 4.00

No. 841 contains four 42x28mm stamps. Aeropex 2009 Philatelic Exhibition, Beijing.

Christmas A302

Designs: 22c, Santa Claus and palm tree. 44c, Christmas ornaments. 98c, Christmas stocking. $4.80, Decorated Christmas tree.

2009, Nov. 30 *Perf. 14x14¾*
843-846 A302 Set of 4 13.00 13.00

Miniature Sheet

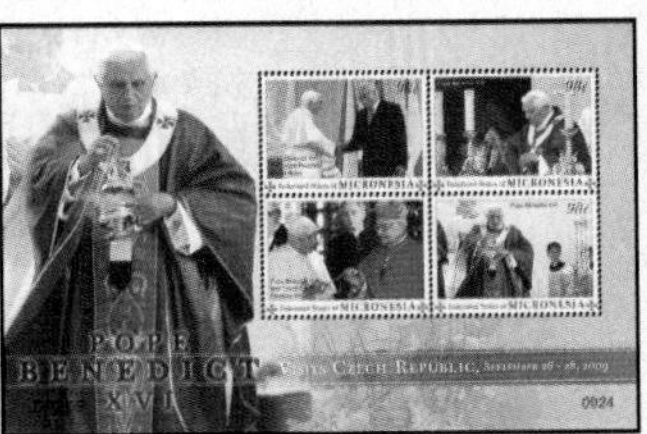
Visit of Pope Benedict XVI to Czech Republic — A303

No. 847: a, Pope and Czech Pres. Vaclav Klaus. b, Pope in red vestments. c, Pope and Miroslav Cardinal Vlk. d, Pope in green vestments.

2009, Dec. 2 *Perf. 13x13¼*
847 A303 98c Sheet of 4, #a-d 8.00 8.00

Worldwide Fund for Nature (WWF) — A304

No. 848 — Mandarinfish: a, Male. b, Female. c, Unspecified gender. d, Unspecified gender, diff.

2009, Dec. 2 *Perf. 13½*
848 Block or strip of 4 4.25 4.25
a. A304 28c orange & multi .60 .60
b. A304 35c yellow & multi .70 .70
c. A304 44c green & multi .90 .90
d. A304 98c blue & multi 2.00 2.00
e. Sheet of 8, 2 each #848a-848d 8.50 8.50

Turtles A305

Designs: 22c, Hawksbill turtle. 88c, Australian flatback turtle. 95c, Loggerhead turtle. $2.80, Green sea turtle.
No. 853: a, Kemp's ridley turtle. b, Leatherback turtle. c, Loggerhead turtle, diff. d, Olive ridley turtle.
No. 854: a, Green sea turtle, diff. b, Hawksbill turtle, diff.

2009, Sept. 4 Litho. *Perf. 14¾x14*
849-852 A305 Set of 4 9.75 9.75
853 A305 98c Sheet of 4, #a-d 8.00 8.00

Souvenir Sheet

854 A305 $1.56 Sheet of 2, #a-b 6.25 6.25

Birds — A306

Designs: 28c, Brown booby. 44c, Sacred kingfisher. 98c, White-face heron. $1.05, Rainbow lorikeet.
No. 859, horiz.: a, Brandt's cormorant. b, Red-footed booby. c, Beach thick-knee. d, Common noddy.
No. 860, horiz.: a, Blue-footed booby. b, Australian pelican.

2009, Sept. 4 *Perf. 14x14¾*
855-858 A306 Set of 4 5.50 5.50

Perf. 14¾x14

859 A306 98c Sheet of 4, #a-d 8.00 8.00

Souvenir Sheet

860 A306 $1.56 Sheet of 2, #a-b 6.25 6.25

Miniature Sheet

Chinese Zodiac Animals — A307

No. 861: a, Rat. b, Ox. c, Tiger. d, Rabbit. e, Dragon. f, Snake. g, Horse. h, Ram. i, Monkey. j, Cock. k, Dog. l, Pig.

2010, Jan. 4 *Perf. 13¼*
861 A307 22c Sheet of 12, #a-l 5.50 5.50

Souvenir Sheet

New Year 2010 (Year of the Tiger) — A308

No. 862: a, Tiger. b, Chinese character for "tiger."

2010, Jan. 4 *Perf. 11½*
862 A308 $2 Sheet of 2, #a-b 8.00 8.00

Miniature Sheet

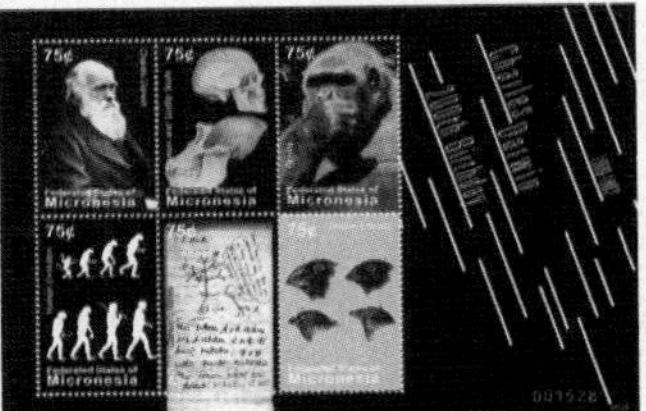
Charles Darwin (1809-82), Naturalist — A309

No. 863: a, Photograph of Darwin. b, Human and gorilla skulls. c, Gorilla. d, Human evolution. e, Darwin's notes. f, Darwin's drawings of finch beaks.

2010, Feb. 17 *Perf. 13¼*
863 A309 75c Sheet of 6, #a-f 9.00 9.00

Miniature Sheet

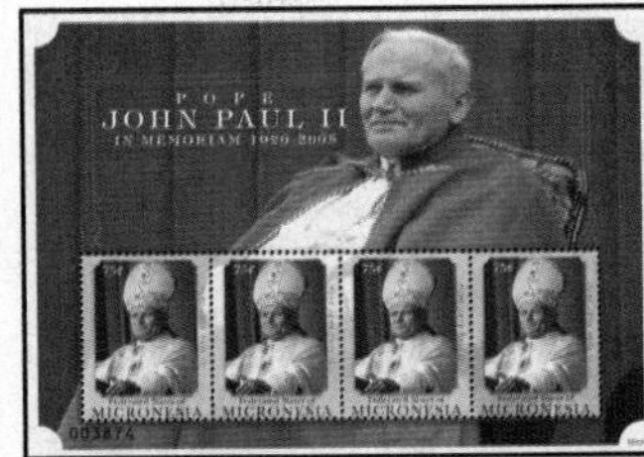

Pope John Paul II (1920-2005) — A310

No. 864 — Pope John Paul II with: a, Faint vertical line at left, white area at right. b, White area at left and top. c, White area at UL corner and at left, gray area at right. d, Gray area at left and bottom, faint vertical line at right.

2010, Apr. 23 *Perf. 11½*
864 A310 75c Sheet of 4, #a-d 6.00 6.00

A311

Mushrooms — A312

Designs: 28c, Galerina decipiens. 44c, Amanita pekeoides. 75c, Rhodocollybia laulaha. 98c, Amanita nothofagi.
No. 869: a, Hygrocybe aff. minutula. b, Hygrocybe pakelo. c, Amanita nehuta. d, Amanita muscaria. e, Amanita australis. f, Hygrocybe constrictospora.

2010, June 8 *Perf. 11½*
865-868 A311 Set of 4 5.00 5.00

Perf. 12x11½

869 A312 75c Sheet of 6, #a-f 9.00 9.00

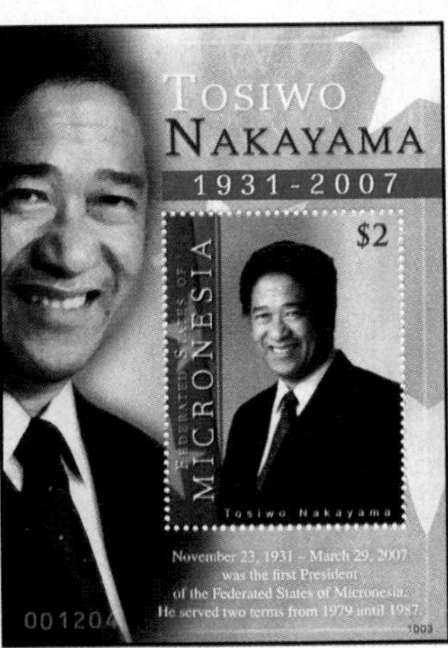

Pres. Tosiwo Nakayama (1931-2007) — A313

No. 870 — Photos of Pres. Nakayama: a, On Saipan, 1970. b, In Washington, DC, 1986. c, On Pohnpei, 1970. d, On Saipan, 1975.
$2, Color photograph.

2010, June 8 *Perf. 11½*
870 A313 80c Sheet of 4, #a-d 6.50 6.50

Souvenir Sheet

Perf. 13½

871 A313 $2 multi 4.00 4.00

No. 870 contains four 30x40mm stamps.

Girl Guides, Cent. — A314

No. 872, horiz.: a, Two Girl Guides holding hands. b, Two Girl Guides with yellow neckerchiefs. c, Three Girl Guides with balloons. d, Three Girl Guides writing.
$2.50, Two Rainbows.

2010, June 8 *Perf. 11½x12*
872 A314 94c Sheet of 4, #a-d 7.75 7.75

Souvenir Sheet

Perf. 11½

873 A314 $2.50 multi 5.00 5.00

Flowers and Fruit — A315

Designs: 1c, Bougainvillea. 2c, Yellow plumeria. 4c, White ginger. 5c, Guettardia speciosa. 10c, Mangat bananas. 19c, Akadahn Weitahta bananas. 20c, Peleu bananas. 22c, Three unopened coconuts. 28c, Utin Kerenis bananas. 40c, Unopened coconut. 44c, Opened coconut. 70c, Coconut out of shell. $1, Opened and unopened coconuts. $3.85, Opened coconut, diff. $4.60, Soursop. $4.80, Partially opened soursop.

2010, June 18 *Perf. 13¼*
874 A315 1c multi .20 .20
875 A315 2c multi .20 .20
876 A315 4c multi .20 .20
877 A315 5c multi .20 .20
878 A315 10c multi .20 .20
879 A315 19c multi .40 .40
880 A315 20c multi .40 .40
881 A315 22c multi .45 .45
882 A315 28c multi .60 .60
883 A315 40c multi .80 .80
884 A315 44c multi .90 .90
885 A315 70c multi 1.40 1.40
886 A315 $1 multi 2.00 2.00
887 A315 $3.85 multi 7.75 7.75
888 A315 $4.60 multi 9.25 9.25
889 A315 $4.80 multi 9.75 9.75
Nos. 874-889 (16) 34.70 34.70

Miniature Sheet

British Monarchs — A316

No. 890: a, Queen Anne. b, King George I. c, King George II. d, King George III. e, King George IV. f, King George V.

2010, Aug. 26 ***Perf. 11½***
890 A316 75c Sheet of 6, #a-f 9.00 9.00

Miniature Sheet

Paintings by Sandro Botticelli (1445-1510) — A317

No. 891: a, Madonna and Two Angels. b, Pallas and the Centaur. c, Portrait of a Man with the Medal. d, St. Augustine in His Cell. e, Scenes from the Life of Moses. f, Adoration of the Magi.

2010, Aug. 26 **Litho.**
891 A317 75c Sheet of 6, #a-f 9.00 9.00

Henri Dunant (1828-1910), Founder of the Red Cross — A318

No. 892 — Various depictions of the Battle of Solferino and Dunant's photograph in: a, Gray green. b, Brown. c, Red violet. d, Gray blue.
$2.50, Violet.

2010, Aug. 26 ***Perf. 11½x12***
892 A318 94c Sheet of 4, #a-d 7.75 7.75

Souvenir Sheet
Perf. 11½

893 A318 $2.50 multi 5.00 5.00

Diplomatic Relations Between Micronesia and People's Republic of China, 15th Anniv. — A212a

Designs: No. 631A, FSM-China Friendship Sports Center. No. 631B, Arms of People's Republic of China and Micronesia.

2004, Dec. 29 **Litho.** ***Perf. 13x13¼***
631A A212a 37c multi —
631B A212a 37c multi —

A306a

A306b

A306c

A306d

A306e

Diplomatic Relations Between Micronesia and People's Republic of China, 20th Anniv. — A306f

2009 **Litho.** ***Perf. 12***
860C A306a 44c multi —
860D A306b 44c multi —
860E A306c 44c multi —
860F A306d 44c multi —
860G A306e 44c multi —
860H A306f 44c multi —

Additional stamps might have been issued in this set. The editors would like to examine any examples.

Miniature Sheet

Princess Diana (1961-97) — A319

No. 894 — Princess Diana: a, In beige dress, embracing child. b, In plaid suit, meeting child. c, In blue green suit, meeting child. d, In pink suit.

2010, Aug. 26 **Litho.** ***Perf. 12x11½***
894 A319 75c Sheet of 4, #a-d 6.00 6.00

Souvenir Sheet

Issuance of the Penny Black, 170th Anniv. — A320

No. 895: a, Great Britain #1. b, Micronesia #2.

2010, Oct. 6 ***Perf. 13x13¼***
895 A320 $2 Sheet of 2, #a-b 8.00 8.00

Christmas A321

Paintings: 22c, Adoration of the Magi, by Corrado Giaquinto. 28c, Polyptych with the Nativity, by Rogier van der Weiden. 44c, The Nativity, by Federico Barocci. 98c, The Newborn Christ, by Georges de La Tour. $4.95, The Flight into Egypt, by Giotto di Bondone.

2010, Nov. 1 ***Perf. 13¼x13***
896-900 A321 Set of 5 14.00 14.00

Pope John Paul II (1920-2005) A322

2010, Dec. 16 ***Perf. 12***
901 A322 75c multi 1.50 1.50

Printed in sheets of 4.

Miniature Sheet

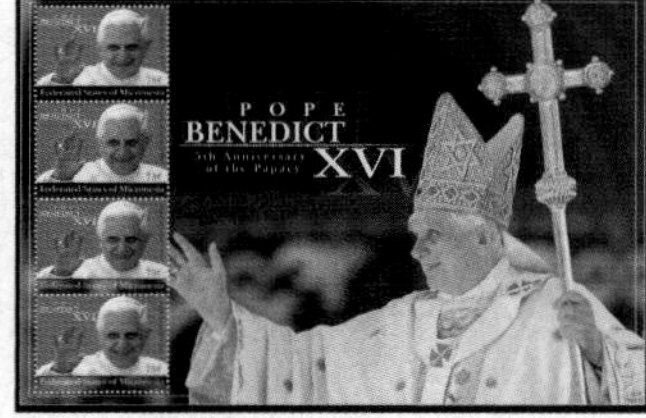

Pope Benedict XVI — A323

No. 902 — Pope Benedict XVI with lower panel: a, In solid black. b, In black and dark gray at LR. c, In brown and black with "d" over black area, finger partially visible at right. d, In brown and black with "of" over black area.

2010, Dec. 16
902 A323 75c Sheet of 4, #a-d 6.00 6.00

Miniature Sheet

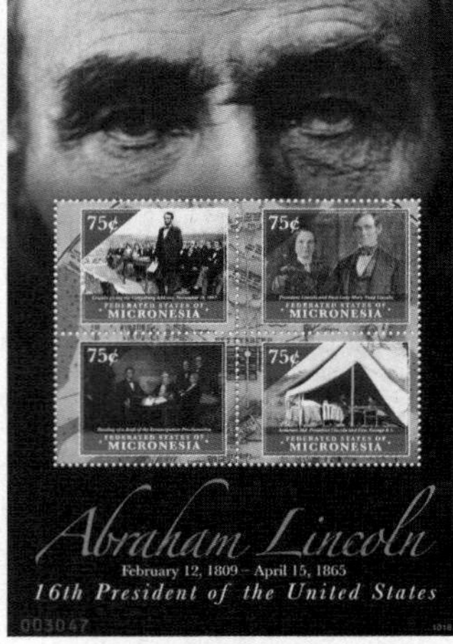

Pres. Abraham Lincoln (1809-65) — A324

No. 903 — Lincoln: a, Giving Gettysburg Address. b, With wife, Mary. c, Reading draft of the Emancipation Proclamation. d, Meeting General George McClellan in tent at Antietam.

2010, Dec. 16 ***Perf. 12½x12***
903 A324 75c Sheet of 4, #a-d 6.00 6.00

AIR POST STAMPS

Boeing 727, 1968 AP1

1984, July 12 **Litho.** ***Perf. 13½***
C1 AP1 28c shown .60 .60
C2 AP1 35c SA-16 Albatross, 1960 .80 .80
C3 AP1 40c PBY-5A Catalina, 1951 1.00 1.00
Nos. C1-C3 (3) 2.40 2.40

Ausipex Type of 1984

Ausipex '84 emblem and: 28c, Caroline Islands No. 4. 35c, No. 7. 40c, No. 19.

1984, Sept. 21 **Litho.** ***Perf. 13½***
C4 A4 28c multicolored .65 .65
C5 A4 35c multicolored .85 .85
C6 A4 40c multicolored 1.10 1.10
Nos. C4-C6 (3) 2.60 2.60

Christmas Type

Children's drawings.

1984, Dec. 20
C7 A5 28c Illustrated Christmas text .65 .65
C8 A5 35c Decorated palm tree .90 .90
C9 A5 40c Feast preparation 1.10 1.10
Nos. C7-C9 (3) 2.65 2.65

Ships Type

1985, Aug. 19
C10 A6 33c L'Astrolabe .65 .65
C11 A6 39c La Coquille .80 .80
C12 A6 44c Shenandoah 1.00 1.00
Nos. C10-C12 (3) 2.45 2.45

Christmas Type

1985, Oct. 15 **Litho.** ***Perf. 13½***
C13 A7 33c Dublon Protestant Church .90 .90
C14 A7 44c Pohnpei Catholic Church 1.25 1.25

Audubon Type

1985, Oct. 31 ***Perf. 14½***
C15 A8 44c Sooty tern 1.00 1.00

Ruins Type

1985, Dec. Litho. *Perf. 13½*

C16 A16 33c Nan Tauas inner courtyard .70 .70
C17 A16 39c Outer wall .80 .80
C18 A16 44c Tomb .90 .90
Nos. C16-C18 (3) 2.40 2.40

Halley's Comet AP2

1986, May 16

C19 AP2 44c dk bl, bl & blk 1.40 1.25

Return of Nauruans from Truk, 40th Anniv. AP3

1986, May 16

C20 AP3 44c Ship in port 1.40 1.25

AMERIPEX '86 Type

Bully Hayes (1829-1877), buccanneer.

1986, May 22

C21 A18 33c Forging Hawaiian stamp .55 .55
C22 A18 39c Sinking of the Leonora, Kosrae .70 .70
C23 A18 44c Hayes escapes capture .75 .75
C24 A18 75c Biography, by Louis Becke 1.50 1.50
Nos. C21-C24 (4) 3.50 3.50

Souvenir Sheet

C25 A18 $1 Hayes ransoming chief 3.25 3.25

Christmas Type

Virgin and child paintings: 33c, Austria, 19th cent. 44c, Italy, 18th cent., diff.

1986, Oct. 15 Litho. *Perf. 14½*

C26 A20 33c multicolored 1.00 1.00
C27 A20 44c multicolored 1.40 1.40

Anniversaries and Events Type

1987, June 13 Litho. *Perf. 14½*

C28 A21 33c US currency, bicent. .60 .60
C29 A21 39c 1st American in orbit, 25th anniv. 1.00 1.00
C30 A21 44c US Constitution, bicent. 1.10 1.10
Nos. C28-C30 (3) 2.70 2.70

Christmas Type

1987, Nov. 16 Litho. *Perf. 14½*

C31 A22 33c Holy Family .80 .80
C32 A22 39c Shepherds .90 .90
C33 A22 44c Three Wise Men 1.00 1.00
Nos. C31-C33 (3) 2.70 2.70

Bird Type

1988, Aug. 1 Litho. *Perf. 13½*

C34 A9 33c Great truk white-eye .55 .55
C35 A9 44c Blue-faced parrotfinch .70 .70
C36 A9 $1 Yap monarch 1.75 1.75
Nos. C34-C36 (3) 3.00 3.00

Colonial Era Type

1988, July 20 *Perf. 13x13½*

C37 A23 44c Traditional skills (boat-building) .95 .95
C38 A23 44c Modern Micronesia (tourism) .95 .95
a. Pair, #C37-C38 1.90 1.90

Printed se-tenant in sheets of 28 plus 4 center labels picturing flags of Kosrae (UL), Truk (UR), Pohnpei (LL) and Yap ((LR).

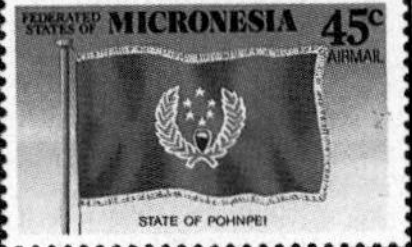

Flags of the Federated States of Micronesia AP4

1989, Jan. 19 Litho. *Perf. 13x13½*

C39 AP4 45c Pohnpei .70 .70
C40 AP4 45c Truk .70 .70
C41 AP4 45c Kosrae .70 .70
C42 AP4 45c Yap .70 .70
a. Block of 4, #C39-C42 2.80 2.80

This issue exists with 44c denominations but was not issued.

Aircraft Serving Micronesia AP5

1990, July 16 Litho. *Perf. 14*

C43 AP5 22c shown .40 .40
C44 AP5 36c multi, diff. .65 .65
C45 AP5 39c multi, diff. .75 .75
C46 AP5 45c multi, diff. .85 .85

1992, Mar. 27

C47 AP5 40c Propeller plane, outrigger canoe .70 .70
C48 AP5 50c Passenger jet, sailboat .85 .85
Nos. C43-C48 (6) 4.20 4.20

Souvenir Sheet

First Manned Moon Landing, 25th Anniv. — AP6

1994, July 20 Litho. *Perf. 13½*

C49 AP6 $2.90 US #C76 4.25 4.25

MIDDLE CONGO

'mi-dəl 'käŋ-ₒgō

LOCATION — Western Africa at the Equator, bordering on the Atlantic Ocean
GOVT. — Former French Colony
AREA — 166,069
POP. — 746,805 (1936)
CAPITAL — Brazzaville

In 1910 Middle Congo, formerly a part of French Congo, was declared a separate colony. It was grouped with Gabon and the Ubangi-Shari and Chad Territories and officially designated French Equatorial Africa. This group became a single administrative unit in 1934. See Gabon.

See Congo People's Republic for issues of 1959 onward.

100 Centimes = 1 Franc

See French Equatorial Africa No. 191 for additional stamp inscribed "Moyen Congo" and "Afrique Equatoriale Francaise."

Leopard — A1

Bakalois Woman — A2

Coconut Grove — A3

Perf. 14x13½

1907-22 Typo. Unwmk.

1 A1 1c ol gray & brn .40 .45
2 A1 2c vio & brn .40 .45
3 A1 4c blue & brn .80 *1.00*
4 A1 5c dk grn & bl .90 .80
5 A1 5c yel & bl ('22) .90 .90
6 A1 10c car & bl 1.10 .80
7 A1 10c dp grn & bl grn ('22) 4.00 4.00
8 A1 15c brn vio & rose ('17) 2.50 1.25
9 A1 20c brown & bl 3.25 3.25
10 A2 25c blue & grn 1.60 1.25
11 A2 25c bl grn & gray ('22) 1.10 1.10
12 A2 30c scar & grn 2.40 2.00
13 A2 30c dp rose & rose ('22) 2.00 *2.40*
14 A2 35c vio brn & bl 2.00 1.60
15 A2 40c dl grn & brn 2.00 2.00
16 A2 45c violet & red 6.00 4.25
17 A2 50c bl grn & red 2.50 2.40
18 A2 50c bl & grn ('22) 2.50 2.40
19 A2 75c brown & bl 10.00 5.75
20 A3 1fr dp grn & vio 15.00 10.50
21 A3 2fr vio & gray grn 16.00 12.50
22 A3 5fr blue & rose 50.00 35.00
Nos. 1-22 (22) 127.35 96.05

For stamps of types A1-A3 in changed colors, see Chad and Ubangi-Shari. French Congo A4-A6 are similar but inscribed "Congo Francais."

For overprints and surcharges see Nos. 23-60, B1-B2.

Stamps and Types of 1907-22 Overprinted in Black, Blue or Red

1924-30

23 A1 1c ol gray & brn .30 .50
a. Double surcharge 150.00
24 A1 2c violet & brn .30 .50
25 A1 4c blue & brn .30 .50
26 A1 5c yellow & bl .50 .50
27 A1 10c grn & bl grn (R) 1.00 .40
28 A1 10c car & gray ('25) .40 *.55*
29 A1 15c brn vio & rose (Bl) .80 .50
a. Double surcharge 130.00
30 A1 20c brown & blue .70 .70
31 A1 20c bl grn & yel grn ('26) .40 .45
32 A1 20c dp brn & rose lil ('27) 1.60 1.20

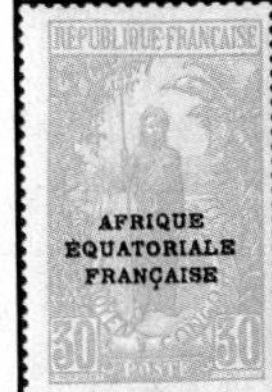

Overprinted

33 A2 25c bl grn & gray 1.00 .50
34 A2 30c rose & pale rose (Bl) 1.60 .80
35 A2 30c gray & bl vio (R) ('25) .80 .70
36 A2 30c dk grn & grn ('27) 2.00 1.60
37 A2 35c choc & bl .70 .80
38 A2 40c ol grn & brn 1.60 1.60
a. Double overprint 275.00
39 A2 45c vio & pale red (Bl) 1.60 1.20
a. Inverted overprint 160.00
40 A2 50c blue & grn (R) 1.60 1.20
41 A2 50c org & blk ('25) .80 .70
a. Without overprint 250.00 *275.00*
42 A2 65c org brn & bl ('27) 2.75 2.40
43 A2 75c brown & blue 1.25 1.25
44 A2 90c brn red & pink ('30) 5.00 4.00
45 A3 1fr green & vio 2.00 1.60
a. Double overprint 250.00
46 A3 1.10fr vio & brn ('28) 5.00 4.75
47 A3 1.50fr ultra & bl ('30) 8.00 5.50
48 A3 2fr vio & gray grn 2.00 1.60
49 A3 3fr red violet ('30) 9.00 7.25
50 A3 5fr blue & rose 6.50 5.25
Nos. 23-50 (28) 59.50 48.50

Nos. 48 and 50 Surcharged with New Values

1924

51 A3 25c on 2fr vio & gray grn 1.20 1.20
52 A3 25c on 5fr bl & rose (Bl) 1.20 1.20

Types of 1924-27 Surcharged with New Values in Black or Red

1925-27

53 A3 65c on 1fr red org & ol brn 1.20 1.20
a. Without surcharge 250.00
54 A3 85c on 1fr red org & ol brn 1.20 1.20
a. Double surcharge 175.00
55 A2 90c on 75c brn red & rose red ('27) 2.00 *2.40*
56 A3 1.25fr on 1fr dl bl & ultra (R) 1.20 1.20
a. Without surcharge 180.00 200.00
57 A3 1.50fr on 1fr ultra & bl ('27) 2.00 2.00
a. Without surcharge 200.00 *225.00*
58 A3 3fr on 5fr org brn & dl red ('27) 4.50 *4.00*
a. Without surcharge 325.00
59 A3 10fr on 5fr ver & bl grn ('27) 13.00 13.00
60 A3 20fr on 5fr org brn & vio ('27) 13.50 13.50
Nos. 53-60 (8) 38.60 38.50

Bars cover old values on Nos. 56-60.

Common Design Types pictured following the introduction.

Colonial Exposition Issue

Common Design Types

1931 Engr. *Perf. 12½*

Name of Country in Black

61 CD70 40c deep green 5.00 5.00
62 CD71 50c violet 4.00 4.00
63 CD72 90c red orange 4.00 4.00
64 CD73 1.50fr dull blue 5.50 5.50
Nos. 61-64 (4) 18.50 18.50

Viaduct at Mindouli A4

Pasteur Institute at Brazzaville A5

Government Building, Brazzaville — A6

1933 Photo. *Perf. 13½*

65 A4 1c lt brown .25 .25
66 A4 2c dull blue .25 .25
67 A4 4c olive grn .30 .30
68 A4 5c red violet .55 .40
69 A4 10c slate .80 .50
70 A4 15c dk violet 1.60 1.20
71 A4 20c red, *pink* 8.50 7.25
72 A4 25c orange 1.20 1.10
73 A4 30c yellow grn 2.75 2.00
74 A5 40c orange brn 2.75 2.00
75 A5 45c blk, *green* 2.75 2.00
76 A5 50c black violet 1.00 .80
77 A5 65c brn red, *grn* 2.75 2.00
78 A5 75c black, *pink* 15.00 11.00
79 A5 90c carmine 2.75 2.00
80 A5 1fr dark red 1.20 .80
81 A5 1.25fr Prus blue 2.40 1.60
82 A5 1.50fr dk blue 13.50 6.50
83 A6 1.75fr dk violet 3.25 1.60
84 A6 2fr grnsh blk 2.40 1.60
85 A6 3fr orange 6.00 4.75
86 A6 5fr slate blue 32.50 25.00

87 A6 10fr black 55.00 36.00
88 A6 20fr dark brown 36.00 32.50
Nos. 65-88 (24) 195.45 143.40

SEMI-POSTAL STAMPS

No. 6 Surcharged in Black

1916 **Unwmk.** ***Perf. 14x13½***
B1 A1 10c + 5c car & blue 1.60 1.60
a. Double surcharge 160.00 160.00
b. Inverted surcharge 140.00 140.00
e. As "a," One inverted 200.00 200.00
f. In pair with unsurcharged stamp 425.00

A printing with the surcharge placed lower and more to the left was made and used in Ubangi.

No. 6 Surcharged in Red

B2 A1 10c + 5c car & blue 1.60 1.60

POSTAGE DUE STAMPS

Postage Due Stamps of France Overprinted

1928 **Unwmk.** ***Perf. 14x13½***
J1 D2 5c light blue .50 *.80*
J2 D2 10c gray brn .70 *.80*
J3 D2 20c olive grn 1.20 *1.60*
J4 D2 25c brt rose 1.60 *2.00*
J5 D2 30c lt red 1.60 *2.00*
J6 D2 45c blue grn 1.60 *2.00*
J7 D2 50c brown vio 1.60 *2.00*
J8 D2 60c yellow brn 2.00 2.00
a. Period after "F" omitted 16.00 *20.00*
J9 D2 1fr red brn 2.75 *3.25*
J10 D2 2fr orange red 4.00 *4.75*
J11 D2 3fr brt violet 5.50 *8.00*
Nos. J1-J11 (11) 23.05 29.20

Village on Ubangi, Dance Mask — D3

Steamer on Ubangi River — D4

1930 **Typo.**
J12 D3 5c dp bl & ol .80 *1.20*
J13 D3 10c dp red & brn 1.20 *1.60*
J14 D3 20c green & brn 2.25 *3.25*
J15 D3 25c lt bl & brn 3.50 *4.00*
J16 D3 30c bis brn & Prus bl 5.25 *5.50*
J17 D3 45c Prus bl & ol 6.00 *6.50*
J18 D3 50c red vio & brn 6.00 *6.75*
J19 D3 60c gray lil & bl blk 8.00 *8.75*
J20 D4 1fr bis brn & bl blk 12.00 *13.50*
J21 D4 2fr violet & brn 13.00 *15.00*
J22 D4 3fr dk red & brn 13.50 *17.50*
Nos. J12-J22 (11) 71.50 *83.55*

Rubber Trees and Djoué River — D5

1933 **Photo.** ***Perf. 13½***
J23 D5 5c apple green .80 .80
J24 D5 10c dk bl, *bl* .80 .80
J25 D5 20c red, *yel* 1.60 1.60
J26 D5 25c chocolate 1.60 1.60
J27 D5 30c orange red 2.00 *2.40*
J28 D5 45c dk violet 2.00 *2.40*
J29 D5 50c gray black 2.75 *3.25*
J30 D5 60c blk, *orange* 4.50 *4.75*
J31 D5 1fr brown rose 6.50 *7.25*
J32 D5 2fr orange yel 8.00 *9.50*
J33 D5 3fr Prus blue 13.50 *17.50*
Nos. J23-J33 (11) 44.05 51.85

MOHELI

mo-'ā-lē

LOCATION — One of the Comoro Islands, situated in the Mozambique Channel midway between Madagascar and Mozambique (Africa)
GOVT. — French Colony
AREA — 89 sq. mi.
POP. — 4,000
CAPITAL — Fomboni
See Comoro Islands

100 Centimes = 1 Franc

Navigation and Commerce — A1

Perf. 14x13½
1906-07 **Typo.** **Unwmk.**
Name of Colony in Blue or Carmine
1 A1 1c blk, *lil bl* 3.75 2.40
2 A1 2c brn, *buff* 2.00 1.75
3 A1 4c claret, *lav* 3.25 2.40
4 A1 5c yellow grn 4.25 2.40
5 A1 10c carmine 5.50 2.40
6 A1 20c red, *green* 13.00 7.25
7 A1 25c blue 13.00 5.50
8 A1 30c brn, *bister* 17.50 14.50
9 A1 35c blk, *yellow* 10.50 4.00
10 A1 40c red, *straw* 17.50 13.50
11 A1 45c blk, *gray grn* ('07) 75.00 60.00
12 A1 50c brn, *az* 24.00 14.50
13 A1 75c dp vio, *org* 26.00 24.00
14 A1 1fr brnz grn, *straw* 24.00 17.50
15 A1 2fr vio, *rose* 35.00 35.00
16 A1 5fr lil, *lavender* 130.00 130.00
Nos. 1-16 (16) 404.25 337.10

Perf. 13½x14 stamps are counterfeits.
No. 12, affixed to pressboard with animals printed on the back, was used as emergency currency in the Comoro Islands in 1920.

Issue of 1906-07 Surcharged in Carmine or Black

1912
17 A1 5c on 4c cl, *lav* (C) 2.40 *3.25*
18 A1 5c on 20c red, *grn* 4.00 *4.75*
19 A1 5c on 30c brn, *bis* (C) 2.75 *3.50*
20 A1 10c on 40c red, *straw* 2.75 *3.50*
21 A1 10c on 45c blk, *gray grn* (C) 2.00 2.00
a. "Moheli" double 475.00
b. "Moheli" triple 475.00
22 A1 10c on 50c brn, *az* (C) 3.50 *4.50*
Nos. 17-22 (6) 17.40 21.50

Two spacings between the surcharged numerals are found on Nos. 17 to 22. For detailed listings, see the *Scott Classic Specialized Catalogue of Stamps and Covers.*

The stamps of Mohéli were supposed to have been superseded by those of Madagascar, January, 1908. However, Nos. 17-22 were surcharged in 1912 to use up remainders. These were available for use in Madagascar and the entire Comoro archipelago. In 1950 stamps of Comoro Islands came into use.

MOLDOVA

mäl-'dō-və

(Moldavia)

LOCATION — Southeastern Europe, bounded by Romania and the Ukraine
GOVT. — Independent republic, member of the Commonwealth of Independent States
AREA — 13,012 sq. mi.
POP. — 4,460,838 (1999 est.)
CAPITAL — Chisinau

With the breakup of the Soviet Union on Dec. 26, 1991, Moldova and ten former Soviet republics established the Commonwealth of Independent States.

100 Kopecks = 1 Ruble
100 Bani = 1 Leu (1993)

Catalogue values for all unused stamps in this country are for Never Hinged items.

Coat of Arms — A1

Flag — A2

1991, June 23 **Litho.** ***Imperf.***
Without Gum
1 A1 7k grn & multi .20 .20
2 A1 13k blue & multi .25 .40
3 A2 30k multi .40 .40
Nos. 1-3 (3) .85 1.00

Codrii Nature Preserve — A6

1992, Feb. 8 **Litho.** ***Perf. 12***
25 A6 25k multicolored .40 .40

For surcharge see No. 547.

Natl. Arms — A7

1992, May 24 **Photo.** ***Perf. 13½***
26 A7 35k green .20 .20
27 A7 50k red .20 .20
28 A7 65k brown .20 .20
29 A7 1r purple .20 .20
30 A7 1.50r blue .20 .20
Nos. 26-30 (5) 1.00 1.00

Birds — A8

Designs: 50k, Merops apiaster. 65k, Oriolus oriolus. 2.50r, Picus viridis. 6r, Coracias garrulus. 7.50r, Upupa epops. 15r, Cuculus canorus.

1992, Aug. 5 **Litho.** ***Perf. 13½x14***
31 A8 50k multicolored .30 .30
32 A8 65k multicolored .30 .30
33 A8 2.50r multicolored .45 .45
34 A8 6r multicolored .75 .75
35 A8 7.50r multicolored .95 .95
36 A8 15r multicolored 2.00 2.00
Nos. 31-36 (6) 4.75 4.75

No. 31 incorrectly inscribed "ariaster."
See Nos. 75-81.

Church of St. Panteleimon, Cent. — A9

1992, Aug. 10 **Photo.** ***Perf. 11½***
37 A9 1.50r multicolored .40 .40

She-Wolf Suckling Romulus and Remus — A10

1992, Aug. 10 ***Perf. 12x11½***
38 A10 5r multicolored .50 .50

Russia Nos. 4598-4599, 5839 Surcharged "MOLDOVA" and New Value in Black or Red

1992, Aug. 31 **Litho.** ***Perf. 12x12½***
39 A2138 2.50r on 4k #4599 .40 .40
40 A2139 6r on 3k #4598 .45 .45
41 A2138 8.50r on 4k #4599 .60 .60
42 A2765 10r on 3k #5839 (R) .70 .70
a. Black surcharge .70 .70
b. Brown red surcharge .70 .70
Nos. 39-42 (4) 2.15 2.15

Sheets of Nos. 39, 41 had row 5 inverted. On No. 40 only the 1st 5 stamps of row 5 were inverted. Counterfeit inverts were made using the original plates but with all 100 surcharges inverted. All inverts on No. 42 are fakes.

Russia Nos. 4596-4598 Surcharged in Black, Green or Red

1992, Oct. 20 **Litho.** ***Perf. 12x12½***
43 A2138 45k on 2k #4597 (G) .40 .40
44 A2138 46k on 2k #4597 .40 .40
45 A2138 63k on 1k #4596 (R) .40 .40
46 A2138 63k on 3k #4598 .70 .70
47 A2138 70k on 1k #4596 (R) .40 .40
50 A2138 4r on 1k #4596 .70 .70
a. Red surcharge .70 .70
Nos. 43-50 (6) 3.00 3.00

Nos. 45-46 exist with overprint inverted (6th row of sheet).

1992 Summer Olympics, Barcelona — A11

1992, Oct. 24 **Litho.** ***Perf. 13***
53 A11 35k High jump .30 .30
54 A11 65k Wrestling .35 .35
55 A11 1r Archery .35 .35
56 A11 2.50r Swimming .75 .75
57 A11 10r Equestrian 2.50 2.50
a. Souvenir sheet, #53-57 + label 4.75 4.75
Nos. 53-57 (5) 4.25 4.25

Nos. 55-56 Ovptd. with Name of Medalist, Medal and Olympic Rings in Bronze or Silver

1992, Oct. 24

58 A11 1r "NATALIA VALEEV / bronz" (BR) .55 .55
59 A11 2.50r "IURIE BAS-CATOV / argint" 1.00 1.00

Souvenir Sheet

Tudor Casapu, 1992 Weight Lifting Gold Medalist — A12

1992, Oct. 24 *Perf. 14½*

60 A12 25r multicolored 6.00 6.00

Admission of Moldova to UN — A13

Designs: 12r, UN Headquarters at left, Statue of Liberty, UN emblem, Moldovan flag.

1992, Oct. 24 *Perf. 13*

61 A13 1.30r multicolored .55 .55
62 A13 12r multicolored 1.00 1.00

Moldovan Participation in Conference on European Security and Cooperation — A14

1992, Oct. 24

63 A14 2.50r Flag, Prague Castle .50 .50
64 A14 25r Helsinki Cathedral, flag 1.50 1.50

Traditional Folk Art — A15

1992, Nov. 21 *Perf. 12x11½*

65 A15 7.50r Rug, pottery .45 .45

Admission of Moldova to UPU A16

1992, Dec. 26 *Perf. 12*

66 A16 5r Train, flag, emblem .50 .50
67 A16 10r Plane, flag, emblem 1.00 1.00

Discovery of America, 500th Anniv. — A17

1992, Dec. 26 **Litho.** *Perf. 12*

68 A17 1r Galleon .20 .20
69 A17 6r Carrack .75 .75
70 A17 6r Caravel .75 .75
a. Pair, #69-70 3.25 3.25
Nos. 68-70 (3) 1.70 1.70

Souvenir Sheet

71 A17 25r Columbus 5.00 5.00

Elaphe Longissima A18

Denominations at: a, UL. b, UR. c, LL. d, LR.

1993, July 3 **Litho.** *Perf. 13½*

72 A18 3r Block of 4, #a.-d. 2.50 2.50
73 A18 15r Natrix natrix 1.00 1.00
74 A18 25r Vipera berus 1.40 1.40
Nos. 72-74 (3) 4.90 4.90

Bird Type of 1992

1993, July 24 **Litho.** *Perf. 13x13½*

75 A8 2r like #31 .30 .30
76 A8 3r like #32 .30 .30
77 A8 5r like #33 .30 .30
78 A8 10r like #34 .30 .30
79 A8 15r like #35 .35 .35
80 A8 50r like #36 .90 .90
81 A8 100r Hirundo rustica 2.00 2.00
Nos. 75-81 (7) 4.45 4.45

Natl. Arms — A19

1993, Aug. 7 **Photo.** *Perf. 12x12½*

82 A19 2k blue .25 .25
83 A19 3k purple .25 .25
84 A19 6k green .25 .25
85 A19 10k olive & purple .25 .25
86 A19 15k olive & purple .25 .25
87 A19 20k gray & purple .25 .25
88 A19 30k yellow & purple .25 .25
89 A19 50k pink & purple .25 .25

Size: 21x32½mm

Perf. 12½x12

90 A19 100k multicolored .60 .60
91 A19 250k multicolored 1.40 1.40
Nos. 82-91 (10) 4.00 4.00

For surcharges see Nos. 558-559.

Butterflies — A20

Flowers — A21

1993, Dec. 22 **Litho.** *Perf. 13*

94 A20 6b Pyrameis atalanta .20 .20
95 A20 10b Papilio machaon .20 .20
96 A20 50b Vanessa jo .60 .60
97 A20 250b Saturnia pavonia 2.75 2.75
Nos. 94-97 (4) 3.75 3.75

1993, Dec. 25 **Litho.** *Perf. 13½*

Designs: 6b, Tulipa bibersteiniana. 15b, Convallaria majalis. 25b, Galanthus nivalis. 30b, Paeonia peregrina. 50b, Galanthus plicatus. 90b, Pulsatilla grandis. 250b, Cypripedium calceolus.

98 A21 6b multicolored .20 .20
99 A21 15b multicolored .20 .20
100 A21 25b multicolored .35 .35
101 A21 30b multicolored .40 .40
102 A21 50b multicolored .65 .65
103 A21 90b multicolored 1.10 1.10
Nos. 98-103 (6) 2.90 2.90

Souvenir Sheet

104 A21 250b multicolored 3.00 3.00

No. 104 contains one 30x45mm stamp.

A22

A23

Famous Men: 6b, Dragos Voda. 25b, Bogdan Voda I. 50b, Latcu Voda. 100b, Petru I Musat. 150b, Roman Voda Musat. 200b, Stefan I.

1993, Dec. 29 **Litho.** *Perf. 13*

105 A22 6b multicolored .20 .20
106 A22 25b multicolored .20 .20
107 A22 50b multicolored .25 .25
108 A22 100b multicolored .45 .45
109 A22 150b multicolored .65 .65
110 A22 200b multicolored 1.10 1.10
Nos. 105-110 (6) 2.85 2.85

1993, Dec. 29 **Litho.** *Perf. 13*

Europa (Contemporary art): 3b, History of Man, by M. Grecu. 150b, Springtime, by I. Vieru.

111 A23 3b multicolored .75 .75
112 A23 150b multicolored 5.75 5.75
a. Souvenir sheet, 4 each #111-112 + label 26.00 26.00

1994 Winter Olympics, Lillehammer A24

1994, Feb. 12 **Litho.** *Perf. 13½*

113 A24 3b Biathlete, skiiers .35 .35
114 A24 150b Biathlete, diff. 1.50 1.50

Russia No. 4596 Surcharged in Dark Blue

1994, Apr. 11 **Litho.** *Perf. 12x12½*

114A A2138 3b on 1k olive grn .20 .20
114B A2138 25b on 1k olive grn .20 .20
114C A2138 50b on 1k olive grn .35 .35
Nos. 114A-114C (3) .75 .75

First Manned Moon Landing, 25th anniv. — A25

1994, June 18 **Litho.** *Perf. 14*

Europa: 1b, Gemini space mission, Titan II rocket. 45b, Ed White, Gemini IV. 2.50 l, Lunar landing module.

115 A25 1b multicolored .60 .60
116 A25 45b multicolored 3.00 3.00
117 A25 2.50 l multicolored 6.50 6.50
Nos. 115-117 (3) 10.10 10.10

Natl. Arms — A26

1994 *Perf. 13½x14*

118 A26 1b multicolored .25 .25
119 A26 10b multicolored .25 .25
120 A26 30b multicolored .25 .25
121 A26 38b multicolored .25 .25
122 A26 45b multicolored .50 .50
123 A26 75b multicolored .60 .60
125 A26 1.50 l multicolored 1.10 1.10
126 A26 1.80 l multicolored 1.10 1.10
127 A26 2.50 l multi, size: 23½x29mm 1.75 1.75
128 A26 4.50 l multicolored 3.50 3.50
128A A26 5.40 l multicolored 3.75 3.75
128B A26 6.90 l multicolored 4.50 4.50

Size: 23½x29mm

128C A26 7.20 l multicolored 4.50 4.50
129 A26 13 l multicolored 8.50 8.50
130 A26 24 l multicolored 16.00 16.00
Nos. 118-130 (15) 46.80 46.80

Issued: 1b, 45b, 1.50 l, 4.50 l, 6/11/94; 10b, 20b, 5.40 l, 6.90 l, 13 l, 7/16/94; 38b, 75b, 1.80 l, 2.50 l, 7.20 l, 8/13/94.

This is a expanding set. Numbers may change.

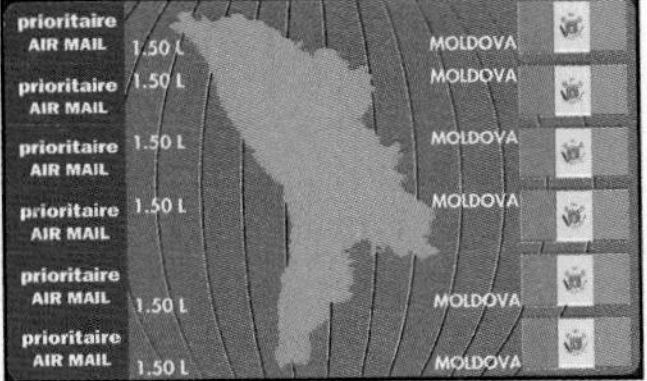

Stamp Card — A27

Designs: 1.50 l, 4.50 l, Map of Moldova.

Rouletted 26 on 2 or 3 Sides

1994, Dec. 22 **Litho.**

Self-Adhesive

Cards of 6 + 6 labels

131 A27 1.50 l #a.-f., lt vio & multi 6.00
132 A27 4.50 l #a.-f., dp red vio & multi 17.50

Individual stamps measure 70x9mm and have a card backing. Se-tenant labels inscribed "AIR MAIL."

Famous People A28

Designs: 3b, Maria Cibotari (1910-49), singer. 90b, Dumitru Caraciobanu (1937-80), actor. 150b, Eugeniu Coca (1893-1954), composer. 250b, Igor Vieru (1923-83), actor.

1994, June 30 **Litho.** *Perf. 13½*

133 A28 3b multicolored .30 .30
134 A28 90b multicolored .40 .40
135 A28 150b multicolored .80 .80
136 A28 250b multicolored 1.40 1.40
Nos. 133-136 (4) 2.90 2.90

Stamp Day A29

Designs: 10b, Designing stamp. 45b, Printing stamps. 2 l, Inspecting finished sheets.

1994, July 22 Litho. *Perf. 14*

137	A29	10b multicolored	.40	.40
138	A29	45b multicolored	.85	.85
139	A29	2 l multicolored	2.75	2.75
		Nos. 137-139 (3)	4.00	4.00

Intl. Olympic Committee, Cent. — A30

1994, Aug. 29 Litho. *Perf. 13½x14*

140	A30	60b Pierre de Coubertin	.65	.65
141	A30	1.50 l Olympic rings, symbol	1.50	1.50

Moldova's Entrance into NATO — A31

Intl. Year of the Family — A32

Designs: 60b, Moldova Pres. Mircea Snegur, NATO Secretary General Manfred Worner signing documents. 2.50 l, World map centered on Europe.

1994, Nov. 8 Litho. *Perf. 13½*

142	A31	60b multicolored	1.10	1.10
143	A31	2.50 l multicolored	4.25	4.25

1994, Nov. 26 *Perf. 14*

144	A32	30b Family	.60	.60
145	A32	60b Mother breast-feeding	1.25	1.25
146	A32	1.50 l Child painting	2.40	2.40
		Nos. 144-146 (3)	4.25	4.25

1996 European Soccer Championships, England — A33

Designs: 10b, Handshaking. 40b, Players legs, soccer ball. 1.20 l, Goalie.

No. 150: a, 1.10 l, Soccer federation, German flags. b, 2.20 l, Soccer ball, German, Moldovan flags. c, 2.40 l, Players.

1994, Dec. 10

147	A33	10b multicolored	.40	.40
148	A33	40b multicolored	.70	.70
149	A33	2.40 l multicolored	3.00	3.00
		Nos. 147-149 (3)	4.10	4.10

Souvenir Sheet

150	A33	Sheet of 3, #a.-c.	5.75	5.75

Christmas A34

Mushrooms — A35

Paintings of Birth of Christ by: 20b, unknown artist, 18th cent. 3.60 l, Gherasim, 1808.

1994, Dec. 29

151	A34	20b multicolored	.50	.50
152	A34	3.60 l multicolored	4.50	4.50

1995, Feb. 8

153	A35	4b Russula virescens	.50	.50
154	A35	10b Boletus luridus	.80	.80
155	A35	20b Cantherellus cibarius	1.60	1.60
156	A35	90b Leccinum aurantiacum	4.75	4.75
157	A35	1.80 l Leccinum duriusculum	9.00	9.00
		Nos. 153-157 (5)	16.65	16.65

European Nature Conservation Year — A36

Designs: 4b, Hieraaetus pennatus. 45b, Capreolus capreolus. 90b, Sus scrofa.

1995, Mar. 18 Litho. *Perf. 14*

158	A36	4b multicolored	.95	.95
159	A36	45b multicolored	4.50	4.50
160	A36	90b multicolored	9.25	9.25
		Nos. 158-160 (3)	14.70	14.70

Museum of Natural Sciences — A37

Designs: 4b, Jars. 10b+2b, Dinotherium gigantissimum. 1.80 l+30b, Silver coin, 3rd-2nd cent. BC.

1995 Litho. *Perf. 14*

161	A37	4b multicolored	.55	.55
162	A37	10b +2b multi	1.10	1.10
163	A37	1.80 l +30b multi	7.75	7.75
		Nos. 161-163 (3)	9.40	9.40

Peace & Freedom — A38

Paintings: 10b, May 1945, by Igor Vieru. 40b, Linistea, by Sergiu Cuciuc. 2.20 l, Primavara 1944, by Cuciuc.

1995, May 9 Litho. *Perf. 14*

164	A38	10b multicolored	.45	.45
165	A38	40b multicolored	2.75	2.75
166	A38	2.20 l multicolored	5.25	5.25
		Nos. 164-166 (3)	8.45	8.45

Europa.

A39 A40

Famous People: 90b, Constantin Stere (1865-1936), writer. 10b, Tamara Ceban (1914-90), musician. 40b, Alexandru Plamadeala (1888-1940), artist. 1.80 l, Lucian Blaga (1895-1961), writer.

1995, June 17 Litho. *Perf. 14*

167	A39	9b dp cl & gray	.30	.30
168	A39	10b brt mag & gray	.30	.30
169	A39	40b violet & gray	.95	.95
170	A39	1.80 l dk grn & gray	4.75	4.75
		Nos. 167-170 (4)	6.30	6.30

1995, July 2 Litho. *Perf. 14*

Kings of Moldova, reign: No. 171, Alexandru Cel Bun, 1400-32. No. 172, Petru Aron, 1451-52, 1454-57. No. 173, Stefan Cel Mare, 1457-1504. 45 l, Petru Rares, 1527-38, 1541-46. 90 l, Alexandru Lapusneanu, 1552-61, 1564-68. 1.80 l, Ion Voda Cel Cumplit, 1572-74. 5 l, Stefan Cel Mare, 1457-1504.

171	A40	10 b multicolored	.45	.45
172	A40	10 b multicolored	.45	.45
173	A40	10 b multicolored	.45	.45
174	A40	45 b multicolored	1.90	1.90
175	A40	90 b multicolored	3.50	3.50
176	A40	1.80 l multicolored	7.75	7.75
		Nos. 171-176 (6)	14.50	14.50

Souvenir Sheet

177	A40	5 l multicolored	4.00	4.00

No. 177 contains one 24x29mm stamp.

Citadels of Moldova A41

1995, July 29

178	A41	10 b Soroca	.35	.35
179	A41	20 b Tighina	.65	.65
180	A41	60 b Alba	1.40	1.40
181	A41	1.30 l Hotin	3.75	3.75
		Nos. 178-181 (4)	6.15	6.15

A42

UN, 50th Anniv. — A43

Designs inside of stylized eye: No. 182, Devastation of war. No. 183, Fighter plane. No. 184, Prisoner of war.

Nos. 185-186: a, 1. b, 2. c, 3. d, 4. e, 5. f, 6. g, 7. h, 8. i, 9. j, 10.

1995, Oct. 24 Litho. *Perf. 14*

182	A42	10b yellow & multi	.50	.50
183	A42	10b blue & multi	.50	.50
184	A42	1.50 l green & multi	6.50	6.50
		Nos. 182-184 (3)	7.50	7.50

Stamp Cards

Rouletted 15 on 2 or 3 Sides

Self-Adhesive

Cards of 10

185	A43	90b #a.-j.	*15.00*	*15.00*
186	A43	1.50 l #a.-j.	*25.00*	*25.00*

Background color of stamps gradually shifts from light blue (#1) to dark blue (#10). Each stamp is individually numbered.

Motion Pictures, Cent. — A44

Films: 10b, Last Moon of Autumn. 40b, Lautarii. 2.40 l, Dimitrie Cantemir.

1995, Dec. 28 Litho. *Perf. 14*

187	A44	10b red brn & blk	.80	.80
188	A44	40b olive & black	2.50	2.50
189	A44	2.40 l ultra & black	8.00	8.00
		Nos. 187-189 (3)	11.30	11.30

Mushrooms A45

1996 Summer Olympic Games, Atlanta A46

No. 190, Amanita muscaria. No. 191, Boletus satanas. 65b, Amanita phalloides. 1.30 l, Hypholoma fasciculare. 2.40 l, Amanita virosa.

1996, Mar. 23 Litho. *Perf. 14*

190	A45	10b multicolored	.70	.70
191	A45	10b multicolored	.70	.70
192	A45	65b multicolored	1.10	1.10
193	A45	1.30 l multicolored	1.75	1.75
194	A45	2.40 l multicolored	4.75	4.75
		Nos. 190-194 (5)	9.00	9.00

Moldova Grapes — A208

2009, Oct. 9 ***Perf. 14½x14***
647 A208 4.50 l multi 1.25 1.25

European Day Against Human Trafficking — A209

2009, Oct. 18 ***Perf. 14x14½***
648 A209 4.50 l multi 1.25 1.25

Famous People A210

Designs: No. 649, 1.20 l, Eugene Ionescu (1909-94), playwright. No. 650, 1.20 l, Eufrosinia Kersnovskaia (1907-95), writer. 4.50 l, Nicolai Gogol (1809-52), writer. 7 l, Charles Darwin (1809-92), naturalist.

2009, Nov. 26 **Litho.** ***Perf. 14x14½***
649-652 A210 Set of 4 3.50 3.50

Christmas — A211

Designs: 1.20 l, Capra. 4.50 l, Plugusorul.

2009, Dec. 1
653-654 A211 Set of 2 1.40 1.40

Famous People A212

Designs: No. 655, 1.20 l, Grigore Vieru (1935-2009), writer. No. 656, 1.20 l, Natalia Dadiani (1865-1903), founder of school for girls. 5.40 l, Ivan Zaikin (1880-1948), wrestler and aviator. 7 l, Maria Cebotari (1910-49), singer and actress.
4.50 l, Mihai Eminescu (1850-89), writer, vert.

2010, Jan. 15 **Litho.** ***Perf. 14x14½***
655-658 A212 Set of 4 3.00 3.00

Souvenir Sheet
Perf. 14½x14
659 A212 4.50 l multi + label .90 .90

2010 Winter Olympics, Vancouver — A213

Designs: 1.20 l, Alpine skiing. 8.50 l, Biathlon, vert.

2010, Feb. 12 ***Perf. 14x14½, 14½x14***
660-661 A213 Set of 2 1.90 1.90

Jewelry in National Museum of Archaeology and History A214

Designs: 1.20 l, Shell necklace, 5th cent. B.C. 7 l, Ring and pendant, 5th cent. B.C.

2010, Feb. 23 ***Perf. 13 Syncopated***
662-663 A214 Set of 2 1.60 1.60

Frédéric Chopin (1810-49), Composer — A215

2010, Mar. 1 ***Perf. 14x14½***
664 A215 5.40 l multi 1.10 1.10

Mushrooms A216

Designs: 1.20 l, Lactarius piperatus. 2 l, Amanita panherina. 5.40 l, Russula sanguinea. 7 l, Coprinus picaceus.

2010, Mar. 27 ***Perf. 14½x14***
665-668 A216 Set of 4 3.25 3.25
668a Souvenir sheet, #665-668 3.25 3.25

Birds — A217

Designs: 85b, Carduelis carduelis. 1 l, Passer domesticus. 1.20 l, Strix uralensis. 4.50 l, Pica pica.
8.50 l, Columba livia.

2010, Apr. 8 ***Perf. 13 Syncopated***
669-672 A217 Set of 4 1.50 1.50

Souvenir Sheet
673 A217 8.50 l multi 1.75 1.75

Europa A218

Children's books: 1.20 l, Punguta cu doi Bani, by Ion Creanga. 5.40 l, Guguta Si Prietenii Sai, by Spiridon Vangheli.

2010, Apr. 30 ***Perf. 14x14½***
674-675 A218 Set of 2 1.40 1.40
675a Sheet, 3 each #674-675 4.25 4.25

No. 675a was sold with, but unattached to, a booklet cover.

End of World War II, 65th Anniv. — A219

2010, May 9 ***Perf. 14½x14***
676 A219 4.50 l multi .90 .90

2010 World Cup Soccer Championships, South Africa — A220

Soccer player and: 1.20 l, Mascot. 8.50 l, Emblem, vert.

Perf. 14x14½, 14½x14
2010, June 11
677-678 A220 Set of 2 1.90 1.90

Campaign Against AIDS — A221

2010, July 1 ***Perf. 14x14½***
679 A221 1.20 l multi .25 .25

Paintings Depicting Flowers A222

Designs: 1 l, Flowers, by Ion Tabirta. 1.20 l, Bouquet of Poppies, by Oleg Cojocari. 2 l, Flowers, by Mihail Statnii. 5.40 l, Chrysanthemums, by Leonid Grigorasenco.

Perf. 13 Syncopated
2010, Aug. 6 **Litho.**
680-683 A222 Set of 4 2.10 2.10

Dances — A223

Designs: 85b, Moldovanesca. 5.40 l, Calusarii, vert.

Perf. 14x14½, 14½x14
2010, Sept. 18
684-685 A223 Set of 2 1.40 1.40

Feteasca Grapes — A224

2010, Oct. 9 ***Perf. 14½x14***
686 A224 4.50 l multi 1.00 1.00

National Symbols A225

Perf. 13 Syncopated at Top
2010, Nov. 3
687 A225 1.20 l Arms .25 .25
a. Perf. 13, syncopation at sides .25 .25
688 A225 4.50 l Flag 1.00 1.00
a. Perf. 13, syncopation at sides 1.00 1.00
b. Sheet of 6, 3 each #687a, 688a 3.75 3.75

AIR POST STAMPS

TU-144 — AP1

1992-93 **Litho.** ***Perf. 12***

C1	AP1	1.75r maroon	.30	.30
C2	AP1	2.50r red vio	.35	.35
C3	AP1	7.75r blue	1.20	1.20
C4	AP1	8.50r blue green	1.50	1.50
C5	AP1	25r red brown	.45	.45
C6	AP1	45r brown	.75	.75
C7	AP1	50r olive green	.90	.90
C8	AP1	90r blue	1.90	1.90
		Nos. C1-C8 (8)	7.35	7.35

Issued: #C1-C4, 7/20/92; #C5-C8, 7/24/93.

POSTAGE DUE STAMPS

Dove, Envelope — D1

1994, Nov. 12 **Litho.** ***Perf. 14***
J1 D1 30b lt olive & brown .55 .55
J2 D1 40b pale vio & slate .65 .65

In use, Nos. J1-J2 were torn apart, one half being affixed to the postage due item and the other half being pasted into the postman's record book. Values are for unused and canceled-to-order pairs.

MONACO

'mä-nə-ˌkō

LOCATION — Southern coast of France, bordering on the Mediterranean Sea
GOVT. — Principality
AREA — 481 acres
POP. — 31,842 (2001 est.)
CAPITAL — Monaco

100 Centimes = 1 Franc
100 Cents = 1 Euro (2002)

Catalogue values for unused stamps in this country are for Never Hinged items, beginning with Scott 182 in the regular postage section, Scott B51 in the semi-postal section, Scott C2 in the airpost section, Scott CB1 in the airpost semi-postal section, and Scott J28 in the postage due section.

Values for unused stamps are for examples with original gum as defined in the catalogue introduction. Very fine examples of Nos. 1-181, B1-B50, C1 and J1-J27 will have perforations clear of the design and/or frameline. Very well centered are worth more than the values quoted.

Prince Charles III — A1

Prince Albert I — A2

1885 Unwmk. Typo. *Perf. 14x13½*

No.	Type	Description	Unused	Used
1	A1	1c olive green	25.00	17.50
2	A1	2c dull lilac	57.50	27.50
3	A1	5c blue	70.00	35.00
4	A1	10c brown, *straw*	85.00	40.00
5	A1	15c rose	350.00	18.00
6	A1	25c green	700.00	75.00
7	A1	40c slate, *rose*	85.00	45.00
8	A1	75c black, *rose*	275.00	125.00
9	A1	1fr black, *yellow*	1,750.	500.00
10	A1	5fr rose, *green*	3,000.	2,000.

1891-1921

No.	Type	Description	Unused	Used
11	A2	1c olive green	.70	.70
12	A2	2c dull violet	.80	.80
13	A2	5c blue	50.00	6.00
14	A2	5c yellow grn ('01)	.40	.35
15	A2	10c brown, *straw*	100.00	16.00
16	A2	10c carmine ('01)	3.25	.70
17	A2	15c rose	175.00	10.00
a.		Double impression	1,400.	
18	A2	15c vio brn, *straw* ('01)	3.00	1.00
19	A2	15c gray green ('21)	2.00	*2.50*
20	A2	25c green	275.00	32.50
21	A2	25c deep blue ('01)	15.00	5.00
22	A2	40c slate, *rose* ('94)	3.50	2.40
23	A2	50c violet brown (shades), *orange*	7.00	4.75
24	A2	75c vio brn, *buff* ('94)	27.50	18.00
25	A2	75c ol brn, *buff* ('21)	20.00	*24.00*
26	A2	1fr black, *yellow*	19.00	11.00
27	A2	5fr rose, *grn*	100.00	87.50
c.		Double impression	1,500.	
28	A2	5fr dull violet ('21)	200.00	*250.00*
29	A2	5fr dark green ('21)	22.50	*27.50*
		Nos. 11-29 (19)	1,024.	500.70

The handstamp "OL" in a circle of dots is a cancellation, not an overprint.

For shades, see the *Scott Classic Specialized Catalogue of Stamps and Covers.*

See No. 1782. For overprints and surcharges see Nos. 30-35, 57-59, B1.

Stamps of 1901-21 Overprinted or Surcharged:

1921, Mar. 5

No.	Type	Description	Unused	Used
30	A2	5c lt green	.70	*.70*
31	A2	75c brown, *buff*	5.25	*6.25*
32	A2	2fr on 5fr dull vio	32.50	*52.50*
		Nos. 30-32 (3)	38.45	*59.45*

Issued to commemorate the birth of Princess Antoinette, daughter of Princess Charlotte and Prince Pierre, Comte de Polignac.

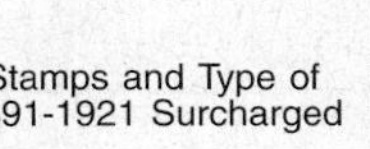
Stamps and Type of 1891-1921 Surcharged

1922

No.	Type	Description	Unused	Used
33	A2	20c on 15c gray green	1.10	*1.40*
34	A2	25c on 10c rose	.70	*.90*
35	A2	50c on 1fr black, *yel*	6.00	*6.50*
		Nos. 33-35 (3)	7.80	*8.80*

Prince Albert I — A5

Oceanographic Museum — A6

"The Rock" of Monaco — A7

Royal Palace — A8

1922-24 Engr. *Perf. 11*

No.	Type	Description	Unused	Used
40	A5	25c deep brown	4.00	*4.75*
41	A6	30c dark green	.90	.90
42	A6	30c scarlet ('23)	.50	.45
43	A6	50c ultra	4.25	4.25
44	A7	60c black brown	.35	.35
45	A7	1fr black, *yellow*	.25	.25
46	A7	2fr scarlet ver	.50	.45
47	A8	5fr red brown	32.50	*37.50*
48	A8	5fr green, *bluish*	10.50	10.50
49	A8	10fr carmine	14.00	18.00
		Nos. 40-49 (10)	67.75	*77.40*

Nos. 40-49 exist imperf.

For shades, see the *Scott Classic Specialized Catalogue of Stamps and Covers.*

Prince Louis II
A9 A10

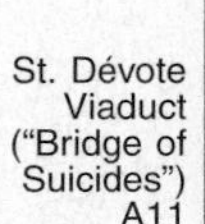
St. Dévote Viaduct ("Bridge of Suicides") A11

1923-24 Engr.

No.	Type	Description	Unused	Used
50	A9	10c deep green	.35	*.55*
51	A9	15c car rose ('24)	.45	*.70*
52	A9	20c red brown	.35	*.55*
53	A9	25c violet	.25	*.45*
a.		Without engraver's name	27.50	27.50
54	A11	40c orange brn ('24)	.65	.55
55	A10	50c ultra	.35	*.45*
		Nos. 50-55 (6)	2.40	*3.25*

The 25c comes in 2 types, one with larger "5" and "c" touching frame of numeral tablet.

Stamps of the 1922-24 issues sometimes show parts of the letters of a papermaker's watermark.

The engraved stamps of type A11 measure 31x21½mm. The typographed stamps of that design measure 36x21½mm.

See #86-88. For surcharges see #95-96.

Stamps and Type of 1891-1921 Surcharged

1924, Aug. 5 *Perf. 14x13½*

No.	Type	Description	Unused	Used
57	A2	45c on 50c brn ol, *buff*	.50	*.70*
a.		Double surcharge	775.00	775.00
58	A2	75c on 1fr blk, *yel*	.50	*.70*
a.		Double surcharge	550.00	*550.00*
59	A2	85c on 5fr dk green	.50	*.70*
a.		Double surcharge	*650.00*	*650.00*
		Nos. 57-59 (3)	1.50	2.10
		Set, never hinged	2.25	

Grimaldi Family Coat of Arms — A12

Prince Louis II — A13

Louis II — A14

View of Monaco A15

1924-33 Typo.

No.	Type	Description	Unused	Used
60	A12	1c gray black	.20	.20
61	A12	2c red brown	.20	.20
62	A12	3c brt violet ('33)	2.75	1.90
63	A12	5c orange ('26)	.35	.30
64	A12	10c blue	.20	.20
65	A13	15c apple green	.20	.20
66	A13	15c dull vio ('29)	2.75	1.90
67	A13	20c violet	.20	.20
68	A13	20c rose	.35	.25
69	A13	25c rose	.20	.20
70	A13	25c red, *yel*	.20	*.25*
71	A13	30c orange	.20	.20
72	A13	40c black brown	.25	.20
73	A13	40c lt bl, *bluish*	.35	.35
74	A13	45c gray black ('26)	.90	.70
75	A14	50c myrtle grn ('25)	.20	*.25*
76	A13	50c brown, *org*	.20	.20
77	A14	60c yellow brn ('25)	.20	*.25*
78	A13	60c ol grn, *grnsh*	.20	*.25*
79	A13	75c ol grn, *grnsh* ('26)	.70	.35
80	A13	75c car, *straw* ('26)	.35	.20
81	A13	75c slate	.90	.55
82	A13	80c red, *yel* ('26)	.40	.30
83	A13	90c rose, *straw* ('27)	2.00	1.60
84	A13	1.25fr bl, *bluish* ('26)	.20	.20
85	A13	1.50fr bl, *bluish* ('27)	3.75	1.90

Size: 36x21½mm

No.	Type	Description	Unused	Used
86	A11	1fr blk, *orange*	.20	*.25*
87	A11	1.05fr red violet ('26)	.20	*.25*
88	A11	1.10fr blue grn ('27)	8.00	6.00
89	A15	2fr vio & ol brn ('25)	2.75	1.00
90	A15	3fr rose & ultra, *yel* ('27)	25.00	12.00
91	A15	5fr green & rose ('25)	8.50	6.00
92	A15	10fr yel brn & bl ('25)	25.00	17.50
		Nos. 60-92 (33)	88.05	56.30
		Set, never hinged	175.00	

Nos. 60 to 74 and 76 exist imperforate.

For surcharges see Nos. 93-94, 97-99, C1.

Type of 1924-33 Surcharged with New Value and Bars

1926-31

No.	Type	Description	Unused	Used
93	A13	30c on 25c rose	.30	.25
94	A13	50c on 60c ol grn, *grnsh* ('28)	1.50	.35
95	A11	50c on 1.05fr red vio ('28)	1.10	.70
a.		Double surcharge	65.00	
96	A11	50c on 1.10fr bl grn ('31)	14.00	8.75
97	A13	50c on 1.25fr bl, *bluish* (R) ('28)	1.60	.65
98	A13	1.25fr on 1fr bl, *bluish*	.80	.50
99	A15	1.50fr on 2fr vio & ol brn ('28)	7.00	5.25
		Nos. 93-99 (7)	26.30	16.45
		Set, never hinged	40.00	

Princes Charles III, Louis II and Albert I A17

1928, Feb. 18 Engr. *Perf. 11*

No.	Type	Description	Unused	Used
100	A17	50c dull carmine	2.50	*4.75*
101	A17	1.50fr dark blue	2.50	*4.75*
102	A17	3fr dark violet	2.50	*4.75*
		Nos. 100-102 (3)	7.50	14.25
		Set, never hinged	18.00	

Nos. 100-102 were sold exclusively at the Intl. Phil. Exhib. at Monte Carlo, Feb., 1928. One set was sold to each purchaser of a ticket of admission to the exhibition which cost 5fr. Exist imperf. Value, set $27.50.

Old Watchtower A20

Royal Palace A21

Church of St. Dévote — A22

Prince Louis II — A23

"The Rock" of Monaco A24

Gardens of Monaco A25

Fortifications and Harbor — A26

1932-37 ***Perf. 13, 14x13½***

No.	Type	Description	Unused	Used
110	A20	15c lilac rose	.80	.25
111	A20	20c orange brn	.80	.25
112	A21	25c olive blk	1.10	.35
113	A22	30c yellow grn	1.40	.35
114	A23	40c dark brown	3.25	1.40
115	A24	45c brown red	3.50	1.10
a.		45c red	425.00	425.00
116	A23	50c purple	3.25	.85
117	A25	65c blue green	3.50	1.10
118	A26	75c deep blue	4.00	1.75
119	A23	90c red	9.50	3.25
120	A22	1fr red brown ('33)	27.50	7.75
121	A26	1.25fr rose lilac	6.75	4.50
122	A23	1.50fr ultra	40.00	10.50
123	A21	1.75fr rose lilac	35.00	9.50
124	A21	1.75fr car rose ('37)	24.00	13.00
125	A24	2fr dark blue	13.50	4.75
126	A20	3fr purple	20.00	9.00
127	A21	3.50fr orange ('35)	47.50	32.50
128	A22	5fr violet	27.50	20.00
129	A21	10fr deep blue	125.00	70.00
130	A25	20fr black	175.00	140.00
		Nos. 110-130 (21)	572.85	332.15
		Set, never hinged	1,150.	

Postage Due Stamps of 1925-32 Surcharged or Overprinted in Black:

1937-38 ***Perf. 14x13***

No.	Type	Description	Unused	Used
131	D3	5c on 10c violet	1.00	1.00
132	D3	10c violet	1.00	1.00
133	D3	15c on 30c bister	1.00	1.00
134	D3	20c on 30c bister	1.00	1.00
135	D3	25c on 60c red	1.50	1.50
136	D3	30c bister	2.40	2.40
137	D3	40c on 60c red	2.40	2.40
138	D3	50c on 60c red	2.40	2.40
139	D3	65c on 1fr lt bl	2.25	2.00
140	D3	85c on 1fr lt bl	5.00	4.50
141	D3	1fr light blue	7.75	7.75
142	D3	2.15fr on 2fr dl red	7.75	7.75
143	D3	2.25fr on 2fr dl red ('38)	19.00	19.00
144	D3	2.50fr on 2fr dl red ('38)	29.00	29.00
		Nos. 131-144 (14)	83.45	82.70
		Set, never hinged	175.00	

Grimaldi Arms — A27

Prince Louis II — A28

1937-43 **Engr.**

No.	Type	Description	Unused	Used
145	A27	1c dk vio brn ('38)	.20	.20
146	A27	2c emerald	.20	.20
147	A27	3c brt red violet	.20	.20
148	A27	5c red	.20	.20
149	A27	10c ultra	.20	.20
149A	A27	10c black ('43)	.20	.20
150	A27	15c violet ('39)	1.75	1.50
150A	A27	30c dull green ('43)	.20	.20
150B	A27	40c rose car ('43)	.20	.20
150C	A27	50c brt violet ('43)	.20	.20
151	A28	55c red brown ('38)	5.75	2.25
151A	A27	60c Prus blue ('43)	.20	.20
152	A28	65c violet ('38)	30.00	13.00
153	A28	70c red brown ('39)	.35	.35
153A	A27	70c red brown ('43)	.20	.20
154	A28	90c violet ('39)	.35	.30
155	A28	1fr rose red ('38)	18.50	10.50
156	A28	1.25fr rose red ('39)	.35	.35

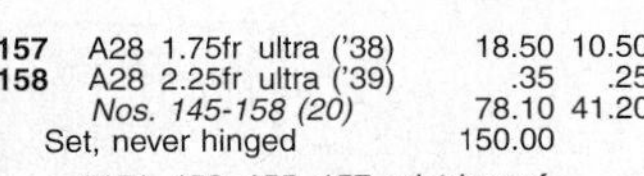

No.	Type	Description	Unused	Used
157	A28	1.75fr ultra ('38)	18.50	10.50
158	A28	2.25fr ultra ('39)	.35	.25
		Nos. 145-158 (20)	78.10	41.20
		Set, never hinged	150.00	

#151, 152, 155, 157 exist imperf.

Souvenir Sheet

Prince Louis II — A29

1938, Jan. 17 **Unwmk.** ***Imperf.***

No.	Type	Description	Unused	Used
159	A29	10fr magenta	65.00	65.00
		Never hinged	175.00	

"Fête Nationale" 1/17/38. Size: 99x120mm.

Cathedral of Monaco — A30

St. Nicholas Square — A31

Palace Gate — A32

Palace of Monaco — A34

Panorama of Monaco A33

Harbor of Monte Carlo A35

1939-46 ***Perf. 13***

No.	Type	Description	Unused	Used
160	A30	20c rose lilac	.25	.25
161	A31	25c gldn brown	.45	.30
162	A32	30c dk blue grn	.35	.30
162A	A32	30c brown red ('40)	.35	.25
163	A31	40c henna brn	.70	.50
164	A33	45c brt red vio	.50	.50
165	A34	50c dk blue grn	.35	.25
166	A32	60c rose carmine	.40	.35
166A	A32	60c dk green ('40)	.90	.70
166B	A35	70c brt red vio ('41)	.40	.25
167	A35	75c dark green	.40	.25
167A	A30	80c dull green ('43)	.20	*.25*
168	A34	1fr brown black	.40	.25
168A	A33	1fr claret ('43)	.20	.20
168B	A35	1.20fr ultra ('46)	.25	*.35*
168C	A34	1.30fr brown blk ('41)	.40	.35
168D	A31	1.50fr ultra ('46)	.40	.40
169	A31	2fr rose violet	.40	.30
169A	A35	2fr lt ultra ('43)	.20	.20
169B	A34	2fr green ('46)	.35	.25
170	A33	2.50fr red	27.50	17.50
171	A33	2.50fr dp blue ('40)	1.75	1.75
172	A35	3fr brown red	.45	.35
172A	A31	3fr black ('43)	.20	.20
172B	A30	4fr rose lilac ('46)	1.25	.55
172C	A34	4.50fr brt violet ('43)	.20	.20
173	A30	5fr Prus blue	5.25	4.00
173A	A32	5fr deep green ('43)	.20	.20
173B	A34	6fr lt violet ('46)	.70	.55
174	A33	10fr green	1.40	*1.60*
174A	A30	10fr deep blue ('43)	.20	*.25*
174B	A35	15fr rose pink ('43)	.40	*.25*
175	A32	20fr brt ultra	1.60	1.25
175A	A33	20fr sepia ('43)	.40	.25
175B	A35	25fr blue green ('46)	1.40	1.25
		Nos. 160-175B (35)	50.75	36.60
		Set, never hinged	100.00	

See Nos. 214-221, 228-232, 274-275, 319-320, 407-408, 423, 426, 428-429, B36-B50.

Louis II Stadium A36

1939, Apr. 23 **Engr.**

No.	Type	Description	Unused	Used
176	A36	10fr dark green	100.00	*110.00*
		Never hinged	175.00	

Inauguration of Louis II Stadium.

Louis II Stadium A37

1939, Aug. 15

No.	Type	Description	Unused	Used
177	A37	40c dull green	1.25	1.25
178	A37	70c brown black	1.60	1.60
179	A37	90c dark violet	2.25	2.25
180	A37	1.25fr copper red	3.00	3.00
181	A37	2.25fr dark blue	4.25	4.25
		Nos. 177-181 (5)	12.35	12.35
		Set, never hinged	22.50	

8th International University Games.

Imperforates

Many Monaco stamps from 1940 to 1999 exist imperforate. Officially 20 sheets, ranging from 25 to 100 subjects, were left imperforate.

Catalogue values for unused stamps in this section, from this point to the end of the section, are for Never Hinged items.

Prince Louis II — A38

1941-46 ***Perf. 14x13***

No.	Type	Description	Unused	Used
182	A38	40c brown carmine	.65	.50
183	A38	80c deep green	.65	.50
184	A38	1fr rose violet	.25	.20
185	A38	1.20fr green ('42)	.25	.20
186	A38	1.50fr rose	.25	.20
187	A38	1.50fr violet ('42)	.25	.20
187A	A38	2fr lt green ('46)	.65	.35
188	A38	2.40fr red ('42)	.25	.20
189	A38	2.50fr deep ultra	1.10	*1.25*
190	A38	4fr blue ('42)	.20	.20
		Nos. 182-190 (10)	4.50	3.80

Prince Louis II — A39

1943 ***Perf. 13***

No.	Type	Description	Unused	Used
191	A39	50fr purple	2.00	1.10

A40

Prince Louis II — A41

1946 **Unwmk.** **Engr.** ***Perf. 14x13***

No.	Type	Description	Unused	Used
192	A40	2.50fr dk blue green	.70	.25
193	A40	3fr brt red violet	.70	.25
194	A40	6fr brt red	.70	.35
195	A40	10fr brt ultra	.70	.35
		Perf. 13		
196	A41	50fr dp Prus green	4.00	2.10
197	A41	100fr red	5.25	2.75
		Nos. 192-197 (6)	12.05	6.05

Nos. 196-197 exist imperforate.

See Nos. 222-227, 233-236. For overprints see Nos. C8-C9.

Franklin D. Roosevelt — A42

Harbor of Monte Carlo A43

Palace of Monaco A44

Map of Monaco — A45

Prince Louis II — A46

1946, Dec. 13 Unwmk. *Perf. 13*

198	A42	10c red violet	.50	.45
199	A43	30c deep blue	.50	.45
200	A44	60c blue black	.50	.45
201	A45	1fr sepia	1.50	1.25
202	A45	3fr lt violet	2.25	1.75
		Nos. 198-202,B93,C14-C15,CB6 (9)	10.35	8.65

Issued in tribute to the memory of Franklin D. Roosevelt.

1947, May 15

203	A46	10fr dark blue green	4.50	4.50

25th anniv. of the reign of Prince Louis II.
See Nos. B94, C20a.

Hurdler A47

Runner — A48

Designs: 2fr, Discus thrower. 2.50fr, Basketball. 4fr, Swimmer.

1948, July 1 *Perf. 13*

204	A47	50c blue green	.25	.25
205	A48	1fr rose brown	.25	.25
206	A48	2fr grnsh blue	1.25	.85
207	A48	2.50fr vermilion	3.50	2.50
208	A48	4fr slate gray	4.00	3.25
		Nos. 204-208,CB7-CB10 (9)	91.25	89.10

Issued to publicize Monaco's participation in the 1948 Olympic Games held at Wembley, England, during July and August.

Nymph Salmacis A49

Hercules — A50

Aristaeus — A51

Hyacinthus A52

François J. Bosio and Louis XIV Statue — A53

1948, July 12

209	A49	50c dark green	.55	.35
210	A50	1fr red	.55	.35
211	A51	2fr deep ultra	1.90	.75
212	A52	2.50fr deep violet	4.75	2.25
213	A53	4fr purple	4.75	2.50
		Nos. 209-213,CB11-CB14 (9)	94.50	88.20

Issued to honor François J. Bosio (1768-1845), sculptor. No. 213 inscribed "J F Bosio."

Scenic Types of 1939

1948 Engr.

214	A30	50c sepia	.35	.25
215	A31	60c rose pink	.35	.25
216	A32	3fr violet rose	1.10	.35
217	A31	4fr emerald	1.10	.35
218	A34	8fr red brown	4.25	2.00
219	A34	10fr brown red	6.00	2.00
220	A33	20fr carmine rose	1.50	.65
221	A35	25fr gray black	35.00	17.50
		Nos. 214-221 (8)	49.65	23.35

Louis II Type of 1946

1948, July *Perf. 14x13*

222	A40	30c black	.30	.20
223	A40	5fr orange brown	.45	.30
224	A40	6fr purple	5.00	1.75
225	A40	10fr orange	.45	.30
226	A40	12fr deep carmine	6.00	2.50
227	A40	18fr dark blue	9.50	6.00
		Nos. 222-227 (6)	21.70	11.05

Scenic Types of 1939

1949 *Perf. 13*

228	A33	5fr blue green	.85	.35
229	A35	10fr orange	1.75	.65
230	A32	25fr blue	52.50	16.00
231	A30	40fr brown red	9.25	4.75
232	A30	50fr purple	5.75	1.00
		Nos. 228-232 (5)	70.10	22.75

Louis II Type of 1946

1949, Mar. 10 *Perf. 14x13*

233	A40	50c olive	.35	.20
234	A40	1fr dk violet bl	.25	.25
235	A40	12fr dk slate grn	10.00	7.00
236	A40	15fr brown carmine	10.00	3.75
		Nos. 233-236 (4)	20.60	11.20

Hirondelle I A54

Cactus Plants — A55

Designs: 4fr, Oceanographic Museum. 5fr, Princess Alice II at Spitzbergen. 6fr, Albert I Monument. 10fr, Hirondelle II. 12fr, Albert I whaling. 18fr, Bison.

1949, Mar. 5 *Perf. 13*

237	A54	2fr brt blue	.25	.25
238	A55	3fr dark green	.25	.25
239	A54	4fr blk brn & bl	.25	.25
240	A54	5fr crimson	1.10	1.10
241	A55	6fr dark violet	1.00	1.00
242	A54	10fr black brown	1.25	1.25
243	A54	12fr brt red violet	2.75	2.75
244	A54	18fr dk brn & org brn	4.00	4.00
		Nos. 237-244 (8)	10.85	10.85

See Nos. C21-C26.

Palace, Globe and Pigeon A56

1949-50 Engr. Unwmk.

245	A56	5fr blue green	.60	.60
245A	A56	10fr orange	7.00	7.00
246	A56	15fr carmine	.60	.60
		Nos. 245-246,C30-C33 (7)	21.35	21.35

75th anniversary of the UPU.
Nos. 245, 245A and 246 exist imperf.
Issued: 5fr, 15fr, 12/27; 10fr, 9/12/50.

Prince Rainier III
A57 A58

1950, Apr. 11

247	A57	10c red & blk brn	.20	.20
248	A57	50c dp yel & dk brn	.20	.20
249	A57	1fr purple	.45	.35
250	A57	5fr dark green	3.50	1.90
251	A57	15fr carmine	5.25	5.25
252	A57	25fr ultra, ol grn & ind	5.25	5.25
		Nos. 247-252,C34-C35 (8)	33.60	30.15

Enthronement of Prince Rainier III.

1950, Apr. Engr. *Perf. 14x13*

253	A58	50c purple	.35	.20
254	A58	1fr orange brown	.35	.30
255	A58	8fr blue green	9.00	2.40
256	A58	12fr blue	2.25	.50
257	A58	15fr crimson	4.25	.70
		Nos. 253-257 (5)	16.20	4.10

1951, Apr. 31 Typo.

258	A58	5fr emerald	12.00	4.75
259	A58	10fr orange	20.00	7.75

See Nos. 276-279.

Statue of Prince Albert I — A59

1951, Apr. 11 Engr. *Perf. 13*

260	A59	15fr deep blue	11.00	6.50

Edmond and Jules de Goncourt A60

1951, Apr. 11

261	A60	15fr violet brown	11.00	6.50

50th anniversary of the foundation of Goncourt Academy.

St. Vincent de Paul — A61

Judgment of St. Dévote — A62

Symbolizing Monaco's Adoption of Catholicism — A63

Mosaic of the Immaculate Conception A64

Blessed Rainier of Westphalia A65

Holy Year, 1951: 50c, Pope Pius XII. 12fr, Prince Rainier III at Prayer. 15fr, St. Nicholas de Patare. 20fr, St. Roman. 25fr, St. Charles Borromée. 40fr, Cross, arms and Roman Coliseum. 50fr, Chapel of St. Dévote.

Inscribed: "Anno Santo"

1951, June 4 **Unwmk.** ***Perf. 13***
262 A61 10c ultra & red .25 .25
263 A61 50c dk rose lake & pur .25 .25
264 A62 1fr brown & dk grn .30 .30
265 A63 2fr vio brn & ver .35 .35
266 A64 5fr blue green .45 .45
267 A63 12fr rose violet .70 .70
268 A63 15fr vermilion 4.50 4.50
269 A63 20fr red brown 6.50 6.50
270 A63 25fr ultra 9.00 9.00
271 A63 40fr dk car rose & pur 10.50 10.50
272 A63 50fr ol grn & dk vio brn 14.00 14.00
273 A65 100fr dk violet brn 27.50 27.50
Nos. 262-273 (12) 74.30 74.30

Scenic Types of 1939-46

1951, Dec. 22 ***Perf. 13***
274 A31 3fr deep turq green 2.75 .90
275 A32 30fr slate black 8.50 3.50

Rainier Type of 1950

1951, Dec. 22 ***Perf. 14x13***
276 A58 6fr blue green 1.75 .75
277 A58 8fr orange 1.75 .75
278 A58 15fr indigo 2.50 .45
279 A58 18fr crimson 6.25 1.50
Nos. 276-279 (4) 12.25 3.45

Radio Monte Carlo — A66

Knight in Armor — A67

1951, Dec. 22 ***Perf. 13***
280 A66 1fr blue, car & org 1.10 .35
281 A66 15fr pur, car & rose vio 4.25 1.25
282 A66 30fr indigo & red brn 21.00 6.50
Nos. 280-282 (3) 26.35 8.10

1951, Dec. 22
283 A67 1fr purple 1.25 .55
284 A67 5fr gray black 3.75 2.25
285 A67 8fr deep carmine 7.75 3.75
286 A67 15fr emerald 12.50 7.50
287 A67 30fr slate black 21.00 15.00
Nos. 283-287 (5) 46.25 29.05

See Nos. 328-332, 2025-2026.

Nos. B96-B99a Surcharged with New Values and Bars in Black

1951, Dec. ***Perf. 13½x13, Imperf.***
288 SP51 1fr on 10fr + 5fr 12.50 12.50
289 SP52 3fr on 15fr + 5fr 12.50 12.50
290 SP52 5fr on 25fr + 5fr 13.00 12.50
291 SP51 6fr on 40fr + 5fr 13.00 12.50
b. Block of 4, #288-291 51.00 50.00

Gallery of Hercules, Royal Palace A68

1952, Apr. 26 **Engr.** ***Perf. 13***
292 A68 5fr red brn & brn 2.25 .55
293 A68 15fr purple & lil rose 2.75 .75
294 A68 30fr indigo & ultra 3.25 .90
Nos. 292-294 (3) 8.25 2.20

Opening of a philatelic museum at the royal palace, Apr. 26, 1952.

Basketball — A69

2fr, Soccer. 3fr, Sailing. 5fr, Cyclist. 8fr, Gymnastics. 15fr, Louis II Stadium.

1953, Feb. 23 **Unwmk.** ***Perf. 11***
295 A69 1fr dk purple & mag .25 .25
296 A69 2fr dk grn & sl bl .25 .25
297 A69 3fr blue & lt blue .25 .25
298 A69 5fr dk brn & grnsh blk .90 .45
299 A69 8fr brown lake & red 2.25 1.00
300 A69 15fr bl, brn blk & dk grn 1.25 .90
Nos. 295-300,C36-C39 (10) 78.15 53.10

Issued to publicize Monaco's participation in the Helsinki Olympic Games.

Books, Pens and Proof Pages A70

1953, June 29 ***Perf. 13***
301 A70 5fr dark green .55 .45
302 A70 15fr red brown 3.75 .70

Publication of a first edition of the unexpurgated diary of Edmond and Jules Goncourt.

Physalia and Laboratory Ship Hirondelle II — A71

1953, June 29
303 A71 2fr Prus green, pur & choc .25 .20
304 A71 5fr dp mag, red & Prus grn .90 .40
305 A71 15fr ultra, vio brn & Prus grn 3.25 1.75
Nos. 303-305 (3) 4.40 2.35

50th anniversary of the discovery of anaphylaxis by Charles Richet and Paul Portier.

Frederic Ozanam — A72

Nun — A73

1954, Apr. 12 **Engr.** ***Perf. 13***
306 A72 1fr bright red .25 .25
307 A73 5fr dark blue .50 .50
308 A72 15fr black 2.10 1.90
Nos. 306-308 (3) 2.85 2.65

Centenary of the death of Frederic Ozanam, founder of the Society of Saint Vincent de Paul.

Jean Baptiste de la Salle
A74 A75

1954, Apr. 12
309 A74 1fr dark carmine .25 .25
310 A75 5fr black brown .50 .50
311 A74 15fr bright ultra 2.10 1.90
Nos. 309-311 (3) 2.85 2.65

Jean Baptiste de la Salle, founder of the Christian Brothers Institute and saint.

A76

A77

Grimaldi Arms — A78

Knight in Armor — A79

Perf. 13½x14, 14x13½

1954, Apr. 12 **Typo.**

Various Forms of Grimaldi Arms in Black and Red or Black, Red and Deep Plum (5fr)

312 A76 50c black & mag .20 .20
313 A77 70c black & aqua .20 .20
314 A76 80c black, red & dk grn .20 .20
315 A77 1fr violet blue .20 .20
316 A77 2fr black & dp org .25 .25
317 A77 3fr black & green .25 .25
318 A78 5fr black & lt grn .25 .25
Nos. 312-318 (7) 1.55 1.55

Scenic Types of 1939-46

1954, Apr. 12 **Engr.** ***Perf. 13***
319 A34 25fr bright red 3.75 .75
320 A31 75fr dark green 25.00 8.50

1954, Apr. 12 **Unwmk.** ***Perf. 13***
321 A79 4fr dark red 1.50 .40
322 A79 8fr dark green 1.50 .80
323 A79 12fr dark purple 6.00 1.75
324 A79 24fr dark maroon 11.00 4.75
Nos. 321-324 (4) 20.00 7.70

Nos. 321-324 were issued precanceled only. Values for precanceled stamps in first column are for those which have not been through the post and have original gum. Values in the second column are for postally used, gumless stamps.

See Nos. 400-404, 430-433, 466-469.

Lambarene Landing, Gabon — A80

Dr. Albert Schweitzer — A81

Design: 15fr, Lambarene hospital.

1955, Jan. 14 ***Perf. 11x11½***
325 A80 2fr ol grn, bl grn & ind .30 .25
326 A81 5fr dk grnsh bl & grn 1.40 1.40
327 A81 15fr dk bl grn, dp cl & brn blk 3.75 3.00
Nos. 325-327 (3) 5.45 4.65

Issued to honor Dr. Albert Schweitzer, medical missionary. See No. C40.

Knight Type of 1951

1955, Jan. 14 ***Perf. 13***
328 A67 5fr purple 3.50 1.10
329 A67 6fr red 6.25 2.25
330 A67 8fr red brown 6.25 3.25
331 A67 15fr ultra 15.00 5.00
332 A67 30fr dark green 25.00 15.00
Nos. 328-332 (5) 56.00 26.60

Automobile and Representation of Eight European Cities — A82

Prince Rainier III — A83

1955, Jan. 14 **Unwmk.**

333	A82	100fr dk brown & red	90.00	65.00

25th Monte Carlo Automobile Rally.

1955, June 7 **Engr.** ***Perf. 13***

334	A83	6fr green & vio brn	.70	.40
335	A83	8fr red & violet	.70	.40
336	A83	12fr carmine & green	.70	.40
337	A83	15fr purple & blue	1.40	.40
338	A83	18fr orange & blue	4.50	.40
339	A83	30fr ultra & gray	14.00	7.75
		Nos. 334-339 (6)	22.00	9.75

See Nos. 405-406, 424-425, 427, 462-465, 586, 603-604A, 725-728, 730, 789, 791.

"Five Weeks in a Balloon" — A84

"A Floating City" and Jules Verne — A85

"Michael Strogoff" A86

"Around the World in 80 Days" — A87

USS Nautilus and Verne — A88

Designs (Scenes from Jules Verne's Books): 3fr, The House of Vapors. 6fr, The 500 Millions of the Begum. 8fr, The Magnificent Orinoco. 10fr, A Journey to the Center of the Earth. 25fr, Twenty Thousand Leagues under the Sea.

1955, June 7

340	A84	1fr red brn & bl gray	.20	.20
341	A85	2fr blue, ind & brn	.20	.20
342	A85	3fr red brn, gray & sl	.20	.20
343	A86	5fr car & blk brn	.25	.25
344	A84	6fr blk brn & bluish gray	.45	.45
345	A86	8fr ol grn & aqua	.35	.35
346	A85	10fr indigo, turq & brn	1.25	1.00
347	A87	15fr rose brn & ver	1.00	.70
348	A85	25fr bl grn, grn & gray	2.50	1.75
349	A88	30fr violet, turq & blk	6.25	5.25
		Nos. 340-349,C45 (11)	40.15	35.35

50th anniv. of the death of Jules Verne.

Virgin by Francois Brea A89

Blessed Rainier — A90

Marian Year: 10fr, Pieta by Louis Brea.

1955, June 7

350	A89	5fr vio brn, gray & dk grn	.25	.25
351	A89	10fr vio brn, gray & dk grn	.40	.35
352	A90	15fr black brn & org brn	.60	.55
		Nos. 350-352 (3)	1.25	1.15

Rotary Emblem, World Map — A91

1955, June 7

353	A91	30fr blue & orange	1.10	1.10

50th anniv. of the founding of Rotary Intl.

George Washington A92

Franklin D. Roosevelt — A93

Dwight D. Eisenhower — A94

Palace of Monaco, c. 1790 — A95

Palace of Monaco, c. 1750 — A96

Designs: 3fr, Abraham Lincoln. 30fr, Columbus landing in America. 40fr, Prince Rainier III. 100fr, Early Louisiana scene.

1956, Apr. 3 **Engr.** ***Perf. 13***

354	A92	1fr dark purple	.20	.20
355	A93	2fr claret & dk pur	.30	.30
356	A93	3fr vio & dp ultra	.30	.30
357	A94	5fr brown lake	.40	.40
358	A95	15fr brn blk & vio brn	1.00	1.00
359	A95	30fr ind, blk & ultra	3.75	2.00
360	A94	40fr dk brn & vio brn	6.00	2.50
361	A96	50fr vermilion	6.00	2.50
362	A96	100fr Prus green	6.00	3.50
a.		Strip of 3, #360-362	19.00	19.00
		Nos. 354-362 (9)	23.95	12.70

5th Intl. Phil. Exhib. (FIPEX), NYC, Apr. 28-May 6, 1956.

Ski Jump, Cortina d'Ampezzo — A97

Design: 30fr, Olympic Scenes.

1956, Apr. 3

363	A97	15fr brn vio, brn & dk grn	1.10	.55
364	A97	30fr red orange	2.25	1.60

Issued to publicize Monaco's participation in the 1956 Olympic Games.

"Glasgow to Monte Carlo" A98

1956, Apr. 3 **Unwmk.**

365	A98	100fr red brn & red	25.00	25.00

The 26th Monte Carlo Automobile Rally.

See Nos. 411, 437, 460, 483, 500, 539, 549, 600, 629.

Princess Grace and Prince Rainier III — A99

1956, Apr. 19 **Engr.** ***Perf. 13***

Portraits in Black

366	A99	1fr dark green	.20	.20
367	A99	2fr dark carmine	.35	.25
368	A99	3fr ultra	.45	.35
369	A99	5fr brt yellow grn	1.00	.55
370	A99	15fr redsh brown	1.40	.65
		Nos. 366-370,C46-C48 (8)	10.00	8.60

Wedding of Prince Rainier III to Grace Kelly, Apr. 19, 1956.

Nos. J41-J47, J50-J56 Overprinted with Bars and Surcharged in Indigo, Red or Black

Unwmk.

1956, Apr. 3 **Engr.** ***Perf. 11***

Designs: Early Transportation.

371	D6	2fr on 4fr (I)	.50	.45
a.		Pair, #371, 381	1.00	1.00
372	D6	3fr (R)	.50	.45
a.		Pair, #372, 382	1.00	1.00
373	D6	5fr on 4fr	.70	.70
a.		Pair, #373, 383	1.40	1.40
374	D6	10fr on 4fr (R)	1.40	1.10
a.		Pair, #374, 384	2.75	2.75
375	D6	15fr on 5fr (I)	1.75	1.75
a.		Pair, #375, 385	3.50	3.50
376	D6	20fr (R)	2.75	2.75
a.		Pair, #376, 386	5.50	5.50
377	D6	25fr on 20fr	5.00	5.00
a.		Pair, #377, 387	10.00	10.00
378	D6	30fr on 10fr (I)	9.50	9.50
a.		Pair, #378, 388	19.00	19.00
379	D6	40fr on 50fr (R)	13.50	13.50
a.		Pair, #379, 389	27.00	27.00
380	D6	50fr on 100fr	16.00	16.00
a.		Pair, #380, 390	32.00	32.00

Designs: Modern Transportation.

381	D7	2fr on 4fr (I)	.50	.50
382	D7	3fr (R)	.50	.45
383	D7	5fr on 4fr	.70	.70
384	D7	10fr on 4fr (R)	1.40	1.10
385	D7	15fr on 5fr (I)	1.75	1.75
386	D7	20fr (R)	2.75	2.75
387	D7	25fr on 20fr	5.00	5.00
388	D7	30fr on 10fr (I)	9.50	9.50
389	D7	40fr on 50fr (R)	13.50	13.50
390	D7	50fr on 100fr	16.00	16.00
		Nos. 371-390,C49-C50 (22)	124.20	123.45

Pairs se-tenant at the base.

Princess Grace — A100

1957, May 11 **Engr.** ***Perf. 13***

391	A100	1fr blue violet	.20	.20
392	A100	2fr lt olive grn	.20	.20
393	A100	3fr yellow brown	.25	.20
394	A100	5fr magenta	.35	.25
395	A100	15fr pink	.35	.25
396	A100	25fr Prus blue	1.10	.65
397	A100	30fr purple	1.10	.90
398	A100	50fr scarlet	1.75	.90
399	A100	75fr orange	3.00	2.50
		Nos. 391-399 (9)	8.30	6.05

Birth of Princess Caroline of Monaco.

Knight Type of 1954

1957 **Unwmk.** ***Perf. 13***

400 A79 5fr dark blue .40 .25
401 A79 10fr yellow green .30 .20
402 A79 15fr brt orange 1.40 .90
403 A79 30fr brt blue 2.00 .90
404 A79 45fr crimson 3.25 1.75
Nos. 400-404 (5) 7.35 4.00

Nos. 400-404 were issued precanceled only. See note after No. 324.

Types of 1955 and 1939-46

1957

405 A83 20fr greenish blue 2.00 .50
406 A83 35fr red brown 4.00 1.60
407 A33 65fr brt violet 10.00 6.50
408 A30 70fr orange yellow 9.50 6.00
Nos. 405-408 (4) 25.50 14.60

Princesses Grace and Caroline A101

1958, May 15 **Engr.** ***Perf. 13***

409 A101 100fr bluish black 8.50 6.00

Birth of Prince Albert Alexander Louis, Mar. 14.

Order of St. Charles — A102

1958, May 15

410 A102 100fr carmine, grn & bis 2.25 2.00

Cent. of the Natl. Order of St. Charles.

Rally Type of 1956

Design: 100fr, "Munich to Monte Carlo."

1958, May 15

411 A98 100fr red, grn & sepia 8.00 7.00

27th Monte Carlo Automobile Rally.

Virgin Mary, Popes Pius IX and XII — A103

Bernadette Soubirous A104

Tomb of Bernadette, Nevers A105

Designs: 3fr, Shepherdess Bernadette at Bartres. 5fr, Bouriette kneeling (first miracle). 8fr, Stained glass window showing apparition. 10fr, Empty grotto at Lourdes. 12fr, Grotto with statue and altar. 20fr, Bernadette praying. 35fr, High Altar at St. Peter's during canonization of Bernadette. 50fr, Bernadette, Pope Pius XI, Mgr. Laurence and Abbe Peyramale.

1958, May 15 **Unwmk.**

412 A103 1fr lilac gray & vio brn .20 .20
413 A104 2fr blue & violet .20 .20
414 A104 3fr green & sepia .20 .20
415 A104 5fr gray brn & vio bl .20 .20
416 A104 8fr blk, ol bis & ind .35 .25
417 A105 10fr multicolored .35 .35
418 A105 12fr ind, ol bis & ol grn .45 .25
a. Strip of 3, #416-418 3.50 3.50
419 A104 20fr dk sl grn & rose .45 .35
420 A104 35fr ol, gray ol & dk sl grn .55 .45
421 A103 50fr lake, ol grn & ind .90 .55
422 A105 65fr indigo & grnsh bl 1.25 .85
Nos. 412-422,C51-C52 (13) 9.35 7.75

Centenary of the apparition of the Virgin Mary at Lourdes.

Sizes: Nos. 413-415, 419-420 26x36mm. No. 416 22x36mm. Nos. 417-418 48x36mm. No. 422 36x26mm.

Types of 1939-46 and 1955

1959 **Engr.** ***Perf. 13***

423 A32 5fr copper red 1.10 .55
424 A83 25fr orange & blk 1.10 .55
425 A83 30fr dark violet 4.25 2.10
426 A34 35fr dark blue 8.50 3.25
427 A83 50fr bl grn & rose cl 5.50 2.10
428 A31 85fr dk carmine rose 12.50 6.50
429 A33 100fr brt grnsh blue 12.50 6.50
Nos. 423-429 (7) 45.45 21.55

Knight Type of 1954

1959

430 A79 8fr deep magenta .75 .35
431 A79 20fr bright green 1.40 1.25
432 A79 40fr chocolate 2.75 1.10
433 A79 55fr ultra 4.50 2.75
Nos. 430-433 (4) 9.40 5.45

Nos. 430-433 were issued precanceled only. See note after No. 324.

Princess Grace Polyclinic — A106

1959, May 16

434 A106 100fr gray, brn & grn 3.75 2.25

Opening of Princess Grace Hospital.

UNESCO Building, Paris, and Cultural Emblems — A107

50fr, UNESCO Building, children of various races.

1959, May 16

435 A107 25fr multicolored .30 .30
436 A107 50fr ol, bl grn & blk brn .40 .40

Opening of UNESCO Headquarters in Paris, Nov. 3, 1958.

Rally Type of 1956

Design: 100fr, "Athens to Monaco."

1959, May 16

437 A98 100fr vio bl, red & sl grn, *bl* 6.50 5.50

28th Monte Carlo Automobile Rally.

Carnations — A108

Bougainvillea — A109

Flowers: 10fr on 3fr, Princess Grace Carnations. 15fr on 1fr, Mimosa, vert. 25fr on 6fr, Geranium, vert. 35fr, Oleander. 50fr, Jasmine. 85fr on 65fr, Lavender. 100fr, Grace de Monaco Rose.

1959, May 16

438 A108 5fr brn, Prus grn & rose car .25 .20
439 A108 10fr on 3fr brn, grn & rose .35 .25
440 A109 15fr on 1fr dk grn & cit .35 .25
441 A109 20fr ol grn & mag .90 .55
442 A109 25fr on 6fr yel grn & red 1.25 .75
443 A109 35fr dk grn & pink 2.50 1.75
444 A109 50fr dk brn & dk grn 3.00 2.10
445 A109 85fr on 65fr ol grn & gray vio 3.50 3.00
446 A108 100fr green & pink 4.75 4.25
Nos. 438-446 (9) 16.85 13.10

Nos. 439-440, 442 and 445 were not issued without surcharge.

View of Monaco and Uprooted Oak Emblem — A110

1960, June 1 **Unwmk.** ***Perf. 13***

447 A110 25c bl, olive grn & sepia .35 .25

World Refugee Year, 7/1/59-6/30/60.

Entrance to Oceanographic Museum — A111

Museum and Aquarium — A112

Designs: 15c, Museum conference room. 20c, Arrival of equipment, designed by Prince Albert I. 25c, Research on electrical qualities of cephalopodes. 50c, Albert I and vessels Hirondelle I and Princesse Alice.

1960, June 1 **Engr.** ***Perf. 13***

448 A111 5c blue, sepia & cl .55 .25
449 A112 10c multicolored .70 .35
450 A112 15c sep, ultra & bis .70 .35
451 A112 20c rose lil, blk & bl 1.10 .55
452 A112 25c grnsh blue 2.25 1.60
453 A112 50c lt ultra & brown 2.50 1.75
Nos. 448-453 (6) 7.80 4.85

Inauguration of the Oceanographic Museum of Monaco, 50th anniv. See #475.

Horse Jumping — A113

Sports: 10c, Women swimmers. 15c, Broad jumper. 20c, Javelin thrower. 25c, Girl figure skater. 50c, Skier.

1960, June 1

454 A113 5c dk brn, car & emer .25 .25
455 A113 10c red brn, bl & grn .25 .25
456 A113 15c dl red brn, ol & mag .35 .35
457 A113 20c black, bl & grn 2.75 2.75
458 A113 25c dk grn & dull pur .90 .90
459 A113 50c dk bl, grnsh bl & dl pur 1.10 1.10
Nos. 454-459 (6) 5.60 5.60

Nos. 454-457 for the 17th Olympic Games, Rome, Aug. 25-Sept. 11; Nos. 458-459 for the 8th Winter Olympic Games, Squaw Valley, Feb. 18-29.

Rally Type of 1956

Design: 25c, "Lisbon to Monte Carlo."

1960, June 1

460 A98 25c bl, brn & car, *bluish* 2.25 2.00

29th Monte Carlo Automobile Rally.

Stamps of Sardinia and France, 1860, and Stamp of Monaco, 1885 A114

1960, June 1 **Engr. & Embossed**

461 A114 25c violet, blue & ol .80 .70

75th anniv. of postage stamps of Monaco.

Prince Rainier Type of 1955

1960 **Engr.** ***Perf. 13***

462 A83 25c orange & blk .55 .20
463 A83 30c dark violet .55 .20
464 A83 50c bl grn & rose lil 2.25 .35
465 A83 65c yel brn & slate 14.00 4.25
Nos. 462-465 (4) 17.35 5.00

Knight Type of 1954

1960

466 A79 8c deep magenta 1.60 .55
467 A79 20c brt green 2.75 .55
468 A79 40c chocolate 4.50 1.10
469 A79 55c ultra 6.75 1.60
Nos. 466-469 (4) 15.60 3.80

Nos. 466-469 were issued precanceled only. See note after No. 324.

Sea Horse — A115

#471 Cactus (Cereanee). #472, Cactus (Nopalea dejecta). #473, Scorpion fish, horiz.

1960, June 1

470 A115 15c org brn & sl grn .80 .25
471 A115 15c ol grn, yel & brn .95 .20
472 A115 20c maroon & ol grn .95 .25
473 A115 20c brn, red brn, red & ol .80 .35
Nos. 470-473 (4) 3.50 1.05

See Nos. 581-584.

Type of 1960 and

Palace of Monaco A116

Designs: 10c, Type A111 without inscription. 45c, Aerial view of Palace. 85c, Honor court. 1fr, Palace at night.

1960, June 1 **Engr.**

474 A116 5c green & sepia .20 .20
475 A111 10c dk bl & vio brn .55 .35
476 A116 45c dk bl, sep & grn 6.75 .70
477 A116 85c slate, gray & bis 8.75 2.10
478 A116 1fr dk bl, red brn & sl grn 1.10 .40
Nos. 474-478 (5) 17.35 3.75

See #585, 602, 729, 731, 731A, 790, 792.

Sphinx of Wadi-es-Sebua — A117

1961, June 3 **Unwmk.** ***Perf. 13***

479 A117 50c choc, dk bl & ocher 1.25 .80

Issued as publicity to save historic monuments in Nubia.

Murena, Starfish, Sea Urchin, Sea Cucumber and Coral — A118

1961, June 3

480 A118 25c vio buff & dk red .25 .25

Issued to commemorate the World Congress of Aquariology, Monaco, Nov. 1960.

Medieval Town and Leper — A119

1961, June 3

481 A119 25c ol gray, ocher & car .25 .25

Issued to honor the Sovereign Order of the Knights of Malta.

Hand and Ant A120

1961, June 3

482 A120 25c magenta & dp car .40 .40

Issued to publicize "Respect for Life."

Rally Type of 1956

Design: 1fr, "Stockholm to Monte Carlo."

1961, June 3

483 A98 1fr multicolored 1.50 1.50

30th Monte Carlo Automobile Rally.

Turcat-Mery, 1911 Winner, and 1961 Car — A121

1961, June 3

484 A121 1fr org brn, vio & rose red 1.60 1.60

50th anniv. of the founding of the Monte Carlo Automobile Rally.

Chevrolet, 1912 A122

Automobiles (pre-1912): 2c, Peugeot. 3c, Fiat. 4c, Mercedes. 5c, Rolls Royce. 10c, Panhard-Levassor. 15c, Renault. 20c, Ford. 25c, Rochet-Schneider. 30c, FN-Herstal. 45c, De Dion Bouton. 50c, Buick. 65c, Delahaye. 1fr, Cadillac.

1961, June 13 **Engr.**

485 A122 1c org brn, dk brn & grn .20 .20
486 A122 2c org red, dk bl & brn .20 .20
487 A122 3c multicolored .20 .20
488 A122 4c multicolored .20 .20
489 A122 5c ol bis, sl grn & car .20 .20
490 A122 10c brn, sl & red .25 .25
491 A122 15c grnsh bl & dk sl grn .25 .25
492 A122 20c pur, blk & red .25 .25
493 A122 25c dk brn lil & red .45 .45
494 A122 30c ol grn & dl pur 1.10 1.10
495 A122 45c multicolored 2.10 2.10
496 A122 50c brn blk, red & ultra 2.10 2.10
497 A122 65c multicolored 3.25 3.25
498 A122 1fr brt pur, ind & red 3.75 3.75
Nos. 485-498 (14) 14.50 14.50

See Nos. 648-661.

Bugatti, First Winner, and Course — A123

1962, June 6 **Unwmk.** ***Perf. 13***

499 A123 1fr lilac rose 1.50 1.50

20th Automobile Grand Prix of Monaco.

Rally Type of 1956

Design: 1fr, "Oslo to Monte Carlo."

1962, June 6

500 A98 1fr multicolored 1.50 1.50

31st Monte Carlo Automobile Rally.

Louis XII and Lucien Grimaldi A124

50c, Document granting sovereignty. 1fr, Seals of Louis XII & Lucien Grimaldi.

1962, June 6 **Engr.**

501 A124 25c ver, blk & vio bl .30 .30
502 A124 50c dk bl, brn & mag .45 .45
503 A124 1fr dk brn, grn & car .70 .70
Nos. 501-503 (3) 1.45 1.45

450th anniversary of Monaco's reception of sovereignty from Louis XII.

Mosquito and Swamp A125

1962, June 6

504 A125 1fr brn ol & lt grn .60 .60

WHO drive to eradicate malaria.

Aquatic Stadium at Night A126

1962, June 6

505 A126 10c dk bl, ind & grn .25 .20

Sun, Flowers and Hope Chest A127

1962, June 6

506 A127 20c multicolored .25 .25

Issued to publicize the National Multiple Sclerosis Society of New York.

Wheat Harvest A128

1962, June 6

507 A128 25c dk bl, red brn & brn *.50 .30*
508 A128 50c ind, ol bis & dk bl grn *.50 .35*
509 A128 1fr red lil & olive bister *1.00 .65*
Nos. 507-509,C61 (4) 4.00 2.30

Europa. See No. C61.

Blood Donor's Arm and Globe A129

1962, Nov. 15 **Engr.** ***Perf. 13***

510 A129 1fr dk red, blk & orange .90 .90

3rd International Blood Donors' Congress, Nov. 15-18 at Monaco.

Yellow Wagtails — A130

Birds: 10c, European robins. 15c, European goldfinches. 20c, Blackcaps. 25c, Great spotted woodpeckers. 30c, Nightingale. 45c, Barn owls. 50c, Common starlings. 85c, Red crossbills. 1fr, White storks.

1962, Dec. 12 **Unwmk.**

511 A130 5c green, sep & yel .25 .25
512 A130 10c bis, dk pur & red .25 .25
513 A130 15c multicolored .35 .35
514 A130 20c mag, grn & blk .45 .35
515 A130 25c multicolored .55 .45
516 A130 30c brn, sl grn & bl .85 .65
517 A130 45c vio & gldn brn 1.40 1.25
518 A130 50c bl grn, blk & yel 2.25 1.40
519 A130 85c multicolored 2.75 2.00
520 A130 1fr blk, grn & red 3.25 2.25
Nos. 511-520 (10) 12.35 9.20

Protection of useful birds.

Divers A131

10c, Galeazzi's turret, vert. 25c, Williamson's photosphere, 1914 & bathyscape "Trieste," 1962. 45c, Diving suits. 50c, Diving chamber. 85c, Fulton's "Nautilus," 1800 and modern submarine. 1fr, Alexander the Great's underwater chamber and bathysphere of the N. Y. Zoological Society.

1962, Dec. 12

521 A131 5c bluish grn, vio & blk .20 .20
522 A131 10c multicolored .25 .25
523 A131 25c bis, bluish grn & sl grn .25 .25
524 A131 45c green, ind & blk .45 .45
525 A131 50c cit & dk bl .70 .70
526 A131 85c Prus grn & dk vio bl 1.25 1.25
527 A131 1fr dk bl, dk brn & dk grn 2.00 2.00
Nos. 521-527 (7) 5.10 5.10

Issued in connection with an exhibition at the Oceanographic Museum "Man Under Water," showing ancient and modern methods of under-water exploration.

Dancing Children and UN Emblem — A132

Children on Scales A133

Designs: 10c, Bird feeding nestlings, vert. 20c, Sun shining on children of different races, vert. 25c, Mother and child, vert. 50c, House and child. 95c, African mother and child, vert. 1fr, Prince Albert and Princess Caroline.

1963, May 3 **Unwmk.** ***Perf. 13***

528 A132 5c ocher, dk red & ultra .20 .20
529 A133 10c vio bl, emer & ol gray .25 .20
530 A133 15c ultra, red & grn .25 .25
531 A133 20c multicolored .25 .25
532 A133 25c blue, brn & pink .25 .25
533 A133 50c multicolored .70 .45
534 A133 95c multicolored 1.25 .70
535 A132 1fr multicolored 2.00 1.25
Nos. 528-535 (8) 5.15 3.55

Publicizing the UN Children's Charter.

Figurehead with Red Cross, Red Crescent and Red Lion and Sun — A134

1fr, Centenary emblem, Gustave Moynier, Henri Dunant and Gen. Henri Dufour, horiz.

1963, May 3 **Engr.**

536 A134 50c bluish grn, red & red brn .50 .50
537 A134 1fr blue, sl grn & red .75 .75

Centenary of International Red Cross.

Racing Cars on Monte Carlo Course and Map of Europe A135

1963, May 3

538 A135 50c multicolored .70 .45

European Automobile Grand Prix.

Rally Type of 1956

Design: 1fr, "Warsaw to Monte Carlo."

1963, May 3

539 A98 1fr multicolored 1.50 1.50

32nd Monte Carlo Auto Race.

Lions International Emblem — A136

1963, May 3

540 A136 50c bis, lt vio & bl .75 .60

Issued to commemorate the founding of the Lions Club of Monaco, Mar. 24, 1962.

Hôtel des Postes, Paris, and UPU Allegory — A137

1963, May 3

541 A137 50c multicolored .60 .40

1st Intl. Postal Conference, Paris, 1863.

Globe and Telstar A138

1963, May 3

542 A138 50c grn, dk pur & maroon .75 .50

1st television connection of the US and Europe through the Telstar satellite, July 11-12, 1962.

Holy Spirit over St. Peter's and World A139

1963, May 3

543 A139 1fr grn, red brn & bl .75 .60

Vatican II, the 21st Ecumenical Council of the Roman Catholic Church.

Wheat Emblem and Dove Feeding Nestlings A140

1963, May 3 **Engr.**

544 A140 1fr multicolored .80 .80

FAO "Freedom from Hunger" campaign.

Henry Ford and 1903 Model A — A141

1963, Dec. 12 **Unwmk.** ***Perf. 13***

545 A141 20c slate grn & lil rose .75 .50

Centenary of the birth of Henry Ford, American automobile manufacturer.

Bicyle Racer in Town A142

Design: 50c, Bicyclist on country road.

1963, Dec. 12

546 A142 25c bl, sl grn & red brn .50 .50
547 A142 50c bl, gray grn, & blk brn .50 .50

50th anniv. of the Bicycle Tour de France.

Pierre de Coubertin and Myron's Discobolus A143

1963, Dec. 12

548 A143 1fr dp cl, car & ocher .75 .75

Baron Pierre de Coubertin, organizer of the modern Olympic Games, birth cent.

Rally Type of 1956

Design: 1fr, "Paris to Monte Carlo."

1963, Dec. 12

549 A98 1fr multicolored 1.10 1.10

33rd Monte Carlo Automobile Rally.

Children with Stamp Album and UNESCO Emblem A144

1963, Dec. 12

550 A144 50c dp ultra, red & vio .45 .45

International Philatelic and Educational Exposition, Monaco, Nov.-Dec., 1963.

Europa Issue, 1963

Woman, Dove and Lyre — A145

1963, Dec. 12

551 A145 25c brn, grn & car *1.50* .35
552 A145 50c dk brn, bl & car *2.00* *.60*

Wembley Stadium and British Football Association Emblem — A146

Overhead Kick A147

Soccer Game, Florence, 16th Century A148

Tackle A149

Designs: 3c, Goalkeeper. 4c, Louis II Stadium and emblem of Sports Association of Monaco, with black overprint: "Championnat /1962-1963/Coupe de France." 15c, Soule Game, Brittany, 19th century. 20c, Soccer, England, 1827. 25c, Soccer, England, 1890. 50c, Clearing goal area. 95c, Heading the ball. 1fr, Kicking the ball.

1963, Dec. 12

553 A146 1c grn, vio & dk red .20 .20
554 A147 2c black, red & grn .20 .20
555 A147 3c gray ol, org & red .20 .20
556 A146 4c bl, red, grn, pur & blk .20 .20
557 A148 10c dk bl, car & sep .20 .20
558 A148 15c sepia & car .20 .20
559 A148 20c sepia & dk bl .25 .25
560 A148 25c sepia & lilac .25 .25
a. Block of 4 1.00 1.00
561 A149 30c green, sep & red .45 .45
562 A149 50c sepia, grn & red .70 .70
563 A149 95c sepia, grn & red 1.00 1.00
564 A149 1fr sepia, grn & red 1.25 1.25
a. Block of 4 4.00 4.00
Nos. 553-564 (12) 5.10 5.10

Cent. of British Football Assoc. (organized soccer). No. 556 also for the successes of the soccer team of Monaco, 1962-63 (overprint typographed). No. 556 was not regularly issued without overprint. Value $750.

The 4 stamps of No. 560a are connected by an 1863 soccer ball in red brown; the stamps of No. 564a by a modern soccer ball.

Design from 1914 Rally Post Card — A150

Farman Biplane over Monaco — A151

Designs: 3c, Nieuport monoplane. 4c, Breguet biplane. 5c, Morane-Saulnier monoplane. 10c, Albatros biplane. 15c, Deperdussin monoplane. 20c, Vickers-Vimy biplane and map (Ross Smith's flight London-Port Darwin, 1919). 25c, Douglas Liberty biplane (first American around-the-world flight. 4 planes, 1924). 30c, Savoia S-16 hydroplane (De Pinedo's Rome-Australia-Japan-Rome flight, 1925). 45c, Trimotor Fokker F-7 monoplane (first aerial survey of North Pole, Richard E. Byrd and James Gordon Bennett, 1925). 50c, Spirit of St. Louis (first crossing of Atlantic, New York-Paris, Charles Lindbergh, 1927). 65c, Breguet 19 (Paris-New York, Coste and Bellonte, 1930). 95c, Laté 28 hydroplane (first South Atlantic airmail route, Dakar-Natal, 1930). 1fr, Dornier DO-X, (Germany-Rio de Janeiro, 1930).

1964, May 22 Engr. *Perf. 13*

565 A150 1c green, bl & ol .20 .20
566 A151 2c bl, bis & red brn .20 .20
567 A151 3c olive, grn & bl .20 .20
568 A151 4c red brn, bl & Prus grn .20 .20
569 A151 5c gray ol, vio & mag .20 .20
570 A151 10c violet, bl & ol .25 .20
571 A151 15c blue, org & brn .25 .20
572 A151 20c brt grn, blk & bl .35 .25
573 A151 25c red, bl & ol .35 .35
574 A151 30c bl, sl grn & dp cl .45 .45
575 A151 45c red brn, grnsh bl & blk .75 .55
576 A151 50c purple, ol & bis .90 .75
577 A151 65c steel bl, blk & red 1.20 1.00
578 A151 95c ocher, sl grn & red 1.60 1.25
579 A151 1fr sl grn, bl & vio brn 2.25 1.60
Nos. 565-579,C64 (16) 12.10 10.35

50th anniv. of the 1st airplane rally of Monte Carlo. Nos. 565-571 show planes which took part in the 1914 rally, Nos. 572-579 and C64 show important flights from 1919 to 1961.

Ancient Egyptian Message Transmitters and Rocket — A152

1964, May 22 Unwmk.

580 A152 1fr dk bl, indigo & org brn .70 .70

Issued to publicize "PHILATEC", International Philatelic and Postal Techniques Exhibition, Paris, June 5-21, 1964.

Types of 1955-60

1c, Crab (Macrocheira Kampferi), horiz. 2c, Flowering cactus (Selenicereus Gr.). 12c, Shell (Fasciolaria trapezium). 18c, Aloe ciliaris. 70c, Honor court of palace (like #477). 95c, Prince Rainier III.

1964, May 19 *Perf. 13*

581 A115 1c bl grn & dk red .20 .20
582 A115 2c dk grn & multi .20 .20
583 A115 12c vio & brn red .50 .20
584 A115 18c grn, yel & car .55 .20
585 A116 70c lt grn, choc & red org .70 .40
586 A83 95c ultra 1.50 .50
Nos. 581-586 (6) 3.65 1.70

Rainier III Aquatic Stadium A153

1964-67 Engr. *Perf. 13*

587 A153 10c dk car, rose, bl & blk 1.75 .25
587A A153 15c dk car, rose, brt bl & blk ('67) 1.00 .25
588 A153 25c dl grn, dk bl & blk 1.00 .25
589 A153 50c lil, bl grn & blk 1.75 1.00
Nos. 587-589 (4) 5.50 1.75

Nos. 587-589 were issued precanceled only. See note after No. 324. The "1962" date has been obliterated with 2 bars. See Nos. 732-734, 793-796, 976-979.

Common Design Types pictured following the introduction.

Europa Issue, 1964
Common Design Type

1964, Sept. 12
Size: 22x34½mm

590 CD7 25c brt red, brt grn & dk grn *1.00* .20
591 CD7 50c ultra, ol bis & dk red brn *1.50* .45

Weight Lifter — A154

1964, Dec. 3 Unwmk. *Perf. 13*

592 A154 1c shown .20 .20
593 A154 2c Judo .20 .20
594 A154 3c Pole vault .20 .20
595 A154 4c Archery .20 .20
Nos. 592-595 (4) .80 .80

18th Olympic Games, Tokyo, 10/10-25. See #C65.

Pres. John F. Kennedy and Mercury Capsule — A155

1964, Dec. 3

596 A155 50c brt bl & indigo .60 .60

Pres. John F. Kennedy (1917-63).

Television Set and View of Monte Carlo A156

1964, Dec. 3

597 A156 50c dk car rose, dk bl & brn .50 .50

Fifth International Television Festival.

Frédéric Mistral, (1830-1914), Provençal Poet — A157

1964, Dec. 3 Engr.

598 A157 1fr gray olive & brn red .55 .55

Scales of Justice and Code A158

1964, Dec. 3

599 A158 1fr gldn brn & slate grn .60 .60

Universal Declaration of Human Rights.

Rally Type of 1956

Design: 1fr, "Minsk to Monte Carlo."

1964, Dec. 3

600 A98 1fr bl grn, ocher & brn 1.00 1.00

34th Monte Carlo Automobile Rally.

International Football Association Emblem — A159

1964, Dec. 3

601 A159 1fr red, bl & ol bister .85 .85

60th anniv. of FIFA, the Federation Internationale de Football (soccer).

Types of 1955 and 1960

Designs: 40c, Aerial view of palace. 60c, 1.30fr, 2.30fr, Prince Rainier III.

1965-66 Engr. *Perf. 13*

602 A116 40c sl grn, dl cl & brt grn .75 .25
603 A83 60c sl grn & blk 1.10 .35
604 A83 1.30fr dk red & blk 3.25 .75
604A A83 2.30fr org & rose lil ('66) 2.75 .75
Nos. 602-604A (4) 7.85 2.10

Telstar and Pleumeur-Bodou Relay Station — A160

Alexander Graham Bell and Telephone A161

Designs (ITU Emblem and): 5c, Syncom II and Earth. 10c, Echo II and Earth. 12c, Relay satellite and Earth, vert. 18c, Lunik III and Moon. 50c, Samuel Morse and telegraph. 60c, Edouard Belin, belinograph and newspaper. 70c, Roman signal towers and Chappe telegraph. 95c, Cable laying ships; "The Great Eastern" (British, 1858) and "Alsace" (French, modern). 1fr, Edouard Branly, Guglielmo Marconi and map of English Channel.

1965, May 17

605 A161 5c vio bl & slate grn .20 .20
606 A161 10c dk bl & sepia .20 .20
607 A161 12c gray, brn & dk car .25 .25
608 A161 18c ind, dk car & plum .25 .25
609 A160 25c vio, ol & rose brn .25 .25
610 A161 30c dk brn, ol & bis brn .35 .35
611 A161 50c green & indigo .35 .35
612 A161 60c dl red brn & brt bl .70 .70
613 A160 70c brn blk, org & dk bl .85 .85
614 A160 95c indigo, blk & bl 1.00 1.00
615 A160 1fr brn, blk & ultra 1.40 1.40
Nos. 605-615,C66 (12) 10.55 10.55

International Telecommunication Union, cent.

Europa Issue, 1965
Common Design Type

1965, Sept. 25 Engr. *Perf. 13*
Size: 36x22mm

616 CD8 30c red brn & grn *1.25* *.65*
617 CD8 60c violet & dk car *2.00* *1.00*

Palace of Monaco, 18th Century A162

Views of Palace: 12c, From the Bay, 17th century. 18c, Bay with sailboats, 18th century. 30c, From distance, 19th century. 60c, Close-up, 19th century. 1.30fr, Aerial view, 20th century.

1966, Feb. 1 Engr. *Perf. 13*

618 A162 10c vio, dl grn & ind .20 .20
619 A162 12c bl, bis brn & dk brn .20 .20
620 A162 18c blk, grn & bl .25 .25
621 A162 30c vio bl, sep & red brn .35 .35
622 A162 60c bl, grn & brn .70 .70
623 A162 1.30fr dk grn & red brn 1.25 1.25
Nos. 618-623 (6) 2.95 2.95

750th anniversary of Palace of Monaco.

Dante Alighieri — A163

Designs: 60c, Dante facing Panther of Envy. 70c, Dante and Virgil boating across muddy swamp of 5th Circle. 95c, Dante watching the arrogant and Cross of Salvation. 1fr, Invocation of St. Bernard; Dante and Beatrice.

1966, Feb. 1

624 A163 30c crimson & dp grn .40 .40
625 A163 60c dl grn, Prus bl & ind .75 .75
626 A163 70c black, sep & car .90 .90
627 A163 95c red lilac & blue 1.40 1.40
628 A163 1fr ultra & bluish grn 1.50 1.50
Nos. 624-628 (5) 4.95 4.95

700th anniv. (in 1965) of the birth of Dante (1265-1321), poet.

Rally Type of 1956

Design: 1fr, "London to Monte Carlo."

1966, Feb. 1

629 A98 1fr purple, red & indigo .95 .75

The 35th Monte Carlo Automobile Rally.

St. Vincent de Paul, View of Monaco A294

1976, Nov. 9
1038 A294 60c multicolored .55 .45

St. Vincent de Paul Conference, Monaco, July 31, 1876, centenary.

Marquise de Sevigné — A295

1976, Nov. 9
1039 A295 80c multicolored .55 .35

Marie de Rabutin-Chantal, Marquise de Sevigné (1626-1696), writer.

Coin Type of 1975

Design: 80c, Honoré II 2-gros coin.

1976, Nov. 9
1040 A281 80c grn & steel bl .75 .45

Richard E. Byrd, Roald Amundsen, North Pole — A296

1976, Nov. 9
1041 A296 85c olive, blk & bl 1.75 1.25

1st flights over the North Pole, 50th anniv.

Gulliver Holding King, Queen and Enemy Fleet — A297

1976, Nov. 9
1042 A297 1.20fr indigo, bl & brn .80 .55

250th anniversary of the publication of Gulliver's Travels, by Jonathan Swift.

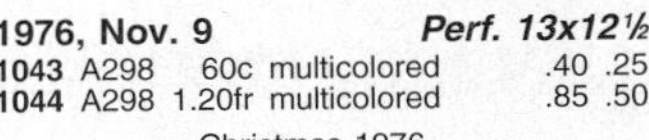
Child and Christmas Decorations A298

1976, Nov. 9 *Perf. 13x12½*
1043 A298 60c multicolored .40 .25
1044 A298 1.20fr multicolored .85 .50

Christmas 1976.

"Trapped by Drugs" A299

1976, Nov. 9
1045 A299 80c grn, ultra & org .60 .35
1046 A299 1.20fr red brn, vio & car .85 .50

Fight against drug abuse.

Floral Arrangement A300

Design: 1fr, Floral arrangement. Designs by Princess Grace.

1976, Nov. 9 Photo. *Perf. 13½x13*
1047 A300 80c yellow grn & multi 1.50 .90
1048 A300 1fr lt blue & multi 2.25 1.50

International Flower Show, Monte Carlo, May 1977. See Nos. 1124-1125, 1191.

Clown and Circus Acts — A301

1976, Nov. 9
1049 A301 1fr multi 1.90 1.10

3rd Intl. Circus Festival, Dec. 26-30.

L'Hirondelle I — A302

Prince Albert I — A303

Designs (Gouaches by Louis Tinayre): 30c, Crew of L'Hirondelle. 80c, L'Hirondelle in Storm. 1fr, The Helmsman, vert. 1.25fr, L'Hirondelle in Storm. 1.40fr, Shrimp Fishermen in Boat. 1.90fr, Hauling in the Net, vert. 2.50fr, Catching Opah Fish.

1977, May 3 Engr. *Perf. 13*
1050 A302 10c multicolored .20 .20
1051 A303 20c multicolored .25 .20
1052 A302 30c multicolored .30 .25
1053 A302 80c multicolored .45 .45
1054 A302 1fr multicolored .75 .55
1055 A302 1.25fr multicolored 1.10 .90
1056 A302 1.40fr multicolored 1.60 .25
1057 A302 1.90fr multicolored 2.75 2.25
1058 A302 2.50fr multicolored 2.25 1.50
Nos. 1050-1058 (9) 9.65 6.55

75th anniversary of publication of "The Career of a Sailor," by Prince Albert I. See Nos. 1073-1081.

Pyreneean Mountain Dogs — A304

1977, May 3 Photo.
1059 A304 80c multicolored 6.25 3.75

International Dog Show, Monte Carlo. See No. 1199.

Motherhood, by Mary Cassatt — A305

1977, May 3 Engr.
1060 A305 80c multicolored 1.10 .90

World Association of the Friends of Children.

Archers, Target and Monte Carlo — A306

1977, May 3
1061 A306 1.10fr multicolored .80 .55

10th Intl. Rainier III Archery Championships.

Spirit of St. Louis and Lindbergh — A307

1977, May 3
1062 A307 1.90fr multicolored 1.75 1.25

50th anniversary of first transatlantic flight by Charles Lindbergh.

The Dock at Deauville, by Dufy — A308

1977, May 3 Photo.
1063 A308 2fr multicolored 4.50 3.00

Raoul Dufy (1877-1953), painter, birth centenary.

Young Girl, by Rubens — A309

Rubens Paintings: 1fr, Duke of Buckingham. 1.40fr, Rubens' son Nicolas, 2 years old.

1977, May 3 Engr.
1064 A309 80c multicolored .75 .55
1065 A309 1fr multicolored 1.10 .70
1066 A309 1.40fr multicolored 2.00 1.25
Nos. 1064-1066 (3) 3.85 2.50

Peter Paul Rubens (1577-1640).

Helmet Tower, Monaco — A310

Europa: 1.40fr, St. Michael's Church, Menton.

1977, May 3
1067 A310 1fr multicolored *1.25 .50*
1068 A310 1.40fr multicolored *3.00 .80*
a. Souv. sheet, 5 each #1067-1068 *35.00 25.00*

Clock Tower Type of 1974

1977, Apr. 1 Engr. *Perf. 13*
1069 A263 54c brt green .45 .35
1070 A263 68c orange .55 .45
1071 A263 1.05fr olive 1.10 .55
1072 A263 1.85fr brown 1.75 1.00
Nos. 1069-1072 (4) 3.85 2.35

Nos. 1069-1072 were issued precanceled only. See note after No. 324.

Career of a Sailor Types of 1977

Designs (Gouaches by Louis Tinayre): 10c, Yacht Princess Alice II, Kiel harbor. 20c, Laboratory on board ship. 30c, Yacht amidst ice floes. 80c, Crew in arctic outfits. 1fr, Yacht in polar region. 1.25fr, Yacht in snow storm. 1.40fr, Building camp on ice. 1.90fr, Yacht under steam amidst ice floes. 3fr, Yacht passing iceberg.

1977, Nov. Engr. *Perf. 13*
1073 A302 10c blk & brt bl .20 .20
1074 A302 20c Prus blue .25 .20
1075 A302 30c blk & brt bl .25 .25
1076 A303 80c multicolored .55 .45
1077 A302 1fr brt grn & blk .70 .55
1078 A302 1.25fr vio, sep & blk 1.00 .75
1079 A302 1.40fr ol, bl & pur 1.60 1.25
1080 A302 1.90fr blk & brt bl 2.75 2.25
1081 A302 3fr dk grn, ol & brt bl 4.00 3.00
Nos. 1073-1081 (9) 11.30 8.90

75th anniversary of publication of "The Career of a Sailor," by Prince Albert I.

Santa Claus A311

1977, Nov.
1082 A311 80c multicolored .60 .25
1083 A311 1.40fr multicolored .80 .40

Christmas 1977.

Flowers Types of 1974

Designs: 80c, Snapdragons and bellflowers. 1fr, Ikebana arrangement.

1977, Nov. Photo. *Perf. 13½x13*
1084 A259 80c multicolored 1.25 .70
1085 A260 1fr multicolored 1.75 1.10

Intl. Flower Show, Monte Carlo, May 1978.

Face (Van Gogh), Syringe, Hallucination Pattern — A312

1977, Nov. **Engr.** ***Perf. 13***
1086 A312 1fr multicolored .75 .45

Fight against drug abuse.

Clown, Flags of Participants A313

1977, Nov. **Photo.** ***Perf. 13½x13***
1087 A313 1fr multicolored 1.75 1.25

Fourth International Circus Festival. Monte Carlo, December 1977.

Coin Type of 1975

Design: 80c, Doubloon of Honoré II, 1648.

1977, Nov. **Engr.** ***Perf. 13***
1088 A281 80c lil & brn .70 .45

Mediterranean Landscape and Industrial Pollution — A314

1977, Nov.
1089 A314 1fr multicolored .85 .50

Protection of the Mediterranean. Meeting of the UN Mediterranean Environmental Protection Group, Monte Carlo, Nov. 28-Dec. 6.

Men Spreading Tar, Dr. Guglielminetti, 1903 Car — A315

1977, Nov.
1090 A315 1.10fr multicolored .80 .45

75th anniversary of first tarred roads, invented by Swiss Dr. Guglielminetti.

View of Monaco and Tennis Emblem — A316

First Match at Wimbledon and Stadium — A317

1977, Nov.
1091 A316 1fr multicolored 1.40 .70
1092 A317 1.40fr multicolored 1.50 1.00

Lawn Tennis Federation of Monaco, 50th anniv. and cent. of 1st intl. tennis match at Wimbledon.

Prince of Monaco Type of 1967

Honoré V (1819-1841), by Marie Verroust.

1977, Nov. ***Perf. 12½x13***
1093 A182 6fr multicolored 4.50 3.25

Red Cross Type of 1969

Design: 4fr, St. John Bosco and boys.

1977, Nov. ***Perf. 13***
1094 A194 4fr multicolored 2.50 2.00

Nos. 1069-1072 Surcharged

1978, Jan. 17
1095 A263 58c on 54c brt grn .55 .40
1096 A263 73c on 68c orange .90 .55
1097 A263 1.15fr on 1.05fr olive 1.25 .90
1098 A263 2fr on 1.85fr brn 2.10 1.40
Nos. 1095-1098 (4) 4.80 3.25

See note after No. 324.

Illustrations, Novels by Jules Verne — A318

5c, Shipwreck. 25c, The Abandoned Ship, from "Mysterious Island". 30c, Secret of the Island. 80c, Robur, the Conqueror. 1fr, Master Zacharius. 1.40fr, The Castle in the Carpathians. 1.70fr, The Children of Capt. Grant. 5.50fr, Jules Verne and allegories.

1978, May 2 **Engr.** ***Perf. 13***
1099 A318 5c multicolored .20 .20
1100 A318 25c multicolored .30 .20
1101 A318 30c multicolored .30 .25
1102 A318 80c multicolored .55 .50
1103 A318 1fr multicolored 1.00 .60
1104 A318 1.40fr multicolored 1.20 .85
1105 A318 1.70fr multicolored 1.75 1.40
1106 A318 5.50fr multicolored 4.25 3.25
Nos. 1099-1106 (8) 9.55 7.25

Jules Verne (1828-1905), science fiction writer, birth sesquicentennial.

Congress Center and Monte Carlo A319

1.40fr, Congress Center, view from the sea.

1978, May 2
1107 A319 1fr multicolored .60 .50
1108 A319 1.40fr multicolored .80 .50

Inauguration of Monaco Congress Center.

Soccer Players and Globe — A320

1978, May 2
1109 A320 1fr multicolored .75 .75

11th World Soccer Cup Championship, Argentina, June 1-25.

Vivaldi and St. Mark's Place, Venice — A321

1978, May 2
1110 A321 1fr dk brown & red .90 .80

Antonio Vivaldi (1675?-1741), Italian violinist and composer.

Control Ship and Grimaldi Palace — A322

1fr, Map of coastal area and city emblems.

1978, May 2
Size: 26x36mm
1111 A322 80c multi .60 .50
Size: 48x27mm
1112 A322 1fr multi, horiz. .60 .50

Protection of the environment, signing of "Ra Mo Ge" agreement for the protection of the Mediterranean Coast between Saint-Raphael, France, and Genoa, Italy (including Monaco).

Monaco Cathedral A323

Europa: 1.40fr, View of Principality from East.

1978, May 2 ***Perf. 12½x13***
1113 A323 1fr multicolored *1.75* *.40*
1114 A323 1.40fr multicolored *3.25* *.70*
a. Souv. sheet, 5 each #1113-1114 *40.00* *25.00*

Cinderella — A324

Mother Goose Tales: 25c, Puss in Boots. 30c, Sleeping Beauty. 80c, Fairy tale princess. 1fr, Little Red Riding Hood. 1.40fr, Bluebeard. 1.70fr, Tom Thumb. 1.90fr, Riquet with the Tuft of Hair. 2.50fr, The Fairies.

1978, Nov. 8 **Engr.** ***Perf. 13***
1115 A324 5c multicolored .20 .20
1116 A324 25c multicolored .25 .20
1117 A324 30c multicolored .25 .25
1118 A324 80c multicolored .60 .50
1119 A324 1fr multicolored .80 .60
1120 A324 1.40fr multicolored 1.00 .85
1121 A324 1.70fr multicolored 1.25 1.10
1122 A324 1.90fr multicolored 1.75 1.25
1123 A324 2.50fr multicolored 2.40 1.75
Nos. 1115-1123 (9) 8.50 6.70

Charles Perrault (1628-1703), compiler of Mother Goose Tales.

Flower Type of 1976

Van Gogh Paintings: 1fr, Sunflowers. 1.70fr, Iris.

1978, Nov. 8 **Photo.** ***Perf. 12½x13***
1124 A300 1fr multicolored 2.75 2.25
1125 A300 1.70fr multicolored 3.75 2.25

Intl. Flower show, Monte Carlo, May 1979, and 125th birth anniv. of Vincent van Gogh (1853-1890), Dutch painter.

Afghan Hound A325

Design: 1.20fr, Russian wolfhound.

1978, Nov. 8 ***Perf. 13x12½***
1126 A325 1fr multicolored 3.00 2.40
1127 A325 1.20fr multicolored 4.50 3.00

International Dog Show, Monte Carlo.

Child Holding Gift of Shoes — A326

1978, Nov. 8 **Engr.** ***Perf. 12½x13***
1128 A326 1fr multicolored .80 .50

Christmas 1978.

Catherine and William Booth, Salvation Army Band — A327

1978, Nov. 8 **Engr.** ***Perf. 13***
1129 A327 1.70fr multicolored 1.20 1.00

Centenary of founding of Salvation Army.

Trained Seals A328

1fr, Lions, vert. 1.40fr, Equestrian act. 1.90fr, Monkey music band. 2.40fr, Trapeze act.

1978, Nov. 8 ***Perf. 13x12½***
1130 A328 80c multicolored .70 .50
1131 A328 1fr multicolored 1.00 .80
1132 A328 1.40fr multicolored 1.40 1.00
1133 A328 1.90fr multicolored 2.40 2.00
1134 A328 2.40fr multicolored 3.50 2.40
Nos. 1130-1134 (5) 9.00 6.70

5th Intl. Circus Festival, Monte Carlo.

Princes of Monaco Type of 1967

Paintings: 2fr, Florestan I (1841-1856), by G. Dauphin. 4fr, Caroline Gilbert de Lametz (1793-1879), by Marie Verroust.

1978, Nov. 8 Engr. *Perf. 12½x13*

1135 A182 2fr multicolored 2.00 1.40
1136 A182 4fr multicolored 3.50 3.00

Souvenir Sheet

Henri Dunant and Battle Scene — A329

1978, Nov. 8 Engr. *Perf. 13*

1137 A329 5fr multicolored 4.25 4.25

Henri Dunant (1828-1910), founder of Red Cross.

View Types of 1974

1978-80

1138 A262 25c All Saints' Tower .35 .35
1139 A262 65c Monte Carlo Beach .35 .35
1140 A263 70c Exotic Garden, cacti ('80) .70 .55
1142 A262 1.10fr Palais de Justice ('80) .75 .55
1144 A263 1.30fr Cathedral .75 .45
1145 A264 1.50fr Prince Albert Statue and Museum ('80) 1.25 1.10
1146 A262 1.80fr La Condamine 1.25 1.00
1148 A262 2.30fr Palace ('80) 2.25 1.60
1152 A262 6.50fr Monte Carlo Auditorium 3.75 2.75
Nos. 1138-1152 (9) 11.40 8.70

Convention Center, Monte Carlo A330

1978-79

1154 A330 61c vermilion .40 .20
1155 A330 64c green .40 .20
1156 A330 68c brt blue .40 .20
1157 A330 78c dp rose lilac .55 .20
1158 A330 83c violet blue .45 .20
1159 A330 88c orange .45 .20
1160 A330 1.25fr brown .90 .45
1161 A330 1.30fr purple .75 .45
1162 A330 1.40fr brt yel grn .70 .40
1163 A330 2.10fr violet blue 1.10 .80
1164 A330 2.25fr brown org 1.25 .75
1165 A330 2.35fr lilac rose 1.40 .75
Nos. 1154-1165 (12) 8.75 4.80

Issued precanceled only. See note after No. 324.

Issue dates: 61c, 78c, 1.25fr, 2.10fr, July 10, 1978. Others, 1979.

Souvenir Sheet

Prince Albert — A331

1979, Apr. 30 Engr. *Perf. 12½x13*

1166 A331 10fr multicolored 8.25 8.25

21st birthday of Hereditary Prince Albert.

The Juggler of Notre Dame, by Jules Massenet A332

1.20fr, Hans, the Flute Player, by Gaston L. Ganne. 1.50fr, Don Quichotte, by Massenet. 1.70fr, L'Aiglon, by Jacques Ibert & Arthur Honegger, vert. 2.10fr, The Child & the Sorcerer, by Maurice Ravel. 3fr, Monte Carlo Opera & Charles Garnier, architect.

1979, Apr. 30 *Perf. 13*

1167 A332 1fr multicolored .55 .45
1168 A332 1.20fr multicolored .75 .55
1169 A332 1.50fr multicolored 1.10 .90
1170 A332 1.70fr multicolored 1.40 1.25
1171 A332 2.10fr multicolored 2.25 2.00
1172 A332 3fr multicolored 3.25 3.00
Nos. 1167-1172 (6) 9.30 8.15

Centenary of the Salle Garnier, Monte Carlo Opera.

Flower, Bird, Butterfly, IYC Emblem A333

Children's Drawings (IYC Emblem and): 1fr, Horse and child. 1.20fr, Children shaking hands, and heart. 1.50fr, Children of the world for peace. 1.70fr, Children against pollution.

1979, Apr. 30

1173 A333 50c multicolored .25 .25
1174 A333 1fr multicolored .65 .50
1175 A333 1.20fr multicolored .85 .80
1176 A333 1.50fr multicolored 1.50 1.25
1177 A333 1.70fr multicolored 1.75 1.60
Nos. 1173-1177 (5) 5.00 4.40

International Year of the Child.

Armed Messenger, 15th-16th Centuries A334

Europa (designs similar to 1960 postage dues); 1.50fr, Felucca, 18th cent. 1.70fr, Arrival of 1st train, Dec. 12, 1868.

1979, Apr. 30

1178 A334 1.20fr multicolored *1.25* .40
1179 A334 1.50fr multicolored 5.00 *.60*
1180 A334 1.70fr multicolored 5.00 *.85*
a. Souv. sheet of 6, 2 each #1178-1180, perf. 13x12½ *27.50* *18.00*
Nos. 1178-1180 (3) 11.25 1.85

Les Biches, by Francis Poulenc A335

Ballets: 1.20fr, Les Matelots, by George Auric. 1.50fr, Le Spectre de 1a Rose, by Carl Maria Weber, vert. 1.70fr, Gaieté Parisienne, by Jacques Offenbach. 2.10fr, Dance of Salomé, by Richard Strauss, vert. 3fr, Instrumental Music, ceiling decoration of Salle Garnier.

1979, Nov. 12

Size: 26x36mm, 36x26mm

1181 A335 1fr multicolored .70 .50
1182 A335 1.20fr multicolored .85 .65
1183 A335 1.50fr multicolored 1.25 1.00
1184 A335 1.70fr multicolored 1.60 1.40
1185 A335 2.10fr multicolored 2.75 2.25

Size: 48x27mm

1186 A335 3fr multicolored 4.00 3.25
Nos. 1181-1186 (6) 11.15 9.05

Salle Garnier, Monte Carlo Opera, cent.

Princes of Monaco Type of 1967

Paintings: 3fr, Charles III (1856-1889). 4fr, Antoinette de Merode (1828-1864).

1979, Nov. 12 *Perf. 12½x13*

1187 A182 3fr multicolored 2.25 1.75
1188 A182 4fr multicolored 3.25 2.40

Red Cross Type of 1969

5fr, St. Peter Claver preaching to slaves.

1979, Nov. 12 *Perf. 13*

1189 A194 5fr multicolored 3.25 2.40

Princess Grace Orchid — A336

1979, Nov. 12 Photo.

1190 A336 1fr multicolored 2.75 1.75

Intl. Orchid Exhibition, Monte Carlo, Apr. 1980.

Flower Type of 1976

Design: 1.20fr, Princess Grace rose.

1979, Nov. 12

1191 A300 1.20fr multicolored 2.75 1.75

Intl. Flower Show, Monte Carlo, May 1980.

Clown Balancing on Globe — A337

1979, Nov. 12

1192 A337 1.20fr multicolored 2.00 1.25

6th International Circus Festival, Monte Carlo, Dec. 6-10.

Rowland Hill, Penny Black — A338

1979, Nov. 12 Engr. *Perf. 13*

1193 A338 1.70fr multicolored 1.00 .65

Sir Rowland Hill (1795-1879), originator of penny postage.

Albert Einstein, Equations A339

1979, Nov. 12

1194 A339 1.70fr multicolored 1.40 .80

Albert Einstein (1879-1955), theoretical physicist.

St. Patrick's Cathedral, New York City, Cent. — A340

1979, Nov. 12

1195 A340 2.10fr multicolored 1.25 .75

Nativity A341

1979, Nov. 12

1196 A341 1.20fr multicolored .80 .65

Christmas 1979.

Bugatti, Monte Carlo, 1929 Winner A342

1979, Nov. 12

1197 A342 1fr multicolored 1.10 .70

50th anniv. of Grand Prix auto race, Monte Carlo.

Arms of Charles V and Monaco, View of Monaco — A343

1979, Nov. 12

1198 A343 1.50fr multicolored .90 .65

Emperor Charles V visit to Monaco, 450th anniversary.

Dog Type of 1977

Design: 1.20fr, Setter and pointer.

1979, Nov. 12 **Photo.**

1199	A304	1.20fr multicolored	5.00	3.50

International Dog Show, Monte Carlo.

Prince Rainier Type of 1974

1980, Jan. 17 **Engr.** ***Perf. 13***

1200	A261	1.10fr emerald	.70	.25
1201	A261	1.30fr rose red	.70	.25
1202	A261	1.60fr dk blue gray	1.25	.55
1203	A261	1.80fr grnsh blue	2.00	1.90
1204	A261	2.30fr red lilac	2.50	1.40
		Nos. 1200-1204 (5)	7.15	4.35

Chestnut Branch in Spring A344

Designs of 1980, 1981 stamps show chestnut branch. 1982 stamps show peach branch. 1983 stamps show apple branch.

1980-83 **Engr.** ***Perf. 13x12½***

1205	A344	76c shown	.50	.40
1206	A344	88c Spring ('81)	.50	.40
1207	A344	97c Spring ('82)	.50	.40
1208	A344	99c Summer	.80	.60
1209	A344	1.05fr Spring ('83)	.80	.60
1210	A344	1.14fr Summer ('81)	.80	.60
1211	A344	1.25fr Summer ('82)	.80	.60
1212	A344	1.35fr Summer ('83)	.85	.60
1213	A344	1.60fr Autumn	1.25	.85
1214	A344	1.84fr Autumn ('81)	1.25	.85
1215	A344	2.03fr Autumn ('82)	1.25	.85
1216	A344	2.19fr Autumn ('83)	1.40	1.00
1217	A344	2.65fr Winter	1.75	1.20
1218	A344	3.05fr Winter ('81)	1.60	1.25
1219	A344	3.36fr Winter ('82)	1.75	1.25
1220	A344	3.63fr Winter ('83)	1.60	1.60
		Nos. 1205-1220 (16)	17.40	13.05

Issued precanceled only. See note after No. 324. See Nos. 1406-1409, 1457-1460.

Gymnast — A345

1980, Apr. 28

1221	A345	1.10fr shown	.40	.25
1222	A345	1.30fr Handball	.50	.35
1223	A345	1.60fr Shooting	.65	.45
1224	A345	1.80fr Volleyball	.85	.60
1225	A345	2.30fr Ice hockey	1.00	.85
1226	A345	4fr Slalom	1.60	1.25
		Nos. 1221-1226 (6)	5.00	3.75

22nd Summer Olympic Games, Moscow, July 19-Aug. 3; 13th Winter Olympic Games, Lake Placid, NY, Feb. 12-24.

Colette, Novelist — A346

Europa: 1.80fr, Marcel Pagnol (1895-1974), French playwright.

1980, Apr. 28 ***Perf. 12½x13***

1227	A346	1.30fr multicolored	1.00	*.35*
1228	A346	1.80fr multicolored	1.50	*.35*
a.		Souv. sheet, 5 each #1227-1228	*15.00*	*10.00*

The Source, by Ingres A347

1980, Apr. 28

1229	A347	4fr multicolored	8.00	5.50

Jean Auguste Dominique Ingres (1780-1867).

Michel Eyquem de Montaigne A348

1980, Apr. 28 ***Perf. 13***

1230	A348	1.30fr multicolored	.70	.45

Essays of Montaigne (1533-1592), 400th anniversary of publication.

Guillaume Apollinaire (1880-1918), French Writer — A349

1980, Apr. 28

1231	A349	1.10fr multicolored	.70	.45

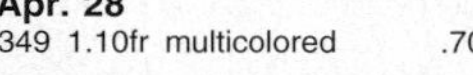

Paul P. Harris, Chicago Skyline, Rotary Emblem — A350

1980, Apr. 28

1232	A350	1.80fr multicolored	.75	.55

Rotary International, 75th anniversary.

Convention Center, Map of Europe, Kiwanis Emblem — A351

1980, Apr. 28

1233	A351	1.30fr multicolored	.70	.50

Kiwanis International, European Convention, Monte Carlo, June.

Coin Type of 1975

Design: 1.50fr, Honoré II silver ecu, 1649.

1980, Apr. 28

1234	A281	1.50fr multicolored	.75	.55

Lhasa Apso and Shih-Tzu — A352

1980, Apr. 28 **Photo.**

1235	A352	1.30fr multicolored	5.00	3.25

International Dog Show, Monte Carlo.

The Princess and the Pea — A353

Hans Christian Andersen (1805-1875) Fairy Tales: 1.30fr, The Little Mermaid. 1.50fr, The Chimneysweep and the Shepherdess. 1.60fr, The Brave Little Tin Soldier. 1.80fr, The Little Match Girl. 2.30fr, The Nightingale.

1980, Nov. 6 **Engr.** ***Perf. 13***

1236	A353	70c multicolored	.50	.25
1237	A353	1.30fr multicolored	.70	.60
1238	A353	1.50fr multicolored	1.00	.85
1239	A353	1.60fr multicolored	1.40	.85
1240	A353	1.80fr multicolored	1.40	1.10
1241	A353	2.30fr multicolored	2.00	1.20
		Nos. 1236-1241 (6)	7.00	4.85

Women on Balcony, by Van Dongen — A354

Paintings from 1905 Paris Fall Salon: 2fr, The Road, by de Vlaminck. 4fr, Woman Reading, by Matisse. 5fr, Three Women in a Meadow, by Andrè Derain.

1980, Nov. 6 ***Perf. 13x12***

1242	A354	2fr multicolored	2.50	1.75
1243	A354	3fr multicolored	3.75	2.50
1244	A354	4fr multicolored	5.00	4.25
1245	A354	5fr multicolored	6.00	5.00
		Nos. 1242-1245 (4)	17.25	13.50

Princes of Monaco Type of 1967

Paintings: No. 1246, Prince Albert I (1848-1922), by Leon Bonnat. No. 1247, Princess Alice (1857-1925), by L. Maeterlinck.

1980, Nov. 6 ***Perf. 12½x13***

1246	A182	4fr multicolored	3.00	2.40
1247	A182	4fr multicolored	3.00	2.40

Sun and Birds, by Perrette Lambert — A355

1980, Nov. 6 ***Perf. 13***

1248	A355	6fr multicolored	4.00	3.25

Red Cross.

7th International Circus Festival — A356

1980, Nov. 6 ***Perf. 13x12½***

1249	A356	1.30fr multicolored	2.00	1.25

Christmas 1980 A357

1980, Nov. 6

1250	A357	1.10fr multicolored	.55	.35
1251	A357	2.30fr multicolored	1.20	.75

Princess Stephanie of Monaco Rose — A358

1980, Nov. 6 **Photo.** ***Perf. 12½x13***

1252	A358	1.30fr shown	1.40	.65
1253	A358	1.80fr Ikebana	2.25	1.40

International Flower Show, Monte Carlo, May 1981.

Prince Rainier Type of 1974

1980 **Engr.** ***Perf. 13***

1255	A261	1.20fr bright green	1.10	.25
1256	A261	1.40fr red	1.25	.20

Issue dates: 1.20fr, Aug. 19; 1.40fr, Aug. 11.

Paramuricea Clavata — A359

5c-20c, 40c, 50c, vert.

1980, Nov. 6 ***Perf. 13x12½***

1259	A359	5c Spirographis spallanzanii	.20	.20
1260	A359	10c Anemonia sulcata	.20	.20
1261	A359	15c Leptosammia pruvoti	.20	.20
1262	A359	20c Pteroides	.25	.20
1263	A359	30c shown	.25	.25
1264	A359	40c Alcyonium	.35	.25
1265	A359	50c Corallium rubrum	.55	.45
1266	A359	60c Caliactis parisitica	1.00	.65
1267	A359	70c Cerianthus membranaceus	1.25	.90
1268	A359	1fr Actinia equina	1.25	.90
1269	A359	2fr Protula	2.50	1.10
		Nos. 1259-1269 (11)	8.00	5.30

See Nos. 1316-1321, 1380.

25th Wedding Anniversary of Prince Rainier and Princess Grace — A360

1981, May 4 *Perf. 13*
1270 A360 1.20fr green & blk 1.50 1.00
1271 A360 1.40fr carmine & blk 2.00 1.50
1272 A360 1.70fr olive grn & blk 2.50 1.90
1273 A360 1.80fr brown & blk 2.75 2.25
1274 A360 2fr brt blue & blk 3.75 2.75
Nos. 1270-1274 (5) 12.50 9.40

Mozart with his Father and Sister, by Carmontelle — A361

Wolfgang Amadeus Mozart (1756-1791), 225th Birth Anniversary (Paintings): 2fr, Portrait, by Lorenz Vogel (26x36mm). 3.50fr, Conducting his Requiem Two Days Before his Death, by F.C. Baude.

1981, May 4 Engr. *Perf. 13½x13*
1275 A361 2fr multicolored 1.65 1.50
1276 A361 2.50fr multicolored 2.40 2.00
1277 A361 3.50fr multicolored 3.25 2.50
a. Strip of 3, #1275-1277 8.50 8.50

Cross of Palms — A362

Europa (Palm Sunday Traditions): 2fr, Children with palms at benediction.

1981, May 4 *Perf. 12½x13*
1278 A362 1.40fr multicolored .75 *.35*
1279 A362 2fr multicolored 1.25 *.55*
a. Souv. sheet, 5 ea #1278-1279 *18.00 9.00*

European Soccer Cup, 25th Anniversary A363

1981, May 4 *Perf. 13*
1280 A363 2fr black & blue 1.25 .85

International Year of the Disabled — A364

1981, May 4
1281 A364 1.40fr brt grn & bl 1.00 .60

Monegasque National Pavilion Centenary — A365

1981, May 4
1282 A365 2fr multicolored 1.25 .85

Oceanographic Institute, Monaco and Museum, Paris — A366

1981, May 4
1283 A366 1.20fr multicolored .95 .80

75th anniversary of the Oceanographic Institute (Monaco-France).

50th Anniversary of the International Hydrographic Bureau — A367

1981, May 4
1284 A367 2.50fr multicolored 1.75 1.25

Rough Collies and Shetland Sheepdogs — A368

1981, May 4 Photo.
1285 A368 1.40fr multicolored 5.50 4.00

International Dog Show, Monte Carlo.

Marine Life Preservation A369

1981, Mar. 21 Photo.
1286 A369 1.20fr multicolored 1.00 .70

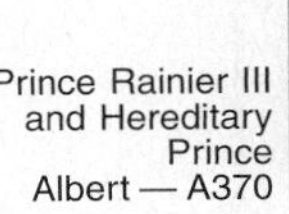

Prince Rainier III and Hereditary Prince Albert — A370

1981-84 Engr. *Perf. 13*
1287 A370 1.40fr dark green 1.00 .25
1288 A370 1.60fr carmine 1.40 .25
1289 A370 1.60fr olive grn ('82) .75 .25
1290 A370 1.70fr bluish grn ('84) 1.00 .25
1291 A370 1.80fr magenta ('82) .95 .20
1292 A370 2fr red ('83) 1.10 .20
1293 A370 2.10fr red ('84) 1.10 .20
1294 A370 2.30fr blue 3.50 2.75
1295 A370 2.60fr violet bl ('82) 2.25 1.90
1296 A370 2.80fr steel bl ('83) 2.25 1.60
1297 A370 3fr sky blue ('84) 2.25 1.60
1298 A370 4fr brown 1.75 .75
1299 A370 5.50fr black 2.10 1.50
Nos. 1287-1299 (13) 21.40 11.70

See Nos. 1505-1515.

Hauling Ice Floes, 17th Cent. Map Arctic A371

1981, Oct. 5
1301 A371 1.50fr multicolored 1.60 1.25

First Intl. Arctic Committee Congress, Rome, Oct. 5-9.

Princes of Monaco Type of 1967

Paintings by P.A. de Laszlo, 1929: 3fr, Prince Louis II. 5fr, Princess Charlotte.

1981, Nov. 5 Engr. *Perf. 12½x13*
1302 A182 3fr multicolored 2.50 1.25
1303 A182 5fr multicolored 3.50 2.40

Ettore Bugatti, Auto Designer and Racer, Birth Centenary A372

1981, Nov. 5 *Perf. 13*
1304 A372 1fr multicolored 1.25 .85

George Bernard Shaw (1856-1950) A373

1981, Nov. 5

2.50fr, Fernand Leger, painter, birth cent.

1305 A373 2fr multicolored 1.25 1.00
1306 A373 2.50fr multicolored 1.25 1.00

Self-portrait, by Pablo Picasso (1881-1973) — A374

#1308, Self-portrait, by Rembrandt (1606-69).

1981, Nov. 5 *Perf. 12½x13*
1307 A374 4fr multicolored 4.50 3.25
1308 A374 4fr multicolored 4.50 3.25

Ikebana, Painting by Ikenobo, 1673 — A375

Intl. Flower Show, Monte Carlo, 1982: 1.40fr, Elegantines, morning glories.

1981, Nov. 5 Photo. *Perf. 12½*
1309 A375 1.40fr multicolored 1.40 1.00
1310 A375 2fr multicolored 2.25 1.75

Catherine Deneuve Rose A376

1981, Nov. 5 *Perf. 13x12½*
1311 A376 1.80fr multicolored 4.00 2.50

First Intl. Rose Competition, Monte Carlo, June 12-14.

8th Intl. Circus Festival, Monte Carlo, Dec. 10-14 — A377

1981, Nov. 5 Engr. *Perf. 13*
1312 A377 1.40fr multicolored 2.50 1.40

Christmas 1981 A378

1981, Nov. 5
1313 A378 1.20fr multicolored .75 .60

50th Monte Carlo Auto Race — A379

1981, Nov. 5
1314 A379 1fr Lancia-Stratos 1.50 1.10

Souvenir Sheet

Persimmon Branch in Spring A380

1981, Nov. 5 *Perf. 13x12½*

1315 Sheet of 4 8.50 8.50
- *a.* A380 1fr shown .80 .80
- *b.* A380 2fr Summer 1.50 1.50
- *c.* A380 3fr Autumn 2.50 2.50
- *d.* A380 4fr Winter 3.00 3.00

Coral Type of 1980

Exotic Plants. 1.40fr, 1.60fr, 2.30fr vert.

Perf. 12½x13, 13x12½

1981-82 **Photo.**

1316 A359 1.40fr Hoya bella 3.25 1.60
1317 A359 1.60fr Bolivicereus samaipatanus 2.75 1.10
1317A A359 1.80fr Trichocereus grandi-florus 2.25 1.10
1318 A359 2.30fr Euphorbia milii 2.75 1.10
1319 A359 2.60fr Echinocereus fitchii 2.75 1.10
1320 A359 2.90fr Rebutia heliosa 2.75 1.10
1321 A359 4.10fr Echinopsis multiplex 3.25 2.75
Nos. 1316-1321 (7) 19.75 9.85

Issued: 1.80fr, June 7; others Dec. 10.

Miniature Sheet

1982 World Cup A381

Designs: Various soccer players.

1982, May 3 *Perf. 13*

1322 Sheet of 4 8.00 8.00
- *a.* A381 1fr multicolored .75 .75
- *b.* A381 2fr multicolored 1.50 1.50
- *c.* A381 3fr multicolored 2.25 2.25
- *d.* A381 4fr multicolored 2.75 2.75

Mercantour Natl. Park Birds — A382

1982, May 3 *Perf. 12½x13, 13x12½*

1323 A382 60c Nutcracker 1.00 .85
1324 A382 70c Black grouse 1.20 1.10
1325 A382 80c Rock partridge 1.20 1.10
1326 A382 90c Wall creeper, horiz. 2.25 1.75
1327 A382 1.40fr Ptarmigan, horiz. 3.00 2.40
1328 A382 1.60fr Golden eagle 3.75 2.40
Nos. 1323-1328 (6) 12.40 9.60

Europa — A383

1982, May 3 *Perf. 12½x13*

1329 A383 1.60fr Guelph attacking Fortress of Monaco, 1297 *1.50* .40
1330 A383 2.30fr Treaty of Peronne, 1641 *1.50* .50
- *a.* Souv. sheet, 5 ea #1329-1330 *18.00* *9.00*

Fontvielle Landfill Project A384

1982, May 3 *Perf. 13x12½*

1331 A384 1.40fr Old coastline 1.00 .50
1332 A384 1.60fr Landfill site 1.00 .60
1333 A384 2.30fr Completed site 1.50 1.00
Nos. 1331-1333 (3) 3.50 2.10

Fontvielle Stadium — A385

1982, May 3 *Perf. 13*

1334 A385 2.30fr multicolored 1.25 1.00

PHILEXFRANCE '82 Stamp Exhibition,Paris, June 11-21 — A386

1982, May 3

1335 A386 1.40fr multicolored 1.00 .80

Intl. Dog Show, Monte Carlo A387

1982, May 3 **Photo.** *Perf. 13x12½*

1336 A387 60c Old English sheepdog 3.25 1.75
1337 A387 1fr Briard terrier 3.25 1.75

See Nos. 1366, 1431, 1479, 1539, 1676, 1704, 1756, 1806, 1855, 1900, 1940, 1990, 2035, 2069A, 2108.

Monaco Cathedral, Arms of Pope John Paul II and Monaco A388

1982, May 3 **Engr.**

1338 A388 1.60fr multicolored .85 .80

Creation of archbishopric of Monaco, July 25, 1981.

800th Birth Anniv. of St. Francis of Assisi — A389

1982, May 3 *Perf. 12½x13*

1339 A389 1.40fr multicolored 1.00 .80

TB Bacillus Cent. — A390

1982, May 3

1340 A390 1.40fr multicolored 1.00 .85

Scouting Year — A391

1982, May 3

1341 A391 1.60fr dk brown & blk 1.60 1.00

Intl. Hunting Council, 29th Meeting — A392

1982, June 11 **Photo.** *Perf. 12½*

1342 A392 1.60fr St. Hubert 1.20 1.00

Intl. Bibliophile Assoc. General Assembly — A393

1982, Sept. 30 **Engr.** *Perf. 13*

1343 A393 1.60fr multicolored .80 .60

Monte Carlo and Monaco During the Belle Epoch (1870-1925), by Hubert Clerissi — A394

1982, Nov. 8 **Engr.** *Perf. 13x12½*

1344 A394 3fr Casino, 1870 1.75 1.25
1345 A394 5fr Palace, 1893 3.75 2.00

See Nos. 1385-1386, 1436-1437, 1488-1489, 1546-1547, 1605-1606, 1638-1639, 1695-1696.

Nicolo Paganini (1782-1840), Composer and Violinist — A395

1.80fr, Anna Pavlova (1881-1931), ballerina. 2.60fr, Igor Stravinsky (1882-1971), composer.

1982, Nov. 8 **Engr.** *Perf. 12½x13*

1346 A395 1.60fr multicolored 1.25 1.00
1347 A395 1.80fr multicolored 1.75 1.20
1348 A395 2.60fr multicolored 2.00 1.40
Nos. 1346-1348 (3) 5.00 3.60

In a Boat, by Manet (1832-1883) — A396

Design: No. 1350, Les Poissons Noir, by Georges Braque (1882-1963).

1982, Nov. 8 **Engr.** *Perf. 13x12½*

1349 A396 4fr multicolored 4.00 3.00
1350 A396 4fr multicolored 4.00 3.00

Intl. Flower Show, Monte Carlo — A397

Designs: Various floral arrangements.

1982, Nov. 8 **Photo.** *Perf. 12½x13*

1351 A397 1.60fr multicolored 2.10 1.25
1352 A397 2.60fr multicolored 2.10 1.25

Bouquet — A398

1982 *Perf. 13*

1353 A398 1.60fr multicolored 2.50 1.75

Christmas 1982 — A399

1982, Nov. 8 **Engr.** *Perf. 12½x13*

1354 A399 1.60fr Three Kings .60 .35
1355 A399 1.80fr Holy Family .75 .35
1356 A399 2.60fr Shepherds 1.10 .50
- *a.* Souv. sheet of 3, #1354-1356 3.25 3.25

Nos. 1354-1356 (3) 2.45 1.20

Intl. Polar Year Centenary — A400

1982, Nov. 8 **Engr.** *Perf. 13*

1358 A400 1.60fr Prince Louis, Discovery 2.25 1.60

Discovery of Greenland Millenium — A401

1982, Nov. 8
1359 A401 1.60fr Erik the Red's longship 2.25 1.60

Death Bimillenium of Virgil — A402

1982, Nov. 8
1360 A402 1.80fr Scene from Aeneid, Book 6 2.25 1.60

50th Anniv. of Botanical Garden A403

1983, Feb. 11 Photo. *Perf. 12½x13*
1361 A403 1.80fr Cacti, vert. 1.50 1.10
1362 A403 2fr Exotic plants, vert. 1.75 1.20
1363 A403 2.30fr Intl. exhibits, vert. 2.00 1.75
1364 A403 2.60fr Cave 2.50 1.75
1365 A403 3.30fr Prehistoric Anthropology Museum 3.50 2.75
Nos. 1361-1365 (5) 11.25 8.55

Monte Carlo Dog Show Type

1983, Apr. 13 *Perf. 13x12½*
1366 A387 1.80fr Alaskan malamute 7.25 4.75

Souvenir Sheet

Princess Grace (1929-1982) — A405

1983, Apr. 19 Engr. *Perf. 13*
1367 A405 10fr black 8.25 8.25

Europa — A406

1983, Apr. 27 *Perf. 12½x13*
1368 A406 1.80fr Montgolfiere balloon flight, 1783 1.75 *.35*
1369 A406 2.60fr Columbia space shuttle 1.75 *.50*
a. Souv. sheet, 5 ea #1368-1369 20.00 *8.00*

St. Charles' Church, Monte Carlo, Cent. — A407

1983, Apr. 27 Engr.
1370 A407 2.60fr St. Charles Borromeo 1.00 .90

Franciscan College Centenary A408

1983, Apr. 27 *Perf. 13x12½*
1371 A408 2fr Church, medallion .90 .70

Fontvielle Stadium Interior — A409

1983, Apr. 28 *Perf. 13*
1372 A409 2fr multicolored .90 .70

Automobile Centenary — A410

1983, Apr. 27
1373 A410 2.90fr Benz, 1883, Formula One racer 3.25 1.90

Save the Whales Campaign — A411

1983, Apr. 27
1374 A411 3.30fr Blue whale 3.75 3.00

World Communications Year — A412

1983, Apr. 27
1375 A412 4fr lil rose & brn vio 1.60 1.20

Souvenir Sheet

Fig Branch in Spring A413

1983, Nov. 9 Engr. *Perf. 13x12½*
1376 Sheet of 4 8.00 8.00
a. A413 1fr shown .75 .75
b. A413 2fr Summer 1.40 1.40
c. A413 3fr Autumn 2.25 2.25
d. A413 4fr Winter 2.75 2.75

Exotic Plant Type of 1980

1983, Nov. 9 Photo. *Perf. 13*
1380 A359 2fr Argyroderma roseum 1.75 .65

Belle Epoch Type of 1982

Paintings by Hubert Clerissi: 3fr, Thermes Valentia from the Beach, 1902. 5fr, Cafe de Paris and Place du Casino, 1905.

1983, Nov. 9 Engr. *Perf. 13x12½*
1385 A394 3fr multicolored 3.00 2.40
1386 A394 5fr multicolored 4.25 3.50

Portrait of a Young Man, by Raphael (1483-1520) — A414

Passage Cottin, by Maurice Utrillo (1883-1955) — A415

1983, Nov. 9 Engr. *Perf. 13*
1387 A414 4fr multicolored 3.25 2.40
1388 A415 4fr multicolored 3.25 2.40

Johannes Brahms (1833-1897), Composer — A416

#1390, Giacomo Puccini (1858-1924), composer, scene from Madame Butterfly.

1983, Nov. 9 Engr. *Perf. 13½x13*
1389 A416 3fr multicolored 1.40 1.20
1390 A416 3fr multicolored 1.60 1.20

9th Intl. Circus Festival, Monte Carlo, Dec. 8-12 — A417

1983, Nov. 9 *Perf. 13*
1391 A417 2fr multicolored 1.75 1.40

Intl. Flower Show, Monte Carlo — A418

1983, Nov. 9 Photo.
1392 A418 1.60fr Pansies, convolvulus, carnations 1.50 1.00
1393 A418 2.60fr Oriental poppies 2.25 1.50

Christmas 1983 — A419

1983, Nov. 9 Photo.
1394 A419 2fr Provencal creche figures 1.60 1.10

Alfred Nobel (1833-1896), Literature Medal — A420

1983, Nov. 9 Engr.
1395 A420 2fr multicolored 1.00 .80

Sesquicentenary of Society of St. Vincent de Paul — A421

1983, Nov. 9 Engr.
1396 A421 1.80fr F. Ozanam, founder, Paris headquarters 1.00 .60

A422

1983, Nov. 9

1397 A422 5fr Offshore petroleum plant 2.25 1.25

19th Cent. Figurines, Galea Toy Collection A423

1983, Nov. 9 Photo. ***Perf. 12½x13***

1398	A423	50c	Water pipe smoker	.25	.25
1399	A423	60c	Clown with yo-yo	.40	.25
1400	A423	70c	Smoking monkey	.40	.25
1401	A423	80c	Farmer and pig	.50	.50
1402	A423	90c	Buffalo Bill	.60	.60
1403	A423	1fr	Snake charmer	.60	.60
1404	A423	1.50fr	Piano and harp player	1.00	.80
1405	A423	2fr	Girl powdering her face	1.75	1.00
			Nos. 1398-1405 (8)	5.50	4.25

Quince Branch in Spring A424

1984, May 10 Photo. ***Perf. 13x12½***

1406	A424	1.14fr	shown	.80	.50
1407	A424	1.47fr	Summer	.85	.60
1408	A424	2.38fr	Autumn	1.50	1.00
1409	A424	3.95fr	Winter	1.90	1.50
			Nos. 1406-1409 (4)	5.05	3.60

Issued precanceled only. See note after No. 324.

Place de la Visitation, by Hubert Clerissi — A425

Drawings by Hubert Clerissi: 10c, Town Hall. 15c, Rue Basse. 20c, Place Saint-Nicolas. 30c, Quai du Commerce. 40c, Rue des Iris. 3fr, Bandstand. 6fr, Opera House.

1984, May 10 Engr. ***Perf. 12½x13***

1410	A425	5c	brown	.20	.20
1411	A425	10c	claret	.20	.20
1412	A425	15c	violet	.20	.20
1413	A425	20c	dark blue	.25	.20
1414	A425	30c	deep blue	.25	.20
1415	A425	40c	dark green	.70	.25
1416	A425	3fr	red brown	2.25	.90
1417	A425	6fr	yellow green	1.25	1.10
			Nos. 1410-1417 (8)	5.30	3.25

See #1516-1524, 1750-1755, 1821-1825.

Souvenir Sheet

1984 Los Angeles Olympics A426

Rhythmic Gymnastics.

1984, May 10 ***Perf. 13***

1418	Sheet of 4	7.50	7.50
a.	A426 2fr Ball	.95	.95
b.	A426 3fr Clubs	1.40	1.40
c.	A426 4fr Ribbon	1.75	1.75
d.	A426 5fr Hoop	2.40	2.40

1984 Winter Olympics — A427

1984, May 10

1422	A427	2fr	Rink, speed skater	.90	.55
1423	A427	4fr	Skater, snowflake	1.60	1.10

Europa (1959-84) A428

1984, May 10 ***Perf. 13x12½***

1424	A428	2fr blue	1.50	*.40*
1425	A428	3fr yel grn	2.50	*.85*
a.		Souv. sheet, 4 ea #1424-1425	*20.00*	8.50

Butterflies and Rare Flowers, Mercantour Natl. Park A429

1.60fr, Boloria graeca tendensis, ranunculus montanus. 2fr, Zygaena vesubiana, saxifraga aizoides. 2.80fr, Erebia aethiopella, myosotis alpestris. 3fr, Parnassius phoebus gazeli, rhododendron ferrugineum. 3.60fr, Papilio alexanor, myrrhis odorata. Nos. 1426-1428 vert.

Perf. 12½x13, 13x12½

1984, May 10 Photo.

1426	A429	1.60fr	multicolored	1.50	1.25
1427	A429	2fr	multicolored	2.40	1.40
1428	A429	2.80fr	multicolored	2.25	1.75
1429	A429	3fr	multicolored	3.00	2.25
1430	A429	3.60fr	multicolored	4.00	2.50
			Nos. 1426-1430 (5)	13.15	9.15

Monte Carlo Dog Show Type

1984, May 10 ***Perf. 13x12½***

1431 A387 1.60fr Auvergne pointer 4.00 2.50

Sanctuary of Our Lady of Laghet — A431

1984, May 10 Engr. ***Perf. 12½x13***

1432 A431 2fr Statue, rosary, pilgrimage sanctuary .90 .45

Auguste Piccard, Birth Cent. — A432

1984, May 10

1433	A432	2.80fr	Stratosphere balloon	1.10	.60
1434	A432	4fr	Bathyscaphe	1.50	.85

25th Anniv. of Princely Palace Concerts A433

1984, May 10 ***Perf. 13x12½***

1435 A433 3.60fr Orchestra 1.60 .90

Belle Epoch Type of 1982

Paintings by Hubert Clerissi: 4fr, Rue Grimaldi, 1908. 5fr, Train Entering Monte Carlo Station, 1910.

1984, Nov. 8 Engr. ***Perf. 12½x13***

1436	A394	4fr multicolored	3.50	2.40
1437	A394	5fr multicolored	5.50	3.75

25th Intl. Television Festival, Monte Carlo, Feb. 1985 — A434

1984, Nov. 8 Engr. ***Perf. 13***

1438	A434	2.10fr	Lights	1.00	.60
1439	A434	3fr	Golden nymph (prize)	1.40	.85

Intl. Flower Show, Monte Carlo — A435

1984, Nov. 8 Photo. ***Perf. 12½x13***

1440	A435	2.10fr	Mixed bouquet	1.60	1.00
1441	A435	3fr	Ikebana	2.40	1.25

See Nos. 1491-1492, 1552-1553.

Pharmaceuticals, Cosmetics Industry — A436

1984, Nov. 8 Engr. ***Perf. 13***

1442 A436 2.40fr multicolored 1.10 .85

Illustration from Gargantua, by Rabelais — A437

Francois Rabelais (1490-1553), 17th Cent. Drawing — A438

1984, Nov. 8 ***Perf. 13x12½, 12½x13***

1443	A437	2fr	With animals	1.10	.60
1444	A437	2fr	With sheep of Panurge	1.10	.60
1445	A438	4fr	multicolored	2.50	1.25
			Nos. 1443-1445 (3)	4.70	2.45

Souvenir Sheet

PRINCIPAUTÉ DE MONACO

10ᵉ festival international du cirque de Monte-Carlo

10th Intl. Circus Festival, Dec. 6-10 — A439

1984, Nov. 8 Photo. ***Perf. 13***

1446 A439 5fr Poster 4.00 4.00

La Femme a la Potiche, by Degas A440

1984, Nov. 8 Engr. ***Perf. 12x13***

1447 A440 6fr multicolored 5.00 2.75

Christmas 1984 — A441

Figurines from Provence.

1984, Nov. 8 ***Perf. 12½x13***

1448	A441	70c	Shepherd	.45	.40
1449	A441	1fr	Blind man	.55	.50
1450	A441	1.70fr	Happy man	1.20	1.00
1451	A441	2fr	Woman spinning	1.25	1.10
1452	A441	2.10fr	Angel	1.40	1.20
1453	A441	2.40fr	Garlic seller	1.60	1.40
1454	A441	3fr	Drummer	1.90	1.60
1455	A441	3.70fr	Knife grinder	2.40	2.00

1456 A441 4fr Elderly couple 2.75 2.40
Nos. 1448-1456 (9) 13.50 11.60

See Nos. 1737-1739, 1766-1768, 1838-1840, 1883-1885, 1919-1921, 1976-1978.

Cherry Tree A442

1985, Mar. 1 Engr. *Perf. 13*

1457 A442 1.22fr Spring .80 .50
1458 A442 1.57fr Summer 1.00 .60
1459 A442 2.55fr Fall 1.60 1.10
1460 A442 4.23fr Winter 2.10 1.75
Nos. 1457-1460 (4) 5.50 3.95

Issued precanceled only. See note after No. 324.

No. 1 in Green A443

1985, Mar. 25

1461 A443 1.70fr shown .85 .50
1462 A443 2.10fr #1 in scarlet 1.00 .25
1463 A443 3fr #1 in lt peacock bl 1.20 .85
Nos. 1461-1463 (3) 3.05 1.60

Stamp centenary, Natl. Stamp Exhibition, Dec. 5-8, Monte Carlo.

Europa 1985 — A444

Portraits: 2.10fr Prince Antoine I (1661-1731), Founder of Monaco Palace, music library. 3fr, Jean-Baptiste Lully (1632-1687), composer, violinist, superintendent of music to King Louis XIV.

1985, May 23 *Perf. 12½x13*

1464 A444 2.10fr brt blue 1.75 *.50*
1465 A444 3fr dark carmine 3.00 *.75*
a. Souv. sheet, 5 #1464, 5 #1465 *25.00 15.00*

Flowers in Mercantour Park A444a

Perf. 13x12½, 12½x13

1985, May 23 Photo.

1466 A444a 1.70fr Berardia subacaulis .85 .80
1467 A444a 2.10fr Saxifraga florulenta, vert. 1.00 .85
1468 A444a 2.40fr Fritillaria moggridgei, vert. 1.20 1.00
1469 A444a 3fr Sempervivum allionii, vert. 1.75 1.20
1470 A444a 3.60fr Silene cordifolia, vert. 2.40 1.60
1471 A444a 4fr Primula allionii 3.00 2.00
Nos. 1466-1471 (6) 10.20 7.45

Japanese Medlar A445

1985, May 23 Engr. *Perf. 13x12½*

1472 Sheet of 4 6.50 6.50
a. A445 1fr Spring .55 .55
b. A445 2fr Summer 1.25 1.25
c. A445 3fr Autumn 1.90 1.90
d. A445 4fr Winter 2.40 2.40

Nadia Boulanger (1887-1979), Musician, Composer, Conductor A446

Portraits, manuscripts and music: 2.10fr, Georges Auric (1899-1983), composer of film, ballet music, Music Foundation council president.

1985, May 23 *Perf. 13*

1473 A446 1.70fr brown 1.00 .60
1474 A446 2.10fr brt ultra 1.25 .90

Prince Pierre de Monaco Music Foundation composition prize, 25th anniv.

Natl. Oceanographic Museum, 75th Anniv. — A447

1985, May 23

1475 A447 2.10fr brt bl, grn & blk 1.00 .80

Graphs, Fish, Molecular Structures, Lab Apparatus — A448

1985, May 23

1476 A448 3fr dk bl grn, blk & dk rose lil 1.25 .70

Prince Rainier III Scientific Research Center, 25th anniv.

Intl. Athletic Championships, May 25-26 — A449

1985, May 23

1477 A449 1.70fr Running .70 .55
1478 A449 2.10fr Swimming 1.00 .55

Opening of Louis II Stadium, May 25.

Monte Carlo Dog Show Type

1985, May 3 Photo. *Perf. 13x12½*

1479 A387 2.10fr Boxer 3.25 2.00

Intl. Youth Year A450

1985, May 23 Engr. *Perf. 13*

1480 A450 3fr fawn, sepia & dp grn 1.25 .75

Fish, Natl. Oceanographic Museum Aquarium A451

1985, Aug. 13 Photo. *Perf. 12½x13*

1481 A451 1.80fr Pygoplites diacanthus 1.40 1.10
1482 A451 2.20fr Acanthurus leucosternon 1.40 1.10
1483 A451 3.20fr Chaetodon collare 2.25 1.60
1484 A451 3.90fr Balistoides conspicillum 2.75 2.25

Size: 40x52mm

Perf. 13

1485 A451 7fr Aquarium 4.75 3.50
Nos. 1481-1485 (5) 12.55 9.55

See Nos. 1560-1561, 1610-1615.

Souvenir Sheet

Transatlantic Yachting Race, Oct. 13 — A452

Yacht classes: a, Catamaran. b, Monocoque. c, Trimaran.

1985, Oct. Engr. *Perf. 13*

1486 Sheet of 3 6.00 6.00
a.-c. A452 4fr, any single 1.75 1.75

Monaco-New York competition.

ITALIA '85, Rome, Oct. 25-Nov. 3 — A453

Design: Exhibition emblem, St. Peter's Cathedral and Temple of Castor ruins.

1985, Oct. 25 *Perf. 13½x13*

1487 A453 4fr int blk, brt grn & red rose 1.75 1.00

Belle Epoch Type of 1982

Illustrations by Hubert Clerissi.

1985, Nov. 7 Engr. *Perf. 13x12½*

1488 A394 4fr Port of Monaco, 1912 3.00 1.75
1489 A394 6fr La Gare Vers Avenue, 1920 3.50 3.00

11th Intl. Circus Festival, Dec. 5-9 — A454

1985, Nov. 7 Photo. *Perf. 13*

1490 A454 1.80fr multi 1.50 1.10

Intl. Flower Show Type of 1984

1985, Nov. 7

1491 A435 2.20fr Roses, tulips, jonquils 1.40 1.00
1492 A435 3.20fr Ikebana of chrysanthemums, bryony 2.10 1.90

Dated 1986.

Factory, Ship, Fish, Crustaceans A455

1985, Nov. 7 Engr. *Perf. 13x13½*

1493 A455 2.20fr brt bl, dp brn & dk grnsh bl 1.00 .60

Monagasque fishing industry, Fontvieille District. See No. 1555.

Christmas 1985 — A456

1985, Nov. 7 Photo. *Perf. 12½x13*

1494 A456 2.20fr multi 1.25 .50

EUTELSAT Orbiting Earth — A457

1985, Nov. 7 Engr. *Perf. 13*

1495 A457 3fr int blk, dp rose lil & dk bl 1.40 1.00

European Telecommunications Satellite Org.

Sacha Guitry (1885-1957), Actor, Dramatist — A458

Authors, composers: 4fr, Brothers Grimm. 5fr, Frederic Chopin and Robert Schumann, composers. 6fr, Johann Sebastian Bach and George Frideric Handel, composers.

1985, Nov. 7

1496 A458 3fr brn blk & gldn brn 1.50 1.20
1497 A458 4fr dp rose lil, sep & turq bl 2.00 1.20
1498 A458 5fr stl bl, dp bl & grnsh bl 2.50 1.90
1499 A458 6fr blk, brn & stl bl 3.00 2.40
Nos. 1496-1499 (4) 9.00 6.70

Souvenir Sheet

Natl. Postage Stamp Cent. — A459

Altered designs: a, Type A1. b, Type A2. c, Type A13. d, Type A83.

1985, Dec. 5

1500 Sheet of 4 8.00 8.00
a.-d. A459 5fr, any single 2.00 2.00

Rainier and Albert Type of 1981-84

1985-88 Engr. *Perf. 13*

1505 A370 1.80fr brt grn 1.10 .25
1506 A370 1.90fr ol grn ('86) 1.90 .55
1507 A370 2fr emer grn ('87) 1.25 .25
1508 A370 2.20fr red rose 1.25 .20
1509 A370 2.50fr dk brn 1.50 .75
1510 A370 3.20fr brt bl 2.75 2.25
1511 A370 3.40fr ind ('86) 4.25 2.25
1512 A370 3.60fr dp ultra ('87) 2.75 1.25
1513 A370 10fr claret ('86) 4.75 1.10
1514 A370 15fr dk bl grn ('86) 9.25 2.25
1515 A370 20fr brt blue ('88) 11.00 2.75
Nos. 1505-1515 (11) 41.75 13.85

Views of Old Monaco Type of 1984

Illustrations by Hubert Clerissi: 50c, Port of Monaco. 60c, St. Charles Church. 70c, Promenade. 80c, Harbor, olive trees. 90c, Quay. 1fr, Palace Square. 2fr, Ships, harbor mouth. 4fr, Monaco Tram Station. 5fr, Mail coach.

1986, Jan. 23

1516 A425 50c red .25 .20
1517 A425 60c Prus blue .25 .20
1518 A425 70c orange .55 .35
1519 A425 80c brt yel grn .35 .25
1520 A425 90c rose violet .35 .25
1521 A425 1fr brt blue .45 .20
1522 A425 2fr black .95 .45
1523 A425 4fr ultramarine 1.90 .75
1524 A425 5fr olive green 2.40 .75
Nos. 1516-1524 (9) 7.45 3.40

Hazel Nut Tree A460

1986, Feb. 24 Engr. *Perf. 13x12½*

1525 A460 1.28fr Spring .70 .45
1526 A460 1.65fr Summer .90 .55
1527 A460 2.67fr Fall 1.40 1.00
1528 A460 4.44fr Winter 2.00 1.60
Nos. 1525-1528 (4) 5.00 3.60

Nos. 1525-1528 known only precanceled. See note after No. 324.

See Nos. 1580-1583, 1616-1619, 1685-1688, 1719-1722, 1809-1812.

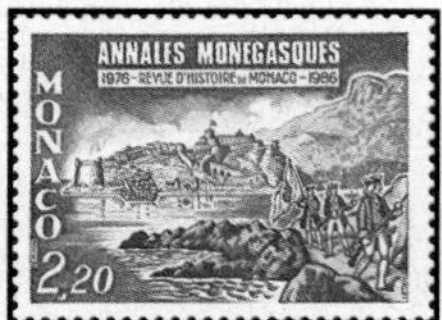

Port of Monaco, 18th Cent. A461

1986, Feb. 24

1529 A461 2.20fr ultra, gray & brown 1.10 .45

Publication of Annales Monegasques, 10th anniv.

Europa 1986 — A462

1986, May 22 Engr. *Perf. 12½x13*

1530 A462 2.20fr Ramoge Nature Protection Treaty 1.75 *.40*
1531 A462 3.20fr Natl. marine reserve 2.25 *.75*
a. Souv. sheet, 5 each #1530-1531 25.00 *14.00*

Souvenir Sheet

1986 World Cup Soccer Championships, Mexico — A463

1986, May 22

1532 Sheet of 2 6.50 6.50
a. A463 5fr Player 2.50 2.50
b. A463 7fr Goalie 3.50 3.50

Ovis Musimon A464

1986, May 22 *Perf. 13x12½*

1533 A464 2.20fr shown 1.25 .60
1534 A464 2.50fr Capra ibex 1.25 1.00
1535 A464 3.20fr Rupicapra rupicapra 1.75 1.60
1536 A464 3.90fr Marmota marmota 2.50 2.00
1537 A464 5fr Lepus timidus varronis 3.00 2.75
1538 A464 7.20fr Mustela erminea 3.75 3.25
Nos. 1533-1538 (6) 13.50 11.20

Nos. 1536-1538 vert.

Monte Carlo Dog Show Type

1986, May 22 Photo. *Perf. 13x12½*

1539 A387 1.80fr Terriers 5.00 3.25

Prince Albert I, Parliament — A465

1986, May 22 *Perf. 13*

1540 A465 2.50fr brn & ol grn 1.10 .75

First Constitution, 75th anniv.

Serge Diaghilev, Founder — A466

1986, May 22 *Perf. 13*

1541 A466 3.20fr brn blk, carm rose & blk 1.90 1.60

Diaghilev's first permanent ballet company, 75th anniv., and creation of Monte Carlo Ballet Company, 1986.

1st Monte Carlo Auto Rally, 75 Anniv. — A467

Winner Henri Rougier and Turcat-Mery, 1911.

1986, May 22

1542 A467 3.90fr rose mag & car 2.50 2.00

Statue of Liberty, Cent. — A468

1986, May 22

1543 A468 5fr multi 2.00 1.40

Halley's Comet — A469

1986, May 22

1544 A469 10fr Sightings, 1986, 1352 4.25 3.00

AMERIPEX '86, Chicago, May 22-June 1 — A470

1986, May 22

1545 A470 5fr US flag, skyline 2.00 1.20

Belle Epoch Type of 1982

Illustrations by Hubert Clerissi.

1986, Oct. 28 Engr. *Perf. 12½x13*

1546 A394 6fr Pavilion, 1920, vert. 4.00 2.40
1547 A394 7fr Beau Rivage Avenue, 1925, vert. 5.75 3.00

Premiere of El Cid, by Pierre Corneille, 350th Anniv. — A471

1986, Oct. 28 Engr. *Perf. 13*

1548 A471 4fr Scenes 1.75 1.20

Franz Liszt, Composer — A472

1986, Oct. 28

1549 A472 5fr dk red brn & brt ultra 2.00 1.40

The Olympic Swimmer, 1961, by Emma de Sigaldi A473

1986, Oct. 28 *Perf. 12½x13*

1550 A473 6fr multi 2.50 1.60

Intl. Insurers Congress, Monte Carlo, Sept. 30 — A474

1986, Oct. 28 *Perf. 13½x13*

1551 A474 3.20fr brn, dp grn & brt bl 1.50 1.00

Intl. Flower Show Type of 1984

2.20fr, Bouquet of roses, acidenthera. 3.90fr, Ikebana of lilies, beech branches.

1986, Oct. 28 Photo. *Perf. 12½x13*

1552 A435 2.20fr multi 1.90 .80
1553 A435 3.90fr multi 2.75 1.75

Dated 1987.

12th Intl. Circus Festival, Dec. 4-8 — A475

1986, Oct. 28 *Perf. 13*

1554 A475 2.20fr multi 1.75 1.00

Industries Type of 1985

Design: 3.90fr, Plastics industry.

1986, Oct. 28 Engr.

1555 A455 3.90fr dk red, dk gray & bl grn 1.75 1.20

Christmas A476

1986, Oct. 28 Photo. *Perf. 12½x13*

1556 A476 1.80fr Holly .85 .30
1557 A476 2.50fr Poinsettia 1.25 .50

Ascent of Mt. Blanc by J. Balmat and M.G. Paccard, Bicent. — A477

1986, Oct. 28 Engr. *Perf. 13*
1558 A477 5.80fr red, brt bl & slate bl 2.50 1.75

Miniature Sheet

Arbutus Tree A478

1986, Oct. 28 *Perf. 13x12½*
1559 Sheet of 4 9.50 9.50
a. A478 3fr Spring 1.25 1.25
b. A478 4fr Summer 1.90 1.90
c. A478 5fr Fall 2.75 2.75
d. A478 6fr Winter 2.50 2.50

See Nos. 1645, 1680, 1736, 1775, 1804, 1852, 1934, 1943.

Aquarium Type of 1985

1986, Sept. 25 Photo. *Perf. 12½x13*
1560 A451 1.90fr like No. 1481 2.25 1.00
1561 A451 3.40fr like No. 1483 4.00 2.50

Prince Rainier III — A479

Villa Miraflores, Seat of the Philatelic Bureau — A480

#1562b, Prince Louis II, founder of the bureau.

1987, Apr. 23 Engr. *Perf. 12½x13*
1562 Strip of 3 8.50 8.50
a. A479 4fr bright blue 1.90 1.90
b. A479 4fr dark red 1.90 1.90
c. A480 8fr multi 3.75 3.75

Philatelic Bureau, 50th anniv.
See No. 1607.

Louis II Stadium A481

1987, Apr. 23 *Perf. 13x12½*
1563 A481 2.20fr Exterior 1.75 *.40*
1564 A481 3.40fr Interior 2.00 *.75*
a. Min. sheet, 5 each #1563-1564 25.00 *13.00*

Europa 1987.

Insects — A482

1987, Apr. 23 Photo.
1565 A482 1fr Carabe de solier .55 .55
1566 A482 1.90fr Guepe dorec 1.00 .90
1567 A482 2fr Cicindele 1.25 1.00
1568 A482 2.20fr Grande aeschne 1.50 1.00
1569 A482 3fr Chrysomele 2.40 1.75
1570 A482 3.40fr Grande sauterelle verte 3.25 2.50
Nos. 1565-1570 (6) 9.95 7.70

Nos. 1565, 1567 and 1569 horiz.

St. Devote Parish, Cent. — A483

1987, Apr. 23 Engr. *Perf. 12½x13*
1571 A483 1.90fr black .90 .45

Monaco Diocese, Cent. — A484

1987, Apr. 23
1572 A484 2.50fr dk yellow grn 1.00 .55

50th Intl. Dog Show, Monte Carlo A485

1987, Apr. 23 *Perf. 13x12½*
1573 A485 1.90fr Dog breeds 2.00 1.25
1574 A485 2.70fr Poodle 3.50 1.90

Stamp Day — A486

1987, Apr. 23 *Perf. 13*
1575 A486 2.20fr multi 1.00 .45

Red Curley Tail, Mobile by Alexander Calder (1898-1976), Sculptor — A487

1987, Apr. 23 Photo.
1576 A487 3.70fr multi 1.60 1.00

Sculpture Exhibition, Monte Carlo.

2nd Small European Countries Games, May 14-17 — A488

1987, Apr. 23 Engr.
1577 A488 3fr Tennis 2.00 1.60
1578 A488 5fr Windsurfing 2.50 1.75

Miniature Sheet

Grape Vines A489

1987, Apr. 23 *Perf. 13x12½*
1579 Sheet of 4 12.00 12.00
a. A489 3fr Spring 1.60 1.60
b. A489 4fr Summer 2.25 2.25
c. A489 5fr Autumn 3.25 3.25
d. A489 6fr Winter 3.75 3.75

Four Seasons Type of 1986

Life cycle of the chestnut tree.

1987, Mar. 17 Engr. *Perf. 13x12½*
1580 A460 1.31fr Spring .70 .45
1581 A460 1.69fr Summer .90 .70
1582 A460 2.74fr Fall 1.40 1.10
1583 A460 4.56fr Winter 2.00 1.60
Nos. 1580-1583 (4) 5.00 3.85

Nos. 1580-1583 known only precanceled. See note after No. 324.

The Life of St. Devote, Patron Saint of Monaco A490

Text: 4fr, Born in 283, in Quercio, Devote was martyred in Mariana, Corsica. 5fr, Devote's nurse teaches the saint about Christianity.

1987, Nov. 13 Photo. *Perf. 13x12½*
1584 A490 4fr multi 1.90 .85
1585 A490 5fr multi 2.40 1.40

Red Cross of Monaco.
See Nos. 1643-1644, 1692-1693, 1714-1715, 1776-1777, 1836-1837.

Philately A491

Butterflies and butterflies on simulated stamps.

1987, July 28 Engr.
1586 A491 1.90fr brt grn & dk gray .90 .40
1587 A491 2.20fr rose red & rose lake .95 .50
1588 A491 2.50fr red lil & vio 1.25 .80
1589 A491 3.40fr brt bl & bluish blk 1.90 .85
Nos. 1586-1589 (4) 5.00 2.55

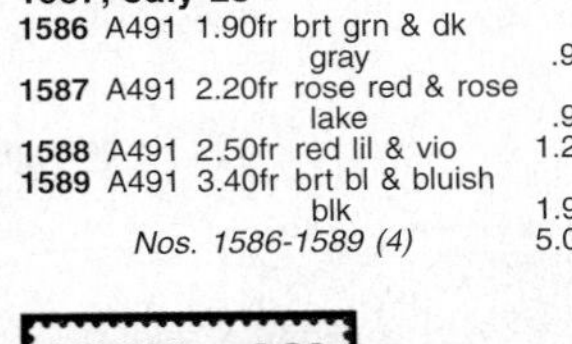

13th Int'l. Circus Festival, Monte Carlo, Jan. 28-Feb. 1 — A492

1987, Nov. 13 Photo. *Perf. 12½x13*
1590 A492 2.20fr multi 2.10 1.00

1988 Int'l Flower Show — A493

1987, Nov. 13
1591 A493 2.20fr Ikebanas 1.25 .60
1592 A493 3.40fr multi, horiz. 2.10 1.20

Dated 1988. See Nos. 1651, 1749.

Christmas A494

1987, Nov. 13 Engr. *Perf. 13x12½*
1593 A494 2.20fr crimson 1.00 .50

5-Franc Prince Honoré V Coin A495

1987, Nov. 13 *Perf. 13*
1594 A495 2.50fr scar & dk gray 1.10 .45

Recapture of the Mint, 150th anniv.

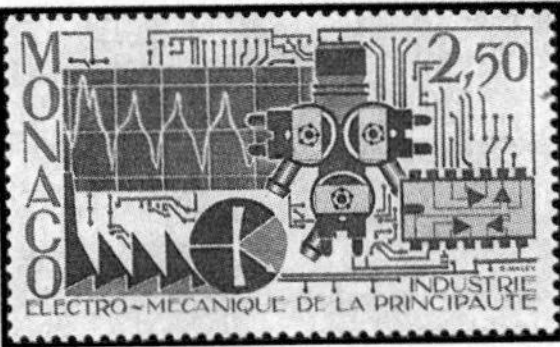
Electronics Industry — A496

1987, Nov. 13
1595 A496 2.50fr henna brn, vio bl & grn 1.10 .80

Int'l. Marine Radioactivity Laboratory, 25th Anniv. — A497

Design: Monaco Oceanographic Museum and Int'l. Agency of Atomic Energy, Vienna.

1987, Nov. 13

1596 A497 5fr brt bl, red brn & blk 2.25 1.40

Louis Jouvet (b.1887), French Actor A498

1987, Nov. 16 ***Perf. 13x12½***

1597 A498 3fr black 1.25 1.10

A499

1987, Nov. 16

1598 A499 3fr The River Crossing 1.25 1.10

Paul and Virginia, by Bernardin de Saint-Pierre, first edition bcent. (in 1988).

Marc Chagall (1887-1985), Painter — A500

1987, Nov. 16 ***Perf. 13***

1599 A500 4fr terra cotta & bl gray 2.25 1.25

Jean Jenneret (Le Corbusier, 1887-1965), French Architect — A501

1987, Nov. 16

1600 A501 4fr Architect, Ronchamp Chapel 1.90 1.20

Newton's Theory of Gravity, 300th Anniv. — A502

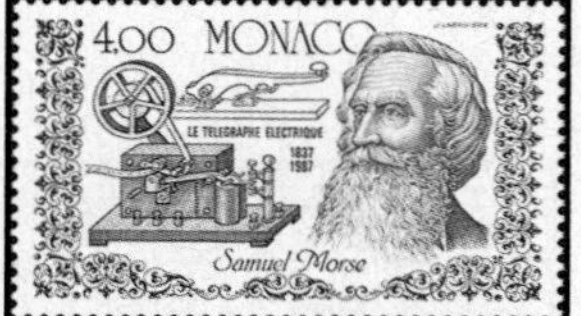

Invention of the Telegraph by Samuel Morse, 150th Anniv. — A503

1987, Nov. 16

1601 A502 4fr magenta & dk bl 2.10 1.10

1602 A503 4fr brt vio, turq bl & brn 2.10 1.10

Don Juan, Opera by Mozart, Bicent. — A504

Mass of the Dead, by Berlioz — A505

1987, Nov. 16

1603 A504 5fr ind, vio brn & sage grn 2.50 1.50

1604 A505 5fr sl grn, vio brn & bl 2.50 1.50

Belle Epoch Type of 1982

Illustrations by Hubert Clerissi. 6fr, 7fr vert.

1987, Nov. 16 Engr. ***Perf. 12½x13***

1605 A394 6fr Rampe Major 3.75 2.50

1606 A394 7fr Old Monte Carlo Station 5.00 3.75

Philatelic Bureau Type of 1987

1987, Nov. 13 Engr. ***Perf. 12½x13***

1607 Sheet of 3 8.00 8.00
- *a.* A479 4fr blk vio, like #1562a 1.90 1.90
- *b.* A479 4fr blk vio, like #1562b 1.90 1.90
- *c.* A480 8fr blk vio, like #1562c 3.75 3.75

Postage Due Arms Type of 1985 Booklet Stamps

1987-88 Photo. ***Perf. 13 on 3 Sides***

Size: 17x23mm

1608 D10 2fr multi ('88) 1.00 .40
- *a.* Bklt. pane of 10 11.00

1609 D10 2.20fr multi 1.00 .60
- *a.* Bklt. pane of 10 11.00

Issued: 2fr, Jan. 15; 2.20fr, Nov. 13.

Aquarium Type of 1985

Perf. 13x12½, 12½x13

1988, Jan. 15 Photo.

1610 A451 2fr Bodianus rufus 1.25 .80

1611 A451 2.20fr Chelmon rostratus 1.75 .50

1612 A451 2.50fr Oxymonacanthus longirostris 2.00 1.10

1613 A451 3fr Ostracion lentiginosum 1.50 .80

1614 A451 3.70fr Pterois volitans 2.50 2.10

1615 A451 7fr Thalassoma lunare, horiz. 3.50 2.25

Nos. 1610-1615 (6) 12.50 7.55

Four Seasons Type of 1986

Life cycle of the pear tree.

1988, Feb. 15 ***Perf. 13x12½***

1616 A460 1.36fr Spring .70 .45

1617 A460 1.75fr Summer .90 .70

1618 A460 2.83fr Fall 1.40 1.10

1619 A460 4.72fr Winter 2.00 1.60

Nos. 1616-1619 (4) 5.00 3.85

Nos. 1616-1619 known only precanceled. See note after No. 324.

Souvenir Sheet

Biathlon, 1988 Winter Olympics, Calgary — A506

1988, Feb. 15 Engr. ***Perf. 13***

1620 Sheet of 2 13.50 13.50
- *a.* A506 4fr Skiing 5.75 5.75
- *b.* A506 6fr Shooting 6.75 6.75

51st Intl. Dog Show, Monte Carlo — A507

1988, Mar. 30 Photo. ***Perf. 12½x13***

1621 A507 3fr Dachshunds 3.00 2.00

World Assoc. of the Friends of Children (AMADE), 25th Anniv. A508

1988, Mar. 30 Engr. ***Perf. 13***

1622 A508 5fr dark vio blue, dark brn & brt olive grn 2.50 1.75

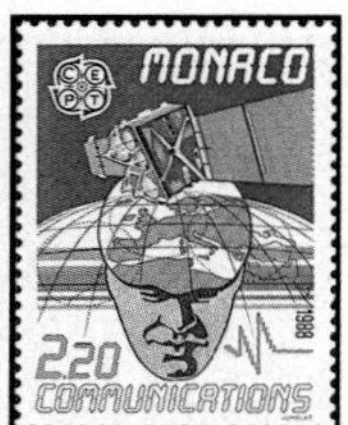

Europa 1988 — A509

Transport and communication: 2.20fr, Globe picturing hemispheres, man, brain, telecommunications satellite. 3.60fr, Plane propeller and high-speed locomotive.

1988, Apr. 21 ***Perf. 12½x13***

1623 A509 2.20fr multi *1.50 .50*

1624 A509 3.60fr multi *2.75 1.00*
- *a.* Souv. sheet, 5 each #1623-1624 *27.50 12.50*

Mushrooms of Mercantour Natl. Park A510

Perf. 13x12½, 12½x13

1988, May 26 Photo.

1625 A510 2fr Leccinum rotundifoliae 1.25 .90

1626 A510 2.20fr Hygrocybe punicea 1.50 .85

1627 A510 2.50fr Pholiota flammans 1.60 1.50

1628 A510 2.70fr Lactarius lignyotus 2.10 1.75

1629 A510 3fr Cortinarius traganus 2.50 2.25

1630 A510 7fr Russula olivacea 4.50 4.25

Nos. 1625-1630 (6) 13.45 11.50

Nos. 1629-1630 vert.

Nautical Soc., Cent. — A511

1988, May 26 Engr. ***Perf. 13***

1631 A511 2fr dk red, lt blue & dk grn 1.10 .70

5th Year of Restoration of Our Lady of Laghet Sanctuary A512

1988, May 26 ***Perf. 12½***

1632 A512 5fr multicolored 2.50 1.40

World Health Organization, 40th Anniv. — A513

1988, May 26 ***Perf. 13***

1633 A513 6fr brt blue & lake 2.75 1.75

Intl. Red Cross and Red Crescent Organizations, 125th Annivs. — A514

1988, May 26 Photo. ***Perf. 13x12½***

1634 A514 6fr dull red, blk & gray 2.75 1.75

Jean Monnet (1888-1979), Nobel Peace Prize Winner in 1922 — A515

Maurice Chevalier (1888-1972), Actor — A516

1988, May 26 Engr. ***Perf. 12½x13***

1635 A515 2fr brt blue, dark olive bister & blk 3.50 1.75

1636 A516 2fr blk & dark blue 3.75 1.75

1st Crossing of Greenland by Fridtjof Nansen (1861-1930), Cent. — A517

1988, May 26 *Perf. 13*

1637 A517 4fr bright violet 2.10 1.60

Belle Epoch Type of 1982

Illustrations by Hubert Clerissi.

1988, Sept. 8 Engr. *Perf. 13x12½*

1638 A394 6fr Packet in Monte Carlo Harbor, 1910 4.00 2.50
1639 A394 7fr Monte Carlo Station, c. 1910 4.50 3.25

Souvenir Sheet

1988 Summer Olympics, Seoul A518

Woman wearing Korean regional costume, Games emblem and event: 2fr, Women's tennis. 3fr, Women's table tennis. 5fr, Women's yachting. 7fr, Women's cycling.

1988, Sept. 8 **Engr.**

1640 Sheet of 4 9.50 9.50
a. A518 2fr blk, light ultra & brown 1.10 1.10
b. A518 3fr blk, light ultra & brown 1.40 1.40
c. A518 5fr blk, light ultra & brown 2.40 2.40
d. A518 7fr blk, light ultra & brown 3.25 3.25

Monte Carlo Congress Center, 10th Anniv. — A519

1988, Sept. 8 *Perf. 13*

1641 2fr dark blue grn 1.00 1.00
1642 3fr henna brn 1.25 1.25
a. A519 Pair, #1641-1642 2.50 2.50

Monegasque Red Cross Type of 1987

The Life of St. Devote, patron saint of Monaco: 4fr, Devote witnessing the arrival of the governor of Rome. 5fr, Devote and the governor.

1988, Oct. 20 Photo. *Perf. 13x12½*

1643 A490 4fr multicolored 2.00 1.00
1644 A490 5fr multicolored 2.50 1.50

Tree Type of 1986

Life cycle of the olive tree.

1988, Oct. 20 Engr. *Perf. 13x12½*

1645 Sheet of 4 12.50 12.50
a. A478 3fr Spring 2.25 2.25
b. A478 4fr Summer 2.75 2.75
c. A478 5fr Fall 3.25 3.25
d. A478 6fr Winter 3.75 3.75

Le Nain and Brothers, Detail of a Painting in the Louvre, by Antoine Le Nain (c. 1588-1648) A521

1988, Oct. 20 *Perf. 12½x13*

1646 A521 5fr ol brn, dull brn & car rose 3.25 1.90

Les Grands Archeologues, Bronze Sculpture by Giorgio De Chirico (1888-1978), Italian Painter and Sculptor — A522

1988, Oct. 20 *Perf. 13*

1647 A522 5fr ol bis, blk brn & dark bl 3.25 1.90

Pierre Carlet de Chamblain de Marivaux (1688-1763), French Playwright, Novelist — A523

1988, Oct. 20

1648 A523 3fr dull ol & ultra 1.75 1.00

Lord Byron (1788-1824), English Poet — A524

1988, Oct. 20

1649 A524 3fr grnsh bl, brn & blk 1.75 .85

14th Intl. Circus Festival, Monte Carlo, Feb. 2-6, 1989 — A525

1988, Oct. 20 Photo. *Perf. 12½x13*

1650 A525 2fr multi 1.50 1.00

Intl. Flower Show Type of 1987

1988, Oct. 20

1651 A493 3fr Ikebana 2.10 1.25

22nd Intl. Flower Show and Flower Arranging Contest, Monte Carlo.

Textile Industry (Ready-to-Wear Clothes by Bettina and Le Squadra) A526

1988, Oct. 20 Engr. *Perf. 13*

1652 A526 3fr blk, yel org & dk ol grn 1.40 1.00

Christmas A527

1988, Oct. 20 Litho. *Perf. 12½x13*

1653 A527 2fr black & lemon 1.25 .70

Petroglyphs, Mercantour Natl. Park — A528

Perf. 13x12½, 12½x13

1989, Feb. 8 **Litho.**

1654 A528 2fr multi 1.00 .80
1655 A528 2.20fr multi, diff. 1.00 .80
1656 A528 3fr multi, diff. 1.40 1.20
1657 A528 3.60fr multi, diff. 2.00 1.50
1658 A528 4fr multi, diff., vert. 2.25 1.75
1659 A528 5fr multi, diff., vert. 2.75 2.00
Nos. 1654-1659 (6) 10.40 8.05

St. Nicolas Place — A528a

1989, Feb. 8 Litho. *Perf. 13½x13*

Booklet Stamps

1660 A528a 2fr Rue des Spelugues 1.00 .50
b. Booklet pane of 10 12.00
1660A A528a 2.20fr shown 1.25 .60
c. Booklet pane of 10 14.00

See Nos. 1702-1703, 1826-1827.

Prince Rainier III — A529

1989-91 Engr. *Perf. 13*

1661 A529 2fr pale blue grn & Prus grn 1.00 .35
1662 A529 2.10fr lt blue & Prus blue 1.00 .25
1663 A529 2.20fr pink & rose brn 1.10 .20
1664 A529 2.20fr pale greenish bl & greenish bl 1.00 .35
1665 A529 2.30fr pale pink & car lake 1.10 .20
1666 A529 2.50fr pale rose & rose lake 1.25 .20
1667 A529 3.20fr pale blue & brt blue 1.50 .90
1668 A529 3.40fr lt bl & dk bl 1.75 1.00
1669 A529 3.60fr lt blue & sapphire 2.00 1.25
1670 A529 3.80fr pale pink & dk lil rose 1.75 .55
1671 A529 4fr pale vio & rose vio 1.90 1.25
1672 A529 5fr buff & dark vio brn 2.40 .55
1673 A529 15fr pale vio & indigo 7.00 1.75
1673A A529 20fr pink & rose car 9.50 2.75
1674 A529 25fr pale gray & blk 11.50 2.00
Nos. 1661-1674 (15) 45.75 13.55

Issued: 2fr, #1663, 3.60fr, 5fr, 15fr, 3/14; 2.10fr, 2.30fr, 25fr, 1/11/90; 3.20fr, 3.80fr, 3/15/90; 20fr, 4/26/91; #1664, 2.50fr, 3.40fr, 4fr, 9/24/91.

See Nos. 1790-1799.

5th Magic Grand Prix, Monte Carlo, Mar. 17-19 A530

1989, Mar. 14 Engr. *Perf. 13x12½*

1675 A530 2.20fr multi 1.40 .80

Dog Show Type of 1982

1989, Mar. 14 **Photo.**

1676 A387 2.20fr Yorkshire terrier 2.00 1.10

Our Lady of Mercy Soc., 350th Anniv. A531

1989, Mar. 14 Engr. *Perf. 13*

1677 A531 3fr choc, dark red & blk 1.25 .75

Theater & Film — A532

Designs: 3fr, Jean Cocteau (1889-1963), French writer, artist. 4fr, Charlie Chaplin (1889-1977), English actor, film producer.

1989, Mar. 14

1678 A532 3fr Prus grn, olive grn & dp rose lil 1.40 1.10
1679 A532 4fr dk grn, dk vio & dk red 2.75 1.60

Tree Type of 1986

Life cycle of the pomegranate tree.

1989, Mar. 14 *Perf. 13x12½*

Miniature Sheet

1680 Sheet of 4 10.00 10.00
a. A478 3fr Spring 1.40 1.40
b. A478 4fr Summer 2.00 2.00
c. A478 5fr Fall 2.75 2.75
d. A478 6fr Winter 3.00 3.00

Souvenir Sheet

Reign of Prince Rainier III, 40th Anniv. — A533

1989, May 9 Engr. *Perf. 13*
1681 A533 20fr rose vio 11.00 11.00

See No. 2128.

Europa 1989 — A534

Children's games.

1989, May 9 *Perf. 12½x13*
1682 A534 2.20fr Marbles 1.50 *.40*
1683 A534 3.60fr Jumping rope 2.75 *.70*
a. Souv. sheet, 5 each #1682-1683 27.50 *14.00*

Souvenir Sheet

French Revolution, Bicent., PHILEXFRANCE '89 — A535

a, Liberty. b, Equality. c, Fraternity.

1989, July 7 Engr. *Perf. 12½x13*
1684 A535 Sheet of 3 7.50 7.50
a. 5fr sapphire 2.40 2.40
b. 5fr black 2.40 2.40
c. 5fr dark red 2.40 2.40

Four Seasons Type of 1986

Life cycle of the pear tree.

1989, July 27 Photo. *Perf. 13x12½*
1685 A460 1.39fr like No. 1616 .80 .50
1686 A460 1.79fr like No. 1617 1.00 .80
1687 A460 2.90fr like No. 1618 1.60 1.25
1688 A460 4.84fr like No. 1619 2.00 1.75
Nos. 1685-1688 (4) 5.40 4.30

Nos. 1685-1688 known only precanceled. See note after No. 324.

Portrait of the Artist's Mother, by Philibert Florence A536

Regatta at Molesey, by Alfred Sisley (1839-1899) — A537

Paintings: 8fr, *Enclosed Courtyard, Auvers,* by Paul Cezanne (1839-1906), vert.

Perf. 13, 13x12½ (6fr), 12½x13 (8fr)
1989, Sept. 7 Engr.
1689 A536 4fr olive black 2.50 1.75
1690 A537 6fr multi 3.25 2.00
1691 A537 8fr multi 4.25 3.00
Nos. 1689-1691 (3) 10.00 6.75

Birth sesquicentennials of painters.

Monegasque Red Cross Type of 1987

The life of St. Devote, patron saint of Monaco: 4fr, Eutychius refuses to betray Devote to Barbarus and is poisoned. 5fr, Devote is condemned to torture by Barbarus when she refuses to make sacrifices to the Gods.

1989, Sept. 7 Photo. *Perf. 13x12½*
1692 A490 4fr multi 1.75 1.20
1693 A490 5fr multi 2.50 1.40

Interparliamentary Union, Cent. — A538

1989, Oct. 26 Engr. *Perf. 13*
1694 A538 4fr multi 2.00 1.00

Belle Epoch Type of 1982

Illustrations by Hubert Clerissi.

1989, Oct. 26 *Perf. 12½x13*
1695 A394 7fr Ship in Monaco Port 3.75 2.50
1696 A394 8fr Gaming hall, Monte Carlo Casino 4.25 3.00

Souvenir Sheet

Princess Grace Foundation, 25th Anniv. — A539

a, Princess Grace. b, Princess Caroline.

1989, Oct. 26
1697 Sheet of 2 9.25 9.25
a.-b. A539 5fr any single 3.50 3.50

20th UPU Congress — A540

Design: Views of the Prince of Monaco's palace and the White House.

1989, Oct. 26 *Perf. 13*
1698 A540 6fr multicolored 2.75 1.75

Christmas A541

1989, Oct. 26 Litho. *Perf. 12½x13*
1699 A541 2fr Poinsettia 2.25 .80

15th Intl. Circus Festival, Monte Carlo, Feb. 1-5, 1990 — A542

1989, Dec. 7 Photo. *Perf. 12½x13*
1700 A542 2.20fr multicolored 3.50 1.00

Monaco Aid and Presence, 10th Anniv. A543

1989, Dec. 7 Engr. *Perf. 13x12½*
1701 A543 2.20fr brown & red 2.25 1.00

Avenues Type of 1989

1990, Feb. 8 Litho. *Perf. 13½x13*
1702 A528a 2.10fr The Great Stairs 1.00 .50
a. Bklt. pane of 10 + 2 labels 10.50
1703 A528a 2.30fr Mayoral Court of Honor 1.25 .50
a. Bklt. pane of 10 + 2 labels 12.50

Dog Show Type of 1982

1990, Mar. 15 *Perf. 13x12½*
1704 A387 2.30fr Bearded collie 2.25 1.25

Sir Rowland Hill, Great Britain No. 1 — A544

1990, Mar. 15 Engr. *Perf. 13*
1705 A544 5fr royal bl & blk 2.75 2.00

Penny Black, 150th anniv.

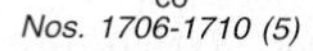

Flowers Named for Members of the Royal Family — A545

1990, Mar. 15 Litho. *Perf. 12½x13*
1706 A545 2fr Princess Grace .95 .55
1707 A545 3fr Prince Rainier III 1.40 .70
1708 A545 3fr Grace Patricia 1.40 .90
1709 A545 4fr Principessa Grace 1.90 1.10
1710 A545 5fr Caroline of Monaco 3.25 1.75
Nos. 1706-1710 (5) 8.90 5.00

Intl. Telecommunications Union, 125th Anniv. — A546

1990, Mar. 15 Engr. *Perf. 13*
1711 A546 4fr pink, deep vio & dull blue grn 2.00 1.50

Antony Noghes (1890-1978), Creator of the Monaco Grand Prix and Monte Carlo Rally — A547

1990, Mar. 15
1712 A547 3fr deep vio, blk & dark red 1.50 1.00

Automobile Club, Cent. — A548

1990, Mar. 15
1713 A548 4fr brt pur, sepia & brt blue 2.10 1.40

Monegasque Red Cross Type of 1987

The life of St. Devote, patron saint of Monaco: 4fr, Devote tortured to death (whipped). 5fr, Body layed out in a small boat.

1990, Mar. 15 Litho. *Perf. 13x12½*
1714 A490 4fr multicolored 1.90 1.25
1715 A490 5fr multicolored 2.50 1.75

Europa — A549

1990, May 3 Engr. *Perf. 12½x12*

1716 A549 2.30fr multicolored 1.50 *.35*
1717 A549 3.70fr multicolored 2.25 *.55*
a. Souv. sheet, 4 each, perf. 12½x13 27.50 *13.00*

Souvenir Sheet

World Cup Soccer Championships, Italy — A550

1990, May 3 *Perf. 13x12½*

1718 A550 Sheet of 4 13.00 13.00
a. 5fr Players, trophy 3.25 3.25
b. 5fr Player dribbling ball 3.25 3.25
c. 5fr Ball 3.25 3.25
d. 5fr Players, stadium 3.25 3.25

Four Seasons Type of 1986

Life cycle of the plum tree.

1990, Sept. 17 *Perf. 13*

1719 A460 1.46fr Spring .80 .50
1720 A460 1.89fr Summer 1.00 .80
1721 A460 3.06fr Fall 1.60 1.25
1722 A460 5.10fr Winter 2.25 1.75
Nos. 1719-1722 (4) 5.65 4.30

Nos. 1719-1722 known only precanceled. See note after No. 324.

Minerals, Mercantour Natl. Park A551

Perf. 13x12½, 12½x13

1990, Sept. 4 Litho.

1723 A551 2.10fr Anatase 1.00 .50
1724 A551 2.30fr Albite 1.00 .50
1725 A551 3.20fr Rutile 1.50 1.10
1726 A551 3.80fr Chlorite 2.00 1.25
1727 A551 4fr Brookite 2.50 1.75
1728 A551 6fr Quartz 3.25 2.75
Nos. 1723-1728 (6) 11.25 7.85

Nos. 1727-1728 vert.

Pierrot Ecrivain — A552

1990, Sept. 4 Engr. *Perf. 12½x13*

1729 A552 3fr dark blue 1.50 .80

Helicopter, Monaco Heliport A553

5fr, Helicopters, Monte Carlo skyline.

1990, Sept. 4 *Perf. 13*

1730 A553 3fr red, brn & blk 1.25 .60
1731 A553 5fr blk, gray bl & brn 2.50 1.40

30th World Congress of Civilian Airports, Monte Carlo.

C. Samuel Hahnemann (1755-1843), Physician — A554

1990, Sept. 4

1732 A554 3fr multicolored 1.40 .85

Homeopathic medicine, bicentennial.

Jean-Francois Champollion (1790-1832), Egyptologist — A555

1990, Sept. 4

1733 A555 5fr blue & brown 2.40 1.25

Offshore Power Boating World Championships A556

6fr, Petanque World Championships.

1990, Sept. 4

1734 A556 2.30fr brt ultra, brn & red 1.10 .70
1735 A556 6fr brn org, brn & bl 2.75 1.60

Tree Type of 1986

Miniature Sheet

Life cycle of the lemon tree.

1990, Oct. 17 Litho. *Perf. 13x12½*

1736 Sheet of 4 9.50 9.50
a. A478 3fr Spring 1.25 1.25
b. A478 4fr Summer 1.75 1.75
c. A478 5fr Fall 2.40 2.40
e. A478 6fr Winter 2.75 2.75

Type of 1984

1990, Oct. 17 Litho. *Perf. 12½x13*

1737 A441 2.30fr Miller riding donkey 1.25 .45
1738 A441 3.20fr Woman carrying firewood 1.60 .80
1739 A441 3.80fr Baker 2.10 1.25
Nos. 1737-1739 (3) 4.95 2.50

The Cathedral, by Auguste Rodin (1840-1917) A558

1990, Oct. 17 Engr. *Perf. 12½*

1740 A558 5fr bl & cream 2.25 1.25

La Pie by Claude Monet (1840-1926) — A559

1990, Oct. 17 *Perf. 13x12*

1741 A559 7fr multicolored 5.00 4.00

Peter Ilich Tchaikovsky (1840-1893), Composer A560

1990, Oct. 17 *Perf. 12½x13*

1742 A560 5fr dark grn & bl 2.25 1.25

16th Intl. Circus Festival, Monte Carlo — A561

1991, Jan. 2 Photo. *Perf. 13*

1743 A561 2.30fr multicolored 1.50 .85

See No. 1801.

Intl. Symposium on Migratory Birds — A562

Migratory birds and their continents: 2fr, Ciconia abdimii, Africa. 3fr, Selasphorus platycercus, America. 4fr, Anas querquedula, Asia. 5fr, Eurystomus orientalis, Australia. 6fr, Merops apiaster, Europe.

1991, Feb. 22 Litho. *Perf. 12½x13*

1744 A562 2fr multicolored 1.00 .60
1745 A562 3fr multicolored 1.25 1.00
1746 A562 4fr multicolored 2.00 1.25
1747 A562 5fr multicolored 2.50 2.00
1748 A562 6fr multicolored 3.25 2.50
Nos. 1744-1748 (5) 10.00 7.35

Intl. Flower Show Type of 1987

1991, Feb. 22

1749 A493 3fr Cyclamen 2.00 .85

Views of Old Monaco Type of 1984

Designs: 20c, Cliffs of Monaco, Port de Fontvieille. 40c, Place du Casino. 50c, Place de la Cremaillere. 70c, Prince's Palace. 80c, Avenue du Beau Rivage. 1fr, Place d'Armes.

1991, Feb. 22 Engr.

1750 A425 20c rose violet .25 .20
1751 A425 40c dk green .25 .20
1752 A425 50c claret .25 .20
1753 A425 70c ol green .25 .20
1754 A425 80c ultramarine .30 .25
1755 A425 1fr dk blue .40 .25
Nos. 1750-1755 (6) 1.70 1.30

Dog Show Type of 1982

1991, Feb. 22 Litho. *Perf. 12*

1756 A387 2.50fr Schnauzer 2.25 1.40

Oceanographic Museum — A563

1991, Feb. 22

1757 A563 2.10fr Phytoplankton 1.25 .80

1992 Olympics A564

Design: No. 1758b, Cross country skiiers, diff. No. 1759a, Relay runner receiving baton. No. 1759b, Runner passing baton.

1991, Apr. 26 Engr. *Perf. 13x12½*

1758 Pair 3.50 3.50
a. A564 3fr dark green, blue & olive 1.40 1.25
b. A564 4fr dark green, blue & olive 2.00 1.60
1759 Pair 4.00 4.00
a. A564 3fr brown & Prussian blue 1.40 1.25
b. A564 5fr brown & Prussian blue 2.50 2.00

Nos. 1758 and 1759 have continuous designs.

Europa A565

1991, Apr. 26

1760 A565 2.30fr Eutelsat 1.75 *.45*
1761 A565 3.20fr Inmarsat 3.00 *.60*
a. Min. sheet, 5 ea. #1760-1761 30.00 *13.00*

25th Intl. Contemporary Art Competition A566

1991, Apr. 26 Engr. *Perf. 12½x13*

1762 A566 4fr multicolored 2.00 1.25

Prince Pierre Foundation, 25th Anniv. — A567

1991, Apr. 26

1763 A567 5fr multicolored 2.25 1.25

Coral — A568

1991, Apr. 26 Photo. *Perf. 12*
1764 A568 2.20fr shown 1.25 .80
1765 A568 2.40fr Coral necklace 1.25 .85

Christmas Type of 1984

1991, Nov. 7 Litho. *Perf. 12*
1766 A441 2.50fr Consul 1.25 .50
1767 A441 3.50fr Woman from Arles 2.00 1.10
1768 A441 4fr Mayor 2.50 1.40
Nos. 1766-1768 (3) 5.75 3.00

Conifers, Mercantour Natl. Park A569

1991, Nov. 7
1769 A569 2.50fr Epicea .95 .35
1770 A569 3.50fr Sapin 1.40 .70
1771 A569 4fr Pin a crochets 1.50 .90
1772 A569 5fr Pin sylvestre, vert. 1.90 1.10
1773 A569 6fr Pin cembro 2.25 1.50
1774 A569 7fr Meleze, vert. 2.75 1.75
Nos. 1769-1774 (6) 10.75 6.30

Tree Type of 1986
Miniature Sheet

Life cycle of an orange tree.

1991, Nov. 7 Engr. *Perf. 13x12½*
1775 Sheet of 4 9.50 9.50
a. A478 3fr Spring 1.25 1.25
b. A478 4fr Summer 1.75 1.75
c. A478 5fr Fall 2.50 2.50
d. A478 6fr Winter 2.75 2.75

Monagasque Red Cross Type of 1987

Life of St. Devote, Monaco's Patron Saint: 4.50fr, The Storm is Rising. 5.50fr, Arrival of the Rock of Monaco.

1991, Nov. 7 Photo.
1776 A490 4.50fr multicolored 2.00 .90
1777 A490 5.50fr multicolored 2.50 1.25

Testudo Hermanni A570

1991, Nov. 7 Litho. *Perf. 12*
1778 A570 1.25fr Two crawling right 1.40 .80
1779 A570 1.25fr Peering from shell 1.40 .80
1780 A570 1.25fr Walking in grass 1.40 .80
1781 A570 1.25fr Walking amid plants 1.40 .80
a. Block or strip of 4, #1778-1781 7.00 7.00

Prince Albert I Type of 1891
Miniature Sheet

1991, Nov. 7 Engr. *Perf. 13*
Stamp size: 22½x28mm
1782 Sheet of 3 13.00 13.00
a. A2 10fr dark red 4.25 4.25
b. A2 10fr dark blue green 4.25 4.25
c. A2 10fr deep violet 4.25 4.25

Portrait of Claude Monet by Auguste Renoir A571

1991, Nov. 7 Engr. *Perf. 12½x13*
1783 A571 5fr multicolored 2.40 1.75

Treaty of Peronne, 350th Anniv. A572

Portraits by Philippe de Champaigne (1602-1674): 6fr, Honore II (1604-1662), Monaco. 7fr, Louis XIII (1610-1643), France.

1991, Nov. 7
1784 A572 6fr multicolored 3.00 2.50
1785 A572 7fr multicolored 3.75 2.50

Princess Grace Theatre, 10th Anniv. A573

1991, Nov. 7 Litho.
1786 A573 8fr Princess Grace 5.00 3.75

Prince Rainier III Type of 1989

1991-96 Engr. *Perf. 13*
1790 A529 2.40fr pale greenish bl & dk Prus bl 1.10 .50
1791 A529 2.70fr pale bl grn, dk bl grn 1.60 .80
1791A A529 (2.70fr) pale & Prus grn 1.25 .50
b. With strengthened lines in military ribbon at LR 1.25 .50
1792 A529 2.80fr pale rose & rose lake 1.25 .60
1793 A529 3fr pale red, red brn 1.75 .90
1793A A529 (3fr) pink & red 1.40 .55
1794 A529 3.70fr pale bl & dk bl 1.75 .80
1795 A529 3.80fr pale bl & dk bl 2.25 1.10
1796 A529 (3.80fr) pale & dk bl 1.75 .70
1797 A529 10fr lt bl grn & dp bl grn 4.75 1.90
1799 A529 40fr pale brn & dk brn 18.00 8.25
Nos. 1790-1799 (11) 36.85 16.60

Nos. 1791A, 1793A, 1796 are dated "1999."

Issued: 10fr, 11/7/91; 2.40fr, 2.80fr, 3.70fr, 40fr, 7/28/93; 2.70fr, 3/18/96; 3fr, 3.80fr, 7/8/96; #1791A, 1793A, 1796, 11/28/98. No. 1791Ab, Apr. 2003.

No. 1791Ab sold for 41c on day of issue and has other strengthened lines other than those in the military ribbon.

See No. 1863b.

This is an expanding set. Numbers will change if necessary.

16th Intl. Circus Festival Type

1992, Jan. 6 Photo. *Perf. 12½x13*
1801 A561 2.50fr multicolored 1.60 1.00

1992 Winter and Summer Olympics, Albertville and Barcelona A574

Designs: 7fr, Two-man bobsled. 8fr, Soccer.

1992, Feb. 7 Engr. *Perf. 13*
1802 A574 7fr multicolored 3.25 1.50
1803 A574 8fr multicolored 3.75 2.00

Tree Type of 1986
Miniature Sheet

Life cycle of a cactus plant.

1992, Apr. 24 Photo. *Perf. 13x12½*
1804 Sheet of 4 10.00 10.00
a. A478 3fr Spring 1.25 1.25
b. A478 4fr Summer 1.75 1.75
c. A478 5fr Fall 2.50 2.50
d. A478 6fr Winter 3.50 3.50

60th Monte Carlo Rally A575

1992, Mar. 13 Engr. *Perf. 13x12½*
1805 A575 4fr dk bl grn, blk & red 2.00 1.25

Intl. Dog Show Type of 1982

1992, Mar. 13 Litho. *Perf. 13x12½*
1806 A387 2.20fr Labrador retriever 1.90 1.00

50th Grand Prix of Monaco A576

1992, Mar. 13 Engr.
1807 A576 2.50fr vio brn, blk & brt bl 1.50 .80

25th Intl. Flower Show, Monte Carlo — A577

1992, Mar. 13 Photo. *Perf. 12½x13*
1808 A577 3.40fr multicolored 1.90 1.25

See No. 1848.

Four Seasons Type of 1986

Life cycle of a walnut tree.

1992, Mar. 13 Photo.
1809 A460 1.60fr Spring .85 .50
1810 A460 2.08fr Summer 1.00 .80
1811 A460 2.98fr Fall 1.50 1.25
1812 A460 5.28fr Winter 2.25 1.75
Nos. 1809-1812 (4) 5.60 4.30

Nos. 1809-1812 known only precanceled. See the note after No. 324.

Souvenir Sheet

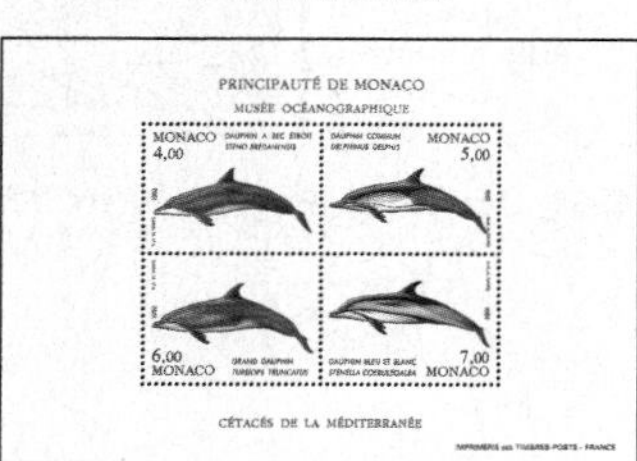

Dolphins — A578

1992, Mar. 13
1813 A578 Sheet of 4 11.50 11.50
a. 4fr Steno bredanensis 1.90 1.90
b. 5fr Delphinus delphis 2.40 2.40
c. 6fr Tursiops truncatus 3.00 3.00
d. 7fr Stenella coeruleoalba 3.50 3.50

See Nos. 1853, 1898.

Discovery of America, 500th Anniv. A579

1992, Apr. 24
1814 A579 2.50fr Pinta 1.50 *.45*
1815 A579 3.40fr Santa Maria 2.75 *.80*
1816 A579 4fr Nina 4.00 *1.25*
a. Sheet, 2 each #1814-1816 30.00 *13.50*
Nos. 1814-1816 (3) 8.25 2.50

Europa.

Ameriflora Intl. Flower Show, Columbus, Ohio A580

1992, Apr. 24 Litho. *Perf. 12½x13*
1817 A580 4fr Fruits & vegetables 1.90 1.10
1818 A580 5fr Vase of flowers 2.40 1.75

Columbus Exposition, Genoa '92 — A581

1992, Apr. 24 Engr. *Perf. 13*
1819 A581 6fr multicolored 3.00 1.75

Expo '92, Seville — A582

1992, Apr. 24
1820 A582 7fr multicolored 3.00 2.00

Views of Old Monaco Type of 1984

Illustrations by Hubert Clerissi: 60c, National Council. 90c, Port of Fontvieille. 2fr, Condamine Market. 3fr, Sailing ship. 7fr, Oceanographic Museum.

1992, May 25 Engr. *Perf. 12½x13*
1821 A425 60c dark blue .25 .20
1822 A425 90c violet brown .35 .25
1823 A425 2fr vermilion .95 .40
1824 A425 3fr black 1.40 .60
1825 A425 7fr gray blue & blk 3.25 1.40
Nos. 1821-1825 (5) 6.20 2.85

Avenues Type of 1989

1992, May 25 Litho. *Perf. 13x13½*
Booklet Stamps
1826 A528a 2.20fr Porte Neuve, horiz. 1.10 .40
a. Bklt. pane of 10 + 2 labels 11.00
1827 A528a 2.50fr Placette Bosio, horiz. 1.10 .45
a. Bklt. pane of 10 + 2 labels 11.00

Genoa '92 — A583

Roses: 3fr, Christopher Columbus. 4fr, Prince of Monaco.

1992, Sept. 18 Litho. *Perf. 12*
1828 A583 3fr multicolored 1.75 1.10
1829 A583 4fr multicolored 1.75 1.10

Gypaetus Barbatus, Mercantour Natl. Park A584

1992, Oct. 20 Engr. *Perf. 13x12½*
1830 A584 2.20fr grn, org & blk 1.25 1.00

Seabus A585

1992, Oct. 20
1831 A585 4fr multicolored 1.75 1.40

Phytoplankton A586

Designs: 2.20fr, Ceratium ranipes. 2.50fr, Ceratium hexacanthum.

1992, Oct. 20 Litho. *Perf. 12*
1832 A586 2.20fr multicolored 1.25 .80
1833 A586 2.50fr multicolored 1.25 .40

Baron de Coubertin's Call for Modern Olympics, Cent. — A587

1992, Oct. 20 Engr. *Perf. 13*
1834 A587 10fr blue 4.75 2.50

Chapel of St. Catherine — A588

Prince of Monaco, the Marquisat of Baux-de-Provence.

1992, Oct. 20 Litho. & Engr.
1835 A588 15fr multicolored 6.50 3.50

Monagasque Red Cross Type of 1987

The life of St. Devote, patron saint of Monaco: 6fr, Fire aboard ship. 8fr, Procession of the reliquary.

1992, Oct. 20 Engr.
Size: 48x36mm
1836 A490 6fr multicolored 2.75 1.75
1837 A490 8fr multicolored 3.50 2.50

Christmas Type of 1984

1992, Oct. 20 Litho. *Perf. 12*
1838 A441 2.50fr Basket maker 1.25 .50
1839 A441 3.40fr Fishmonger 1.90 .85
1840 A441 5fr Drummer 2.50 1.50
Nos. 1838-1840 (3) 5.65 2.85

Miniature Sheet

Postal Museum — A589

Litho. & Engr.
1992, Oct. 20 *Perf. 13*
1841 A589 Sheet of 2 10.50 10.50
a. 10fr Sardinia Type A4 4.75 4.75
b. 10fr France Type A3 4.75 4.75

17th Intl. Circus Festival, Monte Carlo — A590

1993, Jan. 5 Litho. *Perf. 13½x13*
1842 A590 2.50fr multicolored 1.40 .60

Birds, Mercantour Natl. Park — A591

Perf. 13x12½, 12½x13
1993, Feb. 15 Engr.

Designs: 2fr, Circaetus gallicus, horiz. 3fr, Falco peregrinus, horiz. 4fr, Bubo bubo. 5fr, Pernis apivorus. 6fr, Aegolius funereus.

1843 A591 2fr multicolored .95 .55
1844 A591 3fr multicolored 1.40 .70
1845 A591 4fr multicolored 1.90 1.10
1846 A591 5fr multicolored 2.40 1.50
1847 A591 6fr multicolored 2.75 1.75
Nos. 1843-1847 (5) 9.40 5.60

Intl. Flower Show Type of 1992

1993, Mar. 1 Photo. *Perf. 12½x13*
1848 A577 3.40fr multicolored 1.75 .85

10th World Amateur Theater Festival — A592

1993, Mar. 1 Litho. *Perf. 13*
1849 A592 4.20fr multicolored 2.00 .85

Intl. Civil Protection Day — A593

1993, Mar. 1 Engr. *Perf. 12½x13*
1850 A593 6fr multicolored 3.00 1.75

A594

1993, Mar. 24 Engr. *Perf. 13*
1851 A594 5fr Princess Grace 2.40 1.40

See US No. 2749.

Tree Type of 1986
Miniature Sheet

Life cycle of an almond tree: a, Spring. b, Summer. c, Autumn. d, Winter.

1993, Feb. 15 Photo. *Perf. 13x12½*
1852 Sheet of 4 10.50 10.50
a.-d. A478 5fr any single 2.40 2.40

Marine Mammals Type of 1992
Miniature Sheet

1993, Mar. 24
1853 Sheet of 4 11.50 11.50
a. A578 4fr Balaenoptera physalus 1.90 1.90
b. A578 5fr Balaenoptera acutorostrata 2.40 2.40
c. A578 6fr Physeter catodon 3.00 3.00
d. A578 7fr Ziphius cavirostris 3.25 3.25

10th Monte Carlo Open Golf Tournament A595

1993, Mar. 24 Photo. *Perf. 12*
1854 A595 2.20fr multicolored 1.00 .70

Dog Show Type of 1982

1993, Mar. 24 Litho. *Perf. 13x13½*
1855 A387 2.20fr Newfoundland 1.75 1.10

10th Biennial of Antique Dealers of Monte Carlo A596

1993, Mar. 24 *Perf. 12*
1856 A596 7fr multicolored 3.25 1.60

Flowering Cacti — A597

1993, May 4 Engr. *Perf. 13x13½*
Booklet Stamps
1857 A597 2.50fr Echinopsis multiplex 1.10 .70
1858 A597 2.50fr Zygocactus truncatus 1.10 .70
1859 A597 2.50fr Echinocereas procumbens 1.10 .70
1860 A597 2.50fr Euphorbia virosa 1.10 .70
a. Booklet pane, 2 each #1857-1860 9.25
Nos. 1857-1860 (4) 4.40 2.80

See Nos. 1889-1892, 1914-1918, 2007-2009, 2086-2089.

Europa A598

1993, May 4 *Perf. 12½x12*
1861 A598 2.50fr Monte Carlo Ballet .90 *.40*
1862 A598 4.20fr Sigaldi sculpture 1.25 *.70*
a. Souvenir sheet, 3 each, #1861-1862, perf. 13x12½ 7.50 *7.50*

Souvenir Sheet

Admission to the UN — A599

1993, July 28 Engr. *Perf. 13*
1863 A599 Sheet of 3 12.50 12.50
a. 10fr light blue 4.00 4.00
b. 10fr brn vio (Design A529) 4.00 4.00
c. 10fr brown violet & red 4.00 4.00

Intl. Olympic Committee, 101st Session A600

Litho. & Engr.
1993, Sept. 20 *Perf. 13½x13*
Booklet Stamps
1864 A600 2.80fr Coat of arms 1.25 1.25
1865 A600 2.80fr Bobsledding 1.25 1.25
1866 A600 2.80fr Skiing 1.25 1.25
1867 A600 2.80fr Sailing 1.25 1.25
1868 A600 2.80fr Rowing 1.25 1.25
1869 A600 2.80fr Swimming 1.25 1.25
1870 A600 2.80fr Cycling 1.25 1.25
1871 A600 2.80fr shown 1.25 1.25
a. Bklt. pane of 8, #1864-1871 10.00
1872 A600 4.50fr like #1864 2.00 2.00
1873 A600 4.50fr Gymnastics 2.00 2.00
1874 A600 4.50fr Judo 2.00 2.00
1875 A600 4.50fr Fencing 2.00 2.00
1876 A600 4.50fr Hurdles 2.00 2.00
1877 A600 4.50fr Archery 2.00 2.00
1878 A600 4.50fr Weight lifting 2.00 2.00
1879 A600 4.50fr like #1871 2.00 2.00
a. Bklt. pane of 8, #1872-1879 16.00

See No. 1899.

Red Cross of Monaco — A601

Design: 6fr, Red, white crosses.

1993, Nov. 10 Litho. *Perf. 13½x13*
1880 A601 5fr red, black & yellow 2.10 1.25
1881 A601 6fr red & black 2.50 2.00

Monaco Philatelic Union, Cent. A602

1993, Nov. 10 ***Perf. 13x13½***
1882 A602 2.40fr multicolored 1.10 .45

Christmas Type of 1984

1993, Nov. 10 ***Perf. 13½x13***
1883 A441 2.80fr Donkey 1.25 .50
1884 A441 3.70fr Shepherd 1.75 .85
1885 A441 4.40fr Cow 2.10 1.25
Nos. 1883-1885 (3) 5.10 2.60

Edvard Grieg (1843-1907), Composer — A603

Joan Miro (1893-1943), Artist — A604

Georges de La Tour (1593-1652), Painter — A605

Litho. (#1887), Engr.

1993, Dec. 10 ***Perf. 13***
1886 A603 4fr blue 2.50 1.25
1887 A604 5fr multicolored 2.50 1.60

Perf. 12x13
1888 A605 6fr multicolored 2.75 1.75

Flowering Cacti Type of 1993

1994, Jan. 7 **Engr.** ***Perf. 13***
1889 A597 20c like #1857 .20 .20
1890 A597 30c like #1858 .20 .20
1891 A597 40c like #1860 .20 .20
1892 A597 4fr like #1859 1.50 .70
Nos. 1889-1892 (4) 2.10 1.30

18th Intl. Circus Festival, Monte Carlo — A606

1994, Jan. 7 **Litho.** ***Perf. 13½x13***
1893 A606 2.80fr multicolored 1.25 .60

Figurines, Natl. Museum — A607

Designs: No. 1894, Poet. No. 1895, Japanese geisha. No. 1896, Shepherdess with lamb. No. 1897, Parisian woman.

1994, Jan. 7 **Engr.** ***Perf. 12½x13***
1894 A607 2.80fr blue 1.25 .60
1895 A607 2.80fr magenta 1.25 .60
1896 A607 2.80fr purple 1.25 .60
1897 A607 2.80fr blue green 1.25 .60
Nos. 1894-1897 (4) 5.00 2.40

Marine Mammals Type of 1992
Miniature Sheet

1994, Feb. 11 **Photo.** ***Perf. 13x12½***
1898 Sheet of 4 12.00 12.00
a. A578 4fr Orcinus orca 2.10 2.10
b. A578 5fr Grampus griseus 2.50 2.50
c. A578 6fr Pseudorca crassidens 2.90 2.90
d. A578 7fr Globicephala melas 3.50 3.50

Intl. Olympic Committee Type of 1993
Souvenir Sheet

1994, Feb. 11 **Engr.** ***Perf. 13***
1899 Sheet of 2 10.00 10.00
a. A600 10fr like #1866 4.50 4.50
b. A600 10fr like #1865 4.50 4.50

1994 Winter Olympics, Lillehammer.

Intl. Dog Show Type of 1982

1994, Mar. 14 **Litho.** ***Perf. 13x13½***
1900 A387 2.40fr King Charles spaniel 3.50 .80

27th Intl. Flower Show — A608

1994, Mar. 14 ***Perf. 13½x13***
1901 A608 4.40fr Iris 2.50 1.25

See Nos. 1941, 1989, 2028.

10th Grand Prix of Magic, Monte Carlo A609

1994, Mar. 14 **Engr.** ***Perf. 13x12½***
1902 A609 5fr lake, black & blue 2.50 1.50

25th Conference of the Grand Cordon of French Cuisine A610

1994, Mar. 14 ***Perf. 12½***
1903 A610 6fr multicolored 2.75 1.75

Prince Albert I, Research Ship Princess Alice II — A611

Europa: 4.50fr, Opisthoproctus Grimaldii, Eryoneicus Alberti, Oceanographic Museum, Monaco.

1994, May 5 **Engr.** ***Perf. 13x12½***
1904 A611 2.80fr multicolored 1.25 *.75*
1905 A611 4.50fr multicolored 2.10 *1.10*
a. Min. sheet, 3 each #1904-1905 12.00 *9.00*

Intl. Olympic Committee, Cent. — A612

1994, May 17 **Engr.** ***Perf. 12½x12***
1906 A612 3fr multicolored 1.40 .75

Institute for Preservation of the Sea — A613

1994, May 17 **Litho.** ***Perf. 13***
1907 A613 6fr multicolored 2.75 1.75

Intl. Year of the Family — A614

1994, May 17 **Engr.** ***Perf. 13***
1908 A614 7fr multicolored 3.25 2.00

1994 World Cup Soccer Championships, US — A615

1994, May 17 ***Perf. 12½x13***
1909 A615 8fr red & black 3.50 2.25

Intl. Amateur Athletic Federation — A616

1994, June 10 ***Perf. 13***
1910 A616 8fr multicolored 3.50 2.25

1903 De Dion Bouton A617

1994, Aug. 22 **Engr.** ***Perf. 13x12½***
1911 A617 2.80fr lil, blk & brn 1.25 .85

Intl. Assoc. of Philatelic Catalogue Editors (ASCAT) — A618

1994, Aug. 22 **Litho.** ***Perf. 13***
1912 A618 3fr blk, lil rose & grn 1.40 .75

21st UPU Congress, Seoul, Korea — A619

1994, Aug. 22
1913 A619 4.40fr bl, red & blk 2.75 1.25

Flowering Cacti Type of 1993

1994, Oct. 17 **Engr.** ***Perf. 13***
1914 A597 50c Selenicereus grandiflorus .20 .20
1915 A597 60c Opuntia basilaris .30 .20
1916 A597 70c Aloe plicatilis .35 .20
1917 A597 80c Opuntia hybride .35 .20
1918 A597 2fr Aporocactus flagelliformis .95 .40
Nos. 1914-1918 (5) 2.15 1.20

Christmas Type of 1984

1994, Oct. 17 **Litho.** ***Perf. 13***
1919 A441 2.80fr Mary 1.25 .55
1920 A441 4.50fr Christ child 2.10 .90
1921 A441 6fr Joseph 2.75 1.10
Nos. 1919-1921 (3) 6.10 2.55

Currency Museum — A620

1994, Oct. 17 Engr. *Perf. 12½*

1922	A620	3fr Prince Albert	1.40	.85
1923	A620	4fr Arms of Grimaldi	2.00	1.25
1924	A620	7fr Prince Rainier III	3.25	2.00
		Nos. 1922-1924 (3)	6.65	4.10

Souvenir Sheet

Perf. 12½x13

1925		Sheet of 3	14.00	14.00
a.		A620 10fr like #1922	4.50	4.50
b.		A620 10fr like #1923	4.50	4.50
c.		A620 10fr like #1924	4.50	4.50

Red Cross Campaigns — A621

Designs: 6fr, Fight against cancer. 8fr, Fight against AIDS.

1994, Oct. 17 Litho. *Perf. 13*

1926	A621	6fr lake, blue & black	2.75	1.90
1927	A621	8fr lake, grn & blk	3.75	2.50

See Nos. 1983-1984.

ICAO, 50th Anniv. A622

Helicopters and: 5fr, Monaco Heliport. 7fr, Monaco skyline.

1994, Oct. 17 Engr. *Perf. 13*

1928	A622	5fr multicolored	2.40	1.50
1929	A622	7fr multicolored	3.25	2.00

Voltaire (1694-1778), Writer — A623

Sarah Bernhardt (1844-1923), Actress — A624

Publication of Robinson Crusoe, by Daniel Defoe, 275th Anniv. — A625

The Snake Charmer, by Henri Rousseau (1844-1910) — A626

1994, Oct. 17 Engr. *Perf. 13*

1930	A623	5fr olive green	2.40	1.25
1931	A624	6fr multicolored	2.75	1.50

Litho.

1932	A625	7fr multicolored	3.25	1.90
1933	A626	9fr multicolored	4.25	2.25
		Nos. 1930-1933 (4)	12.65	6.90

Tree Type of 1986

Miniature Sheet

Life cycle of an apricot tree.

1994, Oct. 17 Photo. *Perf. 13x12½*

1934		Sheet of 4	14.00	14.00
a.		A478 6fr Spring	2.75	2.75
b.		A478 7fr Summer	3.25	3.25
c.		A478 8fr Autumn	3.75	3.75
d.		A478 9fr Winter	4.25	4.25

19th Intl. Circus Festival, Monte Carlo — A627

1995, Jan. 3 Litho. *Perf. 13½x13*

1935	A627	2.80fr multicolored	1.25	.60

Monte Carlo Television, 35th Festival — A628

1995, Feb. 13 Engr. *Perf. 12½x13*

1936	A628	8fr Prince Albert	3.50	1.75

European Nature Conservation Year — A629

1995, Apr. 3 Litho. *Perf. 13x13½*

1937	A629	2.40fr multicolored	1.10	.55

Intl. Special Olympics A630

1995, Apr. 3

1938	A630	3fr multicolored	1.40	.80

Rotary Intl. Convention, Nice A631

1995, Apr. 3 Engr. *Perf. 13x12½*

1939	A631	4fr blue	2.00	1.00

Intl. Dog Show Type of 1982

1995, Apr. 3 Litho. *Perf. 13x13½*

1940	A387	4fr American cocker spaniel	2.75	1.25

Intl. Flower Show Type of 1993

1995, Apr. 3 *Perf. 13½x13*

1941	A608	5fr Perroquet tulips	2.40	1.25

European Bonsai Congress A632

1995, Apr. 3 *Perf. 12*

1942	A632	6fr Acer palmatum	2.75	1.40

Tree Type of 1986

Miniature Sheet

Life cycle of a jujube tree.

1995, Apr. 3 Photo. *Perf. 12x12½*

1943		Sheet of 4	10.50	10.50
a.		A478 4fr Spring	1.90	1.90
b.		A478 5fr Summer	2.40	2.40
c.		A478 6fr Fall	2.75	2.75
d.		A478 7fr Winter	3.25	3.25

Peace & Liberty A633

Europa: 2.80fr, Dove with olive branch, Alfred Nobel. 5fr, Chain broken over concentration camp, flowers.

Photo. & Engr.

1995, May 8 *Perf. 12x12½*

1944	A633	2.80fr multicolored	1.25	.80
1945	A633	5fr multicolored	2.40	1.25

50th anniversaries: End of World War II (#1944), liberation of the concentration camps (#1945).

A634

Designs: 5fr, Jean Giono (1895-1970), writer. 6fr, Marcel Pagnol (1895-1974), film producer, writer.

1995, May 8 Engr. *Perf. 12½x13*

1946	A634	5fr multicolored	2.40	1.00
1947	A634	6fr multicolored	2.75	1.40

Princess Caroline, Pres. of World Assoc. of Friends of Children — A635

1995, May 8 Photo. *Perf. 13½x13*

1948	A635	7fr blue	3.25	2.00

Intl. Council of Wildlife Conservation — A636

1995, May 8 Engr. *Perf. 13*

1949	A636	6fr St. Hubert, stag	2.75	1.25

IAAF Track & Field Championships, Louis II Stadium — A637

1995, May 8

1950	A637	7fr multicolored	3.25	1.60

Alps Monument A638

1995, May 8

1951	A638	8fr multicolored	3.75	2.00

Prince Pierre of Monaco (1895-1964) A639

1995, May 8

1952	A639	10fr lake	4.50	2.40

Souvenir Sheet

Stamp & Coin Museum — A640

a, #927. b, Museum entrance. c, #294.

1995, May 8

1953 A640 Sheet of 3, #a.-c. 13.50 13.50
a.-c. 10fr any single 4.50 4.50

St. Anthony of Padua (1195-1231) A641

1995, Sept. 25 Litho. *Perf. 13½*

1954 A641 2.80fr multicolored 1.25 .60

UN, 50th Anniv. A642

Designs: #1955, 1963a, Soldiers, UN Charter. #1956, 1963b, Grain, child. #1957, 1963c, Childrens' faces. #1958, 1963d, Musical notes, temple of Abu Simbel. #1959, 1963e, UN Security Council. #1960, 1963f, Hand holding grain, field. #1961, 1963g, Letters from various languages. #1962, 1963h, UNESCO Headquarters.

1995, Oct. 24 Engr. *Perf. 13*

1955 A642 2.50fr multicolored 1.10 .50
1956 A642 2.50fr multicolored 1.10 .50
1957 A642 2.50fr multicolored 1.10 .50
1958 A642 2.50fr multicolored 1.10 .50
1959 A642 3fr multicolored 1.40 .70
1960 A642 3fr multicolored 1.40 .70
1961 A642 3fr multicolored 1.40 .70
1962 A642 3fr multicolored 1.40 .70
Nos. 1955-1962 (8) 10.00 4.80

Miniature Sheet

1963 Sheet of 8 16.00 16.00
a.-d. A642 3fr any single 1.40 1.40
e.-h. A642 4.50fr any single 2.10 2.10

A643

Flowers: No. 1964, Rose *Grace of Monaco.* No. 1965, Fuschia *Lakeland Princess.* No. 1966, Carnation *Century of Monte Carlo.* No. 1967, Fuschia *Grace.* No. 1968, Rose *Princess of Monaco.* No. 1969, Alstroemeria *Gracia.* No. 1970, Lily *Princess Grace.* No. 1971, Carnation *Princess Caroline.* No. 1972, Rose *Stephanie of Monaco.* No. 1973, Carnation *Prince Albert.* No. 1974, Sweet pea *Grace of Monaco.* No. 1975, Gerbera *Gracia.*

1995, Oct. 24 Litho. *Perf. 13½*

Booklet Stamps

1964 A643 3fr multicolored 1.40 .80
1965 A643 3fr multicolored 1.40 .80
1966 A643 3fr multicolored 1.40 .80
1967 A643 3fr multicolored 1.40 .80
1968 A643 3fr multicolored 1.40 .80
1969 A643 3fr multicolored 1.40 .80
1970 A643 3fr multicolored 1.40 .80
1971 A643 3fr multicolored 1.40 .80
1972 A643 3fr multicolored 1.40 .80
1973 A643 3fr multicolored 1.40 .80
1974 A643 3fr multicolored 1.40 .80
1975 A643 3fr multicolored 1.40 .80
a. Bklt. pane, #1964-1975 + 2 labels 17.00
Complete booklet, #1975a 18.00

Christmas Type of 1984

1995, Oct. 24 Litho. *Perf. 13½x13*

1976 A441 3fr Balthazar 1.40 .65
1977 A441 5fr Gaspard 2.40 1.10
1978 A441 6fr Melchior 2.75 1.25
Nos. 1976-1978 (3) 6.55 3.00

Monagasque Assoc. for Protection of Nature, 20th Anniv. — A644

1995, Oct. 24 Engr. *Perf. 13*

1980 A644 4fr green, black & red 1.90 .85

Wilhelm Röntgen (1845-1923), Discovery of X-Rays, Cent. — A645

1995, Oct. 24

1981 A645 6fr multicolored 2.75 1.25

Motion Pictures, Cent. — A646

1995, Oct. 24

1982 A646 7fr dark blue 3.25 1.75

Red Cross Campaigns Type of 1994

Designs: 7fr, World fight against leprosy. 8fr, Drs. Prakash and Mandakini Amte, Indian campaign against leprosy.

1995, Oct. 24 Litho.

1983 A621 7fr multicolored 3.25 1.50
1984 A621 8fr multicolored 3.75 1.75

Pneumatic Automobile Tires, Cent. — A647

1995, Oct. 24 Engr.

1985 A647 8fr claret & dk purple 3.75 1.75

Springtime, by Sandro Botticelli (1445-1510) — A648

1995, Oct. 24

1986 A648 15fr blue 9.25 5.25
a. Souvenir sheet of 1 9.25 5.25

No. 1986 printed in sheets of 10 + 5 labels.

No. 1986a inscribed in sheet margin as a winner of the 4th World Cup of Stamps, portrait of Botticelli. Issued 11/6/97.

20th Intl. Circus Festival, Monte Carlo — A649

1996, Jan. 10 Litho. *Perf. 13*

1987 A649 2.40fr multicolored 1.10 .50

Magic Festival, Monte Carlo A650

1996, Jan. 10 Engr.

1988 A650 2.80fr black & gray 1.25 .55

Intl. Flower Show Type of 1994

1996, Jan. 26 Litho.

1989 A608 3fr Rhododendron 1.40 .65

Intl. Dog Show Type of 1982

1996, Jan. 26

1990 A387 4fr Fox terrier 2.00 1.00

Oceanographic Voyages of Prince Albert I of Monaco and King Charles I of Portugal, Cent. — A652

3fr, Fish in sea, net, Prince Albert I holding binoculars, ship. 4.50fr, Ship, King Charles I holding sextant, microscope, sea life.

1996, Feb. 1 Litho. *Perf. 12*

1992 A652 3fr multicolored 1.40 .70
1993 A652 4.50fr multicolored 2.10 1.25

See Portugal Nos. 2084-2085.

Prince Rainier III Type of 1974 Inscribed "MUSEE DES TIMBRES ET DES MONNAIES"

1996, Mar. 11 Engr. *Perf. 13*

1994 AP37 10fr purple 4.50 2.25
1995 AP37 15fr henna brown 7.00 3.50
1996 AP37 20fr ultra 9.50 4.75
Nos. 1994-1996 (3) 21.00 10.50

Stamp and Currency Museum.

Princess Grace — A653

1996, Apr. 29

1997 A653 3fr red & brown 1.40 .70

Europa.

RAMOGE Agreement Between France, Italy, Monaco, 20th Anniv. A654

Photo. & Engr.

1996, May 14 *Perf. 13*

1998 A654 3fr multicolored 1.40 .65

See France #2524, Italy #2077.

Annales Monegasques, 20th Anniv. — A655

Famous people: a, Saint Nicolas of Myra, by Louis Brea. b, Guillaume Apollinaire (1880-1918), poet. c, Jean-Baptiste Francois Bosio (1764-1827), painter. d, Francois-Joseph Bosio (1768-1845), sculptor. e, Hector Berlioz (1803-69), composer. f, Niccolo Machiavelli (1469-1527), writer. g, Sidonie-Gabrielle Colette (1873-1954), writer. h, Michael Montaigne (1533-92), essayist.

1996, May 14 Engr. *Perf. 12½x13*

1999 Sheet of 8 21.00 21.00
a., e. A655 3fr any single 1.60 1.60
b., f. A655 4fr any single 2.00 2.00
c., g. A655 5fr any single 2.50 2.50
d., h. A655 6fr any single 3.00 3.00

Opening of Chapel of Notre Dame of Miséricorde, 350th Anniv. — A651

1996, Jan. 26 Engr. *Perf. 12x13*

1991 A651 6fr multicolored 2.75 2.00

Souvenir Sheet

CHINA '96, 9th Asian Intl. Philatelic Exhibition — A656

Designs: a, Chinese acrobats in Monaco. b, Fuling Tomb, Shenyang.

1996, May 14 Litho. *Perf. 13*
2000 A656 Sheet of 2 5.00 5.00
a.-b. 5fr any single 2.50 2.50

Introduction of Telephone Area Code 377 for Monaco — A657

1996, June 21 Engr. *Perf. 13*
2001 A657 3fr dark blue 1.75 .90
2002 A657 3.80fr vermilion 2.25 1.10

1996 Summer Olympic Games, Atlanta — A658

1996, July 19 Litho. *Perf. 13½x13*
2003 A658 3fr Javelin, 1896 1.75 .90
2004 A658 3fr Women's soft-ball, 1996 1.75 .90
2005 A658 4.50fr Runners, 1896 2.75 1.40
2006 A658 4.50fr Cycling, 1996 2.75 1.40
Nos. 2003-2006 (4) 9.00 4.60

Flowering Cacti Type of 1993

Designs: 10c, Bromelia brevifolia. 1fr, Stapelia flavirostris. 5fr, Cereus peruvianus.

1996, Sept. 16 Engr. *Perf. 13*
2007 A597 10c multicolored .20 .20
2008 A597 1fr multicolored .40 .20
2009 A597 5fr multicolored 2.40 1.00
Nos. 2007-2009 (3) 3.00 1.40

Tree Type of 1986

Life cycle of thorn (ronce) tree.

1996, Oct. 14 Photo. *Perf. 13*
2010 Sheet of 4 11.00 11.00
a. A478 4fr Spring 1.75 1.75
b. A478 5fr Summer 2.25 2.25
c. A478 6fr Fall 2.75 2.75
d. A478 7fr Winter 3.25 3.25

Red Cross Campaigns Type of 1994

Designs: 7fr, Fight against tuberculosis. 8fr, Camille Guérin, Albert-Leon C. Calmette, developers of BCG vaccine against tuberculosis.

1996, Oct. 14
2011 A621 7fr multicolored 3.25 1.50
2012 A621 8fr multicolored 3.75 2.00

UNICEF, 50th Anniv. — A658a

1996, Oct. 14 Engr. *Perf. 12½x13*
2013 A658a 3fr multicolored 1.40 .70

Discovery of the Planet, Neptune, 150th Anniv. — A659

Photo. & Engr.
1996, Oct. 14 *Perf. 13x12½*
2014 A659 4fr multicolored 1.75 .80

René Descartes (1596-1650), Philosopher, Mathematician — A660

1996, Oct. 14 Engr. *Perf. 13*
2015 A660 5fr blue & carmine 2.50 1.25

Christmas A661

1996, Oct. 14 Litho. *Perf. 13*
2016 A661 3fr Angel 1.40 .65
2017 A661 6fr Angels 2.75 1.25

Self-Portrait, by Corot (1796-1875) — A662

7fr, Self-portrait (detail), by Goya (1746-1828).

Photo. & Engr.
1996, Oct. 14 *Perf. 12x13*
2018 A662 6fr multicolored 2.75 1.50
2019 A662 7fr multicolored 3.25 1.75

Stamp and Coin Museum — A663

Designs: No. 2020, Printing and engraving stamps. No. 2021, Coins, screw press. 10fr, Front entrance to museum.

1996, Oct. 14 Engr. *Perf. 13*
2020 A663 5fr dk olive & violet 2.50 2.50
2021 A663 5fr dk ol & dk bl 2.50 2.50
2022 A663 10fr dk ol & dk bl 4.75 4.75
a. Souvenir sheet, #2020-2022 9.75 9.75
Nos. 2020-2022 (3) 9.75 9.75

No. 2022 is 48x36mm.

Grimaldi Dynasty, 700th Anniv. A664

No. 2023: a, Francois Grimaldi, 1297. b, Rainier I, d. 1314. c, Charles I, d. 1357. d, Rainier II, 1350-1407. e, Jean I, 1382-1454. f, Catalan, d. 1457. g, Lambert, d. 1494. h, Jean II, 1468-1505. i, Lucien, 1481-1523. j, Augustin, d. 1532. k, Honoré I, 1522-1581. l, Charles II, 1555-1589. m, Hercule I, 1562-1604.

No. 2024: a, Honoré II (1597-1662). b, Louis I (1642-1701). c, Antoine (1661-1731). d, Louise-Hippolyte (1697-1731). e, Jacques I (1689-1751). f, Honoré III (1720-95). g, Honoré IV (1758-1819). h, Honoré V (1778-1841). i, Florestan I (1785-1856). j, Charles III (1818-89). k, Albert I (1848-1922). l, Louis II (1870-1949). m, Rainier III.

1997 Litho. *Perf. 13*
2023 Sheet of 13 + 2 labels 35.00 35.00
a. A664 7fr multicolored 3.25 3.25
b.-d. A664 1fr multi, each .45 .45
e, g. A664 2fr multi, each .95 .95
f. A664 9fr multicolored 4.25 4.25
h.-j A664 9fr multi, each 4.25 4.25
k.-m. A664 7fr multi, each 3.25 3.25
2024 Sheet of 13 + 2 labels 35.00 35.00
a.-c. A664 1fr multi, each .45 .45
d. A664 9fr multicolored 4.25 4.25
e. A664 2fr multicolored .95 .95
f.-i. A664 9fr multi, each 4.25 4.25
j.-m. A664 7fr multi, each 3.25 3.25

Portions of the designs on Nos. 2023-2024 were applied by a thermographic process producing a shiny, raised effect.

Issued: #2023, 1/8; #2024, 7/3.

Knight in Armor Type of 1951 Inscribed "1297-1997"

1996-97 Engr. *Perf. 13*
2025 A67 2.70fr bl, brn & red 1.25 .60

Sheet of 8

2026 2 ea #a.-c., 2025 11.00 11.00
a. A67 2.70fr red 1.50 1.50
b. A67 2.70fr brown 1.50 1.50
c. A67 2.70fr blue 1.50 1.50

Issued: #2025, 12/19/96; #2026, 1/8/97.

Yacht Club of Monaco — A665

1996, Dec. 12 Litho. *Perf. 13*
2027 A665 3fr multicolored 1.40 .70

Intl. Flower Show Type of 1993

1996, Dec. 19 *Perf. 13½x13*
2028 A608 3.80fr Camellia 1.75 .75

Tennis Tournaments in Monaco, Cent. — A666

1997, Feb. 1 Litho. *Perf. 13*
2029 A666 4.60fr multicolored 2.10 1.00

Portions of the design on No. 2029 were applied by a thermographic process producing a shiny, raised effect.

For overprint see No. 2049.

37th Festival of Television in Monte Carlo — A667

1996, Dec. 19 *Perf. 13½x13*
2030 A667 4.90fr multicolored 2.25 1.00

Campanula "Medium" — A668

1996, Dec. 19 Litho. *Perf. 13*
2031 A668 5fr multicolored 2.40 1.10

Auto Sports in Monaco — A669

1996, Dec. 19 Litho. *Perf. 13*
2032 A669 3fr multicolored 1.40 .65

Philatelic Events A670

Stamp & Coin Museum and: No. 2033, Pictures, engraving tools, picture on stamps. No. 2034, Stamp, magnifying glass, envelopes.

1996, Dec. 19 Engr. *Perf. 13*
2033 A670 3fr multicolored 1.40 .60
2034 A670 3fr multicolored 1.40 .60
a. Pair, #2033-2034 3.00 3.00

Monaco Philatelic Office, 60th anniv. (#2033). Monaco Intl. Philatelic Exhibition (#2034).

Dog Show Type of 1982

1996, Dec. 19 Litho. *Perf. 13x13½*
2035 A387 4.40fr Afghan hound 2.25 1.00

21st Intl. Circus Festival, Monte Carlo — A671

1996, Dec. 19 Litho. ***Perf. 13½x13***

2036 A671 3fr multicolored 1.40 .60

Intl. Grand Prix of Philately — A672

1997, Apr. 5 Litho. ***Perf. 13***

2041 A672 4.60fr multicolored 2.10 1.25

Red Cross Campaign Against Drug Abuse — A673

1997, May 5 ***Perf. 13½x13***

2042 A673 7fr multicolored 3.25 1.60

Europa (Stories and Legends) A674

No. 2043, Legend of St. Devote. No. 2044, Port Hercules named for mythological Hercules.

1997, May 5 Engr. ***Perf. 12½x13***

2043 A674 3fr multicolored 1.50 .65
2044 A674 3fr multicolored 1.50 .65
a. Pair, #2043-2044 3.00 3.00

PACIFIC 97 Intl. Philatelic Exhibition A675

Design: US types A2 & A1, Monaco #1995.

1997, May 29 ***Perf. 13x12½***

2045 A675 4.90fr multicolored 2.25 1.25

Uniforms of the Carabiniers (Palace Guards) A676

Years uniforms used: 3fr, 1997. 3.50fr, 1750-1853. 5.20fr, 1865-1935.

1997, May 31 Litho. ***Perf. 13x13½***

2046 A676 3fr multicolored 1.40 .50
2047 A676 3.50fr multicolored 1.60 .60
2048 A676 5.20fr multicolored 2.50 .90
Nos. 2046-2048 (3) 5.50 2.00

No. 2029 Ovptd. "M. RIOS"

1997 ***Perf. 13***

2049 A666 4.60fr multicolored 2.10 1.40

13th Grand Prix of Magic, Monte Carlo — A677

1997 Litho. ***Perf. 13½x13***

2050 A677 4.40fr multicolored 2.10 1.25

Monaco Soccer Assoc., 1996 French Division 1 Champions — A678

1997 ***Perf. 13***

2051 A678 3fr multicolored 1.40 .80

Francois Grimaldi, by Ernando Venanzi A679

9fr, Saint Peter and Saint Paul, by Rubens.

1997, Sept. 8 Engr. ***Perf. 13½x13***

2052 A679 8fr multicolored 3.75 2.00
2053 A679 9fr multicolored 4.25 2.50

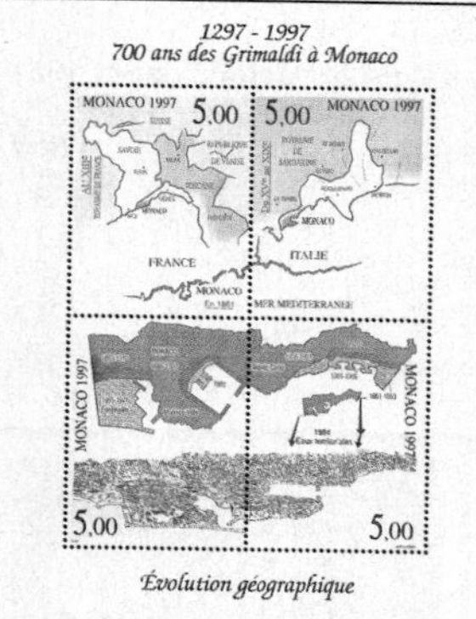

Evolution of the Geographic Territory of Monaco — A680

Designs: a, 13th century. b, 15th-19th century. c, Map of western half of Monaco, panoramic view. d, Map of eastern half of Monaco, panoramic view.

1997, Oct. 6 Litho. & Engr. ***Perf. 13***

2054 A680 5fr Sheet of 4, #a.-d. 9.50 9.50

Grimaldi Dynasty, 700th anniv.

49th Session of Intl. Whaling Commission — A681

1997, Oct. 20 Photo. ***Perf. 13x13½***

2055 A681 6.70fr multicolored 3.00 1.75

22nd Intl. Circus Festival, Monte Carlo — A682

1997, Nov. 30 Litho. ***Perf. 13½x13***

2057 A682 3fr multicolored 1.40 .70

Princess Charlotte (1898-1977) — A683

1997, Nov. 28 Engr. ***Perf. 13x12½***

2058 A683 3.80fr brown 1.75 .90

A684

Designs by Monagasque Students — A685

Perf. 13½x13, 13x13½

1997, Nov. 29 Litho.

2059 A684 4fr Under 13 group 1.90 .90
2060 A685 4.50fr Over 13 group 2.10 .90

31st Intl. Flower Show — A686

1997, Nov. 30 ***Perf. 13½x13***

2061 A686 4.40fr multicolored 2.10 1.25

1998 Winter Olympic Games, Nagano A687

Designs: No. 2062, 4-Man bobsled, speed skating, ice hockey, figure skating. No. 2063, Downhill skiing, biathlon, luge, ski jumping, slalom skiing.

1997, Nov. 28 Photo. ***Perf. 12½***

2062 A687 4.90fr multicolored 2.25 1.25
2063 A687 4.90fr multicolored 2.25 1.25
a. Pair, #2062-2063 4.50 4.50

Moscow '97 — A688

Ballet Russes de Monte Carlo.

1997, Nov. 28 Photo. ***Perf. 13½x13***

2064 A688 5fr multicolored 2.40 1.25

J.L. David (1748-1825), Painter — A689

1997, Nov. 30 Engr. ***Perf. 12½x13***

2065 A689 5.20fr red brn & dk grn 2.40 1.10

Papal Bull for the Parish of Monaco, 750th Anniv. A690

1997, Nov. 30 ***Perf. 12½x13***

2066 A690 7.50fr Pope Innocent IV 3.50 1.90

Prince Albert I (1848-1922) — A691

1997, Nov. 29 Photo. ***Perf. 13x12½***

2067 A691 8fr multicolored 3.75 2.40

38th Television Festival — A692

1998, Feb. 4 Litho. *Perf. 13½x13*
2068 A692 4.50fr multicolored 2.10 1.00

Marcel Kroenlein Arboretum, 10th Anniv. — A693

1997, Nov. 28 Photo. *Perf. 13*
2069 A693 9fr multicolored 4.25 2.50

No. 2069 was issued in sheets of 2.

Dog Show Type of 1987

1998, Mar. 19 Litho. *Perf. 13x13½*
2069A A387 2.70fr Boxer, Doberman 1.50 .80

Intl. Academy of Peace A694

1998, Mar. 19 Litho. *Perf. 13*
2070 A694 3fr green & blue 1.40 .70

Portions of the design of No. 2070 were applied by a thermographic process producing a shiny, raised effect.

15th Spring Arts Festival A695

1998, Mar. 19 Litho. *Perf. 13x13½*
2071 A695 4fr multicolored 1.75 .90

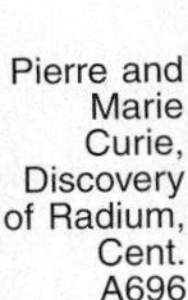

Pierre and Marie Curie, Discovery of Radium, Cent. A696

1998, Mar. 19 Engr. *Perf. 13x12½*
2072 A696 6fr lilac & green blue 2.75 1.40

Monegasque Red Cross, 50th Anniv. — A697

Prince Albert, Prince Louis II, Princess Grace, Prince Rainier III.

1998, Mar. 3 Litho. *Perf. 13*
2073 A697 5fr sepia, red & dk brown 2.40 1.25

Prince Albert I (1848-1922) — A698

1998, May 6 Engr.
2074 A698 7fr dark brown 3.25 1.50

Charles Garnier (1825-98), Architect, Designer of Casino of Monte Carlo — A699

1998, May 6 Litho.
2075 A699 10fr multicolored 4.75 2.25

Festival of St. Dévote — A700

1998, May 6 Litho. *Perf. 13x13½*
2076 A700 3fr multicolored 1.40 .65

Europa.

Portions of the design on No. 2076 were applied by a thermographic process producing a shiny, raised effect.

Joseph Kessel (1898-1979), Writer and Journalist A701

1998, May 6 Engr. *Perf. 13½*
2077 A701 3.90fr multicolored 1.75 .90

Expo '98, Lisbon A702

1998, May 6 Litho. *Perf. 13x13½*
2078 A702 2.70fr multicolored 1.25 .60

1st Formula 3000 Grand Prix in Monaco A703

1998, May 20 Engr. *Perf. 12*
2079 A703 3fr red & black 1.40 .70

European Conference of the Youth Chamber of Economics A705

1998, May 6 Litho. *Perf. 13½x13*
2081 A705 3fr multicolored 1.40 .70

World Music Awards — A706

1998, May 6
2082 A706 10fr multicolored 4.25 2.75

Porcelain — A707

1998, June 24 *Perf. 13*
2083 A707 8fr multicolored 3.75 1.75

Publication of Monaco's Works of Art — A708

1998, June 24
2084 A708 9fr multicolored 4.25 2.00

National Festival — A709

Europa: Prince Albert, Prince Rainier III, national palace.

1998, May 31 Litho. *Perf. 13*
2085 A709 3fr multicolored 1.40 .70

Portions of the design on No. 2085 were applied by a thermographic process producing a shiny, raised, effect.

Flowering Cacti Type of 1993

2.70fr, Opuntia dejecta. 4fr, Echinocereus blanckii. 6fr, Euphorbia milii. 7fr, Stapelia variegata.

1998, Aug. 3 Engr. *Perf. 13*
2086 A597 2.70fr multicolored 1.25 .50
2087 A597 4fr multicolored 1.75 .75
2088 A597 6fr multicolored 2.75 1.10
2089 A597 7fr multicolored 3.25 1.25
Nos. 2086-2089 (4) 9.00 3.60

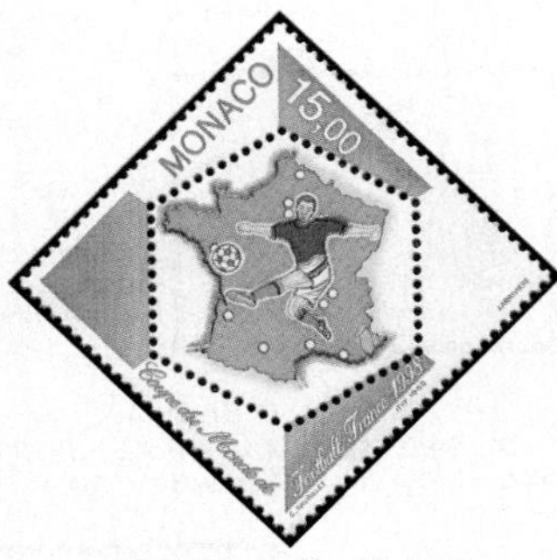

1998 World Cup Soccer Championships, France — A710

1998, Aug. 3
2090 A710 15fr multicolored 7.00 3.50

No. 2090 contains hexagonal perforated label in center.

Enzo Ferrari (1898-1988), Automobile Manufacturer — A711

1998, Aug. 14 Litho.
2091 A711 7fr multicolored 3.25 1.75

George Gershwin (1898-1937), Composer — A712

1998, Aug. 14 Engr. *Perf. 13x12½*
2092 A712 7.50fr bl, bl grn & blk 3.50 1.75

Intl. College for Study of Marine Pollution, Marine Environment Laboratory — A713

1998, Sept. 4 Litho. *Perf. 13x13½*
2093 A713 4.50fr multicolored 2.10 .90

Plenary Assembly of the European Post, Monte Carlo A714

1998, Sept. 4
2094 A714 5fr multicolored 2.40 .90

Expo '98, World Philatelic Exhibition, Lisbon A715

1998, Sept. 4 **Litho. & Engr.**
2095 A715 6.70fr multicolored 3.00 1.50

Intl. Assoc. Against Violence in Sports, 30th Anniv. A716

Photo. & Engr.
1998, Sept. 14 ***Perf. 13x13½***
2096 A716 4.20fr multicolored 2.00 1.00

Magic Stars Magic Festival, Monte Carlo — A717

1998, Sept. 26 **Litho.** ***Perf. 13½x13***
2097 A717 3.50fr red & bister 1.60 .80

See No. 2140.

Giovanni Lorenzo Bernini (1598-1680), Architect, Sculptor — A718

1998, Sept. 26 **Engr.** ***Perf. 13x12½***
2098 A718 11.50fr blue & brown 5.50 3.25

Italia '98, Intl. Philatelic Exhibition, Milan — A719

1998, Oct. 23 ***Perf. 12½x13***
2099 A719 4.90fr Milan Cathedral 2.25 1.10

Christmas A720

3fr, Ornament. 6.70fr, Nativity scene, horiz. 15fr, Icon of Madonna and Child, 18th cent.

Perf. 13½x13, 13x13½
1998, Oct. 26 **Litho.**
2100 A720 3fr multicolored 1.40 .50
2101 A720 6.70fr multicolored 3.00 1.25

Souvenir Sheet
Engr.
Perf. 13
2102 A720 15fr multicolored 5.75 5.75

No. 2102 contains one 36x49mm stamp.

23rd Intl. Circus Festival, Monte Carlo — A721

1998, Nov. 20 **Litho.** ***Perf. 13½x13***
2103 A721 2.70fr multicolored 1.25 .50

Grimaldi Seamounts A722

1998, Nov. 20 ***Perf. 13***
2104 A722 10fr multicolored 4.25 2.00

Souvenir Sheet

Reign of Prince Rainier III, 50th Anniv. — A723

1998, Nov. 20 **Engr.**
2105 A723 25fr red & yel bister 12.00 12.00

Congress Center Auditorium of Monaco, 20th Anniv. A724

1999, Feb. 12 **Litho.** ***Perf. 13x13½***
2106 A724 2.70fr multicolored 1.25 .50

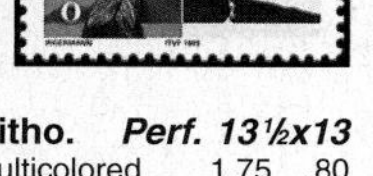

39th Intl. Television Festival, Monte Carlo — A725

1999, Jan. 18 **Litho.** ***Perf. 13½x13***
2107 A725 3.80fr multicolored 1.75 .80

Dog Show Type of 1982

Cocker spaniel and American cocker spaniel.

1999, Jan. 18 **Litho.** ***Perf. 13x13½***
2108 A387 4fr multicolored 2.10 1.10

Geneva Conventions, 50th Anniv. — A726

1999, Jan. 18 **Engr.** ***Perf. 13½x13***
2109 A726 4.40fr black & red 2.10 .80

32nd Intl. Flower Show, Monte Carlo — A727

1999, Jan. 18 **Litho.** ***Perf. 13½x13***
2110 A727 4.50fr multicolored 2.10 1.10

Monaco '99, Intl. Philatelic Exhibition — A728

Photo. & Engr.
1999, Jan. 18 ***Perf. 13x12***
2111 A728 3fr multicolored 1.40 .50

Beginning with No. 2112, denominations are indicated on the stamps in both Francs and Euros. The listing value is shown in Francs.

10th Piano Masters Competition, Monte Carlo — A729

1999, Feb. 12 ***Perf. 13x13½***
2112 A729 4.60fr multicolored 2.10 .80

Flowers — A730

Designs: 4.90fr, Prince of Monaco Jubilee Rose. 6fr, Paphiopedilum Prince Rainier III, Prince of Monaco and Grimaldi Roses.

1999 **Litho.** ***Perf. 13½x13***
2113 A730 4.90fr multicolored 2.25 1.25
2114 A730 6fr multicolored 2.75 1.40

Issued: 4.90fr, 2/14; 6fr, 2/13.

Monaco Charity Assoc., 20th Anniv. A731

1999, Jan. 28 **Litho.** ***Perf. 13***
2115 A731 6.70fr multicolored 3.00 1.50

Formula 1 Grand Prix of Monaco, 70th Anniv. — A732

1999, Apr. 16 **Photo.** ***Perf. 12¼***
2116 A732 3fr multicolored 1.40 .80

Intl. Grand Prix of Philately, Monaco — A733

1999, Apr. 16 ***Perf. 13¼***
2117 A733 4.40fr multicolored 2.00 1.10

Fifth Intl. Show Jumping Championships, Monte Carlo — A734

1999, Apr. 16 **Engr.** ***Perf. 13x12½***
2118 A734 5.20fr blk, dk grn & red 2.40 1.50

ASM Sports Club, 75th Anniv. — A735

Cutouts of soccer players over: No. 2119, Palace. No. 2120, Aerial view of city.

1999, Apr. 16 **Litho.** ***Perf. 13x12¾***
2119 A735 7fr multicolored 3.25 1.90
2120 A735 7fr multicolored 3.25 1.90
a. Pair, #2119-2120 6.50 6.50

Grimaldi Forum A736

1999, Apr. 25 **Photo.** ***Perf. 13¼***
2121 A736 3fr multicolored 1.40 .50

Oceanography Museum, Cent. — A737

1999, Apr. 25 Engr. *Perf. 13¼x13*
2122 A737 5fr multicolored 2.40 1.25

Philexfrance '99, Intl Philatelic Exhibition A738

France #1, Eiffel Tower, map of France, exhibition emblem, arms of Monaco.

1999, May 5 Engr. *Perf. 13¼*
2123 A738 2.70fr multicolored 1.25 .60

See No. 2133.

A739

1999, May 5 Photo. *Perf. 13*
2124 A739 3fr Casino, Cliffs 1.50 .65

Size: 51x28mm

2125 A739 3fr Park in Fontvieille 1.50 .65
a. Pair, #2124-2125 3.25 3.25

Europa.

Monegasque Economic Growth — A740

Chart and: No. 2126, Fontveille and underground train station. No. 2127, Larvotto and Grimaldi Forum.

1999, May 5 Photo. *Perf. 13x13¼*
2126 A740 5fr multi 2.40 .95
2127 A740 5fr multi 2.40 .95
a. Pair, #2126-2127 5.00 5.00

Souvenir Sheet

Reign of Prince Rainier III, 50th Anniv. — A741

1999, May 9 Engr. *Perf. 13*
2128 A741 20fr blue & gold 9.50 9.50

See No. 1681.

Honoré de Balzac (1799-1850), Writer — A742

Design: 5.20fr, Countess of Ségur (1799-1874), children's storyteller.

1999 *Perf. 12¾x13*
2129 A742 4.50fr red & blue 2.10 1.10
2130 A742 5.20fr multicolored 2.40 1.25

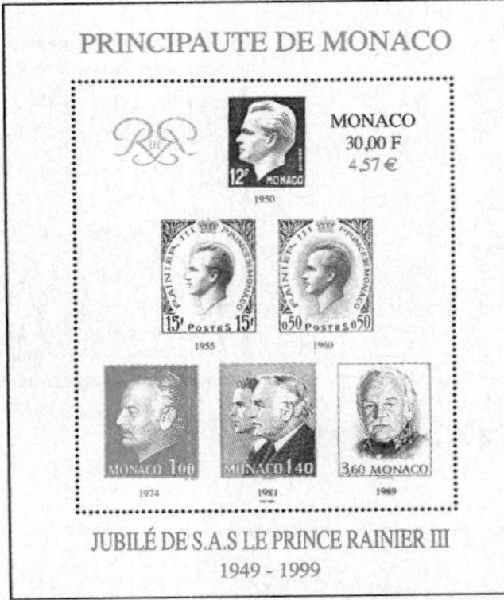

Reign of Prince Rainier III, 50th Anniv. — A743

Design: #256, 337, 427, 937, 1287, 1669.

1999 Engr. *Perf. 12¾x13*
2131 A743 30fr multicolored 14.00 14.00

UNESCO, 50th Anniv. A744

1999, July 2 Engr. *Perf. 13x12½*
2132 A744 4.20fr multicolored 2.00 .80

PhilexFrance Type of 1999

1999, July 2 Engr. *Perf. 13¼*
2133 A738 7fr France #4, 92, Monaco #3 3.25 1.50

Sportel, 10th Anniv. A745

1999, July 2 Litho. *Perf. 12¼*
2134 A745 10fr multicolored 4.75 2.40

Sovereign Military Order of Malta, 900th Anniv. A746

1999, July 2 Engr. *Perf. 11*
2135 A746 11.50fr multicolored 5.50 2.75

UPU, 125th Anniv. — A747

1999, July 2 Engr. *Perf. 13¼*
2136 A747 3fr multicolored 1.40 .70

Rose, Iris Named After Prince Rainier III — A748

1999, July 2 Litho. *Perf. 13¼x13*
2137 A748 4fr multicolored 1.90 .90

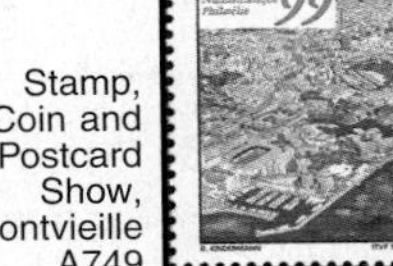

Stamp, Coin and Postcard Show, Fontvieille A749

3fr, Aerial photograph, coin obverse, No. 1793A. 6.50fr, Aerial photograph, 100fr coin, #257.

1999 Photo. *Perf. 13¼*
2138 A749 3fr multicolored 1.40 .50

Perf. 13¼x13½

2139 A749 6.50fr multicolored 3.00 1.75

Jubilee Bourse (#2139).
Issued: 3fr, 7/3; 6.50fr, 9/26.

Magic Stars Type of 1998
Inscribed "99"
Litho. & Typo.

1999, Sept. 6 *Perf. 13¼x13*
2140 A717 4.50fr red & gold 2.10 1.00

Development Projects — A750

Designs: a, Fontveille 1 & 2. b, La Digue (with jetty). c, Grimaldi Forum. d, La Gare.

1999, Sept. 26 Photo. *Perf. 13*
2141 Sheet of 4 + label 20.00 20.00
a. A750 4fr multicolored 1.90 1.90
b.-c. A750 9fr Any single 4.25 4.25
d. A750 19fr multicolored 9.00 9.00

No. 2141d is 80x40mm.

24th Intl. Circus Festival, Monte Carlo — A751

1999, Dec. 13 Litho. *Perf. 13¼x13*
2142 A751 2.70fr multi 1.25 .55

A752

1999, Dec. 13 Engr. *Perf. 13¼*
2143 A752 3fr Christmas 1.40 .60

Holy Year 2000 A753

1999, Dec. 13 Litho. *Perf. 13x13¼*
2144 A753 3.50fr multi 1.60 .95

33rd Intl. Flower Show — A754

1999, Dec. 13 *Perf. 13¼x13*
2145 A754 4.50fr multi 2.10 1.00

Monaco 2000 Intl. Philatelic Exposition A755

1999, Dec. 23 Engr. *Perf. 13¼x13*
2146 A755 3fr multi 1.40 .55

Bust of Napoleon, by Antonio Canova — A756

Litho. & Embossed

2000, Jan. 17 *Perf. 13¼*
2147 A756 4.20fr multi 2.00 .90

40th Intl. Television Festival, Monte Carlo — A757

2000, Jan. 17 Litho. *Perf. 13¼x13*
2148 A757 4.90fr multi 2.25 .95

The Twelve Apostles — A758

Saints: 4fr, Peter and James the Great. 5fr, John and Andrew. 6fr, Philip and Bartholomew. 7fr, Matthew and Thomas. 8fr, James the Less and Judas. 9fr, Simon and Matthias.

Engr. with Foil Application

2000, Apr. 3 *Perf. 13¼*
2149 A758 4fr multi 1.90 .80
2150 A758 5fr multi 2.40 .95
2151 A758 6fr multi 2.75 1.25
2152 A758 7fr multi 3.25 1.50
2153 A758 8fr multi 3.75 2.00
2154 A758 9fr multi 4.25 2.40
Nos. 2149-2154 (6) 18.30 8.90

Labrador Retriever and Golden Retriever A759

2000, Apr. 3 Engr. *Perf. 13¼*
2155 A759 6.50fr multi 3.00 1.50

Intl. Dog Show, Monte Carlo.

1993 Intl. Olympic Committee Meeting Awarding 2000 Games to Sydney A760

2000, Apr. 25 **Photo.**
2156 A760 7fr multi 3.25 1.50

Souvenir Sheet

Art Depicting Monaco and the Sea A761

Artwork by: a, Adami. b, Arman. c, Cane. d, Folon. e, Fuchs. f, E. De Sigaldi. g, Sosno. h, Verkade.

2000, Apr. 25 *Perf. 13x12½*
2157 Sheet of 8 + label 25.00 25.00
a.-h. A761 6.55fr Any single 3.00 1.50

2nd Historic Automobile Grand Prix — A762

2000, May 9 Litho. *Perf. 13½x13*
2158 A762 4.40fr multi 2.10 1.00

Monaco Pavilion, Expo 2000, Hanover A763

2000, May 9 *Perf. 13x13¼*
2159 A763 5fr multi 2.40 1.25

Saints Mark, Matthew, John and Luke — A764

2000, May 9 Engr. *Perf. 12¾x13*
2160 A764 20fr multi 9.50 6.00

Europa, 2000

Common Design Type and

Flags and Map of Europe — A765

2000, May 9 Litho. *Perf. 13¼x13*
2161 CD17 3fr multi 1.40 .70
2162 A765 3fr multi 1.40 .70
a. Pair, #2161-2162 3.00 3.00

WIPA 2000 Philatelic Exhibition, Vienna — A766

2000, May 30 Engr. *Perf. 13¼*
2163 A766 4.50fr multi 2.10 1.00

Professional-Celebrity Golf Tournament, Monte Carlo — A767

2000, June 19 Photo. *Perf. 13¼*
2164 A767 4.40fr multi 2.10 1.00

Club de Monte Carlo Exhibition of Rare Philatelic Material — A768

2000, June 23
2165 A768 3.50fr multi 1.60 .75

Red Cross — A769

2000, June 23
2166 A769 10fr multi 4.75 2.00

2000 Summer Olympics, Sydney A770

Olympic rings and: 2.70fr, Fencing, emblem of Monegasque Fencing Federation. 4.50fr, Rowers, flag of Monegasque Nautical Society.

2000, June 23 Engr. & Embossed
2167-2168 A770 Set of 2 3.50 1.75

Automobiles in Prince Rainier III Collection — A771

Woman and: 3fr, 1911 Humber Type Beeston. 6.70fr, 1947 Jaguar 4 cylinder. 10fr, 1956 Rolls-Royce Silver Cloud. 15fr, 1986 Lamborghini Countach.

2000, June 23 Engr. *Perf. 13x13¼*
2169-2172 A771 Set of 4 16.00 10.50

See Nos. 2186-2188.

World Stamp Expo 2000, Anaheim — A772

2000, July 7 Litho. *Perf. 13¼x13*
2173 A772 4.40fr multi 2.10 .90

Magic Stars Magic Festival, Monte Carlo — A773

2000, Sept. 4 Photo. *Perf. 13¼*
2174 A773 4.60fr multi 2.10 1.25

Intl. Mathematics Year — A774

2000, Sept. 4 **Engr.**
2175 A774 6.50fr brown 3.00 1.50

Souvenir Sheet

Retable of St. Nicholas, by Ludovic Bréa, Monaco Cathedral — A775

2000, Sept. 4 **Photo.**
2176 A775 Sheet of 2 14.00 14.00
a. 10fr Two figures, 31x52mm 4.50 1.75
b. 20fr Three figures, 53x52mm 9.50 4.50

New Aquarium, Oceanographic Museum — A776

2000, Oct. 2 **Engr.**
2177 A776 3fr multi 1.40 .70

España 2000 Intl. Philatelic Exhibition A777

2000, Oct. 2
2178 A777 3.80fr multi 1.75 .80

Observatory Grotto, 50th Anniv. and Anthropological Museum, 40th Anniv. — A778

2000, Oct. 2
2179 A778 5.20fr multi 2.40 .80

Fish A779

5fr, Fish, coral. 9fr, Fish, starfish, seaweed.

2000, Oct. 2 **Photo.**
2180-2181 A779 Set of 2 6.50 3.00

Fifth Congress of Aquariums (No. 2180), Monegasque Nature Protection Association, 25th anniv. (No. 2181).

Fifth Congress of Aquariums — A780

2000, Nov. 25 Photo. ***Perf. 13x12¾***
2182 A780 7fr multi 3.25 1.75

Christmas A781

2000, Dec. 1 Photo. ***Perf. 13¼***
2183 A781 3fr multi 1.40 .50

Princess Stephanie, President of AMAPEI — A782

2000, Dec. 1 **Engr.**
2184 A782 11.50fr red & slate 5.50 3.00

Souvenir Sheet

Monaco 2000 Intl. Philatelic Exhibition — A783

2001, Dec. 1 Photo. ***Imperf.***
2185 A783 Sheet of 2 #2185a 19.00 19.00
a. 20fr multi 9.50 9.50

Prince's Automobiles Type of 2000

Woman and: 5fr, 1989 Ferrari F1. 6fr, 1955 Fiat 600 Type Jolly. 8fr, 1929 Citroen C4F Autochenille.

2000, Dec. 1 Engr. ***Perf. 13x13¼***
2186-2188 A771 Set of 3 9.00 4.50

Exhibit of Chinese Terra-cotta Figures, Grimaldi Forum — A784

2000, Dec. 2 Photo. ***Perf. 13¼***
2189 A784 2.70fr multi 1.25 .40

Postal Museum. 50th Anniv. — A785

2000, Dec. 2
2190 A785 3fr multi 1.40 .50

Coat of Arms — A786

Serpentine Die Cut 11
2000, Dec. 4 **Photo.**
Booklet Stamp
Self-Adhesive
2191 A786 (3fr) red & black 1.40 .30
a. Booklet of 10 14.00

Princess Caroline of Monaco Iris — A787

2000, Dec. 2 Photo. ***Perf. 13¼***
2192 A787 3.80fr multi 1.75 .70

34th Intl. Flower Show.

Sardinian Postage Stamps, 150th Anniv. (in 2001) A788

2000, Dec. 2 Engr. ***Perf. 13x12½***
2193 A788 6.50fr Sardinia #1-3 3.00 1.75

RAMOGE Agreement, 25th Anniv. A789

2000, Dec. 2
2194 A789 6.70fr multi 3.00 1.75

Awarding of ASCAT Grand Prize to Bertrand Piccard — A790

2000, Dec. 2 Photo. ***Perf. 13¼***
2195 A790 9fr Balloon, #1433 4.25 2.00

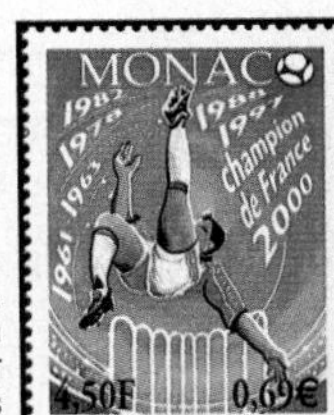
Monaco Team, 2000 French Soccer Champions A791

2000, Dec. 3
2196 A791 4.50fr multi 2.10 .90

French, Italian and Monegasque Marine Mammal Sanctuary — A792

2000, Dec. 3
2197 A792 5.20fr multi 2.40 1.25

Neapolitan Creche, Natl. Museum — A793

2000, Dec. 3 ***Perf. 13x12½***
2198 A793 10fr multi 4.75 3.00

25th Intl. Circus Festival, Monte Carlo — A794

No. 2200: a, Clown with guitar. b, Clown. c, Tiger and tent top. d, Acrobats, tiger, lion, horses, clowns. e, Chimpanzee and high-wire acrobat.

2000, Dec. 3 ***Perf. 13¼***
2199 A794 2.70fr shown 1.25 .60
2200 A794 6fr Sheet of 5, #a-e + label 14.00 14.00

41st Intl. Television Festival, Monte Carlo — A795

2001, Feb. 5 Photo. ***Perf. 13½x13***
2201 A795 3.50fr multi 1.60 .90

Leonberger and Newfoundland — A796

2001, Apr. 14 Litho. ***Perf. 13x13¼***
2202 A796 6.50fr multi 3.00 1.25

Euroflora Flower Show — A797

2001, Apr. 21 Photo. ***Perf. 13¼***
2203 A797 6.70fr multi 3.00 1.25

Europa — A798

Designs: No. 2204, 3fr, Palace of Monaco, water droplets. No. 2205, 3fr, Wash house.

2001, May 7 Litho. ***Perf. 13½x13***
2204-2205 A798 Set of 2 2.75 1.10

Prince Rainier III Literary Prize, 50th Anniv. — A799

2001, May 14 Engr. *Perf. 13¼*
2206 A799 2.70fr multi 1.25 .45

André Malraux (1901-76), Novelist — A800

2001, May 14 Litho. *Perf. 13¼x13*
2207 A800 10fr black & red 4.75 1.75

Belgica 2001 Intl. Stamp Exhibition, Brussels — A801

2001, June 9 Engr. *Perf. 13¼*
2208 A801 4fr brt blue & red 1.90 .70

2001 Philatelic and Numismatic Bourse — A802

2001, July 2 Photo. *Perf. 13¼*
2209 A802 2.70fr multi 1.25 .45

Princess Grace Dance Academy, 25th Anniv. — A803

2001 July 2 Photo. *Perf. 13¼*
2210 A803 4.40fr multi 2.10 .90

Naval Museum A804

2001, July 2 Photo. *Perf. 13¼*
2211 A804 4.50fr multi 2.10 .90

37th Petanque World Championships — A805

2001, July 2 *Perf. 13x13¼*
2212 A805 5fr multi 2.40 .80

Emile Littré, Denis Diderot, and Reference Books A806

2001, Aug. 1 Engr. *Perf. 13¼*
2213 A806 4.20fr multi 2.00 .95

Prince Albert I Oceanography Prize, 30th Anniv. — A807

2001, Aug. 1 Engr. *Perf. 13¼*
2214 A807 9fr bright blue 4.25 1.50

David, by Michelangelo, 500th Anniv. — A808

2001, Aug. 1 Engr. *Perf. 13*
2215 A808 20fr multi 9.50 6.00

Palace of Monaco — A809

Designs: 3fr, Fireplace, Throne Hall. 4.50fr, Blue Hall. 6.70fr, York Chamber. 15fr, Fresco, ceiling of Throne Hall.

2001, Aug. 1 Photo. *Perf. 13x13¼*
2216-2219 A809 Set of 4 13.50 6.50

A810

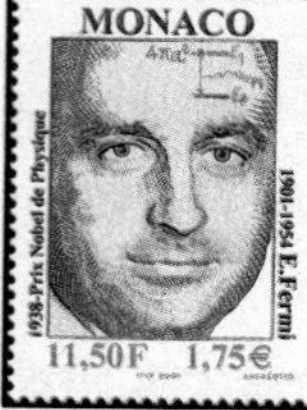

Nobel Prizes, Cent. — A811

Designs: 5fr, Alfred Nobel. 8fr, Jean-Henri Dunant, 1901 Peace laureate. 11.50fr, Enrico Fermi, 1938 Physics laureate.

2001, Sept. 3 Engr. *Perf. 13¼*

2220	A810	5fr multi	2.40	.95
2221	A810	8fr multi	3.75	1.50
2222	A811	11.50fr multi	5.50	3.25
	Nos. 2220-2222 (3)		11.65	5.70

36th Meeting of Intl. Commission for Scientific Exploration of the Mediterranean — A812

2001, Oct. 1 Photo. *Perf. 13x13¼*
2223 A812 3fr multi 1.40 .50

Christmas — A813

2001, Oct. 1 *Perf. 13¼*
2224 A813 3fr multi 1.40 .50

100 Cents = 1 Euro (€)

Flora & Fauna A814

Designs: 1c, Arctia caja, vert. 2c, Luria lurida. 5c, Thunbergia grandiflora, vert. 10c, Parus major. 20c, Anthias anthias. 50c, Charaxes jasius, vert. €1, Mitra zonata. €2, Datura sanguinea, vert. €5, Parus cristatus, vert. €10, Macroamphosus scolopax.

2002, Jan. 1 Engr. *Perf. 13¼*

2225	A814	1c multi	.20	.20
2226	A814	2c multi	.20	.20
2227	A814	5c multi	.20	.20
2228	A814	10c multi	.30	.20
2229	A814	20c multi	.60	.20
2230	A814	50c multi	1.50	.75
2231	A814	€1 multi	3.00	1.50
2232	A814	€2 multi	6.00	3.00
2233	A814	€5 multi	15.00	7.50
2234	A814	€10 multi	30.00	15.00
	Nos. 2225-2234 (10)		57.00	28.75

See No. 2275.

Palace of Monaco A815

Designs: 41c, Gallery of Mirrors, vert. 46c, Throne room. 58c, Painting in Gallery of Mirrors.

2002, Jan. 1 Photo.
2235-2237 A815 Set of 3 4.25 2.00

26th Intl. Circus Festival — A816

2002, Jan. 1
2238 A816 41c multi 1.25 .60

35th Intl. Flower Show A817

2002, Jan. 1
2239 A817 53c multi 1.50 .75

Souvenir Sheet

Automobile Club of Monaco — A818

No. 2240: a, Old and new cars, emblem of 70th Monte Carlo Rally. b, Racing cars in 3rd Historic Grand Prix and 60th Grand Prix races.

2002, Jan. 16 *Perf. 13¼x13*

2240	A818	Sheet of 2	6.75	6.75
a.		€1.07 multi	3.00	1.50
b.		€1.22 multi	3.50	1.75

Prehistoric Anthropology Museum, Cent. — A819

2002, Feb. 8 *Perf. 13¼*
2241 A819 64c multi 1.90 .95

La Carrière d'un Navigateur, by Prince Albert I, Cent. A820

2002, Feb. 8
2242 A820 67c multi 2.00 1.00

2002 Winter Olympics, Salt Lake City — A821

No. 2243: a, Denomination at UL. b, Denomination at UR.

2002, Feb. 8 *Perf. 12¼*
2243 A821 Horiz. pair 1.75 1.75
a.-b. 23c Either single .85 .40

Jules Cardinal Mazarin (1602-61) A822

2002, Feb. 18
2244 A822 69c multi 2.00 1.00

Legion of Honor, Bicent. — A823

2002, Feb. 18 *Perf. 13¼*
2245 A823 70c multi 2.10 1.00

Cetacean Conservation Accord — A824

2002, Feb. 18 **Engr.**
2246 A824 75c multi 2.25 1.10

Leonardo da Vinci (1452-1519) — A825

2002, Mar. 21 **Photo.**
2247 A825 76c multi 2.25 1.10

St. Bernard and Swiss Bouvier A826

2002, Mar. 21 **Engr.**
2248 A826 99c multi 3.00 1.50

Intl. Dog Show.

Police, Cent. — A827

2002, Apr. 23 **Photo.**
2249 A827 53c multi 1.60 .70

European Academy of Philately, 25th Anniv. A828

2002, Apr. 27 **Engr.**
2250 A828 58c multi 1.75 .85

20th Intl. Swimming Meet — A829

2002, May 3 **Photo.** *Perf. 13¼*
2251 A829 64c multi 1.90 .95

Europa — A830

Designs: No. 2252, 46c, Clown on globe, juggler, elephant, tent tops. No. 2253, 46c, "Jours de Cirque," circus acts.

2002, May 3
2252-2253 A830 Set of 2 *2.75 1.25*

First Experiment with Tar Roads, Cent. A831

2002, May 31 **Engr.**
2254 A831 41c multi 1.25 .60

MonacoPhil 2002 Intl. Philatelic Exhibition — A832

2002, May 31
2255 A832 46c multi 1.40 .65

42nd Intl. Television Festival, Monte Carlo — A833

2002, May 31 **Photo.** *Perf. 13¼x13*
2256 A833 70c multi 2.10 1.00

2002 World Cup Soccer Championships, Japan and Korea — A834

2002, May 31 **Engr.** *Perf. 13¼*
2257 A834 75c multi 2.25 1.10

"Pelléas et Mélisande," Opera by Claude Debussy, Cent. of Debut — A835

2002, June 21
2258 A835 69c multi 2.10 1.00

Saint Dévote, Dove and Boat A836

2002, June 21
2259 A836 €1.02 multi 3.00 1.50

Red Cross.

Intl. Year of Mountains A837

2002, June 21 **Litho.** *Perf. 13x13¼*
2260 A837 €1.37 multi 4.00 2.00

Euro Coinage — A838

No. 2261: a, Obverse of 1c, 2c, and 5c coins and reverse. b, Obverse of 10c, 20c, and 50c coins and reverse.
No. 2262: a, Obverse and reverse of €1 coin. b, Obverse and reverse of €2 coin.

Litho. & Embossed

2002, June 21 *Perf. 13¼*
2261 A838 Horiz. pair 3.00 3.00
a.-b. 46c Either single 1.40 .70
2262 A838 Horiz. pair 9.25 9.25
a.-b. €1.50 Either single 4.50 4.50

Victor Hugo (1802-85), Writer — A839

No. 2263: a, Hugo and illustration from *Notre-Dame de Paris*. b, Hugo and illustration from *La Légende de Siécles*.

2002, July 1 **Engr.** *Perf. 13¼*
2263 A839 Horiz. pair 3.25 3.25
a. 50c multi 1.50 .75
b. 57c multi 1.75 .85

Alexandre Dumas (Father) (1802-70), Writer — A840

No. 2264: a, Dumas. b, Characters, manuscript.

2002, July 1 **Photo.**
2264 A840 Horiz. pair 3.50 3.50
a.-b. 61c Either single 1.75 .85

26th Publication of "Annales Monegasques" A841

2002, July 15
2265 A841 €1.75 multi 5.25 2.50

Christmas — A842

2002, Sept. 2
2266 A842 50c multi 1.50 .75

Debut of Movie "Le Voyage dans le Lune," by Georges Méliès, Cent. — A843

2002, Sept. 2 *Perf. 13¼*
2267 A843 76c multi 2.25 1.10

17th Magic Stars Magic Festival, Monte Carlo — A844

2002, Sept. 2

2268 A844 €1.52 multi 4.50 2.25

Awarding of ASCAT Grand Prize to Luis Figo — A845

2002, Nov. 29 **Engr.**

2269 A845 91c multi 2.75 1.25

Automobiles in Prince Rainier III Collection A846

Designs: 46c, 1949 Mercedes 220A Cabriolet. 69c, 1956 Rolls-Royce Silver Cloud I. €1.40, 1974 Citroen DS 21.

2002, Nov. 29 **Photo.**

2270-2272 A846 Set of 3 7.50 3.75

Souvenir Sheet

PRINCIPAUTE DE MONACO

"Quatre Saisons" - Palais Princier

The Four Seasons, Frescos in Prince's Palace — A847

2002, Nov. 29 ***Perf. 13x13¼***

2273	A847	Sheet of 4	15.00	15.00
a.		50c Spring	1.50	.75
b.		€1 Summer	3.00	1.50
c.		€1.50 Autumn	4.50	2.25
d.		€2 Winter	6.00	3.00

Souvenir Sheet

MonacoPhil 2002 Intl. Philatelic Exhibition — A848

No. 2274: a, Monaco attractions. b, Emblem of Club de Monte Carlo.

2002, Nov. 29 ***Imperf.***

2274	A848	Sheet of 2	18.00	18.00
a.-b.		€3 Either single	9.00	4.50

Flora & Fauna Type of 2002

2002, Nov. 30 **Engr.** ***Perf. 13¼***

2275 A814 41c Helix aspersa, vert. 1.25 .60

36th Intl. Flower Show — A849

2002, Nov. 30 **Photo.**

2276 A849 67c multi 2.00 1.00

World Association of Friends of Children, 40th Anniv. (in 2003) A850

2002, Nov. 30

2277 A850 €1.25 multi 3.75 1.75

Martyrdom of St. George, 1700th Anniv. — A851

2002, Dec. 1

2278 A851 53c multi 1.60 .70

Saint Cyr Military School, Bicent. — A852

2002, Dec. 1

2279 A852 61c multi 1.75 .85

27th Intl. Circus Festival — A853

2003, Jan. 2 **Photo.** ***Perf. 13¼***

2280 A853 59c multi 1.75 .70

15th New Circus Artists' Festival — A854

2003, Feb. 1

2281 A854 €2.82 multi 8.50 4.00

10th World Bobsled Push Championships, Ilsenberg, Germany — A855

2003, Feb. 3

2282 A855 80c multi 2.40 .95

Monaco Yacht Club, 50th Anniv. — A856

2003, Feb. 5

2283 A856 46c multi 1.40 .60

Intl. Institute for Peace, Cent. — A857

2003, Mar. 3

2284 A857 €1.19 multi 3.50 1.75

Tennis Tournament at Monte Carlo Country Club, 75th Anniv. — A858

2003, Mar. 3

2285 A858 €1.30 multi 4.00 2.00

Dog Show Type of 2002

2003, Mar. 24 **Litho.** ***Perf. 13x13½***

2286 A826 79c Rough collie 2.50 1.25

Junior Economic Chamber of Monaco, 40th Anniv. A859

2003, Apr. 5 **Photo.** ***Perf. 13¼***

2287 A859 41c multi 1.25 .60

Monte Carlo Country Club, 75th Anniv. A860

2003, Apr. 12

2288 A860 46c multi 1.40 .70

General Bathymetric Charts of the Oceans, Cent. — A861

No. 2289: a, Prince Albert I, map of Arctic region, chart of Northern hemisphere. b, Oceanographic museum, map of Antarctica, chart of Southern hemisphere.

2003, Apr. 14 ***Perf. 13x12½***

2289 A861 €1.25 Vert. pair, #a-b 7.50 7.50

Poster by Alfons Mucha — A862

Poster by Jean-Gabriel Domergue — A863

2003, May 5 ***Perf. 13¼***

2290	A862	50c multi	1.50	.75
2291	A863	50c multi	1.50	.75

Europa.

Grand Bourse 2003 — A864

2003, June 2

2292 A864 45c multi 1.40 .70

43rd Intl. Television Festival, Monte Carlo — A865

2003, June 2 ***Perf. 13¼x13***

2293 A865 90c multi 2.75 1.25

15th Antiques Biennale — A866

2003, June 2 *Perf. 13¼*
2294 A866 €1.80 multi 5.50 2.75

Navigation of Northwest Passage by Roald Amundsen, Cent. A867

2003, June 30
2295 A867 90c multi 2.75 1.40

Powered Flight, Cent. A868

2003, June 30
2296 A868 €1.80 multi 5.50 2.75

Hector Berlioz (1803-69), Composer A869

2003, July 21 **Engr.**
2297 A869 75c red & black 2.25 1.10

Aram Khatchaturian (1903-78), Composer — A870

2003, July 21
2298 A870 €1.60 multi 4.75 2.40

Portrait of a Woman, by François Boucher (1703-70) A871

Self-portrait, by Vincent van Gogh (1853-90) — A872

Self-portrait, by Francesco Mazzola, "Il Parmigianino" (1503-40) — A873

2003, Aug. 6 *Perf. 13¼x13*
2299 A871 €1.30 multi 4.00 1.90
2300 A872 €3 black & pink 9.00 4.25
2301 A873 €3.60 black & tan 10.50 5.00
Nos. 2299-2301 (3) 23.50 11.15

Discovery of Structure of DNA Molecule, 50th Anniv. — A874

2003, Sept. 1 *Perf. 13¼*
2302 A874 58c multi 1.75 .85

Nostradamus (1503-66), Astrologer — A875

2003, Sept. 1 **Photo.**
2303 A875 70c multi 2.00 1.00

2003 Magic Stars Festival, Monte Carlo — A876

2003, Sept. 1 **Litho.** *Perf. 13½x13*
2304 A876 75c multi 2.25 1.10

Discovery of Penicillin by Alexander Fleming, 75th Anniv. — A877

2003, Sept. 1 **Engr.** *Perf. 13¼*
2305 A877 €1.11 multi 3.25 1.60

Awarding of Nobel Physics Prize to Pierre and Marie Curie, Cent. A878

2003, Sept. 1 **Photo.**
2306 A878 €1.20 multi 3.50 1.75

Conquest of Mt. Everest, by Sir Edmund Hillary, 50th Anniv. A879

2003, Sept. 29 **Engr.** *Perf. 13¼*
2307 A879 €1 multi 3.00 1.50

Saint Dévote — A880

No. 2308: a, Kneeling before cross. b, Standing before soldiers. c, Boat and dove. d, Standing in front of church.

2003, Sept. 29
2308 A880 45c Block of 4, #a-d 5.50 5.50

Christmas — A881

2003, Oct. 13 **Photo.**
2309 A881 50c multi 1.50 .75

MonacoPhil 2004 Intl. Philatelic Exhibition — A882

2003, Dec. 15
2310 A882 50c multi 1.50 .75

28th Intl. Circus Festival, Monte Carlo — A883

2003, Dec. 15
2311 A883 70c multi 2.10 1.00

Beausoleil, France, Cent. A884

2004, Jan. 5 **Photo.** *Perf. 13¼*
2312 A884 75c multi 2.25 1.10

Saint Dévote A885

Designs: 50c, Arrest of St. Dévote, vert. 75c, Proceedings against St. Dévote. 90c, Stoning of St. Dévote. €1, St. Dévote in boat, vert. €4, Protection of St. Dévote.

2004, Jan. 5 **Engr.**
2313 A885 50c red brn & red 1.50 .75
2314 A885 75c brn & orange 2.25 1.10
2315 A885 90c dk brn & brn 2.75 1.50
2316 A885 €1 dk brn & yel brn 3.00 1.50
2317 A885 €4 dk brn & red brn 12.00 6.00
Nos. 2313-2317 (5) 21.50 10.85

6th Monegasque Biennale of Cancerology — A886

2004, Jan. 29 **Photo.** *Perf. 13¼*
2318 A886 €1.11 multi 3.25 1.50

Princess Grace Foundation, 40th Anniv. — A887

Princess Grace Irish Library, 20th Anniv. A888

Statue of Princess Grace, by Daphné du Barry — A889

Princess Grace Rose Garden, 20th Anniv. — A890

Photo., Litho. (#2320-2321)

2004, Jan. 29

2319 A887	50c multi		1.50	.75
2320 A888	€1.11 grn & brown		3.25	1.50
2321 A889	€1.45 multi		4.25	2.00
2322 A890	€1.90 multi		5.50	2.75
	Nos. 2319-2322 (4)		14.50	7.00

Flora & Fauna Type of 2002

Designs: 75c, Hyla meridionalis, vert. €4.50, Lacerta viridis, vert.

2004, Mar. 8 Engr. *Perf. 13¼*

2323 A814	75c multi	2.25	1.10
2324 A814	€4.50 multi	13.50	6.75

20th Spring of Arts A891

2004, Apr. 2

2325 A891 €1 multi 3.00 1.50

Cathedral Choir School, Cent. — A892

2004, Apr. 5 Photo.

2326 A892 45c multi 1.40 .70

37th Intl. Flower Show — A893

2004, Apr. 5

2327 A893 58c multi 1.75 .85

Dog Show Type of 2002

2004, Apr. 9 Litho. *Perf. 13x13¼*

2328 A826 90c Cavalier King Charles Spaniel 2.75 1.40

Monaco Grand Prix, 75th Anniv. A894

2004, Apr. 14 Photo. *Perf. 13¼*

2329 A894 €1.20 multi 3.50 1.75

International School of Monaco, 10th Anniv. — A895

2004, Apr. 26 Litho. *Perf. 13x13¼*

2330 A895 50c multi 1.50 .75

Europa — A896

Travel posters: No. 2331, 50c, Shown. No. 2332, 50c, Women in bathing suits at beach.

2004, May 3 Photo. *Perf. 13¼*

2331-2332 A896 Set of 2 3.00 1.50

Order of Grimaldi, 50th Anniv. — A897

Litho. & Embossed

2004, May 3 *Perf. 13¼x13*

2333 A897 90c multi 2.75 1.40

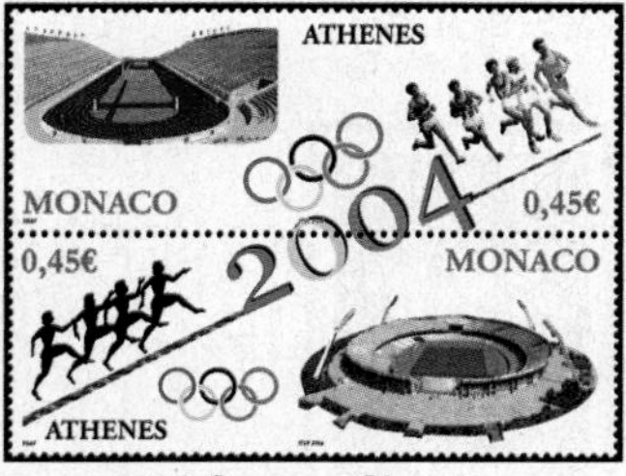
2004 Summer Olympics, Athens — A898

No. 2334: a, Stadium, modern runners. b, Stadium, ancient runners.

2004, May 3 *Perf. 13x13¼*

2334 A898 45c Vert. pair, #a-b 2.75 1.40

Napoleon I and Monegasque Princes in Imperial Army — A899

Stéphanie de Beauharnais, by Baron Gérard — A900

Designs: 75c, Imperial symbols of Napoleon I, horiz. €2.40, Napoleon I, by Gérard.

Perf. 12¼x13, 13x13¼ (75c)

2004, May 28 Photo.

2335 A899	58c multi	1.75	.85
2336 A899	75c multi	2.25	1.10
2337 A900	€1.90 multi	5.75	2.75
2338 A900	€2.40 multi	7.25	3.50
	Nos. 2335-2338 (4)	17.00	8.20

Sergey Diaghilev (1872-1929), George Balanchine (1904-83) and Dancers of Ballet Russes de Monte Carlo — A901

2004, June 14 Engr. *Perf. 13¼*

2339 A901 €1.60 multi 4.75 2.40

44th Television Festival, Monte Carlo — A902

2004, June 14 Litho. *Perf. 13¼x13*

2340 A902 €1.80 multi 5.50 2.75

Frédéric Mistral (1830-1914), 1904 Nobel Laureate in Literature — A903

2004, June 26 Engr. *Perf. 13¼*

2341 A903 45c multi 1.40 .70

23rd UPU Congress, Bucharest, Romania A904

2004, June 26

2342 A904 50c multi 1.50 .75

Marco Polo (1254-1324), Explorer — A905

2004, June 26

2343 A905 50c multi 1.50 .75

Salon du Timbre, Paris A906

2004, June 26

2344 A906 75c multi 2.25 1.10

Translation into French of *A Thousand and One Nights*, 300th Anniv. — A907

Litho. & Silk Screened

2004, June 26 *Perf. 13x13¼*

2345 A907 €1 deep blue & gray 3.00 1.50

Monte Carlo Beach Hotel, 75th Anniv. A908

2004, July 5 Photo. *Perf. 13¼*

2346 A908 45c multi 1.40 .70

FIFA (Fédération Internationale de Football Association), Cent. — A909

2004, Aug. 2

2347 A909 €1.60 multi 4.75 2.40

Magic Stars Magic Festival, Monte Carlo A910

2004, Sept. 6 Litho. ***Perf. 13x13¼***
2348 A910 45c multi 1.40 .70

Souvenir Sheet

Princess Grace (1929-82) — A911

Portraits of Princess Grace engraved by: a, 75c, Pierre Albuisson. b, €1.75, Czeslaw Slania. c, €3.50, Martin Mörck.

2004, Oct. 4 Engr. ***Perf. 13¼x13***
2349 A911 Sheet of 3 + label 18.00 18.00
a. 75c green & blue 2.25 1.10
b. €1.75 green & blue 5.25 2.50
c. €3.50 green & blue 10.50 5.25

Christmas A912

2004, Oct. 4 Photo. ***Perf. 13¼***
2350 A912 50c multi 1.50 .75

Admission to Council of Europe A913

2004, Oct. 5 Engr. ***Perf. 13x12½***
2351 A913 50c red & blue 1.50 .75

29th Intl. Circus Festival, Monte Carlo — A914

2004, Dec. 3 Photo. ***Perf. 13¼***
2352 A914 45c multi 1.40 .70

Louis II Stadium, 20th Anniv. — A915

2004, Dec. 3 Engr. ***Perf. 12½x13***
2353 A915 50c multi 1.50 .75

University of Paris Student Hostel, 70th Anniv. — A916

2004, Dec. 3 ***Perf. 13¼***
2354 A916 58c multi 1.75 .85

Palace of Justice, 75th Anniv. — A917

2004, Dec. 3 Photo.
2355 A917 75c multi 2.25 1.10

French Alliance of Monaco, 25th Anniv. — A918

2004, Dec. 3
2356 A918 75c multi 2.25 1.10

38th Intl. Flower Show — A919

2004, Dec. 3 Photo. ***Perf. 13¼***
2357 A919 90c multi 2.75 1.40

Luigi Valentino Brugnatelli (1761-1818), Inventor of Electroplating — A920

Litho. & Engr.
2004, Dec. 3 ***Perf. 13¼***
2358 A920 €1 blk & brn 3.00 1.50

Jean-Paul Sartre (1905-80), Author A921

2004, Dec. 3 Photo.
2359 A921 €1.11 multi 3.25 1.60

Invention of Safety Matches by Johan Edvard Lundstrom, 150th Anniv. A922

2004, Dec. 3
2360 A922 €1.20 multi 3.50 1.75

Publication of Don Quixote, by Miguel de Cervantes, 400th Anniv. — A923

2004, Dec. 3 Engr.
2361 A923 €1.20 multi 3.50 1.75

Léo Ferré (1916-93), Singer A924

2004, Dec. 3 Photo.
2362 A924 €1.40 multi 4.25 2.10

Invention of Hypodermic Syringe by Alexander Wood, 150th Anniv. — A925

2004, Dec. 3 Engr.
2363 A925 €1.60 multi 4.75 2.40

Development of Carbon 14 Dating by Willard F. Libby, 50th Anniv. — A926

2004, Dec. 3 ***Perf. 12½x13***
2364 A926 €1.80 multi 5.50 2.75

Princes and Palace of Monaco — A927

No. 2365: a, Prince Rainier III (30x31mm). b, Palace of Monaco (60x31mm). c, Hereditary Prince Albert (30x31mm).

2004, Dec. 3 ***Perf. 13¼***
2365 A927 50c Horiz. strip of 3, #a-c 4.50 2.25

First World Cup Soccer Championships, 75th Anniv. — A928

No. 2366: a, World Cup, goalie catching soccer ball. b, Flag of Uruguay, player dribbling ball.

2004, Dec. 3 Photo. ***Perf. 13¼***
2366 A928 €1 Horiz. pair, #a-b 6.00 3.00

Princess Grace Type of 2004 in Changed Colors with "MonacoPhil 2004" Added in Sheet Margin

Souvenir Sheet

Designs like No. 2349.

2004, Dec. 3 Engr. ***Imperf.***
2367 A911 Sheet of 3 18.00 18.00
a. 75c blue & emerald 2.25 2.25
b. €1.75 blue & emerald 5.25 5.25
c. €3.50 blue & emerald 10.50 10.50

Rotary International, Cent. — A929

Designs: 55c, Rotary emblem, founder, president, treasurer and secretary of original club. 70c, Rotary emblem, vert.

Litho. & Engr., Litho. (70c)
Perf. 13¼, 13¼x13 (70c)
2005, Feb. 23
2368-2369 A929 Set of 2 3.75 1.90

UNESCO Fine Arts Committee, 50th Anniv. — A930

2005, Mar. 1 Photo. ***Perf. 13¼***
2370 A930 48c multi 1.40 .70

Publication of Albert Einstein's Theory of Relativity, Cent. — A931

2005, Mar. 1
2371 A931 53c multi 1.60 .80

First Awarding of Diplomas From School of Fine Arts — A932

2005, Mar. 1 Litho. ***Perf. 13¼x13***
2372 A932 64c black & red 1.90 .95

Dog Show Type of 2002

2005, Mar. 1 Photo. ***Perf. 13¼***
2373 A826 82c Dachshund (teckel) 2.50 1.25

Intl. Automobile Federation, Cent. — A933

2005, Apr. 1 Photo. ***Perf. 13¼***
2374 A933 55c multi 1.60 1.60

21st World Exhibition of Hybrid and Electric Vehicles A934

Designs, 75c, Fetish, first electric sports car. €1.30, Stylized automobile with electric plug.

2005, Apr. 1
2375-2376 A934 Set of 2 6.00 6.00

Tenth Horse Jumping International, Monte Carlo — A935

2005, Apr. 1 Engr. ***Perf. 13¼***
2377 A935 90c multi 2.75 1.40

Food — A936

No. 2378, 53c: a, Pissaladière. b, Barbaguians.
No. 2379, 55c: a, Tourte de blettes. b, Desserts.

2005, May 3 Photo.
Horiz. Pairs, #a-b
2378-2379 A936 Set of 2 *6.50 3.25*
Europa (#2378).

Monegasque Special Olympics, 25th Anniv. — A937

2005, June 3 Litho. ***Perf. 13x13¼***
2380 A937 €1.20 multi 3.50 1.75

Early 20th Century Advertising Art A938

Advertisements for: 77c, Bains de Mer de Monaco. €2.50, English Sanitary Co. €3.10, Scapini Biscuits.

2005, June 3 Photo. ***Perf. 12¼x13***
2381-2383 A938 Set of 3 19.00 9.50

Monaco Yacht Show — A939

2005, July 4 ***Perf. 13¼***
2384 A939 82c multi 2.40 1.25

Admission to UPU, 50th Anniv. — A940

2005, July 4 Engr.
2385 A940 €3.03 multi 9.00 4.50

Astronomers A941

Designs: €1.22, Edmond Halley (1656-1742). €1.98, Gerard P. Kuiper (1905-73). €3.80, Clyde Tombaugh (1906-97).

2005, July 4 ***Perf. 12½x13***
2386-2388 A941 Set of 3 21.00 10.50

Coat of Arms Type of 2000
Inscribed "20g Ecopli" at Top
Serpentine Die Cut 11
2005, July 12 Photo.
Booklet Stamp
Self-Adhesive
2389 A786 (48c) grn, blk & red 1.40 1.40
a. Booklet pane of 10 14.00

10th European Patrimony Day — A942

2005, Sept. 5 Engr. ***Perf. 13¼***
2390 A942 48c multi 1.40 1.40

20th Magic Stars Festival, Monte Carlo A943

2005, Sept. 5 Litho. ***Perf. 13x13¼***
2391 A943 €1.45 red, gold & blk 4.25 4.25

Christmas A944

2005, Oct. 3 Engr. ***Perf. 13¼***
2392 A944 53c blk & red 1.60 1.60

Monte Carlo Bay Hotel and Resort A945

2005, Oct. 7 Photo.
2393 A945 55c multi 1.60 1.60

Nadia Boulanger (1887-1979), Conductor, and Lili Boulanger (1893-1918), Composer — A946

2005, Oct. 21 Engr.
2394 A946 90c multi 2.75 2.75

Miniature Sheet

Restoration of Garnier Hall, Monte Carlo Opera — A947

No. 2395: a, "Song." b, Garnier Hall. c, "Comedy." d, "Dance." e, Charles Garnier (1825-98), architect. f, "Music."

2005, Nov. 16
2395 A947 82c Sheet of 6, #a-f 14.50 14.50

Souvenir Sheet

Prince Rainier III (1923-2005) — A948

2005, Nov. 19 ***Perf. 13***
2396 A948 €4 black 12.00 12.00

Prince Albert II — A949

2005, Nov. 19 ***Perf. 13x13¼***
2397 A949 (48c) green 1.40 1.40
2398 A949 (53c) red 1.60 1.60
2399 A949 (75c) blue 2.25 2.25
Nos. 2397-2399 (3) 5.25 5.25

National Day — A950

No. 2400: a, Fontveille (26x27mm, country name at UL). b, Palace (56x27mm). c, La Condamine and Monte Carlo (26x27mm, country name at UR).

2005, Nov. 19 Photo. ***Perf. 13¼***
2400 A950 €1.01 Horiz. strip of 3, #a-c 9.00 9.00

MonacoPhil 2006 Philatelic Exhibition A951

2005, Dec. 12
2401 A951 55c multi 1.60 1.60

30th Intl. Circus Festival, Monte Carlo

A952

A952a

No. 2403: a, Charles Rivel, 1974 Golden Clown. b, Fredy Knie, 1977 Golden Clown. c, Alexis Gruss, Sr., 1975 Golden Clown. d, Golden Clown award. e, Georges Carl, 1979 Golden Clown.

2005, Dec. 14

2402 A952 64c shown 1.90 1.90
2403 A952a 75c Sheet of 5, #a-e, + label 11.00 11.00

The label on No. 2403 has the same vignette as No. 2402, lacking country name and denomination, but with a gray background.

A953

2006 Winter Olympics, Turin A954

No. 2404: a, Red mascot. b, Blue mascot.

2006, Jan. 9 Photo. *Perf. 13¼*

2404 A953 55c Horiz. pair, #a-b 3.25 3.25
2405 A954 82c multi 2.40 2.40

Museum of Postage Stamps and Money, 10th Anniv. A955

2006, Jan. 30 Engr.

2406 A955 53c multi 1.60 1.60

5th Intl. Film and Literature Forum — A956

2006, Feb. 6 Photo. *Perf. 13¼*

2407 A956 82c multi 2.40 2.40

Léopold Sédar Senghor (1906-2001), First President of Senegal — A957

Litho. & Engr.

2006, Mar. 6 *Perf. 13x13¼*

2408 A957 €1.45 multi 4.25 4.25

100th Monte Carlo Tennis Tournament A958

2006, Mar. 8 Photo. *Perf. 13¼*

2409 A958 55c multi 1.60 1.60

Coat of Arms Type of 2000 Inscribed "20g Zone A" at Top

Serpentine Die Cut 11

2006, Apr. 6 Photo.

Self-Adhesive Booklet Stamp

2410 A786 (55c) red & black 1.60 1.60
a. Booklet pane of 10 16.00

Monte Carlo Philharmonic Orchestra, 150th Anniv. — A959

2006, Apr. 6 *Perf. 13¼*

2411 A959 64c multi 1.90 1.90

Arctic Oceanographic Expeditions of Prince Albert I, Cent. — A960

Litho. & Engr.

2006, Apr. 10 *Perf. 13x13¼*

2412 A960 €1.60 multi 4.75 4.75

Dog Show Type of 2002

2006, Apr. 14 Photo. *Perf. 13¼*

2413 A826 64c Special schnauzer 1.90 1.90

39th Intl. Flower Show — A961

2006, Apr. 18

2414 A961 77c multi 2.25 2.25

2006 World Cup Soccer Championships, Germany — A962

No. 2415: a, World Cup, stadium. b, Stadium and 2006 World Cup emblem.

2006, Apr. 18

2415 A962 90c Horiz. pair, #a-b 5.25 5.25

A963

Europa A964

2006, May 5 Photo. *Perf. 13¼*

2416 A963 53c multi 1.60 1.60
2417 A964 55c multi 1.60 1.60

RAMOGE Agreement, 30th Anniv. — A965

2006, May 9 *Perf. 12¼x13*

2418 A965 €1.75 multi 5.25 5.25

Washington 2006 World Philatelic Exhibition A966

2006, May 27 Engr. *Perf. 13¼*

2419 A966 90c blue & red 2.75 2.75

John Huston (1906-87), Film Director — A967

2006, May 27 *Perf. 13x12¼*

2420 A967 €1.80 black & henna brn 5.25 5.25

Prince Albert Challenge Sabre Tournament — A968

2006, June 6 Photo. *Perf. 13¼*

2421 A968 48c multi 1.40 1.40

Pierre Corneille (1606-84), Dramatist A969

2006, June 17

2422 A969 53c multi 1.60 1.60

46th Intl. Television Festival, Monte Carlo — A970

2006, June 17

2423 A970 82c multi 2.40 2.40

Wolfgang Amadeus Mozart (1756-91), Composer — A971

2006, June 17 Engr. *Perf. 13x12¼*

2424 A971 €1.22 org red & blue 3.50 3.50

Prince Pierre Foundation, 40th Anniv. — A972

2006, June 20 *Perf. 12½x13*

2425 A972 €2.50 multi 7.50 7.50

Dino Buzzati (1906-72), Writer A973

2006, July 17 Photo. *Perf. 13¼*

2426 A973 55c multi 1.60 1.60

Cetacean Conservation Accord, 10th Anniv. — A974

2006, July 17 ***Perf. 13x12¼***
2427 A974 90c multi 2.75 2.75

Luchino Visconti (1906-76), Film Director A975

2006, July 17 Engr. ***Perf. 12¼x13***
2428 A975 €1.75 henna brn 5.25 5.25

Rolls-Royce Automobiles, Cent. — A976

2006, Sept. 4 Engr. ***Perf. 13¼***
2429 A976 64c multi 1.90 1.90

2006 Magic Stars Festival, Monte Carlo — A977

2006, Sept. 4 **Photo.**
2430 A977 77c multi 2.25 2.25

Monaco Red Cross — A978

2006, Oct. 2
2431 A978 48c multi 1.40 1.40

Christmas A979

Perf. 13½x13¼
2006, Oct. 2 **Litho. & Engr.**
2432 A979 53c multi 1.60 1.60

Prince Albert II — A980

2006, Dec. 1 Engr. ***Perf. 13x13¼***
2433 A980 (49c) green 1.40 1.40
2434 A980 (54c) red 1.50 1.50
a. Dated "2009" 1.50 1.50
2435 A980 (60c) blue 1.60 1.60
Nos. 2433-2435 (3) 4.50 4.50

Dated 2007.
No. 2434a sold for 56c when issued.

Prince Albert II and Coat of Arms A981

2006, Dec. 1 Photo. ***Perf. 13¼x13***
2436 A981 60c multi 1.60 1.60

Souvenir Sheet
Perf. 13x13¼
2437 A981 €6 multi 16.00 16.00

MonacoPhil 2006 Intl. Philatelic Exhibition. Dated 2007.

World AIDS Day A982

2006, Dec. 1 Litho. ***Perf. 13x13¼***
2438 A982 49c multi 1.40 1.40

Dated 2007.

Josephine Baker (1906-75), Singer and Dancer — A983

2006, Dec. 1 ***Perf. 13¼x13***
2439 A983 49c multi 1.40 1.40

Princess Grace Theater, 25th anniv. Dated 2007.

Philatelic Anniversaries A984

2006, Dec. 1 Photo. ***Perf. 13¼***
2440 A984 54c multi 1.50 1.50

Creation of Philatelic Bureau, 70th anniv. (in 2007), Consultative Commission of the Prince's Philatelic Collection, 20th anniv. (in 2007). Dated 2007.

Les Enfants de Frankie Children's Charity, 10th Anniv. (in 2007) — A985

2006, Dec. 1
2441 A985 70c multi 1.90 1.90

Dated 2007.

Albert Camus (1913-60), 1957 Nobel Literature Laureate — A986

2006, Dec. 1 **Engr.**
2442 A986 84c multi 2.25 2.25

Dated 2007.

Auguste Escoffier (1846-1935), Chef — A987

2006, Dec. 1
2443 A987 85c multi 2.25 2.25

Dated 2007.

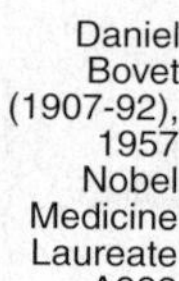

Daniel Bovet (1907-92), 1957 Nobel Medicine Laureate A988

2006, Dec. 1
2444 A988 86c dk blue & red 2.40 2.40

Dated 2007.

Cardiothoracic Center, 20th Anniv. (in 2007) — A989

2006, Dec. 1
2445 A989 €1.15 multi 3.25 3.25

Dated 2007.

Rudyard Kipling (1865-1936), 1907 Nobel Literature Laureate — A990

2006, Dec. 1
2446 A990 €1.57 multi 4.25 4.25

Dated 2007.

Opening of Institute of Sports Medicine and Surgery A991

2006, Dec. 1
2447 A991 €1.70 multi 4.75 4.75

Dated 2007.

Meeting of Prince Albert II and Pope Benedict XVI, 1st Anniv. — A992

2006, Dec. 1 Photo. ***Perf. 13x13¼***
2448 A992 €1.70 multi 4.75 4.75

Dated 2007.

Paul-Emile Victor (1907-95), Explorer — A993

2006, Dec. 1 Engr. ***Perf. 13x12¼***
2449 A993 €2.11 multi 5.75 5.75

Dated 2007.

European Philatelic Academy, 30th Anniv. (in 2007) — A994

2006, Dec. 1 Photo. ***Perf. 13x13¼***
2450 A994 €2.30 multi 6.25 6.25

Dated 2007.

Awarding of 2006 Grand Prix of Philately to Alexander D. Kroo — A995

2006, Dec. 1 Litho. ***Perf. 13¼x13***
2451 A995 €3 multi 8.00 8.00

Dated 2007.

Auto Racing — A996

No. 2452: a, 65th Monaco Grand Prix. b, 75th Monte Carlo Rally.

2006, Dec. 1
2452 A996 60c Horiz. pair, #a-b 3.25 3.25

Dated 2007.

Art in Grimaldi Forum by Nall — A997

No. 2453: a, Purple Flower. b, Yellow Flower

2006, Dec. 1 Photo. ***Perf. 13¼***
2453 A997 €1.70 Pair, #a-b 9.25 9.25

Printed in panes of 2 pairs. Dated 2007.

A998

31st Intl. Circus Festival, Monte Carlo — A999

2006, Dec. 1 Photo. ***Perf. 13¼***
2454 A998 60c multi 1.60 1.60

Litho.

Perf. 13¼x13

2455 A999 84c multi 2.25 2.25

Dated 2007.

Souvenir Sheet

40th Intl. Flower Show — A1000

No. 2456: a, Classic composition. b, Modern composition. c, Contemporary composition. d, Japanese composition.

2006, Dec. 1 Photo. ***Perf. 13¼***
2456 A1000 €1.30 Sheet of 4, #a-d 14.00 14.00

Dated 2007.

Stenella Coeruleoalba — A1001

2007, Jan. 2 Litho. ***Perf. 13x13¼***
2457 A1001 (36c) multi .95 .95

Issued precanceled only. See note after No. 324.

Giuseppe Garibaldi (1807-82), Italian Nationalist Leader A1002

2007, Mar. 16 Engr. ***Perf. 13¼***
2458 A1002 €1.40 ol brn & red 3.75 3.75

Carlo Goldoni (1707-93), Playwright A1003

Litho. & Silk-screened

2007, Mar. 16 ***Perf. 13x13¼***
2459 A1003 €4.54 multi 12.50 12.50

Monaco Olympic Committee, Cent. — A1004

2007, Apr. 2 Photo. ***Perf. 13¼***
2460 A1004 60c multi 1.60 1.60

Dalmatian A1005

2007, Apr. 2 ***Perf. 13x13¼***
2461 A1005 70c multi 1.90 1.90

Intl. Dog Show.

12th Games of Small European States A1006

2007, Apr. 2 ***Perf. 13¼***
2462 A1006 86c multi 2.40 2.40

Princess Grace Exposition, Grimaldi Forum A1007

2007, May 4 Litho. ***Perf. 13***
2463 A1007 85c multi 2.40 2.40

First Flight of Helicopter Designed by Maurice Leger, Cent. — A1008

2007, May 4 Engr. ***Perf. 12½x13***
2464 A1008 €1.15 multi 3.25 3.25

47th Television Festival, Monte Carlo — A1009

2007, May 4 Litho. ***Perf. 13¼x13***
2465 A1009 €2.90 multi 8.00 8.00

Scouting, Cent. — A1010

No. 2466: a, Scouts and campfire. b, Lord Robert Baden-Powell.

2007, May 4 Photo. ***Perf. 13¼***
2466 A1010 60c Horiz. pair, #a-b 3.25 3.25

Cartophily, Numismatics and Philately Grand Bourse — A1011

Litho. & Silk-Screened

2007, June 25 ***Perf. 13¼x13***
2467 A1011 49c multi 1.40 1.40

22nd Magic Stars Festival, Monte Carlo — A1012

2007, June 25 Litho.
2468 A1012 €1.30 red & black 3.50 3.50

Monaco Harbor — A1013

2007, Oct. 1 Engr. ***Perf. 13x12½***
2469 A1013 85c multi 2.40 2.40

Christmas A1014

Litho. & Silk-screened

2007, Oct. 1 ***Perf. 13¼x13***
2470 A1014 54c multi 1.60 1.60

32nd Intl. Circus Festival, Monte Carlo — A1015

2007, Oct. 15 Photo. ***Perf. 13¼***
2471 A1015 60c multi 1.75 1.75

Giacomo Puccini (1858-1924), Composer A1016

2007, Dec. 7 Engr. ***Perf. 13¼***

2472 A1016 €1.40 blue & red 4.25 4.25

41st Intl. Flower Show — A1017

2008, Jan. 3 **Photo.**

2473 A1017 49c multi 1.50 1.50

Reformed Church of Monaco, 50th Anniv. — A1018

2008, Jan. 3 Engr. ***Perf. 13¼***

2474 A1018 49c blue & brown 1.50 1.50

Consecration of St. Charles Church, 125th Anniv. — A1019

2008, Mar. 3

2475 A1019 54c gray blue & red 1.60 1.60

Arc de Triomphe du Carrousel Quadriga, Paris, by François Joseph Bosio A1020

2008, Jan. 3

2476 A1020 54c multi 1.60 1.60

Andrea Palladio (1508-80), Architect A1021

2008, Jan. 3 Photo. ***Perf. 13¼***

2477 A1021 60c multi 1.75 1.75

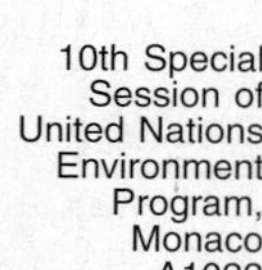

10th Special Session of United Nations Environment Program, Monaco A1022

2008, Jan. 3 Photo. ***Perf. 13¼***

2478 A1022 85c multi 2.50 2.50

Johannes Brahms (1833-97), Composer A1023

2008, Jan. 3 Engr. ***Perf. 13¼***

2479 A1023 €1.15 Prus grn & red 3.50 3.50

Return of Comet Predicted by Edmond Halley, 250th Anniv. A1024

2008, Jan. 3 Photo. ***Perf. 13¼***

2480 A1024 €1.57 multi 4.75 4.75

Marcel Kroenlein Arboretum, Roure, France, 20th Anniv. — A1025

2008, Jan. 3 Engr. ***Perf. 13¼***

2481 A1025 €2.11 multi 6.25 6.25

Poster for Monte Carlo Country Club, by Raymond Gid A1026

Poster for Monte Carlo Beach Hotel, by Raymond Gid A1027

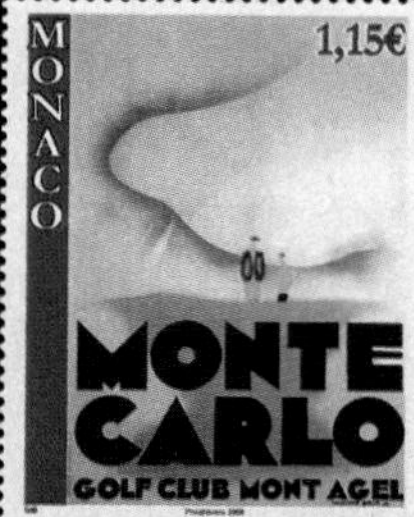

Poster for Monte Carlo Golf Club, by Raymond Gid A1028

Poster for Monte Carlo Tourism, by Louis Rué A1029

Perf. 12¼x13, 13 (#2483)

2008, Jan. 3 Photo., Litho. (#2483)

2482	A1026	70c multi	2.10	2.10
2483	A1027	85c multi	2.50	2.50
2484	A1028	€1.15 multi	3.50	3.50
2485	A1029	€2.90 multi	8.50	8.50
		Nos. 2482-2485 (4)	16.60	16.60

Gen. André Massena (1758-1817) A1030

2008, Jan. 21 Engr. ***Perf. 13¼***

2486 A1030 86c grn & yel brown 2.60 2.60

Apparition at Lourdes, France, 150th Anniv. A1031

2008, Feb. 11 Engr. ***Perf. 13x12¾***

2487 A1031 €1.30 dark blue & blue 4.00 4.00

Introduction of the Ford Model T, Cent. — A1032

2008, Mar. 10 ***Perf. 13¼***

2488 A1032 €1.70 multi 5.50 5.50

National Aeronautics and Space Administration, 50th Anniv. — A1033

2008, Mar. 10

2489 A1033 €2.30 multi 7.25 7.25

Alfred Nobel (1833-1906), Inventor and Philantropist A1034

2008, Mar. 10

2490 A1034 €4 blk & claret 12.50 12.50

Dog Show Type of 2002

2008, Mar. 17 Photo. ***Perf. 13¼***

2491 A826 88c Greyhound, vert. 2.75 2.75

Expo Zaragoza 2008 A1035

2008, Mar. 18 Litho. ***Perf. 13x13¼***

2492 A1035 65c multi 2.10 2.10

Mother's Day — A1036

2008, Apr. 8 ***Perf. 13¼x13***

2493 A1036 55c multi 1.75 1.75

Stendhal (Marie-Henri Beyle) (1783-1842), Writer — A1037

2008, Apr. 8 Engr. ***Perf. 13¼***

2494 A1037 €1.33 multi 4.25 4.25

Boris Pasternak (1890-1960), Writer — A1038

2008, Apr. 8

2495 A1038 €2.18 multi 7.00 7.00

2008 Summer Olympics, Beijing — A1039

No. 2496 — Olympic rings and: a, Pagoda, basketball, tennis, javelin. b, Beijing Olympics emblem, baseball, fencing, shooting.

2008, Apr. 8 ***Perf. 13x12½***
2496 A1039 Horiz. pair 4.50 4.50
a. 55c red & black 1.75 1.75
b. 85c red & black 2.75 2.75

Cap d'Ail, France, Cent. A1040

2008, Apr. 21 Litho. ***Perf. 13x13¼***
2497 A1040 55c multi 1.75 1.75

Exotic Garden, 75th Anniv. A1041

2008, May 2 Engr. ***Perf. 13¼***
2498 A1041 50c multi 1.60 1.60

2008 Magic Stars Festival, Monte Carlo — A1042

2008, May 5 **Photo.**
2499 A1042 72c multi 2.25 2.25

Europa A1043

Designs: 55c, Letters encircling globe. 65c, Postmen, letter, means of postal communication.

2008, May 5 **Engr.**
2500-2501 A1043 Set of 2 3.75 3.75

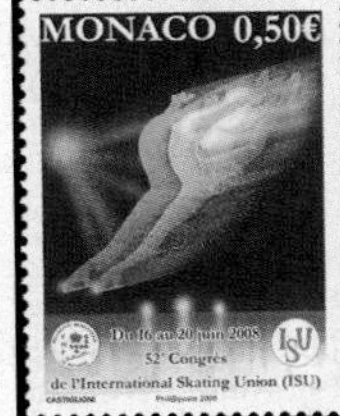

Intl. Skating Union, 52nd Congress A1044

2008, May 16 Litho. ***Perf. 13¼x13***
2502 A1044 50c multi 1.60 1.60

Prince Albert II of Monaco Foundation A1045

Litho. & Engr.

2008, May 16 ***Perf. 13x13¼***
2503 A1045 88c multi 2.75 2.75

48th Intl. Television Festival, Monte Carlo — A1046

2008, June 2 Photo. ***Perf. 13¼***
2504 A1046 €2.80 multi 9.00 9.00

Monegasque International Cooperation — A1047

Designs: 65c, Education. €1, Health. €1.25, Campaign against poverty. €1.70, Campaign against desertification.

2008, June 5 **Engr.**
2505-2508 A1047 Set of 4 14.50 14.50

Monaco 2008 Intl. Numismatic Exhibition A1048

Litho. & Embossed With Foil Application

2008, June 16 ***Perf. 13½x13***
2509 A1048 65c multi 2.10 2.10

Schönbrunn Palace, Vienna — A1049

2008, Sept. 18 Engr. ***Perf. 13¼***
2510 A1049 65c multi 1.90 1.90

WIPA 2008 Intl. Philatelic Exhibition, Vienna.

Order of Saint Charles, 150th Anniv. A1050

Photo. & Embossed With Foil Application

2008, Sept. 18 ***Perf. 13x13¼***
2511 A1050 €1.50 multi 4.25 4.25

Coins of Monaco A1051

Obverse and reverse of: 50c, 1837 Franc. 55c, 1943 Franc. 72c, 1950 Franc. €1.25, 1960 Franc. €1.64, Euro coinage of 2002. €1.70, Euro coinage of 2006.

Litho. & Embossed With Foil Application

2008, Sept. 18
2512-2517 A1051 Set of 6 17.50 17.50

Christmas A1052

2008, Sept. 19 Photo. ***Perf. 13¼***
2518 A1052 55c multi 1.50 1.50

33rd Intl. Circus Festival, Monte Carlo — A1053

2008, Dec. 19 Photo. ***Perf. 13¼***
2519 A1053 85c multi 2.40 2.40

Prince Albert I — A1054

Flag of Monaco and Intl. Polar Year Emblem A1055

Prince Albert II — A1056

2008, Dec. 19 ***Perf. 13x12¼***
2520 Horiz. strip of 3 7.25 7.25
a. A1054 85c multi 2.40 2.40
b. A1055 85c multi 2.40 2.40
c. A1056 85c multi 2.40 2.40

Admiral Robert E. Peary (1856-1920), Arctic Explorer, and Dog Sleds — A1057

Peary, Flag of US and Map of Arctic Area A1058

Matthew Henson (1866-1955), Arctic Explorer and Ship — A1059

Litho. & Engr.

2008, Dec. 19 ***Perf. 13¼***
2521 Horiz. strip of 3 7.25 7.25
a. A1057 87c multi 2.40 2.40
b. A1058 87c multi 2.40 2.40
c. A1059 87c multi 2.40 2.40

Monaco Firefighting Corps, Cent. A1060

Designs: 50c, Railway and road emergency vehicle. 72c, Ladder truck, 1909. 87c, Fireman, ladder truck.

2009, Jan. 5 Photo. ***Perf. 13¼***
2522-2524 A1060 Set of 3 5.75 5.75

Princess Grace Rose Garden, 25th Anniv. — A1061

2009, Jan. 5 ***Perf. 13¼x13***
2525 A1061 €1.25 multi 3.50 3.50

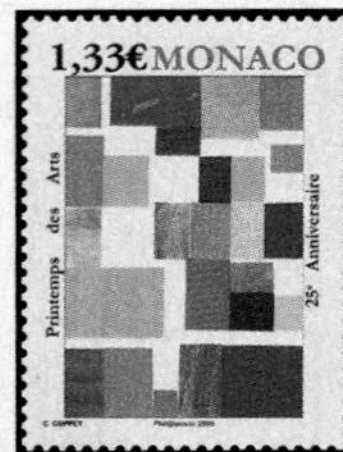

Spring Arts Festival, 25th Anniv. — A1062

2009, Jan. 5
2526 A1062 €1.33 multi 3.75 3.75

First Flight Across English Channel by Louis Blériot, Cent. A1063

Litho. & Engr.
2009, Jan. 29 ***Perf. 13x12½***
2527 A1063 87c multi 2.25 2.25

Felix Mendelssohn Bartholdy (1809-47), Composer A1064

2009, Jan. 29 Engr. ***Perf. 13¼***
2528 A1064 €1.50 olive grn & blue 4.00 4.00

Beatification of Joan of Arc, Cent. — A1065

2009, Jan. 29
2529 A1065 €2.22 multi 5.75 5.75

MonacoPhil 2009 Philatelic Exhibition A1066

2009, Feb. 7 Litho. ***Perf. 13¼x13***
2530 A1066 56c multi 1.50 1.50

Chihuahua and Cavalier King Charles Spaniel A1067

2009, Feb. 7 Photo. ***Perf. 13¼***
2531 A1067 72c multi 1.90 1.90

Intl. Dog Show.

2009 Intl. Cat Show A1068

2009, Feb. 7 Litho. ***Perf. 13x13¼***
2532 A1068 88c multi 2.25 2.25

Association of Members of the Order of Academic Palms World Conference — A1069

2009, Feb. 7 Engr. ***Perf. 13x12½***
2533 A1069 88c multi 2.25 2.25

Barbie Doll, 50th Anniv. — A1070

2009, Feb. 7 Photo. ***Perf. 13¼***
2534 A1070 88c multi 2.25 2.25

42nd Intl. Flower Show — A1071

2009, Feb. 7 Photo. ***Perf. 13¼***
2535 A1071 89c multi 2.25 2.25

Monaco Fencing and Handgun Club, Cent. — A1072

2009, Feb. 16 Litho. & Engr.
2536 A1072 55c multi 1.40 1.40

Giro d'Italia Bicycle Race, Cent. — A1073

2009, Feb. 16 Photo.
2537 A1073 70c multi 1.75 1.75

Sir Arthur Conan Doyle (1859-1930), Writer — A1074

2009, Feb. 16 Engr. ***Perf. 12¼***
2538 A1074 85c multi 2.25 2.25

Edgar Allan Poe (1809-49), Writer — A1075

2009, Feb. 16
2539 A1075 €1.70 red & dark green 4.50 4.50

Coat of Arms — A1076

Serpentine Die Cut 11
2009, Apr. 6 Photo.
Booklet Stamp
Self-Adhesive
2540 A1076 (70c) multi 1.90 1.90
a. Booklet pane of 10 19.00

Louis Notari Library, Cent. A1077

2009, Apr. 29 Engr. ***Perf. 13x12½***
2541 A1077 51c red & purple 1.40 1.40

Monaco Grand Prix Auto Race, Cent. — A1078

2009, Apr. 29 Photo. ***Perf. 13x13¼***
2542 A1078 70c multi 1.90 1.90

Monaco's Admission to UNESCO, 60th Anniv. — A1079

2009, Apr. 29
2543 A1079 €1.70 multi 4.50 4.50

Louis Braille (1809-52), Educator of the Blind A1080

2009, Apr. 29 Engr. ***Perf. 12¼x13***
2544 A1080 €3.80 multi 10.00 10.00

Concerts at the Prince's Palace, 50th Anniv. A1081

2009, May 4 ***Perf. 13x13¼***
2545 A1081 51c purple & black 1.50 1.50

Europa A1082

Astronomers: 56c, Francesco Maria Grimaldi (1618-63), map of Moon showing crater named after Grimaldi. 70c, Galileo Galilei (1564-1642), telescope.

Litho. & Engr.
2009, May 4 ***Perf. 13x12½***
2546-2547 A1082 Set of 2 3.50 3.50

Intl. Year of Astronomy.

Ballets de Monte-Carlo — A1083

2009, May 11 Photo. ***Perf. 13¼x13***
2548 A1083 73c multi 2.10 2.10

Ballets Russes, Cent. A1084

Designs: 89c, Fifteen performers. €1.35, Nine performers.

2009, May 11
2549-2550 A1084 Set of 2 6.25 6.25

Georges Seurat (1859-91), Painter A1085

Litho. & Engr.

2009, May 14 ***Perf. 13x13¼***
2551 A1085 73c multi 2.10 2.10

St. Francis of Assisi (c. 1181-1226) A1086

2009, May 14 Engr. ***Perf. 13¼***
2552 A1086 90c blue & black 2.50 2.50

Franciscan Order, 800th anniv.

John Calvin (1509-64), Theologian and Religious Reformer A1087

2009, May 14 ***Perf. 13x13¼***
2553 A1087 €1.67 multi 4.75 4.75

49th Intl. Television Festival, Monte Carlo — A1088

2009, May 29 Photo. ***Perf. 13¼***
2554 A1088 €1.60 multi 4.50 4.50

Italian Writers A1089

Emblem of Monaco Dante Alighieri Society and: 70c, Niccolò Machiavelli (1469-1527). 85c, Giovanni Boccaccio (1313-75). €1.30, Francesco Petrarca (Petrarch) (1304-74).

2009, June 3 Engr. ***Perf. 12¼x13***
2555-2557 A1089 Set of 3 8.00 8.00

Monaco Dante Alighieri Society, 30th anniv.

Grande Bourse 2009 — A1090

2009, June 17 Photo. ***Perf. 13¼***
2558 A1090 51c multi 1.50 1.50

Youth Hostels, Cent. A1091

2009, June 17 Litho. ***Perf. 13x13¼***
2559 A1091 90c multi 2.50 2.50

Tuiga, Flagship of Monaco Yacht Club, Cent. A1092

2009, June 18 Photo. ***Perf. 13¼***
2560 A1092 70c multi 2.00 2.00

Start of Tour de France Bicycle Race in Monaco A1093

2009, July 2 Litho. ***Perf. 13¼x13***
2561 A1093 56c multi 1.60 1.60

2009 Magic Stars Festival, Monte Carlo — A1094

2009, Sept. 16 Litho. ***Perf. 13¼x13***
2562 A1094 73c multi 2.25 2.25

Place de la Mairie — A1095

2009, Sept. 16 **Photo.**
2563 A1095 85c multi 2.50 2.50

Big Ben, 150th Anniv. — A1096

2009, Sept. 16 **Engr.**
2564 A1096 €1 red & black 3.00 3.00

Christmas A1097

2009, Oct. 5 ***Perf. 13x13¼***
2565 A1097 56c multi 1.75 1.75

2010 Intl. Cat Show — A1098

2009, Dec. 4 Photo. ***Perf. 13¼***
2566 A1098 56c multi 1.75 1.75

Dated 2010.

Jean Anouilh (1910-87), Playwright — A1099

2009, Dec. 4 Engr. ***Perf. 13x12¼***
2567 A1099 73c multi 2.25 2.25

Dated 2010.

Ayrton Senna (1960-94), Race Car Driver — A1100

2009, Dec. 4 Engr. ***Perf. 13x12¼***
2568 A1100 73c multi 2.25 2.25

Dated 2010.

Auguste Rodin (1840-1917), Sculptor — A1101

2009, Dec. 4 Engr. ***Perf. 13x12¼***
2569 A1101 85c multi 2.60 2.60

Dated 2010.

Princess Grace (1929-82) A1102

2009, Dec. 4 Engr. ***Perf. 12¼x13***
2570 A1102 89c red & black 2.75 2.75

Dated 2010.

Gustav Mahler (1860-1911), Composer — A1103

2009, Dec. 4
2571 A1103 90c brown & blue 2.75 2.75

Dated 2010.

2010 Winter Olympics, Vancouver — A1104

No. 2572 — 2010 Winter Olympics emblem and: a, Slalom skier. b, Snowboarder and figure skater.

2009, Dec. 4 Engr. *Perf. 13¼x13½*
2572 A1104 Horiz. pair 5.50 5.50
a.-b. 90c Either single 2.75 2.75

Dated 2010.

Monte Carlo Vu de Roquebrune, by Claude Monet (1840-1926) — A1105

2009, Dec. 4 Photo. *Perf. 13x13¼*
2573 A1105 €1.30 multi 4.00 4.00

Dated 2010.

US No. 85A, Trophy A1106

2009, Dec. 4 Litho.
2574 A1106 €1.35 multi 4.00 4.00

Awarding of Intl. Association of Stamp Catalogue Publishers Grand Prix for Philately to William H. Gross. Dated 2010.

The Birth of Venus, by William Bouguereau (1825-1905) — A1107

2009, Dec. 4 Photo. *Perf. 13¼x13*
2575 A1107 €1.60 multi 4.75 4.75

Dated 2010.

Anton Chekhov (1860-1904), Writer — A1108

2009, Dec. 4 Engr. *Perf. 13x12¼*
2576 A1108 €1.67 multi 5.00 5.00

Dated 2010.

Souvenir Sheet

Prince Albert II — A1109

Litho. (Margin) & Engr.
2009, Dec. 4 *Perf. 13¼x13*
2577 A1109 €4 red & black 12.00 12.00

MonacoPhil 2009 Intl. Philatelic Exhibition. Dated 2010.

Souvenir Sheet

Automobile Club of Monaco, 120th Anniv. — A1110

No. 2578: a, Race car. b, Formula 1 race car.

2009, Dec. 4 Photo. *Perf. 13x13¼*
2578 A1110 Sheet of 2 9.00 9.00
a. €1.30 multi 4.00 4.00
b. €1.70 multi 5.00 5.00

Dated 2010.

34th Intl. Circus Festival, Monte Carlo — A1111

2009, Dec. 10 Photo. *Perf. 13¼*
2579 A1111 70c multi 2.10 2.10

Dated 2010.

Australian Shepherd A1112

2010, Feb. 8 Photo. *Perf. 13¼*
2580 A1112 51c multi 1.40 1.40

Intl. Dog Show.

Intl. Flower Arrangement Festival — A1113

2010, Feb. 8
2581 A1113 70c multi 1.90 1.90

Five Nations Rugby Championships, Cent. — A1114

2010, Feb. 8 Litho. *Perf. 13¼x13*
2582 A1114 70c multi 1.90 1.90

Scenes From "The Seven Samurai," Film by Akira Kurosawa (1910-98) — A1115

2010, Feb. 24 Engr. *Perf. 13x12¼*
2583 A1115 51c ol grn & black 1.40 1.40

Monte Carlo Rolex Masters Tennis Tournament A1116

2010, Mar. 4 Photo. *Perf. 13¼*
2584 A1116 85c multi 2.40 2.40

2010 World Cup Soccer Championships, South Africa — A1117

No. 2585 — Flag of South Africa, players in stadium with denomination at: a, LL. b, UR.

2010, Mar. 4
2585 A1117 Horiz. pair 5.00 5.00
a.-b. 89c Either single 2.50 2.50

Souvenir Sheet

2008 Monaco Coin — A1118

Litho. & Embossed With Foil Application
2010, Mar. 4 *Perf. 13½*
2586 A1118 €1 multi 2.75 2.75

Expo 2010, Shanghai.

Miniature Sheet

Oceanographic Museum of Monaco, Cent. — A1119

No. 2587: a, Prince Albert I. b, Stuffed Ursus maritimus. c, Pterapogon kauderni, horiz. d, Hands pointing at starfish, horiz.

Litho. & Engr.
2010, Mar. 29 *Perf. 13¼x13*
2587 A1119 Sheet of 4 7.50 7.50
a. 51c multi 1.40 1.40
b. 56c multi 1.50 1.50
c. 73c multi 2.00 2.00
d. 90c multi 2.50 2.50

Miniature Sheet

Former Grimaldi Family Fiefs in France — A1120

No. 2588: a, County of Thann. b, Barony of Altkirch. c, County of Rosemont. d, County of Ferrette.

2010, Apr. 23 Photo. *Perf. 13x13¼*
2588 A1120 €1 Sheet of 4, #a-d 11.00 11.00

Flora and Fauna — A1121

Designs: 2c, Pinna nobilis, Submarine Reserve of Larvotto. €2, Lis martagon, Mercantour National Park, France.

2010, Apr. 29 Engr. *Perf. 13¼*
2589 A1121 2c multi .20 .20
2590 A1121 €2 multi 5.50 5.50

Mother Teresa (1910-97), Humanitarian A1122

2010, Apr. 29 Photo. *Perf. 13¼*
2591 A1122 €1.70 multi 4.50 4.50

UNAIDS Program, 15th Anniv. — A1123

2010, May 5 Photo. *Perf. 13¼*
2592 A1123 89c multi 2.25 2.25

Europa A1124

Map of Europe, books and: 56c, Five children. 70c, One child.

2010, May 5 Engr. *Perf. 13x13¼*
2593-2594 A1124 Set of 2 3.25 3.25

London 2010 Festival of Stamps — A1125

2010, May 7
2595 A1125 €1.30 multi 3.50 3.50

50th Television Festival, Monte Carlo — A1126

Litho. With Foil Application

2010, May 26 *Perf. 13¼x13*
2596 A1126 €2.80 multi 6.75 6.75

Human Paleontology Institute, Paris, Cent. — A1127

2010, June 1 Engr. *Perf. 13x12¾*
2597 A1127 56c multi 1.40 1.40

See France No. 3821.

Grimaldi Forum, 10th Anniv. A1128

2010, June 22 Litho. *Perf. 13x13¼*
2598 A1128 75c multi 1.90 1.90

Youth Olympic Games, Singapore — A1129

2010, June 22 Photo.
2599 A1129 87c multi 2.25 2.25

Maritime and Airport Police Division, 50th Anniv. — A1130

2010, July 1 Engr. *Perf. 13¼*
2600 A1130 53c multi 1.40 1.40

Invention of the Food Canning Process, by Nicholas Appert, Bicent. A1131

2010, July 1 *Perf. 12¼*
2601 A1131 95c red & purple 2.40 2.40

Invention of First Practical Internal Combustion Engine by Jean-Joseph-Etienne Lenoir, 150th Anniv. — A1132

2010, July 1
2602 A1132 €1.75 multi 4.50 4.50

Little Africa Gardens, Monaco — A1133

2010, July 1 *Perf. 13x13¼*
2603 A1133 €2.30 multi 5.75 5.75

First International Electric Postal Flight, Monaco to Nice — A1134

2010, Aug. 23 Litho. *Perf. 13*
2604 A1134 95c multi 2.50 2.50

Monaco Scientific Center, 50th Anniv. A1135

2010, Sept. 17 Photo. *Perf. 13¼*
2605 A1135 58c multi 1.50 1.50

25th Magic Stars Festival, Monte Carlo — A1136

2010, Sept. 17 Litho. *Perf. 13¼x13*
2606 A1136 €1.40 multi 3.75 3.75

Monaco Regional Express Transport A1137

2010, Sept. 19 Engr. *Perf. 13x13¼*
2607 A1137 €1.35 multi 3.50 3.50

SEMI-POSTAL STAMPS

No. 16 Surcharged in Red

1914, Oct. Unwmk. *Perf. 14x13½*
B1 A2 10c + 5c carmine 8.00 8.00

View of Monaco — SP2

1919, Sept. 20 Typo.

B2	SP2	2c + 3c lilac	32.50	*35.00*
B3	SP2	5c + 5c green	21.00	*20.00*
B4	SP2	15c + 10c rose	21.00	*20.00*
B5	SP2	25c + 15c blue	39.00	*40.00*
B6	SP2	50c + 50c brn, *buff*	190.00	*175.00*
B7	SP2	1fr + 1fr blk, *yel*	300.00	*375.00*
B8	SP2	5fr + 5fr dull red	1,000.	*1,200.*
		Nos. B2-B8 (7)	1,603.	*1,865.*

Nos. B4-B8 Surcharged

1920, Mar. 20

B9	SP2 2c + 3c on #B4	40.00	*45.00*
a.	"c" of "3c" inverted	*1,500.*	*1,850.*
b.	Pair, Nos. 9, 9a	2,250.	*2,600.*
B10	SP2 2c + 3c on #B5	40.00	*45.00*
a.	"c" of "3c" inverted	*1,500.*	*1,850.*
b.	Pair, Nos. 10, 10a	2,250.	*2,600.*
B11	SP2 2c + 3c on #B6	40.00	*45.00*
a.	"c" of "3c" inverted	*1,500.*	*1,850.*
b.	Pair, Nos. 11, 11a	2,250.	*2,600.*
B12	SP2 5c + 5c on #B7	40.00	*45.00*
B13	SP2 5c + 5c on #B8	40.00	*45.00*

Overprinted

B14	SP2 15c + 10c rose	25.00	25.00
B15	SP2 25c + 15c blue	16.00	16.00
B16	SP2 50c + 50c brown, *buff*	55.00	55.00
B17	SP2 1fr + 1fr black, *yel*	75.00	75.00
B18	SP2 5fr + 5fr red	6,500.	6,500.
	Nos. B9-B17 (9)	371.00	396.00

Marriage of Princess Charlotte to Prince Pierre, Comte de Polignac.

Palace Gardens SP3

"The Rock" of Monaco SP4

Bay of Monaco SP5

Prince Louis II — SP6

1937, Apr. Engr. *Perf. 13*

B19	SP3	50c + 50c green	3.00	3.00
B20	SP4	90c + 90c car	3.00	3.00
B21	SP5	1.50fr + 1.50fr blue	6.00	6.00
B22	SP6	2fr + 2fr violet	11.50	11.50
B23	SP6	5fr + 5fr brn red	100.00	100.00
		Nos. B19-B23 (5)	123.50	123.50
		Set, never hinged	250.00	

The surtax was used for welfare work.

Pierre and Marie Curie — SP7

Monaco Hospital, Date Palms SP8

1938, Nov. 15 *Perf. 13*

B24	SP7	65c + 25c dp bl grn	11.00	11.00
B25	SP8	1.75fr + 50c dp ultra	11.00	11.00
		Set, never hinged	40.00	

B24 and B25 exist imperforate.

The surtax was for the International Union for the Control of Cancer.

Lucien — SP9

Honoré II — SP10

Louis I — SP11

Charlotte de Gramont — SP12

Antoine I — SP13

Marie de Lorraine — SP14

Jacques I SP15

Louise-Hippolyte SP16

Honoré III — SP17

"The Rock," 18th Century SP18

1939, June 26

B26	SP9	5c + 5c brown blk	1.90	1.10
B27	SP10	10c + 10c rose vio	1.90	1.10

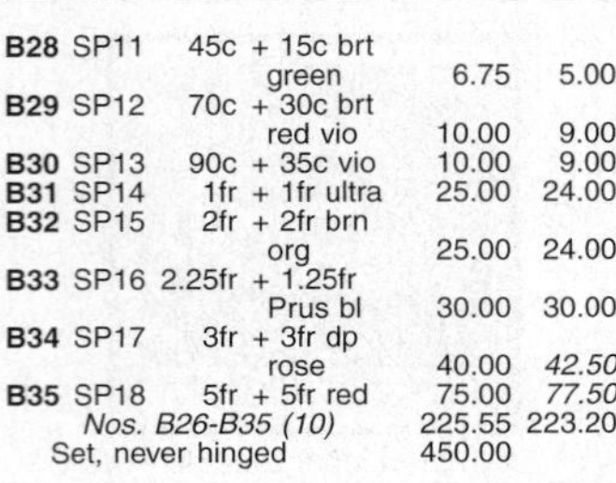

B28	SP11	45c + 15c brt green	6.75	5.00
B29	SP12	70c + 30c brt red vio	10.00	9.00
B30	SP13	90c + 35c vio	10.00	9.00
B31	SP14	1fr + 1fr ultra	25.00	24.00
B32	SP15	2fr + 2fr brn org	25.00	24.00
B33	SP16	2.25fr + 1.25fr Prus bl	30.00	30.00
B34	SP17	3fr + 3fr dp rose	40.00	*42.50*
B35	SP18	5fr + 5fr red	75.00	*77.50*
		Nos. B26-B35 (10)	225.55	223.20
		Set, never hinged	450.00	

Types of Regular Issue, 1939 Surcharged in Red

1940, Feb. 10 **Engr.** *Perf. 13*

B36	A30	20c + 1fr violet	2.75	2.75
B37	A31	25c + 1fr dk grn	2.75	2.75
B38	A32	30c + 1fr brn red	2.75	2.75
B39	A31	40c + 1fr dk blue	2.75	2.75
B40	A33	45c + 1fr rose car	2.75	2.75
B41	A34	50c + 1fr brown	2.75	2.75
B42	A32	60c + 1fr dk grn	3.50	3.50
B43	A35	75c + 1fr brn blk	3.50	3.50
B44	A34	1fr + 1fr scarlet	4.50	4.50
B45	A31	2fr + 1fr indigo	4.50	4.50
B46	A33	2.50fr + 1fr dk grn	11.00	11.00
B47	A35	3fr + 1fr dk blue	11.00	11.00
B48	A30	5fr + 1fr brn blk	15.00	15.00
B49	A33	10fr + 5fr lt blue	28.00	28.00
B50	A32	20fr + 5fr brn vio	29.00	29.00
		Nos. B36-B50 (15)	126.50	126.50
		Set, never hinged	300.00	

The surtax was used to purchase ambulances for the French government.

Catalogue values for unused stamps in this section, from this point to the end of the section, are for Never Hinged items.

Symbol of Charity and View of Monaco SP19

Symbol of Charity and View of Monaco — SP20

1941, May 15

B51	SP19	25c + 25c brt red vio	3.50	1.75
B52	SP20	50c + 25c dk brown	3.50	1.75
B53	SP20	75c + 50c rose vio	6.50	2.25
B54	SP19	1fr + 1fr dk blue	6.50	2.25
B55	SP20	1.50fr + 1.50fr rose red	6.50	2.25
B56	SP19	2fr + 2fr Prus grn	7.00	3.00
B57	SP20	2.50fr + 2fr brt ultra	8.50	4.00
B58	SP19	3fr + 3fr dl red brn	11.00	4.50
B59	SP20	5fr + 5fr dk bl grn	16.00	6.50
B60	SP19	10fr + 8fr brn blk	24.00	13.00
		Nos. B51-B60 (10)	93.00	41.25

The surtax was for various charities.

Rainier Grimaldi — SP21

Designs: 5c, Charles II. 10c, Jeanne Grimaldi. 20c, Charles-August Goyon de Matignon. 30c, Jacques I. 40c, Louise-Hippolyte. 50c, Charlotte Grimaldi. 75c, Marie-Charles Grimaldi. 1fr, Honore III. 1.50fr, Honore IV. 2.50fr, Honore V. 3fr, Florestan I. 5fr, Charles III. 10fr, Albert I. 20fr, Marie-Victoire. Frames differ.

1942, Dec. 10

B61	SP21	2c + 3c ultra	.50	.50
B62	SP21	5c + 5c org ver	.50	.50
B63	SP21	10c + 5c blk	.50	.50
B64	SP21	20c + 10c brt grn	.50	.50
B65	SP21	30c + 30c brn vio	.50	.50
B66	SP21	40c + 40c rose red	.50	.50
B67	SP21	50c + 50c vio	.50	.50
B68	SP21	75c + 75c brt red vio	.50	.50
B69	SP21	1fr + 1fr dk grn	.50	.50
B70	SP21	1.50fr + 1fr car brn	.50	.50
B71	SP21	2.50fr + 2.50fr pur	5.50	4.75
B72	SP21	3fr + 3fr turq bl	6.00	4.75
B73	SP21	5fr + 5fr sepia	6.75	6.00
B74	SP21	10fr + 5fr rose lil	7.25	6.75
B75	SP21	20fr + 5fr ultra	8.75	7.75
		Nos. B61-B75 (15)	39.25	35.00

Saint Dévote SP36

Procession SP37

Procession SP38

Church of St. Dévote — SP39

Burning of Symbolic Boat — SP40

Blessing of the Sea SP41

Church of St. Dévote SP42

Trial of St. Barbara — SP43

Arrival of St. Dévote at Monaco — SP44

1944, Jan. 27 **Unwmk.** *Perf. 13*

B76	SP36	50c + 50c sepia	.25	.25
B77	SP37	70c + 80c dp ultra	.25	.25
B78	SP38	80c + 70c green	.25	.25
B79	SP39	1fr + 1fr rose vio	.25	.25
B80	SP40	1.50fr + 1.50fr red	.45	.45
B81	SP41	2fr + 2fr brn vio	.85	.85
B82	SP42	5fr + 2fr violet	.85	.85
B83	SP43	10fr + 40fr royal bl	.85	.85
B84	SP44	20fr + 60fr chlky bl	6.00	6.00
		Nos. B76-B84 (9)	10.00	10.00

Issued in honor of St. Dévote.

Type SP43 is inscribed "Jugement de Sainte Dévote," but actually shows the trial of St. Barbara in 235 A.D.

Needy Child — SP45

Nurse and Child — SP46

1946, Feb. 18 **Engr.**

B85	SP45	1fr + 3fr dp bl grn	.35	.35
B86	SP45	2fr + 4fr rose pink	.35	.35
B87	SP45	4fr + 6fr dk bl	.35	.35
B88	SP45	5fr + 40fr dk vio	1.10	.90
B89	SP45	10fr + 60fr brn red	1.10	.90
B90	SP45	15fr + 100fr indigo	1.60	1.40
		Nos. B85-B90 (6)	4.85	4.25

The surtax was for child welfare.

1946, Feb. 18

B91	SP46	2fr + 8fr brt blue	.75	.70

The surtax was used for prevention of tuberculosis.

19th Century Steamer and Map SP47

1946

B92	SP47	3fr + 2fr deep blue	.50	.50

Stamp Day, June 23, 1946.

Harbor of Monte Carlo SP48

1946, Dec. 13

B93	SP48	2fr + 3fr dk bluish grn	1.40	1.40

Issued in tribute to the memory of Franklin D. Roosevelt. The surtax was for a fund to erect a monument in his honor.

Prince Louis II Type
Souvenir Sheet
Unwmk.

1947, May 15 **Engr.** ***Imperf.***
B94 A46 200fr + 300fr dk red & choc 42.50 24.00

Prince Charles III — SP50

1948, Mar. 6 ***Perf. 14x13***
B95 SP50 6fr + 4fr dk bl grn, *lt bl* .55 .55

Issued for Stamp Day, Mar. 6.

Princess Charlotte SP51

Prince Rainier III SP52

Perf. 13½x13, Imperf.
1949, Dec. 27 **Engr.**
Cross Typo. in Red

B96	SP51	10fr + 5fr red brown	12.00	12.00
B97	SP52	15fr + 5fr brt red	12.00	12.00
B98	SP52	25fr + 5fr dk vio bl	12.00	12.00
B99	SP51	40fr + 5fr dull green	12.00	12.00
a.		Block of 4, #B96-B99	50.00	50.00

Printed in sheets measuring 151x173mm, perf. and imperf., containing 4 of No. B99a.
The surtax was for the Red Cross.
For surcharges see Nos. 288-291.

Hercules Strangling the Lion of Nemea — SP53

Twelve Labors of Hercules: No. B101, Killing the Hydra of Lerna. No. B102, Capturing the Erymanthean boar. No. B103, Killing Stymphalian birds. No. B104, Hercules and the Ceryneian Hind. No. B105, The Augean Stables. No. B106, Hercules and the Cretan Bull. No. B107, Wild horses of Diomedes. No. B108, Hercules and the Oxen of Geryon. No. B109, Hercules and the Belt of Hippolytus. No. B110, Winning the golden apple of Hesperides. No. B111, Battling Cerberus.

1981, Nov. 5 **Engr.** ***Perf. 13***

B100	SP53	2.50fr + 50c multi	1.60	1.60
B101	SP53	3.50fr + 50c multi	1.60	1.60

1982, Nov. 8

B102	SP53	2.50fr + 50c multi	1.60	1.60
B103	SP53	3.50fr + 50c multi	1.60	1.60

1983, Nov. 9

B104	SP53	2.50fr + 50c multi	1.60	1.60
B105	SP53	3.50fr + 50c multi	1.60	1.60

1984, Nov. 8

B106	SP53	3fr + 50c multi	1.50	1.50
B107	SP53	4fr + 50c multi	1.90	1.90

1985, Nov. 7

B108	SP53	3fr + 70c multi	1.50	1.50
B109	SP53	4fr + 80c multi	1.90	1.90

1986, Oct. 28

B110	SP53	3fr + 70c multi	1.50	1.50
B111	SP53	4fr + 80c multi	1.90	1.90
		Nos. B100-B111 (12)	19.80	19.80

Surtax on #B100-B111 for the Red Cross.

Monegasque Committee to Fight Tuberculosis and Respiratory Diseases — SP54

1994, Mar. 14 **Litho.** ***Perf. 13½x13***
B112 SP54 2.40fr +60c multi 1.25 1.25

AIR POST STAMPS

No. 91 Surcharged in Black

Perf. 14x13½
1933, Aug. 22 **Unwmk.**
C1 A15 1.50fr on 5fr 25.00 25.00
a. Imperf., pair 375.00

Catalogue values for unused stamps in this section, from this point to the end of the section, are for Never Hinged items.

Plane over Monaco — AP1

Plane Propeller and Buildings — AP2

Pegasus — AP3

Sea Gull — AP4

Plane, Globe and Arms of Monaco AP5

1942, Apr. 15 **Engr.** ***Perf. 13***

C2	AP1	5fr blue green	.35	.35
C3	AP1	10fr ultra	.35	.35
C4	AP2	15fr sepia	.70	.70
C5	AP3	20fr henna brown	1.00	1.00
C6	AP4	50fr red violet	5.00	4.00
C7	AP5	100fr red & vio brn	5.00	4.00
		Nos. C2-C7 (6)	12.40	10.40

For surcharges see Nos. CB1-CB5.

Nos. 196-197 Overprinted in Blue

1946, May 20

C8	A41	50fr dp Prus green	4.75	4.25
C9	A41	100fr red	4.75	4.25
a.		Inverted overprint	37,500.	
b.		Double overprint	22,500.	

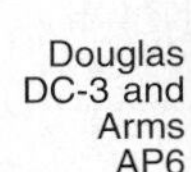

Douglas DC-3 and Arms AP6

1946, May 20

C10	AP6	40fr red	1.25	.60
C11	AP6	50fr red brown	2.00	.85
C12	AP6	100fr dp blue grn	3.00	1.60
C13	AP6	200fr violet	3.25	2.40
		Nos. C10-C13 (4)	9.50	5.45

Exist imperforate. See Nos. C27-C29.

Harbor of Monte Carlo AP7

Map of Monaco — AP8

1946, Dec. 13

C14	AP7	5fr carmine rose	.65	.65
C15	AP8	10fr violet black	.65	.65

Issued in tribute to the memory of Franklin D. Roosevelt.

Franklin D. Roosevelt Examining his Stamp Collection AP9

Main Post Office, New York City AP10

Oceanographic Museum, Monaco — AP11

Harbor of Monte Carlo — AP12

Statue of Liberty and New York City Skyline — AP13

1947, May 15 **Unwmk.**

C16	AP9	50c violet	1.25	1.25
C17	AP10	1.50fr rose violet	.55	.55
C18	AP11	3fr henna brown	.55	.55
C19	AP12	10fr deep blue	4.00	4.00
C20	AP13	15fr rose carmine	7.50	7.50
a.		Strip of 3, #C20, 203, C19	16.00	16.00
		Nos. C16-C20 (5)	13.85	13.85

Monaco's participation in the Centenary Intl. Philatelic Exhibition, NYC, May, 1947.

Crowd Acclaiming Constitution of 1911 AP14

Anthropological Museum — AP15

Designs: 25fr, Institute of Human Paleontology, Paris. 50fr, Albert I. 100fr, Oceanographic Institute, Paris. 200fr, Albert I medal.

1949, Mar. 5 **Engr.** ***Perf. 13***

C21	AP14	20fr brown red	.75	.75
C22	AP14	25fr indigo	.75	.75
C23	AP15	40fr blue green	2.00	2.00
C24	AP15	50fr blk, brn & grn	2.75	2.75
C25	AP15	100fr cerise	9.25	9.25
C26	AP14	200fr deep orange	15.00	15.00
		Nos. C21-C26 (6)	30.50	30.50

Plane-Arms Type of 1946
1949, Mar. 10

C27	AP6	300fr dp ultra & ind	70.00	70.00
C28	AP6	500fr grnsh blk & bl grn	45.00	45.00
C29	AP6	1000fr black & red vio	75.00	70.00
		Nos. C27-C29 (3)	190.00	185.00

UPU Type of Regular Issue
1949-50

C30	A56	25fr deep blue	.65	.65
C31	A56	40fr red brown & sep	2.50	2.50
C32	A56	50fr dk green & ultra	4.00	4.00
C33	A56	100fr dk car & dk grn	6.00	6.00
		Nos. C30-C33 (4)	13.15	13.15

75th anniv. of the UPU.
Nos. C30-C33 exist imperforate, also No. C30 in deep plum and violet, imperforate.
Issued: 25fr, 12/27; others, 9/12/50.

Rainier Type of Regular Issue
1950, Apr. 11 **Unwmk.**

C34	A57	50fr black & red brn	7.75	6.50
C35	A57	100fr red brn, sep & ind	11.00	10.50

Enthronement of Prince Rainier III.

Runner — AP18

Designs: 50fr, Fencing. 100fr, Target Shooting. 200fr, Olympic Torch.

1953, Feb. 23 *Perf. 11*

C36 AP18	40fr black		12.00	9.00
C37 AP18	50fr brt purple		15.00	10.00
C38 AP18	100fr dk slate grn		20.00	15.00
C39 AP18	200fr deep carmine		26.00	16.00
	Nos. C36-C39 (4)		73.00	50.00

Issued to publicize Monaco's participation in the Helsinki Olympic Games.

Dr. Albert Schweitzer and Ogowe River Scene, Gabon — AP19

1955, Jan. 14 *Perf. 13*

C40 AP19 200fr multicolored 42.50 35.00

Dr. Albert Schweitzer, medical missionary.

Mediterranean Sea Swallows — AP20

Birds: 200fr, Sea gulls. 500fr, Albatross. 1000fr, Great cormorants.

1955-57 *Perf. 11*

C41 AP20	100fr dp blue & indigo	32.50	13.50
a.	Perf. 13	32.50	22.00
C42 AP20	200fr bl & blk	32.50	14.50
a.	Perf. 13	375.00	175.00
C43 AP20	500fr gray & dk grn	50.00	32.50

Perf. 13

C44 AP20	1000fr dk bl grn & blk brn	110.00	67.50
a.	Perf. 11	350.00	225.00
	Nos. C41-C44 (4)	225.00	128.00

Issued: Perf. 11, 1/14/55; Perf. 13, 1957.

"From the Earth to the Moon" and Jules Verne — AP21

1955, June 7 **Unwmk.**

C45 AP21 200fr dp blue & slate 27.50 25.00

50th anniv. of the death of Jules Verne.

Wedding Type of Regular Issue

1956, Apr. 19 **Engr.**

Portraits in Brown

C46 A99	100fr purple	1.25	1.25
C47 A99	200fr carmine	1.60	1.60
C48 A99	500fr gray violet	3.75	3.75
	Nos. C46-C48 (3)	6.60	6.60

Wedding of Prince Rainier III to Grace Kelly, Apr. 19, 1956.

Nos. J45 and J54 Surcharged and Overprinted "Poste Aerienne" and bars

1956, Apr. *Perf. 11*

C49 D6	100fr on 20fr	10.50	10.50
a.	Double surcharge	*475.00*	
C50 D7	100fr on 20fr	10.50	10.50
a.	Double surcharge	*475.00*	
b.	Pair, #C49, C50	22.50	22.50

See footnote after No. 390.

Basilica of Lourdes — AP23

200fr, Pope Pius X, underground basilica.

1958, May 15 **Unwmk.** *Perf. 13*

C51 AP23	100fr dk bl, grn & gray	1.75	1.40
C52 AP23	200fr red brn & sepia	2.50	2.50

Centenary of the apparition of the Virgin Mary at Lourdes.

Prince Rainier III and Princess Grace — AP24

1959, May 16

C53 AP24	300fr dark purple	14.00	9.25
C54 AP24	500fr blue	20.00	16.00

St. Dévote AP25

1960, June 1 **Engr.** *Perf. 13*

C55 AP25	2fr green, bl & vio	1.10	.75
C56 AP24	3fr dark purple	39.00	19.00
C57 AP24	5fr blue	39.00	27.50
C58 AP25	10fr green & brown	6.50	4.00
	Nos. C55-C58 (4)	85.60	51.25

1961, June 3

C59 AP25	3fr ultra, grn & gray ol	2.10	1.10
C60 AP25	5fr rose carmine	4.50	2.10

Europa Issue, 1962

Mercury over Map of Europe AP26

1962, June 6 **Unwmk.** *Perf. 13*

C61 AP26 2fr dk grn, sl grn & brn *2.00 1.00*

Oceanographic Museum, Atom Symbol and Princes Albert I and Rainier III — AP27

1962, June 6

C62 AP27 10fr violet, bl & bis 6.00 6.50

Establishment of a scientific research center by agreement with the Intl. Atomic Energy Commission.

Roland Garros AP28

1963, Dec. 12 **Engr.** *Perf. 13*

C63 AP28 2fr dk blue & dk brn 1.25 1.25

50th anniversary of the first airplane crossing of the Mediterranean by Roland Garros (1888-1918).

Type of Regular Issue, 1964

Design: 5fr, Convair B-58 Hustler (New York-Paris in 3 hours, 19 minutes, 41 seconds, Maj. William R. Payne, USAF, 1961).

1964, May 22 **Unwmk.** *Perf. 13*

C64 A151 5fr brown, blk & bl 2.75 2.75

1st airplane rally of Monte Carlo, 50th anniv.

Bobsledding — AP29

1964, Dec. 3 **Engr.** *Perf. 13*

C65 AP29 5fr multicolored 2.75 2.75

9th Winter Olympic Games, Innsbruck, Austria, Jan. 29-Feb. 9, 1964.

ITU Type of Regular Issue

Design: 10fr, ITU Emblem and Monte Carlo television station on Mount Agel, vert.

1965, May 17 **Engr.** *Perf. 13*

C66 A161 10fr bis brn, sl grn & bl 4.75 4.75

Princess Grace with Albert Alexander Louis, Caroline and Stephanie — AP30

1966, Feb. 1 **Engr.** *Perf. 13*

C67 AP30 3fr pur, red brn & Prus bl 2.25 1.50

Birth of Princess Stephanie, Feb. 1, 1965.

Opera House Interior AP31

1966, June 1 **Engr.** *Perf. 13*

C68 AP31 5fr Prus bl, bis & dk car rose 2.75 2.75

Centenary of founding of Monte Carlo.

Prince Rainier III and Princess Grace — AP32

1966-71 **Engr.** *Perf. 13*

C69 AP32	2fr pink & slate	1.10	.40
C70 AP32	3fr emerald & slate	2.10	.80
C71 AP32	5fr lt blue & slate	2.75	1.10
C72 AP32	10fr lemon & sl ('67)	5.00	3.50
C72A AP32	20fr orange & brn ('71)	42.50	35.00
	Nos. C69-C72A (5)	53.45	40.80

Issue dates: 10fr, Dec. 7, 1967; 20fr, Sept. 6, 1971. Others, Dec. 12, 1966.

Panhard-Phenix, 1895 — AP33

1967, Apr. 28 **Engr.** *Perf. 13*

C73 AP33 3fr Prus blue & blk 2.40 2.40

25th Grand Prix of Monaco.

Olympic Games Type of Regular Issue

1968, Apr. 29 **Engr.** *Perf. 13*

C74 A183 3fr Field hockey 1.75 1.75

Berlioz Monument, Monte Carlo — AP34

1969, Apr. 26 **Engr.** *Perf. 13*

C75 AP34 2fr green, blk & ultra 1.25 1.25

Hector Berlioz (1803-69), French composer.

Napoleon, by Paul Delaroche AP35

1969, Apr. 26 Photo. *Perf. 12x13*
C76 AP35 3fr multicolored 1.60 1.60

Bicentenary of birth of Napoleon I.

Horses, Prehistoric Drawing from Lascaux Cave — AP36

1970, Dec. 15 Engr. *Perf. 13*
C77 AP36 3fr multicolored 2.00 2.00

Nativity Type of Regular Issue

Design: 3fr, Nativity, Flemish School, 15th century, vert.

1973, Nov. 12 Engr. *Perf. 12x13*
C78 A243 3fr Prus green 2.25 1.75

Prince Rainier III — AP37

1974, Dec. 23 Engr. *Perf. 12½x13*
C81 AP37 10fr dark purple 6.75 3.00
C82 AP37 15fr henna brown 9.25 6.25
C83 AP37 20fr ultra 15.00 8.50
Nos. C81-C83 (3) 31.00 17.75

See Nos. 1994-1996.

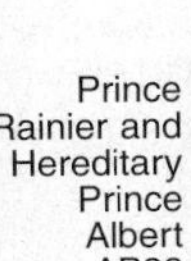

Prince Rainier and Hereditary Prince Albert AP38

1982-84 Engr. *Perf. 13x13½*
C84 AP38 5fr deep violet 1.60 .60
C85 AP38 10fr red 5.00 1.10
C86 AP38 15fr dk blue grn 6.00 1.75
C87 AP38 20fr brt blue 7.00 2.25
C88 AP38 30fr brown ('84) 11.00 4.50
Nos. C84-C88 (5) 30.60 10.20

AIR POST SEMI-POSTAL STAMPS

Catalogue values for unused stamps in this section are for Never Hinged items.

Types of 1942 Air Post Stamps Surcharged with New Values and Bars

Unwmk.

1945, Mar. 27 Engr. *Perf. 13*
CB1 AP1 1fr + 4fr on 10fr rose red .60 .60
CB2 AP2 1fr + 4fr on 15fr red brown .60 .60
CB3 AP3 1fr + 4fr on 20fr sepia .60 .60
CB4 AP4 1fr + 4fr on 50fr ultra .60 .60
CB5 AP5 1fr + 4fr on 100fr bright red violet .60 .60
Nos. CB1-CB5 (5) 3.00 3.00

Surtax for the benefit of prisoners of war.

Franklin D. Roosevelt Type

1946, Dec. 13
CB6 A42 15fr + 10fr red 2.40 1.60

The surtax was for a fund to erect a monument in his honor.

1948 Olympic Type

1948, July
CB7 A48 5fr +5fr Rowing 11.00 11.00
CB8 A48 6fr +9fr Skiing 16.00 16.00
CB9 A48 10fr +15fr Tennis 22.50 22.50
CB10 A47 15fr +25fr Sailing 32.50 32.50
Nos. CB7-CB10 (4) 82.00 82.00

Salmacis Nymph SPAP4

Designs similar to regular issue.

1948, July
CB11 A50 5fr + 5fr blk bl 19.00 19.00
CB12 A51 6fr + 9fr dk grn 19.00 19.00
CB13 A52 10fr + 15fr crim 20.00 20.00
CB14 SPAP4 15fr + 25fr red brown 24.00 24.00
Nos. CB11-CB14 (4) 82.00 82.00

François J. Bosio (1769-1845), sculptor.

POSTAGE DUE STAMPS

D1

Prince Albert I — D2

Perf. 14x13½

1905-43 Unwmk. Typo.
J1 D1 1c olive green .45 .55
J2 D1 5c green .45 .55
J3 D1 10c rose .45 .55
J4 D1 10c brn ('09) 350.00 125.00
J5 D1 15c vio brn, *straw* 3.50 1.75
J6 D1 20c bis brn, *buff* ('26) .35 .35
J7 D1 30c blue .45 .55
J8 D1 40c red vio ('26) .35 .35
J9 D1 50c brn, *org* 4.50 4.00
J10 D1 50c blue grn ('27) .35 .35
J11 D1 60c gray blk ('26) .35 .65
J12 D1 60c brt vio ('34) 21.00 27.50
J13 D1 1fr red brn, *straw* ('26) .35 .25
J14 D1 2fr red org ('27) 1.00 1.50
J15 D1 3fr mag ('27) 1.00 1.50
J15A D1 5fr ultra ('43) .80 1.00
Nos. J1-J15A (16) 385.35 166.40

For surcharge see No. J27.

1910
J16 D2 1c olive green .25 .45
J17 D2 10c light violet .45 .60
J18 D2 30c bister 190.00 160.00

In January, 1917, regular postage stamps overprinted "T" in a triangle were used as postage due stamps.

Nos. J17 and J18 Surcharged

1918
J19 D2 20c on 10c lt vio 4.00 7.50
a. Double surcharge 1,000.
J20 D2 40c on 30c bister 4.50 8.50

D3

1925-32
J21 D3 1c gray green .40 .50
J22 D3 10c violet .40 .55
J23 D3 30c bister .50 .75
J24 D3 60c red .70 .75
J25 D3 1fr lt bl ('32) 80.00 80.00
J26 D3 2fr dull red ('32) 80.00 80.00
Nos. J21-J26 (6) 162.00 162.55

Nos. J25 and J26 have the numerals of value double-lined.

"Recouvrements" stamps were used to recover charges due on undelivered or refused mail which was returned to the sender.

No. J9 Surcharged

1925
J27 D1 1fr on 50c brn, *org* .80 .55
a. Double surcharge 750.00

Catalogue values for unused stamps in this section, from this point to the end of the section, are for Never Hinged items.

D4

D5

1946-57 Engr. *Perf. 14x13, 13*
J28 D4 10c sepia .20 .20
J29 D4 30c dark violet .20 .20
J30 D4 50c deep blue .20 .20
J31 D4 1fr dark green .20 .20
J32 D4 2fr yellow brn .20 .20
J33 D4 3fr brt red vio .30 .30
J34 D4 4fr carmine .45 .45
J35 D5 5fr chocolate .35 .35
J36 D5 10fr deep ultra .65 .65
J37 D5 20fr grnsh blue .70 .70
J38 D5 50fr red vio & red ('50) 55.00 55.00
J38A D5 100fr dk grn & red ('57) 12.00 12.00
Nos. J28-J38A (12) 70.45 70.45

Sailing Vessel — D6

S. S. United States — D7

Early Postal Transport (D6): 1fr, Carrier pigeons. 3fr, Old railroad engine. 4fr, Old monoplane. 5fr, Steam automobile. 10fr, daVinci's flying machine. 20fr, Balloon. 50fr, Post rider. 100fr, Old mail coach.

Modern Postal Transport (D7): 1fr, Sikorsky S-51 helicopter. 3fr, Modern locomotive. 4fr, Comet airliner. 5fr, Sabre sports car. 10fr, Rocket. 20fr, Graf Zeppelin. 50fr, Motorcyclist. 100fr, Railroad mail car.

1953-54 *Perf. 11*
J39 D6 1fr dk grn & brt red ('54) .20 .20
a. Pair, Nos. J39, J48 .20 .20
J40 D6 2fr dp ultra & bl grn .20 .20
a. Pair, Nos. J40, J49 .40 .40
J41 D6 3fr Prus grn & brn lake .20 .20
a. Pair, Nos. J41, J50 .40 .40
J42 D6 4fr dk brn & Prus grn .35 .35
a. Pair, Nos. J42, J51 .70 .70
J43 D6 5fr ultra & pur .85 .85
a. Pair, Nos. J43, J52 1.75 1.75
J44 D6 10fr dp ultra & dk bl 9.00 9.00
a. Pair, Nos. J44, J53 18.00 18.00
J45 D6 20fr indigo & pur 6.00 6.00
a. Pair, Nos. J45, J54 12.00 12.00
J46 D6 50fr red & dk brn 12.00 12.00
a. Pair, Nos. J46, J55 24.00 24.00
J47 D6 100fr vio brn & dp grn 20.00 20.00
a. Pair, Nos. J47, J56 40.00 40.00
J48 D7 1fr brt red & dk grn ('54) .20 .20
J49 D7 2fr bl grn & dp ultra .20 .20
J50 D7 3fr brn lake & Prus grn .20 .20
J51 D7 4fr Prus grn & dk brn .35 .35
J52 D7 5fr purple & ultra .85 .85
J53 D7 10fr dk bl & dp ultra 9.00 9.00
J54 D7 20fr purple & indigo 6.00 6.00
J55 D7 50fr dk brn & red 12.00 12.00
J56 D7 100fr dp grn & vio brn 20.00 20.00
Nos. J39-J56 (18) 97.60 97.60

Pairs se-tenant at the base.

For overprints see Nos. 371-390.

Felucca, 18th Century D8

2c, Paddle steamer La Palmaria, 19th cent. 5c, Arrival of 1st train. 10c, Armed messenger, 15th-16th cent. 20c, Monaco-Nice courier, 18th cent. 30c, "Charles III," 1866. 50c, Courier on horseback, 17th cent. 1fr, Diligence, 19th cent.

1960-69 Engr. *Perf. 13*
J57 D8 1c bl grn, bis brn & bl .20 .20
J58 D8 2c sl grn, sep & ultra .20 .20
J59 D8 5c grnsh bl, gray & red brn .20 .20
J60 D8 10c vio bl, blk & grn .20 .20
J61 D8 20c blue, brn & grn .90 .90
J62 D8 30c brn, brt grn & brt bl ('69) 1.40 1.40
J63 D8 50c dk bl, brn & sl grn 1.90 1.90
J64 D8 1fr sl grn, bl & brn 2.50 2.50
Nos. J57-J64 (8) 7.50 7.50

Knight in Armor D9

1980-83	**Engr.**		*Perf. 13*	
J65	D9	5c red & gray	.20	.20
J66	D9	10c salmon & red	.20	.20
J67	D9	15c violet & red	.20	.20
J68	D9	20c lt green & red	.20	.20
J69	D9	30c blue & red	.20	.20
J70	D9	40c lt brown & red	.35	.35
J71	D9	50c lilac & red	.45	.45
J72	D9	1fr black & blue	.70	.70
J73	D9	2fr dk brn & org ('82)	1.10	1.10
J74	D9	3fr sl bl & rose car ('83)	1.60	1.60
J75	D9	4fr red & dk grn ('82)	2.25	2.25
J76	D9	5fr magenta & brn ('83)	2.75	2.75
		Nos. J65-J76 (12)	10.20	10.20

Nos. J65-J76 printed in horizontal rows with princely coat of arms between stamps. Sold in strips of 3 only.

Issued: #J65-J72, 2/8; #J73, J75, 2/15; 3J74, J76, 1/3.

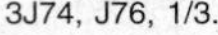

Natl. Coat of Arms — D10

1985-86	**Photo.**		*Perf. 13x12½*	
J77	D10	5c multicolored	.20	.20
J78	D10	10c multicolored	.20	.20
J79	D10	15c multicolored	.20	.20
J80	D10	20c multicolored	.20	.20
J81	D10	30c multicolored	.20	.20
J82	D10	40c multicolored	.20	.20
J83	D10	50c multicolored ('86)	.20	.20
J84	D10	1fr multicolored ('86)	.45	.45
J85	D10	2fr multicolored ('86)	.75	.75
J86	D10	3fr multicolored	1.25	1.25
J87	D10	4fr multicolored ('86)	1.60	1.60
J88	D10	5fr multicolored	2.25	2.25
		Nos. J77-J88 (12)	7.70	7.70

See Nos. 1608-1609.

MONGOLIA

män-'gōl-yə

(Mongolian People's Republic)

(Outer Mongolia)

LOCATION — Central Asia, bounded on the north by Siberia, on the west by Sinkiang, on the south and east by China proper and Manchuria
GOVT. — Republic
AREA — 604,250 sq. mi.
POP. — 2,617,379 (1999 est.)
CAPITAL — Ulan Bator

Outer Mongolia, which had long been under Russian influence although nominally a dependency of China, voted at a plebescite on October 20, 1945, to sever all ties with China and become an independent nation. See Tannu Tuva.

100 Cents = 1 Dollar
100 Mung = 1 Tugrik (1926)

Catalogue values for unused stamps in this country are for Never Hinged items, beginning with Scott 149 in the regular postage section, Scott B1 in the semi-postal section, Scott C1 in the airpost section, and Scott CB1 in the airpost semi-postal section.

Watermark

Wmk. 170 — Greek Border and Rosettes

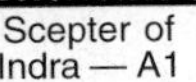

Scepter of Indra — A1

A2

1924 Litho. Unwmk. *Perf. 10, 13½*
Surface Tinted Paper

No.	Type	Description	Unused	Used
1	A1	1c multi, *bister*	12.00	12.00
2	A1	2c multi, *brnsh*	10.50	5.50
a.		Perf. 13½	47.50	40.00
3	A1	5c multi	40.00	24.00
a.		Perf. 10	47.50	35.00
4	A1	10c multi, *gray bl*	20.00	16.00
a.		Perf. 10	20.00	16.00
5	A1	20c multi, *gray*	27.50	17.50
6	A1	50c multi, *salmon*	40.00	24.00
7	A1	$1 multi, *yellow*	55.00	40.00
b.		Perf. 10	650.00	190.00
		Nos. 1-7 (7)	205.00	139.00

These stamps vary in size from 19x25mm (1c) to 30x39mm ($1). They also differ in details of the design.

Errors of perforating and printing exist.

Some quantities of Nos. 1-2, 4-7 were defaced with horizontal perforation across the center.

The 5c exists perf 11½. Value, $325 unused, hinged, $190 used.

Revenue Stamps Handstamp Overprinted "POSTAGE" in Violet

Sizes: 1c to 20c: 22x36mm
50c, $1: 26x43½mm
$5: 30x45½mm

1926 ***Perf. 11***

No.	Type	Description	Unused	Used
16	A2	1c blue	12.00	12.00
17	A2	2c orange	16.00	11.00
18	A2	5c plum	16.00	13.00
19	A2	10c green	20.00	17.00
20	A2	20c yel brn	24.00	20.00
21	A2	50c brn & ol grn	*190.00*	*175.00*
22	A2	$1 brn & salmon	*550.00*	*475.00*
23	A2	$5 red, yel & gray	*650.00*	—
		Nos. 16-23 (8)	*1,478.*	*723.00*

Black Overprint

No.	Type	Description	Unused	Used
16a	A2	1c blue	20.00	13.50
17a	A2	2c orange	32.50	20.00
18a	A2	5c plum	36.00	20.00
19a	A2	10c green	47.50	24.00
20a	A2	20c yellow brown	65.00	45.00
21a	A2	50c brown & olive grn	*1,200.*	*325.00*
22a	A2	$1 brown & salmon	*600.00*	*400.00*
23a	A2	$5 red, yellow & gray		
		Nos. 16a-22a (7)	*2,001.*	*847.50*

Red Overprint

16b	A2	1c blue
17b	A2	2c orange
18b	A2	5c plum
19b	A2	10c green
20b	A2	20c yellow brown

The preceding handstamped overprints may be found inverted, double, etc. Counterfeits abound.

For overprints and surcharges see #48-61.

A3

A4

Soyombo

TYPE I — The pearl above the crescent is solid. The devices in the middle of the stamp are not outlined.

TYPE II — The pearl is open. The devices and panels are all outlined in black.

1926-29 ***Perf. 11***

Type I
Size: 22x28mm

No.	Type	Description	Unused	Used
32	A3	5m lilac & blk	12.00	12.00
33	A3	20m blue & blk	20.00	24.00

Type II
Size: 22x29mm

No.	Type	Description	Unused	Used
34	A3	1m yellow & blk	3.25	3.25
35	A3	2m brn org & blk	4.00	3.25
36	A3	5m lilac & blk	4.75	4.00
37	A3	10m lt blue & blk	4.00	2.00
a.		Imperf, pair		
39	A3	25m yel grn & blk	8.00	4.00
a.		Imperf, pair	125.00	110.00

Size: 26x34mm

No.	Type	Description	Unused	Used
40	A3	40m lemon & blk	11.00	4.75
41	A3	50m buff & blk	16.00	6.50

Size: 28x37mm

No.	Type	Description	Unused	Used
42	A4	1t brown, grn & blk	32.50	12.00
43	A4	3t red, yel & blk	72.50	47.50
44	A4	5t brn vio, rose & blk	95.00	60.00
		Nos. 32-44 (12)	283.00	183.25

In 1929 a change was made in the perforating machine. Every fourth pin was removed, which left the perforation holes in groups of three with blank spaces between the groups. Nos. 44A-44D have only this interrupted perforation. Nos. 37 and 39 are found with both perforations.

For overprints and surcharges see #45-47.

Soyombo — A5

1929, July ***Interrupted Perf 11***

No.	Type	Description	Unused	Used
44A	A5	5m lilac & black	25.00	20.00
44B	A5	10m lt grnish blue & black	100.00	65.00
a.		imperf, pair	—	
44C	A5	20m blue & black	35.00	27.50
a.		imperf, pair	—	
b.		Horiz. pair, imperf btwn.		—
44D	A5	25m yel grn & black	32.50	27.50
a.		imperf, pair	—	

See note after No. 44.

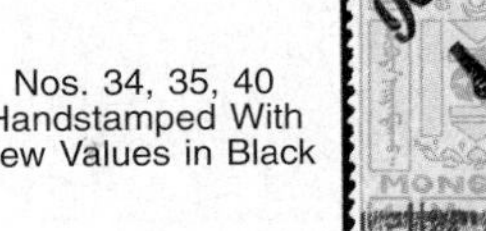

Nos. 34, 35, 40 Handstamped With New Values in Black

1930

No.	Type	Description	Unused	Used
45	A3	10m on 1m	32.50	30.00
46	A3	20m on 2m	45.00	40.00
47	A3	25m on 40m	52.50	47.50
		Nos. 45-47 (3)	130.00	117.50

Soyombo

A6 A7

Violet Overprint, Handstamped

1931

No.	Type	Description	Unused	Used
48	A6	1c blue	24.00	12.00
a.		Blue overprint	87.50	47.50
49	A6	2c orange	27.50	9.50
50	A6	5c brown vio	35.00	9.50
a.		Blue overprint	65.00	22.50
51	A6	10c green	32.50	9.50
a.		Blue overprint	65.00	37.50
52	A6	20c bister brn	47.50	12.00
53	A6	50c brown & ol yel	130.00	120.00
54	A6	$1 brown & salmon	200.00	160.00
		Nos. 48-54 (7)	496.50	332.50

Revenue Stamps Surcharged in Black, Red or Blue

1931

No.	Type	Description	Unused	Used
59	A7	5m on 5c brn vio (Bk)	40.00	16.00
a.		Inverted surcharge		35.00
b.		Imperf., pair	225.00	225.00
60	A7	10m on 10c green (R)	55.00	27.50
a.		Inverted surcharge	90.00	50.00
b.		Imperf., pair	225.00	225.00
61	A7	20m on 20c bis brn (Bl)	65.00	35.00
a.		Inverted surcharge		55.00
b.		Imperf., pair	225.00	225.00
		Nos. 59-61 (3)	160.00	78.50

On Nos. 59-61, "Postage" is always diagonal, and may read up or down.

Weaver at Loom — A8

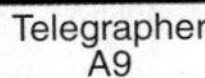

Telegrapher A9

Sukhe Bator A10

Lake and Mountains — A11

Designs: 5m, Mongol at lathe. 10m, Government building, Ulan Bator. 15m, Young Mongolian revolutionary. 20m, Studying Latin alphabet. 25m, Mongolian soldier. 50m, Monument to Sukhe Bator. 3t, Sheep shearing. 5t, Camel caravan. 10t, Chasing wild horses.

Perf. 12½x12

1932 Photo. Wmk. 170

No.	Type	Description	Unused	Used
62	A8	1m brown	3.25	1.50
63	A9	2m red violet	3.25	1.50
64	A8	5m indigo	2.00	.80
65	A8	10m dull green	2.00	.80
66	A9	15m dp brown	2.00	.80
67	A9	20m rose red	2.40	.80
68	A9	25m dull violet	2.40	.80
69	A10	40m gray black	2.00	1.20
70	A10	50m dull blue	2.40	.80

Perf. 11x12

No.	Type	Description	Unused	Used
71	A11	1t dull green	2.75	1.20
72	A11	3t dull violet	5.50	2.00
73	A11	5t brown	19.50	12.00
74	A11	10t ultra	40.00	20.00
		Nos. 62-74 (13)	89.45	44.20

Used values are for c-t-o's.

Nos. 70-74 Handstamped With New Values in Black or Violet

1941

Black handstamp

No.	Type	Description	Unused	Used
74A	A11	5m on 5t	—	—
74B	A10	10m on 50m	—	—
74C	A11	10m on 10t	—	—
74D	A11	15m on 5t	—	—
74E	A11	20m on 1t	—	—
74F	A11	30m on 3t	—	—

Violet handstamp

No.	Type	Description	Unused	Used
74G	A11	5m on 5t	—	—
74H	A11	15m on 5t	—	—
74I	A11	20m on 1t	—	—
74J	A11	30m on 3t	—	—

Mongolian Man — A12

Mongolian Woman — A13

Soldier — A14

Camel Caravan A15

Modern School A16

Arms of the Republic — A17

Sukhe Bator — A18

Pasture Scene — A19

Paper with network as in italics

1943 **Typo.** ***Perf. 12½***

No.	Type	Denom.	Color	Unused	Used
75	A12	5m	green, *green*	12.00	10.00
76	A13	10m	dp blue, *lt bl*	20.00	11.00
77	A14	15m	rose, *lt rose*	22.50	15.00
78	A15	20m	org brn, *org*	32.50	27.50
79	A16	25m	red brn, *buff*	32.50	32.50
80	A17	30m	carmine, *red*	37.50	37.50
81	A18	45m	purple, *mauve*	50.00	50.00
82	A19	60m	dp green, *grn*	90.00	90.00
			Nos. 75-82 (8)	297.00	273.50

Marshal Kharloin Choibalsan — A21

1945 **Unwmk.** ***Perf. 12½***

No.	Type	Denom.	Color	Unused	Used
83	A21	1t	black brown	60.00	30.00

Choibalsan A22

Victory Medal A24

Sukhe Bator and Choibalsan A23

Designs: #86, Choibalsan as young man. #87, Choibalsan University, Ulan Bator. 1t, Anniversary medal. 2t, Sukhe Bator.

1946, July **Photo.** ***Perf. 12½***

No.	Type	Denom.	Color	Unused	Used
84	A22	30m	olive bister	6.50	6.50
85	A23	50m	dull purple	7.75	7.75
86	A24	60m	black	8.00	8.00
87	A23	60m	orange brown	14.00	14.00
88	A24	80m	dk orange brn	12.50	12.50
89	A24	1t	indigo	16.00	16.00
90	A24	2t	deep brown	22.50	22.50
			Nos. 84-90 (7)	87.25	87.25

25th anniversary of independence.

New Housing A25

School Children — A26

Mongolian Arms and Flag — A27

Sukhe Bator — A28

Flags of Communist Countries — A29

Lenin — A30

Designs: 15m, Altai Hotel. No. 94, State Store. No. 95, Like 30m. 25m, University. 40m, National Theater. 50m, Pedagogical Institute. 60m, Sukhe Bator monument. Sizes of type A25: Nos. 91, 93-94, 98-99, 32½x22mm. 25m, 55x26mm.

1951, July

No.	Type	Denom.	Color	Unused	Used
91	A25	5m	brn, *pink*	6.75	6.75
92	A26	10m	dp bl, *pink*	8.25	8.25
93	A25	15m	grn, *grnsh*	10.00	10.00
94	A25	20m	red org	10.00	10.00
95	A27	20m	dk bl & multi	10.00	10.00
96	A25	25m	bl, *bluish*	10.00	10.00
97	A27	30m	red & multi	10.00	10.00
98	A25	40m	pur, *pink*	10.00	10.00
99	A25	50m	brn, *grysh*	20.00	20.00
100	A28	60m	brn blk	20.00	20.00
101	A29	1t	multi	20.00	20.00
102	A28	2t	dk brn & org brn	25.00	25.00
103	A30	3t	multi	25.00	25.00
			Nos. 91-103 (13)	185.00	185.00

30th anniversary of independence.

Choibalsan — A31

Choibalsan and Farmer — A32

Choibalsan in uniform — A32a

Choibalsan and Sukhe Bator — A33

Designs: No. 108, 30m, Choibalsan and factory worker (47x33mm). 50m, Choibalsan and Young Pioneer. No. 112, 2t, Choibalsan in uniform.

1953, Dec. **Photo.** ***Perf. 12½***

No.	Type	Denom.	Color	Unused	Used
104	A31	15m	dull blue	5.00	5.00
105	A32	15m	dull green	5.00	5.00
106	A31	20m	dull green	10.00	10.00
107	A32	20m	sepia	10.00	10.00
108	A32	20m	violet blue	10.00	10.00
109	A32	30m	dark brown	10.00	10.00
110	A33	50m	orange brn	10.00	10.00
111	A33	1t	carmine rose	10.00	10.00
112	A32a	1t	sepia	15.00	15.00
113	A32a	2t	red	15.00	15.00
114	A33	3t	sepia	20.00	20.00
115	A33	5t	red	40.00	40.00
			Nos. 104-115 (12)	160.00	160.00

First anniversary of death of Marshal Karloin Choibalsan (1895-1952).

Arms of Mongolia — A34

1954, Mar. **Litho.** ***Perf. 12½***

No.	Type	Denom.	Color	Unused	Used
116	A34	10m	carmine	12.00	7.00
117	A34	20m	carmine	60.00	50.00
118	A34	30m	carmine	12.00	8.00
119	A34	40m	carmine	40.00	40.00
120	A34	60m	carmine	12.00	10.00
			Nos. 116-120 (5)	136.00	115.00

Sukhe Bator and Choibalsan — A35

Lake Hubsugul A36

Guard with Dog — A37

#122, Lenin Statue, Ulan Bator. 50m, Choibalsan University. 1t, Arms and flag of Mongolia.

1955, June **Photo.** ***Perf. 12½***

No.	Type	Denom.	Color	Unused	Used
121	A35	30m	green	1.25	1.00
122	A35	30m	orange ver	2.50	1.00
123	A36	30m	brt blue	2.25	1.25
124	A37	40m	dp red lilac	5.00	1.75
125	A36	50m	ocher	5.00	2.25
126	A37	1t	red & multi	9.00	7.00
			Nos. 121-126 (6)	25.00	14.25

35th anniversary of independence.

1955

Design: 2t, Lenin.

No.	Type	Denom.	Color	Unused	Used
127	A35	2t	bright blue	10.00	5.00

85th anniversary of birth of Lenin.

Flags of Communist Countries A38

Arms of Mongolia A39

1955

No.	Type	Denom.	Color	Unused	Used
128	A38	60m	blue & multi	5.00	4.00

Fight for peace.

1956 **Photo.** ***Perf. 12½***

No.	Type	Denom.	Color	Unused	Used
129	A39	20m	dark brown	3.00	2.00
130	A39	30m	dark olive	4.00	3.00
131	A39	40m	bright blue	5.00	4.00
132	A39	60m	blue green	6.00	4.50
133	A39	1t	deep carmine	10.00	8.00
			Nos. 129-133 (5)	28.00	21.50

Kremlin, Moscow, Train and Sukhe Bator Monument A40

Design: 2t, Flags of Mongolia and USSR.

1956

No.	Type	Denom.	Color	Unused	Used
134	A40	1t	dk blue & multi	25.00	15.00
135	A40	2t	red & multi	10.00	8.00

Establishment of railroad connection between Moscow and Ulan Bator.

Mongolian Arms and Flag — A41

Hunter with Golden Eagle — A42

Wrestlers A43

Designs: No. 138, 3 children (33x26½mm).

1956, July **Typo.** ***Perf. 9***

136	A41	30m blue	10.00	5.00
137	A42	30m pale brown	50.00	50.00
138	A42	60m orange	20.00	20.00
139	A43	60m yellow green	20.00	20.00
		Nos. 136-139 (4)	100.00	95.00

35th anniversary of independence.

Types A41 and A43 without "XXXV"

1958

140	A41	20m red	5.00	3.00
141	A43	50m brown, *pink*	12.50	3.00

Nos. 140-143 were issued both with and without gum.

Poster — A44

Globe and Dove — A45

1958, Mar. **Litho.** ***Perf. 9***

142	A44	30m maroon & salmon	5.00	4.00

13th Congress of Mongolian People's Party.

1958, May

143	A45	60m deep blue	5.00	4.00

4th Congress of International Democratic Women's Federation, Vienna, June, 1958.
Nos. 142-143 exist imperf.

Yak — A46

No. 144, Pelicans, vert. No. 145, Siberian ibex, vert. No. 147, Yak. No. 148, Camels.

1958, July **Typo.** ***Perf. 9***

144	A46	30m lt blue	25.00	5.00
145	A46	30m brt green	5.00	4.00
146	A46	60m orange	5.00	4.00
147	A46	1t blue	6.00	5.00
148	A46	1t rose	6.00	5.00
		Nos. 144-148 (5)	47.00	23.00

Shades exist.

Canceled to Order

Some quantity of all issues not printed by the State Printing Works, Ulan Bator, except Nos. 296-303, were canceled to order.

Used values are for c-t-o. Postally used stamps sell for considerably more.

Catalogue values for unused stamps in this section, from this point to the end of the section, are for Never Hinged items.

Stallion A47

Holy Flame (Tulaga) — A48

Designs: 5m, 40m, Goat. 10m, 30m, Ram. 15m, 60m, Stallion. 20m, 50m, Bull. 25m, 1t, Bactrian camel.

Perf. 10½x11½

1958, Nov. 11 **Litho.**

149	A47	5m yellow & brn	.25	.20
150	A47	10m lt grn & brn	.25	.20
151	A47	15m lilac & brn	.40	.20
152	A47	20m lt bl & brn	.40	.20
153	A47	25m rose & brn	.55	.20
154	A47	30m lilac & pur	.65	.20
155	A47	40m lt & dk green	.65	.20
156	A47	50m salmon & brn	.75	.25
157	A47	60m lt blue & ind	1.25	.35
158	A47	1t yellow & brn	3.00	1.00
		Nos. 149-158 (10)	8.15	3.00

1959, May 1 **Litho.** ***Perf. 9***

159	A48	1t multi	5.00	2.00

See No. C36.

Archer — A49

Mongol Sports: 5m, Taming wild horse. 10m, Wrestlers. 15m, Horseback riding. 25m, Horse race. 30m, Archers. 70m, Hunting wild horse. 80m, Proclaiming a champion.

1959, June 6 **Photo.** ***Perf. 11***

160	A49	5m multi	.25	.20
161	A49	10m multi	.25	.20
162	A49	15m multi	.25	.20
163	A49	20m multi	.40	.20
164	A49	25m multi	.50	.20
165	A49	30m multi	.50	.20
166	A49	70m multi	.75	.35
167	A49	80m multi	1.50	.75
		Nos. 160-167 (8)	4.40	2.30

Young Wrestlers A50

Youth Festival Emblem — A51

Designs: 5m, Young musician, horiz. 20m, Boy on horseback. 25m, Two opera singers. 40m, Young Pioneers with flags, horiz.

Photo.; Litho. (30m)

1959, July ***Perf. 12, 11 (30m)***

168	A50	5m vio bl & rose car	.20	.20
169	A50	10m bl grn & brn	.30	.20
170	A50	20m claret & grn	.30	.20
171	A50	25m green & vio bl	.30	.20
172	A51	30m lil & lt bl	.50	.25
173	A50	40m green & pur	2.00	1.00
		Nos. 168-173 (6)	3.60	2.05

Mongolian Youth Festival.

The 30m was printed by State Printing Works, Ulan Bator.

Issue dates: 30m, July 11; others July 10.

"Mongol" in Stylized Uighur Script — A52

"Mongol" in Various Scripts: 40m, Soyombo. 50m, Kalmuck. 60m, Square (Pagspa). 1t, Cyrillic.

Printed by State Printing Works, Ulan Bator.

1959, Sept. 1 **Litho.** ***Perf. 11***

Size: 29x42½mm

174	A52	30m black & multi	6.50	6.50
175	A52	40m black & multi	6.50	6.50
a.		Horiz. pair, imperf between and at right	*150.00*	
176	A52	50m black & multi	8.50	8.50
177	A52	60m black & multi	14.00	14.00

Size: 21x31mm

Perf. 9

178	A52	1t black & multi	17.50	17.50
		Nos. 174-178 (5)	53.00	53.00

1st Intl. Mongolian Language Congress.

Battle Emblem A53

Battle Monument A54

1959, Sept. 15 **Photo.** ***Perf. 12½x12***

179	A53	40m yellow, brn & car	1.00	.50
180	A54	50m multicolored	1.00	.50

Ha-lo-hsin (Khalka) River Battle, 20th anniv.

Congress Emblem A55

Printed by State Printing Works, Ulan Bator.

1959, Dec. **Litho.** ***Perf. 11***

181	A55	30m green	4.50	4.50

2nd meeting of rural economy cooperatives of Mongolia.

Sable — A56

Pheasants — A57

Perf. 15, 11x13

1959, Dec. 21 **Photo.**

182	A56	5m shown	.25	.20
183	A57	10m shown	.25	.20
184	A56	15m Muskrat	.25	.20
185	A57	20m Otter	.55	.20
186	A56	30m Argali	.55	.25
187	A57	50m Saigas	1.00	.35
188	A57	1t Musk deer	2.00	.75
		Nos. 182-188 (7)	4.85	2.15

Lunik 3 — A58

50m, Lunik 3 with path around moon, horiz.

1959, Dec. 30 **Photo.** ***Perf. 12***

189	A58	30m violet & yel grn	1.00	.40
190	A58	50m red, dk bl & grn	1.50	.40

Lunik 3 Russian moon mission, Oct. 7, 1959.

Motherhood Badge — A59

Flower Emblem — A60

1960, Mar. 8 ***Perf. 11, 12½x11½***

191	A59	40m blue & bister	1.00	.30
192	A60	50m blue, grn & yel	1.50	.50

International Women's Day.

Lenin — A61

Jacob's-ladder — A62

1960, Apr. 22 Photo. *Perf. 11½x12*

193 A61 40m dk rose car 1.00 .30
194 A61 50m rose violet 1.25 .50

90th anniversary, birth of Lenin.

1960, May 31 *Perf. 11½x12*

195 A62 5m Larkspur .25 .20
196 A62 10m Tulips .25 .20
197 A62 15m shown .25 .20
198 A62 20m Globeflowers .25 .20
199 A62 30m Bellflowers .35 .20
200 A62 40m Parnassia .75 .25
201 A62 50m Geranium 1.00 .50
202 A62 1t Begonia 1.50 1.00
Nos. 195-202 (8) 4.60 2.75

For overprints see Nos. 296-303.

Equestrian — A63

Running — A64

1960, Aug. 1 *Perf. 15, 11*

203 A63 5m shown .20 .20
204 A64 10m shown .25 .20
205 A63 15m Diving .25 .20
206 A64 20m Wrestling .30 .20
207 A63 30m Hurdling .50 .20
208 A64 50m Gymnastics, women's .65 .30
209 A63 70m High jump 1.00 .50
210 A64 1t Discus, women's 1.25 .70
Nos. 203-210 (8) 4.40 2.50

17th Olympic Games, Rome, 8/25-9/11.

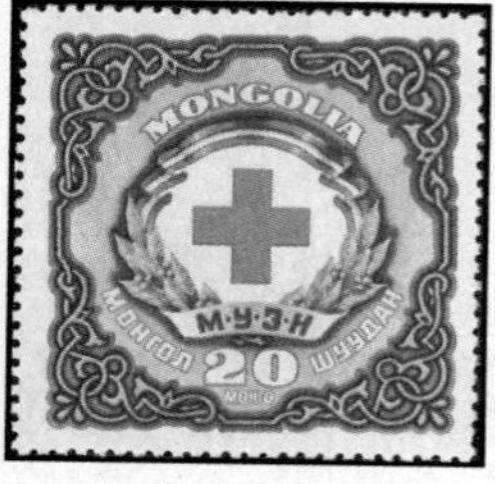

Red Cross A65

1960, Aug. 29 *Perf. 11*

211 A65 20m blue, red & yel 1.00 .50

Newspaper "Unen" (Truth) — A66

1960, Dec. 19 *Perf. 12x11½*

212 A66 20m red, yel & sl grn .75 .50
213 A66 30m grn, yel & red .75 .50

40th anniversary of Mongolian press.

Golden Orioles — A67

Songbirds: 5m, Rose-colored starling. 10m, Hoopoe. 20m, Black-billed capercaillie. 50m, Oriental broad-billed roller. 70m, Tibetan sandgrouse. 1t, Mandarin duck.
Triangle points down on 5m, 50m, 70m, 1t.

1961, Jan. 3 *Perf. 11*

214 A67 5m multi .60 .20
215 A67 10m multi .85 .20
216 A67 15m multi 1.00 .20
217 A67 20m multi 1.40 .25
218 A67 50m multi 1.60 .50
219 A67 70m multi 2.00 .70
220 A67 1t multi 2.50 1.00
Nos. 214-220 (7) 9.95 3.05

Federation Emblem — A68

Design: 30m, Worker and emblem, vert.

Perf. 11½x12, 12x11½

1961, Jan. 29 Photo.

221 A68 30m dk gray & rose .50 .20
222 A68 50m ultra & red .75 .30

World Federation of Trade Unions, 15th anniv.

Patrice Lumumba (1925-1961), Premier of Congo — A69

1961, Apr. 8 *Perf. 11½x12*

223 A69 30m brown 1.00 .50
224 A69 50m violet gray 2.00 .50

Bridge A70

Designs: 10m, Shoemaker. 15m, Department Store, Ulan Bator. 20m, Government building. 30m, State Theater, Ulan Bator. 50m, Machinist. 1t, Modern and old buildings.

1961, Apr. 30 *Perf. 11½x12, 15*
Sizes: 31½x21mm, 59x20mm (20m)

225 A70 5m emerald .20 .20
226 A70 10m blue .20 .20
227 A70 15m rose red .25 .20
228 A70 20m brown .25 .20
229 A70 30m blue .35 .20
230 A70 50m olive green .50 .25
231 A70 1t violet 1.00 .35
Nos. 225-231 (7) 2.75 1.60

40th anniversary of independence; modernization of Mongolia.

Yuri Gagarin and Globe — A71

Designs: 20m, Gagarin with rocket, vert. 50m, Gagarin making parachute descent, vert. 1t, Gagarin wearing helmet, globe.

1961, May 31 *Perf. 15*

232 A71 20m multi .60 .25
233 A71 30m multi .90 .40
234 A71 50m multi 1.00 .60
235 A71 1t multi 1.75 .80
Nos. 232-235 (4) 4.25 2.05

Yuri A. Gagarin, 1st man in space, 4/12/61.

Postman on Reindeer A72

15m, #241a, Postman on camel. 10m, 20m, Postman with yaks. 25m, #241c, Postman with ship. 30m, 50m, Diesel train.

1961, June 5 *Perf. 15*

236 A72 5m multi .20 .20
237 A72 15m multi .25 .20
238 A72 20m multi .25 .20
239 A72 25m multi .25 .20
240 A72 30m multi 4.00 2.00
Nos. 236-240,C1-C3 (8) 6.95 3.60

Souvenir Sheet

Perf. 11

241 Sheet of 4 6.00 6.00
a. A72 5m light blue & brown 1.50 1.00
b. A72 10m green, brown & blue 1.50 1.00
c. A72 15m green, violet & brown 1.50 1.00
d. A72 50m violet, green & black 1.50 1.00

40th anniv. of independence; postal modernization. See No. C4b for 25m, perf. 11.

Souvenir Sheet

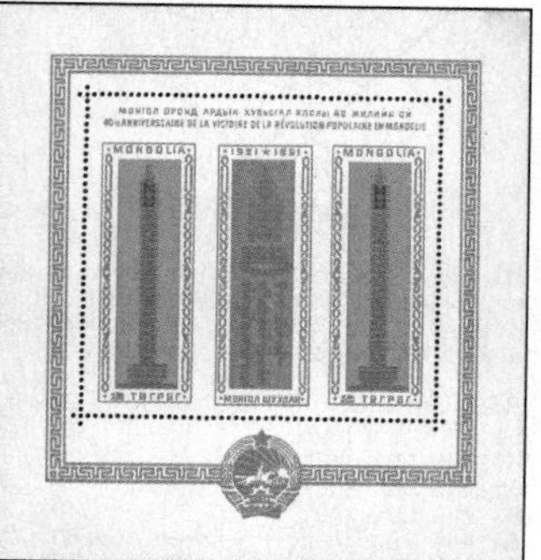

Ornamental Column — A73

1961, June 20 *Perf. 12*

242 A73 Sheet of 2 + label 6.00 6.00
a. 2t blue, red & gold 2.75 2.00

40th anniversary of the Mongolian People's Revolution. No. 242 contains two No. 242a and label, imperf. between.

Herdsman and Oxen — A74

Designs: Herdsmen and domestic animals (except 1t and No. 252a).

1961, July 10 *Perf. 13*

243 A74 5m Rams .20 .20
244 A74 10m shown .20 .20
245 A74 15m Camels .25 .20
246 A74 20m Pigs and geese .25 .20
247 A74 25m Angora goats .30 .25
248 A74 30m Horses .40 .25
249 A74 40m Sheep .50 .25
250 A74 50m Cows .75 .30
251 A74 1t Combine harvester 1.10 .75
Nos. 243-251 (9) 3.95 2.60

Souvenir Sheets

Perf. 12

252 Sheet of 3 2.50 2.50
a. A74 5m Combine harvester .75 .50
b. A74 15m Angora goats .75 .50
c. A74 40m Oxen .75 .50
253 Sheet of 3 2.50 2.50
a. A74 10m Pigs and geese .75 .50
b. A74 20m Horses .75 .50
c. A74 30m Cows .75 .50
254 Sheet of 3 3.00 3.00
a. A74 25m Camels .90 .75
b. A74 50m Rams .90 .75
c. A74 1t Sheep .90 .75

40th anniversary of independence. Nos. 252-254 each contain 3 stamps imperf. between.

Horseback Riders — A75

5m, Young wrestlers & instructor. 15m, Camel & pony riders. 20m, Falconers. 30m, Skier. 50m, Archers. 1t, Male dancers.

1961, Aug. 10 *Perf. 11*

255 A75 5m multi .25 .20
256 A75 10m multi .25 .20
257 A75 15m multi .25 .20
258 A75 20m multi 1.10 .35
259 A75 30m multi .55 .45
260 A75 50m multi .65 .50
261 A75 1t multi 1.10 .70
Nos. 255-261 (7) 4.15 2.60

Independence, 4th anniv.; Mongolian youth sports.

Statue of Sukhe Bator — A76

Arms of Mongolia — A77

Designs: 5m, Mongol youth. 10m, Mongol chieftain. 20m, Singer. 30m, Dancer. 50m, Dombra player. 70m, Musicians. 1t, Gymnast. 5m, 10m, 70m, 1t, horiz.

Perf. 12x11½, 11½x12

1961, Sept. 16

262 A76 5m brt grn & red lil .20 .20
263 A76 10m red & dk bl .20 .20
264 A76 15m bl & lt brn .25 .20
265 A76 20m pur & brt grn .25 .20
266 A76 30m vio bl & car .35 .25
267 A76 50m ol & vio .65 .35
268 A76 70m brt lil rose & ol .80 .45
269 A76 1t dk bl & ver 1.50 .75
Nos. 262-269 (8) 4.20 2.60

40th anniv. of independence; Mongolian culture.

1961, Nov. 17 *Perf. 11½x12*

270 A77 5m multi .40 .40
271 A77 10m multi .40 .40
272 A77 15m multi .40 .40
273 A77 20m multi .40 .40
274 A77 30m multi .50 .50
275 A77 50m multi 1.00 1.00

276 A77 70m multi 1.50 1.50
277 A77 1t multi 2.00 2.00
Nos. 270-277 (8) 6.60 6.60

For surcharges see Nos. 2144A, 2302D.

Congress Emblem A78

1961, Dec. 4 Litho. *Perf. 11½*
278 A78 30m vio bl, yel & red .40 .30
279 A78 50m brn, yel & red .60 .50

5th World Congress of Trade Unions, Moscow, Dec. 4-16.

UN Emblem and Arms of Mongolia — A79

10m, Globe, map of Mongolia, dove. 50m, Flags of UN & Mongolia. 60m, UN Headquarters, New York. Parliament, Ulan Bator. 70m, UN assembly, UN & Mongolian flags.

1962, Mar. 15 Photo. *Perf. 11*
280 A79 10m gold & multi .20 .20
281 A79 30m gold & multi .30 .25
282 A79 50m gold & multi .60 .45
283 A79 60m gold & multi .75 .50
284 A79 70m gold & multi .80 .60
Nos. 280-284 (5) 2.65 2.00

Mongolia's admission to UN.

Soccer — A80

Designs: 10m, Soccer ball, globe and flags. 30m, Soccer players, globe and ball. 60m, Goalkeeper. 70m, Stadium.

1962, May 15 Litho. *Perf. 10½*
285 A80 10m multi .70 .20
286 A80 30m multi .70 .30
287 A80 50m multi .70 .45
288 A80 60m multi 1.00 .50
289 A80 70m multi 1.40 .50
Nos. 285-289 (5) 4.50 1.95

World Soccer Championship, Chile, 5/30-6/17.

D. Natsagdorji A81

Solidarity Emblem A82

1962, May 15 Photo. *Perf. 15x14½*
290 A81 30m brown .40 .25
291 A81 50m bluish grn .75 .50

Mongolian writers' congress.
For overprints see Nos. 430-431.

1962, May 22 Litho. *Perf. 11½x10½*
292 A82 20m yel grn & multi .35 .20
293 A82 30m bl & multi .60 .40

Afro-Asian Peoples' solidarity.

Flags of USSR and Mongolia — A83

Perf. 11½x10½
1962, June 25 Litho.
294 A83 30m brn & multi .40 .20
295 A83 50m vio bl & multi .75 .40

Mongol-Soviet friendship.

Nos. 195-202 Overprinted

1962, July 20 Photo. *Perf. 11½x12*
296 A62 5m multi .35 .25
297 A62 10m multi .35 .25
298 A62 15m multi .45 .25
299 A62 20m multi .45 .25
300 A62 30m multi .60 .40
301 A62 40m multi .75 .60
302 A62 50m multi 1.25 .90
303 A62 1t multi 2.00 1.25
Nos. 296-303 (8) 6.20 4.15

WHO drive to eradicate malaria.

Military Field Emblem — A84

Designs: 30m, Tablets with inscriptions. 50m, Stone column. 60m, Genghis Khan.

1962, July 20 *Perf. 11½x12*
304 A84 20m blue & multi 7.50 7.50
305 A84 30m red & multi 7.50 7.50
306 A84 50m pink, brn & blk 15.00 15.00
307 A84 60m blue & multi 15.00 15.00
Nos. 304-307 (4) 45.00 45.00

Genghis Khan (1162-1227), Mongol conqueror.
For overprints see Nos. 1846-1849. For surcharge, see No. 2378A.

River Perch — A85

1962, Dec. 28 *Perf. 11*
308 A85 5m shown .20 .20
309 A85 10m Burbot .20 .20
310 A85 15m Arctic grayling .30 .20
311 A85 20m Shorthorn sculpin .45 .25
312 A85 30m Marine zander .65 .30
313 A85 50m Siberian sturgeon .90 .45
314 A85 70m Waleck's chub minnow 1.25 .85
315 A85 1.50t Cottocomephorid 2.00 1.25
Nos. 308-315 (8) 5.95 3.70

Sukhe Bator (1893-1923), National Hero — A86

1963, Feb. 2 Photo. *Perf. 11½x12*
316 A86 30m blue .25 .20
317 A86 60m rose car .60 .50

Laika and Rocket — A87

Designs: 15m, Rocket launching, vert. 25m, Lunik 2, vert. 70m, Andrian G. Nikolayev and Pavel R. Popovich. 1t, Mars rocket.

1963, Apr. 1 Litho. *Perf. 12½x12*
Size: 46x32mm
318 A87 5m multicolored .20 .20
Size: 20x68mm
319 A87 15m multicolored .25 .20
320 A87 25m multicolored .40 .35
Size: 46x32mm
321 A87 70m multicolored 1.25 .80
322 A87 1t multicolored 1.60 1.10
Nos. 318-322 (5) 3.70 2.65

Soviet space explorations.

Blood Transfusion — A88

1963, Aug. 15 *Perf. 10½*
323 A88 20m Packing Red Cross parcels .30 .20
324 A88 30m shown .50 .25
325 A88 50m Vaccination .75 .40
326 A88 60m Ambulance service 1.00 .60
327 A88 1.30t Centenary emblem 1.50 .80
Nos. 323-327 (5) 4.05 2.25

Red Cross centenary.

Karl Marx — A89

Mongolian Woman — A90

1963, Sept. 16 Photo. *Perf. 11½x12*
328 A89 30m blue .35 .20
329 A89 60m dk car rose .70 .50

145th anniversary of birth of Karl Marx.

1963, Sept. 26
330 A90 30m blue & multi .50 .35

5th Intl. Women's Cong., Moscow, 6/24-29.

Inachis A91

Designs: Mongolian butterflies.

1963, Nov. 7 Litho. *Perf. 11½*
331 A91 5m shown .50 .25
332 A91 10m Gonepteryxrhamni .75 .40
333 A91 15m Aglais urticae 1.00 .50
334 A91 20m Parnassius apollo 1.25 .65
335 A91 30m Papilio machaon 1.75 .90
336 A91 60m Agrodiaetus damon 2.25 1.10
337 A91 1t Limenitis populi 3.00 1.50
Nos. 331-337 (7) 10.50 5.30

UNESCO Emblem, Globe and Scales — A92

1963, Dec. 10 Photo. *Perf. 12*
338 A92 30m multicolored .40 .20
339 A92 60m multicolored .60 .40

Universal Declaration of Human Rights, 15th anniversary.

Coprinus Comatus — A93

Designs: Mushrooms.

1964, Jan. 1 Litho. *Perf. 10½*

340	A93	5m	shown	.50	.25
341	A93	10m	Lactarius torminosus	.75	.40
342	A93	15m	Psalliota campestris	.95	.50
343	A93	20m	Russula delica	1.10	.55
344	A93	30m	Ixocomus granulatus	1.25	.60
345	A93	50m	Lactarius scrobiculatus	1.50	.75
346	A93	70m	Lactarius deliciosus	1.75	.90
347	A93	1t	Ixocomus variegatus	2.25	2.10
			Nos. 340-347 (8)	10.05	6.05

Souvenir Sheet

Skier — A94

1964, Feb. 12 Photo. *Perf. 12x11½*

348	A94	4t	gray	4.50	4.50

9th Winter Olympic Games, Innsbruck, Jan. 29-Feb. 9.

Lenin — A95

1964 Photo. *Perf. 11½x12*

349	A95	30m	salmon & multi	.75	.40
350	A95	50m	blue & multi	1.00	.50

60th anniversary of Communist Party. Nos. 349-350 printed with alternating label showing Lenin quotation.

Javelin — A96

1964, Apr. 30 Litho. *Perf. 10½*

351	A96	5m	Gymnastics, women's	.20	.20
352	A96	10m	shown	.25	.20
353	A96	15m	Wrestling	.30	.20
354	A96	20m	Running, women's	.35	.25
355	A96	30m	Equestrian	.40	.30
356	A96	50m	Diving, women's	.75	.40
357	A96	60m	Bicycling	1.00	.50
358	A96	1t	Olympic Games emblem	1.25	.75
			Nos. 351-358 (8)	4.50	2.80

Souvenir Sheet

Perf. 12x11½

359	A96	4t	Wrestling	4.50	4.50

18th Olympic Games, Toyko, Oct. 10-25. No. 359 contains one horizontal stamp, 37x27½mm. Issued Sept. 1.

Congress Emblem — A97

1964, Sept. 30 Photo. *Perf. 11*

360	A97	30m	multicolored	.40	.30

4th Mongolian Women's Congress.

Lunik 1 — A98

Space Research: 10m, Vostok 1 and 2. 15m, Tiros weather satellite, vert. 20m, Cosmos circling earth, vert. 30m, Mars probe, vert. 60m, Luna 4, vert. 80m, Echo 2. 1t, Radar and rockets.

1964, Oct. 30

361	A98	5m	multicolored	.20	.20
362	A98	10m	multicolored	.20	.20
363	A98	15m	multicolored	.25	.20
364	A98	20m	multicolored	.35	.25
365	A98	30m	multicolored	.50	.35
366	A98	60m	multicolored	.65	.40
367	A98	80m	multicolored	.95	.45
368	A98	1t	multicolored	1.25	.55
			Nos. 361-368 (8)	4.35	2.60

Rider Carrying Flag — A99

1964, Nov. 26 Photo. *Perf. 11½x12*

369	A99	25m	multicolored	.40	.20
370	A99	50m	multicolored	.50	.40

40th anniversary of Mongolian constitution.

Weather Balloon A100

Designs: 5m, Oceanographic exploration. 60m, Northern lights and polar bears. 80m, Geomagnetism. 1t, I.Q.S.Y. emblem and Mercator map.

1965, May 15 Photo. *Perf. 13½*

371	A100	5m	gray & multi	.20	.20
372	A100	10m	grn & multi	.25	.30
373	A100	60m	blue, blk & pink	.85	.50
374	A100	80m	citron & multi	1.00	.60
375	A100	1t	brt green & multi	1.50	.90
			Nos. 371-375,C6-C8 (8)	7.70	3.55

International Quiet Sun Year.

Horses — A101

Designs: Mares and Foals.

1965, Aug. 25 *Perf. 11*

376	A101	5m	shown	.20	.20
377	A101	10m	Falconers	.20	.20
378	A101	15m	Taming wild horse	.25	.20
379	A101	20m	Horse race	.35	.25
380	A101	30m	Hurdles	.50	.35
381	A101	60m	Wolf hunt	.65	.40
382	A101	80m	Milking a mare	.95	.45
383	A101	1t	Mare and foal	1.25	.55
			Nos. 376-383 (8)	4.35	2.60

Girl Holding Lambs — A102

1965, Oct. 10 Photo. *Perf. 11*

384	A102	5m	shown	.20	.20
385	A102	10m	Boy and girl drummers	.30	.20
386	A102	20m	Camp fire	.60	.20
387	A102	30m	Wrestlers	.90	.35
388	A102	50m	Emblem	1.50	.90
			Nos. 384-388 (5)	3.50	1.85

40th anniv. of Mongolian Youth Org.

Chinese Perch — A103

1965, Nov. 25

389	A103	5m	shown	.30	.20
390	A103	10m	Lenok trout	.35	.25
391	A103	15m	Siberian sturgeon	.40	.35
392	A103	20m	Amur salmon	.45	.40
393	A103	30m	Bagrid catfish	.55	.45
394	A103	60m	Siluri catfish	1.00	.50
395	A103	80m	Northern pike	1.40	.60
396	A103	1t	River perch	2.00	.75
			Nos. 389-396 (8)	6.45	3.50

Marx and Lenin — A104

1965, Dec. 15 *Perf. 11½x12*

397	A104	10m	red & blk	.35	.25

6th Conference of Postal Ministers of Communist Countries, Peking, June 21-July 15.

Sable — A105

1966, Feb. 15 Photo. *Perf. 12½*

398	A105	5m	shown	.40	.20
399	A105	10m	Fox	.40	.20
400	A105	15m	Otter, vert.	.40	.20
401	A105	20m	Cheetah, vert.	.40	.25
402	A105	30m	Pallas's cat	.40	.25
403	A105	60m	Stone marten	.75	.30
404	A105	80m	Ermine, vert.	1.00	.40
405	A105	1t	Woman in mink coat, vert.	1.25	.75
			Nos. 398-405 (8)	5.00	2.55

Opening of WHO Headquarters, Geneva — A106

1966, May 3 Photo. *Perf. 12x11½*

406	A106	30m	bl grn, bl & gold	.40	.20
407	A106	50m	red, bl & gold	.60	.40

For overprints see Nos. 483-484.

Soccer — A107

Designs: 30m, 60m, 80m, Various soccer plays. 1t, British flag and World Soccer Cup emblem. 4t, Wembley Stadium, horiz.

1966, May 31 Photo. *Perf. 11*

408	A107	10m	multicolored	.20	.20
409	A107	30m	multicolored	.30	.25
410	A107	60m	multicolored	.40	.30
411	A107	80m	multicolored	.50	.40
412	A107	1t	multicolored	1.10	.60
			Nos. 408-412 (5)	2.50	1.75

Souvenir Sheet

Perf. 12½, Imperf.

413	A107	4t	gray & brown	2.75	2.00

World Soccer Championship for Jules Rimet Cup, Wembley, England, July 11-30. No. 413 contains one stamp 61x83mm.

Sukhe Bator, Parliament Building, Ulan Bator — A108

1966, June 7 Litho. *Perf. 12x12½*

414	A108	30m	red, bl & brn	.40	.20

15th Congress of Mongolian Communist Party.

Wrestling A109

Designs: Various wrestling holds.

1966, June 15 Photo. *Perf. 11½x12*

415 A109 10m multicolored .20 .20
416 A109 30m multicolored .20 .20
417 A109 60m multicolored .25 .20
418 A109 80m multicolored .30 .20
419 A109 1t multicolored .35 .20
Nos. 415-419 (5) 1.30 1.00

World Wrestling Championship, Toledo, Spain.

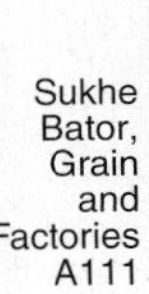

Emblem and Map of Mongolia A110

Sukhe Bator, Grain and Factories A111

Perf. 11½x12, 12x11½

1966, July 11 Litho.

420 A110 30m red & multi 1.10 .80
421 A111 50m red & multi 2.75 1.00

45th anniversary of independence.
For overprints see Nos. 552-553.

Lilium Tenuifolium — A112

1966, Oct. 15 Photo. *Perf. 12x11½*

422 A112 5m Physochlaena physaloides .20 .20
423 A112 10m Allium polyrrchizum .30 .20
424 A112 15m shown .40 .20
425 A112 20m Thermopsis lanceolata .50 .20
426 A112 30m Amygdalus mongolica .60 .30
427 A112 60m Caryopteris mongolica .85 .40
428 A112 80m Piptanthus mongolicus 1.00 .55
429 A112 1t Iris bungei 1.25 .75
Nos. 422-429 (8) 5.10 2.80

Nos. 290-291 Overprinted: "1906/1966"

1966, Oct. 26 Photo. *Perf. 15x14½*

430 A81 30m brown 10.00 10.00
431 A81 50m bluish grn 14.00 14.00

60th anniv. of birth of D. Natsagdorji, writer.
50m exists double, one inverted.

Child with Dove — A113

1966, Dec. 2 *Perf. 11½x12, 12x11½*

432 A113 10m shown .25 .20
433 A113 15m Children with reindeer .35 .20
434 A113 20m Boys wrestling, vert. .40 .20
435 A113 30m Horseback riding .45 .25
436 A113 60m Children riding camel, vert. .70 .40
437 A113 80m Child with sheep .95 .50
438 A113 1t Boy archer, vert. 1.25 .75
Nos. 432-438 (7) 4.35 2.50

Children's Day.

Proton 1 — A114

Perf. 11½x12½, 12½x11½

1966, Dec. 28 Photo.

439 A114 5m Vostok 2, vert. .20 .20
440 A114 10m shown .20 .20
441 A114 15m Telstar 1, vert. .25 .20
442 A114 20m Molnija 1, vert. .40 .25
443 A114 30m Syncom 3, vert. .50 .35
444 A114 60m Luna 9 .70 .20
445 A114 80m Luna 12, vert. 1.00 .40
446 A114 1t Mariner 4 1.25 .70
Nos. 439-446 (8) 4.50 2.50

Space exploration.

Tarbosaurus — A115

1967, Mar. 31 *Perf. 12x11½*

447 A115 5m shown .50 .25
448 A115 10m Talarurus .55 .30
449 A115 15m Proceratops .60 .35
450 A115 20m Indricotherium .70 .40
451 A115 30m Saurolophus 1.00 .50
452 A115 60m Mastodon 2.00 .90
453 A115 80m Mongolotherium 2.25 1.00
454 A115 1t Mammoth 2.50 1.25
Nos. 447-454 (8) 10.10 4.95

Prehistoric animals.

A116

A117

Congress emblem.

1967, June 9 Litho. *Perf. 12*

455 A116 30m lt blue & multi .40 .20
456 A116 50m pink & multi .60 .40

9th Youth Festival for Peace and Friendship, Sofia.

1967, Oct. 25 Litho. *Perf. 11½x12*

Design: 40m, Sukhe Bator and soldiers. 60m, Lenin and soldiers.

457 A117 40m red & multi .50 .20
458 A117 60m red & multi .80 .50

Russian October Revolution, 50th anniv.

Ice Hockey and Olympic Rings A118

1967, Dec. 29 *Perf. 12x12½*

459 A118 5m Figure skating .20 .20
460 A118 10m Speed skating .25 .20
461 A118 15m shown .35 .20
462 A118 20m Ski jump .45 .25
463 A118 30m Bobsledding .75 .35
464 A118 60m Figure skating, pair 1.00 .50
465 A118 80m Slalom 1.50 .80
Nos. 459-465 (7) 4.50 2.50

Souvenir Sheet

Perf. 12

466 A118 4t Women's figure skating 4.00 4.00

10th Winter Olympic Games, Grenoble, France, Feb. 6-18.

Bactrian Camels A119

1968, Jan. 15 Photo. *Perf. 12*

467 A119 5m shown .20 .20
468 A119 10m Yak .20 .20
469 A119 15m Lamb .25 .20
470 A119 20m Foal .40 .20
471 A119 30m Calf .50 .25
472 A119 60m Bison .65 .35
473 A119 80m Roe deer .90 .40
474 A119 1t Reindeer 1.40 .70
Nos. 467-474 (8) 4.50 2.50

Young animals.

Black Currants — A120

Berries: 5m, Rosa acicularis. 15m, Gooseberries. 20m, Malus. 30m, Strawberries. 60m, Ribes altissimum. 80m, Blueberries. 1t, Hippophae rhamnoides.

Lithographed & Engraved

1968, Feb. 15

475 A120 5m blue & ultra .20 .20
476 A120 10m buff & brn .20 .20
477 A120 15m lt grn & grn .25 .20
478 A120 20m yel & red .40 .20
479 A120 30m pink & car .50 .25
480 A120 60m sal & org brn .80 .35
481 A120 80m pale & dl bl 1.10 .40
482 A120 1t lt yel & red 1.20 .75
Nos. 475-482 (8) 4.65 2.55

Nos. 406-407 Overprinted

1968, Apr. 16 Photo. *Perf. 12x11½*

483 A106 30m bl grn, bl & gold 6.50 6.50
484 A106 50m red, blue & gold 6.50 6.50

WHO, 20th anniversary.

Human Rights Flame — A121

1968, June 20 Litho. *Perf. 12*

485 A121 30m turq & vio bl .50 .25

International Human Rights Year.

"Das Kapital," by Karl Marx A122

Design: 50m, Karl Marx.

1968, July 1 Litho. *Perf. 12*

486 A122 30m blue & multi .40 .20
487 A122 50m red & multi .60 .40

Karl Marx (1818-1883).

Artist, by A. Sangatzohyo — A123

Paintings: 10m, On Remote Roads, by Sangatzohyo. 15m, Camel calf, by B. Avarzad. 20m, Milk, by Avarzad. 30m, The Bowman, by B. Gombosuren. 80m, Girl Sitting on Yak, by Sangatzohyo. 1.40t, Cagan Dara Eke, by Janaivajara. 4t, Meeting, by Sangatzohyo, horiz.

1968, July 11 Litho. *Perf. 12*

488 A123 5m brown & multi .25 .20
489 A123 10m brown & multi .30 .20
490 A123 15m brown & multi .35 .20
491 A123 20m brown & multi .45 .40
492 A123 30m brown & multi .65 .50
493 A123 80m brown & multi 1.25 .75
494 A123 1.40t brown & multi 2.25 1.40
Nos. 488-494 (7) 5.50 3.65

Miniature Sheets

Perf. 11½, Imperf.

495 A123 4t brown & multi 5.50 5.50

Paintings from national museum, Ulan Bator. #495 contains one 54x84mm stamp.

Volleyball — A124

Olympic Rings and: 10m, Wrestling. 15m, Bicycling. 20m, Javelin, women's. 30m, Soccer. 60m, Running. 80m, Gymnastics, women's. 1t, Weight lifting. 4t, Equestrian.

1968, Sept. 1 Litho. *Perf. 12*

496 A124 5m multicolored .20 .20
497 A124 10m multicolored .20 .20
498 A124 15m multicolored .20 .20

499 A124 20m multicolored .25 .20
500 A124 30m multicolored .40 .25
501 A124 60m multicolored .75 .35
502 A124 80m multicolored 1.00 .45
503 A124 1t multicolored 1.50 .65
Nos. 496-503 (8) 4.50 2.50

Souvenir Sheets

Perf. 11½, Imperf.

504 A124 4t orange & multi 4.00 4.00

19th Olympic Games, Mexico City, Oct. 12-27. #504 contains one 52x44mm stamp.

A125

A126

Hammer, spade & cogwheel.

1968, Sept. 17 Litho. *Perf. 11½*
505 A125 50m blue & vermilion .40 .20

Industrial development in town of Darhan.

1968, Nov. 6 Litho. *Perf. 12*
506 A126 60m turquoise & sepia .40 .25

Maxim Gorki (1868-1936), Russian writer.

Madonna and Child, by Boltraffio A127

Paintings: 10m, St. Roch Healed by an Angel, by Brescia. 15m, Madonna and Child with St. Anne, by Macchietti. 20m, St. John on Patmos, by Cano. 30m, Lady with Viola da Gamba, by Kupetzky. 80m, Boy, by Amerling. 1.40t, Death of Adonis, by Furini. 4t, Portrait of a Lady, by Renoir.

1968, Nov. 20 Litho. *Perf. 12*
507 A127 5m gray & multi .25 .20
508 A127 10m gray & multi .30 .20
509 A127 15m gray & multi .40 .25
510 A127 20m gray & multi .50 .25
511 A127 30m gray & multi .60 .30
512 A127 80m gray & multi 1.00 .40
513 A127 1.40t gray & multi 1.50 .90
Nos. 507-513 (7) 4.55 2.50

Miniature Sheet

514 A127 4t gray & multi 4.50 4.50

UNESCO, 22nd anniv.

Jesse Owens, US — A128

Olympic Gold Medal Winners: 5m, Paavo Nurmi, Finland. 15m, Fanny Blankers-Koen, Netherlands. 20m, Laszlo Papp, Hungary. 30m, Wilma Rudolph, US. 60m, Boris Shakhlin, USSR. 80m, Donald Schollander, US. 1t Akinori Nakayama, Japan. 4t, Jigjidin Munkhbat, Mongolia.

1969, Mar. 25 Litho. *Perf. 12*
515 A128 5m multicolored .20 .20
516 A128 10m multicolored .20 .20
517 A128 15m multicolored .20 .20
518 A128 20m multicolored .25 .20
519 A128 30m multicolored .40 .25
520 A128 60m multicolored .75 .35
521 A128 80m multicolored 1.00 .45
522 A128 1t multicolored 1.50 .65
Nos. 515-522 (8) 4.50 2.50

Souvenir Sheet

523 A128 4t green & multi 4.50 4.50

Bayit Woman A129

Regional Costumes: 10m, Torgut man. 15m, Dzakhachin woman. 20m, Khalkha woman. 30m, Dariganga woman. 60m, Mingat woman. 80m, Khalkha man. 1t, Bargut woman.

1969, Apr. 20 Litho. *Perf. 12*
524 A129 5m multicolored .25 .20
525 A129 10m multicolored .25 .20
526 A129 15m multicolored .30 .20
527 A129 20m multicolored .50 .20
528 A129 30m multicolored .60 .25
529 A129 60m multicolored .70 .25
530 A129 80m multicolored .90 .40
531 A129 1t multicolored 1.25 .75
Nos. 524-531 (8) 4.75 2.45

Red Cross Emblem and Helicopter — A130

50m, Emblem, Red Cross car, shepherd.

1969, May 15 Litho. *Perf. 12*
532 A130 30m multicolored 1.25 .30
533 A130 50m multicolored 1.25 .40

30th anniversary of Mongolian Red Cross.

Landscape and Edelweiss — A131

Mongolian landscapes and flowers.

1969, May 20
534 A131 5m shown .25 .20
535 A131 10m Pinks .25 .20
536 A131 15m Dianthus superbus .30 .20
537 A131 20m Geranium .50 .20
538 A131 30m Dianthus ramosissimus .60 .25
539 A131 60m Globeflowers .70 .25
540 A131 80m Delphinium .80 .40
541 A131 1t Haloxylon 1.25 .80
Nos. 534-541 (8) 4.65 2.50

See No. 1105.

Bull Fight, by Tsewegdjaw — A132

Paintings from National Museum: 10m, Fighting Colts, by O. Tsewegdjaw. 15m, Horseman and Herd, by A. Sangatzohyo. 20m, Camel Caravan, by D. Damdinsuren. 30m, On the Steppe, by N. Tsultem. 60m, Milking Mares, by Tsewegdjaw. 80m, Going to School, by B. Avarzad. 1t, After Work, by G. Odon. 4t, Horses, by Damdinsuren.

1969, July 11 Litho. *Perf. 12*
542 A132 5m multicolored .20 .20
543 A132 10m multicolored .20 .20
544 A132 15m multicolored .20 .20
545 A132 20m multicolored .50 .20
546 A132 30m multicolored .60 .25
547 A132 60m multicolored .75 .25
548 A132 80m multicolored .90 .40
549 A132 1t multicolored 1.25 .75
Nos. 542-549 (8) 4.60 2.45

Souvenir Sheet

550 A132 4t multicolored 4.50 4.50

10th anniversary of cooperative movement. No. 550 contains one stamp 65x42mm.

Mongolian Flag and Emblem A133

1969, Sept. 20 Litho. *Perf. 11½*
551 A133 50m multicolored .50 .30

Battle of Ha-lo-hsin (Khalka) River, 30th anniversary.
For surcharge, see No. 2384A.

Nos. 420-421 Overprinted

Perf. 11½x12, 12x11½

1969, Nov. 26 Photo.
552 A110 30m red & multi *8.00 8.00*
553 A111 50m red & multi *10.00 10.00*

45th anniv. of Mongolian People's Republic.

Mercury 7 — A134

Designs: 5m, Sputnik 3. 10m, Vostok 1. 20m, Voskhod 2. 30m, Apollo 8. 60m, Soyuz 5. 80m, Apollo 12.

1969, Dec. 6 Photo. *Perf. 12x11½*
554 A134 5m multicolored .20 .20
555 A134 10m multicolored .20 .20
556 A134 15m multicolored .20 .20
557 A134 20m multicolored .20 .20
558 A134 30m multicolored .25 .20
559 A134 60m multicolored .40 .20
560 A134 80m multicolored .55 .20
Nos. 554-560 (7) 2.00 1.40

Souvenir Sheet

561 A134 4t multicolored 4.50 4.50

Space achievements of US and USSR.

Wolf — A135

Designs: 10m, Brown bear. 15m, Lynx. 20m, Wild boar. 30m, Moose. 60m, Bobac marmot. 80m, Argali. 1t, Old wall carpet showing hunter and dog.

1970, Mar. 25 Photo. *Perf. 12*
562 A135 5m multicolored .25 .20
563 A135 10m multicolored .25 .20
564 A135 15m multicolored .35 .20
565 A135 20m multicolored .40 .20
566 A135 30m multicolored .45 .25
567 A135 60m multicolored .75 .40
568 A135 80m multicolored 1.00 .60
569 A135 1t multicolored 1.25 .80
Nos. 562-569 (8) 4.70 2.85

Lenin and Mongolian Delegation, by Sangatzohyo — A136

Designs: 20m, Lenin, embroidered panel, by Cerenhuu, vert. 1t, Lenin, by Mazhig, vert.

1970, Apr. 22 Photo. & Litho.
570 A136 20m multicolored .40 .20
571 A136 50m multicolored .75 .25
572 A136 1t lt bl, blk & red 1.25 .50
Nos. 570-572 (3) 2.40 .95

Centenary of the birth of Lenin.

Souvenir Sheet

EXPO '70 Pavilion of Matsushita Electric Co. and Time Capsule — A137

1970, May 26 Photo. *Perf. 12½*
573 A137 4t gold & multi 4.50 4.50

EXPO '70 International Exposition, Osaka, Japan, Mar. 15-Sept. 13.

Sumitomo Fairy Tale Pavilion — A138

1970, June 5 **Photo.** ***Perf. 12x11½***
574 A138 1.50t multi + label 1.00 1.00

EXPO '70 International Exposition, Osaka. No. 574 printed in sheets of 20 (5x4) with alternating horizontal rows of tabs showing various fairy tales and EXPO '70 emblem.

Soccer, Rimet Cup — A139

Soccer players of various teams in action.

1970, June 20 ***Perf. 12½x11½***
575 A139 10m multi .25 .20
576 A139 20m multi .30 .20
577 A139 30m multi .40 .25
578 A139 50m multi .50 .25
579 A139 60m multi .60 .30
580 A139 1t multi 1.00 .40
581 A139 1.30t multi 1.50 .90
Nos. 575-581 (7) 4.55 2.50

Souvenir Sheet
Perf. 12½

582 A139 4t multi 3.50 3.50

World Soccer Championship for Jules Rimet Cup, Mexico City, May 30-June 21. No. 582 contains one stamp 51x37mm.

Old World Buzzard A140

Birds of Prey: 20m, Tawny owls. 30m, Northern goshawk. 50m, White-tailed sea eagle. 60m, Peregrine falcon. 1t, Old world kestrel. 1.30t, Black kite.

1970, June 30 **Litho.** ***Perf. 12***
583 A140 10m bl & multi .75 .25
584 A140 20m pink & multi 1.00 .30
585 A140 30m yel grn & multi 1.25 .50
586 A140 50m bl & multi 1.50 .75
587 A140 60m yel & multi 1.75 1.00
588 A140 1t grn & multi 2.25 1.25
589 A140 1.30t bl & multi 2.50 1.50
Nos. 583-589 (7) 11.00 5.55

Russian War Memorial, Berlin — A141

1970, July 11 **Litho.** ***Perf. 12***
590 A141 60m blue & multi .75 .40

25th anniversary of end of World War II.

Bogdo-Gegen Palace — A142

Designs: 10m, Archer. 30m, Horseman. 40m, "White Mother" Goddess. 50m, Girl in national costume. 60m, Lion statue. 70m, Dancer's mask. 80m, Detail from Bogdo-Gegen Palace, Ulan Bator.

1970, Sept. 20 **Litho.** ***Perf. 12***
591 A142 10m multi .35 .25
592 A142 20m multi .35 .25
593 A142 30m multi .35 .25
594 A142 40m multi .35 .30
595 A142 50m multi .75 .65
596 A142 60m multi .90 .75
597 A142 70m multi 1.00 .85
598 A142 80m multi 1.25 1.10
a. Block of 4, #595-598
Nos. 591-598 (8) 5.30 4.40

Souvenir Sheet

Recovery of Apollo 13 Capsule — A143

1970, Nov. 1 **Litho.** ***Perf. 12***
599 A143 4t blue & multi 4.50 4.50

Space missions of Apollo 13, Apr. 11-17, and Soyuz 9, June 1-10, 1970.

Mongolian Flag, UN and Education Year Emblems — A144

1970, Nov. 7
600 A144 60m multi .80 .40

International Education Year.

Mounted Herald A145

1970, Nov. 7 **Litho.** ***Perf. 12***
601 A145 30m gold & multi .75 .40

50th anniv. of newspaper Unen (Truth).

Apollo 11 Lunar Landing Module — A146

Designs: 10m, Vostok 2 & 3. 20m, Voskhod 2, space walk. 30m, Gemini 6 & 7 capsules. 50m, Soyuz 4 & 5 docking in space. 60m, Soyuz 6, 7 & 8 group flight. 1t, Apollo 13 with damaged capsule. 1.30t, Luna 16 unmanned moon landing. 4t, Radar ground tracking station.

1971, Feb. 25 **Litho.** ***Perf. 12***
602 A146 10m multi .20 .20
603 A146 20m multi .20 .20
604 A146 30m multi .20 .20
605 A146 50m multi .50 .20
606 A146 60m multi .60 .25
607 A146 80m multi .75 .25
608 A146 1t multi .90 .40
609 A146 1.30t multi 1.25 .75
Nos. 602-609 (8) 4.60 2.45

Souvenir Sheet

610 A146 4t vio bl & multi 4.00 4.00

US and USSR space explorations.

Rider with Mongolian Flag — A147

Designs: 30m, Party meeting. 90m, Lenin with Mongolian leader. 1.20t, Marchers, pictures of Lenin and Marx.

1971, Mar. 1 **Photo.** ***Perf. 12½***
611 A147 30m gold & multi .30 .20
612 A147 60m gold & multi .40 .30
613 A147 90m gold & multi .50 .40
614 A147 1.20t gold & multi .60 .50
Nos. 611-614 (4) 1.80 1.40

Mongolian Revolutionary Party, 50th anniv.

Souvenir Sheet

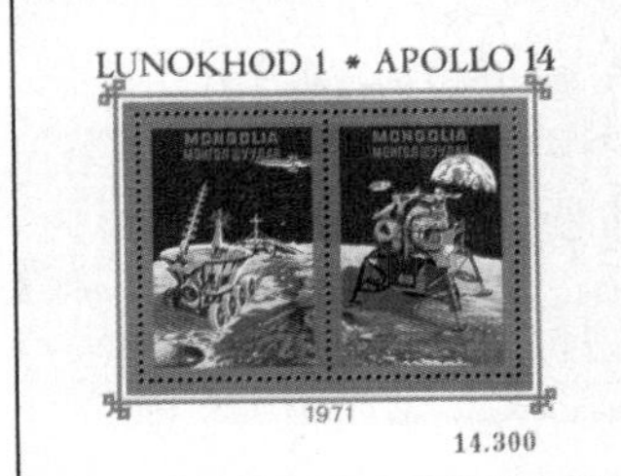

Lunokhod 1 on Moon — A148

Design: No. 615b, Apollo 14 on moon.

1971, Apr. 15 **Photo.** ***Perf. 14***
615 A148 Sheet of 2 4.00 4.00
a.-b. 2t any single 1.75 1.75

Luna 17 unmanned automated moon mission, Nov. 10-17, 1970, and Apollo 14 moon landing, Jan. 31-Feb. 9, 1971.

Dancer's Mask A149

Designs: Various masks for dancers.

1971, Apr. 25 **Litho.** ***Perf. 12***
616 A149 10m gold & multi .20 .20
617 A149 20m gold & multi .30 .20
618 A149 30m gold & multi .50 .20
619 A149 50m gold & multi .55 .25
620 A149 60m gold & multi .60 .30
621 A149 1t gold & multi 1.10 .70
622 A149 1.30t gold & multi 1.40 1.00
Nos. 616-622 (7) 4.65 2.85

Red Flag and Emblems A150

1971, May 31 **Photo.** ***Perf. 12x11½***
623 A150 60m bl, red & gold .40 .25

16th Congress of Mongolian Revolutionary Party.

Steam Locomotive — A151

1971, July 11 **Litho.** ***Perf. 12***
624 A151 20m shown .50 .20
625 A151 30m Diesel locomotive .50 .20
626 A151 40m Truck .65 .20
627 A151 50m Automobile .75 .25
628 A151 60m Biplane PO-2 1.00 .35
629 A151 80m AN-24 plane 1.25 .60
630 A151 1t Fishing boat 1.75 1.00
Nos. 624-630 (7) 6.40 2.80

50th anniversary of modern transportation.
For overprints see Nos. 850A-850G.

Arms of Mongolia and Soldier — A152

Design: 1.50t, Arms, policeman and child.

1971, July 11 **Litho.** ***Perf. 12***
631 A152 60m multi .50 .20
632 A152 1.50t multi .75 .40

50th anniversary of the people's army and police.

Mongolian Flag and Emblem — A153

1971, Aug. 25 Photo. ***Perf. 12x11½***

633	A153	60m lt bl & multi	.40	.25

International Year Against Racial discrimination.

Flag of Youth Organization — A154

1971, Aug. 25 Litho. ***Perf. 12***

634	A154	60m org & multi	.60	.30

50th anniversary of Mongolian revolutionary youth organization.

The Woodsman and the Tiger A155

Designs: Various Mongolian fairy tales.

1971, Sept. 15 Litho. ***Perf. 12***

635	A155	10m gold & multi	.20	.20
636	A155	20m gold & multi	.20	.20
637	A155	30m gold & multi	.30	.20
638	A155	50m gold & multi	.40	.25
639	A155	60m gold & multi	.60	.25
640	A155	80m gold & multi	.80	.30
641	A155	1t gold & multi	1.00	.40
642	A155	1.30t gold & multi	1.25	.65
		Nos. 635-642 (8)	4.75	2.45

Bactrian Camel — A156

1971, Nov. 1 Litho. ***Perf. 12½***

643	A156	20m Yaks	.25	.20
644	A156	30m shown	.25	.20
645	A156	40m Sheep	.35	.25
646	A156	50m Goats	.50	.25
647	A156	60m Cattle	.75	.40
648	A156	80m Horses	.85	.40
649	A156	1t White horse	1.40	.75
		Nos. 643-649 (7)	4.35	2.45

Mongolian livestock breeding.

Cross-country Skiing — A157

Designs (Sapporo Olympic Emblem and): 20m, Bobsledding. 30m, Women's figure skating. 50m, Slalom. 60m, Speed skating. 80m, Downhill skiing. 1t, Ice hockey. 1.30t, Figure skating, pairs. 4t, Ski jump.

Perf. 12½x11½

1972, Jan. 20 **Photo.**

650	A157	10m multi	.25	.20
651	A157	20m ol & multi	.25	.20
652	A157	30m ultra & multi	.35	.20
653	A157	50m brt bl & multi	.45	.25
654	A157	60m multi	.55	.25
655	A157	80m grn & multi	.65	.25
656	A157	1t bl & multi	.85	.35
657	A157	1.30t vio & multi	1.10	.60
		Nos. 650-657 (8)	4.45	2.30

Souvenir Sheet

Perf. 12½

658	A157	4t lt bl & multi	4.00	4.00

11th Winter Olympic Games, Sapporo, Japan, Feb. 3-13.

Taming Wild Horse A158

Paintings: 20m, Mythological animal in winter. 30m, Lancer on horseback. 50m, Athletes. 60m, Waterfall and horses. 80m, The Wise Musician, by Sarav. 1t, Young musician. 1.30t, Old sage with animals.

1972, Apr. 15 Litho. ***Perf. 12***

659	A158	10m multi	.20	.20
660	A158	20m multi	.20	.20
661	A158	30m multi	.30	.20
662	A158	50m multi	.40	.25
663	A158	60m multi	.50	.25
664	A158	80m multi	.80	.45
665	A158	1t multi	.90	.45
666	A158	1.30t multi	1.25	.55
		Nos. 659-666 (8)	4.55	2.55

Paintings by contemporary artists in Ulan Bator Museum.

Calosoma Fischeri A159

Designs: Various insects.

1972, Apr. 30 Litho. ***Perf. 12***

667	A159	10m multi	.20	.20
668	A159	20m multi	.30	.20
669	A159	30m multi	.40	.20
670	A159	50m multi	.50	.25
671	A159	60m multi	.70	.25
672	A159	80m multi	1.00	.50
673	A159	1t multi	1.25	.75
674	A159	1.30t multi	1.75	.95
		Nos. 667-674 (8)	6.10	3.30

UN Emblem A160

1972, Aug. 30 Photo. ***Perf. 12***

675	A160	60m multi	.60	.40

ECAFE (UN Economic Commission for Asia and the Far East), 25th anniv.

Slow Lizard — A161

Designs: 15m, Radd's toad. 20m, Pallas's viper. 25m, Toad-headed agamid. 30m, Siberian wood frog. 60m, Przewalski's lizard. 80m, Taphrometopon lineolatum (snake). 1t, Stoliczka's agamid.

1972, Sept. 5 Litho. ***Perf. 12***

676	A161	10m multi	.25	.20
677	A161	15m multi	.30	.20
678	A161	20m multi	.35	.20
679	A161	25m multi	.50	.20
680	A161	30m multi	.60	.25
681	A161	60m multi	.75	.50
682	A161	80m multi	1.25	.75
683	A161	1t multi	1.50	1.10
		Nos. 676-683 (8)	5.50	3.40

Symbols of Technical Knowledge — A162

Design: 60m, University of Mongolia.

1972, Sept. 25

684	A162	50m org & multi	.55	.20
685	A162	60m lil & multi	.75	.30

30th anniversary of Mongolian State University.

Virgin and Child with St. John, by Bellini — A163

Paintings by Venetian Masters: 20m, Transfiguration, by Bellini, vert. 30m, Virgin and Child, by Bellini, vert. 50m, Presentation in the Temple, by Bellini. 60m, St. George, by Mantegna, vert. 80m, Departure of St. Ursula, by Carpaccio, vert. 1t, Departure of St. Ursula, by Carpaccio.

1972, Oct. 1

686	A163	10m multi	.25	.20
687	A163	20m multi	.25	.20
688	A163	30m multi	.45	.25
689	A163	50m multi	.60	.25
690	A163	60m multi	.90	.40
691	A163	80m multi	1.25	.80
692	A163	1t multi	1.40	1.00
		Nos. 686-692 (7)	5.10	3.10

Save Venice campaign. See No. B3.

Manlay Bator Damdinsuren — A164

Designs: 20m, Ard Ayus, horiz. 50m, Hatan Bator Magsarzhav. 60m, Has Bator, horiz. 1t, Sukhe Bator.

1972, Oct. 20 Litho. ***Perf. 12***

693	A164	10m gold & multi	.20	.20
694	A164	20m gold & multi	.35	.30
695	A164	50m gold & multi	.55	.40
696	A164	60m gold & multi	.75	.50
697	A164	1t gold & multi	1.25	.60
		Nos. 693-697 (5)	3.10	2.00

Paintings of national heroes.

Spasski Tower, Moscow — A165

1972, Nov. 7 Photo. ***Perf. 11***

698	A165	60m multi + label	.75	.40

50th anniversary of USSR.

Mark Spitz, US, Gold Medal — A166

Designs (Medal and): 10m, Ulrike Meyfarth, Germany. 20m, Sawao Kato, Japan. 30m, András Balczó, Hungary. 60m, Lasse Viren, Finland. 80m, Shane Gould, Australia. 1t, Anatoli Bondarchuk, USSR. 4t, Khorloo Baianmunk, Mongolia.

1972, Dec. 15 Photo. ***Perf. 12½***

699	A166	5m grn & multi	.20	.20
700	A166	10m ver & multi	.25	.20
701	A166	20m bl & multi	.40	.20
702	A166	30m multi	.60	.25
703	A166	60m lt vio & multi	1.00	.25
704	A166	80m ol & multi	1.10	.40
705	A166	1t lem & multi	1.25	.60
		Nos. 699-705 (7)	4.80	2.10

Souvenir Sheet

706	A166	4t red & multi	2.00	2.00

Winners in 20th Olympic Games, Munich.

Chimpanzee on Bicycle — A167

Circus Scenes: 10m, Seal playing ball. 15m, Bear riding wheel. 20m, Woman acrobat on camel. 30m, Woman equestrian. 50m, Clown playing flute. 60m, Woman gymnast. 1t, Circus building, Ulan Bator, horiz.

1973, Jan. 29 Litho. *Perf. 12*

707 A167 5m multi .20 .20
708 A167 10m multi .25 .20
709 A167 15m multi .35 .20
710 A167 20m multi .45 .20
711 A167 30m multi .55 .25
712 A167 50m multi .70 .35
713 A167 60m multi .90 .45
714 A167 1t multi 1.25 .75
Nos. 707-714 (8) 4.65 2.60

Postrider A168

Designs: 60m, Diesel locomotive. 1t, Truck.

1973, Jan. 31 Photo. *Perf. 12x11½*

715 A168 50m brown 1.00 .20
716 A168 60m green 3.50 .40
717 A168 1t rose claret 1.75 .60
Nos. 715-717,C34 (4) 7.05 1.40

For surcharges, see Nos. 2405-2407.

Sukhe Bator and Merchants A169

Paintings of Sukhe Bator: 20m, With elders. 50m, Leading partisans. 60m, With revolutionary council. 1t, Receiving deputation, horiz.

1973, Feb. 2 Photo. *Perf. 11½x12*

718 A169 10m gold & multi .20 .20
719 A169 20m gold & multi .30 .20
720 A169 50m gold & multi .70 .30
721 A169 60m gold & multi 1.00 .40
722 A169 1t gold & multi 1.50 .60
Nos. 718-722 (5) 3.70 1.70

Sukhe Bator (1893-1923).

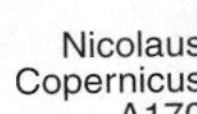

Nicolaus Copernicus A170

Marx and Lenin — A171

Designs: 60m, 2t, Copernicus in laboratory, by Jan Matejko, horiz., 55x35mm. Nos. 725, 726b, Portrait. No. 726a, like 50m.

1973, Mar. Litho. *Perf. 12*

723 A170 50m gold & multi .50 .25
724 A170 60m gold & multi .70 .40
725 A170 1t gold & multi 1.25 .60
Nos. 723-725 (3) 2.45 1.25

Souvenir Sheet

726 Sheet of 3 4.00 3.00
a. A170 1t multi .60 .60
b. A170 1t multi .60 .60
c. A170 2t multi 1.50 1.50

500th anniversary of the birth of Nicolaus Copernicus (1473-1543), Polish astronomer.

1973, July 15 Photo. *Perf. 11½x12*

727 A171 60m gold, car & ultra .75 .40

9th meeting of postal administrations of socialist countries, Ulan Bator.

Common Shelducks — A172

Designs: Aquatic birds.

1973, Aug. 10 Litho. *Perf. 12x11*

728 A172 5m shown .40 .25
729 A172 10m Arctic loons .75 .25
730 A172 15m Bar-headed geese 1.25 .25
731 A172 30m Great crested grebe 1.50 .40
732 A172 50m Mallards 2.00 .60
733 A172 60m Mute swans 2.50 .80
734 A172 1t Greater scaups 2.75 1.25
Nos. 728-734 (7) 11.15 3.80

1973, Aug. 25 Litho. *Perf. 12x11*

Designs: Fur-bearing animals.

735 A172 5m Siberian weasel .25 .20
736 A172 10m Siberian chipmunk .25 .20
737 A172 15m Flying squirrel .30 .20
738 A172 20m Eurasian badger .40 .20
739 A172 30m Eurasian red squirrel .60 .25
740 A172 60m Wolverine 1.00 .50
741 A172 80m Mink 1.25 .70
742 A172 1t White hare 1.60 .90
Nos. 735-742 (8) 5.65 3.15

1973, Dec. 15 Litho. *Perf. 12x11*

Designs: Flowers.

743 A172 5m Alpine aster .25 .20
744 A172 10m Mongolian silene .25 .20
745 A172 15m Rosa davurica .30 .20
746 A172 20m Mongolian dandelion .40 .20
747 A172 30m Rhododendron dahuricum .60 .25
748 A172 50m Clematis tangutica 1.00 .50
749 A172 60m Siberian primula 1.25 .70
750 A172 1t Pasqueflower 1.60 .90
Nos. 743-750 (8) 5.65 3.15

Globe and Red Flag Emblem — A173

1973, Dec. 10 Photo. *Perf. 12x12½*

751 A173 60m gold, red & blue .60 .30

15th anniversary of the review "Problems of Peace and Socialism," published in Prague.

Limenitis Populi A174

Butterflies: 10m, Arctia hebe. 15m, Rhyparia purpurata. 20m, Catocala pacta. 30m, Isoceras kaszabi. 50m, Celerio costata. 60m, Arctia caja. 1t, Diacrisia sannio.

1974, Jan. 15 Litho. *Perf. 11*

752 A174 5m lil & multi .50 .25
753 A174 10m brn & multi .60 .25
754 A174 15m bl & multi .75 .25
755 A174 20m brn org & multi .90 .25
756 A174 30m lt vio & multi 1.10 .30
757 A174 50m dl red & multi 1.50 .60
758 A174 60m yel grn & multi 1.75 .90
759 A174 1t ultra & multi 2.50 1.25
Nos. 752-759 (8) 9.60 4.05

"Hehe Namshil" by L. Merdorsh A175

Designs (Various Scenes from): 20m, "Sive Hiagt," by D. Luvsansharav. 25m, 80m, 1t, "Edre," by D. Namdag. 30m, "The 3 Khans of Sara-Gol" (legend). 60m, "Amarsana," by B. Damdinsuren. 20m and 30m horizontal.

1974, Feb. 20 Litho. *Perf. 12*

760 A175 15m sil & multi .25 .20
761 A175 20m sil & multi .35 .25
762 A175 25m sil & multi .50 .25
763 A175 30m sil & multi .60 .30
764 A175 60m sil & multi .70 .30
765 A175 80m sil & multi .95 .40
766 A175 1t sil & multi 1.25 .80
Nos. 760-766 (7) 4.60 2.50

Mongolian operas and dramas.

Government Building and Sukhe Bator — A176

1974, Mar. 1 Photo. *Perf. 11*

767 A176 60m gold & multi .75 .40

50th anniv. of renaming capital Ulan Bator.

Juggler A177

10m, Circus horses, horiz. 30m, Trained elephant. 40m, Yak pushing ball, horiz. 60m, Acrobats with ring. 80m, Woman acrobat on unicycle.

1974, May 4 Litho. *Perf. 12*

768 A177 10m multi .25 .20
769 A177 20m multi .40 .20
770 A177 30m multi .50 .30
771 A177 40m multi .80 .40
772 A177 60m multi 1.00 .50
773 A177 80m multi 1.60 .75
Nos. 768-773,C65 (7) 5.55 2.85

Mongolian Circus. No. 773 has se-tenant label, with similar design.

Girl on Bronco — A178

Children's Activities: 20m, Boy roping calf. 30m, 40m, Boy taming horse (different designs). 60m, Girl with doves. 80m, Wrestling. 1t, Dancing.

1974, June 2 Litho. *Perf. 12*

774 A178 10m dl yel & multi .20 .20
775 A178 20m lt bl & multi .25 .20
776 A178 30m grn & multi .35 .20
777 A178 40m yel & multi .50 .30
778 A178 60m pink & multi .75 .30
779 A178 80m bl & multi .95 .50
780 A178 1t dl bl & multi 1.50 .75
Nos. 774-780 (7) 4.50 2.45

Children's Day.
For surcharges see Nos. 2577-2578.

Archer — A179

National Sports: 20m, Two horsemen fighting for goatskin. 30m, Archer on horseback. 40m, Horse race. 60m, Riding wild horse. 80m, Rider chasing riderless horse. 1t, Boys wrestling.

1974, July 11 **Photo.** ***Perf. 11***

781	A179	10m	vio bl & multi	.20	.20
782	A179	20m	yel & multi	.25	.20
783	A179	30m	lil & multi	.35	.20
784	A179	40m	multi	.50	.30
785	A179	60m	multi	.75	.30
786	A179	80m	multi	.95	.50
787	A179	1t	multi	1.50	.75
			Nos. 781-787 (7)	4.50	2.45

Nadom, Mongolian national festival.

Grizzly Bear A180

1974, July **Litho.** ***Perf. 12***

788	A180	10m	shown	.25	.25
789	A180	20m	Common panda	.30	.25
790	A180	30m	Giant panda	.35	.25
791	A180	40m	Two brown bears	.50	.35
792	A180	60m	Sloth bear	.75	.35
793	A180	80m	Asiatic black bears	1.00	.50
794	A180	1t	Giant brown bear	1.50	.75
			Nos. 788-794 (7)	4.65	2.70

Stag in Zuun Araat Wildlife Preserve — A181

1974, Sept. **Litho.** ***Perf. 12***

795	A181	10m	shown	.25	.25
796	A181	20m	Beaver	.30	.25
797	A181	30m	Leopard	.35	.25
798	A181	40m	Great black-backed gull	.50	.35
799	A181	60m	Deer	.75	.35
800	A181	80m	Mouflon	1.00	.50
801	A181	1t	Deer and entrance to Bogd-uul Preserve	1.50	.75
			Nos. 795-801 (7)	4.65	2.70

Protected fauna in Mongolian wildlife preserves.

Buddhist Temple, Bogdo Gegen Palace — A182

Mongolian Architecture: 15m, Buddhist Temple, now Museum. 30m, Entrance to Charity Temple, Ulan Bator. 50m, Mongolian yurta. 80m, Gazebo in convent yard.

1974, Oct. 15 **Litho.** ***Perf. 12***

802	A182	10m	bl & multi	.30	.20
803	A182	15m	multi	.35	.20
804	A182	30m	grn & multi	.45	.30
805	A182	50m	multi	.60	.40
806	A182	80m	yel & multi	1.00	.50
			Nos. 802-806 (5)	2.70	1.60

Spasski Tower, Sukhe Bator Statue A183

1974, Nov. 26 **Photo.** ***Perf. 11½x12***

807	A183	60m	multi	.75	.40

Visit of General Secretary Brezhnev and a delegation from the USSR to participate in celebration of 50th anniversary of People's Republic of Mongolia.

Sukhe Bator Proclaiming Republic A184

Designs: No. 808, "First Constitution," symbolic embroidery. No. 809, Flag over landscape, plane and communications tower.

1974, Nov. 28 **Litho.**

808	A184	60m	multi	.75	.40
809	A184	60m	multi	.75	.40
810	A184	60m	multi	.75	.40
			Nos. 808-810 (3)	2.25	1.20

50th anniv. of People's Republic of Mongolia.

Decanter A185

Designs: 20m, Silver jar. 30m, Night lamp. 40m, Tea jug. 60m, Candelabra. 80m, Teapot. 1t, Silver bowl on 3-legged stand.

1974, Dec. 1 **Photo.**

811	A185	10m	blue & multi	.25	.25
812	A185	20m	claret & multi	.30	.25
813	A185	30m	multi	.35	.25
814	A185	40m	dp bl & multi	.50	.35
815	A185	60m	multi	.75	.35
816	A185	80m	grn & multi	1.00	.50
817	A185	1t	lilac & multi	1.50	.75
			Nos. 811-817 (7)	4.65	2.70

Mongolian 19th century goldsmiths' work.

Lapwing (plover) — A186

1974, Dec. **Litho.** ***Perf. 11***

818	A186	10m	shown	.60	.25
819	A186	20m	Fish	.70	.25
820	A186	30m	Marsh marigolds	.90	.30
821	A186	40m	White pelican	1.00	.30
822	A186	60m	Perch	1.10	.50
823	A186	80m	Mink	1.25	.75
			Nos. 818-823,C66 (7)	6.55	2.85

Water and nature protection.

American Mail Coach, UPU Emblem — A187

Designs (UPU Emblem and): 20m, French two-wheeled coach. 30m, Changing horses, Russian coach. 40m, Swedish caterpillar mail truck. 50m, First Hungarian mail truck. 60m, German Daimler-Benz mail truck. 1t, Mongolian dispatch rider.

1974, Dec. **Litho.** ***Perf. 12***

824	A187	10m	multi	.25	.20
825	A187	20m	multi	.30	.20
826	A187	30m	multi	.35	.25
827	A187	40m	multi	.50	.35
828	A187	50m	multi	.75	.45
829	A187	60m	multi	1.00	.60
830	A187	1t	multi	1.50	.80
			Nos. 824-830 (7)	4.65	2.85

Cent. of the UPU and Stockholmia 74.

Soviet Flag, Broken Swastika A188

1975, May 9 **Photo.** ***Perf. 11½x12***

832	A188	60m	multi	.75	.40

30th anniversary of the end of World War II and victory over fascism.

Mongolian Woman A189

1975, May

833	A189	60m	multi	.75	.45

International Women's Year 1975.

Zygophyllum Xanthoxylon — A190

Medicinal Plants: 20m, Ingarvillea potaninii. 30m, Lancea tibetica. 40m, Jurinea mongolica. 50m, Saussurea involucrata. 60m, Allium mongolicum. 1t, Adonis mongolica.

1975, May 24 **Photo.** ***Perf. 11x11½***

834	A190	10m	dp org & multi	.25	.20
835	A190	20m	grn & multi	.40	.20
836	A190	30m	yel & multi	.60	.25
837	A190	40m	vio & multi	.75	.35
838	A190	50m	brn & multi	.85	.60
839	A190	60m	bl & multi	1.10	.90
840	A190	1t	multi	1.75	1.25
			Nos. 834-840 (7)	5.70	3.75

12th International Botanists' Conference.

Shepherd — A191

Puppet Theater: 20m, Boy on horseback. 30m, Boy and disobedient bull calf. 40m, Little orphan camel's tale. 50m, Boy and obedient little yak. 60m, Boy riding swan. 1t, Children's choir.

1975, June 30 **Litho.** ***Perf. 12***

841	A191	10m	multi	.25	.20
842	A191	20m	multi	.30	.20
843	A191	30m	multi	.35	.30
844	A191	40m	multi	.50	.30
845	A191	50m	multi	.75	.40
846	A191	60m	multi	1.00	.50
847	A191	1t	multi	1.50	.75
			Nos. 841-847 (7)	4.65	2.65

For surcharges see Nos. 2575-2576.

Pioneers Tending Fruit Tree — A192

60m, Pioneers studying, and flying model plane. 1t, New emblem of Mongolian Pioneers.

1975, July 15 ***Perf. 12x11½***

848	A192	50m	multi	.60	.30
849	A192	60m	multi	.85	.30
850	A192	1t	multi	1.00	.60
			Nos. 848-850 (3)	2.45	1.20

Mongolian Pioneers, 50th anniversary.

Nos. 624-630 Overprinted

1975, July 15 Litho. *Perf. 12*
850A A151 20m multi 5.00 5.00
850B A151 30m multi 5.00 5.00
850C A151 40m multi 4.00 4.00
850D A151 50m multi 4.00 4.00
850E A151 60m multi 5.00 5.00
850F A151 80m multi 5.00 5.00
850G A151 1t multi 6.00 6.00
Nos. 850A-850G (7) 34.00 34.00

Fifty years of communication.

Golden Eagle Hunting Fox — A193

Hunting Scenes: 20m, Dogs treeing lynx, vert. 30m, Hunter stalking marmots. 40m, Hunter riding reindeer, vert. 50m, Boar hunt. 60m, Trapped wolf, vert. 1t, Bear hunt.

1975, Aug. 25 Litho. *Perf. 12*
851 A193 10m multi .50 .20
852 A193 20m multi .60 .25
853 A193 30m multi .70 .30
854 A193 40m multi .80 .40
855 A193 50m multi .90 .50
856 A193 60m multi 1.00 .70
857 A193 1t multi 1.10 .90
Nos. 851-857 (7) 5.60 3.25

Hunting in Mongolia.

Mesocottus Haitej — A194

Various Fish: 20m, Pseudaspius lepto cephalus. 30m, Oreoleuciscus potanini. 40m, Tinca tinca. 50m, Coregonus lavaretus pidschian. 60m, Erythroculter mongolicus. 1t, Carassius auratus.

1975, Sept. 15 Photo. *Perf. 11*
858 A194 10m multi .25 .20
859 A194 20m multi .35 .20
860 A194 30m multi .50 .30
861 A194 40m bl & multi .75 .30
862 A194 50m grn & multi .90 .40
863 A194 60m lil & multi 1.00 .70
864 A194 1t vio bl & multi 1.75 .90
Nos. 858-864 (7) 5.50 3.00

Neck and Bow of Musical Instrument (Morin Hur) — A195

National Handicraft: 20m, Saddle. 30m, Silver headgear. 40m, Boots. 50m, Tasseled Woman's cap. 60m, Pipe and tobacco pouch. 1t, Sable cap.

1975, Oct. 10 Litho. *Perf. 11½x12½*
865 A195 10m multi .20 .20
866 A195 20m multi .25 .20
867 A195 30m multi .50 .30
868 A195 40m multi .65 .30
869 A195 50m multi .85 .40
870 A195 60m multi .95 .45
871 A195 1t multi 1.10 .65
Nos. 865-871 (7) 4.50 2.50

Revolutionists with Flags — A196

1975, Nov. 15 Litho. *Perf. 11½x12*
872 A196 60m multi .75 .40

70th anniversary of Russian Revolution.

Ski Jump, Olympic Games Emblem A197

Winter Olympic Games Emblem and: 20m, Ice hockey. 30m, Skiing. 40m, Bobsled. 50m, Biathlon. 60m, Speed skating. 1t, Figure skating, women's. 4t, Skier carrying torch.

Perf. 11½x12½
1975, Dec. 20 Litho.
873 A197 10m multi .20 .20
874 A197 20m multi .25 .20
875 A197 30m brn & multi .50 .30
876 A197 40m grn & multi .65 .30
877 A197 50m multi .85 .40
878 A197 60m ol & multi .95 .45
879 A197 1t multi 1.10 .65
Nos. 873-879 (7) 4.50 2.50

Souvenir Sheet

880 A197 4t multi 4.00 4.00

12th Winter Olympic Games, Innsbruck, Austria, Feb. 4-15, 1976.

Taming Wild Horse A198

Mongolian Paintings: 20m, Camel caravan, horiz. 30m, Man playing lute. 40m, Woman adjusting headdress, horiz. 50m, Woman wearing ceremonial costume. 60m, Women fetching water. 1t, Woman musician. 4t, Warrior on horseback.

1975, Nov. 30 *Perf. 12*
881 A198 10m brown & multi .20 .20
882 A198 20m blue & multi .25 .20
883 A198 30m olive & multi .50 .30
884 A198 40m lilac & multi .65 .30
885 A198 50m blue & multi .85 .40
886 A198 60m lilac & multi .95 .45
887 A198 1t silver & multi 1.25 .65
Nos. 881-887 (7) 4.65 2.50

Souvenir Sheet

888 A198 4t bl & multi 4.50 4.00

House of Young Technicians A199

Designs: 60m, Hotel Ulan Bator. 1t, Museum of the Revolution.

1975, Dec. 30 Photo. *Perf. 12x11½*
893 A199 50m ultra .65 .20
894 A199 60m bl grn .75 .30
895 A199 1t brick red 1.10 .60
Nos. 893-895 (3) 2.50 1.10

Camels in Gobi Desert — A200

20m, Horse taming. 30m, Herding. 40m, Pioneers' camp. 60m, Young musician. 80m, Children's festival. 1t, Mongolian wrestling.

1976, June 1 Litho. *Perf. 12*
896 A200 10m multi .25 .20
897 A200 20m multi .30 .20
898 A200 30m multi .35 .20
899 A200 40m multi .50 .30
900 A200 60m multi .75 .30
901 A200 80m multi 1.00 .50
902 A200 1t multi 1.50 .75
Nos. 896-902 (7) 4.65 2.45

International Children's Day.

Red Star — A201

1976, May 1 Photo. *Perf. 11x12½*
903 A201 60m red, maroon & silver .75 .40

17th Congress of the Mongolian People's Revolutionary Party, June 14.

Archery, Montreal Games' Emblem, Canadian Flag — A202

20m, Judo. 30m, Boxing. 40m, Vaulting. 60m, Weight lifting. 80m, High Jump. 1t, Target shooting.

1976, May 20 Litho. *Perf. 12½x11½*
904 A202 10m yel & multi .20 .20
905 A202 20m yel & multi .25 .20
906 A202 30m yel & multi .50 .20
907 A202 40m yel & multi .65 .30
908 A202 60m yel & multi .85 .30
909 A202 80m yel & multi .95 .50
910 A202 1t yel & multi 1.10 .75
Nos. 904-910 (7) 4.50 2.45

21st Olympic Games, Montreal, Canada, July 17-Aug. 1. See No. C81.

Partisans A203

Fighter and Sojombo Independence Symbol — A204

Perf. 12x11½, 11½x12
1976, June 15 Litho.
911 A203 60m multi 1.00 .50
912 A204 60m multi 1.00 .50

55th anniversary of Mongolia's independence. See No. C82.

Souvenir Sheet

Sukhe Bator Medal — A205

1976, July 11 *Perf. 11½*
913 A205 4t multi 4.00 4.00

Mongolian honors medals.

Osprey — A206

Protected Birds: 20m, Griffon vulture. 30m, Bearded lammergeier. 40m, Marsh harrier. 60m, Black vulture. 80m, Golden eagle. 1t, Tawny eagle.

1976, Aug. 16 Litho. *Perf. 12*

No.	Type	Value	Unused	Used
914	A206	10m multi	.75	.25
915	A206	20m multi	1.00	.25
916	A206	30m multi	1.25	.35
917	A206	40m multi	1.50	.55
918	A206	60m multi	1.75	.75
919	A206	80m multi	2.00	.95
920	A206	1t multi	2.50	1.10
		Nos. 914-920 (7)	10.75	4.20

"Nadom" Military Game — A207

Paintings by O. Cevegshava: 10m, Taming Wild Horse, vert. 30m, Hubsugul Lake Harbor. 40m, The Steppe Awakening. 80m, Wrestlers. 1.60t, Yak Descending in Snow, vert.

1976, Sept. Litho. *Perf. 12*

No.	Type	Value	Unused	Used
921	A207	10m multi	.25	.20
922	A207	20m multi	.40	.20
923	A207	30m multi	.50	.20
924	A207	40m multi	.60	.30
925	A207	80m multi	1.00	.60
926	A207	1.60t multi	1.75	1.00
		Nos. 921-926 (6)	4.50	2.50

Interlocking Circles, Industry and Transport — A208

1976, Oct. 15 Photo. *Perf. 12x11½*

No.	Type	Value	Unused	Used
927	A208	60m brn, bl & red	1.25	.75

Soviet-Mongolian friendship.

John Naber, US Flag, Gold Medals A209

Designs: 20m, Nadia Comaneci, Romanian flag. 30m, Kornelia Ender, East German flag. 40m, Mitsuo Tsukahara, Japanese flag. 60m, Gregor Braun, German flag. 80m, Lasse Viren, Finnish flag. 1t, Nikolai Andrianov, Russian flag.

1976, Nov. 30 Litho. *Perf. 12*

No.	Type	Value	Unused	Used
928	A209	10m multi	.20	.20
929	A209	20m multi	.25	.20
930	A209	30m multi	.50	.20
931	A209	40m multi	.65	.30
932	A209	60m multi	.85	.30
933	A209	80m multi	.85	.50
934	A209	1t multi	1.10	.75
		Nos. 928-934 (7)	4.40	2.45

Gold medal winners, 21st Olympic Games, Montreal. See No. C83.

Stone Tablet on Tortoise A210

Carved Tablet, 6th-8th Centuries A211

1976, Dec. 15 Litho. *Perf. 11½x12*

No.	Type	Value	Unused	Used
935	A210	50m brn & lt bl	1.00	.35
936	A211	60m gray & brt grn	1.50	.40

Intl. Archaeological Conference, Ulan Bator.

R-1 Plane — A212

Designs: Various Mongolian planes.

1976, Dec. 22 *Perf. 12*

No.	Type	Value	Unused	Used
937	A212	10m multi	.25	.20
938	A212	20m multi	.35	.20
939	A212	30m multi	.45	.20
940	A212	40m multi	.55	.25
941	A212	60m multi	.75	.35
942	A212	80m multi	.95	.55
943	A212	1t multi	1.25	.75
		Nos. 937-943 (7)	4.55	2.50

Dancers — A213

Folk Dances: 20m, 13th century costumes. 30m, West Mongolian dance. 40m, "Ekachi," or horse-dance. 60m, "Bielge," West Mongolian trunk dance. 80m, "Hodak," or friendship dance. 1t, "Dojarka."

1977, Mar. 20 Litho. *Perf. 12½*

No.	Type	Value	Unused	Used
944	A213	10m multi	.25	.20
945	A213	20m multi	.35	.20
946	A213	30m multi	.45	.30
947	A213	40m multi	.55	.30
948	A213	60m multi	.75	.40
949	A213	80m multi	1.00	.50
950	A213	1t multi	1.25	.75
		Nos. 944-950 (7)	4.60	2.65

Miniature Sheet

Path of Pioneer from Earth to Jupiter, deflected by Mars — A214

Isaac Newton — A215

1977, Mar. 31 Litho. *Perf. 11½x12*

No.	Description	Unused	Used
951	Sheet of 9	4.50	2.50
a.	A214 60m shown	.40	.25
b.	A215 60m Apple tree	.40	.25
c.	A214 60m Sextant and planets	.40	.25
d.	A214 60m Astronauts in space	.40	.25
e.	A215 60m shown	.40	.25
f.	A214 60m Prism and spectrum	.40	.25
g.	A214 60m Rain falling on earth	.40	.25
h.	A215 60m Motion of celestial bodies	.40	.25
i.	A214 60m Pioneer 10 over Jupiter	.40	.25

Sir Isaac Newton (1642-1727), English natural philosopher and mathematician.

Nos. 951a-951i arranged in 3 rows of 3. Nos. 951d and 951i inscribed AIR MAIL.

D. Natsagdorji, Writer, and Quotation — A216

Design: No. 953, Grazing horses, landscape, ornament and quotation.

1977 *Perf. 11½x12*

No.	Type	Value	Unused	Used
952	A216	60m multi	1.00	.50
953	A216	60m multi	1.00	.50

D. Natsagdorji, founder of modern Mongolian literature. Label and vignette separated by simulated perforations.

Primitive Tortoises — A217

Prehistoric Animals: 20m, Ungulate (titanothere). 30m, Beaked dinosaurs. 40m, Entelodon (swine). 60m, Antelope. 80m, Hipparion. 1t, Aurochs.

1977, May 7 Photo. *Perf. 12½*

No.	Type	Value	Unused	Used
954	A217	10m multi	.35	.20
955	A217	20m multi	.50	.20
956	A217	30m multi	.55	.25
957	A217	40m multi	.75	.30
958	A217	60m multi	1.25	.30
959	A217	80m multi	1.50	.60
960	A217	1t multi	1.75	.90
		Nos. 954-960 (7)	6.65	2.75

Souvenir Sheet

Mongolia, Type A2 and Netherlands No. 1 — A218

1977, May 20

No.	Type	Value	Unused	Used
961	A218	4t multi	4.50	3.50

AMPHILEX '77 International Philatelic Exhibition, Amsterdam, May 27-June 5. No. 961 contains one 37x52mm stamp.

Boys on Horseback — A219

20m, Girl on horseback. 30m, Hunter on horseback. 40m, Grazing horses. 60m, Mare & foal. 80m, Grazing horse & student. 1t, White stallion.

1977, June 15 Litho. *Perf. 12*

No.	Type	Value	Unused	Used
962	A219	10m multi	.25	.20
963	A219	20m multi	.35	.20
964	A219	30m multi	.45	.20
965	A219	40m multi	.55	.25
966	A219	60m multi	.75	.35
967	A219	80m multi	.95	.55
968	A219	1t multi	1.25	.75
		Nos. 962-968 (7)	4.55	2.50

Copper and Molybdenum Plant, Vehicles A220

1977, June 15 Litho. *Perf. 12*

No.	Type	Value	Unused	Used
969	A220	60m multi	1.50	.50

Erdenet, a new industrial town.

Bucket Brigade Fighting Fire — A221

Fire Fighting: 20m, Horse-drawn fire pump. 30m, Horse-drawn steam pump. 40m, Men in protective suits fighting forest fire. 60m, Modern foam extinguisher. 80m, Truck and ladder. 1t, Helicopter fighting fire on steppe.

1977, Aug. Litho. *Perf. 12*

No.	Type	Value	Unused	Used
970	A221	10m multi	.25	.20
971	A221	20m multi	.40	.20
972	A221	30m multi	.55	.30
973	A221	40m multi	.75	.30
974	A221	60m multi	.90	.40
975	A221	80m multi	1.10	.50
976	A221	1t multi	1.25	.60
		Nos. 970-976 (7)	5.20	2.50

Radar and Molnya Satellite on TV Screen — A222

1977, Sept. 12 Photo. *Perf. 12x11½*

No.	Type	Value	Unused	Used
977	A222	60m gray, bl & blk	.80	.50

40th anniversary of Technical Institute.

Lenin Museum, Ulan Bator — A223

1977, Oct. 1 Litho. *Perf. 12*

No.	Type	Value	Unused	Used
978	A223	60m multi	1.00	.40

Inauguration of Lenin Museum in connection with the 60th anniversary of the Russian October Revolution.

Dove, Globe, Decree of Peace A224

Designs: 50m, Cruiser Aurora and Russian flag, vert. 1.50t, Globe and "Freedom."

Perf. 11½x12, 12x11½

1977, Oct. 1				**Photo.**	
979	A224	50m gold & multi		.85	.30
980	A224	60m gold & multi		.75	.30
981	A224	1.50t gold & multi		1.40	.90
		Nos. 979-981 (3)		3.00	1.50

60th anniversary of the Russian Revolution.

Aporia Crataegi — A225

Moths: 20m, Gastropacha quercifolia. 30m, Colias chrysoteme. 40m, Dasychira fascelina. 60m, Malocosoma neustria. 80m, Diacrisia sanno. 1t, Heodes virgaureae.

1977, Sept. 25		**Photo.**	*Perf. 12½*	
982	A225	10m multi	.30	.20
983	A225	20m multi	.50	.25
984	A225	30m multi	.75	.30
985	A225	40m multi	1.10	.35
986	A225	60m multi	1.50	.40
987	A225	80m multi	1.75	.60
988	A225	1t multi	2.25	1.00
		Nos. 982-988 (7)	8.15	3.10

Giant Pandas — A226

Pandas: 10m, Eating bamboo, vert. 30m, Female and cub in washtub, vert. 40m, Male and cub playing with bamboo. 60m, Female and cub, vert. 80m, Family. 1t, Male, vert.

1977, Nov. 25		**Litho.**	*Perf. 12*	
989	A226	10m multi	.25	.20
990	A226	20m multi	.40	.20
991	A226	30m multi	.55	.25
992	A226	40m multi	.75	.35
993	A226	60m multi	1.00	.50
994	A226	80m multi	1.75	.75
995	A226	1t multi	2.00	1.00
		Nos. 989-995 (7)	6.70	3.25

Souvenir Sheet

Helen Fourment and her Children, by Rubens — A227

1977, Dec. 5			*Perf. 11½x10½*	
996	A227	4t multi	4.50	4.50

Peter Paul Rubens (1577-1640).

Ferrari Racing Car — A228

Experimental Racing Cars: 30m, Ford McLaren. 40m, Madi, USSR. 50m, Mazda. 60m, Porsche. 80m, Russian model car. 1.20t, The Blue Flame, US speed car.

1978, Jan. 28		**Litho.**	*Perf. 12*	
997	A228	20m multi	.35	.20
998	A228	30m multi	.45	.25
999	A228	40m multi	.60	.25
1000	A228	50m multi	.80	.35
1001	A228	60m multi	1.00	.35
1002	A228	80m multi	1.25	.50
1003	A228	1.20t multi	1.50	.60
		Nos. 997-1003 (7)	5.95	2.50

Boletus Variegatus — A229

Mushrooms: 30m, Russula cyanoxantha. 40m, Boletus aurantiacus. 50m, Boletus scaber. 60m, Russula flava. 80m, Lactarius resimus. 1.20t, Flammula spumosa.

1978, Feb. 28		**Photo.**	*Perf. 11x11½*	
1004	A229	20m yel & multi	.50	.20
1005	A229	30m yel & multi	.75	.25
1006	A229	40m yel & multi	1.00	.35
1007	A229	50m yel & multi	1.25	.45
1008	A229	60m yel & multi	1.50	.55
1009	A229	80m yel & multi	1.75	.65
1010	A229	1.20t yel & multi	2.50	1.00
		Nos. 1004-1010 (7)	9.25	3.45

Young Couple with Youth Flag — A230

1978, Apr.		**Litho.**	*Perf. 11½x12*	
1011	A230	60m multi	1.00	.40

17th Congress of Mongolian Youth Organization, Ulan Bator, Apr. 1978.

Soccer, Sugar Loaf Mountain, Rio de Janeiro, Brazil 1950 Emblem — A231

Designs (Various Soccer Scenes and): 30m, Old Town Tower, Bern, Switzerland, 1954. 40m, Town Hall, Stockholm, Sweden, 1958. 50m, University of Chile, Chile, 1962. 60m, Parliament and Big Ben, London, 1966. 80m, Degolladeo Theater, Guadalajara, Mexico, 1970. 1.20t, Town Hall and TV Tower, Munich, Germany.

1978, Apr. 15			*Perf. 12*	
1012	A231	20m multi	.25	.20
1013	A231	30m multi	.35	.25
1014	A231	40m multi	.45	.25
1015	A231	50m multi	.55	.35
1016	A231	60m multi	.65	.35
1017	A231	80m multi	.90	.40
1018	A231	1.20t multi	1.40	.60
		Nos. 1012-1018 (7)	4.55	2.40

11th World Cup Soccer Championship, Argentina, June 1-25. See No. C109.

Capex Emblem, Eurasian Beaver and Canada #336 — A232

30m, Tibetan sand grouse & Canada #478. 40m, Red-throated loon & Canada #369. 50m, Argali & Canada #324. 60m, Eurasian brown bear & Canada #322. 80m, Moose & Canada #323. 1.20t, Great black-backed gull & Canada #343.

1978, June		**Litho.**	*Perf. 12*	
1019	A232	20m multi	.30	.20
1020	A232	30m multi	.50	.25
1021	A232	40m multi	.65	.30
1022	A232	50m multi	.90	.40
1023	A232	60m multi	1.00	.50
1024	A232	80m multi	1.10	.60
1025	A232	1.20t multi	1.50	.80
		Nos. 1019-1025 (7)	5.95	3.05

CAPEX '78 International Philatelic Exhibition, Toronto, June 9-18. See No. C110.

Marx, Engels and Lenin A233

1978, July 11		**Photo.**	*Perf. 12x11½*	
1026	A233	60m gold, blk & red	1.00	.50

50th anniversary of publication in Prague of "Problems of Peace and Socialism."

Souvenir Sheet

Outdoor Rest, by Amgalan — A234

Paintings by D. Amgalan: No. 1027b, Winter Night (dromedary and people in snow). No. 1027c, Saddling up.

1978, Aug. 10		**Litho.**	*Perf. 12*	
1027		Sheet of 3	4.50	4.50
a.-c.	A234	1.50t any single	1.25	

Philatelic cooperation between Hungary and Mongolia, 20th anniversary. No. 1027 contains 3 stamps and 3 labels.

Papillon — A235

Dogs: 20m, Black Mongolian sheepdog. 30m, Puli. 40m, St. Bernard. 50m, German shepherd. 60m, Mongolian watchdog. 70m, Samoyed. 80m, Laika (1st dog in space) and rocket. 1.20t, Cocker spaniel and poodles.

1978, Sept. 25		**Litho.**	*Perf. 12*	
1028	A235	10m multi	.35	.20
1029	A235	20m multi	.35	.20
1030	A235	30m multi	.55	.25
1031	A235	40m multi	.65	.35
1032	A235	50m multi	.85	.35
1033	A235	60m multi	1.00	.35
1034	A235	70m multi	1.10	.60
1035	A235	80m multi	1.25	.75
1036	A235	1.20t multi	2.00	.90
		Nos. 1028-1036 (9)	8.10	3.95

Open Book and Pen — A236

1978, Oct. 20		**Photo.**	*Perf. 12x11½*	
1037	A236	60m car & ultra	.75	.45

Mongolian Writers' Association, 50th anniversary.

Souvenir Sheets

Clothed Maya, by Goya — A237

Melancholy, by Dürer — A238

Paintings: No. 1038b, "Ta Matete," by Gauguin. No. 1038c, Bridge at Arles, by Van Gogh.

1978, Oct. 30		**Litho.**	*Perf. 12*	
1038		Sheet of 3 + 3 labels	4.50	4.50
a.-c.	A237	1.50t any single + label	1.25	1.25
		Perf. 11½		
1039	A238	4t black	4.50	4.50

Anniversaries of European painters: Francisco Goya; Paul Gauguin; Vincent van Gogh; Albrecht Dürer.

Camel and Calf — A239

Bactrian Camels: 30m, Young camel. 40m, Two camels. 50m, Woman leading pack camel. 60m, Old camel. 80m, Camel pulling cart. 1.20t, Race.

1978, Nov. 30		**Litho.**	*Perf. 12*	
1040	A239	20m multi	.30	.25
1041	A239	30m multi	.40	.25
1042	A239	40m multi	.55	.35
1043	A239	50m multi	.75	.35
1044	A239	60m multi	.90	.50
1045	A239	80m multi	1.00	.75
1046	A239	1.20t multi	1.60	.90
		Nos. 1040-1046 (7)	5.50	3.35

Flags of Comecon Members, Globe — A240

1979, Jan. 2 Litho. *Perf. 12*

1047	A240 60m multi + label	.75	.40

30th anniversary of the Council of Mutual Assistance (Comecon).

Label and vignette separated by simulated perforations.

Silver Tabby — A241

Domestic Cats: 30m, White Persian. 50m, Red Persian. 60m, Cream Persian. 70m, Siamese. 80m, Smoky Persian. 1t, Burmese.

1979, Feb. 10

1048	A241 10m multi	.30	.20
1049	A241 30m multi	.50	.25
1050	A241 50m multi	.65	.25
1051	A241 60m multi	.90	.35
1052	A241 70m multi	1.10	.45
1053	A241 80m multi	1.25	.60
1054	A241 1t multi	1.40	.80
	Nos. 1048-1054 (7)	6.10	2.90

Potaninia Mongolica — A242

Flowers: 30m, Sophora alopecuroides. 50m, Halimodendron halodendron. 60m, Forget-me-nots. 70m, Pincushion flower. 80m, Leucanthemum Sibiricum. 1t, Edelweiss.

1979, Mar. 10 Litho. *Perf. 12*

1055	A242 10m multi	.40	.20
1056	A242 30m multi	.75	.20
1057	A242 50m multi	.90	.25
1058	A242 60m multi	1.00	.35
1059	A242 70m multi	1.25	.45
1060	A242 80m multi	1.50	.55
1061	A242 1t multi	1.75	.75
	Nos. 1055-1061 (7)	7.55	2.75

Finland-Czechoslovakia, Finnish Flag — A243

Ice Hockey Games and 1980 Olympic Emblems: 30m, German Fed. Rep.-Sweden, German flag. 50m, US-Canada, US flag. 60m, USSR-Sweden, Russian flag. 70m, Canada-USSR, Canadian flag. 80m, Swedish goalie and flag. 1t, Czechoslovakia-USSR, Czechoslovak flag.

1979, Apr. 10 Litho. *Perf. 12*

1062	A243 10m multi	.20	.20
1063	A243 30m multi	.25	.20
1064	A243 50m multi	.35	.25
1065	A243 60m multi	.50	.35
1066	A243 70m multi	.60	.45
1067	A243 80m multi	1.00	.55
1068	A243 1t multi	1.60	.75
	Nos. 1062-1068 (7)	4.50	2.75

Ice Hockey World Championship, Moscow, Apr. 14-27.

Lambs — A244

Paintings: 30m, Milking, camels. 50m, Plane bringing supplies in winter. 60m, Herdsmen and horses. 70m, Milkmaids, vert. 80m, Summer Evening (camels). 1t, Landscape with herd. 4t, After the Storm.

Perf. 12x11½, 11½x12

1979, May 3 Litho.

1069	A244 10m multi	.20	.20
1070	A244 30m multi	.25	.20
1071	A244 50m multi	.45	.25
1072	A244 60m multi	.55	.35
1073	A244 70m multi	.65	.45
1074	A244 80m multi	.95	.50
1075	A244 1t multi	1.10	.55
	Nos. 1069-1075 (7)	4.15	2.50

Souvenir Sheet

1076	A244 4t multi	4.00	4.00

20th anniv. of 1st agricultural cooperative.

Souvenir Sheet

Mongolia No. 4, Bulgaria No. 1, Philaserdica Emblem — A245

Designs (Rowland Hill and): No. 1077b, American mail coach. No. 1077c, Mail car, London-Birmingham railroad, 1838. 1077d, Packet leaving Southampton, Sept. 24, 1842, opening Indian mail service.

1979, May 15 Litho. *Perf. 12*

1077	Sheet of 4, multi	6.00	6.00
a.-d.	A245 1t any single	1.50	1.50

Philaserdica '79, Sofia, May 18-27, and Rowland Hill (1795-1879), originator of penny postage.

Rocket, Manchester, 1829 — A246

Locomotives: 20m, "Adler" Nuremberg-Furth, 1835. 30m, American engine, 1860. 40m, Ulan Bator-Nalajh run, 1931. 50m, Moscow-Ulan Bator run, 1936. 60m, Moscow-Ulan Bator, 1970. 70m, Tokyo-Osaka run, 1963. 80m, Orleans Aerotrain, 1967. 1.20t, Soviet Rapidity, experimental train.

1979, June 8 Litho. *Perf. 12*

1078	A246 10m multi	.25	.20
1079	A246 20m multi	.35	.20
1080	A246 30m multi	.55	.20
1081	A246 40m multi	.65	.25
1082	A246 50m multi	.75	.30
1083	A246 60m multi	.85	.40
1084	A246 70m multi	1.00	.40
1085	A246 80m multi	1.10	.55
1086	A246 1.20t multi	1.25	.75
	Nos. 1078-1086 (9)	6.75	3.25

Intl. Transportation Exhibition, Hamburg.

For surcharge see No. 2144B.

Mongolian and Russian Flags — A247

Battle Scene and Emblem A248

1979, Aug. 10 Photo. *Perf. 11½x12*

1087	A247 60m multi	1.00	.50
1088	A248 60m multi	1.00	.50

Battle of Ha-lo-hsin River, 40th anniversary.

Manuls A249

Wild Cats: 30m, Lynx. 50m, Tigers. 60m, Snow leopards. 70m, Black panthers. 80m, Cheetahs. 1t, Lions.

1979, Sept. 10 Litho. *Perf. 12*

1089	A249 10m multi	.25	.20
1090	A249 30m multi	.45	.25
1091	A249 50m multi	.75	.30
1092	A249 60m multi	.85	.30
1093	A249 70m multi	.95	.40
1094	A249 80m multi	1.10	.50
1095	A249 1t multi	1.25	.60
	Nos. 1089-1095 (7)	5.60	2.55

Souvenir Sheet

Brazil No. 1582 — A250

b, Brazil #1144 (Pele). c, Mongolia #C1.

1979, Sept. 15 Litho. *Perf. 11*

1096	Sheet of 3 + 3 labels	7.50	7.50
a.-c.	A250 1.50t any single + label	2.50	2.50

Brasiliana '79, 3rd World Thematic Stamp Exhibition, Rio de Janeiro, Sept. 15-23.

Cross-Country Skiing, Lake Placid '80 Emblem — A251

30m, Biathlon. 40m, Ice hockey. 50m, Ski jump. 60m, Downhill skiing. 80m, Speed skating. 1.20t, Bobsledding. 4t, Figure skating.

1980, Jan. 20 Litho. *Perf. 11½x12½*

1097	A251 20m multi	.20	.20
1098	A251 30m multi	.25	.20
1099	A251 40m multi	.35	.25
1100	A251 50m multi	.50	.35
1101	A251 60m multi	.75	.40
1102	A251 80m multi	.95	.45
1103	A251 1.20t multi	1.50	.70
	Nos. 1097-1103 (7)	4.50	2.55

Souvenir Sheet

1104	A251 4t multi	2.75	2.75

13th Winter Olympic Games, Lake Placid, NY, Feb. 12-24.

Flower Type of 1969
Souvenir Sheet

Design: Landscape and edelweiss.

1980, May 5 Litho. *Perf. 11*

1105	A131 4t multi	4.50	4.50

London 1980 Intl. Stamp Exhib., May 6-14. No. 1105 contains one stamp 43x26mm.

Weightlifting, Moscow '80 Emblem — A252

1980, June 2 Litho. *Perf. 12*

1106	A252 20m shown	.20	.20
1107	A252 30m Archery	.25	.20
1108	A252 40m Gymnast	.40	.25
1109	A252 50m Running	.50	.25
1110	A252 60m Boxing	.60	.35
1111	A252 80m Judo	.75	.35
1112	A252 1.20t Bicycling	1.00	.70
	Nos. 1106-1112 (7)	3.70	2.30

Souvenir Sheet

1113	A252 4t Wrestling	4.50	4.50

22nd Summer Olympic Games, Moscow, July 19-Aug. 3.

Gold Medal, Swimmer, Moscow '80 Emblem — A253

Gold Medal, Moscow '80 Emblem and Number of Medals won by Top Countries: 30m, Fencing. 50m, Judo. 60m, Track. 80m, Boxing. 1t, Weight lifting. 1.20t, Kayak.

1980, Sept. 15 Litho. *Perf. 12½*

1114	A253 20m multi	.20	.20
1115	A253 30m multi	.25	.20
1116	A253 50m multi	.35	.30
1117	A253 60m multi	.55	.30
1118	A253 80m multi	.75	.40
1119	A253 1t multi	1.00	.50
1120	A253 1.20t multi	1.25	.60
	Nos. 1114-1120 (7)	4.35	2.50

See No. C144.

A254

A255

1980, Sept. 17 ***Perf. 11½x12***

1121 A254 60m Jumdshaigiin Zedenbal .75 .50
1122 A254 60m Zedenbal, 1941, grn .75 .50
1123 A254 60m Zedenbal, 1979, gray grn .75 .50
1124 A254 60m with Brezhnev, horiz. .75 .50
1125 A254 60m with children .75 .50
1126 A254 60m Sukhe Bator, dk brn .75 .50
1127 A254 60m Choibalsan, ultra .75 .50
Nos. 1121-1127 (7) 5.25 3.50

Miniature Sheet

Cosmonauts from various Intercosmos flights: a, A. Gubarjev. b, Czechoslovakia #2222. c, P. Klimuk. d, Poland #2270. e, V. Bykovsky. f, DDR #1947. g, N. Rukavishnikov. h, Bulgaria #2576. i, V. Kubasov. j, Hungary #C417.

1980, Oct. 10 **Litho.** ***Perf. 12***

1128 Sheet of 10 4.50 4.50
a.-j. A255 40m any single .40 .40

Intercosmos cooperative space program. See No. 1232.

Benz, Germany, 1885 — A256

Antique Cars: 30m, President, Austria-Hungary, 1897. 40m, Armstrong Siddley, 1904. 50m, Russo-Balt, 1909. 60m, Packard, United States, 1909. 80m, Lancia, Italy, 1911. 1.60t, Marne taxi, France, 1914. 4t, Nami-1, Russia, 1927.

1980, Nov. 20 **Litho.** ***Perf. 12½***

1129 A256 20m multi .25 .20
1130 A256 30m multi .25 .20
1131 A256 40m multi .45 .25
1132 A256 50m multi .50 .35
1133 A256 60m multi .60 .40
1134 A256 80m multi .80 .50
1135 A256 1.60t multi 1.75 .75
Nos. 1129-1135 (7) 4.60 2.65

Souvenir Sheet

1136 A256 4t multi 4.50 4.50

Penguins A257

1980, Dec. 1 ***Perf. 12***

1137 A257 20m shown .90 .25
1138 A257 30m Giant blue whale 1.25 .40
1139 A257 40m Albatross 1.50 .50
1140 A257 50m Weddell seals 1.75 .60
1141 A257 60m Emperor penguins 2.00 .70
1142 A257 70m Skua 2.25 .80
1143 A257 80m Grampus 2.75 1.00
1144 A257 1.20t Penguins, Soviet plane 3.25 1.25
Nos. 1137-1144 (8) 15.65 5.50

Souvenir Sheet

1145 A257 4t World map showing continental drift 7.50 7.50

Antarctic animals and exploration. No. 1145 contains one 44mm circular stamp.

Souvenir Sheet

A258

1980, Dec. 20 **Litho.** ***Perf. 11***

1146 Sheet of 2 4.00 2.50
a. A258 2t shown 1.75 1.00
b. A258 2t Old Marketplace 1.75 1.00

The Shepherd Speaking the Truth, IYC Emblem A259

IYC Emblem and Nursery Tales: 30m, Above Them the Sky is Always Clear. 40m, Winter's Joys. 50m, Little Musicians. 60m, Happy Birthday. 80m, The First Day of School. 1.20t, May Day. 4t, The Wonder-working Squirrels.

1980, Dec. 29 ***Perf. 12***

1147 A259 20m multi .20 .20
1148 A259 30m multi .25 .20
1149 A259 40m multi .45 .25
1150 A259 50m multi .60 .25
1151 A259 60m multi .90 .40
1152 A259 80m multi 1.10 .60
1153 A259 1.20t multi 1.25 .80
Nos. 1147-1153 (7) 4.75 2.70

Souvenir Sheet

1154 A259 4t multi 4.50 3.50

Intl. Year of the Child (1979).

60th Anniversary of People's Army — A260

1981, Jan. 31 **Litho.** ***Perf. 12***

1155 A260 60m multi 1.00 .40

60th Anniversary of People's Revolutionary Party — A261

1981, Feb. 2

1156 A261 60m multi 1.00 .40

Ice Racing — A262

Designs: Various racing motorcycles.

1981, Feb. 28 ***Perf. 12½***

1157 A262 10m multi .20 .20
1158 A262 20m multi .25 .20
1159 A262 30m multi .30 .25
1160 A262 40m multi .40 .25
1161 A262 50m multi .50 .25
1162 A262 60m multi .60 .30
1163 A262 70m multi .70 .30
1164 A262 80m multi .80 .30
1165 A262 1.20t multi .90 .45
Nos. 1157-1165 (9) 4.65 2.50

Cosmonauts Boarding Soyuz 39 — A263

Designs: 30m, Rocket designer Koroljov. 40m, Vostok I, Yuri Gagarin. 50m, Salyut space station. 60m, Satellite photographing earth. 80m, Light crystallization from Salyut spacecraft. 1.20t, Salyut, Kremlin, Sukhe Bator statue. 4t, Soviet and Mongolian cosmonauts.

1981, Mar. 22 **Litho.** ***Perf. 12***

1166 A263 20m multi .25 .20
1167 A263 30m multi .35 .20
1168 A263 40m multi .40 .25
1169 A263 50m multi .50 .35
1170 A263 60m multi .75 .45
1171 A263 80m multi 1.00 .50
1172 A263 1.20t multi 1.25 .60
Nos. 1166-1172 (7) 4.50 2.55

Souvenir Sheet
Perf. 11½

1173 A263 4t multi 4.50 3.50

Intercosmos cooperative space program (Mongolia-USSR). No. 1173 contains one 29x39mm stamp.

A264

1981, Apr. 28 **Litho.** ***Perf. 12***

1174 Sheet of 4 + 4 labels 6.00 6.00
a. A264 1t No. 240, Ulan Bator + label 1.40 1.25
b. A264 1t Germany #8N4, 8NB10 + label 1.40 1.25
c. A264 1t Austria #B110 + label 1.40 1.25
d. A264 1t Japan #827 + label 1.40 1.25

1981 Stamp Exhibitions: Mongolian Natl., Ulan Bator; Naposta, Stuttgart; WIPA, Vienna; Japex, Tokyo.

Star Shining on Factories and Sheep A265

1981, May 5

1175 A265 60m multi .75 .40

18th Congress of Revolutionary People's Party, May.

Souvenir Sheet

Statue of Sukhe Bator, Mongolian Flag — A266

1981, May 20 ***Perf. 12½***

1176 A266 4t multi 3.50 3.50

Mongolian Revolutionary People's Party, 60th anniv.

Sheep Farming (Economic Development) — A267

1981, June 1 ***Perf. 12½x11½***

1177 A267 20m shown .25 .20
1178 A267 30m Transportation .35 .20
1179 A267 40m Telecommunications .40 .25
1180 A267 50m Public health service .50 .35
1181 A267 60m Agriculture .75 .45
1182 A267 80m Power plant 1.00 .50
1183 A267 1.20t Public housing 1.25 .60
Nos. 1177-1183 (7) 4.50 2.55

A268

Souvenir Sheet

1981, July 11 Litho. ***Perf. 12½x11½***
1184 A268 4t multi 4.50 3.50

20th anniv. of UN membership.

A269

1981, Aug. 1 ***Perf. 12***

Designs: Sailing ships. 10m, 20m, horiz.

1185 A269 10m Egyptian, 15th cent. BC .25 .20
1186 A269 20m Mediterranean, 9th cent. .30 .25
1187 A269 40m Hansa Cog, 12th cent. .40 .30
1188 A269 50m Venitian, 13th cent. .60 .30
1189 A269 60m Santa Maria .70 .40
1190 A269 80m Endeavor .80 .40
1191 A269 1t Poltava, 18th cent. .90 .45
1192 A269 1.20t US schooner, 19th cent. 1.00 .50
Nos. 1185-1192 (8) 4.95 2.80

Mongolian-USSR Friendship Pact — A270

1981, Sept. 1 ***Perf. 11½x12***
1193 A270 60m multi 1.00 .50

Flora, by Rembrandt A271

1981, Sept. 1 ***Perf. 11½x12½***
1194 A271 20m shown .25 .20
1195 A271 30m Hendrickje in the Bed .35 .25
1196 A271 40m Young Woman with Earrings .40 .25
1197 A271 50m Young Girl in the Window .50 .30
1198 A271 60m Hendrickje like Flora .75 .30
1199 A271 80m Saskia with Red Flower 1.00 .50
1200 A271 1.20t Holy Family with Drape 1.25 .60
Nos. 1194-1200 (7) 4.50 2.40

Souvenir Sheet

1201 A271 4t Self-portrait with Saskia 4.50 4.50

375th birth anniv. of Rembrandt.

Goat (Pawn) — A272

Designs: Wood chess pieces.

1981, Sept. 30 Litho. ***Perf. 12½***
1202 A272 20m shown .30 .20
1203 A272 40m Cart (castle) .50 .25
1204 A272 50m Camel (bishop) .60 .35
1205 A272 60m Horse (knight) .70 .45
1206 A272 80m Lion (queen) 1.00 .55
1207 A272 1.20t Man and dog (king) 1.25 .75
Nos. 1202-1207 (6) 4.35 2.55

Souvenir Sheet

1208 A272 4t Men playing 4.50 4.50

Camel and Circus Tent A273

1981, Oct. 30 Litho. ***Perf. 12***
1209 A273 10m shown .20 .20
1210 A273 20m Horsemen .25 .25
1211 A273 40m Wrestlers .35 .25
1212 A273 50m Archers .45 .30
1213 A273 60m Folksinger .55 .30
1214 A273 80m Girl playing jat-ga .75 .35
1215 A273 1t Ballet dancers 1.00 .40
1216 A273 1.20t Statue 1.10 .50
Nos. 1209-1216 (8) 4.65 2.55

Wolfgang Amadeus Mozart and Scene from his Magic Flute — A274

Composers and Scenes from their Works.

1981, Nov. 16
1217 A274 20m shown .30 .20
1218 A274 30m Beethoven, Fidelio .45 .25
1219 A274 40m Bartok, Miraculous Mandarin .45 .25
1220 A274 50m Verdi, Aida .55 .35
1221 A274 60m Tchaikovsky, Sleeping Beauty .65 .35
1222 A274 80m Dvorak, New World Symphony score .85 .45
1223 A274 1.20t Chopin, piano 1.25 .50
Nos. 1217-1223 (7) 4.50 2.35

Ribbon Weaver A275

Designs: Mongolian women.

Perf. 11½x12½

1981, Dec. 10 Litho.
1224 A275 20m multi .35 .20
1225 A275 30m multi .45 .25
1226 A275 40m multi .55 .25
1227 A275 50m multi .65 .25
1228 A275 60m multi .75 .30
1229 A275 80m multi 1.00 .40
1230 A275 1.20t multi 1.10 .50
Nos. 1224-1230 (7) 4.85 2.15

Souvenir Sheet

1231 A275 4t multi 4.50 4.50

Intercosmos Type of 1980

Designs: a, V. Gorbatko. b, Y. Romanenko. c, V. Dzhanibekov. d, L. Popov. e, Vietnamese stamp. f, Cuban stamp. g, No. 1173. h, Romania No. C241.

1981, Dec. 28 ***Perf. 12***
1232 Sheet of 8, multi 4.50 4.50
a.-h. A255 50m, any single .50 .35

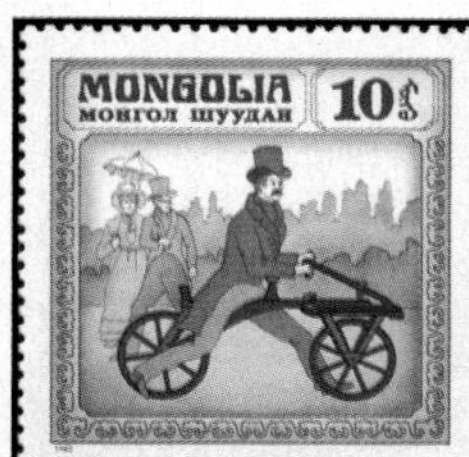

Historic Bicycles A276

1982, Mar. 25 Litho. ***Perf. 11***
1233 A276 10m Germany, 1816 .20 .20
1234 A276 20m Scotland, 1838 .25 .20
1235 A276 40m US, 1866 .35 .25
1236 A276 50m France, 1863 .45 .25
1237 A276 60m "Kangaroo", 1877 .55 .30
1238 A276 80m England, 1870 .75 .30
1239 A276 1t 1878 .90 .40
1240 A276 1.20t Modern bike 1.10 .50
Nos. 1233-1240 (8) 4.55 2.40

Souvenir Sheet

Perf. 12½

1241 A276 4t Racing 4.50 4.50

No. 1241 contains one stamp 47x47mm.

1982 World Cup A277

1982, Apr. 20 ***Perf. 12***
1242 A277 10m Brazil, 1950 .20 .20
1243 A277 20m Switzerland, 1954 .25 .20
1244 A277 40m Sweden, 1958 .35 .25
1245 A277 50m Chile, 1962 .45 .25
1246 A277 60m England, 1966 .55 .30
1247 A277 80m Mexico, 1970 .75 .30
1248 A277 1t Germany, 1974 .90 .40
1249 A277 1.20t Argentina, 1978 1.00 .50
Nos. 1242-1249 (8) 4.45 2.40

Souvenir Sheet

Perf. 11

1250 A277 4t Spain, 1982 4.50 3.50

No. 1250 contains one stamp 48x48mm.

12th Trade Union Congress, Ulan Bator A278

1982, May 20 Litho. ***Perf. 11½x12½***
1251 A278 60m multi 1.00 .50

Souvenir Sheet

PHILEXFRANCE Intl. Stamp Exhibition, Paris, June 11-21 — A279

1982, June 11 ***Imperf.***
1252 A279 4t No. B13 design 4.00 3.00

George Dimitrov (1882-1949), First Prime Minister of Bulgaria — A280

1982, June 18 ***Perf. 12***
1253 A280 60m gold & blk 1.00 .40

Chicks — A281

1982, June 25 ***Perf. 11***
1254 A281 10m shown .25 .20
1255 A281 20m Colt .30 .20
1256 A281 30m Lamb .45 .25
1257 A281 40m Fawn .55 .25
1258 A281 50m Camel calf .65 .25
1259 A281 60m Kid .75 .30
1260 A281 70m Calf .85 .45
1261 A281 1.20t Young boar 1.00 .55
Nos. 1254-1261 (8) 4.80 2.45

Coal Mining Industry — A282

1982, July 5 ***Perf. 12***
1262 A282 60m Mine, truck 1.00 .50

18th Mongolian Youth Org. Congress A283

1982, Aug. 14 ***Perf. 11½x12***
1263 A283 60m multi 1.00 .50

Siberian Pine
A284

1982, Aug. 16

1264 A284 20m shown .25 .20
1265 A284 30m Abies sibirica .35 .20
1266 A284 40m Populus diversifolia .45 .25
1267 A284 50m Larix sibirica .60 .25
1268 A284 60m Pinus silvestris .75 .25
1269 A284 80m Betula platyphylla .90 .35
1270 A284 1.20t Picea obovata 1.00 .45
Nos. 1264-1270 (7) 4.30 1.95

60th Anniv. of Mongolian Youth Org. — A285

1982, Aug. 30

1271 A285 60m multi 1.00 .40

Iseki-6500 Tractor, Japan — A286

1982, Oct. 1 **Litho.** ***Perf. 12½***

1272 A286 10m shown .20 .20
1273 A286 20m Deutz-DX-230, Germany .25 .20
1274 A286 40m Bonser, Gt. Britain .35 .25
1275 A286 50m Intl.-884, US .45 .25
1276 A286 60m Renault TX-145-14, France .60 .35
1277 A286 80m Belarus-611, USSR .75 .35
1278 A286 1t K-7100, USSR .90 .45
1279 A286 1.20t DT-75, USSR 1.00 .50
Nos. 1272-1279 (8) 4.50 2.55

Scenes from The Foal and The Hare Folktale
A287

1983, Jan. 1 **Litho.** ***Perf. 14***

1280 A287 10m multi .20 .20
1281 A287 20m multi .25 .20
1282 A287 30m multi .30 .25
1283 A287 40m multi .35 .30
1284 A287 50m multi .45 .30
1285 A287 60m multi .55 .40
1286 A287 70m multi .75 .40
1287 A287 80m multi .95 .40
1288 A287 1.20t multi 1.10 .50
Nos. 1280-1288 (9) 4.90 2.95

Souvenir Sheet

Imperf

1289 A287 7t multi 4.50 4.50

No. 1289 contains one stamp 58x58mm.

Scenes from Walt Disney's The Sorcerer's Apprentice — A288

1983, Jan. 1

1290 A288 25m multi .25 .20
1291 A288 35m multi .30 .20
1292 A288 45m multi .35 .25
1293 A288 55m multi .45 .30
1294 A288 65m multi .55 .30
1295 A288 75m multi .65 .30
1296 A288 85m multi .85 .30
1297 A288 1.40t multi 1.00 .40
1298 A288 2t multi 1.10 .45
Nos. 1290-1298 (9) 5.50 2.70

Souvenir Sheet

1299 A288 7t multi 4.50 4.50

Fish, Lake Hevsgel — A289

1982, Nov. 30 ***Perf. 12***

1300 A289 20m shown .25 .20
1301 A289 30m Sheep, Zavhan Highlands .25 .25
1302 A289 40m Beaver, Lake Hovd .30 .25
1303 A289 50m Horses, Lake Uvs .40 .35
1304 A289 60m Chamois, Bajanhongor Steppe .50 .45
1305 A289 80m Mounted hunter, eagle, Bajan-Elgij Highlands 1.40 .45
1306 A289 1.20t Camels, Gobi Desert 1.40 .50
Nos. 1300-1306 (7) 4.50 2.45

Mongolian Skin Tent (Yurt) — A290

1983, Mar. 30 **Litho.** ***Perf. 14***

1307 A290 20m Antonov AN-24B plane .30 .20
1308 A290 30m shown .40 .25
1309 A290 40m Deer .50 .25
1310 A290 50m Bighorn sheep .60 .30
1311 A290 60m Eagle .75 .50
1312 A290 80m Museum of the Khans, Ulan Bator .90 .55
1313 A290 1.20t Sukhe Bator monument, Ulan Bator 1.10 .60
Nos. 1307-1313 (7) 4.55 2.65

For surcharge, see No. 2670.

Souvenir Sheet

90th Birth Anniv. of Sukhe Bator — A291

1983 ***Perf. 13x14***

1314 A291 4t multi 4.50 4.50

Local Flowers — A292

1983, Feb. 4 **Photo.** ***Perf. 13***

1315 A292 20m Rose .25 .20
1316 A292 30m Dahlias .35 .20
1317 A292 40m Tagetes faula .45 .20
1318 A292 50m Narcissus .55 .20
1319 A292 60m Violets .75 .30
1320 A292 80m Tulips .90 .30
1321 A292 1.20t Heliopsis helianthoides 1.10 .40
Nos. 1315-1321 (7) 4.35 1.80

50th Anniv. of Border Forces — A293

1983, Feb. 9 **Litho.** ***Perf. 14***

1322 A293 60m multi 1.00 .40

Souvenir Sheet

BRASILIANA, Philatelic Exhibition — A294

1983, July 10 **Litho.** ***Perf. 14***

1323 A294 4t multi 4.00 3.00

Karl Marx — A295

1983, Oct. 1 **Litho.** ***Perf. 14***

1324 A295 60m gold, dp car & bl 1.00 .40

18th Party Congress, Ulan Bator — A296

1983, Nov. 1 **Litho.** ***Perf. 14***

1325 A296 10m Cattle .25 .20
1326 A296 20m Coal .25 .20
1327 A296 30m Garment .30 .20
1328 A296 40m Agricultural .40 .30
1329 A296 60m Communications .60 .30
1330 A296 80m Transportation 1.50 .60
1331 A296 1t Educational System 1.00 .60
Nos. 1325-1331 (7) 4.30 2.40

Souvenir Sheet

Sistine Madonna, by Raphael (1483-1520) — A297

1983, Dec. 15 **Litho.** ***Perf. 14x13½***

1332 A297 4t multi 4.50 4.50

A298

Children in Various Activities.

1984, Jan. 1 **Photo.** ***Perf. 13***

1333 A298 10m multi .25 .20
1334 A298 20m multi .25 .20
1335 A298 30m multi .30 .20
1336 A298 40m multi .45 .25
1337 A298 50m multi .75 .35
1338 A298 70m multi 1.10 .50
1339 A298 1.20t multi 1.50 .75
Nos. 1333-1339 (7) 4.60 2.45

Rodents — A299

Various rodents.

1984, Jan. 15 Litho. ***Perf. 13½x13***

1340 A299 20m multi .30 .20
1341 A299 30m multi .50 .25
1342 A299 40m multi .60 .30
1343 A299 50m multi .70 .40
1344 A299 60m multi .80 .50
1345 A299 80m multi 1.00 .75
1346 A299 1.20t multi 1.25 1.00
Nos. 1340-1346 (7) 5.15 3.40

1984 Winter Olympics — A300

1984, Feb. 15 Litho. ***Perf. 14***

1347 A300 20m Bobsledding .25 .20
1348 A300 30m Cross-country skiing .30 .20
1349 A300 40m Hockey .45 .20
1350 A300 50m Speed skating .55 .20
1351 A300 60m Downhill skiing .75 .25
1352 A300 80m Figure skating 1.00 .25
1353 A300 1.20t Biathlon 1.25 .40
Nos. 1347-1353 (7) 4.55 1.70

Souvenir Sheet

1354 A300 4t Ski jumping 4.00 3.00

Size of No. 1354: 134x106mm. Nos. 1347-1352 vert.

Children Feeding Lambs — A301

1984, Mar. 1 Litho. ***Perf. 12***

1355 A301 20m Ice skating .25 .20
1356 A301 30m shown .30 .20
1357 A301 40m Planting tree .45 .20
1358 A301 50m Playing on beach .55 .20
1359 A301 60m Carrying pail .75 .25
1360 A301 80m Dancing 1.00 .25
1361 A301 1.20t Dancing, diff. 1.25 .35
Nos. 1355-1361 (7) 4.55 1.65

Souvenir Sheet

1362 A301 4t Boy, girl 4.50 3.50

No. 1362 contains one stamp 48x46mm. Compare with Type SP3. For surcharges, see Nos. 2656-2657.

Mail Car, Communications Emblems — A302

1984, Apr. 15 ***Perf. 13½x14***

1363 A302 10m shown .25 .20
1364 A302 20m Earth satellite receiving station .30 .20
1365 A302 40m Airplane .40 .25
1366 A302 50m Central PO .50 .35
1367 A302 1t Radar station .90 .40
1368 A302 1.20t Train 2.00 1.00
Nos. 1363-1368 (6) 4.35 2.40

Souvenir Sheet

Imperf

1369 A302 4t Dish antenna 4.50 3.50

1984 Summer Olympics — A303

1984, June 1 Photo. ***Perf. 14***

1370 A303 20m Gymnastics .25 .20
1371 A303 30m Bicycling .30 .20
1372 A303 40m Weight lifting .45 .20
1373 A303 50m Judo .55 .20
1374 A303 60m Archery .75 .25
1375 A303 80m Boxing 1.00 .25
1376 A303 1.20t High jump 1.25 .35
Nos. 1370-1376 (7) 4.55 1.65

Souvenir Sheet

1377 A303 4t Wrestling 4.50 3.50

Souvenir Sheet

AUSIPEX '84 and ESPANA '84 — A304

1984, May Litho. ***Perf. 14***

1378 A304 4t Jet 4.50 4.50

Cuban Revolution, 25th Anniv. — A304a

1984, June 2 Litho. ***Perf. 14***

1378A A304a 60m multi 1.00 .50

State Bank, 60th Anniv. A304b

1984, Sept. 25 ***Perf. 13½x13***

1378B A304b 60m Commemorative coins, 1981 .75 .40

Radio Broadcasting in Mongolia, 50th Anniv. — A304c

1984, Sept. 1 Litho. ***Perf. 13x13½***

1378C A304c 60m multicolored 1.00 .50

Scenes from Walt Disney's Mickey and the Beanstalk — A305

1984, Dec. 20 Litho. ***Perf. 11***

1379 A305 25m multi .30 .20
1380 A305 35m multi .40 .20
1381 A305 45m multi .55 .25
1382 A305 55m multi .65 .25
1383 A305 65m multi .75 .30
1384 A305 75m multi .85 .40
1385 A305 85m multi .95 .50
1386 A305 1.40t multi 1.10 .65
1387 A305 2t multi 1.40 .80
Nos. 1379-1387 (9) 6.95 3.55

Miniature Sheet

Perf. 14

1388 A305 7t multi 6.00 6.00

Fairy Tales — A306

1984, Dec. 20 Litho. ***Perf. 13½***

1389 A306 10m multi .25 .20
1390 A306 20m multi .30 .20
1391 A306 30m multi .35 .20
1392 A306 40m multi .40 .20
1393 A306 50m multi .45 .25
1394 A306 60m multi .50 .25
1395 A306 70m multi .60 .35
1396 A306 80m multi .75 .40
1397 A306 1.20t multi .90 .55
Nos. 1389-1397 (9) 4.50 2.60

Miniature Sheet

1398 A306 4t multi 4.50 4.50

Souvenir Sheet

60th Anniv. of Mongolian Stamps — A308

1984, Dec. 20 Litho. ***Perf. 14***

1400 A308 4t No. 1 4.50 3.50

Ulan Bator, 60th Anniv. — A309

Mongolian People's Republic, 60th Anniv. — A310

1984, Nov. 26 Litho. ***Perf. 13x13½***

1401 A309 60m multicolored 1.00 .50

Perf. 14

1402 A310 60m multicolored .90 .45

Mongolian People's Party, 60th Anniv. — A311

1984, Nov. 26 Litho. ***Perf. 14***

1403 A311 60m multi .90 .45

Native Masks — A312

1984, Dec. 31 Litho. ***Perf. 14***

1404 A312 20m multi .25 .20
1405 A312 30m multi .30 .20
1406 A312 40m multi .45 .25
1407 A312 50m multi .55 .25
1408 A312 60m multi .75 .30
1409 A312 80m multi 1.00 .30
1410 A312 1.20t multi 1.25 .50
Nos. 1404-1410 (7) 4.55 2.00

Souvenir Sheet

1411 A312 4t multi 4.50 4.50

Dogs A313

1984, Dec. 31 Litho. ***Perf. 13***

1412 A313 20m Collie .25 .20
1413 A313 30m German Sheepdog .30 .20
1414 A313 40m Papillon .45 .25

1415 A313 50m Cocker Spaniel .55 .25
1416 A313 60m Puppy .75 .30
1417 A313 80m Dalmatians 1.00 .30
1418 A313 1.20t Mongolian Sheepdog 1.25 .50
Nos. 1412-1418 (7) 4.55 2.00

Cattle — A314

1985, Jan. ***Perf. 14***

1419 A314 20m Shar tarlan .25 .20
1420 A314 30m Bor khaliun .30 .20
1421 A314 40m Sarlag .45 .20
1422 A314 50m Dornod taliin bukh .55 .25
1423 A314 60m Char tarlan .75 .25
1424 A314 80m Nutgiin uulderiin unee 1.00 .35
1425 A314 1.20t Tsagaan tolgoit 1.25 .35
Nos. 1419-1425 (7) 4.55 1.80

1984 Olympic Winners — A315

Gold medalists: 20m, Gaetan Boucher, Canada, 1500-meter speed skating. 30m, Eirik Kvalfoss, Norway, 10-kilometer biathlon. 40m, Marja-Lissa Haemaelainen, Finland, 5-kilometer Nordic skiing. 50m, Max Julen, Switzerland, men's giant slalom. 60m, Jens Weissflog, German Democratic Republic, 70-meter ski jump. 80m, W. Hoppe and D. Schauerhammer, German Democratic Republic, 2-man bobsled. 1.20t, Elena Valova and Oleg Vasiliev, USSR, pairs figure skating. 4t, USSR, ice hockey. Nos. 1430-1432 vert.

1985, Apr. 25

1426 A315 20m multi .25 .20
1427 A315 30m multi .30 .20
1428 A315 40m multi .45 .25
1429 A315 50m multi .50 .30
1430 A315 60m multi .70 .30
1431 A315 80m multi .95 .40
1432 A315 1.20t multi 1.10 .50
Nos. 1426-1432 (7) 4.25 2.15

Souvenir Sheet

1433 A315 4t multi 4.00 3.00

Souvenir Sheet

Girl, Fawn — A316

1985, Apr. 25

1434 A316 4m multi 4.50 4.50

Birds — A317

World Youth Festival, Moscow A318

1985, May 1 ***Perf. 12½x13***

1435 A317 20m Ciconia nigra .25 .20
1436 A317 30m Haliaetus albicilla .35 .20
1437 A317 40m Grus leucogeranus .50 .25
1438 A317 50m Paradoxornis heudei .60 .25
1439 A317 60m Grus monacha .80 .30
1440 A317 80m Grus vipio 1.00 .40
1441 A317 1.20t Buteo lagopus 1.25 .50
Nos. 1435-1441 (7) 4.75 2.10

National Wildlife Preservation Association.

1985, June ***Perf. 14***

1442 A318 60m Girls in folk costumes .80 .40

Camelus Bactrianus — A319

Panthera Unicias — A320

Cervus Elaphus — A321

Camels, leopards and deer.

1985

1443 A319 50m Adults, young 2.00 1.00
1444 A319 50m Facing right 2.00 1.00
1445 A319 50m Facing left 2.00 1.00
1446 A319 50m Trotting 2.00 1.00
1447 A320 50m Hunting 1.00 .40
1448 A320 50m Standing in snow 1.00 .40
1449 A320 50m Female, young 1.00 .40
1450 A320 50m Adults 1.00 .40
1451 A321 50m Fawn 1.00 .40
1452 A321 50m Doe in woods 1.00 .40
1453 A321 50m Adult male 1.00 .40
1454 A321 50m Adults, fawn 1.00 .40
Nos. 1443-1454 (12) 16.00 7.20

#1443-1446 show the World Wildlife Fund emblem, #1447-1454 the Natl. Wildlife Preservation emblem. Issue dates: #1443-1446, July 1; #1447-1454, Aug. 1.

UN, 40th Anniv. A322

1985, Aug. 1 ***Perf. 13½x13***

1455 A322 60m Flags, UN building .75 .40

Indigenous Flowering Plants — A323

1985, Aug. 1 ***Perf. 14***

1456 A323 20m Rosa davurica .25 .20
1457 A323 30m Matricaria chamomilla .35 .20
1458 A323 40m Taraxacum officinale .55 .20
1459 A323 50m Saxzifraga hirculus .65 .25
1460 A323 60m Vaccinium vitis idaea .75 .25
1461 A323 80m Sanguisorba officinalis .85 .30
1462 A323 1.20t Plantago major .95 .40
Nos. 1456-1462 (7) 4.35 1.80

Souvenir Sheet

1463 A323 4t Hippophae rhamnoides 4.50 4.50

A324

A325

1985, Sept. 15 ***Perf. 13x13½***

1464 A324 60m Monument .30 .25

Defeat of Nazi Germany, 40th anniv.

1985, Oct. 1 ***Perf. 14***

Various soccer plays. No. 1472 horiz.

1465 A325 20m multi .25 .20
1466 A325 30m multi .30 .20
1467 A325 40m multi .40 .20
1468 A325 50m multi .60 .20
1469 A325 60m multi .80 .20
1470 A325 80m multi .90 .25
1471 A325 1.20t multi 1.00 .25
Nos. 1465-1471 (7) 4.25 1.50

Souvenir Sheet

1472 A325 4t multi 4.00 3.00

1985 Junior World Soccer Championships, Moscow.

Souvenir Sheet

ITALIA '85 — A326

1985, Oct. 1

1473 A326 4t Horseman 4.00 3.00

Conquest of Space — A327

Russian spacecraft.

1985, Nov. 1

1474 A327 20m Soyuz .30 .20
1475 A327 30m Cosmos .40 .20
1476 A327 40m Venera 9 .50 .20
1477 A327 50m Salyut .60 .20
1478 A327 60m Luna 9 .70 .25
1479 A327 80m Train .90 .55
1480 A327 1.20t Dish receiver 1.10 .25
Nos. 1474-1480 (7) 4.50 1.85

Souvenir Sheet

1985, Dec. 15

1481 A327 4t Cosmonaut on space walk 4.50 3.50

Mushrooms — A328

1985, Dec. 1 ***Perf. 13½***

1482 A328 20m Tricholoma mongolica .45 .20
1483 A328 30m Cantharellus cibarius .55 .20
1484 A328 40m Armillariella mellea .65 .20
1485 A328 50m Amanita caesarea .75 .25
1486 A328 70m Xerocomus badius .85 .30
1487 A328 80m Agaricus silvaticus .95 .30
1488 A328 1.20t Boletus edulis 2.00 .40
Nos. 1482-1488 (7) 6.20 1.85

Souvenir Sheet

Phalacrocorax Penicillatus — A329

1986, Jan. 15 *Perf. 12½x13*
1489 A329 4t multi 4.50 4.50

No. 1489 contains one stamp plus 2 labels picturing various bird species.

Young Pioneers A330

Victory Monument A331

1985, Dec. 31 **Litho.** *Perf. 13x13½*
1490 A330 60m multi .70 .30

1985, Dec. 31 *Perf. 12½x13*
1491 A331 60m multi .70 .30

Victory over Japan ending WWII, 40th anniv.

Natl. Costumes A332

1986, Mar. 1 **Litho.** *Perf. 14*

Background Color

1492 A332 60m yel grn, shown .60 .30
1493 A332 60m red .60 .30
1494 A332 60m pale yel grn .60 .30
1495 A332 60m violet .60 .30
1496 A332 60m ultra .60 .30
1497 A332 60m bluish grn .60 .30
1498 A332 60m pale org brn .60 .30
Nos. 1492-1498 (7) 4.20 2.10

Ernst Thalmann (1886-1944) A333

1986, May 15 **Litho.** *Perf. 14*
1499 A333 60m gold, redsh brn & dk brn .75 .30

Natl. Revolution, 65th Anniv. — A334

1986, May 15
1500 A334 60m Statue of Sukhe Bator .70 .30

19th Socialist Party Congress A335

1986, May 15
1501 A335 60m multi .70 .30

1986 World Cup Soccer Championships, Mexico — A336

FIFA emblem and various soccer plays. Nos. 1502-1503, 1505-1508 vert.

1986, May 31
1502 A336 20m multi .20 .20
1503 A336 30m multi .25 .20
1504 A336 40m multi .35 .20
1505 A336 50m multi .45 .20
1506 A336 60m multi .55 .25
1507 A336 80m multi .65 .25
1508 A336 1.20t multi .80 .30
Nos. 1502-1508 (7) 3.25 1.60

Souvenir Sheet

1509 A336 4t multi 1.90

Mink, Wildlife Conservation — A337

1986, June 15
1510 A337 60m Spring .75 .40
1511 A337 60m Summer .75 .40
1512 A337 60m Autumn .75 .40
1513 A337 60m Winter .75 .40
Nos. 1510-1513 (4) 3.00 1.60

Flowers — A338

Butterflies — A339

1986, June 1 **Litho.** *Perf. 14*
1514 A338 20m Valeriana officinalis .25 .20
1515 A338 30m Hyoscymus niger .30 .20
1516 A338 40m Ephedra sinica .35 .20
1517 A338 50m Thymus gobica .40 .20
1518 A338 60m Paeonia anomala .50 .25
1519 A338 80m Achilea millefolium .75 .30
1520 A338 1.20t Rhododendron adamsii 1.00 .40
Nos. 1514-1520 (7) 3.55 1.75

1986, Aug. 1 *Perf. 13½*
1521 A339 20m Neptis coenobita .25 .20
1522 A339 30m Colias tycha .30 .20
1523 A339 40m Leptidea amurensis .35 .20
1524 A339 50m Oeneis tarpenledevi .40 .25
1525 A339 60m Mesoacidalia charlotta .50 .25
1526 A339 80m Smerinthus ocellatus .75 .30
1527 A339 1.20t Pericalia matronula 1.00 .40
Nos. 1521-1527 (7) 3.55 1.80

Circus — A340

Animal trainers & acrobats. #1531-1534 vert.

1986, Aug. 1 *Perf. 14*
1528 A340 20m multi .25 .20
1529 A340 30m multi .30 .20
1530 A340 40m multi .35 .20
1531 A340 50m multi .40 .20
1532 A340 60m multi .50 .25
1533 A340 80m multi .75 .25
1534 A340 1.20t multi 1.00 .30
Nos. 1528-1534 (7) 3.55 1.60

Przewalski's Horses — A341

1986, Aug. 1 **Litho.** *Perf. 14*
1535 A341 50m Two horses, foal .75 .40
1536 A341 50m One facing left, two facing right .75 .40
1537 A341 50m Three facing right .75 .40
1538 A341 50m Four in storm .75 .40
Nos. 1535-1538 (4) 3.00 1.60

Pelicans *(Pelecanus)* — A341a

1986, Sept. 1 **Litho.** *Perf. 14*
1538A A341a 60m *crispus* feeding .80 .50
1538B A341a 60m *crispus* wading .80 .50
1538C A341a 60m *onocrotalus* flying .80 .50
1538D A341a 60m *onocrotalus* on land .80 .50
Nos. 1538A-1538D (4) 3.20 2.00

Saiga tatarica mongolica — A341b

1986, Sept. 15
1538E A341b 60m Spring (doe, fawn) .75 .40
1538F A341b 60m Summer (buck, doe) .75 .40
1538G A341b 60m Fall (buck) .75 .40
1538H A341b 60m Winter (buck, doe) .75 .40
Nos. 1538E-1538H (4) 3.00 1.60

Musical Instruments — A342

1986, Sept. 4
1539 A342 20m Morin khuur .25 .20
1540 A342 30m Bishguur .30 .20
1541 A342 40m Ever buree .35 .20
1542 A342 50m Shudarga .40 .25
1543 A342 60m Khiil .50 .25
1544 A342 80m Janchir .75 .30
1545 A342 1.20t Jatga 1.00 .30
Nos. 1539-1545 (7) 3.55 1.70

Souvenir Sheet

1546 A342 4t like 20m, vert. 3.50 3.50

STOCKHOLMIA '86. Nos. 1539-1543 vert.

Intl. Peace Year — A342a

1986, Sept. 20 **Litho.** *Perf. 13x13½*
1546A A342a 10m multicolored .75 .30

North American Bird Species — A343

1986, Oct. 1
1547 A343 60m Anthus spinoletta .80 .50
1548 A343 60m Aythya americana .80 .50

1549 A343 60m Bonasa umbellus .80 .50

1550 A343 60m Olor columbianus .80 .50

Nos. 1547-1550 (4) 3.20 2.00

Eastern Architecture — A343a

Various two-story buildings.

1986, Oct. 1

Color of Border

1551 A343a 60m dark grn & blk .80 .45

1552 A343a 60m beige & blk .80 .45

1553 A343a 60m apple grn & blk .80 .45

1554 A343a 60m red brn & blk .80 .45

Nos. 1551-1554 (4) 3.20 1.80

Classic Automobiles — A344

1986, Oct. 1 Litho. ***Perf. 14***

1554A A344 20m 1922 Alfa Romeo RL Sport, Italy .25 .20

1554B A344 30m 1912 Stutz Bearcat, US .30 .20

1554C A344 40m 1902 Mercedes Simplex, Germany .35 .20

1554D A344 50m 1923 Tatra 11, Czechoslovakia .40 .20

1554E A344 60m 1908 Ford Model T, US .50 .25

1554F A344 80m 1905 Vauxhall, England .75 .30

1554G A344 1.20t 1913 Russo-Baltik, Russia 1.00 .40

Nos. 1554A-1554G (7) 3.55 1.75

Souvenir Sheet

1554H A344 4t like 1.20t 3.50 3.50

Woodpeckers A344a

1986, Nov. 1

1555 A344a 20m Picus canus .25 .20

1556 A344a 30m Jynx torquilla .30 .20

1557 A344a 40m Dryobates major .35 .20

1558 A344a 50m Dryobates leucotos .40 .20

1559 A344a 60m Dryobates minor .50 .25

1560 A344a 80m Dryocopus martius .75 .30

1561 A344a 1.20t Picoides tridactylus 1.00 .40

Nos. 1555-1561 (7) 3.55 1.75

Souvenir Sheet

1562 A344a 4t Saphopipo noguchi 4.50 4.50

Chess Champions — A345

Portraits and chessmen on boards in match-winning configurations. No. 1562H, Chess champions Gary Kasparov, Jose R. Capablanca, Max Euwe, Vassily Smyslow, Mikhail Tal, Tigran Petrosian, Boris Spasski and Bobby Fischer; W. Menchik, L. Rudenko, E. Bykowa and O. Rubzowa.

1986, Nov. 1 ***Perf. 14***

1562A A345 20m Steinitz, Austria .25 .20

1562B A345 30m Lasker, Germany .30 .20

1562C A345 40m Alekhine, France .35 .20

1562D A345 50m Botvinnik, USSR .40 .20

1562E A345 60m Karpov, USSR .50 .25

1562F A345 80m N. Gaprindashvili .75 .25

1562G A345 1.20t M. Chiburdanidze 1.00 .30

Size: 110x100mm

Imperf

1562H A345 4t multi 4.50 4.50

Nos. 1562A-1562H (8) 8.05 6.10

Souvenir Sheet

Halley's Comet — A346

1986, Nov. 30 Litho. ***Perf. 14***

1563 A346 4t multicolored 4.50 4.00

Ovis Ammon Ammon — A347

1987, Jan. 1

1564 A347 60m shown .75 .40

1565 A347 60m In the mountains .75 .40

1566 A347 60m Close-up of head .75 .40

1567 A347 60m Male, female, lamb .75 .40

Nos. 1564-1567 (4) 3.00 1.60

Children's Activities A348

1987, Feb. 1

1568 A348 20m Backpacking, hunting butterflies .25 .20

1569 A348 30m Playing with calves .30 .20

1570 A348 40m Chalk-writing on cement .35 .20

1571 A348 50m Playing soccer .40 .20

1572 A348 60m Go-cart, model rocket, boat .45 .25

1573 A348 80m Agriculture .55 .25

1574 A348 1.20t Playing the morin khuur, dancing .80 .30

Nos. 1568-1574 (7) 3.10 1.60

Int'l. Peace Year (40m); Child Survival Campaign (50m).

13th Trade Unions Congress — A349

1987, Feb. 15 ***Perf. 13½x13***

1575 A349 60m multi 1.50 1.00

Equestrian Sports — A350

1987, Mar. 1

1576 A350 20m Lassoer .30 .20

1577 A350 30m Breaking horse .35 .20

1578 A350 40m Shooting bow .40 .20

1579 A350 50m Race .45 .20

1580 A350 60m Retrieving flags .50 .25

1581 A350 80m Tug-of-war .60 .25

1582 A350 1.20t Racing wolf .90 .30

Nos. 1576-1582 (7) 3.50 1.60

Admission into Comecon, 25th Anniv. — A351

1987, Apr. 15 ***Perf. 13x13½***

1583 A351 60m multi .75 .40

Fruit — A352

A353

1987, June 1 ***Perf. 13½***

1584 A352 20m Hippophae rhamnoides .30 .20

1585 A352 30m Ribes nigrum .35 .20

1586 A352 40m Ribes rubrus .40 .20

1587 A352 50m Ribes altissimum .50 .20

1588 A352 60m Rubus sachalinensis .55 .25

1589 A352 80m Padus asiatica .60 .25

1590 A352 1.20t Fragaria orientalis .90 .25

Nos. 1584-1590 (7) 3.60 1.55

Souvenir Sheet

Perf. 14

1591 A353 4t Malus domestica 3.50 3.50

Soviet-Mongolian Diplomatic Relations, 50th Anniv. — A354

Russian Revolution, 70th Anniv. — A355

1987, July 1 ***Perf. 13x13½***

1592 A354 60m multi .75 .45

1987, July 1

1593 A355 60m multi .75 .45

Folk Dances — A356

1987, Aug. 1 ***Perf. 14***

1594 A356 20m multi .20 .20

1595 A356 30m multi, diff. .25 .20

1596 A356 40m multi, diff. .35 .20

1597 A356 50m multi, diff. .55 .20

1598 A356 60m multi, diff. .65 .25

1599 A356 80m multi, diff. .75 .25

1600 A356 1.20t multi, diff. 1.00 .30

Nos. 1594-1600 (7) 3.75 1.60

Antiques A357

Full costume and accessories.

1987, Aug. 10

1601 A357 20m Folk costumes .20 .20

1602 A357 30m Gilded nunchaku .25 .20

1603 A357 40m Brooches .35 .20

1604 A357 50m Draw-string pouch, rice bowl .55 .20

1605 A357 60m Headdress .65 .25
1606 A357 80m Pouches, bottle, pipe .75 .25
1607 A357 1.20t Sash, brooch 1.00 .30
Nos. 1601-1607 (7) 3.75 1.60

Souvenir Sheet

HAFNIA '87 — A358

1987, Aug. 10
1608 A358 4t multi 4.00 3.00

Swans — A359

1987, Aug. 15
1609 A359 60m Cygnus olor on land .80 .50
1610 A359 60m Cygnus olor in water .80 .50
1611 A359 60m Cygnus bewickii .80 .50
1612 A359 60m Cygnus bewickii, gunus and olor .80 .50
Nos. 1609-1612 (4) 3.20 2.00

Domestic and Wild Cats — A360

1987, Oct. 1 **Litho.** ***Perf. 14***
1613 A360 20m multi, vert. .30 .20
1614 A360 30m multi, vert. .35 .20
1615 A360 40m multi, vert. .40 .20
1616 A360 50m shown .50 .25
1617 A360 60m multi .60 .25
1618 A360 80m multi .75 .30
1619 A360 1.20t multi 1.10 .30
Nos. 1613-1619 (7) 4.00 1.70

Miniature Sheet

1620 A360 4t multi, vert. 4.00 3.00

Helicopter — A361

1987, Oct. 3 ***Perf. 12½x11½***
1621 A361 20m B-12 .20 .20
1622 A361 30m Westland-WG-30 .25 .20
1623 A361 40m Bell-S-206L .45 .20
1624 A361 50m Kawasaki-369HS .50 .20
1625 A361 60m KA-32 .65 .25
1626 A361 80m MI-17 .80 .25
1627 A361 1.20t MI-10K 1.10 .30
Nos. 1621-1627 (7) 3.95 1.60

Disney Cartoons — A362

The Brave Little Tailor (25m-55m, 2t, No. 1637), and The Celebrated Jumping Frog of Calaveras County (65m-1.40t, No. 1638).

1987, Nov. 23 ***Perf. 14***
1628 A362 25m multi .20 .20
1629 A362 35m multi .40 .20
1630 A362 45m multi .50 .20
1631 A362 55m multi .55 .20
1632 A362 65m multi .65 .25
1633 A362 75m multi .75 .25
1634 A362 85m multi 1.00 .30
1635 A362 1.40t multi 1.25 .50
1636 A362 2t multi 2.00 .75
Nos. 1628-1636 (9) 7.30 2.85

Souvenir Sheets

1637 A362 7t multi 5.50 5.50
1638 A362 7t multi 5.50 5.50

A363

Tropical Fish — A364

1987, Oct. ***Perf. 13x12½, 12½x13***
1639 A363 20m Betta splendens .30 .20
1640 A363 30m Carassius auratus .35 .20
1641 A363 40m Rasbora hengeli .40 .20
1642 A363 50m Aequidens .50 .20
1643 A363 60m Xiphophorus macalatus .65 .25
1644 A363 80m Xiphophorus helleri .90 .25
1645 A363 1.20t Pterophyllum scalare, vert. 1.25 .30
Nos. 1639-1645 (7) 4.35 1.60

Miniature Sheet
Perf. 14

1646 A364 4t Crenuchus spilurus 4.50 4.50

19th Communist Party Congress A365

1987, Dec. ***Perf. 14***
1647 A365 60m Family .50 .20
1648 A365 60m Construction .50 .20
1649 A365 60m Jet, harvesting, produce .50 .20
1650 A365 60m Education .50 .20
1651 A365 60m Transportation .50 .20
1652 A365 60m Heavy industry .50 .20
1653 A365 60m Science and technology .50 .20
Nos. 1647-1653 (7) 3.50 1.40

Vulpes Vulpes (Fox) — A366

1987, Dec.
1654 A366 60m Adult in snow .75 .45
1655 A366 60m Adult, young .75 .45
1656 A366 60m Adult in field .75 .45
1657 A366 60m Close-up of head .75 .45
Nos. 1654-1657 (4) 3.00 1.80

Souvenir Sheet

INTERCOSMOS — A367

1987, Dec. 15 **Litho.** ***Perf. 14***
1658 A367 4t multi 3.50 3.00

Souvenir Sheet

PRAGA '88 — A368

1988, Jan. 30
1659 A368 4t 1923 Tatra 11 3.50 3.00

Sukhe Bator — A369

1988, Feb. 2 ***Perf. 13x13½***
1660 A369 60m multi .80 .50

Roses — A370

19th Communist Youth Congress — A371

1988, Feb. 20 ***Perf. 14***
1661 A370 20m Invitation .30 .20
1662 A370 30m Meilland .55 .20
1663 A370 40m Pascali .40 .20
1664 A370 50m Tropicana .50 .20
1665 A370 60m Wendy Cussons .55 .25
1666 A370 80m Blue moon .60 .25
1667 A370 1.20t Diorama .90 .30
Nos. 1661-1667 (7) 3.80 1.60

Souvenir Sheet

1668 A370 4t shown 3.50 3.00

1988, Apr. 15 ***Perf. 12½x13***
1669 A371 60m multicolored .80 .50

Puppets — A372

Folk tales.

1988, Apr. 1 **Litho.** ***Perf. 14***
1670 A372 20m Ukhaant Ekhner .20 .20
1671 A372 30m Altan Everte Mungun Turuut .30 .20
1672 A372 40m Aduuchyn Khuu .40 .20
1673 A372 50m Suulenkhuu .45 .20
1674 A372 60m Khonchyn Khuu .60 .25
1675 A372 80m Argat Byatskhan Baatar .80 .25
1676 A372 1.20t Botgochyn Khuu 1.25 .30
Nos. 1670-1676 (7) 4.00 1.60

1988 Summer Olympics, Seoul — A373

Soviet Space Achievements
A374

1988, Feb. 15

1677 A373 20m Judo .20 .20
1678 A373 30m Women's archery .25 .20
1679 A373 40m Weight lifting .40 .20
1680 A373 50m Women's gymnastics .45 .20
1681 A373 60m Cycling .50 .25
1682 A373 80m Running .60 .25
1683 A373 1.20t Wrestling 1.00 .30
Nos. 1677-1683 (7) 3.40 1.60

Souvenir Sheet

1684 A373 4t Boxing 3.50 3.00

1988, May 15

1685 A374 20m Cosmos .20 .20
1686 A374 30m Meteor .25 .20
1687 A374 40m Salyut-Soyuz .40 .20
1688 A374 50m Prognoz-6 .45 .20
1689 A374 60m Molniya-1 .50 .20
1690 A374 80m Soyuz .60 .20
1691 A374 1.20t Vostok 1.00 .25
Nos. 1685-1691 (7) 3.40 1.45

Effigies of Buddhist Deities — A375

Various statues.

1988, June 15 **Litho.** ***Perf. 14***

1692 A375 20m multi .20 .20
1693 A375 30m multi, diff. .25 .20
1694 A375 40m multi, diff. .35 .20
1695 A375 50m multi, diff. .50 .20
1696 A375 60m multi, diff. .65 .25
1697 A375 70m multi, diff. .85 .25
1698 A375 80m multi, diff. 1.00 .30
1699 A375 1.20t multi, diff. 1.50 .30
Nos. 1692-1699 (8) 5.30 1.90

Wildlife Conservation — A376

Eagles, Haliaeetus albicilla. Nos. 1700-1702 vert.

1988, Aug. 1 **Litho.** ***Perf. 14***

1700 A376 60m Eagle facing left, diff. .80 .50
1701 A376 60m Landing on branch .80 .50
1702 A376 60m Facing right .80 .50
1703 A376 60m shown .80 .50
Nos. 1700-1703 (4) 3.20 2.00

Souvenir Sheet

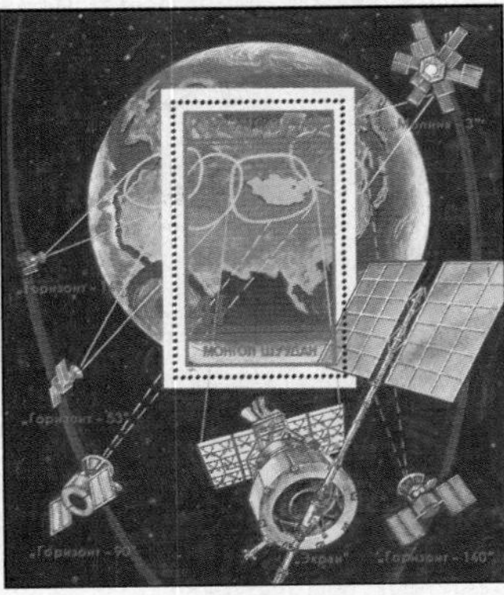

Cosmos — A377

1988, Sept. 15 **Litho.** ***Perf. 14***

1704 A377 4t Satellite links 4.00 4.00

Opera — A378

1988, Oct. 1 **Litho.** ***Perf. 13x12½***

1705 A378 60m multi + label 1.50 .75

Equus hemionus — A380

1988, May 3

1713 A380 60m Mare, foal .80 .50
1714 A380 60m Ass's head .80 .50
1715 A380 60m Ass galloping .80 .50
1716 A380 60m Ass cantering .80 .50
Nos. 1713-1716 (4) 3.20 2.00

Winners of the 1988 Winter Olympics, Calgary — A381

1988, July 1

1717 A381 1.50t Matti Nykaenen, Finland 1.00 .45
1718 A381 1.50t Bonnie Blair, US 1.00 .45
1719 A381 1.50t Alberto Tomba, Italy 1.00 .45
1720 A381 1.50t USSR hockey team 1.00 .45
Nos. 1717-1720 (4) 4.00 1.80

Souvenir Sheet

1721 A381 4t Katarina Witt, DDR 4.00 4.00

Nos. 1718-1720 vert.

A382

A383

1988, Sept. 1

1722 A382 10m shown .20 .20
1723 A382 20m Horsemanship .25 .20
1724 A382 30m Archery .35 .20
1725 A382 40m Wrestling .45 .20
1726 A382 50m Archery, diff. .55 .25
1727 A382 70m Horsemanship, diff. .80 .25
1728 A382 1.20t Horsemanship, wrestling, archery 1.50 .30
Nos. 1722-1728 (7) 4.10 1.60

1988, Dec. 1 ***Perf. 13x13½***

1729 A383 60m multicolored 1.00 .50

Socialism and Peace.

Goats — A384

Various species.

1989, Jan. 15 ***Perf. 14***

1730 A384 20m multi .20 .20
1731 A384 30m multi .35 .20
1732 A384 40m multi .50 .20
1733 A384 50m multi .60 .20
1734 A384 60m multi .75 .25
1735 A384 80m multi .85 .25
1736 A384 1.20t multi 1.25 .30
Nos. 1730-1736 (7) 4.50 1.60

Souvenir Sheet

1737 A384 4t multi, vert. 4.00 4.00

Souvenir Sheet

Child Survival — A385

1989, Jan. 28 **Litho.** ***Perf. 14***

1738 A385 4t Drawing by H. Jargalsuren 4.00 4.00

Karl Marx — A386

1989, Feb. 25 **Litho.** ***Perf. 13x13½***

1739 A386 60m multicolored .80 .30

Miniature Sheet

Statue of Sukhe Bator — A387

Mongolian Airline Jet — A388

1989, July 1 ***Perf. 14***

1740 Sheet of 3 8.00 8.00
a. A387 20m Concorde jet .75 .50
b. A387 60m TGV high-speed train 2.00 1.75
c. A387 1.20t shown 4.50 4.00

Souvenir Sheet

1741 A388 4t shown 4.50 4.50

PHILEXFRANCE '89, BULGARIA '89.
For overprint see No. 1756.

World War II Memorial
A389

1989, Sept. 2

1742 A389 60m multicolored 1.00 .50

For surcharge, see No. 2384B.

Cacti — A390

1989, Sept. 7

1743 A390 20m *O. microdasys* .20 .20
1744 A390 30m *E. multipiex* .25 .20
1745 A390 40m *R. tephracanthus* .45 .20
1746 A390 50m *B. haselbergii* .60 .20
1747 A390 60m *G. mihanovichii* .70 .25
1748 A390 80m *C. strausii* .85 .25
1749 A390 1.20t *Horridocactus tuberisvicatus* 1.10 .30
Nos. 1743-1749 (7) 4.15 1.60

Souvenir Sheet

1750 A390 4t *Astrophytum ornatum* 4.00 4.00

A391

A392

Winners at the 1988 Summer Olympics, Seoul.

1989, Oct. 1

1751 A391 60m Kristin Otto, East Germany .80 .45
1752 A391 60m Florence Griffith-Joyner, US .80 .45
1753 A391 60m Gintaoutas Umaras, USSR .80 .45
1754 A391 60m Stefano Cerioni, Italy .80 .45
Nos. 1751-1754 (4) 3.20 1.80

Souvenir Sheet

1755 A391 4t N. Enkhbat, Mongolia 4.00 4.00

No. 1740 Overprinted for WORLD STAMP EXPO '89

1989, Nov. 17 **Miniature Sheet**

1756 Sheet of 3 8.00 8.00
a. A387 20m multicolored .75 .50
b. A387 60m multicolored 2.00 1.50
c. A387 1.20t multicolored 4.50 4.00

1989, Dec. 1

1757 A392 60m Books, fountain pen .75 .45

Beavers *(Castor fiber birulai)* — A393

1989, Dec. 10

1758 A393 60m Cutting down saplings .80 .50
1759 A393 60m Rolling wood across ground .80 .50
1760 A393 60m Beaver on land, in water .80 .50
1761 A393 60m Beaver and young .80 .50
Nos. 1758-1761 (4) 3.20 2.00

Medals and Military Decorations — A394

1989, Dec. 31 ***Perf. 13x13½***

1762 A394 60m pink & multi 1.25 .75
1763 A394 60m lt blue grn & multi 1.25 .75
1764 A394 60m vio & multi 1.25 .75
1765 A394 60m org & multi 1.25 .75
1766 A394 60m brt blue & multi 1.25 .75
1767 A394 60m ver & multi 1.25 .75
1768 A394 60m vio blue & multi 1.25 .75
Nos. 1762-1768 (7) 8.75 5.25

Bears and Giant Pandas — A395

1990, Jan. 1 ***Perf. 14***

1769 A395 20m *Ursus pruinosis* .20 .20
1770 A395 30m *Ursus arctos syriacus* .30 .20
1771 A395 40m *Ursus thibetanus* .40 .25
1772 A395 50m *Ursus maritimus* .55 .30
1773 A395 60m *Ursus arctos bruinosus* .65 .40
1774 A395 80m *Ailuropus melanoleucus* .85 .50
1775 A395 1.20t *Ursus arctos isabellinus* 1.25 1.00
Nos. 1769-1775 (7) 4.20 2.85

Souvenir Sheet

1776 A395 4t *Ailuropus melanoleucus,* diff. 6.00 4.00

Winter Sports — A396

1990, Jan. 6

1777 A396 20m 4-man bobsled .20 .20
1778 A396 30m Luge .30 .20
1779 A396 40m Women's figure skating .40 .20
1780 A396 50m 1-man bobsled .50 .20
1781 A396 60m Pairs figure skating .60 .25
1782 A396 80m Speed skating .75 .25
1783 A396 1.20t Ice speedway 1.25 .30
Nos. 1777-1783 (7) 4.00 1.60

Souvenir Sheet

1784 A396 4t Ice hockey 4.25 4.25

Space Exploration — A397

Rockets and spacecraft: 20m, Soyuz, USSR. 30m, Apollo-Soyuz, US-USSR. 40m, *Columbia* space shuttle, US, vert. 50m, *Hermes,* France. 60m, *Nippon,* Japan, vert. 80m, *Energy,* USSR, vert. 1.20t, *Buran,* USSR, vert. 4t, *Sanger,* West Germany.

1990, Jan. 30

1785 A397 20m shown .20 .20
1786 A397 30m multicolored .30 .20
1787 A397 40m multicolored .40 .25
1788 A397 50m multicolored .50 .25
1789 A397 60m multicolored .60 .30
1790 A397 80m multicolored .75 .30
1791 A397 1.20t multicolored 1.25 .40
Nos. 1785-1791 (7) 4.00 1.90

Souvenir Sheet

1792 A397 4t multicolored 4.25 4.25

Jawaharlal Nehru, 1st Prime Minister of Independent India — A398

1990, Feb. 10

1793 A398 10m gold, blk & dark red brn 1.50 .75

Mongolian Ballet — A400

Dancers in scenes from various ballets. 40m, 80m, 1.20t vert.

1990, Feb. 28

1795 A400 20m shown .20 .20
1796 A400 30m multi .30 .20
1797 A400 40m multi .45 .20
1798 A400 50m multi .55 .20
1799 A400 60m multi .65 .25
1800 A400 80m multi .75 .25
1801 A400 1.20t multi 1.10 .30
Nos. 1795-1801 (7) 4.00 1.60

Automobiles — A401

1990, Mar. 26

1802 A401 20m Citroen, France .20 .20
1803 A401 30m Volvo 760 GLF, Sweden .30 .20
1804 A401 40m Honda, Japan .40 .20
1805 A401 50m Volga, USSR .50 .20
1806 A401 60m Ford Granada, US .60 .25
1807 A401 80m VAZ 21099, USSR .75 .25
1808 A401 1.20t Mercedes Class 190, West Germany 1.25 .30
Nos. 1802-1808 (7) 4.00 1.60

Souvenir Sheet

1809 A401 4t like 50m 4.50 4.50

Lenin — A402

1990, Mar. 27 ***Perf. 13x13½***

1810 A402 60m gold, black & ver 1.00 .50

Statue of Sukhe Bator — A399

1990, Feb. 27

1794 A399 10m multicolored 1.50 .75

Unen Newspaper, 70th Anniv. — A403

1990, Apr. 1 ***Perf. 14***

1811 A403 60m multicolored 1.00 .50

End of World War II, 45th Anniv. — A404

1990, Apr. 1

1812 A404 60m multicolored 1.25 .60

Buddhist Deities (18th-20th Cent. Paintings)
A405

1990, Apr. 1

1813	A405	20m	Damdin Sandub	.25	.20
1814	A405	30m	Pagwa Lama	.40	.20
1815	A405	40m	Chu Lha	.50	.25
1816	A405	50m	Agwanglobsan	.60	.30
1817	A405	60m	Dorje Dags Dan	.75	.30
1818	A405	80m	Wangchikdorje	.85	.40
1819	A405	1.20t	Buddha	1.10	.50
			Nos. 1813-1819 (7)	4.45	2.15

Souvenir Sheet

1820	A405	4t	Migjed Jang-Rasek	6.50	6.50

A406

Aspects of a Cooperative Settlement — A407

Paintings: 20m, Animals on plain, rainbow. 30m, Workers, reindeer, dog, vert. 40m, Two men, mountains, Bactrian camels. 50m, Man, Bactrian camels. 60m, Huts, animal shelter, corral. 80m, Breaking horses, vert. 1.20t, Sheep, shepherd girl on horse. 4t, Wrestling match.

1990, Apr. 1

1821	A406	20m	shown	.40	.20
1822	A406	30m	multicolored	.50	.20
1823	A406	40m	multicolored	.60	.25
1824	A406	50m	multicolored	.70	.30
1825	A406	60m	multicolored	.90	.40
1826	A406	80m	multicolored	1.25	.50
1827	A406	1.20t	multicolored	1.75	.55
			Nos. 1821-1827 (7)	6.10	2.40

Souvenir Sheet

1828	A407	4t	shown	7.00	7.00

Scenes from Various Mongolian-made Films — A408

1990, Apr. 1

1829	A408	20m	shown	.30	.20
1830	A408	30m	multi, diff.	.40	.25
1831	A408	40m	multi, diff.	.60	.30
1832	A408	50m	multi, diff.	.80	.40
1833	A408	60m	multi, diff.	1.10	.50
1834	A408	80m	multi, diff.	1.25	.65
1835	A408	1.20t	multi, diff.	1.75	1.00
			Nos. 1829-1835 (7)	6.20	3.30

Souvenir Sheet

1836	A408	4t	multi, diff., vert.	7.00	7.00

Souvenir Sheet

Stamp World London '90 — A409

1990, Apr. 1

1837	A409	4t	multicolored	5.50	5.50

1990 World Cup Soccer Championships, Italy — A410

Trophy and various athletes.

1990, Apr. 30

1838	A410	20m	multicolored	.20	.20
1839	A410	30m	multicolored	.30	.20
1840	A410	40m	multicolored	.40	.20
1841	A410	50m	multicolored	.50	.20
1842	A410	60m	multicolored	.60	.20
1843	A410	80m	multicolored	.75	.25
1844	A410	1.20t	multicolored	1.25	.25
			Nos. 1838-1844 (7)	4.00	1.50

Souvenir Sheet

1845	A410	4t	Trophy, vert.	4.50	4.50

Nos. 304-307 Ovptd.

1990, May 1 Photo. ***Perf. 11½x12***

1846	A84	20m	multicolored	*10.00*
1847	A84	30m	multicolored	*12.50*
1848	A84	50m	multicolored	*12.50*
1849	A84	60m	multicolored	*15.00*
			Nos. 1846-1849 (4)	*50.00*

Coronation of Genghis Khan, 800th anniv. (in 1989).

Souvenir Sheet

Genghis Khan — A411

1990, May 8 Litho. ***Perf. 13½***

1850	A411	7t	multicolored	7.50	7.50

Stamp World London '90. Exists imperf. Exists without "Stamp World London '90" and Great Britain No. 1.

Cranes *(Grus vipio pallas)* — A412

1990, May 23 ***Perf. 14***

1851	A412	60m	brt blue & multi	.90	.60
1852	A412	60m	brt rose lil & multi	.90	.60
1853	A412	60m	red lil & multi	.90	.60
1854	A412	60m	car rose & multi	.90	.60
			Nos. 1851-1854 (4)	3.60	2.40

Nos. 1853-1854 are vert.

Marine Mammals — A413

1990, June 20 Litho. ***Perf. 14***

1855	A413	20m	Balaenoptera physalus	.30	.20
1856	A413	30m	Megaptera novaeangliae	.40	.20
1857	A413	40m	Monodon monoceros	.45	.25
1858	A413	50m	Grampus griseus	.55	.30
1859	A413	60m	Tursiops truncatus	.70	.40
1860	A413	80m	Lagenorhynchus acutius	.95	.50
1861	A413	1.20t	Balaena mysticetus	1.40	.55
			Nos. 1855-1861 (7)	4.75	2.40

Souvenir Sheet

1861A	A413	4t	Killer whale	4.50	4.50

A414

Cultural Heritage — A415

1990, Aug. 13 ***Perf. 13x12½***

1862	A414	10m	shown	.25	.20
1863	A414	10m	Like No. 1862, arrows at left	.25	.20
1864	A415	40m	Fire ring	.60	.20
1865	A415	60m	Genghis Khan	.80	.25
1866	A414	60m	Tent	.80	.25
1867	A414	60m	Horses	.80	.25
1868	A414	80m	Royal family (green panel)	1.25	.40
1869	A414	80m	Royal court (dk bl panel)	1.25	.40
a.			Souv. sheet, #1862-1869 + label	8.00	8.00
			Nos. 1862-1869 (8)	6.00	2.15

20th Party Congress
A416

1990, Mar. 1 Litho. ***Perf. 14***

1870	A416	60m	multicolored	1.00	.50

Dinosaurs — A417

1990, Aug. 25

1871	A417	20m	shown	.40	.20
1872	A417	30m	multi, diff.	.50	.20
1873	A417	40m	multi, diff.	.65	.25
1874	A417	50m	multi, diff	.75	.30
1875	A417	60m	multi, vert.	1.00	.40
1876	A417	80m	multi, diff.	1.25	.50

Size: 60x21mm

Perf. 13

1877	A417	1.20t	multi, diff.	1.75	.55
			Nos. 1871-1877 (7)	6.30	2.40

Souvenir Sheet

1878	A417	4t	multi, diff.	6.00	6.00

Giant Pandas — A418

1990, Aug. 15 Litho. ***Perf. 14***

1879	A418	10m	Adult on rock, vert.	.25	.20
1880	A418	20m	Adult, eating, vert.	.30	.20
1881	A418	30m	Adult and cub, vert.	.45	.25
1882	A418	40m	shown	.60	.30
1883	A418	50m	Adult and cub, resting	.70	.40
1884	A418	60m	Adult, mountains	.90	.50
1885	A418	80m	Adult and cub, playing	1.25	.65
1886	A418	1.20t	Adult, in winter	1.75	1.00
			Nos. 1879-1886 (8)	6.20	3.50

Souvenir Sheet

1887	A418	4t	Family	6.00	6.00

Pyramids of Egypt — A419

Seven wonders of the ancient world: 20m, Lighthouse of Alexander, vert. 40m, Statue of Zeus, vert. 50m, Colossus of Rhodes, vert. 60m, Mausoleum of Halicarnassus, vert. 80m, Temple of Artemis. 1.20t, Hanging gardens of Babylon, vert. 4t, Pyramids of Egypt, vert.

1990, Sept. 25

1888	A419	20m	multicolored	.35	.20
1889	A419	30m	shown	.45	.20
1890	A419	40m	multicolored	.65	.25
1891	A419	50m	multicolored	.75	.25
1892	A419	60m	multicolored	1.00	.25
1893	A419	80m	multicolored	1.25	.40
1894	A419	1.20t	multicolored	1.75	.65
			Nos. 1888-1894 (7)	6.20	2.20

Souvenir Sheet

1895	A419	4t	multicolored	6.00	6.00

Moschus Moschiferus — A419a

1990, Sept. 26 Litho. *Perf. 14*

1895A	A419a	60m	shown	.90	.60
1895B	A419a	60m	In snow	.90	.60
1895C	A419a	60m	Facing left	.90	.60
1895D	A419a	60m	Two, one on ground	.90	.60
			Nos. 1895A-1895D (4)	3.60	2.40

Parrots — A420

1990, Oct. 25 Litho. *Perf. 14*

1896	A420	20m	shown	.30	.20
1897	A420	30m	multi, diff.	.40	.20
1898	A420	40m	multi, diff.	.60	.25
1899	A420	50m	multi, diff.	.70	.30
1900	A420	60m	multi, diff.	.90	.40
1901	A420	80m	multi, diff.	1.25	.50
1902	A420	1.20t	multi, diff.	1.50	.55
			Nos. 1896-1902 (7)	5.65	2.40

Souvenir Sheet

1903	A420	4t	multi, diff.	5.50	5.50

Butterflies — A421

Designs: 20m, Purpurbar. 30m, Grosses nachtpfauenauge. 40m, Grosser C-Falter. 50m, Stachelbeerspanner. 60m, Damenbrett. 80m, Schwalbenschwanz. 1.20t, Aurorafalter. 4t, Linienschwarmer, vert.

1990, Nov. 25 Litho. *Perf. 14*

1904	A421	20m	multicolored	.30	.20
1905	A421	30m	multicolored	.40	.20
1906	A421	40m	multicolored	.60	.25
1907	A421	50m	multicolored	.80	.30
1908	A421	60m	multicolored	.90	.40
1909	A421	80m	multicolored	1.10	.50
1910	A421	1.20t	multicolored	1.60	.55
			Nos. 1904-1910 (7)	5.70	2.40

Souvenir Sheet

1911	A421	4t	multicolored	5.50	5.50

Flintstones Visit Mongolia — A422

Designs: 25m, Dino, Bamm-Bamm. 35m, Dino, Bamm-Bamm, diff., vert. 45m, Betty, Wilma, Bamm-Bamm, Pebbles. 55m, Fred, Barney, Dino. 65m, Flintstones & Rubbles. 75m, Bamm-Bamm riding Dino. 85m, Fred, Barney, Bamm-Bamm. 1.40t, Flintstones, Rubbles in car. 2t, Fred, Barney. No. 1921, Wilma, Betty & Bamm-Bamm. No. 1922, Bamm-Bamm, Pebbles riding Dino.

1991, Feb. 10 Litho. *Perf. 14*

1912	A422	25m	multicolored	.30	.20
1913	A422	35m	multicolored	.40	.20
1914	A422	45m	multicolored	.55	.25
1915	A422	55m	multicolored	.65	.25
1916	A422	65m	multicolored	.80	.25
1917	A422	75m	multicolored	.90	.30
1918	A422	85m	multicolored	1.00	.30
1919	A422	1.40t	multicolored	1.70	.40
1920	A422	2t	multicolored	2.40	.40
			Nos. 1912-1920 (9)	8.70	2.55

Souvenir Sheets

1921	A422	7t	multicolored	5.50	5.50
1922	A422	7t	multicolored	5.50	5.50

The Jetsons A423

Designs: 20m, Jetsons blasting off in space-ship. 25m, Jetsons on planet, horiz. 30m, George, Jane, Elroy & Astro. 40m, George, Judy, Elroy & Astro. 50m, Jetsons in space-ship, horiz. 60m, George, Jane, Elroy & Mr. Spacely, horiz. 70m, George, Elroy wearing jet packs. 80m, Elroy. 1.20t, Elroy, Judy & Astro. No. 1932, Elroy, red flowers. No. 1933, Elroy, blue flowers.

1991, Feb. 10

1923	A423	20m	multicolored	.25	.20
1924	A423	25m	multicolored	.30	.20
1925	A423	30m	multicolored	.35	.25
1926	A423	40m	multicolored	.50	.25
1927	A423	50m	multicolored	.60	.30
1928	A423	60m	multicolored	.70	.30
1929	A423	70m	multicolored	.85	.30
1930	A423	80m	multicolored	1.00	.40
1931	A423	1.20t	multicolored	1.50	.40
			Nos. 1923-1931 (9)	6.05	2.60

Souvenir Sheets

1932	A423	7t	multicolored	5.50	5.50
1933	A423	7t	multicolored	5.50	5.50

Mongolian People's Revolutionary Party, 70th Anniv. — A423a

1991, Mar. 1 Litho. *Perf. 14*

1933A	A423a	60m	multicolored	.90	.40

A424

Stamp World London '90 — A425

Various birds.

1991, Mar. 3 Litho. *Perf. 14½*

1934	A424	25m	multicolored	.25	.20
1935	A424	35m	multicolored	.35	.20
1936	A424	45m	multicolored	.50	.20
1937	A424	55m	multicolored	.60	.20
1938	A424	65m	multicolored	.75	.25
1939	A424	75m	multi, horiz.	.80	.30
1940	A424	85m	multicolored	1.00	.40
1941	A424	1.40t	multicolored	1.50	.50
1942	A424	2t	multicolored	2.25	.55
			Nos. 1934-1942 (9)	8.00	2.80

Souvenir Sheets

1943	A424	7t	multicolored	7.00	7.00
1944	A425	7t	multicolored	7.00	7.00

Butterflies and Flowers of Mongolia — A426

Designs: 20m, 30m-60m, various butterflies. Others, various flowers.

1991, Mar. 3 Litho. *Perf. 14½*

1945	A426	20m	multicolored	.45	.20
1946	A426	25m	multicolored	.50	.20
1947	A426	30m	multicolored	.65	.20
1948	A426	40m	multicolored	.85	.20
1949	A426	50m	multicolored	1.00	.25
1950	A426	60m	multicolored	1.25	.25
1951	A426	70m	multicolored	1.50	.30
1952	A426	80m	multicolored	1.75	.30
1953	A426	1.20t	multicolored	2.25	.40
			Nos. 1945-1953 (9)	10.20	2.30

Nos. 1945-1953 and Types Overprinted

1991, Mar. 3

1954	A426	20m	multicolored	.45	.20
1955	A426	25m	multicolored	.50	.20
1956	A426	30m	multicolored	.65	.20
1957	A426	40m	multicolored	.85	.20
1958	A426	50m	multicolored	1.00	.25
1959	A426	60m	multicolored	1.25	.25
1960	A426	70m	multicolored	1.50	.30
1961	A426	80m	multicolored	1.75	.30
1962	A426	1.20t	multicolored	2.25	.40
			Nos. 1954-1962 (9)	10.20	2.30

Souvenir Sheets

1963	A426	7t	Butterfly	10.00	10.00
1964	A426	7t	Flower	10.00	10.00

Nos. 1963-1964 were not issued without overprint which appears in sheet margin only.

Mongolian People's Army, 70th Anniv. — A426a

1991, Mar. 18 Litho. *Perf. 14*

1964A	A426a	60m	multicolored	.80	.50

Birds — A427

1991, Apr. 1 *Perf. 14*

1965	A427	20m	Lururus tetrix	.30	.20
1966	A427	30m	Tadorna tadorna	.50	.20
1967	A427	40m	Phasianus colchicus	.60	.25
1968	A427	50m	Clangula by-emalis	.80	.30
1969	A427	60m	Tetrastes bona-sia	1.00	.40
1970	A427	80m	Mergus serrator	1.25	.50
1971	A427	1.20t	Bucephaia clangula	1.75	.75
			Nos. 1965-1971 (7)	6.20	2.60

Souvenir Sheet

1972	A427	4t	Anas crecca, vert.	6.00	6.00

Flowers — A428

1991, Apr. 15

1973	A428	20m	Dianthus superbus	.25	.20
1974	A428	30m	Gentiana puenmonanthe	.40	.20
1975	A428	40m	Taraxacum of-ficinale	.60	.25
1976	A428	50m	Iris sibrica	.70	.30
1977	A428	60m	Lilium martagon	.80	.40
1978	A428	80m	Aster amellus	1.10	.50
1979	A428	1.20t	Cizsium rivulare	1.60	.55
			Nos. 1973-1979 (7)	5.45	2.40

Souvenir Sheet

1980	A428	4t	Campanula per-sicifolia	5.50	5.50

Buddhist Effigies — A429

1991, May 1

1981	A429	20m	Defend	.35	.20
1982	A429	30m	Badmasanhava	.40	.20
1983	A429	40m	Avalokitecvara	.55	.25
1984	A429	50m	Buddha	.75	.30
1985	A429	60m	Mintugwa	.80	.40

1986 A429 80m Shyamatara 1.10 .50
1987 A429 1.20t Samvara 1.50 .55
Nos. 1981-1987 (7) 5.45 2.40

Souvenir Sheet

1988 A429 4t Lamidhatara 5.50 5.50

For surcharge, see No. 2658.

Insects — A430

1991, May 22

1989 A430 20m Neolamprima adolphinae .35 .20
1990 A430 30m Chelorrhina polyphemus .40 .20
1991 A430 40m Coptolabrus coelestis .55 .25
1992 A430 50m Epepeotes togatus .75 .30
1993 A430 60m Cicindela chinensis .80 .40
1994 A430 80m Macrodontia cervicornis 1.25 .50
1995 A430 1.20t Dynastes hercules 1.50 .55
Nos. 1989-1995 (7) 5.60 2.40

Souvenir Sheet

1991, May 22 Litho. *Perf. 14*

1995A A430 4t Cercopis sanguinolenta, vert. 5.50 5.50

African Animals — A431

1991, May 23

1996 A431 20m Zebras .30 .20
1997 A431 30m Cheetah .40 .20
1998 A431 40m Black rhinos .60 .25
1999 A431 50m Giraffe, vert. .80 .30
2000 A431 60m Gorilla .90 .40
2001 A431 80m Elephants 1.10 .50
2002 A431 1.20t Lion, vert. 1.50 .55
Nos. 1996-2002 (7) 5.60 2.40

Souvenir Sheet

2003 A431 4t Gazelle 5.50 5.50

No. 1997 is incorrectly spelled "Cheetan."

Exhibition of Meiso Mizuhara's Mongolian Stamp Collection — A432

1991, June Litho. *Perf. 13½*

2004 A432 1.20t multicolored 3.00 1.25

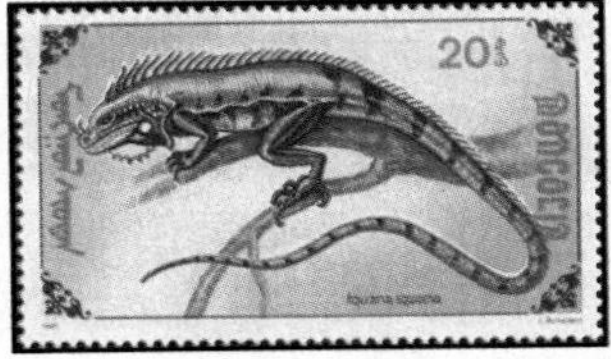

Lizards — A433

1991, Oct. 29 *Perf. 14*

2005 A433 20m Iguana iguana .30 .20
2006 A433 30m Ptychozoon kihli .40 .20
2007 A433 40m Chlamydosaurus kingii .65 .25
2008 A433 50m Cordylus cordylus .75 .30
2009 A433 60m Basiliscus basilisus .80 .40
2010 A433 80m Tupinambis teguixin 1.10 .50
2011 A433 1.20t Amblyrhynchus cristatus 1.75 .55
Nos. 2005-2011 (7) 5.75 2.40

Souvenir Sheet

2012 A433 4t Varanus bengalensis, vert. 5.50 5.50

Masks and Costumes A434

Various masks and costumes.

1991, Oct. 1

2013 A434 35m multicolored .40 .20
2014 A434 45m multicolored .50 .25
2015 A434 55m multicolored .65 .25
2016 A434 65m multicolored .75 .30
2017 A434 85m multicolored 1.00 .50
2018 A434 1.40t multicolored 1.65 .80
2019 A434 2t multicolored 2.35 1.00
Nos. 2013-2019 (7) 7.30 3.30

Souvenir Sheet

2020 A434 4t multicolored 5.50 5.50

Phila Nippon '91 — A435

1991, Oct. 29

2021 A435 1t Pagoda .55 .50
2022 A435 2t Japanese beauty 1.00 .75
2023 A435 3t Mongolian woman 1.75 1.00
2024 A435 4t Mongolian building 2.75 1.25
Nos. 2021-2024 (4) 6.05 3.50

Fantasia, 50th Anniv. A436

Designs: 1.70t, Poster, 1985. 2t, Poster, 1940. 2.30t, Poster, 1982. 2.60t, Poster, 1981. 4.20t, Poster, 1969. 10t, Poster, 1941. 15t, Drawing of Mlle. Upanova, 1940. 16t, Sketch of Mickey as Sorcerer's Apprentice.

No. 2033, Mickey as Sorcerer's Apprentice. No. 2034, Dinosaurs from "The Rite of Spring," horiz. No. 2035, Thistles and orchids from "Russian Dance," horiz. No. 2036, Dancing mushrooms from "Chinese Dance," horiz.

1991, Dec. 31 *Perf. 13½x14, 14x13½*

2025 A436 1.70t multicolored .40 .20
2026 A436 2t multicolored .60 .20
2027 A436 2.30t multicolored .75 .25
2028 A436 2.60t multicolored 1.00 .25
2029 A436 4.20t multicolored 1.25 .40
2030 A436 10t multicolored 1.75 .50
2031 A436 15t multicolored 2.75 1.20
2032 A436 16t multicolored 3.00 1.20
Nos. 2025-2032 (8) 11.50 4.20

Souvenir Sheets

2033 A436 30t multicolored 7.50 7.50
2034 A436 30t multicolored 7.50 7.50
2035 A436 30t multicolored 7.50 7.50
2036 A436 30t multicolored 7.50 7.50

1992 Winter Olympics, Albertville — A437

1992, Feb. 1 *Perf. 14*

2037 A437 60m Speed skating, vert. .40 .20
2038 A437 80m Ski jumping, vert. .50 .20
2039 A437 1t Hockey, vert. .60 .20
2040 A437 1.20t Figure skating, vert. .70 .20
2041 A437 1.50t Biathlon .80 .20
2042 A437 2t Downhill skiing .90 .20
2043 A437 2.40t Two-man bobsled 1.00 .25
Nos. 2037-2043 (7) 4.90 1.45

Souvenir Sheet

2044 A437 8t Four-man bobsled, vert. 5.00 5.00

Dogs — A438

Various breeds of dogs.

1991, Dec. 1 Litho. *Perf. 14*

2045 A438 20m multi .25 .20
2046 A438 30m multi, vert. .40 .20
2047 A438 40m multi, vert. .55 .25
2048 A438 50m multi .75 .30
2049 A438 60m multi 1.00 .40
2050 A438 80m multi 1.25 .50
2051 A438 1.20t multi 1.50 .70
Nos. 2045-2051 (7) 5.70 2.55

Souvenir Sheet

2052 A438 4t multi 5.50 5.50

Cats — A439

Various breeds of cats.

1991, Dec. 27

2053 A439 20m multi .25 .20
2054 A439 30m multi, vert. .40 .20
2055 A439 40m multi .55 .25
2056 A439 50m multi, vert. .75 .30
2057 A439 60m multi, vert. 1.00 .40
2058 A439 80m multi, vert. 1.25 .50
2059 A439 1.20t multi, vert. 1.50 .70
Nos. 2053-2059 (7) 5.70 2.55

Souvenir Sheet

2060 A439 4t multi 5.50 5.50

Alces Alces — A440

1992, May 1 Litho. *Perf. 14*

2061 A440 3t Male 1.00 .65
2062 A440 3t Two females 1.00 .65
2063 A440 3t One female, vert. 1.00 .65
2064 A440 3t Male's head, vert. 1.00 .65
Nos. 2061-2064 (4) 4.00 2.60

Souvenir Sheet

Ferdinand von Zeppelin (1838-1917), Airship Designer — A441

1992, May 1

2065 A441 16t multicolored 4.00 4.00

Souvenir Sheets

People and Events — A442

No. 2066, Pres. Punsalmaagiin Ochirbat visiting Pres. George Bush at White House. No. 2067, Mother Teresa helping poor in Calcutta. No. 2068, Pope John Paul II at mass. Nos. 2069-2070, Boy Scout blowing bugle.

1992, May 22 *Perf. 14x13½*

2066 A442 30t silver & multi 5.50 5.50

Perf. 14

2067 A442 30t silver & multi 5.50 5.50
2068 A442 30t silver & multi 5.50 5.50
2069 A442 30t silver & multi 5.50 5.50
2070 A442 30t silver & multi 5.50 5.50
Nos. 2066-2070 (5) 27.50 27.50

Nos. 2067-2070 each contain one 43x28mm stamp. Nos. 2069-2070 exist with gold inscription and border. No. 2069, 17th World Boy Scout Jamboree, Korea. No. 2070, 18th World Boy Scout Jamboree, Netherlands, 1995.

Souvenir Sheet

Discovery of America, 500th Anniv. — A443

Designs: a, Columbus. b, Sailing ship.

1992, May 22

2071 A443 30t Sheet of 2, #a.-b. 9.25 9.25

World Columbian Stamp Expo '92, Chicago, Genoa '92.

Miniature Sheets

Railways of the World — A444

Designs: No. 2072a, 3t, Tank locomotive, Darjeeling-Himalaya Railway, India. b, 3t, Royal Scot, Great Britain. c, 6t, Bridge on the River Kwai, Burma-Siam Railway. d, 6t, Baltic tank engine, Burma. e, 8t, Baldwin locomotive, Thailand. f, 8t, Western Railway locomotive, Pakistan. g, 16t, P.36 class locomotive, USSR. h, 16t, Shanghai-Beijing Express, China.

Orient Express: No. 2073a, 3t, 1931 Advertising poster. b, 3t, 1928 poster. c, 6t, Dawn departure. d, 6t, Golden Arrow departing Victoria Station. e, 8t, Waiting at station in Yugoslavia. f, 8t, Turn of the century picture of train. g, 16t, Fleche d'Or locomotive approaching Etaples, France. h, 16t, Arrival in Istanbul, Turkey.

No. 2074, New Tokaido line, Japan. No. 2075, TGV, France. No. 2076a, Emblem of Pullman Car Company. b, Emblem of Intl. Wagons-lits Company. No. 2077, Passengers waiting to board Orient Express.

1992, May 24

2072 A444 Sheet of 8, #a.-h. 15.00 11.00
2073 A444 Sheet of 8, #a.-h. 15.00 11.00

Souvenir Sheets

2074 A444 30t multicolored 6.00 5.00
2075 A444 30t multicolored 6.00 5.00
2076 A444 30t Sheet of 2, #a.-b. 12.00 11.00
2077 A444 30t black & gold 6.00 5.00

Nos. 2074-2075 contain one 58x42mm stamp.

Miniature Sheet

Birds — A445

Various birds: a, 3t. b, 3t, Owl. c, 6t, Gull, horiz. d, 6t, horiz. e, 8t. f, 8t, horiz. g, 16t. h, 16t, horiz.

1992, May 24

2078 A445 Sheet of 8, #a.-h. 15.00 10.00

Souvenir Sheet

Perf. 14x13½

2079 A445 30t Ducks, 30t in UR 6.00 6.00
2080 A445 30t Duck, 30t in LR 6.00 6.00

Nos. 2079-2080 contain one 50x38mm stamp.

Miniature Sheet

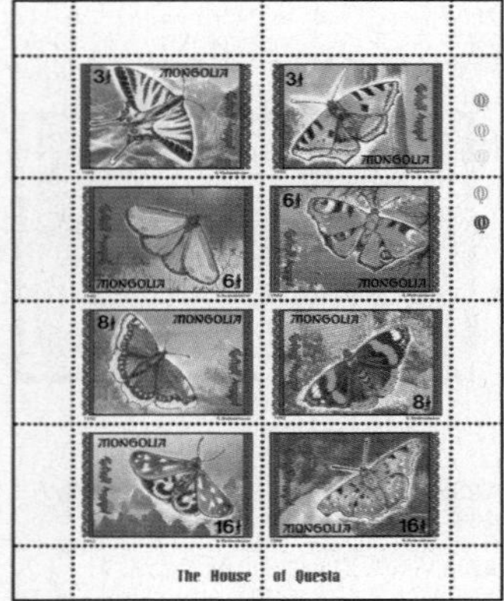

Butterflies and Moths — A446

Various butterflies or moths and: a, 3t, Mountains. b, 3t, Desert. c, 6t, Grass. d, 6t, Lake. e, 8t, Mountain, diff. f, 8t, Flowers. g, 16t, Rocks. h, 16t, Lake, diff.

1992, May 24 ***Perf. 14***

2081 A446 Sheet of 8, #a.-h. 15.00 10.00

Souvenir Sheet

Perf. 14x13½

2082 A446 30t pink & multi 6.00 5.00
2083 A446 30t blue & multi 6.00 5.00

Nos. 2082-2083 contain one 50x38mm stamp.

1992 Summer Olympics, Barcelona — A447

Designs: a, Gold medal. b, Torch.

1992, Jan. 22 Litho. ***Perf. 14***

2084 A447 30t Sheet of 2, #a.-b. 9.50 9.50

Souvenir Sheet

Genghis Khan — A448

1992, June 15 Litho. ***Perf. 14***

2085 A448 16t multicolored *20.00 20.00*

Mushrooms — A449

Designs: 20m, Marasmius oreades. 30m, Boletus luridus. 40m, Hygrophorus marzuelus. 50m, Cantharellus cibarius. 60m, Agaricus campester. 80m, Boletus aereus. 1.20t, Amanita caesarea. 2t, Tricholoma terreum. 4t, Mitrophora hybrida.

1991, June 18 Litho. ***Perf. 13***

2086 A449 20m multicolored .30 .20
2087 A449 30m multicolored .40 .20
2088 A449 40m multicolored .60 .25
2089 A449 50m multicolored .70 .25
2090 A449 60m multicolored .80 .30
2091 A449 80m multicolored 1.00 .40
2092 A449 1.20t multicolored 1.25 .55
2093 A449 2t multicolored 2.00 .80
Nos. 2086-2093 (8) 7.05 2.95

Souvenir Sheet

2094 A449 4t multicolored 6.50 6.50

Dated 1990. No. 2094 contains one 32x40mm stamp.

Discovery of America, 500th Anniv. — A450

Columbus and: 3t, Two sailing ships. 7t, Natives approaching Santa Maria. 10t, Pinta. 16t, Santa Maria, vert. 30t, Santa Maria, diff. 40t, Santa Maria, dolphins. 50t, Nina.

#2102, Ship, vert. #2103, Portrait, vert.

1992, Aug. Litho. ***Perf. 14***

2095 A450 3t multicolored .25 .20
2096 A450 7t multicolored .50 .20
2097 A450 10t multicolored .75 .25
2098 A450 16t multicolored 1.00 .30
2099 A450 30t multicolored 1.75 .80
2100 A450 40t multicolored 2.25 1.40
2101 A450 50t multicolored 3.50 1.75
Nos. 2095-2101 (7) 10.00 4.90

Souvenir Sheets

Perf. 13½x14

2102 A450 80t multicolored 5.50 5.50
2103 A450 80t multicolored 5.50 5.50

Nos. 2102-2103 each contain one 38x52mm stamp.

Miniature Sheet

Butterflies A451

#2104: a, 3t, Anthocharis cardamines. b, 8t, Inachis io. c, 10t, Fabriciana adippe. d, 16t, Limenitis reducta. e, 30t, Agrumaenia carniolica. f, 40t, Polyommatus icarus. g, 50t, Parnassius apollo. h, 60t, Saturnia pyri.

No. 2105, Limenitis populi. No. 2106, Heodes virgaureae.

1992, Dec. Litho. ***Perf. 14***

2104 A451 Sheet of 8, #a.-h. 12.00 11.00

Souvenir Sheets

Perf. 14x13½

2105 A451 80t multicolored 5.50 4.50
2106 A451 80t multicolored 5.50 4.50

Nos. 2105-2106 each contain one 51x38mm stamp.

1992 Summer Olympics, Barcelona — A452

1993, Jan. Litho. ***Perf. 13½***

2107 A452 3t Long jump .20 .20
2108 A452 6t Pommel horse .20 .20
2109 A452 8t Boxing .25 .20
2110 A452 16t Wrestling .60 .20
2111 A452 20t Archery, vert. .70 .25
2112 A452 30t Cycling .80 .25
2113 A452 40t Equestrian .90 .30
2114 A452 50t High jump 1.00 .30
2115 A452 60t Weight lifting 1.25 .40
Nos. 2107-2115 (9) 5.90 2.30

Souvenir Sheet

Perf. 15x14

2116 A452 80t Judo 5.00 4.00
2117 A452 80t Javelin 5.00 4.00

Nos. 2116-2117 contain one 40x30mm stamp.

Miniature Sheet

Birds A453

Designs: No. 2118a, 3t, Tetrae tetrix. b, 8t, Gallinula chloropus. c, 10t, Regulus satrapa. d, 16t, Alcede atthis. e, 30t, Gavia stellata. f, 40t, Ardes cinerea. g, 50t, Upupa epops. h, 60t, Niltava rubeculoides. No. 2119, Gyps fulvus. No. 2120, Podiceps cristatus.

1993, Feb. Litho. ***Perf. 14***

2118 A453 Sheet of 8, #a.-h. 12.00 11.00

Souvenir Sheets

Perf. 14x13½

2119 A453 80t multicolored 5.00 4.00
2120 A453 80t multicolored 5.00 4.00

Nos. 2119-2120 each contain one 51x38mm stamp.

Souvenir Sheets

Polska '93 — A454

#2121a, 2122, Copernicus. #2121b, Chopin. #2121c, 2123, Pope John Paul II.

1993, May 1 Litho. ***Perf. 13½x14***

2121 A454 30t Sheet of 3, #a.-c. 10.00 8.00
2122 A454 80t multicolored 8.00 7.00
2123 A454 80t multicolored 8.00 7.00
Nos. 2121-2123 (3) 26.00 22.00

Animals, Sports, & Transportation — A455

Designs in gold: No. 2124, Cats, dogs. No. 2125, Turtle, bee, wildcat, butterfly. No. 2126, Owl, butterfly, mushroom, dinosaur. Nos. 2127, Chessmen, archer, baseball player, wrestlers, horse and rider. Nos. 2128, Modern transportation.

No. 2129, Dinosaur, whales, butterflies. No. 2130, Mushroom, turtle, flowers.

1993, Jan. 5 Embossed ***Perf. 9***

2124-2128 A455 200t Set of 5

Nos. 2124-2128 exist in silver and in either gold or silver imperf. souvenir sheets of 1.

Embossed

1993, June 1 ***Perf. 8½x9***

Size: 79x53mm

2129 A455 200t silver

Souvenir Sheet
Imperf
Litho. & Embossed

2130 A455 200t gold

No. 2130, Topex '93, Madison, WI. No. 2129 exists in imperf. souvenir sheet of 1. No. 2130 exists in silver.

Souvenir Sheets

Taipei '93 — A456

1993, Aug. 14 Litho. ***Perf. 13½x14***

2137 A456 80t Genghis Khan *15.00*
2138 A456 80t Sun Yat-Sen *20.00*

Dirigible Flight Over Ulan Bator — A457

1993, Aug. 27 Litho. ***Perf. 14***

2139 A457 80t multicolored 3.00 3.00

No. 2139 has a holographic image. Soaking in water may affect the hologram.

Issued in sheets of 4

Buddhist Deities A458

Various statues and paintings.

1993, Oct. 3 ***Perf. 13½x14***

2140 A458 50t multicolored .35 .25
2141 A458 100t multicolored .70 .30
2142 A458 150t multicolored 1.00 .50
2143 A458 200t multicolored 1.40 .65
a. Miniature sheet of 4 5.25 5.25
Nos. 2140-2143 (4) 3.45 1.70

Souvenir Sheet

2144 A458 300t multicolored 2.00 2.00

Bangkok '93.

Nos. 276 & 1084 Surcharged

1993 ***Perfs., Etc. as Before***

2144A A77 8t on 70m #276 *7.50*
2144B A246 15t on 70m #1084 *15.00*

No. 2144A exists with double surcharge. The surcharge on No. 2144B exists with four different type fonts.

New Year 1994 (Year of the Dog) — A459

No. 2146, Stylized dog running, vert.

1994, Jan. 10 ***Perf. 14x13½, 13½x14***

2145 A459 60t multicolored 3.00 .75
2146 A459 60t multicolored 3.00 .75

1994 World Cup Soccer Championships, U.S. — A460

Championship teams: #2147, Uruguay, 1930, 1950. #2148, Italy, 1954. #2149, Brazil, 1959. #2150, West Germany, 1954. #2151, Argentina, 1978, 1986. #2152, Italy, 1938. #2153, Brazil, 1962. #2154, West Germany, 1974. #2155, Brazil, 1970. #2156, Italy, 1982. #2157, West Germany, 1990.

1994, Jan. 15 ***Perf. 14x13½***

2147 A460 150t multicolored 1.00 .25
2148 A460 150t multicolored 1.00 .25
2149 A460 150t multicolored 1.00 .25
2150 A460 150t multicolored 1.00 .25
2151 A460 150t multicolored 1.00 .25
a. Souv. sheet of 2, #2147, 2151 2.00 2.00
2152 A460 200t multicolored 1.40 .40
2153 A460 200t multicolored 1.40 .40
2154 A460 200t multicolored 1.40 .40
2155 A460 250t multicolored 1.75 .55
a. Souvenir sheet of 3, #2149, 2153, 2155 4.25 4.25
2156 A460 250t multicolored 1.75 .55
a. Souvenir sheet of 3, #2148, 2152, 2156 4.25 4.25
2157 A460 250t multicolored 1.75 .55
a. Souvenir sheet of 3, #2150, 2154, 2157 4.25 4.25
b. Miniature sheet of 4, #2151, 2155-2157 6.25 6.25
Nos. 2147-2157 (11) 14.45 4.10

Souvenir Sheet

Punsalmaagiin Ochirbat, First President of Mongolia — A461

1994, Apr. 1 ***Perf. 14***

2158 A461 150t multicolored 2.00 2.00

1994 Winter Olympics, Lillehammer A462

1994, Apr. 10 Litho. ***Perf. 13½***

2159 A462 50t Biathlon .40 .20
2160 A462 60t Two-man bob-sled .50 .25
2161 A462 80t Slalom skiing .60 .40
2162 A462 100t Ski jumping .75 .50
2163 A462 120t Pairs figure skating .95 .55
2164 A462 200t Speed skating 1.40 .90
Nos. 2159-2164 (6) 4.60 2.80

Souvenir Sheet

2165 A462 400t Ice hockey 5.00 5.00

Souvenir Sheet

Dalai Lama, 1989 Nobel Peace Prize Winner — A463

1994, June 27 Litho. ***Perf. 13½***

2166 A463 400t multicolored *30.00*

A464

People's Army — A465

1994 Litho. ***Perf. 14***

2167 A464 60m multicolored .90 .90

Souvenir Sheet

2168 A465 4t multicolored 3.50 3.50

Miniature Sheet of 18

Wildlife A466

Designs: a, Brown raptor. b, Woodpecker. c, Cranes in flight. d, White raptor. e, Yellow bird on tree branch (i). f, Two birds flying left. g, Raptor perched on rock. h, Two birds flying right. i, Squirrel. j, Dragonfly (f). k, Water bird standing near pond (o). l, Duck in flight over pond. m, Brown bird. n, Ground hog. o, Ladybug on flower. p, Bird's eggs. q, Grasshopper (m). r, Butterfly.

1994, July 15

2169 A466 60t #a.-r. + 2 labels 12.00 10.00

First Manned Moon Landing, 25th Anniv. A467

1994, July 20 Litho. ***Perf. 13½***

2170 A467 200t Trans-lunar injection 1.00 .60
2171 A467 200t Astronaut on moon 1.00 .60
2172 A467 200t Space shuttle, earth 1.00 .60
2173 A467 200t Astronaut, shuttle 1.00 .60
a. Miniature sheet of 4, #2170-2173 5.00 4.00
Nos. 2170-2173 (4) 4.00 2.40

Singpex '94 — A468

1994, Aug. 31

2174 A468 300t Butterfly 1.50 1.00

Souvenir Sheet

2175 A468 400t Dog *6.00 5.00*

New Year 1994 (Year of the Dog).

A469

PHILAKOREA '94 — A470

1994 Litho. *Perf. 14*

2176 A469 600t Korea #1749 2.75 1.00
2177 A469 600t #433 2.75 1.00
2178 A470 600t #1 2.75 1.00
2179 A470 600t Korea #1 2.75 1.00
Nos. 2176-2179 (4) 11.00 4.00

Souvenir Sheets

Perf. 13½x14

2180 A470 400t #5 4.00 4.00

Perf. 14

2181 A469 600t Yong Sik Hong 5.00 5.00

First Mongolian Stamp, 70th anniv. (#2180).
No. 2180 contains one 34x46mm stamp.
Issued: No. 2180, 11/23, others, 8/16.
For surcharges see #2247C-2247G.

Dinosaurs — A471

1994, Nov. 30 *Perf. 14*

2182 A471 60t Mammuthus, vert. .40 .25
2183 A471 80t Stegosaurus, vert. .50 .30
2184 A471 100t Talararus .60 .40
2185 A471 120t Gorythosaurus .75 .55
2186 A471 200t Tyrannosaurus 1.25 .90
Nos. 2182-2186 (5) 3.50 2.40

Souvenir Sheet

2187 A471 400t Triceratops *3.50 3.50*

Nos. 2182-2187 exist in imperf. sheets of 1.
No. 2182 is misspelled.

Mongolian-Japanese Friendship — A472

1994, Dec. 15 *Perf. 14x13½*

2188 A472 20t multicolored *1.00* .30

New Year 1995 (Year of the Boar) — A474

1995, Jan. 1 *Perf. 14x13½, 13½x14*

2190 A474 200t shown 1.00 .30
2191 A474 200t Boar, diff, vert. 1.00 .30

A475

Litho. & Typo.

1994, July 25 *Perf. 15x14*

Denomination in Black

2192 A475 10t Flower — —
2192A A475 10t Flower, red denomination — —
2193 A475 18t Ram — —
2194 A475 22t Airplane — —
2195 A475 22t Airplane, red denomination — —
2196 A475 44t like #2193 — —
2197 A475 44t Ram, blue denomination — —

Dated 1993.
No. 2192A issued 1994(?).
This is an expanding set. Numbers may change.

Religious Masked Dancing — A476

Various masked dancers in traditional costumes.

1995, Feb. 25 Litho. *Perf. 14*

2201 A476 20t multicolored .20 .20
2202 A476 50t multicolored .30 .20
2203 A476 60t multicolored .35 .25
2204 A476 100t multicolored .60 .30
2205 A476 120t multicolored .70 .30
2206 A476 150t multicolored .85 .40
2207 A476 200t multicolored 1.10 .50
Nos. 2201-2207 (7) 4.10 2.15

Souvenir Sheet

2208 A476 400t multicolored 4.00 4.00

Saiga Tatarica A477

1995, Mar. 30 Litho. *Perf. 14*

2209 A477 40t shown .40 .20
2210 A477 55t Two adults .50 .25
2211 A477 70t One running left .60 .30
2212 A477 200t One up close 1.60 .80
a. Block of 4, #2209-2212 3.50 3.50

World Wildlife Fund.

Souvenir Sheet

First Philately & Collections Fair, Hong Kong '95 — A478

Designs: a, Butterfly. b, Flowers.

1995, June 6 Litho. *Perf. 14*

2213 A478 200t Sheet of 2, #a.-b. + 2 labels 4.25 4.25

Goldfish — A479

Designs: 20t, Yellow oranda. 50t, Red and white wen-yu. 60t, Brown oranda with red head. 100t, Calico pearl-scale with phoenix tail. 120t, Red lion-head. 150t, Brown oranda. 200t, Red and white oranda with narial.
400t, White and gold unidentified fish.

1995, Sept. 1 Litho. *Perf. 14*

2214-2220 A479 Set of 7 5.50 4.00

Souvenir Sheet

2221 A479 400t multicolored 5.50 4.00

No. 2221 contains one 50x38mm stamp.

Miniature Sheet

Motion Pictures, Cent. A480

Various portraits of Marilyn Monroe (1926-62): No. 2222a, 60t. b, 80t. c, 100t. d, 120t. e, 150t. f, 200t. g, 250t. h, 300t. i, 350t.
No. 2223, In white-collared blouse. No. 2224, With lion. No. 2225, In black lace dress. No. 2226, In scene from movie, Niagara.

1995, Oct. 20

2222 A480 Sheet of 9, #a.-i. 9.00 8.00

Souvenir Sheets

2223 A480 200t multi 5.50 5.50
2224-2226 A480 300t each 5.50 5.50

Miniature Sheet

UN, 50th Anniv. — A481

Exterior views of UN complexes, Secretaries General: a, Trygve Lie. b, Dag Hammarskjold. c, U Thant. d, Kurt Waldheim. e, Jose Perez de Cuellar. f, Boutros Boutros-Ghali.

1995, Oct. 15

2227 A481 60t Sheet of 6, #a.-f. 10.00 9.00

Miniature Sheet

Elvis Presley (1935-77) A482

Various portaits: No. 2228a, 60t. b, 80t. c, 100t. d, 120t. e, 150t. f, 200t. g, 250t. h, 300t. i, 350t.
No. 2229, Wearing yellow sweater. No. 2230, With dancing girl. No. 2231, With guitar. No. 2232, In army uniform, wife Priscilla.

1995, Oct. 20

2228 A482 Sheet of 9, #a.-i. 9.00 8.00

Souvenir Sheets

2229 A482 200t multi 5.00 5.00
2230 A482 300t multi 5.00 5.00
2231-2232 A482 400t each 6.50 5.00

Miniature Sheet

X-Men Comic Characters A483

Designs: No. 2233a, 30t, Bishop. b, 50t, Beast. c, 60t, Rogue. d, 70t, Gambit. e, 80t, Cyclops. f, 100t, Storm. g, 200t, Professor X. h, 250t, Wolverine.
No. 2234: a, Wolverine, horiz. b, Magneto, horiz.

1995, Sept. 15

2233 A483 Sheet of 8, #a.-h. 4.25 4.00

Souvenir Sheet of 2

2234 A483 250t #a.-b. 4.25 4.10

New Year 1996 (Year of the Rat) A484

1996, Jan. 1 Litho. *Perf. 14*

2235 A484 150t Rat, diff., vert. 1.00 .60
2236 A484 200t shown 1.50 .85

CHINA '96 — A485

Designs: a, Monument of Sukhe Bator. b, Temple of Heaven, Beijing. c, Migjed Jang-Rasek. d, Great Wall.

1996, Apr. 25 Litho. *Perf. 13½x14*

2237 A485 65t Sheet of 4, #a.-d. 10.00 10.00

1996 Summer Olympic Games, Atlanta A486

30t, Cycling. 60t, Women's shooting. 80t, Weight lifting. 100t, Boxing. 120t, Women's archery, vert. 150t, Rhythmic gymnastics, vert. 200t, Hurdles, vert. 350t, Equestrian. 400t, Wrestling.
500t, Basketball. 600t, Judo.

1996 Litho. *Perf. 14*

2238 A486 30t multicolored .20 .20
2239 A486 60t multicolored .20 .20
2240 A486 80t multicolored .30 .20
2241 A486 100t multicolored .30 .20
2242 A486 120t multicolored .30 .20
2243 A486 150t multicolored .40 .25
2244 A486 200t multicolored .50 .30
2245 A486 350t multicolored 1.00 .70
2246 A486 400t multicolored 1.10 .80
Nos. 2238-2246 (9) 4.30 3.05

Souvenir Sheets

2246A	A486	500t multicolored	4.00	3.00
2246B	A486	600t multicolored	4.00	4.00

No. 2246A contains one 37x53mm stamp, No. 2246B one 52x39mm stamp.
Olymphilex '96 (#2246A-2246B).

Mongolian postal authorities have declared as "unauthorized" two sheets of nine 350t Train stamps similar to Nos. 2442-2443, two souvenir sheets of one 2000t Train stamps similar to Nos. 2444-2445, and one sheet of six 300t Ferrari stamps similar to No. 2446.

Genghis Khan — A486a

Die Cut Perf. 7½

1996, Aug. 28 **Embossed**

Self-Adhesive

2246C A486a 10,000t gold *60.00 60.00*

CAPEX '96 — A487

Designs: a, 350t, #2. b, 400t, Canada #1.

1996 **Litho.** ***Perf. 12½***

2247 A487 Sheet of 2, #a.-b. 8.00 8.00

No. 2247b is 40x30mm. No. 2247 exists with blue at upper right margin corner and different colored margin picture of CN Tower.

Nos. 2176-2179, 2181 Overprinted

1996, Sept. 8 **Litho.** ***Perf. 14***

2247C	A469	600t On #2176	2.50	2.50
2247D	A469	600t On #2177	2.50	2.50
2247E	A470	600t On #2178	2.50	2.50
2247F	A470	600t On #2179	2.50	2.50
		Nos. 2247C-2247F (4)	10.00	10.00

Souvenir Sheet

2247G A469 600t On No. 2181 4.00 4.00

Mongolian National Democratic and Social Democratic Parties A487a

1996, Sept. 25 **Litho.** ***Perf. 13¾***

2247H A487a 100t multicolored .60 .50

Souvenir Sheet

Taipei '96 — A487b

1996, Oct. 21 **Litho.** ***Perf. 12¾***

2247I	A487b	750t multicolored	5.00	5.00
r.		Overprinted "Taipei 2005" in margin in silver	5.00	5.00

No. 2247Ir issued 8/19/2005.

Children & Scouting Emblem — A487c

1996, Dec. 16 **Litho.** ***Perf. 14***

Country Flags

2247J	A487c	250t Mongolia	1.75	1.75
2247K	A487c	250t US	1.75	1.75
2247L	A487c	250t Germany	1.75	1.75
2247M	A487c	250t Russia	1.75	1.75
2247N	A487c	250t Japan	1.75	1.75
2247O	A487c	250t PRC	1.75	1.75
q.		Souvenir sheet, #2247J-2247O	15.00	15.00
		Nos. 2247J-2247O (6)	10.50	10.50

Souvenir Sheet

Perf. 12¾x12¾

2247P A487c 700t No flag 5.00 5.00

UNICEF (#2247P).

New Year 1997 (Year of the Ox) A488

1997 **Litho.** ***Perf. 14***

2248	A488	300t Ox, vert.	1.25	1.00
2249	A488	350t shown	1.50	1.25

Souvenir Sheet

Total Solar Eclipse Over Mongolia, Mar. 9, 1997 — A489

1997 **Litho.** ***Perf. 12½***

2250 A489 1000t Map of Mongolia 5.00 4.75

Return of Hong Kong to China A490

Designs: 200t, Former Chinese Pres. Deng Xioaping, Queen Elizabeth II. 250t, Chinese Pres. Jiang Zemin and Chief Executive of the Special Administrative Region of Hong Kong, Tung Chee-hwa.

1997 **Litho.** ***Perf. 13½***

2251	A490	200t multicolored	1.00	1.00
2252	A490	250t multicolored	1.50	1.50
a.		Pair, #2251-2252	2.50	2.50

Seven Joys — A491

Designs: a, Wheel. b, Gem. c, Minister. d, Queen. e, Elephant. f, Horse. g, General.

1997 **Litho.** ***Perf. 11***

2253 A491 200t Sheet of 7, #a.-g., + 2 labels 6.00 6.00

Souvenir Sheet

Moscow '97 — A492

1997 ***Perf. 12½x11½***

2254	A492	1000t No. 264	5.00	5.00
a.		With Irkutsk 2007 emblem and inscirption added in sheet margin ('07)	1.75	1.75

No. 2254a issued 6/8/2007.

Monument to the Politically Repressed A493

1997 ***Perf. 13x13½***

2255 A493 150t black & gray .95 .60

Trains A493a

Designs: 20t, VL-80 electric locomotive. 40t, Japanese high speed electric train. 120t, BL-80 Diesel locomotive. 200t, German steam locomotive. 300t, Lass "FDp" steam locomotive. 350t, 0-6-0 tank locomotive. 400t, Diesel locomotive. 500t, T6-106 Diesel locomotive. 600t, Magnetic train.

No. 2255K, "Rocket." No. 2255L, London-Paris train.

1997, Dec. 5 **Litho.** ***Perf. 14x14¼***

2255A	A493a	20t multi	.20	.20
2255B	A493a	40t multi	.20	.20
2255C	A493a	120t multi	.50	.50
2255D	A493a	200t multi	.85	.85
2255E	A493a	300t multi	1.25	1.25
2255F	A493a	350t multi	1.50	1.50
2255G	A493a	400t multi	1.75	1.75
2255H	A493a	500t multi	2.10	2.10
2255I	A493a	600t multi	2.50	2.50
j.		Sheet of 9, #2255A-2255I	11.00	11.00
		Nos. 2255A-2255I (9)	10.85	10.85

Souvenir Sheets

Perf. 11¼

2255K	A493a	800t multi	4.50	4.50
2255L	A493a	800t multi	4.50	4.50

Nos. 2255K, 2255L each contain one 59x43mm stamp.

Emperors of Mongolia A494

a, Genghis Khan. b, Ogadai Khan. c, Guyuk Khan. d, Mangu Khan. e, Kublai Khan.

Perf. 11½x12½

1997, Dec. 25 **Litho.**

2256 A494 1000t Strip of 5, #a.-e. 20.00 20.00

Nos. 2256a-2256e exist in souvenir sheets containing 1 or 2 21x33mm stamps.

New Year 1998 (Year of the Tiger) A495

Various stylized tigers.

1998, Feb. 1 ***Perf. 12***

2257	A495	150t multicolored	1.00	1.00
2258	A495	200t multicolored	1.50	1.50
2259	A495	300t multicolored	2.00	2.00
		Nos. 2257-2259 (3)	4.50	4.50

Design on No. 2259 is oriented point down.

Mongolian Yaks
A496

Various yaks: 20t, Three. 30t, One white. 50t, With carts. 100t, One male. 150t, Female with calf. 200t, Three, campsite. 300t, One with horns, flowing hair. 400t, Brown yak looking back.
800t, Carrying children and supplies.

1998, Mar. 15 Litho. *Perf. 12*

2260 A496 20t multicolored .20 .20
2261 A496 30t multicolored .20 .20
2262 A496 50t multicolored .25 .25
2263 A496 100t multicolored .35 .35
2264 A496 150t multicolored .55 .55
2265 A496 200t multicolored .75 .75

Size: 50x36mm

2266 A496 300t multicolored 1.10 1.10
2267 A496 400t multicolored 1.50 1.50
Nos. 2260-2267 (8) 4.90 4.90

Souvenir Sheet

Perf. 11

2268 A496 800t multicolored 5.50 5.50

No. 2268 contains one 60x47mm stamp.

Butterflies and Orchids — A497

Designs: 100t, Adonis blue, dendrobium cunninghamii. 150t, Brown hairstreak, oncidium ampliatum. 200t, Large skipper, maxillaria triloris. 250t, Orange tip, calypso bulbosa. 300t, Painted lady, catasetum pileatum. 350t, Purple hairstreak, epidedrum fimbratum. 400t, Red admiral, cleistes rosea. 450t, Small copper, ponthieva maculata. 500t, Small tortoiseshell, cypripeium calceolus.
Each 800t: No. 2278, Red admiral, c. macranthum. No. 2279, Adonis blue, c. guttatum.

1997, Dec. 5 Litho. *Perf. 14*

2269-2277 A497 Set of 9 6.00 6.00

Souvenir Sheets

2278-2279 A497 Set of 2 9.00 9.00

Souvenir Sheet

1998 World Cup Soccer Championships, France — A498

1998, June 1 *Perf. 13*

2280 A498 1000t multicolored 5.50 5.50

Souvenir Sheet

Pres. Natsagyn Bagabandi — A499

1998, July 15 Litho. *Perf. 12½*

2281 A499 1000t multicolored 4.50 4.50

Greenpeace, 26th Anniv. — A500

Designs: 200t, Penguin in snow. 400t, Six penguins, water, mountain. 500t, Two penguins at water's edge. 800t, Large group of penguins.
No. 2286: a, like #2282. b. like #2283. c, like #2284. d, like #2285. e, like #2287.
1000t, Greenpeace ship.

1997, Sept. 15 Litho. *Perf. 13½*

2282-2285 A500 Set of 4 6.00 6.00
2286 A500 Sheet of 5, #a.-e. 6.00 6.00

Souvenir Sheet

2287 A500 1000t multicolored 6.00 6.00

Country name, denominations, "Greenpeace" in red on No. 2286. Nos. 2282-2287 exist imperf.

Diana, Princess of Wales (1961-97)
A501

Various portraits with bister background — #2288: a, 50t. b, 100t. c, 150t, d, 200t. e, 250t. f, 300t. g, 350t. h, 400t. i, 450t.
Various portraits with pale brown background — #2289a, 50t. b. 100t. c, 150t. d, 200t. e, 250t. f, 300t. g, 350t. h, 400t. i, 450t.
Each 1000t: No. 2290, Diana holding infant son. No. 2291, Diana wearing tiara. No. 2292, Diana in pink dress. No. 2293, Diana in white (Mother Teresa in margin).

1997, Dec. 15

Sheets of 9, #a-i

2288-2289 A501 Set of 2 12.00 12.00

Souvenir Sheets

2290-2293 A501 Set of 4 16.00 16.00

Nos. 2288-2289 exist imperf.

Genghis Khan's Soldiers
A502

Various soldiers in traditional attire, background color: 100t, tan. 150t, pale violet. 200t, green blue. 250t, green. 300t, gray. 350t, pink. 400t, blue. 600t, pale brown.
Army on the march — #2302: a, 600t, One standing, others on horses. b, 1000t, Leaders riding decorated horses. c, 600t, Two standing, leopards, others on horses.

1997, Dec. 20 *Perf. 12*

2294-2301 A502 Set of 8 8.50 8.50

Souvenir Sheet

2302 A502 Sheet of 3, #a.-c. 8.50 8.50

No. 2302b is 65x56mm.

No. 276 Surcharged

1996, Dec. 25 Photo. *Perf. 11½x12*

2302D A77 200t on 70m multicolored *10.00 5.00*

National Symbols — A503

1998, Jan. 1

2303 A503 300t Natl. flag, horiz. 1.00 .75
2304 A503 300t shown 1.00 .75

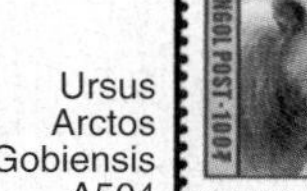

Ursus Arctos Gobiensis
A504

100t, Adult looking forward. 150t, Adult walking left. 200t, Two bears. 250t, Mother, cubs.

1998, July 20

2305-2308 A504 Set of 4 7.00 7.00
2307a Sheet of 2, #2305, 2307 3.00 3.00
2308a Sheet of 2, #2306, 2308 4.00 4.00

Fish
A505

Designs: 20t, Lebistes reticulatus. 30t, Goldfish. 50t, Balistes conspicillum. 100t, Goldfish, diff. 150t, Synchirops splendidus. 200t, Auratus. 300t, Xiphophorus helleri. 400t, Pygoplites diacanthus. 600t, Chaetodon auriga.
Various fish, denomination (800t): No. 2318, At top. No. 2319, At bottom.

1998, July 20 *Perf. 12½*

2309-2317 A505 Set of 9 6.00 6.00

Souvenir Sheets

Perf. 11

2318-2319 A505 Set of 2 12.00 12.00

Nos. 2318-2319 each contain one 95x49mm stamp.

Domestic Cats
A506

Designs: 50t, Red Persian. 100t, Manx cat. 150t, Smoke Persian. 200t, Long-haired white Persian. 250t, Silver tabby. 300t, Siamese.
1000t, Kittens, basket.

1998, Sept. 1 *Perf. 12*

2320-2325 A506 Set of 6 5.00 5.00

Souvenir Sheet

2326 A506 1000t multicolored 5.00 5.00

Jerry Garcia (1942-95) and The Grateful Dead
A507

Nos. 2327-2328, Various portraits of Jerry Garcia.
No. 2328A — Black and white photos: f, 100t. g, 150t. h, 50t.
No. 2328B — Blue guitar: i, 150t. j, 200t. k, 100t.
No. 2328C — Red guitar: l, 200t. m, 250t. n, 150t.
No. 2328D — White guitar: o, 200t. p, 250t. q, 150t.
No. 2328E — Dark background: r, 300t. s, 350t. t, 250t.
No. 2329: Various portraits of Garcia: a, 50t. b, 100t. c, 150t. d, 200t. e, 250t. f, 300t. g, 350t. h, 400t. i, 450t.
No. 2330: Various pictures of bears (Grateful Dead emblem) in sports activities: a, 50t, Dirt biking. b, 100t, Soccer. c, 150t, Basketball. d, 200t, Golf. e, 250t, Baseball. f, 300t, Roller blading. g, 350t, Ice hockey. h, 400t, Football. i, 450t, Skiing.
Each 1000t: No. 2331, Garcia holding guitar. No. 2331A, Garcia with left hand on guitar, right hand in air.

1998-99 *Perf. 12½*

2327 A507 100t multicolored .25 .25
2328 A507 200t multicolored .50 .50

Strips of 3

2328A-2328E A507 Set of 5 9.00 9.00

Sheets of 9, #a-i

2329-2330M A507 Set of 2 11.50 11.50

Souvenir Sheets

2331-2331A A507 Set of 2 5.00 5.00

Nos. 2327-2328 were each issued in sheets of 9. Nos. 2331-2331A contain one 51x76mm.
Dot of "I" in Garcia is a diamond on Nos. 2327-2329, 2331-2331A. "Jerry Garcia" is in pink letters with rose shadowing on Nos. 2328A-2328E.
Issued: No. 2331A, 1/1/99; #2328A-2328E, 1999; others 10/15/98.
See Nos. 2385-2389.

Bob Marley (1947-81) A508

Portraits: 200t, Up close. 1000t, At microphone.

1998, Oct. 15
2332 A508 200t multicolored .50 .50

Souvenir Sheet

2333 A508 1000t multicolored 2.50 2.50

No. 2332 was issued in sheets of 9. No. 2333 contains one 51x76mm stamp.

Carlos Santana A509

1998, Oct. 15
2334 A509 200t multicolored .50 .50

No. 2334 was issued in sheets of 9.

The Three Stooges — A510

Scenes from "The Three Stooges" motion pictures — #2335: a, 50t, Guns, cigars. b, 100t, Road signs. c, 150t, Dynamite. d, 200t, Golf clubs. e, 240t, Medals on uniform. f, 300t, Dove. g, 350t, Flower bouquets. h, 400t, Bright green cap. i. 450t, Whisk broom, cigar.

No. 2336: a, 50t, Doctor's equipment. b, 100t, Musical instruments. c, 150t, Clothes press. d, 200t, Long cord. e, 250t, Vise. f, 300t, Brick wall. g, 350t, Pliers. h, 400t, Turkey. i, 450t, Door.

No. 2337: a, 50t, Union soldiers. b, 100t, French Foreign Legion. c, 150t, Confederate soldiers, women. d, 200t, Horse. e, 250t, Army uniform, grenade. f, 300t, Cannon. g, 350t, Confederate soldiers, whiskey flask. 400t, Army uniforms, officer. 450t, Scarecrow.

Each 800t: No. 2338, like #2335b. No. 2339, like #2336c, vert. No. 2340, With football.

1998, Nov. 25 Litho. *Perf. 13½*

Sheets of 9, #a-i.

2335-2337 A510 Set of 3 22.50 22.50

Souvenir Sheets

2338-2340 A510 Set of 3 9.00 9.00

Nos. 2335-2340 exist imperf. Nos. 2338-2340 each contain one 51x41mm stamp.

Eight Offerings of Buddha — A511

#2341, The White Sign of Luck. #2342, The Auspicious Wheel. #2343, The Auspicious Cup. #2344, The White Couch. #2345, The White Umbrella. #2346, The Duaz of Victory. #2347, The White Lotus. #2348, The Auspicious Fish.

1998, Dec. 10 Litho. *Perf. 12*
2341-2348 A511 200t Set of 8 5.00 5.00

Howdy Doody Television Show — A512

No. 2349: a, 50t, Chief Thunderthud. b, 100t, Princess Summerfall Winterspring. c, 150t, Howdy in Mexican outfit. d, 150t, Buffalo Bob in gray shirt, Howdy. e, 200t, Buffalo Bob in red and white shirt, Howdy. f, 250t, Howdy, Buffalo Bob rubbing noses. g, 450t, Howdy in military uniform. h, 250t, Clarabell the Clown. i, 450t, Howdy lying down.

Each 800t: No. 2350, Howdy. No. 2351, Buffalo Bob, Howdy, horiz. No. 2352, Howdy, Buffalo Bob.

Perf. 13½x14, 14x13½x14

1999, Apr. 1
2349 A512 Sheet of 9, #a.-i. 7.00 7.00

Souvenir Sheets

Perf. 14 (#2352)

2350-2352 A512 Set of 3 9.00 9.00

No. 2352 contains one 48x61mm stamp.

Prime Ministers of Mongolia — A513

a, T. Namnansuren. b, Badamdorj. c, D. Chagdarjav. d, D. Bodoo. e, S. Damdinbazar. f, B. Tserendorj. g, A. Amar. h, Ts. Jigjidjav. i, P. Genden. j, Kh. Ghoibalsan. k, Yu. Tsedenbal. l, J. Batmunkh. m, D. Sodnom. n, Sh. Gungaadorj. o, D. Byambasuren. p, P. Jasrai. q, M. Enkhsaikhan. r, Ts. Elbegdorj.

1998, Dec. 1 *Perf. 12*
2353 A513 200t Sheet of 18, #a.-r. 18.00 18.00

Natl. Wrestling Champions A514

Designs: a, D. Damdin. b, S. Batsuury. c, J. Munkhbat. d, H. Bayanmunkh. e, B. Tubdendorj. f, D. Tserentogtokh. g, B. Baterdne.

1998, Dec. 26 *Perf. 12½*
2354 A514 200t Sheet of 7, #a.-g. 7.00 7.00

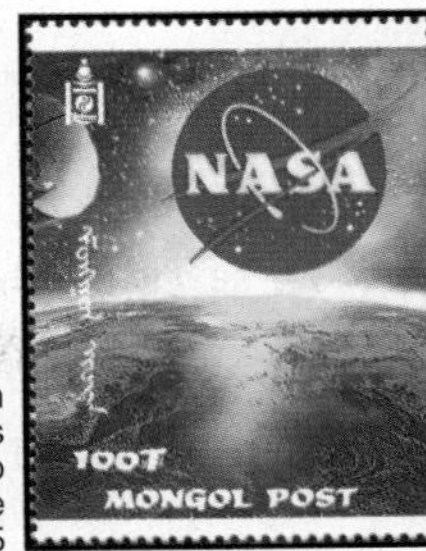
John Glenn's Return to Space A515

Mercury Friendship 7 — #2355: a, 50t, Mercury capsule in outer space. b, 100t, NASA emblem. c, 150t, Friendship 7 mission patch. d, 150t, Launch of Friendship 7. e, 200t, Glenn, 1962. f, 250th, Recovery of capsule. g, 450t, Moon. h, 250t, Capsule re-entering atmosphere. i, 450t, Stars.

Shuttle Discovery mission — #2356: a, 50t, NASA emblem. b, 100t, Glenn in red launch suit. c, 150t, Discovery mission patch. d, 150t, Launch of Discovery. e, 200t, Glenn, 1998. f, 250t, Discovery landing. g, 450t, Sun. h, 250t, Discovery in outer space. i, 450t, NASA "40" emblem.

1998, Dec. 31 *Perf. 14*

Sheets of 9

2355-2356 A515 #a.-i., each 9.00 9.00

Postal Delivery — A516

Post office: a, 100t, Brown. b, 200t, Blue. c, 200t, Blue green. d, 400t, Red lilac. e, 400t, Violet.

Electronic services: f, 100t, Blue. g, 200t, Blue green. h, 200t, Red lilac. i, 400t, Violet. j, 400t, Brown.

EMS delivery: k, 100t, Blue green. l, 200t, Red lilac. m, 200t, Violet. n, 400t, Brown. o, 400t, Blue.

Mail train: p, 100t, Red lilac. q, 200t, Violet. r, 200t, Brown. s, 400t, Blue. t, 400t, Blue green.

Jet plane: u, 100t, Violet. v, 200t, Brown. w, 200t, Blue. x, 400t, Blue green. y, 400t, Red lilac.

1998, Nov. 15 *Perf. 12*
2357 A516 Sheet of 25, #a.-y. 25.00 25.00

Universal Declaration of Human Rights, 50th Anniv. — A517

1998, Dec. 25 Litho. *Perf. 12*
2358 A517 450t multi + label 3.50 3.50

New Year 1999 (Year of the Rabbit) A518

1999, Feb. 17
2359 A518 250t Rabbit, vert. 2.00 2.00
2360 A518 300t shown 2.00 2.00

Buddha Migjed Jankraisig, Ulan Bator A519

Designs: 200t, Temple.

Each 1000t: No. 2363, Statue. No. 2364, Statue, drawing of Temple.

1999, Apr. 15
2361 A519 200t multicolored 1.00 1.00
2362 A519 400t multicolored 2.00 2.00

Souvenir Sheets

Perf. 11

2363-2364 A519 Set of 2 8.00 8.00

Nos. 2363-2364 each contain one 49x106mm stamp.

Falcons — A520

Falcon: a, 300t, Subbuteo. b, 250t, Naumanni. c, 200t, Tinnunculus. d, 170t, Peregrinus. e, 800t, Rusticolus by nest. f, 600t, Rusticolus in flight. g, 400t, Pelegrinoides over kill. h, 350t, Pelegrinoides on branch. i, 150t, Columbarius. j, 100t, Vespertinus. k, 50t, Cherrug. l, 30t, Amurensis.

1999, Mar. 20 *Perf. 12*
2365 A520 Sheet of 12, #a.-l. 12.00 12.00

"I Love Lucy" Television Show — A521

Various scenes — #2366: a, 50t. b, 100t. c, 150t. d, 150t. e, 200t. f, 250t. g, 450t. h, 250t. i, 450t.

Each 800t: No. 2367, Lucy talking with woman. No. 2368, Ethel looking at Lucy locked in cold storage locker.

1999, July 15 Litho. *Perf. 13½x14*
2366 A521 250t Sheet of 9, #a.-i. 7.00 7.00

Souvenir Sheets

2367-2368 A521 Set of 2 6.00 6.00

Nos. 2367-2368 each contain one 38x51mm stamp.

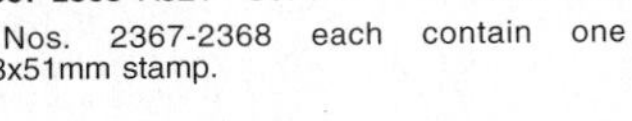

Betty Boop Cartoon Character A522

Various pictures of Betty Boop — #2369: a, 50t. b, 100t. c, 150t. d, 150t. e, 200t. f, 250t. g, 450t. h, 250t. i, 450t.
Each 800t: No. 2370, Betty in dog's eyes, horiz. No. 2371, Up close, horiz.

1999, July 15
2369 A522 Sheet of 9, #a.-i. 7.00 7.00

Souvenir Sheets
Perf. 14x13½
2370-2371 A522 Set of 2 6.00 6.00

Nos. 2370-2371 each contain one 51x38mm stamp.

Folk Tales A523

Designs: 50t, Man, yurt, two demons. 150t, Chess players. 200t, Lion carrying logs. 250t, Flying horse. 300t, Archer, bird, sun. 450t, Horses, cranes.
1000t, Birds, camel in flight.

1999, June 15 Litho. *Perf. 13x13¼*
2372-2377 A523 Set of 6 7.50 7.50

Souvenir Sheet
Perf. 12½
2378 A523 1000t multicolored 7.50 7.50

No. 2378 contains one 41x32mm stamp.

No. 307 Surcharged

Methods and Perfs as Before
1999, June 15
2378A A84 810t on 60m bl & multi *20.00 20.00*

Miniature Sheet

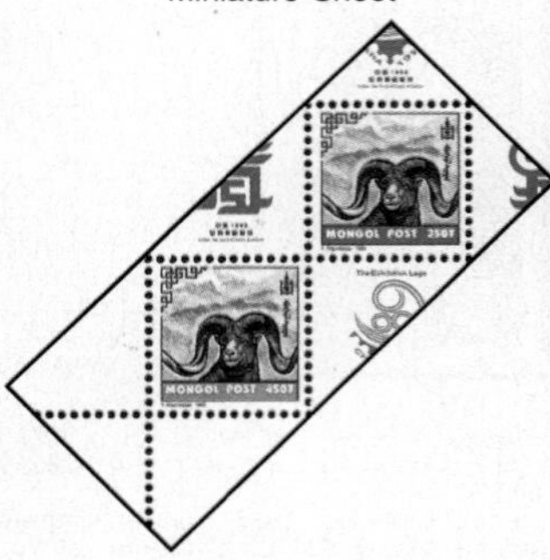

Ram — A524

Panel color: a, 250t, Blue. b, 450t, Red.

1999, Aug. 21 Litho. *Perf. 12½*
2379 A524 Miniature sheet of 2, #a.-b. 2.00 2.00

China 1999 World Philatelic Exhibition. No. 2379 is cut from a larger sheet of alternating stamps and labels. The cutting is through the labels along the diagonal axes.

UPU, 125th Anniv. — A525

Designs: No. 2380, Rider, two horses. No. 2381, Rider, one horse. No. 2382, Train and truck. No. 2382, Airplane and computer.
800t, Ogodei Khan (1186-1241).

1999, Oct. 9
2380-2383 A525 250t Set of 4 4.00 4.00

Souvenir Sheet
2384 A525 800t multi 4.50 4.50

No. 2384 contains one 31x41mm stamp.

Nos. 551, 1742 Surcharged

Methods and Perfs. as Before
1999, Aug. 25
2384A A133 250t on 50m multi 10.00 10.00
2384B A389 250t on 60m multi 10.00 10.00

Victory in Khalkh-gol War, 60th anniv.

Genghis Khan A525a

Die Cut Perf. 11½
1999, Sept. 27 Embossed
Self-Adhesive
2384C A525a 15,000t gold & sil 60.00 —

Jerry Garcia Type of 1998

No. 2385 — Rose and blue speckled background: a, 50t. b, 100t. c, 150t.
No. 2386 — Pink-toned vignette extension backgrounds: a, 100t. b, 150t. c, 200t.
No. 2387 — Pink, blue and purple curved line backgrounds: a, 150t. b, 200t. c, 250t.
No. 2388 — Dark blue and purple straight line backgrounds: a, 150t. b, 200t. c, 250t.
No. 2389 — Blue green and green backgrounds: a, 250t. b, 300t. c, 350t.

1999 Litho. *Perf. 12½*
"Jerry Garcia" In Black-Shadowed Letters
2385-2389 A507 Set of 5 strips of 3 9.00 9.00

Stone Carvings A526

Designs: 50t, Stele with Uigur inscriptions, vert. 150t, Turtle, 13th cent. 200t, Kul Tegin burial site, 7th-8th cent., vert. 250t, Kul Tegin, 8th cent., vert. 300t, Dragon, 8th-9th cent. 450t, Man, 5th-7th cent., vert.

2000, Jan. 17 Litho. *Perf. 12*
2390-2395 A526 Set of 6 5.00 5.00

A527

World Teachers' Day — A528

Academicians: #2396, 2398, Dr. Tsendiin Damdinsuren (1908-86). #2397, 2399, Dr. B. Rinchin (1905-77).

1999, Dec. 5
2396 A527 250t blue & blk .50 .50
2397 A527 250t grn & blk .50 .50
2398 A527 450t pur & blk .85 .85
2399 A527 450t brn & blk .85 .85
2400 A528 600t multi 1.10 1.10
Nos. 2396-2400 (5) 3.80 3.80

Souvenir Sheet

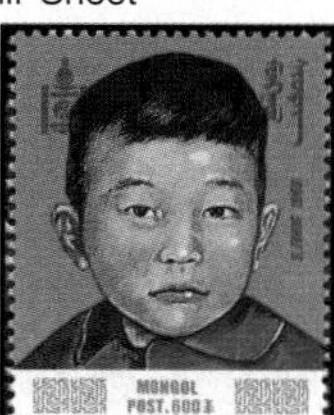

Sanjaasuregin Zorig (1962-98), Politician — A529

Designs: a, 600t, Zorig in 1968. b, 1000t, Three people, flag. c, 600t, Zorig in 1998.

1999, Oct. 1 *Perf. 13¼x13*
2401 A529 Sheet of 3, #a.-c. 6.00 6.00

Size of No. 2401b: 59x39mm.

World Intellectual Property Organization, 20th Anniv. — A529a

No. 2401D: e, 250t, Satellite, airplane. f, 450t, Statue, television. g, 250t, Cauldron, toy. h, 250t, Copier, stamps. i, 450t, Camera, yurt, Mongolian couple. j, 250t, Red automobile. k, 250t, Grille of antique auto, bottles, cellular phones, wristwatch. l, 450t, Perfume bottles. m, 250t, Pack of cigarettes, soccer ball, volley ball, basketball, bottle of motor oil, boom box.

1999, Dec. 24 Litho. *Perf. 12*
2401D A529a Sheet of 9, #e-m 8.00 8.00

Souvenir Sheet

Japan-Mongolia Friendship — A530

a, Sumo wrestler. b, Symbols of countries.

1999, Dec. 28 *Perf. 13½*
2402 A530 450t Sheet of 2, #a.-b. 4.50 4.50

New Year 2000 (Year of the Dragon) — A531

Background color: 250t, Red. 450t, Blue, vert.

2000, Jan. 10 Litho. *Perf. 12*
2403-2404 A531 Set of 2 4.00 4.00

Nos. 715-717, C34 Surcharged

Methods and Perfs as Before
2000, Jan. 19
2405 A168 1000t on 50m brn 7.00 7.00
2406 A168 2000t on 60m grn 8.00 8.00
2407 A168 5000t on 1t rose claret 15.00 15.00
2408 AP12 10,000t on 1.50t bl 30.00 30.00
Nos. 2405-2408 (4) 60.00 60.00

Wolves — A532

Designs: 150t, Pair, one with snout up. 250t, Eating deer. 300t, Nursing young. 450t, Snarling.

2000, Jan. 17 Litho. *Perf. 12*
2409-2412 A532 Set of 4 4.00 4.00

Souvenir Sheet
2413 A532 800t Pair baying 4.00 4.00

No. 2413 contains one 50x30mm stamp.

Sheep — A533

Breeds: 50t, Sumber. 100t, Orkhon. 150t, Baidrag. 250t, Barga. 400t, Uzemchin. 450t, Bayad.

2000, Jan. 20

2414-2419	A533	Set of 6	4.00	4.00

Souvenir Sheet

2420	A533	800t Govi-Altai	4.00	4.00

One Day of Mongolia, by Balduugiin Sharav — A534

Various parts of painting: a, 50t. b, 100t, c, 150t. d, 200t. e, 250t. f, 300t. g, 350t. h, 450t. i, 600t.

2000, Jan. 24

2421	A534	Sheet of 9, #a-i	9.00	9.00

Huts and Yurts A535

Designs: 50t, Hunters returning to hut. 100t, Mother, daughter, animals near hut. 150t, Yurt near hill. 250t, Two yurts, motorcycle, and satellite dish. 450t, Yurt construction.

No. 2427, 800t, Yurt's furnishings. No. 2428, 800t, Yurt and wagon.

2000, Jan. 25

2422-2426	A535	Set of 5	4.00	4.00

Souvenir Sheets

2427-2428	A535	Set of 2	8.00	8.00

Union of Mongolian Production and Service Cooperatives, 10th Anniv. — A536

Panel colors: 300t, Blue. 450t, Green.

2000, Mar. 27 *Perf. 12*

2429-2430	A536	Set of 2	4.00	4.00

A537

A538

A539

A540

A541

A542

A543

Costumes of Mongolian Lords — A544

2000, May 11 *Perf. 13¼*

2431	A537	550t multi	1.50	1.00
2432	A538	550t multi	1.50	1.00
2433	A539	550t multi	1.50	1.00
2434	A540	550t multi	1.50	1.00
2435	A541	550t multi	1.50	1.00
2436	A542	550t multi	1.50	1.00
2437	A543	550t multi	1.50	1.00
2438	A544	550t multi	1.50	1.00
		Nos. 2431-2438 (8)	12.00	8.00

Buddhas A545

No. 2439: a, Jigjid. b, Gombo. c, Tsamba. d, Jamsran. e, Baldanlkham. f, Ochirvani. g, Namsrai. h, Gongor. i, Damdinchoijoo. j, Shalshi.

2000, July 1 *Perf. 13x13½*

2439		Block of 10	15.00	11.00
a.-j.	A545	550t Any single	1.50	1.10

Worldwide Fund for Nature (WWF) — A546

Two Przewalski's horses: No. 2440a, 300t, No. 2441a, 100t, Standing apart. No. 2440b, 150t, No. 2441b, 250t, Galloping. No. 2440c, 100t, No. 2441d, 200t, Grazing. No. 2440d, 200t, No. 2441c, 50t, Standing together.

2000, July 5 **Litho.** *Perf. 13½*

2440	A546	Block or strip of 4, #a-d	4.50	4.50

Litho. & Holography

Size: 50x35mm

2441	A546	Block of 4, #a-d	5.50	5.50

Illustrations on No. 2441 are mirror images of those on No. 2440.

Trains — A547

No. 2442: a, 200t, Guaari-Current electric locomotive, France. b, 400t, 2-10-0 Austerity, Great Britain. c, 300t, ALG Bo-Bo electric locomotive, Great Britain. d, 400t, Diesel-electric locomotive, Australia. e, 300t, E-10 Bo-Bo electric locomotive, Germany. f, 200t, C38 Class Pacific, US. g, 300t, 46 Class electric locomotive, US. h, 200t, Bo-Bo electric locomotive, New Zealand. i, 400t, Bo-Bo electric locomotive, Netherlands.

No. 2443: a, 300t, Italian second-clas carriage. b, 400t, Bodmin & Wadebridge Railway composite carriage. c, 200t, Stephenson 2-2-2, Russia. d, 200t, 2-2-2 Walt, US. e, 300t, The General, US. f, 400t, 4-4-0 Washington, US. g, 400t, Braithwaite 0-4-0, Great Britain. h, 200t, Ross Winans Muddigger locomotive, US. i, 300t, 4-4-0 Ramapo, US.

No. 2444, 800t, The Ringmaster, US. No. 2445, 800t, Deltic electric locomotive, Great Britain.

2000, July 7 **Litho.** *Perf. 14*

Sheets of 9, #a-i

2442-2443	A547	Set of 2	14.00	14.00

Souvenir Sheets

2444-2445	A547	Set of 2	8.00	8.00

Ferrari Race Cars — A548

No. 2446: a, 1975 312 T. b, 1961 156 F1. c, 1979 312 T4. d, 1964 158 F1. e, 1981 126 CK. f, 1974 312 B3.

2000, July 15

2446	A548	350t Sheet of 6, #a-f	18.00	18.00

2000 Summer Olympics, Sydney A549

Designs: 100t, Boxing. 200t, Wrestling. 300t, Judo. 400t, Shooting.

2000, July 21 *Perf. 13x13¼*

2447-2450	A549	Set of 4	4.00	4.00

Albert Einstein (1879-1955) — A550

Einstein: a, 100t, At blackboard. b, 300t, Wearing hat. c, 200t, Wearing green sweater. d, 200t, With violin. e, 550t, Close-up. f, 100t, At lectern. g, 100t, Holding pipe. h, 400t, Receiving award. i, 300t, Holding clock.

2000, Aug. 10 *Perf. 12½*

2451	A550	Sheet of 9, #a-i	7.50	7.50

I Love Lucy — A551

No. 2452, vert.: a, 100t, Lucy, wiping hands, and Ethel. b, 400t, Lucy, reading letter, and Ethel. c, 200t, Lucy, setting table, and Fred. d, 200t, Lucy on telephone. e, 300t, Lucy with chin on fist. f, 100t, Lucy with head on hands. g, 100t, Lucy and Ethel waving. h, 550t, Lucy, holding bowl, and Ethel. i, 300t, Lucy, wearing brown sweater and holding jar, and Ethel.

No. 2453, 800t, Lucy, with mouth open, holding jar, and Ethel. No. 2454, 800t, Lucy. wearing stole, and Ethel.

2000, Aug. 15 Litho. ***Perf. 12½***

2452 A551 Sheet of 9, #a-i 7.00 7.00

Souvenir Sheets

2453-2454 A551 Set of 2 3.00 3.00

The Three Stooges — A552

No. 2455, horiz.: a, 100t, Moe, Larry and woman. b, 400t, Moe, Shemp and Larry attempting jail escape. c, 300t, Moe, with blow torch, Shemp and Larry. d, 200t, Moe, Larry and Joe Besser with musical instruments. e, 300t, Man knocking together heads of Shemp, Larry and Moe. f, 100t, Man with hammer, Moe, Larry and Shemp. g, 100t, Larry, Joe Besser and Moe in kitchen. h, 550t, Moe, Shemp and Larry with large wrench. i, 200t, Larry, Moe and Shemp in kitchen.

No. 2456, 800t, Moe, with fingers in ears, and Shemp. No. 2457, 800t, Shemp and Larry in army uniforms.

2000, Aug. 17

2455 A552 Sheet of 9, #a-i 7.00 7.30

Souvenir Sheets

2456-2457 A552 Set of 2 3.00 3.00

20th Century Events in Mongolia — A553

No. 2458: a, Independence, 1911. b, National revolution, 1921. c, Declaration of Mongolian People's Republic, 1924. d, Political repression, 1937. e, War years, 1939-45. f, Voting for independence, 1945. g, Agricultural reform, 1959. h, Member of UN, 1961. i, Space flight, 1981. j, Democratic revolution, 1990.

2000, Sept. 13 Litho. ***Perf. 13½x13***

2458 A553 300t Sheet of 10, #a-j + 2 labels 8.00 8.00

See No. 2482.

Marmota Sidisica — A554

Number of marmots: 100t, One. 200t, Three. 300t, Two. 400t, Three, diff.

2000, Sept. 15 ***Perf. 13¼x13***

2459-2462 A554 Set of 4 6.00 6.00

Souvenir Sheet

Perf. 13x13¼

2463 A554 800t One marmot, horiz. 5.50 5.50

Traditional Patterns A555

Various designs: 50t, 200t, 250t, 300t, 400t, 550t.

50t, 250t, 550t are horiz.

Perf. 13¼x13, 13x13¼

2000, Sept. 20

2464-2469 A555 Set of 6 10.00 10.00

John F. Kennedy, Jr. (1960-99) — A556

2000, Sept. 25 ***Perf. 14***

2470 A556 300t multi 1.50 1.50

Printed in sheets of 6.

Millennium — A557

Exploration: a, 100t, Charles Darwin. b, 200t, Mollusk. c, 300t, HMS Beagle. d, 400t, Peacock. e, 400t, Dinosaur. f, 100t, Clematis. g, 200t, Orchid. h, 300t, Giant tortoise. i, 200t, Reduviid bug. j, 100t, Down House. k, 300t, Duck. l, 550t, The Origin of Species. m, 100t, Chimpanzee. n, 300t, Turkey. o, 550t, Horse. p, 600t, Ram (60x40mm). q, Vormela peregusna.

2000, Oct. 5 ***Perf. 12¾x12½***

2471 A557 Sheet of 17, #a-q + label 18.00 18.00

State Symbols — A558

No. 2472: a, Headdress on spike. b, Horn. c, Bow, arrows and quiver. d, Robe. e, Crossed swords. f, Saddle. g, Belt. h, Seated man. i, Throne.

2000, Oct. 25 Litho. ***Perf. 12***

2472 A558 300t Sheet of 9, #a-i 15.00 15.00

Queens — A559

No. 2473: a, Oulen. b, Borteujin. c, Turakana. d, Caymish. e, Chinbay.

2000, Oct. 30

2473 Horiz. strip of 5 7.50 7.50

a.-e. A559 300t Any single 1.50 1.50

Trains — A560

No. 2474: a, 200t, TGV, France. b, 100t, X200, Sweden. c, 300t, Regio Runner, Netherlands. d, 100t, Deltic, Great Britain. e, 300t, Type M1200, Burma. f, 200t, ICE, Germany. g, 300t, G Class, Australia. h, 200t, Class E444, Italy. i, 100t, GM F7 Warbonnet, US.

No. 2475: a, 200t, Class 18 4-6-2, Germany. b, 100t, Class GS-4 4-8-4, US. c, 300t, Class 25 4-8-4, South Africa. d, 100t, Class 685 2-6-2, Italy. e, 300t, Class HP, India. f, 200t, Class SY 2-8-2, China. g, 300t, Liner A3 Pacific, Great Britain. h, 200t, Class 231C 4-6-2, France. i, 100t, Class 3700, Netherlands.

No. 2476, 800t, Rocket 0-2-2, Great Britain. No. 2477, 800t, Eurostar, France and Great Britain, vert.

2000, Nov. 25 ***Perf. 14***

Sheets of 9, #a-i

2474-2475 A560 Set of 2 13.50 13.50

Souvenir Sheets

2476-2477 A560 Set of 2 9.00 9.00

Nos. 2474-2475 each contain nine 42x28mm stamps.

Endangered Animals of Gobi Desert — A561

No. 2478: a, 100t, Scarabaeus typhon (40x30mm). b, 400t, Ursus arctos gobiensis (40x40mm). c, 300t, Camelus bactrianus ferus (40x40mm). d, 300t, Saiga tatarica mongolica (40x40mm). e, 550t, Ovis ammon (40x40mm). f, 550t, Uncia uncia (40x40mm). g, 100t, Phrynosephalus helioscopus(40x30mm). h, 200t, Coliber spinalus (40x30mm). i, 200t, Euchoreutes paso (40x30mm). j, 300t, Chlamydotis undulata (40x40mm).

2000, Dec. 25 ***Perf. 12½***

2478 A561 Sheet of 10, #a-j 15.00 15.00

Souvenir Sheet

Advent of New Millennium — A562

Litho. & Embossed with Foil Application

2001, Jan. 1 ***Perf. 13½***

2479 A562 5000t multi 15.00 15.00

New Year 2001 (Year of the Snake) — A563

Color behind snake: 300t, Pink. 400t, green, vert.

2001, Jan. 15 Litho. ***Perf. 13¼***

2480-2481 A563 Set of 2 4.00 4.00

20th Century Events Type of 2000

World events: a, First World War, 1914. b, October Revolution, 1917. c, Power seized by Fascists, 1933. d, Second World War, 1939. e, Nuclear weapons, 1945. f, Establishment of the United Nations, 1945. g, End of colonialism, 1940. h, Space travel, 1961. i, Downfall of socialism, 1989. j, Establishment of Mongolia, 1911.

2001, Mar. 15 ***Perf. 13½x13***

2482 A553 300t Sheet of 10, #a-j, + 2 labels 8.00 8.00

Armed Forces, 80th Anniv. — A564

Designs: No. 2483, 300t, Marshal G. Demid (blue green). No. 2484, 300t, Marshal J.

Lhagvasuren (dark green). No. 2485, 300t, L. Dandar (olive green).

2001, Mar. 18 ***Perf. 13¾x13¼***
2483-2485 A564 Set of 3 3.00 3.00

Souvenir Sheet

Mountaineers — A565

No. 2486: a, Mountaineer waving. b, Mountaineers starting climb.

2001, Apr. 1 ***Perf. 13¼x13***
2486 A565 400t Sheet of 2, #a-b 4.00 4.00

I Love Lucy — A566

No. 2487, horiz.: a, 100t, Lucy drinking from cup, Ricky reading newspaper. b, 400t, Ricky and Fred. c, 300t, Lucy, Ethel and two candy factory workers. d, 200t, Lucy with arms outstretched, candy factory worker. e, 300t, Lucy looking at candy factory worker. f, 100t, Lucy smearing chocolate on worker's face. g, 100t, Worker smearing Lucy's face with chocolate. h, 550t, Ricky holding stocking, Fred. i, 200t, Ethel and Lucy.

No. 2488, 800t, Lucy wrapping chocolates. No. 2489, 800t, Fred and Ricky preparing dinner.

2001, Apr. 15 ***Perf. 12½***
2487 A566 Sheet of 9, #a-i 7.00 7.00

Souvenir Sheets

2488-2489 A566 Set of 2 3.00 3.00

The Three Stooges — A567

No. 2490: a, 100t, Larry. b, 400t, Larry and Shemp inserting instrument into man's mouth. c, 300t, Moe and Shemp. d, 200t, Moe, Larry and Shemp on telephones. e, 300t, Moe with chef's toque, Shemp, Larry. f, 100t, Moe looking in tube. g, 100t, Moe hitting Larry, Shemp. h, 550t, Shemp, Larry, Moe and woman. i, 200t, Moe with gavel, Curly on telephone.

No. 2491, 800t, Shemp and Larry as shown on #2490e. No. 2492, 800t, Shemp as angel, vert.

2001, Apr. 15
2490 A567 Sheet of 9, #a-i 7.00 7.00

Souvenir Sheets

2491-2492 A567 Set of 2 3.00 3.00

Philatelic Exhibitions — A568

Nomading, by T.S. Minjuur and exhibition emblem of: a, Hong Kong 2001. b, Hafnia 01. c, Phila Nippon '01. d, Belgica 2001.

2001, May 15 ***Perf. 13½***
2493 A568 400t Sheet of 4, #a-d 6.00 6.00

Souvenir Sheet

Expo 2001, Kitakyushu, Japan — A569

No. 2494: a, Roses from Gobi Dream, by Shosaku Tasaki (52x24mm). b, Dreamer from Gobi Dream, vert. (32x42mm). c, Tarbosaurus (48x25mm). d, Iguanodon, vert. (30x41mm). e, Triceratops (48x25mm).

Serpentine Die Cut 10¾, 12¼ (#2494c-2494e)

2001, July 1

Self-Adhesive

2494 A569 500t Sheet of 5, #a-e 9.00 9.00

Children and Sports — A570

No. 2495: a, Chess. b, Bicycling. c, Baseball.

No. 2496: a, 200t, Mongolian children on horses. b, 350t, Ice hockey. c, 500t, Flag, Mongolian boy on horse. d, 150t, Children playing soccer. e, 300t, Mongolian girl on horse. f, 450t, Boy playing soccer. g, 100t, Mongolian children on horses. h, 250t, Golf. i, 400t, Mongolian children on horses.

2001, Sept. 1 ***Perf. 12½***
2495 A570 500t Horiz. strip of 3, #a-c 4.00 4.00
2496 A570 Sheet of 9, #a-i 12.00 12.00

Scouting and Nature — A571

No. 2497: a, 100t, Salpingotus. b, 200t, Uncia uncia. c, 300t, Haliaeetus albicilla. d, 400t, Pandion haliatus. e, 450t, Panciawus colchicus.

No. 2498: a, 50t, Butterfly. b, 100t, Bat. c, 200t, Butterfly, diff. d, 300t, Mushrooms. e, 400t, Dinosaur. f, 450t, Puffin.

No. 2499, vert.: a, 150t, Sea shell. b, 300t, Owl. c, 450t, Sea turtle. d, 100t, Frog. e, 250t, Butterfly. f, 400t, Orchid. g, 50t, Penguins. h, 200t, Elephant. i, 350t, Whale.

2001, Sept. 1
2497 A571 Sheet of 5, #a-e, + label 5.00 5.00
2498 A571 Sheet of 6, #a-f 5.00 5.00
2499 A571 Sheet of 9, #a-i 7.50 7.50

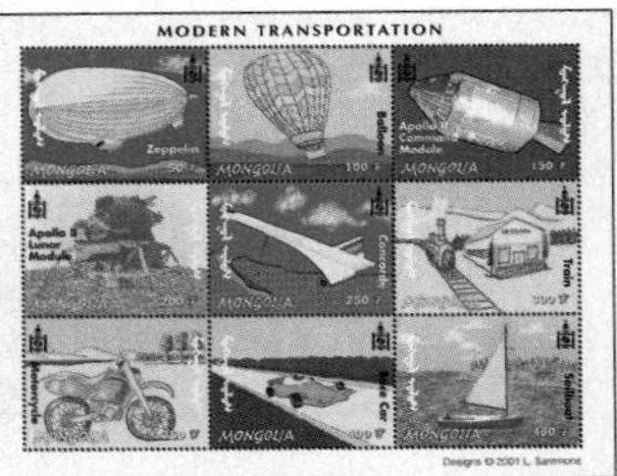

Modern Transportation — A572

No. 2500: a, 50t, Zeppelin. b, 100t, Balloon. c, 150t, Apollo 11 command module. d, 200t, Apollo Lunar Module. e, 250t, Concorde. f, 300t, Train. g, 350t, Motorcycle. h, 400t, Race car. i, 450t, Sailboat.

2001, Sept. 15
2500 A572 Sheet of 9, #a-i 7.50 7.50

Admission to United Nations, 40th Anniv. — A573

No. 2501: a, Dove, map. b, UN and Mongolian flags.

2001, Oct. 27 ***Perf. 13***
2501 A573 400t Horiz. pair, #a-b 3.00 3.00

Year of Dialogue Among Civilizations A574

2001, Dec. 20 ***Perf. 13¼x13***
2502 A574 300t multi 2.50 2.50

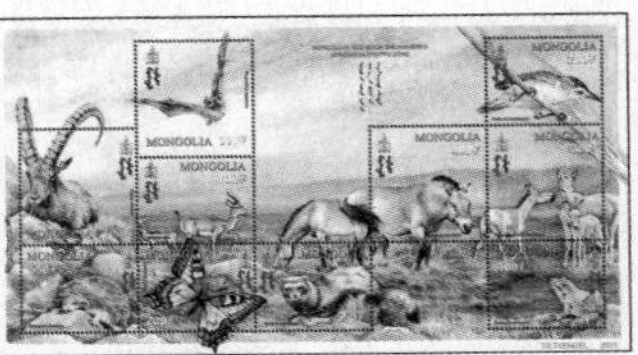

Endangered Species in Steppe Zone — A575

No. 2503: a, 300t, Vespertilio superans (40x40mm). b, 200t, Podoces hendersoni (40x30mm). c, 300t, Capra sibirica (40x40mm). d, 100t, Gazella subgutturosa (40x30mm). e, 400t, Equus przewalskii (40x40mm). f, 300t, Equus hemionus hemionus (40x40mm). g, 550t, Erinaceus dauricus (40x30mm). h, 200t, Papilio machaon (40x30mm). i, 550t, Vormela peregusna (40x30mm). j, 100t, Rana chensinensis (40x30mm).

2001, Dec. 30 ***Perf. 13½x13¼***
2503 A575 Sheet of 10, #a-j 10.00 10.00

History of Humanity — A576

Prominent features of stamps: a, Leaning Tower of Pisa, Romulus and Remus suckling she-wolf. b, Eagle, warrior with shield. c, Great Wall of China. d, Mosque, warrior on horseback. e, Celtic cross, castle, warrior with shield. f, Mona Lisa, by Leonardo da Vinci, David, by Michelangelo, other sculptures and religious paintings. g, Mask, Easter Island statues, boomerang, native, hut. h, Sir Isaac Newton, telescope, planets, Nicolaus Copernicus. i, Eiffel tower, Napoleon bonaparte on horseback, French flag, Arc de Triomphe. j, Astronaut, Earth, DNA molecule, computer. k, Greek soldier and amphora. l, Taj Mahal, Asoka pillar. m, Statue of Buddha. n, Genghis Khan. o, Yurt, Buddhist statue. p, Jesus Christ, Madonna and Child. q, Globe, ship, Christopher Columbus. r, Statue of Liberty, U.S. Capitol, Indian chief, U.S. flag, George Washington, city skyline. s, Printing press, man on horseback, letters of alphabet. t, Tower Bridge, British flag, Penny Black.

2001, Dec. 30 ***Perf. 13¼***
2504 Sheet of 20 20.00 20.00
a.-j. A576 200t Any single 1.00 1.00
k.-t. A576 300t Any single 1.00 1.00

New Year 2002 (Year of the Horse) A577

Mane color: 300t, Gray, vert. 400t, Yellow brown.

2002, Feb. 13 ***Perf. 13¼x13, 13x13¼***
2505-2506 A577 Set of 2 4.00 4.00

Birds of Prey — A578

Designs: 100t, Gyps himalayensis. 150t, Gyps fulvus. 300t, Neophron percnopterus. 400t, Aegypius monachus. 550t, Gypaetus barbatus.

2002, Apr. 1 ***Perf. 12½***
2507-2511 A578 Set of 5 5.00 5.00

Souvenir Sheets

Mongolia - Japan Diplomatic Relations, 30th Anniv. — A579

No. 2512, 550t: a, Camel. b, Przewalski's horse.

No. 2513, 550t, vert. (38x50mm): a, Rider on horseback. b, Face of cartoon character.

2002, Apr. 27 ***Perf. 12***
2512-2513 A579 Set of 2 8.00 8.00

Dogs A580

Dogs with: 100t, Sheep. 200t, Cattle. 300t, Camel and yurt. 400t, Camels. 800t, Dog.

2002, May 1 ***Perf. 13¼x13***

2514-2517 A580 Set of 4 4.00 4.00

Souvenir Sheet

2518 A580 800t multi 3.50 3.50

2002 World Cup Soccer Championships, Japan and Korea — A581

No. 2519: a, 300t, Stadium, Seoul. b, 400t, 1998 French team and flag, World Cup trophy. c, 400t, 1966 English team and flag, Jules Rimet Cup. d, 300t, Stadium, Yokohama.

2002, May 31 ***Perf. 12***

2519 A581 Sheet of 4, #a-d 4.50 4.50

Flowers — A582

Designs: 100t, Thermopsis. No. 2521, 150t, Chelidonium. No. 2522, 150t, Hypencum. 200t, Plantago. 250t, Saussurea. 300t, Rosa acicularis. 450t, Lilium.

2002, June 15 Litho. ***Perf. 12***

2520-2526 A582 Set of 7 7.00 7.00

Rock Paintings — A583

Various paintings with background colors of: 50t, Pink. 100t, Beige. 150t, Greenish blue. 200t, Green. 300t, Blue. 400t, Blue. 800t, Dark blue.

2002, July 1

2527-2532 A583 Set of 6 6.00 6.00

Souvenir Sheet

2533 A583 800t multi 3.50 3.50

New Year 2003 (Year of the Sheep) — A584

Sheep with background colors of: 300t, Yellow. 400t, Green, horiz.

2003, Jan. 1

2534-2535 A584 Set of 2 4.00 4.00

Mushrooms and Birds A585

Designs: 50t, Russula aeruginosa, Coccothraustes coccothraustes. 100t, Boletus edulis, Loxia curvirostra. 150t, Boletus badius, Carpodacus erythrinus. 200t, Agaricus campester, Garrulus glandarius. 250t, Marasmius onreades, Luscinia megarhynchos. 300t, Cantharellus cibarius, Locustella certhiola. 400t, Amanita phalloides, Ardea cinerea. 550t, Suillus granulatus, Accipter gentilis.

No. 2544, 800t, Lactarius tormmosus, Aeqithalos caudatus. No. 2545, 800t, Tricholoma pertentosum, Lanius collurio.

2003, Feb. 1 ***Perf. 13¼x13***

2536-2543 A585 Set of 8 12.00 12.00

Souvenir Sheets

2544-2545 A585 Set of 2 12.00 12.00

Nos. 2544-2545 each contain one 60x40mm stamp.

Visit Mongolia — A586

No. 2546: a, 100t, Statue of Sukhe Bator. b, 200t, City buildings. c, 300t, Rock formation. d, 400t, Yurts.

No. 2547: a, 100t, Camels. b, 200t, Yaks. c, 300t, Hunter with eagle. d, 400t, Snow leopard.

2003, July 11 ***Perf. 12***

Sheets of 4, #a-d

2546-2547 A586 Set of 2 8.00 8.00

Endangered Species in Khangai Zone — A587

No. 2548: a, 300t, Pandion haliaetus (40x30mm). b, 200t, Dryomys nitedula (40x30mm) c, 300t, Rangifer tarandus (40x40mm). d, 100t, Moschus moschiferus (40x40mm). e, 550t, Alces alces pfizenmayeri (40x40mm). f, 400t, Alces alces cameloides (40x40mm). g, 300t, Sus scrofa nigripes (40x40mm). h, 550t, Phasianus colchicus (40x30mm). i, 200t, Lutra lutra (40x30mm). j, 100t, Castor fiber birulai (40x30mm).

2003, Aug. 15 ***Perf. 13½***

2548 A587 Sheet of 10, #a-j 10.00 10.00

Birds, Butterflies, Orchids and Mushrooms — A588

No. 2549, 800t — Birds: a, Common bush tanager. b, Black-headed hemispingus. c, Scarlet-rumped tanager. d, Band-tailed seedeater.

No. 2550, 800t — Butterflies: a, Thecla teresina. b, Theritas cypria. c, Theritas coronata. d, Thecla phaleros.

No. 2551, 800t — Orchids: a, Vanda rothschildiana. b, Paphiopedium parishii. c, Dendrobium nobile. d, Cattleya loddigesii.

No. 2552, 800t — Mushrooms: a, Hypholoma fasciculare. b, Marasmiellus ramealis. c, Collybia fusipes. d, Kuehneromyces mutabilis.

No. 2553, 2500t, Andean hillstar. No. 2554, 2500t, Thecla pedusa. No. 2555, 2500t, Barkeria skinnerii. No. 2556, 2500t, Psathyrella multipedata, vert.

Perf. 13¼x13½, 13½x13¼

2003, Dec. 10

Sheets of 4, #a-d

2549-2552 A588 Set of 4 20.00 20.00

Souvenir Sheets

2553-2556 A588 Set of 4 16.00 16.00

Souvenir Sheet

Yang Liwei, First Chinese Astronaut — A589

2003, Dec. 25 Litho. ***Perf. 12***

2557 A589 800t multi 4.00 4.00

New Year 2004 (Year of the Monkey) — A590

Monkey and background in: 300t, Blue. 400t, Red.

2004, Feb. 21

2558-2559 A590 Set of 2 4.00 4.00

Peace Mandala — A591

No. 2560: a, 50t, Tushita Heaven. b, 100t, Elephant and Lady Maya. c, 150t, Birth of Buddha. d, 200t, Buddha as prince of Shakya clan. e, 250t, Prince shaving off hair. f, 300t, Buddha beating the devil. g, 400t, Buddha preaching for first time. h, 550t, Great Nirvana Sutra. i, 5000t, Various scenes in Buddha's life.

No. 2561, Central details of No. 2560i.

Size of Nos. 2560a-2560h, 41x38mm; No. 2560i, 132x182mm.

Serpentine Die Cut 10, 6¾ (#2560i, 2561)

2004, June 3 Litho.

Self-Adhesive

2560 A591 Sheet of 9, #a-i 18.00 18.00

Souvenir Sheet

Litho. With Foil Application

2561 A591 5000t gold & brn 20.00 20.00

Mammals — A592

Designs: (100t), Equus przewalskii. (300t), Camelus bactrianus ferus. (400t), Ovis ammon. (550t), Capra sibirica.

2004, July 1 Litho. ***Perf. 13¼x13***

2562 A592 (100t) multi .50 .50

2563 A592 (300t) multi .75 .75

2564 A592 (400t) multi 1.25 1.25

2565 A592 (550t) multi 1.50 1.50

Nos. 2562-2565 (4) 4.00 4.00

Genghis Khan (c. 1162-1227) — A593

Various depictions of Genghis Khan: 200t, 300t, 350t, 550t. 300t is horiz.

2004, July 11 ***Perf. 13***

2566-2569 A593 Set of 4 4.00 4.00

Unification of Mongolia, 800th anniv. (in 2006).

2004 Summer Olympics, Athens — A594

Designs: 100t, Judo. 200t, Wrestling, horiz. 300t, Boxing. 400t, Pistol shooting, horiz.

2004, Aug. 13 *Perf. 12*
2570-2573 A594 Set of 4 4.00 4.00

UPU, 130th Anniv. — A595

2004, Sept. 15 *Perf. 12¾*
2574 A595 300t multi 1.50 1.50

Nos. 776, 778, 841, 842 Surcharged

Methods and Perfs as Before

2004, Oct. 5
2575 A191 550t on 10m #841 — —
2576 A191 550t on 20m #842 — —
2577 A178 550t on 30m #776 — —
2578 A178 550t on 60m #778 — —

A596

A597

A598

Soccer A599

Designs: No. 2581, Goalie making save. No. 2582, Player kicking ball. No. 2583, Three players. No. 2584, Player and goalie.

2004, Oct. 15 Litho. *Perf. 12¾x13*
2579 A596 50t multi .25 .25
2580 A597 50t multi .25 .25
2581 A597 100t multi .40 .40
2582 A597 100t multi .40 .40
2583 A597 150t multi .55 .55
2584 A597 150t multi .55 .55
2585 A598 200t multi .80 .80
2586 A599 200t multi .80 .80
Nos. 2579-2586 (8) 4.00 4.00

Souvenir Sheet

First Mongolian Stamp, 80th Anniv. — A600

2004, Dec. 4 *Perf. 13¼x13*
2587 A600 800t multi 3.50 3.50

Miniature Sheets

Insects and Flowers — A601

No. 2588: a, 100t, Mantis religiosa. b, 100t, Aster alpina. c, 200t, Echinops humilis. d, 200t, Apis mellifera. e, 300t, Angaraeris barabensis. f, 300t, Nymphaea candida.

No. 2589: a, 100t, Lytta caraganae. b, 100t, Rosa acicularis. c, 200t, Aguilegia sibirica. d, 200t, Tabanus bovinus. e, 300t, Corizus hyoscyami. f, 300t, Lilium pumilum.

2004, Dec. 25 *Perf. 13*
Sheets of 6, #a-f
2588-2589 A601 Set of 2 10.00 10.00

Women's Headdresses — A602

No. 2590: a, Kazakh headdress, denomination at left. b, Mongol headdress, denomination at right.

2004, Dec. 31 *Perf. 11½x11¾*
2590 A602 550t Horiz. pair, #a-b 5.00 5.00

See Kazakhstan No. 472.

New Year 2005 (Year of the Rooster) A603

Roosters with frame color of: 300t, Red violet. 400t, Blue, vert.

2005, Jan. 1 *Perf. 12*
2591-2592 A603 Set of 2 4.00 4.00

Souvenir Sheet

Expo 2005, Aichi, Japan — A604

No. 2593: a, 100t, Butterfly on flower. b, 150t, Flower. c, 200t, Puppy. d, 550t, Kitten.

2005, Mar. 25
2593 A604 Sheet of 4, #a-d 4.50 4.50

World Vision A605

2005, Apr. 1
2594 A605 550t multi 1.50 1.00

Native Costumes — A606

No. 2595, 200t — Blue frame: a, Man with white and blue costume. b, Woman with green and white costume.

No. 2596, 200t — Green frame: a, Man with stringed instrument. b, Woman with red costume.

No. 2597, 200t — Rose pink frame: a, Man with white and blue costume. b, Woman with green costume.

2005, June 20 *Perf. 13½x13*
Horiz. pairs, #a-b
2595-2597 A606 Set of 3 5.00 5.00

Maharanza A607

No. 2595 — Color of face: a, White. b, Blue. c, Red. d, Yellow brown.

2005, July 8 *Perf. 13x12¾*
2598 Horiz. strip of 4 4.00 4.00
a.-d. A607 400t Any single 1.00 1.00

Souvenir Sheet

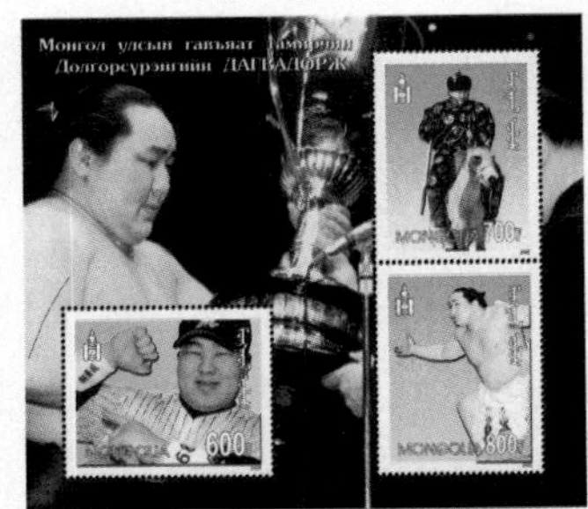

Asashorou, Sumo Wrestling Champion — A608

No. 2599 — Asashorou: a, 600t, Wearing baseball cap. b, 700t, On horse, vert. c, 800t, In wrestling loincloth, vert.

2005, July 18 *Perf. 13*
2599 A608 Sheet of 3, #a-c 5.00 5.00

World Vision A609

2005, Sept. 20 *Perf. 12*
2600 A609 550t multi 1.50 1.00

Headdresses A610

People wearing various headdresses: 50t, 100t, 150t, 200t, 250t, 300t.
800t, National headdress.

2005, Oct. 3 *Perf. 12¾x13*
2601-2606 A610 Set of 6 4.00 4.00

Souvenir Sheet
Perf. 12
2607 A610 800t multi 3.50 3.50

No. 2607 contains one 37x56mm stamp.

Souvenir Sheets

Shenzhou IV Space Flight — A611

No. 2608, 800t, Astronauts waving. No. 2609, 800t, Astronauts in spacecraft.

2005, Dec. 9 *Perf. 12*
2608-2609 A611 Set of 2 8.00 8.00

Souvenir Sheet

Coins of the Mongolian Empire — A612

No. 2610 — Various coins with background color of: a, Blue. b, Grayish lilac. c, Deep bister.

2006, Jan. 11 *Perf. 13x12¾*
2610 A612 550t Sheet of 3, #a-c 5.00 5.00

New Year 2006 (Year of the Dog) A613

Mongolian emblem and "Year of the Dog" at: 300t, Right. 400t, Left.

2006, Jan. 27 *Perf. 13x13¼*
2611-2612 A613 Set of 2 3.50 3.50

Miniature Sheet

Europa Stamps, 50th Anniv. — A614

No. 2613: a, Archer. b, Camels. c, Boys herding livestock. d, Goat. e, Rocks. f, Building spire. g, Dinosaur skeleton. h, Circus performers. i, Yurt. j, Two men in native costumes. k, Airplane. l, Ox.

2006, Feb. 1 ***Perf. 12½x13***

2613 A614 200t Sheet of 12, #a-l 8.00 8.00
- *m.* Souvenir sheet, #2613a-2613b, perf. 13 1.50 1.50
- *n.* Souvenir sheet, #2613c-2613d, perf. 13 1.50 1.50
- *o.* Souvenir sheet, #2613e-2613f, perf. 13 1.50 1.50
- *p.* Souvenir sheet, #2613g-2613h, perf. 13 1.50 1.50
- *q.* Souvenir sheet, #2613i-2613j, perf. 13 1.50 1.50
- *r.* Souvenir sheet, #2613k-2613l, perf. 13 1.50 1.50

World Vision — A615

No. 2614: a, Children riding ox. b, Child riding horse.

2006, May 5 **Litho.** ***Perf. 12***

2614 A615 550t Horiz. pair, #a-b 3.50 3.50

Souvenir Sheet

Morin Khuur — A616

2006, June 16

2615 A616 550t multi 2.00 2.00

Souvenir Sheet

Pres. Nambaryn Enkhbayar — A617

2006, June 21

2616 A617 800t multi 3.50 3.50

Souvenir Sheet

2006 World Cup Soccer Championships, Germany — A618

No. 2617 — Various stylized players: a, 200t. b, 250t. c, 300t. d, 400t.

2006, June 23

2617 A618 Sheet of 4, #a-d 5.00 5.00

Souvenir Sheet

State Visit of US Pres. George W. Bush — A619

2006, June 30 ***Perf. 13x13¼***

2618 A619 600t multi 3.00 3.00

Souvenir Sheets

A620

Famous Mongols — A621

No. 2619 — Various unnamed Mongols: a, 50t (23x33mm). b, 100t (23x33mm). c, 300t (23x33mm). d, 400t (23x33mm). e, 500t (80x56mm).

2006 ***Perf. 13, 11½ (#2619e)***

2619 A620 Sheet of 5, #a-e 6.00 6.00
- *f.* As #2619, with sheet margin overprinted in gold with Mongolian text 1.90 1.90

Perf. 11½x11¾

2620 A621 3800t shown 12.00 12.00

Mongolian stamps, 85th anniv. (#2619). Issued: No. 2619, 7/8; No. 2619f, 7/16/09. No. 2620, 9/19. Mongolian State, 800th anniv.

Souvenir Sheet

Horse Sculptures — A622

No. 2621: a, 300t, Horse and rider. b, 400t, Horse only.

2006, Sept. 28 ***Perf. 12***

2621 A622 Sheet of 2, #a-b 3.50 3.50

See India No. 2167.

Miniature Sheet

Friendly Exchange Philatelic Exhibition — A623

No. 2622: a, 150t, Olympic Stadium, Beijing. b, 200t, Waterfalls. c, 250t, City street at night.

2006, Oct. 25 **Litho.** ***Perf. 12***

2622 A623 Sheet of 3, #a-c 1.10 1.10

Hucho Taimen Fish — A624

No. 2623 — Various depictions of fish: a, 100t. b, 200t. c, 300t. d, 400t.

2006, Dec. 17

2623 A624 Block of 4, #a-d 1.75 1.75

New Year 2007 (Year of the Pig) — A625

Designs: 300t, Two pigs. 400t, Two pigs, diff.

2006, Dec. 17

2624-2625 A625 Set of 2 1.25 1.25

Dutch Royalty — A625a

No. 2625A: b, Prince Willem-Alexander. c, Prince Willem-Alexander and Princess Máxima. d, Princess Máxima.

2007, Jan. 7 ***Perf. 13¼x13½***

2625A Vert. strip of 3 3.75 3.75
- *b.-d.* A625a 700t Any single 1.25 1.25

Printed in sheets containing 2 each of Nos. 2625Ab-2625Ad.

Miniature Sheet

Marilyn Monroe (1926-62), Actress — A625b

No. 2625E — Monroe with: f, Background in orange in white, country name and denomination in orange. g, Background and denomination in orange, country name in white. h, Background in rose and white, country name and denomination in white. i, Background in claret, country name and denomination in white.

2007, Jan. 26

2625E A625b 1050t Sheet of 4, #f-i 7.25 7.25

Miniature Sheet

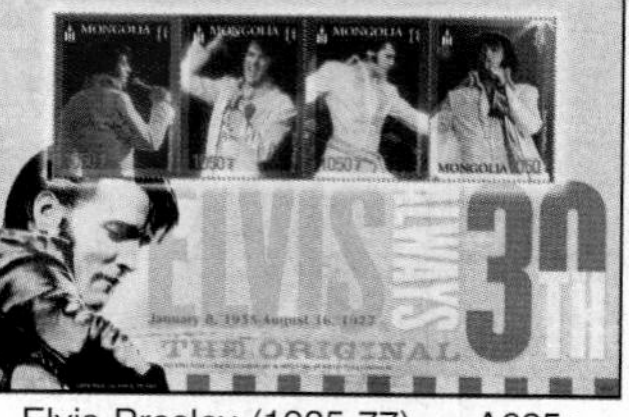

Elvis Presley (1935-77) — A625c

No. 2625J — Presley: k, Facing right, holding microphone. l, Facing forward, country name at top. m, Facing right, without microphone. n, Facing forward, country name at bottom.

2007, Jan. 26 ***Perf. 13¼***

2625J A625c 1050t Sheet of 4, #k-n 7.25 7.25

Betty Boop — A625d

No. 2625O — Betty Boop: p, Holding down dress in breeze. q, With both hands in air. r, With hands clasped. s, With one arm raised, parts of "B," "E," and "T" at top. t, Winking, with leg lifted. u, With one arm raised, parts of "B," "O," and "P" at top.

No. 2625V — Betty Boop lifting dress to expose garter: a, Without part of heart to left of "GO" in country name. b, With part of heart to left of "GO" in country name.

2007, Jan. 26 *Perf. 13¼x13½*

2625O A625d 700t Sheet of 6, #p-u 7.25 7.25

Souvenir Sheet

2625V A625d 1500t Sheet of 2, #w-x 5.25 5.25

Souvenir Sheet

Diplomatic Relations Between Mongolia and the United States, 20th Anniv. — A626

No. 2626: a, 400t, Statue of Genghis Khan, Ulan Bator. b, 550t, Statue of Abraham Lincoln, Washington, DC.

2007, Jan. 29 *Perf. 12*

2626 A626 Sheet of 2, #a-b 1.75 1.75

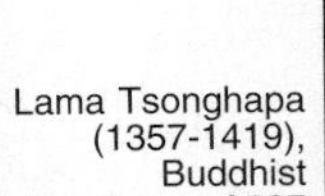
Lama Tsonghapa (1357-1419), Buddhist Teacher — A627

2007, Jan. 30 *Perf. 12¾*

2627 A627 100t multi .20 .20

Souvenir Sheet

Diplomatic Relations Between Mongolia and Japan, 35th Anniv. — A628

No. 2628: a, 550t, Mt. Fuji, Japan. 700t, Mt. Otgontenger, Mongolia.

2007, Feb. 23 *Perf. 12*

2628 A628 Sheet of 2, #a-b 2.25 2.25

Calligraphy A629

Designs: 50t, Light of wisdom. 100t, Butterfly. 150t, Flower. 200t, Horse. 250t, Spring. 300t, Leaves. 400t, Wow. 550t, Wild camel. 800t, Sky.

2007, Aug. 2 *Perf. 13x12¾*

2629-2636 A629 Set of 8 3.50 3.50

Souvenir Sheet

Perf. 12¾

2637 A629 800t multi 1.40 1.40

No. 2637 contains one 43x57mm stamp.

Souvenir Sheets

Modern Art — A630

Art by: No. 2638, 400t, Ts. Tsegmid. No. 2639, 400t, S. Sarantsatsralt. No. 2640, 400t, Ts. Enkhjin. No. 2641, 400t, Do. Bold, horiz. No. 2642, 400t, Sh. Chimeddorj, horiz.

2007, Aug. 21 *Perf. 13*

2638-2642 A630 Set of 5 3.50 3.50

Miniature Sheet

Naotoshi Yamada, Olympic Cheerleader, and Mongolian Sumo Wrestlers — A631

No. 2643 — Yamada and various wrestlers with Mongolian emblem and inscriptions at: a, 500t, Right. b, 500t, Left. c, 600t, Right. d, 600t, Left. e, 700t, Right. f, 700t, Left.

2007, Oct. 3 *Die Cut*

Self-Adhesive

2643 A631 Sheet of 6, #a-f, + 10 labels 6.25 6.25

Genghis Khan (c. 1162-1227) — A632

Perf. 12½x12¾

2007, Nov. 29 **Litho.**

2644 Horiz. strip of 5 5.50 5.50
- *a.* A632 230t black .40 .40
- *b.* A632 400t brown .40 .40
- *c.* A632 650t blue .40 .40
- *d.* A632 800t green .40 .40
- *e.* A632 1000t violet .40 .40

New Year 2008 (Year of the Rat) — A633

No. 2645 — Rat with denomination at: a, UR. b, LL.

2008, Jan. 1 *Perf. 12¾*

2645 A633 800t Vert. pair, #a-b 2.75 2.75

Wedding of Queen Elizabeth II and Prince Philip, 50th Anniv. — A634

No. 2646: a, Queen. b, Queen and Prince.

2008, Jan. 25 *Perf. 13¼*

2646 A634 400t Pair, #a-b 1.40 1.40

Printed in sheets of 6 containing 2 each of Nos. 2646a-2646b.

Princess Diana (1961-97) — A635

No. 2647, vert. — Princess Diana wearing: a, Necklace and black gown. b, Red hat and coat. c, Black and white dress. d, Black and white hat and jacket.

3000t, Prince Charles and Princess Diana.

2008, Jan. 25

2647 A635 1150t Sheet of 4, #a-d 8.00 8.00

Souvenir Sheet

2648 A635 3000t multi 5.25 5.25

First Helicopter Flight, Cent. — A636

No. 2649: a, Belvedere. b, AS 565 Dauphin/Panther. c, Explorer. d, Shark.

3000t, Scout.

2008, Jan. 25

2649 A636 1150t Sheet of 4, #a-d 8.00 8.00

Souvenir Sheet

2650 A636 3000t multi 5.25 5.25

Muhammad Ali, Boxer — A637

No. 2651, 1150t — Ali: a, Wearing shirt. b, Shadow-boxing. c, Punching bag. d, Punching at opponent.

No. 2652, 1150t, horiz. — Ali with: a, Black boxing gloves punching at opponent. b, Red boxing gloves with left arm extended. c, Red boxing gloves, ring rope in background. d, Red boxing gloves, lights and ring rope in background.

No. 2653, 3000t, Ali wearing robe. No. 2654, 3000t, Close-up photograph.

Perf. 13¼, 11½ (#2652)

2008, Jan. 25

Sheets of 4, #a-d

2651-2652 A637 Set of 2 16.00 16.00

Souvenir Sheets

2653-2654 A637 Set of 2 10.50 10.50

Pope John Paul II (1920-2005) — A637a

2008, Jan. 25 **Litho.** *Perf. 13½x13¼*

2654A A637a 880t multi 1.50 1.50

Miniature Sheet

Photomosaic of Pope Benedict XVI — A638

No. 2655 — Part of photomosaic with frame around it: a, At left and top in green. b, At left in green. c, At left in green and white. d, At left and bottom in white.

2008, Jan. 25 ***Perf. 13¼***
2655 A638 1150t Sheet of 4, #a-d 8.00 8.00

Nos. 1355 and 1359 Surcharged

Methods and Perfs As Before
2008, Feb. 29
2656 A301 1000t on 20m #1355 1.75 1.75
2657 A301 1000t on 60m #1359 1.75 1.75

No. 1983 Surcharged

Method and Perf. As Before
2008, Mar. 7
2658 A429 250t on 40m #1983 .45 .45

Campaign Against AIDS — A639

2008, Apr. 10 Litho. ***Perf. 12¾x13***
2659 A639 500t multi .85 .85

Handcrafted Items A640

Designs: No. 2660, 500t, Pipe and tobacco pouch (shown). No. 2661, 500t, Jar and cloth. No. 2662, 500t, Silver bowls. No. 2663, 500t, Sword and sheath. No. 2664, 500t, Saddle.

2008, June 8 ***Perf. 12¾***
2660-2664 A640 Set of 5 4.50 4.50

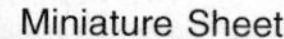
Miniature Sheet

2008 Summer Olympics, Beijing — A641

No. 2665: a, Canoe-kayak. b, Fencing. c, Handball. d, Modern pentathlon.

2008, July 8 ***Perf. 12¾x12½***
2665 A641 600t Sheet of 4, #a-d 4.25 4.25

Wild Boars A642

No. 2666: a, Head of boar. b, Sow and piglets. c, Boar. d, Boar and sow.

2008, Sept. 10 ***Perf. 12½x12¾***
2666 Horiz. strip of 4 5.75 5.75
a.-d. A642 800t Any single 1.40 1.40

New Year 2009 (Year of the Ox) A643

Ox with background color of: 200t, Yellow. 300t, Blue.

2009, Jan. 19 ***Perf. 12***
2667-2668 A643 Set of 2 .75 .75

National Coat of Arms — A644

Great White Banner — A645

National Flag — A646

Soyombo A647

2009, Jan. 28 Litho.
2669 Horiz. strip of 4 4.00 4.00
a. A644 400t multi .60 .60
b. A645 500t multi .75 .75
c. A646 800t multi 1.10 1.10
d. A647 1000t multi 1.50 1.50

No. 1307 Surcharged

Method and Perf. As Before
2009, Apr. 6
2670 A290 1000t on 20m #1307 1.40 1.40

People in Yurt A648

2009, Apr. 6 Litho. ***Perf. 13x12¾***
2671 A648 1000t multi 1.40 1.40

China 2009 World Stamp Exhibition, Luoyang — A649

No. 2672: a, Giant panda. b, Ursus arctos gobiensis.

2009, Apr. 10 ***Perf. 12¾x12½***
2672 A649 300t Pair, #a-b .85 .85

Printed in sheets of 14, 7 each Nos. 2672a-2672b, + 2 labels.

Peonies A650

2009, Apr. 23 ***Perf. 13½x13¼***
2673 A650 700t multi 1.00 1.00

Printed in sheets of 6.

Earrings From Korea, 5th-6th Cent. A651

Earrings From Mongolia, 18th-19th Cent. A652

Earring From Kazakhstan, 2nd-1st Cent. B.C. — A653

2009, June 12 ***Perf. 12***
2674 Horiz. strip of 3 3.50 3.50
a. A651 800t multi 1.10 1.10
b. A652 800t multi 1.10 1.10
c. A653 800t multi 1.10 1.10

See Kazakhstan No. 595, South Korea No. 2313.

Battles of Khalkhiin Gol, 70th Anniv. — A654

2009, Aug. 20 ***Perf. 13x12½***
2675 A654 500t lil & pur .70 .70

Souvenir Sheet

Taras — A655

No. 2676: a, White Tara. b, Green Tara.

2009, Oct. 9 ***Perf. 12***
2676 A655 800t Sheet of 2, #a-b 2.25 2.25

Diplomatic Relations Between Mongolia and People's Republic of China, 60th Anniv. — A656

No. 2677 — Buildings with frame and denomination in: a, Blue. b, Red.

2009, Oct. 9 ***Perf. 12¾***
2677 Horiz. pair with central label 3.00 3.00
a.-b. A656 1000t Either single 1.50 1.50

APU Company, 85th Anniv. — A657

2009, Dec. 1 ***Perf. 12¾x13***
2678 A657 800t multi 1.10 1.10

Camel Polo
A658

2010, Jan. 26 Litho. *Perf. 11½*
2679 A658 1000t multi 1.40 1.40

A659

A660

A661

A662

A663

A664

Secrets of the Mongols — A665

Designs: No. 2686, Black banner. No. 2687, Five arrows.

2010, Feb. 5 *Perf. 13x12¾*
2680 A659 1000t multi 1.40 1.40
2681 A660 1000t multi 1.40 1.40
2682 A661 1000t multi 1.40 1.40
2683 A662 1000t multi 1.40 1.40
2684 A663 1000t multi 1.40 1.40
2685 A664 1000t multi 1.40 1.40
Nos. 2680-2685 (6) 8.40 8.40

Souvenir Sheets
Perf. 12
2686 A665 1500t pur & multi 2.10 2.10
2687 A665 1500t grn & multi 2.10 2.10

New Year 2010 (Year of the Tiger) — A666

No. 2688 — Tiger with background color of: a, Green. b, Blue.

2010, Feb. 14 *Perf. 12*
2688 A666 1000t Vert. pair, #a-b 3.00 3.00

Children
A667

Children with stringed instruments and: 800t, Horse. 1000t, Camel.

2010, Apr. 20 *Perf. 13½*
2689-2690 A667 Set of 2 2.75 2.75

Mountains — A668

No. 2691: a, Sutai Khairkhan. b, Altan Khokhii. c, Khan Khokhii. d, Suvarga Khairkhan.
No. 2692: a, Burkhan Khaldun. b, Bogd Khairkhan. c, Dariganga, Dari Ovoo. d, Otgontenger.

2010 Litho. *Perf. 13¼*
2691 A668 500t Block or horiz. strip of 4, #a-d 3.00 3.00
Perf. 12
2692 A668 500t Block of 4, #a-d 3.00 3.00

Issued: No. 2691, 5/27; No. 2692, 6/15.

Flag of Mongolia
A669

2010, June 15 *Perf. 13*
2693 A669 800t multi 1.25 1.25

2010 World Cup Soccer Championships, South Africa — A670

No. 2694: a, Emblem. b, Mascot.

2010, July 11 *Perf. 13¼x13*
2694 A670 800t Horiz. pair, #a-b, + central label 2.40 2.40

Souvenir Sheet

Chingunjav (1710-57), Leader of Rebellion Against Manchus — A671

2010, Aug. 27 *Perf. 12¼x12*
2695 A671 800t multi 1.25 1.25

Souvenir Sheet

Pres. Tsakhia Elbegdorj — A672

2010, Oct. 22 *Perf. 12½x13*
2696 A672 500t multi .80 .80

SEMI-POSTAL STAMPS

Catalogue values for unused stamps in this section are for Never Hinged items.

Vietnamese Mother and Child — SP1

1967, Dec. 22 Photo. *Perf. 12x11½*
B1 SP1 30m + 20m multi .60 .30
B2 SP1 50m + 30m multi .60 .30

Solidarity with Vietnam.

Save Venice Type of Regular Issue
Souvenir Sheet

Departure of St. Ursula, by Carpaccio.

1972, Oct. 1 Litho. *Perf. 12*
B3 A163 3t + 1t multi 4.00 4.00

Save Venice Campaign. No. B3 contains one horizontal stamp.

Girl Feeding Lambs
SP2

UNICEF Emblem and: 20m+5m, Boy playing flute and dancing girl. 30m+5m, Girl chasing butterflies. 40m+5m, Girl with ribbon. 60m+5m, Girl with flowers. 80m+5m, Girl carrying bucket. 1t+5m, Boy going to school.

1977, June 1 Litho. *Perf. 12*
B4 SP2 10m + 5m multi .25 .20
B5 SP2 20m + 5m multi .25 .20
B6 SP2 30m + 5m multi .35 .20
B7 SP2 40m + 5m multi .50 .30
B8 SP2 60m + 5m multi .75 .35
B9 SP2 80m + 5m multi .85 .55
B10 SP2 1t + 5m multi 1.10 .70
Nos. B4-B10 (7) 4.05 2.50

Surtax was for Mongolian Children's Village. See No. CB1.

Boys on Horseback — SP3

Children and IYC Emblem: 30m+5m, Raising chickens. 50m+5m, With deer. 60m+5m, With flowers. 70m+5m, Planting tree. 80m+5m, Studying space project. 1t+5m, Dancing. 4t+50m, Girl on horseback.

1979, Jan. 10
B11 SP3 10m + 5m multi .30 .20
B12 SP3 30m + 5m multi .30 .20
B13 SP3 50m + 5m multi .45 .20
B14 SP3 60m + 5m multi .50 .25
B15 SP3 70m + 5m multi .65 .35
B16 SP3 80m + 5m multi .80 .40
B17 SP3 1t + 5m multi 1.10 .65
Nos. B11-B17 (7) 4.10 2.25

Souvenir Sheet
B18 SP3 4t + 50m multi 4.00 4.00

International Year of the Child. Compare with Type A301.

1998 Winter Olympic Games, Nagano — SP4

1998 Litho. *Perf. 12*
B19 SP4 150t +15t Speed skating .60 .60
B20 SP4 200t +20t Ski jumping .90 .90
B21 SP4 300t +30t Snowboarding 1.30 1.30
B22 SP4 600t +60t Freestyle skiing 2.75 2.75
Nos. B19-B22 (4) 5.55 5.55

Ulan Bator, 360th Anniv. — SP5

Designs, 300t +30t each: No. B23, Flags and arms. No. B24, Seated man. No. B25, Arms.
No. B26, Various views of Ulan Bator.

1999 Litho. *Perf. 12½*
B23-B25 SP5 Set of 3 3.00 3.00

Sheet of 9

Perf. 12½x12¼

B26 SP5 200t +20t #a.-i. 8.00 8.00

No. B26 contains nine 45x27mm stamps.

Unity Against Terrorism — SP6

World Trade Center, Statue of Liberty, American flag and country name in: 300t+50t, Red. 400t+50t, Blue.

Perf. 13½x13¼

2001, Nov. 11 Litho.
B27-B28 SP6 Set of 2 3.00 3.00

AIR POST STAMPS

Catalogue values for unused stamps in this section are for Never Hinged items.

Postal Modernization Type of Regular Issue

Designs: 10m, 20m, Postman with horses. 25m, Postman with reindeer. 30m, 50m, Plane over map of Mongolia. 1t, Post horn and flag of Mongolia.

1961, June 5 Photo. *Perf. 15*

C1	A72	10m multicolored	.30	.20
C2	A72	50m multicolored	.60	.20
C3	A72	1t multicolored	1.10	.40
		Nos. C1-C3 (3)	2.00	.80

Souvenir Sheet

Perf. 11

C4		Sheet of 4	4.00	4.00
a.		A72 20m lt blue grn & multi	1.00	1.00
b.		A72 25m light blue & multi	1.00	1.00
c.		A72 30m light green & multi	1.00	1.00
d.		A72 1t rose carmine & multi	1.00	1.00

40th anniversary of independence; postal modernization. No. C4b is not inscribed Airmail.

Souvenir Sheet

Austria Type SP55, Austrian and Mongolian Stamps Circling Globe — AP1

1965, May 1 Engr. *Perf. 11½*
C5 AP1 4t brown carmine 4.50 3.50

Vienna Intl. Philatelic Exhibition, WIPA, June 4-13. #C5 contains one 61x38mm stamp.

Weather Satellite AP2

Designs: 20m, Antarctic exploration. 30m, Space exploration.

1965, May 15 Photo. *Perf. 13½*

C6	AP2	15m lilac, gold & blk	.50	.20
C7	AP2	20m blue & multi	2.75	.60
C8	AP2	30m rose & multi	.65	.25
		Nos. C6-C8 (3)	3.90	1.05

International Quiet Sun Year, 1964-65.

ITU Emblem — AP3

Design: 4t, Communications satellite.

1965, Dec. 20 *Perf. 11½x12*

C9	AP3	30m blue & bister	1.00	.50
C10	AP3	50m red & bister	1.00	.50

Souvenir Sheet

Perf. 11, Imperf.

C11 AP3 4t gold, bl & blk 4.50 3.50

ITU, centenary. No. C11 contains one stamp, 38x51mm. Exists imperf. Values: unused $5.50; used $4.50.

Souvenir Sheet

Luna 10, Moon and Earth — AP4

1966, July 10 Photo. *Imperf.*
C12 AP4 4t multicolored 4.50 3.50

Luna 10 Russian moon mission, Apr. 3, 1966.

Souvenir Sheet

Astronaut and Landing Module — AP5

1969, Aug. 20 Litho. *Perf. 11½*
C13 AP5 4t ultra & multi 4.50 3.50

Apollo 11 US moon mission, first man landing on moon.

Souvenir Sheet

Apollo 16 — AP6

Perf. 12½x11½

1972, Apr. 16 Photo.
C14 AP6 4t multicolored 4.00 3.00

Apollo 16 moon mission, Apr. 15-27.

Souvenir Sheet

Mongolian Horse — AP7

1972, May 10 Photo. *Perf. 12½*
C15 AP7 4t multicolored 4.00 3.00

Centenary of the discovery of the Przewalski wild horse, bred in captivity in Berlin Zoo.

Telecommunication — AP8

Designs: 30m, Horse breeding. 40m, Train and plane. 50m, Corn and farm machinery. 60m, Red Cross ambulance and hospital. 80m, Actors. 1t, Factories.

1972, July 11 Litho. *Perf. 12*

C16	AP8	20m olive & multi	.40	.35
C17	AP8	30m violet & multi	.40	.35
C18	AP8	40m rose & multi	.40	.35
C19	AP8	50m red & multi	.40	.35
C20	AP8	60m multicolored	.70	.35
C21	AP8	80m lt blue & multi	.70	.35
C22	AP8	1t green & multi	1.00	.90
		Nos. C16-C22 (7)	4.00	3.00

Mongolian Achievements.

Mongolian Flag, Globe and Radar — AP9

Perf. 12½x11½

1972, July 20 Photo.
C23 AP9 60m olive & multi 1.00 .50

Intl. Telecommunications Day, May 17, 1972.

Running and Olympic Rings — AP10

Olympic Rings and: 15m, Boxing. 20m, Judo. 25m, High jump. 30m, Rifle shooting. 60m, Wrestling. 80m, Weight lifting. 1t, Mongolian flag and sport emblem. 4t, Woman archer, vert.

Perf. 12½x11½

1972, July 30 Photo.

C24	AP10	10m multicolored	.30	.30
C25	AP10	15m multicolored	.30	.30
C26	AP10	20m multicolored	.30	.30
C27	AP10	25m multicolored	.30	.30
C28	AP10	30m multicolored	.30	.30
C29	AP10	60m multicolored	.65	.30
C30	AP10	80m multicolored	.85	.50
C31	AP10	1t multicolored	1.00	.70
		Nos. C24-C31 (8)	4.00	3.00

Souvenir Sheet

Perf. 11½x12½

C32 AP10 4t orange & multi 4.00 3.00

20th Olympic Games, Munich, 8/26-9/11.

U.S./U.S.S.R. Space Achievements — AP11

Astrological Signs of the Eastern Calendar and Space Project: a, Snake, Mars 1. b, Dragon and Mariner 2. c, Hare, Soyuz 5. d, Monkey, Explorer 6. e, Cock, Venus 1. f, Rat, Apollo 15. g, Horse, Apollo 8. h, Boar, Cosmos 110. i, Tiger, Gemini 7. j, Sheep, Electron 2. k, Dog, Ariel 2. l, Ram, Venus 4.

1972, Dec. 4 Photo. *Perf. 12*
C33 Sheet of 12 6.00 5.00
a.-f. AP11 60m any single, size: 55x35mm .50 .40
g.-l. AP11 60m any single, size: 35x35mm .50 .40

Airliner — AP12

1973, Jan. Photo. *Perf. 12*
C34 AP12 1.50t blue .80 .20

For surcharge, see No. 2408.

Weather Satellite, Earth Station, WMO Emblem — AP13

1973, Feb. Photo. *Perf. 12x11½*
C35 AP13 60m multicolored 1.00 .50

Intl. meteorological cooperation, cent.

Holy Flame Type of 1959
Souvenir Sheet

1973, Apr. 15 Photo. *Perf. 12½*
C36 A48 4t gold & multi 4.00 3.00

IBRA München 1973 Intl. Stamp Exhibition, Munich, May 11-20. No. C36 contains one 40x63mm stamp in redrawn design of A48 with simulated perforations and wide gold margin.

Mongolia #236 — AP14

Designs: Stamps (with mail-connected designs) of participating countries.

1973, July 31 Litho. *Perf. 12½*
C37 AP14 30m Russia No. 3100 .65 .30
C38 AP14 30m shown .65 .30
C39 AP14 30m Bulgaria #1047 .65 .30
C40 AP14 30m Hungary #B202 .65 .30
C41 AP14 30m Czechoslavia #C72 .65 .30
C42 AP14 30m German Dem. Rep. #369 .65 .30
C43 AP14 30m Cuba #C31 .65 .30
C44 AP14 30m Romania #2280 .65 .30
C45 AP14 30m Poland #802 .65 .30
Nos. C37-C45 (9) 5.85 2.70

Conference of Permanent Committee for Posts and Telecommunications of Council for Economic Aid (COMECON), Ulan Bator, Aug. 1973.

Launching of Soyuz Spacecraft — AP15

1973, Oct. 26 Litho. *Perf. 12½*
C46 AP15 5m shown .30 .20
C47 AP15 10m Apollo 8 .30 .20
C48 AP15 15m Soyuz 4 & 5 docking .30 .20
C49 AP15 20m Apollo 11 lunar module .30 .20
C50 AP15 30m Apollo 14 splashdown .50 .20
C51 AP15 50m Soyuz 6, 7 & 8 .75 .25
C52 AP15 60m Apollo 16 moon rover .80 .50
C53 AP15 1t Lunokhod 1 on moon 1.25 .75
Nos. C46-C53 (8) 4.50 2.50

Souvenir Sheet

C54 AP15 4t Soyuz and Apollo 4.50 3.50

US and Russian achievements in space.

Comecon Building, Moscow — AP16

1974, Feb. 28 Photo. *Perf. 11½x12*
C55 AP16 60m blue & multi 1.00 .50

25th anniversary of the Council of Mutual Economic Assistance.

Souvenir Sheet

Mongolia No. 4 — AP17

1974, Mar. 15 Photo. *Perf. 12½*
C56 AP17 4t multicolored 4.00 3.00

50th anniv. of 1st stamps of Mongolia.

Postrider and UPU Emblem — AP18

UPU emblem & means of transportation.

1974, Apr. Litho. *Perf. 12*
C57 AP18 50m shown .65 .35
C58 AP18 50m Reindeer post .65 .35
C59 AP18 50m Mail coach .65 .35
C60 AP18 50m Balloon post .65 .35
C61 AP18 50m Steamship and AN-2 plane .65 .35
C62 AP18 50m Train, truck and city .65 .35
C63 AP18 50m Rocket over North Pole .65 .35
Nos. C57-C63 (7) 4.55 2.45

Souvenir Sheet

C64 AP18 4t Globe and post horn, vert. 4.50 3.50

Centenary of Universal Postal Union.

Circus Type of 1974

Design: 1t, Two women contortionists.

1974, May 4 Litho. *Perf. 12*
C65 A177 1t multicolored 1.00 .50

No. C65 has se-tenant label, with similar design.

Nature Type of Regular Issue

1t, Scientist checking water, globe. 4t, Wild rose.

1974, Dec. Litho. *Perf. 11*
C66 A186 1t multicolored 1.00 .50

Souvenir Sheet
Perf. 12½

C67 A186 4t multicolored 4.50 3.50

UPU Type of 1974
Souvenir Sheet

Design: UPU Emblem, vert.

1974, Dec. *Perf. 11½x12*
C68 A187 4t multicolored 5.00 4.00

Soyuz on Launching Pad, Project Emblem — AP19

Project Emblem and: 20m, Radar and Apollo. 30m, Apollo, Soyuz and earth. 40m, Spacecraft before docking. 50m, Spacecraft after docking. 60m, Soyuz circling earth. 1t, Spacecraft, space station and earth. 4t, Russian and American astronauts.

1975, June 14 Litho. *Perf. 12*
C69 AP19 10m blue & multi .25 .20
C70 AP19 20m multicolored .25 .20
C71 AP19 30m sepia & multi .35 .20
C72 AP19 40m silver & multi .50 .30
C73 AP19 50m multicolored .75 .40
C74 AP19 60m multicolored 1.00 .40
C75 AP19 1t multicolored 1.40 .80
Nos. C69-C75 (7) 4.50 2.50

Souvenir Sheet

C76 AP19 4t black & multi 3.00 3.00

Apollo Soyuz space test project (Russo-American space cooperation), launching July 15; link-up July 17.

Mongolian Mountain Sheep — AP20

1975, Aug. 4 Litho. *Perf. 12*
C77 AP20 1.50t multi + label 2.00 1.00

South Asia Tourism Year.

Satellite over Weather Map of Mongolia AP21

1976, Mar. 20 *Perf. 12x11½*
C78 AP21 60m blue & yellow 1.50 .75

40th anniversary of meteorological service.

Souvenir Sheet

Girl with Books and Flowers — AP22

1976, Mar. 30 *Perf. 12*
C79 AP22 4t multicolored 4.00 3.00

30th anniversary of UNESCO.

Souvenir Sheet

The Wise Musician, by Sarav — AP23

1976, May 3 Litho. *Perf. 11½x12½*
C80 AP23 4t multicolored 4.00 3.00

Interphil 76 Phil. Exhib., Philadelphia, Pa., May 29-June 6.

Olympic Games Type of 1976
Souvenir Sheet

1976, May 20 *Perf. 12½x11½*
C81 A202 4t Wrestling 4.50 3.50

Independence Type of 1976

60m, Progress in agriculture and industry.

1976, June 20 Litho. *Perf. 12x11½*
C82 A203 60m multicolored 1.00 .50

Olympic Medalists Type, 1976
Souvenir Sheet

Design: 4t, Oidov Zeveg, Mongolian flag.

1976, Nov. 30 Litho. *Perf. 11x11½*
C83 A209 4t multicolored 4.50 3.50

Mounting Carrier Rocket with Bell-shaped Gear — AP24

Designs: 20m, Launching of Intercosmos 3. 30m, Marine Observatory Gagarin (ship). 40m, Satellite observation of lunar eclipse. 60m, Observatory with multiple antenna system. 80m, Examination of Van Allen Zone, magnetosphere. 1t, Meteorological earth satellite. 4t, Intercosmos satellite with lines showing participating countries on globe.

1977, June 20 Litho. *Perf. 12*
C84 AP24 10m multicolored .20 .20
C85 AP24 20m multicolored .25 .20
C86 AP24 30m multicolored .35 .20

C87 AP24 40m multicolored .55 .20
C88 AP24 60m multicolored .80 .45
C89 AP24 80m multicolored 1.00 .55
C90 AP24 1t multicolored 1.25 .65
Nos. C84-C90 (7) 4.40 2.45

Souvenir Sheet

Perf. 12½

C91 AP24 4t multicolored 4.50 3.50

11th anniv. of Intercosmos program, cooperation of 9 socialist countries for space research. No. C91 contains one stamp 58x37mm.

Trade Union Emblem, Factory and Sheep AP25

1977, June ***Perf. 12x11½***
C92 AP25 60m multicolored 1.25 .75

11th Cong. of Mongolian Trade Unions, May 12.

Montgolfier's Balloon — AP26

Dirigibles: 30m, Zeppelin over North Pole, 1931. 40m, Osoaviahim, Russian Arctic cargo. 50m, North, Russian heavy duty cargo. 60m, Aeron-340, Russian planned. 80m, Machinery transport, Russian planned. 1.20t, Flying crane, French planned. 4t, Russia No. C26 (stamp) and Sukhe Bator statue.

1977, Dec. **Litho.** ***Perf. 12***
C93 AP26 20m multicolored .25 .20
C94 AP26 30m multicolored .25 .20
C95 AP26 40m multicolored .35 .20
C96 AP26 50m multicolored .50 .35
C97 AP26 60m multicolored .75 .35
C98 AP26 80m multicolored 1.00 .50
C99 AP26 1.20t multicolored 1.50 .65
Nos. C93-C99 (7) 4.60 2.45

Souvenir Sheet

Perf. 12½x11½

C100 AP26 4t multicolored 4.00 3.00

History of airships.

A. F. Mozhaiski and his Plane, 1884 — AP27

Designs: 30m, Henry Farman and his plane, 1909. 40m, Geoffrey de Havilland and D. H. 66 Hercules, 1920's. 50m, Charles A. Lindbergh, Spirit of St. Louis and route New York to Paris, 1927. 60m, Mongolian pilots Shagdarsuren and Demberel and plane over Altai Mountains, 1935. 80m, Soviet aviators Chkalov, Baidukov, Beliakov, plane and route Moscow to Vancouver, 1937. 1.20t, A. N. Tupolev, supersonic plane TU 154, route Moscow to Alma-Ata, 1968. 4t, Wilbur and Orville Wright and their plane.

1978, Mar. 25 **Litho.** ***Perf. 12½x11***
C101 AP27 20m multi .25 .20
C102 AP27 30m multi .30 .20
C103 AP27 40m multi .40 .25
C104 AP27 50m multi .50 .35
C105 AP27 60m multi .60 .35
C106 AP27 80m multi .85 .50
C107 AP27 1.20t multi 1.25 .75
Nos. C101-C107 (7) 4.15 2.60

Souvenir Sheet

C108 AP27 4t multi 4.00 4.00

75th anniversary of first powered flight, Wright brothers, 1903.

Soccer Type of 1978

Souvenir Sheet

Design: 4t, Two soccer players.

1978, Apr. 15 ***Perf. 11½***
C109 A231 4t multi 4.25 4.25

World Soccer Championships, Argentina 78, June 1-25. #C109 contains 1 45x38mm stamp.

Souvenir Sheet

Canada No. 553 and Mongolia No. 549 — AP28

1978, June **Litho.** ***Perf. 12½***
C110 AP28 4t multi 4.50 4.50

CAPEX '78, Intl. Phil. Exhibition, Toronto, June 9-18.

Map of Cuba, Ship, Plane and Festival Emblem — AP29

1978, July 28 **Litho.** ***Perf. 12***
C111 AP29 1t multicolored 2.00 .75

11th World Youth Festival, Havana, 7/28-8/5.

Souvenir Sheet

Aleksei Gubarev and Vladimir Remek, PRAGA '78 Emblem — AP30

1978, Sept. 5 **Litho.** ***Perf. 12***
C112 AP30 4t multicolored 4.00 4.00

PRAGA '78 Intl. Phil. Exhib., Prague, Sept. 8-17, and Russian-Czechoslovak space cooperation, Intercosmos.

DDR Flag, TV Tower, Berlin, Satellite AP31

1979, Oct. 9 **Litho.** ***Perf. 11½x12***
C113 AP31 60m multicolored .75 .40

German Democratic Republic, 30th anniv.

Demoiselle Crane AP32

Protected Birds: 30m, Hawk warbler. 50m, Ruddy shelduck. 60m, Blue magpie. 70m, Goldfinch. 80m, Titmouse. 1t, Golden oriole.

1979, Oct. 25
C114 AP32 10m multi .40 .20
C115 AP32 30m multi .60 .20
C116 AP32 50m multi .75 .25
C117 AP32 60m multi 1.00 .25
C118 AP32 70m multi 1.10 .30
C119 AP32 80m multi 1.25 .30
C120 AP32 1t multi 1.50 .35
Nos. C114-C120 (7) 6.60 1.85

Venera 5 and 6 — AP33

American and Russian Space Missions: 30m, Mariner 5. 50m, Mars 3. 60m, Viking 1 and 2. 70m, Luna 1, 2 and 3. 80m, Lunokhod 2. 1t, Apollo 15. 4t, Apollo 11, astronauts on moon.

Perf. 12½x11½

1979, Nov. 24 **Litho.**
C121 AP33 10m multi .20 .20
C122 AP33 30m multi .25 .20
C123 AP33 50m multi .40 .20
C124 AP33 60m multi .55 .25
C125 AP33 70m multi .70 .35
C126 AP33 80m multi .85 .45
C127 AP33 1t multi 1.00 .50
Nos. C121-C127 (7) 3.95 2.15

Souvenir Sheet

C128 AP33 4t multi 4.00 4.00

Apollo 11 moon landing, 10th anniversary.

Andrena Scita — AP34

Insects: 30m, Paravespula germanica. 40m, Perilampus ruficornis. 50m, Bumblebee. 60m, Honey bee. 80m, Stilbum cyanurum. 1.20t, Ruby tail.

1980, Feb. 25 **Litho.** ***Perf. 11x12***
C129 AP34 20m multi .20 .20
C130 AP34 30m multi .30 .20
C131 AP34 40m multi .45 .30
C132 AP34 50m multi .55 .30
C133 AP34 60m multi .65 .40
C134 AP34 80m multi .85 .50
C135 AP34 1.20t multi 1.25 .60
Nos. C129-C135 (7) 4.25 2.50

Z-526 AFS Stunt Planes, Czechoslovakia — AP35

1980, Aug. 4 **Litho.** ***Perf. 12***
C136 AP35 20m shown .20 .20
C137 AP35 30m RS-180 "Sportsman," Germany .30 .20
C138 AP35 40m Yanki-Anu, US .45 .30
C139 AP35 50m MJ-2 "Tempete," France .60 .30
C140 AP35 60m "Pits," Canada .75 .45
C141 AP35 80m "Acrostar," Switzerland .90 .60
C142 AP35 1.20t JAK-50, USSR 1.30 .75
Nos. C136-C142 (7) 4.50 2.80

Souvenir Sheet

C143 AP35 4t JAK-52, USSR 4.00 4.00

10th World Aerobatic Championship, Oshkosh, Wisconsin, Aug. 17-30. No. C143 contains one 50x43mm stamp.

Olympic Type of 1980

Souvenir Sheet

1980, Sept. 15 **Litho.** ***Perf. 12½***
C144 A253 4t Wrestlers 4.00 4.00

J. Davaajav, Mongolian silver medalist, 22nd Summer Olympic Games, Moscow. Inscribed "Los Angeles '84".

Souvenir Sheet

AP36

1980, Dec. 10 **Litho.** ***Perf. 11½x11***
C145 AP36 4t multi 4.00 4.00

Johannes Kepler (1571-1630), German astronomer.

AP37

1981, Oct. 5 **Litho.** ***Perf. 12x11½***

Graf Zeppelin and: 20m, Germany #C40, sea eagle. 30m, Germany #C41, polar fox. 40m, Germany #C42, walrus. 50m, Russia #C26, polar bear. 60m, Russia #C27, snowy owl. 80m, Russia #C28, puffin. 1.20t, Russia #C29, seal. 4t, Icebreaker Maligin.

C146 AP37 20m multi .50 .20
C147 AP37 30m multi .50 .25
C148 AP37 40m multi .75 .40
C149 AP37 50m multi 1.00 .35
C150 AP37 60m multi 1.50 .45
C151 AP37 80m multi 1.75 .70
C152 AP37 1.20t multi 2.00 .85
Nos. C146-C152 (7) 8.00 3.20

Souvenir Sheet

C153 AP37 4t multi 5.50 5.50

Graf Zeppelin polar flight, 50th anniv. No. C153 contains one stamp 36x51mm.

ITU Plenipotentiaries Conference, Nairobi, Sept. — AP38

1982, Sept. 27 Litho. *Perf. 12*

C154	AP38 60m Map		1.00	.60

2nd UN Conference on Peaceful Uses of Outer Space, Vienna, Aug. 9-21 — AP39

1982, Dec. 15 Litho. *Perf. 12*

C155	AP39 60m Sputnik 1	.55	.30
C156	AP39 60m Sputnik 2	.55	.30
C157	AP39 60m Vostok 1	.55	.30
C158	AP39 60m Venera 8	.55	.30
C159	AP39 60m Vostok 6	.55	.30
C160	AP39 60m Voskhod 2	.55	.30
C161	AP39 60m Apollo II	.55	.30
C162	AP39 60m Soyuz 6	.55	.30
	Nos. C155-C162 (8)	4.40	2.40

Souvenir Sheet

Perf. 12½x12

C163	AP39 4t Soyuz 39, Salyut 6	4.00	4.00

Balloon Flight Bicentenary AP40

1982, Dec. 31 *Perf. 11½x12½*

C164	AP40 20m Montgolfiere, 1783	.20	.20
C165	AP40 30m Blanchard, 1785	.30	.20
C166	AP40 40m Royal-Vauzhall, 1836	.45	.30
C167	AP40 50m Oernen, 1897	.60	.30
C168	AP40 60m Gordon Bennett Race, 1906	.75	.30
C169	AP40 80m Paris, 1931	.90	.45
C170	AP40 1.20t USSR-VR-62, 1933	1.50	.60
	Nos. C164-C170 (7)	4.70	2.35

Souvenir Sheet

C171	AP40 4t Mongolia, 1977	4.00	4.00

Souvenir Sheet

Revolutionary Mongolia Monument — AP41

1983 Litho. *Imperf.*

C172	AP41 4t multi	4.50	4.50

Concorde — AP42

1984, Aug. 15 Litho. *Perf. 14*

C173	AP42 20m DC-10, vert.	.25	.20
C174	AP42 30m Airbus A-300 B-2	.35	.25
C175	AP42 40m shown	.55	.35
C176	AP42 50m Boeing 747	.60	.45
C177	AP42 60m IL-62	.70	.45
C178	AP42 80m TU-154	1.00	.70
C179	AP42 1.20t IL-86	1.50	.70
	Nos. C173-C179 (7)	4.95	3.10

Souvenir Sheet

C180	AP42 4t Yak-42	4.75	4.75

1988 Winter Olympics, Calgary AP43

1988, Jan. 20 Litho. *Perf. 14*

C181	AP43 20m Bobsled	.20	.20
C182	AP43 30m Ski jumping	.30	.20
C183	AP43 40m Downhill skiing	.45	.30
C184	AP43 50m Biathlon	.60	.30
C185	AP43 60m Speed skating	.75	.45
C186	AP43 80m Women's figure skating	.90	.45
C187	AP43 1.20t Ice hockey	1.00	.60
	Nos. C181-C187 (7)	4.20	2.50

Souvenir sheet

C188	AP43 4t Cross-country skiing	4.25	4.25

Souvenir Sheet

Hong Kong '94 — AP44

1994, Feb. 18 Litho. *Perf. 14½x15*

C189	AP44 600t multicolored	4.25	4.25
a.	With Hong Kong '97 emblem in sheet margin	4.25	4.25

Issued: #C189a, 1/12/97.

Souvenir Sheet
No. C163 Surcharged in Red

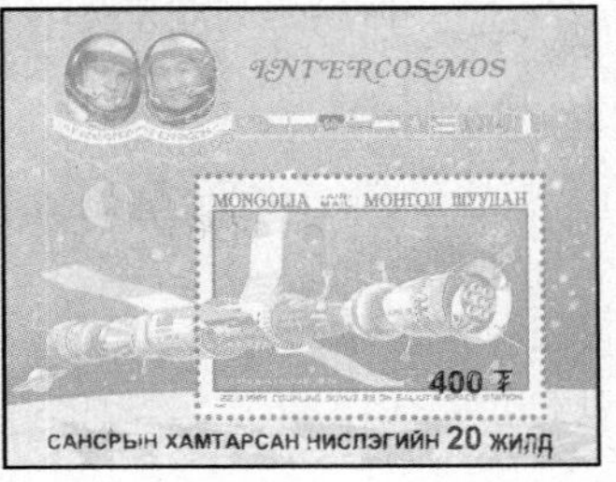

2001, Mar. 22 Litho. *Perf. 12½x12*

C190	AP39 400t on 4t multi	*25.00*	*25.00*

Joint Soviet-Mongolian space flight, 20th anniv.

AIR POST SEMI-POSTAL STAMP

Catalogue values for unused stamps in this section are for Never Hinged items.

UNICEF Type of 1977
Souvenir Sheet

Design: 4t+50m, Balloon with Mongolian flag, children and UNICEF emblem.

1977, June 1 Litho. *Perf. 12*

CB1	SP2 4t + 50m multi	4.25	4.25

First balloon flight in Mongolia. Surtax was for Children's Village.

MONTENEGRO

ˌmän-tə-ˈnē-ˌgrō

LOCATION — Southern Europe, bordering on the Adriatic Sea
GOVT. — Republic in southern Europe.
AREA — 5,415 sq. mi.
POP. — 620,145 (2003)
CAPITAL — Cetinje

Montenegro maintained a precarious independence from the Ottoman Turks during the 16th-19th centuries as a theocracy, under a succession of bishop princes. In 1852 it became an independent principality. On December 1, 1918, Montenegro, along with Bosnia and Herzegovina, Croatia, Dalmatia and Slovenia, was absorbed by Serbia to form the Kingdom of the Serbs, Croats and Slovenes, which became the Kingdom of Yugoslavia in 1929.

During World War II, an Italian satellite regime was established in an enlarged Montenegrin state, but after the war, Montenegro became one of the constituent republics of the Socialist Federal Republic of Yugoslavia.

In 1992, with the dissolution of the greater Yugoslav republic, only Montenegro remained associated with Serbia, first in the Federal Republic of Yugoslavia and, after 2002, in the looser federation of Serbia & Montenego.

On May 21, 2006, Montenegrins endorsed independence and complete separation from Serbia in a national referendum, and

100 Novcic = 1 Florin
100 Helera = 1 Kruna (1902)
100 Para = 1 Kruna (1907)
100 Para = 1 Perper (1910)
100 cents = 1 euro (2003)

Canceled to Order

Used values for Nos. 1-110, H1-H5, J1-J26, are for canceled to order stamps. Postally used specimens sell for considerably more.

Watermark

Wmk. 91 — "BRIEF-MARKEN" (#1-14) or "ZEITUNGS-MARKEN" (#15-21) in Double-lined Capitals once across sheet

Wmk. 140 — Crown

Prince Nicholas I — A1

1874 Typo. Wmk. 91

Early Printings

Perf. 10½ Large Holes, pointed teeth

Narrow Spacing (2-2½mm)

1	A1	2n yellow	40.00	40.00
2	A1	3n green	55.00	40.00
3	A1	5n rose red	50.00	40.00
4	A1	7n lt lilac	50.00	32.50
5	A1	10n blue	120.00	80.00
6	A1	15n yel bister	135.00	120.00
7	A1	25n lilac gray	280.00	210.00
		Nos. 1-7 (7)	730.00	562.50

Middle Printings (1879)

Perf. 12, 12½, 13 and Compound

Narrow spacing

8	A1	2n yellow	10.00	7.00
a.		Perf. 12-13x10½	65.00	65.00
9	A1	3n green	7.50	5.50
10	A1	5n red	7.50	5.50
11	A1	7n rose lilac	7.50	5.50
a.		7n lilac	19.00	14.00
12	A1	10n blue	16.00	11.00
a.		Perf. 12-13x10½	65.00	52.50
13	A1	15n bister brn	19.00	11.00
14	A1	25n gray lilac	25.00	16.00
		Nos. 8-14 (7)	92.50	61.50

Late Printings (1893?)

Perf. 10½, 11½ Small holes, broad teeth

(Perf. 11½ also with pointed teeth)

Narrow and wide spacing

(2¾-3½mm)

15	A1	2n yellow	4.00	2.75
a.		Perf. 11 ('94)	27.50	20.00
16	A1	3n green	4.00	2.75
17	A1	5n red	4.75	3.25
18	A1	7n rose	2.75	2.00
a.		Perf. 11 ('94)	12.00	9.00
19	A1	10n blue	4.00	2.75
20	A1	15n brown	4.00	3.25
21	A1	25n brown violet	4.75	3.00
		Nos. 15-21 (7)	28.25	19.75

Dates of issue of the late printings are still being researched.

Types of 1874-93 Overprinted in Black or Red

1893 *Perf. 10½, 11½*

22	A1	2n yellow	35.00	6.50
a.		Perf. 11	*35.00*	*35.00*
23	A1	3n green	6.50	3.25
24	A1	5n red	2.40	1.60
25	A1	7n rose	4.00	2.50
a.		Perf. 12	60.00	50.00
b.		7n rose lilac	5.00	3.00
c.		7n lilac, perf. 12	*125.00*	
d.		Perf. 11	*40.00*	*30.00*
26	A1	10n blue	4.00	3.25
27	A1	10n blue (R)	6.00	4.00
28	A1	15n brown	4.50	3.25
a.		Perf. 12	50.00	42.50
29	A1	15n brown (R)	*2,400.*	*1,600.*
30	A1	25n brown violet	4.00	2.40
31	A1	25n brn vio (R)	6.00	4.00
a.		Perf. 12½	-	*225.00*
		Nos. 22-28,30-31 (9)	72.40	30.75

Introduction of printing to Montenegro, 400th anniversary.

This overprint had many settings. Several values exist with "1494" or "1495" instead of "1493", or with missing letters or numerals due to wearing of the clichés. Double and inverted overprints exist. Some printings were made after 1893 to supply a philatelic demand, but were available for postage.

The 7n with red overprint was not issued.

1894-98 **Wmk. 91** *Perf. 10½, 11½*

32	A1	1n gray blue	.40	.40
33	A1	2n emerald ('98)	.40	.40
34	A1	3n carmine rose ('98)	.40	.40
35	A1	5n orange ('98)	2.40	.55
36	A1	7n gray lilac ('98)	.50	.50
37	A1	10n magenta ('98)	.50	.50
38	A1	15n red brown ('98)	.40	.40
39	A1	20n brown orange	.40	.40
40	A1	25n dull blue ('98)	.40	.40
41	A1	30n maroon	.40	.20
42	A1	50n ultra	.55	.55
43	A1	1fl deep green	.80	.80
44	A1	2fl red brown	1.25	1.25
		Nos. 32-44 (13)	8.80	6.75

Monastery at Cetinje (Royal Mausoleum) A3

Perf. 10½, 11½

1896, Sept. 1 **Litho.** **Unwmk.**

45	A3	1n dk blue & bis	.40	.40
46	A3	2n magenta & yel	.40	.40
47	A3	3n org brn & yel grn	.40	.40
48	A3	5n bl grn & bis	.40	.40
49	A3	10n yellow & ultra	.40	.40
50	A3	15n dk blue & grn	.40	.40
a.		Perf. 11½	60.00	60.00
51	A3	20n bl grn & ultra	.40	.40
a.		Perf. 11½	40.00	40.00
52	A3	25n dk blue & yel	.50	.50
53	A3	30n magenta & bis	.55	.55
54	A3	50n red brn & gray bl	.55	.55
55	A3	1fl rose & gray bl	.95	.95
56	A3	2fl brown & black	1.25	1.25
		Nos. 45-56 (12)	6.60	6.60

Bicentenary of the ruling dynasty, founded by the Vladika, Danilo Petrovich of Nyegosh.

Inverted centers and other errors exist, but experts believe these to be printer's waste.

Perf. 11½ counterfeits are common.

Prince Nicholas I
A4 A5

Perf. 13x13½, 13x12½ (2h, 5h, 50h, 2k, 5k), 12½ (1h, 25h)

1902, July 12

57	A4	1h ultra	.40	.40
58	A4	2h rose lilac	.40	.40
59	A4	5h green	.40	.40
60	A4	10h rose	.40	.40
61	A4	25h dull blue	.55	.55
62	A4	50h gray green	.80	.80
63	A4	1k chocolate	.80	.80
64	A4	2k pale brown	.80	.80
65	A4	5k buff	.95	.95
		Nos. 57-65 (9)	5.50	5.50

The 2h black brown and 25h indigo were not issued. The 25h, perf. 12½, probably was never issued.

Constitution Issue

Same Overprinted in Red or Black "Constitution" 15mm

1905, Dec. 5

66	A4	1h ultra (R)	.40	.40
67	A4	2h rose lilac	.40	.40
68	A4	5h green (R)	.40	.40
69	A4	10h rose	.40	.40
70	A4	25h dull blue (R)	.40	.40
71	A4	50h gray green (R)	.40	.40
72	A4	1k chocolate (R)	.55	.55
73	A4	2k pale brown (R)	.80	.80
74	A4	5k buff	.95	.95
		Nos. 66-74 (9)	4.70	4.70

Overprints in other colors are proofs.

1906

"Constitution" 16½mm

66a	A4	1h ultra (R)	.40	.40
67a	A4	2h rose lilac	.40	.40
68a	A4	5h green (R)	.40	.40
69a	A4	10h rose	.40	.40
70a	A4	25h dull blue (R)	.40	.40
71a	A4	50h gray green (R)	.40	.40
72a	A4	1k chocolate (R)	.40	.40
73a	A4	2k pale brown (R)	.55	.55
74a	A4	5k buff	.95	.95
		Nos. 66a-74a (9)	4.30	4.30

Three settings of Nos. 66a-74a containing four types of "YCTAB": I, 9¾mm, II, 11¼mm, III, 10¼mm, IV, 8½mm. Type IV occurs only in one setting, at two positions. Nos. 67a, 69a-74a, H3a exist in type IV.

Two errors occur: "Constitutton" and "Coustitution." Many other varieties including reversed color overprints exist.

Values are for types I and II.

1907, June 1 **Engr.** *Perf. 12½*

75	A5	1pa ocher	.30	.30
76	A5	2pa black	.30	.30
77	A5	5pa yellow green	.55	.30
78	A5	10pa rose red	.55	.30
79	A5	15pa ultra	.30	.30
80	A5	20pa red orange	.30	.30
81	A5	25pa indigo	.30	.30
82	A5	35pa bister brown	.30	.30
83	A5	50pa dull violet	.55	.30
84	A5	1kr carmine rose	.55	.35
85	A5	2kr green	.55	.55
86	A5	5kr red brown	1.20	.55
		Nos. 75-86 (12)	5.75	4.15

Many Montenegro stamps exist imperforate or part perforate. Experts believe these to be printer's waste.

King Nicholas I as a Youth — A6

King Nicholas I and Queen Milena — A7

King Nicholas I — A11

Prince Nicholas — A12

5pa, 10pa, 25pa, 35pa, Nicholas in 1910. 15pa, Nicholas in 1878. 20pa, King and Queen, diff.

1910, Aug. 28 **Engr.**

87	A6	1pa black	.65	.65
88	A7	2pa purple brown	.65	.65
89	A6	5pa dark green	.65	.65
90	A6	10pa carmine	.65	.65
91	A6	15pa slate blue	.65	.65
92	A7	20pa olive green	.65	.65
93	A6	25pa deep blue	.65	.65
94	A6	35pa chestnut	.65	.65
95	A11	50pa violet	1.20	1.20
96	A11	1per lake	1.20	1.20
97	A11	2per yellow green	1.25	.70
98	A12	5per pale blue	1.60	1.25
		Nos. 87-98 (12)	10.45	9.55

Proclamation of Montenegro as a kingdom, the 50th anniv. of the reign of King Nicholas and the golden wedding celebration of the King and Queen.

King Nicholas I — A13

1913, Apr. 1 **Typo.**

99	A13	1pa orange	.65	.65
100	A13	2pa plum	.65	.65
101	A13	5pa deep green	.65	.65
102	A13	10pa deep rose	.65	.65
103	A13	15pa blue gray	.65	.65
104	A13	20pa dark brown	.65	.65
105	A13	25pa deep blue	.65	.65
106	A13	35pa vermilion	.65	.65
107	A13	50pa pale blue	.65	.65
108	A13	1per yellow brown	.65	.65
109	A13	2per gray violet	.65	.65
110	A13	5per yellow green	.65	.65
		Nos. 99-110 (12)	7.80	7.80

SERBIA & MONTENEGRO

100 Cents=1 Euro

Yugoslavia became Serbia & Montenegro Feb. 4, 2003, with each section of the country maintaining and operating their own postal service, and each having their own currency. After a referendum on independence on May 21, 2006, Montenegro seceded from Serbia and Montenegro, declaring independence on June 3. Serbia formally recognized Montenegro's independence on June 7.

The stamps below are inscribed only with euro denominations, used solely within Montenegro. Stamps inscribed with dinar denominations, issued for use in Serbia, and those denominated in both dinar and euro currencies, for use in either region, are found under the Serbia listings.

Budva A20

Durmitor A21

2003, Sept. 15 **Litho.** *Perf. 12½*

120	A20	25c multi	1.25	1.25
121	A21	40c multi	2.25	2.25

Christmas — A22

2003, Nov. 21 *Perf. 13¼*

122	A22	25c multi	1.75	1.75
		Complete booklet, 10 #122	17.50	

National Symbols A23

Small coat of arms, outline map of Europe and: 25c, Map of Montenegro. 40c, Parliament Building and map of Montenegro. 50c, Large coat of arms and map of Montenegro. 60c, Flag and map of Montenegro.

2005, Dec. 15 **Litho.** *Perf. 13*

123-126	A23	Set of 4	9.50	9.50

See Nos. 140-142.

Europa A24

Designs: 25c, Fish, shrimp, and mussels. 50c, Meat, olives, cheese and fruit.

No. 128C: d, 25c, Bee, honeycomb and honey. e, 50c, Grapes, grapevine, wine.

2005, Dec. 30 *Perf. 13½x13¾*

127	A24	25c multicolored	*6.00*	*6.00*
a.		As #127, perf. 13½x 13¾x 13½x imperf.	*11.50*	*11.50*
128	A24	50c multicolored	11.50	11.50
a.		As #128, perf. 13½x imperf. x 13½x 13¾	*22.50*	*22.50*
b.		Souvenir sheet, #127a, 128a	*35.00*	*35.00*

Souvenir Sheet

Perf. 13½x13¾

128C	A24	Sheet of 2, #d-e	*35.00*	*35.00*

A25

Europa Stamps, 50th Anniv. — A26

No. 129: a, Montenegro #100, common vignette of 1960 Europa stamps. b, Montenegro #101, common vignette of 1961-62 Europa stamps. c, Montenegro #102, bee and honeycomb. d, Montenegro #105, common vignette of 1956 Europa stamps.

No. 129E: f, Like #129a. g, Like #129b. h, Like #129c. i, Like #129d.

2006, Jan. 3 **Litho.** *Perf. 13½x13¾*

Stamps with Frames

129		Horiz. strip of 4	18.00	18.00
a.		A25 50c multi	1.60	1.60
b.		A25 €1 multi	3.25	3.25
c.-d.		A25 €2 Either single	6.25	6.25

Souvenir Sheet

Stamps Without Frames

129E	A25	Sheet of 4, #f-i	21.00	21.00

Litho. with Foil Application

Imperf

Size: 103x76mm

130	A26	€5.50 multi	15.00	15.00

2006 Winter Olympics, Turin A27

Designs: 60c, Figure skating. 90c, Ski jumping.

2006, Feb. 7 **Litho.** *Perf. 13½x13¾*

131-132	A27	Set of 2	5.50	5.50

Flowers A28

Designs: 25c, Petteria ramentacea. 50c, Viola nikolai.

2006, Mar. 15
133-134 A28 Set of 2 2.75 2.75

Introduction of Perper Currency, Cent. — A29

Central Bank of Montenegro and: 40c, 1906 1-para coin. 50c, 1906 20-para coin.

2006, Apr. 27 Litho. ***Perf. 13½x13¾***
135-136 A29 Set of 2 3.25 3.25

2006 World Cup Soccer Championships, Germany — A30

Designs: No. 137, 60c, Players in match. No. 138, 90c, Players in match, diff.
No. 139: a, 60c, Players, empty stadium in background. b, 90c, Players, empty stadium in background, diff.

2006, May 30 ***Perf. 13¾x13½***
137-138 A30 Set of 2 5.25 5.25

Souvenir Sheet

139 A30 Sheet of 2, #a-b 5.25 5.25

National Symbols Type of 2005 Redrawn With "Posta Crne Gore" Under Postal Emblem

Designs as before.

2006, June Litho. ***Perf. 13¾***
140 A23 25c multi 1.00 1.00
a. Perf. 13 1.00 1.00
141 A23 40c multi 1.50 1.50
a. Perf. 13 1.50 1.50
142 A23 60c multi 2.50 2.50
Nos. 140-142 (3) 5.00 5.00

Nos. 140a and 141a are dated "2005," while Nos. 140-142 are dated "2006."

Independent Republic

Tourism A31

Designs: 25c, Durmitor. 50c, Sveti Stefan.

2006, July 5 ***Perf. 13½x13¾***
143-144 A31 Set of 2 2.75 2.75

Independence Referendum of May 21 — A32

2006, July 13
145 A32 50c multi 1.75 1.75

Europa — A33

Designs: No. 146, 60c, Women linking chain. No. 147, 90c, People and sun, horiz.
No. 148: a, 60c, Man with suitcase. b, 90c, People of different races.

2006, Aug. 30 ***Perf. 13¾***
146-147 A33 Set of 2 5.25 5.25

Souvenir Sheet

148 A33 Sheet of 2, #a-b 5.25 5.25

Capt. Ivo Visin (1806-68), Circumnavigator, and Ship, Splendido — A34

2006, Sept. 5 ***Perf. 13½x13¾***
149 A34 40c multi 1.50 1.50

Stamp Day — A35

2006, Oct. 2 ***Perf. 13¾***
150 A35 25c multi .85 .85

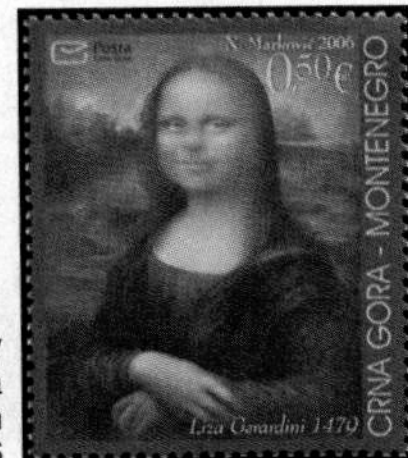
Mona Lisa, by Leonardo da Vinci, 500th Anniv. — A36

2006, Oct. 18 ***Perf. 13¾x13½***
151 A36 50c multi 1.75 1.75

Cultural Heritage A37

Designs: No. 152, 25c, Ruins, Dukla Archaeological Site. No. 153, 25c, Glassware.

2006, Nov. 3 ***Perf. 13¾x13½***
152-153 A37 Set of 2 1.75 1.75

Tara River A38

Perf. 13½x13¾

2006, Nov. 15 **Litho.**
154 A38 40c multi 1.50 1.50

Gregorian Calendar, 425th Anniv. A39

2007, Jan. 4 ***Perf. 13¾x13***
155 A39 50c multi 1.75 1.75

Printed in sheets of 8 + label.

Wildlife Protection A40

2007, Feb. 7
156 A40 50c multi 1.75 1.75

Printed in sheets of 8 + label.

Europa — A41

Map of Montengro and: Nos. 157, 159a, 60c, Montengro Scouting emblem. Nos. 158, 159b, 90c, Tent and campfire.

2007, Apr. 20 Litho. ***Perf. 13¾***
157 A41 60c multi 2.00 2.00
158 A41 90c multi 2.75 2.75
a. Souvenir sheet, #157-158 5.25 5.25

Perf. 13¾ (Imperf. Between Stamps)

159 Sheet of 2 5.25 5.25
a. A41 60c multi, 42x28mm 2.00 2.00
b. A41 90c multi, 42x28mm 2.75 2.75

Nos. 157 and 158 were each printed in sheets of 8 + label. No. 159 was sold with but not attached to a booklet cover.

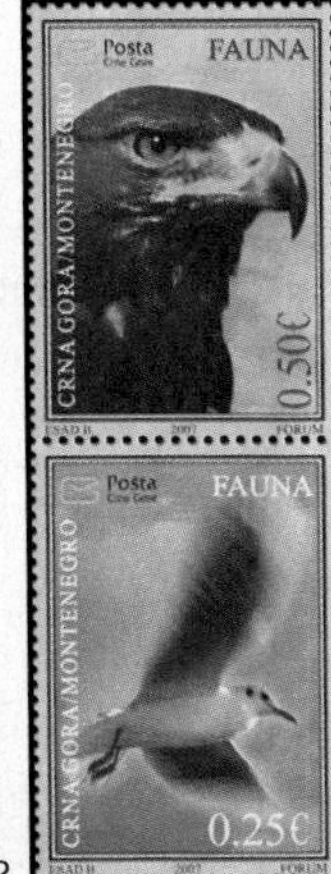
Birds — A42

No. 160: a, 25c, Gull. b, 50c, Eagle.

2007, May 11 Litho. ***Perf. 13¾***
160 A42 Pair, #a-b 2.75 2.75

Migration of Montenegrins to Istria, 350th Anniv. — A43

2007, June 21 ***Perf. 13¾***
161 A43 60c multi 2.10 2.10

Printed in sheets of 8 + label.

Postal History A44

Glagolithic Text — A45

Mountains A46

Stylized Butterfly A47

2007, July 3
162 A44 25c multi .90 .90
163 A45 40c multi 1.40 1.40
164 A46 50c multi 1.75 1.75
165 A47 60c multi 2.25 2.25
Nos. 162-165 (4) 6.30 6.30

Petar Lubarda (1907-74), Painter A48

2007, July 27 *Perf. 13¾*
166 A48 40c multi 1.40 1.40

Ship — A49

2007, Aug. 1
167 A49 60c multi 2.10 2.10

Printed in sheets of 8 + label.

Joy of Europe — A50

2007, Oct. 2
168 A50 50c multi 1.75 1.75

Regional Telephone Service, Cent. — A51

Designs: 25c, Telephone dial. 50c, Telephone dial and red dots.

2007, Nov. 9 **Litho.** *Perf. 13¾*
169-170 A51 Set of 2 2.50 2.50

New Year's Day — A52

Designs: No. 171, 25c, Twisted ribbon. No. 172, 25c, Christmas ornament on tree branch. 50c, Wreath and bells. €1, Lit candle.

2007, Dec. 5 *Perf. 14x13¾*
171-174 A52 Set of 4 7.00 7.00

Stabilization and Association Agreement Between Montenegro and the European Union — A53

Jigsaw puzzle pieces with: 60c, Montenegro coat of arms and European Union ring of stars.

No. 176: a, 40c, Montenegro coat of arms. b, 50c, European Union ring of stars.

2008, Feb. 1 **Litho.** *Perf. 13¾*
175 A53 60c multi 2.00 2.00

Souvenir Sheet

176 A53 Sheet of 2, #a-b 3.25 3.25

Flowers — A54

Designs: 25c, Draba bertiscea. 40c, Edraianthus wettsteinii. 50c, Protoedriantus tarae. 60c, Dianthus nitidus.

2008, Feb. 20
177-180 A54 Set of 4 6.25 6.25

Nos. 177-180 each were printed in sheets of 5 + label.

2008 Summer Olympics, Beijing A55

Stylized athletes, Beijing Olympics emblem and: 60c, Map of Montenegro. 90c, Montenegro coat of arms.

2008, Mar. 26
181-182 A55 Set of 2 5.50 5.50

Europa — A56

Designs: No. 183, 60c, Boy, envelope with stamp. No. 184, 90c, Girl, letter.

No. 185: a, 60c, Boy, right half of envelope. b, 90c, Girl, left half of envelope.

2008, Apr. 2
183-184 A56 Set of 2 5.50 5.50

Souvenir Sheet

185 A56 Sheet of 2, #a-b 5.50 5.50

Nos. 183-184 each were printed in sheets of 8 + label.

Marko Miljanov (1833-1901), Writer — A57

2008, Apr. 24
186 A57 60c multi 2.25 2.25

Battle of Grahovac, 150th Anniv. — A58

2008, Apr. 29
187 A58 25c multi .90 .90

Tourism A59

Designs: 25c, Hillside hut. 40c, Fortress. 50c, Pier and boats. 60c, Boat on lake.

2008, May 21
188-191 A59 Set of 4 5.50 5.50
191a Sheet of 4, #188-191 5.50 5.50

Chess Olympics, Dresden, Germany A60

2008, June 18 **Litho.** *Perf. 13¾*
192 A60 60c multi 2.25 2.25

Ship Jadran, 75th Anniv. A61

2008, July 16
193 A61 50c multi 1.90 1.90

Victory of Montenegrin Team at European Water Polo Championships, Malaga, Spain — A62

2008, Sept. 15
194 A62 50c multi 1.90 1.90

Printed in sheets of 8 + label.

Roman Art — A63

No. 195: a, 25c, Frieze depicting faces. 50c, Mosaic depicting angel.

2008, Sept. 17
195 A63 Horiz. pair, #a-b 2.75 2.75

Stamp Day — A64

2008, Oct. 2
196 A64 60c multi 2.25 2.25

Automobile A65

Hourglass, Map of Montenegro A66

Eagle and Angel — A67

2008, Oct. 20 *Perf. 13¾x13¼*
197 A65 40c multi 1.50 1.50
198 A66 50c multi 1.60 1.60
199 A67 60c multi 2.25 2.25
Nos. 197-199 (3) 5.35 5.35

Alfred Nobel (1833-96), Inventor and Philanthropist — A68

2008, Oct. 21 *Perf. 13¾*
200 A68 50c multi 1.75 1.75

A69

A70

A71

A72

A73

First Railway in Montenegro, Cent. — A74

2008, Nov. 2

201 A69 25c multi	.85	.85
202 A70 25c multi	.85	.85
203 A71 25c multi	.85	.85
204 A72 25c multi	.85	.85
205 A73 25c multi	.85	.85
206 A74 25c multi	.85	.85
a. Souvenir sheet of 6, #201-206	5.50	5.50
Nos. 201-206 (6)	5.10	5.10

Nos. 201-206 each were printed in sheets of 5 + label.

Joy of Europe — A75

Designs: 25c, Shown. 40c, Towers and bridge, horiz.

2008, Nov. 20

207-208 A75 Set of 2 1.75 1.75

Nos. 207-208 each were printed in sheets of 8 + label.

Universal Declaration of Human Rights, 60th Anniv. — A76

2008, Dec. 11 ***Perf. 13¾***

209 A76 50c multi 1.40 1.40

Printed in sheets of 8 + label.

Louis Braille (1809-52), Educator of the Blind A77

2009, Jan. 30

210 A77 60c multi 1.60 1.60

Kotor Churches Honoring St. Tryphon, 1200th Anniv. — A78

No. 211 — St. Tryphon and denomination in: a, Black. b, White.

2009, Feb. 3 ***Perf. 14***

211 A78 50c Horiz. pair, #a-b 2.60 2.60

First Theatrical Performance in Niksic, 125th Anniv. — A79

Vita Nikolic (1934-94), Poet — A80

Zetski Dom Theater, Cetinje, 125th Anniv. A81

Crnojevic Monastery, 525th Anniv. — A82

2010 **Litho.** ***Perf. 13¾***

212 A79 25c multi	.65	.65
213 A80 40c multi	1.10	1.10
214 A81 50c multi	1.40	1.40
215 A82 60c multi	1.60	1.60
Nos. 212-215 (4)	4.75	4.75

Arts through the ages. Issued: 25c, 2/16; others, 4/8.

Fish A83

Designs: 25c, Alburnus scoranza. 40c, Thymallus thymallus. 50c, Salmothymus obtusirostris zetensis. 60c, Cyprinus carpio.

2009, Apr. 16

216-219 A83 Set of 4 4.75 4.75

Nos. 216-219 each were printed in sheets of 5 + label.

Europa A84

Designs: No. 220, 60c, Boy and girl looking at celestial objects. No. 221, 90c, Boy looking through telescope.

No. 222, vert.: a, 60c, Planets and constellations. b, 90c, Comet, asteroids and constellations.

2009, Apr. 16

220-221 A84 Set of 2 4.00 4.00

Souvenir Sheet

222 A84 Sheet of 2, #a-b 4.00 4.00

Intl. Year of Astronomy.

Tourism A85

Designs: 25c, Water skiing. 40c, Rock climbing in Nevidio Canyon. 50c, Paragliding. 60c, Rafting on the Tara River.

2009, Apr. 16

223-226 A85 Set of 4 4.75 4.75

226a Souvenir sheet of 4, #223-226 4.75 4.75

Nos. 223-226 each were printed in sheets of 5 + label.

25th Universiade, Belgrade — A86

2009, June 4 ***Perf. 13¾***

227 A86 50c multi 1.40 1.40

Printed in sheets of 8 + label.

Prince Vasilije Petrovic-Njegos (1709-66), Bishop — A87

2009, June 4 ***Perf. 13¾x13***

228 A87 40c multi 1.10 1.10

Vicko Bujovic (1660-1709), Military Leader, and Ship — A88

2009, July 10 ***Perf. 13¾***

229 A88 60c multi 1.75 1.75

Printed in sheets of 8 + label.

Nature Protection A89

Bandaged plants and: 25c, Lake Plav. 50c Lake Crno.

2009, July 10 **Litho.**

230-231 A89 Set of 2 2.10 2.10

Nos. 230-231 each were printed in sheets of 8 + label.

Stamp Day — A90

2009, Oct. 2 ***Perf. 13x13¾***

232 A90 25c multi .75 .75

Joy of Europe — A91

Children's art with: 40c, Dialogue balloon. 50c, Thought balloon.

2009, Nov. 20 ***Perf. 13¾***

233-234 A91 Set of 2 2.75 2.75

Nos. 233-234 each were printed in sheets of 8 + label.

Valtazar Bogisic (1834-1908), Jurist — A92

2009, Dec. 7 ***Perf. 13x13¾***

235 A92 50c multi 1.50 1.50

700-Year-Old Historical Document in Kotor Archives — A93

2009, Dec. 20 ***Perf. 13¾x13***

236 A93 25c multi .75 .75

Dado Duric (1933-2010), Painter — A94

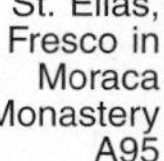

St. Elias, Fresco in Moraca Monastery A95

2010, Jan. 28 *Perf. 13x13¾*

237 A94 50c multi 1.40 1.40
238 A95 50c multi 1.40 1.40

2010 Winter Olympics, Vancouver A96

Designs: €1, Speed skater. €1.50, Snowboarder.

2010, Feb. 12 *Perf. 13¾*

239-240 A96 Set of 2 7.00 7.00

Nos. 239-240 each were printed in sheets of 8 + label.

Danilo Kis (1935-89), Writer — A97

2010, Feb. 22 *Perf. 13¾x13*

241 A97 50c multi 1.40 1.40

Flora — A98

Designs: 25c, Salvia officialis. 50c, Satureja subspicata. 60c, Tilia tomentosa. €1, Epilobium angustifolium.

2010, Mar. 18 **Litho.**

242-245 A98 Set of 4 6.50 6.50

Nos. 242-245 each were printed in sheets of 5 + label.

Europa — A99

Stack of books and: No. 246, 60c, Girl, butterfly, castle, rainbow. No. 247, 90c, Boy, car, star, rope ladder.

No. 248: a, 60c, Books, fairy, crown, dress. b, Books, ship, ladder.

2010, Apr. 22 *Perf. 13¾*

246-247 A99 Set of 2 4.00 4.00

Souvenir Sheet

248 A99 Sheet of 2, #a-b 4.00 4.00

St. Basil of Ostrog (1610-71) A100

2010, May 12 *Perf. 13x13¾*

249 A100 50c multi 1.25 1.25

2010 World Cup Soccer Tournament, South Africa — A101

2010, June 11 *Perf. 13¾*

250 A101 €1.50 multi 3.75 3.75

Printed in sheets of 8 + label.

Tourism A102

Designs: 25c, Canoe and trees. 50c, Mountains. 60c, Waterside straw hut. €1, Beach.

2010, June 24 **Litho.**

251-254 A102 Set of 4 6.00 6.00
254a Souvenir sheet of 4, #251-254 6.00 6.00

Nos. 251-254 each were printed in sheets of 5 + label.

Ship A103

2010, July 8

255 A103 25c multi .65 .65

Printed in sheets of 8 + label.

Balsic Dynasty, 650th Anniv. — A104

2010, July 15 *Perf. 13x13¾*

256 A104 25c multi .65 .65

First Electric Power Network in Montenegro, Cent. — A105

2010, Aug. 19

257 A105 25c multi .65 .65

Kingdom of Montenegro, Cent. — A106

2010, Aug. 28

258 A106 50c multi 1.40 1.40

Bozidar Vukovic (c. 1466-c. 1540), Printer A107

2010, Sept. 16 **Litho.**

259 A107 50c multi 1.40 1.40

Stamp Day — A108

2010, Oct. 2 *Perf. 13¾x13*

260 A108 30c multi .85 .85

Joy of Europe A109

2010, Oct. 21 *Perf. 13¾*

261 A109 90c multi 2.60 2.60

Printed in sheets of 8 + label.

Pasha Husein Mosque, Pljevlja — A110

Ivan Mazuranic (1814-90), Poet — A111

Reverse of Roman Reduced Sestertius Found in Duklja (Podgorica) A112

Miroslav Gospels — A113

Perf. 13¾x13, 13x13¾

2010, Nov. 12

262 A110 30c multi .85 .85
263 A111 40c multi 1.10 1.10
264 A112 80c multi 2.25 2.25
265 A113 90c multi 2.50 2.50
Nos. 262-265 (4) 6.70 6.70

Art through the ages.

Nature Protection — A114

Umbrella over: 30c, Waterfall. 40c, Mountains.

2010, Dec. 16 *Perf. 13¾x13*

266-267 A114 Set of 2 1.90 1.90

ACKNOWLEDGMENT OF RECEIPT STAMPS

Prince Nicholas I
AR1 AR2

Perf. 10½, 11½

1895 **Litho.** **Wmk. 91**

H1 AR1 10n ultra & rose .95 .95

1902 **Unwmk.** *Perf. 12½*

H2 AR2 25h orange & carmine .95 .95

Constitution Issue

#H2 Overprinted in Black Like #66-74

1905

H3 AR2 25h orange & carmine .95 .95
a. "Constitution" 16½mm ('06) .95 .95

See note after 74a.

AR3

Nicholas I — AR4

1907 **Engr.**

H4 AR3 25pa olive .80 .80

1913 **Typo.**

H5 AR4 25pa olive green .80 .80

POSTAGE DUE STAMPS

D1

D2

Perf. 10½, 11, 11½

1894 **Litho.** **Wmk. 91**

J1	D1	1n red	3.25	2.25
J2	D1	2n yellow green	1.10	.65
J3	D1	3n orange	.85	.65
J4	D1	5n olive green	.55	.45
J5	D1	10n violet	.55	.45
J6	D1	20n ultra	.55	.45
J7	D1	30n emerald	.55	.45
J8	D1	50n pale gray grn	.55	.45
		Nos. J1-J8 (8)	7.95	5.80

1902 **Unwmk.** *Perf. 12½*

J9	D2	5h orange	.40	.40
J10	D2	10h olive green	.40	.40
J11	D2	25h dull lilac	.40	.40
J12	D2	50h emerald	.40	.40
J13	D2	1k pale gray green	.40	.40
		Nos. J9-J13 (5)	2.00	2.00

Constitution Issue

Postage Due Stamps of 1902 Overprinted in Black or Red Like Nos. 66-74

1905

J14 D2 5h orange .40 .40
J15 D2 10h olive green (R) .40 .40
J16 D2 25h dull lilac .40 .40
J17 D2 50h emerald .40 .40
J18 D2 1k pale gray green .40 .40
Nos. J14-J18 (5) 2.00 2.00

The 10h with "Constitution" 16½mm is not known used. It is an unissued stamp.

D3

D4

1907 **Typo.** ***Perf. 13x13½***

J19 D3 5pa red brown .40 .40
J20 D3 10pa violet .40 .40
J21 D3 25pa rose .40 .40
J22 D3 50pa green .40 .40
Nos. J19-J22 (4) 1.60 1.60

1913 ***Perf. 12½***

J23 D4 5pa gray .40 .40
J24 D4 10pa violet .40 .40
J25 D4 25pa blue gray .40 .40
J26 D4 50pa lilac rose .40 .40
Nos. J23-J26 (4) 1.60 1.60

ISSUED UNDER AUSTRIAN OCCUPATION

Austrian Military Stamps of 1917 Overprinted

1917 **Unwmk.** ***Perf. 12½***

1N1 M1 10h blue 14.50 12.00
1N2 M1 15h car rose 14.50 12.00

Austrian Military Stamps of 1917 Overprinted in Black

1918

1N3 M1 10h blue 40.00
1N4 M1 15h car rose 1.90

Nos. 1N3-1N4 were never placed in use.
This overprint exists on other stamps of Austria and Bosnia and Herzegovina, and in blue or red.

ISSUED UNDER ITALIAN OCCUPATION

Yugoslavia Nos. 142, 144-154 Overprinted

1941 **Unwmk.** **Typo.** ***Perf. 12½***

2N1 A16 25p black .80 *1.40*
2N2 A16 1d yel grn .80 *1.40*
2N3 A16 1.50d red .80 *1.40*
2N4 A16 2d dp mag .80 *1.40*
2N5 A16 3d dull red brn .80 *1.40*
2N6 A16 4d ultra .80 *1.40*
2N7 A16 5d dark blue 1.20 *3.25*
2N8 A16 5.50d dk vio brn 1.20 *3.25*
2N9 A16 6d slate blue 1.20 *3.25*
2N10 A16 8d sepia 1.20 *3.25*
2N11 A16 12d brt violet 1.20 *3.25*
2N12 A16 16d dull violet 1.20 *3.25*
2N13 A16 20d blue 100.00 *205.00*
2N14 A16 30d brt pink 35.00 *97.50*
Nos. 2N1-2N14 (14) 147.00 *330.40*
Set, never hinged 360.00

The 25p, 1d, 3d, 6d and 8d exist with inverted overprint.

Stamps of Italy, 1929, Overprinted in Red or Black

1941 **Wmk. 140** ***Perf. 14***

2N15 A90 5c ol brn (R) .65 *.95*
2N16 A92 10c dark brn .65 *.95*
2N17 A93 15c sl grn (R) .65 *.95*
2N18 A91 20c rose red .65 *.95*
2N19 A94 25c deep grn .65 *.95*
2N20 A95 30c ol brn (R) .65 *.95*
2N21 A95 50c pur (R) .65 *.95*
2N22 A94 75c rose red .65 *.95*
2N23 A94 1.25 l dp bl (R) .65 *.95*
Nos. 2N15-2N23 (9) 5.85 *8.55*
Set, never hinged 17.50

Yugoslavia Nos. 144-145, 147-148, 148B, 149-152 Overprinted in Black

1942 **Unwmk.** **Typo.** ***Perf. 12½***

2N24 A16 1d yel grn 2.00 2.75
2N25 A16 1.50d red 95.00 65.00
2N26 A16 3d dull red brn 2.00 2.75
2N27 A16 4d ultra 2.00 2.75
2N28 A16 5.50d dk vio brn 2.00 2.75
2N29 A16 6d slate blue 2.00 2.75
2N30 A16 8d sepia 2.00 2.75
2N31 A16 12d brt violet 2.00 2.75
2N32 A16 16d dull violet 2.00 2.75
Nos. 2N24-2N32 (9) 111.00 87.00
Set, never hinged 220.00

Yugoslavia Nos. 142 and 146 with this overprint in red were not officially issued.

Red Overprint

2N24a A16 1d 2.00 *2.75*
2N25a A16 1.50d 145.00 *200.00*
2N26a A16 3d 2.00 *2.75*
2N27a A16 4d 2.00 *2.75*
2N28a A16 5.50d 2.00 *2.75*
2N29a A16 6d 2.00 *2.75*
2N30a A16 8d 2.00 *2.75*
2N31a A16 12d 2.00 *2.75*
2N32a A16 16d 2.00 *2.75*
Nos. 2N24a-2N32a (9) 161.00 *222.00*
Set, never hinged 300.00

Peter Nyegosh and Mt. Lovchen View OS1

Mt. Lovchen Scene OS2

Peter Petrovich Nyegosh — OS3

Designs: 15c, Mountain Church, Eve of Trinity Feast. 20c, Chiefs at Cetinje Monastery. 25c, Folk Dancing at Cetinje Monastery. 50c, Eagle dance. 1.25 l, Chiefs taking loyalty oath. 2 l, Moslem wedding procession. 5 l, Group sitting up with injured standard bearer.

Perf. 14.

1943, May 9 **Unwmk.** **Photo.**

2N33 OS1 5c deep violet 2.40 *4.00*
2N34 OS2 10c dull olive grn 2.40 *4.00*
2N35 OS1 15c brown 2.40 *4.00*
2N36 OS1 20c dull orange 2.40 *4.00*
2N37 OS1 25c dull green 2.40 *4.00*
2N38 OS1 50c rose pink 2.40 *4.00*
2N39 OS1 1.25 l sapphire 2.40 *4.00*
2N40 OS1 2 l blue green 2.40 *4.00*
2N41 OS2 5 l dark red, *sal* 3.60 *14.00*
2N42 OS3 20 l dark vio, *gray* 9.50 *27.50*
Nos. 2N33-2N42 (10) 32.30 *73.50*
Set, never hinged 82.50

Quotations from national poem on backs of stamps.
For overprints and surcharges see Nos. 3N10-3N14, 3NB3-3NB8.

OCCUPATION AIR POST STAMPS

Yugoslavia Nos. C7-C14 Overprinted Like Nos. 2N1-2N14

Perf. 12½, 11½x12½, 12½x11½

1941 **Photo.** **Unwmk.**

2NC1 AP6 50p brown 8.00 7.50
2NC2 AP7 1d yel grn 6.00 7.50
2NC3 AP8 2d blue gray 6.00 7.50
2NC4 AP9 2.50d rose red 8.00 7.50
2NC5 AP6 5d brn vio 47.50 55.00
2NC6 AP7 10d brn lake 47.50 55.00
2NC7 AP8 20d dark grn 92.50 92.50
2NC8 AP9 30d ultra 55.00 55.00
Nos. 2NC1-2NC8 (8) 270.50 287.50
Set, never hinged 660.00

Italy No. C13 Overprinted in Red Like Nos. 2N15-2N23

1941 **Wmk. 140** ***Perf. 14***

2NC9 AP3 50c olive brn .60 .95
Never hinged 1.10

Yugoslavia Nos. C7-C14 Overprinted in Black

a

b

Perf. 12½, 11½x12½, 12½x11½

1942, Jan. 9 **Unwmk.**

2NC10 AP6(a) 50p brown 2.75 *6.00*
2NC11 AP7(a) 1d yel grn 2.75 *6.00*
2NC12 AP8(b) 2d blue gray 2.75 *6.00*
2NC13 AP9(b) 2.50d rose red 2.75 *6.00*
2NC14 AP6(a) 5d brn vio 2.75 *6.00*
2NC15 AP7(a) 10d brn lake 2.75 *6.00*
2NC16 AP8(b) 20d dk grn 110.00 210.00
2NC17 AP9(b) 30d ultra 17.50 42.50
Nos. 2NC10-2NC17 (8) 144.00 288.50
Set, never hinged 365.00

Nos. 2NC10-2NC17 exist with red overprints. Value, each $80 unused, $150 used.

Governatorato
del
Montenegro
c

Overprints *a*, *b* or *c* were applied in 1941-42 to the following Yugoslavia stamps under Italian occupation:
a. or *b*. Nos. B120-B123 (4 values) in black and in red.
c. Nos. B116-B119 (4 values) in black and in red.

Cetinje AP1

Mt. Durmitor — AP6

Designs: 1 l, Seacoast. 2 l, Budus. 5 l, Mt. Lovchen. 10 l, Rieka River.

1943 **Unwmk.** **Photo.** ***Perf. 14***

2NC18 AP1 50c brown .45 *2.40*
2NC19 AP1 1 l ultra .45 *2.40*
2NC20 AP1 2 l rose pink .60 *2.40*
2NC21 AP1 5 l green .75 *2.50*
2NC22 AP1 10 l lake, *rose buff* 3.75 *13.00*
2NC23 AP6 20 l indigo, *rose* 9.00 *27.50*
Nos. 2NC18-2NC23 (6) 15.00 *50.20*
Set, never hinged 37.50

For overprints and surcharges see Nos. 3NC1-3NC5, 3NCB1-3NCB6.

OCCUPATION POSTAGE DUE STAMPS

Yugoslavia Nos. J28-J32 Overprinted Like Nos. 2N1-2N14

1941 **Unwmk.** **Typo.** ***Perf. 12½***

2NJ1 D4 50p violet .50 *1.90*
2NJ2 D4 1d deep magenta .50 *1.90*
2NJ3 D4 2d deep blue .50 *1.90*
2NJ4 D4 5d orange 40.00 *90.00*
2NJ5 D4 10d chocolate 3.25 *9.75*
Nos. 2NJ1-2NJ5 (5) 44.75 *105.45*
Set, never hinged 120.00

Postage Due Stamps of Italy, 1934, Overprinted in Black Like Nos. 2N15-2N23

1942 **Wmk. 140** ***Perf. 14***

2NJ6 D6 10c blue .60 *2.25*
2NJ7 D6 20c rose red .60 *2.25*
2NJ8 D6 30c red orange .60 *2.25*
2NJ9 D6 50c violet .60 *2.25*
2NJ10 D7 1 l red orange .60 *2.25*
Nos. 2NJ6-2NJ10 (5) 3.00 *11.25*
Set, never hinged 7.50

ISSUED UNDER GERMAN OCCUPATION

Yugoslavia Nos. 147-148 Surcharged

1943 **Unwmk.** **Typo.** ***Perf. 12½***

3N1 A16 50c on 3d 3.00 *26.00*
3N2 A16 1 l on 3d 3.00 *26.00*
3N3 A16 1.50 l on 3d 3.00 *26.00*
3N4 A16 2 l on 3d 4.25 *52.50*
3N5 A16 4 l on 3d 4.25 *52.50*
3N6 A16 5 l on 4d 4.50 *52.50*
3N7 A16 8 l on 4d 10.50 *100.00*
3N8 A16 10 l on 4d 15.00 *160.00*
3N9 A16 20 l on 4d 30.00 *375.00*
Nos. 3N1-3N9 (9) 77.50 *870.50*
Set, never hinged 190.00

Montenegro Nos. 2N37-2N41 Ovptd.

1943 Photo. Perf. 14
3N10 OS1 25c dull green 11.00 *175.00*
3N11 OS1 50c rose pink 11.00 *175.00*
3N12 OS1 1.25 l sapphire 11.00 *175.00*
3N13 OS1 2 l blue green 11.00 *175.00*
3N14 OS2 5 l dk red, *sal* 160.00 *2,250.*
Nos. 3N10-3N14 (5) 204.00 *2,950.*
Set, never hinged 500.00

Counterfeits exist.

SEMI-POSTAL STAMPS

Yugoslavia Nos. 147-148 Surcharged

1944 Unwmk. Typo. Perf. 12½
3NB1 A16 15pf + 85pf on 3d 11.00 *160.00*
3NB2 A16 15pf + 85pf on 4d 11.00 *160.00*

Montenegro Nos. 2N37-2N40 Surcharged

d

1944 Photo. Perf. 14
3NB3 OS1 15pf +85pf on 25c 11.00 *160.00*
3NB4 OS1 15pf +1.35m on 50c 11.00 *160.00*
3NB5 OS1 25pf +1.75m on 1.25 l 11.00 *160.00*
3NB6 OS1 25pf +1.75m on 2 l 11.00 *160.00*
Nos. 3NB1-3NB6 (6) 66.00 *960.00*
Set, never hinged 170.00

Surtax on Nos. 3NB1-3NB6 aided refugees.

Montenegro Nos. 2N37-2N38 and Yugoslavia Nos. 147-148 Surcharged

e

f

1944
3NB7 OS1 15pf + 85pf on 25c (e) 9.50 *160.00*
3NB8 OS1 15pf + 1.35m on 50c (e) 9.50 *160.00*
3NB9 A16 50pf + 2.50m on 3d (f) 9.50 *160.00*
3NB10 A16 50pf + 2.50m on 4d (f) 9.50 *160.00*
Nos. 3NB7-3NB10 (4) 38.00 *640.00*
Set, never hinged 95.00

The surtax on Nos. 3NB7-3NB10 aided the Montenegro Red Cross.

AIR POST STAMPS

Montenegro Nos. 2NC18-2NC22 Overprinted Like Nos. 3N10-3N14

1943 Unwmk. Photo. Perf. 14
3NC1 AP1 50c brown 12.50 *175.00*
3NC2 AP1 1 l ultra 12.50 *175.00*
3NC3 AP1 2 l rose pink 12.50 *175.00*
3NC4 AP1 5 l green 12.50 *175.00*
3NC5 AP1 10 l lake, *rose buff* *1,900.* *18,000.*
Nos. 3NC1-3NC5 (5) *1,950.* *18,700.*
Set, never hinged 3,375.

Counterfeits exist.

AIR POST SEMI-POSTAL STAMPS

Montenegro Nos. 2NC18-2NC20 Surcharged Type "d"

1944 Unwmk. Photo. Perf. 14
3NCB1 AP1 15pf +85pf on 50c 11.00 *175.00*
3NCB2 AP1 25pf +1.25m on 1 l 11.00 *175.00*
3NCB3 AP1 50pf +1.50m on 2 l 11.00 *175.00*
Nos. 3NCB1-3NCB3 (3) 33.00 *525.00*
Set, never hinged 80.00

The surtax aided refugees.

Same Surcharged Type "e"

1944
3NCB4 AP1 25pf +1.75m on 50c 9.50 *160.00*
3NCB5 AP1 25pf +2.75m on 1 l 9.50 *160.00*
3NCB6 AP1 50pf +2m on 2 l 9.50 *160.00*
Nos. 3NCB4-3NCB6 (3) 28.50 *480.00*
Set, never hinged 70.00

The surtax aided the Montenegro Red Cross.

MONTSERRAT

ˌmänˌtˌ-sə-ˈrat

LOCATION — West Indies southeast of Puerto Rico
GOVT. — British Crown Colony
AREA — 39 sq. mi.
POP. — 12,853 (1999 est.)

Montserrat was one of the four presidencies of the former Leeward Islands colony until it became a colony itself in 1956.

Montserrat stamps were discontinued in 1890 and resumed in 1903. In the interim, stamps of Leeward Islands were used. In 1903-56, stamps of Montserrat and Leeward Islands were used concurrently.

12 Pence = 1 Shilling
20 Shillings = 1 Pound
100 Cents = 1 Dollar (1951)

Catalogue values for unused stamps in this country are for Never Hinged items, beginning with Scott 104 in the regular postage section, Scott B1 in the semi-postal section, Scott O45 in the officials section.

Watermark

Wmk. 380 — "POST OFFICE"

Values for unused stamps are for examples with original gum as defined in the catalogue introduction. Very fine examples of Nos. 1-2, 6 and 11 will have perforations touching the design on at least one side due to the narrow spacing of the stamps on the plates. Stamps with perfs clear of the framelines on all four sides are scarce and will command higher prices.

Stamps of Antigua Overprinted in Black

a

1876 Engr. Wmk. 1 Perf. 14
1 A1 1p red 27.50 19.00
a. Vert. or diag. half used as ½p on cover 1,650.
c. "S" inverted 1,250. 875.00
2 A1 6p green 75.00 50.00
a. Vertical half used as 3p on cover —
b. Vertical third used as 2p on cover 6,000.
c. "S" inverted 1,450. 1,350.
d. 6p blue green 1,350.
e. As "d," "S" inverted *12,750.*

Some experts consider Nos. 2d, 2e to be from a trial printing.

Queen Victoria — A2

1880 Typo.
3 A2 2½p red brown 300.00 225.00
4 A2 4p blue 160.00 47.50

See Nos. 5, 7-10.

1884 Wmk. 2
5 A2 ½p green 1.25 *8.75*

Antigua No. 18 Overprinted type "a"

1884 Engr.
6 A1 1p rose red 19.00 20.00
a. Vert. half used as ½p on cover 1,550.
b. "S" inverted 1,100. 1,100.

Type of 1880

1884-85 Typo.
7 A2 2½p red brown 275.00 77.50
8 A2 2½p ultra ('85) 25.00 22.50
9 A2 4p blue 2,100. 300.00
10 A2 4p red lilac ('85) 6.00 3.50

Antigua No. 20 Overprinted type "a"

1884 Engr. Perf. 12
11 A1 1p red 82.50 65.00
a. "S" inverted 2,350. 1,550.
b. Vert. half used as ½p on cover 1,900.

Symbol of the Colony — A3

King Edward VII — A4

1903 Wmk. 2 Typo. Perf. 14
12 A3 ½p gray green .90 17.00
13 A3 1p car & black .90 .50
14 A3 2p brown & black 6.50 *45.00*
15 A3 2½p ultra & black 1.75 2.10
16 A3 3p dk vio & brn orange 5.00 *47.50*
17 A3 6p ol grn & vio 8.00 57.50
18 A3 1sh vio & gray grn 12.00 20.00
19 A3 2sh brn org & gray green 30.00 20.00
20 A3 2sh6p blk & gray grn 22.50 *47.50*

Wmk. 1
21 A4 5sh car & black 150.00 *200.00*
Nos. 12-21 (10) 237.55 *457.10*

1904-08 Wmk. 3
Chalky Paper
22 A3 ½p grn & gray grn 7.50 2.25
23 A3 1p car & blk ('08) 17.00 *30.00*
24 A3 2p brown & black 2.50 1.40
25 A3 2½p ultra & blk ('06) 3.00 *7.75*
26 A3 3p dk vio & brn orange 11.00 2.75
27 A3 6p ol grn & vio 11.00 *6.50*
28 A3 1sh violet & gray grn ('08) 11.50 8.50
29 A3 2sh brn org & gray grn ('08) 47.50 *52.50*
30 A3 2sh6p blk & gray grn ('08) 55.00 *57.50*
31 A4 5sh car & blk ('07) 140.00 *150.00*
Nos. 22-31 (10) 306.00 *319.15*

The ½, 2, 3 and 6p are also on ordinary paper.

1908-13
Ordinary Paper
31A A3 ½p deep green 8.25 1.10
32 A3 1p carmine 1.75 .35
33 A3 2p gray 2.00 *18.00*
34 A3 2½p ultramarine 2.50 4.25

Chalky Paper
35 A3 3p vio, *yellow* 1.10 *22.50*
36 A3 6p red vio & gray vio 7.75 *60.00*
37 A3 1sh blk, *green* 10.00 *55.00*
38 A3 2sh bl & vio, *bl* 42.50 *67.50*
39 A3 2sh 6p car & blk, *blue* 35.00 *87.50*
40 A4 5sh grn & scar, *yel* 60.00 92.50

Surface-colored Paper
41 A3 3p vio, *yel* ('13) 4.50 *37.50*
Nos. 31A-41 (11) 175.35 *446.20*

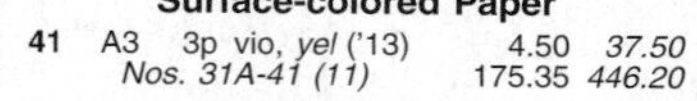

King George V
A5 A6

1913
Chalky Paper
42 A5 5sh green & scar, *yel* 80.00 *130.00*

1916-22 Wmk. 3 Perf. 14
Ordinary Paper
43 A6 ½p green .65 2.75
44 A6 1p scarlet 1.50 .90
45 A6 2p gray 2.25 *5.00*
46 A6 2½p ultramarine 2.50 *24.00*

Chalky Paper
47 A6 3p violet, *yel* 1.40 *17.50*
48 A6 4p blk & red, *yel* ('22) 6.50 *42.50*
49 A6 6p dl vio & red violet 3.50 *27.50*
50 A6 1sh blk, *bl grn,* ol back 3.50 *30.00*
51 A6 2sh vio & ultra, *bl* 17.00 *45.00*
52 A6 2sh 6p blk & red, *bl* 30.00 *80.00*
53 A6 5sh grn & red, *yel* 47.50 *80.00*
Nos. 43-53 (11) 116.30 *355.15*

For overprints see Nos. MR1-MR3.

1922-29 Wmk. 4

Ordinary Paper

54 A6 ¼p brown .35 6.25
55 A6 ½p green ('23) .30 .30
56 A6 1p dp violet ('23) .80 .70
57 A6 1p carmine ('29) 1.10 1.75
58 A6 1½p orange 2.50 *11.00*
59 A6 1½p rose red ('23) .60 *4.25*
60 A6 1½p fawn ('29) 2.25 .55
61 A6 2p gray .80 *2.25*
62 A6 2½p ultramarine 9.25 18.00
63 A6 2½p orange ('23) 2.75 *21.00*
64 A6 3p ultra ('23) .80 *18.00*

Chalky Paper

65 A6 3p vio, *yel* ('26) 2.00 *5.50*
66 A6 4p black & red, *yel* ('23) 1.75 *14.00*
67 A6 5p dull vio & ol grn 4.50 *11.00*
68 A6 6p dull vio & red vio ('23) 3.50 *8.50*
69 A6 1sh blk, *emer* ('23) 3.50 *8.00*
70 A6 2sh vio & ultra, *bl* 8.00 *18.00*
71 A6 2sh 6p blk & red, *bl* ('23) 14.00 *57.50*
72 A6 3sh green & vio 14.00 *21.00*
73 A6 4sh black & scar 17.50 *42.50*
74 A6 5sh grn & red, *yel* ('23) 30.00 *55.00*
Nos. 54-74 (21) 120.25 *325.05*

Tercentenary Issue

New Plymouth and Harbor A7

1932, Apr. 18 Engr.

75 A7 ½p green .85 *11.00*
76 A7 1p red .85 *6.50*
77 A7 1½p orange brown 1.40 *2.75*
78 A7 2p gray 1.90 *19.00*
79 A7 2½p ultra 1.40 *18.00*
80 A7 3p orange 1.90 *21.00*
81 A7 6p violet 2.50 *35.00*
82 A7 1sh olive green 14.50 *47.50*
83 A7 2sh6p lilac rose 52.50 *87.50*
84 A7 5sh dark brown 115.00 *200.00*
Nos. 75-84 (10) 192.80 448.25
Set, never hinged 400.00

300th anniv. of the colonization of Montserrat.

Common Design Types pictured following the introduction.

Silver Jubilee Issue

Common Design Type

1935, May 6 Perf. 11x12

85 CD301 1p car & dk blue 1.25 4.25
86 CD301 1½p gray blk & ultra 2.00 *3.75*
87 CD301 2½p ultra & brn 2.75 *4.25*
88 CD301 1sh brn vio & ind 4.25 *18.00*
Nos. 85-88 (4) 10.25 *30.25*
Set, never hinged 19.00

Coronation Issue

Common Design Type

1937, May 12 Perf. 13½x14

89 CD302 1p carmine .20 1.50
90 CD302 1½p brown .40 .35
91 CD302 2½p bright ultra .35 1.50
Nos. 89-91 (3) .95 3.35
Set, never hinged 1.75

Carr's Bay — A8

Sea Island Cotton — A9

Botanic Station A10

1941-48 Perf. 14

92 A8 ½p dk grn ('42) .20 .20
93 A9 1p car ('42) .40 .35
94 A9 1½p rose vio ('42) .40 *.55*
95 A10 2p red orange 1.20 .80
96 A9 2½p brt ultra ('43) .40 .35
97 A8 3p brown ('42) 1.50 .45
98 A10 6p dull vio ('42) 2.00 .70
99 A8 1sh brn lake ('42) 1.75 .35
100 A10 2sh6p slate bl ('43) 13.50 3.00
101 A8 5sh car rose ('42) 16.00 3.50

Perf. 12

102 A10 10sh blue ('48) 10.00 *30.00*
103 A8 £1 black ('48) 10.00 *35.00*
Nos. 92-103 (12) 57.35 *75.25*
Set, never hinged 85.00

1938, Aug. 2 Perf. 13

92a A8 ½p 2.50 *2.00*
93a A8 1p 2.50 .40
94a A9 1½p 11.00 *1.00*
95a A10 2p 11.00 *1.00*
96a A9 2½p 1.25 *1.50*
97a A8 3p 3.00 *3.25*
98a A10 6p 11.50 *1.25*
99a A8 1sh 11.50 *1.25*
100a A10 2sh6p 20.00 *1.00*
101a A8 5sh 24.00 *10.00*
Nos. 92a-101a (10) 98.25 *22.65*
Set, never hinged 200.00

Catalogue values for unused stamps in this section, from this point to the end of the section, are for Never Hinged items.

Peace Issue

Common Design Type

1946, Nov. 1 Engr. Perf. 13½x14

104 CD303 1½p deep magenta .20 .20
105 CD303 3p brown .20 .20

Silver Wedding Issue

Common Design Types

1949, Jan. 3 Photo. Perf. 14x14½

106 CD304 2½p brt ultra .20 .20

Engraved; Name Typographed

Perf. 11½x11

107 CD305 5sh rose carmine 9.00 *18.00*

UPU Issue

Common Design Types

Engr.; Name Typo. on 3p and 6p

Perf. 13½, 11x11½

1949, Oct. 10 Wmk. 4

108 CD306 2½p ultramarine .45 *.90*
109 CD307 3p chocolate 1.10 .65
110 CD308 6p lilac .75 .75
111 CD309 1sh rose violet 1.10 1.10
Nos. 108-111 (4) 3.40 3.40

University Issue

Common Design Types

1951, Feb. 16 Engr. Perf. 14x14½

112 CD310 3c rose lil & gray blk .25 *.50*
113 CD311 12c violet & black .60 *.80*

Government House A11

Designs (portrait at right on 12c, 24c and $2.40): 2c, $1.20, Cotton field. 3c, Map of Presidency. 4c, 24c, Picking tomatoes. 5c, 12c, St. Anthony's Church. 6c, $4.80, Badge of Presidency. 8c, 60c, Cotton ginning.

Perf. 11½x11

1951, Sept. 17 Engr. Wmk. 4

114 A11 1c gray .20 .20
115 A11 2c green .20 .20
116 A11 3c orange brown .20 .20
117 A11 4c rose carmine .20 .20
118 A11 5c red violet .20 .20
119 A11 6c dark brown .35 .35
120 A11 8c dark blue .50 .50
121 A11 12c red brn & blue 1.00 1.00
122 A11 24c emer & rose carmine 1.40 1.40
123 A11 60c rose car & gray black 2.75 2.75
124 A11 $1.20 dp bl & emer 9.00 9.00
125 A11 $2.40 dp grn & gray black 11.00 *13.00*
126 A11 $4.80 pur & gray blk 22.50 *27.50*
Nos. 114-126 (13) 49.50 *56.50*

Coronation Issue

Common Design Type

1953, June 2 Perf. 13½x13

127 CD312 2c dark green & black .50 .50

Type of 1951 with Portrait of Queen Elizabeth II

½c, 3c, "Map of Presidency." 48c, Cotton field.

1953-57 Perf. 11½x11

128 A11 ½c violet ('56) .20 .20
129 A11 1c gray black .20 .20
130 A11 2c green .20 .20
131 A11 3c orange brown .65 .65
132 A11 4c rose car ('55) .20 .20
133 A11 5c red vio ('55) .20 .20
134 A11 6c dk brown ('55) .70 .70
135 A11 8c dp ultra ('55) .20 .20
136 A11 12c red brn & blue ('55) .20 .20
137 A11 24c emer & rose car ('55) .80 .80
138 A11 48c rose violet & olive ('57) 1.60 1.60
139 A11 60c rose car & blk ('55) 2.00 2.00
140 A11 $1.20 bl & emer ('55) 4.00 4.00
141 A11 $2.40 dp green & blk ('55) 8.00 8.00
142 A11 $4.80 pur & gray black ('55) 35.00 35.00
Nos. 128-142 (15) 54.15 54.15

See Nos. 146-149, 156.

West Indies Federation

Common Design Type

Perf. 11½x11

1958, Apr. 22 Engr. Wmk. 314

143 CD313 3c green .45 .20
144 CD313 6c blue .65 .45
145 CD313 12c carmine rose 1.25 .65
Nos. 143-145 (3) 2.35 1.30

Type of 1953-57

As before, but inscribed: "Map of the Colony" (½c, 3c) "Badge of the Colony" (6c, $4.80).

1958 Wmk. 4 Perf. 11½x11

146 A11 ½c violet .50 .20
147 A11 3c orange brown .50 .75
148 A11 6c dark brown .25 .20
149 A11 $4.80 pur & gray blk 11.00 *9.00*
Nos. 146-149 (4) 12.25 *10.15*

Freedom from Hunger Issue

Common Design Type

Perf. 14x14½

1963, June 4 Photo. Wmk. 314

150 CD314 12c lilac .75 .65

Red Cross Centenary Issue

Common Design Type

1963, Sept. 2 Litho. Perf. 13

151 CD315 4c black & red .20 .20
152 CD315 12c ultra & red .75 .55

Shakespeare Issue

Common Design Type

1964, Apr. 23 Photo. Perf. 14x14½

153 CD316 12c slate blue .35 .25

Type of 1953-57

Perf. 11½x11

1964, Oct. 30 Engr. Wmk. 314

156 A11 2c green 1.00 .20

ITU Issue

Common Design Type

Perf. 11x11½

1965, May 17 Litho. Wmk. 314

157 CD317 4c ver & lilac .20 .20
158 CD317 48c emer & rose red 1.00 .90

Pineapple — A12

Wmk. 314 Upright

1965, Aug. 16 Photo. Perf. 15x14

159 A12 1c shown .20 .20
160 A12 2c Avacado .20 .20
161 A12 3c Soursop .20 .20
162 A12 4c Peppers .20 .20
163 A12 5c Mango .20 .20
164 A12 6c Tomatoes .20 .20
165 A12 8c Guava .20 .20
166 A12 10c Okra .20 .20
167 A12 12c Limes .25 .20
168 A12 20c Oranges .35 .20
169 A12 24c Bananas .55 .40
170 A12 42c Onion 1.10 1.25
171 A12 48c Cabbage 1.40 1.40
172 A12 60c Papayas 1.50 1.60
173 A12 $1.20 Pumpkin 1.75 2.25
174 A12 $2.40 Sweet potato 4.50 5.25
175 A12 $4.80 Eggplant 9.00 11.00
Nos. 159-175 (17) 22.00 25.15

For surcharges see Nos. 193-198.

1969 Wmk. 314 Sideways

159a A12 1c .20 .20
160a A12 2c .45 *.50*
161a A12 3c .30 .40
162a A12 4c .75 .40
163a A12 5c .90 *1.00*
166a A12 10c 1.75 *2.00*
168a A12 20c 2.10 *2.40*
Nos. 159a-168a (7) 6.45 6.90

Intl. Cooperation Year Issue

Common Design Type

1965, Oct. 25 Litho. Perf. 14½

176 CD318 2c lt green & claret .20 .20
177 CD318 12c lt violet & green .40 .40

Churchill Memorial Issue

Common Design Type

1966, Jan. 24 Photo. Perf. 14

Design in Black, Gold and Carmine Rose

178 CD319 1c bright blue .20 .20
179 CD319 2c green .20 .20
180 CD319 24c brown .35 .30
181 CD319 42c violet .75 .75
Nos. 178-181 (4) 1.50 1.45

Royal Visit Issue

Common Design Type

Perf. 11x12

1966, Feb. 4 Litho. Wmk. 314

182 CD320 14c violet blue .50 .20
183 CD320 24c dk carmine rose .95 .95

WHO Headquarters Issue

Common Design Type

1966, Sept. 20 Litho. Perf. 14

184 CD322 12c multicolored .20 .20
185 CD322 60c multicolored .75 .75

UNESCO Anniversary Issue

Common Design Type

1966, Dec. 1 Litho. Perf. 14

186 CD323 4c "Education" .20 .20
a. Orange omitted 50.00
187 CD323 60c "Science" .40 .40
188 CD323 $1.80 "Culture" 1.75 1.75
Nos. 186-188 (3) 2.35 2.35

On No. 186a, the squares of the lowercase letters appear in yellow.

Sailing and ITY Emblem A13

ITY Emblem and: 15c, Waterfall, Chance Mountain, vert. 16c, Beach scene. 24c, Golfers.

1967, Dec. 29 Photo. Wmk. 314

189 A13 5c multicolored .35 .35
190 A13 15c multicolored .35 .35
191 A13 16c multicolored .45 .45
192 A13 24c multicolored .95 .95
Nos. 189-192 (4) 2.10 2.10

Issued for International Tourist Year.

Nos. 167, 169, 171, 173-175 and Type Surcharged

1968, May 6 Perf. 15x14

193 A12 15c on 12c multi .25 .25
a. Wmkd. sideways ('69) 1.50 *1.75*

194 A12 25c on 24c multi .40 .40
a. Wmkd. sideways ('69) 2.50 *3.00*
195 A12 50c on 48c multi .85 .85
a. Wmkd. sideways ('69) 5.25 *6.00*
196 A12 $1 on $1.20 multi 1.25 1.25
197 A12 $2.50 on $2.40 multi 2.75 2.75
198 A12 $5 on $4.80 multi 5.50 5.50
Nos. 193-198 (6) 11.00 11.00

The surcharge bars are slightly thinner on the "Wmkd. sideways" varieties.

Woman Runner A14

Designs: 25c, Weight lifter. 50c, Athlete on rings. $1, Runner and Toltec sculptures, vert.

Perf. 14½x14, 14x14½

1968, July 31 Photo. Wmk. 314

199 A14 15c gold, brt grn & rose claret .20 .20
200 A14 25c gold, org & blue .20 .20
201 A14 50c gold, ver & green .25 .25
202 A14 $1 multicolored .55 .55
Nos. 199-202 (4) 1.20 1.20

19th Olympic Games, Mexico City, 10/12-27.

Albert T. Marryshow — A15

Portraits and Human Rights Flame: 5c, Alexander Hamilton. 25c, William Wilberforce. 50c, Dag Hammarskjold. $1, Rev. Martin Luther King, Jr.

1968, Dec. 2 Photo. *Perf. 14x14½*

203 A15 5c multicolored .20 .20
204 A15 15c multicolored .20 .20
205 A15 25c multicolored .20 .20
206 A15 50c multicolored .20 .20
207 A15 $1 multicolored .50 .50
Nos. 203-207 (5) 1.30 1.30

International Human Rights Year.

The Two Trinities, by Murillo A16

Map of Caribbean A17

Christmas: 15c, 50c, The Adoration of the Magi, by Botticelli.

1968, Dec. 16 *Perf. 14½x14*

208 A16 5c red & multi .20 .20
209 A16 15c dk green & multi .20 .20
210 A16 25c purple & multi .20 .20
211 A16 50c brown & multi .40 .40
Nos. 208-211 (4) 1.00 1.00

1969, May 27 Photo. *Perf. 14*

Design: 35c, 50c, "Strength in Unity," horiz.

212 A17 15c green & multi .20 .20
213 A17 20c brown & multi .20 .20
214 A17 35c dp carmine & multi .25 .25
215 A17 50c multicolored .35 .35
Nos. 212-215 (4) 1.00 1.00

First anniversary of CARIFTA (Caribbean Free Trade Area).

Telephone and Map — A18

Development Projects (Map and): 25c, Book and "New Schools." 50c, Planes (air transport service). $1, Pylon and power lines.

Wmk. 314

1969, July 29 Litho. *Perf. 13½*

216 A18 15c multicolored .20 .20
217 A18 25c multicolored .20 .20
218 A18 50c multicolored .30 .30
219 A18 $1 multicolored .60 .60
Nos. 216-219 (4) 1.30 1.30

Dolphin A19

Fish: 15c, Atlantic sailfish. 25c, Blackfin tuna and fishing boat. 40c, Spanish mackerel.

1969, Nov. 1 Photo. *Perf. 13x14*

220 A19 5c multicolored .20 .20
221 A19 15c multicolored .35 .35
222 A19 25c multicolored .70 .70
223 A19 40c multicolored 1.25 1.25
Nos. 220-223 (4) 2.50 2.50

King Caspar, Virgin and Child (Stained-glass Window) — A20

Christmas: 50c, Nativity, by Leonard Limosin, horiz.

Perf. 12½x13, 13x12½

1969, Dec. 10 Litho. Wmk. 314

224 A20 15c violet & multi .20 .20
225 A20 25c red & multi .25 .25
226 A20 50c orange & multi .45 .45
Nos. 224-226 (3) .90 .90

Red Cross and Distribution of Hearing Aids — A21

Red Cross and: 3c, Fund raising sale and invalid. 15c, Car bringing handicapped to work. 20c, Instruction for blind worker.

1970, Apr. 13 Litho. *Perf. 14½*

227 A21 3c multicolored .20 .20
228 A21 4c multicolored .20 .20
229 A21 15c multicolored .25 .25
230 A21 20c multicolored .35 .35
Nos. 227-230 (4) 1.00 1.00

Centenary of British Red Cross Society.

Red-footed Booby A22

Birds: 2c, Killy hawk, vert. 3c, Frigate bird, vert. 4c, White egret, vert. 5c, Brown pelican, vert. 10c, Bananaquit, vert. 15c, Common ani. 20c, Tropic bird. 25c, Montserrat oriole. 50c, Greenthroated carib, vert. $1, Antillean crested hummingbird. $2.50, Little blue heron, vert. $5, Purple-throated carib. $10, Forest thrush.

Wmk. 314 Upright on Horiz. Stamps, Sideways on Vert. Stamps

Perf. 14x14½, 14½x14

1970-74 Photo.

231 A22 1c yel org & multi .20 .20
232 A22 2c lt vio & multi .20 .20
233 A22 3c multicolored .20 .20
234 A22 4c lt grn & multi .20 .20
235 A22 5c bister & multi .20 .20
236 A22 10c gray & multi .20 .20
237 A22 15c multicolored .50 .40
238 A22 20c rose brn & multi .65 .55
239 A22 25c brown & multi .85 .70
240 A22 50c lt vio & multi 1.75 1.40
241 A22 $1 multicolored 3.00 2.40
242 A22 $2.50 dl bl & multi 6.75 5.50
243 A22 $5 multicolored 13.50 11.00
243A A22 $10 blue & multi 26.00 22.50
Nos. 231-243A (14) 54.20 45.65

Issued: $10, 10/30/74; others 7/2/70.
For surcharges and overprints see Nos. 314, 317, 337-339, O1-O4.

Wmk. Sideways on Horiz. Stamps, Upright on Vert. Stamps

1972-74

231a A22 1c multicolored .75 *1.25*
232a A22 2c multicolored .95 *1.25*
233a A22 3c multicolored .95 *1.25*
234a A22 4c multicolored 1.40 *1.60*
235a A22 5c multicolored 1.75 *2.00*
237a A22 15c multicolored 4.75 *4.75*
238a A22 20c multicolored 6.75 *7.75*
239a A22 25c multicolored 9.50 *9.75*
Nos. 231a-239a (8) 26.80 *29.60*

Issued: 1c, 2c, 3c, 7/21/72; 5c, 15c, 3/8/73; 20c, 10/2/73; 4c, 2/4/74; 25c, 5/17/74.

"Madonna and Child with Animals," after Dürer — A23

Christmas: 15c, $1, Adoration of the Shepherds, by Domenichino (Domenico Zampieri).

1970, Sept. 21 Litho. *Perf. 14*

244 A23 5c lt blue & multi .20 .20
245 A23 15c red orange & multi .20 .20
246 A23 20c ol green & multi .25 .25
247 A23 $1 multicolored 1.00 1.00
Nos. 244-247 (4) 1.65 1.65

War Memorial, Plymouth — A24

Tourist Publicity: 15c, Fort St. George and view of Plymouth. 25c, Beach at Carrs Bay. 50c, Golf Course.

1970, Nov. 30 Litho. *Perf. 14*

248 A24 5c multicolored .20 .20
249 A24 15c multicolored .40 .40
250 A24 25c multicolored .70 .70
251 A24 50c multicolored 1.50 1.50
a. Souvenir sheet of 4, #248-251 7.50 7.50
Nos. 248-251 (4) 2.80 2.80

Girl Guide — A25

"Noli me Tangere," by Orcagna (Andrea di Cione) — A26

Girl Guides' 60th Anniv.: 15c, 25c, Brownie.

1970, Dec. 31

252 A25 10c orange & multi .20 .20
253 A25 15c lt blue & multi .20 .20
254 A25 25c lilac & multi .30 .30
255 A25 40c multicolored .50 .50
Nos. 252-255 (4) 1.20 1.20

Perf. 13½x13

1971, Mar. 22 Photo. Wmk. 314

Easter: 5c, 20c, Descent from the Cross, by Jan van Hemessen.

256 A26 5c orange brn & multi .20 .20
257 A26 15c multicolored .20 .20
258 A26 20c green & multi .25 .25
259 A26 40c blue green & multi .50 .50
Nos. 256-259 (4) 1.15 1.15

Distinguished Flying Cross and Medal — A27

"Nativity with Saints" (detail), by Romanino A28

Highest Awards for Military Personnel: 20c, Military Cross and Medal. 40c, Distinguished Service Cross and Medal. $1, Victoria Cross.

Perf. 14½x14

1971, July 8 Litho. Wmk. 314

260 A27 10c gray, vio & silver .20 .20
261 A27 20c green & multi .25 .25
262 A27 40c lt bl, dk bl & sil .45 .45
263 A27 $1 red, dk brn & gold 1.25 1.25
Nos. 260-263 (4) 2.15 2.15

50th anniversary of the British Commonwealth Ex-services League.

1971, Sept. 16 *Perf. 14x13½*

Christmas (Paintings): 15c, $1, Angels' Choir, by Simon Marmion.

264 A28 5c brown & multi .20 .20
265 A28 15c emerald & multi .20 .20
266 A28 20c ultra & multi .20 .20
267 A28 $1 red & multi 1.10 1.10
Nos. 264-267 (4) 1.70 1.70

Piper Apache, First Landing at Olveston Airfield — A29

Designs: 10c, Beech Twin Bonanza. 15c, De Havilland Heron. 20c, Britten Norman Islander. 40c, De Havilland Twin Otter. 75c, Hawker Siddeley 748 and stewardesses.

1971, Dec. 16 *Perf. 13½x14*

268 A29 5c multicolored .20 .20
269 A29 10c multicolored .30 .30
270 A29 15c multicolored .45 .45
271 A29 20c multicolored .65 .65
272 A29 40c multicolored 1.25 1.25
273 A29 75c multicolored 2.00 2.00
a. Souvenir sheet of 6, #268-273 19.00 19.00
Nos. 268-273 (6) 4.85 4.85

14th anniversary of Leeward Islands Air Transport (LIAT).

Chapel of Christ in Gethsemane, Coventry Cathedral — A30

Easter: 10c, 75c, The Agony in the Garden, by Giovanni Bellini.

1972, Mar. 9 **Litho.** *Perf. 13½x13*

274 A30 5c red & multi .20 .20
275 A30 10c blue & multi .20 .20
276 A30 20c emerald & multi .25 .25
277 A30 75c lilac & multi 1.25 1.25
Nos. 274-277 (4) 1.90 1.90

Iguana A31

Designs: 15c, Spotted ameiva (lizard), vert. 20c, Frog ("mountain chicken"), vert. $1, Redfoot tortoises.

1972, June 8 **Litho.** *Perf. 14½*

278 A31 15c lilac rose & multi .50 .50
279 A31 20c black & multi .60 .60
280 A31 40c blue & multi 1.25 1.25
281 A31 $1 green & multi 2.50 2.50
Nos. 278-281 (4) 4.85 4.85

Madonna of the Chair, by Raphael A32

Christmas (Paintings): 35c, Virgin and Child with Cherubs, by Bernardino Fungai. 50c, Magnificat Madonna, by Botticelli. $1, Virgin and Child with St. John and Angel, by Botticelli.

1972, Oct. 18 *Perf. 13½*

282 A32 10c violet & multi .20 .20
283 A32 35c brt red & multi .40 .40
284 A32 50c red brown & multi .70 .70
285 A32 $1 olive & multi 1.50 1.50
Nos. 282-285 (4) 2.80 2.80

Silver Wedding Issue, 1972

Common Design Type

Design: Queen Elizabeth II, Prince Philip, tomatoes, papayas, limes.

Perf. 14x14½

1972, Nov. 20 **Photo.** **Wmk. 314**

286 CD324 35c car rose & multi .20 .20
287 CD324 $1 ultra & multi .60 .60

Passionflower A33

Designs: 35c, Passiflora vitifolia. 75c, Passiflora amabilis. $1, Passiflora alata caerulea.

1973, Apr. 9 **Litho.** *Perf. 14x13½*

288 A33 20c purple & multi .50 .50
289 A33 35c multicolored .85 .85
290 A33 75c brt blue & multi 1.25 1.25
291 A33 $1 multicolored 2.25 2.25
Nos. 288-291 (4) 4.85 4.85

Easter. Black backprinting gives story of passionflower.

Montserrat Monastery, Spain — A34

35c, Columbus aboard ship sighting Montserrat. 60c, Columbus' ship off Montserrat. $1, Arms and map of Montserrat & neighboring islands.

1973, July 16 **Litho.** *Perf. 13½x14*

292 A34 10c multicolored .45 .45
293 A34 35c multicolored 1.00 1.00
294 A34 60c multicolored 1.60 1.60
295 A34 $1 multicolored 2.50 2.50
a. Souvenir sheet of 4, #292-295 25.00 25.00
Nos. 292-295 (4) 5.55 5.55

480th anniversary of the discovery of Montserrat by Columbus.

Virgin and Child, Studio of David — A35

Masqueraders A36

Christmas (Paintings): 35c, Holy Family with St. John, by Jacob Jordaens. 50c, Virgin and Child, by Bellini. 90c, Virgin and Child by Carlo Dolci.

1973, Oct. 15 **Litho.** *Perf. 14x13½*

296 A35 20c blue & multi .25 .25
297 A35 35c ol bister & multi .40 .40
298 A35 50c brt green & multi .95 .95
299 A35 90c brt rose & multi 1.90 1.90
Nos. 296-299 (4) 3.50 3.50

Princess Anne's Wedding Issue

Common Design Type

1973, Nov. 14 *Perf. 14*

300 CD325 35c brt green & multi .20 .20
301 CD325 $1 multicolored .65 .65

1974, Apr. 8

302 A36 20c Steel band, horiz. .25 .25
303 A36 35c shown .60 .60
304 A36 60c Girl weaving .90 .90
305 A36 $1 University Center, horiz. 1.40 1.40
a. Souvenir sheet of 4, #302-305 11.00 11.00
Nos. 302-305 (4) 3.15 3.15

University of the West Indies, 25th anniv. For surcharge see No. 316.

Hands Holding Letters, UPU Emblem A37

Designs: 2c, 5c, $1, Hands and figures from UPU Monument, Bern; UPU emblem. 3c, 50c, like 1c.

1974, July 3 **Litho.** *Perf. 14*

306 A37 1c violet & multi .20 .20
307 A37 2c red & black .20 .20
308 A37 3c olive & multi .20 .20
309 A37 5c orange & black .20 .20
310 A37 50c brown & multi .35 .35
311 A37 $1 grnsh blue & black .85 .85
Nos. 306-311 (6) 2.00 2.00

Centenary of Universal Postal Union. For surcharges see Nos. 315-318.

Churchill, Parliament, Big Ben — A38

Churchill and Blenheim Palace — A39

Perf. 13x13½

1974, Nov. 30 **Unwmk.**

312 A38 35c ocher & multi .20 .20
313 A39 70c brt green & multi .60 .60
a. Souvenir sheet of 2, #312-313 1.10 1.10

Sir Winston Churchill (1874-1965).

Nos. 241, 304, 310-311 Surcharged with New Value and Two Bars

Perf. 14x14½, 14

Photo., Litho.

1974, Oct. 2 **Wmk. 314**

314 A22 2c on $1 multi .20 .20
315 A37 5c on 50c multi 1.10 1.10
316 A36 10c on 60c multi 3.00 3.00
317 A22 20c on $1 multi 1.00 1.00
a. One bar in surcharge 2.25 2.25
318 A37 35c on $1 multi 2.25 2.25
Nos. 314-318 (5) 7.55 7.55

Carib Carbet (House) A40

Carib Artifacts: 20c, Necklace (caracoli). 35c, Club. 70c, Canoe.

Wmk. 314

1975, Mar. 3 **Litho.** *Perf. 14*

319 A40 5c dk red, ocher & blk .20 .20
320 A40 20c blk, och & dk red .20 .20
321 A40 35c blk, dk red & och .30 .30
322 A40 70c ocher, dk red & blk .55 .55
a. Souvenir booklet 3.00
Nos. 319-322 (4) 1.25 1.25

No. 322a contains 2 self-adhesive panes printed on peelable paper backing with bicolored advertising on back. One pane of 6 contains 3 each similar to Nos. 320-321; the other pane of 4 contains one each similar to Nos. 319-322. Stamps are imperf. x roulette. Panes have commemorative marginal inscription.

One Bitt A41

Old Local Coinage (1785-1801): 10c, Eighth of a dollar. 35c, Quarter dollars. $2, One dollar.

1975, Sept. 1 **Litho.** *Perf. 14*

323 A41 5c ultra, silver & blk .20 .20
324 A41 10c brown org, sil & blk .20 .20
325 A41 35c green, silver & blk .35 .35
326 A41 $2 brt rose, sil & blk 1.75 1.75
a. Souvenir sheet of 4, #323-326 3.00 3.00
Nos. 323-326 (4) 2.50 2.50

Explanation and description of coinage printed in black on back of souvenir sheet.

Montserrat Nos. 1 and 2 — A42

10c, Post Office, Montserrat & #1a with AO8 cancel. 40c, Cover with #1a, 1b. 55c, #A4 (G.B. #27 with AO8 cancel) & #2. 70c, 2 #1, 1 #1a with AO8 cancels. $1.10, Packet "Antelope" & #2.

1976, Jan. 5 *Perf. 13½*

327 A42 5c multicolored .20 .20
328 A42 10c multicolored .20 .20
329 A42 40c multicolored .50 .50
330 A42 55c multicolored .65 .65
331 A42 70c multicolored .85 .85
332 A42 $1.10 multicolored 1.25 1.25
a. Souvenir sheet of 6, #327-332 4.50 4.50
Nos. 327-332 (6) 3.65 3.65

Centenary of Montserrat's postage stamps.

Trinity, by Orcagna — A43

Paintings by Orcagna (Andrea di Cione): 40c, Resurrection. 55c, Ascension. $1.10, Pentecost.

Perf. 14x13½

1976, Apr. 5 **Litho.** **Wmk. 373**

333 A43 15c multicolored .20 .20
334 A43 40c multicolored .25 .25
335 A43 55c multicolored .25 .25
336 A43 $1.10 multicolored .60 .60
a. Souvenir sheet of 4 1.90 1.90
Nos. 333-336 (4) 1.30 1.30

Easter 1976. Nos. 333-336 were prepared, but not issued in 1975. Stamps are surcharged with new values; date "1975" obliterated with heavy bar. No. 336a contains one each of Nos. 333-336; "1975" in margin obliterated with heavy bar.

Nos. 235-236, 233 Surcharged

Perf. 14½x14

1976, Apr. 12 Photo. Wmk. 314

337	A22	2c on 5c multi	.20	.20
338	A22	30c on 10c multi	.50	.50
339	A22	45c on 3c multi	.85	.85
		Nos. 337-339 (3)	1.55	1.55

For overprints see Nos. O3-O4.

White Frangipani — A44

Designs: Flowering trees of Montserrat.

Perf. 13½x14

1976, July 5 Litho. Wmk. 373

340	A44	1c	shown	.20	.20
341	A44	2c	Cannonball tree	.20	.20
342	A44	3c	Lignum vitae	.20	.20
343	A44	5c	Malay apple	.20	.20
344	A44	10c	Jacaranda	.20	.20
345	A44	15c	Orchid tree	.20	.20
346	A44	20c	Manjak	.20	.20
347	A44	25c	Tamarind	.20	.20
348	A44	40c	Flame of the Forest	.20	.20
349	A44	55c	Pink cassia	.30	.30
350	A44	70c	Long John	.35	.35
351	A44	$1	Saman	.50	.50
352	A44	$2.50	Immortelle	1.25	1.25
353	A44	$5	Yellow poui	2.50	2.50
354	A44	$10	Flamboyant	5.00	5.00
			Nos. 340-354 (15)	11.70	11.70

For surcharges and overprints see Nos. 374-376, 420, 435-440, O10-O44.

Mary and Joseph on Road to Bethlehem — A45

Christmas (Map of Montserrat and): 20c, Shepherds. 55c, Virgin and Child. $1.10, Three Kings.

1976, Oct. 4 *Perf. 14½*

355	A45	15c vio blue & multi	.20	.20
356	A45	20c green & multi	.20	.20
357	A45	55c lilac & multi	.40	.40
358	A45	$1.10 multicolored	.90	.90
a.		Souvenir sheet of 4, #355-358	2.50	2.50
		Nos. 355-358 (4)	1.70	1.70

Hudson River Review of Opsail 76 — A46

Designs: 40c, Raleigh. 75c, HMS Druid (Raleigh attacking Druid, 1776).

1976, Dec. 13 Litho. *Perf. 13*

359		15c multicolored	.20	.20
a.	A46	Pair, #359, 362	1.75	1.75
360		40c multicolored	.50	.50
361		75c multicolored	1.00	1.00
a.	A46	Pair, #360-361	1.50	1.50
362		$1.25 multicolored	1.50	1.50
a.	A46	Souvenir sheet of 4, #359-362, perf. 14x13½	3.50	3.50
		Nos. 359-362 (4)	3.20	3.20

American Bicentennial.

Queen Arriving for 1966 Visit, Yacht Britannia — A48

Designs: 45c, Firing of cannons at Tower of London. $1, The crowning.

1977, Feb. 7

363	A48	30c multicolored	.25	.25
364	A48	45c multicolored	.35	.35
365	A48	$1 multicolored	.90	.90
		Nos. 363-365 (3)	1.50	1.50

25th anniv. of the reign of Elizabeth II. #363-365 were issued also in booklet panes of 4.

Epiphyllum Hookeri — A49

Flowers of the Night: 15c, Ipomoea alba, vert. 55c, Cereus hexagonus. $1.50, Cestrum nocturnum, vert.

1977, June 1 Litho. *Perf. 14*

366	A49	15c multicolored	.20	.20
367	A49	40c multicolored	.40	.40
368	A49	55c multicolored	.50	.50
369	A49	$1.50 multicolored	1.50	1.50
a.		Souvenir sheet of 4, #366-369	3.50	3.50
		Nos. 366-369 (4)	2.60	2.60

Princess Anne at Ground-breaking Ceremony, Glendon Hospital — A50

Designs: 40c, New deep-water jetty, Plymouth. 55c, Glendon Hospital. $1.50, Freighter unloading at new jetty.

1977, Oct. 3 Wmk. 373 *Perf. 14½*

370	A50	20c multicolored	.20	.20
371	A50	40c multicolored	.20	.20
372	A50	55c multicolored	.30	.30
373	A50	$1.50 multicolored	.80	.80
a.		Souvenir sheet of 4, #370-373	2.50	2.50
		Nos. 370-373 (4)	1.50	1.50

Development.

Nos. 349-350, 352 Surcharged with New Value and Bars and Overprinted: "SILVER JUBILEE 1977 / ROYAL VISIT / TO THE CARIBBEAN"

1977, Oct. Litho. *Perf. 13½x14*

374	A44	$1 on 55c multi	.60	.60
375	A44	$1 on 70c multi	.60	.60
376	A44	$1 on $2.50 multi	.60	.60
		Nos. 374-376 (3)	1.80	1.80

Caribbean visit of Queen Elizabeth II. Surcharge has bars of differing thickness and length. No. 374 has two settings.

"Silent Night, Holy Night" — A51

Christmas Carols and Map of Montserrat: 40c, "We Three Kings of Orient Are." 55c, "I Saw Three Ships Come Sailing In." $2, "Hark the Herald Angels Sing."

1977, Nov. 14 Litho. *Perf. 14½*

377	A51	5c blue & multi	.20	.20
378	A51	40c bister & multi	.20	.20
379	A51	55c lt blue & multi	.20	.20
380	A51	$2 rose & multi	.85	.85
a.		Souvenir sheet of 4, #377-380	1.50	1.50
		Nos. 377-380 (4)	1.45	1.45

Four-eye Butterflyfish — A52

Fish: 40c, French angelfish. 55c, Blue tang. $1.50, Queen triggerfish.

1978, Feb. 27 Wmk. 373 *Perf. 14*

381	A52	30c multicolored	.30	.30
382	A52	40c multicolored	.40	.40
383	A52	55c multicolored	.55	.55
384	A52	$1.50 multicolored	1.50	1.50
a.		Souvenir sheet of 4, #381-384	5.25	5.25
		Nos. 381-384 (4)	2.75	2.75

Elizabeth II and St. Paul's, London — A53

Designs: 55c, Chichester Cathedral. $1, Lincoln Cathedral. $2.50, Llandaff Cathedral, Cardiff.

1978, June 2 *Perf. 13½*

385	A53	40c multicolored	.20	.20
386	A53	55c multicolored	.20	.20
387	A53	$1 multicolored	.30	.30
388	A53	$2.50 multicolored	.70	.70
a.		Souvenir sheet of 4, #385-388	1.40	1.40
		Nos. 385-388 (4)	1.40	1.40

25th anniversary of coronation of Elizabeth II, Defender of the Faith. Nos. 385-388 printed in sheets of 10 stamps and 2 labels.

#385-388 also issued in bklt. panes of 2.

Alpinia — A54

Private, 1796 — A55

Flowering Plants: 55c, Allamanda cathartica. $1, Blue tree petrea. $2, Amaryllis.

1978, Sept. 18 Litho. *Perf. 13½x13*

389	A54	40c multicolored	.20	.20
390	A54	55c multicolored	.35	.35
391	A54	$1 multicolored	.65	.65
392	A54	$2 multicolored	1.25	1.25
		Nos. 389-392 (4)	2.45	2.45

1978, Nov. 20 Litho. *Perf. 14½*

Uniforms: 40c, Corporal, 1831. 55c, Sergeant, 1837. $1.50, Officer, 1784.

393	A55	30c multicolored	.20	.20
394	A55	40c multicolored	.20	.20
395	A55	55c multicolored	.35	.35
396	A55	$1.50 multicolored	1.00	1.00
a.		Souvenir sheet of 4, #393-396	2.00	2.00
		Nos. 393-396 (4)	1.75	1.75

See Nos. 401-404.

Cub Scouts A56

Boy Scouts: 55c, Signaling. $1.25, Cooking, vert. $2, Flag folding ceremony, vert.

1979, Apr. 2 Litho. *Perf. 14*

397	A56	40c multicolored	.25	.25
398	A56	55c multicolored	.35	.35
399	A56	$1.25 multicolored	.80	.80
400	A56	$2 multicolored	1.25	1.25
a.		Souvenir sheet of 4, #397-400	3.00	3.00
		Nos. 397-400 (4)	2.65	2.65

50th anniversary of Scouting in Montserrat.

Uniform Type of 1978

30c, Private, 1783. 40c, Private, 1819. 55c, Officer, 1819. $2.50, Highlander officer, 1830.

1979, July 4 Wmk. 373 *Perf. 14*

401	A55	30c multicolored	.20	.20
402	A55	40c multicolored	.25	.25
403	A55	55c multicolored	.30	.30
404	A55	$2.50 multicolored	1.50	1.50
a.		Souvenir sheet of 4, #401-404	2.50	2.50
		Nos. 401-404 (4)	2.25	2.25

IYC Emblem, Learning to Walk — A56a

1979, Sept. 17 Litho. *Perf. 13½x14*

405	A56a	$2 brown org & black	.85	.85
a.		Souvenir sheet	2.00	2.00

International Year of the Child.

Hill, Penny Black, Montserrat No. 1 — A57

Designs: 55c, UPU Emblem, charter. $1, UPU Emblem, cover. $2, Hill, Post Office regulations.

1979, Oct. 1 *Perf. 14*

406	A57	40c multicolored	.20	.20
407	A57	55c multicolored	.20	.20
408	A57	$1 multicolored	.40	.40
409	A57	$2 multicolored	.80	.80
a.		Souvenir sheet of 4, #406-409	3.50	3.50
		Nos. 406-409 (4)	1.60	1.60

Sir Rowland Hill (1795-1879), originator of penny postage; UPU membership, centenary.

Tree Lizard A58

1980, Feb. 4 Litho. *Perf. 14*

410 A58 40c Tree frog .20 .20
411 A58 55c shown .35 .35
412 A58 $1 Crapaud .65 .65
413 A58 $2 Wood slave 1.25 1.25
Nos. 410-413 (4) 2.45 2.45

Marquis of Salisbury, 1817; Postmarks, 1838, London 1980 Emblem — A59

Ships or Planes, Stamps of Montserrat: 55c, H.S. 748, #349. #416, La Plata, 1901, type A4. #417, Lady Hawkins, 1929, #84. #418, Avon, 1843, Gt Britain #3. #419, Aeronca, #140.

1980, Apr. 14 Litho. *Perf. 14½*

414 A59 40c multicolored .20 .20
415 A59 55c multicolored .30 .30
416 A59 $1.20 multicolored .55 .60
417 A59 $1.20 multicolored .55 .60
418 A59 $1.20 multicolored .55 .60
419 A59 $1.20 multicolored .55 .60
a. Souvenir sheet of 6, #414-419 2.75 2.75
Nos. 414-419 (6) 2.70 2.90

London 1980 Intl. Stamp Exhib., May 6-14.
For surcharges see Nos. 736-740.

No. 352 Overprinted: 75th Anniversary of / Rotary International

1980, July 7 Litho. *Perf. 13½x14*

420 A44 $2.50 multicolored .90 .90

Discus Thrower, Stadium, Olympic Rings — A60

Flags of Host Countries: 40c, Greece, 1896; France, 1900; U.S., 1904. 55c, Great Britain, 1908; Sweden, 1912; Belgium, 1920. 70c, France, 1924; Netherlands, 1928; US, 1932. $1, Germany, 1936; Great Britain, 1948; Finland, 1952. $1.50, Australia, 1956; Italy, 1960; Japan, 1964. $2, Mexico, 1968,; Fed. Rep. of Germany, 1972; Canada, 1976.

1980, July 7 Litho. *Perf. 14*

421 A60 40c multicolored .20 .20
422 A60 55c multicolored .20 .20
423 A60 70c multicolored .30 .30
424 A60 $1 multicolored .40 .40
425 A60 $1.50 multicolored .50 .50
426 A60 $2 multicolored .70 .70
427 A60 $2.50 multicolored .90 .90
a. Souv. sheet of 7, #421-427 + 2 labels 3.50 3.50
Nos. 421-427 (7) 3.20 3.20

22nd Summer Olympic Games, Moscow, July 19-Aug. 3.

Lady Nelson, 1928 A61

1980 Litho. *Perf. 14*

428 A61 40c shown .20 .20
429 A61 55c Chignecto, 1913 .40 .40
430 A61 $1 Solent, 1878 .75 .75
431 A61 $2 Dee, 1841 1.40 1.40
Nos. 428-431 (4) 2.75 2.75

Plume Worm — A62

1980 Litho. *Perf. 14*

432 A62 40c shown .40 .40
433 A62 55c Sea fans .55 .55
434 A62 $2 Coral, sponges 1.40 1.40
Nos. 432-434 (3) 2.35 2.35

Nos. 340, 342, 345, 348 Surcharged

1980, Sept. 30 Litho. *Perf. 14*

435 A44 5c on 3c (#342) .20 .20
436 A44 35c on 1c (#340) .20 .20
437 A44 35c on 3c (#342) .20 .20
438 A44 35c on 15c (#345) .20 .20
439 A44 55c on 40c (#348) .20 .20
440 A44 $5 on 40c (#348) 1.25 1.40
Nos. 435-440 (6) 2.25 2.40

Zebra Butterfly — A63

Spadefish — A64

1981, Feb. 2 Wmk. 373

441 A63 50c shown .75 .50
442 A63 65c Tropical checkered skipper .90 .55
443 A63 $1.50 Large orange sulphur 1.10 1.00
444 A63 $2.50 Monarch 1.60 1.40
Nos. 441-444 (4) 4.35 3.45

Wmk. 373

1981, Mar. 20 Litho. *Perf. 13½*

445 A64 5c shown .20 .25
446 A64 10c Hogfish .20 .25
447 A64 15c Creole wrasse .20 .25
448 A64 20c Yellow damselfish .20 .25
449 A64 25c Sergeant major .20 .25
450 A64 35c Clown wrasse .20 .25
451 A64 45c Schoolmaster .40 .40
452 A64 55c Striped parrotfish 1.25 1.25
453 A64 65c Bigeye .55 .55
454 A64 75c French grunt .60 .60
455 A64 $1 Rock beauty .85 .85
456 A64 $2 Blue chromis 1.75 1.75
457 A64 $3 Fairy basslet, blueheads 2.75 2.75
458 A64 $5 Cherubfish 4.25 4.25
459 A64 $7.50 Longspine squirrelfish 4.75 4.75
460 A64 $10 Longsnout butterflyfish 7.25 7.25
Nos. 445-460 (16) 25.60 25.90

For surcharges and overprints see Nos. 507-508, 511-512, 515, O45-O55, O95-O97.

Inscribed 1983

1983 Wmk. 380

445a A64 5c .30 .20
446a A64 10c .35 .20
449a A64 25c .40 .20
450a A64 35c .45 .30
454a A64 75c .65 .55
455a A64 $1 .85 .70
458a A64 $5 3.75 3.75
460a A64 $10 6.75 6.75
Nos. 445a-460a (8) 13.50 12.65

Fort St. George (National Trust) — A65

1981, May 18 Wmk. 373 *Perf. 13½*

461 A65 50c shown .20 .20
462 A65 65c Bird Sanctuary, Fox's Bay .25 .25
463 A65 $1.50 The Museum .55 .65
464 A65 $2.50 Bransby Point Battery 1.00 1.10
Nos. 461-464 (4) 2.00 2.20

Prince Charles, Lady Diana, Royal Yacht Charlotte A66

Prince Charles and Lady Diana — A67

Wmk. 380

1981, July 13 Litho. *Perf. 14*

465 A66 90c shown .40 .40
a. Booklet pane of 4, perf. 12 2.00
466 A67 90c shown 1.40 1.40
467 A66 $3 Portsmouth .95 .95
468 A67 $3 like #466 2.40 2.40
a. Booklet pane of 2, perf. 12 4.00
469 A66 $4 Britannia 1.25 1.25
470 A67 $4 like #466 2.75 2.75
Nos. 465-470 (6) 9.15 9.15

Royal wedding. Each denomination issued in sheets of 7 (6 type A66, 1 type A67).
For surcharges and overprints see Nos. 509-510, 513-514, 578-579, O56-O61.

Souvenir Sheet

1981, Dec. *Perf. 12*

471 A67 $5 multicolored 2.50 2.50

50th Anniv. of Airmail Service A68

1981, Aug. 31 Wmk. 373 *Perf. 14*

472 A68 50c Seaplane, Dorsetshire .40 .40
473 A68 65c Beechcraft Twin Bonanza .50 .50
474 A68 $1.50 DeHaviland Dragon Rapide 1.00 1.00
475 A68 $2.50 Hawker Siddeley Avro 748 1.60 1.60
Nos. 472-475 (4) 3.50 3.50

Methodist Church, Bethel — A69

Christmas (Churches): 65c, St. George's Anglican, Harris. $1.50, St. Peter's Anglican, St. Peter's. $2.50, St. Patrick's Roman Catholic, Plymouth.

1981, Nov. 16 Litho. *Perf. 14*

476 A69 50c multicolored .25 .25
477 A69 65c multicolored .35 .35
478 A69 $1.50 multicolored .55 .55
479 A69 $2.50 multicolored 1.00 1.00
a. Souvenir sheet of 4, #476-479 3.00 3.00
Nos. 476-479 (4) 2.15 2.15

Wild Flowers First Discovered on Montserrat — A70

1982, Jan. 18 Litho. *Perf. 14½*

480 A70 50c Rondeletia buxifolia, vert. .20 .20
481 A70 65c Heliotropium ternatum .25 .25
482 A70 $1.50 Picramnia pentandra, vert. .55 .55
483 A70 $2.50 Diospyros revoluta 1.50 1.50
Nos. 480-483 (4) 2.50 2.50

350th Anniv. of Settlement of Montserrat by Sir Thomas Warner — A70a

Jubilee Type of 1932.

Wmk. 373

1982, Apr. 17 Litho. *Perf. 14½*

483A A70a 40c green .20 .20
483B A70a 55c red .30 .30
483C A70a 65c brown .35 .35
483D A70a 75c gray .40 .40
483E A70a 85c ultra .50 .50
483F A70a 95c orange .55 .55
483G A70a $1 purple .60 .60
483H A70a $1.50 olive .85 .85
483I A70a $2 car rose 1.10 1.10
483J A70a $2.50 sepia 1.50 1.50
Nos. 483A-483J (10) 6.35 6.35

A70b

A71

1982, June Wmk. 380 *Perf. 14*

484 A70b 75c Catherine of Aragon, 1501 .30 .30
485 A70b $1 Aragon arms .30 .30
486 A70b $5 Diana 1.75 1.75
Nos. 484-486 (3) 2.35 2.35

21st birthday of Princess Diana, July 1.
For surcharges and overprints see Nos. 574, O62-O64.

1982, Sept. 13 Litho. *Perf. 14*

487 A71 $1.50 Scout .85 .85
488 A71 $2.50 Baden-Powell 1.40 1.40

Scouting Year.

Christmas A72

1982, Nov. 18 Wmk. 373 Perf. 14

489 A72 35c Annunciation .20 .20
490 A72 75c Shepherds' vision .40 .40
491 A72 $1.50 Virgin and Child .70 .70
492 A72 $2.50 Flight into Egypt 1.25 1.25
Nos. 489-492 (4) 2.55 2.55

Dragonflies — A73

1983, Jan. 19 Litho. Perf. 13½x14

493 A73 50c Lepthemis vesiculosa .50 .50
494 A73 65c Orthemis ferruginea .65 .65
495 A73 $1.50 Triacanthagyna trifida 1.40 1.40
496 A73 $2.50 Erythrodiplax umbrata 1.90 1.90
Nos. 493-496 (4) 4.45 4.45

Blue-headed Hummingbird A74

1983, May 24 Wmk. 373 Perf. 14

497 A74 35c shown .90 .90
498 A74 75c Green-throated carib 1.25 1.25
499 A74 $2 Antillean crested hummingbird 3.25 3.25
500 A74 $3 Purple-throated carib 4.50 4.50
Nos. 497-500 (4) 9.90 9.90

Arms — A75

1983, July 25 Litho. Perf. 14½

501 A75 $12 red & black 5.00 *7.50*
502 A75 $30 blue & red 15.00 *20.00*

Manned Flight Bicentenary — A76

Designs: 35c, Montgolfiere, 1783, vert. 75c, De Havilland Twin Otter 310, 1981. $1.50, Lockheed Vega's around the world flight, 1933. $2, British R34 airship transatlantic flight, 1919.

1983, Sept. 19 Litho. Perf. 14

503 A76 35c multicolored .25 .25
504 A76 75c multicolored .35 .35
505 A76 $1.50 multicolored .55 .55
506 A76 $2 multicolored .85 .85
a. Souvenir sheet of 4, #503-506 3.00 3.00
Nos. 503-506 (4) 2.00 2.00

For surcharges see Nos. 573, 577.

Nos. 449, 446, 467-468, 453-454, 469-470, 456 Surcharged

Wmk. 373 (A64), 380

1983, Aug. 15 Litho. Perf. 13½x14

507 A64 40c on 25c multi .50 .50
508 A64 70c on 10c multi .80 .80
509 A66 70c on $3 multi .70 .70
510 A67 70c on $3 multi 1.60 1.60
511 A64 90c on 65c multi .90 .90
512 A64 $1.15 on 75c multi 1.10 1.10
513 A66 $1.15 on $4 multi .90 .90
514 A67 $1.15 on $4 multi 2.10 2.10
515 A64 $1.50 on $2 multi 1.40 1.40
Nos. 507-515 (9) 10.00 10.00

Christmas Carnival 1983 A77

1983, Nov. 18 Wmk. 380 Perf. 14

516 A77 55c Clowns .20 .20
517 A77 90c Star Bursts .25 .25
518 A77 $1.15 Flower Girls .40 .40
519 A77 $2 Masqueraders .65 .65
Nos. 516-519 (4) 1.50 1.50

See Nos. 547-550.

Nos. 503-506 were overprinted "INAUGURAL FLIGHT Montserrat — Nevis — St. Kitts." These exist on souvenir covers with first day cancel of Dec. 15, 1983. No announcement of this set was made nor were mint stamps generally available.

1984 Summer Olympics — A78

1984, Mar. 6 Litho. Perf. 14

520 A78 90c Discobolus .40 .40
521 A78 $1 Torch .50 .50
522 A78 $1.15 Stadium .55 .55
523 A78 $2.50 Flags .90 .90
a. Souvenir sheet of 4, #520-523 2.75 2.75
Nos. 520-523 (4) 2.35 2.35

Cattle Egret A79

1984, May 11

524 A79 5c shown .45 .35
525 A79 10c Carib grackles .45 .35
526 A79 15c Common gallinule .45 .35
527 A79 20c Brown boobys .60 .35
528 A79 25c Black-whiskered vireos .60 .50
529 A79 40c Scaly-breasted thrashers .90 .55
530 A79 55c Laughing gulls 1.10 .35
531 A79 70c Glossy ibis 1.40 .50
532 A79 90c Green heron 1.50 .70
533 A79 $1 Belted kingfisher 1.90 .90
534 A79 $1.15 Bananaquits 2.40 1.60
535 A79 $3 Sparrow hawks 5.00 *6.00*
536 A79 $5 Forest thrush 7.00 *8.00*
537 A79 $7.50 Black-crowned night heron 9.00 *14.50*
538 A79 $10 Bridled quail doves 10.50 *15.00*
Nos. 524-538 (15) 43.25 50.00

For surcharges see Nos. 651-655, 663-666.
For overprints see Nos. O65-O78.

Packet Boats A80

1984, July 9 Wmk. 380 Perf. 14

539 A80 55c Tagus, 1907 .30 .30
540 A80 90c Cobequid, 1913 .45 .45
541 A80 $1.15 Lady Drake, 1942 .55 .55
542 A80 $2 Factor, 1948 .90 .90
a. Souvenir sheet of 4, #539-542 4.00 4.00
Nos. 539-542 (4) 2.20 2.20

Marine Life A81

1984, Sept. Wmk. 380 Perf. 14

543 A81 90c Top shell & hermit crab 1.60 1.60
544 A81 $1.15 Rough file shell 2.00 2.00
545 A81 $1.50 True tulip snail 3.00 3.00
546 A81 $2.50 West Indian fighting conch 4.00 4.00
Nos. 543-546 (4) 10.60 10.60

Christmas Carnival Type of 1983

1984, Nov. 12

547 A77 55c Bull Man .65 .65
548 A77 $1.15 Masquerader Captain 1.60 1.60
549 A77 $1.50 Carnival Queen contestant 1.75 1.75
550 A77 $2.30 Contestant, diff. 2.75 2.75
Nos. 547-550 (4) 6.75 6.75

National Emblems — A82
Indigenous Orchids — A83

1985, Feb. 8 Litho. Perf. 14

551 A82 $1.15 Mango .30 *.60*
552 A82 $1.50 Lobster Claw .40 *.80*
553 A82 $3 Montserrat Oriole .60 *1.25*
Nos. 551-553 (3) 1.30 2.65

1985, May 9 Wmk. 380 Perf. 14

554 A83 90c Oncidium urophyllum .45 *.55*
555 A83 $1.15 Epidendrum difforme .45 *.60*
556 A83 $1.50 Epidendrum ciliare .50 *.65*
557 A83 $2.50 Brassavola cucullata .60 *.75*
a. Souvenir sheet of 4, #554-557 5.00 5.00
Nos. 554-557 (4) 2.00 2.55

Queen Mother, 85th Birthday — A84

#558a, 564a, Facing right. #558b, 564b, Facing forward. #559a, Facing right. #559b, Facing left. #560a, Facing right. #560b, Glancing right. #561a, 563a, Facing right. #561b, 563b, Facing left. #562a, Facing right. #562b, Facing forward.

1985-86 Unwmk. Perf. 12½

558 A84 55c Pair, #a.-b. .40 .40
559 A84 90c Pair, #a.-b. .70 .70
560 A84 $1.15 Pair, #a.-b. .80 .80
561 A84 $1.50 Pair, #a.-b. 1.10 1.10
Nos. 558-561 (4) 3.00 3.00

Souvenir Sheets of 2

562 A84 $2 #a.-b. 1.75 1.75
563 A84 $3.50 #a.-b. 3.50 3.50
564 A84 $6 #a.-b. 5.50 5.50

Issued: #563-564, 1/10/86; others, 8/7/85.
For surcharges see No. 575.

Cotton Industry A85

1985, Sept. 23 Unwmk. Perf. 15

569 A85 90c Cotton plants .20 *.30*
570 A85 $1 Carding .25 *.35*
571 A85 $1.15 Automated loom .25 *.35*
572 A85 $2.50 Hand loom .40 *.50*
a. Souvenir sheet of 4, #569-572 4.25 4.25
Nos. 569-572 (4) 1.10 1.50

Nos. 504, 485, 560, 505, 469-470 Ovptd. or Surcharged "CARIBBEAN ROYAL VISIT 1985" in 2 or 3 Lines

Perf. 14, 12½ ($1.15)

Wmk. as Before

1985, Nov. 14 Litho.

573 A76 75c multi 4.75 4.75
574 A70b $1 multi 6.75 6.75
575 A84 $1.15 Pair, #a.-b. 14.50 14.50
577 A76 $1.50 multi 9.25 9.25
578 A66 $1.60 on $4 multi 4.75 4.75
579 A67 $1.60 on $4 multi 16.00 16.00
Nos. 573-579 (6) 56.00 56.00

No. 579 surcharged but not overprinted.

Audubon Birth Bicentenary — A86

Illustrations of North American bird species by John J. Audubon: #580a, Black-throated blue warbler. #580b, Palm warbler. #581a, Bobolink. #581b, Lark sparrow. #582a, Chipping sparrow. #582b, Northern oriole. #583a, American goldfinch. #583b, Blue grosbeak.

1985, Nov. 29 Unwmk. Perf. 12½

580 A86 15c Pair, #a.-b. .20 .20
581 A86 30c Pair, #a.-b. .25 .25
582 A86 55c Pair, #a.-b. .40 .40
583 A86 $2.50 Pair, #a.-b. 1.40 1.40
Nos. 580-583 (4) 2.25 2.25

Christmas A87

1985, Dec. 2 Wmk. 380 Perf. 15

588 A87 70c Angel of the Lord .20 .20
589 A87 $1.15 Three wise men .35 .35
590 A87 $1.50 Caroling, Plymouth War Memorial .40 .40
591 A87 $2.30 Our Lady of Montserrat .70 .70
Nos. 588-591 (4) 1.65 1.65

A set of 8 stamps for the 1986 World Cup was printed but not issued. Stamps became available with the liquidation of the printer.

Girl Guides, 50th Anniv. — A88

#592a, Lord Baden-Powell. #592b, Guide giving oath. #593a, Lady Baden-Powell. #593b, Guide cutting hair. #594a, Lord and Lady Baden-Powell. #594b, Guides in public service. #595a, Troop inspection, 1936. #595b, Guides saluting.

1986, Apr. 11

592 A88 20c Pair, #a.-b. .20 .20
593 A88 75c Pair, #a.-b. .75 .75
594 A88 90c Pair, #a.-b. .85 .85
595 A88 $1.15 Pair, #a.-b. 1.10 1.10
Nos. 592-595 (4) 2.90 2.90

For overprints see Nos. 966-967.

Queen Elizabeth II, 60th Birthday — A89

Various portraits.

1986, Apr. 11 Unwmk. *Perf. 12½*

600 A89 10c multicolored .20 .20
601 A89 $1.50 multicolored .35 *.35*
602 A89 $3 multicolored .55 *.55*
603 A89 $6 multi, vert. .85 *.85*
Nos. 600-603 (4) 1.95 1.95

Souvenir Sheet

604 A89 $8 multicolored 5.00 5.00

Halley's Comet — A90

Designs: 35c, 40c, #613a, Bayeux Tapestry (detail), 1066 sighting. 50c, $1.75, #613b, Adoration of the Magi, by Giotto. 70c, $2, #613c, Edmond Halley, trajectory diagram, 1531 sighting. $1, $3, #613d, Sightings, 1066 and 1910. $1.15, 55c, #614a, Sighting, 1910. $1.50, 60c, #614b, Giotto space probe, comet, diagram. $2.30, 80c, #614c, U.S. Space Telescope, comet. $4, $5, #614d, Computer picture of photograph, 1910.

1986 *Perf. 14*

605-612 A90 Set of 8 4.50 4.50

Souvenir Sheets

613 A90 Sheet of 4, #a.-d. 3.00 3.00
614 A90 Sheet of 4, #a.-d. 3.00 3.00

Issued: #613-614, 10/10; others, 5/9.
For overprints see Nos. 656-657.

A91

Wedding of Prince Andrew and Sarah Ferguson — A92

No. 615: a, Andrew, vert. b, Sarah, vert.
No. 616: a, Andrew wearing cowboy hat. b, Sarah wearing fur hat.

1986 Litho. *Perf. 12½x13, 13x12½*

615 A91 70c Pair, #a.-b. .70 .70
616 A91 $2 Pair, #a.-b 1.00 1.00
c. Souvenir booklet 5.00

Souvenir Sheet

617 A92 $10 multicolored 5.00 5.00

#616c contains 2 imperf panes. One pane contains 2 #615; the other 2 #616.
Issued: #617, 10/15; others, 7/23.
For overprints see Nos. 628-629.

Clipper Ships A93

1986, Aug. 29 *Perf. 14*

618 A93 90c Antelope, 1793 1.90 1.25
619 A93 $1.15 Montagu, 1840 3.00 3.00
620 A93 $1.50 Little Catherine, 1813 3.25 3.25
621 A93 $2.30 Hinchingbrook, 1813 4.25 4.75
a. Souvenir sheet of 4, #618-621 12.00 12.00
Nos. 618-621 (4) 12.40 12.25

Communications — A94

Designs: 70c, Radio Montserrat, near Dagenham. $1.15, Radio Gem ZGM-FM 94, Plymouth. $1.50, Radio Antilles, O'Garro's. $2.30, Cable & Wireless telegraph office, Plymouth.

1986, Sept. 29 Wmk. 380 *Perf. 14*

622 A94 70c multicolored 1.10 .65
623 A94 $1.15 multicolored 1.60 1.25
624 A94 $1.50 multicolored 1.90 1.90
625 A94 $2.30 multicolored 2.40 *3.00*
Nos. 622-625 (4) 7.00 6.80

Nos. 615-616 Ovptd. in Silver "Congratulations to T.R.H. The Duke & Duchess of York"

Perf. 12½x13, 13x12½

1986, Nov. 14 Litho.

628 A91 70c Pair, #a.-b. 1.75 1.75
629 A91 $2 Pair, #a.-b. 4.00 4.00

Christmas — A95

1986, Dec. 12 Unwmk. *Perf. 14*

632 A95 70c Christmas rose .85 .85
633 A95 $1.15 Candle flower 1.40 1.40
634 A95 $1.50 Christmas tree kalanchoe 2.00 2.00
635 A95 $2.30 Snow on the mountain 3.00 *3.50*
a. Souvenir sheet of 4, #632-635, perf. 12x12½ 11.00 11.00
Nos. 632-635 (4) 7.25 7.75

Souvenir Sheets

Statue of Liberty, Cent. — A96

1986, Nov. 18 Litho. *Perf. 14*

636 A96 $3 Statue, pedestal 2.00 2.00
637 A96 $4.50 Head 2.75 2.75
638 A96 $5 Statue, NYC 3.25 3.25
Nos. 636-638 (3) 8.00 8.00

Sailing A97

1986, Dec. 10 *Perf. 15*

639 A97 70c shown .50 .50
640 A97 $1.15 Golf .75 *1.00*
641 A97 $1.50 Plymouth Public Market .75 *1.00*
642 A97 $2.30 Air Studios 1.50 *2.00*
Nos. 639-642 (4) 3.50 4.50

For surcharge see No. B3.

Sharks A98

1987, Feb. 2 Wmk. 380 *Perf. 14*

643 A98 40c Tiger 1.75 .50
644 A98 90c Lemon 3.00 1.25
645 A98 $1.15 White 3.50 2.00
646 A98 $3.50 Whale 7.00 *8.50*
a. Souvenir sheet of 4, #643-646, perf. 12½x12 16.00 16.00
Nos. 643-646 (4) 15.25 12.25

Butterflies A99

1987, Aug. 10 Wmk. 380 *Perf. 14*

647 A99 90c Straight-line sulpher 2.25 2.25
648 A99 $1.15 Red rim 3.00 3.00
649 A99 $1.50 Hammock skipper 3.75 3.75
650 A99 $2.50 Mimic 6.00 6.00
Nos. 647-650 (4) 15.00 15.00

Nos. 531, 527, 525, 532 and 535 Surcharged

1987, Apr. 6

651 A79 5c on 70c multi .65 .95
652 A79 $1 on 20c multi 2.10 .95
653 A79 $1.15 on 10c multi 2.50 1.60
654 A79 $1.50 on 90c multi 3.00 2.25
655 A79 $2.30 on $3 multi 4.25 *5.25*
Nos. 651-655 (5) 12.50 11.00

Nos. 613-614 Ovptd. for CAPEX '87 in Red and Black
Souvenir Sheets of 4

1987, June 13 Unwmk.

656 A90 #a.-d. 3.25 3.25
657 A90 #a.-d. 3.25 3.25

Orchids — A100

1987, Nov. 13 Unwmk. *Perf. 14*

658 A100 90c Oncidium variegatum, vert. .90 .90
659 A100 $1.15 Vanilla planifolia 1.10 1.10
660 A100 $1.50 Gongora quinquenervis, vert. 1.50 1.50
661 A100 $3.50 Brassavola nodosa 3.75 3.75
Nos. 658-661 (4) 7.25 7.25

Souvenir Sheet

662 A100 $5 Oncidium lanceanum 15.00 15.00

Christmas.

Nos. 525, 528-529 and 532 Surcharged "40th Wedding Anniversary / HM Queen Elizabeth II / HRH Duke of Edinburgh / November 1987." and New Value

Wmk. 380

1987, Nov. 20 Litho. *Perf. 14*

663 A79 5c on 90c No. 532 .55 .55
664 A79 $1.15 on 10c No. 525 .70 .70
665 A79 $2.30 on 25c No. 528 1.60 1.60
666 A79 $5 on 40c No. 529 3.25 3.25
Nos. 663-666 (4) 6.10 6.10

Exists spelled "Edingburgh." Value, set $35.

Tropical Bats — A101

Marine Birds — A102

1988, Feb. 8 Wmk. 380 *Perf. 14*

667 A101 55c Free-tailed bat 1.00 1.00
668 A101 90c Fruit bat 1.75 1.75
669 A101 $1.15 Fisherman bat 2.25 2.25
670 A101 $2.30 Fruit bat, diff. 4.50 4.50
Nos. 667-670 (4) 9.50 9.50

Souvenir Sheet

671 A101 $2.50 Funnel-eared bat 10.00 10.00

1988, Apr. 2 Unwmk.

672 A102 90c Magnificent frigatebird 1.00 1.00
673 A102 $1.15 Caribbean elaenia 1.25 1.25
674 A102 $1.50 Glossy ibis 1.50 1.50
675 A102 $3.50 Purple-throated carib 3.25 3.25
Nos. 672-675 (4) 7.00 7.00

Souvenir Sheet

676 A102 $5 Brown pelican 5.50 5.50

Easter.

1988 Summer Olympics, Seoul — A103

Eastern architecture and events: 90c, Women's discus. $1.15, High jump. $3.50, Women's 200-meter and Seoul university building. $5, Single scull rowing, pagoda.

Unwmk.

1988, July 29 Litho. *Perf. 14*
677 A103 90c multicolored .95 .95
678 A103 $1.15 multicolored 1.00 1.00
679 A103 $3.50 multicolored 3.25 3.25
Nos. 677-679 (3) 5.20 5.20

Souvenir Sheet

680 A103 $5 multicolored 5.25 5.25

Sea Shells A104

1988, Aug. 30
681 A104 5c Golden tulip .20 .25
682 A104 10c Little knobby scallop .20 .25
683 A104 15c Sozoni's cone .20 .25
684 A104 20c Globular coral shell .20 .25
685 A104 25c Sundial .20 .25
686 A104 40c King helmet .40 .45
687 A104 55c Channeled turban .50 .60
688 A104 70c True tulip shell .65 .75
689 A104 90c Music volute .85 1.00
690 A104 $1 Flame auger .90 1.10
691 A104 $1.15 Rooster-tail conch 1.10 1.40
692 A104 $1.50 Queen conch 1.40 1.75
693 A104 $3 Teramachi's slit shell 3.25 3.50
694 A104 $5 Florida crown conch 4.50 5.50
695 A104 $7.50 Beau's murex 7.00 8.50
696 A104 $10 Triton's trumpet 9.75 11.50
Nos. 681-696 (16) 31.30 37.30

For surcharges see Nos. 698-701, 767-770.
For overprints see Nos. O79-O94.

University of the West Indies, 40th Anniv. — A105

1988, Oct. 4 Litho. *Perf. 14*
697 A105 $5 multicolored 4.00 4.00

Nos. 687, 690, 693 and 694 Surcharged

Unwmk.

1988, Nov. 4 Litho. *Perf. 14*
698 A104 40c on 55c No. 687 .40 .40
699 A104 90c on $1 No. 690 1.25 1.25
700 A104 $1.15 on $3 No. 693 1.50 1.50
701 A104 $1.50 on $5 No. 694 2.10 2.10
Nos. 698-701 (4) 5.25 5.25

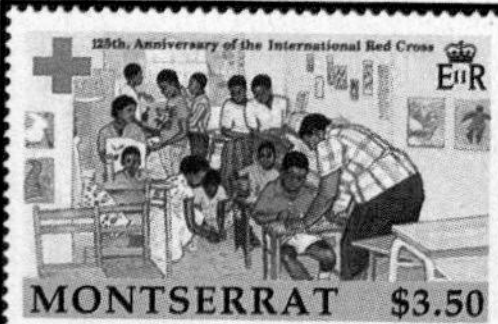

Intl. Red Cross, 125th Anniv. A106

1988, Dec. 16
702 A106 $3.50 multicolored 2.00 2.00

Christmas — A107

Birds.

1988, Nov. 28 *Perf. 14x13½*
703 A107 90c Spotted sandpiper .90 .90
704 A107 $1.15 Ruddy turnstone 1.10 1.10
705 A107 $3.50 Red-footed booby 3.50 3.50
Nos. 703-705 (3) 5.50 5.50

Souvenir Sheet

Perf. 13½x14

706 A107 $5 Aububon's shearwater 5.75 5.75

Uniforms A108

1989, Feb. 24 Litho. *Perf. 14*
707 A108 90c Drum major 1.10 1.10
708 A108 $1.15 Fatigue clothing 1.25 1.25
709 A108 $1.50 Khaki uniform 1.60 1.60
710 A108 $3.50 Dress uniform 4.25 4.25
Nos. 707-710 (4) 8.20 8.20

Souvenir Sheet

711 A108 $5 Cadet (girl), woman 6.25 6.25

Defense Force, 75th anniv.

Easter Lilies A109

1989, Mar. 21 Litho. *Perf. 14*
712 A109 90c Amazon .75 .75
713 A109 $1.15 Salmon blood, vert. .90 .90
714 A109 $1.50 Amaryllis, vert. 1.10 1.10
715 A109 $3.50 Amaryllis, diff., vert. 3.00 3.00
Nos. 712-715 (4) 5.75 5.75

Souvenir Sheet

716 A109 $5 Resurrection, vert. 7.25 7.25

Ships Built in Montserrat — A110

Designs: 90c, Schooner Morning Prince, 1942-1948. $1.15, Cargo boat Western Sun. $1.50, Cargo boat Kim G under construction. $3.50, Cargo and passenger boat MV Romaris.

1989, June 30 Litho. *Perf. 13½x14*
717 A110 90c multicolored 1.40 1.40
718 A110 $1.15 multicolored 1.60 1.60
719 A110 $1.50 multicolored 2.10 2.10
720 A110 $3.50 multicolored 5.00 5.00
Nos. 717-720 (4) 10.10 10.10

For surcharges see Nos. B1-B2.

Making of the Film *The Wizard of Oz*, 50th Anniv. — A111

1989, Sept. 22 Litho. *Perf. 14*
721 A111 90c Scarecrow .70 .70
722 A111 $1.15 Cowardly Lion .80 .80
723 A111 $1.50 Tin Man 1.10 1.10
724 A111 $3.50 Dorothy 2.50 2.50
Nos. 721-724 (4) 5.10 5.10

Souvenir Sheet

725 A111 $5 shown 5.00 5.00

Nos. 721-724 vert.

1st Moon Landing, 20th Anniv. — A112

Designs: $1.15, Armstrong on ladder, descending from lunar module. $1.50, Eagle, astronaut on lunar surface. $3.50, Recovery of command module after splashdown. $5, Astronaut on the Moon, vert.

Perf. 13½x14, 14x13½

1989, Dec. 19 Litho.
726 A112 90c shown .60 .60
727 A112 $1.15 multicolored .75 .75
728 A112 $1.50 multicolored 1.00 1.00
729 A112 $3.50 multicolored 2.10 2.10
Nos. 726-729 (4) 4.45 4.45

Souvenir Sheet

730 A112 $5 multicolored 7.25 7.25

For overprints see Nos. 847-850.

World War II Battle Ships A113

1990, Feb. 12 Litho. *Perf. 14*
731 A113 70c I.J.N. Yamato 2.25 2.25
732 A113 $1.15 USS Arizona 4.25 4.25
733 A113 $1.50 K.M. Bismarck on fire 5.50 5.50
734 A113 $3.50 HMS Hood 12.50 12.50
Nos. 731-734 (4) 24.50 24.50

Souvenir Sheet

735 A113 $5 K.M. Bismarck, map 20.00 20.00

Nos. 414-418 Surcharged in Bright Rose Lilac

1990, May 3 *Perf. 14½*
736 A59 70c on 40c #414 1.10 1.10
737 A59 90c on 55c #415 1.40 1.40
738 A59 $1 on $1.20 #416 1.50 1.50
739 A59 $1.15 on $1.20 #417 1.75 1.75
740 A59 $1.50 on $1.20 #418 2.25 2.25
Nos. 736-740 (5) 8.00 8.00

Stamp World London '90.

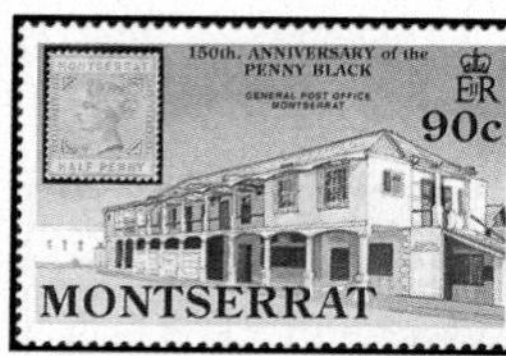

Penny Black, 150th Anniv. A114

Designs: 90c, Montserrat #5, General P.O. $1.15, Montserrat #1, postal workers sorting mail, vert. $1.50, Great Britain #1, man and woman mailing letters, vert. $3.50, Great Britain #2, mailman delivering to residence. $5, Chateau Barrack cover of 1836, Great Britain #1, landscape.

1990, June 1 *Perf. 13½x14, 14x13½*
741 A114 90c shown 1.25 1.25
742 A114 $1.15 multicolored 1.60 1.60
743 A114 $1.50 multicolored 1.90 1.90
744 A114 $3.50 multicolored 4.50 4.50
Nos. 741-744 (4) 9.25 9.25

Souvenir Sheet

745 A114 $5 multicolored 10.00 10.00

Stained-glass Windows — A115

1990, Apr. 12 Litho. *Perf. 14x15*
746 A115 Strip of 3 7.00 7.00
a. $1.15 The Empty Tomb 1.25 1.25
b. $1.50 The Ascension 1.75 1.75
c. $3.50 Risen Christ with Disciples 3.75 3.75

Souvenir Sheet

747 A115 $5 The Crucifixion 7.50 7.50

World Cup Soccer Championships, Italy — A116

Designs: 90c, Montserrat vs. Antigua. $1.15, U.S. vs. Trinidad. $1.50, Montserrat team. $3.50, West Germany vs. Wales. $5, World Cup trophy.

1990, July 8 Litho. *Perf. 14*
748 A116 90c multicolored .90 .90
749 A116 $1.15 multicolored 1.25 1.25
750 A116 $1.50 multicolored 1.60 1.60
751 A116 $3.50 multicolored 3.75 3.75
Nos. 748-751 (4) 7.50 7.50

Souvenir Sheet

752 A116 $5 multicolored 8.50 8.50

Spinner Dolphin A117

1990, Sept. 25 **Litho.** ***Perf. 14***

753 A117 90c shown 2.10 1.10
754 A117 $1.15 Common dolphin 2.50 1.60
755 A117 $1.50 Striped dolphin 3.50 3.25
756 A117 $3.50 Atlantic spotted dolphin 5.75 6.25
Nos. 753-756 (4) 13.85 12.20

Souvenir Sheet

757 A117 $5 Atlantic white-sided dolphin 15.00 12.00

Fish A118

1991, Feb. 7 **Litho.** ***Perf. 14***

758 A118 90c Spotted goatfish 1.75 1.75
759 A118 $1.15 Cushion starfish 2.25 2.25
760 A118 $1.50 Rock beauty 3.00 3.00
761 A118 $3.50 French grunt 6.50 6.50
Nos. 758-761 (4) 13.50 13.50

Souvenir Sheet

762 A118 $5 Trunkfish 14.00 14.00

For surcharges and overprints see Nos. O98-O99, O104, O107.

Birds A119

1991, Apr. 17 **Litho.** ***Perf. 14***

763 A119 90c Duck .95 .95
764 A119 $1.15 Hen, chicks 1.25 1.25
765 A119 $1.50 Rooster 1.50 1.50
766 A119 $3.50 Helmeted guinea fowl 3.50 3.50
Nos. 763-766 (4) 7.20 7.20

For surcharges and overprints see Nos. O100, O102, O105, O108.

Nos. 684-685, 692, 695 Surcharged

1991 **Litho.** ***Perf. 14***

767 A104 5c on 20c #684 .35 .35
768 A104 5c on 25c #685 .35 .35
769 A104 $1.15 on $1.50 #692 4.25 4.25
770 A104 $1.15 on $7.50 #695 4.25 4.25
Nos. 767-770 (4) 9.20 9.20

Mushrooms A120

Lilies — A121

1991, June 13 **Litho.** ***Perf. 14***

771 A120 90c Panaeolus antillarum 1.50 1.50
772 A120 $1.15 Cantharellus cinnabarinus 1.90 1.90
773 A120 $1.50 Gymnopilus chrysopellus 2.50 2.50
774 A120 $2 Psilocybe cubensis 3.50 3.50
775 A120 $3.50 Leptonia caeruleocapitata 5.75 5.75
Nos. 771-775 (5) 15.15 15.15

1991, Aug. 8

776 A121 90c Red water lily .90 .90
777 A121 $1.15 Shell ginger 1.10 1.10
778 A121 $1.50 Early day lily 1.40 1.40
779 A121 $3.50 Anthurium 3.50 3.50
Nos. 776-779 (4) 6.90 6.90

For surcharges and overprints see Nos. O101, O103, O106, O109.

Frogs and Toads — A122

1991, Oct. 9 **Litho.** ***Perf. 14***

780 A122 $1.15 Tree frog 2.75 2.75
781 A122 $2 Crapaud toad 5.00 5.00
782 A122 $3.50 Mountain chicken 8.00 8.00
Nos. 780-782 (3) 15.75 15.75

Souvenir Sheet

Perf. 14½x14

783 A122 $5 Sheet of 1 12.00 12.00

No. 783 contains one 81x48mm stamp that incorporates designs of Nos. 780-782.

Cats A123

1991, Dec. 5

784 A123 90c Black British shorthair 1.50 1.50
785 A123 $1.15 Seal point siamese 1.90 1.90
786 A123 $1.50 Silver tabby persian 2.50 2.50
787 A123 $2.50 Birman temple cat 4.00 4.00
788 A123 $3.50 Egyptian mau 5.50 5.50
Nos. 784-788 (5) 15.40 15.40

Discovery of America, 500th Anniv. A124

No. 789: a, $1.50, Navigating instruments. b, $1.50, Coat of arms, Columbus. c, $1.50, Columbus, Bahamian natives. d, $1.50, Queen Isabella, Columbus with petition. e, $1.50, Exotic birds. f, $1.50, Exotic plants. g, $3.00, Santa Maria, Nina & Pinta.

1992, Jan. 16 **Litho.** ***Perf. 14***

789 A124 Sheet of 7, #a.-g. 17.50 17.50

No. 789g is 85x28mm. See No. 829.

Dinosaurs A125

1992, Aug. 1 **Litho.** ***Perf. 14***

790 A125 $1 Tyrannosaurus 2.10 2.10
791 A125 $1.15 Diplodocus 2.40 2.40
792 A125 $1.50 Apatosaurus 3.00 3.00
793 A125 $3.45 Dimetrodon 7.00 7.00
Nos. 790-793 (4) 14.50 14.50

Souvenir Sheet

794 A125 $4.60 Owen with bone, vert. 12.50 12.50

Sir Richard Owen, cent. of death.

1992 Summer Olympics, Barcelona A126

1992, Apr. 10

795 A126 $1 Torch bearer 1.25 1.25
796 A126 $1.15 Flags 1.50 1.50
797 A126 $2.30 Olympic flame, map 2.75 2.75
798 A126 $3.60 Various events 4.50 4.50
Nos. 795-798 (4) 10.00 10.00

Montserrat Oriole — A127

1992, June 30 **Litho.** ***Perf. 13½x14***

799 A127 $1 Male 1.50 1.50
800 A127 $1.15 Male, female 1.75 1.75
801 A127 $1.50 Female feeding chicks 2.25 2.25
802 A127 $3.60 Map, male 5.50 5.50
Nos. 799-802 (4) 11.00 11.00

Insects A128

1992, Aug. 20 **Litho.** ***Perf. 15x14***

803 A128 5c Grasshopper .20 .20
804 A128 10c Field cricket .20 .20
805 A128 15c Dragonfly .20 .20
806 A128 20c Red skimmer .20 .20
807 A128 25c Pond skater .20 .20
808 A128 40c Leaf weevil .35 .40
809 A128 55c Leaf cutter ants .45 .50
810 A128 70c Paper wasp .60 .65
811 A128 90c Bee fly .80 .90
812 A128 $1 Lacewing .95 1.00
813 A128 $1.15 Orange-barred sulphur 1.00 1.10
814 A128 $1.50 Painted lady 1.25 1.40
815 A128 $3 Bella moth 2.50 3.00
816 A128 $5 Plume moth 4.25 4.75
817 A128 $7.50 White peacock 6.50 7.25
818 A128 $10 Postman 8.75 9.75
Nos. 803-818 (16) 28.40 31.70

For overprints see #871-872, O110-O125.

A used example of No. 806 with a 10c surcharge was shown to the editors, but Montserrat Postal officials were unable to provide any information about it stating "this was prior to the appointment of the present manager." The editors would like to receive information from any knowledgeable source about this stamp, an example of No. 810 with a 5c surcharge, and the possible existence of other similar surcharges.

Christmas — A129

Designs: $1.15, Adoration of the Magi. $4.60, Angel appearing before shepherds.

1992, Nov. 26 **Litho.** ***Perf. 13½x14***

819 A129 $1.15 multicolored 1.75 1.75
820 A129 $4.60 multicolored 7.00 7.00

Coins and Bank Notes — A130

Designs: $1, One-dollar coin, twenty-dollar notes. $1.15, Ten-cent, twenty-five cent coins, ten-dollar notes. $1.50, Five-cent coin, five-dollar notes. $3.60, One-cent, two-cent coins, one-dollar notes.

1993, Feb. 10 ***Perf. 14x13½***

821 A130 $1 multicolored 1.50 1.50
822 A130 $1.15 multicolored 1.60 1.60
823 A130 $1.50 multicolored 2.10 2.10
824 A130 $3.60 multicolored 5.25 5.25
Nos. 821-824 (4) 10.45 10.45

Discovery of America, 500th Anniv. (in 1992) — A131

1993, Mar. 10 **Litho.** ***Perf. 14***

825 A131 $1 Coming ashore 2.25 2.25
826 A131 $2 Natives, ships 4.25 4.25

Organization of East Caribbean States.

Coronation of Queen Elizabeth II, 40th Anniv. — A132

Designs: $1.15, Queen, M.H. Bramble. $4.60, Queen riding in Gold State Coach.

1993, June 2 ***Perf. 13½x14***

827 A132 $1.15 multicolored 1.50 1.50
828 A132 $4.60 multicolored 5.50 5.50

Columbus Type of 1992 with Added Text

No. 829: a, $1.15, like #789a. b, $1.15, like #789b. c, $1.15, like #789c. d, $1.50, like

#789d. e, $1.50, like #789e. f, $1.50, like #789f. g, $3.45, like #789g.

1993, Sept. 7 Litho. *Perf. 14*
829 A124 Sheet of 7, #a.-g. 25.00 25.00

Nos. 829a-829g each have different added text.

Royal Air Force, 75th Anniv.
Common Design Type

Designs: 15c, Boeing Sentry, 1993. 55c, Vickers Valiant, 1962. $1.15, Handley Page Hastings, 1958. $3, 1943 Lockheed Ventura, 1943.

No. 834: a, Felixstowe F5, 1921. b, Armstrong Whitworth Atlas, 1934. c, Fairey Gordon, 1935. d, Boulton Paul Overstrand, 1936.

Wmk. 373

1993, Nov. 17 Litho. *Perf. 14*
830 CD350 15c multicolored .20 .20
831 CD350 55c multicolored .70 .70
832 CD350 $1.15 multicolored 1.60 1.60
833 CD350 $3 multicolored 4.25 4.25
Nos. 830-833 (4) 6.75 6.75

Souvenir Sheet

834 CD350 $1.50 Sheet of 4, #a.-d. 7.25 7.25

Beetles A133

Perf. 15x14

1994, Jan. 21 Litho. Unwmk.
835 A133 $1 Ground beetle 1.25 1.25
836 A133 $1.15 Click beetle 1.60 1.60
837 A133 $1.50 Harlequin beetle 1.90 1.90
838 A133 $3.45 Leaf beetle 4.50 4.50
Nos. 835-838 (4) 9.25 9.25

Souvenir Sheet

839 A133 $4.50 Scarab beetle 5.75 5.75

Hibiscus Flowers and Fruits — A134

Designs: 90c, Cotton. $1.15, Sorrel. $1.50, Okra. $3.50, Hibiscus rosa sinensis.

1994, Mar. 22 Litho. *Perf. 14x13½*
840 A134 90c multicolored 1.25 1.25
841 A134 $1.15 multicolored 1.60 1.60
842 A134 $1.50 multicolored 2.00 2.00
843 A134 $3.50 multicolored 5.00 5.00
Nos. 840-843 (4) 9.85 9.85

Aquatic Dinosaurs A135

No. 844: a, $1, Elasmosaurus. b, $1.15, Plesiosaurus. c, $1.50, Nothosaurus. d, $3.45, Mosasaurus.

1994, May 6 Litho. *Perf. 15x14*
844 A135 Strip of 4, #a.-d. 12.50 12.50

1994 World Cup Soccer Championships, U.S. — A136

No. 845: a, 90c, Montserrat youth soccer. b, $1, 1990 World Cup, US vs. England. c, $1.15, Rose Bowl Stadium, Pasadena, Calif., US. d, $3.45, German team, 1990 World Cup Winners.

No. 846: a, Jules Rimet. b, Bobby Moore, England Team Captain, 1966. c, Lew Jaschin. d, Sepp Herberger, German trainer.

1994, May 20 *Perf. 14*
845 A136 Vert. strip of 4, #a.-d. 10.00 10.00

Souvenir Sheet
Perf. 14x14½

846 A136 $2 Sheet of 4, #a.-d. 11.00 11.00

No. 845 printed in sheets of 2 strips + 4 labels.

Nos. 726-729 Ovptd. in Red or Surcharged in Red and Black

Inscribed "Space Anniversaries" and: 40c, "Yuri Gagarin / First man in space / April 12, 1961." $1.15, "First Joint US / Soviet Mission / July 15, 1975." $1.50, "25th Anniversary / First Moon Landing / Apollo XI-July 20, 1994." $2.30, "Columbia / First Space Shuttle / April 12, 1981."

1994, July 20 *Perf. 13½x14*
847 A112 40c on 90c multi .75 .75
848 A112 $1.15 multi 3.00 3.00
849 A112 $1.50 multi 3.50 3.50
850 A112 $2.30 on $3.50 multi 5.75 5.75
Nos. 847-850 (4) 13.00 13.00

Obliterator on Nos. 847, 850 is black.

Woodstock Festival, 25th Anniv. A137

1994, Oct. 20 *Perf. 12½*
851 A137 $1.15 1969 Poster 1.60 1.60
852 A137 $1.50 1994 Poster 1.75 1.75

Souvenir Sheets

853 A137 $4.50 like #851 6.00 6.00
854 A137 $4.50 like #852 6.00 6.00

Sea Vegetation A138

1995, Feb. 14 *Perf. 14x15*
855 A138 $1 Sea fan .85 .85
856 A138 $1.15 Sea lily 1.00 1.00
857 A138 $1.50 Sea pen 1.40 1.40
858 A138 $3.45 Sea fern 3.25 3.25
Nos. 855-858 (4) 6.50 6.50

Souvenir Sheet

859 A138 $4.50 Sea rose 4.50 4.50

Motion Pictures, Cent. A139

No. 860: a.-i., Various portraits of Marilyn Monroe.
$6, Marilyn Monroe & Elvis Presley.

1995, June 13 Litho. *Perf. 12½*
860 A139 $1.15 Sheet of 9, #a-i 12.00 12.00

Souvenir Sheet

861 A139 $6 multicolored 7.50 7.50

No. 861 contains one 51x57mm stamp.

1995 IAAF World Track & Field Championships, Gothenburg, Sweden — A140

No. 862: a, Jesse Owens, U.S. b, Eric Lemming, Sweden. c, Rudolf Harbig, Germany. d, Montserrat youth.

1995, Aug. 3 *Perf. 14*
862 A140 $1.50 Sheet of 4, #a-d 7.50 7.50

End of World War II, 50th Anniv. A141

No. 863: a, Atmospheric sounding experiments using V-2 rockets. b, Space Shuttle Challenger.

No. 864: a, 1st successful nuclear reactor. b, Calder Hall Atomic Power Station, England.

No. 865: a, Ju88G-7a nightfighter equipped with SN2 radar. b, NATO Boeing E6 AWACS.

No. 866: a, Gloster Meteor III jet aircraft. b, British Airways Concorde.

1995, Aug. 15
863 A141 $1.15 Pair, #a.-b. 3.00 3.00
864 A141 $1.15 Pair, #a.-b. 3.00 3.00
865 A141 $1.50 Pair, #a.-b. 4.25 4.25
866 A141 $1.50 Pair, #a.-b. 4.25 4.25
Nos. 863-866 (4) 14.50 14.50

Nos. 812, 818 Ovptd.

1995 Litho. *Perf. 15x14*
871 A128 $1 multicolored 1.00 1.00
872 A128 $10 multicolored 10.50 10.50

UN, 50th Anniv. — A142

1995, Sept. 4 Litho. *Perf. 14*
873 A142 $1.15 Food 1.25 1.25
874 A142 $1.50 Education 1.50 1.50
875 A142 $2.30 Health 2.50 2.50
876 A142 $3 Peace 3.25 3.25
Nos. 873-876 (4) 8.50 8.50

Souvenir Sheet

877 A142 $6 Justice 7.00 7.00

Natl. Trust, 25th Anniv. A143

Designs: $1.15, Headquarters building. $1.50, 17th cent. cannon, Bransby Point. $2.30, Painting of original Galways sugar mill, vert. $3, Great Alps Falls, vert.

1995, Nov. 15 Litho. *Perf. 14*
878-881 A143 Set of 4 12.50 12.50

Scavengers of the Sea — A144

1996, Feb. 14 Litho. *Perf. 15x14*
882 A144 $1 Bull shark 1.10 1.10
883 A144 $1.15 Sea mouse 1.25 1.25
884 A144 $1.50 Bristleworm 1.60 1.60
885 A144 $3.45 Prawn xiphocaris 3.75 3.75
Nos. 882-885 (4) 7.70 7.70

Souvenir Sheet

886 A144 $4.50 Man o'war 6.00 6.00

Radio, Cent. (in 1995) A145

Designs: $1.15, Guglielmo Marconi, transmitting equipment, 1901. $1.50, Wireless laboratory, Marconi's yacht, Elettra. $2.30, First transatlantic radio message, Newfoundland, 1901. $3, First air/ground radio station, Croydon, 1920.

$4.50, First radio telescope, Jodrell Bank, Cheshire, England.

1996, Mar. 19 Litho. *Perf. 14*
887-890 A145 Set of 4 8.50 8.50

Souvenir Sheet

891 A145 $4.50 multi 5.25 5.25

1996 Summer Olympic Games, Atlanta A146

1896 Medalists: $1.15, Paul Masson, cycling. $1.50, Robert Garrett, discus. $2.30, Spiridon Louis, marathon. $3, John Boland, tennis.

1996, June 24 Litho. *Perf. 14*
892-895 A146 Set of 4 7.50 7.50

Mythical Creatures — A147

1996, Aug. 15 Litho. *Perf. 14*

896	A147	5c	Leprechaun	.20	.20
897	A147	10c	Pegasus	.20	.20
898	A147	15c	Griffin	.20	.20
899	A147	20c	Unicorn	.20	.20
900	A147	25c	Gnome	.20	.20
901	A147	40c	Mermaid	.30	.30
902	A147	55c	Cockatrice	.40	.40
903	A147	70c	Fairy	.55	.55
904	A147	90c	Goblin	.70	.70
905	A147	$1	Faun	.75	.75
906	A147	$1.15	Dragon	.90	.90
907	A147	$1.50	Giant	1.10	1.10
908	A147	$3	Elf	2.25	2.25
909	A147	$5	Centaur	3.75	3.75
910	A147	$7.50	Phoenix	5.75	5.75
911	A147	$10	Erin	7.50	7.50
			Nos. 896-911 (16)	24.95	24.95

For overprints see Nos. O126-O140.

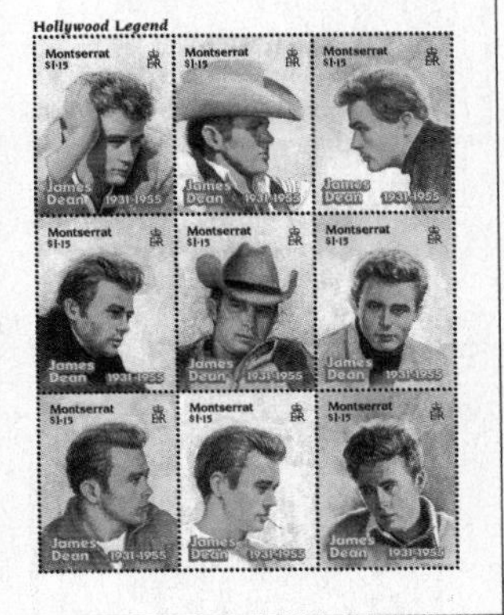

James Dean (1931-55), Actor — A148

Various portraits.

1996, June 28 Litho. *Perf. 12½*

912 A148 $1.15 Sheet of 9, #a.-i. 11.50 11.50

Souvenir Sheet

913 A148 $6 multicolored 7.50 7.50

No. 913 contains one 51x57mm stamp.
For overprint see No. 921.

Dancing Bears, Emblem of "The Grateful Dead" — A149

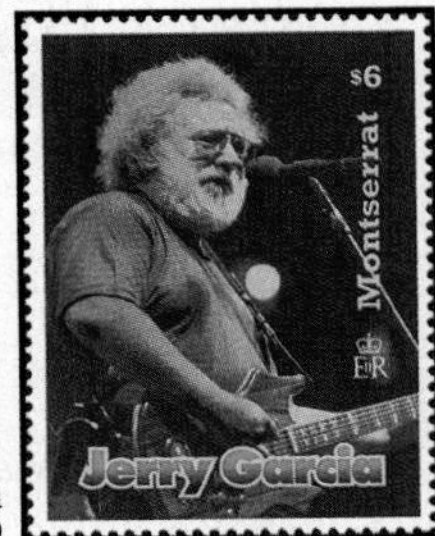

Jerry Garcia A150

No. 914 — Color of bears: a, blue violet, green. b, yellow. c, orange, pink.

1996, Oct. 21 Litho. *Perf. 12½*

914	A149	$1.15	Strip of 3, #a.-c.	3.50	3.50
915	A150	$6	multicolored	6.25	6.25

For overprint and surcharge see #920A, 928. Compare with #955-956 and #970-83.

Scavenger Birds A151

1997, Jan. 28 Litho. *Perf. 14½x14*

916	A151	$1	Turkey vulture	1.00	1.00
917	A151	$1.15	American crow	1.25	1.25
918	A151	$1.50	Great skua	1.50	1.50
919	A151	$3.45	Kittiwake	3.50	3.50
			Nos. 916-919 (4)	7.25	7.25

Souvenir Sheet

920 A151 $4.50 King vulture 5.00 5.00

No. 914 Overprinted "Hong Kong '97" Across Strip in Dark Blue

Methods and Perfs as before

1997, Mar. 26

920A A149 $1.15 Strip of 3, #b-d 3.00 3.00

No. 912 Overprinted

1997, June 2 Litho. *Perf. 12½*

921 A148 $1.15 Sheet of 9, #a.-i. 12.50 12.50

Overprints are placed over vertical perfs separating each column of stamps. Each stamp in the left and right columns has only half the overprint. The stamps in the center column contains two incomplete halves of the overprint. The overprints also appear twice in sheet margin.

Eruption of Mt. Soufriere, Endangered Species — A152

No. 922: a, Heavy ash eruption, Plymouth, 1995. b, First pyroclastic flow entering sea. c, Double venting at Castle Peak. d, Mangrove cuckoo. e, Nocturnal lava flow, Soufriere Hills, 1996. f, Antillean crested hummingbird. g, Ash cloud engulfing Plymouth. h, Lava spine extruded, Soufriere Hills, 1996. i, New land created from pyroclastic flows.

1997, June 23 *Perf. 14*

922 A152 $1.50 Sheet of 9, #a.-i. 10.50 10.50

j. Additional inscription in sheet margin 10.50 10.50

No. 922j is inscribed in sheet margin: "MUSIC FOR" and "IN AID OF THE VICTIMS OF SOUFRIERE HILLS VOLCANO," "ROYAL ALBERT HALL LONDON" and "15th SEPTEMBER 1997."

Elvis Presley (1935-77) A153

American rock stars: No. 924, Jimi Hendrix (1942-70). No. 925, Jerry Garcia (1942-95). No. 926, Janis Joplin (1943-70).

1997, Aug. 29 Litho. *Perf. 12½*

923	A153	$1.15	multicolored	2.00	2.00
924	A153	$1.15	multicolored	2.00	2.00
925	A153	$1.15	multicolored	2.00	2.00
926	A153	$1.15	multicolored	2.00	2.00
			Nos. 923-926 (4)	8.00	8.00

Abstract Art — A154

1997, Aug. 29 Litho. *Perf. 12½*

927 A154 $1.50 multicolored 2.50 2.50

No. 915 Surcharged in Gold and Black

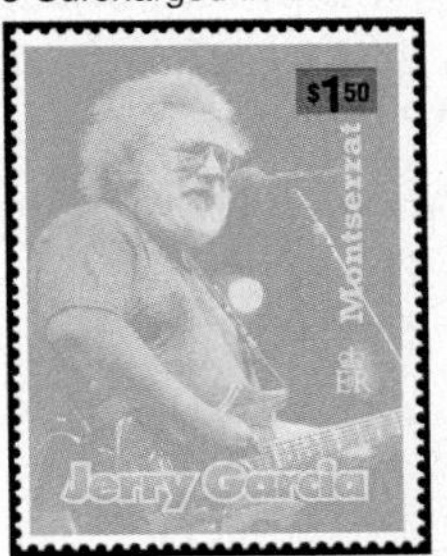

1997 Litho. *Perf. 12½*

928 A150 $1.50 on $6 multi 2.50 2.50

Medicinal Plants — A155

A156

1998, Mar. 30 Litho. *Perf. 15*

929	A155	$1	Prickly pear	.70	.70
930	A155	$1.15	Pomme coolie	.80	.80
931	A155	$1.50	Aloe	1.00	1.00
932	A155	$3.45	Bird pepper	2.50	2.50
			Nos. 929-932 (4)	5.00	5.00

1998, May 18 Litho. *Perf. 12½*

Famous People of the 20th Cent.: No. 933, Jean-Henri Dunant. No. 934, Mohandas Gandhi. No. 935, Pablo Picasso. No. 936, David Ben-Gurion. No. 937, Dwidght D. Eisenhower. No. 938, Wernher von Braun. No. 939, Eva & Juan Perón. No. 940, Konrad Adenauer. No. 941, Mao Tse-tung. No. 942, Lord Mountbatten. No. 943, Charles Lindbergh. No. 944, Anne Frank. $3, John F. Kennedy.

933	A156	$1.15	multicolored	1.50	1.50
934	A156	$1.15	multicolored	1.50	1.50
935	A156	$1.15	multicolored	1.50	1.50
936	A156	$1.15	multicolored	1.50	1.50
937	A156	$1.15	multicolored	1.50	1.50
938	A156	$1.15	multicolored	1.50	1.50
939	A156	$1.15	multicolored	1.50	1.50
940	A156	$1.50	multicolored	2.10	2.10
941	A156	$1.50	multicolored	2.10	2.10
942	A156	$1.50	multicolored	2.10	2.10
943	A156	$1.50	multicolored	2.10	2.10
944	A156	$1.50	multicolored	2.10	2.10
			Nos. 933-944 (12)	21.00	21.00

Souvenir Sheet

945 A156 $3 multicolored 4.00 4.00

No. 945 contains one 51x38mm stamp.
Issued in sheets of 4 with illustrated right margin.

1998, May 18 Litho. *Perf. 12½*

Royalty of the 20th cent.: No. 946, Grand Duchess Charlotte (1896-1985) & Felix, Luxembourg. No. 947, Leopold III (1901-83) & Astrid, Belgium. No. 948, Wilhelmina (1880-1962), Netherlands. No. 949, Gustav V (1858-1950), Sweden. No. 950, Alfonso XIII (1886-1931), Spain. No. 951, Christian X (1870-1947), Denmark. No. 952, Haakon VII (1872-1957) & Olav, Denmark. No. 953, George VI (1895-1952), Great Britain.

946	A156	$1.15	multicolored	1.10	1.10
947	A156	$1.15	multicolored	1.10	1.10
948	A156	$1.50	multicolored	1.25	1.25
949	A156	$1.50	multicolored	1.25	1.25
950	A156	$1.50	multicolored	1.25	1.25
951	A156	$1.50	multicolored	1.25	1.25
952	A156	$1.50	multicolored	1.25	1.25
953	A156	$1.50	multicolored	1.25	1.25
			Nos. 946-953 (8)	9.70	9.70

Issued in sheets of 4 with illustrated right margin.

Bob Marley (1947-81) A157

Various portraits.

1998, Aug. 6

954 A157 $1.15 Sheet of 8, #a.-h. + label 10.00 10.00

Jerry Garcia (1947-95) A158

Various portraits.

1998, Aug. 6

955 A158 $1.15 Sheet of 9, #a.-i. 10.00 10.00

Souvenir Sheet

956 A158 $5 multicolored 6.50 6.50

No. 956 contains one 51x76mm stamp. Compare with #914-915 and #970-983.

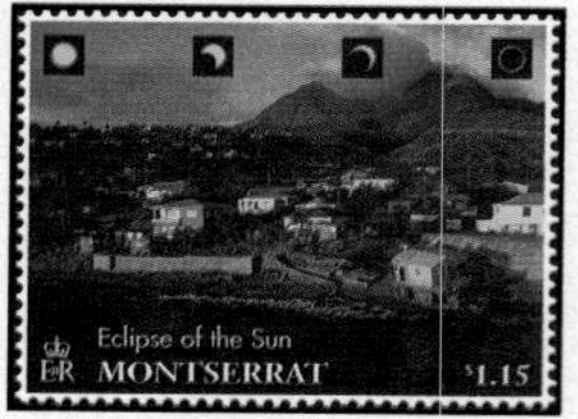

Eclipse of the Sun, Feb. 26, 1998 — A159

Views of Mt. Soufriere volcano: No. 957, Homes near water. No. 958, Looking across mountain tops. No. 959, Ash on mountainside, home. No. 960, Ash, steam rising in air.
$6, View of eclipse, vert.

1998 Litho. *Perf. 12½*
957 A159 $1.15 multicolored 1.75 1.75
958 A159 $1.15 multicolored 1.75 1.75
959 A159 $1.15 multicolored 1.75 1.75
960 A159 $1.15 multicolored 1.75 1.75
Nos. 957-960 (4) 7.00 7.00

Souvenir Sheet

961 A159 $6 multicolored 7.25 7.25

Diana, Princess of Wales (1961-97) A160

1998 Litho. *Perf. 12½*
962 A160 $1.15 As bride 1.50 1.50
963 A160 $1.50 Princess of charities 1.75 1.75
964 A160 $3 At Royal Ascot 3.75 3.75
Nos. 962-964 (3) 7.00 7.00

Souvenir Sheet

965 A160 $6 Rose, Diana 6.50 6.50

No. 965 contains one 51x38mm stamp.

Nos. 592-593 Ovptd. in Red with emblem and "13th WORLD JAMBOREE MONDIALE CHILE 1999"

Wmk. 380

1998, Dec. 29 Litho. *Perf. 15*
966 20c Pair, #a.-b. .60 .60
967 75c Pair, #a.-b. 2.40 2.40

Nos. 873-874 Overprinted

Unwmk.

1999, Apr. 27 Litho. *Perf. 14*
968 A142 $1.15 on #873 2.75 2.75
969 A142 $1.50 on #874 3.25 3.25

Jerry Garcia (1947-95) — A161

Garcia: No. 970, $1.15, Wearing purple shirt, microphone at right, light blue background. No. 971, $1.15, In red light, dark blue background. No. 972, $1.15, Wearing purple shirt, microphone at left. No. 973, $1.15, Like #971, blue green background. No. 974, $1.15, Wearing black shirt, playing guitar. No. 975, $1.15, Wearing red shirt. No. 976, $1.15, Wearing blue shirt, microphone at right, vert. No. 977, $1.15, Wearing blue shirt, microphone to left of face, vert. No. 978, $1.15, Wearing blue shirt, microphone partially covering face, vert. No. 979, $1.15, Wearing black shirt, orange rectangular frame, vert. No. 980, $1.15, Wearing blue shirt, orange and blue frame, vert. No. 981, $1.15, Wearing black shirt, orange and blue frame, vert.

No. 982, $6, Vignette of #980. No. 983, $6, Wearing black shirt, vert.

1999 Litho. Unwmk. *Perf. 12½*
970-981 A161 Set of 12 20.00 20.00

Souvenir Sheets

982-983 A161 Set of 2 20.00 20.00

Issued in sheets of 9 containing 3 each of Nos. 970-972, 973-975, 976-978, 979-981 respectively. Nos. 982-983 contain one 76x51mm or 51x76mm stamp, respectively. Compare with #914-915 and #955-956.

Fruit A162

1999 Litho. Wmk. 380 *Perf. 12½*
984 A162 $1.15 Mango 1.10 1.10
985 A162 $1.50 Breadfruit 1.50 1.50
986 A162 $2.30 Papaya 2.40 2.40
987 A162 $3 Lime 3.00 3.00
988 A162 $6 Akee 6.25 6.25
a. Sheet of 5, #984-988 +label 15.00 15.00
Nos. 984-988 (5) 14.25 14.25

Dogs A163

1999
989 A163 70c Yorkshire terrier 1.10 1.10
990 A163 $1 Welsh corgi 1.90 1.90
991 A163 $1.15 King Charles spaniel 2.00 2.00
992 A163 $1.50 Poodle 2.75 2.75
993 A163 $3 Beagle 5.25 5.25
a. Sheet of 5, #989-993 + label 13.00 13.00
Nos. 989-993 (5) 13.00 13.00

World Teachers' Day — A164

World map and: $1, Ruler, scissors, compass, pencil, paint brush. $1.15, Teacher lecturing, $1.50, Compass, flag, camera, globe, plumb bob, theodolite. $5, Pen, flask, funnel, thermometer, calipers, microscope.

1999 Litho. *Perf. 12½*
994-997 A164 Set of 4 12.50 12.50

Worldwide Fund for Nature A165

No. 998 - Great hammerhead shark: a, Pair swimming. b, Pair near ocean floor. c, Trio swimming. d, One swimming.

Perf. 13¼

1999, Nov. 29 Litho. Unwmk.
998 Horiz. strip of 4 3.50 3.50
a.-d. A165 50c Any single .70 .70

Millennium — A166

2000, Jan. 1 Unwmk.
999 A166 $1.50 multi 2.75 2.75

100th Test Cricket Match at Lord's Ground — A167

Designs: $1, Alfred Valentine. $5, George Headley.
$6, Lord's Ground, horiz.

2000, May 5 Litho. *Perf. 13½x13¼*
1000-1001 A167 Set of 2 6.75 6.75

Souvenir Sheet

Perf. 13¼x13½

1002 A167 $6 multi 8.75 8.75

The Stamp Show 2000, London A168

Battle of Britain, 60th anniv.: 70c, Scramble. $1.15, Hurricane Mk.1 overhaul. $1.50, Hurricane Mk. 1 and enemy plane. $5, Spitfire Mk. 1a of Flight Lt. Frank Howell.
$6, Plane in air.

Wmk. 373

2000, May 22 Litho. *Perf. 14*
1003 A168 70c multi .70 .70
1004 A168 $1.15 multi 1.10 1.10
1005 A168 $1.50 multi 1.50 1.50
1006 A168 $5 multi 5.00 5.00
Nos. 1003-1006 (4) 8.30 8.30

Souvenir Sheet

1007 A168 $6 multi 6.75 6.75

Millennium — A169

People of Montserrat and: 90c, Statue of Liberty. $1.15, Great Wall of China. $1.50, Eiffel Tower. $3.50, Millennium Dome, Great Britain.

Perf. 13½

2000, July 3 Litho. Unwmk.
1008-1011 A169 Set of 4 7.25 7.25

Queen Mother, 100th Birthday A170

Queen Mother and various buildings. Panel color under country name in: 70c, Yellow. $1.15, Purple. $3, Green. $6, Orange.

2000, Aug. 4 *Perf. 13½x13*
1012-1015 A170 Set of 4 11.50 11.50
1015a Souvenir sheet, #1012-1015 12.00 12.00

Christmas A171

Designs: $1, The three Magi. $1.15, Cavalla Hill Methodist Church. $1.50, Shepherds. $3, $6, Mary and Joseph arriving in Bethlehem.

Perf. 14x14¾

2000, Nov. 29 Wmk. 373
1016-1019 A171 Set of 4 7.25 7.25

Souvenir Sheet

1020 A171 $6 multi 4.25 4.25

Birds A172

Designs: $1, Golden swallow, vert. $1.15, Crested quail dove. $1.50, Red-legged thrush. $5, Fernandina's flicker, vert.
$8, St. Vincent parrot.

2001, Mar. 26 Litho. *Perf. 13¼*
1021-1024 A172 Set of 4 7.25 7.25

Souvenir Sheet

1025 A172 $8 St. Vincent parrot 8.25 8.25

Philatelic Personalities — A173

Designs: $1, Edward Stanley Gibbons, Charles J. Phillips. $1.15, John Lister. $1.50, Theodore Champion and 19th cent. French postilion. $3, Thomas de la Rue.
$8, Sir Rowland Hill, Bruce Castle.

2001, Apr. 30 *Perf. 13¼*
1026-1029 A173 Set of 4 8.00 8.00

Souvenir Sheet

1030 A173 $8 multi 8.00 8.00

Queen Elizabeth II, 75th Birthday — A174

Dress color: 90c, Black. $1.15, Yellow. $1.50, Pink. $5, Green.
$6, Lilac.

2001, June 22 *Perf. 13¼*
1031-1034 A174 Set of 4 10.00 10.00

Souvenir Sheet

1035 A174 $6 multi 8.00 8.00

Buildings — A175

Designs: 70c, Lookout community. $1, St. John's Hospital. $1.15, Tropical Mansion Suites. $1.50, Montserrat Secondary School. $3, Golden Years Home.

2001, Aug. 15 **Litho.** ***Perf. 13½***
1036-1040 A175 Set of 5 8.00 8.00

Fruit
A176

Designs: 5c, West Indian cherries. 10c Mammee apples. 15c, Limes. 20c, Grapefruits. 25c, Orange. 40c, Passion fruits. 55c, Bananas. 70c, Papayas. 90c, Pomegranates. $1, Guavas. $1.15, Mangos. $1.50, Sugar apple. $3, Cashews. $5, Soursops. $7.50, Watermelon. $10, Pineapple.

2001, Oct. 10 **Litho.** ***Perf. 13½x13¼***

1041	A176	5c multi	.20	.20
1042	A176	10c multi	.20	.20
1043	A176	15c multi	.20	.20
1044	A176	20c multi	.20	.20
1045	A176	25c multi	.20	.20
1046	A176	40c multi	.40	.40
1047	A176	55c multi	.50	.50
1048	A176	70c multi	.65	.65
1049	A176	90c multi	.85	.85
1050	A176	$1 multi	1.00	1.00
1051	A176	$1.15 multi	1.10	1.10
1052	A176	$1.50 multi	1.40	1.40
1053	A176	$3 multi	3.00	3.00
1054	A176	$5 multi	4.75	4.75
1055	A176	$7.50 multi	7.50	7.50
1056	A176	$10 multi	9.75	9.75
	Nos. 1041-1056 (16)		31.90	31.90

Butterflies — A177

Designs: $1, Common long-tail skipper. $1.15, Straight-line skipper. $1.50, Giant hairstreak. $3, Monarch.
$10, Painted lady.

2001, Dec. 20 **Litho.** ***Perf. 13¼***
1057-1060 A177 Set of 4 8.00 8.00

Souvenir Sheet

1061 A177 $10 multi 10.50 10.50

2002 Winter Olympics, Salt Lake City — A178

No. 1062: a, $3, Downhill skiing. b, $5, Bobsled.

2002, Mar. 12 **Litho.** ***Perf. 13¼***
1062 A178 Horiz. pair, #a-b 8.75 8.75

Fish
A179

Designs: $1, Sergeant major. $1.15, Mutton snapper. $1.50, Lantern bass. $5, Shy hamlet.
$8, Queen angelfish.

Perf. 13¼

2002, July 29 **Litho.** **Unwmk.**
1063-1066 A179 Set of 4 10.00 10.00

Souvenir Sheet

1067 A179 $8 multi 10.00 10.00

Nos. 1012-1015 Overprinted

2002, Sept. 23 **Litho.** ***Perf. 13½x13***

1068	A170	70c on #1012	.75	.75
1069	A170	$1.15 on #1013	1.25	1.25
1070	A170	$3 on #1014	3.25	3.25
1071	A170	$6 on #1015	6.75	6.75
	Nos. 1068-1071 (4)		12.00	12.00

Wild Flowers — A180

Designs: 70c, Allamanda cathartica. $1.15, Lantana camara. $1.50, Leonotis nepetifolia. $5, Plumeria rubra.
$8, Alpinia purpurata.

Perf. 13¼

2002, Nov. 29 **Litho.** **Unwmk.**
1072-1075 A180 Set of 4 9.00 9.00

Souvenir Sheet

1076 A180 $8 multi 9.00 9.00

Coronation of Queen Elizabeth II, 50th Anniv. — A181

No. 1077: a, Queen wearing crown. b, Crown on pillow. c, Queen wearing tiara and purple sash.
$6, Queen wearing crown, diff.

2003, Apr. 30 ***Perf. 14***
1077 A181 $3 Sheet of 3, #a-c 9.00 9.00

Souvenir Sheet

1078 A181 $6 multi 5.25 5.25

Powered Flight, Cent. — A182

No. 1079: a, Wright Flyer II in blue. b, Wright Flyer II in brown. c, Wright Brothers. d, Wright Flyer I.
$6, Wright Flyer II.

2003, June 30 **Litho.** ***Perf. 14***
1079 A182 $2 Sheet of 4, #a-d 6.75 6.75

Souvenir Sheet

1080 A182 $6 multi 6.75 6.75

Prince William, 21st Birthday — A183

No. 1081 — Prince William in suit and tie with: a, Frame obscured at LL and LR by portrait. b, Frame obscured at LL by portrait. c, Frame not obscured.
$6, Wearing sweater and shirt with open collar.

2003, Aug. 20
1081 A183 $3 Sheet of 3, #a-c 8.50 8.50

Souvenir Sheet

1082 A183 $6 multi 7.00 7.00

Fauna — A184

No. 1083: a, Piping frog. b, Land hermit crab. c, Spix's pinche. d, Dwarf gecko. e, Green sea turtle. f, Indian mongoose.
$6, Sally Lightfoot crab.

2003, Nov. 28
1083 A184 $1.50 Sheet of 6, #a-f 8.25 8.25

Souvenir Sheet

1084 A184 $6 multi 6.00 6.00

Mushrooms — A185

No. 1085: a, Slimy lead milk cap. b, Rosy spike cap. c, Stump puffball. d, Parasol. e, Crab russula. f, Scaly vase chanterelle.
$6, Fly agaric.

2003, Nov. 28
1085 A185 $1.50 Sheet of 6, #a-f 8.50 8.50

Souvenir Sheet

1086 A185 $6 multi 6.25 6.25

Birds
A186

Designs: 90c, Belted kingfisher. $1.15, Yellow warbler. No. 1089, $1.50, Hooded warbler. $5, Cedar waxwing.
No. 1091: a, Roseate spoonbill. b, Laughing gull. c, White-tailed tropicbird. d, Bare-eyed thrush. e, Glittering-throated emerald. f, Lesser Antillean grackle.
$6, Bananaquit.

2003, Nov. 28
1087-1090 A186 Set of 4 9.00 9.00
1091 A186 $1.50 Sheet of 6, #a-f 6.75 6.75

Souvenir Sheet

1092 A186 $6 multi 6.00 6.00

2004 Summer Olympics, Greece
A187

Designs: 90c, 1932 Los Angeles Olympics poster. $1.15, 1972 Munich Olympics pin. $1.50, 1976 Montreal Olympics poster. $5, Pankration, horiz.

2004, June 30 **Litho.** ***Perf. 13¼***
1093-1096 A187 Set of 4 8.25 8.25

Butterflies — A188

No. 1097: a, Lacewing. b, Swallowtail. c, Shoemaker. d, White peacock.
$6, Flashing astraptes.

2004, July 6 **Litho.** ***Perf. 14***
1097 A188 $2.30 Sheet of 4, #a-d 8.50 8.50

Souvenir Sheet

1098 A188 $6 multi 4.50 4.50

Cats — A189

Designs: $1.15, Singapura. $1.50, Burmese. $2, Abyssinian. $5, Norwegian.
$6, Russian Blue.

2004, Aug. 23
1099-1102 A189 Set of 4 9.00 9.00

Souvenir Sheet

1103 A189 $6 multi 7.75 7.75

Fish — A190

No. 1104: a, Blue-girdled angelfish. b, Regal angelfish. c, Emperor angelfish. d, Blotch-eyed soldierfish.
$6, Banded butterflyfish.

2004, Sept. 30

1104	A190	$2.30 Sheet of 4, #a-d	8.25	8.25

Souvenir Sheet

1105	A190	$6 multi	6.50	6.50

Locomotives, 200th Anniv. — A191

No. 1106: a, Austerity. b, Deli Vasut. c, Class 424 No. 424.247/287. d, L-1646. e, Steam locomotive 324.1564. f, Class la.
No. 1107: a, Old Class TV. b, Class Va 7111. c, Class 424 No. 424.009. d, Class III.
$6, Class QR1.

2004, Oct. 29 *Perf. 14½x14*

1106	A191	$1.50 Sheet of 6, #a-f	6.75	6.75
1107	A191	$2 Sheet of 4, #a-d	6.00	6.00

Souvenir Sheet

1108	A191	$6 multi	4.50	4.50

World AIDS Day — A192

2004, Dec. 1 *Perf. 13½*

1109	A192	$3 multi	2.25	2.25

Printed in sheets of 4.

D-Day, 60th Anniv. A193

Designs: $1.15, Air assault begins. $1.50, Troops assault beaches of Normandy. $2, Field Marshal Montgomery. $5, HMS Belfast.

2004, Dec. 24 *Perf. 14*

1110-1113	A193	Set of 4	7.25	7.25

National Soccer Team — A194

2004, Dec. 24 **Litho.** *Perf. 12*

1114	A194	$6 multi	4.50	4.50

Nos. 1036-1040 Overprinted

2005, Feb. 21 **Litho.** *Perf. 13½*

1115	A175	70c multi	.55	.55
1116	A175	$1 multi	.75	.75
1117	A175	$1.15 multi	.85	.85
1118	A175	$1.50 multi	1.10	1.10
1119	A175	$3 multi	2.25	2.25
		Nos. 1115-1119 (5)	5.50	5.50

Birds — A195

No. 1120: a, Brown pelican. b, Red-billed tropicbird. c, Galapagos Island cormorant. d, Waved albatross.
$6, Common tern.

2005, Apr. 25 **Litho.** *Perf. 13¼x13½*

1120	A195	$2.30 Sheet of 4, #a-d	7.00	7.00

Souvenir Sheet

1121	A195	$6 multi	4.50	4.50

Orchids — A196

No. 1122: a, Cattleya lueddemanniana. b, Cattleya luteola. c, Cattleya trianaei. d, Cattleya mossiae.
$6, Cattleya mendelii.

2005, Apr. 25

1122	A196	$2.30 Sheet of 4, #a-d	7.00	7.00

Souvenir Sheet

1123	A196	$6 multi	4.50	4.50

Molluscs and Shells A197

Designs: $1.15, Liguus virgineus. $1.50, Liguus fasciatus testudineus. $2, Liguus fasciatus. $5, Cerion striatella.
$6, Liguus fasciatus, vert.

2005, June 1 *Perf. 13¼x13½*

1124-1127	A197	Set of 4	7.25	7.25

Souvenir Sheet
Perf. 13½x13¼

1128	A197	$6 multi	4.50	4.50

Miniature Sheet

Soufriere Hills Volcanic Eruption, 10th Anniv. — A198

No. 1129: a, Dome glow. b, Explosion. c, Tar River Delta. d, Belham River. e, MVO Building. f, Pyroclastic flow entering the sea. g, Blackburne Airport, destroyed in 1997. h, Helicopter maintenance and monitoring. i, Instruments used for monitoring.

2005, July 18 **Litho.** *Perf. 14*

1129	A198	$2 Sheet of 9, #a-i	13.50	13.50

Rotary International, Cent. — A199

Emblem and: $1, Shamrock. $1.15, Heliconia flower. $1.50, Lady and the Harp. $5, Map of Montserrat.
$6, Medical care for children, horiz.

2005, Sept. 12 *Perf. 12¾*

1130-1133	A199	Set of 4	6.50	6.50

Souvenir Sheet

1134	A199	$6 multi	4.50	4.50

Battle of Trafalgar, Bicent. — A200

No. 1135: a, Napoleon Bonaparte. b, Admiral Horatio Nelson. c, Battle of the Nile. d, Battle of Trafalgar.
$6, Nelson, diff.

2005, Nov. 4 **Litho.** *Perf. 12*

1135	A200	$2 Sheet of 4, #a-d	6.00	6.00

Souvenir Sheet

1136	A200	$6 multi	4.50	4.50

Hans Christian Andersen (1805-75), Author — A201

No. 1137: a, Thumbelina. b, The Flying Trunk. c, The Buckwheat.
$6, The Little Mermaid.

2005, Dec. 23 *Perf. 12¾*

1137	A201	$3 Sheet of 3, #a-c	6.75	6.75

Souvenir Sheet
Perf. 12

1138	A201	$6 multi	4.50	4.50

No. 1137 contains three 39x25mm stamps.

Famous People A202

Designs: No. 1139, $1.15, William Henry Bramble (1901-88), first chief minister. No. 1140, $1.15, Michael Simmons Osborne (1902-67), merchant and parliamentarian. No. 1141, $1.15, Robert William Griffith (1904-96), union leader. No. 1142, $1.15, Patricia Griffin (1907-86), social worker. No. 1143, $1.15, Lilian Cadogan (1907-92), nurse. No. 1144, $1.15, Samuel Aymer (1911-79), folk musician.

2005, Dec. 5 **Litho.** *Perf. 12¾*

1139-1144	A202	Set of 6	5.25	5.25
1140a		Inscribed "Symmons" instead of "Simmons"	.85	.85
1144a		Souvenir sheet, #1139, 1140a, 1141-1144	5.25	5.25

Nos. 1022, 1058-1059, 1072 and 1075 Overprinted

Methods and Perfs As Before

2006, Apr. 1

1145	A180	70c on #1072	.55	.55
1146	A172	$1 on #1022	.75	.75
1147	A177	$1.15 on #1058	.90	.90
1148	A177	$1.50 on #1059	1.10	1.10
1149	A180	$5 on #1075	3.75	3.75
		Nos. 1145-1149 (5)	7.05	7.05

Overprint is on four lines on No. 1146.

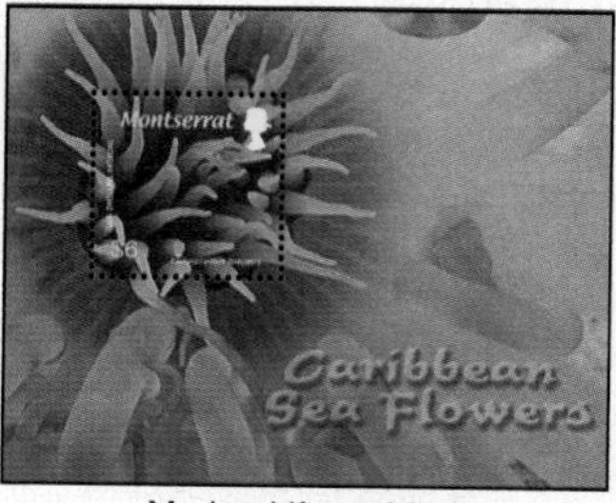

Marine Life — A203

No. 1150: a, Giant Caribbean anemone. b, Beadlet anemone. c, Golden crinoid. d, Oval cup coral.
$6, Tube-dwelling anemone.

2006, May 2 Litho. *Perf. 12*

1150	A203	$2.30 Sheet of 4, #a-d	7.00	7.00

Souvenir Sheet

1151	A203	$6 multi	4.50	4.50

Moths — A204

No. 1152: a, Cecropia moth. b, Madagascan sunset moth. c, Great peacock moth. d, Zodiac moth.
$6, White-lined sphinx moth.

2006, May 2

1152	A204	$2.30 Sheet of 4, #a-d	7.00	7.00

Souvenir Sheet

1153	A204	$6 multi	4.50	4.50

Dogs — A205

Designs: $1.15, Rottweiler. $1.50, Boxer. $2, Corgi. $5, Great Dane.
$6, St. Bernard.

2006, Aug. 16

1154-1157	A205	Set of 4	7.25	7.25

Souvenir Sheet

1158	A205	$6 multi	4.50	4.50

Worldwide Fund for Nature (WWF) — A206

No. 1159 — Various depictions of Mountain chicken frog: a, 70c. b, $1. c, $1.15. d, $1.50.

2006, Aug. 16 *Perf. 13¼*

1159	A206	Block of 4, #a-d	3.75	3.75
e.		Miniature sheet, 2 #1159	7.50	7.50

Souvenir Sheet

2006 World Cup Soccer Championships, Germany — A207

No. 1160 — World Cup, emblem and: a, $1.15, FIFA World Cup Stadium, Hanover. b, $1.50, Sir Stanley Matthews, England team uniform. c, $2, Sir Ralph "Dixie" Dean, England team uniform. d, $5, Bobby Moore, England team uniform.

2006, Aug. 31 *Perf. 12*

1160	A207	Sheet of 4, #a-d	7.25	7.25

Christopher Columbus (1451-1506), Explorer — A208

Designs: $1.15, Map of North and South America, Columbus's vessels. $1.50, Columbus and map of voyage. $2, Ship, Earth, Columbus. $5, Columbus, vert.
$6, Earth, Columbus and crew with flag, vert.

2006, Oct. 27 *Perf. 12¾*

1161-1164	A208	Set of 4	7.25	7.25

Souvenir Sheet

1165	A208	$6 multi	4.50	4.50

A209

Queen Elizabeth II, 80th Birthday — A210

No. 1166: a, Queen wearing crown, country name in black. b, Queen wearing crown, country name in white, c, Queen wearing tiara. d, Queen wearing tiara and sash.

2006, Oct. 27 *Perf. 13¼*

1166	A209	$2.30 Sheet of 4, #a-d	7.00	7.00

Souvenir Sheet

1167	A210	$8 shown	6.00	6.00

2007 Cricket World Cup, West Indies — A211

Designs: $3, 2007 Cricket World Cup emblem, map and flag of Montserrat. $5, Cricket team, horiz.
$8, 2007 Cricket World Cup emblem.

2007, Mar. 9 Litho. *Perf. 13¼*

1168-1169	A211	Set of 2	6.00	6.00

Souvenir Sheet

1170	A211	$8 multi	6.00	6.00

Scouting, Cent. — A212

No. 1171, horiz. — Scouts: a, Looking at flower. b, Working at construction site. c, In sailboat. d, Feeding goat. e, Making campfire. f, Installing birdhouse.
$6, Lord Robert Baden-Powell.

2007, Mar. 9

1171	A212	$2 Sheet of 6, #a-f	9.00	9.00

Souvenir Sheet

1172	A212	$6 multi	4.50	4.50

Flowers — A213

Designs: 10c, Poinsettia. 30c, Periwinkle. 35c, Bougainvillea. 50c, Ixora. 70c, Heliconia. 80c, Morning glory. 90c, Poinciana. $1, Cup of gold. $1.10, Chenille plant. $1.50, Oleander. $2.25, Hibiscus. $2.50, Frangipani. $2.75, Bird of paradise. $5, Madagascar jasmine. $10, Yellow poui. $20, Rose.

2007, May 14 Litho. *Perf. 12½*

1173	A213	10c multi	.20	.20
1174	A213	30c multi	.25	.25
1175	A213	35c multi	.25	.25
1176	A213	50c multi	.40	.40
1177	A213	70c multi	.55	.55
1178	A213	80c multi	.60	.60
1179	A213	90c multi	.70	.70
1180	A213	$1 multi	.75	.75
1181	A213	$1.10 multi	.85	.85
1182	A213	$1.50 multi	1.10	1.10
1183	A213	$2.25 multi	1.75	1.75
1184	A213	$2.50 multi	1.90	1.90
1185	A213	$2.75 multi	2.10	2.10
1186	A213	$5 multi	3.75	3.75
1187	A213	$10 multi	7.50	7.50
1188	A213	$20 multi	15.00	15.00
		Nos. 1173-1188 (16)	37.65	37.65

Princess Diana (1961-97) — A214

No. 1189 — Diana wearing tiara and: a, Blue dress. b, Black dress. c, White dress. d, White dress with high neck.
$7, Diana without tiara.

2007, Aug. 8 Litho. *Perf. 13¼*

1189	A214	$3.40 Sheet of 4, #a-d	10.50	10.50

Souvenir Sheet

1190	A214	$7 multi	5.25	5.25

Turtles — A215

No. 1191: a, Hawksbill turtle. b, Green turtle. c, Leatherback turtle. d, Loggerhead turtle.
$7, Kemp's Ridley sea turtle.

2007, Aug. 8 *Perf. 13¼x13½*

1191	A215	$3.40 Sheet of 4, #a-d	10.50	10.50

Souvenir Sheet

1192	A215	$7 multi	5.25	5.25

Parrots — A216

No. 1193: a, Green-winged macaw. b, Mitred conure. c, Sun conure. d, Blue-and-yellow macaw.
$7, Hyacinth macaw.

2007, Oct. 11 Litho. *Perf. 13½x13¼*

1193	A216	$3.40 Sheet of 4, #a-d	10.50	10.50

Souvenir Sheet

1194	A216	$7 multi	5.25	5.25

Lilies — A217

No. 1195, horiz.: a, Hippeastrum puniceum. b, Hymenocallis caribaea. c, Zephyranthes puertoricensis. d, Belamcanda chinensis.
$7, Crinum erubescens.

2007, Oct. 11 *Perf. 13¼x13½*

1195	A217	$3.40 Sheet of 4, #a-d	10.50	10.50

Souvenir Sheet

Perf. 13½x13¼

1196	A217	$7 multi	5.25	5.25

Miniature Sheet

Charles Wesley (1707-88), Hymn Writer — A218

No. 1197: a, Portrait of Wesley by unknown artist. b, Portrait of Wesley by John Russell. c, Engraving of Wesley by Jonathan Spilsbury. d, Bethany Methodist Church.

2007, Dec. 18 Litho. *Perf. 13¼*

1197	A218	$2.50 Sheet of 4, #a-d	7.50	7.50

Whales — A219

No. 1198: a, Sperm whale. b, Minke whale. c, Cuvier's beaked whale. d, Humpback whale.
$7, Blue whale.

2008, May 2 ***Perf. 12¾***

1198 A219 $3.55 Sheet of 4, #a-d 11.00 11.00

Souvenir Sheet

1199 A219 $7 multi 5.25 5.25

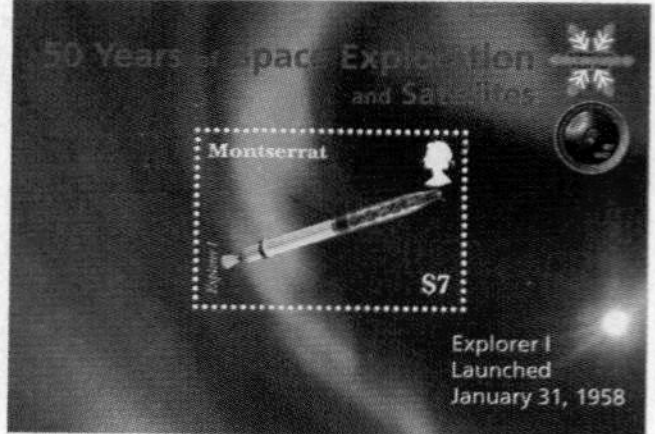

Space Exploration, 50th Anniv. — A220

No. 1200, vert.: a, Explorer I on Juno I launch rocket. b, Dr. James Van Allen, Explorer I. c, Explorer I. d, Drs. William Pickering, James Van Allen and Wernher von Braun with Explorer I model.
$7, Explorer I, diff.

2008, May 29 ***Perf. 13¼***

1200 A220 $3.55 Sheet of 4, #a-d 11.00 11.00

Souvenir Sheet

1201 A220 $7 multi 5.25 5.25

Endangered Animals — A221

No. 1202, vert.: a, African elephant. b, Bald eagle. c, Sumatran tiger. d, Hawksbill turtle. e, Indian rhinoceros. f, Western gorilla.
$7, Rock iguana.

2008, July 3

1202 A221 $2.25 Sheet of 6, #a-f 10.00 10.00

Souvenir Sheet

1203 A221 $7 multi 5.25 5.25

Miniature Sheet

Early Postal History — A222

No. 1204: a, "Lady McLeod" stamp, early paddle packet boat. b, Early Montserrat postal card. c, Great Britain #U1-U2. d, Great Britain #1, Sir Rowland Hill. e, Montserrat #1-2. f, Montserrat cancels.

2008, July 31 **Litho.** ***Perf. 13½***

1204 A222 $2.75 Sheet of 6, #a-f 12.50 12.50

Miniature Sheets

Royal Air Force, 90th Anniv. — A223

No. 1205, $3.55: a, English Electric Lightning P3. b, Hurricane IIC. c, Jet Provost T3A. d, Jaguar GR3A.
No. 1206, $3.55: a, Westland Sea King HAR3 helicopter. b, Gloster Javelin FAW9. c, P-66 Pembroke C1. d, Chinook HC2 helicopter.

2008, Sept. 5 **Litho.** ***Perf. 13¼***

Sheets of 4, #a-d

1205-1206 A223 Set of 2 22.00 22.00

University of the West Indies, 60th Anniv. — A224

Designs: $2, Building on Montserrat campus. $5, University arms, diploma.

2008, Sept. 30

1207-1208 A224 Set of 2 5.50 5.50

Miniature Sheets

Orchids — A225

No. 1209, $2.75: a, Cattleya labiata. b, Phalaenopsis cultivar with pink spots. c, Cymbidium annabelle. d, Phalaenopsis taisuco.
No. 1210, $2.75: a, Phalaenopsis amabilis. b, Cattleya aurantiaca. c, Phalaenopsis cultivar with pink lines. d, Dendrobium nobile.

2008, Nov. 27 ***Perf. 13¼***

Sheets of 4, #a-d

1209-1210 A225 Set of 2 17.00 17.00

Dolphins — A226

No. 1211: a, Common dolphin. b, Bottlenose dolphin. c, Pantropical spotted dolphin. d, Long-snouted spinner dolphin.
$7, Risso's dolphin.

2008, Nov. 27 ***Perf. 12¾***

1211 A226 $3.55 Sheet of 4, #a-d 11.00 11.00

Souvenir Sheet

1212 A226 $7 multi 5.50 5.50

Miniature Sheet

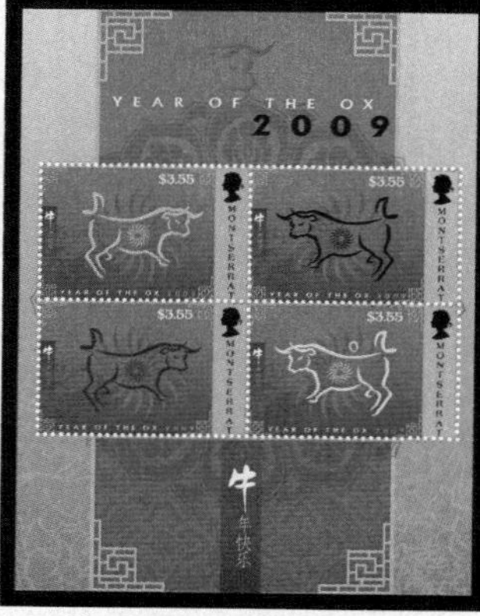

New Year 2009 (Year of the Ox) — A227

No. 1213: a, Yellow orange ox facing right. b, Black ox facing left. c, Gray ox facing right. d, White ox facing left.

2009, Feb. 2 **Litho.** ***Perf. 12¾***

1213 A227 $3.55 Sheet of 4, #a-d 11.00 11.00

Miniature Sheets

Dr. Martin Luther King, Jr. (1929-68), Civil Rights Leader — A228

No. 1214, $2.50: a, King. b, King at desk. c, King wearing hat. d, King's wife, Coretta.
No. 1215, $2.50, horiz.: a, March on Washington crowd. b, King meeting Malcolm X. c, King with Pres. John F. Kennedy and other civil rights leaders. d, King waving to March on Washington crowd.

2009, Feb. 26 ***Perf. 13½***

Sheets of 4, #a-d

1214-1215 A228 Set of 2 15.00 15.00

Birds — A229

No. 1216: a, Smooth-billed ani. b, American kestrel. c, Common moorhen. d, Cattle egret.
$7, Male Montserrat oriole.

2009, Apr. 1

1216 A229 $2.75 Sheet of 4, #a-d 8.50 8.50

Souvenir Sheet

1217 A229 $7 multi 5.50 5.50

Corals A230

Designs: $1.10, Staghorn coral. $2.25, Zoanthid coral. $2.50, Blade fire coral. $2.75, Brain coral.
$7, Orange tube coral, vert.

2009, Apr. 29

1218-1221 A230 Set of 4 6.50 6.50

Souvenir Sheet

1222 A230 $7 multi 5.25 5.25

No. 1222 contains one 37x51mm stamp.

Charles Darwin (1809-82), Naturalist — A231

No. 1223, vert.: a, Darwin. b, Coenobita clypeatus. c, Anolis lividus. d, Epidendrum montserratense.
$7, Darwin, waterfall, emblem of Montserrat Centre Hills Project.

2009, July 28

1223 A231 $2.75 Sheet of 4, #a-d 8.25 8.25

Souvenir Sheet

1224 A231 $7 multi 5.25 5.25

Rain Forest Animals — A232

No. 1225: a, $1.10, Green iguana. b, $2.25, Galliwasp. c, $2.50, Black snake. d, $2.75, Common agouti.
$5, Yellow-shouldered bat.

2009, Sept. 25 **Litho.** ***Perf. 13¼***

1225 A232 Sheet of 4, #a-d 6.50 6.50

Souvenir Sheet

1226 A232 $5 multi 3.75 3.75

Trees — A233

Designs: $1.10, Tamarind. $2.25, Dwarf coconut. $2.50, Breadfruit. $2.75, Calabash. $5, Geiger.

2009, Oct. 30 ***Perf. 14¼x14¾***
1227-1231 A233 Set of 5 10.50 10.50

Miniature Sheet

Naval Aviation, Cent. — A234

No. 1232 — Aircraft carriers: a, 70c, HMS Ark Royal II. b, $1.10, HMS Furious. c, $2.25, HMS Argus. d, $2.50, HMS Illustrious. e, $2.75, HMS Ark Royal IV. f, $5, HMS Invincible.

2009, Dec. 4 Litho. ***Perf. 11½x11¼***
1232 A234 Sheet of 6, #a-f 11.00 11.00

A235

Christmas — A236

Designs: $1.10, Snowflake bush. $2.25, Carnival troupe. $2.50, Masquerade. $2.75, St. Patrick's Roman Catholic Church.
$6, Creche figurines of Holy Family.

2009, Dec. 18 ***Perf. 12¾***
1233-1236 A235 Set of 4 6.75 6.75

Souvenir Sheet

1237 A236 $6 multi 4.75 4.75

Marine Life
A237

Designs: $1.10, Basket star. $2.25, Spiny lobster. $2.50, Spotted drum. $2.75, Sea anemone, vert. $5, Batwing coral crab.

2010, Mar. 15 ***Perf. 14¼***
1238-1242 A237 Set of 5 10.00 10.00

Miniature Sheets

World Landmarks — A238

No. 1243: a, $1.10, Jin Mao Tower, Shanghai, China. b, $2.25, Montserrat Cultural Center, Little Bay, Montserrat. c, $2.50, Assumption Cathedral, Moscow, Russia. d, $2.75, Brooklyn Bridge.

No. 1244: a, $1.10, Fishing villages in Shanghai and Hong Kong. b, $2.25, Camelot Villa, Montserrat. c, $2.50, Buildings at Zaanse Schans Windmill Village, Zaandam, Netherlands. d, $2.75, Reichstag, Berlin, Germany.

2010, Apr. 19 ***Perf. 14¼***
Sheets of 4, #a-d
1243-1244 A238 Set of 2 13.00 13.00

Miniature Sheets

A239

Michael Jackson (1958-2009), Singer — A240

No. 1245 — Jackson: a, Wearing sunglasses. b, Wearing red jacket and white shirt. c, With microphone near mouth. d, Wearing high-collared red jacket.

No. 1246 — Jackson: a, Facing right, no microphone. b, Facing left, holding microphone. c, Wearing black jacket, holding microphone. d, Facing forward, no microphone.

2010, June 25 ***Perf. 13½***
1245 A239 $2.50 Sheet of 4, #a-d 7.50 7.50
1246 A240 $2.50 Sheet of 4, #a-d 7.50 7.50

A241

Flowers — A242

Designs: $1.10, Wild marigold. $2.25, Shrubby toothedthread. $2.50, Wild sweet pea. $2.75, Rosy periwinkle. $5, Measle bush. $7, Pribby.

2010, Aug. 18
1247-1251 A241 Set of 5 10.00 10.00

Souvenir Sheet

1252 A242 $7 multi 5.25 5.25

Worldwide Fund for Nature (WWF) — A243

No. 1253 — Reddish egret: a, $1.10, Two birds in water. b, $2.25, Two birds in flight. c, $2.50, Bird preening feathers. d, $2.75, Bird running in water.

2010, Oct. 29 **Litho.**
1253 A243 Block or strip of 4, #a-d 6.50 6.50
e. Souvenir sheet of 8, 2 each #a-d 13.00 13.00

SEMI-POSTAL STAMPS

Catalogue values for unused stamps in this section, from this point to the end of the section, are for Never Hinged items.

Nos. 719-720 Surcharged

1989, Oct. 20 Litho. ***Perf. 13½x14***
B1 A110 $1.50 +$2.50 multi 2.75 2.75
B2 A110 $3.50 +$2.50 multi 4.25 4.25

Surcharge for hurricane relief.

No. 642 Surcharged

1995, Dec. 29 Litho. ***Perf. 15***
B3 A97 $2.30 +$5 multi 7.00 7.00

Surcharge for volcano relief.

WAR TAX STAMPS

No. 43 Overprinted in Red or Black

1917-18 Wmk. 3 ***Perf. 14***
MR1 A6 ½p green (R) .20 *1.75*
MR2 A6 ½p green ('18) .20 *2.25*

Type of Regular Issue of 1919 Overprinted

1918
MR3 A6 1½p orange & black .30 *.35*

Denomination on No. MR3 in black on white ground. Two dots under "d."

OFFICIAL STAMPS

Nos. O1-O44 used on Post Office and Philatelic Bureau mail. Not sold to public, used or unused.

Nos. 235-236, 338-339 Overprinted **O.H.M.S.**

Perf. 12½x14
1976, Apr. 12 Photo. Wmk. 314
O1 A22 5c multicolored 1.90
O2 A22 10c multicolored 2.50
O3 A22 30c on 10c multi 5.00
O4 A22 45c on 3c multi 6.00
Nos. O1-O4 (4) 15.40

Nos. 243-243A also received this overprint.

Nos. 343-347, 349-351, 353 Overprinted

Perf. 13½x14
1976, Oct. 1 Litho. Wmk. 373
O10 A44 5c multicolored .20
O11 A44 10c multicolored .20
O12 A44 15c multicolored .20
O13 A44 20c multicolored .20
O14 A44 25c multicolored .20
O15 A44 55c multicolored .40
O16 A44 70c multicolored .50
O17 A44 $1 multicolored .70
O18 A44 $5 multicolored 3.50
O19 A44 $10 multicolored 7.00
Nos. O10-O19 (10) 13.10

Nos. 343-347, 349-351, 353-354 Overprinted

1980, Sept. 30 ***Perf. 14***
O20 A44 5c multicolored .20
O21 A44 10c multicolored .20
O22 A44 15c multicolored .20
O23 A44 20c multicolored .20
O24 A44 25c multicolored .20
O25 A44 55c multicolored .35
O26 A44 70c multicolored .45
O27 A44 $1 multicolored .65
O28 A44 $5 multicolored 3.25
O29 A44 $10 multicolored 6.50
Nos. O20-O29 (10) 12.20

Nos. 341-351, 353-354 Overprinted or Surcharged

1980, Sept. 30 Litho. ***Perf. 14***
O30 A44 5c multicolored .20
O31 A44 5c on 3c multi .20
O32 A44 10c multicolored .20
O33 A44 15c multicolored .20
O34 A44 20c multicolored .20
O35 A44 25c multicolored .20
O36 A44 30c on 15c multi .25
O37 A44 35c on 2c multi .40
O38 A44 40c multicolored .30
O39 A44 55c multicolored .45
O40 A44 70c multicolored .60
O41 A44 $1 multicolored .80
O42 A44 $2.50 on 40c multi 2.00

O43 A44 $5 multicolored 4.00
O44 A44 $10 multicolored 8.00
Nos. O30-O44 (15) 18.00

Catalogue values for unused stamps in this section, from this point to the end of the section, are for Never Hinged items.

Fish Issue of 1981 Nos. 445-449, 451, 453, 455, 457-458, 460 Overprinted

1981, Mar. 20 Litho. *Perf. 13½*

O45 A64 5c multicolored .20 .20
O46 A64 10c multicolored .20 .20
O47 A64 15c multicolored .20 .20
O48 A64 20c multicolored .20 .20
O49 A64 25c multicolored .20 .20
O50 A64 45c multicolored .35 .35
O51 A64 65c multicolored .50 .50
O52 A64 $1 multicolored .75 .75
O53 A64 $3 multicolored 2.25 2.25
O54 A64 $5 multicolored 3.75 3.75
O55 A64 $10 multicolored 7.50 7.50
Nos. O45-O55 (11) 16.10 16.10

Nos. 465-470 Surcharged

1982, Nov. 17 Litho. *Perf. 14*

O56 A66 45c on 90c (#465) .40 .40
O57 A67 45c on 90c (#466) .40 .40
O58 A66 75c on $3 (#467) .70 .70
O59 A67 75c on $3 (#468) .70 .70
O60 A66 $1 on $4 (#469) .90 .90
O61 A67 $1 on $4 (#470) .90 .90
Nos. O56-O61 (6) 4.00 4.00

Princess Diana Issue, Nos. 484-486 Overprinted or Surcharged

1983, Oct. 19 Litho. *Perf. 14*

O62 A70b 70c on 75c (#484) 1.00 1.00
O63 A70b $1 (#485) 1.40 1.40
O64 A70b $1.50 on $5 (#486) 2.00 2.00
Nos. O62-O64 (3) 4.40 4.40

Nos. 524-536, 538 Overprinted

1985, Apr. 12 Wmk. 380 *Perf. 14*

O65 A79 5c multicolored .50 .20
O66 A79 10c multicolored .50 .20
O67 A79 15c multicolored .50 .20
O68 A79 20c multicolored .50 .20
O69 A79 25c multicolored .50 .20
O70 A79 40c multicolored .80 .40
O71 A79 55c multicolored .90 .45
O72 A79 70c multicolored 1.25 .65
O73 A79 90c multicolored 1.60 .80
O74 A79 $1 multicolored 1.90 .90
O75 A79 $1.15 multicolored 2.00 1.00
O76 A79 $3 multicolored 5.25 2.50
O77 A79 $5 multicolored 9.25 4.75
O78 A79 $10 multicolored 17.50 9.00
Nos. O65-O78 (14) 42.95 21.45

Nos. 681-694 and 696 Overprinted

Unwmk.

1989, May 9 Litho. *Perf. 14*

O79 A104 5c multicolored .20 .20
O80 A104 10c multicolored .20 .20
O81 A104 15c multicolored .20 .20
O82 A104 20c multicolored .20 .20
O83 A104 25c multicolored .20 .20
O84 A104 40c multicolored .40 .40
O85 A104 55c multicolored .60 .55
O86 A104 70c multicolored .75 .70
O87 A104 90c multicolored .95 .90
O88 A104 $1 multicolored 1.00 .95
O89 A104 $1.15 multicolored 1.25 1.25
O90 A104 $1.50 multicolored 1.60 1.40
O91 A104 $3 multicolored 3.00 2.75
O92 A104 $5 multicolored 5.25 4.75
O94 A104 $10 multicolored 10.50 9.50
Nos. O79-O94 (15) 26.30 24.15

Nos. 446, 454a and 456 Surcharged

1989 Wmk. 373 *Perf. 13½*

O95 A64 70c on 10c multi 1.75 1.75
O96 A64 $1.15 on 75c multi 3.25 3.25
O97 A64 $1.50 on $2 multi 4.00 4.00
Nos. O95-O97 (3) 9.00 9.00

Nos. 758-761, 763-766, 776-779 Surcharged or Overprinted "OHMS"

1992 Litho. *Perf. 14*

O98 A118 70c on 90c #758 1.50 1.50
O99 A118 70c on $3.50 #761 1.50 1.50
O100 A119 70c on 90c #763 1.50 1.50
O101 A121 70c on 90c #776 1.50 1.50
O102 A119 $1 on $3.50 #766 2.00 2.00
O103 A121 $1 on $3.50 #779 2.00 2.00
O104 A118 $1.15 on #759 2.25 2.25
O105 A119 $1.15 on #764 2.25 2.25
O106 A121 $1.15 on #777 2.25 2.25
O107 A118 $1.50 on #760 3.00 3.00
O108 A119 $1.50 on #765 3.00 3.00
O109 A121 $1.50 on #778 3.00 3.00
Nos. O98-O109 (12) 25.75 25.75

Nos. 803-816, 818 Ovptd. "OHMS" in Red

1993, Apr. 14 Litho. *Perf. 15x14*

O110 A128 5c multicolored .20 .20
O111 A128 10c multicolored .20 .20
O112 A128 15c multicolored .20 .20
O113 A128 20c multicolored .20 .20
O114 A128 25c multicolored .20 .20
O115 A128 40c multicolored .40 .40
O116 A128 55c multicolored .60 .60
O117 A128 70c multicolored .70 .70
O118 A128 90c multicolored .85 .85
O119 A128 $1 multicolored .95 .95
O120 A128 $1.15 multicolored 1.10 1.10
O121 A128 $1.50 multicolored 1.40 1.40
O122 A128 $3 multicolored 3.00 3.00
O123 A128 $5 multicolored 4.75 4.75
O125 A128 $10 multicolored 9.75 9.75
Nos. O110-O125 (15) 24.50 24.50

A number has been reserved for an additional value in this set.

Nos. 896-909, 911 Ovptd. "O.H.M.S." In Red

1997 Litho. *Perf. 14*

O126 A147 5c multicolored .20 .20
O127 A147 10c multicolored .20 .20
O128 A147 15c multicolored .20 .20
O129 A147 20c multicolored .20 .20
O130 A147 25c multicolored .20 .20
O131 A147 40c multicolored .40 .40
O132 A147 55c multicolored .50 .50
O133 A147 70c multicolored .70 .70
O134 A147 90c multicolored .90 .90
O135 A147 $1 multicolored .95 .95
O136 A147 $1.15 multicolored 1.10 1.10
O137 A147 $1.50 multicolored 1.40 1.40
O138 A147 $3 multicolored 3.00 3.00
O139 A147 $5 multicolored 4.75 4.75
O140 A147 $10 multicolored 9.75 9.75
Nos. O126-O140 (15) 24.45 24.45

Nos. 1041-1054, 1056 Overprinted

Perf. 13½x13¼

2002, June 14 Litho.

O141 A176 5c multi .20 .20
O142 A176 10c multi .20 .20
O143 A176 15c multi .20 .20
O144 A176 20c multi .20 .20
O145 A176 25c multi .20 .20
O146 A176 40c multi .30 .30
O147 A176 55c multi .40 .40
O148 A176 70c multi .80 .80
O149 A176 90c multi 1.10 1.10
O150 A176 $1 multi 1.25 1.25
O151 A176 $1.15 multi 1.50 1.50
O152 A176 $1.50 multi 1.90 1.90
O153 A176 $3 multi 4.00 4.00
O154 A176 $5 multi 6.50 6.50
O155 A176 $10 multi 13.00 13.00
Nos. O141-O155 (15) 31.75 31.75

Nos. 1173-1186, 1188 Overprinted

2007, May 14 Litho. *Perf. 12½*

O156 A213 10c multi .20 .20
O157 A213 30c multi .25 .25
O158 A213 35c multi .25 .25
O159 A213 50c multi .40 .40
O160 A213 70c multi .55 .55
O161 A213 80c multi .60 .60
O162 A213 90c multi .70 .70
O163 A213 $1 multi .75 .75
O164 A213 $1.10 multi .85 .85
O165 A213 $1.50 multi 1.10 1.10
O166 A213 $2.25 multi 1.75 1.75
O167 A213 $2.50 multi 1.90 1.90
O168 A213 $2.75 multi 2.10 2.10
O169 A213 $5 multi 3.75 3.75
O170 A213 $20 multi 15.00 15.00
Nos. O156-O170 (15) 30.15 30.15

Size and location of overprint varies.

MOROCCO

mə-ˈrä-ˌkō

LOCATION — Northwest coast of Africa
GOVT. — Kingdom
AREA — 171,953 sq. mi.
POP. — 29,661,636 (1999 est.)
CAPITAL — Rabat

A powerful kingdom from the 8th century, during the Middle Ages, Morocco ruled large areas of northwest Africa and Spain. By the turn of the 20th century, it had contracted to roughly its present borders and was the focus of an intense rivalry between France and Germany, who actively competed for control of the country. In 1912 most of Morocco became a French protectorate, with Spain acting as protector of zones in the extreme northern and southern parts of the country. Tangier was designated an international zone, administered by France, Spain, Britain and, later, Italy.

In 1956 the three zones of Morocco, French, Spanish and Tangier, were united to form an independent nation. Nos. 1-24 and C1-C3 were intended for use only in the southern (French currency) zone. Issues of the northern zone (Spanish currency) are listed after Postage Due stamps.

For earlier issues see French Morocco and Spanish Morocco.

400 Moussonats = 1 Rial (1912)
100 Centimes = 1 Franc (1956)
100 Centimes = 1 Dirham (1962)

Catalogue values for all unused stamps in this country are for Never Hinged items, except for Nos. A1-A14.

In 1892 the Sultan of Morocco established a postal service for most of the country's chief towns and cities. This service, utilizing handstuck franks, carried official correspondence, as well as some private correspondence. With French guidance, it was reorganized as the *Administration Cherifienne des Postes, Telegraphes et Telephones* in Sept. 1911. In 1912 Morocco became a French protectorate, and on Oct. 1, 1913, the Cherifian PTT was merged with the French *Administration des Postes et Telegraphes*.

Stamps were issued by the Moroccan post office in 1912, and these remained in use throughout the country until 1915 and in Tangier until 1919.

Aissaouas Mosque, Tangier — A1a

On White Paper

1912, May 25 Litho. *Perf. 11*

Narrow Margins

A1 A1a 1m light gray 9.25 8.50
A2 A1a 2m lilac 10.00 9.25
A3 A1a 5m blue green 12.50 8.50
A4 A1a 10m vermilion 19.00 8.50
A5 A1a 25m blue 29.00 24.00
A6 A1a 50m violet 42.50 37.50
Nos. A1-A6 (6) 122.25 96.25

On Nos. A1-A12, the 5m and 10m values always have the name of the engraver beneath the design, while the 1m, 25m and 50m always lack name, and the 2m value exists both with and without name.

Aissaouas Mosque, Tangier — A1b

On Lightly Tinted Paper

1913, Feb.

Wide Margins

A7 A1b 1m gray 1.25 1.25
A8 A1b 2m brown lilac 1.25 1.25
A9 A1b 5m blue green 1.75 1.75
A10 A1b 10m vermilion 1.75 1.75
A11 A1b 25m blue 3.75 3.75
A12 A1b 50m gray violet 4.50 4.50
Nos. A7-A12 (6) 14.25 14.25

No. A6 Surcharged with New Values

1913, Nov.

A13 A1a .05 on 50c violet 1,750. *2,000.*
A14 A1a .10 on 50c violet 1,750. *2,000.*

Sultan Mohammed V — A1

Men Reading — A2

1956-57 Unwmk. Engr. *Perf. 13*

No.	Type	Description	Unused	Used
1	A1	5fr brt bl & indigo	.25	.20
2	A1	10fr bis brn & choc	.25	.20
3	A1	15fr dp grn & magenta	.25	.20
4	A1	25fr purple ('57)	1.20	.20
5	A1	30fr green ('57)	2.25	.20
6	A1	50fr rose red ('57)	2.75	.20
7	A1	70fr dk brn & brn red ('57)	4.25	.80
		Nos. 1-7 (7)	11.20	2.00

For surcharges see Nos. B1-B5, B8-B9.

1956, Nov. 5

Campaign against illiteracy: 15fr, Girls reading. 20fr, Instructor and pupils. 30fr, Old man and child reading. 50fr, Girl pointing out poster.

No.	Type	Description	Unused	Used
8	A2	10fr pur & vio	1.60	1.20
9	A2	15fr car & rose lake	2.75	1.60
10	A2	20fr bl grn & grn	3.00	2.50
11	A2	30fr rose lake & brt red	5.50	3.00
12	A2	50fr dp bl & bl	7.00	5.25
		Nos. 8-12 (5)	19.85	13.55

Sultan Mohammed V — A3

Prince Moulay el Hassan — A4

1957, Mar. 2 Photo. *Perf. 13½x13*

No.	Type	Description	Unused	Used
13	A3	15fr blue green	1.60	1.20
14	A3	25fr gray olive	2.25	1.20
15	A3	30fr deep rose	4.00	1.90
		Nos. 13-15 (3)	7.85	4.30

Anniversary of independence.

1957, July 9 *Perf. 13*

No.	Type	Description	Unused	Used
16	A4	15fr blue	1.50	1.00
17	A4	25fr green	1.90	1.50
18	A4	30fr car rose	3.00	2.10
		Nos. 16-18 (3)	6.40	4.60

Designation of Prince Moulay el Hassan as heir to the throne.

King Mohammed V — A5

1957, Nov. *Perf. 12½*

No.	Type	Description	Unused	Used
19	A5	15fr blk & brt grn	.80	.70
20	A5	25fr blk & rose red	1.50	.95
21	A5	30fr blk & vio	1.75	1.25
		Nos. 19-21 (3)	4.05	2.90

Enthronement of Mohammed V, 30th anniv.

Morocco Pavilion, Brussels World's Fair — A6

1958, Apr. 20 Engr. *Perf. 13*

No.	Type	Description	Unused	Used
22	A6	15fr brt grnsh bl	.40	.25
23	A6	25fr carmine	.40	.30
24	A6	30fr indigo	.55	.35
		Nos. 22-24 (3)	1.35	.90

World's Fair, Brussels.

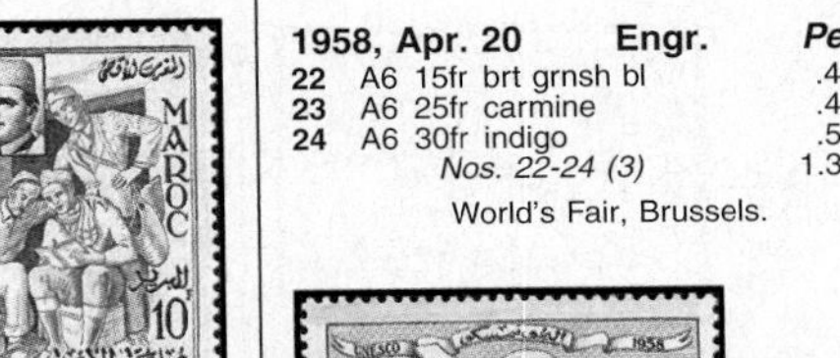

UNESCO Building, Paris, and Mohammed V — A7

1958, Nov. 23

No.	Type	Description	Unused	Used
25	A7	15fr green	.40	.20
26	A7	25fr lake	.40	.25
27	A7	30fr blue	.55	.30
		Nos. 25-27 (3)	1.35	.75

UNESCO Headquarters opening, Paris, Nov. 3.

Ben Smin Sanatorium A8

1959, Jan. 18 Unwmk. *Perf. 13*

No.	Type	Description	Unused	Used
28	A8	50fr dk brn, car & slate grn	.80	.50

Red Cross-Red Crescent Society.

Mohammed V — A9

Princess Lalla Amina — A10

1959, Aug. 18 Engr. *Perf. 13*

No.	Type	Description	Unused	Used
29	A9	15fr dk car rose	.60	.40
30	A9	25fr brt bl	.85	.55
31	A9	45fr dk grn	1.10	.60
		Nos. 29-31 (3)	2.55	1.55

50th birthday of King Mohammed V.

1959, Nov. 17

No.	Type	Description	Unused	Used
32	A10	15fr blue	.40	.20
33	A10	25fr green	.50	.20
34	A10	45fr rose lil	.55	.30
		Nos. 32-34 (3)	1.45	.70

Issued for International Children's Week.

Map of Africa and Symbols of Agriculture, Industry and Commerce — A11

1960, Jan. 31 *Perf. 13*

No.	Type	Description	Unused	Used
35	A11	45fr vio, ocher & emer	.90	.65

Issued to publicize the meeting of the Economic Commission for Africa, Tangier.

Refugees and Uprooted Oak Emblem A12

45fr, Refugee family and uprooted oak emblem.

1960, Apr. 7 Unwmk. *Perf. 13*

No.	Type	Description	Unused	Used
36	A12	15fr ocher, blk & grn	.30	.30
37	A12	45fr blk & grn	.50	.50

World Refugee Year, July 1, 1959-June 30, 1960.

Marrakesh A13

1960, Apr. 25 Engr. *Perf. 13*

No.	Type	Description	Unused	Used
38	A13	100fr grn, bl & red brn	1.25	.90

900th anniversary of Marrakesh.

Lamp — A14

Wrestlers — A16

Arab League Center, Cairo and Mohammed V — A15

Designs: 25fr, Fountain and arched door. 30fr, Minaret. 35fr, Ornamented wall. 45fr, Moorish architecture.

1960, May 12 *Perf. 13½*

No.	Type	Description	Unused	Used
39	A14	15fr rose lil	.55	.50
40	A14	25fr dk bl	.65	.55
41	A14	30fr org red	1.25	.65
42	A14	35fr black	1.50	1.10
43	A14	45fr yel grn	2.25	1.50
		Nos. 39-43 (5)	6.20	4.30

1,100th anniv. of Karaouiyne University, Fez.

1960, June 28 Photo. *Perf. 12½*

No.	Type	Description	Unused	Used
44	A15	15fr grn & blk	.40	.20

Opening of the Arab League Center and the Arab Postal Museum, Cairo.

1960, Sept. 26 Engr. *Perf. 13*

Sports: 10fr, Gymnast. 15fr, Bicyclist. 20fr, Weight lifter. 30fr, Runner. 40fr, Boxers. 45fr, Sailboat. 70fr, Fencers.

No.	Type	Description	Unused	Used
45	A16	5fr ol, vio bl & plum	.20	.20
46	A16	10fr org brn, bl & brn	.20	.20
47	A16	15fr emer, bl & org brn	.30	.20
48	A16	20fr ultra, ol & brn	.35	.20
49	A16	30fr vio bl, mar & sep	.40	.20
50	A16	40fr grnsh bl, dk pur & red brn	.65	.25
51	A16	45fr grn, plum & ultra	.80	.30
52	A16	70fr dk brn, bl & gray	1.10	.40
		Nos. 45-52 (8)	4.00	1.95

17th Olympic Games, Rome, 8/25-9/11.

Runner A17

1961, Aug. 30 Unwmk. *Perf. 13*

No.	Type	Description	Unused	Used
53	A17	20fr dk grn	.20	.20
54	A17	30fr dk car rose	.50	.25
55	A17	50fr brt bl	.65	.40
		Nos. 53-55 (3)	1.35	.85

3rd Pan-Arabic Games, Casablanca.

Post Office, Tangier — A18

View of Tangier and Gibraltar A19

Design: 30fr, Telephone operator.

1961, Dec. 8 Litho. *Perf. 12½*

No.	Type	Description	Unused	Used
56	A18	20fr red vio	.40	.20
57	A18	30fr green	.55	.25
57A	A19	90fr lt bl & vio bl	1.00	.50
		Nos. 56-57A (3)	1.95	.95

Conference of the African Postal and Telecommunications Union, Tangier.

Mohammed V and Map of Africa — A20

Patrice Lumumba and Map of Congo — A21

1962, Jan. 4 Unwmk. *Perf. 11½*

No.	Type	Description	Unused	Used
58	A20	20c buff & vio brn	.25	.20
59	A20	30c lt & dk bl	.30	.20

1st anniv. of the conference of African heads of state at Casablanca.

1962, Feb. 12 *Perf. 12½*

No.	Type	Description	Unused	Used
60	A21	20c bis & blk	.25	.20
61	A21	30c dl red brn & blk	.30	.25

1st death anniv. of Patrice Lumumba, Premier of Congo Democratic Republic.

Moroccan Students — A22

Arab League Building, Cairo — A23

1962, Mar. 5 Engr.

No.	Type	Description	Unused	Used
62	A22	20fr multi	.55	.30
63	A22	30fr multi	.55	.40
64	A22	90fr gray grn, indigo & brn	.90	.70
		Nos. 62-64 (3)	2.00	1.40

Issued to honor the nation's students.

1962, Mar. 22 Photo. *Perf. 13½x13*

No.	Type	Description	Unused	Used
65	A23	20c red brn	.35	.20

Arab Propaganda Week, 3/22-28. See #146.

Malaria Eradication Emblem and Swamp A24

50c, Dagger stabbing mosquito, vert.

1962, Sept. 3 Engr. *Perf. 13*

66 A24 20c dk grn & grnsh blk .20 .20
67 A24 50c dk grn & mag .40 .30

WHO drive to eradicate malaria.

Fish and Aquarium — A25

1962, Nov. 5 Unwmk. *Perf. 13*

68 A25 20c shown .45 .20
69 A25 30c Moray eel .55 .20

Casablanca Aquarium.

Courier and Sherifian Stamp of 1912 A26

Designs: 30c, Courier on foot and round Sherifian cancellation. 50c, Sultan Hassan I and octagonal cancellation.

1962, Dec. 15 Unwmk.

70 A26 20c Prus grn & redsh brn .75 .20
71 A26 30c dk car rose & blk .75 .40
72 A26 50c bl & bister 1.10 .50
Nos. 70-72 (3) 2.60 1.10

Stamp Day; 1st National Stamp Exhibition, Dec. 15-23; 75th anniv. of the Sherifian Post and the 50th anniv. of its reorganization.

Boy Scout — A27

King Hassan II — A28

1962, Aug. 8 Litho. *Perf. 11½*

73 A27 20c vio brn & lt bl .20 .20

5th Arab Boy Scout Jamboree, Rabat.

1962 Engr. *Perf. 13½x13*

75 A28 1c gray olive .20 .20
76 A28 2c violet .20 .20
77 A28 5c black .20 .20
78 A28 10c brn org .20 .20
79 A28 15c Prus grn .20 .20
80 A28 20c purple .25 .20
81 A28 30c dp yel grn .30 .20
82 A28 50c vio brn .60 .20
83 A28 70c deep blue .90 .20
84 A28 80c magenta 1.50 .25
Nos. 75-84 (10) 4.55 2.05

"Mazelin" (designer-engraver) reads down on Nos. 75-84. See Nos. 110-114.

King Moulay Ismail — A29

Al Idrissi, Geographer — A30

1963, Mar. 3 *Perf. 12½*

85 A29 20c sepia .55 .25

Tercentenary of Meknes as Ismaili capital.

1963-66 Engr.

#87, 88A, Ibn Batota, explorer. #88, Ibn Khaldoun, historian and sociologist.

86 A30 20c dk sl grn .40 .30
87 A30 20c dk car rose .40 .30
88 A30 20c black .40 .30
88A A30 40c dk vio bl ('66) .45 .30
Nos. 86-88A (4) 1.65 1.20

Famous medieval men of Morocco (Maghreb). No. 88A also marks the inauguration of the ferryboat "Ibn Batota" connecting Tangier and Malaga.

Issued: #86-88, 5/7/63; #88A, 7/15/66.

Sugar Beet and Sugar Refinery, Sidi Slimane A31

1963, June 10 Unwmk. *Perf. 13*

89 A31 20c shown .35 .20
90 A31 50c Tuna fisherman, vert. .50 .35

FAO "Freedom from Hunger" campaign.

Heads of Ramses II, Abu Simbel A32

Designs: 30c, Isis, Kalabsha Temple, vert. 50c, Temple of Philae.

1963, July 15 Engr. *Perf. 11½*

91 A32 20c black .30 .30
92 A32 30c vio, *grysh* .55 .30
93 A32 50c maroon, *buff* .75 .40
Nos. 91-93 (3) 1.60 1.00

Campaign to save historic monuments in Nubia.

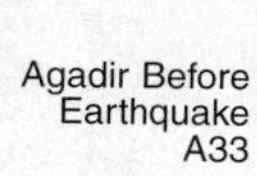

Agadir Before Earthquake A33

30c, Like 20c, with "29 Février 1960" and crossed bars added. 50c, Agadir rebuilt.

Engr.; Engr. & Photo. (No. 95)

1963, Oct. 10 *Perf. 13½x13*

94 A33 20c bl & brn red .45 .30
95 A33 30c bl, brn red & red .50 .40
96 A33 50c bl & brn red 1.00 .60
Nos. 94-96 (3) 1.95 1.30

Issued to publicize the rebuilding of Agadir.

Centenary Emblem and Plan of Agadir Hospital A34

1963, Oct. 28 Photo. *Perf. 12½x13*

97 A34 30c blk, dp car & sil .50 .20

Centenary of the International Red Cross.

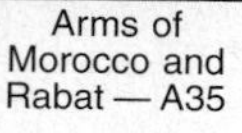

Arms of Morocco and Rabat — A35

Flag — A37

Hands Breaking Chain A36

1963, Nov. 18 *Perf. 13x12½*

98 A35 20c gold, red, blk & emer .40 .20

Installation of Parliament.

1963, Dec. 10 Engr. *Perf. 13*

99 A36 20c dk brn, grn & org .55 .20

15th anniversary of the Universal Declaration of Human Rights.

1963, Dec. 25 Photo. *Perf. 13x12½*

100 A37 20c blk, dp car & grn .60 .20

Evacuation of all foreign military forces from Moroccan territory.

Moulay Abd-er-Rahman, by Delacroix — A38

1964, Mar. 3 Engr. *Perf. 12x13*

101 A38 1d multi 3.00 2.00

Coronation of King Hassan II, 3rd anniv.

Weather Map of Africa and UN Emblem — A39

Children on Vacation A40

30c, World map and barometer trace, horiz.

1964, Mar. 23 Photo. *Perf. 11½*

Granite Paper

102 A39 20c multi .50 .25
103 A39 30c multi .55 .40

UN 4th World Meteorological Day. See No. C10.

1964, July 6 Litho. *Perf. 12½*

30c, Heads of boy and girl, buildings.

104 A40 20c multi .40 .40
105 A40 30c multi .50 .50

Issued for vacation camps for children of P.T.T. employees.

Olympic Torch A41

Cape Spartel Lighthouse, Sultan Mohammed ben Abd-er-Rahman A42

1964, Sept. 22 Engr. *Perf. 13*

106 A41 20c car lake, dk pur & grn .35 .25
107 A41 30c bl, dk grn & red brn .55 .35
108 A41 50c grn, red & brn .70 .60
Nos. 106-108 (3) 1.60 1.20

18th Olympic Games, Tokyo, Oct. 10-25.

Perf. 12½x11½

1964, Oct. 15 Photo.

109 A42 25c multi .55 .20

Centenary of the Cape Spartel lighthouse.

King Type of 1962

1964-65 Engr. *Perf. 12½x13*

Size: 17x23mm

110 A28 20c purple (redrawn) 2.00 .30

Perf. 13½x13

Size: 18x22mm

111 A28 25c rose red ('65) .35 .20
112 A28 35c slate ('65) .55 .20
113 A28 40c ultra ('65) .55 .20
114 A28 60c red lilac ('65) .85 .20
Nos. 110-114 (5) 4.30 1.10

The Arabic inscription touches the frame on No. 110. "Mazelin" (designer-engraver) reads up on No. 110, down on Nos. 111-114. No. 110 is a coil stamp with red control numbers on the back of some copies.

Iris — A43

Mohammed V Arriving by Plane — A44

1965 Photo. *Perf. 11½*

Granite Paper

115 A43 25c shown .90 .50
116 A43 40c Gladiolus segetum 1.20 .60
117 A43 60c Capparis spinosa, horiz. 1.90 1.25
Nos. 115-117 (3) 4.00 2.35

Printed in sheets of 10. Five tête-bêche pairs in every sheet; vertical stamps arranged 5x2, horizontal stamps 2x5.

See Nos. 129-131.

1965, Mar. 15 Litho. *Perf. 12½*

118 A44 25c lt bl & dk grn .50 .30

10th anniv. of the return of King Mohammed V from exile and the restoration of the monarchy.

ITU Emblem, Punched-Tape Writer and Telegraph Wires — A45

Design: 40c, ITU emblem, Syncom satellite, radio waves and "ITU" in Morse code.

Perf. 13x14

1965, May 17 Unwmk. Typo.

119 A45 25c multi	.40	.20
120 A45 40c lt bl, dp bl & bis	.50	.25

ITU, centenary.

ICY Emblem A46

1965, June 14 Engr. *Perf. 13*

121 A46 25c slate grn	.30	.20
122 A46 60c dk car rose	.50	.25

International Cooperation Year.

Royal Prawn A47

#123, Triton shell. #124, Varnish shell (pitaria chione). #125, Great voluted shell (cymbium neptuni). #126, Helmet crab, vert. 40c, Mantis shrimp, vert.

1965 Photo. *Perf. 11½*
Granite Paper

123 A47 25c vio & multi	1.00	.40
124 A47 25c lt bl & multi	1.00	.40
125 A47 25c org & multi	1.00	.40
126 A47 25c lt grn & multi	1.00	.40
127 A47 40c bl & multi	1.75	.60
128 A47 1d yel & multi	2.50	1.25
Nos. 123-128 (6)	8.25	3.45

Printed in sheets of 10. Nos. 126-127 (5x2); others (2x5). Five tête bêche pairs in every sheet.

Flower Type of 1965

Orchids: 25c, Ophrys speculum. 40c, Ophrys fusca. 60c, Ophrys tenthredinifera (front and side view), horiz.

1965, Dec. 13 Photo. *Perf. 11½*
Granite Paper

129 A43 25c yel & multi	.80	.50
130 A43 40c dl rose & multi	1.00	.50
131 A43 60c lt bl & multi	1.75	1.50
Nos. 129-131 (3)	3.55	2.50

Note on tête bêche pairs after No. 117 also applies to Nos. 129-131.

Grain — A48

40c, Various citrus fruit. 60c, Olives, horiz.

1966 Photo. *Perf. 11½*
Granite Paper

133 A48 25c blk & bister	.30	.20
136 A48 40c multi	.50	.25
137 A48 60c gray & multi	.55	.25
Nos. 133-137 (3)	1.35	.70

For surcharge see No. 231.

Flag, Map and Dove A49

1966, Mar. 2 Typo. *Perf. 14x13*

139 A49 25c brt grn & red	.20	.20

Tenth anniversary of Independence.

King Hassan II — A50

1966, Mar. 2 Engr. *Perf. 13*

140 A50 25c red, brt grn & indigo	.20	.20

Coronation of King Hassan II, 5th anniv.

Cross-country Runner — A51

1966, Mar. 20 Engr. *Perf. 13*

141 A51 25c blue green	.30	.20

53rd International Cross-country Race.

WHO Headquarters from West — A52

40c, WHO Headquarters from the East.

1966, May 3 Engr. *Perf. 13*

142 A52 25c rose lil & blk	.30	.20
143 A52 40c dp bl & blk	.50	.25

Inauguration of the WHO Headquarters, Geneva.

Crown Prince Hassan Kissing Hand of King Mohammed V — A53

25c, King Hassan II and parachutist.

Perf. 12½x12

1966, May 14 Photo. Unwmk.

144 A53 25c gold & blk	.30	.25
145 A53 40c gold & blk	.35	.30
a. Strip of 2, #144-145 + label	.70	.55

10th anniv. of the Royal Armed Forces.

Type of 1962 Inscribed: "SEMAINE DE LA PALESTINE"

1966, May 16 *Perf. 11x11½*

146 A23 25c slate blue	.20	.20

Issued for Palestine Week.

Train — A54

1966, Dec. 19 Photo. *Perf. 13½*

147 A54 25c shown	1.00	.30
148 A54 40c Ship	.95	.40
149 A54 1d Autobus	1.20	.55
Nos. 147-149 (3)	3.15	1.25

Twaite Shad A55

Fish: 40c, Plain bonito. 1d, Bluefish, vert.

1967, Feb. 1 Photo. *Perf. 11½*
Granite Paper

150 A55 25c yel & multi	.75	.30
151 A55 40c yel & multi	.85	.30
152 A55 1d lt grn & multi	1.90	.90
Nos. 150-152 (3)	3.50	1.50

Printed tête bêche in sheets of 10. Nos. 150-151 (2x5); No. 152 (5x2).

Ait Aadel Dam — A56

1967, Mar. 3 Engr. *Perf. 13*

153 A56 25c sl grn, Prus bl & gray	.50	.25
154 A56 40c Prus bl & lt brn	.70	.25

Inauguration of Ait Aadel Dam.

Rabat Hilton Hotel, Map of Morocco and Roman Arch — A57

1967, Mar. 3

155 A57 25c brt bl & blk	.40	.25
156 A57 1d brt bl & pur	.90	.25

Opening of the Rabat Hilton Hotel.

Torch, Globe, Town and Lions Emblem — A58

1967, Apr. 22 Photo. *Perf. 12½*

157 A58 40c gold & saph bl	.40	.25
158 A58 1d gold & slate grn	1.10	.25

Lions International, 50th anniversary.

Three Hands Holding Pickax — A59

1967, July 9 Engr. *Perf. 13*

159 A59 25c slate green	.25	.20

Community Development Campaign.

Intl. Tourism Year Emblem A60

1967, Aug. 9 Photo. *Perf. 12½*

160 A60 1d lt ultra & dk bl	.90	.35

Arrow and Map of Mediterranean A61

1967, Sept. 8 *Perf. 13x12*

161 A61 25c dk bl, ultra, red & tan	.50	.20
162 A61 40c blk, bl grn, red & tan	.55	.20

Mediterranean Games, Tunis, Sept. 8-17.

Steeplechase — A62

1967, Oct. 14 Photo. *Perf. 12½*

163 A62 40c yel grn, blk & brt rose lilac	.50	.25
164 A62 1d lt ultra, blk & brt rose lilac	.80	.35

International Horseshow.

Cotton — A63

Human Rights Flame — A64

1967, Nov. 15 Photo. *Perf. 12½*

165 A63 40c lt bl, grn & yel	.50	.25

1968, Jan. 10 Engr. *Perf. 13*

166 A64 25c gray	.40	.20
167 A64 1d rose claret	.50	.25

International Human Rights Year.

King Hassan II — A65

1968-74 Litho. *Perf. 13*
Portrait in Magenta, Brown and Black
Size: 23x30mm

169 A65 1c cream & blk	.20	.20
170 A65 2c lt grnsh bl & blk	.20	.20
171 A65 5c lt ol grn & blk	.20	.20
172 A65 10c pale rose & blk	.20	.20
173 A65 15c gray bl & blk	.20	.20
174 A65 20c pink & blk	.25	.20
175 A65 25c white & blk	.25	.20
176 A65 30c pale rose & blk	.30	.20

177 A65 35c bl & blk .50 .30
178 A65 40c gray & blk .50 .20
179 A65 50c lt bl & blk .60 .20
180 A65 60c salmon & blk .85 .20
181 A65 70c gray & blk 3.50 .90
182 A65 75c pale yel ('74) 1.00 .30
183 A65 80c ocher & blk 1.00 .30

Perf. 13½x14

Size: 26x40mm

184 A65 90c lt bl grn & blk 1.40 .45
185 A65 1d tan & blk 1.75 .30
186 A65 2d lt ultra & blk 2.50 .60
187 A65 3d bluish lil & blk 5.25 1.10
188 A65 5d apple grn & blk 8.50 3.25
Nos. 169-188 (20) 29.15 9.70

For overprints & surcharges see #224, B17-B18.

Nurse and Child — A66

Pendant — A67

1968, Apr. 8 Engr. *Perf. 13*

189 A66 25c ultra, red & olive .30 .20
190 A66 40c slate, red & olive .50 .20

WHO, 20th anniv.

1968, May 15 Photo. *Perf. 11½*

191 A67 25c shown .80 .25
192 A67 40c Bracelet 1.25 .30
a. Pair, #191-192, vertically tête-bêche 4.00 2.40

Moroccan Red Crescent Society. See Nos. 373-374.

Map of Morocco and Rotary Emblem — A68

1968, May 23 *Perf. 13*

193 A68 40c multi .65 .20
194 A68 1d ultra & multi .95 .30

Rotary Intl. District Conference, Casablanca, May 24-25.

Ornamental Design A69

Designs: Various patterns used for sashes.

1968, July 12 Photo. *Perf. 11½*

195 A69 25c multi 2.00 .90
196 A69 40c multi 2.40 1.20
197 A69 60c multi 3.50 2.10
198 A69 1d multi 6.50 3.25
Nos. 195-198 (4) 14.40 7.45

Berber (Riff), North Morocco — A70

Princess Lalla Meryem — A71

Regional Costumes: 10c, Man from Ait Moussa ou Ali. 15c, Woman from Ait Mouhad. No. 200, Bargeman from Rabat Salé. No. 201, Citadin man. 40c, Citadin woman. 60c, Royal Mokhazni. No. 204, Zemmours man. No. 204A, Man from Meknassa. No. 206, Msouffa woman, Sahara.

1968-74 Litho. *Perf. 13x12½*

198A A70 10c multi ('69) .75 .50
199 A70 15c yel & multi ('69) 1.25 .70
200 A70 25c bis & multi 1.25 .75
201 A70 25c tan & multi ('69) 1.40 .75
202 A70 40c lt bl & multi 1.50 1.10
203 A70 60c emer & multi 2.10 1.40
204 A70 1d lt bl & multi 2.75 1.90
204A A70 1d gray & multi ('69) 2.50 1.25

Perf. 15

205 A70 1d bis & multi 1.75 1.00
206 A70 1d grn & multi 1.75 1.00
a. Souvenir sheet of 10, #198A-206, perf. 13 20.00 20.00
b. As "a," with red overprint & surcharge 22.50 20.00
Nos. 198A-206 (10) 17.00 10.35

No. 206a issued June 30, 1970, for the opening of the National P.T.T. Museum, Rabat. Sold for 10d.

No. 206b issued Nov. 22, 1974, for the 8th Cong. of the Intl. Fed. of Blood Donors. Each stamp overprinted vertically "8eme Congres de la F.I.O.D.S." and blood container emblem. Black marginal inscription partially obliterated with lines, new Arabic inscription and price added. Sold for 20d.

1968, Oct. 7 Litho. *Perf. 13½*

Children's Week: 40c, Princess Lalla Asmaa. 1d, Crown Prince Sidi Mohammed.

207 A71 25c red & multi .55 .20
208 A71 40c yel & multi .70 .40
209 A71 1d lt bl & multi .85 .70
Nos. 207-209 (3) 2.10 1.30

Wrestling, Aztec Calendar Stone and Olympic Rings — A72

1968, Oct. 25 Photo. *Perf. 12x11½*

210 A72 15c shown .25 .20
211 A72 20c Basketball .25 .20
212 A72 25c Cycling .60 .30
213 A72 40c Boxing .65 .30
214 A72 60c Running .85 .30
215 A72 1d Soccer 1.10 .50
Nos. 210-215 (6) 3.70 1.80

19th Olympic Games, Mexico City, 10/12-27.

10 Dirham Coin of Tetuan, 1780 — A73

Women from Zagora A74

Coins: 25c, Dirham, Agmat, c. 1138 A.D. 40c, Dirham, El Alya (Fes), c. 840 A.D. 60c, Dirham, Marrakesh, c. 1248 A.D.

1968, Dec. 17 Photo. *Perf. 11½*

Granite Paper

216 A73 20c dp plum, sil & blk .40 .25
217 A73 25c dk rose brn, gold & blk .50 .35
218 A73 40c dk grn, sil & blk 1.00 .45
219 A73 60c dk red, gold & blk 1.25 .65
Nos. 216-219,C16-C17 (6) 17.40 9.30

Issued with tabs.

1969, Jan. 21 Litho. *Perf. 12*

Design: 25c, Women from Ait Adidou.

220 A74 15c multi 1.25 .65
221 A74 25c multi 1.60 .95
Nos. 220-221,C15 (3) 5.25 2.85

Painting by Belkahya — A75

King Hassan II — A76

1969, Mar. 27 Litho. *Perf. 11½x12*

222 A75 1d lt grnsh bl, blk & brn .65 .40

International Day of the Theater.

1969, July 9 Photo. *Perf. 11½*

223 A76 1d gold & multi 1.25 .55

40th birthday of King Hassan II. A souvenir sheet contains one No. 223. Size: 75x105mm. Sold for 2.50d.

No. 185 Overprinted

1969, Sept. 22 Litho. *Perf. 13*

224 A65 1d tan & multi 5.25 3.25

First Arab Summit Conference, Rabat.

Mahatma Gandhi — A77

1969, Oct. 16 Photo. *Perf. 11½*

225 A77 40c pale vio, blk & gray .75 .40

Mohandas K. Gandhi (1869-1948), leader in India's struggle for independence.

ILO Emblem A78

1969, Oct. 29

226 A78 50c multi .40 .25

ILO, 50th anniv.

King Hassan II on Way to Prayer — A79

1969, Nov. 20 Photo. *Perf. 11½*

227 A79 1d multi 1.00 .55

1st Arab Summit Conference, Rabat, Sept. 1969. For overprint see No. 311.

Spahi Horsemen, by Haram al Glaoui A80

1970, Jan. 23 Engr. *Perf. 12x13*

228 A80 1d multi 1.00 .55

Main Sewer, Fez — A81

Guedra Dance, by P. C. Beaubrun A82

1970, Mar. 23 **Litho.** ***Perf. 12***
229 A81 60c multi .50 .20

50th Congress of Municipal Engineers, Rabat, Mar. 1970.

1970, Apr. 15
230 A82 40c multi .55 .25

Folklore Festival, Marrakesh, May 1970.

No. 137 Overprinted "1970", "Census" in Arabic in Red and Surcharged in Black

1970, July 9 **Photo.** ***Perf. 11½***
231 A48 25c on 60c multi .45 .25

Issued to publicize the 1970 census.

Radar Station at Souk El Arba des Sehoul, and Satellite — A83

Ruddy Shelduck — A84

1970, Aug. 20
232 A83 1d lt ultra & multi .80 .30

Revolution of King and People, 17th anniv.

1970, Sept. 25 **Photo.** ***Perf. 11½***
233 A84 25c shown 1.20 .40
234 A84 40c Houbara bustard 1.60 .45

Campaign to save Moroccan wildlife.

Man Reading Book, Intl. Education Year Emblem — A85

1970, Oct. 20 **Litho.** ***Perf. 12x11½***
235 A85 60c dl yel & multi .55 .25

Symbols of Peace, Justice and Progress A86

1970, Oct. 27 ***Perf. 13½***
236 A86 50c multi .40 .25

United Nations, 25th anniversary.

Arab League Countries and Emblem A87

1970, Nov. 13 **Photo.** ***Perf. 11½***
237 A87 50c multi .40 .25

Arab League, 25th anniversary.

Olive Grove, Tree and Branch A88

1970, Dec. 3 **Litho.** ***Perf. 12***
238 A88 50c red brn & grn .80 .40

International Olive Year.

Es Sounna Mosque, Rabat A89

1971, Jan. 5 **Engr.** ***Perf. 13***
239 A89 60c ol bis, bl & sl grn .55 .30

Restoration of Es Sounna Mosque, Rabat, built in 1785.

Heart and Horse — A90

1971, Feb. 23 **Photo.** ***Perf. 12x12½***
240 A90 50c blk & multi .40 .20

European heart research week, Feb. 21-28.

Dam and Hassan II — A91

1971, Mar. 3 ***Perf. 11½***
241 A91 25c multi .35 .20
a. Souv. sheet of 4 2.50 2.00

Accession of King Hassan II, 10th anniv. No. 241a issued Mar. 24. Sold for 2.50d.

Black and White Hands with Dove and Emblem A92

1971, June 16 **Photo.** ***Perf. 13***
242 A92 50c brn & multi .30 .20

Intl. Year against Racial Discrimination.

Children Around the World — A93

Shah Mohammed Riza Pahlavi of Iran — A94

1971, Oct. 4 **Litho.** ***Perf. 13x14***
243 A93 40c emer & multi .25 .20

International Children's Day.

1971, Oct. 11 **Photo.** ***Perf. 11½***
244 A94 1d bl & multi .70 .45

2500th anniv. of the founding of the Persian empire by Cyrus the Great.

Mausoleum of Mohammed V — A95

50c, Mausoleum, close-up view, and Mohammed V. 1d, Decorated interior wall.

1971, Nov. 10 **Litho.** ***Perf. 14***
245 A95 25c multi .35 .20
246 A95 50c multi .45 .20
247 A95 1d multi, vert. .75 .25
Nos. 245-247 (3) 1.55 .65

Soccer Ball and Games Emblem A96

1971, Nov. 30 **Photo.** ***Perf. 13x13½***
248 A96 40c shown .55 .25
249 A96 60c Runner .80 .25

Mediterranean Games, Izmir, Turkey, Oct. 6-17.

Arab Postal Union Emblem A97

1971, Dec. 23 **Litho.** ***Perf. 13x12½***
250 A97 25c dk & lt bl & org .20 .20

25th anniv. of the Conference of Sofar, Lebanon, establishing APU.

Sun over Cultivated Sand Dunes — A98

Torch and Book Year Emblem — A99

1971, Dec. 30 **Photo.** ***Perf. 12½***
251 A98 70c blk, bl & yel .50 .20

Sherifian Phosphate Office (fertilizer production and export), 50th anniversary.

1972, Jan. 12 ***Perf. 11½***
252 A99 1d silver & multi .55 .20

International Book Year.

National Lottery — A100

Bridge of Sighs — A101

1972, Feb. 7 **Photo.** ***Perf. 13***
253 A100 25c tan, blk & gold .20 .20

Creation of a national lottery.

1972, Feb. 25

Designs: 50c, St. Mark's Basilica and waves, horiz. 1d, Lion of St. Mark.

254 A101 25c multi .20 .20
255 A101 50c red, blk & buff .30 .20
256 A101 1d lt bl & multi .50 .35
Nos. 254-256 (3) 1.00 .75

UNESCO campaign to save Venice.

Bridge, Road, Map of Africa — A102

1972, Apr. 21 ***Perf. 13***
257 A102 75c blue & multi .55 .25

2nd African Road Conf., Rabat, Apr. 17-22.

Morocco No. 223 — A103

1972, Apr. 27 ***Perf. 11½***

258 A103 1d lt ultra & multi .65 .25

Stamp Day.

The Engagement of Imilchil, by Tayeb Lahlou A104

1972, May 26 **Litho.** ***Perf. 13x13½***

259 A104 60c blk & multi .90 .50

Folklore Festival, Marrakesh, May 26-June 4.

Map of Africa, Dove and OAU Emblem — A105

1972, June 12 **Photo.** ***Perf. 11½***

260 A105 25c multi .25 .20

9th Summit Conference of Organization for African Unity, Rabat, June 12-15.

Landscape, Environment Emblem — A106

1972, July 20 **Photo.** ***Perf. 12½x12***

261 A106 50c bl & multi .50 .20

UN Conference on Human Environment, Stockholm, June 5-16

Olympic Emblems, Running A107

1972, Aug. 29 **Photo.** ***Perf. 13x13½***

262 A107 25c shown .20 .20
263 A107 50c Wrestling .35 .20
264 A107 75c Soccer .60 .25
265 A107 1d Cycling .75 .50
Nos. 262-265 (4) 1.90 1.15

20th Olympic Games, Munich, 8/26-9/11.

Sow Thistle — A108

Mountain Gazelle — A109

1972, Sept. 15 **Litho.** ***Perf. 14***

266 A108 25c shown .50 .20
267 A108 40c Amberboa crupinoides .65 .25

See No. 305-306.

1972, Sept. 29 **Photo.** ***Perf. 11½***

268 A109 25c shown .80 .35
269 A109 40c Barbary sheep 1.10 .40

Nos. 266-269 issued for nature protection.

Rabat Rug — A110

Child and UNICEF Emblem — A111

25c, High Atlas rug. 70c, Tazenakht rug. 75c, Rabat rug, different pattern.

Perf. 13½ (25fr, 70fr), 11½

1972-73 **Photo.**

270 A110 25c multi .90 .25
270A A110 50c multi 1.00 .20
271 A110 70c multi 1.40 .50
271A A110 75c multi 1.50 .50
Nos. 270-271A (4) 4.80 1.45

Issued: 50c, 75c, 10/27; 25c, 70c, 12/28/73.
See Nos. 326-327.

1972, Dec. 20 **Photo.** ***Perf. 13½x13***

272 A111 75c brt grn & bl .50 .20

International Children's Day.

Symbolic Letter Carrier and Stamp A112

1973, Jan. 30 **Photo.** ***Perf. 13x13½***

273 A112 25c brn & multi .20 .20

Stamp Day.

Weather Map, Northern Hemisphere A113

1973, Feb. 23 **Photo.** ***Perf. 13***

274 A113 70c silver & multi .55 .30

Intl. meteorological cooperation, cent.

King Hassan II, Coat of Arms — A114

1973-76 **Photo.** ***Perf. 14***

275 A114 1c pale yel & multi .20 .20
276 A114 2c pale bl & multi .20 .20
277 A114 5c pale ol & multi .20 .20
278 A114 10c brn org & multi .20 .20
279 A114 15c vio gray & multi .20 .20
280 A114 20c pink & multi .25 .20
281 A114 25c pale bl & multi .20 .20
282 A114 30c rose & multi .25 .20
283 A114 35c org yel & multi .35 .20
284 A114 40c lt gray & multi 4.00 .35
285 A114 50c ultra & multi .50 .20
286 A114 60c sal & multi .60 .20
287 A114 70c yel grn & multi .50 .20
288 A114 75c lem & multi .45 .20
289 A114 80c multi .50 .30
290 A114 90c brt grn & multi .55 .20
291 A114 1d beige & multi 1.75 .20
292 A114 2d gray & multi 3.50 .50
293 A114 3d lt lil & multi 4.50 .75
294 A114 5d lt brn & multi ('75) 3.50 1.00
294A A114 5d pink & multi ('76) 3.50 1.00
Nos. 275-294A (21) 25.90 6.90

Nos. B26-B27 Surcharged to Obliterate Surtax

1973, Mar. 13 ***Perf. 11½***

295 SP1 25c multi 2.50 2.50
296 SP1 70c multi 2.75 2.75
a. Pair, #295-296, vert. tête-bêche 7.25 7.25

Tourism Conference 1973. Arabic overprint and date on one line on No. 296.
See Nos. 351-352.

Holy Ka'aba, Mecca, Mosque and Minaret, Rabat A115

1973, May 3 **Photo.** ***Perf. 13½x14***

297 A115 25c lt bl & multi .20 .20

Mohammed's 1,403rd birthday.

Roses and M'Gouna A116

1973, May 14 ***Perf. 13***

298 A116 25c bl & multi .20 .20

Rose Festival of M'Gouna.

Hands, Torch, OAU Emblem — A117

1973, May 25 **Photo.** ***Perf. 14x13***

299 A117 70c deep claret & multi .30 .20

OAU, 10th anniversary.

Dancers with Tambourines — A118

Design: 1d, Dancer with handbells, Marrakesh Minaret, Atlas Mountain.

1973, May 30 ***Perf. 12½x13***

300 A118 50c multi .50 .20
301 A118 1d multi .65 .30

Folklore Festival, Marrakesh.

Copernicus A119

1973, June 29 ***Perf. 13x13½***

302 A119 70c Heliocentric system .65 .30

Microscope, WHO Emblem, World Map — A120

1973, July 16 **Photo.** ***Perf. 13x12½***

303 A120 70c multi .55 .20

WHO, 25th anniversary.

INTERPOL Emblem, Fingerprint A121

1973, Sept. 12 **Photo.** ***Perf. 13x13½***

304 A121 70c brn, sil & bl .30 .20

50th anniv. of Intl. Criminal Police Org.

Flower Type of 1972

1973, Oct. 12 Litho. *Perf. 14*

305 A108 25c Daisies, horiz.	.65	.20
306 A108 1d Thistle	1.25	.50

Nature protection.

Berber Hyena A122

Design: 50c, Eleonora's falcon, vert.

1973, Nov. 23 Photo. *Perf. 14*

307 A122 25c multi	1.25	.25
308 A122 50c multi	2.50	.40

Nature protection.

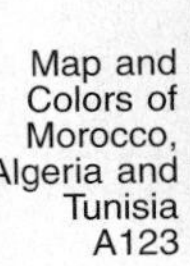

Map and Colors of Morocco, Algeria and Tunisia A123

1973, Dec. 7 *Perf. 13x13½*

309 A123 25c gold & multi	.40	.20

Maghreb Committee for Coordination of Posts and Telecommunications.

Fairway and Drive over Water Hazard — A124

1974, Feb. 8 Photo. *Perf. 14x13*

310 A124 70c multi	1.25	.25

International Golf Grand Prix for the Hassan II Morocco trophy.

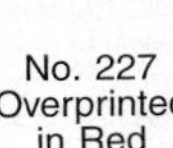

No. 227 Overprinted in Red

1974, Feb. 25 *Perf. 11½*

311 A79 1d multi	3.00	1.75

Islamic Conference, Lahore, India, 1974.

Map of Africa, Scales, Human Rights Flame — A125

1974, Mar. 15 Photo. *Perf. 14x13½*

312 A125 70c gold & multi	.40	.20

25th anniversary of the Universal Declaration of Human Rights.

Vanadinite A126

1974-75 Photo. *Perf. 13*

313 A126 25c shown	2.25	.60
313A A126 50c Aragonite	2.00	.35
314 A126 70c Erythrine	4.00	.75
314A A126 1d Agate	4.00	.60
Nos. 313-314A (4)	12.25	2.30

Issued: 25c, 70c, 4/30/74; 50c, 1d, 2/14/75.

Minaret, Marrakesh Mosque, Rotary Emblem — A127

1974, May 11 Photo. *Perf. 14*

315 A127 70c multi	.55	.20

District 173 Rotary International annual meeting, Marrakesh, May 10-12.

UPU Emblem, Congress Dates — A128

1d, Scroll with UPU emblem, Lausanne coat of arms & 17th UPU Congress emblem, horiz.

1974, May 30 Photo.

316 A128 25c lt grn, org & blk	.30	.20
317 A128 1d dk grn & multi	.70	.25

Centenary of Universal Postal Union.

Drummer and Dancers — A129

1974, June 7 Photo. *Perf. 14*

Design: 70c, Knife juggler and women.

318 A129 25c multi	.50	.20
319 A129 70c multi	1.25	.35

National folklore festival, Marrakesh.

Environment Emblem, Polution, Clean Water and Air — A130

1974, June 25 *Perf. 13*

320 A130 25c multi	.25	.20

World Environment Day.

Simulated Stamps, Cancel and Magnifier A131

1974, Aug. 2 Photo. *Perf. 13*

321 A131 70c sil & multi	.50	.20

Stamp Day.

No. J5 Surcharged

1974, Sept. 25 Photo. *Perf. 14*

322 D2 1d on 5c multi	2.00	1.40

Agricultural census.

World Soccer Cup — A132

Double-spurred Francolin — A133

1974, Oct. 11

323 A132 1d brt bl & multi	.95	.65

World Cup Soccer Championship, Munich, June 13-July 7.

A stamp similar to No. 323, also issued Oct. 11, has gold inscription: "CHAMPION: R.F.A." in French and Arabic, honoring the German Federal Republic as championship winner. Value $32.50.

Perf. 14x13½, 13½x14

1974, Dec. 5 Photo.

324 A133 25c green & multi	.60	.25
325 A133 70c Leopard, horiz.	1.25	.35

Nature protection.

Zemmour Rug A134

Columbine A135

Design: 1d, Beni Mguilo rug.

1974, Dec 20 *Perf. 13*

326 A134 25c multi	.55	.20
327 A134 1d multi	1.20	.30

See Nos. 349-350, 398-400.

1975 Photo. *Perf. 13½*

328 A135 10c Daisies	.20	.20
329 A135 25c Columbine	.50	.20
330 A135 35c Orange lilies	.55	.20
331 A135 50c Anemones	.65	.20
332 A135 60c White starflower	.80	.35
333 A135 70c Poppies	.85	.35
334 A135 90c Carnations	1.20	.50
335 A135 1d Pansies	1.10	.60
Nos. 328-335 (8)	5.85	2.60

Issued: 25c, 35c, 70c, 90c, 1/10; others, 4/29.

Water Carrier, by Feu Tayeb Lahlou A136

1975, Apr. 3 *Perf. 13*

338 A136 1d multicolored	1.20	.50

Stamp Collector, Carrier Pigeon, Globe — A137

Musicians and Dancers — A138

1975, May 21 Photo. *Perf. 13*

339 A137 40c gold & multi	.40	.20

Stamp Day.

1975, June 12 Photo. *Perf. 14x13½*

340 A138 1d multicolored	.95	.30

16th Folklore Festival, Marrakesh, 5/30-6/15.

Guitar and Association for the Blind Emblem A139

1975, July 8 *Perf. 13x13½*

341 A139 1d purple & multi	.90	.50

Week of the Blind.

Animals in Forest — A140

1975, July 25 Photo. *Perf. 13x13½*

342 A140 25c multicolored	.40	.20

Children's Week.

Games' Emblem, Runner, Weight Lifter — A141

1975, Sept. 4 **Photo.** ***Perf. 13***

343 A141 40c gold, maroon & buff .30 .20

7th Mediterranean Games, Algiers, 8/23-9/6.

Bald Ibis A142

1975, Oct. 21 **Photo.** ***Perf. 13***

344 A142 40c shown 1.25 .40
345 A142 1d Persian lynx, vert. 1.60 .80

Nature protection.

King Mohammed V Greeting Crowd, Prince Moulay Hassan at Left — A143

King Hassan II A144

#348, King Mohammed V wearing fez.

1975, Nov. 21 **Photo.** ***Perf. 13½***

346 A143 40c blk, sil & dk bl .55 .25
347 A144 1d blk, gold & dk bl .80 .50
348 A144 1d blk, gold & dk bl .80 .50
a. Sheet of 3, #346-348 12.50 12.50

20th anniversary of independence.

Rug Type of 1974

25c, Ouled Besseba. 1d, Ait Ouaouzguid.

1975, Dec. 11

349 A134 25c red & multi .90 .50
350 A134 1d orange & multi 1.40 .55

A number of issues have been printed se-tenant in sheets of 10 (5x2) arranged vertically tête bêche.

Nos. B29-B30 Surcharged in Green to Obliterate Surtax

1975 ***Perf. 11½***

351 SP1 25c blue & multi 2.50 2.50
352 SP1 70c orange & multi 2.75 2.75
a. Pair, #351-352, vertically tête-bêche 7.25 7.25

March of Moroccan people into Spanish Sahara, Dec. 1975.

"Green March of the People" — A145

1975, Dec. 30 **Photo.** ***Perf. 13½x13***

353 A145 40c multicolored .25 .20

March of Moroccan people into Spanish Sahara, Dec. 1975.

Copper Coin, Fez, 1883-84 — A146

1976 **Photo.** ***Perf. 14x13½***

Coins: 15c, 50c, silver coin, Rabat, 1774-75. 35c, 65c, Gold coin, Sabta, 13th-14th centuries. 1d, Square coin, Sabta, 12th-13th centuries.

354 A146 5c dull rose & multi .20 .20
355 A146 15c brown & multi .20 .20
356 A146 35c gray & multi .50 .20
357 A146 40c ocher & multi .40 .20
358 A146 50c ultra & blk .50 .20
359 A146 65c yellow & multi .55 .30
360 A146 1d multicolored .90 .45
Nos. 354-360 (7) 3.25 1.75

Issued: #354-356, 4/26; #357-360, 1/20.

1976, Sept. 9

Designs: Various Moroccan coins.

361 A146 5c green & multi .20 .20
362 A146 15c dp rose & multi .20 .20
363 A146 20c lt bl & multi .25 .20
364 A146 30c lil rose & multi .25 .20
365 A146 35c green & multi .45 .20
366 A146 70c orange & multi .60 .20
Nos. 361-366 (6) 1.95 1.20

See Nos. 403-406A, 524B-524C.

Family — A147

1976, Feb. 12 ***Perf. 14x13½***

367 A147 40c multicolored .30 .20

Family planning.

Arch, Ibn Zaidoun Mosque — A148

Perf. 13½x14, 14x13½

1976, Feb. 12 **Photo.**

40c, Hall, Ibn Zaidoun Mosque, horiz.

368 A148 40c multicolored .25 .20
369 A148 65c multicolored .40 .25

Ibn Zaidoun Mosque, millennium.

Medersa bou Anania, Fez A149

1976, Feb. 26 ***Perf. 13x14½***

370 A149 1d multicolored .65 .25

Borobudur Temple — A150

Design: 40c, Bas-relief, Borobudur.

1976, Mar. 11 **Photo.** ***Perf. 13***

371 A150 40c multicolored .40 .20
372 A150 1d multicolored .80 .20

UNESCO campaign to save Borobudur Temple, Java.

Islamic Conference, 6th Anniv. — A151

1976 **Litho.** ***Perf. 13½x13***

372A A151 1d Dome of the Rock 1.50 .25

Jewelry Type of 1968

Designs: 40c, Pendant. 1d, Breastplate.

1976, June 29 **Photo.** ***Perf. 14x13½***

373 A67 40c blue & multi .50 .20
374 A67 1d olive & multi .95 .30
a. Pair, #373-374, vertically tête-bêche 1.75 1.75

Moroccan Red Crescent Society.

Bicentennial Emblem, Flags and Map of US and Morocco — A152

Design: 1d, George Washington, King Hassan, Statue of Liberty and Royal Palace, Rabat, vert.

1976, July 27 **Photo.** ***Perf. 14***

375 A152 40c multicolored .50 .20
376 A152 1d multicolored .90 .35

American Bicentennial.

Wrestling A153

1976, Aug. 11 ***Perf. 13x13½***

377 A153 35c shown .20 .20
378 A153 40c Cycling .25 .20
379 A153 50c Boxing .50 .30
380 A153 1d Running .95 .45
Nos. 377-380 (4) 1.90 1.15

21st Olympic Games, Montreal, Canada, July 17-Aug. 1.

Old and New Telephones, Radar — A154

1976, Sept. 29 **Photo.** ***Perf. 14***

381 A154 1d gold & multi .65 .20

Centenary of first telephone call by Alexander Graham Bell, Mar. 10, 1876.

Blind Person's Identification A155

1976, Oct. 12 **Photo.** ***Perf. 13½x14***

382 A155 50c multicolored .30 .20

Week of the Blind.

Chanting Goshawk A156

1976, Oct. 29 ***Perf. 13x13½***

383 A156 40c shown 1.40 .40
384 A156 1d Purple gallinule 2.00 .70

Nature protection.

King Hassan, Star, Torch, Map of Morocco — A157

Africa Cup — A159

Globe and Dove
A158

1976, Nov. 19 Photo. *Perf. 12½x13*
385 A157 40c multicolored .55 .20

Green March into Spanish Sahara, 1st anniv.

Nos. B34-B35 Overprinted with 2 Bars over Surcharge and 4-line Arabic Inscription

1976, Nov. 29 Photo. *Perf. 13½*
386 SP1 25c ultra, blk & org 2.00 2.00
387 SP1 70c red, blk & org 2.40 2.40
a. Pair, #386-387, vert. tête-bêche 5.50 5.50

5th African Tuberculosis Conference, Rabat.

1976, Dec. 16 *Perf. 13*
388 A158 1d blue, blk & red .50 .20

5th Summit Meeting of Non-aligned Countries, Colombo, Aug. 9-19, and 25th anniv. of Org. of Non-aligned Countries.

1976, Dec. 29 Photo. *Perf. 14*
389 A159 1d multicolored .70 .20

African Soccer Cup.

Letters Circling Globe, Postmark
A160

1977, Jan. 24 Photo. *Perf. 13½*
390 A160 40c multicolored .30 .20

Stamp Day.

Aeonium Arboreum
A161

Malope Trifida — A162

1d, Hesperolaburnum platyclarpum.

Perf. 13x13½, 14 (A162)

1977, Feb. 22
391 A161 40c multicolored .55 .40
392 A162 50c multicolored 1.00 .50
393 A161 1d multicolored 1.20 .65
Nos. 391-393 (3) 2.75 1.55

Ornamental Lamps, View of Salé — A163

1977, Mar. 24 Photo. *Perf. 14*
394 A163 40c multicolored .30 .20

Candle procession of Salé.

No. J6 Surcharged in Orange

1977, May 11 Photo. *Perf. 14*
395 D2 40c on 10c multi .80 .40

Cherry Festival.

Map of Arab Countries, Emblem
A164

1977, June 2 Photo. *Perf. 14*
396 A164 50c multicolored .25 .20

5th Congress of Organization of Arab Cities.

APU Emblem, Members' Flags
A165

1977, June 20
397 A165 1d multicolored .50 .20

Arab Postal Union, 25th anniversary.

Rug Type of 1974

Designs: 35c, No. 399A, Marmoucha rug, diff. No. 399, Ait Haddou rug. 1d, Salé rug.

Perf. 11½x12, 13½ (#399A)

1977-79 Photo.
398 A134 35c multicolored .45 .20
399 A134 40c multicolored .60 .20
399A A134 40c multicolored ('79) .85 .25
400 A134 1d multicolored 1.00 .40
Nos. 398-400 (4) 2.90 1.05

Issued: #399A, 3/8/79; others, 7/21/77.

Cithara — A166

Ali Jinnah and Map of Pakistan — A167

1977, Aug. 18 Photo. *Perf. 14*
401 A166 1d multi .80 .30

Week of the Blind.

1977, Oct. 10 Photo. *Perf. 13½x13*
402 A167 70c multi .40 .20

Mohammed Ali Jinnah (1876-1948), first Governor General of Pakistan.

Coin Type of 1976

Designs: Various Moroccan coins.

1977-81 *Perf. 14x13½*
403 A146 10c gray & multi .20 .20
403A A146 25c ap grn & multi ('81) 1.10 .35
404 A146 60c dk red & multi ('78) .35 .20
405 A146 75c citron & multi .30 .20
405A A146 80c pale vio & mult ('81) 2.50 .50
406 A146 2d yel grn & multi 1.00 .35
406A A146 3d beige & multi ('81) 5.00 1.75
Nos. 403-406A (7) 10.45 3.55

Marcher with Flag, Map of Morocco and Spanish Sahara — A168

1977, Nov. 6 Photo. *Perf. 14*
407 A168 1d multi .65 .20

Green March into Spanish Sahara, 2nd anniv.

Chamber of Representatives — A169

1977, Nov. 6 *Perf. 13½*
408 A169 1d multi .65 .20
a. Souvenir sheet 3.00 3.00

Opening of Chamber of Representatives. No. 408a sold for 3d.

Enameled Silver Brooch — A170

Copper Vessel — A171

1977, Dec. 14 Photo. *Perf. 11½*
409 A170 1d multi 1.25 .20

Moroccan Red Crescent Society.

1978, Jan. 5 Photo. *Perf. 13*

1d, Standing filigree copper bowl with cover.

410 A171 40c gold & multi .40 .20
411 A171 1d gold & multi .90 .25
a. Pair, #410-411, vert. tête-bêche 2.00 2.00

Map of Sahara, Cogwheel Emblem — A172

1d, Map of North Africa, fish in net, camels.

1978, Feb. 27 Photo. *Perf. 14*
412 A172 40c multi .40 .20
413 A172 1d multi, horiz .80 .25

Promotion of the Sahara. See Nos. 441-442 for similar stamps overprinted.

Covered Jar — A173

1978, Mar. 27 *Perf. 13½x13*
414 A173 1d shown .90 .50
415 A173 1d Vase .90 .50

Week of the Blind.

Red Crescent, Red Cross, Arab Countries
A174

1978, Apr. 14 *Perf. 13x13½*
416 A174 1d multi .65 .30

10th Conference of Arab Red Crescent and Red Cross Societies, Apr. 10-15.

View of Fez, Rotary Emblem — A175

1978, Apr. 22 Photo. *Perf. 14*
417 A175 1d multi .65 .30

Rotary Intl. Meeting, Fez, District 173.

Dome of the Rock, Jerusalem — A176

1978, May 29 *Perf. 14½*
418 A176 5c multi .20 .20
419 A176 10c multi .20 .20

Palestinian fighters and their families. For overprints see Nos. 502-502A.

Folk Dancers and Flutist — A177

1978, June 15 ***Perf. 13½x13***
420 A177 1d multi .65 .30

National Folklore Festival, Marrakesh.

Sugar Cane Field, and Conveyor Belt A178

1978, July 24 **Photo.** ***Perf. 13***
421 A178 40c multi .25 .20

Sugar industry.

Games Emblem — A179

Bird, Tree, Tent, Scout Emblem — A180

1978, Aug. 25
422 A179 1d multi .80 .25

World sailing championships.

1978, Sept. 26 **Photo.** ***Perf. 13***
423 A180 40c multi 1.00 .50

Pan-Arab Scout Jamboree, Rabat.

View of Fez A181

1978, Oct. 10
424 A181 40c multi .40 .20

Moulay Idriss the Great, Festival, Fez.

Flame Emblem — A182

Houses, Agadir — A183

1978, Dec. 21 **Photo.** ***Perf. 14***
425 A182 1d multi .70 .20

30th anniversary of Universal Declaration of Human Rights.

1979, Jan. 25 **Photo.** ***Perf. 12***
426 A183 40c shown .40 .20
427 A183 1d Old Fort, Marrakesh .80 .25

Soccer and Cup A184

1979, Mar. 2 ***Perf. 13***
428 A184 40c multi .40 .20

Mohammed V Soccer Cup.

Vase — A185

Procession A186

1979, Mar. 29 **Photo.** ***Perf. 14***
429 A185 1d multi .95 .25

Week of the Blind.

1979, Apr. 18 ***Perf. 13x13½, 13½x13***

1d, Festival, by Mohamed Ben Ali Rbati, horiz.

430 A186 40c multi .45 .20
431 A186 1d multi .55 .25

Brass Containers, Red Crescent A187

Perf. 13x13½, 13½x13
1979, May 16 **Photo.**
432 A187 40c shown .30 .20
433 A187 1d Heated coffee urn, vert. .80 .30

Red Crescent Society.

Dancers — A188

Silver Dagger — A189

1979, June 1 **Photo.** ***Perf. 13***
434 A188 40c multi .40 .20

National Festival of Marrakech.

1979, June 20 ***Perf. 14***
435 A189 1d multi .40 .20

King Hassan II, 50th Birthday — A190

1979, July 9 **Photo.** ***Perf. 14***
436 A190 1d multi .65 .20

4th Arab Youth Festival, Rabat A191

1979, July 30 **Photo.** ***Perf. 13½x14***
437 A191 1d multi .65 .20

King Hassan II and Crowd — A192

1979, Aug. 20 ***Perf. 14x13½***
438 A192 1d multi .50 .20

Revolution of the King and the People, 25th anniv.

Intl. Bureau of Education, 50th Anniv. — A193

1979, Sept. 28 **Photo.** ***Perf. 13x13½***
439 A193 1d multi .65 .20

Pilgrimage to Mecca, Mt. Arafat, Holy Ka'aba A194

1979, Oct. 25 ***Perf. 13½***
440 A194 1d multi .65 .20

No. 413 Redrawn in Smaller Size and Overprinted in Red

1979, Nov. 7 **Litho.** ***Perf. 14***
Size: 33x23mm
441 A172 40c multi .40 .20
442 A172 1d multi .80 .40

Return of Oued Eddahab province, Aug. 14.

Leucanthemum Catanance — A195

Children, Globe, IYC Emblem — A196

1979, Nov. 21 **Photo.** ***Perf. 14½***
443 A195 40c Centaurium .25 .20
444 A195 1d shown .80 .20

1979, Dec. 3 ***Perf. 14***
445 A196 40c multi .90 .30

International Year of the Child.

Otter — A197

Traffic Signs and Road — A198

1979, Dec. 18 ***Perf. 13½x13***
446 A197 40c shown .70 .20
447 A197 1d Redstart 1.50 .25

1980, Jan. 3 **Photo.** ***Perf. 14***
448 A198 40c shown .20 .20
449 A198 1d Children at curb .55 .20

Fortress A199

1980, Jan. 29 *Perf. 13x13½*
450 A199 1d multi .55 .20

Copper Bowl and Lid, Red Crescent — A200

Week of the Blind — A201

Red Crescent Soc.: 70c, Copper kettle, brazier.

1980, Feb. 28 **Photo.** *Perf. 14*
451 A200 50c multi .40 .20
452 A200 70c multi .50 .20
a. Pair, #451-452, vert. tête-bêche 1.10 1.10

1980, Mar. 19 **Photo.** *Perf. 14*
453 A201 40c multi .25 .20

Rabat Mechanical Sorting Office — A202

1980, Apr. 17
454 A202 40c multi .25 .20

Stamp Day.

Rotary Intl., 75th Anniv. — A203

Cloth and Leather Goods — A204

1980, May 14 **Photo.** *Perf. 14*
455 A203 1d multi .35 .20

1980, May 31 **Photo.** *Perf. 13½x13*
456 A204 1d multi .40 .20

4th Textile and Leather Exhibition, Casablanca, May 2-9.

Gypsum — A205

Falcon — A206

1980, June 19 **Photo.** *Perf. 13½x13*
457 A205 40c multi .70 .20

See Nos. 477-478.

1980, July 26 *Perf. 11½*
458 A206 40c multi .60 .30

Hunting with falcons.

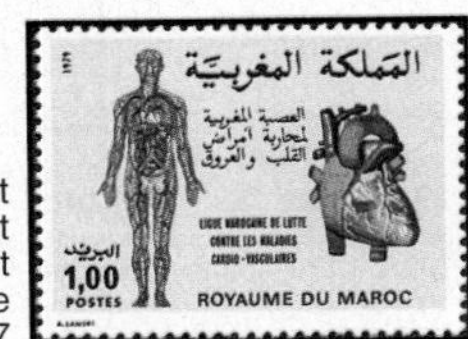
Fight against Heart Disease A207

1980, Aug. 7 **Photo.** *Perf. 13x13½*
459 A207 1d multi .65 .20

A208

A210

Ornamental Saddle and Harness A209

1980, Aug. 18 *Perf. 14*
460 A208 40c shown .20 .20
461 A208 1d Emblems, diff. .55 .20

United Nations Decade for Women.

1980, Sept. 3 *Perf. 14½*
462 A209 40c Saddle, harness, diff. .30 .20
463 A209 1d shown .80 .25

1980, Sept. 18
464 A210 40c multi .20 .20

World Meteorological Day.

Hand Holding Dry Gas Pump A211

1980, Oct. 6 **Photo.** *Perf. 14*
465 A211 40c Light bulb, gas can .30 .20
466 A211 1d shown .65 .20

Energy conservation.

World Tourism Conference, Manila, Sept. 27 — A212

1980, Oct. 22 *Perf. 11½x12*
467 A212 40c multi .20 .20

Symbolic Tree Rooted in Europe and Africa A213

1980, Oct. 30 *Perf. 14*
468 A213 1d multi .80 .25

Straits of Gibraltar linking Europe and Africa.

5th Anniversary of the Green March — A214

1980, Nov. 6
469 A214 1d multi .65 .20

Holy Ka'aba — A215

Senecio Antheuphorbium A216

1980, Nov. 9
470 A215 40c shown .20 .20
471 A215 1d Mecca Mosque .70 .20
a. Souv. sheet of 2, #470-471 1.75 1.75

No. 471a sold for 3d.

1980, Dec. 4 *Perf. 13*
472 A216 50c shown .70 .20
473 A216 1d Periploca laevigata 1.25 .40

Leaves, by Mahjoubi Aherdan — A217

Nejjarine Fountain, Fes — A218

Design: 40c. Untitled painting by Mahjoubi Aherdan (23x38mm).

1980, Dec. 18 *Perf. 12*
474 A217 40c multi .20 .20
475 A217 1d multi .70 .20

1981, Jan. 22 *Perf. 14x13½*
476 A218 40c multi .25 .20

Mineral Type of 1980

1981, Feb. 19 **Photo.** *Perf. 13½x13*
477 A205 40c Onyx .95 .20
478 A205 1d Malachite-azurite 2.00 .40

Inscribed 1980.

King Hassan II — A219

1981, Mar. 2 *Perf. 14*
479 A219 60c shown .25 .20
480 A219 60c Map of Morocco .25 .20
481 A219 60c King Mohammed V .25 .20
a. Strip of 3, #479-481 .95 .50

25th anniv. of independence.

25th Anniv. of King Hassan II Coronation — A220

1981, Mar. 3
482 A220 1.30d multi .65 .25

The Source, by Jillali Gharbaoui — A221

1981, Apr. 8 *Perf. 13x12½*
483 A221 1.30d multi 1.00 .35

Anagalis Monelli — A222

Army Badge — A223

1981, Apr. 23 ***Perf. 13***

484 A222 40c shown .30 .20
485 A222 70c Bubonium intricatum .55 .20

1981, May 14 Photo. ***Perf. 14x13½***

Moroccan Armed Forces, 25th Anniv: No. 486, King Hassan II as army major general; No. 488, King Mohammed V.

486 A223 60c multi .25 .20
487 A223 60c multi .25 .20
488 A223 60c multi .25 .20
a. Strip of 3, #486-488 .95 .50

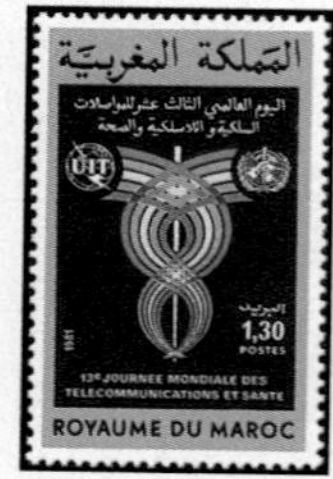

13th World Telecommunications Day — A224

1981, May 18 ***Perf. 14x13***

489 A224 1.30d multi .55 .25

Hand-painted Plate — A225

22nd Marrakesh Arts Festival — A226

1981, June 5 ***Perf. 14***

490 A225 50c shown .30 .20
491 A225 1.30d Plate, diff. .55 .20

Week of the Blind.

1981, June 18 ***Perf. 13½x13***

492 A226 1.30d multi .90 .20

For overprint see No. 579.

Seboula Dagger, Oujda — A227

Copper Mortar and Pestle, Red Crescent — A228

1981, Sept. 7 Photo. ***Perf. 13½***

493 A227 1.30d multi .65 .20

1981, Sept. 24 ***Perf. 14***

494 A228 60c shown .25 .20
495 A228 1.30d Tripod .80 .25

Intl. Year of the Disabled — A229

Iphiclides Feisthamelii A230

1981, Oct. 15 ***Perf. 13½***

496 A229 60c multi .40 .20

1981, Oct. 29 ***Perf. 13½x13***

497 A230 60c shown 2.00 .50
498 A230 1.30d Zerynthia rumina 3.50 1.00

See Nos. 528-529.

6th Anniv. of Green March — A231

Intl. Palestinian Solidarity Day — A232

1981, Nov. 6 ***Perf. 13x13½***

499 A231 1.30d multi .50 .25

1981, Nov. 22 ***Perf. 13½x13***

500 A232 60c multi .40 .25

Congress Emblem — A233

1981, Nov. 22 ***Perf. 13½***

501 A233 1.30d multi .65 .30

World Federation of Twin Cities, 10th Congress, Casablanca, Nov. 15-18.

Nos. 418-419 Overprinted

1981, Nov. 25 Photo. ***Perf. 14½***

502 A176 40c on 5c multi 9.25 6.00
502A A176 40c on 10c multi 7.00 3.75

First Anniv. of Mohammed V Airport — A234

King Hassan II — A236

Al Massirah Dam Opening A235

1981, Dec. 8 Photo. ***Perf. 14x13***

503 A234 1.30d multi .65 .25

1981, Dec. 17 ***Perf. 11½***

504 A235 60c multi .40 .20

1981, Dec. 28 ***Perf. 13x12½***

505 A236 5c multi .20 .20
506 A236 10c multi .20 .20
507 A236 15c multi .20 .20
508 A236 20c multi .20 .20
509 A236 25c multi .20 .20
510 A236 30c multi .20 .20
511 A236 35c multi .20 .20
512 A236 40c multi .40 .20
513 A236 50c multi .20 .20
514 A236 60c multi .20 .20
515 A236 65c multi .20 .20
516 A236 70c multi .20 .20
a. Perf 12x11¾, granite paper .20 .20
517 A236 75c multi .20 .20
518 A236 80c multi .30 .20
519 A236 90c multi .50 .20

No. 516a is dated 1999 and has the denomination and "Postes" closer to the shoulder than to the chin.

1983, Mar. 1 Photo. ***Perf. 14½***
Size: 25x32mm

520 A236 1d multi .30 .20
521 A236 1.40d multi .40 .20
522 A236 2d multi .45 .20
523 A236 3d multi .75 .20
524 A236 5d multi 1.10 .45
524A A236 10d multi 2.25 .80
e. Perf 11½, granite paper 2.00 1.00
Nos. 505-524A (21) 8.85 5.05

No. 524Ae is dated 1999 and has the denomination and "Postes" closer to the shoulder than to the chin.

See Nos. 566-575, 715-724.

Coin Type of 1976

1979-81 Photo. ***Perf. 12½***
Size: 18x23mm

524B A146 40c ocher & multi .20 .20
d. Bklt. pane of 10 1.25
524C A146 50c brt bl, blk & dk brn ('81) .20 .20

Equestrian Sports A237

1981, Dec. 29 ***Perf. 13x13½***

525 A237 1.30d multi 1.25 .40

Traditional Carpet Design — A238

1982, Jan. 21

526 A238 50c Glaoua pattern .20 .20
527 A238 1.30d Ouled Besseba pattern .65 .25

Butterfly Type of 1981

1982, Feb. 25 ***Perf. 13½x13***

528 A230 60c Celerio oken lineata 1.60 .55
529 A230 1.30d Mesoacidalia aglaja lyauteyi 3.25 .85

World Forest Day — A240

Blind Week — A241

1982, Apr. 8 ***Perf. 14***

531 A240 40c multi .20 .20

1982, May 10

532 A241 1d Jug .40 .20

Folk Dancers, Rabat — A242

Copper Candlestick, Red Crescent — A243

1982, June 3
533 A242 1.40d multi .65 .25

1982, July 1
534 A243 1.40d multi .65 .25

Women in Traditional Clothing, by M. Mezian — A244

ITU Conf., Nairobi, Sept. — A246

Natl. Census A245

1982, Aug. 16 **Photo.** ***Perf. 14***
535 A244 1.40d multi .65 .30

1982, Sept. 6 **Photo.** ***Perf. 11½***
536 A245 60c multi .20 .20

1982 ***Perf. 13½x13***
537 A246 1.40d multi .55 .25

TB Bacillus Centenary A247

World Food Day — A248

1982, Sept. 30
538 A247 1.40d multi .80 .30

1982, Oct. 16 ***Perf. 14***
539 A248 60c multi .20 .20

Unity Railroad A249

1982, Nov. 6 ***Perf. 13x13½***
540 A249 1.40d multi 1.40 .50

30th Anniv. of Arab Postal Union A250

1982, Nov. 17 ***Perf. 14***
541 A250 1.40d multi .55 .20

Intl. Palestinian Solidarity Day — A251

Red Coral, Al-Hoceima A252

1982, Nov. 29 ***Perf. 14***
542 A251 1.40d sil & multi .55 .20

1982, Dec. 20 ***Perf. 13½***
543 A252 1.40d multi .95 .30

Stamp Day — A253

Week of the Blind — A254

1983, Jan. 26 ***Perf. 13½x13***
544 A253 1.40d Nos. 3, 178 .55 .20

1983, Apr. 20 **Photo.** ***Perf. 14***
545 A254 1.40d multi .65 .20

Popular Arts A255

1983, June 27 **Photo.** ***Perf. 14***
546 A255 1.40d multi .80 .20

Wrought-Iron Lectern — A256

Moroccan Flora — A258

Economic Commission for Africa, 25th Anniv. — A257

1983, July 7 **Litho.** ***Perf. 13½***
547 A256 1.40d multi .80 .20

1983, July 18 **Photo.** ***Perf. 14***
548 A257 1.40d multi .55 .20

1983, Aug. 1 **Litho.** ***Perf. 14***
549 A258 60c Tecoma .40 .20
550 A258 1.40d Strelitzia .90 .30

Kings Mohammed V and Hassan II — A259

1983, Aug. 20 **Litho.** ***Perf. 14***
551 A259 80c multi .90 .90
a. Souvenir sheet of 1 2.40 2.40

King and People's Revolution, 30th Anniv. No. 551a sold for 5 dinars.

Mediterranean Games — A260

Palestinian Solidarity — A262

Touiza A261

1983, Sept. 3 **Photo.** ***Perf. 14***
552 A260 80c Stylized sportsmen .40 .25
553 A260 1d Emblem .55 .30
554 A260 2d Stylized runner, horiz. 1.60 .45
a. Souv. sheet of 3, #552-554, imperf. 3.00 3.00
Nos. 552-554 (3) 2.55 1.00

No. 554a sold for 5d.

1983, Sept. 30 **Photo.** ***Perf. 13***
555 A261 80c Tractors .20 .20

1983, Nov. 10 **Photo.** ***Perf. 13½x13***
556 A262 80c multi .25 .20

8th Anniv. of the Green March into Spanish Sahara A263

1983, Nov. 17 ***Perf. 13x13½***
557 A263 80c multi .20 .20

Ouzoud Waterfall — A264

1983, Nov. 28 ***Perf. 14***
558 A264 80c multi .20 .20

Children's Day — A265

Zemmouri Carpet — A266

1983, Dec. 5 **Photo.** ***Perf. 13½x13***
559 A265 2d multi .65 .20

1983, Dec. 15 *Perf. 13½*

Various carpets.

560 A266 60c multi .20 .20
561 A266 1.40d multi .55 .20

World Communications Year — A267

1983, Dec. 20 *Perf. 14*
562 A267 2d multi .95 .25

Twin Cities, Jerusalem and Fez A268

1984, Jan. 16 Photo. *Perf. 13x13½*
563 A268 2d multi .95 .25

Desert Fox — A269

1984, Feb. 13 *Perf. 11½x12, 12x11½*
564 A269 80c shown .95 .40
565 A269 2d Jumping mouse, vert. 2.00 .80

King Hassan II Type of 1981

1984-88 Photo. *Perf. 14½*

Size: 25x32mm

566	A236 1.20d multi ('88)	.30	.20
567	A236 1.25d multi	.25	.20
568	A236 1.60d multi ('87)	.45	.25
569	A236 2.50d multi ('87)	.65	.35
570	A236 3.60d multi ('88)	1.25	.40
571	A236 4d multi	1.00	.65
572	A236 5.20d multi ('88)	1.75	.75
573	A236 6.50d multi ('87)	1.75	1.10
574	A236 7d multi ('87)	1.90	1.25
575	A236 8.50d multi ('87)	2.25	1.60
	Nos. 566-575 (10)	11.55	6.75

Dated 1986: 1.60d, 2.50d, 6.50d, 7d, 8.50d. Issued: 1.20d, 3.60d, 5.20d, Dec. 26, 1988.

39th Anniv. of Arab League A270

1984, May 24 *Perf. 14½x14*
578 A270 2d Emblem .65 .20

No. 492 Overprinted

1984, June 12 *Perf. 13½x13*
579 A226 1.30d multi .80 .25

25th Anniv. of Marrakesh Arts Festival.

Local Plants — A271

Red Crescent — A273

Week of the Blind A272

1984, June 13 *Perf. 14*
580 A271 80c Mentha viridis .30 .20
581 A271 2d Aloe .90 .40

See Nos. 602-603.

1984, July 10 *Perf. 13x13½*
582 A272 80c Painted bowl .40 .20

1984, July 16 *Perf. 14*
583 A273 2d Octagonal brass container .80 .35

1984 Summer Olympics — A274

Intl. Child Victims' Day — A275

1984, Aug. 8 *Perf. 13½x13*
584 A274 2d Sports .80 .35

1984, Aug. 22 *Perf. 14*
585 A275 2d Children held by dove .80 .35

UPU Day — A276

World Food Day — A277

1984, Oct. 9 Photo. *Perf. 13½*
586 A276 2d multi .65 .25

1984, Oct. 16 *Perf. 14*
587 A277 80c multi .40 .20

Intl. Civil Aviation Org., 40th Anniv. — A278

Green March, 9th Anniv. — A279

1984, Oct. 20 *Perf. 13½*
588 A278 2d multi .90 .50

1984, Nov. 6 *Perf. 14*
589 A279 80c Scroll, text .40 .20

Palestinian Solidarity — A281

UN Human Rights Declaration, 36th Anniv. — A282

1984, Nov. 29 *Perf. 13½*
591 A281 2d Arab Revolt flag, 1918-19 1.00 .50

1984, Dec. 10 *Perf. 14*
592 A282 2d multi .65 .35

Native Dogs — A283

UN Child Survival Campaign A284

1984, Dec. 21 Photo. *Perf. 14*
593 A283 80c Aidi .55 .20
594 A283 2d Sloughi 1.10 .40

1985, Mar. 5 Photo. *Perf. 14*
595 A284 80c Growth monitoring .30 .20

1st SOS Children's Village in Morocco A285

1985, Mar. 11 *Perf. 13x13½*
596 A285 2d multi .50 .25

Sherifian Hand Stamp, 1892 — A287

World Environment Day — A288

1985, Mar. 25 Photo. *Perf. 14*
597 A287 2d dl pink, blk & gray .50 .25

Souvenir Sheet

Perf. 13½

598	Sheet of 6	4.00	4.00
a.	A287 80c green, black & gray	.55	.40
b.	A287 80c yellow, black & gray	.55	.40
c.	A287 80c blue, black & gray	.55	.40
d.	A287 80c red, black & gray	.55	.40
e.	A287 80c purple, black & gray	.55	.40
f.	A287 80c brown, black & gray	.55	.40

Stamp Day. #598 sold for 5d.

See #615-616, 633-634, 668-669, 684-685, 701-702, 733-734, 756-757, 790-791, 806-807, 821-822, 835-836, 906-907.

1985, June 5 *Perf. 13*
599 A288 80c Emblem, ecosystem .30 .20

Susi Dancers from Marrakesh and Kutabia, Minaret A289

1985, June 7 *Perf. 13x13½*
600 A289 2d multi .95 .40

Folk Arts Festival.

Week of the Blind — A290

Berber Woman — A291

1985, June 24 ***Perf. 14***
601 A290 80c Ceramic bowl .25 .20

See type A316.

Flower Type of 1984

1985, July 1
602 A271 80c Bougainvillea .70 .30
603 A271 2d Red hibiscus 1.60 .50

1985, July 15 ***Perf. 14***
604 A291 2d multi 1.25 .35

Red Crescent Society.

6th Pan-Arab Games — A292

UN, 40th Anniv. — A293

1985, Aug. 2 ***Perf. 14½x13½***
605 A292 2d Torch, emblem, map .90 .35

1985, Oct. 7 ***Perf. 13***
606 A293 2d multi .70 .35

Intl. Youth Year — A294

Green March, 10th Anniv. — A295

1985, Oct. 21
607 A294 2d multi .50 .25

1985, Nov. 6 ***Perf. 14½x13½***
608 A295 2d Commemorative medal .50 .25

Palestinian Solidarity A296

Butterflies A297

1985, Nov. 29 ***Perf. 13½***
609 A296 2d multi .70 .25

1985, Dec. 16 **Photo.** ***Perf. 14***
610 A297 80c Euphydryas desfontainii 1.60 .65
611 A297 2d Colotis evagore 4.00 1.60

Accession of King Hassan II, 25th Anniv. — A298

Perf. 13x13½, 13½x13

1986, Mar. 3 **Litho.**
612 A298 80c Natl. arms, vert. .25 .20
613 A298 2d shown .65 .40
a. Souv. sheet of 2, #612-613, imperf. 1.00 1.00

26th Intl. Military Medicine and Pharmaceutical Congress A299

1986, Mar. 24 **Photo.** ***Perf. 14***
614 A299 2d multi .60 .45

Hand Stamp Type of 1985

Sherifian postal seals of Maghzen-Safi, 1892.

1986, Apr. 7
615 A287 80c orange & blk .20 .20
616 A287 2d green & blk .60 .25

Week of the Blind — A300

1986 World Cup Soccer Championships, Mexico — A301

1986, Apr. 21
617 A300 1d multi .25 .20

1986, May 31 ***Perf. 13½***
618 A301 1d Emblems, horiz. .40 .20
619 A301 2d Soccer cup, emblems .70 .35

Red Crescent Soc. — A302

Flowers — A304

Popular Arts A303

1986, June ***Perf. 14***
620 A302 2d multi .90 .35

1986, June
621 A303 2d Folk band, dancers .65 .30

1986, July 21 **Photo.** ***Perf. 14***
622 A304 1d Warionia saharae .80 .20
623 A304 2d Mandragora autumnalis 1.25 .55

Intl. Peace Year — A305

18th Skydiving Championships A306

1986, Aug. 4 ***Perf. 13***
624 A305 2d multi .65 .40

1986, Aug. 18 ***Perf. 13½x13***
625 A306 2d multi .80 .40

Horse Week A307

1986, Oct. 10 ***Perf. 13***
626 A307 1d multicolored .55 .20

Green March, 11th Anniv. — A308

World Food Day — A309

1986, Nov. 6 **Photo.** ***Perf. 14***
627 A308 1d multicolored .25 .20

1986, Nov. 12
628 A309 2d multicolored .60 .40

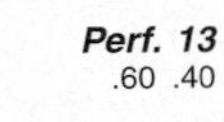
Aga Khan Architecture Prize A310

1986, Nov. 24 **Litho.** ***Perf. 13***
629 A310 2d multicolored .60 .40

Operation Grain: One Million Hectares — A311

Butterflies
A312

1986, Dec. 8
630 A311 1d multicolored .25 .20

1986, Dec. 22 ***Perf. 14***
631 A312 1d Elphinstonia charlonia 1.25 .55
632 A312 2d Anthocharis belia 3.25 1.50

Hand Stamp Type of 1985

Stamp Day: Sherifian postal seals of Maghzen-Tetouan, 1892.

1987, Jan. 26 **Photo.**
633 A287 1d blue & blk .25 .20
634 A287 2d red & black .65 .30

King Mohammed V, Flag, 1947 — A313

1987, Apr. 9 **Photo.** ***Perf. 13½x13***
635 A313 1d shown .30 .20
636 A313 1d King Hassan II, 1987 .30 .20
a. Souvenir sheet of 2, Nos. 635-636 1.00 1.00

Tangiers Conf., 40th anniv. #636a sold for 3d.

Red Crescent Society — A314

UN Child Survival Campaign A315

1987, May 1 **Photo.** ***Perf. 14***
637 A314 2d Brass lamp .65 .35

1987, May 25 ***Perf. 12½x13***
638 A315 1d Oral rehydration .25 .20

See Nos. 647, 687.

Week of the Blind — A316

1987, June 8 ***Perf. 14***
639 A316 1d Porcelain cup .25 .20

Flowering Plants — A317

US-Morocco Diplomatic Relations, 200th Anniv. — A318

1987, July 6 **Photo.**
640 A317 1d Zygophyllum fontanesii .25 .20
641 A317 2d Otanthus maritimus .70 .35

See Nos. 661-662.

1987, July **Litho & Engr.**
642 A318 1d lt bl, blk & scar .25 .20

See United States No. 2349.

Give Blood — A319

1987, Aug. 20 **Photo.** ***Perf. 13x13½***
643 A319 2d King Hassan II, map .80 .45

Desert Costumes, the Sahara — A320

13th Intl. Cong. on Irrigation and Drainage — A321

1987, Sept. 14 ***Perf. 13***
644 A320 1d Woman from Melhfa .30 .25
645 A320 2d Man from Derraa .65 .50

See Nos. 711-712, 740-741.

1987, Sept. 21
646 A321 1d multi .35 .30

UN Child Survival Type of 1987

1987, Sept. 28
647 A315 1d Universal immunization .35 .30

Congress on Mineral Industries, Marrakesh A322

Green March, 12th Anniv. — A323

1987, Oct.
648 A322 1d Azurite .55 .25
649 A322 2d Wulfenite 1.00 .50

See No. 769.

1987, Nov. 6 **Photo.** ***Perf. 14***
650 A323 1d multicolored .30 .25

See Nos. 667, 683, 695, 727, 750, 769, 802, 820, 834, 848, 862, 885.

Royal Armed Forces Social Services Month A324

1987, Nov. 13 ***Perf. 13x12½***
651 A324 1d multicolored .30 .25

Birds — A325

1987, Dec. 1 **Litho.** ***Perf. 14***
652 A325 1d Passer simplex saharae .50 .25
653 A325 2d Alectoris barbara 1.50 .45

Natl. Postage Stamp 75th Anniv. — A326

Design: Postmark and Sherifian postage stamp (French Morocco) of 1912.

1987, Dec. 31 **Photo.** ***Perf. 14x13½***
654 A326 3d pale lil rose, blk & blue grn 1.00 .70

Cetiosaurus Mogrebiensis — A327

1988, Jan. 18 **Photo.** ***Perf. 13½***
655 A327 2d multicolored 3.25 .95

A328

A329

1988, Feb. 16 **Litho.** ***Perf. 14***
656 A328 2d multicolored .60 .45

Intl. Symposium on Mohammed V, Aug. 16-Nov. 20, 1987.

Perf. 14½x13½

1988, Mar. 13 **Photo.**
657 A329 3d multi .95 .75

16th Africa Cup Soccer Championships.

Horse Week A330

1988, Mar. 20 **Litho.** ***Perf. 14***
658 A330 3d multi 1.40 .75

Intl. Red Cross and Red Crescent Orgs., 125th Annivs. — A331

1988, Apr. 30 **Photo.** ***Perf. 12½x13***
659 A331 3d pink, blk & dark red .95 .65

Week of the Blind — A332

UN Child Survival Campaign A333

1988, May 25 Litho. *Perf. 14*
660 A332 3d Pottery bottle .90 .65

Flower Type of 1987

1988, June 27 Litho. *Perf. 14*
661 A317 3.60d Citrullus colocynthis 1.25 .75
662 A317 3.60d Calotropis procera 1.25 .75

1988, July 18 Litho. *Perf. 12½x13*
663 A333 3d multi .90 .60

1988 Summer Olympics, Seoul — A334

Birds — A335

Perf. 14½x13½
1988, Sept. 19 Litho.
664 A334 2d multi .60 .50

1988, Oct. 26 Litho. *Perf. 14*
665 A335 3.60d Grande outarde 1.40 .75
666 A335 3.60d Flamant rose 1.40 .75

Green March Anniv. Type of 1987

1988, Nov. 6
667 A323 2d multi .55 .40

Green March, 13th anniv.

Hand Stamp Type of 1985

Sherifian postal seals of Maghzen-El Jadida, 1892: No. 668, Octagonal. No. 669, Circular.

1988, Nov. 22 Photo. *Perf. 14*
668 A287 3d olive bister & blk .90 .60
669 A287 3d violet & blk .90 .60

Stamp Day.

Housing of the Ksours and Casbahs A336

1989, Jan. 23 *Perf. 13x13½*
670 A336 2d multi .55 .40

Royal Chess Federation, 25th Anniv. — A337

1989, Apr. 17 Litho. *Perf. 14*
671 A337 2d multi .80 .40

Red Crescent Society — A338

Week of the Blind — A339

1989, May 29 Litho. *Perf. 14x13½*
672 A338 2d multi .55 .40

1989, June 12 *Perf. 14*
673 A339 2d multi .55 .40

A340

A341

1989, July 9 Litho. *Perf. 13x13½*
674 A340 2d multi .70 .40
675 A340 2d King Hassan II, diff. .70 .40
a. Souvenir sheet of 2, #674-675, imperf. & embossed 1.75 1.75

King Hassan II, 60th birthday. No. 675a sold for 5d.

1989, Sept. 11 Litho. *Perf. 14*

Flowering plants.

676 A341 2d Narcissus papyraceus .80 .45
677 A341 2d Cerinthe major .80 .45

See Nos. 709-710, 742-743.

World Telecommunications Day — A342

1989, Sept. 25 *Perf. 13x12½*
678 A342 2d multicolored .60 .45

13th World Congress on Fertility and Sterility — A343

1989, Oct. 6 *Perf. 14*
679 A343 2d multicolored .60 .45

Birds A344

1989, Oct. 16 *Perf. 14*
680 A344 2d Desert beater .70 .45
681 A344 3d Gorget lark 1.00 .70

Interparliamentary Union, Cent. — A345

1989, Oct. 27
682 A345 2d multicolored .60 .45

Green March Anniv. Type of 1987

1989, Nov. 6
683 A323 3d multicolored .90 .70

Green March, 14th anniv.

Hand Stamp Type of 1985

Sherifian postal seals of Maghzen-Casablanca, 1892: 2d, Circular. 3d, Octagonal.

1990, Jan. 15 Photo. *Perf. 14*
684 A287 2d orange & blk .65 .45
685 A287 3d green & blk 1.00 .70

Maghreb Union, 1st Anniv. A346

1990, Feb. 17 *Perf. 13½x14*
686 A346 2d multicolored .60 .45
a. Souv. sheet of one, perf. 13½ .95 .95

No. 686a sold for 3d.

UN Child Survival Type of 1987

1990 *Perf. 12½x13*
687 A315 3d Breast feeding .95 .70

3rd World Olive Day A347

1990, May 14 Litho. *Perf. 14*
688 A347 2d Olive press .50 .35
689 A347 3d King Hassan II .75 .55

Week of the Blind A348

1990, May 28 Litho. *Perf. 14*
690 A348 2d multicolored .70 .50

Red Crescent Society A349

1990, June 11
691 A349 2d multicolored .55 .35

A350

A353

Birds A351

1990, Sept. 17 Litho. *Perf. 14*
692 A350 3d blk, yel grn & grn 1.10 .80

Intl. Literacy Year

1990, Oct. 26
693 A351 2d Tourterelle, vert. .85 .50
694 A351 3d Huppe fasciee 1.25 .80

Green March Anniv. Type of 1987

1990, Nov. 5
695 A323 3d multicolored 1.10 .80

Green March, 15th anniv.

1990, Nov. 18
696 A353 3d multicolored 1.10 .80

Independence, 35th anniv.

Dam A354

1990, Nov. 26

697 A354 3d multicolored 1.10 .80

A355

A357

A356

1990, Dec. 28 Litho. *Perf. 14*

698 A355 3d multicolored 1.00 .75

Royal Academy of Morocco, 10th anniv.

1990, Dec. 31 Litho. *Perf. 13½x13*

Opening of Postal Museum, 20th Anniv.: No. 699, Telegraph machine. No. 700, Horse-drawn mail carriage fording river.

699 A356 2d multicolored .65 .50
700 A356 3d multicolored 1.00 .75
a. Souv. sheet of 2, #699-700, imperf. 2.10 2.10

No. 700a sold for 6d, has simulated perforations.

Hand Stamp Type of 1985

Sherifian postal seals of Maghzen-Rabat, 1892: 2d, Circular. 3d, Octagonal.

1991, Jan. 25 *Perf. 14*

701 A287 2d ver & blk .65 .50
702 A287 3d blue & blk 1.00 .75

1991, Feb. 18

703 A357 3d multicolored 1.00 .75

UN Development Program, 40th anniv.

A358

A359

1991, Mar. 3 Litho. *Perf. 14½x13*

704 A358 3d shown 1.00 .75
705 A358 3d Wearing business suit 1.00 .75
a. Souv. sheet of 2, #704-705, imperf. 3.00 2.35

Coronation of King Hassan II, 30th anniv. Nos. 704-705 exist tete beche. No. 705a has simulated perforations and sold for 10d.

1991, Mar. 28 Litho. *Perf. 14*

706 A359 3d multicolored 1.00 .75

Phosphate Mining, 70th anniv.

Week of the Blind — A360

Red Crescent Society — A361

1991, May 15 Photo. *Perf. 14*

707 A360 3d multicolored 1.00 .75

1991, May 27 Litho. *Perf. 14*

708 A361 3d multicolored .95 .70

Flowering Plants Type of 1989

1991, June 27 Litho. *Perf. 14*

709 A341 3d Pyrus mamorensis 1.00 .70
710 A341 3d Cynara humilis 1.00 .70

Desert Costumes Type of 1987

Costumes of Ouarzazate.

1991, July 31 Photo.

711 A320 3d Woman 1.00 .70
712 A320 3d Man 1.00 .70

King Hassan II Type of 1981

1991-98 Photo. *Perf. 14½*

Size: 25x32mm

715 A236 1.35d multicolored .45 .20
717 A236 1.70d multicolored .40 .20
719 A236 2.30d multicolored .50 .25
a. Perf 11½, granite paper .50 .25
722 A236 5.50d multicolored 1.25 1.00
a. Perf 11½, granite paper 2.00 1.00
723 A236 6d multicolored 1.25 .95
724 A236 20d multicolored 5.00 3.50
Nos. 715-724 (6) 8.85 6.10

Issued: 1.35d, Sept. 2; 1.70d, 1994; 2.30d, 6d, 1998.

This is an expanding set. Numbers will change if necessary.

Nos. 719a and 722a are dated 1999, and have the denomination and "Postes" closer to the shoulder than to the chin.

A362

A363

1991, Sept. 23 Litho. *Perf. 14*

725 A362 3d multicolored .95 .70

19th World Congress on Roads, Marrakesh.

1991, Oct. 30 Litho.

726 A363 3d multicolored .95 .70

4th Session of the Council of Presidents of the Maghreb Arab Union.

Green March Anniv. Type of 1987

1991, Nov. 6 Photo. *Perf. 14*

727 A323 3d multicolored .95 .70

Green March, 16th anniv.

Birds — A364

Fight Against AIDS — A365

1991, Nov. 20 Litho. *Perf. 14*

728 A364 3d Merops apiaster 1.00 .80
729 A364 3d Ciconia ciconia 1.00 .80

See Nos. 748-749.

1991, Dec. 16

730 A365 3d multicolored 1.00 .80

Organization of the Islamic Conference, 20th Anniv. — A366

1991, Dec. 16

731 A366 3d multicolored 1.00 .80

A367

A368

1991 Litho. *Perf. 14*

732 A367 3d multicolored 1.00 .80

African Tourism Year.

Hand Stamp Type of 1985

Sherifian postal seals of Maghzen-Essaouira, 1892: No. 733, Circular. No. 734, Octagonal.

1992, Jan. 13

733 A287 3d olive & blk 1.00 .80
734 A287 3d purple & blk 1.00 .80

1992, Feb. 17

735 A368 3d multicolored 1.00 .80

Intl. Space Year.

Week of the Blind — A369

Red Crescent Society — A370

1992, Mar. 19 Photo. *Perf. 14*

736 A369 3d multicolored 1.00 .80

1992, Mar. 30

737 A370 3d multicolored 1.00 .80

Minerals — A371

A372

1992, May 11 Litho. *Perf. 14*
738 A371 1.35d Quartz .50 .40
739 A371 3.40d Calcite 1.25 1.00

Desert Costumes Type of 1987

Costumes of Tata.

1992, May 25 Photo. *Perf. 14*
740 A320 1.35d Woman .50 .40
741 A320 3.40d Man 1.25 1.00

Flowering Plants Type of 1989

1992, July 13
742 A341 1.35d Campanula afra .50 .40
743 A341 3.40d Thymus broussonetii 1.25 1.00

1992, July 24
744 A372 3.40d multicolored 1.25 1.00

1992 Summer Olympics, Barcelona.

Modes of Transportion and Communications, Map of Africa — A373

1992, Sept. 14 Litho. *Perf. 14*
745 A373 3.40d multicolored .95 .75

Expo '92, Seville — A374

1992, Oct. 12
746 A374 3.40d multicolored .95 .75

Discovery of America, 500th Anniv. A375

1992, Oct. 12
747 A375 3.40d multicolored 1.25 .75

Bird Type of 1991

1992, Oct. 26 Litho. *Perf. 14*
748 A364 3d Gyps fulvus .80 .65
749 A364 3d Ganga cata, horiz. .80 .65

Green March Anniv. Type of 1987

1992, Nov. 6 Litho. *Perf. 14*
750 A323 3.40d multicolored .95 .75

Green March, 17th anniv.

Sherifian Post, Cent. A377

Designs: 3.40d, Octagonal Sherifian postal seal, scroll, Sultan Moulay Hassan I. 5d, Scroll, various circular and octagonal Sherifian postal seals, Sultan.

1992, Nov. 22 Litho. *Perf. 14*
751 A377 1.35d multicolored .40 .25
752 A377 3.40d multicolored .95 .75

Size: 165x115mm

Imperf

753 A377 5d multicolored 1.40 1.00
Nos. 751-753 (3) 2.75 2.00

Intl. Conference on Nutrition, Rome — A378

1992, Dec. 7 Litho. *Perf. 14*
754 A378 3.40d multicolored .95 .75

Al Massira Airport, Agadir — A379

1992, Dec. 21 Litho. *Perf. 14*
755 A379 3.40d multicolored 1.00 .80

Hand Stamp Type of 1985

Sherifian postal seals of Maghzen-Tanger, 1892: 1.70, Circular. 3.80d, Octagonal.

1993, Jan. 29 Litho. *Perf. 14*
756 A287 1.70d green & black .45 .35
757 A287 3.80d orange & black 1.00 .80

Stamp Day.

Week of the Blind A380

1993, Mar. 15 Litho. *Perf. 14*
758 A380 4.40d multicolored 1.25 1.00

World Meteorology Day — A381

1993, Mar. 23
759 A381 4.40d multicolored 1.25 1.00

A382

A383

1993, Apr. 26 Litho. *Perf. 14*
760 A382 4.40d multicolored 1.25 1.00

Red Crescent Society.

1993, June 14
761 A383 4.40d multicolored 1.25 1.00

World Telecommunications Day.

A384

A385

Argania spinosa.

1993, July 26 Litho. *Perf. 14*
762 A384 1.70d Extracting oil .45 .35
763 A384 4.80d Tree branch 1.25 1.00

1993, Aug. 21
764 A385 4.80d multicolored 1.25 1.00

Prince Sidi Mohammed, 30th birthday.

Inauguration of the Hassan II Mosque A386

1993, Aug. 30 *Perf. 13*
765 A386 4.80d multicolored 1.25 1.00

A387

A388

1993, Sept. 30 Litho. *Perf. 14*
766 A387 4.80d multicolored 1.25 1.00

King and People's Revolution, 40th Anniv.

1993, Oct. 15
767 A388 4.80d multicolored 1.25 1.00

World Post Day.

New Islamic University — A389

1993, Nov. 1 Litho. *Perf. 14*
768 A389 4.80d multicolored 1.25 1.00

Green March Anniv. Type of 1987

1993, Nov. 6
769 A323 4.80d multicolored 1.25 1.00

Green March, 18th anniv.

Water Birds A390

1993, Dec. 13 Litho. *Perf. 14*
770 A390 1.70d Sarcelle marbree .40 .30
771 A390 4.80d Foulque a crete 1.10 .85

Manifest of Independence, 50th Anniv. — A391

1994, Mar. 31 Litho. *Perf. 14*
772 A391 4.80d multicolored 1.10 .85

A392

General Agreement on Tariffs and Trade (GATT), 1994 Summit, Marrakech A393

No. 774Ab, 1.70d, like #773. c, 4.80d, like #774.

1994, Apr. 29 Litho. *Perf. 14*
773 A392 1.70d multicolored .40 .30
774 A393 4.80d multicolored 1.10 .80

Sheet of 2
Rouletted

774A A393 #b.-c. 3.50 3.00

Buildings and background are all in shades of claret on Nos. 774b-774c. No. 773 has building and background in shades of green. No. 774 has black building with claret background. No. 774A sold for 10d.

Week of the Blind — A394

Red Crescent Society — A395

1994, May 9
775 A394 4.80d multicolored 1.10 .85

1994, May 18
776 A395 4.80d multicolored 1.10 .85

Natl. Conference on Children's Rights — A396

1994, May 25
777 A396 1.70d shown .40 .30
778 A396 4.80d Boy, girl under sun 1.10 .85

1994 World Cup Soccer Championships, US — A397

1994, June 17 *Perf. 13*
779 A397 4.80d multicolored 1.10 .85

King Hassan II, 65th Birthday A398

Designs: 1.70d, Wearing business suit. 4.80d, Wearing traditional costume, vert.

1994 *Perf. 13x12½, 12½x13*
780 A398 1.70d multicolored .40 .30
781 A398 4.80d multicolored 1.10 .45

A399

A400

1994 *Perf. 12½x13*
782 A399 4.80d multicolored 1.10 .45
Intl. Olympic Committee, Cent.

1994
783 A400 4.80d multicolored 1.10 .45

Death of Antoine de Saint-Exupery, 50th anniv.

Flowers A401

1994 *Perf. 13x12½, 12½x13*
784 A401 1.70d Chamaelon gummifer .40 .30
785 A401 4.80d Pancratium maritimum, vert. 1.10 .45

Water Birds A402

1994, Oct. 24 Photo. *Perf. 13x13½*
786 A402 1.70d Courlis a bec grele .40 .30
787 A402 4.80d Goeland d'audouin 1.10 .80

A403

A404

Green March, 19th Anniv.: 4.80d, Marchers, map, inscription.

1994, Nov. 6 Litho. *Perf. 12½*
788 A403 1.70d multicolored .40 .30
789 A403 4.80d multicolored 1.10 .80

Hand Stamp Type of 1985

Sherifan postal seals of Maghzen-Marrakesh: 1.70d, Circular. 4.80d, Octagonal.

1994, Nov. 22 *Perf. 12½*
790 A287 1.70d blue & black .40 .30
791 A287 4.80d vermilion & black 1.10 .80
Stamp Day.

1995, Feb. 27 Litho. *Perf. 13½*
792 A404 4.80d multicolored 1.10 .80
Week of the Blind.

A405

A406

1995, Mar. 22 Litho. *Perf. 13½*
793 A405 4.80d multicolored 1.10 .80
Arab League, 50th anniv.

1995, Apr. 24 Litho. *Perf. 13½x13*
794 A406 4.80d multicolored 1.10 .80
Red Crescent Society.

Flowers — A407

Birds — A408

1995, May 29 Litho. *Perf. 13½x13*
795 A407 2d Malva hispanica .50 .35
796 A407 4.80d Phlomis crinita 1.10 .85

1995, Sept. 18 Litho. *Perf. 13½x13*
797 A408 1.70d Coracias garrulus .40 .30
798 A408 4.80d Carduelis carduelis 1.10 .85

See Nos. 818-819, 832-833, 846-847.

FAO, 50th Anniv. A409

1995, Oct. 16 Photo. *Perf. 13½*
799 A409 4.80d multicolored 1.10 .85

UN, 50th Anniv. A410

1.70d, "50," Moroccan, UN flags. 4.80d, Moroccan flag, UN emblem, map of Africa.

1995, Oct. 24 *Perf. 12½*
800 A410 1.70d multicolored .40 .30
801 A410 4.80d multicolored 1.10 .85

Green March Anniv. Type of 1987 and

Green March, 20th Anniv. — A411

1995, Nov. 6 Photo. *Perf. 12½*
802 A323 1.70d multicolored .40 .30
803 A411 4.80d multicolored 1.10 .85

A412

A413

Independence, 40th anniv.: 4.80d, Crown, national flag. 10d, King Mohammed V, crown over flag, King Hassan II.

1995, Nov. 18 Litho. *Perf. 12½*
804 A412 4.80d multicolored 1.10 .85

Size: 112x83mm

Imperf

805 A412 10d multicolored 2.75 2.00

Hand Stamp Type of 1985

Sherifan postal seals of Maghzen-Meknes, 1892: 1.70d, Circular. 4.80d, Octagonal.

1995, Nov. 22 Photo. *Perf. 12½*
806 A287 1.70d olive & black .40 .30
807 A287 4.80d violet & black 1.10 .85

Stamp Day.

1996, Mar. 3 Litho. *Perf. 13½*
808 A413 2d Natl. arms .45 .35
809 A413 5.50d King Hassan II 1.25 .95

Size: 134x86mm

Imperf

810 A413 10d Crown, King 2.50 1.75

Accession of King Hassan II, 35th anniv.

Traditional Crafts — A414

Flowers — A415

1996, Mar. 25 Photo. *Perf. 13½x13*
811 A414 5.50d Pottery 1.25 1.00
812 A414 5.50d Copper 1.25 1.00

1996, Apr. 25
813 A415 2d Cleonia lusitanica .50 .40
814 A415 5.50d Tulipa sylvestris 1.25 1.00

A416

A417

King Hassan II: 2d, In uniform. 5.50d, Wearing traditional headpiece.

1996, May 14 Photo. *Perf. 13x13½*
815 A416 2d multicolored .50 .40
816 A416 5.50d multicolored 1.25 1.00

Royal Armed Forces, 40th anniv.

1996, July 19 Photo. *Perf. 13½x13*
817 A417 5.50d multicolored 1.25 1.00

1996 Summer Olympics, Atlanta.

Bird Type of 1995

1996, Oct. 21 Photo. *Perf. 13½x13*
818 A408 2d Pandion haliaetus .50 .40
819 A408 5.50d Egretta garzetta 1.25 1.00

Green March Anniv. Type of 1987

1996, Nov. 6 Litho. *Perf. 13½*
820 A323 5.50d multicolored 1.25 1.00

Green March, 21st anniv.

Hand Stamp Type of 1985

Sherifan postal seals of Maghzen-Fes, 1892: 2d, Circular. 5.50d, Octagonal.

1996, Nov. 22 Photo. *Perf. 13½*
821 A287 2d orange & black .45 .35
822 A287 5.50d green & black 1.25 1.00

Stamp Day.

UNICEF, 50th Anniv. A418

1996, Dec. 11 *Perf. 13x13½*
823 A418 5.50d multicolored 1.25 1.00

Moroccan Pottery A419

1997, Feb. 24 Photo. *Perf. 13x13½*
824 A419 5.50d multicolored 1.10 .90

Flowers — A420

A421

1997, Mar. 24 Photo. *Perf. 13½x13*
825 A420 2d Lupinus luteus .50 .20
826 A420 5.50d Silybum marianum 1.25 .60

1997, Apr. 9 Litho. *Perf. 13½x13*

Speakers, 1947: No. 827, Crown Prince Hassan. No. 828, Sultan Mohammed V.

827 A421 2d multicolored .50 .20
828 A421 2d multicolored .50 .20

Speech in Tangier by King Hassan II, 50th anniv.

World Reading and Copyright Day — A422

1997, Apr. 23
829 A422 5.50d multicolored 1.25 .60

Intl. Meeting on Ibn Battuta (1304-77?), Traveler and Writer — A423

1997, May 9 *Perf. 13x13½*
830 A423 5.50d multicolored 1.25 .60

Moroccan Copper — A424

1997, July 21 Photo. *Perf. 13½*
831 A424 5.50d multicolored 1.10 .55

Bird Type of 1995

Designs: 2d, Anthropoides virgo. 5.50d, Parus caeruleus ultramarinus.

1997, Oct. 20 Photo. *Perf. 13½x13*
832 A408 2d multicolored .50 .20
833 A408 5.50d multicolored 1.10 .60

Green March Anniv. Type of 1987

1997, Nov. 6 *Perf. 13½*
834 A323 5.50d multicolored 1.10 .60

Green March, 22nd anniversary.

Hand Stamp Type of 1985

Sherifan postal seals of Maghzen-Larache, 1892: 2d, Circular. 5.50d, Octagonal.

1997 Photo. *Perf. 13½*
835 A287 2d blue & black .50 .20
836 A287 5.50d vermilion & black 1.10 .60

Flowers — A425

A426

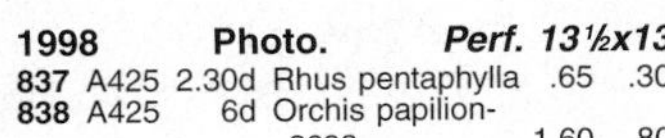

1998 Photo. *Perf. 13½x13*
837 A425 2.30d Rhus pentaphylla .65 .30
838 A425 6d Orchis papilionacea 1.60 .80

1998
839 A426 6d multicolored 1.60 .80

25th Intl. Road Transportation Congress.

A427

A428

1998
840 A427 6d Copper ornament 1.60 .80

1998
841 A428 6d multicolored 1.60 .80

1998 World Cup Soccer Championships, France.

Pottery A429

1998 *Perf. 13x13½*
842 A429 6d multicolored 1.60 .80

Intl. Year of the Ocean A430

1998
843 A430 6d multicolored 1.60 .80

King & People's Revolution, 45th Anniv. A431

1998
844 A431 6d multicolored 1.60 .80

World Stamp Day — A432

1998 Photo. *Perf. 13½x13*
845 A432 6d multicolored 1.60 .80

Bird Type of 1995

Designs: 2.30d, Luscinia megarhynchos. 6d, Struthio camelus.

1998 **Photo.**
846 A408 2.30d multicolored .65 .30
847 A408 6d multicolored 1.60 .80

Green March Anniv. Type

1998, Nov. 6 ***Perf. 13½***
848 A323 6d multicolored 1.60 .80

Green March, 23rd anniv.

A433

A434

1998 **Litho.** ***Perf. 13½x13***
849 A433 6d multicolored 1.60 .80

Public Liberties, 40th anniv.

1998 **Photo.**
850 A434 6d multicolored 1.60 .80

Universal Declaration of Human Rights, 50th anniv.

A435

A436

1999 **Litho.** ***Perf. 13¼***
851 A435 6d multi 1.50 .75

World Theater Day.

1999

Flora: 2.30d, Eryngium triquetrum. 6d, Viscum cruciatum.

852 A436 2.30d multi .60 .30
853 A436 6d multi 1.50 .75

Bab Mansour Laalej — A437

1999 ***Perf. 13x13¼***
854 A437 6d multi 1.50 .75

Jewelry A438

1999 ***Perf. 13¼***
855 A438 6d multi 1.50 .75

A439

A440

1999
856 A439 2.30d On throne .60 .30
857 A439 6d In robes 1.50 .75
a. Souvenir sheet, #856-857, imperf, without gum 2.25 1.10

King Hassan II, 70th birthday.

1999
858 A440 6d multi 1.50 .75

World Environment Day.

UPU, 125th Anniv. — A441

1999, Oct. 9 **Photo.** ***Perf. 13¼***
859 A441 6d multi 1.25 .60

FAO Medal Awarded by King Hassan II — A442

1999, Oct. 16
860 A442 6d multi 1.25 .60

See No. 964.

Anti-poverty Week — A443

1999, Nov. 11 **Photo.** ***Perf. 11¾***
Granite Paper
861 A443 6d multi

Compare with type A461.

Green March Anniv. Type of 1987

1999, Nov. 6 **Photo.** ***Perf. 13¼***
862 A323 6d multi 1.25 .60

Green March, 24th anniv.

Fish A444

Designs: 2.30d, Diplodus cervinus. 6d, Lampris guttatus.

1999, Nov. 29 **Photo.** ***Perf. 13¼***
863 A444 2.30d multi .55 .25
864 A444 6d multi 1.50 .75

Miniature Sheet

Morocco Year in France A445

No. 865: a, Stork on nest. b, People in robes. c, Mandolin, pillars. d, Boat at dock.

1999, Dec. 13 ***Perf. 13¼x13***
865 Sheet of 4 6.25 3.00
a.-d. A445 6d Any single 1.50 .75

African Cup Soccer Tournament — A446

2000, Jan. 25 ***Perf. 11¾x11½***
Granite Paper
866 A446 6d multi 1.50 .75

Year 2000 A447

2000, Jan. 31
Granite Paper
867 A447 6d multi 1.50 .75

Reconstruction of Agadir, 40th Anniv. — A448

2000, Feb. 29 **Photo.** ***Perf. 11¾***
Granite Paper
868 A448 6.50d multi 1.60 .80

Islamic Development Bank — A449

2000, Mar. 6 **Photo.** ***Perf. 11¾x11½***
Granite Paper
869 A449 6.50d multi 1.60 .80

Natl. Day of the Handicapped — A450

2000, Mar. 30
Granite Paper
870 A450 6.50d multi 1.60 .80

Flora A451

Designs: 2.50d, Jasione montana. 6.50d, Pistorica breviflora.

2000, Apr. 27 Photo. *Perf. 11¾*
Granite Paper

871-872 A451 Set of 2 2.50 1.10

World Meteorological Organization, 50th Anniv. — A452

2000, May 15 Granite Paper

873 A452 6.50d multi 1.60 .80

Marrakesh Arts Festival A453

2000, June 5 Photo. *Perf. 11¾*
Granite Paper

874 A453 6.50d multi 1.60 .80

Intl. Peace Year A454

2000 Photo. *Perf. 11¾*
Granite Paper

875 A454 6.50d multi 1.60 .80

Enthronement of King Mohammed VI, 1st Anniv. — A455

King in: 2.50d, Business suit. 6.50d, Robe.

2000, July 30 Photo. *Perf. 11¾*
Granite Paper

877-878 A455 Set of 2 2.10 1.00
878a Souvenir sheet of 2, #877-878, imperf. 2.50 1.25

No. 878a sold for 10d.

Intl. Festival, Volubilis A456

2000, Sept. 8 *Perf. 11¾*
Granite Paper

879 A456 6.50d multi 1.90 1.60

2000 Summer Olympics, Sydney — A457

2000, Sept. 15 Granite Paper

880 A457 6.50d multi 1.90 1.60

SOS Children's Villages — A458

2000, Oct. 12 Granite Paper

881 A458 6.50d multi 1.60 .80

World Teacher's Day — A459

2000, Oct. 25 Photo. *Perf. 11¾*
Granite Paper

882 A459 6.50d multi 1.60 .80

Anti-poverty Week — A461

2000, Nov. 1 Photo. *Perf. 11¾*
Granite Paper

884 A461 6.50d multi 1.60 .80

Compare with type A443. Value is for stamp with surrounding selvage. See Nos. 911, 928, 953, 997, 1027, 1048, 1076, 1098.

Green March Anniv. Type of 1987 and

Map and Inscription A462

2000, Nov. 6 Photo. *Perf. 11¾*
Granite Paper

885 A323 2.50d multi .60 .25
886 A462 6.50d multi 1.60 .80

Green March, 25th anniv.

Antoine de Saint-Exupéry (1900-44), Aviator, Writer — A463

2000, Nov. 13 Photo. *Perf. 11¾*
Granite Paper

887 A463 6.50d multi 1.60 .80

Independence, 45th Anniv. — A464

2000, Nov. 18 Granite Paper

888 A464 6.50d multi 1.60 .80

Fish A465

Designs: 2.50d, Apogon imberbis. 6.50d, Scorpaena loppei.

2000, Dec. 25 Granite Paper

889-890 A465 Set of 2 2.00 1.00

El Gharbi Gate A466

2001, Mar. 22 Photo. *Perf. 11¾*
Granite Paper

891 A466 6.50d multi 1.60 .70

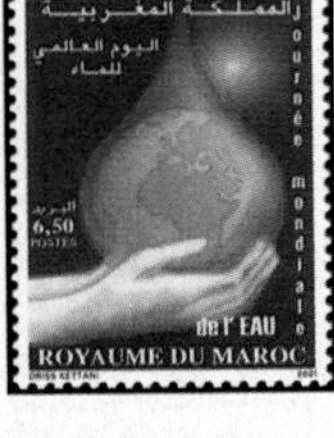

World Water Day — A467

2001, Mar. 30 Granite Paper

892 A467 6.50d multi 1.60 .70

Armed Forces, 45th Anniv. — A468

Designs: 2.50d, Soldier and insignia. 6.50d, Soldier in frame.

2001, May 16 Litho. *Perf. 14¼x13¾*

893-894 A468 Set of 2 2.25 .95

Flora — A469

Designs: 2.50d, Euphorbia rigida. 6.50d, Glaucium flavum.

2001, June 7 Photo. *Perf. 11¾*
Granite Paper

895-896 A469 Set of 2 2.25 .95

Houses of Worship — A470

Designs: 2.50d, Koekelberg Basilica, Belgium. 6.50d, Hassan II Mosque, Casablanca.

2001, June 10 Granite Paper

897-898 A470 Set of 2 1.90 .95

See Belgium Nos. 1855-1856.

Natl. Diplomacy Day — A471

Perf. 14¼x13¾

2001, June 29 Litho.

899 A471 6.50d multi 1.40 .70

A472

A473

A474

King Mohammed VI
A475

Perf. 12¾x13¼, 13¼x12¾

2001, July 31 Litho.

Size: 24x33mm

900	A472	2.50d multi	.55	.25
901	A473	6d multi	1.40	.55
902	A474	6.50d multi	1.50	.60

32x24mm

Arms 9mm Tall

903	A475	10d multi	2.40	.85
		Nos. 900-903 (4)	5.85	2.25

See Nos. 934A-934B, 940-943, 960-962, 1020, 1029A.

Marine Life — A476

Designs: 2.50d, Lophius budegassa. 6.50d, Monachus monachus, horiz.

2001, Sept. 28 Litho. ***Perf. 11¾***

Granite Paper

904-905 A476 Set of 2 2.25 .95

Hand Stamp Type of 1985

Hand stamps of Ksar el Kebir, 1892: 2.50d, Round. 6.50d, Octagonal.

2001, Oct. 9 Litho. ***Perf. 14¼x13¾***

906	A287	2.50d olive & black	.60	.25
907	A287	6.50d violet & black	1.60	.70

World Day to Combat Desertification
A477

2001, Oct. 29 Litho. ***Perf. 13¼***

908 A477 6.50d multi 1.25 .60

7th UN Climate Change Conference
A478

2001, Oct. 29

909 A478 6.50d multi 1.25 .60

Green March, 26th Anniv.
A479

2001, Nov. 7 Photo. ***Perf. 13x13¼***

910 A479 6.50d multi 1.25 .60

Anti-Poverty Week Type of 2000 and

Anti-Poverty Week
A480

2001, Nov. 8 ***Perf. 12½***

911 A461 6.50d multi 1.25 .60

Perf. 13x13¼

912 A480 6.50d multi 1.25 .60

Value of No. 911 is for stamp with surrounding selvage.

Year of Dialogue Among Civilizations
A481

2001, Dec. 14 ***Perf. 13¼x13***

913 A481 6.50d multi 1.25 .60

Fountains — A482

Designs: 2.50d, Wallace Fountain, Paris. 6.50d, Nejjarine Fountain, Fez.

2001, Dec. 14 ***Perf. 13¼***

914-915 A482 Set of 2 2.25 .85

See France Nos. 2847-2848.

Chellah Gate
A483

2002, Feb. 28 ***Perf. 13x13¼***

916 A483 6.50d multi 1.25 .60

Intl. Women's Day — A484

2002, Mar. 8 ***Perf. 13¼x13***

917 A484 6.50d multi 1.25 .60

Cedar Tree — A485

2002, Mar. 29

918 A485 6.50d multi 1.25 .60

2nd World Assembly on the Elderly
A486

2002, Apr. 30 ***Perf. 13x13¼***

919 A486 6.50d multi 1.25 .60

Special Session of UN General Assembly on Children — A487

2002, May 8 ***Perf. 13¼x13***

920 A487 6.50d multi 1.25 .60

Dated 2001.

Flora — A488

Designs: 2.50d, Linaria bipartita. 6.50d, Verbascum pseudocreticum.

2002, June 5 Photo. ***Perf. 13¼x13***

921-922 A488 Set of 2 2.25 .80

Intl. Telecommunications Union Plenipotentiary Conference, Marrakesh — A489

2002, Sept. 23 Photo. ***Perf. 13¼***

923 A489 6.50d multi 1.25 .60

Size: 120x90mm

Imperf

Without Gum

924 A489 10d multi 2.40 1.00

Palestinian Intifada
A490

2002, Sept. 28 ***Perf. 13¼***

925 A490 6.50d multi 1.40 .70

Intl. Year of Ecotourism
A491

2002, Sept. 30

926 A491 6.50d multi 1.40 .70

Green March, 27th Anniv. — A492

2002, Nov. 7

927 A492 6.50d multi 1.40 .70

Anti-Poverty Week Type of 2000 and

Anti-Poverty Week — A493

2002, Nov. 8 ***Perf. 12½***

928 A461 6.50d multi 1.40 .70

Perf. 13¼

929 A493 6.50d multi 1.40 .70

Value of No. 928 is for stamp with surrounding selvage.

Maghzen Post, 110th Anniv.
A494

Sultan Moulay Hassan I and: 2.50d, Circular postal seal. 6.50d, Octagonal postal seal.

2002, Nov. 22 ***Perf. 12½, 13 (6.50d)***

930-931 A494 Set of 2 2.25 .95

Value of Nos. 930-931 are for stamps with surrounding selvage. No. 931 is ocatagonally shaped.

UN Year for Cultural Heritage A495

2002, Dec. 18 *Perf. 13¼x13*
932 A495 6.50d multi 1.40 .70

Fish A496

Designs: 2.50d, Alosa alosa. 6.50d, Epinephelus marginatus.

2002, Dec. 30 *Perf. 13¼*
933-934 A496 Set of 2 2.50 .95

King Mohammed VI Type of 2001

2002 Litho. *Perf. 11½*
Granite Paper
Size: 24x30mm
934A A472 2.50d multi .50 .25
934B A473 6d multi 1.25 .60

Bab el Okla, Tetuan A497

2003, Feb. 28 Photo. *Perf. 13¼*
935 A497 6.50d multi 1.60 .70

Fir Trees A498

2003, Mar. 28
936 A498 6.50d multi 1.60 .70

Intl. Year of Fresh Water — A499

2003, Apr. 28 *Perf. 13¼x13*
937 A499 6.50d multi 1.60 .70

Flora — A500

Designs: 2.50d, Limonium sincatum. 6.50d, Echinops spinosus.

2003, May 30 *Perf. 13¼*
938-939 A500 Set of 2 2.60 1.25

King Mohammed VI Type of 2001

2003 Litho. *Perf. 13¼x12¾*
940 A475 70c lt bl & multi .20 .20
941 A475 80c pur & multi .20 .20
942 A475 5d yel & multi 1.50 .50
943 A475 20d lil & multi 6.00 2.10
Nos. 940-943 (4) 7.90 3.00

Salé Grand Mosque, 1000th Anniv. — A501

2003, July 11 Photo. *Perf. 13x12¼*
944 A501 6.50d multi 1.40 .70

World Youth Congress A502

2003, Aug. 12 *Perf. 13¼*
945 A502 6.50d multi 1.40 .70

Revolution of the King and People, 50th Anniv. A503

2003, Aug. 20
946 A503 6.50d multi 1.40 .70

King Mohammed VI, 40th Birthday — A504

Designs: Nos. 947, 949a, 2.50d, King in suit and tie. Nos. 948, 949b, 6.50d, King in robe.

2003, Aug. 21
947-948 A504 Set of 2 2.00 .95

Souvenir Sheet
Stamps With Pink Frames
949 A504 Sheet of 2, #a-b 2.50 1.25

No. 949 sold for 10d.
Compare with type A545.

Fish A505

Designs: 2.50d, Sparisoma cretense. 6.50d, Anthias anthias.

2003, Sept. 30 Photo. *Perf. 13¼*
950-951 A505 Set of 2 2.25 1.00

World Post Day — A506

2003, Oct. 9
952 A506 6.50d multi 1.90 .95

Anti-Poverty Week Type of 2000 and

King Mohammed VI Visiting Sick Child — A507

2003, Oct. 31 Photo. *Perf. 12¾*
953 A461 6.50d multi 1.90 .95
954 A507 6.50d multi 1.90 .95

Green March, 28th Anniv. — A508

2003, Nov. 5 Photo. *Perf. 13¼*
955 A508 6.50d multi 1.90 .95

Rabat, 2003 Arab Culture Capital — A509

2003, Dec. 19 Litho. *Perf. 13x13¼*
956 A509 6.50d multi 2.00 1.00

Philately at School A510

2003, Dec. 29 *Perf. 13¼*
957 A510 6.50d multi 2.00 1.00

UN Literacy Decade — A511

2003, Dec. 29 *Perf. 13x13¼*
958 A511 6.50d multi 2.00 1.00

Morocco - People's Republic of China Diplomatic Relations, 45th Anniv. — A512

2003, Dec. 31 *Perf. 12*
959 A512 6.50d multi 2.00 1.00

Types of 2001 Redrawn With Added Frame Lines

2002-03 Litho. *Perf. 11½*
Size: 24x30mm
960 A474 6.50d multi — —
Size: 32x23mm
Arms 7mm Tall
961 A475 10d multi 2.40 1.00

Booklet Stamps
Self-Adhesive
Serpentine Die Cut 11
Size: 20x23mm
962 A472 2.50d multi ('03) .60 .25
a. Booklet pane of 10 6.00
963 A482 6.50d Like #915 ('03) 1.60 .70
a. Booklet pane of 10 16.00

Issued: 6.50d, 10d, 2002. 2.50d, 6.50d, 9/3/03.
On No. 903, arms are 9mm tall.

FAO Medal Type of 1999

2003, July Photo. *Perf. 13x13¼*
Size: 48x38mm
964 A442 6d multi *5.00 5.00*

Ibn Battutah (1304-68), Traveler and Author — A513

2004, Feb. 24 Photo. *Perf. 13x12¼*
965 A513 6.50d multi 2.00 1.00

Bab Agnaou, Marrakesh A514

2004, Mar. 18 *Perf. 13¼*
966 A514 6.50d multi 2.00 1.00

Flowers — A515

Designs: 2.50d, Linaria gharbensis. 6.50d, Nigella damascena.

2004, Mar. 29
967-968 A515 Set of 2 2.75 1.25

16th World Military Equestrian Championships, Témara — A516

2004, Apr. 18

969 A516 6.50d multi 2.00 1.00

Hassan II Tennis Grand Prix, 20th Anniv. — A517

2004, May 14

970 A517 6.50d multi 2.00 1.00

10th World Sacred Music Festival, Fez A518

2004, May 28 ***Perf. 12¼x13***

971 A518 6.50d multi 2.00 1.00

Caftan — A519

2004, June 18 ***Perf. 13¼***

972 A519 6.50d multi 2.00 1.00

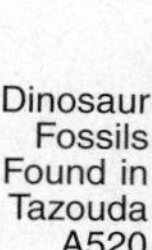

Dinosaur Fossils Found in Tazouda A520

2004, July 12

973 A520 6.50d multi 2.00 1.00

30th Intl. Military History Congress A521

2004, July 29

974 A521 6.50d multi 2.00 1.00

Enthronement of King Mohammed VI, 5th Anniv. — A522

Designs: Nos. 975, 977a, 2.50d, King in suit. Nos. 976, 977b, 6d, King in robe.

2004, July 30

975-976 A522 Set of 2 2.75 2.75

Souvenir Sheet

Stamps With Yellow Frames

977 A522 Sheet of 2, #a-b 3.00 3.00

No. 977 sold for 10d.

Intl. Peace Day — A523

2004, Sept. 21 **Photo.** ***Perf. 13¼***

978 A523 6d multi 1.90 .95

Anti-Poverty Week Type of 2000 and

Anti-Poverty Week — A524

2004, Oct. 22 ***Perf. 12¾***

979 A461 6.50d multi 2.00 1.00

Perf. 13¼

980 A524 6.50d multi 2.00 1.00

Value for No. 979 is for stamp with surrounding selvage.

Green March, 29th Anniv. — A525

2004, Nov. 6 **Photo.** ***Perf. 13¼***

981 A525 6d multi 2.00 1.00

Marine Life A526

Designs: 2.50d, Xiphias gladius. 6.50d, Octopus vulgaris.

2004, Nov. 16 **Photo.** ***Perf. 13¼***

982-983 A526 Set of 2 2.75 1.25

World Children's Day — A527

2004, Nov. 24

984 A527 6.50d multi 2.00 1.00

Rotary International, Cent. — A528

2005, Feb. 23 ***Perf. 13x13¼***

985 A528 6.50d multi 2.00 1.00

Arab League, 60th Anniv. — A529

2005, Mar. 22 ***Perf. 13¼x13***

986 A529 6.50d multi 2.00 1.00

Bab Boujloud, Fez A530

2005, Mar. 30 ***Perf. 13¼***

987 A530 6.50d multi 2.00 1.00

Amnesty International A531

2005, May 6 **Photo.** ***Perf. 13¼***

988 A531 6.50d multi 2.00 1.00

Flora — A532

Designs: 2.50d, Erodium sebaceum. 6.50d, Linaria ventricosa.

2005, May 26 **Photo.** ***Perf. 13¼***

989-990 A532 Set of 2 2.00 1.00

Rock Carvings, Iourarhane A533

2005, May 31

991 A533 6.50d multi 2.00 1.00

13th World Neurosurgery Congress, Marrakesh A534

2005, June 19

992 A534 6.50d multi 2.00 1.00

Phosphates Office, 80th Anniv. — A535

2005, Aug. 31 **Photo.** ***Perf. 13¼***

993 A535 6.50d multi 2.00 1.00

United Nations, 60th Anniv. — A536

2005, Oct. 24

994 A536 6.50d multi 2.00 1.00

Green March, 30th Anniv. A537

Marchers and "30" in: 2.50d, Light blue. 6d, Green.

2005, Nov. 6

995-996 A537 Set of 2 2.75 2.75

Anti-Poverty Week Type of 2000 and

Anti-Poverty Week — A538

2005, Nov. 7 ***Perf. 12¾***

997 A461 6.50d multi 2.00 1.00

Perf. 13¼

998 A538 6.50d multi 2.00 1.00

Values for No. 997 are for stamps with surrounding selvage.

Friendship of Morocco and the Netherlands, 400th Anniv. — A539

Designs: No. 999, 6.50d, Five tourist attractions. No. 1000, 6.50d, Arch and waterway, vert.

2005, Nov. 14 *Perf. 13¼*

999-1000 A539 Set of 2 4.00 1.90

World Summit on the Information Society, Tunis A540

2005, Nov. 16

1001 A540 6d multi 2.00 1.00

Return from Exile of King Mohammed V, 50th Anniv. — A541

Country name in: No. 1002, Red. No. 1003a, Green.

2005, Nov. 16 *Perf. 13¼x13*

1002 A541 6.50d multi 1.90 1.00

Souvenir Sheet

1003 Sheet, #1002, 1003a 4.00 2.25
a. A541 6.50d multi 1.75 .75

Souvenir Sheet

Children's Art — A542

No. 1004: a, Children and flower, by Kaoutar Azizi Alaoui. b, Children and dove, by Sara Bourquiba. c, House and trees, by Mohcine Kahyouchat. d, Sun on horizon, by Anise Anico.

2005, Nov. 21 *Perf. 13x13¼*

1004 A542 2.50d Sheet of 4, #a-d 2.75 2.00

Intl. Year of Microcredit A543

2005, Nov. 30 *Perf. 13¼*

1005 A543 6.50d multi 2.00 1.00

Marine Life A544

Designs: 2.50d, Sparus aurata. 6d, Sepia officinalis.

2005, Dec. 22

1006-1007 A544 Set of 2 2.70 1.00

King Mohammed VI — A545

Designs: No. 1008, King in suit and tie. No. 1009, King in robe.

2005 Litho. ***Serpentine Die Cut 11***

Booklet Stamps

Self-Adhesive

1008 A545 2.50d multi .55 .25
1009 A545 2.50d multi .55 .25
a. Booklet pane, 5 each #1008-1009 5.50

Compare type A545 with A504. See Nos. 1054A-1054B.

Bustard A546

Melierax Metabates A547

Egretta Garzetta A548

Pandion Haliaetus A549

Alectoris Barbara A550

Porphyrio Porphyrio A551

Carduelis Carduelis A552

Bird A553

Duck A554

Falcon A555

2005 ***Serpentine Die Cut 11***

Self-Adhesive

1010 Booklet pane of 10 6.00
a. A546 2.50d multi .60 .25
b. A547 2.50d multi .60 .25
c. A548 2.50d multi .60 .25
d. A549 2.50d multi .60 .25
e. A550 2.50d multi .60 .25
f. A551 2.50d multi .60 .25
g. A552 2.50d multi .60 .25
h. A553 2.50d multi .60 .25
i. A554 2.50d multi .60 .25
j. A555 2.50d multi .60 .25

Two Women A556

Ait Mouhad A557

Saharaoui Derraa A558

Two Women A559

Citadin A560

Saharaoui Melhfa A561

Tata Woman A562

Tata Man A563

Meknassa A564

Mokhazni du Roi A565

2005 ***Serpentine Die Cut 11***

Self-Adhesive

1011 Booklet pane of 10 14.00
a. A556 6d multi 1.40 .65
b. A557 6d multi 1.40 .65
c. A558 6d multi 1.40 .65
d. A559 6d multi 1.40 .65
e. A560 6d multi 1.40 .65
f. A561 6d multi 1.40 .65
g. A562 6d multi 1.40 .65
h. A563 6d multi 1.40 .65
i. A564 6d multi 1.40 .65
j. A565 6d multi 1.40 .65

Traffic Safety Day — A566

2006, Feb. 18 Photo. *Perf. 13½x13*

1012 A566 6.50d multi 2.00 1.00

OPEC Intl. Development Fund, 30th Anniv. — A567

2006, Feb. 28 *Perf. 13¼*

1013 A567 6.50d multi 2.00 1.00

Bab Marshan, Tangiers A568

2006, Mar. 30

1014 A568 6.50d multi 1.90 1.00

Foreign Affairs Ministry, 50th Anniv. A569

2006, Apr. 26

1015 A569 6d multi 1.75 1.00

Flowers — A570

Designs: 2.50d, Narcissus cantabricus. 6.50d, Paeonia mascula.

2006, Apr. 28

1016-1017 A570 Set of 2 2.50 2.50

Royal Armed Forces, 50th Anniv. A571

Kings Mohammed VI, Hassan II, and Mohammed V, anniversary emblem, airplanes and: 2.50d, Tank . 6.50d, Ships.

2006, May 14

1018-1019 A571 Set of 2 2.10 1.10
1019a Souvenir sheet, #1018-1019 2.40 2.40

No. 1019a sold for 10d.

Type of 2001 With Added Frameline and

A572

King Mohammed VI — A573

2006, July 1 Litho. *Perf. 11½*

Granite Paper

1020 A472 3.25d blue & multi .90 .50
1021 A572 7.80d lt grn & multi 2.40 1.20
1022 A573 13d lilac & multi 3.75 1.90
Nos. 1020-1022 (3) 7.05 3.60

Designs size of No. 1020: 25x32mm. See No. 1029A for stamp similar to No. 1020, with 22x32mm design without frameline. Compare types A572 and A573 with types A473 and A475.

Barbary Ape — A574

Atlas Lion — A575

2006, July 31 *Perf. 13¼x13*

1023 A574 3.25d multi .90 .50
1024 A575 7.80d multi 2.25 1.10

Green March, 31st Anniv. A576

Designs: No. 1025, 7.80d, King Mohammed VI waving to crowd. No. 1026, 7.80d, Mohammed VI Mosque, Boujdour.

2006, Nov. 7 **Photo.** *Perf. 13¼*

1025-1026 A576 Set of 2 4.50 2.25

Anti-Poverty Week Type of 2000

2006, Nov. 10

1027 A461 7.80d multi 1.90 .95

Values are for stamps with surrounding selvage.

Stamp Day — A577

2006, Nov. 22

1028 A577 7.80d multi 2.25 1.10

Values are for stamps with surrounding selvage.

Admission to the United Nations, 50th Anniv. — A578

006, Nov. 24

9 A578 7.80d multi 2.25 1.10

Mohammed VI Type of 2001

. Litho. *Perf. 13¼*

Size: 22x32mm

5d blue & multi 1.10 1.10

frame line around design es not. No. 1029A has a "Phil@poste."

World AIDS Day A579

2006, Dec. 1 **Litho.** *Perf. 13¼*

1030 A579 7.80d multi 2.25 1.10

Diplomatic Relations Between Morocco and Japan, 50th Anniv. A580

Designs: 3.25d, Dove, maps and flags. 7.80d, Flags, arches, pottery.

2006, Dec. 20 **Photo.** *Perf. 13¼*

1031-1032 A580 Set of 2 3.25 1.50

Fish A581

Designs: 3.25d, Thunnus thynnus. 7.80d, Sardina pilchardus.

2006, Dec. 25

1033-1034 A581 Set of 2 3.25 1.50

African Soccer Confederation, 50th Anniv. — A582

2007, Feb. 26 **Litho.** *Perf. 13¼*

1035 A582 7.80d multi 2.40 1.10

Values are for stamps with surrounding selvage.

Mohammed V University, 50th Anniv. — A583

2007, Mar. 15

1036 A583 3.25d multi 1.00 .50

Ibn Khaldun (1332-1406), Philosopher — A584

2007, Mar. 28

1037 A584 7.80d multi 2.40 1.10

Souvenir Sheet

Intl. Agricultural Exhibition, Meknès — A585

No. 1038: a, Palm trees. b, Argans. c, Cattle, horiz. d, Olives, horiz.

Perf. 12¾x13¼, 13¼x12¾ (horiz. stamps)

2007, Apr. 19

1038 A585 Sheet of 4 7.00 7.00
a.-b. 3.25d Either single 1.00 .50
c.-d. 7.80d Either single 2.40 1.25

No. 1038 sold for 24d.

Couscous A586

2007, June 1 *Perf. 13¼x13*

1039 A586 7.80d multi 2.40 1.10

Andalusian Music — A587

2007, June 8 *Perf. 13x13¼*

1040 A587 7.80d multi 2.40 1.10

Souvenir Sheet

Paintings — A588

No. 1041: a, Fulgurance, by M. Qotbi, vert. b, Horses and Riders, by, H. Glaoui. c, Symphonie d'Eté, by Qotbi. d, Horses, by Glaoui.

2007, June 21 *Perf. 13*

1041 A588 3.25d Sheet of 4, #a-d 4.00 4.00

Scouting, Cent. — A589

2007, Aug. 7 **Litho.** *Perf. 13¼*

1042 A589 7.80d multi 2.40 1.10

Buildings — A590

Designs: 3.25d, Silves Castle, Portugal. 7.80d, Tower, Arzila, Morocco.

2007, Sept. 26

1043-1044 A590 Set of 2 3.50 1.75

See Portugal Nos. 2955-2956.

World Post Day A591

2007, Oct. 9

1045 A591 3.25d multi 1.25 .90

Fez, 2007 Islamic Cultural Capital A592

2007, Oct. 30

1046 A592 7.80d multi 2.40 1.10

Compare with Type A618.

Green March, 32nd Anniv. A593

2007, Nov. 6

1047 A593 7.80d multi 2.40 1.10

Anti-Poverty Week Type of 2000

2007, Nov. 8

1048 A461 7.80d multi 2.40 1.10

Values are for stamps with surrounding selvage.

National Quality Week — A594

2007, Nov. 12
1049 A594 7.80d multi 2.40 1.10

World Children's Day — A595

2007, Nov. 20
1050 A595 7.80d multi 2.40 1.10

Supreme Court, 50th Anniv. — A596

2007, Nov. 21
1051 A596 3.25d multi 1.00 .50

Bab Lamrissa — A597

2007, Dec. 7 Litho. *Perf. 13¼*
1052 A597 7.80d multi 2.40 1.10

Royal Air Morocco, 50th Anniv. A598

2007, Dec. 19
1053 A598 7.80d multi 2.40 1.10

"Morocco of Champions" — A599

2007, Dec. 28
1054 A599 7.80d multi 2.40 1.10

Values are for stamps with surrounding selvage.

King Mohammed VI Types of 2005, 2006 (Redrawn)

Designs: No. 1054A, King in suit and tie. No. 1054B, King in robe.

2007 Litho. *Serpentine Die Cut 11*
Booklet Stamps
Self-Adhesive

1054A A545 3.25d multi — —
1054B A545 3.25d multi — —
c. Booklet pane, 5 each #1054A-1054B —

Size: 22x32mm
Country Name in White
Water-Activated Gum
Perf. 13

1054D A572 7.80d multi 2.10 1.10

Compare with No. 1021, which is wider and has country name in blue.

Moroccan Travel Market A600

2008, Jan. 17
1055 A600 7.80d multi 2.40 1.10

Africa Cup of Nations Soccer Championships — A601

2008, Jan. 31
1056 A601 7.80d multi 2.40 1.10

Export Trophy — A602

2008, Apr. 4 Litho. *Perf. 13¼*
1057 A602 3.25d multi 1.00 .50

Fez, 1200th Anniv. — A603

2008, Apr. 5
1058 A603 3.25d multi 1.00 .50

Flowers — A604

Designs: 3.25d, Calendula stellata. 7.80d, Convolvulus tricolor.

2008, Apr. 30 Litho. *Perf. 13¼*
1059-1060 A604 Set of 2 3.25 1.60

Buildings in Morocco and Iran — A605

No. 1061: a, 3.25d, Flags of Morocco and Iran, Kasbah, Oudayas, Morocco, and Falak-Ol-Aflak Castle, Iran. b, 3,25d, Scroll and Falak-Ol-Aflak Castle. c, 7.80d, Scroll and Kasbah, Oudayas, Morocco.

2008, May 12 Litho. *Perf. 13¼*
1061 A605 Horiz. strip of 3, #a-c 4.25 2.25

See Iran No. 2955.

Children's Art — A606

No. 1062: a, Earth, by Narjiss Lasfar. b, House and trees, by Chaimae Abbaich. c, Polluted sphere, by Ahmed Anas Bennis, vert. d, House and sun, by Wassim Chakou, vert.

2008, May 26
1062 Horiz. strip of 4 4.00 2.00
a.-d. A606 3.25d Any single .95 .45

World Environment Day — A607

2008, June 5
1063 A607 7.80d multi 2.40 1.10

Rug From Salé A608

Rug From Marmoucha A609

Rug From Ouled Besseba A610

Rug From Haut Atlas A611

Rug From Ait Haddou A612

Rug From Tazenakht A613

Rug From Marmoucha A614

Rug From Rabat A615

Rug From Ait Ouaouzguid A616

Rug From Rabat A617

2008 *Serpentine Die Cut 11*
Self-Adhesive

1064 Booklet pane of 10 22.50
a. A608 7.80d multi 2.25 1.10
b. A609 7.80d multi 2.25 1.10
c. A610 7.80d multi 2.25 1.10
d. A611 7.80d multi 2.25 1.10
e. A612 7.80d multi 2.25 1.10
f. A613 7.80d multi 2.25 1.10
g. A614 7.80d multi 2.25 1.10
h. A615 7.80d multi 2.25 1.10
i. A616 7.80d multi 2.25 1.10
j. A617 7.80d multi 2.25 1.10

Fez, 1200th Anniv. A618

2008, June 23 *Perf. 13¼*
1065 A618 7.80d multi 2.40 1.10

Compare with Type A592.

Bouregreg Valley Light Rail Line — A619

No. 1066: a, 3.25d, Train, bridge. b, 7.80d, Train, fortress.

2008, July 21
1066 A619 Horiz. pair, #a-b 3.25 1.60

2008 Summer Olympics, Beijing — A620

No. 1067 — Olympic rings and: a, Four runners. b, Three hurdlers. c, Boxers. d, Runner.

2008, Aug. 8 Photo. ***Perf. 13¼***
1067 Horiz. strip of 4 4.00 2.00
a.-d. A620 3.25d Any single 1.00 .45

Arab Post Day — A621

No. 1068 — Emblem and: a, World map, pigeon. b, Camel caravan.

2008, Aug. 28 Litho. ***Perf. 12¾***
1068 Sheet of 2 4.50 2.25
a.-b. A621 7.80d Either single 2.25 1.10

Marine Life A622

Designs: 3.25d, Isurus oxyrinchus. 7.80d, Haliotis tuberculata.

2008, Sept. 18 ***Perf. 13¼***
1069-1070 A622 Set of 2 3.25 1.60

Miniature Sheet

Art and Culture — A623

No. 1071: a, Musicians. b, Ezzellij tiles. c, Haik (white garment). d, Koran school.

2008, Oct. 10 Photo. ***Perf. 13¼x13***
1071 A623 3.25d Sheet of 4, #a-d 4.00 2.00

Diplomatic Relations Between Morocco and People's Republic of China — A624

Designs: 3.25r, Vases and flags of Morocco and People's Republic of China. No. 1073, 7.80d, Intertwined arabesque and Chinese emblem. No. 1074, 7.80d, Arabic archway and Great Wall of China, vert.

2009, Oct. 30 Photo. ***Perf. 12***
1072-1074 A624 Set of 3 4.50 2.25

Green March, 33rd Anniv. A625

2008, Nov. 6 Litho. ***Perf. 13¼***
1075 A625 3.25d multi .75 .35

Anti-Poverty Week Type of 2000

2008, Nov. 12 Photo. ***Perf. 13¼***
1076 A461 7.80d multi 1.90 .95

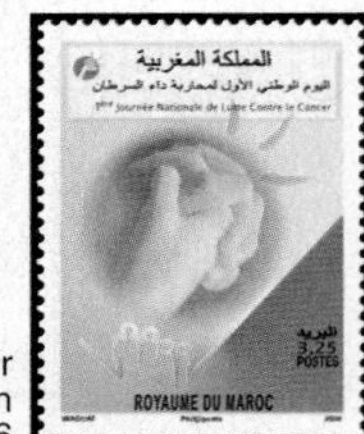

Natl. Cancer Prevention Day — A626

2008, Nov. 22 ***Perf. 13¼***
1077 A626 3.25d multi .75 .35

Universal Declaration of Human Rights, 60th Anniv. A627

2008, Dec. 10 Litho. ***Perf. 13***
1078 A627 7.80d multi 1.90 .95

Bab Al Marsa, Essaouira A628

2008, Dec. 26 Photo. ***Perf. 13¼***
1079 A628 7.80d multi 2.00 1.00

Louis Braille (1809-52), Educator of the Blind — A629

2009, Jan. 16
1080 A629 7.80d multi 1.90 .95

Insurance for Artisans and the Self-Employed — A630

2009, Feb. 16 ***Perf. 13x13¼***
1081 A630 3.25d multi .75 .35

25th Hassan II Grand Prix Tennis Tournament A631

2009, Apr. 6 ***Perf. 13¼***
1082 A631 3.25d multi .80 .40

Cadi Ayyad University, Marrakesh, 30th Anniv. A632

2009, Apr. 20
1083 A632 3.25d multi .80 .40

Sugar Industry — A633

2009, Apr. 22 **Photo.**
1084 A633 3.25d multi .80 .40

Natl. Theater Day A634

2009, May 14 ***Perf. 13¼***
1085 A634 3.25d multi .80 .40

Intl. Year of Astronomy A635

2009, May 15
1086 A635 7.80d multi 2.00 1.00

Protection for Children Using Computers A636

2009, May 17 Litho. ***Perf. 13x13¼***
1087 A636 7.80d multi 2.00 1.00

Al-Maghrib Bank, 50th Anniv. A637

2009, July 2 Photo. ***Perf. 13¼***
1088 A637 3.25d multi .80 .40

A638

Enthronement of King Mohammed VI, 10th Anniv. — A639

King Mohammed VI: 3.25d, On horse. 7.80d, Wearing suit.
15d, With images of Kings Mohammed V and Hassan II.

Photo. & Embossed With Foil Application

2009, July 30 ***Perf. 13¼***

Granite Paper (#1089-1090)

1089 A638 3.25d multi .85 .40
1090 A638 7.80d multi 2.00 1.00

Souvenir Sheet

Litho. with Three-Dimensional Plastic Affixed

Serpentine Die Cut 9½

Self-Adhesive

1091 A639 15d multi 3.75 1.90

Nos. 1089-1090 have gold frames with an orange cast. A souvenir sheet containing Nos. 1089-1090 having gold frames with a yellow cast sold for 36d.

Jerusalem, Capital of Arab Culture — A640

2009, Aug. 3 Litho. ***Perf. 13¼***
1092 A640 3.25d multi .85 .40

Natl. Women's Day — A641

2009, Oct. 10
1093 A641 3.25d multi .85 .40

Mohammedia School of Engineering, 50th Anniv. — A652

2009, Oct. 24 Litho. ***Perf. 13¼***
1095 A652 3.25d multi .85 .40

Mehdia Gate A653

2009, Oct. 30 Photo. *Perf. 13¾*
1096 A653 7.80d multi 2.10 1.10

Anti-Poverty Week Type of 2001

2009, Nov. 15 Photo. *Perf. 13*
1098 A461 7.80d multi 2.10 1.10

Value is for stamp with surrounding selvage.

Port of Tangiers — A655

No. 1099 — Ship in port, gear wheels in: a, 3.25d, Gray. b, 7.80d, Brown.

2009, Dec. 7 Litho. *Perf. 13¼*
1099 A655 Horiz. pair, #a-b 3.00 1.50

Caisse de Dépot et de Gestion, 50th Anniv. — A656

2009, Dec. 19
1100 A656 7.80d dk blue & gold 2.00 1.00

Fish A657

Designs: No. 1101, 7.80d, Sarda sarda. No. 1102, 7.80d, Oblada melanura.

2009, Dec. 28
1101-1102 A657 Set of 2 4.00 2.00

Children's Art A658

No. 1103: a, Horses. b, Trees. c, Lake, mountain and trees. d, Building with smokestacks.

2009, Dec. 31
1103 Vert. strip of 4 3.50 1.75
a.-d. A658 3.25d Any single .85 .40

Rosa Damascena A659

Orange Blossoms A660

2010, Jan. 14 *Perf. 13¼x13*
1104 A659 7.80d multi 2.00 1.00

Perf. 13x13¼
1105 A660 7.80d multi 2.00 1.00

Nos. 1104-1105 are each impregnated with the scent of the depicted flower.

Reconstruction of Agadir, 50th Anniv. — A661

2010, Feb. 28 *Perf. 13¼*
1106 A661 7.80d multi 1.90 .95

Earth Day — A662

2010, Apr. 22
1107 A662 3.25d multi .80 .40

Alfalfa A663

2010, Apr. 22 Litho. & Embossed
1108 A663 10d multi 2.40 1.25

No. 1108 has a circle of adhesive tape covering a small embossed circle containing alfalfa seeds.

Miniature Sheet

Art and Culture — A664

No. 1109 — Paintings of casbahs in: a, Ibeghouzen. b, Oudaias. c, Ait ben Haddou. d, Tinzouline.

2010, May 12 *Perf. 13x13¼*
1109 A664 3.25d Sheet of 4, #a-d 3.00 1.50

Level A Quality Certification for Morocco Post — A665

2010, May 26 *Perf. 13¼*
1110 A665 3.25d multi .75 .35

National Day of Resistance A666

2010, June 18
1111 A666 3.25d multi .75 .35

Bab al Bahr, Abilah — A667

2010, July 10
1112 A667 7.80d multi 1.90 .95

OCP Groupe, 90th Anniv. — A668

2010, Aug. 7 *Perf. 12¼*
1113 A668 7.80d multi 1.90 .95

Intl. Year of Biodiversity A669

2010, Oct. 11 Litho. *Perf. 13¼*
1114 A669 7.80d multi 2.00 1.00

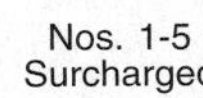

SEMI-POSTAL STAMPS

Nos. 1-5 Surcharged

1960, Mar. Unwmk. Engr. *Perf. 13*

B1	A1	5fr + 10fr brt bl & ind	.45	.40
B2	A1	10fr + 10fr bis brn & choc	.55	.55
B3	A1	15fr + 10fr dp grn & mag	1.25	1.10
B4	A1	25fr + 15fr purple	1.40	1.15
B5	A1	30fr + 20fr green	2.25	2.25
		Nos. B1-B5 (5)	5.90	5.45

The surtax aided families whose members consumed adulterated cooking oil with crippling or fatal results.

French Morocco Nos. 321 and 322 Surcharged

1960, Sept. 12
B6 A71 15fr + 3fr on 18fr dk grn .80 .80
B7 A71 20fr + 5fr brown lake 1.25 1.25

Nos. 1 and 6 Surcharged in Red or Black

1963, Jan. 28 Engr. *Perf. 13*
B8 A1 20c + 5c on 5fr brt bl & ind (R) .70 .70
B9 A1 30c + 10c on 50fr rose red .80 .45

The surtax was for flood victims.

Moroccan Brooch — SP1

Design: 40c+10c, Brooch with pendants.

1966, May 23 Photo. *Perf. 11½*
Granite Paper
B10 SP1 25c + 5c ultra, sil, blk & red .90 .55
B11 SP1 40c + 10c mag, sil, blk, ultra & bl 1.40 .70
a. Pair, #B10-B11, vertically tête-bêche 3.25 3.25

Meeting in Morocco of the Middle East and North African Red Cross-Red Crescent Seminar. The surtax was for the Moroccan Red Crescent Society.

See Nos. B12-B13, B15-B16, B19-B22, B26-B27, B29-B30, B34-B35.

1967, May 15 Granite Paper

Designs: 60c+5c, Two brooches, by silver drapery. 1d+10c, Two bracelets.

B12 SP1 60c + 5c yel bis & multi .95 .95
a. Pair, vertically tête-bêche 3.00 3.00
B13 SP1 1d + 10c emer & multi 1.90 1.90
a. Pair, vertically tête-bêche 4.75 4.75

Surtax for the Moroccan Red Crescent Society.

Hands Reading Braille and Map of Morocco — SP2

1969, Mar. 21 Photo. *Perf. 12½*
B14 SP2 25c + 10c multi .50 .20

Week of the Blind, Mar. 21-29.

Jewelry Type of 1966

Designs: 25c+5c, Silver earrings. 40c+10c, Gold ear pendant.

1969, May 9 Photo. *Perf. 11½*
Granite Paper

B15 SP1 25c + 5c gray grn & multi 1.25 .65
B16 SP1 40c + 10c tan & multi 1.60 .80
a. Pair, #B15-B16, vert. tête-bêche 6.00 6.00

50th anniv. of the League of Red Cross Societies. Surtax was for Moroccan Red Crescent Society.

Nos. 173-174 Surcharged

1970, Feb. 26 Litho. *Perf. 13*

B17 A65 10c + 25c multi 3.50 3.50
B18 A65 15c + 25c multi 3.50 3.50

The surtax was for flood victims.

Jewelry Type of 1966

Designs: 25c+5c, Necklace with pendants. 50c+10c, Earring with 5 pendants.

1970, May 25 Photo. *Perf. 11½*
Granite Paper

B19 SP1 25c + 5c gray & multi 1.00 .90
B20 SP1 50c + 10c brt vio & multi 1.50 1.25
a. Pair, #B19-B20, vert. tête-bêche 4.00 4.00

Surtax for Moroccan Red Crescent Society.

1971, May 10

25c+5c, Brooch. 40c+10c, Stomacher.

Granite Paper

B21 SP1 25c + 5c gray & multi .80 .65
B22 SP1 40c + 10c yel & multi 1.15 1.00
a. Pair, #B21-B22, vertically tête-bêche 2.50 2.50

Globe and Map of Palestine SP3

1971, Apr. 30 *Perf. 13*

B23 SP3 25c + 10c multi .60 .30

Palestine Week, May 3-8.

String Instrument and Bow — SP4

1971, June 28 Photo. *Perf. 12*

B24 SP4 40c + 10c multi .55 .40

Week of the Blind.

Mizmar (Double Flute) — SP5

1972, Mar. 31 Photo. *Perf. 13x13½*

B25 SP5 25c + 10c multi .55 .55

Week of the Blind.

Jewelry Type of 1966

Designs: 25c+5c, Jeweled bracelets. 70c+10c, Rectangular pendant with ball drop.

1972, May 8 Photo. *Perf. 11½*
Granite Paper

B26 SP1 25c + 5c brn & multi .80 .80
B27 SP1 70c + 10c dp grn & multi 1.25 1.25
a. Pair, #B26-B27, vert. tête-bêche 3.25 3.25

For overprints see Nos. 295-296.

Drums SP6

1973, Mar. 30 Photo. *Perf. 13x14*

B28 SP6 70c + 10c multi .65 .50

Week of the Blind.

Jewelry Type of 1966

25c+5c, Silver box pendant. 70c+10c, Bracelet.

1973, June 15 Photo. *Perf. 11½*

B29 SP1 25c + 5c bl & multi 1.00 .60
B30 SP1 70c + 10c org & multi 1.25 .95
a. Pair, #B29-B30, vert. tête-bêche 4.00 4.00

Moroccan Red Crescent Society. For overprints see Nos. 351-352.

Pistol — SP7

Erbab (Fiddle) — SP8

70c+10c, Decorated antique powder box.

1974, July 8 Photo. *Perf. 14x13½*

B31 SP7 25c + 5c multi .80 .80
B32 SP7 70c + 10c multi 1.25 1.25
a. Pair, #B31-B32, vert. tête-bêche 2.50 2.50

Moroccan Red Crescent Society.

1975, Jan. 10 Photo. *Perf. 13*

B33 SP8 70c + 10c multi .80 .50

Week of the Blind.

Jewelry Type of 1966

25c+5c, Silver pendant. 70c+10c, Earring.

1975, Mar. 13 Photo. *Perf. 13½*

B34 SP1 25c + 5c multi .80 .80
B35 SP1 70c + 10c multi 1.25 1.25
a. Pair, #B34-B35, vert. tête-bêche 2.50 2.50

Moroccan Red Crescent Society. For overprints see #386-387.

AIR POST STAMPS

Sultan's Star over Casablanca AP1

King Hassan II AP2

Unwmk.

1957, May 4 Engr. *Perf. 13*

C1 AP1 15fr car & brt grn 1.40 1.10
C2 AP1 25fr brt grnsh bl 2.10 1.40
C3 AP1 30fr red brn 3.00 1.90
Nos. C1-C3 (3) 6.50 4.40

Intl. Fair, Casablanca, May 4-19.

1962

C5 AP2 90c black .70 .20
C6 AP2 1d rose red 1.00 .25
C7 AP2 2d deep blue 1.15 .60
C8 AP2 3d dl bl grn 2.25 1.00
C9 AP2 5d purple 4.50 1.60
Nos. C5-C9 (5) 9.60 3.65

Meteorological Day Type of Regular Issue

1964, Mar. 23 Photo. *Perf. 11½*
Granite Paper

C10 A39 90c Anemometer & globe .95 .70

Intl. Fair, Casablanca, 20th Anniv. — AP3

1964, Apr. 30 Photo. *Perf. 12½*

C11 AP3 1d bl, bis & org .80 .70

Moroccan Pavilion and Unisphere AP4

1964, May 25 Unwmk. *Perf. 12½*

C12 AP4 1d dk grn, red & bl 1.10 .80

New York World's Fair, 1964-65.

Ramses II and UNESCO Emblem — AP5

Litho. & Engr.

1966, Oct. 3 *Perf. 12x11½*

C13 AP5 1d magenta, *yel* 1.25 .80

UNESCO, 20th anniv.

Jet Plane — AP6

Perf. 12½x13½

1966, Dec. 19 Photo.

C14 AP6 3d multi 4.50 2.00

Costume Type of Regular Issue

Design: 1d, Women from Ait Ouaouzguit.

1969, Jan. 21 Litho. *Perf. 12*

C15 A74 1d multi 2.40 1.25

Coin Type of Regular Issue, 1968

Coins: 1d, King Mohammed V, 1960. 5d, King Hassan II, 1965.

1969, Mar. 3 Photo. *Perf. 11½*
Granite Paper

C16 A73 1d brt bl, sil & blk 4.75 1.60
C17 A73 5d vio blk, sil & blk 9.50 6.00

King Hassan II — AP7

1983, Mar. 1 Photo. *Perf. 12*
Granite Paper

C18 AP7 1.40d multi .60 .20
C19 AP7 2d multi .65 .20
C20 AP7 3d multi .90 .30
C21 AP7 5d multi 1.40 .50
C22 AP7 10d multi 3.00 .95
Nos. C18-C22 (5) 6.55 2.15

No. C19 Overprinted

1987, Mar. 23 Photo. *Perf. 12*
Granite Paper

C23 AP7 2d multi .90 .65

1st World Congress of Friday Preachers, Al Joumouaa.

No. C18 Overprinted

1989, Mar. 27 Photo. *Perf. 12*
Granite Paper

C24 AP7 1.40d multi .50 .40

Maghreb Union, agreement between Morocco, Algeria and Tunisia.

No. C18 Surcharged

2000, July 6 Photo. *Perf. 12*
Granite Paper

C25 AP7 6.50d on 1.40d multi 1.25 .60

Intl. Colloquium on King Hassan II.

POSTAGE DUE STAMPS

D1

Oranges — D2

1965 Unwmk. Typo. *Perf. 14x13½*

J1	D1	5c green	13.00	1.10
J2	D1	10c bister brown	.65	.30
J3	D1	20c red	.65	.30
J4	D1	30c brown black	1.50	.65
		Nos. J1-J4 (4)	15.80	2.35

See French Morocco Nos. J27-J34, J46-J56.

1974-96 Photo. *Perf. 14*

J5	D2	5c shown	.20	.20
J6	D2	10c Cherries	.30	.20
J7	D2	20c Grapes	.40	.20
J8	D2	30c Peaches, horiz.	.55	.20
J9	D2	40c Grapes ('78)	.35	.20
J10	D2	60c Peaches, horiz. ('78)	.50	.20
J11	D2	80c Oranges ('78)	.70	.20
J12	D2	1d Apples ('86)	.40	.20
J13	D2	1.20d Cherries ('84)	.70	.20
J14	D2	1.60d Peaches ('85)	.70	.25
J15	D2	2d Strawberries ('86)	.75	.35

Litho.

J16	D2	5d like #J12 ('96)	1.25	1.00
		Nos. J5-J16 (12)	6.80	3.40

For surcharges see Nos. 322, 395.

Strawberries — D3

Strawberries — D3a

Grapes D4

Apples D5

Cherries — D6

2003 Photo. *Perf. 13x13½*

J17	D3	1.50d multi	.30	.20
J17A	D3a	1.50d multi	.35	.20
J18	D4	2d multi	.40	.20
J19	D5	5d multi	1.10	.55
J20	D6	2d multi	.45	.20
		Nos. J17-J20 (5)	2.60	1.35

Fruit Type of 1974-96

2005 ? Litho. *Perf. 14*

J21	D2	60c Peaches	.20	.20

No. J21 has a background of solid color. No. J10 has a background of dots. The text is thicker and heavier on No. J10 than on No. J21.

NORTHERN ZONE

100 Centimos = 1 Peseta

All Northern Zone issues except Nos. 21-22 were also sold imperforate in limited quantities.

Sultan Mohammed V — A1

Villa Sanjurjo Harbor A2

Designs: 25c, Polytechnic school. 50c, 10p, Institute of Culture, Tetuan.

Perf. 13x12½, 12½x13

1956, Aug. 23 Photo. Unwmk.

1	A1	10c deep rose	.20	.20
2	A2	15c yellow brn	.20	.20
3	A2	25c dk bl gray	.20	.20
4	A1	50c dark olive	.20	.20
5	A1	80c brt green	.20	.20
6	A2	2p brt red lil	2.00	1.25
7	A2	3p brt blue	5.00	2.25
8	A1	10p green	17.50	9.00
		Nos. 1-8 (8)	25.50	13.50

A3

Sultan Mohammed V — A4

1957, Mar. 2 *Perf. 13½x13*

9	A3	80c blue green	.55	.40
10	A3	1.50p gray olive	2.25	1.00
11	A3	3p deep rose	6.00	3.50
		Nos. 9-11 (3)	8.80	4.90

1st anniv. of independence. See Morocco #13-15.

1957 Engr. *Perf. 13*

12	A4	30c brt bl & indigo	.25	.20
13	A4	70c bis, brn & choc	.25	.20
14	A4	80c brt violet	.90	.20
15	A4	1.50p dp grn & mag	.25	.20
16	A4	3p green	.35	.25
17	A4	7p rose red	1.50	.40
		Nos. 12-17 (6)	3.50	1.45

Prince Moulay el Hassan — A5

King Mohammed V — A6

1957, July 15 Photo. *Perf. 13*

18	A5	80c blue	.35	.35
19	A5	1.50p green	2.10	1.00
20	A5	3p carmine rose	6.75	4.00
		Nos. 18-20 (3)	9.20	5.35

Exist imperf. Value, set $250.

Nos. 13 and 15 Surcharged in Carmine or Black

1957 Engr.

21	A4	15c on 70c (C)	.30	.25
22	A4	1.20p on 1.50p (Bk)	.75	.25

1957, Nov. Photo. *Perf. 12½*

23	A6	1.20p blk & brt grn	.65	.30
24	A6	1.80p blk & rose red	.65	.40
25	A6	3p black & violet	2.00	.60
		Nos. 23-25 (3)	3.30	1.30

Enthronement of Mohammed V, 30th anniv.

NORTHERN ZONE AIR POST STAMPS

Plane over Lau Dam AP1

1.40p, 4.80p, Plane over Nekor bridge.

Perf. 12½x13

1956, Dec. 17 Photo. Unwmk.

C1	AP1	25c rose violet	.25	.20
C2	AP1	1.40p lilac rose	.25	.20
C3	AP1	3.40p org vermilion	1.25	.75
C4	AP1	4.80p dull violet	1.75	1.10
		Nos. C1-C4 (4)	3.50	2.25

MOZAMBIQUE

mō-zəm-'bēk

LOCATION — Southeastern Africa, bordering on the Mozambique Channel
GOVT. — Republic
AREA — 308,642 sq. mi.
POP. — 16,542,800 (1997)
CAPITAL — Maputo

Formerly a Portuguese colony, Mozambique, or Portuguese East Africa, was divided into eight districts: Lourenco Marques, Inhambane, Quelimane, Tete, Mozambique, Zambezia, Nyassa and the Manica and Sofala region formerly administered by the Mozambique Company. At various times the districts issued their own stamps which were eventually replaced by those inscribed "Mocambique."

Mozambique achieved independence June 25, 1975, taking the name People's Republic of Mozambique.

1000 Reis = 1 Milreis
100 Centavos = 1 Escudo (1913)
100 Centavos = 1 Metical (1980)

Catalogue values for unused stamps in this country are for Never Hinged items, beginning with Scott 330 in the regular postage section, Scott C29 in the airpost section, Scott J51 in the postage due section, and Scott RA55 in the postal tax section.

Portuguese Crown — A1

King Luiz — A2

Perf. 12½, 13½

1877-85 Typo. Unwmk.

1	A1	5r black	2.00	1.00
a.		Perf. 13½	3.00	1.60
2	A1	10r yellow	15.00	4.50
3	A1	10r green ('81)	1.50	.60
4	A1	20r bister	1.50	.75
a.		Perf. 13½	3.00	2.00
5	A1	20r rose ('85)	275.00	*125.00*
6	A1	25r rose	1.00	.35
a.		Perf. 13½	6.75	1.60
7	A1	25r violet ('85)	3.00	2.00
8	A1	40r blue	25.00	15.00
9	A1	40r yel buff ('81)	2.00	1.60
a.		Perf. 12½	3.50	3.00
10	A1	50r green	60.00	20.00
a.		Perf. 13½	125.00	60.00
11	A1	50r blue ('81)	.75	.40
12	A1	100r lilac	1.00	.50
13	A1	200r orange	2.00	1.40
a.		Perf. 12½	5.25	4.50
14	A1	300r chocolate	2.25	2.00
		Nos. 1-4,6-14 (13)	117.00	50.10

The reprints of the 1877-85 issues are printed on a smooth white chalky paper, ungummed, with rough perforation 13½, also on thin white paper, with shiny white gum and clean-cut perforation 13½.

Typographed and Embossed

1886 *Perf. 12½*

15	A2	5r black	1.50	.60
16	A2	10r green	1.50	.70
17	A2	20r rose	2.00	1.50
18	A2	25r dull lilac	9.00	1.40
19	A2	40r chocolate	1.75	.85
20	A2	50r blue	2.25	.50
21	A2	100r yellow brn	2.50	.50
22	A2	200r gray violet	4.25	1.75
23	A2	300r orange	4.50	2.00
		Nos. 15-23 (9)	29.25	9.80

Perf. 13½

15a	A2	5r	4.00	2.75
16a	A2	10r	4.25	2.75
17a	A2	20r	13.00	6.00
18a	A2	25r	13.00	6.00
19a	A2	40r	15.00	9.50
20a	A2	50r	16.00	4.50
22a	A2	200r	15.00	12.50
		Nos. 15a-22a (7)	80.25	44.00

Nos. 15, 18, 19, 20, 21 and 23 have been reprinted. The reprints have shiny white gum and clean-cut perforation 13½. Many of the colors are paler than those of the originals.

For surcharges and overprints see Nos. 23A, 36-44, 46-48, 72-80, 192, P1-P5.

PROVISORIO

No. 19 Surcharged in Black

5 5

1893, Jan. *Perf. 12½*

Without Gum

23A	A2	5r on 40r choc	125.00	50.00

There are three varieties of No. 23A:

I — "PROVISORIO" 19mm long, numerals 4½mm high.

II — "PROVISORIO" 19½mm long, numerals 5mm high.

III — "PROVISORIO" 19½mm long, numerals of both sizes.

King Carlos I — A3

1894 Typo. *Perf. 11½, 12½*

24	A3	5r yellow	.50	.45
25	A3	10r red lilac	.50	.35
26	A3	15r red brown	1.25	.75
27	A3	20r gray lilac	1.25	.50
28	A3	25r blue green	1.25	.20
29	A3	50r lt blue	5.00	1.50
a.		Perf. 12½	7.50	2.00

No.	Type	Description	Unused	Used
30	A3	75r rose	1.75	1.25
31	A3	80r yellow grn	2.00	1.00
32	A3	100r brown, *buff*	1.75	1.25
33	A3	150r car, *rose*	8.00	4.00
a.		Perf. 11½		
34	A3	200r dk blue, *blue*	5.00	3.00
35	A3	300r dk blue, *salmon*	7.00	3.00
		Nos. 24-35 (12)	35.25	17.25

Nos. 28 and 31-33 have been reprinted with shiny white gum and clean-cut perf. 13½.

For surcharges and overprints see Nos. 45, 81-92, 193-198, 201-205, 226-228, 238-239.

Stamps of 1886 Overprinted in Red or Black

1895, July 1 ***Perf. 12½***

Without Gum

No.	Type	Description	Unused	Used
36	A2	5r black (R)	11.00	5.50
37	A2	10r green	12.50	6.50
38	A2	20r rose	14.00	6.00
39	A2	25r violet	16.00	6.50
a.		Double overprint		
40	A2	40r chocolate	17.50	7.50
41	A2	50r blue	17.50	7.50
a.		Perf. 13½	80.00	55.00
42	A2	100r yellow brown	17.50	8.25
43	A2	200r gray violet	27.50	13.00
a.		Perf. 13½	100.00	65.00
44	A2	300r orange	37.50	17.50
		Nos. 36-44 (9)	171.00	78.25

Birth of Saint Anthony of Padua, 7th cent.

No. 35 Surcharged in Black

50 réis

1897, Jan. 2 ***Perf. 12½***

Without Gum

No.	Type	Description	Unused	Used
45	A3	50r on 300r dk bl, *sal*	150.00	40.00

Nos. 17, 19 Surcharged

MOCAMBIQUE 2 1/2 REIS

a

MOCAMBIQUE 2½ RÉIS

b

c

1898

Without Gum

No.	Type	Description	Unused	Used
46	A2 (a)	2½r on 20r rose	42.50	11.00
47	A2 (b)	2½r on 20r rose	27.50	10.00
a.		Inverted surcharge	55.00	45.00
48	A2 (c)	5r on 40r choc	35.00	10.00
a.		Inverted surcharge	90.00	45.00
		Nos. 46-48 (3)	105.00	31.00

King Carlos I — A4

1898-1903 **Typo.** ***Perf. 11½***

Name and Value in Black except 500r

No.	Type	Description	Unused	Used
49	A4	2½r gray	.20	.20
50	A4	5r orange	.20	.20
51	A4	10r lt green	.25	.20
52	A4	15r brown	3.00	1.50
53	A4	15r gray grn ('03)	.70	.55
54	A4	20r gray violet	.85	.40
55	A4	25r sea green	.85	.40
56	A4	25r carmine ('03)	.70	.30
57	A4	50r dark blue	1.50	.50
58	A4	50r brown ('03)	2.00	1.50
59	A4	65r dull blue ('03)	15.00	12.00
60	A4	75r rose	7.00	2.75
61	A4	75r red lilac ('03)	3.00	1.75
62	A4	80r violet	6.00	3.25
63	A4	100r dk blue, *bl*	2.00	1.00
64	A4	115r org brn, *pink* ('03)	10.00	5.00
65	A4	130r brown, *straw* ('03)	10.00	5.00
66	A4	150r brown, *straw*	10.00	2.75
67	A4	200r red lilac, *pnksh*	2.00	1.40
68	A4	300r dk blue, *rose*	8.00	3.25
69	A4	400r dl bl, *straw* ('03)	13.00	7.50
70	A4	500r blk & red, *bl* ('01)	20.00	8.00
71	A4	700r vio, *yelsh* ('01)	25.00	9.00
		Nos. 49-71 (23)	141.25	68.40

For overprints and surcharges see Nos. 94-113, 200, 207-220.

Stamps of 1886-94 Surcharged

1902 ***Perf. 12½, 13½***

On Stamps of 1886

Red Surcharge

No.	Type	Description	Unused	Used
72	A2	115r on 5r blk	5.00	2.00

Black Surcharge

No.	Type	Description	Unused	Used
73	A2	65r on 20r rose	5.00	2.50
a.		Double surcharge	50.00	50.00
74	A2	65r on 40r choc	6.00	4.00
75	A2	65r on 200r violet	5.00	1.75
76	A2	115r on 50r blue	2.00	1.00
77	A2	130r on 25r red vio	3.00	.90
78	A2	130r on 300r orange	3.00	.90
79	A2	400r on 10r green	7.50	3.25
80	A2	400r on 100r yel brn	40.00	25.00
		Nos. 72-80 (9)	76.50	41.30

The reprints of Nos. 74, 75, 76, 77, 79 and 80 have shiny white gum and clean-cut perforation 13½.

On Stamps of 1894

Perf. 11½

No.	Type	Description	Unused	Used
81	A3	65r on 10r red lil	3.50	2.00
82	A3	65r on 15r red brn	3.50	2.00
a.		Pair, one without surcharge		
83	A3	65r on 20r gray lil	3.75	2.00
84	A3	115r on 5r yel	4.00	2.00
a.		Inverted surcharge		
85	A3	115r on 25r bl grn	3.50	2.00
86	A3	130r on 75r rose	4.00	2.25
87	A3	130r on 100r brn, *buff*	6.00	5.00
88	A3	130r on 150r car, *rose*	4.00	2.00
89	A3	130r on 200r bl, *bl*	5.00	3.50
90	A3	400r on 50r lt bl	1.00	1.40
91	A3	400r on 80r yel grn	1.00	1.40
92	A3	400r on 300r bl, *sal*	1.00	1.40

On Newspaper Stamp of 1893

Perf. 13½

No.	Type	Description	Unused	Used
93	N3	115r on 2½r brn	2.00	2.25
		Nos. 81-93 (13)	42.25	29.20

Reprints of No. 87 have shiny white gum and clean-cut perforation 13½.

Overprinted in Black

On Stamps of 1898

Perf. 11½

No.	Type	Description	Unused	Used
94	A4	15r brown	2.00	.85
95	A4	25r sea green	2.50	.85
96	A4	50r blue	3.00	1.75
97	A4	75r rose	5.00	2.00
		Nos. 94-97 (4)	12.50	5.45

No. 59 Surcharged in Black

1905

No.	Type	Description	Unused	Used
98	A4	50r on 65r dull blue	3.00	2.00

Stamps of 1898-1903 Overprinted in Carmine or Green

1911

No.	Type	Description	Unused	Used
99	A4	2½r gray	.30	.20
a.		Inverted overprint	15.00	15.00
100	A4	5r orange	.30	.20
101	A4	10r lt green	2.00	.50
102	A4	15r gray grn	.30	.20
103	A4	20r gray vio	2.00	.40
104	A4	25r carmine (G)	.30	.20
a.		25r gray violet (error)		
105	A4	50r brown	.50	.20
106	A4	75r red lilac	1.00	.50
107	A4	100r dk blue, *bl*	1.00	.50
108	A4	115r org brn, *pink*	1.50	.85
109	A4	130r brown, *straw*	1.50	.85
a.		Double overprint		
110	A4	200r red lil, *pnksh*	3.00	.70
111	A4	400r dull bl, *straw*	3.50	.85
112	A4	500r blk & red, *bl*	4.00	.85
113	A4	700r vio, *straw*	4.50	.85
		Nos. 99-113 (15)	25.70	7.85

King Manoel — A5

Overprinted in Carmine or Green

1912 ***Perf. 11½x12***

No.	Type	Description	Unused	Used
114	A5	2½r violet	.20	.20
115	A5	5r black	.20	.20
116	A5	10r gray grn	.20	.20
117	A5	20r carmine (G)	.55	.40
118	A5	25r vio brn	.20	.20
119	A5	50r dp blue	.50	.35
120	A5	75r bis brn	.50	.35
121	A5	100r brn, *lt grn*	.50	.35
122	A5	200r dk grn, *salmon*	1.00	.70
123	A5	300r black, *azure*	1.00	.70

Perf. 14x15

No.	Type	Description	Unused	Used
124	A5	500r ol grn & vio brn	2.00	1.25
		Nos. 114-124 (11)	6.85	4.90

Vasco da Gama Issue of Various Portuguese Colonies Common Design Types Surcharged

1913

On Stamps of Macao

No.	Type	Description	Unused	Used
125	CD20	¼c on ½a bl grn	1.50	1.50
126	CD21	½c on 1a red	1.50	1.50
127	CD22	1c on 2a red vio	1.50	1.50
128	CD23	2½c on 4a yel grn	1.50	1.50
a.		Double surcharge	50.00	50.00
129	CD24	5c on 8a dk bl	2.50	2.50
130	CD25	7½c on 12a vio brn	2.00	2.00
131	CD26	10c on 16a bis brn	1.75	1.50
132	CD27	15c on 24a bis	1.50	1.50
		Nos. 125-132 (8)	13.75	13.50

On Stamps of Portuguese Africa

No.	Type	Description	Unused	Used
133	CD20	¼c on 2½r bl grn	1.25	1.25
134	CD21	½c on 5r red	1.25	1.25
135	CD22	1c on 10r red vio	1.25	1.25
a.		Inverted surcharge	45.00	45.00
136	CD23	2½c on 25r yel grn	1.25	1.25
137	CD24	5c on 50r dk bl	1.25	1.25
138	CD25	7½c on 75r vio brn	1.75	1.75
139	CD26	10c on 100r bis brn	1.50	1.50
140	CD27	15c on 150r bis	1.50	1.50
		Nos. 133-140 (8)	11.00	11.00

On Stamps of Timor

No.	Type	Description	Unused	Used
141	CD20	¼c on ½a bl grn	1.50	1.50
142	CD21	½c on 1a red	1.50	1.50
143	CD22	1c on 2a red vio	1.50	1.50
144	CD23	2½c on 4a yel grn	1.50	1.50
145	CD24	5c on 8a dk bl	1.50	1.50
146	CD25	7½c on 12a vio brn	3.00	3.00
147	CD26	10c on 16a bis brn	1.50	1.50
148	CD27	15c on 24a bis	2.00	2.00
		Nos. 141-148 (8)	14.00	14.00
		Nos. 125-148 (24)	38.75	38.50

Ceres — A6

1914-26 **Typo.** ***Perf. 15x14, 12x11½***

Name and Value in Black

No.	Type	Description	Unused	Used
149	A6	¼c olive brown	.20	.20
a.		Name and value printed twice	12.00	
b.		Name and value printed triple	—	
150	A6	½c black	.20	.20
151	A6	1c blue green	.20	.20
a.		Name and value printed twice	16.00	
152	A6	1½c lilac brown	.20	.20
153	A6	2c carmine	.20	.20
154	A6	2c gray ('26)	.20	.20
155	A6	2½c lt vio	.20	.20
156	A6	3c org ('21)	.20	.20
a.		Name and value printed twice	—	
157	A6	4c pale rose ('21)	.20	.20
a.		Name and value printed twice	16.00	
b.		Value omitted	15.00	
158	A6	4½c gray ('21)	.20	.20
159	A6	5c deep blue	.20	.20
160	A6	6c lilac ('21)	.20	.20
a.		Name and value printed twice		
161	A6	7c ultra ('21)	.20	.20
162	A6	7½c yel brn	.20	.20
163	A6	8c slate	.20	.20
164	A6	10c org brn	.20	.20
165	A6	12c gray brn ('21)	.25	.20
166	A6	12c blue grn ('22)	.20	.20
167	A6	15c plum	1.40	1.00
a.		Perf. 12x11½ ('30)	.65	.35
168	A6	15c brn rose ('22)	.20	.20
169	A6	20c yel grn	.20	.20
170	A6	24c ultra ('26)	4.50	2.00
171	A6	25c choc ('26)	1.50	1.25
172	A6	30c brown, *grn*	1.50	1.10
173	A6	30c deep green ('21)	1.00	.20
174	A6	30c gray bl, *pink* ('21)	1.50	1.25
175	A6	40c brn, *pink*	1.25	.85
176	A6	40c turq blue ('22)	1.00	.30
177	A6	50c org, *salmon*	2.75	3.00
178	A6	50c lt violet ('26)	.50	.20
179	A6	60c red brn, *pink* ('21)	1.00	.85
180	A6	60c dk blue ('22)	1.00	.30
181	A6	60c rose ('26)	1.10	.25
182	A6	80c dk brn, *bl* ('21)	1.10	.85
183	A6	80c brt rose ('22)	1.00	.25
184	A6	1e grn, *bl*, perf. 12x11½ ('21)	1.40	.60
a.		Perf. 15x14	6.00	2.00
185	A6	1e rose ('21)	1.60	.50
186	A6	1e blue ('26)	1.60	.65
187	A6	2e brt vio, *pink* ('21)	1.40	.60
188	A6	2e dk violet ('22)	1.00	.35
189	A6	5e buff ('26)	7.25	2.50
190	A6	10e pink ('26)	15.00	5.00
191	A6	20e pale turq ('26)	40.00	17.50
		Nos. 149-191 (43)	95.40	45.35

For surcharges see Nos. 232-234, 236-237, 249-250, J46-50.

Stamps of 1902 Overprinted Locally in Carmine

1915

On Provisional Stamps of 1902

No.	Type	Description	Unused	Used
192	A2	115r on 5r black	150.00	100.00
193	A3	115r on 5r yellow	1.25	.75
194	A3	115r on 25r bl grn	1.25	.75
195	A3	130r on 75r rose	1.25	.75
196	A3	130r on 100r brn, *buff*	1.25	.75
197	A3	130r on 150r car, *rose*	1.25	.75
198	A3	130r on 200r bl, *bl*	1.25	.75
199	N3	115r on 2½r brn	.80	.40

On No. 97

No.	Type	Description	Unused	Used
200	A4	75r rose	1.50	1.10
		Nos. 192-200 (9)	159.80	106.00

Stamps of 1902-05 Overprinted in Carmine

1915

On Provisional Stamps of 1902

No.	Type	Description	Unused	Used
201	A3	115r on 5r yellow	.80	.50
202	A3	115r on 25r bl grn	.80	.55
203	A3	130r on 75r rose	.80	.55
204	A3	130r on 150r car, *rose*	1.00	.50
205	A3	130r on 200r bl, *bl*	1.00	.50
206	N3	115r on 2½r brn	1.00	.50

On No. 96

No.	Type	Description	Unused	Used
207	A4	50r blue	1.00	.50

On No. 98

No.	Type	Description	Unused	Used
208	A4	50r on 65r dull blue	1.00	.50
		Nos. 201-208 (8)	7.40	4.10

Stamps of 1898-1903 Overprinted Locally in Carmine Like Nos. 192-200

1917

No.	Type	Description	Unused	Used
209	A4	2½r gray	20.00	17.50
210	A4	15r gray grn	15.00	12.50
211	A4	20r gray vio	15.00	12.50
212	A4	50r brown	14.00	11.00
213	A4	75r red lilac	32.50	25.00
214	A4	100r blue, *bl*	6.00	2.50
215	A4	115r org brn, *pink*	8.00	3.00
216	A4	130r brown, *straw*	7.50	3.00
217	A4	200r red lil, *pnksh*	7.50	2.50
218	A4	400r dull bl, *straw*	7.50	3.00
219	A4	500r blk & red, *bl*	7.00	2.50
220	A4	700r vio, *yelsh*	15.00	6.00
		Nos. 209-220 (12)	155.00	101.00

War Tax Stamps of 1916-18 Surcharged

1918 ***Rouletted 7***

No.	Type	Description	Unused	Used
221	WT2	2½c on 5c rose	2.50	1.50

Perf. 11, 12

No.	Type	Description	Unused	Used
222	WT2	2½c on 5c red	1.10	.70
a.		"PETRIA"	2.00	2.00
b.		"PEPUBLICA"	2.00	2.00
c.		"1910" for "1916"	9.00	4.00

War Tax Stamps of 1916-18 Surcharged

1919 ***Perf. 11***

No.	Type	Description	Unused	Used
224	WT1	1c on 1c gray grn	.75	.40
a.		"PEPUBLICA"	4.75	4.00
b.		Rouletted 7	*300.00*	*100.00*

Perf. 12

No.	Type	Description	Unused	Used
225	WT2	1½c on 5c red	.40	.35
a.		"PETRIA"	3.00	2.00
b.		"PEPUBLICA"	3.00	2.50
c.		"1910" for "1916"	7.50	3.75

Stamps of 1902 Overprinted Locally in Carmine Like Nos. 192-200

1920

No.	Type	Description	Unused	Used
226	A3	400r on 50r lt blue	1.25	1.25
227	A3	400r on 80r yel grn	1.25	1.25
228	A3	400r on 300r bl, *sal*	1.25	1.25
		Nos. 226-228 (3)	3.75	3.75

War Tax Stamp of 1918 Surcharged in Green

1920 ***Perf. 12***

No.	Type	Description	Unused	Used
229	WT2	6c on 5c red	.60	.48
a.		"1910" for "1916"	8.00	5.00
b.		"PETRIA"	2.50	2.00
c.		"PEPUBLICA"	2.50	2.00

Lourenco Marques Nos. 117, 119 Surcharged in Red or Bue

1921 ***Perf. 15x14***

No.	Type	Description	Unused	Used
230	A4	10c on ½c blk (R)	.75	.40
231	A4	30c on 1½c brn (Bl)	1.25	.70

Same Surcharge on Mozambique Nos. 150, 152, 155 in Red, Blue or Green

No.	Type	Description	Unused	Used
232	A6	10c on ½c blk (R)	1.00	.85
233	A6	30c on 1½c brn (Bl)	1.10	.70
234	A6	60c on 2½c vio (G)	1.50	.80
		Nos. 230-234 (5)	5.60	3.45

War Tax Stamp of 1918 Surcharged in Green

1921 ***Perf. 12***

No.	Type	Description	Unused	Used
235	WT2	2e on 5c red	1.00	.50
a.		"PETRIA"	2.50	2.25
b.		"PEPUBLICA"	4.25	2.50
c.		"1910" for "1916"	8.00	6.50

No. 157 Surcharged

1923 ***Perf. 12x11½***

No.	Type	Description	Unused	Used
236	A6	50c on 4c pale rose	1.00	.55

No. 183 Overprinted in Green

1924

No.	Type	Description	Unused	Used
237	A6	80c bright rose	1.00	.60

4th centenary of the death of Vasco da Gama.

Nos. 90 and 91 Surcharged

1925 ***Perf. 11½***

No.	Type	Description	Unused	Used
238	A3	40c on 400r on 50r	.70	.70
239	A3	40c on 400r on 80r	.60	.50
a.		"a" omitted	42.50	42.50

Postage Due Stamp of 1917 Overprinted in Black and Bars in Red

1929, Jan. ***Perf. 12***

No.	Type	Description	Unused	Used
247	D1	50c gray	.85	.55

No. 188 Surcharged

1931 ***Perf. 11½***

No.	Type	Description	Unused	Used
249	A6	70c on 2e dk vio	1.00	.50
250	A6	1.40e on 2e dk vio	1.50	.50

"Portugal" Holding Volume of the "Lusiads" — A7

Wmk. Maltese Cross (232)

1933, July 13 **Typo.** ***Perf. 14***

Value in Red or Black

No.	Type	Description	Unused	Used
251	A7	1c bister brn (R)	.20	.20
252	A7	5c black brn	.20	.20
253	A7	10c dp violet	.20	.20
254	A7	15c black (R)	.20	.20
255	A7	20c light gray	.20	.20
256	A7	30c blue green	.20	.20
257	A7	40c orange red	.20	.20
258	A7	45c brt blue	.40	.20
259	A7	50c dk brown	.30	.20
260	A7	60c olive grn	.25	.20
261	A7	70c orange brn	.20	.20
262	A7	80c emerald	.20	.20
263	A7	85c deep rose	1.00	.50
264	A7	1e red brown	.75	.25
265	A7	1.40e dk blue (R)	7.00	1.10
266	A7	2e dk violet	2.00	.35
267	A7	5e apple green	3.00	.50
268	A7	10e olive bister	7.00	1.00
269	A7	20e orange	22.50	2.00
		Nos. 251-269 (19)	46.00	8.10

See Nos. 298-299.

Common Design Types pictured following the introduction.

Common Design Types

Perf. 13½x13

1938, Aug. **Engr.** **Unwmk.**

Name and Value in Black

No.	Type	Description	Unused	Used
270	CD34	1c gray green	.20	.20
271	CD34	5c orange brn	.20	.20
272	CD34	10c dk carmine	.20	.20
273	CD34	15c dk vio brn	.20	.20
274	CD34	20c slate	.20	.20
275	CD35	30c rose vio	.20	.20
276	CD35	35c brt green	.30	.20
277	CD35	40c brown	.40	.20
278	CD35	50c brt red vio	.40	.20
279	CD36	60c gray black	.50	.20
280	CD36	70c brown vio	.50	.20
281	CD36	80c orange	.75	.20
282	CD36	1e red	.70	.20
283	CD37	1.75e blue	1.75	.30
284	CD37	2e brown car	1.50	.30
285	CD37	5e olive green	3.50	.50
286	CD38	10e blue vio	9.00	1.00
287	CD38	20e red brown	22.50	1.40
		Nos. 270-287 (18)	43.00	6.10

For surcharges see Nos. 297, 301.

No. 258 Surcharged in Black

1938, Jan. 16 **Wmk. 232** ***Perf. 14***

No.	Type	Description	Unused	Used
288	A7	40c on 45c brt blue	2.50	1.40

Map of Africa — A7a

Perf. 11½x12

1939, July 17 **Litho.** **Unwmk.**

No.	Type	Description	Unused	Used
289	A7a	80c vio, *pale rose*	1.50	1.25
290	A7a	1.75e bl, *pale bl*	4.00	2.75
291	A7a	3e grn, *yel grn*	6.00	4.00
292	A7a	20e brn, *buff*	*30.00*	*50.00*
		Nos. 289-292 (4)	*41.50*	*58.00*

Presidential visit.

New Cathedral, Lourenço Marques — A8

Railroad Station A9

Municipal Hall — A10

1944, Dec. Litho. *Perf. 11½*

293	A8	50c	dk brown	.70	.40
294	A8	50c	dk green	.70	.40
295	A9	1.75e	ultra	4.00	.85
296	A10	20e	dk gray	8.50	.85
		Nos. 293-296 (4)		13.90	2.50

4th cent. of the founding of Lourenço Marques. See No. 302. For surcharge see No. 300.

No. 283 Surcharged in Carmine

1946 Engr. *Perf. 13½x13*

297 CD37 60c on 1.75e blue 1.00 .40

Lusiads Type of 1933

1947 Wmk. 232 Typo. *Perf. 14*

Value in Black

298	A7	35c	yellow grn	4.00	2.00
299	A7	1.75e	deep blue	4.50	2.00

No. 296 Surcharged in Pink

1946 Unwmk. *Perf. 11½*

300 A10 2e on 20e dk gray 1.40 .40

No. 273 Surcharged with New Value and Wavy Lines

Perf. 13½x13

301 CD34 10c on 15c dk vio brn .70 .40
a. Inverted surcharge 30.00

Cathedral Type of 1944
Commemorative Inscription Omitted

1948 Litho. *Perf. 11½*

302 A8 4.50e brt vermilion 1.75 .40

Antonio Enes — A11

1948, Oct. 4 *Perf. 14*

303	A11	50c	black & cream	1.00	.35
304	A11	5e	vio brn & cream	3.00	.85

Birth centenary of Antonio Enes.

Gogogo Peak — A12

Zambezi River Bridge — A13

Zumbo River A14

Waterfall at Nhanhangare A15

Lourenço Marques A16

Plantation, Baixa Zambezia A17

Pungwe River at Beira — A18

Lourenço Marques A19

Polana Beach — A20

Malema River — A21

Perf. 13½x13, 13x13½

1948-49 Typo. Unwmk.

305	A12	5c	orange brn	.25	*.50*
306	A13	10c	violet brn	.25	.20
307	A14	20c	dk brown	.25	.20
308	A12	30c	plum	.25	.20
309	A14	40c	dull green	.25	.20
310	A16	50c	slate	.25	.20
311	A15	60c	brown car	.25	.20
312	A16	80c	violet blk	.25	.20
313	A17	1e	carmine	.35	.20
314	A13	1.20e	slate gray	.35	.20
315	A18	1.50e	dk purple	.50	.20
316	A20	1.75e	dk blue ('49)	.75	.25
317	A18	2e	brown	.50	.20
318	A19	2.50e	dk slate ('49)	1.50	.20
319	A20	3e	gray ol ('49)	1.00	.20
320	A15	3.50e	olive gray	1.10	.20
321	A17	5e	blue grn	1.10	.20
322	A19	10e	choc ('49)	2.50	.35
323	A21	15e	dp carmine ('49)	7.25	1.75
324	A21	20e	orange ('49)	12.00	1.75
		Nos. 305-324 (20)		30.90	7.60

On No. 320 the "$" is reversed.

Lady of Fatima Issue

Common Design Type

1948, Oct. Litho. *Perf. 14½*

325	CD40	50c	blue	1.00	.50
326	CD40	1.20e	red violet	3.00	1.00
327	CD40	4.50e	emerald	6.00	1.50
328	CD40	20e	chocolate	10.00	1.50
		Nos. 325-328 (4)		20.00	4.50

Symbols of the UPU — A21a

1949, Apr. 11 *Perf. 14*

329 A21a 4.50e ultra & pale gray 1.00 .50

75th anniversary of UPU.

Catalogue values for unused stamps in this section, from this point to the end of the section, are for Never Hinged items.

Holy Year Issue

Common Design Types

1950, May *Perf. 13x13½*

330	CD41	1.50e	red orange	.70	.25
331	CD42	3e	brt blue	.75	.30

Spotted Triggerfish A22

Pennant Coral Fish — A22a

Fish: 10c, Golden butterflyfish. 15c, Orange butterflyfish. 20c, Lionfish. 30c, Sharpnose puffer. 40c, Porky filefish. 50c, Dark brown surgeonfish. 1.50e Rainbow wrasse. 2e, Orange-spotted gray-skin. 2.50e, Kasmir snapper. 3e, Convict fish. 3.50e, Stellar triggerfish. 4e, Cornetfish. 4.50e, Vagabond butterflyfish. 5e, Mail-cheeked fish. 6e, Pinnate batfish. 8e, Moorish idol. 9e, Triangulate boxfish. 10e, Flying gurnard. 15e, Redtooth triggerfish. 20e, Striped triggerfish. 30e, Horned cowfish. 50e, Spotted cowfish.

Photogravure and Lithographed

1951 Unwmk. *Perf. 14x14½*

Fish in Natural Colors

332	A22	5c	dp yellow	.30	*.75*
333	A22	10c	lt blue	.20	*.50*
334	A22	15c	yellow	.80	*1.00*
335	A22	20c	pale olive	.40	.20
336	A22	30c	gray	.40	.20
337	A22	40c	pale green	.30	.20
338	A22	50c	pale buff	.30	.20
339	A22a	1e	aqua	.30	.20
340	A22	1.50e	olive	.25	.20
341	A22	2e	blue	.30	.20
342	A22	2.50e	brnsh lilac	.60	.20
343	A22	3e	aqua	.60	.20
344	A22	3.50e	olive grn	.60	.20
345	A22	4e	blue gray	1.40	1.00
346	A22	4.50e	green	.90	2.00
347	A22	5e	buff	.90	.20
348	A22a	6e	salmon pink	.90	.20
349	A22a	8e	gray blue	.90	.25
350	A22	9e	lilac rose	3.75	.30
351	A22	10e	gray lilac	13.50	2.00
352	A22	15e	gray	27.50	5.75
353	A22	20e	lemon	22.25	3.75
354	A22	30e	yellow grn	22.50	4.25
355	A22	50e	gray vio	32.50	6.75
		Nos. 332-355 (24)		132.35	30.70

Holy Year Extension Issue

Common Design Type

1951, Oct. Litho. *Perf. 14*

356 CD43 5e carmine & rose + label 2.25 1.00

No. 356 without label attached sells for less.

Victor Cordon — A23

Plane and Ship — A24

1951, Oct. *Perf. 11½*

357	A23	1e	dk brown	1.00	.35
358	A23	5e	black & slate	2.00	1.00

Centenary of the birth of Victor Cordon, explorer.

Medical Congress Issue

Common Design Type

Design: Miguel Bombarda Hospital.

1952, June 19 Litho. *Perf. 13½*

359 CD44 3e dk bl & brn buff .85 .35

1952, Sept. 15 Unwmk.

360 A24 1.50e multi .50 .35

4th African Tourism Congress.

Missionary A25

Papilio Demodocus A26

1953

361	A25	10c	red brn & pale vio	.20	.20
362	A25	1e	red brn & pale yel grn	.50	.20
363	A25	5e	blk & lt bl	1.40	.35
		Nos. 361-363 (3)		2.10	.75

Exhibition of Sacred Missionary Art, held at Lisbon in 1951.

Canceled to Order

Certain issues, including Nos. 364-383, were canceled to order under Republican administration.

Photogravure and Lithographed

1953, May 28 *Perf. 13x14*

Various Butterflies and Moths in Natural Colors

364	A26	10c	lt blue	.20	.20
365	A26	15c	cream	.20	.20
366	A26	20c	yellow grn	.20	.20
367	A26	30c	lt violet	.20	.20
368	A26	40c	brown	.20	.20
369	A26	50c	bluish gray	.20	.20
370	A26	80c	brt blue	.20	.20
371	A26	1e	gray bl	.20	.20
372	A26	1.50e	ocher	.25	.20
373	A26	2e	orange brn	3.50	.50
374	A26	2.30e	blue	3.50	.35
375	A26	2.50e	citron	5.25	.35
376	A26	3e	lilac rose	1.90	.20
377	A26	4e	light blue	.35	.20
378	A26	4.50e	orange	.35	.20
379	A26	5e	green	.35	.20
380	A26	6e	pale vio	.50	.20
381	A26	7.50e	buff	4.00	.30
382	A26	10e	pink	6.25	.75
383	A26	20e	grnsh gray	8.00	.70
		Nos. 364-383 (20)		35.80	5.75

Value of set canceled-to-order, $1.00. For overprints see Nos. 517, 527.

Stamps of Portugal and Mozambique A27

Stamp of Portugal and Arms of Colonies A27a

1953, July 23 Litho. Perf. 14

384 A27 1e multicolored .55 .40
385 A27 3e multicolored 1.90 .70

Issued in connection with the Lourenço Marques philatelic exhibition, July 1953.

Stamp Centenary Issue

1953 Photo. Perf. 13

386 A27a 50c multicolored .55 .40

Map — A28

1954, Oct. 15 Litho.

Color of Colony

387 A28 10c pale rose lilac .20 .20
388 A28 20c pale yellow .20 .20
389 A28 50c lilac .20 .20
390 A28 1e orange yel .20 .20
391 A28 2.30e white .45 .20
392 A28 4e pale salmon .60 .20
393 A28 10e lt green 1.90 .20
394 A28 20e brown buff 2.50 .35
Nos. 387-394 (8) 6.25 1.75

For overprints see Nos. 516, 530.

Sao Paulo Issue

Common Design Type

1954, July 2

395 CD46 3.50e dk gray, cream & ol .35 .30

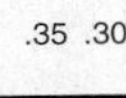

Arms of Beira A29

Mousinho de Albuquerque A30

Paper with network as in parenthesis

1954, Dec. 1 Perf. 13x13½

Arms in Silver, Gold, Red and Pale Green

396 A29 1.50e dk bl *(bl)* .35 .30
397 A29 3.50e brn *(buff)* .75 .35

Issued to publicize the first philatelic exhibition of Manica and Sofala.

1955, Feb. 1 Litho. Perf. 11½x12

2.50e, Statue of Mousinho de Albuquerque.

398 A30 1e gray, blk & buff .75 .35
399 A30 2.50e ol bis, blk & bl 1.25 .50

100th anniversary of the birth of Mousinho de Albuquerque, statesman.

A31

A32

Eight Races Holding Arms of Portugal

1956, Aug. 4 Unwmk. Perf. 14½

Central Design in Multicolored

400 A31 1e pale yellow & multi .30 .20
401 A31 2.50e lt blue & multi .70 .30

Issued to commemorate the visit of President Antonio Oscar de Fragoso Carmona.

1957, Aug. 15 Litho.

402 A32 2.50e View of Beira .50 .30

50th anniversary of the city of Beira.

Brussels Fair Issue

Exhibition Emblems and View — A32a

1958, Oct. 8 Unwmk. Perf. 14½

403 A32a 3.50c blk, grn, yel, red & bl .25 .20

Tropical Medicine Congress Issue

Common Design Type

Design: Strophanthus grandiflorus.

1958, Sept. 14 Perf. 13½

404 CD47 1.50e sal brn, grn & red 1.75 .50

Caravel — A33

Technical Instruction A34

1960, June 25 Litho. Perf. 13½

405 A33 5e multicolored .30 .20

500th anniversary of the death of Prince Henry the Navigator.

1960, Nov. 21 Unwmk. Perf. 14½

406 A34 3e multicolored .30 .20

Commission for Technical Co-operation in Africa South of the Sahara (C.C.T.A.), 10th anniv.

Arms of Lourenço Marques — A35

Arms of various cities of Mozambique.

1961, Jan. 30 Litho. Perf. 13½

Arms in Original Colors; Black, Ultramarine and Red Inscriptions

407 A35 5c salmon .20 .20
408 A35 15c pale green .20 .20
409 A35 20c lt vio gray .20 .20
410 A35 30c buff .20 .20
411 A35 50c bluish gray .20 .20
412 A35 1e pale ol .20 .20
413 A35 1.50e lt blue .20 .20
414 A35 2e pale pink .20 .20
415 A35 2.50e lt bl grn .70 .20
416 A35 3e beige .25 .20
417 A35 4e yellow .25 .20
418 A35 4.50e pale gray .25 .20
419 A35 5e pale bluish grn .25 .20
420 A35 7.50e rose .55 .25
a. "CORREIOS 7$50" omitted
421 A35 10e lt yel grn .90 .25
422 A35 20e beige 1.90 .35
423 A35 50e gray 4.00 .75
Nos. 407-423 (17) 10.65 4.20

Sports Issue

Common Design Type

50c, Water skiing. 1e, Wrestling. 1.50e, Woman gymnast. 2.50e, Field hockey. 4.50e, Women's basketball. 15e, Speedboat racing.

1962, Feb. 10 Unwmk. Perf. 13½

Multicolored Designs

424 CD48 50c gray green .30 .20
425 CD48 1e dk gray .65 .20
426 CD48 1.50e pink .35 .20
427 CD48 2.50e buff .55 .25
428 CD48 4.50e gray .85 .40
429 CD48 15e gray green 1.40 .80
Nos. 424-429 (6) 4.10 2.05

For overprints see Nos. 522, 526, 529.

Anti-Malaria Issue

Common Design Type

Design: Anopheles funestus.

1962, Apr. 5 Perf. 13½

430 CD49 2.50e multicolored 1.00 .20

Planes over Mozambique A36

Lourenço Marques 1887 and 1962 A37

1962, Oct. 15 Litho. Perf. 14½

431 A36 3e multicolored .35 .20

25th anniversary of DETA airlines.

1962, Nov. 1 Perf. 13

432 A37 1e multicolored .25 .20

75th anniversary of Lourenço Marques.

Vasco da Gama Statue and Arms — A38

1963, Apr. 25 Unwmk. Perf. 14½

433 A38 3e multicolored .20 .20

Founding of Mozambique City, 200th anniv.

Airline Anniversary Issue

Common Design Type

1963, Oct. 21 Litho. Perf. 14½

434 CD50 2.50e brt pink & multi .20 .20

Barque, 1430 — A39

Caravel, 1436 — A40

Development of Sailing Ships: 30c, Lateen-rigged caravel, 1460. 50c, "Sao Gabriel," 1497. 1e, Dom Manuel's ship, 1498. 1.50e, Warship, 1500. 2e, "Flor de la Mar," 1511. 2.50e, Redonda caravel, 1519. 3.50e, 800-ton ship, 1520. 4e, Portuguese India galley, 1521. 4.50e, "Santa Tereza," 1639. 5e, "Nostra Senhora da Conceiçao," 1716. 6e, "Nostra Senhora do Bom Sucesso," 1764. 7.50e, Launch with mortar, 1788. 8e, Brigantine, 1793. 10e, Corvette, 1799. 12.50e, Schooner "Maria Teresa," 1820. 15e, "Vasco da Gama," 1841. 20e, Frigate "Dom Fernando II," 1843. 30e, Training Ship "Sagres," 1924.

1963, Dec. 1 Litho. Perf. 14½

435 A39 10c multicolored .20 .20
436 A40 20c multicolored .20 .20
437 A40 30c multicolored .20 .20
438 A40 50c multicolored .20 .20
439 A40 1e multicolored .35 .20
440 A40 1.50e multicolored .20 .20
441 A40 2e multicolored .30 .20
442 A39 2.50e multicolored .50 .20
443 A40 3.50e multicolored .45 .30
444 A39 4e multicolored .60 .20
445 A40 4.50e multicolored 1.10 .25
446 A40 5e multicolored 3.00 .20
447 A39 6e multicolored 1.00 .25
448 A39 7.50e multicolored 1.10 .30
449 A39 8e multicolored 1.10 .30
450 A39 10e multicolored 1.25 .60
451 A39 12.50e multicolored 1.40 .75
452 A39 15e multicolored 1.40 .60
453 A40 20e multicolored 2.00 .70
454 A40 30e multicolored 2.75 1.25
Nos. 435-454 (20) 19.30 7.30

National Overseas Bank Issue

Modern Bank Building, Luanda A40a

1964, May 16 Perf. 13½

455 A40a 1.50e bl, yel gray & grn .20 .20

National Overseas Bank of Portugal, cent.

Pres. Americo Rodrigues Thomaz — A41

1964, July 23 Litho. Perf. 13½x12½

456 A41 2.50e multicolored .20 .20

Visit of Pres. Americo Rodrigues Thomaz of Portugal to Mozambique, in July.

Royal Barge of King John V, 1728 A42

Designs: 35c, Barge of Dom Jose I, 1753. 1e, Customs barge, 1768. 1.50e, Sailor, 1780, vert. 2.50e, Royal barge, 1780. 5e, Barge of Dona Carlota Joaquina, 1790. 9e, Barge of Dom Miguel, 1831.

1964, Dec. 18 Litho. Perf. 14½

457 A42 15c multicolored .20 .20
458 A42 35c lt bl & multi .20 .20
459 A42 1e gray & multi .50 .20
460 A42 1.50e gray & multi .30 .20
461 A42 2.50e multicolored .25 .20
462 A42 5e multicolored .30 .20
463 A42 9e multicolored .50 .40
Nos. 457-463 (7) 2.25 1.60

ITU Issue

Common Design Type

1965, May 17 Unwmk. ***Perf. 14½***

464	CD52	1e yellow & multi	.30	.20

National Revolution Issue

Common Design Type

Design: 1e, Beira Railroad Station, and Antonio Enes School.

1966, May 28 Litho. ***Perf. 11½***

465	CD53	1e multicolored	.20	.20

Harquebusier, 1560 — A42a

30c, Harquebusier, 1640. 40c, Infantry soldier, 1777. 50c, Infantry officer, 1777. 80c, Drummer, 1777. 1e, Infantry sergeant, 1777. 2e, Infantry major, 1784. 2.50e, Colonial officer, 1788. 3e, Infantry soldier, 1789. 5e, Colonial bugler, 1801. 10e, Colonial officer, 1807. 15e, Colonial infantry soldier, 1817.

1967, Jan. 12 Photo. ***Perf. 14***

466	A42a	20c	multicolored	.20	.20
467	A42a	30c	multicolored	.20	.20
468	A42a	40c	multicolored	.20	.20
469	A42a	50c	multicolored	.20	.20
470	A42a	80c	multicolored	.20	.20
471	A42a	1e	multicolored	.20	.20
472	A42a	2e	multicolored	.25	.20
473	A42a	2.50e	multicolored	.30	.20
474	A42a	3e	multicolored	.30	.25
475	A42a	5e	multicolored	.40	.25
476	A42a	10e	multicolored	.50	.30
477	A42a	15e	multicolored	.75	.40
			Nos. 466-477 (12)	3.70	2.80

Navy Club Issue

Common Design Type

Designs: 3e, Capt. Azevedo Coutinho and gunboat (stern-wheeler) Tete. 10e, Capt. Joao Roby and gunboat (paddle steamer) Granada.

1967, Jan. 31 Litho. ***Perf. 13***

478	CD54	3e multicolored	.20	.20
479	CD54	10e multicolored	.45	.25

Virgin's Crown, Presented by Portuguese Women — A43

1967, May 13 Litho. ***Perf. 12½x13***

480	A43	50c multicolored	.20	.20

50th anniversary of the appearance of the Virgin Mary to 3 shepherd children at Fatima.

Cabral Issue

Raising the Cross at Porto Seguro — A44

Designs: 1.50e, First mission to Brazil. 3e, Grace Church, Santarem, vert.

1968, Apr. 22 Litho. ***Perf. 14***

481	A44	1e multicolored	.20	.20
482	A44	1.50e multicolored	.20	.20
483	A44	3e multicolored	.30	.20
		Nos. 481-483 (3)	.70	.60

500th birth anniv. of Pedro Alvares Cabral, navigator who took possession of Brazil for Portugal.

Admiral Coutinho Issue

Common Design Type

Design: 70c, Adm. Coutinho and Adm. Gago Coutinho Airport.

1969, Feb. 17 Litho. ***Perf. 14***

484	CD55	70c multicolored	.20	.20

Luiz Vaz de Camoens — A45

Sailing Ship, 1553 — A46

Designs: 1.50e, Map of Mozambique, 1554. 2.50e, Chapel of Our Lady of Baluarte, 1552. 5e, Excerpt from Lusiads about Mozambique (1st Song, 14th Stanza).

Perf. 12½x13, 13x12½

1969, June 10 Litho.

485	A45	15c	multicolored	.20	.20
486	A46	50c	multicolored	.20	.20
487	A45	1.50e	multicolored	.20	.20
488	A46	2.50e	multicolored	.20	.20
489	A45	5e	multicolored	.30	.20
			Nos. 485-489 (5)	1.10	1.00

Visit to Mozambique of Luiz Vaz de Camoens (1524-80), poet, 400th anniv.

Vasco da Gama Issue

Map Showing Voyage to Mozambique and India — A47

1969, Aug. 29 Litho. ***Perf. 14***

490	A47	1e multicolored	.20	.20

Vasco da Gama (1469-1524), navigator.

Administration Reform Issue

Common Design Type

1969, Sept. 25 Litho. ***Perf. 14***

491	CD56	1.50e multicolored	.20	.20

King Manuel I Issue

Illuminated Miniature of King's Arms — A48

1969, Dec. 1 Litho. ***Perf. 14***

492	A48	80c multicolored	.20	.20

500th anniversary of the birth of King Manuel I.

Marshal Carmona Issue

Common Design Type

5e, Antonio Oscar Carmona in marshal's uniform.

1970, Nov. 15 Litho. ***Perf. 14***

493	CD57	5e multicolored	.20	.20

Fossil Fern A49

Fossils and Minerals: 50c, Fossil snail. 1e, Stibnite. 1.50e, Pink beryl. 2e, Dinosaur. 3e, Tantalocolumbite. 3.50e, Verdelite. 4e, Zircon. 10e, Petrified wood.

1971, Jan. 15 Litho. ***Perf. 13***

494	A49	15c	gray & multi	.20	.20
495	A49	50c	lt ultra & multi	.20	.20
496	A49	1e	green & multi	.30	.20
497	A49	1.50e	multicolored	.40	.20
498	A49	2e	multicolored	.75	.20
499	A49	3e	lt bl & multi	1.50	.20
500	A49	3.50e	lilac & multi	2.00	.20
501	A49	4e	multicolored	3.00	.20
502	A49	10e	dl red & multi	4.00	.40
			Nos. 494-502 (9)	12.35	2.00

For overprints see Nos. 525, 528.

Mozambique Island — A49a

1972, May 25 Litho. ***Perf. 13***

503	A49a	4e ultra & multi	.30	.20

4th centenary of publication of The Lusiads by Luiz Camoens.

Olympic Games Issue

Common Design Type

3e, Hurdles and swimming, Olympic emblem.

1972, June 20 ***Perf. 14x13½***

504	CD59	3e multi	.20	.20

For overprint see No. 523.

Lisbon-Rio de Janeiro Flight Issue

Common Design Type

1e, "Santa Cruz" over Recife harbor.

1972, Sept. 20 Litho. ***Perf. 13½***

505	CD60	1e multi	.20	.20

Sailboats A50

Designs: Various sailboats.

1973, Aug. 21 Litho. ***Perf. 12x11½***

506	A50	1e	multi	.20	.20
507	A50	1.50e	multi	.20	.20
508	A50	3e	multi	.30	.20
			Nos. 506-508 (3)	.70	.60

World Sailing Championships, Vauriens Class, Lourenço Marques, Aug. 21-30.
For overprints see Nos. 519-520, 524.

WMO Centenary Issue

Common Design Type

1973, Dec. 15 Litho. ***Perf. 13***

509	CD61	2e rose red & multi	.20	.20

For overprint see No. 521.

Radar Station A51

1974, June 25 Litho. ***Perf. 13***

510	A51	50c multi	.20	.20

Establishment of satellite communications network via Intelsat among Portugal, Angola and Mozambique.
For overprint see No. 518.

"Bird" Made of Flags of Portugal and Mozambique — A52

1975, Jan. Litho. ***Perf. 14½***

511	A52	1e	pink & multi	.20	.20
512	A52	1.50e	yel & multi	.20	.20
513	A52	2e	gray & multi	.20	.20
514	A52	3.50e	lem & multi	.30	.20
515	A52	6e	lt bl & multi	.75	.30
a.			Souv. sheet of 5, #511-515 + label	3.25	3.25
			Nos. 511-515 (5)	1.65	1.10

Lusaka Agreement, Sept. 7, 1974, which gave Mozambique independence from Portugal, effective June 25, 1975.
No. 515a sold for 25e.
For overprints see Nos. 543-545.

Republic

Issues of 1953-74 Overprinted in Red or Black:

a

b

1975, June 25

516	A28 (a)	10c	(R; #387)	.20	.20
517	A26 (a)	40c	(R; #368)	.20	.20
518	A51 (b)	50c	(B; #510)	.20	.20
519	A50 (b)	1e	(B; #506)	.20	.20
520	A50 (b)	1.50e	(B; #507)	.20	.20
521	CD61 (a)	2e	(B; #509)	.20	.20
522	CD48 (b)	2.50e	(B; #427)	.40	.20
523	CD59 (a)	3e	(R; #504)	.40	.20
524	A50 (b)	3e	(B; #508)	.40	.40
525	A49 (b)	3.50e	(B; #500)	.40	.40
526	CD48 (b)	4.50e	(B; #428)	2.50	1.75
527	A26 (a)	7.50e	(R; #381)	.85	.40
528	A49 (b)	10e	(B; #502)	1.75	.60
529	CD48 (b)	15e	(B; #429)	1.75	.85
530	A28 (a)	20e	(R; #394)	1.00	.60
			Nos. 516-530,C35-C38 (19)	13.80	7.60

Workers, Farmers and Children A53

Designs: 30c, 50c, 2.50e, like 20c. 4.50e, 5e, 10e, 50e, Dancers, workers, armed family.

1975 Litho. ***Perf. 12x11½***

531	A53	20c	pink & multi	.20	.20
532	A53	30c	bis & multi	.20	.20
533	A53	50c	bl & multi	.20	.20
534	A53	2.50e	grn & multi	.20	.20
535	A53	4.50e	brn & multi	.20	.20
536	A53	5e	bis & multi	.20	.20
537	A53	10e	bl & multi	.35	.20
538	A53	50e	yel & multi	1.60	.80
a.			Souvenir sheet of 8	3.25	3.25
			Nos. 531-538 (8)	3.15	2.20

No. 538a contains 8 stamps similar to Nos. 531-538 with simulated perforation. Sold for 75e.
For overprint see No. 554.

Farm Woman — A54

1976, Apr. 7 Litho. ***Perf. 14½***

539	A54	1e	shown	.20	.20
540	A54	1.50e	Teacher	.20	.20
541	A54	2.50e	Nurse	.25	.25
542	A54	10e	Mother	.50	.35
			Nos. 539-542 (4)	1.15	1.00

Day of the Mozambique Woman, Apr. 7.

Nos. 513-515 Overprinted in Red: "PRESIDENTE KENNETH KAUNDA / PRIMEIRA VISITA 20/4/1976"

1976, Apr. 20 Litho. ***Perf. 14½***

543 A52 2e gray & multi .20 .20
544 A52 3.50e lem & multi .30 .30
545 A52 6e lt bl & multi .50 .50
Nos. 543-545 (3) 1.00 1.00

Visit of President Kaunda of Zambia.

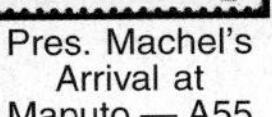

Pres. Machel's Arrival at Maputo — A55

Mozambique No. 1 — A56

Designs: 1e, Independence proclamation ceremony. 2.50e, Pres. Samora Moises Machel taking office. 7.50e, Military parade. 20e, Flame of Unity and festival.

1976, June 25

546 A55 50c multi .20 .20
547 A55 1e multi .20 .20
548 A55 2.50e multi .20 .20
549 A55 7.50e multi .40 .25
550 A55 20e multi 1.00 .50
Nos. 546-550 (5) 2.00 1.35

First anniversary of independence.

1976, July ***Perf. 11½x12***

551 A56 1.50e ocher & multi .20 .20
552 A56 6e red & multi .35 .30

Centenary of Mozambique postage stamps.

Flag and Weapons A57

1976, Sept. 25 Litho. ***Perf. 14½***

553 A57 3e multi .25 .20

Army Day 1976.

No. 534 Overprinted in Silver: "FACIM"

1976 Litho. ***Perf. 12x11½***

554 A53 2.50e multi .30 .20

FACIM, Industrial Fair.

Bush Baby — A58

Animals: 1e, Honey badger. 1.50e, Pangolin. 2e, Steinbok. 2.50e, Guenon (monkey). 3e, Cape hunting dog. 4e, Cheetah. 5e, Spotted hyena. 7.50e, Wart hog. 8e, Hippopotamus. 10e, Rhinoceros. 15e, Sable antelope. 1e, 2e, 3e, 4e, 7.50e, 8e, 10e horiz.

1977, Jan. Litho. ***Perf. 14½***

555 A58 50c multi .20 .20
556 A58 1e multi .20 .20
557 A58 1.50e multi .20 .20
558 A58 2e multi .20 .20
559 A58 2.50e multi .20 .20
560 A58 3e multi .20 .20
561 A58 4e multi .30 .20
562 A58 5e multi .35 .20
563 A58 7.50e multi .50 .20
564 A58 8e multi .55 .30
565 A58 10e multi .70 .30
566 A58 15e multi 1.00 .40
Nos. 555-566 (12) 4.60 2.80

Congress Emblem — A59

Monument in Maputo — A60

Design: 3.50e, Monument in Macheje, site of 2nd Frelimo Congress, horiz.

1977, Feb. 7 ***Perf. 14½***

567 A59 3e multi .20 .20

Perf. 12x11½, 11½x12

568 A60 3.50e multi .30 .30
569 A60 20e multi 1.00 .35
Nos. 567-569 (3) 1.50 .85

3rd FRELIMO Party Congress, Maputo, Feb. 3-7.

Women, Child's Design — A61

Worker and Farmer — A62

1977, Apr. 7 Litho. ***Perf. 14½***

570 A61 5e dp org & multi .30 .20
571 A61 15e lt grn & multi .70 .20

Mozambique Women's Day 1977.

1977, May 1 Litho. ***Perf. 14½***

572 A62 5e red, blk & yel .40 .30

Labor Day.

People, Flags and Rising Sun — A63

1977, June 25 Litho. ***Perf. 11½x12***

573 A63 50c multi .20 .20
574 A63 1.50e multi .20 .20
575 A63 3e multi .20 .20
576 A63 15e multi .70 .20
Nos. 573-576 (4) 1.30 .80

2nd anniversary of independence.

Bread Palm A64

1977, Dec. 21 Litho. ***Perf. 12x11½***

577 A64 1e shown .25 .20
578 A64 10e Nyala .60 .25

Nature protection and Stamp Day.

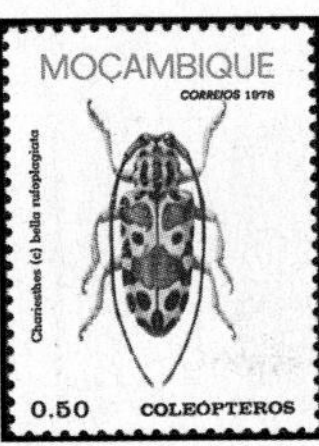

Chariesthes Bella Rufoplagiata A65

Violet-crested Touraco — A66

Beetles: 1e, Tragocephalus variegata. 1.50e, Monochamus leuconotus. 3e, Prosopocera lactator meridionalis. 5e, Dinocephalus ornatus. 10e, Tragiscoschema nigroscriptum maculata.

1978, Jan. 20 Litho. ***Perf. 11½x12***

579 A65 50c multi .25 .20
580 A65 1e multi .25 .20
581 A65 1.50e multi .30 .20
582 A65 3e multi .35 .20
583 A65 5e multi .45 .40
584 A65 10e multi .75 .40
Nos. 579-584 (6) 2.35 1.60

1978, Mar. 20 Litho. ***Perf. 11½***

Birds of Mozambique: 1e, Lilac-breasted roller. 1.50e, Weaver. 2.50e, Violet-backed starling. 3e, Peter's twinspot. 15e, European bee-eater.

585 A66 50c multi .25 .20
586 A66 1e multi .30 .20
587 A66 1.50e multi .50 .20
588 A66 2.50e multi .75 .25
589 A66 3e multi 1.00 .30
590 A66 15e multi 1.75 .50
Nos. 585-590 (6) 4.55 1.65

Mother and Child, WHO Emblem A67

1978, Apr. 17 ***Perf. 12***

591 A67 15e multi .50 .30

Smallpox eradication campaign.

Crinum Delagoense A68

No. 1, Canada No. 1 — A69

Flowers of Mozambique: 1e, Gloriosa superba. 1.50e, Eulophia speciosa. 3e, Erithrina humeana. 5e, Astripomoea malvacea. 10e, Kigelia africana.

1978, May 16 ***Perf. 11½x12***

592 A68 50c multi .20 .20
593 A68 1e multi .20 .20
594 A68 1.50e multi .20 .20
595 A68 3e multi .20 .20
596 A68 5e multi .25 .25
597 A68 10e multi .50 .30
Nos. 592-597 (6) 1.55 1.35

1978, June 9

598 A69 15e multi .50 .30

CAPEX Canadian International Philatelic Exhibition, Toronto, Ont., June 9-18.

National Flag — A70

Soldiers, Festival Emblem — A71

1.50e, Coat of arms. 7.50e, Page of Constitution people. 10e, Music band & natl. anthem.

1978, June 25 ***Perf. 11½x12***

599 A70 1e multi .20 .20
600 A70 1.50e multi .20 .20
601 A70 7.50e multi .30 .20
602 A70 10e multi .50 .25
a. Souvenir sheet of 4 2.00 1.75
Nos. 599-602 (4) 1.20 .85

3rd anniversary of proclamation of independence. No. 602a contains 4 stamps similar to Nos. 599-602 with simulated perforations. Sold for 30e.

1978, July 28

2.50e, Student. 7.50e, Farmworkers.

603 A71 2.50e multi .20 .20
604 A71 3e multi .20 .20
605 A71 7.50e multi .25 .20
Nos. 603-605 (3) .65 .60

11th World Youth Festival, Havana, 7/28-8/5.

Czechoslovakia No. B126 and PRAGA '78 Emblem — A72

1978, Sept. 8 Litho. ***Perf. 12x11½***

606 A72 15e multi .50 .25
a. Souvenir sheet 3.00 3.00

PRAGA '78 International Philatelic Exhibition, Prague, Sept. 8-17.

No. 606a contains one stamp with simulated perforations. Sold for 30e.

Soccer A73

Stamp Day: 1.50e, Shotput. 3e, Hurdling. 7.50e, Fieldball. 12.50e, Swimming. 25e, Roller skate hockey.

1978, Dec. 21 Litho. ***Perf. 12x11½***

607 A73 50c multi .20 .20
608 A73 1.50e multi .20 .20
609 A73 3e multi .20 .20
610 A73 7.50e multi .30 .20
611 A73 12.50e multi .35 .20
612 A73 25e multi .75 .35
Nos. 607-612 (6) 2.00 1.35

Carrier Pigeon, UPU Emblem
A74

1979, Jan. 1 Litho. *Perf. 11x11½*

613 A74 20e multi .55 .40

Membership in Universal Postal Union.

Soldier Giving Gourd to Woman — A75

Edward Chivambo Mondlane
A76

Designs: 3e, Frelimo soldiers. 7.50e, Mozambique children in school.

1979, Feb. 3 *Perf. 11½x11, 11x11½*

614 A75 1e multi .20 .20
615 A75 3e multi .20 .20
616 A75 7.50e multi .30 .20
617 A76 12.50e multi .55 .20
Nos. 614-617 (4) 1.25 .80

Dr. Edward Chivambo Mondlane (1920-1969), educator, founder of Frelimo Party.

Shaded Silver Cat — A77

Cats: 1.50e, Manx. 2.50e, English blue. 3e, Turkish. 12.50e, Long-haired Mid-East tabby. 20e, African wild cat.

1979, Mar. 27 Litho. *Perf. 11*

618 A77 50c multi .20 .20
619 A77 1.50e multi .25 .20
620 A77 2.50e multi .25 .20
621 A77 3e multi .30 .20
622 A77 12.50e multi .65 .20
623 A77 20e multi 1.00 .30
Nos. 618-623 (6) 2.65 1.30

Wrestling and Moscow '80 Emblem — A78

Sport and Moscow '80 Emblem: 2e, Running. 3e, Equestrian. 5e, Canoeing. 10e, High jump. 15e, Archery.

1979, Apr. 24 Litho. *Perf. 11*

624 A78 1e gray grn & blk .20 .20
625 A78 2e brt bl & blk .25 .20
626 A78 3e lt brn & blk .35 .20
627 A78 5e multi .50 .20
628 A78 10e grn & blk .60 .20
629 A78 15e lil rose & blk 1.00 .20
Nos. 624-629 (6) 2.90 1.20

Souvenir Sheet

Imperf

630 A78 30e rose & dk brn 3.50 3.50

22nd Olympic Games, Moscow, July 10-Aug. 3, 1980. No. 630 contains one 47x37mm stamp.

Garden and IYC Emblem
A79

Children's Drawings and IYC Emblem: 1.50e, Dancers. 3e, City. 5e, Farmers. 7.50e, Village. 12.50e, Automobiles, train and flowers.

1979, June 1 Litho. *Perf. 11*

631 A79 50c multi .20 .20
632 A79 1.50e multi .20 .20
633 A79 3e multi .25 .20
634 A79 5e multi .30 .20
635 A79 7.50e multi .40 .20
636 A79 12.50e multi .65 .20
Nos. 631-636 (6) 2.00 1.20

International Year of the Child.

Flight from Colonialism — A80

Designs: 2e, Founding of FRELIMO and Pres. Eduardo Chivambo Mondlane. 3e, Advance of armed strruggle and death of Mondlane. 7.50e, Final fight for liberation. 15e, Proclamation of victory, Pres. Samora Moises Machel, flag and torch. Designs after mural in Heroes' Square, Maputo. 30e, Building up the country.

1979, June 25

637 A80 50c multi .20 .20
638 A80 2e multi .20 .20
639 A80 3e multi .20 .20
640 A80 7.50e multi .20 .20
641 A80 15e multi .50 .20
b. Strip of 5, #537-641 1.25 1.00

Souvenir Sheet

Imperf

641A A80 30e multi 3.25 3.25

4th anniversary of independence. No. 641A contains one stamp with simulated perforations. No. 641b has continuous design.

Scorpion Fish
A81

Tropical Fish: 1.50e, King fish. 2.50e, Gobius inhaca. 3e, Acanthurus lineatus. 10e, Gobuchthys lemayi. 12.50e, Variola louti.

1979, Aug. 7 Litho. *Perf. 11*

642 A81 50c multi .20 .20
643 A81 1.50e multi .20 .20
644 A81 2.50e multi .20 .20
645 A81 3e multi .20 .20
646 A81 10e multi .50 .20
647 A81 12.50e multi .60 .20
Nos. 642-647 (6) 1.90 1.20

For surcharge see No. 1254.

Quartz
A82

Mozambique Minerals.

1979, Sept. 10

648 A82 1e shown .20 .20
649 A82 1.50e Beryl .30 .20
650 A82 2.50e Magnetite .40 .20
651 A82 5e Tourmaline .60 .20
652 A82 10e Euxenite .70 .20
653 A82 20e Fluorite 1.00 .35
Nos. 648-653 (6) 3.20 1.35

Citizens Gathering Arms — A83

1979, Sept. 25

654 A83 5e multi .30 .20

15th anniversary of independence.

Locomotive — A85

Designs: Historic Locomotives.

1979, Nov. 11 Litho. *Perf. 11*

656 A85 50c multi .20 .20
657 A85 1.50e multi .25 .20
658 A85 3e multi .30 .20
659 A85 7.50e multi .40 .20
660 A85 12.50e multi .50 .20
661 A85 15e multi .75 .20
Nos. 656-661 (6) 2.40 1.20

For surcharge see No. 1298.

Dalmatian — A86

Perf. 11½x11, 11x11½

1979, Dec. 17 Litho.

662 A86 50c Basenji, vert. .20 .20
663 A86 1.50e shown .20 .20
664 A86 3e Boxer .25 .20
665 A86 7.50e Blue gasconha braco .40 .20
666 A86 12.50e Cocker spaniel .50 .20
667 A86 15e Pointer .75 .20
Nos. 662-667 (6) 2.30 1.20

For surcharge see No. 1299.

Nireus Lyaeus — A87

Butterflies: 1.50e, Amauris ochlea. 2.50e, Pinacopterix eriphia. 5e, Junonia hierta cebrene. 10e, Nephronia argia. 20e, Catacroptera cloanthe.

1979, Dec. 21

668 A87 1e multi .20 .20
669 A87 1.50e multi .25 .20
670 A87 2.50e multi .30 .20
671 A87 5e multi .40 .20
672 A87 10e multi .60 .25
673 A87 20e multi 1.25 .50
Nos. 668-673 (6) 3.00 1.55

Dermacentor Rhinocerinus, Rhinoceros — A88

Ticks and Animals: 50c, Dermacentor circumguttatus cunhasilvai, elephant. 2.50e, Green tick, giraffe. 3e, Red tick, antelope. 5e, Ambloymma theilerae, cattle. 7.50e, Buffalo tick, buffalo.

1980, Jan. 29 Litho. *Perf. 11½x11*

674 A88 50c multi .20 .20
675 A88 1.50e multi .20 .20
676 A88 2.50e multi .25 .20
677 A88 3e multi .35 .20
678 A88 5e multi .40 .20
679 A88 7.50e multi .50 .20
Nos. 674-679 (6) 1.90 1.20

Ford Hercules, 1950 — A89

Public Transportation: 1.50e, Scania Marcopolo, 1978. 3e, Bussing Nag, 1936. 5e, Articulated Ikarus, 1978. 7.50e, Ford taxi, 1929. 12.50e, Fiat 131 taxi, 1978.

1980, Feb. 29 Litho. *Perf. 11*

680 A89 50c multi .20 .20
681 A89 1.50e multi .20 .20
682 A89 3e multi .20 .20
683 A89 5e multi .20 .20
684 A89 7.50e multi .35 .20
685 A89 12.50e multi .50 .20
Nos. 680-685 (6) 1.65 1.20

Marx, Engels, and Lenin A90

1980, May 1 **Litho.** ***Perf. 11***
686 A90 10e multi .30 .20

Workers' Day.

"Heads," by Malangatana, London 1980 Emblem — A91

Paintings by Mozambique Artists: 1.50e, Crowded Market, by Moises Simbine. 3e, Heads with Helmets, by Malangatana. 5e, Women with Goods, by Machiana. 7.50e, Crowd with Masks, by Malangatana. 12.50e, Man and Woman with Spear, by Mankeu.

1980, May 6
687 A91 50c multi .20 .20
688 A91 1.50e multi .20 .20
689 A91 3e multi .20 .20
690 A91 5e multi .20 .20
691 A91 7.50e multi .30 .20
692 A91 12.50e multi .50 .20
Nos. 687-692 (6) 1.60 1.20

London 1980 Intl. Stamp Exhibition, 5/6-14.

World Telecommunications Day — A92

1980, May 17 **Litho.** ***Perf. 12***
693 A92 15e multi .50 .30

Mueda Massacre, 20th Anniv. — A93

People with Weapons and Flag — A94

1980, June 16 **Litho.** ***Perf. 11***
694 A93 15e multi .50 .30

1980, June 25
695 A94 1e Development projects, 1975 .20 .20
696 A94 2e shown .20 .20
697 A94 3e Arms, flags, 1977 .20 .20
698 A94 4e Raised fists, 1978 .20 .20
699 A94 5e Hand holding grain, flags, 1979 .25 .20
700 A94 10e Year banners, 1980 .40 .20
Nos. 695-700 (6) 1.45 1.20

Souvenir Sheet

Litho. ***Imperf.***
700A A94 30e Soldiers 3.00

5th anniv. of independence. No. 700A contains one stamp with simulated perforations.

Gymnast, Moscow '80 Emblem — A95

1980, July 19
701 A95 50c shown .20 .20
702 A95 1.50e Soccer .20 .20
703 A95 2.50e Running .20 .20
704 A95 3e Volleyball .20 .20
705 A95 10e Bicycling .40 .20
706 A95 12.50e Boxing .50 .30
Nos. 701-706 (6) 1.70 1.30

22nd Summer Olympic Games, Moscow, July 19-Aug. 3.

Soldier, Map of Southern Africa Showing Zimbabwe — A96

1980, Apr. 18
707 A96 10e multi .30 .20

Establishment of independent Zimbabwe, Apr. 18.

Narina Trogon — A97

1980, July 30 **Litho.** ***Perf. 11***
708 A97 1m shown .25 .20
709 A97 1.50m Crowned crane .50 .20
710 A97 2.50m Red-necked francolin .75 .20
711 A97 5m Ostrich 1.25 .25
712 A97 7.50m Spur-winged goose 1.50 .30
713 A97 12.50m Fish eagle 2.00 .40
Nos. 708-713 (6) 6.25 1.55

For surcharges see Nos. 1253A, 1255.

First Census, Aug. 1-15 A98

1980, Aug. 12 ***Perf. 11***
714 A98 3.5m multi .20 .20

Brush Fire Control Campaign — A99

1980, Sept. 7
715 A99 3.5m multi .25 .20

Harpa Major A100

1980, Dec. 12 **Litho.** ***Perf. 11***
716 A100 1m shown .20 .20
717 A100 1.50m Lambis chiragra .25 .20
718 A100 2.50m Murex pecten .30 .20
719 A100 5m Architectonia perspectiva .40 .20
720 A100 7.50m Murex ramosus .50 .20
721 A100 12.50m Strombus aurisdinae .80 .25
Nos. 716-721 (6) 2.45 1.25

Pres. Machel and Symbols of Industry and Transportation — A101

Decade of Development, 1981-1990 (Pres. Machel and): 7.50m, Soldiers. 12.50m, Symbols of education.

1981, Jan. 1 **Litho.** ***Perf. 11x11½***
722 A101 3.50m red & bl .20 .20
723 A101 7.50m grn & red brn .30 .20
724 A101 12.50m dk bl & lil rose .50 .20
Nos. 722-724 (3) 1.00 .60

Bilbao Soccer Stadium, Soccer Player — A102

Soccer players and various stadiums.

1981, Jan. 30 **Litho.** ***Perf. 11***
725 A102 1m multi .20 .20
726 A102 1.50m multi .20 .20
727 A102 2.50m multi .20 .20
728 A102 5m multi .25 .20
729 A102 7.50m multi .40 .20
730 A102 12.50m multi .75 .30
c. Souvenir sheet of 6 1.75 1.75
Nos. 725-730 (6) 2.00 1.30

Souvenir Sheets

Imperf
730A A102 20m multi 1.25 1.25
730B A102 20m multi 1.25 1.25

ESPANA '82 World Cup Soccer Championship. No. 730c contains Nos. 725-730 with simulated perforations. Sizes: No. 730A, 105x85mm; 730B, 141x111mm.

For surcharge see No. 1303.

Giraffe — A103

1981, Mar. 3 ***Perf. 11***
731 A103 50c shown .25 .20
732 A103 1.50m Tsessebe .30 .20
733 A103 2.50m Aardvark .35 .20
734 A103 3m African python .40 .20
735 A103 5m Loggerhead turtle .45 .20
736 A103 10m Marabou .55 .20
737 A103 12.50m Saddlebill stork .75 .25
738 A103 15m Kori bustard .85 .35
Nos. 731-738 (8) 3.90 1.80

Pankwe A104

1981, Apr. 8 **Litho.** ***Perf. 11***
739 A104 50c Chitende, vert. .20 .20
740 A104 2m shown .20 .20
741 A104 2.50m Kanyembe, vert. .30 .20
742 A104 7m Nyanga .50 .30
743 A104 10m Likuti and m'petheni .75 .40
Nos. 739-743 (5) 1.95 1.30

International Year of the Disabled — A105

1981, Apr. 18
744 A105 5m multi .30 .20

African Buffalo and Helicopter, Exhibition Emblem — A106

1981, June 14 ***Perf. 11***
745 A106 2m shown .20 .20
746 A106 5m Hunters, blue kids .25 .20
747 A106 6m Hunter, impala .35 .20
748 A106 7.50m Hunters shooting .45 .20
749 A106 12.50m Elephants .60 .25
750 A106 20m Trap 1.25 .40
a. Souv. sheet of 6, #745-750, imperf. 3.50 3.00
Nos. 745-750 (6) 3.10 1.45

World Hunting Exhibition, Plovdiv, Bulgaria. No. 750a sold for 60m.

For surcharge see No. 1258.

50-centavo Coin, Obverse and Reverse A107

First Anniversary of New Currency (Coins on stamps of matching denomination).

1981, June 16

751	A107	50c	multi	.20	.20
752	A107	1m	multi	.25	.20
753	A107	2.50m	multi	.35	.20
754	A107	5m	multi	.40	.20
755	A107	10m	multi	.60	.20
756	A107	20m	multi	.90	.30
a.			Souv. sheet of 6, #751-756, imperf.	2.50	1.75
			Nos. 751-756 (6)	2.70	1.30

No. 756a sold for 40m.

Sunflower — A108

1981, July 24 Litho. *Perf. 14½*

757	A108	50c	shown	.20	.20
758	A108	1m	Cotton	.20	.20
759	A108	1.50m	Sisal	.20	.20
760	A108	2.50m	Cashews	.20	.20
761	A108	3.50m	Tea leaves	.20	.20
762	A108	4.50m	Sugar cane	.20	.20
763	A108	10m	Castor-oil plant	.40	.20
764	A108	12.50m	Coconut	.50	.20
765	A108	15m	Tobacco leaves	.60	.20
766	A108	25m	Rice	1.00	.40
767	A108	40m	Corn	1.60	.60
768	A108	60m	Peanut	2.50	.85
			Nos. 757-768 (12)	7.80	3.65

For surcharges see Nos. 1034A, 1185, 1216, 1218, 1252, 1300, 1399, 1420.

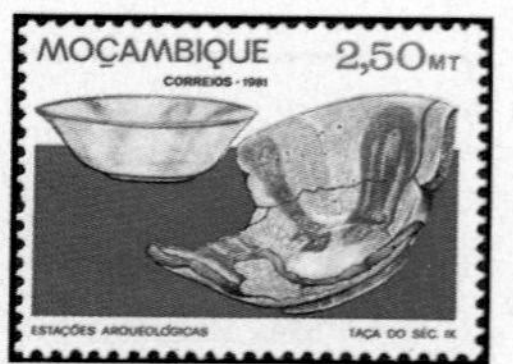

9th Cent. Persian Bowl, Chibuene Excavation Site — A109

1981, Aug. 30 *Perf. 11*

769	A109	1m	Manyikeni Museum	.20	.20
770	A109	1.50m	Hand ax, Massingir Dam	.20	.20
771	A109	2.50m	shown	.20	.20
772	A109	7.50m	Pot, Chibuene, 9th cent.	.30	.20
773	A109	12.50m	Gold beads, Manyikeni	.50	.20
774	A109	20m	Iron, Manyikeni, 15th cent.	.80	.30
			Nos. 769-774 (6)	2.20	1.30

For surcharge see No. 1213.

Sculptures A110

1981, Sept. 25 Litho. *Perf. 11*

775	A110	50c	Mapiko mask	.20	.20
776	A110	1m	Suffering woman	.20	.20
777	A110	2.50m	Mother and child	.20	.20
778	A110	3.50m	Man making fire	.20	.20
779	A110	5m	Chietane	.50	.30
780	A110	12.50m	Chietane, diff.	.50	.50
			Nos. 775-780 (6)	1.80	1.60

World Food Day A111

1981, Oct. 16 Litho. *Perf. 11*

781	A111	10m	multi	.40	.20

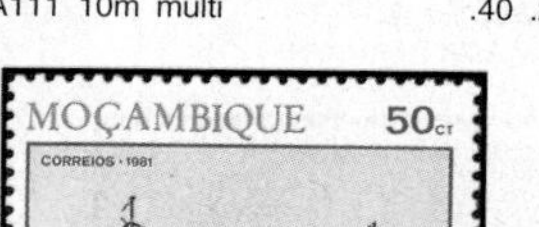

Ocean Tanker Matchedje — A112

1981, Nov. 22 Litho. *Perf. 11*

782	A112	50c	shown	.20	.20
783	A112	1.50m	Tugboat Macuti	.20	.20
784	A112	3m	Prawn trawler Vega 7	.20	.20
785	A112	5m	Freighter Linde	.20	.20
786	A112	7.50m	Ocean freighter Pemba	.30	.20
787	A112	12.50m	Dredger Rovuma	.50	.25
			Nos. 782-787 (6)	1.60	1.25

Chinaman Crab — A113

1981, Dec. 6

788	A113	50c	Portunus pelagieus	.20	.20
789	A113	1.50m	Scylla serrata	.20	.20
790	A113	3m	Penaeus indicus	.20	.20
791	A113	7.50m	Palinurus delagoae	.30	.20
792	A113	12.50m	Lusiosquilla maculata	.50	.20
793	A113	15m	Panulirus ornatus	.60	.30
			Nos. 788-793 (6)	2.00	1.30

For surcharges see Nos. 1214, 1219, 1253, 1392.

Hypoxis Multiceps A114

1981, Dec. 21 Litho. *Perf. 11*

794	A114	1m	shown	.20	.20
795	A114	1.50m	Pelargonium luridum	.20	.20
796	A114	2.50m	Caralluma melananthera	.20	.20
797	A114	7.50m	Ansellia gigantea	.30	.20
798	A114	12.50m	Stapelia leendertsiae	.50	.20
799	A114	25m	Adenium multiflorium	1.00	.30
			Nos. 794-799 (6)	2.40	1.30

For surcharges see Nos. 1215, 1217, 1251, 1301, 1390.

First Anniv. of Posts and Telecommunications Dept. — A115

1982, Jan. 1 Litho. *Perf. 11*

800	A115	6m	Phone, globe	.25	.20
801	A115	15m	Envelope	.60	.20

Gasoline Conservation — A116

1982, Jan. 25

802	A116	5m	Piston	.20	.20
803	A116	7.50m	Car	.30	.20
804	A116	10m	Truck	.40	.20
			Nos. 802-804 (3)	.90	.60

Sea Snake A117

1982, Feb. 27 Litho. *Perf. 11*

805	A117	50c	shown	.20	.20
806	A117	1.50m	Mozambique spitting cobra	.20	.20
807	A117	3m	Savanna vine snake	.20	.20
808	A117	6m	Black mamba	.25	.20
809	A117	15m	Boomslang	.60	.20
810	A117	20m	Bitis arietans	.80	.30
			Nos. 805-810 (6)	2.25	1.30

TB Bacillus Centenary — A118

1982, Mar. 15 Litho. *Perf. 11*

811	A118	20m	multi	.80	.30

ITU Plenipotentiary Conference, Nairobi, Sept. 28-Nov. 5 — A119

1982, Mar. 31 *Perf. 13½*

812	A119	20m	multi	.80	.35

1982 World Cup — A120

Designs: Various soccer players.

1982, Apr. 19 Litho. *Perf. 13½*

813	A120	1.5m	multi	.20	.20
814	A120	3.5m	multi	.20	.20
815	A120	7m	multi	.30	.20
816	A120	10m	multi	.40	.20
817	A120	20m	multi	.80	.30
			Nos. 813-817 (5)	1.90	1.10

Souvenir Sheet

Imperf

818	A120	50m	multi	2.00	2.00

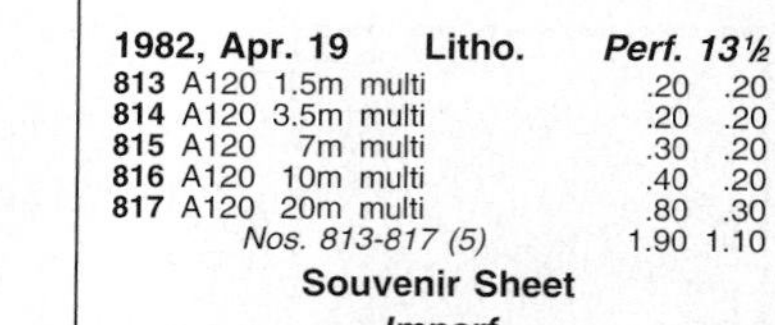

Souvenir Sheet

Two Tahitian Women, by Gauguin — A121

1982, June 11 Litho. *Imperf.*

819	A121	35m	multi	4.00	2.50

PHILEXFRANCE '82 Intl. Stamp Exhibition, Paris, June 11-21.

Natl. Liberation Front, 20th Anniv. — A122

Vangueria Infausta A123

1982, June 25 *Perf. 13*

820	A122	4m	Pres. Mondland addressing crowd	.20	.20
821	A122	8m	Guarded fields	.30	.20
822	A122	12m	Procession	.50	.20
			Nos. 820-822 (3)	1.00	.60

1982, Sept. 13 *Perf. 11*

Designs: Fruits.

823	A123	1m	shown	.20	.20
824	A123	2m	Mimusops caffra	.20	.20
825	A123	4m	Sclerocarya caffra	.20	.20
826	A123	8m	Strychnos spinosa	.35	.20
827	A123	12m	Salacia kraussi	.50	.20
828	A123	32m	Trichilia emetica	1.40	.40
			Nos. 823-828 (6)	2.85	1.40

25th Anniv. of Sputnik 1 Flight A124

1982, Oct. 4 Litho. *Perf. 11*

829	A124	1m	Sputnik, 1957	.20	.20
830	A124	2m	Yuri Gagarin's flight, 1961	.20	.20
831	A124	4m	A. Leonov's spacewalk, 1965	.20	.20
832	A124	8m	Apollo 11, 1969	.35	.20
833	A124	16m	Apollo-Soyuz, 1975	.70	.25
834	A124	20m	Salyut-6, 1978	.85	.30
a.			Min. sheet of 6, #829-834	2.50	2.50
			Nos. 829-834 (6)	2.50	1.35

People's Vigilance Day — A125

Caique — A126

1982, Oct. 11 *Perf. 13½*

835 A125 4m multi .20 .20

1982, Nov. 29

Traditional boats. 4m, 8m, 12m, 16m horiz.

836 A126 1m shown .20 .20
837 A126 2m Machua .20 .20
838 A126 4m Calaua .20 .20
839 A126 8m Chitatarro .35 .20
840 A126 12m Cangaia .50 .20
841 A126 16m Chata (flatboat) .70 .25
Nos. 836-841 (6) 2.15 1.25

Marine Life — A127

1982, Dec. 21 **Litho.** *Perf. 11*

842 A127 1m Ophiomastix venosa .20 .20
843 A127 2m Protoreaster lincki .20 .20
844 A127 4m Tropiometra carinata .25 .20
845 A127 8m Holothuria scabra .40 .20
846 A127 12m Prionocidaris baculosa .60 .25
847 A127 16m Colobocentrotus atnatus .80 .40
Nos. 842-847 (6) 2.45 1.45

Frelimo Party 4th Congress — A128

1983, Jan. 17

848 A128 4m Map, soldier .20 .20
849 A128 8m Voters .35 .20
850 A128 16m Farm workers .70 .20
Nos. 848-850 (3) 1.25 .60

Seaweed A129

1983, Feb. 28 **Litho.** *Perf. 11*

851 A129 1m Codium duthierae .20 .20
852 A129 2m Halimeda cuncata .20 .20
853 A129 4m Dictyota liturata .20 .20
854 A129 8m Encorachne binghamiae .35 .20
855 A129 12m Laurencia flexuosa .50 .20
856 A129 20m Acrosorium sp. .85 .35
Nos. 851-856 (6) 2.30 1.35

1984 Olympic Games, Los Angeles A130

1983, Mar. 31 **Litho.** *Perf. 11*

857 A130 1m Diving .20 .20
858 A130 2m Boxing .20 .20
859 A130 4m Basketball .20 .20
860 A130 8m Handball .35 .20
861 A130 12m Volleyball .50 .20
862 A130 16m Running .70 .25
863 A130 20m Sailing .85 .35
Nos. 857-863 (7) 3.00 1.60

Souvenir Sheet

Imperf

864 A130 50m Discus 2.00 2.00

For surcharge see No. 1257.

Steam Locomotives — A131

1983, Apr. 29 **Litho.** *Perf. 11*

865 A131 1m 1912 .20 .20
866 A131 2m 1947 .20 .20
867 A131 4m 1923 .20 .20
868 A131 8m 1924 .30 .20
869 A131 16m 1924, diff. .70 .30
870 A131 32m 1950 1.40 .40
Nos. 865-870 (6) 3.00 1.50

20th Anniv. of Org. of African Unity A132

1983, May 25 **Litho.** *Perf. 11*

871 A132 4m multi .20 .20

Mammals A133

1983, May 30

872 A133 1m Petrodromus tetradactylus .20 .20
873 A133 2m Rhabdomys pumilio .20 .20
874 A133 4m Paraxerus vincenti .20 .20
875 A133 8m Cryptomys hottentotus .35 .20
876 A133 12m Pronolagus crassicaudatus .50 .20
877 A133 16m Eidolon helvum .70 .30
Nos. 872-877 (6) 2.15 1.30

Souvenir Sheet

Marimba Players — A134

1983, July 29 **Litho.** *Perf. 11*

878 A134 30m multi 1.50 1.50

BRASILIANA '83 Intl. Stamp Show, Rio de Janeiro, July 29-Aug. 7.

World Communications Year — A135

1983, Aug. 26 **Litho.** *Perf. 11*

879 A135 8m multi .35 .20

Fishing Techniques — A136

1983, Oct. 29 **Litho.** *Perf. 11*

880 A136 50c Line fishing .20 .20
881 A136 2m Chifonho .20 .20
882 A136 4m Momba .20 .20
883 A136 8m Gamboa .30 .20
884 A136 16m Mono .55 .20
885 A136 20m Lema .70 .30
Nos. 880-885 (6) 2.15 1.30

World Communications Year, Stamp Day — A137

1983, Dec. 21 **Litho.**

886 A137 50c Horn .20 .20
887 A137 1m Drum .20 .20
888 A137 4m Native mail carriers .20 .20
889 A137 8m Boat .30 .20
890 A137 16m Truck .55 .20
891 A137 20m Train .70 .30
Nos. 886-891 (6) 2.15 1.30

2nd Anniv. of Mozambique Red Cross (July 10) — A138

1983, Oct. 29 **Litho.** *Perf. 11*

892 A138 4m Flood relief .20 .20
893 A138 8m Rescue truck .30 .20
894 A138 16m First aid .55 .20
895 A138 32m Field first aid 1.10 .40
Nos. 892-895 (4) 2.15 1.00

Olympic Games 1984, Los Angeles A139

1984, Jan. 2 **Litho.** *Perf. 11*

896 A139 50c Swimming .20 .20
897 A139 4m Soccer .20 .20
898 A139 8m Hurdles .30 .20
899 A139 16m Basketball .55 .25
900 A139 32m Handball 1.10 .30
901 A139 60m Boxing 2.00 .50
Nos. 896-901 (6) 4.35 1.65

Indigenous Trees — A140

1984, Mar. 30 **Litho.** *Perf. 11*

902 A140 50c Trichilia emetica .20 .20
903 A140 2m Brachystegia spiciformis .20 .20
904 A140 4m Androstachys johnsonii .20 .20
905 A140 8m Pterocarpus angolensis .20 .20
906 A140 16m Milletia stuhlmannii .30 .20
907 A140 50m Dalbergia melanoxylon 1.00 .40
Nos. 902-907 (6) 2.10 1.40

Nkomati Accord, Mar. 16 — A141

1984, Mar. 16

908 A141 4m Dove .20 .20

Natl. Arms A142

1984, May 1

909 A142 4m shown .20 .20
910 A142 8m Natl. flag .20 .20

Traditional Dances A143

1984, May 9

911 A143 4m Makway .20 .20
912 A143 8m Mapiko .20 .20
913 A143 16m Wadjaba .30 .20
Nos. 911-913 (3) .70 .60

LUBRAPEX '84, May 9-17.

Museums and Artifacts — A144

Designs: 50c, Nampula Museum, African carrying water jar, wooden statue. 4m, Museum of Natural History, preserved bird. 8m, Revolution Museum, guerrilla fighter statue. 16m, Colonial Occupation Museum, fort and cannon. 20m, Numismatic Museum, coins. 30m, Palace of St. Paul, char, 19th cent.

1984, June 25

914 A144 50c multi .20 .20
915 A144 4m multi .20 .20
916 A144 8m multi .20 .20
917 A144 16m multi .30 .20
918 A144 20m multi .40 .25
919 A144 30m multi .60 .30
Nos. 914-919 (6) 1.90 1.35

Freshwater Fish — A145

1984, Aug. 24

920 A145 50c Alestes imberi .20 .20
921 A145 4m Labeo congoro .20 .20
922 A145 12m Syndontis zambezensis .40 .20
923 A145 16m Notobranchius zachovii .55 .30
924 A145 40m Barbus paludinosus 1.40 .40
925 A145 60m Barilius zambezensis 2.00 .60
Nos. 920-925 (6) 4.75 1.90

For surcharge see No. 1311.

Intl. Fair, Maputo — A145a — 925A

1984, Aug. 24 Litho. *Perf. 11*

925A A145a 16m multicolored 1.25 .40

Traditional Weapons A146

1984, Sept. 25

926 A146 50c Knife, cudgel *.45* .20
927 A146 4m Axes *.60* .20
928 A146 8m Shield, assagai *1.25* .20
929 A146 16m Bow and arrow *2.40* .30
930 A146 32m Muzzleloader *3.00* .40
931 A146 50m Assagai, arrow *5.00* .50
Nos. 926-931 (6) *12.70* 1.80

Natl. Revolution, 20th anniv.
For surcharge see No. 1256.

Natl. Trade Unions, 1st Anniv. — A147

1984, Oct. 13 *Perf. 13½*

932 A147 4m Workers, emblem .20 .20

Stamp Day — A149

Cancellations on altered stamps and stationery: 4m, Barue cancel on 1885 20r postal card. 8m, Zumbo cancel on design similar to No. 52. 12m, Mozambique Co. cancel on design similar to Mozambique Company Type API. 16m, Macequece cancel on design similar to Mozambique Company No. 190.

1984, Dec. 21 *Perf. 11½x11*

936 A149 4m multi .20 .20
937 A149 8m multi .30 .20
938 A149 12m multi .40 .20
939 A149 16m multi .55 .25
Nos. 936-939 (4) 1.45 .85

African Development Bank, 20th Anniv. — A150

1984, Sept. 16 Photo. *Perf. 11½x11*

940 A150 4m multi .20 .20

Apiculture A151

1985, Feb. 3

941 A151 4m Beekeeper .30 .20
942 A151 8m Bee gathering pollen .50 .20
943 A151 16m Entering nest 1.00 .25
944 A151 20m Building honeycomb 1.50 .30
Nos. 941-944 (4) 3.30 .95

OLYMPHILEX '85, Lausanne A152

1985, Mar. 18 *Perf. 11*

945 A152 16m Shot putter .25 .20

World Meteorology Day — A153

1985, Mar. 23 Litho. *Perf. 11*

946 A153 4m multi .20 .20

Southern African Development Coordination Conference, 5th Anniv. — A154

1985, Apr. 1

947 A154 4m Map .20 .20
948 A154 8m Map, transmission tower .20 .20
949 A154 16m Industry .25 .20
950 A154 32m Flags .45 .20
Nos. 947-950 (4) 1.10 .80

Independence, 10th Anniv. — A155

Colonial resistance battles: 1m, Mujenga, 1896. 4m, Mungari, 1917. 8m, Massangano, 1868. 16m, Marracuene, 1895, and Gungunhana (c. 1840-1906), resistance leader.

1985, June 25 Litho. *Perf. 11*

951 A155 1m multi .20 .20
952 A155 4m multi .20 .20
953 A155 8m multi .20 .20
954 A155 16m multi .25 .20
Nos. 951-954 (4) .85 .80

UN, 40th Anniv. — A156

1985, June 26

955 A156 16m multi *9.00 9.00*

Traditional Games — A157

1985, Aug. 28 Litho. *Perf. 11*

956 A157 50c Mathacuzana .20 .20
957 A157 4m Mudzobo .20 .20
958 A157 8m Muravarava .35 .35
959 A157 16m N'Tshuwa .70 .70
Nos. 956-959 (4) 1.45 1.45

Frogs and Toads A158

1985, Oct. 25 Litho. *Perf. 11*

960 A158 50c Rana angolensis .20 .20
961 A158 1m Hyperolius pictus .20 .20
962 A158 4m Ptychadena porosissima .30 .20
963 A158 8m Afrixalus formasinii .40 .25
964 A158 16m Bufo regularis .75 .30
965 A158 32m Hyperolius marmoratus .90 .40
Nos. 960-965 (6) 2.75 1.55

Medicinal Plants — A159

1985, Nov. 28 Litho. *Perf. 11*

966 A159 50c Aloe ferox .20 .20
967 A159 1m Boophone disticha .30 .20
968 A159 3.50m Gloriosa superba .50 .20
969 A159 4m Cotyledon orbiculata .75 .25
970 A159 8m Homeria breyniana 1.25 .30
970A A159 50m Haemanthus coccineus 3.00 .75
Nos. 966-970A (6) 6.00 1.90

Stamp Day A160

Stamps: 1m, Mozambique Company No. 126. 4m, Nyassa Type A6. 8m, Mozambique Company No. 110. 16m, Nyassa No. J2.

1985, Dec. 21

971 A160 1m multi .20 .20
972 A160 4m multi .20 .20
973 A160 8m multi .20 .20
974 A160 16m multi .25 .20
Nos. 971-974 (4) .85 .80

Halley's Comet — A161

Comet and: 4m, Space probe. 8m, Trajectory diagram. 16m, Newton's telescope, observatory, probe. 30m, Earth.

1986, Jan. 2

975 A161 4m multi .20 .20
976 A161 8m multi .25 .20
977 A161 16m multi .40 .20
978 A161 30m multi .90 .25
Nos. 975-978 (4) 1.75 .85

1986 World Cup Soccer Championships, Mexico — A162

Players.

1986, Feb. 28 Litho. ***Perf. 11½x11***

979	A162	3m	Vicente	.20	.20
980	A162	4m	Coluna	.20	.20
981	A162	8m	Costa Pereira	.20	.20
982	A162	12m	Hilario	.20	.20
983	A162	16m	Matateu	.25	.20
984	A162	50m	Eusebio	.70	.40
			Nos. 979-984 (6)	1.75	1.40

Intl. Peace Year — A163

1986, Mar. 18 ***Perf. 11***

985 A163 16m multi .25 .20

Mushrooms A164

1986, Apr. 8

986	A164	4m	Amanita muscaria	.20	.20
987	A164	8m	Lactarius deliciosus	.25	.20
988	A164	16m	Amanita phaloides	.45	.20
989	A164	30m	Tricholoma nudum	.90	.35
			Nos. 986-989 (4)	1.80	.95

Souvenir Sheet

Statue of Liberty, Cent. — A165

1986, May 22 ***Imperf.***

990 A165 100m multi 2.00 2.00

AMERIPEX '86. #990 has simulated perfs.

Traditional Women's Hair Styles — A166

1986, June Litho. ***Perf. 11½x11***

991	A166	1m	Tanzanian	.20	.20
992	A166	4m	Miriam	.20	.20
993	A166	8m	Estrelinhas	.20	.20
994	A166	16m	Toto	.25	.20
			Nos. 991-994 (4)	.85	.80

Marine Mammals — A167

1986, Aug. ***Perf. 11***

995	A167	1m	Dugongo dugon	.20	.20
996	A167	8m	Delphinus delphis	.25	.20
997	A167	16m	Neobalena marginata	.35	.20
998	A167	50m	Balaenoptera physalus	1.00	.25
			Nos. 995-998 (4)	1.80	.85

Continuing Youth Education Organization, 1st Anniv. — A168

1986, Sept. 16 Litho. ***Perf. 11½x11***

999 A168 4m multi .20 .20

Natl. Savings Campaign — A169

Bank notes, front and back.

1986, Oct. 22 Litho. ***Perf. 11½x11***

1000	A169	4m	50m note	.20	.20
1001	A169	8m	100m note	.30	.20
1002	A169	16m	500m note	.40	.20
1003	A169	30m	1000m note	1.00	.20
			Nos. 1000-1003 (4)	1.90	.80

For surcharge see No. 1302.

Stamp Day A170

Post offices.

1986, Dec. 21 Litho. ***Perf. 11***

1004	A170	3m	Quelimane	.20	.20
1005	A170	4m	Maputo	.25	.20
1006	A170	8m	Beira	.30	.20
1007	A170	16m	Nampula	.50	.20
			Nos. 1004-1007 (4)	1.25	.80

Minerals A171

1987, Jan. 2 ***Perf. 11x11½***

1008	A171	4m	Pyrite	.25	.20
1009	A171	8m	Emerald	.30	.20
1010	A171	12m	Agate	.40	.20
1011	A171	16m	Malachite	.50	.20
1012	A171	30m	Garnet	.75	.25
1013	A171	50m	Amethyst	1.00	.40
			Nos. 1008-1013 (6)	3.20	1.45

For surcharges see #1304-1305.

Frelimo Party, 10th Anniv. — A172

1987, Feb. 3 ***Perf. 11***

1014 A172 4m multi .20 .20

Pequenos Libombos Dam — A173

1987, Feb. 17 ***Perf. 11½x11***

1015 A173 16m multi .25 .20

World Health Day A174

1987, Apr. 7 Litho. ***Perf. 11x11½***

1016 A174 50m multi .70 .25

Birds — A175

1987, Apr. 27 Litho. ***Perf. 11½x11***

1017	A175	3m	Granatina granatina	.20	.20
1018	A175	4m	Halcyon senegalensis	.20	.20
1019	A175	8m	Mellittophagus bullockoides	.20	.20
1020	A175	12m	Perinestes minor	.20	.20
1021	A175	16m	Coracias naevia mosambica	.25	.25
1022	A175	30m	Cimmyris neergardi	.40	.30
			Nos. 1017-1022 (6)	1.45	1.35

Souvenir Sheet

CAPEX '87, Toronto, June 13-21 — A176

1987, June ***Imperf.***

1023 A176 200m multi 2.00 2.00

No. 1023 contains one stamp having simulated perforations.

1988 Summer Olympics, Seoul — A177

1987, May Litho. ***Perf. 11½x11***

1024	A177	12.50m	Soccer players and ball	.20	.20
1025	A177	25m	Runner's legs	.25	.20
1026	A177	50m	Volleyball	.50	.30
1027	A177	75m	Chess	.75	.40
1028	A177	100m	Basketball	1.00	.50
1029	A177	200m	Swimming	2.00	.75
			Nos. 1024-1029 (6)	4.70	2.35

Tapestries — A178

1987, Aug. ***Perf. 11***

1030	A178	20m	Incomplete pattern on loom	.20	.20
1031	A178	40m	Diamond-shaped pattern	.20	.20
1032	A178	80m	Landscape pattern	.30	.25
1033	A178	200m	Oriental pattern	.80	.35
			Nos. 1030-1033 (4)	1.50	1.00

Maputo City A179

Early Portuguese map of Lourenco Marques.

1987, Nov. 10 Litho. ***Perf. 11***

1034 A179 20m multi .20 .20

No. 762 Surcharged in Silver and Dark Red

1987 Litho. ***Perf. 14½***

1034A A108 4m on 4.50m multi *5.00 5.00*

1988 Summer Olympics, Seoul — A180

1988, Feb. 10 Litho. ***Perf. 11***

1035 A180 10m Javelin .20 .20
1036 A180 20m Baseball .30 .20
1037 A180 40m Boxing .60 .25
1038 A180 80m Field hockey 1.10 .40
1039 A180 100m Gymnastic rings 1.40 .50
1040 A180 400m Cycling 5.75 1.90
Nos. 1035-1040 (6) 9.35 3.45

Nos. 1036-1040 horiz.

Flowering Plants — A181

1988, Mar. 18 ***Perf. 11½x11***

1041 A181 10m Heamanthus nelsonii .20 .20
1042 A181 20m Crinum polyphyllum .30 .20
1043 A181 40m Boophane disticha .60 .25
1044 A181 80m Cyrtanthus contractus 1.10 .40
1045 A181 100m Nerine angustifolia 1.40 .50
1046 A181 400m Cyrtanthus galpinnii 5.75 1.90
Nos. 1041-1046 (6) 9.35 3.45

World Health Organization, 40th Anniv. — A182

1988, Apr. 7

1047 A182 20m multi .30 .30

Anti-smoking campaign.

Wickerwork — A183

1988, June 16 Litho. ***Perf. 11***

1048 A183 20m Mat .20 .20
1049 A183 25m Lidded container .20 .20
1050 A183 80m Market basket .60 .20
1051 A183 100m Fan .75 .25
1052 A183 400m Flat basket 2.00 1.00
1053 A183 500m Funnel basket 3.00 1.25
Nos. 1048-1053 (6) 6.75 3.10

Souvenir Sheet

FINLANDIA '88 — A184

1988, June 12 Litho. ***Imperf.***

1054 A184 500m multi 3.00 1.00

Stamp in No. 1054 has simulated perfs.

Souvenir Sheet

State Visit of Pope John Paul II, Sept. 16-19 — A185

1988 Litho. ***Perf. 13½***

1055 A185 500m multi 3.00 1.50

Horses A186

1988, Sept. 20 Litho. ***Perf. 11***

1056 A186 20m Percheron .25 .20
1057 A186 40m Arab .50 .20
1058 A186 80m Thoroughbred 1.00 .25
1059 A186 100m Pony 1.50 .35
Nos. 1056-1059 (4) 3.25 1.00

Pres. Samora Machel (1933-1986) A187

1988, Oct. 19 Litho. ***Perf. 11***

1060 A187 20m multi .20 .20

Stamp Day A188

1988, Dec. 21 ***Perf. 11x11½, 11½x11***

1061 A188 20m P.O. trailer .20 .20
1062 A188 40m Mailbox, vert. .20 .20

Ports A189

1988, Nov. 30 ***Perf. 11***

1063 A189 25m Inhambane .20 .20
1064 A189 50m Quelimane, vert. .20 .20
1065 A189 75m Pemba .30 .20
1066 A189 100m Beira .40 .20
1067 A189 250m Nacala, vert. 1.00 .25
1068 A189 500m Maputo 2.10 .50
Nos. 1063-1068 (6) 4.20 1.55

5th Frelimo Party Congress A190

1989, Jan. 19

1069 Strip of 5 2.60 1.25
a. A190 25m Corn .20 .20
b. A190 50m Axe .25 .20
c. A190 75m Abstract shapes .35 .20
d. A190 100m 2½ Gearwheels .50 .25
e. A190 250m ½ Gearwheel 1.25 .60

Printed se-tenant in a continuous design.

French Revolution Bicent. — A191

Designs: 100m, *Storming of the Bastille,* by Thevenin. 250m, *Liberty Guiding the People,* by Delacroix. 500m, *Declaration of the Rights of Man and the Citizen,* a print by Blanchard.

1989, Feb. 16 ***Perf. 11***

1070 A191 100m multi .30 .20
1071 A191 250m multi .75 .25

Souvenir Sheet

1072 A191 500m multi 1.50 .75

No. 1072 is a continuous design.

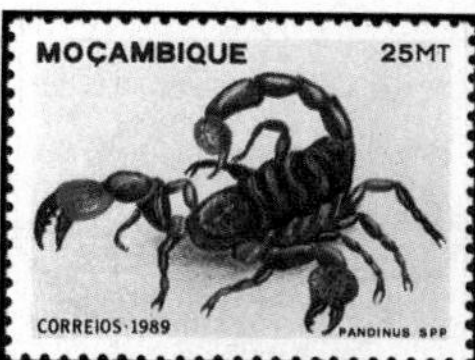

Venomous Species — A193

1989, Mar. 23

1074 A193 25m Pandinus .20 .20
1075 A193 50m Naja haje .20 .20
1076 A193 75m Bombus .30 .20
1077 A193 100m Paraphysa .40 .20
1078 A193 250m Conus marmoreus 1.00 .25
1079 A193 500m Pterois volitans 2.10 .50
Nos. 1074-1079 (6) 4.20 1.55

Coral A194

1989, May 2 Litho. ***Perf. 11***

1080 A194 25m Acropora pulchra .20 .20
1081 A194 50m Eunicella papilosa .20 .20
1082 A194 100m Dendrophyla migrantus .30 .20
1083 A194 250m Favia fragum .70 .25
Nos. 1080-1083 (4) 1.40 .85

1990 World Cup Soccer Championships, Italy — A195

Athletes executing various plays.

1989, June 22 Litho. ***Perf. 11½x11***

1084 A195 30m multi .20 .20
1085 A195 60m multi .20 .20
1086 A195 125m multi .30 .20
1087 A195 200m multi .55 .20
1088 A195 250m multi .70 .25
1089 A195 500m multi 1.40 .45
Nos. 1084-1089 (6) 3.35 1.50

Lighthouses A196

1989, July 24 Litho. ***Perf. 11***

1090 A196 30m Macuti .20 .20
1091 A196 60m Pinda .20 .20
1092 A196 125m Cape Delgado .35 .20
1093 A196 200m Isle of Goa .55 .20
1094 A196 250m Caldeira Point .70 .25
1095 A196 500m Vilhena 1.40 .45
Nos. 1090-1095 (6) 3.40 1.50

Filigree Workmanship in Silver — A197

Eduardo Chivambo Mondlane (1920-1969), Frelimo Party Founder, 20th Death Anniv. — A192

1989, Feb. 3 Litho. ***Perf. 11***

1073 A192 25m blk, gold & dark red .20 .20

1989, Aug. 30 Litho. *Perf. 11x11½*

1096 A197 30m shown .20 .20
1097 A197 60m Flower on band .20 .20
1098 A197 125m Necklace .30 .20
1099 A197 200m Decorative box .50 .20
1100 A197 250m Utensils .60 .25
1101 A197 500m Butterfly 1.25 .45
Nos. 1096-1101 (6) 3.05 1.50

Natl. Liberation War, 25th Anniv. A198

1989, Sept. 25

1102 A198 30m multicolored .20 .20

Meteorological Instruments A199

Designs: 30m, Rain gauge. 60m, Weather system on radar. 125m, Instrument shelter. 200m, Computer monitor and keyboard.

1989, Oct. 12 *Perf. 11½x11*

1103 A199 30m multicolored .20 .20
1104 A199 60m multicolored .25 .20
1105 A199 125m multicolored .40 .20
1106 A199 200m multicolored .75 .25
Nos. 1103-1106 (4) 1.60 .85

Souvenir Sheet

World Stamp Expo '89, Washington, DC — A200

1989, Nov. 17 *Perf. 13½*

1107 A200 500m Washington Monument 2.50 1.50

Stamp Day — A201

1989, Dec. 21 Litho. *Perf. 11½x11*

1108 A201 30m UPU emblem .20 .20
1109 A201 60m P.O. emblem .20 .20

Southern African Development Coordination Conf. (SADCC), 10th Anniv. — A201a

1990, Jan. 31 *Perf. 11½x11*

1109A A201a 35m multicolored .20 .20

Textile Designs A202

1990, Feb. 28 Litho. *Perf. 11x11½*

1110 A202 42m multi, diff. .20 .20
1111 A202 90m multi, diff. .30 .20
1112 A202 150m multi, diff. .45 .25
1113 A202 200m multi, diff. .60 .30
1114 A202 400m multi, diff. 1.25 .60
1115 A202 500m multi, diff. 1.50 .75
Nos. 1110-1115 (6) 4.30 2.30

Forts A203

1990, Mar. 20 *Perf. 11x11½*

1116 A203 45m Sena .20 .20
1117 A203 90m Santo Antonio .30 .20
1118 A203 150m Santo Sebastiao .45 .25
1119 A203 200m Santo Caetano .60 .30
1120 A203 400m Our Lady of Conceicao 1.25 .60
1121 A203 500m Santo Luis 1.50 .75
Nos. 1116-1121 (6) 4.30 2.30

Souvenir Sheet

Penny Black, Mozambique No. 1 — A204

1990, May 3 Litho. *Perf. 11½x11*

1122 A204 1000m red, blk & bl 4.00 3.00

Penny Black, 150th anniversary. Stamp World London '90.

Bank of Mozambique, 15th Anniv. — A205

1990, May 17 Litho. *Perf. 11x11½*

1123 A205 100m multicolored .30 .20

Natl. Independence, 15th Anniv. — A206

1990, June 25 *Perf. 11*

1124 A206 42.50m Eduardo Mondlane .20 .20
1125 A206 150m Samora Machel .45 .25

Endangered Species — A207

1990, Aug. 20 Litho. *Perf. 11x11½*

1126 A207 42.50m Ceratotherium simum .20 .20
1127 A207 100m Dugong dugong .30 .20
1128 A207 150m Loxodonta africana .45 .25
1129 A207 200m Acinonix jubatus .60 .30
1130 A207 400m Lutra maculicollis 1.25 .60
1131 A207 500m Eretmochelys imbricata 1.50 .70
Nos. 1126-1131 (6) 4.30 2.25

Trees and Plants — A208

1990, Oct. 15 Litho. *Perf. 11½x11*

1132 A208 42.50m Dichrostachys cinerea .20 .20
1133 A208 100m Queimadas .30 .20
1134 A208 150m Casuariana equisetifolia .45 .25
1135 A208 200m Rhizophora muronata .60 .30
1136 A208 400m Estrato herbaceo 1.25 .60
1137 A208 500m Atzelia cuanzensis 1.50 .70
Nos. 1132-1137 (6) 4.30 2.25

Stamp Day — A209

No. 1138: a, Pick-up at letter box. b, Canceling letters. c, Letter carrier. d, Delivery to recipient.

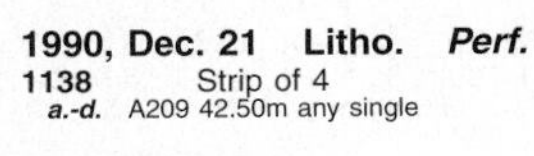

1990, Dec. 21 Litho. *Perf. 11½x11*

1138 Strip of 4 .60 .40
a.-d. A209 42.50m any single .20 .20

Governmental Departments A210

Designs: No. 1139, Post Office Dept., 10th anniv. No. 1140, Telecommunications Dept.

1991, Jan. 2

1139 A210 50m dk bl, red & blk .20 .20
1140 A210 50m grn, blk & brn .20 .20

Flowers — A211

1991, Feb. 25 Litho. *Perf. 11½x11*

1141 A211 50m Strilitzia reginae .20 .20
1142 A211 125m Anthurium andraeanum .55 .25
1143 A211 250m Zantedeschia pentlandii 1.00 .50
1144 A211 300m Canna indica 1.25 .60
Nos. 1141-1144 (4) 3.00 1.55

Alcelaphus Lichtensteini A212

1991, Mar. 27 *Perf. 14*

1145 Strip of 4 12.50 7.50
a. A212 50m Two adults .50 .30
b. A212 100m Adult 1.25 .30
c. A212 250m Adult grazing 3.00 .75
d. A212 500m Nursing calf 6.00 2.00

Fountains of Maputo — A213

Designs: 50m, Mpompine. 125m, Chinhambanine. 250m, Sao Pedro-Zaza. 300m, Xipamanine.

1991, Apr. 15 Litho. *Perf. 11½x11*

1146 A213 50m multicolored .20 .20
1147 A213 125m multicolored .30 .20
1148 A213 250m multicolored .55 .30
1149 A213 300m multicolored .65 .30
Nos. 1146-1149 (4) 1.70 1.00

For surcharge see No. 1394.

Paintings by Mozambican Artists — A214

1991, May 18 Litho. *Perf. 11½x11*
1150 A214 180m Samale .40 .20
1151 A214 250m Malangatana .55 .30
1152 A214 560m Malangatana, diff. 1.25 .60
Nos. 1150-1152 (3) 2.20 1.10

1992 Summer Olympics, Barcelona A215

1991, June 25 Litho. *Perf. 11½x11*
1153 A215 10m Swimming .20 .20
1154 A215 50m Roller hockey .20 .20
1155 A215 100m Tennis .25 .20
1156 A215 200m Table tennis .45 .25
1157 A215 500m Running 1.10 .55
1158 A215 1000m Badminton 2.25 1.10
Nos. 1153-1158 (6) 4.45 2.50

For surcharges, see Nos. 1393, 1393A, 1395-1396.

British-Portuguese Agreement on Mozambique Borders, Cent. — A216

1991, Oct. 9 Litho. *Perf. 11½x11*
1159 A216 600m Map of 1890 .85 .40
1160 A216 800m Map of 1891 1.10 .60

Souvenir Sheet

Phila Nippon '91 — A217

1991, Nov. 15 Litho. *Perf. 11½x11*
1161 A217 1500m Map of Japan 1.75 1.75

Children's Games — A218

1991, Dec. 21
1162 A218 40m Jumping rope .20 .20
1163 A218 150m Spinning top .20 .20
1164 A218 400m Marbles .35 .20
1165 A218 900m Hopscotch .80 .40
Nos. 1162-1165 (4) 1.55 1.00

Stained Glass Windows — A219

No. 1166 — Various designs: a, 40m. b, 150m. c, 400m. d, 900m.

1992, Jan. 22
1166 A219 Block of 4, #a.-d. 1.40 .70

Plants — A220

1992, Mar. 23 Litho. *Perf. 11½x11*
1167 A220 300m Rhisophora mucronata .50 .30
1168 A220 600m Cymodocea ciliata 1.10 .50
1169 A220 1000m Sophora inhambanensis 1.75 .90
Nos. 1167-1169 (3) 3.35 1.70

Traditional Tools — A221

1992, May 9
1170 A221 100m Spear, spear-thrower .20 .20
1171 A221 300m Pitch forks .50 .25
1172 A221 500m Hatchet .90 .45
1173 A221 1000m Dagger 1.75 .90
Nos. 1170-1173 (4) 3.35 1.80

Lubrapex '92, Lisbon.

A222

Birds: 150m, Chalcomitra amethystina. 200m, Ceropis senegalensis. 300m, Cossypha natalensis. 400m, Lamprocolius chloropterus. 500m, Malaconotus poliocephalus. 800m, Oriolus auratus.

1992, July 24 Litho. *Perf. 11½x11*
1174 A222 150m multicolored .30 .20
1175 A222 200m multicolored .35 .20
1176 A222 300m multicolored .50 .25
1177 A222 400m multicolored .70 .35
1178 A222 500m multicolored .85 .40
1179 A222 800m multicolored 1.40 .70
Nos. 1174-1179 (6) 4.10 2.10

Eduardo Mondlane University, 30th Anniv. — A223

1992, Aug. 21
1180 A223 150m grn, brn & blk .30 .20

Traditional Musical Instruments A224

1992, Sept. 18
1181 A224 200m Phiane .35 .20
1182 A224 300m Xirupe .50 .25
1183 A224 500m Ngulula .85 .40
1184 A224 1500m Malimba 2.50 1.25
a. Souvenir sheet of 4, #1181-1184, imperf. 4.25 2.10
Nos. 1181-1184 (4) 4.20 2.10

Genoa '92. #1184a has simulated perfs.

No. 757 Surcharged

1992, Oct. Litho. *Perf. 14½*
1185 A108 50m on 50c #757 .80 .40

Intl. Conference on Nutrition — A225

1992, Oct. 16 *Perf. 11½x11*
1186 A225 450m multicolored .75 .40

Parachuting A226

Various parchutists descending from sky.

1992, Nov. 10 Litho. *Perf. 11½x11*
1187 A226 50m multicolored .20 .20
1188 A226 400m multicolored .60 .30
1189 A226 500m multicolored .80 .40
1190 A226 1500m multicolored 2.40 1.10
Nos. 1187-1190 (4) 4.00 2.00

Medals — A227

1993, Feb. 3 Litho. *Perf. 11½x11*
1191 A227 400m Order of Peace & Amity .30 .20
1192 A227 800m Baga moyo .55 .30
1193 A227 1000m Order of Eduardo Mondlane .70 .35
1194 A227 1500m War veterans 1.00 .50
Nos. 1191-1194 (4) 2.55 1.35

Pollution A228

1993, Apr. 8 *Perf. 11x11½*
1195 A228 200m Deforestation .20 .20
1196 A228 750m Factory smoke .50 .25
1197 A228 1000m Oil spill from ship .70 .35
1198 A228 1500m Automobile exhaust 1.00 .50
Nos. 1195-1198 (4) 2.40 1.30

Natl. Parks A229

Park, animal, map: 200m, Gorongosa, lion. 800m, Banhine, giraffes. 1000m, Bazaruto, manatees. 1500m, Zinave, ostriches.

1993, May 25 Litho. *Perf. 11x11½*
1199 A229 200m multicolored .20 .20
1200 A229 800m multicolored .60 .30
1201 A229 1000m multicolored .70 .35
1202 A229 1500m multicolored 1.00 .50
Nos. 1199-1202 (4) 2.50 1.35

Natl. Conference on Culture — A230

1993, Sept. 27 Litho. *Perf. 11½x11*
1203 A230 200m multicolored .20 .20

Union of Portuguese Speaking Capitals A231

1993, July 30 Litho. *Perf. 11x11½*
1204 A231 1500m multicolored 1.75 .85

Brasilana '93.

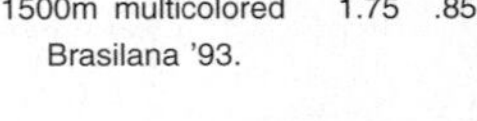

Forest Plants — A232

Designs: 200m, Cycas cercinalis. 250m, Cycas revoluta. 900m, Encephalartos ferox. 2000m, Equisetum ramosissimum.

1993, Dec. 29 Litho. *Perf. 11½x11*
1205 A232 200m multicolored .20 .20
1206 A232 250m multicolored .20 .20
1207 A232 900m multicolored .55 .30
1208 A232 2000m multicolored 1.25 .60
Nos. 1205-1208 (4) 2.20 1.30

Medicinal Plants — A233

1994 Litho. *Perf. 11½x11*

1209 A233 200m Anacardium occidentale .20 .20
1210 A233 250m Sclerocarya caffra .20 .20
1211 A233 900m Annona senegalensis .55 .30
1212 A233 2000m Crinum delagoense 1.25 .65
Nos. 1209-1212 (4) 2.20 1.35

Nos. 763-764, 772, 791-792, 797-798 Surcharged

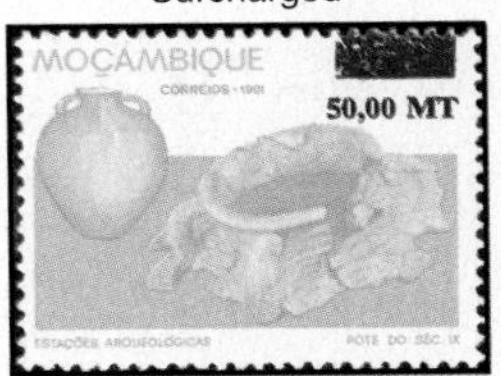

1994
Perfs. and Printing Methods as Before

1213 A109 50m on 7.50m #772 .20 .20
1214 A113 50m on 7.50m #791 .20 .20
1215 A114 50m on 7.50m #797 .20 .20
1216 A108 100m on 10m #763 .20 .20
1217 A114 100m on 12.50m #798 .20 .20
1218 A108 200m on 12.50m #764 .20 .20
1219 A113 250m on 12.50m #792 .20 .20
Nos. 1213-1219 (7) 1.40 1.40

Size and location of surcharge varies. Surcharge on Nos. 1214-1215, 1219 does not contain an obliterator.

For additional surcharge, see No. 1391.

PHILAKOREA '94 — A234

Reptiles: 300m, Ichnotropis squamulosa. 500m, Lepidachelys olivacea. 2000m, Prosyma frontalis. 3500m, Rampholeon marshalli. 4000m, Snake eating a lizard.

1994, Aug. 16 Litho. *Perf. 11½x11*

1220 A234 300m multicolored .20 .20
1221 A234 500m multicolored .20 .20
1222 A234 2000m multicolored .85 .40
1223 A234 3500m multicolored 1.40 .70
Nos. 1220-1223 (4) 2.65 1.50

Souvenir Sheet

1224 A234 4000m multicolored 1.75 .90

ICAO, 50th Anniv. A235

Designs: 300d, Crop dusting. 500m, Airport terminal. 2000m, Passenger jet in flight. 3500m, Maintenance man inspecting jet engine.

1994, Oct. 12 Litho. *Perf. 11x11½*

1225 A235 300m multicolored .20 .20
1226 A235 500m multicolored .30 .20
1227 A235 2000m multicolored 1.25 .60
1228 A235 3500m multicolored 2.00 1.00
Nos. 1225-1228 (4) 3.75 2.00

World Food Day — A236

1994, Oct. 24 *Perf. 11½x11*

1229 A236 2000m multicolored 1.25 .60

Lubrapex '94.

National Elections — A237

1994, Oct. 26

1230 A237 900m multicolored .70 .35

Fight Against Illegal Drugs — A238

Designs: 500m, Couple using drugs. 1000m, Hypodermic needle, couple tied in rope, skeleton. 2000m, Man with drug dependency. 5000m, Dog apprehending man with contraband.

1994, Dec. 7

1231 A238 500m multicolored .30 .20
1232 A238 1000m multicolored .60 .30
1233 A238 2000m multicolored 1.25 .60
1234 A238 5000m multicolored 3.00 1.50
Nos. 1231-1234 (4) 5.15 2.60

Lusaka Accord, 20th Anniv. — A239

1994, Nov. 9

1235 A239 1500m multicolored .90 .45

Basketry — A240

1995, Apr. 15 Litho. *Perf. 11½x11*

1236 A240 250m shown .20 .20
1237 A240 300m Two-handled basket .20 .20
1238 A240 1200m Round purse .55 .35
1239 A240 5000m Purse, diff. 2.25 1.25
Nos. 1236-1239 (4) 3.20 2.00

Clothing — A241

Various styles of women's traditional clothing.

1995, May 25

1240 A241 250m blue & multi .20 .20
1241 A241 300m pink & multi .20 .20
1242 A241 1200m blue & multi .55 .35
1243 A241 5000m red & multi 2.25 1.25
Nos. 1240-1243 (4) 3.20 2.00

Inauguration of Pres. Joaquim A. Chissano, Dec. 9, 1994 — A242

No. 1244: a, 900m, Natl. arms. b, 5000m, Pres. Chissano. c, 2500m, Natl. flag.

1995, June 25 Litho. *Perf. 11½x11*

1244 A242 Strip of 3, #a.-c. 2.25 1.25

No. 1244 has a common inscription across the bottom.

Wild Animals — A243

Designs: 500m, Crassicadautus lombergi. 2000m, Tragelaphus strepsceros, horiz. 3000m, Potamochoerus porcus nyasae, horiz. 5000m, Tragelaphus scriptus.

Perf. 11½x11, 11x11½

1995, Aug. 29 Litho.

1245 A243 500m multicolored .20 .20
1246 A243 2000m multicolored .45 .25
1247 A243 3000m multicolored .65 .35
1248 A243 5000m multicolored 1.10 .55
Nos. 1245-1248 (4) 2.40 1.35

FAO, 50th Anniv. — A244

1995, Oct. 16 *Perf. 11½x11*

1249 A244 5000m multicolored 1.10 .55

UN, 50th Anniv. — A245

1995, Oct. 24

1250 A245 5000m blue & black 1.10 .55

Nos. 647, 711, 713, 749, 763, 792, 798, 862, 929 Surcharged

Perfs. and Printing Methods as Before

1995, Oct. 4

1251 A114 250m on 12.50m #798 .20 .20
1252 A108 300m on 10m #763 .20 .20
1253 A113 500m on 12.50m #792 .20 .20
1253A A97 600m on 5m #711 — —
1254 A81 900m on 12.50m #647 .20 .20
1255 A97 1000m on 12.50m #713 .25 .20
1256 A146 1500m on 16m #929 .35 .20
1257 A130 2000m on 16m #862 .45 .25
1258 A106 2500m on 12.50m #749 .55 .30
Nos. 1251-1258 (9) 2.40 1.75

UNICEF, 20th Anniv. — A246

1995, Nov. 22 Litho. *Perf. 11½*

1259 A246 5000m multicolored 1.10 .55

Mozambique-South Africa Soccer Match — A247

Various soccer plays.

1996, Apr. 5 Litho. *Perf. 11x11½*

1260 A247 1000m multicolored .20 .20
1261 A247 2000m multicolored .40 .20
1262 A247 4000m multicolored .80 .40
1263 A247 6000m multicolored 1.25 .60
Nos. 1260-1263 (4) 2.65 1.40

Masks — A248

Various masks.

1996, July 2 Litho. *Perf. 11½x11*

1264 A248 1000m multicolored .20 .20
1265 A248 2000m multicolored .40 .20
1266 A248 4000m multicolored .80 .40
1267 A248 6000m multicolored 1.25 .60
Nos. 1264-1267 (4) 2.65 1.40

Red Cross of Mozambique, 15th Anniv. — A249

1996, July 10
1268 A249 5000m multicolored .90 .45

Endangered Wildlife — A250

1996, Sept. 3 Litho. *Perf. 11½x11*
1269 A250 1000m Loxodona africana .20 .20
1270 A250 2000m Ceratotherum simum .40 .20
1271 A250 4000m Panthera pardus .80 .40
1272 A250 6000m Scotopelia peli 1.25 .60
Nos. 1269-1272 (4) 2.65 1.40

Removal of Land Mines — A251

Designs: 2000m, Mine, tripwire across path. 6000m, Warning sign posted. 8000m, Using mine detector. 10,000m, Removing mine.

1996, Nov. 9 Litho. *Perf. 11½x11*
1273 A251 2000m multicolored .35 .20
1274 A251 6000m multicolored 1.10 .55
1275 A251 8000m multicolored 1.40 .70
1276 A251 10,000m multicolored 1.75 .90
Nos. 1273-1276 (4) 4.60 2.35

Keep The City Clean Campaign A252

1996, Dec. 16 Litho. *Perf. 11½x11*
1277 A252 2000m multicolored .40 .20

Mozambique Postage Stamps, 120th Anniv. — A253

1996, Dec. 16 Litho. *Perf. 11½x11*
1278 A253 2000m No. 1 .35 .20

Mozambique Boats — A254

1997, Apr. 10 Litho. *Perf. 11x11½*
1279 A254 2000m Mitumbui .35 .20
1280 A254 6000m Muterere 1.10 .55
1281 A254 8000m Lancha 1.40 .70
1282 A254 10,000m Dau 1.75 .90
Nos. 1279-1282 (4) 4.60 2.35

Children's Day A255

1997, June 1 Litho. *Perf. 11x11½*
1283 A255 2000m multicolored .35 .20

Aquatic Birds A256

Designs: 2000m, Mycteria ibis. 4000m, Himantopus himantopus. 8000m, Calidris subminuta. 10,000m, Pelecanus onocrotalus.

Perf. 11½x11, 11x11½
1997, June 10
1284 A256 2000m multi, vert. .35 .20
1285 A256 4000m multi, vert. .65 .30
1286 A256 8000m multi 1.40 .65
1287 A256 10,000m multi, vert. 1.75 .85
Nos. 1284-1287 (4) 4.15 2.00

Independence of India, 50th Anniv. — A258a

1997 Litho. *Perf. 11x11½*
1287A A258a 2000m multi .95 .45

Insects A257

Designs: 2000m, Enaretta conifera. 6000m, Zographus heiroglyphicus. 8000m, Tragiscoschema bertolonii. 10,000m, Tragocephala ducalis.

1997, July 5 Litho. *Perf. 11x11½*
1288 A257 2000m multicolored .35 .20
1289 A257 6000m multicolored 1.00 .50
1290 A257 8000m multicolored 1.40 .70
1291 A257 10,000m multicolored 1.70 .85
a. Souvenir sheet, #1288-1291 4.50 2.25
Nos. 1288-1291 (4) 4.45 2.25

Labrapex '97 (#1291a).

Joao Ferreira dos Santos Group, Cent. — A258

1997, Sept. 5 Litho. *Perf. 11x11½*
1292 A258 2000m multi .40 .20

Protection of the Ozone Layer — A259

1997, Sept. 16 Litho. *Perf. 11½x11*
1293 A259 2000m multicolored .40 .20

Peace Accord, 5th Anniv. — A260

1997, Oct. 4 Litho. *Perf. 11½x11*
1294 A260 2000m multi .45 .25

Souvenir Sheet

Anhinga — A261

1997 Litho. *Perf. 11½x11*
1295 A261 5000m multi 3.00 .75

Food Products A262

1998, June 1 Litho. *Perf. 11x11½*
1296 A262 2000m multicolored .75 .20

Expo '98, Lisbon A263

1998, May 22
1297 A263 2000m Coelacanth .35 .20

Nos. 660, 666, 730, 764, 797, 1002, 1009, 1011 Surcharged

Printing Methods and Perfs as before

1998 (?)
1298 A85 2000m on 12.50e #660 1.25 1.25
1299 A86 2000m on 12.50e #666 1.25 1.25
1300 A108 4000m on 12.50m #764 1.00 1.00
1301 A114 6000m on 7.50m #797 2.00 2.00
1302 A169 7500m on 16m #1002 2.75 2.50
1303 A102 10,000m on 12.50m #730 2.00 1.00
1304 A171 12,500m on 8m #1009 3.00 3.00
1305 A171 12,500m on 16m #1011 2.25 2.25
Nos. 1298-1305 (8) 15.50 14.25

For surcharges, see Nos. 1400-1400A.

Diana, Princess of Wales (1961-97) A264

Nos. 1306-1308: Various portraits.
No. 1309, 30,000m, Wearing Red Cross vest. No. 1310, 30,000m, Wearing purple dress.

1998 Litho. *Perf. 13½*
1306 A264 2000m Sheet of 9, #a.-i. *3.50 2.50*
1307 A264 5000m Sheet of 9, #a.-i. *6.00 3.50*
1308 A264 8000m Sheet of 9, #a.-i. *8.00 6.00*

Souvenir Sheets
1309-1310 A264 Set of 2 9.50 6.00

Nos. 1309-1310 each contain one 42x60mm stamp.

No. 923 Surcharged in Silver

1998 Litho. *Perf. 14*
1311 A145 500m on 16m multi — —

Promotion of Breast Feeding — A265

1998 Litho. *Perf. 11½x11*
1312 A265 2000m multi .45 .25

Mother Teresa (1910-97) A266

1998 ***Perf. 11x11½***

1313 A266 2000m multi .45 .25

UPAP, 18th Anniv. A267

1998, Oct. 9 ***Perf. 11½x11***

1314 A267 2000m multi .45 .25

Mother's Day — A268

Designs: 2000m, Breast feeding. 4000m, Teacher. 8000m, Using computer. 10,000m, Woman in field.

1998, June 25 ***Perf. 11½x11***

1315-1318 A268 Set of 4 *5.25 5.25*

For surcharge, see No. 1417.

Plants — A269

Designs: 2000m Garcinia livingstonei. 7500m, Tabernaemontana elegans. 12,500m, Ximenia caffra. 25,000m, Syzygium guineense.
50,000m, Uapaca kirkiana.

1998, Oct. 9 ***Perf. 11¾x12***

1319-1322 A269 Set of 4 *6.50 6.50*

Souvenir Sheet

1323 A269 50,000m multi *7.50 7.50*

For surcharges, see Nos. 1418-1419, 1741-1742.

Dwellings A270

Various dwellings: 2000m, 4000m, 6000m, 8000m, 10,000m, 15,000m, 20,000m, 30,000m, 50,000m, 100,000m.

1998 **Litho.** ***Perf. 11x11¼***

1324-1333 A270 Set of 10 *25.00 25.00*

For surcharges, see Nos. 1399A, 1418-1419.

Souvenir Sheets

I Love Lucy — A270a

Designs: No. 1333A, 35,000m, Lucy wearing hat. No. 1333B, 35,000m, Lucy as ballet dancer.

1999 **Litho.** ***Perf. 13½***

1333A-1333B A270a Set of 2 *6.50 3.00*

A271

Diana, Princess of Wales (1961-97) — A272

No. 1334: a, purple, shown. b, Dull brown, looking left. c, Orange brown, wearing pearls. d, Olive green. e, Purple, wearing feathers & hat, looking right. f, Red brown, wearing round earring.

No. 1335 — Diana with: a, Large white collar, earring (purple vignette). b, Hat, looking left (red violet vignette). c, White dress (red brown vignette). d, Dangling earrings (brown vignette). e, Patterned dress (blue violet vignette). f, Flower bouquet (olive green vignette).

1999 ***Perf. 14***

1334 A271 6500m Sheet of 6, #a.-f. *5.00 2.00*

1335 A271 6500m Sheet of 6, #a.-f. *5.00 2.00*

Litho. & Embossed

Die Cut Perf. 7

1336 A272 25,000m gold & multi

Issued: #1336, 6/30.

The Three Stooges — A272a

No. 1336A: b, Joe Besser, Larry, Moe, frying pan. c, Shemp wearing hat. d, Moe and Larry putting pan on Joe Besser's head. e, Moe with pipe. f, Larry and Moe pouring liquids on Curly's head. g, Larry wearing hat. h, Joe Besser and Larry, pulling Moe's tooth. i, Curly. j, Shemp, Larry and Moe.

No. 1336K, 35,000m, Larry in pink shirt. No. 1336L, 35,000m, Larry holding shovel.

1999 **Litho.** ***Perf. 13½***

1336A A272a 5000m Sheet of 9, #b-j *4.50 2.00*

Souvenir Sheets

1336K-1336L A272a Set of 2 *7.50 3.00*

Trains — A273

2000m, DE-AC Blue Tiger, Germany. #1338, 2500m, DB 218 (red & black), Germany. #1339, 3000m, Mt. Pilatus inclined railroad car, Switzerland. 3500m, Berlin subway train, Germany.

No. 1341: a, DB V200, Germany. b, Union Pacific, US. c, Class 613, Germany. d, Canadian Pacific 4242, Canada. e, Duchess of Hamilton, Great Britain. f, Pacific Delhi, India. g, ISA, South Africa. h, DR VT 18-16-07, Germany. i, DB-DE, Australia.

No. 1342: a, DB 218 (green & yellow), Germany. b, QJ Class 2-10-2, China. c, 232 232.9, Germany. d, Flying Scotsman, Scotland. e, WR 360 CH, Germany. f, Henschel 2-8-2. g, Santa Fe 39C, US. h, Balkan Express, Greece. i, DB 218 (red & white), Germany.

No. 1343, 25,000m, Steam 2-8-2, Germany. No. 1344, 25,000m, DMU, Germany.

1999, Oct. 12 **Litho.** ***Perf. 14***

1337-1340 A273 Set of 4 1.90 1.90

1341 A273 2500m Sheet of 9, #a.-i. 4.00 4.00

1342 A273 3000m Sheet of 9, #a.-i. 4.75 4.75

Souvenir Sheets

1343-1344 A273 Set of 2 9.00 9.00

Betty Boop — A273a

No. 1344A: b, Seated on motorcycle, winking, wearing cap. c, Seated on motocycle, winking, without cap. d, Wearing cap. e, Seated on motorcycle, wearing cap, not winking. f, Hands folded across handlebars. g, Riding motorcycle. h, Hitchhiking. i, Seated on motorcycle, wearing bandana. j, Seated on motorcycle, hand raised.

No. 1344K, 35,000m, Seated on motorcycle, hand raised. No. 1344L, 35,000m, Seated next to motorcycle.

1999 **Litho.** ***Perf. 13½***

1344A A273a 3500m Sheet of 9, #b-j *6.50 6.00*

Souvenir Sheets

1344K-1344L A273a Set of 2 *12.00 10.00*

Cats — A274

No. 1345, 4000m, : a, Chartreux. b, Australian Mist. c, Egyptian Mau. d, Scottish Fold. e, Cornish Rex. f, Abyssinian.

No. 1346, 4000m: a, Himalayan. b, Balinese. c, Persian. d, Turkish Van. e, Norwegian Forest Cat. f, Maine Coon Cat.

No. 1347, 25,000m, Ragdoll. No. 1348, 25,000m, Siamese.

2000, Mar. 29 **Litho.** ***Perf. 14***

Sheets of 6, #a-f

1345-1346 A274 Set of 2 9.50 9.50

Souvenir Sheets

1347-1348 A274 Set of 2 9.50 9.50

Dated 1999.

Dogs — A275

No. 1349, 4500m, vert.: a, Shetland sheepdog. b, Basenji. c, Poodle. d, St. Bernard. e, Shar Pei. f, Spinone Italiano.

No. 1350, 4500m, vert.: a, Jack Russell terrier. b, Schweizer Laufhund. c, Japanese Spitz. d, Australian Shepherd. e, Saluki. f, Siberian Husky.

No. 1351, 25,000m, Border Collie. No. 1352, 25,000m, Eurasier.

2000, Mar. 29 **Litho.** ***Perf. 14***

Sheets of 6, #a-f

1349-1350 A275 Set of 2 10.00 10.00

Souvenir Sheets

1351-1352 A275 Set of 2 9.50 9.50

Dated 1999.

Dinosaurs — A276

No. 1353, 3000m: a, Pteranodon. b, Bothriospondylus. c, Iguanodon. d, Stegosaurus. e, Nodosaurus. f, Elaphrosaurus. g, "Petrolaccisaurus." h, Procompsognathus. i, Dimetrodon.
No. 1354, 3000m, : a, Plesiosaur. b, "Ceresiosaurus." c, Cryptoclidus. d, Placochelys. e, Plotosaurus. f, Ichthyosaurus. g, Platecarpus. h, Archelon. i, Mosasaur.
No. 1355, 20,000m, Tyrannosaurus Rex. No. 1356, 20,000m, "Honodus."

2000, Apr. 28

Sheets of 9, #a-i

1353-1354 A276 Set of 2 9.50 9.50

Souvenir Sheets

1355-1356 A276 Set of 2 6.50 6.50

Dated 1999.

A277

Butterflies — A278

Designs: 2000m, Palla ussheri. 2500m, Euschemon rafflesia. No. 1359, 3000m, Buttus philenor. No. 1360, 3000m, Hypolimnas bolina. 3500m, Lycorea cleobaea. 4000m, Dynastor napoleon. No. 1363, 4500m, Callimorpha dominula. 5000m, Pereute leucodrosime.
No. 1365, 4500m: a, Tisiphone abeone. b, Pseudacraea boisduvali. c, Mylothris chloris. d, Papilio glaucus. e, Mimacraea marshalli. f, Gonepteryx cleopatra.
No. 1366, 4500m: a, Palla ussheri, diff. b, Hypolimnas salmacis. c, Pereute leucodrosime, diff. d, Anteos clorinde. e, Colias eurytheme. f, Hebomoia glaucippe.
No. 1367, 4500m, horiz.: a, Thauria aliris. b, Catocala ilia. c, Colotis danae. d, Agrias claudia. e, Euploe core. f, Scoptes alphaeus.
No. 1368, 4500m, horiz.: a, Phoebis philea. b, Anteos clorinde, diff. c, Arhopala amantes. d, Mesene phareus. e, Euploea mulciber. f, Heliconius ricini.
No. 1369, 4500m, vert.: a, Euphaedra neophorn. b, Catopsilia florella. c, Charaxes bohemani. d, Junonia orithya. e, Colotis danae, diff. f, Eurytela dryope.
No. 1370, 4500m, vert.: a, Papilio demodocus. b, Kallimoides rumia. c, Danaus chrysippus. d, Palla ussheri, diff. e, Hypolimnas salmacis, diff. f, Zinina otis.
No. 1371, 20,000m, Papilio glaucus, diff. No. 1372, 20,000m, Delias mysis, horiz. No. 1373, 20,000m, Mylothris chloris, horiz. No. 1374, 20,000m, Loxura atymnus, horiz. No. 1375, 20,000m, Hemiolaus coeculus. No. 1376, 20,000m, Euxanthe wakefieldii.

2000, Apr. 28

1357-1364 A277 Set of 8 4.50 4.50

Sheets of 6, #a-f

1365-1368 A277 Set of 4 17.50 17.50
1369-1370 A278 Set of 2 9.50 9.50

Souvenir Sheets

1371-1374 A277 Set of 4 12.00 12.00
1375-1376 A278 Set of 2 7.00 7.00

Dated 1999.

Worldwide Fund for Nature — A279

No. 1377: a, Two adult gnus. b, Adult and juvenile gnus. c, Lion catching gnu. d, Adult gnu.
Illustration reduced.

2000, Apr. 28

1377 A279 6500m Block of 4, #a-d *8.50 8.50*

Dated 1999.

Wild Cats — A280

No. 1378, 3000m: a, Leptailurus several. b, Panthera onca. c, Panthera tigris corbetti. d, Puma concolor. e, Panthera leo persica. f, Felis pardina. g, Lepardus pardalia. h, Acinonyx jubatus. i, Felis wrangeli.
No. 1379, 3000m: a, Felis silvestris grampia. b, Felis ourata. c, Panthera tigris tigris. d, Panthera uncia. e, Felis caracal. f, Panthera pardus. g, Panthera tigris amoyensis. h, Panthera onca (spotted). i, Neofelis nabuloso.
No. 1380, 25,000m, Panthera tigris altaica. No. 1381, 25,000m, Panthera tigris, horiz.

2000, Apr. 28

Sheets of 9, #a-i

1378-1379 A280 Set of 2 9.50 9.50

Souvenir Sheets

1380-1381 A280 Set of 2 8.00 8.00

Dated 1999.

Flowers — A281

No. 1382, 3000m: a, Laetiocattleya. b, Papaver oriental. c, Anemone blanda. d, Ipoema alba. e, Phalaenopsis luma. f, Iris ensata. g, Coenagrion puella. h, Rosa raubritter. i, Iris x daylilies hybridizers.
No. 1383, 3000m: a, Lilium auratum. b, Oncidium macianthum. c, Dendrobium. d, Cobaea scandens. e, Paphiopedilum gilda. f, Papaver nudicaule. g, Colocasia esculenta. h, Carinatum tricolor. i, Phalaenopsis.
No. 1384, vert.: a, Euanthe sanderiana. b, Torenia fourleri. c, "Amor Perfeito." d, Borboleto matizada. e, Dendrobium primulinum. f, "Lasurstern" Clematite. g, Helianthus annuus. h, Jacinto grana.
No. 1385, 20,000m, Viola x wittrockiana. No. 1386, 20,000m, Nelimbo nucifera. No. 1387, 20,000m, Gerbera jamesonii. No. 1388, 20,000m, Narcissuses and anemones.
Illustration reduced.

2000, Apr. 28

Sheets of 9, #a-i

1382-1383 A281 Set of 2 9.00 9.00
1384 A281 3500m Sheet of 8, #a-h 5.00 5.00

Souvenir Sheets

1385-1388 A281 Set of 4 10.50 10.50

Dated 1999.

Nos. 792, 797, 1147, 1153, 1154, 1156, 1214 Surcharged

2000 Methods & Perfs. As Before

1390 A114 10,000m on 7.50m #797 — —
1391 A113 10,000m on 50m on 7.50m #1214 — —
1392 A113 10,000m on 12.50m #792 —
1393 A215 17,000m on 10m #1153 — —
1393A A215 17,000m on 50m #1154 — —
1394 A213 17,000m on 125m #1147 — —
1395 A215 17,000m on 200m #1156 — —
1396 A215 17,000m on 1000m #1158 — —

No. 1393A and 1396 lack "2000" date in surcharge. No. 1391 contains "Correios — 2000) in surcharge.
The editors suspect that other surcharges may exist and would like to examine any examples.

No. 764 Surcharged in Black and Brown

2000 Litho. *Perf. 14½*

1399 A108 2000m on 12.50m #764 — —

No. 1325 Overprinted

2000 Method and Perf. as Before

1399A A270 4000m on #1325 — —

Nos. 1300, 1301 Ovptd. in Brown or Black

2000 Litho. *Perf. 14½*

1400 A108 4000m on 12.50m #1300 (BR) — —
1400A A114 6000m on 7.50m #1301 — —

Sports and Chess — A282

No. 1401, 6500m: a, Cycling. b, Volleyball. c, Boxing. d, Weight lifting. e, Fencing. f, Judo.
No. 1402, 9000m — Chess pieces: a, Six pieces, red queen at left. b, Six pieces, gray bishop fifth from left. c, Five knights. d, Six rooks, elephant rook at left. e, Six pawns. f, Six pawns, spearholder pawn at right.
No. 1403, 9500m — Chess champions: a, Paul Morphy. b, Mikhail Botvinnik. c, Emanuel Lasker. d, Wilhelm Steinitz. e, José Raul Capablanca. f, Howard Staunton.
No. 1404, 12,500m: a, Cricket batsmen and bowler. b, Three cricket batsman, one fielder. c, Polo, rider with red shirt at left. d, Polo, player wearing #1 at right. e, Golf, flag stick at right. f, Golf, woman golfer at right.
No. 1405, 14,000m: a, Tennis, woman with headband at right. b, Table tennis, players with blue shirts. c, Table tennis, player with pink shirt in center. d, Tennis, two men at left. e, Tennis, man with cap at left. f, Table tennis, player with red shirt at left.
No. 1406, 35,000m, Table tennis. No. 1407, 35,000m, Chess player Garry Kasparov.

2000 Litho. *Perf. 13¼*

Sheets of 6, #a-f

1401-1405 A282 Set of 5 *60.00 60.00*

Souvenir Sheets

1406-1407 A282 Set of 2 *16.00 16.00*

Nos. 1401-1405 each contain six 59x29mm stamps.

A283

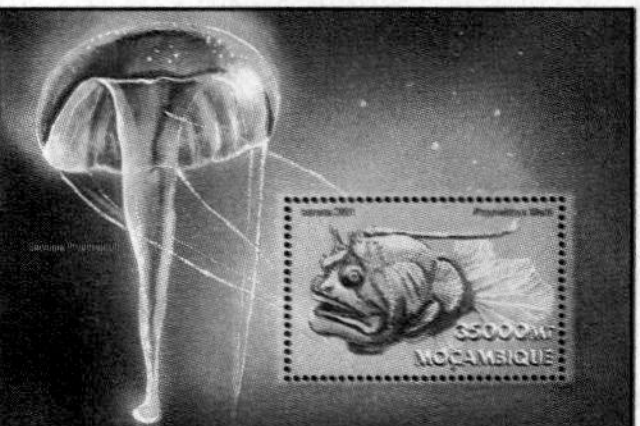

Marine Life — A284

No. 1408: a, Threadfin butterflyfish. b, Common clownfish. c, Regal tang. d, Regal angelfish. e, Copperbanded butterflyfish. f, Blue-girdled angelfish. g, Sharpnosed pufferfish. h, Humbug damselfish. i, Tailbar lionfish. j, Forcepsfish. k, Powder blue surgeon. l, Moorish idol.
No. 1409, 9500m: a, Oceanic whitetip shark. b, Gray reef shark. c, Tiger shark. d, Silky shark. e, Basking shark. f, Epaulette shark.

No. 1410, 9500m: a, Sperm whale. b, Giant squid. c, Killer whale. d, Great white shark. e, Manta ray. f, Octopus.
No. 1411, 9500m: a, Blue whale. b, Dolphinfish. c, Hammerhead shark. d, Whale shark. e, Leatherback turtle. f, Porkfish.
No. 1412, 35,000m, Wimple fish. No. 1413, 35,000m, Queen angelfish.
No. 1414, 35,000m, Phryniethys wedli. No. 1415, 35,000m, Bull shark. No. 1416, 35,000m, Spotted trunkfish.

2001, Aug. 8 *Perf. 14*

1408 A283 4550m Sheet of 12, #a-l *9.00 9.00*

Sheets of 6, #a-f

1409-1411 A284 Set of 3 *17.50 17.50*

Souvenir Sheets

1412-1413 A283 Set of 2 *8.00 8.00*
1414-1416 A284 Set of 3 *10.50 10.50*

Nos. 763, 1317, 1329 and 1330 Surcharged

Methods and Perfs As Before

2001 ?

1417 A268 3000m on 8000m #1317 — —
1418 A270 3000m on 15,000m #1329 — —
1419 A270 3000m on 20,000m #1330 — —
1420 A108 5000m on 10m #763 — —

2000 European Soccer Championships — A285

No. 1421, 10,000m: a, Luis Figo dribbling ball. b, Fernando Couto. c, Figo diving. d, Sergio Conceicao. e, Nuno Gomes. f, Rui Costa.
No. 1422, 17,000m: a, Nicolas Anelka. b, Didier Deschamps. c, Emmanuel Petit. d, Thierry Henry. e, Marcel Desailly. f, Zinedine Zidane.
No. 1422G, 75,000m, Zinedine Zidane. No. 1422H, 75,000m, Rivaldo.

2001 **Litho.** *Perf. 13¼x12¾*

Sheets of 6, #a-f

1421-1422 A285 Set of 2 *20.00 20.00*

Souvenir Sheets

1422G-1422H A285 Set of 2 *16.00 16.00*

2000 Summer Olympics Medalists — A286

No. 1423, 8500m: a, Domenico Fioravanti. b, Stacy Dragila. c, Pieter van den Hoogenband. d, David O'Connor. e, Venus Williams. f, Maurice Greene. g, Joy Fawcett. h, Marion Jones. i, Patricio Ormazabal and Jeff Agoos.
No. 1424, 10,000m: a, Agnes Kovacs. b, Youila Raskina. c, Kong Linghui and Liu Guoliang. d, Nicolas Gill. e, Anky van Grunsven. f, Brian Olson. g, Wang Nan. h, Megan Quann. i, Venus Williams.
No. 1425, 17,000m: a, Vince Carter. b, Blaine Wilson. c, Steve Keir. d, Wen Xiao Wang and Chris Xu. e, Venus and Serena Williams. f, Gu Jun and Ge Fei.
No. 1426, 20,000m: a, Clara Hughes. b, Martina Hingis. c, Otilla Badescu. d, Isabel Fernandez. e, Coralie Simmons. f, Mia Hamm.
No. 1427, 28,000m: a, Patrick Rafter. b, Tadahiro Nomura. c, Seiko Iseki. d, Michael Dodge. e, Ann Dow. f, David Beckham.
No. 1428, 50,000m, Andre Agassi. No. 1429, 50,000m, Chang Jun Gao and Michelle Do. No. 1430, 50,000m, Kong Linghui. No. 1431, 100,000m, Michelle Do. No. 1432, 100,000m, Serena Williams. No. 1433, Christophe Legout.

2001 **Litho.**

Sheets of 9, #a-i

1423-1424 A286 Set of 2 14.00 14.00

Sheets of 6, #a-f

1425-1427 A286 Set of 3 16.00 16.00

Souvenir Sheets

1428-1433 A286 Set of 6 24.00 24.00

Chess Champions — A287

No. 1434, 10,000m: a, Mikhail Botvinnik. b, Garry Kasparov. c, Wilhelm Steinitz. d, Emanuel Lasker. e, Paul Morphy. f, Anatoly Karpov. g, Tigran Petrossian. h, Mikhail Tal. i, José Raul Capablanca.
No. 1435, 10,000m: a, Judith Polgar (wearing brown sweater). b, Xie Jun. c, Zsuza Polgar. d, Nana Ioseliani. e, Alisa Galliamova. f, Judith Polgar (head in hands). g, Judith Polgar (wearing blouse). h, Monica Calzetta. i, Anjelina Belakovskaia.
No. 1436, 100,000m, Kasparov. No. 1437, 100,000m, Judith Polgar.

2001 *Perf. 13¼x12¾*

Sheets of 9, #a-i

1434-1435 A287 Set of 2 *20.00 20.00*

Souvenir Sheets

1436-1437 A287 Set of 2 *22.00 22.00*

2002 Winter Olympics, Salt Lake City — A288

No. 1438, 17,000m: a, Martin Brodeur. b, Svetlana Vysokova. c, Ray Bourque and Patrik Elias. d, Rachel Belliveau. e, Scott Gomez and Janne Laukkanen. f, Sonja Nef.
No. 1439, 20,000m: a, Rusty Smith. b, Sandra Schmirler. c, Totmianina and Marinin. d, Brigitte Obermoser. e, Roman Turek. f, Jennifer Heil.
No. 1440, 28,000m: a, Kovarikova and Novotny. b, Li Song. c, Armin Zoeggeler. d, Michael von Gruenigen. e, Tami Bradley. f, Chris Drury, Turner Stevenson and Greg de Vries.
No. 1441, 50,000m, Armin Zoeggeler. No. 1442, 75,000m, Tommy Salo. No. 1443, 100,000m, Jayne Torvill and Christopher Dean.

2001 **Litho.**

Sheets of 6, #a-f

1438-1440 A288 Set of 3 *20.00 20.00*

Souvenir Sheets

1441-1443 A288 Set of 3 *17.50 17.50*

On illustrated sheets lacking design information the lettering of minors starts with the upper left stamp, goes right and down and ends with the lower right stamp.

2002 World Cup Soccer Championships, Japan and Korea — A289

No. 1444: a, Filippo Inzaghi. b, Georghe Hagi. c, Gabriel Batistuta pointing. d, Mateja Kezman. e, Ivan Zamorano. f, Michael Owen wearing blue uniform.
No. 1445: a, Marcio Amoroso. b, Alessandro Nesta. c, Robbie Keane. d, Michel Owen kicking ball. e, Stefan Effenberg. f, Oliver Kahn.
No. 1446: a, Zinedine Zidane without ball. b, Zoran Mirkovic. c, Robbie Fowler with fist raised. d, Romario wearing red jersey. e, Francesco Totti. f, Ryan Giggs.
No. 1447: a, Javier Saviola. b, Alan Smith. c, Raul Gonzalez. d, Dwight Yorke. e, Joe Cole. f, David Beckham wearing red jersey.
No. 1448: a, Angelo Peruzzi. b, Jaap Stam. c, Jamie Redknapp. d, Rivaldo with ball at feet. e, Alan Shearer. f, Boudewijn Zenden.
No. 1449: a, Hernan Jorge Crespo. b, Gianluigi Buffon. c, Arnold Bruggink. d, Antonio Cassano. e, Mohamed Kallon. f, Jonathan Bachini.
No. 1450: a, Didier Deschamps. b, Cafu wearing green jersey. c, Dennis Bergkamp. d, Lilian Thuram. e, David Beckham wearing red jersey, diff. f, Francesco Totti, diff. g, Carsten Jancker. h, Martin Palermo. i, Andy Cole running left.
No. 1451: a, David Beckham sitting on ball. b, Edgar Davids wearing orange shirt. c, Michael Owen with hands on ball. d, Andy Cole with one leg raised. e, Ronaldo sitting. f, Emmanuel Petit with ball. g, Rivaldo with ball at chest. h, Robbie Fowler looking at ball. i, Romario wearing blue jacket.
No. 1452: a, César Manuel Rui Costa. b, Hidetoshi Nakata. c, Luis Figo. d, Michael Owen. e, Leonardo. f, Thierry Henry. g, Fabien Barthez. h, Oliver Kahn. i, Antonio Conte.
No. 1453: a, Shinji Ono. b, Rigobert Song. c, Matias Jesus Almeyda. d, Ronaldinho. e, Gabriel Batistuta wearing striped jersey. f, Rivaldo sitting on ground. g, Thierry Henry. h, Zinedine Zidane kicking ball. i, Ronaldo with ball.
No. 1454: a, Florain Maurice. b, Nicolas Anelka. c, Zinedine Zidane without ball, wearing striped jersey. d, Kazuyoshi Miura. e, Patrick Vieira. f, Gianfranco Zola. g, Emmanuel Petit without ball. h, Roberto Carlos. i, Teddy Sheringham.
No. 1455, 75,000m, Fabien Barthez. No. 1456, 75,000m, Edgar Davids wearing striped shirt. No. 1457, 75,000m, Cafu wearing red shirt.
No. 1458, 100,000m, Ronaldo wearing striped uniform. No. 1459, 100,000m, Romario wearing yellow shirt. No. 1460, 100,000m, Rivaldo dribbling ball. No. 1461, 100,000m, Nwankwo Kanu. No. 1462, 100,000m, Michael Owen wearing yellow shirt. No. 1463, 100,000m, Franz Beckenbauer. No. 1464, 100,000m, Pelé. No. 1465, 100,000m, Diego Maradona.

2001 **Litho.** *Perf. 13¼x12¾*

1444 A289 5000m Sheet of 6, #a-f 2.60 2.60
1445 A289 10,000m Sheet of 6, #a-f 5.25 5.25
1446 A289 12,000m Sheet of 6, #a-f 6.25 6.25
1447 A289 15,000m Sheet of 6, #a-f 8.00 8.00
1448 A289 17,000m Sheet of 6, #a-f 9.00 9.00
1449 A289 20,000m Sheet of 6, #a-f 10.50 10.50
Nos. 1444-1449 (6) 41.60 41.60
1450 A289 5000m Sheet of 9, #a-i 4.00 4.00
1451 A289 5000m Sheet of 9, #a-i 4.00 4.00
1452 A289 5000m Sheet of 9, #a-i 4.00 4.00
1453 A289 8500m Sheet of 9, #a-i 6.75 6.75
1454 A289 8500m Sheet of 9, #a-i 6.75 6.75
Nos. 1450-1454 (4) 21.50 21.50

Souvenir Sheets

1455-1457 A289 Set of 3 2.00 2.00
1458-1465 A289 Set of 8 70.00 70.00

On illustrated sheets lacking design information, the lettering of minors starts with the upper left stamp, continues right and down and ends with the lower right stamp.

Paintings

Madonna Paintings — A290

Alfred Sisley — A291

Hieronymus Bosch — A292

Pieter Brueghel — A293

Paul Cézanne — A294

Salvador Dali — A295

Henri Matisse — A296

Michelangelo — A297

Vincent van Gogh — A298

Johannes Vermeer — A299

Michelangelo — A300

Amadeo Modigliani — A301

Paintings of Angels — A302

Gustav Klimt — A303

Perf. 13¼x12¾

2001, Dec. 28 **Litho.**

1466	A290	5000m Sheet of 6 #a-f	2.60	2.60
1467	A291	10,000m Sheet of 6, #a-f	5.25	5.25
1468	A292	12,000m Sheet of 6, #a-f	6.25	6.25
1469	A293	12,000m Sheet of 6, #a-f	6.25	6.25
1470	A294	12,000m Sheet of 6, #a-f	6.25	6.25
1471	A295	12,000m Sheet of 6, #a-f	6.25	6.25
1472	A296	12,000m Sheet of 6, #a-f	6.25	6.25
1473	A297	12,000m Sheet of 6, #a-f	6.25	6.25
1474	A298	12,000m Sheet of 6, #a-f	6.25	6.25
1475	A299	12,000m Sheet of 6, #a-f	6.25	6.25
1476	A300	15,000m Sheet of 6, #a-f	8.00	8.00
1477	A301	15,000m Sheet of 6, #a-f	8.00	8.00
1478	A302	17,000m Sheet of 6, #a-f	9.25	9.25
1479	A303	28,000m Sheet of 6, #a-f	15.00	15.00
	Nos. 1466-1479 (13)		88.85	88.85

Paintings

Marc Chagall — A304

Salvador Dali — A305

Edgar Degas — A306

Paul Delvaux — A307

Paul Gauguin — A308

Pablo Picasso — A309

Pierre Auguste Renoir — A310

Henri de Toulouse-Lautrec — A311

Vincent van Gogh — A312

Pablo Picasso — A313

Individual stamps depicting various works of art lack titles. On Nos. 1489-1512 artist name is in margin.

No. 1489, Pieter Breughel. No. 1490, Lucas Cranach. No. 1491, Paul Delvaux. No. 1492, El Greco. No. 1493, Wassily Kandinsky. No. 1494, Gustav Klimt. No. 1495, Johannes Vermeer. No. 1496, Paul Cézanne. No. 1497, Marc Chagall. No. 1498, Albrecht Dürer. No. 1499, Thomas Gainsborough. No. 1500, Francisco de Goya. No. 1501, Edouard Manet. No. 1502, Claude Monet. No. 1503, Henri Matisse. No. 1504, Camille Pissarro. No. 1505, Vincent van Gogh. No. 1506, Salvador Dali. No. 1507, Paul Gauguin. No. 1508, Joan Miró. No. 1509, Amadeo Modigliani. No. 1511, Picasso, diff. No. 1512, Henri de Toulouse-Lautrec. No. 1513, Religious icon.

Perf. 13¾x12¾

2001, Dec. 28 **Litho.**

1480 A304 10,000m Sheet of 9, #a-i 6.75 6.75
1481 A305 10,000m Sheet of 9, #a-i 6.75 6.75
1482 A306 10,000m Sheet of 9, #a-i 6.75 6.75
1483 A307 10,000m Sheet of 9, #a-i 6.75 6.75
1484 A308 10,000m Sheet of 9, #a-i 6.75 6.75
1485 A309 10,000m Sheet of 9, #a-i 6.75 6.75
1486 A310 10,000m Sheet of 9, #a-i 6.75 6.75
1487 A311 10,000m Sheet of 9, #a-i 6.75 6.75
1488 A312 10,000m Sheet of 9, #a-i 6.75 6.75
Nos. 1480-1488 (9) 60.75 60.75

Souvenir Sheets

1489 A313 50,000m multi 3.75 3.75
1490 A313 50,000m multi 3.75 3.75
1491 A313 50,000m multi 3.75 3.75
1492 A313 50,000m multi 3.75 3.75
1493 A313 50,000m multi 3.75 3.75
1494 A313 50,000m multi 3.75 3.75
1495 A313 50,000m multi 3.75 3.75
1496 A313 75,000m multi 5.75 5.75
1497 A313 75,000m multi 5.75 5.75
1498 A313 75,000m multi 5.75 5.75
1499 A313 75,000m multi 5.75 5.75
1500 A313 75,000m multi 5.75 5.75
1501 A313 75,000m multi 5.75 5.75
1502 A313 75,000m multi 5.75 5.75
1503 A313 75,000m multi 5.75 5.75
1504 A313 75,000m multi 5.75 5.75
1505 A313 75,000m multi 5.75 5.75
1506 A313 100,000m multi 7.50 7.50
1507 A313 100,000m multi 7.50 7.50
1508 A313 100,000m multi 7.50 7.50
1509 A313 100,000m multi 7.50 7.50
1510 A313 100,000m shown 7.50 7.50
1511 A313 100,000m multi 7.50 7.50
1512 A313 100,000m multi 7.50 7.50
1513 A313 100,000m multi 7.50 7.50
Nos. 1489-1513 (25) 143.75 143.75

Souvenir Sheet

Lance Armstrong, Cyclist — A314

2001 **Litho.** *Perf. 13¼x12¾*

1514 A314 100,000m multi 8.75 8.75

2004 Olympic Games, Athens.

New Year 2002 (Year of the Horse) — A315

No. 1515 — Chinese characters in: a, Yellow. b, Purple. c, Pink. d, Brown.

22,000m, Maroon, vert.

2002, May 6 **Litho.** *Perf. 13¼*

1515 A315 11,000m Sheet of 4, #a-d 5.25 5.25

Souvenir Sheet

Perf. 13½x13¼

1516 A315 22,000m multi 2.75 2.75

No. 1516 contains one 28x42mm stamp.

2002 Winter Olympics, Salt Lake City A316

Designs: 10,000m, Freestyle skiing. 17,000m, Freestyle skiing, vert.

Perf. 13¼x13½, 13½x13¼

2002, May 6

1517-1518 A316 Set of 2 2.75 2.75

Intl. Year of Mountains A317

Designs: No. 1519, 17,000m, Mt. Namuli. No. 1520, 17,000m, Mt. Binga.

No. 1521: a, Mt. Kenya, Kenya. b, Mt. Cook, New Zealand. c, Mt. Ararat, Turkey. d, Mt. Paine, Chile. e, Mt. Everest, Nepal. f, Mt. Kilimanjaro, Tanzania.

50,000m, Zugspitze, Germany.

2002, May 6 *Perf. 13¼x13½*

1519-1520 A317 Set of 2 3.00 3.00
1521 A317 17,000m Sheet of 6, #a-f 9.50 9.50

Souvenir Sheet

1522 A317 50,000m multi 4.75 4.75

20th World Scout Jamboree, Thailand — A318

No. 1523, horiz.: a, 1933 Jamboree patch. b, 19th World Jamboree patch. c, Patch and mascot. d, Jamboree emblem, scout.

No. 1524, Scout.

2002, May 6 *Perf. 13¼x13½*

1523 A318 28,000m Sheet of 4, #a-d 11.50 11.50

Souvenir Sheet

Perf. 13½x13¼

1524 A318 28,000m multi 3.00 3.00

Amerigo Vespucci (1452-1512), Explorer — A319

No. 1525, horiz.: a, Vespucci observing stars. b, Brotogeris chiriri, ship. c, Huts, ship.

50,000m, Map of voyages to South America.

2002, May 6 *Perf. 13¼x13½*

1525 A319 30,000m Sheet of 3, #a-c 8.50 8.50

Souvenir Sheet

Perf. 13½x13¼

1526 A319 50,000m multi 5.00 5.00

Ships — A320

No. 1527, 13,500m: a-f, Various unnamed ships (shown).

No. 1528, 13,500m: a, Viking ship. b, Kayak. c, Gondola, bridge. d, Fishing boat. e, Light ship. f, Tugboat.

No. 1529, 40,000m, Aircraft carrier. No. 1530, 40,000m, Ship's figurehead, vert.

Perf. 13¼x13½, 13½x13¼

2002, May 6

Sheets of 6, #a-f

1527-1528 A320 Set of 2 14.50 14.50

Souvenir Sheets

1529-1530 A320 Set of 2 7.50 7.50

2002 World Cup Soccer Championships, Japan and Korea — A321

No. 1531, 28,000m: a, Zico. b, 1958 World Cup poster. c, Flag, player from Nigeria. d, Flag, player from Morocco. e, Gwangju Stadium, Korea, horiz. (56x42mm).

No. 1532, 28,000m: a, 1966 World Cup poster. b, Paolo Rossi. c, Flag, player from Denmark. d, Flag, player from Colombia. e, Inchon Munhak Stadium, Korea, horiz. (56x42mm)

No. 1533, 50,000m, Pele. No. 1534, 50,000m, Morlock, horiz.

Perf. 13½x13¼, 13¼x13½

2002, May 6

Sheets of 5, #a-e

1532-1533 A321 Set of 2 24.00 24.00

Souvenir Sheets

1534-1534A A321 Set of 2 9.50 9.50

A322

A323

Princess Diana (1961-97) — A324

No. 1538, 50,000m, Brown background. No. 1539, 50,000m, Purple background. No. 1540, 50,000m, Pink lilac background.

2002, May 6 *Perf. 13½x13¼*

1535 A322 28,000m Sheet of 4, #a-d 10.50 10.50
1536 A323 28,000m Sheet of 4, #a-d 10.50 10.50
1537 A324 28,000m Sheet of 4, #a-d 10.50 10.50
Nos. 1535-1537 (3) 31.50 31.50

Souvenir Sheets

1538-1540 A324 Set of 3 14.50 14.50

Butterflies — A325

Designs: 5000m, Papilio demoleus. No, 1542, 10,000m, Euschemom rafflesia. 17,000m, Liphyra brassolis. 28,000m, Mimacraea marshalli.

No. 1545, 10,000m: a, Eurema brigitta. b, Loxura atymunus. c, Arhopala amantes. d, Junonia coenia. e, Eurides isabella. f, Hiliconius ricini. g, Zipaetis scylax. h, Cepheuptychia cephus. i, Philaethria dido.

No. 1546, 10,000m: a, Parides coon. b, Delias mysis. c, Troides brookiana. d, Syrmatia dorilas. e, Danis danis. f, Lycaena dispar. g, Mesene phareus. h, Kallima inachus. i, Morpho rhetenor.

No. 1547, 50,000m, Papilio cresphontes. No. 1548, 50,000m, Ornithoptera alexandrae caterpillar.

2002, June 17 *Perf. 14*

1541-1544 A325 Set of 4 5.25 5.25

Sheets of 9, #a-i

1545-1546 A325 Set of 2 16.00 16.00

Souvenir Sheets

1547-1548 A325 Set of 2 11.00 11.00

Fauna, Flora and Mushrooms — A326

No. 1549, 10,000m: a, Pandion haliaetus. b, Flying squirrel. c, Fox squirrel. d, Agelaius phoeniceus. e, Papilio polyxenes. f, Didelphus virginiana. g, Hyla crucifer. h, Odocoileus virginianus, standing. i, Procyon lotor.

No. 1550, 10,000m: a, Heraclides cresphontes. b, Tyto alba. c, Drocopus pileatus. d, Cypripedium parviflorum, Archilochus colobris. e, Vulpes vulpes. f, Odocoileus virginianus. g, Enallagma sp. h, Amanita muscaria. i, Tamiasciurus hudsonicus.

2002, June 17 ***Perf. 14***

Sheets of 9, #a-i

1549-1550 A326 Set of 2 16.00 16.00

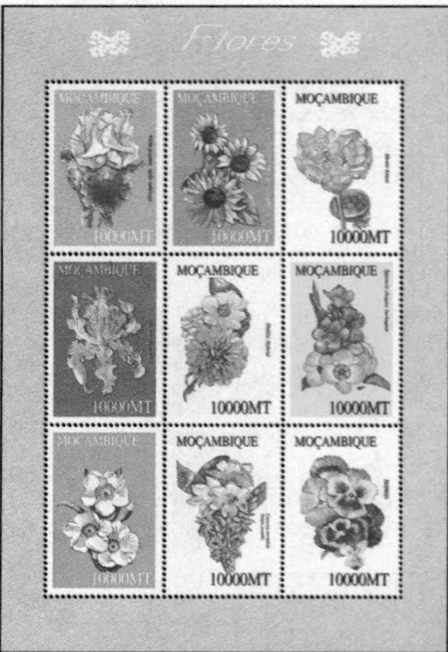

Flowers — A327

No. 1551, 10,000m: a, Viola jeannie, Viola cultivar. b, Sunflower Moonshadow. c, Momo botan. d, Schomburgkia orchid. e, Dahlia hybrid. f, Sparaxis elegans harlequin. g, Dianhus. h, Camassia leichtlinii, Tulipa saxatilis. i, Pansy hybrid.

No. 1552, 10,000m, horiz.: a, Hemerocallis. b, Narcissus (Nazcissys). c, Hybrid tea rose. d, Rainbow Promised Cayenne Capers and flying insect. e, Anemone cordnazia. f, Hymenocallis narcissiflora. g, Hymenocallis. h, Tulipa. i, Lachenalia aloides, Meconopsis poppies.

No. 1553, 10,000m, horiz.: a, Narcissus. b, L. bulbiferun var. Croceum. c, Iris purpureobractea. d, Neomarica caerulea. e, Peonia lactiflora, Primula chungensis, Viola cornuta. f, Rainbow Promised Cayenne Capers and beetle. g, Iris purpureobractea (puzpuzeobractea). h, Tuberous begonia cultivar. i, Oriental hybrid lily.

2002, June 17 ***Perf. 14***

Sheets of 9, #a-i

1551-1553 A327 Set of 3 10.00 10.00

Dogs, Cats and Horses — A328

No. 1554, 17,000m — Dogs: a, Labrador retriever. b, Bulldog. c, Cocker spaniel. d, Golden retriever. e, Boxer. f, Bloodhound.

No. 1555, 17,000m — Cats: a, Maine Coon. b, Cornish Rex. c, La Perm. d, Sphynx. e, Siamese. f, Persian.

No. 1556, 17,000m — Horses: a, Hanoverian. b, Haflinger. c, Nonius. d, Belgian heavy drafts. e, Australian-bred Arab. f, Thoroughbred.

No. 1557, 40,000m, Basset hound. No. 1558, 50,000m, Chestnut Oriental Longhair cat. No. 1559, 50,000m, Don horses.

2002, June 17 ***Perf. 13¼***

Sheets of 6, #a-f

1554-1556 A328 Set of 3 10.00 10.00

Souvenir Sheets

1557-1559 A328 Set of 3 6.00 6.00

Dinosaurs A329

Designs: 5000m, Protosaurus. No. 1561, 10,000m, Psittacosaurus. 17,000m, Torosaurus. 28,000m, Triceratops.

No. 1564, 10,000m: a, Diplodocus head. b, Pterosaurs. c, Diplodocuses. d, Afrovenator. e, Parasaurolophus. f, Ramphorhynchus. g, Lambeosaur. h, Euoplocephalus. i, Cynodont.

No. 1565, 10,000m: a, Brachiosaur. b, Monoclonius. c, Homalocephalus. d, Pterodactyl. e, Deinonychus. f, Archaeopteryx. g, Cretaceous landscape. h, Hypsilophodon. i, Lystrosaur.

No. 1566, 50,000m, Baryonyx. No. 1567, 50,000m, Styracosaurus, vert.

2002, June 17 ***Perf. 14***

1560-1563 A329 Set of 4 5.25 5.25

Sheets of 9, #a-i, + 3 labels

1564-1565 A329 Set of 2 10.00 10.00

Souvenir Sheets

1566-1567 A329 Set of 2 6.00 6.00

A330

Birds — A331

Designs: No. 1568, 5000m, Tachymarptis melba. No. 1569, 5000m, Falco tinnunculus. No. 1570, 10,000m, Pitta angolensis. No. 1571, 10,000m, Ardea cinerea. No. 1572, 17,000m, Corythaeola cristata. No. 1573, 28,000m, Butastur rufipennis.

No. 1574, 5000m, Creagrus furcatus. No. 1575, 10,000m, Larosterna inca. No. 1576, 17,000m, Pelecanus crispus. No. 1577, 28,000m, Morus bassanus.

No. 1578, 10,000m: a, Phaeton aethereus. b, Catharacta maccormicki. c, Diomedea bulleri. d, Puffinus iherminieri. e, Oceanites oceanicus. f, Pterodroma hasitata. g, Fregata magnificens. h, Sula nebouxii. i, Uria aagle.

No. 1579, 17,000m: a, Psittacus erithacus. b, Ficedula hypleuca. c, Tchagra senegala. d, Oriolus oriolus. e, Luscinia megarhynchos. f, Halcyon malimbica.

No. 1580, 17,000m: a, Coracias garrulus. b, Estrilda astrild. c, Upupa epops. d, Merops apiaster. e, Ploceus cucullatus. f, Clamator glandarius.

No. 1581, 50,000m, Falco subbuteo. No. 1582, 50,000m, Strix varia. No. 1583, 50,000m, Butorides striatus. No. 1584, 50,000m, Actophilornis africanus, horiz.

No. 1585, 50,000m, Spheniscus demersus. No. 1586, 50,000m, Rhynchops niger, horiz.

2002, June 17

1568-1573 A330 Set of 6 6.50 6.50
1574-1577 A331 Set of 4 5.25 5.25
1578 A331 10,000m Sheet of 9, #a-i 7.75 7.75

Sheets of 6, #a-f

1579-1580 A330 Set of 2 17.50 17.50

Souvenir Sheets

1581-1584 A330 Set of 4 17.00 17.00
1585-1586 A331 Set of 2 8.50 8.50

For surcharges see Nos. 1740, 1748.

Worldwide Fund for Nature (WWF) A332

African savannah elephant: Nos. 1587a, 1588a, Herd. Nos. 1587b, 1588b, And birds. Nos. 1587c, 1588c, With juvenile. Nos. 1587d, 1588d, With rainbow.

2002, Sept. 20 ***Perf. 13¼x13½***

Size: 40x26½mm

Large Year

1587 Strip of 4 8.50 8.50
a.-d. A332 19,000m Any single 1.90 1.75

Size: 39x25mm

Small Year

1588 Miniature sheet of 4 + 4 labels 12.00 12.00
a.-d. A332 19,000m Any single 2.50 2.25

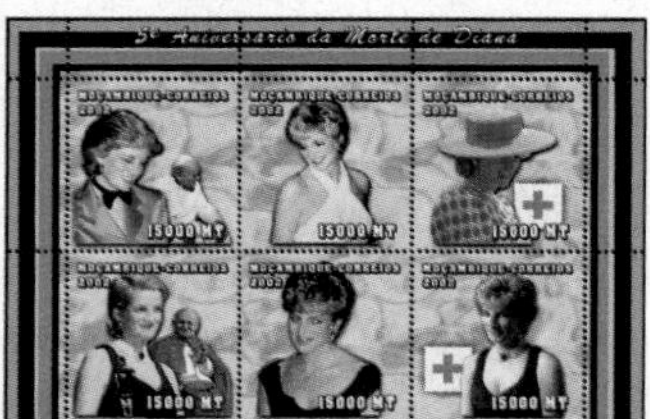

Princess Diana — A333

Pope John Paul II — A334

Elvis Presley — A335

Marilyn Monroe — A336

Marilyn Monroe — A337

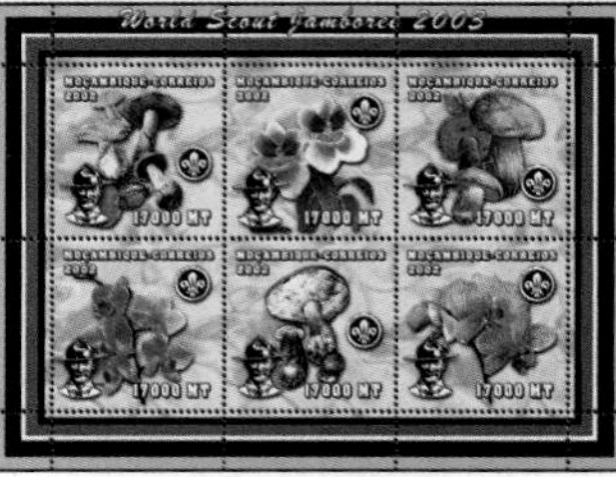

Lord Robert Baden-Powell, Scout Emblem, Mushrooms and Flowers — A338

Astronauts and the Concorde — A339

Composers — A340

Louis Pasteur and Dogs — A341

Robert Stephenson and Locomotives — A342

Pope John Paul II — A343

Pope John Paul II, Madonna and Child — A344

Pope John Paul II, Madonna and Child — A345

Robert Stephenson — A346

Robert Stephenson — A347

No. 1593 — Famous men: a, Henri Dunant. b, Theodore Roosevelt. c, Albert Einstein. d, Ernest Hemingway. e, Thomas Nast. f, Albert Camus.

No. 1594 — Egyptian rulers: a, Seti I. b, Djedefre. c, Smekhkare. d, Seti II. e, Senusret III. f, Tutankhamun.

No. 1597: a, Michael Collins. b, Concorde. c, John Glenn. d, Concorde, diff. e, Neil Armstrong. f, Concorde, diff.

No. 1598 — Chess players and pieces: a, Tigran Petrosian, Lions emblem. b, Robert Fischer, Rotary emblem. c, Boris Spassky, Lions emblem. d, Raul Capablanca, Rotary emblem. e, Max Euwe, Lions emblem. f, Emanuel Lasker, Rotary emblem.

No. 1599 — Nobel Prize winners: a, Albert Einstein. b, Dalai Lama. c, Winston Churchill. d, Hideki Yukawa. e, Albert Schweitzer. f, Linus Pauling.

No. 1600 — Scout emblem and: a, Lord Robert Baden-Powell. b, Morpho aega, Baden-Powell. c, Prepona meander, Baden-Powell. d, Charaxes bernardus, Baden-Powell. e, Hypolimnas salmacis, Baden-Powell. f, Morpho rhetenor, Baden-Powell.

No. 1601 — Egyptian rulers: a, Netjenkhet Djoser. b, Tutankhamun. c, Neferefre. d, Amenhotep III. e, Pepi I. f, Amenmesses.

No. 1602 — Composers: a, Antonio Vivaldi. b, Franz Liszt. c, Ludwig van Beethoven. d, Wolfgang Mozart.

No. 1603 — Famous Men: a, Che Guevara. b, Pope John Paul II (blue gray background). c, Dr. Martin Luther King, Jr. d, Mao Zedong.

No. 1604 — Princess Diana and Pope John Paul II: a, Princess Diana in deep blue dress. b, Diana holding flowers. c, Pope John Paul II, hand showing. d, Pope John Paul II.

No. 1605 — Nelson Mandela and: a, Heulandite. b, Adamite. c, Wulfenite. d, Hemimorphite.

No. 1606 — Auto racing: a, Ayrton Senna. b, Modern race car. c, Old race car. d, Juan Manuel Fangio.

No. 1607 — Egyptian queens (tan background): a, Nefertiti facing right. b, Cleopatra VII. c, Nefertiti facing left. d, Nefertiti facing forward.

No. 1608 — Egyptian rulers (gray background): a, Nefertari. b, Tutankhamun. c, Tuthmosis. d, Nefertiti.

No. 1609 — Egyptian rulers (green background): a, Amenhotemp II. b, Merenptah. c, Amenophis IV. d, Tuthmosis.

No. 1610 — Famous people: a, Dalai Lama. b, Mother Teresa. c, Pope John Paul II. d, Mahatma Gandhi.

No. 1611 — Explorers: a, Vasco da Gama. b, Ferdinand Magellan. c, Christopher Columbus. d, Amerigo Vespucci.

No. 1612 — Aviation: a, Antoine de Saint-Exupéry. b, Charles Lindbergh standing. c, Lindbergh seated. d, Concorde.

No. 1613 — Lions and Rotary Founders: a, Paul Harris (color picture), Rotary emblem. b, Melvin Jones (sepia picture), Lions emblem. c, Harris (sepia picture), Rotary emblem. d, Jones (color picture), Lions emblem.

No. 1614 — Film personalities: a, Charlie Chaplin. b, Frank Sinatra. c, Alfred Hitchcock. d, Walt Disney.

No. 1615: a, Scipionyx. b, Beipiaosaurus. c, Haroun Tazieff and vanadinite. d, Tazieff and adamite.

No. 1616 — Famous men: a, Winston Churchill. b, John F. Kennedy. c, Konrad Adenauer. d, Charles de Gaulle.

No. 1619 — Scientists: a, Charles Darwin, Byronosaurus. b, Alexander Fleming, Tricholoma terreum. c, Fleming, Boletus edulis. d, Darwin, Irratator.

No. 1620 — Famous men: a, Albert Schweitzer. b, Claude Bernard. c, Henri Dunant. d, Raoul Follerau.

No. 1621: a, John J. Audubon. b, Audubon, Aix sponsa. c, Audubon, Toxastoma montanum, Ixoreus naevius. d, Audubon, Loxia leucoptera.

No. 1625, John Glenn. No. 1626, Lord Robert Baden-Powell. No. 1627, Victor Hugo. No. 1628, John F. Kennedy. No. 1629, Princess Diana. No. 1630, Wolfgang Mozart. No. 1631, Alexander Fleming. No. 1632, Garry Kasparov. Nos. 1633, 1634, Marilyn Monroe. No. 1635, Mother Teresa. No. 1636, Henri Dunant. No. 1637, Nelson Mandela. No. 1638, Elvis Presley. No. 1639, Vasco da Gama. No. 1640, Paul Emile Victor. No. 1641, Tutankhamun. No. 1642, Nefertiti. No. 1643, John J. Audubon, Patagioenas leucophal. No. 1644, Audubon, Quiscalus quiscula.

2002, Sept. 30 ***Perf. 13¼x12¾***

No.	Type	Value	Description	Unused	Used
1589	A333	15,000m	Sheet of 6, #a-f	7.75	7.75
1590	A334	15,000m	Sheet of 6, #a-f	7.75	7.75
1591	A335	15,000m	Sheet of 6, #a-f	7.75	7.75
1592	A336	15,000m	Sheet of 6, #a-f	7.75	7.75
1593	A336	15,000m	Sheet of 6, #a-f	7.75	7.75
1594	A336	15,000m	Sheet of 6, #a-f	7.75	7.75
1595	A337	17,000m	Sheet of 6, #a-f	8.75	8.75
1596	A338	17,000m	Sheet of 6, #a-f	8.75	8.75
1597	A339	17,000m	Sheet of 6, #a-f	8.75	8.75
1598	A339	17,000m	Sheet of 6, #a-f	8.75	8.75
1599	A339	17,000m	Sheet of 6, #a-f	8.75	8.75
1600	A339	17,000m	Sheet of 6, #a-f	8.75	8.75
1601	A339	17,000m	Sheet of 6, #a-f	8.75	8.75
1602	A340	5000m	Sheet of 4, #a-d	1.75	1.75
1603	A340	20,000m	Sheet of 4, #a-d	6.75	6.75
1604	A340	20,000m	Sheet of 4, #a-d	6.75	6.75
1605	A340	20,000m	Sheet of 4, #a-d	6.75	6.75
1606	A340	20,000m	Sheet of 4, #a-d	6.75	6.75
1607	A340	20,000m	Sheet of 4, #a-d	6.75	6.75
1608	A340	20,000m	Sheet of 4, #a-d	6.75	6.75
1609	A340	20,000m	Sheet of 4, #a-d	6.75	6.75
1610	A340	22,000m	Sheet of 4, #a-d	7.50	7.50
1611	A340	22,000m	Sheet of 4, #a-d	7.50	7.50
1612	A340	22,000m	Sheet of 4, #a-d	7.50	7.50
1613	A340	25,000m	Sheet of 4, #a-d	8.50	8.50
1614	A340	25,000m	Sheet of 4, #a-d	8.50	8.50
1615	A340	25,000m	Sheet of 4, #a-d	8.50	8.50
1616	A340	25,000m	Sheet of 4, #a-d	8.50	8.50
1617	A341	25,000m	Sheet of 4, #a-d	8.50	8.50
1618	A342	25,000m	Sheet of 4, #a-d	8.50	8.50
1619	A342	33,000m	Sheet of 4, #a-d	11.50	11.50
1620	A342	33,000m	Sheet of 4, #a-d	11.50	11.50
1621	A342	33,000m	Sheet of 4, #a-d	11.50	11.50
			Nos. 1589-1621 (33)	264.75	264.75

Souvenir Sheets

No.	Type	Value	Description	Unused	Used
1622	A343	88,000m	shown	7.50	7.50
1623	A344	88,000m	shown	7.50	7.50
1624	A345	88,000m	shown	7.50	7.50
1625	A345	88,000m	multi	7.50	7.50
1626	A345	88,000m	multi	7.50	7.50
1627	A345	88,000m	multi	7.50	7.50
1628	A345	88,000m	multi	7.50	7.50
1629	A345	88,000m	multi	7.50	7.50
1630	A345	88,000m	multi	7.50	7.50
1631	A345	88,000m	multi	7.50	7.50
1632	A345	88,000m	multi	7.50	7.50
1633	A345	88,000m	multi	7.50	7.50
1634	A345	110,000m	multi	9.50	9.50
1635	A345	110,000m	multi	9.50	9.50
1636	A345	110,000m	multi	9.50	9.50
1637	A345	110,000m	multi	9.50	9.50
1638	A345	110,000m	multi	9.50	9.50
1639	A345	110,000m	multi	9.50	9.50
1640	A345	110,000m	multi	9.50	9.50
1641	A345	110,000m	multi	9.50	9.50
1642	A345	110,000m	multi	9.50	9.50
1643	A345	110,000m	multi	9.50	9.50
1644	A345	110,000m	multi	9.50	9.50
1645	A346	110,000m	shown	9.50	9.50
1646	A347	110,000m	shown	9.50	9.50
			Nos. 1622-1646 (25)	213.50	213.50

World of the Sea

Ships — A348

Aircraft — A349

Sea Lions — A350

Polar Bears — A351

Killer Whales — A352

Whales — A353

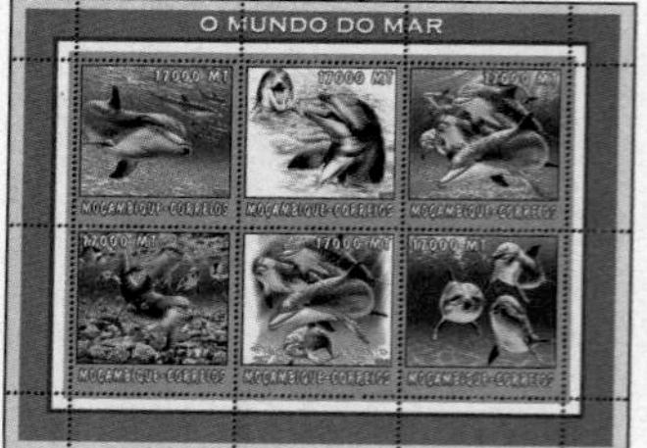

Dolphins — A354

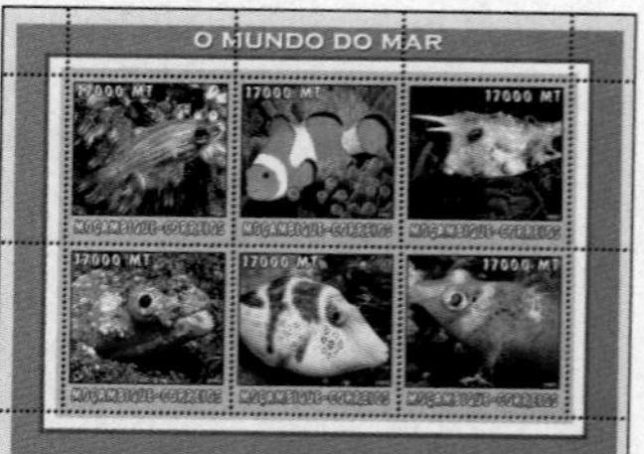

Fish — A355

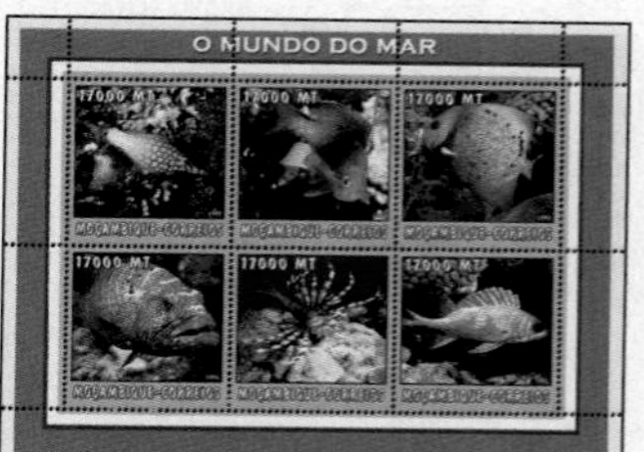

Fish — A356

Fish — A357

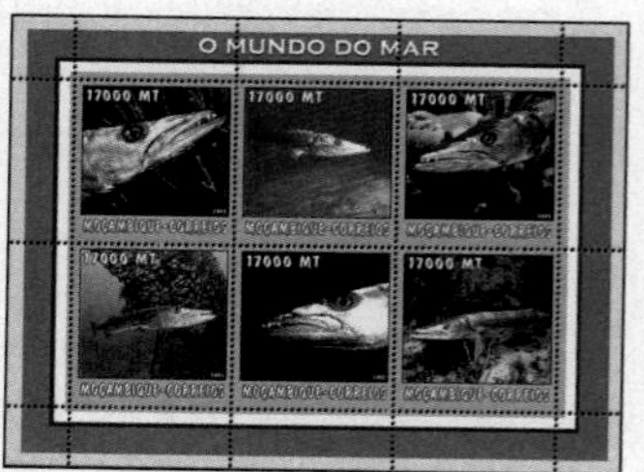

Fish — A358

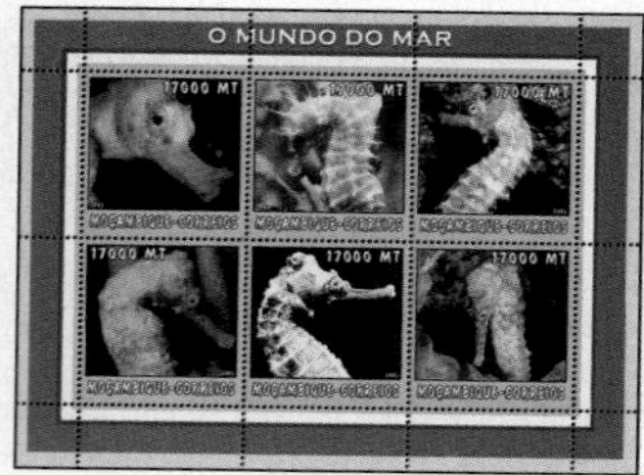

Sea Horses — A359

Penguins — A360

Penguins — A361

Sea Birds — A362

Sea Birds — A363

Sea Birds — A364

Crustaceans — A365

Snails — A366

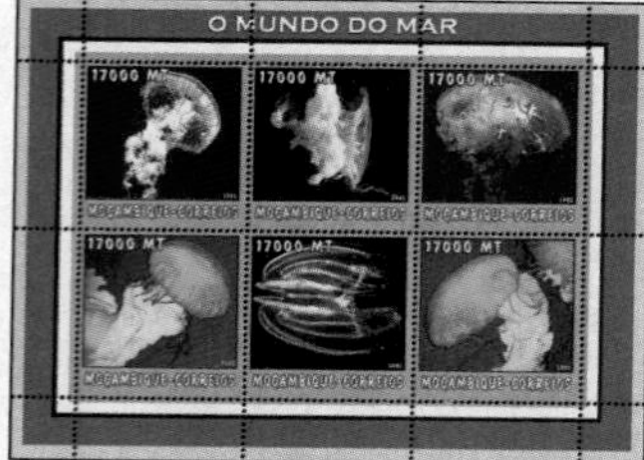

Jellyfish — A367

Coral — A368

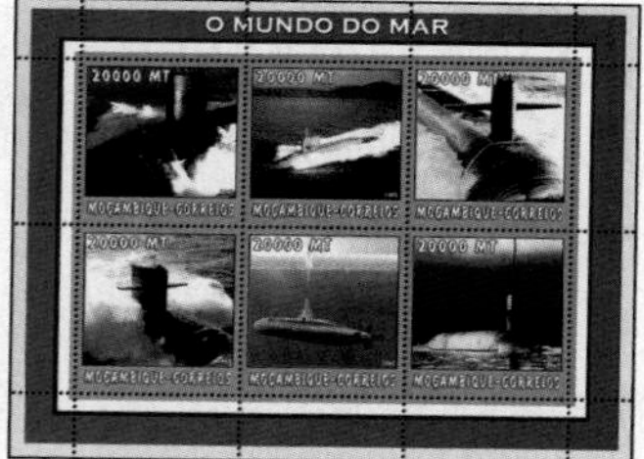

Submarines — A369

Lighthouses — A370

Ship — A371

Ship — A372

Fish — A373

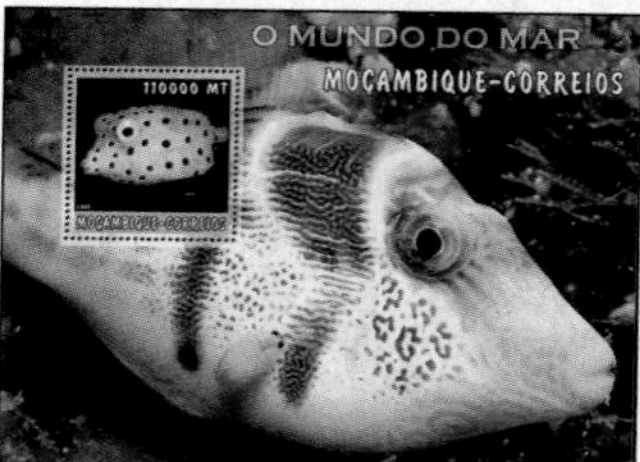

Fish — A374

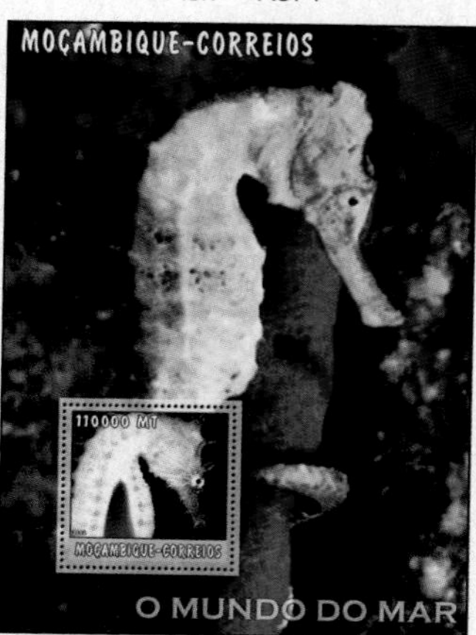

Sea Horse — A375

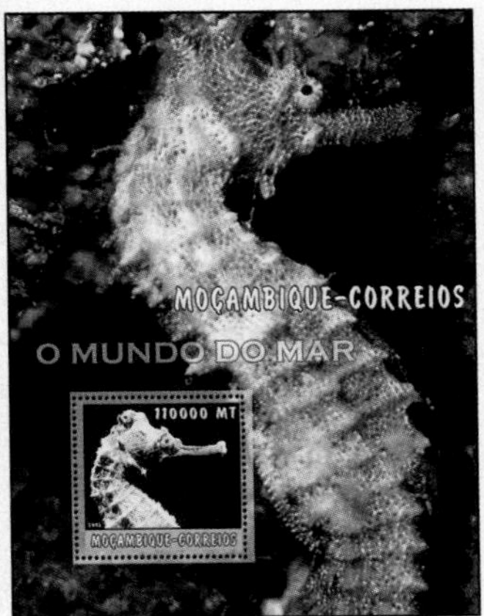

Sea Horse — A376

Penguin — A377

Penguin — A378

Sea Bird — A379

Sea Bird — A380

Sea Bird — A381

No. 1668 — Marine invertebrates: a, Phyllidia elegans. b, Phyllidia coelestis. c, Hypselodoris bullocki. d, Glossodoris hikuerensis. e, Glossodoris cruentus. f, Chromodoris leopardus.

No. 1669 — Shells: a, Murex brassica (showing shell opening). b, Cassis cornuta. c, Strombus gigas. d, Rapana rapiformis (showing shell opening). e, Chicoreus ramosus. f, Bursa bubo.

No. 1670 — Shells: a, Chicoreus virgineus. b, Tonna galea. c, Murex erythrostomus. d, Strombus gigas. e, Murex brassica (showing front of shell). f, Rapana rapiformis (showing front of shell).

No. 1671 — Tubeworms and seaweed: a, Kallymenia cribosa. b, Ulva lactuca. c, Chondrus crispus. d, Gigartina disticha. e, Palmaria palmata. f, Filogranella elatensis.

No. 1685, Seal flensing. No. 1686, Polar bear. No. 1687, Killer whale breaching surface. No. 1688, Whales underwater. No. 1689, Dolphins with open mouths. No. 1690, Lobster. No. 1691, Jellyfish. No. 1692 Coral and fish. No. 1693, Filogranella elatensis. No. 1694, Chromodoris leopardus. No. 1695, Tonna galea. No. 1696, Turbo marmoratus. No. 1697, Submarine. No. 1698, Christopher Columbus.

Perf. 12¾x13¼, 13¼x12¾

2002, Nov. 1

1647	A348	5000m Sheet of 6, #a-f	2.60	2.60
1648	A349	17,000m Sheet of 6, #a-f	8.75	8.75
1649	A350	17,000m Sheet of 6, #a-f	8.75	8.75
1650	A351	17,000m Sheet of 6, #a-f	8.75	8.75
1651	A352	17,000m Sheet of 6, #a-f	8.75	8.75
1652	A353	17,000m Sheet of 6, #a-f	8.75	8.75
1653	A354	17,000m Sheet of 6, #a-f	8.75	8.75
1654	A355	17,000m Sheet of 6, #a-f	8.75	8.75
1655	A356	17,000m Sheet of 6, #a-f	8.75	8.75
1656	A357	17,000m Sheet of 6, #a-f	8.75	8.75
1657	A358	17,000m Sheet of 6, #a-f	8.75	8.75
1658	A359	17,000m Sheet of 6, #a-f	8.75	8.75
1659	A360	17,000m Sheet of 6, #a-f	8.75	8.75
1660	A361	17,000m Sheet of 6, #a-f	8.75	8.75
1661	A362	17,000m Sheet of 6, #a-f	8.75	8.75
1662	A363	17,000m Sheet of 6, #a-f	8.75	8.75
1663	A364	17,000m Sheet of 6, #a-f	8.75	8.75
1664	A365	17,000m Sheet of 6, #a-f	8.75	8.75
1665	A366	17,000m Sheet of 6, #a-f	8.75	8.75
1666	A367	17,000m Sheet of 6, #a-f	8.75	8.75
1667	A368	17,000m Sheet of 6, #a-f	8.75	8.75
1668	A368	17,000m Sheet of 6, #a-f	8.75	8.75
1669	A368	17,000m Sheet of 6, #a-f	8.75	8.75
1670	A368	17,000m Sheet of 6, #a-f	8.75	8.75
1671	A368	17,000m Sheet of 6, #a-f	8.75	8.75
1672	A369	20,000m Sheet of 6, #a-f	10.50	10.50
1673	A370	33,000m Sheet of 6, #a-f	17.00	17.00
		Nos. 1647-1673 (27)	240.10	240.10

Souvenir Sheets

1674	A371	110,000m shown	9.50	9.50
1675	A372	110,000m shown	9.50	9.50
1676	A373	110,000m shown	9.50	9.50
1677	A374	110,000m shown	9.50	9.50
1678	A375	110,000m shown	9.50	9.50
1679	A376	110,000m shown	9.50	9.50
1680	A377	110,000m shown	9.50	9.50
1681	A378	110,000m shown	9.50	9.50
1682	A379	110,000m shown	9.50	9.50
1683	A380	110,000m shown	9.50	9.50
1684	A381	110,000m shown	9.50	9.50
1685	A350	110,000m multi	9.50	9.50
1686	A351	110,000m multi	9.50	9.50
1687	A352	110,000m multi	9.50	9.50
1688	A353	110,000m multi	9.50	9.50
1689	A354	110,000m multi	9.50	9.50
1690	A365	110,000m multi	9.50	9.50
1691	A367	110,000m multi	9.50	9.50
1692	A368	110,000m multi	9.50	9.50
1693	A368	110,000m multi	9.50	9.50
1694	A368	110,000m multi	9.50	9.50
1695	A368	110,000m multi	9.50	9.50
1696	A368	110,000m multi	9.50	9.50
1697	A369	110,000m multi	9.50	9.50
1698	A369	110,000m multi	9.50	9.50
		Nos. 1674-1698 (25)	237.50	237.50

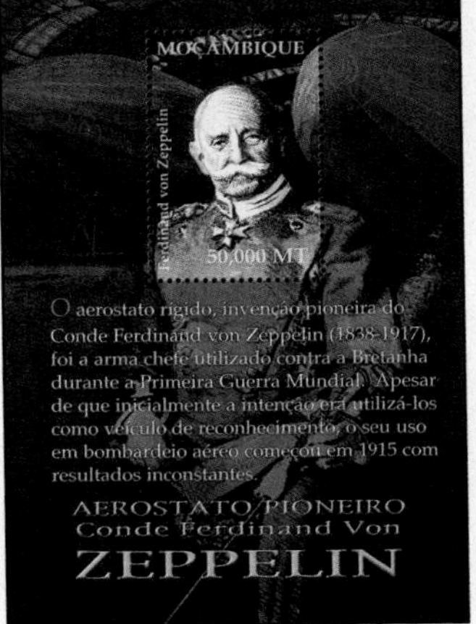

Zeppelins — A382

No. 1699, 28,000m, horiz.: a, Ferdinand von Zeppelin, brown and yellow background. b, LZ-2 in flight. c, LZ-10 in flight. d, LZ-1, purple background.

No. 1700, 28,000m, horiz.: a, LZ-1, blue and yellow background. b, LZ-2 tethered. c, LZ-10 above sheep. d, Ferdinand von Zeppelin with binoculars.

No. 1701, 50,000m, Ferdinand von Zeppelin, in military uniform. No. 1702, 50,000m, Ferdinand von Zeppelin, in suit.

2002, Nov. 18 ***Perf. 13¼x13½***

Sheets of 4, #a-d

1699-1700	A382	Set of 2	12.00	12.00

Souvenir Sheets

Perf. 13½x13¼

1701-1702	A382	Set of 2	6.00	6.00

Locomotives — A383

No. 1703, 17,000m, horiz.: a, London, Midland and Scottish Railway, England. b, Great Northern Railway, Ireland. c, Southern Railway, England. d, Great Northern Railway, US. e, Chicago, Milwaukee, St. Paul and Pacific Railroad, US. f, London and Northeastern Railway, England.

No. 1704, 17,000m, horiz.: a, Great Southern Railway, Spain. b, Shantung Railway, China. c, Shanghai-Nanking Railway, China. d, Austrian State Railway. e, Victorian Government Railways, Australia. f, London and Northwester Railways, England.

No. 1705, 17,000m, horiz.: a, Western Railways, France. b, Netherlands State Railway (green locomotive on bridge). c, Great Indian Peninsula Railway. d, Paris-Orleans Railway, France. e, Madras and Southern Mahratta Railway, India. f, Netherlands State Railway (green locomotive).

No. 1706, 50,000m, London, Brighton and South Coast Railway, England. No. 1707, 50,000m, New York Central, US.

2002, Nov. 18 ***Perf. 13¼x13½***

Sheets of 6, #a-f

1703-1705	A383	Set of 3	12.00	12.00

Souvenir Sheets

1706-1707	A383	Set of 2	6.00	6.00

A384

Automobiles — A385

No. 1708, 13,000m: a, 1912 Bentley. b, 1914 Delage Grand Prix. c, 1949, Healey Silverstone. d, 1922 Duesenberg. e, Delage 1500cc Grand Prix. f, 1961 Ferrari 375/F1.

No. 1709, 13,000m: a, 1906 Mercedes. b, 1951 Morgan. c, 1912 Sunbeam. d, 1922 Sunbeam. e, 1925 Sunbeam Tiger. f, 1908 Austin 100hp.

No. 1710, 17,000m: a, 1937, Bugatti Type 57 Alalante coupe. b, 1948 Tucker Torpedo. c, 1966 Honda S 800m. d, 1946 Cisitalia 202 GT. e, 1958 Chevrolet Impala. f, 1934 Cadillac LaSalle convertible.

No. 1711, 17,000m: a, 1908 Austin. b, 1937 Studebaker coupe. c, 1930 Bugatti Type 40GP. d, 1931 Ford Model A roadster. e, 1937 Alfa Romeo 2900B. f, 1937 Cord 812.

No. 1712, 40,000m, 1931 Alfa Romeo. No. 1713, 40,000m, 1911 Marmon Wasp.

No. 1714, 50,000m, 1957 Plymouth Fury. No. 1715, 50,000m, 1928 Mercedes-Benz SSK.

Perf. 13¼x13½, 13½x13¼

2002, Nov. 18

Sheets of 6, #a-f

1708-1709	A384	Set of 2	9.00	9.00
1710-1711	A385	Set of 2	10.00	10.00

Souvenir Sheets

1712-1713	A384	Set of 2	5.00	5.00
1714-1715	A385	Set of 2	6.00	6.00

Pottery — A386

Designs: 1000m, Pote. 2000m, Chaleira. 4000m, Taças. 5000m, Cantaro. 17,000m, Panela. 28,000m, Alguidar. 50,000m, Jarra. 100,000m, Bilhas.

2002, Dec. 2 ***Perf. 12¾***

1716-1723	A386	Set of 8	8.00	8.00

Dated 2001.

For surcharge see No. 1739.

Justino Chemane, Composer of National Anthem — A387

2003, July 11
1724 A387 6000m multi .55 .55

Minerals — A388

Designs: 5000m, Bauxite. 14,000m, Marble. 19,000m, shown. 33,000m, Gold.

2004, Apr. 30
1725-1728 A388 Set of 4 6.00 6.00

Dated 2003.

Paintings by Jean-Auguste Ingres — A389

Paintings by James Tissot — A390

Paintings by Pierre-Auguste Renoir — A391

Paintings by Edgar Degas — A392

Various unnamed paintings.

2004, June 17 Litho. ***Perf. 13½x13***
1729 A389 6500m Sheet of 6, #a-f 3.50 3.50
1730 A390 6500m Sheet of 6, #a-f 3.50 3.50
g. Souvenir sheet, #1730e .60 .60
1731 A391 10,000m Sheet of 6, #a-f 5.50 5.50
1732 A392 17,000m Sheet of 6, #a-f 9.25 9.25
Nos. 1729-1732 (4) 21.75 21.75

Diplomatic Relations Between Mozambique and People's Republic of China, 30th Anniv. — A395

No. 1735: a, Flags, buildings and animals. b, Arms, Admiral Zheng He, building, vase, sculpture.
Illustration reduced.

2005, June 25 Litho. ***Perf. 13¼***
1735 A395 33,000m Pair, #a-b 5.50 5.50

Exists imperf.

Southern African Development Community, 25th Anniv. — A396

2005, Aug. 11 ***Perf. 11¼x11***
1736 A396 8000m multi .65 .65

Traditional African Medicine Day A397

2005, Aug. 31 ***Perf. 11x11¼***
1737 A397 8000m multi .65 .65

World Summit on the Information Society, Tunis — A398

2005, Oct. 9 ***Perf. 11¼x11***
1738 A398 8000m multi .65 .65

Nos. 1320, 1576, 1717 Surcharged Like No. 1417 and

No. 1321 Surcharged in Black and Silver

Methods and Perfs as Before

2005 ?
1739 A386 6000m on 2000m #1717 .50 .50
1740 A331 8000m on 17,000m #1576 .70 .70
1741 A269 33,000m on 7500m #1320 2.75 2.75
1742 A269 33,000m on 12,500m #1321 (B&S) 2.75 2.75
Nos. 1739-1742 (4) 6.70 6.70

Mozambique Telecommunications Company, 25th Anniv. — A399

2006, June 10 Litho. ***Perf. 11½x11***
1743 A399 8000m multi .65 .65

No. 1743 also has denomination expressed in revalued meticals, which were put into service on July 1.
For surcharge, see No. 1747.

Presidential Initiative Against AIDS — A400

Pres. Armando Guebuza: 8m, Holding gavel. 16m, Behind microphones. 33m, With arm raised.

2006, Oct. 9 ***Perf. 11x11½***
1744-1746 A400 Set of 3 4.50 4.50

No. 1743 Surcharged

2006 Litho. ***Perf. 11½x11***
1747 A399 33m on 8000m #1743 —

The following items inscribed "Moçambique Correios" have been declared "illegal" by Mozambique postal officials:
Sheet of nine stamps of various denominations depicting Princess Diana;
Sheet of six 5000m stamps depicting the art of Paul Delvaux;
Sheet of six 17,000m stamps depicting the art of Edgar Degas;
Stamps depicting the art of Lucas Cranach;
Six different 15,000m souvenir sheets of one depicting Pope John Paul II;
Souvenir sheet of one 30,000m stamp depicting French Pres. Nicolas Sarkozy.
A set of 12 stamps with denominations of 5,000m, 19,000m, and 33,000m depicting Europa stamps, 50th anniv.
Stamps depicting Wolfgang Amadeus Mozart; Pierre Auguste Renoir; Jean Auguste Ingres Bessieres; Marilyn Monroe; Rotary International; Lions International; Formula 1 Racing; Astronauts; 2007 Rugby World Cup.

No. 1575 Surcharged

Methods and Perfs As Before

2006 ?
1748 A331 33m on 10,000m #1575 *6.75 6.75*

Cahora Bassa Dam A401

Designs: 8m, Dam and reservoir. 20m, Dignitaries shaking hands. 33m, Dam and flag of Mozambique.

2007, Nov. 26 Litho. ***Perf. 11x11¼***
1749-1751 A401 Set of 3 4.75 4.75

Reign of Aga Khan, 50th Anniv. — A402

Designs: 8m, Building. No. 1753, 20m, People on beach. No. 1754, 20m, People under shelter. No. 1755, 33m, Polana Serena Hotel. No. 1756, 33m, Students in classroom, vert. (30x40mm).

Perf. 12¾, 11¼x11 (#1756)

2007, Nov.
1752-1756 A402 Set of 5 9.00 9.00

Fauna, Flora and Minerals — A403

No. 1757 — Map of Africa and wild cats: a, 8m, Acionyx jubatus. b, 8m, Panthera leo with closed mouth. c, 8m, Panthera leo with open mouth. d, 33m, Male Panthera leo. e, 33m, Female Panthera leo, diff. f, 33m, Panthera pardus.

No. 1758 — Map of Africa and elephants: a, 8m, Loxodonta cyclotis facing right. b, 8m, Loxodonta africana. c, 8m, Loxodonta cyclotis facing left. d, 33m, Loxodonta africana facing right. e, 33m, Loxodonta cyclotis, diff. f, 33m, Loxodonta africana facing left.

No. 1759 — Lighthouses and marine mammals: a, 8m, Sousa teuszii. b, 8m, Stenella frontalis. c, 8m, Stenella clymene. d, 33m, Sotalia fluviatilis. e, 33m, Stenella longirostris. f, 33m, Tursiops truncatus.

No. 1760 — Map of Africa and birds of prey: a, 8m, Haliaeetus leucocephalus. b, 8m, Terathopius ecaudatus. c, 8m, Accipiter gentilis. d, 33m, Buteo lagopus. e, 33m, Head of Aquila verreauxii. f, 33m, Aquila verreauxi on branch.

No. 1761 — Hummingbirds and orchids: a, 8m, Tachybaptus, Malaxis uniflora. b, 8m, Fregata magnificus, Coryanthes speciosa. c, 8m, Gallinula, Calochilus robertsonii. d, 33m, Veniliornis, Stanhopea. e, 33m, Basilinna leucotis, Habaneria saccata. f, 33m, Actitis macularia, Diuris filifolia.

No. 1762 — Map of Africa and bees: a, 8m, Polubia. b, 8m, Apis mellifera scutellata. c, 8m, Pompilus. d, 33m, Tiphiidae. e, 33m, Vespula vulgaris. f, 33m, Scoliidae.

No. 1763 — Map of Africa and butterflies: a, 8m, Danaus chrysippus. b, 8m, Libytheana carineta. c, 8m, Papilio morondavana. d, 33m, Danaus gilippus. e, 33m, Amblypodia tyrannus. f, 33m, Lycaena cupreus.

No. 1764 — Map of Africa and crocodiles: a, 8m, Crocodylus porosus. b, 8m, Crocodylus novaeguineae. c, 8m, Crocodylus rhombifer. d, 33m, Crocodylus niloticus. e, 33m, Osteolaemus tetraspis. f, 33m, Crocodylus siamensis.

No. 1765 — Map of Africa and frogs: a, 8m, Gastrotheca. b, 8m, Mantella. c, 8m, Rana esculenta. d, 33m, Litoria rubella. e, 33m, Dendrobatidae. f, 33m, Pyxicephalus.

No. 1766 — Dinosaurs: a, 8m, Aublysodon. b, 8m, Ornithomimus. c, 8m, Coelurus. d, 33m, Velociraptor. e, 33m, Abelisaurus. f, 33m, Saurornithoides.

No. 1767 — Map of Africa and cacti: a, 8m, Hoodia gordonii. b, 8m, Hoodia officinalis. c, 8m, Hoodia ruschii. d, 33m, Hoodia flava. e, 33m, Hoodia officinalis, diff. f, 33m, Hoodia currorii.

No. 1768 — Fruit: a, 8m, Citrus vulgaris. b, 8m, Cola acuminata. c, 8m, Cocos nucifera. d, 33m, Citrus limonum. e, 33m, Cocos nucifera, diff. f, 33m, Citrus bergamia.

No. 1769 — Map of Africa, diamonds and minerals: a, 8m, Fluorite, quartz. b, 8m, Elbaite tourmaline, quartz. c, 8m, Staurolite. d, 33m, Fluorite, pyrite. e, 33m, Benitoite, neptunite. f, 33m, Celestine.

No. 1770, 20m — Map of Africa and primates: a, Cebidae. b, Nomascus leucogenys. c, Borneo proboscis monkey. d, Symphalangus syndactylus. e, Pan troglodytes. f, Cercopithecidae.

No. 1771, 20m — Lighthouses and whales: a, Balaenoptera borealis. b, Orcinus orca. c, Eschrichtius robustus. d, Balaenoptera physalus. e, Three Orcinus orca. f, Megaptera novaeangliae.

No. 1772, 20m — Map of Africa and owls: a, Strix woodfordii. b, Tyto capensis. c, Phodilus badius on thin branch. d, Phodilus badius on thick branch. e, Tytonidae. f, Otus senegalensis.

No. 1773, 20m — Map of Africa and parrots: a, Psittacopes. b, Serudaptus. c, Pseudasturidae. d, Quercypsittidae. e, Xenopsitta. f, Palaeopsittacus.

No. 1774, 20m — Butterflies or moths and unnamed flowers: a, Inachis io. b, Saturnia pavonia. c, Papilio xuthus. d, Prepona praeneste. e, Speyeria cybele. f, Nymphalidae.

No. 1775, 20m — Map of Africa and fish: a, Scorpaenidae. b, Balistodae. c, Antennarius. d, Triglidae. e, Hydrocynus. f, Lophius.

No. 1776, 20m — Map of Africa and marine life: a, Birgus latro. b, Panulirus. c, Gecarcoidea natalis. d, Loligo opalescens. e, Genus ocypode. f, Hapalochlaena.

No. 1777, 20m — Map of Africa and reptiles: a, Vaanus niloticus. b, Chamaeleo jacksonii. c, Veranus exanthematicus. d, Scincus. e, Brookesia. f, Furcifer pardalis.

No. 1778, 20m — Map of Africa and turtles: a, Natator depressus. b, Eretmochelys imbricata. c, Lepidochelys olivacea with dark neck. d, Lepidochelys olivacea with light neck. e, Caretta caretta. f, Chelonia mydas.

No. 1779, 20m — Map of Africa and snakes: a, Bitis nasicornis. b, Bitis gabonica. c, Ophiophagus hannah. d, Thelolornis kirtlandii. e, Dendroaspis angusticeps. f, Atheris.

No. 1780, 20m — Dinosaurs: a, Therizinosaurus. b, Heterdontosaurus. c, Prosaurolophus. d, Melanorosaurus. e, Megalosaurus. f, Proceratosaurus.

No. 1781, 20m — Trees: a, Punica granatum, fruit split, and on branch. b, Elaeis guineensis. c, Cola acuminata. d, Areca catechu. e, Hevea brasiliensis. f, Punica granatum, flowers on branches and split.

No. 1782, 20m — Map of Africa and orchids: a, Purple Cattleya lueddemanniana. b, Paphiopedilum delenatii. c, Vanda coerulea. d, Pink Cattleya lueddmanniana. e, Paphiopedilum. f, Spathoglottis.

No. 1783, 20m — Map of Africa and minerals: a, Carrollite. b, Ettringite. c, Cerrusite, barite. d, Malachite. e, Carrolite, calcite. f, Dioptase.

No. 1784, 132m, Map of Africa and Nomascus nasutus. No. 1785, 132m, Map of Africa and Panthera leo. No. 1786, 132m, Loxodonta africana. No. 1787, 132m, Stenella logirostris, diff. No. 1788, 132m, Orcinus orca and lighthouse, diff. No. 1789, 132m, Lepidocolaptes, Spathoglottis plicata. No. 1790, 132m, Pulchrapollia. No. 1791, 132m, Accipiter nisus. No. 1792, 132m, Map of Africa and Polubia. No. 1793, 132m, Arctia hebe. No. 1794, 132m, Papilio homerus, Caladeria reptans. No. 1795, 132m, Map of Africa and Thassophryninae. No. 1796, 132m, Map of Africa and Chauliodus. No. 1797, 132m, Map of Africa and Dendroaspis polylepis. No. 1798, 132m, Map of Africa and Pogona vitticeps. No. 1799, 132m, Map of Africa and Crocodylus niloticus, diff. No. 1800, 132m, Map of Africa and Eretmochelys imbircata, diff. No. 1801, 132m, Map of Africa and Pychicephalus adspersus. No. 1802, 132m, Hadrosaurus. No. 1803, 132m, Adansonia tree. No. 1804, 132m, Map of Africa and Euphorbia enopla. No. 1805, 132m, Map of Africa, Diuris filifolia, Malaxis uniflora. No. 1806, 132m, Cirtus vulgaris, diff. No. 1807, 132m, Vanadinite, poldervaartite. No. 1808, 132m, Malachite, barite and malachite.

Perf. 12¾x13¼

2007, Dec. 10 **Litho.**

Sheets of 6, #a-f

1757-1769 A403 Set of 13 125.00 125.00
1770-1783 A403 Set of 14 130.00 130.00

Souvenir Sheets

Perf. 13¼ Syncopated

1784-1808 A403 Set of 25 260.00 260.00

Minerva Central Publishers, Cent. — A404

Background color: 8m, Red. 20m, Olive green. 33m, Purple.

2008, Apr. 10 **Litho.** ***Perf. 11x11¼***
1809-1811 A404 Set of 3 4.75 4.75

Second Frelimo Party Congress, 40th Anniv. — A405

2008, July 25 ***Perf. 11¼x11***
1812 A405 8m multi .65 .65

Miniature Sheets

2008 Summer Olympics, Beijing — A406

No. 1813 Surcharged

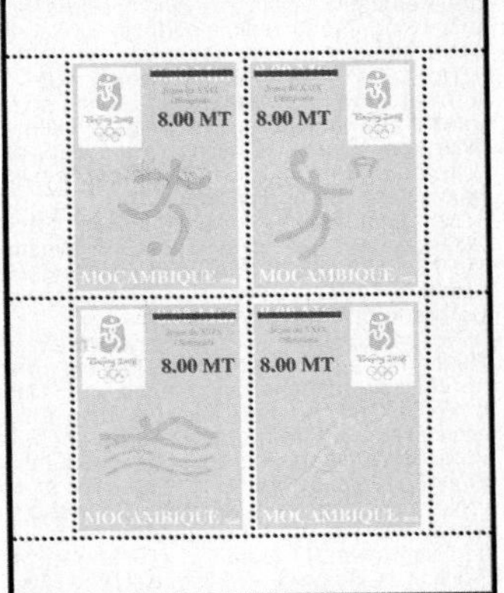

Nos. 1813 and 1814: a, Soccer. b, Basketball. c, Swimming. d, Running.

2008 ***Perf. 13¼x12¾***
1813 A406 8m Sheet of 4, #a-d 5.00 5.00
1814 A406 8m on 8m Sheet of 4, #a-d 2.50 2.50

No. 1813 shows an incorrect abbreviation for the currency, which was corrected by the surcharge.

Food — A407

Designs: 8m, Bolo de milho (corn cake). 20m, Mathapa com caranguejo (cassava with crab). 33m, Quiabo com camarao (Okra and shrimp).

2008, Oct. 9 ***Perf. 11¼x11***
1815-1817 A407 Set of 3 4.75 4.75

Maria de Lurdes Mutola, 800-Meter Gold Medalist in 2000 Summer Olympics — A408

2009, Jan. 21 ***Perf. 11x11¼***
1818 A408 8m multi .65 .65

Mozambique postal officials have declared as "illegal" stamps dated 2008 depicting chess grandmaster Bobby Fischer.

Eduardo Mondlane (1920-69), President of Mozambique Liberation Front — A409

2009, June 20 **Litho.** ***Perf. 11¼x11***
1819 A409 33m black & red 2.40 2.40

Transportation — A410

No. 1820, 33m — Transportation with animals: a, Elephants and howdah. b, Reindeer pulling sled. c, Camel and rider. d, Horse-drawn carriage. e, Donkey and rider. f, Dog sled.

No. 1821, 33m — Two-wheeled transportation: a, Rickshaw. b, Bicycle. c, Motor scooter. d, Motorcycle. e, Foot-powered scooter. f, Segway.

No. 1822, 33m — Old automobiles: a, Citroen BL 11. b, Jaguar XK-140. c, Chrysler Imperial. d, Dodge Royal Lancer. e, Mercedes-Benz 300 SL. f, Ford Custom.

No. 1823, 33m — Modern automobiles: a, Hyundai QuarmaQ. b, Lamborghini Murcielago. c, Buick Invicta. d, Ford Verve. e, Mazda RX-8. f, Cadillac CTS Sport Wagon.

No. 1824, 33m — Modern electric automobiles: a, Mitsubishi iMiEV Sport. b, Opel Meriva. c, Pickup truck (incorrectly identified as InterCity 225). d, Nissan Navara. e, Opel Insignia. f, Tesla Roadster.

No. 1825, 33m — Ancient sailing vessels: a, Phoenician bark. b, Egyptian wooden ship. c, Arab ship. d, Chinese junk. e, Greek galley. f, Roman galley.

No. 1826, 33m — Ships and maps: a, Independence, map of United States. b, Great Harry, map of Great Britain and Ireland. c, Vespucci, map of Spain. d, Norske Löwe, map of Denmark. e, Brederoe, map of Netherlands. f, Madre di Dio, map of Italy.

No. 1827, 33m — Steam-powered ships: a, SS Martha's Vineyard. b, SS America. c, SS Statendam. d, SS Brazil. e, SS Ryndam. f, SS Nieuw Amsterdam.

No. 1828, 33m — Warships: a, Warrior. b, Merrimack. c, Dreadnought. d, Lightning. e, MEKO frigate. f, Yamato.

No. 1829, 33m — Warships: a, HMS Astute. b, NS Yamal. c, USS Harry S Truman. d, Trafalgar. e, Vaygach. f, Nimitz class aircraft carrier.

No. 1830, 33m — Modern ships: a, Surcouf. b, Sea Shadow. c, Skjold class patrol boat. d, MS Radiance of the Seas. e, MS Pacific Princess. f, MS Mariner of the Seas.

No. 1831, 33m — Early locomotives: a, Trevithick. b, Blenkinsop. c, Marc Seguin. d, Puffing Billy. e, Rocket. f, Liverpool.

No. 1832, 33m — Locomotives: a, Evening Star. b, LMS Princess Royal Class. c, Russian 2TE10U. d, Atlantis. e, Cock o' the North. f, LMS Compound 4-4-0.

No. 1833, 33m — Locomotives: a, ALCO RS-1 (bister panel). b, British Rail Class 03. c, 643 Class. d, 661 Class. e, 641 Class. f, Hudswell Clarke 0-4-2ST.

No. 1834, 33m — Locomotives: a, ALCO RS-1 (gray panel). b, Re420. c, TAGAB Re2. d, EuroSprinter DB AG Class 182. e, SKODA 109. f, Re4.

No. 1835, 33m — High-speed trains: a, Thalys. b, Eurostar. c, InterCity 225. d, ICE. e, TGV. f, Pendolino.

No. 1836, 33m — High-speed trains: a, JR-Maglev. b, KTX. c, Maglev. d, 100 Series Shinkansen. e, E1 Series Shinkansen. f, N700 Series Shinkansen.

No. 1837, 33m — Pioneer aircraft: a, 1868 Albatros II glider of Jean-Marie LeBris. b, 1852 Henry Giffard balloon. c, 1849 glider of George Cayley. d, 1897 Avion III airplane of Clément Ader. e, 1874 monoplane of Félix du Temple. f, 1901 flying machine of Traian Vuia.

No. 1838, 33m — Pioneer aircraft: a, 1902 Number 21 airplane of Gustave Whitehead. b, 1904 Wright Flyer II. c, 14 Bis, 1906. c, 1908 Henry Farman biplane. d, 1909 Louis Blériot monoplane. f, 1910 Rumpler Taube.

No. 1839, 33m — Airplanes: a, Fokker D.1. b, Handley Page. c, Winstead Special. d, Boeing P26-B. e, Mitsubishi Ki-15. f, Nakajima Ki-27.

No. 1840, 33m — Military airplanes: a, Messerschmitt Bf-109. b, B-29 Superfortress. c, Yak-9. d, Avro Lancaster. e, Kawasaki Ki-61. f, Northrop P-61 Black Widow.

No. 1841, 33m — Military airplanes: a, Saab J35J. b, Sukhoi SU-30MKI. c, A-7 Corsair. d, Boeing 747 carrying Space Shuttle. e, Myasishchev M-55. f, Aero L-39 Albatros.

No. 1842, 33m — Supersonic airplanes: a, TU-144. b, F-105 Thunderbird. c, North American XB-70A. d, SR-71 Blackbird. e, Concorde 102. f, F16XL.

No. 1843, 33m — Fire vehicles: a, 1963 Magirus-Deutz Mercur 126 DL. b, 1979 Mercedes-Benz LA 1113 BR. c, 1958 Magirus-Deutz V6 Ladder. d, 1976 Dodge K1050 Somati MONIA. e, 2002 Scania 91 G310 Rosenbauer. f, 1984 Renault G300-17 Riffaul.

No. 1844, 33m — Ambulances: a, 1942 Morris Y Series. b, 1974 Citroen HB2AS 1600.

c, 1942 Dodge WC54. d, 1981 Land Rover. e, 1966 Cadillac S&S48. f, 1955 Ford Kaiser V8.

No. 1845, 33m — Spacecraft: a, Sputnik I. b, Vostok I. c, Explorer I. d, Skylab. e, Mir. f, Apollo 11.

No. 1846, 33m — Spacecraft: a, Venture Star. b, Ares V. c, Space Shuttle Discovery. d, Dawn. e, SpaceShip One. f, Phoenix.

No. 1847, 175m, Camels and rider. No. 1848, 175m, Rickshaw and Segway. No. 1849, 175m, Cadillac Eldorado. No. 1850, 175m, Citroen 2CV. No. 1851, 175m, Renault Z17. No. 1852, 175m, Egyptian canoe. No. 1853, 175m, Portuguese carrack Santa Catarina do Monte Sinai and map of Portugal. No. 1854, 175m, SS Great Britain. No. 1855, 175m, Italian battleship Littorio. No. 1856, 175m, PFS Polarstern. No. 1857, 175m, F261 Magdeburg. No. 1858, 175m, North Star locomotive. No. 1859, 175m, Pannier locomotive. No. 1860, 175m, 10000 locomotive. No. 1861, 175m, CC7102 locomotive. No. 1862, 175m, Thalys, diff. No. 1863, 175m, KTX, diff. No. 1864, 175m, Triplane of John Stringfellow. No. 1865, 175m, Nieuport 28. No. 1866, 175m, Aichi D3A. No. 1867, 175m, Corsair F4U. No. 1868, 175m, EF-111. No. 1869, 175m, A2 airplane. No. 1870, 175m, 1996-2001 Mercedes Unimog 2450 L38 fire truck. No. 1871, 175m, 1956 Gurkha Red Cross Ambulance. No. 1872, 175m, Salyut 1 and Telstar. No. 1873, 175m, V-2 rocket and SS-6 Sapwood. Nos. 1847-1873 are vert.

Perf. 12¾x13¼

2009, Sept. 30 Litho.

Sheets of 6, #a-f

1820-1846 A410 Set of 27 425.00 425.00

Souvenir Sheets

Perf. 13¼ Syncopated

1847-1873 A410 Set of 27 375.00 375.00

Nos. 1847-1873 each contain one 37x38mm stamp.

Famous People and Events — A411

No. 1874, 8m — Year of the Tiger (in 2010): a, Tiger with head at bottom, Temple of Heaven. b, Tiger running, Forbidden City. c, Tiger with head at top, Temple of Heaven. d, Tiger walking, Forbidden City. e, Tiger, Yong He Gong Lama Temple. f, Tiger, Great Wall of China.

No. 1875, 8m — Shen Chou (1427-1509), painter: a, Painting of forest, sketch of tree branch with calligraphy. b, Shen Chou at R, painting at L. c, 14x19mm landscape and 13x26mm landscape. d, 17x21mm landscape and 16x20mm landscape. e, Shen Chou at L, painting at R. f, 13x15mm landscape and 16x23mm painting of man on bridge.

No. 1876, 8m — Pope John Paul II (1920-2005) and: a, Arms, sculpture. b, Dove, St. Peter's Basilica. c, Arms, dome interior. d, Arms, St. Peter's Basilica. e, Dove in flight, St. Peter's Square. f, Arms, buildings in distance.

No. 1877, 8m — Mohandas Gandhi (1869-1948) and: a, Ganesha. b, Spinning wheel. c, Taj Mahal. d, Naja naja (cobra). e, Meditating woman. f, Panthera tigris tigris (tiger).

No. 1878, 8m — Chinese film personalities: a, Sun Daolin. b, Zhao Dan. c, Ge You. d, Bai Yang. e, Ruan Lingyu. f, Zhang Yu.

No. 1879, 8m — People's Republic of China, 60th Anniv.: a, Hand holding Chinese flag, Chinese soldiers. b, Mao Zedong. c, Qian Sanqiang, Tianwan Nuclear Center. d, Deng Xiaoping, Great Wall of China. e, Hu Jintao, fireworks above Olympic Stadium. f, Jiang Zemin, Hong Kong skyline, ruins of St. Paul's Church, Macao.

No. 1880, 20m — Charlie Chaplin (1889-1977), actor, in scene from film from: a, 1915. b, 1925 (clapboard in background). c, 1918 (film reel in background). d, 1925 (film reel in background). e, 1918 (strip of film in background). f, 1925 (standing next to actress).

No. 1881, 20m — Hirohito (1901-89), emperor of Japan, in suit and tie, and in background: a, Japanese flag, Hirohito in military uniform. b, Hirohito, waving, standing next to Empress Nakano. c, Japanese flag. d, Hirohito as child, pagoda. e, Hirohito on horse, Japanese flag. f, Hirohito and Empress Nakano in gown.

No. 1882, 20m — Pres. John F. Kennedy (1917-63) and: a, Astronaut on moon. b, Kennedy at typewriter. c, Kennedy presidential campaign button. d, Family. e, Wife, Jacqueline, holding baby. f, Wedding photo.

No. 1883, 20m — Marilyn Monroe (1926-62), actress: a, Wearing costume from 1954 movie, wearing striped blouse. b, Wearing swimsuit, wearing green coat. c, Wearing top hat, wearing necklace. d, Wearing blue shorts. e, Looking through ship's porthole. f, Wearing short skirt and wearing red dress.

No. 1884, 20m — Elvis Presley (1935-77): a, Wearing white jacket and lei. b, Wearing red jacket, and jumping in air wearing cape. c, With four women. d, With arms raised, and with arms at neck. e, On telephone, wearing blue striped jacket. f, With guitar.

No. 1885, 20m — Michael Jackson (1958-2009), singer: a, Holding on to rail. b, Wearing top hat. c, Holding woman. d, As boy, with brothers. e, Speaking into microphone. f, Behind lectern, raising both arms.

No. 1886, 20m — Pope Benedict XVI: a, Facing forward, wearing miter, holding cross, arms at left. b, Wearing red hat, dove in flight. c, Facing left, wearing miter, holding cross, arms at left. d, Waving censer, arms at UR. e, With arms extended, dove on pedestal. f, Wearing red stole and zucchetto, arms at left.

No. 1887, 20m — Expo 2010, Shanghai: a, Nepal Pavilion. b, Africa Pavilion, with text beginning with "O tema." c, United Kingdom Pavilion. d, Romania Pavilion. e, African Pavilion, with text beginning with "A fachada." f, Japan Pavilion.

No. 1888, 33m — Galileo Galilei (1564-1642), astronomer, and: a, Leaning Tower of Pisa. b, Three people around telescope. c, Gear mechanism. d, Galileo's telescope. e, Telescope on wooden stand. f, Globe.

No. 1889, 33m — Johannes Kepler (1571-1630), astronomer, and: a, Moon. b, Kepler's model of the solar system and book, Mysterium Cosmographicum. c, Austrian coin depicting Kepler. d, Horoscope for General Wallenstein. e, Model of solar system. f, Model inscribed with Kepler's name.

No. 1890, 33m — George Frideric Handel (1685-1759), composer, and: a, Bust. b, Sculpture of Handel. c, Musical notes and orchestra hall in background. d, Engraving of Handel. e, Sculpture of lyre player. f, Handel's house in London.

No. 1891, 33m — William Kirby (1759-1850), entomologist: a, Kirby and Hypochrysops epicurus. b, Nicrophorus vespillo and Dytiscus marginalis. c, Kirby and unnamed butterfly. d, Kirby and Delias ninus. e, Polistes dominula and Philanthus triangulum. f, Kirby and Chilasa agestor.

No. 1892, 33m — Napoleon Bonaparte (1769-1821), emperor of France, and: a, French army. b, Battle of the Pyramids, 1798. c, Battle of Borodino, 1812. d, Imperial arms. e, Napoleon's bed. f, Battle of Arcola Bridge, 1796.

No. 1893, 33m — Joseph Haydn (1732-1809), composer, and: a, Haydn's house, Eisenstadt, Germany. b, Haydn's birthplace. c, Piano. d, Musicians. e, Esterházy Theater. f, Pianist.

No. 1894, 33m — Charles Darwin (1809-82), naturalist, and: a, Mimus trifasciatus. b, Allosaurus. c, Darwin's notes and sketches. d, Desmodus d'Orbignyi. e, Lesothosaurus. f, Microraptor gui.

No. 1895, 33m — Louis Braille (1809-52), educator of the blind: a, Braille, at left, and blind boy reading book, at right. b, Braille Institute. c, Braille, at right, and blind boy writing in Braille, at left. d, Woman and seeing-eye dogs. e, Hands and book in Braille, at left, Braille, at right. f, Braille alphabet.

No. 1896, 33m — Katsushika Hokusai (1760-1849), artist: a, Poppies, ocean waves. b, Man, red mountain. c, Sumo wrestlers. d, Man on horseback. e, Palanquin carriers. f, Man and falcon.

No. 1897, 33m — Alexander von Humboldt (1769-1859), naturalist, and: a, Simia melanocephala. b, Rhexia speciosa. c, Simia leonina. d, Hibiscus. e, Convolvulus. f, Melastoma.

No. 1898, 33m — Georges-Pierre Seurat (1859-91), painter, and paintings on tripod: a, Young woman Powdering Herself (Muher jovem a maquilhar-se). b, The Reaper (O debulhador). c, The Stonebreaker. d, Chahut (O Chabut). e, A Sunday Afternoon on the Island of La Grande Jatte (Tarde de Domingo na Ilha da Grande Jatte). f, The Bridge - View of the Seine (A vista da ponte de Seine).

No. 1899, 33m — Sir Peter Scott (1909-89), founder of Worldwide Fund for Nature: a, Scott holding dog, painting of birds in flight. b, Scott feeding ducks, painting of ducks in flight. c, Scott facing left, painting of birds in flight. d, Scott with camera, painting of birds in flight. e, Scott facing forward, painting of birds in flight. f, Scott with binoculars, painting of ducks on water.

No. 1900, 33m — First man on the Moon, 40th anniv.: a, Moon, Apollo 11 on launch pad. b, Neil Armstrong, Moon, Apollo 11 in flight. c, Apollo 11 Lunar Module above Moon. d, Apollo 11 above Moon, Edwin E. Aldrin. e, Apollo 11, astronaut and American flag on Moon. f, Apollo 11 Command Module, Michael Collins.

No. 1901, 33m — International Polar Year: a, Iceberg and Odobenus rosmarus. b, Map of Antarctica, Belgium's Princess Elisabeth Antarctic Station. c, Map of Arctic Ocean and CCGS Amundsen. d, Intl. Polar Year emblem, iceberg, Ovibos moschatus. e, Map of Antarctica, Georg von Neumayer (1826-1909) and Karl Weyprecht (1838-81), polar explorers. f, Intl. Polar Year emblem, iceberg, Ursus maritimus.

No. 1902, 175m, Tiger and Forbidden City. No. 1903, 175m, Shen Chou and painting. No. 1904, 175m, Pope John Paul II giving communion to man. No. 1905, 175m, Gandhi. No. 1906, 175m, Xie Jin (1923-2008), Chinese film director. No. 1907, 175m, Ceremony of founding of the People's Republic of China. No. 1908, 175m, Chaplin. No. 1909, 175m, Emperor Hirohito, Empress Nakano and Queen Elizabeth II. No. 1910, 175m, Pres. Kennedy, White House. No. 1911, 175m, Monroe. No. 1912, 175m, Presley. No. 1913, 175m, Jackson and Slash. No. 1914, 175m, Pope Benedict XVI. No. 1915, 175m, Chinese Pavilion at Expo 2010, Shanghai. No. 1916, 175m, Galileo Galilei and men around globe. No. 1917, 175m, Kepler, telescope, planets. No. 1918, 175m, Handel. No. 1919, 175m, Kirby and Psuedotergumia pisidice. No. 1920, 175m, Map, Napoleon on horse. No. 1921, 175m, Haydn, harpsichord. No. 1922, 175m, Darwin and Rhea darwinii. No. 1923, 175m, Braille, teacher and blind students. No. 1924, 175m, Hokusai paintings of server of sake and mountain. No. 1925, 175m, Humboldt and specimens of flora and fauna. No. 1926, 175m, Artist's palette, Bathers at Asniers, by Seurat. No. 1927, 175m, Scott with camera on tripod, painting of birds in flight. No. 1928, 175m, Astronauts on moon, American flag. No. 1929, 175m, Iceberg, Alopes lagopus.

Perf. 12¾x13¼

2009, Nov. 30 Litho.

Sheets of 6, #a-f

1874-1901 A411 Set of 28 375.00 375.00

Souvenir Sheets

Perf. 13¼ Syncopated

1902-1929 A411 Set of 28 375.00 375.00

On Nos. 1874-1901, stamps "a," "c," "d" and "f" are 37x38mm, stamps "b" and "e" are 50x38mm. Nos. 1902-1929 each contain one 50x38mm stamp.

Worldwide Fund for Nature (WWF) — A412

No. 1930 — Hippotragus equinus: a, Adult. b, Adult and juvenile. c, Adults at watering hole. d, Adults in grass.

175m, Adult grazing.

2010, Jan. 30 ***Perf. 13x13¼***

1930 A412 33m Block or strip of 4, #a-d 10.50 10.50

e. Souvenir sheet of 8, 2 each #1930a-1930d + 2 labels 21.00 21.00

Souvenir Sheet

Perf. 12¾x13¼

1931 A412 175m multi 13.50 13.50

No. 1931 contains one 37x38mm stamp.

The Natural World — A413

No. 1932, 8m — Giraffes (Giraffa camelopardalis): a, Two giraffes, giraffe at right on ground. b, Herd of giraffes. c, Two giraffes, giraffe at left on ground. d, Adult and juvenile giraffes. e, Two giraffes, giraffe at left with front legs extended. f, Two adult giraffes standing.

No. 1933, 8m — Wild pigs: a, Sus scrofa facing right. b, Brown Sus scrofa facing left. c, Gray Sus scrofa facing left. d, Phacochoerus aethiopicus. e, Potamochoerus porcus. f, Phacochoerus africanus.

No. 1934, 8m — Zebras: a, Two Equus quagga boehmi with heads pointed to left. b, Two Equus quagga burchellii standing. c, Three Equus quagga burchellii. d, Two Equus quagga crawshayi. e, Two Equus quagga burchellii, zebra on left on ground. f, Two Equus quagga boehmi, zebra at right facing right.

No. 1935, 8m — Squirrels: a, Heliosciurus gambianus. b, Atlantoxerus getulus. c, Funisciurus isabella. d, Funisciurus pyrropus. e, Funisciurus substriatus. f, Geosciurus princeps.

No. 1936, 8m — Elephants (Loxodonta africana): a, Juvenile at left with trunk raised, adult at right. b, Adult at left, juvenile at right facing right. c, Adult facing right. d, Adult facing left. e, Juvenile at left with trunk down, adult at right. f, Adult at left, juvenile at right facing forward.

No. 1937, 20m — Peonies: a, Paeonia lactiflora and Paeonia moutan. b, Paeonia albiflora and Paeonia foemina. c, Paeonia peregrina and Paeonia moutan. d, Paeonia moutan and Paeonia tenuifolia. e, Paeonia nezhnyi and Paeonia officinalis. f, Paeonia arborea and Paeonia mascula.

No. 1938, 20m — Tropical birds and plants: a, Apaloderna vittatum, Sesuvium portulacastrum. b, Corythaeola cristata, Premna leucostoma. c, Lybius bidentatus, Ehretia rigida. d, Ceyx picta, Tamarind. e, Trachyphonus erythrocephalus, Pterocarpus indicus. f, Indicator indicator, Dracaena fragrans.

No. 1939, 20m — Pigeons: a, Columba arquatrix on branch that extends to right. b, Columba guinea. c, Streptopelia senegalensis on bare branch. d, Streptopelia senegalensis on branch with foliage. e, Columba livia. f, Columba arquatrix on branch that extends to bottom.

No. 1940, 20m — Rabbits and hares: a, Oryctolagus cuniculus, three paws visible. b, Poelagus rupestris, four paws visible. c, Poelagus majorita. d, Lepus capensis. e, Oryctolagus cuniculus, two paws visible. f, Poelagus rupestris, two paws visible.

No. 1941, 20m — Wild dogs and hyenas: a, Crocuta crocuta. b, Hyaena brunnea. c, Hyaena hyaena facing right. d, Lycaon pictus. e, Proteles cristata. f, Hyaena hyaena facing left.

No. 1942, 20m — Wild cats: a, Acinonyx jubatus. b, Panthera leo. c, Leptailurus serval. d, Profelis aurata. e, Panthera pardus. f, Felis caracal.

No. 1943, 20m — Aardvarks (Orycteropus afer): a, Facing right, tail extending to left of "2." b, Facing left, tip of ear at left under "c" of "Orycteropus." c, Facing right, tip of tail below "20." d, Facing left, snout in air, tip of ear at left under "p" of "Orycteropus." e, Facing right, tip of tail under decimal point in denomination. f, Facing left, snout on ground, tip of ear at left under "p" of "Orycteropus."

No. 1944, 20m — Bats: a, Two Rousettus aegyptiacus, bat at right with wing tip under last "0" in denomination. b, Two Rousettus aegyptiacus, bat at left hanging onto branch. c, Eidolon helvum. d, Otonycteris hemprichii. e, Two Rousettus aegyptiacus hanging onto branches. f, Barbastella barbastellus.

No. 1945, 20m — Rhinoceroses: a, Ceratotherium simum facing left. b, Diceros bicornis facing left, with all legs on ground. c, Ceratotherium simum facing right. d, Diceros bicornis with front legs raised. e, Ceratotherium simum facing forward. f, Diceros bicornis facing right.

No. 1946, 20m — Antelopes and gazelles: a, Tragelaphus buxtoni. b, Taurotragus derbianus. c, Kobus megaceros. d, Damaliscus lunatus. e, Alcelaphus buselaphus. f, Connochaetes gnou.

No. 1947, 33m — Marine birds: a, Morus capensis. b, Rynchops flavirostris. c, Thalasseus bergii. d, Sterna dougallii. e, Laurs dominicanus. f, Leucophaeus pipixcan.

No. 1948, 33m — Parrots: a, Psittacus erithacus. b, Agapornis nigrigenis. c, Psittacula krameri. d, Agapornis personatus. e, Poicephalus gulielmi. f, Poicephalus senegalus.

No. 1949, 33m — Birds of prey: a, Circaetus gallicus. b, Terathopius ecaudatus. c, Melierax metabates. d, Melierax canorus. e, Pandion haliaetus, f, Elanus caeruleus.

No. 1950, 33m — Hippopotami (Hippopotamus amphibius): a, Juvenile at left, adult at right with mouth open. b, Adult at left with mouth open, juvenile at right. c, Juvenile at left, adult at right with mouth closed. d, Adult and juvenile facing right. e, Adult. f, Adult at left facing forward, juvenile at right facing right.

No. 1951, 33m — Pangolins: a, Phataginus tricuspis in ball and facing right. b, Manis gigantea facing right. c, Manis gigantea facing left. d, Uromanis tetradactyla. e, Smutsia temminckii. f, Phataginus tricuspis on branch.

No. 1952, 33m — Seals and sea lions: a, Mirounga leonina. b, Gray Monachus monachus, head at left, denomination at right. c, Monachus monachus, denomination at left. d, Brown Monachus monachus, denomination at right. e, Gray Monachus monachus, head at upper right, denomination at left. f, Hydrurga leptonyx.

No. 1953, 33m — Dolphins: a, Delphinus delphis. b, Tursiops truncatus. c, Grampus griseus. d, Stenella coeruleoalba, denomination at right. e, Stenella coeruleoalba, denomination at left. f, Delphinus capensis.

No. 1954, 33m — Whales: a, Eubalaena australis. b, Balaenoptera musculus, denomination at right. c, Caperea marginata. d, Kogia simus, Kogia breviceps. e, Balaenoptera musculus, denomination at left. f, Balaenoptera edeni.

No. 1955, 33m — Monkeys: a, Piliocolobus kirkii. b, Colobus angolensis. c, Cercopithecus solatus. d, Papio cynocephalus. e, Cercocebus torquatus. f, Cercopithecus denti.

No. 1956, 33m — Orchids: a, Neobenthamia gracilis. b, Aeranga distincta. c, Disa cardinalis. d, Mystacidium venosum. e, Phalaenopsis equestris. f, Vanda luzonica.

No. 1957, 33m — Volcanoes: a, Cattle near volcanoes. b, Lava tunnel. c, Robot exploring volcano. d, Mt. Vesuvius, Italy. e, Volcanic island. f, Sadiman Volcano, Tanzania, Goddess Pélé.

No. 1958, 33m — Global warming: a, Iceberg, Ursus maritimus. b, Haliaeetus vocifer, smokestacks. c, Panthera tigris sumatrae, forest fire. d, Sterna paradisaea, iceberg. e, Pandion haliaetus, smokestacks. f, Canis rufus, forest fire.

No. 1959, 175m, Giraffa camelopardalis, diff. No. 1960, 175m, Potamocherus porcus, diff. No. 1961, 175m, Equus quagga boehmi, diff. No. 1962, 175m, Heliosciurus rufobrachium, Funisciurus lemniscatus. No. 1963, 175m, Three Loxodonta africana. No. 1964, 175m, Paeonia tenuifolia. No. 1965, 175m, Vidua paradisaea, Dracaena fragrans. No. 1966, 175m, Columba livia, diff. No. 1967, 175m, Pronolagus randensis. No. 1968, 175m, Lycaon pictus, diff. No. 1969, 175m, Panthera leo, diff. No. 1970, 175m, Orycteropus afer, diff. No. 1971, 175m, Eidolon helvum, diff. No. 1972, 175m, Ceratotherium simum, diff. No. 1973, 175m, Syncerus caffer. No. 1974, 175m, Pelecanus rufescens. No. 1975, 175m, Psittacus erithacus, diff. No. 1976, 175m, Haliaeetus vocifer, diff. No. 1977, 175m, Hippopotamus amphibius, diff. No. 1978, 175m, Smutsia gigantea. No. 1979, 175m, Hydrurga leptonyx, diff. No. 1980, 175m, Delphinus delphis, diff. No. 1981, 175m, Megaptera novaeangliae. No. 1982, 175m, Theropithecus gelada, Mandrillus sphinx. No. 1983, 175m, Dendrobium gonzalesii. No. 1984, 175m, Piton de la Fournaise Volcano, Reunion. No. 1985, 175m, Copenhagen Congress Center, Little Mermaid Statue, Copenhagen.

2010, Jan. 30 ***Perf. 13¼x12¾***

Sheets of 6, #a-f

1932-1958 A413 Set of 27 300.00 300.00

Souvenir Sheets

Perf. 12¾x13¼

1959-1985 A413 Set of 27 375.00 375.00

Miniature Sheet

2010 World Cup Soccer Championships, South Africa — A414

No. 1986 — Soccer players wearing: a, Dark blue shirt, orange shirt. b, Pink shirt, Light green shirt. c, Lilac shirt, light blue shirt. d, Red shirt, white shirt.

2010, Mar. 31 ***Perf. 13¼x13***

1986 A414 33m Sheet of 4, #a-d 10.50 10.50

Sports — A415

No. 1987, 8m — 2010 World Cup venues, South Africa: a, Green Point Stadium, Cape Town. b, Nelson Mandela Bay Stadium, Port Elizabeth. c, Ellis Park Stadium, Johannesburg. d, Free State Stadium, Mangaung-Bloemfontein. e, Soccer City Stadium, Johannesburg. f, Royal Bafokeng Stadium, Rustenburg.

No. 1988, 20m — 2010 Men's Winter Olympic Gold Medalists: a, Alexei Grishin, Freestyle skiing aerials. b, Felix Loch, Luge. c, Bill Demong, Large hill Nordic combined skiing. d, Jung-Su Lee, 1500-meter short-track speed skating. e, Jon Montgomery, Skeleton. f, Jasey Jay Anderson, Snowboard.

No. 1989, 20m — 2010 Women's Winter Olympic Gold Medalists: a, Lydia Lassila, Freestyle skiing aerials (incorrectly inscribed Alexei Grishin). b, Canadian team, Ice hockey. c, Amy Williams, Skeleton. d, Tatjana Huefner, Luge. e, Nicolien Sauerbreij, Snowboard. f, Martina Sablikova, 3000- and 5000-meter long track speed skating.

No. 1990, 20m — Female Table Tennis players: a, Wang Nan, denomination at left. b, Zhang Yining, denomination at right. c, Zhang Yining, denomination at left. d, Guo Yue. e, Li Xiaoxia. f, Wang Nan, denomination at right.

No. 1991, 20m — Female Cyclists: a, Linda Villumsen. b, Marianne Vos. c, Nicole Cooke. d, Victoria Pendleton. e, Simona Krupeckaite. f, Jeannie Longo.

No. 1992, 20m — Female Chess players: a, Antoaneta Stefanova. b, Xu Yuhua. c, Pia Cramling. d, Alexandra Kosteniuk. e, Viktorija Cmilyte. f, Judit Polgar.

No. 1993, 33m — Male Chess players: a, Garry Kasparov. b, Viswanathan Anand. c, Vasily Smyslov. d, Bobby Fischer. e, Anatoly Karpov. f, Veselin Topalov.

No. 1994, 33m — Male Table Tennis players: a, Wang Hao. b, Ma Lin, denomination at right. c, Ma Lin, denomination at left. d, Jorg Rosskopf. e, Wang Liqin. f, Jean-Philippe Gatien.

No. 1995, 33m — 2010 Men's Winter Olympic Gold Medalists: a, Didier Defago, Downhill skiing. b, Evgeny Ustyugov, 15-kilometer biathlon. c, Andre Lange and Kevin Kuske, two-man bobsled. d, Peter Northug, 50-kilometer cross-country skiing. e, Canadian team, Curling. f, Evan Lysacek, Figure skating.

No. 1996, 33m — 2010 Women's Winter Olympic Gold Medalists: a, Maria Riesch, Slalom and Super Combined skiing. b, Magdalena Neuner, 10-kilometer biathlon. c, Kaille Humphries and Heather Moyse, bobsled. d, Justyna Kowalczyk, 30-kilometer cross-country skiing. e, Kim Yu-Na, Figure skating. f, Canadian team, Curling.

No. 1997, 33m — Golfers: a, Angel Cabrera. b, Padraig Harrington. c, Vijay Singh. d, Tiger Woods. e, Phil Mickelson. f, Ernie Els.

No. 1998, 33m — Tennis players: a, Dinara Safina. b, Caroline Wozniacki. c, Roger Federer wearing blue shirt. d, Rafael Nadal. e, Novak Djokovic. f, Serena Williams.

No. 1999, 33m — Baseball players: a, Ichiro Suzuki. b, Doug Mientkiewicz. c, Hideo Nomo. d, Ryan Franklin. e, Nomar Garciaparra. f, Adam Everett.

No. 2000, 33m — Ice Hockey players: a, Alexander Ovechkin. b, Sidney Crosby. c, Teemu Selanne. d, Steve Yzerman. e, Mats Sundin. f, Mario Lemieux.

No. 2001, 33m — Male Cyclists: a, Cadel Evans. b, Jan Ullrich. c, Bernard Hinault. d, Mario Cipollini. e, Marco Pantani. f, Miguel Indurain.

No. 2002, 33m — Judo: a, Alina Alexandra Dumitru. b, Ole Bischof. c, Tang Wen. d, Irakli Tsirekidze. e, Masae Ueno. f, Kosei Inoue.

No. 2003, 33m — Taekwondo: a, Cha Dong-Min. b, Guillermo Perez. c, Hadi Sari. d, Lim Su-Jeong. e, Maria Espinoza. f, Son Tae-Jin.

No. 2004, 33m — Polo players: a, Hilario Ulloa. b, Bartolomé Castagnola. c, Juan Martin Nero. d, Gonzalo Pieres. e, Nacho Figueras. f, Charles, Prince of Wales.

No. 2005, 33m — Horse racing: a, Horse #14 and rival horse. b, Horses #8 and #10. c, Horse #2. d, Horse #3. e, Horse #9 and rival horse. f, Horses #4 and #1.

No. 2006, 33m — Dog racing: a, Dog #9. b, Dog #8. c, Dog without visible number. d, Dogs #3 and #4. e, Dog #2. f, Dog #6.

No. 2007, 33m — Rugby players: a, Richie McCaw. b, Matt Giteau. c, Sergio Parisse. d, Bryan Habana. e, Victor Matfield. f, Juan Smith.

No. 2008, 33m — African soccer players: a, Player with orange shirt. b, Player with blue shirt. c, Player #17 in red shirt, player #19 in white shirt. d, Player #15 in white shirt, player in red shirt. e, Player #8 in red shirt, player #20 in blue green shirt. f, Player #5 in orange shirt, player in white shirt.

No. 2009, 33m — Soccer players: a, Samuel Eto'o. b, Kaka. c, Cesc Fabregas. d, Wayne Rooney. e, Cristiano Ronaldo. f, Lionel Messi wearing #70 on pants.

No. 2010, 33m — Lionel Messi, soccer player, dribbling soccer ball, and wearing: a, Red shirt with wide blue vertical stripe in center, at left. b, Red and blue vertically striped shirt with wide stripes, at right. c, Dark blue shirt with white trim, at left. d, Horizontally striped shirt, at right. e, Light blue shirt, at left. f, Red and blue vertically striped shirt with narrow stripes, at right.

No. 2011, 33m — Roger Federer, tennis player, with two images: a, Wearing black shirt at left, white shirt at right. b, Black shirt with blue trim at left and right. c, White shirt at left, red shirt at right. d, White shirt at left, black shirt at right. e, White shirt at left and right. f, Black shirt at left, red shirt at right.

No. 2012, 33m — Alberto Contador, cyclist, on bicycle at left, and wearing, at right: a, White shirt with blue trim. b, Yellow shirt with collar buttoned. c, Yellow shirt with open collar. d, White shirt with blue and red trim. e, Yellow shirt and blue cap. f, Yellow shirt and cap, sunglasses on cap.

No. 2013, 33m — Valentino Rossi, motorcyclist: a, Wearing blue racing uniform at left, on motorcycle at right. b, On motorcycle at left, wearing green racing uniform at right. c, On motorcycle, facing right. d, On motorcycle, facing left. e, On motorcycle at left, wearing yellow sun visor at right. f, Wearing horizontally striped shirt at left, on motorcycle at right.

No. 2014, 175m, Loftus Versfeld Stadium, Tshwane-Pretoria. No. 2015, 175m, Mark Tuitert, 1500-meter long track speed skating gold medalist. No. 2016, 175m, Torah Bright, Halfpipe gold medalist. No. 2017, 175m, Guo Yue, diff. No. 2018, 175m, Jeannie Longo, diff. No. 2019, 175m, Alexandra Kosteniuk, diff. No. 2020, 175m, Vasily Smyslov, diff. No. 2021, 175m, Wang Liqin, diff. No. 2022, 175m, Evgeny Ustygov, diff. No. 2023, 175m, Marit Bjoergen, Individual sprint and 15-kilometer biathlon gold medalist. No. 2024, 175m, Tiger Woods, diff. No. 2025, 175m, Roger Federer (one image), diff. No. 2026, 175m, Ken Griffey, Jr., baseball player. No. 2027, 175m, Wayne Gretzky, hockey player. No. 2028, 175m, Lance Armstrong, cyclist. No. 2029, 175m, Choi Min-Ho, judo. No. 2030, 175m, Wu Jingyu, taekwondo. No. 2031, 175m, Pablo Mac Donough, polo player. No. 2032, 175m, Two race horses. No. 2033, 175m, Dog #8, diff. No. 2034, 175m, Shane Williams, rugby player. No. 2035, 175m, Soccer players wearing red and white shirts. No. 2036, 175m, Didier Drogba, soccer player. No. 2037, 175m, Messi, diff. No. 2038, 175m, Federer (two images), diff. No. 2039, 175m, Contador, diff. No. 2040, Rossi, diff.

2010, Mar. 30 ***Perf. 13¼x12¾***

Sheets of 6, #a-f

1987-2013 A415 Set of 27 375.00 375.00

Souvenir Sheets

Perf. 12¾x13¼

2014-2040 A415 Set of 27 375.00 375.00

Mozambique Airlines, 30th Anniv. — A416

Denominations: 8m, 20m, 33m.

2010, Apr. 14 ***Perf. 11x11¼***

2041-2043 A416 Set of 3 4.75 4.75

SEMI-POSTAL STAMPS

"History" Pointing out to "the Republic" Need for Charity SP1

Nurse Leading Wounded Soldiers SP2

Veteran Relating Experiences — SP3

Perf. 11½

1920, Dec. 1 **Litho.** **Unwmk.**

B1	SP1	¼c	olive	3.50	3.50
B2	SP1	½c	olive blk	3.50	3.50
B3	SP1	1c	dp bister	3.50	3.50
B4	SP1	2c	lilac brn	3.50	3.50
B5	SP1	3c	lilac	3.50	3.50
B6	SP1	4c	green	3.50	3.50
B7	SP2	5c	grnsh blue	3.50	3.50
B8	SP2	6c	light blue	3.50	3.50
B9	SP2	7½c	red brown	3.50	3.50
B10	SP2	8c	lemon	3.50	3.50
B11	SP2	10c	gray lilac	3.50	3.50
B12	SP2	12c	pink	3.50	3.50
B13	SP3	18c	rose	3.50	3.50
B14	SP3	24c	vio brn	3.50	3.50
B15	SP3	30c	pale ol grn	3.50	3.50
B16	SP3	40c	dull red	3.50	3.50
B17	SP3	50c	yellow	3.50	3.50
B18	SP3	1e	ultra	3.50	3.50
			Nos. B1-B18 (18)	63.00	63.00

Nos. B1-B18 were used Dec. 1, 1920, in place of ordinary stamps. The proceeds were for war victims.

AIR POST STAMPS

Common Design Type

Perf. 13½x13

1938, Aug. **Engr.** **Unwmk.**

Name and Value in Black

C1	CD39	10c	scarlet	.30	.20
C2	CD39	20c	purple	.30	.20
C3	CD39	50c	orange	.30	.20
C4	CD39	1e	ultra	.40	.30
C5	CD39	2e	lilac brn	1.00	.30
C6	CD39	3e	dk green	1.75	.40
C7	CD39	5e	red brown	2.00	.70
C8	CD39	9e	rose car	4.25	.75
C9	CD39	10e	magenta	5.50	1.10
			Nos. C1-C9 (9)	15.80	4.15

No. C7 exists with overprint "Exposicao Internacional de Nova York, 1939-1940" and Trylon and Perisphere.

No. C7 Surcharged in Black

1946, Nov. 2 ***Perf. 13½x13***

C10 CD39 3e on 5e red brn 6.00 1.75
a. Inverted surcharge

Plane — AP1

1946, Nov. 2 **Typo.** ***Perf. 11½***

Denomination in Black

C11	AP1	1.20e	carmine	1.10	.85
C12	AP1	1.60e	blue	1.40	.90
C13	AP1	1.70e	plum	3.50	1.40
C14	AP1	2.90e	brown	3.50	1.90
C15	AP1	3e	green	3.00	1.75
			Nos. C11-C15 (5)	12.50	6.80

Inscribed "Taxe perçue" and Denomination in Brown Carmine or Black

1947, May 20

C16	AP1	50c blk (BrC)	.50	.25
C17	AP1	1e pink	.50	.25
C18	AP1	3e green	1.00	.40
C19	AP1	4.50e yel grn	2.50	.75
C20	AP1	5e red brown	2.50	.90
C21	AP1	10e ultra	6.00	1.25
C22	AP1	20e violet	11.00	4.00
C23	AP1	50e orange	15.00	6.00
		Nos. C16-C23 (8)	39.00	13.80

Dangerous counterfeits exist.

Planes Circling Globe — AP2

Oil Refinery, Sonarep AP3

1949, Mar.

C24	AP2	50c sepia	.30	.20
C25	AP2	1.20e violet	.50	.30
C26	AP2	4.50e dull blue	1.25	.50
C27	AP2	5e blue green	1.75	.50
C28	AP2	20e chocolate	4.00	.85
		Nos. C24-C28 (5)	7.80	2.35

Catalogue values for unused stamps in this section, from this point to the end of the section, are for Never Hinged items.

1963, Mar. 5 Litho. *Perf. 13*

Designs: 2e, Salazar High School, Lourenço Marques. 3.50e, Lourenço Marques harbor. 4.50e, Salazar dam. 5e, Trigo de Morais bridge. 20e, Marcelo Caetano bridge.

C29	AP3	1.50e multi	.60	.20
C30	AP3	2e multi	.30	.20
C31	AP3	3.50e multi	.60	.20
C32	AP3	4.50e multi	.40	.20
C33	AP3	5e multi	.50	.20
C34	AP3	20e multi	1.10	.50
		Nos. C29-C34 (6)	3.50	1.50

Republic

Nos. C31-C34 Overprinted in Red

1975, June 25 Litho. *Perf. 13*

C35	AP3	3.50e multi	.20	.20
C36	AP3	4.50e multi	.35	.20
C37	AP3	5e multi	.85	.20
C38	AP3	20e multi	1.75	.40
		Nos. C35-C38 (4)	3.15	1.00

DeHavilland Dragonfly, 1937 — AP4

Designs: 1.50m, Junker JU-52-3M, 1938. 3m, Lockheed Lodestar L-18-08, 1940. 7.50m, DeHavilland Dove DH-104, 1948. 10m, Douglas Dakota DC-3, 1956. 12.5m, Fokker Friendship F-27, 1962.

1981, May 14 Litho. *Perf. 11*

C39	AP4	50c multi	.90	.20
C40	AP4	1.50m multi	1.10	.20
C41	AP4	3m multi	1.75	.20
C42	AP4	7.50m multi	2.50	.20
C43	AP4	10m multi	3.00	.35
C44	AP4	12.5m multi	4.50	.50
		Nos. C39-C44 (6)	13.75	1.65

Piper Navajo Over Hydroelectric Dam — AP5

Designs: 40m, De Havilland Hornet trainer, 1936. 80m, Boeing 737, Maputo Airport, 1973. 120m, Beechcraft King-Air. 160m, Piper Aztec. 320m, Douglas DC-10, 1982.

1987, Oct. 28 Litho. *Perf. 11*

C45	AP5	20m multi	.20	.20
C46	AP5	40m multi	.20	.20
C47	AP5	80m multi	.30	.20
C48	AP5	120m multi	.50	.25
C49	AP5	160m multi	.65	.35
C50	AP5	320m multi	1.25	.40
		Nos. C45-C50 (6)	3.10	1.60

POSTAGE DUE STAMPS

D1

1904 Unwmk. Typo. *Perf. 11½x12*

Name and Value in Black

J1	D1	5r yellow grn	.40	.20
J2	D1	10r slate	.40	.20
J3	D1	20r yellow brn	.40	.25
J4	D1	30r orange	.75	.60
J5	D1	50r gray brn	.70	.40
J6	D1	60r red brown	3.25	1.60
J7	D1	100r red lilac	2.75	1.60
J8	D1	130r dull blue	1.25	.85
J9	D1	200r carmine	1.75	1.00
J10	D1	500r violet	2.25	1.00
		Nos. J1-J10 (10)	13.90	7.70

See J34-J43. For overprints see Nos. 247, J11-J30.

Same Overprinted in Carmine or Green

1911

J11	D1	5r yellow green	.20	.20
J12	D1	10r slate	.20	.20
J13	D1	20r yellow brn	.30	.20
J14	D1	30r orange	.30	.20
J15	D1	50r gray brown	.40	.30
J16	D1	60r red brown	.50	.35
J17	D1	100r red lilac	.55	.45
J18	D1	130r dull blue	1.10	.80
J19	D1	200r carmine (G)	1.10	.90
J20	D1	500r violet	1.25	.85
		Nos. J11-J20 (10)	5.90	4.45

Nos. J1-J10 Overprinted Locally in Carmine

1916

J21	D1	5r yellow grn	3.75	3.00
J22	D1	10r slate	5.00	1.75
J23	D1	20r yellow brn	75.00	52.50
J24	D1	30r orange	20.00	11.00
J25	D1	50r gray brown	75.00	52.50
J26	D1	60r red brown	60.00	40.00
J27	D1	100r red lilac	75.00	50.00
J28	D1	130r dull blue	2.25	2.00
J29	D1	200r carmine	2.50	2.75
J30	D1	500r violet	5.25	4.50
		Nos. J21-J30 (10)	323.75	220.00

War Tax Stamps of 1916 Overprinted Diagonally

1918 *Rouletted 7*

J31	WT1	1c gray green	.85	.70
J32	WT2	5c rose	.85	.70
a.		Inverted overprint	8.25	7.50

Perf. 11

J33	WT1	1c gray green	.85	.70
a.		"PEPUBLICA"	50.00	40.00
		Nos. J31-J33 (3)	2.55	2.10

Type of 1904 Issue With Value in Centavos

1917 *Perf. 12*

J34	D1	½c yellow green	.20	.20
J35	D1	1c slate	.20	.20
J36	D1	2c orange brown	.20	.20
J37	D1	3c orange	.20	.20
J38	D1	5c gray brown	.20	.20
J39	D1	6c pale brn	.20	.20
J40	D1	10c red violet	.20	.20
J41	D1	13c deep blue	.20	.20
J42	D1	20c rose	.20	.20
J43	D1	50c gray	.20	.20
		Nos. J34-J43 (10)	2.00	2.00

Lourenco Marques Nos. 117, 119 Surcharged in Red

1921

J44	A4	5c on ½c blk	1.50	.70
J45	A4	10c on 1½c brn	1.50	.70

Same Surcharge on Mozambique Nos. 151, 155, 157 in Red or Green

J46	A6	6c on 1c bl grn (R)	1.50	.85
J47	A6	20c on 2½c vio (R)	1.00	.70
J48	A6	50c on 4c rose (G)	1.00	.70
		Nos. J44-J48 (5)	6.50	3.65

Regular Issues of 1921-22 Surcharged in Black or Red

1924 *Perf. 12x11½*

J49	A6	20c on 30c ol grn (Bk)	1.00	.40
a.		Perf. 15x14	19.00	4.50
J50	A6	50c on 60c dk bl (R)	1.00	.55

Catalogue values for unused stamps in this section, from this point to the end of the section, are for Never Hinged items.

Common Design Type

Photo. and Typo.

1952 Unwmk. *Perf. 14*

Numeral in Red Orange or Red; Frame Multicolored

J51	CD45	10c carmine (RO)	.20	.20
J52	CD45	30c black brn	.20	.20
J53	CD45	50c black	.20	.20
J54	CD45	1e violet blue	.20	.20
J55	CD45	2e olive green	.20	.20
J56	CD45	5e orange brown	.50	.30
		Nos. J51-J56 (6)	1.50	1.30

WAR TAX STAMPS

Coats of Arms of Portugal and Mozambique on Columns, Allegorical Figures of History of Portugal and the Republic Holding Scroll with Date of Declaration of War — WT1

Prow of Galley of Discoveries. Left, "Republic" Teaching History of Portugal; Right "History" with Laurels (Victory) and Sword (Symbolical of Declaration of War) — WT2

1916 Unwmk. Litho. *Rouletted 7*

MR1	WT1	1c gray green	2.00	.50
a.		Imperf., pair	15.00	
MR2	WT2	5c rose	2.00	.50
a.		Imperf., pair	15.00	

1918 *Perf. 11, 12*

MR3	WT1	1c gray green	.50	.50
a.		"PEPUBLICA"	8.50	4.75
MR4	WT2	5c red	.70	.60
a.		"PETRIA"	2.25	2.25
b.		"PEPUBLICA"	2.50	2.25
c.		"1910" for "1916"	10.00	5.00
d.		Imperf., pair		
		Nos. MR1-MR4 (4)	5.20	2.10

For surcharges and overprints see Nos. 221-225, 229, 235, J31-J33.

NEWSPAPER STAMPS

No. 19 Surcharged in Black, Red or Blue:

JORNAES JORNAES

2 ½ REIS (a) 2½ 2½ (b)

1893 Unwmk. *Perf. 11½, 12½, 13½*

P1	A2 (a)	2½r on 40r	200.00	90.00
P2	A2 (a)	5r on 40r	175.00	90.00
P3	A2 (a)	5r on 40r (R)	150.00	75.00
P4	A2 (a)	5r on 40r (Bl)	180.00	75.00
P5	A2 (b)	2½r on 40r	22.50	16.00
		Nos. P1-P5 (5)	727.50	346.00

Nos. P1-P5 exist with double surcharge, Nos. P2-P4 with inverted surcharge.

N3

1893 Typo. *Perf. 11½, 13½*

P6	N3	2½r brown	.35	.30

For surcharge and overprint see Nos. 93, 199, 206.

No. P6 has been reprinted on chalk-surfaced paper with clean-cut perforation 13½. Value, 50 cents.

POSTAL TAX STAMPS

Pombal Commemorative Issue

Common Design Types

1925 **Engr.** ***Perf. 12½***

RA1 CD28 15c brown & black .30 .25
RA2 CD29 15c brown & black .30 .25
RA3 CD30 15c brown & black .30 .25
Nos. RA1-RA3 (3) .90 .75

Seal of Local Red Cross Society
PT7 PT8

Surcharged in Various Colors

1925 **Typo.** ***Perf. 11½***

RA4 PT7 50c slate & yel (Bk) 1.40 1.40

1926

RA5 PT8 40c slate & yel (Bk) 3.00 3.00
RA6 PT8 50c slate & yel (R) 3.00 3.00
RA7 PT8 60c slate & yel (V) 3.00 3.00
RA8 PT8 80c slate & yel (Br) 3.00 3.00
RA9 PT8 1e slate & yel (Bl) 3.00 3.00
RA10 PT8 2e slate & yel (G) 3.00 3.00
Nos. RA5-RA10 (6) 18.00 18.00

Obligatory on mail certain days of the year. The tax benefited the Cross of the Orient Society.

Type of 1926 Issue

1927

Black Surcharge

RA11 PT8 5c red & yel 3.00 3.00
RA12 PT8 10c green & yel 3.00 3.00
RA13 PT8 20c gray & yel 3.00 3.00
RA14 PT8 30c lt bl & yel 3.00 3.00
RA15 PT8 40c vio & yel 3.00 3.00
RA16 PT8 50c car & yel 3.00 3.00
RA17 PT8 60c brown & yel 3.00 3.00
RA18 PT8 80c blue & yel 3.00 3.00
RA19 PT8 1e olive & yel 3.00 3.00
RA20 PT8 2e yel brn & yel 3.00 3.00
Nos. RA11-RA20 (10) 30.00 30.00

See note after No. RA10.

PT9

1928 **Litho.**

RA21 PT9 5c grn, yel & blk 4.00 4.00
RA22 PT9 10c sl bl, yel & blk 4.00 4.00
RA23 PT9 20c gray blk, yel & blk 4.00 4.00
RA24 PT9 30c brn rose, yel & blk 4.00 4.00
RA25 PT9 40c cl brn, yel & blk 4.00 4.00
RA26 PT9 50c red org, yel & blk 4.00 4.00
RA27 PT9 60c brn, yel & blk 4.00 4.00
RA28 PT9 80c dk brn, yel & blk 4.00 4.00
RA29 PT9 1e gray, yel & blk 4.00 4.00
RA30 PT9 2e red, yel & blk 4.00 4.00
Nos. RA21-RA30 (10) 40.00 40.00

See note after RA10.

Mother and Children
PT10

Mousinho de Albuquerque
PT11

1929 **Photo.** ***Perf. 14***

RA31 PT10 40c ultra, cl & blk 2.50 2.50

The use of this stamp was compulsory on all correspondence to Portugal and Portuguese Colonies for eight days beginning July 24, 1929.

See Nos.RA39-RA47.

1930-31 ***Perf. 14½x14***

Inscribed: "MACONTENE"

RA32 PT11 50c lake, red & gray 3.50 4.00

Inscribed: "COOLELA"

RA33 PT11 50c red vio, red brn & gray 3.50 4.00

Inscribed: "MUJENGA"

RA34 PT11 50c org red, red & gray 3.50 4.00

Inscribed: "CHAIMITE"

RA35 PT11 50c dp grn, bl grn & gray 3.50 4.00

Inscribed: "IBRAHIMO"

RA36 PT11 50c dk bl, blk & gray 3.50 4.00

Inscribed: "MUCUTO-MUNO"

RA37 PT11 50c ultra, blk & gray 3.50 4.00

Inscribed: "NAGUEMA"

RA38 PT11 50c dk vio, lt vio & gray 3.50 4.00
Nos. RA32-RA38 (7) 24.50 28.00

The portrait is that of Mousinho de Albuquerque, the celebrated Portuguese warrior, and the names of seven battles in which he took part appear at the foot of the stamps. The stamps were issued for the memorial fund bearing his name and their use was obligatory on all correspondence posted on eight specific days in the year.

Type of 1929 Issue
Denominations in Black
No. RA40 Without Denomination

1931 ***Perf. 14***

RA39 PT10 40c rose & vio 4.00 3.25
RA40 PT10 40c ol grn & vio ('32) 5.00 4.00
RA41 PT10 40c bis brn & rose ('33) 5.00 4.00
RA42 PT10 bl grn & rose ('34) 3.50 2.75
RA43 PT10 40c org & ultra ('36) 5.00 4.00
RA44 PT10 40c choc & ultra ('37) 5.00 4.00
RA45 PT10 40c grn & brn car ('38) 7.00 5.00
RA46 PT10 40c yel & blk ('39) 7.00 5.00
RA47 PT10 40c gray brn ('40) 7.00 5.00
Nos. RA39-RA47 (9) 48.50 37.00

Allegory of Charity
PT12

White Pelican — PT13

1942 **Unwmk.** **Litho.** ***Perf. 11½***

Denomination in Black

RA48 PT12 50c rose carmine 8.25 1.40

1943-51 ***Perf. 11½, 14***

Denomination in Black

RA49 PT13 50c rose carmine 17.00 1.25
RA50 PT13 50c emerald 10.00 1.25
RA51 PT13 50c purple 15.00 1.25
RA52 PT13 50c blue 12.00 1.25
RA53 PT13 50c red brown 50.00 1.25
RA54 PT13 50c olive bister 18.00 1.25
Nos. RA49-RA54 (6) 122.00 7.50

There are two sizes of the numeral on No. RA49.

Catalogue values for unused stamps in this section, from this point to the end of the section, are for Never Hinged items.

Inscribed: "Provincia de Mocambique"

1954-56 ***Perf. 14½x14***

RA55 PT13 50c orange 1.40 .30
RA56 PT13 50c olive grn ('56) 1.40 .30
RA57 PT13 50c brown ('56) 1.40 .30
Nos. RA55-RA57 (3) 4.20 .90

No. RA57 Surcharged with New Value and Wavy Lines

1956

RA58 PT13 30c on 50c brown .85 .35

Pelican Type of 1954-56

1958 **Litho.** ***Perf. 14***

Denomination in Black

RA59 PT13 30c yellow .70 .35
RA60 PT13 50c salmon .70 .35

Imprint: "Imprensa Nacional de Mocambique"

1963-64

Denomination Typographed in Black

RA61 PT13 30c yellow ('64) .50 .20
RA62 PT13 50c salmon .35 .20

Women and Children
PT14

Lineman on Pole and Map of Mozambique
PT15

1963-65 **Litho.** ***Perf. 14***

RA63 PT14 50c blk, bis & red .30 .25
RA64 PT14 50c blk, pink & red ('65) .30 .25

See Nos. RA68-RA76.

1965, Apr. 1 **Unwmk.** ***Perf. 14***

30c, Telegraph poles and map of Mozambique.

Size: 23x30mm

RA65 PT15 30c blk, salmon & lil .20 .20

Size: 19x36mm

RA66 PT15 50c blk, bl & sepia .20 .20
RA67 PT15 1e blk, yel & org .20 .20

The tax was for improvement of the telecommunications system. Obligatory on inland mail. A 2.50e in the design of the 30c was issued for use on telegrams.

Type of 1963

1967-70 **Litho.** ***Perf. 14***

RA68 PT14 50c blk, lt yel grn & red .40 .25
RA69 PT14 50c blk, lt bl & red ('69) .40 .20
RA70 PT14 50c blk, buff & brt red ('70) .40 .20
Nos. RA68-RA70 (3) 1.20 .65

1972-73

RA71 PT14 30c blk, lt grn & red .20 .20
RA72 PT14 50c blk, gray & red ('73) 1.00 .20
RA73 PT14 1e blk, bis & red ('73) .20 .20
Nos. RA71-RA73 (3) 1.40 .60

1974-75

RA74 PT14 50c blue, yel & red .20 .20
RA75 PT14 1e blk, gray & ver .85 .20
RA76 PT14 1e blk, lil rose & red ('75) .40 .20
Nos. RA74-RA76 (3) 1.45 .60

Intl. Year of the Child — PT16

1979 **Litho.** ***Perf. 14¼***

RA77 PT16 50e red 1.50 1.50

POSTAL TAX DUE STAMPS

Pombal Commemorative Issue

Common Design Types

1925 **Unwmk.** ***Perf. 12½***

RAJ1 CD28 30c brown & black .50 .60
RAJ2 CD29 30c brown & black .50 .60
RAJ3 CD30 30c brown & black .50 .60
Nos. RAJ1-RAJ3 (3) 1.50 1.80

MOZAMBIQUE COMPANY

mō-zəm-'bēk 'kəmp-nē

LOCATION — Comprises the territory of Manica and Sofala of the Mozambique Colony in southeastern Africa
GOVT. — A part of the Portuguese Colony of Mozambique
AREA — 51,881 sq. mi.
POP. — 368,447 (1939)
CAPITAL — Beira

The Mozambique Company was chartered by Portugal in 1891 for 50 years. The territory was under direct administration of the Company until July 18, 1941.

1000 Reis = 1 Milreis
100 Centavos = 1 Escudo (1916)

Mozambique Nos. 15-23 Overprinted in Carmine or Black

1892 Unwmk. *Perf. 12½, 13½*

1 A2 5r black (C) 1.25 .25
a. Pair, one without overprint 50.00 22.50
2 A2 10r green 1.25 .25
3 A2 20r rose 1.25 .25
a. Perf. 13½ 45.00 30.00
4 A2 25r violet 1.50 .35
a. Double overprint 27.50
5 A2 40r chocolate 1.25 .30
a. Double overprint 20.00
6 A2 50r blue 1.50 .25
7 A2 100r yellow brown 1.25 .35
8 A2 200r gray violet 2.50 .45
9 A2 300r orange 3.50 .70
Nos. 1-9 (9) 15.25 3.15

Nos. 1 to 6, 8-9 were reprinted in 1905. These reprints have white gum and clean-cut perf. 13½ and the colors are usually paler than those of the originals.

Company Coat of Arms — A2

Perf. 11½, 12½, 13½

1895-1907 Typo.

Black or Red Numerals

10 A2 2½r olive yellow .25 .25
11 A2 2½r gray ('07) 1.50 1.50
12 A2 5r orange .25 .20
a. Value omitted 15.00
b. Perf. 13½ 2.00 1.10
13 A2 10r red lilac .40 .30
14 A2 10r yel grn ('07) 2.50 .40
a. Value inverted at top of stamp 20.00 20.00
15 A2 15r red brown 1.00 .30
16 A2 15r dk green ('07) 2.50 .40
17 A2 20r gray lilac 1.50 .30
18 A2 25r green .75 .30
a. Perf. 13½ 1.90 1.25
19 A2 25r carmine ('07) 2.50 .60
a. Value omitted 15.00 10.00
20 A2 50r blue .90 .30
21 A2 50r brown ('07) 2.50 .60
a. Value omitted 15.00
22 A2 65r slate blue ('02) .75 .35
23 A2 75r rose .55 .30
24 A2 75r red lilac ('07) 5.00 1.00
25 A2 80r yellow green .35 .30
26 A2 100r brown, *buff* .40 .30
27 A2 100r dk bl, *bl* ('07) 4.00 1.00
28 A2 115r car, *pink* ('04) 1.00 .70
29 A2 115r org brn, *pink* ('07) 6.00 1.40
30 A2 130r grn, *pink* ('04) 1.50 .70
31 A2 130r brn, *yel* ('07) 6.00 1.40
32 A2 150r org brn, *pink* .35 .35
33 A2 200r dk blue, *bl* .35 .35
a. Perf. 13½ 2.00 1.60
34 A2 200r red lil, *pink* ('07) 7.00 1.40
35 A2 300r dk bl, *salmon* .50 .30
a. Perf. 13½ 2.50 1.40
36 A2 400r brn, *bl* ('04) 2.50 .70
37 A2 400r dl bl, *yel* ('07) 8.00 1.90
38 A2 500r blk & red .55 .40
39 A2 500r blk & red, *bl* ('07) 8.00 1.90
a. 500r pur & red, *yel* (error)
40 A2 700r slate, *buff* ('04) 8.50 2.00
41 A2 700r pur, *yel* ('07) 5.00 2.00
42 A2 1000r violet & red .90 .40
Nos. 10-42 (33) 83.75 24.60

#12b, 18a, 33a, 35a were issued without gum.

For overprints & surcharges see #43-107, B1-B7.

Nos. 25 and 6 Surcharged or Overprinted in Red:

25

b

c

1895 *Perf. 12½, 13½*

43 A2(b) 25r on 80r yel grn 22.50 15.00
44 A2(c) 50r blue 9.00 4.00

Overprint "c" on No. 44 also exists reading from upper left to lower right.

Stamps of 1895 Overprinted in Bister, Orange, Violet, Green, Black or Brown

1898 *Perf. 12½, 13½*

Without Gum

45 A2 2½r olive yel (Bi) 5.00 1.50
a. Double overprint 40.00 25.00
b. Red overprint 60.00 50.00
46 A2 5r orange (O) 7.00 1.50
47 A2 10r red lilac (V) 7.00 1.50
48 A2 15r red brown (V) 10.00 3.00
a. Red overprint
49 A2 20r gray lilac (V) 10.00 3.00
50 A2 25r green (G) 12.00 3.00
a. Inverted overprint 65.00 40.00
51 A2 50r blue (Bk) 12.00 4.00
a. Inverted overprint 60.00 40.00
52 A2 75r rose (V) 12.50 5.00
a. Inverted overprint 75.00 40.00
b. Red overprint
53 A2 80r yellow grn (G) 17.50 5.00
a. Inverted overprint
54 A2 100r brn, *buff* (Br) 17.50 5.00
55 A2 150r org brn, *pink* (O) 17.50 5.00
a. Inverted overprint 75.00 30.00
b. Double overprint
56 A2 200r dk blue, *bl* (Bk) 16.00 7.50
57 A2 300r dk blue, *sal* (Bk) 20.00 10.00
a. Inverted overprint 60.00 50.00
b. Green overprint
Nos. 45-57 (13) 164.00 55.00

Vasco da Gama's discovery of route to India, 400th anniversary.

No. 57b was prepared but not issued.

Nos. 45 and 49 were also issued with gum.

The "Centenario" overprint on stamps perf. 11½ is forged.

Nos. 23, 12, 17 Surcharged in Black, Carmine or Violet

25

PROVISORIO

e

25
Réis

f

g

1899 *Perf. 12½*

59 A2(e) 25r on 75r rose (Bk) 4.00 2.00

1900 *Perf. 12½, 12½x11½*

60 A2(f) 25r on 5r org (C) 1.75 1.25
61 A2(g) 50r on half of 20r gray lil (V) 2.00 1.00
b. Entire stamp 15.00 9.00

No. 61b is perf. 11½ vertically through center.

Stamps of 1895-1907 Overprinted Locally in Carmine or Green

1911 *Perf. 11½, 13½*

61A A2 2½r gray (C) 7.00 3.00
62 A2 5r orange (G) 6.00 3.00
63 A2 10r yellow grn (C) .70 .50
64 A2 15r dk green (C) .90 .50
a. Double overprint 40.00 20.00
65 A2 20r gray lilac (G) 1.25 .50
a. Perf. 13½ 1.40 .80
66 A2 25r carmine (G) 1.25 .60
67 A2 50r brown (G) .70 .45
68 A2 75r red lilac (G) 1.10 .45
69 A2 100r dk bl, *bl* (C) 1.25 .50
70 A2 115r org brn, *pink* (G) 2.00 .60
71 A2 130r brn, *yel* (G) 3.00 .60
72 A2 200r red lil, *pink* (G) 3.00 .60
73 A2 400r dull bl, *yel* (C) 3.00 .60
74 A2 500r blk & red, *bl* (C) 4.00 .95
75 A2 700r pur, *yel* (G) 4.00 .95
Nos. 61A-75 (15) 39.15 13.80

Nos. 63, 67 and 71 exist with inverted overprint; Nos. 63, 72 and 75 with double overprint.

Overprinted in Lisbon in Carmine or Green

1911 *Perf. 11½, 12½*

75B A2 2½r gray .30 .20
76 A2 5r orange .30 .20
77 A2 10r yellow grn .25 .20
78 A2 15r dark green .35 .20
79 A2 20r gray lilac .40 .20
80 A2 25r carmine (G) .35 .20
a. Value inverted at top of stamp 18.00
81 A2 50r brown .70 .20
82 A2 75r red lilac .70 .20
a. Value omitted 15.00
83 A2 100r dk blue, *bl* 1.00 .20
84 A2 115r org brn, *pink* 2.50 .30
85 A2 130r brown, *yel* 3.00 .35
a. Double overprint 30.00
86 A2 200r red lil, *pink* 3.00 .25
87 A2 400r dull bl, *yel* 5.00 .30
88 A2 500r blk & red, *bl* 7.50 .30
89 A2 700r pur, *yel* 5.00 .50
Nos. 75B-89 (15) 30.35 3.80

Nos. 75B-89 Surcharged

1916 *Perf. 11½*

90 A2 ¼c on 2½r gray .20 .20
91 A2 ½c on 5r org .20 .20
a. "½c" double 20.00
92 A2 1c on 10r yel grn .40 .20
93 A2 1½c on 15r dk grn .40 .20
a. Imperf., pair 35.00
94 A2 2c on 20r gray lil .50 .20
95 A2 2½c on 25r car 1.00 .25
96 A2 5c on 50r brn .40 .20
a. Imperf., pair 40.00
97 A2 7½c on 75r red lil .65 .20
98 A2 10c on 100r dk bl, *bl* 1.25 .30
a. Inverted surcharge 40.00 40.00
99 A2 11½c on 115r org brn, *pink* 3.50 .35
a. Inverted surcharge 50.00 50.00
100 A2 13c on 130r brn, *yel* 6.50 .30
101 A2 20c on 200r red lil, *pink* 5.50 .30
102 A2 40c on 400r dl bl, *yel* 6.50 .35
103 A2 50c on 500r blk & red, *bl* (R) 8.00 .70
104 A2 70c on 700r pur, *yel* 8.00 .75
Nos. 90-104 (15) 43.00 4.70

Nos. 87 to 89 Surcharged

1918 *Perf. 11½*

105 A2 ½c on 700r pur, *yel* 2.50 .95
106 A2 2½c on 500r blk & red, *bl* (Bl) 3.50 .95
107 A2 5c on 400r dl bl, *yel* 4.50 .95
Nos. 105-107 (3) 10.50 2.85

Native and Village — A9

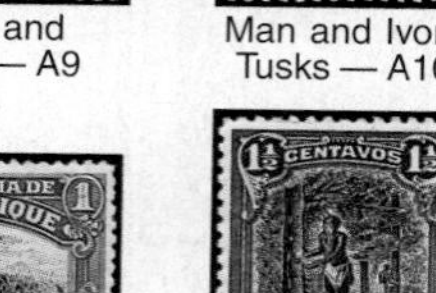

Man and Ivory Tusks — A10

Corn — A11

Tapping Rubber Tree — A12

Sugar Refinery — A13

Buzi River Scene — A14

Tobacco Field — A15

View of Beira — A16

Coffee Plantation A17

Orange Tree A18

Cotton Field A19

Sisal Plantation A20

Scene on Beira R. R. — A21

Court House at Beira — A22

Coconut Palm A23

Mangroves A24

Cattle — A25

Company Arms — A26

1918-31 Engr. *Perf. 14, 15, 12½*

No.	Type	Description	Unused	Used
108	A9	¼c brn & yel grn	.25	.20
109	A9	¼c ol grn & blk ('25)	.20	.20
110	A10	½c black	.25	.20
111	A11	1c green & blk	.25	.20
112	A12	1½c black & grn	.25	.25
113	A13	2c carmine & blk	.25	.20
114	A13	2c ol blk & blk ('25)	.25	.25
115	A14	2½c lilac & blk	.20	.20
116	A11	3c ocher & blk ('23)	.25	.20
117	A15	4c grn & brn ('21)	.25	.20
118	A15	4c red & blk ('25)	.20	.20
119	A9	4½c gray & blk ('23)	.20	.20
120	A16	5c blue & blk	.20	.20
121	A17	6c claret & bl ('21)	.80	.30
122	A17	6c lilac & blk ('25)	.25	.20
123	A21	7c ultra & blk ('23)	1.00	.50
124	A18	7½c orange & grn	.75	.30
125	A19	8c violet & blk	.20	.20
126	A20	10c red org & blk	.20	.20
128	A19	12c brn & blk ('23)	1.00	.35
129	A19	12c bl grn & blk ('25)	2.00	.35
130	A21	15c carmine & blk	.40	.30
131	A22	20c dp green & blk	.35	.20
132	A23	30c red brn & blk	3.50	.70
133	A23	30c gray grn & blk ('25)	2.00	.25
134	A23	30c bl grn & blk ('31)	3.50	.40
135	A24	40c yel grn & blk	.85	.45
136	A24	40c grnsh bl & blk ('25)	.70	.30
137	A25	50c orange & blk	2.25	.75
138	A25	50c lt vio & blk ('25)	2.25	.45
139	A25	60c rose & brn ('23)	1.50	.50
140	A20	80c ultra & brn ('23)	4.00	.70
141	A20	80c car & blk ('25)	1.00	.35
142	A26	1e dk green & blk	2.25	.45
143	A26	1e blue & blk ('25)	2.25	.35
144	A16	2e rose & vio ('23)	5.00	.70
145	A16	2e lilac & blk ('25)	4.00	.45
		Nos. 108-145 (37)	45.00	12.40

Shades exist of several denominations.
For surcharges see Nos. 146-154, RA1.

Nos. 132, 142, 115, 120, 131, 135, 125, 137 Surcharged with New Values in Red, Blue, Violet or Black:

h

i

j

1920 *Perf. 14, 15*

No.	Type	Description	Unused	Used
146	A23(h)	½c on 30c (Bk)	6.00	4.50
147	A26(h)	½c on 1e (R)	6.00	4.50
148	A14(h)	1½c on 2½c (Bl)	4.00	2.25
149	A16(h)	1½c on 5c (V)	4.00	3.50
150	A14(h)	2c on 2½c (R)	1.75	1.75
151	A22(i)	4c on 20c (V)	7.50	4.50
152	A24(i)	4c on 40c (V)	8.50	5.00
153	A19(j)	6c on 8c (R)	8.00	5.50
154	A25(j)	6c on 50c (Bk)	9.00	5.50
		Nos. 146-154 (9)	54.75	37.00

The surcharge on No. 148 is placed vertically between two bars. On No. 154 the two words of the surcharge are 13mm apart.

Native — A27

View of Beira — A28

Tapping Rubber Tree — A29

Picking Tea — A30

Zambezi River — A31

1925-31 Engr. *Perf. 12*

No.	Type	Description	Unused	Used
155	A27	24c ultra & blk	1.00	.50
156	A28	25c choc & ultra	1.00	.50
157	A27	85c brn red & blk ('31)	.85	.45
158	A28	1.40e dl bl & blk ('31)	.85	.45
159	A29	5e yel brn & ultra	1.25	.30
160	A30	10e rose & blk	1.75	.75
161	A31	20e green & blk	1.75	.75
		Nos. 155-161 (7)	8.45	3.70

Ivory Tusks — A32

Panning Gold — A33

1931 Litho. *Perf. 14*

No.	Type	Description	Unused	Used
162	A32	45c lt blue	2.00	.85
163	A33	70c yellow brn	1.40	.35

Zambezi Railroad Bridge A34

1935 Engr. *Perf. 12½*

No.	Type	Description	Unused	Used
164	A34	1e dk blue & blk	2.00	1.40

Opening of a new bridge over the Zambezi River.

Airplane over Beira — A35

1935

No.	Type	Description	Unused	Used
165	A35	5c blue & blk	.45	.35
166	A35	10c red org & blk	.45	.35
a.		Square pair, imperf. between	50.00	
167	A35	15c red & blk	.45	.35
a.		Square pair, imperf. between	50.00	
168	A35	20c yel grn & blk	.45	.35
169	A35	30c green & blk	.45	.35
170	A35	40c gray bl & blk	.45	.35
171	A35	45c blue & blk	.45	.35
172	A35	50c violet & blk	.45	.35
a.		Square pair, imperf. btwn.	60.00	
173	A35	60c carmine & brn	.60	.35
174	A35	80c carmine & blk	.60	.35
		Nos. 165-174 (10)	4.80	3.50

Issued to commemorate the opening of the Blantyre-Beira Salisbury air service.

Giraffe — A36

Thatched Huts — A37

Rock Python — A41

Coconut Palms A50

Zambezi Railroad Bridge A52

Sena Gate — A53

Company Arms — A54

Designs: 10c, Dhow. 15c, St. Caetano Fortress, Sofala. 20c, Zebra. 40c, Black rhinoceros. 45c, Lion. 50c, Crocodile. 60c, Leopard. 70c, Mozambique woman. 80c, Hippopotami. 85c, Vasco da Gama's flagship. 1e, Man in canoe. 2e, Greater kudu.

1937, May 16 *Perf. 12½*

No.	Type	Description	Unused	Used
175	A36	1c yel grn & vio	.20	*.20*
176	A37	5c blue & yel grn	.20	*.20*
177	A36	10c ver & ultra	.20	*.20*
178	A37	15c carmine & blk	.20	*.20*
179	A36	20c green & ultra	.20	*.20*
180	A41	30c dk grn & ind	.20	*.30*
181	A41	40c gray bl & blk	.20	*.30*
182	A41	45c blue & brn	.20	*.30*
183	A41	50c dk vio & emer	.20	*.30*
184	A37	60c carmine & bl	.20	*.20*
185	A36	70c yel brn & pale grn	.20	*.20*
186	A37	80c car & pale grn	.40	.30
187	A41	85c org red & blk	.40	.40
188	A41	1e dp bl & blk	.40	.20
189	A50	1.40e dk bl & pale grn	.40	.20
190	A41	2e pale lilac & brn	.85	.20
191	A52	5e yel brn & bl	1.25	.75
192	A53	10e carmine & blk	2.25	1.50
193	A54	20e grn & brn vio	3.00	2.75
		Nos. 175-193 (19)	11.15	8.90

Stamps of 1937 Overprinted in Red or Black

1939, Aug. 28

No.	Type	Description	Unused	Used
194	A41	30c dk grn & ind (R)	1.50	.85
195	A41	40c gray bl & blk (R)	1.50	.85
196	A41	45c blue & brn (Bk)	1.50	.85
197	A41	50c dk vio & emer (R)	2.25	1.00
198	A41	85c org red & blk (Bk)	2.25	1.00
199	A41	1e dp bl & blk (R)	1.75	1.25
200	A41	2e pale lil & brn (Bk)	2.75	1.60
		Nos. 194-200 (7)	13.50	7.40

Visit of the President of Portugal to Beira in 1939.

King Alfonso Henriques A55

King John IV A56

1940, Feb. 16 Typo. *Perf. 11½x12*

No.	Type	Description	Unused	Used
201	A55	1.75e blue & lt blue	.70	.70

800th anniv. of Portuguese independence.

1941 Engr. *Perf. 12½*

No.	Type	Description	Unused	Used
202	A56	40c gray grn & blk	.30	.20
203	A56	50c dk vio & brt grn	.30	.20
204	A56	60c brt car & dp bl	.30	.20
205	A56	70c brn org & dk grn	.30	.20
206	A56	80c car & dp grn	.30	.20
207	A56	1e dk bl & blk	.30	.20
		Nos. 202-207 (6)	1.80	1.20

300th anniv. of the restoration of the Portuguese Monarchy.

Mozambique Company's charter terminated July 18th, 1941 after which date its stamps were superseded by those of the territory of Mozambique.

SEMI-POSTAL STAMPS

Lisbon Issue of 1911 Overprinted in Red

1917 Unwmk. *Perf. 11½*

No.	Type	Description	Unused	Used
B1	A2	2½r gray	7.50	*10.50*
a.		Double overprint	75.00	*75.00*
B2	A2	10r yellow grn	8.75	*15.00*
B3	A2	20r gray lilac	12.00	*20.00*
B4	A2	50r brown	20.00	*25.00*
B5	A2	75r red lilac	65.00	*70.00*
B6	A2	100r dk blue, *bl*	65.00	*70.00*
B7	A2	700r purple, *yel*	160.00	*225.00*
		Nos. B1-B7 (7)	338.25	*435.50*

Nos. B1-B7 were used on July 31, 1917, in place of ordinary stamps. The proceeds were given to the Red Cross.

AIR POST STAMPS

Airplane over Beira — AP1

1935 Unwmk. Engr. *Perf. 12½*

No.	Type	Description	Unused	Used
C1	AP1	5c blue & blk	.20	.20
C2	AP1	10c org red & blk	.20	.20
C3	AP1	15c red & blk	.20	.20
C4	AP1	20c yel grn & blk	.20	.20
C5	AP1	30c green & blk	.20	.20
C6	AP1	40c gray bl & blk	.20	.20
C7	AP1	45c blue & blk	.20	.20
C8	AP1	50c dk vio & blk	.40	.20
C9	AP1	60c car & brn	.40	.20
C10	AP1	80c car & blk	.50	.20
C11	AP1	1e blue & blk	.50	.20
C12	AP1	2e mauve & blk	1.25	.25
C13	AP1	5e bis brn & bl	1.25	.40
C14	AP1	10e car & blk	1.40	.60
C15	AP1	20e bl grn & blk	2.75	.85
		Nos. C1-C15 (15)	9.85	4.30

POSTAGE DUE STAMPS

D1

1906 Unwmk. Typo. ***Perf. 11½x12***
Denominations in Black

J1	D1	5r yellow grn	.70	.30
J2	D1	10r slate	.70	.30
J3	D1	20r yellow brn	1.25	.30
J4	D1	30r orange	1.50	1.00
J5	D1	50r gray brown	1.50	1.00
J6	D1	60r red brown	22.50	9.00
J7	D1	100r red lilac	4.00	2.50
J8	D1	130r dull blue	32.50	12.00
J9	D1	200r carmine	13.00	4.00
J10	D1	500r violet	18.00	5.00
		Nos. J1-J10 (10)	95.65	35.40

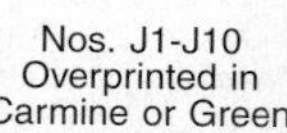
Nos. J1-J10 Overprinted in Carmine or Green

1911

J11	D1	5r yellow grn	.20	.20
J12	D1	10r slate	.20	.20
J13	D1	20r yellow brn	.20	.20
J14	D1	30r orange	.20	.20
J15	D1	50r gray brown	.30	.20
J16	D1	60r red brown	.40	.30
J17	D1	100r red lilac	.40	.30
J18	D1	130r dull blue	2.00	1.00
J19	D1	200r carmine (G)	1.25	.85
J20	D1	500r violet	2.50	1.00
		Nos. J11-J20 (10)	7.65	4.45

D2

Company Arms — D3

1916 **Typo.**
With Value in Centavos in Black

J21	D2	½c yellow grn	.30	.20
J22	D2	1c slate	.30	.20
J23	D2	2c orange brn	.30	.20
J24	D2	3c orange	.60	.25
J25	D2	5c gray brown	.60	.25
J26	D2	6c pale brown	.60	.25
J27	D2	10c red lilac	.60	.30
J28	D2	13c gray blue	.90	.55
J29	D2	20c rose	1.25	.65
J30	D2	50c gray	3.00	.85
		Nos. J21-J30 (10)	8.45	3.70

1919 Engr. ***Perf. 12½, 13½, 14, 15***

J31	D3	½c green	.20	.20
J32	D3	1c slate	.20	.20
J33	D3	2c red brown	.20	.20
J34	D3	3c orange	.20	.20
J35	D3	5c gray brown	.20	.20
J36	D3	6c lt brown	.45	.45
J37	D3	10c lilac rose	.45	.45
J38	D3	13c dull blue	.45	.45
J39	D3	20c rose	.45	.45
J40	D3	50c gray	.45	.45
		Nos. J31-J40 (10)	3.25	3.25

NEWSPAPER STAMP

Newspaper Stamp of Mozambique Overprinted

1894 Unwmk. ***Perf. 11½***

P1	N3	2½r brown	.50	.40
a.		Inverted overprint	30.00	30.00
b.		Perf. 12½	.85	.50

Reprints are on stout white paper with clean-cut perf. 13½. Value $1.

POSTAL TAX STAMPS

No. 116 Surcharged in Black

1932 ***Perf. 12½***

RA1	A11	2c on 3c org & blk	1.40	*2.00*

Charity — PT2

1933 Litho. ***Perf. 11***

RA2	PT2	2c magenta & blk	1.00	*2.00*

PT3

PT4

1940 Unwmk. ***Perf. 10½***

RA3	PT3	2c black & ultra	15.00	*16.00*

1941

RA4	PT4	2c black & brt red	15.00	*16.00*

Vol. 4 Number Additions, Deletions & Changes

Jordan

Number in 2011 Catalogue	Number in 2012 Catalogue
new	113a
new	114b
new	116a
new	118a
new	119a
new	119b
new	121a
new	121b
new	122a
new	123a
new	124a
new	126a
new	128a
new	129a
1471a	1471b
1472A	1472E
1474b	1474d
1476Ac	1476Ad
1477Ac	1477Ad
new	J2a
new	J2b
new	J3a
new	J3b
new	J4b
new	J5a
new	J5b

Korea (North)

Number in 2011 Catalogue	Number in 2012 Catalogue
new	727
727	727a
728	727b
729	727c
new	1190
1190	1190a
1191	1190b
1192	1190c
new	3113
3113	3113a
3114	3113b
3115	3113c
3116	3113d
3117	3113e
3117a	3113f
3118	3114
3163c	3163C
3294a	deleted
3478	3426a
3609	3607a
3610	3608b
new	3770
3770	3770a
3771	3770b
3772	3770c
new	3792
3792	3792a
3793	3792b
3794	3792c
3795	3792d
new	3811
3811	3811a
3812	3811b
3813	3811c
3814	3811d
3814a	3811e
3814b	3811f
new	3863
3863	3863a
3864	3863b
3865	3863c
3866	3863d
3867	3863e
3868	3864
new	3874
3874	3874a
3875	3874b
3876	3874c
3877	3874d
new	3890
new	3879
3879	3879a
3880	3879b
3881	3879c
3882	3879d
new	3890
3890	3890a
3891	3890b
new	3907
3907	3907a
3908	3907b
3909	3907c
3910	3907d
3911	3907e
3912	3907f
new	3913
3913	3913a
3914	3913b
3915	3913c
3916	3913d
new	3923
3923	3923a
new	3924
3924	3923b
3925	3923c
3926	3923d
3927	3923e
3928	3923f
3929	3924a
3930	3924b
3931	3924c
3932	3924d
3933	3924e
3934	3924f
new	3949
3949	3949a
3950	3949b
3951	3949c
3952	3949d
new	3956
3956	3956a
3957	3956b
3958	3956c
3962	3962a
3963	3962b
3964	3962c
3965	3962d
3965a	3962
3966	3963a
3967	3963b
3968	3963c
3969	3963d
3969a	3963
3970	3964a
3971	3964b
3972	3964c
3973	3964d
3973a	3964
3974	3965a
3975	3965b
3976	3965c
3977	3965d
3977a	3965
3978	3966a
3979	3966b
3980	3966c
3981	3966d
3981a	3966
3982	3967a
3983	3967b
3984	3967c
3985	3967d
3985a	3967
3986	3968a
3987	3968b
3988	3968c
3989	3968d
3989a	3968
3990	3969a
3991	3969b
3992	3969c
3993	3969d
3993a	3969
3994	3970a
3995	3970b
3996	3970c
3997	3970d
3997a	3970
3998	3971a
3999	3971b
4000	3971c
4001	3971d
4001a	3971
4002	3972a
4003	3972b
4004	3972c
4005	3972d
4005a	3972
4006	3973a
4007	3973b
4008	3973c
4009	3973d
4009a	3973
4010	3974a
4011	3974b
4012	3974c
4013	3974d
4013a	3974
4014	3975a
4015	3975b
4016	3975c
4017	3975d
4017a	3975
4018	3976a
4019	3976b
4020	3976c
4021	3976d
4021a	3976
new	4023
4023	4023a
4024	4023b
4025	4023c
new	4029
4029	4029a
4030	4029b
4031	4029c
4032	4029d
new	4046
4046	4046a
4047	4047b
4048	4047c
new	4074
4074	4074a
4075	4074b
4076	4074c
4080	4023d
new	4090
4090	4090a
4091	4090b
4092	4090c
4093	4090d
4094	4090e
4117a	deleted
4159a	deleted
4163a	deleted
4169a	deleted
4182a	deleted
4190a	deleted
new	4192
4192	4192a
4193	4192b
4194	4192c
4195	4192d
4196	4192e
new	4242
4242	4242a
4243	4242b
4244	4242c
4245	4242d
new	4324
4324	4324a
4325	4324b
4326	4324c
4327	4324d
4356	4350d

Lebanon

Number in 2011 Catalogue	Number in 2012 Catalogue
new	C2a
new	C3b
new	C4b
new	C5a
new	C6a

Libya

Number in 2011 Catalogue	Number in 2012 Catalogue
new	1286-1297

Macao

Number in 2011 Catalogue	Number in 2012 Catalogue
new	RA20A

Malawi

Number in 2011 Catalogue	Number in 2012 Catalogue
743	744

Malaya

Number in 2011 Catalogue	Number in 2012 Catalogue
new	66a
new	J21b
new	J23b
new	J27b
new	NJ1a
new	NJ1b
new	NJ2a
new	NJ3a
new	NJ3b
new	NJ4a
new	NJ4b
new	NJ5a
new	NJ5b
new	NJ6a
new	NJ7a

Johore

Number in 2011 Catalogue	Number in 2012 Catalogue
new	59a
new	60a
new	65a

Penang

Number in 2011 Catalogue	Number in 2012 Catalogue
new	N4b
new	N5b
new	N7c

Malaysia

Number in 2011 Catalogue	Number in 2012 Catalogue
new	543b
new	545b
new	781e

Johore

Number in 2011 Catalogue	Number in 2012 Catalogue
new	175a
new	193c
new	195c

Perlis

Number in 2011 Catalogue	Number in 2012 Catalogue
new	70b

Sabah

Number in 2011 Catalogue	Number in 2012 Catalogue
new	30a

Martinique

Number in 2011 Catalogue	Number in 2012 Catalogue
new	177a

Mexico

Number in 2011 Catalogue	Number in 2012 Catalogue
new	62e
new	393F

Guadalajara

Number in 2011 Catalogue	Number in 2012 Catalogue
42a	deleted
new	47c

Moldova

Number in 2011 Catalogue	Number in 2012 Catalogue
new	112a

Monaco

Number in 2011 Catalogue	Number in 2012 Catalogue
new	27c

Illustrated Identifier

This section pictures stamps or parts of stamp designs that will help identify postage stamps that do not have English words on them.

Many of the symbols that identify stamps of countries are shown here as well as typical examples of their stamps.

See the Index and Identifier on the previous pages for stamps with inscriptions such as "sen," "posta," "Baja Porto," "Helvetia," "K.S.A.", etc.

Linn's Stamp Identifier is now available. The 144 pages include more 2,000 inscriptions and over 500 large stamp illustrations. Available from Linn's Stamp News, P.O. Box 29, Sidney, OH 45365-0029.

1. HEADS, PICTURES AND NUMERALS

GREAT BRITAIN

Great Britain stamps never show the country name, but, except for postage dues, show a picture of the reigning monarch.

Victoria

Edward VII George V Edward VIII

George VI

Elizabeth II

Some George VI and Elizabeth II stamps are surcharged in annas, new paisa or rupees. These are listed under Oman.

Silhouette (sometimes facing right, generally at the top of stamp)

The silhouette indicates this is a British stamp. It is not a U.S. stamp.

VICTORIA

Queen Victoria

INDIA

Other stamps of India show this portrait of Queen Victoria and the words "Service" (or "Postage") and "Annas."

AUSTRIA

YUGOSLAVIA

(Also BOSNIA & HERZEGOVINA if imperf.)

BOSNIA & HERZEGOVINA

Denominations also appear in top corners instead of bottom corners.

HUNGARY

Another stamp has posthorn facing left

BRAZIL

AUSTRALIA

Kangaroo and Emu

GERMANY

Mecklenburg-Vorpommern

SWITZERLAND

PALAU

2. ORIENTAL INSCRIPTIONS

CHINA

Any stamp with this one character is from China (Imperial, Republic or People's Republic).
This character appears in a four-character overprint on stamps of Manchukuo. These stamps are local provisionals, which are unlisted. Other overprinted Manchukuo stamps show this character, but have more than four characters in the overprints. These are listed in People's Republic of China.

Some Chinese stamps show the Sun.

Most stamps of Republic of China show this series of characters.

Stamps with the China character and this character are from People's Republic of China. 人

Calligraphic form of People's Republic of China

(一)	(二)	(三)	(四)	(五)	(六)
1	2	3	4	5	6
(七)	(八)	(九)	(十)	(一十)	(二十)
7	8	9	10	11	12

Chinese stamps without China character

REPUBLIC OF CHINA

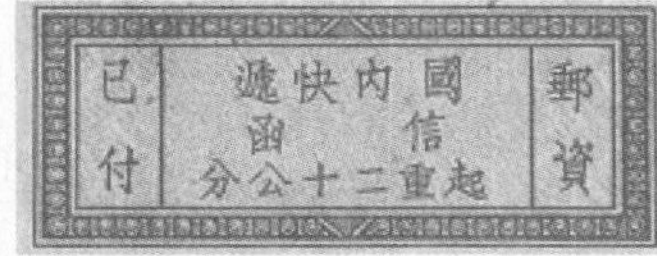

PEOPLE'S REPUBLIC OF CHINA

Mao Tse-tung

MANCHUKUO

Temple

Emperor Pu-Yi

The first 3 characters are common to many Manchukuo stamps.

The last 3 characters are common to other Manchukuo stamps.

Orchid Crest

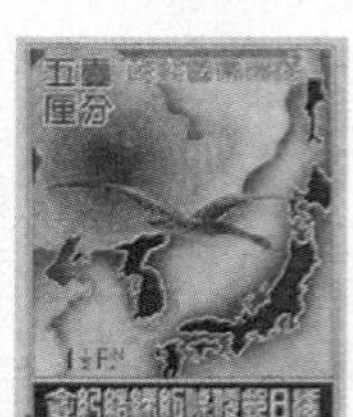

Manchukuo stamp without these elements

JAPAN

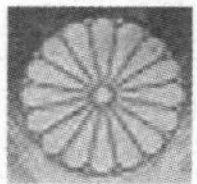

Chrysanthemum Crest Country Name

Japanese stamps without these elements

The number of characters in the center and the design of dragons on the sides will vary.

RYUKYU ISLANDS

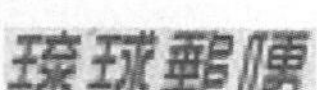

Country Name

PHILIPPINES (Japanese Occupation)

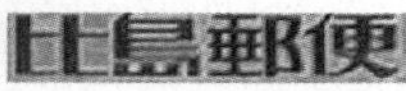

Country Name

NETHERLANDS INDIES (Japanese Occupation)

JAVA

SUMATRA

Java

Sumatra

MOLUCCAS, CELEBES AND SOUTH BORNEO

NORTH BORNEO (Japanese Occupation)

Indicates Japanese Occupation

Country Name

MALAYA (Japanese Occupation)

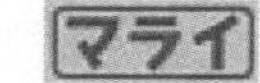

Indicates Japanese Occupation

Country Name

BURMA

Union of Myanmar

ပြည်ထောင်စုမြန်မာနိုင်ငံတော်

Union of Myanmar

(Japanese Occupation)

Indicates Japanese Occupation Country Name

Other Burma Japanese Occupation stamps without these elements

Burmese Script

KOREA

These two characters, in any order, are common to stamps from the Republic of Korea (South Korea) or of the People's Democratic Republic of Korea (North Korea).

This series of four characters can be found on the stamps of both Koreas. Most stamps of the Democratic People's Republic of Korea (North Korea) have just this inscription.

대한민국우표

Indicates Republic of Korea (South Korea)

South Korean postage stamps issed after 1952 do not show currency expressed in Latin letters. Stamps wiith "HW," "HWAN," "WON," "WN," "W" or "W" with two lines through it, if not illustrated in listings of stamps before this date, are revenues. North Korean postage stamps do not have currency expressed in Latin letters.

Yin Yang appears on some stamps.

South Korean stamps show Yin Yang and starting in 1966, 'KOREA" in Latin letters

Example of South Korean stamps lacking Latin text, Yin Yang and standard Korean text of country name. North Korean stamps never show Yin Yang and starting in 1976 are inscribed "DPRK" or "DPR KOREA" in Latin letters.

THAILAND

Country Name

King Chulalongkorn

King Prajadhipok and Chao P'ya Chakri

3. CENTRAL AND EASTERN ASIAN INSCRIPTIONS

INDIA - FEUDATORY STATES

Alwar

Bhor

Bundi

Similar stamps come with different designs in corners and differently drawn daggers (at center of circle).

Dhar

Duttia

Faridkot

Hyderabad

Similar stamps exist with different central design which is inscribed "Postage" or "Post & Receipt."

Indore

Jammu & Kashmir

Text varies.

Jasdan

Jhalawar

Kotah

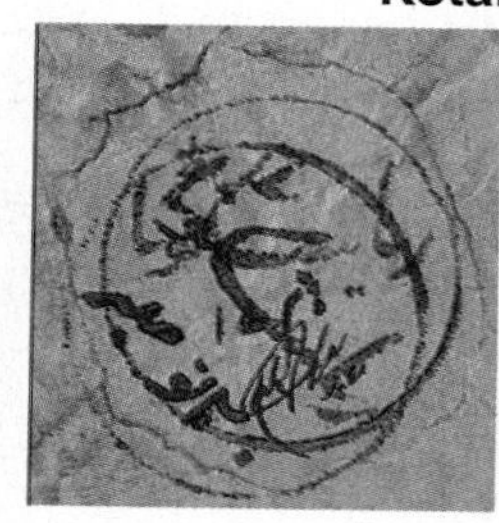

Size and text varies

Nandgaon

Nowanuggur

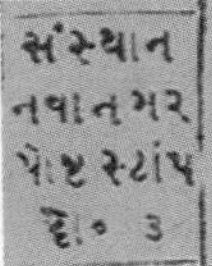

Poonch

Similar stamps exist in various sizes with different text

Rajasthan

Rajpeepla

Soruth

Tonk

BANGLADESH

Country Name

NEPAL

Similar stamps are smaller, have squares in upper corners and have five or nine characters in central bottom panel.

TANNU TUVA

ISRAEL

GEORGIA

This inscription is found on other pictorial stamps.

Country Name

ARMENIA

The four characters are found somewhere on pictorial stamps. On some stamps only the middle two are found.

4. AFRICAN INSCRIPTIONS

ETHIOPIA

5. ARABIC INSCRIPTIONS

١ ٢ ٣ ٤ ٥
1 2 3 4 5

٦ ٧ ٨ ٩ ٠
6 7 8 9 0

AFGHANISTAN

Many early Afghanistan stamps show Tiger's head, many of these have ornaments protruding from outer ring, others show inscriptions in black.

Arabic Script

Crest of King Amanullah

Mosque Gate & Crossed Cannons

The four characters are found somewhere on pictorial stamps. On some stamps only the middle two are found.

BAHRAIN

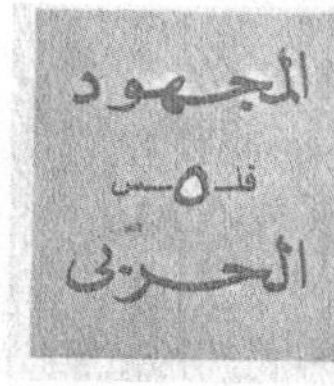

EGYPT

Postage

IRAN

Country Name

Royal Crown

Lion with Sword

Symbol

IRAQ

JORDAN

LEBANON

Similar types have denominations at top and slightly different design.

LIBYA

Country Name in various styles

Other Libya stamps show Eagle and Shield (head facing either direction) or Red, White and Black Shield (with or without eagle in center).

Without Country Name

SAUDI ARABIA

Tughra (Central design)

Palm Tree and Swords

SYRIA

Arab Government Issues

THRACE

YEMEN

PAKISTAN

PAKISTAN - BAHAWALPUR

Country Name in top panel, star and crescent

TURKEY

Star & Crescent is a device found on many Turkish stamps, but is also found on stamps from other Arabic areas (see Pakistan-Bahawalpur)

Tughra (similar tughras can be found on stamps of Turkey in Asia, Afghanistan and Saudi Arabia)

Mohammed V

Mustafa Kemal

Plane, Star and Crescent

TURKEY IN ASIA

Other Turkey in Asia pictorials show star & crescent.
Other stamps show tughra shown under Turkey.

6. GREEK INSCRIPTIONS

GREECE

Country Name in various styles
(Some Crete stamps overprinted with the Greece country name are listed in Crete.)

Lepta

ΔΡΑΧΜΑΙ ΛΕΠΤΟΝ

Drachma Drachmas Lepton

Abbreviated Country Name ΕΛΛ

Other forms of Country Name

No country name

CRETE

Country Name

Crete stamps with a surcharge that have the year "1922" are listed under Greeece.

EPIRUS

Similar stamps have text above the eagle.

IONIAN IS.

7. CYRILLIC INSCRIPTIONS

RUSSIA

Postage Stamp

Imperial Eagle

Postage in various styles

Abbreviation for Kopeck | Abbreviation for Ruble | Russia

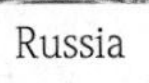

Abbreviation for Russian Soviet Federated Socialist Republic
RSFSR stamps were overprinted (see below)

Abbreviation for Union of Soviet Socialist Republics

This item is footnoted in Latvia

RUSSIA - Army of the North

"OKCA"

RUSSIA - Wenden

RUSSIAN OFFICES IN THE TURKISH EMPIRE

These letters appear on other stamps of the Russian offices.

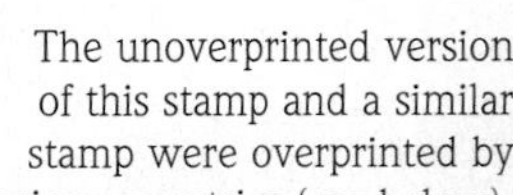
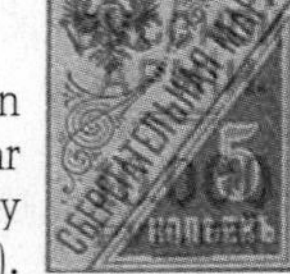

The unoverprinted version of this stamp and a similar stamp were overprinted by various countries (see below).

ARMENIA

BELARUS

FAR EASTERN REPUBLIC

Country Name

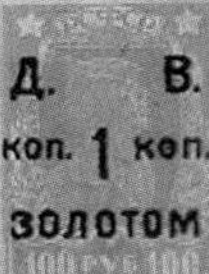

SOUTH RUSSIA

Country Name

FINLAND

Circles and Dots on stamps similar to Imperial Russia issues

BATUM

Forms of Country Name

TRANSCAUCASIAN FEDERATED REPUBLICS

Abbreviation for Country Name

KAZAKHSTAN

КАЗАКСТАН

Country Name

KYRGYZSTAN

КЫРГЫЗСТАН

Country Name

ROMANIA

TADJIKISTAN

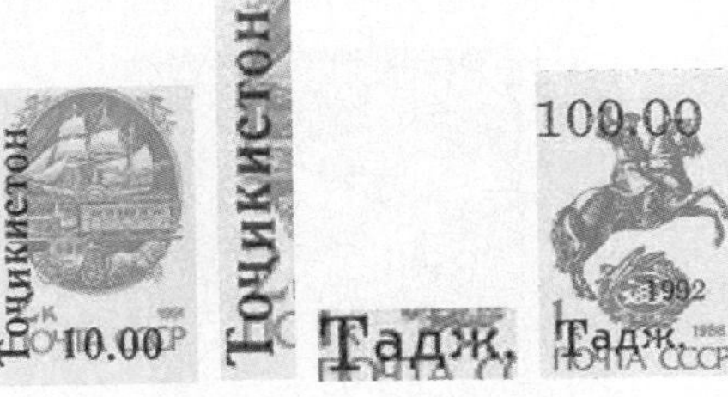

Country Name & Abbreviation

UKRAINE

Украïни

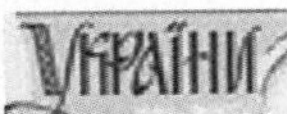

Украïни

Country Name in various forms

The trident appears on many stamps, usually as an overprint.

Abbreviation for Ukrainian Soviet Socialist Republic

WESTERN UKRAINE

Abbreviation for Country Name

AZERBAIJAN

AZƏRBAYCAN

Country Name

Abbreviation for Azerbaijan Soviet Socialist Republic

MONTENEGRO

ЦРНА ГОРА

Country Name in various forms

ЦР. ГОРЕ

Abbreviation for country name

No country name (A similar Montenegro stamp without country name has same vignette.)

SERBIA

СРПСКА СРБИЈА

Country Name in various forms

СРП. К.С.

Abbreviation for country name

No country name

SERBIA & MONTENEGRO

YUGOSLAVIA

ЈУГОСЛАВИЈА

Showing country name

No Country Name

MACEDONIA

МАКЕДОНИЈА

МАКЕДОНИЈА

Country Name

МАКЕДОНСКИ

Different form of Country Name

BOSNIA & HERZEGOVINA (Serb Administration)

РЕПУБЛИКА СРПСКА

Country Name

РЕПУБЛИКЕ СРПСКЕ

Different form of Country Name

No Country Name

BULGARIA

Country Name Postage

Stotinka

Stotinki (plural)

Abbreviation for Stotinki

Country Name in various forms and styles

No country name

Abbreviation for Lev, leva

MONGOLIA

Country name in one word

Tugrik in Cyrillic

Country name in two words

Mung in Cyrillic

Mung in Mongolian

Tugrik in Mongolian

Arms

No Country Name

INDEX AND IDENTIFIER

All page numbers shown are those in this Volume 4.

Postage stamps that do not have English words on them are shown in the Illustrated Identifier.

Pronunciation Symbols

ə .... banana, collide, abut

ˈə, ˌə .... humdrum, abut

^{ə} .... immediately preceding \l\, \n\, \m\, \ŋ\, as in battle, mitten, eaten, and sometimes open \ˈō-p^{ə}m\, lock and key \-^{ə}ŋ-\; immediately following \l\, \m\, \r\, as often in French table, prisme, titre

ər .... further, merger, bird

ˈər- / ˈə-r .... as in two different pronunciations of hurry \ˈhər-ē, ˈhə-rē\

a .... mat, map, mad, gag, snap, patch

ā .... day, fade, date, aorta, drape, cape

ä .... bother, cot, and, with most American speakers, father, cart

ȧ .... father as pronounced by speakers who do not rhyme it with *bother*; French patte

au̇ .... now, loud, out

b .... baby, rib

ch .... chin, nature \ˈnā-chər\

d .... did, adder

e .... bet, bed, peck

ˈē, ˌē .... beat, nosebleed, evenly, easy

ē .... easy, mealy

f .... fifty, cuff

g .... go, big, gift

h .... hat, ahead

hw .... whale as pronounced by those who do not have the same pronunciation for both *whale* and *wail*

i .... tip, banish, active

ī .... site, side, buy, tripe

j .... job, gem, edge, join, judge

k .... kin, cook, ache

k̲ .... German ich, Buch; one pronunciation of loch

l .... lily, pool

m .... murmur, dim, nymph

n .... no, own

^{n} .... indicates that a preceding vowel or diphthong is pronounced with the nasal passages open, as in French *un bon vin blanc* \œ^{n} -bō^{n} -va^{n} -blä^{n}\

ŋ .... sing \ˈsiŋ\, singer \ˈsiŋ-ər\, finger \ˈfiŋ-gər\, ink \ˈiŋk \

ō .... bone, know, beau

ȯ .... saw, all, gnaw, caught

œ .... French boeuf, German Hölle

œ̄ .... French feu, German Höhle

ȯi .... coin, destroy

p .... pepper, lip

r .... red, car, rarity

s .... source, less

sh .... as in shy, mission, machine, special (actually, this is a single sound, not two); with a hyphen between, two sounds as in *grasshopper* \ˈgras-ˌhä-pər\

t .... tie, attack, late, later, latter

th .... as in thin, ether (actually, this is a single sound, not two); with a hyphen between, two sounds as in *knighthood* \ˈnīt-ˌhu̇d\

t̲h̲ .... then, either, this (actually, this is a single sound, not two)

ü .... rule, youth, union \ˈyün-yən\, few \ˈfyü\

u̇ .... pull, wood, book, curable \ˈkyu̇r-ə-bəl\, fury \ˈfyu̇r-ē\

ue .... German füllen, hübsch

ue̅ .... French rue, German fühlen

v .... vivid, give

w .... we, away

y .... yard, young, cue \ˈkyü\, mute \ˈmyüt\, union \ˈyün-yən\

^{y} .... indicates that during the articulation of the sound represented by the preceding character the front of the tongue has substantially the position it has for the articulation of the first sound of *yard*, as in French *digne* \dēn^{y}\

z .... zone, raise

zh .... as in vision, azure \ˈa-zhər\ (actually, this is a single sound, not two); with a hyphen between, two sounds as in *hogshead* \ˈhȯgz-ˌhed, ˈhägz-\

\ .... slant line used in pairs to mark the beginning and end of a transcription: \ˈpen\

ˈ .... mark preceding a syllable with primary (strongest) stress: \ˈpen-mən-ˌship\

ˌ .... mark preceding a syllable with secondary (medium) stress: \ˈpen-mən-ˌship\

- .... mark of syllable division

( ) .... indicate that what is symbolized between is present in some utterances but not in others: *factory* \ˈfak-t(ə-)rē\

÷ .... indicates that many regard as unacceptable the pronunciation variant immediately following: *cupola* \ˈkyü-pə-lə, ÷-ˌlō\

SCOTT®

Specialty Series

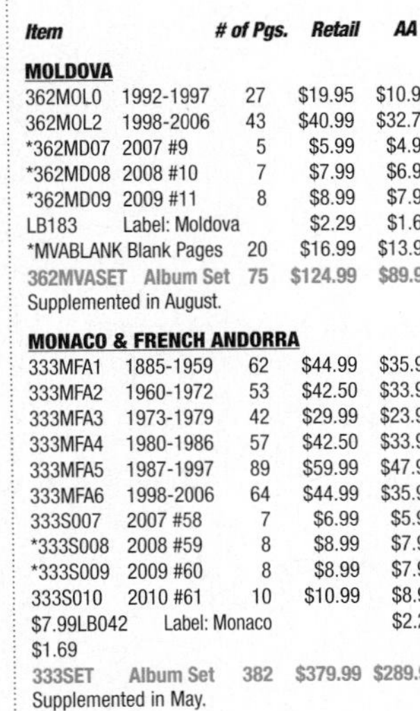

Embark on a new collecting journey. There are Specialty pages available for more than 140 countries with some of them back in print after many years thanks to on-demand printing technology. Start a new collecting adventure with countries featured in Volume 4 of the new Scott Standard Postage Stamp Catalogue!

Specialty Series pages are sold as page units only. Binders, labels and slipcases are sold separately.

ALBUM SETS

These money-saving album sets include pages, binders and self-adhesive binder labels. Some set contents may vary, please call or visit or web site for specific information.

JAPAN

Item		# of Pgs.	Retail	AA
510JAP1	1871-1953	78	$49.99	$37.99
510JAP2	1954-1974	71	$49.99	$37.99
510JAP3	1975-1988	62	$44.99	$35.99
510JAP4	1989-1994	66	$44.99	$35.99
510JAP5	1995-1999	49	$39.99	$31.99
510JAP6	2000-2004	100	$69.99	$55.99
510S005	2005 #39	15	$12.99	$10.99
510S006	2006 #40	20	$14.99	$11.99
*510S007	2007 #41	18	$16.99	$13.99
*510S008	2008 #42	29	$21.99	$17.99
*510S009	2008 #43	48	$37.50	$29.99
LB036	Label: Japan		$2.29	$1.69
*510BLANK	Blank Pages	20	$16.99	$13.99
510SET	Album Set	508	$474.99	$349.99

Supplemented in July.

JERSEY

Item		# of Pgs.	Retail	AA
202JRS0	1958-1998	92	$59.95	$32.99
202JRS2	1999-2006	72	35.99	29.99
202JR07	2007 #9	12	$11.99	$9.99
*202JR08	2008 #10	7	$7.99	$6.99
*202JR09	2009 #11	13	$14.99	$11.99
202JR10	2010 #12	12	$14.99	$11.99
LB198	Label: Jersey		$2.29	$1.69
*JRSBLANK	Blank Pages	20	$16.99	$13.99
202JRSET	Album Set	164	$199.99	$134.99

Supplemented in May.

KAZAKHSTAN

Item		# of Pgs.	Retail	AA
362KAZ0	1992-1997	20	$15.95	$11.16
362KAZ2	1998-2006	48	$37.50	$29.99
*362KZ07	2007 #10	4	$5.99	$4.99
*362KZ08	2008 #11	5	$5.99	$4.99
*362KZ09	2009 #12	5	$5.99	$4.99
LB181	Label: Kazakhstan		$2.29	$1.69
*KAZBLANK	Blank Pages	20	$16.99	$13.99
362KAZSET	Album Set	68	$129.99	$94.99

Supplemented in August.

KIRIBATI

Item		# of Pgs.	Retail	AA
628KIR1	1979-2006	91	$59.99	$47.99
*628S007	2007 #12	4	$5.99	$4.99
*628S008	2008 #13	7	$7.99	$6.99
*628S009	2009 #14	4	$5.99	$4.99
LB173	Label: Kiribati		$2.29	$1.69

Supplemented in August.

KOREA

Item		# of Pgs.	Retail	AA
515KOR1	1884-1980	94	$64.99	$51.99
515KOR2	1981-1999	76	$52.50	$41.99
515KOR3	2000-2006	83	$65.99	$51.99
*515S008	2007-08 #29	13	$14.99	$11.99
515S009	2009 #30	13	$10.99	$8.99
515S010	2010 #31	9	$9.99	$7.99
LB037	Label: Korea		$2.29	$1.69
*515BLANK	Blank Pages	20	$16.99	$13.99
515SET	Album Set	266	$299.99	$229.99

Supplemented in June.

Indicates special order item. May take 4-6 weeks for delivery.

KUWAIT

Item		# of Pgs.	Retail	AA
623KWT1	1923-1986	84	$47.95	$26.99
623KWT2	1987-1998	51	$35.95	$19.99
623KWT3	1999-2006	36	$35.95	$25.95
*623S007	2007 #12	3	$4.99	$3.99
623S009	2008-09 #13	8	$8.99	$7.99
623S010	2010 #14	3	$4.99	$3.99
LB102	Label: Kuwait		$2.29	$1.69
623SET	Album Set	174	$174.99	$113.99

Supplemented in June.

KYRGYZSTAN

Item		# of Pgs.	Retail	AA
362KYR0	1992-1997	19	$15.95	$8.99
362KYR2	1998-2006	54	$46.99	$37.99
*362KY07	2007 #9	5	$5.99	$4.99
*362KY08	2008 #10	6	$6.99	$5.99
*362KY09	2009 #11	8	$8.99	$7.99
LB182	Label: Kyrgyzstan		$2.29	$1.69
362KYRSET	Album Set	73	$139.99	$99.99

Supplemented in August.

LAOS

Item		# of Pgs.	Retail	AA
619LAS1	1951-1984	107	$59.95	$38.99
619LAS2	1985-1993	74	$44.95	$29.99
619LAS3	1994-2004	78	$44.95	$29.99
619S005	2005 #11	3	$3.99	$3.29
619S006	2006 #12	6	$5.99	$4.99
*619S007	2007 #13	10	$10.99	$8.99
619S009	2008-09 #14	7	$7.99	$6.99
LB145	Label: Laos		$2.29	$1.69
619SET	Album Set	268	$279.99	$199.99

Supplemented in July.

LEBANON

Item		# of Pgs.	Retail	AA
610LBN0	1924-1994	118	$69.95	$55.99
610S095	1995 #1	4	$5.99	$4.99
610S098	1996-1997 #2	3	$3.95	$3.16
610S001	1998-2001 #3	4	$4.99	$3.99
610S002	2002 #4	4	$4.99	$3.99
610S003	2003 #5	2	$2.99	$2.49
*610S005	2004-05 #6	4	$5.99	$4.99
*610S007	2006-07 #7	8	$8.99	$7.99
610S009	2008-09 #8	6	$6.99	$5.99
LB143	Label: Lebanon		$2.29	$1.69
610SET	Album Set	149	$178.99	$129.99

Supplemented in June.

LIECHTENSTEIN

Item		# of Pgs.	Retail	AA
367LCH1	1912-1996	106	$64.99	$51.99
367LCH2	1997-1999	12	$11.95	$6.99
367LCH3	2000-2006	33	$32.99	$25.25
*367S007	2007 #58	4	$5.99	$4.99
*367S008	2008 #59	5	$5.99	$4.99
367S009	2009 #60	5	$5.99	$4.99
*367BLANK	Blank Pages	20	$16.99	$13.99
LB039	Label		$2.29	$1.69
367SET	Album Set	160	$179.99	$129.99

Supplemented in June.

LUXEMBOURG

Item		# of Pgs.	Retail	AA
330LUX1	1852-1986	99	$64.99	$51.99
330LUX2	1987-1999	36	$26.99	$21.99
330LUX3	2000-2006	25	$18.99	$15.99
*330S007	2007 #56	5	$5.99	$4.99
*330S008	2008 #57	6	$6.99	$5.99
*330S009	2009 #58	6	$6.99	$5.99
LB040	Label: Luxembourg		$2.29	$1.69
*330BLANK	Blank Pages	20	$16.99	$13.99
330SET	Album Set	171	$189.99	$139.99

Supplemented in August

MALDIVE ISLANDS

Item		# of Pgs.	Retail	AA
706MDV1	1906-1975	72	$39.95	$21.99
706MDV2	1976-1986	100	$54.95	$30.99
706MDV3	1987-1991	71	$39.95	$21.99
706MDV4	1992-1993	98	$54.95	$30.99
706MDV5	1994-1996	108	$69.99	$38.99
706MDV6	1997-1999	84	$49.99	$27.99
*706S000	2000 #7	4	$5.99	$4.99
706S001	2001 #8	3	$3.99	$3.19
706S002	2002 #9	4	$4.99	$3.99
706S003	2003 #10	5	$4.99	$3.99
706S004	2004 #11	6	$5.99	$4.99
706S006	2005-2006 #13	6	$5.99	$4.99
LB118	Label: Maldive Islands		$2.29	$1.69
706SET	Album Set	561	$499.99	$319.99

Supplemented in December.

MALAYSIA

Item		# of Pgs.	Retail	AA
620MLS1	SE Asia: 1867-1963	56	$42.50	$33.99
620MLS2	Malaya: 1876-1965	91	$59.99	$47.99
620MLS3	Malaysia: 1963-1993	77	$52.50	$41.99
620MLS4	1994-2002	72	$57.99	$43.49
620S003	2003 #9	5	$4.99	$3.99
*620S004	2004 #10	15	$14.99	$11.99
620S005	2005 #11	13	$11.99	$9.99
620S006	2006 #12	15	$12.99	$10.99
*620S007	2007 #13	7	$7.99	$6.99
*620S008	2008 #14	14	$14.99	$11.99
620S009	2009 #15	29	$21.99	$17.99
LB117	Label: Malaysia		$2.29	$1.69
620SET	Album Set	351	$364.99	$274.99

Supplemented in July.

MALTA

Item		# of Pgs.	Retail	AA
203MLT0	1860-1997	99	$59.95	$32.99
203MLT2	1998-2006	60	$29.99	$25.99
203ML07	2007 #10	8	$7.99	$6.99
*203ML08	2008 #11	14	$14.99	$11.99
203ML09	2009 #12	6	$6.99	$5.99
LB190	Label: Malta		$2.29	$1.69
*MLTBLANK	Blank Pages	20	$16.99	$13.99
203MLTSET	Album Set	181	$169.99	$109.99

Supplemented in May.

MEXICO

Item		# of Pgs.	Retail	AA
430MEX1	1856-1978	151	89.99	67.99
430MEX2	1979-1999	113	79.99	59.99
430MEX3	2000-2004	31	$27.99	$20.99
430S005	2005 #57	12	$11.99	$9.99
430S006	2006 #58	8	$7.99	$6.99
*430S007	2007 #59	11	$13.99	$11.99
*430S008	2008 #60	11	$13.99	$11.99
*430S009	2009 #61	11	$13.99	$11.99
LB041	Label: Mexico		$2.29	$1.69
*430BLANK	Blank Pages	20	$16.99	$13.99
430SET	Album Set	315	$320.99	$237.99

Supplemented in September.

MOLDOVA

Item		# of Pgs.	Retail	AA
362MOL0	1992-1997	27	$19.95	$10.99
362MOL2	1998-2006	43	$40.99	$32.75
*362MD07	2007 #9	5	$5.99	$4.99
*362MD08	2008 #10	7	$7.99	$6.99
*362MD09	2009 #11	8	$8.99	$7.99
LB183	Label: Moldova		$2.29	$1.69
*MVABLANK	Blank Pages	20	$16.99	$13.99
362MVASET	Album Set	75	$124.99	$89.99

Supplemented in August.

MONACO & FRENCH ANDORRA

Item		# of Pgs.	Retail	AA
333MFA1	1885-1959	62	$44.99	$35.99
333MFA2	1960-1972	53	$42.50	$33.99
333MFA3	1973-1979	42	$29.99	$23.99
333MFA4	1980-1986	57	$42.50	$33.99
333MFA5	1987-1997	89	$59.99	$47.99
333MFA6	1998-2006	64	$44.99	$35.99
333S007	2007 #58	7	$6.99	$5.99
*333S008	2008 #59	8	$8.99	$7.99
*333S009	2009 #60	8	$8.99	$7.99
333S010	2010 #61	10	$10.99	$8.99
$7.99LB042	Label: Monaco			$2.29
$1.69				
333SET	Album Set	382	$379.99	$289.99

Supplemented in May.

ORDERING INFORMATION

*AA prices apply to paid subscribers of Amos Hobby titles and orders placed online.

Prices, terms and product availability subject to change.

Shipping & Handling:

United States: 10% of order total. Minimum charge $6.99 Maximum charge $45.00.

Canada: 15% of order total. Minimum charge $19.99 Maximum charge $50.00.

Foreign orders are shipped via FedEx Economy Intl. and billed actual freight.

To Order

Call **1-800-572-6885**

Visit **www.amosadvantage.com**

INDEX TO ADVERTISERS 2012 VOLUME 4

2012
VOLUME 4
DEALER DIRECTORY YELLOW PAGE LISTINGS

This section of your Scott Catalogue contains advertisements to help you conveniently find what you need, when you need it...!

Accessories

BROOKLYN GALLERY COIN & STAMP, INC.
8725 4th Ave.
Brooklyn, NY 11209
PH: 718-745-5701
FAX: 718-745-2775
info@brooklyngallery.com
www.brooklyngallery.com

Appraisals

PHILIP WEISS AUCTIONS
1 Neil Ct.
Oceanside, NY 11572
PH: 516-594-0731
FAX: 516-594-9414
phil@prwauctions.com
www.prwauctions.com

Asia

MICHAEL ROGERS, INC.
Suite 4-1
415 S. Orlando Ave.
Winter Park, FL 32789-3683
PH: 407-644-2290
PH: 800-843-3751
FAX: 407-645-4434
Stamps@michaelrogersinc.com
www.michaelrogersinc.com

THE STAMP ACT
PO Box 1136
Belmont, CA 94002
PH: 650-703-2342
PH: 650-592-3315
FAX: 650-508-8104
thestampact@sbcglobal.net
www.thestampact.com

Auctions

DANIEL F. KELLEHER AUCTIONS LLC
PMB 44
60 Newtown Rd
Danbury, CT 06810
PH: 203-297-6056
FAX: 203-297-6059
info@kelleherauctions.com
www.kelleherauctions.com

JACQUES C. SCHIFF, JR., INC.
195 Main St.
Ridgefield Park, NJ 07660
PH: 201-641-5566
FAX: 201-641-5705

MICHAEL ROGERS, INC.
Suite 4-1
415 S. Orlando Ave.
Winter Park, FL 32789-3683
PH: 407-644-2290
PH: 800-843-3751
FAX: 407-645-4434
Stamps@michaelrogersinc.com
www.michaelrogersinc.com

PHILIP WEISS AUCTIONS
1 Neil Ct.
Oceanside, NY 11572
PH: 516-594-0731
FAX: 516-594-9414
phil@prwauctions.com
www.prwauctions.com

R. MARESCH & SON LTD.
5th Floor - 6075 Yonge St.
Toronto, ON M2M 3W2
CANADA
PH: 416-363-7777
FAX: 416-363-6511
www.maresch.com

Auctions

THE STAMP CENTER DUTCH COUNTRY AUCTIONS
4115 Concord Pike
Wilmington, DE 19803
PH: 302-478-8740
FAX: 302-478-8779
auctions@thestampcenter.com
www.thestampcenter.com

Auctions - Public

ALAN BLAIR AUCTIONS, L.L.C.
Suite 1
5405 Lakeside Ave.
Richmond, VA 23228-6060
PH: 800-689-5602
FAX: 804-262-9307
alanblair@verizon.net
www.alanblairstamps.com

British Asia

THE STAMP ACT
PO Box 1136
Belmont, CA 94002
PH: 650-703-2342
PH: 650-592-3315
FAX: 650-508-8104
thestampact@sbcglobal.net
www.thestampact.com

British Commonwealth

ARON R. HALBERSTAM PHILATELISTS, LTD.
PO Box 150168
Van Brunt Station
Brooklyn, NY 11215-0168
PH: 718-788-3978
FAX: 718-965-3099
arh@arhstamps.com
www.arhstamps.com

WWW.WORLDSTAMPS.COM
PO Box 4743
Pinehurst, NC 28374
PH: 910-295-2048
FAX: 910-295-2049
by mail:
Frank Geiger Philatelists
info@WorldStamps.com
www.WorldStamps.com

Central America

GUY SHAW
PO Box 27138
San Diego, CA 92198
PH/FAX: 858-485-8269
guyshaw@guyshaw.com
www.guyshaw.com

China

MICHAEL ROGERS, INC.
Suite 4-1
415 S. Orlando Ave.
Winter Park, FL 32789-3683
PH: 407-644-2290
PH: 800-843-3751
FAX: 407-645-4434
Stamps@michaelrogersinc.com
www.michaelrogersinc.com

Auctions

Schiff Auctions

Buyers, Auctioneers & Appraisers of U.S. & Worldwide Stamps & Covers

We have been catering to the individual buyer and seller since 1947. Let us put our over **60 years** of experience to work for you when selling your stamps, covers or your collection. Whether you prefer consigning to public auction or selling outright, call us first. Describe your material before sending. Please include your address and telephone numbers.

CATALOG SUBSCRIPTIONS	N. AMERICA	OVERSEAS
1 Year Catalogs & Prices Realized	$10.00	$18.00
1 Year Catalog Only	$7.50	$15.00
1 Catalog with Prices Realized	$2.00	$3.50
1 Catalog Only	$1.50	$3.00

Send a self-addressed, stamped envelope for our complimentary brochure "How to auction your stamps and covers".

JACQUES C. SCHIFF, JR., INC.

195 Main St., Ridgefield Park, NJ 07660 USA
Telephone 201-641-5566 FAX 201-641-5705

OFFICIAL AUCTIONEERS:
AMERIPEX 1986.
WORLD STAMP EXPO 1989.
WORLD COLUMBIAN STAMP EXPO 1992.
AMERICAN PHILATELIC SOCIETY 2000-2003

Qualified Auctioneer

British Commonwealth

Aden to Zululand Mint & Used
Most complete stock in North America

For over 35 years we have helped our customers build some of the worlds finest known collections. Our expert ***Want Lists Services*** can do the same for you. With over 50 volumes filled with singles, sets and rare stamps, I am sure we have what you need. We welcome your Want Lists in Scott or Gibbons numbers. Monthly payment plans available for larger purchases.

Put our expertise to work for you today!
You'll be glad you did!!

Colonial Stamp Company
5757 Wilshire Blvd., Penthouse 8
Los Angeles, CA 90036 USA
Tel: +1 (323) 933-9435 Fax: +1 (323) 939-9930
Toll Free in North America
Tel: 1 (877) 272-6693 Fax: 1 (877) 272-6694
E-Mail: *info@colonialstampcompany.com*
URL: *www.colonialstampcompany.com*

Ask for your free Public Auction Catalogue today!

CCNY, IFSDA, INTERNATIONAL SOCIETY OF APPRAISERS

Ducks

MICHAEL JAFFE
PO Box 61484
Vancouver, WA 98666
PH: 360-695-6161
PH: 800-782-6770
FAX: 360-695-1616
mjaffe@brookmanstamps.com
www.brookmanstamps.com

German Colonies

COLONIAL STAMP COMPANY
5757 Wilshire Blvd. PH #8
Los Angeles, CA 90036
PH: 323-933-9435
FAX: 323-939-9930
Toll Free in North America
PH: 877-272-6693
FAX: 877-272-6694
info@colonialstampcompany.com
www.colonialstampcompany.com

Great Britain

COLONIAL STAMP COMPANY
5757 Wilshire Blvd. PH #8
Los Angeles, CA 90036
PH: 323-933-9435
FAX: 323-939-9930
Toll Free in North America
PH: 877-272-6693
FAX: 877-272-6694
info@colonialstampcompany.com
www.colonialstampcompany.com

Japan

MICHAEL ROGERS, INC.
Suite 4-1
415 S. Orlando Ave.
Winter Park, FL 32789-3683
PH: 407-644-2290
PH: 800-843-3751
FAX: 407-645-4434
Stamps@michaelrogersinc.com
www.michaelrogersinc.com

THE STAMP ACT
PO Box 1136
Belmont, CA 94002
PH: 650-703-2342
PH: 650-592-3315
FAX: 650-508-8104
thestampact@sbcglobal.net
www.thestampact.com

Kenya, Uganda, Tanzania

COLONIAL STAMP COMPANY
5757 Wilshire Blvd. PH #8
Los Angeles, CA 90036
PH: 323-933-9435
FAX: 323-939-9930
Toll Free in North America
PH: 877-272-6693
FAX: 877-272-6694
info@colonialstampcompany.com
www.colonialstampcompany.com

Kiauchau (German)

COLONIAL STAMP COMPANY
5757 Wilshire Blvd. PH #8
Los Angeles, CA 90036
PH: 323-933-9435
FAX: 323-939-9930
Toll Free in North America
PH: 877-272-6693
FAX: 877-272-6694
info@colonialstampcompany.com
www.colonialstampcompany.com

Korea

MICHAEL ROGERS, INC.
Suite 4-1
415 S. Orlando Ave.
Winter Park, FL 32789-3683
PH: 407-644-2290
PH: 800-843-3751
FAX: 407-645-4434
Stamps@michaelrogersinc.com
www.michaelrogersinc.com

THE STAMP ACT
PO Box 1136
Belmont, CA 94002
PH: 650-703-2342
PH: 650-592-3315
FAX: 650-508-8104
thestampact@sbcglobal.net
www.thestampact.com

WWW.WORLDSTAMPS.COM
PO Box 4743
Pinehurst, NC 28374
PH: 910-295-2048
FAX: 910-295-2049
by mail:
Frank Geiger Philatelists
info@WorldStamps.com
www.WorldStamps.com

Latin America

GUY SHAW
PO Box 27138
San Diego, CA 92198
PH/FAX: 858-485-8269
guyshaw@guyshaw.com
www.guyshaw.com

Leeward Islands

COLONIAL STAMP COMPANY
5757 Wilshire Blvd. PH #8
Los Angeles, CA 90036
PH: 323-933-9435
FAX: 323-939-9930
Toll Free in North America
PH: 877-272-6693
FAX: 877-272-6694
info@colonialstampcompany.com
www.colonialstampcompany.com

Liechtenstein

HENRY GITNER PHILATELISTS, INC.
PO Box 3077-S
Middletown, NY 10940
PH: 845-343-5151
PH: 800-947-8267
FAX: 845-343-0068
hgitner@hgitner.com
www.hgitner.com

Luxembourg

HENRY GITNER PHILATELISTS, INC.
PO Box 3077-S
Middletown, NY 10940
PH: 845-343-5151
PH: 800-947-8267
FAX: 845-343-0068
hgitner@hgitner.com
www.hgitner.com

WWW.WORLDSTAMPS.COM
PO Box 4743
Pinehurst, NC 28374
PH: 910-295-2048
FAX: 910-295-2049
by mail:
Frank Geiger Philatelists
info@WorldStamps.com
www.WorldStamps.com

Madagascar (British Issues)

COLONIAL STAMP COMPANY
5757 Wilshire Blvd. PH #8
Los Angeles, CA 90036
PH: 323-933-9435
FAX: 323-939-9930
Toll Free in North America
PH: 877-272-6693
FAX: 877-272-6694
info@colonialstampcompany.com
www.colonialstampcompany.com

Malaya

COLONIAL STAMP COMPANY
5757 Wilshire Blvd. PH #8
Los Angeles, CA 90036
PH: 323-933-9435
FAX: 323-939-9930
Toll Free in North America
PH: 877-272-6693
FAX: 877-272-6694
info@colonialstampcompany.com
www.colonialstampcompany.com

THE STAMP ACT
PO Box 1136
Belmont, CA 94002
PH: 650-703-2342
PH: 650-592-3315
FAX: 650-508-8104
thestampact@sbcglobal.net
www.thestampact.com

Manchukuo

MICHAEL ROGERS, INC.
Suite 4-1
415 S. Orlando Ave.
Winter Park, FL 32789-3683
PH: 407-644-2290
PH: 800-843-3751
FAX: 407-645-4434
Stamps@michaelrogersinc.com
www.michaelrogersinc.com

Mariana Islands (Ger & Sp)

COLONIAL STAMP COMPANY
5757 Wilshire Blvd. PH #8
Los Angeles, CA 90036
PH: 323-933-9435
FAX: 323-939-9930
Toll Free in North America
PH: 877-272-6693
FAX: 877-272-6694
info@colonialstampcompany.com
www.colonialstampcompany.com

British Commonwealth

THE BRITISH COMMONWEALTH
O·F N·A·T·I·O·N·S

We are active buyers and sellers of stamps and postal history of all areas of pre-1960 British Commonwealth, including individual items, collections or estates. Want lists from all reigns are accepted with references.

L. W. Martin, Jr.

"VISIT OUR BOOTH AT MOST MAJOR SHOWS"

CROWN COLONY STAMPS
P.O. Box 1198
BELLAIRE, TEXAS 77402
PH. (713) 781-6563 • FAX (713) 789-9998
E-mail: lwm@crowncolony.com

Stamp Shows

Looking For Stamp Entertainment?

QUALITY STAMPSHOWS

See Our Website For Upcoming Events at:
www.stampshowsteve.com

We BUY & SELL All Philatelic And Stamp Related Material. Appraisals At Your Home Or Bank.

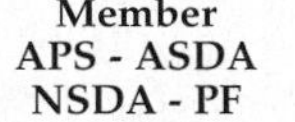

Member
APS - ASDA
NSDA - PF

Contact: Stephen Pattillo
888-995-0548
Fax 562-694-2323

P.O. Box 604
Fullerton, CA
92832

Marshall Islands

COLONIAL STAMP COMPANY
5757 Wilshire Blvd. PH #8
Los Angeles, CA 90036
PH: 323-933-9435
FAX: 323-939-9930
Toll Free in North America
PH: 877-272-6693
FAX: 877-272-6694
info@colonialstampcompany.com
www.colonialstampcompany.com

Mauritius

COLONIAL STAMP COMPANY
5757 Wilshire Blvd. PH #8
Los Angeles, CA 90036
PH: 323-933-9435
FAX: 323-939-9930
Toll Free in North America
PH: 877-272-6693
FAX: 877-272-6694
info@colonialstampcompany.com
www.colonialstampcompany.com

Mesopotamia

COLONIAL STAMP COMPANY
5757 Wilshire Blvd. PH #8
Los Angeles, CA 90036
PH: 323-933-9435
FAX: 323-939-9930
Toll Free in North America
PH: 877-272-6693
FAX: 877-272-6694
info@colonialstampcompany.com
www.colonialstampcompany.com

Middle East-Arab

MICHAEL ROGERS, INC.
Suite 4-1
415 S. Orlando Ave.
Winter Park, FL 32789-3683
PH: 407-644-2290
PH: 800-843-3751
FAX: 407-645-4434
Stamps@michaelrogersinc.com
www.michaelrogersinc.com

Monaco

WULFF'S STAMPS
PO Box 661746
Sacramento, CA 95866
PH/FAX: 800-884-0656
PH/FAX: 916-489-0656
service@wulffstamps.com
www.wulffstamps.com

Natal

COLONIAL STAMP COMPANY
5757 Wilshire Blvd. PH #8
Los Angeles, CA 90036
PH: 323-933-9435
FAX: 323-939-9930
Toll Free in North America
PH: 877-272-6693
FAX: 877-272-6694
info@colonialstampcompany.com
www.colonialstampcompany.com

New Britain

COLONIAL STAMP COMPANY
5757 Wilshire Blvd. PH #8
Los Angeles, CA 90036
PH: 323-933-9435
FAX: 323-939-9930
Toll Free in North America
PH: 877-272-6693
FAX: 877-272-6694
info@colonialstampcompany.com
www.colonialstampcompany.com

New Issues

DAVIDSON'S STAMP SERVICE
PO Box 36355
Indianapolis, IN 46236-0355
PH: 317-826-2620
ed-davidson@earthlink.net
www.newstampissues.com

New Issues - Retail

BOMBAY PHILATELIC INC.
PO Box 301
Wake Forest, NC 27588
PH: 561-499-7990
FAX: 561-499-7553
sales@bombaystamps.com
www.bombaystamps.com

New Zealand

ARON R. HALBERSTAM PHILATELISTS, LTD.
PO Box 150168
Van Brunt Station
Brooklyn, NY 11215-0168
PH: 718-788-3978
FAX: 718-965-3099
arh@arhstamps.com
www.arhstamps.com

COLONIAL STAMP COMPANY
5757 Wilshire Blvd. PH #8
Los Angeles, CA 90036
PH: 323-933-9435
FAX: 323-939-9930
Toll Free in North America
PH: 877-272-6693
FAX: 877-272-6694
info@colonialstampcompany.com
www.colonialstampcompany.com

Niger Coast Protectorate

COLONIAL STAMP COMPANY
5757 Wilshire Blvd. PH #8
Los Angeles, CA 90036
PH: 323-933-9435
FAX: 323-939-9930
Toll Free in North America
PH: 877-272-6693
FAX: 877-272-6694
info@colonialstampcompany.com
www.colonialstampcompany.com

Orange River Colony

COLONIAL STAMP COMPANY
5757 Wilshire Blvd. PH #8
Los Angeles, CA 90036
PH: 323-933-9435
FAX: 323-939-9930
Toll Free in North America
PH: 877-272-6693
FAX: 877-272-6694
info@colonialstampcompany.com
www.colonialstampcompany.com

Proofs & Essays

HENRY GITNER PHILATELISTS, INC.
PO Box 3077-S
Middletown, NY 10940
PH: 845-343-5151
PH: 800-947-8267
FAX: 845-343-0068
hgitner@hgitner.com
www.hgitner.com

Rhodesia

COLONIAL STAMP COMPANY
5757 Wilshire Blvd. PH #8
Los Angeles, CA 90036
PH: 323-933-9435
FAX: 323-939-9930
Toll Free in North America
PH: 877-272-6693
FAX: 877-272-6694
info@colonialstampcompany.com
www.colonialstampcompany.com

South America

GUY SHAW
PO Box 27138
San Diego, CA 92198
PH/FAX: 858-485-8269
guyshaw@guyshaw.com
www.guyshaw.com

Stamp Stores

Arizona

A TO Z STAMPS & COINS
4950 E. Thomas Rd.
Phoenix, AZ 85018
OFFICE: 480-844-9878
CELL: 248-709-8939
michael@azstampcoin.com
www.WorldwideStamps.com

California

BROSIUS STAMP, COIN & SUPPLIES
2105 Main St.
Santa Monica, CA 90405
PH: 310-396-7480
FAX: 310-396-7455
brosius.stamp.coin@hotmail.com

COLONIAL STAMP CO./ BRITISH EMPIRE SPECIALIST
5757 Wilshire Blvd. PH #8
(by appt.)
Los Angeles, CA 90036
PH: 323-933-9435
FAX: 323-939-9930
Toll Free in North America
PH: 877-272-6693
FAX: 877-272-6694
info@colonialstampcompany.com
www.colonialstampcompany.com

FISCHER-WOLK PHILATELICS
Suite 211
22762 Aspan St.
Lake Forest, CA 92630
PH: 949-837-2932
fischerwolk@fw.occoxmail.com

NATICK STAMPS & HOBBIES
PO Box 80613
San Marino, CA 91118
PH: 626-285-1384
natickco@att.net
Ebay ID: attickmwj

Connecticut

SILVER CITY COIN & STAMP
41 Colony St.
Meriden, CT 06451
PH: 203-235-7634
FAX: 203-237-4915

Stamp Stores

Georgia

STAMPS UNLIMITED OF GEORGIA, INC.
Suite 1460
100 Peachtree St.
Atlanta, GA 30303
PH: 404-688-9161
tonyroozen@yahoo.com

Illinois

DR. ROBERT FRIEDMAN & SONS
2029 W. 75th St.
Woodridge, IL 60517
PH: 800-588-8100
FAX: 630-985-1588
drbobstamps@yahoo.com
www.drbobfriedmanstamps.com

Indiana

KNIGHT STAMP & COIN CO.
237 Main St.
Hobart, IN 46342
PH: 219-942-4341
PH: 800-634-2646
knight@knightcoin.com
www.knightcoin.com

Missouri

DAVID SEMSROTT STAMPS
11235 Manchester Rd.
St. Louis (Kirkwood), MO 63122
PH: 314-984-8361
fixodine@sbcglobal.net
www.DavidSemsrott.com

New Jersey

BERGEN STAMPS & COLLECTIBLES
306 Queen Anne Rd.
Teaneck, NJ 07666
PH: 201-836-8987

TRENTON STAMP & COIN CO.
Thomas DeLuca
Store: Forest Glen Plaza
1804 Route 33
Hamilton Square, NJ 08690
Mail: PO Box 8574
Trenton, NJ 08650
PH: 800-446-8664
PH: 609-584-8100
FAX: 609-587-8664
TOMD4TSC@aol.com

New York

CHAMPION STAMP CO., INC.
432 W. 54th St.
New York, NY 10019
PH: 212-489-8130
FAX: 212-581-8130
championstamp@aol.com
www.championstamp.com

Ohio

HILLTOP STAMP SERVICE
Richard A. Peterson
PO Box 626
Wooster, OH 44691
PH: 330-262-8907 (0)
PH: 330-262-5378
hilltop@bright.net

THE LINK STAMP CO.
3461 E. Livingston Ave.
Columbus, OH 43227
PH/FAX: 614-237-4125
PH/FAX: 800-546-5726

Stamp Stores

Virginia

KENNEDY'S STAMPS & COINS, INC.
7059 Brookfield Plaza
Springfield, VA 22150
PH: 703-569-7300
FAX: 703-569-7644
j.w.kennedy@verizon.net

LATHEROW & CO., INC.
5054 Lee Hwy.
Arlington, VA 22207
PH: 703-538-2727
PH: 800-647-4624
FAX: 703-538-5210
latherow@filatco.com

Topicals

E. JOSEPH McCONNELL, INC.
PO Box 683
Monroe, NY 10949
PH: 845-783-9791
FAX: 845-782-0347
ejstamps@gmail.com
www.EJMcConnell.com

Topicals-Columbus

MR. COLUMBUS
PO Box 1492
Fennville, MI 49408
PH: 269-543-4755
Mr.Columbus1492@gmail.com

United States

ACS STAMP COMPANY
10831 Chambers Way
Commerce City, CO 80022
PH: 303-841-8666
ACS@ACSStamp.com
www.acsstamp.com

A TO Z STAMPS & COINS
4950 E. Thomas Rd.
Phoenix, AZ 85018
OFFICE: 480-844-9878
CELL: 248-709-8939
michael@azstampcoin.com
www.WorldwideStamps.com

United States

BROOKMAN STAMP CO.
PO Box 90
Vancouver, WA 98666
PH: 360-695-1391
PH: 800-545-4871
FAX: 360-695-1616
larry@brookmanstamps.com
www.brookmanstamps.com

U.S.-Collections Wanted

DR. ROBERT FRIEDMAN & SONS
2029 W. 75th St.
Woodridge, IL 60517
PH: 800-588-8100
FAX: 630-985-1588
drbobstamps@yahoo.com
www.drbobfriedmanstamps.com

U.S.-Trust Territories

HENRY GITNER PHILATELISTS, INC.
PO Box 3077-S
Middletown, NY 10940
PH: 845-343-5151
PH: 800-947-8267
FAX: 845-343-0068
hgitner@hgitner.com
www.hgitner.com

Want Lists

CHARLES P. SCHWARTZ
PO Box 165
Mora, MN 55051
PH: 320-679-4705
cpschw@yahoo.com

Want Lists-British Empire 1840-1935 German Cols./Offices

COLONIAL STAMP COMPANY
5757 Wilshire Blvd. PH #8
Los Angeles, CA 90036
PH: 323-933-9435
FAX: 323-939-9930
Toll Free in North America
PH: 877-272-6693
FAX: 877-272-6694
info@colonialstampcompany.com
www.colonialstampcompany.com

Wanted-Worldwide Collections

A TO Z STAMPS & COINS
4950 E. Thomas Rd.
Phoenix, AZ 85018
OFFICE: 480-844-9878
CELL: 248-709-8939
michael@azstampcoin.com
www.WorldwideStamps.com

DANIEL F. KELLEHER AUCTIONS LLC
PMB 44
60 Newtown Rd
Danbury, CT 06810
PH: 203-297-6056
FAX: 203-297-6059
info@kelleherauctions.com
www.kelleherauctions.com

DR. ROBERT FRIEDMAN & SONS
2029 W. 75th St.
Woodridge, IL 60517
PH: 800-588-8100
FAX: 630-985-1588
drbobstamps@yahoo.com
www.drbobfriedmanstamps.com

THE STAMP CENTER DUTCH COUNTRY AUCTIONS
4115 Concord Pike
Wilmington, DE 19803
PH: 302-478-8740
FAX: 302-478-8779
auctions@thestampcenter.com
www.thestampcenter.com

Websites

ACS STAMP COMPANY
10831 Chambers Way
Commerce City, CO 80022
PH: 303-841-8666
ACS@ACSStamp.com
www.acsstamp.com

Worldwide

A TO Z STAMPS & COINS
4950 E. Thomas Rd.
Phoenix, AZ 85018
OFFICE: 480-844-9878
CELL: 248-709-8939
michael@azstampcoin.com
www.WorldwideStamps.com

WWW.WORLDSTAMPS.COM
PO Box 4743
Pinehurst, NC 28374
PH: 910-295-2048
FAX: 910-295-2049
by mail:
Frank Geiger Philatelists
info@WorldStamps.com
www.WorldStamps.com

Worldwide

Marshall Goldberg
Academy Stamp & Autograph
139 South Beverly Drive, Suite 313
Beverly Hills, CA 90212-3040
Phone: 310-275-5922 • Fax: 310-275-8804
Want Lists filled for the World.
http://www.academystamp.com

Worldwide

All Countries A-Z
ALL TOPICS
VERY LARGE WORLDWIDE STOCK
including varieties, cancels, covers, etc.
Search online: www.ercolegloria.it
WANT LISTS WELCOME!
any catalogue #, any main language.
ERCOLE GLORIA srl - Zuskis Family
Piazza Pio XI 1, 20123 Milan, ITALY
TEL. +39.02804106 • FAX +39.02864217 • E-MAIL: info@ercolegloria.it

SHOWGARD MOUNTS

Showgard mounts are manufactured with the highest archival qualities in mind. The foil used to produce the mounts is acid free and stronger than other mounts for maximum protection and durability. Selecting the right size mount for your stamp is easy. Simply use a millimeter ruler to measure the stamps width then the height. Showgard incorporates these measurements into their product numbers to insure you get the right size. Mounts available with clear (c) or black (b) backgrounds. Please specify background preference when ordering.

Item	*Description*	*Mounts*	*Retail*	*AA**
SGC50/31	50/31 U.S. Jumbo Singles - Horizontal	40	$3.85	**$2.75**
SGCV31/50	31/50 U.S. Jumbo Singles - Vertical	40	$3.85	**$2.75**
SGJ40/25	40/25 U.S. Commem. - Horizontal	40	$3.85	**$2.75**
SGJV25/40	25/40 U.S. Commem. - Vertical	40	$3.85	**$2.75**
SGE22/25	22/25 U.S. Regular Issues - Vertical	40	$3.85	**$2.75**
SGEH25/22	25/22 U.S. Regular Issues - Horizontal	40	$3.85	**$2.75**
SGT25/27	25/27 U.S. Famous Americans	40	$3.85	**$2.75**
SGU33/27	33/27 U.N., Germany	40	$3.85	**$2.75**
SGN40/27	40/27 United Nations	40	$3.85	**$2.75**
SGAH41/31	41/31 U.S. Semi Jumbo - Horizontal	40	$3.85	**$2.75**
SGAV31/41	31/41 U.S. Semi Jumbo - Vertical	40	$3.85	**$2.75**
SGDH52/36	52/36 U.S. Duck Stamps	30	$3.85	**$2.75**
SGS31/31	31/31 U.S. Celebrate the Century	30	$3.85	**$2.75**
SGUS2	Cut Style with Tray-8 Sizes	320	$29.50	**$21.25**
SGUS3	Strip Style w/Tray-No. 22 thru No. 52	75	$43.95	**$31.50**
SGUS1	U.S. Strip Sizes No. 22 thru No. 52	50	$22.50	**$16.25**
SG50VPB	50th Anniversary Value Pack	50	$24.95	**$19.96**
SG67/25	67/25 U.S. Coil Strips of 3	40	$7.50	**$5.50**
SG57/55	57/55 U.S. Regular Issue	25	$7.50	**$5.50**
SG106/55	106/55 U.S. 3¢, 4¢ Commemoratives	20	$7.50	**$5.50**
SG105/57	105/57 U.S. Giori Press Issues	20	$7.50	**$5.50**
SG127/70	127/70 U.S. Jumbo Issues	10	$7.50	**$5.50**
SG140/89	140/89 Postcards, Souvenir Sheets	10	$7.50	**$5.50**
SG165/94	165/94 First Day Covers	10	$7.50	**$5.50**
SG20	215/20 U.S. Mini Stamps, etc.	22	$8.95	**$6.50**
SG22	215/22 Narrow U.S. Airs	22	$8.95	**$6.50**
SG24	215/24 U.K. and Canada, early U.S.	22	$8.95	**$6.50**
SG25	215/25 U.S. Commem. & Regular Issues	22	$8.95	**$6.50**
SG27	215/27 U.S. Famous Americans, U.N.	22	$8.95	**$6.50**
SG28	215/28 Switzerland, Liechtenstein	22	$8.95	**$6.50**
SG30	215/30 U.S. Special Stamps, Jamestown	22	$8.95	**$6.50**
SG31	315/31 U.S. Squares & Semi Jumbo	22	$8.95	**$6.50**
SG33	215/33 U.K. Issues, Misc. Foreign	22	$8.95	**$6.50**
SG36	215/36 Duck Stamps, Misc. Foreign	15	$8.95	**$6.50**
SG39	215/39 U.S. Magsaysay, Misc. Foreign	15	$8.95	**$6.50**
SG41	215/41 U.S. Vertical Commem. Israel Tabs	15	$8.95	**$6.50**
SG44	215/44 Booklet Panes, Hatteras Quartet	15	$8.95	**$6.50**
SG48	215/48 Canada Reg. Issue & Comm Blocks	15	$8.95	**$6.50**
SG50	215/50 U.S. Plain Blocks of 4	15	$8.95	**$6.50**
SG52	215/52 France Paintings, Misc. Foreign	15	$8.95	**$6.50**
SG57	215/57 U.S. Commem. Plate Blocks	15	$8.95	**$6.50**
SG61	215/61 Souvenir Sheets, Tab Singles, etc.	15	$8.95	**$6.50**
SG63	240/63 U.S. Semi Jumbo Blocks	10	$11.25	**$8.25**
SG66	240/66 U.S. ATM Panes, SA Duck Panes	10	$11.25	**$8.25**
SG68	240/68 Canadian Plate Blocks, etc.	10	$11.25	**$8.25**
SG74	240/74 U.N. Inscription Blocks of 4	10	$11.25	**$8.25**
SG80	240/80 U.S. Commem. Blocks	10	$11.25	**$8.25**
SG82	240/82 U.N. Chagall SS, Canada Plate Blocks	10	$11.25	**$8.25**
SG84	240/84 Israel Plate Blocks, etc.	10	$11.25	**$8.25**
SG89	240/89 U.N. Inscription Blocks of 6	10	$11.25	**$8.25**
SG100	240/100 U.S. Squares Plate Blocks	7	$11.25	**$8.25**
SG120	240/120 Miniature Sheets	7	$11.25	**$8.25**
SG70	264/70 U.S. Jumbo Plate Blocks	10	$14.85	**$10.65**
SG91	264/91 U.K. Souvenir Sheets	10	$14.85	**$10.65**
SG105	264/105 U.K. Blocks, Covers, etc.	10	$14.85	**$10.65**
SG107	264/107 U.S. Plate No. Strip of 20	10	$14.85	**$10.65**
SGMPK	Assortment No. 22 thru No. 41	12	$7.15	**$5.25**
SGMPK2	Assortment No. 76 thru No. 171	15	$29.95	**$22.50**
SGAB	U.S. SS to 1975-except White Plains	11	$7.65	**$5.50**
SGWSE	World Stamp Expo Souvenir Sheets	3	$2.50	**$1.75**
SG265/231	265/231 U.S. Full Sheets & Souvenir Cards	5	$21.25	**$15.25**
SGRP94	U.S. 1994 Souvenir Sheets	5	$9.75	**$6.95**
SGRPAC97	Pacific 97 Issues	7	$4.75	**$3.50**
SGDC2006	Washington 2006 Souvenir Sheets (4)	11	$7.75	**$5.50**
SGTM	Trans-Mississippi Issues	11	$4.75	**$3.50**
SGSPC	Space Exploration Sheets	5	$6.50	**$4.75**
SG111	264/111 U.S. Floating Plate No. Strips of 20	5	$9.75	**$6.95**
SG127	264/127 Modern U.S. Definitive Sheets of 20	5	$10.75	**$7.75**

Item	*Description*	*Mounts*	*Retail*	*AA**
SG137	264/137 U.N. SS, U.K. Coronation	5	$11.75	**$8.50**
SG158	264/158 Miniature Sheets, Apoll Soyuz PB	5	$13.50	**$9.75**
SG175	264/175 U.S. Sheets-Pan American Reissues	5	$14.50	**$10.50**
SG188	264/188 U.S. Miniature Sheets-Hollywood, etc.	5	$15.25	**$10.95**
SG198	264/198 U.S. Miniature Sheets	5	$15.95	**$11.50**
SG260/25	260/25 U.S. Coil Strips of up to 11 stamps	25	$11.95	**$8.50**
SG293/30	293/30 U.S. American Eagle Coil Strips of up to 11 stamps	5	$3.50	**$2.50**
SG260/40	260/40 U.S. Postal People Full Strip	10	$9.75	**$6.95**
SG260/46	260/46 U.S. Vending Booklets	10	$9.75	**$6.95**
SG260/55	260/55 U.S. 13¢ Eagle Full Strip	10	$9.75	**$6.95**
SG260/59	260/59 U.S. Double Press Reg. Iss. Strips of 20	10	$9.75	**$6.95**
SG111/91	111/91 U.S. Columbian Souvenir Sheets	6	$4.50	**$3.25**
SG229/131	229/131 U.S. WWII Sheets, Looney Tunes	5	$9.87	**$7.00**
SG187/144	187/144 U.N. Flag Sheetlets	10	$17.50	**$12.50**
SG204/153	204/153 U.S. Commem. Sheets, Bicentennial	5	$10.25	**$7.25**
SG120/207	120/207 U.S. Ameripex Presidential Sheetlets	4	$5.75	**$4.25**
SG192/201	192/201 U.S. Classics Mini-Sheets	5	$12.50	**$8.95**
SG280/228	280/228 U.S. Greetings From America Sheets	5	$18.50	**$13.25**
SG191/229	191/229 U.S. Celebrate The Century Sheets	5	$14.50	**$10.50**
SG76	264/76 BEP SS, Booklets, Plate Blocks	5	$10.95	**$7.50**
SG96	264/96 Souvenir Sheets, Panes	5	$10.95	**$7.50**
SG109	264/109 Foreign Miniature Sheets	5	$10.95	**$7.50**
SG115	264/115 Foreign Miniature Sheets	5	$10.95	**$7.95**
SG117	264/117 Foreign Miniature Sheets	5	$10.95	**$7.95**
SG121	264/121 Foreign Miniature Sheets	5	$10.95	**$7.95**
SG131	264/131 Looney Toons, Misc. Sheetlets	5	$10.95	**$7.95**
SG135	264/135 Foreign Miniature Sheets	5	$10.95	**$7.95**
SG139	264/139 White House Pane, etc.	5	$10.95	**$7.95**
SG143	264/143 Victorian Love, Misc. Sheets	5	$10.95	**$7.95**
SG147	264/147 Cinco de Mayo, etc.	5	$13.95	**$9.97**
SG151	264/151 Antique Auto, Communication, etc.	5	$13.95	**$9.97**
SG163	264/163 Tropical Flowers, UN Human Rights	5	$13.95	**$9.97**
SG167	264/167 Misc. U.S. Sheetlets	5	$13.95	**$9.97**
SG171	264/171 Helping Children Learn, etc.	5	$13.95	**$9.97**
SG181	264/181 U.S. Sheets– Calder, All Aboard, etc.	5	$16.95	**$12.25**
SG201	264/201 Dinosaurs, etc.	5	$16.95	**$12.25**
SG215	264/215 U.S. Sheets–Arctic Animals, Ballet, etc.	5	$16.95	**$12.25**

7" LIGHTHOUSE STAMP MOUNT CUTTER

This affordable and versatile mount cutter features an attachable measuring scale up to 7" (180mm) with an adjustable stop for accurate and clean cuts every time.

Item	*Retail*	*AA*
LH180MC	$19.95	**$17.99**

Call **1-800-572-6885**

Visit **www.amosadvantage.com**

ORDERING INFORMATION

*AA prices apply to paid subscribers of Amos Hobby titles and orders placed online. Prices, terms and product availability subject to change.

Shipping & Handling:
United States: 10% of order total. Minimum charge $6.99 Maximum charge $45.00.
Canada: 15% of order total. Minimum charge $19.99 Maximum charge $50.00.
Foreign orders are shipped via FedEx Economny Intl. and billed actual freight.